GET ACQUAINTED with Linn's

13 weeks FOR $7.95

OUTSIDE U.S. $15

Linn's Stamp News

$1.50 U.S.

MARCH 28, 1988 WORLD'S LARGEST WEEKLY STAMP NEWS AND MARKETPLACE VOL. 61 ISSUE 3099

Jack London definitive to become first Great Americans stamp in booklet format

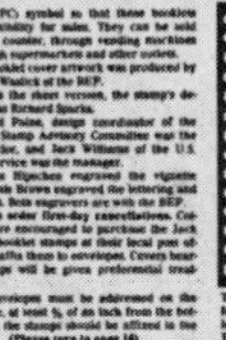

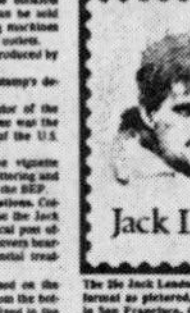

Jack London USA 25

Royal couple visit British stamp display

Test coil use grows

Britain to issue Europa stamps

Contents on page 3

- Fun
- Knowledge
- New Issues
- Stamp Trends
- Errors

Linn's is the world's largest weekly stamp newspaper and mail order marketplace, with thousands of buy, sell, and trade ads for your collecting enjoyment.

SEND YOUR ORDER AND REMITTANCE TO:

Linn's Stamp News

P. O. BOX 29 • SIDNEY, OHIO 45365

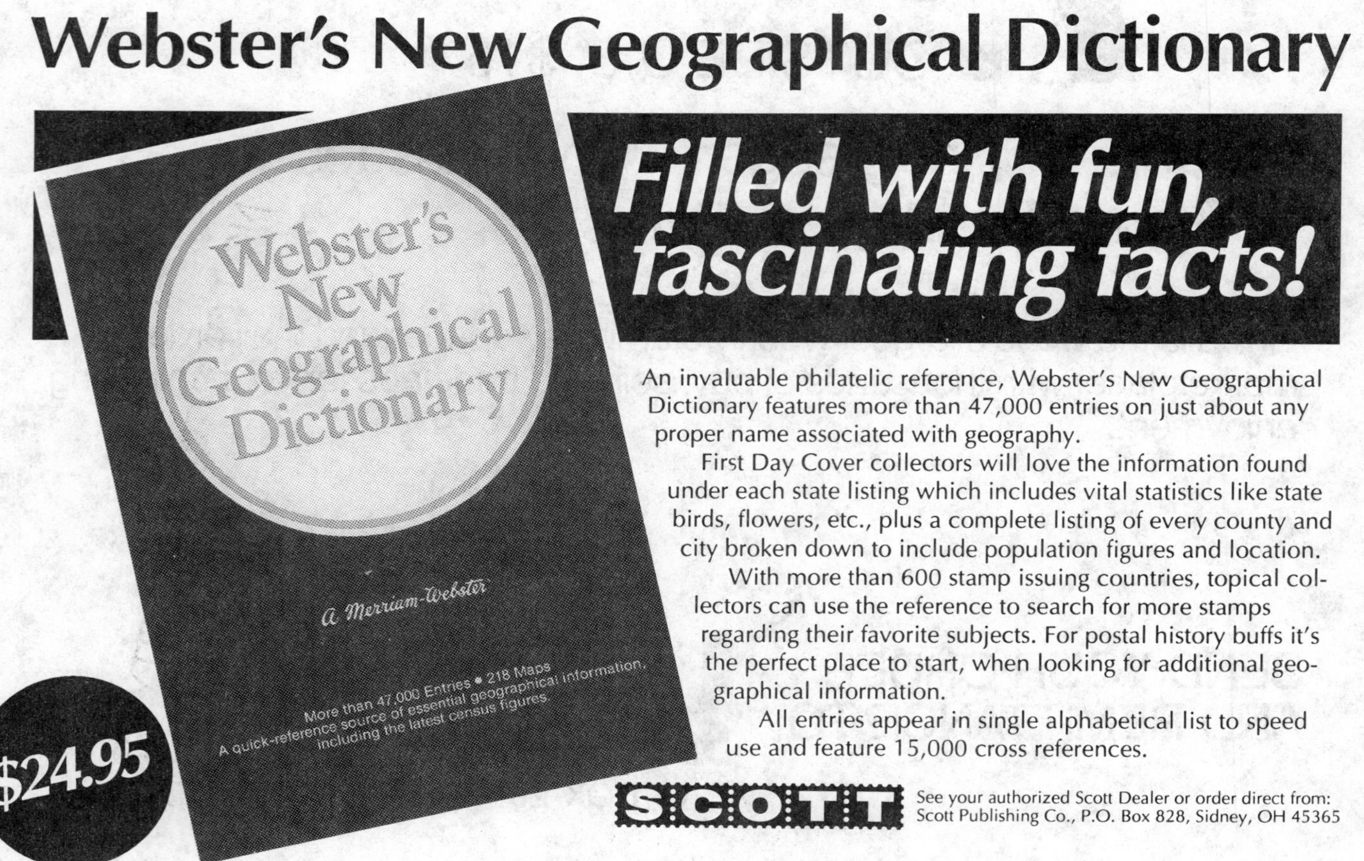
Webster's New Geographical Dictionary
Filled with fun, fascinating facts!
Webster's New Geographical Dictionary
A Merriam-Webster
More than 47,000 Entries • 218 Maps
A quick-reference source of essential geographical information, including the latest census figures.
$24.95
An invaluable philatelic reference, Webster's New Geographical Dictionary features more than 47,000 entries on just about any proper name associated with geography.
First Day Cover collectors will love the information found under each state listing which includes vital statistics like state birds, flowers, etc., plus a complete listing of every county and city broken down to include population figures and location.
With more than 600 stamp issuing countries, topical collectors can use the reference to search for more stamps regarding their favorite subjects. For postal history buffs it's the perfect place to start, when looking for additional geographical information.
All entries appear in single alphabetical list to speed use and feature 15,000 cross references.
SCOTT
See your authorized Scott Dealer or order direct from: Scott Publishing Co., P.O. Box 828, Sidney, OH 45365

SCOTT®

1994 Standard Postage Stamp Catalogue

ONE HUNDRED AND FIFTIETH EDITION IN FIVE VOLUMES

VOLUME 4

EUROPEAN COUNTRIES AND COLONIES,
INDEPENDENT NATIONS of
AFRICA, ASIA, LATIN AMERICA

J-Q

VICE PRESIDENT/PUBLISHER Stuart J. Morrissey
EDITOR William W. Cummings
ASSISTANT EDITOR William H. Hatton
VALUING EDITOR Martin J. Frankevicz
NEW ISSUES EDITOR David C. Akin
COMPUTER CONTROL COORDINATOR Denise Oder
VALUING ANALYSTS Jose R. Capote, Roger L. Listwan
EDITORIAL ASSISTANTS Judith E. Bertrand, Beth Brown
CONTRIBUTING EDITOR Joyce Nelson
ART/PRODUCTION DIRECTOR Janine S. Apple
PRODUCTION COORDINATOR Nancy S. Martin
SALES MANAGER Bill Fay
ADVERTISING David Lodge
CIRCULATION/PRODUCT PROMOTION MANAGER Tim Wagner

Scott Publishing Co.

911 Vandemark Road, Sidney, OH 45365

A division of AMOS PRESS, INC., publishers of *Linn's Stamp News*, *Coin World*, *Cars & Parts* magazine and *The Sidney Daily News*.

Table of Contents

Letter from the Publisher 5A
Auction-House Bulletin Board 6A
Acknowledgments 8A
Catalogue Information 10A
Catalogue Listing Policy 11A
Understanding the Listings 12A
Special Notices 14A
Abbreviations 15A
Basic Stamp Information 18A
Terminology 25A
Currency Conversion 26A
Colonies, Former Colonies, Offices, Territories Controlled by Parent States 27A
Common Designs 28A

The Topical Cross Reference 37A
Butterflies 37A
Ships 40A
American Topical Association Handbooks and Checklists.......... 47A

Countries of the World J-Q 1

1994 Volume 4 Number Changes 908
Numerical Index of Volume 4 Watermark Illustrations.......... 908
Index and Identifier 914
Index to Advertisers 920
Reader Service Card Advertiser's Index 920

See Volumes 2, 3 and 5 for nations of Africa, Asia, Europe, Latin America A-C, D-I and R-Z and their affiliated territories.

See Volume 1 for United States and its affiliated territories, United Nations and the British Commonwealth of Nations.

ISBN 0-89487-193-5

Library of Congress Card No. 2-3301

Scott Publishing Co.

SCOTT 911 VANDEMARK ROAD, SIDNEY, OHIO 45365 513-498-0802

Dear Catalogue User:

What's new in the 1994 edition? Plenty. As a matter of fact, there is such an awesome amount to tell you about, I'm almost not sure where to begin. So, I've employed an imaginary reporter to ask a few questions. And, to make sure this doesn't become a self-promoting, rah-rah exercise, I made sure our reporter was a big-city "just the facts, mister" type.

What do you view as the single most important change in the 1994 edition?

Dual valuing of never-hinged stamps. Many collectors were dissatisfied with the former arrangement where we valued hinged stamps up to a certain year, and then made a clean break and valued all stamps after the breakpoint as never-hinged. Now we value stamps, both hinged and never-hinged, for many countries from the early 20th century to the 1940's or 1950's. In Volume 4, seven countries have the added never-hinged listings. The number of stamps covered by the added values in some of these countries is often quite large.

The added listings in **Netherlands** cover over 25 years of listings, and start with the 1913 Centenary of Dutch Independence set, Scott 90-101. In semi-postals, air mails and marine insurance stamps, the added listings stretch back to the first stamps in each category. In semi-postals, the first listing is the 1906 Tuberculosis set.

In **Luxembourg,** over 30 years of dual coverage starts with the Clervaux 2fr and its perforation variety minor, Scott 194 and 194a, issued in 1928-34. In semi-postals, the additions start with the first issue of 1921. Air mails and occupation stamps also have the added listings.

In **Norway,** dual coverage starts with the 1925 Polar Bear and Airplane set, Scott 104-110, and continues to cover 20 years of issues. Additions in semi-postals and air mails start with the first listings. In postage dues, the additions start with the 1922-23 issue, Scott J7-J12.

Liechtenstein's added never-hinged listings cover more than 25 years and start with the 1933 Francis I 3fr, Scott 114. In postage dues, the listings start with the first issue of 1920. Additions in semi-postals and air mails start with the first issues, and in Officials, with the 1937-41 overprints, Scott O21-O29.

Over 20 years of issues have dual coverage in **Lithuania.** Additions start with the first issue with gum, the 1919 Vytis set, Scott 30-39. Other sections with additions are semi-postals, air mails and occupation stamps.

Added never hinged listings in **Latvia** cover all sets from the pre-war era except for the 1919 German and Russian occupation issues. Latvia's first issue was in 1918.

Monaco's added listings start with the 1937-43 set showing the Arms or Prince Louis II, Scott 145-158. Added listings are also found in semi-postals.

Thanks, but we need to move on. Is there anything else that is truly dramatic that users will notice right off the bat?

Yes. **The type style has changed** for the first time in decades. And the good news is that it is easier to read. Although the type appears larger, it actually takes up no more space than the old. Give it a test drive and see for yourself.

Let's get down to the real important stuff - like trends in values. You guys really shook things up a few years ago when you went to retail values. Seems like now just about everyone likes the retail value system - are there any surprises?

Well, that depends...

Just the facts, please.

Korea shows substantial increases. There are many values that increase dramatically at all levels. The 1903 Falcon set, Scott 39-51, increases to $1,410 unused from $580. Scott 90, the 1940 Syngman Rhee 5-weun, jumps to $70 unused from $25. The sheet for President Park's inauguration, Scott 579a, rises to $17.50 from $8.

Are there any stamps with large differences between hinged and never-hinged values?

Netherlands shows many sharp differences between hinged and never-hinged. For instance, Scott 212-213, the 1939 St. Willibrord issue, is $4.95 hinged, but weighs in at $16 never-hinged. Scott 202-203, the 1934 Curacao Tercentenary, is $20 hinged and $80 never-hinged. And, in Netherlands semi-postals, Scott B118-B122, the 1939 issue to aid destitute children, is $6.98 hinged and $32.50 never-hinged.

Any new features we should be aware of? Remember, just the facts.

More explanatory footnotes have been added to the catalogue. Footnotes are intended to help users by providing additional information, such as the special situations regarding condition, or the circumstances under which a stamp was issued. For example, in Mexico, a note has been added to make it easier to distinguish the three 35-cent airmail definitives issued between 1950 and 1955, Scott C191, C191a and C220C.

The new listings program continues, as we have added many stamps that were not listed in the recent past. This is part of our multi-year program to list all stamps that were officially sanctioned and valid for postage. Katanga is now listed for the first time. The country was formerly a province of the Congo Republic (previously known as the Belgian Congo, and currently known as Zaire) that seceded in July of 1960. The United Nations declared the secession over in September of 1961. Although no other nations recognized Katanga's independence, stamps were issued for the country that were tolerated in the international mails.

The topical cross reference returns with butterflies and ships. Each year we select two new topics. The cross reference includes butterfly and ship stamps in this volume. For a complete definition of what is included for each topic (yes, we do include moths and some related insects), see the introduction prior to the section. The lists are organized by country, and there is a brief description after each catalogue number of the butterfly species or type of boat (watercraft or whatever, as long as it floats).

Any final comments?

Happy collecting, have fun searching for those elusive items on your wantlist and let us know if there are any improvements you'd like to see from us in the future.

Stuart Morrissey

Stuart Morrissey
Publisher

SCOTT®

AUCTION HOUSE DIRECTORY

A LISTING OF WORLDWIDE AUCTION-HOUSES COMPILED AS A SERVICE TO OUR READERS.

ABBEY STAMP AUCTIONS
P.O. Box 25-043, St. Heliers, Auckland 5, NEW ZEALAND

MICHAEL ALDRICH
P.O. Box 130484, St. Paul, MN 55113 USA

GEORGE ALEVIZOS
2800 28th Street, Suite 323, Santa Monica, CA 90405 USA

ALPHA STAMPS, LTD.
54 Tsimiski Str., Thessaloniki, GREECE

EARL P.L. APFELBAUM, INC.
2006 Walnut Street, Philadelphia PA 19103 USA

THE AUCTION HOUSE
P.O. Box 1129, La Porte, TX 77572 USA

B TRADING CO.
114 Quail St., Albany, NY 12206 USA

WILLY BALASSE SA GENEVA
1 Rue Pedro Meylan, CH1208, Geneva, SWITZERLAND

RICK BASINI STAMPS
312 E. Oakland Park Blvd., Ft. Lauderdale, FL 33334 USA

BECK STAMP AUCTIONS
P.O. Box 2506, Mesa, Arizona 85214 USA

MATTHEW BENNETT
31 W. Chesapeake Avenue, Baltimore, MD 21204 USA

BEXAR STAMP AUCTIONS
P.O. Box 39838, San Antonio, TX 78218 USA
See our display ad on this page and on page 339.

ALAN BLAIR AUCTIONS
6413 McLean St., Richmond, VA 23231 USA

ROELF BOEKEMA
P.O. Box 45, 2501 CA, The Hague, NETHERLANDS

• ATTENTION ADVERTISERS •

This Public-Auction-House Directory is designed to provide, as a service to the users of this catalog, the names and addresses of auction houses worldwide. The company name and address line-listing is **provided FREE** to all bona fide public-auction-houses. If your auction house is not on these pages, we urge you to contact us for inclusion.

You can improve your visibility and present a more complete message about your company with an **"AUCTION BLOCK" ad.** The "AUCTION BLOCK" display ads on these pages are $232 net with additional discounts available when it appears in other volumes (copy can be different). If you place a display ad, minimum size 1/4 page, elsewhere in a given volume your Auction-House Directory **"AUCTION BLOCK"** ad, in that volume is **FREE**!

For further details Ph. 513-498-0832 or write Scott Publishing Company P.O. Box 828, Sidney, OH 45365 USA

JOHN BULL STAMPS, LTD.
P.O. Box 10009, GPO, HONG KONG

BUTTERFIELD & BUTTERFIELD
164 Utah St., San Francisco, CA 94103 USA

CEE-JAY STAMP AUCTIONS
P.O. Box 321, Waldorf, MD 20604 USA

CHERRYSTONE STAMP CENTER, INC.
119 W. 57th Street, New York, NY 10019 USA

CHRISTIE'S
8 King St., St. James's London SW1Y 6QT
UNITED KINGDOM

CHRISTIE'S ROBSON LOWE
502 Park Avenue, New York, NY 10022 USA

CINDERELLA STAMP AUCTIONS
P.O. Box 315, Willoughby, NSW, 2068, AUSTRALIA

COLONIAL STAMP CO.
5410 Wilshire Blvd., Los Angeles, CA 90036 USA

TED CONWAY
P.O. Box 520, Lynbrook, NY 11563 USA

CORINPHILA
Bellerivestrasse, Ferrohaus, Zurich CH8034, SWITZERLAND

H.J.W. DAUGHERTY
P.O. Box 1146, Eastham, MA 02642 USA

DOWNEAST STAMPS
52 Fern St., Bangor, ME 04401 USA

E & F STAMP AUCTIONS
P.O. Box 737, Marshalltown, IA 50158 USA

EASTERN AUCTIONS, LTD.
Box 250 L., Bathurst, NB E2A 3Z2, CANADA

EASTLAND STAMP AUCTIONS
Concourse-Eastland Center, Harper Woods, MI 48225 USA

ELLIOT LINDSAY AUCTIONS
1624 Seabright Ave., Santa Cruz, CA 95062 USA

EXPRESS STAMP AUCTIONS
35 Eaton Rise, London W5 2HE, UNITED KINGDOM

DAVID FELDMAN SA
175 Route De Chancy, P.O.Box 81, Geneva CH1213, SWITZERLAND

CHARLES G. FIRBY AUCTIONS
6695 Highland Rd., Suite 106, Waterford, MI 48327 USA

WILLIAM A. FOX AUCTIONS, INC.
676 Morris Avenue, Springfield, NJ 07081 USA

RICHARD C. FRAJOLA, INC.
125 W. Park Ave., Box 608, Empire, CO 80438 USA

FRIMARKSHUSET AB
Master Samuelsgatan 5, Stockholm S11144, SWEDEN

STANLEY GIBBONS (Australia), LTD.
343 Little Collins Street, Melbourne, Victoria 3000
AUSTRALIA

H.R. HARMER, INC.
14 E. 33rd Street, New York, NY 10016 USA

HARMERS AUCTIONS SA
Pocobelli 16, 6815-MELIDE, SWITZERLAND

HARMERS OF LONDON
91 New Bond St., London W1A 4EH, UNITED KINGDOM

J. STUART HARPER
P.O. Box 188, Naramata, BC VOH 1NO, CANADA

HEINRICH STAMP AUCTIONS
735 S.W. St. Clair, Portland, OR 97205 USA

JIM A. HENNOK, LTD.
185 Queen East, Toronto, Ontario M5A 1S2 CANADA

IMPERIAL AUCTIONEERS & VALUERS, LTD.
5 Cross Chapel St., Headingley, Leeds LS6 3JE
UNITED KINGDOM

INTERSTAMPS
4 Woods View Rd., Bournemouth BH9 2LN
UNITED KINGDOM

INTERPHILA
3 Hannover, Postfach 55 67, GERMANY

STEVE IVY PHILATELIC AUCTIONS, INC.
100 Highland Park Village, Dallas, TX 75205 USA

J & M PHILATELIC AUCTION
106 West Broadway, Vancouver, BC V5Y 1P3, CANADA

D.I. JORGENSEN
P.O. Box 4485 Station C, London, Ontario N5W 5J5, CANADA

DANIEL F. KELLEHER CO., INC.
50 Congress St., Suite 314, Boston, MA 02109 USA

IAN KIMMERLY STAMPS
240 Catherine St. #100, Ottawa, Ontario K2P2G8 CANADA

HEINRICH KOHLER
Bahnhofstr., 63 Postfach 3680, D6200 Wiesbaden 1, GERMANY

KUKSTIS AUCTIONS
Box 130, Scituate, MA 02066 USA

ADRIANO LANDINI s.r.l.
Via Dell'Orso 7/A, 20121 Milano, ITALY

LANG & FIALKOWSKI
Briefmarken Versteigerungen, Friedrichstr 29, D6200 Wiesbaden, GERMANY

HERB LATUCHIE AUCTIONS
Box 67099, Cuyahoga Falls, OH 44222 USA

LAWSONS
212 Cumberland Street, Sydney, 2000, AUSTRALIA

CHARLES LESKI & ASSOC.
83 Riverdale Rd., Hawthorn 3122, Victoria, AUSTRALIA

ALLAN LEVY
4th Floor, 343 Little Collins St., Melbourne 3000, AUSTRALIA

BENGT LILJA STAMP AUCTION
Stora Nygatan 31, S211 37 Malmo, SWEDEN

ROBERT E. LIPPERT
23800 Greater Mack, St. Clair Shores, MI 48080 USA

GUNTER LOTH
Neubrunnenstr 12, D6500 Mainz 1, GERMANY

MACDONNELL & WHYTE, LTD.
102 Leinster Rd., Dublin 6, IRELAND

MACRAY WATSON AUCTIONS
156 Nicholson Street, Fitzroy, Vic., 3065, AUSTRALIA

GREG MANNING AUCTIONS
115 Main Rd., Montville, NJ 07045 USA

R. MARESCH & SON
330 Bay St., Suite 703, Toronto, Ontario M5H 2S9, CANADA

L. D. MAYO, JR.
P.O. Box 20837, Indianapolis, IN 46220 USA

McBRIDE STAMP AUCTIONS, INC.
4557 N. Channel Avenue, Portland, OR 97217 USA

JAMES T. McCUSKER, INC.
P.O. Box 121, Raynham Ctr., MA 02768 USA

METRO-SIMMY AUCTIONS
440 Forsgate Drive, Cranbury, NJ 08512 USA

MONTREAL STAMPS AND COINS
1878 Ste. Catherine East, Montreal, Quebec H2K 2H5CANADA

J.R. MOWBRAY
P.O. Box 63, Otaki Railway, NEW ZEALAND

LOWELL S. NEWMAN & CO.
1500 Harbor Blvd., Weehawken, NJ 07087 USA

NORTH COAST STAMP AUCTIONS
4132 Erie Street, Room 208, Willoughby, OH 44094

NORTHLAND AUCTIONS
Box 34, Vernon, NJ 07044 USA
See our display advertisement on page 633

SCOTT

AUCTION HOUSE DIRECTORY

A LISTING OF WORLDWIDE AUCTION-HOUSES COMPILED AS A SERVICE TO OUR READERS.

JAMES NORWICH AUCTIONS
33 Timberhill, Norwich, Norfolk NR1 3LA, UNITED KINGDOM

OTTAWA STAMP AUCTIONS
P.O. Box 5083 Station F, Ottawa, Ontario K2C 3H3 CANADA

PARCEL POSTE COMPANY
Moody Lane, Danbury, CT 06810 USA

RODNEY PERRY
79 Bourke St., Melbourne 3000, AUSTRALIA

PHILAS STAMP AUCTIONS
17 Brisbane Street, Sydney, NSW, 2000, AUSTRALIA

PHILLIPS
Blenstock House, 7 Blenheim St., London W1Y 0AS UNITED KINGDOM

DAVID G. PHILLIPS CO.
P.O. Box 611388, North Miami, FL 33161 USA

PHOENIX INTERNATIONAL
Ashleigh, Monument Lane, Condnor Park, Notts NG16 5PJ UNITED KINGDOM

NORM POSTAL
P.O. Box 13008, Sunrise, FL 33313 USA

POSTILJONEN AB
Sodra Tullgatan 3, S 211 40 Malmo, SWEDEN

QUALITY AUCTIONS, LTD.
P.O. Box 3116, Middletown, NY 10940 USA

PETER RAPP
P.O. Box 2924, CH9500 Wil. SWITZERLAND

RASDALE STAMP CO.
36 South State Street, Chicago, IL 60603 USA

RAVEN STAMPS
16 Bridge Street, Cork, IRELAND

BRIAN REEVE STAMP AUCTIONS
27 Maiden Lane, London WC2E 7JS, UNITED KINGDOM

MICHAEL ROGERS, INC.
199 E. Welbourne Ave., Winter Park, FL 32789 USA

SAM HOUSTON PHILATELICS
13310 Westheimer #150, Houston, TX 77077 USA

SCANIA FRIMARKEN
Box 13029, S200 44 Malmo, SWEDEN

JACQUES C. SCHIFF JR., INC.
195 Main St., Ridgefield Park, NJ 07660 USA
See our display ad on this page and in the Yellow Pages.

SCHLITT & CO.
Postfach 2100, Burgermeister-Mahr, Strasse 2-4, 6053 Obertshausen-Hausen, GERMANY

SCHWANKE & SOHN
Kleine Reichenstrabe 1, D2000 Hamburg 11, GERMANY

SEAWAY AUCTIONS
P.O. Box 551, Brockville, Ontario K6V 5V7, CANADA

JOHN SHEFFIELD PHILATELIST, LTD.
P.O. Box 2014, Lambeth, Ontario N0L 1S0 CANADA

IRWIN SIEGEL
P.O. Box 368, Columbus, NJ 08022 USA

ROBERT A. SIEGEL AUCTIONS
65 E. 55th St., New York, NY 10022 USA

J.N. SISSONS, INC.
Suite 119, Box 513, 220 Yonge, Toronto, Ontario M5B 2H1, CANADA

SKANDIA POSTILLONEN
Trommesalen 7, DK1614 Copenhagen V. DENMARK

SOTHEBY'S
1334 York Ave., New York, NY 10021 USA

ST. LOUIS STAMP & COIN
351 Paul Brown Bldg., 818 Olive St., St. Louis, MO 63101 USA

STAMP CENTER/DUTCH COUNTRY AUCTIONS
4115 Concord Pike, Wilmington, DE 19803 USA

STAMP ENTERPRISES
4 Chandni Chowk St., Calcutta 700072, INDIA

STATUS STAMPS PTY., LIMITED
14th Floor, Hilton Building, 225 Pitt Street, Sydney, NSW, 2000, AUSTRALIA

RUDOLF STELTZER
Rudolfstr 13-17, D6000 Frankfurt Main 11, GERMANY

SUBURBAN STAMP, INC.
P.O. Box 715, 1071 St. James Ave., Springfield, MA 01101 USA

SUPERIOR GALLERIES
9478 W. Olympic Blvd., Beverly Hills, CA 90212 USA
See our display ad on this page and on page 2A.

JOHN TALMAN AUCTIONS
P.O. Box 70 Adelaide St., Toronto, Ontario M5C 2H8, CANADA

THAMES STAMP AUCTIONS
35 Wheathill Road, Anerley, London SE20 7XQ, UNITED KINGDOM

TREASURE-HUNTERS, LTD.
G.P.O. Box 11446, HONG KONG

TROPICAL STAMPS, INC.
P.O. Box 6261, Fort Lauderdale, FL 33310 USA

URSULA PHILATELIX AUCTIONS
819 Townsend Blvd., Suite 11, Jacksonville, FL 32211 USA

FRANK VOGEL
Box 38, Snowdon PO, Montreal H3X 3T3, CANADA

WARWICK & WARWICK
Pageant House, Jury St., Warwick CV 34 4EW, UNITED KINGDOM

WEISS PHILATELICS
P.O. Box 5358, Bethelem, PA 18015 USA

WESTERN AUCTIONS, LTD.
Bank House, 225 City Rd., Cardiff, Wales CF2 3JD, UNITED KINGDOM

WILD ROSE PHILATELICS
P.O. Box 1442, Edmonton, Alberta T5J 2N5, CANADA

RICHARD WOLFFERS, INC.
127 Kearny St., San Francisco, CA 94108 USA

MENTION THE 1994 SCOTT CATALOGUE WHEN CONTACTING AUCTION HOUSES

• ATTENTION ADVERTISERS •

This Public-Auction-House Directory is designed to provide, as a service to the users of this catalog, the names and addresses of auction houses worldwide. The company name and address line-listing is **provided FREE** to all bona fide public-auction-houses. If your auction house is not on these pages, we urge you to contact us for inclusion.

You can improve your visibility and present a more complete message about your company with an **"AUCTION BLOCK" ad.** The "AUCTION BLOCK" display ads on these pages are $232 net with additional discounts available when it appears in other volumes (copy can be different). If you place a display ad, minimum size 1/4 page, elsewhere in a given volume your Auction-House Directory **"AUCTION BLOCK"** ad, in that volume is **FREE**!

For further details Ph. 513-498-0832 or write Scott Publishing Company P.O. Box 828, Sidney, OH 45365 USA

Acknowledgments

Our appreciation and gratitude go to the following individuals and organizations who have assisted us in preparing information included in the 1994 Scott Catalogues. Some helpers prefer anonymity. Those individuals have generously shared their stamp knowledge with others through the medium of the Scott Catalogue.

Those who follow provided information that is in addition to the hundreds of dealer price lists and advertisements and scores of auction catalogues and realizations which were used in producing the Catalogue Values used herein. It is from those noted here that we have been able to obtain information on items not normally seen in published lists and advertisements. Support from these people of course goes beyond data leading to Catalogue Values, for they also are key to editorial changes.

Michael E. Aldrich
B. J. Ammel
Mike Armus
Jules K. Beck
Vladimir Berrio-Lemm
John Birkinbine II
Torbjorn Bjork
Brian M. Bleckwenn
Al Boerger
John R. Boker, Jr.
George W. Brett
William C. Brooks VI
Michael Bryne
Joseph V. Bush
Lawrence A. Bustillo
Nathan Carlin
E. J. Chamberlin
Albert F. Chang
Andrew Cronin
James A. Cross
P.J. Drossos
Bob Dumaine
Donald East
Victor E. Engstrom
J. A. Farrington
Peter Feltus
Henry Fisher
William Fletcher
Joseph E. Foley
Marvin Frey
Peter Georgiadis
Brian M. Green
Rudolf Hamar
Robert R. Hegland
Clifford O. Herrick
Lee H. Hill, Jr.
Rollin C. Huggins, Jr.
Peter C. Jeannopoulos
Clyde Jennings
A. E. Buzz Jehle
Jack Jonza
Henry Karen
Stanford M. Katz
Dr. James Kerr
Charles Kezbers
Katherine Kirk
Stanley Kronenberg
William Langs
Ken Lawrence
Pedro Llach
William Thomas Lockard
Stanley J. Luft
Walter J. Mader
Jason H. Manchester
Clyde R. Maxwell
Menachim Mayo
P. J. McGowan
Timothy M. McRee
Dr. Hector Mena
Robert Meyersburg
Jack Molesworth
Gary Morris
Peter Mosiondz, Jr.
Bruce M. Moyer
Richard H. Muller
James Natale
Gregg Nelson
Victor Ostolaza
Souren Panirian
Sheldon Paris
Bob Penn
Donald J. Peterson
Vernon Pickering
Stanley M. Piller
Gilbert N. Plass
Peter A. Robertson
Jon Rose
Frans H. A. Rummens
Richard H. Salz
Byron Sandfield
Jacques C. Schiff, Jr.
Richard Schwartz
F. Burton Sellers
Michael Shamilzadeh
William E. Shelton
Dr. Hubert Skinner
Roger D. Skinner
Sherwood Springer
Scott Trepel
Corey K. Tsang
A. John Ultee
George P. Wagner
Jerome S. Wagshal
Richard A. Washburn
Irwin Weinberg
Larry S. Weiss
William R. Weiss, Jr.
Hans A. Westphal
John M. Wilson
Don Wright
Nathan Zankel

American Air Mail Society
John J. Smith
102 Arbor Road
Cinnaminson, NJ 08077

American Philatelic Society
PO Box 8000
State College, PA 16803

American Revenue Association
Bruce Miller
Suite 332, 701 South First Ave.
Arcadia, CA 91006

Booklet Collectors Club
James Natale
PO Box 2461
Cinnaminson, NJ 08077-5461

Bureau Issues Association
George V.H. Godin
PO Box 23707
Belleville, IL 62223

Carriers and Locals Society
William T. Crowe
PO Box 2090
Danbury, CT 06813

Confederate Stamp Alliance
Richard L. Calhoun
1749 W. Golf Rd., Suite 366
Mt. Prospect, IL 60056

Errors, Freaks, and Oddities Collectors Club
Jim McDevitt
1903 Village Road West
Norwood, MA 02062-2516

Fine and Performing Arts Philatelists
Dorothy E. Weihrauch
Nine Island Ave., Apt. 906
Miami Beach, FL 33139

Junior Philatelists of America
Sally Horn
PO Box 557
Boalsburg, PA 16827

Masonic Stamp Club of New York
Bernard Nathan
22 East 35th Street
New York, NY 10016

Official Mail Study Group
Sherman L. Pompey
725 S.E. Division
Albany, OR 97321

Plate Number Coil Collectors Club
Rob Washburn
PO Box 840
Skowhegan, ME 04976

Precancel Stamp Society
1750 Skippack Pk. #1603
Center Square, PA 19422

Royal Philatelic Society
Francis Kiddle
41 Devonshire Place
London, U.K. W1N 1PE

Royal Philatelic Society of Canada
PO Box 100
First Canadian Place
Toronto ONT, CANADA M6A 1T6

Scouts on Stamps Society International
Kenneth A. Shuker
20 Cedar Lane
Cornwall, NY 12518

United Postal Stationery Society
Joann Thomas
PO Box 48
Redlands, CA 92373

US Philatelic Classics Society
Patricia S. Walker
Briarwood
Lisbon, MD 21765

US Possessions Philatelic Society
Kenneth M. Koller
217 Tyler Ave.
Cuyahoga Falls, OH 44221

Austria Philatelic Society of New York
Henry W. Houser
1206 Racebrook Rd.
Woodbridge, CT 06525

American Belgian Philatelic Society
Kenneth L. Costilow
621 Virginius Dr.
Virginia Beach, VA 23452

Belize Philatelic Study Circle
Charles R. Gambill
730 Collingswood
Corpus Christi, TX 78412

Bermuda Collectors Society
Thomas J. McMahon
86 Nash Road
Purdys, NY 10578

Brazil Philatelic Association
Kurt Ottenheimer
464 West Walnut St.
Long Beach, NY 11561

British Caribbean Philatelic Study Group
Gale J. Raymond
PO Box 35695
Houston, TX 77235

British North America Philatelic Society
Jerome C. Jarnick
108 Duncan Drive
Troy, MI 48098

Canal Zone Study Group
Richard H. Salz
60 27th Ave.
San Francisco, CA 94121

Club of Channel Islands Collectors
Matthew Trachinsky
PO Box 579
Gracie Station
New York, NY 10028

China Stamp Society
Paul H. Gault
140 West 18th Ave.
Columbus, OH 43210

COPAPHIL (Colombia & Panama)
David Leeds
PO Box 2245
El Cajon, CA 92021

Society of Costa Rica Collectors
Dr. Hector Mena
PO Box 14831
Baton Rouge, LA 70808

Croatian Philatelic Society
Eck Spahich
1512 Lancelot Rd.
Borger, TX 79007

Cuban Philatelic Society of America
PO Box 450207
Miami, FL 33245-0207

Society for Czechoslovak Philately
Jane Sterba
6624 Windsor Ave.
Berwyn, IL 60402

Estonian Philatelic Society
Rudolf Hamar
31 Addison Terrace
Old Tappan, NJ 07675

Ethiopian Philatelic Society
Huguette Gagnon
PO Box 8110-45
Blaine, WA 98230

Falkland Islands Philatelic Study Group
James Driscoll
PO Box 172
South Dennis, NJ 08245

France & Colonies Philatelic Society
Stanley J. Luft
16291 West 56th Place
Golden, CO 80403

Germany Philatelic Society
PO Box 779
Arnold, MD 21012

GDR Study Group of German Philatelic Society
Ken Lawrence
1227 First Avenue
PO Box 3568
Jackson, MS 39203

Great Britain Collectors Club
Frank Koch
PO Box 309
Batavia, OH 45301

Hellenic Philatelic Society of America (Greece and related areas)
Dr. Nicholas Asimakopulos
541 Cedar Hill Ave.
Wyckoff, NJ 07481

International Society of Guatemala Collectors
Mrs. Mae Vignola
105 22nd Ave.
San Francisco, CA 94116

Haiti Philatelic Society
Dwight Bishop
16434 Shamhart Dr.
Granada Hills, CA 91344

Hong Kong Stamp Society
Corey K. Tsang
PO Box 206
Glenside, PA 19038

Hungary Philatelic Society
Thomas Phillips
PO Box 1162
Fairfield, CT 06432

India Study Circle
John Warren
PO Box 70775
Washington, DC 20024

Society of Indochina Philatelists
Paul Blake
1466 Hamilton Way
San Jose, CA 95125

Iran Philatelic Circle
A. John Ultee
816 Gwynne Ave.
Waynesboro, VA 22980

Eire Philatelic Association (Ireland)
Michael J. Conway
74 Woodside Circle
Fairfield, CT 06430

Society of Israel Philatelists
Howard D. Chapman
28650 Settlers Lane
Pepper Pike, OH 44124

Italy and Colonies Study Circle
David F. Emery
PO Box 86
Philipsburg, NJ 08865

International Society for Japanese Philately
Kenneth Kamholz
PO Box 1283
Haddonfield, NJ 08033

Korea Stamp Society
Harold L. Klein
PO Box 750
Lebanon, PA 17042

Latin American Philatelic Society
Piet Steen
PO Box 820
Hinton, AB, CANADA T0E 1B0

Liberian Philatelic Society
William Thomas Lockard
PO Box 267
Wellston, OH 45692

Plebiscite-Memel-Saar Study Group
Clay Wallace
158 Arapahoe Circle
San Ramon, CA 94583

Mexico-Elmhurst Philatelic Society International
William E. Shelton
PO Box 39838
San Antonio, TX 78218

Nepal & Tibet Philatelic Study Group
Roger D. Skinner
1020 Covington Road
Los Altos, CA 94022

American Society of Netherlands Philately
Frans H.A. Rummens
94 Munroe Pl.
Regina, SK, CANADA S4S 4P7

Nicaragua Study Group
Clyde R. Maxwell
Airport Plaza
2041 Business Center Drive, Suite 101
Irvine, CA 92715

Society of Australasian Specialists/Oceania
Henry Bateman
PO Box 4862
Monroe, LA 71211

Orange Free State Study Circle
Alan MacGregor
PO Box 330
Croydon, Surrey, U.K. CR9 2ZF

International Philippine Philatelic Society
Eugene A. Garrett
446 Stratford Ave.
Elmhurst, IL 60126-4123

Pitcairn Islands Study Group
Nelson A.L. Weller
2940 Wesleyan Lane
Winston-Salem, NC 27106

Polonus Philatelic Society (Poland)
864 N. Ashland Ave.
Chicago, IL 60622

International Society for Portuguese Philately
Nancy M. Gaylord
1116 Marineway West
North Palm Beach, FL 33408

Rhodesian Study Circle
William R. Wallace
PO Box 16381
San Francisco, CA 94116

Rossica Society of Russian Philately
Norman Epstein
33 Crooke Ave.
Brooklyn, NY 11226

Canadian Society of Russian Philately
Andrew Cronin
PO Box 5722, Station A
Toronto, ON, CANADA M5W 1P2

Ryukyu Philatelic Specialist Society
Carmine J. Di Vincenzo
PO Box 381
Clayton, CA 94517-0381

St. Helena, Ascension & Tristan Society
R.V. Skavaril
222 East Torrance Road
Columbus, OH 43214

Associated Collectors of El Salvador
Jeff Brasor
7365 NW 68th Way
Pompano Beach, FL 33067-3918

Sarawak Specialists' Society
C. Jackson Selsor
Apt. 402, 2300 Front St.
San Diego, CA 92101

Arabian Philatelic Society
ARAMCO Box 1929
Dhahran, SAUDI ARABIA 31311

Scandinavia Collectors Club
Jared H. Richter
PO Box 302
Lawrenceville, GA 30246-0302

Philatelic Society for Greater South Africa
William C. Brooks VI
PO Box 2698
San Bernardino, CA 92406-2698

Spanish Philatelic Society
Bob Penn
PO Box 3804
Gettysburg, PA 17325

American Helvetia Philatelic Society (Switzerland)
E. Ben Henson
102 Adams St.
Burlington, VT 05401

Society for Thai Philately
H.R. Blakeney
PO Box 25644
Oklahoma City, OK 73125

Tonga/Tin Can Mail Study Circle
Paul Stanton
10016 Wolfriver Dr.
Plymouth, MI 48170

Turkey and Ottoman Philatelic Society
Gary F. Paiste
4249 Berritt St.
Fairfax, VA 22030

Tuvalu & Kiribati Philatelic Society
Michael Butkiss
PO Box 1209
Temple Hills, MD 20757

Ukrainian Philatelic & Numismatic Society
Val Zabijaka
PO Box 3711
Silver Spring, MD 20918

United Nations Philatelists
Helen Benedict
408 S. Orange Grove Blvd.
Pasadena, CA 91105

Vatican Philatelic Society
Louis Padavan
PO Box 127
Remsenburg, NY 11960

Yugoslavia Study Group
Michael Lenard
1514 North 3rd Ave.
Wausau, WI 54401 ❑

Catalogue Information

Catalogue Value

The Scott Catalogue value is a retail price, what you could expect to pay for the stamp in a grade of Fine-Very Fine. The value listed is a reference which reflects recent actual dealer selling prices.

Dealer retail price lists, public auction results, published prices in advertising, and individual solicitation of retail prices from dealers, collectors, and specialty organizations have been used in establishing the values found in this catalogue.

Use this catalogue as a guide in your own buying and selling. The actual price you pay for a stamp may be higher or lower than the catalogue value because of one or more of the following: the amount of personal service a dealer offers, increased interest in the country or topic represented by the stamp or set, whether an item is a "loss leader," part of a special sale, or otherwise is being sold for a short period of time at a lower price, or if at a public auction you are able to obtain an item inexpensively because of little interest in the item at that time.

For unused stamps, more recent issues are valued as never-hinged, with the beginning point determined on a country-by-country basis. Notes to show the beginning points are prominently noted in the text.

Grade

A stamp's grade and condition are crucial to its value. Values quoted in this catalogue are for stamps graded at Fine-Very Fine and with no faults. Exceptions are noted in the text. The accompanying illustrations show an example of a Fine-Very Fine grade between the grades immediately below and above it: Fine and Very Fine.

FINE stamps have the design noticeably off-center on two sides. Imperforate stamps may have small margins and earlier issues may show the design touching one edge of the stamp. Used stamps may have heavier than usual cancellations.

FINE-VERY FINE stamps may be somewhat off-center on one side, or only slightly off-center on two sides. Imperforate stamps will have two margins at least normal size and the design will not touch the edge. *Early issues of a country may be printed in such a way that the design naturally is very close to the edges.* Used stamps will not have a cancellation that detracts from the design. This is the grade used to establish Scott Catalogue values.

VERY FINE stamps may be slightly off-center on one side, with the design well clear of the edge. Imperforate stamps will have three margins at least normal size. Used stamps will have light or otherwise neat cancellations.

Condition

The above definitions describe *grade,* which is centering and (for used stamps) cancellation. *Condition* refers to the soundness of the stamp, i.e., faults, repairs, and other factors influencing price.

Copies of a stamp which are of a lesser grade and/or condition trade at lower prices. Those of exceptional quality often command higher prices.

Factors that can increase the value of a stamp include exceptionally wide margins, particularly fresh color, and the presence of selvage.

Factors other than faults that decrease the value of a stamp include loss of gum or regumming, hinge remnant, foreign object adhering to gum, natural inclusion, or a straight edge.

Faults include a missing piece, tear, clipped perforation, pin or other hole, surface scuff, thin spot, crease, toning, oxidation or other form of color changeling, short or pulled perforation, stains or such man-made changes as reperforation or the chemical removal or lightening of a cancellation.

Scott Publishing Co. recognizes that there is no formal, enforced grading scheme for postage stamps, and that the final price you pay for a stamp or obtain for a stamp you are selling will be determined by individual agreement at the time of the transaction.

Catalogue Listing Policy

It is the intent of Scott Publishing to list all postage stamps of the world in the *Scott Standard Postage Stamp Catalogue.* The only strict criteria for listing is that stamps be decreed legal for postage by the issuing country. Whether the primary intent of issuing a given stamp or set was for sale to postal patrons or to stamp collectors is not part of our listing criteria. Scott's role is to provide comprehensive stamp information. It is up to each stamp collector to choose which items to include in a collection.

It is Scott's objective to seek reasons why a stamp should be listed, rather than why it should not. Nevertheless, there are certain types of items which will not be listed:

1. Unissued items, even if they ''accidentally'' are distributed to the philatelic or even postal market. If such items later are officially issued by the country, they will be listed. Unissued items consist of those which have been printed and then held from sale for reasons such as change in government, error found on stamp, or even something objectionable about a stamp subject or design.
2. Stamps ''issued'' by non-existent entities or fantasy countries, such as Nagaland, Occusi-Ambeno, South Moluccas and others.
3. Semi-official or unofficial items not required for postage. Examples are items issued by private agencies for their own express services. When such items are required or valid as prepayment of postage, they will be listed.
4. Local stamps issued for local use only. Stamps issued by government specifically for ''domestic'' use, such as Haiti Scott 219-228 or the U.S. non-denominated stamps, are not considered to be locals.
5. Items not valid for postal use. For example, a few countries have issued souvenir sheets not valid for postage.
6. Intentional varieties, such as imperforate stamps issued in very small quantities with the same design as perforate stamps.
7. Items distributed by the issuing government only to a limited group, such as a stamp club or a single stamp dealer, and then brought to market at inflated prices. These items normally will be included in a footnote.

The fact that a stamp has been used successfully as postage, even on international mail, is not sufficient to prove that it was legitimately issued. Numerous examples of ''stamps'' from non-existent countries are known to have been used to post letters that have passed through the international mail.

Those items that will still not appear in the catalogue represent a very small percentage, perhaps as little as two percent, of the more than 400,000 stamps currently listed in the Scott catalogue system, or the 8,000 or so new issues that are listed each year.

There are certain items that are subject to interpretation. When a stamp falls outside our specifications, it will be listed and a cautionary footnote added.

A series of factors are considered in our approach to how a stamp is listed. Following is a list of various factors, presented here primarily to share with catalogue users the complexity of the listing process.

Additional printings — ''additional printings'' of a previously issued stamp may range from something that is totally different to cases where it is virtually impossible to differentiate it from the original. We will assign at least a minor number (a small-letter suffix) if there is a distinct change in stamp color, the design is noticeably redrawn, or the perforation measurement is different. A major number (numeral or numeral and capital-letter combination) will be assigned if we believe the ''additional printing'' is sufficiently different from the original that it constitutes a whole new issue.

Commemoratives — where practical, or where advance information is available, like commemoratives will be placed in a set, for example, the U.S. Credo issue of 1960-61 and the Constitution Bicentennial series of 1989-90. Japan and Korea issue such material on a regular basis, with an announced or, at least, predictable number of stamps known in advance.

Definitive sets — blocks of numbers are reserved for definitive sets, based on previous experience with that country. If more stamps are issued than expected, but it looks as if only a few more stamps will be issued for that series, they will be inserted into the original set with a capital-letter suffix, such as U.S. Scott 1059A. If it appears that many more stamps are yet to be issued in the set, a new block of numbers will be reserved, and the original grouping closed off, as in the case of the U.S. Transportation coil series and the Great Americans series.

New country — the important consideration is correct placement of the listings within the catalogue, either as a separate country listing or as a ''state'' following the ''mother country'' listing, for example, Aland Islands following Finland. Membership in the Univeral Postal Union is not a consideration for listing status or order of placement in the Catalogue.

''No release date'' items — very complete information is readily available from certain countries for new issues before the stamps are issued; in some cases no information is available; while others fall somewhere in between. Often countries will provide denominations of upcoming stamps or souvenir sheets not released at the time of issue. Sometimes philatelic agencies, private firms employed by postal administrations, will add these later-issued items to sets months or years after the formal release date. If the items are officially issued by the country, the later material will be inserted into the proper set.

In order to understand how new issues come to market, it is important to know how philatelic agents operate. A philatelic agent is employed by a postal administration to perform duties ranging from complete development of all new issues including concept, design, printing and philatelic distribution to simply publicizing and selling new issues. Many countries do not have agents, or use them only for special projects.

Overprints — color of an overprint is always noted if it is other than black. Where more than one color ink is used on overprints of a set, the color used for a particular stamp is noted in the description line of that stamp.

Early overprint and surcharge illustrations were altered to prevent their use for counterfeiting.

Se-tenants — including pairs and blocks, will be listed in the format most commonly collected. If the stamps are collected as a unit, the major number will be assigned to the multiple and the minor numbers to the individual increments. When the items are usually collected as singles, then each individual stamp is given a major number and the entire se-tenant item is given a minor number of the last item in sequence. The manner in which an item is listed generally depends on the stamp's usage in the country of issue. Where stamps are used widely for postal purposes, even if se-tenant issues will be collected as a unit, each stamp will be given a major number, such as the stamps of the United States, Canada, Germany, and Great Britain.

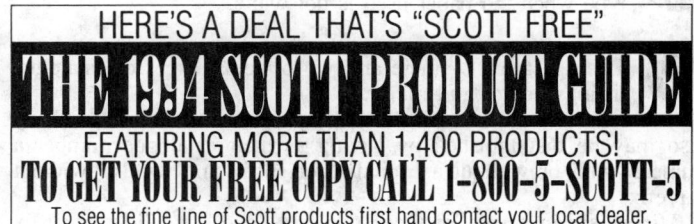

Understanding the Listings

On the following page is an enlarged ''typical'' listing from this catalogue. Following are detailed explanations of each of the high-lighted parts of the listing.

1 **Scott number** — Stamp collectors use Scott numbers to identify specific stamps when buying, selling, or trading stamps, and for ease in organizing their collections. Each stamp issued by a country has a unique number. Therefore, Germany Scott 99 can only refer to a single stamp. Although the Scott Catalogue usually lists stamps in chronological order by date of issue, when a country issues a set of stamps over a period of time the stamps within that set are kept together without regard of date of issue. This follows the normal collecting approach of keeping stamps in their natural sets.

When a country is known to be issuing a set of stamps over a period of time, a group of consecutive catalogue numbers is reserved for the stamps in that set, as issued. If that group of numbers proves to be too few, capital-letter suffixes are added to numbers to create enough catalogue numbers to cover all items in the set. Scott uses a suffix letter, e.g., ''A,'' ''b,'' etc., only once. If there is a Scott 16A in a set, there will not be a Scott 16a also. Suffix letters are not cumulative. A minor variety of Scott 16A would be Scott 16b, not Scott 16Ab. Any exceptions, such as Great Britain Scott 358cp, are clearly shown.

There are times when the block of numbers is too large for the set, leaving some numbers unused. Such gaps in the sequence also occur when the editors move an item elsewhere in the catalogue or removed from the listings entirely. Scott does not attempt to account for every possible number, but rather it does attempt to assure that each stamp is assigned its own number.

Scott numbers designating regular postage normally are only numerals. Scott numbers for other types of stamps, i.e., air post, semi-postal, and so on, will have a prefix of either a capital letter or a combination of numerals and capital letters.

2 **Illustration number** — used to identify each illustration. For most sets, the lowest face-value stamp is shown. It then serves as an example of the basic design approach for the set. Where more than one stamp in a set uses the same illustration number but has no different design, that number needs to be used with the design paragraph or description line (noted below) to be certain of the exact design on each stamp within the set. Where there are both vertical and horizontal designs in a set, a single illustration may be used, with the exceptions noted in the design paragraph or description line. When an illustration is followed by a lower-case letter in parentheses, such as ''A2(b),'' the trailing letter indicates which overprint illustration applies from those shown.

Illustrations normally are 75 percent of the original size of the stamp. An effort has been made to note all illustrations not at that percentage. Overprints are shown at 100 percent of the original, unless otherwise noted. In some cases, the illustration will be placed above the set, between listings, or omitted completely. Overprint and surcharge illustrations are not placed in this catalogue for purposes of expertizing stamps.

3 **Paper color** — The color of the paper is noted in italic type when the paper used is not white.

4 **Listing styles** — there are two principal types of catalogue listings: major and minor.

Majors normally are in a larger type style than minor listings. They also may be distinguished by having as their catalogue number a numeral with or without a capital-letter suffix and with or without a prefix.

Minors are in a smaller type style and have a small-letter suffix (or, only have the small letter itself shown if the listing is immediately beneath its major listing). These listings show a variety of the ''normal,'' or major item. Examples include color variation or a different watermark used for that stamp only.

Examples of major numbers are 16, 28A, B97, C13A, 10N5, and 10N6A. Examples of minor numbers are 16a and C13b.

5 **Basic information on stamp or set** — introducing each stamp issue, this section normally includes the date of issue, method of printing, perforation, watermark, and sometimes some additional information. *New information on method of printing, watermark or perforation measurement will appear when that information changes in the sequential order of the listings.* Stamps created by overprinting or surcharging previous stamps are assumed to have the same perforation, watermark and printing method as the original. Dates of issue are as precise as Scott is able to confirm and often reflect the dates on First Day Covers, not the actual date of release.

6 **Denomination** — normally the face value of the stamp, i.e., the cost of the stamp at the post office at the time of issue. When the denomination is shown in parentheses, it does not appear on the stamp.

7 **Color or other description** — this line provides information to solidify identification of the stamp. In many cases, a description of the stamp design appears in this space instead of the colors.

8 **Year of issue** — in stamp sets issued over more than one year, the number in parentheses is the year that stamp appeared. Stamps without a date appeared during the first year of the span. Dates are not always given for minor varieties.

9 **Value unused** and **Value used** — the catalogue values are based on stamps which are in a grade of Fine-Very Fine unless stated otherwise. Unused values refer to items which have not seen postal or other duty for which they were intended. For pre-1900 issue, unused stamps must have at least most of their original gum; for later issues full original gum is expected. It is probably that they will show evidence of hinging if issued before the never-hinged breakpoint. Stamps issued without gum are noted. Modern issues with PVA gum may appear ungummed. Unused values are for never-hinged stamps beginning at the point immediately following a prominent notice in the actual listing. The same information also appears at the beginning of the country's information. See the section ''Catalogue Values'' for an explanation of the meaning of these values. Information about catalogue values shown in italics may be found in the section ''Understanding Valuing Notations.''

10 **Changes in basic set information** — bold type is used to show any change in the basic data on within a set of stamps, i.e., perforation from one stamp to the next or a different paper or printing method or watermark.

11 **Total value of set** — the total value of sets of five or more stamps, issued after 1900, are shown. The line also notes the range of Scott numbers and total number of stamps included in the total. *Set value* is the term used to indicate the value of a set when it is less than the total of the individual stamps.

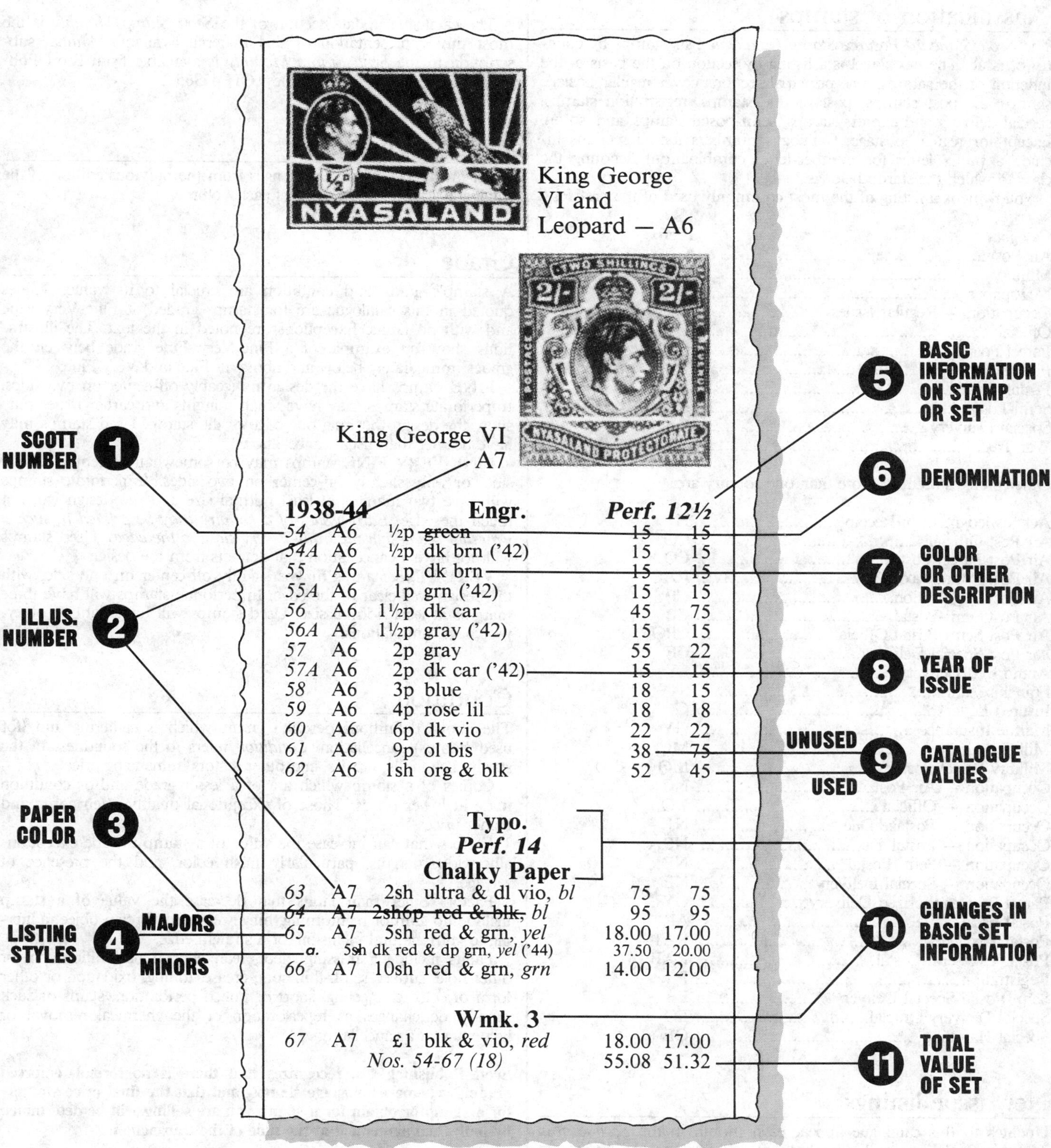

1938-44 Engr. *Perf. 12½*

54	A6	½p green	15	15
54A	A6	½p dk brn ('42)	15	15
55	A6	1p dk brn	15	15
55A	A6	1p grn ('42)	15	15
56	A6	1½p dk car	45	75
56A	A6	1½p gray ('42)	15	15
57	A6	2p gray	55	22
57A	A6	2p dk car ('42)	15	15
58	A6	3p blue	18	15
59	A6	4p rose lil	18	18
60	A6	6p dk vio	22	22
61	A6	9p ol bis	38	75
62	A6	1sh org & blk	52	45

Typo.
Perf. 14
Chalky Paper

63	A7	2sh ultra & dl vio, *bl*	75	75
64	A7	2sh6p red & blk, *bl*	95	95
65	A7	5sh red & grn, *yel*	18.00	17.00
a.		5sh dk red & dp grn, *yel* ('44)	37.50	20.00
66	A7	10sh red & grn, *grn*	14.00	12.00

Wmk. 3

67	A7	£1 blk & vio, *red*	18.00	17.00
		Nos. 54-67 (18)	55.08	51.32

Special Notices

Classification of stamps

The *Scott Standard Postage Stamp Catalogue* lists stamps by country of issue. The next level is a listing by section on the basis of the function of the stamps. The principal sections cover regular postage stamps; air post stamps; postage due stamps, registration stamps, special delivery and express stamps, semi-postal stamps, and, so on. Except for regular postage, Catalogue numbers for all sections include a prefix letter (or number-letter combination) denoting the class to which the stamp belongs.

Following is a listing of the most commonly used of the prefixes.

Category	**Prefix**
Air Post	C
Military	M
Newspaper	P
Occupation — Regular Issues	N
Official	O
Parcel Post	Q
Postage Due	J
Postal Tax	RA
Semi-Postal	B
Special Delivery	E
War Tax	MR

Other prefixes used by more than one country are:

Acknowledgment of Receipt	H
Air Post Official	CO
Air Post Parcel Post	CQ
Air Post Postal Tax	RAC
Air Post Registration	CF
Air Post Semi-Postal	CB
Air Post Semi-Postal Official	CBO
Air Post Special Delivery	CE
Authorized Delivery	EY
Franchise	S
Insured Letter	G
Marine Insurance	GY
Military Air Post	MC
Military Parcel Post	MQ
Occupation — Air Post	NC
Occupation — Official	NO
Occupation — Postage Due	NJ
Occupation — Postal Tax	NRA
Occupation — Semi-Postal	NB
Occupation — Special Delivery	NE
Parcel Post Authorized Delivery	QY
Postal-fiscal	AR
Postal Tax Due	RAJ
Postal Tax Semi-Postal	RAB
Registration	F
Semi-Postal Special Delivery	EB
Special Delivery Official	EO
Special Handling	QE

New issue listings

Updates to this catalogue appear each month in the *Scott Stamp Monthly.* Included in this update are additions to the listings of countries found in *Scott Standard Postage Stamp Catalogue* and the *Specialized Catalogue of United States Stamps,* new issues of countries not listed in the catalogues, and corrections and updates to current editions of this catalogue.

From time to time there will be changes in the listings from the *Scott Stamp Monthly* to the next edition of the catalogue, as additional information becomes available.

The catalogue update section of the *Scott Stamp Monthly* is the most timely presentation of this material available. Annual subscription to the *Scott Stamp Monthly* is available from Scott Publishing Co., P.O. Box 828, Sidney, OH 45365.

Number changes

A list of catalogue number changes from the previous edition of the catalogue appears at the back of each volume.

Grade

A stamp's grade and condition are crucial to its value. Values quoted in this catalogue are for stamps graded at Fine-Very Fine and with no faults. Exceptions are noted in the text. The illustrations show an example of a Fine-Very Fine grade between the grades immediately below and above it: Fine and Very Fine.

FINE stamps have the design noticeably off-center on two sides. Imperforate stamps may have small margins and earlier issues may show the design touching one edge of the stamp. Used stamps may have heavier than usual cancellations.

FINE-VERY FINE stamps may be somewhat off-center on one side, or only slightly off-center on two sides. Imperforate stamps will have two margins at least normal size and the design will not touch the edge. *Early issues of a country may be printed in such a way that the design naturally is very close to the edges.* Used stamps will not have a cancellation that detracts from the design.

VERY FINE stamps maybe slightly off-center on one side, with the design well clear of the edge. Imperforate stamps will have three margins at least normal size. Used stamps will have light or otherwise neat cancellations.

Condition

The above definitions describe *grade,* which is centering and (for used stamps) cancellation. *Condition* refers to the soundness of the stamp, i.e., faults, repairs, and other factors influencing price.

Copies of a stamp which are of a lesser grade and/or condition trade at lower prices. Those of exceptional quality often command higher prices.

Factors that can increase the value of a stamp include exceptionally wide margins, particularly fresh color, and the presence of selvage.

Factors other than faults that decrease the value of a stamp include no gum or regumming, hinge remnant, foreign object adhering to gum, natural inclusion, or a straight edge.

Faults include a missing piece, tear, clipped perforation, pin or other hole, surface scuff, thin spot, crease, toning, oxidation or other form of color changeling, short or pulled perforation, stains or such man-made changes as reperforation or the chemical removal or lightening of a cancellation.

Scott Publishing Co. recognizes that there is no formal, enforced grading scheme for postage stamps, and that the final price you pay for a stamp or obtain for a stamp you are selling will be determined by individual agreement at the time of the transaction.

Catalogue Value

The Scott Catalogue value is a retail price, what you could expect to pay for the stamp in a grade of Fine-Very Fine. The value listed is a reference which reflects recent actual dealer selling prices.

Dealer retail price lists, public auction results, published prices in advertising, and individual solicitation of retail prices from dealers, collectors, and specialty organizations have been used in establishing the values found in this catalogue.

Use this catalogue as a guide in your own buying and selling. The actual price you pay for a stamp may be higher or lower than the catalogue value because of one or more of the following: the amount of personal service a dealer offers, increased interest in the country or topic represented by the stamp or set, whether an item is a "loss leader," part of a special sale, or otherwise is being sold for a short period of time at a lower price, or if at a public auction you are able to obtain an item inexpensively because of little interest in the item at that time.

For unused stamps, more recent issues are valued as never-hinged, with the beginning point determined on a country-by-country basis. Notes in the text prominently show the beginning points of these designations.

As a point of philatelic-economic fact, the lower the value shown for an item in this catalogue, the greater the percentage of that value which is attributed to dealer mark-up and profit margin. Thus, a packet of 1,000 different items — each of which has a catalogue value of 15 cents — normally sells for considerably less than 150 dollars!

Persons wishing to establish the specific value of a stamp or other philatelic item may wish to consult with recognized stamp experts (collectors or dealers) and review current information or recent developments which would affect stamp prices.

Scott Publishing Co. assumes no obligation to revise the values during the distribution period of this catalogue or to advise users of other facts, such as stamp availability, political and economic conditions, or collecting preferences, any of which may have an immediate positive or negative impact on values.

Understanding valuing notations

The *absence of a value* does not necessarily suggest that a stamp is scarce or rare. In the U.S. listings, a dash in the value column means that the stamp is known in a stated form or variety, but information is lacking or insufficient for purposes of establishing a usable catalogue value.

Stamp values in *italics* generally refer to items which are difficult to value accurately. For expensive items, i.e., value at $1,000 or more, a value in italics represents an item which trades very seldom, such as a unique item. For inexpensive items, a value in italics represents a warning. One example is a "blocked" issue where the issuing postal administration controlled one stamp in a set in an attempt to make the whole set more valuable. Another example is a single item with a very low face value which sells in the marketplace, at the time of issue, at an extreme multiple of face value. Some countries have released back issues of stamps in a canceled-to-order form, sometimes covering at much as 10 years.

The Scott Catalogue values for used stamps reflect canceled-to-order material when such are found to predominate in the marketplace for the issue involved. Frequently notes appear in the stamp listings to specify items which are valued as canceled-to-order or if there is a premium for postally used examples.

Another example of a warning to collectors is a stamp that used has a value considerably higher than the unused version. Here, the collector is cautioned to be certain the used version has a readable, contemporary cancellation. The type of cancellation on a stamp can be an important factor in determining its sale price. Catalogue values do not apply to fiscal or telegraph cancels, unless otherwise noted.

The *minimum catalogue value* of a stamp is 15 cents, to cover a dealer's costs and then preparing it for resale. As noted, the sum of these values does not properly represent the "value" of sets with a number of minimum-value stamps, or packets of stamps.

Values in the "unused" column are for stamps that have been hinged, unless there is a specific note in a listing after which unused stamps are valued as never-hinged. A similar note will appear at the beginning of the country's listings, noting exactly where the dividing point between hinged and never-hinged is for each section of the listings. Where a value for a used stamp is considerably higher than for the unused stamp, the value applies to a stamp showing a distinct contemporary postmark of origin.

Many countries sell canceled-to-order stamps at a marked reduction of face value. Countries which sell or have sold canceled-to-order stamps at *full* face value include Australia, Netherlands, France, and Switzerland. It may be almost impossible to identify such stamps, if the gum has been removed, because official government canceling devices are used. Postally used copies on cover, of these items, are usually worth more than the canceled-to-order stamps with original gum.

Abbreviations

Scott Publishing Co. uses a consistent set of abbreviations throughout this catalogue to conserve space while still providing necessary information. The first block shown here refers to color names only:

COLOR ABBREVIATIONS

amb....... amber
anil....... aniline
ap....... apple
aqua....... aquamarine
az....... azure
bis....... bister
bl....... blue
bld....... blood
blk....... black
bril....... brilliant
brn....... brown
brnsh....... brownish
brnz....... bronze
brt....... bright
brnt....... burnt
car....... carmine
cer....... cerise
chlky....... chalky
cham....... chamois
chnt....... chestnut
choc....... chocolate
chr....... chrome
cit....... citron
cl....... claret
cob....... cobalt
cop....... copper
crim....... crimson
cr....... cream
dk....... dark
dl....... dull
dp....... deep
db....... drab
emer....... emerald
gldn....... golden
grysh....... grayish
grn....... green
grnsh....... greenish
hel....... heliotrope
hn....... henna
ind....... indigo
int....... intense
lav....... lavender
lem....... lemon
lil....... lilac
lt....... light
mag....... magenta
man....... manila
mar....... maroon
mv....... mauve
multi....... multicolored
mlky....... milky
myr....... myrtle
ol....... olive
olvn....... olivine
org....... orange
pck....... peacock
pnksh....... pinkish
Prus....... Prussian
pur....... purple
redsh....... reddish
res....... reseda
ros....... rosine
ryl....... royal
sal....... salmon
saph....... sapphire
scar....... scarlet
sep....... sepia
sien....... sienna
sil....... silver
sl....... slate
stl....... steel
turq....... turquoise
ultra....... ultramarine
ven....... Venetian
ver....... vermilion
vio....... violet
yel....... yellow
yelsh....... yellowish

When no color is given for an overprint or surcharge, black is the color used. Abbreviations for colors used for overprints and surcharges are: "(B)" or "(Blk)," black; "(Bl)," blue; "(R)," red; "(G)," green; etc.

Additional abbreviations in this catalogue are shown below:

Adm. .... Administration
AFL .... American Federation of Labor
Anniv. .... Anniversary
APU .... Arab Postal Union
APS .... American Philatelic Society
ASEAN .... Association of South East Asian Nations
ASPCA .... American Society for the Prevention of Cruelty to Animals
Assoc. .... Association
ASSR .... Autonomous Soviet Socialist Republic

b. .... Born
BEP .... Bureau of Engraving and Printing
Bicent. .... Bicentennial
Bklt. .... Booklet
Brit. .... British
btwn. .... Between
Bur. .... Bureau

c. or ca. .... Circa
CAR .... Central African Republic
Cat. .... Catalogue
CCTA. .... Commission for Technical Cooperation in Africa South of the Sahara
Cent. .... Centennial, century, centenary
CEPT .... Conference Europeenne des Administrations des Postes et des Telecommunications
CIO .... Congress of Industrial Organizations
Conf. .... Conference
Cong. .... Congress
Cpl. .... Corporal
CTO .... Canceled to order

d. .... Died
Dbl. .... Double
DDR .... German Democratic Republic (East Germany)

ECU .... European currency unit
EEC .... European Economic Community
EKU .... Earliest known use
Engr. .... Engraved
Exhib. .... Exhibition
Expo. .... Exposition

FAO .... Food and Agricultural Organization of the United Nations
Fed. .... Federation
FIP .... Federation International de Philatelie

GB .... Great Britain
Gen. .... General
GPO .... General post office

Horiz. .... Horizontal

ICAO .... International Civil Aviation Organization
ICY .... International Cooperation Year
IEY .... International Education Year
ILO .... International Labor Organization
Imperf. .... Imperforate
Impt. .... Imprint

Intl. .... International
Invtd. .... Inverted
INTELSAT... International Telecommunications Satellite Consortium
IQSY .... International Quiet Sun Year
ITU .... International Telecommunications Union
ITY .... International Tourism Year
IWY .... International Women's Year
IYC .... International Year of the Child
IYD .... International Year of the Disabled
IYP .... International Year of Peace
IYSH .... International Year of Shelter for the Homeless
IYY .... International Youth Year

L .... Left
Lieut., lt. .... Lieutenant
Litho. .... Lithographed
LL .... Lower left
LR .... Lower right

mm .... Millimeter
Ms. .... Manuscript

NASA .... National Aeronautics and Space Administration
Natl. .... National
NATO .... North Atlantic Treaty Organization
No. .... Number
NY .... New York
NYC .... New York City

OAU .... Organization of African Unity
OPEC .... Organization of Petroleum Exporting Countries
Ovpt. .... Overprint
Ovptd. .... Overprinted

P .... Plate number
Perf. .... Perforated, perforation
Phil. .... Philatelic
Photo. .... Photogravure
PO .... Post office
Pr. .... Pair
P.R. .... Puerto Rico
PRC .... People's Republic of China (Mainland China)
Prec. .... Precancel, precanceled
Pres. .... President
PTT .... Post, Telephone and Telegraph
PUAS .... Postal Union of the Americas and Spain
PUASP .... Postal Union of the Americas, Spain and Portugal

Rio .... Rio de Janeiro
ROC .... Republic of China (Taiwan)

SEATO .... South East Asia Treaty Organization
Sgt. .... Sergeant
Soc. .... Society
Souv. .... Souvenir
SSR .... Soviet Socialist Republic, see ASSR
St. .... Saint, street
Surch. .... Surcharge

Typo. .... Typographed

UAE .... United Arab Emirates
UAMPT .... Union of African and Malagasy Posts and Telecommunications
UAR. .... United Arab Republic
UL .... Upper left

UN .... United Nations
UNCTAD ..... United Nations Conference on Trade and Development
UNESCO ...... United Nations Educational, Scientific and Cultural Organization
UNICEF........ United Nations Children's Fund
UAR .... United Arab Republic
UNPA........... United Nations Postal Administration
Unwmkd. ...... Unwatermarked
UPAE .... Union Postal de las Americas y Espana
UPU............. Universal Postal Union
UR .... Upper Right
US................ United States
USPO........... United States Post Office Department
USPS .... United States Postal Service
USSR............ Union of Soviet Socialist Republics

Vert.............. Vertical
VP................. Vice president

WCY .... World Communications Year
WFUNA .... World Federation of United Nations Associations
WHO .... World Health Organization
Wmk............. Watermark
Wmkd............ Watermarked
WMO............ World Meteorological Organization
WRY .... World Refugee Year
WWF............ World Wildlife Fund
WWI............. World War I
WWII............ World War II

YAR .... Yemen Arab Republic
Yemen PDR . Yemen People's Democratic Republic

Examination

Scott Publishing Co. will not pass upon the genuiness, grade or condition of stamps, because of the time and responsibility involved. Rather, there are several expertizing groups which undertake this work for both collectors and dealers. Neither can Scott Publishing Co. appraise or identify philatelic material. The Company cannot take responsibility for unsolicited stamps or covers.

How to order from your dealer

It is not necessary to write the full description of a stamp as listed in this catalogue. All that you need is the name of the country, the Scott Catalogue number and whether the item is unused or used. For example, ''Japan Scott 422 unused'' is sufficient to identify the stamp of Japan listed as ''422 A206 5y brown.''

Basic Stamp Information

A stamp collector's knowledge of the combined elements that make a given issue of a stamp unique determines his or her ability to identify stamps. These elements include paper, watermark, method of separation, printing, design and gum. On the following pages each of these important areas is described.

PAPER

Paper is a material composed of a compacted web of cellulose fibers formed into sheets. Paper may be manufactured in sheets, or may have been part of a roll before being cut to size. The fibers most often used for the paper on which stamps are printed are bark, wood, straw and certain grasses with linen or cotton rags added for greater strength. Grinding and bleaching these fibers reduces them to a slushy pulp. Sizing and sometimes coloring matter are added to the pulp. Thin coatings of pulp are poured onto sieve-like frames, which allow the water to run off while retaining the matted pulp. Mechanical processes convert the pulp, when it is almost dry, by passing it through smooth or engraved rollers — dandy rolls — or placed between cloth in a press then flattens and dries the product under pressure.

Stamp paper falls broadly into two types: wove and laid. The nature of the surface of the frame onto which the pulp is first fed causes the differences in appearance between the two. If the surface is smooth and even the paper will be of uniform texture throughout, showing no light and dark areas when held to a light. This is known as *wove paper.* Early paper-making machines poured the pulp onto continuously circulating web of felt, but modern machines feed the pulp onto a cloth-like screen made of closely interwoven fine wires. This paper, when held to a light, will show little dots or points very close together. The proper name for this is "wire wove," but the type is still considered wove. Any U.S. or British stamp printed after 1880 will serve as an example of wire wove paper.

Closed spaced parallel wires, with cross wires at wider intervals, make up the frames used for *laid paper.* A greater thickness of the pulp will settle between the wires. The paper, when held to a light, will show alternate light and dark lines. The spacing and the thickess of the lines may vary, but on any one sheet of paper they are all alike. See Russia Scott 31-38 for an example of laid paper.

Batonne, from the French word meaning "a staff," is used if the lines are spaced quite far apart, like the ruling on a writing tablet. Batonne paper may be either wove or laid. If laid, fine laid lines can be seen between the batons. The laid lines, which are a form of watermark, may be geometrical figures such as squares, diamonds, rectangles, or wavy lines.

Quadrille is the term used when the lines form little squares. *Oblong quadrille* is the term used when rectangles rather than squares are formed. See Mexico-Guadalajara Scott 35-37.

Paper also is classified as thick or thin, hard or soft, and by color if dye is added during manufacture. Such colors may be yellowish, greenish, bluish and reddish. Following are brief explanations of other types of paper used for stamps:

Pelure — A very thin, hard and often brittle paper, it is sometimes bluish or grayish. See Serbia Scott 169-170.

Native — A term applied to handmade papers used to produce some of the early stamps of the Indian states. Japanese paper, originally made of mulberry fibers and rice flour, is part of this group. See Japan Scott 1-18.

Manila — Often used to make stamped envelopes and wrappers, it is a coarse textured stock, usually smooth on one side and rough on the other. A variety of colors are known.

Silk — Introduced by the British in 1847 as a safeguard against counterfeiting, bits of colored silk thread are scattered throughout it. Silk-thread paper has uninterrupted threads of colored silk arranged so that one or more threads run through the stamp or postal stationery. See Great Britain Scott 5-6.

Granite — Filled with minute fibers of various colors and lengths, this should not be confused with either type of silk paper. See Austria Scott 172-175.

Chalky — A chalk-like substance coats the surface to discourage the cleaning and reuse of canceled stamps. Because the design is imprinted on the water-soluble coating of the stamp, any attempt to remove a cancellation will destroy the stamp. *Do not soak these stamps in any fluid.* To remove a stamp printed on chalky paper from an envelope, wet the paper from underneath the stamp until the gum dissolves enough to release the stamp from the paper. See St. Kitts-Nevis Scott 89-90.

India — Another name for this paper, originally introduced from China about 1750, is "China Paper." It is a thin, opaque paper often used for plate and die proofs by many countries.

Double — In philately, this has two distinct meanings. The first, used experimentally as a means to discourage reuse, is two-ply paper, usually a combination of a thick and a thin sheet, joined during manufacture. The design is printed on the thin paper. Any attempt to remove a cancellation would destroy the design. The second occurs on the rotary press, when the end of one paper roll is glued to the next roll to save time feeding the paper through the press. Stamp designs are printed over the joined paper and, if overlooked by inspectors, may get into post office stocks.

Goldbeater's Skin — Used for the 1866 issue of Prussia, it was made of a tough translucent paper. The design was printed in reverse on the back of the stamp, and the gum applied over the printing. It is impossible to remove stamps printed on this type of paper from the paper to which they are affixed without destroying the design.

Ribbed — An uneven, corrugated surface made by passing the paper through ridged roller. This type exists on some copies of U.S. Scott 156-165.

Various other substances have been used for stamp manufacture, including wood, aluminum, copper, silver and gold foil; plastic; and silk and cotton fabrics. Stamp collectors and dealers consider most of these as novelties designed for sale to collectors.

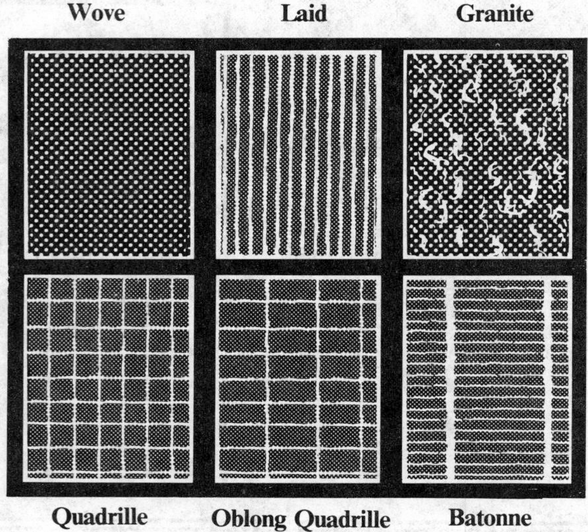

WATERMARKS

Watermarks are an integral part of the paper, for they are formed in the process of paper manufacture. They consist of small designs formed of wire or cut from metal and soldered to the surface of the dandy roll or mold. The designs may be in the form of crowns, stars, anchors, letters, etc. These pieces of metal — known in the paper-making industry as "bits" — impress a design into the paper. The design may be seen by holding the stamp to the light. Some are more easily seen with a watermark detector. This important tool is a small black tray into which the stamp is placed face down and dampened with a watermark detection fluid that brings up the watermark in the form of dark lines against a lighter background.

Multiple watermarks of Crown Agents and Burma

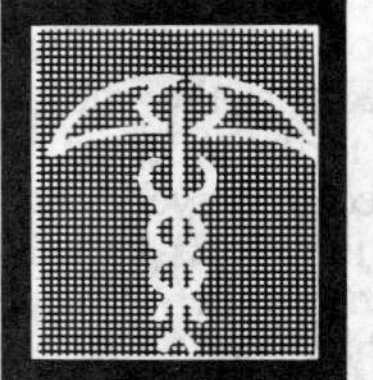

Watermarks of Uruguay, Vatican and Jamaica

WARNING: Some inks used in the photogravure process dissolve in watermark fluids. (See section below on Soluble Printing Inks.) Also, see "chalky paper." There also are electric watermark detectors, which come with plastic filter disks of various colors. The disks neutralize the color of the stamp, permitting the watermark to be seen more easily.

Watermarks may be found reversed, inverted, sideways or diagonal, as seen from the back of the stamp. The relationship of watermark to stamp design depends on the position of the printing plates or how paper is fed through the press. On machine-made paper, watermarks normally are read from right to left. The design is repeated closely throughout the sheet in a "multiple-watermark design." In a "sheet watermark," the design appears only once on the sheet, but extends over many stamps. Individual stamps may carry only a small fraction or none of the watermark.

"Marginal watermarks" occur in the margins of sheets or panes of stamps. They occur outside the border of paper (ostensibly outside the area where stamps are to be printed) a large row of letters may spell the name of the country or the manufacturer of the paper. Careless press feeding may cause parts of these letters to show on stamps of the outer row of a pane.

For easier reference, Scott Publishing Co. identifies and assigns a number to watermarks. See the numerical index of watermarks at the back of this volume.

Soluble Printing Inks

WARNING: Most stamp colors are permanent. That is, they are not seriously affected by light or water. Some colors may fade from excessive exposure to light. There are stamps printed with inks which dissolve easily in water or fluids used to detect watermarks. Use of these inks is intentional to prevent the removal of cancellations. Water affects all aniline prints, those on safety paper, and some photogravure printings — all known as *fugitive colors.*

Separation

"Separation" is the general term used to describe methods of separating stamps. The earliest issues, such as the 1840 Penny Black of Great Britain (Scott 1), did not have any means provided for separating. It was expected they would be cut apart with scissors. These are imperforate stamps. Many stamps first issued imperforate were later issued perforated. Care therefore must be observed in buying imperforate stamps to be certain they were issued imperforate and are not perforated copies that have been altered by having the perforations trimmed away. Imperforate stamps sometimes are valued as singles, as within this catalogue. But, imperforate varieties of normally perforated stamps should be collected in pairs or larger pieces as indisputable evidence of their imperforate character.

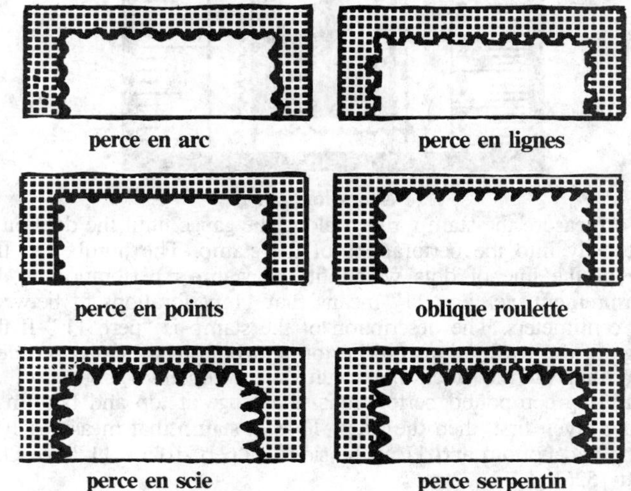

ROULETTING

Separation is brought about by two general methods during stamp production, rouletting and perforating. In rouletting, the paper is cut partly or wholly through, with no paper removed. In perforating, a part of the paper is removed. Rouletting derives its name from the French roulette, a spur-like wheel. As the wheel is rolled over the paper, each point makes a small cut. The number of cuts made in two centimeters determines the gauge of the roulette, just as the number of perforations in two centimeters determines the gauge of the perforation (see below).

The shape and arrangement of the teeth on the wheels varies. Various roulette types generally carry French names:

Perce en lignes — rouletted in lines. The paper receives short, straight cuts in lines. See Mexico Scott 500.

Perce en points — pin-perforated. This differs from a small perforation because no paper is removed, although round, equidistant holes are pricked through the paper. See Mexico Scott 242-256.

Perce en arc and *perce en scie* — pierced in an arc or sawtoothed designs, forming half circles or small triangles. See Hanover (German States) Scott 25-29.

Perce en serpentin — serpentine roulettes. The cuts form a serpentine or wavy line. See Brunswick (German States) Scott 13-18.

PERFORATION

The other chief style of separation of stamps, and the one which is in universal use today, is perforating. By this process, paper between the stamps is cut away in a line of holes, usually round, leaving little bridges of paper between the stamps to hold them together. These little bridges, which project from the stamp when it is torn from the pane are called the teeth of the perforation. As the size of the perforation is sometimes the only way to differentiate between two otherwise identical stamps, it is necessary to be able to measure and describe them. This is done with a perforation gauge, usually a ruler-like device that has dots to show how many perforations may be counted in the space of two centimeters. Two centimeters is the space universally adopted in which to measure perforations.

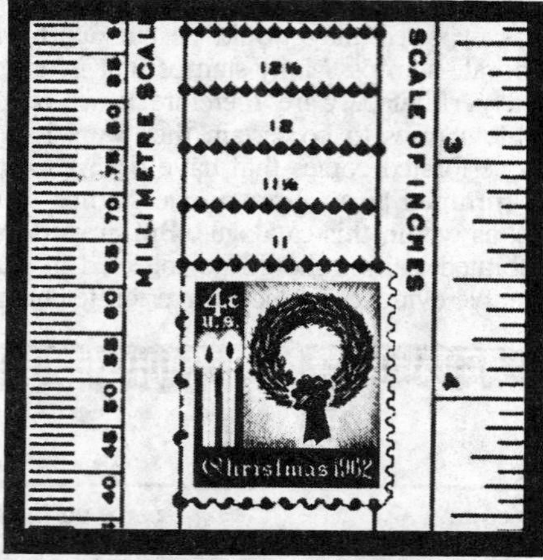

Perforation gauge

To measure the stamp, run it along the gauge until the dots on it fit exactly into the perforations of the stamp. The number to the side of the line of dots which fit the stamp's perforation is the measurement, i.e., an "11" means that 11 perforations fit between two centimeters. The description of the stamp is "perf. 11." If the gauge of the perforations on the top and bottom of a stamp differs from that on the sides, the result is a *compound perforation.* In measuring compound perforations, the gauge at top and bottom is always given first, then the sides. Thus, a stamp that measures 10½ at top and bottom and 11 at the sides is "perf. 10½ x 11." See U.S. Scott 1526.

There are stamps known with perforations different on three or all four sides. Descriptions of such items are in clockwise order, beginning with the top of the stamp.

A perforation with small holes and teeth close together is a "fine perforation." One with large holes and teeth far apart is a "coarse perforation." Holes jagged rather than clean cut, are "rough perforations." *Blind perforations* are the slight impressions left by the perforating pins if they fail to puncture the paper. Multiples of stamps showing blind perforations may command a slight premium over normally perforated stamps.

Printing Processes

ENGRAVING (Intaglio)

Master die — The initial operation in the engraving process is making of the master die. The die is a small flat block of soft steel on which the stamp design is recess engraved in reverse.

Master die

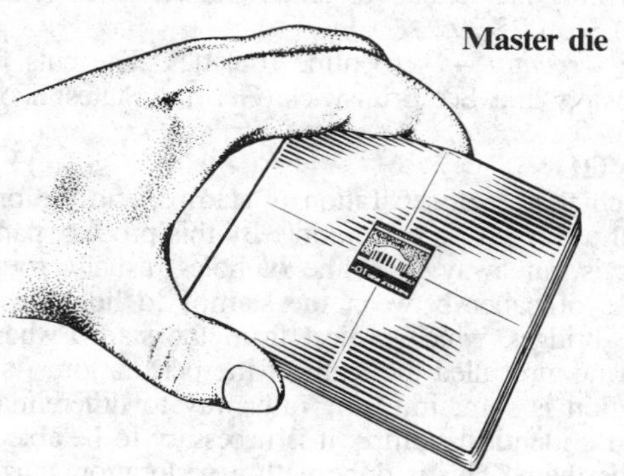

Photographic reduction of the original art is made to the appropriate size, and it serves as a tracing guide for the initial outline of the design. After completion of the engraving, the die is hardened to withstand the stress and pressures of later transfer operations.

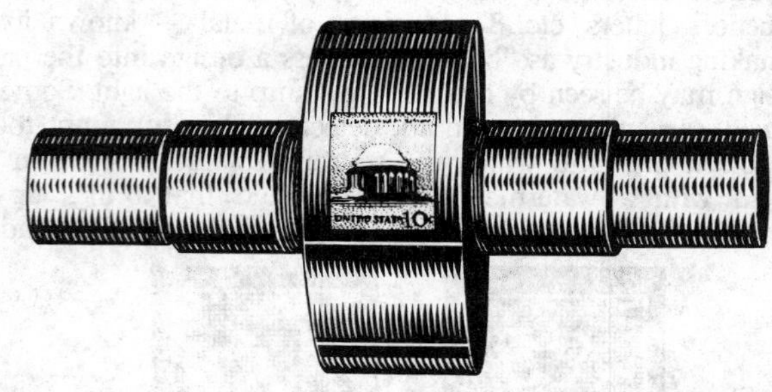

Transfer roll

Transfer roll — Next is production of the transfer roll which, as the name implies, is the medium used to transfer the subject from the die to the plate. A blank roll of soft steel, mounted on a mandrel, is placed under the bearers of the transfer press to allow it to roll freely on its axis. The hardened die is placed on the bed of the press and the face of the transfer roll is applied on the die, under pressure. The bed is then rocked back and forth under increasing pressure until the soft steel of the roll is forced into every engraved line of the die. The resulting impression on the roll is known as a "relief" or a "relief transfer." After the required number of reliefs are "rocked in," the soft steel transfer roll is also hardened.

A "relief" is the normal reproduction of the design on the die in reverse. A "defective relief" may occur during the "rocking in" process because of a minute piece of foreign material lodging on the die, or some other cause. Imperfections in the steel of the transfer roll may result in a breaking away of parts of the design. A damaged relief continued in use will transfer a repeating defect to the plate. Deliberate alterations of reliefs sometimes occur. "Broken reliefs" and "altered reliefs" designate these changed conditions.

Plate — The final step in the procedure is the making of the printing plate. A flat piece of soft steel replaces the die on the bed of the transfer press. One of the reliefs on the transfer roll is applied on this soft steel. "Position dots" determine the position on the plate. The dots have been lightly marked in advance. After the correct position of the relief is determined, pressure is applied. By following the same method used in making the transfer roll, a transfer is entered. This transfer reproduces the design of the relief in reverse and in detail. There are as many transfers entered on the plate as there are subjects printed on the sheet of stamps.

Transferring the design to the plate

Following the entering of the required transfers, the position dots, layout dots and lines, scratches, etc., generally are burnished out. Added at this time are any required *guide lines, plate numbers* or other *marginal markings.* A proof impression is then taken and, if approved, the plate machined for fitting to the press, hardened and sent to the plate vault ready for use.

On press, the plate is inked and the surface automatically wiped clean, leaving the ink in the depressed lines only. Paper under pressure is forced down into the engraved depressed lines, thereby receiving the ink. Thus, the ink lines on engraved stamps are slightly raised; and, conversely, slight depressions occur on the back of the stamp. Historically, paper had been dampened before inking. Newer processes do not require this procedure. Thus, there are both *wet* and *dry printings* of some stamps.

Rotary Press — Until 1915, only flat plates were used to print engraved stamps. Rotary press printing was introduced in 1915. After approval, *rotary press plates* require additional machining. They are curved to fit the press cylinder. "Gripper slots" are cut into the back of each plate to receive the "grippers," which hold the plate securely on the press. The plate is then hardened. Stamps printed from rotary press plates are usually longer or wider than the same stamps printed from flat press plates. The stretching of the plate during the curving process causes this enlargement.

Re-entry — In order to execute a re-entry, the transfer roll is reapplied to the plate, usually at some time after its first use on the press. Worn-out designs can be resharpened by carefully re-entering the transfer roll. If the transfer roll is not precisely in line with the impression of the plate, the registration will not be true and a double transfer will result. After a plate has been curved for the rotary press, it is impossible to make a re-entry.

Double Transfer — This is a description of the condition of a transfer on a plate that shows evidence of a duplication of all, or a portion of the design. It is usually the result of the changing of the registration between the transfer roll and the plate during the rocking-in of the original entry.

It is sometimes necessary to remove the original transfer from a plate and repeat the process a second time. If the finished re-transfer shows indications of the original impression attributable to incomplete erasure, the result is a double transfer.

Re-engraved — Either the die that has been used to make a plate or the plate itself may have it's "temper" drawn (softened) and be re-cut. The resulting impressions from such a re-engraved die or plate may differ slightly from the original issue, and are known as "re-engraved."

Short Transfer — Sometimes the transfer roll is not rocked its entire length in entering a transfer onto a plate, so that the finished transfer fails to show the complete design. This is known as a "short transfer." See U.S. Scott 8.

TYPOGRAPHY (Letterpress, Surface Printing)

As it relates to the printing of postage stamps, typography is the reverse of engraving. Typography includes all printing where the design is above the surface area, whether it is wood, metal, or in some instances hard rubber.

The master die and the engraved die are made in much the same manner. In this instance, however, the area not used as a printing surface is cut away, leaving the surface area raised. The original die is then reproduced by stereotyping or electrotyping. The resulting electrotypes are assembled in the required number and format of the desired sheet of stamps. The plate used in printing the stamps is an electroplate of these assembled electrotypes.

Ink is applied to the raised surface and the pressure of the press transfers the ink impression to the paper. In contrast with engraving, the fine lines of typography are impressed on the surface of the stamp. When viewed from the back (as on a typewritten page), the corresponding linework will be raised slightly above the surface.

PHOTOGRAVURE (Rotogravure, Heliogravure)

In this process, the basic principles of photography are applied to a sensitized metal plate, as opposed to photographic paper. The design is transferred photographically to the plate through a halftone screen, breaking the reproduction into tiny dots. The plate is treated chemically and the dots form depressions of varying depths, depending on the degrees of shade in the design. Ink is lifted out of the depressions in the plate when the paper is pressed against the plate in a manner similar to that of engraved printing.

LITHOGRAPHY

The principle that oil and water will not mix is the basis for lithography. The stamp design is drawn by hand or transferred from engraving to the surface of a lithographic stone or metal plate in a greasy (oily) ink. The stone (or plate) is wet with an acid fluid, causing it to repel the printing ink in all areas not covered by the greasy ink.

Transfer paper is used to transfer the design from the original stone of plate. A series of duplicate transfers are grouped and, in turn, transferred to the final printing plate.

Photolithography — The application of photographic processes to lithography. This process allows greater flexibility of design, related to use of halftone screens combined with linework.

Offset — A development of the lithographic process. A rubber-covered blanket cylinder takes up the impression from the inked lithographic plate. From the "blanket" the impression is *offset* or transferred to the paper. Greater flexibility and speed are the principal reasons offset printing has largely displaced lithography. The term "lithography" covers both processes, and results are almost identical.

Sometimes two or even three printing methods are combined in producing stamps.

EMBOSSED (Relief) Printing

Embossing is a method in which the design first is sunk into the metal of the die. Printing is done against a yielding platen, such as leather or linoleum. The platen is forced into the depression of the die, thus forming the design on the paper in relief.

Embossing may be done without color (see Sardinia Scott 4-6); with color printed around the embossed area (see Great Britain Scott 5 and most U.S. envelopes); and with color in exact registration with the embossed subject (see Canada Scott 656-657).

INK COLORS

Inks or colored papers used in stamp printing usually are of mineral origin. The tone of any given color may be affected by many aspects: heavier pressure will cause a more intense color, slight interruptions in the ink feed will cause a lighter tint.

Hand-mixed ink formulas produced under different conditions (humidity and temperature) at different times account for notable color variations in early printings, mostly 19th century, of the same stamp (see U.S. Scott 248-250, 279B, etc.).

Papers of different quality and consistency used for the same stamp printing may affect color shade. Most pelure papers, for example, show a richer color when compared with wove or laid papers. See Russia Scott 181a.

The very nature of the printing processes can cause a variety of differences in shades or hues of the same stamp. Some of these shades are scarcer than others and are of particular interest to the advanced collector.

Tagged Stamps

Tagging also is known as *luminescence, fluorescence,* and *phosphorescence.* Some tagged stamps have bars (Great Britain and Canada), frames (South Africa), or an overall coating of luminescent material applied after the stamps have been printed (United States). Another tagging method is to incorporate the luminescent material into some or all colors of the printing ink. See Australia Scott 366 and Netherlands Scott 478. A third is to mix the luminescent material with the pulp during the paper manufacturing process or apply it as a surface coating afterwards: "fluorescent" papers. See Switzerland Scott 510-514 and Germany Scott 848.

The treated stamps show up in specific colors when exposed to ultraviolet light. The wave length of light radiated by the luminescent material determines the colors and activates the triggering mechanism of the electronic machinery for sorting, facing or canceling letters.

Various fluorescent substances have been used as paper whiteners, but the resulting "hi-brite papers" show up differently under ultraviolet light and do not trigger the machines. The Scott Catalogue does not recognize these papers.

Many countries now use tagging in its various forms to expedite mail handling, following introduction by Great Britain, on an experimental basis, in 1959. Among these countries, and dates of their introduction, are Germany, 1961; Canada and Denmark, 1962; United States, Australia, Netherlands and Switzerland, 1963; Belgium and Japan, 1966; Sweden and Norway, 1967; Italy, 1968; and Russia, 1969.

Certain stamps were issued with and without the luminescent feature. In those instances, Scott lists the "tagged" variety in the United States, Canada, Great Britain and Switzerland listings and notes the situation in some of the other countries.

Gum

The gum on the back of a stamp may be smooth, rough, dark, white, colored or tinted. It may be either obvious or virtually invisible as on Canada Scott 453 or Rwanda Scott 287-294. Most stamp gumming adhesives use gum arabic or dextrine as a base. Certain polymers such as polyvinyl alcohol (PVA) have been used extensively since World War II. The PVA gum which the security printers Harrison & Sons of Great Britain introduced in 1968 is dull, slightly yellowish and almost invisible.

The *Scott Standard Postage Stamp Catalogue* does not list items by types of gum. The *Scott Specialized Catalogue of United States Stamps* does differentiate among some types of gum for certain issues.

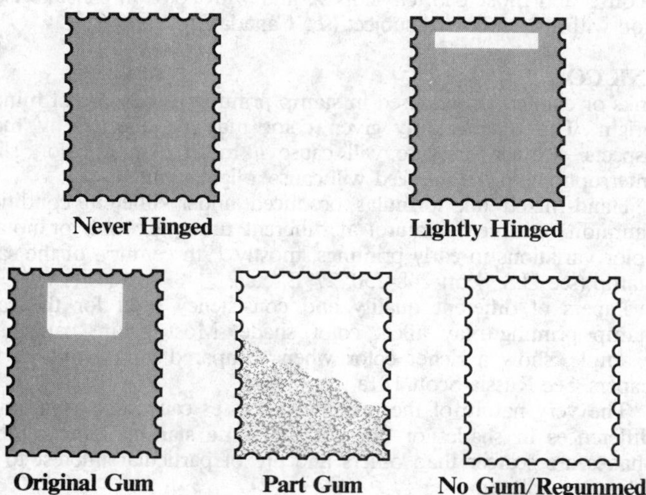

For purposes of determining the grade of an unused stamp, Scott Publishing Co. presents the following (with accompanying illustrations) definitions: **Never Hinged (NH)** — Full original gum with no hinge mark or other blemish or disturbance. The presence of an expertizer's mark does not disqualify a stamp from this designation; **Lightly Hinged (LH)** — Full original gum with a light disturbance of the gum from the removal of a peelable hinge; **Original Gum (OG)** — Hinging and other disturbances should affect 20 percent or less of the original gum. A stamp issued without gum also fits this category; **Part Gum (PG)** — Between 20 and 80 percent of the original gum remains. The stamp may have hinge remnants; **No Gum (NG) or Regummed (RE)** — A stamp with no gum or less than 20 percent of the original gum. A regummed stamp, considered the same as a stamp with none of its original gum, fits this category.

Stamps having full *original gum* sell for more than those from which the gum has been removed. Reprints of stamps may have gum differing from the original issues.

Many stamps have been issued without gum and the catalogue will note this fact. See China Scott 1438-1440. Sometimes, gum may have been removed to preserve the stamp. Germany Scott B68 is valued in the catalogue with gum removed.

Reprints and Reissues

These are impressions of stamps (usually obsolete) made from the original plates or stones. If valid for postage and from obsolete issues, they are *reissues.* If they are from current issues, they are *second, third,* etc., *printings.* If designated for a particular purpose, they are *special printings.*

Scott normally lists those reissues and reprints that are valid for postage.

When reprints are not valid for postage, but made from original dies and plates by authorized persons, they are *official reprints. Private reprints* are made from original plates and dies by private hands. *Official reproductions* or imitations are made from new dies and plates by government authorization.

For the United States' 1876 Centennial, the U.S. government made official imitations of its first postage stamps. Produced were copies of the first two stamps (listed as Scott 3-4), reprints of the demonetized pre-1861 issues and reissues of the 1861 stamps, the 1869 stamps and the then-current 1875 denominations. An example of the private reprint is that of the New Haven, Connecticut, postmaster's provisional.

Most reprints differ slightly from the original stamp in some characteristic, such as gum, paper, perforation, color or watermark. Sometimes the details are followed so meticulously that only a student of that specific stamp is able to distinguish the reprint from the original.

Remainders and Canceled to Order

Some countries sell their stock of old stamps when a new issue replaces them. To avoid postal use, the *remainders* usually are canceled with a punch hole, a heavy line or bar, or a more-or-less regular cancellation. The most famous merchant of remainders was Nicholas F. Seebeck. In the 1880's and 1890's, he arranged printing contracts between the Hamilton Bank Note Co., of which he was a director, and several Central and South American countries. The contracts provided that the plates and all remainders of the yearly issues became the property of Hamilton. Seebeck saw to it that ample stock remained. The "Seebecks," both remainders and reprints, were standard packet fillers for decades.

Some countries also issue stamps *canceled to order (CTO),* either in sheets with original gum or stuck onto pieces of paper or envelopes and canceled. Such CTO items generally are worth less than postally used stamps. Most can be detected by the presence of gum. However, as the CTO practice goes back at least to 1885, the gum inevitably has been washed off some stamps so they could pass for postally used. The normally applied postmarks usually differ slightly and specialists are able to tell the difference. When applied individually to envelopes by philatelically minded persons, CTO material is known as *favor canceled* and generally sells at large discounts.

Cinderellas and Facsimiles

Cinderella is a catchall term used by stamp collectors to describe phantoms, fantasies, bogus items, municipal issues, exhibition seals, local revenues, transportation stamps, labels, poster stamps, and so on. Some cinderella collectors include in their collections local postage issues, telegraph stamps, essays and proofs, forgeries and counterfeits.

A *fantasy* is an adhesive created for a nonexistent stamp issuing authority. Fantasy items range from imaginary countries (Kingdom of Sedang, Principality of Trinidad, or Occusi-Ambeno), to nonexistent locals (Winans City Post), or nonexistent transportation lines (McRobish & Co.'s Acapulco-San Francisco Line).

On the other hand, if the entity exists and might have issued stamps or did issue other stamps, the items are *bogus* stamps. These would include the Mormon postage stamps of Utah, S. Allan Taylor's Guatemala and Paraguay inventions, the propaganda issues for the South Moluccas and the adhesives of the Page & Keyes local post of Boston.

Phantoms is another term for both fantasy and bogus issues.

Facsimiles are copies or imitations made to represent original stamps, but which do not pretend to be originals. A catalogue illustration is such a facsimile. Illustrations from the Moens catalogue of the last century were occasionally colored and passed off as stamps. Since the beginning of stamp collecting, facsimiles have been made for collectors as space fillers or for reference. They often carry the word "facsimile," "falsch" (German), "sanko" or "mozo" (Japanese), or "faux" (French) overprinted on the face or stamped on the back.

Counterfeits or Forgeries

Unauthorized imitations of stamps, intended to deprive the post office of revenue, are *postal counterfeits* or *postal forgeries.* These items often command higher prices in the philatelic marketplace than the genuine stamps they imitate. Sales are illegal. Governments can, and do, prosecute those who trade in them.

The first postal forgery was of Spain's 4-cuarto carmine of 1854 (the real one is Scott 25). The forgers lithographed it, though the original was typographed. Apparently they were not satisfied and soon made an engraved forgery, which is common, unlike the scarce lithographed counterfeit. Postal forgeries quickly followed in Spain, Austria, Naples, Sardinia and the Roman States.

An infamous counterfeit to defraud is the 1-shilling Great Britain "Stock Exchange" forgery of 1872, used on telegraphs at the exchange that year. It escaped detection until a stamp dealer noticed it in 1898. Many postal counterfeits are known of U.S. stamps.

Wartime propaganda stamps of World War I and World War II may be classed as postal counterfeits. They were distributed by enemy governments or resistance groups.

Philatelic forgeries or *counterfeits* are unauthorized imitations of stamps designed to deceive and defraud stamp collectors. Such spurious items first appeared on the market around 1860 and most old-time collections contain one or more. Many are crude and easily spotted, but some can deceive the experts.

An important supplier of these early philatelic forgeries was the Hamburg printer Gebruder Spiro. Many others with reputations in this craft were S. Allan Taylor, George Hussey, James Chute, George Forune, Benjamin & Sarpy, Julius Goldner, E. Oneglia and L.H. Mercier. Among the noted 20th century forgers were Francois Fournier, Jean Sperati, and the prolific Raoul DeThuin.

Fraudulently produced copies are known of most classic rarities, many medium-priced stamps and, in this century, cheap stamps destined for beginners' packets. Few new philatelic forgeries have appeared in recent decades. Successful imitation of engraved work is virtually impossible.

It has proven far easier to produce a fake by altering a genuine stamp than to duplicate a stamp completely.

Repairs, Restoration and Fakes

Scott Publishing Co. bases its catalogue values on stamps which are free of defects and otherwise meet the standards set forth earlier in this introduction. Stamp collectors desire to have the finest copy of an item possible. Even within given grading categories there are variances. This leads to practice that is not universally defined, nor accepted, that of stamp *restoration.*

There are differences of opinion about what is "permissible" when it comes to restoration. Applying a soft eraser carefully to a stamp to remove dirt marks is one form of restoration, as is the washing of the stamp in mild soap and water. More severe forms of restoration are the pressing out of creases, or the removal of stains caused by tape. To what degree each of the above is "acceptable" is dependent on the individual situation. Further along the spectrum is the freshening of a stamp's color by removing oxide build-up or removing toning or the effects of wax paper left next to stamps shipped to the tropics.

At some point along this spectrum the concept of *repair* replaces that of "restoration." Repairs include filling in thin spots, mending tears by reweaving, adding a missing perforation tooth. Regumming stamps may have been acceptable as a restoration technique decades ago, but today it is considered a form of fakery.

Restored stamps may not sell at a discount, and it is possible that the value of individual restored items may be enhanced over that of their pre-restoration state. Specific situations will dictate the resultant value of such an item. Repaired stamps sell at substantial discounts.

When the purchaser of an item has any reason to suspect an item has been repaired, and the detection of such a repair is beyond his own ability, he should seek expert advice. There are services that specialize in such advice.

Fakes are genuine stamps altered in some way to make them more desirable. One student of this part of stamp collecting has estimated that by the 1950's more than 30,000 varieties of fakes were known. That number has grown. The widespread existence of fakes makes it important for stamp collectors to study their philatelic holdings and use relevant literature. Likewise, they should buy from reputable dealers who will guarantee their stamps and make full and prompt refund should a purchase be declared not genuine by some mutually agreed-upon authority. Because fakes always have some genuine characteristics, it is not always possible to obtain unanimous agreement among experts regarding specific items. These students may change their opinions as philatelic knowledge increases. More than 80 percent of all fakes on the philatelic market today are regummed, reperforated (or, perforated for the first time), or bear altered overprints, surcharges or cancellations.

Stamps can be chemically treated to alter or eliminate colors. For example, a pale rose stamp can be recolored into a blue of high market value, or a "missing color" variety can be created. Designs may be changed by "painting," or a stroke or a dot added or bleached out to turn an ordinary variety into a seemingly scarcer stamp. Part of a stamp can be bleached and reprinted in a different version, achieving an inverted center or frame. Margins can be added or repairs done so deceptively that the stamps move from the "repaired" into the "fake" category.

The fakers have not left the backs of the stamps untouched. They may create false watermarks, add fake grills or press out genuine grills. A thin India paper proof may be glued onto a thicker backing to "create" an issued stamp, or a proof printed on cardboard may be shaved down. Silk threads are impressed into paper and stamps have been split so that a rare paper variety is "added" to an otherwise inexpensive stamp. The most common treatment to the back of a stamp, however, is regumming.

Some in the business of faking stamps openly advertise "fool-proof" application of "original gum" to stamps that lack it. This is faking, not counterfeiting. It is believed that few early stamps have survived without being hinged. The large number of never-hinged examples of such earlier material offered for sale thus suggests the widespread extent of regumming activity. Regumming also may be used to hide repairs or thin spots. Dipping the stamp into watermark fluid often will reveal these flaws.

Fakers also tamper with separations. Ingenious ways to add margins are known. Perforated wide-margin stamps may be falsely represented as imperforate when trimmed. Reperforating is commonly done to create scarce coil or perforation varieties and to eliminate the straight-edge stamps found in sheet margin positions of many earlier issues. Custom has made straight edges less desirable. Fakers have obliged by perforating straight-edged stamps so that many are now uncommon, if not rare.

Another fertile field of the faker is that of the overprint, surcharge and cancellation. The forging of rare surcharges or overprints began in the 1880's or 1890's. These forgeries are sometimes difficult to detect, but the experts have identified almost all. Only occasionally are overprints or cancellations removed to create unoverprinted stamps or seemingly unused items. "SPECIMEN" overprints may be removed — scraping and repainting is one way — to create unoverprinted varieties. Fakers use inexpensive revenues or pen-canceled stamps to generate "unused" stamps for further faking by adding other markings. The quartz lamp and a high-powered magnifying glass help in detecting cancellation removal.

The bigger problem, however, is the addition of overprints, surcharges or cancellations — many with such precision that they are very difficult to ascertain. Plating of the stamps or the overprint can be an important method of detection.

Fake postmarks may range from many spurious fancy cancellations, to the host of markings applied to transatlantic covers, to adding "normal" postmarks to World War II-vintage definitives of some countries whose stamps are valued at far more used than unused. With the advance of cover collecting and the widespread interest in postal history, a fertile new field for fakers has come about. Some have tried to create entire covers. Others specialize in adding stamps, tied by fake cancellations, to genuine stampless covers, or replacing less expensive or damaged stamps with more valuable ones. Detailed study of postal rates in effect at the time of the cover in question, including the analysis of each handstamp in the period, ink analysis and similar techniques, usually will unmask the fraud.

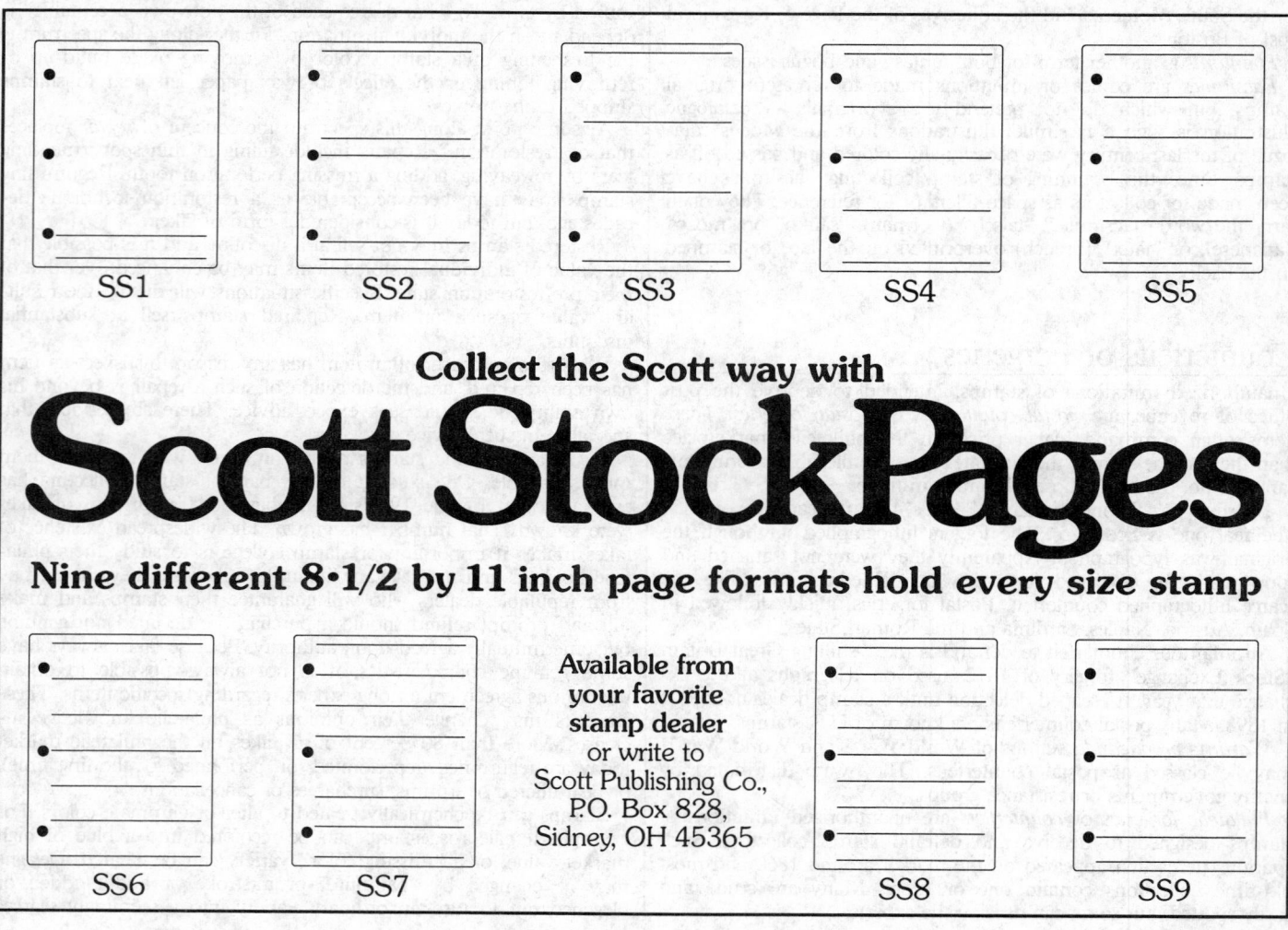

Terminology

Booklets — Many countries have issued stamps in small booklets for the convenience of users. This idea is becoming increasingly more popular today in many countries. Booklets have been issued in all sizes and forms, often with advertising on the covers, on the panes of stamps or on the interleaving.

The panes may be printed from special plates or made from regular sheets. All panes from booklets issued by the United States and many from those of other countries contain stamps that are straight edged on the bottom and both sides, but perforated between. Any stamp-like unit in the pane, either printed or blank, which is not a postage stamp, is considered a *label* in the catalogue listings.

Scott lists and values panes only. Complete booklets are listed only in a very few cases. See Grenada Scott 1055. Panes are listed only when they are not fashioned from existing sheet stamps and, therefore, are identifiable from their sheet-stamp counterparts.

Panes usually do not have a "used" value because there is little market activity in used panes, even though many exist used.

Cancellations — the marks or obliterations put on a stamp by the postal authorities to show that the stamp has done service and is no long valid for postage. If made with a pen, the marking is a "pen cancellation." When the location of the post office appears in the cancellation, it is a "town cancellation." When calling attention to a cause or celebration, it is a "slogan cancellation." Many other types and styles of cancellations exist, such as duplex, numerals, targets, etc.

Coil Stamps — stamps issued in rolls for use in dispensers, affixing and vending machines. Those of the United States, Canada, Sweden and some other countries are perforated horizontally or vertically only, with the outer edges imperforate. Coil stamps of some countries, such as Great Britain, are perforated on all four sides.

Covers — envelopes, with or without adhesive postage stamps, which have passed through the mail and bear postal or other markings of philatelic interest. Before the introduction of envelopes in about 1840, people folded letters and wrote the address on the outside. Many people covered their letters with an extra sheet of paper on the outside for the address, producing the term "cover." Used airletter sheets, stamped envelopes, and other items of postal stationery also are considered covers.

Errors — stamps having some unintentional deviation from the normal. Errors include, but are not limited to, mistakes in color, paper, or watermark; inverted centers or frames on multicolor printing, surcharges or overprints, and double impressions. Factually wrong or misspelled information, if it appears on all examples of a stamp, even if corrected later, is not classified as a philatelic error.

Overprinted and Surcharged Stamps — Overprinting is a wording or design placed on stamps to alter the place of use (i.e., "Canal Zone" on U.S. stamps), to adapt them for a special purpose ("Porto" on Denmark's 1913-20 regular issues for use as postage due stamps, Scott J1-J7), or for a special occasion (Guatemala Scott 374-378).

A *surcharge* is an overprint which changes or restates the face value of the item.

Surcharges and overprints may be handstamped, typeset or, occasionally, lithographed or engraved. A few hand-written overprints and surcharges are known.

Precancels — stamps canceled before they are placed in the mail. Precanceling is done to expedite the handling of large mailings.

In the United States, precancellations generally identified the point of origin. That is, the city and state names or initials appeared, usually centered between parallel lines. More recently, bureau precancels retained the parallel lines, but the city and state designation was dropped. Recent coils have a "service inscription" to show the mail service paid for by the stamp. Since these stamps do not receive any further cancellation when used as intended, they fall under the general precancel umbrella.

Such items may not have parallel lines as part of the precancellation.

In France, the abbreviation *Affranchts* in a semicircle together with the word *Postes* is the general form. Belgian precancellations are usually a box in which the name of the city appears. Netherlands' precancellations have the name of the city enclosed between concentric circles, sometimes called a "lifesaver."

Precancellations of other countries usually follow these patterns, but may be any arrangement of bars, boxes and city names.

Precancels are listed in the catalogue only if the precancel changes the denomination (Belgium Scott 477-478); the precanceled stamp is different from the non-precancel version (untagged U.S. stamps); or, if the stamp only exists precanceled (France Scott 1096-1099, U.S. Scott 2265).

Proofs and Essays — Proofs are impressions taken from an approved die, plate or stone in which the design and color are the same as the stamp issued to the public. Trial color proofs are impressions taken from approved dies, plates or stones in varying colors. An essay is the impression of a design that differs in some way from the stamp as issued.

Provisionals — stamps issued on short notice and intended for temporary use pending the arrival of regular issues. They usually are issued to meet such contingencies as changes in government or currency, shortage of necessary postage values, or military occupation.

In the 1840's, postmasters in certain American cities issued stamps that were valid only at specific post offices. In 1861, postmasters of the Confederate States also issued stamps with limited validity. Both of these examples are known as "postmaster's provisionals."

Se-tenant — joined, referring to an unsevered pair, strip or block of stamps differing in design, denomination or overprint. See U.S. Scott 2158a.

Unless the se-tenant item has a continuous design (see U.S. Scott 1451a, 1694a) the stamps do not have to be in the same order as shown in the catalogue (see U.S. Scott 2158a).

Specimens — One of the regulations of the Universal Postal Union requires member nations to send samples of all stamps they put into service to the International Bureau in Switzerland. Member nations of the UPU receive these specimens as samples of what stamps are valid for postage. Many are overprinted, handstamped or initial-perforated "Specimen," "Canceled" or "Muestra." Some are marked with bars across the denominations (China-Taiwan), punched holes (Czechoslovakia) or back inscriptions (Mongolia).

Stamps distributed to government officials or for publicity purposes, and stamps submitted by private security printers for official approval, also may receive such defacements.

These markings prevent postal use, and all such items generally are known as "specimens."

Tete Beche — A pair of stamps in which one is upside down in relation to the other. Some of these are the result of intentional sheet arrangements, e.g. Morocco Scott B10-B11. Others occurred when one or more electrotypes accidentally were placed upside down on the plate. See Colombia Scott 57a. Separation of the stamps, of course, destroys the tete beche variety.

Currency Conversion

Country	Value on 4/02/93	Dollar	Pound	Swiss Franc	Guilder	Yen	Lira	HK Dollar	D-Mark	French Franc	Canadian Dollar	Australian Dollar
Australia	1.4331	1.4331	2.2022	0.9628	0.79798	0.0126	0.0009	0.185359	0.89709	0.263438	1.133423	....
Canada	1.2644	1.2644	1.9429	0.8494	0.70405	0.01112	0.0008	0.163539	0.79149	0.232426	....	0.88228
France	5.44	5.44	8.3594	3.6547	3.02912	0.04782	0.00343	0.703615	3.40532	....	4.302436	3.79597
Germany	1.5975	1.5975	2.4548	1.0732	0.88953	0.01404	0.00101	0.206622	....	0.293658	1.263445	1.11472
Hong Kong	7.7315	7.7315	11.881	5.1942	4.30508	0.06797	0.00488	....	4.83975	1.421232	6.114758	5.39495
Italy	1584	1584	2434.1	1064.2	882.009	13.9253	....	204.8762	991.549	291.1765	1252.768	1105.3
Japan	113.75	113.75	174.79	76.419	63.3387	....	0.07181	14.71254	71.205	20.90993	89.96362	79.3734
Netherlands	1.7959	1.7959	2.7597	1.2065	....	0.01579	0.00113	0.232284	1.12419	0.330129	1.420357	1.25316
Switzerland	1.4885	1.4885	2.2873	....	0.82883	0.01309	0.00094	0.192524	0.93177	0.273621	1.177238	1.03866
U.K.	1.5367	1.5367	....	0.4372	0.36236	0.00572	0.00041	0.084171	0.40737	0.119626	0.514684	0.4541
U.S.	1.0000	....	1.5367	0.6718	0.55682	0.00879	0.00063	0.129341	0.62598	0.183824	0.790889	0.69779

Country	Currency	U.S. $ Equiv.
Japan	yen	.00877
Jordan	dollar	1.4577
Kazakhstan	ruble	.001445
Korea	won	.001257
Kyrgyzstan	ruble	.001445
Laos	kip	.001388
Latvia	ruble	.001445
Lebanon	pound	.00057
Liberia	U.S. dollar	1.00
Libya	dinar	3.386
Liechtenstein	Swiss franc	.6782
Lithuania	ruble	.001445
Luxembourg	franc	.03053
Macao	pataca	.1252
Madagascar	franc	.00052
Mali	Community of French Africa (CFA) franc	.0037
Mauritania	ouguiya	.00878
Mexico	new peso	.3233
Moldova	ruble	.001445
Monaco	French franc	.18547
Mongolia	tugrik	.00666
Mozambique	metical	.00036
Netherlands	guilder	.5595
Netherlands Antilles	guilder	.5586
New Caledonia	Community of French Pacific (CFP) franc	.0102
Nicaragua	gold cordoba	.16487
Niger	CFA franc	.0037
Norway	krone	.1477
Panama	balboa	1.00
Paraguay	guarani	.00058
Peru	new sol	.5391
Philippines	peso	.0388
Poland	zloty	.00006
Portugal	escudo	.00677
Qatar	riyal	.2747

*Source: **Wall Street Journal** April 5, 1993. Figures reflect values as of April 2, 1993.*

Colonies, Former Colonies, Offices, Territories Controlled by Parent States

Belgium

Belgian Congo
Ruanda-Urundi

Denmark

Danish West Indies
Faroe Islands
Greenland
Iceland

Finland

Aland Islands

France

COLONIES PAST AND PRESENT, CONTROLLED TERRITORIES

Afars & Issas, Territory of
Alaouites
Alexandretta
Algeria
Alsace & Lorraine
Ajouan
Annam & Tonkin
Benin
Cambodia (Khmer)
Cameroun
Castellorizo
Chad
Cilicia
Cochin China
Comoro Islands
Dahomey
Diego Suarez
Djibouti (Somali Coast)
Fezzan
French Congo
French Equatorial Africa
French Guiana
French Guinea
French India
French Morocco
French Polynesia (Oceania)
French Southern & Antarctic Territories
French Sudan
French West Africa
Gabon
Germany
Ghadames
Grand Comoro
Guadeloupe
Indo-China
Inini
Ivory Coast
Laos
Latakia
Lebanon
Madagascar
Martinique
Mauritania
Mayotte
Memel
Middle Congo
Moheli
New Caledonia
New Hebrides
Niger Territory
Nossi-Be
Obock
Reunion
Rouad, Ile
Ste.-Marie de Madagascar
St. Pierre & Miquelon
Senegal
Senegambia & Niger
Somali Coast
Syria
Tahiti
Togo
Tunisia
Ubangi-Shari
Upper Senegal & Niger
Upper Volta
Viet Nam
Wallis & Futuna Islands

POST OFFICES IN FOREIGN COUNTRIES

China
Crete
Egypt
Turkish Empire
Zanzibar

Germany

EARLY STATES

Baden
Bavaria
Bergedorf
Bremen
Brunswick
Hamburg
Hanover
Lubeck
Mecklenburg-Schwerin
Mecklenburg-Strelitz
Oldenburg
Prussia
Saxony
Schleswig-Holstein
Wurttemberg

FORMER COLONIES

Cameroun (Kamerun)
Caroline Islands
German East Africa
German New Guinea
German South-West Africa
Kiauchau
Mariana Islands
Marshall Islands
Samoa
Togo

Italy

EARLY STATES

Modena
Parma
Romagna
Roman States
Sardinia
Tuscany
Two Sicilies
  Naples
  Neapolitan Provinces
  Sicily

FORMER COLONIES, CONTROLLED TERRITORIES, OCCUPATION AREAS

Aegean Islands
  Calimno (Calino)
  Caso
  Cos (Coo)
  Karki (Carchi)
  Leros (Lero)
  Lipso
  Nisiros (Nisiro)
  Patmos (Patmo)
  Piscopi
  Rodi (Rhodes)
  Scarpanto
  Simi
  Stampalia
Castellorizo
Corfu
Cyrenaica
Eritrea
Ethiopia (Abyssinia)
Fiume
Ionian Islands
  Cephalonia
  Ithaca
  Paxos
Italian East Africa
Libya
Oltre Giuba
Saseno
Somalia (Italian Somaliland)
Tripolitania

POST OFFICES IN FOREIGN COUNTRIES

"ESTERO"*
Austria
China
  Peking
  Tientsin
Crete
Tripoli
Turkish Empire
  Constantinople
  Durazzo
  Janina
Jerusalem
Salonika
Scutari
Smyrna
Valona

* Stamps overprinted "ESTERO" were used in various parts of the world.

Netherlands

Aruba
Netherlands Antilles (Curacao)
Netherlands Indies
Netherlands New Guinea
Surinam (Dutch Guiana)

Portugal

COLONIES PAST AND PRESENT, CONTROLLED TERRITORIES

Angola
Angra
Azores
Cape Verde
Funchal
Horta
Inhambane
Kionga
Lourenco Marques
Macao
Madeira
Mozambique
Mozambique Co.
Nyassa
Ponta Delgada
Portuguese Africa
Portuguese Congo
Portuguese Guinea
Portuguese India
Quelimane
St. Thomas & Prince Islands
Tete
Timor
Zambezia

Russia

ALLIED TERRITORIES AND REPUBLICS, OCCUPATION AREAS

Armenia
Aunus (Olonets)
Azerbaijan
Batum
Estonia
Far Eastern Republic
Georgia
Karelia
Latvia
Lithuania
North Ingermanland
Ostland
Russian Turkestan
Siberia
South Russia
Tannu Tuva
Transcaucasian Fed. Republics
Ukraine
Wenden (Livonia)
Western Ukraine

Spain

COLONIES PAST AND PRESENT, CONTROLLED TERRITORIES

Aguera, La
Cape Juby
Cuba
Elobey, Annobon & Corisco
Fernando Po
Ifni
Mariana Islands
Philippines
Puerto Rico
Rio de Oro
Rio Muni
Spanish Guinea
Spanish Morocco
Spanish Sahara
Spanish West Africa

POST OFFICES IN FOREIGN COUNTRIES

Morocco
Tangier
Tetuan

Common Design Types

Pictured in this section are issues where one illustration has been used for a number of countries in the Catalogue. Not included in this section are overprinted stamps or those issues which are illustrated in each country.

EUROPA

Europa Issue, 1956

The design symbolizing the cooperation among the six countries comprising the Coal and Steel Community is illustrated in each country.

Belgium ... 496-497
France ... 805-806
Germany ... 748-749
Italy ... 715-716
Luxembourg ... 318-320
Netherlands ... 368-369

Europa Issue, 1958

"E" and Dove
CD1

European Postal Union at the service of European integration.

1958, Sept. 13

Belgium ... 527-528
France ... 889-890
Germany ... 790-791
Italy ... 750-751
Luxembourg ... 341-343
Netherlands ... 375-376
Saar ... 317-318

Europa Issue, 1959

6-Link Endless Chain
CD2

1959, Sept. 19

Belgium ... 536-537
France ... 929-930
Germany ... 805-806
Italy ... 791-792
Luxembourg ... 354-355
Netherlands ... 379-380

Europa Issue, 1960

19-Spoke Wheel
CD3

First anniversary of the establishment of C.E.P.T. (Conference Europeenne des Administrations des Postes et des Telecommunications.)

The spokes symbolize the 19 founding members of the Conference.

1960, Sept.

Belgium ... 553-554
Denmark ... 379
Finland ... 376-377
France ... 970-971
Germany ... 818-820
Great Britain ... 377-378
Greece ... 688
Iceland ... 327-328
Ireland ... 175-176
Italy ... 809-810
Luxembourg ... 374-375
Netherlands ... 385-386
Norway ... 387
Portugal ... 866-867
Spain ... 941-942
Sweden ... 562-563
Switzerland ... 400-401
Turkey ... 1493-1494

Europa Issue, 1961

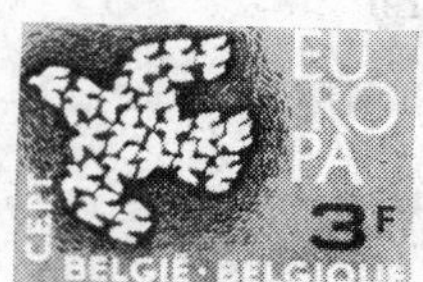

19 Doves Flying as One
CD4

The 19 doves represent the 19 members of the Conference of European Postal and Telecommunications Administrations C.E.P.T.

1961-62

Belgium ... 572-573
Cyprus ... 201-203
France ... 1005-1006
Germany ... 844-845
Great Britain ... 383-384
Greece ... 718-719
Iceland ... 340-341
Italy ... 845-846
Luxembourg ... 382-383
Netherlands ... 387-388
Spain ... 1010-1011
Switzerland ... 410-411
Turkey ... 1518-1520

Europa Issue 1962

Young Tree with 19 Leaves
CD5

The 19 leaves represent the 19 original members of C.E.P.T.

1962-63

Belgium ... 582-583
Cyprus ... 219-221
France ... 1045-1046
Germany ... 852-853
Greece ... 739-740
Iceland ... 348-349
Ireland ... 184-185
Italy ... 860-861
Luxembourg ... 386-387
Netherlands ... 394-395
Norway ... 414-415
Switzerland ... 416-417
Turkey ... 1553-1555

Europa Issue, 1963

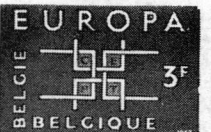

Stylized Links, Symbolizing Unity
CD6

1963, Sept.

Belgium ... 598-599
Cyprus ... 229-231
Finland ... 419
France ... 1074-1075
Germany ... 867-868
Greece ... 768-769
Iceland ... 357-358
Ireland ... 188-189
Italy ... 880-881
Luxembourg ... 403-404
Netherlands ... 416-417
Norway ... 441-442
Switzerland ... 429
Turkey ... 1602-1603

Europa Issue, 1964

Symbolic Daisy
CD7

5th anniversary of the establishment of C.E.P.T. The 22 petals of the flower symbolize the 22 members of the Conference.

1964, Sept.

Austria ... 738
Belgium ... 614-615
Cyprus ... 244-246
France ... 1109-1110
Germany ... 897-898
Greece ... 801-802
Iceland ... 367-368
Ireland ... 196-197
Italy ... 894-895
Luxembourg ... 411-412
Monaco ... 590-591
Netherlands ... 428-429
Norway ... 458
Portugal ... 931-933
Spain ... 1262-1263
Switzerland ... 438-439
Turkey ... 1628-1629

Europa Issue, 1965

Leaves and "Fruit"
CD8

1965

Belgium ... 636-637
Cyprus ... 262-264
Finland ... 437
France ... 1131-1132
Germany ... 934-935
Greece ... 833-834
Iceland ... 375-376
Ireland ... 204-205
Italy ... 915-916
Luxembourg ... 432-433
Monaco ... 616-617
Netherlands ... 438-439
Norway ... 475-476
Portugal ... 958-960
Switzerland ... 469
Turkey ... 1665-1666

Europa Issue, 1966

Symbolic Sailboat
CD9

1966, Sept.

Andorra, French ... 172
Belgium ... 675-676
Cyprus ... 275-277
France ... 1163-1164
Germany ... 963-964
Greece ... 862-863
Iceland ... 384-385
Ireland ... 216-217
Italy ... 942-943
Liechtenstein ... 415
Luxembourg ... 440-441
Monaco ... 639-640
Netherlands ... 441-442
Norway ... 496-497
Portugal ... 980-982
Switzerland ... 477-478
Turkey ... 1718-1719

Europa Issue, 1967

Cogwheels
CD10

1967

Andorra, French ... 174-175
Belgium ... 688-689
Cyprus ... 297-299
France ... 1178-1179
Greece ... 891-892
Germany ... 969-970
Iceland ... 389-390
Ireland ... 232-233
Italy ... 951-952
Liechtenstein ... 420
Luxembourg ... 449-450
Monaco ... 669-670
Netherlands ... 444-447
Norway ... 504-505
Portugal ... 994-996
Spain ... 1465-1466
Switzerland ... 482
Turkey ... B120-B121

Europa Issue, 1968

Golden Key with C.E.P.T. Emblem
CD11

1968

Andorra, French ... 182-183
Belgium ... 705-706
Cyprus ... 314-316
France ... 1209-1210
Germany ... 983-984
Greece ... 916-917
Iceland ... 395-396

Ireland	242-243
Italy	979-980
Liechtenstein	442
Luxembourg	466-467
Monaco	689-691
Netherlands	452-453
Portugal	1019-1021
San Marino	687
Spain	1526
Turkey	1775-1776

Europa Issue, 1969

"EUROPA" and "CEPT"
CD12

Tenth anniversary of C.E.P.T.

1969

Andorra, French	188-189
Austria	837
Belgium	718-719
Cyprus	326-328
Denmark	458
Finland	483
France	1245-1246
Germany	996-997
Great Britain	585
Greece	947-948
Iceland	406-407
Ireland	270-271
Italy	1000-1001
Liechtenstein	453
Luxembourg	474-475
Monaco	722-724
Netherlands	475-476
Norway	533-534
Portugal	1038-1040
San Marino	701-702
Spain	1567
Sweden	814-816
Switzerland	500-501
Turkey	1799-1800
Vatican	470-472
Yugoslavia	1003-1004

Europa Issue, 1970

Interwoven Threads
CD13

1970

Andorra, French	196-197
Belgium	741-742
Cyprus	340-342
France	1271-1272
Germany	1018-1019
Greece	985, 987
Iceland	420-421
Ireland	279-281
Italy	1013-1014
Liechtenstein	470
Luxembourg	489-490
Monaco	768-770
Netherlands	483-484
Portugal	1060-1062
San Marino	729-730
Spain	1607
Switzerland	515-516
Turkey	1848-1849
Yugoslavia	1024-1025

Europa Issue, 1971

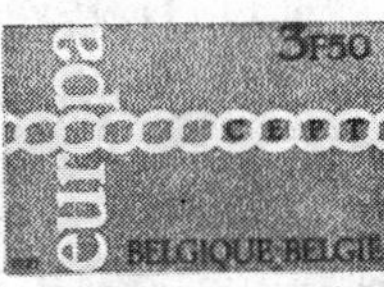

"Fraternity, Cooperation, Common Effort"—CD14

1971

Andorra, French	205-206
Belgium	803-804
Cyprus	365-367
Finland	504
France	1304
Germany	1064-1065
Greece	1029-1030
Iceland	429-430
Ireland	305-306
Italy	1038-1039
Liechtenstein	485
Luxembourg	500-501
Malta	425-427
Monaco	797-799
Netherlands	488-489
Portugal	1094-1096
San Marino	749-750
Spain	1675-1676
Switzerland	531-532
Turkey	1876-1877
Yugoslavia	1052-1053

Europa Issue, 1972

Sparkles, Symbolic of Communications
CD15

1972

Andorra, French	210-211
Andorra, Spanish	62
Belgium	825-826
Cyprus	380-382
Finland	512-513
France	1341
Germany	1089-1090
Greece	1049-1050
Iceland	439-440
Ireland	316-317
Italy	1065-1066
Liechtenstein	504
Luxembourg	512-513
Malta	450-453
Monaco	831-832
Netherlands	494-495
Portugal	1141-1143
San Marino	771-772
Spain	1718
Switzerland	544-545
Turkey	1907-1908
Yugoslavia	1100-1101

Europa Issue, 1973

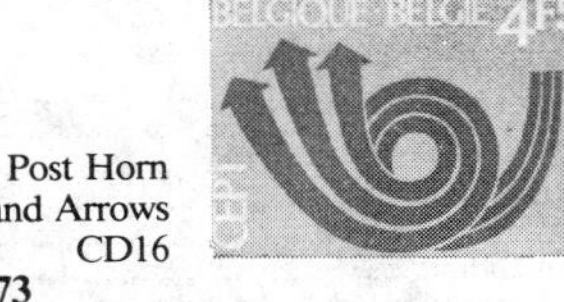

Post Horn and Arrows
CD16

1973

Andorra, French	319-320
Andorra, Spanish	76
Belgium	839-840
Cyprus	396-398
Finland	526
France	1367
Germany	1114-1115
Greece	1090-1092
Iceland	447-448
Ireland	329-330
Italy	1108-1109
Liechtenstein	528-529
Luxembourg	523-524
Malta	469-471
Monaco	866-867
Netherlands	504-505
Norway	604-605
Portugal	1170-1172
San Marino	802-803
Spain	1753
Switzerland	580-581
Turkey	1935-1936
Yugoslavia	1138-1139

PORTUGAL & COLONIES

Vasco da Gama Issue

Fleet Departing—CD20

Fleet Arriving at Calicut
CD21

Embarking at Rastello—CD22

Muse of History
CD23

Flagship San Gabriel, da Gama and Camoens
CD24

Archangel Gabriel, the Patron Saint
CD25

Flagship San Gabriel
CD26

Vasco da Gama
CD27

Fourth centenary of Vasco da Gama's discovery of the route to India.

1898

Azores	93-100
Macao	67-74
Madeira	37-44
Portugal	147-154
Port. Africa	1-8
Port. india	189-196
Timor	45-52

Pombal Issue

POSTAL TAX

Marquis de Pombal
CD28

Planning Reconstruction of Lisbon, 1755
CD29

Pombal Monument, Lisbon
CD30

Sebastiao Jose' de Carvalho e Mello, Marquis de Pombal (1699-1782), statesman, rebuilt Lisbon after earthquake of 1755. Tax was for the erection of Pombal monument. Obligatory on all mail on certain days throughout the year.

1925

Angola	RA1-RA3
Azores	RA9-RA11
Cape Verde	RA1-RA3
Macao	RA1-RA3
Madeira	RA1-RA3
Mozambique	RA1-RA3
Portugal	RA11-RA13
Port. Guinea	RA1-RA3
Port. India	RA1-RA3
St. Thomas & Prince Islands	RA1-RA3
Timor	RA1-RA3

Pombal Issue

POSTAL TAX DUES

Marquis de Pombal
CD31

Planning Reconstruction of Lisbon, 1755
CD32

Pombal Monument, Lisbon
CD33

1925

Angola	RAJ1-RAJ3

Azores	RAJ2-RAJ4
Cape Verde	RAJ1-RAJ3
Macao	RAJ1-RAJ3
Madeira	RAJ1-RAJ3
Mozambique	RAJ1-RAJ3
Portugal	RAJ2-RAJ4
Port. Guinea	RAJ1-RAJ3
Port. India	RAJ1-RAJ3
St. Thomas & Prince Islands	RAJ1-RAJ3
Timor	RAJ1-RAJ3

Vasco da Gama
CD34

Mousinho de Albuquerque
CD35

Dam
CD36

Prince Henry the Navigator
CD37

Affonso de Albuquerque
CD38

1938-39

Angola	274-291
Cape Verde	234-251
Macao	289-305
Mozambique	270-287
Port. Guinea	233-250
Port. India	439-453
St. Thomas & Prince Islands	302-319, 323-340
Timor	223-239

Plane over Globe
CD39

1938-39

Angola	C1-C9
Cape Verde	C1-C9
Macao	C7-C15
Mozambique	C1-C9
Port. Guinea	C1-C9
Port. India	C1-C8
St. Thomas & Prince Islands	C1-C18
Timor	C1-C9

Lady of Fatima Issue

Our Lady of the Rosary, Fatima, Portugal
CD40

1948-49

Angola	315-318
Cape Verde	266
Macao	336
Mozambique	325-328
Port. Guinea	271
Port. India	480
St. Thomas & Prince Islands	351
Timor	254

A souvenir sheet of 9 stamps was issued in 1951 to mark the extension of the 1950 Holy Year. The sheet contains: Angola No. 316, Cape Verde No. 266, Macao No. 336, Mozambique No. 325, Portuguese Guinea No. 271, Portugese India Nos. 480, 485, St. Thomas & Prince Islands No. 351, Timor No. 254.

The sheet also contains a portrait of Pope Pius XII and is inscribed "Encerramento do Ano Santo, Fatima 1951." It was sold for 11 escudos.

Holy Year Issue

Church Bells and Dove
CD41

Angel Holding Candelabra
CD42

Holy Year, 1950.

1950-51

Angola	331-332
Cape Verde	268-269
Macao	339-340
Mozambique	330-331
Port. Guinea	273-274
Port. India	490-491, 496-503
St. Thomas & Prince Islands	353-354
Timor	258-259

A souvenir sheet of 8 stamps was issued in 1951 to mark the extension of the Holy Year. The sheet contains: Angola No. 331, Cape Verde No. 269, Macao No. 340, Mozambique No. 331, Portuguese Guinea No. 275, Portuguese India No. 490, St. Thomas & Prince Islands No. 354, Timor No. 258, some with colors changed. The sheet contains doves and is inscribed "Encerramento do Ano Santo, Fatima 1951." It was sold for 17 escudos.

Holy Year Conclusion Issue

Our Lady of Fatima
CD43

Conclusion of Holy Year. Sheets contain alternate vertical rows of stamps and labels bearing quotation from Pope Pius XII, different for each colony.

1951

Angola	357
Cape Verde	270
Macao	352
Mozambique	356
Port. Guinea	275
Port. India	506
St. Thomas & Prince Islands	355
Timor	270

Medical Congress Issue

Medical Examination
CD44

First National Congress of Tropical Medicine, Lisbon, 1952.

Each stamp has a different design.

1952

Angola	358
Cape Verde	287
Macao	364
Mozambique	359
Port. Guinea	276
Port. India	516
St. Thomas & Prince Islands	356
Timor	271

POSTAGE DUE STAMPS

CD45

1952

Angola	J37-J42
Cape Verde	J31-J36
Macao	J53-J58
Mozambique	J51-J56
Port. Guinea	J40-J45
Port. India	J47-J52
St. Thomas & Prince Islands	J52-J57
Timor	J31-J36

Sao Paulo Issue

Father Manuel de Nobrega and View of Sao Paulo
CD46

400th anniversary of the founding of Sao Paulo, Brazil.

1954

Angola	385
Cape Verde	297
Macao	382
Mozambique	395
Port. Guinea	291
Port. India	530
St. Thomas & Prince Islands	369
Timor	279

Tropical Medicine Congress Issue

Securidaca Longipedunculata
CD47

Sixth International Congress for Tropical Medicine and Malaria, Lisbon, Sept. 1958.

Each stamp shows a different plant.

1958

Angola	409
Cape Verde	303
Macao	392
Mozambique	404
Port. Guinea	295
Port. India	569
St. Thomas & Prince Islands	371
Timor	289

Sports Issue

Flying
CD48

Each stamp shows a different sport.

1962

Angola	433-438
Cape Verde	320-325
Macao	394-399
Mozambique	424-429
Port. Guinea	299-304
St. Thomas & Prince Islands	374-379
Timor	313-318

Anti-Malaria Issue

Anopheles Funestus and Malaria Eradication Symbol
CD49

World Health Organization drive to eradicate malaria.

1962

Angola	439
Cape Verde	326
Macao	400
Mozambique	430
Port. Guinea	305
St. Thomas & Prince Islands	380
Timor	319

Airline Anniversary Issue

Map of Africa, Super Constellation and Jet Liner
CD50

Tenth anniversary of Transportes Aereos Portugueses (TAP).

1963

Angola	490
Cape Verde	327
Mozambique	434
Port. Guinea	318
St. Thomas & Prince Islands	381

National Overseas Bank Issue

Antonio Teixeira de Sousa
CD51

Centenary of the National Overseas Bank of Portugal.

1964, May 16

Angola 509
Cape Verde 328
Port. Guinea 319
St. Thomas & Prince Islands 382
Timor 320

ITU Issue

ITU Emblem and St. Gabriel
CD52

Centenary of the International Communications Union.

1965, May 17

Angola 511
Cape Verde 329
Macao 402
Mozambique 464
Port. Guinea 320
St. Thomas & Prince Islands 383
Timor 321

National Revolution Issue

St. Paul's Hospital, and Commercial and Industrial School
CD53

40th anniversary of the National Revolution.
Different buildings on each stamp.

1966, May 28

Angola 525
Cape Verde 338
Macao 403
Mozambique 465
Port. Guinea 329
St. Thomas & Prince Islands 392
Timor 322

Navy Club Issue

Mendes Barata and Cruiser Dom Carlos I
CD54

Centenary of Portugal's Navy Club.
Each stamp has a different design.

1967, Jan. 31

Angola 527-528
Cape Verde 339-340
Macao 412-413
Mozambique 478-479
Port. Guinea 330-331
St. Thomas & Prince Islands 393-394
Timor 323-324

Admiral Coutinho Issue

Admiral Gago Coutinho and his First Ship
CD55

Centenary of the birth of Admiral Carlos Viegas Gago Coutinho (1869-1959), explorer and aviation pioneer.
Each stamp has a different design.

1969, Feb. 17

Angola 547
Cape Verde 355
Macao 417
Mozambique 484
Port. Guinea 335
St. Thomas & Prince Islands 397
Timor 335

Administration Reform Issue

Luiz Augusto Rebello da Silva
CD56

Centenary of the administration reforms of the overseas territories.

1969, Sept. 25

Angola 549
Cape Verde 357
Macao 419
Mozambique 491
Port. Guinea 337
St. Thomas & Prince Islands 399
Timor 338

Marshal Carmona Issue

Marshal A.O. Carmona
CD57

Birth centenary of Marshal Antonio Oscar Carmona de Fragoso (1869-1951), President of Portugal.
Each stamp has a different design.

1970, Nov. 15

Angola 563
Cape Verde 359
Macao 422
Mozambique 493
Port. Guinea 340
St. Thomas & Prince Islands 403
Timor 341

Olympic Games Issue

Racing Yachts and Olympic Emblem
CD59

20th Olympic Games, Munich, Aug. 26-Sept. 11.
Each stamp shows a different sport.

1972, June 20

Angola 569
Cape Verde 361
Macao 426
Mozambique 504
Port. Guinea 342
St. Thomas & Prince Islands 408
Timor 343

Lisbon-Rio de Janeiro Flight Issue

"Santa Cruz" over Fernando de Noronha
CD60

50th anniversary of the Lisbon to Rio de Janeiro flight by Arturo de Sacadura and Coutinho, March 30-June 5, 1922.
Each stamp shows a different stage of the flight.

1972, Sept. 20

Angola 570
Cape Verde 362
Macao 427
Mozambique 505
Port. Guinea 343
St. Thomas & Prince Islands 409
Timor 344

WMO Centenary Issue

WMO Emblem
CD61

Centenary of international meterological cooperation.

1973, Dec. 15

Angola 571
Cape Verde 363
Macao 429
Mozambique 509
Port. Guinea 344
St. Thomas & Prince Islands 410
Timor 345

FRENCH COMMUNITY

Upper Volta sets can be found under Burkina Faso in Vol. 2.

Colonial Exposition Issue

People of French Empire
CD70

Women's Heads
CD71

France Showing Way to Civilization
CD72

"Colonial Commerce"
CD73

International Colonial Exposition, Paris 1931.

1931

Cameroun 213-216
Chad 60-63
Dahomey 97-100
Fr. Guiana 152-155
Fr. Guinea 116-119
Fr. India 100-103
Fr. Polynesia 76-79
Fr. Sudan 102-105
Gabon 120-123
Guadeloupe 138-141
Indo-China 140-142
Ivory Coast 92-95
Madagascar 169-172
Martinique 129-132
Mauritania 65-68
Middle Congo 61-64
New Caledonia 176-179
Niger 73-76
Reunion 122-125
St. Pierre & Miquelon 132-135
Senegal 138-141
Somali Coast 135-138
Togo 254-257
Ubangi-Shari 82-85
Upper Volta 66-69
Wallis & Futuna Isls. 85-88

Paris International Exposition Issue

Colonial Arts Exposition Issue

"Colonial Resources"
CD74 CD77

Overseas Commerce
CD75

Exposition Building and Women
CD76

"France and the Empire"
CD78

Cultural Treasures of the Colonies
CD79

Souvenir sheets contain one imperf. stamp.

1937	
Cameroun	217-222A
Dahomey	101-107
Fr. Equatorial Africa	27-32, 73
Fr. Guiana	162-168
Fr. Guinea	120-126
Fr. India	104-110
Fr. Polynesia	117-123
Fr. Sudan	106-112
Guadeloupe	148-154
Indo-China	193-199
Inini	41
Ivory Coast	152-158
Kwangchowan	132
Madagascar	191-197
Martinique	179-185
Mauritania	69-75
New Caledonia	208-214
Niger	72-83
Reunion	167-173
St. Pierre & Miquelon	165-171
Senegal	172-178
Somali Coast	139-145
Togo	258-264
Wallis & Futuna Isls.	89

Curie Issue

Pierre and Marie Curie
CD80

40th anniversary of the discovery of radium. The surtax was for the benefit of the International Union for the Control of Cancer.

1938	
Cameroun	B1
Dahomey	B2
France	B76
Fr. Equatorial Africa	B1
Fr. Guiana	B3
Fr. Guinea	B2
Fr. India	B6
Fr. Polynesia	B5
Fr. Sudan	B1
Guadeloupe	B3
Indo-China	B14
Ivory Coast	B2
Madagascar	B2
Martinique	B2
Mauritania	B3
New Caledonia	B4
Niger	B1
Reunion	B4
St. Pierre & Miquelon	B3
Senegal	B3
Somali Coast	B2
Togo	B1

Caillie Issue

Rene Caille and Map of Northwestern Africa
CD81

Death centenary of Rene Caillie (1799-1838), French explorer.

All three denominations exist with colony name omitted.

1939	
Dahomey	108-110
Fr. Guinea	161-163
Fr. Sudan	113-115
Ivory Coast	160-162
Mauritania	109-111
Niger	84-86
Senegal	188-190
Togo	265-267

New York World's Fair Issue

Natives and New York Skyline
CD82

1939	
Cameroun	223-224
Dahomey	111-112
Fr. Equatorial Africa	78-79
Fr. Guiana	169-170
Fr. Guinea	164-165
Fr. India	111-112
Fr. Polynesia	124-125
Fr. Sudan	116-117
Guadeloupe	155-156
Indo-China	203-204
Inini	42-43
Ivory Coast	163-164
Kwangchowan	121-122
Madagascar	209-210
Martinique	186-187
Mauritania	112-113
New Caledonia	215-216
Niger	87-88
Reunion	174-175
St. Pierre & Miquelon	205-206
Senegal	191-192
Somali Coast	179-180
Togo	268-269
Wallis & Futuna Isls.	90-91

French Revolution Issue

Storming of the Bastille
CD83

150th anniversary of the French Revolution. The surtax was for the defense of the colonies.

1939	
Cameroun	B2-B6
Dahomey	B3-B7
Fr. Equatorial Africa	B4-B8, CB1
Fr. Guiana	B4-B8, CB1
Fr. Guinea	B3-B7
Fr. India	B7-B11
Fr. Polynesia	B6-B10, CB1
Fr. Sudan	B2-B6
Guadeloupe	B4-B8
Indo-China	B15-B19, CB1
Inini	B1-B5
Ivory Coast	B3-B7
Kwangchowan	B1-B5
Madagascar	B3-B7, CB1
Martinique	B3-B7
Mauritania	B4-B8
New Caledonia	B5-B9, CB1
Niger	B2-B6
Reunion	B5-B9, CB1
St. Pierre & Miquelon	B4-B8
Senegal	B4-B8, CB1
Somali Coast	B3-B7
Togo	B2-B6
Wallis & Futuna Isls.	B1-B5

Plane over Coastal Area
CD85

All five denominations exist with colony name omitted.

1940	
Dahomey	C1-C5
Fr. Guinea	C1-C5
Fr. Sudan	C1-C5
Ivory Coast	C1-C5
Mauritania	C1-C5
Niger	C1-C5
Senegal	C12-C16
Togo	C1-C5

Colonial Infantryman—CD86

1941	
Cameroun	B13B
Dahomey	B13
Fr. Equatorial Africa	B8B
Fr. Guiana	B10
Fr. Guinea	B13
Fr. India	B13
Fr. Polynesia	B12
Fr. Sudan	B12
Guadeloupe	B10
Indo-China	B19B
Inini	B7
Ivory Coast	B13
Kwangchowan	B7
Madagascar	B9
Martinique	B9
Mauritania	B14
New Caledonia	B11
Niger	B12
Reunion	B11
St. Pierre & Miquelon	B8B
Senegal	B14
Somali Coast	B9
Togo	B10B
Wallis & Futuna Isls.	B7

Cross of Lorraine and Four-motor Plane—CD87

1941-5	
Cameroun	C1-C7
Fr. Equatorial Africa	C17-C23
Fr. Guiana	C9-C10
Fr. India	C1-C6
Fr. Polynesia	C3-C9
Fr. West Africa	C1-C3
Guadeloupe	C1-C2
Madagascar	C37-C43
Martinique	C1-C2
New Caledonia	C7-C13
Reunion	C18-C24
St. Pierre & Miquelon	C1-C7
Somali Coast	C1-C7

Transport Plane—CD88

Caravan and Plane—CD89

1942	
Dahomey	C6-C13
Fr. Guinea	C6-C13
Fr. Sudan	C6-C13
Ivory Coast	C6-C13
Mauritania	C6-C13
Niger	C6-C13
Senegal	C17-C25
Togo	C6-C13

Red Cross Issue

Marianne—CD90

The surtax was for the French Red Cross and national relief.

1944	
Cameroun	B28
Fr. Equatorial Africa	B38
Fr. Guiana	B12
Fr. India	B14
Fr. Polynesia	B13
Fr. West Africa	B1
Guadeloupe	B12
Madagascar	B15
Martinique	B11
New Caledonia	B13
Reunion	B15
St. Pierre & Miquelon	B13
Somali Coast	B13
Wallis & Futuna Isls.	B9

Eboue Issue

Felix Eboue—CD91

Felix Eboue, first French colonial administrator to proclaim resistance to Germany after French surrender in World War II.

1945	
Cameroun	296-297
Fr. Equatorial Africa	156-157
Fr. Guiana	171-172
Fr. India	210-211
Fr. Polynesia	150-151
Fr. West Africa	15-16
Guadeloupe	187-188
Madagascar	259-260
Martinique	196-197
New Caledonia	274-275
Reunion	238-239
St. Pierre & Miquelon	322-323
Somali Coast	238-239

Victory Issue

Victory—CD92

European victory of the Allied Nations in World War II.

1946, May 8

Cameroun	C8
Fr. Equatorial Africa	C24
Fr. Guiana	C11
Fr. India	C7
Fr. Polynesia	C10
Fr. West Africa	C4
Guadeloupe	C3
Indo-China	C19
Madagascar	C44
Martinique	C3
New Caledonia	C14
Reunion	C25
St. Pierre & Miquelon	C8
Somali Coast	C8
Wallis & Futuna Isls.	C1

Chad to Rhine Issue

Leclerc's Departure from Chad
CD93

Battle at Cufra Oasis
CD94

Tanks in Action, Mareth
CD95

Normandy Invasion
CD96

Entering Paris
CD97

Liberation of Strasbourg
CD98

"Chad to the Rhine" march, 1942-44, by Gen. Jacques Leclerc's column, later French 2nd Armored Division.

1946, June 6

Cameroun	C9-C14
Fr. Equatorial Africa	C25-C30
Fr. Guiana	C12-C17
Fr. India	C8-C13
Fr. Polynesia	C11-C16
Fr. West Africa	C5-C10
Guadeloupe	C4-C9
Indo-China	C20-C25
Madagascar	C45-C50
Martinique	C4-C9
New Caledonia	C15-C20
Reunion	C26-C31
St. Pierre & Miquelon	C9-C14
Somali Coast	C9-C14
Wallis & Futuna Isls.	C2-C7

UPU Issue

French Colonials, Globe and Plane
CD99

75th anniversary of the Universal Postal Union.

1949, July 4

Cameroun	C29
Fr. Equatorial Africa	C34
Fr. India	C17
Fr. Polynesia	C20
Fr. West Africa	C15
Indo-China	C26
Madagascar	C55
New Caledonia	C24
St. Pierre & Miquelon	C18
Somali Coast	C18
Togo	C18
Wallis & Futuna Isls.	C10

Tropical Medicine Issue

Doctor Treating Infant
CD100

The surtax was for charitable work.

1950

Cameroun	B29
Fr. Equatorial Africa	B39
Fr. India	B15
Fr. Polynesia	B14
Fr. West Africa	B3
Madagascar	B17
New Caledonia	B14
St. Pierre & Miquelon	B14
Somali Coast	B14
Togo	B11

Military Medal Issue

Medal, Early Marine and Colonial Soldier
CD101

Centenary of the creation of the French Military Medal.

1952

Cameroun	332
Comoro Isls.	39
Fr. Equatorial Africa	186
Fr. India	233
Fr. Polynesia	179
Fr. West Africa	57
Madagascar	286
New Caledonia	295
St. Pierre & Miquelon	345
Somali Coast	267
Togo	327
Wallis & Futuna Isls.	149

Liberation Issue

Allied Landing, Victory Sign and Cross of Lorraine
CD102

10th anniversary of the liberation of France.

1954, June 6

Cameroun	C32
Comoro Isls.	C4
Fr. Equatorial Africa	C38
Fr. India	C18
Fr. Polynesia	C23
Fr. West Africa	C17
Madagascar	C57
New Caledonia	C25
St. Pierre & Miquelon	C19
Somali Coast	C19
Togo	C19
Wallis & Futuna Isls.	C11

FIDES Issue

Plowmen
CD103

Efforts of FIDES, the Economic and Social Development Fund for Overseas Possessions (Fonds d' Investissement pour le Developpement Economique et Social).

Each stamp has a different design.

1956

Cameroun	326-329
Comoro Isls.	43
Fr. Polynesia	181
Madagascar	292-295
New Caledonia	303
Somali Coast	268
Togo	331

Flower Issue

Euadania
CD104

Each stamp shows a different flower.

1958-9

Cameroun	333
Comoro Isls.	45
Fr. Equatorial Africa	200-201
Fr. Polynesia	192
Fr. So. & Antarctic Terr.	11
Fr. West Africa	79-83
Madagascar	301-302
New Caledonia	304-305
St. Pierre & Miquelon	357
Somali Coast	270
Togo	348-349
Wallis & Futuna Isls.	152

Human Rights Issue

Sun, Dove and U.N. Emblem
CD105

10th anniversary of the signing of the Universal Declaration of Human Rights.

1958

Comoro Isls.	44
Fr. Equatorial Africa	202
Fr. Polynesia	191
Fr. West Africa	85
Madagascar	300
New Caledonia	306
St. Pierre & Miquelon	356
Somali Coast	274
Wallis & Futuna Isls.	153

C.C.T.A. Issue

Map of Africa & Cogwheels—CD106

10th anniversary of the Commission for Technical Cooperation in Africa south of the Sahara.

1960

Cameroun	335
Cent. African Rep.	3
Chad	66
Congo, P.R.	90
Dahomey	138
Gabon	150
Ivory Coast	180
Madagascar	317
Mali	9
Mauritania	117
Niger	104
Upper Volta	89

Air Afrique Issue, 1961

Modern and Ancient Africa, Map and Planes—CD107

Founding of Air Afrique (African Airlines).

1961-62

Cameroun	C37
Cent. African Rep.	C5
Chad	C7
Congo, P.R.	C5
Dahomey	C17
Gabon	C5
Ivory Coast	C18
Mauritania	C17
Niger	C22
Senegal	C31
Upper Volta	C4

Anti-Malaria Issue

Malaria Eradication Emblem—CD108

World Heatlh Organization drive to eradicate malaria.

1962, Apr. 7

Cameroun B36
Cent. African Rep. B1
Chad B1
Comoro Isls. B1
Congo, P.R. B3
Dahomey B15
Gabon B4
Ivory Coast B15
Madagascar B19
Mali B1
Mauritania B16
Niger B14
Senegal B16
Somali Coast B15
Upper Volta B1

Abidjan Games Issue

Relay Race
CD109

Abidjan Games, Ivory Coast, Dec. 24-31, 1961.
Each stamp shows a different sport.

1962

Chad 83-84
Cent. African Rep. 19-20
Congo, P.R. 103-104
Gabon 163-164
Niger 109-111
Upper Volta 103-105

African and Malagasy Union Issue

Flag of African and Malagasy Union
CD110

First anniversary of the Union.

1962, Sept. 8

Cameroun 373
Cent. African Rep. 21
Chad 85
Congo, P.R. 105
Dahomey 155
Gabon 165
Ivory Coast 198
Madagascar 332
Mauritania 170
Niger 112
Senegal 211
Upper Volta 106

Telstar Issue

Telstar and Globe Showing Andover and Pleumeur-Bodou
CD111

First television connection of the United States and Europe through the Telstar satellite, July 11-12, 1962.

1962-63

Andorra, French 154
Comoro Isls. C7
Fr. Polynesia C29
Fr. So. & Antarctic Terr. C5
New Caledonia C33
Somali Coast C31
St. Pierre & Miquelon C26
Wallis & Futuna Isls. C17

Freedom From Hunger Issue

World Map and Wheat Emblem
CD112

United Nations Food and Agriculture Organization's "Freedom from Hunger" campaign.

1963, Mar. 21

Cameroun B37-B38
Cent. African Rep. B2
Chad B2
Congo, P.R. B4
Dahomey B16
Gabon B5
Ivory Coast B16
Madagascar B21
Mauritania B17
Niger B15
Senegal B17
Upper Volta B2

Red Cross Centenary Issue

Centenary Emblem—CD113

Centenary of the International Red Cross.

1963, Sept. 2

Comoro Isls. 55
Fr. Polynesia 205
New Caledonia 328
St. Pierre & Miquelon 367
Somali Coast 297
Wallis & Futuna Isls. 165

African Postal Union Issue

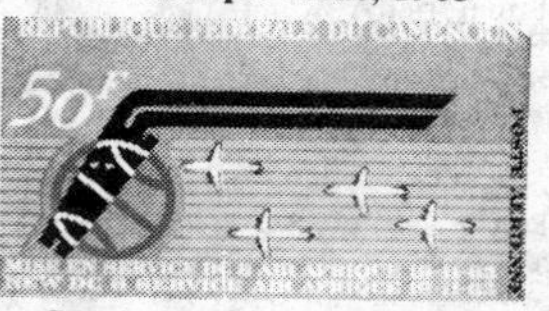

UAMPT Emblem, Radio Masts, Plane and Mail—CD114

Establishment of the African and Malagasy Posts and Telecommunications Union, UAMPT.

1963, Sept. 8

Cameroun C47
Cent. African Rep. C10
Chad C9
Congo, P.R. C13
Dahomey C19
Gabon C13
Ivory Coast C25
Madagascar C75
Mauritania C22
Niger C27
Rwanda 36
Senegal C32
Upper Volta C9

Air Afrique Issue, 1963

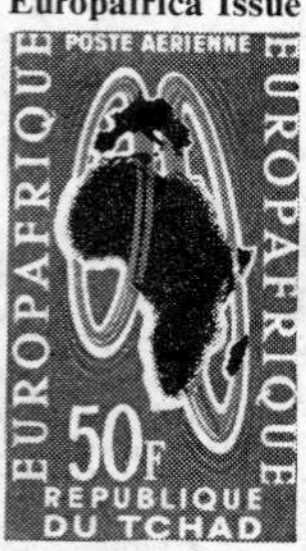

Symbols of Flight—CD115

First anniversary of Air Afrique and inauguration of DC-8 service.

1963, Nov. 19

Cameroun C48
Chad C10
Congo, P.R. C14
Gabon C18
Ivory Coast C26
Mauritania C26
Niger C35
Senegal C33

Europafrica Issue

Europe and Africa Linked Together
CD116

Signing of an economic agreement between the European Economic Community and the African and Malagasy Union, Yaounde, Cameroun, July 20, 1963.

Human Rights Issue

Scales of Justice and Globe
CD117

15th anniversary of the Universal Declaration of Human Rights.

1963, Dec. 10

Comoro Isls. 58
Fr. Polynesia 206
New Caledonia 329
St. Pierre & Miquelon 368
Somali Coast 300
Wallis & Futuna Isls. 166

PHILATEC Issue

Stamp Album, Champs Elysees Palace and Horses of Marly
CD118

"PHILATEC," International Philatelic and Postal Techniques Exhibition, Paris, June 5-21, 1964.

1963-64

Comoro Isls. 60
France 1078
Fr. Polynesia 207
New Caledonia 341
St. Pierre & Miquelon 369
Somali Coast 301
Wallis & Futuna Isls. 167

Cooperation Issue

Maps of France and Africa and Clasped Hands
CD119

Cooperation between France and the French-speaking countries of Africa and Madagascar.

1964

Cameroun 409-410
Cent. African Rep. 39
Chad 103
Congo, P.R. 121
Dahomey 193
France 1111
Gabon 175
Ivory Coast 221
Madagascar 360
Mauritania 181
Niger 143
Senegal 236
Togo 495

ITU Issue

Telegraph, Syncom Satellite and ITU Emblem
CD120

Centenary of the International Telecommunication Union.

1965, May 17

Comoro Isls. C14
Fr. Polynesia C33
Fr. So. & Antarctic Terr. C8
New Caledonia C40
New Hebrides 124-125
St. Pierre & Miquelon C29
Somali Coast C36
Wallis & Futuna Isls. C20

French Satellite A-1 Issue

Diamant Rocket and Launching Installation
CD121

Launching of France's first satellite, Nov. 26, 1965.

1965-66

Comoro Isls. C15-C16
France 1137-1138
Fr. Polynesia C40-C41
Fr. So. & Antarctic Terr. C9-C10
New Caledonia C44-C45
St. Pierre & Miquelon C30-C31
Somali Coast C39-C40
Wallis & Futuna Isls. C22-C23

French Satellite D-1 Issue

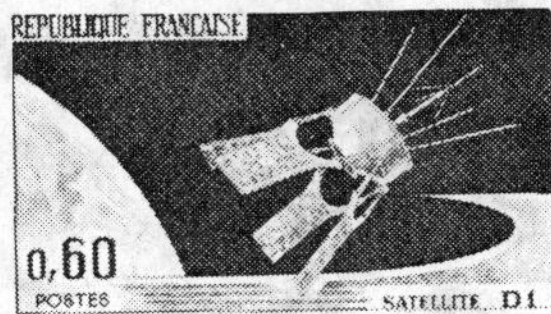

D-1 Satellite in Orbit
CD122

Launching of the D-1 satellite at Hammaguir, Algeria, Feb. 17, 1966.

1966

Comoro Isls. C17
France 1148
Fr. Polynesia C42
Fr. So. & Antarctic Terr. C11
New Caledonia C46
St. Pierre & Miquelon C32
Somali Coast C49
Wallis & Futuna Isls. C24

Air Afrique Issue, 1966

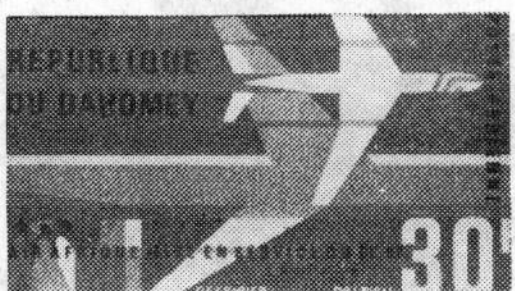

Planes and Air Afrique Emblem
CD123

Introduction of DC-8F planes by Air Afrique.

1966

Cameroun C79
Cent. African Rep. C35
Chad C26
Congo, P.R. C42
Dahomey C42
Gabon C47
Ivory Coast C32
Mauritania C57
Niger C63
Senegal C47
Togo C54
Upper Volta C31

African Postal Union, 1967

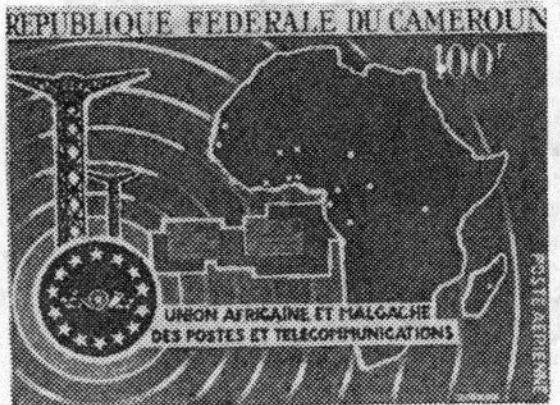

Telecommunications Symbols and Map of Africa
CD124

Fifth anniversary of the establishment of the African and Malagasy Union of Posts and Telecommunications, UAMPT.

1967

Cameroun C90
Cent. African Rep. C46
Chad C37
Congo, P.R. C57
Dahomey C61
Gabon C58
Ivory Coast C34
Madagascar C85
Mauritania C65
Niger C75
Rwanda C1-C3
Senegal C60
Togo C81
Upper Volta C50

Monetary Union Issue

Gold Token of the Ashantis, 17-18th Centuries
CD125

Fifth anniversary of the West African Monetary Union.

1967, Nov. 4

Dahomey 244
Ivory Coast 259
Mauritania 238
Niger 204
Senegal 294
Togo 623
Upper Volta 181

WHO Anniversary Issue

Sun, Flowers and WHO Emblem
CD126

20th anniversary of the World Health Organization.

1968, May 4

Afars & Issas 317
Comoro Isls. 73
Fr. Polynesia 241-242
Fr. So. & Antarctic Terr. 31
New Caledonia 367
St. Pierre & Miquelon 377
Wallis & Futuna Isls. 169

Human Rights Year Issue

Human Rights Flame
CD127

International Human Rights Year.

1968, Aug. 10

Afars & Issas 322-323
Comoro Isls. 76
Fr. Polynesia 243-244
Fr. So. & Antarctic Terr. 32
New Caledonia 369
St. Pierre & Miquelon 382
Wallis & Futuna Isls. 170

2nd PHILEXAFRIQUE Issue

Gabon No. 131 and Industrial Plant
CD128

Opening of PHILEXAFRIQUE, Abidjan, Feb. 14. Each stamp shows a local scene and stamp.

1969, Feb. 14

Cameroun C118
Cent. African Rep. C65
Chad C48
Congo, P.R. C77
Dahomey C94
Gabon C82
Ivory Coast C38-C40
Madagascar C92
Mali C65
Mauritania C80
Niger C104
Senegal C68
Togo C104
Upper Volta C62

Concorde Issue

Concorde in Flight
CD129

First flight of the prototpye Concorde super-sonic plane at Toulouse, Mar. 1, 1969.

1969

Afars & Issas C56
Comoro Isls. C29
France C42
Fr. Polynesia C50
Fr. So. & Antarctic Terr. C18
New Caledonia C63
St. Pierre & Miquelon C40
Wallis & Futuna Isls. C30

Development Bank Issue

Bank Emblem—CD130

Fifth anniversary of the African Development Bank.

1969

Cameroun 499
Chad 217
Congo, P.R. 181-182
Ivory Coast 281
Mali 127-128
Mauritania 267
Niger 220
Senegal 317-318
Upper Volta 201

ILO Issue

ILO Headquarters, Geneva, and Emblem
CD131

50th anniversary of the International Labor Organization.

1969-70

Afars & Issas 337
Comoro Isls. 83
Fr. Polynesia 251-252
Fr. So. & Antarctic Terr. 35
New Caledonia 379
St. Pierre & Miquelon 396
Wallis & Futuna Isls. 172

ASECNA Issue

Map of Africa, Plane and Airport
CD132

10th anniversary of the Agency for the Security of Aerial Navigation in Africa and Madagascar (ASECNA, Agence pour la Securite de la Navigation Aerienne en Afrique et a Madagascar).

1969-70

Cameroun 500
Cent. African Rep. 119
Chad 222
Congo, P.R. 197
Dahomey 269
Gabon 260
Ivory Coast 287
Mali 130
Niger 221
Senegal 321
Upper Volta 204

U.P.U. Headquarters Issue

U.P.U. Headquarters and Emblem
CD133

New Universal Postal Union headquarters, Bern, Switzerland.

1970

Afars & Issas 342
Algeria 443
Cameroun 503-504
Cent. African Rep. 125
Chad 225
Comoro Isls. 84
Congo, P.R. 216
Fr. Polynesia 261-262
Fr. So. & Antarctic Terr. 36
Gabon 258
Ivory Coast 295
Madagascar 444
Mali 134-135
Mauritania 283
New Caledonia 382
Niger 231-232
St. Pierre & Miquelon 397-398
Senegal 328-329
Tunisia 535
Wallis & Futuna Isls. 173

De Gaulle Issue

General de Gaulle 1940
CD134

First anniversary of the death of Charles de Gaulle, (1890-1970), President of France.

1971-72

Afars & Issas 356-357
Comoro Isls. 104-105
France 1322-1325
Fr. Polynesia 270-271
Fr. So. & Antarctic Terr. 52-53
New Caledonia 393-394
Reunion 377, 380
St. Pierre & Miquelon 417-418
Wallis & Futuna Isls. 177-178

African Postal Union Issue, 1971

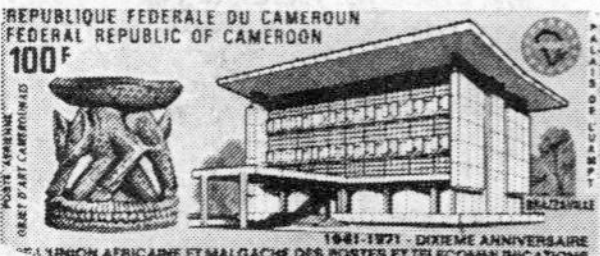

Carved Stool, UAMPT Building, Brazzaville, Congo
CD135

10th anniversary of the establishment of the African and Malagasy Posts and Telecommunications Union, UAMPT.

Each stamp has a different native design.

1971, Nov. 13

Cameroun	C177
Cent. African Rep.	C89
Chad	C94
Congo, P.R.	C136
Dahomey	C146
Gabon	C120
Ivory Coast	C47
Mauritania	C113
Niger	C164
Rwanda	C8
Senegal	C105
Togo	C166
Upper Volta	C97

West African Monetary Union Issue

African Couple, City, Village and Commemorative Coin
CD136

10th anniversary of the West African Monetary Union.

1972, Nov. 2

Dahomey	300
Ivory Coat	331
Mauritania	299
Niger	258
Senegal	374
Togo	825
Upper Volta	280

African Postal Union Issue, 1973

Telecommunications Symbols and Map of Africa
CD137

11th anniversary of the African and Malagasy Posts and Telecommunications Union (UAMPT).

1973, Sept. 12

Cameroun	574
Cent. African Rep.	194
Chad	272
Congo, P.R.	289
Dahomey	311
Gabon	320
Ivory Coast	361
Madagascar	500
Mauritania	304
Niger	287
Rwanda	540
Senegal	393
Togo	849
Upper Volta	285

Philexafrique II—Essen Issue

Buffalo and Dahomey No. C33
CD138

Wild Ducks and Baden No. 1
CD139

Designs: Indigenous fauna, local and German stamps.

Types CD138-CD139 printed horizontally and vertically se-tenant in sheets of 10 (2x5). Label between horizontal pairs alternately commemoratives Philexafrique II, Libreville, Gabon, June 1978, and 2nd International Stamp Fair, Essen, Germany, Nov. 1-5.

1978-1979

Benin	C285-C286
Central Africa	C200-C201
Chad	C238-C239
Congo Republic	C245-C246
Djibouti	C121-C122
Gabon	C215-C216
Ivory Coast	C64-C65
Mali	C356-C357
Mauritania	C185-C186
Niger	C291-C292
Rwanda	C12-C13
Senegal	C146-C147
Togo	C363-C364
Upper Volta	C253-C254

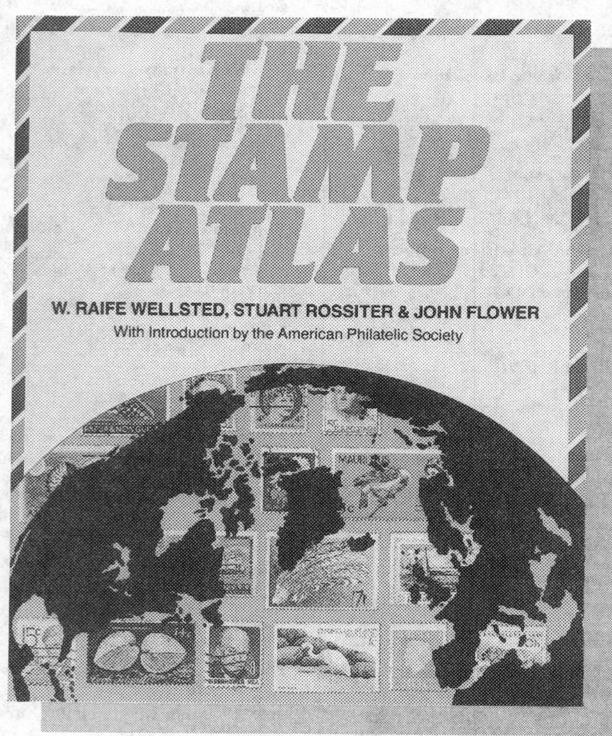

The Topical Cross Reference

The topical cross reference is a listing of stamps relating to a specific topic or theme. Each year, two topics are selected for this treatment. The topics chosen for this edition are butterflies and ships. The listings are organized by country and sequentially by Scott number. After each Scott number a brief subject description follows.

Topical collections are based on the design of the stamp. As is the case for any type of stamp collection, you may extend your collection as far as you like, including perforation differences, paper differences, related cancellations and so on. Or, you may wish to narrowly collect within a topic. For the ship topic, as an example, you may choose to limit your collection to ocean liners, military ships, sailboats or to those used in sporting events.

The listings we present are based on individual handbooks published by the American Topical Association (ATA). Since it is our intent to present topical listings as current as the stamp listings in our catalogue, we have supplemented that which is found in the ATA-published listings with more current information.

Topical listings found in each volume of the 1994 edition will include items issued by countries found in that volume. Thus, the listings that follow will cover only Volume 4 (J-Q) countries.

Following the topical listings is information on the ATA, including a list of its available handbooks and checklists. The ATA is a membership organization, offering a variety of services. This information and listing begins on page 47A.

Catching Butterflies

The listings for butterflies also contain moths and related insects. Both stylized and unidentified insects, as well as at least 2,138 identified species, are found on stamps. Our listings are based on the ATA handbook, *Lepidoptera on Stamps,* and its supplement, *Insects on Stamps,* both by Don Wright.

Ship Stamps Ahoy

Although we call the topic ships, as do most collectors and topical new issue services, the purists refer to the topic as watercraft on stamps. Our listings include everything from ocean liners and battleships to canoes and rafts. If you collect more narrowly (for example, you collect only outrigger canoes), just check the description next to the catalogue number. The listings are compiled from *Watercraft on Stamps* by Katherine A. Kirk. We would also like to thank the Ships on Stamps Society (a unit of the ATA) and the Ship Stamp Society of Great Britain.

To keep up-to-date on topical listings for new stamps, you'll want to take a look at the *Scott Stamp Monthly.* Each issue features topical listings for those stamps appearing for the first time in that issue. In addition to butterflies and ships, you'll find information on subjects as diverse as Americana, astronomy, baseball, castles, computers, hands, minerals, theater and many more.

Butterflies

Japan

154, Bombyx mori L., Bombycidae; 383, Bombyx mori L., Bombycidae - No insect, only shows silk; 431, Bobbins of silk, Bombyx mori L., Bombycidae; 622, 887A, Sasakia charonda Hewitson, Apaturidae; 879, Papilio bianor Cramer, Papilio memnon L., Atrophaneura alcinous Klug, all Papilionidae, Inachis io L., Hypolimnas bolina L., Vanessa canace L., all 3 are Nymphalidae; Hebomoia glaucippe L., Gonepteryx mahaguru Gistel, Anthocharis cardamines L., last 3 are Pieridae. Painting by Fujishima; 1052, Stylized butterfly, actor with wings, "Kocho, the butterfly"; 1293, Graphium doson albidum Wileman, Papilionidae; 1361, moths at flame, "Fire Dance"; 1374, Stylized butterfly, child with net, dragonfly; 1381, Stylized butterfly; 1412, Luehdorfia japonica Leech, Papilionidae; 1416, Pieris rapae crucivora Boisduval, Pieridae; 1399, Stylized butterflies; 1437A, Pieris rapae crucivora Boisduval, Pieridae; 1448, Stylized butterfly & boy; 1680, 1699A, Parnassius eversmanni Menetries, Papilionidae.

1685, Thermozephyrus ataxus Doubleday & Hewitson, Lycaenidae; 1688, Elcysma westwoodi Vollenhoven, Zygaenidae; 1692, 1699A, Danaus sita Kollar, Danaidae; 1698, Kallima inachus Boisduval, Nymphalidae; 1699b, 1699A, Anthocharis cardamines L., Pieridae; 1699c, 1699A, Sasakia charonda Hewitson, Apaturidae; 1722, 1723a, Pieris rapae L., Pieridae; 1772, Stylized butterfly in dress; 2024, Fabriciana nerippe Felder, Nymphalidae; 2059, 2059a, Boy with butterfly wings, on horse; 2090, 2116, 2117b, Stylized butterfly; B10-B11, Caterpillar in beak.

Jordan

1431, 1435, Danaus chrysippus; 1432, 1435, Aporia cartaegi; 1433, 1435, Papilio machaon; 1434, 1435, Pseudochazara telephassa.

Korea

202A, Metopta rectifasciata Menetries, Noctuidae; 501, Sericinus telemon Donovan, Papilionidae; 573, Bombyx mori L., Bombycidae; 722A, Stylized butterflies; 802, Bombyx mori L., Bombycidae; 817, Aporia hippia Bremer, Pieridae; 934, butterfly dance; 1004, Dilipa fenestra Leech, Apaturidae; 1005, Luehdorfia puziloi Leech, Papilionidae; 1006, Papilio xuthus L., Papilionidae; 1007, Parnassius bremeri Felder, Papilionidae; 1008, Colias erate Esper, Pieridae; 1009, Atrophaneura alcinous Klug, Papilionidae; 1010, Hestina assimilis L., Apaturidae; 1011, Graphium sarpedon L., Papilionidae; 1012, Fabriciana nerippe Felder, Nymphalidae.

1013, Nymphalis xanthomelas Denis & Schiffermuller, Nymphalidae; 1261, Stylized butterflies, hand and cane inside heart; 1467a, Papilio xuthus L., Papilionidae; 1467b, Papilio maackii Menetries, Papilionidae & Pierid; 1467c, Papilio xuthus L., Papilionidae & stylized butterfly; 1467d, Papilio xuthus L., Papilionidae; 1467e, Papilio xuthus L., Papilionidae; 1467f, Papilio maackii Menetries, Papilionidae, Scott 1467a-1467e in souvenir sheet showing folk paintings of butterflies; 1530, Stylized butterfly; 1584, 1594A, Stylized butterfly and collecting net; 1625, Mimeusemia persimilis, Agaristidae; 1627, Anthocharis scolymus Butler, Pieridae.

Laos

101, Cethosia biblis Drury, Nymphalidae; 102, Precis hierta Fabr., Nymphalidae; 103, Euschema militaris L., Geometridae; 201-202, Weaving silk of Bombyx mori L., Bombycidae; 386, Herona marathus angustata Moore, Apaturidae; 387, Pantoporia paraka Butler, Nymphalidae; 388, Euripus halitherses Doubleday, Apaturidae; 389, Lebadea martha Fabr., Nymphalidae; 390, Iton semamora Moore, Hesperiidae; 391, Elymnias hypermnestra L., Satyridae; 692, Aporia hippia Bremer, Pieridae; 693, Euthalia irrubescens, Nymphalidae; 694, Shirozua lutea Hewitson, Lycaenidae; 695, Camena ctesia Hewitson, Lycaenidae; 696, Kallima inachus L., Nymphalidae; 697, Ixias pyrene L., Pieridae; 698, Danaus sita Kollar, Danaidae (Flowers & butterflies); 870, Polyura eudamippus Doubleday, Nymphalidae; 871, Papilio memnon L., Papilionidae; 872, Graphium doson Felder, Papilionidae; 873, Danaus chrysippus L., Danaidae; 874, Unidentified Nymphalidae; 875, Unidentified Lycaenidae; 876, Danaus sp., Danaidae; 1048A, Sasakia charonda Hewitson, Apaturidae; 1048B, Luehdorfia puziloi Erschoff, Papilionidae; 1048C, Papilio bianor Cramer, Papilionidae; 1048D, Papilio machaon L., Papilionidae; 1048E, Graphium doson Felder, Papilionidae; 1048F, Cyrestis thyodamas Boisduval, Nymphalidae; C46, Attacus atlas L., Saturniidae; C69, Bombyx mori L., Bombycidae.

Lebanon

108-113, Bombyx mori L., Bombycidae; C427, Pericallia matronula L., Arctiidae; C428, Heliconius cyrbia Godart, Heliconiidae; C429, Vanessa atalanta L., Nymphalidae; C430, Hipparchia semele L., Satyridae; C431, Papilio machaon L., Papilionidae; C432, Anthocharis cardamines L., Pieridae; C433, Morpho cypris Westwood, Morphidae; C434, Erasmia sanguiflua Drury, Zygaenidae; C435, C654, C656, Battus crassus Cramer, Papilionidae; C436, C655, Charaxes ameliae Doumet, Nymphalidae; C439-C441, Bombyx mori B L., Bombycidae; C442-C445, Weaving silk at loom, Bombyx mori L., Bombycidae.

Liberia

683, Chrysiridia madagascariensis Lesson, Uraniidae; 684, Callicore sorana Godart, Nymphalidae; 685, Erasmia pulchella Hope, Zygaenidae; 686, Morpho cypris Westwood, Morphidae; 687, Agrias amydon Hewitson, Nymphalidae; 688, Vanessa cardui L., Nymphalidae; C204, Pierella nereis Drury, Satyridae, Margin: Morpho hecuba L. & Morpho cypris Westwood, Morphidae, Graphium weiskei Ribbe, Papilionidae.

Libya

249-251, Bombyx mori L., Bombycidae; 811, Stylized butterfly, painting; 966a, Pseudotergumia fidia L., Satyridae; 966b, Chazara prieuri Pierret, Satyridae; 966c, Polygonia c-album L., Nymphalidae; 966d, Colias crocea Geoffroy, Pieridae; 966e, Anthocharis belia L., Pieridae; 966f, Pandoriana pandora Schiffermuller, Nymphalidae; 966g, Melanargia ines Hofmannsegg, Satyridae; 966h, Charaxes jasius L., Nymphalidae; 966i, Nymphalis antiopa L., Nymphalidae; 966j, Euphydryas desfontainii Godart, Nymphalidae; 966k, Iphiclides podalirius feisthameli Duponchel, Papilionidae; 966l, Glaucopsyche melanops algerica Heyne, Lycaenidae; 966m, Spialia sertorius ali Oberthur, Hesperiidae; 966n, Pieris brassicae L., Pieridae; 966o, Lysandra albicans Herrich-Schaeffer, Lycaenidae; 966p, Celestrina argiolus L., Lycaenidae; 966, sheet of 16, Scott 966a-966p; 1302c, "Catching butterflies," Children's Day; 1330e, White butterfly, Pieridae & combine harvester; 1330h, Colias sp., Pieridae in irrigation design; 1330h, 1330l, Polygonia c-album L., Nymphalidae, across 2 stamps; 1393, Stylized butterflies.

Liechtenstein
536, Coenonympha oedippus Fabr., Satyridae; 539, Euphydryas cynthia Denis & Schiffermuller, Nymphalidae; 608, Stylized butterfly.

Luxembourg
734, Vanessa atalanta L., Nymphalidae.

Macao
512, 517a, Euploea midamas L., Danaidae; 513, 517a, Hebomoia glaucippe L., Pieridae; 514, 517a, Lethe confusa Aurivillius, Satyridae; 515, 517a, Heliophorus epicles Godart, Lycaenidae; 516, 517a, Euthalia phemius seitzi Fruhstorfer, Nymphalidae; 517, 517a, Troides helena L., Papilionidae.

Madagascar
306, Colotis zoe Grandidier, Pieridae; 307, Acraea hova Boisduval, Acraeidae; 308, Salamis anacardi duprei Vinson, Nymphalidae; 309, Chionaema saalmulleri pauliani Tougoet, Arctiidae; 310, Hypolimnas dexithea Hewitson, Nymphalidae; 343, caterpillar in bird's beak; 698, Eudaphaenura splendens Viette, Noctuidae; 699, Othreis boseae, Noctuidae; 700, Atrophaneura antenor Drury, Papilionidae; 701, Acraea hova Boisduval, Acraeidae; 702, Epicausis smithi Mabille, Noctuidae; 703, Papilio delalandei Godart, Papilionidae; 736, Nephele oenopion Hubner, Sphingidae; 738, Xanthopan morgani praedicta Rothschild & Jordan, Sphingidae; 739, Hippotion batschi Keferstein, Sphingidae; 740, Daphnis nerii L., Sphingidae; 863, Chrysiridia madagascariensis Lesson, Uraniidae; 865, Papilio dardanus Brown, Papilionidae; 867, Argema mittrei Guerin, Saturniidae; 868, Salamis anteva Ward, Nymphalidae Margin: Charaxes analava Ward; Graphium cyrnus Boisduval, Papilionidae; Precis rhadama Boisduval; Hypolimnas dexithea Hewitson; Euxanthe wakefieldi Ward. All Nymphalidae unless noted; C63, Charaxes antamboulou Lucas, Nymphalidae; C64, Chrysiridia madagascariensis Lesson, Uraniidae; C65, Argema mittrei Guerin, Saturniidae.

Mali
348, Eurema brigitta Cramer, Pieridae; 349, Graphium pylades Fabr., Papilionidae; 350, Melanitis leda L., Satyridae; 351, Gonimbrasia belina occidentalis, Rothschild, Saturniidae; 352, Bunaea alcinoe Stoll, Saturniidae; 391, Utetheisa pulchella L., Arctiidae; 392, Mylothris chloris Fabr., Pieridae; 393, Hypolimnas misippus L., Nymphalidae; 394, Papilio demodocus Esper, Papilionidae; C402, Danaus chrysippus L., Danaidae; J21, Polyptychus roseus Druce, Sphingidae; J22, Deilephila nerii L., Sphingidae; J23, Gynanisa maja Klug, Saturniidae; J24, Bunaea alcinoe Stoll, Saturniidae; J25, Colotis eris Klug, Pieridae; J26, Colotis evippe Boisduval, Pieridae; J27, Charaxes jasius epijasius Reiche, Nymphalid; J28, Manatha microcera Bourgogne, Psychidae; J29, Hypokopelates otraeda Hewitson, Lycaenidae; J30, Lipaphnaeus leonina Sharpe, Lycaenidae; J31, Gonimbrasia hecate Rougeot, Saturniidae; J32, Lobobunaea christyi Sharpe, Saturniidae; J33, Hypolimnas misippus L., Nymphalidae; J34, Catopsilia florella Fabr., Pieridae.

Manchukuo
136, Stylized butterfly.

Mauritania
212, Myrina silenus silenus Fabr., Lycaenidae; 213, Colotis danae Fabr., Pieridae; 214, Hypolimnas misippus L., Nymphalidae; 215, Danaus chrysippus L., Danaidae; 647, Heliothis armigera Hubner, Noctuidae; 650, Agrotis ipsilon Hufnagel, Noctuidae; 651, Chilo sp., Pyralidae; 654, Plutella xylostella L., Plutellidae; 657, Trichoplusia ni Hubner, Noctuidae; 681, No insect on stamp - Margin: Mylothris chloris Fabr., Pieridae, Antanartia hippomene, Hubner, Nymphalidae, Melanitis leda L., Satyridae; 682, No insect on stamp - Margin: Acraea bonasia Fabr., Acraeidae Graphium antheus Cramer, Papilionidae Precis octavia Cramer, Nymphalidae Precis westermanni Wwd., Nymphalidae; 683, Bunaea alcinoe Stoll, Saturniidae, Margin: Colotis regina Trimen, Pieridae, Antanartia delius Doubleday, Nymphalidae, Papilio demoleus L., Papilionidae.

Papilio machaon L., Papilionidae; 684, Cyrestis camillus Fabr., Nymphalidae, Margin: Colotis evagore Klug, Pieridae, Precis sophia Fabr. & P. oenone L., both Nymphalidae, Graphium pylades Fabr., Papilionidae; 685, Salamis cytora Doubleday, Nymphalidae, Margin: Papilio demodocus Esper, Papilionidae, Acherontia atropos L., Sphingidae, Hypolimnas misippus L., Nymphalidae, Vanessula milca Hewitson, Nymphalidae Mesoacidalia aglaja L., Nymphalidae; Margin: Charaxes jasius L., Nymphalidae, Myrina silenus Fabr., Lycaenidae, Iphiclides podalirius L., Papilionidae, Precis hierta Fabr., Nymphalidae; 686, No insect on stamp, Margin: Deilephila nerii L., Sphingidae; Papilio dardanus Brown, Papilionidae; Pseudacraea boisduvali Doubleday, Nymphalidae; Phalanta columbina Cramer, Nymphalidae; C95, Stylized butterfly on fan.

Mexico
1327, Papilio machaon L., Papilionidae; 1345, Stylized butterfly; 1559-1562, Danaus plexippus L., Danaidae; 1733, Butterfly, flower, etc.; RA1-RA3, No insect, but funds from sales used to fight a plague of locusts. Required on mail 1925-31.

Monaco
529, caterpillar in bird's beak; 760, Parnassius apollo L., Papilionidae; 872, Colias sp., Pieridae and Zygaena sp., Zygaenidae. Colette & cat; 874, Nyctaon pyri Schiffermuller, Saturniidae; 1119, Stylized butterfly; 1173, Very stylized Nymphalidae; 1390, Stylized Madame butterfly; 1426, Boloria graeca tendensis Higgins, Nymphalidae; 1427, Zygaena brisae vesubiana Esper, Zygaenidae; 1428, Erebia aethiops Esper, Satyridae; 1429, Parnassius phoebus gazeli, Papilionidae; 1430, Papilio alexanor Esper, Papilionidae; 1498, Stylized butterfly, Chopin & Schubert issue; 1586-1589, Papilio machaon L., Papilionidae; 1680b, Stylized butterfly with pomegranate.

Mongolia
218, caterpillar in bird's beak; 331, Inachis io L., Nymphalidae; 332, Gonepteryx rhamni L., Pieridae; 333, Aglais urticae L., Nymphalidae; 334, Parnassius apollo L., Papilionidae; 335, Papilio machaon L., Papilionidae; 336, Agrodiaetus damon Denis & Schiffermuller, Lycaenidae; 337, Limenitis populi L., Nymphalidae; 752, Limenitis populi L., Nymphalidae; 753, Ammobiota festiva Hufnagel, Arctiidae; 754, Diacrisis purpurata L., Arctiidae; 755, Catocala electa View, Noctuidae; 756, Isoceras kaszabi Daniel, Cossidae; 757, Hyles euphorbiae L., Sphingidae; 758, Arctia caja L., Arctiidae; 759, Diacrisia sannio L., Arctiidae; 982, Aporia crataegi L., Pieridae; 983, Gastropacha quercifolia L., Lasiocampidae; 984, Colias chrysotheme Esper, Pieridae; 985, Dasychira fascelina L., Lymantriidae; 986, Malacosoma neustria L., Lasiocampidae; 987, Diacrisia sannio L., Arctiidae; 988, Heodes virgaureae L., Lycaenidae; 1176, Stylized butterfly; 1281, Stylized butterfly, pony; 1488, Stylized butterfly on mushroom; 1521, Pseudoneptis coenobita Fabr., Nymphalidae; 1522, Colias tycha, Pieridae; 1523, Leptidea amurensis Menetries, Pieridae; 1524, Oeneis tarpenledevi, Satyridae; 1525, Mesoacidalia aglaja L., Nymphalidae; 1526, Smerinthus ocellata L., Sphingidae; 1527, Pericallia matronula L., Arctiidae; 1568, Children backpacking, hunting butterflies UNICEF, stylized butterflies; 1904, Diacrisia purpurata L., Arctiidae; 1905, Nyctaon pyri Denis & Schiffermuller, Saturniidae; 1906, Polygonia c-album L., Nymphalidae; 1907, Abraxas grossulariata L., Geometridae; 1908, Melanargia galathea L., Satyridae; 1909, Papilio machaon L., Papilionidae; 1910, Anthocharis cardamines L., Pieridae; 1911, Hyles lineata Fabr., Sphingidae, Margin: Papilio machaon L., Papilionidae; 1944, No insect, stylized butterflies in margin; 1945, 1954, Colotis pleione Klug, Pieridae; 1947, 1956, Parnassius charltonius Gray, Papilionidae; 1948, Diacrisia purpurata L., Arctiidae; 1949, 1957, Pseudochazara regeli Alpheraky, Satyridae; 1950, 1958, Colotis fausta Olivier, Pieridae; 1963, Diacrisia sannio L., Arctiidae; 2081a-2081h, Moths & Butterflies; 2082, Butterfly; 2083, Moth, Arctiidae; B6, Girl chasing butterflies; C5, Stylized butterfly; 2104a, Anthocharis cardamines; 2104b, Inachis io; 2104c, Fabriciana adippe; 2104d, Limenitis reducta; 2104e, Agrumaenia carniolica; 2104f, Polyommatus icarus; 2104g, Parnassius apollo; 2104h, Saturnia pyri; 2105, Limenitis populi; 2106, Heodes virgaureae.

Morocco
497, Iphiclides podalirius feisthameli Duponchel, Papilionidae; 498, Parnalius rumina ornatior Blachier, Papilionidae; 528, Hyles lineata livornica Esper, Sphingidae; 529, Mesoacidalia aglaja lyauteyi Oberthur, Nymphalidae; 610, Euphydryas desfontainii Godart, Nymphalidae; 611, Colotis evagore Klug, Pieridae; 631, Elphinstonia charlonia Donzel, Pieridae; 632, Anthocharis belia L., Pieridae.

Mozambique
364, Papilio demodocus Esper, Papilionidae; 365, Amphicallia thewalli Druce, Arctiidae; 366, Euxanthe wakefieldi Ward, Nymphalidae; 367, Axiocerses harpax Fabr., Lycaenidae; 368, 517, Colotis omphale Godart, Pieridae; 369, Papilio dardanus tibullus Kirby, Papilionidae; 370, Bunaeopsis hersilia dido M&W, Saturniidae; 371, Argema mimosae Boisduval, Saturniidae; 372, Graphium antheus evombaroides Eimer, Papilionidae; 373, Athletes ethra Westwood, Saturniidae; 374, Danaus chrysippus L., Danaidae; 375, Papilio phorcas ansorgei Rothschild, Papilionidae; 376, Arniocera ericata Butler, Zygaenidae; 377, Pseudaphelia apollinaris Boisduval, Saturniidae; 378, Egybollis vaillantina Stoll, Noctuidae; 379, Hebena lateritia Herrich-Schaeffer, Thyretidae; 380, Heraclia mozambica Mabille, Agaristidae; 381, 527, Nyctemera leuconoe Hopffer, Arctiidae; 382, Charaxes protoclea azota Hewitson, Nymphalidae; 383, Aegocera fervida Walker, Agaristidae; 384-385, Papilio dardanus tibullus Kirby, Papilionidae, shows Scott 369; 635, Stylized butterfly, scene; 668, Papilio nireus lyaeus Doubleday, Papilionidae; 669, Amauris ochlea Boisduval, Danaidae; 670, Pinacopteryx eriphia Godart, Pieridae; 671, Precis hierta cebrene Trimen, Nymphalidae; 672, Colotis ione Godart, Pieridae; 673, Catacroptera cloanthe Cramer, Nymphalidae; 1101, butterfly done in silver.

Netherlands
B207, Stylized butterfly, girl; B223, Stylized butterfly, girl; B361, Stylized butterfly; B370, Stylized butterfly; B386, Stylized butterflies; B387, Stylized butterfly; B393, butterfly dancer; B477, Stylized butterfly.

Netherlands Antilles
36-42, Stylized Hippotion celerio L., Sphingidae, in corners; 414, Polythysana rubrescens Blanchard, Saturniidae; 415, Caligo eurilochus Cramer, Brassolidae; 416, Prepona omphale amesia Fruhstorfer, Nymphalidae; 417, Morpho aega Hubner, Morphidae.

Netherlands Indies
48-58, 70-78, 88-96, 139, O10-O18, Stylized Hippotion celerio L., Sphingidae.

Netherlands New Guinea
B23, Ornithoptera paradisea Staudinger, Papilionidae; B24, Thysonotis danis Cramer, Lycaenidae; B25, Cethosia chrysippe cydippe L., Nymphalidae; B26, Taenaris catops Westwood, Amathusiidae.

New Caledonia
357, Papilio montrouzieri Boisduval, Papilionidae; 358, Polyura clitarchus Hewitson, Nymphalidae; 359-360, Hypolimnas bolina L., Nymphalidae, male & female; 552, "Butterfly Chase," painting by B. Morisot; 555, Graphium gelon Boisduval, Papilionidae; 556, Polyura gamma Lathy, Nymphalidae; 626-628, Paratisiphone lyrnessa Holloway, Satyridae; 651, butterflies, ladybugs, flora, fauna, etc.; 658, Eurema hecabe novae- caledoniae, Pieridae; 659, Hypolimnas octocula elsina Butler, Nymphalidae; 660, Precis villida calybe, Nymphalidae; 661, Cyrestis achates whitmei Butler, Nymphalidae; 662a, 661, flying in jungle; 662b, 659, flying in Jungle; 662c, 658, flying in jungle; 662d, 660, flying in jungle; C51, Danaus genutia

Cramer, Danaidae; C52, Hippotion celerio L., Sphingidae; C53, Delias ellipsis deJoannis, Pieridae; C152, Stylized butterfly.

New Hebrides
203, Lyssa curvata Skinner, Uraniidae.

Nicaragua
1148, Dynamine myrrhina Doubleday, Nymphalidae; 1149, Eunica alcmena Doubleday & Hewitson, Nymphalidae; 1150, Callizona acesta L., Nymphalidae; 1151, Adelpha leuceria Druce, Nymphalidae; C1000, Parides iphidamas Fabr., Papilionidae; 1230, Xylophanes chiron Walker, Sphingidae; 1231, Manduca ochus Klug, Sphingidae; 1232, Eumorpha labruscae L., Sphingidae; 1233, Amphypterus gannascus Stoll, Sphingidae; 1234, Eumorpha satellita licaon Cramer, Sphingidae; 1235, Agrius cingulata Fabr., Sphingidae; 1236, Rothschildia jorulla Westwood, Saturniidae; 1567, Evenus coronata Hewitson, Lycaenidae; 1568, Charaxes nitebis Hewitson, Nymphalidae; 1569, Salamis cacta Fabr., Nymphalidae; 1570, Papilio maackii Menetries, Papilionidae; 1571, Euphaedra cyparissa Cramer, Nymphalidae; 1572, Palaeochrysophanus hippothoe L., Lycaenidae; 1573, Ritra aurea Druce, Lycaenidae; 1853, Prepona praeneste Hewitson, Nymphalidae; 1854, Anartia fatima Fabr., Nymphalidae; 1855, Eryphanis aesacus Herrich-Schaeffer, Brassolidae; 1856, Heliconius melpomene L., Heliconiidae; 1857, Chlosyne janais Druce, Nymphalidae; 1858, Marpesia iole Drury, Nymphalidae; 1859, Siproeta epaphus Latreille, Nymphalidae; 1860, Morpho peleides Kollar, Morphidae; 1861p, Doxocopa clothilda Felder, Apaturidae; 1861q, Dismorphia deione Hewitson, Pieridae; 1861s, Callithomia hezia Hewitson, Ithomiidae; 1870, No insect, Margin: Ithomia derasa Hewitson, Ithomiidae; 1917, flora and fauna of the rainforest; 1917d, Marposa morpho; C606, Heliconius petiverana Doubleday & Hewitson, Heliconiidae; C607, Dryas iulia Fabr., Nymphalidae; C608, Marpesia petreus Cramer, Nymphalidae; C609, Ancyluris jurgenseni Saunders, Riodinidae; C610, Evenus regalis Cramer, Lycaenidae; C611, Rhetus arcius L., Riodinidae; C612, Lymnas pixe Boisduval, Riodinidae; C613, Philaethria dido L., Heliconiidae; C614, Parides arcas Cramer, Papilionidae; C615, Anaea cleomestra Hewitson, Nymphalidae; C616, Siproeta epaphus Latreille, Nymphalidae; C617, Prepona demophon L., Nymphalidae; C967, Morpho cypris Westwood, Morphidae; C1001, Anaea fabius Cramer, Nymphalidae; C1002, Morpho peleides Kollar, Morphidae.

Niger
643, Hypolimnas misippus L., Nymphalidae; 644, Papilio demodocus Esper, Papilionidae; 645, Nymphalis antiopa L., Nymphalidae; 646, Charaxes jasius L., Nymphalidae; 647, Danaus chrysippus L., Danaidae; 810, Cymothoe sangaris Godart, Nymphalidae; 823, Graphium pylades Fabr., Papilionidae; 824, Pseudacraea hostilia Drury, Nymphalidae; 827, Precis octavia Cramer, Nymphalidae, dry season form; 828, Pseudacraea boisduvali Doubleday, Nymphalidae, Margin: Sallya amulia Cramer, Neptis saclava marpessa Hopffer, Aterica galene Brown, Pseudacraea clarki Butler, Precis octavia Cramer (wet season form), all Nymphalidae; Bematistes alcinoe Felder, Acraeidae; Graphium agamedes Westwood, Papilionidae.

Norway
893, Aporia crataegi L., Pieridae.

Panama
500, Apodemia albinus Felder, Riodinidae; 501, Caligo ilioneus Cramer, Brassolidae; 502, Mesosemia tenaera Westwood, Riodinidae; 503, Anthoptus epictetus Fabr., Hesperiidae; C368, Entheus priassus L., Hesperiidae; C369, Brachyglenis drymo Godman & Salvin, Ithomiidae; C370, Urbanus chalco Hubner, Hesperiidae.

Paraguay
1302, 1304, Stylized butterfly; 1498a, Callicore pastazza Staudinger, Nymphalidae; 1498b, Agrias narcissus Staudinger, Nymphalidae; 1498c, Papilio zagreus Doubleday, Papilionidae; 1498d, Heliconius chestertoni Hewitson, Heliconiidae; 1498e, Philaethria dido L., Heliconiidae; 1498f, Callicore astarte Cramer, Nymphalidae; 1498g, Papilio thoas brasiliensis Rothschild & Jordan, Papilionidae; 1499a, Agrias sardanapalus Bates, Nymphalidae; 1499b, Callithea sapphira Hubner, Nymphalidae; 1499c, Jemadia hospita Butler, Hesperiidae; 1532f, Stylized butterfly; 1655a, Prepona praeneste Hewitson, Nymphalidae; 1655b, Prepona pylene proschion Fruhstorfer, Nymphalidae; 1655c, Pereute leucodrosime Kollar, Pieridae; 1655d, Agrias amydon Hewitson, Nymphalidae; 1655e, Morpho aega Hubner, Morphidae; 1655f, Pseudatteria leopardina Butler, Tortricidae; 1655g, Morpho helena Staudinger, Morphidae; 1655h, Morpho hecuba L., Morphidae; 1886, Stylized butterfly, IYC; 1968, Stylized butterfly, Christmas & IYC; 2137d, 2138 Stylized butterfly with fungi; C401, Hypolimnas bolina L., Nymphalidae.

Peru
978, Agrias amydon Hewitson, Nymphalidae, female; 979, Agrias beata Staudinger, Nymphalidae, male; 980, Agrias sardanapalus Bates, Nymphalidae, male; 981, Agrias sardanapalus Bates, Nymphalidae, female; 982, Agrias beata Staudinger, Nymphalidae, female; 1033, Amydon; 1034, Agrias beata, female; 1037, Agrias beata, male; 1035, Sardanapalus, male; 1036, Sardanapalus, female.

Philippines
1031, Troides magellanus Felder, Papilionidae; 1032, Graphium agamemnon L., Papilionidae; 1033, Papilio helena hystaspes Felder, Papilionidae; 1034, Trogonoptera trojana Staudinger, Papilionidae; 1693, Euthalia satrapes amlana Jumulon, Nymphalidae; 1694, Papilio palinurus daedalus Felder, Papilionidae; 1695, Prothoe franck semperi Honrath, Nymphalidae; 1696, Troides magellanus Felder, Papilionidae; 1697, Yoma sabina vasuki Lindemans, Nymphalidae; 1698, Graphium idaeoides Hewitson, Papilionidae; 1820, Cepora sp., Pieridae.

Poland
830, Printed on silk, Bombyx mori L., Bombycidae; 1035, Parnassius mnemosyne L., Papilionidae; 1036, Acherontia atropos L., Sphingidae; 1037, Iphiclides podalirius L., Papilionidae; 1105, Pieris sp., Pieridae; 1543, Inachis io L., Nymphalidae; 1543, Papilio machaon L., Papilionidae; 1544, Aglais urticae L., Nymphalidae; 1545, Nymphalis antiopa L., Nymphalidae; 1546, Apatura iris L., Apaturidae; 1547, Vanessa atalanta L., Nymphalidae; 1548, Colias hyale L., Pieridae; 1549, Melanargia galathea L., Satyridae; 1550, Maculinea arion L., Lycaenidae; 1813, Stylized butterfly; 1866, Stylized butterfly; 2030, Stylized butterfly; 2113, Stylized butterfly; 2227, Parnassius apollo L., Papilionidae; 2228, Nymphalis polychloros L., Nymphalidae; 2229, Papilio machaon L., Papilionidae; 2230, Nymphalis antiopa L., Nymphalidae; 2231, Fabriciana adippe Schiffermuller, Nymphalidae; 2232, Argynnis paphia L., Nymphalidae; 2556, butterfly with flowers; 3050, Papilio machaon L., Papilionidae; 3051, Catocala sponsa L., Noctuidae; 3052, Vanessa cardui L., Nymphalidae; 3053, Iphiclides podalirius L., Papilionidae; 3054, Callimorpha dominula L., Arctiidae; 3055, Inachis io L., Nymphalidae; 3056, Aporia crataegi L., Pierdae; 3094, Butterfly, dog, sun & person. Child's drawing.

Portugal
1924, Stylized butterfly; 1925, 1925a, unidentified butterfly.

Portugal – Azores
346, Pieris brassicae azorensis Rebel, Pieridae; 348, Phlogophora interrupta Warren, Noctuidae; 351, Colias crocea Geoffroy, Pieridae; 352, Hipparchia azorina Strecker, Satyridae.

Ships

Japan
167-170, Battleships KATORI Japanese Navy; 218, 220, Cruiser HIEI Japanese Navy; 257, 276, Trading ship, "goshuinbune"; 328, Shipbuilding; 392, Bow of whaling vessel; 409-411, 426, 439-441, Bow of whaling vessel; 446-447, Train ferry KOAN MARU Japanese Gov't. Railways; 452, 453a, Log raft; 453, 453a, Sampans; 466, Sailing vessel; 471, Racing yacht; 475, 475a, 477, Stylized steamer; 532, Steamer; 533, Motorboat; 535, Indistinct freighter; 552, Lifeboat in davits; 578, Indistinct sampan; 584, Cormorant fishing boat; 632, Sampans, junks; 633, Freighter NISSHO MARU Tokyo Sempaku; 637, Research ship SOYA Japanese Maritime Safety Board; 647, Paddle frigate POWHATTAN US Navy, modern freighter; 652, Passenger/cargo ship KASATO MARU Japanese Gov't.; 677, Tourist boat; 679, Fishing junks; 688, Sampan; 691, Sailboats; 693, 703, Sailing steamer KANRIN MARU Japanese Gov't.; 737, Racing shells; 760, Sampan; 769, Small vessels; 800, Sampans; 809, Motorboat; 846, Training ship MEIJI MARU Japanese Gov't.; 850, Sampan; 857, Icebreaker FUJI Japanese Gov't.; 894, Motor cruiser; 908, Liner SUMOTO MARU Kansai Kisen Kaisha; 942, Rowing boat; 943, Liner/exhibition ship SAKURA MARU Japan Industry Floating Fair Ass'n.; 960, Open boat; 972, Barque SHOHEI MARU Toko gawa Shogunate; 991, Nuclear ship MUTSU Japanese Gov't.; 993, Cableship KDD MARU Kokusai Cable Ship; 1101-1102, Treasure ship; 1126, Sailing vessels; 1131, Sailing ships; 1134, Tour boat; 1147, Open boat; 1151, Ship; 1167, Rice bowl boat (folk tale); 1186, Sailing vessels; 1218, Aircraft carrier; 1218a, Contains 1218; 1219, "Kentoshi-sen"; 1220, "Kenmin-sen"; 1221, Trader, "goshuin-sen" NIPPON MARU Hideyoshi Toyotomi; 1222, State barge TENCHI MARU Tokugawa Gov't.; 1223, "Sengoku-bune," small fishing boat; 1224, Barque SHOHEI MARU Tokogawa Shogunate; 1225, Training ship TAISEI MARU Japanese Gov't.; 1226, Liner TENYO MARU Toyo Kisen Kaisha; 1227, Liner ASAMA MARU Nippon Yusen Kaisha; 1228, Freighter KINAI MARU Osaka Shosen Kaisha; 1229, Container ship KAMAKURA MARU Nippon Yusen Kaisha; 1230, Tanker NISSEI MARU Tokyo Tanker K.K.; 1266, Cableship KDD MARU Kokusai Cable Ship; 1285, Boats; 1331, Various vessels; 1339, "Sengoku bune"; 1369, Quarantine boat, ship; 1379, Harbor, various; 1391, Ship; 1407, Composite of training ships NIPPON MARU Nautical Training Institute; 1456, Stylized container ship; 1485, Sloop; 1495, Ship; 1508, Carrack; 1554, Icebreaker SHIRASE Japanese Navy; 1626C, Cargo ship; 1644, Sailing vessel; 1679, Training ship NIPPON MARU Nautical Training Institute; 1767, Boat; 1768, Ship; 1769, Ship; 1770, Boat; 1775, Small river boat; 1829, Dutch East Indiaman; 1847a, Junk and sailboats; 1917, Sailing ship; 1931, Boats; 1967, dragon boats; 2139, kayak; B7, Battleships NEVADA, repair ship VESTAL, battleships TENNESSEE, MARYLAND, CALIFORNIA, sea plane tender AVOCET, other ships of US Navy; B20, B20a, Portion of racing scull; B21, B23a, Racing yachts; B30, B31a, Racing kayaks.

Jordan
245-248, N18-N21, Steamer; 383-384, 384a, Freighter RIDA Kheireddine Abdul-Wahhab & Sons; 489, Sailboat; 674, Ship; 1004, Stylized liner; 1190, Patrol boat; 1237, Sailboats.

Karelia
N6, N13, Finland Scott 177 ovptd.

Kiauchau
10-42, Designs as Cameroun 7, 16 (HOHENZOLLERN).

Korea
79, Armoured warship, "tortoise boat" KWI-SUN Korean Navy; 113, KWI-SUN; 225, KWI-SUN; 263-264, 264a, Freighters; 291, 291a, Landing craft; 301, 301a, Stylized ship; 329, 329a, Warship; 356, KWI-SUN; 357, KWI-SUN; 375, Trawler; 405, Trawlers; 406, Freighter KOREA Far Eastern Marine Transport; 409, Freighter; 432, Stylized freighter; 438, 439a, Sampan; 452, 452a, 8-oared racing shell; 575, Freighters; 611, Stylized destroyer CHUNG MU Korean Navy; 633, Tortoise boats; 721, 721a, Boat; 726, Ships; 739, 739a, Ships; 746,

746a, Stylized ship; 781, 781a, Boat; 814, Tanker; 847, Ships; 851, Patrol craft; 907, Ships; 913, Stylized sculls; 994A, Destroyer; 1053, Portion of bulk carrier; 1058, Ship; 1061, Warship; 1117, Ship; 1118, Freighters; 1139, Ship; 1140, Destroyer; 1217, Stylized freighters; 1225, Boat with square sail; 1231, Cable ship; 1235, Tanker KOREA STAR Asia Merchant Marine Co.; 1236, Freighter ASIA YUKHO Asia Merchant Marine Co.; 1237, Bulk carrier SATURN Saturn Bulk Carriers; 1238, Container ship HANJIN SEOUL Hanjin Container Lines; 1239, Tug CHUNG RYONG NO. 3 Hyundai Construction Co.; 1240, Stern trawler SOO GONG NO. 71 Korea Marine Industry Dev't. Corp.; 1241, Log carrier ALDEBARAN Finland Steamship Co.; 1242, Auto carrier HYUNDAI NO. 1 Asia Merchant Marine Co.; 1243, Chemical carrier STOLT HAWK Stolt Hawk; 1244, Passenger boat Tortoise boats; 1321, Freighter; 1371, Ship; 1431, Leaf as boat; 1440, Rowboat; 1470a, Yacht, power; 1470b, Excursion ship; 1470c, Kayak; 1493, Stylized ship's bow; B22, B22a, Portion of single scull; B25, B26a, Racing kayak; B51, B51a, Yachts racing; C6-C8, C9-C11, Steamer.

Laos
1-3, Pirogue; 77, Pirogues; 211, Boat building; 249, Mekong river ferry; 317, 320, Pirogues; 393, Punt; 395, Houseboat; 396, Passenger steamer; 397, Car ferry; 398, Self-propelled wooden barge; 460, Sailing ship; 480, Rice boat, pirogues in S/S, rice boats in margin; 487, Nau VITORIA Ferdinand Magellan; 488, Carrack LA GRANDE HERMINE Jacques Cartier; 489, SANTA MARIA; 490, Caravel EL RAY Cabral; 491, Barque ENDEAVOUR British Navy; 492, Aux. barque POURQUOI PAS? J.B. Charcot; 608, Water taxi; 665a, PINTA in S/S; 665b, NINA in S/S; 665c, SANTA MARIA in S/S; 788, Design as Canada Scott 745; 789, Design as Canada Scott 746; 790, Design as Canada Scott 670; 791, Design as Canada Scott 672; 792, Design as Canada Scott 703; 793, Design as Canada Scott 701; 795, Canada Scott 282 depicted on stamp in S/S; 886, Canoe; 895, Canal boat; 896, Ferry; 1014, Sailing ship; 1016, 1026, 2-person canoe; 1017, Kayak; 1023, Sailboat; 1086, sailing ships; 1085, PINTA; 1087, Magellan's ship; 1088, Vasco de Gama's ship; 1089, Portuguese caravelle; B8, B8a, Canoe; C28, Portion of canoe; C117, Riverboat; J7, Boat, raft.

Latakia
C4, C6 Syria Scott C49, C51 ovptd.

Latvia
70-73, Helm of boat; 159, Small vessel; 161, Sailing vessels; 162, Steamers; 308, 308a, Russia Scott 5984a ovptd.; 309, 309a, 310, 310a, 311, 311a, Russia Scott 5981 ovptd.; B24, Steamer, sailing vessels.

Lebanon
56, 75, 89, Indistinct vessel; 114, Sailing vessel; 119-120, Sailing vessel; 128, Harbor, various vessels; 139-141, 145-146A, 160, Phoenician galley; 444, Sailboat; 445, Rowing boats; 475, Stylized galley; C50, C52, C54-C55, C119-C125, Sailboat; C132-C134, Phoenician galley; C207-C210, C210a, Steamer; C245-C249, Stylized liner; C313, Tourist boat; C317-C321, C341, Open boats; C477, Roman corbita; C478, Phoenician galley; C481, Rowboat; C513, Boat; C515, Small boats; C518, Boats; C520, Indistinct boats; C550, Lateen-rigged vessels; C577, Phoenician ship; C589, Ancient ship (coin); C597, Sailboat; C598, Yacht regatta; C632, Harbor, various; C645, Patrol boat TARABLOUS Lebanese Navy; C688, Lebanese galley; C709, Container ship; C754, Roman grain ship; C797, Raft; J30, Roman corbita.

Liberia
1-3, 7-9, 13-15, 16-20, 157-159, Sailing ship (arms); 31, Full-rigged ship; 41-42, 45-46, 73-74, 77, 86, 89-90, 95, 97, 100, O7, O9, O20, O22, O39, O41,O 45, Sailing ship (arms); 52-53, 69, O26-O27, Dugout; 117, 152, 152B, O61, O88-O89, O99, Gunboat LARK Liberian Navy; 123, 133, 142-143, 150, O67, O80, O86, Dugout; 165, 249, 260,B5, O100,; 173, 256, 267, B13, O108, Steamer; 183, 195, O116, O127, Indistinct vessel; 185, 199, O118, O131; 189, 203, O121, O135, Dugout; 190, 204, O122, O136, Dugout; 194, 208, O126, O140, Dugout; 209-213, Full-rigged AUGUSTA US Gov't.; 277, 280, B16, C14, CB1, Sailing ships; 278, 281, B17, C15, CB2, CE1, CF1, E1, F35, Dugouts; 279, 282, B18, C16, CB3, Dugouts; 300, C54-C56, C56a, Sailing ship (arms); 307, Sailing ship (arms); 309, Sailing ship (arms); 311, Sailing ship; 332, Sailing ship (arms); 340, 340a, Sailing ship (arms); 368-370, Sailing ship (arms); 391, Racing shell, dugout; 393-394, C128-C129, Scott #1-3 depicted on stamps; 459, Canoe; 494, Sailing yachts; 552, Helicopter carrier NEW ORLEANS US Navy; 553, Recovery raft, Apollo 14; 560, Stylized canoe; 585, 587, Full-rigged ELIZABETH US Gov't.; 586, Sailing ship (arms); 608, British Navy, figurehead; 609, 3rd Rate HOGUE British Navy, figurehead; 610, 6th Rate ARIADNE British Navy, figurehead; 611, 1st Rate ROYAL ADELAIDE British Navy, figurehead; 612, Steam sloop RINALDO British Navy, figurehead.

613, Steam sloop NYMPHE British Navy, figurehead; 663, Full-rigged THOMAS COUTTS British East India Co., liner AUREOL Elder Dempster; 664, Naval launch, merchant convoy; 695, Portion of landing craft; 707, US 618 on stamp; 708, SANTA MARIA, US Scott 231 depicted on stamp; 709, Dugouts; 710, Dugouts; 739, Racing yachts; 745, Cableship DOMINIA Telegraph Const. & Maint. Co.; 749, 944, Open boat; 755, 759, 952, Sailboat, sport fishing boat; 845, Mail steamer JOHN PENN London, Chatham & Dover Railway; 851, Tanker WORLD PEACE World Peace Corp.; 852, WORLD PEACE; 874-877, Canoe; 911, Open boats, in margin; 1006, Ship; 1046, Boats; 1066a, Training ship in S/S; 1066b, Ferry in S/S; 1066d, Tug, training ship in S/S; 1068b, Yachts, cabin cruisers in S/S; 1082-1084, Ship; 1095, Yachts; 1103, Tanker CHEVRON ANTWERP Chevron Transport; 1104, Cruise ship LAKONIA Greek Line, on fire; 1118, Sailing vessel (coin); 1123, Sailing ship (arms); 1124, Sailing ship (arms); 1125, OKINAWA US Navy; 1132, Scott 165 & 185 on border; 1139, Sailing ship (arms); C64, Sailing vessel; C72, C83, Freighter AFRICAN GLEN Farrell Lines; C114-C117, Sailing ship; C141-C143, Shipboard scene, freighter AFRICAN CRESCENT Farrell˜20Lines; C169, C169a,; C187a, C187b Racing yachts in S/S; C191, Full-rigged ELIZABETH US Gov't. in S/S; C194, 1st Rate VICTORY British Navy, figurehead in S/S; C195, Sailing ship (arms) in margin; C207, Sailing ship MAYFLOWER Pilgrims, US 548 on stamp; F15-F19, Patrol vessel QUAIL (?); F30, Surfboat with sail; F31, Steamer, tug, surfboat; F32, Sailing vessel; F33, Liner GEORGE WASHINGTON United States Line; F34, Kru dugout.

Libya
26-28, 54-56, 59, Bow of Roman galley; 209-211, Tanker ESSO CANTER BURY Esso Petroleum; 316, Tanker; 338-339, Stylized tanker; 366-371, 379-384, Warship; 626, Tanker in S/S; 742, Warship; 805-809, Stylized boat (emblem); 813, Boat in storm (child's drawing); 894, Warships of 1911; 898, Warships of 1911; 904, Cruise ship; 907, Cruise ship in S/S; 916, Boat (mosaic); 965, Naval vessels in S/S; 975e, Open boat (mosaic) in S/S; 1041, Ships; 1043, Ships; 1045, Ships in S/S; 1090, Ancient Phoenician ship; 1091, Viking ship; 1092, Ancient Greek ship; 1093, Ancient Roman ship; 1094, Libyan sailing galley; 1095, Ancient Egyptian ship; 1115, Sailboards; 1164a, Sailboards in S/S; 1164b, Sailboat in S/S; 1164c, Sailboat in S/S; 1164f, Boat in S/S; 1164g, Motorboat in S/S; 1164j, Kayak in S/S; 1164k, Surfboard in S/S; 1208, Sailboards; 1214p, Freighter; 1265a, Frigate PHILADELPHIA US Navy, blowing up; 1265c, Ship's rigging; 1406, Ship; 1435, cargo ship and tugboat; B5-B6, Steamer; J45, Reed boats (mosaic).

Lithuania
185, Steamers; 316, 316a, Sailboat; B45, Racing yacht; C80, Steamers.

Lourenco Marques
92-99, Macao Scott 187-194 ovptd.; 100-107, Portuguese Africa Scott 1-8 ovptd.; 108-115, Timor Scott 45-52 ovptd.

Luxembourg
410, Barge; 440-441, Design as Belgium Scott 675; 459, River barges; 503, Sailboats; 560, Rowboat; 600, Barges; 784, Barge; B117, Ancient ship (arms); B237, Ancient sailing vessel.

Macao
67, 187, Design as Portugal Scott 147; 68-70, 188-90, Designs as Portugal Scott 148-150; 71, 191, Design as Portugal Scott 151; 72, 192, Design as Portugal Scott 152; 73, 193, Design as Portugal Scott 153; 74, 194, Design as Portugal Scott 154; 268-288, 306-315, 316-323, Carrack SAO GABRIEL Vasco da Gama; 289-292, Design as Angola Scott 274; 331, 347, Junk; 353, 358 Ancient sailing ship; 361, Trading junk; 363, Junk, "tsat-pon"; 371, Sailing vessel (arms); 401, Design as Angola Scott 509; 412, Patrol launch VEGA Portu guese Navy (stamp depicts ANTARES, a sistership); 413, Frigate DOM FERNANDO II E GLORIA Portuguese Navy; 425, Sailing ship; 433-434, Boat; 447-450, Sailing ship; 483, Portuguese ships; 484, Portuguese ships; 500, Rowing boat, "hok lou t'eng"; 501, Fishing boat, "tai t'ong"; 502, Trawler, "tai mei chai"; 503, Trawler, "ch'at pong t'o"; 507, Sailing junk; 509, Boat; 518, Sailing vessel, "tou" or "sa't'ay"; 519, Motor junk VENG SENG LEI; 520, Motor junk TONG HENG LONG NO. 2; 521, Freighter FONG VON SANG; 530, Hydrofoil; 531, Hovercraft Sealink Ferries; 532, Jetfoil TERCEIRA Far East Hydrofoil; 533, High speed ferry JU KONG or CHEUNG KONG Hi-Speed Ferries; 534, Junk; 545, Dragon boat; 546, Bow of dragon boat; 585, Stern of "tan-kia," junk; 603, Junk; 607, Portuguese ship (deck); 615, Junk; 630-634, Sailing ship; 656, 657a, Open boat; 677, 677A, racing sailboat.

Madagascar
1-7, Fr. Colonies Scott 50, 54, 57 ovptd.; 28-47, 48-55, 58-60, 127-128, Design as Anjouan 1; 172, Design as Cameroun Scott 216; 191-193, 197, Designs as Cameroun Scott 217-219; 294, Dredge; 330, C70a, Canoe; 331, C70a, Indistinct vessels; 337, Tanker ESSO GASIKARA Esso Standard (Madagascar); 350, Lateen-rigged vessels (arms); 353, Sailing vessel (arms); 374, Pirogue; 378, Hydrofoil PORTMOS; 390, Sailing vessels (arms); 438, Sailing ship (arms); 439, Stylized sailing vessel (arms); 461, Outrigger canoe; 525, 564, Frigate RANDOLPH Continental Navy, sailing ship; 526, 565, Brigantine LEXINGTON Continental Navy, sloop EDWARD British Navy; 541, Pirogue; 542, Coastal vessel, "boutre"; 543, Racing canoe, kayak; 547, Ships; 556, Cableship êMILE BAUDOT French Gov't.; 604, Stylized ship; 729, Sailboats; 788, Replica of pirogue SARIMANOK Bob Hobman; 789, Replica of SARIMANOK; 814, Fleet of Bartolomeu Dias; 815, Sailing ship Henry the Navigator; 816, Boat; 819, Columbus, NINA; 820, Sailing ships Columbus in margin; 827, Ship's boat; 878, Ships; 879, Sailboats; 880, Sailing ship LESNOIE (?); 881, Merchantman OREL (?); 882, Ships; 883, Sailing ship in S/S, sailing ships in margin; 968, Boats; 979, Ship; 1001, Ship of Columbus in S/S margin; 1014, galley; 1015, clipper ship; 1016, GOLDEN HINDE; 1017, galley; 1018, galleon OSTRUST; 1019, caravel AMSTERDAM; 1020, SANTA MARIA; 1021, Columbus' fleet, pictured on label; B17, Design as Cameroun Scott B29; C48, Design as Cameroun Scott C12; C51, Harbor, various vessels; C52, C54, Canoes; C57, Design as Cameroun Scott C32; C70, C70a, Harbor, various vessels; C93, Open boat; C123, Rowboat; C137, C164, 1st Rate LE LANGUEDOC French Navy; C138, C165, Frigate BONHOMME RICHARD Continental Navy, 5th Rate SERAPIS British Navy; C139, C166, Privateer MONTGOMERY Continental Navy; C140, C167, Schooner HANNAH Continental Navy in S/S; C158, Ships; C159, Ships.

Mali
88, 91, Pirogue; 89, 92, Pirogue; 90, 93, Pirogues; 147, Canoes; 216, 229, Sailing ship, liner; 269, Muscat fishing boat; 270, Chinese coaster; 271, Lightship RUYTINGEN; 272, Nile barge; 288, Stylized ship; 440, Freighter; 465-467, Sailboards (different designs); 482, Bow of liner; C14, Harbor, various; C118, Racing yacht; C125, SANTA MARIA; C126, Sailing ship MAYFLOWER Pilgrims; C127, Battleship KNIAZ POTEMKIN TAVRITCHESKY Russian Navy; C128, Liner NORMANDIE Cie. GÇnÇrale Transatlantique; C133, Sailing ves-

sels; C136, Sailing vessels; C142, Gondolas; C143, Gondolas; C199, Helicopter carrier IWO JIMA US Navy; C243, Submarine NAUTILUS (fictional) Jules Verne; C255, Rowboat; C256, Naval battle; C278, Warships; C289, Freighter; C302, Sailboat; C324, Deck scene, ship-sloop RESOLUTION British Navy; C325, RESOLUTION; C366, RESOLUTION; C367, RESOLUTION; C384, C385a, C400, C401a, Finn-class yachts; C393, French fleet; C396, Sailing ship, paddle steamer (attached label); C426, SANTA MARIA, NINA, PINTA, US Scott 233 depicted on stamp; C427, Spain Scott 418 depicted on stamp (SANTA MARIA); C428, Spain Scott 421 depicted on stamp (SANTA MARIA); C429, US Scott 232 depicted on stamp (SANTA MARIA); C474, Sailboard; C478b, Ship; C500, C510, Sailboard in S/S; C522, Mississippi river steamer.

Manchukuo
132-133, Mast, flag of flagship; 146, Indistinct vessel; C3-C4, Sailing vessels.

Mariana Islands
17-31, Designs as Cameroun Scott 7, 16 (HOHENZOLLERN).

Marshall Islands
13-27, Designs as Cameroun Scott 7, 16 (HOHENZOLLERN); 31, Sailing outrigger canoe; 51, 53, Scott #13, 25 depicted on stamp; 59, Sailing canoe; 60, Aircraft carrier; 61, Liberty ship; 62, Container ship; 82, Mission ship MORNING STAR American Board of Commissioners for Foreign Missions; 83, Launching MORNING STAR; 84, MORNING STAR; 85, MORNING STAR; 90, Tracking ship; 115, Tibinal sailing canoe; 116, Amphibious DUKW and submarine tender SUMNER US Navy; 117, Landing ship LST 1108 US Navy; 132, Whaler JAMES ARNOLD Henry Tabor & Co.; 133, Whaler GENERAL SCOTT Capt. J.R. Huntting; 134, Whaler CHARLES W. MORGAN Charles W. Morgan, et al.; 135, Whaler LUCRETIA Capt. J.S. Carter; 142, Gunboat ITASCA US Coast Guard in S/S, sailboat in margin; 190, FLYING SCUD (fictional) Robert Louis Stevenson, sail boat in margin; 190, 190a, Schooner CASCO Dr. Samuel Merritt; 190, 190b, CASCO; 190, 190c, Schooner EQUATOR John Wightman; 190, 190d, Canoe; 190, 190f, Steamer JANET NICOLL G.W. Nicoll, outrigger canoe; 190, 190h, Samoan outrigger canoe; 191, Galleon SANTA MARIA DE LA VICTORIA Spanish Navy; 192, Transports CHARLOTTE and SCARBOROUGH; 193, Schooner FLYING FISH and sloop-of-war PEACOCK British Navy; 194, Steam schooner PLANET; 199, Outrigger canoe; 207, Recovery ship; 210, Japanese warship; 211, Japanese fishing boats; C3, Bow of canoe; C4, Traditional boat; C7, Aircraft carrier SARATOGA US Navy in S/S, ships in margin; C18, ITASCA; C19, Rubber raft; C20, Research ship KOSHU Japanese Navy.

Martinique
1-21, 29-32, Fr. Colonies Scott 47-48, 50, 52, 54-58, ovptd.; 33-53, 54-61, 101-104, Design as Anjouan Scott 1; 74-92, 111-113, 116-119, 123, Harbor, various vessels; 132, Design as Cameroun Scott 216; 179-182, Design as Cameroun Scott 217; 188-189, Harbor, various vessels; 198-216, Indistinct sailing vessels; 217-219, Canoes; 220-222, Harbor lighters; C7, Design as Cameroun Scott C12; C10, Canoe; J37-J46, Sailing vessels, canoes.

Mauritania
68, Design as Cameroun Scott 216; 69-71, Designs as Cameroun Scott 217-219; 75, Design as Cameroun Scott 219 in S/S; 126, Fishing boats; 200, Freighters; 271, Ships; 299, Design as Dahomey Scott 300; 415, Paddle steamer SIRIUS St. George Steam Packet Co.; 416, Paddle steamer GREAT REPUBLIC Pacific Mail Steamship Co.; 417, Liner MAURETANIA Cunard Line; 418, Liner STIRLING CASTLE Union-Castle Line; 419, Ships in margin; 421, Ship; 490, Naval battle; 491, PINTA; 492, SANTA MARIA; 496, Rowboat; 497, Longboat; 498, Sailboat; 499, Sailboat, rowboat in margin; 562, Boat building; 592, Bow of fishing boat; 604, SANTA MARIA; 605, NINA; 606, PINTA; 641, Cargo ship; 689, Container ship; C21, Ore carrier; C58, Raft from frigate MEDUSA shipwreck survivors; C96, Boat; C118, Sailing ships; C119, Gondolas; C120, Gondolas; C153, Dugout canoe; C210, Harbor, sailboats; C218, Ships; C229, Sailboards; C230, Finn-class yachts; C231, 470-class yachts; C232, Soling-class yachts; C233, Flying Dutchman-class yachts; J1-J8, Design as Dahomey Scott J1.

Mayotte
1-20, 22-32, Design as Anjouan Scott 1.

Memel
N31-N34, N70-N73, N83-N84, Steamer; N40-N43, N79-N82, Part of vessels.

Mexico
254-256, 266-268, 278, 278A, 289-291, O20-O22, O39, Small vessel; 764-766, C114-C116, Ship's helm; 865, 883, 929, 951, 1099, Stylized ancient sailing ship; 981, Kayaks; 1010, Sailboats; 1041, Training ship ZARAGOSA Mexican Navy; 1046, Stylized caravel; 1312, Training freighter NAUTICUS MEXICO Mexican Gov't.; 1485, Section through ship's hull; 1514, Harbor, boats; 1519, SANTA MARIA; 1535, Ship; 1552, Freighter; 1678, Stern of galleon; 1679, Bow of galleon; 1683, Stylized liner; 1694, Freighter; 1695o, Freighter; 1695p, Bow of freighter; 1707-1708, Stylized sailing ship; 1735, Ships in S/S; 1745, Rowing; 1751, stylized sailing ship; 1779, Navy Day: sailing ship, modern warship; C111, Galleon; C186, C447, Harbor, small boats; C300, Galleon SAN PEDRO Miguel Lopez de Legaspi; C335, C336a, Racing yachts; C336, C336a, 8-oared shells; C343, C344a, Stylized sailboat; C458, Balsa raft ACALI Sailing ships (arms); C547, Freighter RIO YAQUI Spanish galleon in S/S.

Middle Congo
64, Design as Cameroun Scott 216; J20-J22, River steamer WILLIAM GUINET Cia. Galftransaf.

Moheli
1-22, Design as Anjouan Scott 1.

Moldova
42, cruiser AURORA.

Monaco
44-46, Sailing vessels; 89-92, 99, Sailing vessels; 118, 121, Harbor, various vessels; 166B, 167, 168B, 169A, 172, 174B, 175B, 221, 229, Yacht HUSSAR E.F. Hutton, other vessels; 199, C14, Harbor, various vessels; 208, Sailboat; 237, Schooner HIRONDELLE Albert I of Monaco; 240, Research yacht PRINCESS ALICE II Albert I of Monaco; 242, Research yacht HIRONDELLE II Albert I of Monaco; 243, Whaleboat; 280, Harbor, ship; 297, Racing yachts; 303-305, HIRONDELLE II; 325, Dugouts; 327, Portions of dugouts; 341, Steamer GREAT EASTERN Eastern Steam Navigation Co., tanker; 345, Dugouts with shelter; 346, Raft; 348, Submarine NAUTILUS (fictional) Jules Verne; 349, Nuclear submarine NAUTILUS US Navy; 359, Fleet of Columbus; 362, River steamer; 450, PRINCESS ALICE II in painting; 451, Shipboard scene, PRINCESS ALICE Albert I of Monaco; 453, Schooner HIRONDELLE Albert I of Monaco, PRINCESS ALICE; 483, Portion of steamer; 522, Butoscopic turret; 523, Bathyscaphe TRIESTE August & Jacques Piccard, observation chamber WILLIAMSON PHOTOSPHERE J.E. Williamson; 525, Diving saucer DENISE Jacques Cousteau; 526, Submarine NAUTILUS Robert Fulton, modern US Fleet-type submarine; 527, Bathysphere Alexander the Great, bathysphere Dr. William Beebe; 536, Ship's bow with figurehead; 565, Harbor, various vessels.

587-589, 587A, Yachts; 612, Steamer; 614, Cableships GREAT EASTERN Telegraph Construction & Maintenance, and ALSACE French Gov't. PTT; 618, Sailing vessels; 619, Indistinct vessel; 620, Sailboats; 626, Open boat; 632, Sailboat; 639-640, Design as Belgium Scott 675; 641, Schooner HIRONDELLE Albert I of Monaco, PRINCESS ALICE Albert I of Monaco; 645, Bathysphere PRECONTINENT III Jacques Cousteau; 667, Sailboat; 696, Sailboats; 824, Holy League and Turkish warships; 827, Tanker; 833, Gondolas; 834, State barge BUCENTAUR Venetian State; 890, Sailboats; 907, Ships; 916, Indistinct vessels; 919, Boats; 1028, 1029a, Portion of racing scull; 1038, Indistinct vessels; 1042, Sailing ship; 1050, HIRONDELLE, other vessels; 1052, Deck scene; 1053, Deck scene; 1054, Ship's helm; 1055, Deck scene, lifeboat; 1056, Open boat; 1057, Shrouds, ship's side; 1058, Open boat, ship's side; 1063, Sailboats; 1073, Research yacht PRINCESS ALICE II Albert I of Monaco, state yacht HOHENZOLLERN German Government, other vessels; 1074, Laboratory aboard PRINCESS ALICE II; 1075, PRINCESS ALICE II; 1077, Steam launch; 1078, Bridge of PRINCESS ALICE II; 1080, Steam launch; 1081, PRINCESS ALICE II; 1099, Shipwreck; 1100, Sailing ship, submarine NAUTILUS (fictional) Jules Verne; 1101, NAUTILUS; 1105, Sinking ship; 1106, NAUTILUS; 1110, Gondolas; 1111, Research vessel RAMOGE Centre Scientifique de Monaco; 1178, 1180a, J60, Sailing vessels; 1179, 1180a, J57, Felucca; 1198, Ship; 1284, Hydrographic ship FADDEY BELLINGHAUSEN Russian Gov't.; 1301, Dutch whaling ships; 1333, Marina, small craft; 1335, Sailing ship (arms); 1349, Portion of sailboat.

1358, Research yacht PRINCESS ALICE II Albert I of Monaco; 1359, Viking longships; 1360, Roman galley; 1385, Sailboat; 1397, Oil storage barge TAZERKA Shell Tunirex; 1414, Open boats; 1434, Bathyscaphe TRIESTE August Piccard; 1444, Sailing ship; 1475, Schooner HIRONDELLE Albert I of Monaco, diving saucer DENISE Jacques Cousteau; 1486, yacht in margin; 1486, 1486a, Catamaran in S/S; 1486, 1486b, Monocoque in S/S; 1486, 1486c, Trimaran in S/S; 1488, Harbor, various vessels; 1493, Fishing boat; 1516, Boats; 1519, Harbor; 1520, Wharf; 1522, Vessels; 1529, Sailing ship; 1530, 1531a, Research vessel RAMOGE Centre Scientifique de Monaco; 1550, Sailing yachts; 1578, Sailboards; 1605, Passenger ship, small craft; 1631, 4-man scull; 1638, boats; 1640c, Sailboat in S/S; 1643, Galleys; 1690, Regatta; 1695, Boat; 1734, Powerboat; 1759b, Ship; 1761, Ship; 1776-1777, Boat; 1814, PINTA; 1815, SANTA MARIA; 1816, NINA; 1819, Naval fleet; 1821, Sailboats; 1824, Sailboat; 1831, Seabus; 1836, Sailboat; B19, Indistinct sailboats; B21, Indistinct sailboats; B35, Sailboat; B80, Burning symbolic boat; B81, Sailing vessels; B84, Sailing boat; B92, Paddle steamer IL COMMERCIO DI GENOVA Societa Anonima dei Pacchetti a Vapore Sardi; B93, Harbor, various vessels; C19, Harbor, various vessels; C20, Harbor, various vessels; C40, Portion of dugouts; C55, C58, Small vessel; CB7, 8-oared racing shell; CB10, 8m-class yachts UNITY R.H. Anstruther, Gough Calthorpe, VIM M. Bordenave, MARGARET A. Ballentine, and OLD CHAP Sailing vessel; J49, Liner UNITED STATES United States Line; J57, Felucca; J58, Packet LA PALMARIA Sailing vessels; J61, Sailing vessels; J62, Packet CHARLES III; J63, Sailing vessels; J64, Sailing vessels.

Mongolia
239, 241c, Mail boat SUKNATAR Russian Gov't.; 371, Fishing boat SUKHE-BATOR; 923, Small cargo vessel; 961, Sailing ship in margin; 979, Cruiser AURORA Russian Navy; 1077d, Passenger/cargo ship HINDOSTAN; 1120, Kayak; 1139, Research ship CALYPSO Jacques Cousteau, bathyscaphe; 1185, Egyptian ship; 1186, Mediterranean ship; 1187, Hansa cog; 1188, Venetian ship; 1189, SANTA MARIA; 1190, Barque ENDEAVOUR British Navy; 1191, Battleship POLTAVA Russia Scottn Navy; 1192, American schooner; 1300, Fishing boat; 1378A, Bow of ship; 1572, Sailboat; 1845, Fishing boats; 1888, Galley; 1894, Sailing craft; 2095, Columbus' fleet; 2096, SANTA MARIA, at anchor; 2098-2100, SANTA MARIA, at sea; 2097, PINTA; 2101, NINA; 2102-2103, sailing ship; 2116, sailboats, pictured in sheet margin; C7, Russia Scott 3100 depicted on stamp; C61, Research ship KOSMONAUT YURI GAGARIN Russian Gov't.; C110, Canada Scott 553 depicted on stamp in S/S; C111, Russia Scott C26 depicted on stamp (MALYGIN); C150, Russia Scott C27 depicted on stamp; C151, Russia Scott C28 depicted on stamp; C152, Russia Scott C29 depicted on stamp; C153, Icebreaker MALYGIN .

Morocco
51, Sailboat; 57A, Freighter; 104, Stylized sailboats; 148, Cie. GÇnÇrale Transatlantique;

422, Stylized yachts; 501, Bow of freighter; 562, Liner; 745, cruise ship; 747, Columbus' fleet.

Morocco – Northern Zone
2, 6-7, Harbor, various vessels.

Mozambique
125-132, Macao Scott 187-194 ovptd.; 133-140, Portuguese Africa Scott 1-8 ovptd.; 141-148, Timor Scott 45-52 ovptd.; 270-274, 301, Design as Angola Scott 287; 360, Stylized liner; 384-385, Scott 360 depicted on stamp; 386, Design as Macao Scott 371; 402, Freighters DAMARALAND South African Lines, CLAN MACKINNON Clan Line, MOCAMEDES Cia. Nacional de Navegacao, coaster TAGUS Cia. Nacional de Navegacao, liner ORANJEFONTEIN United Netherlands Navigation Co.; 405, Portuguese caravela; 407, Sailing ship (arms); 423, Sailing vessel (arms); 429, 529, Speed boat; 431, Sailing ship; 432, Sailing vessels; 435, Portuguese barca; 436, Caravel; 437, Caravela latina; 438, Carrack SAO GABRIEL Vasco da Gama; 439, Don Manuel I; 440, Armed carrack Portuguese Navy; 441, Galleon FLOR DE LA MAR Portuguese Navy; 442, Caravela redonda; 443, Nau; 444, Portuguese India galley Portuguese Governor at Calicut; 445, Galleon SANTA TERESA Portuguese Navy; 446, 80-gun ship NOSSA SENHORA DA CONCEICAO Portuguese Navy; 447, 64-gun ship NOSSA SENHORA DO BOM SUCESSO Portuguese Navy; 448, Launch with mortar Portuguese Navy; 449, Brigantine LEBRE Portuguese Navy; 450, Frigate ANDORINHA Portu guese Navy; 451, Schooner MARIA TERESA Portuguese Navy; 452, Nau VASCO DA GAMA Portu guese Navy; 453, Frigate DOM FERNANDO II E GLORIA Portuguese Navy.

454, Training ship SAGRES Portuguese Navy; 455, Design as Angola Scott 509; 457, Galeota grande King John V; 458, Small galliot Dom Jose I; 459, Galeota da Alfandega Royal barge PINTO DA FONSECA Portuguese State; 462, Dona Carlota Joaquina; 463, Dom Miguel; 478, River gunboat TETE Portuguese Navy; 479, River gunboat GRANADA Portuguese Navy; 482, Sailing vessels; 486, Nau; 487, Caravels; 490, Sailing ships; 503, Sailing ships; 505, Open boats; 506, 519, Vauriens-class racing yachts; 507, 520, Racing yacht; 508, 524, Racing yachts; 627, Tanker MATCHEDJE Empresa Nacional Petroleos de Mozambique; 783, Min. of Overseas Provinces, Portuguese Gov't.; 784, Trawler VEGA 7 Entreposto Frigorifique de Pesca; 785, Empresa de Limpopo A Couto; 786, Freighter PEMBA Cia. Mocambicana de Navegacao; 787, Suction dredge ROVUMA Cia. Nacional de Navegacao; 836, Machua; 838, Chitatarro; 840, Cangaia; 841, Chata; 863, Stylized yachts; 879, Ship; 880, Canoe; 892, Rowboat; 949, Oil tankers; 1063, Sailboats; 1064, Freighters; 1065, Freighter; 1067, Container ship; 1068, Freighter; B1-B6, Sailing vessels; C31, Harbor, various vessels; J32, MR2, MR4, Prow of galley.

Mozambique Company
115, 148, 150, Sailing boat; 120, 144-145, 149, Harbor, various vessels; 135-136, 152, Portion of canoe; 156, 158, Steamer; 161, Small boat; 164, 191, Steamer; 165-174, Harbor, boats; 177, Dhow, "sambuk"; 187, 198, Carrack SAO GABRIEL Vasco da Gama; 188, 199, Portion of dugout; C1-C15, Indistinct vessels.

Netherlands
87-89, Fleet of Admiral de Ruyter; 140, Racing yachts; 141, Lifeboat; 201, Liner BALOERAN Rotterdam Lloyd, bow of liner CHRISTIAAN HUYGENS Netherlands Royal Mail Line; 202, Bows of two freighters; 203, Van Walbeeck's ship; 212, Boat with sail; 252-261, Dutch warships (different designs); 263, Liner NIEUW AMSTERDAM Holland-America Line; 265, Cruiser DE RUYTER Netherlands Navy; 370, Sailing ships; 371, Ship-of-the-line DE ZEVEN PROVINCIEN Netherlands Navy; 403, Suction dredge; 418-419, Bow of vessel; 441-442, Design as Belgium Scott 675; 512c, Rowboat; 517, Lifeboat SUZANNA Royal Dutch Lifeboat Society; 529, Packet STAD MIDDELBURG Maats. Zeeland; 530, Portion of canoe; 561, Fishing boat, "tjalk" (silhouette); 588, River/canal barge ALRINA A. Korsten; 617, Harbor, ships; 672, Model ships; 673, Rigging of sailing vessel, "botter"; 732, Sailing ship; 736, Sailing ship; 813, sailing ship; 761, East Indiaman, wreck of merchantman AMSTERDAM Dutch East India Co.; 762, Ship's rigging; 806, 4-man shell without coxswain; B25, Single scull; B28, Racing yacht; B62, Monument with ship-like base; B63, Hospital schooner DE HOOP Netherlands Seamen's Society; B64, Lifeboat; B144, Sails of vessel; B189, Kayak; B198, Sailboats; B212, Tugs STORMVOGEL Maas Co., ADELAAR Mueller, JAN BLANKEN JZN Ministry of Waterways.

B213, Market barge OVERIJSSEL Van der Schuyt; B228, Bow of open boat; B262, Sailing vessel, "tjalk"; B273, Toy sailboat; B296, Sailboat; B306, Freighter GAASTERLAND Royal Holland Lloyd; B307, Coaster; B308, Whale factory ship WILLEM BARENDSZ Maats. voor de Walvisvaart; B309, Trawler CURAÄAO N.V. Viss. Maats. Batavia; B310, Liner NIEUW AMSTERDAM Holland-America Line; B312, Hospital cruise ship J. HENRY DUNANT Neth. Red Cross Society; B331, Tugs; B332, Dredge; B334, Floating cranes; B366, Figurehead from ship model Netherlands Navy; B397, Small vessel; B399, Small vessel; B400, Small vessel; B403, Stylized steamer (child's drawing); B493, Ship-of-the-line DE ZEVEN PROVINCIEN Netherlands Navy; B494, Liner W.A. SCHOLTEN Holland-America Line; B495, Liner VEENDAM Holland America Line; B496, Fish-well boat; B528, B529a, Ship (child's drawing); B533, Part of ancient Roman ferry; B539, B541a, Overturned boat; B562, Sailboats; B633, B634a, Boats (child's drawing); B644, Boyer; B645, Smack; B646, Clipper; B657, Open boat.

Netherlands Antilles
43-44, Sailing vessel; 59-69, 74, Steamer; 95-106, Liner MAASDAM Holland-America Line; 119-121, Galleon GROOT HOORN Van Walbeeck; 164, Schooner; 169, Harbor, various vessels; 203, 205, Caravela latina LA GORDA A. de Ojeda; 235, Pontoon bridge; 238, Sailboats; 239, Sailboats; 273, Brig ANDREW DORIA Continental Navy; 293, Tanker ASPRELLA; 295, Floating market; 308, Cruiser GELDERLAND Netherlands Navy; 309, Schooner PIONIER S.E. Maduro & Sons; 310, Tanker OSCILLA; 311, Liner SANTA ROSA Grace Line; 337, Portion of ship in drydock; 366, Sailboat; 379, Sailboat; 380, Sailboat; 386, ANDREW DORIA; 422, Ship's bridge; 423, Ships; 458a, Ship in margin; 472, Bow of ship, pilot boat; 473, Ship, pilot boat; 474, Portion of pilot boat, ship's ladder; 490, Cruise ship SOUTHWARD Kloster Cruise Line; 492, 492a, Cruise ship SOUTHWARD Kloster Cruise Line; 493, Paddle steamer CURAÄAO Netherlands Navy; 514, Cruise ship; 577, Cruise ship EMERALD SEAS Eastern Cruise Lines; 610, Cruise ship SUN VIKING; 611, Cruise ship EUGENIO COSTA Costa Crociere; 619, ANDREA DORIA; 635, Dutch West Indiaman; 673, Ship; 675-676, Container ships; B15, Deck view of ship; B17, Bow of sailing vessel; B18, Tanker; B19, Steamer; B152, Sailboat; B162-B165, B165a, Stylized yachts (different designs); B208, Sailboard; B257, Harbour, ships.

Netherlands Indies
59-62, 79, 80, 97-98, 140, Sailing vessel; 117-130, 121a, 123a, 145a, 144-146, 158, 194-195, B3, C1-C2, Steamer; 173-188, 208-225, 271, 272-274, 275, B48, B57, Bow of vessel; 251, Pleasure barge; 266, Canoe; B9, Fishing boat, "proa".

Netherlands New Guinea
B11, B13, Outrigger canoe.

New Caledonia
8-9, 12-13, 23-33, 35-39, French Colonies Scott 46-59 ovptd.; 40-58, 59-80, 117-121, Design as Anjouan Scott 1; 97-112, 127-130, Small boat; 113-116, 125-126, 131-135, Q1-Q3, Barque PRESIDENT FELIX FAURE Cie. Havraise de Nav. Ŏ Voile; 136-143, 182-189, 217-225, Native sailing boat; 158-175, 199-207, 239-251, Q5-Q6, Frigates L'ASTROLABE French Navy; 179, Design as Cameroun Scott 216; 208-210, Designs as Cameroun Scott 217-219; 282-284, Sailing canoe; 285-288, Steamer; 296, Flute LA RECHERCHE and frigate L'ESPERANCE French Navy; 299, Sailing vessels; 316-317, 317a, Sailing vessels; 318, Melanesian pirogues; 320, Sailboats; 321, Design as French Polynesia Scott 198; 355, Sailboats; 368, River ferry; 387, Cie. des Messageries Maritimes; 389, Racing yachts; 443, Canoe; 447, Catamarans; 466, Corvette CONSTANTINE French Navy; 467, Aviso LE PHOQUE French Navy; 476, Barque LE CHER French Navy; 477, Dispatch vessel KERSAINT French Navy; 481, Sailboat; 498, Freighter SAINT JOSEPH Cie. Navale de l'Oceanie; 499, Freighter SAINT ANTOINE Union Commerciale de Nav. Caledonienne; 500, Sailing ship (arms); 501, Ships; 523, Ship; 528-529, Pirogue; 553, Yacht CHALLENGE FRANCE France; 554, Yacht FRENCH KISS Isle of Pines outrigger canoe; 558, Ouvea double canoe; 567, Boats; 571, Frigates L'ASTROLABE French Navy; 582, 583a, On board LA BOUSSOLE, ships of First Fleet British Navy.

583, 583a, LA BOUSSOLE and L'ASTROLABE; 583a, Ship in margin; 605, Sailing ships; 618, Ferry; 620, Hobie-Cat 14s; 657, Sailing ship CAMDEN; 668, cargo ships in harbor; B10, Frigate LA ZELéE French Navy; B14, Design as Cameroun Scott B29; C18, Design as Cameroun Scott C12; C25, Design as Cameroun Scott C32; C27, Sailing outrigger canoe; C47, Sailing vessels; C50, Sailing yachts; C69, Outrigger canoe; C80, Racing yachts; C84, Harbor, sailboats; C92, Stylized canoe; C100, Liner EL KANTARA Cie. des Messageries Maritimes; C114, Barque ENDEAVOUR British Navy; C115, Frigate L'ASTROLABE French Navy; C116, Shipboard scene; C117, Frigate L'ESPERANCE French Navy; C118, Corvette L'ASTROLABE French Navy; C136, Sailboats; C151, Sailing ship, container ship; C155, Sailing ships; C160, Pirogue; C162, Portion of deep sea fishing boat; C165, Native sailing boat; C174, Transport ZEALANDIA British Navy; C198, Sailboards; C203, Ship-sloop RESOLUTION British Navy; C204, Sailboat; C212, Ship; C231, C233a-C233b, PINTA; C232, C233a-C233b, SANTA MARIA; C233, C233a-C233b, NINA; C234, C234a, Viking longboat, Sailing ship (border); C238, Sailing ships; C241b, Comic strip character in rowboat with outboard motor; J9-J16, J17-J18, Native boat.

Nicaragua
40-49, O21-O30, Columbus aboard ship; 121-136, 144-151, 159-161, 162-163, 175-178, 1L1-1L13, 1L16-1L20, 2L1-2L10, 2L16-2L23, 2L36-2L38, Steamers; 668, Sailboat; 669, Steamer; 726, C300, Sailboats; 736, 739a, C318, C320a, Fleet of Columbus; 737, 739a, C319, C320a, SANTA MARIA; 794, Freighter HONDURAS Mamenic Line; 795, Freighter; 796, Freighter GUATEMALA Mamenic Line; 797, Freighter EL SALVADOR Mamenic Line; 798, Freighter; 799, Freighter; 800, C411, C415a, Sailing ship (arms); 984, Sailing ships; 990, Canoe; 1022, 4-oared shell without coxswain; 1023, 2-oared shell without coxswain; 1024, 2-oared shell with coxswain; 1025, Double sculls; 1026, 2-oared shell with coxswain; 1027, Single scull; 1086, Submarine NAUTILUS (fictional) Jules Verne; 1087, Sailing ship; 1158, Steamship; 1187, SANTA MARIA; 1188, NINA; 1189, PINTA; 1190, Fleet of Columbus; 1208, Sailboat in S/S; 1248, Bow of inflatable boat; 1261, Container ship; 1296, Sinking ship, lifeboat.

1755, Ships in S/S margin; 1762, Sailboards; 1764, Sailboat; 1781, Sidewheel paddle steamer DIRECTOR; 1782, Barque-rigged steamer INDEPENDENCE; 1783, Sidewheel paddle steamer ORIZABA; 1784, Liner S.S. LEWIS (1851) Ocean Steamship Co. of New England; 1785, Sidewheel paddle steamer GOLDEN RULE; 1786, Sidewheel paddle steamer SANTIAGO DE CUBA; 1787, Sidewheel paddle steamer NORTH STAR Cornelius Vanderbilt; 1788, Schooner, ship in S/S margin; 1892, Rowboat; 1907, Ships; 1933, Two-man canoe; C88-C91, Indistinct sailboats; C222-C228, Rowing boats; C266-C270, Fleet of Columbus; C271, Fleet of Columbus; C398, Freighter MANAGUA Mamenic Line; C401, Freighter COSTA RICA Mamenic Line; C402, Freighter NICARAO Mamenic Line; C403, Freighter; C541, Floating Red Cross station; C681-C685, C685a, Sailboat; C700, Freighter; C822, Galleon REVENGE British Navy; C829, Ships; C878, Ship's boat, ships; C902, Single scull; C903, 8-oared shell; C904, 4-oared shell with coxswain; C905, 8-oared shell; C906, 8-oared shell in S/S; C909, Frigate BONHOMME RICHARD Continental Navy, 5th Rate SERAPIS British Navy; C910, Nuclear submarine; C915, British Guiana Scott 13 depicted on stamp (SANDBACH); C942, Submarine NAUTILUS (fictional) Jules Verne; C974, Ships;

C985, Ship; C1015, Open boat; C1030, Fleet of Columbus; C1046, Freighter; C1048, Ship-sloop DISCOVERY British Navy.

Niger
37-54, B7-B8, Native boat; 76, Design as Cameroun Scott 216; 77-79, 83, Designs as Cameroun Scott 217-219; 253, Sailing ship; 258, Design as Dahomey Scott 300; 303, Yacht ELETTRA Guglielmo Marconi; 322, Dugout canoes; 339, Dugout canoe; 352, Portion of open boat; 356, Ship; 475, Canoes; 576, Sailboat, rowboats; 586, Canoe; 587, Rubber raft; 588, Poling boats; 589, Raft; 593, Boat; 614, Open fishing boat; 655, Liner PARIS Cie. GÇnÇrale Transatlantique; 657, 3-master JACQUES COEUR Cie. GÇnÇrale Transatlantique; 659, Barque BOSPHORUS Rathbones; 661, Clipper COMET Bucklin & Crane; 663, Full-rigged RICKMER RICKMERS Rickmers ReismÅlen Reederei; 665, Pirogue; 714, Motorboats; 715, Motorboat; 716, Motorboat; 796-797, Ships; 830, SANTA MARIA; 831-832, Caravel; 833, ESTREMADURA; 834, VIJA; 835, PINTA; 835A, NINA; 848, Columbus' fleet preparing to sail from Palos; C15, Canoe; C26, Building reed-bundle canoe, "kadei"; C55, Weather ship FRANCE I or FRANCE II French Gov't.; C71, Meterological vessel; C83, Canoe; C103, River boats; C127, Sailing boat; C224, Ferry barge; C225, Tug BABAN MAZA Soc. de Nav. Transport Fluvial, barges; C242, Ships; C270, On board frigate BONHOMME RICHARD Continental Navy; C273, Sailing yachts; C275, Ship, sailboats; C373, One-man kayak; C374, Kayaks; C375, Two-man kayak; C376, One-man kayak; C377, One-man kayak.

Norway
243, Viking galleys; 248, Viking galleys; 259, 261, Destroyer SLEIPNER Norwegian Navy; 260, 264, Merchant convoy; 281, Flat-bottomed "stykprams" ARKEN NOA and HIELPEREN Danish Navy, artillery ship STEENBUKKEN Swedish Navy; 283, Sloop RESTAURATIONEN Norwegian emigrants to US; 284, Paddle steamer CONSTITUTIONEN Norwegian Post Office; 286, Whaler SPES AND FIDES Svend Foyn; 287, Aux. schooner FRAM of Nansen, Sverdrup, Amundsen; 299, Fishing boat; 382, Viking longship; 383, Merchant ship; 384, Barque SKOMVAER J.C. Knudsen; 385, Tanker DALFONN Skibs A-S Dalfonn; 386, Liner BERGENSFJORD Norwegian-America Line; 392, Sailboat; 399, Aux. schooner FRAM Roald Amundsen; 433-434, Rowing boat; 437, Postal river boat; 438, Northland postal sailing boat; 456-457, Harbor, various vessels; 477, Ancient vessels; 478, Ancient vessels; 496-497, Design as Belgium Scott 675; 523-524, Design as Denmark Scott 454; 531, Ferry PRINSESSE RAGNHILD Jahre Line; 556, Freighters, in convoy; 559, Stylized ships; 568-569, Ancient ship; 588, Dragon head from Oseberg Viking ship; 596, Aux. schooner MAUD Roald Amundsen; 597, FRAM; 598, Aux. sloop GJO-A Roald Amundsen; 633, Open ferry; 651, Fishing boats; 693, Harbor, various vessels; 698, Paddle steamer CONSTITUTIONEN Norwegian P.O.; 699, Steamer VESTERAALEN Vesteraalens D-S; 700, Steamer KONG HAAKON Stavangerske D-S, steamer DRONNINGEN; 701, Coastal ferries NORDSTJERNEN Det Bergenske D-S and HARALD JARL Det Nordenfjeldske D-S; 702, Fishing boat, rowboats; 731, Portion of sailboat.

747, Open boat; 752, Tanker POLYTRADER; 765a, Sailing steamer BERGEN Det Bergenske D-S in S/S; 783, Deck scene; 784, Ship's rigging; 785, Training ship CHRISTIAN RADICH Ostlandets Skoleskib; 786, Lake passenger steamer SKIBLADNER Oplandske D-S; 787, Lake passenger steamer VICTORIA A-S Turisttrafikk; 788, Motor launch FAEMUND II; 789, Ferry STOREGUT; 805, Deck scene, royal yacht HEIMDAL Norwegian Navy; 806, Ship's launch; 820, Stylized cruise ship; 829, Sailing vessel, "Nordlandsfemboring"; 830, Sailing vessel, "Nordlandsjekt"; 838, Rowboat; 850, Raft with sail; 869, Dredge BERGHAVN Norwegian Government; 894, Motorboats; 895, Fishing boats; 915, Cockpit of sailboat; 927, Pontoon boat; 928, Passenger steamer PRINDS GUSTAV Norwegian Government; 929, Boat; 938-939, Boats; 975-976, Naval ships; 988, Tanker; 991-992, Sailboats; 993, SKOMVAER III; 994, COLIN ARCHER; 1024, RESTAURATIONEN; 1025, STAVANGERFJORD; 1022, Boat; 1023, Boat, oil platform; 1026, Boat; B1-B3, B28-B30, B54-B56, B59-B61, Liner BERGENSFJORD Norwegian-America Line; B9-B10, BERGENSFJORD; B19, Norwegian "jaegt"; B20-B21, Lifeboat COLIN ARCHER Norwegian Lifeboat Inst.; B22-B23, Lifeboat OSLOSKOYTA Norwegian Lifeboat Inst.; B32, Fishing boats; B35, Freighter BARRO-Y Trondhjems Ofotens S.S. Co.; B36, Liner SANCT SVITHUN Stavanger S.S. Co.; B37, Steamer IRMA Det Bergenske D-S; B68b, Tug-supply ship ODIN VIKING K-S Viking Supply Ships in S/S; B68c, Tugs TEMPEST and TYPHOON˜20 Bureau Weismuller, tugs OCEANIC and ARCTIC Bugsier, tug SMIT SINGAPORE Smit-Tak International in S/S.

Nossi-Be
3-21, 23-31, French Colonies Scott 49-52, 55, 57-59 ovptd.; 32-44, Design as Anjouan Scott 1; J1-J17, French Colonies Scott 46-52, 55-56, 58 ovptd.

Nyassa
60-62, 85, 88, 92, 97, 100, 104, 115-119, J5-J7, Carrack SAO GABRIEL Vasco da Gama; 124-125, Dhow, "sambuk".

Obock
1-31, French Colonies Scott 46-52, 54, 56-59 ovptd.; 32-44, Design as Anjouan Scott 1.

Panama
1-7, Full-rigged ship (arms); 214, Passenger-cargo ship PANAMA Panama Railroad S.S. Co.; 215, PANAMA; 216, Passenger-cargo ship CRISTOBAL Panama Canal Railroad Co.; 218, Freighters GENERAL W.C. GORGAS and GENERAL GEORGE W. GOETHALS Panama Railroad S.S. Co.; 219, C37, Collier NEREUS US Navy; 220, Heraldic ship; 286, 296, Liner RESOLUTE Atlantic Mail Corp. (United American Lines); 322, Freighter ANCON Panama Canal Railroad Co.; 323, Liner SANTA ELENA or SANTA˜20LUCIA Grace Line; 325, Passenger-cargo ship RANGITATA˜20New Zealand Shipping Co.; 326, Ferry boat; 342, 357, 374, 381, Sailing vessel; 438, Sailing vessel; 548, Bow of ship; 594, Cruise ship; 597, Cruise ship; 669, Ship; 681, Freighter; 785, Ship (railing, rigging); 800, Columbus' fleet; 800a, Columbus' fleet at sea; 800b, Columbus' fleet at anchor; C73, Sailing vessel (arms); C156, ANCON and tug GATUN Panama Canal Railroad Co.; C448, ANCON; C449, Bulk carrier CENTURY HOPE Kowin Shipping Co.

Paraguay
260, Fleet of Columbus; 304-306, Ship of Columbus; 319, L33, Gunboat HUMAITA Paraguayan Navy; 330-337, Fleet of Columbus; 370, Motorboat; 395-396, C131-C132, Sailing vessels; 399-402, 405, Columbus aboard ship; 410, 435, Armed paddle steamer TACUARI Paraguayan Navy; 411, C134, C136, C159, Steamers; 453-458, Freighter PARAGUARI Flota Mercante del Estado; 578, 580, C279, Motorized timber barge; 666, Motor coaster; 667, Bow of liner; 668, Trawler; 669, Bow of ore-carrier; 670, Trawler (design as 668, reversed); 2393, line drawing of sailing ship; 2262d, Kayak; 2263, Yacht (labels); 2267, Scott 1454 ovptd.; 2278, Scott 1972 ovptd.; 2279, Scott 2122a ovptd.; 2393, Ship; C39-C53, Gunboat PARAGUAY Paraguayan Navy; C179-C183, Stylized steamer; C342-C347, Stylized sailboat; C398, Liner PRESIDENTE STROESSNER Flota Mercante del Estado; C764, Finn-class sailboat; C767, 8-oared shells in S/S; C781, Galleon; C782, Windjammer; C783, Barque; C784, Ferry, ship; C785, Cruise ship, BAVARIA; C786, Sailing ships; C809, NINA, PINTA, SANTA MARIA; C811-C812, Sailing ship; C813, Galleon, SANTA URSULA, SANTA MARIA.

Peru
1, Paddle steamer PERU Pacific Steam Navigation Co.; 2, Paddle steamer CHILE Pacific Steam Navigation Co.; 272-275, Sailing vessel (arms); 341, Caravel SAN CRISTOBAL Francisco Pizarro; 344, Harbor, steamer; 345, Liner REINA DEL PACIFICO Pacific Steam Navigation Co.; 348, Schooner SACRAMENTO Peruvian Navy; 395, 400, Portion of ship; 397, 401, Spanish carrack; 399, 404, Bergantin SAN PEDRO Francisco de Orellana; 458, Fishing boat; 459, 484, 498, Steamer; 485, 499, C115, River gunboat MARANON Peruvian Navy; 517, C238-C241, Raft KON-TIKI Thor Heyerdahl; 520, Turret ship HUASCAR Peruvian Navy; 566, Fishing boat; 687, Corvette ESMERALDA Chilean Navy, HUASCAR; 689, Corvette UNION Peruvian Navy; 690, HUASCAR; 692, HUASCAR, Chilean vessels; 801, Cruiser ALMIRANTE GRAU Peruvian Navy; 802, Submarine FERRE Peruvian Navy; 812, Freighter; 813, Freighter; 824b, Naval battle; 824d, Naval battle; 825, Destroyer ALMIRANTE GUISE Peruvian Navy; 826, Gunboat AMERICA Peruvian Navy; 869, Reed-bundle canoe; 873, Submarine R-1 Peruvian Navy; 874, Submarine ABTAO Peruvian Navy; 897, Brigantine GAMARRA Peruvian Navy; 898, Monitor MANCO CAPAC Peruvian Navy; 917, Scott 1 and Scott 2 depicted on stamp; 935, Research-survey ship HUMBOLDT Government of Peru.

950, Sailing ship; 991, Ships; 992, Hospital ship B.A.P. MORONA Peruvian Navy; 997, Scott 1 depicted on stamp, container ship; 998, Scott 2 depicted on stamp, container ship; 1002, Sailboats; 1024, sailing ship in emblem of Catholic University of Peru; C18-C19, Lake steamer INCA Lake Titicaca Nav. Co. (Peruvian Gov't.); C51, Harbor, various; C99, Indistinct vessels; C124, C126 Fleet of Columbus; C129, Screw frigate LA VICTORIEUSE French Navy; C132, Scott 1 depicted on stamp; C133, Scott 2 depicted on stamp; C140, Various ship stamps depicted on stamp; C143, Harbor, various; C147, Balsa; C169-C171, Training ship AMAZONAS Peruvian Navy; C310, Ancient models of reed boats; C329, Schooner SACRAMENTO Peruvian Navy; C383, Freighter ILO Peruvian Ministry of Marine; C384, Fishing boats; C389, Reed boats, "totoras"; C464, Tanker; J2-J5, J7-J10, J12-J15, J18-J21, J23-J26, J29-J31, 8N15, 14N18, Sailing steamer ADRIATIC Collins Line; RA1-RA3, RA6-RA13, Steamers.

Philippines
356, C31, C48, Harbor, various vessels; 386, 414, 436, 472, 488, O18, O30, Moro vinta, sailing vessel; 387, 415, 437, 473-474, 489, C52, O19, O31, O41, Harbor, sailing vessels; 389, 417, 439, 478-480, 491, O21, O33, N3, Nau VITORIA Ferdinand Magellan, other vessels; 394, 422, 444, Cruiser OLYMPIA, followed by cruisers BALTIMORE, RALEIGH, and other ships of US Navy, battleship REINA CHRISTINA Spanish Navy, in flames; 506, Various types; 508, 614, O54, Steamer; 554-556, Portion of canoe; 563-565, 635, Moro vinta (arms); 566-568, 636, Sailing vessel (arms); 605-607, 829, C74-C76, Indistinct vessel; 618-619, 827, C77, Moro vinta; 817-818, Sailing outriggers; 892, Moro vinta; 893-895, Portion of freighter; 896-897, 1166, Sailing vessel; 973-975, River boats; 1074, Ferry boat; 1087, Canoes; 1088, Canoe; 1089, Sailboat; 1091, Native boats; 1094, Moro vintas; 1105-1106, Sailing ship; 1149, Ferry of Charon; 1152, Open boat; 1242, Sailing canoes; 1262, Sailing ship, junk; 1303-1304, Galleon EL ALMIRANTE; 1330, Cableship; 1349, Moro vinta; 1350a, Design as 1349 in S/S; 1350d, Sailing ship in S/S; 1360, Cableship; 1420-1421, Fast patrol boat; 1452, Landing craft in S/S; 1453-1454, Ships of Columbus; 1484-1485, Sailing canoe; 1631, Stylized bow of liner; 1690b, Galleon; 1718, Caracao; 1719, Chinese junk; 1720, Spanish galleon; 1721, Casco; 1722, Steamboat; 1723, Cruise ship; 1751, Galleon; 1752, Galleon; 1770, Boat; 1892, Wrecked Spanish galleon; 1907b, Ship's bow; 1935, Yachts; 1988, Boat, skiff, power boat; 1997, Sailing vessels; 2010, Ship; 2105, Boat; 2190-2192, sailing ship; 2199-2200, outrigger canoes; C59-C62, N10-N11, N35-N36, NO7, Moro vinta; C91, C92a, C108, Sailing vessels; C92, C92a, C108, Galleons; C93, Portion of ship; C94, Canoes; N18-N19, N24-N25, NB5, Moro vinta; N26-N27, Battleship MUTSU Japanese Navy.

Poland
138, Sailing vessel; 233, 237, 1K17, Sailing vessel; 296, 1K29, Liner PILSUDSKI Gdynia-America Line; 309, Liner BATORY Gdynia-America Line; 420, Launching of freighter OLIWA Polish Ocean Lines; 421, Freighter; 422, Training ship GENERAL ZARUSKI Polish Merchant Navy; 458, Steamer; 548, Shipbuilding; 560-561, Shipbuilding; 580, Fishing vessel DALMOR; Polish State Fisheries Board; 581, Freighter CZECH Polish Ocean Lines; 642, Single-masted sailing ship; 655, Freighter SOLDEK Polish S.S. Co.; 703, Racing scull; 719, Freighter KILINSKI Polish Ocean Lines; 720, Towboat, barges; 721, Freighter POKOJ Polish

Ocean Lines; 722, Launching freighter MARCELI NOWOTKO Polish Ocean Lines; 723, Fisheries parent ship FRYDERYK CHOPIN Polish Ocean Lines, trawler RADUNIA Polish State Fisheries; 731, Canoe; 752, Racing sculls; 797-798, Full-rigged TORRENS A.L. Elder; 804, Medieval sailing vessel, stylized modern liners; 826, Sailing ship MARY AND MARGARET Virginia Co., London; 835, Sailing yacht; 854, Sailing vessels, sand barges; 951, River steamer; 952A, Boat; 954, Sailing vessel; 955, Galleons, may represent two of the following: CZARNY ORZEL, PROROK SAMUEL, WIELKIE SLONCE Polish Navy; 957, Carrack; 959, Galleon; 960, River barge; 961, Small ships; 985, Fish factory LESKOV Russian Gov't.; 986, Fish factory SEVERODVINSK Russian Gov't.; 987, Coaster RAMBUTAN Republik Indonesia; 988, Freighter KRYNICA Polish Ocean Lines; 989, Freighter MARCELI NOWOTKO Polish Ocean Lines; 990, Tanker PROFESSOR HUBER Polish Ocean Lines; 1001, Tug, floating crane; 1005, Bow of freighter EMELIA PLATER Polish Ocean Lines; 1006, Kayaks; 1007, 4-man racing sculls; 1097, Cruiser AURORA Russian Navy; 1124, 1299, Egyptian galley Queen Hatshepsut; 1125, 1300, Phoenician merchantman; 1126, 1301, Greek trireme; 1127, 1302, Roman corbita; 1128, 1303, Scandinavian longship; 1129, 1304, Hansa cog; 1130, 1305, Danzig holk; 1131, 1306, Carrack; 1167, Destroyer BLYSKAWICA Polish Navy; 1172, Amphibious troop carrier; 1206, Caravel of Columbus; 1207, Galleon ARK ROYAL British Navy; 1208, Warship WODNIK Polish Navy; 1209, Dutch flute.

1210, Ship-of-the-line; 1211, Frigate; 1212, Clipper FLYING CLOUD Grinnel, Minturn & Co.; 1213, Training ship DAR POMORZA Polish Navy; 1246, Shipyard construction; 1258, Racing scull; 1265b, Racing kayak in S/S; 1276, Open boats; 1324, Dragon-class racing yachts; 1325, 5.5m-class racing yacht; 1326, Finn-class racing yachts; 1327, Vega-class racing yachts; 1328, Cadet-class racing yachts; 1329, Star-class racing yachts; 1330, Flying Dutchman-class racing yacht; 1331, Amethyst-class racing yacht; 1332, Finn-class racing yachts; 1387, Stylized freighter; 1389, Freighter; 1439, Indistinct vessel; 1441, Amethyst-class yacht; 1442, Sailboat; 1444, Indistinct boat; 1447, Liner BATORY Polish Ocean Lines; 1532, Cruiser AURORA Russian Navy; 1618, Destroyer BLYSKAWICA Polish Navy; 1652, Sailing yacht; 1653, Freighter; 1658, Yawl OPTY Leonid Teliga; 1673, Stern of ship; 1760, Destroyer PIORUN Polish Navy; 1761, Submarine ORZEL Polish Navy; 1762, Destroyer GARLAND Polish Navy; 1780, Training ship DAR POMORZA Polish Navy; 1781, Liner STEFAN BATORY Polish Ocean Lines; 1782, Icebreaker PERKUN Polish Ship Salvage; 1783, Rescue ship R-1 Polish Ship Salvage; 1784, Bulk carrier ZIEMIA SZCZECINSKA Polish S.S. Co.; 1785, Tanker BESKIDY Polish S.S. Co.; 1786, Freighter HEL Polish Ocean Lines; 1787, Ferry GRYF Polish Ocean Lines; 1843, Sailboat; 1852, Ship's helm; 1854, Bulk carrier MANIFEST LIPCOWY Polish S.S. Co., under construction; 1929, Sailboat; 1990, Small boats; 1999, OSA-class missile boat.

2005, Lugger LUCJA-MALGORZATA Stefan Szolc-Rogozinski; 2007, Submarine Stefan Drzewiecki; 2038, 16th c. vessel; 2039, Sloop DAL Lt. J. Swiechowski, Lt. A. Bohomolec; 2040, Yawl OPTY Leonid Teliga; 2041, Training ship DAR POMORZA Polish Navy; 2042, Yacht POLONEZ Capt. Chris Baranowski; 2093, Raft; 2117, Sailing ship MARY AND MARGARET Virginia Co., London; 2188, Tanker ZAWRAT Polish Ocean Lines; 2189, Ferry GRYF Polish S.S. Co.; 2190, Container ship GENERAL BEM Polska Zegluga; 2191, Liner STEFAN BATORY Polish Ocean Lines; 2192, Bulk carrier ZIEMIA SZCZECINSKA Polish S.S. Co., barge; 2193, Freighter; 2194, Hydrofoil, river passenger ship; 2195, Ships; 2240, Sailing ship (coin); 2249, Iceboats; 2250, Iceboat; 2328, Rowboat; 2341, Paddle steamer KSIAZE KSAWERY Konstanty Wolicki and Piotr Steinkeller; 2342, Paddle steamer GENERAL SWIERCZEWSKI Fajans River Co.; 2343, Pusher tug ZUBR Zegluga Warszawska; 2344, Motorship SYRENA Zegluga Warszawska; 2404, Training ship LWOW Polish Merchant Marine; 2405, Freighter-training ship ANTONI GARNUSZEWSKI Polish Ocean Lines; 2406, Fishery training ship ZENIT Wyzsza Szkola Morska; 2407, Fishery training ship JAN TURLEJSKI Rederei Dalmor; 2408, Fishery training ship HORYZONT'20; 2409, Training ship DAR POMORZA Polish Navy; 2461, Rafts; 2466, Harbor, sailing vessels; 2474, Model of tug ATLAS II, other model boats; 2478, Model sailing yachts; 2559, Ship; 2581, 2581a, Harbor, various vessels; 2624, Boats on river; 2625, Boats, rafts; 2626, Rowboat; 2688, Schooner ISKRA Polish Navy; 2729, 2730a, Ferry WILANOW Polish Baltic Shipping Co.; 2730, 2730a, Ferry WAWEL Polish Baltic Shipping Co.; 2731, 2732a, Ferry POMERANIA Polish Baltic Shipping Co.; 2732, 2732a, Ferry ROGALIN Polish Baltic Shipping Co.; 2733, Research ship KOPERNIK Polish Government.

2734, Research-fishing vessel PROFESSOR SIEDLECKI Morski Instytut Rybacki; 2751, Sailboards; 2782, Freighter-training ship ANTONI GARNUSZEWSKI Polish Ocean Lines; 2783, Fishing vessel ZULAWY Transocean; 2784, Training ship POGORIA Iron Shackle Fraternity; 2785, Yacht GEDANIA (?); 2786, Sealer DZIUNIA (?); 2787, Freighter-training ship KAPITAN LEDOCHOWSKI Polish Steamship Co.; 2821, Kayak; 2857, 2-man kayak; 2881, Freighter; 2888, Fire boat BLYSK Zarzad Portu Gdansk; 2889, Fire fighting tug ZAR Zarzad Portu Gdansk; 2890, Fire boat PLOMIEN Zarzad Portu Gdansk; 2891, Fire boat STRAZAK 4 Morski, Port Handlowy, Gdansk; 2892, Fire boat STRAZAK 11 Morski, Port Handlowy, Gdansk; 2893, Fire boat STRAZAK 25 Aarzad Portu Szczecin-Swinoujscie; 2922, Training ship SCHLESWIG HOLSTEIN; 2923, Warships; 2959, Yachts; 2980-2981, Kayaks; 3040, PIORUN, warship; 3085, SANTA MARIA; B36, Cruiser DRAGON Polish Navy; B37, Training ship DAR POMORZA Polish Navy; B39, Small sailing boat; B41, Battleship SCHLESWIG-HOLSTEIN German Navy; B46, Canal barge; B47, Sailing vessels; B48, Floating crane; B77, Sailing yachts; B78, DAR POMORZA; B128, B128a, Various vessels in S/S; B138, Kayak in S/S; C28, Harbor, various vessels; C51, Liner BATORY Polish Ocean Lines; 1K33-1K36, Portion of sailboat; 3K8, 3K20, Submarine ORZEL Polish Navy; 3K9, Submarine; 3K10, Convoy of merchant ships; 3K12, Steamer.

Portugal

97-100, Bow view of sailing vessel; 101-105, Sailing vessels; 147, 185, 199, Carracks SAO GABRIEL and SAO RAPHAEL, caravel BERRIO Vasco da Gama; 148, 186, 200, Fleet of da Gama; 149, 192, 206, Fleet of da Gama; 150, 187, 201, Fleet of da Gama; 151, 188, 202, SAO GABRIEL; 152, 189, 203, Sailing vessels; 153, 191, 205, SAO GABRIEL; 154, 190, 204, Model of sailing vessel; 299-314, Sailing vessel; 320-324, Sailing vessel sinking; 587, 592, 594a, Sailing vessel; 589, 593, 594a, Symbolic caravel; 608, 614a, Fishing boat; 610, 614a, Fishing boat, "saveiro"; 615-631, 702-710, Caravela latina; 644, 649a, Sails of vessel; 735-736, Portuguese caravel; 792-793, Symbolic barge; 838-839, Liner SANTA MARIA Cia. Colonial de Nav.; 861, Portuguese caravel; 864, Portuguese bark Prince Henry the Navigator; 868-869, Stylized ship; 873-874, Sailing vessels; 925-927, Sailing vessel; 976-977, Liner FRANCE Cie. GÇnÇrale Transatlantique; 980-982, Design as Belgium Scott 675; 1004, 1006, Ships; 1005, 1007, Ship's lines; 1037, Fleet of Cabral; 1058, Sailing ships; 1059, Fleet of da Gama; 1080-1081, Cableship GREAT EASTERN Telegraph Const. & Maint.; 1086, Douro wine boat, "barcos rabelas"; 1116-1118, Carrack SANTIAGO Portuguese missionaries; 1144, Portion of freighter; 1151, Racing yachts; 1182, Ship; 1206, Ship; 1222, 1225a, Sailing ship, steamer; 1258, Rubber raft; 1281, Ship's hull; 1295, 1297b, Ship; 1339, 1341a, Boat; 1350, 1355a, Fishing boat, "barco poveiro"; 1351, 1355a, Fishing boat, "barco do mar"; 1352, 1355a, Fishing boat, "barco do nazare"; 1353, 1355a, Fishing boat, "caique do algarve".

1354, 1355a, Fishing boat, "barco da xavega"; 1355, 1355a, Coastal boat, "bateira de buarcos"; 1365, Fishing boat, trawler; 1378, Wooden fishing boat, supertanker; 1396, Canoes, sailboats; 1400-1403, Trawlers (different designs); 1461, 1461a, Sailing ships; 1469, Naval battle; 1474, Aveiro river boats; 1476, 1479a, Caravel; 1477, 1479a, Nau; 1478, 1479a, Galleon; 1479, 1479a, Sailing steamer; 1488, River boat, "fragata"; 1489, Wine boat, "rabelo"; 1490, Fishing boat, "moliceiro"; 1491, Cargo boat, "barco"; 1492, River boat, "carocho"; 1493, River boat, "varino"; 1505, Ships; 1506, 1507a, Bow of boat, model; 1507, 1507a, Bow of boat; 1510, Ships; 1525, Sailing ship (arms); 1526, Hull on ways, fishing boat; 1532, Training ship SAGRES Portuguese Navy; 1534, 470-class yachts; 1554, Container ship, tug; 1559, 1562a, Ship-of-the-line VASCO DA GAMA Portuguese Navy; 1560, 1562a, Steam corvette ESTEFANIA Portuguese Navy; 1561, 1562a, Cruiser ADAMASTOR Portuguese Navy; 1562, 1562a, Frigate COMANDANTE JOAO BELO Portuguese Navy; 1569, 1572a, Caravel (tapestry); 1604, 1605a, Harbor, various vessels; 1618, 1618a, Sailing ship; 1697, Fishing boats; 1710, Stylized caravels Bartolomeu Dias; 1711, Stylized caravels Bartolomeu Dias; 1721, Stylized caravel Bartolomeu Dias; 1745, Racing yachts in S/S; 1752-1753, Caravel; 1781, River boat CACILHEIRO Transtejo Co. in S/S, boat in margin; 1815, 1815a, Barca; 1816, 1816a, Caravela pescareza; 1817, 1817a, Barinel; 1818, 1818a, Caravela; 1862, 1862a, Caravel; 1863-1864, 1863a-1864a, Nau; 1865, 1865a, Galleon; 1872, Sailing ships; 1880, Racing yachts; 1907, Boat; 1918, US 230 revalued, US 233 unvalued and shipboard scene (border); 1919, US 231, 232 revalued (border); RA14, Sailing vessel.

Portugal – Azores

333, 333a, Ships' boats ships; 354, Sailing vessel, "jeque"; 355, Sailing vessel, "bote"; 381, 382, 382a Tin boat (toy); 384, Sailing vessel; 401, Schooner HELENA; 403, Yacht CRUZEIRO DO CANAL; 405, PINTA or SANTA MARIA; 409, 409a-409b, boat builders; 410, INSULANO; 411, CARVALHO ARAUJO; 412, FUNCHAL; 413, TERCEIRENSE.

Portugal – Madeira

37, Design as Portugal Scott 147; 38-40, Designs as Portugal Scott 148-50; 41, Design as Portugal Scott 151; 42, Design as Portugal Scott 152; 43, Design as Portugal Scott 153; 44, Design as Portugal Scott 154; 73, Madeira fishing boat; 75, Joao Goncalves Zarco; 76, Caravels; 100, Carreria boat; 106, Fishing boat; 107, Motor launch; 110, 110a, Tanker; 122, Passenger/cargo ship MARIA CHRISTINA; 128, SANTA MARIA; 143, Tuna boat; 144, Desert Island boat; 145, Maneiro boat; 146, Chevelha boat; 162, steam coaster GAVIAO; 163, catamaran-type passenger ferry INDEPENDENCIA; 164, freighter MADEIRENSE; 165, freighter FUNCHALENSE.

Portuguese Africa

1, Design as Portugal Scott 147; 2-4, Designs as Portugal Scott 148-150; 5, Design as Portugal Scott 151; 6, Design as Portugal Scott 152; 7, Design as Portugal Scott 153; 8, Design as Portugal Scott 154.

Portuguese Congo

75-82, Macao Scott 187-94 ovptd.; 83-90, Portuguese Africa Scott 1-8 ovptd.; 91-98, Timor Scott 45-52 ovptd.

Portuguese Guinea

116-123, Macao Scott 187-194 ovptd.; 124-131, Port. Africa Scott 1-8 ovptd.; 132-139, Timor Scott 45-52 ovptd.; 233-237, Design as Angola Scott 274; 280, Design as Angola Scott 382; 292-293, Design as Cape Verde Scott 298-299; 319, Design as Angola Scott 509; 330, Cruiser REPUBLICA Portuguese Navy; 331, Destroyer GUADIANA Portuguese Navy.

Portuguese India

189, 290, Design as Portugal Scott 147; 190-192, 291-293, 384-385, Designs as Portugal Scott 148-150; 193, 294, 386, Design as Portugal 151; 195, 295, 387, Design as Portugal 152; 196, 296, 388, Design as Portugal 153; 197, 297, 389, Design as Portugal 154; 411-412, Carrack SAO GABRIEL Vasco da Gama; 417, Sailing vessel; 424-438, 454-463, 472-474,"20J34-J36, Galeasse; 439-442, Design as Angola Scott 274; 527, Design as Macao Scott 371.

Puerto Rico

133, Ship's boat, stern of ship, Columbus.

Qatar

32, 38, 43, Dhow; 112, Kayak; 116, Norman longship MORN William the Conqueror; 117, SANTA MARIA; 118, Carrack SAO GABRIEL Vasco da Gama; 119, Nau VITORIA Ferdinand

Magellan; 120, Galleon GOLDEN HIND Sir Francis Drake; 121, Yacht GIPSY MOTH IV Francis Chichester; 125, Open boat; 150, Dhow; 152, Oil tanker; 166, Trawler ROSS RAYYAN Qatar Natl. Fishing Co.; 178, Tanker SIVELLA Soc. Maritime Shell; 180, Oil rig supply vessel SHELL DOLPHIN Shell Intl. Marine; 183, Oil tankers; 184, 187a, Boatbuilding; 197, Liner PRESIDENT WILSON American President Lines; 222, 223a, Fishing boat; 234, Sailboat; 245, Cableship C.S. ARIEL British P.O.; 314, Oil rig support ship; 347, Weather ship; 386, Liner IBERIA P&O Line, paddle steamer HINDOSTAN P&O Line; 418, Sailboats; 419, Dhow; 478-483, Dhow (different designs); 485, Olympic sailboat; 631-632, Container ship BAR'ZAN United Arab Shipping Co.; 641-642, Symbolic ship; 651-653, Dhow; 684, Container ship QATARI IBN AL FUJA'A United Arab Shipping; 685, Container ship AL WAJBA United Arab Shipping; 742, Dhow; 789, ships shown in child's painting; 790, fishing boats shown in child's painting.

Quelimane

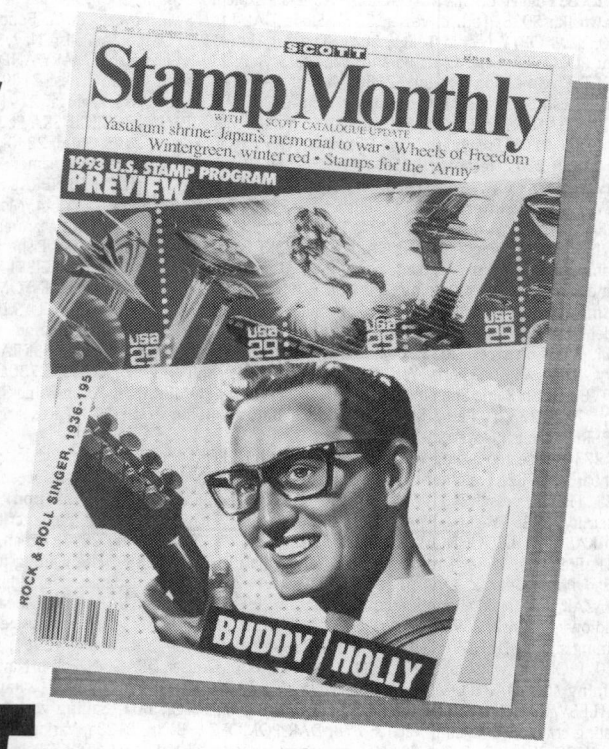

1-8, Macao Scott 187-194 ovptd.; 9-16, Port. Africa Scott 1-8 ovptd.; 17-24, Timor Scott 45-52 ovptd. END OF LISTING

American Topical Association

In addition to the specific American Topical Association (ATA) handbooks used in developing the listings above, considerably more material is available for a wide variety of topics. Following are two sets of such information, one showing handbooks and their prices from ATA and the other showing checklists. Handbooks are large and normally more broad in scope. Checklists may deal with much tighter specialties.

Only ATA members may take advantage of the checklist service, and therefore cost information on checklists is not included here. Membership information is available for a SASE from the ATA Central Office, P.O. Box 630, Johnstown, PA 15907.

Handbooks may not be current, based on the publication date of each.

ATA Handbooks

Adventures in Topical Stamp Collecting (HB96), $8.
Americana on Foreign Stamps, volume 1 (HB58), $6.
Americana on Foreign Stamps, volume 2 (HB85), $6.
Astronomy and Philately (HB90), $5.
Bicentennial of American Independence (HB97), $6.
Bicentennial of Postmarks 1972-1984 (HB110), $5.
Birds of the World in Philately (HB106), $14.
Birds of the World in Philately, supplement 1 (HB106-1), $6.
Birds of the World in Philately, supplement 2 (HB106-2), $6.
Christmas Stamps of the World (HB120), $17.
Christopher Columbus in Philately (HB121), $5.
Cooking with Stamps (HB56), $6.
Education on Stamps (HB68), $4.
Fairy Tales and Folk Tales on Stamps (HB73), $4.
Fishes, Amphibia, and Reptiles on Stamps of the World (HB91), $8.
Holy Family on Stamps (HB92), $8.
Horses & Horse Relatives (HB116), $16.
Insects & other Invertebrates of the World on Stamps (HB98), $10.
Lions International Philately (HB59), $4.
Mammals of the World on Stamps (HB79), $5.
Map Stamps of the World (HB104), $7.
Medical Stamps (HB63), $5.
Medicine Stamps (HB66), $7.
Music World of Stamps (HB84), $6.
Old Glory Around the World (HB75), $3.
Orchids on Stamps (HB118), $9.
Pharmaceutical Philately (HB114), $9.
Plants on Stamps, volume 1 (HB94), $10.
Plants on Stamps, volume 2 (HB112), $12.
Railway Stamps (HB102), $11.
Railway Stamps, supplement 1 (HB102-1), $5.
Science Stamps (HB87), $7.
Space Stamps (HB99), $11.
Sports & Recreation Checklist (HB83), $4.
Stamps on Stamps (HB122), $17.
Statue of Liberty Stamps and Postmarks (HB111), $5.
Theatre Philatelic (HB67), $5.
Watercraft on Stamps (HB117), $17.
Women on Stamps, volume 1 (HB71), $4.
Women on Stamps, volume 2 (HB93), $7.

ATA Checklists

African Postal Union, 2 pages
AIDS, 1 page
Airlines, 7 pages
Airports, 5 pages
Airships (Zeppelins), 8 pages
Anti-Alcohol, 1 page
Anti-Drug, 2 pages
Anti-Polio, 2 pages
Anti-Malaria (WHO), 4 pages
Anti-Smoking, 2 pages
Arab Postal Union, 1 page
Archery, 7 pages
Audubon, 4 pages
Automobiles, 31 pages
Bach, Johann Sebastian, 1 page
Badger, 1 page
Badminton, 2 pages
Bagpipes, 2 pages
Ballet, 3 pages
Balloons, 13 pages
Balloons – Toy, 2 pages
Balloons – Weather, 2 pages
Bananas, 3 pages
Baseball, 7 pages
Basketball, 8 pages
Bats, 2 pages
Bears, 8 pages
Bears – Pandas, 1 page
Bears – Teddy Bears, 2 pages
Beauty Queens, 2 pages
Bees, 8 pages
Beethoven, 2 pages
Bells, 19 pages
Biathlon, 2 pages
Birds of Prey, 14 pages
Birds – Cockatoos, Lories, Parrots, Parakeets, 7 pages
Birds – Ducks, 6 pages
Birds – Geese, 3 pages
Birds – Hummingbirds, 4 pages
Birds – Loons, 1 page
Birds – Penguins, 4 pages
Birds – Swans, 3 pages
Birds – Woodpeckers, 4 pages
Bison, 2 pages
Black Americans, 3 pages
Blacksmiths, 3 pages
Blood Donations, 3 pages
Bobsled, Luge, Sled & Toboggan, 3 pages
Bonsai, 2 pages
Bowling, 1 page
Boxing, 9 pages
Braille, Louis, 1 page
Breast Feeding, 3 pages
Bridges, 15 pages
Bromeliads (Pineapple Plant), 2 pages
Buffalo, 2 pages
Butterflies, 11 pages
Cameras & Photography, 6 pages
Captain Cook, 4 pages
Carnivals, 2 pages
Castles, 16 pages
Cattle, 9 pages
Cats – Domestic, 11 pages
Cats – Feral, 21 pages
Chess, 8 pages
Civets & Genets, 1 page
Children, Caring for, 8 pages
Children's Drawings, 6 pages
Chopin, 1 page
Churchill, Sir Winston, 4 pages
Circus, 5 pages
Clocks (Timepieces), 11 pages
Clowns, 3 pages
Coffee, 5 pages
Coffee & Tea Service, 4 pages
Columbus, 7 pages
Computers, 5 pages
Copernicus, 4 pages
Costumes, 7 pages
Costumes – Folk (Full Length), 2 pages
Cotton, 3 pages
Crabs, 6 pages
Cricket (Sport), 6 pages
Crocodile, 4 pages
Curies, The, 2 pages
Dams & Hydroelectric Plants, 10 pages
Dance (no Ballet), 11 pages
Darwin, 1 page
Dentistry, 3 pages
Detectives, Fictional, 1 page
Diamonds, 2 pages
Dinosaurs & Flying Reptiles, 5 pages
Diving Competition, 3 pages
Dogs, 11 pages
Dog Sleds, 2 pages
Dolls, 5 pages
Dolphins, 4 pages
Dragonflies (Odonata), 3 pages
Einstein, Albert, 1 page
Elephants, 14 pages
Elvis Presley, 1 page
Esperanto, 2 pages
Europa, 14 pages
Fables, 2 pages
Fairy Tales, Children's Stories, Etc.
Fairy Tales – African & Asian, 1 page
Fairy Tales – Andersen, Hans Christian, 2 pages
Fairy Tales – Arabian Nights, 1 page
Fairy Tales – Baltic Fairy Tales, 1 page
Fairy Tales – Children's Classics, 2 pages
Fairy Tales – Children's Stories, 1 page
Fairy Tales – Dickens, Charles, 2 pages
Fairy Tales – Disney, Walt, 6 pages
Fairy Tales – Don Quixote, 2 pages

Fairy Tales – European Fairy Tales, 1 page
Fairy Tales – Folktales, 2 pages
Fairy Tales – Grimm Brothers, 2 pages
Fairy Tales – Hercules: Life and Labors, 1 page
Fairy Tales – Japanese Fairy Tales, 1 page
Fairy Tales – Legends, 3 pages
Fairy Tales – Nursery Rhymes, 1 page
Fairy Tales – Perrault, Charles, 1 page
Fairy Tales – Pinocchio, 1 page
Fairy Tales – Russian Folklore, 1 page
Fairy Tales – Scandinavian Fairy Tales, 1 page
Fairy Tales – South & Central American, 1 page
Fairy Tales – Twain, Mark, 1 page
Fairy Tales – Verne, Jules, 2 pages
Fans – Hand Held, 4 pages
Fencing, 8 pages
Field Hockey, 3 pages
Firearms, Hunting & Shooting, 6 pages
Fire Fighting, 8 pages
Fireworks, 2 pages
Fleming, 1 page
Flowers, 22 pages
Flowers – Hibiscus, 9 pages
Flowers – Iris, 4 pages
Flowers – Peonies, 2 pages
Flowers – Poinsettias, 1 page
Flowers – Roses, 11 pages
Fossils & Prehistoric Animals, 11 pages
Foxes, 3 pages
Frogs & Toads, 5 pages
Fruits & Berries, 18 pages
Galileo, 1 page
Gandhi, Mahatma, 2 pages
Geese, 3 pages
Gems & Minerals, 11 pages
Giraffes, 2 pages
Girl Guides & Scouts, 4 pages
Glass, 2 pages
Goats, 3 pages
Golf, 2 pages
Gymnastics – Men, 6 pages
Gymnastics – Women, 8 pages
Halley's Comet, 2 pages
Hammarskjold, Dag, 1 page
Helicopters (Vertical Flight), 7 pages
Hermes (Mercury), 6 pages
Hippopotamus, 2 pages
Horse Racing, 4 pages
Hugo, Victor, 1 page
Hummel Figurines, 1 page
Hunting Scenes, 2 pages
Ice Hockey, 6 pages
International Education Year, 1 page
International Labor Organization 50th Anniversary, 2 pages
International Letter Writing Week, 2 pages
International Quiet Sun Year, 1 page
International Telecommunications Union Centenary, 4 pages
International Year of the Child, 6 pages
International Year of the Disabled, 3 pages
Jaycees, 1 page
Jazz Musicians, 1 page
Jesuits, 7 pages
Jewelry, 2 pages
Joint Issues, 4 pages
Joint Issues – U.S., 2 pages
Judo, 4 pages
Karate, 2 pages
Kennedy, J.F. Memorial, 5 pages
King, Martin Luther, Jr., 2 pages
Kites, 1 page
Koalas, 2 pages
Koch, Dr. Robert, 2 pages
Leonardo da Vinci, 3 pages
Liberty Bell, 1 page
Lifesaving, 1 page
Lindbergh, 2 pages
Lizards, 6 pages
Lobsters & Crayfish, 3 pages
Magnifying Glasses, 2 pages
Maritime Disasters, 6 pages
Martial Arts, 6 pages
Masks, 16 pages
Masks – Comedy/Tragedy, 2 pages
Mermaids, 2 pages
Methodist Religion, 2 pages
Mice & Rats, 2 pages
Microscopes, 7 pages
Mining, 4 pages
Mosaics, 6 pages
Motorcycles, 10 pages
Mountain Climbing, 3 pages
Mozart, 3 pages
Mushrooms, 21 pages
Musical Instruments – Bagpipes, 2 pages
Musical Instruments – Brasses, 2 pages
Musical Instruments – Drums, 5 pages
Musical Instruments – Guitar, Mandolin & Zither, 2 pages
Musical Instruments – Keyboard, 1 page
Musical Instruments – Lute, 2 pages
Musical Instruments – Violin Family, 4 pages
Musical Instruments – Wood Winds, 2 pages
Musical Instruments – Xylophone, 1 page
Nobel Chemistry Prize, 3 pages
Nobel Literature Prize, 8 pages
Nobel Medicine Prize, 5 pages
Nobel Peace Prize, 8 pages
Nobel Physics Prize, 6 pages
North American Indians, 5 pages
Nubian Monuments, 3 pages
Nurses & Nursing, 18 pages
Octopus & Squid, 2 pages
Opera, 23 pages
Owls, 5 pages
Parachute, 3 pages
Pasteur, Louis, 1 page
Peace, 7 pages
Pegasus & Winged Horses, 2 pages
Phoenix, 2 pages
Phonographs & Records, 1 page
Picasso, 7 pages
Pigs, Hogs & Wild Boar, 5 pages
Pinnipeds (Seals & Walruses), 4 pages
Pipe Organs, 3 pages
Pirates, 3 pages
Playing Cards, 1 page
Polo, 1 page
Pope John Paul II, 3 pages
Popes, 7 pages
Primates (Apes & Monkeys), 6 pages
Puffins, 2 pages
Puppets, 2 pages
Rabbits, 5 pages
Rainbows, 4 pages
Red Cross Societies, 30 pages
Red Cross Societies, supplement 1, 4 pages
Rockwell, Norman, 3 pages
Roller Skating, 1 page
Rotary International, 6 pages
Rowing, 4 pages
Rugby, 2 pages
St. George & Dragon, 4 pages
Sailing, 8 pages
Salvation Army, 2 pages
Santa Claus, 3 pages
Scales (Measuring & Weighing), 9 pages
Schweitzer, Albert, 2 pages
Scuba, 5 pages
Sea Horses, 1 page
Seaplanes & Flying Boats, 10 pages
Shakespeare, 3 pages
Sheep, 4 pages
Shells, 6 pages
Side-Saddle Riders, 2 pages
Skating (no Ice Hockey), 8 pages
Skiing, (no Biathlon), 16 pages
Smoking & Tobacco, 6 pages
Snakes, 9 pages
Snakes: Caduceus & WHO Emblem, 2 pages
Soccer, 28 pages
Spiders, 1 page
Stained Glass, 6 pages
Streetcars, 4 pages
Submarines, 3 pages
Sugar, 7 pages
Surveying, 6 pages
Swimming, 7 pages
Table Tennis, 3 pages
Telephone Centenary, 2 pages
Tennis, 10 pages
3-D & Holograms, 2 pages
Toys, 4 pages
Track and Field Events – Discus, 5 pages
Track and Field Events – Hammer Throw, 2 pages
Track and Field Events – High Jump, 4 pages
Track and Field Events – Hurdles, 6 pages
Track and Field Events – Javelin, 5 pages
Track and Field Events – Long Jump, 3 pages
Track and Field Events – Pole Vault, 3 pages
Track and Field Events – Relay Race, 2 pages
Track and Field Events – Running, 18 pages
Track and Field Events – Shot Put, 3 pages
Track and Field Events – Triple Jump, 1 page
Track and Field Events – Walking, 1 page
Traffic Safety, 9 pages
Turtles, 9 pages
Umbrellas, 7 pages
Unesco Building in Paris, 1 page
Uniforms, 4 pages
Universal Postal Union, 13 pages
Universities, 11 pages
U.S. Stage & Screen Stars, 6 pages
Vegetables, 5 pages
Volleyball, 5 pages
Wagner, Richard, 2 pages
Waterfalls, 9 pages
Water Polo, 1 page
Water Skiing & Surfing, 2 pages
Whales, 6 pages
Whaleboats, 2 pages
Whisks, Fly, 1 page
Windmills, 6 pages
Windsurfing, 2 pages
Wine, 9 pages
Wolves, 3 pages
World Refugees Year, 2 pages
World Wildlife Fund, 3 pages
Wrestling, 7 pages
X-Ray, 1 page
Zebras, 3 pages
Zodiac: Eastern & Western, 4 pages ❑

JAPAN

LOCATION — North Pacific Ocean, east of China
GOVT. — Constitutional monarchy
AREA — 142,726 sq. mi.
POP. — 120,020,000 (est. 1984)
CAPITAL — Tokyo

1000 Mon = 10 Sen
100 Sen = 1 Yen (or En)
10 Rin = 1 Sen

Catalogue values for unused stamps in this country are for Never Hinged items, beginning with Scott 362 in the regular postage section, Scott B8 in the semi-postal section, and Scott C9 in the airpost section.

Watermarks

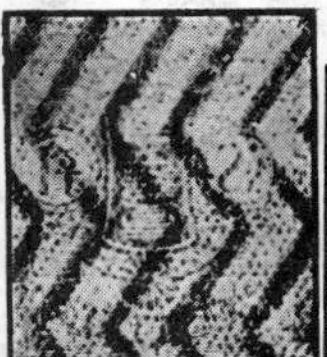
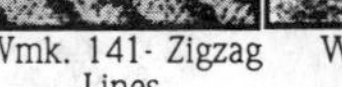
Wmk. 141- Zigzag Lines

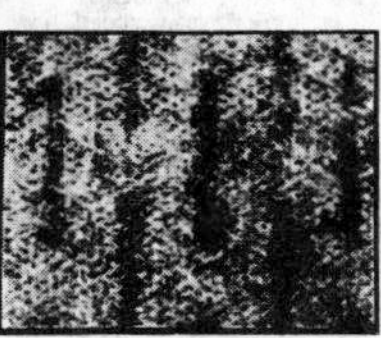
Wmk. 142- Parallel Lines

Wmk. 257- Curved Wavy Lines

After 1945, Wmk. 257 exists also in a narrow spacing on a small number of issues.

Counterfeits of Nos. 1-71 are plentiful. Some are excellent and deceive many collectors.

Nos. 1-54A were printed from hand engraved plates of 40. Each stamp in the sheet is slightly different.

Pair of Dragons Facing Characters of Value — A1

Plate I Plate II

48 mon:
Plate I- Solid dots in inner border.
Plate II- Tiny circles replace dots.

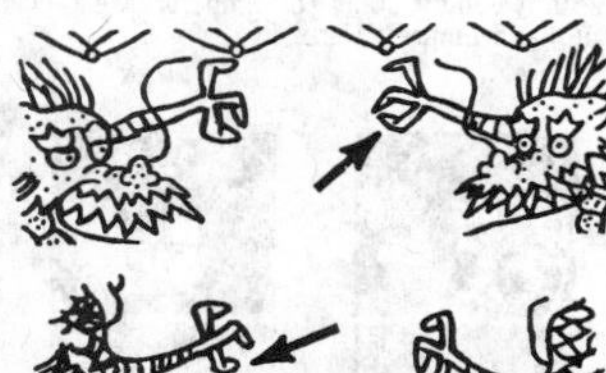
Plate I

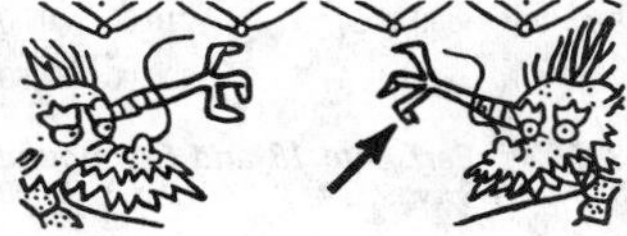
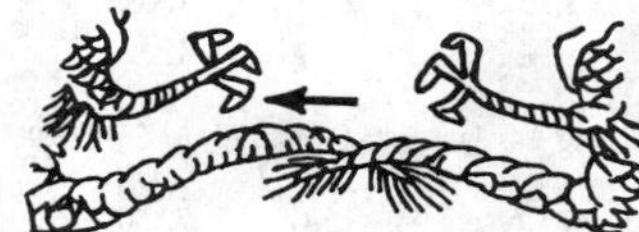
Plate II

100 mon:
Plate I- Lowest dragon claw at upper right and at lower left point upward.
Plate II- Same two claws point downward.

Plate I

Plate II

200 mon:
Plate I- Dot in upper left corner.
Plate II- No dot. (Some Plate I copies show dot faintly; these can be mistaken for Plate II.)

Plate I

Plate II

500 mon:
Plate I- Lower right corner of Greek-type border incomplete
Plate II- Short horizontal line completes corner border pattern.

Unwmk.

1871, Apr. 20 Engr. *Imperf.*

Native Laid Paper Without Gum
Denomination in Black

1	A1	48m brn (I)	225.00	210.00
a.		48m red brown (I)	225.00	210.00
b.		Wove paper (I)	230.00	240.00
c.		48m brown (II)	250.00	260.00
d.		Wove paper (II)	260.00	260.00
2	A1	100m blue (I)	215.00	200.00
a.		Wove paper (I)	220.00	220.00
b.		Plate II	500.00	425.00
c.		Wove paper (II)	600.00	600.00
3	A1	200m ver (I)	300.00	210.00
a.		Wove paper (I)	315.00	275.00
b.		Plate II	2,000.	1,200.
c.		Wove paper (II)		3,000.
4	A1	500m bl grn (I)	375.00	350.00
a.		500m greenish blue (I)	360.00	340.00
b.		500m green (I)	800.00	800.00
c.		500m yellow green (I)	850.00	825.00
d.		Wove paper (I)	360.00	360.00
e.		500m blue green (II)	400.00	*2,100.*
f.		500m greenish blue (II)	400.00	*2,100.*
g.		Wove paper (II)	1,650.	*3,000.*
h.		Denomination inverted (I)		*95,000.*

Perforations

Values are for copies with damaged perfs. on Nos. 5-8 because of the perforating equipment used and the quality of the paper. The perfs. also touch the design.

Dragons and Denomination — A1a

½ sen:
Plate I- Same as 48m Plate II. Measures not less than 19.8x19.8mm. Some subjects on this plate measure 20.3x20.2mm.
Plate II- Same as 48m Plate II. Measures not more than 19.7x19.3mm. Some subjects measure 19.3x18.7mm.

Plates I & II

Plate III

1 sen:
Plate I- Same as 100m Plate I. Narrow space between frameline and Greek-type border.
Plate II- Same as 100m Plate II. Same narrow space between frameline and border.
Plate III- Space between frameline and border is much wider. Frameline thinner. Shading on dragon heads heavier than on Plates I and II.

Native Laid Paper
With or Without Gum

1872 *Perf. 9-12 & compound*

Denomination in Black

5	A1a	½s brown (II)	77.50	85.00
a.		½s red brown (II)	77.50	85.00
b.		½s gray brown (II)	77.50	85.00
c.		Wove paper (II)	675.00	600.00
d.		½s brown (I)	95.00	130.00
e.		½s red brown (I)	95.00	130.00
f.		½s gray brown (I)	95.00	130.00
g.		Wove paper (I)	130.00	200.00
6	A1a	1s blue (II)	195.00	195.00
a.		Wove paper (II)	380.00	400.00
b.		Plate I	850.00	*1,900.*
c.		Wove paper (I)	*3,750.*	
d.		Plate III	*6,500.*	1,300.
e.		Wove paper (III)		*3,000.*
7	A1a	2s vermilion	300.00	300.00
a.		Wove paper	315.00	315.00
8	A1a	5s bl grn	400.00	400.00
a.		5s yellow green	400.00	400.00
b.		Wove paper	775.00	775.00

In 1896 the government made imperforate imitations of Nos. 6-7 to include in a presentation book.

Perforations on Nos. 9-52 frequently are very rough and irregular. Values are for copies that have perfs. touching the design.

Imperial Crest and Branches of Kiri Tree — A2

Dragons and Chrysanthemum Crest — A3

Imperial Chrysanthemum Crest — A4

Imperial Crest and Branches of Kiri Tree — A5

1872-73 *Perf. 9 to 13 and Compound*

Native Wove or Laid Paper
of Varying Thickness

9	A2	½s brown, *wove*	18.00	18.00
a.		Upper character in left label has 2 diagonal top strokes missing	1,800.	1,400.
b.		Laid paper	60.00	
c.		As "a," laid paper	2,000.	

Nos. 9, 9a are on stiff, brittle wove paper. Nos. 9b, 9c on a soft, fibrous paper. Nos. 9b and 9c probably were never put in use.

10	A2	1s blue, *wove*	45.00	27.50
a.		Laid paper	45.00	27.50
11	A2	2s ver, *wove*	110.00	45.00
12	A2	2s dl rose, *laid*	72.50	27.50
a.		Wove paper	100.00	37.50
13	A2	2s yel, *laid* ('73)	72.50	18.00
a.		Wove paper ('73)	190.00	24.00
14	A2	4s rose, *laid* ('73)	60.00	20.00
a.		Wove paper ('73)	190.00	27.50
15	A3	10s bl grn, *wove*	225.00	150.00
16	A3	10s yel grn, *laid*	465.00	300.00
a.		Wove paper ('73)	600.00	550.00
17	A4	20s lil, *wove*	360.00	250.00
a.		20s violet, *wove*	360.00	250.00
b.		20s red violet, *laid*		
18	A5	30s gray, *wove*	500.00	400.00

See Nos. 24-25, 30-31, 37-39, 51-52.

1874

Foreign Wove Paper

24	A2	4s rose	525.00	180.00
25	A5	30s gray		*5,250.*

A6

A7

A8

Type A6 differs from A2 by the addition of a syllabic character in a box covering crossed kiri branches above SEN. Stamps of type A6 differ for each value in border and spandrel designs.

In type A7, the syllabic character appears just below the buckle. In type A8, it appears in an oval frame at bottom center below SE of SEN.

With Syllabic Characters

イ	ロ	ハ	ニ	ホ	ヘ	ト	チ
i	ro	ha	ni	ho	he	to	chi
1	2	3	4	5	6	7	8

リ	ヌ	ル	ヲ	ワ	カ	ヨ	タ
ri	nu	ru	wo	wa	ka	yo	ta
9	10	11	12	13	14	15	16

レ	ソ	ツ	子	ナ	ラ	ム
re	so	tsu	ne	na	ra	mu
17	18	19	20	21	22	23

Perf. 9½ to 12½ and Compound

1874

Native Laid or Wove Paper

28	A6 2s yellow	210.00	300.00

Unused value is for copies with syll. 16, used value for copies with syll. 1.

29	A7 6s vio brn (Syll. 1)	1,000.	340.00
	Syllabic 2	1,250.	360.00
	Syllabic 3		900.00
	Syllabic 4,5,7		465.00
	Syllabic 6		550.00
	Syllabic 8		425.00
	Syllabic 9		500.00
	Syllabic 10		3,000.
	Syllabic 11		2,750.
	Syllabic 12		1,600.
30	A4 20s red vio (Syll. 3)	*7,250.*	
	Syllabic 2	*7,500.*	
31	A5 30s gray (Syll. 1)	2,500.	3,000.
a.	Very thin laid paper	2,500.	3,000.

No. 30, syll. 1, comes only with specimen dot. Value $22,500.

Perf. 11 to 12½ and Compound

1874

Foreign Wove Paper

32	A6 ½s brn (Syll. 1)	19.00	16.00
	Syllabic 2	35.00	35.00
33	A6 1s bl (Syll. 4,6,9)	125.00	27.50
	Syllabic 1,2,3	140.00	27.50
	Syllabic 5	450.00	105.00
	Syllabic 7	200.00	27.50
	Syllabic 8	125.00	27.50
	Syllabic 10	150.00	40.00
	Syllabic 11	150.00	40.00
	Syllabic 12	165.00	40.00
34	A6 2s yel (Syll. 2-4, 9, 15, 17, 20)	125.00	25.00
	Syllabic 1	250.00	25.00
	Syllabic 5	305.00	25.00
	Syllabic 6	1,800.	35.00
	Syllabic 7	1,750.	20.00
	Syllabic 8	125.00	27.50
	Syllabic 10	*2,500.*	37.50
	Syllabic 11	125.00	20.00
	Syllabic 12,22	*2,500.*	20.00
	Syllabic 13	*2,000.*	20.00
	Syllabic 14	*2,500.*	27.50
	Syllabic 16	*2,100.*	20.00
	Syllabic 18,19	125.00	20.00
	Syllabic 21	200.00	20.00
	Syllabic 23	210.00	20.00
35	A6 4s rose (Syll. 1)	2,000.	315.00
36	A7 6s vio brn (Syll. 16)	125.00	42.50
	Syllabic 10	475.00	500.00
	Syllabic 11	425.00	
	Syllabic 13		*4,750.*
	Syllabic 14	250.00	200.00
	Syllabic 15		*2,500.*
	Syllabic 17	150.00	65.00
	Syllabic 18	225.00	87.50
37	A3 10s yel grn (Syll. 2)	75.00	45.00
	Syllabic 1	250.00	80.00
	Syllabic 3	550.00	315.00
38	A4 20s vio (Syll. 5)	210.00	60.00
	Syllabic 4	210.00	60.00
39	A5 30s gray (Syll. 1)	200.00	57.50

1875 *Perf. 9 to 13 and Compound*

40	A6 ½s gray (Syll. 2, 3)	16.00	14.00
	Syllabic 4	24.00	
41	A6 1s brn (Syll. 15-17)	30.00	16.00
	Syllabic 5	315.00	40.00
	Syllabic 7,8		225.00
	Syllabic 12	525.00	150.00
	Syllabic 13	37.50	16.00
	Syllabic 14	40.00	16.00
42	A6 4s grn (Syll. 1)	87.50	18.00
	Syllabic 2	135.00	18.00
	Syllabic 3	110.00	18.00
43	A7 6s org (Syll. 16,17)	72.50	16.00
	Syllabic 10	150.00	40.00
	Syllabic 11	130.00	30.00
	Syllabic 13	135.00	27.50
	Syllabic 14	175.00	30.00
	Syllabic 15		
44	A8 6s org (Syll. 20)	72.50	16.00
	Syllabic 19	80.00	14.00
	Syllabic 21	100.00	18.00
	Syllabic 22	3,750.	1,500.

Dragons — A9

Wild Goose — A10

Wagtail — A11

Imperial Crest — A11a

Kiri Branches — A11b

Goshawk — A12

45	A9 10s ultra (Syll. 4)	105.00	16.00
	Syllabic 5	*3,350.*	300.00
46	A10 12s rose (Syll. 1)	230.00	105.00
	Syllabic 2	235.00	130.00
	Syllabic 3	*3,250.*	425.00
47	A11 15s lil (Syll. 1)	210.00	140.00
	Syllabic 2	220.00	125.00
	Syllabic 3	250.00	140.00
48	A11a 20s rose (Syll. 8)	57.50	14.00
49	A11b 30s vio (Syll. 2-4)	110.00	45.00
50	A12 45s lake (Syll. 1)	250.00	130.00
	Syllabic 2	1,350.	425.00
	Syllabic 3	1,250.	380.00

Issue dates: No. 46, syll. 2, 1882. No. 46, syll. 3, 1883. Others, 1875.

The 1s brown on laid paper, type A6, formerly listed as No. 50A, is one of several stamps of the preceding issue which exist on a laid type paper. They are difficult to identify and mainly of interest to specialists.

Without Syllabic Characters

1875

51	A2 1s brown	*5,750.*	600.00
52	A2 4s green	235.00	60.00

Branches of Kiri Tree Tied with Ribbon — A13

Imperial Crest and Kiri Branches — A14

1875-76

53	A13 1s brown	47.50	13.00
54	A13 2s yellow	77.50	13.00
54A	A14 5s green ('76)	190.00	95.00

A15

A16

Imperial Crest, Star and Kiri Branches — A17

Sun, Kikumon and Kiri Branches — A18

Imperial Crest and Kiri Branches — A19

Kikumon — A20

Perf. 8 to 14 and Compound

1876-77 **Typo.**

55	A15 5r slate	15.00	12.00
56	A16 1s black	32.50	4.50
a.	Horiz. pair, imperf. btwn.		
57	A16 2s brn ol	47.50	3.00
58	A16 4s bl grn	40.00	4.00
a.	4s green	40.00	4.00
59	A17 5s brown	60.00	24.00
60	A17 6s org ('77)	150.00	55.00
61	A17 8s vio brn ('77)	60.00	6.00
62	A17 10s blue ('77)	47.50	2.50
63	A17 12s rose ('77)	210.00	150.00
64	A18 15s yel grn ('77)	130.00	3.00
65	A18 20s dk bl ('77)	155.00	12.50
66	A18 30s vio ('77)	200.00	100.00
a.	30s red violet	195.00	90.00
67	A18 45s car ('77)	550.00	525.00

1879

68	A16 1s maroon	12.00	1.10
69	A16 2s dk vio	27.50	1.40
70	A16 3s orange	47.50	22.50
71	A18 50s carmine	175.00	13.00

1883

72	A16 1s green	8.75	50
73	A16 2s car rose	11.00	20
74	A17 5s ultra	18.00	50

1888-92

75	A15 5r gray blk ('89)	4.75	42
76	A16 3s lil rose ('92)	14.00	42
77	A16 4s ol bis	12.00	42
78	A17 8s bl lil	18.00	1.65
79	A17 10s brn org	16.00	42
80	A18 15s purple	50.00	45
81	A18 20s orange	70.00	1.65
a.	20s yellow	70.00	1.65
82	A19 25s bl grn	125.00	1.75
83	A18 50s brown	100.00	3.50
84	A20 1y carmine	150.00	4.50

Stamps of types A16-A18 differ for each value, in backgrounds and ornaments.

Nos. 58, 61-62, 65, 71-84 are found with telegraph or telephone office cancellations. These sell at considerably lower prices than postally used copies.

Cranes and Imperial Crest — A21

Perf. 11½ to 13 and Compound

1894, Mar. 9

85	A21 2s carmine	22.50	2.75
86	A21 5s ultra	37.50	12.50

25th wedding anniv. of Emperor Meiji (Mutsuhito) and Empress Haru.

Gen. Yoshihisa Kitashirakawa

A22 A23

Field Marshal Akihito Arisugawa
A24 A25

1896, Aug. 1 **Engr.**

87	A22 2s rose		24.00	2.50
88	A23 5s deep ultra		55.00	2.25
89	A24 2s rose		24.00	2.50
90	A25 5s deep ultra		55.00	2.25

Victory in Chinese-Japanese War (1894-95).

A26

A27

A28

A29

Perf. 11½ to 14 and Compound

1899-1907 **Typo.**

91	A26	5r gray	5.00	60
92	A26	½s gray ('01)	2.75	15
93	A26	1s lt red brn	3.50	15
94	A26	1½s ultra ('00)	12.50	90
95	A26	1½s vio ('06)	8.75	20
96	A26	2s lt grn	8.75	16
97	A26	3s vio brn	8.75	20
a.		Double impression		
98	A26	3s rose ('06)	5.00	20
99	A26	4s rose	5.50	95
a.		4s pink ('06)	5.50	1.00
100	A26	5s org yel	18.00	20
101	A27	6s mar ('07)	27.50	3.50
102	A27	8s olive grn	30.00	3.75
103	A27	10s dp bl	10.50	15
104	A27	15s purple	42.50	1.40
105	A27	20s red org	22.50	15
106	A28	25s blue grn	60.00	90
107	A28	50s red brn	60.00	1.10
108	A29	1y carmine	70.00	1.25
		Nos. 91-108 (18)	401.50	15.91

For overprints see Nos. M1, Offices in China, 1-18, Offices in Korea, 1-14.

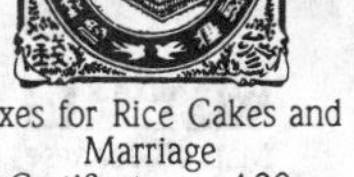

Boxes for Rice Cakes and Marriage Certificates — A30

Symbols of Korea and Japan — A31

Perf. 11½ to 12½ and Compound

1900, May 10

109	A30 3s carmine	19.00	75

Wedding of the Crown Prince Yoshihito and Princess Sadako.

For overprints see Offices in China No. 19, Offices in Korea, 15.

1905, July 1

110	A31 3s rose red	90.00	20.00

Issued to commemorate the amalgamation of the postal services of Japan and Korea. Korean stamps were withdrawn from sale June 30, 1905, but remained valid until Aug. 31. No. 110 was used in the Korea and China Offices of Japan, as well as in Japan proper.

Field-piece and Japanese Flag — A32

Empress Jingo — A33

1906, Apr. 29

111	A32 1½s blue	30.00	3.75
112	A32 3s car rose	62.50	17.50

Triumphal military review following the Russo-Japanese War.

1908 **Engr.**

113	A33 5y green	600.00	3.50
114	A33 10y dk vio	825.00	5.75

The frame of No. 114 differs slightly from the illustration.

For overprints see Offices in China Nos. 20-21, 48-49.

A34

A35

A36

Perf. 12, 12x13, 13x13½

1913 **Typo.** **Unwmk.**

115	A34	½s brown	6.00	75
116	A34	1s orange	7.25	75
117	A34	1½s lt bl	7.25	1.10
a.		Bklt. pane of 6	210.00	
118	A34	2s green	9.00	75
119	A34	3s rose	10.50	38
a.		Bklt. pane of 6	210.00	
120	A35	4s red	18.00	9.00
121	A35	5s violet	22.50	1.10
122	A35	10s dp bl	60.00	75
123	A35	20s claret	97.50	1.25
124	A35	25s olive grn	100.00	2.25
125	A36	1y yel grn & mar	575.00	20.00
		Nos. 115-125 (11)	913.00	38.08

1914-25 **Wmk. 141** **Granite Paper**
Size: 19x22½mm ("Old Die")

127	A34	½s brown	1.90	15
128	A34	1s orange	2.00	15
129	A34	1½s blue	2.00	15
a.		Bklt. pane of 6	85.00	
d.		As "a," imperf.		
130	A34	2s green	3.25	15
a.		Bklt. pane of 6	85.00	
131	A34	3s rose	1.50	15
a.		Bklt. pane of 6	72.50	
132	A35	4s red	10.50	1.25
a.		Bklt. pane of 6	85.00	
133	A35	5s violet	10.00	52
134	A35	6s brn ('19)	14.00	2.75
136	A35	8s gray ('19)	13.00	10.50
137	A35	10s dp bl	7.00	15
a.		Bklt. pane of 6	85.00	
138	A35	13s ol brn ('25)	25.00	2.25
139	A35	20s claret	35.00	70
140	A35	25s ol grn	11.00	1.00
141	A36	30s org brn ('19)	12.50	60
143	A36	50s dk brn ('19)	19.00	1.00
145	A36	1y yel grn & mar	77.50	1.00
b.		Imperf., pair		
146	A33	5y green	350.00	2.75
147	A33	10y violet	500.00	5.25
		Nos. 127-147 (18)	1,095.	30.47

1924-33
"New Die" Size: 18½x22mm (Flat Plate)
or 18½x22½mm (Rotary)

127a	A34	½s brown	2.00	1.00
128a	A34	1s orange	2.00	1.00
129b	A34	1½s blue	3.25	28
c.		Bklt. pane of 6 ('30)	21.00	
131b	A34	3s rose	1.40	15
c.		Bklt. pane of 6 ('28)	50.00	
133a	A35	5s violet	17.50	15
135	A35	7s red org ('30)	8.75	15
138a	A35	13s bis brn ('25)	7.00	15
140a	A35	25s olive green	50.00	16
142	A36	30s org & grn ('29)	19.00	28
144	A36	50s yel brn & dk bl ('29)	13.00	55
145a	A36	1y yel grn & mar	80.00	60
		Nos. 127a-145a (11)	203.90	4.47

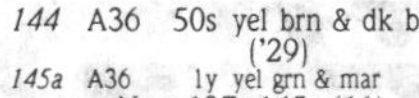

See Nos. 212-213, 239-241, 243, 245, 249-252, 255. For overprints see Nos. C1-C2, M2-M5, Offices in China, 22-47.

Ceremonial Cap — A37

Imperial Throne — A38

Enthronement Hall, Kyoto — A39

Perf. 12½

1915, Nov. 10 **Typo.** **Unwmk.**

148	A37 1½s red & blk	1.90	50
149	A38 3s org & vio	2.00	60

Engr.

Perf. 12x12½

150	A39 4s car rose	11.00	9.25
151	A39 10s ultra	22.50	17.00

Enthronement of Emperor Yoshihito.

Mandarin Duck — A40

Ceremonial Cap — A41

1916, Nov. 3 **Typo.** ***Perf. 12½***

152	A40 1½s grn, red & yel	1.65	80
153	A40 3s red & yel	3.00	1.00
154	A41 10s ultra & dk bl	525.00	240.00

Nomination of the Prince Heir Apparent, later Emperor Hirohito.

Dove and Olive Branch
A42 A43

Perf. 12, 12½, 13½x13

1919, July 1 **Engr.**

155	A42 1½s dk brn	1.90	65
156	A43 3s gray grn	2.25	95
157	A42 4s rose	5.25	3.00
158	A43 10s dk bl	21.00	11.00

Restoration of peace after World War I.

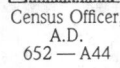

Census Officer, A.D. 652 — A44

Meiji Shrine, Tokyo — A45

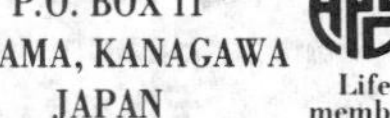

Perf. 12½

1920, Sept. 25 Typo. Unwmk.

159 A44	1½s red vio	7.00	3.00
160 A44	3s vermilion	7.75	3.00

Taking of the 1st modern census in Japan. Not available for foreign postage except to China.

1920, Nov. 1 Engr.

161 A45	1½s dull violet	2.50	1.25
162 A45	3s rose	2.50	1.25

Dedication of the Meiji Shrine. Not available for foreign postage except to China.

National and Postal Flags — A46

Ministry of Communications Building, Tokyo — A47

Typographed (A46), Engraved (A47)

1921, Apr. 20 *Perf. 12½, 13x13½*

163 A46	1½s gray grn & red	1.50	90
164 A47	3s vio brn	2.00	1.10
165 A46	4s rose & red	32.50	15.00
166 A47	10s dk bl	175.00	125.00

50th anniv. of the establishment of postal service and Japanese postage stamps.

Battleships "Katori" and "Kashima" — A48

1921, Sept. 3 Litho. *Perf. 12½*

167 A48	1½s violet	2.00	90
168 A48	3s ol grn	2.75	90
169 A48	4s rose red	37.50	18.00
170 A48	10s dp bl	42.50	21.00

Return of Crown Prince Hirohito from his European visit.

Mount Fuji — A49

Mt. Niitaka, Taiwan — A50

Perf. 13x13½

1930-37 Typo. Wmk. 141

Granite Paper

Size: 18½x22mm ("New Die")

171 A49	4s grn ('37)	2.75	32
172 A49	4s orange	6.50	25
174 A49	8s ol grn	10.00	15
175a A49	20s blue ('37)	20.00	25.00
176 A49	20s brn vio	30.00	20
	Nos. 171-176 (5)	69.25	25.92

1922-29

Size: 19x22½mm ("Old Die")

171a A49	4s green	9.00	3.00
172a A49	4s orange ('29)	90.00	9.00
173 A49	8s rose	18.00	6.00
174a A49	8s olive green ('29)	250.00	80.00
175 A49	20s deep blue	20.00	60
176a A49	20s brn vio ('29)	90.00	1.50
	Nos. 171a-176a (6)	477.00	100.10

See Nos. 242, 246, 248.

Perf. 12½

1923, Apr. 16 Unwmk. Engr.

177 A50	1½s orange	10.00	8.00
178 A50	3s dk vio	15.00	7.00

1st visit of Crown Prince Hirohito to Taiwan. The stamps were sold only in Taiwan, but were valid throughout the empire.

Cherry Blossoms A51

Sun and Dragonflies A52

Empress Jingo — A53

1923 Wmk. 142 Litho. *Imperf.*

Without Gum; Granite Paper

179 A51	½s gray	2.25	2.00
180 A51	1½s lt bl	3.00	1.00
181 A51	2s red brn	2.75	1.00
182 A51	3s brt rose	1.90	70
183 A51	4s gray grn	19.00	14.00
184 A51	5s dl vio	9.00	1.00
185 A51	8s red org	32.50	25.00
186 A52	10s dp brn	19.00	1.00
187 A52	20s dp bl	22.50	1.40
	Nos. 179-187 (9)	111.90	47.10

#179-187 exist rouletted and with various perforations. These were made privately.

Perf. 12, 13x13½

1924 Engr. Wmk. 141

Granite Paper

188 A53	5y gray grn	165.00	2.00
189 A53	10y dl vio	275.00	1.50

See Nos. 253-254.

Cranes — A54

Phoenix — A55

Perf. 10½ to 13½ and Compound

1925, May 10 Litho. Unwmk.

190 A54	1½s gray vio	1.50	75
191 A55	3s sil & brn org	2.50	1.50
a.	Vert. pair, imperf. btwn.	500.00	
192 A54	8s lt red	20.00	9.75
193 A55	20s sil & gray grn	50.00	24.00

25th wedding anniv. of the Emperor Yoshihito (Taisho) and Empress Sadako.

Mt. Fuji — A56

Yomei Gate, Nikko — A57

Nagoya Castle — A58

Perf. 13½x13

1926-37 Typo. Wmk. 141

Granite Paper

194 A56	2s green	1.90	15
195 A57	6s carmine	6.75	15
196 A58	10s dk bl	8.25	15
197 A58	10s car ('37)	8.00	6.00

See Nos. 244, 247. For surcharges see People's Republic of China No. 2L5-2L6.

Baron Hisoka Maejima — A59

Map of World on Mollweide's Projection — A60

Perf. 12½, 13x13½

1927, June 20 Unwmk.

198 A59	1½s lilac	2.25	90
199 A59	3s olive grn	2.25	90
200 A60	6s car rose	65.00	40.00
201 A60	10s blue	80.00	40.00

50th anniv. of Japan's joining the UPU. Baron Maejima (1835-1919) organized Japan's modern postal system and was postmaster general.

Phoenix — A61

Enthronement Hall, Kyoto — A62

1928, Nov. 10 Engr. *Perf. 12½*

Yellow Paper

202 A61	1½s dp grn	90	50
203 A62	3s red vio	90	50
204 A61	6s car rose	2.75	2.00
205 A62	10s dp bl	3.50	2.50

Enthronement of Emperor Hirohito.

Great Shrines of Ise — A63

Map of Japanese Empire — A64

1929, Oct. 2 *Perf. 12½*

206 A63	1½s gray vio	1.25	1.00
207 A63	3s carmine	1.75	1.25

58th rebuilding of the Ise Shrines.

1930, Sept. 25 Unwmk.

208 A64	1½s dp vio	2.50	1.25
209 A64	3s dp red	2.75	1.65

2nd census in the Japanese Empire.

Meiji Shrine — A65

1930, Nov. 1 — **Litho.**

No.	Type	Value	Color	Unused	Used
210	A65	1½s	green	1.75	1.00
211	A65	3s	brn org	2.25	1.25

10th anniv. of dedication of Meiji Shrine.

Coil Stamps

Wmk. Zigzag Lines (141)

1933 — **Typo.** — ***Perf. 13 Horiz.***

No.	Type	Value	Color	Unused	Used
212	A34	1½s	light blue	13.00	18.00
213	A34	3s	rose	15.00	22.00

Japanese Red Cross Badge — A66

Red Cross Building, Tokyo — A67

Perf. 12½

1934, Oct. 1 — **Engr.** — **Unwmk.**

No.	Type	Value	Color	Unused	Used
214	A66	1½s	grn & red	1.65	1.10
215	A67	3s	dl vio & red	1.90	1.25
216	A66	6s	dk car & red	9.00	5.50
217	A67	10s	bl & red	12.00	8.50

15th International Red Cross Congress. Sheets of 20 with commemorative marginal inscription. One side of sheet is perf. 13.

White Tower of Liaoyang and Warship "Hiei" — A68

Akasaka Detached Palace, Tokyo — A69

1935, Apr. 2

No.	Type	Value	Color	Unused	Used
218	A68	1½s	olive green	1.10	75
219	A69	3s	red brown	1.65	1.00
220	A68	6s	carmine	7.25	3.75
221	A69	10s	blue	10.00	6.00

Visit of Emperor Kang Teh of Manchukuo (Henry Pu-yi) to Tokyo, April 6, 1935. Sheets of 20 with commemorative marginal inscription. One side of sheet is perf. 13.

Mt. Fuji — A70

Perf. 13x13½

1935 — **Typo.** — **Granite Paper**

No.	Type	Value	Color	Unused	Used
222	A70	1½s	rose car	10.00	25
a.			Miniature sheet of 20	475.00	450.00

Issued to pay postage on New Year's cards from Dec. 1-31, 1935. After Jan. 1, 1936, used for ordinary letter postage. No. 222 was issued in sheets of 100.

Mt. Fuji — A71

Fuji from Lake Ashi A72

Fuji from Lake Kawaguchi A73

Fuji from Mishima A74

1936, July 10 — **Photo.** — **Wmk. 141**

Granite Paper

No.	Type	Value	Color	Unused	Used
223	A71	1½s	red brn	2.75	2.25
224	A72	3s	dk grn	5.00	3.75
225	A73	6s	car rose	11.00	9.00
226	A74	10s	dk bl	13.00	11.00

Fuji-Hakone National Park.

Dove, Map of Manchuria and Kwantung — A75

Shinto Shrine, Port Arthur — A76

Headquarters of Kwantung Government — A77

1936, Sept. 1 — **Litho.** — ***Perf. 12½***

Granite Paper

No.	Type	Value	Color	Unused	Used
227	A75	1½s	gray vio	17.00	12.00
228	A76	3s	red brn	12.50	12.50
229	A77	10s	dull grn	165.00	165.00

30th anniv. of Japanese administration of Kwantung Leased Territory and the South Manchuria Railway Zone. Sold only in Kwantung Territory and South Manchuria Railway Zone, but valid throughout Japan.

Imperial Diet Building A78

Grand Staircase A79

1936, Nov. 7 — **Engr.** — ***Perf. 13***

No.	Type	Value	Color	Unused	Used
230	A78	1½s	green	1.50	1.00
231	A79	3s	brn vio	1.75	1.25
232	A79	6s	car	4.75	4.00
233	A78	10s	blue	7.25	5.25

Opening of the new Diet Building, Tokyo.

"Wedded Rocks," Futamigaura — A80

1936, Dec. 10 — **Photo.**

No.	Type	Value	Color	Unused	Used
234	A80	1½s	rose car	4.25	20

Issued to pay postage on New Year's greeting cards.

Types of 1913-26

Perf. 13½x13, 13x13½

1937 — **Typo.** — **Wmk. 257**

No.	Type	Value	Color	Unused	Used
239	A34	½s	brown	1.65	1.10
240	A34	1s	org yel	2.50	1.50
241	A34	3s	rose	95	15
242	A49	4s	green	3.50	22
243	A35	5s	violet	4.50	15
244	A57	6s	crimson	6.75	1.10
245	A35	7s	red org	6.75	15
246	A49	8s	olive bister	7.50	55
247	A58	10s	carmine	6.00	15
248	A49	20s	blue	11.00	30
249	A35	25s	olive grn	30.00	1.25
250	A36	30s	org & grn	18.00	25
251	A36	50s	brn org & dk bl	95.00	1.10
252	A36	1y	yel grn & mar	52.50	45
			Nos. 239-252 (14)	246.60	8.42

Engr.

No.	Type	Value	Color	Unused	Used
253	A53	5y	gray grn	300.00	4.00
254	A53	10y	dl vio	350.00	3.50

For overprint see People's Republic of China No. 2L6.

Coil Stamp

1938 — **Typo.** — ***Perf. 13 Horiz.***

No.	Type	Value	Color	Unused	Used
255	A34	3s	rose	3.75	3.75

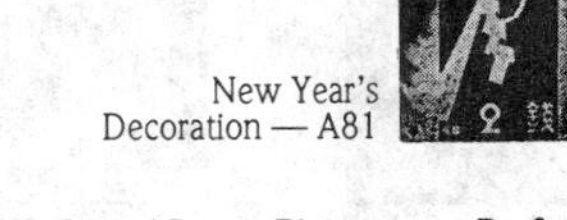

New Year's Decoration — A81

1937, Dec. 15 — **Photo.** — ***Perf. 13***

No.	Type	Value	Color	Unused	Used
256	A81	2s	scarlet	8.00	20

Issued to pay postage on New Year's cards, later for ordinary use.

Trading Ship — A82

Rice Harvest — A83

Gen. Maresuke Nogi — A84

Power Plant — A85

Admiral Heihachiro Togo — A86

Mount Hodaka — A87

Garambi Lighthouse, Taiwan — A88

Diamond Mountains, Korea — A89

Meiji Shrine, Tokyo — A90

Yomei Gate, Nikko — A91

Plane and Map of Japan — A92

Kasuga Shrine, Nara — A93

Mount Fuji and Cherry Blossoms — A94

Horyu Temple, Nara — A95

Miyajima Torii, Itsukushima Shrine — A96

Golden Pavilion, Kyoto — A97

Great Buddha, Kamakura — A98

Kamatari Fujiwara — A99

Plum Blossoms — A100

Typographed or Engraved

1937-45 — **Wmk. 257** — ***Perf. 13***

No.	Type	Value	Color	Unused	Used
257	A82	½s	purple	60	28
258	A83	1s	fawn	1.75	24
259	A84	2s	crimson	42	15
a.			Bklt. pane of 20	50.00	
b.			2s pink, perf. 12 ('45)	1.50	1.00
c.			2s ver ('44)	2.50	2.00
260	A85	3s	grn ('39)	42	15
261	A86	4s	dk grn	90	15
a.			Bklt. pane of 20	15.00	
262	A87	5s	dk ultra ('39)	90	15
263	A88	6s	org ('39)	1.75	70
264	A89	7s	dp grn ('39)	52	15
265	A90	8s	dk pur & pale vio ('39)	50	20
266	A91	10s	lake ('38)	2.75	15
267	A92	12s	ind ('39)	52	35
268	A93	14s	rose lake & pale rose ('38)	52	24
269	A94	20s	ultra ('40)	55	15
270	A95	25s	dk brn & pale brn ('38)	52	15
271	A96	30s	pck bl ('39)	1.40	15
a.			Imperf., pair	375.00	
272	A97	50s	ol & pale ol ('39)	70	15
a.			Pale olive (forest) omitted		
273	A98	1y	brn & pale brn ('39)	2.75	35
274	A99	5y	dp gray grn ('39)	20.00	1.40
275	A100	10y	dk brn vio ('39)	13.00	1.00
			Nos. 257-275 (19)	50.47	6.26

Nos. 257 to 261, 265, 268, 270, 272 and 273 are typographed; the others are engraved.

Coil Stamps

1938-39 — **Typo.** — ***Perf. 13 Horiz.***

No.	Type	Value	Color	Unused	Used
276	A82	½s	pur ('39)	3.00	3.75
277	A84	2s	crimson	3.25	4.00
278	A86	4s	dk grn	3.25	4.00
279	A93	14s	rose lake & pale rose	85.00	60.00

See Nos. 329, 331, 333, 341, 351, 360 and 351. For surcharges see Nos. B4-B5, Burma 2N4-2N27, China-Taiwan, 8-9, People's Republic of China 2L3, 2L7, 2L9-2L10, 2L39, Korea 55-56. For overprints see Ryukyu Islands (US Specialized) Nos. 2X1-2X2, 2X4-2X7, 2X10, 2X13-2X14, 2X17, 2X20, 2X23, 2X27, 2X29, 2X33-2X34, 3X2-3X7, 3X10-3X11, 3X14, 3X17, 3X19, 3X21, 3X23, 3X26-3X30, 5X1-5X3, 5X5-5X8, 5X10.

Footnotes often refer to other stamps of the same design.

Mount Nantai — A101

Kegon Falls — A102

Sacred Bridge, Nikko A103

Mount Hiuchi A104

Unwmk.

1938, Dec. 25 **Photo.** ***Perf. 13***

280	A101	2s brn org	70	60
281	A102	4s ol grn	70	60
282	A103	10s dp rose	5.50	4.50
283	A104	20s dk bl	5.50	4.50
a.		Souvenir sheet of 4, #280-283	40.00	45.00

Nikko National Park.
No. 283a sold for 50s.

Mount Daisen A106

Yashima Plateau, Inland Sea A107

Abuto Kwannon Temple A108

Tomo Bay, Inland Sea — A109

1939, Apr. 20

285	A106	2s lt brn	65	60
286	A107	4s yel grn	1.25	1.25
287	A108	10s dl rose	5.75	4.75
288	A109	20s blue	5.75	4.75
a.		Souvenir sheet of 4, #285-288	20.00	22.50

Daisen and Inland Sea National Parks.
No. 288a sold for 50s.

View from Kuju Village, Kyushu A111

Mount Naka A112

Crater of Mount Naka A113

Volcanic Cones of Mt. Aso A114

1939, Aug. 15

290	A111	2s ol brn	85	50
291	A112	4s yel grn	2.75	1.90
292	A113	10s carmine	17.50	10.00
293	A114	20s sapphire	25.00	11.00
a.		Souvenir sheet of 4, #290-293	75.00	70.00

Aso National Park.
No. 293a sold for 50s.

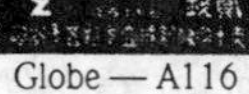
Globe — A116

Tsunetami Sano — A117

1939, Nov. 15 ***Perf. 12½***

Cross in Carmine

295	A116	2s brown	1.25	90
296	A117	4s yel grn	1.40	1.00
297	A116	10s crimson	8.50	7.75
298	A117	20s sapphire	8.50	7.75

75th anniv. of the founding of the Intl. Red Cross Society.

Sacred Golden Kite — A118

Mount Takachiho — A119

Five Ayu Fish and Sake Jar — A120

Kashiwara Shrine — A121

1940 **Engr.** ***Perf. 12***

299	A118	2s brn org	80	80
300	A119	4s dk grn	60	48
301	A120	10s dk car	3.75	3.50
302	A121	20s dk ultra	80	80

2,600th anniv. of the legendary date of the founding of Japan.

Mt. Hokuchin, Hokkaido A122

Mt. Asahi, Hokkaido A123

Sounkyo Gorge — A124

Tokachi Mountain Range A125

1940, Apr. 20 **Photo.** ***Perf. 13***

303	A122	2s brown	75	75
304	A123	4s yel grn	2.75	2.00
305	A124	10s carmine	7.50	6.00
306	A125	20s sapphire	7.50	6.50
a.		Souvenir sheet of 4, #303-306	200.00	200.00

Daisetsuzan National Park.
No. 306a sold for 50s.

Mt. Karakuni, Kyushu A127

Mt. Takachiho A128

Torii of Kirishima Shrine A129

Lake of the Six Kwannon A130

1940, Aug. 21

308	A127	2s brown	80	55
309	A128	4s green	1.75	1.40
310	A129	10s carmine	6.00	4.50
311	A130	20s dp ultra	7.25	5.50
a.		Souvenir sheet of 4, #308-311	185.00	185.00

Kirishima National Park.
No. 311a sold for 50s.

Education Minister with Rescript on Education A132

Characters Signifying Loyalty and Filial Piety A133

1940, Oct. 25 **Engr.** ***Perf. 12½***

313	A132	2s purple	75	75
314	A133	4s green	90	90

50th anniv. of the imperial rescript on education, given by Emperor Meiji to clarify Japan's educational policy.

Mt. Daiton, Taiwan A134

Central Peak of Mt. Niitaka A135

Buddhist Temple on Mt. Kwannon A136

View from Mt. Niitaka A137

1941, Mar. 10 **Photo.** ***Perf. 13***

315	A134	2s brown	60	52
316	A135	4s brt grn	1.00	85
317	A136	10s rose red	3.50	2.00
318	A137	20s bril ultra	4.50	2.00
a.		Souv. sheet of 4, #315-318	30.00	32.50

Daiton and Niitaka-Arisan National Parks.
#318a sold with #323a in same folder for 90s.

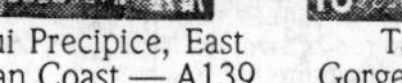
Seisui Precipice, East Taiwan Coast — A139

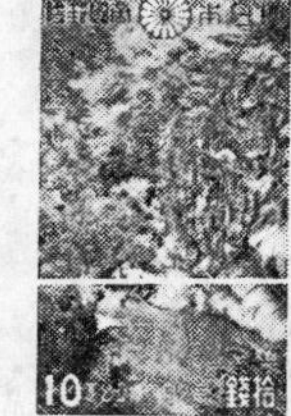
Taroko Gorge — A141

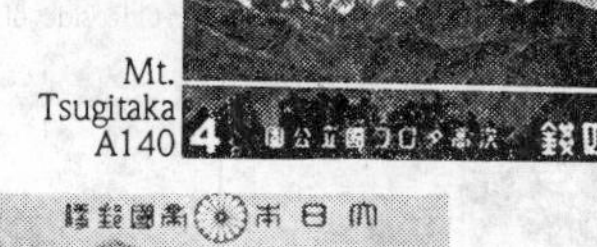
Mt. Tsugitaka A140

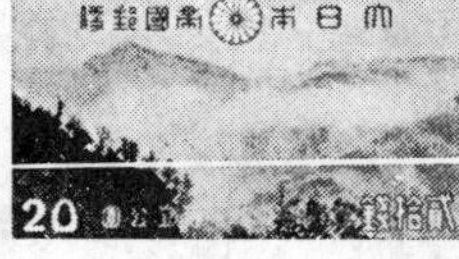
Upper River Takkiri District A142

1941, Mar. 10

320	A139	2s brown	70	52
321	A140	4s brt grn	1.00	90
322	A141	10s rose red	3.25	1.50
323	A142	20s bril ultra	4.50	2.25
a.		Souv. sheet of 4, #320-323	55.00	25.00

Tsugitaka-Taroko National Park.
See note after No. 318.

War Factory Girl — A144

Building of Wooden Ship — A145

Hyuga Monument and Mt. Fuji — A146

War Worker and Planes — A147

Palms and Map of "Greater East Asia" — A148

"Enemy Country Surrender" — A149

Aviator Saluting and Japanese Flag — A150

Torii of Yasukuni Shrine — A151

Mt. Fuji and Cherry Blossoms — A152

Torii of Miyajima — A153

Garambi Lighthouse, Taiwan — A154

Typographed; Engraved

1942-45 Wmk. 257 *Perf. 13*

No.	Type	Description	Unused	Used
325	A144	1s org brn ('43)	15	15
328	A145	2s green	28	25
329	A84	3s brown ('44)	45	20
330	A146	4s emerald	15	15
331	A86	5s brn lake	16	15
332	A147	6s lt ultra ('44)	28	24
a.		Imperf., pair		
333	A86	7s org ver ('44)	16	15
334	A148	10s crim & dl rose	35	15
a.		Dull rose (map) omitted	350.00	350.00
335	A149	10s lt gray ('45)	2.00	2.00
336	A150	15s dl bl	1.40	85
337	A151	17s gray vio ('43)	42	32
338	A152	20s blue ('44)	42	15
339	A151	27s rose brn ('45)	45	35
340	A153	30s bluish grn ('44)	1.40	52
341	A88	40s dl vio	35	15
342	A154	40s dk vio ('44)	1.00	85
		Nos. 325,328-342 (16)	9.42	6.63

Nos. 325-335, 337-340 and 342 are typo. Nos. 336 and 341 are engr. Nos. 329, 331, 333, 334 and 342 were issued with and without gum. No. 335 was issued only without gum.

#328, 342 exist with watermark sideways. #328 exists printed on gummed side.

Most stamps of the above series exist in numerous shades.

For overprints and surcharges see North Borneo Nos. N34, N37, N41-N42, People's Republic of China 2L4, 2L8, Korea 57-60, Ryukyu Islands (US Specialized) Nos. 2X3, 2X9, 2X12, 2X15-2X16, 2X18-2X19, 2X21-2X22, 2X24-2X26, 2X28, 3X1, 3X8-3X9, 3X12-3X13, 3X15-3X16, 3X18, 3X20, 3X25, 3X31, 4X1-4X2, 5X4.

Kenkoku Shrine, Hsinking — A155

Boys of Japan and Manchukuo A156

Orchid Crest of Manchukuo A157

1942 Unwmk. Engr. *Perf. 12*

No.	Type	Description	Unused	Used
343	A155	2s brown	90	90
344	A156	5s olive	50	35
345	A155	10s red	80	80
346	A157	20s dk bl	2.00	2.00

The 2s and 10s were issued Mar. 1 for the 10th anniv. of the creation of Manchukuo; 5s and 20s on Sept. 15 for the 10th anniv. of Japanese diplomatic recognition of Manchukuo.

C-59 Locomotive — A158

Yasukuni Shrine, Tokyo — A159

1942, Oct. 14 Photo.

No.	Type	Description	Unused	Used
347	A158	5s Prus grn	3.50	3.50

70th anniv. of Japan's 1st railway.

1944, June 29 *Perf. 13*

No.	Type	Description	Unused	Used
348	A159	7s Prus grn	60	60

75th anniversary of Yasukuni Shrine.

Kwantung Shrine and Map of Kwantung Peninsula — A160

1944, Oct. 1

No.	Type	Description	Unused	Used
349	A160	3s red brn	3.00	5.25
350	A160	7s gray vio	3.25	5.25

Dedication of Kwantung Shrine, Port Arthur.

Sun and Cherry Blossoms — A161

Sunrise at Sea and Plane — A162

Coal Miners — A163

Yasukuni Shrine — A164

Lithographed, Typographed

1945-47 Wmk. 257 *Imperf.*

Without Gum

No.	Type	Description	Unused	Used
351	A84	2s rose red	35	35
352	A161	3s rose car	20	30
353	A162	5s green	20	20
a.		5s blue	8.00	8.00
354	A149	10s lt gray	9.00	9.00
354A	A149	10s blue	22.50	
355	A152	10s red org	20	15
356	A152	20s ultra ('46)	40	15
357	A153	30s brt bl ('46)	1.50	90
358	A163	50s dk brn ('46)	30	15
a.		Souvenir sheet of 5 ('47)	11.00	13.00
359	A164	1y dp ol grn ('46)	90	90
360	A99	5y dp gray grn	5.00	80
361	A100	10y dk brn vio	35.00	90
		Nos. 351-354,355-361 (11)	53.05	13.80

Nos. 351 and 354 are typographed. The other stamps in this set are printed by offset lithography.

No. 358a was issued with marginal inscriptions to commemorate the Sapporo (Hokkaido) Philatelic Exhibition, Nov., 1947.

Nos. 351 to 361 are on grayish paper, and Nos. 355 to 361 also exist on white paper.

Most stamps of the above series exist in numerous shades and with private perforation or roulette.

See No. 404. For overprints see Ryukyu Islands (US Specialized) Nos. 2X8, 2X11, 2X30, 3X22, 4X3, 5X9.

Catalogue values for unused stamps in this section, from this point to the end of the section, are for Never Hinged items.

Baron Hisoka Maejima — A165

Horyu Temple Pagoda — A166

"Thunderstorm below Fuji," by Hokusai — A167

"First Geese," Print by Hokusai — A168

Kintai Bridge, Iwakuni — A169

Kiyomizu Temple, Kyoto — A170

Goldfish — A171

Noh Mask — A172

Plum Blossoms — A173

Characters Read Right to Left

1946-47 Wmk. 257 Litho. *Imperf.*

Without Gum

No.	Type	Description	Unused	Used
362	A165	15s dk grn	38	25
363	A166	30s dl lil	50	15
364	A167	1y dp ultra	1.90	15
a.		1y ultramarine	65	18
b.		1y light blue	75	15
365	A168	1.30y ol bis	2.25	52
366	A169	1.50y dk gray	2.25	38
367	A170	2y vermilion	2.00	15
a.		Souvenir sheet of 5 ('47)	22.50	21.00
368	A171	5y lil rose	7.25	48
		Nos. 362-368 (7)	16.53	2.08

Nos. 363, 368 exist with and without gum.

No. 367a was issued in sheets measuring 113x71mm, with marginal inscriptions and ornaments, to commemorate the "Know Your Stamps" exhibition, Kyoto, Aug. 19-24, 1947.

#362, 369 exist with watermark horizontal.

See Nos. 384-387, 512A. For overprints see Ryukyu Islands (US Specialized) Nos. 2X32, 3X24, 4X4.

Engr.

No.	Type	Description	Unused	Used
369	A172	50y bis brn	70.00	75
370	A173	100y brn car ('47)	70.00	75

Perf. 13

No.	Type	Description	Unused	Used
371	A172	50y bis brn, with gum ('47)	70.00	75
372	A173	100y brn car, with gum ('47)	70.00	38

Litho.

Perf. 13x13½, 12, 12x12½

No.	Type	Description	Unused	Used
373	A166	30s dull lilac	2.75	2.75

Rouletted in Colored Lines

Typo. Unwmk.

With Gum

No.	Type	Description	Unused	Used
374	A166	30s deep lilac	1.00	1.50

Medieval Postman's Bell A175

Baron Hisoka Maejima A176

Design of First Japanese Stamp — A177

Communication Symbols — A178

Perf. 12½, 13½x13

1946, Dec. 12 Engr. Unwmk.

With Gum

No.	Type	Description	Unused	Used
375	A175	15s orange	4.50	3.25
376	A176	30s dp grn	5.25	4.25
377	A177	50s carmine	2.25	2.25
378	A178	1y dp bl	2.25	2.25
a.		Souvenir sheet of 4, #375-378, imperf.	125.00	110.00

75th anniversary of government postal service in Japan.

No. 378a measures 183x125mm and is ungummed. There were 2 printings: I - The 4 colors were printed simultaneously. Arched top inscription in high relief (2,000 sheets). II - Stamps were printed in one step, sheet inscriptions in another. Top inscription flat, almost level with paper's surface (49,000 sheets). 1st printing value $700.

Mother and Child, Diet Building A180

Bouquet of Japanese May Flowers A181

Perf. 12½

1947, May 3 Litho. Wmk. 257

No.	Type	Description	Unused	Used
380	A180	50s rose brn	25	30
381	A181	1y brt ultra	52	42
a.		Souv. sheet of 2, #380-381, imperf.	11.00	6.00
b.		As "a," 50s omitted	1,000.	
c.		As "a," 1y omitted	1,000.	

Inauguration of the constitution of May 3, 1947.

A182

1947, Aug. 15 Photo. *Perf. 12½*

No.	Type	Description	Unused	Used
382	A182	1.20y brown	2.25	1.10
383	A182	4y brt ultra	4.50	1.50

Reopening of foreign trade on a private basis.

The ornaments on No. 383 differ from those shown in the illustration.

Types of 1946 Redrawn
Characters Read Left to Right

1947-48 Wmk. 257 Typo. *Perf. 13*

384 A166 30s dp lil 1.50 1.40
385 A166 1.20y lt ol grn 95 35
a. Souvenir sheet of 15 125.00 135.00
386 A170 2y ver ('48) 3.75 20
387 A168 4y lt ultra 2.50 28

No. 385a was issued with marginal inscriptions to commemorate the "Know Your Stamps" Exhibition, Tokyo, May, 1947.

On No. 386, the chrysanthemum crest has been eliminated and the top inscription centered.

Plum Blossoms — A183

1947 Typo. *Imperf.*

388 A183 10y dk brn vio 25.00 80

This stamp is similar to type A100 but with new inscription "Nippon Yubin" (Japan Post), reading from left to right. The characters for the denomination are likewise transposed.

A184

A185

Baron Hisoka Maejima
A186

Whaling
A187

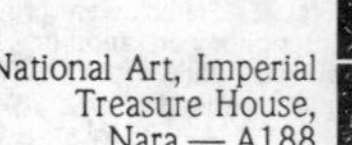

National Art, Imperial Treasure House, Nara — A188

1947 Typo. *Perf. 13x13½*

389 A184 35s green 40 30

Litho.

390 A185 45s lilac rose 55 55
a. Imperf., pair 700.00
b. Perf. 11x13½ 4.50 4.50
391 A186 1y dl brn 2.50 40

Typo.

392 A187 5y blue 6.00 15
a. Imperf., pair 600.00
b. Perf. 11x13½ 22.50 2.75

Engr.

Perf. 13½x13

393 A188 10y lilac 13.00 15
a. Imperf., pair
Nos. 389-393 (5) 22.45 1.55

No. 389 was produced on both rotary and flat press. Sheets of the rotary press printing have a border. Those of the flat press printing have none.

Lily of the Valley — A188a

1947, Sept. 13 Unwmk. *Perf. 12½*

394 A188a 2y dk Prus grn 3.25 1.40

Relief of Ex-convicts Day, Sept. 13, 1947.

Souvenir Sheet

A189

1947 Wmk. 257 Litho. *Imperf.*
Without Gum

395 A189 Sheet of 5, ultra 2.75 3.00

Stamp Hobby Week, Nov. 1-7, 1947. Sheet size: 113½x71½mm, on white or grayish paper.

"Benkei," 1880 Locomotive — A190

1947, Oct. 14 Unwmk. Engr.

396 A190 4y dp ultra 15.00 15.00

75th anniv. of railway service in Japan.

Hurdling
A191

Diving
A192

Discus Throwing
A193

Volleyball
A194

1947, Oct. 25 Photo. *Perf. 12½*
With Gum

397 A191 1.20y red violet 7.00 6.50
398 A192 1.20y red violet 7.00 6.50
399 A193 1.20y red violet 7.00 6.50
400 A194 1.20y red violet 7.00 6.50
a. Block of 4, #397-400 37.50 30.00

2nd Natl. Athletic Meet, held in Kanazawa, Oct. 30-Nov. 3.

Souvenir Sheets

A195

1948 Wmk. 257 Litho. *Imperf.*
Without Gum

401 A195 Sheet of 2, #368 12.00 14.00

Same, Inscribed with Three instead of Two Japanese Characters at Bottom Center

402 A195 Sheet of 2, #368 13.00 14.00

Philatelic exhibitions at Osaka (No. 401) and Nagoya (No. 402).

Stylized Tree — A196

National Art Treasure, Nara — A197

Perf. 12½

1948, Apr. 1 Unwmk. Photo.

403 A196 1.20y dp yel grn 80 60

Forestation movement. Sheets of 30, marginal inscription.

Coal Miners Type of 1946, and Type A197
Wmk. 257

1948 Litho. With Gum *Perf. 13*

404 A163 50s dk brn 1.00 50

Typo.

405 A197 10y rose violet 10.00 15
a. Imperf., pair

See No. 515A.

School Children — A198

Perf. 12½

1948, May 3 Unwmk. Photo.

406 A198 1.20y dk car 75 60

Reorganization of Japan's educational system. Sheets of 30, marginal inscription.

Souvenir Sheets
No. 402 Overprinted at Top, Bottom and Sides with Japanese Characters and Flowers in Green

1948, Apr. 3 Wmk. 257 *Imperf.*

407 A195 Sheet of 2 50.00 35.00
a. Overprint inverted 250.00
b. Overprint on No. 401 175.00

Mishima Philatelic Exhibition, Apr. 3-9.

No. 395 Overprinted at Top and Bottom With Japanese Characters in Plum

1948, Apr. 18

408 A189 Sheet of 5, ultra 16.00 17.50

Issued to commemorate the centenary of the death of Katsushika Hokusai, painter.

Sampans on Inland Sea, Near Suma — A199

Engr. & Litho.

1948, Apr. 22 Unwmk. *Imperf.*
Without Gum

409 A199 Sheet of 2 10.50 5.50

Communications Exhib., Tokyo, Apr. 27-May 3, 1948. Sheet contains two 2y deep carmine stamps. Sheet exists with green border omitted.

1948, May 20

410 A199 Sheet of 2, ultra border 12.00 12.00

Aomori Newspaper and Stamp Exhibition. Border design of apples and apple blossoms.

Type A199 With Altered Border and Inscriptions

1948, May 23

411 A199 Sheet of 2, blue border 12.00 12.00

Fukushima Stamp Exhibition. Border design of cherries and crossed lines.

Horse Race — A200

1948, June 6 Photo. *Perf. 12½*
With Gum

412 A200 5y brown 2.10 60

25th anniv. of the enforcement of Japan's horse racing laws. Each sheet contains 30 stamps and 2 labels, with marginal inscription.

A201

A202

Wmk. 257

1948, Sept. 10 Litho. *Perf. 13*

413 A201 1.50y blue 1.20 45
414 A202 3.80y lt brn 4.50 3.50

Souvenir Sheet
Imperf

415 Sheet of 4 22.50 22.50

Kumamoto Stamp Exhibition, Sept. 20. Souvenir sheet, issued Sept. 20, contains two each of 1.50y deep blue (A201) and 3.80y brown (A202).

Rectifying Tower — A203

Perf. 12½

1948, Sept. 14 Photo. Unwmk.

416 A203 5y dk olive bister 2.50 1.25

Government alcohol monopoly.

Swimmer — A204

Runner — A205

Designs: No. 419, High jumper. No. 420, Baseball players. No. 421, Bicycle racers.

1948

417 A204 5y blue 3.00 1.50
418 A205 5y green 7.00 3.00
419 A205 5y green 7.00 3.00
420 A205 5y green 7.00 3.00
421 A205 5y green 7.00 3.00
a. Block of 4, #418-421 35.00 15.00
Nos. 417-421 (5) 31.00 13.50

3rd Natl. Athletic Meet. Swimming matches held at Yawata, Sept. 16-19, field events, Fukuoka, Oct. 29-Nov. 3.

"Beauty Looking Back," Print by Moronobu — A206

1948, Nov. 29 *Perf. 13*

422 A206 5y brown 47.50 40.00
a. Sheet of 5 275.00 175.00

Philatelic Week, Nov. 29-Dec. 5.

Souvenir Sheet

1948, Dec. 3 *Imperf.*

Without Gum

423 A206 5y brn, sheet of 1 30.00 21.00

Kanazawa and Takaoka stamp exhibitions.

Child Playing Hane-tsuki — A207

1948, Dec. 13 **Litho.** *Perf. 13*

424 A207 2y scarlet 3.50 2.00

Issued to pay postage on New Year's cards, later for ordinary use.

Farm Woman A208

Whaling A209

Miner A210

Tea Picking A211

Girl Printer A212

Factory Girl with Cotton Bobbin A213

Mt. Hodaka A214

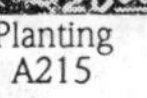

Planting A215

Postman A216

Blast Furnace A217

Locomotive Assembly A218

Typographed, Engraved

1948-49 **Wmk. 257** *Perf. 13x13½*

425 A208 2y green 1.00 15
a. Overprinted with 4 characters in frame 50 60
b. As "a," ovpt. inverted *150.00*
426 A209 3y lt grnsh bl ('49) 5.00 15
427 A210 5y ol bis 14.00 15
a. Booklet pane of 20 90.00
428 A211 5y bl grn ('49) 27.50 4.50
429 A212 6y red org ('49) 5.50 15
430 A210 8y brn org ('49) 5.50 15
a. Booklet pane of 20 *100.00*
431 A213 15y blue 2.25 15
432 A214 16y ultra ('49) 6.00 3.00
433 A215 20y dk grn ('49) 22.50 15
434 A216 30y vio bl ('49) 30.00 15
435 A217 100y car lake ('49) 250.00 80
436 A218 500y dp bl ('49) 240.00 1.40
Nos. 425-436 (12) 609.25 10.90

No. 425a has a red control overprint of four characters ("Senkyo Jimu," or "Election Business") arranged vertically in a rectangular frame. Each candidate received 1,000 copies.

Nos. 432, 435-436 are engraved.

See Nos. 511-512, 514-515, 518, 520, 521A-521B.

Souvenir Sheets

Typo. and Litho.

1948, Oct. 16 *Imperf.*

437 A213 15y bl, sheet of 1 30.00 32.50

Nagano Stamp Exhibition, Oct. 16.

1948, Nov. 2 *Imperf.*

438 A210 5y ol bis, sheet of 2 32.50 32.50

Shikoku Traveling Stamp Exhib., Nov. 1948.

Sampans on Inland Sea A219

Perf. 13x13½

1949 **Wmk. 257** **Engr.**

439 A219 10y rose lake 27.50 10.50
440 A219 10y car rose 20.00 8.50
441 A219 10y org ver 20.00 9.50
442 A214 16y brt bl 9.25 4.25

Issued in sheets of 20 stamps with marginal inscription publicizing expositions at Takamatsu (#439), Okayama (#440) and Matsuyama (#441), Nagano Peace Exposition, Apr. 1-May 31, 1949 (#442).

Ice Skater — A221

Ski Jumper — A222

1949 **Unwmk.** **Photo.** *Perf. 12*

444 A221 5y violet 1.90 1.00
445 A222 5y ultra 2.25 1.00

Issued for the winter events of the 4th National Athletic Meet - skating at Suwa Jan. 27-30 and skiing at Sapporo Mar. 3-6. Issue dates: No. 444, Jan. 27; No. 445, Mar. 3.

Steamer in Beppu Bay — A223

1949, Mar. 10 **Engr.** *Perf. 13x13½*

446 A223 2y carmine & ultra 85 60
447 A223 5y green & ultra 3.25 80

Scene at Fair — A224

Stylized Trees — A225

1949, Mar. 15 **Photo.** *Perf. 13*

448 A224 5y brt rose 2.50 1.00
a. Imperf. 1.75 90
b. Sheet of 20, imperf. 55.00 55.00

Issued to publicize the Japan Foreign Trade Fair, Yokohama, 1949.

No. 448 was printed in sheets of 50 (10x5); No. 448a in sheets of 20 (4x5) with marginal inscriptions (No. 448b).

1949, Apr. 1 **Unwmk.** *Perf. 12*

449 A225 5y brt grn 8.00 90

Issued to publicize the forestation movement.

Lion Rock A226

Daiho-zan (Mt. Ohmine) A227

Doro Gorge A228

Bridge Pier Rocks A229

1949, Apr. 10 **Photo.** *Perf. 13*

450 A226 2y brown 1.00 50
451 A227 5y yel grn 2.50 1.00
452 A228 10y scarlet 11.00 4.00
453 A229 16y blue 5.00 1.50
a. Souv. sheet of 4, #450-453, no gum 22.50 22.50
b. As "a," 10y omitted

Yoshino-Kumano National Park.

No. 453a sold for 40y.

Boy — A230

Radio Tower and Star — A231

1949, May 5 *Perf. 12*

455 A230 5y rose brn & org 4.00 1.25
a. Orange omitted 200.00

Children's Day, May 5, 1949.

Souvenir Sheets

1949, May 5 *Imperf.*

456 A230 5y rose brn & org, sheet of 10 225.00 250.00

Children's Exhib., Inuyama, Apr. 1-May 31.

1949, May 11 *Perf. 13*

457 A231 20y dp bl, sheet of one 100.00 80.00

Electrical Communication Week, May 11-18.

Symbols of Communication A232

Central Meteorological Observatory, Tokyo A233

Wmk. 257

1949, June 1 **Engr.** *Perf. 12*

458 A232 8y brt ultra 3.50 1.10

Establishment of the Post Ministry and the Ministry of Electricity and Communication.

1949, June 1 **Unwmk.** *Perf. 12½*

459 A233 8y dp grn 3.50 1.10

57th anniv. of the establishment of the Central Meteorological Observatory.

Mt. Fuji in Autumn A234

Lake Kawaguchi A235

Fiji from Mt. Shichimen A236

Shinobuno Village and Mt. Fuji A237

1949, July 15 **Photo.** *Perf. 13*

460 A234 2y yel brn 1.50 65
461 A235 8y yel grn 2.75 1.00
462 A236 14y car lake 1.50 40
463 A237 24y blue 2.25 60
a. Souvenir sheet of 4, #460-463 26.00 30.00

Fuji-Hakone National Park.

No. 463a sold for 55y.

Allegory of Peace A238

Doves over Nagasaki — A239

Perf. 13x13½, 13½x13

1949 Photo. Unwmk.

465 A238 8y yel brn	4.75	1.50
466 A239 8y green	3.50	1.25

Establishment of Hiroshima as the City of Eternal Peace and of Nagasaki as the International City of Culture. Issue dates: No. 465, Aug. 6; No. 466, Aug. 9.

Boy Scout — A240

Pen Nib of Newspaper Stereotype Matrix — A241

1949, Sept. 22 ***Perf. 13x13½***

467 A240 8y brown	5.25	2.00

Natl. Boy Scout Jamboree.

1949, Oct. 1 ***Perf. 13½x13***

468 A241 8y dp bl	3.25	1.50

Natl. Newspaper Week.

Racing Swimmer Poised for Dive — A242

Javelin Thrower — A243

1949 ***Perf. 13½***

469 A242 8y dl bl	2.50	1.10

Perf. 12

470 A243 8y shown	3.50	1.90
471 A243 8y Yacht Racing	3.50	1.90
472 A243 8y Relay Race	3.50	1.90
473 A243 8y Tennis	3.50	1.90
a. Block of 4, #470-473	19.00	9.50
Nos. 469-473 (5)	16.50	8.70

4th Natl. Athletic Meet. The swimming matches were held at Yokohama, Sept. 15-18 and the fall events at Tokyo, Oct. 30.

Issue dates: No. 469, Sept. 15; Nos. 470-473, Oct. 30.

Map and Envelopes Forming "75" — A244

Symbols of UPU — A245

1949, Oct. 10 Engr. ***Perf. 12, 13½***

474 A244 2y dl grn	1.75	48
475 A245 8y maroon	2.00	48
a. Souv. sheet of 2, #474-475, imperf.	3.25	4.00

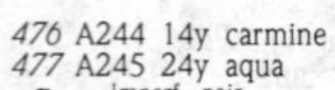

476 A244 14y carmine	6.75	2.50
477 A245 24y aqua	10.00	2.50
a. Imperf., pair		

75th anniv. of the UPU.

Floating Zenith Telescope A246

"Moon and Geese," Print by Hiroshige A247

1949, Oct. 30 Photo. ***Perf. 12***

478 A246 8y dk bl grn	2.25	1.00

50th anniv. of the Mizusawa Latitudinal Observatory.

1949, Nov. 1 ***Perf. 13x13½***

479 A247 8y purple	75.00	27.50
a. Sheet of 5	475.00	165.00

Postal Week, Nov. 1-7.

Dr. Hideyo Noguchi A248

Yukichi Fukuzawa A249

Soseki Natsume A250

Shoyo Tsubouchi A251

Danjuro Ichikawa A252

Joseph Hardy Niijima A253

Hogai Kano A254

Kanzo Uchimura A255

Ichiyo Higuchi — A256

Ogai Mori — A257

Shiki Masaoka — A258

Shunso Hishida — A259

Amane Nishi — A260

Kenjiro Ume — A261

Hisashi Kimura — A262

Inazo Nitobe — A263

Torahiko Terada — A264

Tenshin Okakura — A265

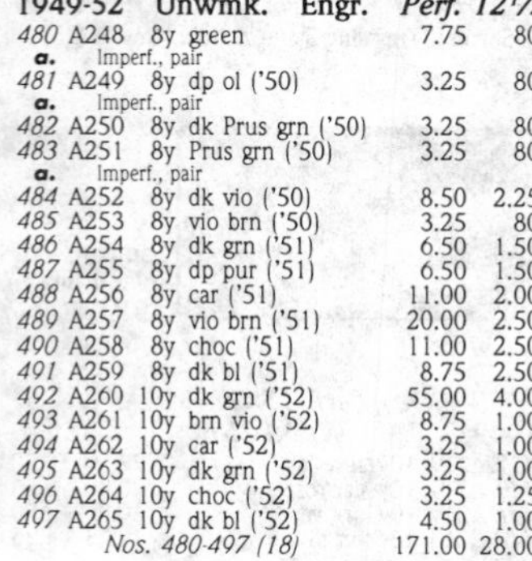

1949-52 Unwmk. Engr. ***Perf. 12½***

480 A248 8y green	7.75	80
a. Imperf., pair		
481 A249 8y dp ol ('50)	3.25	80
a. Imperf., pair		
482 A250 8y dk Prus grn ('50)	3.25	80
483 A251 8y Prus grn ('50)	3.25	80
a. Imperf., pair		
484 A252 8y dk vio ('50)	8.50	2.25
485 A253 8y vio brn ('50)	3.25	80
486 A254 8y dk grn ('51)	6.50	1.50
487 A255 8y dp pur ('51)	6.50	1.50
488 A256 8y car ('51)	11.00	2.00
489 A257 8y vio brn ('51)	20.00	2.50
490 A258 8y choc ('51)	11.00	2.50
491 A259 8y dk bl ('51)	8.75	2.50
492 A260 10y dk grn ('52)	55.00	4.00
493 A261 10y brn vio ('52)	8.75	1.00
494 A262 10y car ('52)	3.25	1.00
495 A263 10y dk grn ('52)	3.25	1.00
496 A264 10y choc ('52)	3.25	1.25
497 A265 10y dk bl ('52)	4.50	1.00
Nos. 480-497 (18)	171.00	28.00

Tiger — A266

Microphones of 1925 and 1950 — A267

1950, Feb. 1 Photo. ***Perf. 12***

498 A266 2y dk red	5.00	1.25

6th prize (lottery), sheet of 5, value $125.

1950, Mar. 21 ***Perf. 13***

499 A267 8y ultra	2.75	1.00

25th anniversary of broadcasting in Japan. Sheets of 20 with marginal inscription.

Dove and Olive Twig on Letter Box — A268

1950, Apr. 20 ***Perf. 12***

500 A268 8y dp yel grn	2.25	1.00

Day of Posts, Apr. 20.

Lake Akan and Mt. Akan A269

Lake Kutcharo, Hokkaido A270

Mt. Akan-Fuji A271

Lake Mashu A272

1950, July 15 Unwmk. ***Perf. 13***

501 A269 2y yel brn	1.50	50
502 A270 8y dp yel grn	1.90	1.00
503 A271 14y rose car	8.25	3.00
504 A272 24y brt bl	10.50	4.00
a. Souvenir sheet of 4, #501-504	27.50	30.00

Akan National Park.

No. 504a sold for 55y.

Gymnast on Rings — A273

Designs: No. 506, Pole vault. No. 507, Soccer. No. 508, Equestrian.

1950, Oct. 28 ***Perf. 13½x13***

505 A273 8y rose brown	20.00	6.00
506 A273 8y rose brown	20.00	6.00
507 A273 8y rose brown	20.00	6.00
508 A273 8y rose brown	20.00	6.00
a. Strip of 4, Nos. 505-508	95.00	
b. Block of 4, Nos. 505-508	150.00	

5th National Athletic Meet. Sheets of 20 stamps in which each horizontal row contains all four designs.

Types of 1947-49 and

Ishiyama-dera Pagoda — A274

Hisoka Maejima — A275

Long-tailed Cock of Tosa — A276

Goddess Kannon — A277

Himeji Castle — A278

Nyoirin Kannon of Chuguji — A280

Phoenix Hall, Byodoin Temple A279

Perf. 13x13½, 13½x13 (14y)

1950-52 Typo. Unwmk.

509 A274 80s car ('51) 1.25 1.25
a. Sheet of 1 5.50 6.50

Photo.

510 A275 1y dk brn ('51) 1.75 30
a. Souvenir sheet of 4 9.25 9.00

Typo.

511 A208 2y grn ('51) 1.65 15
512 A209 3y lt grnsh bl ('51) 40.00 1.00
512A A168 4y lt ultra ('52) 32.50 80
513 A276 5y dp grn & org brn ('51) 4.75 15
a. Orange brown omitted 175.00
514 A212 6y red org ('51) 4.50 25
515 A210 8y dk org brn ('51) 35.00 40
515A A197 10y rose vio ('51) 57.50 4.50
516 A277 10y red brn & lil ('51) 12.00 15

Engr.

517 A278 14y brn & car ('51) 37.50 20.00
a. Sheet of 1 45.00 50.00

Typo.

518 A215 20y dk grn ('51) 40.00 70

Engr.

519 A279 24y dp ultra 26.00 10.00
a. Sheet of 1 27.50 32.50

Typo.

520 A216 30y vio bl ('52) 92.50 1.00

Photo.

521 A280 50y dk brn ('51) 92.50 90
c. Sheet of 1 175.00 195.00

Engr.

521A A217 100y car lake ('52) 275.00 1.00
521B A218 500y dp bl ('52) 250.00 1.50
Nos. 509-521B (17) 1,004. 44.05

No. 510a for the 80th anniv. of Japan's postal service. On No. 512A, characters read from left to right.

See Nos. 557-559, 580, 623, 636-636A, 672, 879A, 885, 916, 1244, 1256.

Girl and Rabbit — A281

1951, Jan. 1 Photo. *Perf. 12*

522 A281 2y rose pink 4.25 60

9th prize (lottery), sheet of 5, value $32.50.

Scenic Spots Issue

Skiers on Mt. Zao
A282 A283

1951, Feb. 15 *Perf. 13*

523 A282 8y olive 12.00 1.40
524 A283 24y blue 14.00 3.50

Tea Picking — A284

Mt. Fuji Seen from Nihon Plateau — A285

Nihon-daira Plateau.

1951, Apr. 2

525 A284 8y ol grn 14.00 3.00
526 A285 24y brt bl 60.00 12.00

Hot Springs, Hakone — A286

Lake Ashi, Hakone — A287

1951, May 25

527 A286 8y chnt brn 7.75 1.75
528 A287 24y dp bl 6.00 2.00

Senju Waterfall A288

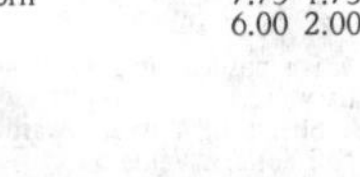

Ninai Waterfall A289

Akame 48 Waterfalls.

1951, June 1

529 A288 8y dp grn 6.00 2.00
530 A289 24y dp bl 9.00 1.40

Pavilion, Wakanoura Bay — A290

Wakanoura Bay — A291

Wakanoura & Tomogashima.

1951, June 25

531 A290 8y brown 5.50 1.10
532 A291 24y brt bl 5.00 1.25

Uji River — A292

View from Uji Bridge — A293

Perf. 13x13½, 13½x13

1951, Aug. 1 Engr.

533 A292 8y brown 5.50 1.50
534 A293 24y dp bl 5.00 1.75

Oura Catholic Church, Nagasaki A294

Sofuku Temple A295

1951, Sept. 15 Photo. *Perf. 13½*

535 A294 8y car rose 8.50 90
536 A295 24y dl bl 6.25 1.50

Marunuma A296

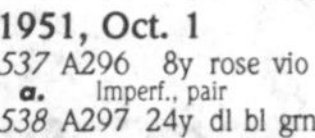
Sugenuma A297

1951, Oct. 1

537 A296 8y rose vio 8.50 1.00
a. Imperf., pair
538 A297 24y dl bl grn 4.75 1.25

Kakuenpo (peak) — A298

Nagatoro Bridge — A299

Shosenkyo Gorge.

1951, Oct. 15

539 A298 8y brn red 7.25 1.00
540 A299 24y dp Prus grn 6.75 1.25
Nos. 523-540 (18) 191.75 39.55

Boy's Head and Seedling — A300

1951, May 5 *Perf. 13½*

541 A300 8y org brn 17.00 1.75

Issued to publicize Children's Day, May 5, 1951.

Oirase River A301

Lake Towada A302

View from Kankodai A303

Mt. Hakkoda from Mt. Yokodake A304

1951, July 20 Photo. *Perf. 13x13½*

542 A301 2y brown 1.65 50
543 A302 8y green 7.00 85
544 A303 14y dk red 5.00 2.00
545 A304 24y blue 5.75 3.00
a. Souv. sheet of 4, #542-545 27.50 27.50

Towada Natl. Park. No. 545a sold for 55y.

Chrysanthemum A305

National Flag A306

1951, Sept. 9 *Perf. 13½*

546 A305 2y org brn 1.75 60
547 A306 8y sl bl & red 4.25 1.25
548 A305 24y bl grn 9.50 3.25

Signing of the peace treaty of 1951.

Putting the Shot A307

Hockey A308

1951, Oct. 27

549 A307 2y org brn 2.75 1.25
550 A308 2y gray bl 2.75 1.25
a. Pair, #549-550 6.00 3.00

6th Natl. Athletic Meet, Hiroshima, Oct. 27-31.

Okina Mask — A309

1952, Jan. 16 Photo. *Perf. 13½x13*

551 A309 5y crimson rose 6.75 40

Sheets reproducing four of these stamps with Japanese inscriptions and floral ornament at left were awarded as sixth prize in the national lottery. Value $75.

Southern Cross from Ship — A310

Earth and Big Dipper — A311

1952, Feb. 19

552 A310 5y purple 5.50 60
553 A311 10y dk grn 11.00 1.25

75th anniv. of Japan's admission to the UPU.

Red Cross and Lilies — A312

Red Cross Nurse — A313

1952, May 1

554 A312 5y rose red & dk red 4.00 65
555 A313 10y dk grn & red 9.25 1.25
a. Red cross omitted
b. Imperf., pair

75th anniv. of the formation of the Japanese Red Cross Society.

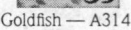

Goldfish — A314

A314a

A314b

A314c

Japanese Serow — A315

1952 ***Perf. 13x13½***

556 A314 35y red org 8.00 15
a. Imperf., pair

Types of 1951
Redrawn; Zeros Omitted
Unwmk.

557 A314a 1y dk brn 22 15
558 A314b 50y dk brn 3.25 15

Typo.

559 A314c 4y dp cl & pale rose 1.10 15
a. Background (pale rose) omitted

Ornamental frame and background added, denomination at upper left, Japanese characters at upper right.

Photo.

560 A315 8y brown 15 15
Set value, #556-560 25

Mt. Yari — A316

Kurobe Valley — A317

Mt. Shirouma A318

Mt. Norikura A319

1952, July 5 ***Perf. 13½x13, 13x13½***

561 A316 5y brown 3.75 32
562 A317 10y bl grn 17.00 1.25
563 A318 14y brt red 5.50 1.10
564 A319 24y brt bl 11.00 2.00
a. Souv. sheet of 4, #561-564, imperf. 40.00 45.00

Japan Alps (Chubu-Sangaku) National Park. No. 564a sold for 60y.

Yasuda Hall, Tokyo University A320

Yomei Gate, Nikko A321

1952, Oct. 1 **Engr.** ***Perf. 13***

565 A320 10y dl grn 12.00 1.25

75th anniversary of the founding of Tokyo University.

1952, Oct. 15 **Photo.** ***Perf. 13x13½***

566 A321 45y blue 3.00 15

Mountain Climber — A322

1952, Oct. 18
Dated "1952"

567 A322 5y shown 4.00 1.50
568 A322 5y Wrestlers 4.00 1.50
a. Pair, #567-568 17.00 4.00

7th Nat.l Athletic Meet, Fukushima, Oct. 18-22.

Mt. Azuma A323

Mt. Asahi A324

Mt. Bandai A325

Mt. Gatsun A326

Unwmk.

1952, Oct. 18 **Photo.** ***Perf. 13***

569 A323 5y brown 2.25 45
570 A324 10y ol grn 9.50 1.25
571 A325 14y rose red 5.00 1.65
572 A326 24y blue 7.75 3.25
a. Souv. sheet of 4, #569-572, imperf. 50.00 55.00

Bandai-Asahi National Park. No. 572a sold for 60y.

Kirin — A327

Flag of Crown Prince — A328

Engr. and Photo.

1952, Nov. 10 ***Perf. 13½***

573 A327 5y red org & pur 2.25 32
574 A327 10y red org & dk grn 2.75 50
575 A328 24y dp bl 11.00 4.00
a. Souv. sheet of 3, #573-575, imperf. 62.50 125.00

Issued to commemorate the nomination of Crown Prince Akihito as Heir Apparent.

No. 575a measures 130x129mm, and has a background design of phoenix and clouds in violet brown and blue. Sold for 50y.

Sambaso Doll — A329

First Electric Lamp in Japan — A330

Perf. 13½x13

1953, Jan. 1 **Photo.** **Unwmk.**

576 A329 5y carmine 5.00 40

For postage on New Year's cards, later for ordinary use.

Sheets of 4 were awarded as 6th prize in the natl. lottery. Value $55.

1953, Mar. 25

577 A330 10y brown 5.25 1.25

75th anniv. of electric lighting in Japan.

"Kintai Bridge," Print by Hiroshige A331

Kintai Bridge as Rebuilt in 1953 A332

1953, May 3 ***Perf. 13***

578 A331 10y chestnut 5.75 2.00
579 A332 24y blue 5.75 2.25

Kannon Type of 1951
Redrawn; Zeros Omitted

A332a

1953-54 **Typo.**

580 A332a 10y red brn & lil 3.25 15
a. Booklet pane 10 + 2 labels (souvenir) ('54) 150.00 150.00
b. Bklt. pane 10 + 2 labels ('54) 50.00

No. 580a was issued in honor of Philatelic Week 1954. The inscriptions on the two labels are arranged in two rows of boldface characters.

On No. 580b, the label inscriptions are arranged in three rows of mixed heavy and thin characters.

See Nos. 611a and 672.

Lake Shikotsu, Hokkaido A333

Mt. Yotei A334

1953, July 25 **Photo.** ***Perf. 13***

581 A333 5y ultra 1.45 45
582 A334 10y green 4.00 1.00
a. Souv. sheet of 2, #581-582, imperf., no gum 25.00 27.50

Shikotsu-Toya National Park.
No. 582a sold for 20 yen.

Akita Dog — A335

Cormorant Fishing — A336

1953 **Unwmk.**

583 A335 2y gray 15 15

Engr.

584 A336 100y dk red 27.50 15
a. Imperf., pair 600.00
Set value 15

See No. 1621A.

Futamigaura Beach A337

Namikiri Coast A338

1953, Oct. 2 **Photo.**

585 A337 5y red 1.50 50
586 A338 10y blue 3.50 75
a. Souv. sheet of 2, #585-586, imperf., no gum 16.00 16.00

Ise-Shima National Park.

Phoenix — A339

Design: 10y, Japanese crane in flight.

1953, Oct. 12 **Engr.** ***Perf. 12½***

587 A339 5y brn car 2.00 1.00

Photo.

588 A339 10y dark blue 5.00 1.75

Nos. 587-588 were issued on the occasion of the return of Crown Prince Akihito from his visit to Europe and America. Issued in sheets of 20 with marginal inscription.

Rugby Match — A340

Judo — A341

1953, Oct. 22 *Perf. 13½*

589 A340 5y black 3.00 1.00
590 A341 5y bl grn 3.00 1.00
a. Pair, #589-590 14.00 3.00

8th Natl. Athletic Meet, Matsuyama, Oct. 22-26.

Sky and Top of Observatory — A342

1953, Oct. 29

591 A342 10y dk gray bl 8.00 1.00

75th anniversary of the Tokyo Astronomical Observatory.

Mt. Unzen from Golf Course A343

Mt. Unzen from Chijiwa Beach A344

1953, Nov. 20 *Perf. 13*

592 A343 5y red 1.45 32
593 A344 10y blue 3.75 50
a. Souv. sheet of 2, #592-593, imperf., no gum 16.00 17.50

Unzen National Park.

Toy Horse — A345

Racing Skaters — A346

1953, Dec. 25 *Perf. 13½x13*

594 A345 5y rose 5.50 40

Issued to pay postage on New Year's cards, later for ordinary use. A sheet reproducing four of these stamps was awarded as sixth prize in the national lottery. Value $40.

1954, Jan. 16

595 A346 10y blue 4.00 1.00

World Speed Skating Matches for Men, Sapporo City, Jan. 16-17, 1954.

> ***Set Values***
> *A 15-cent minimum now applies to individual stamps and sets. Where the 15-cent minimum per stamp would increase the "value" of a set beyond retail, there is a "Set Value" notation giving the retail value of the set.*

Golden Hall, Chusonji Temple — A347

Thread, Pearls, Gears, Buttons and Globe — A348

1954, Jan. 20

596 A347 20y ol grn 85 15

1954, Apr. 10

597 A348 10y dk red 3.00 65

International Trade Fair, Osaka, Apr. 10-23.

Little Cuckoo A349

Wrestlers A350

1954, May 10 *Perf. 13x13½*

598 A349 3y bl grn 15 15
a. Imperf., pair 350.00

1954, May 22 **Engr.**

599 A350 10y dp grn 2.25 65

World Free Style Wrestling Championship Matches, Tokyo, 1954.

Mt. Asama A351

Mt. Tanikawa A352

1954, June 25 *Perf. 13*

600 A351 5y dk gray brn 1.65 40
601 A352 10y dk bl grn 3.25 90
a. Souvenir sheet of 2, #600-601, no gum 16.00 16.00

Jo-Shin-etsu National Park.

Table Tennis — A353

Archery — A354

1954, Aug. 22 **Engr.** *Perf. 12*

602 A353 5y dl brn 3.00 70
603 A354 5y gray grn 3.00 70
a. Se-tenant pair, #602-603 7.00

9th Natl. Athletic Meet, Sapporo, Aug. 22-26.

Morse Telegraph Instrument A355

ITU Monument A356

Perf. 13x13½, 13½x13

1954, Oct. 13

604 A355 5y dk pur brn 1.75 35
605 A356 10y dp bl 4.00 60

75th anniv. of Japanese membership in the ITU.

Daruma Doll — A357

1954, Dec. 20 **Photo.** *Perf. 13½x13*

606 A357 5y blk & red 3.50 35

Sheets reproducing four of these stamps with Japanese inscriptions and ornaments were awarded as fifth prize in the national lottery. Value $40.

Mountain Stream, Tama Gorge — A358

Chichibu Mountains A359

1955, Mar. 1 **Engr.** *Perf. 13*

607 A358 5y blue 1.25 35
608 A359 10y red brn 1.65 42
a. Souv. sheet of 2, #607-608, imperf., no gum 15.00 13.00

Chichibu-Tama National Park.

Bridge and Iris — A360

1955, Mar. 15 *Perf. 13x13½*

609 A360 500y dp plum 75.00 25

Paper Carp as Flown on Boys' Day A361

Mandarin Ducks A362

Unwmk.

1955, May 16 **Photo.** *Perf. 13*

610 A361 10y multi 3.75 70

15th congress of the International Chamber of Commerce, Tokyo, May 16-21, 1955.

1955-64

611 A362 5y lt bl & red brn 25 15
a. Bklt. pane, 4 #611, 8 #580 ('59) 20.00
b. Bklt. pane, 4 #611, 8 #725 ('63) 18.00
c. Bklt. pane of 4 ('64) 7.00
d. Imperf., pair 650.00

See Nos. 738, 881d, 914b.

Benten Cape — A363

Jodo Beach A364

1955, Sept. 30

612 A363 5y dp grn 1.25 22
613 A364 10y rose lake 1.75 40
a. Souv. sheet of 2, #612-613, imperf., no gum 16.00 12.00

Rikuchu-Kaigan National Park.
No. 613a sold for 20y.

Girl Athletes A365

Runners A366

1955, Oct. 30 **Engr.**

614 A365 5y brn lake 1.00 40
615 A366 5y bluish blk 1.00 40
a. Se-tenant pair, #614-615 3.50

10th National Athletic Meet, Kanagawa Prefecture.

See Nos. 639-640, 657.

"A Girl Blowing Glass Toy," by Utamaro A367

1955, Nov. 1 **Photo.**

616 A367 10y multi 9.50 4.00

150th anniv. of the death of Utamaro, woodcut artist, and to publicize Philatelic Week, Nov., 1955. Issued in sheets of 10.

Kokeshi Dolls — A368

Table Tennis — A369

1955, Dec. 30 **Unwmk.** *Perf. 13*

617 A368 5y ol grn & red 1.75 18

Sheets reproducing four of these stamps, were awarded as fifth prize in the New Year's lottery. Value $22.50.

1956, Apr. 2 *Perf. 13x13½*

618 A369 10y red brown 1.10 35

International Table Tennis Championship, Tokyo, Apr. 2-11.

Judo — A370

1956, May 2 *Perf. 13*
619 A370 10y green & lilac 1.50 35

Issued to publicize the first World Judo Championship Meet, Tokyo, May 3, 1956.

Boy and Girl with Paper Carp A371

1956, May 5
620 A371 5y lt bl & blk 90 25

Issued to commemorate the establishment of World Children's Day, May 5, 1956.

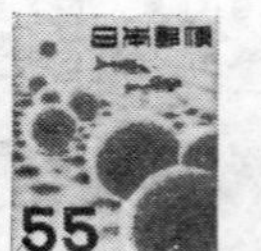

Water Plants, Lake Akan A372 — Big Purple Butterfly A373

1956 **Unwmk.** *Perf. 13*
621 A372 55y lt bl, grn & blk 13.00 15
622 A373 75y multi 7.75 25

See Nos. 887A, 917.

Castle Type of 1951
Redrawn; Zeros Omitted

A373a

1956 **Engr.** *Perf. 13½x13*
623 A373a 14y gray olive 5.50 1.65

Osezaki Promontory A374

Kujuku Island A375

1956, Oct. 1 **Photo.**
624 A374 5y red brn 85 30

Engr. & Photo.
625 A375 10y lt bl & ind 1.10 40
a. Souv. sheet of 2, #624-625, imperf., no gum 15.00 16.00

Saikai National Park.
No. 625a sold for 20y.

> *Scott's editorial staff cannot undertake to identify, authenticate or appraise stamps and postal markings.*

Palace Moat and Modern Tokyo A376

1956, Oct. 1 **Engr.**
626 A376 10y dl pur 2.00 40

500th anniv. of the founding of Tokyo.

Sakuma Dam — A377

1956, Oct. 15 **Unwmk.** *Perf. 13*
627 A377 10y dk bl 2.00 50

Completion of Sakuma Dam.

Long Jump A378

Basketball A379

1956, Oct. 28 *Perf. 13½x13*
628 A378 5y brn vio 75 30
629 A379 5y steel blue 75 30
a. Pair, #628-629 2.25

11th Natl. Athletic Meet, Hyogo Prefecture.
See No. 658.

Kabuki Actor Ebizo Ichikawa by Sharaku — A380

1956, Nov. 1 **Photo.** *Perf. 13*
630 A380 10y multi 9.50 4.25

Stamp Week. Sheets of 10.

Mount Manaslu A381

1956, Nov. 3
631 A381 10y multi 3.00 1.25

Issued in honor of the Japanese expedition which climbed Mount Manaslu in the Himalayas on May 9 and 11, 1956.

Electric Locomotive and Hiroshige's "Yui Stage" A382

1956, Nov. 19 **Unwmk.** *Perf. 13*
632 A382 10y dk ol bis, blk & grn 3.75 1.00

Electrification of Tokaido Line.

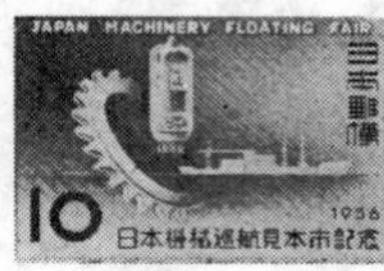
Cogwheel, Vacuum Tube and Ship — A383

1956, Dec. 18 **Engr.**
633 A383 10y ultra 75 35

Japanese Machinery Floating Fair.

Toy Whale — A384

United Nations Emblem — A385

1956, Dec. 20 **Photo.**
634 A384 5y multi 1.00 15
a. Imperf., pair

Sheets reproducing four of these stamps, with inscriptions and ornaments, were awarded as sixth prize in the national lottery. Value $12.

Photogravure and Engraved
1957, Mar. 8 **Unwmk.** *Perf. 13½x13*
635 A385 10y lt bl & dk car 65 40

Japan's admission to the UN, Dec. 18, 1956.

Temple Type of 1950
Redrawn; Zeros Omitted

A385a

1957-59 **Engr.** *Perf. 13x13½*
636 A385a 24y violet 16.00 2.00
636A A385a 30y rose lil ('59) 35.00 35
b. Imperf., pair

IGY Emblem, Penguin and "Soya" — A386

Atomic Reactor — A387

1957, July 1 **Photo.** *Perf. 13*
637 A386 10y bl, yel & blk 60 35

International Geophysical Year.

1957, Sept. 18 **Engr.** *Perf. 13*
638 A387 10y dk pur 38 15

Completion of Japan's atomic reactor at Tokai-Mura, Ibaraki Prefecture.

Sports Type of 1955

Designs: No. 639, Girl on parallel bars. No. 640, Boxers.

1957, Oct. 26 **Unwmk.** *Perf. 13*
639 A366 5y ultra 35 15
640 A366 5y dk red 35 15
a. Pair, #639-640 1.00
Set value 20

12th Natl. Athletic Meet, Shizuoka Prefecture.

"Girl Bouncing Ball," by Suzuki Harunobu A388

1957, Nov. 1 **Photo.**
641 A388 10y multi 2.50 1.00

1957 Stamp Week. Issued in sheets of 10. See Nos. 646, 671, 728, 757.

Lake Okutama and Ogochi Dam — A389

1957, Nov. 26 **Engr.** *Perf. 13½*
642 A389 10y ultra 30 15

Completion of Ogochi Dam, part of the Tokyo water supply system.

Modern and First Japanese Blast Furnaces A390

Toy Dog (Inu-hariko) A391

1957, Dec. 1 **Photo.** **Unwmk.**
643 A390 10y org & dk pur 25 15

Centenary of Japan's iron industry.

1957, Dec. 20 *Perf. 13½x13*
644 A391 5y multi 28 15

New Year 1958. Sheets reproducing 4 #644, with inscriptions and ornaments, were awarded as 5th prize in the New Year lottery. Value $4.75.

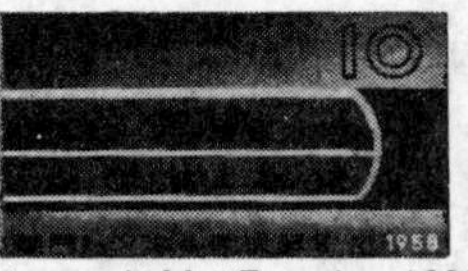
Shimonoseki-Moji Tunnel — A392

1958, Mar. 9 *Perf. 13x13½*
645 A392 10y multi 30 15

Completion of the Kan-Mon Underwater Highway connecting Honshu and Kyushu Islands.

Stamp Week Type of 1957

Design: 10y, Woman with Umbrella, woodcut by Kiyonaga.

1958, Apr. 20 **Unwmk.** *Perf. 13*
646 A388 10y multi 80 20

Stamp Week, 1958. Sheets of 10.

Statue of Ii Naosuke and Harbor A393

Unwmk.

1958, May 10 Engr. *Perf. 13*

647 A393 10y gray bl & car 18 15

Cent. of the opening of the ports of Yokohama, Nagasaki and Hakodate to foreign powers.

National Stadium — A394

3rd Asian Games, Tokyo: 10y, Torch and emblem. 14y, Runner. 24y, Woman diver.

1958, May 24 Photo.

648 A394 5y bl grn, bis & pink	15	15
649 A394 10y multi	25	15
650 A394 14y multi	32	15
651 A394 24y multi	40	15
Set value		42

Kasato Maru, Map and Brazilian Flag A395

1958, June 18

652 A395 10y multi 18 15

50 years of Japanese emigration to Brazil.

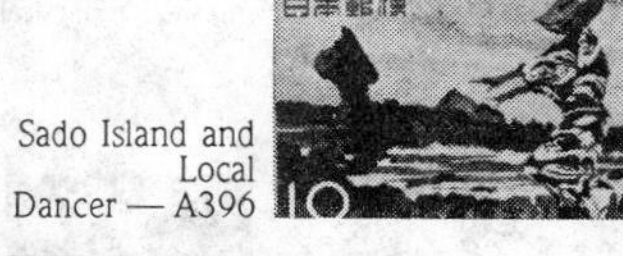
Sado Island and Local Dancer — A396

Mt. Yahiko and Echigo Plain — A397

1958, Aug. 20 Unwmk. *Perf. 13*

653 A396 10y multi	60	15
654 A397 10y multi	60	15
Set value		24

Sado-Yahiko Quasi-National Park.

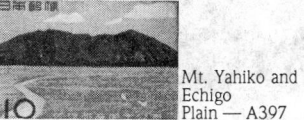

Stethoscope A398

1958, Sept. 7 Photo. *Perf. 13*

655 A398 10y Prus grn 30 15

5th Intl. Cong. on Diseases of the Chest and the 7th Intl. Cong. of Bronchoesophagology.

"Kyoto" (Sanjo Bridge), Print by Hiroshige A399

1958, Oct. 5

656 A399 24y multi 2.75 40

Issued for International Letter Writing Week, Oct. 5-11. See No. 679.

Sports Types of 1955-56

Designs: No. 657, Weight lifter. No. 658, Girl badminton player.

1958, Oct. 19 Engr.

657 A365 5y gray blue	35	15
658 A379 5y claret	35	15
a. Pair, #657-658	1.00	

13th Natl. Athletic Meet, Toyama Prefecture.

Keio University and Yukichi Fukuzawa — A400

1958, Nov. 8 Engr. *Perf. 13½*

659 A400 10y magenta 28 15

Centenary of Keio University.

Globe and Playing Children A401

1958, Nov. 23 Photo. *Perf. 13*

660 A401 10y dp grn 28 15

9th Intl. Conf. of Social Work and the 2nd Intl. Study Conf. on Child Welfare.

Flame: Symbol of Human Rights — A402

1958, Dec. 10 Unwmk. *Perf. 13*

661 A402 10y multi 32 15

10th anniv. of the signing of the Universal Declaration of Human Rights.

Toy of Takamatsu (Tai-Ebisu) A403

Tractor and Map of Kojima Bay A404

1958, Dec. 20 *Perf. 13½*

662 A403 5y multi 38 15

New Year 1959. Sheets reproducing 4 #662, with inscriptions and ornaments, were awarded as prizes in the New Year lottery. Size: 103x89mm. Value $4.

1959, Feb. 1 *Perf. 12½*

663 A404 10y claret & bis brn 30 15

Completion of the embankment closing Kojima Bay for reclamation.

Karst Plateau — A405

Akiyoshi Cave — A406

1959, Mar. 16 Photo. *Perf. 13½*

664 A405 10y grn, bl & ocher	1.00	15
665 A406 10y multi	1.60	15
Set value		24

Akiyoshidai Quasi-National Park.

Map of Southeast Asia — A407

1959, Mar. 27

666 A407 10y dp car 28 15

Asian Cultural Cong., Tokyo, Mar. 27-31, marking the 2,500th anniv. of the death of Buddha.

Ceremonial Fan — A408

Prince Akihito and Princess Michiko — A409

Photogravure; Portraits Engraved

1959, Apr. 10

667 A408 5y mag & vio	16	15
668 A409 10y red brn & dl pur	50	15
a. Souv. sheet of 2, #667-668, imperf.	3.00	3.00
669 A408 20y org brn & brn	60	15
670 A409 30y yel grn & dk grn	1.25	25

Wedding of Crown Prince Akihito and Princess Michiko, Apr. 10, 1959.

Type of 1957

Design: 10y, Women Reading Poetry Print by Eishi Fujiwara.

1959, May 20 Photo. *Perf. 13*

671 A388 10y multi 3.50 1.25

Issued to publicize Stamp Week, 1959. Issued in sheets of 10.

Redrawn Kannon Type of 1953
Coil Stamp
Perf. 13 Horiz.

1959, Jan. 20 Typo. Unwmk.

672 A332a 10y red brn & lil 22.50 22.50

Measuring Glass, Tape Measure and Scales — A410

Nurses Carrying Stretcher — A411

1959, June 5 Photo. *Perf. 13*

673 A410 10y lt bl & blk 30 15

Adoption of the metric system.

1959, June 24

674 A411 10y ol grn & red 28 15

Centenary of the Red Cross idea.

Mt. Fuji and Lake Motosu — A412

1959, July 21 Engr. *Perf. 13*

675 A412 10y grn, bl & sep 52 15

Establishment of Natural Park Day and 1st Natural Park Convention, Yumoto, Nikko, July 21, 1959.

Ao Cave Area of Yabakei — A413

Hita, Mt. Hiko and Great Cormorant A414

1959, Sept. 25 Photo. *Perf. 13*

676 A413 10y multi	1.25	15
677 A414 10y multi	1.25	15

Yaba-Hita-Hiko Quasi National Park.

Golden Dolphin, Nagoya Castle — A415

Japanese Crane, IATA Emblem — A416

1959, Oct. 1

678 A415 10y brt bl, gold & blk 60 15

350th anniversary of Nagoya.

Hiroshige Type of 1958

Design: 30y, "Kuwana," the 7-ri Crossing Point, print by Hiroshige.

1959, Oct. 4 Unwmk.

679 A399 30y multi 5.25 1.00

Intl. Letter Writing Week, Oct. 4-10.

1959, Oct. 12 Engr.

680 A416 10y brt grnsh bl 32 15

15th General Meeting of the International Air Transport Association.

Shoin Yoshida and PTA Symbol — A417

Throwing the Hammer — A418

1959, Oct. 27 Photo. *Perf. 13*

681 A417 10y brown 32 15

Centenary of the death of Shoin Yoshida, educator, and in connection with the Parent-Teachers Association convention.

1959, Oct. 25 Engr.

Design: No. 683, Woman Fencer.

682 A418 5y gray bl 52 15
683 A418 5y ol bis 52 15
a. Pair, #682-683 1.25
Set value 24

14th National Athletic Meet, Tokyo.

Globes — A419

1959, Nov. 2 Photo.

684 A419 5y brn red 38 15

15th session of GATT (General Agreement on Tariffs & Trade), Tokyo, Oct. 12-Nov. 21.

Toy Mouse of Kanazawa — A420

1959, Dec. 19 Unwmk. *Perf. 13½*

685 A420 5y gold, red, grn & blk 60 15

New Year 1960. Sheets reproducing 4 #685, with marginal inscription and ornaments, were awarded as prizes in natl. lottery. Value $5.

Yukio Ozaki and Clock Tower, Ozaki Memorial Hall — A421

Nara Period Artwork, Shosoin Treasure House — A422

1960, Feb. 25 Photo. *Perf. 13½*

686 A421 10y red brn & dk brn 28 15

Completion of Ozaki Memorial Hall, erected in memory of Yukio Ozaki (1858-1954), statesman.

1960, Mar. 10

687 A422 10y ol gray 32 15

1250th anniversary of the transfer of the capital to Nara.

Scenic Trio Issue

Bay of Matsushima A423

Ama-no-hashidate (Heavenly Bridge) — A424

Miyajima from the Sea — A425

1960 Engr.

688 A423 10y mar & bl grn 1.25 40
689 A424 10y grn & lt bl 1.50 40
690 A425 10y vio blk & bl grn 1.50 40

Issue dates: No. 688, Mar. 15. No. 689, July 15. No. 690, Nov. 15.

Takeshima, off Gamagori A426

1960, Mar. 20 Photo. *Perf. 13½*

691 A426 10y multi 75 15

Mikawa Bay Quasi-National Park.

Poetess Isé, 13th Century Painting — A427

1960, Apr. 20 Unwmk. *Perf. 13*

692 A427 10y multi 2.50 1.25

Stamp Week, 1960.

Kanrin Maru — A428

Design: 30y, Pres. Buchanan receiving first Japanese diplomatic mission.

1960, May 17 Engr.

693 A428 10y bl grn & brn 65 20
694 A428 30y car & indigo 1.00 20

Cent. of the Japan-US Treaty of Amity and Commerce. Nos. 694 and 693 form pages of an open book when placed next to each other. Souvenir sheet is No. 703.

Crested Ibis (Toki) — A429

Radio Waves Encircling Globe — A430

1960, May 24 Photo. *Perf. 13½*

695 A429 10y gray, pink & red 52 20

12th Intl. Congress for Bird Preservation.

1960, June 1 Engr.

696 A430 10y car rose 28 15

25th anniv. of the Intl. Radio Program by the Japanese Broadcasting Corporation.

Flower Garden (Gensei Kaen) — A431

1960, June 15 Photo.

697 A431 10y multi 1.00 20

Abashiri Quasi-National Park.

Cape Ashizuri — A432

1960, Aug. 1 Unwmk.

698 A432 10y multi 1.00 20

Ashizuri Quasi-National Park.

Rainbow Spanning Pacific, Cherry Blossoms and Pineapples — A433

Henri Farman's Biplane and Jet — A434

1960, Aug. 20 *Perf. 13½*

699 A433 10y multi 60 25

75th anniversary of Japanese contract emigration to Hawaii.

1960, Sept. 20 *Perf. 13*

700 A434 10y brn & chlky bl 48 15

50th anniversary of Japanese aviation.

Seat Plan of Diet — A435

"Red Fuji" by Hokusai and Diet Building — A436

1960, Sept. 27

701 A435 5y indigo & org 28 15
702 A436 10y bl & red brn 65 15
Set value 24

49th Inter-Parliamentary Conference.

Souvenir Sheet
Type A428

1960, Sept. 27 Engr.

703 Sheet of 2, #693-694 15.00 15.00

Visit of Prince Akihito and Princess Michiko to the US.

"Night Snow at Kambara," by Hiroshige A437

1960, Oct. 9 Photo.

704 A437 30y multi 10.50 2.00

Issued for International Letter Writing Week, Oct. 9-15. See Nos. 735, 769.

Japanese Fencing (Kendo) — A438

Okayama Astrophysical Observatory — A439

Design: No. 706, Girl gymnast and vaulting horse.

1960, Oct. 23 Engr. *Perf. 13½*

705 A438 5y dull blue 55 15
706 A438 5y rose vio 55 15
a. Pair, #705-706 1.25

15th National Athletic Meet, Kumamoto.

1960, Oct. 19

707 A439 10y brt vio 60 15

Opening of the Okayama Astrophysical Observatory.

Lt. Naoshi Shirase and Map of Antarctica — A440

Little Red Calf of Aizu, Gold Calf of Iwate — A441

1960, Nov. 29 Photo.

708 A440 10y fawn & blk 38 15

50th anniv. of the 1st Japanese Antarctic expedition.

1960, Dec. 20 Unwmk. *Perf. 13½*

709 A441 5y multi 60 15

New Year 1961. Sheets reproducing 4 #709 were awarded as prizes in the New Year lottery. Size: 102x89mm. Value $5.50.

Diet Building at Night — A442

Opening of First Session — A443

1960, Dec. 24 Photo.; Engr. (10y)

710 A442 5y gray & dk bl 45 15
711 A443 10y carmine 45 15
Set value 24

70th anniversary of the Japanese Diet.

Narcissus
A444

Nojima Cape Lighthouse and Fisherwomen
A445

Designs: No. 713, Plum blossoms. No. 714, Camellia japonica. No. 715, Cherry blossoms. No. 716, Peony. No. 717, Iris. No. 718, Lily. No. 719, Morning glory. No. 720, Bellflower. No. 721, Gentian. No. 722, Chrysanthemum. No. 723, Camellia sasanqua.

1961 Photo. *Perf. 13½*

712 A444 10y lil, yel & grn 2.25 60
713 A444 10y brn, grn & yel 1.50 60
714 A444 10y lem, grn, pink & yel 1.10 50
715 A444 10y gray, brn, pink, yel & blk 1.10 65
716 A444 10y blk, grn, pink & yel 1.10 65
717 A444 10y gray, pur, grn & yel 75 45
718 A444 10y gray grn, yel & brn 55 25
719 A444 10y lt bl, grn & lil 55 25
720 A444 10y lt yel grn, vio & grn 55 25
721 A444 10y org, vio bl & grn 55 25
722 A444 10y bl, yel & grn 55 25
723 A444 10y sl, pink, yel & grn 55 25
Nos. 712-723 (12) 11.10 4.95

1961, Mar. 15

724 A445 10y multi 52 10

South Boso Quasi-National Park.

Cherry Blossoms
A446

Hisoka Maejima
A447

Unwmk.

1961, Apr. 1 Photo. *Perf. 13*

725 A446 10y lil rose & gray 18 15
a. Lilac rose omitted 350.00
b. Imperf., pair 500.00
c. Booklet pane of 4 7.50
d. Gray omitted 300.00

See No. 611b.

Coil Stamp

1961, Apr. 25 *Perf. 13 Horiz.*

726 A446 10y lil rose & gray 4.50 1.65

1961, Apr. 20 *Perf. 13*

727 A447 10y ol & blk 65 15

90th anniv. of Japan's modern postal service from Tokyo to Osaka, inaugurated by Deputy Postmaster General Hisoka Maejima.

Type of 1957

Design: "Dancing Girl" from a "Screen of Dancers."

1961, Apr. 20 *Perf. 13½*

728 A388 10y multi 1.25 65

Stamp Week, 1961. Sheets of 10 (5x2).

Lake Biwa — A448

1961, Apr. 25

729 A448 10y blk, dk bl & yel grn 60 15

Lake Biwa Quasi-National Park.

Rotary Emblem and People of Various Races — A449

1961, May 29 Engr. *Perf. 13*

730 A449 10y gray & org 22 15

52nd convention of Rotary Intl., Tokyo, May 29-June 1, 1961.

Faucet, Wheat, Insulator & Cogwheel
A450

Sun, Earth and Meridian
A451

1961, July 7 Photo. *Perf. 13½*

731 A450 10y vio & aqua 30 15

Aichi irrigation system, Kiso river.

1961, July 12

732 A451 10y yel, red & blk 28 15

75th anniv. of Japanese standard time.

Parasol Dance on Dunes of Tottori — A452

1961, Aug. 15

733 A452 10y multi 60 18

San'in Kaigan Quasi-National Park.

Onuma Lake and Komagatake Volcano — A453

Gymnast on Horizontal Bar — A454

1961, Sept. 15

734 A453 10y grn, red brn & bl 60 18

Onuma Quasi-National Park.

Hiroshige Type of 1960

1961, Oct. 8 *Perf. 13*

Design: 30y, "Hakone," print by Hiroshige from the 53 Stages of the Tokaido.

735 A437 30y multi 5.50 2.25

Intl. Letter Writing Week, Oct. 8-14.

1961, Oct. 8 Engr. *Perf. 13½*

Design: No. 737, Women rowing.

736 A454 5y bl grn 45 15
737 A454 5y ultra 45 15
a. Pair, #736-737 1.00
Set value 24

16th National Athletic Meet, Akita.
See Nos. 770-771, 816-817, 852-853.

Duck Type of 1955
Coil Stamp

1961, Oct. 2 Photo. *Perf. 13 Horiz.*

738 A362 5y lt bl & red brn 3.00 3.00

National Diet Library and Book — A455

Papier Maché Tiger — A456

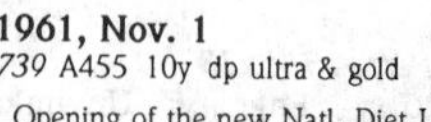

1961, Nov. 1 *Perf. 13½*

739 A455 10y dp ultra & gold 32 15

Opening of the new Natl. Diet Library, Tokyo.

1961, Dec. 15 *Perf. 13½*

740 A456 5y multi 38 15

New Year 1962. Sheets reproducing 4 #740 were awarded as 5th prize in the New Year lottery. Size: 102x90. Value $6.

Mt. Fuji from Lake Ashi — A457

Minokake-Iwa at Irozaki — A458

Mt. Fuji from Mitsu Pass — A459

Mt. Fuji from Cape of Ose — A460

1962, Jan. 16 Unwmk. Photo.

741 A457 5y dp grn 70 15
742 A458 5y dk bl 45 15
743 A459 10y red brn 1.75 20
744 A460 10y black 1.50 25

Fuji-Hakone-Izu National Park.

Omishima A461

1962, Feb. 15 *Perf. 13½*

745 A461 10y ultra, red & yel 48 15

Kitanagato-Kaigan Quasi-National Park.

Perotrochus Hirasei — A462

Sacred Bamboo — A463

Shari-den of Engakuji — A464

Yomei Gate, Nikko — A465

Noh Mask — A466

Copper Pheasant — A466a

Wind God, Fujin, by Sotatsu — A467

Japanese Crane — A468

Mythical Winged Woman, Chusonji — A469

1962-65 Unwmk. *Perf. 13*

746 A462 4y dk brn & red ('63) 15 15
747 A463 6y gray grn & car 15 15
748 A464 30y vio blk 3.25 15
749 A465 40y rose red 3.25 15
750 A466 70y yel brn & blk ('65) 1.95 15
751 A466a 80y crim & brn ('65) 1.25 15
752 A467 90y brt bl grn 30.00 20
753 A468 100y pink & blk ('63) 8.75 15
754 A469 120y purple 7.75 15
Nos. 746-754 (9) 56.50
Set value 90

See Nos. 888, 888A, 890, 1076, 1079, 1257.

Coil Stamp

755 A464 30y dl vio ('63) 3.50 1.25

Hinamatsuri, Doll Festival — A470

1962, Mar. 3 *Perf. 13½*

756 A470 10y brn, blk, bl & car 1.25 35

The Doll Festival is celebrated Mar. 3 in honor of young girls.

Type of 1957

Design: Dancer from "Flower Viewing Party" by Naganobu Kano.

1962, Apr. 20 Photo. *Perf. 13½*

757 A388 10y multi 1.40 90

Stamp Week, 1962. Sheets of 10.

Sakurajima Volcano and Kagoshima Bay — A471

1962, Apr. 30

758 A471 10y multi 42 15

Kinkowan Quasi-National Park.

Mount Kongo — A472

1962, May 15 *Perf. 13½*

759 A472 10y gray bl, dk grn & sal 42 15

Kongo-Ikoma Quasi-National Park.

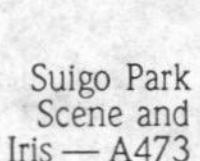

Suigo Park Scene and Iris — A473

1962, June 1 ***Perf. 13½***

760 A473 10y multi 52 15

Suigo Quasi-National Park.

Train Emerging from Hokuriku Tunnel — A474

1962, June 10 **Photo.**

761 A474 10y olive gray 80 15

Opening of Hokuriku Tunnel between Tsuruga and Imajo, Fukui Prefecture.

Star Festival (Tanabata Matsuri) A475

Boy Scout Hat on Map of Southeast Asia A476

1962, July 7 **Unwmk.** ***Perf. 13½***

762 A475 10y multi 42 15

The Tanabata festival is celebrated on the evening of July 7.

1962, Aug. 3

763 A476 10y red org, blk & bis 22 15

Asian Boy Scout Jamboree, Mt. Fuji, Aug. 3-7.

Ozegahara Swampland and Mt. Shibutsu A477

Fumes on Mt. Chausu, Nasu — A478

Lake Chuzenji and Mt. Nantai — A479

Senryu-kyo Narrows, Shiobara A480

1962, Sept. 1

764 A477 5y greenish blue 25 15
765 A478 5y maroon 25 15
766 A479 10y purple 38 15
767 A480 10y olive 38 15
Set value 32

Nikko National Park.

Wakato Suspension Bridge — A481

Perf. 13½x13

1962, Sept. 26 **Engr.** **Unwmk.**

768 A481 10y rose red 75 25

Opening of Wakato Bridge over Dokai Bay in North Kyushu.

Hiroshige Type of 1960

Design: 40y, "Nihonbashi," print by Hiroshige from the 53 Stages of the Tokaido.

1962, Oct. 7 **Photo.** ***Perf. 13***

769 A437 40y multi 4.50 1.65

Intl. Letter Writing Week, Oct. 7-13.

Sports Type of 1961

Design: No. 770, Woman softball pitcher. No. 771, Rifle shooting.

1962, Oct. 21 **Engr.** ***Perf. 13½***

770 A454 5y bluish blk 25 15
771 A454 5y brn vio 25 15
a. Pair, #770-771 60
Set value 16

17th National Athletic Meeting, Okayama.

Shichi-go-san Festival A482

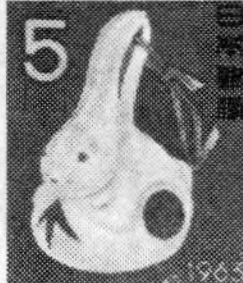

Rabbit Bell A483

1962, Nov. 15 **Photo.** ***Perf. 13½***

772 A482 10y multi 40 15

This festival for 7 and 3-year-old girls and 5-year-old boys is celebrated on Nov. 15.

1962, Dec. 15

773 A483 5y multi 22 15

New Year 1963. Sheets reproducing 4 #773 were awarded as prizes in the New Year lottery. Value $6.25.

Mt. Ishizuchi A484

1963, Jan. 11 **Unwmk.** ***Perf. 13½***

774 A484 10y multi 28 15

Ishizuchi Quasi-National Park.

Setsubun, Spring Festival, Bean Scattering Ceremony — A485

Map of City, Birds, Ship and Factory — A486

1963, Feb. 3 **Photo.**

775 A485 10y multi 30 15

1963, Feb. 10

776 A486 10y chocolate 18 15

Consolidation of the communities of Moji, Kokura, Wakamatsu, Yawata and Tobata into Kita-Kyushu City.

"Frost Flowers" on Mt. Fugen — A487

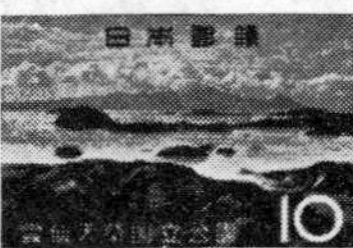

Amakusa Island and Mt. Unzen — A488

1963, Feb. 15

777 A487 5y gray blue 25 15
778 A488 10y carmine rose 25 15
Set value 16

Unzen-Amakusa National Park.

Green Pond, Midorigaike A489

Hakusan Range — A490

Perf. 13½

1963, Mar. 1 **Unwmk.** **Photo.**

779 A489 5y vio brn 20 15
780 A490 10y dk grn 20 15
Set value 16

Hakusan National Park.

Keya-no-Oto Rock — A491

1963, Mar. 15

781 A491 10y multi 22 15

Genkai Quasi-National Park.

Wheat Emblem and Globe — A492

1963, Mar. 21

782 A492 10y dk grn 18 15

FAO "Freedom from Hunger" campaign.

"Girl Reading Letter," Yedo Screen — A493

1963, Apr. 20 ***Perf. 13½***

783 A493 10y multi 65 65

Issued to publicize Stamp Week, 1963.

World Map and Centenary Emblem — A494

1963, May 8

784 A494 10y multi 15 15

Centenary of the International Red Cross.

Globe and Leaf with Symbolic River System — A495

1963, May 15 **Photo.**

785 A495 10y blue 15 15

5th Congress of the Intl. Commission on Irrigation and Drainage.

Ito-dake, Asahi Range — A496

Lake Hibara and Mt. Bandai — A497

1963, May 25 **Unwmk.** ***Perf. 13½***

786 A496 5y green 20 15
787 A497 10y red brn 20 15
Set value 16

Bandai-Asahi National Park.

Lidth's Jay — A498

Designs: No. 789, Rock ptarmigan. No. 790, Eastern turtle dove. No. 791, Japanese white stork. No. 792, Bush warbler. No. 792A, Meadow bunting.

1963-64 ***Perf. 13½***

Design and Inscription

788 A498 10y lt grn 85 55
789 A498 10y blue 24 15
790 A498 10y pale yel 24 15
791 A498 10y grnsh bl ('64) 24 15

792	A498 10y grn ('64)	24	15
792A	A498 10y lt rose brn ('64)	22	15
	Nos. 788-792A (6)	2.03	
	Set value		95

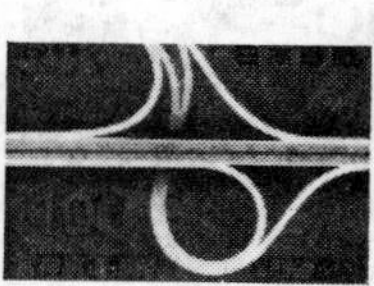

Intersection at Ritto, Shiga — A499

Girl Scout and Flag — A500

1963, July 15 Unwmk. *Perf. 13½*

793	A499 10y bl grn, blk & org	15	15

Opening of the Nagoya-Kobe expressway, linking Nagoya with Kyoto, Osaka and Kobe.

1963, Aug. 1 Photo.

794	A500 10y multi	15	15

Asian Girl Scout and Girl Guides Camp, Togakushi Heights, Nagano, Aug. 1-7.

View of Nashu — A501

Whirlpool at Naruto — A502

1963, Aug. 20

795	A501 5y ol bis	18	15
796	A502 10y dk grn	18	15
	Set value		16

Inland Sea National Park.

Lake Shikaribetsu, Hokkaido A503

Mt. Kurodake from Sounkyo Valley — A504

1963, Sept. 1 Unwmk. *Perf. 13½*

797	A503 5y dp Prus bl	18	15
798	A504 10y rose vio	18	15
	Set value		16

Daisetsuzan National Park.

Parabolic Antenna for Space Communications A505

1963, Sept. 9 Photo.

799	A505 10y multi	15	15

14th General Assembly of the International Scientific Radio Union, Tokyo.

"Great Wave off Kanagawa," by Hokusai A506

1963, Oct. 10 *Perf. 13*

800	A506 40y gray, dk bl & yel	2.50	55

Issued for International Letter Writing Week, Oct. 6-12. Design from Hokusai's "36 Views of Fuji." Printed in sheets of 10 (5x2).

Diver, Pole Vaulter and Relay Runner — A507

Woman Gymnast — A508

1963, Oct. 11 *Perf. 13½*

801	A507 10y bl, ocher, blk & red	15	15

Tokyo Intl. (Pre-Olympic) Sports Meet, Tokyo, Oct. 11-16.

Perf. 13½

1963, Oct. 27 Unwmk. Engr.

Design: #803, Japanese wrestling (sumo).

802	A508 5y slate green	15	15
803	A508 5y brown	15	15
a.	Pair, #802-803	40	
	Set value		15

18th National Athletic Meet, Yamaguchi.

Phoenix Tree and Hachijo Island A509

Toy Dragons of Tottori and Yamanashi A510

1963, Dec. 10 Photo.

804	A509 10y multi	18	15

Izu Islands Quasi-National Park.

1963, Dec. 16

805	A510 5y gold, pink, aqua, indigo & red	15	15
a.	Aqua omitted		

New Year 1964. Sheets containing 4 #805 were awarded as 5th prize in the New Year lottery. Value $3.75.

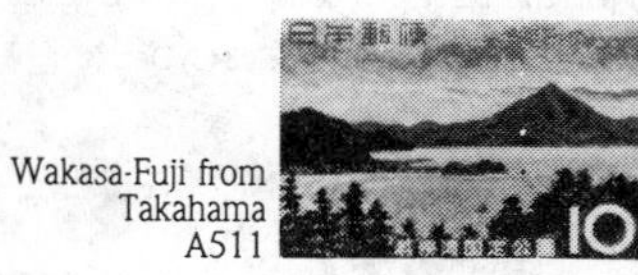

Wakasa-Fuji from Takahama A511

1964, Jan 25 *Perf. 13½*

806	A511 10y multi	18	15

Wakasa Bay Quasi-National Park.

Agave and View from Horikiri Pass — A512

1964, Feb. 20 Unwmk.

807	A512 10y multi	18	15

Nichinan-Kaigan Quasi-National Park.

Uji Bridge — A513

View of Toba — A514

1964, Mar. 15 Photo.

808	A513 5y sepia	15	15
809	A514 10y red lilac	15	15
	Set value		15

Ise-Shima National Park.

Takayama Festival Float and Mt. Norikura — A515

Design: No. 811, Yamaboko floats and Gion Shrine, Kyoto.

1964 Photo. *Perf. 13½*

810	A515 10y lt grn & multi	20	15
811	A515 10y grnsh bl & multi	20	15
	Set value		15

No. 810 issued for the annual Takayama spring and autumn festivals, Takayama City, Gifu Prefecture. No. 811 for the annual Gion festival of Kyoto, July 10-30.

Issue dates: #810, Apr. 15. #811, July 15.

Yadorigi Scene from Genji Monogatari Scroll — A516

1964, Apr. 20

814	A516 10y multi	32	15

Stamp Week, 1964. Sheets of 10 (2x5).

Himeji Castle — A517

1964, June 1 *Perf. 13½*

815	A517 10y dk brn	15	15

Restoration of Himeji Castle.

Sports Type of 1961

1964, June 6 *Perf. 13½*

816	A454 5y Handball	15	15
817	A454 5y Woman on beam	15	15
a.	Pair, #816-817	40	
	Set value	24	20

19th National Athletic Meeting, Niigata.

Cable Cross Section, Map of Pacific Ocean A518

Tokyo Expressway Crossing Nihonbashi A519

1964, June 19

818	A518 10y gray grn, dp mag & yel	15	15

Opening of the transpacific cable.

1964, Aug. 1 Photo.

819	A519 10y grn, sil & blk	15	15

Opening of the Tokyo Expressway.

Coin-like Emblems A520

1964, Sept. 7 Unwmk. *Perf. 13½*

820	A520 10y scar, gold & blk	15	15

Annual general meeting of the Intl. Monetary Fund, Intl. Bank for Reconstruction and Development, Intl. Financial Corporation and the Intl. Development Assoc., Tokyo, Sept. 7-11.

Athletes, Olympic Flame and Rings — A521

National Stadium, Tokyo — A522

Designs: 30y, Nippon Bodokan (fencing hall). 40y, National Gymnasium. 50y, Komazawa Gymnasium.

1964

821	A521 5y multi	15	15
822	A522 10y multi	15	15
823	A522 30y multi	40	15
824	A522 40y multi	40	15
825	A522 50y multi	52	18
a.	Souvenir sheet of 5, #821-825	2.75	3.00
	Nos. 821-825 (5)	1.62	
	Set value		45

18th Olympic Games, Tokyo, Oct. 10-25.

Issue dates: 5y, Sept. 9. Others, Oct. 10.

Foreign postal stationery (stamped envelopes, postal cards and air letter sheets) lies beyond the scope of this Catalogue, which is limited to adhesive postage stamps.

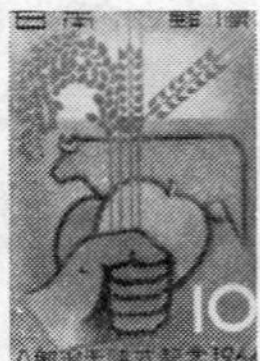

Hand with Grain, Cow and Fruit — A523

Express Train — A524

1964, Sept. 15 *Perf. $13^1/_2$*

826 A523 10y vio brn & gold 15 15

Draining of Hachirogata Lagoon, providing new farmland for the future.

1964, Oct. 1

827 A524 10y bl & blk 20 15

Opening of the new Tokaido railroad line.

Mt. Fuji Seen from Tokaido, by Hokusai A525

1964, Oct. 4 *Perf. 13*

828 A525 40y multi 1.25 35

Issued for International Letter Writing Week, Oct. 4-10. Issued in sheets of 10 (5x2). See Nos. 850, 896, 932, 971, 1016.

"Straw Snake" Mascot — A526

1964, Dec. 15 **Photo.** *Perf. $13^1/_2$*

829 A526 5y crim, blk & yel 15 15

New Year 1965. Sheets containing 4 #829 were awarded as prizes in the New Year lottery (issued Jan. 20, 1965). Value $2.

Mt. Daisen — A527

Paradise Cove, Oki Islands — A528

1965, Jan. 20 **Unwmk.** *Perf. $13^1/_2$*

830 A527 5y dk bl 15 15
831 A528 10y brn org 15 15
Set value 15

Daisen-Oki National Park.

Niseko-Annupuri A529

1965, Feb. 15 **Photo.**

832 A529 10y multi 15 15

Niseko-Shakotan-Otarukaigan Quasi-Natl. Park.

Meteorological Radar Station on Mt. Fuji — A530

1965, Mar. 10 **Photo.** *Perf. $13^1/_2$*

833 A530 10y multi 15 15

Completion of the Meteorological Radar Station on Kengamine Heights of Mt. Fuji.

Kiyotsu Gorge — A531

Lake Nojiri and Mt. Myoko — A532

1965, Mar. 15

834 A531 5y brown 15 15
835 A532 10y magenta 15 15
Set value 15

Jo-Shin-etsu Kogen National Park.

Communications Museum, Tokyo — A533

1965, Mar. 25 **Unwmk.** *Perf. $13^1/_2$*

836 A533 10y green 15 15

Philatelic Exhibition celebrating the completion of the Communications Museum.

"The Prelude" by Shoen Uemura A534

1965, Apr. 20 **Photo.**

837 A534 10y gray & multi 35 15

Issued for Stamp Week, 1965.

Playing Children, Cows and Swan — A535

Stylized Tree and Sun — A536

1965, May 5 **Unwmk.** *Perf. $13^1/_2$*

838 A535 10y pink & multi 15 15

Opening of the National Garden for Children, Tokyo-Yokohama.

1965, May 9

839 A536 10y multi 15 15

Issued to publicize the forestation movement and the forestation ceremony, Tottori Prefecture.

Globe, Old and New Communication Equipment A537

1965, May 17

840 A537 10y brt bl, yel & blk 15 15

Cent. of the ITU.

Crater of Mt. Naka, Kyushu — A538

Five Central Peaks of Aso and Mountain Road — A539

1965, June 15 **Photo.** *Perf. $13^1/_2$*

841 A538 5y car rose 15 15
842 A539 10y dp grn 15 15
Set value 15

Aso National Park.

ICY Emblem and Doves — A540

1965, June 26 **Unwmk.**

843 A540 40y multi 50 15

Intl. Cooperation Year, 1965, and 20th anniv. of the UN.

Horse Chase, Soma A541

Chichibu Festival Scene A542

1965 **Photo.** *Perf. $13x13^1/_2$*

844 A541 10y multi 18 15
845 A542 10y multi 20 15
Set value 20

No. 844 issued to publicize the ancient Soma Nomaoi Festival, Fukushima Prefecture; No. 845, to publicize the festival dedicated to the Chichibu Myoken Shrine (built 1584).

Issue dates: #844, July 16. #845, Dec. 3.

Meiji Maru, Black-tailed Gulls — A543

1965, July 20 *Perf. $13^1/_2$*

846 A543 10y grn, gray, blk & yel 15 15

25th Maritime Day, July 20.

Drop of Blood, Girl's Face and Bloodmobile A544

1965, Sept. 1 *Perf. $13^1/_2$*

847 A544 10y yel, grn, blk & red 15 15

Issued to publicize the national campaign for blood donations, Sept. 1-30.

Tokai Atomic Power Station and Structure of Alpha Uranium — A545

1965, Sept. 21 **Photo.**

848 A545 10y multi 15 15

9th General Conf. of the Intl. Atomic Energy Agency, IAEA, Tokyo, Sept. 21-30.

People and Flag — A546

1965, Oct. 1

849 A546 10y multi 15 15

Tenth national census.

Hokusai Type of 1964

Design: No. 850, "Waters at Misaka" by Hokusai (Mt. Fuji seen across Lake Kawaguchi).

1965, Oct. 6 **Unwmk.** *Perf. 13*

850 A525 40y multi 75 20

Issued for International Letter Writing Week, Oct. 6-12. Issued in sheets of 10 (5x2).

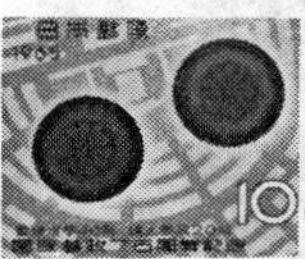

Emblems and Diagram of Seats in National Diet — A547

1965, Oct. 15 *Perf. $13^1/_2$*

851 A547 10y multi 15 15

75th anniv. of natl. suffrage, 40th anniv. of universal suffrage and 20th anniv. of women's suffrage.

Sports Type of 1961

Designs: No. 852, Gymnast on vaulting horse. No. 853, Walking race.

1965, Oct. 24 **Engr.** *Perf. $13^1/_2$*

852 A454 5y red brn 15 15
853 A454 5y yel grn 15 15
Set value 15
a. Pair, #852-853 30 20

20th National Athletic Meeting, Gifu.

Profile and Infant — A548

1965, Oct. 30 **Photo.** *Perf. 13*

854 A548 30y car lake, yel & lt bl 35 15

8th Intl. Conf. of Otorhinolaryngology and the 11th Intl. Conf. of Pediatrics.

Mt. Iwo from Shari Coast, Hokkaido
A549

Rausu Lake and Mt. Rausu
A550

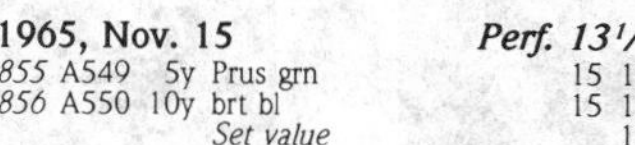

1965, Nov. 15 *Perf. 13½*

855 A549 5y Prus grn 15 15
856 A550 10y brt bl 15 15
Set value 15

Shiretoko National Park.

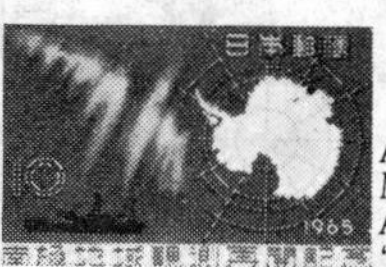

Aurora Australis, Map of Antarctica and "Fuji" — A551

1965, Nov. 20

857 A551 10y bl, yel & dk bl 15 15

Issued to publicize the Antarctic expedition, which left on the observation ship "Fuji," Nov. 20, 1965.

"Secret Horse" Straw Toy, Iwate Prefecture
A552

Telephone Dial and 1890 Switchboard
A553

1965, Dec. 10

858 A552 5y lt bl & multi 15 15

Issued for New Year 1966. Sheets containing four of No. 858 were awarded as prizes in the New Year lottery (issued Jan. 20, 1966). Value $1.75.

1965, Dec. 16

859 A553 10y multi 15 15

Issued to commemorate the 75th anniversary of telephone service in Japan.

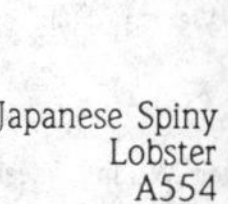

Japanese Spiny Lobster
A554

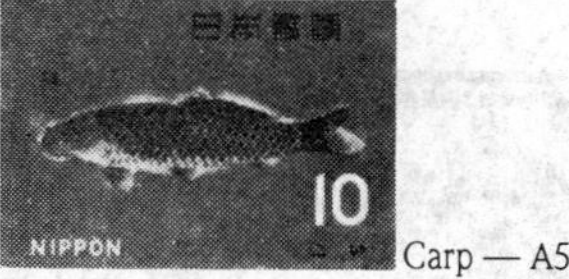

Carp — A555

1966-67 **Photo.** *Perf. 13*

Multicolored; Background in Colors Indicated

860 A554 10y grn & ultra 16 15
861 A555 10y bl grn 16 15
862 A555 10y dk bl *(Bream)* 16 15
863 A555 10y dk ultra *(Skipjack tuna)* 16 15
864 A555 10y bis & dk grn *(3 Ayu)* 16 15
865 A555 15y grnsh bl & yel *(Eel)* 25 15
866 A555 15y brt grn *(Jack mackerel)* 25 15
867 A555 15y brt grn & bl *(Chum salmon)* 25 15
868 A555 15y lt bl grn *(Yellowtail)* ('67) 30 15
869 A555 15y brt grn *(Tiger puffer)* ('67) 32 15

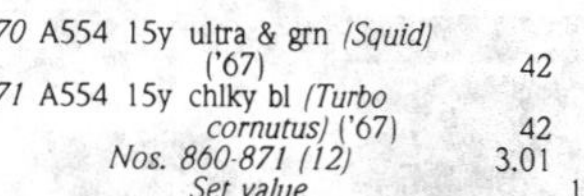

870 A554 15y ultra & grn *(Squid)* ('67) 42 15
871 A554 15y chlky bl *(Turbo cornutus)* ('67) 42 15
Nos. 860-871 (12) 3.01
Set value 1.00

Famous Gardens Issue

Kobuntei Pavilion and Plum Blossoms, Kairakuen Garden, Ibaragi — A556

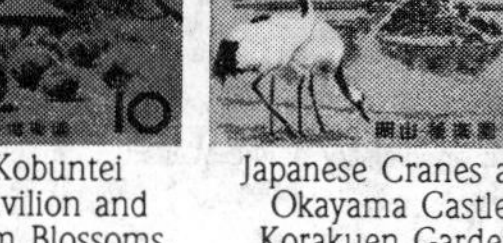

Japanese Cranes and Okayama Castle, Korakuen Garden, Okayama — A557

Kenrokuen Garden in the Snow — A558

1966-67 *Perf. 13½*

872 A556 10y gold, blk & grn 20 15
873 A557 15y bl, blk & mag 22 15
874 A558 15y sil, grn & dk brn 22 15
Set value 24

Dates of issue: 10y, Feb. 25; No. 873, Nov. 3; No. 874, Jan. 25, 1967.

Crater Lake, Zao — A559

1966, Mar. 15

875 A559 10y multi 16 15

Zao Quasi-National Park.

Muroto Cape — A560

Senba Cliffs, Anan Coast — A561

1966, Mar. 22 *Perf. 13½*

876 A560 10y multi 16 15
877 A561 10y multi 16 15
Set value 15

Muroto-Anan Coast Quasi-National Park.

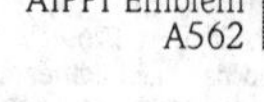

AIPPI Emblem
A562

1966, Apr. 11 *Perf. 13*

878 A562 40y multi 50 15

26th General Assembly of the Intl. Association for the Protection of Industrial Properties, Tokyo, Apr. 11-16.

"Butterflies" by Takeji Fujishima — A563

Photogravure and Engraved

1966, Apr. 20 *Perf. 13½*

879 A563 10y gray & multi 32 15

Stamp Week, 1966. Sheets of 10 (2x5). See No. 907.

Hisoka Maejima — A563a

Goldfish — A564

Chrysanthemums
A565

Wistaria
A565a

Hydrangea
A565b

Golden Hall, Chusonji
A565c

Yomei Gate, Nikko — A565d

Nyoirin Kannon of Chuguji — A565f

Central Hall, Enryakuji Temple — A566

Ancient Clay Horse (Haniwa) — A567

A567a

A567b

A567c

Katsura Palace Garden — A568

A569

Bodhisattva Playing Flute (from Todaiji Lantern) — A570

Designs: 20y, Wistaria. 25y, Hydrangea. 35y, Luminescent squid. 45y, Lysichiton camtschatsense (white flowers). 500y, Deva King statue, South Gate, Todaiji.

1966-69 **Photo.** *Perf. 13*

879A A563a 1y ol bis ('68) 15 15
880 A564 7y ol & dp org 1.00 15
881 A565 15y bl & yel (bl "15") 90 15
b. Bklt. pane of 2 + label ('67) 3.25
c. Bklt. pane of 4 ('67) 2.25
d. Bklt. pane of 4 (2 #881 + 2 #611) ('67) 6.00
e. Imperf., pair 350.00
881A A565a 20y vio & multi ('67) 1.65 1.00
882 A565b 25y grn & lt ultra 50 15
882A A565c 30y dp ultra & gold ('68) 60 15
883 A564 35y bl, gray & blk 85 15
883A A565d 40y bl grn & brn ('68) 60 15
884 A565 45y bl & multi ('67) 60 15
885 A565f 50y dk car rose 10.50 15

Engr.

886 A566 60y sl grn 1.40 15

Photo.

887 A567 65y org brn 13.00 15
887A A567a 75y rose, blk, yel & pur 1.40 15
888 A567b 90y gold & brn 2.50 15
888A A567c 100y ver & blk ('68) 1.65 15

Engr.

889 A568 110y brown 1.90 15
890 A569 120y red 3.25 15
891 A570 200y Prus grn (22x33mm) 6.50 15
891A A570 500y dl pur ('69) 9.50 15
Nos. 879A-891A (19) 58.45
Set value 1.60

Nos. 880-881 were also issued with fluorescent frame on July 18, 1966.
See Nos. 913-916, 918, 926, 1072, 1081.

UNESCO Emblem
A571

Map of Pacific Ocean
A572

1966, July 2 **Photo.** *Perf. 13*

892 A571 15y multi 22 15

20th anniv. of UNESCO.

1966, Aug. 22 *Perf. 13*

893 A572 15y bis brn, dl bl & rose 22 15

11th Pacific Science Congress, Tokyo, Aug. 22-Sept. 10.

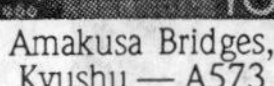

Amakusa Bridges, Kyushu — A573

Emblem of Post Office Life Insurance and Family — A574

1966, Sept. 24 **Photo.** ***Perf. 13***
894 A573 15y multi 22 15

Completion of five bridges linking Misumi Harbor, Kyushu, with Amakusa islands.

1966, Oct. 1
895 A574 15y yel grn & multi 22 15

Post office life insurance service, 50th anniv.

Hokusai Type of 1964

Design: 50y, "Sekiya on the Sumida" (horseback riders and Mt. Fuji) from Hokusai's "36 Views of Fuji."

1966, Oct. 6
896 A525 50y multi 1.00 40

Intl. Letter Writing Week, Oct. 6-12. Printed in sheets of 10 (5x2).

Sharpshooter — A575

Design: No. 898, Hop, skip and jump.

1966, Oct. 23 **Engr.** ***Perf. 13½***
897 A575 7y ultra 15 15
898 A575 7y car rose 15 15
a. Pair, #897-898 40
Set value 15

21st Natl. Athletic Meet, Oita, Oct. 23-28.

National Theater A576

Kabuki Scene — A577

Bunraku Puppet Show — A578

1966, Nov. 1 ***Perf. 13, 13½***
899 A576 15y multi 20 15
900 A577 25y multi 52 20
901 A578 50y multi 52 25
Set value 50

Inauguration of first National Theater in Japan. Nos. 900-901 issued in sheets of 10.

Rice Year Emblem A579

Ittobori Carved Sheep, Nara Prefecture A580

1966, Nov. 21 ***Perf. 13½***
902 A579 15y red, blk & ocher 18 15

FAO International Rice Year.

1966, Dec. 10 **Photo.** ***Perf. 13½***
903 A580 7y bl, gold, blk & pink 15 15

New Year 1967. Sheets containing 4 #903 were awarded as prizes in the New Year lottery. Value $1.25.

International Communications Satellite, Lani Bird 2 — A581

1967, Jan. 27 ***Perf. 13½***
904 A581 15y dk Prus bl & sep 18 15

Inauguration in Japan of Intl. commercial communications service via satellite.

Around the World Air Route and Jet Plane — A582

1967, Mar. 6 **Photo.** ***Perf. 13½***
905 A582 15y multi 18 15

Issued to publicize the inauguration of Japan Air Lines Tokyo-London service via New York, which completes the around the world air route.

Library of Modern Japanese Literature A583

1967, Apr. 11
906 A583 15y grnsh bl, lt & dk brn 18 15

Opening of the Library of Modern Japanese Literature, Komaba Park, Meguro-ku, Tokyo.

Painting Type of 1966

Design: 15y, Lakeside (seated woman), by Seiki (Kiyoteru) Kuroda.

1967, Apr. 20
907 A563 15y multi 60 20

Stamp Week, 1967. Sheets of 10 (2x5).

Kobe Harbor A584

1967, May 8 **Photo.** ***Perf. 13x13½***
908 A584 50y multi 70 18

5th Cong. of the Intl. Association of Ports and Harbors, Tokyo, May 8-13.

Welfare Commissioner's Emblem — A585

Traffic Light, Automobile and Children — A586

1967, May 12 ***Perf. 13½***
909 A585 15y dk brn & gold 18 15

50th anniversary of the Welfare Commissioner System.

1967, May 22 ***Perf. 13x13½***
910 A586 15y emer, red, blk & yel 18 15

Issued to publicize traffic safety.

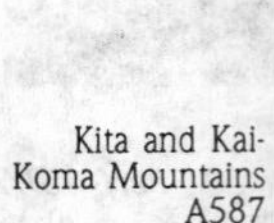

Kita and Kai-Koma Mountains A587

Akaishi and Hijiri Mountains A588

1967, July 10
911 A587 7y Prus bl 15 15
912 A588 15y rose lil 24 15
Set value 15

South Japan Alps National Park.

Types of 1966-69 Redrawn and

A588a

Original 20y No. 881A

Redrawn 20y No. 915

1967-69 **Photo.** ***Perf. 13***
913 A564 7y brt yel grn & dp org 22 15
914 A565 15y bl & yel (white "15") 35 15
a. Pane of 10 (5x2) ('68) 2.75
b. Bklt. panes of 4 with gutter (6 #914 + 2 #611) ('68) 3.25
c. Imperf., pair 225.00
d. Blue shading omitted
e. Bklt. panes of 2 & 4 with gutter ('68) 17.50
915 A565 20y vio & multi ('69) 1.50 15
916 A565f 50y brt car 1.10 15
917 A588a 55y lt bl, grn & blk ('69) 1.25 15
918 A567 65y dp org 1.50 15
Nos. 913-918 (6) 5.92
Set value 30

Issued for use in facer-canceling machines. Issue dates: 7y, Aug. 1; 15y, 50y, July 1; 65y, July 20, 1967; 20y, Apr. 1, 1969; 55y, Sept. 1, 1969.

On No. 913 the background has been lightened and a frame line of shading added at top and right side.

No. 914a is imperf. on four sides.

The two panes of Nos. 914b and 914e are connected by a vertical creased gutter 21mm wide. The left pane of No. 914b consists of 2 No. 914 and 2 No. 611; the right pane, 4 of No. 914. The left pane of 2 of No. 914e includes a 4-line inscription.

On No. 915 the wistaria leaves do not touch frame at left and top. On No. 881A they do.

Coil Stamp

1968, Jan. 9 ***Perf. 13 Horiz.***
926 A565 15y bl & yel (white "15") 80 45

Mitochondria and Protein Model — A589

1967, Aug. 19 **Photo.** ***Perf. 13***
927 A589 15y gray & multi 20 15

7th Intl. Biochemistry Cong., Tokyo, Aug. 19-25.

Gymnast on Horizontal Bar — A590

Universiade Emblem — A591

1967, Aug. 26
928 A590 15y red & multi 24 15
929 A591 50y yel & multi 65 24
Set value 28

World University Games, Universiade 1967, Tokyo, Aug. 26-Sept. 4.

Paper Lantern, ITY Emblem — A592

"Sacred Mt. Fuji" by Taikan Yokoyama — A593

1967, Oct. 2 **Photo.** ***Perf. 13***
930 A592 15y ultra & multi 22 15
931 A593 50y multi 1.75 1.10

International Tourist Year, 1967. No. 931 issued in sheets of 10.

Hokusai Type of 1964

Design: 50y, "Kajikazawa, Koshu" (fisherman and waves) from Hokusai's "36 Views of Fuji."

1967, Oct. 6
932 A525 50y multi 1.75 50

Issued for International Letter Writing Week, Oct. 6-12. Sheets of 10 (5x2).

Athlete, Wild Primrose and Chichibu Mountains — A594

1967, Oct. 22 **Photo.** ***Perf. 13***
933 A594 15y gold & multi 30 15

22nd Natl. Athletic Meet, Saitama, Oct. 22-27.

Miroku Bosatsu, Koryuji Temple, Kyoto — A595

Kudara Kannon, Horyuji Temple, Nara — A596

Golden Hall and Pagoda, Horyuji Temple, Nara — A597

1967, Nov. 1 **Photo.**

934 A595 15y multi 32 24

Engr.

935 A596 15y pale grn, blk & red 32 24

Photo. & Engr.

936 A597 50y multi 2.00 65

National treasures of Asuka Period (6th-7th centuries). No. 936 issued in sheets of 10.

Highway and Congress Emblem A598

1967, Nov. 5 **Photo.** ***Perf. 13***

937 A598 50y multi 65 15

Issued to publicize the 13th World Road Congress, Tokyo, Nov. 5-11.

Mt. Kumotori A599

Lake Chichibu A600

1967, Nov. 27

938 A599 7y olive 15 15
939 A600 15y red lilac 25 15
Set value 15

Chichibu-Tama National Park

Climbing Monkey Toy (Noborizaru), Miyazaki Prefecture — A601

1967, Dec. 11 **Photo.** ***Perf. 13***

940 A601 7y multi 15 15

New Year 1968. Sheets containing 4 #940 were awarded as prizes in the New Year lottery. Value $1.25.

Mt. Sobo — A602

Takachiho Gorge — A603

1967, Dec. 20

941 A602 15y multi 22 15
942 A603 15y multi 22 15
Set value 20

Sobo Katamuki Quasi-National Park.

Girl, Boy and Sakura Maru — A604

1968, Jan. 19 **Photo.** ***Perf. 13***

943 A604 15y ultra, ocher & blk 18 15

Cent. of the Meiji Era, and 1st Japanese Youth Good Will Cruise in celebration of the centenary.

Ashura, Kofukuji Temple, Nara — A605

Gakko Bosatsu, Todaiji Temple, Nara — A606

Kichijo Ten, Yakushiji Temple, Nara — A607

1968, Feb. 1 **Engr.** ***Perf. 13***

944 A605 15y sep & car 28 30

Engr. & Photo.

945 A606 15y dk brn, pale grn & org 50 35

Photo.

946 A607 50y multi 1.50 70

Issued to show National Treasures of the Nara Period (710-784).

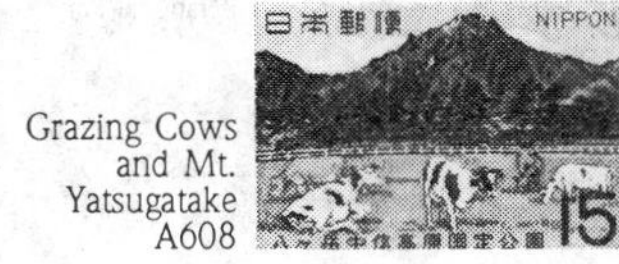

Grazing Cows and Mt. Yatsugatake A608

Mt. Tateshina A609

1968, Mar. 21 **Photo.** ***Perf. 13***

947 A608 15y multi 24 15
948 A609 15y multi 24 15
Set value 24

Yatsugatake-Chushin-Kogen Quasi-Natl. Park.

Young Dancer (Maiko) in Tenjuan Garden, by Bakusen Tsuchida — A610

1968, Apr. 20 **Photo.** ***Perf. 13***

949 A610 15y multi 45 15

Stamp Week, 1968. Sheets of 10 (5x2).

Rishiri Isl. Seen from Rebun Isl. — A611

1968, May 10 **Photo.** ***Perf. 13***

950 A611 15y multi 18 15

Rishiri-Rebun Quasi-National Park.

Gold Lacquer and Mother-of-Pearl Box — A612

"The Origin of Shigisan" Painting from Chogo-sonshiji, Nara — A613

Bodhisattva Samantabhadra A614

1968, June 1 **Engr. & Photo.**

951 A612 15y lt bl & multi 45 20

Photo.

952 A613 15y tan & multi 45 35
953 A614 50y sep & multi 3.25 1.00

Issued to show national treasures of the Heian Period (8-12th centuries).

Memorial Tower and Badge of Hokkaido — A615

1968, June 14

954 A615 15y grn, vio bl, bis & red 22 15

Centenary of development of Hokkaido.

Sunrise over Pacific and Fan Palms — A616

1968, June 26 **Photo.** ***Perf. 13***

955 A616 15y blk, org & red org 22 15

Return of Bonin Islands to Japan by US.

Map of Japan Showing Postal Codes — A617

Two types of inscription:
Type I (enlarged)

あなたの住所にも郵便番号を

"Postal code also on your address"

Type II (enlarged)

あて名に郵便番号を

"Don't omit postal code on the address"

1968, July 1

956 A617 7y yel grn & red (I) 1.40 35
957 A617 7y yel grn & red (II) 1.40 35
a. Pair, #956-957 4.50
958 A617 15y sky bl & car (I) 1.00 15
a. Bklt. panes of 4 with gutter (3 #958 + 3 #959 + 2 #611) 35.00
959 A617 15y sky bl & car (II) 1.00 15
a. Pair, #958-959 3.00

Introduction of the postal code system.

The double booklet pane, No. 958a, comes in two forms, the positions of the Postal Code types being transposed.

Coil Stamps
Perf. 13 Horiz.

959A A617 15y sky bl & car (I) 1.10 65
959B A617 15y sky bl & car (II) 1.10 65
a. Pair, #959A-959B 2.25 1.59

Kiso River — A618

Inuyama Castle — A619

1968, July 20 ***Perf. 13½***

960 A618 15y multi 20 15
961 A619 15y multi 20 15
Set value 15

Hida-Kisogawa Quasi-National Park.

Youth Hostel Emblem, Trees and Sun — A620

1968, Aug. 6 **Photo.** ***Perf. 13***
962 A620 15y cit & multi 22 15

Issued to publicize the 27th International Youth Hostel Congress, Tokyo, Aug. 6-20.

Boys Forming Tournament Emblem — A621

Pitcher and Tournament Flag — A622

1968, Aug. 9
963 A621 15y yel grn, yel, blk & red 30 15
964 A622 15y red, yel & blk 30 15
a. Pair, #963-964 65 30
Set value 24

50th All-Japan High School Baseball Championship Tournament, Koshi-en Baseball Grounds, Aug. 9. Nos. 963-964 printed checkerwise.

Minamoto Yoritomo, Jingoji, Kyoto — A623

Heiji Monogatari Scroll Painting — A624

Red-threaded Armor, Kasuga Shrine, Nara — A625

1968, Sept. 16 **Photo.** ***Perf. 13***
965 A623 15y blk & multi 55 30
966 A624 15y tan & multi 65 35

Photo. & Engr.
967 A625 50y multi 2.00 1.35

National treasures of Kamakura period (1180-1192 to 1333).

Mt. Iwate, seen from Hachimantai A626

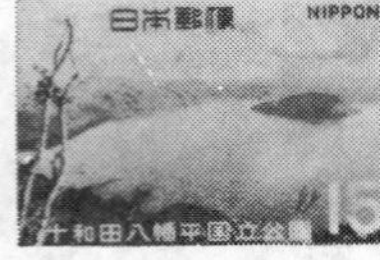

Lake Towada, seen from Mt. Ohanabe A627

1968, Sept. 16 **Photo.**
968 A626 7y red brn 15 15
969 A627 15y green 24 15
Set value 15

Towada-Hachimantai National Park.

Gymnast, Tojimbo Cliff and Narcissus — A628

1968, Oct. 1 **Photo.** ***Perf. 13***
970 A628 15y multi 30 15

23rd National Athletic Meet, Fukui Prefecture, Oct. 1-6.

Hokusai Type of 1964

Design: 50y, "Fujimihara in Owari Province" (cooper working on a barrel) from Hokusai's "36 Views of Fuji."

1968, Oct. 7
971 A525 50y multi 1.25 45

Issued for International Letter Writing Week, Oct. 7-13. Sheets of 10 (5x2).

Centenary Emblem, Sun and First Western Style Warship — A629

Imperial Carriage Arriving in Tokyo (1868), by Tomone Kobori A630

1968, Oct. 23
972 A629 15y vio bl, red, gold & gray 20 15
973 A630 15y multi 24 15
a. Imperf., pair
Set value 15

Meiji Centenary Festival.

Old and New Lighthouses — A631

1968, Nov. 1 **Photo.** ***Perf. 13***
974 A631 15y multi 22 15

Issued to commemorate the centenary of the first western style lighthouse in Japan.

Ryo'o Court Dance and State Hall, Imperial Palace — A632

1968, Nov. 14
975 A632 15y multi 22 15

Completion of the new Imperial Palace.

Mt. Takachiho A633

Mt. Motobu, Yaku Island — A634

1968, Nov. 20
976 A633 7y purple 15 15
977 A634 15y orange 24 15
Set value 15

Kirishima-Yaku National Park.

Carved Toy Cock of Yonezawa, Yamagata Prefecture — A635

Human Rights Flame, Dancing Children and Globe — A636

1968, Dec. 5 **Photo.** ***Perf. 13***
978 A635 7y lt bl & multi 15 15

New Year 1969. Sheets containing 4 #978 were awarded as prizes in the New Year lottery. Value $1.25.

1968, Dec. 10
979 A636 50y org & multi 75 15

International Human Rights Year.

Striped Squirrel A637

Kochomon Cave and Road A638

1968, Dec. 14
980 A637 15y emer & blk 30 15

Issued to promote saving.

1969, Jan. 27 **Photo.**
981 A638 15y multi 30 15

Echizen-Kaga-Kaigan Quasi-National Park.

Silver Pavilion, Jishoji Temple, Kyoto — A639

Pagoda, Anrakuji Temple, Nagano — A640

Winter Landscape by Sesshu — A641

1969, Feb. 10 **Photo.** ***Perf. 13***
982 A639 15y multi 30 15

Photo. & Engr.
983 A640 15y lt grn & multi 30 15

Photo.
984 A641 50y tan, blk & ver 1.50 1.20

Issued to show national treasures of the Muromachi Period (1333-1572).

Mt. Chokai, seen from Tobishima Island — A642

1969, Feb. 25 **Photo.**
985 A642 15y brt bl & multi 22 15

Chokai Quasi-National Park.

Mt. Koya Seen from Jinnogamine A643

Mt. Gomadan and Rhododendron A644

1969, Mar. 25 **Photo.** ***Perf. 13***
986 A643 15y multi 20 15
987 A644 15y multi 20 15
Set value 15

Koya-Ryujin Quasi-National Park.

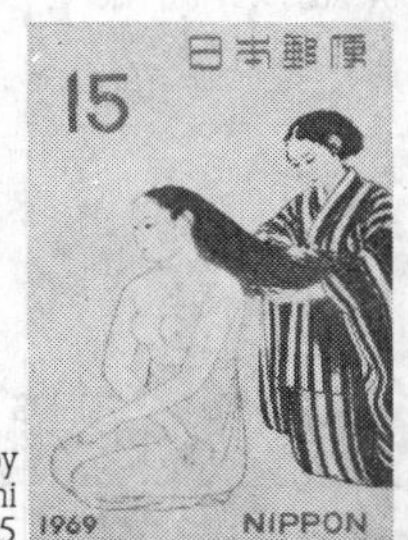

Hair (Kami), by Kokei Kobayashi A645

1969, Apr. 20 **Photo.** ***Perf. 13***
988 A645 15y multi 40 22

Issued for Philatelic Week.

Mother, Son Crossing Street — A646

Tokyo-Nagoya Expressway and Sakawagawa Bridge — A647

1969, May 10 Photo. *Perf. 13*

989 A646 15y lt bl, red & grn 22 15

National traffic safety campaign.

1969, May 26

990 A647 15y multi 22 15

Completion of Tokyo-Nagoya Expressway.

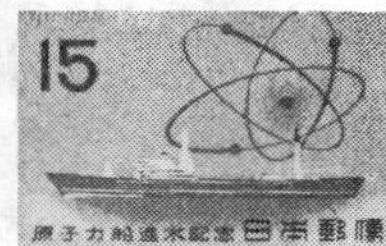

Nuclear Ship Mutsu and Atom Diagram A648

1969, June 12

991 A648 15y gray, blk, pink & bl 22 15

Issued to publicize the launching of the first Japanese nuclear ship, Mutsu.

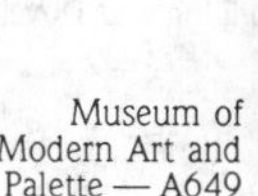

Museum of Modern Art and Palette — A649

1969, June 11 Photo. *Perf. 13½*

992 A649 15y lt bl, brn, yel & blk 22 15

Opening of the new National Museum of Modern Art, Tokyo.

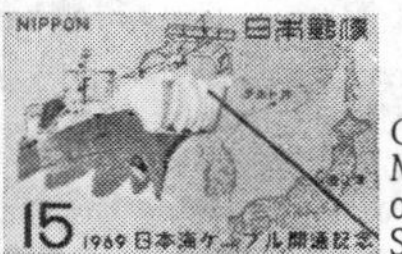

Cable Ship KKD Maru and Map of Japan Sea — A650

1969, June 25

993 A650 15y lt bl, blk & ocher 22 15

Completion of the Japan sea cable between Naoetsu, Japan, and Nakhodka, Russia.

Postcards, Postal Code Symbol — A651

Mailbox, Postal Code Symbol — A652

1969, July 1 Photo. *Perf. 13*

997 A651 7y yel grn & car 40 15

998 A652 15y sky bl & car 40 15

Set value 24

1st anniv. of the postal code system and to promote its use.

Lions Emblem and Rose — A653

1969, July 2

999 A653 15y bl, blk, rose & gold 22 15

Issued to publicize the 52nd Convention of Lions International, Tokyo, July 2-5.

Hotoke-ga-ura on Shimokita Peninsula, Northern Honshu — A654

1969, July 15

1000 A654 15y multi 22 15

Shimokita Hanto Quasi-National Park.

Himeji Castle, Hyogo Prefecture A655

"Pine Forest" (Detail), by Tohaku Hasegawa — A656

"Cypresses," Attributed to Eitoku Kano — A657

1969, July 21 Photo. & Engr.

1001 A655 15y lt bl & multi 28 20

Photo.

1002 A656 15y pale brn & blk 28 20

1003 A657 50y gold & multi 1.25 80

Issued to show national treasures of the Momoyama period (1573-1614). The 50y is in sheets of 10 (2x5); Nos. 1001-1002 in sheets of 20 (5x4).

Harano-fudo Waterfall A658

Mt. Nagisan A659

1969, Aug. 20

1004 A658 15y multi 20 15

1005 A659 15y multi 20 15

Set value 15

Hyobosen-Ushiroyama-Nagisan Quasi-Natl. Park.

Mt. O-akan, Hokkaido A660

Mt. Iwo A661

1969, Aug. 25 Photo. *Perf. 13*

1006 A660 7y bright blue 15 15

1007 A661 15y sepia 20 15

Set value 15

Akan National Park.

Angling, by Taiga Ikeno — A662

The Red Plum, by Korin Ogata — A663

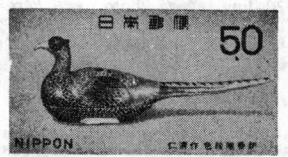

Pheasant-shaped Incense Burner — A664

Design: No. 1010, The White Plum, by Korin Ogata.

1969, Sept. 25 Photo. *Perf. 13x13½*

1008 A662 15y multi 30 15

Perf. 13

1009 A663 15y gold & multi 35 15

1010 A663 15y gold & multi 35 15

a. Pair, #1009-1010 75 25

Photo. & Engr.

1011 A664 50y multi 1.00 35

Set value 58

Natl. treasures, Edo Period (1615-1867).

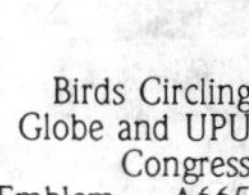

Birds Circling Globe and UPU Congress Emblem — A665

Woman Reading Letter, by Utamaro A666

Designs (UPU Congress Emblem and): 50y, Two Women Reading a Letter, by Harunobu. 60y, Man Reading a Letter (Miyako Dennai), by Sharaku.

1969, Oct. 1 Photo. *Perf. 13*

1012 A665 15y red & multi 22 15

1013 A666 30y multi 55 38

1014 A666 50y multi 65 48

1015 A666 60y multi 95 65

16th Congress of the UPU, Tokyo, Oct. 1-Nov. 16. 15y issued in sheets of 20, others in sheets of 10.

Hokusai Type of 1964

Design: 50y, "Passing through Koshu down to Mishima" from Hokusai's 36 Views of Fuji.

1969, Oct. 7 Photo. *Perf. 13*

1016 A525 50y multi 1.00 55

Issued for International Letter Writing Week Oct. 7-13. Sheets of 10 (5x2).

Rugby Player, Camellia and Oura Catholic Church — A667

1969, Oct. 26

1017 A667 15y lt ultra & multi 22 15

24th National Athletic Meet, Nagasaki, Oct. 26-31.

Cape Kitayama A668

Goishi Coast A669

1969, Nov. 20 Photo. *Perf. 13*

1018 A668 7y gray & dk bl 15 15

1019 A669 15y sal & dk red 24 15

Set value 32 15

Rikuchu Coast National Park.

Worker in Hard Hat — A670

Dog Amulet, Hokkeji, Nara — A671

1969, Nov. 26

1020 A670 15y ultra, blk yel & brn 22 15

50th anniv. of the ILO.

1969, Dec. 10

1021 A671 7y org & multi 15 15

New Year 1970. Sheets containing 4 #1021 were awarded as prizes in the New Year lottery. Value $1.25.

Aso Bay and Tsutsu Women with Horse — A672

1970, Feb. 25 Photo. *Perf. 13*

1022 A672 15y multi 22 15

Iki-Tsushima Quasi-National Park.

The lack of a value for a listed item does not necessarily indicate rarity.

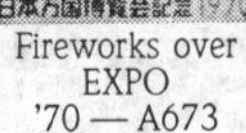

Fireworks over EXPO '70 — A673

Cherry Blossoms Around Globe — A674

Irises, by Korin Ogata (1658-1716) — A675

1970, Mar. 14 **Photo.** ***Perf. 13***

1023	A673	7y red & multi	15	15
1024	A674	15y gold & multi	15	15
1025	A675	50y gold & multi	65	65
a.		Souv. sheet of 3, #1023-1025	1.40	1.40
b.		Bklt. pane of 4 & 3 with gutter	3.00	
		Set value		75

EXPO '70 Intl. Exposition, Senri, Osaka, Mar. 15-Sept. 13.

No. 1025b contains a pane of 4 No. 1023 and a pane with Nos. 1023-1025. A 35mm gutter separates the panes.

Woman with Hand Drum, by Saburosuke Okada — A676

1970, Apr. 20 **Photo.** ***Perf. 13***

1026	A676	15y multi	45	15

Issued for Stamp Week, Apr. 20-26.

Mt. Yoshino — A677

Nachi Waterfall — A678

1970, Apr. 30 **Photo.** ***Perf. 13***

1027	A677	7y gray & pink	15	15
1028	A678	15y pale bl & grn	24	15
		Set value	32	15

Yoshino-Kumano National Park.

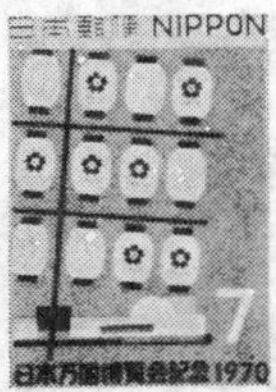

Pole Lanterns at EXPO — A679

View of EXPO Within Globe — A680

Grass in Autumn Wind, by Hoitsu Sakai (1761-1828) — A681

1970, June 15 **Photo.** ***Perf. 13***

1029	A679	7y red & multi	15	15
1030	A680	15y bl & multi	24	15
1031	A681	50y sil & multi	60	15
a.		Souv. sheet of 3, #1029-1031	1.40	
b.		Bklt. panes of 4 & 3 with gutter	3.00	
		Set value		20

EXPO '70, 2nd issue.

No. 1031b contains a pane of 4 No. 1029 and a pane with Nos. 1029-1031. A 35mm gutter separates the panes.

Buildings and Postal Code Symbol — A682

1970, July 1 **Photo.** ***Perf. 13***

1032	A682	7y emer & vio	35	15
1033	A682	15y brt bl & choc	48	15
		Set value		20

Postal code system.

"Maiden at Dojo Temple" A683

Scene from "Sukeroku" A684

"The Subscription List" (Kanjincho) — A685

1970, July 10

1034	A683	15y multi	24	15
1035	A684	15y multi	24	16
1036	A685	50y multi	65	40

Issued to publicize the Kabuki Theater.

Girl Scout — A686

1970, July 26

1037	A686	15y multi	18	15

50th anniversary of Japanese Girl Scouts.

Kinoura Coast and Festival Drum — A687

Tate Mountains Seen from Himi Coast — A688

1970, Aug. 1

1038	A687	15y multi	20	15
1039	A688	15y multi	20	15
		Set value		15

Noto Hanto Quasi-National Park.

Sunflower and UN Emblem — A689

1970, Aug. 17

1040	A689	15y lt bl & multi	22	15

Issued to publicize the 4th United Nations Congress on the Prevention of Crime and the Treatment of Offenders, Kyoto, Aug. 17-26.

Mt. Myogi — A690

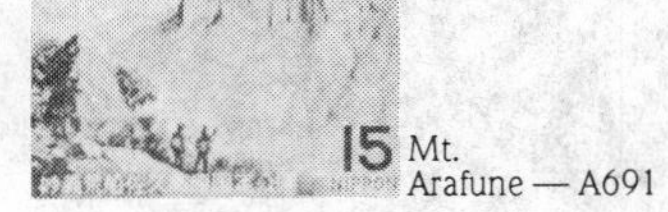

Mt. Arafune — A691

1970, Sept. 11 **Photo.** ***Perf. 13***

1041	A690	15y multi	20	15
1042	A691	15y multi	20	15
		Set value		15

Myogi-Arafune-Sakukogen Quasi-Natl. Park.

G.P.O., Tokyo, by Hiroshige III — A692

Equestrian, Mt. Iwate and Paulownia — A693

1970, Oct. 6

1043	A692	50y multi	70	30

Intl. Letter Writing Week, Oct. 6-12. Sheets of 10 (5x2). Design from wood block series, "Noted Places in Tokyo."

1970, Oct. 10 **Photo.** ***Perf. 13***

1044	A693	15y sil & multi	22	15

25th Natl. Athletic Meet, Morioka, Oct. 10-16.

Hodogaya Stage, by Hiroshige III — A694

Tree and UN Emblem — A695

1970, Oct. 20

1045	A694	15y silver & multi	22	15

Centenary of telegraph service in Japan.

1970, Oct. 24

Design: 50y, UN emblem and Headquarters with flags.

1046	A695	15y ol, ap grn & gold	20	15
1047	A695	50y multi	60	15
		Set value		20

25th anniversary of United Nations.

Vocational Training Competition Emblem A696

Diet Building and Doves A697

1970, Nov. 10 **Photo.** ***Perf. 13***

1048	A696	15y multi	22	15

The 19th International Vocational Training Competition, Chiba City, Nov. 10-19.

1970, Nov. 29

1049	A697	15y multi	22	15

80th anniversary of Japanese Diet.

Wild Boar, Folk Art, Arai City, Niigata Prefecture — A698

1970, Dec. 10

1050	A698	7y multi	15	15

New Year 1971. Sheets containing 4 #1050 were awarded as prizes in the New Year lottery. Value $1.25.

Gen-jo-raku A699

Ko-cho A700

Tai-hei-raku — A701

1971, Apr. 1 Photo. *Perf. 13*

1051 A699 15y multi 24 15
1052 A700 15y multi 24 15
1053 A701 50y multi 65 15
Set value 24

Gagaku, classical Japanese court entertainment.

Woman Voter and Parliament A702

Pines and Maple Leaves A703

1971, Apr. 10 Photo. *Perf. 13*

1054 A702 15y org & multi 22 15

25th anniversary of woman suffrage.

1971, Apr. 18

1055 A703 7y emerald & vio 15 15

National forestation campaign.

Woman of Tokyo, by Kiyokata Kaburagi — A704

1971, Apr. 19

1056 A704 15y gray & multi 32 15

Philatelic Week, Apr. 19-25.

Mailman A705

Mailbox A706

Railroad Post Office — A707

1971, Apr. 20

1057 A705 15y blk & org brn 20 15
1058 A706 15y multi 20 15
1059 A707 15y multi 20 15
Set value 15

Centenary of Japanese postage stamps.

Titmouse A708

Penguins A709

1971, May 10 Photo. *Perf. 13*

1060 A708 15y emer, blk & bis 22 15

25th Bird Week.

1971, June 23 Photo. *Perf. 13*

1061 A709 15y dk bl, yel & grn 25 15

Tenth anniversary of the Antarctic Treaty pledging peaceful uses of and scientific co-operation in Antarctica.

Goto Wakamatsu Seto Region — A710

Kujukushima ("99 Islands"), Kyushu — A711

1971, June 26 Photo. *Perf. 13*

1062 A710 7y dk grn 15 15
1063 A711 15y dp brn 22 15
Set value 15

Saikai National Park.

Arabic Numerals and Postal Code Symbol — A712

1971, July 1

1064 A712 7y emer & red 20 15
1065 A712 15y bl & car 28 15
Set value 22

Promotion for postal code system.

Inscribed "NIPPON"
Types of 1962-67 and

Little Cuckoo — A713

Mute Swan — A714

Sika Deer — A715

Beetle — A716

Pine — A717

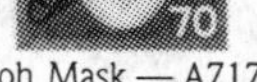

Noh Mask — A717a

Pheasant — A717b

Golden Eagle — A717c

Bronze Phoenix, Uji — A718

Burial Statue of Warrior, Ota — A718a

Buddha, Sculpture, 685 — A718b

Tentoki Sculpture, 11th Century — A718c

Bazara-Taisho, c. 710-794 — A718d

Goddess Kissho — A718e

Designs: 25y, Hydrangea. No. 1076, Wind God Fujin. 120y, Mythical winged woman. 1081, Bodhisattva.

1971-75 Photo. *Perf. 13*

1067 A713 3y emerald 15 15
a. Bklt. pane of 20 ('72) 2.00
1068 A714 5y brt bl 15 15
1069 A715 10y yel grn & sep ('72) 16 15
a. Bklt. pane of 6 (2 #1069, 4 #1071 with gutter btwn.) ('72) 1.40
1070 A716 12y dp brn 16 15
1071 A717 20y grn & sep ('72) 25 15
a. Pane of 10 (5x2) ('72) 2.75
1072 A565 25y emer & lt ultra ('72) 30 15
1074 A717a 70y dp org & blk 95 15
1075 A717b 80y crim & brn 1.25 15
1076 A467 90y org & dk brn 1.40 15
1077 A717c 90y org & brn ('73) 1.40 15
1079 A469 120y dk brn & lt grn ('72) 1.65 15
1080 A718 150y lt & dk grn 1.90 15
1081 A570 200y dp car (18x22mm; '72) 3.00 15
1082 A718a 200y red brn ('74) 3.00 15
1083 A718b 300y dk bl ('74) 3.75 15
1084 A718c 400y car rose ('74) 5.25 15
1085 A718d 500y grn ('74) 6.25 25
1087 A718e 1000y multi ('75) 14.00 1.00
a. Miniature sheet of 1 14.00 9.00
Nos. 1067-1087 (18) 44.97
Set value 2.25

No. 1071a is imperf. on four sides.
See Nos. 1249-1250, 1254, 1631.

Coil Stamp
Perf. 13 Horiz.

1088 A717 20y grn & sep ('72) 42 30

Boy Scout Bugler — A719

Rose and Rings — A720

1971, Aug. 2

1090 A719 15y lt bl & multi 22 15

13th World Boy Scout Jamboree, Asagiri Plain, Aug. 2-10.

1971, Oct. 1

1091 A720 15y ultra & multi 22 15

50th anniv. of Japanese Conciliation System.

Tokyo Horsedrawn Streetcar, by Yoshimura A721

1971, Oct. 6

1092 A721 50y multi 75 30

Intl. Letter Writing Week. Sheets of 10 (5x2).

Emperor's Flag, Chrysanthemums and Phoenix — A722

"Beyond the Sea," by Empress Nagako A723

1971, Oct. 14

1093 A722 15y gold, vio, red & bl 24 15
1094 A723 15y gold, vio, red & bl 24 15
a. Souvenir sheet of 2, #1093-1094, imperf. 85 85
b. Pair, #1093-1094 50 25
Set value 15

European trip of Emperor Hirohito and Empress Nagako, Sept. 28-Oct. 15. No. 1094a has violet map of Asia, Africa and Europe in background.

Tennis, Cape Shiono-misaki, Plum Blossoms — A724

Child's Face and "100" — A725

1971, Oct. 24 Photo. *Perf. 13*

1095 A724 15y org & multi 22 15

26th National Athletic Meet, Wakayama Prefecture, Oct. 24-29.

1971, Oct. 27

1096 A725 15y pink, car & blk 22 15

Centenary of Japanese Family Registration System.

Tiger, by Gaho Hashimoto
A726

Design: No. 1098, Dragon, from "Dragon and Tiger," by Gaho Hashimoto.

1971, Nov. 1 **Engr.** ***Perf. 13***
1097 A726 15y ol & multi 28 15
1098 A726 15y ol & multi 28 15
a. Pair, #1097-1098 75
Set value 15

Centenary of Government Printing Works. Nos. 1097-1098 printed checkerwise.

Mt. Yotei from Lake Toya — A727

Mt. Showa-Shinzan — A728

Treasure Ship — A729

1971, Dec. 6
1099 A727 7y sl grn & yel 15 15
1100 A728 15y pink & vio bl 24 15
Set value 16

Shikotsu-Toya National Park.

1971-72
1101 A729 7y emer, gold & org 15 15
1102 A729 10y lt bl, org & gold 16 15
Set value 16

New Year 1972. Sheets containing 3 #1102 were awarded as prizes in the New Year lottery. Value $1.75.
Issued: 7y, Dec. 10; 10y, Jan. 11, 1972.

Downhill Skiing — A730

Designs (Olympic Rings and): No. 1104, Bobsledding. 50y, Figure skating, pairs.

1972, Feb. 3 **Photo.** ***Perf. 13***
Size: 24x34mm
1103 A730 20y ultra & multi 25 15
1104 A730 20y ultra & multi 25 15
Size: 49x34mm
1105 A730 50y ultra & multi 65 22
a. Souv. sheet of 3, #1103-1105 1.50 1.40
Set value 34

11th Winter Olympic Games, Sapporo, Feb. 3-13. No. 1105a has continuous design extending into margin.

Bunraku, Ningyo Jyoruri Puppet Theater
A731 A732

A733

1972, Mar. 1 **Photo.** ***Perf. 13½***
1106 A731 20y gray & multi 32 15
Perf. 12½x13
1107 A732 20y multi 32 15

Lithographed and Engraved
Perf. 13½x13
1108 A733 50y multi 65 18
Set value 28

Japanese classical entertainment.

Express Train on New Sanyo Line — A734

Taishaku-kyo Valley — A735

Hiba Mountains Seen from Mt. Dogo — A736

1972, Mar. 15 **Photo.** ***Perf. 13***
1109 A734 20y multi 30 15

Centenary of first Japanese railroad.

1972, Mar. 24
1110 A735 20y gray & multi 25 15
1111 A736 20y grn & multi 25 15
Set value 15

Hiba-Dogo-Taishaku Quasi-National Park.

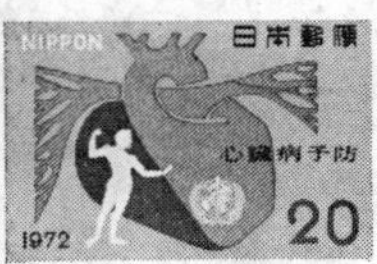
Heart and UN Emblem — A737

1972, Apr. 15
1112 A737 20y gray, red & blk 30 15

"Your heart is your health," World Health Day.

"A Balloon Rising," by Gakuryo Nakamura — A738

1972, Apr. 20
1113 A738 20y vio bl & multi 32 15

Philatelic Week, Apr. 20-26.

Shurei Gate, Okinawa
A739

Camellia
A740

1972, May 15
1114 A739 20y ultra & multi 30 15

Ratification of the Reversion Agreement with US under which the Ryukyu Islands were returned to Japan.

1972, May 20
1115 A740 20y brt grn, vio bl & yel 30 15

National forestation campaign and 23rd Arbor Day, May 21.

Mt. Kurikoma and Kijiyama Kokeshi Doll — A741

Naruko-kyo Gorge and Naruko Kokeshi Doll — A742

1972, June 20 **Photo.** ***Perf. 13***
1116 A741 20y bl & multi 25 15
1117 A742 20y red & multi 25 15
Set value 24

Kurikoma Quasi-National Park.

Envelope, Postal Code Symbol — A743

Mailbox, Postal Code Symbol — A744

1972, July 1
1118 A743 10y bl, blk & gray 22 15
1119 A744 20y emer & org 40 15
Set value 20

Publicity for the postal code system.

Mt. Hodaka — A745

Mt. Tate — A746

1972, Aug. 10 **Photo.** ***Perf. 13***
1120 A745 10y rose & vio 15 15
1121 A746 20y bl & buff 28 15
Set value 20

Chubu Sangaku National Park.

Ghost in "Tamura"
A747

Lady Rokujo in "Lady Hollyhock"
A748

"Hagoromo" (Feather Robe) — A749

1972, Sept. 20 **Engr.**
1122 A747 20y multi 30 15
Photo.
1123 A748 20y multi 30 15
Perf. 13½x13
1124 A749 50y multi 75 15
Set value 30

Noh, classical public entertainment.

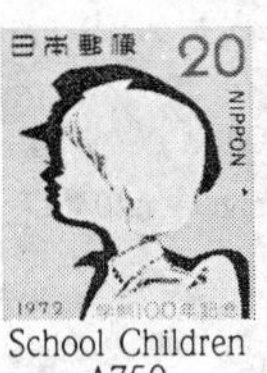
School Children
A750

Eitai Bridge, Tokyo, by Hiroshige III
A751

1972, Oct. 5 **Photo.** ***Perf. 13***
1125 A750 20y lt ultra, vio bl & car 28 15

Centenary of modern education system.

1972, Oct. 9
1126 A751 50y multi 70 15

Intl. Letter Writing Week, Oct. 9-15.

Inauguration of Railway Service, by Hiroshige III — A752

Locomotive, Class C62 — A753

1972, Oct. 14
1127 A752 20y multi 32 15
1128 A753 20y multi 32 15
Set value 15

Centenary of Japanese railroad system.

Kendo (Fencing) and Sakurajima Volcano — A754

1972, Oct. 22
1129 A754 10y yel & multi 18 15

27th National Athletic Meet, Kagoshima Prefecture, Oct. 22-27.

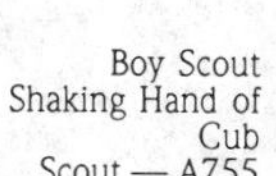

Boy Scout Shaking Hand of Cub Scout — A755

1972, Nov. 4
1130 A755 20y yel & multi 28 15

50th anniversary of the Boy Scouts of Japan.

US Ship, Yokohama Harbor — A756

"Clay Plate with Plum Blossoms" — A757

1972, Nov. 28 **Photo.** ***Perf. 13***
1131 A756 20y multi 30 15

Centenary of Japanese customs. Wood block by Hiroshige III (d. 1896).

1972, Dec. 11
1132 A757 10y bl & multi 15 15

New Year 1973. Art work by Kenzan Ogata (1663-1743). Sheets containing 3 #1132 were awarded as prizes in the New Year lottery. Value $1.75.

Mt. Tsurugi — A758

Oboke Valley — A759

1973, Feb. 20 **Photo.** ***Perf. 13***
1133 A758 20y multi 25 15
1134 A759 20y multi 25 15
Set value 15

Mt. Tsurugi Quasi-National Park.

Mt. Takao — A760

Minoo Falls — A761

1973, Mar. 12 **Photo.** ***Perf. 13***
1135 A760 20y multi 25 15
1136 A761 20y multi 25 15
Set value 15

Meiji Forests Quasi-National Park.

Phoenix Tree — A762

Sumiyoshi Shrine Visitor — A763

1973, Apr. 7 **Photo.** ***Perf. 13***
1137 A762 20y brt grn, yel & dk bl 30 15

National forestation campaign.

1973, Apr. 20
1138 A763 20y multi 30 15

Philatelic Week, Apr. 20-26. Design from painting by Ryusei Kishida (1891-1929) of his daughter, "A Portrait of Reiko Visiting Sumiyoshi Shrine."

Mt. Kamagatake A764

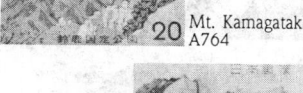

Mt. Haguro — A765

1973, May 25 **Photo.** ***Perf. 13***
1139 A764 20y multi 25 15
1140 A765 20y multi 25 15
Set value 20

Suzuka Quasi-National Park.

Chichijima Beach — A766

Coral Reef on Minami Island — A767

1973, June 26
1141 A766 10y grnsh bl & Prus bl 16 15
1142 A767 20y lil & dk pur 24 15
Set value 15

Ogasawara National Park.
5th anniversary of the return of the Bonin (Ogasawara Islands) to Japan.

Tree, Postal Code Symbol — A768

Mailman, Postal Code Symbol — A769

1973, July 1 **Photo.** ***Perf. 13***
1143 A768 10y brt grn & gold 20 15
1144 A769 20y bl, pur & car 30 15
Set value 20

Postal code system, 5th anniversary.

Sandan Gorge — A770

Mt. Shinnyu — A771

1973, Aug. 28 **Photo.** ***Perf. 13***
1145 A770 20y multi 25 15
1146 A771 20y multi 25 15
Set value 15

Nishi-Chugoku-Sanchi Quasi-National Park.

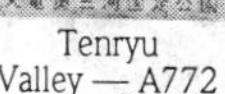

Tenryu Valley — A772

Mt. Horaiji — A773

1973, Sept. 18 **Photo.** ***Perf. 13***
1147 A772 20y lil & multi 25 15
1148 A773 20y vio bl, lt bl & sil 25 15
Set value 15

Tenryu-Okumikawa Quasi-National Park.

Cock, by Jakuchu Ito (1716-1800) — A774

Woman Runner at Start — A775

1973, Oct. 6
1149 A774 50y gold & multi 70 25

International Letter Writing Week, Oct. 7-13. Sheets of 10.

1973, Oct. 14
1150 A775 10y sil & multi 20 15

28th National Athletic Meet, Chiba Prefecture, Oct. 14-19.

Kan Mon Bridge A776

1973, Nov. 14 **Engr.** ***Perf. 13***
1151 A776 20y blk, rose & yel 28 15

Opening of Kan Mon Bridge connecting Honshu and Kyushu.

Old Man and Dog — A777

Designs: No. 1153, Old man and wife pounding rice mortar, which yields gold. No. 1154, Old man sitting in tree and landlord admiring tree.

1973, Nov. 20 **Photo.**
1152 A777 20y multi 24 15
1153 A777 20y multi 24 15
1154 A777 20y multi 24 15
Set value 15

Folk tale "Hanasaka-jiiji" (The Old Man Who Made Trees Bloom).

Bronze Lantern, Muromachi Period — A778

1973, Dec. 10
1155 A778 10y emer, blk & org 20 15

New Year 1974. Sheets containing 3 #1155 were awarded as prizes in the New Year lottery. Value $1.50.

Nijubashi, Tokyo — A779

Imperial Palace, Tokyo — A780

1974, Jan. 26 **Photo.** ***Perf. 13***
1156 A779 20y gold & multi 25 15
1157 A780 20y gold & multi 25 15
a. Souv. sheet of 2, #1156-1157 90 40
Set value 15

50th anniversary of the wedding of Emperor Hirohito and Empress Nagako.

Young Wife — A781

Crane Weaving A782

Cranes in Flight — A783

1974, Feb. 20 **Photo.** ***Perf. 13***
1158 A781 20y multi 25 15
1159 A782 20y multi 25 15
1160 A783 20y multi 25 15
Set value 15

Folk tale "Tsuru-nyobo" (Crane becomes wife of peasant).

The Scott Catalogue value is a retail price, what you could expect to pay for the stamp in a grade of Fine-Very Fine. The value listed is a reference which reflects recent actual dealer selling price.

Marudu Falls — A784

Marine Scene — A785

1974, Mar. 15

1161 A784 20y multi 25 15
1162 A785 20y multi 25 15
Set value 15

Iriomote National Park.

"Finger," by Ito Shinsui — A786

Nambu Red Pine Sapling & Mt. Iwate — A787

1974, Apr. 20 **Photo.** ***Perf. 13***

1163 A786 20y multi 30 15

Philatelic Week, Apr. 20-27.

1974, May 18

1164 A787 20y multi 30 15

National forestation campaign.

Supreme Court Building A788

1974, May 23 **Engr.**

1165 A788 20y redsh brn 30 15

Completion of Supreme Court Building, Tokyo.

Midget Using Bowl as Boat — A789

Designs: No. 1167, Midget fighting demon. No. 1168, Princess and midget changed into prince with magic hammer.

1974, June 10 **Photo.** ***Perf. 13***

1166 A789 20y yel & multi 25 15
1167 A789 20y bis & multi 25 15
1168 A789 20y bis & multi 25 15
Set value 15

Folk tale "Issun Hoschi" (The Story of the Mini-mini Boy).

"Police," by Kunimasa Baido — A790

1974, June 17 ***Perf. 13***

1169 A790 20y multi 30 15

Centenary of the Tokyo Metropolitan Police Department.

Iriomote Wildcat A791

Japanese Otter — A792

Ogasawara Flying Fox — A793

Litho. and Engr.; Photo. and Engr. (Nos. 1172-1173)

1974

1170 A791 20y shown 30 15
1171 A792 20y shown 30 15
1172 A792 20y Black hare 30 15
1173 A793 20y shown 30 15
Set value 40

Nature conservation.
Issue dates: #1170, Mar. 25; #1171, June 25; #1172, Aug. 30; #1173, Nov. 15.

Transfusion Bottle, Globe, Doves — A794

1974, July 1 **Photo.**

1174 A794 20y brt bl & multi 30 15

Intl. Red Cross Blood Donations Year.

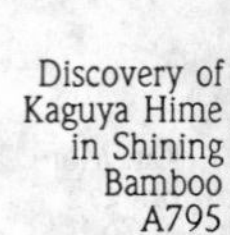

Discovery of Kaguya Hime in Shining Bamboo A795

Kaguya Hime as Grown-up Beauty — A796

Kaguya Hime and Escorts Returning to Moon — A797

1974, July 29 **Photo.** ***Perf. 13***

1175 A795 20y multi 25 15
1176 A796 20y multi 25 15
1177 A797 20y multi 25 15
Set value 15

Folk tale "Kaguya Hime" or "Tale of the Bamboo Cutter."

Rich and Poor Men with Wens — A798

Poor Man Dancing With Spirits A798a

Design: No. 1180, Rich man with two wens, poor man without wen, spirits.

1974, Sept. 9 **Photo.** ***Perf. 13***

1178 A798 20y multi 25 15
1179 A798a 20y multi 25 15
1180 A798 20y multi 25 15
Set value 15

Folk tale "Kobutori Jiisan," or "The Old Man who had his Wen Taken by Spirits."

Goode's Projection and Diet — A799

"Aizen" by Ryushi Kawabata — A800

1974, Oct. 1 **Photo.** ***Perf. 13***

1181 A799 20y multi 25 15
1182 A800 50y multi 60 15
Set value 24

Interparliamentary Union, 61st Meeting, Tokyo, Nov. 2-11.

Pine and Hawk, by Sesson A801

UPU Emblem A802

Tending Cow, Fan by Sotatsu Tawaraya — A803

1974, Oct. 7

1183 A801 50y sep, blk & dk brn 65 15

Intl. Letter Writing Week, Oct. 6-12.

1974, Oct. 9

1184 A802 20y multi 25 15
1185 A803 50y multi 60 15
Set value 15

Centenary of Universal Postal Union.

Soccer Players and Sailboat A804

Various Mushrooms A805

1974, Oct. 20 **Photo.**

1186 A804 10y multi 18 15

29th National Athletic Meet, Ibaraki Prefecture, Oct. 20-25.

1974, Nov. 2

1187 A805 20y multi 30 15

9th International Congress on the Cultivation of Edible Fungi, Japan, Nov. 4-13.

Steam Locomotive Class D51 — A806

Class C57 — A807

Class 8620 — A808

Class C11 — A809

Designs: Steam locomotives.

1974, Nov. 26 **Photo.** ***Perf. 13***

1188 A806 20y shown 40 15
1189 A807 20y shown 40 15
a. Pair, #1188-1189 80 15

1975, Feb. 25

1190 A806 20y Class D52 40 15
1191 A807 20y Class C58 40 15
a. Pair, #1190-1191 80 15

1975, Apr. 3

1192 A808 20y shown 40 15
1193 A809 20y shown 40 15
a. Pair, #1192-1193 80 15

1975, May 15

1194 A806 20y Class 9600 40 15
1195 A807 20y Class C51 40 15
a. Pair, #1194-1195 80 15

1975, June 10 **Photo. & Engr.**

1196 A806 20y Class 7100 40 15
1197 A806 20y Class 150 40 15
a. Pair, #1196-1197 80 15
Nos. 1188-1197 (10) 4.00
Set value 50

Japanese National Railways.

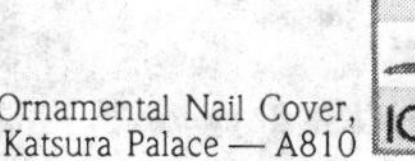
Ornamental Nail Cover, Katsura Palace — A810

1974, Dec. 10
1198 A810 10y bl & multi 20 15

New Year 1975. Sheets containing 3 #1198 were awarded as prizes in the New Year Lottery. Value $1.50.

Short-tailed Albatrosses — A811

Bonin Island Honey-eater A812

Temminck's Robin — A813

Ryukyu-Yamagame Tortoise — A814

Design: No. 1200, Japanese cranes.

1975-76 Photo. & Engr. *Perf. 13*
1199 A811 20y multi 28 15
1200 A811 20y multi 28 15
1201 A812 20y multi 28 15
1202 A813 50y multi 65 15
1203 A814 50y multi 65 15
Nos. 1199-1203 (5) 2.14
Set value 35

Nature conservation.
Issue dates: No. 1199, Jan. 16; No. 1200, Feb. 13; No. 1201, Aug. 8; No. 1202, Feb. 27, 1976; No. 1203, Mar. 25, 1976.

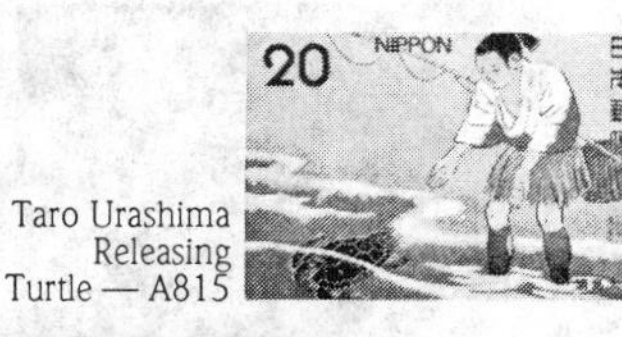
Taro Urashima Releasing Turtle — A815

Palace of the Sea God and Fish — A816

Smoke from Casket Making Taro an Old Man — A817

1975, Jan. 28 Photo. *Perf. 13*
1204 A815 20y multi 25 15
1205 A816 20y multi 25 15
1206 A817 20y multi 25 15
Set value 15

Folk tale "Legend of Taro Urashima."

Kan-mon-sho (Seeing and Hearing), by Shiko Munakata — A818

1975, Mar. 20 Photo. *Perf. 13*
1207 A818 20y brn & multi 30 15

Japan Broadcasting Corp., 50th anniv.

Old Man Feeding Mouse A819

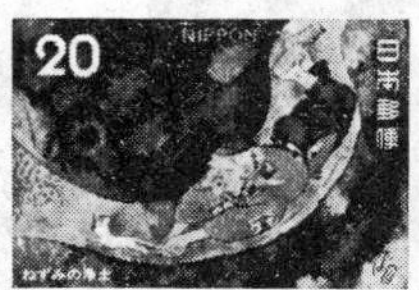
Man Following Mouse Underground A820

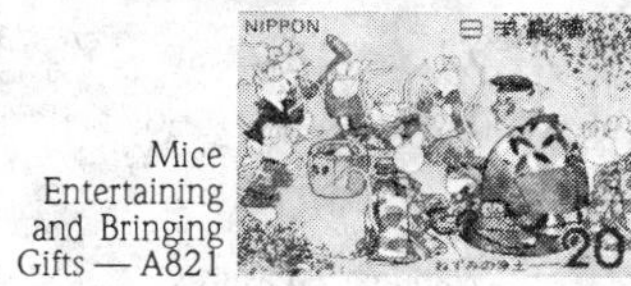
Mice Entertaining and Bringing Gifts — A821

1975, Apr. 15 Photo. *Perf. 13*
1208 A819 20y multi 25 15
1209 A820 20y multi 25 15
1210 A821 20y multi 25 15
Set value 15

Folk tale "Paradise for the Mice."

Matsuura Screen (detail), 16th Century
A822 A823

1975, Apr. 21
1211 A822 20y gold & multi 30 15
1212 A823 20y gold & multi 30 15
a. Pair, #1211-1212 60 15
Set value 15

Philatelic Week, Apr. 21-27.

Oil Derricks, Congress Emblem — A824

1975, May 10 Photo. *Perf. 13*
1213 A824 20y multi 30 15

9th World Petroleum Cong., Tokyo, May 11-16.

Trees and River — A825

IWY Emblem, Sun and Woman — A826

1975, May 24
1214 A825 20y grn & multi 30 15

National forestation campaign.

1975, June 23
1215 A826 20y org & multi 30 15

International Women's Year 1975.

Okinawan Dancer, EXPO 75 Emblem A827

Birds in Flight (Bingata) A828

Aquapolice and Globe — A829

1975, July 19 Photo. *Perf. 13*
1216 A827 20y ultra & multi 25 15
1217 A828 30y bl grn & multi 35 15
1218 A829 50y ultra & multi 60 15
a. Souv. sheet of 3, #1216-1218 1.50 90
Set value 24

Oceanexpo 75, 1st Intl. Ocean Exposition, Okinawa, July 20, 1975-Jan. 18, 1976.

Historic Ship Issue

Kentoshi-sen 7th-9th Centuries A830

Ships: No. 1220, Kenmin-sen, 7th-9th centuries. No. 1221, Goshuin-sen, merchant ship, 16th-17th centuries. No. 1222, Tenchi-maru, state barge, built 1630. No. 1223, Sengoku-bune (cargo ship) and fishing vessel. No. 1224, Shoheimaru, 1852, European-type sailing ship. No. 1225, Taisei-maru, four-mast bark training ship, 1903. No. 1226, Tenyomaru, first Japanese passenger liner, 1907. No. 1227, Asama-maru, passenger liner. No. 1228, Kinai-maru, transpacific freighter and Statue of Liberty. No. 1229, Container ship. No. 1230, Tanker.

1975-76 Engr. *Perf. 13*
1219 A830 20y rose red 28 15
1220 A830 20y sepia 28 15
a. Pair, #1219-1220 56 15
1221 A830 20y lt ol 28 15
1222 A830 20y dk bl 28 15
a. Pair, #1221-1222 56 15
1223 A830 50y vio bl 65 15
1224 A830 50y lilac 65 15
a. Pair, #1223-1224 1.30 25
1225 A830 50y gray 65 15
1226 A830 50y dk brn 65 15
a. Pair, #1225-1226 1.30 25
1227 A830 50y ol grn 65 15
1228 A830 50y ol brn 65 15
a. Pair, #1227-1228 1.30 25
1229 A830 50y ultra 65 15
1230 A830 50y vio bl 65 15
a. Pair, #1229-1230 1.30 25
Nos. 1219-1230 (12) 6.32
Set value 1.00

Printed checkerwise in sheets of 20.
Issued: #1219-1220, Aug. 30; #1221-1222, Sept. 25, 1975; #1223-1224, Mar. 11; #1225-1226, Apr. 12; #1227-1228, June 1, 1976; #1229-1230, Aug. 18, 1976.

Apple and Apple Tree — A831

Peacock, by Korin Ogata — A832

1975, Sept. 17 Photo. *Perf. 13*
1231 A831 20y gray, blk & red 30 15

Centenary of apple cultivation in Japan.

1975, Oct. 6 Photo. *Perf. 13*
1232 A832 50y gold & multi 70 15

Intl. Letter Writing Week, Oct. 6-12.

American Flag and Cherry Blossoms A833

Japanese Flag and Dogwood A834

1975, Oct. 14
1233 A833 20y ultra & multi 25 15
1234 A834 20y grn & multi 25 15
a. Souv. sheet of 2, #1233-1234 90 60
Set value 15

Visit of Emperor Hirohito and Empress Nagako to the United States, Oct. 1-14.

Savings Box and Coins — A835

Weight Lifter — A836

1975, Oct. 24
1235 A835 20y multi 30 15

Japan's Postal Savings System, centenary.

1975, Oct. 25
1236 A836 10y multi 20 15

30th National Athletic Meet, Mie Prefecture, Oct. 26-31.

Papier-mache Dragon, Fukushima Prefecture — A837

1975, Dec. 13 **Photo.** ***Perf. 13***

1237 A837 10y multi	18	15

New Year 1976. Sheets containing 3 #1237 were awarded as prizes in the New Year Lottery. Value $1.50.

Inscribed "NIPPON"
Types of 1951-1974 and

Japanese Narcissus — A841

Noh Mask, Old Man — A843

Guardian Dog, Katori Shrine — A845

Sho-Kannon, Yakushiji Temple — A846

Designs: 50y, Nyoirin Kannon, Chuguji Temple. 150y, Bronze phoenix, Uji. 200y, Clay burial figure of warrior, Ota.

1976-79 **Photo.** ***Perf. 13***

1244 A280 50y emerald	80	15
a. Bklt. panes of 2 & 4 with gutter	5.00	
1245 A841 60y multi	1.00	15
1248 A843 140y lil rose & lil	2.00	15
1249 A718 150y red org & brn	2.00	15
1250 A718a 200y red org	2.75	15
1251 A845 250y blue	3.50	15
1253 A846 350y dk vio brn	4.25	15
Nos. 1244-1253 (7)	16.30	
Set value		50

Coil Stamps
Perf. 13 Horiz.

1254 A715 10y yel grn & sep ('79)	20	15
1256 A280 50y emerald	1.25	15
1257 A468 100y ver & blk ('79)	1.50	30
Set value		50

See No. 1635.

Hikone Folding Screen (detail), 17th Century
A850 A851

1976, Apr. 20 **Photo.** ***Perf. 13***

1258 A850 50y gold & multi	75	15
1259 A851 50y gold & multi	75	15
a. Pair, #1258-1259	1.75	
Set value		20

Philatelic Week, Apr. 20-26.

Plum Blossoms, Cedars, Mt. Tsukuba — A852

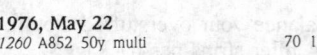

1976, May 22

1260 A852 50y multi	70	15

National forestation campaign.

Green Tree Frog — A853

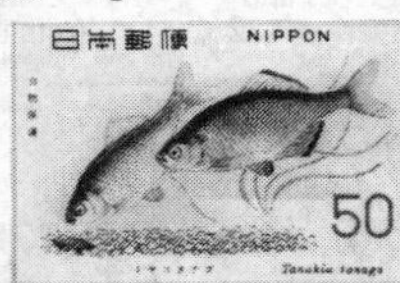

Bitterlings A854

Sticklebacks A855

1976 **Photo. & Engr.** ***Perf. 13***

1261 A853 50y multi	60	15
1262 A854 50y multi	60	15
1263 A855 50y multi	60	15
Set value		30

Nature conservation.
Issue dates: No. 1261, July 20; No. 1262, Aug. 26; No. 1263, Sept. 16.

Crows, by Yosa Buson — A856

Gymnasts and Stadium — A857

1976, Oct. 6 **Photo.** ***Perf. 13***

1264 A856 100y gray, blk & buff	1.25	20

Intl. Letter Writing Week, Oct. 6-12.

1976, Oct. 23 **Photo.** ***Perf. 13***

1265 A857 20y multi	30	15

31st National Athletic Meet, Saga Prefecture, Oct. 24-29.

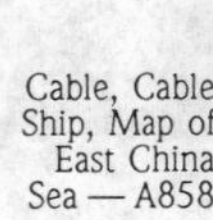

Cable, Cable Ship, Map of East China Sea — A858

1976, Oct. 25

1266 A858 50y bl, blk & sil	65	15

Opening of Sino-Japanese cable between Shanghai and Reihoku-cho, Kumamoto Prefecture.

Classical Court Dance A859

Imperial Coach A860

1976, Nov. 10 **Photo.** ***Perf. 13***

1267 A859 50y multi	65	15
1268 A860 50y multi	65	15
a. Souv. sheet of 2, #1267-1268	1.40	80
Set value		20

Emperor Hirohito's accession to the throne, 50th anniversary.

Kindergarten Class — A861

1976, Nov. 16

1269 A861 50y multi	60	15

Centenary of first Kindergarten in Japan.

Healthy Family A862

Bamboo Toy Snake A863

1976, Nov. 24

1270 A862 50y multi	60	15

Natl. Health Insurance, 50th anniv.

1976, Dec. 1 **Photo.** ***Perf. 13***

1271 A863 20y multi	30	15

New Year 1977. Sheets containing 2 #1271 were awarded as prizes in the New Year lottery. Value $1.65.

National Treasures

East Pagoda, Yakushiji Temple, c. 730 — A864

Deva King in Armor Holding Spear, Nara Period — A865

1976, Dec. 9 **Photo.** ***Perf. 13***

1272 A864 50y multi	60	15

Engr.

1273 A865 100y grn & multi	1.25	20

Golden Pavilion, Toshodai-ji Temple, 8th Century — A866

Praying Women, from Heike Nokyo Sutra, 12th Century — A867

Photogravure and Engraved
1977, Jan. 20 ***Perf. 13***

1274 A866 50y multi	65	15

Photo.

1275 A867 100y multi	1.40	20

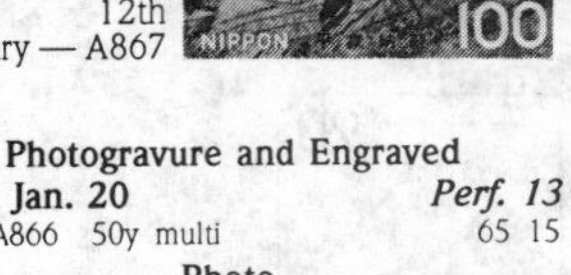

Comic Picture Scroll, Attributed to Toba Sojo Kakuyu (1053-1140) — A868

Saint on Cloud, 11th Century Wood Carving, Byodoin Temple A869

1977, Mar. 25 **Photo.** ***Perf. 13***

1276 A868 50y multi	65	15

Engr.

1277 A869 100y multi	1.40	20

Noblemen on Way to Court, from Picture Scroll, Heian Period — A870

Statue of Seitaka-doji, Messenger, Kamakura Period — A871

1977, June 27 **Photo.** ***Perf. 13***

1278 A870 50y multi	65	15

Engr.

1279 A871 100y multi	1.40	20

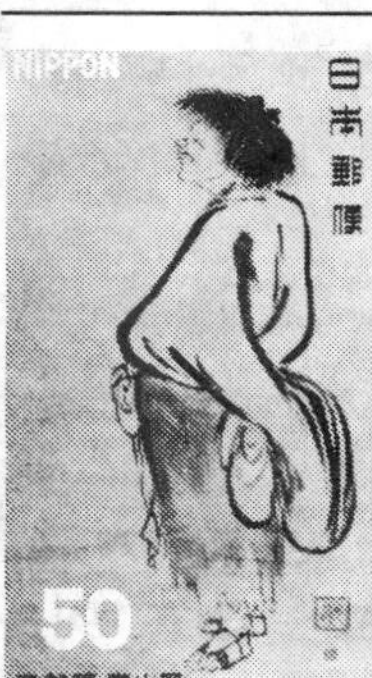
The Recluse Han Shan, 14th Century Painting — A872

Tower, Matsumoto Castle, 16th Century — A873

1977, Aug. 25 Photo. *Perf. 13*
1280 A872 50y multi 65 15

Photogravure and Engraved
1281 A873 100y blk & multi 1.40 20

Pine and Flowers, Chishakuin Temple, Kyoto, 1591 — A874

Main Hall, Kiyomizu Temple, 1633 — A875

1977, Nov. 16 Photo. *Perf. 13*
1282 A874 50y multi 65 15

Engr.
1283 A875 100y multi 1.40 20

Scene from Tale of Genji, by Sotatsu Tawaraya — A876

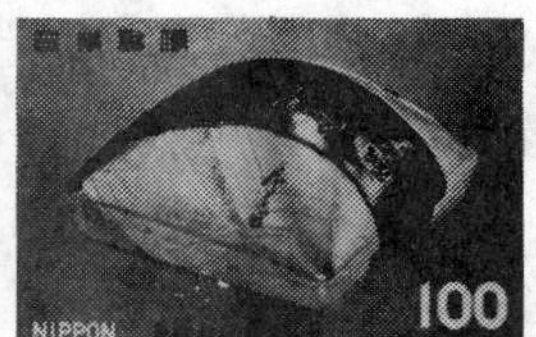
Inkstone Case, by Koetsu Honami — A877

1978, Jan. 26 Photo. *Perf. 13*
1284 A876 50y multi 65 15

Photogravure and Engraved
1285 A877 100y blk & multi 1.40 25

Family Enjoying Cool Evening, by Morikage Kusumi — A878

Yomeimon, Toshogu Shrine, 1636 — A879

1978, Mar. 3 Photo. *Perf. 13*
1286 A878 50y gray & multi 65 15

Photogravure and Engraved
1287 A879 100y multi 1.40 25

Horseshoe Crabs — A884

Graphium Doson Albidum — A885

Firefly — A886

Cicada — A887

Dragonfly — A888

1977 Photo. *Perf. 13*
1292 A884 50y multi 60 15

Photogravure and Engraved
1293 A885 50y multi 60 15
1294 A886 50y multi 60 15
1295 A887 50y multi 60 15

Photo.
1296 A888 50y multi 60 15
Nos. 1292-1296 (5) 3.00
Set value 50

Issue dates: No. 1292, Feb. 18; No. 1293, May 18; No. 1294, July 22; No. 1295, Aug. 15; No. 1296, Sept. 14.

Figure Skating — A889

Figure Skating Pair — A890

1977, Mar. 1
1297 A889 50y sil & multi 65 15
1298 A890 50y sil & multi 65 15
Set value 20

World Figure Skating Championships, National Yoyogi Stadium, March 1-6.

Sun Shining on Forest — A891

1977, Apr. 16 Photo. *Perf. 13*
1299 A891 50y grn & multi 65 15

National forestation campaign.

Weavers and Dyers (Detail from Folding Screen)
A892 A893

1977, Apr. 20
1300 A892 50y gold & multi 65 15
1301 A893 50y gold & multi 65 15
a. Pair, #1300-1301 1.50
Set value 20

Philatelic Week, Apr. 20-26.

Nurses — A894

1977, May 30 Photo. *Perf. 13*
1302 A894 50y multi 65 15

16th Quadrennial Congress of the Intl. Council of Nurses, Tokyo, May 30-June 3.

Fast Breeder Reactor, Central Part — A895

1977, June 6
1303 A895 50y multi 65 15

Experimental fast breeder reactor "Joyo," which began operating Apr. 24, 1977.

Workers and Safety Emblems A896

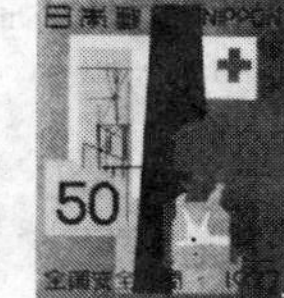
Work on High-rise Buildings A897

Cargo Unloading A898

Machinery Work A899

1977, July 1
1304 A896 50y multi 70 15
1305 A897 50y multi 70 15
1306 A898 50y multi 70 15
1307 A899 50y multi 70 15
a. Strip of 4, #1304-1307 3.00
Set value 40

National Safety Week, July 1-July 7.

Carrier Pigeons, Mail Box, UPU Emblem — A900

Design: 100y, UPU emblem, Postal Service flag of Meiji era, world map.

1977, June 20 Photo. *Perf. 13*
1308 A900 50y multi 60 15
1309 A900 100y multi 1.25 20
a. Souv. sheet of 2, #1308-1309 2.00 1.00

Cent. of Japan's admission to the UPU.

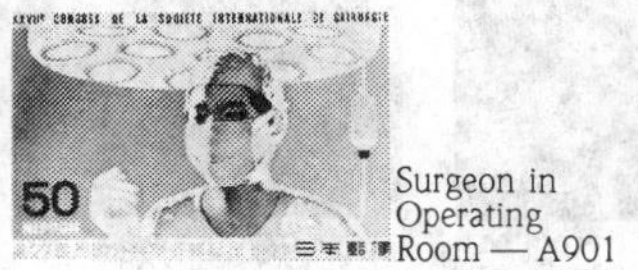
Surgeon in Operating Room — A901

1977, Sept. 3 Photo. *Perf. 13*
1310 A901 50y multi 65 15

27th Cong. of the Intl. Surgeon's Society on the 75th anniv. of its founding, Kyoto, Sept. 3-8.

Child Using Telephone, Map of New Cable Route — A902

1977, Aug. 26
1311 A902 50y multi 65 15

Inauguration of underwater telephone cable linking Okinawa, Luzon and Hong Kong.

Early Speaker, Waves and Telegraph Key — A903

1977, Sept. 24 Photo. *Perf. 13*
1312 A903 50y multi 65 15

50th anniversary of amateur radio in Japan.

Bicyclist, Mt. Iwaki and Iwaki River — A904

Flowers and Ducks, Attributed to Hasegawa Tohaku — A905

1977, Oct. 1

1313 A904 20y multi 30 15

32nd National Athletic Meet, Aomori Prefecture, Oct. 2-7.

1977, Oct. 6

1314 A905 100y multi 1.40 20

Intl. Letter Writing Week, Oct. 6-12.

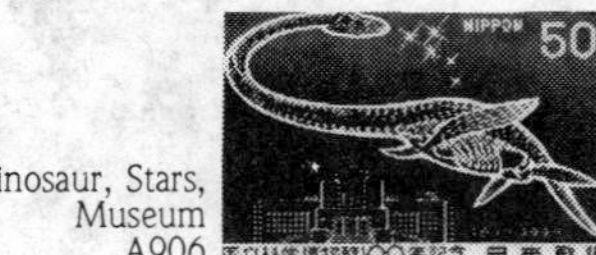

Dinosaur, Stars, Museum A906

1977, Nov. 2 Photo. *Perf. 13*

1315 A906 50y multi 65 15

Centenary of National Science Museum.

Decorated Horse, Fushimi Toy — A907

Tokyo Subway, 1927 — A908

1977, Dec. 1 Photo. *Perf. 13*

1316 A907 20y multi 30 15

New Year 1978. Sheets containing 2 #1316 were awarded as prizes in the New Year lottery. Value $1.50.

1977, Dec. 6

1317 A908 50y shown 65 15
1318 A908 50y Subway, 1977 65 15
a. Pair, #1317-1318 1.50
Set value 20

Tokyo Subway, 50th anniversary.

Primrose — A909

Pinguicula Ramosa — A910

Dicentra — A911

1978 Photo. & Engr. *Perf. 13*

1319 A909 50y multi 65 15
1320 A910 50y multi 65 15
1321 A911 50y multi 65 15
Set value 36

Nature protection.
Issue dates: No. 1319, Apr. 12. No. 1320, June 8. No. 1321, July 25.

Kanbun Bijinzu Folding Screen, Edo Period
A912 A913

1978, Apr. 20 Photo. *Perf. 13*

1322 A912 50y multi 65 15
1323 A913 50y multi 65 15
a. Pair, #1322-1323 1.50
Set value 24

Philatelic Week, Apr. 16-22.

Rotary Emblem, Mt. Fuji A914

Congress Emblem, by Taro Okamoto A915

1978, May 13 Photo. *Perf. 13*

1324 A914 50y multi 65 15

69th Rotary International Convention, Tokyo, May 14-18.

1978, May 15

1325 A915 50y multi 65 15

23rd International Ophthalmological Congress, Kyoto, May 14-20.

Narita International Airport, Tokyo — A916

1978, May 20

1326 A916 50y multi 65 15

Opening of Tokyo International Airport.

Rainbow, Japanese Cedars, Cape Ashizuri — A917

Lion, by Sotatsu Tawaraya, Lions Emblem — A918

1978, May 20

1327 A917 50y multi 65 15

National forestation campaign.

1978, June 21 Photo. *Perf. 13*

1328 A918 50y multi 65 15

61st Lions International Convention, Tokyo, June 21-24.

Sumo Print Issues

Grand Champion Hidenoyama with Sword Bearer and Herald, by Kunisada I (Toyokuni III)
A919 A920

Ekoin Drum Tower, Ryogoku, by Hiroshige — A921

Photogravure and Engraved

1978, July 1 *Perf. 13*

1329 A919 50y multi 70 15
1330 A920 50y multi 70 15
a. Pair, #1329-1330 1.40 30

Photo.

1331 A921 50y multi 70 15
Set value 36

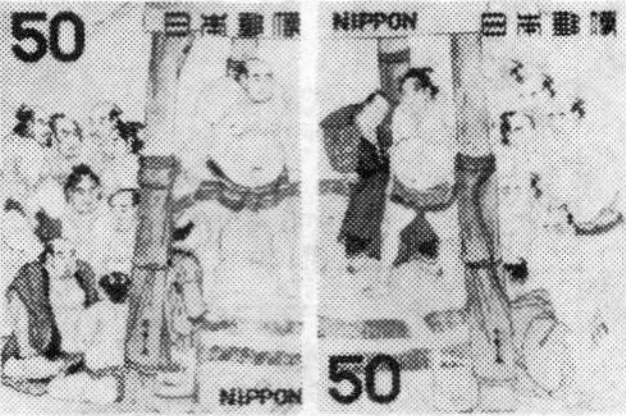

Champions Tanikaze and Onogawa in Ring-entry Ceremony, 1782, by Shunsho
A922 A923

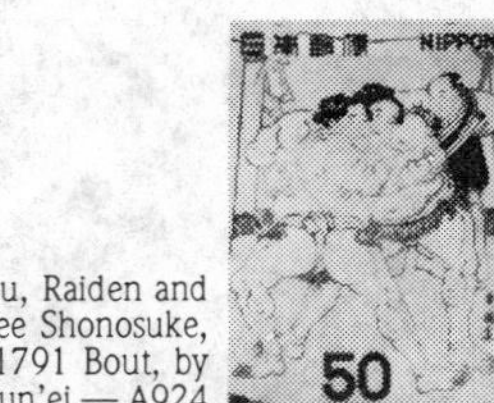

Jimmaku, Raiden and Referee Shonosuke, 1791 Bout, by Shun'ei — A924

Photogravure and Engraved

1978, Sept. 9 *Perf. 13*

1332 A922 50y multi 70 15
1333 A923 50y multi 70 15
a. Pair, #1332-1333 1.40 30
1334 A924 50y multi 70 15
Set value 36

Referee Shonosuke and Champion Onomatsu, by Kunisada I
A925 A926

Children's Sumo Play, by Utamaro — A927

1978, Nov. 11 *Perf. 13*

1335 A925 50y multi 70 15
1336 A926 50y multi 70 15
a. Pair, #1335-1336 1.40 30
1337 A927 50y multi 70 15
Set value 36

Wrestlers on Ryogoku Bridge, by Kunisada I
A928 A929

Bow-receiving Ceremony at Tournament, by Kunisada II — A930

1979, Jan. 13 *Perf. 13*

1338 A928 50y multi 70 15
1339 A929 50y multi 70 15
a. Pair, #1338-1339 1.40 30
1340 A930 50y multi 70 15
Set value 36

Takekuma and Iwamigata (Hidenoyama) Wrestling, by Kuniyoshi
A931 A932

Daidozan (Great Child Mountain) in Ring-entry Ceremony, by Sharaku — A933

1979, Mar. 10 *Perf. 13*

1341 A931 50y multi 70 15
1342 A932 50y multi 70 15
a. Pair, #1341-1342 1.40 30
1343 A933 50y multi 70 15
Set value 36

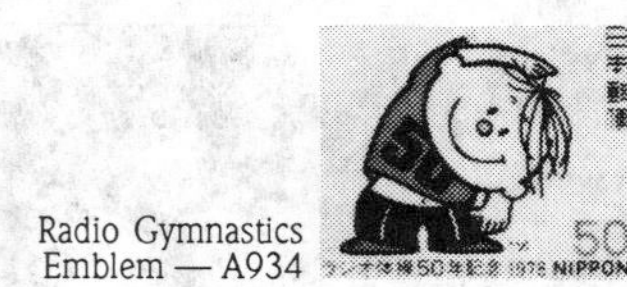

Radio Gymnastics Emblem — A934

1978, Aug. 1 **Photo.** *Perf. 13*
1344 A934 50y multi 65 15

Radio gymnastics program exercises, 50th anniversary.

Chamber of Commerce and Industry A935

1978, Aug. 28 **Photo.** *Perf. 13*
1345 A935 50y multi 65 15

Tokyo Chamber of Commerce, centenary.

Symbolic Sculptures, Tokyo Stock Exchange — A936

Flowering Plum with Pheasant, from Screen, Tenkyuin Temple — A937

1978, Sept. 14 **Engr.** *Perf. 13*
1346 A936 50y lil, grn & brn 65 15

Centenary of the Tokyo and Osaka Stock Exchanges.

1978, Oct. 6 **Photo.** *Perf. 13*
1347 A937 100y multi 1.40 25

Intl. Letter Writing Week, Oct. 6-12.

Softball and Mt. Yarigatake A938

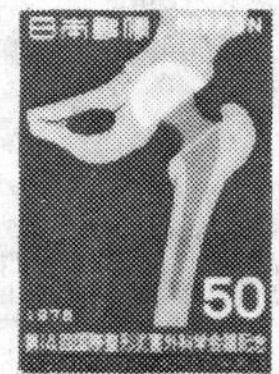

Artificial Hip, Orthopedists' Emblem A939

1978, Oct. 14
1348 A938 20y multi 30 15

33rd National Athletic Meet, Nagano Prefecture, Oct. 15-20.

1978, Oct. 16
1349 A939 50y multi 65 15

14th World Cong. of Intl. Soc. of Orthopedic Surgeons (50th anniv.), Kyoto, Oct. 15-20.

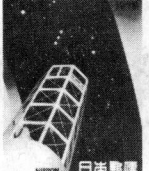

Telescope and Stars — A940

Sheep Bell, Nakayama Toy — A941

1978, Dec. 1 **Photo.**
1350 A940 50y multi 65 15

Tokyo Astronomical Observatory, cent.

1978, Dec. 4
1351 A941 20y multi 30 15

New Year 1979. Sheets containing 2 #1351 were awarded as prizes in the New Year Lottery. Value $1.50.

Family, Human Rights Emblem — A942

Hands Shielding Children — A943

1978, Dec. 4
1352 A942 50y multi 65 15

Human Rights Week, Dec. 4-10.

1979, Feb. 16 **Photo.** *Perf. 13*
1353 A943 50y multi 65 15

Education of the handicapped, centenary.

Telephone Dials — A944

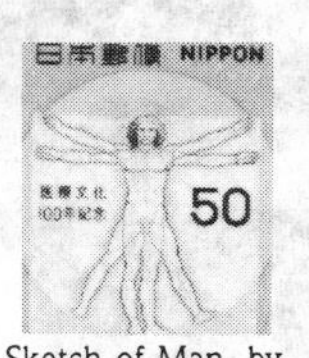

Sketch of Man, by Leonardo da Vinci — A945

1979, Mar. 14 **Photo.** *Perf. 13*
1354 A944 50y multi 65 15

Completion of nation-wide telephone automatization.

Photogravure and Engraved

1979, Apr. 7 *Perf. 13*
1355 A945 50y multi 65 15

Centenary of, promulgation of State Medical Act, initiating modern medicine.

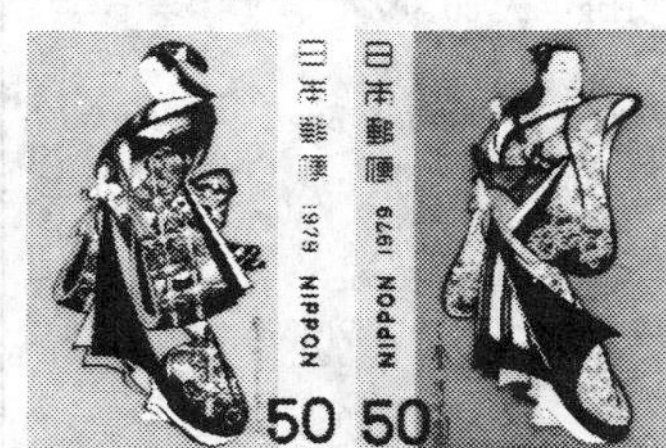

Standing Beauties, Middle Edo Period A946 A947

1979, Apr. 20 **Photo.**
1356 A946 50y multi 65 15
1357 A947 50y multi 65 15
a. Pair, #1356-1357 1.50
Set value 24

Philatelic Week, Apr. 16-22.

Mt. Horaiji and Maple — A948

1979, May 26 **Photo.** *Perf. 13*
1358 A948 50y multi 65 15

National forestation campaign.

Modern Japanese Art Issue

Merciful Mother Goddess, by Kano Hogai — A949

Sea God's Princess, by Aoki Shigeru — A950

1979, May 30 **Photo.** *Perf. 13*
1359 A949 50y multi 70 15
1360 A950 50y multi 70 15
Set value 24

Fire Dance, by Gyoshu Hayami — A951

Leaning Figure, by Tetsugoro Yorozu — A952

1979, June 25 **Photo.** *Perf. 13*
1361 A951 50y red & multi 65 15

Photogravure and Engraved

1362 A952 50y red & multi 65 15
Set value 24

The Black Cat, by Shunso Hishida — A953

Kinyo, by Sotaro Yasui — A954

1979, Sept. 21 **Photo.** *Perf. 13*
1363 A953 50y multi 65 15
1364 A954 50y multi 65 15
Set value 24

Nude, by Kagaku Murakami — A955

Harvest, by Asai Chu — A956

Photogravure and Engraved

1979, Nov. 22 *Perf. 13*
1365 A955 50y multi 65 15
1366 A956 50y multi 65 15
Set value 24

Salmon — A956a

Hall of the Supreme Buddha — A956b

Photogravure and Engraved

1980, Feb. 22 *Perf. 13½*
1367 A956a 50y multi 65 15

Photo.

1368 A956b 50y multi 65 15
Set value 24

Quarantine Officers, Ships, Plane, Microscope A957

1979, July 14 **Photo.**
1369 A957 50y multi 65 15

Centenary of Japanese Quarantine system.

Girl Mailing Letter A958

Hakata Doll with Letter-paper Roll A959

1979, July 23
1370 A958 20y multi 32 15
1371 A959 50y multi 65 15
Set value 17

Letter Writing Day.

Pitcher, Baseball with Black Lion Emblem — A960

1979, July 27

1372 A960 50y multi	65	15

50th National Inter-city Amateur Baseball Tournament, Tokyo, August.

Girl Floating in Space — A961

Design: No. 1374, Boy floating in space.

1979, Aug. 1

1373 A961 50y mag & multi	65	15
1374 A961 50y bl & multi	65	15
a. Souv. sheet of 2, #1373-1374	1.50	
Set value		24

International Year of the Child.

Japanese Song Issue

Moon over Castle, by Rentaro Taki — A962

Evening Glow, by Shin Kusakawa — A963

Maple Leaves, by Teiichi Okano — A964

The Birthplace, by Teiichi Okano — A965

Winter Landscape A966

Mt. Fuji — A967

Spring Brook — A968

Cherry Blossoms A969

1979, Aug. 24 **Photo. & Engr.**

1375 A962 50y multi	65	15
1376 A963 50y multi	65	15
Set value		24

1979, Nov. 26

1377 A964 50y multi	65	15
1378 A965 50y multi	65	15
Set value		24

1980, Jan. 28 ***Perf. 13***

1379 A966 50y multi	65	15
1380 A967 50y multi	65	15
Set value		24

1980, Mar. 21 ***Perf. 13***

1381 A968 50y multi	65	15
1382 A969 50y multi	65	15
Set value		24

Great Owl, by Okyo Maruyama — A970

1979, Oct. 8 **Photo.** ***Perf. 13***

1383 A970 100y multi	1.25	24

Intl. Letter Writing Week, Oct. 8-14.

Runner — A971

"ITU," Globe — A972

1979, Oct. 13

1384 A971 20y multi	32	15

34th National Athletic Meet, Miyazaki, Oct. 4-19.

1979, Oct. 13 **Litho.** ***Perf. 13½***

1385 A972 50y multi	65	15

Admission to ITU, cent.

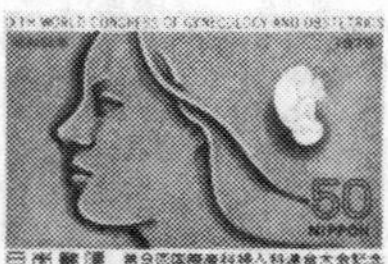

Woman and Fetus — A973

1979, Nov. 12 **Photo.**

1386 A973 50y multi	65	15

9th World Congress of Gynecology and Obstetrics, Tokyo, Oct. 25-31.

> ***Buying Sets***
> *Frequently it is less expensive to purchase complete sets rather than the individual stamps that make up the set. "Set Values" are provided for many such sets.*

Happy Monkeys, Osaka Toy — A974

Government Auditing Centenary — A975

1979, Dec. 1 **Photo.** ***Perf. 13x13½***

1387 A974 20y multi	30	15

New Year 1980. Sheets of 2 #1387 were New Year Lottery prizes. Value $1.40.

1980, Mar. 5 **Photo.** ***Perf. 13½***

1388 A975 50y multi	65	15

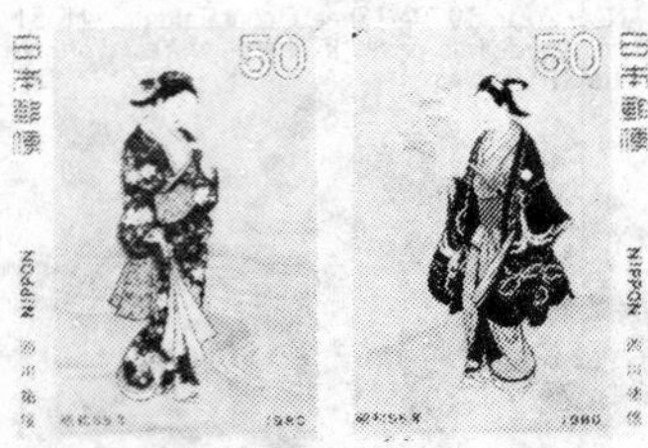

Scenes of Outdoor Play in Spring, by Sukenobu Nishikawa
A976 A977

1980, Apr. 21 **Photo.** ***Perf. 13½***

1389 A976 50y multi	65	15
1390 A977 50y multi	65	15
a. Pair, #1389-1390	1.30	50
Set value		24

Philatelic Week, Apr. 21-27. Sheets of 10.

Japanese Song Issue

The Sea — A978

The Night of the Hazy Moon — A979

Memories of Summer — A981

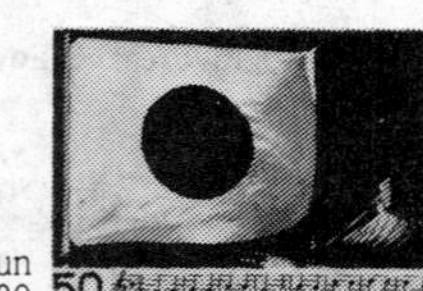

The Sun Flag — A980

1980 **Photo. & Engr.** ***Perf. 13***

1391 A978 50y multi	70	15
1392 A979 50y multi	70	15
1393 A980 50y multi	70	15
1394 A981 50y multi	70	15
Set value		48

Issue dates: Nos. 1391-1392, Apr. 28; Nos. 1393-1394, June 16.

Song by the Sea — A982

The Red Dragonfly — A983

1980, Sept. 18 ***Perf. 13***

1395 A982 50y multi	65	15
1396 A983 50y multi	65	15
Set value		24

Lullaby — A984

Coconut, by Toraji Ohnaka — A985

1981, Feb. 9 ***Perf. 13***

1397 A984 60y multi	70	15
1398 A985 60y multi	70	15
Set value		20

Spring Has Come, by Tatsuyuki Takano — A986

Cherry Blossoms, by Hagoromo Takeshima A987

1981, Mar. 10 ***Perf. 13***

1399 A986 60y multi	70	15
1400 A987 60y multi	70	15
Set value		20

Modern Japanese Art Issue

Dancers, by Seiki Kuroda — A988

Mother and Child, by Shoen Uemura — A989

1980, May 12 Photo. *Perf. 13½*

1401 A988 50y multi	70	15
1402 A989 50y multi	70	15
Set value		24

The Black Fan, by Takeji Fujishima — A990

Dear Me . . . It's a Shower, by Seiho Takeuchi — A991

1980, July 7 Photo. *Perf. 13½*

1403 A990 50y multi	70	15
1404 A991 50y multi	70	15
Set value		24

Woman, by Morie Ogiwara — A992

Kurofuneya, by Yumeji Takehisa — A993

1980, Oct. 27 Photo. *Perf. 13½*

1405 A992 50y multi	70	15
1406 A993 50y multi	70	15
Set value		24

Nippon Maru, Institute Emblem — A994

1980, May 17

1407 A994 50y multi	65	15

Institute for Nautical Training, training ships Nippon Maru and Kaio Maru, 50th anniversary.

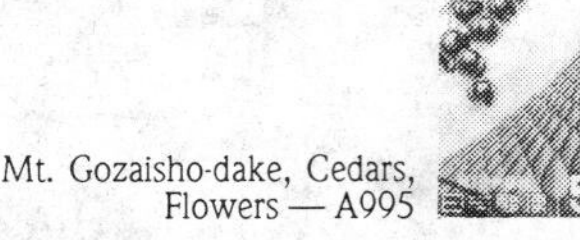

Mt. Gozaisho-dake, Cedars, Flowers — A995

1980, May 24 *Perf. 13x13½*

1408 A995 50y multi	65	15

National forestation campaign.

Yayosu Fire Brigade Review, by Hiroshige III — A996

Teddy Bear Holding Letter — A997

1980, May 31

1409 A996 50y multi	65	15

Fire fighting centenary.

Perf. 13x13½, 13½x13
1980, July 23

Letter Writing Day: 50y, Folded and tied letter of good wishes, horiz.

1410 A997 20y multi	30	15
1411 A997 50y multi	60	15
Set value		18

Lühdorfla Japonica A998

1980, Aug. 2 *Perf. 13½*

1412 A998 50y multi	65	15

16th Intl. Congress of Entomology, Kyoto, Aug. 3-9.

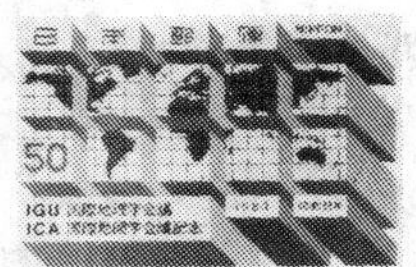

Three-dimensional World Map — A999

1980, Aug. 25 Photo.

1413 A999 50y multi	65	15

24th Intl. Geographic Cong. and 10th Intl. Cartographic Conf., Tokyo, August.

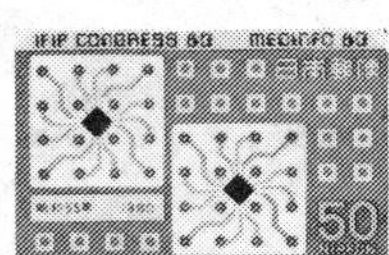

Integrated Circuit A1000

Camellia A1001

1980, Sept. 29

1414 A1000 50y multi	65	15

Intl. Federation for Information Processing Cong. '80, Tokyo, Oct. 6-9 and World Conf. on Medical Informatics '80, Tokyo, Sept. 29-Oct. 4.

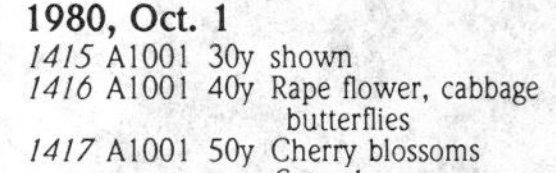

1980, Oct. 1

1415 A1001 30y shown	42	15
1416 A1001 40y Rape flower, cabbage butterflies	50	15
1417 A1001 50y Cherry blossoms	70	15
Set value		24

See No. 1437.

Cranes, by Motooki Watanabe A1002

Archery, Mt. Nantai A1003

1980, Oct. 6 *Perf. 13*

1418 A1002 100y multi	1.25	24

24th Intl. Letter Writing Week, Oct. 6-12.

1980, Oct. 11

1419 A1003 20y multi	32	15

35th Natonal Athletic Meet, Tochigi, Oct.

Globe, Jaycee Emblem — A1004

Diet Building and Doves — A1005

1980, Nov. 8 *Perf. 13*

1420 A1004 50y multi	65	24

35th Jaycee (Intl. Junior Chamber of Commerce) World Congress, Osaka, Nov. 9-15.

1980, Nov. 29 *Perf. 13½*

1421 A1005 50y multi	65	15

90th anniversary of Japanese Diet.

Type of 1980 and:

Amur Adonis — A1006

White Trumpet Lily — A1007

Hanging Bell, Byodoin Temple — A1008

Bronze Buddhist Ornament, 7th Century — A1009

Writing Box Cover — A1010

Mirror with Figures — A1011

Heart-shaped Figurine — A1012

Silver Crane — A1013

Maitreya, Horyuji Temple — A1014

Ichiji Kinrin, Chusonji Temple — A1015

Komokuten, Todaiji Temple — A1016

Lady Maya — A1017

Enamel Jar, by Ninsei Nonomura A1018

Miroku Bosatsu, Koryuji Temple A1019

1980-82 Photo. *Perf. 13x13½*

1422 A1006 10y multi	25	15
1423 A1007 20y multi	30	15
1424 A1008 60y multi	90	15
a. Bklt. pane (#1424, 4 #1424 with gutter btwn.) ('81)	4.00	
1425 A1009 70y multi	1.10	20
1426 A1010 70y multi	1.10	15
1427 A1011 80y multi	1.25	15
1428 A1012 90y multi	1.40	16
1429 A1013 100y multi	1.50	18
1430 A1014 170y multi	2.50	25
1431 A1015 260y multi	3.75	40
1432 A1016 310y multi	4.50	65
1433 A1017 410y multi	5.75	1.15
1434 A1018 410y multi	5.75	1.15
1435 A1019 600y multi	8.50	1.40
Nos. 1422-1435 (14)	38.55	6.29

Coil Stamps
Perf. 13 Horiz.

1436 A1006 10y multi ('82)	25	15
1437 A1001 40y as #1416	60	15
1438 A1008 60y multi ('82)	90	15
1439 A1013 100y multi ('82)	1.50	18
Set value		42

See Nos. 1627, 1629.

Clay Chicken, Folk Toy — A1026

1980, Dec. 1 *Perf. 13 Horiz.*

1442 A1026 20y multi	30	15

New Year 1981.
Sheets of two were New Year Lottery Prizes. Value $1.25.

Modern Japanese Art Issue

Snow-Covered Power Station, by Shikanosuke Oka — A1027

NuKada-no-Ohkimi and Nara in Spring, by Yukihiko Yasuda — A1028

1981, Feb. 26 *Perf. 13½*
1443 A1027 60y multi 75 15

Photo.

1444 A1028 60y multi 75 15
Set value 20

Artist's Family, by Narashige Koide — A1029

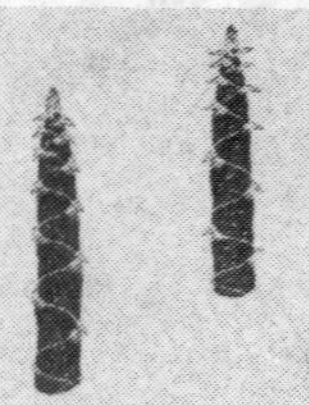
Bamboo Shoots, by Heihachiro Fukuda — A1030

Photo. & Engr., Photo.

1981, June 18 *Perf. 13½*
1445 A1029 60y multi 75 15
1446 A1030 60y multi 75 15
Set value 20

Portrait of Ichiyo, by Kiyokata Kaburagi (1878-1972) A1031

Portrait of Reiko, by Ryusei Kishida (1891-1929) A1032

Photo., Photo. and Engr.

1981, Nov. 27 **Engr.** *Perf. 13½*
1447 A1031 60y multi 75 15
1448 A1032 60y multi 75 15
Set value 20

Yoritomo in a Cave, by Seison Maeda — A1033

Advertisement of a Terrace, by Yuzo Saeki — A1034

1982, Feb. 25 **Photo.** *Perf. 13½*
1449 A1033 60y multi 75 15
1450 A1034 60y multi 75 15
Set value 20

Emblem, Port Island A1035

1981, Mar. 20 *Perf. 13*
1451 A1035 60y multi 70 15

Portopia '81, Kobe Port Island Exhibition, Mar. 20-Sept. 15.

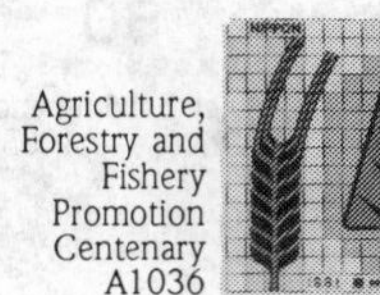
Agriculture, Forestry and Fishery Promotion Centenary A1036

1981, Apr. 7
1452 A1036 60y multi 70 15

Moonflower, by Harunobu Suzuki
A1037 A1038

1981, Apr. 20 **Photo.** *Perf. 13½*
1453 A1037 60y multi 75 15
1454 A1038 60y multi 75 15
a. Pair, #1453-1454 1.50 30
Set value 20

Philatelic Week, Apr. 21-27.

Cherry Blossoms A1039

Cargo Ship and Crane A1040

1981, May 23 **Photo.** *Perf. 13x13½*
1455 A1039 60y multi 70 15

1981, May 25 *Perf. 13*
1456 A1040 60y multi 70 15

International Port and Harbor Association, 12th Convention, Nagoya, May 23-30.

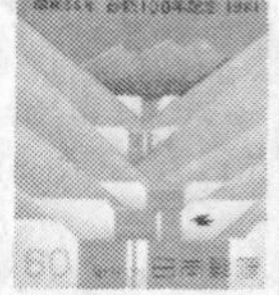
Land Erosion Control Cent. — A1041

Stylized Man and Spinal Cord Dose Response Curve — A1042

1981, June 27 *Perf. 13½*
1457 A1041 60y multi 70 15

1981, July 18 **Photo.** *Perf. 13*
1458 A1042 60y multi 70 15

8th Intl. Pharmacology Congress, Tokyo, July 19-24.

Girl Writing Letter A1043

Japanese Crested Ibis A1044

1981, July 23
1459 A1043 40y shown 48 15
1460 A1043 60y Boy, stamp 70 15
Set value 16

Letter Writing Day (23rd of each month).

1981, July 27 **Litho.**
1461 A1044 60y multi 70 15

Energy Conservation — A1045

1981, Aug. 1 **Photo.**
1462 A1045 40y Plug, faucet 48 15
1463 A1045 60y shown 70 15
Set value 16

Western Architecture Issue

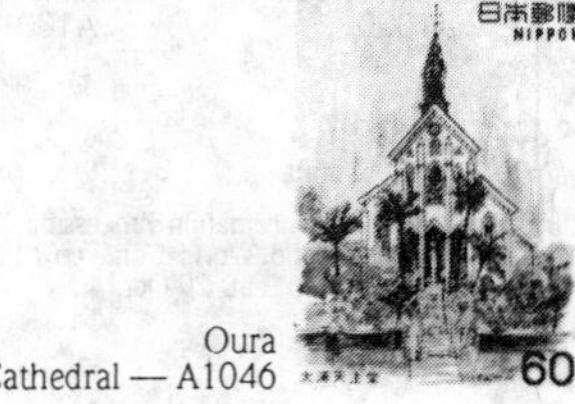
Oura Cathedral — A1046

Hyokei Hall, Tokyo A1047

Photogravure and Engraved

1981, Aug. 22
1464 A1046 60y multi 70 15
1465 A1047 60y multi 70 15
Set value 20

Old Kaichi School, Nagano A1048

Doshisha University Chapel, Kyoto A1049

1981, Nov. 9 *Perf. 13*
1466 A1048 60y multi 70 15
1467 A1049 60y multi 70 15
Set value 20

St. John's Church, Meiji-mura — A1050

Military Exercise Hall (Former Sapporo Agricultural School), Sapporo A1051

1982, Jan. 29 *Perf. 13*
1468 A1050 60y multi 70 15
1469 A1051 60y multi 70 15
Set value 20

Former Kyoto Branch of Bank of Japan A1052

Main Building, Former Saiseikan Hospital — A1053

1982, Mar. 10 *Perf. 13*
1470 A1052 60y multi 70 15
1471 A1053 60y multi 70 15
Set value 20

Oyama Shrine Gate, Kanazawa — A1054

Former Iwasaki Family Residence, Tokyo A1055

1982, June 12 *Perf. 13*

1472 A1054 60y multi		70	15
1473 A1055 60y multi		70	15
Set value			20

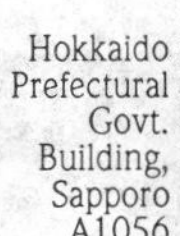

Hokkaido Prefectural Govt. Building, Sapporo A1056

Former Residence of Tsugumichi Saigo A1057

1982, Sept. 10 *Perf. 13*

1474 A1056 60y multi		70	15
1475 A1057 60y multi		70	15
Set value			20

Old Mutsuzawa School — A1058

Sakuranomiya Public Hall — A1059

1983, Feb. 15

1476 A1058 60y multi		70	15
1477 A1059 60y multi		70	15
Set value			20

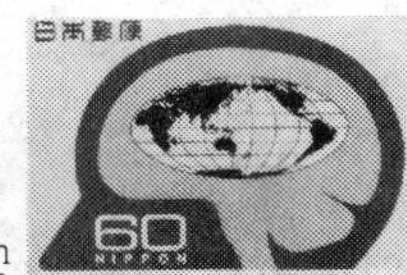

Globe on Brain — A1060

1981, Sept. 12 **Photo.**

1478 A1060 60y multi		70	15

Intl. medical conferences, Kyoto: 12th Neurology, Sept. 20-25; 10th Brainwaves and Clinical Neurophysiology, Sept. 13-17; 1981 Intl. Epilepsy Conference, Sept. 17-21.

Congress Emblem — A1061

1981, Sept. 16

1479 A1061 60y multi		70	15

24th World PTTI (Post, Telegraph and Telephone Intl. Labor Federation) Congress, Tokyo, Sept. 16-22.

Plum Trees and Fowl, by Sanraku Kano A1062

No. 1, Philatokyo '81 Emblem A1063

1981, Oct. 6 **Photo.**

1480 A1062 130y multi		1.75	18

25th Intl. Letter Writing Week, Oct. 6-12.

1981, Oct. 9 **Photo. & Engr.**

1481 A1063 60y shown		85	15
1482 A1063 60y No. 2		85	15
1483 A1063 60y No. 3		85	15
1484 A1063 60y No. 4		85	15
a. Strip or block of 4, #1481-1484		3.50	1.00

Philatokyo '81 Intl. Stamp Exhibition, Tokyo, Oct. 9-18.

36th Natl. Athletic Meet, Oct. 13-18 — A1064

1981, Oct. 13 **Photo.**

1485 A1064 40y multi		50	15

New Year of 1982 (Year of the Dog) — A1065

1981, Dec. 1 **Photo.** *Perf. 13x13½*

1486 A1065 40y multicolored		48	15

Sheets of 2 were lottery prizes. Value $1.50.

Ueno Zoo Centenary — A1066

Designs: a, Gorilla, flamingo. b, Penguins, lion. c, Panda, elephants. d, Zebras, giraffe.

1982, Mar. 20 **Photo.**

1487 Strip of 4		3.25	1.40
a.-d. A1066 60y any single		70	32

Views of the Snow on Matsuchiyama, by Kiyonago Torii
A1067 A1068

1982, Apr. 20 **Photo.** *Perf. 13½*

1488 A1067 60y multi		75	35
1489 A1068 60y multi		75	35
a. Pair, #1488-1489		1.50	70

Philatelic Week.

Shisa (Lion-shaped Guard Dog) A1069

Natl. Forestation Campaign A1070

1982, May 15 **Photo.**

1490 A1069 60y multi		70	32

10th anniv. of Reversion Agreement returning Ryukyu Islands.

1982, May 22 *Perf. 13x13½*

1491 A1070 60y multi		70	32

16th Intl. Dermatology Conference Tokyo, May 23-28 — A1071

1982, May 24 *Perf. 13*

1492 A1071 60y Noh mask		70	32

Tohoku-Shinkansen Railroad Line Opening — A1072

1982, June 23

1493 A1072 60y Diesel locomotive		70	32
1494 A1072 60y Steam model 1290		70	32
a. Pair, #1493-1494		1.50	

Letter Writing Day — A1073

Perf. 13x13½, 13½x13

1982, July 23

1495 A1073 40y Sea gull, letter		50	15
1496 A1073 60y Fairy, letter, horiz.		75	35

Modern Japanese Art Issue

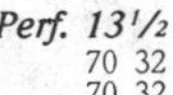

Kimono Patterned with Irises, by Saburosuke Okada (1869-1939) A1074

Bodhisattva Kuan-yin on Potalaka Island, by Tessai Tomioka (1837-1924) A1075

1982, Aug. 5 **Photo.** *Perf. 13½*

1497 A1074 60y multi		70	32
1498 A1075 60y multi		70	32

The Sarasvati, by Shiko Munakata (1903-1975) A1076

Saltim- banque, by Seiji Togo (1897-1978) A1077

1982, Nov. 24

1499 A1076 60y multi		70	32
1500 A1077 60y multi		70	32

Snowstorm, by Shinsui Ito — A1078

Spiraeas and Callas with Persian Pot, by Zenzaburo Kojima — A1079

1983, Jan. 24 **Photo.**

1501 A1078 60y multi		70	32
1502 A1079 60y multi		70	32

Muga, by Taikan Yokoyama (1868-1958) A1080

Roen, by Koun Takamura (1852-1934)
A1081

Photo., Photo. and Engr.

1983, Mar. 10 *Perf. 13½*

1503 A1080 60y multi 70 32
1504 A1081 60y multi 70 32

A1082 A1083 A1084

1982, Aug. 23 *Perf. 13x13½*

1505 A1082 60y Wreath 75 35
1506 A1083 60y Crane 75 35
1507 A1084 70y Tortoise 85 38

For use on greeting (Nos. 1506-1507) and condolence (No. 1505) cards.

See Nos. 1555-1556, 1836-1839 and footnote after No. 1765.

400th Anniv. of Boys' Delegation to Europe, Tensho Era — A1085

1982, Sept. 20 **Photo.** *Perf. 13*

1508 A1085 60y 16th cent. ship, map 70 32

10th Anniv. of Japanese-Chinese Relations Normalization — A1086

Design: Hall of Prayer for Good Harvests, Temple of Heaven, Peking, by Ryuzaburo Umehara.

1982, Sept. 29

1509 A1086 60y multi 70 32

Table Tennis — A1087

"Amusement," Doll by Goyo Hirata — A1088

1982, Oct. 2

1510 A1087 40y multi 50 25

37th Natl. Athletic Meet, Matsue, Oct. 3-8.

1982, Oct. 6

1511 A1088 130y multi 1.65 60

Intl. Letter Writing Week, Oct. 6-12.

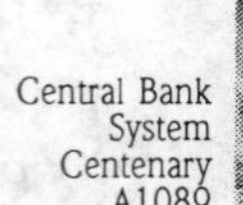

Central Bank System Centenary
A1089

Design: The Bank of Japan near Eitaibashi in Snow, by Yasuji Inoue.

Photogravure and Engraved

1982, Oct. 12 *Perf. 13½*

1512 A1089 60y multi 70 32

A1090

A1091

Opening of Joetsu Shinkansen Railroad Line

1982, Nov. 15

1513 A1090 60y Locomotive, 1982 70 32
1514 A1091 60y Locomotive, 1931 70 32
a. Pair, #1513-1514 1.50

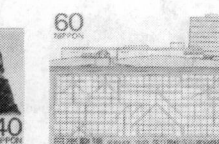

New Year 1983
A1092

Natl. Museum of History and Folklore Opening
A1093

1982, Dec. 1 *Perf. 13x13½*

1515 A1092 40y Kintaro on Wild Boar 50 15

Sheets of 2 were lottery prizes. Value, $1.50.

1983, Mar. 16 **Photo.** *Perf. 13½x13*

1516 A1093 60y multi 70 32

Women Working in the Kitchen, by Utamaro Kitagawa (1753-1806)
A1094 A1095

1983, Apr. 20 **Photo.** *Perf. 13*

1517 A1094 60y multi 70 32
1518 A1095 60y multi 70 32
a. Pair, #1517-1518 1.40 70

Philatelic Week.

Natl. Forestation Campaign — A1096

50th Nippon Derby — A1097

1983, May 21 *Perf. 13*

1519 A1096 60y Hakusan Mountains, black lily, forest 70 32

1983, May 28

1520 A1097 60y Colt, racing horse 70 32

Islands Cleanup Campaign — A1098

1983, June 13 **Photo.** *Perf. 13½*

1521 A1098 60y multi 70 32

Western Architecture Series

Hohei Hall Sapporo
A1099

Old Glover House, Nagasaki
A1100

Gojyuku Bank, Hirosaki
A1101

Gakushuin Elementary School, Tokyo
A1102

Bank of Japan, Tokyo
A1103

Old Hunter House, Kobe
A1104

Photogravure and Engraved

1983, June 23 *Perf. 13*

1522 A1099 60y multi 75 35
1523 A1100 60y multi 75 35

1983, Aug. 15 *Perf. 13*

1524 A1101 60y multi 75 35
1525 A1102 60y multi 75 35

1984, Feb. 16 *Perf. 13*

1526 A1103 60y multi 75 35
1527 A1104 60y multi 75 35

Official Gazette Centenary
A1107

Letter Writing Day
A1108

Design: First issue, Drawing of the Government Bulletin Board at Nihonbashi, by Hiroshige Ando III.

1983, July 2 **Photo.** *Perf. 13*

1530 A1107 60y multi 70 32

Perf. 13x13½, 13½x13

1983, July 23

1531 A1108 40y Boy writing letter 50 22
1532 A1108 60y Fairy bringing letter, horiz. 75 35

Opening of Natl. Noh Theater, Tokyo — A1109

1983, Sept. 14 **Photo.** *Perf. 13*

1533 A1109 60y Masked actor, theater 70 32

Endangered Birds Issue

Rallus Okinawae — A1110

Ketupa Blakistoni
A1111

Photo. and Engr., Photo.

1983, Sept. 22 *Perf. 13*

1534 A1110 60y multi 75 35
1535 A1111 60y multi 75 35

Photo., Photo. & Engr.

1983, Nov. 25 *Perf. 13*

1536 A1110 60y Sapheopipo noguchii 75 35
1537 A1111 60y Branta canadensis leucopareia 75 35

Photo., Photo. and Engr.

1984, Jan. 26 *Perf. 13*

1538 A1111 60y Megalurus pryeri pryeri 75 35
1539 A1110 60y Spilornis cheela perplexus 75 35

1984, Mar. 15 **Photo.** *Perf. 13*

1540 A1110 60y Columba janthina nitens 75 35
1541 A1111 60y Tringa guttifer 75 35

1984, June 22 **Photo.** *Perf. 13*

1542 A1110 60y Falco peregrinus frutti 75 35

Photo. and Engr.

1543 A1111 60y Dendrocopus leucutus austoni 75 35

Souvenir Sheet

1984, Dec. 10 **Photo. & Engr.**

1544 Sheet of 3 2.75 1.10
a. A1111 60y Prus grn, engr., #1535 80 35
b. A1110 60y vio brn, engr., #1539 80 35
c. A1110 60y ol blk, engr., #1542 80 35

Intl. Letter Writing Week — A1124

38th Natl. Athletic Meet — A1125

Design: Chikyu Doll by Juzo Kagoshima (1898-1982).

1983, Oct. 6 Photo. *Perf. 13*
1548 A1124 130y multi 1.75 70

1983, Oct. 15 *Perf. 13*
1549 A1125 40y Naginata event 50 26

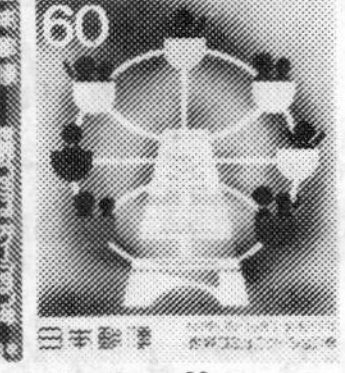

World Communications Year
A1126 A1127

1983, Oct. 17 Photo. *Perf. 13*
1550 A1126 60y multi 70 32
1551 A1127 60y multi 70 32

Showa Memorial National Park Opening A1128

1983, Oct. 26 Photo. *Perf. 13*
1552 A1128 60y multi 70 32

A1129 A1130

1983, Nov. 14 Photo.
1553 A1129 60y multi 70 32

71st World Dentistry Congress.

1983, Nov. 14 Photo. *Perf. 13*
1554 A1130 60y multi 70 32

Shirase, Antarctic observation ship, maiden voyage.

Type of 1982

1983, Nov. 22 Photo. *Perf. 12½*
1555 A1082 40y Wreath 60 26
1556 A1083 40y Crane 60 26

For use on condolence and greeting cards.

New Year 1984 — A1131

1983, Dec. 1 Photo. *Perf. 13x13½*
1557 A1131 40y Rat riding hammer 50 26

Sheets of 2 were lottery prizes. Value, $1.45.

Universal Declaration of Human Rights, 35th Anniv. — A1132

1983, Dec. 5 Photo. *Perf. 13½*
1558 A1132 60y Emblem 70 32

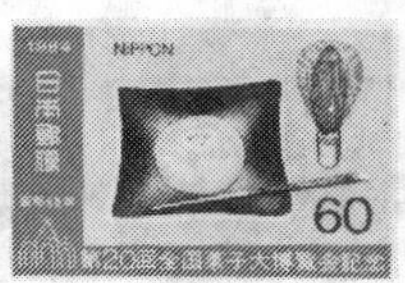

20th Grand Confectionery Fair, Tokyo, Feb. 24-Mar. 12 — A1133

1984, Feb. 24 Photo.
1559 A1133 60y Confection, tea whisk 70 32

Natl. Bunraku Theater Opening, Osaka — A1134

1984, Apr. 6 Photo. *Perf. 13*
1560 A1134 60y Bunraku puppet 70 32

A1135

A1136

Philatelic Week (Sharaku Prints): No. 1561, Hanshiro Iwai IV Playing Shigenoi. No. 1562, Oniji Otani Playing Edobe.

Photogravure and Engraved

1984, Apr. 20 *Perf. 13½*
1561 A1135 60y multi 70 32
1562 A1136 60y multi 70 32
a. Pair, #1561-1562 1.40 70

Natl. Forestation Campaign A1137

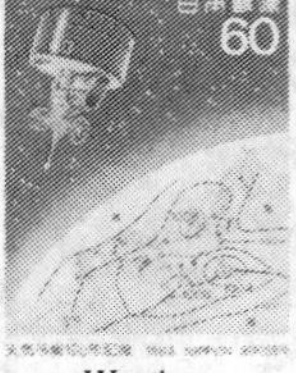

Weather Forecasting Centenary A1138

1984, May 19 Photo.
1563 A1137 60y Cedar Forest, Sakurajima 70 32

1984, June 1 *Perf. 13x13½*
1564 A1138 60y Himawari satellite, map 70 32

UNESCO Emblem, Doves A1139

Letter Writing Day A1140

1984, July 16 Photo.
1565 A1139 60y multi 70 32

UNESCO Clubs and Associations World Congress, July 16-24.

Perf. 13x13½, 13½x13

1984, July 23
1566 A1140 40y Birds in tree 48 20
1567 A1140 60y Bird holding letter, horiz. 70 32

Disaster Relief — A1141

Perf. 13x12½, 12½x13

1984, Aug. 23 Photo.
1568 A1141 40y Fire, wind 48 20
1569 A1141 60y Mother, child, vert. 70 32

Alpine Plant Series

Leontopodium Fauriei — A1142

Lagotis Glauca A1143

Photogravure and Engraved

Perf. 12½x13, 13x12½

1984, Aug. 27
1570 A1142 60y multi 75 35
1571 A1143 60y multi 75 35

Trollius Riederianus A1144

Primula Cuneifolia A1145

1984, Sept. 21 *Perf. 13*
1572 A1144 60y multi 75 35
1573 A1145 60y multi 75 35

Rhododendron Aureum — A1146

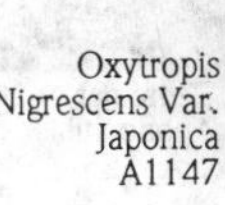

Oxytropis Nigrescens Var. Japonica A1147

1985, Jan. 25 *Perf. 13*
1574 A1146 60y multi 75 35
1575 A1147 60y multi 75 35

Draba Japonica — A1148

Dryas Octopetala A1149

1985, Feb. 28
1576 A1148 60y multi 75 35
1577 A1149 60y multi 75 35

Callianthemum Insigne Var. Miyabeanum A1150

Gentiana Nipponica A1151

1985, July 31 *Perf. 13*
1578 A1150 60y multi 75 35
1579 A1151 60y multi 75 35

Campanula Chamissonis — A1152

Viola Crassa A1153

1985, Sept. 27
1580 A1152 60y multi 75 35
1581 A1153 60y multi 75 35

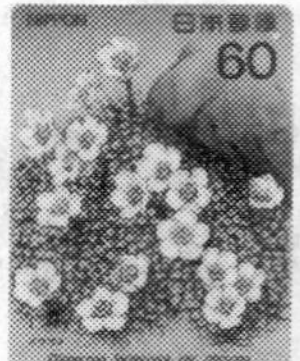

Deapensia Lapponica A1154

Pedicularis Apodochila A1155

1986, Feb. 13 ***Perf. 13***
1582 A1154 60y multi 75 35
1583 A1155 60y multi 75 35

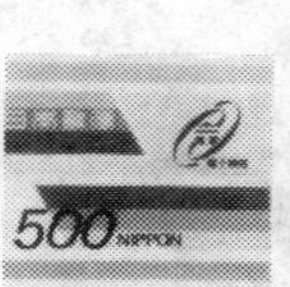
Basho's Street, Sendai — A1156

1984, Sept. 1 **Photo.** ***Perf. 13***
1584 A1156 60y multi 70 32

Intl. Microbiological Association's 6th Intl. Congress of Virology, Sendai, Sept. 1-7.

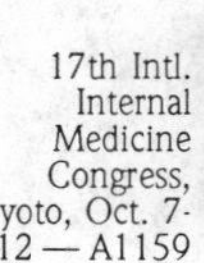
Electronic Mail — A1157

28th Intl. Letter Writing Week, Oct. 6-12 — A1158

1984, Oct. 1 **Photo.**
1585 A1157 500y multi 10.00 4.00

1984, Oct. 6
1586 A1158 130y Wooden doll 1.65 70

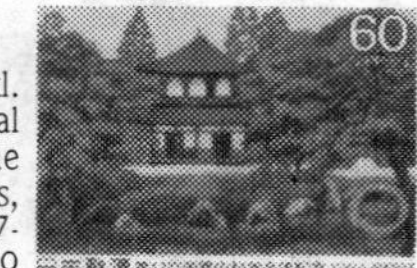
17th Intl. Internal Medicine Congress, Kyoto, Oct. 7-12 — A1159

1984, Oct. 8
1587 A1159 60y Ginkakuji Temple 70 32

39th Natl. Athletic Meet, Nara City, Oct. 12-17 — A1160

1984, Oct. 12
1588 A1160 40y Field hockey 50 25

Traditional Crafts Series

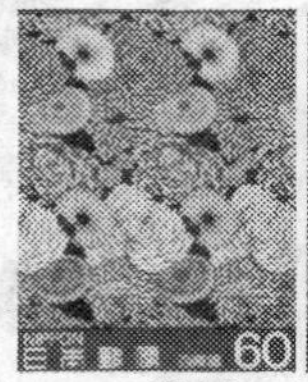

Kutaniyaki Plates
A1161 A1162

Nishijinori Weavings
A1163 A1164

1984, Nov. 2 **Photo.** ***Perf. 12½x13***
1589 A1161 60y Birds 75 35
1590 A1162 60y Flowers 75 35
a. Pair, #1589-1590 1.50 75
1591 A1163 60y Flowers 75 35
1592 A1164 60y Leaves 75 35
a. Pair, #1591-1592 1.50 75

Edokimekomi Dolls
A1165 A1166

Ryukyubingata Cloth
A1167 A1168

1985, Feb. 15 **Photo.** ***Perf. 13***
1593 A1165 60y Adult figures 75 35
1594 A1166 60y Child and pet 75 35
a. Pair, #1593-1594 1.50 75
1595 A1167 60y Bird and branch 75 35
1596 A1168 60y Birds 75 35
a. Pair, #1595-1596 1.50 75

Ichii-ittobori Carved Birds
A1169 A1170

Imariyaki & Aritayaki Ceramic Ware
A1171 A1172

Kamakurabori Wood Carvings
A1173 A1174

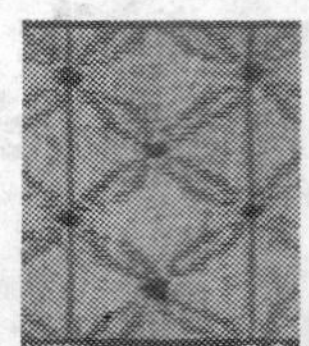
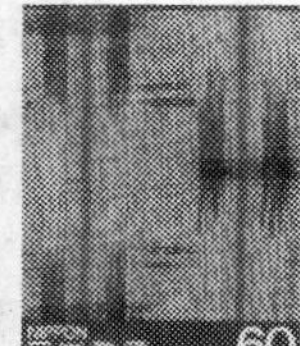
Ojiyachijimi Weavings
A1175 A1176

Hakata Ningyo Clay Figures
A1177 A1178

Nanbu Tekki Iron Ware
A1179 A1180

1985, May 23 **Photo.** ***Perf. 13***
1597 A1169 60y Bird 75 35
1598 A1170 60y Birds 75 35
a. Pair, #1597-1598 1.50 75
1599 A1171 60y Bowl 75 35
1600 A1172 60y Plate 75 35
a. Pair, #1599-1600 1.50 75

1985, June 24 **Photo. & Engr.**
1601 A1173 60y Bird and flower panel 75 35
1602 A1174 60y Round flower panel 75 35
a. Pair, #1601-1602 1.50 75

Litho.
1603 A1175 60y Hemp star pattern 75 35
1604 A1176 60y Hemp linear pattern 75 35
a. Pair, #1603-1604 1.50 75

1985, Aug. 8 **Photo.**
1605 A1177 60y Man 75 38
1606 A1178 60y Woman and child 75 38
a. Pair, #1605-1606 1.50 80

Photogravure and Engraved
1607 A1179 60y Silver kettle 75 38
1608 A1180 60y Black kettle 75 38
a. Pair, #1607-1608 1.50 80

Wajimanuri Lacquerware
A1181 A1182

Izumo-ishidoro Sandstone Sculptures
A1183 A1184

Photo., Photo. & Engr. (#1611-1612)
1985, Nov. 15
1609 A1181 60y Bowl on table 75 38
1610 A1182 60y Bowl 75 38
1611 A1183 60y Columnar lantern 75 38
1612 A1184 60y Lantern on four legs 75 38

Kyo-sensu Silk Fans
A1185 A1186

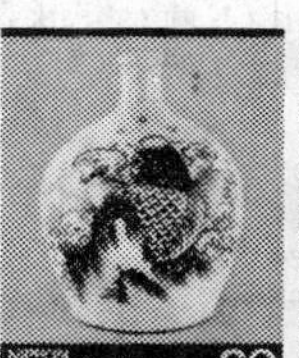

Tobeyaki Porcelain
A1187 A1188

1986, Mar. 13 **Photo.** ***Perf. 13***
1613 A1185 60y Flower bouquets 75 38
1614 A1186 60y Sun and trees 75 38
1615 A1187 60y Jug 75 38
1616 A1188 60y Jar 75 38

Japanese Professional Baseball, 50th Anniv. — A1189

1984, Nov. 15 ***Perf. 13½***
1617 A1189 60y Batter 80 35
1618 A1189 60y Pitcher 80 35
1619 A1189 60y Matsutaro Shoriki 80 35

Industrial Education Centenary — A1190

New Year 1984 — A1191

1984, Nov. 20 ***Perf. 13x12½***
1620 A1190 60y Workers, symbols 70 32

1984, Dec. 1 Photo. *Perf. 13½x13*
1621 A1191 40y Sakushu Cattle Folk Toy 50 25

Sheets of 2 were lottery prizes. Value, $1.25.

A1191a

Ivory Shell — A1192

Hiougi-gai (Bivalve) — A1192a

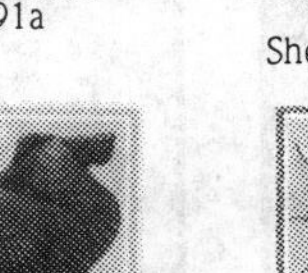

Rinbo Shell — A1193

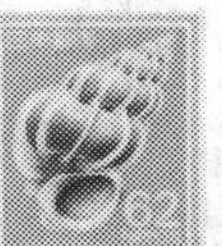
Ooitokake-gai (Conch) — A1194

A1196

A1198

A1200

Keiki-doji Statue, Kongobuki A1203

Temple A1205

1984-89 Photo. *Perf. 13x13½*
1621A A1191a 2y turq blue ('89) 15 15
1622 A1192 40y multi ('88) 52 15
1622A A1192a 41y multi ('89) 62 15
b. Imperf., self-adhesive 62 15
1623 A1193 60y multi ('88) 80 15
a. Bklt. pane, 5 each #1622-1623 6.75
1624 A1194 62y multi ('89) 92 15
a. Bklt. pane, 2 #1622A, 4 #1624 5.00
b. Imperf., self-adhesive 92 15
c. Bklt. pane, 2 #1622b, 4 #1624b ('89) 5.00
1627 A1196 72y dark vio, blk & org yel ('89) 1.10 20
1629 A1198 175y multi ('89) 2.65 25
1631 A1200 210y multi ('89) 3.15 30

Engr.

1633 A1203 300y dk red brn 4.25 1.40
1635 A1205 360y ('89) 5.50 80
Nos. 1621A-1635 (10) 19.66
Set value 3.10

Coil Stamps

Perf. 13 Horiz.

1636 A1192a 41y multi ('89) 62 15
1637 A1194 62y multi ('89) 92 15
Set value 15

No. 1621A inscribed "Nippon," unlike No. 583.

No. 1624c is adhered to the booklet cover, made of peelable paper, folded in half and rouletted down the center fold.

Issue dates: 40y, 60y, Apr. 1. 300y, Apr. 3. 2y, 72y, Apr. 1; 42y, Nos. 1624, 1624a, 41y, No. 1637, Mar. 24; 175y, 210y, 360y, June 1. No. 1624d, July 3.

This is an expanding set. Numbers will change if necessary.

A1210

EXPO '85 — A1211

1985, Mar. 16 Photo. *Perf. 13*
1640 A1210 40y multi 50 22
1641 A1211 60y multi 75 35
a. Souv. sheet of 2, #1640-1641 1.65

University of the Air — A1212

1985, Apr. 1 Photo. *Perf. 13½*
1642 A1212 60y University broadcast tower 70 35

Inauguration of adult education through broadcasting.

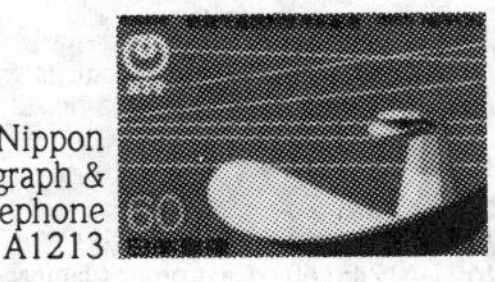
Nippon Telegraph & Telephone Co. — A1213

1985, Apr. 1
1643 A1213 60y Satellite receiver 70 35

Inauguration of Japan's new telecommunications system.

World Import Fair, Nagoya A1214

1985, Apr. 5 Photo. *Perf. 13*
1644 A1214 60y 16th century map of Japan 70 35

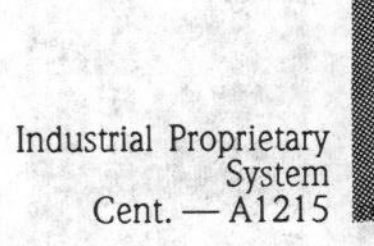
Industrial Proprietary System Cent. — A1215

Design: Portrait of Korekiyo Takashashi, system promulgator, inscriptions in English.

1985, Apr. 18 Photo. *Perf. 13½*
1645 A1215 60y multi 70 35

Winter in the North — A1216

To the Morning Light — A1217

Paintings by Yumeji Takehisa (1884-1934).

1985, Apr. 20 *Perf. 13*
1646 A1216 60y multi 70 35
1647 A1217 60y multi 70 35

Philatelic Week. Printed in sheets of 10.

Natl. Land Forestation Project — A1218

Intl. Year of the Forest: Autumn bellflower, camphor tree, cattle and Mt. Aso.

1985, May 10 *Perf. 13½*
1648 A1218 60y multi 70 35

Radio Japan, 50th Anniv. — A1219

Painting: Cherry Blossoms at Night, by Taikan Yokoyama.

1985, June 1 Photo. *Perf. 13*
1649 A1219 60y multi (Left) 75 35
1650 A1219 60y multi (Right) 75 35
a. Pair, #1649-1650 1.60

Hisoko Maejima, 1st Postmaster General — A1220

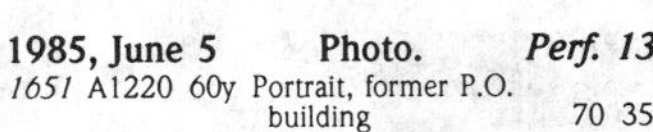

1985, June 5 Photo. *Perf. 13*
1651 A1220 60y Portrait, former P.O. building 70 35

Oonaruto Bridge Opening A1221

1985, June 7 *Perf. 13½*
1652 A1221 60y multi 70 35

Intl. Youth Year A1222

Owl Carrying Letter A1223

1985, July 20 Photo. *Perf. 13*
1653 A1222 60y Emblem, silhouette 70 35

Perf. 13½x13, 13x13½

1985, July 23 Photo.
1654 A1223 40y shown 60 28
1655 A1223 60y Girl, cat, bird, letter 75 45

Letter Writing Day (23rd of each month).

Electronic Mail — A1224

Meson Theory, 50th Anniv. — A1225

1985, Aug. 1 Photo. *Perf. 13x13½*
1656 A1224 500y multi 7.00 3.00

1985, Aug. 15 Photo. *Perf. 13*
1657 A1225 60y Portrait, nuclear particles 70 35

Dr. Hideki Yukawa was presented the Nobel Prize for Physics for the Meson Theory in 1949, which is the foundation for high-energy physics.

A1226

A1227

1985, Aug. 24 Photo. *Perf. 13½*
1658 A1226 60y Gymnast, horse 70 35

Universiade 1985, Kobe.

1985, Sept. 13 Photo.
1659 A1227 40y Emblem, competitor 50 25

28th Intl. Vocational Training Competition, Oct. 21-27.

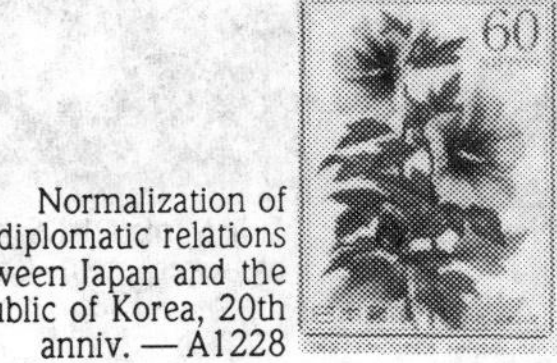
Normalization of diplomatic relations between Japan and the Republic of Korea, 20th anniv. — A1228

1985, Sept. 18
1660 A1228 60y Rose of Sharon 70 30

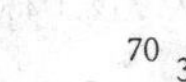

Kan-Etsu Tunnel Opening A1229

1985, Oct. 2 *Perf. 13*
1661 A1229 60y Mountains, diagram, cross sections 70 35

Seisen Doll by Goyo Hirata (1903-1981) — A1230

1985, Oct. 7
1662 A1230 130y multi 1.75 85

Intl. Letter Writing Week, Oct. 6-12.

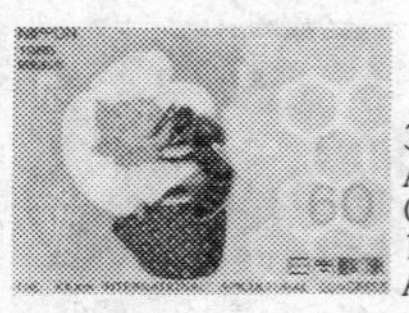

30th Intl. Apicultural Congress, Oct. 10-16, Nagoya A1231

1985, Oct. 9
1663 A1231 60y Honeybee, strawberry plants 70 35

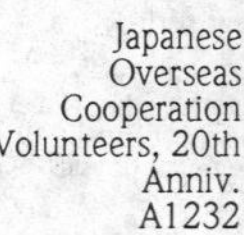

Japanese Overseas Cooperation Volunteers, 20th Anniv. A1232

1985, Oct. 9 **Litho.**
1664 A1232 60y Planting crop 70 35

40th Natl. Athletic Meet, Oct. 20-25, Tottori City Sports Arena — A1233

1985, Oct. 19 **Photo.**
1665 A1233 40y Handball player, Mt. Daisen 50 25

New Year 1986 A1234

Natl. Ministerial System of Government, Cent. A1235

1985, Dec. 2 **Photo.** ***Perf. 13x13½***
1666 A1234 40y Shinno papier-mache tiger 50 25

Sheets of 2 were lottery prizes. Value, $1.40.

1985, Dec. 20 **Litho.** ***Perf. 13½***
1667 A1235 60y Official seal, Cabinet emblem 70 35

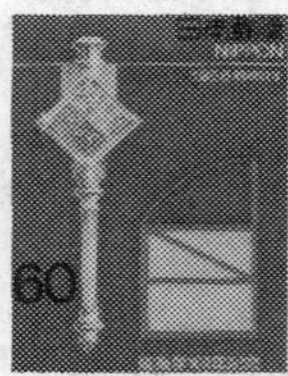
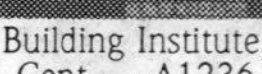

Building Institute, Cent. — A1236

Philately Week — A1237

1986, Apr. 9 **Photo.** ***Perf. 13***
1668 A1236 60y multi 70 42

1986, Apr. 15

Southern Hateroma (details), by Keigetsu Kikuchi.

1669 A1237 60y Woman standing 75 42
1670 A1237 60y Seated woman 75 42
a. Pair, #1669-1670 1.60

Kyoto Imperial Palace, Phoenix A1238

Designs: No. 1672, Imperial chrysanthemum crest and partridges.

1986, Apr. 28
1671 A1238 60y multi 75 42
1672 A1238 60y multi 75 42
a. Souv. sheet of 2, #1671-1672 1.65 1.25

Reign of Emperor Hirohito, 60th anniv.

6th Intl. Summit, Tokyo — A1239

1986, May 2
1673 A1239 60y Mt. Fuji 70 42

Shrike on Reed, Emperor Nintoku's Mausoleum A1240

1986, May 9 ***Perf. 13½***
1674 A1240 60y multi 70 42

Natl. Land Afforestation Campaign.

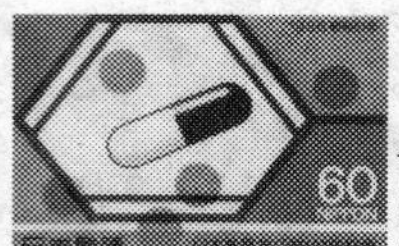

Japanese Pharmaceutical Regulatory Syst., Cent. — A1241

1986, June 25 **Photo.** ***Perf. 13½***
1675 A1241 60y multi 70 45

Japanese Standard Time, Cent. A1242

Letter Writing Day A1243

1986, July 11 **Litho.** ***Perf. 13***
1676 A1242 60y Meridian, clock 70 45

1986, July 23 **Photo.** ***Perf. 13x13½***
1677 A1243 40y Bird 55 35
1678 A1243 60y Girl, rabbit, birds 80 52
a. Bklt. pane, 5 each #1677-1678 7.50

Sheets of 2 were lottery prizes. Value, *$50.*

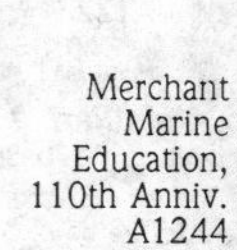

Merchant Marine Education, 110th Anniv. A1244

Design: Training ship Nihonmaru and navigation training institute founders Makoto Kondo, Yataro Iwasaki.

1986, July 26 ***Perf. 13***
1679 A1244 60y multi 75 48

Insects

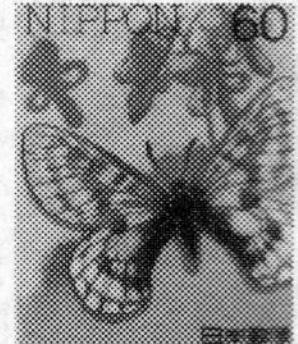

Parnassius Eversmanni — A1245

Photogravure and Engraved

1986, July 30 ***Perf. 13***
1680 A1245 60y shown 80 48
1681 A1245 60y Poecilocoris Lewisi 80 48
a. Pair, #1680-1681 1.60 1.00
1682 A1245 60y Rasalia Batesi 80 48
1683 A1245 60y Epiophlebia Superstes 80 48
a. Pair, #1682-1683 1.60 1.00

1986, Sept. 26 ***Perf. 13***
1684 A1245 60y Dorcus hopei 80 55
1685 A1245 60y Thermo- zephyrus ataxus 80 55
a. Pair, #1684-1685 1.60 1.10
1686 A1245 60y Sympetrum pedemontanum 80 55
1687 A1245 60y Damaster blaptoides 80 55
a. Pair, #1686-1687 1.60 1.10

1986, Nov. 21 ***Perf. 13***
1688 A1245 60y Elcysma westwoodii 80 52
1689 A1245 60y Rhyothemis variegata 80 52
a. Pair, #1688-1689 1.60 1.10
1690 A1245 60y Tibicen japonicus 80 52
1691 A1245 60y Chrysochroa holstii 80 52
a. Pair, #1690-1691 1.60 1.10

1987, Jan. 23 ***Perf. 13***
1692 A1245 60y Parantica sita 80 55
1693 A1245 60y Cheirotonus jambar 80 55
a. Pair, #1692-1693 1.60 1.10
1694 A1245 60y Lucanus maculifemoratus 80 55
1695 A1245 60y Anotogaster sieboldii 80 55
a. Pair, #1694-1695 1.60 1.10

1987, Mar. 12 ***Perf. 13***
1696 A1245 60y Ascaraphus ramburi 80 55
1697 A1245 60y Polyphylla laticollis 80 55
a. Pair, #1696-1697 1.60 1.10
1698 A1245 60y Kallima inachus 80 55
1699 A1245 60y Calopteryx cornelia 80 55
a. Pair, #1698-1699 1.60 1.10

Miniature Sheet

1699A Sheet of 4 (#1680, 1692, 1699b-1699c) 3.50 2.75
b. A1245 40y Anthocaris cardamines 75 55
c. A1245 40y Sasakia charonda 75 55
d. Bklt. pane, 5 #1680, 5 #1699b 8.50
e. Bklt. pane, 5 #1692, 5 #1699c 8.50

Booklet panes are perf. 13x13½ on 2 or 3 sides.

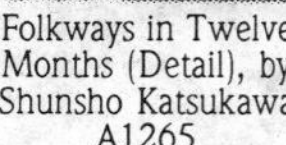

Folkways in Twelve Months (Detail), by Shunsho Katsukawa A1265

Electron Microscope A1266

1986, Aug. 23 **Photo.** ***Perf. 13***
1700 A1265 60y multi 70 48

52nd conference of the Intl. Federation of Library Associations, Tokyo, Aug. 24-29.

1986, Aug. 30
1701 A1266 60y multi 70 48

11th Int. Congress of Electron Microscopy, Kyoto, Aug. 31-Sept. 7.

23rd Intl. Conference on Social Welfare, Tokyo, Aug. 31-Sept. 5 — A1267

1986, Aug. 30 **Litho.**
1702 A1267 60y multi 70 48

Ohmorimiyage Doll, by Juzoh Kagoshima A1268

41st Natl. Athletic Meet, Oct. 12-17, Kofu A1269

1986, Oct. 6 **Photo.**
1703 A1268 130y multi 1.75 1.10

Intl. Letter Writing Week.

1986, Oct. 9
1704 A1269 40y multi 52 38

5th World Ikebana Convention A1270

Painting: Flower in Autumn and a Girl in Rakuhoku.

1986, Oct. 17 **Photo.** ***Perf. 13½x13***
1705 A1270 60y multi 70 48

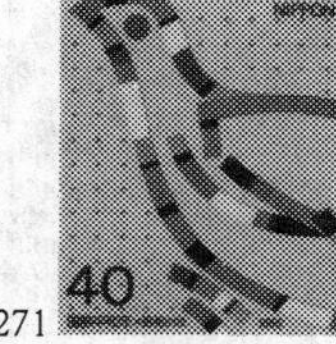

A1271

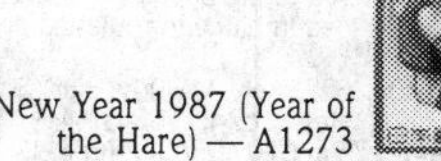

Intl. Peace Year — A1272

Lithographed, Photogravure (#1707)

1986, Nov. 28
1706 A1271 40y multi 55 35
1707 A1272 60y multi 80 52

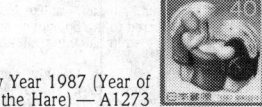

New Year 1987 (Year of the Hare) — A1273

Design: A Couple of Rabbits Making Rice Cake, Nagoya clay figurine.

1986, Dec. 1 **Photo.** ***Perf. 13x13½***
1708 A1273 40y multi 52 32

Sheets of two containing one each of Nos. 1506 and 1708 were lottery prizes. Value, $1.75.

Real Estate Registry System, Cent. — A1274

1987, Jan. 30 Photo. *Perf. 13½*
1709 A1274 60y multi 70 48

Literature Series

Basho — A1275

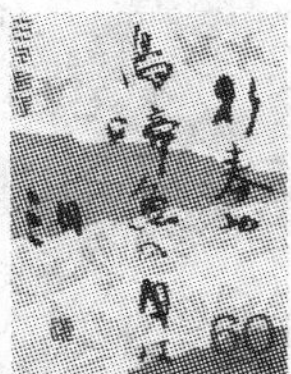
Verse from Basho's Haiku — A1276

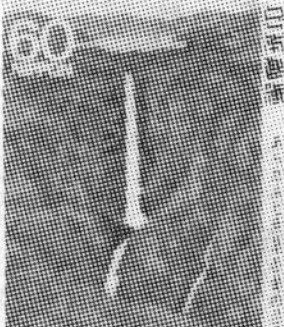
Kegon Falls — A1277

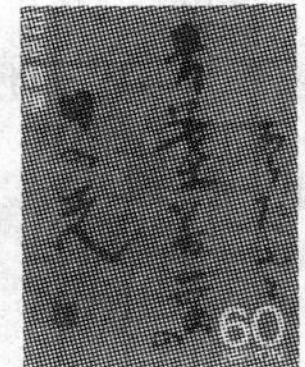
Haiku Verse — A1278

Cuckoo — A1279

Horse and Verse — A1280

Willow Tree — A1281

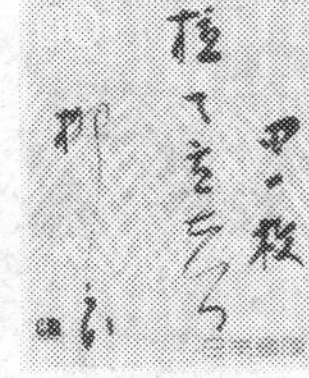
Rice Paddy and Verse — A1282

Chestnut Tree in Bloom — A1283

Chestnut Leaves and Verse — A1284

Planting Rice Paddy — A1285

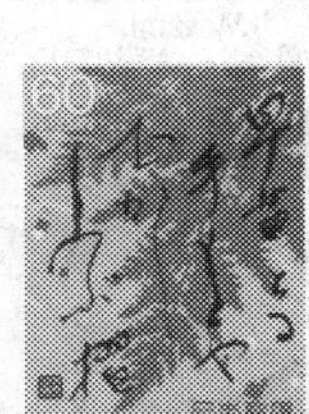
Fern Leaves and Verse — A1286

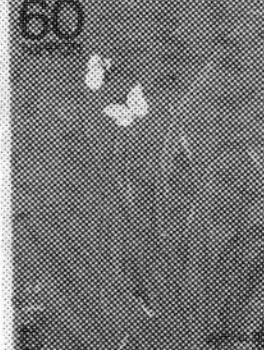
Sweetflags — A1287

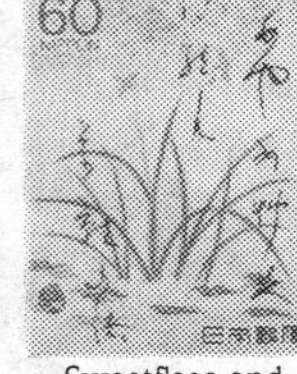
Sweetflags and Verse — A1288

Prosperous Man, 17th Cent. — A1289

Summer Grass and Verse — A1290

Safflowers in Bloom — A1291

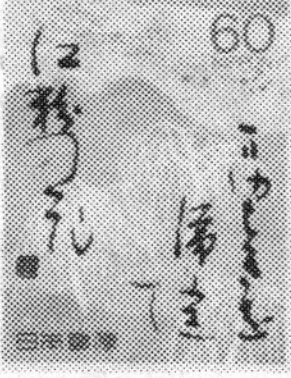
Verse — A1292

Yamadera (Temple) — A1293

Forest and Verse — A1294

1987-89 Photo. *Perf. 13x13½*
1710 A1275 60y multi 90 60
1711 A1276 60y multi 90 60
a. Sheet of 2, #1710-1711, imperf. ('89) 1.80
b. Pair, #1710-1711 1.80 1.25
1712 A1277 60y multi 90 60
1713 A1278 60y multi 90 60
a. Sheet of 2, #1712-1713, imperf. ('89) 1.80
b. Pair, #1712-1713 1.80 1.25
1714 A1279 60y multi 90 60
1715 A1280 60y multi 90 60
a. Sheet of 2, #1714-1715, imperf. ('89) 1.80
b. Pair, #1714-1715 1.80 1.25
1716 A1281 60y multi 90 60
1717 A1282 60y multi 90 60
a. Sheet of 2, #1716-1717, imperf. ('89) 1.80
b. Pair, #1716-1717 1.80 1.25
1718 A1283 60y multi 90 60
1719 A1284 60y multi 90 60
a. Sheet of 2, #1718-1719, imperf. ('89) 1.80
b. Pair, #1718-1719 1.80 1.25
1720 A1285 60y multi 90 60
1721 A1286 60y multi 90 60
a. Sheet of 2, #1720-1721, imperf. ('89) 1.80
b. Pair, #1720-1721 1.80 1.25
1722 A1287 60y multi ('88) 90 60
1723 A1288 60y multi ('88) 90 60
a. Sheet of 2, #1722-1723, imperf. ('89) 1.80
b. Pair, #1722-1723 1.80 1.25
1724 A1289 60y multi ('88) 90 60
1725 A1290 60y multi ('88) 90 60
a. Sheet of 2, #1724-1725, imperf. ('89) 1.80
b. Pair, #1724-1725 1.80 1.25
1726 A1291 60y multi ('88) 90 60
1727 A1292 60y multi ('88) 90 60
a. Sheet of 2, #1726-1727, imperf. ('89) 1.80
b. Pair, #1726-1727 1.80 1.25
1728 A1293 60y multi ('88) 90 60
1729 A1294 60y multi ('88) 90 60
a. Sheet of 2, #1728-1729, imperf. ('89) 1.80
b. Pair, #1728-1729 1.80 1.25
Nos. 1710-1729 (20) 18.00 12.00

Illustrations and text from Oku-no hosomichi, 1694, a travel description haiku written by Munefus "Basho" Matsuo (1644-1694), poet.

Issue dates: #1710-1713, Feb. 26. #1714-1717, June 23. #1718-1721, Aug. 25. #1722-1725, Jan. 3. #1726-1729, Mar. 26.

12th World Orchid Congress, Tokyo
A1295 A1296

1987, Mar. 19 Photo. *Perf. 13*
1730 A1295 60y multi 80 60
1731 A1296 60y multi 80 60

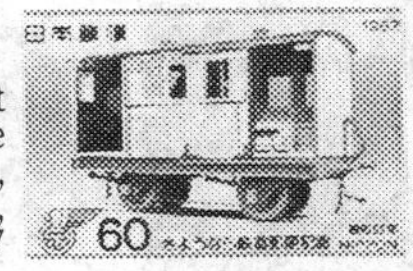
Railway Post Office Termination, Oct. 1, 1986 — A1297

1987, Mar. 26 Litho. *Perf. 13½*
1732 A1297 60y Mail car 80 60
1733 A1297 60y Loading mail on car 80 60
a. Pair, #1732-1733 1.60 1.25

Privatization of Japan Railways A1298

1987, Apr. 1 Photo. *Perf. 13½*
1734 A1298 60y Locomotive No. 137, c. 1900 80 60
1735 A1298 60y Linear induction train, 1987 80 60

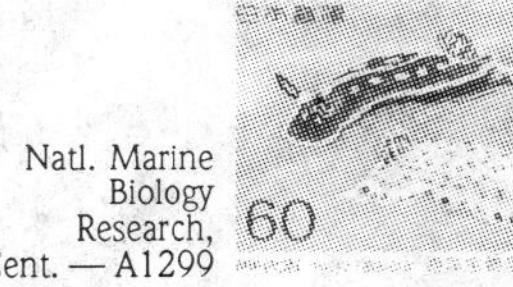
Natl. Marine Biology Research, Cent. — A1299

1987, Apr. 2 *Perf. 13*
1736 A1299 60y Sea slugs 80 60

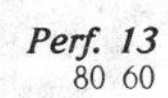

Philately Week
A1300 A1301

1987, Apr. 14
1737 A1300 60y multi 80 60
1738 A1301 60y multi 80 60
a. Pair, #1737-1738 1.60 1.25

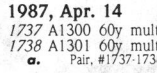

Map of Asia and Oceania A1302

1987, Apr. 27 Photo. *Perf. 13½*
1739 A1302 60y multi 80 60

20th annual meeting of the Asian Development Bank.

Nat'l. Land Afforestation Campaign — A1303

1987, May 23
1740 A1303 60y Magpie, seashore 80 60

National Treasures Series

A1304

A1305

Golden Turtle Sharito — A1306

Imuyama Dastle Donjon, 1469 — A1307

Kongo Sanmai in Tahotoh Temple, Kamakura Era — A1308

Wood Ekoh-Dohji Statue in the Likeness of Kongobuji Fudodo, Kamakura Era, by Unkei — A1309

Itsukushima Shrine, Heian Period A1310

Kozakura-gawa, Braided Armor Worn by Minamoto-no-Yoshimitsu, Heian Period War Lord, Kai Province — A1311

Statue of *Nakatsu-hime-no-mikoto*, a Hachiman Goddess, Heian Period, Yakushiji Temple — A1312

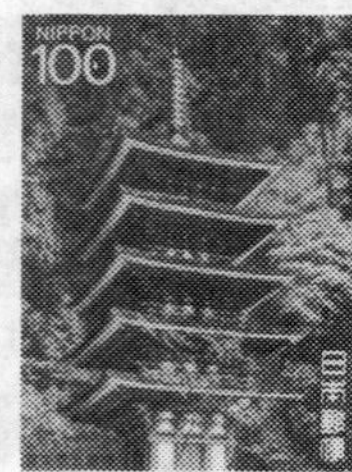

Murou-ji Temple Pagoda, 9th Cent. — A1313

Designs: No. 1741, Yatuhashi gold inkstone box, by Kohrin Ogata. No. 1742, Donjon of Hikone Castle, c. 1573-1592.

1987, May 26 Photo. *Perf. 13*
1741 A1304 60y multi 90 60

Photo. & Engr.
Perf. 13½
1742 A1305 110y multi 1.65 1.15

1987, July 17 Photo. *Perf. 13*
1743 A1306 60y multi 90 62

Photo. & Engr.
Perf. 13½
1744 A1307 110y multi 1.65 1.15

1988, Feb. 12 Photo. *Perf. 13*
1745 A1308 60y multi 90 62

Photo. & Engr.
Perf. 13½
1746 A1309 110y multi 1.65 1.15

1988, June 23 Photo. *Perf. 13*
1747 A1310 60y multi 90 68

Photo. & Engr.
Perf. 13½
1748 A1311 100y multi 1.50 1.15

1988, Sept. 26 Photo. *Perf. 13*
1749 A1312 60y multi 92 70

Photo. & Engr.
Perf. 13½
1750 A1313 100y multi 1.50 1.15
Nos. 1741-1750 (10) 12.47 8.97

Letter Writing Day — A1314

1987, July 23 Photo. *Perf. 13x13½*
1751 A1314 40y Flowers, envelope 55 42
1752 A1314 60y Elephant 82 62
a. Bklt. pane, 5 each #1751-1752 7.00

Sheets of 2, Nos. 1751-1752, were lottery prizes. Value, *$20.*

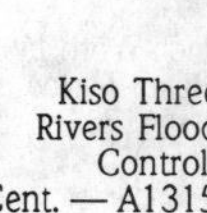

Kiso Three Rivers Flood Control, Cent. — A1315

1987, Aug. 7 Photo. *Perf. 13½*
1753 A1315 60y Kiso, Nagara and Ibi Rivers 82 62

Japan - Thailand Diplomatic Relations, Cent. — A1316

Design: Temple of the Emerald Buddha and cherry blossoms.

1987, Sept. 26 *Perf. 13*
1754 A1316 60y multi 85 65

Intl. Letter Writing Week — A1317

13th World Congress of Certified Public Accountants, Tokyo, Oct. 11-15 — A1318

Dolls by Goyo Hirata: 130y, Gensho Kanto, by Royojo Hori (1898-1984). 150y, Utage-no-Hana (Fair Woman at the Party).

1987, Oct. 6 Photo. *Perf. 13*
1755 A1317 130y multi 1.85 1.40
1756 A1317 150y multi 2.10 1.60

1987, Oct. 9 *Perf. 13*

Design: Three Beauties (adaptation), by Toyokuni Utagawa (1769-1825).

1757 A1318 60y multi 85 65

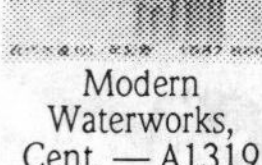

Modern Waterworks, Cent. — A1319

Shurei Gate, Okinawa, Basketball Players — A1320

Design: Lion's head public fountain, 1887, Waterworks Museum, Yokohama.

1987, Oct. 16 Engr.
1758 A1319 60y multi 88 65

1987, Oct. 24 Photo.
1759 A1320 40y multi 88 65

42nd Natl. Athletic Meet, Okinawa.

6th World Cong. on Smoking & Health, Nov. 9-12, Tokyo — A1321

World Telecommunications Conf., Nov. 15-18, Tokyo — A1322

1987, Nov. 9
1760 A1321 60y multi 90 68

1987, Nov. 13 *Perf. 13½*

Design: Microwave dish antenna at Kashima Station Radio Research Laboratory.

1761 A1322 60y multi 90 68

World Conference on Large Historic Cities, Nov. 18-21, Kyoto A1323

Design: Nijo Castle guardhouse roof and Ninomaru Hall, 17th cent.

1987, Nov. 18 *Perf. 13*
1762 A1323 60y multi 90 68

Intl. Year of Shelter for the Homeless A1324

Prize-winning illustrations by: 40y, Takahiro Nahahama. 60y, Yoko Sasaki.

1987, Nov. 25
1763 A1324 40y multi 60 45
1764 A1324 60y multi 90 68

New Year 1988 (Year of the Dragon) — A1325

Design: Kurashiki papier-mache dragon, 1869, by Tajuro Omizu.

1987, Dec. 1 *Perf. 13x13½*
1765 A1325 40y multi 60 45

Sheets of 2, Nos. 1506, 1765, were lottery prizes. Value, $2.25.

Seikan Tunnel Opening A1326

1988, Mar. 11 Engr. *Perf. 13½*
1766 A1326 60y ED 79 locomotive, map 95 72

Opening of Seto-Oohashi Bridge

Kagawa Side
A1327 A1328

Okayama Side
A1329 A1330

1988, Apr. 8 Engr. *Perf. 13½*
1767 A1327 60y multi 98 75
1768 A1328 60y multi 98 75
1769 A1329 60y multi 98 75
1770 A1330 60y multi 98 75
a. Strip of 4, #1767-1770 4.00 3.00

Nos. 1767-1768 and 1769-1770 have continuous designs.

Philately Week
A1331 A1332

Prints by Kotondo Torii (b. 1900): No. 1771, Long Undergarment. No. 1772, Kimono Sash.

1988, Apr. 19 Photo. *Perf. 13*
1771 A1331 60y multi 98 75
1772 A1332 60y multi 98 75
a. Pair, #1771-1772 2.00

Souv. sheet of 2 exists. Value $9.

Silk Road Exposition, Apr. 24-Oct. 23, Nara — A1333

Design: Plectrum guard playing the biwa, detail of Raden-Shitan-no-Gogen-Biwa, a five-panel work of gold lacquer nacre on sandalwood preserved at Shosoin.

1988, Apr. 23 Photo. & Engr.
1773 A1333 60y multi 98 75

Natl. Afforestation Campaign — A1334

Design: Yahsima, site of the Genji-Heike war, and cuckoo on olive tree branch.

1988, May 20 Photo. *Perf. 13½*
1774 A1334 60y multi 98 75

Literature Series

Mogami River — A1335

Verse and Flower — A1336

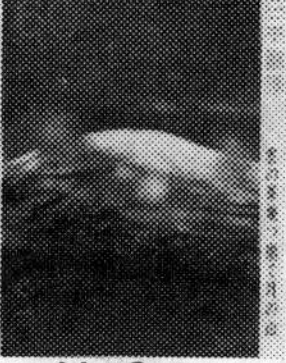

Mt. Gassan A1337

Verse and Mountain A1338

Mimosa in Bloom — A1339

Verse, Birds, Kisagata Inlet — A1340

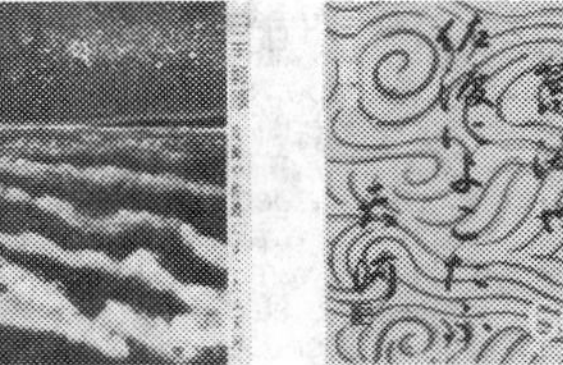
Ocean Waves — A1341

Verse and Current — A1342

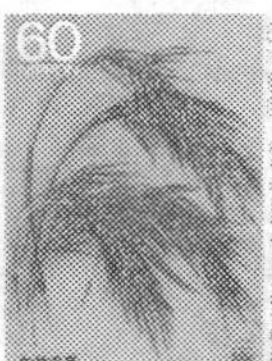
Rice — A1343

Birds in Flight, Verse — A1344

Sun Glow — A1345

Rice, Verse — A1346

Nata-dera Temple — A1347

Verse, White Grass — A1348

Trees — A1349

Verse, Moonlit Forest — A1350

Autumn on the Beach — A1351

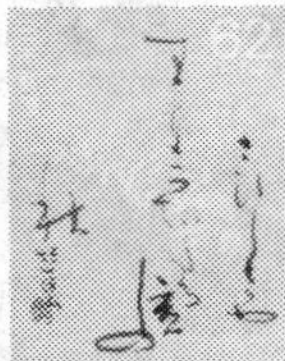
Verse — A1352

Clams — A1353

Verse — A1354

1988, May 30 Photo. *Perf. 13x13½*

1775 A1335 60y multi 98 75
1776 A1336 60y multi 98 75
a. Souv. sheet of 2, #1775-1776, imperf. ('89) 2.00
b. Pair, #1775-1776 2.00 1.50
1777 A1337 60y multi 98 75
1778 A1338 60y multi 98 75
a. Souv. sheet of 2, #1777-1778, imperf. ('89) 2.00
b. Pair, #1777-1778 2.00 1.50

1988, Aug. 23

1779 A1339 60y multi 92 70
1780 A1340 60y multi 92 70
a. Souv. sheet of 2, #1779-1780, imperf ('89) 2.00
b. Pair, #1779-1780 1.90 1.50
1781 A1341 60y multi 92 70
1782 A1342 60y multi 92 70
a. Souv. sheet of 2, #1781-1782, imperf. ('89) 2.00
b. Pair, #1781-1782 1.90 1.50

1988, Nov. 11

1783 A1343 60y multi 92 70
1784 A1344 60y multi 92 70
a. Souv. sheet of 2, #1783-1784, imperf. ('89) 2.00
b. Pair, #1783-1784 1.90 1.50
1785 A1345 60y multi 92 70
1786 A1346 60y multi 92 70
a. Souv. sheet of 2, #1785-1786, imperf. ('89) 2.00
b. Pair, #1785-1786 1.90 1.50

1989, Feb. 13

1787 A1347 60y multi 95 72
1788 A1348 60y multi 95 72
a. Souv. sheet of 2, #1787-1788, imperf. 2.00
b. Pair, #1787-1788 2.00 1.50
1789 A1349 60y multi 95 72
1790 A1350 60y multi 95 72
a. Souv. sheet of 2, #1789-1790, imperf. 2.00
b. Pair, #1789-1790 2.00 1.50

1989, May 12

1791 A1351 62y multi 92 68
1792 A1352 62y multi 92 68
a. Souv. sheet of 2, #1791-1792, imperf. 2.00
b. Pair, #1791-1792 1.90 1.40
1793 A1353 62y multi 92 68
1794 A1354 62y multi 92 68
a. Souv. sheet of 2, #1793-1794, imperf. 2.00
b. Pair, #1793-1794 1.90 1.40

Illustrations and text from *Oku-no-hosomichi,* "Narrow Road to a Far Province," 1694, a travel description written in haiku by munefus "Basho" Matsuo (1644-94), poet.

Issue date: Nos. 1776a-1794a, Aug. 1, 1989.

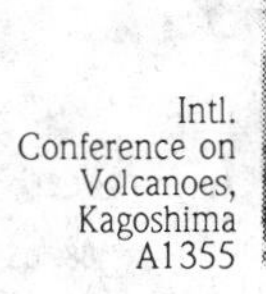
Intl. Conference on Volcanoes, Kagoshima A1355

1988, July 19 Photo. *Perf. 14*

1795 A1355 60y multi 92 70

A1356

A1357

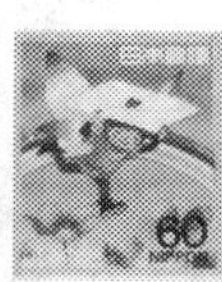
A1358

Letter Writing Day, 10th Anniv. — A1359

Designs and contest-winning children's drawings: No. 1796, Cat and letter. No. 1797, *Crab and Letter,* by Katsuyuki Yamada. No. 1798, Fairy and letter. No. 1799, *Girl and Letter,* by Takashi Ukai.

Photo., Litho. (Nos. 1797, 1799)

1988, July 23 *Perf. 13x13½*

1796 A1356 40y multi 62 48
a. Imperf., self-adhesive 62 48
1797 A1357 40y multi 62 48
1798 A1358 60y multi 92 70
a. Bklt. pane, 5 each #1796, 1798 7.75
b. Imperf., self-adhesive 92 70
c. Bklt. pane, 3 each #1796a, 1798b 4.65
1799 A1359 60y multi 92 70

No. 1798c is adhered to the booklet cover, made of peelable paper, folded in half and rouletted down the center fold, with No. 1796a at left and No. 1798b at right of the roulette.

Sheets of 2 containing Nos. 1796, 1798 were lottery prizes. Value, $9.

A1360 A1361

A1362 A1363

15th World Puppetry Festival, July 27-Aug. 11

Puppets: No. 1800, *Ohana,* string puppet from the film *Spring and Fall in the Meiji Era,* by Kinosuke Takeda (1923-1979), Japan. No. 1801, Girl, stick puppet from the Natl. Radost Puppet Theater, Brno, Czechoslovakia. No. 1802, Woman, shadow puppet from China. No. 1803, Knight, a marionette from Sicily.

1988, July 27 Photo. *Perf. 13*

1800 A1360 60y multi 92 70
1801 A1361 60y multi 92 70
1802 A1362 60y multi 92 70
1803 A1363 60y multi 92 70
a. Block of 4, #1800-1803 4.00 3.00

Japan-China Treaty, 10th Anniv.
A1364 A1365

1988, Aug. 12 Photo.

1804 A1364 60y Peony 92 70
1805 A1365 60y Panda 92 70

18th World Poultry Congress, Nagoya, Sept. 4-9 — A1366

1988, Sept. 3 *Perf. 13½*

1806 A1366 60y multi 92 70

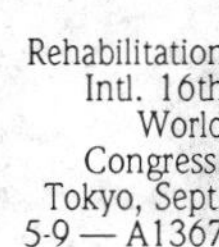

Rehabilitation Intl. 16th World Congress, Tokyo, Sept. 5-9 — A1367

Photo. & Embossed

1988, Sept. 5 *Perf. 13*

1807 A1367 60y multi 92 70

A1368 A1369

Prints: 80y, *Kumesaburo Iwai as Chiyo,* by Kunimasa Utagawa (1773-1810), late Edo Period. 120y, *Komazo Ichikawa III as Ganryu Sasaki,* by Toyokuni Utagawa (1769-1825).

1988, Oct. 6 Photo.

1808 A1368 80y multi 1.30 1.00
1809 A1368 120y multi 2.00 1.50

Intl. Letter-Writing Week.

1988, Oct. 14

Design: Gymnast on parallel bars and "Kinkakuji," Temple of the Golden Pavilion.

1810 A1369 40y multi 65 50

43rd Natl. Athletic Meet, Kyoto.

Japan-Mexico Trade Agreement, Cent. A1370

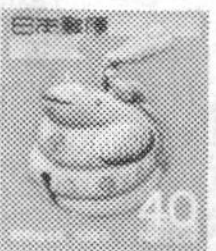
New Year 1989 (Year of the Snake) A1371

1988, Nov. 30 Photo.

1811 A1370 60y multi 98 75

1988, Dec. 1

Design: Clay bell snake by Masanobu Ogawa.

1812 A1371 40y multi 65 50

Sheets of two containing Nos. 1506, 1812 were lottery prizes. Value, $2.50.

UN Declaration of Human Rights, 40th Anniv. — A1372

1988, Dec. 5 **Litho.** ***Perf. 13½***

1813 A1372 60y multi			98	75

National Treasures Series

Votive Silver Lidded Bowl Used in Todai-ji Temple Ground-Breaking Ceremony, 8th Cent. — A1373

Bronze Yakusi-nyorai Buddha, Asuka Period, 7th Cent. — A1374

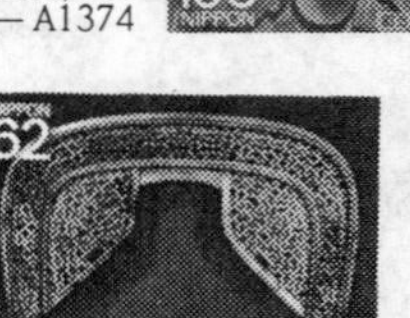
Kondo-Sukashibori-Kurakanagu, Bronze Saddle from Ohjin Imperial Mausoleum — A1375

Tamamushi-no-Zushi, Buddhist Altar in Lacquered Cypress from the Azuka Era — A1376

Kin-in, a Gokan Era Gold Seal Given to the King of Na by Emperor Kobutai — A1377

Shinninshaba-gazokyo, a 5th Cent. European Bronze Plate — A1378

Photo., Photo & Engr. (100y)

1989, Jan. 20 ***Perf. 13, 13½ (100y)***

1814 A1373 60y multi 95 72
1815 A1374 100y multi 1.60 1.20

1989, June 30

1816 A1375 62y multi 88 65
1817 A1376 100y multi 1.40 1.05

1989, Aug. 15

1818 A1377 62y multi 88 65
1819 A1378 100y multi 1.40 1.05

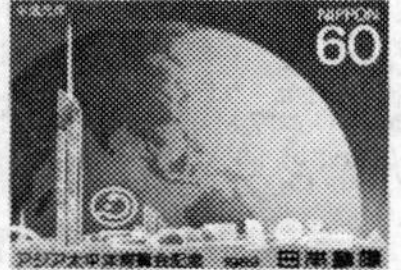
Asian-Pacific Expo, Fukuoka, Mar. 17-Sept. 3 — A1383

1989 **Photo.** ***Perf. 13***

1822 A1383 60y multicolored 95 72
1823 A1383 62y multicolored 1.25 95

Issue dates: 60y, Mar. 16. 62y, Apr. 18.

Yokohama Exposition (Space and Children), Yokohama City, Mar. 25 to Oct. 1 — A1384

Design: Detail of *Russian Lady Sight-seeing at the Port*, by Yoshitora, and entrance to the Yokohama City Art Museum.

1989, Mar. 24 **Litho.**

1824 A1384 60y multicolored 95 72
1825 A1384 62y multicolored 95 72

World Bonsai Convention, Omiya, Apr. 6-9 — A1385

1989, Apr. 6 **Photo.** ***Perf. 13***

1826 A1385 62y multi 92 68

Awa-odori, by Tsunetomi Kitano (b. 1880)

A1386 A1387

1989, Apr. 18 ***Perf. 13***

1827 A1386 62y multi 92 68
1828 A1387 62y multi 92 68
a. Pair, #1827-1828 2.00

Philately Week. Sheets of 2 containing #1827-1828 were lottery prizes. Value, $5.

Values quoted in this catalogue are for stamps graded at Fine-Very Fine and with no faults. An illustrated guide to grade is provided in introductory material, beginning on Page 5A.

Holland Festival 1989 — A1388

1989, Apr. 19 ***Perf. 13½***

1829 A1388 62y Ship 92 68

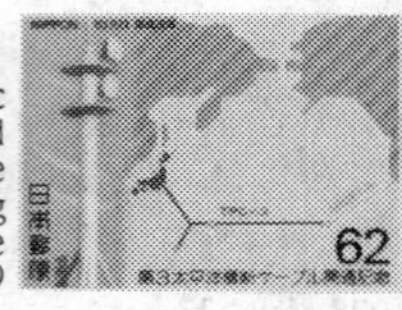
Fiber-optic Cable, the 3rd Transpacific Line Relay Linking Japan and the US — A1389

1989, May 10 ***Perf. 13½x13***

1830 A1389 62y Station tower, map 92 68

Natl. Afforestation Campaign — A1390

1989, May 19 ***Perf. 13½***

1831 A1390 62y Bayberry, lime, Mt. Tsurugi 92 68

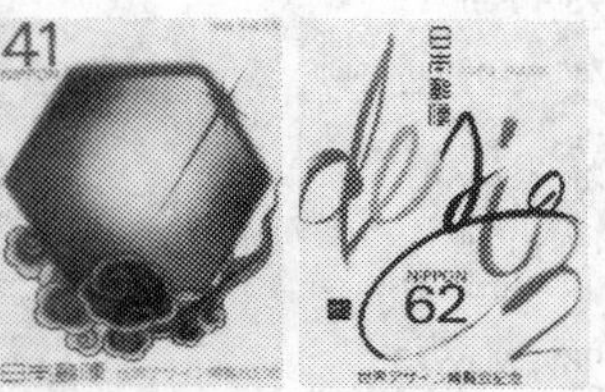
World Design Exposition, Nagoya, July 15-Nov. 26

A1391 A1392

1989, July 14

1832 A1391 41y multi 58 42
1833 A1392 62y multi 88 65

Letter Writing Day

A1393 A1394

1989, July 21 ***Perf. 13x13½***

1834 A1393 41y multi 58 42
1835 A1394 62y multi 88 65
a. Bklt. pane, 5 each #1834-1835 7.30

Sheets of 2 containing Nos. 1834-1835 were lottery prizes. Value, $5.25.

Congratulations and Condolances Types of 1982

1989, Aug. 10 **Photo.** ***Perf. 13x13½***

1836 A1082 41y Wreath 58 42
1837 A1083 41y Crane 58 42
1838 A1083 62y Crane 88 65
1839 A1084 72y Tortoise 1.05 78

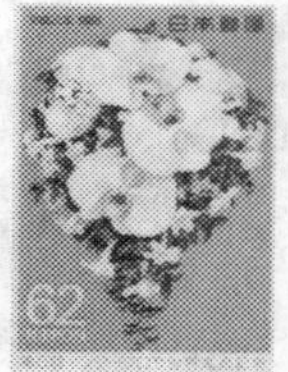
6th Interflora World Congress, Tokyo, Aug. 27-30 — A1395

1989, Aug. 25 **Photo.** ***Perf. 13½***

1840 A1395 62y multi 88 65

Prefecture Issues

Nos. 1841-1990 have been reserved for issues for Japan's 47 prefectures (political subdivisions). These stamps were available only in the prefecture for which they were issued, except for No. 1909a, which was available nationwide. All of the stamps were valid throughout Japan. Prefecture stamps are distinguishable from other Japanese issues by the calligraphic style of the four characters which represent the country name.

Monkeys (Nagano) A1396

Cherries on Tree (Yamagata) A1397

Shurei-mon, Gate of Courtesy (Okinawa) A1398

Dogo Hot Spa (Ehime) A1399

Blue-eyed Doll (Kanagawa) — A1400

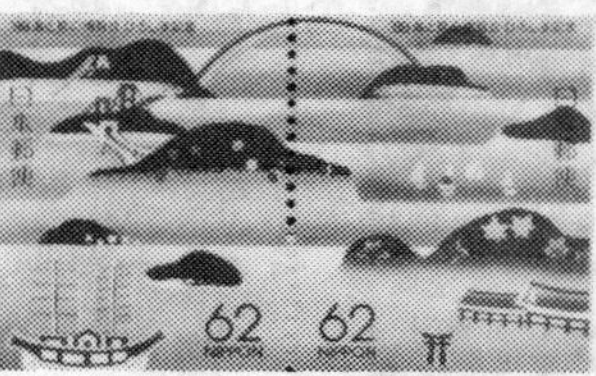
Seto Inland Sea (Hiroshima)

A1401 A1402

Memorial Hall and Mandai Bridge (Niigata) — A1403

Nagoya Castle and *Shachihoko* (Aichi)
A1404

Mt. Takasaki Monkey Holding Perilla Leaf, Fruit (Oita) — A1405

City Hall, 1888 (Hokkaido) — A1406

Runner, Flower (Hokkaido)
A1407

Kumamoto Castle (Kumamoto)
A1408

Stone Lantern, Kenroku-en Park (Ishikawa)
A1409

Bunraku Puppets and Theater (Osaka)
A1410

Shigaraki Ware Raccoon Dog and Lake Biwa (Shiga)
A1411

Apples and Blossoms (Aomori) — A1412

Raccoon Dogs Dancing (Chiba) — A1413

Blowfish Lanterns (Yamaguchi)
A1414

Tokyo Station (Tokyo)
A1415

2nd Asian Winter Olympics (Hokkaido)
A1416

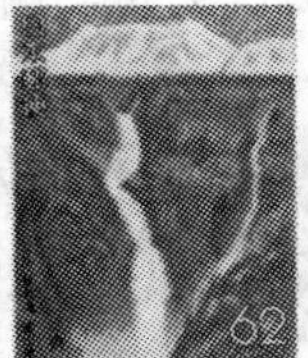
Waterfalls (Toyama)
A1417

Perf. 13, 13½ (#1844, 1851, 1860), 13x13½ (#1852-1859)

1989-90 Photo., Litho. (#1856-1857)

1841	A1396	62y multi		88	65
1842	A1397	62y multi		88	65
1843	A1398	62y multi		88	65
1844	A1399	62y multi		88	65
1845	A1400	62y multi		88	65
1846	A1401	62y multi		88	65
1847	A1402	62y multi		88	65
a.		Pair, #1846-1847		2.00	1.50
1848	A1403	62y multi		88	65
1849	A1404	62y multi		88	65
1850	A1405	62y multi		88	65
1851	A1406	62y multi		88	65
1852	A1407	62y multi		88	65
1853	A1408	62y multi		88	65
1854	A1409	62y multi		88	65
1855	A1410	62y multi		88	65
1856	A1411	62y multi		88	65
1857	A1412	62y multi		88	65
1858	A1413	62y multi		88	65
1859	A1414	62y multi		88	65
1860	A1415	62y multi		88	65
1861	A1416	62y multi		88	65
1862	A1417	62y multi		82	62

Sheets containing 4 #1841, 1842, 1844, 1851 or 3 #1854 + label, 3 #1859 + label were lottery prizes.

Issued: #1841-1842, Apr. 1; #1843, May 15; #1844, June 1; #1845, June 2; #1846-1847, July 7; #1848, July 14. #1849, Aug. 1; #1850-1851, Aug. 15. #1852, Sept. 1; #1853, Sept. 29; #1854-1857, Oct. 2; #1858, Oct. 27; #1859-1860, Nov. 1; #1861, Mar. 1, 1990; #1862, Apr. 18, 1990.

Nos. 1863-1909 were issued as one set. It is broken into sections for ease of reference.

Hokkaido
A1418

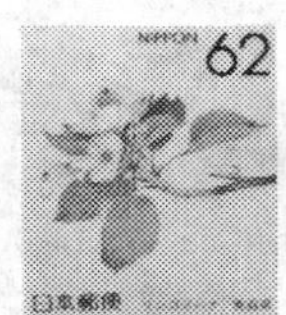
Aomori
A1419

Iwate — A1420

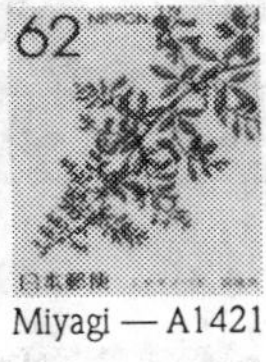
Miyagi — A1421

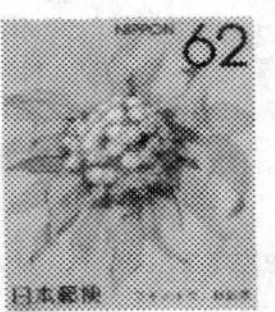
Akita
A1422

Yamagata
A1423

Fukushima
A1424

Ibaraki
A1425

Flowers of the Prefectures.

1990, Apr. 27 Litho. *Perf. 13½*

1863	A1418	62y	Sweet briar	82	62
1864	A1419	62y	Apple blossom	82	62
1865	A1420	62y	Paulowina	82	62
1866	A1421	62y	Japanese bush clover	82	62
1867	A1422	62y	Butterbur flower	82	62
1868	A1423	62y	Safflower	82	62
1869	A1424	62y	Alpine rose	82	62
1870	A1425	62y	Rose	82	62

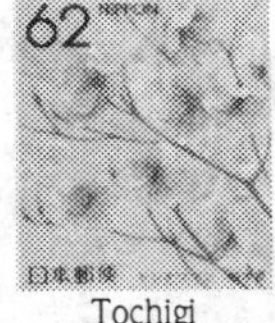
Tochigi
A1426

Gunma
A1427

Saitama
A1428

Chiba
A1429

Kanagawa
A1430

Yamanashi
A1431

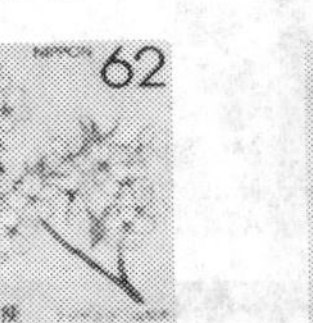
Tokyo
A1432

Nagano
A1433

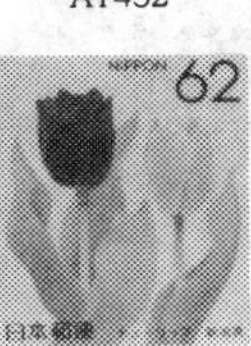
Niigata
A1434

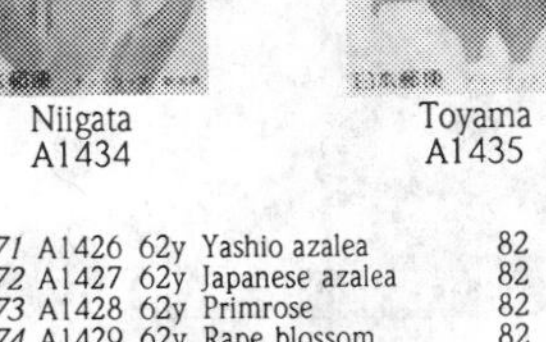
Toyama
A1435

1871	A1426	62y	Yashio azalea	82	62
1872	A1427	62y	Japanese azalea	82	62
1873	A1428	62y	Primrose	82	62
1874	A1429	62y	Rape blossom	82	62
1875	A1430	62y	Gold-banded lily	82	62
1876	A1431	62y	Cherry blossom	82	62
1877	A1432	62y	Cherry blossom	82	62
1878	A1433	62y	Autumn bellflower	82	62
1879	A1434	62y	Tulip	82	62
1880	A1435	62y	Tulip	82	62

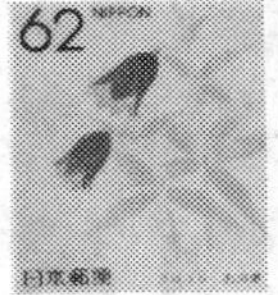
Ishikawa
A1436

Fukui
A1437

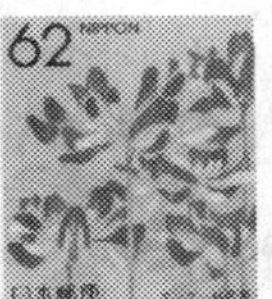
Gifu
A1438

Shizuoka
A1439

Aichi — A1440

Mie — A1441

Shiga — A1442

Kyoto — A1443

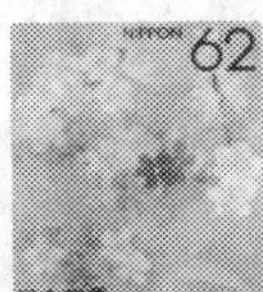
Osaka — A1444

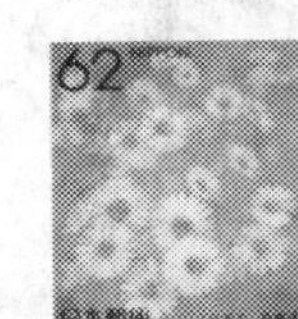
Hyogo — A1445

1881	A1436	62y	Black lily	82	62
1882	A1437	62y	Daffodil	82	62
1883	A1438	62y	Chinese milk vetch	82	62
1884	A1439	62y	Azalea	82	62
1885	A1440	62y	Rabbit-ear iris	82	62
1886	A1441	62y	Iris	82	62
1887	A1442	62y	Alpine rose	82	62
1888	A1443	62y	Drooping cherry blossom	82	62
1889	A1444	62y	Japanese apricot and primrose	82	62
1890	A1445	62y	Chrysanthemum	82	62

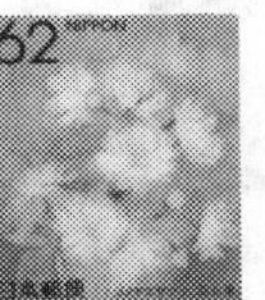
Nara
A1446

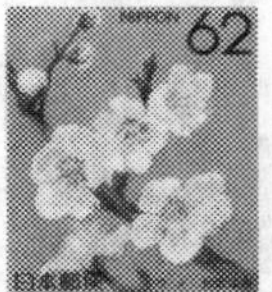
Wakayama
A1447

Tottori
A1448

Shimane
A1449

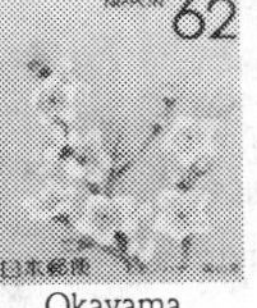
Okayama
A1450

Hiroshima
A1451

Yamaguchi
A1452

Tokushima
A1453

Kagawa
A1454

Ehime
A1455

1891 A1446 62y Double cherry blossom 82 62
1892 A1447 62y Japanese apricot 82 62
1893 A1448 62y Pear blossom 82 62
1894 A1449 62y Peony 82 62
1895 A1450 62y Peach blossom 82 62
1896 A1451 62y Japanese Mmple 82 62
1897 A1452 62y Summer orange blossom 82 62
1898 A1453 62y Sudachi orange blossom 82 62
1899 A1454 62y Olive blossom 82 62
1900 A1455 62y Mandarin orange blossom 82 62

Kochi
A1456

Fukuoka
A1457

Saga
A1458

Nagasaki
A1459

Kumamoto
A1460

Oita
A1461

Miyazaki
A1462

Kagoshima
A1463

Okinawa — A1464

1901 A1456 62y Myrica 82 62
1902 A1457 62y Japanese apricot 82 62
1903 A1458 62y Laurel 82 62
1904 A1459 62y Unzen azalea 82 62
1905 A1460 62y Autumn bellflower 82 62
1906 A1461 62y Japanese apricot of bungo 82 62
1907 A1462 62y Crinum 82 62
1908 A1463 62y Rosebay 82 62
1909 A1464 62y Coral tree 82 62
a. Sheet of 47 + 3 labels, #1863-1909 39.00

Nos. 1863-1909 were issued in sheets of 20.

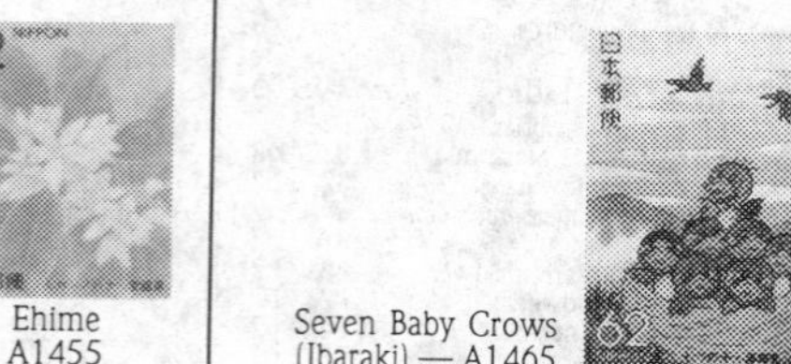
Seven Baby Crows (Ibaraki) — A1465

Inns of Tsumago & Magome (Nagano)
A1466 A1467

Mt. Fuji and Tea Picking (Shizuoka)
A1468

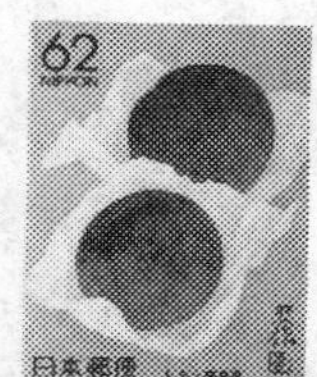
Two Peaches (Fukushima)
A1469

Mt. Sakurajima (Kagoshima)
A1470

Fireworks Festival of Omagari (Akita)
A1471

Travel Expo '90, Nagasaki (Nagasaki) — A1472

Tokyo Shin Post Office (Tokyo)
A1473

Yasukibushi Folk Song (Shimane)
A1474

Ryukyu Dancer (Okinawa)
A1475

Litho., Litho. & Engr. (#1911-1912)

1990 ***Perf. 13***

1910 A1465 62y multicolored 82 62
1911 A1466 62y blk & buff 82 62
1912 A1467 62y blk & pale grn 82 62
a. Pair, #1911-1912 1.65 1.25
1913 A1468 62y multicolored 82 62
1914 A1469 62y multicolored 95 72
1915 A1470 62y multicolored 95 72
1916 A1471 62y multicolored 95 72
1917 A1472 62y multicolored 95 72
1918 A1473 62y multicolored 95 72
1919 A1474 62y multicolored 95 72
1920 A1475 62y multicolored 95 72

Issued: #1910-1912, May 1. #1913, May 2. #1914, June 1. #1915-1916, July 2. #1917, Aug. 1. #1918, Aug. 6. #1919-1920, Aug. 15.

Sheets of 3 + label of #1910, 1913, 1920 were lottery prizes. Value, each $3.25.

Dancing Girl (Kyoto)
A1476

Old Path of Kumano (Wakayama)
A1477

45th Natl. Athletic Meet (Fukuoka)
A1478

Izu Swamp, Swans (Miyagi)
A1479

Spring (Gifu) — A1480

Summer (Gifu) — A1481

Autumn (Gifu) — A1482

Winter (Gifu) — A1483

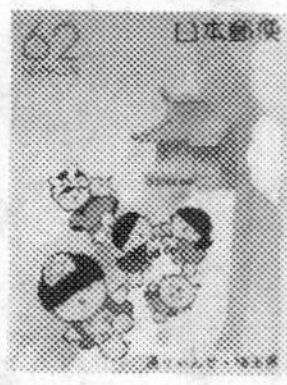
Nursery Rhyme, Toryanse (Saitama) — A1484

Japanese Cranes (Hokkaido)
A1485

1990

1921 A1476 62y multicolored 95 72
1922 A1477 62y multicolored 95 72
1923 A1478 62y multicolored 95 72
1924 A1479 62y multicolored 1.00 75
1925 A1480 62y multicolored 1.00 75
1926 A1481 62y multicolored 1.00 75
1927 A1482 62y multicolored 1.00 75
1928 A1483 62y multicolored 1.00 75
a. Strip of 4, #1925-1928 4.00 3.00
1929 A1484 62y multicolored 1.00 75
1930 A1485 62y multicolored 1.00 75

Issued: #1921-1923, Sept. 3. #1924, Oct. 1. #1925-1928, Oct. 9. #1929, Oct. 12. #1930, Oct. 30.

Sheets of 3 #1922 + label were lottery prizes. Value, $3.25.

Bizen Ware (Okayama)
A1487 A1488

Battle of Yashima (Kagawa) — A1486

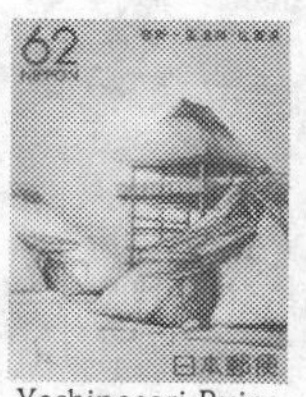
Yoshinogari Ruins (Saga) — A1489

Bride Under Cherry Blossoms (Yamanashi)
A1490

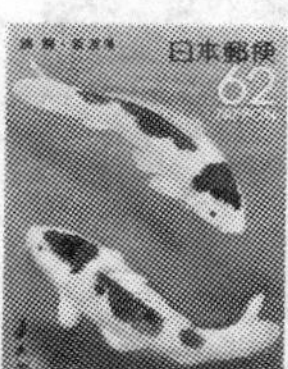
Carp (Niigata)
A1491

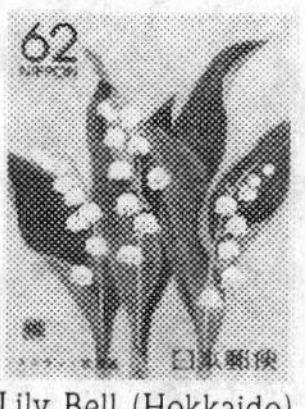
Lily Bell (Hokkaido)
A1492

Lilac (Hokkaido)
A1493

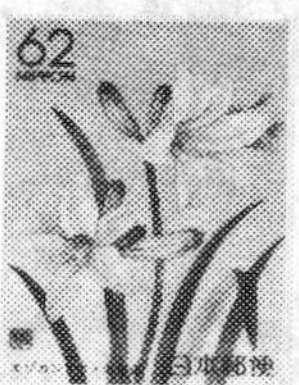
Day Lily (Hokkaido)
A1494

Rowanberry (Hokkaido)
A1495

Litho., Photo. (#1934-1935)

1991 ***Perf. 13***

1931 A1486 62y multicolored 1.00 75
1932 A1487 62y multicolored 95 70
1933 A1488 62y multicolored 95 70
a. Pair, #1932-1933 1.90 1.50
1934 A1489 62y multicolored 95 70
1935 A1490 62y multicolored 95 70
1936 A1491 62y multicolored 95 70
1937 A1492 62y multicolored 95 70
1938 A1493 62y multicolored 95 70
1939 A1494 62y multicolored 95 70
1940 A1495 62y multicolored 95 70
a. Strip of 4, #1937-1940 3.80 2.50

Issued: #1931, Feb. 19. #1932-1933, Apr. 5. #1934, Apr. 12. #1935, Apr. 18. #1936, May 1. #1937-1940, May 31.

Nikkou Mountains (Tochigi) — A1496

Mt. Iwate by Yaoji Hashimoto (Iwate) — A1497

Wooden Puppet (Tokushima) A1498

Whales (Kochi) A1499

Fringed Orchids (Tokyo) A1500

Cape Toi, Horses (Miyazaki) A1501

Black Pearls of Kabira Bay (Okinawa) A1502

Japanese Pears (Tottori) A1504

Tsujun-kyo Bridge (Kumamoto) A1503

1991 **Photo.**

1941 A1496 62y multicolored 95 70
1942 A1497 62y multicolored 95 70
a. Booklet pane of 10 9.50
1943 A1498 62y multicolored 95 70
a. Booklet pane of 10 9.50
1944 A1499 62y multicolored 95 70
a. Booklet pane of 10 9.50
1945 A1500 41y multicolored 68 50
a. Booklet pane of 10 15.00
1946 A1501 62y multicolored 95 70
a. Booklet pane of 10 15.00
1947 A1502 41y multicolored 68 50
1948 A1503 62y multicolored 95 70
a. Bklt. pane of 10 15.00
1949 A1504 62y multicolored 95 70

Issued: #1941, May 29. #1942, June 10. #1943-1944, June 26. #1945-1946, July 1. #1947-1948, Aug. 1. #1949, Aug. 26.

Sheets of 3 #1946 + label were lottery prizes. Value, $3.

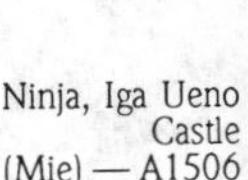

Ninja, Iga Ueno Castle (Mie) — A1506

46th Natl. Athletic Meet (Ishikawa) — A1505

Eyeglass Industry (Fukui) — A1507

Nursery Rhyme, Tortoise and the Hare — A1508

Kobe City Weathervane (Hyogo) — A1509

Spring (Nara) — A1510

Autumn (Nara) (Gunma) — A1511

Litho., Photo. (#1950, 1952)

1991 ***Perf. 13, 13½ (#1950)***

1950 A1505 41y multicolored 68 50
1951 A1506 62y multicolored 95 70
a. Bklt. pane of 10 14.00
1952 A1507 62y multicolored 1.00 75
a. Booklet pane of 10 14.00 10.50
1953 A1508 62y multicolored 1.00 75
a. Booklet pane of 10 14.00
1954 A1509 62y multicolored 1.00 75
a. Booklet pane of 10 14.00
1955 A1510 62y multicolored 1.00 75
1956 A1511 62y multicolored 1.00 75
a. Pair, #1955-1956 2.00 1.50
b. Bklt. pane of 5 #1956a 14.00

Issued: #1950, Sept. 2. #1951, Sept. 10. #1952, Oct. 1. #1953-1956, Oct.

Gogo-An Temple, Sea of Japan (Niigata) — A1512

Natl. Land Afforestation Campaign (Fukuoka) — A1513

Arctic Fox (Hokkaido) A1514

Tateyama Mountain Range (Toyama) A1515

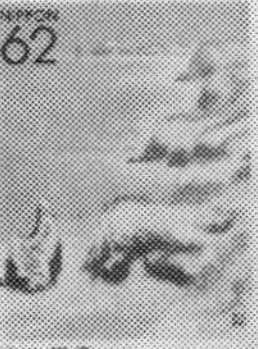
Rikuchu Coast (Iwate) A1516

Kurushima Strait (Ehime) A1517

Tsurusaki Dance (Oita) A1518

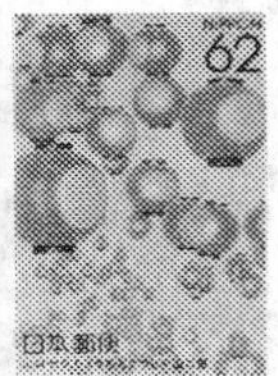
Tanabata Lantern Festival (Yamaguchi) A1519

1992 **Litho.** ***Perf. 13½***

1957 A1512 41y multicolored 65 48
a. Booklet pane of 10 6.50

Photo.

1958 A1513 41y multicolored 65 48
1959 A1514 62y multicolored 1.00 75
a. Souvenir sheet of 3 3.00 2.25

Litho.

1960 A1515 62y multicolored 1.00 75
a. Booklet pane of 10 10.00

Photo.

1961 A1516 62y multicolored 1.00 75
a. Booklet pane of 10 10.00
1962 A1517 62y multicolored 1.00 75
1963 A1518 62y multicolored 1.05 78
1964 A1519 62y multicolored 1.05 78

Issued: #1957, May. 1. #1958, May 8. #1961-1962, June 23. #1959, May 29. #1963, July 23. #1964, July 7.

Shasui-no-taki Waterfall (Kanagawa) A1520

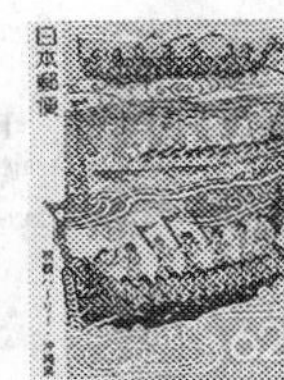
Boat Race (Okinawa) A1522

Osaka Castle, Business Park (Osaka) — A1523

Owl, Mt. Horaiji (Aichi) — A1524

Oga Peninsula (Akita) — A1525

1992 **Photo.** ***Perf. 13½***

1965 A1520 62y multicolored 1.05 78
a. Booklet pane of 10 10.50
b. Souvenir sheet of 3 3.00 2.25

Litho.

1967 A1522 62y multicolored 1.00 75
1968 A1523 41y multicolored 70 52

Photo.

1969 A1524 62y multicolored 1.00 75
a. Souvenir sheet of 3 3.00 2.25

Litho.

1970 A1525 41y multicolored 70 52

Issued: #1965, July 24. #1967, Aug. 17. #1969, Oct. 15.

This is an expanding set. Format and numbers will change if necessary.

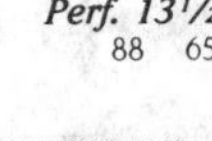
Far East and South Pacific Games for the Disabled (FESPIC), Kobe, Sept. 15-20 A1546

1989, Sept. 14 **Photo.** ***Perf. 13½***

1991 A1546 62y multicolored 88 65

Okuni Kabuki Screen
A1547 A1548

1989, Sept. 18 ***Perf. 13***

1992 A1547 62y multicolored 88 65
1993 A1548 70y multicolored 98 75

EUROPALIA '89, Japan.

A1549

A1550

Scenes from the Yadori and Takekawa Chapters of the Tales of the Genji picture scroll, attributed to Fujiwara-no-Takeyoshi, late Heian Period (897-1185).

1989, Oct. 6 **Photo.** ***Perf. 13½***

1994 A1549 80y multicolored 1.15 88
1995 A1550 120y multicolored 1.70 1.25

Intl. Letter Writing Day.

Intl. Conference on Irrigation and Drainage A1551

100th Tenno Sho Horse Race A1552

1989, Oct. 13

1996 A1551 62y Rice 90 68

1989, Oct. 27 ***Perf. 13***

1997 A1552 62y Jockey riding Shinzan 90 68

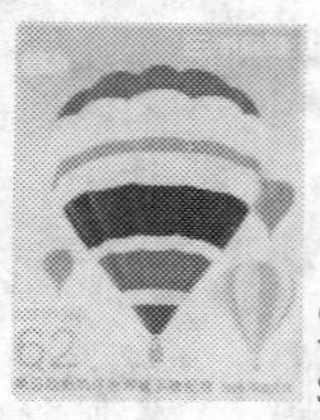

9th Hot Air Balloon World Championships, Saga — A1553

1989, Nov. 17 Photo. *Perf. 13x13½*

1998 A1553 62y multicolored 88 65

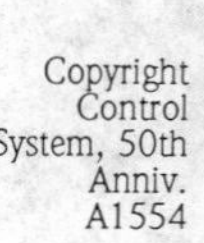

Copyright Control System, 50th Anniv. A1554

1989, Nov. 17 *Perf. 13*

1999 A1554 62y Conductor 88 65

New Year 1990 (Year of the Horse)

A1555 A1556

1989, Dec. 1 *Perf. 13x13½, 13½*

2000 A1555 41y *Yawata-Uma* festival horse 58 42

2001 A1556 62y *Kazari-Uma*, Meiji Period 88 65

No. 2001 was sold through Jan. 10, 1990, serving as a lottery ticket.

Sheets of two containing Nos. 1838, 2000 were lottery prizes. Value, $2.

Electric Locomotives

10,000 A1557

1990 Photo. & Engr., Photo. *Perf. 13*

2002 A1557 62y shown	88	65
2003 A1557 62y EF58	88	65
2004 A1557 62y ED40	88	65
2005 A1557 62y EH10	88	65
2006 A1557 62y EF53	88	65
2007 A1557 62y ED70	88	65
2008 A1557 62y EF55	82	62
2009 A1557 62y ED61	82	62
2010 A1557 62y EF57	82	62
2011 A1557 62y EF30	82	62
Nos. 2002-2011 (10)	8.56	6.38

Issued two stamps at a time, the first photo. & engr., the second photo.

Issue dates: Nos. 2002-2003, Jan. 31; Nos. 2004-2005, Feb. 28; Nos. 2006-2007, Apr. 23; Nos. 2008-2009, May 23; Nos. 2010-2011, July 18.

Intl. Garden and Greenery Exposition, Osaka A1558

1990, Mar. 30 Photo. *Perf. 13*

2021 A1558 62y multicolored 88 65

See No. B45.

A1559 A1560

Painting: *Women Gazing at the Stars*, by Chou Ohta.

1990, Apr. 20 Photo. *Perf. 13*

2022 A1559 62y multicolored 88 65
 a. Souvenir sheet of 1 88

Philately Week.

1990, May 18 Photo. *Perf. 13½*

2023 A1560 62y Azalea, Mt. Unzen 82 62

Natl. Land Afforestation Campaign.

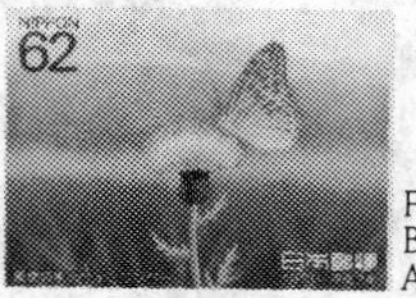

Flower, Butterfly A1561

Designs: 70y, Abstract art.

1990, June 1 Photo. *Perf. 13*

2024 A1561 62y multicolored 82 62

2025 A1561 70y multicolored 88 66

Japan-Turkey Relations, Cent. — A1562

1990, June 13

2026 A1562 62y multicolored 82 62

Horses Series

Horse at Stable from Umaya-zu Byobu — A1563 Ponies — A1564

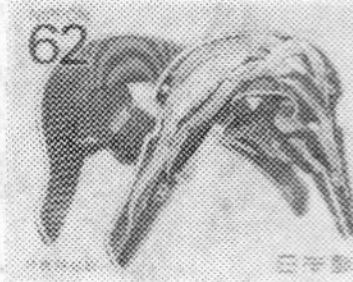

Lacquered Saddle, 16th Cent. — A1565

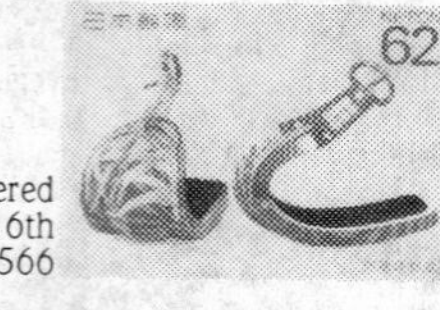

Lacquered Stirrups, 16th Cent. — A1566

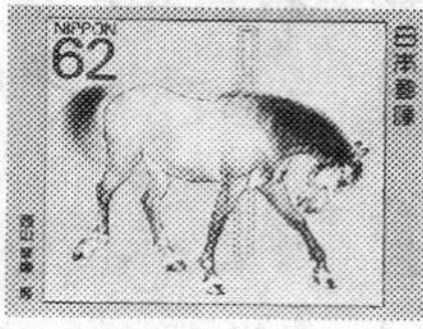

Horse by S. Nishiyama A1567

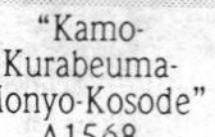

"Kamo-Kurabeuma-Monyo-Kosode" A1568 Kettei A1569

Postal Carriages

A1569a A1569b

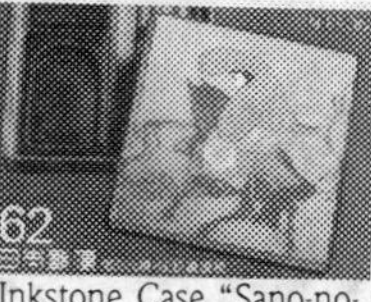

Inkstone Case "Sano-no-Watashi" — A1570

"Bushu-Senju-zu" by Hokusai — A1571

"Shudan" by Kogetsu Saigo A1571a

Designs: Nos. 2027-2031 each show a panel of folding screen with a different horse tied up at a stable.

Perf. 13x13½, 13

1990, June 20 Litho. & Engr.

Color of Horse

2027 A1563 62y red brown	82	62
2028 A1563 62y gray	82	62
2029 A1563 62y beige	82	62
2030 A1563 62y tan	82	62
2031 A1563 62y mottled	82	62
a. Strip of 5, #2027-2031	4.10	

Photo.

2032 A1564 62y shown 82 62

Photo. & Engr.

2033 A1565 62y shown	82	62
2034 A1566 62y shown	82	62
a. Pair, #2033-2034	1.65	1.25

Photo.

2035 A1567 62y multicolored	82	62
2036 A1568 62y multicolored	82	62
2037 A1569 62y multicolored	82	62

Photo. & Engr., photo. (#2040, 2042)

1991 *Perf. 12½x13*

2038 A1569a 62y multicolored	1.00	75
2039 A1569b 62y multicolored	1.00	75
a. Pair, #2038-2039	2.00	1.50

Perf. 13½x13

2040 A1570 62y multicolored	1.00	75
2041 A1571 62y multicolored	1.00	75
2042 A1571a 62y multicolored	1.00	75
Nos. 2027-2037 (11)	9.02	6.82

Issue dates: Nos. 2038-2040, Jan. 31. Nos. 2041-2042, Feb. 28.

38th Intl. Youth Hostel Fed. Conference — A1573

1990, June 25 Litho. *Perf. 13*

2057 A1573 62y multicolored 82 62

Letter Writing Day

A1574 A1575

1990, July 23 Photo. *Perf. 13½*

2058 A1574 41y multicolored	54	40
2059 A1575 62y multicolored	82	62
a. Souv. sheet of 1	90	70
b. Bklt. pane, 5 each #2058-2059	7.50	

See No. 2117.

21st Intl. Congress of Mathematicians A1576

1990, Aug. 17 Photo. *Perf. 13*

2060 A1576 62y multicolored 82 62

World Cycling Championships A1577

1990, Aug. 20 Litho. *Perf. 13½*

2061 A1577 62y multicolored 82 62

Ogai Mori, Educator A1578

1990, Aug. 27 **Photo.**
2062 A1578 62y multicolored 82 62

Intl. Assoc. for Germanic Studies (IVG), 8th Congress.

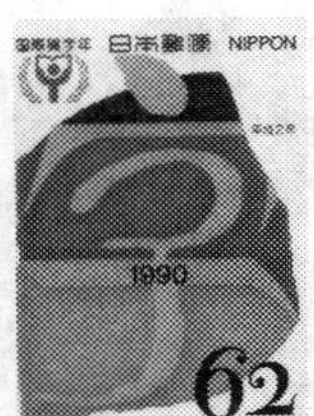

Character "Ji" in Shape of Rosetta Stone — A1579

1990, Sept. 7 ***Perf. 13***
2063 A1579 62y multicolored 82 62

Intl. Literacy Year.

Decade for Natural Disaster Reduction A1580

1990, Sept. 27 **Photo.**
2064 A1580 62y multicolored 82 62

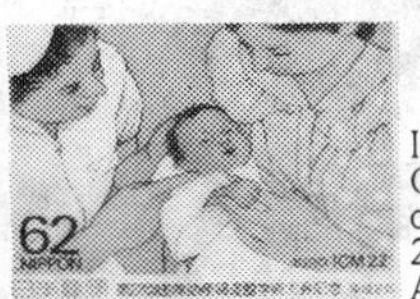

Intl. Confederation of Midwives, 22nd Congress A1581

1990, Oct. 5 **Photo.**
2065 A1581 62y multicolored 90 65

A1582

"Choju-Jinbutsu-Giga" — A1583

Photo. & Engr.

1990, Oct. 5 ***Perf. 13½***
2066 A1582 80y multicolored 1.15 90
2067 A1583 120y multicolored 1.75 1.30

Intl. Letter Writing Week.

"Fumizukai-zu" by Harunobu Suiendo — A1584

1990, Oct. 16 **Photo.**
2068 A1584 100y multicolored 1.45 1.10
a. Souv. sheet of 1 1.45 1.10

No. 2068a exists with surcharge which paid admission to PHILANIPPON '91. These were not sold by the post office.

Court System, Cent. — A1585

1990, Nov. 1 **Photo.** ***Perf. 13x13½***
2069 A1585 62y "Justice" 90 65

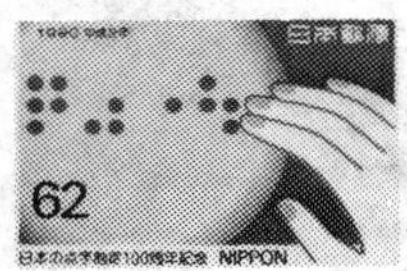

Japanese Braille, Cent. — A1586

Photo & Embossed

1990, Nov. 1 ***Perf. 13½***
2070 A1586 62y multicolored 90 65

Enthronement of Akihito A1587

Designs: No. 2071, Chinese phoenix depicted on Emperor's chair. No. 2072, Diamond pattern for costume worn at banquet ceremony.

1990, Nov. 9 **Photo.** ***Perf. 13***
2071 A1587 62y multicolored 90 65
2072 A1587 62y multicolored 90 65
a. Souv. sheet of 2, #2071-2072 1.80 1.30

Japanese Diet, Cent. — A1588

1990, Nov. 29 **Litho.**
2073 A1588 62y multicolored 90 65

New Year 1991 (Year of the Sheep)

A1589 A1590

1990, Dec. 3 **Photo.** ***Perf. 13x13½***
2074 A1589 41y multicolored 62 42

Photo. & Engr.
Perf. 13½
2075 A1590 41y multicolored 62 42
2076 A1590 62y multi, diff. 90 65

Sheets of 2 No. 2074 were lottery prizes. Value, $1.50.

Dr. Yoshio Nishina, Physicist — A1591

Telephone Service, Cent. — A1592

1990, Dec. 6 **Photo.** ***Perf. 13***
2077 A1591 62y multicolored 90 65

Use of radio isotopes in Japan, 50th anniv.

1990, Dec. 14
2078 A1592 62y multicolored 90 65

A1593 A1594

1991, Mar. 1 **Photo.** ***Perf. 13½***
2079 A1593 41y Figure skating 60 45

Perf. 13½x13
2080 A1593 62y Speed skating, horiz. 1.00 75

1991 Winter Universiade.

1991, Apr. 1 **Photo.** ***Perf. 13***
2081 A1594 62y multicolored 95 70

Postal Life Insurance System.

Philately Week

A1595 A1596

Designs: No. 2082, Beauty Looking Back by Moronobu. No. 2083, Opening Dance by Shuho Yamakawa.

1991, Apr. 19
2082 A1595 62y multicolored 95 70
2083 A1596 62y multicolored 95 70
a. Souv. sheet of 2, #2082-2083 1.90 1.50

Postal Service, 120th anniv.

Pairs of Nos. 2082-2083 with label between are available from sheets of 20.

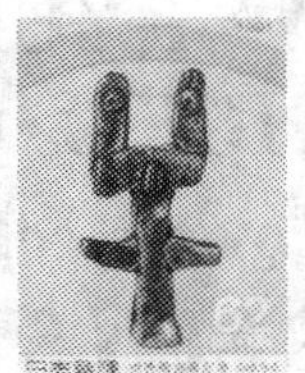

A1597 A1598

1991, Apr. 19 ***Perf. 13½***
2084 A1597 62y multicolored 95 70

Ceramic World Shigaraki '91.

1991, May 24 **Photo.** ***Perf. 13½***
2085 A1598 41y multicolored 65 48

Natl. Land Afforestation Campaign.

Standard Datum of Leveling, Cent. — A1599

1991, May 30 **Photo.** ***Perf. 13***
2086 A1599 62y mutlicolored 95 70

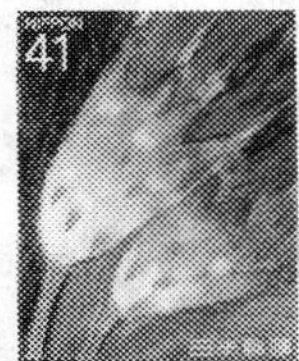

Flowers — A1600

Couple in Ethnic Dress — A1601

1991, May 31 **Photo.** ***Perf. 13***
2087 A1600 41y shown 62 30
2088 A1601 62y shown 95 70
2089 A1600 70y World peace 1.05 80
2090 A1601 100y Butterfly 1.50 1.15

Intl. Stamp Design Contest winning entries.

Kabuki Series

Kagamijishi A1602

Yaegakihime A1603

Koshiro Matsumoto VII A1604

Danjuro Ichikawa XI A1605

Baigyoku Nakamura III A1606

Ganjiro Nakamura II A1607

Kichiemon Nakamura I — A1608

Nizaemon Kataoka XIII — A1609

Enjaku Jitsukawa II A1610

Hakuo Matsumoto I A1611

Fuji-Musume A1612

Kotobuki-Soganotaimen — A1613

Perf. 13 (62y), 13½ (100y)

1991-92 **Photo.**

2091	A1602	62y	dp bl grn & gold	95	70
2092	A1603	100y	multicolored	1.50	1.15
2093	A1604	62y	multicolored	1.00	75
2094	A1605	100y	multicolored	1.60	1.20
2095	A1606	62y	multicolored	1.00	75
2096	A1607	100y	multicolored	1.60	1.20
2097	A1608	62y	multicolored	1.00	75
2098	A1609	100y	multicolored	1.55	1.15
2099	A1610	62y	multicolored	1.00	75
2100	A1611	100y	multicolored	1.60	1.20
2101	A1612	62y	multicolored	1.05	78
2102	A1613	100y	multicolored	1.60	1.20
	Nos. 2091-2102 (12)			15.45	11.58

Issue dates: #2091-2092, June 28. #2093-2094, Sept. 27. #2095-2096, Nov. 20. #2097-2098, Feb. 20, 1992. #2099-2100, Apr. 10, 1992. #2101-2102, June 30, 1992.

Waterbird Series

Gallinago Hardwickii (Latham's Snipe) A1614

1991-93 **Photo.** ***Perf. 13½***

2103	A1614	62y	shown	95	70
2104	A1614	62y	Sula leucogaster	95	70
2105	A1614	62y	Larus crassirostris	1.00	75
2106	A1614	62y	Podiceps ruficollis	1.00	75
2107	A1614	62y	Lunda cirrhata	1.00	75
2108	A1614	62y	Grus monacha	1.00	75
2109	A1614	62y	Cygnus cygnus	1.00	75
2110	A1614	62y	Rostratula benghalensis	1.00	75
2111	A1614	62y	Calonectris leucomelas	1.00	75
2112	A1614	62y	Halcyon coromanda	1.00	75
2113	A1614	62y	Alcedo atthis	1.00	75
2114	A1614	62y	Bubulcus ibis	1.00	75
	Nos. 2103-2115 (13)			12.85	9.60

#2103-2104 printed in blocks of 12 with gutter between in sheet of 24.

Issued: #2103-2104, June 28. #2105-2106, Sept. 27. #2107-2108, Jan. 30, 1992. #2109-2110, Mar. 25, 1992. #2111-2112, Aug. 31, 1992. #2113-2114, Jan. 29, 1993.

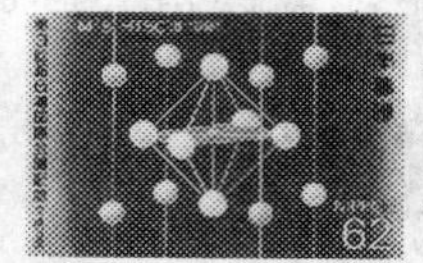

Intl. Conf. on Superconductivity — A1620

1991, July 19 **Litho.** ***Perf. 13½***

2115	A1620	62y	multicolored	95	70

Type of Letter Writing Day of 1990 and

A1621

1991, July 23 **Photo.** ***Perf. 13x13½***

2116	A1621	41y	multicolored	68	50
2117	A1575	62y	multicolored	95	70
a.			Souvenir sheet of 1	95	70
b.			Bklt. pane, 5 each #2116-2117	8.00	

Nos. 2117, 2117a have light blue frameline and inscription and violet denomination.

3rd IAAF World Track & Field Championships, Tokyo — A1622

1991, Aug. 23 ***Perf. 13***

2118	A1622	41y	High jump	68	50
2119	A1622	62y	Shot put	95	70

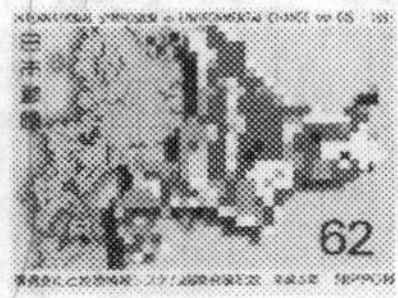

Intl. Symposium on Environmental Change and Geographical Information Systems A1623

1991, Aug. 23

2120	A1623	62y	multicolored	95	70

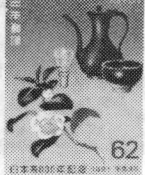

Intl. Letter Writing Week A1624

Bandainagon-emaki picture scroll probably by Mitsunaga Tokiwa: 80y, Crowd of people. 120y, People, house.

Photo. & Engr.

1991, Oct. 7 ***Perf. 13½***

2121	A1624	80y	multicolored	1.30	95
2122	A1624	100y	multicolored	1.60	1.20

A1625 A1626

Design: 62y, Breezy Fine Weather by Hokusai.

1991, Oct. 8 **Photo.** ***Perf. 13***

2123	A1625	62y	multicolored	1.00	75

Summit Conf. on Earthquake and Natural Disasters Countermeasures.

1991, Oct. 31 **Litho.** ***Perf. 13***

2124	A1626	62y	multicolored	1.00	75

Japanese Green Tea, 800th anniv.

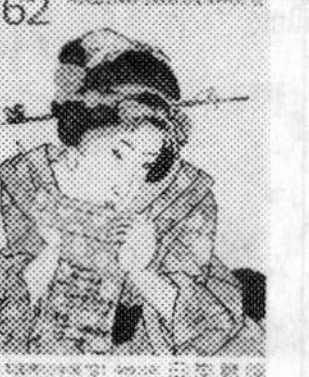

A1627 A1628

Design: Koshaku-Musume by Kunisada Utagawa.

Photo. & Engr.

1991, Nov. 15 *Perf. 13*
2125 A1627 62y multicolored 1.05 80
a. Sheet of 2 2.10 1.60

World Stamp Exhibition, Nippon '91.

1991, Nov. 20 **Photo.**
2126 A1628 62y multicolored 1.05 80

Administrative Counselors System, 30th anniv.

A1629

A1630

New Year 1992 (Year of the Monkey)
A1631 A1632

1991, Dec. 2 **Photo.** *Perf. 13½*
2127 A1629 41y multicolored 70 52
2128 A1630 62y multicolored 1.00 75
2129 A1631 41y +3y, multi 75 58
2130 A1632 62y +3y, multi 1.05 80

8th Conference on Intl. Trade in Endangered Species (CITES) A1633

1992, Mar. 2 **Photo.** *Perf. 13*
2131 A1633 62y multicolored 1.00 75

A1634

A1635

Design: Flowers on the Chair, by Hushum Yamaguchi.

1992, Apr. 20
2132 A1634 62y multicolored 1.00 75

Philately Week.

1992, May 15
2133 A1635 62y multicolored 1.00 75

Return of Ryukyu Islands to Japan, 20th anniv.

Intl. Space Year
A1636 A1637

1992, July 7 **Photo.** *Perf. 13*
2134 A1636 62y multicolored 1.05 78
2135 A1637 62y multicolored 1.05 78
a. Pair, #2134-2135 2.10 1.56

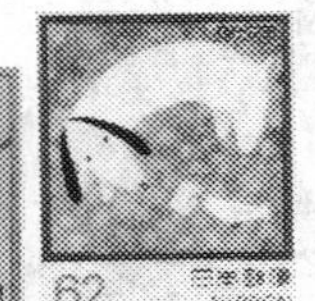

Letter Writing Day
A1638 A1639

1992, July 23 *Perf. 13x13½*
2136 A1638 41y multicolored 70 52

Perf. 13½

2137 A1639 62y multicolored 1.05 78
a. Souvenir sheet of 1 1.05 78
b. Bklt. pane, 5 each #2136-2137 8.50

29th Intl. Geological Congress, Kyoto — A1640

1992, Aug. 24 **Photo.** *Perf. 13½x13*
2138 A1640 62y multicolored 1.00 75

47th Natl. Athletic Meet, Yamagata Prefecture — A1641

1992, Sept. 4 *Perf. 13½*
2139 A1641 41y multicolored 70 50

Normalization of Japanese-Chinese Relations, 20th Anniv.
A1642 A1643

Photo. & Engr.

1992, Sept. 29 *Perf. 13*
2140 A1642 62y multicolored 1.00 75
2141 A1643 62y multicolored 1.00 75
a. Pair, #2140-2141 2.00 1.50

Intl. Letter Writing Week — A1644

Heiji picture scroll: 80y, Nobles, servants in carriages by Taikenmon gate. 120y, Fujiwara-no Nobuyori seated before samurai.

Photo. & Engr.

1992, Oct. 6 *Perf. 13½*
2142 A1644 80y multicolored 1.35 1.00
2143 A1644 120y multicolored 2.00 1.50

Cat and Birds A1644a

Design: 70y, Santa Claus, snow scene.

Perf. 13½x13, 13x13½

1992, Oct. 9 **Photo.**
2144 A1644a 62y multicolored 1.00 75
2145 A1644a 70y multicolored 1.15 85

Winners of Third Postage Stamp Design contest.

30th Congress of Intl. Cooperative Alliance, Tokyo — A1644b

1992, Oct. 27 *Perf. 13x13½*
2146 A1644b 62y multicolored 1.00 75

A1645

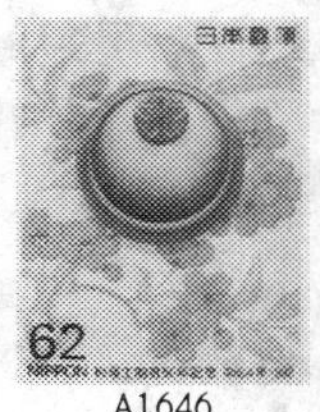

A1646

Cultural Pioneers: No. 2147, Takakazu Seki (1642?-1708), mathematician. No. 2148, Akiko Yosano (1878-1942), poet.

1992, Nov. 4 **Photo. & Engr.** *Perf. 13*
2147 A1645 62y multicolored 1.00 75
2148 A1645 62y multicolored 1.00 75

1992, Nov. 9 **Photo.** *Perf. 13x13½*
2149 A1646 62y multicolored 1.00 75

Certified Public Tax Accountant System, 50th anniv.

A1647

A1648

New Year 1993 (Year of the Rooster)
A1649 A1650

1992, Nov. 16 *Perf. 13x13½*
2150 A1647 41y multicolored 70 50
2151 A1648 62y multicolored 1.00 75
a. Souvenir sheet of 2, #2150-2151 2.00 1.50

Perf. 13½
2152 A1649 41y +3y multi 70 50
2153 A1650 62y +3y multi 1.00 75

Surtax on Nos. 2152-2153 for lottery.

Wildlife — A1651

1992, Nov. 30 *Perf. 13x13½*
2156 A1651 41y Mandarin duck 70 50
2159 A1651 62y Rufous turtle dove 1.00 75
a. Booklet pane, 5 each #2156, 2159 8.50
2162 A1651 72y Varied tit 1.20 90

This is an expanding set. Numbers may change.

World Alpine Skiing Championships, Morioka-Shizukuishi — A1657

1993, Feb. 3 Photo. *Perf. 13*
2174 A1657 41y shown 75 58
2175 A1657 62y Skier, diff. 1.10 82

SEMI-POSTAL STAMPS

Douglas Plane over Japan Alps — SP1

Wmk. Zigzag Lines (141)
1937, June 1 Photo. *Perf. 13*
B1 SP1 2s + 2s rose carmine 1.75 80
B2 SP1 3s + 2s purple 1.75 1.40
B3 SP1 4s + 2s green 2.75 1.15

The surtax was for the Patriotic Aviation Fund to build civil airports.

Nos. 259 and 261 Surcharged in Blue or Red

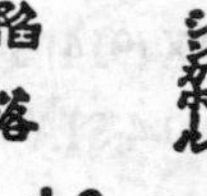

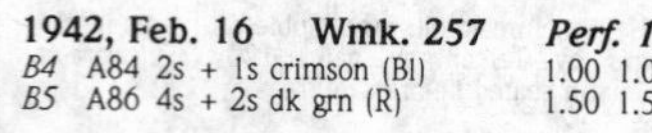

1942, Feb. 16 Wmk. 257 *Perf. 13*
B4 A84 2s + 1s crimson (Bl) 1.00 1.00
B5 A86 4s + 2s dk grn (R) 1.50 1.50

Fall of Singapore to Japanese forces.

Tank Corps Attack, Bataan — SP2
Pearl Harbor under Japanese Attack — SP3

Unwmk.
1942, Dec. 8 Photo. *Perf. 12*
B6 SP2 2s + 1s rose brn 1.50 1.10
B7 SP3 5s + 2s sapphire 2.00 1.65

1st anniv. of the "Greater East Asia War." The surtax was for national defense.

Catalogue values for unused stamps in this section, from this point to the end of the section, are for Never Hinged items.

SP4

1947, Nov. 25 Wmk. 257 *Perf. 12½*
B8 SP4 1.20y + 80s dk rose red 1.25 1.00

Japan's 1st Community Chest drive. The surtax was for charitable purposes.

Nurse — SP5

Bird Feeding Young — SP6

1948, Oct. 1 Unwmk. *Perf. 12½*
B9 SP5 5y + 2.50y brt red 8.50 8.50
B10 SP6 5y + 2.50y emer 8.50 8.50

Souvenir Sheet
Wmk. 257
Imperf
B11 SP7 Sheet of 2 40.00 45.00

The surtax on Nos. B9-B11 was divided between the Red Cross and Community Chest organizations.

No. B11 contains Nos. B9-B10, imperf.

Javelin Thrower SP8

Designs: No. B13, Wrestlers. No. B14, Diver. No. B15, Water polo. No. B16, Woman gymnast. No. B17, Judo. No. B18, Fencing. No. B19, Basketball. No. B20, Rowing. No. B21, Sailing. No. B22, Boxing. No. B23, Volleyball. No. B24, Bicyclist. No. B25, Equestrian. No. B26, Field hockey. No. B27, Pistol shooting. No. B28, Modern pentathlon. No. B29, Weight lifter. No. B30, Women's kayak doubles. No. B31, Soccer.

Perf. 13½
1961, Oct. 11 Unwmk. Engr.
B12 SP8 5y + 5y bister 1.00 52
B13 SP8 5y + 5y dk grn 1.00 52
B14 SP8 5y + 5y car 1.00 52
a. Souv. sheet of 3 ('64) 4.50 5.00

1962, June 23
B15 SP8 5y + 5y green 52 28
B16 SP8 5y + 5y dk pur 52 28
B17 SP8 5y + 5y dk car 52 28
a. Souv. sheet of 3 ('64) 3.00 3.50

1962, Oct. 10
B18 SP8 5y + 5y brick red 35 28
B19 SP8 5y + 5y slate grn 35 28
B20 SP8 5y + 5y vio 35 28
a. Souv. sheet of 3 ('64) 2.50 2.75

1963, June 23
B21 SP8 5y + 5y blue 45 28
B22 SP8 5y + 5y dk brn 45 28
B23 SP8 5y + 5y brown 45 28
a. Souv. sheet of 3 ('64) 4.00 4.25

1963, Nov. 11
B24 SP8 5y + 5y dk bl 20 15
B25 SP8 5y + 5y olive 20 15
B26 SP8 5y + 5y blk 20 15
B27 SP8 5y + 5y claret 20 15
a. Souv. sheet of 4 ('64) 4.00 4.25

1964, June 23
B28 SP8 5y + 5y bluish vio 24 15
B29 SP8 5y + 5y dp olive 24 15
B30 SP8 5y + 5y grnsh bl 24 15
B31 SP8 5y + 5y rose claret 24 15
a. Souv. sheet of 4 ('64) 4.00 4.25
Nos. B12-B31 (20) 8.72 5.28

Issued to raise funds for the 1964 Olympic Games in Tokyo.

The souvenir sheets were issued Aug. 20, 1964. Each contains one each of the stamps in the set it follows. Nos. B14a, B20a, B23a and B27a, exist imperf.

Cobalt Treatment Unit — SP9
Early Cancer Detection with X-rays — SP10

1966, Oct. 21 Photo. *Perf. 13*
B32 SP9 7y + 3y yel org & blk 22 15
B33 SP10 15y + 5y multi 42 20

9th Intl. Anticancer Congress, Tokyo, Oct. 23-29. The surtax was for the fight against cancer and for research.

EXPO '70 Emblem and Globe — SP11

Cherry Blossoms, Screen, Chishakuin Temple — SP12

1969, Mar. 15 Photo. *Perf. 13*
B34 SP11 15y + 5y bl, ocher & ver 80 80
B35 SP12 50y + 10y gold, brn & grn 1.50 1.50

Issued to publicize EXPO '70, International Exhibition, Osaka, 1970.

Ice Hockey, Sapporo Olympic Emblem SP13

Design: No. B37, Ski jump and Sapporo Olympic Games emblem, vert.

1971, Feb. 6 Photo. *Perf. 13*
B36 SP13 15y + 5y multi 35 15
B37 SP13 15y + 5y multi 35 15

To promote the 11th Winter Olympic Games, Sapporo, Japan, 1972.

Blue Dragon, East Wall — SP14

Murals from ancient tomb mound: No. B39, Two men, east wall, vert. 50y+10y, Four women, west wall, vert.

1973, Mar. 26 Photo. *Perf. 13*
Size: 48x27mm, 27x48mm
B38 SP14 20y + 5y multi 35 15
B39 SP14 20y + 5y multi 35 15

Photogravure and Engraved
Size: 33x48mm
B40 SP14 50y + 10y multi 75 25

Surtax was for restoration work on the murals of the Takamatsu-zuka tomb mound, discovered in March, 1972, and excavated in Nara Prefecture.

Reefs, by Hyakusui Hirafuku — SP15

1974, Mar. 2 Photo. *Perf. 13*
B41 SP15 20y + 5y multi 30 15

The surtax was for the International Ocean Exposition, Okinawa, 1975.

Intl. Year of the Disabled — SP16

Photogravure and Embossed
1981, Sept. 1 *Perf. 13½*
B42 SP16 60y + 10y multi 1.00 20

Surtax was for education of the disabled.

TSUKUBA '85 Intl. Exposition, Mar. 17-Sept. 16, 1985 — SP17

1984, Feb. 19 Photo. *Perf. 13½*
B43 SP17 60y + 10y multi 1.10 45

Intl. Garden and Greenery Exposition, Osaka — SP18

1989, June 1 Photo. *Perf. 13*

B44	SP18	62y +10y multi	1.10	82

Surtax for the preparation and management of the exposition.

Intl. Garden and Greenery Exposition, Osaka SP19

1990, Mar. 30

B45	SP19	41y +4y multi	60	45

11th World Congress of the World Federation of the Deaf — SP20

1991, July 5 Photo. *Perf. 13*

B46	SP20	62y +10y multi	1.20	90

AIR POST STAMPS

Regular Issue of 1914 Overprinted in Red or Blue

Wmk. Zigzag Lines (141)

1919, Oct. 3 *Perf. 13x13½*

Granite Paper

C1	A34	1½s blue (R)	250.00	85.00
C2	A34	3s rose (Bl)	450.00	250.00

Excellent counterfeits exist.

Passenger Plane over Lake Ashi — AP1

1929-34 Engr. *Perf. 13½x13*

Granite Paper

C3	AP1	8½s org brn	22.50	13.50
C4	AP1	9½s rose	6.75	3.50
C5	AP1	16½s yel grn	7.75	4.25
C6	AP1	18s ultra	8.25	3.50
C7	AP1	33s gray	16.00	3.00
		Nos. C3-C7 (5)	61.25	27.75

Souvenir Sheet

C8	AP1	Sheet of 4, #C4-C7	900.00	1,200.

Issue dates: 9½s, Mar. 1, 1934; No. C8, Apr. 20, 1934; others, Oct. 6, 1929. No. C8 for Communications Commemoration Day (1st observance of establishment of the postal service and issuance of Nos. 1-4). Sold only at Phil. Exhib. p.o., Tokyo, Apr. 20-27. Size: 110x100mm.

Catalogue values for unused stamps in this section, from this point to the end of the section, are for Never Hinged items.

Southern Green Pheasant AP3

Perf. 13x13½

1950, Jan. 10 Engr. Unwmk.

C9	AP3	16y gray	14.00	5.50
C10	AP3	34y brn vio	35.00	10.00
C11	AP3	59y carmine	50.00	8.00
C12	AP3	103y org yel	37.50	14.00
C13	AP3	144y olive	42.50	14.00
		Nos. C9-C13 (5)	179.00	51.50

Pagoda and Plane — AP4

Plane and Mt. Tsurugi-dake — AP5

1951-52 Photo.

C14	AP4	15y purple	2.50	2.75
C15	AP4	20y blue	22.50	90
C16	AP4	25y yel grn	20.00	32
C17	AP4	30y brn red	15.00	32
C18	AP4	40y gray blk	5.75	40
C19	AP5	55y brt bl	150.00	42.50
C20	AP5	75y brnsh red	110.00	17.00
C21	AP5	80y magenta	17.50	3.00
C22	AP5	85y black	12.00	6.00
C23	AP5	125y ol bis	12.00	3.50
C24	AP5	160y Prus grn	25.00	4.25
		Nos. C14-C24 (11)	392.25	80.94

Issue dates: 25y, 30y, Dec. 20. 15y, 20y, 40y, Sept. 1. 55y-160y, Feb. 11, 1952.

Redrawn; Underlined Zeros Omitted

1952-62

C25	AP4	15y pur ('62)	1.10	60
C26	AP4	20y blue	35.00	70
C27	AP4	25y yel grn ('53)	70	15
C28	AP4	30y brn red	4.50	15
C29	AP4	40y gray blk ('53)	3.00	15
C30	AP5	55y brt bl	45.00	4.00
C31	AP5	75y brnsh red	90.00	10.00
C32	AP5	80y magenta	70.00	4.00
C34	AP5	85y black	3.50	1.40
C36	AP5	125y ol bis	5.50	1.50
C38	AP5	160y Prus grn	22.50	2.00
		Nos. C25-C38 (11)	280.80	24.65

See No. C43.

Great Buddha of Kamakura — AP6

1953, Aug. 15 *Perf. 13½*

C39	AP6	70y red brn	3.00	15
C40	AP6	80y blue	4.50	15
C41	AP6	115y olive grn	2.75	40
C42	AP6	145y Prus grn	11.00	1.40

Coil Stamp
Redrawn Type of 1952-62

1961, Oct. 2 *Perf. 13 Horiz.*

C43	AP4	30y brown red	30.00	22.50

MILITARY STAMPS

Nos. 98, 119, 131 Overprinted

Perf. 11½ to 13½

1910-14 Unwmk.

M1	A26	3s rose	175.00	35.00
M2	A34	3s rose ('13)	250.00	160.00

Wmk. 141

M3	A34	3s rose ('14)	30.00	17.50

Nos. M1-M3 overprint type I has 3.85mm between characters; type II, 4-4.5mm (movable type).

1921 On Offices in China No. 37

M4	A34	3s rose	*6,000.*	*5,000.*

No. M4 is a provisional military stamp issued at the Japanese Post Office, Tsingtao, China. The overprint differs from the illustration, being 12mm high with thicker characters. Counterfeits are plentiful.

Overprint 16mm High

1924 On No. 131

M5	A34	3s rose	80.00	70.00
a.		3s rose (#131b)	85.00	75.00

Excellent forgeries exist of Nos. M1-M5.

JAPANESE OFFICES ABROAD

Offices in China

Regular Issues of Japan Overprinted in Red or Black 那 支

Perf. 11½, 12, 12½, 13½, 13x13½

1900-06 Unwmk.

1	A26	5r gray (R)	3.50	3.25
2	A26	½s gray (R) ('01)	2.00	85
3	A26	1s lt red brn (R)	2.00	85
4	A26	1½s ultra	9.00	2.50
5	A26	1½s vio ('06)	5.00	1.15
6	A26	2s lt grn (R)	5.00	85
7	A26	3s vio brn	5.50	85
8	A26	3s rose ('06)	4.00	60
9	A26	4s rose	4.50	1.50
10	A26	5s org yel (R)	9.00	1.50
11	A27	6s mar ('06)	16.00	12.00
12	A27	8s ol grn (R)	8.00	7.00
13	A27	10s dp bl	8.00	70
14	A27	15s purple	18.50	1.50
15	A27	20s red org	16.50	70
16	A28	25s bl grn (R)	35.00	4.00
17	A28	50s red brn	37.50	2.25
18	A29	1y carmine	55.00	2.25
		Nos. 1-18 (18)	244.00	44.30

No. 6 with black overprint is bogus.

1900

19	A30	3s carmine	25.00	16.00

Wedding of Crown Prince Yoshihito and Princess Sadako.

1908

20	A33	5y green	375.00	40.00
21	A33	10y dark violet	700.00	100.00

On #20-21 the space between characters of the overprint is 6½mm instead of 1½mm.

1913 *Perf. 12, 12x13, 13x13½*

22	A34	½s brown	14.00	14.00
23	A34	1s orange	15.00	15.00
24	A34	1½s lt bl	40.00	17.50
a.		Bklt. pane of 6	350.00	
25	A34	2s green	45.00	20.00
26	A34	3s rose	22.50	7.50
a.		Bklt. pane of 6	350.00	
27	A35	4s red	60.00	60.00
28	A35	5s violet	60.00	45.00
29	A35	10s dp bl	60.00	18.00
30	A35	20s claret	240.00	130.00
31	A35	25s ol grn	90.00	20.00
32	A36	1y yel grn & mar	750.00	500.00
		Nos. 22-32 (11)	1,396.	847.00

1914-21 Wmk. 141

Granite Paper

33	A34	½s brown	2.50	85
34	A34	1s orange	2.75	85
35	A34	1½s blue	3.00	85
a.		Booklet pane of 6	250.00	
36	A34	2s green	2.00	1.00
a.		Booklet pane of 6	250.00	
37	A34	3s rose	1.75	85
a.		Booklet pane of 6	250.00	
38	A35	4s red	7.50	5.00
a.		Booklet pane of 6	250.00	
39	A35	5s violet	14.00	1.85
40	A35	6s brn ('20)	25.00	20.00
41	A35	8s gray ('20)	28.50	22.50
42	A35	10s dp bl	10.00	1.40
a.		Booklet pane of 6		
43	A35	20s claret	32.50	3.50
44	A35	25s ol grn	40.00	3.75
45	A36	30s org brn ('20)	70.00	30.00
46	A36	50s dk brn ('20)	75.00	35.00
47	A36	1y yel grn & mar ('18)	110.00	7.00
48	A33	5y green	1,200.	500.00
49	A33	10y vio ('21)	1,800.	1,100.
		Nos. 33-49 (17)	3,424.	1,734.

On Nos. 48-49 the space between characters of overprint is 4½mm, instead of 6½mm on Nos. 20-21 and 1½mm on all lower values. See No. M4.

Counterfeit overprints exist of Nos. 1-49.

Offices in Korea

Regular Issue of Japan Overprinted in Red or Black 鮮 朝

1900 Unwmk. *Perf. 11½, 12, 12½*

1	A26	5r gray (R)	17.50	10.00
2	A26	1s lt red brn (R)	18.50	5.50
3	A26	1½ ultra	225.00	160.00
4	A26	2s lt grn (R)	17.50	11.00
5	A26	3s vio brn	15.00	5.00
6	A26	4s rose	57.50	30.00
7	A26	5s org yel (R)	60.00	30.00
8	A27	8s ol grn (R)	225.00	160.00
9	A27	10s dp bl	30.00	10.00
10	A27	15s purple	75.00	6.50
11	A27	20s red org	75.00	5.50
12	A28	25s bl grn (R)	200.00	60.00
13	A28	50s red brn	150.00	20.00
14	A29	1y carmine	425.00	15.00
		Nos. 1-14 (14)	1,591.	528.50

1900

15	A30	3s carmine	85.00	35.00

Wedding of Crown Prince Yoshihito and Princess Sadako.

Counterfeit overprints exist of Nos. 1-15.

Taiwan (Formosa)

Numeral of Value and Imperial Crest — A1

1945 Unwmk. Litho. *Imperf.*

No.	Type	Description	Unused	Used
1	A1	3s carmine	25.00	25.00
2	A1	5s blue green	20.00	20.00
3	A1	10s pale blue	30.00	30.00

Additional values, prepared, but not issued, were: 30s, 40s, 50s, 1y, 5y and 10y. The entire set of nine was overprinted by Chinese authorities after World War II and issued for use in Taiwan.

For overprints see China-Taiwan Nos. 1-7.

JORDAN

Trans-Jordan

LOCATION — In the Near East, separated from the Mediterranean Sea by Israel
GOVT. — Kingdom
AREA — 38,400 sq. mi.
POP. — 3,750,000 (est. 1982)
CAPITAL — Amman

The former Turkish territory was mandated to Great Britain following World War I. It became an independent state in 1946.

10 Milliemes = 1 Piaster
1000 Mils = 1 Palestine Pound (1930)
1000 Fils = 1 Jordan Dinar (1951)

Catalogue values for unused stamps in this country are for Never Hinged items, beginning with Scott 221 in the regular postage section, Scott C1 in the air post section, Scott J47 in the postage due section, Scott RA1 in the postal tax section, Scott N1 in the occupation section, Scott NJ1 in the occupation postage due section, and Scott NRA1 in the occupation postal tax section.

Watermarks

Wmk. 305 - Roman and Arabic Initials

Wmk. 328 - UAR

British Mandate

Stamps and Type of Palestine 1918 Overprinted in Black or Silver

شرقي الاردن

1920, Nov. Wmk. 33 *Perf. 14, 15x14*

No.	Type	Description	Unused	Used
1	A1	1m dark brown	15	28
a.		Inverted overprint	87.50	87.50
b.		Perf. 15x14	25	38
c.		As "b," inverted overprint	75.00	65.00
2	A1	2m blue green	15	20
a.		Perf. 15x14	1.90	2.25
3	A1	3m light brown	20	30
a.		Perf. 14	2.75	3.25
4	A1	4m scarlet	30	38
a.		Perf. 14	5.00	6.25
5	A1	5m orange	30	25
a.		Perf. 15x14	50	65
6	A1	1pi dark blue (S)	35	45
a.		Perf. 15x14		
7	A1	2pi olive green	90	90
a.		Perf. 15x14	1.10	1.25
8	A1	5pi plum	1.00	2.00
a.		Perf. 15x14	7.50	10.00
9	A1	9pi bister	2.50	3.50
a.		Perf. 15x14	875.00	875.00
10	A1	10pi ultramarine	2.75	5.00
11	A1	20pi gray	4.25	6.25
		Nos. 1-11 (11)	12.85	19.51

The overprint reads "Sharqi al-ardan" (East of Jordan).

For overprints, see Nos. 12-63, 83A.

Stamps of 1920 Issue Handstamp Surcharged "Ashir el qirsh" (tenth of piaster) and numeral in Black, Red or Violet

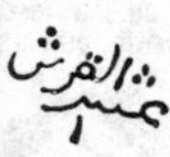

1922

No.	Type	Description	Unused	Used
12	A1	1/10pi on 1m dk brn	17.50	20.00
13	A1	1/10pi on 1m dk brn (R)	67.50	67.50
13A	A1	1/10pi on 1m dk brn (V)	67.50	67.50
14	A1	2/10pi on 2m bl grn	17.50	20.00
a.		3/10pi on 2m bl grn (error)	75.00	75.00
15	A1	2/10pi on 2m bl grn (R)	75.00	60.00
16	A1	2/10pi on 2m bl grn (V)	75.00	75.00
17	A1	3/10pi on 3m lt brn	6.25	6.25
17A	A1	3/10pi on 3m lt brn (V)	165.00	165.00
18	A1	4/10pi on 4m scar	32.50	35.00
19	A1	5/10pi on 5m org	100.00	87.50
c.		Perf. 15x14	140.00	140.00
19A	A1	5/10pi on 5m dp org (R)	225.00	
19B	A1	5/10pi on 5m org (V)	250.00	

For overprint, see No. 83B.

Handstamp Surcharged "El qirsh" (piaster) and numeral in Black, Red or Violet

No.	Type	Description	Unused	Used
20	A1	1pi dk bl (R)	87.50	42.50
20A	A1	1pi dk bl (V)	180.00	175.00
21	A1	2pi ol grn (Bk)	150.00	22.50
22	A1	2pi ol grn (R)	150.00	42.50
22A	A1	2pi ol grn (V)	165.00	55.00
23	A1	5pi plum (Bk)	30.00	32.50
23A	A1	5pi plum (V)	*250.00*	
24	A1	9pi bister (Bk)	150.00	145.00
25	A1	9pi bister (R)	60.00	62.50
a.		Perf. 14	175.00	175.00
26	A1	10pi ultra (Bk)	750.00	750.00
27	A1	20pi gray (Bk)	600.00	600.00
27A	A1	20pi gray (V)	625.00	625.00

Same Surcharge in Black on Palestine Nos. 13-14

No.	Type	Description	Unused	Used
28	A1	10pi on 10pi ultra	*1,500.*	
29	A1	20pi on 20pi gray	*1,900.*	

For overprints, see Nos. 86, 88, 94, 97, 98.

Stamps of 1920 Handstamped in Violet, Black or Red

1922, Dec. *Perf. 15x14, 14*

No.	Type	Description	Unused	Used
30	A1	1m dk brn (V)	15.00	15.00
31	A1	1m dk brn (Bk)	15.00	15.00
32	A1	1m dk brn (R)	6.00	6.00
33	A1	2m bl grn (V)	3.00	3.00
34	A1	2m bl grn (Bk)	4.50	4.50
35	A1	2m bl grn (R)	15.00	15.00
36	A1	3m lt brn (V)	3.75	3.75
37	A1	3m lt brn (Bk)	4.50	4.50
38	A1	3m lt brn (R)	17.50	17.50
39	A1	4m scar (V)	32.50	32.50
39A	A1	4m scar (Bk)	32.50	32.50
40	A1	4m scar (R)	32.50	32.50
41	A1	5m orange (V)	8.25	8.25
42	A1	5m orange (R)	22.50	19.00
a.		Perf. 14	225.00	55.00
43	A1	1pi dk blue (V)	8.25	8.25
44	A1	1pi dk blue (R)	14.00	14.00
45	A1	2pi ol grn (V)	14.00	11.50
a.		Perf. 14	47.50	47.50
46	A1	2pi ol grn (Bk)	7.50	7.50
47	A1	2pi ol grn (R)	40.00	40.00
48	A1	5pi plum (V)	37.50	37.50
a.		Perf. 14	67.50	67.50
49	A1	5pi plum (R)	60.00	60.00
50	A1	9pi bister (V)	150.00	150.00
50A	A1	9pi bister (Bk)	45.00	45.00
50B	A1	9pi bister (R)	225.00	225.00
51	A1	10pi ultra (V)	950.00	950.00
51A	A1	10pi ultra (R)	*1,750.*	*1,750.*
52	A1	20pi gray (V)	950.00	950.00
52A	A1	20pi gray (R)	*2,000.*	*2,000.*

The overprint reads "Hukumat al Sharqi al Arabia" (Arab Government of the East) and date, 1923. The surcharges or overprints on Nos. 12 to 52A inclusive are handstamped and, as usual, are found inverted and double.

Ink pads of several colors were in use at the same time and the surcharges and overprints frequently show a mixture of two colors.

For overprints, see Nos. 84, 87, 89, 92-93, 95-96.

Stamps of 1920 Overprinted in Gold

حكومة الشرق
العربية
نيسان سنة ١٩٢١

1923, Mar. 1 *Perf. 14, 15x14*

No.	Type	Description	Unused	Used
53	A1	1m dark brn (G)	8.75	10.00
a.		Perf. 15x14	1,000.	1,000.
54	A1	2m blue grn (G)	10.00	15.00
a.		Double overprint	200.00	
b.		Inverted overprint	200.00	
55	A1	3m lt brn (G)	6.00	7.00
a.		Black overprint	50.00	50.00
56	A1	4m scarlet (Bk)	6.00	6.00
57	A1	5m orange (Bk)	6.00	6.00
a.		Perf. 15x14	25.00	25.00
58	A1	1pi dk blue (G)	6.00	6.00
a.		Double overprint	300.00	300.00
b.		Black overprint	*300.00*	*300.00*
59	A1	2pi ol grn (G)	7.50	7.50
a.		Black overprint	200.00	
b.		Overprint on back	175.00	
60	A1	5pi plum (G)	27.50	30.00
a.		Inverted overprint	225.00	175.00
b.		"922" for "921"		
61	A1	9pi bister (Bk)	32.50	40.00
a.		Perf. 15x14	*200.00*	*200.00*
62	A1	10pi ultra (G)	40.00	42.50
63	A1	20pi gray (G)	40.00	42.50
a.		Inverted overprint	300.00	
b.		Double overprint	350.00	
c.		Double ovpt., one inverted	450.00	

The overprint reads "Hukumat al Sharqi al Arabia, Nissan Sanat 921" (Arab Government of the East, April, 1921).

For overprints, see Nos. 85, 99, 100, 102.

Stamps of Hejaz, 1922, Overprinted in Black

حكومة
الشرق العربية
٩ شعبان ١٣٤١

Coat of Arms (Hejaz A7)

1923, Apr. Unwmk. *Perf. 11½*

No.	Type	Description	Unused	Used
64	A7	1/8pi orange brn	1.40	1.50
a.		Double overprint	100.00	
65	A7	1/2pi red	1.40	50
a.		Inverted overprint	100.00	
66	A7	1pi dark blue	28	28
a.		Inverted overprint	105.00	
67	A7	1 1/2pi violet	45	50
a.		Double overprint	125.00	
68	A7	2pi orange	45	50
a.		Inverted overprint		
b.		Pair, one without overprint		
69	A7	3pi olive brn	1.10	1.40
a.		Inverted overprint	125.00	
b.		Double overprint	150.00	
c.		Pair, one without overprint	*300.00*	
70	A7	5pi olive green	1.90	2.25
		Nos. 64-70 (7)	6.98	6.93

The overprint is similar to that on the preceding group but is differently arranged. There are numerous varieties in the Arabic letters.

For overprints, see Nos. 71-72, 91, J1-J5.

With Additional Surcharge of New Value in Arabic:

No.	Type	Description	Unused	Used
71	A7(a)	1/4pi on 1/8pi	2.50	2.75
a.		Inverted surcharge	175.00	
72	A7(b)	10pi on 5pi	5.00	6.25

Independence Issue

Palestine Stamps and Type of 1918 Overprinted Vertically in Black or Gold

1923, May Wmk. 33 *Perf. 15x14*

No.	Type	Description	Unused	Used
73	A1	1m dark brn (Bk)	7.00	8.00
a.		Double ovpt., one reversed	425.00	425.00
73B	A1	1m dark brn (G)	225.00	225.00
c.		Double ovpt., one reversed	625.00	625.00
74	A1	2m blue grn	22.50	24.50
75	A1	3m lt brown	5.00	5.50
76	A1	4m scarlet	5.00	5.50
77	A1	5m orange	37.50	40.00
78	A1	1pi dk blue (G)	37.50	40.00
a.		Double overprint	*550.00*	*550.00*
79	A1	2pi olive grn	37.50	40.00
80	A1	5pi plum (G)	37.50	40.00
a.		Double overprint	*360.00*	
81	A1	9pi bis, perf. 14	37.50	40.00
82	A1	10pi ultra, perf. 14	37.50	40.00
83	A1	20pi gray	37.50	40.00

The overprint reads, "Arab Government of the East (abbreviated), Souvenir of Independence, 25th, May, 1923 ('923')".

There were printed 480 complete sets and a larger number of the 1, 2, 3 and 4m. A large number of these sets were distributed to high officials. The overprint was in a setting of twenty-four and the error "933" instead of "923" occurs once in the setting.

The overprint exists reading downward on all values, as illustrated, and reading upward on all except the 5m and 2pi.

Forged overprints exist.

For overprint, see No. 101.

Stamps of Preceding Issues, Handstamp Surcharged

No.	Type	Description	Unused	Used
83A	A1	2½ /10pi on 5m dp org	175.00	190.00
83B	A1	5/10pi on 3m (#17)	*8,000.*	
84	A1	5/10pi on 3m (#36)	20.00	20.00
85	A1	5/10pi on 3m (#55)	8.75	8.75
86	A1	5/10pi on 5pi (#23)	42.50	42.50
87	A1	5/10pi on 5pi (#48)	4.00	4.00
88	A1	1pi on 5pi (#23)	42.50	42.50
89	A1	1pi on 5pi (#48)	*1,500.*	

Same Surcharge on Palestine Stamp of 1918

No.	Type	Description	Unused	Used
90	A1	5/10pi on 3m lt brn	*6,500.*	

As is usual with handstamped surcharges these are found double, inverted, etc.

No. 67 Surcharged by Handstamp

نصف قرش

Unwmk. *Perf. 11½*

No.	Type	Description	Unused	Used
91	A7	1/2pi on 1 1/2pi vio	3.50	3.75
a.		Surcharge typographed	30.00	32.50

The surcharge reads: "Nusf el qirsh" (half piastre). See note after No. 90.

Stamps of Preceding Issues Surcharged by Handstamp

1923, Nov. Wmk. 33 *Perf. 14, 15x14*

No.	Type	Description	Unused	Used
92	A1	1/2pi on 2pi (#45)	45.00	45.00
93	A1	1/2pi on 2pi (#47)	87.50	87.50
94	A1	1/2pi on 5pi (#23)	27.50	27.50
95	A1	1/2pi on 5pi (#48)	2,250.	2,000.
96	A1	1/2pi on 5pi (#49)	1,800.	1,750.
97	A1	1/2pi on 9pi (#24)	*6,500.*	
98	A1	1/2pi on 9pi (#25)	87.50	87.50
99	A1	1/2pi on 9pi (#61)	165.00	165.00

Surcharged by Handstamp

100 A1 1pi on 10pi (#62) *2,000.* *2,000.*
101 A1 1pi on 10pi (#82) *3,000.* *3,000.*
102 A1 2pi on 20pi (#63) 22.50 24.00

Of the 25 copies made of No. 100, a few were handstamped in violet.

Stamp of Hejaz, 1922, Overprinted by Handstamp

الشرق العربية

1923, Dec. Unwmk. *Perf. 11½*
103 A7 ½pi red 3.00 3.25

Stamp of Hejaz, 1922, Overprinted

1924
104 A7 ½pi red 3.25 3.75

King Hussein Issue

Stamps of Hejaz, 1922, Overprinted

مالك العرب

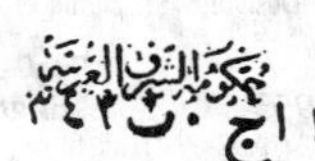

1924

Gold Overprint

105 A7 ½pi red 1.25 1.25
106 A7 1pi dark blue 1.75 1.75
107 A7 1½pi violet 1.50 1.50
108 A7 2pi orange 2.00 2.00

Black Overprint

109 A7 ½pi red 65 65
110 A7 1pi dark blue 75 75
111 A7 1½pi violet 90 90
112 A7 2pi orange 1.00 1.00
Nos. 105-112 (8) 9.80 9.80

The overprint reads: "Arab Government of the East. In commemoration of the visit of H. M. the King of the Arabs, 11 Jemad el Than i 1342 (17th Jan. 1924)." The overprint was in a setting of thirty-six and the error "432" instead of "342" occurs once in the setting and is found on all values.

Stamps of Hejaz, 1922-24, Overprinted in Black or Red

Coat of Arms (Hejaz A8)

حكومة الشرق العربي ١٣٤٢

1924
113 A7 ⅛pi red brown 20 15
114 A7 ¼pi yellow green 15 15
a. Tête bêche pair 2.00 2.00
115 A7 ½pi red 15 15
116 A7 1pi dark blue 2.50 2.50
117 A7 1½pi violet 1.40 1.40
118 A7 2pi orange 75 75
119 A7 3pi red brown 50 50
120 A7 5pi olive green 75 75
121 A8 10pi vio & dk brn (R) 1.10 1.40
a. Pair, one without overprint
Nos. 113-121 (9) 7.50 7.75

The overprint reads: "Hukumat al Sharqi al Arabia, 1342." (Arab Government of the East, 1924).

Stamps of Hejaz, 1925, Overprinted in Black or Red

(Hejaz A9)

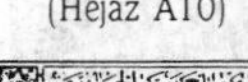

(Hejaz A10)

(Hejaz A11)

1925, Aug.
122 A9 ⅛pi chocolate 15 15
123 A9 ¼pi ultramarine 15 15
124 A9 ½pi carmine rose 15 15
125 A10 1pi yellow green 15 15
126 A10 1½pi orange 20 20
127 A10 2pi deep blue 25 25
128 A11 3pi dark green (R) 38 38
129 A11 5pi orange brn 75 75
Nos. 122-129 (8) 2.18 2.18

The overprint reads: "Hukumat al Sharqi al Arabi. 1343 Sanat." (Arab Government of the East, 1925). Nos. 122-129 exist imperforate, and with overprint inverted or double.

Type of Palestine, 1918, Overprinted in Black

شرق الاردن

1925, Nov. 1 Wmk. 4 *Perf. 14*
130 A1 1m dark brown 15 15
131 A1 2m yellow 15 15
132 A1 3m Prussian bl 15 15
133 A1 4m rose 15 15
134 A1 5m orange 15 15
135 A1 6m blue green 15 15
136 A1 7m yel brown 15 15
137 A1 8m red 20 20
138 A1 1pi gray 28 16
139 A1 13m ultramarine 28 30
140 A1 2pi olive green 40 48
141 A1 5pi plum 85 1.00
142 A1 9pi bister 3.25 2.75
143 A1 10pi light blue 2.75 2.00
144 A1 20pi violet 6.50 5.50
Nos. 130-144 (15) 15.56 13.44

This overprint reads: "Sharqi al-ardan" (East of Jordan).
For overprints, see Nos. J12-J23.

Perf. 15x14
142a A1 9pi 600.00 400.00
143a A1 10pi 50.00 55.00
144a A1 20pi 825.00 500.00

Amir Abdullah ibn Hussein
A1 A2

1927-29 Engr. *Perf. 14*
145 A1 2(m) Prus blue 15 15
146 A1 3(m) rose 15 15
147 A1 4(m) green 28 22
148 A1 5(m) orange 15 15
149 A1 10(m) red 15 18
150 A1 15(m) ultra 32 15
151 A1 20(m) olive grn 55 65
152 A2 50(m) claret 1.10 1.10
153 A2 90(m) bister 3.25 3.00
154 A2 100(m) lt blue 3.25 2.25
155 A2 200(m) violet 7.00 5.00
156 A2 500(m) dp brn ('29) 32.50 20.00
157 A2 1000(m) gray ('29) 85.00 10.00
Nos. 145-157 (13) 133.85 43.00

For overprints, see Nos. 158-168, B1-B12, J24-J29.

Stamps of 1927 Overprinted in Black

دستور

1928, Sept. 1
158 A1 2(m) Prus blue 30 30
159 A1 3(m) rose 30 30
160 A1 4(m) green 32 32
161 A1 5(m) orange 15 15
162 A1 10(m) red 35 35
163 A1 15(m) ultra 1.25 70
164 A1 20(m) olive grn 2.50 2.50
165 A2 50(m) claret 4.25 4.25
166 A2 90(m) bister 9.00 9.00
167 A2 100(m) lt blue 12.00 12.00
168 A2 200(m) violet 30.00 30.00
Nos. 158-168 (11) 60.42 59.87

The overprint is the Arabic word "Dastour," meaning "Constitution." The stamps were in commemoration of the enactment of the law setting forth the Constitution.

A3

"MILS" or "L. P." at lower right and Arabic equivalents at upper left.

1930-36 Engr. *Perf. 14*

Size: 17¼x21mm

169 A3 1m red brn ('34) 15 15
170 A3 2m Prus blue 15 15
171 A3 3m rose 15 15
172 A3 3m green ('34) 42 15
173 A3 4m green 15 15
174 A3 4m rose ('34) 55 15
175 A3 5m orange 15 15
a. Perf. 13½x14 (coil) ('36) 2.00 55
176 A3 10m red 15 15
177 A3 15m ultra 25 16
a. Perf. 13½x14 (coil) ('36) 2.00 70
178 A3 20m olive grn 38 15

Size: 19¼x23½mm

179 A3 50m red violet 38 32
180 A3 90m bister 55 50
181 A3 100m light blue 1.10 1.00
182 A3 200m violet 1.90 1.50
183 A3 500m deep brown 8.75 4.00
184 A3 £1 gray 20.00 7.50
Nos. 169-184 (16) 35.18 16.33

See Nos. 199-220, 230-235. For overprint, see No. N15a.

1939 *Perf. 13½x13*

Size: 17¼x21mm

169a A3 1m red brown 25 15
170a A3 2m Prussian blue 25 15
172a A3 3m green 65 25
174a A3 4m rose 3.00 2.50
175b A3 5m orange 5.00 35
176a A3 10m red 20.00 1.00
177b A3 15m ultramarine 65 30
178a A3 20m olive green 9.00 3.00
Nos. 169a-178a (8) 38.80 7.70

For overprint, see No. N3a.

Mushetta — A4

Nymphaeum, Jerash — A5

Kasr Kharana — A6

Kerak Castle — A7

Temple of Artemis, Jerash — A8

Aijalon Castle — A9

Khazneh, Rock-hewn Temple, Petra — A10

Allenby Bridge, River Jordan — A11

Amir Abdullah ibn Hussein — A13

Ancient Threshing Floor — A12

1933, Feb. 1 *Perf. 12*
185 A4 1m dk brn & blk 22 28
186 A5 2m claret & blk 30 32
187 A6 3m blue green 55 42
188 A7 4m bister & blk 55 50
189 A8 5m orange & blk 55 52
190 A9 10m brown red 70 65
191 A10 15m dull blue 1.50 85
192 A11 20m ol grn & blk 1.75 1.00
193 A12 50m brn vio & blk 3.00 2.25
194 A6 90m yel & black 4.75 3.50
195 A8 100m blue & blk 5.75 4.25
196 A9 200m dk vio & blk 26.00 30.00
197 A10 500m brn & ver 70.00 72.50
198 A13 £1 green & blk 325.00 350.00
Nos. 185-198 (14) 440.62 467.04

Nos. 194-197 are larger than the lower values in the same designs.

Amir Abdullah ibn Hussein — A14

Perf. 13x13½

1942, May 18 Litho. Unwmk.
199 A14 1m dull red brn 15 15
200 A14 2m dull green 15 15
201 A14 3m dp yel green 18 15
202 A14 4m rose pink 26 15
203 A14 5m orange yel 30 18
204 A14 10m dull ver 45 30
205 A14 15m deep blue 60 30
206 A14 20m dull ol grn 1.00 75
Nos. 199-206 (8) 3.09 2.13

Type A14 differs from A3 in the redrawn inscription above the head and in the form of the "millieme" character at upper left.
For overprint, see No. N1.

Abdullah Type of 1930-39
White Paper

1943-44 Engr. Wmk. 4 *Perf. 12*

Size: 17¾x21½mm

207 A3 1m red brown 15 15
208 A3 2m Prussian grn 15 15
209 A3 3m blue green 15 15

210 A3 4m deep rose 15 15
211 A3 5m orange 15 15
212 A3 10m scarlet 15 15
213 A3 15m blue 15 15
214 A3 20m olive ('44) 18 15

Size: 20x24mm

215 A3 50m red lil ('44) 22 20
216 A3 90m ocher 50 50
217 A3 100m dp bl ('44) 75 42
218 A3 200m dk vio ('44) 1.50 1.00
219 A3 500m dk brn ('44) 5.00 1.75
220 A3 £1 black ('44) 12.50 2.50
Nos. 207-220 (14) 21.70 7.57

See Nos. 230-235. For overprints, see Nos. 255-256, 259, 264-269, RA23, N2-N4, N7, N12-N17.

Catalogue values for unused stamps in this section, from this point to the end of the section, are for Never Hinged items.

Independent Kingdom

Symbols of Peace and Liberty — A15

Perf. 11½

1946, May 25 Unwmk. Litho.

221 A15 1m sepia 15 15
222 A15 2m yel orange 15 15
223 A15 3m dl ol grn 15 15
224 A15 4m lt violet 15 15
225 A15 10m orange brn 15 15
226 A15 12m rose red 15 15
227 A15 20m dark blue 15 15
228 A15 50m ultra 55 45
229 A15 200m green 1.00 1.00
Set value 2.15 2.00

Independence of the Kingdom of Trans-Jordan.
Nos. 221 to 229 exist imperforate.

Abdullah Type of 1930-39

1947 Wmk. 4 Engr. *Perf. 12*

230 A3 3m rose carmine 15 15
231 A3 4m deep yel green 15 15
232 A3 10m violet 15 15
233 A3 12m deep rose 65 65
234 A3 15m dull olive grn 16 16
235 A3 20m deep blue 20 20
Set value 1.20 1.20

For overprints, see Nos. 257-258, 260-263, RA24-RA25, N5-N6, N8-N11.

Parliament Building, Amman A16

1947, Nov. 1 Engr. Unwmk.

236 A16 1m purple 15 15
237 A16 3m red orange 15 15
238 A16 4m yel green 15 15
239 A16 10m dk vio brn 15 15
240 A16 12m carmine 15 15
241 A16 20m deep blue 15 15
242 A16 50m red vio 20 20
243 A16 100m rose 35 35
244 A16 200m dark green 75 75
Set value 1.70 1.70

Founding of the new Trans-Jordan parliament, 1947.
Nos. 236 to 244 exist imperforate.

Symbols of the UPU — A17

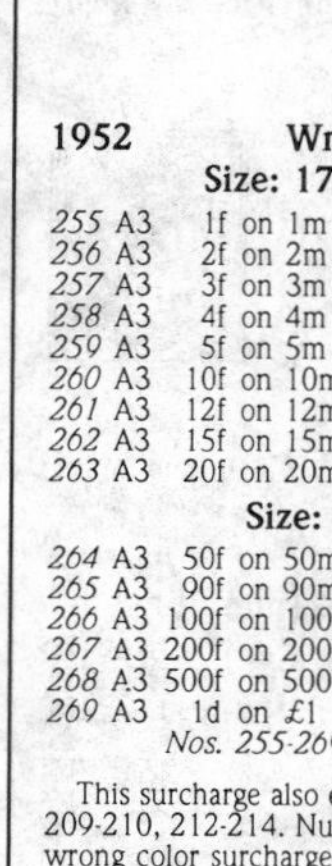

King Abdullah ibn Hussein A18

1949, Aug. 1 Wmk. 4 *Perf. 13*

245 A17 1m brown 15 15
246 A17 4m green 15 15
247 A17 10m red 15 15
248 A17 20m ultramarine 16 16
249 A18 50m dull green 28 28
Set value 64 62

75th anniv. of the UPU. For overprints, see Nos. N18-N22.

Nos. 207-208, 211, 215-220, 230-235 Surcharged in Carmine, Black or Green

= فلس FILS =

1952 Wmk. 4 *Perf. 12*

Size: 17¾x21½mm

255 A3 1f on 1m red brn (Bk) 15 15
256 A3 2f on 2m Prus grn 15 15
257 A3 3f on 3m rose car (Bk) 15 15
258 A3 4f on 4m dp yel grn 20 15
259 A3 5f on 5m org (G) 65 20
260 A3 10f on 10m vio 48 48
261 A3 12f on 12m dp rose (Bk) 48 48
262 A3 15f on 15m dl ol grn 52 30
263 A3 20f on 20m dp bl 75 45

Size: 20x24mm

264 A3 50f on 50m red lil (G) 1.10 65
265 A3 90f on 90m ocher (G) 5.75 5.50
266 A3 100f on 100m dp bl 3.50 1.10
267 A3 200f on 200m dk vio 4.75 1.00
268 A3 500f on 500m dk brn 10.00 2.75
269 A3 1d on £1 black 21.00 4.75
Nos. 255-269 (15) 49.63 18.26

This surcharge also exists on Nos. 199-203, 205, 209-210, 212-214. Numerous inverted, double and wrong color surcharges exist.

Relief Map — A19

Amir Abdullah ibn Hussein — A20

Perf. 13½x13

1952, Apr. 1 Engr. Wmk. 4

270 A19 1f red brn & yel grn 15 15
271 A19 2f dk bl grn & red 15 15
272 A19 3f car & gray blk 15 15
273 A19 4f green & orange 15 15
274 A19 5f choc & rose vio 15 15
275 A19 10f violet & brown 15 15
276 A19 20f dark bl & blk 20 20
277 A19 100f dp blue & brn 1.10 80
278 A19 200f purple & orange 1.40 1.40
Nos. 270-278 (9) 3.60 3.30

Unity of Jordan, Apr. 24, 1950.
For overprints, see Nos. 297-305.

1952 Wmk. 4 *Perf. 11½*

279 A20 5f orange 15 15
280 A20 10f violet 15 15
281 A20 12f carmine 35 35
282 A20 15f olive 15 15
283 A20 20f deep blue 20 15

Size: 20x24½mm

Perf. 12x12½

284 A20 50f plum 48 48
285 A20 90f brn orange 1.40 1.10
286 A20 100f deep blue 1.10 52
Nos. 279-286 (8) 3.98 3.05

Nos. RA5-RA7 Overprinted in Black or Carmine

Perf. 11½x12½

1953 Unwmk. Engr.

286A PT1 10m carmine 27.50 27.50
286B PT1 15m gray (C) 2.75 1.25
286C PT1 20m dark brown 35.00 35.00

Same Overprint on Nos. NRA4-NRA7

286D PT1 5m plum 35.00 35.00
286E PT1 10m carmine 35.00 35.00
286F PT1 15m gray (C) 35.00 35.00
286G PT1 20m dk brn (C) 35.00 35.00

In addition a few sheets of Nos. RA9, NRA1, NRA3, NRA8-NRA9 and RA37-RA41 have been reported with this overprint. It is doubtful whether they were regularly issued. See Nos. 344-347.

Same Overprint on Nos. RA28 to RA31 in Black or Carmine

1953 Wmk. 4 *Perf. 11½x12½*

287 PT1 5f plum 15 15
288 PT1 10f carmine 18 18
289 PT1 15f gray (C) 35 25
290 PT1 20f dark brown (C) 55 40

King Hussein A21

1953, Oct. 1 Unwmk. Engr. *Perf. 12*

Portrait in Black

291 A21 1f dark green 15 15
292 A21 4f deep plum 15 15
293 A21 15f deep ultra 20 15
294 A21 20f dark purple 24 15
295 A21 50f dark blue grn 75 35
296 A21 100f dark blue 1.10 70
Nos. 291-296 (6) 2.59
Set value 1.40

Accession of King Hussein, May 2, 1953.

Nos. 270 to 278 Overprinted in Black with Two Bars Through Center Inscription

1953 Wmk. 4 *Perf. 13½x13*

297 A19 1f red brn & yel grn 15 15
298 A19 2f dk bl grn & red 15 15
299 A19 3f car & gray blk 15 15
300 A19 4f green & orange 15 15
301 A19 5f choc & rose vio 18 18
302 A19 10f violet & brown 45 20
303 A19 20f dark bl & blk 45 38
304 A19 100f dp blue & brn 2.00 1.00
305 A19 200f purple & org 3.75 1.65
Nos. 297-305 (9) 7.43 4.01

Two main settings of the bars exist on Nos. 297-300 and 304—the "normal" 1½mm spacing, and the "narrow" ½mm spacing.

El Deir Temple, Petra — A22

Dome of the Rock — A23

Designs: 2f, 4f, 500f, 1d, King Hussein. 3f, 5f, Treasury Bldg., Petra. 12f, 50f, 100f, 200f, Al Aqsa Mosque. 20f, as 10f.

1954 Unwmk. Engr. *Perf. 12½*

306 A22 1f dk bl grn & red brn 15 15
307 A22 2f red & black 15 15
308 A22 3f dp plum & vio bl 15 15
309 A22 4f org brn & dk grn 15 15
310 A22 5f vio & dk grn 1.25 15
311 A23 10f pur & dk grn 25 15
312 A23 12f car rose & sep 60 40
313 A23 20f dp bl & dk grn 25 15
314 A23 50f dk bl & dp rose 2.25 2.25
315 A23 100f dk grn & dp bl 1.10 45
316 A23 200f dp cl & pck bl 3.50 75
317 A22 500f choc & purple 9.00 4.50
318 A22 1d dk ol grn & rose brn 17.50 10.00
Nos. 306-318 (13) 36.30 19.40

See Nos. 324-337. For overprint, see No. 425.

Globe — A23a

Perf. 13½x13

1955, Jan. 1 Photo. Wmk. 195

319 A23a 15f green 15 15
320 A23a 20f violet 15 15
321 A23a 25f yellow brown 18 15
Set value 35

Founding of the APU, July 1, 1954.

Princess Dina Abdul Hamid and King Hussein — A24

1955, Apr. 19 *Perf. 11x11½*

322 A24 15f ultramarine 18 15
323 A24 100f rose brown 75 75

Marriage of King Hussein and Princess Dina Abdul Hamid.

Types of 1954

Design: 15f, Dome of the Rock.

Perf. 12½

1955-64 Engr. Wmk. 305

324 A22 1f dk bl grn & red brn ('57) 15 15
325 A22 2f red & blk ('57) 15 15
326 A22 3f dp plum & vio bl ('56) 15 15
327 A22 4f org brn & dk grn ('56) 15 15
328 A22 5f vio & dk grn ('56) 15 15
329 A23 10f pur & grn ('57) 15 15
330 A23 12f car rose & sep 15 15
331 A23 15f dp brn & rose red 15 15
332 A23 20f dp bl & dk grn ('57) 15 15
333 A23 50f dk bl & dp rose 30 18
334 A23 100f dk grn & dp bl ('62) 60 35
335 A23 200f dp cl & pck bl ('65) 2.00 50
336 A22 500f choc & pur ('65) 7.50 3.00
337 A22 1d dk ol grn & rose brn ('65) 20.00 4.00
Nos. 324-337 (14) 31.75 9.38

Envelope A25

Wmk. 305

1956, Jan. 15 Engr. *Perf. 14*

"Postmarks" in Black

338 A25 1f light brown 15 15
339 A25 4f dark car rose 15 15
340 A25 15f blue 15 15
341 A25 20f yellow olive 15 15
342 A25 50f slate blue 38 20
343 A25 100f vermilion 65 38
Set value 1.40 90

1st Arab Postal Congress in Amman.

Nos. RA1, RA3, RA8 and RA33 Overprinted in Carmine or Black

بريد POSTAGE

Perf. 11½x12½

1956, Jan. 5 Unwmk.

344 PT1 1m ultramarine 15 15
345 PT1 3m emerald 15 15
346 PT1 50m purple 30 18

Wmk. 4

347 PT1 100f orange (Bk) 1.00 55
Set value 1.40 80

Numerous inverted, double and wrong color surcharges exist.

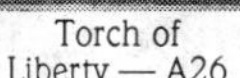

Torch of Liberty — A26

King Hussein — A27

1958 Wmk. 305 Engr. *Perf. 12½*

348 A26 5f blue & red brown 15 15
349 A26 15f bister brn & blk 15 15
350 A26 35f blue grn & plum 20 16
351 A26 45f car & olive grn 28 20
Set value 65 55

10th anniv. of the Universal Declaration of Human Rights.

Perf. 12x11½

1959 Wmk. 305 Engr.

Centers in Black

352 A27 1f deep green 15 15
353 A27 2f violet 15 15
354 A27 3f deep carmine 15 15
355 A27 4f brown black 15 15
356 A27 7f dark green 15 15
357 A27 12f deep carmine 15 15
358 A27 15f dark red 15 15
359 A27 21f green 32 28
360 A27 25f ocher 20 15
361 A27 35f dark blue 20 15
362 A27 40f olive green 28 15
363 A27 50f red 35 16
364 A27 100f blue green 80 20
365 A27 200f rose lake 1.20 40
366 A27 500f gray blue 3.00 1.40
367 A27 1d dark purple 7.25 3.50
Nos. 352-367 (16) 14.65 7.44

For overprints, see Nos. 423-424, 425a, 426-427.

Arab League Center, Cairo, and King Hussein A28

Perf. 13x13½

1960, Mar. 22 Photo. Wmk. 328

368 A28 15f dull green & blk 15 15

Opening of the Arab League Center and the Arab Postal Museum in Cairo.

World Refugee Year Emblem A29

Perf. 13½

1960, Apr. 7 Wmk. 305 Litho.

369 A29 15f pale blue & red 16 15
370 A29 35f bister & blue 26 26

World Refugee Year, July 1, 1959-June 30, 1960.
For overprints, see Nos. 377-378.

Shah of Iran, King Hussein and Flags A30

Perf. 13x13½

1960, May 15 Wmk. 305

Flags in Green, Red & Black

371 A30 15f yellow & black 15 15
372 A30 35f blue & black 18 15
373 A30 50f salmon & black 26 15
Set value 34

Visit of Mohammed Riza Pahlavi, Shah of Iran, to Jordan, Nov. 2, 1959.

Oil Refinery, Zarka A31

1961, May 1 Engr. *Perf. 14x13*

374 A31 15f dull vio & blue 15 15
375 A31 35f dl vio & brick red 20 15
Set value 21

Opening of oil refinery at Zarka.

Urban and Nomad Families and Chart — A32

Perf. 13x13½

1961, Oct. 15 Photo. Unwmk.

376 A32 15f orange brown 20 15

First Jordanian census, 1961.

Nos. 369-370 Overprinted in English and Arabic, "In Memorial of Dag Hammarskjoeld 1904-1961," and Laurel Leaf Border

1961 Wmk. 305 Litho. *Perf. 13½*

377 A29 15f pale blue & red 2.75 1.40
378 A29 35f bister & blue 2.75 1.40

Dag Hammarskjold, Secretary General of the UN, 1953-1961.

Malaria Eradication Emblem — A33

Perf. 11x11½

1962, Apr. 15 Unwmk.

379 A33 15f bright pink 15 15
380 A33 35f blue 22 22

WHO drive to eradicate malaria. A souvenir sheet exists with one each of Nos. 379-380. Value $2.

Dial and Exchange Building, Amman A34

1962, Dec. 11 Engr. Wmk. 305

381 A34 15f blue & lilac 15 15
382 A34 35f lilac & emer 22 22

Telephone automation in Amman (in 1960).

Opening of the Port of 'Aqaba A35

1962, Dec. 11

383 A35 15f lil & blk 16 16
384 A35 35f vio bl & blk 25 25
a. Souvenir sheet of 2, #383-384 75 75

No. 384a imperf., same value.

Dag Hammarskjold and UN Headquarters, NY — A36

Perf. 14x14½

1963, Jan. 24 Photo. Unwmk.

385 A36 15f ultra, ol grn & brn red 20 16
386 A36 35f ol, brn red & ultra 42 40
387 A36 50f brn red, ol & ultra 65 65

17th anniv. of the UN and in memory of Dag Hammarskjold, Secretary General of the UN, 1953-61. An imperf. souvenir sheet contains one each of Nos. 385-387 with simulated perforations. Value $5.

Imperforates

Starting with No. 385, imperforates exist of many Jordanian stamps.

Church of St. Virgin's Tomb, Jerusalem — A37

Arab League Building, Cairo — A38

Designs: No. 389, Basilica of the Agony, Gethsemane. No. 390, Church of the Holy Sepulcher, Jerusalem. No. 391, Church of the Nativity, Bethlehem. No. 392, Haram el-Khalil (tomb of Abraham), Hebron. No. 393, Dome of the Rock, Jerusalem. No. 394, Mosque of Omar el-Khatab, Jerusalem. No. 395, Al Aqsa Mosque, Jerusalem.

1963, Feb. 5 *Perf. 14½x14*

Center Multicolored

388 A37 50f blue 45 38
389 A37 50f dull red 45 38
390 A37 50f bright blue 45 38
391 A37 50f olive green 45 38
a. Vert. strip of 4, #388-391 1.90
392 A37 50f gray 60 38
393 A37 50f purple 60 38
394 A37 50f dull red 60 38
395 A37 50f light purple 60 38
a. Vert. strip of 4, #392-395 2.50
Nos. 388-395 (8) 4.20 3.04

1963, July 16 Photo. *Perf. 13½x13*

396 A38 15f slate blue 15 15
397 A38 35f orange red 22 15
Set value 20

Arab League.

Wheat and UN Emblem — A39

Perf. 11½x12½

1963, Sept. Litho. Wmk. 305

398 A39 15f lt bl, grn & black 15 15
399 A39 35f lt grn, grn & blk 18 15
a. Souv. sheet of 2, #398-399 75 75
Set value 24

FAO "Freedom from Hunger" campaign. No. 399a imperf., same value.

East Ghor Canal, Pylon, Gear Wheel and Wheat A40

1963, Sept. 20 *Perf. 14½x14*

400 A40 1f dull yel & black 15 15
401 A40 4f blue & black 15 15
402 A40 5f lilac & black 15 15
403 A40 10f brt yel grn & blk 15 15
404 A40 35f orange & black 15 15
Set value 35 32

East Ghor Canal Project.

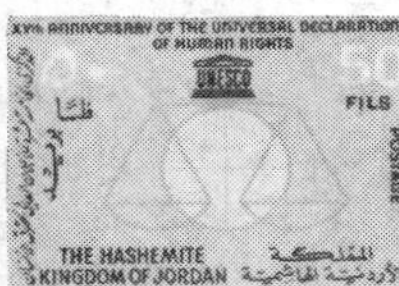

UNESCO Emblem, Scales and Globe — A41

Perf. 13½x13

1963, Dec. 10 Unwmk.

405 A41 50f pale vio bl & red 32 32
406 A41 50f rose red & blue 32 32

15th anniv. of the Universal Declaration of Human Rights.

Red Crescent and King Hussein — A42

1963, Dec. 24 Photo. *Perf. 14x14½*

407 A42 1f red & red lilac 15 15
408 A42 2f red & bl green 15 15
409 A42 3f red & dk blue 15 15
410 A42 4f red & dk green 15 15
411 A42 5f red & dk brown 15 15
412 A42 85f red & dp green 95 95

Design: Red Cross at right, no portrait

413 A42 1f red lilac & red 15 15
414 A42 2f blue grn & red 15 15
415 A42 3f dk blue & red 15 15
416 A42 4f dk green & red 15 15
417 A42 5f dk brown & red 15 15
418 A42 85f dp green & red 3.75 3.75
Set value, #407-418 5.00 5.00

Centenary of the Intl. Red Cross. Two 100f imperf. souvenir sheets, red and red lilac, exist in the Red Crescent and Red Cross designs. Value $15.

Hussein ibn Ali and King Hussein A43

Perf. 11x11½

1963, Dec. 25 Litho. Unwmk.

419 A43 15f yellow & multi 15 15
420 A43 25f multicolored 16 15
421 A43 35f brt pink & multi 35 28
422 A43 50f lt blue & multi 50 50

Arab Renaissance Day, June 10, 1916. Perf. and imperf. souvenir sheets exist containing one each of Nos. 419-422. Value for both, $3.

Nos. 359, 312, 357 and 361 Surcharged

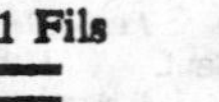

Perf. 12x11½, 12½
Wmk. 305, Unwmk.

1963, Dec. 16 **Engr.**

423 A27 1f on 21f grn & blk 15 15
424 A27 2f on 21f grn & blk 15 *1.00*
425 A23 4f on 12f car rose & sepia 15 15
a. 4f on 12f dp car & blk (#357) 6.50 5.00
426 A27 5f on 21f grn & blk 16 15
427 A27 25f on 35f dk bl & blk 35 15
Set value 75

Pope Paul VI, King Hussein and Al Aqsa Mosque, Jerusalem — A44

Portraits and: 35f, Dome of the Rock. 50f, Church of the Holy Sepulcher. 80f, Church of the Nativity, Bethlehem.

1964, Jan. 4 Litho. ***Perf. 13x13½***

428 A44 15f emerald & blk 15 15
429 A44 35f car rose & blk 25 25
430 A44 50f brown & black 45 45
431 A44 80f vio bl & blk 75 75

Visit of Pope Paul VI to the Holy Land, Jan. 4-6. An imperf. souvenir sheet contains 4 stamps similar to Nos. 428-431. Value $3.

A45

Crown Prince Abdullah ben Al-Hussein — A46

Design: 5f, Crown Prince standing, vert.

1964, Mar. 30 Photo. ***Perf. 14***

432 A46 5f multicolored 15 15
433 A45 10f multicolored 15 15
434 A46 35f multicolored 25 25
Set value 35 35

2nd birthday of Crown Prince Abdullah ben Al-Hussein (b. Jan. 30, 1962).

A47

Mercury Astronauts, Spacecraft — A48

Designs: b, M. Scott Carpenter. c, Entering space. d, Alan Shepard. e, At launch pad. f, Virgil Grissom. g, After separation. h, Walter Schirra. i, Lift-off. j, John Glenn. Stamp has point down on b, d, f, h, j.

1964, Mar. 25 Photo. ***Perf. 14***

435 A47 20f Block of 10, #a.-j. 5.00 5.00

Imperf
Size: 111x80mm

436 A48 100f multicolored 6.50 6.50

Table Tennis A49

Designs: 1f, 2, 3f, 5f vertical.

Perf. 14½x14, 14x14½

1964, June 1 Litho. Unwmk.

446 A49 1f Basketball 15 15
447 A49 2f Volleyball 15 15
448 A49 3f Soccer 15 15
449 A49 4f shown 15 15
450 A49 5f Running 15 15
451 A49 35f Bicycling 70 70
452 A49 50f Fencing 1.00 1.00
453 A49 100f High jump 1.75 1.75
Nos. 446-453 (8) 4.20 4.20

1964 Olympic Games, Tokyo, Oct. 10-25. An imperf. 200f greenish blue souvenir sheet in design of 100f exists. Value $6.

Mother and Child — A50

1964, June 1 Wmk. 305 ***Perf. 14***

454 A50 5f multicolored 15 15
455 A50 10f multicolored 15 15
456 A50 25f multicolored 16 15
Set value 28 20

Social Studies Seminar, fourth session.

Pres. John F. Kennedy — A51

1964, July 15 Unwmk.

457 A51 1f brt violet 15 15
458 A51 2f carmine rose 15 15
459 A51 3f ultramarine 15 15
460 A51 4f orange brn 15 15
461 A51 5f bright green 15 15
462 A51 85f rose red 2.50 2.50
Set value 2.75 2.75

President John F. Kennedy (1917-1963). An imperf. 100f brown souvenir sheet exists. Size of stamp: 58x83mm. Value $5.

Ramses II — A52

Perf. 14½x14

1964, July Litho. Wmk. 305

463 A52 4f lt blue & dark brn 15 15
464 A52 15f yellow & violet 15 15
465 A52 25f lt yel grn & dk red 15 15
Set value 28 22

UNESCO world campaign to save historic monuments in Nubia.

King Hussein and Map of Jordan and Israel — A53

1964, Sept. 5 Unwmk. ***Perf. 12***

466 A53 10f multicolored 15 15
467 A53 15f multicolored 15 15
468 A53 25f multicolored 16 15
469 A53 50f multicolored 35 26
470 A53 80f multicolored 50 45
Set value 1.15 90

Council of the Heads of State of the Arab League (Arab Summit Conference), Cairo, Jan. 13, 1964. An imperf. souvenir sheet contains Nos. 466-470 with simulated perforations. Value $1.

Pope Paul VI, King Hussein and Patriarch Athenagoras; Church of St. Savior, Church of the Holy Sepulcher and Dome of the Rock — A54

1964, Aug. 17 Litho.

471 A54 10f dk grn, sep & org 15 15
472 A54 15f claret, sep & org 15 15
473 A54 25f choc, sepia & org 20 18
474 A54 50f blue, sepia & org 42 38
475 A54 80f brt grn, sep & org 60 52
Nos. 471-475 (5) 1.52 1.38

Meeting between Pope Paul VI and Patriarch Athenagoras of the Greek Orthodox Church in Jerusalem, Jan. 5, 1964. An imperf. souvenir sheet contains Nos. 471-475 with simulated perforations. Value $3.

A two-line bilingual overprint, "Papa Paulus VI World Peace Visit to United Nations 1965", was applied to Nos. 471-475 and the souvenir sheet. These overprints were issued Apr. 27, 1966.

Pagoda, Olympic Torch and Emblem — A55

1964, Nov. 21 Litho. ***Perf. 14***

476 A55 1f dark red 15 15
477 A55 2f bright vio 15 15
478 A55 3f blue green 15 15
479 A55 4f brown 15 15
480 A55 5f henna brown 15 15
481 A55 35f indigo 45 45
482 A55 50f olive 65 65
483 A55 100f violet bl 1.40 1.40
Set value 2.75 2.75

18th Olympic Games, Tokyo, Oct. 10-25. An imperf. 100f carmine rose souvenir sheet exists. Size of stamp: 82mm at the base. Value $7.

Scouts Crossing Stream on Log Bridge — A56

Designs: 2f, First aid. 3f, Calisthenics. 4f, Instruction in knot tying. 5f, Outdoor cooking. 35f, Sailing. 50f, Campfire.

1964, Dec. 7 Unwmk.

484 A56 1f brown 25 15
485 A56 2f bright vio 25 15
486 A56 3f ocher 25 15
487 A56 4f maroon 25 15
488 A56 5f yel green 25 15
489 A56 35f bright blue 1.00 1.00
490 A56 50f dk slate grn 1.75 1.50
Nos. 484-490 (7) 4.00 3.25

Jordanian Boy Scouts. An imperf. 100f dark blue souvenir sheet in campfire design exists. Size of stamp: 104mm at the base. Value $8.

Yuri A. Gagarin — A57

Russian Cosmonauts: No. 492, Gherman Titov. No. 493, Andrian G. Nikolayev. No. 494, Pavel R. Popovich. No. 495, Valeri Bykovski. No. 496, Valentina Tereshkova.

1965, Jan. 20 Litho. ***Perf. 14***

491 A57 40f sepia & vio bl 40 40
492 A57 40f pink & dk grn 40 40
493 A57 40f lt bl & vio blk 40 40
494 A57 40f olive & dk vio 40 40
495 A57 40f lt grn & red brn 40 40
496 A57 40f chlky bl & blk 40 40
Nos. 491-496 (6) 2.40 2.40

Russian cosmonauts. A blue 100f souvenir sheet exists showing portraits of the 6 astronauts and space-ship circling globe. This sheet received later an additional overprint honoring the space flight of Komarov, Feoktistov and Yegorov. Value $10, each.

For overprints see Nos. 527-527E.

UN Headquarters and Emblem — A58

1965, Feb. 15 ***Perf. 14x15***

497 A58 30f yel brn, pur & lt bl 15 15
498 A58 70f vio, lt bl & yel brn 35 35

19th anniv. of the UN (in 1964). A souvenir sheet contains Nos. 497-498, imperf. Value $9.

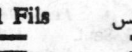

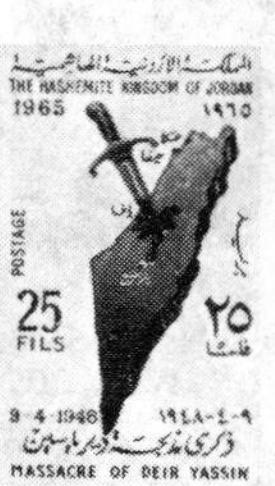

Dagger in Map of Palestine — A59

Volleyball Player and Cup — A60

1965, Apr. 9 Photo. *Perf. 11x11½*

499	A59	25f red & olive	65	20

Deir Yassin massacre, Apr. 9, 1948.

1965, June Litho. *Perf. 14½x14*

500	A60	15f lemon	15	15
501	A60	35f rose brown	22	18
502	A60	50f greenish blue	32	26

Arab Volleyball Championships. An imperf. 100f orange brown souvenir sheet exists. Size of stamp: 33x57mm. Value $7.

Cavalry Horsemanship — A61

Army Day: 10f, Tank. 35f, King Hussein and aides standing in army car.

1965, May 24

503	A61	5f green	15	15
504	A61	10f violet blue	15	15
505	A61	35f brown red	32	24
		Set value	42	34

John F. Kennedy — A62

1965, June 1 Wmk. 305 *Perf. 14*

506	A62	10f blk & brt green	15	15
507	A62	15f vio & orange	30	20
508	A62	25f brn & lt blue	30	30
509	A62	50f deep cl & emer	1.00	60

John F. Kennedy (1917-63). An imperf. 50f salmon and dark blue souv. sheet exists. Value $8.

Pope Paul VI, King Hussein and Dome of the Rock — A63

Perf. 13½x14

1965, June 15 Litho. Wmk. 305

510	A63	5f brown & rose lil	15	15
511	A63	10f vio brn & lt yel grn	22	15
512	A63	15f ultra & salmon	22	18
513	A63	50f black & rose	75	52

1st anniversary of the visit of Pope Paul VI to the Holy Land. An imperf. 50f violet and light blue souvenir sheet exists with simulated perforations. Value $7.50.

Jordan's Pavilion and Unisphere — A64

Perf. 14x13½

1965, Aug. Unwmk. Photo.

514	A64	15f silver & multi	15	15
515	A64	25f bronze & multi	15	15
516	A64	50f gold & multi	30	26
a.		Souvenir sheet of 1, 100f	1.00	1.00
		Set value		42

New York World's Fair, 1964-65.

No. 516a contains a 100f gold and multicolored stamp, type A64, imperf.

Library Aflame and Lamp A64a

1965, Aug. Wmk. 305 *Perf. 11½x11*

517	A64a	25f black, grn & red	15	15

Burning of the Library of Algiers, June 2, 1962.

ITU Emblem, Old and New Telecommunication Equipment — A65

1965, Aug. Litho. *Perf. 14x13½*

518	A65	25f lt blue & dk bl	15	15
519	A65	45f grnsh gray & blk	26	22

ITU, centenary. An imperf. 100f salmon and carmine rose souvenir sheet exists with carmine rose border. Size of stamp: 39x32mm. Value $1.

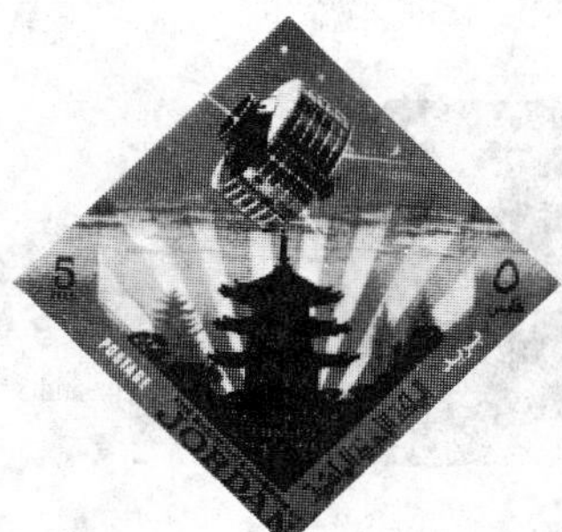

Syncom Satellite over Pagoda — A66

Designs: 10f, 20f, Rocket in space. 15f, Astronauts in cabin.

1965, Sept. *Perf. 14*

521	A66	5f brt ultra, org & grnsh blk	15	15
521A	A66	10f multicolored	20	15
521B	A66	15f multicolored	30	25
521C	A66	20f multicolored	38	30
521D	A66	50f brt ultra, brt & dp yel grn	1.00	75
		Nos. 521-521D (5)	2.03	
		Set value		1.35

Achievements in space research. A 50f multicolored imperf. souvenir sheet shows earth and Syncom satellite. Value $5.

Dead Sea A66a

Designs: b, Qumran Caves. c, Dead Sea. d, Dead Sea Scrolls.

1965, Sept. 23 Photo. *Perf. 14*

522	A66a	35f Strip of 4, #a.-d.		

Visit of King Hussein to France and US — A66b

Wmk. 305

1965, Oct. 5 Litho. *Perf. 14*

523	A66b	5f shown	15	15
523A	A66b	10f With Charles DeGaulle	18	18
523B	A66b	20f With Lyndon Johnson	35	35
523C	A66b	50f like #523	90	90

No. 523C exists in a 50f imperf. souvenir sheet.

Intl. Cooperation Year — A66c

1965, Oct. 24 *Perf. 14x13½*

524	A66c	5f brt org & dk org	15	15
524A	A66c	10f brt bl & dk bl	22	22
524B	A66c	45f brt grn & dk violet	1.00	1.00

Arab Postal Union, 10th Anniv. — A66d

1965, Nov. 5 *Perf. 15x14*

525	A66d	15f violet bl & blk	20	20
525A	A66d	25f brt yel grn & blk	35	35

Dome of the Rock A66e

1965, Nov. 20 *Perf. 14x15*

526	A66e	15f multicolored		
526A	A66e	25f multicolored		

Nos. 491-496 with Spaceship and Bilingual Ovpt. in Blue "Alexei Leonov / Pavel Belyaev / 18-3-65"

1966, Jan. 15 Litho. *Perf. 14*

527	A57	40f on No. 491	2.25	2.25
527A	A57	40f on No. 492	2.25	2.25
527B	A57	40f on No. 493	2.25	2.25
527C	A57	40f on No. 494	2.25	2.25
527D	A57	40f on No. 495	2.25	2.25
527E	A57	40f on No. 496	2.25	2.25

Both souvenir sheets mentioned after No. 496 exist overprinted in red violet.

King Hussein — A67

Perf. 14½x14

1966, Jan. 15 Photo. Unwmk.

Portrait in Slate Blue

528	A67	1f orange	15	15
528A	A67	2f ultramarine	15	15
528B	A67	3f dk purple	15	15
528C	A67	4f plum	15	15
528D	A67	7f brn orange	15	15
528E	A67	12f cerise	15	15
528F	A67	15f olive brn	15	15

Portrait in Violet Brown

528G	A67	21f green	22	15
528H	A67	25f greenish bl	26	15
528I	A67	35f yel bister	38	22
528J	A67	40f orange yel	45	26
528K	A67	50f olive grn	55	15
528L	A67	100f lt yel grn	1.10	32
528M	A67	150f violet	1.90	75
		Nos. 528-528M,C43-C45 (17)	18.66	9.55

Anti-tuberculosis Campaign — A67a

1966, May 17 Photo. *Perf. 14x15*

Blue Overprint

529	A67a	15f multicolored	25	25
529A	A67a	35f multicolored	60	60
529B	A67a	50f multicolored	85	85

Unissued Freedom from Hunger stamps overprinted. Two imperf. souvenir sheets exist, one with simulated perforations.

Nos. 529-529B with Added Surcharge Obliterated with Black Bars

1966, May 17 Photo. *Perf. 14x15*

530	A67a	15f on 15f + 15f	25	25
530A	A67a	35f on 35f + 35f	60	60
530B	A67a	50f on 50f + 50f	85	85

Stations of the Cross — A67b

Designs: Stations on Jesus' walk to Calvary along Via Dolorosa. Denominations expressed in Roman numerals.

1966, Sept. 14 Photo. *Perf. 15x14*

531	1f Condemned to death	15	15
531A	2f Takes up cross	15	15
531B	3f Falls the 1st time	16	16
531C	4f Meets His mother	22	22
531D	5f Simon helps carry cross	28	28
531E	6f Woman wipes Jesus' brow	32	32
531F	7f Falls 2nd time	38	38
531G	8f Tells women not to weep	45	45
531H	9f Falls 3rd time	50	50
531I	10f Stripped of His garment	55	55
531J	11f Nailed to cross	60	60
531K	12f Death on cross	65	65
531L	13f Removal from cross	70	70
531M	14f Burial	75	75
	Nos. 531-531M (14)	5.86	5.86

Souvenir Sheet

Imperf

531N	100f like #551	*13.00*	*13.00*

Gemini Astronauts, Spacecraft — A67c

Astronauts and spacecraft from Gemini Missions 6-8.

1966, Nov. 15 Photo. *Perf. 15x14*

532	1f Walter M. Schirra	15	15
532A	2f Thomas P. Stafford	15	15
532B	3f Frank Borman	15	15
532C	4f James A. Lovell	15	15
532D	30f Neil Armstrong	60	60
532E	60f David R. Scott	1.25	1.25
	Set value	2.00	2.00

Imperf

Size: 119x89mm

532F	100f Gemini 6-8 astronauts	*12.00*	*12.00*

Christmas — A67d

Perf. 14x15, 15x14

1966, Dec. 21 Photo.

533	5f Magi following star	15	15
533A	10f Adoration of the Magi	20	20
533B	35f Flight to Egypt, vert.	70	70

Souvenir Sheet

Imperf

533C	50f like #533A	*12.50*	*12.50*

King Hussein — A67e

Builders of World Peace: No. 534, Dag Hammarskjold. No. 534A, U Thant. No. 534B, Jawaharlal Nehru. No. 534C, Charles DeGaulle. No. 534D, John F. Kennedy. No. 534E, Lyndon B. Johnson. No. 534F, Pope John XXIII. No. 534G, Pope Paul VI. No. 534H, King Abdullah of Jordan.

1967, Jan. 5 Photo. *Perf. 15x14*

Background Color

534	A67e	5f gray	15	15
534A	A67e	5f brt yel grn	15	15
534B	A67e	10f rose lilac	18	18
534C	A67e	10f red brown	18	18
534D	A67e	35f olive green	60	60
534E	A67e	35f orange	60	60
534F	A67e	50f rose claret	85	85
534G	A67e	50f yel bister	85	85
534H	A67e	100f brt blue	1.75	1.75
534I	A67e	100f dull blue	1.75	1.75

Imperf

Size: 99x64mm

534J	A67e	100f Kennedy, etc.	*12.50*	*12.50*
534K	A67e	100f DeGaulle, etc.	*12.50*	*12.50*

King Hussein A67f

Photo. & Embossed

1967, Feb. 7 *Imperf.*

Gold Portrait and Border

Diameter: 50f, 100f, 48mm; 200f, 54mm

Portrait of King Hussein

535	A67f	5f dk bl & salmon	15	15
535A	A67f	10f purple & salmon	15	15
535B	A67f	50f blk brn & vio	75	75
535C	A67f	100f dk ol grn & pink	1.50	1.50
535D	A67f	200f dp bl & bl	3.00	3.00

Portrait of Crown Prince Hassan

536	A67f	5f brt yel grn & blk	15	15
536A	A67f	10f vio & blk	15	15
536B	A67f	50f bl & blk	75	75
536C	A67f	100f bister & blk	1.50	1.50
536D	A67f	200f brt pink & blk	3.00	3.00

Portrait of John F. Kennedy

537	A67f	5f brt bl & lt grn	15	15
537A	A67f	10f dp grn & pink	15	15
537B	A67f	50f brt rose & org yel	75	75
537C	A67f	100f brn & apple grn	1.50	1.50
537D	A67f	200f dk purple & pale grn	3.00	3.00
		Nos. 535-537D (15)	16.65	16.65

1968 Summer Olympic Games, Mexico — A67g

Olympic torch and: 1f, Natl. University Library with O'Gormans mosaics, statue, Mexico City. 2f, Fishermen on Lake Patzcuaro. 3f, Natl. University buildings. 4f, Paseo de la Reforma, Mexico City. 30f, Guadalajara Cathedral. 60f, 100f, Palace of Fine Arts, Mexico City.

Perf. 14x15

1967, Mar. Photo. Unwmk.

538	A67g	1f lake, dk bl vio & blk	15	15
538A	A67g	2f blk, lake & dk bl vio	15	15
538B	A67g	3f dark bl vio, blk & lake	15	15
538C	A67g	4f bl, grn & brn	15	15
538D	A67g	30f grn, brn & bl	45	45
538E	A67g	60f brn, bl & grn	90	90
		Set value	1.50	1.50

Souvenir Sheet

Imperf

538F	A67g	100f brn, dark bl & grn	

Symbolic Water Cycle A68

Perf. 14½x14

1967, Mar. 1 Litho. Wmk. 305

539	A68	10f dp org, blk & gray	15	15
540	A68	15f grnsh bl, blk & gray	15	15
541	A68	25f brt rose lil, blk & gray	18	18
		Set value	35	35

Hydrological Decade (UNESCO), 1965-74.

UNESCO Emblem A69

1967, Mar. 16

542	A69	100f multicolored	65	65

20th anniv. of UNESCO.

Dromedary — A70

Animals: 2f, Karakul. 3f, Angora goat.

Perf. 14x15

1967, Feb. 11 Photo. Unwmk.

543	A70	1f dark brn & multi	15	15
544	A70	2f yellow & multi	15	15
545	A70	3f lt blue & multi	15	15
		Set value, #543-545, C46-C48	85	65

A souvenir sheet exists with a 100f in design and colors of No. C47, simulated perforation and marginal animal design. Value $6.

Inauguration of WHO Headquarters, Geneva — A71

1967, Apr. 7 Wmk. 305

546	A71	5f emerald & blk	15	15
547	A71	45f dl orange & blk	32	32
		Set value	36	36

Arab League Emblem and Hands Reaching for Knowledge — A72

1968, May 5 Unwmk. *Perf. 11*

548	A72	20f org & slate grn	15	15
549	A72	20f brt pink & dk bl	15	15
		Set value	20	20

Issued to publicize the literacy campaign.

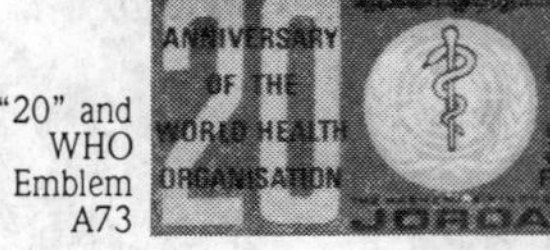

"20" and WHO Emblem A73

Perf. 14½x14

1968, Aug. 10 Wmk. 305

550	A73	30f multicolored	22	18
551	A73	100f multicolored	75	60

20th anniv. of the WHO.

European Goldfinch A74

Protected Game: 10f, Rock partridge, vert. 15f, Ostriches, vert. 20f, Sand partridge. 30f, Dorcas gazelle. 40f, Oryxes. 50f, Houbara bustard.

1968, Oct. 5 Unwmk. *Perf. 13½*

552	A74	5f multicolored	15	15
553	A74	10f multicolored	18	15
554	A74	15f multicolored	20	15
555	A74	20f multicolored	32	15
556	A74	30f multicolored	45	18
557	A74	40f multicolored	60	25
558	A74	50f multicolored	85	30
		Nos. 552-558,C49-C50 (9)	4.90	3.48

Human Rights Flame — A75

1968, Dec. 10 Litho. *Perf. 13*

559	A75	20f dp org, lt org & blk	18	15
560	A75	60f grn, lt blue & blk	50	45

International Human Rights Year.

Dome of the Rock, Jerusalem A76

Designs: 5f, 45f, Holy Kaaba, Mecca, and Dome of the Rock.

1969, Oct. 8 Photo. *Perf. 12*

Size: 56x25mm

561	A76	5f dull vio & multi	15	15

Size: 36x25mm

562	A76	10f vio blue & multi	18	15
563	A76	20f Prus bl & multi	38	15

Size: 56x25mm

564	A76	45f Prus bl & multi	75	22
		Set value		44

ILO Emblem — A77

1969, June 10 *Perf. 13½x14*

565	A77	10f blue & black	15	15
566	A77	20f bister brn & blk	15	15
567	A77	25f lt olive & black	15	15

568 A77 45f lil rose & black 26 25
569 A77 60f orange & black 38 32
Nos. 565-569 (5) 1.09
Set value 84

ILO, 50th anniversary.

Horses — A78

Designs: 20f, White stallion. 45f, Mare and foal.

1969, July 6 Unwmk. *Perf. 13½*
570 A78 10f dark bl & multi 15 15
571 A78 20f dl green & multi 18 15
572 A78 45f red & multi 45 30
Set value 46

Prince Hassan and Princess Tharwat A79

Designs: 60f, 100f, Prince Hassan and bride in western bridal gown.

1969, Dec. 2 Photo. *Perf. 12½*
573 A79 20f gold & multi 15 15
573A A79 60f gold & multi 45 38
573B A79 100f gold & multi 75 75
c. Strip of 3, #573-573B 1.50

Wedding of Crown Prince Hassan, Nov. 14, 1968.

The Tragedy and the Flight of the Refugees A79a

Different design on each stamp. Each strip of 5 has five consecutive denominations.

Perf. 14½x13½
1969, Dec. 10 Photo.
574 A79a 1f-5f multi
574A A79a 6f-10f multi
574B A79a 11f-15f multi
574C A79a 16f-20f multi
574D A79a 21f-25f multi
574E A79a 26f-30f multi

For surcharges see Nos. 870-875.

Inscribed: Tragedy in the Holy Lands

Different design on each stamp. Each strip of 5 has five consecutive denominations.

Perf. 14½x13½
1969, Dec. 10 Photo.
575 A79a 1f-5f multi
575A A79a 6f-10f multi
575B A79a 11f-15f multi
575C A79a 16f-20f multi
575D A79a 21f-25f multi
575E A79a 26f-30f multi

For surcharges see Nos. 876-881.

Pomegranate Flower (inscribed "Desert Scabius") — A80

Oranges — A81

Black Bush Robin — A82

Designs: 15f, Wattle flower ("Caper"). 20f, Melon. 25f, Caper flower ("Pomegranate"). 30f, Lemons. 35f, Morning glory. 40f, Grapes. 45f, Desert scabius ("Wattle"). 50f, Olive-laden branch. 75f, Black iris. 100f, Apples. 180f, Masked shrike. 200f, Palestine sunbird. (Inscriptions incorrect on 5f, 15f, 25f and 45f.)

Perf. 14x13½ (flowers), 12 (fruit), 13½x14 (birds)

1969-70 Photo.
576 A80 5f yel & multi ('70) 15 15
577 A81 10f blue & multi 15 15
578 A80 15f tan & multi ('70) 20 15
579 A81 20f sepia & multi 30 15
580 A80 25f multi ('70) 38 15
581 A81 30f vio bl & multi 42 15
582 A80 35f multi ('70) 45 15
583 A81 40f dull yel & multi 52 15
584 A80 45f gray & multi ('70) 55 15
585 A81 50f car rose & multi 60 15
586 A80 75f multi ('70) 1.00 22
587 A81 100f dk gray & multi 1.25 38
588 A82 120f org & multi ('70) 1.90 45
589 A82 180f multi ('70) 2.25 1.00
590 A82 200f multi ('70) 2.75 1.25
Nos. 576-590 (15) 12.87
Set value 4.10

Issue dates: Fruits, Nov. 22; flowers, Mar. 21; birds, Sept. 1.

Soccer — A83

Designs: 10f, Diver. 15f, Boxers. 50f, Runner. 100f, Bicyclist, vert. 150f, Basketball, vert.

1970, Aug. *Perf. 13½x14, 14x13½*
651 A83 5f green & multi 15 15
652 A83 10f lt bl & multi 15 15
653 A83 15f gray & multi 15 15
654 A83 50f gray & multi 38 30
655 A83 100f yellow & multi 75 60
656 A83 150f multicolored 1.10 1.00
Nos. 651-656 (6) 2.68 2.35

Boy Fetching Water, UNICEF and Refugee Emblems — A84

UNICEF and Refugee Emblems and: 5f, Refugee children, horiz. 15f, Girl and tents. 20f, Boy in front of tent.

1970, Aug.
657 A84 5f multicolored 15 15
658 A84 10f multicolored 30 20
659 A84 15f multicolored 42 20
660 A84 20f multicolored 60 20
Set value 65

Issued for Childhood Day.

Nativity Grotto, Bethlehem A85

Church of the Nativity, Bethlehem: 10f, Manger. 20f, Altar. 25f, Interior.

1970, Dec. 25 Photo. *Perf. 13½*
661 A85 5f blue & multi 15 15
662 A85 10f scarlet & multi 15 15
663 A85 20f rose lilac & multi 15 15
664 A85 25f green & multi 20 15
Set value 45 30

Christmas.

Flag and Map of Arab League Countries A85a

1971, May 10 Photo. *Perf. 11½x11*
665 A85a 10f orange & multi 15 15
666 A85a 20f lt blue & multi 15 15
667 A85a 30f olive & multi 20 15
Set value 40 25

25th anniversary of the Arab League.

Emblem and Doves — A86

Designs: 5f, Emblem and 4 races, vert. 10f, Emblem as flower, vert.

1971, July
668 A86 5f green & multi 15 15
669 A86 10f brick red & multi 15 15
670 A86 15f dk blue & multi 20 15
Set value 40 18

Intl. Year Against Racial Discrimination.

Dead Sea — A87

Views of the Holy Land: 30f, Excavated building, Petra. 45f, Via Dolorosa, Jerusalem, vert. 60f, Jordan River. 100f, Christmas bell, Bethlehem, vert.

1971, Aug. *Perf. 14x13½, 13½x14*
671 A87 5f blue & multi 15 15
672 A87 30f pink & multi 38 20
673 A87 45f blue & multi 50 38
674 A87 60f gray & multi 75 50
675 A87 100f gray & multi 1.25 90
Nos. 671-675 (5) 3.03 2.13

Tourist publicity.

Opening of UPU Headquarters, Bern in 1970 — A88

1971, Oct. *Perf. 11*
676 A88 10f brn, brn & yel grn 15 15
677 A88 20f dk vio, grn & yel grn 28 15
Set value 17

Avicenna (980-1037) — A89

Child Learning to Write — A90

Arab Scholars: 10f, Averroes (1126-1198). 20f, ibn-Khaldun (1332-1406). 25f, ibn-Tufail (?-1185). 30f, Alhazen (965?-1039?).

1971, Sept. *Perf. 12*
678 A89 5f gold & multi 15 15
679 A89 10f gold & multi 15 15
680 A89 20f gold & multi 28 15
681 A89 25f gold & multi 30 15
682 A89 30f gold & multi 40 20
Nos. 678-682 (5) 1.28
Set value 52

1972, Feb. 9 Photo. *Perf. 11*
683 A90 5f ultra, brn & grn 15 15
684 A90 15f mag, brn & blue 15 15
685 A90 20f grn, brn & blue 20 15
686 A90 30f org, brn & blue 30 20
Set value 50

International Education Year.

Mother and Child — A91

Pope Paul VI and Holy Sepulcher — A92

Mother's Day: 10f, Mothers and children, horiz. 30f, Arab mother and child.

1972, Mar. *Perf. 14x13½*
687 A91 10f lt grn & multi 15 15
688 A91 20f red brown & blk 16 15
689 A91 30f blue, brn & blk 25 16
Set value 32

1972, Apr. Photo. *Perf. 14x13½*
690 A92 30f black & multi 20 15

Easter. See Nos. C51-C52.

UNICEF Emblem, Children A93

UNICEF Emblem and: 20f, Child playing with blocks spelling "UNICEF," vert. 30f, Mother and child.

1972, May *Perf. 11½x11, 11x11½*
691 A93 10f bl, vio bl & blk 15 15
692 A93 20f multicolored 16 15
693 A93 30f blue & multi 25 16
Set value 30

25th anniv. (in 1971) of UNICEF.

UN Emblem, Dove and Grain — A94

1972, July *Perf. 11x11½*

No.	Type	Description	Unused	Used
694	A94	5f vio & multi	15	15
695	A94	10f multicolored	15	15
696	A94	15f black & multi	16	15
697	A94	20f green & multi	20	15
698	A94	30f multicolored	35	20
		Nos. 694-698 (5)	1.01	
		Set value		50

25th anniv. (in 1970) of the UN.

Al Aqsa Mosque, Jerusalem A95

Designs: 60f, Al Aqsa Mosque on fire. 100f, Al Aqsa Mosque, interior.

1972, Aug. 21 **Litho.** *Perf. 14½*

No.	Type	Description	Unused	Used
699	A95	30f green & multi	25	20
700	A95	60f blue & multi	50	35
701	A95	100f ocher & multi	80	52

3rd anniversary of the burning of Al Aqsa Mosque, Jerusalem.

House in Desert — A96

1972, Nov. *Perf. 14x13½, 13½x14*

No.	Type	Description	Unused	Used
702	A96	5f Falconer, vert	15	15
703	A96	10f shown	15	15
704	A96	15f Man on camel	20	15
705	A96	20f Pipe line construction	28	15
706	A96	25f Shepherd	30	15
707	A96	30f Camels at water trough	48	20
708	A96	35f Chicken farm	52	20
709	A96	45f Irrigation canal	75	35
		Nos. 702-709 (8)	2.83	
		Set value		1.15

Life in the Arab desert.

Wasfi el Tell and Dome of the Rock — A97

Wasfi el Tell, Map of Palestine and Jordan — A98

Perf. 13x13½, 13½x13

1972, Dec. **Photo.**

No.	Type	Description	Unused	Used
710	A97	5f citron & multi	15	15
711	A98	10f red & multi	15	15
712	A97	20f dl blue & multi	25	18
713	A98	30f green & multi	45	25
		Set value	86	52

In memory of Prime Minister Wasfi el Tell, who was assassinated in Cairo by Black September terrorists.

Trapshooting — A99

Designs: 75f, Trapshooter facing right, horiz. 120f, Trapshooter facing left, horiz.

1972, Dec. *Perf. 14x13½, 13½x14*

No.	Type	Description	Unused	Used
714	A99	25f multicolored	15	15
715	A99	75f multicolored	42	35
716	A99	120f multicolored	75	50

World Trapshooting Championships.

Aero Club Emblem A100

1973, Jan. **Photo.** *Perf. 13½x14*

No.	Type	Description	Unused	Used
717	A100	5f blue, blk & yel	15	15
718	A100	10f blue, blk & yel	20	15
		Nos. 717-718,C53-C55 (5)	1.06	
		Set value		52

Royal Jordanian Aero Club.

Peace Dove and Jordanian Flag — A101

Designs: 10f, Emblem. 15f, King Hussein. 30f, Map of Jordan.

1973, Mar. *Perf. 11½*

No.	Type	Description	Unused	Used
719	A101	5f blue & multi	15	15
720	A101	10f pale grn & multi	15	15
721	A101	15f olive & multi	18	15
722	A101	30f yel grn & multi	35	30
		Set value	70	45

Hashemite Kingdom of Jordan, 50th anniv.

Battle, Flag and Map of Palestine — A102

Designs: 10f, Two soldiers in combat, map of Palestine. 15f, Map of Palestine, olive branch, soldier on tank.

1973, Apr. 10 **Photo.** *Perf. 11*

No.	Type	Description	Unused	Used
723	A102	5f crimson & multi	16	15
724	A102	10f crimson & multi	30	16
725	A102	15f grn, blue & brn	50	20
		Set value		40

5th anniversary of Karama Battle.

Father and Child — A103

Father's Day: 20f, Father and infant. 30f, Family.

1973, Apr. 20 *Perf. 13½*

No.	Type	Description	Unused	Used
726	A103	10f citron & multi	15	15
727	A103	20f lt blue & multi	15	15
728	A103	30f multicolored	22	15
		Set value		30

Phosphate Mine — A104

1973, June 25 **Litho.** *Perf. 13½x14*

No.	Type	Description	Unused	Used
729	A104	5f shown	15	15
730	A104	10f Cement factory	16	15
731	A104	15f Sharmasil Dam	25	15
732	A104	20f Kafrein Dam	30	20
		Set value		50

Development projects.

Camel Racer — A105

Designs: Camel racing.

1973, July 21

No.	Type	Description	Unused	Used
733	A105	5f multicolored	15	15
734	A105	10f multicolored	15	15
735	A105	15f multicolored	15	15
736	A105	20f multicolored	16	15
		Set value	35	22

Book Year Emblem — A106

1973, Aug. 25 **Photo.** *Perf. 13x13½*

No.	Type	Description	Unused	Used
737	A106	30f dk grn & multi	32	15
738	A106	60f purple & multi	65	25

Intl. Book Year. For overprints see #781-782.

Family A107

Family Day: 30f, Family around fire. 60f, Large family outdoors.

1973, Sept. 18 **Litho.** *Perf. 13½*

No.	Type	Description	Unused	Used
739	A107	20f multicolored	15	15
740	A107	30f multicolored	20	15
741	A107	60f multicolored	42	25
		Set value		46

Kings of Iran and Jordan, Tomb of Cyrus the Great and Mosque of Omar — A108

1973, Oct. **Litho.** *Perf. 13*

No.	Type	Description	Unused	Used
742	A108	5f ver & multi	15	15
743	A108	10f brown & multi	20	15
744	A108	15f gray & multi	32	18
745	A108	30f blue & multi	60	35
		Set value		70

2500th anniversary of the founding of the Persian Empire by Cyrus the Great.

Palestine Week Emblem A109

Palestine Week: 10f, Torch and laurel. 15f, Refugee family behind barbed wire, vert. 30f, Children, Map of Palestine, globe. Sizes: 5f, 10f, 30f; 38½x22mm. 15f, 25x46mm.

1973, Nov. 17 **Photo.** *Perf. 11*

No.	Type	Description	Unused	Used
746	A109	5f multicolored	15	15
747	A109	10f dl bl & multi	25	15
748	A109	15f yel grn & multi	30	15
749	A109	30f brt grn & multi	65	25
		Set value		50

Traditional Harvest A110

Designs: Traditional and modern agricultural methods.

1973, Dec. 25 *Perf. 13½*

No.	Type	Description	Unused	Used
750	A110	5f shown	15	15
751	A110	10f Harvesting machine	15	15
752	A110	15f Traditional seeding	15	15
753	A110	20f Seeding machine	18	15
754	A110	30f Ox plow	25	22
755	A110	35f Plowing machine	30	22
756	A110	45f Pest control	38	32
757	A110	60f Horticulture	55	50
		Nos. 750-757,C56 (9)	2.76	2.31

Red Sea Fish — A111

Designs: Various Red Sea fishes.

1974, Feb. 15 **Photo.** *Perf. 14*

No.	Type	Description	Unused	Used
758	A111	5f multicolored	15	15
759	A111	10f multicolored	15	15
760	A111	15f multicolored	18	15
761	A111	20f multicolored	22	15
762	A111	25f multicolored	25	15
763	A111	30f multicolored	30	18
764	A111	35f multicolored	32	22
765	A111	40f multicolored	38	25
766	A111	45f multicolored	45	30
767	A111	50f multicolored	52	38
768	A111	60f multicolored	75	48
		Nos. 758-768 (11)	3.67	2.56

Battle of Muta, 1250 A112

1974, Mar. 15 **Photo.** *Perf. 13½*

No.	Type	Description	Unused	Used
769	A112	10f shown	30	15
770	A112	20f Yarmouk Battle, 636	60	30
771	A112	30f Hitteen Battle, 1187	90	45

Clubfooted Boy, by Murillo — A113

Paintings: 10f, Praying Hands, by Dürer. 15f, St. George and the Dragon, by Paolo Uccello. 20f, Mona Lisa, by Da Vinci. 30f, Hope, by Frederic Watts. 40f, Angelus, by Jean F. Millet, horiz. 50f, The Artist and her Daughter, by Angelica Kauffmann. 60f, Portrait of my Mother, by James Whistler, horiz. 100f, Master Hare, by Reynolds.

Perf. 14x13½, 13½x14

1974, Apr. 15 Litho.

772 A113 5f black & multi 15 15
773 A113 10f black & gray 15 15
774 A113 15f black & multi 15 15
775 A113 20f black & multi 15 15
776 A113 30f black & multi 20 15
777 A113 40f black & multi 25 15
778 A113 50f black & multi 32 22
779 A113 60f black & multi 42 25
780 A113 100f black & multi 65 45
Nos. 772-780 (9) 2.44
Set value 1.40

Nos. 737-738 Overprinted

المؤتمر الدولي لتاريخ بلاد الشام
٢٠ – ١٩٧٤/٤/٢٥
الجامعة الاردنية

1974, Apr. 20 Photo. *Perf. 13x13½*

781 A106 30f dk grn & multi 35 20
782 A106 60f purple & multi 75 50

International Conference for Damascus History, Apr. 20-25.

UPU Emblem — A114

1974 *Perf. 13x12½*

783 A114 10f yel grn & multi 15 15
784 A114 30f blue & multi 30 15
785 A114 60f multicolored 60 30
Set value 48

Centenary of Universal Postal Union.

Camel Caravan at Sunset A115

Designs: 3f, 30f, Palm at shore of Dead Sea. 4f, 40f, Hotel at shore. 5f, 50f, Jars from Qumran Caves. 6f, 60f, Copper scrolls, vert. 10f, 100f, Cracked cistern steps, vert. 20f, like 2f.

1974, June 25 Photo. *Perf. 14*

786 A115 2f multicolored 15 15
787 A115 3f multicolored 15 15
788 A115 4f multicolored 15 15
789 A115 5f multicolored 15 15
790 A115 6f multicolored 15 15
791 A115 10f multicolored 15 15
792 A115 20f multicolored 18 15
793 A115 30f multicolored 26 15
794 A115 40f multicolored 38 18
795 A115 50f multicolored 42 25
796 A115 60f multicolored 62 32
797 A115 100f multicolored 1.00 50
Set value 3.10 1.70

WPY Emblem — A116

Water Skiing — A117

1974, Aug. 20 Photo. *Perf. 11*

798 A116 5f lt green, blk & pur 15 15
799 A116 10f lt green, blk & car 15 15
800 A116 20f lt green, blk & org 20 15
Set value 35 20

World Population Year.

Perf. 14x13½, 13½x14

1974, Sept. 20

Water Skiing: 10f, 100f, Side view, horiz. 20f, 200f, Turning, horiz. 50f, like 5f.

801 A117 5f multicolored 15 15
802 A117 10f multicolored 15 15
803 A117 20f multicolored 15 15
804 A117 50f multicolored 35 20
805 A117 100f multicolored 65 40
806 A117 200f multicolored 1.40 80
Nos. 801-806 (6) 2.85
Set value 1.55

Holy Kaaba, Mecca, and Pilgrims — A118

1974, Nov. Photo. *Perf. 11*

807 A118 10f blue & multi 15 15
808 A118 20f yellow & multi 25 15
Set value 20

Pilgrimage season.

Amrah Palace A119

Ruins: 20f, Hisham Palace. 30f, Kharraneh Castle.

1974, Nov. 25 Photo. *Perf. 14x13½*

809 A119 10f black & multi 25 15
810 A119 20f black & multi 50 30
811 A119 30f black & multi 75 50

Jordanian Woman — A120

Designs: Various women's costumes.

1975, Feb. 1 Photo. *Perf. 12*

812 A120 5f lt green & multi 15 15
813 A120 10f yellow & multi 15 15
814 A120 15f lt blue & multi 15 15
815 A120 20f ultra & multi 15 15
816 A120 25f green & multi 18 15
Set value 50 35

Treasury, Petra — A121

Ommayyad Palace, Amman A122

Designs: 30f, Dome of the Rock, Jerusalem. 40f, Columns, Forum of Jerash.

Perf. 14x13½, 13½x14

1975, Mar. 1 Photo.

824 A121 15f lt blue & multi 15 15
825 A122 20f pink & multi 18 15
826 A122 30f yellow & multi 30 15
827 A122 40f lt blue & multi 38 18
Nos. 824-827,C59-C61 (7) 2.27 1.47

King Hussein — A123

1975, Apr. 8 Photo. *Perf. 14*

Size: 19x23mm

831 A123 5f green & ind 15 15
832 A123 10f vio & indigo 15 15
833 A123 15f car & indigo 15 15
834 A123 20f brn ol & ind 15 15
835 A123 25f vio bl & ind 15 15
836 A123 30f brown & ind 15 15
837 A123 35f vio & indigo 16 15
838 A123 40f orange & ind 18 15
839 A123 45f red lil & ind 20 15
840 A123 50f bl green & ind 22 15
Nos. 831-840,C62-C68 (17) 8.61 5.84

Globe, "alia" and Plane — A125

Designs: 30f, Boeing 727 connecting Jordan with world, horiz. 60f, Globe and "alia."

1975, June 15 Photo. *Perf. 11*

853 A125 10f multicolored 15 15
854 A125 30f multicolored 26 18
855 A125 60f multicolored 55 38
Set value 85 60

Royal Jordanian Airline, 30th anniversary.

Satellite Transmission System, Map of Mediterranean — A126

1975, Aug. 1 Photo. *Perf. 11*

856 A126 20f vio bl & multi 25 15
857 A126 30f green & multi 32 18

Opening of satellite earth station.

Chamber of Commerce Emblem — A127

1975, Oct. 15 Photo. *Perf. 11*

858 A127 10f yellow & blue 15 15
859 A127 15f yel, red & blue 15 15
860 A127 20f yel, grn & blue 16 15
Set value 38 18

Amman Chamber of Commerce, 50th anniv.

Hand Holding Wrench, Wall and Emblem — A128

1975, Nov. Photo. *Perf. 11½*

861 A128 5f green, car & blk 15 15
862 A128 10f car, green & blk 15 15
863 A128 20f blk, green & car 20 15
Set value 35 20

Three-year development plan.

Family and IWY Emblem A129

Salt Industry A130

IWY Emblem and: 25f, Woman scientist with microscope. 60f, Woman graduate.

1976, Apr. 27 Litho. *Perf. 14x13½*

864 A129 5f multicolored 15 15
865 A129 25f multicolored 15 15
866 A129 60f multicolored 38 25
Set value 58 40

International Women's Year.

1976, June 1 Litho. *Perf. 13½x14*

Arab Labor Organization Emblem and: 30f, Welders. 60f, Ship at 'Aqaba.

867 A130 10f gray & multi 15 15
868 A130 30f bister & multi 18 15
869 A130 60f brown & multi 38 25
Set value 60 40

Arab Labor Organization.

Nos. 574-574E Surcharged

Perf. 14½x13½

1976, July 18 Photo.

Strips of 5

870 A79a 25f on 1f-5f
871 A79a 25f on 6f-10f
872 A79a 40f on 11f-15f
873 A79a 50f on 16f-20f
874 A79a 75f on 21f-25f
875 A79a 125f on 26f-30f

Nos. 575-575E Surcharged

876 A79a 25f on 1f-5f
877 A79a 25f on 6f-10f
878 A79a 40f on 11f-15f
879 A79a 50f on 16f-20f
880 A79a 75f on 21f-25f
881 A79a 125f on 26f-30f

Tennis — A132

Designs: 10f, Athlete and wreath. 15f, Soccer. 20f, Equestrian and Jordanian flag. 30f, Weight lifting. 100f, Stadium, Amman.

1976, Nov. 1 Litho. *Perf. 14x13½*

990 A132 5f buff & multi 15 15
991 A132 10f lt bl & multi 15 15
992 A132 15f green & multi 15 15
993 A132 20f green & multi 16 15
994 A132 30f green & multi 25 15
995 A132 100f multicolored 80 48
Nos. 990-995 (6) 1.66
Set value 88

Sports and youth.

Dam — A133

Telephones, 1876 and 1976 — A134

Designs: Various dams.

1976, Dec. 7 Litho. *Perf. 14x13½*

996 A133 30f multicolored 22 15
997 A133 60f multicolored 45 32
998 A133 100f multicolored 75 50

1977, Feb. 17 Litho. *Perf. 11½x12*

Design: 125f, 1876 telephone and 1976 receiver.

999 A134 75f rose & multi 60 45
1000 A134 125f blue & multi 90 75

Centenary of first telephone call by Alexander Graham Bell, Mar. 10, 1876.

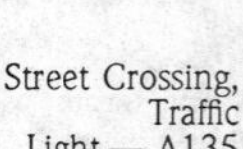

Street Crossing, Traffic Light — A135

Designs: 75f, Traffic circle and light. 125f, Traffic light and signs, motorcycle policeman.

1977, May 4 Litho. *Perf. 11x12*

1001 A135 5f rose & multi 15 15
1002 A135 75f black & multi 60 45
1003 A135 125f yellow & multi 1.00 75

International Traffic Day.

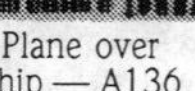

Plane over Ship — A136

Child with Toy Bank — A137

Coat of Arms and: 25f, Factories and power lines. 40f, Fertilizer plant and trucks. 50f, Ground to air missile. 75f, Mosque and worshippers. 125f, Radar station and TV emblem.

1977, Aug. 11 Photo. *Perf. 11½x12*

1004 A136 10f sil & multi 15 15
1005 A136 25f sil & multi 20 15
1006 A136 40f sil & multi 30 24
1007 A136 50f sil & multi 42 30
1008 A136 75f sil & multi 60 45
1009 A136 125f sil & multi 1.10 75
Nos. 1004-1009 (6) 2.77 2.04

Imperf

Size: 100x70mm

1009A A136 100f multicolored

25th anniv. of the reign of King Hussein.

1977, Sept. 1 Litho. *Perf. 11½x12*

Postal Savings Bank: 25f, Boy with piggy bank. 50f, Postal Savings Bank emblem. 75f, Boy talking to teller.

1010 A137 10f multicolored 15 15
1011 A137 25f multicolored 22 15
1012 A137 50f multicolored 45 30
1013 A137 75f multicolored 65 45

King Hussein and Queen Alia — A138

Queen Alia — A139

1977, Nov. 1 Litho. *Perf. 11½x12*

1014 A138 10f lt grn & multi 15 15
1015 A138 25f rose & multi 15 15
1016 A138 40f yellow & multi 28 16
1017 A138 50f blue & multi 35 20
Set value 50

1977, Dec. 1 Litho. *Perf. 11½x12*

1018 A139 10f green & multi 15 15
1019 A139 25f brown & multi 20 15
1020 A139 40f blue & multi 35 20
1021 A139 50f yellow & multi 42 25
Set value 60

Queen Alia, died in 1977 air crash.

Jinnah, Flags of Pakistan and Jordan — A140

APU Emblem, Members' Flags — A141

1977, Dec. 20 *Perf. 11½*

1022 A140 25f multicolored 20 15
1023 A140 75f multicolored 60 40

Mohammed Ali Jinnah (1876-1948), 1st Governor General of Pakistan.

1978, Apr. 12 Litho. *Perf. 12x11½*

1024 A141 25f yellow & multi 45 30
1025 A141 40f buff & multi 75 50

25th anniv. (in 1977), of Arab Postal Union.

Copper Coffee Set — A142

Roman Amphitheater, Jerash — A143

Handicraft: 40f, Porcelain plate and ashtray. 75f, Vase and jewelry. 125f, Pipe holder.

1978, May 30 Photo. *Perf. 11½x12*

1026 A142 25f olive & multi 20 15
1027 A142 40f lilac & multi 32 20
1028 A142 75f ultra & multi 60 40
1029 A142 125f orange & multi 1.00 65

1978, July 30 Litho. *Perf. 12*

Tourist Views: 20f, Roman Columns, Jerash. 40f, Goat, grapes and man, Roman mosaic, Madaba. 75f, Rock formations, Rum, and camel rider.

1030 A143 5f multicolored 15 15
1031 A143 20f multicolored 16 15
1032 A143 40f multicolored 32 20
1033 A143 75f multicolored 60 40
Set value 75

King Hussein and Pres. Sadat — A144

Designs: No. 1035, King Hussein and Pres. Assad, Jordanian and Syrian flags, horiz. No. 1036, King Hussein, King Khalid, Jordanian and Saudi Arabian flags, horiz.

1978, Aug. 20 *Perf. 11½x12*

1034 A144 40f multicolored 32 20
1035 A144 40f multicolored 32 20
1036 A144 40f multicolored 32 20

Visits of Arab leaders to Jordan.

Cement Factory — A145

Designs: 10f, Science laboratory. 25f, Printing press. 75f, Artificial fertilizer plant.

1978, Sept. 25 Litho. *Perf. 12*

1037 A145 5f multicolored 15 15
1038 A145 10f multicolored 15 15
1039 A145 25f multicolored 30 20
1040 A145 75f multicolored 90 60

Industrial development.

"UNESCO" Scales and Globe — A146

1978, Dec. 5 Litho. *Perf. 12x11½*

1041 A146 40f multicolored 40 30
1042 A146 75f multicolored 90 65

30th anniversary of UNESCO.

1976-1980 Development Plan — A147

1979, Oct. 25 Litho. *Perf. 12½x12*

1043 A147 25f multicolored 22 15
1044 A147 40f multicolored 36 24
1045 A147 50f multicolored 45 25

IYC Emblem, Flag of Jordan — A148

1979, Nov. 15 Litho. *Perf. 12x12½*

1046 A148 25f multicolored 20 15
1047 A148 40f multicolored 32 20
1048 A148 50f multicolored 40 24

International Year of the Child.

1979 Population and Housing Census — A149

1979, Dec. 25 Litho. *Perf. 12½x12*

1049 A149 25f multicolored 22 15
1050 A149 40f multicolored 38 24
1051 A149 50f multicolored 45 30

King Hussein — A150

1980 Litho. *Perf. 13½x13*

1052 A150 5f multicolored 15 15
1053 A150 10f multicolored 15 15
1055 A150 20f multicolored 16 15
1056 A150 25f multicolored 20 15
a. Inscribed 1979 20 15
1058 A150 40f multicolored 32 20
a. Inscribed 1979 32 20
1059 A150 50f multicolored 40 25
1060 A150 75f multicolored 55 32
1061 A150 125f multicolored 1.00 65
Nos. 1052-1061 (8) 2.93
Set value 1.70

The 5f, 10f, 20f, 25f and 40f also come inscribed 1981.

International Nursing Day — A151

El Deir Temple, Petra — A152

1980, May 12 Litho. *Perf. 12x12½*

1062 A151 25f multicolored 22 15
1063 A151 40f multicolored 35 22
1064 A151 50f multicolored 40 25

1980 Litho. *Perf. 14½*

1065 A152 25f multicolored 24 16
1066 A152 40f multicolored 35 24
1067 A152 50f multicolored 45 30

World Tourism Conf., Manila, Sept. 27.

Hegira (Pilgrimage Year) — A153

1980, Nov. 11 Litho. *Perf. 14½*

1068 A153 25f multicolored 22 15
1069 A153 40f multicolored 40 22
1070 A153 50f multicolored 50 28
1071 A153 75f multicolored 90 42
1072 A153 100f multicolored 90 55
Nos. 1068-1072 (5) 2.92 1.62

Souvenir Sheet

Imperf

1073 A153 290f multicolored 4.25 2.75

#1073 contains designs of #1068-1071.

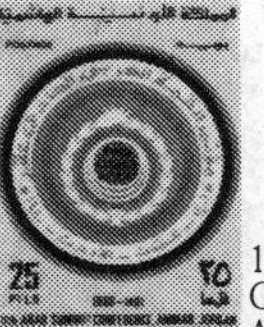

11th Arab Summit Conference, Amman — A153a

1980, Nov. 25 Litho. *Perf. 14½*
1073A A153a 25f multi 20 15
1073B A153a 40f multi 30 25
1073C A153a 50f multi 45 32
1073D A153a 75f multi 75 45
1073E A153a 100f multi 90 65
f. Souv. sheet of 5, #1073A-1073E, imperf. 4.00 4.00
Nos. 1073A-1073E (5) 2.60 1.82

A154

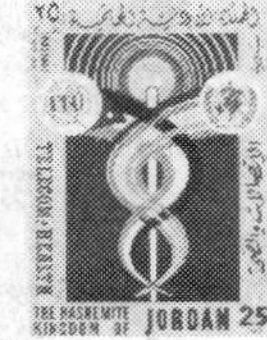
A155

1981, May 8 Litho. *Perf. 14½*
1074 A154 25f multicolored 25 15
1075 A154 40f multicolored 40 28
1076 A154 50f multicolored 45 35

Red Crescent Society.

1981, June 17 Litho. *Perf. 14x14½*
1077 A155 25f multicolored 25 15
1078 A155 40f multicolored 32 28
1079 A155 50f multicolored 45 32

13th World Telecommunications Day.

Nos. 174 and 832 — A156

Perf. 13½x14½, 14½x13½
1981, July 1 Litho.
1080 A156 25f shown 25 18
1081 A156 40f Nos. 313, 189, vert. 45 30
1082 A156 50f Nos. 272, 222 50 38

Postal Museum opening.

A157

A158

Arab Women: 25f, Khawla Bint El-Azwar, Ancient Warrior. 40f, El-Khansa (d.645), writer. 50f, Rabia El-Adawiyeh, religious leader.

1981, Aug. 25 Litho. *Perf. 14½x14*
1083 A157 25f multicolored 22 15
1084 A157 40f multicolored 36 24
1085 A157 50f multicolored 45 30

1981, Oct. 16 Litho. *Perf. 14x14½*
1086 A158 25f multicolored 22 15
1087 A158 40f multicolored 36 24
1088 A158 50f multicolored 45 30

World Food Day.

Intl. Year of the Disabled — A159

Hands Reading Braille — A160

1981, Nov. 14 Litho. *Perf. 14½x14*
1089 A159 25f multicolored 22 15
1090 A159 40f multicolored 36 24
1091 A159 50f multicolored 45 30

1981, Nov. 14 *Perf. 14x14½*
1092 A160 25f multicolored 22 15
1093 A160 40f multicolored 36 24
1094 A160 50f multicolored 45 30

A161

A162

Design: Hand holding jug and stone. Tablet.

1982, Mar. 10 Litho. *Perf. 14x14½*
1095 A161 25f multicolored 32 22
1096 A161 40f multicolored 55 35
1097 A161 50f multicolored 70 45

Nos. 1095-1097 inscribed 1981.

1982, Apr. 12 Litho. *Perf. 14x14½*
1098 A162 10f multicolored 15 15
1099 A162 25f multicolored 22 15
1100 A162 40f multicolored 36 24
1101 A162 50f multicolored 45 30
1102 A162 100f multicolored 90 60
Nos. 1098-1102 (5) 2.08 1.44

30th anniv. of Arab Postal Union.

King Hussein and Rockets A163

1982, May 25 Litho. *Perf. 14½x14*
1103 A163 10f shown 15 15
1104 A163 25f Tanks crossing bridge 22 15
1105 A163 40f Jet 36 24
1106 A163 50f Tanks, diff. 45 30
1107 A163 100f Raising flag 90 60
Nos. 1103-1107 (5) 2.08 1.44

Independence and Army Day; 30th anniv. of King Hussein's accession to the throne.

Salt Secondary School — A164

1982, Sept. 12 Litho. *Perf. 14½x14*
1108 A164 10f multicolored 15 15
1109 A164 25f multicolored 22 15
1110 A164 40f multicolored 36 24
1111 A164 50f multicolored 45 30
1112 A164 100f multicolored 90 60
Nos. 1108-1112 (5) 2.08 1.44

International Heritage of Jerusalem — A165

1982, Nov. 14 Litho. *Perf. 14x14½*
1113 A165 10f Gate to Old City 20 15
1114 A165 25f Minaret 55 30
1115 A165 40f Al Aqsa 90 50
1116 A165 50f Dome of the Rock 1.10 60
1117 A165 100f Dome of the Rock, diff. 2.25 1.25
Nos. 1113-1117 (5) 5.00 2.80

Yarmouk Forces — A166

1982, Nov. 14 *Perf. 14½x14*
1118 A166 10f multicolored 15 15
1119 A166 25f multicolored 30 20
1120 A166 40f multicolored 48 30
1121 A166 50f multicolored 60 40
1122 A166 100f multicolored 1.20 90

Size: 71x51mm
Imperf
1123 A166 100f Armed Forces emblem 11.50 11.50

2nd UN Conf. on Peaceful Uses of Outer Space, Vienna, Aug. 9-21 — A167

1982, Dec. 1 *Perf. 14½x14*
1124 A167 10f multicolored 15 15
1125 A167 25f multicolored 22 15
1126 A167 40f multicolored 36 24
1127 A167 50f multicolored 45 30
1128 A167 100f multicolored 90 60
Nos. 1124-1128 (5) 2.08 1.44

Birth Centenary of Amir Abdullah ibn Hussein — A168

1982, Dec. 13 Litho. *Perf. 14½*
1129 A168 10f multicolored 15 15
1130 A168 25f multicolored 25 15
1131 A168 40f multicolored 40 30
1132 A168 50f multicolored 60 50
1133 A168 100f multicolored 1.40 90
Nos. 1129-1133 (5) 2.80 2.00

Roman Ruins of Jerash A169

1982, Dec. 29 Litho. *Perf. 15*
1134 A169 10f Temple colonnade 15 15
1135 A169 25f Arch 22 15
1136 A169 40f Columns 36 24
1137 A169 50f Ampitheater 45 30
1138 A169 100f Hippodrome 90 60
Nos. 1134-1138 (5) 2.08 1.44

King Hussein — A170

1983 Litho. *Perf. 14½x14*
1139 A170 10f multicolored 15 15
1140 A170 25f multicolored 25 15
1141 A170 40f multicolored 40 30
1142 A170 60f multicolored 60 40
1143 A170 100f multicolored 1.00 65
1144 A170 125f multicolored 1.25 70
Nos. 1139-1144 (6) 3.65 2.35

Issue dates: 10f, 60f, Feb. 1; 40f, Feb. 8; 25f, 100f, 125f, Mar. 3. Inscribed 1982.

Massacre at Shatilla and Sabra Palestinian Refugee Camps — A171

Designs: 10f, 25f, 50f, No. 1149, Various victims. 40f, Children. No. 1150, Wounded child.

1983, Apr. 9 Litho. *Perf. 14½*
1145 A171 10f multicolored *25 20*
1146 A171 25f multicolored *45 40*
1147 A171 40f multicolored *70 50*
1148 A171 50f multicolored *85 70*
1149 A171 100f multicolored *1.25 1.00*
Nos. 1145-1149 (5) 3.50 2.80

Souvenir Sheet
Imperf
1150 A171 100f multicolored *15.00*

Opening of Queen Alia Intl. Airport A172

1983, May 25 Litho. *Perf. 12½*
1151 A172 10f Aerial view 15 15
1152 A172 25f Terminal buildings 22 15
1153 A172 40f Hangar 36 24
1154 A172 50f Terminal buildings, diff. 45 30
1155 A172 100f Embarkation Bridge 90 60
Nos. 1151-1155 (5) 2.08 1.44

Royal Jordanian Radio Amateurs' Society A173

1983, Aug. 11 Litho. *Perf. 12*
1156 A173 10f multicolored 15 15
1157 A173 25f multicolored 22 15
1158 A173 40f multicolored 36 24
1159 A173 50f multicolored 45 30
1160 A173 100f multicolored 90 60
Nos. 1156-1160 (5) 2.08 1.44

Royal Academy for Islamic Cultural Research A174

1983, Sept. 16 Litho. *Perf. 12*
1161 A174 10f Academy Bldg. 20 16
1162 A174 25f Silk carpet 45 30
1163 A174 40f Mosque, Amman 65 45
1164 A174 50f Dome of the Rock 85 55
1165 A174 100f Islamic city views 1.75 1.10
Nos. 1161-1165 (5) 3.90 2.56

A 100f souvenir sheet shows letter from Mohammed.

World Food Day — A175

1983, Oct. 16 Litho. *Perf. 12*
1166 A175 10f Irrigation canal 15 15
1167 A175 25f Greenhouses 25 15
1168 A175 40f Light-grown crops 40 24
1169 A175 50f Harvest 50 30
1170 A175 100f Sheep farm 1.00 60
Nos. 1166-1170 (5) 2.30 1.44

World Communications Year — A176

1983, Nov. 14
1171 A176 10f Radio switchboard operators 15 15
1172 A176 25f Earth satellite station 28 15

1173 A176 40f Symbols of communication 42 28
1174 A176 50f Emblems 52 32
1175 A176 100f Airmail letter 1.10 65
Nos. 1171-1175 (5) 2.47 1.55

Intl. Palestinian Solidarity Day — A177

Dome of the Rock, Jerusalem.

1983, Nov. 29 *Perf. 12*

1176 A177 5f multicolored 35 15
1177 A177 10f multicolored 65 30

35th Anniv. of UN Declaration of Human Rights — A178

1983, Dec. 10

1178 A178 10f multicolored 15 15
1179 A178 25f multicolored 25 15
1180 A178 40f multicolored 32 25
1181 A178 50f multicolored 45 30
1182 A178 100f multicolored 1.00 60
Nos. 1178-1182 (5) 2.17 1.45

Anti-Paralysis — A179

1984, Apr. 7 *Perf. 13½x11½*

1183 A179 40f multicolored 40 24
1184 A179 60f multicolored 60 36
1185 A179 100f multicolored 1.00 60

Anti-Polio Campaign.

Israeli Bombing of Iraq Nuclear Reactor A180

Various designs.

1984, June 7 Litho. *Perf. 13½x11½*

1186 A180 40f multicolored 60 24
1187 A180 60f multicolored 80 35
1188 A180 100f multicolored 1.25 60

Independence and Army Day — A181

King Hussein and various armed forces.

1984, June 10

1189 A181 10f multicolored 15 15
1190 A181 25f multicolored 25 15
1191 A181 40f multicolored 40 24
1192 A181 60f multicolored 60 35
1193 A181 100f multicolored 1.00 60
Nos. 1189-1193 (5) 2.40 1.49

1984 Summer Olympics, Los Angeles A182

1984, July 28

1194 A182 25f shown 25 15
1195 A182 40f Swimming 40 24
1196 A182 60f Shooting, archery 60 35
1197 A182 100f Gymnastics 1.00 60

An imperf. 100f souvenir sheet exists picturing pole vaulting.

Water and Electricity Year A183

1984, Aug. 11

1198 A183 25f Power lines, factory 25 15
1199 A183 40f Amman Power Station 40 24
1200 A183 60f Irrigation 60 35
1201 A183 100f Hydro-electric dam 1.00 60

Coins A184

1984, Sept. 26 Photo. *Perf. 13*

1202 A184 40f Omayyad gold dinar 40 24
1203 A184 60f Abbasid gold dinar 60 35
1204 A184 125f Hashemite silver dinar 1.25 75

Royal Society for the Conservation of Nature — A185

1984, Oct. 18

1205 A185 25f Four antelopes 25 15
1206 A185 40f Grazing 40 24
1207 A185 60f Three antelopes 60 35
1208 A185 100f King Hussein, Queen Alia, Duke of Edinburgh 1.00 60

Natl. Universities A186

Designs: 40f, Mu'ta Military University, Karak. 60f, Yarmouk University, Irbib. 125f, Jordan University, Amman.

1984, Nov. 14 *Perf. 13x13½*

1209 A186 40f multicolored 40 24
1210 A186 60f multicolored 60 35
1211 A186 125f multicolored 1.25 75

Al Sahaba Tombs A187

Designs: 10f, El Harath bin Omier el-Azdi and Derer bin El-Azwar. 25f, Sharhabil bin Hasna and Abu Obaidah Amer bin el-Jarrah. 40f, Muath bin Jabal. 50f, Zaid bin Haretha and Abdullah bin Rawaha. 60f, Amer bin Abi Waqqas. 100f, Jafar bin Abi Taleb.

1984, Dec. 5 Litho. *Perf. 13½x11½*

1212 A187 10f multicolored 15 15
1213 A187 25f multicolored 25 15
1214 A187 40f multicolored 40 24
1215 A187 50f multicolored 50 30
1216 A187 60f multicolored 60 35
1217 A187 100f multicolored 1.00 60
Nos. 1212-1217 (6) 2.90 1.79

Independence and Army Day — A188

Designs: 25f, King Hussein, soldier descending mountain. 40f, Hussein, Arab revolt flag, globe, King Abdullah. 60f, Flag, natl. arms, equestrian. 100f, Natl. flag, arms, King Abdullah.

1985, June 10 *Perf. 13x13½*

1218 A188 25f multicolored 25 15
1219 A188 40f multicolored 40 24
1220 A188 60f multicolored 60 35
1221 A188 100f multicolored 1.00 60

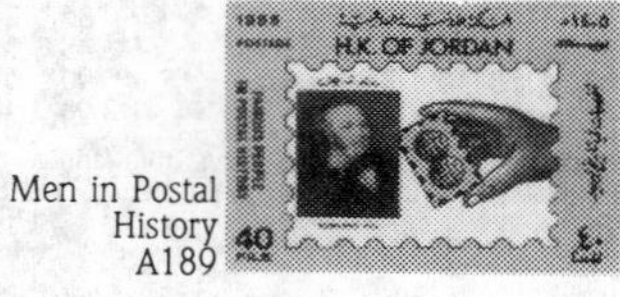

Men in Postal History A189

1985, July 1

1222 A189 40f Sir Rowland Hill 40 24
1223 A189 60f Heinrich von Stephan 60 35
1224 A189 125f Yacoub al-Sukkar 1.25 75

1st Convention of Jordanian Expatriates A190

Various designs.

1985, July 20 **Photo.**

1225 A190 40f multicolored 40 24
1226 A190 60f multicolored 60 35
1227 A190 125f multicolored 1.25 75

Intl. Youth Year — A191

Various designs.

1985, Aug. 11 Litho. *Perf. 13½x13*

1228 A191 10f multicolored 15 15
1229 A191 25f multicolored 25 15
1230 A191 40f multicolored 40 24
1231 A191 60f multicolored 60 35
1232 A191 125f multicolored 1.25 75
Nos. 1228-1232 (5) 2.65 1.64

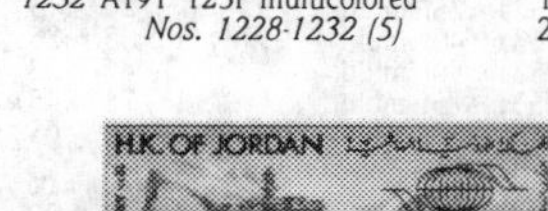

World Tourism Organization, 10th Anniv. — A192

1985, Sept. 13 *Perf. 13½x13*

1233 A192 10f Ruins of the Treasury, Petra 15 15
1234 A192 25f Jerash Temple 25 15
1235 A192 40f Roman baths 40 24
1236 A192 50f Jordanian valley town 50 30
1237 A192 60f Aqaba Bay 60 35
1238 A192 125f Roman amphitheater 1.25 75
Nos. 1233-1238 (6) 3.15 1.94

An imperf. 100f souvenir sheet exists picturing flower, 10 and natl. flag.

UN Child Survival Campaign — A193

Various designs.

1985, Oct. 7

1239 A193 25f multicolored 25 15
1240 A193 40f multicolored 40 24
1241 A193 60f multicolored 60 35
1242 A193 125f multicolored 1.25 75

An imperf. 100f souvenir sheet exists picturing campaign emblem and the faces of healthy children.

5th Jerash Festival A194

1985, Oct. 21

1243 A194 10f Opening ceremony, 1980 15 15
1244 A194 25f Folk dancers 25 15
1245 A194 40f Dancers 40 24
1246 A194 60f Choir, Roman theater 60 35
1247 A194 100f King and Queen 1.00 60
Nos. 1243-1247 (5) 2.40 1.49

UN, 40th Anniv. A195

1985, Oct. 25 Photo. *Perf. 13x13½*

1248 A195 60f multicolored 60 35
1249 A195 125f multicolored 1.25 75

King Hussein, 50th Birthday A196

Various photos of King.

1985, Nov. 14 Litho. *Perf. 14½*

1250 A196 10f multicolored 15 15
1251 A196 25f multicolored 25 15
1252 A196 40f multicolored 40 24
1253 A196 60f multicolored 60 35
1254 A196 100f multicolored 1.00 60
Nos. 1250-1254 (5) 2.40 1.49

An imperf. 200f souvenir sheet exists picturing flags, King Hussein and Dome of the Rock.

Restoration of Al Aqsa Mosque, Jerusalem A196a

1985, Nov. 25 Litho. *Perf. 13x13½*

1254A A196a 5f multicolored *65 65*
1254B A196a 10f multicolored *1.40 1.00*

Police A197

1985, Dec. 18

1255 A197 40f Patrol car 30 20
1256 A197 60f Crossing guard 42 28
1257 A197 125f Police academy 90 60

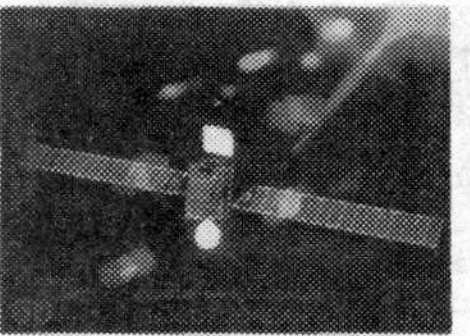
Launch of ARABSAT-1, 1st Anniv. — A198

1986, Feb. 8 Litho. *Perf. 13½x13*

1258 A198 60f Satellite in orbit 32 20
1259 A198 100f Over map of Arab countries 55 32

Arabization of the Army, 30th Anniv. — A199

Designs: 40f, King Hussein presenting flag. 60f, Greeting army sergeant. 100f, Hussein addressing army.

1986, Mar. 1 *Perf. 11½x12½*

1260 A199 40f multicolored 22 15
1261 A199 60f multicolored 32 20
1262 A199 100f multicolored 55 32

An imperf. souvenir sheet exists with design of 100f.

Natl. Independence, 40th Anniv. — A200

Design: King Abdullah decorating soldier.

1986, May 25 *Perf. 12½x11½*

1263 A200 160f multicolored 88 52

Arab Revolt against Turkey, 70th Anniv. — A201

Unattributed paintings (details): 40f, The four sons of King Hussein, Prince of Mecca, vert. 60f, Abdullah, retainers and bodyguard. 160f, Abdullah and followers on horseback.

Perf. 12½x11½, 11½x12½

1986, June 10

1264 A201 40f multicolored 22 15
1265 A201 60f multicolored 32 20
1266 A201 160f multicolored 88 52

An imperf. 200f souvenir sheet exists picturing the Arab Revolt flag, King Abdullah and text from independence declaration.

Intl. Peace Year A202

1986, July 1 Litho. *Perf. 13½x13*

1267 A202 160f multicolored 90 55
1268 A202 240f multicolored 1.35 80

King Hussein Medical City Cardiac Center A203

1986, Aug. 11

1269 A203 40f Cardiac Center 22 15
1270 A203 60f Surgery 35 22
1271 A203 100f Surgery, diff. 55 32

UN, 40th Anniv. — A204

Excerpts from King Hussein's speech: 40f, In Arabic. 80f, Arabic, diff. 100f, English.

1986, Sept. 27 *Perf. 12½x11½*

1272 A204 40f multicolored 22 15
1273 A204 80f multicolored 45 28
1274 A204 100f multicolored 55 32

An imperf. 200f stamp 90x70mm exists picturing speech in Arabic and English, King Hussein at podium.

Arab Postal Union, 35th Anniv. A205

1987, Apr. 12 Litho. *Perf. 13½x13*

1275 A205 80f Old post office 45 28
1276 A205 160f New post office 90 55

Chemical Soc. Emblem and Chemists A206

Designs: 60f, Jaber ibn Hayyan al-Azdi (720-813). 80f, Abu-al-Qasem al-Majreeti (950-1007). 240f, Abu-Bakr al-Razi (864-932).

1987, Apr. 24

1277 A206 60f multicolored 35 22
1278 A206 80f multicolored 45 28
1279 A206 240f multicolored 1.35 80

SOS Children's Village A207

1987, May 7

1280 A207 80f Village in Amman 45 28
1281 A207 240f Child, bird mural 1.35 80

4th Brigade, 40th Anniv. A208

1987, June 10

1282 A208 60f shown 35 22
1283 A208 80f Soldiers in armored vehicle 45 28

Size: 70x91mm

Imperf

1284 A208 160f Four veterans 90 55

Indigenous Birds A209

1987, June 24

1285 A209 10f Hoopoe 15 15
1286 A209 40f Palestine sunbird 30 20
1287 A209 50f Black-headed bunting 38 25
1288 A209 60f Spur-winged plover 45 30
1289 A209 80f Greenfinch 60 40
1290 A209 100f Black-winged stilt 75 50
Nos. 1285-1290 (6) 2.63 1.80

King Hussein — A210

1987, June 24 Litho. *Perf. 13x13½*

1291 A210 60f multicolored 45 30
1292 A210 80f multicolored 60 40
1293 A210 160f multicolored 1.20 80
1294 A210 240f multicolored 1.80 1.20

Battle of Hittin, 800th Anniv. A211

Dome of the Rock and Saladin (1137-1193), Conqueror of Jerusalem — A212

1987, July 4

1295 A211 60f Battle, Jerusalem 35 24
1296 A211 80f Horseman, Jerusalem, Dome of the Rock 45 30
1297 A211 100f Saladin 75 50

Souvenir Sheet

Perf. 12x12½

1298 A212 100f shown 75 50

No. 1298 exists imperf.

Natl. Coat of Arms — A213

Perf. 11½x12½

1987, Aug. 11 Litho.

1299 A213 80f multicolored 60 40
1300 A213 160f multicolored 1.20 80

Amman Industrial Park at Sahab A214

1987, Aug. 11 *Perf. 13½x13*

1301 A214 80f multicolored 60 40

University Crest A215

University Entrance — A216

Perf. 11½x11, 12½x11½

1987, Sept. 2

1302 A215 60f multicolored 45 30
1303 A216 80f multicolored 60 40

University of Jordan, 25th anniv.

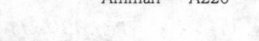

UN Child Survival Campaign A217

1987, Oct. 5 Litho. ***Perf. 13x13½***

1304 A217 60f Oral vaccine 45 30
1305 A217 80f Natl. flag, child 60 40
1306 A217 160f Growth monitoring 1.20 80

Parliament, 40th Anniv. — A218

1987, Oct. 20 ***Perf. 13½x13***

1307 A218 60f Opening ceremony, 1947 45 30
1308 A218 80f In session, 1987 60 40

A219

Special Arab Summit Conference, Amman — A220

1987, Nov. 8

1309 A219 60f multicolored 45 30
1310 A219 80f multicolored 60 40
1311 A219 160f multicolored 1.20 80
1312 A219 240f multicolored 1.80 1.20

Size: 90x66mm

Imperf

1313 A220 100f multicolored

King Hussein, Dag Hammarskjold Peace Prize Winner for 1987 — A221

1988, Feb. 6 Litho. ***Perf. 12½***

1314 A221 80f Hussein, woman, vert. 60 40
1315 A221 160f shown 1.20 80

Natl. Victory at the 1987 Arab Military Basketball Championships — A222

1988, Mar. 1 ***Perf. 13½x13***

1316 A222 60f Golden Sword Award 45 30
1317 A222 80f Hussein congratulating team 60 40
1318 A222 160f Jump ball 1.20 80

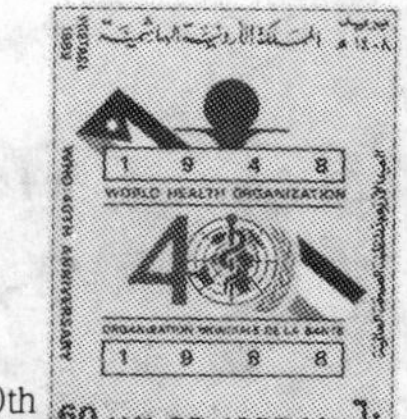

WHO, 40th Anniv. — A223

1988, Apr. 7 Photo. ***Perf. 13x13½***

1319 A223 60f multicolored 55 38
1320 A223 80f multicolored 72 48

Arab Scouts, 75th Anniv. — A224

1988, July 2 Litho. ***Perf. 13x13½***

1321 A224 60f multicolored 45 35
1322 A224 80f multicolored 60 45

Birds A225

1988, July 21 Litho. ***Perf. 11½x12***

1323 A225 10f Crested lark 15 15
1324 A225 20f Stone curlew 15 15
1325 A225 30f Redstart 20 15
1326 A225 40f Blackbird 28 22
1327 A225 50f Rock dove 35 28
1328 A225 160f Smyrna kingfisher 1.10 82

Size: 71x90mm

Imperf

1328A A225 310f Six species 3.75 2.75
Nos. 1323-1328A (7) 5.98 4.52

Restoration of San'a, Yemen Arab Republic A226

1988, Aug. 11 Litho. ***Perf. 12x11½***

1329 A226 80f multicolored 60 45
1330 A226 160f multicolored 1.20 90

Historic Natl. Sites A227

1988, Aug. 11 ***Perf. 13½x13***

1331 A227 60f Umm Al-rasas 45 35
1332 A227 80f Umm Qais 60 45
1333 A227 160f Iraq Al-amir 1.20 90

An imperf. souvenir sheet of 3 exists containing one each Nos. 1331-1333.

1988 Summer Olympics, Seoul — A228

1988, Sept. 17 Litho. ***Perf. 13x13½***

1334 A228 10f Tennis 15 15
1335 A228 60f Character trademark 45 35
1336 A228 80f Running, swimming 60 45
1337 A228 120f Basketball 90 68
1338 A228 160f Soccer 1.20 90
Nos. 1334-1338 (5) 3.30 2.53

Size: 70x91mm

Imperf

1339 A228 100f Emblems

Royal Jordanian Airlines, 25th Anniv. — A229

1988, Dec. 15 Litho. ***Perf. 11½x12***

1340 A229 60f Ruins of Petra 42 32
1341 A229 80f Aircraft, world map 55 42

UN Declaration of Human Rights, 40th Anniv. — A230

1988, Dec. 10

1342 A230 80f multicolored 55 42
1343 A230 160f multicolored 1.10 82

Arab Cooperation Council, Feb. 16 — A231

1989 Litho. ***Perf. 13½x13***

1344 A231 10f shown 15 15
1345 A231 30f multi, diff. 15 15
1346 A231 40f multi, diff. 20 15
1347 A231 60f multi, diff. 30 22
Set value 54

Martyrs of Palestine and Their Families A232

1989 ***Perf. 14½***

1348 A232 5f multi 15 15
1349 A232 10f multi 15 15
Set value 20 16

Interparliamentary Union, Cent. — A233

1989 Litho. ***Perf. 12***

1350 A233 40f multicolored 22 16
1351 A233 60f multicolored 35 25

Arab Housing Day and World Refuge Day A234

Designs: 5f, Housing complex, emblems, vert. 60f, Housing complex, emblem.

1989

1352 A234 5f multicolored 15 15
1353 A234 40f shown 22 16
1354 A234 60f multicolored 35 25
Set value 60 55

Ministry of Agriculture, 50th Anniv. A235

1989 Litho. ***Perf. 12***

1355 A235 5f shown 15 15
1356 A235 40f Tree, anniv. emblem 17 15
1357 A235 60f Fruit tree, emblem, apiary 25 16
Set value 46 30

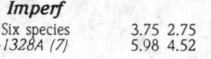

Arabian Horse Festival A236

1989 *Perf. 12*

1358	A236	5f shown	15	15
1359	A236	40f Horse, building facade	17	15
1360	A236	60f Horse's head, vert.	25	16

Size: 90x70mm

Imperf

1361	A236	100f Mare and foal	7.50	5.00

Natl. Library Assoc. A237

1989 *Perf. 12*

1362	A237	40f multicolored	15	15
1363	A237	60f multicolored	22	15
		Set value		24

Mosque of the Martyr King Abdullah — A238

1989 *Perf. 12*

1364	A238	40f multicolored	15	15
1365	A238	60f multicolored	22	15

Size: 90x70mm

Imperf

1366	A238	100f multicolored	5.25	5.25

Mosaics A239

1989, Dec. 23 **Litho.** *Perf. 12*

1367	A239	5f Man with Basket	15	15
1368	A239	10f Building	15	15
1369	A239	40f Deer	42	28
1370	A239	60f shown	62	40
1371	A239	80f Town, horiz.	82	55

Size: 90x70mm

Imperf

1372	A239	100f like #1371, horiz.	6.00	4.00

Arab Cooperation Council, 1st Anniv. — A240

1990, Feb. 16 *Perf. 13*

1373	A240	5f multicolored	15	15
1374	A240	20f multicolored	18	15
1375	A240	60f multicolored	55	36
1376	A240	80f multicolored	72	48

Nature Conservation — A241

1990, Apr. 22

1377	A241	40f Horses	20	15
1378	A241	60f Mountain	30	15
1379	A241	80f Oasis	40	25

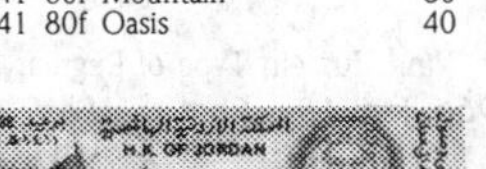

Prince Abdullah's Arrival in Ma'an, 70th Anniv. — A243

1990 **Litho.** *Perf. 13½x13*

1382	A243	40f org & multi	15	15
1383	A243	60f grn & multi	22	15

Size: 90x70mm

Imperf

1384	A243	200f multicolored	2.75	1.80

UN Development Program, 40th Anniv. A244

1990 *Perf. 13*

1385	A244	60f multicolored	22	15
1386	A244	80f multicolored	30	20

King Hussein — A245

1991 **Litho.** *Perf. 12x13½*

1387	A245	5f yel org & multi	15	15
1393	A245	60f blue & multi	30	15
1395	A245	80f pink & multi	45	22
		Set value		42

This is an expanding set. Numbers will change if necessary.

Endangered Animals — A246

1991, Sept. 1 **Litho.** *Perf. 13x13½*

1401	A246	5f Nubian ibex	15	15
1402	A246	40f Onager	18	15
1403	A246	80f Arabian gazelle	35	18
1404	A246	160f Arabian oryx	70	25
		Set value		60

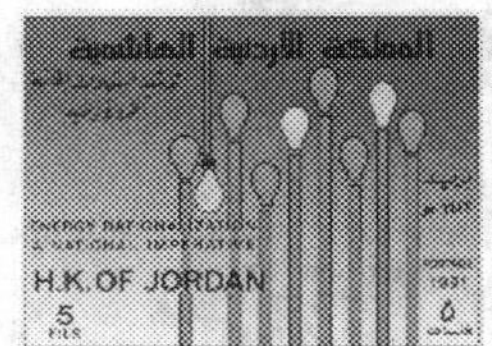

Energy Rationalization Program — A247

Designs: 5f, Light bulbs. 40f, Solar panels, sun, vert. 80f, Electric table lamp, vert.

Perf. 13½x13, 13x13½

1991, Oct. 3 **Litho.**

1405	A247	5f multicolored	15	15
1406	A247	40f multicolored	18	15
1407	A247	80f multicolored	35	18
		Set value	56	28

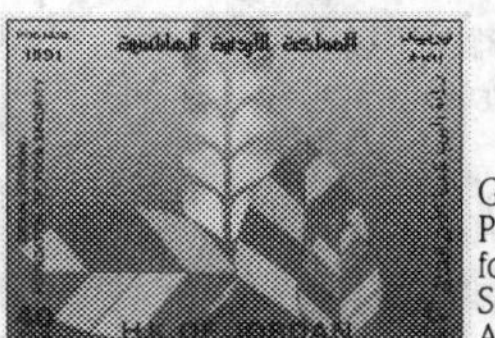

Grain Production for Food Security A248

1991, Oct. 16 *Perf. 13½x13*

1408	A248	5f Different grains	15	15
1409	A248	40f shown	18	15
1410	A248	80f Wheat stalk, kernels	35	18
		Set value	56	28

Palestinian Uprising — A249

1991 **Litho.** *Perf. 11*

1411	A249	20f multicolored	68	35

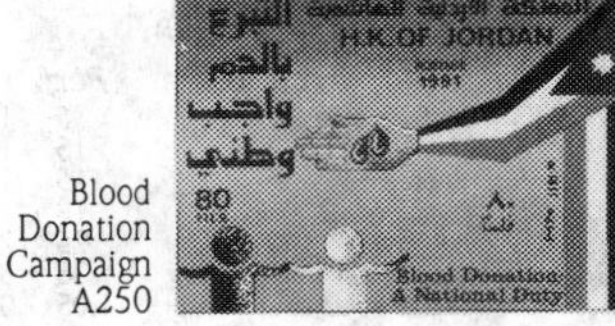

Blood Donation Campaign A250

1991 **Litho.** *Perf. 13½x13*

1412	A250	80f multicolored	30	15
1413	A250	160f multicolored	60	30

Expo '92, Seville A251

1992

1414	A251	80f multicolored	30	15
1415	A251	320f multicolored	1.20	60

Healthy Hearts A252

Design: 80f, Man and woman, heart at center of scale, vert.

1992 **Litho.** *Perf. 13x13½, 13½x13*

1416	A252	80f multicolored	38	20
1417	A252	125f multicolored	60	30

SOS Children's Village, 'Aqaba A253

1992 **Litho.** *Perf. 13½x13*

1418	A253	80f shown	40	20
1419	A253	125f Village	60	30

1992 Summer Olympics, Barcelona A254

Stylized designs with Barcelona Olympic emblem: 5fr, Judo, 40f, Runner, vert. 80f, Diver. 125f, Flag, Cobi, map, vert. 160f, Table tennis. 100f, Incorporates all designs of set.

1992 **Litho.** *Perf. 13½x13, 13x13½*

1420	A254	5f multicolored	15	15
1421	A254	40f multicolored	16	15
1422	A254	80f multicolored	32	16
1423	A254	125f multicolored	50	25
1424	A254	160f multicolored	65	32
		Nos. 1420-1424 (5)	1.78	
		Set value		82

Size: 70x90mm

Imperf

1425	A254	100f multicolored	11.00	5.50

King Hussein, 40th Anniv. of Accession A255

Designs: 40f, Flags, King in full dress uniform, vert. 125f, King wearing headdress, flags. 160f, King in business suit, crown. 200f, Portrait.

1992 *Perf. 13x13½*

1426	A255	40f multicolored	16	15

Perf. 13½x13

1427	A255	80f shown	32	16
1428	A255	125f multicolored	50	25
1429	A255	160f multicolored	65	32

Size: 90x70mm

Imperf

1430 A255 200f multicolored 6.00 3.00

Butterflies A256

Designs: 5f, Danaus chrysippus. 40f, Aporia cartaegi. 80f, Papilio machaon. 160f, Pseudochazara telephassa. 200f, Same designs as #1431-1434.

1992 Litho. *Perf. 13½x13*

1431 A256 5f multicolored 15 15
1432 A256 40f multicolored 15 15
1433 A256 80f multicolored 32 16
1434 A256 160f multicolored 65 32

Imperf

Size: 90x70mm

1435 A256 200f multicolored *9.00 4.50*

SEMI-POSTAL STAMPS

Locust Campaign Issue

Nos. 145-156 Overprinted

مكافحة الجراد
LOCUST CAMPAIGN

1930, Apr. 1 Wmk. 4 *Perf. 14*

1 A1 2(m) Prus blue 1.10 1.25
a. Inverted overprint 175.00
2 A1 3(m) rose 1.40 1.50
3 A1 4(m) green 20 22
4 A1 5(m) orange 5.50 5.75
a. Double overprint 250.00
5 A1 10(m) red 28 32
6 A1 15(m) ultra 32 35
a. Inverted overprint 150.00
7 A1 20(m) olive grn 38 45
8 A2 50(m) claret 1.50 1.65
9 A2 90(m) bister 5.50 6.00
10 A2 100(m) lt blue 3.75 3.75
11 A2 200(m) violet 16.00 16.00
12 A2 500(m) brown 45.00 45.00
a. "C" of "Locust" omitted 600.00
Nos. B1-B12 (12) 80.93 82.24

These stamps were issued to raise funds to help combat a plague of locusts.

AIR POST STAMPS

Catalogue values for unused stamps in this section are for Never Hinged items.

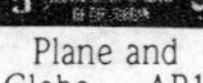

Plane and Globe — AP1

Temple of Artemis, Jerash — AP2

Perf. 13½x13

1950, Sept. 16 Engr. Wmk. 4

C1 AP1 5f org & red vio 15 15
C2 AP1 10f pur & brown 16 16
C3 AP1 15f ol grn & rose car 20 20
C4 AP1 20f deep blue & blk 30 30
C5 AP1 50f rose pink & dl grn 40 30
C6 AP1 100f blue & brown 70 70
C7 AP1 150f blk & red org 1.00 1.00
Nos. C1-C7 (7) 2.91 2.81

1954 Unwmk. *Perf. 12*

C8 AP2 5f blue blk & org 15 15
C9 AP2 10f vio brn & ver 15 15
C10 AP2 25f bl grn & ultra 15 15
C11 AP2 35f dp plum & grnsh bl 18 15
C12 AP2 40f car rose & blk 22 15
C13 AP2 50f dp ultra & org yel 25 25
C14 AP2 100f dk bl & vio brn 45 45
C15 AP2 150f stl bl & red brn 60 60
Nos. C8-C15 (8) 2.15 2.05

1958-59 Wmk. 305 *Perf. 12*

C16 AP2 5f blue blk & org 15 15
C17 AP2 10f vio brn & ver 15 15
C18 AP2 25f bl grn & ultra 20 15
C19 AP2 35f dp plum grnsh bl 20 20
C20 AP2 40f car rose & blk 25 25
C21 AP2 50f dp ultra & org yel ('59) 60 60
Set value 1.30 1.25

Stadium and Torch — AP3

Perf. 11x11½

1964, July 12 Litho. Wmk. 305

C22 AP3 1f yellow & multi 15 15
C23 AP3 4f red & multi 15 15
C24 AP3 10f blue & multi 15 15
C25 AP3 35f yel grn & multi 42 42
a. Souvenir sheet of 4, #C22-C25 1.00 1.00
Set value 65 65

Opening of Hussein Sports City. No. C25a also exists imperf.

Gorgeous Bush-Shrike — AP4

Birds: 500f, Ornate hawk-eagle, vert. 1d, Gray-headed kingfisher, vert.

Perf. 14x14½

1964, Dec. 18 Photo. Unwmk.

Birds in Natural Colors

C26 AP4 150f lt grn, blk & car 1.65 40
C27 AP4 500f brt bl, blk & grn 8.25 2.75
C28 AP4 1d lt ol grn & blk 16.00 8.25

Pagoda, Olympic Torch and Emblem — AP5

1965, Mar. 5 Litho. *Perf. 14*

C29 AP5 10f deep rose 15 15
C30 AP5 15f violet 15 15
C31 AP5 20f blue 15 15
C32 AP5 30f green 18 18
C33 AP5 40f brown 25 25
C34 AP5 60f carmine rose 38 38
Set value 1.05 1.05

18th Olympic Games, Tokyo, Oct. 10-25, 1964. An imperf. 100f violet blue souvenir sheet exists. Size of stamp: 60x60mm. Value $9.

For overprints see Nos. C42A-C42F.

Forum, Jerash AP6

Antiquities of Jerash: No. C36, South Theater. No. C37, Triumphal arch. No. C38, Temple of Artemis. No. C39, Cathedral steps. No. C40, Artemis Temple, gate. No. C41, Columns. No. C42, Columns and niche, South Theater. Nos. C39-C42 are vertical.

1965, June 22 Photo. *Perf. 14x15*

Center Multicolored

C35 AP6 55f bright pink 45 45
C36 AP6 55f light blue 45 45
C37 AP6 55f green 45 45
C38 AP6 55f black 45 45
C39 AP6 55f light green 45 45
C40 AP6 55f carmine rose 45 45
C41 AP6 55f gray 45 45
C42 AP6 55f blue 45 45
Nos. C35-C42 (8) 3.60 3.60

Nos. C35-C38 are printed in horizontal rows of four; Nos. C39-C42 in vertical rows of four; sheets of 16.

Nos. C29-C34 with Bilingual Ovpt. "James McDivitt / Edward White / 2-6-1965" and Rocket

1965, Sept. 25 Litho. *Perf. 14*

C42A AP5 10f deep rose 30 30
C42B AP5 15f violet 45 45
C42C AP5 20f blue 60 60
C42D AP5 30f green 90 90
C42E AP5 40f brown 1.25 1.25
C42F AP5 60f carmine rose 1.75 1.75

The imperf. 100f blue souvenir sheet exists overprinted.

King Hussein Type of Regular Issue

1966, Jan. 15 Photo. *Perf. 14½x14*

Portrait in Brown

C43 A67 200f brt blue grn 1.50 75
C44 A67 500f light green 3.75 2.00
C45 A67 1d light ultra 7.50 3.75

Animal Type of Regular Issue, 1967

Animals: 4f, Striped hyena. 30f, Arabian stallion. 60f, Persian gazelle.

1967, Feb. 11 Photo. *Perf. 14x15*

C46 A70 4f dk brn & multi 15 15
C47 A70 30f lt bl & multi 22 15
C48 A70 60f yellow & multi 45 30
Set value 70 50

Game Type of Regular Issue, 1968

Protected Game: 60f, Nubian ibex, vert. 100f, Wild ducks.

1968, Oct. 5 Litho. *Perf. 13½*

C49 A74 60f multicolored 75 75
C50 A74 100f multicolored 1.40 1.40

Easter Type of Regular Issue

Designs: 60f, Altar, Holy Sepulcher. 100f, Feet Washing, Holy Gate, Jerusalem.

1972, Apr. Photo. *Perf. 14x13½*

C51 A92 60f dk bl & multi 45 45
C52 A92 100f multicolored 75 75

Aero Club Type of Regular Issue

Designs: 15f, Two Piper 140s. 20f, R.J.A.C. Beechcraft. 40f, Aero Club emblem with winged horse.

1973, Jan. Photo. *Perf. 13½x14*

C53 A100 15f blue, blk & red 15 15
C54 A100 20f blue, blk & red 18 15
C55 A100 40f mag, blk & yel 38 22
Set value 38

Agriculture Type of Regular Issue

Design: 100f, Soil conservation.

1973, Dec. 25 *Perf. 13½*

C56 A110 100f multicolored 65 45

King Hussein Driving Car — AP7

1974, Dec. 20 *Perf. 12*

C57 AP7 30f multicolored 20 15
C58 AP7 60f multicolored 45 32

Royal Jordanian Automobile Club.

Building Type of Regular Issue

Designs: 50f, Palms, Aqaba. 60f, Obelisk tomb. 80f, Fort of Wadi Rum.

1975, Mar. 1 Photo. *Perf. 13½x14*

C59 A121 50f pink & multi 32 22
C60 A121 60f lt bl & multi 42 30
C61 A121 80f yellow & multi 52 32

Hussein Type of Regular Issue

1975, Apr. 8 Photo. *Perf. 14x13½*

Size: 22x27mm

C62 A123 60f dk grn & brn 28 18
C63 A123 100f org brn & brn 42 30
C64 A123 120f dp bl & brn 50 36
C65 A123 180f brt mag & brn 85 50
C66 A123 200f grnsh bl & brn 90 50
C67 A123 400f pur & brown 1.75 1.10
C68 A123 500f orange & brn 2.25 1.40
Nos. C62-C68 (7) 6.95 4.34

POSTAGE DUE STAMPS

Stamps of Regular Issue (Nos. 69, 66-68 Surcharged with New Value like No. 91) Overprinted

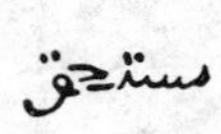

This overprint reads: "Mustahaq" (Tax or Due)

1923 Unwmk. *Perf. 11½*

Typo. Ovpt. "Mustahaq" 10mm long

J1 A7 ½pi on 3pi ol brn 62.50 65.00
a. Inverted overprint 120.00 120.00
b. Double overprint 160.00 150.00

Handstamped Overprints "Mustahaq" 12mm long

J2 A7 ½pi on 3pi ol brn 24.00 25.00
J3 A7 1pi dark blue 12.00 12.50
J4 A7 1½pi violet 12.00 12.50
J5 A7 2pi orange 12.00 12.50

These overprints are found double, inverted, etc. as is usual with handstamps.

Stamps of Hejaz Handstamped

J6 A7 ½pi red 45 45
J7 A7 1pi dark blue 52 52
J8 A7 1½pi violet 65 65
J9 A7 2pi orange 85 85
J10 A7 3pi olive brown 1.40 1.40
J11 A7 5pi olive green 1.90 1.90
Nos. J6-J11 (6) 5.77 5.77

Type of Palestine, 1918, Overprinted

1925 Wmk. 4 *Perf. 14*

J12 A1 1m dark brown 25 38
J13 A1 2m yellow 30 60
J14 A1 4m rose 45 75
J15 A1 8m red 52 75
J16 A1 13m ultramarine 75 80
J17 A1 5pi plum 1.25 1.50
a. Perf. 15x14 5.00 5.50
Nos. J12-J17 (6) 3.52 4.78

The overprint reads: "Mustahaq. Sharqi al'Ardan." (Tax. Eastern Jordan).

Stamps of Palestine, 1918, Surcharged

1926

J18 A1 1m on 1m dk brn 65 80
J19 A1 2m on 1m dk brn 65 80
J20 A1 4m on 3m Prus bl 1.25 1.40
J21 A1 8m on 3m Prus bl 1.00 1.25

J22 A1 13m on 13m ultra 1.40 1.90
J23 A1 5pi on 13m ultra 1.40 1.90
Nos. J18-J23 (6) 6.35 8.05

The surcharge reads "Tax—Eastern Jordan" and New Value.

Stamps of Regular Issue, 1927, Overprinted مستحق

1929
J24 A1 2m Prussian bl 38 25
J25 A1 10m red 90 45
J26 A2 50m claret 1.65 1.25

With Additional Surcharge
J27 A1 4(m) on 3(m) rose 25 25
J28 A1 4(m) on 15(m) ultra 65 42
a. Inverted surch. and ovpt. 90.00
J29 A2 20(m) on 100(m) lt bl 1.40 1.20

D1

D2

1929 Engr. *Perf. 14*
Size: 17¼x21mm
J30 D1 1m brown 15 15
a. Perf. 13½x13 90.00 45.00
J31 D1 2m orange 20 20
J32 D1 4m green 20 20
J33 D1 10m carmine 40 40
J34 D1 20m olive green 40 40
J35 D1 50m blue 65 65
Nos. J30-J35 (6) 2.00 2.00

See Nos. J39-J43. For surcharge, see No. J52. For overprints, see Nos. NJ1a, NJ3, NJ5a, NJ6-NJ7.

1942 Unwmk. Litho. *Perf. 13x13½*
J36 D2 1m dull red brn 15 15
J37 D2 2m dl orange yel 25 25
J38 D2 10m dark carmine 50 50

For overprints, see Nos. NJ8-NJ10.

Type of 1929

1943-44 Engr. Wmk. 4 *Perf. 12*
Size: 17¾x21¼mm
J39 D1 1m orange brn 15 15
J40 D1 2m yel orange 15 15
J41 D1 4m yel green 15 15
J42 D1 10m rose carmine 15 15
J43 D1 20m olive green 4.50 4.50
Nos. J39-J43 (5) 5.10 5.10

For overprints, see Nos. J47-J51, NJ1-NJ2, NJ3a, NJ5, NJ6a.

Catalogue values for unused stamps in this section, from this point to the end of the section, are for Never Hinged items.

Nos. J39-J43, J35 Surcharged "FILS" and its Arabic Equivalent in Black, Green or Carmine

1952 Wmk. 4 *Perf. 12*
J47 D1 1f on 1m org brn (Bk) 15 15
J48 D1 2f on 2m yel org (G) 15 15
J49 D1 4f on 4m yel grn 15 15
J50 D1 10f on 10m rose car (Bk) 40 35
J51 D1 20f on 20m ol grn 50 50

Perf. 14
J52 D1 50f on 50m blue 65 65
Nos. J47-J52 (6) 2.00 1.95

This overprint exists on Nos. J34, J36-J38. Exists inverted, double and in wrong color.

D3

Inscribed: "The Hashemite Kingdom of the Jordan"

1952 Engr. *Perf. 11½*
J53 D3 1f orange brown 15 15
J54 D3 2f yel orange 15 15
J55 D3 4f yel green 15 15
J56 D3 10f rose carmine 15 15
J57 D3 20f yel brown 15 15
J58 D3 50f blue 52 30
Set value 90 60

Type of 1952 Redrawn

Inscribed: "The Hashemite Kingdom of Jordan"

1957 Wmk. 305 *Perf. 11½*
J59 D3 1f orange brown 15 15
J60 D3 2f yel orange 15 15
J61 D3 4f yel green 15 15
J62 D3 10f rose carmine 18 15
J63 D3 20f yel brown 35 25
Set value 70 50

OFFICIAL STAMP

Saudi Arabia No. L34 Overprinted (حكومة) الشرق العربي ١٣٤٢

1924, Jan. Typo. *Perf. 11½*
O1 A7 ½pi red 45.00

Overprint reads: "(Government) the Arabian East 1342."

POSTAL TAX STAMPS

Catalogue values for unused stamps in this section are for Never Hinged items.

Mosque at Hebron — PT1

Designs: 10m, 15m, 20m, 50m, Dome of the Rock. 100m, 200m, 500m, £1, Acre.

Perf. 11½x12½
1947 Unwmk. Engr.
RA1 PT1 1m ultra 22 15
RA2 PT1 2m carmine 22 20
RA3 PT1 3m emerald 30 28
RA4 PT1 5m plum 42 20
RA5 PT1 10m carmine 45 30
RA6 PT1 15m gray 65 30
RA7 PT1 20m dk brown 80 45
RA8 PT1 50m purple 2.25 1.10
RA9 PT1 100m orange red 4.00 2.50
RA10 PT1 200m dp blue 10.00 7.50
RA11 PT1 500m green 16.00 12.50
RA12 PT1 £1 dk brown 27.50 27.50
Nos. RA1-RA12 (12) 62.81 52.98

Issued to help the Welfare Fund for Arabs in Palestine. Required on foreign-bound letters to the amount of half the regular postage.

For overprints and surcharges see #286A-286C, 344-346, RA37-RA46, NRA1-NRA12.

Nos. 211, 232 and 234 Overprinted in Black اعانة Aid

1950 Wmk. 4 *Perf. 12*
RA23 A3 5m orange 6.50
RA24 A3 10m violet 10.00
RA25 A3 15m dull olive grn 12.00

Arch and Colonnade, Palmyra, Syria — PT2

Two types of 5m:
Type I - "A" with serifs. Arabic ovpt. 8mm wide.
Type II - "A" without serifs. Arabic ovpt. 5mm wide.

Black or Carmine Overprint

1950-51 Engr. *Perf. 13½x13*
RA26 PT2 5m orange (I) 6.50
a. Type II ('51) 27.50
RA27 PT2 10m violet (C) 6.50

The overprint on No. RA27 is similar to that on RA23-RA25 but slightly bolder.

Type of 1947

Designs: 5f, Hebron Mosque. 10f, 15f, 20f, Dome of the Rock. 100f, Acre.

1951 Wmk. 4 *Perf. 11½x12½*
RA28 PT1 5f plum 15 15
RA29 PT1 10f carmine 15 15
RA30 PT1 15f gray 16 16
RA31 PT1 20f dk brown 22 22
RA33 PT1 100f orange 1.50 1.50
Nos. RA28-RA33 (5) 2.18 2.18

The tax on Nos. RA1-RA33 was for Arab aid in Palestine.
For overprints, see Nos. 287-290.

Postal Tax Stamps of 1947 Surcharged "FILS" or "J.D." and Their Arabic Equivalents and Bars in Carmine or Black

1952 Unwmk.
RA37 PT1 1f on 1m ultra 38 15
RA38 PT1 3f on 3m emer 38 15
RA39 PT1 10f on 10m car 60 42
RA40 PT1 15f on 15m gray 80 60
RA41 PT1 20f on 20m dk brown 1.25 80
RA42 PT1 50f on 50m pur 3.00 2.00
RA43 PT1 100f on 100m org red 8.25 5.25
RA44 PT1 200f on 200m dp blue 21.00 6.50
RA45 PT1 500f on 500m grn 35.00 13.00
RA46 PT1 1d on £1 dk brn 55.00 32.50
Nos. RA37-RA46 (10) 125.66 61.37

"J.D." stands for Jordanian Dinar.

OCCUPATION STAMPS

Catalogue values for unused stamps in this section are for Never Hinged items.

For Use in Palestine

Stamps of Jordan Overprinted in Red, Black, Dark Green, Green or Orange Red فلسطين PALESTINE

On No. 200

1948 Unwmk. *Perf. 13x13½*
N1 A14 2m dull green (R) 75 75

On #207-209, 211, 230-235, 215-220

1948 Wmk. 4 *Perf. 12, 13½x13, 14*
N2 A3 1m red brown 20 20
N3 A3 2m Prus green (R) 30 30
a. 2m Prussian blue, perf. 13½x13 (R) (#170a) 30 50
N4 A3 3m blue green (R) 50 50
N5 A3 3m rose carmine 25 25
N6 A3 4m dp yel grn (R) 25 25
N7 A3 5m orange (G) 60 25
N8 A3 10m violet (OR) 75 35
N9 A3 12m deep rose 60 60
N10 A3 15m dl ol grn (R) 70 50
N11 A3 20m dp blue (R) 60 60
N12 A3 50m red lil (Dk G) 1.25 1.25
N13 A3 90m ocher (Dk G) 4.00 3.50
N14 A3 100m dp blue (R) 4.50 4.00
N15 A3 200m dk vio (R) 8.00 7.00
a. 200m vio, perf. 14 (R) (#182) 15.00 15.00
N16 A3 500m dk brn (R) 13.00 5.00
N17 A3 £1 black (R) 20.00 10.00
Nos. N2-N17 (16) 55.50 34.55

The first overprinting of these stamps include Nos. N1-N6, N9-N17. The second overprinting includes Nos. N1, N3, N5-N17, in inks differing in shade from the originals.

Many values exist with inverted or double overprint.

Jordan Nos. 245-249 Overprinted in Black or Red فلسطين PALESTINE

1949, Aug. Wmk. 4 *Perf. 13*
N18 A17 1m brown (Bk) 15 15
N19 A17 4m green 18 18
a. "PLAESTINE" 20.00
N20 A17 10m ultra 28 28
N21 A17 20m ultra 28 28
N22 A18 50m dull green 70 70
a. "PLAESTINE" 20.00
Nos. N18-N22 (5) 1.59 1.59

The overprint is in one line on No. N22.
UPU, 75th anniversary.

OCCUPATIONSTAMPSOCCUPATION POSTAGE DUE STAMPS

Catalogue values for unused stamps in this section are for Never Hinged items.

Jordan Nos. J39, J30a, J40, J32, J41-J43, J34 and J35 Overprinted in Black, Red or Carmine فلسطين PALESTINE

1948-49 Wmk. 4 *Perf. 12, 14*
NJ1 D1 1m org brn, perf. 12 15 15
a. Perf. 13½x13 (#J30a) 15.00 10.00
NJ2 D1 2m yel orange 15 15
NJ3 D1 4m grn (R) (#J32) 50 50
a. 4m yel grn (C) (#J41) 3.75
NJ5 D1 10m rose car (#J42) ('49) 80 80
a. Perf. 14 (#J33) 80.00
NJ6 D1 20m ol grn (R), perf. 14 50 50
a. Perf. 12 (R) (#J43) 20.00
NJ7 D1 50m blue (R) 50 50
Nos. NJ1-NJ3, NJ5-NJ7 (6) 2.60 2.60

The second overprinting of these stamps includes Nos. NJ1-NJ3, NJ3a and NJ5-NJ7, in inks differing in shade from the originals.

Double and inverted overprints exist.

Same Overprint in Black on Jordan Nos. J36-J38

1948-49 Unwmk. *Perf. 13x13½*
NJ8 D2 1m dl red brn *100.00 100.00*
NJ9 D2 2m dl org yel ('49) 5.00 5.00
NJ10 D2 10m dark car 2.00 2.00

OCCUPATION POSTAL TAX STAMPS

Catalogue values for unused stamps in this section are for Never Hinged items.

Postal Tax Stamps of 1947 Overprinted in Red or Black فلسطين PALESTINE

1950
NRA1 PT1 1m ultra (R) 24 16
NRA2 PT1 2m carmine 24 16
NRA3 PT1 3m emerald (R) 32 20
NRA4 PT1 5m plum 48 28
NRA5 PT1 10m carmine 1.10 40
NRA6 PT1 15m gray (R) 1.65 60
NRA7 PT1 20m dk brown (R) 2.50 75
NRA8 PT1 50m purple (R) 3.25 1.40
NRA9 PT1 100m org red 4.25 1.75
NRA10 PT1 200m dp blue (R) 12.00 4.00
NRA11 PT1 500m green (R) 24.00 10.00
NRA12 PT1 £1 dk brown (R) 45.00 20.00
Nos. NRA1-NRA12 (12) 95.03 39.70

For overprints, see Nos. 286D-286G.

KARELIA

LOCATION — In northwestern Soviet Russia.
GOVT. — An autonomous republic of the Soviet Union.
AREA — 55,198 sq. mi. (approx.).
POP. — 270,000 (approx.).
CAPITAL — Petrozavodsk (Kalininsk).

In 1921 the Karelians rebelled and for a short period a form of sovereignty independent of Russia was maintained.

100 Pennia = 1 Markka

Bear — A1

1922 Unwmk. Litho. *Perf. 11½, 12*

No.	Type	Value	Color	Unused	Used
1	A1	5p	dk gray	8.00	*27.50*
2	A1	10p	light blue	8.00	*27.50*
3	A1	20p	rose red	8.00	*27.50*
4	A1	25p	yel brown	8.00	*27.50*
5	A1	40p	magenta	8.00	*27.50*
6	A1	50p	gray green	8.00	*27.50*
7	A1	75p	org yel	8.00	*27.50*
8	A1	1m	pink & gray	8.00	*27.50*
9	A1	2m	yel grn & gray	20.00	*35.00*
10	A1	3m	lt bl & gray	25.00	*35.00*
11	A1	5m	red lil & gray	25.00	*65.00*
12	A1	10m	lt brn & gray	25.00	*90.00*
13	A1	15m	grn & car	25.00	*90.00*
14	A1	20m	rose & grn	25.00	*90.00*
15	A1	25m	yel & blue	25.00	*90.00*
			Nos. 1-15 (15)	234.00	

Nos. 1-15 were valid Jan. 31-Feb. 16, 1922. Counterfeits abound.

OCCUPATION STAMPS

Issued under Finnish Occupation

Issued in the Russian territory of Eastern Karelia under Finnish military administration.

Types of Finland Stamps, 1930 Overprinted in Black:

ITÄ-KARJALA Sot.hallinto On A26 — **ITÄ-KARJALA Sot.hallinto** On A27-A28

1941 Unwmk. *Perf. 14*

No.	Type	Value	Color	Unused	Used
N1	A26	50p	brt yel grn	35	*85*
N2	A26	1.75m	dk gray	75	*1.25*
N3	A26	2m	dp org	1.50	*2.25*
N4	A26	2.75m	yel org	70	*1.25*
N5	A26	3½m	lt ultra	1.50	*2.25*
N6	A27	5m	rose vio	3.50	*6.75*
N7	A28	10m	pale brn	3.50	*7.75*
			Nos. N1-N7 (7)	11.80	*22.35*

Types of Finland Stamps, 1930 Overprinted in Green:

ITÄ-KARJALA Sot. hallinto On A26 — **ITÄ-KARJALA Sot. hallinto** On A27-A29

No.	Type	Value	Color	Unused	Used
N8	A26	50p	brt yel grn	35	*65*
N9	A26	1.75m	dk gray	52	*70*
N10	A26	2m	dp org	70	*1.10*
N11	A26	2.75m	yel org	52	*70*
N12	A26	3½m	lt ultra	70	*1.25*
N13	A27	5m	rose vio	1.50	*3.25*
N14	A28	10m	pale brn	3.50	*6.00*
N15	A29	25m	green	3.50	*6.00*
			Nos. N8-N15 (8)	11.29	*19.65*

Mannerheim Type of Finland Overprinted **ITÄ-KARJALA Sot.hallinto**

1942

No.	Type	Value	Color	Unused	Used
N16	A48	50p	dk yel grn	60	*1.40*
N17	A48	1.75m	slate bl	60	*1.40*
N18	A48	2m	red org	60	*1.40*
N19	A48	2.75m	brn org	48	*1.25*
N20	A48	3.50m	brt ultra	48	*1.25*
N21	A48	5m	brn vio	48	*1.25*
			Nos. N16-N21 (6)	3.24	*7.95*

Same Overprint on Ryti Type of Finland

No.	Type	Value	Color	Unused	Used
N22	A49	50p	dk yel grn	48	*1.24*
N23	A49	1.75m	slate bl	48	*1.24*
N24	A49	2m	red org	48	*1.24*
N25	A49	2.75m	brn org	60	*1.40*
N26	A49	3.50m	brt ultra	60	*1.40*
N27	A49	5m	brn vio	60	*1.40*
			Nos. N22-N27 (6)	3.24	*7.92*

The overprint translates, "East Karelia Military Administration."

OCCUPATION SEMI-POSTAL STAMP

Arms of East Karelia — SP1

1943 Unwmk. Engr. *Perf. 14*

No.	Type	Value	Color	Unused	Used
NB1	SP1	3.50m + 1.50m	dk ol	60	*2.50*

This surtax aided war victims in East Karelia.

KATANGA

LOCATION — Central Africa
GOVT. — Republic
CAPITAL — Elisabethville

Katanga province seceded from the Congo (ex-Belgian) Republic in July, 1960, but established nations did not recognize it as an independent state. The UN declared the secession ended in Sept., 1961.

During the secession Katanga stamps were tolerated in the international mails, but the government authorizing them was not recognized.

100 Centimes = 1 Franc

Catalogue values for all unused stamps in this country are for Never Hinged items.

Belgian Congo Nos. 318-322 Overprinted "KATANGA"

Perf. 11½

1960, Sept. 12 Photo. Unwmk.

No.	Type	Value	Color
1	A94	50c	golden brn, ocher & red brn
2	A94	1fr	dk bl, pur & red brn
3	A94	2fr	gray, brt bl & red brn

Inscription in French

No.	Type	Value	Color
4	A95	3fr	gray & red

Inscription in Flemish

No.	Type	Value	Color
5	A95	3fr	gray & red

For surcharges see Nos. 50-51.

Animal Type of Belgian Congo, Nos. 306-317, Overprinted "KATANGA"

1960, Sept. 19

Granite Paper

No.	Type	Value	Color
6	A92	10c	bl & brn
7	A93	20c	red org & slate
8	A92	40c	brn & bl
9	A93	50c	brt ultra, red & sep
10	A92	1fr	brn, grn & blk
11	A93	1.50fr	blk & org yel
12	A92	2fr	crim, blk & brn
13	A93	3fr	blk, gray & lil rose
14	A92	5fr	brn, dk brn & brt grn
15	A93	6.50fr	bl, brn & org yel
16	A92	8fr	org brn, ol bis & lil
17	A93	10fr	multi

Inverted overprints exist.

Flower Type of Belgian Congo, Nos. 263-271, 274-281, Overprinted "KATANGA"

1960, Sept. 22

Granite Paper

Flowers in Natural Colors

No.	Type	Value	Color
18	A86	10c	dp plum & ocher
19	A86	15c	red & yel grn
20	A86	20c	grn & gray
21	A86	25c	dk grn & dl org
22	A86	40c	grn & sal
23	A86	50c	dk car & aqua
24	A86	60c	bl grn & pink
25	A86	75c	dp plum & gray
26	A86	1fr	car & yel
27	A86	2fr	ol grn & buff
28	A86	3fr	ol grn & pink
29	A86	4fr	choc & lil
30	A86	5fr	dp plum & lt bl grn
31	A86	6.50fr	dk car & lil
32	A86	7fr	dk grn & fawn
33	A86	8fr	grn & lt yel
34	A86	10fr	dp plum & pale ol

Inverted overprints exist.

Carving and Mask Type of Belgian Congo, Nos. 241, 246, 254-256, Surcharged or Overprinted "KATANGA"

1960, Sept. 22 *Perf. 12½*

No.	Type	Value	Color
35	A82	1.50fr	on 1.25fr
36	A82	3.50fr	on 2.50fr
37	A82	20fr	red org & vio brn
38	A82	50fr	dp org & blk
39	A82	100fr	crim & blk brn

Inverted surcharges and overprints exist.

Map Type of Congo Democratic Republic, Nos. 356-365, Overprinted "11 / JUILLET / DE / L'ETAT DU KATANGA"

1960, Oct. 26 *Perf. 11½*

Granite Paper

No.	Type	Value	Color	Unused	Used
40	A93a	20c	brown	15	15
41	A93a	50c	rose red	15	15
42	A93a	1fr	green	15	15
43	A93a	1.50fr	red brn	15	15
44	A93a	2fr	rose car	15	15
45	A93a	3.50fr	lilac	16	16
46	A93a	5fr	brt bl	18	18
47	A93a	6.50fr	gray	25	25
48	A93a	10fr	orange	35	35
49	A93a	20fr	ultra	65	65
			Nos. 40-49 (10)	2.34	2.34

Nos. 4-5 Surcharged

1961, Jan. 16

No.	Type	Value	Color
50	A95	3.50fr	on 3fr #4
51	A95	3.50fr	on 3fr #5

A1

A2

Katangan Wood Carvings: 3.50fr-8fr, Preparing meal. 10fr-100fr, Family group.

1961, Mar. 1 *Perf. 11½*

Granite Paper

No.	Type	Value	Color	Unused	Used
52	A1	10c	grn & lt grn	18	18
53	A1	20c	purple & lil	18	18
54	A1	50c	blue & lt bl	18	18
55	A1	1.50fr	ol grn & lt ol grn	18	18
56	A1	2fr	red brn & lt brn	18	18
57	A1	3.50fr	dk blue & lt bl	18	18
58	A1	5fr	bl grn & lt bl grn	18	18
59	A1	6fr	org brn & tan	18	18
60	A1	6.50fr	bl vio & gray vio	18	18
61	A1	8fr	claret & pink	25	25
62	A1	10fr	dk brn & lt brn	30	30
63	A1	20fr	dk ol & lt grn	45	45
64	A1	50fr	brn & lt brn	90	90
65	A1	100fr	Prus bl & lt bl	1.75	1.75
			Nos. 52-65 (14)	5.27	5.27

1961, July 11 *Perf. 11½*

Designs: 1fr, 5fr, Abstract vehicle. 2,50fr, 6.50fr, Gear.

Granite Paper

No.	Type	Value	Color	Unused	Used
66	A2	50c	blk, grn & red	18	18
67	A2	1fr	blk & blue	18	18
68	A2	2.50fr	blk & yellow	20	20
69	A2	3.50fr	blk, brn & scar	30	30
70	A2	5fr	blk & purple	50	50
71	A2	6.50fr	blk & orange	65	65
			Nos. 66-71 (6)	2.01	2.01

Katanga International Fair.

Air Katanga A3

Design: 6.50fr, 10fr, Plane on ground.

1961, Aug. 1 *Perf. 11½*

Granite Paper

No.	Type	Value	Color
72	A3	3.50fr	multicolored
73	A3	6.50fr	multicolored
74	A3	8fr	multicolored
75	A3	10fr	multicolored

Katanga Gendarmerie — A4

1961, Oct. 1 *Perf. 11½*

Granite Paper

No.	Type	Value	Color
76	A4	6fr	multicolored
77	A4	8fr	multicolored
78	A4	10fr	multicolored

SEMI-POSTAL STAMPS

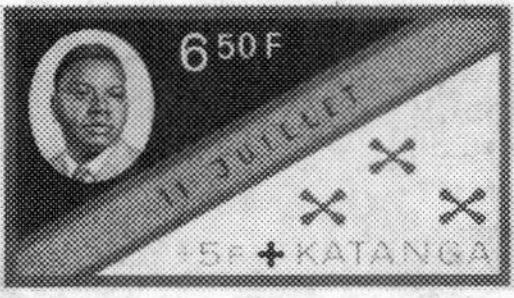

Pres. Moise Tshombe — SP1

1961, July 8 *Perf. 11½*

Granite Paper

No.	Type	Value	Color
B1	SP1	6.50fr + 5fr	multi
B2	SP1	8fr + 5fr	multi
B3	SP1	10fr + 5fr	multi

POSTAGE DUE STAMPS

Belgian Congo Nos. J8a-J10a, J16-J19 Handstamped "KATANGA" in Blue

1960, Dec. 30 Unwmk. *Perf. 12½*

No.	Type	Value	Color
J1	D2	10c	olive green
J2	D2	20c	dark ultra
J3	D2	50c	green

Perf. 11½

No.	Type	Value	Color
J4	D3	1fr	light blue
J5	D3	2fr	vermilion
J6	D3	4fr	purple
J7	D3	6fr	violet blue

This overprint also exists on Belgian Congo Nos. J11a-J12a, J13-J15.

KAZAKHSTAN

(Kazahstan)

LOCATION — Bounded by southern Russia, Uzbekistan, Kyrgyzstan, and China.
GOVT. — Independent republic, member of the Commonwealth of Independent States.
AREA — 1,049,200 sq. mi.
POP. — 16,500,000 (1989)
CAPITAL — Alma Ata

With the breakup of the Soviet Union on Dec. 26, 1991, Kazakhstan and ten former Soviet republics established the Commonwealth of Independent States.

100 Kopecks = 1 Ruble

Catalogue values for all unused stamps in this country are for Never Hinged items.

Overprinted Stamps

The Philatelic Club of Alta Ata, Kazakhstan, has announced that various overprinted stamps of the USSR were not generally available nor were they in values reflecting actual postal rates.

A1

Perf. 12x12½

1992, Mar. 23 Litho. Unwmk.

1 A1 50k multicolored *1.00*

Space Ship and Yurt — A4

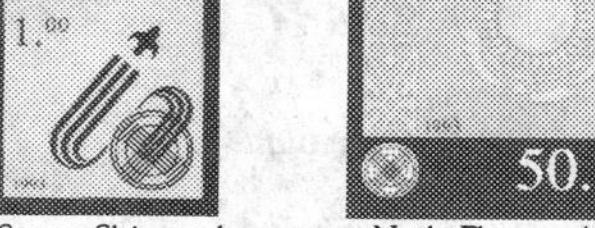

Natl. Flag — A5

1993 Litho. *Perf. 13x12½*

22 A4 1r green *15*
23 A4 3r red *15*
24 A4 10r golden brown *20*
25 A4 25r purple *50*

Perf. 14

27 A5 50r multicolored *1.00*

Issue date: 1r, 3r, 10r, 25r, 50r, Jan. 24.
This is an expanding set. Numbers may change.

Space Mail — A6

1993, Mar. 5 Litho. *Perf. 13½*

35 A6 100r multicolored *2.00*

KIAUCHAU

(Kiautschou)

LOCATION — A district of China on the south side of the Shantung peninsula.
GOVT. — A former German colony.
AREA — 200 sq. mi.
POP. — 192,000 (approx. 1914).

The area was seized by Germany in 1897 and through negotiations that followed was leased to Germany by China.

100 Pfennig = 1 Mark
100 Cents = 1 Dollar (1905)

Tsingtau Issues

Stamps of Germany, Offices in China 1898, with Additional Surcharge:

5 Pfg. *a* 5 Pfg. *b* 5 Pfg. *c*

1900

"China" Overprint at 56 degree Angle

1 A10(a) 5pfg on 10pf car 40.00 40.00
c. Dbl. surch., one inverted 300.00
2 A10(b) 5pfg on 10pf car 40.00 40.00
c. Dbl. surch., one inverted 300.00
3 A10(c) 5pfg on 10pf car 42.50 45.00
c. Dbl. surch., one inverted 350.00

"China" Overprint at 48 degree Angle

1a A10(a) 5pfg on 10pf car 110.00 125.00
b. Double surcharge 450.00 575.00
2a A10(b) 5pfg on 10pf car 110.00 125.00
b. Double surcharge 450.00 575.00
3a A10(c) 5pfg on 10pf car 125.00 140.00
b. Double surcharge 500.00 600.00

Surcharged:

5 Pf. *d* 5 Pf. *e* 5 Pf. *f*

"China" Overprint at 48 degree Angle on Nos. 4-9

4 A10(d) 5pf on 10pf car *2,500. 2,750.*
a. Double surcharge
5 A10(e) 5pf pn 10pf car *2,500. 2,750.*
a. Double surcharge
6 A10(f) 5pf on 10pf car *3,000. 3,650.*
a. Double surcharge
b. 5fP
c. As "b," double surcharge

With Additional Handstamp **5**

7 A10(d) 5pf on 10pf car *30,000. 37,500.*
8 A10(f) 5pf on 10pf car *30,000. 37,500.*
a. On No. 6b

With Additional Handstamp **5 Pf.**

9 A10(f) 5pf on 10pf car *4,000. 6,000.*
a. Double surcharge *9,500. 10,500.*
b. On No. 6a
c. On No. 6b
d. On No. 6c

On Nos. 1-9, a blue or violet line is drawn through "PF. 10 PF." All exist without this line. All copies of Nos. 1b, 2b and 3b lack the colored line.

Kaiser's Yacht "Hohenzollern"
A1 A2

1900 Unwmk. Typo. *Perf. 14*

10 A1 3pf brown 1.90 1.75
11 A1 5pf green 1.50 65
12 A1 10pf carmine 2.50 1.50
13 A1 20pf ultra 6.50 7.25
14 A1 25pf org & blk, *yel* 13.00 16.00
15 A1 30pf org & blk, *sal* 13.00 16.00
16 A1 40pf lake & blk 15.00 20.00
17 A1 50pf pur & blk, *sal* 15.00 20.00
18 A1 80pf lake & blk, *rose* 25.00 45.00

Engr. *Perf. 14½x14*

19 A2 1m carmine 45.00 62.50
20 A2 2m blue 62.50 90.00
21 A2 3m blk vio 62.50 *160.00*
22 A2 5m slate & car 205.00 *500.00*
Nos. 10-22 (13) 468.40 *940.65*

A3

A4

1905 Typo.

23 A3 1c brown 1.10 1.10
24 A3 2c green 1.75 90
25 A3 4c carmine 3.75 85
26 A3 10c ultra 9.00 4.00
27 A3 20c lake & blk 25.00 16.00
28 A3 40c lake & blk, *rose* 70.00 100.00

Engr.

29 A4 $½ carmine 62.50 95.00
30 A4 $1 blue 125.00 95.00
31 A4 $1½ blk vio 625.00 *1,300.*
32 A4 $2½ slate & car 950.00 *3,500.*

1905-09 Wmk. 125 Typo.

33 A3 1c brown ('06) 65 90
34 A3 2c green ('09) 65 70
35 A3 4c carmine ('09) 90 90
36 A3 10c ultra ('09) 90 *1.90*
37 A3 20c lake & blk ('08) 1.75 *14.00*
38 A3 40c lake & blk, *rose* 3.00 *57.50*

Engr.

39 A4 $½ car ('07) 4.25 *60.00*
40 A4 $1 blue ('06) 6.00 *62.50*
41 A4 $1½ blk violet 7.00 *150.00*
42 A4 $2½ slate & car 18.00 *400.00*
Nos. 33-42 (10) 43.10

KIONGA

LOCATION — Southeast Africa and northeast Mozambique, on Indian Ocean south of Rovuma River
GOVT. — Formerly part of German East Africa
AREA — 400 sq. mi.

This territory, occupied by Portuguese troops during World War I was allotted to Portugal by the Treaty of Versailles. Later it became part of Mozambique.

100 Centavos = 1 Escudo

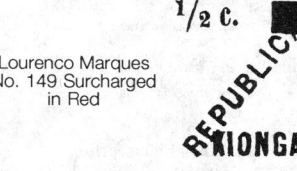

Lourenco Marques No. 149 Surcharged in Red

½ C. REPUBLICA KIONGA

1916, May 29 Unwmk. *Perf. 11½*

1 A2 ½c on 100r bl, *bl* 17.50 12.50
2 A2 1c on 100r bl, *bl* 17.50 12.50
3 A2 2½c on 100r bl, *bl* 17.50 12.50
4 A2 5c on 100r bl, *bl* 17.50 12.50

Most of the stock of Loureno Marques No. 149 used for these surcharges lacked gum.

KOREA

(Corea)

(Chosen, Tyosen, Tae Han)

LOCATION — Peninsula extending from Manchuria between the Yellow Sea and the Sea of Japan
GOVT. — Republic
AREA — 38,221 sq. mi.
POP. — 39,950,743 (1983)
CAPITAL — Seoul

Korea (or Corea) an independent monarchy for centuries under Chinese influence, came under Japanese influence in 1895. Japanese stamps were used there as early as 1875. Administrative control was assumed by Japan in 1904 and annexation followed in 1910. Postage stamps of Japan were used in Korea from 1905 to early 1946.

At the end of World War II, American forces occupied South Korea and Russian forces occupied North Korea, with the 38th parallel of latitude as the dividing line. A republic was established in 1948 following an election in South Korea. North Korea issues its own stamps. See note following air post listings.

100 Mon = 1 Tempo
5 Poon = 1 Cheun
100 Sen = 1 Yen
1000 Re = 100 Cheun = Weun
100 Weun = 1 Hwan (1953)
100 Chun = 1 Won (1962)

Catalogue values for unused stamps in this country are for Never Hinged items, beginning with Scott 283 in the regular postage section, Scott B5 in the semi-postal section, and Scott C23 in the airpost section.

Watermarks

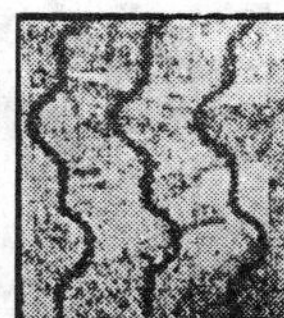
Wmk. 257- Curved Wavy Lines

Wmk. 312- Zigzag Lines

Wmk. 317- Communications Department Emblem

Stylized Yin Yang
A1 A2

Perf. 8½ to 11½

1884 Typo. Unwmk.

1 A1 5m rose 35.00
2 A2 10m blue 9.00

Reprints and counterfeits of Nos. 1-2 exist.

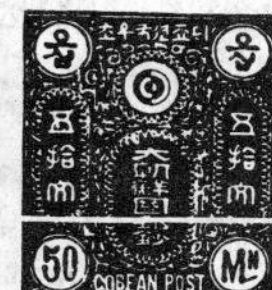

These stamps were never placed in use. Value, each $6.
Counterfeits exist.

Yin Yang — A6

Two types of 50p:
I- No period after "50."
II- Period after "50."

Perf. 11½, 12, 12½, 13 and Compound

1895 Litho.

6 A6 5p green 18.00 12.00
a. 5p pale yellow green 25.00 15.00
b. Vert. pair, imperf horiz. 50.00 50.00
c. Horiz. pair, imperf. vert. 50.00 50.00
d. Vertical pair, imperf. between 55.00 55.00
e. Horiz. pair, imperf. btwn. 55.00 55.00
7 A6 10p deep blue 19.00 12.00
a. Horiz. pair, imperf. between 50.00 50.00
b. Vert. pair, imperf. horiz. 40.00 40.00
8 A6 25p maroon 30.00 19.00
a. Horiz. pair, imperf. between 65.00 65.00
b. Vert. pair, imperf. horiz. 60.00 60.00
9 A6 50p purple (II) 18.00 12.00
a. Horiz. pair, imperf. between 70.00 70.00
b. Vert, pair, imperf. horiz. 40.00 40.00
c. Horiz. pair, imperf. vert. 40.00 40.00
d. Type I 20.00 14.00

For overprints and surcharges see Nos. 10-17C, 35-38.

Counterfeits exist of Nos. 6-9 and all surcharges and overprints.

Overprinted "Tae Han" in Korean and Chinese Characters

1897

Red Overprint

No.	Type	Description	Unused	Used
10	A6	5p green	52.50	10.00
a.		5p pale yellow green	120.00	100.00
b.		Inverted overprint	100.00	100.00
c.		Without ovpt. at bottom	90.00	90.00
d.		Without overprint at top	90.00	90.00
f.		Double overprint at top	100.00	100.00
g.		Overprint at bottom in blk	120.00	120.00
h.		Pair, one without overprint	350.00	350.00
i.		Double overprint at top, inverted at bottom	400.00	
11	A6	10p deep blue	57.50	15.00
a.		Without ovpt. at bottom	75.00	75.00
b.		Without overprint at top	75.00	75.00
c.		Double overprint at top	80.00	80.00

No.	Type	Description	Unused	Used
d.		Bottom overprint inverted	75.00	75.00
e.		Top ovpt. dbl., one in blk	125.00	125.00
f.		Top overprint omitted, bottom overprint inverted	275.00	
12	A6	25p maroon	57.50	17.00
a.		Overprint at bottom invtd.	75.00	75.00
b.		Overprint at bottom in blk	110.00	110.00
c.		Bottom overprint omitted	65.00	65.00
e.		Top ovpt. dbl., one in blk	125.00	125.00
f.		Top and bottom overprints double, one of each in blk	150.00	150.00
g.		Pair, one without overprint	250.00	250.00
13	A6	50p purple	57.50	12.00
a.		Without ovpt. at bottom	90.00	90.00
b.		Without overprint at top	90.00	90.00
c.		Bottom overprint double	80.00	80.00
e.		Pair, one without overprint	250.00	250.00

1900

Black Overprint

No.	Type	Description	Unused	Used
13F	A6	5p green	200.00	
13G	A6	10p deep blue	200.00	
h.		Without ovpt. at bottom	250.00	
14	A6	25p maroon	200.00	
a.		Without ovpt. at bottom	210.00	
b.		Without overprint at top	210.00	
c.		Double overprint at bottom	210.00	
15	A6	50p purple	200.00	
a.		Without ovpt. at bottom	225.00	

These stamps with black overprint, also No. 16A, are said not to have been officially authorized.

Nos. 6, 6a and 8 Surcharged in Red or Black

1900

No.	Type	Description	Unused	Used
15B	A6	1ch on 5p grn (R)	*1,500.*	*500.00*
c.		Yellow green		
16	A6	1ch on 25p mar	80.00	55.00

Same Surcharge in Red or Black on Nos. 10, 12, 12c and 14

No.	Type	Description	Unused	Used
16A	A6	1ch on 5p grn (R)	900.00	
b.		1ch on 5p pale yel grn	900.00	
17	A6	1ch on 25p mar	32.50	17.50
a.		Figure "1" omitted	65.00	
b.		Overprint at bottom omitted (No. 12c)	55.00	55.00
17C	A6	1ch on 25p mar (on No. 14)	350.00	160.00

Counterfeit overprints and surcharges of Nos. 10-17C exist.

A8

A9

A10

A11

A12

A13

A14

A15

A16

A17

1900 Typo. *Perf. 11*

No.	Type	Description	Unused	Used
18	A8	2re gray	9.00	3.00
19	A9	1ch yellow grn	10.00	3.50
21	A11	3ch orange red	12.00	4.00
a.		Imperf. horiz.	85.00	85.00
22	A12	4ch carmine	32.50	12.50
23	A13	5ch pink	15.00	5.00
24	A14	6ch dp blue	16.00	5.50
25	A15	10ch purple	22.50	7.50
26	A16	15ch gray vio	20.00	7.50
27	A17	20ch red brown	24.00	9.00
		Nos. 18-27 (9)	161.00	57.50

Nos. 22, 23, 25, 26 exist imperf.

Reprints of No. 24 were made in light blue, perf. 12x13, in 1905 for a souvenir booklet. See note after No. 54.

Perf. 10

No.	Type	Description	Unused	Used
18a	A8	2re	12.50	3.00
19a	A9	1ch	12.00	4.00
20	A10	2ch blue	30.00	14.00
a.		Horiz. pair, imperf. btwn.	150.00	
21b	A11	3ch	12.50	4.00
22a	A12	4ch	40.00	15.00
23a	A13	5ch	17.50	7.00
24a	A14	6ch	19.00	8.50
26a	A16	15ch	135.00	100.00
27a	A17	20ch	185.00	150.00

A18

A19

A20

A21

1901 *Perf. 11*

No.	Type	Description	Unused	Used
30	A18	2ch pale blue	12.00	7.00
a.		Perf. 10	50.00	40.00
31	A19	50ch ol grn & pink	200.00	60.00
32	A20	1wn rose, blk & bl	600.00	125.00
33	A21	2wn pur & yel grn	900.00	175.00

No. 33 exists imperf.

See Nos. 52-54.

Emperor's Crown — A22

1902, Oct. 18 *Perf. 11½*

No.	Type	Description	Unused	Used
34	A22	3ch orange	32.50	15.00

40th year of the reign of Emperor Kojong. An imperf. single was part of the 1905 souvenir booklet. See note following No. 54.

Counterfeits exist.

Nos. 8 and 9 Handstamp Surcharged in Black

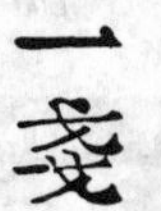
1ch

2ch

3ch

Perf. 11½, 12, 12½, 13 and Compound

1902

No.	Type	Description	Unused	Used
35	A6	1ch on 25p maroon	16.00	5.00
b.		Horiz. pair, imperf. btwn.	80.00	
c.		Imperf.	50.00	
d.		Vert. pair, imperf. horiz.	50.00	
e.		On No. 12	90.00	70.00
36	A6	2ch on 25p maroon	20.00	6.00
b.		Imperf.	45.00	
d.		On No. 12	90.00	70.00
e.		2ch on 50p pur	165.00	125.00
f.		As "e," character "cheun" unabbreviated (in two rows instead of one)	250.00	150.00
37	A6	3ch on 50p purple	20.00	6.00
b.		With character "cheun" unabbreviated (in two rows instead of one)	100.00	75.00
d.		Horiz. pair, imperf. btwn.	60.00	
e.		Vert. pair, imperf. btwn.	60.00	
g.		On No. 13	50.00	50.00
38	A6	3ch on 25p maroon	60.00	45.00

There are several sizes of these surcharges. Being handstamped inverted and double surcharges exist. Counterfeit surcharges exist.

Falcon — A23

1903 *Perf. 13½x14*

No.	Type	Description	Unused	Used
39	A23	2re slate	22.50	3.50
40	A23	1ch violet brn	22.50	3.50
41	A23	2ch green	22.50	3.50
42	A23	3ch orange	37.50	3.50
43	A23	4ch rose	45.00	6.00
44	A23	5ch yellow brn	45.00	7.00
45	A23	6ch lilac	45.00	7.00
46	A23	10ch blue	45.00	7.00
47	A23	15ch red, *straw*	125.00	16.00
48	A23	20ch vio brn, *straw*	125.00	15.00
49	A23	50ch red, *grn*	175.00	50.00
50	A23	1wn vio, *lav*	300.00	75.00
51	A23	2wn vio, *org*	400.00	110.00
		Nos. 39-51 (13)	1,410.	307.00

Values are for copies with perfs touching the design.

Types of 1901

1903 *Perf. 12½*

Thin, Semi-Transparent Paper

No.	Type	Description	Unused	Used
52	A19	50ch pale ol grn & pale pink	*275.00*	*125.00*
53	A20	1wn rose, blk & bl	*550.00*	*160.00*
54	A21	2wn lt vio & lt grn	*575.00*	*160.00*

No. 24, perf. 12x13, No. 34 imperf. and most examples of Nos. 52-54 unused are from souvenir booklets made up in 1905 when the Japanese withdrew all Korean stamps from circulation.

Nos. 1-54 Watermarked In 1957 the Ministry of Communications issued 4000 presentation booklets containing Nos. 1-54 reproduced on watermark 312 paper.

Issued under US Military Rule

Stamps of Japan Nos. 331, 268, 342, 332, 339 and 337 Surcharged in Black

1946, Feb. 1 Wmk. 257 *Perf. 13*

No.	Type	Description	Unused	Used
55	A86	5ch on 5s brn lake	4.50	10.00
56	A93	5ch on 14s rose lake & pale rose	52	90
a.		5ch on 40s dark vio (error)	110.00	

57	A154	10ch on 40s dk vio	45	65
58	A147	20ch on 6s lt ultra	45	65
a.		20ch on 27s rose brn (error)	80.00	
b.		Double surcharge	30.00	
59	A151	30ch on 27s rose brn	45	65
a.		30ch on 6s light ultra (error)	40.00	
b.		Double surcharge	25.00	
60	A151	5wn on 17s gray vio	2.50	6.00
		Nos. 55-60 (6)	8.87	18.85

Five essays for this provisional issue exist both with and without additional overprint of two Chinese characters ("specimen") in vermilion. The essays are: 20ch on Japan No. 269; 50ch on No. 272; 1wn on No. 336; 1wn on No. 273; 10wn on No. 265. Other denominations have been reported.

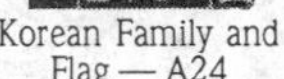

Korean Family and Flag — A24

Arms of Korea — A25

Perf. 10½

1946, May 1 Litho. Wmk. 257

61	A24	3ch orange yel	15	30
62	A24	5ch green	15	20
63	A24	10ch carmine	15	20
64	A24	20ch dk blue	18	25
65	A25	50ch brown vio	28	50
66	A25	1wn lt brown	38	75
		Nos. 61-66 (6)	1.29	2.20

Liberation from Japan.

Imperfs., Part Perfs.

Imperforate and part-perforate examples of a great many Korean stamps from No. 61 onward exist.

The imperfs. include Nos. 61-90, 93-97, 116-117, 119-126, 132-173, 182-186, 195, 197-199, 202A, 203, 204-205, 217, etc.

The part-perfs. include Nos. 62-65, 69, 72-73, 109, 111-113, 132, etc.

Printers waste includes printed on both sides, etc.

As the field is so extensive, the editors believe that they belong more properly in a specialized catalogue.

Dove — A26

1946, Aug. 15 Unwmk.

67	A26	50ch dp violet	1.25	2.50

First anniversary of liberation.

Perforations often are rough on stamps issued between Aug. 1946 and the end of 1954.

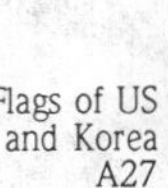

Flags of US and Korea A27

1946, Sept. 9 ***Perf. 11***

68	A27	10wn carmine	1.75	2.50

Issued to commemorate the resumption of postal communication with the United States.

Astronomical Observatory, Kyongju — A28

Hibiscus with Rice — A29

Map of Korea — A30

Gold Crown of Silla Dynasty — A31

Admiral Li Sun-sin — A32

1946 ***Rouletted 12***

69	A28	50ch dk blue	24	40
70	A29	1wn buff	20	40
71	A30	2wn indigo	50	50
72	A31	5wn magenta	2.00	3.00
73	A32	10wn emerald	3.00	2.25
		Nos. 69-73 (5)	5.94	6.55

Perf. 11

70a	A29	1wn	1.00	1.00
71a	A30	2wn	20.00	20.00
72a	A31	5wn	15.00	20.00

Korean Phonetic Alphabet — A33

1946, Oct. 9 ***Perf. 11***

74	A33	50ch deep blue	60	1.25

500th anniv. of the introduction of the Korean phonetic alphabet (Hangul).

Li Jun — A34

Admiral Li Sun-sin — A35

Perf. 11½x11, 11½

1947, Aug. 1 Litho. Wmk. 257

75	A34	5wn lt blue grn	2.00	3.50
76	A35	10wn light blue	2.00	3.50

Presentation Sheets

Starting in 1947 with No. 75, nearly 100 Korean stamps were printed in miniature or souvenir sheets and given to government officials and others. These sheets were released in quantities of 300 to 4,000. In 1957 the Ministry of Communications began to sell the souvenir sheets at post offices at face value to be used for postage. They are listed from No. 244a onward.

Letter-encircled Globe — A36

1947, Aug. 1 ***Perf. 11½x11***

77	A36	10wn light blue	2.00	3.50

Resumption of international mail service between Korea and all countries of the world.

Granite Paper

Starting with No. 77, most Korean stamps, except those on Laid Paper, are on Granite Paper. Granite Paper is noted above listing if the issue was printed on both ordinary and Granite Paper, such as Nos. 360a-374A.

Arch of Independence, Seoul — A37

Tortoise Ship, First Ironclad War Vessel — A38

1948, Apr.

78	A37	20wn rose	12.00	6.00
79	A38	50wn dull red brn	12.00	7.50

Republic

Flag and Ballot — A39

Woman and Man Casting Ballots — A40

Perf. 11x11½

1948, May 10 Litho. Wmk. 257

80	A39	2wn orange	2.00	60
81	A39	5wn lilac rose	4.00	1.50
82	A39	10wn lt violet	10.00	4.00
83	A40	20wn carmine	15.00	8.00
84	A40	50wn blue	20.00	12.50
		Nos. 80-84 (5)	51.00	26.60

South Korea election of May 10, 1948.

Korean Flag and Olive Branches A41

Olympic Torchbearer and Map of Korea — A42

1948, June 1 ***Perf. 11x11½, 11½x11***

85	A41	5wn green	40.00	32.50
86	A42	10wn purple	20.00	8.00

Issued to commemorate Korea's participation in the 1948 Olympic Games.

National Assembly A43

1948, July 1 Wmk. 257 ***Perf. 11½***

87	A43	4wn orange brown	7.00	6.00

Opening of the Assembly July 1, 1948. Exists without period between "5" and "31."

Korean Family and Capitol — A44

Pres. Syngman Rhee — A46

Flag of Korea A45

1948, Aug. 1 Litho.

88	A44	4wn emerald	24.00	5.00
89	A45	10wn orange brn	10.00	5.00

Issued to commemorate the signing of the new constitution, July 17, 1948.

1948, Aug. 5

90	A46	5wn deep blue	70.00	6.00

Inauguration of Korea's first president, Syngman Rhee.

Dove — A47

Hibiscus — A48

Two types of 5wn:
I- "1948" 3mm wide; top inscription 9mm wide; periods in "8.15." barely visible.
II- "1948" 4mm wide; top inscription 9½mm; periods in "8.15." bold and strong.

1948 *Perf. 11, 11x11½*

91	A47	4wn blue	15.00	15.00
92	A48	5wn rose lil (II)	11.00	12.50
a.		Type I	70.00	60.00

Issued to commemorate the establishment of Korea's republican government.

Li Jun A49

Observatory, Kyongju A50

1948, Oct. 1 *Perf. 11½x11*

93	A49	4wn rose car	20	20
94	A50	14wn deep blue	38	30
a.		14wn light blue	60.00	30.00

For surcharges see Nos. 127, 174, 176.

Doves over UN Emblem — A51

Korean Citizen and Census Date — A52

1949, Feb. 12 **Wmk. 257** *Perf. 11*

95	A51	10wn blue	*9.00*	12.50

Arrival of the UN Commission on Korea, Feb. 12, 1949.

1949, Apr. 25

96	A52	15wn purple	10.00	9.00

Census of May 1, 1949.

Korean Boy and Girl — A53

1949, May 5

97	A53	15wn purple	7.00	8.00

20th anniversary of Children's Day, May 5, 1949.

Postman — A54

Worker and Factory — A55

Rice Harvesting — A56

Japanese Cranes — A57

Diamond Mountains — A58

Ginseng Plant — A59

South Gate, Seoul — A60

Tabo Pagoda, Kyongju — A61

1949 **Litho.** *Perf. 11*

98	A54	1wn rose	1.25	1.50
99	A55	2wn dk bl gray	45	30
100	A56	5wn yellow grn	1.75	1.50
101	A57	10wn blue grn	45	50
102	A58	20wn orange brn	38	35
103	A59	30wn blue grn	70	50
104	A60	50wn violet bl	55	50
105	A61	100wn dull yel grn	55	50
		Nos. 98-105 (8)	6.08	5.65

For surcharges see Nos. 129-131, 175, 177B-179, 181.

Phoenix and Yin Yang — A62

1949, Aug. 25

106	A62	15wn deep blue	8.00	7.00

1st anniv. of Korea's independence.

Express Train "Sam Chun Li" — A63

1949, Sept. 18 *Perf. 11½x12*

107	A63	15wn violet blue	25.00	15.00

50th anniversary of Korean railroads.

Korean Flag — A64

Perf. 11½x11

1949, Oct. 15 **Wmk. 257**

108	A64	15wn red org, yel & dk bl	6.00	8.50

75th anniv. of the UPU.

No. 108 exists unwatermarked. These are counterfeit.

Hibiscus A65

Magpies and Map of Korea A66

Stylized Bird and Globe — A67

Diamond Mountains A68

Admiral Li Sun-sin — A69

1949 **Wmk. 257** **Litho.** *Perf. 11*

109	A65	15wn vermilion	16	25
110	A66	65wn dp blue	16	25
111	A67	200wn green	20	25
112	A68	400wn brown	20	35
113	A69	500wn dp blue	20	25
		Nos. 109-113 (5)	92	1.35

For surcharges see Nos. 128, 177, 180.

Canceled to Order

More than 100 Korean stamps and souvenir sheets were canceled to order, the cancellation incorporating the date "67.9.20." These include 81 stamps between Nos. 111 and 327, 18 airmail stamps between Nos. C6 and C26, and 5 souvenir sheets between Nos. 313 and 332, etc.

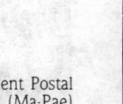

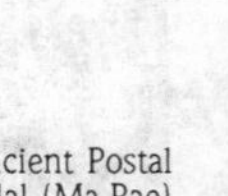
Ancient Postal Medal (Ma-Pae) A70

1950, Jan. 1

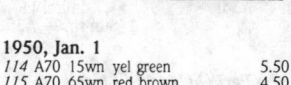

114	A70	15wn yel green	5.50	5.00
115	A70	65wn red brown	4.50	4.00

50th anniv. of Korea's entrance into the UPU.

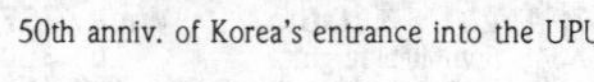

Revolutionists — A71

1950, Mar. 10 *Perf. 11½*

116	A71	15wn olive	7.00	4.00
117	A71	65wn lt violet	5.00	4.00

41st anniversary of Korea's declaration of Independence.

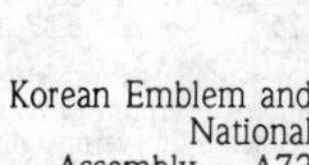

Korean Emblem and National Assembly — A72

1950, May 30

118	A72	30wn bl, red, brn & grn	4.50	5.00

2nd natl. election of the Korean Republic.

Syngman Rhee A73

Korean Flag and White Mountains A74

Flags of UN and Korea, Map of Korea — A75

1950, Nov. 20 **Wmk. 257** *Perf. 11*

119	A73	100wn blue	75	1.00
120	A74	100wn green	1.00	1.00
121	A75	200wn dk green	1.00	1.00

Crane — A76

Tiger Mural — A77

Dove and Flag — A78

Postal Medal — A79

Mural from Ancient Tomb — A80

1951 **Unwmk.** *Perf. 11*

Ordinary Paper

122	A76	5wn orange brn	70	75
123	A77	20wn purple	60	75
124	A78	50wn green	1.50	1.00
125	A79	100wn dp blue	4.00	2.00
126	A80	1000wn green	10.00	2.50
		Nos. 122-126 (5)	16.80	7.00

Rouletted 12

122a	A76	5wn orange brn	45	75
123a	A77	20wn purple	70	1.50
124a	A78	50wn green	85	75
125a	A79	100wn blue	1.10	2.00

No. 126 also exists perforated 12½. See Nos. 187-189.

No. 93 Surcharged with New Value and Wavy Lines in Blue

1951 **Wmk. 257** *Perf. 11½x11*

127	A49	100wn on 4wn rose car	70	60
a.		Inverted surcharge	35.00	

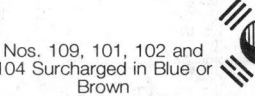

Nos. 109, 101, 102 and 104 Surcharged in Blue or Brown

200원

Perf. 11

No.	Type	Description	Unused	Used
128	A65	200wn on 15wn	2.00	75
a.		Inverted surcharge	10.00	10.00
129	A57	300wn on 10wn (Br)	4.00	2.00
a.		Inverted surcharge	17.50	
130	A58	300wn on 20wn	2.75	1.50
a.		Inverted surcharge	17.50	
131	A60	300wn on 50wn (Br)	6.00	2.50
		Nos. 127-131 (5)	15.45	7.35

Size of surcharge varies. Numeral upright on Nos. 129 and 131; numeral slanted on Nos. 175 and 179. See Nos. 174-181.

On No. 130, the zeros in "300" are octagonal; on No. 177B they are oval.

Flags of US and Korea and Statue of Liberty — A81

Design (blue stamps): Flag of same country as preceding green stamp, UN emblem and doves.

1951-52 Wmk. 257 *Perf. 11*

Flags in Natural Colors, Participating Country at Left

No.	Type	Description	Unused	Used
132	A81	500wn green	8.00	5.00
133	A81	500wn blue	8.00	5.00
134	A81	500wn grn *(Australia)*	6.50	4.00
135	A81	500wn blue	8.00	5.00
136	A81	500wn grn *(Belgium)*	6.50	4.00
137	A81	500wn blue	6.50	4.00
138	A81	500wn grn *(Britain)*	8.00	5.00
139	A81	500wn blue	8.00	5.00
140	A81	500wn grn *(Canada)*	8.00	5.00
141	A81	500wn blue	6.50	4.00
142	A81	500wn grn *(Colombia)*	6.50	4.00
143	A81	500wn blue	8.00	5.00
144	A81	500wn grn *(Denmark)*	12.50	15.00
145	A81	500wn blue	13.00	15.00
146	A81	500wn grn *(Ethiopia)*	6.50	4.00
147	A81	500wn blue	8.00	5.00
148	A81	500wn grn *(France)*	6.50	4.00
149	A81	500wn blue	8.00	5.00
150	A81	500wn grn *(Greece)*	8.00	5.00
151	A81	500wn blue	8.00	5.00
152	A81	500wn grn *(India)*	10.00	6.00
153	A81	500wn blue	10.00	6.00
154	A81	500wn grn *(Italy)*	10.00	6.00
a.		Flag without crown ('52)	11.50	
155	A81	500wn blue	10.00	6.00
a.		Flag without crown ('52)	11.50	
156	A81	500wn grn *(Luxembourg)*	10.00	6.00
157	A81	500wn blue	8.00	5.00
158	A81	500wn grn *(Netherlands)*	6.50	4.00
159	A81	500wn blue	6.50	4.00
160	A81	500wn grn *(New Zealand)*	8.00	5.00
161	A81	500wn blue	8.00	5.00
162	A81	500wn grn *(Norway)*	10.00	6.00
163	A81	500wn blue	10.00	6.00
164	A81	500wn grn *(Philippines)*	8.00	5.00
165	A81	500wn blue	8.00	5.00
166	A81	500wn grn *(Sweden)*	6.50	4.00
167	A81	500wn blue	8.00	5.00
168	A81	500wn grn *(Thailand)*	6.50	4.00
169	A81	500wn blue	8.00	5.00
170	A81	500wn grn *(Turkey)*	8.00	5.00
171	A81	500wn blue	8.00	5.00
172	A81	500wn grn *(Union of So. Africa)*	8.00	5.00
173	A81	500wn blue	8.00	5.00
		Nos. 132-173 (42)	343.00	226.00

Twenty-two imperf. souvenir sheets of two, containing the green and the blue stamps for each participating country (including both types of Italy) were issued. Size: 140x90mm. Value, set $500.

Nos. 93-94, 101-105, 109-110 Surcharged Like Nos. 128-131 in Blue or Brown

1951 Wmk. 257 *Perf. 11½x11, 11*

No.	Type	Description	Unused	Used
174	A49	300wn on 4wn	1.25	90
a.		Inverted surcharge	70.00	50.00
175	A57	300wn on 10wn (Br)	90	75
a.		Inverted surcharge	50.00	40.00
176	A50	300wn on 14wn (Br)	1.50	1.25
a.		300wn on 14wn lt bl	650.00	125.00
b.		Inverted surcharge	50.00	50.00
177	A65	300wn on 15wn	1.25	90
a.		Inverted surcharge	40.00	40.00
177B	A58	300wn on 20wn	3.50	3.50
178	A59	300wn on 30wn (Br)	1.25	90
a.		Inverted surcharge	42.50	40.00
179	A60	300wn on 50wn (Br)	1.25	90
180	A66	300wn on 65wn (Br)	90	75
a.		Inverted monad	52.50	50.00
181	A61	300wn on 100wn	1.50	1.25
a.		Inverted surcharge	50.00	40.00
		Nos. 174-181 (9)	13.30	11.10

"300" slanted on Nos. 175, 177B and 179; "300" upright on Nos. 129 and 131. The surcharge exists double on several of these stamps.

No. 177B differs from No. 130 in detail noted after No. 131.

Syngman Rhee and "Happiness" — A82

1952, Sept. 10 Litho. *Perf. 12½*

No.	Type	Description	Unused	Used
182	A82	1000wn dk grn	1.25	1.00

Second inauguration of President Syngman Rhee, Aug. 15, 1952.

Sok Kul Am, Near Kyongju — A83

Bool Gook Temple, Kyongju — A84

Tombstone of Mu Yal Wang — A85

Choong Yul Sa Shrine, Tongyung — A86

1952 Wmk. 257 Typo. *Perf. 12½*

No.	Type	Description	Unused	Used
183	A83	200wn henna brn	45	15
184	A84	300wn green	45	15
185	A85	500wn carmine	65	60
186	A86	2000wn dp blue	75	15

Rough Perf. 10-11, 11½x11 and Compound

Litho.

No.	Type	Description	Unused	Used
186A	A83	200wn henna brn	75	50
186B	A84	300wn green	1.25	60
		Nos. 183-186B (6)	4.30	2.15

Types of 1951

(Designs Slightly Smaller)

1952-53 *Rough Perf. 10-11*

No.	Type	Description	Unused	Used
187	A77	20wn purple	2.25	90
187A	A78	50wn green	4.50	30
187B	A79	100wn dp blue	1.75	40
187C	A80	1000wn green	52.50	4.00

(Designs Slightly Larger)

Perf. 12½

No.	Type	Description	Unused	Used
187D	A78	50wn green	1.00	50
188	A79	100wn dp blue	1.00	50
189	A80	1000wn grn ('53)	3.25	75

Type of 1952

1953

No.	Type	Description	Unused	Used
189A	A85	500wn deep blue	11.00	*50.00*

All copies of No. 189A were affixed to postal cards before sale.

See Nos. 191-192, 203B, 248.

Types of 1952 and

Planting Trees — A87

Perf. 12½

1953, Apr. 5 Wmk. 257 Litho.

No.	Type	Description	Unused	Used
190	A87	1h aqua	25	28
191	A85	2h aqua	25	32
192	A85	5h brt green	45	32
193	A87	10h brt green	65	18
194	A86	20h brown	1.40	65
		Nos. 190-194 (5)	3.00	1.75

See Nos. 203A, 247.

Map and YMCA Emblem — A88

1953, Oct. 25 *Perf. 13½*

No.	Type	Description	Unused	Used
195	A88	10h dk sl bl & red	1.25	1.25

50th anniv. of the Korean YMCA.

Tombstone of Mu Yal Wang — A88a

Sika Deer

A89 A90

1954, Apr. *Perf. 12½*

No.	Type	Description	Unused	Used
196	A88a	5h dk green	38	15
197	A89	100h brown car	7.00	50
198	A90	500h brown org	19.00	1.25
199	A90	1000h bister brn	50.00	1.50

See Nos. 203C, 203D, 238-239, 248A, 250-251, 259, 261-262, 269-270, 279, 281-282.

Dok Do (Dok Island) — A91

Design: 10h, Dok Do, lateral view.

1954, Sept. 15

No.	Type	Description	Unused	Used
200	A91	2h claret	20	15
201	A91	5h blue	42	20
202	A91	10h blue green	60	25

Moth and Flag — A92

Pagoda Park, Seoul — A92a

1954, Apr. 16 Wmk. 257 *Perf. 12½*

No.	Type	Description	Unused	Used
202A	A92	10h brown	80	50
203	A92a	30h dk blue	1.00	50

See Nos. 203E, 260, 280.

Types of 1952-54

1955-56 Unwmk. *Perf. 12½*

Laid Paper

No.	Type	Description	Unused	Used
203A	A87	1h aqua ('56)	25	20
203B	A85	2h aqua ('56)	25	20
203C	A88a	5h brt grn ('56)	25	20
203D	A89	100h brown car	3.00	75
203E	A92a	200h violet	2.50	1.00
		Nos. 203A-203E (5)	6.25	2.35

On No. 203C the right hand character is redrawn as in illustration above No. 212D.

Nos. 203A and 203C are found on horizontally and vertically laid paper.

Erosion Control on Mountainside — A93

1954, Dec. 12 Wmk. 257

No.	Type	Description	Unused	Used
204	A93	10h dk grn & yel grn	38	20
205	A93	19h dk grn & yel grn	60	40

Issued to publicize the 1954 forestation campaign.

Presidents Rhee and Eisenhower Shaking Hands — A94

1954, Dec. 25 *Perf. 13½*

No.	Type	Description	Unused	Used
206	A94	10h violet blue	40	25
207	A94	19h brown	60	40
208	A94	71h dull green	1.40	75

Issued to publicize the adoption of the United States-Korea mutual defense treaty.

"Reconstruction" — A95

Perf. 12½

1955, Feb. 10 Wmk. 257 Litho.

No.	Type	Description	Unused	Used
209	A95	10h brown	80	50
210	A95	15h violet	60	50
211	A95	20h blue	400.00	7.50
212	A95	50h plum	1.90	40

Issued to publicize Korea's industrial reconstruction.

1955, Oct. 19 Unwmk. *Perf. 12½*

Laid Paper

No.	Type	Description	Unused	Used
212A	A95	15h violet	70	35
212B	A95	20h blue	95	60
212C	A95	50h plum	1.40	35

No. 212B is found on horizontally and vertically laid paper.

Same with Right Character at Top Redrawn

Original

Redrawn

1956, June 5 Unwmk. *Perf. 12½*

Laid Paper

No.	Type	Description	Unused	Used
212D	A95	10h brown	1.25	35
212E	A95	15h violet	80	35
212F	A95	20h blue	80	30
a.		Booklet pane of 6	22.50	

Nos. 212D-212F are found on horizontally and vertically laid paper. See Nos. 248B, 256, 272, 276.

Rotary Emblem — A96

Syngman Rhee — A98

1955, Feb. 23 Wmk. 257 *Perf. 13½*

213	A96	20h	violet	55	35
214	A96	25h	dull green	70	50
215	A96	71h	magenta	95	85

Rotary International, 50th anniversary.

1955, Mar. 26

217	A98	20h	deep blue	2.75	1.75

80th birthday of Pres. Syngman Rhee, Apr. 26.

Flag and Arch of Independence — A99

1955, Aug. 15 Litho. *Perf. 13½*

218	A99	40h	Prus green	85	60
219	A99	100h	lake	1.25	90

Tenth anniversary of independence.

UN Emblem in Circle of Clasped Hands — A100

Olympic Torch and Runners — A101

1955, Oct. 24

221	A100	20h	bluish green	95	60
222	A100	55h	aqua	1.40	1.00

United Nations, 10th anniversary.

1955, Oct. 23

223	A101	20h	claret	1.00	60
224	A101	55h	dk green	1.50	1.00

36th National Athletic Meet.

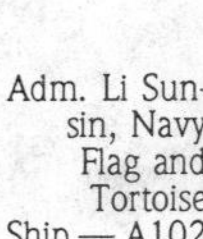

Adm. Li Sun-sin, Navy Flag and Tortoise Ship — A102

Perf. 13x13½

1955, Nov. 11 Unwmk.

Laid Paper

225	A102	20h	violet blue	1.50	1.75

Korean Navy, 10th anniversary.

Rhee Monument near Seoul — A103

Syngman Rhee — A104

1956 *Perf. 13½x13*

226	A103	20h	dull green	1.40	1.25

81st birthday of Pres. Syngman Rhee.

No. 226 is found on horizontally and vertically laid paper.

1956, Aug. 15 *Perf. 13x13½*

227	A104	20h	brown	17.50	1.10
228	A104	55h	violet blue	7.50	1.50

Third inauguration of Pres. Syngman Rhee.

Olympic Rings and Torch — A105

1956, Nov. 1 Litho. *Perf. 12½*

Laid Paper

229	A105	20h	red orange	1.10	1.00
230	A105	55h	brt green	1.90	1.75

16th Olympic Games in Melbourne, Nov. 22-Dec. 8, 1956.

Central Post Office, Seoul — A107

Stamp of 1884 — A108

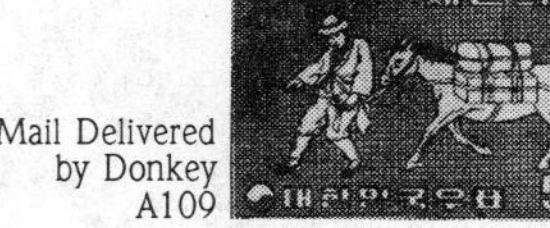

Mail Delivered by Donkey A109

1956, Dec. 4 Laid Paper Unwmk.

232	A107	20h	lt blue grn	85	60
233	A108	50h	lt carmine	1.10	90
234	A109	55h	green	1.40	1.25

Issued to commemorate Postal Day.

Types of 1954 Redrawn and

Hibiscus A110

King Sejong A111

Kyongju Observatory — A112

No Hwan Symbol; Redrawn Character

1956, Dec. 4 Unwmk. *Perf. 12½*

Laid Paper

235	A110	10h	lilac rose	75	20
236	A111	20h	lilac	1.25	20
237	A112	50h	violet	1.50	20
238	A89	100h	brown car	2.00	50
239	A90	500h	brown org	14.00	75
			Nos. 235-239 (5)	19.50	1.85

On Nos. 238-239, the character after numeral has been omitted and the last character of the inscription has been redrawn as illustrated above No. 212D.

Nos. 235-236 are found on horizontally and vertically laid paper.

See Nos. 240-242, 253, 255, 258, 273, 275, 278, 291d, 291f, B3-B4.

Types of 1956

1957, Jan. 21 Wmk. 312 *Perf. 12½*

240	A110	10h	lilac rose	45	30
241	A111	20h	red lilac	55	60
242	A112	50h	violet	1.10	30

Telecommunication Symbols — A117

1957, Jan. 31 *Perf. 13½*

243	A117	40h	lt ultra	65	50
244	A117	55h	brt green	85	75
a.			Souv. sheet of 2, #243-244, imperf.	400.00	

5th anniv. of Korea's joining the ITU.

Boy Scout and Emblem A118

1957, Feb. 27 Wmk. 312

245	A118	40h	pale purple	65	60
246	A118	55h	lt magenta	1.40	1.00
a.			Souv. sheet of 2, #245-246, imperf.	1,750.	

50th anniversary of Boy Scout movement.

Types of 1953-56

Top Right Character Redrawn; Hwan Symbol Retained

1957 Wmk. 312 *Perf. 12½*

247	A87	1h	aqua	35	20
248	A85	2h	aqua	26	25
248A	A88a	5h	brt green	70	25
248B	A95	15h	violet	1.25	40

Redrawn Types of 1954, 1956 and

Planting Trees — A119

South Gate, Seoul — A120

Tiger A121

Diamond Mountains A122

No Hwan Symbol; Redrawn Character

1957 Wmk. 312 Litho. *Perf. 12½*

249	A119	2h	aqua	24	20
250	A88a	4h	aqua	24	20
251	A88a	5h	emerald	30	20
252	A120	10h	green	30	20
253	A110	20h	lilac rose	55	20
254	A121	30h	pale lilac	55	25
255	A111	40h	red lilac	85	25
a.			Booklet pane of 6	45.00	
256	A95	50h	lake	1.50	30
257	A122	55h	violet brn	3.00	1.50
258	A112	100h	violet	2.50	40
259	A89	200h	brown car	6.75	40
260	A92a	400h	brt violet	10.50	1.25
261	A90	500h	ocher	25.00	3.50
262	A90	1000h	dk ol bis	35.00	8.00
			Nos. 249-262 (14)	87.28	16.85

The "redrawn character" is illustrated above No. 212D.

See Nos. 268, 271, 274, 277, 291c, 291e.

Miniature Sheet of 1, Imperf.

249a	A119	2h	35.00
250a	A88a	4h	35.00
252a	A120	10h	35.00
253a	A110	20h	35.00
254a	A121	30h	42.50
255b	A111	40h	35.00
257a	A122	55h	42.50
258a	A112	100h	145.00
259a	A89	200h	25.00
260a	A92a	400h	55.00

Mercury and Flags of Korea and US — A123

1957, Nov. 7 Wmk. 312 *Perf. 13½*

263	A123	40h	dp orange	45	35
264	A123	205h	emerald	1.40	90
a.			Souv. sheet of 2, #263-264, imperf.	750.00	

Treaty of friendship, commerce and navigation between Korea and the US.

Star of Bethlehem and Pine Cone — A124

Designs: 25h, Christmas tree and tassel. 30h, Christmas tree, window and dog.

1957, Dec. 11 Litho. *Perf. 12½*

265	A124	15h	org, brn & grn	95	75
a.			Souv. sheet of 1, imperf.	650.00	
266	A124	25h	lt grn, yel & red	1.10	1.00
a.			Souv. sheet of 1, imperf.	650.00	
267	A124	30h	bl, lt grn & yel	1.50	1.25
a.			Souv. sheet of 1, imperf.	650.00	

Issued for Christmas and the New Year.

Redrawn Types of 1954-57

Perf. 12½

1957-59 Litho. Wmk. 317

268	A119	2h	aqua	30	15
269	A88a	4h	aqua	30	15
270	A88a	5h	emerald ('58)	40	20
271	A120	10h	green	52	20
272	A95	15h	violet ('58)	42	20
273	A110	20h	lil rose	52	20
274	A121	30h	pale lilac ('58)	65	20
275	A111	40h	red lilac	1.40	25
276	A95	50h	lake ('58)	2.75	20
277	A122	55h	vio brn ('59)	4.00	2.25
278	A112	100h	violet	4.00	60
279	A89	200h	brn car ('59)	6.50	75
280	A92a	400h	brt vio ('59)	16.00	4.50
281	A90	500h	ocher ('58)	22.50	2.50
282	A90	1000h	dk ol bis ('58)	35.00	3.00
			Nos. 268-282 (15)	95.26	15.35

Nos. 268-282 have no hwan symbol, and final character of inscription is the redrawn one illustrated above No. 212D.

See No. 291B.

Catalogue values for unused stamps in this section, from this point to the end of the section, are for Never Hinged items.

Winged Envelope — A125

1958, May 20 **Wmk. 317**

283 A125 40h dk blue & red 1.00 60

a. Souv. sheet of 1, imperf. *1,100.*

Issued for the Second Postal Week.

Children Looking at Industrial Growth A126

Design: 40h, Hibiscus forming "10".

1958, Aug. 15 ***Perf. 13½***

284 A126 20h gray 75 30

285 A126 40h dk carmine 1.00 45

a. Souv. sheet of 2, # 284-285, imperf. 325.00

10th anniversary of Republic of Korea.

UNESCO Building, Paris A127

1958, Nov. 3 **Wmk. 317**

286 A127 40h orange & green 75 60

a. Souv. sheet of 1, imperf. 150.00

Opening of UNESCO. headquarters in Paris, Nov. 3.

Children Flying Kites — A128

Christmas Tree and Fortune Screen — A129

Children in Costume — A130

1958, Dec. 11 **Litho.** ***Perf. 12½***

287 A128 15h yellow green 75 60

a. Souv. sheet of 1, imperf. 50.00

288 A129 25h blue, red & yel 75 60

a. Souv. sheet of 1, imperf. 50.00

289 A130 30h yellow, ultra & red 1.25 85

a. Souv. sheet of 1, imperf. 50.00

Issued for Christmas and the New Year.

Flag and Pagoda Park A131

1959, Mar. 1 ***Perf. 13½***

290 A131 40h rose lilac & brn 90 50

a. Souv. sheet of 1, imperf. 20.00

40th anniv. of Independence Movement Day.

Korean Marines Landing A132

1959, Apr. 15

291 A132 40h olive grn 90 50

a. Souv. sheet of 1, imperf. 6.00

Korean Marine Corps, 10th anniversary.

Souvenir Sheet

Types of 1956-57

Wmk. 317

1959, May 20 **Litho.** ***Imperf.***

291B Sheet of 4 6.00 7.50

c. A120 10h green 90 50

d. A110 20h lilac rose 90 50

e. A121 30h pale lilac 90 50

f. A111 40h red lilac 90 50

3rd Postal Week, May 20-26.

WHO Emblem and Family A133

1959, Aug. 17 **Wmk. 317** ***Perf. 13½***

292 A133 40h pink & rose vio 65 35

a. Souv. sheet of 1, imperf. 6.00

10th anniv. of Korea's joining the WHO.

Diesel Train A134

1959, Sept. 18 **Litho.**

293 A134 40h brown & bister 80 50

a. Souv. sheet of 1, imperf. 6.00

60th anniversary of Korean railroads.

Relay Race and Emblem A135

1959, Oct. 3

294 A135 40h lt bl & red brn 80 60

a. Souv. sheet of 1, imperf. 7.00

40th National Athletic Meet.

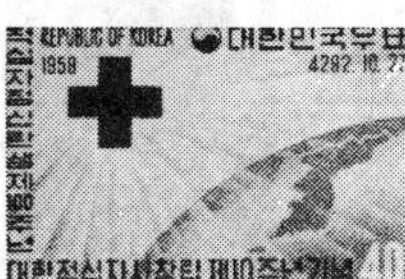

Red Cross and Korea Map — A136

Design: 55h, Red Cross superimposed on globe.

1959, Oct. 27 ***Perf. 13½***

295 A136 40h red & bl grn 50 20

296 A136 55h pale lilac & red 75 30

a. Souv. sheet of 2, #295-296, imperf. 15.00

Centenary of the Red Cross idea.

Old Postal Flag and New Communications Flag — A137

1959, Dec. 4

297 A137 40h blue & red 80 50

a. Souv. sheet of 1, imperf. 7.00

75th anniv. of the Korean postal system.

Mice and Chinese Happy New Year Character — A138

Designs: 25h, Children singing Christmas hymns. 30h, Red-crested crane.

1959, Dec. 15 ***Perf. 12½***

298 A138 15h gray, vio bl & pink 50 30

a. Souv. sheet of 1, imperf. 9.00

299 A138 25h blue, red & emer 60 30

a. Souv. sheet of 1, imperf. 9.00

300 A138 30h lt lilac, blk & red 75 30

a. Souv. sheet of 1, imperf. 9.00

Issued for Christmas and the New Year.

UPU Monument and Means of Transportation A139

Perf. 13½

1960, Jan. 1 **Wmk. 317** **Litho.**

301 A139 40h grnsh bl & brn 65 35

a. Souv. sheet of 1, imperf. 7.00

60th anniv. of Korean membership in the UPU.

Bee, Honeycomb and Clover — A140

Snail and Money Bag — A141

1960, Apr. 1 **Wmk. 317** ***Perf. 12½***

302 A140 10h emer, brn & org 20 15

303 A141 20h pink, bl & brn 40 25

Issued to encourage systematic saving by children. See No. 313, souvenir sheet.

See Nos. 377-380.

Uprooted Oak Emblem and Yin Yang A142

Dwight D. Eisenhower A143

1960, Apr. 7 **Wmk. 312** ***Perf. 13½***

304 A142 40h emer, car & ultra 65 35

a. Souv. sheet of 1, imperf. 15.00

Issued to publicize World Refugee Year, July 1, 1959-June 30, 1960.

1960, June 19 **Litho.** **Wmk. 317**

305 A143 40h bl, red & bluish grn 1.40 75

a. Souv. sheet of 1, imperf. 8.50

Pres. Eisenhower's visit to Korea, June 19.

Children in School and Ancient Home Teaching A144

1960, Aug. 3 **Wmk. 317** ***Perf. 13½***

306 A144 40h cit, cl & org brn 65 35

a. Souv. sheet of 1, imperf. 3.00

75th anniv. of the modern educational system.

Hibiscus and House of Councilors A145

1960, Aug. 8

307 A145 40h blue 65 35

a. Souv. sheet of 1, imperf. 3.00

Inaugural session, House of Councilors.

Woman Holding Torch and Man with Flag — A146

1960, Aug. 15

308 A146 40h bis, lt bl & brn 55 35

a. Souv. sheet of 1, imperf. 2.75

15th anniversary of liberation.

Weight Lifter — A147

Design: 40h, South Gate, Seoul, and Olympic emblem.

1960, Aug. 25 **Litho.**

309 A147 20h brn, lt bl & sal 42 25

310 A147 40h brn, lt bl & dk bl 80 40

a. Souv. sheet of 2, #309-310, imperf. 7.00

Issued to commemorate the 17th Olympic Games, Rome, Aug. 25-Sept. 11.

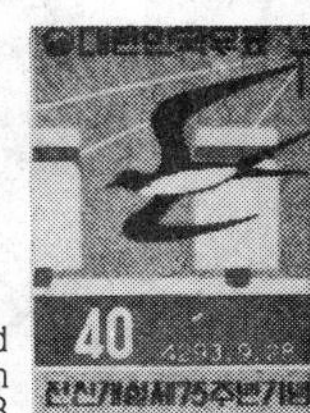

Swallow and Telegraph Pole — A148

1960, Sept. 28 ***Perf. 13½***

311 A148 40h lt bl, lil & gray 65 35

a. Souv. sheet of 1, imperf. 2.00

75th anniv. of the establishment of telegraph service.

Students and Sprout
A149

1960, Oct. 1 **Wmk. 317**
312 A149 40h bl, sal pink & emer 65 35
a. Souv. sheet of 1, imperf. 2.00

Rebirth of the Republic.

Souvenir Sheet
Savings Types of 1960

1960, Oct. 7 ***Imperf.***
313 Sheet of two 1.75 1.75
a. A140 10h emer, brn & org 75 75
b. A141 20h pink, bl & brn 75 75

4th Postal Week, Oct. 7-13, and Intl. Letter Writing Week, Oct. 3-9.

Torch — A150

1960, Oct. 15 ***Perf. 13½***
314 A150 40h dk bl, lt bl & yel 65 35
a. Souv. sheet of 1, imperf. 2.00

Cultural Month (October).

UN Flag, Globe and Laurel — A151

UN Emblem and Grave Markers — A152

1960, Oct. 24 **Litho.**
315 A151 40h rose lil, bl & grn 65 35
a. Souv. sheet of 1, imperf. 2.75

15th anniversary of United Nations.

1960, Nov. 1 **Wmk. 317**
316 A152 40h salmon & brn 65 35
a. Souv. sheet of 1, imperf. 2.50

Establishment of the UN Memorial Cemetery, Tanggok, Pusan, Korea.

"Housing, Agriculture, Population"
A153

1960, Nov. 15 ***Perf. 13½***
317 A153 40h multicolored 65 35
a. Souv. sheet of 1, imperf. 2.00

Issued to publicize the 1960 census.

Boy and Head of Ox — A154

Star of Bethlehem and Korean Sock — A155

Girl Giving New Year's Greeting — A156

1960, Dec. 15 **Litho.** ***Perf. 12½***
318 A154 15h gray, brn & org yel 40 30
a. Souv. sheet of 1, imperf. 4.00
319 A155 25h vio bl, red & grn 50 30
a. Souv. sheet of 1, imperf. 4.00
320 A156 30h red, vio bl & yel 60 40
a. Souv. sheet of 1, imperf. 4.00

Issued for Christmas and the New Year.

UN Emblem, Windsock and Ancient Rain Gauge
A157

1961, Mar. 23 ***Perf. 13½***
321 A157 40h lt blue & ultra 65 35
a. Souv. sheet of 1, imperf. 1.40

1st World Meteorological Day.

Children, Globe and UN Emblem
A158

1961, Apr. 7 **Wmk. 317**
322 A158 40h salmon & brown 65 35
a. Souv. sheet of 1, imperf. 1.40

10th World Health Day.

Students Demonstrating
A159

1961, Apr. 19 **Litho.**
323 A159 40h red, grn & ultra 75 40
a. Souv. sheet of 1, imperf. 2.00

1st anniv. of the Korean April revolution.

Workers — A160

1961, May 6
324 A160 40h brt green 60 35
a. Souv. sheet of 1, imperf. 2.00

International Conference on Community Development, Seoul.

Girl Scout
A161

1961, May 10
325 A161 40h brt green 75 50
a. Souv. sheet of 1, imperf. 6.00

15th anniversary of Korea's Girl Scouts.

Soldier's Grave — A162

Soldier with Torch — A163

Perf. 13½

1961, June 6 **Wmk. 317** **Litho.**
326 A162 40h blk & ol gray 75 35
a. Souv. sheet of 1, imperf. 2.00

6th National Mourning Day.

1961, June 16
327 A163 40h brown & yellow 75 50
a. Souv. sheet of 1, imperf. 2.00

Military Revolution of May 16, 1961.

Map of Korea, Torch and Broken Chain — A164

1961, Aug. 15 **Wmk. 317** ***Perf. 13½***
328 A164 40h dk bl, ver & aqua 75 50
a. Souv. sheet of 1, imperf. 1.40

16th anniv. of liberation.

Flag and Servicemen
A165

1961, Oct. 1 **Litho.**
329 A165 40h vio bl, red & brn 65 50
a. Souv. sheet of 1, imperf. 1.40

Issued for Armed Forces Day.

Kyongbok Palace Art Museum — A166

1961, Nov. 1 **Wmk. 317** ***Perf. 13½***
330 A166 40h beige & dk brn 65 35
a. Souv. sheet of 1, imperf. 1.40

10th Natl. Exhibition of Fine Arts.

"UNESCO," Candle and Laurel
A167

1961, Nov. 4
331 A167 40h lt grn & dk bl 65 35
a. Souv. sheet of 1, imperf. 1.40

15th anniv. of UNESCO.

Mobile X-Ray Unit — A168

1961, Nov. 16
332 A168 40h rose beige & red brn 65 35
a. Souv. sheet of 1, imperf. 1.40

Tuberculosis Prevention Week.

Ginseng
A169

King Sejong and Hangul Alphabet
A170

Tristram's Woodpecker
A171

Rice Farmer
A172

Ancient Drums — A173

1961-62 **Unwmk.** **Litho.** ***Perf. 12½***
338 A169 20h rose brn ('62) 1.00 25
339 A170 30h pale pur 1.25 25
340 A171 40h dk blue & red 1.25 25
341 A172 40h dk green ('62) 1.50 25
342 A173 100h red brown 1.50 60
Nos. 338-342 (5) 6.50 1.60

See #363-366, 368, 388-392, 517-519, B5-B7.

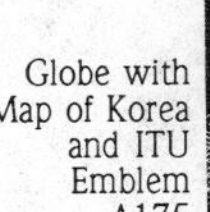

Globe with Map of Korea and ITU Emblem
A175

1962, Jan. 31 **Unwmk.** ***Perf. 13½***
348 A175 40h ver & dk blue 75 35
a. Souv. sheet of 1, imperf. 2.00

10th anniv. of Korea's joining the ITU.

Atomic Reactor and Atom Symbol
A176

1962, Mar. 30 **Litho.** ***Perf. 13½***
349 A176 40h lt bl, sl grn & ol gray 50 35

Inauguration of the Triga Mark II atomic reactor.

Malaria Eradication Emblem and Mosquito A177

1962, Apr. 7 **Unwmk.**

350 A177 40h green & red org 65 40
a. Souv. sheet of 1, imperf. 1.50

WHO drive to eradicate malaria.

YWCA Emblem and Girl — A178

1962, Apr. 20 ***Perf. 13½***

351 A178 40h pink & dk blue 65 40

40th anniv. of the Korean Young Women's Christian Association.

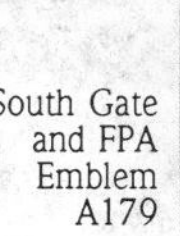

South Gate and FPA Emblem A179

1962, May 12 **Wmk. 317**

352 A179 40h lt bl, dk vio & red 60 35

Meeting of the Federation of Motion Picture Producers in Asia, May 12-16.

Men Pushing Cogwheel A180

Soldiers on Hang Kang Bridge — A181

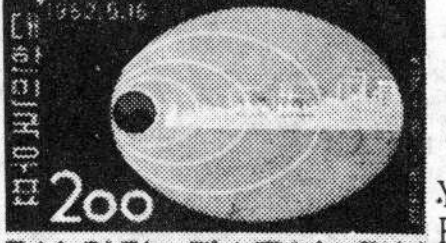

Yin Yang and Factory A182

Perf. 13½

1962, May 16 **Wmk. 317** **Litho.**

353 A180 30h brn & pale olive 1.40 50
a. Souv. sheet of 1, Korean text 4.50
b. Souv. sheet of 1, English text 22.50
354 A181 40h brn, lt bl & cit 1.40 50
a. Souv. sheet of 1, Korean text 4.50
b. Souv. sheet of 1, English text 22.50
355 A182 200h ultra, yel & red 2.75 75
a. Souv. sheet of 1, Korean text 4.50
b. Souv. sheet of 1, English text 22.50

1st anniv. of the May 16th Revolution.

The souvenir sheets are imperf.

The sheets with English text also exist with "E" in "POSTAGE" omitted. The English-text sheets are not watermarked except those with "E" omitted. Value, each $20.

Tortoise Warship, 16th Century A183

Design: 4w, Tortoise ship, heading right.

1962, Aug. 14 **Unwmk.** ***Perf. 13½***

356 A183 2w dk bl & pale bl 1.25 75
357 A183 4w blk, bluish grn & lil 2.25 1.25

370th anniv. of Korea's victory in the naval battle with the Japanese off Hansan Island.

Flag, Scout Emblem and Tents — A184

Perf. 13½

1962, Oct. 5 **Wmk. 312** **Litho.**

358 A184 4w brown, bl & red 75 40
a. Souv. sheet of 1, imperf., unwmkd. 1.75

Wmk. 317

359 A184 4w green, bl & red 75 40
a. Souv. sheet of 1, imperf., unwmkd. 1.75

40th anniv. of Korean Boy Scouts.

Types of 1961-62 and

Hanabusaya Asiatica — A185

Miruk Bosal — A186

Long-horned Beetle A186a

Symbols of Thrift and Development A186b

Meesun Blossoms and Fruit A186c

Library of Early Buddhist Scriptures A186d

Sika Deer — A186e

King Songdok Bell, 8th Cent. — A186f

Bodhisattva in Cavern Temple, Silla Dynasty — A187

Tile of Silla Dynasty — A187a

Designs: 20ch, Jin-Do dog. 1w, Folk dancers. 1.50w, Miruk Bosal. 2w, Ginseng. 3w, King Sejong. 4w, Rice farmer. 5w, Dragon waterpot. 10w, Ancient drums. 500w, Blue dragon fresco, Koguryo dynasty.

1962-66 **Unwmk.** **Litho.** ***Perf. 12½***

Ordinary Paper

Size: 22x25mm, 25x22mm

360 A186 20ch gldn brown 2.50 65
361 A185 40ch blue 2.50 65
362 A186 50ch claret brn 2.50 65
363 A169 1w brt blue ('63) 3.00 65
364 A169 2w red brown 3.00 65
365 A170 3w violet brown 3.75 65
366 A172 4w green 5.00 75
367 A186 5w grnsh blue 5.00 1.00
368 A173 10w red brown 27.50 1.50
369 A186c 20w lil rose ('63) 15.00 3.00
370 A186d 40w dl pur ('63) 40.00 5.00
Nos. 360-370 (11) 109.75 15.15

1964-66

Granite Paper

360a A186 20ch orange brn 2.50 40
361a A185 40ch blue 2.50 40
362a A186 50ch claret brn 2.50 40
362B A186a 60ch black ('66) 2.50 40
363a A169 1w bright blue 2.50 40
363B A186 1.50w dk sl grn ('66) 2.50 40
364a A169 2w red brown 2.50 40
365a A170 3w vio brown 6.00 40
366a A172 4w green 2.50 40
367a A186 5w grnsh blue 10.00 40
367B A186b 7w lilac rose ('66) 5.00 75
368a A173 10w red brown 6.25 75
369a A186c 20w lilac rose 6.25 75
370a A186d 40w vio brown 21.00 1.50
371 A186e 50w red brown 10.00 1.50
372 A186f 100w slate grn 40.00 1.50
373 A187 200w dk & lt grn ('65) 21.00 2.00
374 A187a 300w sl grn & buff ('65) 30.00 3.50
374A A187a 500w dk & lt bl ('65) 45.00 5.00
Nos. 360a-374A (19) 220.50 21.25

The paper of Nos. 360a to 374A contains a few colored fibers; the paper of Nos. 385-396 contains many fibers.

Counterfeits exist of Nos. 369a, 370a and 371.

See Nos. 385-396, 516, 521-522, 582-584, 1076-1079, B8.

Map, Mackerel and Trawler A188

1962, Oct. 10 ***Perf. 13½***

375 A188 4w dk bl & grnsh bl 52 40

10th anniv. of the Pacific Fishery Council.

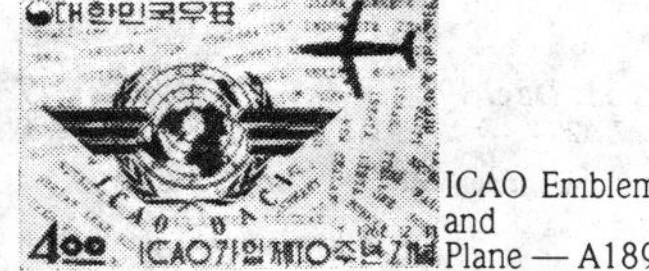

ICAO Emblem and Plane — A189

1962, Dec. 11 ***Perf. 13½***

376 A189 4w blue & brown 65 40
a. Souv. sheet of 1, imperf. 1.75

10th anniv. of Korea's joining the ICAO.

Savings Types of 1960

1962-64 **Unwmk.** ***Perf. 12½***

377 A140 1w emer, brn & org ('63) 1.25 50
a. Granite paper 25.00 65
378 A141 2w pink, bl & brn 1.65 75
a. Granite paper 12.00 75

Wmk. 317

379 A140 1w emer, brn & org ('64) 6.50 4.00
380 A141 2w pink, bl & brn ('64) 3.00 1.25

Wheat Emblem A190

Perf. 13½

1963, Mar. 21 **Wmk. 317** **Litho.**

381 A190 4w emer, dk bl & ocher 52 30
a. Souv. sheet of 1, imperf. 1.20

FAO "Freedom from Hunger" campaign.

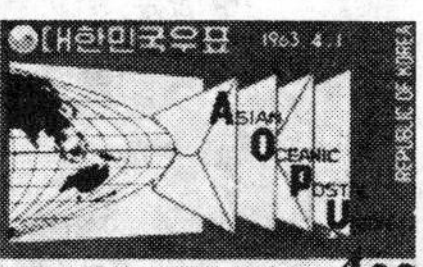

Globe and Letters A191

1963, Apr. 1

382 A191 4w rose lil, ol & dk bl 52 30
a. Souv. sheet of 1, imperf. 1.20

1st anniv. of the formation of the Asian-Oceanic Postal Union, AOPU.

Centenary Emblem and World Map — A192

1963, May 8 **Litho.**

383 A192 4w org, red & gray 70 30
384 A192 4w lt bl, red & gray 70 30
a. Souv. sheet of 2, #383-384, imperf. 2.00

Cent. of the Intl. Red Cross.

Types of 1961-63

Designs: 20ch, Jin-Do dog. 40ch, Hanabusaya. 50ch, Miruk Bosal. 1w, Folk dancers. 2w, Ginseng. 3w, King Sejong. 4w, Rice farmer. 10w, Ancient drums. 20w, Meesun blossoms and fruit. 40w, Library of early Buddhist scriptures. 50w, Deer. 100w, King Songdok bell, 8th century.

1963-64 **Wmk. 317** ***Perf. 12½***

Granite Paper

Size: 22x25mm, 25x22mm

385 A186 20ch gldn brn ('64) 90 25
386 A185 40ch blue 90 25
387 A186 50ch cl brn ('64) 90 25
388 A169 1w brt blue 1.25 35
389 A169 2w red brown 1.25 35
390 A170 3w vio brown 2.50 35
391 A172 4w green 2.50 60
392 A173 10w red brown 5.50 60
393 A186c 20w lil rose ('64) 6.00 1.75
394 A186d 40w dull purple 18.00 1.50
395 A186e 50w brown 18.00 2.00
396 A186f 100w slate grn 37.50 4.00
Nos. 385-396 (12) 95.20 12.25

Hibiscus and "15" A193

1963, Aug. 15 **Wmk. 317** ***Perf. 13½***

398 A193 4w vio bl, pale bl & red 75 35

15th anniversary of the Republic.

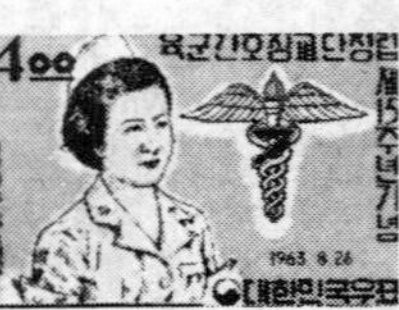

Army Nurse and Corps Emblem A194

1963, Aug. 26 **Litho.**

399 A194 4w citron, grn & blk 65 35

Army Nurses Corps, 15th anniversary.

First Five-Year Plan Issue

Transformer and Power Transmission Tower — A195

Irrigated Rice Fields — A196

Designs: No. 402, Cement factory. No. 403, Coal Miner. No. 404, Oil refinery. No. 405, Fishing industry (ships). No. 406, Cargo ship and cargo. No. 407, Fertilizer plant and grain. No. 408, Radar and telephone. No. 409, Transportation (plane, train, ship and map).

1962-66 **Unwmk.** ***Perf. 12½***

400 A195 4w org & dk vio 1.40 70
401 A196 4w lt bl & vio bl 1.40 70

Wmk. 317

402 A195 4w dk bl & gray 1.40 70
403 A196 4w buff & brn 1.40 70
404 A195 4w yel & ultra 1.10 55
405 A196 4w lt bl & blk 1.10 55

Unwmk.

406 A195 4w pale pink & vio bl 1.00 55
407 A196 4w bis brn & blk 1.00 55
408 A195 7w yel bis & blk 1.25 55
409 A196 7w vio bl & lt bl 1.25 55
Nos. 400-409 (10) 12.30 6.10

Issued to publicize the Economic Development Five-Year Plan.

Issue dates: Nos. 400-401, Dec. 28, 1962. Nos. 402-403, Sept. 1, 1963. Nos. 404-405, June 15, 1964. Nos. 406-407, June 1, 1965. Nos. 408-409, June 1, 1966.

Ramses Temple, Abu Simbel
A197 A198

Perf. 13½

1963, Oct. 1 **Wmk. 317** **Litho.**

410 A197 3w gray & ol gray 75 30
411 A198 4w gray & ol gray 90 50
a. Souv. sheet of 2, #410-411, imperf. 2.50
b. Pair, #410-411 1.75 1.25

UNESCO world campaign to save historic monuments in Nubia.

Rugby and Torch Bearer A199

1963, Oct. 4 **Wmk. 317** ***Perf. 13½***

412 A199 4w pale bl, red brn & dk grn 75 40

44th National Athletic Games.

Nurse & Mobile X-Ray Unit — A200

Eleanor Roosevelt — A201

1963, Nov. 6 ***Perf. 13½***

413 A200 4w org & bluish blk 60 35

10h anniv. of the Korean Natl. Tuberculosis Association.

1963, Dec. 10 **Litho.** **Wmk. 317**

Design: 4w, Hands holding torch and globe.

414 A201 3w lt red brn & dk bl 45 25
415 A201 4w dl org, ol & dk bl 70 40
a. Souv. sheet of 2, 414-415, imperf. 1.75

Issued to honor Eleanor Roosevelt on the 15th anniv. of the Universary Declaration of Human Rights.

Korean Flag and UN Headquarters A202

Tang-piri (Recorder) A203

1963, Dec. 12 **Wmk. 317** ***Perf. 13½***

416 A202 4w grnsh bl, ol & blk 65 35
a. Souv. sheet of 1, imperf. 1.75

15th anniv. of Korea's recognition by the UN.

1963, Dec. 17 **Unwmk.**

Musical Instruments: No. 418, Pyen-kyeng (chimes). No. 419, Chang-ko (drums). No. 420, Tai-keum (large flute). No. 421, Taipyeng-so (Chinese oboe). No. 422, Na-bal (brass trumpet). No. 423, Hyang-pipa (Chinese short lute). No. 424, Wul-keum (banjo). No. 425, Kaya-ko (zither), horiz. No. 426, Wa-kong-hu (harp), horiz.

417 A203 4w pink, blk & car 1.25 35
418 A203 4w bl, bl grn & blk 1.25 35
419 A203 4w rose, vio bl & brn 1.25 35
420 A203 4w tan, dk grn & brn 1.25 35
421 A203 4w yel, vio bl & brn 1.25 35
422 A203 4w gray, brn & vio 1.25 35
423 A203 4w pink, vio bl & red brn 1.25 35
424 A203 4w grnsh bl, blk & bl 1.25 35
425 A203 4w rose, red brn & blk 1.25 35
426 A203 4w lil, blk & bl 1.25 35
Nos. 417-426 (10) 12.50 3.50

Pres. Park and Capitol A204

1963, Dec. 17 **Wmk. 317**

427 A204 4w blk & brt grn 16.00 1.00

Inauguration of Pres. Park Chung Hee.

Symbols of Metric System A205

1964, Jan. 1 **Litho.**

428 A205 4w multicolored 52 35
a. Imperf., pair 75.00

Introduction of the metric system.

UNESCO Emblem and Yin Yang — A206

1964, Jan. 30 **Wmk. 317** ***Perf. 13½***

429 A206 4w red, lt bl & ultra 52 30

10th anniversary of the Korean National Commission for UNESCO.

Industrial Census A207

1964, Mar. 23 **Wmk. 317** ***Perf. 13½***

430 A207 4w gray, blk & red brn 60 35

National Mining and Industrial Census.

YMCA Emblem and Head — A208

1964, Apr. 12 **Litho.**

431 A208 4w ap grn, dk bl & red 60 35

50th anniv. of the Korean YMCA.

Unisphere, Ginseng and Cargo Ship — A209

Design: 100w, Korean pavilion and globe.

1964, Apr. 22 **Wmk. 317** ***Perf. 13½***

432 A209 40w buff, red brn & grn 3.50 60
433 A209 100w bl red brn & ultra 5.50 1.75
a. Souv. sheet of 1, imperf. 10.00

New York World's Fair, 1964-65.

Secret Garden, Changdok Palace, Seoul — A210

Views: 2w, Whahong Gate, Suwon. 3w, Uisang Pavilion, Yangyang-gun. 4w, Maitreya Buddha, Bopju Temple at Mt. Songni. 5w, Paekma River and Rock of Falling Flowers. 6w, Anab Pond, Kyongju. 7w, Choksok Pavilion, Chinju. 8w, Kwanghan Pavilion. 9w, Whaom Temple, Mt. Chiri. 10w, Chonjeyon Falls, Soguipo.

1964, May 25 **Wmk. 317** ***Perf. 13½***

Light Blue Background

434 A210 1w green 50 15
435 A210 2w gray 50 15
436 A210 3w dk green 90 25
437 A210 4w emerald 90 25
438 A210 5w violet 1.25 25
439 A210 6w vio blue 1.75 30
a. Souv. sheet of 2 (5w, 6w) 3.25
440 A210 7w dk brown 1.75 30
a. Souv. sheet of 2 (4w, 7w) 3.25
441 A210 8w brown 1.75 35
a. Souv. sheet of 2 (3w, 8w) 3.25
442 A210 9w lt violet 3.25 50
a. Souv. sheet of 2 (2w, 9w) 4.00
443 A210 10w slate grn 3.25 60
a. Souv. sheet of 2 (1w, 10w) 4.00
Nos. 434-443 (10) 15.80 3.10
Nos. 439a-443a (5) 17.75

The five souvenir sheets are imperf.

Globe and Wheel A211

1964, July 1 **Litho.** ***Perf. 13½***

444 A211 4w lt ol grn, dl brn & ocher 65 35
a. Souv. sheet of 1, imperf. 1.40

Issued to honor the Colombo Plan for co-operative economic development of south and southeast Asia.

Hands and World Health Organization Emblem A212

1964, Aug. 17 **Wmk. 317** ***Perf. 13½***

445 A212 4w brt yel grn, yel grn & blk 65 35
a. Souv. sheet of 1, imperf. 1.40

15th anniv. of Korea's joining the UN.

Runner A213

1964, Sept. 3

446 A213 4w red lil, grn & pink 75 35

45th Natl. Athletic Meet, Inchon, Sept. 3-8.

UPU Monument, Bern A214

1964, Sept. 15

447 A214 4w pink, red brn & bl 65 40
a. Souv. sheet of 1, imperf. 1.40

90th anniv. of the 1st Intl. Cong. for establishing the UPU.

Crane Hook and Emblem — A215

1964, Sept. 29 **Wmk. 317** ***Perf. 13½***

448 A215 4w red brn & dull grn 52 35

5th Convention of the Intl. Federation of Asian and Western Pacific Contractors' Assoc. (IFAWPCA), Seoul, Sept. 29-Oct. 7.

Marathon Runners A216

Design: No. 453, "V," Olympic rings, laurel and track, vert.

1964, Oct. 10 **Litho.**

449	A216	4w	shown	65	25
450	A216	4w	Equestrian	65	25
451	A216	4w	Gymnast	65	25
452	A216	4w	Rowing	65	25
453	A216	4w	multicolored	65	25
			Nos. 449-453 (5)	3.25	1.25

18th Olympic Games, Tokyo, Oct. 10-25.

Souvenir Sheets of 1, Imperf., Unwmk.

449a	A216	4w	90
450a	A216	4w	90
451a	A216	4w	90
452a	A216	4w	90
453a	A216	4w	90
	Nos. 449a-453a (5)		4.50

Stamp of 1885 — A217

Yong Sik Hong — A218

1964, Dec. 4 **Unwmk.** ***Perf. 13½***

454	A217 3w lil, vio & dl bl grn	60	35
455	A218 4w gray, vio bl & blk	80	50

80th anniv. of the Korean postal system. Yong Sik Hong (1855-84) was Korea's 1st general postmaster.

Pine Branch and Cones — A219

Designs: No. 457, Plum Blossoms. No. 458, Forsythia. No. 459, Azalea. No. 460, Lilac. No. 461, Sweetbrier. No. 462, Garden balsam. No. 463, Hibiscus. No. 464, Crape myrtle. No. 465, Chrysanthemum lucidum. No. 466, Paulownia coreana. No. 467, Bamboo.

1965 **Litho.** ***Perf. 13½***

456	A219	4w	pale grn, dp grn & brn	60	18
457	A219	4w	gray, blk, rose & yel	60	18
458	A219	4w	lt bl, yel & brn	60	18
459	A219	4w	brt grn, lil rose & sal	75	18
460	A219	4w	red lil & brt grn	60	15
461	A219	4w	yel grn, grn, car & brn	60	18
462	A219	4w	bl, grn & red	60	18
463	A219	4w	bluish gray, rose red & grn	60	18
464	A219	4w	multicolored	65	15
465	A219	4w	pale grn, dk brn, grn & car rose	75	15
466	A219	4w	buff, ol grn & brn	75	15
467	A219	4w	ultra & emer	65	15
			Nos. 456-467 (12)	7.75	2.01

Souvenir Sheets of 1, Imperf.

456a	A219	4w	90
457a	A219	4w	90
458a	A219	4w	90
459a	A219	4w	90
460a	A219	4w	90
461a	A219	4w	90
462a	A219	4w	90
463a	A219	4w	90
464a	A219	4w	90
465a	A219	4w	90
466a	A219	4w	90
467a	A219	4w	90
	Nos. 456a-467a (12)		10.80

Dancing Women, PATA Emblem and Tabo Tower A220

1965, Mar. 26

468 A220 4w lt bl grn, dk brn & dk vio bl — 65 35
a. Souv. sheet of 1, imperf. — 1.10

14th conf. of the Pacific Travel Association, Seoul, Mar. 26-Apr. 2.

Map of Viet Nam and Flag of Korean Assistance Group A221

1965, Apr. 20 ***Perf. 13½***

469 A221 4w blk, lt yel grn & grnsh bl — 65 35
a. Souv. sheet of 1, imperf. — 1.10

Issued to honor the Korean military assistance group in Viet Nam.

Symbols of 7-Year Plan — A222

1965, May 1 **Litho.**

470 A222 4w emer, dk grn & dk brn — 40 25

Issued to publicize the 7-year plan for increased food production.

Scales with Families and Homes A223

1965, May 8

471 A223 4w lt & dk grn & gray — 45 30
a. Souv. sheet of 1, imperf. — 1.10

May as Month of Family Planning.

ITU Emblem, Old and New Communication Equipment — A224

1965, May 17

472 A224 4w lt bl, car & blk — 45 30
a. Souv. sheet of 1, imperf. — 1.10

Cent. of the ITU.

UN Emblem and Flags of Australia, Belgium, Great Britain, Canada and Colombia A225

Gen. Douglas MacArthur and Flags of Korea, UN and US — A226

UN Emblem and Flags: No. 474, Denmark, Ethiopia, France, Greece and India. No. 475, Italy, Luxembourg, Netherlands, New Zealand and Norway. No. 476, Philippines, Sweden, Thailand, Turkey and South Africa.

1965, June 25

Flags in Original Colors

473	A225	4w	gray & vio bl	40	15
474	A225	4w	grnsh bl & vio bl	40	15
475	A225	4w	grnsh bl & vio bl	40	15
476	A225	4w	grnsh bl & vio bl	40	15
477	A226	10w	lt bl, blk, vio bl & red	75	45
			Nos. 473-477 (5)	2.35	1.05

15th anniv. of the participation of UN Forces in the Korean war.

Souvenir Sheets of 1, Imperf.

473a	A225	4w	50
474a	A225	4w	50
475a	A225	4w	50
476a	A225	4w	50
477a	A226	10w	1.10
	Nos. 473a-477a (5)		3.10

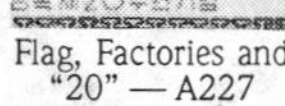

Flag, Factories and "20" — A227

South Gate, Seoul, Fireworks and Yin Yang — A228

1965, Aug. 15 **Litho.**

478 A227 4w lt bl, vio bl & red — 30 20
479 A228 10w vio bl, lt bl & red — 75 40

20th anniv. of liberation from the Japanese.

Factory, Leaf and Ants — A229

1965, Sept. 20 ***Perf. 13½***

480 A229 4w brt yel grn, brn & bis — 52 30

Issued to publicize the importance of saving.

Parabolic Antenna, Telephone Dial and Punched Tape — A230

Telegraph Operator, 1885 A231

1965, Sept. 28

481 A230 3w lt bl, blk & ol — 30 20
482 A231 10w cit, Prus bl & blk — 60 35

80th anniv. of telegraph service between Seoul and Inchon.

Korean Flag and Capitol, Seoul — A232

1965, Sept. 28

483 A232 3w org, sl grn & bl grn — 65 25

15th anniversary of recapture of Seoul.

Pole Vault A233

1965, Oct. 5

484 A233 3w blk, lil & sal — 55 25

Issued to publicize the 46th National Athletic Meet, Kwangju, Oct. 5-10.

ICY Emblem A234

UN Flag and Headquarters, NY — A235

1965, Oct. 24 **Litho.**

485 A234 3w lt & dk grn & org brn — 40 25
a. Souv. sheet of 1, imperf. — 95
486 A235 10w lt bl, vio bl & grn — 70 40
a. Souv. sheet of 1, imperf. — 1.10

ICY, 1965, and 20th anniv. of the UN.

Child Posting Letter A236

Design: 10w, Airmail envelope, telephone.

1965, Dec. 4 ***Perf. 13½***

487 A236 3w bl grn, blk, grn & red — 40 20
488 A236 10w ol, dk bl & red — 70 35

Tenth Communications Day.

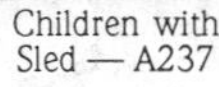

Children with Sled — A237

Children and South Gate — A238

1965, Dec. 11 Litho. *Perf. 12½*
489 A237 3w pale grn, vio bl & red 35 25
490 A238 4w lt bl, grn, vio bl & red 85 60
a. Souv. sheet of 2, #489-490, imperf. 1.25

Issued for Christmas and the New Year.

Freedom House — A239

1966, Feb. 15 Unwmk. *Perf. 12½*
491 A239 7w brt grn, blk & cit 75 30
492 A239 39w lil, blk & pale grn 1.65 65
a. Souv. sheet of 1, imperf. 3.50

Opening of "Freedom House" at Panmunjom.

Wildlife Issue

Mandarin Ducks — A240

Alaska Pollack — A241

Firefly — A242

Badger — A243

Birds: 5w, Japanese cranes. 7w, Ringnecked pheasants.

1966, Mar. 15 Litho. *Perf. 12½*
493 A240 3w multicolored 85 25
494 A240 5w multicolored 1.25 30
495 A240 7w multicolored 1.50 35

1966, June 15

Fish: 5w, Manchurian trout. 7w, Yellow corvina.

496 A241 3w bl, dk brn & yel 85 20
497 A241 5w grnsh bl, blk & mag 1.10 25
498 A241 7w brt grnsh bl, blk & yel 1.50 30

1966, Sept. 15

Insects: 5w, Grasshopper. 7w, Silk butterfly (sericinus telamon).

499 A242 3w multicolored 75 20
500 A242 5w dp yellow & multi 1.00 25
501 A242 7w lt blue & multi 1.50 30

1966, Dec. 15

Animals: 5w, Asiatic black bear. 7w, Tiger.

502 A243 3w multicolored 75 20
503 A243 5w multicolored 1.00 25
504 A243 7w multicolored 1.10 30
Nos. 493-504 (12) 13.15 3.15

Souvenir Sheets of 1, Imperf.

493a	A240	3w	1.25
494a	A240	5w	1.90
495a	A240	7w	2.25
496a	A241	3w	1.25
497a	A241	5w	1.65
498a	A241	7w	2.25
499a	A242	3w	1.10
500a	A242	5w	1.50
501a	A242	7w	2.25
502a	A243	3w	1.10
503a	A243	5w	1.50
504a	A243	7w	1.65
Nos. 493a-504a (12)			19.65

Hwansung-gun and Kwangnung Forests — A244

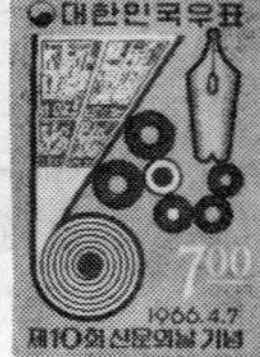
Symbolic Newspaper Printing and Pen — A245

1966, Apr. 5 Unwmk. *Perf. 12½*
505 A244 7w green & brown 40 20

Forestation Movement.

1966, Apr. 7 Litho.
506 A245 7w lt bl, vio brn & yel 40 20

Tenth Newspaper Day.

Children and Bell — A246

1966, May 1 Unwmk. *Perf. 12½*
507 A246 7w org, grn & bl 40 20

Proper guidance of young people.

WHO Headquarters, Geneva — A247

1966, May 3 Litho.
508 A247 7w lt bl, blk & yel 65 15
a. Souv. sheet of 1, imperf. 1.25
509 A247 39w bluish gray, yel & red 2.00 45

Inauguration of the WHO Headquarters, Geneva.

Girl Scout and Flag — A248

1966, May 10
510 A248 7w yel, emer & dk bl 1.00 40

Girl Scouts of Korea, 20th anniversary.

Pres. Park and Flags of Korea, Malaysia, Thailand and China — A249

1966, May 10
511 A249 7w multicolored 1.00 50

State visit of President Chung Hee Park to Malaysia, Thailand and China.

Women's Ewha University, Seoul, and Student A250

1966, May 31
512 A250 7w lt bl, vio bl & dp org 60 30

80th anniv. of modern education for women.

Types of 1961-66 Inscribed "Republic of Korea," and

Porcelain Incense Burner, 11th-12th Centuries A253

Celadon Vessel, 12th Century A254

Unjin Miruk Buddha, Kwanchok Temple — A255

Designs: 60ch, Long-horned beetle. 1w, Folk dancers. 2w, Ginseng. 3w, King Sejong. 5w, Dragon waterpot. 7w, Symbols of thrift and development.

Perf. 12½
1966, Aug. 20 Unwmk. Litho.
Size: 22x19mm, 19x22mm
Granite Paper

516	A186a	60ch	gray green	35	15
517	A169	1w	green	42	15
518	A169	2w	blue green	42	15
519	A170	3w	dull red brn	42	15
521	A186	5w	gray green	45	15
522	A186b	7w	grnsh blue	85	15

Size: 22x25mm

523	A253	13w	vio blue	1.25	15
524	A254	60w	green	3.50	30
525	A255	80w	slate grn	6.25	40
			Nos. 516-525 (9)	13.91	
			Set value		1.40

Souvenir Sheet

Carrier Pigeons — A258

1966, July 13 Wmk. 317 *Imperf.*
Red Brown Surcharge
534 A258 7w on 40h emer & dk grn 1.00 50

6th Intl. Letter Writing Week, June 13-19. No. 534 was not issued without surcharge.

Children and World Map Projection A259

1966, July 28 Unwmk. *Perf. 12½*
535 A259 7w lt & dk vio bl & gray 40 20
a. Souv. sheet of 1, imperf. 1.10

15th annual assembly of WCOTP (World Conf. of Teaching Profession), Seoul, July 28-Aug. 9.

Factory, Money Bag and Honeycomb A260

1966, Sept. 1 Unwmk. *Perf. 12½*
536 A260 7w multicolored 40 20

Issued to publicize systematic saving.

Map of Korea, and People — A261

1966, Sept. 1 Litho.
537 A261 7w multicolored 40 20

Ninth national census.

CISM Emblem and Round-Table Conference A262

1966, Sept. 29 Unwmk. *Perf. 12½*
538 A262 7w multicolored 40 20
a. Souv. sheet of 1, imperf. 1.00

21st General Assembly of the Intl. Military Sports Council (CISM), Seoul, Sept. 29-Oct. 9.

Flags of Korea and Viet Nam and Korean Soldiers — A263

1966, Oct. 1
539 A263 7w multicolored 90 40

1st anniversary of Korean combat troops in Viet Nam.

Wrestlers A264

1966, Oct. 10
540 A264 7w red brn, buff & blk 60 30

47th Natl. Athletic Meet, Seoul, Oct. 10-15.

Lions Emblem and Map of Southeast Asia — A265

1966, Oct. 15
541 A265 7w multicolored 48 20
a. Souv. sheet of 1, imperf. 1.25

5th East and Southeast Asia Lions Convention, Seoul, Oct. 15-17.

Seoul University Emblem — A266

1966, Oct. 15 **Litho.**

542 A266 7w multicolored 40 25

20th anniversary of Seoul University.

Anticommunist League Emblem A267

1966, Oct. 31 **Unwmk.** ***Perf. 12½***

543 A267 7w multicolored 40 25
a. Souv. sheet of 1, imperf. 90

12th Conf. of the Asian Anticommunist League, Seoul, Oct. 31-Nov. 7.

Presidents Park and Johnson, Flags of US and Korea — A268

1966, Oct. 31 **Litho.** ***Perf. 12½***

544 A268 7w multicolored 1.00 30
545 A268 83w multicolored 2.00 1.20
a. Souv. sheet of 2, #544-545, imperf. 5.00

Visit of Pres. Lyndon B. Johnson to Korea.

UNESCO Emblem and Symbols of Learning — A269

1966, Nov. 4

546 A269 7w multicolored 40 30
a. Souvenir sheets 1.10

20th anniv. of UNESCO.

Good Luck Bag and "Joy" A270

Ram and "Completion" A271

Perf. 12½x13, 13x12½

1966, Dec. 10

547 A270 5w multicolored 30 20
a. Souv. sheet of 1, imperf. 75
548 A271 7w multicolored 40 30
a. Souv. sheet of 1, imperf. 1.00

Issued for Christmas and the New Year.

Syncom Satellite over Globe — A272

1967, Jan. 31 **Litho.** ***Perf. 12½***

549 A272 7w dk blue & multi 55 25
a. Souv. sheet of 1, imperf. 1.25

15th anniv. of Korea's membership in the ITU.

Presidents Park and Lübke — A273

Perf. 12½

1967, Mar. 2 **Litho.** **Unwmk.**

550 A273 7w multicolored 90 50
a. Souv. sheet of 1, imperf. 3.00

Issued to commemorate the visit of Pres. Heinrich Lübke of Germany, March 2-6.

Hand Holding Coin, Industrial and Private Buildings A274

1967, Mar. 3

551 A274 7w lt green & blk brn 40 25

1st anniv. of the Natl. Taxation Office.

Folklore Series

Okwangdae Clown — A275

Perfect Peace Dance — A276

Girls on Seesaw A277

Korean Shuttlecock A278

Designs: 5w, Sandi mask and dance, horiz. 7w, Hafoe mask.

1967, Mar. 15 **Litho.** ***Perf. 12½***

552 A275 4w gray, blk & yel 45 15
553 A275 5w multicolored 65 20
554 A275 7w multicolored 90 30

1967, June 15

Designs: 4w, Sword dance, horiz. 7w, Buddhist Monk dance.

555 A276 4w multicolored 45 15
556 A276 5w multicolored 65 20
557 A276 7w multicolored 90 30

1967, Sept. 15

Designs: 4w, Girls on swing, horiz. 7w, Girls dancing in the moonlight.

558 A277 4w multicolored 45 15
559 A277 5w multicolored 65 20
560 A277 7w multicolored 90 30

1967, Dec. 15

Designs: 5w, Girls celebrating full moon, horiz. 7w, Archery.

561 A278 4w multicolored 45 15
562 A278 5w multicolored 65 20
563 A278 7w multicolored 90 30
Nos. 552-563 (12) 8.00 2.60

Souvenir Sheets of 1, Imperf.

552a A275 4w 80
553a A275 5w 1.00
554a A275 7w 1.65
555a A276 4w 80
556a A276 5w 1.00
557a A276 7w 1.65
558a A277 4w 80
559a A277 5w 1.00
560a A277 7w 1.65
561a A278 4w 80
562a A278 5w 1.00
563a A278 7w 1.65
Nos. 552a-563a (12) 13.80

JCI Emblem and Kyunghoe Pavilion — A279

1967, Apr. 13 **Litho.** ***Perf. 12½***

564 A279 7w dk brn, brt grn, bl & red 40 30
a. Souv. sheet of 1, imperf. 1.40

Intl. Junior Chamber of Commerce Conf., Seoul, Apr. 13-16.

Emblem, Map of Far East — A280

1967, Apr. 24 **Unwmk.** ***Perf. 12½***

565 A280 7w vio bl & multi 40 25
a. Souv. sheet of 1, imperf. 1.40

Issued to publicize the 5th Asian Pacific Dental Congress, Seoul, Apr. 24-28.

EXPO '67 Korean Pavilion A281

1967, Apr. 28

566 A281 7w yel, blk & red 1.10 50
567 A281 83w lt bl, blk & red 3.25 1.10
a. Souv. sheet of 1, imperf. 4.00

EXPO '67, Intl. Exhibition, Montreal, Apr. 28-Oct. 27, 1967.

Worker, Soldier, Emblem and Buildings — A282

1967, May 1

568 A282 7w multicolored 40 25

Veterans' Day, May 1.

Second Five-Year Plan Issue

Nut and Arrows A283

Designs: No. 570, Iron wheel and rail. No. 571, Express highway. No. 572, Cloverleaf intersection. No. 573, Rising income for fishermen and farmers (oysters, silk worm, mushrooms and bull's head). No. 574, Machine industry (cogwheels, automobile, wrench and motor). No. 575, Harbor. No. 576, Housing projects plans. No. 577, Atomic power plant. No. 578, Four Great River Valley development.

1967-71 **Litho.** ***Perf. 12½***

569 A283 7w blk, red brn & dl org 90 35
570 A283 7w dl org, yel & blk 90 35
571 A283 7w grn, bl & ol 60 30
572 A283 7w dk brn, yel & grn 60 30

Perf. 13x12½

573 A283 7w brn, grn, yel & org 42 25
574 A283 7w dk bl, lil rose & buff 42 25
575 A283 10w dk bl, bl, yel & grn 40 25
576 A283 10w lt bl, bl, grn & red 40 25

Photo. ***Perf. 13***

577 A283 10w blk, car & bl 40 15
578 A283 10w blk, grn & brn 40 15
Nos. 569-578 (10) 5.44 2.60

Issued to publicize the Second Economic Development Five-Year Plan.

Issue dates: Nos. 569-570, June 1, 1967. Nos. 571-572, Dec. 5, 1968. Nos. 573-574, Dec. 5, 1969. Nos. 575-576, Dec. 5, 1970. Nos. 577-578, Dec. 5, 1971.

President Park and Phoenix — A284

1967, July 1 **Unwmk.** ***Perf. 12½***

579 A284 7w multicolored 2.50 1.00
a. Souv. sheet of 1, imperf. 17.50

Inauguration of President Park Chung Hee for a 2nd term, July 1, 1967.

Korean Boy Scout, Emblem and Tents — A285

Design: 20w, Korean Boy Scout emblem, bridge and tents.

1967, Aug. 10 **Litho.** ***Perf. 12½***

580 A285 7w multicolored 55 25
a. Souv. sheet of 1, imperf. 1.00
581 A285 20w multicolored 1.00 60
a. Souv. sheet of 1, imperf. 2.25

3rd Korean Boy Scout Jamboree, Hwarangdae, Seoul, Aug. 10-15.

Types of 1962-66 Redrawn (Inscribed "Republic of Korea")

Designs: 20w, Meesun blossoms and fruit. 40w, Library of early Buddhist scriptures. 50w, Deer.

1967, Aug. 25

Granite Paper

582 A186c 20w green & lt bl grn 5.00 20
583 A186d 40w dk grn & lt ol 4.50 30
584 A186e 50w dk brn & bis 4.00 50

The printing of redrawn designs of the regular issue of 1962-66 became necessary upon discovery of large quantities of counterfeits, made to defraud the post. The position of the denominations was changed and elaborate fine background tracings were added.

Freedom Center and Emblem — A286

Hand Breaking Chain — A287

The Catalogue editors cannot undertake to appraise, identify or judge the genuineness or condition of stamps.

Boxing — A288

1967, Sept. 25 Litho. *Perf. 12½*

586 A286 5w multicolored	30	15
a. Souv. sheet of 1, imperf.	50	
587 A287 7w multicolored	40	25
a. Souv. sheet of 1, imperf.	1.25	

1st Conf. of the World Anti-Communist League, WACL, Taipei, China, Sept. 25-29.

1967, Oct. 5

Design: 7w, Women's basketball.

588 A288 5w tan & multi	40	35
589 A288 7w pale rose & multi	75	50

48th Natl. Athletic Meet, Seoul, Oct. 5-10.

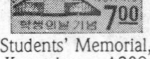

Students' Memorial, Kwangjoo — A289

Symbolic Water Cycle — A290

1967, Nov. 3 Litho. *Perf. 12½*

590 A289 7w lt green & multi	40	25

Issued for Student Day commemorating 1929 students' uprising against Japan.

1967, Nov. 20

591 A290 7w multicolored	40	25

Hydrological Decade (UNESCO), 1965-74.

Children Spinning Top — A291

Monkey and Oriental Zodiac — A292

1967, Dec. 10

592 A291 5w sal, org & vio bl	30	20
a. Souv. sheet of 1, imperf.	60	
593 A292 7w yel bis, brn & vio bl	48	35
a. Souv. sheet of 1, imperf.	1.25	

Issued for Christmas and New Year.

Parabolic Antenna and Electric Waves — A293

1967, Dec. 21

594 A293 7w lt bl, blk & yel	48	25
a. Souv. sheet of 1, imperf.	1.10	

Opening of the natl. microwave communications network, Dec. 21.

Carving from King Songdok Bell — A294

Earrings, 6th Cent. — A295

Flag — A296

Perf. 13x12½

1968, Feb. 1 Litho. Unwmk.

Granite Paper

595 A294 1w yellow & brown	28	15
596 A295 5w dk green & yellow	32	15
597 A296 7w dark blue & red	55	20

WHO Emblem A297

EATA Emblem and Korean Buildings A298

1968, Apr. 7 Unwmk. *Perf. 12½*

598 A297 7w multicolored	40	25
a. Souv. sheet of 1, imperf.	1.40	

20th anniv. of the WHO.

1968, Apr. 9 Litho.

599 A298 7w multicolored	40	25
a. Souv. sheet of 1, imperf.	1.40	

2nd General Meeting of the East Asia Travel Association (EATA), Seoul, Apr. 9-13.

Door Knocker, Factories and Emblem — A299

1968, May 6 Unwmk. *Perf. 12½*

600 A299 7w multicolored	50	30
a. Souv. sheet of 1, imperf.	1.40	

2nd Conf. of the Confederation of Asian Chambers of Commerce and Industry, Seoul.

Pres. Park and Emperor Haile Selassie — A300

1968, May 18 Litho.

601 A300 7w multicolored	90	50
a. Souv. sheet of 1, imperf.	2.75	

Visit of Haile Selassie I, May 18-20.

Mailman's Pouch — A301

Mailman A302

1968, May 31 Unwmk. *Perf. 12½*

602 A301 5w multicolored	30	15
603 A302 7w multicolored	45	25

First Postman's Day, May 31, 1968.

Atom Diagram and Symbols of Development A303

1968, June 1 Litho.

604 A303 7w dk bl, cit & ver	45	25

Issued to promote science and technology.

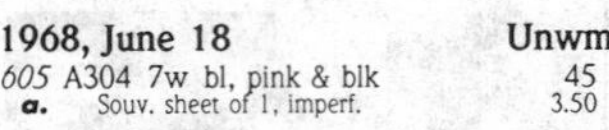
Kyung Hee University and Conference Emblem — A304

1968, June 18 Unwmk.

605 A304 7w bl, pink & blk	45	35
a. Souv. sheet of 1, imperf.	3.50	

2nd Conf. of the Intl. Association of University Presidents.

Liberated People — A305

1968, July 1 Litho. *Perf. 12½*

606 A305 7w multicolored	40	25

Issued to publicize the movement to liberate people under communist rule.

Peacock and Industrial Plant — A306

1968, Aug. 15 Unwmk. *Perf. 12½*

607 A306 7w multicolored	40	30

Republic of Korea, 20th anniversary.

Fair Entrance A307

1968, Sept. 9 Unwmk. *Perf. 12½*

608 A307 7w lilac & multi	50	25

Issued to publicize the first Korean Trade Fair, Seoul, Sept. 9-Oct. 18.

Assembly Emblem and Pills — A308

Soldier, Insigne and Battle Scene — A309

1968, Sept. 16 Litho.

609 A308 7w multicolored	40	25

3rd General Assembly of the Federation of Asian Pharmaceutical Associations, Seoul, Sept. 16-21.

1968, Oct. 1

Designs: No. 611, Sailor, insigne and ship's guns. No. 612, Servicemen and flags. No. 613, Aviator, insigne and planes. No. 614, Marine, insigne and landing group.

610 A309 7w green & org	2.00	35
611 A309 7w lt & dk blue	2.00	35
612 A309 7w dk blue & org	2.00	35
613 A309 7w dk & lt blue	2.00	35
614 A309 7w orange & grn	2.00	35
a. Vert. strip of 5, #610-614	11.00	2.50
Nos. 610-614 (5)	10.00	1.75

20th anniv. of the Korean armed forces.

Colombo Plan Emblem and Globe — A310

1968, Oct. 8 Litho. *Perf. 12½*

615 A310 7w dk brn, pale sal & grn	40	25

19th meeting of the Consultative Committee of the Colombo Plan, Seoul, Oct. 8-28.

Bicycling (Type I) — A311

제19회 올림픽대회기념
대한민국우표

Type II (2nd line flush left)

Designs (Olympic Rings and): No. 617, Bicycling, Type II. Nos. 618-619, Wrestling. Nos. 620-621, Boxing. Nos. 622-623, Olympic flame, "68" and symbols of various sports events.

1968, Oct. 12 Unwmk. *Perf. 12½*

616 A311 7w pink & multi (I)	1.25	40
617 A311 7w pink & multi (II)	1.25	40
a. Souv. sheet of 2, #616-617, imperf.	2.75	
b. Pair, #616-617	11.00	4.50
618 A311 7w olive & multi (I)	1.25	40
619 A311 7w olive & multi (II)	1.25	40
a. Souv. sheet of 2, #618-619, imperf.	2.75	
b. Pair, #618-619	11.00	4.50
620 A311 7w orange & multi (I)	1.25	40
621 A311 7w orange & multi (II)	1.25	40
a. Souv. sheet of 2, #620-621, imperf.	2.75	
b. Pair, #620-621	11.00	4.50
622 A311 7w bluish grn & multi (I)	1.25	40
623 A311 7w bluish grn & multi (II)	1.25	40
a. Souv. sheet of 2, #622-623, imperf.	2.75	
b. Pair, #622-623	11.00	4.50
Nos. 616-623 (8)	10.00	3.20

19th Olympic Games, Mexico City, Oct. 12-27.

The position of the "7" is reversed on Nos. 619, 621 and 623 as are the designs of Nos. 619 and 621.

"Search for Knowledge" and School Girls — A312

1968, Oct. 15

624 A312 7w multicolored 35 25

60th anniv. of public secondary education for women.

Coin and Statistics A313

1968, Nov. 1

625 A313 7w multicolored 35 25

National Wealth Survey.

Memorial to Students' Uprising — A314

1968, Nov. 23

626 A314 7w gray & multi 35 25

Issued to commemorate the anti-communist students' uprising, Nov. 23, 1945.

Men With Banners Declaring Human Rights — A315

1968, Dec. 10

627 A315 7w multicolored 40 30

Issued for the 20th anniversary of the Declaration of Human Rights.

Christmas Decorations A316

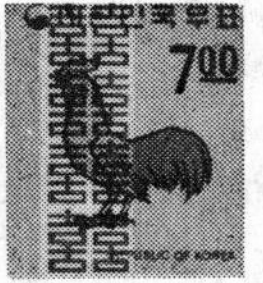

Cock and Good Luck Characters A317

1968, Dec. 11

628 A316 5w salmon & multi 90 60
- **a.** Souv. sheet of 1, imperf. 1.50

629 A317 7w multicolored 90 60
- **a.** Souv. sheet of 1, imperf. 1.50

Issued for Christmas and the New Year.

UN Emblems and Korean House — A318

1968, Dec. 12

630 A318 7w lt blue & multi 40 25

20th anniv. of the recognition of the Republic of Korea by the UN.

A319 A320

Design: Boy Scout Emblem.

1968, Sept. 30 Litho. ***Perf. 12½***

631 A319 7w black & multi 50 25

Regional Boy Scout conference.

1969, Mar. 1 Unwmk. ***Perf. 12½***

Design: Torch, map and students Demonstrating against Japan, 1919.

632 A320 7w multicolored 40 25

50th anniversary of Sam-il movement.

Hyun Choong Sa Shrine and Tortoise Ships — A321

1969, Apr. 28 Unwmk. ***Perf. 12½***

633 A321 7w deep bl, grn & brn 50 40

Issued to commemorate the completion of the Hyun Choong Sa Shrine at Onyang, dedicated to the memory of Adm. Li Sun-sin.

Pres. Park and Tuanku Nasiruddin of Malaysia A322

1969, Apr. 29 Litho.

634 A322 7w yellow & multi 85 40
- **a.** Souv. sheet of 1, imperf. *17.00*

Visit of Tuanku Ismail Nasiruddin, ruler of Malaysia, Apr. 29, 1969.

Hanabusaya Asiatica — A323

Flag of Korea — A324

Ancient Drums — A325

Red-crested Cranes — A326

Highway and Farm — A327

Pitcher (12-13th Centuries) — A328

Ceramic Duck (Water Jar) — A329

Library of Early Buddhist Scriptures — A330

Miruk Bosal — A333

Designs: 1w, Old man's mask. No. 637, Stone lamp, 8th century. No. 638, Chipmunk. No. 644, Tiger lily. No. 649, Bee. No. 651, Vase, Yi dynasty, 17th-18th centuries. No. 653, Gold crown, Silla Dynasty.

Zeros Omitted except 7w, No. 639

Perf. 13x12, 12x13 (Litho.); 13½x12½, 12½x13½ (Photo.)

Litho. (40ch, Nos. 641, 650); Photo.

1969-74 Unwmk.

Granite Paper (Lithographed); Ordinary Paper (Photogravure)

No.	Type	Value	Color	Unused	Used
635	A323	40ch	green	15	15
636	A326	1w	dk rose brn ('74)	15	15
637	A328	5w	brt plum	25	15
638	A326	5w	maroon ('74)	25	15
639	A324	7w	blue ("7.00")	50	15
640	A324	7w	blue ("7")	50	15
641	A325	10w	ultra	1.50	15
642	A324	10w	ultra ("10") ('70)	1.25	15
643	A326	10w	bl & dk bl ('73)	1.00	15
644	A323	10w	grn & multi ('73)	1.00	15
645	A327	10w	grn, red & gray ('73)	1.00	15
647	A328	20w	green	3.00	20
648	A329	30w	dull grn ('70)	3.50	35
649	A326	30w	yel & dk brn ('74)	3.00	35
650	A330	40w	vio bl & pink	6.50	50
651	A328	40w	ultra & lilac	6.50	40
652	A333	100w	dp claret & yel	45.00	1.75
653	A333	100w	brn & yel ('74)	10.00	1.25
			Nos. 635-653 (18)	85.05	
			Set value		5.25

See No. 1090. For surcharge see No. B18.

Red Cross, Faces and Doves — A336

1969, May 5 Litho. ***Perf. 12½***

654 A336 7w multicolored 40 25
- **a.** Souv. sheet of 1, imperf. 1.35

50th anniv. of the League of Red Cross Societies.

Savings Bank, Factories and Highway — A337

1969, May 20 Unwmk. ***Perf. 12½***

655 A337 7w yellow grn & multi 40 20

Second Economy Drive.

Pres. Park, Pres. Thieu and Flags of Korea and Viet Nam — A338

1969, May 27 Litho.

656 A338 7w pink & multi 80 40
- **a.** Souv. sheet of 1, imperf. 2.50

Issued to commemorate the visit of Pres. Nguyen Van Thieu of Viet Nam, May 27.

"Reforestation and Parched Fields" — A339

Growing and Withering Plants — A340

1969, June 10

657 A339 7w multicolored 40 20

658 A340 7w multicolored 40 20

Issued to publicize the need for prevention of damages from floods and droughts.

Apollo 11, Separation of Second Stage — A341

Designs: No. 660, Apollo 11, separation of 3rd Stage. No. 661, Orbits of command and landing modules around moon. No. 662, Astronauts gathering rock samples on moon. 40w, Spacecraft splashdown.

1969, Aug. 15 Unwmk. ***Perf. 12½***

No.	Type	Value	Color	Unused	Used
659	A341	10w	indigo, bl & red	30	20
660	A341	10w	indigo, bl & red	30	20
661	A341	20w	indigo, bl, red & lem	60	30
662	A341	20w	indigo, bl, red & lem	60	30
663	A341	40w	indigo, bl & red	1.25	60
a.			Souv. sheet of 5, #659-663, imperf.	3.50	
b.			Strip of 5, #659-663	3.25	2.00
			Nos. 659-663 (5)	3.05	1.60

Man's 1st landing on the moon, July 20, 1969. US astronauts Neil A. Armstrong and Col. Edwin E. Aldrin, Jr., with Lieut. Col. Michael Collins piloting Apollo 11.

Fable Issue

Girl and Stepmother A342

The Sick Princess A343

Mother Meeting Tiger — A344

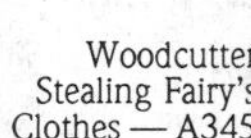

Woodcutter Stealing Fairy's Clothes — A345

Heungbu and Wife Release Healed Swallow A346

Kongji and Patji (Cinderella): 7w, Sparrows help Kongji separate rice. 10w, Ox helps Kongji to weed a field. 20w, Kongji in a sedan chair on the way to the palace.

1969, Sept. 1 Litho. *Perf. 12½*

664 A342 5w apple grn & multi 35 15
665 A342 7w yellow & multi 40 15
666 A342 10w lt violet & multi 60 20
667 A342 20w lt green & multi 1.00 35

1969, Nov. 1 *Perf. 13x12½*

"The Hare's Liver": 7w, Hare riding to the palace on back of turtle. 10w, Hare telling a lie to the King to save his life. 20w, Hare mocking the turtle.

668 A343 5w yellow & multi 30 15
669 A343 7w lt vio & multi 30 15
670 A343 10w lt grnsh bl & multi 50 20
671 A343 20w lt yel grn & multi 90 35

1970, Jan. 5

"The Sun and the Moon": 7w, Tiger disguised as mother at children's house. 10w, Tiger, and children on tree. 20w, Children safe on cloud, and tiger falling to his death.

672 A344 5w orange & multi 50 15
673 A344 7w gray grn & multi 60 15
674 A344 10w lt green & multi 90 20
675 A344 20w gray & multi 1.50 35

1970, Mar. 5

Designs: No. 677, Woodcutter with wife and children. No. 678, Wife taking children to heaven. No. 679, Husband joining family in heaven.

676 A345 10w dull bl grn & multi 90 20
677 A345 10w buff & multi 90 20
678 A345 10w lt grnsh bl & multi 90 20
679 A345 10w pink & multi 90 20

1970, May 5 *Perf. 12½*

Designs: No. 681, Heungbu and wife finding gold treasure in gourd. No. 682, Nolbu and wife with large gourd. No. 683, Demon emerging from gourd punishing evil Nolbu and wife.

680 A346 10w lt grnsh bl & multi 1.25 20
681 A346 10w orange & multi 1.25 20
682 A346 10w apple grn & multi 1.25 20
683 A346 10w tan & multi 1.25 20
Nos. 664-683 (20) 16.45 4.15

Souvenir Sheets of 1, Imperf.

664a A342 5w 50
665a A342 7w 60
666a A342 10w 85
667a A342 20w 1.40
668a A343 5w 50
669a A343 7w 50
670a A343 10w 70
671a A343 20w 1.25
672a A344 5w 70
673a A344 7w 90
674a A344 10w 1.25
675a A344 20w 2.25
676a A345 10w 1.25
677a A345 10w 1.25
678a A345 10w 1.25
679a A345 10w 1.25
680a A346 10w 1.75
681a A346 10w 1.75
682a A346 10w 1.75
683a A346 10w 1.75
Nos. 664a-683a (20) 23.40

1869 Locomotive and Diesel Train — A347

Design: No. 685, Early locomotive.

Perf. 12½
1969, Sept. 18 Litho. Unwmk.

684 A347 7w yellow & multi 40 20
685 A347 7w green & multi 40 20

70th anniversary of Korean Railroads.

Formation of F-5A Planes — A348

Design: No. 687, F-4D Phantom.

1969, Oct. 1 Photo. *Perf. 13½x13*

686 A348 10w blue, blk & car 50 25

Litho. *Perf. 13x12½*

687 A348 10w multicolored 50 25

20th anniversary of Korean Air Force.

Cha-jun Game — A349

1969, Oct. 3

688 A349 7w ap grn, dk bl & blk 40 25

10th National Festival of Traditional Skills.

Institute of Science and Technology A350

1969, Oct. 23

689 A350 7w bister, grn & choc 40 25

Completion of the Korean Institute of Science and Technology, Hongnung, Seoul.

Pres. Park and Diori Hamani A351

1969, Oct. 27

690 A351 7w yellow grn & multi 70 25
a. Souv. sheet of 1, imperf. 2.00

Visit of Diori Hamani, Pres. of Niger, Oct. 27.

Korean Wrestling A352

Sports: No. 692, Fencing. No. 693, Korean karate (taekwondo). No. 694, Volleyball, vert. No. 695, Soccer, vert.

Perf. 13x12½, 12½x13
1969, Oct. 28

691 A352 10w yellow grn & multi 50 20
692 A352 10w blue & multi 50 20
693 A352 10w green & multi 50 20
694 A352 10w olive & multi 50 20
695 A352 10w ultra & multi 50 20
Nos. 691-695 (5) 2.50 1.00

50th Natl. Athletic Meet, Seoul, Oct. 28-Nov. 2.

Allegory of National Education Charter — A353

1969, Dec. 5 Litho. *Perf. 12½x13*

696 A353 7w dull yel & multi 40 25

1st anniv. of the proclamation of the Natl. Education Charter.

Toy Dogs and Lattice Pattern — A354

Candle, Lattice Door and Fence — A355

1969, Dec. 11 Photo. *Perf. 13½*

697 A354 5w green & multi 30 15
698 A355 7w blue & multi 40 25

Issued for New Year 1970.

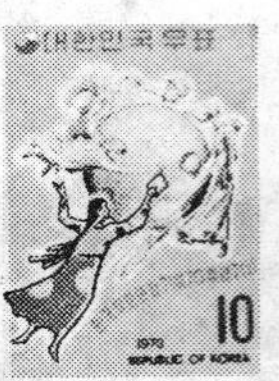

UPU Monument, Bern, and Korean Woman — A356

Education Year Emblem and Book — A357

1970, Jan. 1 Photo. *Perf. 13x13½*

699 A356 10w multicolored 3.50 25

70th anniv. of Korea's admission to the UPU.

1970, Mar. 10 Litho. *Perf. 12½x13*

700 A357 10w pink & multi 75 25

International Education Year 1970.

EXPO '70 Emblem, Seated Buddha, Korean Pavilion A358

1970, Mar. 15 *Perf. 13x12½*

701 A358 10w multicolored 60 25

Issued to publicize EXPO '70 International Exhibition, Osaka, Japan, March 15-Sept. 13.

Korean Youths and 4-H Club Emblem — A359

1970, Mar. 28 *Perf. 12½x13*

702 A359 10w yellow & multi 40 25

Issued to publicize the 15th Korean 4-H Club Central Contest, Suwon, March 28.

Money and Bank Emblem A360

1970, Apr. 9 Litho. *Perf. 13x12½*

703 A360 10w yellow & multi 40 25

3rd annual Board of Governors' meeting of the Asian Development Bank, Seoul, Apr. 9-11.

Royal Palanquin A361

1899 Streetcar A362

Historic Means of Transportation: No. 706, Emperor Sunjong's Cadillac, 1903. No. 707, Nieuport biplane, 1922.

Perf. 13x13½, 13½x13
1970, May 20 Photo.

704 A361 10w citron & multi 50 15
705 A362 10w yellow & multi 50 15
706 A362 10w ocher & multi 50 15
707 A362 10w aqua & multi 50 15

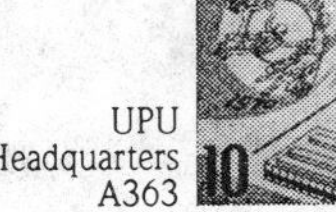

UPU Headquarters A363

1970, May 30 *Perf. 13½x13*

708 A363 10w multicolored 40 25

New UPU Headquarters in Bern, Switzerland.

Map, Radar and Satellite — A364

1970, June 2 *Perf. 13x13½*

709 A364 10w sky bl, vio bl & blk 60 25

Issued to commemorate the completion of the Kum San Earth Station of the International Satellite Consortium (INTELSAT).

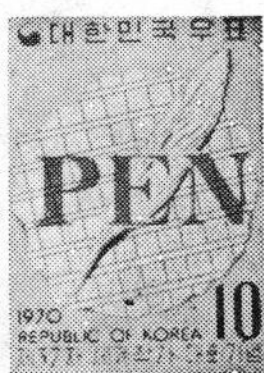

"PEN" and Manuscript Paper — A365

1970, June 28 Photo. *Perf. 13x13½*

710 A365 10w bl grn, bl & car 35 25

37th Intl. P.E.N. Cong. (Poets, Playwrights, Editors, Essayists and Novelists), Seoul, June 28-July 4.

Seoul-Pusan Expressway — A366

1970, June 30

711 A366 10w multicolored 65 30

Opening of Seoul-Pusan Expressway.

Postal Code Symbol and Number A367

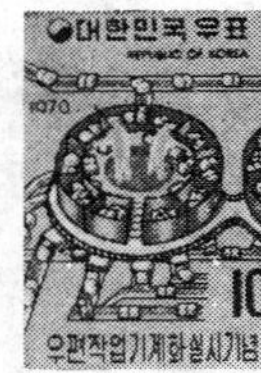

Mail Sorting Machine A368

1970, July 1

712 A367 10w multicolored 40 20

Issued to publicize the introduction of postal zone numbers, July 1, 1970.

1970, July 2

713 A368 10w lt violet & multi 40 20
a. Souv. sheet, 2 each #712-713 *30.00*

Mechanization of Korean postal system.

Boy and Children's Hall — A369

1970, July 25

714 A369 10w pink & multi 40 25

Paintings Issue

Jongyangsa Temple and Mt. Kumgang, by Chong Son (1676-1759) — A370

The Fierce Tiger, by Shim Sa-yung (1707-1769) A371

Paintings: No. 716, Mountains and Rivers, by Yi In-moon (1745-1821). No. 717, Mountains and Rivers in Moonlight, by Kim Doo-ryang (1696-1763).

Perf. 13x13¹/₂, 13¹/₂x13

1970, Aug. 31 **Photo.**

715 A370 10w blue & multi 65 35
716 A370 10w buff & multi 65 35
717 A371 10w multicolored 65 35

1970, Oct. 30

Paintings: No. 719, Cats and Sparrows, by Pyun Sang-byuk (18th century). No. 720, Dog with puppies, by Yi Am (1499-?).

718 A371 30w multicolored 1.65 65
719 A371 30w multicolored 1.65 65
720 A371 30w multicolored 1.65 65

Nos. 718-720 exist imperf., same values.

1970, Dec. 30

Paintings: No. 721, Cliff and Boat, by Kim Hong-do (1745-?). No. 722, Cock, Hens and Chick, by Pyun Sang-byuk (early 18th century). No. 723, Woman Playing Flute, by Shin Yun-bok (late 18th century).

721 A371 10w yel brn, blk & red 65 35
722 A371 10w pale rose, blk & grn 65 35
723 A371 10w multi 65 35
Nos. 715-723 (9) 8.85 4.05

Souvenir Sheets of 2

715a A370 10w 2.00
716a A370 10w 2.00
717a A371 10w 2.00
718a A371 30w 8.50
719a A371 30w 8.50
720a A371 30w 8.50
721a A371 10w 2.50
722a A371 10w 2.50
723a A371 10w 2.50
Nos. 715a-723a (9) 39.00

Nos. 715a-717a have simulated perforations. Background color of stamps on No. 717a is yellow instead of greenish gray as on No. 717.

Nos. 718a-720a exist imperf., half the perf values.

Nos. 721a-723a exist imperf.

P.T.T.I. Emblem and Map of Far East — A372

1970, Sept. 6 Litho. ***Perf. 13x12¹/₂***

724 A372 10w lt yel grn, bl & dk bl 35 25

Opening of the Councillors' Meeting of the Asian Chapter of the Postal, Telegraph and Telephone Intl. Org., Sept. 6-12.

Korean WAC and Emblem — A373

1970, Sept. 6 Photo. ***Perf. 13x13¹/₂***

725 A373 10w blue & multi 45 25

20th anniv. of the founding of the Korean Women's Army Corps.

Pres. Park, Korean Flag and Means of Transportation — A374

Pres. Park, Highways, Factories A375

1970 ***Perf. 13x13¹/₂, 13¹/₂x13***

726 A374 10w vio bl, blk & car 1.00 40
727 A375 10w dk bl, grnsh bl & blk 95 40

Presidents Park and Hernandez, Flags of Korea, Salvador A376

1970, Sept. 28 Litho. ***Perf. 13x12¹/₂***

728 A376 10w dk bl, red & blk 90 25
a. Souv. sheet of 1, imperf. *32.50*

Visit of Gen. Fidel Sanchez Hernandez, President of El Salvador.

People and Houses — A377

1970, Oct. 1 Litho. ***Perf. 13x12¹/₂***

729 A377 10w lilac & multi 35 20

Issued to publicize the national census of population and housing, Oct. 1.

Diver A378

1970, Oct. 6 Photo. ***Perf. 12¹/₂x13¹/₂***

730 A378 10w shown 60 20
a. Souv. sheet of 2, imperf. 2.25
731 A378 10w Field hockey 60 20
a. Souv. sheet of 2, imperf. 2.25
732 A378 10w Baseball 60 20
a. Souv. sheet of 2, imperf. 2.25

51st Natl. Athletic Games, Seoul, Oct. 6-11.

Police Emblem and Activities A379

1970, Oct. 21 Litho. ***Perf. 12¹/₂***

733 A379 10w ultra & multi 45 25

The 25th Policemen's Day.

Freedom Bell, UN Emblem over Globe — A380

1970, Oct. 24 Photo. ***Perf. 13x13¹/₂***

734 A380 10w blue & multi 40 25

25th anniversary of United Nations.

Kite and Holly — A380a

Boar — A381

1970, Dec. 1 Litho. ***Perf. 13***

735 A380a 10w lt blue & multi 30 18
a. Souvenir sheet of 3 2.25
736 A381 10w green & multi 30 18
a. Souvenir sheet of 3 2.25

New Year 1971.

Pres. Park Quotation, Globe and Telecommunications Emblems — A382

1970, Dec. 4 **Photo.**

737 A382 10w multicolored 40 25

For the 15th Communications Day.

Power Dam — A383

Coal Mining A384

Highway Intersection A385

Designs: No. 739, Crate wrapped in world map, and ships. No. 740, Irrigation project and farm, vert. No. 742, Cement factory, vert. No. 743, Fertilizer factory. No. 744, Increased national income (scales). No. 745, Increased savings (factories, bee and coins).

1971 ***Perf. 13x13¹/₂, 13¹/₂x13***

738 A383 10w blue & multi 25 15
739 A383 10w pale lil & multi 25 15
740 A383 10w green & multi 25 15
741 A384 10w bl grn, lt bl & blk 25 15
742 A384 10w lt bl, vio & brt mag 25 15
743 A384 10w vio, grn & bis 25 15
744 A384 10w pink & multi 25 15
745 A384 10w lt bl grn & multi 25 15
746 A385 10w violet & multi 25 15
Nos. 738-746 (9) 2.25 1.35

Economic Development.

Souvenir Sheets of 1, Imperf.

738a A383 10w 1.75
739a A383 10w 1.75
740a A383 10w 1.75

Souvenir Sheets of 2, Imperf.

741a A384 10w 2.00
742a A384 10w 2.00
743a A384 10w 2.00
744a A384 10w 2.00
745a A384 10w 2.00
746a A385 10w 2.00
Nos. 738a-746a (9) 17.25

Torch, Globe and Spider — A386

1971, Mar. 1 Litho. ***Perf. 12¹/₂x13***

747 A386 10w gray & multi 35 25

March, the month for anti-espionage and victory over communism.

Reservist, Reserve Forces Emblem — A387

1971, Apr. 3 Photo. *Perf. 13½x13*
748 A387 10w lt ultra & multi 35 25

Home Reserve Forces Day, Apr. 3.

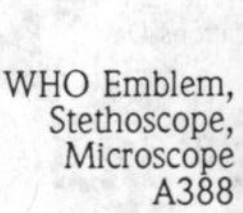

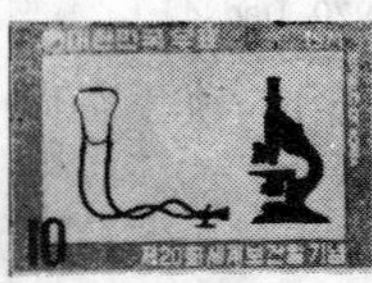

WHO Emblem, Stethoscope, Microscope A388

1971, Apr. 7
749 A388 10w lt bl, pur & yel 35 25

20th World Health Day, Apr. 7.

Subway Tunnel and Train — A389

Soccer Player — A390

1971, Apr. 12 Litho. *Perf. 12½x13*
750 A389 10w multicolored 40 25

Seoul subway construction start.

1971, May 2
751 A390 10w grn, dk brn & blk 40 30

First Asian Soccer Games, Seoul, May 2-13.

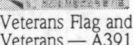

Veterans Flag and Veterans — A391

Girl Scouts and Emblem — A392

1971, May 8 Photo. *Perf. 13x13½*
752 A391 10w ultra & multi 40 25

20th Korean Veterans Day.

1971, May 10
753 A392 10w lilac & multi 40 30

25th anniversary of the Korean Federation of Girl Scouts.

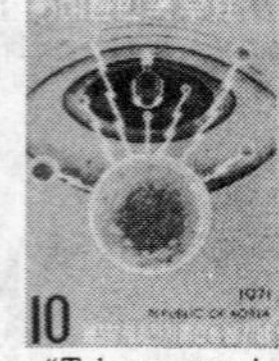

Torch and Development A393

"Telecommunication" A394

1971, May 16
754 A393 10w lt blue & multi 35 25

10th anniversary of May 16th revolution.

1971, May 17
755 A394 10w blue & multi 35 25

3rd World Telecommunications Day.

Security Council — A395

Korean Flag — A396

UN Organizations: No. 756, ILO. No. 757, FAO. No. 758, General Assembly (UN Headquarters). No. 759, UNESCO. No. 760, WHO. No. 761, World Bank. No. 762, Intl. Development Association (IDA). No. 763, Security Council. No. 764, Intl. Finance Corp. (IFC). No. 765, Intl. Monetary Fund. No. 766, ICAO. No. 767, Economic and Social Council. No. 768, Korean Flag. No. 769, Trusteeship Council. No. 770, UPU. No. 771, ITU. No. 772, World Meteorological Org. (WMO). No. 773, Intl. Court of Justice. No. 774, Intl. Maritime Consultative Org. No. 775, UNICEF. No. 776, Intl. Atomic Energy Agency. No. 777, UN Industrial Development Org. No. 778, UN Commission for the Unification and Rehabilitation of Korea. No. 779, UN Development Program. No. 780, UN Conf. on Trade and Development.

1971, May 30 *Perf. 13½x13*

756	A395 10w grn, blk & pink	1.25	25
757	A395 10w pink, blk & bl	1.25	25
758	A395 10w bl, blk, grn & pink	1.25	25
759	A395 10w pink, blk & bl	1.25	25
760	A395 10w grn, blk & pink	1.25	25
761	A395 10w pink, blk & bl	1.25	25
762	A395 10w bl, blk & pink	1.25	25
763	A395 10w grn, blk & pink	1.25	25
764	A395 10w bl, blk & pink	1.25	25
765	A395 10w pink, blk & bl	1.25	25
766	A395 10w bl, blk & pink	1.25	25
767	A395 10w grn, blk & pink	1.25	25
768	A396 10w bl, blk & pink	1.25	25
769	A395 10w grn, blk & pink	1.25	25
770	A395 10w bl, blk & pink	1.25	25
771	A395 10w pink, blk & bl	1.25	25
772	A395 10w bl, blk & pink	1.25	25
773	A395 10w grn, blk & pink	1.25	25
774	A395 10w bl, blk & pink	1.25	25
775	A395 10w pink, blk & bl	1.25	25
776	A395 10w grn, blk & pink	1.25	25
777	A395 10w pink, blk & bl	1.25	25
778	A395 10w bl, blk & pink	1.25	25
779	A395 10w pink, blk & bl	1.25	25
780	A395 10w grn, blk & pink	1.25	25
	Nos. 756-780 (25)	31.25	6.25

Sheet of 50 incorporates 2 each of #756-780.

Boat Ride, by Shin Yun-bok — A397

Man and Boy under Pine Tree — A398

Paintings by Shin Yun-bok: No. 782, Greeting travelers. No. 783, Tea ceremony. No. 784, Lady traveling with servants. No. 785, Man and woman on the road.

Perf. 13x13½, 13½x13

1971, June 20 **Photo.**

781	A397 10w multicolored	80	20
782	A397 10w multicolored	80	20
783	A397 10w multicolored	80	20
784	A397 10w multicolored	80	20
785	A397 10w multicolored	80	20
786	A398 10w multicolored	80	20
b.	Vert. strip of 5, #781-785	5.00	3.00
	Nos. 781-786 (6)	4.80	1.20

Souvenir Sheets of 2

781a	A397 10w	3.00	
782a	A397 10w	3.00	
783a	A397 10w	3.00	
784a	A397 10w	3.00	
785a	A397 10w	3.00	
786a	A398 10w	3.00	
	Nos. 781a-786a (6)	18.00	

Types A397-A398 with Inscription at Left

1971, July 20

Paintings: No. 787, Farmyard scene, by Kim Deuk-shin. No. 788, Family living in valley, by Lee Chae-kwan. No. 789, Man reading book under pine tree, by Lee Chae-kwan.

787	A397 10w pale grn & multi	60	25
788	A398 10w pale grn & multi	60	25
789	A398 10w lt yel grn & multi	60	25

Souvenir Sheets of 2

787a	A397 10w	2.00
788a	A398 10w	2.00
789a	A398 10w	2.00

Teacher and Students, by Kim Hong-do A399

Paintings by Kim Hong-do (Yi Dynasty): No. 791, Wrestlers. No. 792, Dancer and musicians. No. 793, Weavers. No. 794, At the Well.

1971, Aug. 20 *Perf. 13½x13*

790	A399 10w blk, lt grn & rose	90	25
791	A399 10w blk, lt grn & rose	90	25
792	A399 10w blk, lt grn & rose	90	25
793	A399 10w blk, lt grn & rose	90	25
794	A399 10w blk, lt grn & rose	90	25
b.	Horiz. strip of 5, #790-794	4.50	2.50
	Nos. 790-794 (5)	4.50	1.25

Souvenir Sheets of 2

790a	A399 10w	3.00
791a	A399 10w	3.00
792a	A399 10w	3.00
793a	A399 10w	3.00
794a	A399 10w	3.00
	Nos. 790a-794a (5)	15.00

Pres. Park, Highway and Phoenix — A400

1971, July 1 *Perf. 13½x13*
795 A400 10w grn, blk & org 1.40 50
a. Souvenir sheet of 2 *27.50*

Inauguration of President Park Chung Hee for a third term, July 1.

Campfire and Tents — A401

1971, Aug. 2 Photo. *Perf. 13x13½*
796 A401 10w blue grn & multi 40 25

13th Boy Scout World Jamboree, Asagiri Plain, Japan, Aug. 2-10.

Symbol of Conference A402

1971, Sept. 27 *Perf. 13*
797 A402 10w multicolored 40 25
a. Souvenir sheet of 2 *25.00*

Asian Labor Ministers' Conference, Seoul, Sept. 27-30.

Archers — A403

1971, Oct. 8 Photo. *Perf. 13x13½*
798 A403 10w shown 60 20
a. Souvenir sheet of 3 *12.50*
799 A403 10w Judo 60 20
a. Souvenir sheet of 3 *12.50*

52nd National Athletic Meet.

Taeguk on Palette — A404

1971, Oct. 11 *Perf. 13½x13*
800 A404 10w yellow & multi 35 25

20th National Fine Arts Exhibition.

Physician, Globe and Emblem — A405

1971, Oct. 13
801 A405 10w multicolored 35 25

7th Congress of the Confederation of Medical Associations in Asia and Oceania.

Symbols of Contest Events — A406

1971, Oct. 20 Photo. *Perf. 13x13½*
802 A406 10w multicolored 35 25
a. Souvenir sheet of 2 *14.00*

2nd National Skill Contest for High School Students.

Slide Caliper and KS Emblem — A407

1971, Nov. 11 *Perf. 13x13½*
803 A407 10w multicolored 35 25

10th anniversary of industrial standardization in Korea.

Rats — A408

Japanese Crane — A409

1971, Dec. 1
804 A408 10w multicolored 35 18
a. Souvenir sheet of 3 *12.50*
805 A409 10w multicolored 35 18
a. Souvenir sheet of 3 *12.50*

New Year 1972.

Emblem of Hangul Hakhoe and Hangul Letters — A410

1971, Dec. 3 Photo.
806 A410 10w dk blue & multi 35 20

50th anniversary of Korean Language Research Society (Hangul Hakhoe).

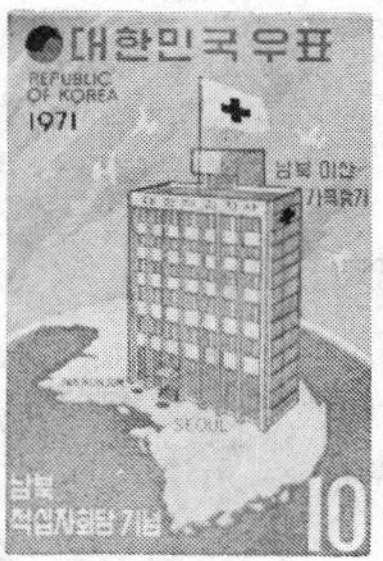

Red Cross Headquarters and Map of Korea — A411

1971, Dec. 31 *Perf. 13½x13*
807 A411 10w multicolored 40 20
a. Souvenir sheet of 2 2.50

First South and North Korean Red Cross Conference, Panmunjom, Aug. 20, 1971.

Globe and Book — A412

1972, Jan. 5 *Perf. 13x13½*
808 A412 10w multicolored 45 30
a. Souvenir sheet of 2 3.50

International Book Year 1972.

Intelsat 4 Sending Signals to Korea — A413

1972, Jan. 31 *Perf. 13½x13*
809 A413 10w dk blue & multi 35 25

Korea's entry into ITU, 20th anniv.

Figure Skating, Sapporo '72 Emblem A414

Map of Korea with Forest Sites A415

Design: No. 811, Speed skating.

1972, Feb. 3 *Perf. 13x13½*
810 A414 10w lt & dk bl & car 35 15
811 A414 10w lt & dk bl & car 35 15
a. Souvenir sheet of 2, #810-811 7.00

11th Winter Olympic Games, Sapporo, Japan, Feb. 3-13.

1972, Mar. 10 Photo. *Perf. 13x13*
812 A415 10w buff, bl grn & red 35 20

Publicity for forests planted to mark hope for reunification of Korea.

Junior Chamber of Commerce Emblem and Beetles — A416

1972, Mar. 19 *Perf. 13½x13*
813 A416 10w pink & multi 35 20

Junior Chamber of Commerce, 20th anniversary.

U.N. Emblem, Agriculture and Industry — A417

1972, Mar. 28 *Perf. 13x13½*
814 A417 10w violet, grn & car 35 20

Economic Commission for Asia and the Far East (ECAFE), 25th anniversary.

Flags — A418

1972, Apr. 1 *Perf. 13½x13*
815 A418 10w blue & multi 35 20

Asian-Oceanic Postal Union, 10th anniv.

Korean Flag — A419

YWCA Emblem, Butterflies — A420

1972, Apr. 1 Photo. *Perf. 13x13½*
816 A419 10w yellow & multi 35 25

Homeland Reserve Forces Day, Apr. 1.

1972, Apr. 20
817 A420 10w violet & multi 40 20

50th anniv. of the YWCA of Korea.

Community Projects — A421

Korean Flag & Inscription — A422

1972, May 1 *Perf. 13x13½*
818 A421 10w pink & multi 35 20

Rural rehabilitation and construction movement.

1972, May 1
819 A422 10w green & multi 35 20

Anti-espionage and victory over communism month.

Children with Balloons — A423

1972, May 5 *Perf. 13½x13*
820 A423 10w yellow & multi 35 20

Children's Day, May 5.

King Munyong's Gold Earrings — A424

Design: No. 822, Gold ornament from King's crown, vert.

Perf. 13½x13, 13x13½
1972, May 10
821 A424 10w green & multi 30 20
822 A424 10w green & multi 30 20

National treasures from tomb of King Munyong of Paekche, who reigned 501-523.

Kojo Island — A425

National parks: No. 823, Crater Lake.

1972, May 30 *Perf. 13½x13*
823 A425 10w blue grn & multi 30 20
824 A425 10w green & multi 30 20

Daisy, Environment Emblem — A426

1972, May 30 Litho. *Perf. 13x13½*
825 A426 10w green & multi 35 20
a. Souvenir sheet of 2 1.90

UN Conference on Human Environment, Stockholm, June 5-16.

Gwanghwa Gate, Flags of Participants — A427

1972, June 14
826 A427 10w yellow & multi 35 20

7th Meeting of Asian-Pacific Council (ASPAC).

Farm and Fish Hatchery — A428

Weight Lifting — A429

Third Five-Year Plan Issue

1972, July 1 Photo. *Perf. 13½x13*
827 A428 10w shown 30 15
828 A428 10w Steel industry and products 30 15
829 A428 10w Globe and cargo 30 15

3rd Economic Development Five-Year Plan.

1972, Aug. 26 Photo. *Perf. 13x13½*
830 A429 20w shown 30 15
831 A429 20w Judo 30 15
a. Souvenir sheet of 2, #830-831 2.50
b. Pair, #830-831 65 35
832 A429 20w Boxing 30 15
833 A429 20w Wrestling 30 15
a. Souvenir sheet of 2, #832-833 2.50
b. Pair, #832-833 65 35

20th Olympic Games, Munich, Aug. 26-Sept. 11. Nos. 831b, 833b each printed checkerwise.

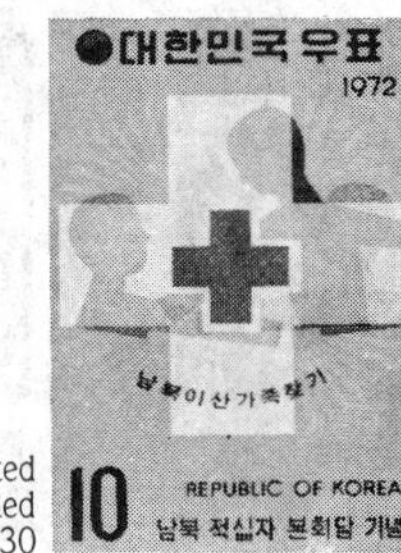

Families Reunited by Red Cross — A430

1972, Aug. 30 Photo. *Perf. 13½x13*
834 A430 10w lt blue & multi 48 20
a. Souvenir sheet of 2 7.00

Plenary meeting of the South-North Red Cross Conference, Pyongyang, Aug. 30, 1972.

Bulkuk-sa Temple, Kyongju Park — A431

Bopju-sa Temple, Mt. Sokri Park — A432

1972, Sept. 20 Photo. ***Perf. 13½x13***

835 A431 10w brown & multi 30 20
836 A432 10w blue & multi 30 20

National parks.

"5" and Conference Emblem — A433

1972, Sept. 25 ***Perf. 13x13½***

837 A433 10w vio blue & multi 35 15

Fifth Asian Judicial Conf., Seoul, Sept. 25-29.

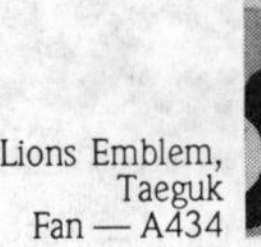

Lions Emblem, Taeguk Fan — A434

1972, Sept. 28 ***Perf. 13½x13***

838 A434 10w multicolored 35 15

11th Orient and Southeast Asian Lions Convention, Seoul, Sept. 28-30.

Scout Taking Oath, Korean Flag and Scout Emblem — A435

1972, Oct. 5

839 A435 10w yellow & multi 35 15

Boy Scouts of Korea, 50th anniversary.

Children and Ox — A436

Children in Balloon — A437

1972, Dec. 1 Photo. ***Perf. 13x13½***

840 A436 10w green & multi 30 15
  a. Souvenir sheet of 2 1.25
841 A437 10w blue & multi 30 15
  a. Souvenir sheet of 2 1.25
  Set value 24

New Year 1973.

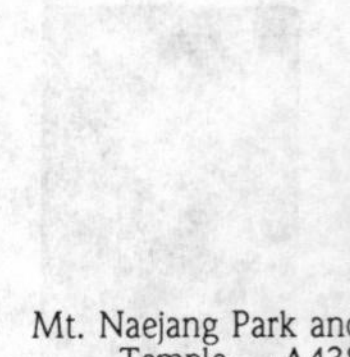

Mt. Naejang Park and Temple — A438

Mt. Sorang and Madeungryong Pass — A439

Perf. 13x13½, 13½x13

1972, Dec. 10

842 A438 10w multicolored 25 20
843 A439 10w multicolored 25 20

National parks.

Pres. Park, Korean Flag and Modern Landscape — A440

1972, Dec. 27 ***Perf. 13x13½***

844 A440 10w multicolored 90 20
  a. Souvenir sheet of 2 *17.50*

Inauguration of Park Chung Hee for a 4th term as president of Korea.

Tourism Issue

Kyongbok Palace (National Museum) A441

Mt. Sorak and Kejo-am Temple — A442

Palmi Island and Beach — A443

Sain-am Rock, Mt. Dokjol — A444

Shrine for Adm. Li Sun-sin — A445

Limestone Cavern, Kusan-ni A446

Namhae Bridge A447

Hongdo Island — A448

Mt. Mai — A449

Tangerine Orchard, Cheju Island — A450

1973, Feb. 20 Photo. ***Perf. 13½x13***

845 A441 10w multicolored 25 15
846 A442 10w multicolored 25 15

1973, Apr. 20 ***Perf. 13x13½***

847 A443 10w multicolored 25 15
848 A444 10w multicolored 25 15

1973, June 20

849 A445 10w multicolored 25 15
850 A446 10w multicolored 25 15

1973, Aug. 20 ***Perf. 13½x13***

851 A447 10w multicolored 25 15
852 A448 10w multicolored 25 15

1973, Oct. 20

853 A449 10w multicolored 25 15
854 A450 10w multicolored 25 15
  Nos. 845-854 (10) 2.50 1.50

Praying Family — A451

Flags of Korea and South Viet Nam, Victory Sign — A452

1973, Mar. 1 ***Perf. 13x13½***

855 A451 10w yellow & multi 25 15

Prayer for national unification.

1973, Mar. 1

856 A452 10w violet & multi 25 15

Return of Korean Expeditionary Force from South Viet Nam.

Workers, Factory, Cogwheel A453

Satellite, WMO Emblem A454

1973, Mar. 10 **Unwmk.**

857 A453 10w blue & multi 25 15

10th Labor Day.

1973, Mar. 23

858 A454 10w blue & multi 25 15
  a. Souvenir sheet of 2 1.50

Cent. of Intl. Meteorological Cooperation.

King's Ceremonial Robe — A455

Traditional Korean Costumes (Yi dynasty): No. 860, Queen's ceremonial dress. No. 861, King's robe. No. 862, Queen's robe. No. 863, Crown Prince. No. 864, Princess. No. 865, Courtier. No. 866, Royal bridal gown. No. 867, Official's wife. No. 868, Military official.

1973 Photo. ***Perf. 13½x13***

859 A455 10w ocher & multi 40 15
860 A455 10w salmon & multi 40 15
861 A455 10w rose lilac & multi 40 15
862 A455 10w apple grn & multi 40 15
863 A455 10w lt blue & multi 40 15
864 A455 10w lilac rose & multi 40 15
865 A455 10w yellow & multi 40 15
866 A455 10w lt blue & multi 40 15
867 A455 10w ocher & multi 40 15
868 A455 10w lil rose & multi 40 15
  Nos. 859-868 (10) 4.00
  Set value 1.20

Issue dates: #859-860, Mar. 30. #861-862, May 30. #863-864, July 30. #865-866, Sept. 30. #867-868, Nov. 30.

Souvenir Sheets of 2

859a A455 10w (#1) 1.75
860a A455 10w (#2) 1.75
861a A455 10w (#3) 1.75
862a A455 10w (#4) 1.75
863a A455 10w (#5) 1.75
864a A455 10w (#6) 1.75
865a A455 10w (#7) 1.75
866a A455 10w (#8) 1.75
867a A455 10w (#9) 1.75
868a A455 10w (#10) 1.75
  Nos. 859a-868a (10) 17.50

Parenthetical numbers after souvenir sheet listings appear in top marginal inscriptions.

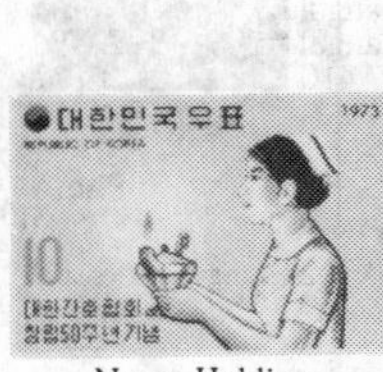

Nurse Holding Lamp — A456

Homeland Reservists and Flag — A457

1973, Apr. 1 ***Perf. 13½x13***

869 A456 10w rose & multi 25 15

50th anniv. of Korean Nurses Association.

1973, Apr. 7 ***Perf. 13x13½***

870 A457 10w yellow & multi 35 15

Homeland Reserve Forces Day on 5th anniversary of their establishment.

Table Tennis Player, and Globe — A458

1973, May 23 ***Perf. 13x13½***

871 A458 10w pink & multi 42 15

Victory of Korean women's table tennis team, 32nd Intl. Table Tennis Championships, Sarajevo, Yugoslavia, Apr. 5-15.

World Vision Children's Choir — A459

1973, June 25 *Perf. 13x13½*
872 A459 10w multicolored 38 15

20th anniversary of World Vision International, a Christian service organization.

Converter, Pohang Steel Works — A460

1973, July 3 *Perf. 13x13½*
873 A460 10w blue & multi 25 15

Inauguration of Pohang iron and steel plant.

INTERPOL Emblem A461

1973, Sept. 3 *Perf. 13½x13*
874 A461 10w lt violet & multi 25 15

50th anniversary of the International Criminal Police Organization (INTERPOL).

Children with Stamp Albums — A462

1973, Oct. 12 *Perf. 13½x13*
875 A462 10w dp green & multi 25 15
a. Souvenir sheet of 2 2.00

Philatelic Week, Oct. 12-18.

Woman Hurdler — A463

1973, Oct. 12 *Perf. 12½x13½*
876 A463 10w shown 25 15
877 A463 10w Tennis player 25 15
Set value 24

54th Natl. Athletic Meet, Pusan, Oct. 12-17.

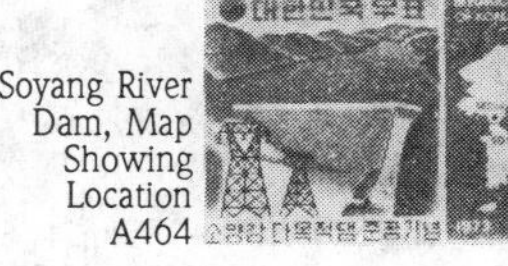

Soyang River Dam, Map Showing Location A464

1973, Oct. 15 *Perf. 13½x13*
878 A464 10w blue & multi 30 15

Inauguration of Soyang River Dam and hydroelectric plant.

Fire from Match and Cigarette — A465

1973, Nov. 1 *Perf. 13x13½*
879 A465 10w multicolored 30 15

10th Fire Prevention Day.

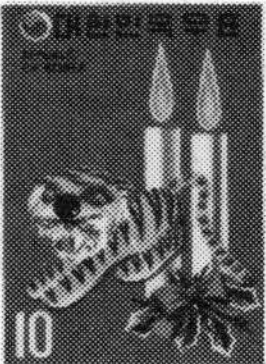

Tiger and Candles — A466

Toys — A467

1973, Dec. 1 Photo. *Perf. 13x13½*
880 A466 10w emerald & multi 25 15
a. Souvenir sheet of 2 80
881 A467 10w blue & multi 25 15
a. Souvenir sheet of 2 80
Set value 24

New Year 1974.

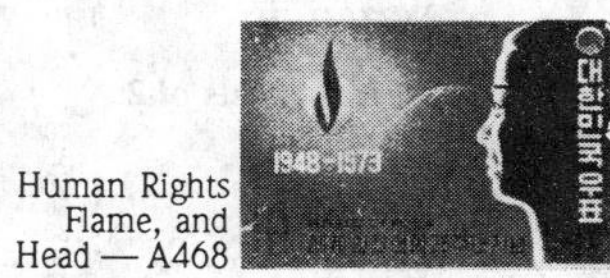

Human Rights Flame, and Head — A468

1973, Dec. 10 *Perf. 13½x13*
882 A468 10w orange & multi 25 15

25th anniversary of Universal Declaration of Human Rights.

Musical Instruments Issue

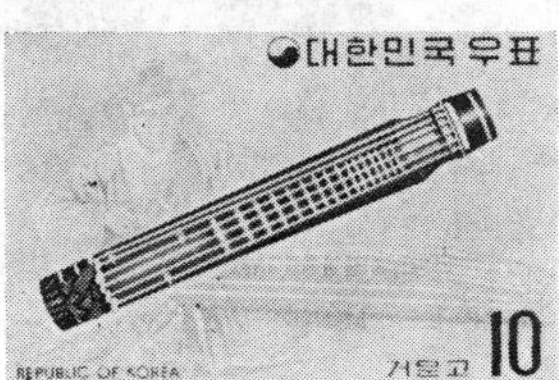

Komunko, Six-stringed Zither — A469

Design: 30w, Nagak, shell trumpet.

1974, Feb. 20 Photo. *Perf. 13x13½*
883 A469 10w lt bl, blk & brn 20 15
884 A469 30w orange & multi 30 20

1974, Apr. 20

Designs: 10w, Tchouk; wooden hammer in slanted box, used to start orchestra. 30w, Eu; crouching tiger, used to stop orchestra.

885 A469 10w brt blue & multi 15 15
886 A469 30w lt green & multi 30 20

1974, June 20

Designs: 10w, A-chaing, 7-stringed instrument. 30w, Kyobang-ko, drum.

887 A469 10w dull yel & multi 15 15
888 A469 30w sal pink & multi 30 20

1974, Aug. 20

Designs: 10w, So, 16-pipe ritual instrument. 30w, Kaikeum, 2-stringed fiddle.

889 A469 10w lt blue & multi 15 15
890 A469 30w brt pink & multi 30 20

1974, Oct. 20

Designs: 10w, Pak (clappers). 30w, Pyenchong (bell chimes).

891 A469 10w lt lilac & multi 15 15
892 A469 30w lemon & multi 30 20
Nos. 883-892 (10) 2.30 1.75

Souvenir Sheets of 2

883a A469 10w (#1) 1.25
884a A469 30w (#2) 1.75
885a A469 10w (#3) 90
886a A469 30w (#4) 1.75
887a A469 10w (#5) 90
888a A469 30w (#6) 1.75
889a A469 10w (#7) 90
890a A469 30w (#8) 1.75
891a A469 10w (#9) 90
892a A469 30w (#10) 1.75
Nos. 883a-892a (10) 13.60

Fruit Issue

Apricots — A470

1974, Mar. 30 Photo. *Perf. 13x13½*
893 A470 10w shown 15 15
894 A470 30w Strawberries 30 20

1974, May 30
895 A470 10w Peaches 15 15
896 A470 30w Grapes 30 20

1974, July 30
897 A470 10w Pears 15 15
898 A470 30w Apples 30 20

1974, Sept. 30
899 A470 10w Cherries 15 15
900 A470 30w Persimmons 30 20

1974, Nov. 30
901 A470 10w Tangerines 15 15
902 A470 30w Chestnuts 30 20
Nos. 893-902 (10) 2.25 1.75

Souvenir Sheets of 2

893a A470 10w (#1) 70
894a A470 30w (#2) 1.40
895a A470 10w (#3) 60
896a A470 30w (#4) 1.25
897a A470 10w (#5) 60
898a A470 30w (#6) 1.25
899a A470 10w (#7) 60
900a A470 30w (#8) 1.25
901a A470 10w (#9) 60
902a A470 30w (#10) 1.25
Nos. 893a-902a (10) 9.50

Reservist and Factory — A471

1974, Apr. 6 Photo. *Perf. 13½x13*
903 A471 10w yellow & multi 25 15

Homeland Reserve Forces Day.

WPY Emblem and Scales — A472

1974, Apr. 10 *Perf. 13x13½*
904 A472 10w salmon & multi 20 15
a. Souvenir sheet of 2 75

World Population Year 1974.

Train and Communications Emblem — A473

1974, Apr. 22 *Perf. 13½x13*
905 A473 10w multicolored 20 15

19th Communications Day.

Emblem and Stylized Globe — A474

1974, May 6 Photo. *Perf. 13*
906 A474 10w red lilac & multi 20 15

22nd Session of Intl. Chamber of Commerce (Eastern Division), Seoul, May 6-8.

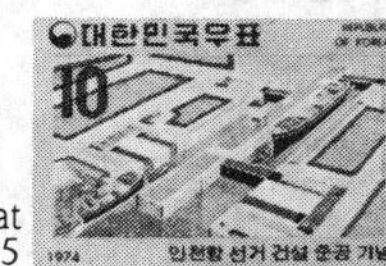

New Dock at Inchon — A475

1974, May 10
907 A475 10w yellow & multi 20 15

Dedication of dock, Inchon.

UNESCO Emblem, "20" and Yin Yang — A476

1974, June 14 Photo. *Perf. 13*
908 A476 10w org yel & multi 20 15

20th anniversary of the Korean National Commission for UNESCO.

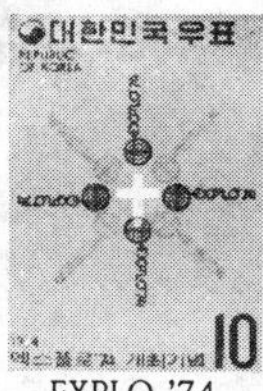

EXPLO '74 Emblems A477

Subway, Bus and Plane A478

Design: No. 910, EXPLO emblem rising from map of Korea.

1974, Aug. 13 Photo. *Perf. 13*
909 A477 10w orange & multi 25 15
910 A477 10w blue & multi 25 15
Set value 20

EXPLO '74, International Christian Congress, Yoido Islet, Seoul, Aug. 13-18.

1974, Aug. 15
911 A478 10w green & multi 25 15

Inauguration of Seoul subway (first in Korea), Aug. 15, 1974.

Target Shooting — A479

1974, Oct. 8 Photo. *Perf. 13x13½*

912 A479 10w shown 25 15
913 A479 30w Rowing 30 15

55th National Athletic Meet.

UPU Emblem A480

1974, Oct. 9 *Perf. 13*

914 A480 10w yellow & multi 25 15
a. Souvenir sheet of 2 1.25

Cent. of UPU. See No. C43.

International Landmarks — A481

1974, Oct. 11

915 A481 10w multicolored 25 15

International People to People Conference, Seoul, Oct. 11-14.

Korea Nos. 1-2 — A482

1974, Oct. 17

916 A482 10w lilac & multi 25 15
a. Souvenir sheet of 2 1.50

Philatelic Week, Oct. 17-23 and 90th anniversary of first Korean postage stamps.

Taekwondo and Kukkiwon Center — A483

1974, Oct. 18

917 A483 10w yellow grn & multi 25 15

First Asian Taekwondo (self-defense) Games, Seoul, Oct. 18-20.

Presidents Park and Ford, Flags and Globe — A484

1974, Nov. 22 Photo. *Perf. 13*

918 A484 10y multicolored 60 20
a. Souvenir sheet of 2 2.75

Visit of Pres. Gerald R. Ford to South Korea.

Yook Young Soo — A485

1974, Nov. 29

919 A485 10w green 45 20
920 A485 10w orange 45 20
921 A485 10w lilac 45 20
922 A485 10w blue 45 20
a. Souvenir sheet of 4, #919-922 14.00
b. Block of 4, #919-922 1.80 1.00

Yook Young Soo (1925-1974), wife of Pres. Park.

Rabbits — A486

Good-luck Purse — A487

1974, Dec. 1 Litho. *Perf. 12½x13*

923 A486 10w multicolored 22 15
a. Souvenir sheet of 2 65
924 A487 10w multicolored 22 15
a. Souvenir sheet of 2 65
Set value 24

New Year 1975.

Good-luck Key and Pigeon — A488

1975, Jan. 1 Photo. *Perf. 13*

925 A488 10w lt blue & multi 22 15

Introduction of National Welfare Insurance System.

UPU Emblem and "75" — A489

UPU Emblem and Paper Plane — A490

1975, Jan. 1

926 A489 10w yellow & multi 15 15
927 A490 10w lt blue & multi 15 15
Set value 20

75th anniv. of Korea's membership in UPU.

Dr. Schweitzer, Map of Africa, Hypodermic Needle — A491

1975, Jan. 14

928 A491 10w olive 15 15
929 A491 10w brt rose 15 15
930 A491 10w orange 15 15
931 A491 10w brt green 15 15
a. Block of 4, #928-931 50 40
Set value 40 32

Dr. Albert Schweitzer (1875-1965), medical missionary, birth centenary.

Folk Dance Issue

Dancer — A492

Bupo Nori — A492a

Designs: No. 933, Dancer with fan. No. 934, Woman with butterfly sleeves. No. 935, Group of Women. No. 936, Pongsan mask dance. No. 937, Pusan mask dance. No. 938, Buddhist drum dance. No. 939, Bara (cymbals) dance. No. 940, Sogo dance.

1975, Feb. 20 Photo. *Perf. 13*

932 A492 10w emerald & multi 15 15
933 A492 10w brt blue & multi 15 15

1975, Apr. 20

934 A492 10w yel grn & multi 15 15
935 A492 10w yellow & multi 15 15

1975, June 20

936 A492 10w pink & multi 15 15
937 A492 10w blue & multi 15 15

1975, Aug. 20

938 A492 20w yellow & multi 20 15
939 A492 20w salmon & multi 20 15

1975, Oct. 20

940 A492 20w blue & multi 20 15
941 A492a 20w yellow & multi 20 15
Nos. 932-941 (10) 1.70
Set value 1.00

Souvenir Sheets of 2

932a A492 10w (#1) 30
933a A492 10w (#2) 30
934a A492 10w (#3) 30
935a A492 10w (#4) 30
936a A492 10w (#5) 30
937a A492 10w (#6) 30
938a A492 20w (#7) 40
939a A492 20w (#8) 40
940a A492 20w (#9) 40
941a A492 20w (#10) 40
Nos. 932a-941a (10) 3.40

Globe and Rotary Emblem — A493

1975, Feb. 23

942 A493 10w multicolored 15 15

Rotary International, 70th anniversary.

Women and IWY Emblem A494

1975, Mar. 8

943 A494 10w multicolored 15 15

International Women's Year 1975.

Flower Issue

Violets — A495

Anemones — A496

Clematis Patens — A496a

Broad-bell Flowers — A496b

Designs: No. 946, Rhododendron. No. 948, Thistle. No. 949, Iris. No. 951, Bush clover. No. 952, Camellia. No. 953, Gentian.

1975, Mar. 15

944 A495 10w orange & multi 15 15
945 A496 10w yellow & multi 15 15

1975, May 15

946 A495 10w dk green & multi 15 15
947 A496a 10w yellow grn & multi 15 15

1975, July 15

948 A495 10w emerald & multi 15 15
949 A495 10w blue & multi 15 15

1975, Sept. 15

950 A496b 20w yellow & multi 15 15
951 A495 20w blue grn & multi 15 15

1975, Nov. 15

952 A495 20w yellow & multi 15 15
953 A496 20w salmon & multi 15 15
Nos. 944-953 (10) 1.50
Set value 1.00

Forest and Water Resources — A497

Reduced illustration.

1975, Mar. 20

954 A497 Strip of 4 40 30
a. 10w Saemaeul forest 15 15
b. 10w Dam and reservoir 15 15
c. 10w Green forest 15 15
d. 10w Timber industry 15 15

Natl. Tree Planting Month, Mar. 21-Apr. 20.

Map of Korea, HRF Emblem — A498

1975, Apr. 12 Photo. *Perf. 13*

955 A498 10w blue & multi 40 20

Homeland Reserve Forces Day.

Lily — A499

Ceramic Jar — A500

Ceramic Vase A501

Adm. Li Sun-sin A502

1975, Oct. 10 Photo. *Perf.* 13½x13

963 A499 6w green & bl grn 20 15
964 A500 50w gray grn & brn 45 30
965 A501 60w brown & yellow 54 52
966 A502 100w carmine 60 40

Metric System Symbols — A507

1975, May 20 *Perf.* 13

975 A507 10w salmon & multi 15 15

Centenary of International Meter Convention, Paris, 1875.

Praying Soldier, Incense Burner — A508

1975, June 6 Photo. *Perf.* 13

976 A508 10w multicolored 15 15

20th Memorial Day.

Flags of Korea, UN and US — A509

Designs (Flags of): No. 978, Ethiopia, France, Greece, Canada, South Africa. No. 979, Luxembourg, Australia, Great Britain, Colombia, Turkey. No. 980, Netherlands, Belgium, Philippines, New Zealand, Thailand.

1975, June 25 Photo. *Perf.* 13

977 A509 10w dk blue & multi 15 15
978 A509 10w dk blue & multi 15 15
979 A509 10w dk blue & multi 15 15
980 A509 10w dk blue & multi 15 15
a. Strip of 4, #977-980 45 40
Set value 40 24

25th anniv. of beginning of Korean War.

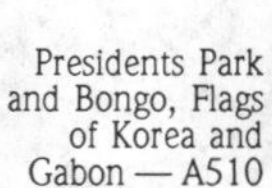

Presidents Park and Bongo, Flags of Korea and Gabon — A510

1975, July 5

981 A510 10w blue & multi 15 15
a. Souvenir sheet of 2 75

Visit of Pres. Albert Bongo of Gabon, July 5-8.

Scout Emblem, Tents and Neckerchief — A511

1975, July 29 Photo. *Perf.* 13

982 A511 10w shown 15 15
983 A511 10w Pick and oath 15 15
984 A511 10w Tents 15 15
985 A511 10w Ax, rope and tree 15 15
986 A511 10w Campfire 15 15
a. Strip of 4, #982-986 65 45
Set value 60 30

Nordjamb 75, 14th Boy Scout Jamboree, Lillehammer, Norway, July 29-Aug. 7.

Flame and Broken Chain — A512

Balloons with Symbols of Development over Map — A513

1975, Aug. 15 *Perf.* 13½x13

987 A512 20w gold & multi 15 15
988 A513 20w silver & multi 15 15
Set value 20

30th anniversary of liberation.

Taekwondo — A514

1975, Aug. 26 *Perf.* 13

989 A514 20w multicolored 15 15

2nd World Taekwondo Championships, Seoul, Aug. 25-Sept. 1.

National Assembly and Emblem — A515

1975, Sept. 1 Photo. *Perf.* 13½x13

990 A515 20w multicolored 15 15

Completion of National Assembly Building.

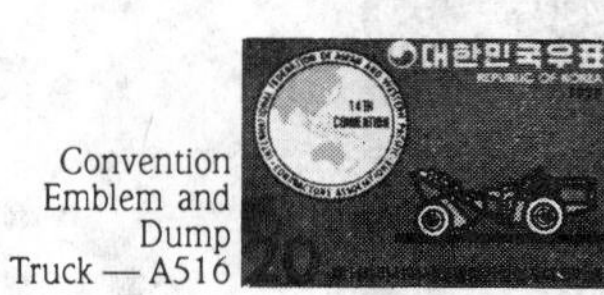

Convention Emblem and Dump Truck — A516

1975, Sept. 7 Photo. *Perf.* 13½x13

991 A516 20w ultra & multi 15 15

14th Convention of the Intl. Fed. of Asian and Western Pacific Contractors.

Cassegrainian Telescope and Morse Key — A517

1975, Sept. 28

992 A517 20w red lil, org & blk 15 15

90th anniversary of Korean telecommunications system.

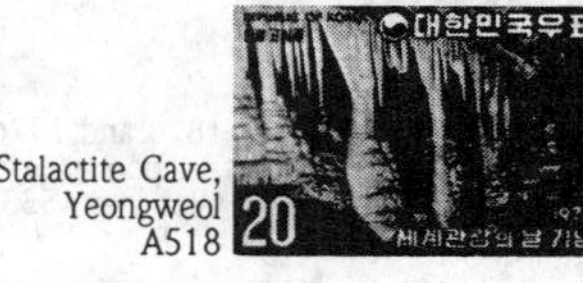

Stalactite Cave, Yeongweol A518

View of Mt. Sorak — A519

1975, Sept. 28

993 A518 20w multicolored 15 15
994 A519 20w multicolored 15 15
Set value 20

International Tourism Day.

Armed Forces Flag and Missiles — A519a

1975, Oct. 1 Photo. *Perf.* 13

994A A519a 20w multicolored 15 15

Armed Forces Day.

Gymnastics A520

Handball A521

1975, Oct. 7 Photo. *Perf.* 13

995 A520 20w yellow & multi 15 15
996 A521 20w multicolored 15 15
Set value 20

56th Natl. Athletic Meet, Taegu, Oct. 7-12.

An enhanced introduction to the Scott Catalogue begins on Page 5A. A thorough understanding of the material presented there will greatly aid your use of the catalogue itself.

Stamp Collecting Kangaroo A522

Hands and UN Emblem A523

1975, Oct. 8

997 A522 20w multicolored 15 15

Philatelic Week, Oct. 8-14.

1975, Oct. 24

998 A523 20w multicolored 15 15

United Nations, 30th anniversary.

Red Cross and Activities A524

Emblem and Dove A525

1975, Oct. 30

999 A524 20w orange, red & brn 15 15

Korean Red Cross, 70th anniversary.

1975, Nov. 30 Photo. *Perf.* 13

1000 A525 20w multicolored 15 15

Asian Parliamentary Union, 10th anniv.

Children Playing — A526

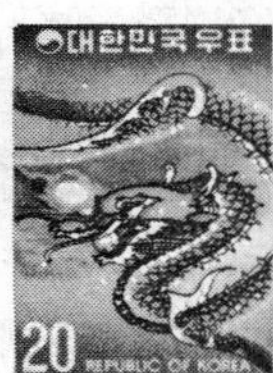

Dragon — A527

1975, Dec. 1

1001 A526 20w multicolored 15 15
a. Souvenir sheet of 2 30
1002 A527 20w multicolored 15 15
a. Souvenir sheet of 2 30
Set value 20

New Year 1976.

Inchong-Bukpyong Railroad — A528

1975, Dec. 5 Photo. *Perf.* 13

1003 A528 20w multicolored 15 15

Opening of electric cross-country railroad.

Butterfly Issue

Dilipa Fenestra A529

Byasa Alcinous Klug — A529a

Graphium Sarpedon A529b

Fabriciana Nerippe A529c

Nymphalis Xanthomelas A529d

Butterflies: No. 1005, Luehdorfia puzilōi. No. 1006, Papilio xuthus linne. No. 1007, Parnassius bremeri. No. 1008, Colias erate esper. No. 1010, Hestina assimilis.

1976, Jan. 20 Photo. *Perf. 13*

1004 A529 20w dp rose & multi 40 15
1005 A529 20w dp blue & multi 40 15

1976, Mar. 20

1006 A529 20w yellow & multi 40 15
1007 A529 20w yel grn & multi 40 15

1976, June 20

1008 A529 20w lt violet & multi 40 15
1009 A529a 20w citron & multi 40 15

1976, Aug. 20

1010 A529 20w tan & multi 40 15
1011 A529b 20w lt gray & multi 40 15

1976, Oct. 20

1012 A529c 20w lt green & multi 40 15
1013 A529d 20w lilac & multi 40 15
Nos. 1004-1013 (10) 4.00
Set value 1.00

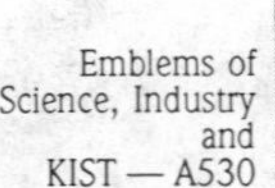

Emblems of Science, Industry and KIST — A530

1976, Feb. 10 Photo. *Perf. 13*

1014 A530 20w multicolored 15 15

Korean Institute of Science and Technology (KIST), 10th anniversary.

Siberian Bustard — A531

White-naped Crane — A532

1976, Feb. 20 Photo. *Perf. 13x13½*

1015 A531 20w shown 15 15
1016 A532 20w shown 15 15

1976, May 20

1017 A531 20w Blue-winged pitta 15 15
1018 A532 20w Tristam's woodpecker 15 15

1976, July 20

1019 A531 20w Wood pigeon 15 15
1020 A532 20w Oyster catcher 15 15

1976, Sept. 20

1021 A531 20w Black-faced spoonbill 15 15
1022 A532 20w Black stork 15 15

1976, Nov. 20

1023 A531 20w Whooper swan 15 15
1024 A532 20w Black vulture 15 15
Nos. 1015-1024 (10) 1.50
Set value 1.00

1876 and 1976 Telephones, Globe — A533

1976, Mar. 10

1025 A533 20w multicolored 15 15

Centenary of first telephone call by Alexander Graham Bell, Mar. 10, 1876.

Homeland Reserves A534

1976, Apr. 3 Photo. *Perf. 13½x13*

1026 A534 20w multicolored 15 15

8th Homeland Reserve Forces Day.

"People and Eye" — A535

1976, Apr. 7 *Perf. 13x13½*

1027 A535 20w multicolored 15 15

World Health Day; "Foresight prevents blindness."

Pres. Park, Village Movement Flag — A536

Intellectual Pursuits — A537

1976, Apr. 22

1028 A536 20w shown 15 15
1029 A537 20w shown 15 15
1030 A537 20w Village improvement 15 15
1031 A537 20w Agriculture 15 15
1032 A537 20w Income from production 15 15
a. Strip of 5, #1028-1032 80
Set value 50

6th anniv. of Pres. Park's New Village Movement for National Prosperity.

Mohenjo-Daro A538

1976, May 1 *Perf. 13½x13*

1033 A538 20w multicolored 15 15

UNESCO campaign to save the Mohenjo-Daro excavations in Pakistan.

13-Star and 50-Star Flags A539

Girl Scouts, Campfire and Emblem A540

American Bicentennial (Bicentennial Emblem and): No. 1035, Statue of Liberty. No. 1036, Map of US and Mt. Rushmore monument. No. 1037, Liberty Bell. No. 1038, First astronaut on moon.

1976, May 8 *Perf. 13x13½*

1034 A539 100w blk, dp bl & red 1.00 30
a. Souvenir sheet of 1 2.00
1035 A539 100w blk, dp bl & red 1.00 30
1036 A539 100w blk, dp bl & red 1.00 30
1037 A539 100w blk, dp bl & red 1.00 30
1038 A539 100w blk, dp bl & red 1.00 30
Nos. 1034-1038 (5) 5.00 1.50

1976, May 10

1039 A540 20w orange & multi 15 15

Korean Federation of Girl Scouts, 30th anniversary.

Stupas, Buddha of Borobudur A541

"Life Insurance" A542

1976, June 10

1040 A541 20w multicolored 15 15

UNESCO campaign to save the Borobudur Temple, Java.

1976, July 1 Photo. *Perf. 13x13½*

1041 A542 20w multicolored 15 15

National Life Insurance policies: "Over 100 billion-won," Apr. 30, 1976.

Volleyball — A543

1976, July 17

1042 A543 20w shown 15 15
1043 A543 20w Boxing 15 15
Set value 20

21st Olympic Games, Montreal, Canada, July 17-Aug. 1.

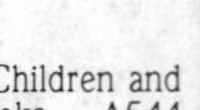

Children and Books — A544

1976, Aug. 10 *Perf. 13½x13*

1044 A544 20w brown & multi 15 15

Books for children.

Civil Defense Corps, Flag and Members — A545

1976, Sept. 15 *Perf. 13x13½*

1045 A545 20w multicolored 15 15

Civil Defense Corps, first anniversary.

Chamsungdan, Mani Mountain A546

Front Gate, Tongdosa Temple — A547

1976, Sept. 28 *Perf. 13½x13*

1046 A546 20w multicolored 15 15
1047 A547 20w multicolored 15 15
Set value 20

International Tourism Day.

Cadets and Academy A548

1976, Oct. 1

1048 A548 20w multicolored 15 15

Korean Military Academy, 30th anniversary.

Leaves and Stones, by Cheong Ju — A549

1976, Oct. 5 *Perf. 13x13½*

1049 A549 20w blk, gray & red 15 15
a. Souvenir sheet of 2 60

Philatelic Week, Oct. 5-11.

Snake-headed Figure, Bas-relief — A550

Door-pull and Cranes — A551

1976, Dec. 1 Photo. *Perf. 13x13½*

1050 A550 20w multicolored 20 15
  a. Souvenir sheet of 2 50
1051 A551 20w multicolored 20 15
  a. Souvenir sheet of 2 50
  Set value 20

New Year 1977.

Arrows, Cogwheels, Worker at Lathe — A552

Design: No. 1053, Arrows, Cogwheels, ship in dock.

1977, Jan. 20 Photo. *Perf. 13½x13*

1052 A552 20w multicolored 15 15
1053 A552 20w multicolored 15 15
  Set value 20

4th Economic Development Five-Year Plan.

Satellite Antenna and Microwaves — A553

1977, Jan. 31 *Perf. 13x13½*

1054 A553 20w multicolored 15 15

Membership in ITU, 25th anniv.

Korean Broadcasting Center A554

Parents and Two Children A555

1977, Feb. 16 *Perf. 13½x13*

1055 A554 20w multicolored 15 15

50th anniversary of broadcasting in Korea.

1977, Apr. 1 Photo. *Perf. 13½x13*

1056 A555 20w brt grn & orange 15 15

Family planning.

Reservist on Duty A556

Head with Symbols A557

1977, Apr. 2 *Perf. 13x13½*

1057 A556 20w multicolored 15 15

9th Homeland Reserve Forces Day.

1977, Apr. 21 Photo. *Perf. 13x13½*

1058 A557 20w dp lilac & multi 15 15

10th anniversary of Science Day.

Book, Map, Syringe — A558

1977, Apr. 25

1059 A558 20w blue & multi 15 15

35th International Meeting on Military Medicine.

Boy with Flowers and Dog — A559

Veteran's Emblem and Flag — A560

1977, May 5

1060 A559 20w multicolored 15 15

Proclamation of Children's Charter, 20th anniversary.

1977, May 8

1061 A560 20w multicolored 15 15

25th anniversary of Korean Veterans' Day.

Buddha, 8th Century, Sokkulam Grotto — A561

1977, May 25 Photo. *Perf. 13x13½*

1062 A561 20w sepia & olive 15 15
  a. Souvenir sheet of 2 45

"2600th" anniversary of birth of Buddha.

Ceramic Issues

Jar with Grape Design, 17th Century — A562

Celadon Vase, Bamboo Design, 12th Century — A563

Celadon Jar with Peonies A564

Vase with Willow Reed Peony Pattern — A565

Celadon Manshaped Wine Jug — A566

Celadon Melon-shaped Vase — A567

1977, Mar. 15 Photo. *Perf. 13x13½*

1063 A562 20w vio brn & multi 15 15
1064 A563 20w gray, grn & bis 15 15
  Set value 20

Perf. 13x13½, 13½x13

1977, June 15 Photo.

1065 A564 20w multicolored 15 15
1066 A565 20w multicolored 15 15
  Set value 20

1977, July 15

1067 A566 20w multicolored 15 15
1068 A567 20w multicolored 15 15
  Set value 20

1977, Aug. 15

Designs: No. 1069, White porcelain bowl with inlaid lotus vine design. No. 1070, Black Koryo ware vase with plum blossom vine.

1069 A564 20w multicolored 15 15
1070 A565 20w multicolored 15 15
  Set value 20

Punch'ong Jar — A568

Celadon Cylindrical Vase — A569

1977, Nov. 15

1071 A568 20w multicolored 15 15
1072 A569 20w multicolored 15 15
  Set value 20

Ceramic, national treasures.

Types of 1962-66
Designs as Before

1976-77 Litho. *Perf. 12½*
Granite Paper

1076 A187 200w brown & lt grn
1077 A187a 300w sl grn & sal ('76)
1078 A187a 300w brown & salmon
1079 A187a 500w purple & lt grn

Magpie A570

Nature Protection A571

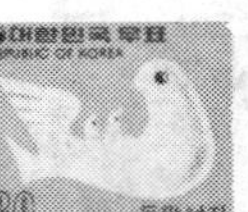
"Family Planning" A572

Children on Swing A573

Ceramic Horseman A574

Muryangsu Hall, Busok Temple A575

Pagoda, Pobjusa Temple A576

Gold Crown, from Chonmachong Mound A577

Monster Mask Tile, 6th or 7th Century A578

Flying Angels from Bronze Bell from Sangwon-sa, 725 A.D. A579

Perf. 12½x13½, 13½x12½

1977-79 Photo.

1088 A570 3w lt blue & blk 15 15
1090 A326 10w emerald & blk 15 15
1091 A571 20w multicolored 15 15
1092 A572 20w emer & blk ('78) 15 15
1093 A573 20w grn & org ('79) 15 15
1097 A574 80w lt brn & sep 48 40
1099 A575 200w salmon & brn 1.00 50
1100 A576 300w brn purple 1.50 60
1101 A577 500w multicolored 3.25 1.00

Perf. 13½x13

1102 A578 500w brown & purple 2.50 1.00

Perf. 13

1103 A579 1000w slate grn ('78) 5.00 2.00
  Nos. 1088-1103 (11) 14.48 6.25

Ulleung Island — A580

Armed Forces — A581

Design: No. 1105, Haeundae Beach.

1977, Sept. 28 Photo. *Perf. 13*

1104 A580 20w multicolored 15 15
1105 A580 20w multicolored 15 15
  Set value 20

World Tourism Day.

1977, Oct. 1 Photo. *Perf. 13*

1106 A581 20w green & multi 15 15

Armed Forces Day.

Mt. Inwang after the Rain, by Chung Seon (1676-1759)
A582 A583

1977, Oct. 4

1107 A582 20w multicolored 15 15
1108 A583 20w multicolored 15 15
a. Souvenir sheet of 2 75
Set value 20

Philatelic Week, Oct. 4-10.

Rotary Emblem on Bronze Bell, Koryo Dynasty — A584

1977, Nov. 10 Photo. *Perf. 13*

1109 A584 20w multicolored 15 15

Korean Rotary Club, 50th anniversary.

Korean Flag on Mt. Everest — A585

1977, Nov. 11

1110 A585 20w multicolored 15 15

Korean Mt. Everest Expedition, reached peak, Sept. 15, 1977.

Children and Kites
A586

Horse-headed Figure, Bas-relief
A587

1977, Dec. 1 Photo. *Perf. 13*

1111 A586 20w multicolored 22 15
a. Souvenir sheet of 2 42
1112 A587 20w multicolored 22 15
a. Souvenir sheet of 2 42
Set value 20

New Year 1978.

Clay Pigeon Shooting
A588

Designs: No. 1114, Air pistol shooting. No. 1115, Air rifle shooting and target.

1977, Dec. 3

1113 A588 20w multicolored 15 15
a. Souvenir sheet of 2 ('78) 85
1114 A588 20w multicolored 15 15
a. Souvenir sheet of 2 ('78) 85
1115 A588 20w multicolored 15 15
a. Souvenir sheet of 2 ('78) 85
Set value 30

42nd World Shooting Championships, Seoul, 1978.

Boeing 727 over Globe, ICAO Emblem
A589

1977, Dec. 11

1116 A589 20w multicolored 15 15

25th anniv. of Korea's membership in the ICAO.

Plane, Cargo, Freighter and Globe — A590

1977, Dec. 22 Photo. *Perf. 13*

1117 A590 20w multicolored 15 15

Korean exports.

Ships and World Map — A591

1978, Mar. 13 Photo. *Perf. 13*

1118 A591 20w multicolored 15 15

Maritime Day.

Stone Pagoda Issue

Four Lions Pagoda, Hwaom-sa — A592

Punhwang-sa Temple
A593

Kyongch'on sa Temple
A594

Design: No. 1120, Seven-storied pagoda, T'appyongri.

1978, Mar. 20 Photo. *Perf. 13*

1119 A592 20w lt green & multi 15 15
1120 A592 20w ocher & multi 15 15

1978, May 20

Design: No. 1122, Miruk-sa Temple.

1121 A593 20w lt green & blk 15 15
1122 A593 20w grn, brn & yel 15 15

1978, June 20

Designs: #1123, Tabo Pagoda, Pulguk-sa. #1124, Three-storied pagoda, Pulguk-sa.

1123 A592 20w gray, lt grn & blk 15 15
1124 A592 20w lilac & black 15 15

1978, July 20 *Perf. 13½x12½*

Design: No. 1126, Octagonal Pagoda, Wolchong-sa Temple.

1125 A594 20w gray & brn 15 15
1126 A594 20w lt green & blk 15 15

1978, Nov. 20 *Perf. 13x13½*

Designs: No. 1127, 13-storied pagoda, Jeonghye-sa. No. 1128, Three-storied pagoda, Jinjeon-sa.

1127 A592 20w pale grn & multi 15 15
1128 A592 20w lilac & multi 15 15
Nos. 1119-1128 (10) 1.50
Set value 1.00

Ants and Coins — A595

Reservist with Flag — A596

1978, Apr. 1

1129 A595 20w multicolored 15 15

Importance of saving.

1978, Apr. 1

1130 A596 20w multicolored 15 15

10th Homeland Reserve Forces Day.

Seoul Cultural Center — A597

1978, Apr. 1

1131 A597 20w multicolored 15 15

Opening of Seoul Cultural Center.

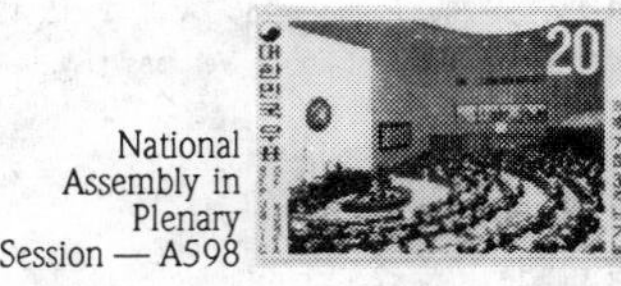
National Assembly in Plenary Session — A598

1978, May 31

1132 A598 20w multicolored 15 15

30th anniversary of National Assembly.

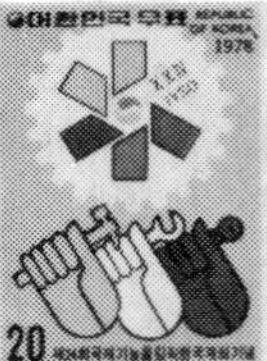
Hands Holding Tools, Competition Emblem — A599

Bell of Joy and Crater Lake, Mt. Baegdu — A600

1978, Aug. 5 Photo. *Perf. 13*

1133 A599 20w multicolored 15 15
a. Souvenir sheet of 2 60

24th World Youth Skill Olympics, Busan, Aug. 30-Sept. 15.

1978, Aug. 15

1134 A600 20w multicolored 15 15

Founding of republic, 30th anniversary.

Nurse, Badge and Flowers
A601

Sobaeksan Observatory
A602

1978, Aug. 26

1135 A601 20w multicolored 15 15

Army Nurse Corps, 30th anniversary.

1978, Sept. 13 Photo. *Perf. 13*

1136 A602 20w multicolored 15 15

Opening of Sobaeksan Natl. Observatory.

Kyunghoeru Pavilion, Kyongbok Palace, Seoul — A603

Design: No. 1138, Baeg Do (island).

1978, Sept. 28

1137 A603 20w multicolored 15 15
1138 A603 20w multicolored 15 15
Set value 20

Tourist publicity.

Customs Flag and Officers
A604

1978, Sept. 28

1139 A604 20w multicolored 15 15

Cent. of 1st Korean Custom House, Busan.

Armed Forces — A605

1978, Oct. 1 Photo. *Perf. 13*

1140 A605 20w multicolored 15 15

Armed Forces, 30th anniversary.

Clay Figurines, Silla Dynasty A606

Portrait of a Lady, by Shin Yoon-bok A607

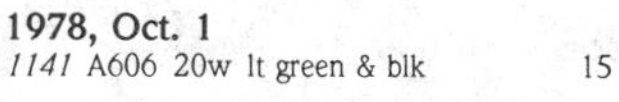

1978, Oct. 1
1141 A606 20w lt green & blk 15 15

Culture Month, October 1978.

1978, Oct. 24
1142 A607 20w multicolored 15 15
a. Souvenir sheet of 2 40

Philatelic Week, Oct. 24-29.

Young Men, YMCA Emblem — A608

1978, Oct. 28
1143 A608 20w multicolored 15 15

75th anniv. of founding of Korean YMCA.

Hand Protecting Against Fire — A609

1978, Nov. 1 Photo. *Perf. 13*
1144 A609 20w multicolored 15 15

Fire Prevention Day, Nov. 1.

Winter Landscape A610

Ram-headed Figure, Bas-relief A611

1978, Dec. 1 Photo. *Perf. 13x13½*
1145 A610 20w multicolored 15 15
a. Souvenir sheet of 2 30
1146 A611 20w multicolored 15 15
a. Souvenir sheet of 2 30
Set value 20

New Year 1979.

Hibiscus, Students, Globe — A612

President Park — A613

1978, Dec. 5
1147 A612 20w multicolored 15 15

Proclamation of National Education Charter, 10th anniversary.

1978, Dec. 27
1148 A613 20w multicolored 15 15
a. Souvenir sheet of 2 2.00

Inauguration of Park Chung Hee for fifth term as president.

Nature Conservation Issue

Golden Mandarinfish A614

Lace-bark Pines A615

Mandarin Ducks — A616

Neofinettia Orchid — A617

Goral — A618

Lilies of the Valley — A619

Rain Frog A620

Asian Polypody A621

Firefly — A622

Meesun Tree — A623

1979, Feb. 20 Photo. *Perf. 13x13½*
1149 A614 20w multicolored 15 15
1150 A615 20w multicolored 15 15

1979, May 20
1151 A616 20w multicolored 15 15
1152 A617 20w multicolored 15 15

1979, June 20
1153 A618 20w multicolored 15 15
1154 A619 20w multicolored 15 15

1979, Nov. 25
1155 A620 20w multicolored 15 15
1156 A621 20w multicolored 15 15

1980, Jan. 20
1157 A622 30w multicolored 18 15
1158 A623 30w multicolored 18 15
Nos. 1149-1158 (10) 1.56
Set value 90

Samil Monument — A624

1979, Mar. 1 Photo. *Perf. 13x13½*
1159 A624 20w multicolored 15 15

60th anniversary of Samil independence movement.

Worker and Bulldozer A625

1979, Mar. 10 *Perf. 13½x13*
1160 A625 20w multicolored 15 15

Labor Day.

Hand Holding Tools, Gun and Grain — A626

Tabo Pagoda, Pulguk-sa Temple — A627

Women, Silk Screen — A628

1979, Apr. 1 *Perf. 13x13½*
1161 A626 20w multicolored 15 15

Strengthening national security.

1979, Apr. 1

Art Treasures: No. 1163, Statue. No. 1164, Crown. No. 1165, Celadon Vase.

1162 A627 20w gray bl & multi 15 15
1163 A627 20w bister & multi 15 15
1164 A627 20w violet & multi 15 15
1165 A627 20w brt grn & multi 15 15
1166 A628 60w multicolored 35 30
a. Souvenir sheet of 2 1.00
Set value 82 70

5000 years of Korean art.
See Nos. 1175-1179, 1190.

Pulguk-sa Temple and PATA Emblem — A629

1979, Apr. 16 *Perf. 13½x13*
1167 A629 20w multicolored 15 15

28th Pacific Area Travel Association (PATA) Conference, Seoul, Apr. 16-18, and Gyeongju, Apr. 20-21.

Presidents Park and Senghor A630

1979, Apr. 22 *Perf. 13½x13*
1168 A630 20w multicolored 15 15
a. Souvenir sheet of 2 42

Visit of Pres. Leopold Sedar Senghor of Senegal.

Basketball — A631

1979, Apr. 29 *Perf. 13x13½*
1169 A631 20w multicolored 15 15

8th World Women's Basketball Championship, Seoul, Apr. 29-May 13.

Children and IYC Emblem A632

1979, May 5 Photo. *Perf. 13½x13*
1170 A632 20w multicolored 15 15
a. Souvenir sheet of 2 60

International Year of the Child.

Traffic Pollution — A633

1979, June 5 Photo. *Perf. 13x13½*
1171 A633 20w green & dk brn 15 15

Pollution control.

Flags, Presidents Park and Carter — A634

1979, June 29 *Perf. 13½x13*
1172 A634 20w multicolored 15 15
a. Souvenir sheet of 2 60

Visit of Pres. Jimmy Carter.

Korean Exhibition Center — A635

1979, July 3
1173 A635 20w multicolored 15 15

Opening of Korean Exhibition Center.

Jet, Globe, Pagoda — A636

1979, Aug. 1 Photo. *Perf. 13½x13*
1174 A636 20w multicolored 15 15

10th anniversary of Korean airlines.

Art Treasure Types

Designs: No. 1175, Porcelain jar, 17th century. No. 1176, Man on horseback, ceremonial pitcher, horiz. No. 1177, Sword Dance, by Shin Yuk-bok. No. 1178, Golden Amitabha with halo, 8th century. No. 1179, Hahoe ritual mask.

1979 Photo. *Perf. 13x13½, 13½x13*
1175 A627 20w lilac & multi 15 15
1176 A627 20w multicolored 15 15
1177 A628 60w multicolored 35 30
a. Souvenir sheet of 2 1.00
Set value 50

Issue dates: No. 1177, Sept. 1. Nos. 1175-1176, Oct. 15.

1979, Nov. 15
1178 A627 20w dp green & multi 15 15
1179 A627 20w multicolored 15 15
Set value 24 20

Yongdu Rock — A637

1979, Sept. 28
1180 A637 20w shown 15 15
1181 A637 20w Mt. Mai, vert. 15 15
Set value 24 20

World Tourism Day.

People, Blood and Heart — A637a

1979, Oct. 1 *Perf. 13½x13*
1182 A637a 20w multicolored 15 15

Blood Banks, 4th anniversary.

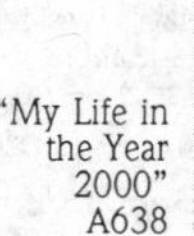

"My Life in the Year 2000" A638

1979, Oct. 30 *Perf. 13½x13*
1183 A638 20w multicolored 15 15
a. Souvenir sheet of 2 50

Philatelic Week, Oct. 30-Nov. 4.

Monkey-headed Figure, Bas-relief A639

Children Playing Yut A640

1979, Dec. 1
1184 A639 20w multicolored 15 15
a. Souvenir sheet of 2 42
1185 A640 20w multicolored 15 15
a. Souvenir sheet of 2 42
Set value 24 20

New Year 1980.

Inauguration of Pres. Choi Kyu-hah — A641

1979, Dec. 21
1186 A641 20w multicolored 15 15
a. Souvenir sheet of 2 60

President Park — A642

1980, Feb. 2 Photo. *Perf. 13x13½*
1187 A642 30w orange brn 18 15
1188 A642 30w dull purple 18 15
a. Souvenir sheet of 2 52
b. Pair, #1187-1188 36 30

President Park Chung Hee (1917-1979) memorial.

Art Treasure Type of 1979 and

Dragon-shaped Kettle — A643

Design: 60w, Landscape, by Kim Hong-do.

Perf. 13½x13, 13x13½
1980, Feb. 20 Photo.
1189 A643 30w multicolored 18 15
1190 A628 60w multicolored 35 30
a. Souvenir sheet of 2 90

Art Treasure Issue

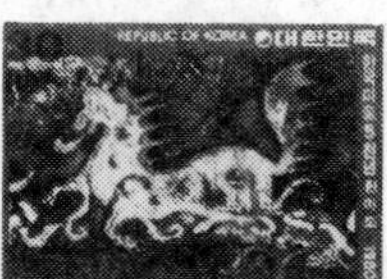

Heavenly Horse, Saddle — A644

Dragon Head, Banner Staff — A645

Tiger, Granite Sculpture — A647

Mounted Nobleman Mural — A646

Human Face, Roof Tile — A648

Deva King Sculpture — A650

White Tiger Mural — A649

Earthenware Ducks
A651 A652

Tiger, Folk Painting — A653

1980 Photo. *Perf. 13½x13, 13x13½*
1191 A644 30w multicolored 18 15
1192 A645 30w multicolored 18 15
1193 A646 30w multicolored 18 15
1194 A647 30w multicolored 18 15
1195 A648 30w multicolored 18 15
1196 A649 30w multicolored 18 15

Engr. *Perf. 12½x13*
1197 A650 30w black 18 15
1198 A650 30w red 18 15
Nos. 1191-1198 (8) 1.44
Set value 40

Issue dates: Nos. 1191-1192, Apr. 20. Nos. 1193-1194, May 20; Nos. 1195-1196, Aug. 20; Nos. 1197-1198, Nov. 20.

1983 Litho. Engr. *Perf. 13*
1199 A651 1000w bis brn & red brn 3.75 75
1200 A652 1000w bis brn & red brn 3.75 75
a. Pair, #1199-1200 7.50 2.50
1201 A653 5000w multicolored 16.00 4.00
a. Souvenir sheet, perf. 13½x13 18.00

Issued: #1199-1200, Nov. 25; #1201, Dec. 1.
No. 1201a for PHILAKOREA '84. No. 1201a exists imperf.

15-Cent Minimum Value
The minimum value for a single stamp is 15 cents. This value reflects the costs of the handlling of inexpensive stamps.

Lotus Blossoms and Ducks — A656

Tiger and Magpie — A657

Perf. 13x13½, 13½x13
1980, Mar. 10
1203 A656 30w multicolored 18 15
1204 A657 60w multicolored 35 30

Red Phoenix (in Form of Rooster) — A658

Moon Over Mt. Konryun — A659

Design: No. 1207, Sun over Mt. Konryun. No. 1207a has continuous design.

1980, May 10 *Perf. 13x13½*
1205 A658 30w multicolored 18 15
1206 A659 60w multicolored 35 30
1207 A659 60w multicolored 35 30
a. Souvenir sheet of 2, #1206-1207 75
b. Pair, #1206-1207 70 60
Set value 65

Rabbits Pounding Grain in a Mortar — A660

Dragon in the Clouds — A661

1980, July 10 Photo. *Perf. 13x13½*
1208 A660 30w multicolored 18 15
1209 A661 30w multicolored 18 15
Set value 15

Pine Tree, Pavilion, Mountain A662

Flowers and Birds, Bridal Room Screen A663

1980, Aug. 9 Photo. *Perf. 13x13½*

1210 A662 30w multicolored 18 15
1211 A663 30w multicolored 18 15
Set value 15

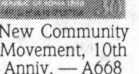

Tortoises and Cranes — A664

Designs: Symbols of longevity.

1980, Nov. 10 Photo. *Perf. 13½x13*

1212 Strip of 4 75 20
a. A664 30w any single 18 15

New Community Movement, 10th Anniv. — A668

Freighters at Sea — A669

1980, Apr. 22 *Perf. 13x13½*

1216 A668 30w multicolored 18 15

1980, Mar. 13

1217 A669 30w multicolored 18 15

Increase of Korea's shipping tonnage to 5 million tons.

Soccer — A670

1980, Aug. 23 *Perf. 13x13½*

1218 A670 30w multicolored 18 15

10th President's Cup Soccer Tournament, Aug. 23-Sept. 5.

Mt. Sorak — A671

Paikryung Island — A672

Perf. 12½x13½

1980, Apr. 10 Photo.

1219 A671 15w multicolored 15 15
1220 A672 90w multicolored 60 15
Set value 16

Flag — A673

1980 *Perf. 13½x13*

1221 A673 30w multicolored 18 15

Coil Stamp

Perf. Vert.

1221A A673 30w multicolored 18 15

UN Intervention, 30th Anniv. — A674

Election of Miss World in Seoul — A675

1980, June 25 *Perf. 13x13½*

1222 A674 30w multicolored 18 15

1980, July 8

1223 A675 30w multicolored 18 15

Women's Army Corps, 30th Anniversary A676

1980, Sept. 6 *Perf. 13½x13*

1224 A676 30w multicolored 18 15

Baegma River — A677

Three Peaks of Dodam A678

1980, Sept. 28

1225 A677 30w multicolored 18 15
1226 A678 30w multicolored 18 15
Set value 15

Inauguration of Pres. Chun Doo-hwan A679

1980, Sept. 1

1227 A679 30w multicolored 18 15
a. Souvenir sheet of 2 75

Ear of Corn — A680

Symbolic Tree — A681

1980, Oct. 20 *Perf. 13x13½*

1228 A680 30w multicolored 18 15

12th population and housing census.

1980, Oct. 27

1229 A681 30w multicolored 18 15

National Red Cross, 75th anniversary.

"Mail-Delivering Angels" A682

1980, Nov. 6 *Perf. 13½x13*

1230 A682 30w multicolored 18 15
a. Souvenir sheet of 2 45

Philatelic Week, Nov. 6-11.

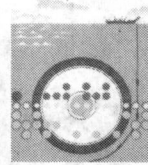

Korea-Japan Submarine Cable System Inauguration — A683

1980, Nov. 28 *Perf. 13x13½*

1231 A683 30w multicolored 18 15

Rooster — A684

Cranes — A685

1980, Dec. 1

1232 A684 30w multicolored 22 15
a. Souvenir sheet of 2 45
1233 A685 30w multicolored 22 15
a. Souvenir sheet of 2 45
Set value 15

New Year 1981.

Second Inauguration of Pres. Chun Doo-hwan A686

1981, Mar. 3 Photo. *Perf. 13½x13*

1234 A686 30w multicolored 18 15
a. Souvenir sheet of 2 55

Ship Issue

Oil Tanker — A687

Cargo Ship — A688

Oil Tanker — A689

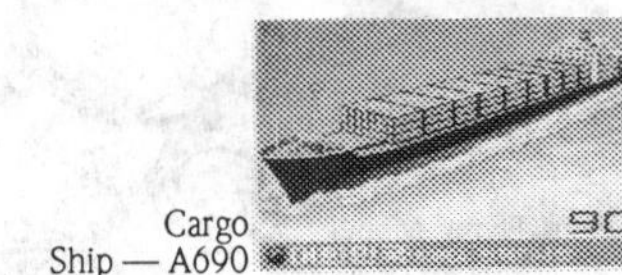

Cargo Ship — A690

Tug Boat — A691

Stern Trawler — A692

Log Carrier — A693

Auto Carrier — A694

Chemical Carrier A695

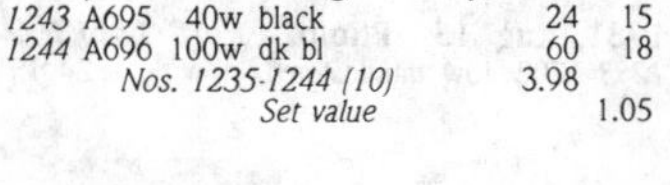

Passenger Boat — A696

Perf. 13½x13, 13x13½

1981, Mar. 13

1235 A687 30w multicolored 18 15
1236 A688 90w multicolored 55 15

5th Maritime Day.

1981, May 10 Photo. *Perf. 13½x13*

1237 A689 30w multicolored 18 15
1238 A690 90w multicolored 55 15

1981, July 10 *Perf. 13½x13*

1239 A691 40w multicolored 24 15
1240 A692 100w multicolored 60 18

1981, Aug. 10

1241 A693 40w multicolored 24 15
1242 A694 100w multicolored 60 18

1981, Nov. 10 Engr. *Perf. 13x12½*

1243 A695 40w black 24 15
1244 A696 100w dk bl 60 18
Nos. 1235-1244 (10) 3.98
Set value 1.05

11th Natl. Assembly Opening Session — A697

1981, Apr. 17 Photo. *Perf. 13½x13*

1245 A697 30w gold & dk brn 18 15

Hand Reading Braille, Helping Hands — A698

1981, Apr. 30 Photo. ***Perf. 13x13½***

1246 A698 30w shown 18 15
1247 A698 90w Man in wheelchair 55 15
Set value 20

International Year of the Disabled.

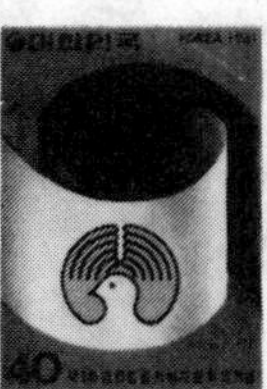

Ribbon and Council Emblem A699

Clena River and Mountains A700

1981, June 5 Photo. ***Perf. 13x13½***

1248 A699 40w multicolored 24 15

Advisory Council on Peaceful Unification Policy (North and South Korea) anniv.

1981, June 5

1249 A700 30w shown 18 15
1250 A700 90w Seagulls 55 15
Set value 20

10th World Environment Day.

Pres. Chun and Pres. Suharto of Indonesia A701

Pres. Chun Visit to Asia: b, King of Malaysia. c, Korean, Singapore flags. d, King Bhumibol Adulyadej of Thailand. e, Pres. Marcos of Philippines.

1981, June 25 ***Perf. 13½x13***

1251 Strip of 5 1.25 25
a.-e. A701 40w any single 24 15
f. Souvenir sheet of 5, imperf. 1.25

Size: 49x33mm
Perf. 13x13½

1252 A701 40w multicolored 24 15
a. Souvenir sheet of 2, imperf. 60
Set value 30

36th Anniv. of Liberation — A702

1981, Aug. 15 Photo. ***Perf. 13x13½***

1253 A702 40w multicolored 24 15

Tolharubang, "Stone Grandfather" A704

Rose of Sharon A705

Porcelain Jar, 17th Cent. — A706

Chomsongdae Observatory, 7th Cent. — A707

Mounted Warrior, Earthenware Jug, 5th Cent. A708

Family Planning A709

Walking Stick — A710

Ryu Kwan-soon (1904-20), Martyr — A711

"Tasan" Chung Yak-yong, Lee Dynasty Scholar — A712

Ahn Joong-guen (1879-1910), Martyr — A713

Ahn Chang-ho (1878-1938), Independence Fighter — A714

Koryo Celadon Incense Burner — A715

Kim Ku (1876-1949), Statesman — A716

Mountain Landscape Brick Bas-relief — A717

Mandarin Duck, Celadon Incense Burner — A718

Perf. 13½x12½ (Nos. 1256, 1257, 1266), 13, 13½x13, 13x13½

1981-89 **Photo., Engr.**

1255	A704	20w	multi ('86)	15	15
1256	A705	40w	multi	24	15
1257	A706	60w	multi	36	15
1258	A707	70w	multi	42	15
1259	A708	80w	multi ('83)	48	15
1260	A709	80w	multi ('86)	25	15
1261	A710	80w	multi ('89)	24	15
1262	A711	100w	lilac	65	15
1263	A712	100w	gray blk ('86)	30	15
1264	A713	200w	lt ol grn & ol	1.25	25
1265	A714	300w	dl lil ('83)	1.10	22
1266	A715	400w	multi	2.75	50
1267	A715	400w	pale grn & multi ('83)	2.40	40
1268	A716	450w	dk vio brn ('86)	1.20	40
1269	A717	500w	multi	3.00	75
1270	A718	700w	multi ('83)	4.25	80
			Nos. 1255-1270 (16)	19.04	
			Set value		3.95

Inscription and denomination of No. 1267, colorless, No. 1267, dark brown.

See Nos. 1449, 1449C.

Coil Stamp

Photo. ***Perf. 13 Horiz.***

1271 A707 70w multicolored 18 15

Girl Flying Model Plane — A721

Air Force Chief of Staff Cup, 3rd Aeronautic Competition: Various model planes.

1981, Sept. 20 ***Perf. 13½x13***

1272 Strip of 5 1.25 30
a. A721 10w multi 15 15
b. A721 20w multi 15 15
c. A721 40w multi 24 15
d. A721 50w multi 30 15
e. A721 80w multi 50 15

WHO Emblem, Citizens — A722

World Tourism Day — A723

1981, Sept. 22 ***Perf. 13x13½***

1273 A722 40w multicolored 24 15

WHO, 32nd Western Pacific Regional Committee Meeting, Seoul, Sept. 22-28.

1981, Sept. 28

1274 A723 40w Seoul Tower 24 15
1275 A723 40w Ulreung Isld. 24 15
Set value 15

Bicycle Racing — A724

1981, Oct. 10 ***Perf. 13½x13***

1276 A724 40w shown 24 15
1277 A724 40w Swimming 24 15
Set value 15

62nd Natl. Sports Festival, Seoul, Oct. 10-15.

Flags, Presidents Chun and Carazo — A725

1981, Oct. 12 ***Perf. 13½x13***

1278 A725 40w multicolored 24 15

Visit of Pres. Rodrigo Carazo Odio of Costa Rica, Oct. 12-14.

World Food Day — A726

First Natl. Aviation Day — A727

1981, Oct. 16 ***Perf. 13x13½***

1279 A726 40w multicolored 24 15

1981, Oct. 30 ***Perf. 13½x13***

1280 A727 40w multicolored 24 15

1988 Olympic Games, Seoul — A728

9th Philatelic Week, Nov. 18-24 — A729

1981, Oct. 30 ***Perf. 13x13½***

1281 A728 40w multicolored 24 15

1981, Nov. 18 ***Perf. 13½x13***

1282 A729 40w multicolored 24 15
a. Souvenir sheet of 2 50

Camellia and Dog — A730

Children Flying Kite — A731

1981, Dec. 1 ***Perf. 13x13½***

1283 A730 40w multicolored 24 15
a. Souvenir sheet of 2 50
1284 A731 40w multicolored 24 15
a. Souvenir sheet of 2 50
Set value 15

New Year 1982 (Year of the Dog).

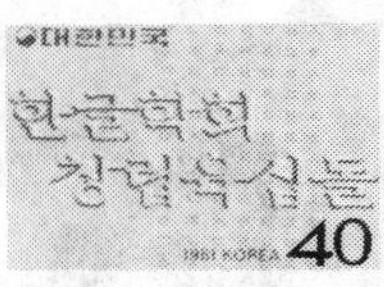

Hangul Hakhoe Language Society, 60th Anniv. — A732

1981, Dec. 3 ***Perf. 13½x13***

1285 A732 40w multicolored 24 15

Telecommunications Authority Inauguration A733

Scouting Year A734

1982, Jan. 4 Photo. ***Perf. 13x13½***

1286 A733 60w multicolored 36 15

1982, Feb. 22

1287 A734 60w multicolored 36 15

60th Anniv. of YWCA in Korea — A735

Intl. Polar Year Centenary — A736

1982, Apr. 20 Photo. ***Perf. 13x13½***

1288 A735 60w multicolored 36 15

1982, Apr. 21 ***Perf. 13½x13***

1289 A736 60w multicolored 36 15

60th Children's Day — A737

1982, May 5 *Perf. 13½x13*

1290	A737 60w multicolored	36	15

Visit of Liberian Pres. Samuel K. Doe, May 9-13 A738

1982, May 9 Litho. *Perf. 13x12½*

1291	A738 60w multicolored	36	15
a.	Souvenir sheet of 2, imperf.	75	

Centenary of US-Korea Treaty of Amity — A739

1982, May 18 Photo. *Perf. 13½x13*

1292	A739 60w Statue of Liberty, pagoda	36	15
1293	A739 60w Emblem	36	15
a.	Souvenir sheet of 2	75	
	Set value		15

Nos. 1292-1293 se-tenant.

Visit of Zaire Pres. Mobutu Sese Seko, June 7-10 — A740

1982, June 7 Litho. *Perf. 13x12½*

1294	A740 60w multicolored	36	15
a.	Souvenir sheet of 2, imperf.	75	

Historical Painting Issue

Gen. Kwon Yul's Victory at Haengju, by Oh Seung-woo — A747

Designs: No. 1295, Territorial Expansion by Kwanggaeto the Great, by Lee Chong-sang, 1975. No. 1296, Gen. Euljimunduck's Victory at Salsoo, by Park Kak-soon, 1975. No. 1297, Shilla's Repulse of Tang's Army, by Oh Seung-woo. No. 1298, Gen. Kang Kam-chan's Victory at Kyiju, by Lee Yong-hwan. No. 1299, Admiral Yi Sun-sin's Victory at Hansan, 1592, by Kim Hyung-ku. No. 1300, Gen. Kim Chwa-jin's Battle at Chungsanri, by Sohn Soo-kwang. No. 1302, Kim Chong-suh's Exploitation of Yukjin, 1434, by Kim Tae.

1982 Photo. *Perf. 13x13½*

1295	A747 60w multicolored	36	24
1296	A747 60w multicolored	36	24
1297	A747 60w multicolored	36	24
1298	A747 60w multicolored	36	24
1299	A747 60w multicolored	36	15
1300	A747 60w multicolored	36	15
1301	A747 60w multicolored	36	15
1302	A747 60w multicolored	36	15
	Nos. 1295-1302 (8)	2.88	
	Set value		1.20

Issue dates: Nos. 1295-1296, June 15; Nos. 1297-1298, July 15; Nos. 1299-1300, Oct. 15, Nos. 1301-1302, Dec. 15.

55th Intl. YMCA Convention, Seoul, July 20-23 — A749

Flags, Presidents Chun and Arap Moi — A750

1982, July 20

1303	A749 60w multicolored	36	24

1982, Aug. 17 *Perf. 13½x13*

Pres. Chun's Visit to Africa and Canada: No. 1304, Kenya (Pres. Daniel T. Arap Moi), Aug. 17-19. No. 1305, Nigeria (Pres. Alhaji Shehe Shagari), Aug. 19-22. No. 1306, Gabon (Pres. El Hadj Omar Bongo), Aug. 22-24. No. 1307, Senegal (Pres. Abdou Diouf), Aug. 24-26. No. 1308, Canada, Aug. 28-31.

1304	A750 60w multicolored	36	24
1305	A750 60w multicolored	36	24
1306	A750 60w multicolored	36	24
1307	A750 60w multicolored	36	24
1308	A750 60w multicolored	36	24
	Nos. 1304-1308 (5)	1.80	1.20

Souvenir Sheets of 2

1304a	A750 60w	75	
1305a	A750 60w	75	
1306a	A750 60w	75	
1307a	A750 60w	75	
1308a	A750 60w	75	
	Nos. 1304a-1308a (5)	3.75	

Natl. Flag Centenary A751

1982, Aug. 22

1309	A751 60w multicolored	36	24
a.	Souvenir sheet of 2	75	

2nd Seoul Open Intl. Table Tennis Championship, Aug. 25-31 — A752

1982, Aug. 25

1310	A752 60w multicolored	36	24

27th World Amateur Baseball Championship Series, Seoul, Sept. 4-18 — A753

1982, Sept. 4 Engr. *Perf. 13*

1311	A753 60w red brn	36	15

Seoul Intl. Trade Fair (SITRA '82), Sept. 24-Oct. 18 — A754

1982, Sept. 17 Photo. *Perf. 13½x13*

1312	A754 60w multicolored	36	15

Philatelic Week, Oct. 15-21 — A755

Design: Miners reading consolatory letters.

1982, Oct. 15

1313	A755 60w multicolored	36	15
a.	Souvenir sheet of 2	75	

Visit of Indonesian Pres. Suharto, Oct. 16-19 A756

1982, Oct. 16 Litho. *Perf. 13x12½*

1314	A756 60w multicolored	36	15
a.	Souvenir sheet of 2, imperf.	75	

37th Jaycee (Intl. Junior Chamber of Commerce) World Congress, Seoul, Nov. 3-18 — A757

1982, Nov. 3 *Perf. 13½x13*

1315	A757 60w multicolored	36	15

2nd UN Conference on Peaceful Uses of Outer Space, Vienna, Aug. 9-21 — A758

1982, Nov. 20 *Perf. 13x13½*

1316	A758 60w multicolored	36	15

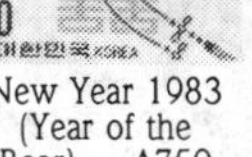

New Year 1983 (Year of the Boar) — A759

Flags of Korea and Turkey — A760

1982, Dec. 1

1317	A759 60w Magpies, money bag	36	15
a.	Souvenir sheet of 2	75	
1318	A759 60w Boar, bas-relief	36	15
a.	Souvenir sheet of 2	75	
	Set value		15

1982, Dec. 20 *Perf. 13*

1319	A760 60w multicolored	36	15
a.	Souvenir sheet of 2, imperf.	75	

Visit of Pres. Kenan Evren of Turkey, Dec. 20-23.

Letter Writing Campaign A761

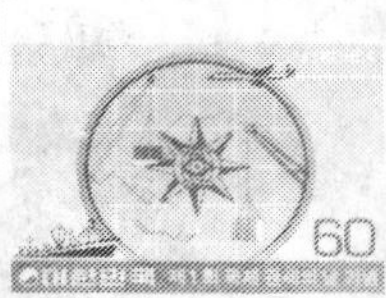

First Intl. Customs Day A762

1982, Dec. 31 Photo. *Perf. 13x13½*

1320	A761 60w multicolored	36	15

1983, Jan. 26 *Perf. 13½x13*

1321	A762 60w multicolored	36	15

Korean-made Vehicle Issue

Hyundai Pony-2 — A764

Daewoo Maepsy — A765

Super Titan Truck — A768

Flat-bed Truck — A770

1983 Photo. *Perf. 13½x13*

1322	A764 60w Keohwa Jeep	36	15
1323	A764 60w shown	36	15
a.	Pair, #1322-1323	75	30
1324	A765 60w shown	36	15
1325	A764 60w Kia minibus	36	15
a.	Pair, #1324-1325	75	30
1326	A764 60w Highway bus	36	15
1327	A768 60w shown	36	15
1328	A764 70w Dump truck	42	15
1329	A770 70w shown	42	15
1330	A764 70w Cement mixer	42	15
1331	A764 70w Oil truck	42	15
	Nos. 1322-1331 (10)	3.84	
	Set value		68

Issue dates: Nos. 1322-1323, Feb. 25; Nos. 1324-1325, Mar. 25; Nos. 1326-1327, May 25; Nos. 1328-1329, July 25; Nos. 1330-1331, Aug. 25.

Visit of Malaysian Seri Paduka Baginda, Mar. 22-26 — A773

1983, Mar. 22

1332	A773 60w multicolored	36	15
a.	Souvenir sheet of 2	75	

The indexes in each volume of the Scott Catalogue contain many listings which help to identify stamps.

Postal Service Issue

General Bureau of Postal Administration Building — A774

Mailman, 1884 — A776

Ancient Mail Carrier — A778

Nos. 1-2 — A780

Pre-modern Period Postal Symbol, Mailbox — A782

Designs: #1334, Seoul Central PO. #1336, Mailman on motorcycle, 1983. #1338, Modern mail transport. #1340, No. 1201. #1342, Current postal symbol, mailbox.

1983, Apr. 22 Photo. *Perf. 13½x13*

1333 A774 60w multicolored 36 15
1334 A774 60w multicolored 36 15
1335 A776 70w multicolored 42 15
1336 A776 70w multicolored 42 15
1337 A778 70w multicolored 42 15
1338 A778 70w multicolored 42 15
1339 A780 70w multi ('84) 25 15
1340 A780 70w multi ('84) 25 15
1341 A782 70w multi ('84) 25 15
1342 A782 70w multi ('84) 25 15
Nos. 1333-1342 (10) 3.40
Set value 64

PHILAKOREA '84, Seoul, Oct. 22-31, 1984.

Issue dates: #1333-1334, Apr. 22; #1335-1336, June 10; #1337-1338, Aug. 10; #1339-1340, Feb. 10; #1341-1342, Mar. 10.

Teachers' Day — A784

1983, May 15 Photo. *Perf. 13x13½*

1343 A784 60w Village schoolhouse, score 36 15
a. Souvenir sheet of 2 75

World Communications Year — A785

1983, June 20

1344 A785 70w multicolored 42 15
a. Souvenir sheet of 2 1.00

Communications Life Insurance Inauguration A786

1983, July 1 Photo. *Perf. 13½x13*

1345 A786 70w multicolored 42 15

Science and Technology Symposium, Seoul, July 4-8 — A787

1983, July 4

1346 A787 70w multicolored 42 15

Visit of Jordan's King Hussein, Sept. 10-13 A788

1983, Sept. 10 Litho. *Perf. 13x12½*

1347 A788 70w Pres. Hwan, King Hussein, flags 42 15
a. Souvenir sheet of 2, imperf. 85

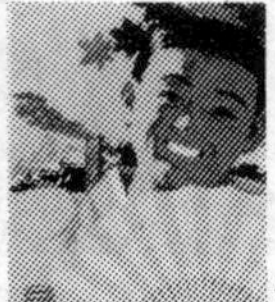
ASTA, 53rd World Travel Congress, Seoul — A789

1983, Sept. 25 Photo. *Perf. 13*

1348 A789 70w multicolored 42 15

70th Inter-Parliamentary Union Conference — A790

1983, Oct. 4 Photo. *Perf. 13*

1349 A790 70w multicolored 42 15
a. Souvenir sheet of 2 85

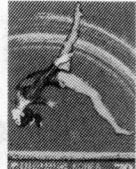

64th National Sports Festival — A791

1983, Oct. 6 Photo. *Perf. 13*

1350 A791 70w Gymnastics 42 15
1351 A791 70w Soccer 42 15
Set value 16

Pres. Chun and Pres. U San Yu of Burma — A791a

Pres. Chun's Curtailed Visit to Southwest Asia: No. 1351B, India. No. 1351C, Pres. Junius R. Jayawardene, Sri Lanka. No. 1351D, Australia, flag. No. 1351E, New Zealand, flag. Withdrawn after one day due to political assassination.

1983, Oct. 8 Photo. *Perf. 13½x13*

1351A A791a 70w multicolored 1.50
1351B A791a 70w multicolored 1.50
1351C A791a 70w multicolored 1.50
1351D A791a 70w multicolored 1.50
1351E A791a 70w multicolored 1.50
Nos. 1351A-1351E (5) 7.50

Souvenir Sheets of 2

1351f A791a 70w 2.25
1351g A791a 70w 2.25
1351h A791a 70w 2.25
1351i A791a 70w 2.25
1351j A791a 70w 2.25
Nos. 1351f-1351j (5) 11.25

Water Resource Development A792

Newspaper Publication Cent. A793

1983, Oct. 15 Litho. *Perf. 13*

1352 A792 70w multicolored 42 15

1983, Oct. 31 Litho. *Perf. 13*

1353 A793 70w multicolored 25 15

Natl. Tuberculosis Assoc., 30th Anniv. — A794

1983, Nov. 6 Photo. *Perf. 13*

1354 A794 70w multicolored 25 15

Presidents Chun and Reagan, Natl. Flags — A795

1983, Nov. 12 Photo. *Perf. 13*

1355 A795 70w multicolored 25 15
a. Souvenir sheet of 2 50

Visit of Pres. Ronald Reagan, Nov. 12-14.

11th Philatelic Week — A796

1983, Nov. 18 Photo. *Perf. 13*

1356 A796 70w multicolored 25 15
a. Souvenir sheet of 2 50

New Year 1984
A797 A798

1983, Dec. 1 Photo. *Perf. 13*

1357 A797 70w Mouse, stone wall relief 25 15
a. Souvenir sheet of 2 50
1358 A798 70w Cranes, pine tree 25 15
a. Souvenir sheet of 2 50
Set value 15

Bicentenary of Catholic Church in Korea — A799

1984, Jan. 4 Photo. *Perf. 13x13½*

1359 A799 70w Cross 25 15
a. Souvenir sheet of 2 50

Visit of Brunei's Sultan Bolkiah-Apr. 7-9 — A800

1984, Apr. 7 Litho. *Perf. 13x12½*

1360 A800 70w multicolored 18 15
a. Souvenir sheet of 2, imperf. 50

Visit of Qatar's Sheik Khalifa, Apr. 20-22 A801

1984, Apr. 20

1361 A801 70w multicolored 18 15
a. Souvenir sheet of 2, imperf. 50

Girl Mailing Letter — A802

Mailman in City — A803

1984, Apr. 22 Photo. *Perf. 13½x13*
1362 A802 70w multicolored 18 15
a. Souvenir sheet of 2 50
1363 A803 70w multicolored 18 15
a. Souvenir sheet of 2 50
Set value 15

Korean postal service.

Visit of Pope John Paul II, May 3-7 — A808

Engraved, Photogravure and Engraved
1984, May 3 *Perf. 12½*
1368 A808 70w dk brn 18 15
1369 A808 70w multicolored 18 15
a. Souvenir sheet of 2, #1368-1369, perf. 13½ 50
Set value 15

A809

A810

1984, May 11 Photo. *Perf. 13x13½*
1370 A809 70w Tools, brushes, flower 18 15

Workers' Cultural Festival.

1984, May 21 Photo. *Perf. 13x13½*
1371 A810 70w Jet, ship, Asia map 18 15

Customs Cooperation Council 63rd-64th Sessions, Seoul, May 21-25.

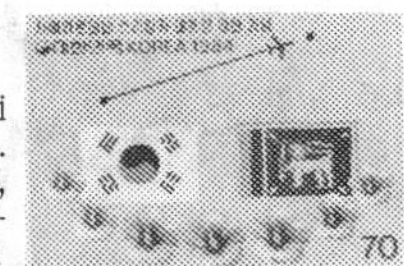
Visit of Sri Lanka's Pres. Jayewardene, May 27-30 — A811

1984, May 27 *Perf. 13½x13*
1372 A811 70w Asia map, flags, flowers 18 15
a. Souvenir sheet of 2 50

Advertising Congress Emblem A812

'88 Olympic Expressway Opening A813

1984, June 18 Photo. *Perf. 13x13½*
1373 A812 70w ADASIA '84 emblem 18 15

14th Asian Advertising Cong., Seoul, June 18-21.

1984, June 22
1374 A813 70w multicolored 18 15

Intl. Olympic Committee, 90th Anniv. — A814

1984, June 23
1375 A814 70w multicolored 18 15

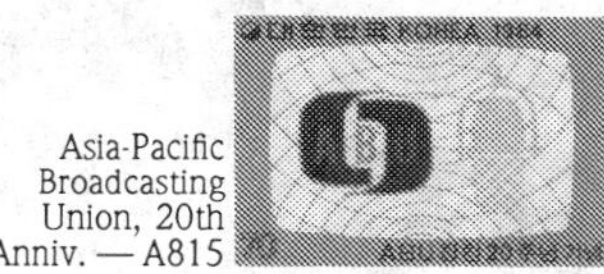
Asia-Pacific Broadcasting Union, 20th Anniv. — A815

1984, June 30 *Perf. 13½x13*
1376 A815 70w Emblem, microphone 18 15

Visit of Senegal's Pres. Diouf, July 9-12 A816

1984, July 9 Litho. *Perf. 13x12½*
1377 A816 70w Flags of Korea & Senegal 18 15
a. Souvenir sheet of 2, imperf. 50

1984 Summer Olympics A817

Lithographed and Engraved
1984, July 28 *Perf. 12½*
1378 A817 70w Archery 18 15
1379 A817 440w Fencing 1.15 25
Set value 30

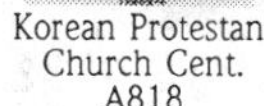
Korean Protestant Church Cent. A818

Groom on Horseback A819

Stained glass windows. Se-tenant.

1984, Aug. 16 *Perf. 13*
1380 A818 70w Crucifixion 18 15
1381 A818 70w Cross, dove 18 15
a. Souvenir sheet of 2 50
Set value 15

1984, Sept. 1 Photo. *Perf. 13x13½*

Wedding Procession: a, Lantern carrier. b, Groom. c, Musician. d, Bride in sedan chair (52x33mm).

1382 Strip of 4 75 20
a.-d. A819 70w any single 18 15
e. Souvenir sheet 25

No. 1382e contains No. 1382d.

Pres. Chun's Visit to Japan, Sept. 6-8 — A820

1984, Sept. 6 Litho. *Perf. 13x12½*
1383 A820 70w Chun, flag, Mt. Fuji 18 15
a. Souvenir sheet of 2, imperf. 50

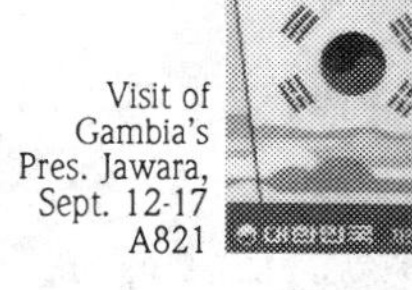
Visit of Gambia's Pres. Jawara, Sept. 12-17 A821

1984, Sept. 12
1384 A821 70w Flags of Korea & Gambia 18 15
a. Souvenir sheet of 2, imperf. 50

A822

A823

1984, Sept. 21 *Perf. 13*
1385 A822 70w Flags of Korea & Gabon 18 15
a. Souvenir sheet of 2, imperf. 50

Visit of Gabon's Pres. Bongo, Sept. 21-23.

1984, Sept. 18 Photo. *Perf. 13x13½*
1386 A823 70w Products 18 15

Seoul Intl. Trade Fair.

65th Natl. Sports Festival, Taegu, Oct. 11-16 — A824

1984, Oct. 11 Photo. *Perf. 13½x13*
1387 A824 70w Badminton 18 15
1388 A824 70w Wrestling 18 15
Set value 15

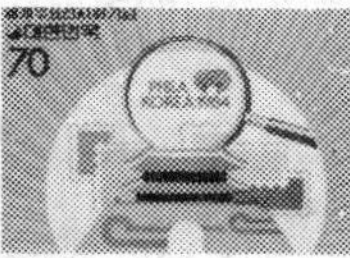
Philakorea '84 Stamp Show, Seoul, Oct. 22-31 — A825

Perf. 13½x13, 13x13½
1984, Oct. 22
1389 A825 70w South Gate, stamps 18 15
a. Souvenir sheet of 4 75
1390 A825 70w Emblem under magnifier, vert. 18 15
a. Souvenir sheet of 4 75
Set value 15

Visit of Maldives Pres. Maumoon Abdul Gayoom, Oct. 29-Nov. 1 — A826

1984, Oct. 29 Litho. *Perf. 13x12½*
1392 A826 70w multicolored 18 15
a. Souvenir sheet of 2, imperf. 50

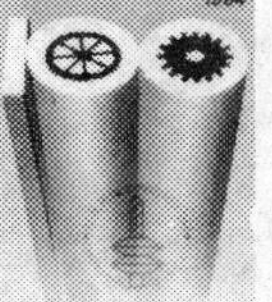
Chamber of Commerce and Industry Cent. — A827

Children Playing Jaegi-chagi — A828

1984, Oct. 31 Photo. *Perf. 13x13½*
1393 A827 70w "100" 18 15

1984, Dec. 1 Photo. *Perf. 13x13½*

New Year 1985 (Year of the ox).

1394 A828 70w Ox, bas-relief 18 15
a. Souvenir sheet of 2 36
1395 A828 70w shown 18 15
a. Souvenir sheet of 2 36
Set value 15

Intl. Youth Year — A829

1985, Jan. 25 Photo. *Perf. 13½x13*
1396 A829 70w IYY emblem 18 15

Folkways — A830

1985, Feb. 19 Photo. *Perf. 13x13½*
1397 A830 70w Pounding rice 18 15
1398 A830 70w Welcoming full moon 18 15
Set value 15

1985, Aug. 20
1399 A830 70w Wrestling 18 15
1400 A830 70w Janggi, Korean chess 18 15
Set value 15

Modern Art Series

Rocky Mountain in the Early Spring, 1915, by Shimjoen, (Ahn Jung-shik) A831

Still-life with a Doll, 1927, by Suhlcho, (Lee Chong-woo) A832

Spring Day on a Farm, 1961, by Eijai, (Huh Paik-ryun, 1903-1977) A833

The Exorcist, 1941, by Chulma, (Kim Chung-hyun, 1901-1953) — A834

Chunhyang-do, by Kim Un-ho — A835

Flowers, by Lee Sang-bum — A836

Image of A Friend, by Ku Bon-wung A837

Woman in a Ski Suit, by Son Ung-seng A838

Valley of the Peach Blossoms, 1964, by Pyen Kwan-Sik (1899-1976) A839

Rural Landscape, 1940, by Lee Yong-Wu (1904-1952) A840

Male, 1932, by Lee Ma-Dong A841

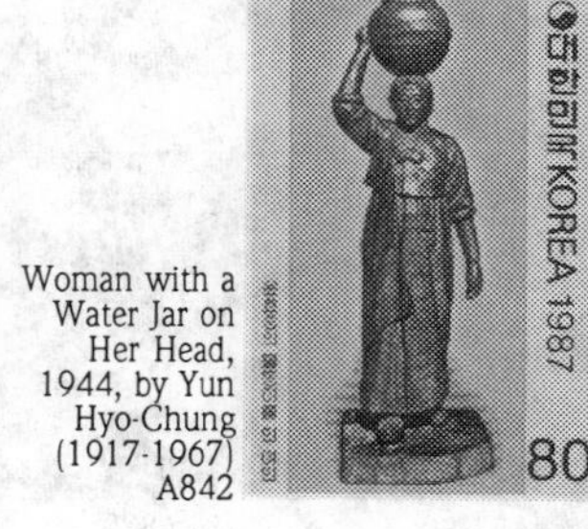
Woman with a Water Jar on Her Head, 1944, by Yun Hyo-Chung (1917-1967) A842

Photo.; Litho. & Engr. (#1411-1412)

1985-87 *Perf. 13½x13, 13x13½*

1401	A831 70w multicolored	18	15
1402	A832 70w multicolored	18	15
1403	A833 70w multicolored	18	15
1404	A834 70w multicolored	18	15
1405	A835 80w multi ('86)	22	15
1406	A836 80w multi ('86)	22	15
1407	A837 80w multi ('86)	22	15
1408	A838 80w multi ('86)	22	15
1409	A839 80w multi ('87)	28	15
1410	A840 80w multi ('87)	28	15
1411	A841 80w multi ('87)	28	15
1412	A842 80w multi ('87)	28	15
	Nos. 1401-1412 (12)	2.72	
	Set value		84

Issue dates: Nos. 1401-1402, Apr. 10. Nos. 1403-1404, July 5. Nos. 1405-1408, Dec. 1. Nos. 1409-1412, June 12.

State Visit of Pres. Chun to the US — A843

Photo. & Engr.

1985, Apr. 24 *Perf. 13*

1413	A843 70w multicolored	20	15
a.	Souvenir sheet of 2	40	

Coastal and Inland Fish Series

Gak-si- Bung-eo (silver carp) — A844

Dot-sac-chi (sword fish) — A845

Eoreumchi A846

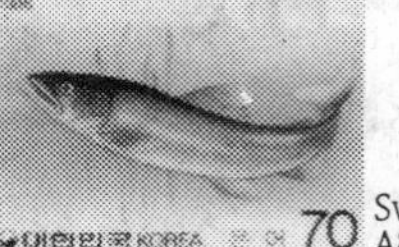
Sweetfish A847

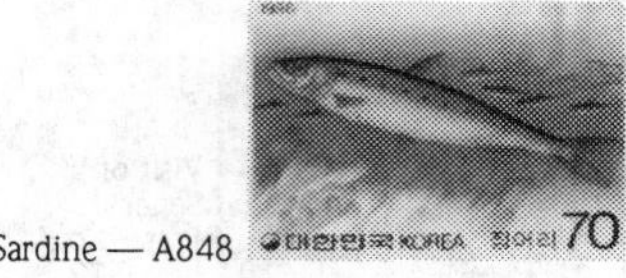
Sardine — A848

Hammerhead Shark — A849

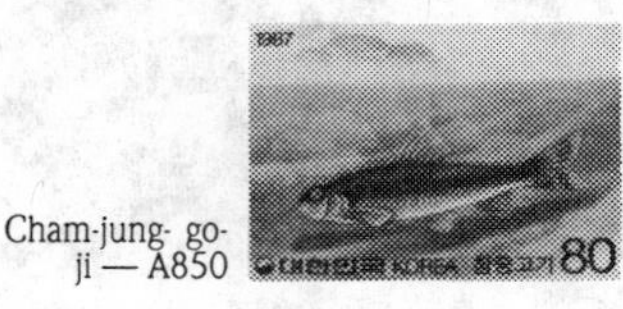
Cham-jung- go-ji — A850

Swi-ri — A851

Oar Fish — A852

Devil-ray A853

1985-87 Photo. *Perf. 13½x13*

1414	A844 70w multicolored	18	15
1415	A845 70w multicolored	18	15
1416	A846 70w multi ('86)	20	15
1417	A847 70w multi ('86)	20	15
1418	A848 70w multi ('86)	20	15
1419	A849 70w multi ('86)	20	15
1420	A850 80w multi ('87)	30	15
1421	A851 80w multi ('87)	30	15
1422	A852 80w multi ('87)	30	15
1423	A853 80w multi ('87)	30	15
	Nos. 1414-1423 (10)	2.36	
	Set value		65

Issue dates: Nos. 1414-1415, May 30. Nos. 1416-1423, July 25.

Yonsei University and Medical School, Cent. A854

Photogravure and Engraved

1985, May 6 *Perf. 13*

1424	A854 70w Underwood Hall	20	15

State Visit of Pres. Mohammad Zia-Ul-Haq of Pakistan, May 6-10 — A855

State Visit of Pres. Luis Alberto Monge of Costa Rica, May 19-23 — A856

1985, May 6 Photo. *Perf. 13x13½*

1425	A855 70w multicolored	20	15
a.	Souvenir sheet of 2	40	

1985, May 18 *Perf. 13½x13*

1426	A856 70w multicolored	20	15
a.	Souvenir sheet of 2	40	

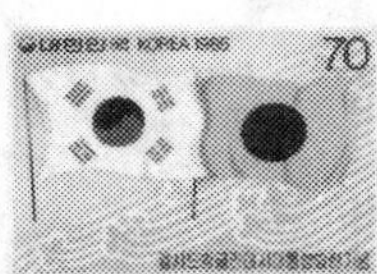
State Visit of Pres. Hussain Muhammad Eshrad of Bangladesh, June 15-19 — A857

1985, June 15

1427	A857 70w multicolored	20	15
a.	Souvenir sheet of 2, imperf.	40	

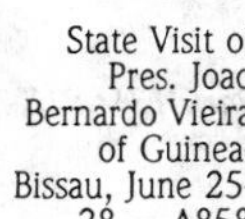
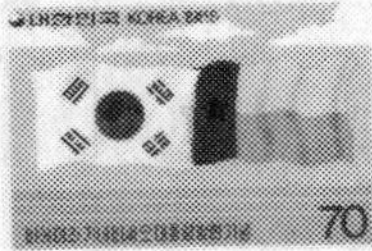
State Visit of Pres. Joao Bernardo Vieira of Guinea-Bissau, June 25-28 — A858

1985, June 25

1428	A858 70w multicolored	20	15
a.	Souvenir sheet of 2, imperf.	40	

Liberation from Japanese Occupation Forces, 40th Anniv. A859

Design: Heavenly Lake, Mt. Paektu, natl. flower.

1985, Aug. 14 Litho. *Perf. 13x12½*

1429 A859 70w multicolored 20 15

Folk Music Series

The Spring of My Home, Music by Hong Nan-pa and Lyrics by Lee Won-su — A860

A Leaf Boat, Music by Yun Yong-ha and Lyrics by Park Hong-Keun — A861

Half Moon, 1924, by Yun Keuk-Young A862

Let's Go and Pick the Moon, by Yun Seok-Jung and Park Tae Hyun A863

Korean Farm Music — A864

Barley Field, by Park Wha-mok and Yun Yong-ha — A865

Magnolia, by Cho Young-Shik and Kim Dong-jin — A866

Chusok, Harvest Moon Festival — A867

1985, Sept. 10 Photo. *Perf. 13x13½*

1430 A860 70w multicolored 20 15

1431 A861 70w multicolored 20 15

Set value 15

1986, June 25 Photo. *Perf. 13x13½*

1432 A862 70w multicolored 20 15

1433 A863 70w multicolored 20 15

Set value 15

1986, Aug. 26 Photo. *Perf. 13½x13*

Musicians with: a, Flag, hand gong. b, Drum flute. c, Drum, hand gong. d, Taborets, ribbons. e, Taboret, sun, woman, child. Has continuous design.

1434 Strip of 5 1.00 32

a.-e. A864 70w, any single 20 15

1987, Mar. 25 Photo. *Perf. 13x13½*

1435 A865 80w multicolored 24 15

1436 A866 80w multicolored 24 15

Set value 16

1987, Sept. 10 Photo. *Perf. 13x13½*

Harvest moon dance: No. 1437a, Eight dancers, harvest moon. No. 1437b, Four dancers, festival wheels, balloons. No. 1437c, Three dancers, children on see-saw. No. 1437d, Four dancers, women preparing meal.

1437 Strip of 4 1.20 32

a.-d. A867 80w any single 30 15

Folklore Series

Tano, Spring Harvest Festival — A868

Sick for Home, by Lee Eun-sang and Kim Kong-jin A869

Pioneer, by Yoon Hae-young and Cho Doo-nam A870

Mask Dance (Talchum) — A871

Designs: a, Woman on shore, riding a swing. b, Sweet flag coiffures. c, Boy picking flowers, girl on swing. d, Boys wrestling.
Illustration reduced.

1988, Aug. 25 Photo. *Perf. 13x13½*

1438 A868 Strip of 4 88 24

a.-d. 80w multicolored 22 15

1988, Nov. 15

1439 A869 80w multicolored 24 15

1440 A870 80w multicolored 24 15

Set value 15

1989, Feb. 25

Designs: a, Two mask dancers with scarves. b, Dancers with fans. c, Dancers with scarf and laurel or fan. d, Three dancers, first as an animal and two more carrying fan and bells or torch.

1441 Strip of 4 96 24

a.-d. A871 80w any single 24 15

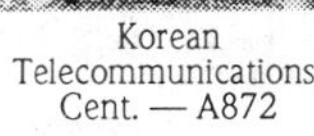

Korean Telecommunications, Cent. — A872

World Bank Conference, Seoul, Oct. 8-11 — A873

1985, Sept. 28 *Perf. 13½x13*

1442 A872 70w Satellite, emblem, dish receiver 20 15

1985, Oct. 8 *Perf. 13x13½*

1443 A873 70w Emblem 20 15

Intl. Bank for Reconstruction & Development, 40th Anniv.

UN, 40th Anniv. — A874

1985, Oct. 24 *Perf. 13½x13*

1444 A874 70w Emblem, doves 20 15

Natl. Red Cross, 80th Anniv. — A875

1985, Oct. 26

1445 A875 70w red, blk & bl 20 15

Segment of Canceled Cover — A876

New Year 1986 — A877

1985, Nov. 18 Photo. *Perf. 13½x13*

1446 A876 70w multicolored 20 15

12th Philatelic Week, Nov. 18-23.

Lithographed and Engraved

1985, Dec. 2 *Perf. 13x13½*

1447 A877 70w multicolored 20 15

Mt. Fuji, Korean Airlines Jet — A878

1985, Dec. 18 Photo.

1448 A878 70w brt bl, blk & red 20 15

Normalization of diplomatic relations between Korea and Japan, 20th anniv.
See No. C44.

Statesman Type of 1986 and Types of 1981-86

1986-87 Engr., Photo. (40w) *Perf. 13*

1449 A716 550w indigo 2.00 68

Coil Stamps

Perf. 13 Vert.

1449A A704 20w multicolored 15 15

1449B A705 40w multicolored 20 15

1449C A708 80w multicolored 48 15

Set value, #1449A-1449C 16

Issue dates: 550w, Dec. 10; others, 1987.

Intl. Peace Year — A879

State Visits of Pres. Chun — A880

1986, Jan. 15 Photo. *Perf. 13x13½*

1450 A879 70w multicolored 20 15

1451 A879 400w multicolored 1.15 35

a. Souvenir sheet of 4 4.60

Set value 40

1986, Apr. 4 Litho. *Perf. 12½x13*

Portrait, natl. flags and: No. 1452, Parliament, Brussels. No. 1453, Eiffel Tower, Paris. No. 1454, Cathedral, Cologne. No. 1455, Big Ben, London.

1452 A880 70w multicolored 16 15

1453 A880 70w multicolored 16 15

1454 A880 70w multicolored 16 15

1455 A880 70w multicolored 16 15

Set value 20

Souvenir Sheets of 2

Perf. 13½

1452a A880 70w 35

1453a A880 70w 35

1454a A880 70w 35

1455a A880 70w 35

Science Series

Chomsongdae Observatory, Satellites — A881

Kwanchondae Observatory, Halley's Comet — A882

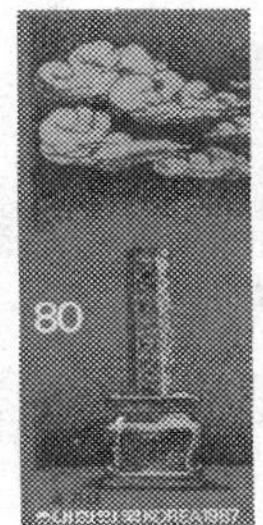

Weather

A883 A884

Clocks

A885 A886

Early Printing Methods

A887 A888

A889

A890

1986, Apr. 21 *Perf. 13½x13*

1456 A881 70w multicolored 16 15
1457 A882 70w multicolored 16 15
 a. Pair, #1456-1457 32 15

1987, Apr. 21 Photo. *Perf. 13½*

Designs: No. 1458, Wind observatory stone foundation, Chosun Dynasty. No. 1459, Rain gauge, Sejong Period to Chosun Dynasty.

1458 A883 80w multicolored 28 15
1459 A884 80w multicolored 28 15
 a. Pair, #1458-1459 56 20

1988, Apr. 21 Photo. *Perf. 13½x13*

Designs: No. 1460, *Chagyokru,* water clock invented by Chang Yongshil and Kim Bin in 1434. No. 1461, *Angbuilgu,* sundial completed during King Sejong's reign (1418-1450).

1460 A885 80w multicolored 26 15
1461 A886 80w multicolored 26 15
 a. Pair, #1460-1461 52 18

Designs: No. 1462, Sutra manuscript (detail) printed from wood type, Shila Dynasty, c.704-751. No. 1463, Character from a manuscript printed from metal type, Koryo, c.1237.

1989, Apr. 21

1462 A887 80w buff & sepia 24 15
1463 A888 80w buff & sepia 24 15
 a. Pair, #1462-1463 48 16

Designs: No. 1464, 7th century gilt bronze Buddha. No. 1465, Bronze Age dagger, spear molds.

1990, Apr. 21

1464 A889 100w multicolored 45 15
1465 A890 100w multicolored 45 15
 a. Pair, #1464-1465 90 30
 Set value 24

Pairs have continuous designs.

Assoc. of Natl. Olympic Committees, 5th General Assembly, Seoul, Apr. 21-25 — A891

1986, Apr. 21 *Perf. 13x13½*

1466 A891 70w multicolored 16 15

Souvenir Sheet

Butterflies A892

1986, May 22 Litho. *Perf. 13½*

1467 Sheet of 6 6.05 2.10
 a. A892 70w multicolored 20 15
 b. A892 370w multicolored 1.00 35
 c. A892 400w multicolored 1.10 38
 d. A892 440w multicolored 1.20 42
 e. A892 450w multicolored 1.25 42
 f. A892 470w multicolored 1.30 45

AMERIPEX '86, Chicago, May 22-June 1. No. 1467 contains stamps of different sizes (370w, 42x41mm; 400w, 42x33mm; 440w, 39x45mm; 450w, 32x42mm; 470w, 33x44mm); margin continues the designs.

Women's Education, Cent. A893

1986, May 31 *Perf. 13x12½*

1468 A893 70w multicolored 20 15

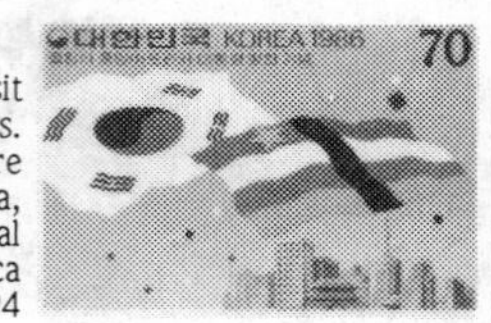
State Visit of Pres. Andre Kolingba, Central Africa A894

1986, June 10 *Perf. 13*

1469 A894 70w multicolored 20 15
 a. Souvenir sheet of 2, imperf. 40

Completion of Han River Development Project — A895

1986, Sept. 10 Litho. *Perf. 13*

1470 Strip of 3 58 22
 a. A895 30w Bridge 15 15
 b. A895 60w Buildings 20 15
 c. A895 80w Seoul Tower, buildings 28 15

Printed in a continuous design.

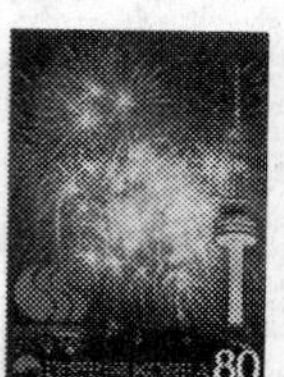

Fireworks, Seoul Tower — A896

Games Emblem — A897

10th Asian Games, Seoul, Sept. 20-Oct. 5 — A898

Illustration A898 reduced.

1986, Sept. 20 Photo. *Perf. 13x13½*

1471 A896 80w multicolored 25 15
 a. Souvenir sheet of 2 1.10
1472 A897 80w multicolored 25 15
 a. Souvenir sheet of 2 1.10
 Set value 16

Souvenir Sheet

1986, Oct. 31

1473 A898 550w multicolored 1.60

Juan Antonio Samaranch, Korean IOC Delegation, 1981 — A899

1986, Sept. 30

1474 A899 80w multicolored 25 15

Intl. Olympic Committee decision to hold 24th Olympic Games in Seoul, 5th anniv.

Philatelic Week — A900

1986, Nov. 18 Photo. *Perf. 13½x13*

1475 A900 80w Boy fishing for stamp 22 15

New Year 1987 (Year of the Hare) — A901

Birds — A902

1986, Dec. 1 Photo. *Perf. 13x13½*

1476 A901 80w multicolored 22 15

1986, Dec. 20 *Perf. 13x14*

1477 A902 80w Waxwing 22 15
1478 A902 80w Oriole 22 15
1479 A902 80w Kingfisher 22 15
1480 A902 80w Hoopoe 22 15
1481 A902 80w Roller 22 15
 a. Strip of 5, #1477-1481 1.10 40
 Set value 40

Coil Stamps
Perf. 14 Horiz.

1481B A902 80w like No. 1479 22 15
1481C A902 80w like No. 1480 22 15
1481D A902 80w like No. 1481 22 15
1481E A902 80w like No. 1477 22 15
1481F A902 80w like No. 1478 22 15
 g. Strip of 5, #1481B-1481F 1.10 40
 Set value 40

Wildlife Conservation A903

Endangered species: No. 1482, Panthera tigris altaica. No. 1483, Felis bengalensis. No. 1484, Vulpes vulpes. No. 1485, Sus scrofa.

1987, Feb. 25 Photo. *Perf. 13½x13*

1482 A903 80w multicolored 22 15
1483 A903 80w multicolored 22 15
1484 A903 80w multicolored 22 15
1485 A903 80w multicolored 22 15
 a. Strip of 4, #1482-1485 88 32
 Set value 32

Flowers — A904

1987, Mar. 20 Photo. *Perf. 14x13*

1486 A904 550w Dicentra spectabilis 1.65 55
1487 A904 550w Hanabusaya asiatica 1.65 55
1488 A904 550w Erythronium japonicum 1.65 55
1489 A904 550w Dianthus chinensis 1.65 55
1490 A904 550w Chrysanthemum zawadskii coreanum 1.65 55
 a. Strip of 5, #1486-1490 8.25 2.75

Coil Stamps
Perf. 13 Vert.

1490B A904 550w like No. 1486 1.65 55
1490C A904 550w like No. 1487 1.65 55
1490D A904 550w like No. 1488 1.65 55
1490E A904 550w like No. 1489 1.65 55
1490F A904 550w like No. 1490 1.65 55
 g. Strip of 5, #1490B-1490F 8.25 2.75

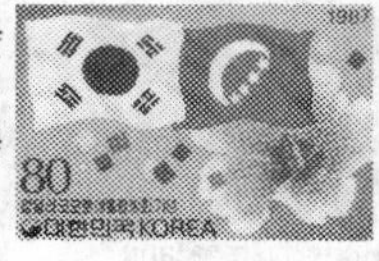
State Visit of Pres. Ahmed Abdallah Abderemane of the Comoro Isls., Apr. 6-9 — A905

1987, Apr. 6 Litho. *Perf. 13½x13*

1491 A905 80w multicolored 28 15
 a. Souvenir sheet of 2 60

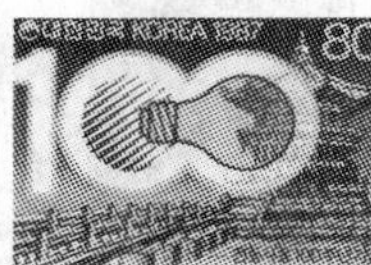
Electrification of Korea, Cent. — A906

1987, Apr. 10 **Photo.**

1492 A906 80w multicolored 28 15

Int'l. Assoc. of Ports and Harbors, 15th General Session, Seoul — A907

1987, Apr. 25 Photo. *Perf. 13½x13*

1493 A907 80w multicolored 28 15

State Visit of Pres. U San Yu of Burma — A908

1987, June 8 Litho. *Perf. 13½x13*

1494 A908 80w multicolored 28 15
 a. Souvenir sheet of 2 60

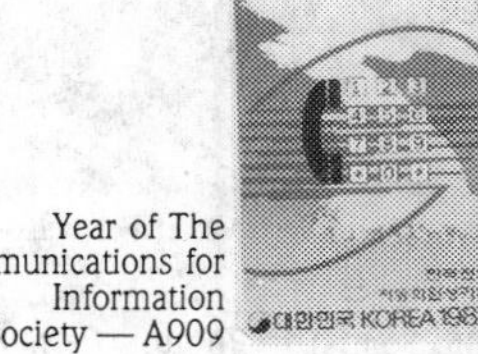
Year of The Communications for Information Society — A909

1987, June 30 *Perf. 13x13½*

1495 A909 80w Map, digital telephone 28 15
1496 A909 80w Emblem 28 15
 Set value 16

Introduction of automatic switching telephone system.

Independence Hall, Monument to the Nation — A910

Statue of Indomitable Koreans, Nat'l. Flag — A911

1987, Aug. 14 Photo. *Perf. 13½x13*

1497 A910 80w multicolored	30	15
a. Souvenir sheet of 2	60	
1498 A911 80w multicolored	30	15
a. Souvenir sheet of 2	60	
Set value		16

Opening of Independence Hall, Aug. 15.

16th Pacific Science Congress, Seoul, Aug. 20-30 — A912

1987, Aug. 20 *Perf. 13x13½*

1499 A912 80w multicolored	30	15
a. Souvenir sheet of 2	60	

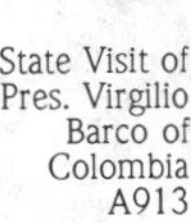

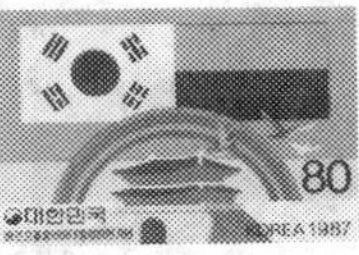

State Visit of Pres. Virgilio Barco of Colombia A913

1987, Sept. 8 Litho. *Perf. 13½x13*

1500 A913 80w multicolored	30	15
a. Souvenir sheet of 2	60	

Installation of 10-millionth Telephone A914

1987, Sept. 28 *Perf. 13½x13*

1501 A914 80w multicolored	30	15

Servicemen, Flags of Three Military Services — A915

1987, Sept. 30 Litho. *Perf. 13*

1502 A915 80w multicolored	30	15

Armed Forces Day, Armed Forces 39th Anniv.

14th Philatelic Week, Nov. 18-24 — A916

Signing of the Antarctic Treaty by Korea, 1st Anniv. — A917

1987, Nov. 18 Photo. *Perf. 13½*

1503 A916 80w Boy playing the nalrali	30	15

1987, Nov. 28 Litho.

1504 A917 80w multicolored	30	15

New Year 1988 (Year of the Dragon) — A918

1987, Dec. 1 Photo.

1505 A918 80w multicolored	30	15

Natl. Social Security Program — A919

1988, Jan. 4 Litho. *Perf. 13½x13*

1506 A919 80w multicolored	26	15

Completion of the Korean Antarctic Base — A919a

1988, Feb. Photo. *Perf. 13x13½*

1506A A919a 80w multicolored	26	15

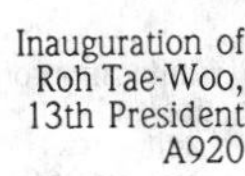

Inauguration of Roh Tae-Woo, 13th President A920

1988, Feb. 24 Photo. *Perf. 13½x13*

1507 A920 80w multicolored	26	15
a. Souvenir sheet of 2	55	

World Wildlife Fund — A921

White-naped crane *(Grus vipio)* displaying various behaviors: a, Calling (1). b, Running (2). c, Spreading wings (3). d, Flying (4).

1988, Apr. 1 *Perf. 13x13½*

1508 Strip of 4	1.05	25
a.-d. A921 80w any single	26	15

Intl. Red Cross & Red Crescent Organizations, 125th Annivs. — A922

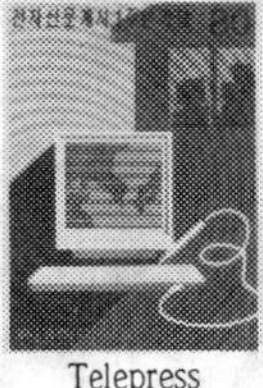

Telepress Medium, 1st Anniv. — A923

1988, May 7 Photo. *Perf. 13x13½*

1509 A922 80w multicolored	28	15

1988, June 1 Litho.

1510 A923 80w multicolored	28	15

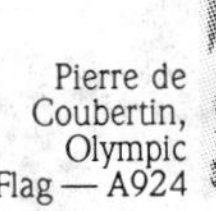

Pierre de Coubertin, Olympic Flag — A924

Olympic Temple — A925

View of Seoul — A926

Folk Dancers — A927

Perf. 13½x13

1988, Sept. 16 Litho. & Engr.

1511 A924 80w multicolored	25	15
1512 A925 80w multicolored	25	15

Photo.

Perf. 13x13½

1513 A926 80w multicolored	25	15
1514 A927 80w multicolored	25	15
Set value		24

1988 Summer Olympics, Seoul.

Souvenir Sheets of 2

1511a	A924 80w	50
1512a	A925 80w	50
1513a	A926 80w	50
1514a	A927 80w	50

Margin inscriptions on Nos. 1511a-1512a are photo.

OLYMPHILEX '88, Sept. 19-28, Seoul — A928

1988, Sept. 19 Photo. *Perf. 13x13½*

1515 A928 80w multicolored	25	15
a. Souvenir sheet of 2	50	

22nd Congress of the Intl. Iron and Steel Institute, Seoul — A929

1988, Oct. 8 *Perf. 13½x13*

1516 A929 80w multicolored	25	15

1988 Natl. Special Olympics (Paralympics), Seoul — A930

1988, Oct. 15 *Perf. 13x13½*

1517 A930 80w shown	25	15
1518 A930 80w Archer seated in wheelchair	25	15
Set value		15

New Year 1989 (Year of the Snake) — A931

1988, Dec. 1 Photo. *Perf. 13x13½*

1519 A931 80w multicolored	24	15

Souvenir Sheet

Successful Completion of the 1988 Summer Olympics, Seoul — A932

1988, Dec. 20 Litho. *Perf. 13x12½*

1520 A932 550w Opening ceremony	1.75

Folklore Series

Arirang — A933

Doraji — A934

Pakyon Falls A935

Chonan-Samkori A936

Willowing Bow — A937

Spinning Wheel — A938

Treating Threads A939

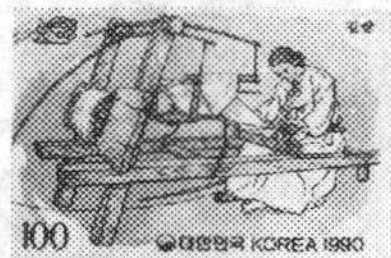
Weaving Fabric — A940

Orchard Avenue — A941

In Flower Garden — A942

A Swing — A943

Longing for Mt. Keumkang — A944

Natl. ballads.

1989, Mar. 27 Photo. *Perf. 13x13¹/2*
1521 A933 80w multicolored 24 15
1522 A934 80w multicolored 24 15

1990, Feb. 26 Litho.
1523 A935 80w multicolored 42 15
1524 A936 80w multicolored 42 15

Perf. 13¹/2x13
1990, Sept. 25 Litho. & Engr.
1525 A937 100w multicolored 45 15
1526 A938 100w multicolored 45 15
1527 A939 100w multicolored 45 15
1528 A940 100w multicolored 45 15
a. Strip of 4, #1525-1528 1.80 60

1991, Mar. 27 Litho. *Perf. 13x13¹/2*
1529 A941 100w multicolored 42 15
1530 A942 100w multicolored 42 15

1992, July 13 Litho. *Perf. 13x13¹/2*
1531 A943 100w multicolored 28 15
1532 A944 100w multicolored 28 15
Nos. 1555-1566 (12) 4.44
Set value 1.50

14th Asian-Pacific Dental Congress — A945

1989, Apr. 26 Photo. *Perf. 13x13¹/2*
1533 A945 80w multicolored 24 15

15-Cent Minimum Value
The minimum catalogue value is 15 cents. Separating se-tenant pieces into individual stamps does not increase the "value" of the stamps... since demand for the separated stamps may be small.

Rotary Intl. Convention, Seoul, May 21-25 — A946

19th Cong. of the Intl. Council of Nurses, Seoul, May 28-June 2 — A947

1989, May 20 Photo. *Perf. 13x13¹/2*
1534 A946 80w multicolored 24 15

1989, May 27
1535 A947 80w multicolored 24 15

Information Industry Month — A948

World Environment Day — A949

1989, June 1
1536 A948 80w multicolored 24 15

1989, June 5
1537 A949 80w multicolored 24 15

Asia-Pacific Telecommunity, 10th Anniv. — A950

1989, July 1 Photo. *Perf. 13x13¹/2*
1538 A950 80w multicolored 24 15

French Revolution, Bicent. — A951

1989, July 14 Litho. *Perf. 13¹/2x13*
1539 A951 80w multicolored 24 15

Federation of Asian and Oceanian Biochemists 5th Congress A952

1989, Aug. 12 Photo.
1540 A952 80w multicolored 24 15

Modern Art Series

A White Ox, by Lee Joong-Sub — A953

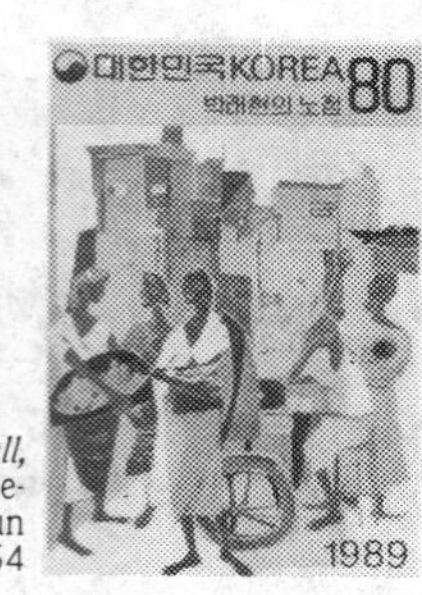
A Street Stall, by Park Lae-hyun A954

A Little Girl, by Lee Bong-Sang A955

An Autumn Scene, by Oh Ji-ho — A956

Litho. & Engr.; Photo. (#1542, 1544)
Perf. 13x13¹/2, 13¹/2x13
1989, Sept. 4
1541 A953 80w multicolored 24 15
1542 A954 80w multicolored 24 15
1543 A955 80w multicolored 24 15
1544 A956 80w multicolored 24 15
Set value 24

Allegory: The Valiant Spirit of Koreans — A965

1989, Sept. 12 Litho. *Perf. 13¹/2x13*
1553 A965 80w multicolored 24 15

1988 Seoul Olympics and the World Korean Sports Festival.

Personification of Justice and Ancient Codex — A966

1989, Sept. 18
1554 A966 80w multicolored 24 15

Constitutional Court, 1st anniv.

Fish

A967

A968

A969

A970

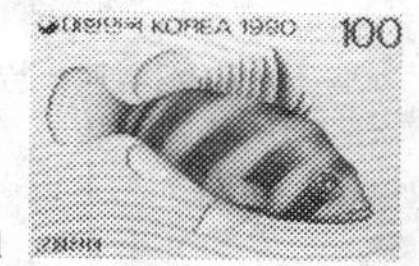
A971

A972

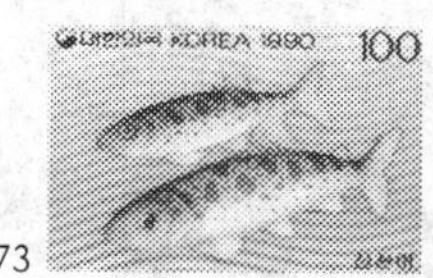
A973

A974

A975

A976

A977

A978

1989, Sept. 30 Photo. *Perf. 13¹/2x13*
1555 A967 80w Oplegnathus fasciatus 24 15
1556 A968 80w Cobitis multifasciata 24 15
1557 A969 80w Liobagrus mediadiposalis 24 15
1558 A970 80w Monocentris japonicus 24 15

1990, July 2
1559 A971 100w Hapalogenys mucronatus 45 15
1560 A972 100w Fugu niphobles 45 15

1561 A973 100w Oncorhynchus masou 45 15
1562 A974 100w Rhodeus ocellatus 45 15

1991, June 8

1563 A975 100w Microphysogobio longidorsalis 42 15
1564 A976 100w Gnathopogon majimae 42 15
1565 A977 100w Therapon oxyrhnchus 42 15
1566 A978 100w Psettina ijimae 42 15
Nos. 1555-1566 (12) 4.44 1.80

Light of Peace Illuminating the World — A979

1989, Oct. 4

1567 A979 80w multicolored 24 15

44th Intl. Eucharistic Cong., Seoul, Oct. 4-8.

29th World Congress of the Intl. Civil Airports Assoc., Seoul, Oct. 17-19 — A980

1989, Oct. 17

1568 A980 80w multicolored 24 15

Philatelic Week — A981

Two Cranes — A982

Folk Festival Customs A983

1989, Nov. 18 Photo. ***Perf. 13x13½***

1569 A981 80w Lantern 24 15
a. Souvenir sheet of 2 60

1989, Dec. 1 ***Perf. 13x13½, 13½x13***

1570 A982 80w multicolored 24 15
a. Souvenir sheet of 2 60
1571 A983 80w multicolored 24 15
a. Souvenir sheet of 2 60
Set value 15

New Year 1990.

World Meteorological Day — A984

1990, Mar. 23 ***Perf. 13½x13***

1572 A984 80w multicolored 42 15

UNICEF in Korea, 40th Anniv. — A985

1990, Mar. 24 ***Perf. 13x13½***

1573 A985 80w multicolored 42 15

Cheju-Kohung Fiber Optic Submarine Cable — A986

1990, Apr. 21 ***Perf. 13½x13***

1574 A986 80w multicolored 42 15

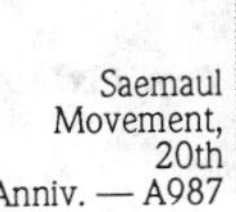

Saemaul Movement, 20th Anniv. — A987

1990, Apr. 21

1575 A987 100w multicolored 45 15

Youth Month — A988

1990, May 1

1576 A988 100w multicolored 45 15

Cart-shaped Earthenware A992

Fire Safety A995

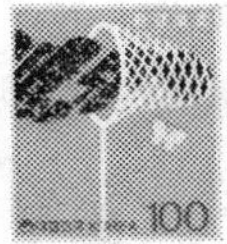

Environ- mental Protection — A996

Traffic Safety — A997

Waiting One's Turn — A997a

Saving Energy — A997b

Child Protection — A997c

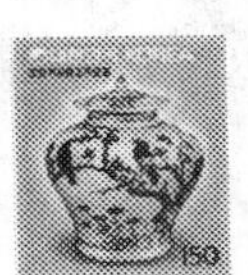

Ginger Jar — A998

Hong Yung Sik — A1004

Dragon Head, Banner Staff — A1006

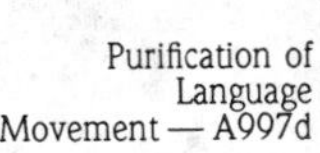

Purification of Language Movement — A997d

Perf. 13½x13, 13x13½

1990-92 Photo., Litho. (#1584)

1580 A992 50w multicolored 22 15
1583 A995 80w multicolored 40 15
1584 A996 100w multicolored 45 15
1585 A997 100w multicolored 42 15
1585A A997a 100w multicolored 42 15
1585B A997b 100w multicolored 42 15
1585C A997c 100w multicolored 30 15
1585D A997d 100w multicolored 30 15
1586 A998 150w multicolored 65 22
1592 A1004 600w multicolored 2.55 85

Perf. 13x13½

1594 A1006 800w multicolored 3.00 1.00
Nos. 1580-1594 (11) 9.13 3.27

Issue dates: No. 1584, June 5. 600w, June 25. 150w, July 2. 800w, July 10. No. 1585, July 25. 50w, Sept. 28. 80w, Nov. 1. 1585A, June 26, 1991. No. 1585B, Nov. 1, 1991. No. 1585C, Apr. 5, 1992. No. 1585D, Nov. 2, 1992.

This is an expanding set. Numbers will change if necessary.

Coil Stamp

1990 Litho. ***Perf. 13 Vert.***

1594A A996 100w multicolored 45 15

Seoul Mail Center — A1007

1990, July 4 Litho. ***Perf. 13½x13***

1595 A1007 100w multicolored 45 15

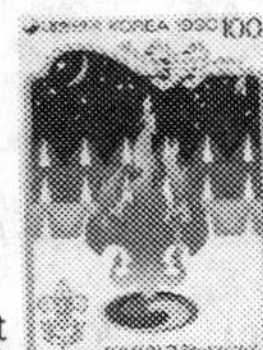

8th Korean Boy Scout Jamboree — A1008

1990, Aug. 8 ***Perf. 13x13½***

1596 A1008 100w multicolored 45 15

Wild Flowers

A1009

A1010

A1011

A1012

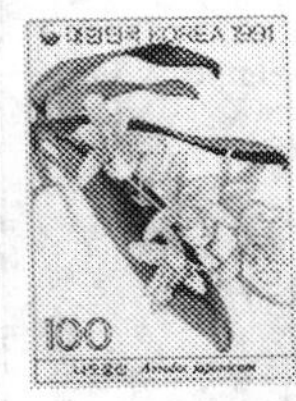

A1013

1990, Aug. 25 **Photo.**

1597 A1009 370w Lilium 1.65 55
1598 A1010 400w Aster 1.80 60
1599 A1011 440w Adonis 2.00 65
1600 A1012 470w Scabiosa 2.10 70

1991, July 26

1601 A1013 100w Aerides japonicum 35 15
1602 A1013 100w Heloniopsis orientalis 35 15
1603 A1013 370w Aquilegia buergeriana 1.15 40
1604 A1013 440w Gentiana zollingeri 1.40 50

1992, June 22 Photo. ***Perf. 13x13½***

1605 A1013 100w Lychnis wilfordii 28 15
1606 A1013 100w Lycoris radiata 28 15
1607 A1013 370w Commelina communis 1.05 28
1608 A1013 440w Calanthe striata 1.25 32
Nos. 1597-1608 (12) 13.66 4.60

A1021

A1022

1990, Sept. 29 Litho. ***Perf. 13x13½***

1609 A1021 100w 42 15

Anglican Church of Korea, cent.

1990, Oct. 15

1610 A1022 100w blk, red & bl 42 15

Opening of Seoul Tower, 10th anniv.

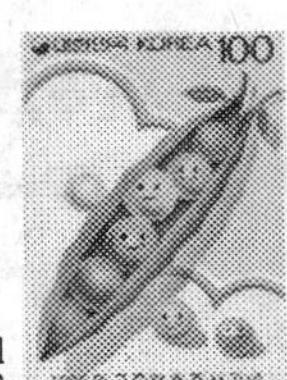

National Census — A1023

1990, Oct. 20 ***Perf. 13x13½***

1611 A1023 100w multicolored 42 15

UN Development Program, 40th Anniv. — A1024

1990, Oct. 24

1612 A1024 100w multicolored 42 15

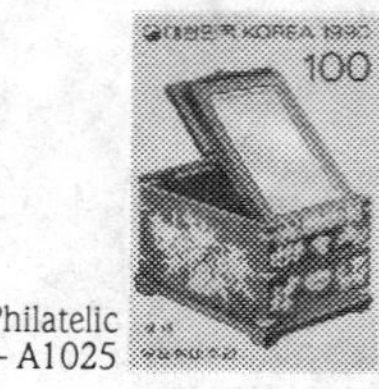

Philatelic Week — A1025

Perf. 13x13½

1990, Nov. 16 **Litho. & Engr.**

1613 A1025 100w multicolored 42 15
  a. Souvenir sheet of 2 85

New Year 1991 (Year of the Sheep) — A1026

Two Cranes — A1027

1990, Dec. 1 **Litho.** ***Perf. 13x13½***

1614 A1026 100w multicolored 42 15
1615 A1027 100w multicolored 42 15
  a. Souv. sheet of 2, #1614-1615 84

Taejon Expo '93

A1028

A1029

A1030

A1031

A1032

A1033

1990, Dec. 12

1616 A1028 100w multicolored 42 15
  a. Souvenir sheet of 2 84
1617 A1029 440w multicolored 1.85 65
  a. Souvenir sheet of 2 3.75

1991, Mar. 23

1618 A1030 100w multicolored 42 15
  a. Souvenir sheet of 2 84
1619 A1031 100w multicolored 42 15
  a. Souvenir sheet of 2 84

1992, Aug. 7 **Photo.** ***Perf. 13½x13***

1620 A1032 100w multicolored 28 15
  a. Souvenir sheet of 2 56
1621 A1033 100w multicolored 28 15
  a. Souvenir sheet of 2 56

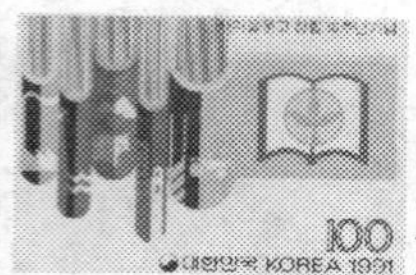

Saemaul Minilibrary, 30th Anniv. A1036

1991, Jan. 2 **Litho.** ***Perf. 13½x13***

1624 A1036 100w multicolored 42 15

Moth A1037

Beetle A1038

Butterfly A1039

Beetle A1040

Cicada — A1041

1991, Apr. 8 **Photo.** ***Perf. 13½x13***

1625 A1037 100w shown 42 15
1626 A1038 100w shown 42 15
1627 A1039 100w shown 42 15
1628 A1040 100w shown 42 15
1629 A1041 100w shown 42 15
1630 A1040 100w Water beetle 42 15
1631 A1040 100w Bee 42 15
1632 A1040 100w Lady bug 42 15
1633 A1037 100w Dragonfly 42 15
1634 A1037 100w Grasshopper 42 15
  a. Strip of 10, #1625-1634 4.25 2.00
  Nos. 1625-1634 (10) 4.20 1.50

Printed in sheets of 100 with each row shifted one design.

Traditional Performing Arts Center, 40th Anniv. — A1042

1991, Apr. 10 ***Perf. 13x13½***

1635 A1042 100w multicolored 42 15

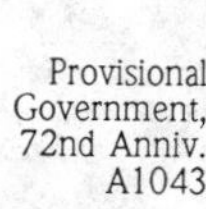

Provisional Government, 72nd Anniv. A1043

1991, Apr. 13 ***Perf. 13½x13***

1636 A1043 100w multicolored 42 15

Hire the Handicapped A1044

1991, Apr. 20

1637 A1044 100w multicolored 42 15

Teachers' Day, 10th Anniv. A1045

1991, May 15 **Litho.** ***Perf. 13½x13***

1638 A1045 100w multicolored 42 15

A1046

A1047

1991, Aug. 8 **Litho.** ***Perf. 13x13½***

1639 A1046 100w multicolored 42 15
  a. Souvenir sheet of 2 1.15 40

17th World Scouting Jamboree.

1991, Aug. 22 **Litho.** ***Perf. 13x13½***

1640 A1047 100w multicolored 42 15

YMCA World Assembly.

Natl. Desire for Reunification — A1048

1991, Sept. 11 **Litho.** ***Perf. 13x13½***

1641 A1048 100w multicolored 42 15

Admission to UN — A1049

1991, Sept. 18 ***Perf. 13½x13***

1642 A1049 100w multicolored 42 15

Musical Instruments

Deerskin Drum (Galgo) A1050

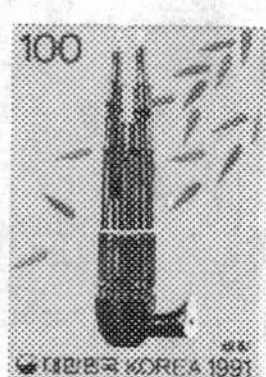

Mouth Organ (Saenghwang) A1051

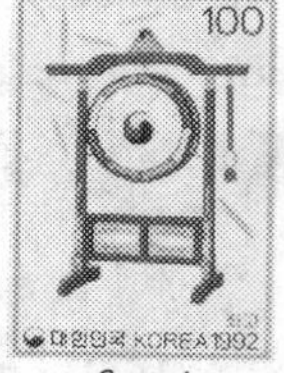

Seated Drum — A1052

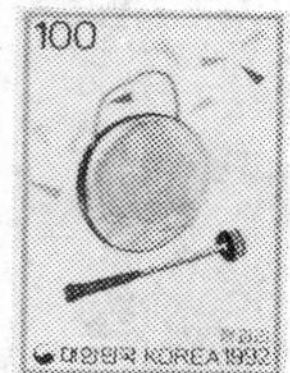

Small Gong — A1053

Designs: No. 1645, Brass chimes (Unra). No. 1646, Large gong (Jing). No. 1649, Dragon drum. No. 1650, Single bell chime.

1991-92 **Photo.** ***Perf. 13x13½***

Background color

1643 A1050 100w gray 42 15
1644 A1051 100w tan 42 15
1645 A1050 100w lt violet 42 15
1646 A1050 100w pale green 42 15
1647 A1052 100w gray 42 15
1648 A1053 100w tan 42 15
1649 A1052 100w pale violet 42 15
1650 A1053 100w pale green 42 15
  Nos. 1643-1650 (8) 3.36 1.20

Issued: #1643-1646, Sept.26; #1647-1650, Feb. 24, 1992.

Month of Culture A1056

Telecom '91 A1057

1991, Oct. 1 **Litho.** ***Perf. 13x13½***

1655 A1056 100w multicolored 42 15

1991, Oct. 7 **Photo.**

1656 A1057 100w multicolored 42 15

Sixth World Telecommunication Exhibition & Forum, Geneva, Switzerland.

Beauty Series

A1058

A1059

Kottam Architectural Patterns
A1060 A1061

A1062 A1063

Norigae
A1064 A1065

1991, Oct. 18

1657 A1058 100w multicolored 42 15
1658 A1059 100w multicolored 42 15
1659 A1060 100w multicolored 42 15
1660 A1061 100w multicolored 42 15
  a. Block or strip of 4, #1657-1660 1.70 60

1992, Sept. 21 **Photo. & Engr.**

1661 A1062 100y multicolored 28 15
1662 A1063 100y multicolored 28 15
1663 A1064 100y multicolored 28 15
1664 A1065 100y multicolored 28 15
a. Block or strip of 4, #1661-1664 1.15
Set value 28

Philatelic Week — A1070

1991, Nov. 16 **Photo.** ***Perf.* 13x13½**

1669 A1070 100w multicolored 42 15
a. Souvenir sheet of 2 85 30

New Year 1992, Year of the Monkey
A1071 A1072

1991, Dec. 2 **Photo. & Engr.**

1670 A1071 100w multicolored 42 15
a. Souvenir sheet of 2 85 30
1671 A1072 100w multicolored 42 15
a. Souvenir sheet of 2 85 30

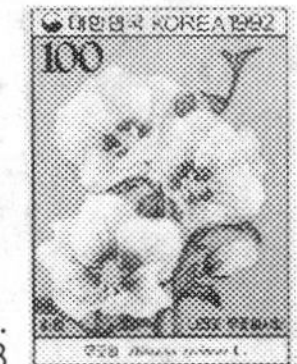

Hibiscus Syriacus, Natl. Flower — A1073

1992, Mar. 9 **Photo.** ***Perf.* 13x13½**
Background color

1672 A1073 100w lt green 30 15
1673 A1073 100w lt blue 30 15

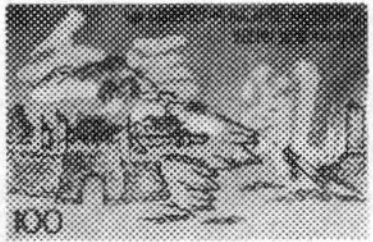

Im-Jin War, 400th Anniv. — A1074

1992, May 23 **Photo.** ***Perf.* 13½x13**

1674 A1074 100w multicolored 30 15

Science Day, 25th Anniv. A1075

1992, Apr. 21 **Photo.** ***Perf.* 13½x13**

1675 A1075 100w multicolored 30 15

Pong-Gil Yoon, Assassin of Japanese Occupation Leaders, 60th Anniv. of Execution — A1076

Photo. & Engr.
1992, Apr. 29 ***Perf.* 13x13½**

1676 A1076 100w multicolored 28 15

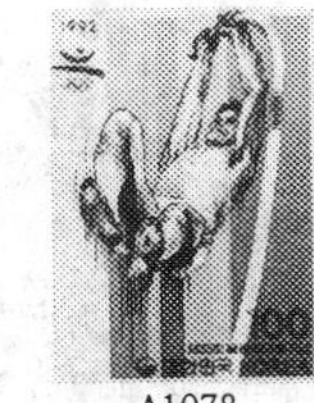

A1077 A1078

***Perf.* 13x13½**
1992, May 25 **Photo & Engr.**

1678 A1077 100w multicolored 30 15

60th Intl. Fertilizer Assoc. conf.

1992, July 25 **Photo.** ***Perf.* 13x13½**

1679 A1078 100w Pole vault 28 15
1680 A1078 100w Rhythmic gymnastics 28 15
Set value 15

1992 Summer Olympics, Barcelona.

21st Universal Postal Congress, Seoul, 1994 — A1079

Designs: No. 1681, Korean Exhibition Center, Namdae-mun Gate. No. 1682, Stone statue of Tolharubang, Songsan Ilchulbong Peak.

1992, Aug. 22 **Photo.** ***Perf.* 13½x13**

1681 A1079 100y red vio & multi 28 15
a. Souvenir sheet of 2 56
1682 A1079 100y brown & multi 28 15
a. Souvenir sheet of 2 56
Set value 15

A1086 A1087

***Perf.* 13x13½**
1992, Oct. 10 **Litho. & Engr.**

1683 A1086 100w salmon & red brn 30 15

Pong-Chang Yi (1900-1932), would-be assassin of Japanese Emperor Hirohito.

1992, Oct. 10 **Litho.**

Design: No. 1684, Hwang Young-Jo, 1992 Olympic marathon winner. No. 1685, Shon Kee-Chung, 1936 Olympic Marathon Winner.

1684 A1087 100w multicolored 30 15
1685 A1087 100w grn & multi 30 15
a. Pair, #1684-1685 60
b. Souv. sheet of 2, #1684-1685 60
Set value 15

Discovery of America, 500th Anniv. — A1088

1992, Oct. 12 **Photo.**

1686 A1088 100w multicolored 30 15

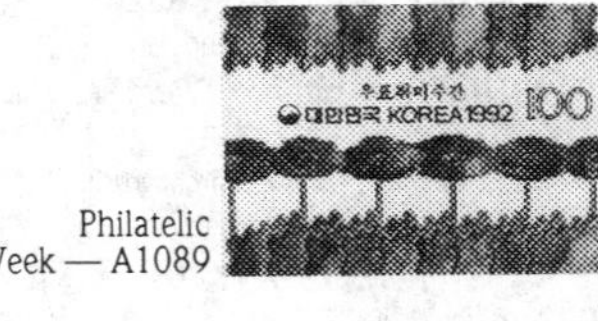

Philatelic Week — A1089

1992, Nov. 14 **Photo.** ***Perf.* 13½x13**

1687 A1089 100w multicolored 30 15
a. Souvenir sheet of 2 60

New Year 1993 (Year of the Rooster)
A1090 A1091

1992, Dec. 1 **Photo.** ***Perf.* 13x13½**

1688 A1090 100w multicolored 28 15
a. Souvenir sheet of 2 55
1689 A1091 100w multicolored 28 15
a. Souvenir sheet of 2 55
Set value 15

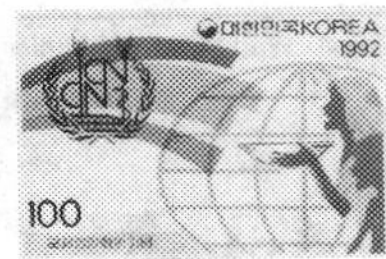

Intl. Conference on Nutrition, Rome — A1092

1992, Dec. 5 ***Perf.* 13½x13**

1690 A1092 100w multicolored 28 15

Seoul Art Center, Grand Opening A1093

1993, Feb. 15 **Photo.** ***Perf.* 13½x13**

1691 A1093 110w multicolored 30 15

Inauguration of Kim Young Sam, 14th President A1094

1993, Feb. 24

1692 A1094 110w multicolored 30 15
a. Souvenir sheet of 2 60

SEMI-POSTAL STAMPS

Field Hospital SP1

Nurses Supporting Patient — SP2

Perf. 13½x14, 14x13½

1953, Aug. 1 Litho. Wmk. 257

Crosses in Red

B1 SP1 10h + 5h bl grn 2.00 1.25
B2 SP2 10h + 5h blue 2.00 1.25

The surtax was for the Red Cross. Nos. B1-B2 exist imperf.

Type of Regular Issue, 1956, with Added inscription at Upper Left

1957, Sept. 1 Wmk. 312 *Perf. 12½*

Granite Paper

B3 A111 40h + 10h lt bl grn 80 60

Wmk. 317

B4 A111 40h + 10h lt bl grn 80 60

The surtax was for flood relief.

Catalogue values for unused stamps in this section, from this point to the end of the section, are for Never Hinged items.

Rice Farmer Type of Regular Issue, 1961-62

1963, July 10 Wmk. 317 *Perf. 12½*

B5 A172 4w + 1w dk bl 65 35

The surtax was for flood victims in southern Korea.

1965, Oct. 1 Unwmk. *Perf. 12½*

B6 A172 4w + 2w indigo 60 35

The surtax was for flood relief.

1965, Oct. 11

B7 A172 4w + 2w magenta 52 30

The surtax was for a scholarship fund.

Type of Regular Issue 1964-66

1966, Nov. 10 Litho. *Perf. 12½*

Granite Paper

B8 A186b 7w + 2w car rose 60 30

The surtax was to help the needy.

Soldier with Wife and Child SP3

Reservist SP4

1967, June 20 *Perf. 12½x13*

B9 SP3 7w + 3w rose lil & blk 65 30

The surtax was for veterans of the war in Viet Nam and their families.

1968, Aug. 1 Litho. *Perf. 13x12½*

B10 SP4 7w + 3w grn & blk 2.00 1.50

Issued for the fund-raising drive to arm reservists.

Flag — SP5

"Pin of Love" — SP6

1968, Nov. 1 Litho. Unwmk.

B11 SP5 7w + 3w dk bl & red 7.00 3.00

The surtax was for disaster relief.

1969, Feb. 15

B12 SP5 7w + 3w lt grn, dk bl & red 2.25 85

Surtax for military helicopter fund.

Flag Type of 1968 Redrawn Zeros Omitted

1969, Nov. 1 Litho. *Perf. 13x12½*

B13 SP5 7w + 3w dk bl & red 1.65 75

The surtax was for the searchlight fund.

Perf. 13½x12½

1972, Aug. 1 Photo.

B14 SP6 10w + 5w bl & car 60 25

Disaster relief.

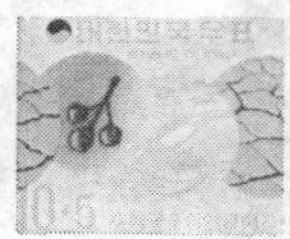

"Pin of Love" — SP7

Paddle and Ball — SP8

1973, July 1 Photo. *Perf. 12½x13½*

B15 SP7 10w + 5w multi 60 25

Disaster relief.

Perf. 13½x12½

1973, Aug. 1 Photo.

B16 SP8 10w + 5w multi 60 25

Surtax was for gymnasium to be built to commemorate the victory of the Korean women's table tennis team at the 32nd World Table Tennis Championships.

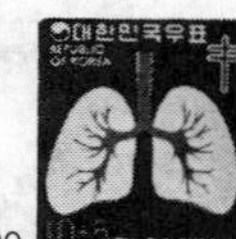

Lungs — SP9

1974, Nov. 1 *Perf. 13½x12½*

B17 SP9 10w + 5w grn & red 60 25

Surtax was for tuberculosis control.

No. 647 Surcharged 수해구제 + 10

Perf. 13½x12½

1977, July 25 Photo.

B18 A328 20w + 10w grn *2.50 2.00*

Surtax was for flood relief.

Seoul 1988 Olympic Games Series

'88 Seoul Games Emblem — SP10

Korean Tiger, Mascot — SP11

Track and Field — SP12

Equestrian — SP18

1985, Mar. 20 Photo. *Perf. 13x13½*

B19 SP10 70w + 30w blk & multi 35 30
B20 SP11 70w + 30w blk & multi 35 30
a. Souvenir sheet of 2, #B19-20 75

1985, June 10

B21 SP12 70w + 30w shown 35 30
B22 SP12 70w + 30w Rowing 35 30
a. Souvenir sheet of 2, #B21-B22 75

1985, Sept. 16

B23 SP12 70w + 30w Boxing 35 30
B24 SP12 70w + 30w Women's basketball 35 30
a. Souvenir sheet of 2, #B23-B24 75

1985, Nov. 1

B25 SP12 70w + 30w Canoeing 35 25
B26 SP12 70w + 30w Cycling 35 25
a. Souvenir sheet of 2, #B25-B26 75

Surtax for the 24th Summer Olympic Games, Sept. 17-Oct. 2, 1988.

1986, Mar. 25 Photo. *Perf. 13x13½*

Designs: No. B28, Fencing. No. B29, Soccer. No. B30, Gymnastic rings.

B27 SP18 70w + 30w multi 25 20
B28 SP18 70w + 30w multi 25 20
B29 SP18 70w + 30w multi 25 20
B30 SP18 70w + 30w multi 25 20

Souvenir Sheets

B31 Sheet of 4 4.25 1.25
a. SP18 370w + 100w like #B27 1.05 32
B32 Sheet of 4 4.75 1.50
a. SP18 400w + 100w like #B28 1.15 35
B33 Sheet of 4 5.00 1.50
a. SP18 440w + 100w like #B29 1.25 38
B34 Sheet of 4 5.25 1.60
a. SP18 470w + 100w like #B30 1.30 40

1986 Photo. *Perf. 13x13½*

B35 SP18 80w +50w Weight lifting 50 30
B36 SP18 80w +50w Team handball 50 30
B37 SP18 80w +50w Judo 50 30
B38 SP18 80w +50w Field hockey 50 30

Souvenir Sheets

B39 Sheet of 4 5.40
a. SP18 370w + 100w like #B35 1.35 1.00
B40 Sheet of 4 5.80
a. SP18 400w + 100w like #B36 1.45 1.10
B41 Sheet of 4 6.20
a. SP18 440w + 100w like #B37 1.55 1.25
B42 Sheet of 4 6.60
a. SP18 470w + 100w like #B38 1.65 1.35

Issue dates: Nos. B35-B36, B39-B40, Oct. 10; others, Nov. 1.

1987, May 25 Photo. *Perf. 13x13½*

B43 SP18 80w +50w Women's tennis 50 35
B44 SP18 80w +50w Wrestling 50 35
B45 SP18 80w +50w Dressage 50 35
B46 SP18 80w +50w Diving 50 35

1987, Oct. 10

B47 SP18 80w +50w Table Tennis 42 32
B48 SP18 80w +50w Men's shooting 42 32
B49 SP18 80w +50w Women's archery 42 32
B50 SP18 80w +50w Women's volleyball 42 32

1988, Mar. 5 Photo. *Perf. 13x13½*

B51 SP18 80w +20w Sailing 35 25
B52 SP18 80w +20w Taekwondo 35 25

1988, May 6 Photo. *Perf. 13½x13*

B53 SP18 80w +20w Torch relay, horiz. 35 25

Litho. & Engr.

B54 SP18 80w +20w Olympic Stadium, horiz. 35 25

See Greece No. 1627.

Souvenir Sheets of 2

B43a SP18 80w +50w 1.00
B44a SP18 80w +50w 1.00
B45a SP18 80w +50w 1.00
B46a SP18 80w +50w 1.00
B47a SP18 80w +50w 85
B48a SP18 80w +50w 85
B49a SP18 80w +50w 85
B50a SP18 80w +50w 85
B51a SP18 80w +20w 70
B52a SP18 80w +20w 70
B53a SP18 80w +20w 70
B54a SP18 80w +20w 70

AIR POST STAMPS

Four-motor Plane and Globe AP1

Perf. 11½x11

1947-50 Litho. Wmk. 257

C1 AP1 50wn car rose 1.75 1.50
a. Horiz. pair, imperf. btwn. 55.00

Perf. 11

C2 AP1 150wn blue ('49) 45 1.25
a. "KORFA" 14.00 10.00
C3 AP1 150wn grn ('50) 1.25

Nos. C2-C3 are redrawn. Issue date: 50wn, Oct. 1.

For surcharge see No. C5.

Plane and Korea Map — AP2

Douglas C-47 and Ship — AP3

1950, Jan. 1

C4 AP2 60wn light blue 3.00 4.50

No. C2 Surcharged with New Value and Wavy Lines in Black

1951, Oct. 10

C5 AP1 500wn on 150wn bl 65 1.00
a. "KORFA" 15.00 12.50
b. Surcharge inverted 125.00

Perf. 13x12½

1952, Oct. 15 Litho. Wmk. 257

C6 AP3 1200wn red brown 15 15
C7 AP3 1800wn lt blue 18 15
C8 AP3 4200wn purple 30 25

Nos. C6-C8 exist imperf.

1953, Apr. 5

C9 AP3 12h dp blue 15 30
C10 AP3 18h purple 25 30
C11 AP3 42h Prus green 50 42

Douglas DC-7 over East Gate, Seoul — AP4

1954, June 15 *Perf. 12½*

C12 AP4 25h brown 20 15
C13 AP4 35h dp pink 30 20
C14 AP4 38h dk green 45 20
C15 AP4 58h ultra 50 25
C16 AP4 71h dp blue 50 35
Nos. C12-C16 (5) 1.95 1.15

Nos. C12-C16 exist imperf.

Type of 1954 Redrawn

1956, July 20 Unwmk.

Laid Paper

C17 AP4 70h brt bluish grn 50 60
C18 AP4 110h brown 85 1.00
C19 AP4 205h magenta 1.00 1.00

Nos. C18-C19 are found on horizontally and vertically laid paper.

1957, July Wmk. 312 *Perf. 12½*

Granite Paper

C20 AP4 70h brt bluish grn 50 50
C21 AP4 110h brown 75 65
C22 AP4 205h magenta 1.25 1.00

On the redrawn stamps, Nos. C17-C22, the lines of the entire design are lighter, and the colorless character at right end of bottom row has been redrawn as in illustration above No. 212D.

Catalogue values for unused stamps in this section, from this point to the end of the section, are for Never Hinged items.

Girl on Palace Balcony — AP5

Designs: 100h, Suwon Castle. 200h, Songnyu Gate, Tuksu Palace. 400h, Kyunghoeru Pavilion.

Perf. 12½

1961, Dec. 1 Unwmk. Litho.

No.	Type	Description	Unused	Used
C23	AP5	50h lt blue & vio	3.00	20
C24	AP5	100h pale grn & sep	5.75	25
C25	AP5	200h pale grn & brn	11.00	50
C26	AP5	400h grn & pale bl	14.00	85

Values in Won; Same Designs; Underlined Zeros Added

1962-63

No.	Type	Description	Unused	Used
C27	AP5	5w lt bl & vio ('63)	20.00	15
C28	AP5	10w pale grn & sep	32.50	25
C29	AP5	20w pale grn & brn ('63)	42.50	50
C30	AP5	40w grn & pale bl ('63)	75.00	80

1964, May 10 Wmk. 317 *Perf. 12½*

Granite Paper

No.	Type	Description	Unused	Used
C32	AP5	10w pale grn & sep	2.75	25
C33	AP5	20w pale grn & brn	4.50	50
C34	AP5	40w pale bl & grn	7.50	1.00

1964, Oct. Unwmk. *Perf. 12½*

Designs: 39w, Girl on palace balcony. 64w, Suwon Castle. 78w, Songnyu Gate, Tuksu Palace. 112w, Kyunghoeru Pavilion.

Granite Paper

No.	Type	Description	Unused	Used
C35	AP5	39w vio bl & gray ol	1.90	25
C36	AP5	64w bl & grnsh gray	2.75	35
C37	AP5	78w grnsh bl & ultra	3.25	45
C38	AP5	112w blue & green	4.75	65

World Map and Plane — AP6

Designs: 135w, Plane over eastern hemisphere. 145w, Plane over world map. 180w, Plane over world map.

1973, Dec. 30 Photo. *Perf. 13x12½*

No.	Type	Description	Unused	Used
C39	AP6	110w pink & multi	5.50	50
C40	AP6	135w yel grn & red	7.00	60
C41	AP6	145w lt bl & rose	8.00	65
C42	AP6	180w lilac & yel	10.00	75

UPU Type of 1974

1974, Oct. 9 Photo. *Perf. 13*

No.	Type	Description	Unused	Used
C43	A480	110w blue & multi	3.00	50
a.		Souvenir sheet of 2	1.75	

Mt. Fuji, Korean Airlines Jet Type

1985, Dec. 18 Photo. *Perf. 13x13½*

No.	Type	Description	Unused	Used
C44	A878	370w brt bl, blk & red	1.50	32

North Korea

Stamps issued by the Korean People's Republic have not been listed because the US Treasury Department (Foreign Assets Control Section) has prohibited their purchase abroad and importation.

KYRGYZSTAN

(Kirghizia)

LOCATION — Bounded by Kazakhstan, Uzbekistan, Tadjikistan and China.
GOVT. — Independent republic, member of the Commonwealth of Independent States.
AREA — 76,642 sq. mi.
POP. — 4,300,000 (1989)
CAPITAL — Pishpek

With the breakup of the Soviet Union on Dec. 26, 1991, Kyrgyzstan and ten former Soviet republics established the Commonwealth of Independent States.

100 Kopecks = 1 Ruble

Catalogue values for all unused stamps in this country are for Never Hinged items.

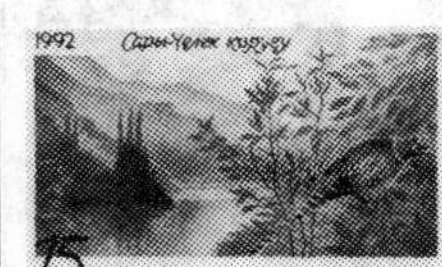
Sary-Chelek Nature Preserve A1

Unwmk.

1992, Feb. 4 Litho. *Perf. 12*

No.	Type	Description	Unused	Used
1	A1	15k multicolored	*60*	

Hawk — A2

1992 Litho. *Perf. 12½x12*

No.	Type	Description	Unused	Used
2	A2	50o multicolored	*32*	

Man with Cattle, by G.A. Aytiev — A3

1992

No.	Type	Description	Unused	Used
3	A3	1r multicolored	*38*	

Handicrafts A4

1992 Litho. *Perf. 12x11½*

No.	Type	Description	Unused	Used
4	A4	1.50r multicolored	*18*	

Kyrgyzstan stamps can be mounted in Scott's annual Russia Supplement.

LAOS

LOCATION — In northwestern Indo-China
GOVT. — Republic
AREA — 89,320 sq. mi.
POP. — 3,460,000 (est. 1977)
CAPITAL — Vientiane

Before 1949, Laos was part of the French colony of Indo-China and used its stamps until 1951. The kingdom was replaced by the Lao Peoples Democratic Republic Dec. 2, 1975.

100 Cents = 1 Piaster
100 Cents = 1 Kip (1955)

Imperforates

Most Laos stamps exist imperforate in issued and trial colors, and also in small presentation sheets in issued colors.

Catalogue values for all unused stamps in this country are for Never Hinged items.

Boat on Mekong River — A1

King Sisavang-Vong — A2

Laotian Woman — A3

Designs: 50c, 60c, 70c, Luang Prabang. 1pi, 2pi, 3pi, 5pi, 10pi, Temple at Vientiane.

1951-52 Unwmk. Engr. *Perf. 13*

No.	Type	Description	Unused	Used
1	A1	10c dk grn & emer	15	15
2	A1	20c dk car & car	15	15
3	A1	30c ind & dp ultra	55	15
4	A3	30c ind & pur ('52)	15	15
5	A1	50c dark brown	15	15
6	A1	60c red & red org	15	15
7	A1	70c ultra & bl grn	15	15
8	A3	80c brt grn & dk bl green ('52)	15	15
9	A1	1pi dk pur & pur	20	18
10	A3	1.10pi dark plum & carmine ('52)	28	15
11	A2	1.50pi blk brn & vio brown	32	18
12	A3	1.90pi indigo & dp blue ('52)	45	35
13	A1	2pi dk grn & gray green	8.75	1.10
14	A1	3pi dk car & red	35	25
15	A3	3pi choc & black brown ('52)	70	32
16	A1	5pi ind & dp ultra	50	32
17	A1	10pi blk brn & vio brown	1.40	50
		Nos. 1-17 (17)	14.55	4.55

A booklet containing 26 souvenir sheets was issued in 1952 on the anniversary of the first issue of Laos stamps. Each sheet contains a single stamp in the center (Nos. 1-17, C2-C4, J1-J6). Value $100.

See No. 223.

UPU Monument and King Sisavang-Vong — A4

1952, Dec. 7

No.	Type	Description	Unused	Used
18	A4	80c ind, blue & pur	25	22
19	A4	1pi dk car, car & org brown	25	22
20	A4	1.20pi dk pur, purple & ultra	25	22
21	A4	1.50pi dk grn, bl grn & dk brn	25	22
22	A4	1.90pi blk brn, vio brn & dk Prus grn	25	22
		Nos. 18-22,C5-C6 (7)	5.25	3.90

Laos' admission to the UPU, May 13, 1952.

Court of Love — A5

1953, July 14

No.	Type	Description	Unused	Used
23	A5	4.50pi indigo & bl grn	42	40
24	A5	6pi gray & dark brn	60	40

Composite of Laotian Temples — A6

1954, Mar. 4

No.	Type	Description	Unused	Used
25	A6	2pi indigo & purple	17.00	12.00
26	A6	3pi blk brn & dk red	18.00	15.00

Accession of King Sisavang-Vong, 50th anniv. See No. C13.

Buddha Statue and Monks — A7

1956, May 24 Engr. *Perf. 13*

No.	Type	Description	Unused	Used
27	A7	2k reddish brown	1.40	1.00
28	A7	3k black	1.40	1.00
29	A7	5k chocolate	1.75	1.40
		Nos. 27-29,C20-C21 (5)	26.55	19.40

2500th anniversary of birth of Buddha.

UN Emblem — A8

1956, Dec. 14 *Perf. 13½x13*

No.	Type	Description	Unused	Used
30	A8	1k black	30	24
31	A8	2k blue	42	42
32	A8	4k bright red	48	45
33	A8	6k purple	65	55
		Nos. 30-33,C22-C23 (6)	6.25	6.06

Admission of Laos to the UN, 1st anniv.

Khouy Player — A9

Khene Player — A10

Musical Instrument: 8k, Ranat.

1957, Mar. 25 **Unwmk.** ***Perf. 13***

34	A9	2k multicolored	75	55
35	A10	4k multicolored	75	65
36	A9	8k org, bl & red brn	75	65
		Nos. 34-36,C24-C26 (6)	5.40	4.10

See No. 224.

Harvesting Rice — A11

Drying Rice — A12

1957, July 22 **Engr.** ***Perf. 13***

37	A11	3k shown	50	35
38	A12	5k shown	65	40
39	A11	16k Winnowing rice	1.10	80
40	A11	26k Polishing rice	2.00	1.25

Elephants — A13

Various Elephants: 30c, 5k, 10k, 13k, vert.

1958, Mar. 17

41	A13	10c multi	16	15
42	A13	20c multi	16	15
43	A13	30c multi	16	15
44	A13	2k multi	16	15
45	A13	5k multi	60	50
46	A13	10k multi	65	60
47	A13	13k multi	1.00	80
		Nos. 41-47 (7)	2.89	2.50

For surcharge see No. B5.

Globe and Goddess — A14

UNESCO Building and Mother with Children — A15

Designs: 70c, UNESCO building, globe and mother with children. 1k, UNESCO building and Eiffel tower.

1958, Nov. 3 **Engr.** ***Perf. 13***

48	A14	50c multi	15	15
49	A15	60c emer, vio & maroon	15	15
50	A15	70c ultra, rose red & brn	15	15
51	A14	1k ol bis, cl & grnsh bl	15	15
		Set value	40	30

Opening of UNESCO Headquarters in Paris, Nov. 3.

King Sisavang-Vong A16

1959, Sept. 16 **Unwmk.**

52	A16	4k rose claret	15	15
53	A16	6.50k orange red	15	15
54	A16	9k bright pink	15	15
55	A16	13k green	15	15

For surcharges see Nos. 112-113, B4.

Dancers A17

Student and Torch of Learning — A18

Portal of Wat Phou, Pakse — A19

Education and Fine Arts: 3k, Globe, key of knowledge and girl student. 5k, Dancers and temple.

1959, Oct. 1 **Engr.** ***Perf. 13***

56	A17	1k vio blk, ol & bl	15	15
57	A18	2k maroon & black	15	15
58	A17	3k slate grn & vio	15	15
59	A18	5k rose vio, yel & brt grn	25	20
		Set value	58	48

1959, Nov. 2 **Unwmk.** ***Perf. 13***

Historic Monuments: 1.50k, That Inghang, Savannakhet, horiz. 2.50k, Phou Temple, Pakse, horiz. 7k, That Luang, Vientiane. 11k, That Luang, Vientiane, horiz. 12.50k, Phousi, Luang Prabang.

60	A19	50c sep, grn & org	15	15
61	A19	1.50k multi	15	15
62	A19	2.50k pur, vio bl & ol	15	15
63	A19	7k vio, olive & cl	15	15
64	A19	11k brn, car & grn	15	15
65	A19	12.50k bl, vio & bis	15	15
		Set value	42	42

Funeral Urn and Monks A20

King Sisavang-Vong A21

Designs: 6.50k, Urn under canopy. 9k, Catafalque on 7-headed dragon carriage.

1961, Apr. 29 **Engr.** ***Perf. 13***

66	A20	4k black, bis & org	16	16
67	A20	6.50k black & bister	16	16
68	A20	9k black & bister	16	16
69	A21	25k black	42	42

Issued in memory of King Sisavang-Vong (1885-1959) and to commemorate the funeral, Apr. 23-29, 1961.

King Savang Vatthana — A22

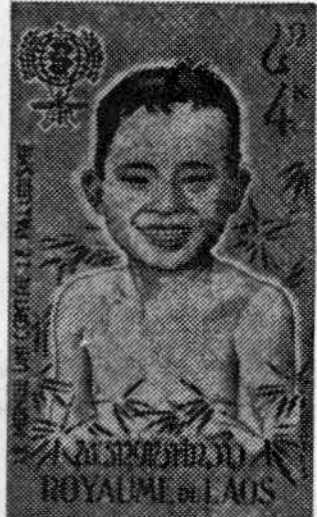

Boy and Malaria Eradication Emblem — A23

1962, Apr. 16 ***Perf. 13***

Portrait in Brown and Carmine

70	A22	1k ultramarine	15	15
71	A22	2k lilac rose	15	15
72	A22	5k greenish blue	15	15
73	A22	10k olive	22	22
		Set value	45	45

1962, July 19 **Engr.**

Designs: 9k, Girl. 10k, Malaria eradication emblem.

74	A23	4k bluish grn, blk & buff	15	15
75	A23	9k lt bl, blk & lt brn	16	15
76	A23	10k ol, bis & rose red	30	25
		Set value	52	45

WHO drive to eradicate malaria. A souvenir sheet exists.

Stamp Day A24

Royal Messenger — A25

Designs: 50c, Modern mail service (truck, train, plane). 1k, Ancient mail service (messenger on elephant).

1962, Nov. 15 **Unwmk.** ***Perf. 13***

77	A24	50c multi	15	15
78	A24	70c multi	15	15
79	A25	1k dp cl, grn & blk	16	16
80	A25	1.50k multi	16	16

Souvenir sheets exist. One contains the 50c and 70c; the other, the 1k and 1.50k. The sheets exist both perf. and imperf.

Fishermen with Nets — A26

Threshing Rice — A27

Designs: 5k, Plowing and planting in rice paddy. 9k, Woman with infant harvesting rice.

1963, Mar. 21 ***Perf. 13***

81	A26	1k grn, bister & pur	15	15
82	A27	4k bister, bl & grn	15	15
83	A26	5k grn, bis & indigo	15	15
84	A27	9k grn, vio bl & ocher	20	20
a.		Min. sheet of 4, #81-84, imperf.	2.00	1.75
		Set value	50	50

FAO "Freedom from Hunger" campaign.

Queen Khamphouy Handing out Gifts — A28

1963, Oct. 10 **Engr.**

85	A28	4k brn, dp car & blue	15	15
86	A28	6k grn, red, yel & bl	15	15
87	A28	10k bl, dp car & dk brn	16	16
a.		Miniature sheet of 3, #85-87	1.25	1.10

Centenary of the International Red Cross.

Man Holding UN Emblem — A29

1963, Dec. 10 **Unwmk.** ***Perf. 13***

88	A29	4k dk bl, dp org & vio brn	25	15

15th anniv. of the Universal Declaration of Human Rights.

Temple of That Luang, Map of Nubia and Ramses II — A30

1964, Mar. 8 **Engr.**

89	A30	4k multicolored	15	15
90	A30	6k multicolored	15	15
91	A30	10k multicolored	16	16
a.		Miniature sheet of 3, #89-91	1.00	90

UNESCO world campaign to save historic monuments in Nubia. No. 91a sold for 25k.

Ceremonial Chalice — A31

Designs: 15k, Buddha. 20k, Soldier leading people through Mekong River Valley. 40k, Royal Palace, Luang Prabang.

1964, July 30 **Unwmk.** ***Perf. 13***

92	A31	10k multicolored	15	15
93	A31	15k multicolored	15	15
94	A31	20k multicolored	25	16
95	A31	40k multicolored	45	30
a.		Miniature sheet of 4, #92-95	1.90	1.75

"Neutral and Constitutional Laos." When the stamps are arranged in a block of four with 40k and 15k in first row and 10k and 20k in second row, the map of Laos appears.

Prince Vet and Wife Mathie — A32

Lao Women — A33

Scenes from Buddhist Legend of Phra Vet Sandone: 32k, God of the Skies sending his son to earth. 45k, Phaune's daughter with beggar husband. 55k, Beggar cornered by guard and dogs.

1964, Nov. 17 **Photo.** ***Perf. 13x12½***

96	A32	10k multicolored	18	18
97	A32	32k multicolored	22	22
98	A32	45k multicolored	35	35
99	A32	55k multicolored	45	45
a.		Miniature sheet of 4	2.25	2.00

No. 99a contains 4 imperf. stamps similar to Nos. 96-99.

1964, Dec. 15 **Engr.** ***Perf. 13***

100	A33	25k blk, org brn & pale ol	22	22

See Nos. C43-C45, C45a.

Teacher and School, American Aid — A35

1965, Mar. 13 **Unwmk.** ***Perf. 13***

Size: 36x36mm

101	A34	10k Cethosia biblis	38	16
102	A34	25k Precis cebrene	42	25

Size: 48x27mm

103	A34	40k Dysphania militaris	70	38

See No. C46.

Designs: 25k, Woman at Wattay Airport, French aid, horiz. 45k, Woman bathing child and food basket, Japanese aid. 55k, Musicians broadcasting, British aid, horiz.

1965, Mar. 30 **Engr.** ***Perf. 13***

104	A35	25k bl grn, brn & car rose	15	15
105	A35	45k ol grn & brn	30	30
106	A35	55k brt bl & bis	35	35
107	A35	75k multicolored	45	45

Issued to publicize foreign aid to Laos.

Hophabang Temple A36

1965, Apr. 23 **Unwmk.** ***Perf. 13***

108	A36	10k multicolored	25	16

Telewriter, Map of Laos and Globe — A37

Designs: 30k, Communication by satellite and map of Laos. 50k, Globe, map of Laos and radio.

1965, June 15 **Engr.** ***Perf. 13***

109	A37	5k vio bl, brn & red lil	15	15
110	A37	30k bl, org brn & sl grn	22	20
111	A37	50k crim, lt bl & bis	35	30
a.		Miniature sheet of 3, #109-111	2.75	2.50

ITU, centenary.

Nos. 52-53 Surcharged in Dark Blue with New Value and Bars

1965, July 5 **Unwmk.** ***Perf. 13***

112	A16	1k on 4k rose claret	15	15
113	A16	5k on 6.50k org red	16	15
		Set value		16

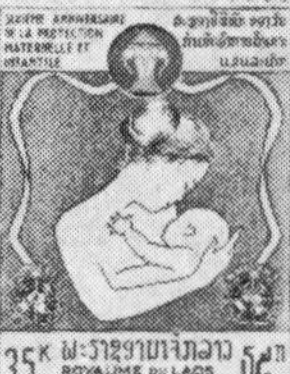

Mother and Child, UNICEF and WHO Emblems — A38

Map of Laos and UN Emblem — A39

Butterflies A34

1965, Sept. 1 **Engr.** ***Perf. 13***

114	A38	35k lt ultra & dk red	50	25
a.		Miniature sheet	3.00	1.75

Mother and Child Protection movement, 6th anniv.

1965, Nov. 3 ***Perf. 12½x13***

115	A39	5k emer, gray & vio bl	15	15
116	A39	25k lil rose, gray & vio bl	16	15
117	A39	40k bl, gray & vio bl	25	25

UN, 20th anniv. Although first day covers were canceled "Oct. 24," the actual day of issue is reported to have been Nov. 3.

Tikhy (Hockey) A40

Pastimes: 10k, Two bulls fighting. 25k, Canoe race. 50k, Rocket festival.

1965, Dec. 23 **Engr.** ***Perf. 13***

118	A40	10k org, brn & gray	15	15
119	A40	20k grn, ver & dk bl	16	16
120	A40	25k brt blue & multi	16	15
121	A40	50k orange & multi	35	35

Slaty-headed Parakeet A41

Birds: 15k, White-crested laughing thrush. 20k, Osprey. 45k, Bengal roller.

1966, Feb. 10 **Engr.** ***Perf. 13***

122	A41	5k car rose, ol & brn	16	15
123	A41	15k bluish grn, brn & blk	22	15
124	A41	20k dl bl, sep & bis	30	15
125	A41	45k vio, Prus bl & sep	60	38
		Set value		70

WHO Headquarters, Geneva A42

1966, May 3 **Engr.** ***Perf. 13***

126	A42	10k bl grn & indigo	15	15
127	A42	25k car & dk green	20	16
128	A42	50k ultra & black	40	40
a.		Miniature sheet of 3, #126-128	2.25	2.00

Inauguration of the WHO Headquarters, Geneva. No. 128a sold for 150k.

Ordination of Buddhist Monk — A43

Folklore: 25k, Women building ceremonial sand hills. 30k, Procession of the Wax Pagoda, vert. 40k, Wrist-tying ceremony (3 men, 3 women), vert.

1966, May 20 ***Perf. 13***

129	A43	10k multicolored	15	15
130	A43	25k multicolored	20	16
131	A43	30k multicolored	22	22
132	A43	40k multicolored	25	25

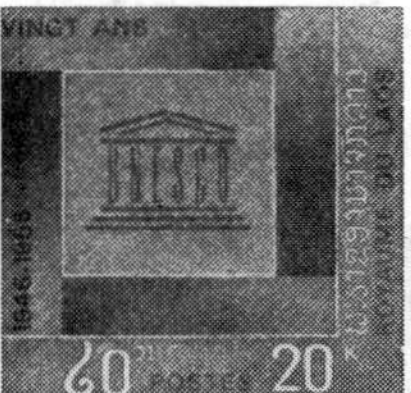

UNESCO Emblem A44

1966, July 7 **Engr.** ***Perf. 13***

133	A44	20k ocher & gray	15	15
134	A44	30k brt blue & gray	20	16
135	A44	40k brt green & gray	25	16
136	A44	60k crimson & gray	38	20
a.		Miniature sheet, #133-136	3.25	3.25

UNESCO, 20th anniv. No. 136a sold for 250k.

Addressed Envelope Carrier Pigeon, Globe and Hand with Quill Pen — A45

1966, Sept. 7 **Engr.** ***Perf. 13***

137	A45	5k red, brn & bl	15	15
138	A45	20k bl grn, blk & lil	16	15
139	A45	40k bl, red brn & dk ol bister	22	20
140	A45	45k brt rose lil, bl grn & black	25	22
a.		Min. sheet of 4, #137-140	2.25	2.25

Intl. Letter Writing Week, Oct. 6-12. No. 140a sold for 250k.

Sculpture from Siprapouthbat Temple — A46

Sculptures: 20k, from Visoun Temple. 50k, from Xiengthong Temple. 70k, from Visoun Temple.

1967, Feb. 21 **Engr.** ***Perf. 12½x13***

141	A46	5k olive grn & grn	15	15
142	A46	20k brn ol & gray bl	15	15
143	A46	50k dk brn & dp cl	20	20
144	A46	70k dk brn & dk mag	28	28
		Set value	65	65

General Post Office — A47

1967, Apr. 6 **Engr.** ***Perf. 13***

145	A47	25k brn, grn & vio brn	15	15
146	A47	50k ind, brt blue & grn	25	20
147	A47	70k dk red, grn & brn	35	25

Inauguration of the new Post and Telegraph Headquarters.

Snakehead A48

Fish: 35k, Giant catfish. 45k, Spiny eel. 60k, Knifefish.

1967, June 8 Engr. *Perf. 13x12½*

148 A48	20k dl bl, bis & blk	15	15
149 A48	35k aqua, bis & gray	22	15
150 A48	45k pale grn, bis & ol brn	38	18
151 A48	60k sl grn, bis & blk	42	20

Drumstick Tree Flower — A49

Blossoms: 55k, Turmeric. 75k, Peacock flower. 80k, Pagoda tree.

1967, Aug. 10 Engr. *Perf. 12½x13*

152 A49	30k red lil, yel & grn	15	15
153 A49	55k org, mag & lt grn	40	20
154 A49	75k bl, red & lt grn	42	20
155 A49	80k brt grn, mag & yel	55	28

Banded Krait — A50

Reptiles: 40k, Marsh crocodile. 100k, Malayan moccasin. 200k, Water monitor.

1967, Dec. 7 Engr. *Perf. 13*

156 A50	5k emer, ind & yel	22	15
157 A50	40k sep, lt grn & yel	28	15
158 A50	100k lt grn, brn & ocher	60	35
159 A50	200k grn, blk & bister	90	80

Human Rights Flame — A51

1968, Feb. 8 Engr. *Perf. 13*

160 A51	20k brt grn, red & grn	15	15
161 A51	30k brn, red & grn	20	16
162 A51	50k brt bl, red & grn	38	28
a.	Souv. sheet of 3, #160-162	1.50	1.50

Intl. Human Rights Year. No. 162a sold for 250k.

WHO Emblem — A52

1968, July 5 Engr. *Perf. 12½x13*

163 A52	15k rose vio, ver & ocher	15	15
164 A52	30k brt bl, brt grn & ocher	15	15
165 A52	70k ver, plum & ocher	35	15
166 A52	110k brn, brt rose lil & ocher	55	38
167 A52	250k brt grn, brt bl & ocher	1.60	70
a.	Souv. sheet of 5, #163-167	4.50	3.50
	Nos. 163-167 (5)	2.80	1.53

WHO, 20th anniv. No. 167a sold for 500k.

Parade and Memorial Arch — A53

Designs: 20k, Armored Corps with tanks. 60k, Three soldiers with Laotian flag.

1968, July 15 *Perf. 13*

168 A53	15k multicolored	15	15
169 A53	20k multicolored	15	15
170 A53	60k multicolored	30	16
	Nos. 168-170,C52-C53 (5)	2.25	1.56

Laotian Army. For souvenir sheet see No. C53a.

Chrysochroa Mnizechi — A54

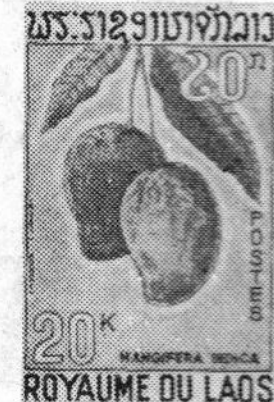
Mangoes — A55

Insects: 50k, Aristobia approximator. 90k, Eutaenia corbetti.

1968, Aug. 28 Engr. *Perf. 13*

171 A54	30k vio bl, grn & yel	22	15
172 A54	50k lil, blk & ocher	38	25
173 A54	90k bis, blk & org	55	40
	Nos. 171-173,C54-C55 (5)	2.60	1.57

1968, Oct. 3 Engr. *Perf. 13*

Fruits: 50k, Tamarind. 180k, Jackfruit, horiz. 250k, Watermelon, horiz.

174 A55	20k ind, lt bl & emer	15	15
175 A55	50k lt bl, emer & brn	25	20
176 A55	180k sep, org & yel grn	70	60
177 A55	250k sep, bis & emer	1.00	70

Hurdling — A56

1968, Nov. 15 Engr. *Perf. 13*

178 A56	15k shown	15	15
179 A56	80k Tennis	50	22
180 A56	100k Soccer	60	30
181 A56	110k High jump	65	35

19th Olympic Games, Mexico City, Oct. 12-27.

Wedding of Kathanam and Nang Sida — A57

Design: 200k, Thao Khathanam battling the serpent Ngou Xouang and the giant bird Phanga Houng. Design from panels of the central gate of Ongtu Temple, Vientiane. Design of 150k is from east gate.

1969, Feb. 28 Photo. *Perf. 12x13*

182 A57	150k blk, gold & red	80	40
183 A57	200k blk, gold & red	1.20	60

Soukhib Ordered to Attack — A58

Scenes from Royal Ballet: 15k, Pharak pleading for Nang Sita. 20k, Thotsakan reviewing his troops. 30k, Nang Sita awaiting punishment. 40k, Pharam inspecting troops. 60k, Hanuman preparing to rescue Nang Sita.

1969 Photo. *Perf. 14*

184 A58	10k multicolored	15	15
185 A58	15k blue & multi	15	15
186 A58	20k lt bl & multi	15	15
187 A58	30k salmon & multi	16	15
188 A58	40k salmon & multi	20	16
189 A58	60k pink & multi	35	25
	Nos. 184-189,C56-C57 (8)	3.81	2.53

For surcharges see Nos. B12-B17, CB1-CB2.

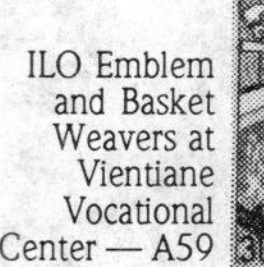

ILO Emblem and Basket Weavers at Vientiane Vocational Center — A59

1969, May 7 Engr. *Perf. 13*

190 A59	30k claret & violet	20	15
191 A59	60k sl grn & vio brn	40	25

ILO, 50th anniv. See No. C58.

Chinese Pangolin — A60

1969, Nov. 6 Photo. *Perf. 13x12*

192 A60	15k multicolored	15	15
193 A60	30k multicolored	15	15
	Nos. 192-193,C59-C61 (5)	1.14	1.08

That Luang, Luang Prabang A61

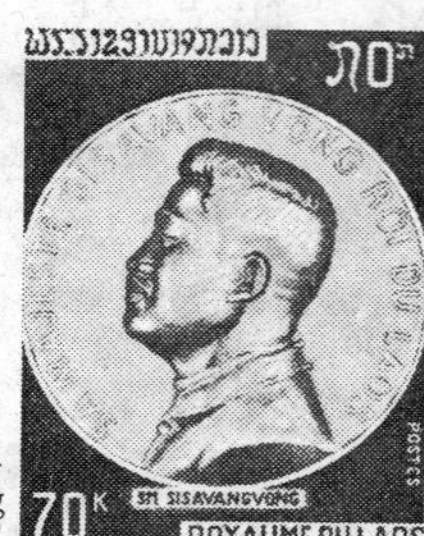
King Sisavang-Vong A62

1969, Nov. 19 Engr. *Perf. 13*

194 A61	50k dk brn, bl & bis	35	15
195 A62	70k maroon & buff	45	22

Death of King Sisavang-Vong, 10th anniv. Nos. 194-195 are printed se-tenant with connecting label with dark green commemorative inscription.

Carved Capital from Wat Xiengthong A63

1970, Jan. 10 Photo. *Perf. 12x13*

196 A63	70k multicolored	45	45

See Nos. C65-C66.

Kongphene (Midday) Drum — A64

Designs: 55k, Kongthong (bronze) drum.

1970, Mar. 30 Engr. *Perf. 13*

197 A64	30k bl gray, ol & org	38	15
198 A64	55k ocher, blk & yel grn	70	40

See No. C67.

Lenin Explaining Electrification Plan, by L. Shmatko — A65

1970, Apr. 22 Litho. *Perf. 12½x12*

199 A65	30k blue & multi	16	15
200 A65	70k rose red & multi	45	28

Lenin (1870-1924), Russian communist leader.

Silk Weaver and EXPO Emblem A66

1970, July 7 **Engr.** ***Perf. 13***

201 A66 30k shown 15 15
202 A66 70k Woman winding thread 35 35

Laotian silk industry; EXPO '70 Intl. Exposition, Osaka, Japan, Mar. 15-Sept. 13. See No. C69.

Wild Boar — A67

1970, Sept. 7 **Engr.** ***Perf. 13***

203 A67 20k green & dp brn 15 15
204 A67 60k dp brn & ol bis 20 20
Set value 27 27

See Nos. C70-C71.

Buddha, UN Headquarters and Emblem — A68

1970, Oct. 24
Size: 22x36mm

205 A68 30k ultra, brn & rose red 20 15
206 A68 70k brt grn, sep & vio 38 22

UN, 25th anniv. See No. C75.

Nakhanet, Symbol of Arts and Culture — A69

1971, Feb. 5

207 A69 70k shown 55 30
208 A69 85k Rahu swallowing the moon 65 40

See No. C76.

Silversmithing A70

1971, Apr. 12 **Engr.** ***Perf. 13***
Size: 36x36mm

209 A70 30k shown 18 15
210 A70 50k Pottery 30 20

Size: 47x36mm

211 A70 70k Boat building 48 22

Laotian and African Children, UN Emblem — A71

Design: 60k, Women musicians, elephants and UN emblem.

1971, May 1 **Engr.** ***Perf. 13***

212 A71 30k lt grn, brn & blk 16 15
213 A71 60k yel, pur & dl red 38 25

Intl. year against racial discrimination.

Miss Rotary, Wat Ho Phrakeo — A72

Dendrobium Aggregatum — A73

Design: 30k, Monk on roof of That Luang and Rotary emblem, horiz.

1971, June 28 **Engr.** ***Perf. 13***

214 A72 30k purple & ocher 35 15
215 A72 70k gray ol, dk bl & rose 65 25

Rotary International, 50th anniversary.

Perf. 12½x13, 13x12½

1971, July 7 **Photo.**
Size: 26x36, 36x26mm

216 A73 30k shown 15 15
217 A73 50k Asocentrum ampullaceum, horiz. 20 15
218 A73 70k Trichoglottis fasciata, horiz. 30 15
Set value 36

See Nos. 230-232, C79, C89.

Palm Civet — A74

Animals: 40k, like 25k. 50k, Lesser Malay chevrotain. 85k, Sika deer.

1971, Sept. 16 **Engr.** ***Perf. 13***

219 A74 25k pur, dk bl & blk 15 15
220 A74 40k grn, ol bis & blk 15 15
221 A74 50k brt grn & ocher 15 15
222 A74 85k sl grn, grn & brn orange 20 20
Nos. 219-222,C83 (5) 1.45 1.05

Types of 1952-57 with Ornamental Panels and Inscriptions

Designs: 30k, Laotian woman. 40k, So player (like #C25). 50k, Rama (like #C19).

1971, Nov. 2

223 A3 30k brn vio & brn 15 15
a. Souvenir sheet of 3 1.75 1.75
224 A10 40k sep, blk & ver 15 15
225 AP7 50k ultra, blk & sal 20 20

20th anniv. of Laotian independent postal service. All stamps inscribed: "Vingtième Anniversaire de la Philatélie Lao," "Postes" and "1971." No. 223a contains No. 223 and 60k and 85k in design of 30k, sold for 250k. See No. C84.

Children Learning to Read — A75

1972, Jan. 30 **Engr.** ***Perf. 13***
Size: 36x22mm

226 A75 30k shown 15 15
227 A75 70k Scribe writing on palm leaves 22 22

Intl. Book Year. See No. C87.

Nam Ngum Hydroelectric Dam, Monument and ECAFE Emblem — A76

1972, Mar. 28 **Engr.** ***Perf. 13***

228 A76 40k grn, ultra & lt brn 15 15
229 A76 80k grn, brn ol & dk bl 22 22

25th anniv. of the Economic Commission for Asia and the Far East (ECAFE), which helped build the Nam Ngum Hydroelectric Dam. See No. C88.

Orchid Type of 1971

Orchids: 40k, Rynchostylis giganterum. 60k, Paphiopedilum exul. 80k, Cattleya (horiz.).

1972, May 1 **Photo.** ***Perf. 13***
Size: 26x36mm, 36x26mm

230 A73 40k lt bl & multi 16 15
231 A73 60k multicolored 20 15
232 A73 80k lt bl & multi 30 15
Set value 32

Woman Carrying Water, UNICEF Emblem — A77

Children's drawings: 80k, Child learning bamboo-weaving, UNICEF emblem.

1972, July 20 **Engr.** ***Perf. 13***

233 A77 50k blue & multi 15 15
234 A77 80k brown & multi 22 22

25th anniv. (in 1971) of UNICEF. See No. C90.

Attopeu Costume, Religious Ceremony — A78

Lion from Wat That Luang and Lions Emblem — A79

Design: 90k, Phongsaly festival costume.

1973, Feb. 16 **Engr.** ***Perf. 13***

235 A78 40k mar & multi 15 15
236 A78 90k multicolored 16 16
Set value 24 24

See Nos. C101-C102.

1973, Mar. 30 **Engr.** ***Perf. 13***

237 A79 40k vio bl, rose cl & lil 16 15
238 A79 80k pur, org brn & yel 25 16

Lions International of Laos. See No. C103.

Dr. Hansen, Map of Laos, "Dok Hak" Flowers — A80

1973, June 28 **Engr.** ***Perf. 13***

239 A80 40k multicolored 16 15
240 A80 80k multicolored 35 20

Centenary of the discovery by Dr. Armauer G. Hansen of the Hansen bacillus, the cause of leprosy.

Wat Vixun, Monk Blessing Girl Scouts — A81

1973, Sept. 1 **Engr.** ***Perf. 13***

241 A81 70k ocher & brown 22 22

25th anniv. of Laotian Scout Movement. See Nos. C106-C107.

INTERPOL Headquarters A82

1973, Dec. 22 **Engr.** ***Perf. 13x12½***

242 A82 40k greenish bl 15 15
243 A82 80k brown 22 22

50th anniv. of Intl. Criminal Police Org. See No. C110.

Boy Mailing Letter — A83

Eranthemum Nervosum — A84

1974, Apr. 30 **Engr.** ***Perf. 13***

244 A83 70k bl, lt grn & ocher 15 15
245 A83 80k lt grn, bl & ocher 20 20

UPU, cent. See Nos. C114-C115.

1974, May 31
Size: 26x36mm, 36x26mm

246 A84 30k grn & vio 15 15
247 A84 50k Water lilies, horiz. 15 15
248 A84 80k Scheffler's kapokier, horiz. 15 20
Set value 26 32

See No. C116.

Mekong River Ferry — A85

Design: 90k, Samlo (passenger tricycle; vert.).

1974, July 31 Engr. *Perf. 13*

249 A85 25k red brn & choc 15 15
250 A85 90k brown ol & lt ol 16 16
Set value 20 20

See No. C117.

Marconi, Indigenous Transmission Methods, Transistor Radio — A86

1974, Aug. 28 Engr. *Perf. 13*

251 A86 60k multicolored 15 15
252 A86 90k multicolored 16 16

Guglielmo Marconi (1874-1937), Italian electrical engineer and inventor. See No. C118.

Diastocera Wallichi Tonkinensis A87

1974, Oct. 23 Engr. *Perf. 13*

253 A87 50k shown 15 15
254 A87 90k Macrochenus isabellunus 20 20
255 A87 100k Purpuricenus malaccensis 22 22

See No. C119.

Temple, Houeisai, and Sapphire A88

1975, Feb. 12 Engr. *Perf. 13x12½*

256 A88 100k bl, brn & grn 22 22
257 A88 110k Sapphire panning at Attopeu 30 30

King Sisavang-Vong, Princes Souvanna Phouma and Souphanou-Vong — A89

1975, Feb. 21 Engr. *Perf. 13*

258 A89 80k ol & multi 25 20
259 A89 300k multicolored 60 45
260 A89 420k multicolored 70 70

1st anniv. of Peace Treaty of Vientiane.

Fortuneteller Working on Forecast for New Year (Size of pair: 100x27mm)
A90 A91

New Year Riding Rabbit, and Tiger (Old Year) — A92

1975, Apr. 14 Engr. *Perf. 13*

261 A90 40k bister & red brn 15 15
262 A91 200k bis, red brn & sl 35 25
263 A92 350k blue & multi 62 50

New Year 1975, Year of the Rabbit. Nos. 261-262 printed se-tenant.

UN Emblem, "Equality" — A93

Design: 200k, IWY emblem, man and woman.

1975, June 19 Engr.

264 A93 100k dl bl & vio bl 20 20
265 A93 200k multi 40 40
a. Miniature sheet of 2, #264-265 80 80

International Women's Year.

UPU, Cent. — A93a

Designs: 15k, Runner, rocket reaching orbit, vert. 30k, Docked Soyuz capsules, chariot, vert. 40k, Biplane, Concorde. 1000k, Apollo spacecraft in orbit. 1500k, Apollo spacecraft, astronaut, vert. No. 266G, Mail truck, Concorde. No. 266H, Stagecoach. No. 266I, Zeppelin, locomotive.

Perf. 13x14, 14x13

1975, July 7 Litho.

266 A93a 10k multicolored
266A A93a 15k multicolored
266B A93a 30k multicolored
266C A93a 40k multicolored
266D A93a 1000k multicolored
266E A93a 1500k multicolored

Litho. & Embossed

Perf. 13½

266G A93a 3000k gold & multi

Souvenir Sheets

266H A93a 2500k gold & multi
266I A93a 3000k gold & multi

Nos. 266D-266E, 266G-266I are airmail.

Apollo-Soyuz Mission — A93b

Designs: 125k, Astronauts, Thomas Stafford, Vance D. Brand, Donald Slayton. 150k, Cosmonauts Alexei Leonov, Valery Koubasov. 200k, Apollo-Soyuz link-up. 300k, Handshake in space. 450k, Preparation for re-entry. 700k, Apollo splashdown.

1975, July 7 Litho. *Perf. 14x13*

267 A93b 125k multicolored
267A A93b 150k multicolored
267B A93b 200k multicolored
267C A93b 300k multicolored
267D A93b 450k multicolored
267E A93b 700k multicolored

Nos. 267D-267E are airmail.

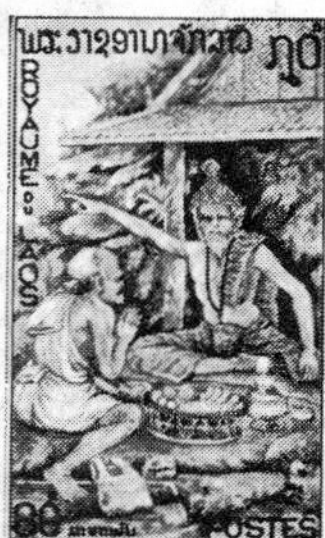

Scene from Vet Sandone Legend — A94

Designs: Scenes from Buddhist legend of Prince Vet Sandone.

1975, July 22 Photo. *Perf. 13*

268 A94 80k multicolored 22 16
268A A94 110k multicolored 30 22
268B A94 120k multicolored 35 25
268C A94 130k multicolored 38 28

American Revolution, Bicent. — A94a

Presidents: 10k, Washington, J. Adams, Jefferson, Madison. 15k, Monroe, J.Q. Adams, Jackson, Van Buren. 40k, Harrison, Tyler, Polk, Taylor. 1000k, Truman, Eisenhower, Kennedy. 1500k, L. Johnson, Nixon, Ford.

1975, July 30 Litho. *Perf. 13½*

269 A94a 10k multicolored
269A A94a 15k multicolored
269B A94a 40k multicolored
269C A94a 1000k multicolored
269D A94a 1500k multicolored

Nos. 269C-269D are airmail. Stamps of similar design in denominations of 50k, 100k, 125k, 150k, and 200k exist but were not available in Laotian post offices.

Buddha, Stupas of Borobudur — A95

Design: 200k, Borobudur sculptures and UNESCO emblem.

1975, Aug. 20 Engr. *Perf. 13*

270 A95 100k ind & multi 18 15
271 A95 200k multicolored 35 22
a. Miniature sheet of 2, #270-271 1.25 90

UNESCO campaign to save Borobudur Temple, Java.

Coat of Arms of Republic — A96

Thathiang Pagoda, Vientiane — A97

1976, Dec. 2 Litho. *Perf. 14*

272 A96 1k blue & multi 15 15
273 A96 2k rose & multi 15 15
274 A96 5k brt grn & multi 15 15
275 A96 10k lilac & multi 15 15
276 A96 200k orange & multi 80 80
a. Min. sheet of 5, #272-276 3.00 2.75
Set value 1.00 1.00

1976, Dec. 18 *Perf. 13½*

Designs: 2k, 80k, 100k, Phonsi Pagoda, Luang Prabang. 30k, 300k, like 1k.

277 A97 1k multicolored 15 15
278 A97 2k multicolored 15 15
279 A97 30k multicolored 15 15
280 A97 80k multicolored 25 25
281 A97 100k multicolored 35 35
282 A97 300k multicolored 1.00 1.00
Nos. 277-282 (6) 2.05 2.05

Silversmith A98

Perf. 13x12½, 12½x13

1977, Apr. 1 Litho.

283 A98 1k shown 15 15
284 A98 2k Weaver 15 15
285 A98 20k Potter 15 15
286 A98 50k Basket weaver, vert. 20 20
Set value 40 40

Miniature sheets of 2 exist, perf. and imperf.

Cosmonauts A.A. Gubarev, G.M. Grechko — A99

Government Palace, Vientiane, Kremlin, Moscow — A100

Designs: 20k, 50k, Lenin speaking on Red Square. 60k, like 5k. 250k, like 100k.

Perf. 12x12½, 12½x12

1977, Oct. 25 **Litho.**

287 A99	5k	multicolored	15	15
288 A99	20k	multicolored	15	15
289 A99	50k	multicolored	15	15
290 A99	60k	multicolored	15	15
291 A100	100k	multicolored	25	25
a.		Souv. sheet of 3, #288, 290-291	1.25	1.00
292 A100	250k	multicolored	70	70
a.		Souv. sheet of 3, #287, 289, 292	2.00	1.75
		Set value	1.30	1.30

60th anniv. of Russian October Revolution.

Natl. Arms — A101

1978, May 26 **Litho.** *Perf. 12½*

293 A101	5k	dull org & blk	15	15
294 A101	10k	tan & black	15	15
295 A101	50k	brt pink & blk	15	15
296 A101	100k	yel grn & blk	25	25
297 A101	250k	violet & blk	65	65
		Set value	1.10	1.10

Soldiers with Flag — A102

Army Day: 40k, Fighters and burning house, horiz. 300k, Anti-aircraft battery.

Perf. 12½x12, 12x12½

1978, Sept. 15 **Litho.**

298 A102	20k	multicolored	15	15
299 A102	40k	multicolored	15	15
300 A102	300k	multicolored	70	70
		Set value	80	80

Marchers with Banner — A103

1978, Dec. 2 **Litho.** *Perf. 11½*

301 A103	20k	shown	15	15
302 A103	50k	Women with flag	15	15
303 A103	400k	Dancer	80	80
a.		Sheet of 3, #301-303, imperf.		

National Day. A second printing in slightly different colors and with rough perforation exists. Stamps in souvenir sheet are in reverse order.

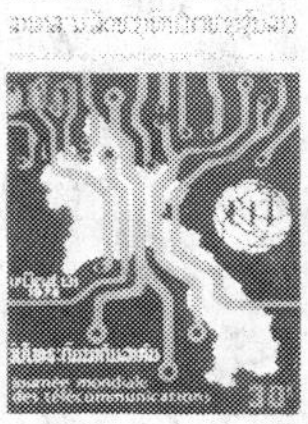

Electronic Tree, Map of Laos, ITU Emblem — A104

Design: 250k, Electronic tree, map of Laos and broadcast tower.

1979, Jan. 18 **Litho.** *Perf. 12½*

304 A104	30k	multicolored	15	15
305 A104	250k	multicolored	55	55

World Telecommunications Day, 1978.

Woman Mailing Letter A105

Designs: 10k, 80k, Processing mail. 100k, like 5k.

1979, Jan. 18

306 A105	5k	multicolored	15	15
307 A105	10k	multicolored	15	15
308 A105	80k	multicolored	20	20
309 A105	100k	multicolored	25	25
		Set value	50	50

Asian-Oceanic Postal Union, 15th anniv.

Intl. Year of the Child A106

1979 **Litho.** *Perf. 11*

Without Gum

310 A106	20k	Playing with ball, vert.	15
311 A106	50k	Studying	18
312 A106	100k	Playing musical instruments	35
313 A106	200k	Breast-feeding, vert.	70
314 A106	200k	Map, globe, vert.	70
315 A106	500k	Immunization, vert.	1.75
316 A106	600k	Girl dancing, vert.	2.25
		Nos. 310-316 (7)	6.08

Issue dates: Nos. 310-311, 313, 315, Aug. 1. Others, Dec. 25. Imperf. sheets of 4 containing Nos. 310-311, 313, 315 issued Aug. 1; imperf. sheet of 3 containing Nos. 312, 314, 316 issued on Dec. 25.

Traditional Modes of Transportation — A107

1979, Oct. 9 *Perf. 12½x13*

317 A107	5k	Elephants, buffalo, pirogues	15
318 A107	10k	Buffalo, carts	15
319 A107	70k	like 10k	25
320 A107	500k	like 5k	1.75

5th Anniv. of the Republic A108

1980, May 30 *Perf. 11*

321 A108	30c	Agriculture, vert.	15
322 A108	50c	Education, health services	15
323 A108	1k	Three women, vert.	60
324 A108	2k	Hydroelectric energy	1.25

Imperf. souvenir sheet of 4 exists.

Lenin, 110th Birth Anniv. A109

1980, July 5 *Perf. 12x12½, 12½x12*

325 A109	1k	Lenin reading	15
326 A109	2k	Writing	30
327 A109	3k	Lenin, red flag, vert.	50
328 A109	4k	Orating, vert.	65

Imperf. souvenir sheet of 4 exists.

5th Anniv. of the Republic — A110

1980, Dec. 2 *Perf. 11*

Without Gum

329 A110	50c	Threshing rice	15
330 A110	1.60k	Logging	25
331 A110	4.60k	Veterinary medicine	60
332 A110	5.40k	Rice paddy	70

Imperf. souvenir sheet of 4 exists.

26th Communist Party (PCUS) Congress A111

1981, June 26 *Perf. 12x12½*

Without Gum

333 A111	60c	shown	15
334 A111	4.60k	Globe, broken chains	60
335 A111	5.40k	Grain, cracked bomb	70
a.		Souv. sheet of 3, Nos. 333-335, imperf.	4.00

No. 335a sold for 15k.

Souvenir Sheet

PHILATOKYO '81 — A112

1981, Sept. 20 *Perf. 13*

Without Gum

336 A112	10k	Pandas	2.25

1982 World Cup Soccer Championships, Spain — A113

Intl. Year of the Disabled — A114

1981, Oct. 15 *Perf. 12½*

Without Gum

337 A113	1k	Heading ball	22
338 A113	2k	Dribble	45
339 A113	3k	Kick	65
340 A113	4k	Goal, horiz.	85
341 A113	5k	Dribble, diff.	1.10
342 A113	6k	Kick, diff.	1.35
		Nos. 337-342 (6)	4.62

1981 *Perf. 13*

Without Gum

343 A114	3k	Office worker	70
344 A114	5k	Teacher	1.10
345 A114	12k	Weaver, fishing net	2.75

Wildcats A115

1981 *Perf. 12½*

Without Gum

346 A115	10c	Felis silvestris ornata	15
347 A115	20c	Felis viverrinus	15
348 A115	30c	Felis caracal	15
349 A115	40c	Neofelis nebulosa	15
350 A115	50c	Felis planiceps	15
351 A115	9k	Felis chaus	2.50
		Nos. 346-351 (6)	3.25

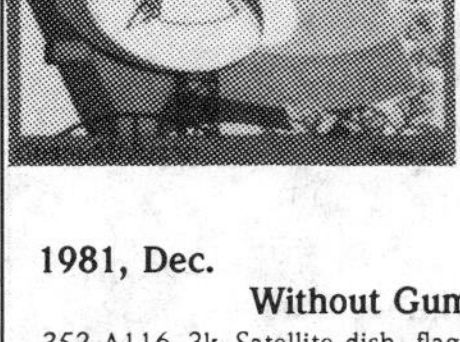

6th Anniv. of the Republic A116

1981, Dec. *Perf. 13*

Without Gum

352 A116	3k	Satellite dish, flag	50
353 A116	4k	Soldier, flag	65
354 A116	5k	Map, flag, women, soldier	85

Indian Elephants
A117

1982, Jan. 23 *Perf. 12½x13*

Without Gum

355	A117	1k	Head	25
356	A117	2k	Carrying log in trunk	50
357	A117	3k	Transporting people	75
358	A117	4k	In trap	1.00
359	A117	5k	Adult and young	1.25
360	A117	5.50k	Herd	1.40
			Nos. 355-360 (6)	5.15

Laotian Wrestling — A118

Various moves.

1982, Jan. 30 *Perf. 13*

Without Gum

361	A118	50c	multicolored	15
362	A118	1.20k	multi, diff.	25
363	A118	2k	multi, diff.	42
364	A118	2.50k	multi, diff.	55
365	A118	4k	multi, diff.	85
366	A118	5k	multi, diff.	1.10
			Nos. 361-366 (6)	3.32

Water Lilies — A119

1982, Feb. 10 *Perf. 12½x13*

Without Gum

367	A119	30c	Nymphaea zanzibariensis	15
368	A119	40c	Nelumbo nucifera gaertn rose	15
369	A119	60c	Nymphaea rosea	15
370	A119	3k	Nymphaea nouchali	65
371	A119	4k	Nymphaea white	85
372	A119	7k	Nelumbo nucifera gaertn white	1.50
			Nos. 367-372 (6)	3.45

Birds
A120

1982, Mar. 9 *Perf. 13*

Without Gum

373	A120	50c	Hirundo rustica, vert.	15
374	A120	1k	Upupa epops, vert.	25
375	A120	2k	Alcedo atthis, vert.	50
376	A120	3k	Hypothymis azurea	75
377	A120	4k	Motacilla cinerea	1.00
378	A120	10k	Orthotomus sutorius	2.50
			Nos. 373-378 (6)	5.15

A121

1982 World Cup Soccer Championships, Spain — A122

Various match scenes.

1982, Apr. 7

Without Gum

379	A121	1k	multicolored	25
380	A121	2k	multicolored	50
381	A121	3k	multicolored	75
382	A121	4k	multicolored	1.00
383	A121	5k	multicolored	1.25
384	A121	6k	multicolored	1.50
			Nos. 379-384 (6)	5.25

Souvenir Sheet

385	A122	15k	multicolored	5.75

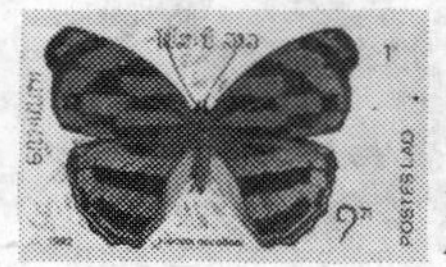

Butterflies
A123

1982, May 5 *Perf. 12½x13*

Without Gum

386	A123	1k	Herona marathus	25
387	A123	2k	Neptis paraka	50
388	A123	3k	Euripus halitherses	75
389	A123	4k	Lebadea martha	1.00

Size: 42x26mm

Perf. 12½

390	A123	5k	Iton semamora	1.25

Size: 54x36½mm

Perf. 13x12½

391	A123	6k	Elymnias hypermnestra	1.50
			Nos. 386-391 (6)	5.25

Souvenir Sheet

PHILEXFRANCE '82 — A124

1982, June 9 *Perf. 13*

Without Gum

392	A124	10k	Temple, Vientiane	3.00

River
Vessels
A125

1982, June 24

Without Gum

393	A125	50c	Raft	15
394	A125	60c	River punt	18
395	A125	1k	Houseboat	28
396	A125	2k	Passenger steamer	55
397	A125	3k	Ferry	85
398	A125	8k	Self-propelled barge	2.00
			Nos. 393-398 (6)	4.01

Pagodas
A126

1982, Aug. 2

Without Gum

399	A126	50c	Chanh	15
400	A126	60c	Inpeng	18
401	A126	1k	Dong Mieng	28
402	A126	2k	Ho Tay	55
403	A126	3k	Ho Pha Keo	85
404	A126	8k	Sisaket	2.25
			Nos. 399-404 (6)	4.26

Dogs
A127

1982, Oct. 13

Without Gum

405	A127	50c	Poodle	15
406	A127	60c	Samoyed	18
407	A127	1k	Boston terrier	30
408	A127	2k	Cairn terrier	60
409	A127	3k	Chihuahua	90
410	A127	8k	Bulldog	2.50
			Nos. 405-410 (6)	4.63

World Food Day — A128

1982, Oct. 16

Without Gum

411	A128	7k	Watering seedlings	2.00
412	A128	8k	Planting rice	2.25

Classic Automobiles — A129

1982, Nov. 7

Without Gum

413	A129	50c	1925 Fiat	15
414	A129	60c	1925 Peugeot	18
415	A129	1k	1925 Berliet	30
416	A129	2k	1925 Ballot	60
417	A129	3k	1926 Renault	90
418	A129	8k	1925 Ford	2.50
			Nos. 413-418 (6)	4.63

7th Anniv.
of the
Republic
A130

1982, Dec. 2

Without Gum

419	A130	50c	Souphanouvong, vert.	15
420	A130	1k	Tractors, field, industry	25
421	A130	2k	Cows, farm	50
422	A130	3k	Truck, microwave dish	75
423	A130	4k	Nurse, child, vert.	1.00
424	A130	5k	Education	1.25
425	A130	6k	Folk dancer, vert.	1.50
			Nos. 419-425 (7)	5.40

Bulgarian Flag, Coat of Arms and George Dimitrov (1882-1949), Bulgarian Statesman — A131

1982, Dec. 15 *Perf. 12½*

Without Gum

426	A131	10k	multicolored	2.75

Constitution of the USSR, 60th Anniv. — A132

1982, Dec. 30

Without Gum

427	A132	3k	shown	90
428	A132	4k	Maps	1.25

Souvenir Sheet

Perf. 13½x13

428A		Sheet of 2	4.00
b.	A132	5k like 3k	1.25
c.	A132	10k like 4k	2.50

Nos. 428b-428c not inscribed in Laotian at top; buff and gold decorative margin contains the inscription.

1984 Summer Olympics, Los Angeles — A133

1983, Jan. 25 *Perf. 13*

Without Gum

429	A133	50c	Hurdling	15
430	A133	1k	Women's javelin	25
431	A133	2k	Basketball	50
432	A133	3k	Diving	75
433	A133	4k	Gymnastics	1.00
434	A133	10k	Weight lifting	2.50
			Nos. 429-434 (6)	5.15

Souvenir Sheet

435	A133	15k	Soccer	4.00

No. 435 contains one stamp 32x40mm.

Horses A134

Various breeds.

1983, Feb. 1

Without Gum

436	A134	50c	multicolored	15
437	A134	1k	multi, diff.	25
438	A134	2k	multi, diff.	50
439	A134	3k	multi, diff.	75
440	A134	4k	multi, diff.	1.00
441	A134	10k	multi, diff.	2.50
			Nos. 436-441 (6)	5.15

A135

Raphael, 500th Birth Anniv. A136

Paintings (details) by Raphael: 50c, St. Catherine of Alexandra, Natl. Gallery, London. 1k, Adoration of the Kings (spectators), Vatican. 2k, Granduca Madonna, Pitti Gallery, Florence. 3k, St. George and the Dragon, The Louvre, Paris. 4k, Vision of Ezekiel, Pitti Gallery. No. 447, Adoration of the Kings (Holy Family), Vatican. No. 448, Coronation of the Virgin, Vatican.

1983, Mar. 9 *Perf. 12½x13*

Without Gum

442	A135	50c	multicolored	15
443	A135	1k	multicolored	28
444	A135	2k	multicolored	55
445	A135	3k	multicolored	85
446	A135	4k	multicolored	1.10
447	A135	10k	multicolored	2.75
			Nos. 442-447 (6)	5.68

Souvenir Sheet

Perf. 13x13½

448	A136	10k	multicolored	2.75

INTERCOSMOS Space Cooperation Program — A137

Cosmonaut and flags of USSR and participating nations.

1983, Apr. 12 *Perf. 12½*

449	A137	50c	Czechoslovakia	15
450	A137	50c	Poland	15
451	A137	1k	East Germany	25
452	A137	1k	Bulgaria	25
453	A137	2k	Hungary	50
454	A137	3k	Mongolia	80
455	A137	4k	Romania	1.10
456	A137	6k	Cuba	1.65
457	A137	10k	France	2.50
			Nos. 449-457 (9)	7.35

Souvenir Sheet

Perf. 13½x13

458	A137	10k	Vietnam	3.00

No. 458 contains one stamp 32x40mm.

A138

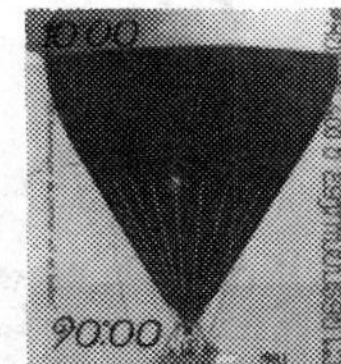

First Manned Balloon Flight, Bicent. — A139

Various balloons.

1983, May 4 *Perf. 12½x13*

459	A138	50c	shown	15
460	A138	1k	multi, diff.	25
461	A138	2k	multi, diff.	50
462	A138	3k	multi, diff.	75
463	A138	4k	multi, diff.	1.00
464	A138	10k	multi, diff.	2.50
			Nos. 459-464 (6)	5.15

Souvenir Sheet

Perf. 13½x13

465	A139	10k	shown	3.50

Souvenir Sheet

TEMBAL '83, Basel — A140

1983, May 21 *Perf. 13x13½*

Without Gum

466	A140	10k	German Maybach	3.00

Flora A141

1983, June 10 *Perf. 13*

Without Gum

467	A141	1k	Dendrobium sp.	25
468	A141	2k	Aerides odoratum	50
469	A141	3k	Dendrobium aggregatum	75
470	A141	4k	Dendrobium	1.00
471	A141	5k	Moschatum	1.25
472	A141	6k	Dendrobium sp., diff.	1.50
			Nos. 467-472 (6)	5.25

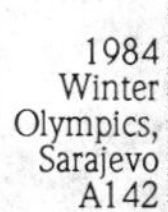

1984 Winter Olympics, Sarajevo A142

1983, July 2

Without Gum

473	A142	50c	Downhill skiing	15
474	A142	1k	Slalom	30
475	A142	2k	Ice hockey	60
476	A142	3k	Speed skating	90
477	A142	4k	Ski jumping	1.25
478	A142	10k	Luge	3.00
			Nos. 473-478 (6)	6.20

Souvenir Sheet

Perf. 13x13½

479	A142	15k	2-Man bobsled	4.50

No. 479 contains one 40x32mm stamp.

Souvenir Sheet

BANGKOK '83 — A143

1983, Aug. 4 *Perf. 13½x13*

480	A143	10k	Boats on river	2.50

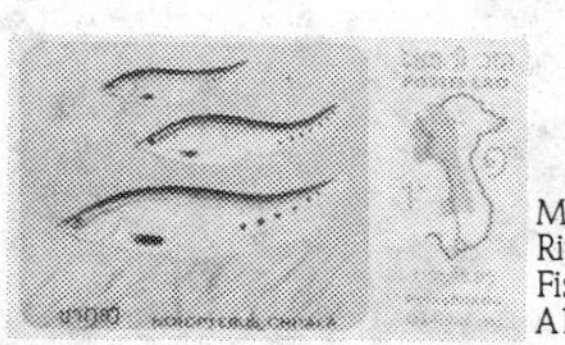

Mekong River Fish A144

1983, Sept. 5 *Perf. 12½*

Without Gum

481	A144	1k	Notopterus chitala	25
482	A144	2k	Cyprinus carpio	50
483	A144	3k	Pangasius sp.	75
484	A144	4k	Catlocarpio siamensis	1.00
485	A144	5k	Morulius sp.	1.25
486	A144	6k	Tilapia nilotica	1.50
			Nos. 481-486 (6)	5.25

Explorers and Their Ships — A145

1983, Oct. 8 *Perf. 13x12½*

Without Gum

487	A145	1k	Victoria, Magellan	25
488	A145	2k	Grand Hermine, Cartier	50
489	A145	3k	Santa Maria, Columbus	75
490	A145	4k	Cabral and caravel	1.00
491	A145	5k	Endeavor, Capt. Cook	1.25
492	A145	6k	Pourquoi-Pas, Charcot	1.50
			Nos. 487-492 (6)	5.25

No. 492 incorrectly inscribed "CABOT".

Domestic Cats — A146

1983, Nov. 9 *Perf. 12½x13*

Without Gum

493	A146	1k	Tabby	25
494	A146	2k	Long-haired Persian	50
495	A146	3k	Siamese	75
496	A146	4k	Burmese	1.00
497	A146	5k	Persian	1.25
498	A146	6k	Tortoiseshell	1.50
			Nos. 493-498 (6)	5.25

Karl Marx (1818-1883) — A147

1983, Nov. 30 *Perf. 13*

Without Gum

499	A147	1k	shown	25
500	A147	4k	Marx, 3 flags, diff., vert.	1.00
501	A147	6k	Marx, flag of Laos	1.50

8th Anniv. of the Republic — A148

1983, Dec. 2 *Perf. 12½x13, 13x12½*

Without Gum

502	A148	1k	Elephant dragging log, vert.	28
503	A148	4k	Oxen, pig	1.10
504	A148	6k	Produce, vert.	1.75
a.			Souv. sheet of 6 with gutter between	5.55

World Communications Year — A149

1983, Dec. 15 *Perf. 13*

505	A149	50c	Teletype	15
506	A149	1k	Telephone	25
507	A149	4k	Television	1.00
508	A149	6k	Satellite, dish receiver	1.50

1984 Winter Olympics, Sarajevo A150

1984, Jan. 16

509 A150 50c Women's figure skating 15
510 A150 1k Speed skating 25
511 A150 2k Biathlon 50
512 A150 4k Luge 1.00
513 A150 5k Downhill skiing 1.25
514 A150 6k Ski jumping 1.50
515 A150 7k Slalom 1.75
Nos. 509-515 (7) 6.40

Souvenir Sheet

Perf. 13½x13

516 A150 10k Ice hockey 2.75

Nos. 509-511, 514-515 vert. No. 516 contains one stamp 32x40mm.

World Wildlife Fund A151

Panthera tigris.

1984, Feb. 1 ***Perf. 13***

517 A151 25c Adult, vert. 15
518 A151 25c shown 15
519 A151 3k Nursing cubs 75
520 A151 4k Two cubs, vert. 1.00

1984 Summer Olympics, Los Angeles — A152

Gold medals awarded during previous games, and athletes. 50c, Athens 1896, women's diving. 1k, Paris 1900, women's volleyball. 2k, St. Louis 1904, running. 4k, London 1908, basketball. 5k, Stockholm 1912, judo. 6k, Antwerp 1920, soccer. 7k, Paris 1924, gymnastics. 10k, Moscow 1980, wrestling.

1984, Mar 26

521 A152 50c multicolored 15
522 A152 1k multicolored 25
523 A152 2k multicolored 50
524 A152 4k multicolored 1.00
525 A152 5k multicolored 1.25
526 A152 6k multicolored 1.50
527 A152 7k multicolored 1.75
Nos. 521-527 (7) 6.40

Souvenir Sheet

Perf. 12½

528 A152 10k multicolored 3.00

No. 528 contains one stamp 32x40mm.

Musical Instruments — A153

1984, Mar. 27 ***Perf. 13***

529 A153 1k Tuned drums 25
530 A153 2k Xylophone 55
531 A153 3k Pair of drums 80
532 A153 4k Hand drum 1.10
533 A153 5k Barrel drum 1.40
534 A153 6k Pipes, string instrument 1.65
Nos. 529-534 (6) 5.75

Natl. Day — A154

Chess — A155

1984, Mar. 30 ***Perf. 12½***

535 A154 60c Natl. flag 15
536 A154 1k Natl. arms 18
537 A154 2k like 1k 38

1984, Apr. 14 ***Perf. 12½x13***

Illustrations of various medieval and Renaissance chess games.

538 A155 50c multi 15
539 A155 1k multi, diff. 28
540 A155 2k multi, red brn board, diff. 55
541 A155 2k multi, blk board, diff. 55
542 A155 3k multi, diff. 65
543 A155 4k multi, diff. 1.10
544 A155 8k multi, diff. 2.25
a. Souv. sheet of 6 with gutter between 5.55
Nos. 538-544 (7) 5.53

Souvenir Sheet

Perf. 13½x13

545 A155 10k Royal game, human chessmen 3.00

World Chess Federation, 60th anniv. No. 545 contains one stamp 32x40mm.

ESPANA '84, Madrid — A156

Woodland Flowers — A157

Paintings: 50c, Cardinal Nino de Guevara, by El Greco. 1k, Gaspar de Guzman, Duke of Olivares, on Horseback, by Velazquez. No. 548, The Annunciation, by Murillo. No. 549, Portrait of a Lady, by Francisco de Zurburan (1598-1664). 3k, The Family of Charles IV, by Goya. 4k, Two Harlequins, by Picasso. 8k, Abstract, by Miro. 10k, Burial of the Count of Orgaz, by El Greco.

1984, Apr. 27 ***Perf. 12½***

546 A156 50c multicolored 15
547 A156 1k multicolored 25
548 A156 2k multicolored 50
549 A156 2k multicolored 50
550 A156 3k multicolored 75
551 A156 4k multicolored 1.00
552 A156 8k multicolored 2.00
Nos. 546-552 (7) 5.15

Souvenir Sheet

Perf. 13½x13

553 A156 10k multicolored 3.00

No. 553 contains one stamp 32x40mm.

1984, May 11 ***Perf. 13***

554 A157 50c Adonis aestivalis 15
555 A157 1k Alpinia speciosa 25
556 A157 2k Aeschynanthus speciosus 50
557 A157 2k Cassia lechenaultiana 50
558 A157 3k Datura meteloides 75
559 A157 4k Quamoclit pennata 1.00
560 A157 8k Commelina benghalensis 2.00
Nos. 554-560 (7) 5.15

A158

19th UPU Congress, Hamburg — A159

Classic sport and race cars.

1984, June 19

561 A158 50c Nazzaro 15
562 A158 1k Daimler 25
563 A158 2k Delage 50
564 A158 2k Fiat S 57/14B 50
565 A158 3k Bugatti 75
566 A158 4k Itala 1.00
567 A158 8k Blitzen Benz 2.00
Nos. 561-567 (7) 5.15

Souvenir Sheet

Perf. 12½

568 A159 10k Winton Bullet 2.75

Paintings by Corregio (1494-1534) A160

Designs: 50c, Madonna and Child (Holy Family). 1k, Madonna and Child (spectators). No. 571, Madonna and Child (Holy Family, diff.). No. 572, Mystical Marriage of St. Catherine (Catherine, child, two women). 3k, The Four Saints. 4k, Noli Me Tangere. 8k, Christ Bids Farewell to the Virgin Mary. 10k, Madonna and Child, diff.

1984, June 26 ***Perf. 13***

569 A160 50c multicolored 15
570 A160 1k multicolored 16
571 A160 2k multicolored 32
572 A160 2k multicolored 32
573 A160 3k multicolored 50
574 A160 4k multicolored 65
575 A160 8k multicolored 1.40
Nos. 569-575 (7) 3.50

Souvenir Sheet

Perf. 13½x13

576 A160 10k multicolored 4.00

No. 576 contains one stamp 32x40mm.

Space Exploration A161

1984, July 12 ***Perf. 13***

577 A161 50c Luna 1 15
578 A161 1k Luna 2 22
579 A161 2k Luna 3 45
580 A161 2k Sputnik 2, Kepler 45
581 A161 3k Lunokhod 2, Newton 65
582 A161 4k Luna 13, Jules Verne 90
583 A161 8k Space station, Copernicus 1.75
Nos. 577-583 (7) 4.57

Reptiles A162

1984, Aug. 20

584 A162 50c Malaclemys terrapin 15
585 A162 1k Bungarus fasciatus 25
586 A162 2k Python reticulatus 50
587 A162 2k Python molurus, vert. 50
588 A162 3k Gekko gecko 75
589 A162 4k Natrix subminiata 1.00
590 A162 8k Eublepharis macumiliaris 2.00
Nos. 584-590 (7) 5.15

Marsupials — A163

1984, Sept. 21

591 A163 50c Schoinobates volans 15
592 A163 1k Ornithorhynchus anatinus 25
593 A163 2k Sarcophilus harrisii 55
594 A163 2k Lasiorhinus latifrons 55
595 A163 3k Thylacinus cynocephalus 80
596 A163 4k Dasyurops maculatus 1.00
597 A163 8k Wallabia isabelinus 2.00
Nos. 591-597 (7) 5.30

Souvenir Sheet

Perf. 12½

598 A163 10k Macropus rufus 3.00

AUSIPEX '84, Melbourne. No. 598 contains one stamp 32x40mm.

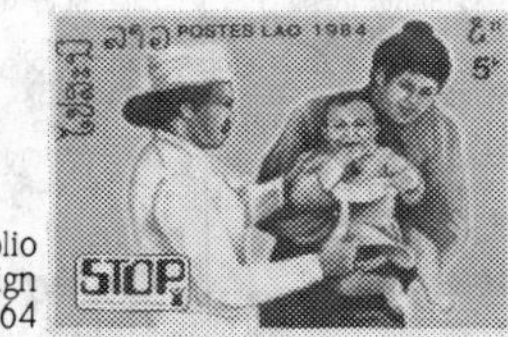

Stop Polio Campaign A164

1984, Sept. 29 ***Perf. 13***

599 A164 5k shown 1.25
600 A164 6k Vaccinating child 1.50

Art — A165

1984, Oct. 26

601 A165 50c Dragon (hand rail) 15
602 A165 1k Capital 28
603 A165 2k Oval panel 55
604 A165 2k Deity 55
605 A165 3k Leaves 80
606 A165 4k Floral pattern 1.00
607 A165 8k Lotus flower (round panel) 2.00
Nos. 601-607 (7) 5.33

Nos. 601-604 and 607 vert.

9th Anniv. of the Republic A166

1984, Dec. 17
608 A166 1k River boats 25
609 A166 2k Aircraft 50
610 A166 4k Bridge building 1.00
611 A166 10k Surveying, construction 2.50

1986 World Cup Soccer Championships, Mexico — A167

Various match scenes and flag of Mexico.

1985, Jan. 18
612 A167 50c multicolored 15
613 A167 1k multi, diff. 25
614 A167 2k multi, diff. 50
615 A167 3k multi, diff. 75
616 A167 4k multi, diff. 1.00
617 A167 5k multi, diff. 1.25
618 A167 6k multi, diff. 1.50
Nos. 612-618 (7) 5.40

Souvenir Sheet
Perf. 12½
619 A167 10k multi, diff. 2.75

No. 619 contains one stamp 32x40mm.

Motorcycle, Cent. — A168

1985, Feb. 25 ***Perf. 12½***
620 A168 50c shown 15
621 A168 1k 1920 Gnome Rhone 25
622 A168 2k 1928 F.N. M67C 50
623 A168 3k 1930 Indian Chief 75
624 A168 4k 1914 Rudge Multi 1.00
625 A168 5k 1953 Honda Benly J 1.25
626 A168 6k 1938 CZ 1.50
Nos. 620-626 (7) 5.40

Mushrooms A169

Lenin, 115th Birth Anniv. A170

1985, Apr. 8 ***Perf. 13***
627 A169 50c Amanita muscaria 15
628 A169 1k Boletus edulis 25
629 A169 2k Coprinus comatus 50
630 A169 2k Amanita rubescens 50
631 A169 3k Xerocomus subtomentosus 75
632 A169 4k Lepiota procera 1.00
633 A169 8k Paxillus involutus 2.00
Nos. 627-633 (7) 5.15

End of World War II, 40th Anniv. A169a

Designs: 1k, Battle of Kursk. 2k, Red Army parade, Moscow. 4k, Battle of Stalingrad. 5k, Battle for Berlin. 6k, Victory parade through Brandenburg Gate.

1985, May **Litho.** ***Perf. 12½x12***
633A A169a 1k multicolored 28
633B A169a 2k multicolored 55
633C A169a 4k multicolored 1.10
633D A169a 5k multicolored 1.40
633E A169a 6k multicolored 1.65

1985, June 28 ***Perf. 12½***
634 A170 1k Reading Pravda, horiz. 30
635 A170 2k shown 60
636 A170 10k Addressing revolutionaries 2.00

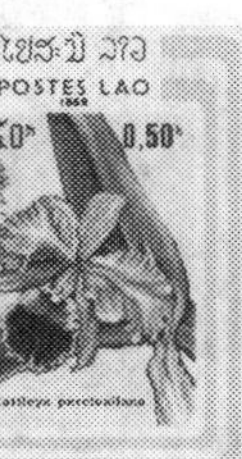

Orchids — A171

Fauna — A172

1985, July 5 ***Perf. 13***
637 A171 50c Cattleya percivaliana 15
638 A171 1k Odontoglossum luteopurpureum 25
639 A171 2k Cattleya lueddemanniana 50
640 A171 2k Maxillaria sanderiana 50
641 A171 3k Miltonia vexillaria 75
642 A171 4k Oncidium varicosum 1.00
643 A171 8k Cattleya dowiana aurea 2.00
Nos. 637-643 (7) 5.15

Souvenir Sheet
Perf. 13½x13
644 A171 10k Catasetum fimbriatum 3.00

ARGENTINA '85, Buenos Aires. No. 644 contains one stamp 32x40mm.

1985, Aug. 15 ***Perf. 13***
645 A172 2k Macaca mulatta 45
646 A172 3k Bos sauveli 65
647 A172 4k Hystrix leucura, horiz. 90
648 A172 5k Selenarctos thibotanus, horiz. 1.10
649 A172 10k Manis pentadactyla 2.25
Nos. 645-649 (5) 5.35

Apollo-Soyuz Flight, 10th Anniv. — A173

1985, Sept. 6
650 A173 50c Apollo launch pad, vert. 15
651 A173 1k Soyuz launch pad, vert. 25
652 A173 2k Apollo approaching Soyuz 50
653 A173 2k Soyuz approaching Apollo 50
654 A173 3k Apollo, astronauts 75
655 A173 4k Soyuz, cosmonauts 1.00
656 A173 8k Docked spacecrafts 2.00
Nos. 650-656 (7) 5.15

Aircraft A174

1985, Oct. 25
657 A174 50c Fiat 15
658 A174 1k Cant z.501 30
659 A174 2k MF-5 60
660 A174 3k Macchi Castoldi 90
661 A174 4k Anzani 1.20
662 A174 5k Ambrosini 1.50
663 A174 6k Piaggio 1.75
Nos. 657-663 (7) 6.40

Souvenir Sheet
Perf. 13x13½
664 A174 10k MF-4 6.50

ITALIA '85, Rome. No. 664 contains one stamp 40x32mm.

Miniature Sheet

Columbus's Fleet A175

1985, Oct. 25 ***Perf. 13***
665 Sheet of 5 + 4 labels 3.00
a. A175 1k Pinta 18
b. A175 2k Nina 35
c. A175 3k Santa Maria 55
d. A175 4k Columbus 75
e. A175 5k Map of 1st voyage 90

ITALIA '85.

UN, 40th Anniv. — A176

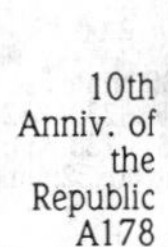

Health — A177

1985, Oct.
666 A176 2k UN and natl. flag 65
667 A176 3k Coats of arms 1.00
668 A176 10k Map, globe 3.00

1985, Nov. 15
669 A177 1k Mother feeding child 25
670 A177 3k Immunization, horiz. 75
671 A177 4k Hospital care, horiz. 1.00
672 A177 10k Breast-feeding 2.50

10th Anniv. of the Republic A178

1985, Dec. 2
673 A178 3k shown 90
674 A178 10k multi, diff. 3.00

People's Revolutionary Party, 30th Anniv. — A179

1985, Dec. 30
675 A179 2k shown 70
676 A179 8k multi, diff. 2.75

1986 World Cup Soccer Championships, Mexico — A180

Flowering Plants — A181

Various match scenes.

1986, Jan. 20
677 A180 50c multicolored 15
678 A180 1k multi, diff. 22
679 A180 2k multi, diff. 45
680 A180 3k multi, diff. 60
681 A180 4k multi, diff. 80
682 A180 5k multi, diff. 1.00
683 A180 6k multi, diff. 1.25
Nos. 677-683 (7) 4.47

Souvenir Sheet
Perf. 13x13½
684 A180 10k multi, diff. 2.30

No. 684 contains one stamp 40x32mm.

27th Congress of the Communist Party of the Soviet Union — A180a

1986, Jan. **Litho.** ***Perf. 12x12½***
684A A180a 4k Cosmonaut, spacecraft 85
684B A180a 20k Lenin 4.25

1986, Feb. 28 ***Perf. 13***
685 A181 50c Pelargonium grandiflorum 15
686 A181 1k Aquilegia vulgaris 24
687 A181 2k Fuchsia globosa 48
688 A181 3k Crocus aureus 70
689 A181 4k Althaea rosea 92
690 A181 5k Gladiolus purpureo 1.15
691 A181 6k Hyacinthus orientalis 1.40
Nos. 685-691 (7) 5.04

Butterflies A182

1986, Mar. 30
692 A182 50c Aporia hippia 15
693 A182 1k Euthalia irrubescens 20
694 A182 2k Japonica lutea 40
695 A182 3k Pratapa ctesia 60
696 A182 4k Kallina inachus 80
697 A182 5k Ixias pyrene 1.00
698 A182 6k Parantica sita 1.20
Nos. 692-698 (7) 4.35

A particular stamp may be scarce, but if few collectors want it, its market value may remain relatively low.

A183

First Man in Space, 25th Anniv. — A184

Designs: 50c, Launch, Baikonur Space Center, vert. 1k, Molniya communications satellite, vert. 2k, Salyut space station. 3k, Yuri Gagarin, Sputnik 1 disengaging stage. 4k, Luna 3, the Moon, vert. 5k, Komarov on first space walk, vert. 6k, Luna 16 lifting off Moon, vert. 10k, Spacecrafts docking.

1986, Apr. 12

699 A183 50c multicolored 15
700 A183 1k multicolored 25
701 A183 2k multicolored 50
702 A183 3k multicolored 75
703 A183 4k multicolored 98
704 A183 5k multicolored 1.25
705 A183 6k multicolored 1.40
Nos. 699-705 (7) 5.28

Souvenir Sheet

Perf. 13x13½

706 A184 10k multicolored 3.00

Fauna A185

AMERIPEX '86, Chicago — A186

Perf. 12½x13, 13x12½

1986, May 22

707 A185 50c Giraffa camelopardalis 15
708 A185 1k Panthera leo 20
709 A185 2k Loxodonta africana africana 42
710 A185 3k Macropus rufus 62
711 A185 4k Gymnobelideus leadbeateri 85
712 A185 5k Phoenicopterus ruber 1.05
713 A185 6k Ailuropoda melanoleucus 1.25
Nos. 707-713 (7) 4.54

Souvenir Sheet

Perf. 13½x13

714 A186 10k Bison 3.00

Nos. 707-712 vert.

Pheasants — A187

1986, June 29 ***Perf. 12½x13***

715 A187 50c Argusianus argus 15
716 A187 1k Cennaeus nycthemerus 24
717 A187 2k Phasianus colchicus 48
718 A187 3k Chrysolophus amherstiae 70
719 A187 4k Symaticus reevesii 92
720 A187 5k Chrysolophus pictus 1.15
721 A187 6k Syrmaticus soemmerringii 1.40
Nos. 715-721 (7) 5.04

Snakes — A188

Perf. 12½x13, 13x12½

1986, July 21

722 A188 50c Elaphe guttata 15
723 A188 1k Thalerophis richardi 20
724 A188 1k Lampropeltis doliata annulata 20
725 A188 2k Diadophis amabilis 40
726 A188 4k Boiga dendrophila 80
727 A188 5k Python molurus 1.00
728 A188 8k Naja naja 1.60
Nos. 722-728 (7) 4.35

Nos. 722-723 and 728 vert.

Halley's Comet — A189

1986, Aug. 22 ***Perf. 12½x13***

729 A189 50c Acropolis, Athens 15
730 A189 1k Bayeux Tapestry 24
731 A189 2k Edmond Halley 48
732 A189 3k Vega space probe 68
733 A189 4k Galileo 95
734 A189 5k Comet 1.20
735 A189 6k Giotto probe 1.90
Nos. 729-735 (7) 5.60

Souvenir Sheet

Perf. 13x13½

736 A189 10k Comet, diff. 3.00

Nos. 730-731, 732-733 and 734-735 printed se-tenant in continuous designs. Size of Nos. 730, 732 and 735: 46x25mm. Size of Nos. 731, 733-734: 23x25mm. No. 736 contains one stamp 40x32mm.

Dogs — A190 Cacti — A191

1986, Aug. 28 ***Perf. 13***

737 A190 50c Keeshond 15
738 A190 1k Elkhound 20
739 A190 2k Bernese 42
740 A190 3k Pointing griffon 62
741 A190 4k Sheep dog (border collie) 85
742 A190 5k Irish water spaniel 1.05
743 A190 6k Briard 1.25
Nos. 737-743 (7) 4.54

Souvenir Sheet

Perf. 13x13½

744 A190 10k Brittany spaniels 2.00

STOCKHOLMIA '86. Nos. 738-743 horiz. No. 744 contains one stamp 40x32mm.

1986, Sept. 28 ***Perf. 13***

Designs: 50c, Mammillaria matudae. 1k, Mammillaria theresae. 2k, Ariocarpus trigonus. 3k, Notocactus crassigibbus. 4k, Astrophytum asterias hybridum. 5k, Melocactus manzanus. 6k, Astrophytum ornatum hybridum.

745 A191 50c multicolored 15
746 A191 1k multicolored 20
747 A191 2k multicolored 42
748 A191 3k multicolored 62
749 A191 4k multicolored 85
750 A191 5k multicolored 1.05
751 A191 6k multicolored 1.25
Nos. 745-751 (7) 4.54

Intl. Peace Year — A192

UNESCO Programs in Laos — A193

1986, Oct. 24

752 A192 3k Natl. arms, dove, globe 68
753 A192 5k Dove, shattered bomb 1.10
754 A192 10k Emblem held aloft 2.20

1986, Nov. 4

755 A193 3k Vat Phu Champasak ruins 60
756 A193 4k Satellite dish, map, globe 80
757 A193 9k Laotians learning to read, horiz. 1.75

1988 Winter Olympics, Calgary A194

1987, Jan. 14

758 A194 50c Speed skating 15
759 A194 1k Biathlon 20
760 A194 2k Pairs figure skating 40
761 A194 3k Luge 60
762 A194 4k 4-Man bobsled 80
763 A194 5k Ice hockey 1.00
764 A194 6k Ski jumping 1.20
Nos. 758-764 (7) 4.35

Souvenir Sheet

Perf. 13½x13

765 A194 10k Slalom 2.50

Nos. 758-760 vert. No. 765 contains one stamp 32x40mm.

1988 Summer Olympics, Seoul — A195

1987, Feb. 2 ***Perf. 12½x13, 13x13½***

766 A195 50c Women's gymnastics 15
767 A195 1k Women's discus 22
768 A195 2k Running 45
769 A195 3k Equestrian 68
770 A195 4k Women's javelin 90
771 A195 5k High jump 1.10
772 A195 6k Wrestling 1.35
Nos. 766-772 (7) 4.85

Souvenir Sheet

Perf. 12½

773 A195 10k Runners leaving start 2.25

Nos. 766, 768, 770 and 772 vert. No. 773 contains one stamp 40x32mm.

Dogs — A196

1987, Mar. 5 ***Perf. 12½x13***

774 A196 50c Great Dane 15
775 A196 1k Labrador retriever 22
776 A196 2k St. Bernard 45
777 A196 3k Schippercke 68
778 A196 4k Alsatian (German shepherd) 90
779 A196 5k Beagle 1.10
780 A196 6k Spaniel 1.35
Nos. 774-780 (7) 4.85

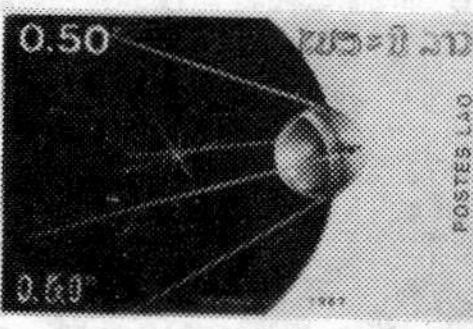

Manned Space Flight, 30th Anniv. A197

1987, Apr. 12 ***Perf. 13***

781 A197 50c Sputnik 1 15
782 A197 1k Sputnik 2 18
783 A197 2k Cosmos 87 35
784 A197 3k Cosmos 55
785 A197 4k Mars 75
786 A197 5k Luna 1 90
787 A197 9k Luna 3, vert. 1.65
Nos. 781-787 (7) 4.53

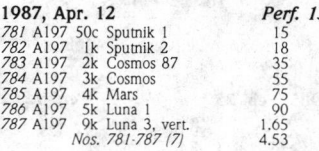

Packet Ships and Stampless Packet Letters A198

Canada No. 282 A199

1987, May 12

788 A198 50c "Montreal" 15
789 A198 1k "Paid Montreal" 20
790 A198 2k "Paid" and "Montreal Nov 24" 40
791 A198 3k "Williamsbvrg" and "Forwarded" 60
792 A198 4k "Montreal Fe 18 1844" 80
793 A198 5k "Paid" and "Montreal Jy 10 1848" 1.00
794 A198 6k "Paid" and "Montreal Paid Ap 16 1861 Canada" 1.20
Nos. 788-794 (7) 4.35

Souvenir Sheet

Perf. 12½

795 A199 10k multicolored 2.50

CAPEX '87.

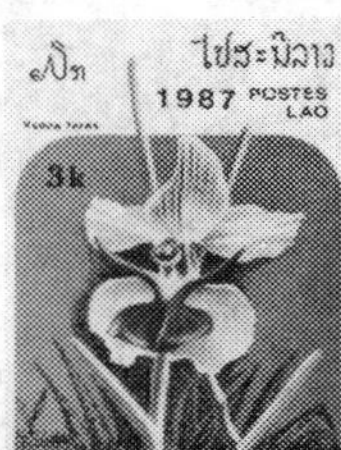

Orchids — A200

1987, Aug. 10 Litho. *Perf. 13*

796 A200 3k *Vanda teres* 15
796A A200 7k *Laeliocattleya* 16
796B A200 10k *Paphiopedilum hibrido* 22
796C A200 39k *Sobralia* 88
796D A200 44k *Paphiopedilum hibrido*, diff. 1.00
796E A200 47k *Paphiopedilum hibrido*, diff. 1.10
796F A200 50k *Cattleya trianaei* 1.15
Nos. 796-796F (7) 4.66

Souvenir Sheet

Perf. 12½

796G A200 95k *Vanda tricolor* 2.50

No. 796G contains one 32x40mm stamp.

Automobiles A201

1987, July 2 Litho. *Perf. 12½*

797 A201 50c Toyota 480 15
798 A201 1k Alfa 33 22
799 A201 2k Ford Fiesta 45
800 A201 3k Datsun 68
801 A201 4k Vauxhall Cavalier 90
802 A201 5k Renault 5 1.10
803 A201 6k Rover-800 1.35
Nos. 797-803 (7) 4.85

Miniature Sheet

Perf. 13

804 A201 10k Talbot 2.25

HAFNIA '87, Denmark A202

Various Indian elephants.

1987, Sept. 2 *Perf. 13*

805 A202 50c Adult, calf 15
806 A202 1k Two adults, calf 22
807 A202 2k Adult eating grass 45
808 A202 3k Adult, diff. 68
809 A202 4k Adult, calf drinking 90
810 A202 5k Adult, diff. 1.10
811 A202 6k Adult, vert. 1.35
Nos. 805-811 (7) 4.85

Souvenir Sheet

812 A202 10k Herd, diff. 2.50

No. 812 contains one stamp 40x32mm.

Horses A203

Perf. 13x12½, 12½x13

1987, June 3 Litho.

813 A203 50c multicolored 15
814 A203 1k multi, diff. 28
815 A203 2k multi, diff. 55
816 A203 3k multi, diff. 85
817 A203 4k multi, diff. 1.15
818 A203 5k multi, diff. 1.40
819 A203 6k multi, diff. 1.70
Nos. 813-819 (7) 6.08

Nos. 814-819 vert.

Fish A204

Designs: 3k, Botia macracantha. 7k, Oxymocanthus longirostris. 10k, Adioryx caudimaculatus. 39k, Synchiropus splendidus. 44k, Cephalopolis miniatus. 47k, Dendrochirus zebra. 50k, Pomacantus semicirculatus.

1987, Oct. 14 Litho. *Perf. 13x12½*

820 A204 3k multicolored 15
821 A204 7k multicolored 16
822 A204 10k multicolored 22
823 A204 39k multicolored 88
824 A204 44k multicolored 1.00
825 A204 47k multicolored 1.05
826 A204 50k multicolored 1.15
Nos. 820-826 (7) 4.61

World Food Day A205

1987, Oct. 16 *Perf. 13*

827 A205 1k Tending crops 15
828 A205 3k Harvesting corn, vert. 15
829 A205 5k Harvesting wheat 15
830 A205 63k Youths, fish, vert. 1.45
831 A205 142k Tending pigs, chickens 3.25
Nos. 827-831 (5) 5.15

Cultivation of Rice in Mountainous Regions — A206

1987, Nov. 9 *Perf. 13*

832 A206 64k Tilling soil 1.50
833 A206 100k Rice paddy 2.30

October Revolution, Russia, 70th Anniv. — A207

Paintings: 1k, Wounded soldier on battlefield. 2k, Mother and child. 4k, Storming the Winter Palace. 8k, Lenin and revolutionaries. 10k, Rebuilding Red Square.

1987, Nov. *Perf. 12x12½*

834 A207 1k multicolored 20
835 A207 2k multicolored 40
836 A207 4k multicolored 75
837 A207 8k multicolored 1.50
838 A207 10k multicolored 2.00
Nos. 834-838 (5) 4.85

Women Wearing Regional Costumes — A208

1987, Dec. 2

839 A208 7k Mountain 16
840 A208 38k Urban 88
841 A208 144k Mountain, diff. 3.35

A209

1988 Winter Olympics, Calgary — A210

1988, Jan.10 *Perf. 13x12½*

842 A209 1k Bobsled 15
843 A209 4k Biathlon 15
844 A209 20k Skiing 48
845 A209 42k Ice hockey 1.00
846 A209 63k Speed skating 1.50
847 A209 70k Slalom 1.65
Nos. 842-847 (6) 4.93

Souvenir Sheet

Perf. 13

848 A210 95k Slalom, diff. 2.50

No. 848 contains one stamp 40x32mm.

ESSEN '88 — A211

Locomotives: 6k, Nonpareil, vert. 15k, Rocket, vert. 20k, Royal George. 25k, Trevithick. 30k, Novelty. 100k, Tom Thumb. 95k, Locomotion.

1988 *Perf. 12½x13, 13x12½*

849 A211 6k multicolored 15
850 A211 15k multicolored 35
851 A211 20k multicolored 48
852 A211 25k multicolored 58
853 A211 30k multicolored 70
854 A211 100k multicolored 2.30
Nos. 849-854 (6) 4.56

Souvenir Sheet

Perf. 13

855 A211 95k multicolored 2.50

No. 855 contains one stamp 40x32mm.

Intl. Year of Shelter for the Homeless A212

1988 Litho. *Perf. 13*

856 A212 1k Building frame of house 15
857 A212 27k Cutting lumber 62
858 A212 46k Completed house 1.15
859 A212 70k Community 1.75

Dinosaurs — A213

Perf. 13x12½, 12½x13

1988, Mar. 3 Litho.

860 A213 3k Tyrannosaurus 15
861 A213 7k Ceratosaurus nasicornis 16
862 A213 39k Iguanodon bernissartensis 88
863 A213 44k Scolosaurus 1.00
864 A213 47k Phororhacus 1.10
865 A213 50k Trachodon 1.15
Nos. 860-865 (6) 4.44

Souvenir Sheet

Perf. 12½

866 A213 95k Pteranodon 2.50

JUVALUX '88. Nos. 861-864 vert.

Identifications on Nos. 860 and No. 865 are switched.

No. 866 contains one 40x32mm stamp.

WHO, 40th Anniv. A214

1988, Apr. 8 *Perf. 12½*

867 A214 5k Students, teacher 15
868 A214 27k Pest control 62
869 A214 164k Public water supply, vert. 3.75

Flowers — A215 Birds — A216

1988 *Perf. 13x12½*

870 A215 8k *Plumieria rubra* 18
871 A215 9k *Althaea rosea* 22
872 A215 15k *Ixora coccinea* 40
873 A215 33k *Cassia fistula* 78
874 A215 64k *Dahlia coccinea* (pink) 1.50
875 A215 69k *Dahlia coccinea* (yellow) 1.65
Nos. 870-875 (6) 4.73

Souvenir Sheet

Perf. 13

876 A215 95k Plumieria, Althaea, Ixora 2.50

FINLANDIA '88. No. 876 contains one 32x40mm stamp.

1988 ***Perf. 13***

877	A216	6k	*Pelargopsis capensis*	15
878	A216	10k	*Coturnix japonica*	24
879	A216	13k	*Psittacula roseata*	32
880	A216	44k	*Treron bicincta*	1.05
881	A216	63k	*Pycnonotus melanicterus*	1.50
882	A216	64k	*Ducula badia*	1.55
			Nos. 877-882 (6)	4.81

1988 Summer Olympics, Seoul — A217

1988 ***Perf. 12½x12***

883	A217	2k	Javelin	15
884	A217	5k	Long jump	15
885	A217	10k	Horizontal bar	24
886	A217	12k	Canoeing	30
887	A217	38k	Balance beam	90
888	A217	46k	Fencing	1.10
889	A217	100k	Wrestling	2.35
			Nos. 883-889 (7)	5.19

Souvenir Sheet

Perf. 13

889A A217 95k Horizontal bar, diff. 2.25

No. 889A contains one 40x32mm stamp.

Decorative Stencils A218

1988 ***Perf. 13***

890	A218	1k	Scarf	15
891	A218	2k	Pagoda entrance, vert.	15
892	A218	3k	Pagoda wall, vert.	15
893	A218	25k	Pagoda pillar	60
894	A218	163k	Skirt	4.00
			Nos. 890-894 (5)	5.05

Completion of the 5-Year Plan (1981-85) — A219

1988 **Litho.** ***Perf. 13***

895	A219	20k	Health care	45
896	A219	40k	Literacy	88
897	A219	50k	Irrigation	1.10
898	A219	100k	Communication, transport	2.20

Intl. Red Cross and Red Crescent Organizations, 125th Annivs. — A220

Designs: 4k, Dove, 3 stylized figures representing mankind, vert. 52k, Giving aid to the handicapped, vert. 144k, Child immunization.

1988

899	A220	4k	multi	15
900	A220	52k	multi	1.15
901	A220	144k	multi	3.20

Chess Champions — A220a

1988 **Litho.** ***Perf. 13***

901A	A220a	1k	R. Segura	15
901B	A220a	2k	Adolph Anderssen	15
901C	A220a	3k	P. Morphy	15
901D	A220a	6k	W. Steinitz	15
901E	A220a	7k	E. Lasker	16
901F	A220a	12k	J.R. Capablanca	28
901G	A220a	172k	A. Alekhine	3.90
			Nos. 901A-901G (7)	4.94

Nos. 901C is incorrectly inscribed "Murphy."

1990 World Cup Soccer Championships, Italy — A221

Various plays.

1989 ***Perf. 13x12½***

902	A221	10k	multi	22
903	A221	15k	multi, diff.	35
904	A221	20k	multi, diff.	45
905	A221	25k	multi, diff.	58
906	A221	45k	multi, diff.	1.00
907	A221	105k	multi, diff.	2.40
			Nos. 902-907 (6)	5.00

Souvenir Sheet

Perf. 13

907A A221 95k multi, diff. 2.25

No. 907A contains one 40x32mm stamp.

INDIA '89 A222

Cats.

1989, Jan. 7 ***Perf. 12½***

908	A222	5k	multi	15
909	A222	6k	multi, diff.	15
910	A222	10k	multi, diff.	22
911	A222	20k	multi, diff.	45
912	A222	50k	multi, diff.	1.15
913	A222	172k	multi, diff.	3.90
			Nos. 908-913 (6)	6.02

Souvenir Sheet

Perf. 13

914 A222 95k multi, diff. 2.25

No. 914 contains one 32x40mm stamp.

1992 Winter Olympics, Albertville A223

Various figure skaters.

1989, May 1 ***Perf. 13***

915	A223	9k	multi, vert.	20
916	A223	10k	shown	22
917	A223	15k	multi, diff., vert.	32
918	A223	24k	multi, diff., vert.	55
919	A223	29k	multi, diff., vert.	65
920	A223	114k	multi, diff., vert.	2.55
			Nos. 915-920 (6)	4.49

Souvenir Sheet

Perf. 12½

921 A223 95k Pairs figure skating 2.25

No. 921 contains one 32x40mm stamp.

People's Army, 40th Anniv. A224

1989, Jan. 20 ***Perf. 13***

922	A224	1k	shown	15
923	A224	2k	Military school, vert.	15
924	A224	3k	Health care	15
925	A224	250k	Ready for combat	5.50

1992 Summer Olympics, Barcelona — A225

Perf. 12x12½, 12½x12

1989, June 1 **Litho.**

926	A225	5k	Pole vault, vert.	15
927	A225	15k	Gymnastic rings, vert.	35
928	A225	20k	Cycling	45
929	A225	25k	Boxing	58
930	A225	70k	Archery, vert.	1.60
931	A225	120k	Swimming, vert.	2.70
			Nos. 926-932 (7)	8.08

Souvenir Sheet

Perf. 13

932 A225 95k Baseball 2.25

No. 932 contains one 32x40mm stamp.

PHILEXFRANCE '89 — A226

Paintings by Picasso: 5k, *Beggars by the Edge of the Sea.* 7k, *Maternity.* 8k, *Portrait of Jaime S. Le Bock.* 9k, *Harlequins.* 105k, *Dog with Boy.* 114k, *Girl Balancing on Ball.*

1989, July 17 ***Perf. 12½x13***

933	A226	5k	multi	15
934	A226	7k	multi	15
935	A226	8k	multi	18
936	A226	9k	multi	20
937	A226	105k	multi	2.35
938	A226	114k	multi	2.55
			Nos. 933-938 (6)	5.58

Souvenir Sheet

Perf. 12½

939 A226 95k shown 2.25

No. 939 contains one 32x40mm stamp.

Cuban Revolution, 30th Anniv. — A227

1989, Apr. 20 **Litho.** ***Perf. 13***

940	A227	45k	shown	1.00
941	A227	50k	Flags	1.15

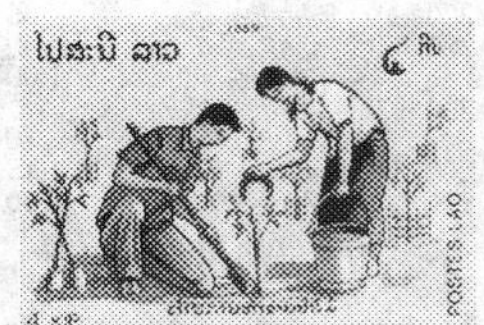

Fight the Destruction of Forests — A228

1989, Mar. 30 **Litho.** ***Perf. 13***

942	A228	4k	Planting saplings	15
943	A228	10k	Fight forest fires	22
944	A228	12k	Do not chop down trees	28
945	A228	200k	Map of woodland	4.50

Nos. 944-945 are vert.

Jawaharlal Nehru (1889-1964), Indian Statesman — A229

1989, Nov. 9 **Litho.** ***Perf. 12½***

946	A229	1k	multicolored	15
947	A229	60k	multi, horiz.	1.35
948	A229	200k	multi, diff.	4.50

Mani Ikara Zapota — A230

A231

1989, Sept. 18 ***Perf. 12½x13***

949	A230	5k	shown	15
950	A230	20k	Psidium guajava	45
951	A230	20k	Annona sguamosa	45
952	A230	30k	Durio zibethinus	68
953	A230	50k	Punica granatum	1.15
954	A230	172k	Moridica charautia	4.00
			Nos. 949-954 (6)	6.88

1989, Oct. 19 **Litho.** ***Perf. 12½***

Historic Monuments: No. 955, That Sikhotabong, Khammouane. No. 956, That Dam, Vientiane. No. 957, That Ing Hang, Savannakhet. No. 958, Ho Vay Phra Thatluang, Vientiane.

955	A231	5k	multicolored	15
956	A231	15k	multicolored	35
957	A231	61k	multicolored	1.40
958	A231	161k	multicolored	3.70

1992 Summer Olympics, Barcelona A232

1990, Mar. 5 Litho. *Perf. 12½x13*
959 A232 10k Basketball 24
960 A232 30k Hurdles 70
961 A232 45k High jump 1.03
962 A232 50k Cycling 1.15
963 A232 60k Javelin 1.40
964 A232 90k Tennis 2.00
Nos. 959-964 (6) 6.52

Souvenir Sheet

965 A232 95k Rhythmic gymnastics 2.20

1992 Winter Olympics, Albertville A233

1990, June 20 *Perf. 13*
966 A233 10k Speed skating 24
967 A233 25k Cross country skiing, vert. 60
968 A233 30k Slalom skiing 70
969 A233 35k Luge 80
970 A233 80k Ice dancing, vert. 1.85
971 A233 90k Biathlon 2.00
Nos. 966-971 (6) 6.19

Souvenir Sheet

972 A233 95k Hockey, vert. 2.20

New Zealand Birds A234

Designs: 10k, Prosthemadera novaeseelandie. 15k, Alauda arvensis. 20k, Haemotopus unicolor. 50k, Phalacrocorax carbo. 50k, Demigretta sacra. 100k Apteryx australis mantelli. 95k, Phalacrocorax corunculatus.

1990, Aug. 24 *Perf. 12½*
973 A234 10k multicolored 24
974 A234 15k multicolored 35
975 A234 20k multicolored 45
976 A234 50k multicolored 1.15
977 A234 60k multicolored 1.40
978 A234 100k multicolored 2.30
Nos. 973-978 (6) 5.89

Souvenir Sheet

979 A234 95k multicolored 2.20

World Stamp Expo, New Zealand '90. No. 979 contains one 32x40mm stamp.

That Luang Temple, 430th Anniv. A235

Perf. 13x12½, 12½x13
1990, July 25
980 A235 60k 1867 1.40
981 A235 70k 1930 1.60
982 A235 130k 1990, vert. 3.00

Ho Chi Minh (1890-1969), Vietnamese Leader — A236

1990, May 11 *Perf. 13*
983 A236 40k Addressing people 90
984 A236 60k With Laotian President 1.40
985 A236 160k Waving, vert. 3.65

UN Development Program, 40th Anniv. — A237

1990, Oct. 24 Litho. *Perf. 13*
986 A237 30k Surgeons 68
987 A237 45k Fishermen 1.00
988 A237 80k Flight controller, vert. 1.80
989 A237 90k Power plant 2.00

15th Anniv. of the Republic A238

Designs: 15k, Placing flowers at monument. 20k, Celebratory parade. 80k, Visiting sick. 120k, Women marching with banner.

1990, Dec. 2 Litho. *Perf. 13*
990 A238 15k multicolored 35
991 A238 20k multicolored 45
992 A238 80k multicolored 1.80
993 A238 120k multicolored 2.75

New Year's Day A239

1990, Nov. 20
994 A239 5k shown 15
995 A239 10k Parade 25
996 A239 50k Ceremony 1.15

Size: 40x29mm

997 A239 150k Ceremomy, diff. 3.35

World Cup Soccer Championships, Italy — A240

Designs: Various soccer players in action.

1990 Litho. *Perf. 13*
998 A240 10k multicolored 25
999 A240 15k multicolored 35
1000 A240 20k multicolored 50
1001 A240 25k multicolored 60
1002 A240 45k multicolored 1.05
1003 A240 105k multicolored 2.50
Nos. 998-1003 (6) 5.25

Souvenir Sheet

Perf. 12½

1004 A240 95k multi, horiz. 2.25

No. 1004 contains one 39x31mm stamp.

Intl. Literacy Year — A241

1990, Feb. 27 Litho. *Perf. 12½*
1005 A241 10k shown 50
1006 A241 50k Woman with child, vert. 2.40
1007 A241 60k Monk teaching class 2.85
1008 A241 150k Two women, man reading 7.00

Stamp World London '90 — A242

Stamps, modes of mail transport: 15k, Great Britain #1, stagecoach. 20k, US #1, train. 40k, France #3, balloons. 50k, Sardinia #1, post rider. 60k, Indo-China #3, elephant. 95k, Laos #272, jet. 100k, Spain #1, sailing ship.

1990, Apr. 26 Litho. *Perf. 13x12½*
1009 A242 15k multicolored 42
1010 A242 20k multicolroed 58
1011 A242 40k multicolored 1.15
1012 A242 50k multicolored 1.40
1013 A242 60k multicolored 1.70
1014 A242 100k multicolored 2.90
Nos. 1009-1014 (6) 8.15

Souvenir Sheet

Perf. 13

1015 A242 95k multicolored 2.85

No. 1015 contains one 40x32mm stamp.

Endangered Animals — A242a

1990, Sept. 15 Litho. *Perf. 12½*
1015A A242a 10k Brow-antlered deer 16
1015B A242a 20k Gaur 32
1015C A242a 40k Wild water buffalo 65
1015D A242a 45k Kouprey 72
1015E A242a 120k Javan rhinoceros 1.95
Nos. 1015A-1015E (5) 3.80

A243

1992 Olympics, Barcelona and Albertville A244

Perf. 12½x12, 12x12½, 13 (A244)
1991, Jan. 25
1016 A243 22k 2-man canoe 15
1017 A243 32k 1-man kayak 15
1018 A244 32k Bobsled, vert. 15
1019 A244 135k Cross country skiing 42
1020 A244 250k Ski jumping 78
1021 A244 275k Biathlon 85
1022 A243 285k Diving, vert. 90
1023 A243 330k Sailing, vert. 1.05
1024 A244 900k Speed skating 2.75
1025 A243 1000k Swimming 3.10
Nos. 1016-1025 (10) 10.30

Souvenir Sheets

Perf. 12½, 13½x13

1026 A243 700k 2-man kayak 2.20
1027 A244 700k Slalom skiing, vert. 2.20

No. 1026 contains one 40x32mm stamp. No. 1027 contains one 32x40mm stamp.

Tourism — A245

Designs: 155k, Rapids, Champassak. 220k, Vangvieng. 235k, Waterfalls, Saravane, vert. 1000k Plain of Jars, Xieng Khouang, vert.

1991 *Perf. 13x12½, 12½x13*
1028 A245 155k multicolored 50
1029 A245 220k multicolored 70
1030 A245 235k multicolored 75
1031 A245 1000k multicolored 3.10

1994 World Cup Soccer Championships — A246

Designs: Various players in action.

1991 Litho. *Perf. 13*
1032 A246 32k multicolored 15
1033 A246 330k multicolored 1.00
1034 A246 340k multi, vert. 1.05
1035 A246 400k multicolored 1.25
1036 A246 500k multicolored 1.55
Nos. 1032-1036 (5) 5.00

Souvenir Sheet

Perf. 13½x13

1037 A246 700k multi, vert. 2.15

No. 1037 contains one 32x40mm stamp.

Espamer '91, Buenos Aires — A247

Espamer '91 Type

1991, June 30 Litho. *Perf. 12½x12*

1038	A247	25k Mallard 4-4-2	15
1039	A247	32k Pacific 231 4-6-2	15
1040	A247	285k American style 4-8-4	1.15
1041	A247	650k Canadian Pacific 4-6-2	2.65
1042	A247	750k Beyer-Garrant 4-8-2 2-8-4	3.00
		Nos. 1038-1042 (5)	7.10

Souvenir Sheet

Perf. 12½

1043	A247	700k Inter-city diesel	2.60

Espamer '91, Buenos Aires. No. 1039 does not show denomination or country in Latin characters. Size of Nos. 1038, 1040-1042: 44x28mm.

Musical Celebrations — A248

Designs: 220k, Man playing mong, vert. 275k, Man, woman singing Siphandone, vert. 545k, Man, woman singing Khapngum. 690k, People dancing.

1991 Litho. *Perf. 13*

1044	A248	20k multicolored	15
1045	A248	220k multicolored	68
1046	A248	275k multicolored	85
1047	A248	545k multicolored	1.70
1048	A248	690k multicolored	2.15
		Nos. 1044-1048 (5)	5.53

Butterflies — A248a

1991 Litho. *Perf. 12½x12*

1048A	A248a	55k Sasakia charonda	18
1048B	A248a	90k Luendorfia puziloi	28
1048C	A248a	255k Papilio bianor	80
1048D	A248a	285k Papilio machaon	90
1048E	A248a	900k Graphium doson	2.80
		Nos. 1048A-1048E (5)	4.96

Souvenir Sheet

Perf. 13

1048F	A248a	700k Cyrestis thyodamas	2.20

No. 1048F contains one 40x32mm stamp. Phila Nippon '91.

Arbor Day — A249

Designs: 700k, Six people planting trees. 800k, Nursery.

1991 *Perf. 12½*

1049	A249	250k multicolored	80
1050	A249	700k multicolored	2.20
1051	A249	800k multicolored	2.50

1992 Winter Olympics, Albertville — A250

Perf. 12½x12, 12x12½

1992, Jan. 12 Litho.

1052	A250	200k Bobsled	65
1053	A250	220k Skiing	68
1054	A250	250k Skiing, horiz.	80
1055	A250	500k Luge	1.60
1056	A250	600k Figure skater	1.90
		Nos. 1052-1056 (5)	5.63

Souvenir Sheet

Perf. 12½

1057	A250	700k Speed skater	2.20

No. 1057 contains one 32x40mm stamp.

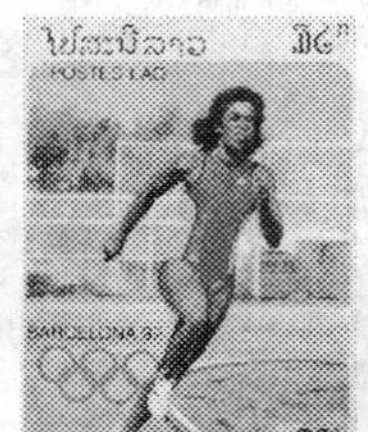

1992 Summer Olympics, Barcelona — A251

1992, Feb. 21 Litho. *Perf. 12½*

1058	A251	32k Women's running	15
1059	A251	245k Baseball	78
1060	A251	275k Tennis	85
1061	A251	285k Basketball	90
1062	A251	900k Boxing, horiz.	2.85
		Nos. 1058-1062 (5)	5.53

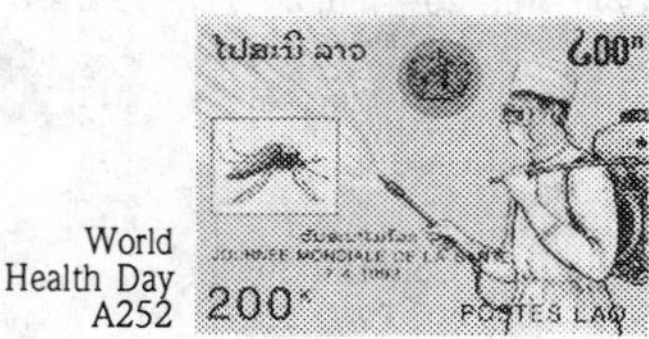

World Health Day — A252

Designs: 200k, Spraying for mosquitoes. 255k, Campaign against smoking. 330k, Receiving blood donation. 1000k, Immunizing child, vert.

1992

1063	A252	200k multicolored	62
1064	A252	255k multicolored	80
1065	A252	330k multicolored	1.05
1066	A252	1000k multicolored	3.10

1994 World Cup Soccer Championships, US — A253

Flags, ball and players: 260k, Argentina, Italy. 305k, Germany, Great Britain. 310k, US, World Cup trophy (no players). 350k, Italy, Great Britain. 800k, Germany, Argentina.

1992, May 1 Litho. *Perf. 13*

1067	A253	260k multicolored	80
1068	A253	305k multicolored	90
1069	A253	310k multicolored	95
1070	A253	350k multicolored	1.10
1071	A253	800k multicolored	2.50
		Nos. 1067-1071 (5)	6.25

Souvenir Sheet

Perf. 12½

1072	A253	700k Goalie	3.75

Restoration of Wat Phou — A256

Different views of Wat Phou.

Perf. 13x12½, 12½x13

1992, Aug. 22 Litho.

1082	A256	185k multicolored	55
1083	A256	220k multicolored	65
1084	A256	1200k multi, horiz.	3.65

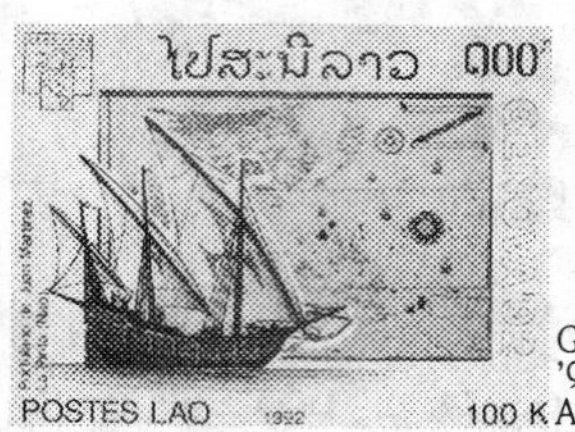

Genoa '92 A257

Sailing ships and maps by: 100k, Juan Martinez. 300k, Piri Reis, vert. 350k, Paolo del Pozo Toscanelli. 400k, Gabriel de Vallseca. 455k, Juan Martinez, diff.

Perf. 13x12½, 12½x13

1992, Sept. 12

1085	A257	100k multicolored	32
1086	A257	300k multicolored	95
1087	A257	350k multicolored	1.15
1088	A257	400k multicolored	1.30
1089	A257	455k multicolored	1.50
		Nos. 1085-1089 (5)	5.22

A number has been reserved for a souvenir sheet in this set.

Traditional Costumes of the Montagnards A258

Various costumes.

1992 Litho. *Perf. 13*

1091	A258	25k multicolored	15
1092	A258	55k multicolored	18
1093	A258	400k multicolored	1.25
1094	A258	1200k multicolored	3.75

A259 A260

UN, UNESCO emblems, stylized faces and: 330k, Drum. 1000k, Traditional flute.

1992 Litho. *Perf. 13*

1095	A259	285k shown	90
1096	A259	330k multicolored	1.05
1097	A259	1000k multicolored	3.00

Cultural Development Decade, 1988-1997.

1992

Designs: Monkeys.

1098	A260	10k Black gibbon	15
1099	A260	100k Douc langur	32
1100	A260	250k Pileated gibbon	78
1101	A260	430k Francois langur	1.35
1102	A260	800k Pygmy loris	2.50
		Nos. 1098-1102 (5)	5.10

Natl. Customs A261

Designs: 100k, Woman praying before Buddha, vert. 160k, Procession. 1500k, People giving food to monks.

1992 *Perf. 12½*

1103	A261	100k multicolored	42
1104	A261	140k multicolored	60
1105	A261	160k multicolored	68
1106	A261	1500k multicolored	6.30

First Subway System, 130th Anniv. A262

1993 Litho. *Perf. 13*

1107	A262	15k New York	15
1108	A262	50k Berlin	20
1109	A262	100k Paris	42
1110	A262	200k London	85
1111	A262	900k Moscow	3.70
		Nos. 1107-1111 (5)	5.32

Souvenir Sheet

Perf. 13x13½

1112	A262	700k Antique engine, vert.	3.00

No. 1112 contains one 32x40mm stamp.

SEMI-POSTAL STAMPS

Laotian Children — SP1

Unwmk.

1953, July 14 Engr. *Perf. 13*

B1	SP1	1.50pi + 1pi multi	90	65
B2	SP1	3pi + 1.50pi multi	90	65
B3	SP1	3.90pi + 2.50pi multi	90	65

The surtax was for the Red Cross.

Nos. 52 and 46 Surcharged: "1k ANNEE MONDIALE DU REFUGIE 1959-1960"

1960, Apr. 7

B4	A16	4k + 1k rose claret	35	40
B5	A13	10k + 1k multicolored	35	40

World Refugee Year, July 1, 1959-June 30, 1960. The surcharge was for aid to refugees.

Flooded Village — SP2

Designs: 40k+10k, Flooded market place and truck. 60k+15k, Flooded airport and plane.

1967, Jan. 18 Engr. *Perf. 13*

B6	SP2	20k + 5k multi	16	16
B7	SP2	40k + 10k multi	25	25
B8	SP2	60k + 15k multi	38	38
a.		Miniature sheet of 3	1.50	1.50

The surtax was for victims of the Mekong Delta flood. No. B8a contains one each of Nos. B6-B8. Size: 148x99mm. Sold for 250k.

Women Working in Tobacco Field — SP3

1967, Oct. 5 Engr. *Perf. 13*

B9	SP3	20k + 5k multi	15	15
B10	SP3	50k + 10k multi	25	25
B11	SP3	60k + 15k multi	35	35
a.		Souv. sheet of 3, #B9-B11	1.50	1.50

Laotian Red Cross, 10th anniv. No. B11a sold for 250k+30k.

Nos. 184-189 Surcharged: "Soutien aux Victimes / de la Guerre / + 5k"

1970, May 1 Photo. *Perf. 14*

B12	A58	10k + 5k multi	16	15
B13	A58	15k + 5k multi	16	15
B14	A58	20k + 5k multi	20	15
B15	A58	30k + 5k multi	25	16
B16	A58	40k + 5k multi	35	20
B17	A58	60k + 5k multi	45	25
		Nos. B12-B17,CB1-CB2 (8)	3.97	2.76

AIR POST STAMPS

Weaving — AP1

Design: 3.30pi, Wat Pra Keo.

Unwmk.

1952, Apr. 13 Engr. *Perf. 13*

C1	AP1	3.30pi dk pur & pur	55	25
C2	AP1	10pi ultra & bl grn	1.10	70
C3	AP1	20pi deep cl & red	1.75	1.25
C4	AP1	30pi blk brn & dk brn violet	2.75	1.90

See note following No. 17.

UPU Monument and King Sisavang-Vong — AP2

1952, Dec. 7

C5	AP2	25pi vio bl & indigo	2.00	1.40
C6	AP2	50pi dk brn & vio brn	2.00	1.40

Laos' admission to the UPU, May 13, 1952.

AP3

AP4

Designs: Various Buddha statues.

1953, Nov. 18

C7	AP3	4pi dark green	16	15
C8	AP4	6.50pi dk bl green	15	15
C9	AP4	9pi blue green	30	15
C10	AP3	11.50pi red, yel & dk vio brn	32	15
C11	AP4	40pi purple	60	45
C12	AP4	100pi olive	1.75	1.40
		Nos. C7-C12 (6)	3.28	2.45

Great Oath of Laos ceremony.

Composite of Laotian Temples — AP5

1954, Mar. 4 Unwmk.

C13	AP5	50pi ind & bl grn	47.50	47.50

Accession of King Sisavang-Vong, 50th anniv.

Ravana — AP6

Sita and Rama — AP7

Scenes from the Ramayana: 4k, Hanuman, the white monkey. 5k, Ninh Laphath, the black monkey. 20k, Lucy with a friend of Ravana. 30k, Rama.

1955, Oct. 28 Engr. *Perf. 13*

C14	AP6	2k bl grn, emer & ind	30	24
C15	AP6	4k red brn, dk red brn & ver	42	35
C16	AP6	5k scar, sep & ol	65	45
C17	AP7	10k blk, org & brn	1.10	80
C18	AP7	20k vio, dk grn & ol	1.50	1.10
C19	AP7	30k ultra, blk & sal	2.00	1.65
		Nos. C14-C19 (6)	5.97	4.59

See No. 225.

Buddha Type of Regular Issue, 1956

1956, May 24

C20	A7	20k carmine rose	11.00	8.00
C21	A7	30k ol & ol bis	11.00	8.00

2500th anniversary of birth of Buddha.

UN Emblem AP8

1956, Dec. 14

C22	AP8	15k light blue	1.90	1.90
C23	AP8	30k deep claret	2.50	2.50

Admission of Laos to the UN, 1st anniv.

Types of Regular Issue, 1957

Musical Instruments: 12k, Khong vong. 14k, So. 20k, Kong.

1957, Mar. 25 Unwmk. *Perf. 13*

C24	A9	12k multicolored	95	65
C25	A10	14k multicolored	95	65
C26	A10	20k bl grn, yel grn & pur	1.25	95

Monk Receiving Alms — AP9

Monks Meditating in Boat — AP10

Designs: 18k, Smiling Buddha. 24k, Ancient temple painting (horse and mythological figures.)

1957, Nov. 5

C27	AP9	10k dk pur, pale brn & dk grn	35	35
C28	AP10	15k dk vio brn, brn org & yel	35	35
C29	AP9	18k sl grn & ol	50	48
C30	AP10	24k cl, org yel & blk	80	70

No. C28 measures 48x27mm. No. C30, 48x36mm. See No. C84.

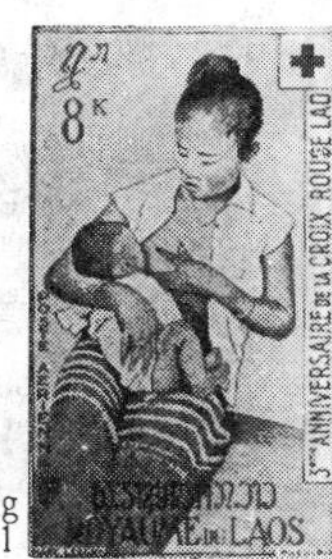
Mother Nursing Infant — AP11

1958, May 2

Cross in Red

C31	AP11	8k lil gray & dk gray	70	45
C32	AP11	12k red brn & brn	1.00	62
C33	AP11	15k sl grn & bluish green	1.25	70
C34	AP11	20k bister & vio	1.50	80

3rd anniversary of Laotian Red Cross.

Plain of Stones, Xieng Khouang — AP12

Papheng Falls, Champassak — AP13

Natl. Tourism Industry: 15k, Buffalo cart. 19k, Buddhist monk and village.

1960, July 1 Engr. *Perf. 13*

C35	AP12	9.50k bl, ol & cl	16	16
C36	AP13	12k vio bl, red brn & gray	22	22
C37	AP13	15k yel grn, ol gray & cl	25	25
C38	AP12	19k multicolored	35	35

Pou Gneu Nha Gneu Legend — AP14

Garuda — AP15

Hanuman, the White Monkey — AP16

Nang Teng One Legend AP17

1962, Feb. 19 Unwmk. *Perf. 13*

C39	AP14	11k grn, car & ocher	20	20
C40	AP15	14k ultra & org	20	20
C41	AP16	20k multicolored	30	30
C42	AP17	25k multicolored	30	30

Makha Bousa festival.

Yao Hunter — AP18

Phayre's Flying Squirrel — AP19

1964, Dec. 15 Engr. *Perf. 13*

C43 AP18 5k shown 15 15
C44 AP18 10k Kha hunter 15 15
C45 AP18 50k Meo woman 50 50
a. Min. sheet of 4, #100, C43-C45 4.00 3.50

No. C45a exists imperf.

Butterfly Type of 1965

1965, Mar. 13
Size: 48x27mm

C46 A34 20k Atlas moth 50 30

1965, Oct. 7 Engr. *Perf. 13*

Designs: 25k, Leopard cat. 75k, Javan mongoose. 100k, Crestless porcupine. 200k, Binturong.

C47 AP19 25k dk brn, yel grn & ocher 30 16
C48 AP19 55k brown & blue 50 25
C49 AP19 75k brt grn & brn 65 35
C50 AP19 100k ocher, brn & blk 80 55
C51 AP19 200k red & black 1.60 1.20
Nos. C47-C51 (5) 3.85 2.51

Army Type of Regular Issue

Design: 200k, 300k, Parading service flags before National Assembly Hall.

1968, July 15 Engr. *Perf. 13*

C52 A53 200k multicolored 65 45
C53 A53 300k multicolored 1.00 65
a. Souvenir sheet of 5, #168-170, C52-C53 4.00 3.50

No. C53a sold for 600k.

Insect Type of Regular Issue

Insects: 120k, Dorysthenes walkeri, horiz. 160k, Megaloxantha bicolor, horiz.

1968, Aug. 28 Engr. *Perf. 13*

C54 A54 120k brn, org & blk 65 35
C55 A54 160k rose car, Prus bl & yel 80 42

Ballet Type of Regular Issue

Designs: 110k, Sudagnu battling Thotsakan. 300k, Pharam dancing with Thotsakan.

1969 Photo. *Perf. 14*

C56 A58 110k multicolored 65 42
a. Souv. sheet of 4, #187-189, C56, imperf. 3.50 1.75
C57 A58 300k multicolored 2.00 1.10
a. Souv. sheet of 4, #184-186, C57, imperf. 11.00 6.50

No. C56a sold for 480k; No. C57a for 650k. For surcharges see Nos. CB1-CB2.

Timber Industry, Paksane AP20

1969, May 7 Engr. *Perf. 13*

C58 AP20 300k ol bis & blk 2.00 1.50

ILO, 50th anniversary.

Animal Type of Regular Issue

Animals: 70k, Asiatic black bear. 120k, White-handed gibbon, vert. 150k, Tiger.

1969, Nov. 6 Photo. *Perf. 12x13*

C59 A60 70k multicolored 16 15
C60 A60 120k multicolored 30 25
C61 A60 150k multicolored 38 38

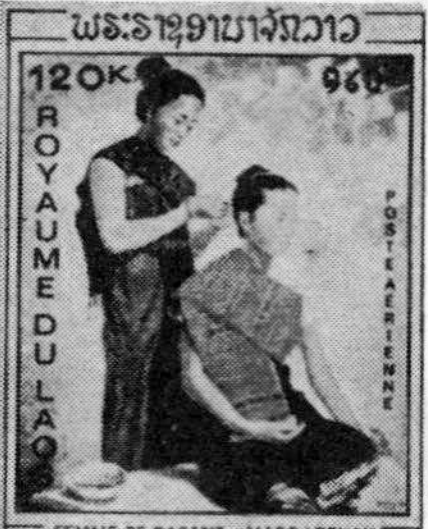

Hairdressing, by Marc Leguay AP21

Paintings: No. C63, Village Market, by Marc Leguay, horiz. No. C64, Tree on the Bank of the Mekong, by Marc Leguay, horiz.

1969-70 Photo. *Perf. 12x13, 13x12*

C62 AP21 120k multicolored 80 40
C63 AP21 150k multicolored 1.25 62
C64 AP21 150k multi ('70) 1.25 62

See Nos. C72-C74.

Wat Xiengthong, Luang Prabang — AP22

1970, Jan. 10 *Perf. 12x13, 13x12*

C65 AP22 100k Library, Wat Sisaket, vert. 85 40
C66 AP22 120k shown 95 55

Drum Type of 1970

1970, Mar. 30 Engr. *Perf. 13*

C67 A64 125k Pong wooden drum, vert. 2.00 1.20

Franklin D. Roosevelt (1882-1945) AP23

1970, Apr. 12

C68 AP23 120k olive & slate 1.00 65

EXPO '70 Type of Regular Issue

Design: 125k, Woman boiling cocoons in kettle, and spinning silk thread.

1970, July 7 Engr. *Perf. 13*

C69 A66 125k ol & multi 55 55

See note after No. 202.

Animal Type of Regular Issue

1970, Sept. 7 Engr. *Perf. 13*

C70 A67 210k Leopard 35 55
C71 A67 500k Gaur 2.25 2.00

Painting Type of 1969-70

Paintings by Marc Leguay: 100k, Village Foot Path. 120k, Rice Field in Rainy Season, horiz. 150k, Village Elder.

Perf. 11½x13, 13x11½

1970, Dec. 21 Photo.

C72 AP21 100k multicolored 40 40
C73 AP21 120k multicolored 35 35
C74 AP21 150k multicolored 50 50

UN Type of Regular Issue

Design: 125k, Earth Goddess Nang Thorani wringing her hair; UN Headquarters and emblem.

1970, Oct. 24
Size: 26x36mm

C75 A68 125k brt bl, pink & dk grn 50 50

Hanuman and Nang Matsa — AP24

1971, Feb. 5

C76 AP24 125k multicolored 1.00 60

Orchid Type of Regular Issue

Design: 125k, Brasilian cattleya.

1971, July Photo. *Perf. 13x12½*
Size: 48x27mm

C79 A73 125k Brasilian cattleya 60 30

Laotian and French Women, That Luang Pagoda and Arms — AP25

1971, Aug. 6 Engr. *Perf. 13*

C80 AP25 30k brn & dl red 22 15
C81 AP25 70k vio & lilac 40 35
C82 AP25 100k sl grn & grn 60 45

Kinship between the cities Keng Kok, Laos, and Saint Astier, France.

Animal Type of Regular Issue

1971, Sept. 16

C83 A74 300k Javan rhinoceros 80 40

Type of 1957 with Ornamental Panel and Inscription

Design: 125k, Monk receiving alms (like No. C27).

1971, Nov. 2 Engr. *Perf. 13*

C84 AP9 125k dk pur, pale brn & dk grn 35 35

20th anniv. of Laotian independent postal service. No. C84 inscribed: "Vingtième Anniversaire de la Philatélie Lao," "Poste Aerienne" and "1971."

Sunset Over the Mekong, by Chamnane Prisayane — AP26

Design: 150k, "Quiet Morning" (village scene), by Chamnane Prisayane.

1971, Dec. 20 Photo. *Perf. 13x12*

C85 AP26 125k black & multi 35 35
C86 AP26 150k black & multi 42 42

Book Year Type of Regular Issue

Design: 125k, Father teaching children to read palm leaf book.

1972, Jan. 30 Engr. *Perf. 13*
Size: 48x27mm

C87 A75 125k bright purple 50 50

Dam Type of Regular Issue

Design: 145k, Nam Ngum Hydroelectric Dam and ECAFE emblem.

1972, Mar. 28 Engr. *Perf. 13*

C88 A76 145k brn, bl & grn 60 60

Orchid Type of Regular Issue 1971

1972, May 1 Photo. *Perf. 13x12½*
Size: 48x27mm

C89 A73 150k Vanda trees, horiz. 55 28

UNICEF Type of Regular Issue

Design: 120k, Boy riding buffalo to water hole (child's drawing).

1972, July Engr. *Perf. 13*

C90 A77 120k multicolored 42 42

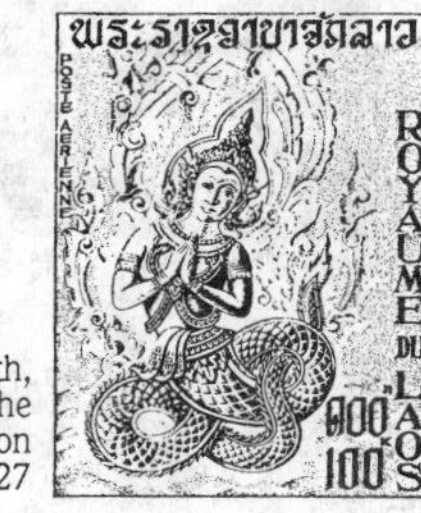

Nakharath, Daughter of the Dragon King — AP27

Wood carvings from Wat Sikhounvieng Dongmieng, Vientiane: 120k, Nang Kinnali, Goddess from Mt. Kailath. 150k, Norasing, Lion King from Himalayas.

1972, Sept. 15 Engr. *Perf. 13*

C91 AP27 100k blue green 20 20
C92 AP27 120k violet 22 22
C93 AP27 150k brn orange 30 30

That Luang Religious Festival — AP28

1972, Nov. 18 Engr. *Perf. 13*

C94 AP28 110k Presentation of wax castles 42 42
C95 AP28 125k Procession 55 55

Workers in Rice Field, by Leguay AP29

Paintings by Mark Leguay: No. C97, Women and water buffalo in rice field. Nos. C98, Rainy Season in Village (Water buffalo in water). No. C99, Rainy Season in Village (Water buffalo on land). 120k, Mother and Child.

1972, Dec. 23 Photo. *Perf. 13*

C96 AP29 50k multicolored 16 16
C97 AP29 50k multicolored 16 16
C98 AP29 70k multicolored 22 22
C99 AP29 70k multicolored 22 22
C100 AP29 120k yel & multi 35 35
Nos. C96-C100 (5) 1.11 1.11

Nos. C97, C99 have denomination and frame at right.

Costume Type of Regular Issue

Women's Costumes: 120k, Luang Prabang marriage costume. 150k, Vientiane evening costume.

1973, Feb. 16 **Engr.** ***Perf. 13***

C101 A78	120k multicolored	22	22
C102 A78	150k brn & multi	28	28

Lions Club Emblems, King Sayasettha-Thirath — AP30

1973, Mar. 30 **Engr.** ***Perf. 13***

C103 AP30	150k rose & multi	38	25

Lions Club of Vientiane.

Rahu with Rockets and Sputnik — AP31

Space achievements: 150k, Laotian festival rocket and US lunar excursion module.

1973, May 11 **Engr.** ***Perf. 13***

C104 AP31	80k ultra & multi	25	16
C105 AP31	150k buff & ultra	45	25

Dancing Around Campfire — AP32

Design: 125k, Boy Scouts helping during Vientiane Flood, 1966.

1973, Sept. 1 **Engr.** ***Perf. 13***

C106 AP32	110k vio & orange	45	20
C107 AP32	125k Prus grn & bis	55	22

Laotian Scout Movement, 25th anniv.

Sun Chariot and WMO Emblem — AP33

Design: 90k, Nang Mékhala, the weather goddess, and WMO emblem, vert.

1973, Oct. 24 **Engr.** ***Perf. 13***

C108 AP33	90k vio, red & ocher	35	20
C109 AP33	150k ocher, red & brn ol	40	30

Intl. meteorological cooperation, cent.

Set Values
A 15-cent minimum now applies to individual stamps and sets. Where the 15-cent minimum per stamp would increase the "value" of a set beyond retail, there is a "Set Value" notation giving the retail value of the set.

Woman in Poppy Field, INTERPOL Emblem — AP34

1973, Dec. 22 **Engr.** ***Perf. 13***

C110 AP34	150k vio, yel grn & red	1.00	40

Intl. Criminal Police Org., 50th anniv.

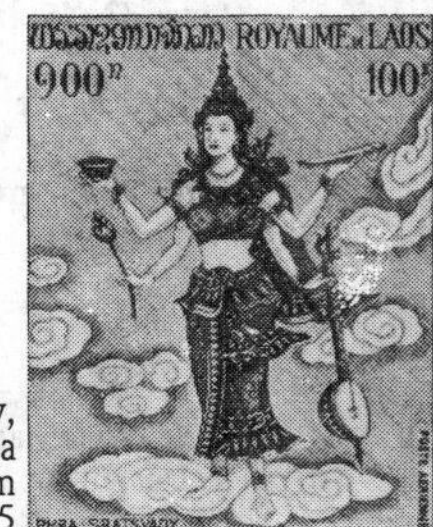

Phra Sratsvady, Wife of Phra Phrom AP35

Designs: 110k, Phra Indra on 3-headed elephant Erawan. 150k, Phra Phrom, the Creator, on phoenix. Designs show giant sculptures in park at Thadeua.

1974, Mar. 23 **Engr.** ***Perf. 13***

C111 AP35	100k lilac, red & blk	42	25
C112 AP35	110k car, vio & brn	50	40
C113 AP35	150k ocher, vio & sep	65	45

UPU Emblem, Women Reading Letter — AP36

1974 **Engr.** ***Perf. 13***

C114 AP36	200k lt brn & car	60	55
C115 AP36	500k lil & red	1.40	1.10
a.	Souvenir sheet	5.00	5.00

Centenary of Universal Postal Union. Issue dates: 200k, Apr. 30; 500k, Oct. 9.

Flower Type of 1974

1974, May 31

Size: 36x36mm

C116 A84	500k Pitcher plant	1.10	80

Transportation Type of Regular Issue

1974, July 31 **Engr.** ***Perf. 13***

C117 A85	250k Sampan	40	30

Marconi Type of 1974

Design: Old and new means of communications.

1974, Aug. 28 **Engr.** ***Perf. 13***

C118 A86	200k vio bl & brn	40	35

Insect Type of 1974

1974, Oct. 23 **Engr.** ***Perf. 13***

C119 A87	110k Sternocera multipunctata	38	22

Boeing 747 AP37

1986, June 2 **Litho.** ***Perf. 12½***

C120 AP37	20k shown	3.00	
C121 AP37	50k IL86	7.00	

AIR POST SEMI-POSTAL STAMPS

Nos. C56-C57 Surcharged: "Soutien aux Victimes / de la Guerre / + 5k"

1970, May 1 **Photo.** ***Perf. 13***

CB1 A58	110k + 5k multi	80	60
CB2 A58	300k + 5k multi	1.60	1.10

The surtax was for war victims.

POSTAGE DUE STAMPS

Vat-Sisaket Monument D1

Boat and Raft D2

Perf. 13½x13

1952-53 **Unwmk.** **Engr.**

J1	D1	10c dark brown	15	15
J2	D1	20c purple	15	15
J3	D1	50c carmine	15	15
J4	D1	1pi dark green	15	15
J5	D1	2pi deep ultra	15	15
J6	D1	5pi rose violet	45	45
J7	D2	10pi indigo ('53)	60	60
		Set value	1.50	1.50

Serpent — D3

1973, Oct. 31 **Photo.** ***Perf. 13***

J8 D3	10k yellow & multi	15	15
J9 D3	15k emerald & multi	15	15
J10 D3	20k blue & multi	15	15
J11 D3	50k scarlet & multi	15	15
	Set value	30	30

LATAKIA

LOCATION — A division of Syria in Western Asia
GOVT. — French Mandate
AREA — 2,500 sq. mi.
POP. — 278,000 (approx. 1930)
CAPITAL — Latakia

This territory, included in the Syrian Mandate to France under the Versailles Treaty, was formerly known as Alaouites. The name Latakia was adopted in 1930. See Alaouites and Syria.

100 Centimes = 1 Piaster

Stamps of Syria Overprinted in Black or Red

or

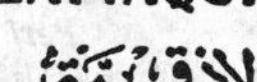

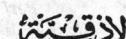

Perf. 12x12½, 13½

1931-33 **Unwmk.**

1	A6	10c red vio	25	25
2	A6	10c vio brn ('33)	30	30
3	A7	20c dk bl (R)	25	25
4	A7	20c brn org ('33)	30	30
5	A8	25c gray grn (R)	25	25
6	A8	25c dk bl gray (R) ('33)	50	50
7	A9	50c violet	60	60
8	A15	75c org red ('32)	60	60
9	A10	1p grn (R)	60	60
10	A11	1.50p bis brn (R)	90	90
11	A11	1.50p dp grn ('33)	1.00	1.00
12	A12	2p dk vio (R)	1.00	1.00
13	A13	3p yel grn (R)	1.75	1.75
14	A14	4p orange	1.75	1.75
15	A15	4.50p rose car	1.75	1.75
16	A16	6p grnsh blk (R)	1.75	1.75
17	A17	7.50p dl bl (R)	1.75	1.75
18	A18	10p dp brn (R)	2.50	2.50
19	A19	15p dp grn (R)	3.75	3.75
20	A20	25p vio brn	7.00	7.00
21	A21	50p dk brn (R)	6.50	6.50
22	A22	100p red org	20.00	20.00
		Nos. 1-22 (22)	55.05	55.05

AIR POST STAMPS

Air Post Stamps of Syria, 1931, Overprinted in Black or Red

LATTAQUIE

1931-33 **Unwmk.** ***Perf. 13½***

C1	AP2	50c ocher	35	35
a.		Inverted overprint	300.00	300.00
C2	AP2	50c blk brn (R) ('33)	45	45
C3	AP2	1p chnt brn	80	80
C4	AP2	2p Prus bl (R)	1.10	1.10
C5	AP2	3p bl grn (R)	1.40	1.40
C6	AP2	5p red vio	3.25	3.25
C7	AP2	10p sl grn (R)	4.00	4.00
C8	AP2	15p org red	4.75	4.75
C9	AP2	25p org brn	9.00	9.00
C10	AP2	50p black (R)	14.00	14.00
C11	AP2	100p magenta	14.00	14.00
		Nos. C1-C11 (11)	53.10	53.10

POSTAGE DUE STAMPS

Postage Due Stamps of Syria, 1931, Overprinted like Regular Issue

1931 **Unwmk.** ***Perf. 13½***

J1	D7	8p blk, *gray bl* (R)	9.00	9.00
J2	D8	15p blk, *dl rose* (R)	7.00	7.00

Stamps of Latakia were superseded in 1937 by those of Syria.

LATVIA

(Lettonia, Lettland)

LOCATION — Northern Europe, bordering on the Baltic Sea and the Gulf of Riga
GOVT. — Independent Republic
AREA — 25,395 sq. mi.
POP. — 1,994,506 (estimated 1939)
CAPITAL — Riga

Latvia was created a sovereign state following World War I and was admitted to the League of Nations in 1922. In 1940 it became a republic in the Union of Soviet Socialist Republics. Latvian independence was recognized by the Soviet Union on Sept. 6, 1991.

100 Kapeikas = 1 Rublis
100 Santims = 1 Lat (1923)
100 Kopecks = 1 Ruble (1991)

Catalogue values for unused stamps in this country are for Never Hinged items, beginning with Scott 300 in the regular postage section, and Scott B150 in the semi-postal section.

Watermarks

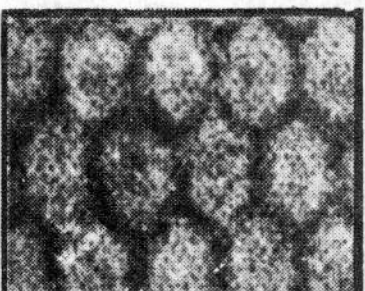

Wmk. 108-Honeycomb

Wmk. 145- Wavy Lines

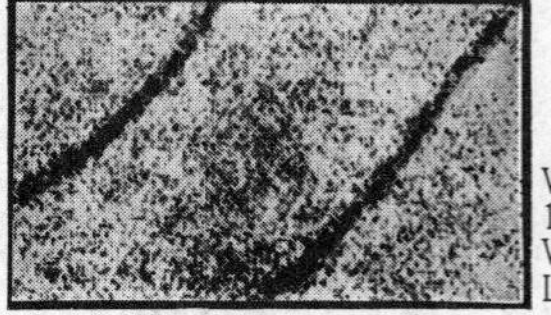

Wmk. 181- Wavy Lines

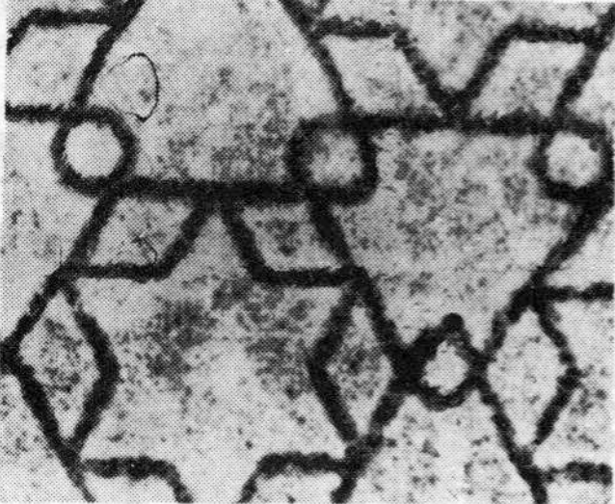

Wmk. 197- Star and Triangles

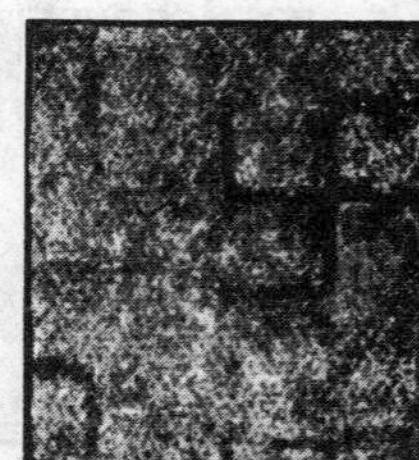

Wmk. 212- Multiple Swastikas

Wmk. 265- Multiple Waves

Arms — A1

Printed on the Backs of German Military Maps

Unwmk.

1918, Dec. 18 Litho. ***Imperf.***

1	A1	5k carmine	38	38

Perf. 11½

2	A1	5k carmine	38	38
		Set, never hinged	95	

Stamps from outer rows of the sheets sometimes have no printing on the back.

Redrawn

Paper with Ruled Lines

1919 ***Imperf.***

3	A1	5k carmine	50	50
4	A1	10k dk bl	50	50
5	A1	15k green	50	50

Perf. 11½

6	A1	5k carmine	1.00	1.00
7	A1	10k dk bl	1.00	1.00
8	A1	15k dp grn	1.50	1.50
		Nos. 3-8 (6)	5.00	5.00
		Set, never hinged	6.50	

In the redrawn design the wheat heads are thicker, the ornament at lower left has five points instead of four, and there are minor changes in other parts of the design.

The sheets of this and subsequent issues were usually divided in half by a single line of perforation gauging 10. Thus stamps are found with this perforation on one side.

1919 Pelure Paper ***Imperf.***

9	A1	3k lilac	3.75	3.75
10	A1	5k carmine	15	15
11	A1	10k dp bl	15	15
12	A1	15k dk grn	15	15
13	A1	20k orange	15	15
13A	A1	25k gray	25.00	25.00
14	A1	35k dk brn	15	15
15	A1	50k purple	18	18
16	A1	75k emerald	3.00	4.00
		Nos. 9-16 (9)	32.68	33.68
		Set, never hinged	40.00	

Perf. 11½, 9½

17	A1	3k lilac	15.00	15.00
18	A1	5k carmine	90	90
19	A1	10k dp bl	1.90	1.90
20	A1	15k dk grn	1.90	1.90
21	A1	20k orange	1.80	1.90
22	A1	35k dk brn	2.50	2.50
23	A1	50k purple	3.75	3.75
24	A1	75k emerald	7.25	7.25
		Nos. 17-24 (8)	35.00	35.10
		Set, never hinged	40.00	

Nos. 17 to 24 are said to be unofficially perforated varieties of Nos. 9 to 16.

1919 Wmk. 108 ***Imperf.***

25	A1	3k lilac	15	15
26	A1	5k carmine	15	15
27	A1	10k dp bl	15	15
28	A1	15k dp grn	15	15
29	A1	20k orange	18	18
30	A1	25k gray	45	45
31	A1	35k dk brn	45	45
32	A1	50k purple	30	30
33	A1	75k emerald	60	60
		Nos. 25-33 (9)	2.58	2.58
		Set, never hinged	3.00	

The variety "printed on both sides" exists for 3k, 10k, 15k, 20k and 35k.

See Nos. 57-58, 76-82. For surcharges and overprints see Nos. 86, 132-133, 2N1-2N8, 2N12-2N19.

Liberation of Riga — A2

Rising Sun — A4

1919 Wmk. 108

43	A2	5k carmine	30	30
44	A2	15k dp grn	30	30
45	A2	35k brown	45	45

Unwmk.

Pelure Paper

49	A2	5k carmine	9.00	12.00
50	A2	15k dp grn	9.00	12.00
51	A2	35k brown	9.00	12.00
		Set, #43-51, never hinged	35.00	

For surcharge and overprints see Nos. 87, 2N9-2N11, 2N20-2N22.

1919 ***Imperf.***

55	A4	10k gray blue	18	18

Perf. 11½

56	A4	10k gray blue	50	50
		Set, never hinged	90	

Type of 1918

1919 Laid Paper ***Perf. 11½***

57	A1	3r slate & org	85	85
58	A1	5r gray brn & org	75	52
		Set, never hinged	2.00	

Independence Issue

Allegory of One Year of Independence — A5

1919, Nov. 18 Unwmk.

Wove Paper

Size: 33x45mm

59	A5	10k brn & rose	60	60

Laid Paper

60	A5	10k brn & rose	85	85

Size: 28x38mm

61	A5	10k brn & rose	26	26
a.		Imperf.		
62	A5	35k ind & grn	22	22
a.		Vertical pair, imperf. between	20.00	20.00

Wmk. 197

Thick Wove Paper

Blue Design on Back

63	A5	1r grn & red	60	60
		Nos. 59-63 (5)	2.53	2.53
		Set, never hinged	3.25	

There are two types of Nos. 59 and 60. In type I the trunk of the tree is not outlined. In type II it has a distinct white outline.

No. 63 was printed on the backs of unfinished 5r bank notes of the Workers and Soldiers Council, Riga.

For surcharges see Nos. 83-85, 88, 94.

Warrior Slaying Dragon — A6

1919-20 Unwmk. ***Perf. 11½***

Wove Paper

64	A6	10k brn & car	20	20
a.		Horiz. pair, imperf. btwn.	25.00	25.00
65	A6	25k ind & yel grn	30	30
a.		Pair, imperf. between	25.00	25.00
66	A6	35k blk & bl ('20)	30	30
a.		Horiz. pair, imperf. btwn.	25.00	25.00
67	A6	1r dk grn & brn ('20)	60	60
a.		Horiz. pair, imperf. vert.	25.00	25.00
b.		Horiz. pair, imperf. btwn.	25.00	25.00
		Set, never hinged	1.75	

Issued in honor of the liberation of Kurzeme (Kurland). The paper sometimes shows impressed quadrille lines.

For surcharges see Nos. 91-93.

Latgale Relief Issue

Latvia Welcoming Home Latgale Province — A7

1920, Mar.

Brown and Green Design on Back

68	A7	50k dk grn & rose	38	38
a.		Horiz. pair, imperf. vert.	25.00	
69	A7	1r slate grn & brn	38	38
a.		Horiz. pair, imperf. vert.	25.00	
		Set, never hinged	90	

No. 68-69 were printed on the backs of unfinished bank notes of the government of Colonel Bermondt-Avalov and on the so-called German "Ober-Ost" money.

For surcharges see Nos. 95-99.

First National Assembly Issue

Latvia Hears Call to Assemble — A8

1920

70	A8	50k rose	35	20
a.		Imperf., pair	6.00	6.00
71	A8	1r blue	35	20
a.		Vertical pair, imperf. between	25.00	25.00
b.		Imperf., pair	6.00	6.00
72	A8	3r dk brn & grn	60	60
73	A8	5r slate & vio brn	75	60
		Set, never hinged	2.50	

For surcharges see Nos. 90, 134.

Type of 1918 Issue

Wove Paper

1920-21 Unwmk. ***Perf. 11½***

76	A1	5k carmine	15	15
78	A1	20k orange	15	15
79	A1	40k lilac ('21)	18	15
80	A1	50k violet	18	15
81	A1	75k emerald	18	15
82	A1	5r gray brn & org ('21)	1.40	20
		Nos. 76-82 (6)	2.24	95
		Set, never hinged	2.75	

No. 63 Surcharged in Black, Brown or Blue

1920, Sept. 1

83	A5	10r on 1r grn & red (Bk)	1.40	1.10
84	A5	20r on 1r grn & red (Br)	4.00	3.50
85	A5	30r on 1r grn & red (Bl)	5.25	4.25
		Set, never hinged	14.50	

Types of 1919 Surcharged

2
DIWI
RUBLI

1920-21 Wmk. 108 ***Perf. 11½***

86	A1	2r on 10k dp bl	1.10	85
87	A2	2r on 35k brown	55	55
		Set, never hinged	1.90	

No. 62 Surcharged in Red

DIWI
RUBLI
2

Unwmk.

88	A5	2r on 35k ind & grn	48	48
		Never hinged	70	

No. 70 Surcharged in Blue

DIVI
2 RUB. 2

1921

90	A8	2r on 50k rose	48	48
		Never hinged	70	

Nos. 64-66 Surcharged in Red or Blue

WEENS
1
RUBLIS

1920-21

91 A6 1r on 35k blk & bl (R) 42 28
92 A6 2r on 10k brn & rose (Bl) 42 28
93 A6 2r on 25k ind & grn (R) 55 20
a. Imperf.
Set, never hinged 1.50

On Nos. 92 and 93 the surcharge reads "DIVI 2 RUBLI."

No. 83 with Added Surcharge

1921 **Wmk. 197**

94 A5 10r on 10r on 1r 1.40 1.00
Never hinged 1.75 —

Latgale Relief Issue of 1920 Surcharged in Black or Blue

DESMIT RBL

1921, May 31 **Unwmk.**

95 A7 10r on 50k grn & rose 1.00 80
a. Imperf.
96 A7 20r on 50k grn & rose 3.75 3.00
97 A7 30r on 50k grn & rose 3.00 2.00
98 A7 50r on 50k grn & rose 6.00 4.75
99 A7 100r on 50k grn & rose (Bl) 12.50 11.00
Nos. 95-99 (5) 26.25 21.55
Set, never hinged 35.00

Excellent counterfeits exist.

Arms and Stars for Vidzeme, Kurzeme & Latgale — A10

Coat of Arms — A11

Type I, slanting cipher in value.
Type II, upright cipher in value.

Perf. 10, 11½ and Compound
Wmk. Similar to 181

1921-22 **Typo.**

101 A10 50k vio (II) 38 15
102 A10 1r org yel 38 20
103 A10 2r dp grn 38 15
104 A10 3r brt grn 20 20
105 A10 5r rose 65 15
106 A10 6r dp claret 1.25 30
107 A10 9r orange 75 25
108 A10 10r blue (I) 75 15
109 A10 15r ultra 1.75 85
a. Printed on both sides 25.00
110 A10 20r dl lil (II) 7.50 2.25

1922, Aug. 21 ***Perf. 11½***

111 A11 50r dk brn & pale brn (I) 17.00 3.50
112 A11 100r dk bl & pale bl (I) 19.00 4.50
Nos. 101-112 (12) 49.99 12.65
Set, never hinged 75.00

Nos. 101 to 131 sometimes show letters of a paper maker's watermark "PACTIEN LIGAT MILLS."
See Nos. 126-131, 152-154.

A12

2 SANTIMS
Type A, tail of "2" ends in an upstroke.
Type B, tail of "2" is nearly horizontal.

1923-25 ***Perf. 10, 11, 11½***

113 A12 1s violet 42 15
114 A12 2s org yel (A) 42 15
115 A12 4s dk grn 55 15
a. Horiz. pair, imperf. btwn. 25.00 25.00
116 A12 5s lt grn ('25) 1.10 15
117 A12 6s grn, *yel* ('25) 2.25 15
118 A12 10s rose red (I) 85 15
a. Horiz. pair, imperf. btwn. 25.00 25.00
119 A12 12s claret 15 15
120 A12 15s brn, *sal* 1.90 15
a. Horiz. pair, imperf. btwn. 25.00 25.00
121 A12 20s dp bl (II) 1.40 15
122 A12 25s ultra ('25) 15 15
123 A12 30s pink (I) ('25) 2.50 15
124 A12 40s lilac (I) 1.10 15
125 A12 50s lil gray (II) 2.25 18
126 A11 1 l dk brn & pale brn 6.75 50
127 A11 2 l dk bl & bl 11.00 1.00
130 A11 5 l dp grn & pale grn 37.50 6.00
131 A11 10 l car rose & pale rose (I) 3.25 3.00
Nos. 113-131 (17) 73.54 12.48
Set, never hinged 125.00

Value in "Santims" (1s); "Santimi" (2s-6s) or "Santimu" (others).
See note after No. 110.
See Nos. 135-151, 155-157. For overprints and surcharges see Nos. 164-167, B21-B23.

Nos. 79-80 Surcharged

15 SANTIMU

1927 **Unwmk.** ***Perf. 11½***

132 A1 15s on 40k lilac 55 42
133 A1 15s on 50k violet 85 85

No. 72 Surcharged

1Ls

134 A8 1 l on 3r brn & grn 4.75 4.75
Set, never hinged 7.50

Types of 1923-25 Issue

1927-33 **Wmk. 212** ***Perf. 10, 11½***

135 A12 1s dl vio 18 15
136 A12 2s org yel (A) 18 15
137 A12 2s org yel (B) ('33) 15 15
138 A12 3s org red ('31) 18 15
139 A12 4s dk grn ('29) 2.00 1.25
140 A12 5s lt grn ('31) 60 15
141 A12 6s grn, *yel* 15 15
142 A12 7s dk grn ('31) 60 22
143 A12 10s red (I) 1.50 15
144 A12 10s grn, *yel* (I) ('32) 6.00 15
145 A12 15s brn, *sal* 3.75 15
146 A12 20s pink (I) 4.25 15
147 A12 20s pink (II) 3.00 15
148 A12 30s lt bl (I) 1.50 15
149 A12 35s dk bl ('31) 1.25 15
150 A12 40s dl lil (I) ('29) 1.50 15
151 A12 50s gray (II) 2.25 15
152 A11 1 l dk brn & pale brn 6.50 28
153 A11 2 l dk bl & bl ('31) 15.00 1.10
154 A11 5 l grn & pale grn ('33) 125.00 21.00
Nos. 135-154 (20) 175.54 26.10
Set, never hinged 250.00

The paper of Nos. 141, 144 and 145 is colored on the surface only.
See note above No. 113 for types A and B, and note above No. 101 for types I and II.

Type of 1927-33 Issue
Paper Colored Through

1931-33 ***Perf. 10***

155 A12 6s grn, *yel* 15 15
156 A12 10s grn, *yel* (I) ('33) 19.00 18
157 A12 15s brn, *sal* 3.50 15
Set, never hinged 25.00

View of Rezekne — A13

Designs (Views of Cities): 15s, Jelgava. 20s, Cesis (Wenden). 30s, Liepaja (Libau). 50s, Riga. 1 l, Riga Theater.

1928, Nov. 18 **Litho.** ***Perf. 10, 11½***

158 A13 6s dp grn & vio 75 30
159 A13 15s dk brn & ol grn 75 30
160 A13 20s cer & bl grn 1.25 38
161 A13 30s ultra & vio brn 1.25 50
162 A13 50s dk gray & plum 1.50 1.25
163 A13 1 l blk brn & brn 2.50 1.50
Nos. 158-163 (6) 8.00 4.23
Set, never hinged 9.50

10th anniv. of Latvian Independence.

Riga Exhibition Issue

Stamps of 1927-33 Overprinted

Latvijas ražojumu izstāde Rigā. 1932.g.10.—18.IX.

1932, Aug. 30 ***Perf. 10, 11***

164 A12 3s orange 1.90 90
165 A12 10s grn, *yel* 1.90 1.25
166 A12 20s pink (I) 1.90 60
167 A12 35s dk bl 2.50 1.40
Set, never hinged 10.00

Riga Castle — A19

Arms and Shield — A20

Allegory of Latvia — A21

Ministry of Foreign Affairs — A22

1934, Dec. 15 **Litho.** ***Perf. 10½, 10***

174 A19 3s red org 15 15
175 A20 5s yel grn 60 15
176 A20 10s gray grn 2.50 15
177 A21 20s dp rose 2.75 15
178 A22 35s dk bl 18 18
179 A19 40s brown 15 15
Nos. 174-179 (6) 6.33
Set value 78
Set, never hinged 8.00

Atis Kronvalds — A23

A. Pumpurs — A24

Juris Maters — A25

Mikus Krogzemis (Auseklis) — A26

1936, Jan. 4 **Wmk. 212** ***Perf. 11½***

180 A23 3s vermilion 2.75 2.75
181 A24 10s green 2.75 2.75
182 A25 20s rose pink 2.75 2.75
183 A26 35s dk bl 2.75 2.75
Set, never hinged 14.00

President Karlis Ulmanis — A27

1937, Sept. 4 **Litho.** ***Perf. 10, 11½***

184 A27 3s org red & brn org 65 52
185 A27 5s yel grn 65 52
186 A27 10s dk sl grn 65 52
187 A27 20s rose lake & brn lake 1.00 52
188 A27 25s blk vio 1.25 65
189 A27 30s dk bl 1.25 65
190 A27 35s indigo 2.00 2.00
191 A27 40s lt brn 1.50 1.50
192 A27 50s ol blk 2.00 1.75
Nos. 184-192 (9) 10.95 8.63
Set, never hinged 14.00

60th birthday of President Ulmanis.

Independence Monument, Rauna (Ronneburg) — A28

Independence Monument, Jelgava — A30

Monument Entrance to Cemetery at Riga — A29

War Memorial, Valka — A31

Independence Monument, Iecava — A32

Independence Monument, Riga — A33

Tomb of Col. Kalpaks — A34

Unwmk.
1937, July 12 **Litho.** ***Perf. 10***
Thick Paper

193 A28 3s vermilion 55 80
194 A29 5s yel grn 55 80
195 A30 10s dp grn 55 80
196 A31 20s carmine 2.00 1.90
197 A32 30s lt bl 1.65 2.25

Perf. 11½
Engr. **Wmk. 212**
Thin Paper

198 A33 35s dk bl 1.65 2.25
199 A34 40s brown 2.50 2.75
Nos. 193-199 (7) 9.45 11.55
Set, never hinged 11.50

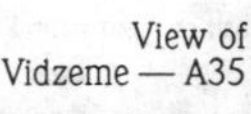

View of Vidzeme — A35

General J. Balodis — A37

President Karlis Ulmanis A38

Views: 5s, Latgale. 30s, Riga waterfront. 35s, Kurzeme. 40s, Zemgale.

1938, Nov. 17 *Perf. 10, 10½x10*

200 A35 3s brn org 15 15
a. Booklet pane of 4 *20.00*
201 A35 5s yel grn 28 15
a. Booklet pane of 4 *20.00*
202 A37 10s dk grn 40 15
a. Booklet pane of 2 *20.00*
203 A38 20s red lil 55 15
a. Booklet pane of 2 *15.00*
204 A35 30s dp bl 95 20
205 A35 35s indigo 70 20
a. Booklet pane of 2 *20.00*
206 A35 40s rose vio 1.10 28
Nos. 200-206 (7) 4.13
Set value 1.05
Set, never hinged 5.50

The 20th anniversary of the Republic.

School, Riga — A42

Independence Monument, Riga — A45

President Karlis Ulmanis — A49

Designs: 5s, Castle of Jelgava. 10s, Riga Castle. 30s, Symbol of Freedom. 35s, Community House Daugavpils. 40s, Powder Tower and War Museum, Riga.

1939, May 13 **Photo.** *Perf. 10*

207 A42 3s brn org 70 55
208 A42 5s dp grn 70 55
209 A42 10s dk sl grn 85 55
210 A45 20s dk car rose 1.10 70
211 A42 30s brt ultra 1.25 55
212 A42 35s dk bl 1.40 1.40
213 A45 40s brn vio 1.65 1.10
214 A49 50s grnsh blk 2.00 1.10
Nos. 207-214 (8) 9.65 6.50
Set, never hinged 11.50

5th anniv. of National Unity Day.

Harvesting Wheat — A50

Apple — A51

1939, Oct. 8

215 A50 10s slate green 65 65
216 A51 20s rose lake 85 85
Set, never hinged 1.90

8th Agricultural Exposition held near Riga.

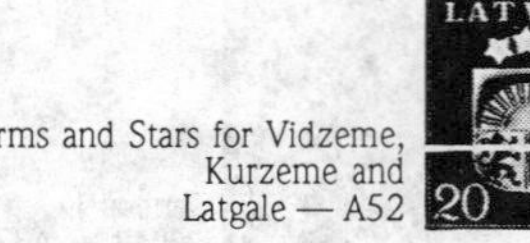

Arms and Stars for Vidzeme, Kurzeme and Latgale — A52

1940

217 A52 1s dk vio brn 15 15
218 A52 2s ocher 15 15
219 A52 3s red org 15 15
220 A52 5s dk ol brn 15 15
221 A52 7s dk grn 15 15
222 A52 10s dk bl grn 65 15
224 A52 20s rose brown 65 15
225 A52 30s dp red brn 70 22
226 A52 35s brt ultra 22 55
228 A52 50s dk slate grn 65 42
229 A52 1 l olive green 1.40 1.10
Nos. 217-229 (11) 5.02
Set value 2.70
Set, never hinged 6.00

Catalogue values for unused stamps in this section, from this point to the end of the section, are for Never Hinged items.

Natl. Arms — A70

1991, Oct. 19 **Litho.** *Perf. 13x12½*

300 A70 5k multicolored 20 15
301 A70 10k multicolored 40 15
302 A70 15k multicolored 60 15
303 A70 20k multicolored 80 20
304 A70 40k multicolored 1.65 40
305 A70 50k multicolored 2.00 50

Size: 28x32mm

Perf. 13½x14

306 A70 100k silver & multi 4.00 1.00
307 A70 200k gold & multi 8.25 2.00
Nos. 300-307 (8) 17.90 4.55

Russia Nos. 5981, 5984a Ovptd. "LATVIJA" and Surcharged in Red Lilac, Orange, Green, Violet, Brown, Red, Emerald

1991, Dec. 23 **Photo.** *Perf. 12x11½*

308 A2765 100k on 7k (RL) 62 15
a. Vert. pair, one without ovpt.

Perf. 12x12½

Litho.

309 A2765 300k on 2k (O) 1.90 38
a. Vert. pair, one without ovpt.
310 A2765 500k on 2k (G) 3.10 62
a. Vert. pair, one without ovpt.
311 A2765 1000k on 2k (V) 6.25 1.25
a. Vert. pair, one without ovpt.

On Nos. 308-311 the sixth row of the sheet was not surcharged.

Liberty Monument, Riga — A71

1991, Dec. 28 *Perf. 12½x13*

312 A71 10k ol brn & multi 20 15
313 A71 15k vio & multi 30 15
314 A71 20k bl grn & multi 40 15
315 A71 30k ol grn & multi 60 15
316 A71 50k choc & multi 1.00 20
317 A71 100k dp bl & multi 2.00 40
Nos. 312-317 (6) 4.50
Set value 90

A72 A73

Latvia stamps can be mounted in Scott's annual Baltic States Supplement.

Monuments — A74

1992, Feb. 29 *Perf. 14*

318 A72 10k black 20 15
319 A73 20k violet black 40 15
320 A73 30k brown 60 15
321 A72 30k purple 60 15
322 A74 40k violet blue 80 16
323 A74 50k green 1.00 20
324 A73 50k olive green 1.00 20
325 A74 100k red brown 2.00 40
326 A72 200k blue 4.00 80
Nos. 318-326 (9) 10.60
Set value 2.10

Russia Nos. 4599, 5981, 5984a Ovptd. "LATVIJA" and Surcharged in Red, Brown, Emerald and Violet

1992, Apr. 4 **Photo.** *Perf. 12x11½*

327 A2765 1r on 7k (R) 32 15

Perf. 12x12½

Litho.

328 A2765 3r on 2k (Br) 1.00 20
329 A2765 5r on 2k (E) 1.60 32
330 A2765 10r on 2k (V) 3.20 65
331 A2138 25r on 4k 8.00 1.60
Nos. 327-331 (5) 14.12 2.92

Surcharged denominations expressed in rubles (large numerals) and kopecks (small zeros).

Birds of the Baltic Shores — A75

Perf. 12½x13

1992, Oct. 3 **Litho. & Engr.**

332 A75 5r Pandion haliaetus 42 15
333 A75 5r Limosa limosa 42 15
334 A75 5r Mergus merganser 42 15
335 A75 5r Tadorna tadorna 42 15
a. Booklet pane of 4, #332-335 1.70

See Estonia Nos. 231-234a and Sweden Nos. 1975-1978a.

Christmas A76

Designs: 2r, 10r Angels with children around Christmas tree. 3r, Angels with musical instruments, Christmas tree. 15r, Nativity scene.

1992 **Litho.** *Perf. 13½x13*

336 A76 2r silver & multi *78* *15*
337 A76 3r multicolored *1.18* *24*
338 A76 10r gold & multi *3.90* *78*
339 A76 15r multicolored *5.85* *1.20*

SEMI-POSTAL STAMPS

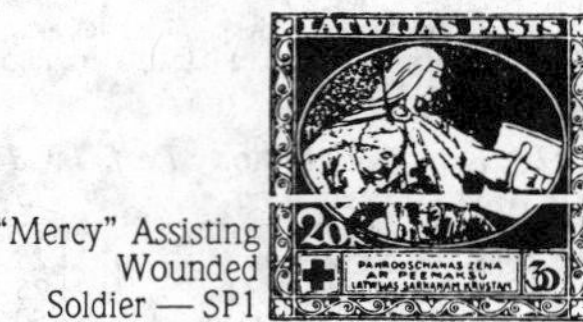

"Mercy" Assisting Wounded Soldier — SP1

1920 **Unwmk.** **Typo.** *Perf. 11½*

Brown and Green Design on Back

B1 SP1 20(30)k dk brn & red 30 50
B2 SP1 40(55)k dk bl & red 30 50
B3 SP1 50(70)k dk grn & red 30 50
B4 SP1 1(1.30)r dl sl & red 30 75

Wmk. Star and Triangles (197)

Blue Design on Back

B5 SP1 20(30)k dk brn & red 50 75
B6 SP1 40(55)k dk bl & red 50 75
a. Vert. pair, imperf. btwn. 25.00
B7 SP1 50(70)k dk grn & red 50 1.00
B8 SP1 1(1.30)r dk sl & red 50 1.00

Wmk. Similar to 145

Pink Paper *Imperf.*

Brown, Green and Red Design on Back

B9 SP1 20(30)k dk brn & red 50 1.40
B10 SP1 40(55)k dk bl & red 50 1.40
B11 SP1 50(70)k dk grn & red 50 1.40
B12 SP1 1(1.30)r dk sl & red 50 1.40
Nos. B1-B12 (12) 5.20 11.35
Set, never hinged 6.25

These semi-postal stamps were printed on the backs of unfinished bank notes of the Workers and Soldiers Council, Riga, and the Bermondt-Avalov Army.

Nos. B1-B8 Surcharged RUB. 2 RUB.

1921 **Unwmk.** *Perf. 11½*

Brown and Green Design on Back

B13 SP1 20k + 2r dk brn & red 1.00 1.65
B14 SP1 40k + 2r dk bl & red 1.00 1.65
B15 SP1 50k + 2r dk grn & red 1.00 1.65
B16 SP1 1r + 2r dk sl & red 1.00 1.65

Wmk. Star and Triangles (197)

Blue Design on Back

B17 SP1 20k + 2r dk brn & red 7.50 6.00
B18 SP1 40k + 2r dk bl & red 7.50 6.00
B19 SP1 50k + 2r dk grn & red 7.50 6.00
B20 SP1 1r + 2r dk sl & red 7.50 6.00
Nos. B13-B20 (8) 34.00 30.60
Set, never hinged 40.00

Regular Issue of 1923-25 Surcharged in Blue

1923 **Wmk. Similar to 181** *Perf. 10*

B21 A12 1s + 10s vio 65 75
B22 A12 2s + 10s yel 65 75
B23 A12 4s + 10s dk grn 65 75
Set, never hinged 2.25

The surtax benefited the Latvian War Invalids Society.

Lighthouse and Harbor, Liepaja (Libau) — SP2

Church at Liepaja — SP5

Coat of Arms of Liepaja — SP6

Designs: 15s (25s), City Hall, Liepaja. 25s (35s), Public Bathing Pavilion, Liepaja.

1925, May 29 *Perf. 11½*

B24 SP2 6s (12s) red brn & dp bl 1.40 65
B25 SP2 15s (25s) dk bl & brn 75 1.00
B26 SP2 25s (35s) vio & dk grn 1.25 1.00
B27 SP5 30s (40s) dk bl & lake 2.75 3.75
B28 SP6 50s (60s) dk grn & vio 4.00 6.00
Nos. B24-B28 (5) 10.15 12.40
Set, never hinged 12.50

Tercentenary of Liepaja (Libau). The surtax benefited that city. Exist imperf.

President Janis Cakste — SP7

1928, Apr. 18 **Engr.**

B29 SP7 2s (12s) red org 1.65 2.00
B30 SP7 6s (16s) dp grn 1.65 2.00
B31 SP7 15s (25s) red brn 1.65 2.00
B32 SP7 25s (35s) dp bl 2.25 2.75
B33 SP7 30s (40s) claret 1.65 2.00
Nos. B29-B33 (5) 8.85 10.75
Set, never hinged 11.00

The surtax helped erect a monument to Janis Cakste, 1st pres. of the Latvian Republic.

Venta River — SP8

Allegory, "Latvia" — SP9

View of Jelgava — SP10

National Theater, Riga — SP11

View of Cesis (Wenden) — SP12

Riga Bridge and Trenches — SP13

Perf. 11½, Imperf.

1928, Nov. 18 **Wmk. 212** **Litho.**

B34 SP8 6s (16s) grn 1.65 1.65
B35 SP9 10s (20s) scar 1.65 1.65
B36 SP10 15s (25s) mar 1.90 1.90
B37 SP11 30s (40s) ultra 2.25 2.25
B38 SP12 50s (60s) dk gray 2.25 2.25
B39 SP13 1 l (1.10 l) choc 3.25 3.25
Nos. B34-B39 (6) 12.95 12.95
Set, never hinged 14.50

The surtax was given to a committee for the erection of a Liberty Memorial.

Z. A. Meierovics — SP14

1929, Aug. 22 ***Perf. 11½, Imperf.***

B46 SP14 2s (4s) org 1.75 1.50
B47 SP14 6s (12s) dp grn 1.75 2.50
B48 SP14 15s (25s) red brn 1.75 2.50
B49 SP14 25s (35s) dp bl 2.25 2.50
B50 SP14 30s (40s) ultra 2.25 2.50
Nos. B46-B50 (5) 9.75 11.50
Set, never hinged 12.00

The surtax was used to erect a monument to Z. A. Meierovics, Latvian statesman.

Tuberculosis Cross — SP15

Allegory of Hope for the Sick — SP16

Gustavs Zemgals SP17

Riga Castle SP18

Daisies and Double-barred Cross — SP20

Tuberculosis Sanatorium, near Riga — SP22

Cakste, Kviesis and Zemgals SP23

Designs: No. B61, Janis Cakste, 1st pres. of Latvia. No. B63, Pres. Alberts Kviesis.

1930, Dec. 4 **Typo.** ***Perf. 10, 11½***

B56 SP15 1s (2s) dk vio & red org 1.00 1.00
B57 SP15 2s (4s) org & red org 1.00 1.00
a. Cliché of 1s (2s) in plate of 2s (4s) *450.00 600.00*
B58 SP16 4s (8s) dk grn & red 1.25 1.25
B59 SP17 5s (10s) brt grn & dk brn 1.25 1.25
B60 SP18 6s (12s) ol grn & bis 1.25 1.65
B61 SP17 10s (20s) dp red & blk 1.50 1.50
B62 SP20 15s (30s) mar & dl grn 1.40 1.90
B63 SP17 20s (40s) rose lake & ind 1.90 1.90
B64 SP22 25s (50s) multi 3.00 3.00
B65 SP23 30s (60s) multi 3.75 4.50
Nos. B56-B65 (10) 17.30 18.95
Set, never hinged 22.50

Surtax for the Latvian Anti-Tuberculosis Soc. For surcharges see Nos. B72-B81.

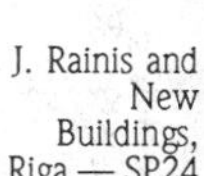
J. Rainis and New Buildings, Riga — SP24

Character from Play and Rainis SP25

Characters from Plays — SP26

Rainis and Lyre — SP27

Flames, Flag and Rainis SP28

1930, May 23 **Wmk. 212** ***Perf. 11½***

B66 SP24 1s (2s) dl vio 65 65
B67 SP25 2s (4s) yel org 65 65
B68 SP26 4s (8s) dp grn 65 65
B69 SP27 6s (12s) yel grn & red brn 65 65
B70 SP28 10s (20s) dk red 6.25 14.00
B71 SP27 15s (30s) red brn & yel grn 6.25 12.50
Nos. B66-B71 (6) 15.10 29.10
Set, never hinged 18.50

Sold at double face value, surtax going to memorial fund for J. Rainis (Jan Plieksans, 1865-1929), writer and politician.
Exist imperf. Value twice that of perf. stamps.

Nos. B56 to B65 Surcharged in Black

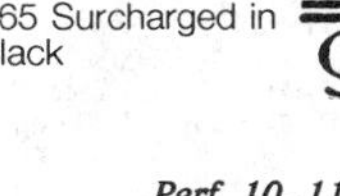

1931, Aug. 19 ***Perf. 10, 11½***

B72 SP18 9s on 6s (12s) 60 1.10
B73 SP15 16s on 1s (2s) 9.00 8.00
B74 SP15 17s on 2s (4s) 1.25 1.40
B75 SP16 19s on 4s (8s) 3.00 3.25
B76 SP17 20s on 5s (10s) 1.75 2.25
B77 SP20 23s on 15s (30s) 1.25 1.10
B78 SP17 25s on 10s (20s) 2.50 2.75
B79 SP17 35s on 20s (40s) 3.50 3.25
B80 SP22 45s on 25s (50s) 11.00 14.00
B81 SP23 55s on 30s (60s) 11.00 14.00
Nos. B72-B81 (10) 44.85 51.10
Set, never hinged 50.00

The surcharge replaces the original total price, including surtax.
Nos. B73 to B81 have no bars in the surcharge. The surtax aided the Latvian Anti-Tuberculosis Society.

Lacplesis, the Deliverer SP29

Designs: 1s, Kriva telling stories under Holy Oak. 2s, Enslaved Latvians building Riga under knight's supervision. 4s, Death of Black Knight. 5s, Spirit of Lacplesis over freed Riga.

Inscribed: "AIZSARGI" (Army Reserve)

1932, Feb. 10 ***Perf. 10½, Imperf.***

B82 SP29 1s (11s) vio brn & bluish 1.50 1.75
B83 SP29 2s (17s) ocher & ol grn 1.50 1.75
B84 SP29 3s (23s) red brn & org brn 1.50 2.00
B85 SP29 4s (34s) dk grn & grn 1.75 2.25
B86 SP29 5s (45s) grn & emer 2.50 3.25
Nos. B82-B86 (5) 8.75 11.00
Set, never hinged 10.50

Surtax aided the Militia Maintenance Fund.

Marching Troops — SP30

Infantry in Action — SP31

Nurse Binding Soldier's Wound — SP32

Army Soup Kitchen — SP33

Gen. J. Balodis — SP34

1932, May ***Perf. 10½, Imperf.***

B87 SP30 6s (25s) ol brn & red vio 2.75 3.00
B88 SP31 7s (35s) dk bl grn & dk bl 2.75 3.00
B89 SP32 10s (45s) ol grn & blk brn 2.75 3.00
B90 SP33 12s (55s) lake & ol grn 3.00 3.75
B91 SP34 15s (75s) red org & brn vio 4.50 5.00
Nos. B87-B91 (5) 15.75 17.75
Set, never hinged 18.50

The surtax aided the Latvian Home Guards.

Symbolical of Unified Latvia — SP35

Aid to the Sick — SP37

Symbolical of the Strength of the Latvian Union SP36

"Charity" SP38

Wmk. Multiple Swastikas (212)

1936, Dec. 28 **Litho.** ***Perf. 11½***

B92 SP35 3s org red 1.50 2.00
B93 SP36 10s green 1.50 2.00
B94 SP37 20s rose pink 1.50 2.00
B95 SP38 35s blue 1.50 2.00
Set, never hinged 7.50

Souvenir Sheets

SP39

1938, May 12 **Wmk. 212** ***Perf. 11***
B96 SP39 Sheet of 2 5.50 12.00
a. 35s Justice Palace, Riga 1.50 2.00
b. 40s Power Station, Kegums 1.50 2.00
Never hinged 6.00

Sold for 2 l. The surtax of 1.25 l was for the National Reconstruction Fund.

Overprinted in Blue with Dates 1934 1939 and "15" over "V"

1939
B97 SP39 Sheet of 2 7.50 15.00
Never hinged 8.00

5th anniv. of Natl. Unity Day. Sold for 2 lats. Surtax for the Natl. Reconstruction Fund.

Catalogue values for unused stamps in this section, from this point to the end of the section, are for Never Hinged items.

Natl. Olympic Committee SP50

1992, Feb. 8 **Litho.** ***Perf. 13½x13***
Background Color
B150 SP50 50k +25k gray 1.50 1.50
B151 SP50 50k +25k buff 1.50 1.50
B152 SP50 100k +50k bister 3.00 3.00

No. B150 inscribed "Berlin 18.09.91."

AIR POST STAMPS

Blériot XI — AP1

Wmk. Wavy Lines Similar to 181
1921, July 30 **Litho.** ***Perf. 11½***
C1 AP1 10r emerald 1.75 1.25
a. Imperf. 7.50 10.50
C2 AP1 20r dark blue 1.75 1.25
a. Imperf. 7.50 10.50
Set, never hinged 4.25
Set, imperf, never hinged 18.00

1928, May 1
C3 AP1 10s dp grn 1.50 1.10
C4 AP1 15s red 1.50 1.10
C5 AP1 25s ultra 2.00 3.50
a. Pair, imperf. between 25.00
Set, never hinged 5.75

Nos. C1 to C5 sometimes show letters of a paper maker's watermark "PACTIEN LIGAT MILLS."

1931-32 **Wmk. 212** ***Perf. 11, 11½***
C6 AP1 10s dp grn 1.25 90
C7 AP1 15s red 1.90 1.40
C8 AP1 25s dp bl ('32) 2.50 1.65
Set, never hinged 6.50

Type of 1921 Overprinted or Surcharged in Black

LATVIJA-AFRIKA
1933.

1933, May 26 **Wmk. 212** ***Imperf.***
C9 AP1 10s dp grn 5.75 8.00
C10 AP1 15s red 5.75 8.00
C11 AP1 25s dp bl 10.50 16.00
C12 AP1 50s on 15s red 72.50 92.50
C13 AP1 100s on 25s dp bl 82.50 92.50
Nos. C9-C13 (5) 177.00 217.00
Set, never hinged 250.00

Issued to commemorate and finance a flight from Riga to Bathurst, Gambia. The plane crashed at Neustettin, Germany.

Counterfeits exist of Nos. C1-C13.

AIR POST SEMI-POSTAL STAMPS

Durbes Castle, Rainis Birthplace — SPAP1

Perf. 11½
1930, May 26 **Litho.** **Wmk. 212**
CB1 SPAP1 10s (20s) red & ol grn 3.75 5.00
CB2 SPAP1 15s (30s) dk yel grn & cop red 3.75 5.00
Set, never hinged 9.50

Surtax for the Rainis Memorial Fund.

Imperf.
CB1a SPAP1 10s (20s) 7.00 15.00
CB2a SPAP1 15s (30s) 7.00 15.00
Set, never hinged 16.00

Nos. C6-C8 Surcharged in Magenta, Blue or Red

1931, Dec. 5
CB3 AP1 10s + 50s dp grn (M) 4.50 7.75
CB4 AP1 15s + 1 l red (Bl) 4.50 7.75
CB5 AP1 25s + 1.50 l dp bl 4.50 7.75
Set, never hinged 16.00

Surtax for the Latvian Home Guards.

Imperf.
CB3a AP1 10s + 50s 7.75 7.75
CB4a AP1 15s + 1 l 7.75 7.75
CB5a AP1 25s + 1.50 l 7.75 7.75
Set, never hinged 24.00

SPAP2

1932, June 17 ***Perf. 10½***
CB6 SPAP2 10s (20s) dk sl grn & grn 11.00 14.00
CB7 SPAP2 15s (30s) brt red & buff 11.00 14.00
CB8 SPAP2 25s (50s) dp bl & gray 11.00 14.00
Set, never hinged 37.50

Surtax for the Latvian Home Guards.

Imperf.
CB6a SPAP2 10s (20s) 14.00 16.00
CB7a SPAP2 15s (30s) 14.00 16.00
CB8a SPAP2 25s (50s) 14.00 16.00
Set, never hinged 50.00

Latvia German Occupation Stamps can be mounted in Scott's Germany Part II Album.

Icarus — SPAP3 Leonardo da Vinci — SPAP4

Charles Balloon — SPAP5

Wright Brothers Biplane SPAP6

Bleriot Monoplane SPAP7

1932, Dec. ***Perf. 10, 11½***
CB9 SPAP3 5s (25s) ol bis & grn 8.50 8.50
CB10 SPAP4 10s (50s) ol brn & gray grn 8.50 8.50
CB11 SPAP5 15s (75s) red brn & gray grn 7.75 8.50
CB12 SPAP6 20s (1 l) gray grn & lil rose 6.50 7.50
CB13 SPAP7 25s (1.25 l) brn & bl 6.50 7.50
Nos. CB9-CB13 (5) 37.75 40.50
Set, never hinged 47.50

Issued to honor pioneers of aviation. The surtax of four times the face value was for wounded Latvian aviators.

Imperf.
CB9a SPAP3 5s (25s) 12.00 13.00
CB10a SPAP4 10s (50s) 12.00 13.00
CB11a SPAP5 15s (75s) 12.00 11.00
CB12a SPAP6 20s (1 l) 9.25 11.00
CB13a SPAP7 25s (1.25 l) 9.25 11.00
Nos. CB9a-CB13a (5) 54.50 59.00
Set, never hinged 62.50

Icarus Falling SPAP8

Monument to Aviators SPAP9

Proposed Tombs for Aviators
SPAP10 SPAP11

1933, Mar. 15 ***Perf. 11½***
CB14 SPAP8 2s (52s) blk & ocher 8.25 15.00
CB15 SPAP9 3s (53s) blk & red org 8.25 15.00
CB16 SPAP10 10s (60s) blk & dk yel grn 8.25 12.00
CB17 SPAP11 20s (70s) blk & cer 8.25 15.00
Set, never hinged 37.50

50s surtax for wounded Latvian aviators.

Imperf.
CB14a SPAP8 2s (52s) 11.00 14.00
CB15a SPAP9 3s (53s) 11.00 14.00
CB16a SPAP10 10s (60s) 11.00 14.00
CB17a SPAP11 20s (70s) 11.00 14.00
Set, never hinged 52.50

Monoplane Taking Off — SPAP12

Designs: 7s (57s), Biplane under fire at Riga. 35s (1.35 l), Map and planes.

1933, June 15 **Wmk. 212** ***Perf. 11½***
CB18 SPAP12 3s (53s) org & sl bl 14.00 17.00
CB19 SPAP12 7s (57s) sl bl & dk brn 14.00 17.00
CB20 SPAP12 35s (1.35 l) dp ultra & ol blk 14.00 17.00
Set, never hinged 47.50

Surtax for wounded Latvian aviators. Counterfeits exist.

Imperf.
CB18a SPAP12 3s (53s) 17.50 21.00
CB19a SPAP12 7s (57s) 17.50 21.00
CB20a SPAP12 35s (1.35 l) 17.50 21.00
Set, never hinged 62.50

American Gee-Bee SPAP13

English Seaplane S6B — SPAP14

Graf Zeppelin over Riga — SPAP15

DO-X SPAP16

1933, Sept. 5 ***Perf. 11½***
CB21 SPAP13 8s (68s) brn & gray blk 40.00 50.00
CB22 SPAP14 12s (1.12 l) brn car & ol grn 40.00 50.00
CB23 SPAP15 30s (1.30 l) bl & gray blk 40.00 50.00
CB24 SPAP16 40s (1.90 l) brn vio & ind 40.00 50.00
Set, never hinged 175.00

Surtax for wounded Latvian aviators.

Imperf.
CB21a SPAP13 8s (68s) 40.00 55.00
CB22a SPAP14 12s (1.12 l) 40.00 55.00
CB23a SPAP15 30s (1.30 l) 40.00 55.00
CB24a SPAP16 40s (1.90 l) 40.00 55.00
Set, never hinged 210.00

OCCUPATION STAMPS

Issued under German Occupation

German Stamps of 1905-18 Handstamped

1919 Wmk. 125 *Perf. 14, 14½*

Red Overprint

No.	Type	Description	Unused	Used
1N1	A22	2½pf gray	225.00	225.00
1N2	A16	5pf green	180.00	90.00
1N3	A22	15pf dk vio	275.00	90.00
1N4	A16	20pf blue vio	110.00	37.50
1N5	A16	25pf org & blk, *yel*	375.00	275.00
1N6	A16	50pf pur & blk, *buff*	375.00	275.00

Blue Overprint

No.	Type	Description	Unused	Used
1N7	A22	2½pf gray	225.00	225.00
1N8	A16	5pf green	110.00	57.50
1N9	A16	10pf carmine	92.50	27.50
1N10	A22	15pf dk vio	275.00	150.00
1N11	A16	20pf bl vio	110.00	27.50
1N12	A16	25pf org & blk, *yel*	375.00	275.00
1N13	A16	50pf pur & blk, *buff*	375.00	275.00

Inverted and double overprints exist, as well as counterfeit overprints.

Some experts believe that Nos. 1N1-1N7 were not officially issued. All used copies are canceled to order.

LATVIJA
1941.
1. VII

Russia Nos. 734, 616, 735, 617, 736 and 619A were overprinted in black or dark green with the three lines above in 1941. They were used in Latvia under the German occupation in July-September, 1941, and were replaced by German stamps in October, 1941.

Kurland

Four stamps of Germany were surcharged for use in Kurzeme in April, 1945, during World War II. Those are Germany Nos. 509, 511A and 516 (5pf, 10pf, 20pf with Hitler's head), surcharged "KURLAND" and "6", and No. MQ1 (red brown military parcel post stamp) surcharged "Kurland" and "12". After the Germans capitulated to the Russians May 8, 1945, in the territory of Latvia, these surcharged stamps were replaced by stamps of Russia.

ISSUED UNDER RUSSIAN OCCUPATION

The following stamps were issued at Mitau during the occupation of Kurland by the West Russian Army under Colonel Bermondt-Avalov.

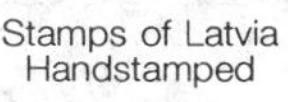
Stamps of Latvia Handstamped

1919 Wmk. 108 *Imperf.*

On Stamps of 1919

No.	Type	Description	Unused	Used
2N1	A1	3k lilac	12.50	17.50
2N2	A1	5k carmine	12.50	17.50
2N3	A1	10k dp blue	67.50	92.50
2N4	A1	20k orange	12.50	17.50
2N5	A1	25k gray	12.50	17.50
2N6	A1	35k dk brown	12.50	17.50
2N7	A1	50k purple	12.50	17.50
2N8	A1	75k emerald	15.00	22.50

On Riga Liberation Stamps

No.	Type	Description	Unused	Used
2N9	A2	5k carmine	7.50	12.50
2N10	A2	15k dp green	7.50	12.50
2N11	A2	35k brown	7.50	12.50

Stamps of Latvia Overprinted

On Stamps of 1919

No.	Type	Description	Unused	Used
2N12	A1	3k lilac	5.00	7.50
2N13	A1	5k carmine	5.00	7.50
2N14	A1	10k dp blue	60.00	92.50
2N15	A1	20k orange	10.00	15.00
2N16	A1	25k gray	17.50	32.50
2N17	A1	35k dk brown	12.50	17.50
2N18	A1	50k purple	12.50	17.50
2N19	A1	75k emerald	12.50	17.50

On Riga Liberation Stamps

No.	Type	Description	Unused	Used
2N20	A2	5k carmine	4.00	5.00
2N21	A2	15k dp green	4.00	5.00
2N22	A2	35k brown	4.00	5.00
a.		Inverted overprint	*115.00*	

The letters "Z. A." are the initials of "Zapadnaya Armiya"-i.e. Western Army.

Russian Stamps of 1909-17 Surcharged Like Illustration

Perf. 14, 14½x15

Unwmk.

On Stamps of 1909-12

No.	Type	Description	Unused	Used
2N23	A14	10k on 2k grn	4.00	5.00
a.		Inverted surcharge	*25.00*	
2N24	A15	30k on 4k car	3.50	4.50
2N25	A14	40k on 5k cl	3.50	4.50
2N26	A15	50k pn 10k dk bl	3.50	4.50
2N27	A11	70k on 15k red brn & bl	3.50	4.50
a.		Inverted surcharge	*50.00*	
2N28	A8	90k on 20k bl & car	3.50	4.50
2N29	A11	1r on 25k grn & vio	3.50	4.50
2N30	A11	1½r on 35k red brn & grn	22.50	37.50
2N31	A8	2r on 50k vio & grn	4.50	6.50
a.		Inverted surcharge	*30.00*	
2N32	A11	4r on 70k brn & org	12.50	15.00

Perf. 13½

No.	Type	Description	Unused	Used
2N33	A9	6r on 1r pale brn, brn & org	12.50	15.00

On Stamps of 1917

Imperf

No.	Type	Description	Unused	Used
2N34	A14	20k on 3k red	4.50	5.00
2N35	A14	40k on 5k claret	32.50	42.50
2N36	A12	10r on 3.50r mar & lt grn	32.50	42.55
a.		Inverted surcharge	*100.00*	
		Nos. 2N1-2N36 (36)	473.50	676.05

Eight typographed stamps of this design were prepared in 1919, but never placed in use. They exist both perforated and imperforate. Value, set, imperf. $1, perf. $2.

Reprints and counterfeits exist.

Arms of Soviet Latvia — OS1

1940 Typo. Wmk. 265 *Perf. 10*

No.	Type	Description	Unused	Used
2N45	OS1	1s dk violet	15	15
2N46	OS1	2s orange yel	15	15
2N47	OS1	3s orange ver	15	15
2N48	OS1	5s dk olive grn	15	15
2N49	OS1	7s turq green	15	15
2N50	OS1	10s slate grn	38	15
2N51	OS1	20s brown lake	65	15
2N52	OS1	30s light blue	75	25
2N53	OS1	35s brt ultra	15	15
2N54	OS1	40s chocolate	50	15
2N55	OS1	50s lt gray	65	15
2N56	OS1	1 l brown	1.25	25
2N57	OS1	5 l brt green	10.00	4.50
		Nos. 2N45-2N57 (13)	15.08	6.50
		Set, never hinged	17.00	

Used values of #2N45-2N57 are for CTOs. Commercially use are worth three times as much.

LEBANON

(Grand Liban)

LOCATION — Asia Minor, bordering on the Mediterranean Sea
GOVT. — Republic
AREA — 4,036 sq. mi.
POP. — 3,500,000 (est. 1984)
CAPITAL — Beirut

Formerly a part of the Syrian province of Turkey, Lebanon was occupied by French forces after World War I. It was mandated to France after it had been declared a separate state. Limited autonomy was granted in 1927 and full independence achieved in 1941. The French issued two sets of occupation stamps (with T.E.O. overprint) for Lebanon in late 1919. The use of these and later occupation issues (of 1920-24, with overprints "O.M.F." and "Syrie-Grand Liban") was extended to Syria, Cilicia, Alaouites and Alexandretta. By custom, these are all listed under Syria.

100 Centimes = 1 Piaster
100 Piasters = 1 Pound

Catalogue values for unused stamps in this country are for Never Hinged items, beginning with Scott 177 in the regular postage section, Scott B13 in the semi-postal section, Scott C97 in the airpost section, Scott CB5 in the airpost semi-postal section, Scott J37 in the postage due section, and Scott RA11 in the postal tax section.

Issued under French Mandate

Stamps of France 1900-21 Surcharged

GRAND
LIBAN
50
CENTIEMES

1924 Unwmk. *Perf. 14x13½*

No.	Type	Description	Unused	Used
1	A16	10c on 2c vio brn	60	35
a.		Inverted surcharge	15.00	9.00
2	A22	25c on 5c orange	60	16
3	A22	50c on 10c green	42	15
4	A20	75c on 15c sl grn	1.10	65
5	A22	1p on 20c red brn	65	22
a.		Double surcharge	15.00	9.00
b.		Inverted surcharge	15.00	9.00
6	A22	1.25p on 25c blue	1.75	80
7	A22	1.50p on 30c org	85	50
8	A22	1.50p on 30c red	85	50
9	A20	2.50p on 50c dl bl	85	35
a.		Inverted surcharge	15.00	9.00

Surcharged

GRAND LIBAN
2 PIASTRES

No.	Type	Description	Unused	Used
10	A18	2p on 40c red & pale bl	2.25	80
a.		Inverted surcharge	20.00	12.00
11	A18	3p on 60c violet & ultra	4.25	2.25
12	A18	5p on 1fr cl & ol green	4.25	2.25
13	A18	10p on 2fr org & pale bl	7.50	4.00
a.		Inverted surcharge	30.00	18.00
14	A18	25p on 5fr dk bl & buff	12.50	6.50
a.		Inverted surcharge	57.50	35.00
		Nos. 1-14 (14)	38.42	19.48

Broken and missing letters and varieties of spacing are numerous in these surcharges.

For overprints see Nos. C1-C4.

Stamps of France, 1923, (Pasteur) Surcharged "GRAND LIBAN" and New Values

No.	Type	Description	Unused	Used
15	A23	50c on 10c green	60	25
a.		Inverted surcharge	17.50	11.00
16	A23	1.50p on 30c red	80	42
17	A23	2.50p on 50c blue	60	25
a.		Inverted surcharge	17.50	11.00

Commemorative Stamps of France, 1924, (Olympic Games) Surcharged "GRAND LIBAN" and New Values

No.	Type	Description	Unused	Used
18	A24	50c on 10c gray grn & yel grn	14.00	14.00
a.		Inverted surcharge	100.00	
19	A25	1.25p on 25c rose & dk rose	14.00	14.00
a.		Inverted surcharge	100.00	
20	A26	1.50p on 30c brn red & blk	14.00	14.00
a.		Inverted surcharge	100.00	
21	A27	2.50p on 50c ultra & dk bl	14.00	14.00
a.		Inverted surcharge	100.00	

Stamps of France, 1900-24, Surcharged

C

Gᵃ Liban
0, P. 25
لبنان الكبير
١/٤ الغرش

1924-25

No.	Type	Description	Unused	Used
22	A16	10c on 2c vio brn	18	15
23	A22	25c on 5c orange	45	25
24	A22	50c on 10c green	65	35
25	A20	75c on 15c gray grn	45	25
26	A22	1p on 20c red brn	35	20
27	A22	1.25p on 25c blue	75	40
28	A22	1.50p on 30c red	65	35
29	A22	1.50p on 30c orange	35.00	22.50
30	A22	2p on 35c vio ('25)	80	45
31	A20	3p on 60c lt vio ('25)	1.00	55
32	A20	4p on 85c ver	1.50	80

Surcharged

Grand Liban
2 Piastres
لبنان الكبير
غرش ٢

No.	Type	Description	Unused	Used
33	A18	2p on 40c red & pale bl	35	20
a.		Second line of Arabic reads "2 Piastre" (singular)	90	50
34	A18	2p on 45c green & blue ('25)	18.00	10.00
35	A18	3p on 60c violet & ultra	1.00	55
36	A18	5p on 1fr cl & ol green	1.50	80
37	A18	10p on 2fr org & pale bl	4.50	2.50
38	A18	25p on 5fr dk bl & buff	7.25	3.50
		Nos. 22-38 (17)	74.38	43.80

Last line of surcharge on No. 33 has four characters, with a 9-like character between the third and fourth in illustration. Last line on No. 33a is as illustrated.

The surcharge may be found inverted on most of Nos. 22-38, and double on some values.

For overprints see Nos. C5-C8.

Stamps of France 1923-24 (Pasteur) Surcharged Type "c"

No.	Type	Description	Unused	Used
39	A23	50c on 10c green	32	22
a.		Inverted surcharge	9.25	7.00
b.		Double surcharge	8.00	6.00
40	A23	75c on 15c green	45	30
41	A23	1.50p on 30c red	55	35
a.		Inverted surcharge	12.00	9.00
42	A23	2p on 45c red	1.00	65
a.		Inverted surcharge	10.50	8.00
43	A23	2.50p on 50c blue	32	22
a.		Inverted surcharge	10.50	8.00
b.		Double surcharge	9.25	7.00
44	A23	4p on 75c blue	85	55
		Nos. 39-44 (6)	3.49	2.29

France Nos. 198 to 201 (Olympics) Surcharged Type "c"

No.	Type	Description	Unused	Used
45	A24	50c on 10c gray grn & yel grn	9.50	9.50
46	A25	1.25p on 25c rose & dk rose	9.50	9.50
47	A26	1.50p on 30c brn red & black	9.50	9.50
48	A27	2.50p on 50c ultra & dk bl	9.50	9.50

France No. 219 (Ronsard) Surcharged Type "c"

No.	Type	Description	Unused	Used
49	A28	4p on 75c bl, *bluish*	1.25	62
a.		Inverted surcharge	35.00	18.00

Cedar of Lebanon — A1

Crusader Castle, Tripoli — A3

View of Beirut — A2

Designs: 50c, Crusader Castle, Tripoli. 75c, Beit-ed-Din Palace. 1p, Temple of Jupiter, Baalbek. 1.25p, Mouktara Palace. 1.50p, Harbor of Tyre. 2p, View of Zahle. 2.50p, Ruins at Baalbek. 3p, Square at Deir-el-Kamar. 5p, Castle at Sidon. 25p, Square at Beirut.

1925 Litho. *Perf. 12½, 13½*

No.	Type	Description	Unused	Used
50	A1	10c dark violet	18	15

Photo.

No.	Type	Description	Unused	Used
51	A2	25c olive black	55	20
52	A2	50c yellow grn	18	15
53	A2	75c brn orange	38	15
54	A2	1p magenta	75	30
55	A2	1.25p deep green	1.00	50
56	A2	1.50p rose red	35	15
57	A2	2p dark brown	60	15
58	A2	2.50p peacock bl	75	30
59	A2	3p orange brn	1.10	40
60	A2	5p violet	1.10	50
61	A3	10p violet brn	2.25	80
62	A2	25p ultramarine	9.50	4.50
		Nos. 50-62 (13)	18.69	8.25

For surcharges and overprints see Nos. 63-107, B1-B12, C9-C38, CB1-CB4.

Stamps of 1925 with Bars and Surcharged **3P·50 غ٣ ١/٢**

1926

No.	Type	Description	Unused	Used
63	A2	3.50p on 75c brn org	35	25
64	A2	4p on 25c ol blk	55	40
65	A2	6p on 2.50p pck bl	45	35
66	A2	12p on 1.25p dp grn	55	40
67	A2	20p on 1.25p dp grn	1.90	1.40

Stamps of 1925 with Bars and Surcharged **4P·50 غ٤ ١/٢**

No.	Type	Description	Unused	Used
68	A2	4.50p on 75c brn org	65	50
69	A2	7.50p on 2.50p pck bl	65	50
70	A2	15p on 25p ultra	80	60
		Nos. 63-70 (8)	5.90	4.40

No. 51 with Bars and Surcharged **4P. غ٤**

1927

No.	Type	Description	Unused	Used
71	A2	4p on 25c ol blk	1.00	65

Issues of Republic under French Mandate

Stamps of 1925 Issue Overprinted in Black or Red **République Libanaise**

1927

No.	Type	Description	Unused	Used
72	A1	10c dark vio (R)	15	15
a.		Black overprint	18.00	11.00
73	A2	50c yellow grn	15	15
74	A2	1p magenta	20	15
75	A2	1.50p rose red	32	20
76	A2	2p dark brown	1.25	20
77	A2	3p orange brn	52	15
78	A2	5p violet	95	30
79	A3	10p violet brn	1.40	30
80	A2	25p ultramarine	6.00	65
		Nos. 72-80 (9)	10.94	
		Set value		1.90

On Nos. 72 and 79 the overprint is set in two lines. On all stamps the double bar obliterates GRAND LIBAN.

Same Overprint on Provisional Issues of 1926-27

15 PIASTERS ON 25 PIASTERS

TYPE I - "République Libanaise" at foot of stamp.

TYPE II - "République Libanaise" near top of stamp.

No.	Type	Description	Unused	Used
81	A2	4p on 25c ol blk	20	15
82	A2	4.50p on 75c brn org	35	15
83	A2	7.50p on 2.50p pck bl	52	15
84	A2	15p on 25p ultra (I)	4.50	1.40
a.		Type II	7.00	2.00

Most of Nos. 72-84 are known with overprint double, inverted or on back as well as face.

Stamps of 1927 Overprinted in Black or Red **الجمهورية اللبنانية**

1928

No.	Type	Description	Unused	Used
86	A1	10c dark vio (R)	25	16
a.		French overprint omitted	6.50	4.00
87	A2	50c yel grn (Bk)	75	45
a.		Arabic overprint inverted	3.25	2.00
88	A2	1p magenta (Bk)	32	20
a.		Inverted overprint	16.00	10.00
89	A2	1.50p rose red (Bk)	1.10	50
90	A2	2p dark brown (R)	1.25	80
90A	A2	2p dk brn (Bk+R)	65.00	40.00
91	A2	3p org brown (Bk)	55	35
92	A2	5p violet (Bk+R)	1.25	80
93	A2	5p violet (R)	7.50	6.00
a.		French ovpt. above Arabic	8.00	6.50
94	A3	10p vio brn (Bk)	2.25	1.40
a.		Double overprint	11.00	7.00
b.		Double overprint inverted		
c.		Inverted overprint	40.00	25.00
95	A2	25p ultra (Bk+R)	5.75	2.50
95A	A2	25p ultra (R)	8.25	4.00
		Nos. 86-95A (12)	94.22	57.16

On all stamps the double bar with Arabic overprint obliterates Arabic inscription.

Same Overprint on Nos. 81-84

No.	Type	Description	Unused	Used
96	A2	4p on 25c (Bk+R)	35	35
97	A2	4.50p on 75c (Bk)	65	50
98	A2	7.50p on 2.50p (Bk+R)	80	80
99	A2	7.50p on 2.50p (R)	4.00	4.00
100	A2	15p on 25p (II) (Bk+R)	2.50	2.50
a.		Arabic overprint inverted		
101	A2	15p on 25p (I) (R)	4.00	4.00
		Nos. 96-101 (6)	12.30	12.15

The new values are surcharged in black. The initials in ( ) refer to the colors of the overprints.

Stamps of 1925 Surcharged in Red or Black

Republique Libanaise
= 4P. غ٤ =
الجمهورية اللبنانية

1928-29 *Perf. 13½*

No.	Type	Description	Unused	Used
102	A2	50c on 75c brn org (Bk) ('29)	75	38
103	A2	2p on 1.25p dp grn	75	38
104	A2	4p on 25c ol blk	75	38
a.		Double surcharge	18.00	9.00
105	A2	7.50p on 2.50p pck bl	1.25	60
a.		Double surcharge	18.00	9.00
b.		Inverted surcharge	18.00	9.00
106	A2	15p on 25p ultra	10.50	5.25
		Nos. 102-106 (5)	14.00	6.99

On Nos. 103, 104 and 105 the surcharged numerals are 3¼mm high, and have thick strokes.

No. 86 Surcharged in Red **05 ٠٥**

1928

No.	Type	Description	Unused	Used
107	A1	5c on 10c dk vio	32	16

Silkworm, Cocoon and Moth — A4

1930, Feb. 11 Typo. *Perf. 11*

No.	Type	Description	Unused	Used
108	A4	4p black brown	7.50	5.25
109	A4	4½p vermilion	7.50	5.25
110	A4	7½p dark blue	7.50	5.25
111	A4	10p dk violet	7.50	5.25
112	A4	15p dark green	7.50	5.25
113	A4	25p claret	7.50	5.25
		Nos. 108-113 (6)	45.00	31.50

Sericultural Congress, Beirut. Presentation imperfs exist.

Pigeon Rocks, Ras Beirut — A5

View of Bickfaya — A8

Beit-ed-Din Palace — A10

Crusader Castle, Tripoli — A11

Ruins of Venus Temple, Baalbek A12

Ancient Bridge, Dog River — A13

Belfort Castle — A14

Afka Falls — A19

Designs: 20c, Cedars of Lebanon. 25c, Ruins of Bacchus Temple, Baalbek. 1p, Crusader Castle, Sidon Harbor. 5p, Arcade of Beit-ed-Din Palace. 6p, Tyre Harbor. 7.50p, Ruins of Sun Temple, Baalbek. 10p, View of Hasbeya. 25p, Government House, Beirut. 50p, View of Deir-el-Kamar. 75c, 100p, Ruins at Baalbek.

1930-35 Litho. *Perf. 12½, 13½*

No.	Type	Description	Unused	Used
114	A5	10c brn orange	15	15
115	A5	20c yellow brn	18	15
116	A5	25c deep blue	20	15

Photo.

No.	Type	Description	Unused	Used
117	A8	50c orange brn	65	30
118	A11	75c ol brn ('32)	22	15
119	A8	1p deep green	45	20
120	A8	1p brn vio ('35)	45	20
121	A10	1.50p violet brn	75	30
122	A10	1.50p dp grn ('32)	2.25	25
123	A11	2p Prussian bl	1.25	30
124	A12	3p black brown	95	30
125	A13	4p orange brn	95	15
126	A14	4.50p carmine	95	40
127	A14	5p greenish blk	65	20
128	A13	6p brn violet	2.50	45
129	A10	7.50p deep blue	95	25
130	A10	10p dk ol grn	3.25	25
131	A19	15p blk violet	3.00	42
132	A19	25p blue green	4.00	55
133	A8	50p apple grn	16.00	2.50
134	A11	100p black	16.00	7.00
		Nos. 114-134 (21)	55.75	14.62

See Nos. 135, 144, 152-155. For surcharges see Nos. 147-149, 161, 173-174.

Pigeon Rocks Type of 1930-35 Redrawn

1934 Litho. *Perf. 12½x12*

No.	Type	Description	Unused	Used
135	A5	10c dull orange	3.50	1.00

Lines in rocks and water more distinct. Printer's name "Hélio Vaugirard, Paris," in larger letters.

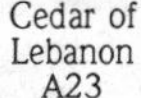
Cedar of Lebanon A23

President Emile Eddé A24

Dog River Panorama A25

1937-40 Typo. *Perf. 14x13½*

No.	Type	Description	Unused	Used
137	A23	10c rose car	15	15
137A	A23	20c aqua ('40)	15	15
137B	A23	25c pale rose lilac ('40)	15	15
138	A23	50c magenta	16	15
138A	A23	75c brown ('40)	18	15

Engr.
Perf. 13

No.	Type	Description	Unused	Used
139	A24	3p dark vio	1.40	30
140	A24	4p black brown	18	15
141	A24	4.50p carmine	30	15
142	A25	10p brn carmine	75	20
142A	A25	12½p dp ultra ('40)	25	15
143	A25	15p dk grn ('38)	1.25	30
143A	A25	20p chestnut ('40)	35	22
143B	A25	25p crimson ('40)	40	25
143C	A25	50p dk vio ('40)	2.25	65
143D	A25	100p sepia ('40)	1.40	90
		Nos. 137-143D (15)	9.32	4.02

Nos. 137A, 137B, 138A, 142A, 143A, 143B, 143C, and 143D exist imperforate.

For surcharges see Nos. 145-146A, 150-151, 160, 162, 175-176.

View of Bickfaya A26

Type A8 Redrawn

1937 Photo. *Perf. 13½*

No.	Type	Description	Unused	Used
144	A26	50c org brown	9.50	3.50

Arabic inscriptions more condensed.

Stamps of 1930-37 Surcharged in Black or Red

1937-42 *Perf. 13, 13½*

No.	Type	Description	Unused	Used
145	A24	2p on 3p dk vio	40	25
146	A24	2½p on 4p blk brn	40	25
146A	A24	2½p on 4p black brown (R) ('42)	40	25
147	A10	6p on 7.50p dp bl (R)	1.65	42

Stamps of 1930-35 and Type of 1937-40 Surcharged in Black or Red

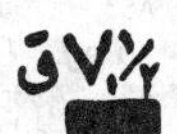

Perf. 13½, 13

No.	Type	Description	Unused	Used
148	A8	7.50p on 50p ap grn	95	60
149	A11	7.50p on 100p black (R)	95	60
150	A25	12.50p on 7.50p dark blue (R)	2.25	1.40

Type of 1937-40 Surcharged in Red with Bars and

12½

1939 Engr. *Perf. 13*

No.	Type	Description	Unused	Used
151	A25	12½p on 7.50p dk bl	65	35
		Nos. 145-151 (8)	7.65	4.12

Type of 1930-35 Redrawn

Imprint: "Beiteddine-Imp.-Catholique-Beyrouth-Liban."

1939 Litho. *Perf. 11½*

No.	Type	Description	Unused	Used
152	A10	1p dk slate grn	65	15
153	A10	1.50p brn violet	65	35
154	A10	7.50p carmine lake	65	40

Bridge Type of 1930-35

Imprint: "Degorce" instead of "Hélio Vaugirard"

1940 Engr. *Perf. 13*

No.	Type	Description	Unused	Used
155	A13	5p grnsh blue	45	15

Exists imperforate.

Independent Republic

Amir Beshir Shehab — A27

1942, Sept. 18 Litho. *Perf. 11½*

No.	Type	Description	Unused	Used
156	A27	50c emerald	1.10	1.10
157	A27	1.50p sepia	1.10	1.10
158	A27	6p rose pink	1.10	1.10
159	A27	15p dull blue	1.10	1.10

1st anniv. of the Proclamation of Independence, Nov. 26, 1941.

Nos. 156-159 exist imperforate.

Nos. 140, 154 and 142A Surcharged in Blue, Green or Black

10 P.

1943 *Perf. 13, 11½*

No.	Type	Description	Unused	Used
160	A24	2p on 4p (Bl)	2.50	2.00
161	A10	6p on 7.50p (G)	40	20
162	A25	10p on 12½p (Bk)	40	30

The surcharge is arranged differently on each value.

Parliament Building A28

Government House, Beirut — A29

1943 Litho. *Perf. 11½*

No.	Type	Description	Unused	Used
163	A28	25p salmon rose	8.00	5.00
164	A29	50p bluish green	8.00	5.00
165	A28	150p light ultra	8.00	5.00
166	A29	200p dull vio brn	8.00	5.00

2nd anniv. of Proclamation of Independence. Nos. 163-166 exist imperforate. See Nos. C82-C87. For overprints see Nos. 169-172.

Quarantine Station, Beirut — A30

1943, July 8 Photo.

Black Overprint

No.	Type	Description	Unused	Used
167	A30	10p cerise	2.75	2.00
168	A30	20p light blue	2.75	2.00
		Nos. 167-168,C88-C90 (5)	11.55	8.50

Arab Medical Congress, Beirut.

Nos. 163 to 166 Overprinted in Blue, Violet, Red or Black

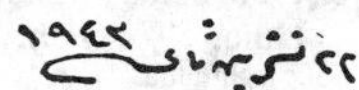

1944

No.	Type	Description	Unused	Used
169	A28	25p sal rose (Bl)	9.50	5.00
170	A29	50p bluish green (V)	9.50	5.00
171	A28	150p lt ultra (R)	9.50	5.00
172	A29	200p dull vio brn (Bk)	13.00	7.00
		Nos. 169-172,C91-C96 (10)	102.50	83.00

Return to office of the president and his ministers, Nov. 22, 1943.

Type of 1930 and No. 142A Surcharged in Violet, Black or Carmine

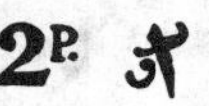

1945 Unwmk. Engr. *Perf. 13*

No.	Type	Description	Unused	Used
173	A13	2p on 5p dk bl grn (V)	35	16
174	A13	3p on 5p dk bl grn (Bk)	35	22
175	A25	6p on 12½p deep ultra (Bk)	45	25
176	A25	7½p on 12½p deep ultra (C)	80	65

Trees at bottom on Nos. 175 and 176.

Catalogue values for unused stamps in this section, from this point to the end of the section, are for Never Hinged items.

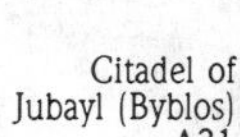

Citadel of Jubayl (Byblos) A31

Crusader Castle, Tripoli — A32

1945 Litho. *Perf. 11½*

No.	Type	Description	Unused	Used
177	A31	15p violet brown	1.90	1.10
178	A31	20p deep green	1.90	1.10
179	A32	25p deep blue	1.90	1.10
180	A32	50p dp carmine	3.50	1.25

See Nos. 229-233.

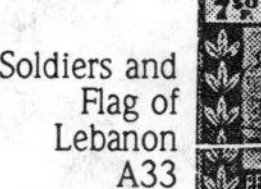

Soldiers and Flag of Lebanon A33

1946 Litho.

Stripes of Flag in Red Orange

No.	Type	Description	Unused	Used
181	A33	7.50p red & pale lil	40	15
182	A33	10p lil & pale lilac	50	15
183	A33	12.50p choc & yel grn	60	15
184	A33	15p sepia & pink	1.25	15
185	A33	20p ultra & pink	1.10	15
186	A33	25p dk grn & yel green	1.90	25
187	A33	50p dk bl & pale bl	3.00	90
188	A33	100p gray blk & pale bl	5.00	2.25
		Nos. 181-188 (8)	13.75	4.15

Type of 1946 Overprinted in Red

1946, May 8

Stripes of Flag in Red

No.	Type	Description	Unused	Used
189	A33	7.50p choc & pink	52	15
190	A33	10p dk vio & pink	75	15
191	A33	12.50p brn red & pale lilac	90	38
192	A33	15p lt grn & yel green	1.75	50
193	A33	20p sl grn & yel green	1.50	55
194	A33	25p sl bl & pale bl	2.50	75
195	A33	50p ultra & gray	4.50	70
196	A33	100p blk & pale bl	7.00	1.75
		Nos. 189-196 (8)	19.42	4.93

See Nos. C101-C106, note after No. C106.

Cedar of Lebanon A34

Night Herons over Mt. Sanin A35

1946-47 Unwmk. *Perf. 10½*

No.	Type	Description	Unused	Used
197	A34	50c red brn ('47)	48	15
198	A34	1p purple ('47)	48	15
199	A34	2.50p violet	90	15
200	A34	5p red	1.50	15
201	A34	6p gray ('47)	1.50	15

Perf. 11½

No.	Type	Description	Unused	Used
202	A35	12.50p deep car	11.00	15
		Nos. 197-202,C107-C110 (10)	32.86	4.64

For surcharge see No. 246.

A36

Crusader Castle, Tripoli — A37

1947 Litho. *Perf. 14x13½*

No.	Type	Description	Unused	Used
203	A36	50c dark brown	70	15
204	A36	2.50p bright green	1.40	15
205	A36	5p car rose	1.50	15

Perf. 11½

No.	Type	Description	Unused	Used
206	A37	12.50p rose pink	4.00	15
207	A37	25p ultramarine	6.25	18
208	A37	50p turq green	18.00	35
209	A37	100p violet	25.00	2.25
		Nos. 203-209 (7)	56.85	3.38

A38

Zebaide Aqueduct — A39

1948 *Perf. 14x13½*

No.	Type	Description	Unused	Used
210	A38	50c blue	15	15
211	A38	1p yel brown	18	15
212	A38	2.50p rose violet	38	15
213	A38	3p emerald	65	15
214	A38	5p crimson	75	15

Perf. 11½

No.	Type	Description	Unused	Used
215	A39	7.50p rose red	3.00	15
216	A39	10p dl violet	1.65	15
217	A39	12.50p blue	4.50	15
218	A39	25p blue vio	5.50	25
219	A39	50p green	12.00	1.75
		Nos. 210-219 (10)	28.76	
		Set value		2.45

See Nos. 227A-228A, 234-237. For surcharge see No. 245.

Europa A40

Avicenna A41

1948 Litho.

No.	Type	Description	Unused	Used
220	A40	10p dk red & org red	2.50	1.40
221	A40	12.50p pur & rose	3.25	1.90
222	A40	25p ol grn & pale green	4.00	1.50
223	A41	30p org brn & buff	5.75	1.50
224	A41	40p Prus grn & buff	7.25	1.50
		Nos. 220-224 (5)	22.75	7.80

UNESCO. Nos. 220 to 224 exist imperforate (see note after No. C145).

Camel Post Rider — A42

1949, Aug. 16 Unwmk. *Perf. 11½*

No.	Type	Description	Unused	Used
225	A42	5p violet	1.10	40
226	A42	7.50p red	1.65	60
227	A42	12.50p blue	2.75	1.00
		Nos. 225-227,C148-C149 (5)	12.50	5.25

UPU, 75th anniv. See note after No. C149.

Cedar Type of 1948 Redrawn and Jubayl Type of 1945

1949 Litho. *Perf. 14x13½*

No.	Type	Description	Unused	Used
227A	A38	50c blue	70	15
228	A38	1p red orange	1.00	15
228A	A38	2.50p rose lilac	7.50	35

Perf. 11½

No.	Type	Description	Unused	Used
229	A31	7.50p rose red	1.75	15
230	A31	10p violet brn	3.25	15
231	A31	12.50p deep blue	7.50	20
232	A31	25p violet	14.00	40
233	A31	50p green	30.00	1.90
		Nos. 227A-233 (8)	65.70	3.45

On No. 227A in left numeral tablet, top of "P" stands higher than flag of the 1¼mm high "5." On No. 210, tops of "P" and the 2mm "5" are on same line.

On No. 228, "1 P." is smaller than on No. 211, and has no line below "P."

On No. 228A, the "O" does not touch tablet frame; on No. 212, it does. No. 228A exists on gray paper.

Cedar Type of 1948 Redrawn and

Ancient Bridge across Dog River — A43

1950 Litho. *Perf. 14x13½*

234 A38 50c rose red 15 15
235 A38 1p salmon 30 15
236 A38 2.50p violet 60 15
237 A38 5p claret 1.10 15

Cedar slightly altered and mountains eliminated.

Perf. 11½

238 A43 7.50p rose red 65 15
239 A43 10p rose vio 1.10 15
240 A43 12.50p light blue 1.60 15
241 A43 25p deep blue 3.75 38
242 A43 50p emerald 8.75 1.65
Nos. 234-242 (9) 18.00
Set value 2.40

See Nos. 251-255, 310-312.

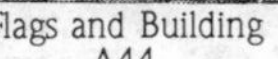

Flags and Building
A44

Cedar
A45

1950, Aug. 8 *Perf. 11½*

243 A44 7.50p gray 70 20
244 A44 12.50p lilac rose 70 20
Nos. 243-244,C150-C153 (6) 4.37 2.40

Conference of Emigrants, 1950. See note after No. C153.

Nos. 213 and 201 Surcharged with New Value and Bars in Carmine

1950 Unwmk. *Perf. 14x13½, 10½*

245 A38 1p on 3p emerald 20 15
246 A34 2.50p on 6p gray 95 15
Set value 15

1951 Litho. *Perf. 14x13½*

247 A45 50c rose red 20 15
248 A45 1p light brown 50 15
249 A45 2.50p slate gray 2.25 15
250 A45 5p rose lake 2.25 15

Bridge Type of 1950, Redrawn

Typo. *Perf. 11½*

251 A43 7.50p red 2.50 16
252 A43 10p dl rose vio 4.00 15
253 A43 12.50p blue 7.00 20
254 A43 25p dull blue 9.00 50
255 A43 50p green 20.00 3.50
Nos. 247-255 (9) 47.70 5.11

Nos. 238-242 are lithographed from a fine-screen halftone; "P" in the denomination has serifs. Nos. 251-255 are typographed and much coarser; "P" without serifs.

Cedar
A46

Ruins at Baalbek
A47

Design: 50p, 100p, Beaufort Castle.

1952 Litho. *Perf. 14x13½*

256 A46 50c emerald 42 15
257 A46 1p orange brn 42 15
258 A46 2.50p grnsh blue 65 15
259 A46 5p car rose 95 15

Perf. 11½

260 A47 7.50p red 1.40 20
261 A47 10p brt violet 2.75 22
262 A47 12.50p blue 2.75 22
263 A47 25p violet bl 3.75 45
264 A47 50p dk blue grn 10.00 90
265 A47 100p chocolate 20.00 2.50
Nos. 256-265 (10) 43.09 5.09

For unused stamps, more recent issues are valued as never hinged, with the beginning point determined on a country-by-country basis. Notes to show the beginning points are prominently placed in the text.

Cedar of Lebanon
A48

Postal Administration Building
A49

1953 *Perf. 14x13½*

266 A48 50c blue 32 15
267 A48 1p rose lake 32 15
268 A48 2.50p lilac 45 15
269 A48 5p emerald 80 15

Perf. 11½

270 A49 7.50p car rose 1.25 16
271 A49 10p dp yel grn 1.65 25
272 A49 12.50p aquamarine 2.75 30
273 A49 25p ultra 3.75 40
274 A49 50p violet brn 6.50 1.00
Nos. 266-274 (9) 17.79 2.71

See No. 306.

A50

Gallery, Beit-ed-Din Palace — A51

1954 *Perf. 14x13½*

275 A50 50c blue 15 15
276 A50 1p dp orange 18 15
277 A50 2.50p purple 52 15
278 A50 5p blue green 1.25 15

Perf. 11½

279 A51 7.50p dp carmine 2.50 20
280 A51 10p dl ol grn 3.00 20
281 A51 12.50p blue 6.25 25
282 A51 25p vio blue 7.75 80
283 A51 50p aqua 11.00 1.40
284 A51 100p black brn 25.00 2.50
Nos. 275-284 (10) 57.60 5.95

Arab Postal Union Issue

Globe — A52

1955, Jan. 1 Litho. *Perf. 13½x13*

285 A52 12.50p blue green 28 20
286 A52 25p violet 35 25

Founding of the APU, July 1, 1954. See No. C197.

Cedar
A53

Jeita Cave
A54

1955 *Perf. 14x13½*

287 A53 50c violet blue 15 15
288 A53 1p vermilion 15 15
289 A53 2.50p purple 18 15
290 A53 5p emerald 30 15

Perf. 11½

291 A54 7.50p deep orange 40 15
292 A54 10p yellow grn 60 15
293 A54 12.50p blue 65 15
294 A54 25p dp vio blue 1.60 15
295 A54 50p dk gray grn 2.25 25
Nos. 287-295 (9) 6.28
Set value 70

See Nos. 308-309, 315-318, 341-343A. For overprint see No. 351.

Cedar of Lebanon
A55

Globe and Columns
A56

1955 Unwmk. *Perf. 13x13½*

296 A55 50c dark blue 15 15
297 A55 1p deep orange 15 15
298 A55 2.50p deep violet 16 15
299 A55 5p green 16 15
300 A56 7.50p yel org & cop red 25 15
301 A56 10p emer & sal 35 15
302 A56 12.50p ultra & bl grn 50 15
303 A56 25p dp ultra & brt pink 1.00 15
304 A56 50p dk grn & lt bl 1.40 16
305 A56 100p dk brn & sal 2.00 40
Nos. 296-305 (10) 6.12
Set value 90

For surcharge see No. 333.

Cedar Type of 1953 Redrawn

1956 Litho. *Perf. 13x13½*

306 A48 2.50p violet 3.75 1.40

No. 306 measures 17x20½mm. The "2p.50" is in Roman (upright) type face.

Cedar Type of 1955 Redrawn and Bridge Type of 1950, Second Redrawing

1957 Litho. *Perf. 13x13½*

308 A53 50c light ultra 20 15
309 A53 2.50p claret 55 22

Perf. 11½

310 A43 7.50p vermilion 80 35
311 A43 10p brn orange 1.10 40
312 A43 12.50p blue 1.50 50
Nos. 308-312 (5) 4.15 1.62

On Nos. 308 and 309 numerals are slanted and clouds slightly changed.

Nos. 310-312 inscribed "Liban" instead of "Republique Libanaise," and different Arabic characters.

Runners — A57

1957, Sept. 12 Litho. *Perf. 13*

313 A57 2.50p shown 38 20
314 A57 12.50p Soccer players 65 35

Second Pan-Arab Games, Beirut. See Nos. C243-C244.

A souvenir sheet of four contains one each of Nos. 313-314, C243-C244.

Cedar Type of 1955 Redrawn and

Workers
A58

Ancient Potter
A59

1957 Unwmk. *Perf. 13x13½*

315 A53 50c light blue 15 15
316 A53 1p light brown 16 15
317 A53 2.50p bright vio 32 15
318 A53 5p light green 75 15

Perf. 11½, 13½x13 (A59)

319 A58 7.50p crim rose 65 15
320 A58 10p dull red brn 85 15
321 A58 12.50p bright blue 1.25 15
322 A59 25p dull blue 90 15
323 A59 50p yellow grn 1.90 16
324 A59 100p sepia 2.75 60
Nos. 315-324 (10) 9.68
Set value 1.20

The word "piaster" is omitted on No. 315; on Nos. 316 and 318 there is a line below "P"; on No. 317 there is a period between "2" and "50."

Nos. 315-318 are 16mm wide and have three shading lines above tip of cedar. See No. 343A and footnote.

For surcharges see Nos. 334-335, 339.

Cedar of Lebanon
A60

Soldier and Flag
A61

1958 Litho. *Perf. 13*

325 A60 50c blue 15 15
326 A60 1p dull orange 15 15
327 A60 2.50p violet 16 15
328 A60 5p yellow grn 30 15
329 A61 12.50p bright blue 60 15
330 A61 25p dark blue 70 15
331 A61 50p orange brn 1.00 15
332 A61 100p black brn 2.00 25
Nos. 325-332 (8) 5.06
Set value 75

For surcharges see Nos. 336-338.

مؤتمر المحامين العرب
من ١ الى ٥ ايلول ١٩٥٩

No. 304 Surcharged

30P. ٣٠ق

1959, Sept. 1

333 A56 30p on 50p dk grn & lt bl 65 25

Arab Lawyers Congress. See No. C265.

No. 323 Surcharged

مؤتمر المغتربين
صيف - ١٩٥٩
30P. ٣٠ق

1959 *Perf. 13½x13*

334 A59 30p on 50p yel grn 50 22
335 A59 40p on 50p yel grn 75 35

Convention of the Assoc. of Arab Emigrants in the United States.

Nos. 329-330 and 323 Surcharged with New Value and Bars

1959 *Perf. 13, 13½x13*

336 A61 7.50p on 12.50p brt bl 20 15
337 A61 10p on 12.50p brt bl 24 15
338 A61 15p on 25p dark blue 32 15
339 A59 40p on 50p yel grn 80 16
Nos. 336-339,C271 (5) 3.21
Set value 60

Arab League Center, Cairo — A62

1960 Unwmk. Litho. *Perf. 13x13½*

340 A62 15p light blue grn 55 15

Opening of the Arab League Center and the Arab Postal Museum in Cairo.
For overprint see No. 352.

Cedar Type of 1955, Second Redrawing

1960 Litho. *Perf. 13x13½*

341 A53 50c light violet 15 15
342 A53 1p rose claret 16 15
343 A53 2.50p ultramarine 26 15
343A A53 5p light green 35 15
Set value 22

Nos. 341-343A are 16½-17mm wide and have two shading lines above cedar. In other details they resemble the redrawn A53 type of 1957 (Nos. 315-318).

President Fuad Chehab
A63 A64

1960 Photo. *Perf. 13½*

344 A63 50c deep green 15 15
345 A63 2.50p olive 15 15
346 A63 5p green 15 15
347 A63 7.50p rose brown 18 15
348 A63 15p bright blue 28 15
349 A63 50p lilac 70 15
350 A63 100p brown 1.25 18
Nos. 344-350 (7) 2.86
Set value 55

Nos. 343A and 340 Overprinted in Red

1960, Nov. Litho. *Perf. 13x13½*

351 A53 5p light green 16 15
352 A62 15p lt blue green 50 18
Set value 24

Arabian Oil Conference, Beirut.

1961, Feb. Litho. *Perf. 13½x13*

353 A64 2.50p blue & light bl 15 15
354 A64 7.50p dark vio & pink 15 15
355 A64 10p red brn & yel 20 15
Set value 40 20

Cedar
A65

Post Office, Beirut
A66

1961 Unwmk. Litho. *Perf. 13*

356 A65 2.50p green 75 15

Redrawn

357 A65 2.50p orange 1.00 25
358 A65 5p maroon 18 15
359 A65 10p black 24 15

Nos. 357-359 have no clouds.

Perf. 11½

361 A66 2.50p rose carmine 24 15
362 A66 5p bright green 75 15
363 A66 15p dark blue 45 15
Nos. 356-363 (7) 3.61
Set value 65

Cedars — A67

Design: 10p, 15p, 50p, 100p, View of Zahle.

1961 Litho. *Perf. 13*

365 A67 50c yellow green 15 15
366 A67 1p brown 15 15
367 A67 2.50p ultramarine 20 15
368 A67 5p carmine 40 15
369 A67 7.50p violet 60 15
370 A67 10p dark brown 85 15
371 A67 15p dark blue 95 15
372 A67 50p dark green 1.50 22
373 A67 100p black 1.75 35
Set value 90

See Nos. 381-384.

Unknown Soldier Monument — A68

1961, Dec. 30 Unwmk. *Perf. 12*

374 A68 10p shown 55 15
375 A68 15p Soldier & flag 80 18

Anniv. of Lebanon's independence; evacuation of foreign troops, Dec. 31, 1946.
See Nos. C329-C330.

Bugler — A69

Scout Carrying Flag and Scout Emblem
A70

Designs: 2.50p, First aid. 6p, Lord Baden-Powell. 10p, Scouts building campfire.

1962, Mar. 1 Litho. *Perf. 12*

376 A69 50c yel grn, blk & yel 15 15
377 A70 1p multicolored 15 15
378 A70 2.50p dk red, blk & grn 15 15
379 A69 6p multicolored 15 15
380 A70 10p dp bl, blk & yel 15 15
Nos. 376-380,C331-C333 (8) 1.95
Set value 80

50th anniversary of Lebanese Boy Scouts.

Type of 1961 Redrawn

Designs as before.

1962 Unwmk. *Perf. 13*

381 A67 50c yellow green 16 15
382 A67 1p brown 16 15
383 A67 2.50p ultramarine 24 15
384 A67 15p dark blue 2.00 20
Nos. 381-384,C341-C342 (6) 8.66
Set value 84

Temple of Nefertari, Abu Simbel — A71

Cherries — A72

1962, Aug. 1 Unwmk. *Perf. 13*

390 A71 5p light ultra 42 15
391 A71 15p brn lake & mar 60 15

Campaign to save the historic monuments in Nubia. See Nos. C351-C352.

1962 Litho.

Designs: 50c, 2.50p, 7.50p, Cherries. 1p, 5p, Figs. 10p, 17.50p, 30p, Grapes. 50p, Oranges. 100p, Pomegranates.

Vignette Multicolored

392 A72 50c violet blue 15 15
393 A72 1p gray blue 15 15
394 A72 2.50p brown 15 15
395 A72 5p bright blue 16 15
396 A72 7.50p lilac rose 20 15
397 A72 10p chocolate 25 15
398 A72 17.50p slate 40 15
399 A72 30p slate grn 75 15
400 A72 50p green 1.10 16
401 A72 100p brown blk 2.75 50
Nos. 392-401,C359-C366 (18) 12.40
Set value 2.40

Elementary Schoolboy — A73

1962, Oct. 1 Litho. *Perf. 12*

404 A73 30p multicolored 40 18

Students' Day, Oct. 1. See No. C355.

Cedar of Lebanon
A74 A75

1963-64 Unwmk. *Perf. 13x13½*

405 A74 50c green 1.20 15
406 A75 50c gray grn ('64) 25 15
407 A75 2.50p ultra ('64) 25 15
408 A75 5p brt pink ('64) 38 15
409 A75 7.50p orange ('64) 45 15
410 A75 17.50p rose lil ('64) 85 18
Nos. 405-410 (6) 3.38
Set value 66

Bicyclist — A76 Hyacinth — A77

1964, Feb. 11 Litho. *Perf. 13*

415 A76 2.50p shown 15 15
416 A76 5p Basketball 16 15
417 A76 10p Track 18 15
Nos. 415-417,C385-C387 (6) 1.51
Set value 58

4th Mediterranean Games, Naples, Sept. 21-29, 1963.

1964 Unwmk. *Perf. 13x13½*

Size: 26x27mm

418 A77 50c shown 15 15
419 A77 1p Hyacinth 15 15
420 A77 2.50p Hyacinth 15 15
421 A77 5p Cyclamen 15 15
422 A77 7.50p Cyclamen 16 15

Perf. 13

Size: 26x37mm

423 A77 10p Poinsettia 30 15
424 A77 17.50p Anemone 80 15
425 A77 30p Iris 1.10 22
426 A77 50p Poppy 2.50 45
Nos. 418-426 (9) 5.46
Set value 1.00

See Nos. C391-C397.

Temple of the Sun, Baalbek
A78

1965, Jan. 11 Litho. *Perf. 13x13½*

429 A78 2.50p blk & red org 16 15
430 A78 7.50p black & blue 50 15
Nos. 429-430,C420-C423 (6) 3.21 1.50

International Festival at Baalbek.

Swimmer
A79

1965, Jan. 23 Engr. *Perf. 13*

431 A79 2.50p shown 15 15
432 A79 7.50p Fencer 40 15
433 A79 10p Basketball, vert. 50 22
Nos. 431-433,C424-C426 (6) 2.22
Set value 78

18th Olympic Games, Toyko, Oct. 10-25, 1964.

Golden Oriole — A80

1965 Engr. *Perf. 13*

434 A80 5p Bullfinch 15 15
435 A80 10p European goldfinch 75 15
436 A80 15p Hoopoe 35 15
437 A80 17.50p Rock partridge 60 15
438 A80 20p shown 75 15
439 A80 32.50p European bee-eater 1.10 15
Nos. 434-439 (6) 3.70
Set value 40

For surcharge see No. 459.

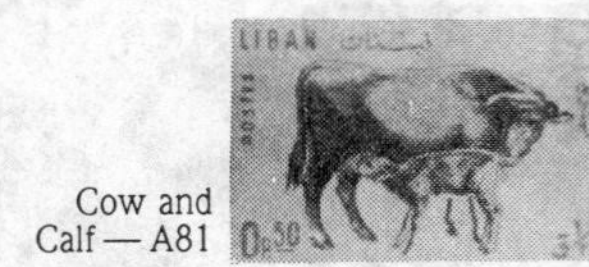

Cow and Calf — A81

1965 Photo. *Perf. 11x12*

440 A81	50c	shown	15	15
441 A81	1p	Rabbit	20	15
442 A81	2.50p	Ewe & lamb	26	15
		Set value		32

Hippodrome, Beirut — A82

Designs: 1p, Pigeon Rocks. 2.50p, Tabarja. 5p, Ruins, Beit-Méry. 7.50p, Statue and ruins, Anjar.

1966 Unwmk. *Perf. 12x11½*

443 A82	50c	gold & multi	15	15
444 A82	1p	gold & multi	16	15
445 A82	2.50p	gold & multi	20	15
446 A82	5p	gold & multi	25	15
447 A82	7.50p	gold & multi	30	15
		Nos. 443-447 (5)	1.06	
		Set value		40

See #C486-C492. For surcharge see #460.

ITY Emblem and Cedars — A83

1967 Photo. *Perf. 11x12*

448 A83	50c	lem, blk & brt bl	15	15
449 A83	1p	sal, blk & brt bl	15	15
450 A83	2.50p	gray, blk & brt bl	15	15
451 A83	5p	lt rose lil, blk & brt bl	15	15
452 A83	7.50p	yel, blk & brt bl	15	15
		Nos. 448-452 (5)	75	
		Set value		40

Intl. Tourist Year; used as a regular issue. See #C515-C522. For surcharge see #461.

Goat and Kid — A84

1968, Feb. Photo. *Perf. 12x11½*

453 A84	50c	shown	15	15
454 A84	1p	Cattle	24	15
455 A84	2.50p	Sheep	35	15
456 A84	5p	Camels	45	15
457 A84	10p	Donkey	55	15
458 A84	15p	Horses	75	15
		Nos. 453-458 (6)	2.49	
		Set value		30

See Nos. C534-C539.

No. 439 Surcharged

1972, Apr. Engr. *Perf. 13*

459 A80	25p on 32.50p multi	60	15

Nos. 447 and 452 Surcharged with New Value and Bars

Perf. 12x11½, 11x12

1972, May Photo.

460 A82	5p on 7.50p multi	38	15
461 A83	5p on 7.50p multi	38	15
	Set value		16

Cedar — A85

Army Badge — A86

1974 Litho. *Perf. 11*

462 A85	50c orange & olive	2.00	25

1980, Dec. 28 Litho. *Perf. 11½*

463 A86	25p multicolored	45	15

Army Day. See Nos. C792-C793.

Pres. Elias Sarkis — A87

World Communications Year — A89

World Food Day, Oct. 16, 1981 A88

1981, Sept. 23 Photo. *Perf. 14x13½*

464 A87	125p multicolored	1.00	50
465 A87	300p multicolored	1.00	1.00
466 A87	500p multicolored	2.75	1.50

1982, Nov. 23 Photo. *Perf. 12x11½*

467 A88	50p Stork carrying food packages	40	25
468 A88	75p Wheat, globe	55	38
469 A88	100p Produce	80	50

1983, Dec. 19 Photo. *Perf. 14*

470 A89	300p multicolored	1.75

Illustrations from Khalil Gibran's The Prophet A90

1983, Dec. 19 *Perf. 13½x14*

471 A90	200p	The Soul Is Back	90	
472 A90	300p	The Family	1.40	
473 A90	500p	Self-portrait	2.25	
474 A90	1000p	The Prophet	5.00	
a.		Souvenir sheet, #471-474	12.50	

No. 474a sold for £25.

Scouting Year — A91

Cedar of Lebanon — A93

1983, Dec. 19 *Perf. 14*

475 A91	200p	Rowing	1.25
476 A91	300p	Signaling	1.65
477 A91	500p	Camp	3.00

1984, Dec. Photo. *Perf. 14½x13½*

481 A93	5p multicolored	60

Flowers — A94

Defense — A95

1984, Dec. Photo. *Perf. 14½x13½*

482 A94	10p	Iris of Sofar	22
483 A94	25p	Periwinkle	45
484 A94	50p	Flowering thorn	80

1984, Dec. Photo. *Perf. 14½x13½*

485 A95	75p	Dove over city	35
486 A95	150p	Soldier, cedar	75
487 A95	300p	Olive wreath, cedar	1.40

Temple Ruins — A96

1985 Photo. *Perf. 13½x14½*

488 A96	100p	Fakra	38
489 A96	200p	Bziza	65
490 A96	500p	Tyre	1.40

Pres. Gemayel, Map of Lebanon, Dove, Text — A97

Pres. Gemayel, Military Academy Graduate — A98

1988, Feb. 1 Litho. *Perf. 14*

491 A97	£50 multicolored	3.25

1988, Mar. 9

492 A98	£25 multicolored	2.75

Arab Scouts, 75th Anniv. — A99

1988, Mar. 9 *Perf. 13½x14½*

493 A99	£20 multicolored	2.25

UN Child Survival Campaign — A100

1988, Mar. 9 *Perf. 14½x13½*

494 A100	£15 multicolored	1.25

Prime Minister Rashid Karame (1921-1987), Satellite, Flags, Earth — A101

1988, Mar. 9 *Perf. 13½x14½*

495 A101	£10 multicolored	1.00

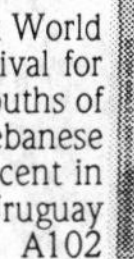

1st World Festival for Youths of Lebanese Descent in Uruguay A102

1988, Mar. 9

496 A102	£5 multicolored	1.00

Cedar — A103

1989 Photo. *Perf. 13x13½*

497 A103	£50	dk grn & vio	65
498 A103	£70	dk grn & brn	95
499 A103	£100	dk grn & brt yel	1.25
500 A103	£200	dk grn & bluish grn	2.75
501 A103	£500	dk grn & brt yel grn	6.75

SEMI-POSTAL STAMPS

Regular Issue of 1925 Surcharged in Red or Black

Secours aux Réfugiés

اعانات للاجئين

Aff^{t} الاجرة

0^{P}.25 ¼ غ

1926 Unwmk. *Perf. 14x13½*

B1	A2	25c + 25c ol blk	1.40	1.40
B2	A2	50c + 25c yellow green (B)	1.40	1.40
B3	A2	75c + 25c brown orange (B)	1.40	1.40
B4	A2	1p + 50c mag	1.40	1.40
B5	A2	1.25p + 50c dp grn	1.60	1.60
B6	A2	1.50p + 50c rose red (B)	1.60	1.60
a.		Double surcharge	14.00	14.00
B7	A2	2p + 75c dk brn	1.40	1.40
B8	A2	2.50p + 75c pck bl	1.60	1.60
B9	A2	3p + 1p org brn	1.60	1.60
B10	A2	5p + 1p vio (B)	1.60	1.60
B11	A3	10p + 2p violet brown (B)	1.60	1.60
B12	A2	25p + 5p ultra	1.60	1.60
		Nos. B1-B12 (12)	18.20	18.20

On No. B11 the surcharge is set in six lines to fit the shape of the stamp. All values of this series exist with inverted surcharge. Value each, $14.

See Nos. CB1-CB4.

Catalogue values for unused stamps in this section, from this point to the end of the section, are for Never Hinged items.

Boxing — SP1

1961, Jan. 12 Litho. *Perf. 13*

B13 SP1 2.50p + 2.50p shown 15 15
B14 SP1 5p + 5p Wrestling 15 15
B15 SP1 7.50p + 7.50p Shot put 18 20
Nos. B13-B15,CB12-CB14 (6) 4.68 3.50

17th Olympic Games, Rome, Aug. 25-Sept. 11, 1960.

Nos. B13-B15 with Arabic and French Overprint in Black, Blue or Green and two Bars through Olympic Inscription: "CHAMPIONNAT D'EUROPE DE TIR, 2 JUIN 1962"

1962, June 2

B16 SP1 2.50p + 2.50p blue & brn (Bk) 22 15
B17 SP1 5p + 5p org & brn (G) 42 16
B18 SP1 7.50p + 7.50p vio & brn (Bl) 60 42
Nos. B16-B18,CB15-CB17 (6) 5.69 3.28

European Marksmanship Championships held in Lebanon.

Red Cross — SP2

1988, June 8 Litho. *Perf. 14*

B19 SP2 £10 + £1 shown 1.00
B20 SP2 £20 + £2 Stylized profile 2.00
B21 SP2 £30 + £3 Globe, emblems, dove 3.00

AIR POST STAMPS

Nos. 10 to 13 with Additional Overprint

Poste par Avion

1924 Unwmk. *Perf. 14x13½*

C1 A18 2p on 40c 4.25 *4.00*
a. Double surcharge 15.00
C2 A18 3p on 60c 4.25 *4.00*
C3 A18 5p on 1fr 4.25 *4.00*
a. Dbl. surch. and ovpt. 18.00
C4 A18 10p on 2fr 4.25 *4.00*
a. Invtd. surch. and ovpt. 55.00 35.00

Nos. 33, 35-37 Overprinted

Avion طيارة

C5 A18 2p on 40c 6.00 4.00
C6 A18 3p on 60c 6.00 4.00
C7 A18 5p on 1fr 6.00 4.00
a. Overprint reversed 21.00
C8 A18 10p on 2fr 6.00 4.00
a. Overprint reversed 21.00
b. Double surcharge 21.00

Nos. 57, 59-61 Overprinted in Green

AVION طيارة

1925

C9 A2 2p dark brown 1.65 1.25
C10 A2 3p orange brown 1.65 1.25
C11 A2 5p violet 1.65 1.25
a. Inverted overprint 7.75
C12 A3 10p violet brown 1.65 1.25

Nos. 57, 59-61 Overprinted in Red

c

1926

C13 A2 2p dark brown 1.75 1.25
C14 A2 3p orange brown 1.75 1.25
C15 A2 5p violet 1.75 1.25
C16 A3 10p violet brown 1.75 1.25

Exist with inverted overprint. Value, each $14.

Issues of Republic under French Mandate

Nos. C13-C16 Overprinted

République Libanaise

d

1927

C17 A2 2p dark brown 1.75 1.25
C18 A2 3p orange brown 1.75 1.25
C19 A2 5p violet 1.75 1.25
C20 A3 10p violet brown 1.75 1.25

Overprint set in two lines on No. C20.

Nos. C17-C20 with Additional Overprint

الجمهورية اللبنانية

e

1928

Black Overprint

C21 A2 2p dark brown 6.00 3.00
a. Double overprint 20.00
b. Inverted overprint 20.00
C22 A2 3p orange brown 6.00 3.00
a. Double overprint 20.00
C23 A2 5p violet 6.00 3.00
a. Double overprint 13.00
C24 A3 10p violet brown 6.00 3.00
a. Double overprint 13.00

Red Overprint

C25 A2 2p dark brown 1.25 65
C26 A2 3p orange brown 1.25 65
C27 A2 5p violet 1.25 65
C28 A3 10p violet brown 2.00 65
Nos. C21-C28 (8) 29.75 14.60

On Nos. C21-C28 the airplane is always in red.
The red overprint of a silhouetted plane and "Republique Libanaise," as on Nos. C25-C27, was also applied to Nos. C9-C12. These are believed to have been essays, and were not regularly issued.

Nos. 52, 54 and 62 Overprinted Type "e" in Red or Black

1929

C33 A2 50c yel green (R) 42 35
a. Inverted overprint 17.50 14.00
C34 A2 1p magenta (Bk) 50 42
a. Inverted overprint 17.50 14.00
C35 A2 25p ultra (R) 80.00 65.00
a. Inverted overprint 225.00 190.00

No. 62 with Surcharge Added in Red

Two types of surcharge:
I- The "5" of "15 P." is italic. The "15" is 4mm high. Arabic characters for "Lebanese Republic" and for "15 P." are on same line in that order.
II- The "5" is in Roman type (upright) and smaller; "15" is 3½mm high. Arabic for "Lebanese Republic" is centered on line by itself, with Arabic for "15 P." below right end of line.

C36 A2 15p on 25p ultra (I) 100.00 100.00
a. Type II (#106) *500.00 500.00*

Nos. 102 Overprinted Type "c" in Blue

C37 A2 50c on 75c 30 22
a. Airplane inverted 19.00
b. French and Arabic surcharge inverted 19.00
c. "P" omitted 8.75
d. Airplane double 19.00

No. 55 Surcharged in Red

1930

C38 A2 2p on 1.25p dp grn 50 42
a. Inverted surcharge 16.00 14.00

Airplane over Racheya — AP2

Designs: 1p, Plane over Broumana. 2p, Baalbek. 3p, Hasroun. 5p, Byblos. 10p, Kadicha River. 15p, Beirut. 25p, Tripoli. 50p, Kabeljas. 100p, Zahle.

1930-31 Photo. *Perf. 13½*

C39 AP2 50c dk vio ('31) 15 15
C40 AP2 1p yel grn ('31) 25 15
C41 AP2 2p dp org ('31) 50 30
C42 AP2 3p magenta ('31) 50 30
C43 AP2 5p indigo 50 30
C44 AP2 10p orange red 1.25 50
C45 AP2 15p orange brn 65 40
C46 AP2 25p gray vio ('31) 1.10 65
C47 AP2 50p dp claret 4.00 2.25
C48 AP2 100p olive brown 5.00 2.75
Nos. C39-C48 (10) 13.90 7.75

Nos. C39 to C48 exist imperforate.

Tourist Publicity Issue

Skiing in Lebanon AP12

Bay of Jounie AP13

1936, Oct. 12

C49 AP12 50c slate grn 1.00 1.00
C50 AP13 1p red orange 1.20 1.20
C51 AP12 2p blk violet 1.20 1.20
C52 AP13 3p yellow grn 1.20 1.20
C53 AP12 5p brown car 1.20 1.20
C54 AP13 10p orange brn 1.20 1.20
C55 AP13 15p dk carmine 16.00 16.00
C56 AP12 25p green 45.00 45.00
Nos. C49-C56 (8) 68.00 68.00

Nos. C49 to C56 exist imperforate.

Lebanese Pavilion at Exposition AP14

1937, July 1 *Perf. 13½*

C57 AP14 50c olive blk 50 50
C58 AP14 1p yellow grn 50 50
C59 AP14 2p dk red org 50 50
C60 AP14 3p dk ol grn 50 50
C61 AP14 5p dp green 65 65
C62 AP14 10p car lake 3.50 3.50
C63 AP14 15p rose lake 3.75 3.75
C64 AP14 25p orange brn 6.50 6.50
Nos. C57-C64 (8) 16.40 16.40

Paris International Exposition.

Arcade of Beit-ed-Din Palace AP15

Ruins of Baalbek AP16

1937-40 Engr. *Perf. 13*

C65 AP15 50c ultra ('38) 15 15
C66 AP15 1p hn brn ('40) 22 16
C67 AP15 2p sepia ('40) 20 15
C68 AP15 3p rose ('40) 90 35
C69 AP15 5p lt grn ('40) 22 15
C70 AP16 10p dull vio 22 15
C71 AP16 15p turq bl ('40) 75 50
C72 AP16 25p violet ('40) 1.90 1.40
C73 AP16 50p yel grn ('40) 3.50 2.00
C74 AP16 100p brown ('40) 1.90 1.00
Nos. C65-C74 (10) 9.96 6.01

Nos. C65-C74 exist imperforate.

Medical College of Beirut AP17

1938, May 9 Photo. *Perf. 13*

C75 AP17 2p green 80 1.00
C76 AP17 3p orange 80 1.00
C77 AP17 5p lilac gray 1.60 2.00
C78 AP17 10p lake 4.00 5.50

Medical Congress.

Maurice Noguès and View of Beirut AP18

1938, July 15 *Perf. 11*

C79 AP18 10p brn carmine 2.50 1.25
a. Souv. sheet of 4, perf. 13½ 16.00 16.00
b. Perf. 13½ 5.00 2.50

10th anniversary of first Marseille-Beirut flight, by Maurice Noguès.
No. C79a has marginal inscriptions in French and Arabic. Exists imperf.; value $250.

Independent Republic

Plane Over Mt. Lebanon AP19

1942, Sept. 18 Litho. *Perf. 11½*

C80 AP19 10p dk brown vio 1.25 2.00
C81 AP19 50p dk gray grn 1.25 2.00

1st anniv. of the Proclamation of Independence, Nov. 26, 1941.
Nos. C80 and C81 exist imperforate.

Bechamoun AP20

Rachaya Citadel — AP21

Air View of Beirut — AP22

1943, May 1 *Perf. 11½*

C82	AP20	25p yellow grn	1.10	1.00
C83	AP20	50p orange	1.65	1.25
C84	AP21	100p buff	1.65	1.10
C85	AP21	200p blue vio	2.25	1.90
C86	AP22	300p sage green	7.25	6.25
C87	AP22	500p sepia	15.00	13.00
		Nos. C82-C87 (6)	28.90	24.50

2nd anniv. of the Proclamation of Independence. Nos. C82-C87 exist imperforate.

For overprints see Nos. C91-C96.

Bhannes Sanatorium AP23

1943, July 8 **Photo.**

Black Overprint

C88	AP23	20p orange	1.65	1.25
C89	AP23	50p steel blue	1.65	1.25
C90	AP23	100p rose violet	2.75	2.00

Arab Medical Congress, Beirut.

Nos. C82 to C87 Overprinted in Red, Blue or Violet

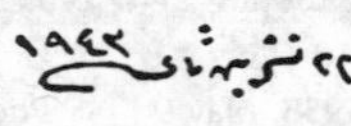

1944, Nov. 23

C91	AP20	25p yel grn (R)	2.50	2.50
C92	AP20	50p orange (Bl)	4.50	4.50
C93	AP21	100p buff (V)	5.00	5.00
C94	AP21	200p blue vio (R)	10.00	10.00
C95	AP22	300p sage grn (R)	14.00	14.00
C96	AP22	500p sepia (Bl)	25.00	25.00
		Nos. C91-C96 (6)	61.00	61.00

Return to office of the President and his ministers, Nov. 22, 1943.

Catalogue values for unused stamps in this section, from this point to the end of the section, are for Never Hinged items.

Falls of Litani — AP24 The Cedars — AP25

1945, July **Unwmk.** **Litho.**

C97	AP24	25p gray brown	1.65	60
C98	AP24	50p rose violet	2.50	80
C99	AP25	200p violet	8.50	1.50
C100	AP25	300p brown black	16.00	3.00

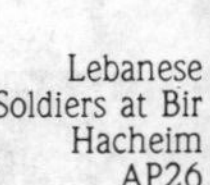

Lebanese Soldiers at Bir Hacheim AP26

1946, May 8

C101	AP26	15p bl blk, org & red org	35	22
C102	AP26	20p red, lil & bl	35	30
C103	AP26	25p brt bl, org & red	40	20
C104	AP26	50p gray blk, bl & red	60	25
C105	AP26	100p pur, pink & red	1.90	60
C106	AP26	150p brn, pink & red	2.25	1.90
		Nos. C101-C106 (6)	5.85	3.47

Victory of the Allied Nations in WWII, 1st anniv.

Three imperf. souvenir sheets of 14 exist. They contain one each of Nos. C101-C106 and 189-196 in changed colors. One has sepia inscriptions, and one on thin white card has blue inscriptions. Value $30 each. The third, with blue inscriptions, is on thick honeycombed chamois card. Value $110.

Night Herons Type

1946, Sept. 11

C107	A35	10p orange	1.50	42
C108	A35	25p ultra	1.75	20
C109	A35	50p blue green	5.50	62
C110	A35	100p dk vio brn	8.25	2.50

Symbols of Communications — AP28

1946, Nov. 22

C111	AP28	25p deep blue	65	40
C112	AP28	50p green	1.00	50
C113	AP28	75p orange red	1.90	1.00
C114	AP28	150p brown black	3.25	1.60

Arab Postal Congress, Sofar, 1946.

Stone Tablet, Dog River and Pres. Bechara el-Khoury AP29

1947, Feb. 11

C115	AP29	25p ultra	1.10	40
C116	AP29	50p dull rose	1.75	60
C117	AP29	75p gray black	2.25	65
C118	AP29	150p blue green	4.50	1.40

Evacuation of foreign troops from Lebanon, Dec. 31, 1946.

Bay of Jounie AP30

Government House, Beirut AP31

1947, Feb. 11

Grayish Paper

C119	AP30	5p dp blue grn	16	15
C120	AP30	10p rose vio	32	15
C121	AP30	15p vermilion	70	15
C122	AP30	20p orange	85	15
a.		20p red org, white paper	90	15
C123	AP30	25p deep blue	1.00	15
C124	AP30	50p henna brn	1.75	15
C125	AP30	100p chocolate	4.50	25
C126	AP31	150p dk vio brn	8.50	45
C127	AP31	200p slate	12.00	2.00
C128	AP31	300p black	20.00	5.00
		Nos. C119-C128 (10)	49.78	8.60

See Nos. C145A-C147B.

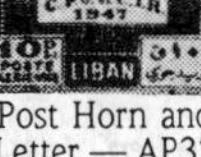

Post Horn and Letter — AP32 Phoenician Galley — AP33

1947, June 17 **Litho.**

C129	AP32	10p brt ultra	48	35
C130	AP32	15p rose car	55	35
C131	AP32	25p bright blue	75	60
C132	AP33	50p dark sl grn	2.25	65
C133	AP33	75p purple	3.00	1.40
C134	AP33	100p dark brown	4.25	1.90
		Nos. C129-C134 (6)	11.28	5.25

Lebanon's participation in the 12th UPU congress, Paris.

Lebanese Village AP34

1948, Sept. 1 *Perf. 11½*

C135	AP34	5p dp orange	20	15
C136	AP34	10p rose lilac	42	15
C137	AP34	15p orange brn	1.10	16
C138	AP34	20p slate	1.60	15
C139	AP34	25p Prussian bl	4.00	55
C140	AP34	50p gray black	6.50	80
		Nos. C135-C140 (6)	13.82	1.96

Apollo AP35 Minerva AP36

1948, Nov. 23 **Unwmk.**

C141	AP35	7.50p bl & lt bl	1.25	80
C142	AP35	15p blk & gray	1.50	1.00
C143	AP35	20p rose brn & rose	2.50	1.50
C144	AP36	35p car rose & rose	4.50	2.00
C145	AP36	75p bl grn & lt green	8.75	4.00
		Nos. C141-C145 (5)	18.50	9.30

UNESCO. Nos. C141-C145 exist imperforate, and combined with Nos. 220-224 in an imperforate souvenir sheet on thin buff cardboard, with black inscriptions in top margin in Arabic and at bottom in French. Value $175.

Bay Type of 1947 Redrawn

1949

White Paper

C145A	AP30	10p rose lilac	3.00	42
C146	AP30	15p dark green	3.75	50
C147	AP30	20p orange	8.25	3.50
C147A	AP30	25p dark blue	22.50	1.25
C147B	AP30	50p brick red	100.00	14.00
		Nos. C145A-C147B (5)	137.50	19.67

In the redrawn designs, Nos. C145A, C147 and C147B have zeros with broader centers than in the 1947 issue (Nos. C120, C122 and C124).

Helicopter Mail Delivery — AP37

1949, Aug. 16 **Unwmk.** *Perf. 11½*

C148	AP37	25p deep blue	2.75	1.50
C149	AP37	50p green	4.25	1.75
a.		Souvenir sheet of 5, #225-227, C148-C149	22.50	11.00

UPU, 75th anniv. No. 149a exists on thin cardboard.

Homing Birds — AP38

Pres. Bechara el-Khoury AP39

1950, Aug. 8 **Litho.**

C150	AP38	5p violet blue	50	35
C151	AP38	15p rose vio	75	40
C152	AP39	25p chocolate	62	50
C153	AP39	35p gray green	1.10	75
a.		Souvenir sheet of 6, #243-244, C150-C153, chamois paper	20.00	20.00

Conference of Emigrants, 1950.

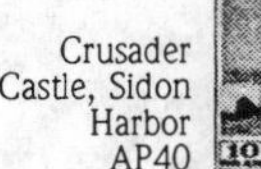

Crusader Castle, Sidon Harbor AP40

1950, Sept. 7

C154	AP40	10p chocolate	25	16
C155	AP40	15p dark green	52	15
C156	AP40	20p crimson	1.40	20
C157	AP40	25p ultra	2.50	50
C158	AP40	50p gray black	3.75	1.40
		Nos. C154-C158 (5)	8.42	2.41

1951, June 9 **Redrawn** **Typo.**

C159	AP40	10p grnsh black	32	15
C160	AP40	15p black brown	60	15
C161	AP40	20p vermilion	60	15
C162	AP40	25p deep blue	80	15
C163	AP40	35p lilac rose	2.25	1.00
C164	AP40	50p indigo	3.50	1.00
		Nos. C159-C164 (6)	8.07	2.60

Nos. C154-C158 are lithographed from a fine-screen halftone; Nos. C159-C164 are typographed and much coarser, with larger plane and many other differences.

Khaldé International Airport, Beirut AP41

Design: 50p to 300p, Amphitheater, Byblos.

1952 **Litho.** *Perf. 11½*

C165	AP41	5p crimson	15	15
C166	AP41	10p dark gray	15	15
C167	AP41	15p rose lilac	26	15
C168	AP41	20p brown org	42	16
C169	AP41	25p grnsh blue	45	20
C170	AP41	35p violet bl	60	20
C171	AP41	50p blue green	4.00	22
C172	AP41	100p deep blue	21.00	1.00
C173	AP41	200p dk bl grn	11.00	1.60
C174	AP41	300p black brn	17.00	3.25
		Nos. C165-C174 (10)	55.03	7.08

Lockheed Constellation — AP42

1953, Oct. 1

C175	AP42	5p yel green	15	15
C176	AP42	10p deep plum	20	15
C177	AP42	15p scarlet	30	15
C178	AP42	20p aqua	42	15
C179	AP42	25p blue	1.00	15
C180	AP42	35p orange brn	1.50	15
C181	AP42	50p vio blue	3.00	25
C182	AP42	100p black brn	5.25	2.00
		Nos. C175-C182 (8)	11.82	
		Set value		2.65

Ruins at Baalbek AP43

Irrigation Canal, Litani — AP44

1954, Mar.

C183	AP43	5p	yel green	15	15
C184	AP43	10p	dull purple	22	15
C185	AP43	15p	carmine	30	15
C186	AP43	20p	brown	38	15
C187	AP43	25p	dull blue	45	15
C188	AP43	35p	black brn	75	16
C189	AP44	50p	dk ol grn	3.75	25
C190	AP44	100p	deep car	7.50	35
C191	AP44	200p	dark brown	11.00	65
C192	AP44	300p	dk gray bl	20.00	1.50
			Nos. C183-C192 (10)	44.50	3.66

Khaldé International Airport, Beirut AP45

1954, Apr. 23 ***Perf. 11½***

C193	AP45	10p	pink & rose red	35	20
C194	AP45	25p	dp bl & gray bl	95	35
C195	AP45	35p	dl brn & yel brn	1.25	60
C196	AP45	65p	dp grn & grn	3.00	1.20

Opening of Beirut's International Airport. Exist imperf.

Arab Postal Union Type of Regular Issue, 1955

1955, Jan. 1 ***Perf. 13½x13***

C197	A52	2.50p	yellow brn	35	20

Rotary Emblem AP47

1955, Feb. 23 ***Perf. 11½***

C198	AP47	35p	dull green	75	42
C199	AP47	65p	dull blue	1.50	55

Rotary International, 50th anniversary.

Skiing Among the Cedars — AP48

1955, Feb. 24 **Litho.**

C200	AP48	5p	blue green	20	15
C201	AP48	15p	crimson	30	15
C202	AP48	20p	lilac	50	15
C203	AP48	25p	blue	1.00	15
C204	AP48	35p	olive brn	1.50	22
C205	AP48	50p	chocolate	3.00	32
C206	AP48	65p	deep blue	4.75	75
			Nos. C200-C206 (7)	11.25	1.89

See Nos. C233-C235. For surcharge see No. C271.

Tourist — AP49

1955, Sept. 10 **Unwmk.** ***Perf. 13***

C207	AP49	2.50p	brn vio & lt bl	15	15
C208	AP49	12.50p	ultra & lt bl	35	15
C209	AP49	25p	ind & lt bl	95	16
C210	AP49	35p	ol grn & lt bl	1.10	22
a.			Sheet of 4, #C207-C210, imperf.	20.00	6.50
			Set value		55

Tourist Year. No. C210a is printed on cardboard.

Oranges AP50

Designs: 25p, 35p, 50p, Grapes, vert. 65p, 100p, 200p, Apples.

1955, Oct. 15

C211	AP50	5p	yel grn & yel	15	15
C212	AP50	10p	dk grn & dp orange	20	15
C213	AP50	15p	yel grn & red orange	25	15
C214	AP50	20p	ol & yel org	42	15
C215	AP50	25p	bl & vio bl	60	15
C216	AP50	35p	green & cl	80	15
C217	AP50	50p	blk brn & dl yellow	80	15
C218	AP50	65p	grn & lemon	1.90	16
C219	AP50	100p	yel grn & dp orange	2.50	42
C220	AP50	200p	green & car	4.00	2.00
			Nos. C211-C220 (10)	11.62	
			Set value		3.00

For surcharge see No. C265.

United Nations Emblem AP52

1956, Jan. 23 ***Perf. 11½***

C221	AP52	35p	violet blue	3.50	1.50
C222	AP52	65p	green	4.00	1.75

UN, 10th anniv. (in 1955).

An imperf. souvenir sheet contains one each of Nos. C221 and C222. Value $40.

Temple of the Sun Colonnade, Masks and Lion's Head — AP53

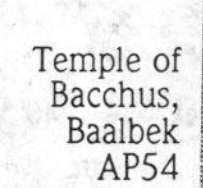

Temple of Bacchus, Baalbek AP54

Design: 35p, 65p, Temple of the Sun colonnade, masks and violincello.

1956, Dec. 10 **Litho.** ***Perf. 13***

C223	AP53	2.50p	dark brown	55	15
C224	AP53	10p	green	80	18
C225	AP54	12.50p	light blue	80	22
C226	AP54	25p	brt vio bl	1.25	35
C227	AP53	35p	red lilac	2.50	45
C228	AP53	65p	slate blue	3.50	90
			Nos. C223-C228 (6)	9.40	2.25

International Festival at Baalbek.

Skiing Type of 1955 Redrawn and

Irrigation Canal, Litani — AP55

1957 **Litho.** ***Perf. 11½***

C229	AP55	10p	brt violet	20	15
C230	AP55	15p	orange	32	15
C231	AP55	20p	yel green	35	15
C232	AP55	25p	slate blue	55	15
C233	AP48	35p	gray green	1.65	15
C234	AP48	65p	dp claret	2.25	22
C235	AP48	100p	brown	4.00	50
			Nos. C229-C235 (7)	9.32	
			Set value		1.00

Different Arabic characters used for the country name; letters in "Liban" larger.

For surcharge see No. C271.

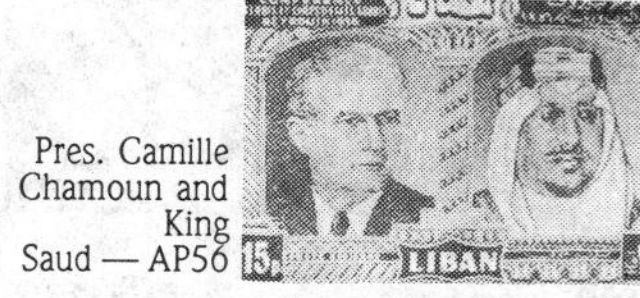

Pres. Camille Chamoun and King Saud — AP56

King Saud, Pres. Chamoun, King Hussein, Pres. Kouatly, King Faisal, Pres. Nasser — AP57

Pres. Chamoun and: No. C237, King Hussein. No. C238, Pres. Kouatly. No. C239, King Faisal. No. C240, Pres. Nasser. 25p, Map of Lebanon.

1957, July 15 **Litho.** ***Perf. 13***

C236	AP56	15p	green	45	20
C237	AP56	15p	blue	45	20
C238	AP56	15p	red lilac	45	20
C239	AP56	15p	red orange	45	20
C240	AP56	15p	claret	45	20
C241	AP56	25p	blue	45	20
C242	AP57	100p	dl red brn	4.00	1.40
			Nos. C236-C242 (7)	6.70	2.60

Issued to commemorate the Congress of Arab Leaders, Beirut, Nov. 12-15, 1956.

Fencing AP58

Design: 50p, Pres. Chamoun and stadium with flags.

1957, Sept. 12 **Unwmk.** ***Perf. 13***

C243	AP58	35p	claret	95	60
C244	AP58	50p	lt green	1.25	90

2nd Pan-Arab Games, Beirut. See note on souvenir sheet below No. 314.

Symbols of Communications — AP59

Power Plant, Chamoun AP60

1957 ***Perf. 13x13½, 11½ (AP60)***

C245	AP59	5p	brt green	15	15
C246	AP59	10p	yel orange	18	15
C247	AP59	15p	brown	25	15
C248	AP59	20p	maroon	38	15
C249	AP59	25p	vio blue	38	15
C250	AP60	35p	violet brn	75	15
C251	AP60	50p	green	1.25	18
C252	AP60	65p	sepia	1.65	18
C253	AP60	100p	dark gray	2.25	50
			Nos. C245-C253 (9)	7.24	
			Set value		1.40

Plane at Airport AP61

Cogwheel AP62

1958-59 **Unwmk.** ***Perf. 13***

C254	AP61	5p	green	20	15
C255	AP61	10p	magenta	24	15
C256	AP61	15p	dull violet	40	15
C257	AP61	20p	orange ver	60	15
C258	AP61	25p	dk vio bl	70	16
C259	AP62	35p	grnsh gray	1.00	16
C260	AP62	50p	aquamarine	1.20	16
C261	AP62	65p	pale brown	2.25	25
C262	AP62	100p	brt ultra	2.75	15
			Nos. C254-C262 (9)	9.34	
			Set value		1.00

Nos. C259 and C261 Surcharged in Black or Dark Blue

30P

1959 **Unwmk.** **Litho.** ***Perf. 13***

C263	AP62	30p	on 35p grnsh gray	50	22
C264	AP62	40p	on 65p pale brn (Bl)	75	38

Arab Engineers Congress.

No. C217 Overprinted as Illustrated and Surcharged with New Value and Bars

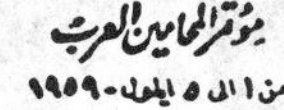

1959, Sept. 1

C265	AP50	40p	on 50p blk brn & dull yel	70	32

Arab Lawyers Congress.

Myron's Discobolus — AP63

Wreath and Hand Holding Torch AP64

1959, Oct. 11 **Litho.** ***Perf. 11½***

C266	AP63	15p	shown	38	15
C267	AP63	30p	Weight lifter	60	20
C268	AP64	40p	shown	1.10	30

3rd Mediterranean Games, Beirut.

A souvenir sheet on white cardboard contains one each of Nos. C266-C268, imperf. Sold for 100p. Value *$25*.

Soldiers and Flag — AP65

Hands Planting Tree — AP66

1959, Nov. 25 *Perf. 13½x13*
C269 AP65 40p sep, brick red & sl 65 28
C270 AP65 60p sep, dk grn & brick red 1.00 32

Lebanon's independence, 1941-1959.

No. C234 Surcharged with New Value and Bars

1959, Dec. 15 *Perf. 11½*
C271 AP48 40p on 65p dp claret 1.65 22

1960, Jan. 18 **Litho.** *Perf. 11½*
C272 AP66 20p rose vio & grn 60 20
C273 AP66 40p dk brn & green 80 32

Friends of the Tree Society, 25th anniv.

Postal Administration Building — AP67

1960, Feb. **Unwmk.** *Perf. 13*
C274 AP67 20p green 45 15

President Fuad Chehab AP68

Uprooted Oak Emblem AP69

1960, Mar. 12 **Photo.** *Perf. 13½*
C275 AP68 5p green 15 15
C276 AP68 10p Prus blue 15 15
C277 AP68 15p orange brn 16 15
C278 AP68 20p brown 20 15
C279 AP68 30p olive 30 15
C280 AP68 40p dull red 40 15
C281 AP68 50p blue 45 15
C282 AP68 70p red lilac 85 15
C283 AP68 100p dark green 1.50 32
Nos. C275-C283 (9) 4.16
Set value 90

1960, Apr. 7 **Litho.** *Perf. 13½x13*
Size: 20½x36½mm
C284 AP69 25p yellow brn 55 20
C285 AP69 40p green 75 28
a. Souv. sheet of 2, #C284-C285, imperf. 13.00 6.50

Size: 20x36mm
C284b AP69 25p yellow brown 80 40
C285b AP69 40p green 1.25 60

World Refugee Year, July 1, 1959-June 30, 1960.
No. C285a sold for 150p.
Nos. C284b-C285b appear fuzzy and pale when compared to the bolder, clear-cut printing of Nos. C284-C285. Issue date: July 18.
Nos. C284b-C285b exist with carmine surcharges of "30P.+15P." (on C284b) and "20P.+10P." (on C285b), repeated in Arabic, with ornaments covering original denominations.

Martyrs' Monument — AP70

Martyrs of May 6th: 70p, Statues from Martyrs' monument, vert.

1960, May 6 *Perf. 13x13½, 13½x13*
C286 AP70 20p rose lilac & grn 38 15
C287 AP70 40p Prus grn & dk grn 50 22
C288 AP70 70p gray olive & blk 1.25 50

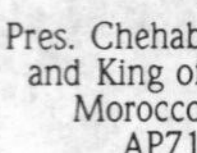

Pres. Chehab and King of Morocco AP71

1960, June 1 *Perf. 13x13½*
C289 AP71 30p choc & dk brn 65 28
C290 AP71 70p blk, dk brn & buff 1.25 35

Visit of King Mohammed V of Morocco.
A souvenir sheet of 2 on white cardboard contains Nos. C289-C290, imperf.

Child Learning to Walk — AP72

Bird, Ribbon of Flags and Map of Beirut — AP73

1960, Aug. 16 **Litho.** *Perf. 13½x13*
C291 AP72 20p shown 38 16
C292 AP72 60p Mother & child 1.00 42

Day of Mother and Child, Mar. 21-22. See Nos. CB10-CB11.

Perf. 13½x13, 13x13½
1960, Sept. 20 **Unwmk.**

Designs: 40p, Cedar and birds. 70p, Globes and cedar, horiz.

C293 AP73 20p multicolored 18 15
C294 AP73 40p vio, bl & grn 35 15
C295 AP73 70p multicolored 55 20
Set value 40

Union of Lebanese Emigrants in the World. A souvenir sheet of 3 contains Nos. C293-C295, imperf., printed on cardboard. Sold for 150p. Value $8.

Pres. Chehab and Map of — AP74

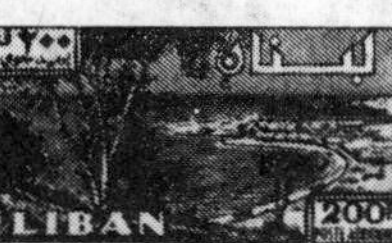
Casino, Maameltein Lebanon AP75

1961, Feb. **Litho.** *Perf. 13½x13*
C296 AP74 5p bl grn & yel grn 15 15
C297 AP74 10p brown & bister 18 15
C298 AP74 70p vio & rose lilac 1.00 25

1961 *Perf. 13x13½*
C299 AP75 15p rose claret 40 15
C300 AP75 30p greenish blue 60 15
C301 AP75 40p brown 70 15
C302 AP75 200p bis brn & dl bl 4.00 1.00
Nos. C296-C302 (7) 7.03
Set value 1.70

On Nos. C299-C301, the denomination, inscription and trees differ from type AP75.

UN Headquarters, New York — AP76

Designs: 20p, UN Emblem and map of Lebanon. 30p, UN Emblem and symbolic building. 20p, 30p are vertical.

1961, May 5 *Perf. 13½x13, 13x13½*
C306 AP76 20p lake & lt blue 20 15
C307 AP76 30p green & beige 28 15
C308 AP76 50p vio bl & grnsh bl 45 20
a. Souvenir sheet of 3 4.00 4.00
Set value 36

UN, 15th anniv. (in 1960).
No. C308a contains one each of Nos. C306-C308, imperf., against a light blue background showing UN emblem. Sold for 125p.

Pottery Workers AP77

1961, July 11 **Litho.** *Perf. 13x13½*
C309 AP77 30p shown 45 18
C310 AP77 70p Weaver 20 15

Issued for Labor Day, 1961.

Fireworks — AP78

Water Skiing — AP79

Design: 70p, Tourists on boat ride through cave.

1961, Aug. 8 *Perf. 13½x13, 13x13½*
C311 AP78 15p lt pur & dk bl 80 28
C312 AP79 40p blue & pink 1.25 42
C313 AP79 70p dull brn & pink 40 15

Issued to publicize tourist month.

Highway Circle at Dora, Beirut Suburb AP80

1961, Aug. *Perf. 11½*
C314 AP80 35p yellow green 65 18
C315 AP80 50p orange brown 85 28
C316 AP80 100p gray 85 32

Beach at Tyre — AP81

Afka Falls — AP82

1961, Sept. **Litho.** *Perf. 13*
C317 AP81 5p carmine rose 20 15
C318 AP81 10p brt violet 40 15
C319 AP81 15p bright blue 60 15
C320 AP81 20p orange 75 15
C321 AP81 30p brt green 95 15
C322 AP82 40p dp claret 45 15
C323 AP82 50p ultramarine 65 16
C324 AP82 70p yellow green 85 24
C325 AP82 100p dark brown 1.50 35
Nos. C317-C325 (9) 6.35
Set value 1.20

See Nos. C341-C342.

Entrance to UNESCO Building AP83

"UNESCO" and Cedar — AP84

Design: 50p, UNESCO headquarters, Paris.

1961, Nov. 20 **Unwmk.** *Perf. 12*
C326 AP83 20p bl, buff & blk 25 15
C327 AP84 30p lt grn, blk & mag 35 15
C328 AP83 50p multicolored 75 20
Set value 40

UNESCO, 15th anniv.

Emir Bechir and Fakhr-el-Din El Maani AP85

Design: 25p, Cedar emblem.

1961, Dec. 30 **Litho.**
C329 AP85 25p Cedar emblem 35 15
C330 AP85 50p shown 65 28

See note after No. 375.

Scout Types of Regular Issue, 1962

Designs: 15p, Trefoil and cedar emblem. 20p, Hand making Scout sign. 25p, Lebanese Scout emblem.

1962, Mar. 1 **Unwmk.** *Perf. 12*
C331 A70 15p grn, blk & red 25 15
C332 A69 20p lil, blk & yel 35 16
C333 A70 25p multicolored 60 24

Arab League Building, Cairo — AP86

1962, Mar. 22 *Perf. 13*
C334 AP86 20p ultra & lt bl 28 15
C335 AP86 30p red brn & pink 45 16
C336 AP86 50p grn & grnsh bl 70 28

Arab League Week, Mar. 22-28. See Nos. C372-C375.

Blacksmith — AP87

Farm Tractor AP88

Perf. 13½x13, 13x13½

1962, May 1 **Litho.**

C337 AP87	5p	green & lt blue	15	15
C338 AP87	10p	blue & pink	15	15
C339 AP88	25p	brt vio & pink	25	15
C340 AP88	35p	car rose & blue	35	18
		Set value		40

Issued for Labor Day.

Types of 1961 Redrawn with Large Numerals Similar to Redrawn Regular Issue of 1962

1962 ***Perf. 13***

C341 AP81	5p	carmine rose	60	15
C342 AP82	40p	deep claret	5.50	35
		Set value		40

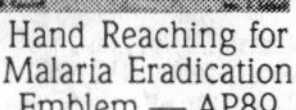

Hand Reaching for Malaria Eradication Emblem — AP89

Bas-relief of Isis, Kalabsha Temple, Nubia — AP90

Design: 70p, Malaria eradication emblem.

1962, July 2 **Litho.** ***Perf. 13½x13***

C349 AP89	30p	tan & brown	35	20
C350 AP89	70p	bluish lil & vio	50	40

WHO drive to eradicate malaria.

1962, Aug. 1 **Unwmk.** ***Perf. 13***

C351 AP90	30p	yellow green	1.10	25
C352 AP90	50p	slate	1.90	60

Campaign to save historic monuments in Nubia.

Spade, Heart, Diamond, Club — AP91

College Student — AP92

1962, Sept.

C353 AP91	25p	car rose, blk & red	1.10	80
C354 AP91	40p	multicolored	1.20	80

European Bridge Championship Tournament.

1962, Oct. 1 ***Perf. 12***

C355 AP92	45p	multicolored	50	20

Issued for Students' Day, Oct. 1.

Sword Severing Chain — AP93

Harvest — AP94

1962, Nov. 22 **Litho.** ***Perf. 13***

C356 AP93	25p	vio, lt bl & red	42	25
C357 AP93	25p	bl, lt bl & red	42	25
C358 AP93	25p	grn, lt bl & red	42	25

19th anniversary of independence.

Fruit Type of Regular Issue, 1962

Designs: 5p, Apricots. 10p, 30p, Plums. 20p, 40p, Apples. 50p, Pears. 70p, Medlar. 100p, Lemons.

1962

Vignette Multicolored

C359 A72	5p	orange brown	15	15
C360 A72	10p	black	22	15
C361 A72	20p	brown	42	15
C362 A72	30p	gray	55	16
C363 A72	40p	dark gray	65	16
C364 A72	50p	light brown	85	20
C365 A72	70p	gray olive	1.25	28
C366 A72	100p	blue	2.25	45
		Nos. C359-C366 (8)	6.34	
		Set value		1.40

1963, Mar. 21 **Litho.** ***Perf. 13***

Design: 15p, 20p, UN Emblem and hand holding Wheat Emblem, horiz.

C367 AP94	2.50p	ultra & yel	15	15
C368 AP94	5p	gray grn & yel	16	15
C369 AP94	7.50p	rose lil & yel	20	15
C370 AP94	15p	rose brn & pale grn	40	15
C371 AP94	20p	rose & pale grn	55	16
		Nos. C367-C371 (5)	1.46	
		Set value		42

FAO "Freedom from Hunger" campaign.

Redrawn Type of 1962, Dated "1963"

Design: Arab League Building, Cairo.

1963, Mar. **Unwmk.** ***Perf. 12***

C372 AP86	5p	violet & lt blue	15	15
C373 AP86	10p	green & lt blue	16	15
C374 AP86	15p	claret & lt blue	25	16
C375 AP86	20p	gray & lt blue	45	25
		Set value		56

Issued for Arab League Week.

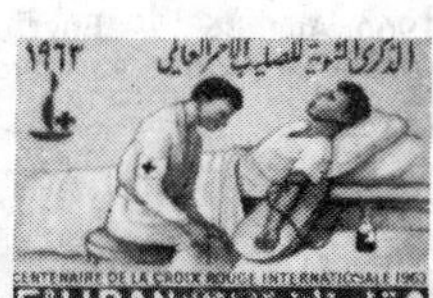

Blood Transfusion AP95

Design: 35p, 40p, Nurse and infant, vert.

1963, Oct. 5 **Unwmk.** ***Perf. 13***

C376 AP95	5p	green & red	15	15
C377 AP95	20p	grnsh bl & red	25	15
C378 AP95	35p	org, red & blk	45	16
C379 AP95	40p	purple & red	65	20
		Set value		48

Centenary of International Red Cross.

Lyre Player and Columns — AP96

Lebanon Flag, Rising Sun — AP97

1963, Nov. 7 **Unwmk.** ***Perf. 13***

C380 AP96	35p	lt bl, org & blk	1.00	28

International Festival at Baalbek.

1964, Jan. 8 **Litho.**

C381 AP97	5p	bluish grn, ver & yel	15	15
C382 AP97	10p	yel grn, ver & yel	22	16
C383 AP97	25p	ultra, ver & yel	50	25
C384 AP97	40p	gray, ver & yel	85	40

20th anniversary of Independence.

Sports Type of Regular Issue, 1964

1964, Feb. 11 **Unwmk.** ***Perf. 13***

C385 A76	15p	Tennis	22	15
C386 A76	17.50p	Swimming, horiz.	30	15
C387 A76	30p	Skiing, horiz.	50	20
a.		Souvenir sheet of 3	7.00	5.50
		Set value		40

No. C387a contains three imperf. stamps similar to Nos. C385-C387 with simulated orange brown perforations and green marginal inscription. Sold for 100p.

Anemone — AP98

Flame and UN Emblem — AP100

Girls Jumping Rope — AP99

1964, June 9 **Unwmk.** ***Perf. 13***

C391 AP98	5p	Lily	24	15
C392 AP98	10p	Ranunculus	32	15
C393 AP98	20p	shown	50	15
C394 AP98	40p	Tuberose	75	20
C395 AP98	45p	Rhododendron	80	20
C396 AP98	50p	Jasmine	90	20
C397 AP98	70p	Yellow broom	1.40	30
		Nos. C391-C397 (7)	4.91	1.35

1964, Apr. 8

Children's Day: 20p, 40p, Boy on hobbyhorse, vert.

C398 AP99	5p	emer, org & red	15	15
C399 AP99	10p	yel brn, org & red	16	15
C400 AP99	20p	dp ultra, lt bl & org	28	16
C401 AP99	40p	lil, lt bl & yel	55	30
		Set value		62

1964, May 15 **Litho.** **Unwmk.**

Design: 40p, Flame, UN emblem and broken chain.

C402 AP100	20p	salmon, org & brn	18	15
C403 AP100	40p	lt bl, gray bl & org	38	16
		Set value		24

15th anniv. (in 1963) of the Universal Declaration of Human Rights.

Arab League Conference — AP101

1964, Apr. 20 ***Perf. 13x13½***

C404 AP101	5p	blk & pale sal	60	20
C405 AP101	10p	black	1.00	35
C406 AP101	15p	green	1.25	50
C407 AP101	20p	dk brn & pink	2.00	65

Arab League meeting.

Child in Crib — AP102

Beit-ed-Din Palace and Children — AP103

1964, July 20 ***Perf. 13½x13, 13½***

C408 AP102	2.50p	multicolored	15	15
C409 AP102	5p	multicolored	15	15
C410 AP102	15p	multicolored	30	15
C411 AP103	17.50p	multicolored	35	15
C412 AP103	20p	multicolored	45	15
C413 AP103	40p	multicolored	55	16
		Nos. C408-C413 (6)	1.95	
		Set value		55

Ball of the Little White Beds, Beirut, for the benefit of children's hospital beds.

Clasped Hands and Map of Lebanon — AP104

1964, Oct. 16 **Litho.** ***Perf. 13½x13***

C414 AP104	20p	yel grn, yel & gray	35	16
C415 AP104	40p	slate, yel & gray	55	35

Issued to publicize the Congress of the International Lebanese Union.

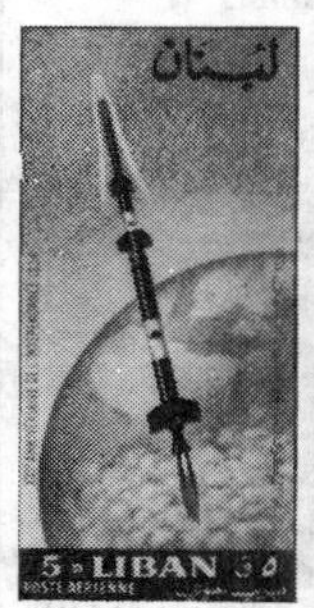

Rocket Leaving Earth — AP105

Woman in Costume — AP107

Battle Scene — AP106

1964, Nov. 24 **Unwmk.** ***Perf. 13½***

C416 AP105	5p	multicolored	24	15
C417 AP105	10p	multicolored	24	15
C418 AP106	40p	sl blue & blk	80	28
C419 AP106	70p	dp claret & blk	1.25	50

21st anniversary of independence.

1965, Jan. 11 **Litho.** ***Perf. 13½***

Design: 10p, 15p, Man in costume.

C420 AP107	10p	multicolored	30	15
C421 AP107	15p	multicolored	50	20
C422 AP107	25p	green & multi	75	35
C423 AP107	40p	brown & multi	1.00	50

International Festival at Baalbek.

Equestrian AP108

1965, Jan. 23 Engr. *Perf. 13*

C424 AP108 15p shown 22 15
C425 AP108 25p Target shooting, vert. 35 15
C426 AP108 40p Gymnast on rings 60 20
a. Souvenir sheet of 3, #C424-C426, imperf. 9.50 5.00
Set value 40

18th Olympic Games, Tokyo, Oct. 10-25, 1964. No. 426a sold for 100p.

Heliconius Cybria AP109

Designs: 30p, Pericallia matronula. 40p, Red admiral. 45p, Satyrus semele. 70p, Machaon. 85p, Aurore. 100p, Morpho cypris. 200p, Erasmia sanguiflua. 300p, Papilio crassus. 500p, Charaxes ameliae.

1965 Unwmk. *Perf. 13*

Size: 36x22mm

C427 AP109 30p ver, yel & dk brown 25 15
C428 AP109 35p ol bis, dk bl & red 32 15
C429 AP109 40p sl grn, org & brown 38 15
C430 AP109 45p blk, Prus bl & yellow 52 16
C431 AP109 70p multicolored 70 25
C432 AP109 85p blk, grn & orange 1.00 25
C433 AP109 100p dk pur & blue 1.40 25
C434 AP109 200p dl pur, blk & blue 3.00 42
C435 AP109 300p brn, sl grn & yellow 4.00 80

Engr. and Litho.

Perf. 12

Size: 35x25mm

C436 AP109 500p lt ultra & blk 8.75 2.00
Nos. C427-C436 (10) 20.32 4.58

For surcharges see Nos. C654-C656.

Pope Paul VI and Pres. Chehab — AP110

1965, June 28 Photo. *Perf. 12*

C437 AP110 45p gold & brt vio 4.50 80
a. Souv. sheet of 1, imperf. 40.00 25.00

Visit of Pope Paul VI to Lebanon. No. C437a sold for 50p.

Cedars of Friendship AP111

1965, Oct. 16 Photo. *Perf. 13x12½*

C438 AP111 40p multicolored 70 15

Cocoon, Spindle and Silk — AP112

Design: 15p, 30p, 40p, 50p, Silk weaver at loom.

1965, Oct. 16 *Perf. 12½x13*

Design in Buff and Bright Green

C439 AP112 2.50p brown 15 15
C440 AP112 5p dk olive grn 15 15
C441 AP112 7.50p Prus blue 15 15
C442 AP112 15p deep ultra 16 15
C443 AP112 30p deep claret 32 15
C444 AP112 40p brown 50 20
C445 AP112 50p rose brown 1.00 25
Nos. C439-C445 (7) 2.43
Set value 70

Parliament Building AP113

1965, Oct. 26 *Perf. 13x12½*

C446 AP113 35p red, buff & brn 45 15
C447 AP113 40p emer, buff & brn 65 16

Centenary of the Lebanese parliament.

UN Headquarters, NYC, UN Emblem and Lebanese Flags — AP114

1965, Nov. 10 Engr. *Perf. 12*

C448 AP114 2.50p dull blue 15 15
C449 AP114 10p magenta 15 15
C450 AP114 17.50p dull vio 18 15
C451 AP114 30p green 30 15
C452 AP114 40p brown 45 20
Nos. C448-C452 (5) 1.23
Set value 45

UN, 20th anniv. A souvenir sheet contains one 40p imperf. stamp in bright rose lilac. Sold for 50p. Value $8.

Playing Card King, Laurel and Cedar AP115

Dagger in Map of Palestine AP116

1965, Nov. 15 Photo. *Perf. 12½x13*

C453 AP115 2.50p multicolored 15 15
C454 AP115 15p multicolored 38 15
C455 AP115 17.50p multicolored 45 15
C456 AP115 40p multicolored 85 20
Set value 40

Intl. Bridge Championships. A souvenir sheet contains two imperf. stamps similar to Nos. C454 and C456. Sold for 75p. Value $9.

1965, Dec. 13 *Perf. 12½x11*

C457 AP116 50p multicolored 2.00 50

Deir Yassin massacre, Apr. 9, 1948.

ITU Emblem, Old and New Communication Equipment and Syncom Satellite — AP117

1966, Apr. 13 *Perf. 13x12½*

C458 AP117 2.50p multi 15 15
C459 AP117 15p multi 22 15
C460 AP117 17.50p multi 25 15
C461 AP117 25p multi 55 15
C462 AP117 40p multi 65 20
Nos. C458-C462 (5) 1.82
Set value 55

ITU, centenary (in 1965).

Folk Dancers Before Temple of Bacchus — AP118

Designs: 7.50p, 15p, Dancers before Temple of Jupiter, vert. 30p, 40p, Orchestra before Temple of Bacchus.

1966, July 20 Unwmk. *Perf. 12*

Gold Frame

C463 AP118 2.50p brn vio, bl & orange 16 15
C464 AP118 5p mag, bl & org 16 15
C465 AP118 7.50p vio bl, bl & pink 16 15
C466 AP118 15p pur, bl & pink 28 15
C467 AP118 30p dk grn, org & blue 40 15
C468 AP118 40p vio, org & bl 75 20
Nos. C463-C468 (6) 1.91
Set value 55

11th International Festival at Baalbek.

Opening of WHO Headquarters, Geneva AP119

1966, Aug. 25 Engr. *Perf. 12*

C469 AP119 7.50p dp yel grn 15 15
C470 AP119 17.50p car rose 35 15
C471 AP119 25p blue 50 15
Set value 24

Skier AP120

Designs: 5p, Children on toboggan. 17.50p, Cedar in snow. 25p, Ski lift.

1966, Sept. 15 Photo. *Perf. 12x11½*

C472 AP120 2.50p multi 24 15
C473 AP120 5p multi 24 15
C474 AP120 17.50p multi 45 15
C475 AP120 25p multi 90 16
Set value 35

International Festival of Cedars.

Sarcophagus of King Ahiram with Early Alphabet — AP121

Designs: 15p, Phoenician ship. 20p, Map of the Mediterranean Sea showing Phoenician travel routes, and ship. 30p, Phoenician with alphabet tablet.

Litho. & Engr.

1966, Sept. 25 *Perf. 12*

C476 AP121 10p dl grn, blk & lt brn 15 15
C477 AP121 15p rose lil, brn & ocher 24 15
C478 AP121 20p tan, dk brn & bl 32 15
C479 AP121 30p org, dk brn & yel 70 20
Set value 46

Invention of alphabet by Phoenicians.

Child in Bathtub and UNICEF Emblem AP122

UNICEF Emblem and: 5p, Boy in rowboat. 7.50p, Girl skier. 12p, Girl feeding bird. 20p, Boy doing homework. 50p, Children of various races, horiz.

1966, Oct. 10 Photo. *Perf. 11½x12*

C480 AP122 2.50p multi 15 15
C481 AP122 5p multi 15 15
C482 AP122 7.50p multi 18 15
C483 AP122 15p multi 35 15
C484 AP122 20p multi 50 16
Nos. C480-C484 (5) 1.33
Set value 36

Miniature Sheet

Imperf

C485 AP122 50p dl yellow & multi 2.75 1.90

UNICEF; World Children's Day. No. C485 contains one horizontal stamp 43x33mm.

Scenic Type of Regular Issue, 1966

Designs: 10p, Waterfall, Djezzine. 15p, Castle of the Sea, Saida. 20p, Amphitheater, Jubayl (Byblos). 30p, Temple of the Sun, Baalbek. 50p, Beit-ed-Din Palace. 60p, Church of Christ the King, Nahr-el-Kalb. 75p, Abu Bakr Mosque, Tripoli.

1966, Oct. 12 *Perf. 12x11½*

C486 A82 10p gold & multi 15 15
C487 A82 15p gold & multi 16 15
C488 A82 20p gold & multi 24 15
C489 A82 30p gold & multi 32 15
C490 A82 50p gold & multi 70 15
C491 A82 60p gold & multi 90 15
C492 A82 75p gold & multi 1.25 18
Nos. C486-C492 (7) 3.72
Set value 58

Symbolic Water Cycle — AP123

Daniel Bliss — AP124

Designs: 15p, 20p, Different wave pattern without sun.

1966, Nov. 15 Photo. *Perf. 12½*

C493 AP123 5p red, bl & vio bl 15 15
C494 AP123 10p org, bl & brn 20 15
C495 AP123 15p org, emer & dk brn 28 15
C496 AP123 20p org, emer & grnsh blue 42 15
Set value 30

Hydrological Decade (UNESCO), 1965-74.

1966, Dec. 3

Designs: 30p, Chapel, American University, Beirut. 50p, Daniel Bliss, D.D., and American University, horiz.

C497 AP124 20p grn, yel & brn 32 15
C498 AP124 30p red brn, grn & blue 40 15
Set value 20

Souvenir Sheet

Imperf

C499 AP124 50p grn, brn & org brown 2.00 1.00

Cent. of American University, Beirut, founded by the Rev. Daniel Bliss (1823-1916). Nos. C497-

C498 are printed each with alternating labels showing University emblem.

No. C499 contains one stamp 59x37mm.

Flags of Arab League Members, Hand Signing Scroll — AP125

1967, Aug. 2 Photo. *Perf. 12x11½*

C500 AP125 5p brown & multi 15 15
C501 AP125 10p multicolored 18 15
C502 AP125 15p black & multi 28 15
C503 AP125 20p multicolored 38 16
Set value 38

Signing of Arab League Pact in 1945.

Veteran's War Memorial Building, San Francisco — AP126

Design: 10p, 20p, 30p, Scroll, flags of Lebanon and United Nations.

1967, Sept. 1 Photo. *Perf. 12x11½*

C504 AP126 2.50p blue & multi 15 15
C505 AP126 5p multicolored 15 15
C506 AP126 7.50p multicolored 15 15
C507 AP126 10p blue & multi 20 15
C508 AP126 20p multicolored 28 15
C509 AP126 30p multicolored 45 15
Nos. C504-C609 (108) 59.38
Set value 40

22nd anniv. of the San Francisco Pact, the United Nations Charter.

Ruins at Baalbek — AP127

Intl. Tourist Year: 10p, Ruins at Anjar. 15p, Bridge over Ibrahim River and ruins. 20p, Boat on underground lake, Jaita cave. 50p, St. George's Bay, Beirut.

1967, Sept. 25 *Perf. 12½*

C510 AP127 5p multicolored 15 15
C511 AP127 10p multicolored 20 15
C512 AP127 15p violet & multi 28 15
C513 AP127 20p brown & multi 40 15
Set value 25

Souvenir Sheet

Imperf

C514 AP127 50p multicolored *25.00 20.00*

View of Tabarja AP128

Views: 15p, Pigeon Rock and shore, Beirut. 17.50p, Beit-ed-Din Palace. 20p, Ship at Sidon. 25p, Tripoli. 30p, Beach at Byblos. 35p, Ruins, Tyre. 40p, Temple of Bacchus, Baalbek.

1967, Oct. *Perf. 12x11½*

C515 AP128 10p multi 15 15
C516 AP128 15p multi 16 15
C517 AP128 17.50p multi 22 15
C518 AP128 20p multi 22 15
C519 AP128 25p multi 22 15
C520 AP128 30p multi 35 15
C521 AP128 35p multi 40 15
C522 AP128 40p multi 65 16
Nos. C515-C522 (8) 2.37
Set value 1.00

Intl. Tourist Year; used as a regular airmail issue.

India Day AP129

1967, Oct. 30 Engr. *Perf. 12*

C523 AP129 2.50p orange 15 15
C524 AP129 5p magenta 15 15
C525 AP129 7.50p brown 16 15
C526 AP129 10p blue 22 15
C527 AP129 15p green 32 15
Set value 75 26

Globe and Arabic Inscription — AP130

Design: 10p, 20p, 30p, UN emblem.

1967, Nov. 25 Engr. *Perf. 12*

C528 AP130 2.50p rose 15 15
C529 AP130 5p gray blue 15 15
C530 AP130 7.50p green 15 15
C531 AP130 10p brt carmine 15 15
C532 AP130 20p violet blue 30 15
C533 AP130 30p dark green 40 15
Set value 1.10 32

Lebanon's admission to the UN. A 100p rose red souvenir sheet in the globe design exists. Value $3.50.

Basking Shark AP131

Fish: 30p, Needlefish. 40p, Pollack. 50p, Cuckoo wrasse. 70p, Red mullet. 100p, Rainbow trout.

1968, Feb. Photo. *Perf. 12x11½*

C534 AP131 20p multi 30 15
C535 AP131 30p multi 30 15
C536 AP131 40p multi 60 15
C537 AP131 50p multi 75 15
C538 AP131 70p multi 1.50 15
C539 AP131 100p multi 2.00 15
Nos. C534-C539 (6) 5.45
Set value 45

Ski Jump AP132

Designs: 5p, 7.50p, 10p, Downhill skiers (various). 25p, Congress emblem (skis and cedar).

1968 *Perf. 12½x11½*

C540 AP132 2.50p multicolored 15 15
C541 AP132 5p multicolored 15 15
C542 AP132 7.50p multicolored 15 15
C543 AP132 10p multicolored 20 15
C544 AP132 25p multicolored 42 15
Nos. C540-C544 (5) 1.07
Set value 32

26th Intl. Ski Congress, Beirut. A 50p imperf. souvenir sheet exists in design of the 25p. Value $4.50.

Emir Fakhr al-Din II — AP133

Designs: 2.50p, Emira Khaskiah. 10p, Citadel of Sidon, horiz. 15p, Citadel of Chekif and grazing sheep, horiz. 17.50p, Citadel of Beirut and harbor, horiz.

Perf. 11½x12, 12x11½

1968, Feb. 20 Litho.

C546 AP133 2.50p multicolored 15 15
C547 AP133 5p multicolored 15 15
C548 AP133 10p multicolored 16 15
C549 AP133 15p multicolored 45 15
C550 AP133 17.50p multicolored 45 15
Nos. C546-C550 (5) 1.36
Set value 35

In memory of the Emir Fakhr al-Din II. A 50p imperf. souvenir sheet exists showing the Battle of Anjar. Value $5.50.

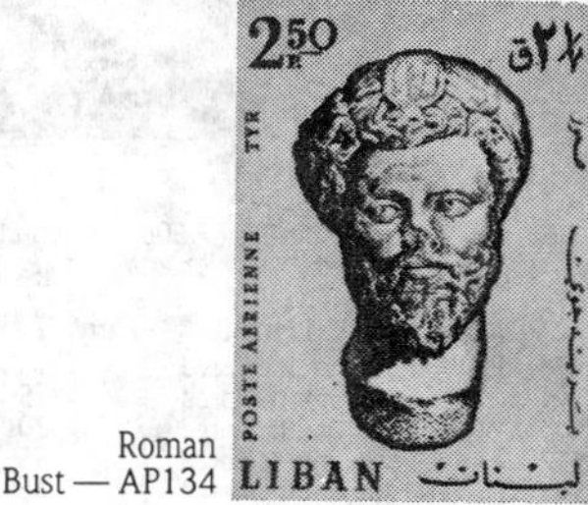

Roman Bust — AP134

Ruins of Tyre: 5p, Colonnade, horiz. 7.50p, Arch, horiz. 10p, Banquet, bas-relief.

Litho. & Engr.

1968, Mar. 20 *Perf. 12*

C552 AP134 2.50p pink, brn & buff 18 15
C553 AP134 5p yel, brn & lt bl 24 15
C554 AP134 7.50p lt grnsh bl, brn & yel 30 15
C555 AP134 10p sal, brn & lt bl 42 15
a. Souvenir sheet 15.00 11.00
Set value 40

No. C555a contains one dark brown and light blue stamp, perf. 10½x11½. Sold for 50p. Exists imperf.

For surcharge see No. C657.

Emperor Justinian AP135

Design: 15p, 20p, Justinian and map of the Mediterranean, horiz.

Perf. 11½x12, 12x11½

1968, May 10 Photo.

C556 AP135 5p blue & multi 15 15
C557 AP135 10p blue & multi 20 15
C558 AP135 15p red & multi 24 15
C559 AP135 20p blue & multi 35 15
Set value 24

Beirut, site of one of the greatest law schools in antiquity; Emperor Justinian (483-565), who compiled and preserved the Roman law.

Arab League Emblem — AP136

1968, June 6 Photo. *Perf. 12x11½*

C560 AP136 5p orange & multi 15 15
C561 AP136 10p multicolored 15 15
C562 AP136 15p pink & multi 28 15
C563 AP136 20p multicolored 45 15
Set value 22

Issued for Arab League Week.

Cedar and Globe Emblem — AP137

1968, July 10

C564 AP137 2.50p sal pink, brn & green 18 15
C565 AP137 5p gray, brn & grn 22 15
C566 AP137 7.50p brt bl, brn & grn 25 15
C567 AP137 10p yel grn, brn & green 40 15
Set value 40

3rd Congress of Lebanese World Union.

Temple of Jupiter, Baalbek AP138

Designs: 10p, Fluted pilasters, cella of Bacchus Temple. 15p, Corniche, south peristyle of Jupiter Temple, horiz. 20p, Gate, Bacchus Temple. 25p, Ceiling detail, south peristyle of Bacchus Temple.

1968, Sept. 25 Photo. *Perf. 12½*

C568 AP138 5p gold & multi 15 15
C569 AP138 10p gold & multi 15 15
C570 AP138 15p gold & multi 20 15
C571 AP138 20p gold & multi 32 15
C572 AP138 25p gold & multi 50 16
Nos. C568-C572 (5) 1.32
Set value 42

13th Baalbek International Festival.

Broad Jump and Phoenician Statue — AP139

Designs: 10p, High jump and votive stele, Phoenician, 6th century B.C. 15p, Fencing and Olmec jade head, 500-400 B.C. 20p, Weight lifting and axe in shape of human head, Vera Cruz region. 25p, Aztec stone calendar and Phoenician ship.

1968, Oct. 19 Photo. *Perf. 12x11½*

C573	AP139	5p	lt ultra, yel & gray	15	15
C574	AP139	10p	mag, lt ultra & blk	15	15
C575	AP139	15p	cit, ocher & brn	15	15
C576	AP139	20p	dp org, brn & ocher	24	15
C577	AP139	25p	light brown	38	18
			Nos. C573-C577 (5)	1.07	
			Set value		45

19th Olympic Games, Mexico City, Oct. 12-27.

Human Rights Flame and Tractor — AP140

Human Rights Flame and: 15p, People. 25p, Boys of 3 races placing hands on globe.

1968, Dec. 10 Litho. *Perf. 11½*

C578	AP140	10p	multicolored	20	15
C579	AP140	15p	yellow & multi	32	15
C580	AP140	25p	lilac & multi	70	15
			Set value		20

International Human Rights Year.

Minshiya Stairs, Deir El-Kamar AP141

Views in Deir El-Kamar: 15p, The Seraglio Kiosk. 25p, Old paved city road.

1968, Dec. 26

C581	AP141	10p	multicolored	15	15
C582	AP141	15p	multicolored	22	15
C583	AP141	25p	multicolored	38	15
			Set value		20

1st Municipal Council in Lebanon, established in Deir El-Kamar by Daoud Pasha, cent.

Nurse Treating Child, and UN Emblem — AP142

Designs: 10p, Grain, fish, grapes and jug. 15p, Mother and children. 20p, Reading girl and Phoenician alphabet. 25p, Playing children.

1969, Jan. 20 Litho. *Perf. 12*

C584	AP142	5p	blk, lt bl & sep	15	15
C585	AP142	10p	blk, brt yel & grn	15	15
C586	AP142	15p	blk, red lil & ver	16	15
C587	AP142	20p	blk, citron & bl	20	15
C588	AP142	25p	blk, pink & bis brn	32	15
			Set value	88	30

UNICEF, 22nd anniversary.

Silver Coin from Byblos, 5th Century B.C. — AP143

Designs (National Museum, Beirut): 5p, Gold dagger, Byblos, 18th century B.C. 7.50p, King Dining in the Land of the Dead, sarcophagus of Ahiram, 13-12th century B.C. 30p, Breastplate with cartouche of Amenemhat III (1849-1801 B.C.). 40p, Phoenician bird vase from Khalde, 8th century B.C.

Photogravure; Gold Impressed

1969, Feb. 20 *Perf. 12*

C589	AP143	2.50p	grn, yel & lt bl	16	15
C590	AP143	5p	vio, brn & yel	22	15
C591	AP143	7.50p	dl yel, brn & pink	30	15
C592	AP143	30p	blue & multi	42	15
C593	AP143	40p	multicolored	55	20
			Nos. C589-C593 (5)	1.65	
			Set value		45

Intl. Congress of Museum Councils; 20th anniv. of the Intl. Council of Museums.

Water Skier AP144

Designs: 5p, Water ballet. 7.50p, Parachutist, vert. 30p, Yachting, vert. 40p, Regatta.

1969, Mar. 3 Litho. *Perf. 11½*

C594	AP144	2.50p	multicolored	15	15
C595	AP144	5p	multicolored	15	15
C596	AP144	7.50p	multicolored	20	15
C597	AP144	30p	multicolored	55	18
C598	AP144	40p	multicolored	85	28
			Nos. C594-C598 (5)	1.90	
			Set value		62

Tomb of Unknown Soldier at Military School — AP145

Designs: 2.50p, Frontier guard. 7.50p, Soldiers doing forestry work. 15p, Army engineers building road. 30p, Ambulance and helicopter. 40p, Ski patrol.

1969, Aug. 1 Litho. *Perf. 12x11½*

C599	AP145	2.50p	multicolored	15	15
C600	AP145	5p	multicolored	15	15
C601	AP145	7.50p	multicolored	15	15
C602	AP145	15p	multicolored	15	15
C603	AP145	30p	multicolored	30	15
C604	AP145	40p	multicolored	35	18
			Set value	1.10	50

25th anniversary of independence.

Crosses and Circles — AP146

1971, Jan. 6 Photo. *Perf. 11½x12*

C605	AP146	15p	shown	15	15
C606	AP146	85p	Crosses, cedar	60	45

Lebanese Red Cross, 25th anniversary.

Foil Fencing AP147

Designs: 10p, Flags of participating Arab countries. 15p, Flags of participating non-Arab countries. 40p, Sword fencing. 50p, Saber fencing.

1971, Jan. 15 Litho. *Perf. 12*

C607	AP147	10p	yellow & multi	15	15
C608	AP147	15p	yellow & multi	15	15
C609	AP147	35p	yellow & multi	24	16
C610	AP147	40p	yellow & multi	32	20
C611	AP147	50p	yellow & multi	38	25
			Set value	1.10	72

10th World Fencing Championships, held in Lebanon.

Agricultural Workers, Arab Painting, 12th Century AP148

1971, Feb. 1

C612	AP148	10p	silver & multi	35	15
C613	AP148	40p	gold & multi	65	15
			Set value		17

International Labor Organization.

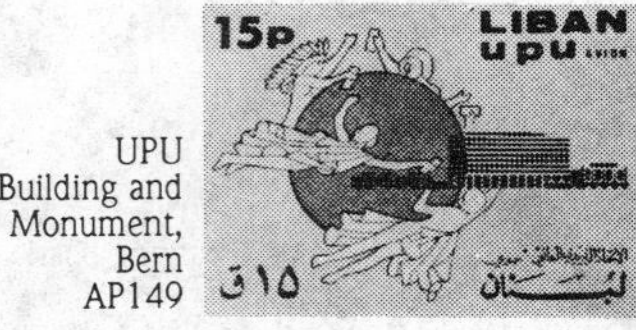

UPU Building and Monument, Bern AP149

1971, Feb. 15 Litho. *Perf. 12*

C614	AP149	15p	yel, blk & dp org	60	16
C615	AP149	35p	dp org, yel & blk	1.10	35

Opening of new UPU Headquarters in Bern, Switzerland.

Ravens Burning Owls — AP150

Children's Day: 85p, Jackal and lion. Designs of the 15p and 85p are after 13th-14th century paintings, illustrations for the "Kalila wa Dumna."

1971, Mar. 1 Photo. *Perf. 11*

Size: 30x30mm

C616	AP150	15p	gold & multi	15	15

Perf. 12x11½

Size: 38½x29mm

C617	AP150	85p	gold & multi	75	30
			Set value		36

Map and Flag of Arab League AP151

1971, Mar. 20 *Perf. 12x11½*

C618	AP151	30p	orange & multi	26	15
C619	AP151	70p	yellow & multi	70	25

Arab League, 25th anniv.

Kahlil Gibran AP152

Famous Lebanese Men: No. C620, Symbolic design for Imam al Ouzai. No. C621, Bechara el Khoury. No. C622, Hassan Kamel al Sabbah.

1971, Apr. 10

C620	AP152	25p	lt grn, gold & brn	20	15
C621	AP152	25p	yel, gold & brn	26	15
C622	AP152	25p	yel, gold & brn	26	15
C623	AP152	25p	lt grn, gold & brn	26	15
			Set value		32

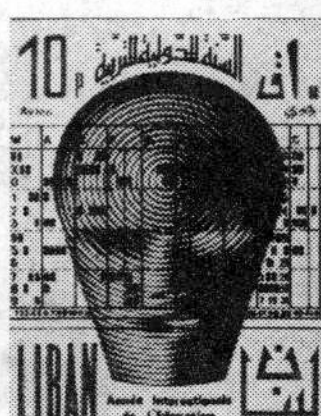

Education Year Emblem, Computer Card — AP153

1971, Apr. 30 Photo. *Perf. 11½x12*

C624	AP153	10p	blk, vio & bl	32	15
C625	AP153	40p	blk, org & yel	70	15
			Set value		18

Intl. Education Year.

Jamhour Substation AP154

Designs: 10p, Maameltein Bridge. 15p, Hotel Management School. 20p, Litani Dam. 25p, Television set wiring. 35p, Temple of Bziza. 40p, Jounieh Port. 45p, Airport radar. 50p, Flower. 70p, New School of Sciences. 85p, Oranges. 100p, Arbanieh earth satellite station.

1971, May Litho. *Perf. 12*

C626	AP154	5p	multi	15	15
C627	AP154	10p	multi	15	15
C628	AP154	15p	multi	15	15
C629	AP154	20p	multi	30	15
C630	AP154	25p	multi	45	15
C631	AP154	35p	multi	60	15
C632	AP154	40p	multi	60	15
C633	AP154	45p	multi	65	15
C634	AP154	50p	multi	1.00	15
C635	AP154	70p	multi	1.50	15
C636	AP154	85p	multi	2.00	20
C637	AP154	100p	multi	2.50	38
			Nos. C626-C637 (12)	10.05	
			Set value		1.35

For overprints see Nos. C771, C775, C779.

Dahr-el-Bacheq Sanatorium AP155

1971, June 1
C638 AP155 50p shown 42 16
C639 AP155 100p multi, diff. 60 35

Campaign against tuberculosis.

Solar Wheel (Festival Emblem) AP156

1971, July 1 Photo. *Perf. 11*
C640 AP156 15p ultra & org 16 15
C641 AP156 85p Corinthian capital 85 30
Set value 36

16th Baalbek International Festival.

155mm Cannon AP157

Army Day: 25p, Mirage fighters flying over Baalbek ruins. 40p, Army Headquarters. 70p, Naval patrol boat.

1971, Aug. 1 *Perf. 12x11½*
C642 AP157 15p gold & multi 65 15
C643 AP157 25p gold & multi 1.10 15
C644 AP157 40p gold & multi 1.50 16
C645 AP157 70p gold & multi 2.50 25
Set value 58

Wooden Console, Al Aqsa Mosque — AP158

1971, Aug. 21 *Perf. 12*
C646 AP158 15p dk brown & ocher 50 15
C647 AP158 35p dk brown & ocher 75 16
Set value 24

2nd anniversary of the burning of Al Aqsa Mosque in Jerusalem.

Lenin (1870-1924) AP159

1971, Oct. 1 *Perf. 12x11½*
C648 AP159 30p gold & multi 40 15
C649 AP159 70p multicolored 85 30

UN Emblem, World Map — AP160

1971, Oct. 24 *Perf. 13x12½*
C650 AP160 15p multicolored 18 15
C651 AP160 85p multicolored 85 25
Set value 30

UN, 25th anniv. (in 1970).

The Rape of Europa, Mosaic from Byblos AP161

1971, Nov 20 Litho. *Perf. 12*
C652 AP161 10p slate & multi 18 15
C653 AP161 40p gold & multi 80 16
Set value 20

Publicity for World Lebanese Union (ULM).

Nos. C435-C436 Surcharged

١٠٠ق

Engr.; Engr. & Litho.
1972, May *Perf. 13, 12*
C654 AP109 100p on 300p multi 3.00 40
C655 AP109 100p on 500p multi 3.00 40
C656 AP109 200p on 300p multi 4.50 80

The numerals on No. C655 are taller (5mm) and bars spaced 1½mm apart.

No. C554 Surcharged

5P. ٥ق

(Reduced)

1972, June Litho. & Engr. *Perf. 12*
C657 AP134 5p on 7.50p multi 75 16

Hibiscus AP162

Lebanese House AP163

1973 Litho. *Perf. 12*
C658 AP162 2.50p shown 15 15
C659 AP162 5p Roses 15 15
C660 AP162 15p Tulips 28 15
C661 AP162 25p Lilies 80 15
C662 AP162 40p Carnations 90 15
C663 AP162 50p Iris 1.25 15
C664 AP162 70p Apples 1.00 15
C665 AP162 75p Grapes 1.10 16
C666 AP162 100p Peaches 1.50 35
C667 AP162 200p Pears 5.25 25
C668 AP162 300p Cherries 5.75 55
C669 AP162 500p Oranges 9.25 90
Nos. C658-C669 (12) 27.38
Set value 2.70

For overprints see Nos. C758-C759, C763, C766, C769, C772, C776, C778, C782, C785-C787.

1973 *Perf. 14*

Designs: Old Lebanese houses.

C670 AP163 35p yellow & multi 2.00 16
C671 AP163 50p lt blue & multi 2.75 20
C672 AP163 85p buff & multi 4.50 28
C673 AP163 100p multicolored 6.00 40

For overprints see Nos. C768, C773, C780, C783.

Woman with Rose — AP164

Lebanese Costumes: 10p, Man. 20p, Man on horseback. 25p, Woman playing mandolin.

1973, Sept. 1 Litho. *Perf. 14*
C674 AP164 5p yellow & multi 22 15
C675 AP164 10p yellow & multi 80 15
C676 AP164 20p yellow & multi 1.25 15
C677 AP164 25p yellow & multi 1.75 15
Set value 25

For overprints see Nos. C760-C761, C764, C767.

Swimming, Temple at Baalbek — AP165

Designs: 10p, Running and portal. 15p, Woman athlete and castle. 20p, Women's volleyball and columns. 25p, Basketball and aqueduct. 50p, Women's table tennis and buildings. 75p, Handball and building. 100p, Soccer and cedar.

1973, Sept. 25 Photo. *Perf. 11½x12*
C678 AP165 5p multicolored 15 15
C679 AP165 10p multicolored 15 15
C680 AP165 15p grn & multi 16 15
C681 AP165 20p multicolored 16 15
C682 AP165 25p ultra & multi 22 15
C683 AP165 50p org & multi 50 30
C684 AP165 75p vio & multi 65 40
C685 AP165 100p multicolored 1.10 80
a. Souvenir sheet 1.75 1.25
Nos. C678-C685 (8) 3.09 2.25

5th Pan-Arabic Scholastic Games, Beirut. No. C685a contains one stamp with simulated perforations similar to No. C685; gold inscription and denomination.

View of Brasilia AP166

Designs: 20p, Old Salvador (Bahia). 25p, Lebanese sailing ship enroute from the Old World to South America. 50p, Dom Pedro I and Emir Fakhr al-Din II.

1973, Nov. 15 Litho. *Perf. 12*
C686 AP166 5p gold & multi 15 15
C687 AP166 20p gold & multi 70 35
C688 AP166 25p gold & multi 70 35
C689 AP166 50p gold & multi 1.40 65

Sesquicentennial of Brazil's independence.

Inlay Worker AP167

1973, Dec. 1
C690 AP167 10p shown 40 15
C691 AP167 20p Weaver 65 25
C692 AP167 35p Glass blower 1.00 35
C693 AP167 40p Potter 1.40 50
C694 AP167 50p Metal worker 1.60 50
C695 AP167 70p Cutlery maker 2.50 65
C696 AP167 85p Lace maker 3.50 1.00
C697 AP167 100p Handicraft Museum 4.00 1.40
Nos. C690-C697 (8) 15.05 4.80

Lebanese handicrafts.
For overprints see Nos. C762, C765, C770, C774, C777, C781, C784.

Camp Site, Log Fire and Scout Emblem AP168

Designs: 5p, Lebanese Scout emblem and map. 7½p, Lebanese Scout emblem and map of Middle East. 10p, Lord Baden-Powell, ruins of Baalbek. 15p, Girl Guide, camp and emblem. 20p, Lebanese Girl Guide and Scout emblems. 25p, Scouts around camp fire. 30p, Symbolic globe with Lebanese flag and Scout emblem. 35p, Flags of participating nations. 50p, Old man, and Scout chopping wood.

1974, Aug. 24 Litho. *Perf. 12*
C698 AP168 2.50p multi 25 25
C699 AP168 5p multi 25 25
C700 AP168 7.50p multi 55 25
C701 AP168 10p multi 55 25
C702 AP168 15p multi 65 55
a. Vert. strip of 5, #C698-C702 2.25
C703 AP168 20p multi 90 65
C704 AP168 25p multi 1.20 65
C705 AP168 30p multi 1.50 65
C706 AP168 35p multi 2.00 90
C707 AP168 50p multi 2.50 1.40
a. Vert. strip of 5, #C703-C707 8.25
Nos. C698-C707 (10) 10.35 5.80

11th Arab Boy Scout Jamboree, Smar-Jubeil, Aug. 1974. Nos. C702-C703 are for the 5th Girl Guide Jamboree, Deir-el-Kamar.

Mail Train and Postman Loading Mail, UPU Emblem — AP169

UPU Emblem and: 20p, Postal container hoisted onto ship. 25p, Postal Union Congress Building, Lausanne, and UPU Headquarters, Bern. 50p, Fork-lift truck loading mail on plane.

1974, Nov. 4 Photo. *Perf. 11½x12*
C708 AP169 5p multicolored 20 15
C709 AP169 20p multicolored 1.00 25
C710 AP169 25p multicolored 1.50 22
C711 AP169 50p ultra & multi 3.00 70

Centenary of Universal Postal Union.

Congress Building, Sofar — AP170

Arab Postal Union Emblem and: 20p, View of Sofar. 25p, APU Headquarters, Cairo. 50p, Ministry of Post, Beirut.

1974, Dec. 4 Litho. *Perf. 13x12½*
C712 AP170 5p orange & multi 15 15
C713 AP170 20p yellow & multi 30 20
C714 AP170 25p blue & multi 42 22
C715 AP170 50p multicolored 1.90 1.00

Arab Postal Union, 25th anniversary.

Mountain Road, by Omar Onsi — AP171

Paintings by Lebanese artists: No. C717, Clouds, by Moustapha Farroukh. No. C718, Woman, by Gebran Kahlil Gebran. No. C719, Embrace, by Cesar Gemayel. No. C720, Self-portrait, by Habib Serour. No. C721, Portrait of a Man, by Daoud Corm.

1974, Dec. 6 Litho. *Perf. 13x12¹/₂*

C716	AP171	50p lilac & multi	1.10	50
C717	AP171	50p blue & multi	1.10	50
C718	AP171	50p green & multi	1.10	50
C719	AP171	50p lt vio & multi	1.10	50
C720	AP171	50p brown & multi	1.10	50
C721	AP171	50p gray brn & multi	1.10	50
		Nos. C716-C721 (6)	6.60	3.00

Hunter Spearing Lion — AP172

Excavations at Hermel: 10p, Statue of Astarte. 25p, Dogs hunting boar, tiled panel. 35p, Greco-Roman tomb.

1974, Dec. 13

C722	AP172	5p blue & multi	15	15
C723	AP172	10p lilac & multi	25	15
C724	AP172	25p multicolored	65	22
C725	AP172	35p multicolored	85	38
		Set value		76

UNESCO Emblems and Globe AP173

1974, Dec. 16 *Perf. 12¹/₂x13*

C726	AP173	5p violet & multi	15	15
C727	AP173	10p bister & multi	26	15
C728	AP173	25p blue & multi	65	30
C729	AP173	35p multicolored	80	40

International Book Year.

Symbolic Stamp under Magnifying Glass — AP174

Designs (Symbolic): 10p, Post horns. 15p, Stamp printing. 20p, Mounted stamp.

1974, Dec. 20 *Perf. 13x12¹/₂*

C730	AP174	5p blue & multi	15	15
C731	AP174	10p olive & multi	24	15
C732	AP174	15p brown & multi	45	22
C733	AP174	20p lilac & multi	60	22
		Set value		62

Georgina Rizk — AP175

Designs: 5p, 25p, Georgina Rizk in Lebanese costume. 50p, Like 20p.

1974, Dec. 21

C734	AP175	5p multicolored	15	15
C735	AP175	20p violet & multi	18	15
C736	AP175	25p yellow & multi	28	15
C737	AP175	50p blue & multi	55	20
a.		Souvenir sheet of 4	1.25	80
		Set value		40

Georgina Rizk, Miss Universe 1971. No. C737a contains 4 stamps similar to Nos. C734-C737 with simulated perforations.

UNICEF Emblem, Helicopter, Camel, Supplies AP176

UNICEF Emblem and: 25p, Child welfare clinic. 35p, Kindergarten class. 70p, Girls in chemistry laboratory.

1974, Dec. 28 Litho. *Perf. 12¹/₂x13*

C738	AP176	20p multicolored	15	15
C739	AP176	25p multicolored	18	15
C740	AP176	35p blue & multi	28	15
C741	AP176	70p blue & multi	65	15
a.		Souvenir sheet of 4	3.25	1.90
		Set value		45

UNICEF, 25th anniv. No. C741a contains 4 stamps similar to Nos. C738-C741 with simulated perforations. Sold for 200p.

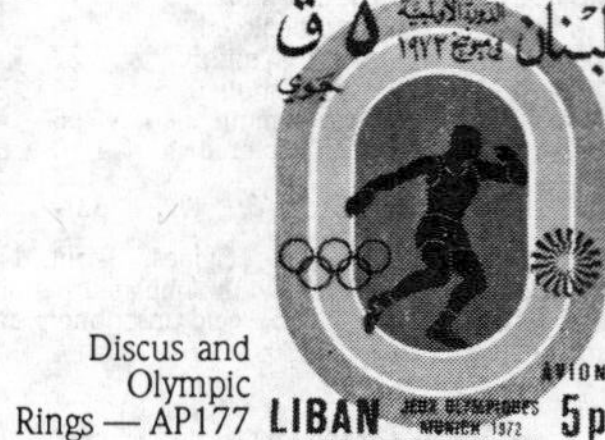

Discus and Olympic Rings — AP177

1974, Dec. 30 *Perf. 13x12¹/₂*

C742	AP177	5p shown	15	15
C743	AP177	10p Shot put	15	15
C744	AP177	15p Weight lifting	15	15
C745	AP177	35p Running	30	22
C746	AP177	50p Wrestling	42	22
C747	AP177	85p Javelin	70	35
a.		Souvenir sheet of 6	3.00	2.00
		Nos. C742-C747 (6)	1.87	
		Set value		90

20th Olympic Games, Munich, Aug. 26-Sept. 11, 1972. No. C747a contains 6 stamps similar to Nos. C742-C747 with simulated perforations.

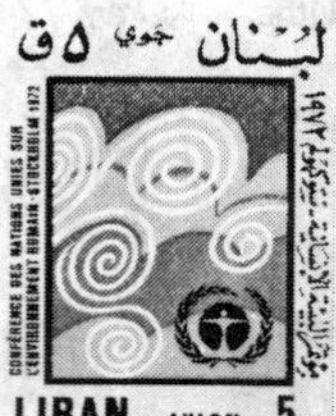

Clouds and Environment Emblem — AP178

1975

C748	AP178	5p shown	15	15
C749	AP178	25p Landscape	32	15
C750	AP178	30p Flowers and tree	32	15
C751	AP178	40p Waves	50	20
a.		Souvenir sheet of 4	2.00	1.40
		Set value		40

UN Conf. on Human Environment, Stockholm, June 5-16, 1972. No. C751a contains four stamps similar to Nos. C748-C751 with simulated perforations. Sold for 150p.

Archaeology AP179

Designs (Symbols of): 25p, Science and medicine. 35p, Justice and commerce. 70p, Industry and commerce.

1975, Aug. Litho. *Perf. 12¹/₂x13*

C752	AP179	20p multicolored	30	20
C753	AP179	25p multicolored	42	22
C754	AP179	35p blue & multi	60	38
C755	AP179	70p buff & multi	1.40	70

Beirut, University City.

Stamps of 1971-73 Overprinted with Various Overall Patterns Including Cedars in Blue, Red, Orange, Lilac, Brown or Green

1978 Litho. *Perf. 12, 14*

C758	AP162	2.50p	(#C658;B)	15	15
C759	AP162	5p	(#C659;R)	15	15
C760	AP164	5p	(#C674;B)	15	15
C761	AP164	10p	(#C675;B)	15	15
C762	AP167	10p	(#C690;O)	15	15
C763	AP162	15p	(#C660;R)	30	15
C764	AP164	20p	(#C676;B)	20	15
C765	AP167	20p	(#C691;B)	20	15
C766	AP162	25p	(#C661;L)	20	15
C767	AP164	25p	(#C677;B)	42	15
C768	AP163	35p	(#C670;Br)	50	15
C769	AP162	40p	(#C662;L)	50	16
C770	AP167	40p	(#C693;G)	50	16
C771	AP154	45p	(#C633;L)	50	20
C772	AP162	50p	(#C663;L)	70	20
C773	AP163	50p	(#C671;L)	70	20
C774	AP167	50p	(#C694;Br)	70	20
C775	AP154	70p	(#C635;L)	80	30
C776	AP162	70p	(#C664;L)	80	30
C777	AP167	70p	(#C695;B)	80	30
C778	AP162	75p	(#C665;B)	1.25	30
C779	AP154	85p	(#C636;R)	1.00	35
C780	AP163	85p	(#C672;B)	1.00	35
C781	AP167	85p	(#C696;G)	1.00	35
C782	AP162	100p	(#C666;O)	1.50	42
C783	AP163	100p	(#C673;B)	1.50	42
C784	AP167	100p	(#C697;L)	1.50	42
C785	AP162	200p	(#C667;O)	3.00	1.60
C786	AP162	300p	(#C668;O)	4.25	3.00
C787	AP162	500p	(#C669;O)	6.50	4.25
		Nos. C758-C787 (30)		31.07	15.13

Heart and Arrow — AP180

1978, Apr. 7 Litho. *Perf. 12*

C788	AP180	50p blue, blk & red	80	65

World Health Day; drive against hypertension.

Poet Mikhail Naimy and Sannine Mountains — AP181

Designs: 50p, Naimy and view of Al Chakhroub Baskinta. 75p, Naimy portrait in sunburst, vert.

1978, May 17

C789	AP181	25p gold & multi	55	24
C790	AP181	50p gold & multi	1.00	55
C791	AP181	75p gold & multi	1.60	80

Mikhail Naimy Festival.

Army Day Type of 1980

Designs: 50p, Emir Fakhr al-Din statue, vert. 75p, Soldiers and flag.

1980, Dec. 28 Litho. *Perf. 11¹/₂*

C792	A86	50p multicolored	50	25
C793	A86	75p multicolored	65	40

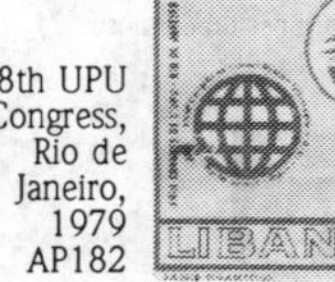

28th UPU Congress, Rio de Janeiro, 1979 AP182

1981, Feb. 17 Photo. *Perf. 12x11¹/₂*

C794	AP182	25p multicolored	25	15
C795	AP182	50p multicolored	65	30
C796	AP182	75p multicolored	1.10	45

Intl. Year of the Child (1979) AP183

1981, Mar. 25 Litho. *Perf. 12x11¹/₂*

C797	AP183	100p multicolored	1.00	65

1974 Chess Championships — AP184

Designs: Various chess pieces. Nos. C799-C802 vert.

Perf. 12x11¹/₂, 11¹/₂x12

1980-81 Photo.

C798	AP184	50p multicolored	1.10	50
C799	AP184	75p multicolored	1.25	65
C800	AP184	100p multicolored	1.65	1.00
C801	AP184	150p multicolored	2.50	1.90
C802	AP184	200p multicolored	3.50	2.50
		Nos. C798-C802 (5)	10.00	6.55

Makassed Islamic Institute Centenary (1978) AP185

1981 Photo. *Perf. 13¹/₂x14*

C803	AP185	50p Children	60	15
C804	AP185	75p Institute	1.00	20
C805	AP185	100p Makassed	1.25	38

AIR POST SEMI-POSTAL STAMPS

Nos. C13-C16 Surcharged Like Nos. B1-B12

1926 *Perf. 13¹/₂*

CB1	A2	2pi + 1pi dk brown	2.75	2.25
CB2	A2	3pi + 2pi org brown	2.75	2.25
CB3	A2	5pi + 3pi violet	2.75	2.25
CB4	A3	10pi + 5pi vio brown	2.75	2.25

These stamps were sold for their combined values, original and surcharged. The latter represented their postal franking value and the former was a contribution to the relief of refugees from the Djebel Druze War.

Catalogue values for unused stamps in this section, from this point to the end of the section, are for Never Hinged items.

Independent Republic

Natural Bridge, Faraya SPAP1

Bay of Jounie SPAP2

Perf. 11½

1947, June 27 Unwmk. Litho.

Cross in Carmine

No.	Type	Description	Unused	Used
CB5	SPAP1	12.50 + 25pi brt bl grn	5.25	3.00
CB6	SPAP1	25 + 50pi blue	6.00	3.50
CB7	SPAP2	50 + 100pi choc	7.50	4.00
CB8	SPAP2	75 + 150pi brt pur	15.00	8.00
CB9	SPAP2	100 + 200pi sl	22.50	11.00
		Nos. CB5-CB9 (5)	56.25	29.50

The surtax was for the Red Cross.

Mother & Child Type of Air Post Stamps, 1960

1960, Aug. 16 *Perf. 13½x13*

No.	Type	Description	Unused	Used
CB10	AP72	20p + 10p dk red & buff	70	16
CB11	AP72	60p + 15p bl & lt bl	1.75	50

Olympic Games Type of Semi-Postal Issue, 1961

1961, Jan. 12 Unwmk. *Perf. 13*

No.	Type	Description	Unused	Used
CB12	SP1	15p + 15p Fencing	1.40	1.00
CB13	SP1	25p + 25p Bicycling	1.40	1.00
CB14	SP1	35p + 35p Swimming	1.40	1.00

An imperf. souvenir sheet exists, containing one each of Nos. CB12-CB14. Value $22.50.

Nos. CB12-CB14 with Arabic and French Overprint in Green, Red or Maroon and two Bars through Olympic Inscription: "CHAMPIONNAT D'EUROPE DE TIR, 2 JUIN 1962"

1962, June 2

No.	Type	Description	Unused	Used
CB15	SP1	15p + 15p (G)	80	45
CB16	SP1	25p + 25p (M)	1.65	90
CB17	SP1	35p + 35p (R)	2.00	1.20

European Marksmanship Championships held in Lebanon.

POSTAGE DUE STAMPS

Postage Due Stamps of France, 1893-1920, Surcharged like Regular Issue

1924 Unwmk. *Perf. 14x13½*

No.	Type	Description	Unused	Used
J1	D2	50c on 10c choc	3.00	1.60
J2	D2	1p on 20c ol grn	3.00	1.60
J3	D2	2p on 30c red	3.00	1.60
J4	D2	3p on 50c vio brn	3.00	1.60
J5	D2	5p on 1fr red brn, *straw*	3.00	1.60
		Nos. J1-J5 (5)	15.00	8.00

Postage Due Stamps of France, 1893-1920, Surcharged

G^d Liban
2 Piastres
لبنان الكبير
غرش ٢

1924

No.	Type	Description	Unused	Used
J6	D2	50c on 10c choc	3.50	1.60
J7	D2	1p on 20c ol grn	3.50	1.60
J8	D2	2p on 30c red	3.50	1.60
J9	D2	3p on 50c vio brn	3.50	1.60
J10	D2	5p on 1fr red brn, *straw*	3.50	1.60
		Nos. J6-J10 (5)	17.50	8.00

Ancient Bridge across Dog River — D3

Designs: 1p, Village scene. 2p, Pigeon Rocks, near Beirut. 3p, Belfort Castle. 5p, Venus Temple at Baalbek.

1925 Photo. *Perf. 13½*

No.	Type	Description	Unused	Used
J11	D3	50c brown, *yellow*	30	16
J12	D3	1p violet, *rose*	50	25
J13	D3	2p black, *blue*	80	42
J14	D3	3p black, *red org*	1.50	80
J15	D3	5p black, *bl grn*	2.75	1.40
		Nos. J11-J15 (5)	5.85	3.03

Nos. J11 to J15 Overprinted

1927

No.	Type	Description	Unused	Used
J16	D3	50c brown, *yellow*	40	22
J17	D3	1p violet, *rose*	65	35
J18	D3	2p black, *blue*	90	50
J19	D3	3p black, *red org*	2.50	1.40
J20	D3	5p black, *bl grn*	3.00	1.60
		Nos. J16-J20 (5)	7.45	4.07

Nos. J16 to J20 with Additional Overprint

= =

الجمهورية اللبنانية

1928

No.	Type	Description	Unused	Used
J21	D3	50c brn, *yel* (Bk+R)	1.00	50
J22	D3	1p vio, *rose* (Bk)	1.00	50
J23	D3	2p blk, *bl* (Bk+R)	2.00	1.00
J24	D3	3p blk, *red org* (Bk)	4.00	2.00
J25	D3	5p blk, *bl grn* (Bk+R)	4.50	2.25
		Nos. J21-J25 (5)	12.50	6.25

No. J23 has not the short bars in the upper corners.

Postage Due Stamps of 1925 Overprinted in Red like Nos. J21-J25

1928

No.	Type	Description	Unused	Used
J26	D3	50c brn, *yel* (R)	45	22
J27	D3	2p blk, *bl* (R)	2.75	1.40
J28	D3	5p blk, *bl grn* (R)	8.00	4.00

No. J28 has not the short bars in the upper corners.

D4

Bas-relief of a Ship — D5

D6

D7

D8

Bas-relief from Sarcophagus of King Ahiram — D9

D10

1930-40 Photo.; Engr. (No. J35)

No.	Type	Description	Unused	Used
J29	D4	50c black, *rose*	26	16
J30	D5	1p blk, *gray bl*	55	35
J31	D6	2p blk, *yellow*	80	50
J32	D7	3p blk, *bl grn*	80	50
J33	D8	5p blk, *orange*	3.75	2.25
J34	D9	8p blk, *lt rose*	2.50	1.50
J35	D8	10p dk green ('40)	4.00	2.00
J36	D10	15p black	3.25	1.40
		Nos. J29-J36 (8)	15.91	8.66

Nos. J29-J36 exist imperf.

Catalogue values for unused stamps in this section, from this point to the end of the section, are for Never Hinged items.

Independent Republic

National Museum, Beirut — D11

1945 Unwmk. Litho. *Perf. 11½*

No.	Type	Description	Unused	Used
J37	D11	2p brn black, *yel*	2.75	1.40
J38	D11	5p ultra, *rose*	4.00	1.60
J39	D11	25p blue, *bl green*	6.00	2.50
J40	D11	50p dark bl, *blue*	6.25	2.50

D12

1947

No.	Type	Description	Unused	Used
J41	D12	5p black, *green*	4.00	50
J42	D12	25p blk, *yellow*	40.00	1.40
J43	D12	50p black, *blue*	20.00	2.00

Hermel Monument D13

1948

No.	Type	Description	Unused	Used
J44	D13	2p blk, *yellow*	1.40	35
J45	D13	3p black, *pink*	2.50	1.25
J46	D13	10p black, *blue*	6.50	2.25

D14

1950

No.	Type	Description	Unused	Used
J47	D14	1p carmine rose	1.25	15
J48	D14	5p violet blue	4.50	35
J49	D14	10p gray green	9.25	65

D15

1952

No.	Type	Description	Unused	Used
J50	D15	1p dp rose lilac	15	15
J51	D15	2p bright violet	15	15
J52	D15	3p dk blue green	26	15
J53	D15	5p blue	38	15
J54	D15	10p chocolate	52	20
J55	D15	25p black	4.50	65
		Nos. J50-J55 (6)	5.96	
		Set value		1.20

D16

D17

1953

No.	Type	Description	Unused	Used
J56	D16	1p carmine rose	15	15
J57	D16	2p blue green	15	15
J58	D16	3p orange	15	15
J59	D16	5p lilac rose	32	15
J60	D16	10p brown	70	15
J61	D16	15p deep blue	1.25	35
		Nos. J56-J61 (6)	2.72	
		Set value		75

1955 Unwmk. *Perf. 13*

No.	Type	Description	Unused	Used
J62	D17	1p orange brown	15	15
J63	D17	2p yellow green	15	15
J64	D17	3p blue green	15	15
J65	D17	5p carmine lake	20	15
J66	D17	10p gray green	28	15
J67	D17	15p ultramarine	40	15
J68	D17	25p red lilac	85	25
		Nos. J62-J68 (7)	2.18	
		Set value		60

Cedar of Lebanon — D18

Emir Fakhr al-Din II — D19

1966 Photo. *Perf. 11½*

No.	Type	Description	Unused	Used
J69	D18	1p bright green	20	15
J70	D18	5p rose lilac	20	15
J71	D18	15p ultramarine	32	15
		Set value		24

1968 Litho. *Perf. 11*

No.	Type	Description	Unused	Used
J72	D19	1p dk & lt gray	32	15
J73	D19	2p dk & lt blue grn	32	15
J74	D19	3p deep org & yel	32	15
J75	D19	5p brt rose lil & pink	32	15
J76	D19	10p olive & lemon	32	15
J77	D19	15p vio & pale violet	40	15
J78	D19	25p brt & lt blue	70	20
		Nos. J72-J78 (7)	2.70	
		Set value		65

POSTAL TAX STAMPS

Fiscal Stamp Surcharged in Violet

R1

Wmk. A T 39 Multiple

1945 *Perf. 13½*

No.	Type	Description	Unused	Used
RA1	R1	5pi on 30c red brn	16.50	1.40

The tax was for the Lebanese Army.

No. RA1 Overprinted in Black

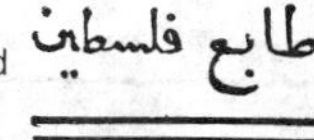

1948

No.	Type	Description	Unused	Used
RA2	R1	5pi on 30c red brn	16.50	1.40

Fiscal Stamps Surcharged in Various Colors

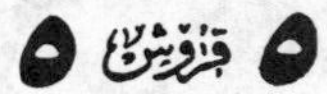

RA3 R1 5pi on 15pi dk vio bl (R) 14.00 1.60
a. Brown surcharge 18.00 2.25
RA4 R1 5pi on 25c dk blue green (R) 14.00 1.60
RA5 R1 5pi on 30c red brn (Bl) 16.00 1.60
RA6 R1 5pi on 60c lt ultra (Br) 22.50 1.60
RA7 R1 5pi on 3pi salmon rose (Ult) 14.00 1.60

Same With Additional Overprint طابع قضائي

RA8 R1 5pi on 10pi red *65.00* 5.00

Fiscal Stamp Surcharged Like Nos. RA3-RA7 with Top Arabic Characters Replaced by

ضريبة فلسطين

RA9 R1 5pi on 3pi rose (Bk+V) 16.50 1.40

Fiscal Stamp Surcharged in Black and Violet

RA10 R1 5pi on 3pi sal rose *190.00* 15.00

The tax was to aid the war in Palestine.

Catalogue values for unused stamps in this section, from this point to the end of the section, are for Never Hinged items.

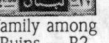

Family among Ruins — R2

Building a House — R3

1956 Unwmk. Litho. ***Perf. 13***
RA11 R2 2.50pi brown 1.75 16

The tax was for earthquake victims. These stamps were obligatory on all inland mail and all mail going to Arab countries.

1957-58 ***Perf. 13¹/₂x13***
RA12 R3 2.50p brown 1.10 15
RA13 R3 2.50p dk blue grn ('58) 85 15

Type of 1957 Redrawn

1959
RA14 R3 2.50p light brown 2.00 16

On No. RA14 the denomination is on top and the Arabic lines are at the bottom of design.

Demand, as well as supply, determines a stamp's market value. One is as important as the other.

Building a House
R4 R5

1961 Unwmk. ***Perf. 13¹/₂x13***
RA15 R4 2.50p yellow brown 1.00 15

1962 ***Perf. 13¹/₂x14***
RA16 R5 2.50p blue green 3.75 15

The tax was for the relief of earthquake victims.

LIBERIA

LOCATION — West coast of Africa, between Ivory Coast and Sierra Leone
GOVT. — Republic
AREA — 43,000 sq. mi.
POP. — 1,900,000 (est. 1984)
CAPITAL — Monrovia

100 Cents = 1 Dollar

Catalogue values for unused stamps in this country are for Never Hinged items, beginning with Scott 330 in the regular postage section, Scott B19 in the semi-postal section, Scott C67 in the airpost section, and Scott CB4 in the airpost semi-postal section.

Watermarks

Wmk. 116- Crosses and Circles

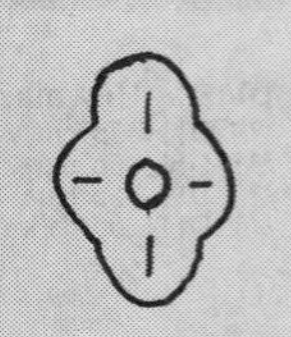

Wmk. 143

"Liberia" — A1

1860 Unwmk. Litho. ***Perf. 12***
Thick Paper

1 A1 6c red 125.00 125.00
a. Imperf. 140.00
2 A1 12c deep blue 22.50 35.00
a. Imperf. 90.00
3 A1 24c green 22.50 35.00
a. Imperf. 90.00

Stamps set very close together. Margins small and perforation close to or touching the design. Copies of the 12c occasionally show traces of a frame line around the design.

Medium to Thin Paper
With a single-line frame around each stamp, about 1mm from the border

1864 ***Perf. 11, 12***
7 A1 6c red 52.50 67.50
a. Imperf. 90.00
8 A1 12c blue 52.50 67.50
a. Imperf. 90.00
9 A1 24c lt grn 52.50 67.50
a. Imperf. 90.00

Stamps set about 5mm apart. Margins large and perforation usually outside the frame line.

Without Frame Line

1866-69
13 A1 6c lt red 17.50 30.00
14 A1 12c lt bl 15.00 30.00
15 A1 24c lt yel grn 15.00 30.00

Stamps set 2-2¹/₂mm apart with small margins. Stamps are usually without frame line but those from one transfer show broken and irregular parts of a frame.

With Frame Line

1880 ***Perf. 10¹/₂***
16 A1 1c ultra 3.25 5.00
17 A1 2c rose 3.25 3.00
a. Imperf., pair 150.00
18 A1 6c violet 3.25 3.00
19 A1 12c yellow 3.25 3.00
20 A1 24c rose red 3.25 3.50

Unused values for Nos. 16-20 are for copies without gum.
For surcharges see Nos. 157-159.

Counterfeits
Counterfeits exist of Nos. 1-28, 32 and 64.

From Arms of Liberia — A2

1881
21 A2 3c black 3.50 3.50

Unused value is for copies without gum.

A3

A4

1882 ***Perf. 11¹/₂, 12, 14***
22 A3 8c blue 25.00 4.00
23 A4 16c red 4.00 2.50

On No. 22 the openings in the figure "8" enclose a pattern of slanting lines. Compare with No. 32.

Canceled to Order
Beginning with the issue of 1885, values in the used column are for "canceled to order" stamps. Postally used copies sell for much more.

A5

A6

From Arms of Liberia — A7

A8

Perf. 10¹/₂, 11, 12, 11¹/₂x10¹/₂, 14, 14¹/₂

1885
24 A5 1c carmine 1.00 1.00
a. 1c rose 1.00 1.00
25 A5 2c green 1.00 1.00
26 A5 3c violet 1.00 1.00
27 A5 4c brown 1.00 1.00
28 A5 6c olive gray 1.00 1.00
29 A6 8c bluish gray 2.50 2.50
a. 8c lilac 2.50 2.50
30 A6 16c yellow 3.50 3.50
31 A7 32c deep blue 12.00 12.00
Nos. 24-31 (8) 23.00 23.00

In the 1885 printing, the stamps are spaced 2mm apart and the paper is medium. In the 1892 printing, the stamps are 4¹/₂mm apart.
For surcharges see Nos. J1-J2.

Imperf., Pair

24b A5 1c 2.50
25a A5 2c 3.50
26a A5 3c 4.00
27a A5 4c 4.00
28a A5 6c 3.50 3.50
29b A6 8c 10.00
30a A6 16c 12.50
31a A7 32c 25.00

Imperf. pairs with 2mm spacing sell for higher prices.

1889 ***Perf. 12, 14***
32 A8 8c blue 3.50 3.50
a. Imperf., pair 15.00

The openings in the figure "8" are filled with network. See No. 22.

A9

Elephant — A10

Oil Palm — A11

Pres. Hilary R. W. Johnson — A12

Vai Woman in Full Dress — A13

Coat of Arms — A14

Liberian Star — A15

Coat of Arms — A16

Hippopotamus A17

Liberian Star A18

President Johnson — A19

1892-96 Wmk. 143 Engr. ***Perf. 15***
33 A9 1c vermilion 32 24
a. 1c blue (error) 30.00
34 A9 2c blue 32 24
a. 2c vermilion (error) 30.00
35 A10 4c grn & blk 1.25 60
a. Center inverted 75.00 75.00
36 A11 6c bl grn 50 35
37 A12 8c brn & blk 60 60
a. Center inverted 300.00 300.00
38 A12 10c chrome yel & indigo ('96) 60 45
39 A13 12c rose red 60 45
40 A13 15c slate ('96) 60 45
41 A14 16c lilac 1.75 1.25
42 A14 20c ver ('96) 1.75 1.25
43 A15 24c ol grn, *yel* 1.00 75
44 A15 25c yel grn ('96) 1.25 90
45 A16 30c steel bl ('96) 4.25 3.00
46 A16 32c grnsh bl 2.50 1.75
47 A17 $1 ultra & blk 4.75 3.25
a. $1 blue & black 5.25 4.00

48 A18 $2 brn, *yel* 2.75 2.50
49 A19 $5 car & blk 5.00 4.25
a. Center inverted 225.00 225.00
Nos. 33-49 (17) 29.79 22.28

Many misperforated and part-perforated varieties exist.

The 1c, 2c and 4c were issued in sheets of 60; 6c, sheet of 40; 8c, 10c, sheets of 30; 12c, 15c, 24c, 25c, sheets of 20; 16c, 20c, 30c, sheets of 15; $1, $2, $5, sheets of 10.

For overprints see Nos. 64B-64F, 66, 71-77, 79-81, 85-90, O1-O12, O15-O25, O37-O41. For surcharges see Nos. 50, 91-93, 95-100, 160, O13, O44-O45.

No. 36 Surcharged:

5 5 5 5

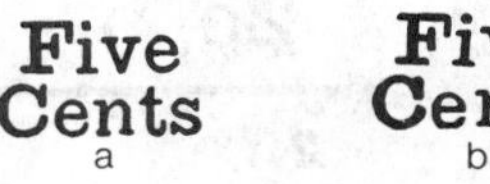

a b

1893
50 A11 (a) 5c on 6c bl grn 1.50 90
a. "5" with short flag 4.00 4.00
b. Both 5's with short flags 2.00 2.00
c. "i" dot omitted 15.00 15.00
d. Surcharge "b" 25.00 25.00

"Commerce," Globe and Krumen — A22

1894 Unwmk. Engr. *Imperf.*
52 A22 5c car & blk 2.50 1.75

Rouletted
53 A22 5c car & blk 4.00 2.75

For overprints see Nos. 69, O26-O27.

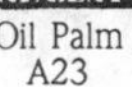

Oil Palm
A23

Hippopotamus
A24

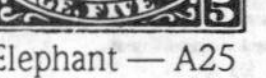

Elephant — A25

Liberty — A26

1897-1905 Wmk. 143 *Perf. 14 to 16*
54 A23 1c lilac rose 65 38
a. 1c violet 65 40
55 A23 1c dp grn ('00) 80 52
56 A23 1c lt grn ('05) 1.40 70
57 A24 2c bister & blk 1.65 95
58 A24 2c org red & blk ('00) 2.25 95
59 A24 2c rose & blk ('05) 1.65 95
60 A25 5c lake & blk 1.65 95
a. 5c lilac rose & black 1.65 95
61 A25 5c gray bl & blk ('00) 3.25 1.50
62 A25 5c ultra & blk ('05) 2.50 1.50
a. Center inverted 500.00
63 A26 50c red brn & blk 2.25 1.50
Nos. 54-63 (10) 18.05 9.90

For overprints see Nos. 65, 66A-66, 70, 78, 82-84, O28-O36, O42. For surcharges see Nos. M1, O92.

A27

Two types:
I - 13 pearls above "Republic Liberia."
II - 10 pearls.

1897 Unwmk. Litho. *Perf. 14*
64 A27 3c red & green (I) 20 40
a. Type II *10.00* 15

No. 64a is considered a reprint, unissued. "Used" copies are CTO.

For surcharge see No. 128.

Official Stamps Handstamped in Black ***ORDINARY***

1901-02 Wmk. 143

On Nos. O7-O8, O10-O12
64B A14 16c lilac *325.00 325.00*
64C A15 24c ol grn, *yel* *300.00 300.00*
64D A17 $1 bl & blk *1,350. 1,350.*
64E A18 $2 brn, *yel*
64F A19 $5 car & blk

On Stamps with "O S" Printed
65 A23 1c green 27.50 32.50
66 A9 2c blue 77.50 82.50
66A A24 2c bis & blk 60.00
67 A24 2c org red & blk 27.50 32.50
68 A25 5c gray bl & blk 22.50 27.50
69 A22 5c vio & grn (No. O26) 225.00 235.00
70 A25 5c lake & blk 150.00 155.00
71 A12 10c yel & bl blk 27.50 32.50
a. "O S" omitted
72 A13 15c slate 27.50 32.50
73 A14 16c lilac 225.00 235.00
74 A14 20c vermilion 32.50 37.50
75 A15 24c ol grn,*yel* 32.50 37.50
76 A15 25c yel grn 32.50 37.50
a. "O S" omitted
77 A16 30c steel blue 27.50 32.50
78 A26 50c red brn & blk 37.50 42.50
79 A17 $1 ultra & blk 225.00 225.00
a. "O S" omitted
80 A18 $2 brn, *yel* *1,200. 1,200.*
81 A19 $5 car & blk *1,500. 1,500.*
a. "O S" omitted *2,250. 2,250.*

On Stamps with "O S" Handstamped
82 A23 1c dp grn 50.00
83 A24 2c org red & blk 60.00
84 A25 5c lake & blk 100.00
85 A12 10c yel & bl blk 90.00
86 A14 20c vermilion 100.00
87 A15 24c ol grn, *yel* 100.00
88 A15 25c yel grn 125.00
89 A16 30c steel blue 250.00
90 A16 32c grnsh bl 140.00

Varieties of Nos. 65-90 include double and inverted overprints.

Nos. 47, O10, O23a Surcharged in Carmine **75c.**

1902
91 A17 75c on $1 #47 8.50 7.50
a. Thin "C" and comma 15.00 15.00
b. Inverted surcharge 50.00 50.00
c. As "a," inverted
92 A17 75c on $1 #O10 *1,750.*
a. Thin "C" and comma *2,500.*
93 A17 75c on $1 #O23a *1,900.*
a. Thin "C" and comma *2,500.*

Liberty — A29

1903 Unwmk. Engr. *Perf. 14*
94 A29 3c black 30 15
a. Printed on both sides 45.00
b. Perf. 12 5.00 3.00

For overprint see No. O43.

Stamps of 1892 Surcharged in Blue

TEN **FIFTEEN**
Cents. **Cents.**
a b

1903 Wmk. 143
95 A14 (a) 10c on 16c lilac 2.50 3.25
96 A15 (b) 15c on 24c ol grn, *yel* 3.50 4.50
97 A16 (b) 20c on 32c grnsh bl 5.00 6.25

Nos. 50, O3 and 45 Surcharged in Black or Red

1904
98 A11 1c on 5c on 6c bl grn 50 45
a. "5" with short flag 3.50 3.50
b. Both 5's with short flags 7.00 7.00
c. "i" dot omitted
d. Surcharge on #50d 10.00 10.00
e. Inverted surcharge 5.50 5.50
99 A10 2c on 4c grn & blk 1.25 2.25
a. Pair, one without surcharge 27.50
b. Double surcharge
c. Double surcharge, red and blk 50.00
d. Surcharged on back also 15.00
e. "Official" overprint missing 25.00
100 A16 2c on 30c stl bl (R) 7.00 11.00

African Elephant — A33 Mercury — A34

Chimpanzee
A35

Great Blue Touraco
A36

Agama — A37

Egret — A38

Head of Liberty From Coin — A39

A40

Liberian Flag
A41

Pygmy Hippopotamus
A42

Liberty with Star of Liberia on Cap
A43

Mandingos
A44

Executive Mansion and Pres. Arthur Barclay — A45

1906 Unwmk. Engr. *Perf. 14*
101 A33 1c grn & blk 65 30
102 A34 2c car & blk 15 15
103 A35 5c ultra & blk 1.40 45
104 A36 10c red brn & blk 2.00 45
105 A37 15c pur & dp grn 5.00 1.65
106 A38 20c org & blk 4.25 1.40
107 A39 25c dl bl & gray 45 15
108 A40 30c dp vio 50 15
109 A41 50c dp grn & blk 50 15
110 A42 75c brn & blk 5.00 1.40
111 A43 $1 rose & gray 1.40 18
112 A44 $2 dp grn & blk 2.00 20
113 A45 $5 red brn & blk 4.00 30
Nos. 101-113 (13) 27.30 6.93

For surcharges see Nos. 114, 129, 130, 141, 145-149, 161, M2, M5, O72-O73, O82-O85, O96. For overprints see Nos. O46-O58.

Center Inverted

101a	A33	1c	32.50	32.50
102a	A34	2c	25.00	25.00
103a	A35	5c	110.00	110.00
104a	A36	10c	50.00	50.00
105a	A37	15c	110.00	110.00
106b	A38	20c	110.00	110.00
107a	A39	25c	47.50	47.50
109b	A41	50c	47.50	47.50
110b	A42	75c	80.00	80.00
111a	A43	$1	65.00	65.00
112a	A44	$2	62.50	62.50

Imperf., Pairs

101b	A33	1c	10.00	
102b	A34	2c	4.00	
106a	A38	20c	15.00	
107b	A39	25c	40.00	40.00
109a	A41	50c	15.00	
110a	A42	75c	15.00	
113a	A45	$5	20.00	

No. 104 Surcharged in Black

1909
114 A36 3c on 10c red brn & blk 4.00 4.00

Coffee Plantation — A46

Pres. Barclay — A47

S. S. Pres. Daniel E. Howard, former Gunboat Lark — A48

Commerce with Caduceus — A49

Vai Woman Spinning Cotton — A50

Blossom and Fruit of Pepper Plant — A51

Circular House — A52

President Barclay — A53

Men in Canoe — A54

Liberian Village — A55

1909-12 *Perf. 14*

115	A46	1c yel grn & blk	30	30
116	A47	2c lake & blk	30	30
117	A48	5c ultra & blk	30	30
118	A49	10c plum & blk, perf. 12½ ('12)	30	30
a.		Imperf., pair	10.00	
119	A50	15c ind & blk	40	35
120	A51	20c rose & grn	1.90	35
b.		Imperf.		
121	A52	25c dk brn & blk	55	35
a.		Imperf.		
122	A53	30c dk brn	1.90	35
123	A54	50c grn & blk	1.50	35
124	A55	75c red brn & blk	1.10	35
		Nos. 115-124 (10)	8.55	3.30

Rouletted

125	A49	10c plum & blk	60	38

For surcharges see Nos. 126-127E, 131-133, 136-140, 142-144, 151-156, 162, B1-B2, M3-M4, M6-M7, O70-O1, O74-O81, O86-O91, O97.
For overprints see Nos. O59-O69.

Center Inverted

116a	A47	2c	60.00	52.50
117a	A48	5c	55.00	47.50
119a	A50	15c	42.50	42.50
120a	A51	20c	62.50	47.50
121b	A52	25c	42.50	37.50
123a	A54	50c	65.00	55.00

Stamps and Types of 1909-12 Surcharged in Blue or Red

3 CENTS INLAND POSTAGE

1910-12 *Rouletted*

126	A49	3c on 10c plum & blk (Bl)	35	20
a.		"3" inverted		
126B	A49	3c on 10c blk & ultra (R)	20.00	2.50

No. 126B is roulette 7. It also exists in roulette 13.

Perf. 12½, 14, 12½x14

127	A49	3c on 10c plum & blk (Bl) ('12)	35	20
a.		Imperf., pair	20.00	
b.		Double surcharge, one invtd.	20.00	
c.		Double vertical surcharge		
127E	A49	3c on 10c blk & ultra (R) ('12)	12.00	50

Nos. 64, 64a Surcharged in Dark Green

1913

128	A27	8c on 3c red & grn (I)	25	15
a.		Surcharge on No. 64a	2.50	15
b.		Double surcharge	5.00	
c.		Imperf., pair	16.00	
d.		Inverted surcharge	20.00	

Stamps of Preceding Issues Surcharged

1914

2
CENTS
a

b

1914

On Issue of 1906

129	A39 (a)	2c on 25c dl bl & gray	7.50	2.00
130	A40 (b)	5c on 30c dp vio	7.50	2.00

On Issue of 1909

131	A52 (a)	2c on 25c brn & blk	7.50	2.00
132	A53 (b)	5c on 30c dk brn	7.50	2.00
133	A54 (a)	10c on 50c grn & blk	7.50	2.00
		Nos. 129-133 (5)	37.50	10.00

Liberian House — A57

Providence Island, Monrovia Harbor — A58

1915 Engr. Wmk. 116 *Perf. 14*

134	A57	2c red	15	15
135	A58	3c dull violet	15	15
		Set value		16

For overprints see Nos. 196-197, O113-O114, O128-O129.

Nos. 109, 111-113, 119-124 Surcharged with New Values in Dark Blue, Black or Red:

c

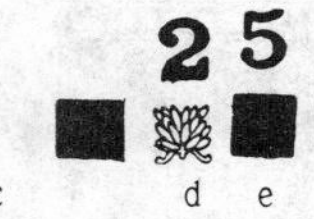

d e

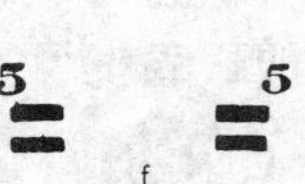

f

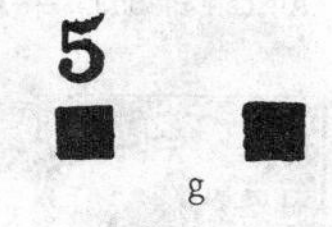

g

1915-16 **Unwmk.**

136	A50 (c)	2c on 15c (R)	80	80
137	A52 (d)	2c on 25c (R)	6.00	6.00
138	A51 (e)	5c on 20c (Bk)	1.00	5.00
139	A53 (f)	5c on 30c (R)	4.00	4.00
a.		Double surcharge	12.00	12.00
140	A53 (g)	5c on 30c (R)	35.00	35.00

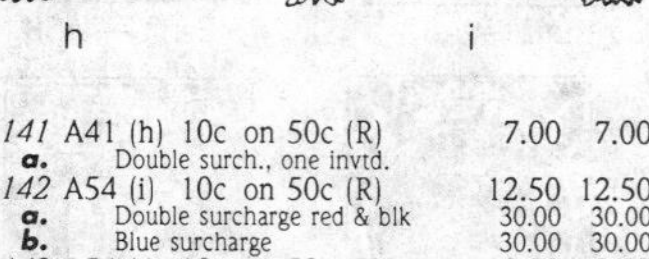

h i

141	A41 (h)	10c on 50c (R)	7.00	7.00
a.		Double surch., one invtd.		
142	A54 (i)	10c on 50c (R)	12.50	12.50
a.		Double surcharge red & blk	30.00	30.00
b.		Blue surcharge	30.00	30.00
143	A54 (i)	10c on 50c (Bk)	12.50	12.50

144	A55 (j)	20c on 75c (Bk)	3.00	5.00
145	A43 (k)	25c on $1 (Bk)	37.50	37.50

146	A44 (l)	50c on $2 (R)	10.00	10.00
a.		"Ceuts"	15.00	15.00
147	A44 (m)	50c on $2 (R)	700.00	700.00

148	A45	$1 on $5 (Bk)	50.00	50.00
a.		Double surcharge	75.00	75.00

o

149	A45	$1 on $5 (R)	45.00	45.00

The color of the red surcharge varies from light dull red to almost brown.

Handstamped Surcharge, Type "i"

150	A54	10c on 50c (Dk Bl)	12.50	12.50

No. 119 Surcharged in Black

2

151	A50	2c on 15c	325.00	325.00

No. 119 Surcharged in Red

2

152	A50	2c on 15c	40.00	35.00
a.		Double surcharge	80.00	

Nos. 116-117 Surcharged in Black or Red

1 a1 **1c** b1

one cemt c1

1ct d1 **one one** e1

1c (inverted) f1 **1cent** * * * * * * g1

1 c 1 h1

one c one i1 **1cts** j1

Two cemts k2

Two cents l2

2cents m2

Two cts (inverted) n2

2c o2

2. **2.** p2

two c two q2

2 2 r2

two s2

2cent t2

153	A47	1c on 2c lake & blk	2.25	2.25
a.		Strip of 10 types	30.00	
154	A48	2c on 5c ultra & blk (R)	2.25	2.25
a.		Black surcharge	12.00	12.00
b.		Strip of 10 types (R)	30.00	
c.		Strip of 10 types (Bk)	140.00	

The 10 types of surcharge are repeated in illustrated sequence on 1c on 2c in each horiz. row and on 2c on 5c in each vert. row of sheets of 100 (10x10).

No. 116 and Type of 1909 Surcharged:

one ct.

155	A47	1c on 2c lake & blk	100.00	100.00

2ct

156	A48	2c on 5c turq & blk	100.00	100.00

1916

Nos. 18-20 Surcharged

5

1916

157	A1	3c on 6c vio	35.00	35.00
a.		Inverted surcharge	60.00	60.00
158	A1	5c on 12c yel	2.50	2.50
a.		Inverted surcharge	10.00	10.00
b.		Surcharge sideways	10.00	
159	A1	10c on 24c rose red	2.25	2.50
a.		Inverted surcharge	12.00	12.00
b.		Surcharge sideways		

Unused values for Nos. 157-159 are for copies without gum.

Nos. 44 and 108 Surcharged

FOUR 1917 CENTS
p

1917 FIVE CENTS
r

1917 **Wmk. 143**

160 A15 (p) 4c on 25c yel grn	9.00	9.00
a. "OUR"	20.00	20.00
b. "FCUR"	20.00	20.00

Unwmk.

161 A40 (r) 5c on 30c dp vio	70.00	70.00

No. 118 Surcharged in Red 3 CENTS

1918

162 A49 3c on 10c plum & blk	2.00	2.00
a. "3" inverted	8.00	8.00

Bongo Antelope — A59

Symbols of Liberia — A61

Two-spot Palm Civet — A60

A62

Palm-nut Vulture — A66

Oil Palm — A63

Mercury — A64

Traveler's Tree A65

"Mudskipper" or Bommi Fish — A67

Mandingos — A68

"Liberia" — A71

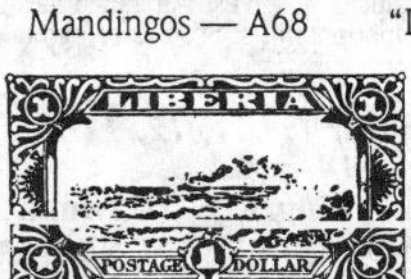

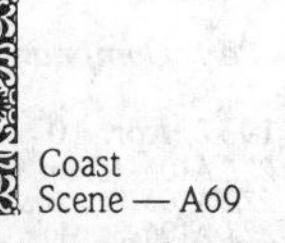

Coast Scene — A69

Liberia College — A70

1918 **Engr.** ***Perf. 12½, 14***

163 A59 1c dp grn & blk	48	15
164 A60 2c rose & blk	60	15
165 A61 5c gray bl & blk	15	15
166 A62 10c dk grn	16	15
167 A63 15c blk & dk grn	2.25	15
168 A64 20c claret & blk	25	15
169 A65 25c dk grn & grn	2.50	15
170 A66 30c red vio & blk	7.50	42
171 A67 50c ultra & blk	12.00	70
172 A68 75c ol bis & blk	65	15
173 A69 $1 yel brn & bl	4.00	15
174 A70 $2 lt vio & blk	4.75	15
175 A71 $5 dk brn	5.00	30
Nos. 163-175 (13)	40.29	2.92

For surcharges see Nos. 176-177, 228-229, 248-270, B3-B15, O111-O112, O155-O157.
For overprints see Nos. O98-O110.

Nos. 163-164, F10-F14 Surcharged

1920 1920

THREE CENTS

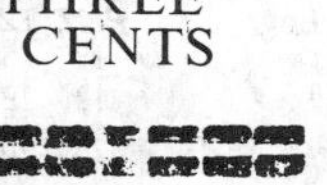

1920 FOUR CENTS

1920

176 A59 3c on 1c grn & blk	85	85
a. "CEETS"	15.00	15.00
b. Double surcharge	6.00	6.00
c. Triple surcharge	7.50	7.50
177 A60 4c on 2c rose & blk	85	85
a. Inverted surcharge	12.00	12.00
b. Double surcharge	4.75	4.75
c. Double surcharge, one invtd.	12.00	
d. Triple surcharge, one inverted	12.00	12.00
e. Quadruple surcharge	15.00	15.00
f. Typewritten surcharge		
g. Same as "f" but inverted		
h. Printed and typewritten surcharges, both inverted		
178 R6 5c on 10c bl & blk	2.25	2.25
a. Inverted surcharge	4.50	4.50
b. Double surcharge	7.25	7.25
c. Double surcharge, one invtd.	7.25	7.25
d. Typewritten surcharge ("five")		62.50
e. Printed and typewritten surcharges	62.50	
179 R6 5c on 10c org red & blk	2.25	2.25
a. 5c on 10c orange & black	3.50	2.50
b. Inverted surcharge	7.25	
c. Double surcharge	7.25	
d. Double surcharge, one invtd.	9.00	8.50
e. Typewritten surch. in violet	62.50	62.50
f. Typewritten surch. in black		
g. Printed and typewritten surcharges	62.50	
180 R6 5c on 10c grn & blk	2.25	2.25
a. Double surcharge	7.25	7.25
b. Double surcharge, one invtd.	11.00	11.00
c. Inverted surcharge		11.00
d. Quadruple surcharge	18.50	18.50
e. Typewritten surcharge		62.50
f. Printed and typewritten surcharges		
181 R6 5c on 10c vio & blk (Monrovia)	3.50	3.50
a. Double surcharge, one invtd.	11.00	11.00
182 R6 5c on 10c mag & blk (Robertsport)	1.75	1.75
a. Double surcharge	11.00	11.00
b. Double surcharge, one invtd.	11.00	11.00
c. Double surcharge, both invtd.	18.50	
Nos. 176-182 (7)	13.70	13.70

Cape Mesurado A75

Pres. Daniel E. Howard — A76

Arms of Liberia — A77

Crocodile A78

Pepper Plant — A79

Leopard — A80

Village Scene — A81

Krumen in Dugout — A82

Rapids in St. Paul's River — A83

Bongo Antelope — A84

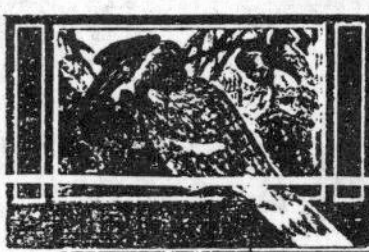

Hornbill — A85

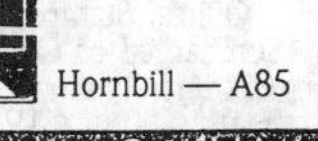

Elephant — A86

1921 **Wmk. 116** ***Perf. 14***

183 A75 1c green	15	15
184 A76 5c dp bl & blk	15	15
185 A77 10c red & dl bl	15	15
186 A78 15c dl vio & grn	3.25	25
187 A79 20c rose red & grn	1.40	15
188 A80 25c org & blk	3.75	25
189 A81 30c grn & dl vio	20	15
190 A82 50c org & ultra	26	15
191 A83 75c red & blk brn	40	15
a. Center inverted		50.00
192 A84 $1 red & blk	16.00	90
193 A85 $2 yel & ultra	5.25	38
194 A86 $5 car rose & vio	16.00	50
Nos. 183-194 (12)	46.96	
Set value		2.75

For overprints see Nos. 195, 198-208, O115-O127, O130-O140.

Nos. 134-135, 183-194 Overprinted "1921"

195 A75 1c green	13.00	22
196 A57 2c red	13.00	22
197 A58 3c dl vio	17.50	22
198 A76 5c dp bl & blk	2.75	22
199 A77 10c red & dl bl	27.50	22
200 A78 15c dl vio & grn	13.00	70
201 A79 20c rose red & grn, ovpt. invtd.	5.75	48
202 A80 25c org & blk	13.00	70
203 A81 30c grn & dl vio	2.00	22
204 A82 50c org & ultra	2.75	22
205 A83 75c red & blk brn	3.75	22
206 A84 $1 red & blk	37.50	1.10
207 A85 $2 yel & ultra	13.00	1.10
208 A86 $5 car rose & vio	35.00	1.40
Nos. 195-208 (14)	199.50	7.24

Overprint exists inverted in Nos. 195-208 and normal on No. 201.

First Settlers Landing at Cape Mesurado from U. S. S. Alligator A87

1923 **Litho.**

209 A87 1c lt bl & blk	12.00	20
210 A87 2c claret & ol gray	17.50	20
211 A87 5c ol grn & ind	17.50	20
212 A87 10c bl grn & vio	65	20
213 A87 $1 rose & brn	2.25	20
Nos. 209-213 (5)	49.90	1.00

Centenary of founding of Liberia.

Memorial to J. J. Roberts, 1st Pres. — A88

Liberian Star — A90

Hall of Representatives, Monrovia A89

Pres. Charles Dunbar Burgess King
A91 A92

Hippopotamus A93

Antelope — A94

West African Buffalo — A95

Grebos Making Dumboy — A96

Pineapple — A97

Carrying Ivory Tusk — A98

Rubber Planter's House — A99

Stockton Lagoon — A100

Grebo Houses A101

1923 ***Perf. 13½x14½, 14½x13½***

White Paper

214	A88	1c yel grn & dp grn	3.50	15
215	A89	2c cl & brn	3.50	15
216	A90	3c lil & blk	25	15
217	A91	5c bl vio & blk	50.00	15
218	A92	10c slate & brn	25	15
219	A93	15c bister & bl	17.50	25
220	A94	20c bl grn & vio	2.00	25
221	A95	25c org red & brn	75.00	30

White, Buff or Brownish Paper

222	A96	30c dk brn & vio	50	15
223	A97	50c dl vio & org	1.00	15
224	A98	75c gray & bl	1.50	32
225	A99	$1 dp red & dk vio	3.50	50
a.		White paper	25.00	
226	A100	$2 org & bl	4.00	45
a.		Buff or brownish paper		
227	A101	$5 dp grn & brn	10.00	45
a.		White paper	25.00	
		Nos. 214-227 (14)	172.50	
		Set value		3.00

Nos. 222-224 on buff or brownish paper sell for about 10% more.

For overprints see Nos. O141-O154.

No. 163 Surcharged

1926 **Unwmk.** ***Perf. 14***

228	A59	2c on 1c dp grn & blk	2.25	2.25
a.		Surch. with ornamental design as on #O155	9.00	

No. 163 Surcharged in Red

1927

229	A59	2c on 1c dp grn & blk	6.00	6.00
a.		"Ceuts"	8.50	
b.		"Vwo"	8.50	
c.		"Twc"	8.50	
d.		Double surcharge	17.00	
e.		Wavy lines omitted	11.00	

Palms — A102

Map of Africa — A103

President King — A104

1928 **Engr.** ***Perf. 12***

230	A102	1c green	20	15
231	A102	2c dk vio	30	22
232	A102	3c bis brn	30	22
233	A103	5c ultra	75	38
234	A104	10c ol gray	1.00	38
235	A103	15c dl vio	4.00	1.50
236	A103	$1 red brn	40.00	15.00
		Nos. 230-236 (7)	46.55	17.85

For surcharges see Nos. 288A, 289A, 290A-291, 292A, C1-C3, O165. For overprints see Nos. O158-O164.

Nos. 164-168, 170-175 Surcharged in Various Colors and Styles, "1936" and New Values

1936 ***Perf. 12½, 14***

248	A60	1c on 2c (Bl)	22	22
249	A61	3c on 5c (Bl)	15	15
250	A62	4c on 10c (Br)	15	15
251	A63	6c on 15c (Bl)	22	22
252	A64	8c on 20c (V)	15	15
253	A66	12c on 30c (V)	40	40
254	A67	14c on 50c (Bl)	45	45
255	A68	16c on 75c (Br)	24	24
256	A69	18c on $1 (Bk)	24	24
a.		22c on $1 yel brn & bl	3.25	
257	A70	22c on $2 (V)	32	32
258	A71	24c on $5 (Bk)	40	40
		Nos. 248-258 (11)	2.94	2.94

Official Stamps, Nos. O99-O110, Surcharged or Overprinted in various colors and styles with 6 pointed star and "1936"

1936

259	A60	1c on 2c (Bl)	16	16
260	A61	3c on 5c (Bl)	15	15
261	A62	4c on 10c (Bl)	15	15
262	A63	6c on 15c (Bl)	16	16
263	A64	8c on 20c (V)	15	15
264	A66	12c on 30c (V)	32	32
a.		"193" instead of "1936"	8.25	
265	A67	14c on 50c (Bl)	42	42
266	A68	16c on 75c (Bk)	22	22
267	A69	18c on $1 (Bk)	22	22
268	A70	22c on $2 (Bl)	28	28
269	A71	24c on $5 (Bk)	32	32
270	A65	25c (Bk)	38	38
		Nos. 259-270 (12)	2.93	2.93

Hornbill — A106

Designs: 2c, Bushbuck. 3c, West African dwarf buffalo. 4c, Pygmy hippopotamus. 5c, Lesser egret. 6c, Pres. E. J. Barclay.

Perf. Compound of 11½, 12, 12½, 14

1937, Apr. 10 **Engr.** **Unwmk.**

271	A106	1c grn & blk	50	25
272	A106	2c car & blk	50	18
273	A106	3c vio & blk	50	25
274	A106	4c org & blk	75	42
275	A106	5c bl & blk	75	30
276	A106	6c grn & blk	25	15
		Nos. 271-276 (6)	3.25	1.55

Coast Line of Liberia, 1839 A107

Seal of Liberia, Map and Farming Scenes A108

Thomas Buchanan and Residence at Bassa Cove A109

1940, July 29 **Engr.** ***Perf. 12***

277	A107	3c dk bl	15	15
278	A108	5c dl red brn	15	15
279	A109	10c dk grn	15	15
		Set value	26	20

100th anniv. of the founding of the Commonwealth of Liberia.

For overprints see Nos. 280-282, B16-B18, C14-C16. For surcharges see Nos. CB1-CB3, CE1, CF1, E1, F35.

Nos. 277-279 Overprinted in Red or Blue

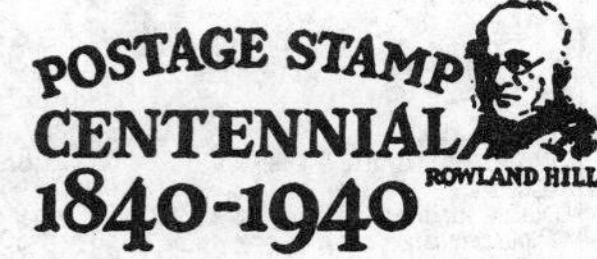

1941, Feb. 21

280	A107	3c dk bl (R)	1.25	1.25
281	A108	5c dl red brn (Bl)	1.25	1.25
282	A109	10c dk grn (R)	1.25	1.25
		Nos. 280-282,C14-C16 (6)	7.05	7.05

Royal Antelope A110

Bay-thighed Diana Monkey A115

Designs: 2c, Water chevrotain. 3c, White-shouldered duiker. 4c, Bushbuck. 5c, Zebra antelope.

1942 **Engr.**

283	A110	1c vio & fawn	25	15
284	A110	2c brt ultra & yel brn	25	15
285	A110	3c brt grn & yel brn	48	24
286	A110	4c blk & red org	60	48
287	A110	5c ol & fawn	75	48
288	A115	10c red & blk	1.25	60
		Nos. 283-288 (6)	3.58	2.10

Nos. 231, 233-234, 271-276 Surcharged with New Values and Bars or X's in Violet, Black, Red Brown or Blue

Perf. 12, 12x12½, 14

1944-46 **Unwmk.**

288A	A102	1c on 2c (Bk)	7.00	5.00
289	A106	1c on 4c (Bk)	37.50	35.00
289A	A104	1c on 10c (R Br)	9.50	6.50
290	A106	2c on 3c	45.00	37.50
290A	A103	2c on 5c (Bk)	2.00	2.00
290B	A103	2c on 5c (Bl)	16.00	7.00
291	A102	3c on 2c	22.50	
292	A106	4c on 5c	8.00	5.25
292A	A104	4c on 10c (Bk)	2.50	2.50
b.		Double surch., one inverted		
293	A106	5c on 1c (Bk)	60.00	37.50
294	A106	6c on 2c (Bk)	8.00	7.00
295	A106	10c on 6c	8.00	7.00

Surcharges on Nos. 289, 290, 293, 294 are found inverted. Values same as normal.

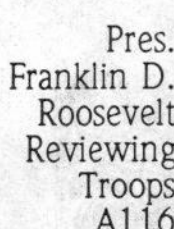

Pres. Franklin D. Roosevelt Reviewing Troops A116

1945, Nov. 26 **Engr.** ***Perf. 12½***

Grayish Paper

296	A116	3c brt vio & blk	15	15
297	A116	5c dk bl & blk	25	25

In memory of Pres. Franklin D. Roosevelt (1882-1945).

See No. C51.

Monrovia Harbor A117

1947, Jan. 2

298	A117	5c deep blue	15	15

Opening of the Monrovia Harbor Project, Feb. 16, 1946. See No. C52.

Without Inscription at Top

1947, May 16

299	A117	5c violet	15	15

See No. C53.

1st US Postage Stamps and Arms of Liberia A118

1947, June 6

300	A118	5c car rose	15	15

Cent. of US postage stamps and the 87th anniv. of Liberian postal issues.

See Nos. C54-C56, C56a.

Matilda Newport Firing Cannon A119

1947, Dec. 1 Engr. & Photo.
Center in Gray Black

301	A119	1c brt bl grn	15	15
302	A119	3c brt red vio	16	15
303	A119	5c brt ultra	32	15
304	A119	10c yellow	1.65	42
		Nos. 301-304,C57 (5)	3.38	
		Set value		90

125th anniv. of Matilda Newport's defense of Monrovia, Dec. 1, 1822.

Liberian Star — A120

Cent. of Independence: 2c, Liberty. 3c, Liberian Arms. 5c, Map of Liberia.

1947, Dec. 22 Engr.

305	A120	1c dk grn	15	15
306	A120	2c brt red vio	15	15
307	A120	3c brt pur	15	15
308	A120	5c dk bl	15	15
		Set value, #305-308, C58-C60	1.15	85

Centenary of independence.

Natives Approaching Village A124

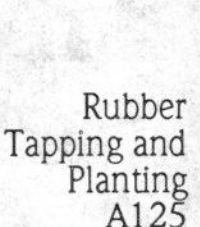

Rubber Tapping and Planting A125

Landing of First Colonists A126

Jehudi Ashmun and Defenders A127

1949, Apr. 4 Litho. *Perf. 11½*

309	A124	1c multi	25	45
310	A125	2c multi	25	45
311	A126	3c multi	25	45
312	A127	5c multi	25	45
		Nos. 309-312,C63-C64 (6)	1.64	3.00

Nos. 309-312 exist perf. 12½ and sell at a much lower price. The status of the perf. 12½ set is indefinite.

Pres. Joseph J. Roberts A128

Designs (Liberian Presidents): 2c, Stephen Benson. 3c, Daniel B. Warner. 4c, James S. Payne. 5c, Executive mansion. 6c, Edward J. Roye. 7c, A. W. Gardner and A. F. Russell. 8c, Hilary R. W. Johnson. 9c, Joseph J. Cheeseman. 10c, William D. Coleman. 15c, Garretson W. Gibson. 20c, Arthur Barclay. 25c, Daniel E. Howard. 50c, Charles D. B. King. $1, Edwin J. Barclay.

1948-50 Unwmk. Engr. *Perf. 12½*
Caption and Portrait in Black

313	A128	1c green ('48)	1.25	*3.75*
314	A128	2c salmon pink	28	*40*
315	A128	3c rose vio	28	*40*
a.		"1876-1878" added	6.50	*19.00*
316	A128	4c lt ol grn	28	*60*
317	A128	5c ultra	32	*60*
318	A128	6c red org	42	*1.00*
319	A128	7c lt bl ('50)	55	*1.40*
320	A128	8c carmine	55	*1.65*
321	A128	9c red vio	80	*1.25*
322	A128	10c yel ('50)	55	35
323	A128	15c yel org	65	45
324	A128	20c blue gray	95	80
325	A128	25c cerise	1.25	1.25
326	A128	50c aqua	2.50	85
327	A128	$1 rose lilac	4.00	80
		Nos. 313-327,C65 (16)	15.18	*16.15*

Issue dates: 1c, Nov. 18. 7c, 10c, 1950. Others, July 21, 1949.
See Nos. 328, 371-378, C118.

Pres. Joseph J. Roberts A129

1950

328	A129	1c grn & blk	15	15

Hand Holding Book — A130

1950, Feb. 14

329	A130	5c deep blue	28	15

National Literacy Campaign. See No. C66.

Catalogue values for unused stamps in this section, from this point to the end of the section, are for Never Hinged items.

UPU Monument A131

First UPU Building, Bern A132

1950, Apr. 21 Engr. Unwmk.

330	A131	5c grn & blk	15	15
331	A132	10c red vio & blk	18	18

UPU, 75th anniv. (in 1949).
Nos. 330-331 exist imperf., same value.
See Nos. C67, C67a.

Jehudi Ashmun and Seal of Liberia — A133

John Marshall, Ashmun and Map of Town of Marshall A134

Designs (Map or View and Two Portraits): 2c, Careysburg, Gov. Lott Carey (1780-1828), freed American slave, and Jehudi Ashmun (1794-1828), American missionary credited as founder of Liberia. 3c, Town of Harper, Robert Goodlow Harper (1765-1825), American statesman, and Ashmun. 5c, Upper Buchanan, Gov. Thomas Buchanan and Ashmun. 10c, Robertsport, Pres. Joseph J. Roberts and Ashmun.

1952, Apr. 10 *Perf. 10½*

332	A133	1c dp grn	15	15
333	A133	2c scar & ind	15	15
334	A133	3c pur & grn	15	15
335	A134	4c brn & grn	15	15
336	A133	5c ultra & org red	15	15
337	A134	10c org red & dk bl	15	15
		Set value, #332-337, C68-C69	1.00	95

Nos. 332-337 exist imperf. Value about two and one-half times that of the perf. set.
See No. C69a.

UN Headquarters Building — A135

Scroll and Flags A136

Design: 10c, Liberia arms, letters "UN" and emblem.

1952, Dec. 20 Unwmk. *Perf. 12½*

338	A135	1c ultra	15	15
339	A136	4c car & ultra	15	15
340	A136	10c red brn & yel	15	15
a.		Souv. sheet of 3, #338-340	1.25	1.25
		Set value	25	25

See No. C70.
Nos. 338-340 and 340a exist imperforate. Same values as above.

Pepper Bird — A137

The only foreign revenue stamps listed in this Catalogue are those authorized for prepayment of postage.

Roller A138

1953, Nov. 18 *Perf. 10½*

341	A137	1c shown	15	15
342	A138	3c shown	15	15
343	A137	4c Hornbill	15	15
344	A137	5c Kingfisher	15	15
345	A138	10c Jacana	24	15
346	A138	12c Weaver	38	15
		Set value	1.00	30

Exist imperf. Value, set unused $2.75.

Tennis A139

Callichilia Stenosepala A140

1955, Jan. 26 Litho. *Perf. 12½*

347	A139	3c shown	15	15
348	A139	5c Soccer	15	15
349	A139	25c Boxing	16	15
		Set value, #347-349, C88-C90	54	52

See No. C90a.

1955, Sept. 28 Unwmk.

Various Native Flowers: 7c, Gomphia subcordata. 8c, Listrostachys caudata. 9c, Musaenda isertiana.

350	A140	6c yel grn, org & yel	15	15
351	A140	7c emer, yel & car	15	15
352	A140	8c yel grn, buff & bl	15	15
353	A140	9c org & grn	15	15
		Set value, #350-353, C91-C92	55	55

Rubber Tapping — A141

1955, Dec. 5 *Perf. 12½*

354	A141	5c emer & yel	15	15

50th anniv. of Rotary Intl. No. 354 exists printed entirely in emerald. See Nos. C97-C99.

Statue of Liberty — A142

Coliseum, New York City A143

Design: 6c, Globe inscribed FIPEX.

1956, Apr. 28 *Perf. 12*

355 A142	3c brt grn & dk red brn	15	15
356 A143	4c Prus grn & bis brn	15	15
357 A143	6c gray & red lil	15	15
	Set value, #355-357, C100-C102	72	40

Fifth International Philatelic Exhibition (FIPEX), NYC, Apr. 28-May 6, 1956.

Kangaroo and Emu A144

Discus Thrower — A145

Designs: 8c, Goddess of Victory and Olympic symbols. 10c, Classic chariot race.

1956, Nov. 15 **Litho.** **Unwmk.**

358 A144	4c lt ol grn & gldn brn	15	15
359 A145	6c emer & gray	15	15
360 A144	8c lt ultra & redsh brn	15	15
361 A144	10c rose red & blk	15	15
	Set value, #358-361, C104-C105	64	35

16th Olympic Games at Melbourne, Nov. 22-Dec. 8, 1956.

Idlewild Airport, New York A146

Design: 5c, Roberts Field, Liberia, plane and Pres. Tubman.

Lithographed and Engraved

1957, May 4 *Perf. 12*

362 A146	3c org & dk bl	15	15
363 A146	5c red lil & blk	15	15
	Set value, #362-363, C107-C110	1.00	50

1st anniv. of direct air service between Roberts Field, Liberia, and Idlewild (Kennedy), NY.

Orphanage Playground A147

Orphanage and: 5c, Teacher and pupil. 6c, Singing boys and natl. anthem. 10c, Children and flag.

1957, Nov. 25 **Litho.** *Perf. 12*

364 A147	4c grn & red	15	15
365 A147	5c bl grn & red brn	15	15
366 A147	6c brt vio & bis	15	15
367 A147	10c ultra & rose car	15	15
	Set value, #364-367, C111-C112	62	42

Founding of the Antoinette Tubman Child Welfare Foundation.

Windmill and Dutch Flag — A148

Designs: No. 369, German flag and Brandenburg Gate. No. 370, Swedish flag, palace and crowns.

Engraved and Lithographed

1958, Jan. 10 **Unwmk.** *Perf. 10½*

Flags in Original Colors

368 A148	5c reddish brn	15	15
369 A148	5c blue	15	15
370 A148	5c lilac rose	15	15
	Set value, #368-370, C114-C117	58	40

European tour of Pres. Tubman in 1956.

Presidential Types of 1948-50

Designs as before.

1958-60 **Engr.** *Perf. 12*

Caption and Portrait in Black

371 A129	1c sal pink	25	20
372 A128	2c brt yel	25	20
373 A128	10c bl gray	28	28
374 A128	15c brt bl & blk ('59)	15	15
375 A128	20c dk red	35	32
376 A128	25c blue	35	32
377 A128	50c red lil & blk ('59)	38	32
378 A128	$1 bister brn ('60)	2.50	40
	Nos. 371-378,C118 (9)	4.89	2.47

Many shades of 1c.

Open Globe Projection A149

Designs: 5c, UN Emblem and building. 10c, UN Emblem. 12c, UN Emblem and initials of agencies.

1958, Dec. 10 **Litho.** *Perf. 12*

379 A149	3c gray, bl & blk	15	15
380 A149	5c bl & choc	15	15
381 A149	10c blk & org	16	16
382 A149	12c blk & car	22	22
	Set value	52	52

10th anniv. of the Universal Declaration of Human Rights. See No. C119.

People of Africa on the March — A150

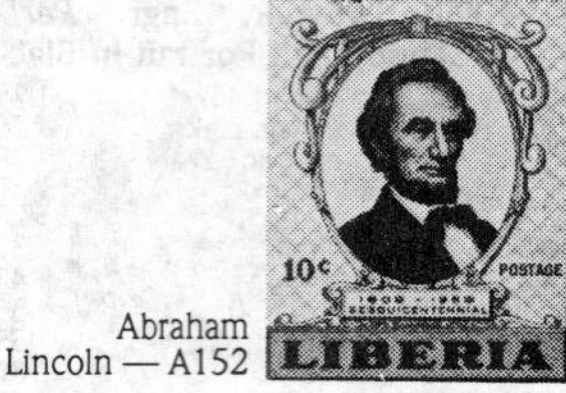

Symbols of UNESCO — A151

1959, Apr. 15

383 A150	20c org & brn	24	24

African Freedom Day, Apr. 15. See No. C120.

1959, May 11 **Unwmk.**

384 A151	25c dp plum & emer	30	35

Opening of UNESCO Headquarters in Paris, Nov. 3, 1958.

See Nos. C121, C121a.

Abraham Lincoln — A152

1959, Nov. 20 **Engr.** *Perf. 12*

385 A152	10c ultra & blk	15	15
386 A152	15c org & blk	18	18
a.	Souv. sheet of 3, Nos. 385-386, C122, imperf.	90	1.50

150th anniv. of the birth of Abraham Lincoln. See No. C122.

Touré, Tubman and Nkrumah A153

1960, Jan. 27 **Litho.** **Unwmk.**

387 A153	25c crim & blk	30	30

1959 "Big Three" conference of Pres. Sékou Touré of Guinea, Pres. William V. S. Tubman of Liberia and Prime Minister Kwame Nkrumah of Ghana at Saniquellie, Liberia. See No. C123.

World Refugee Year Emblem — A154

Map of Africa — A155

1960, Apr. 7 *Perf. 11½*

388 A154	25c emer & blk	30	45

World Refuge Year, July 1, 1959-June 30, 1960. See No. C124, C124a.

1960, May 11 **Litho.** *Perf. 11½*

389 A155	25c grn & blk	30	30

10th anniv. of the Commission for Technical Cooperation in Africa South of the Sahara (C.C.T.A.). See No. C125.

Weight Lifter and Porter — A156

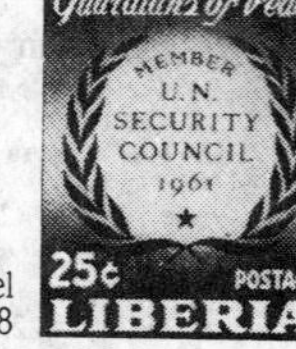

Liberian Stamps of 1860 — A157

Designs: 10c, Rower and canoeists, horiz. 15c, Walker and porter.

1960, Sept. 6 **Unwmk.**

390 A156	5c dk brn & emer	15	15
391 A156	10c brn & red lil	15	18
392 A156	15c brn & org	25	30

17th Olympic Games, Rome, Aug. 25-Sept. 11. See Nos. C126-C127.

1960, Dec. 1 **Litho.** *Perf. 11½*

393 A157	5c multi	15	15
394 A157	20c multi	32	32

Cent. of Liberian postage stamps. See Nos. C128-C129.

Laurel Wreath — A158

1961, May 19 **Unwmk.** *Perf. 11½*

395 A158	25c red & dk bl	26	38

Liberia's membership in the UN Security Council. Exists imperf. See Nos. C130-C131 and note after No. C131.

Anatomy Class — A159

1961, Sept. 8 *Perf. 11½*

396 A159	25c grn & brn	35	35

15th anniv. of UNESCO. See #C132-C133.

Joseph J. Roberts Monument, Monrovia — A160

Design: 10c, Pres. Roberts and old and new presidential mansions, horiz.

1961, Oct. 25 **Litho.**

397 A160	5c org & sep	15	15
398 A160	10c ultra & sep	15	15
	Set value	20	20

150th anniv. of the birth of Joseph J. Roberts, 1st pres. of Liberia.

See No. C134, C134a.

Boy Scout — A161

Design: Insignia and Scouts camping.

1961, Dec. 4 **Unwmk.** *Perf. 11½*

399 A161	5c lil & sep	15	15
400 A161	10c ultra & bis	25	25
	Set value	28	28

Issued to honor the Boy Scouts of Liberia. Exist imperf. See Nos. C135-C136.

Dag Hammarskjold and UN Emblem A162

1962, Feb. 1 *Perf. 12*

401 A162	20c blk & ultra	26	26

Issued in memory of Dag Hammarskjold, Secretary General of the United Nations, 1953-61. See Nos. C137-C138.

Malaria Eradication Emblem — A163

1962, Apr. 7 Litho. *Perf. 12½*
402 A163 25c dk grn & red 32 22

WHO drive to eradicate malaria. See Nos. C139-C140.

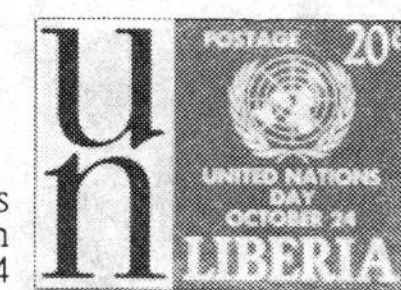

United Nations Emblem A164

1962, Oct. 22 *Perf. 12x12½*
403 A164 20c grn & yel bis 24 24

Issued to mark the observance of United Nations Day, Oct. 24, as a national holiday.
See Nos. C144-C145.

Treasury Department Building, Monrovia A165

Buildings: 1c, 80c, Executive Mansion, Monrovia. 10c, Information Service. 15c, Capitol.

1962-64
403A A165 1c vio bl & dp org ('64) 15 15
404 A165 5c lt bl & pur 15 15
405 A165 10c bis & brn 15 15
406 A165 15c sal & dk bl 18 18
406A A165 80c brn & yel ('64) 1.00 1.00
Nos. 403A-406A,C146-C148 (9) 4.58 3.68

"FAO" Emblem and Food Bowl — A166

1963, Mar. 21 *Perf. 12½*
407 A166 5c aqua & dk car 15 15

FAO "Freedom from Hunger" campaign. See Nos. C149-C150.

Rocket in Space — A167

Design: 15c, Space capsule and globe.

1963, May 27 Litho. *Perf. 12½*
408 A167 10c dp vio bl & yel 15 15
409 A167 15c bl & red brn 22 22

Achievements in space exploration for peaceful purposes. See Nos. C151-C152.

Red Cross — A168

Design: 10c, Centenary emblem and torch, vert.

1963, Aug. 26 Unwmk. *Perf. 11½*
410 A168 5c bl grn & red 15 15
411 A168 10c gray & red 15 15
Set value 15 15

Cent. of the Intl. Red Cross. See Nos. C153-C154.

Palm Tree and Scroll — A169

Ski Jump — A170

1963, Oct. 28 *Perf. 12½*
412 A169 20c brn & grn 25 25

Issued to commemorate the conference of African heads of state for African Unity, Addis Ababa, May, 1963. See No. C156.

1963, Dec. 11 Unwmk. *Perf. 12½*
413 A170 5c rose red & dk vio bl 15 15

Issued to publicize the 9th Winter Olympic Games, Innsbruck, Austria, Jan. 29-Feb. 9, 1964. See Nos. C157-C159.

John F. Kennedy A171

1964, Apr. 6 Litho.
414 A171 20c blk & brt bl 26 26

Issued in memory of John F. Kennedy (1917-63). See Nos. C160-C161.

Syncom Satellite — A172

Designs (Satellites): 15c, Relay I, vert. 25c, Mariner II.

1964, June 22 Unwmk. *Perf. 12½*
415 A172 10c org & emer 15 15
416 A172 15c brt car rose & vio 15 15
417 A172 25c bl, org & blk 32 32

Issued to publicize progress in space communications and the peaceful uses of outer space. See No. C162.

Mt. Fuji — A173

Designs: 15c, Torii and Olympic flame. 25c, Cherry blossoms and stadium.

1964, Sept. 15 Litho.
418 A173 10c org yel & emer 15 15
419 A173 15c lt red & pur 18 18
420 A173 25c ocher & red 45 45

Issued for the 18th Olympic Games, Tokyo, Oct. 10-25, 1964. See No. C163.

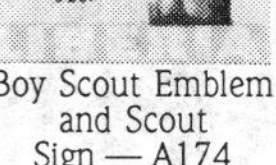
Boy Scout Emblem and Scout Sign — A174

"Emancipation" by Thomas Ball — A175

Design: 10c, Bugle and Liberian Scout emblem, horiz.

1965, Mar. 8 Litho. *Perf. 12½*
421 A174 5c lt bl & brn 15 15
422 A174 10c dk grn & ocher 20 20
Set value 28 28

Issued to honor the Liberian Boy Scouts. See Nos. C164-C165.

1965, May 3 Unwmk. *Perf. 12½*

Designs: 20c, Abraham Lincoln and John F. Kennedy, horiz. 25c, Lincoln by Augustus St. Gaudens, Lincoln Park, Chicago.

423 A175 5c dk gray & brn org 15 15
424 A175 20c emer & lt gray 28 28
425 A175 25c mar & bl 35 35

Centenary of the death of Abraham Lincoln. See No. C166.

ICY Emblem A176

1965, June 21 Litho. *Perf. 12½*
426 A176 12c org & brn 15 15
427 A176 25c vio bl & brn 28 28
428 A176 50c emer & brn 60 60

Intl. Cooperation Year. See No. C167.

ITU Emblem, Old and New Communication Equipment A177

1965, Sept. 21 Unwmk. *Perf. 12½*
429 A177 25c brt grn & red brn 25 25
430 A177 35c blk & car rose 35 35

Cent. of the ITU. See No. C168.

Pres. Tubman and Liberian Flag — A178

1965, Nov. 29 Litho.
431 A178 25c red, ultra & brn 40 40

Pres. William V. S. Tubman's 70th birthday. See No. C169, C169a.

Churchill in Admiral's Uniform A179

Pres. Joseph J. Roberts A180

Designs: 15c, Churchill giving "V" sign, vert.

1966, Jan. 18 Litho. *Perf. 12½*
432 A179 15c org & blk 18 15
433 A179 20c blk & brt grn 26 15

Issued in memory of Sir Winston Spencer Churchill (1874-1965), statesman and World War II leader. See Nos. C170-C171.

1966-69 Litho. *Perf. 12½*

Presidents: 2c, Stephen Benson. 3c, Daniel Bashiel Warner. 4c, James S. Payne. 5c, Edward James Roye. 10c, William D. Coleman. 25c, Daniel Edward Howard. 50c, Charles Dunbar Burgess King. 80c, Hilary R. W. Johnson. $1, Edwin J. Barclay. $2, Joseph James Cheeseman ("Cheesman" on stamp).

434 A180 1c blk & brick red 15 15
435 A180 2c blk & yel 15 15
436 A180 3c blk & lil 15 15
437 A180 4c ap grn & blk ('67) 15 15
438 A180 5c blk & dl org 15 15
439 A180 10c pale grn & blk ('67) 15 15
440 A180 25c blk & lt bl 30 15
441 A180 50c blk & brt lil rose 60 48
442 A180 80c dp rose & blk ('67) 1.00 65
443 A180 $1 blk & ocher 1.25 15

Perf. 11½x11
443A A180 $2 blk & dp red lil ('69) 2.50 1.75
Nos. 434-443A,C182 (12) 6.95
Set value 3.60

Soccer Players and Globe — A181

Designs: 25c, World Championships Cup, ball and shoes, vert. 35c, Soccer player dribbling, vert.

1966, May 3 Litho. *Perf. 12½*
444 A181 10c brt grn & dk brn 15 15
445 A181 25c brt pink & brn 30 20
446 A181 35c brn & org 42 26

Issued to publicize the World Cup Soccer Championships, Wembley, England, July 11-30. See No. C172.

Pres. Kennedy Taking Oath of Office — A182

Designs: 20c, 1964 Kennedy stamps, Nos. 414 and C160.

1966, Aug. 16 Litho. *Perf. 12½*
447 A182 15c red & blk 18 15
448 A182 20c brt bl & red lil 22 15
Set value 16

3rd anniv. of Pres. Kennedy's death (Nov. 22). See Nos. C173-C175.

Children on Seesaw and UNICEF Emblem — A183

Design: 80c, Boy playing doctor.

1966, Oct. 25 Unwmk. *Perf. 12½*

449 A183	5c	brt bl & red	15	15
450 A183	80c	org brn & yel grn	75	75

20th anniv. of UNICEF.

Giraffe — A184

Jamboree Badge — A185

Designs: 3c, Lion. 5c, Slender-nosed crocodile, horiz. 10c, Baby chimpanzees. 15c, Leopard, horiz. 20c, Black rhinoceros, horiz. 25c, Elephant.

1966, Dec. 20

451 A184	2c	multi	15	15
452 A184	3c	multi	15	15
453 A184	5c	multi	15	15
a.		Black omitted ("5¢ LIBERIA" and imprint)		*50.00*
454 A184	10c	multi	15	15
455 A184	15c	multi	25	15
456 A184	20c	multi	32	16
457 A184	25c	multi	45	20
		Set value	1.30	70

1967, Mar. 23 Litho. *Perf. 12½*

Designs: 25c, Boy Scout emblem and various sports, horiz. 40c, Scout at campfire and vision of moon landing, horiz.

458 A185	10c	brt lil rose & grn	15	15
459 A185	25c	brt red & bl	32	24
460 A185	40c	brt grn & brn org	45	35

Issued to publicize the 12th Boy Scout World Jamboree, Farragut State Park, Idaho, Aug. 1-9. See No. C176.

A186

— A187

Pre-Hispanic Sculpture of Mexico: 25c, Aztec Calendar and Olympic rings. 40c, Mexican pottery, sombrero and guitar, horiz.

1967, June 20 Litho. *Perf. 12½*

461 A186	10c	ocher & vio	15	15
462 A186	25c	lt bl, org & blk	30	24
463 A186	40c	yel grn & car	45	38

Issued to publicize the 19th Olympic Games, Mexico City. See No. C177.

1967, Aug. 28 Litho. *Perf. 12½*

Designs: 5c, WHO Office for Africa, horiz. 80c, WHO Office for Africa.

464 A187	5c	bl & yel	15	15
465 A187	80c	brt grn & yel	1.00	1.00

Inauguration of the WHO Regional Office for Africa in Brazzaville, Congo.

Boy Playing African Rattle — A188

Africans Playing Native Instruments: 3c, Tom-tom and soko violin, horiz. 5c, Mang harp, horiz. 10c, Alimilim. 15c, Xylophone drums. 25c, Large tom-toms. 35c, Large harp.

1967, Oct. 16 Litho. *Perf. 14*

466 A188	2c	vio & multi	15	15
467 A188	3c	bl & multi	15	15
468 A188	5c	lil rose & multi	15	15
469 A188	10c	yel grn & multi	18	15
470 A188	15c	vio & multi	24	15
471 A188	25c	ocher & multi	52	22
472 A188	35c	dp rose & multi	75	35
		Nos. 466-472 (7)	2.14	
		Set value		1.00

Ice Hockey — A189

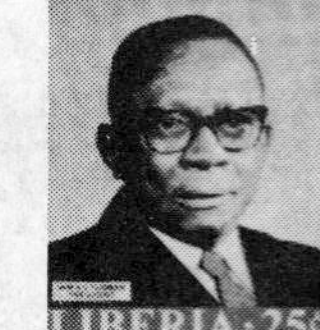

Pres. William Tubman — A190

Designs: 25c, Ski jump. 40c, Bobsledding.

1967, Nov. 20 Litho. *Perf. 12½*

473 A189	10c	emer & vio bl	15	15
474 A189	25c	grnsh bl & dp plum	24	20
475 A189	40c	ocher & org brn	35	32

10th Winter Olympic Games, Grenoble, France, Feb. 6-18, 1968. See No. C178.

1967, Dec. 22 Litho. *Perf. 12½*

476 A190	25c	ultra & brn	40	24

Souvenir Sheet

Imperf

477 A190	50c	ultra & brn	80	80

Inauguration of President Tubman, Jan. 1, 1968. No. 477 contains one stamp with simulated perforations and picture frame.

Human Rights Flame — A191

Martin Luther King, Jr. — A192

1968, Apr. 26 Litho. *Perf. 12½*

478 A191	3c	ver & dp bl	15	15
479 A191	80c	brn & emer	75	75

Issued for International Human Rights Year. See No. C179.

1968, July 11 Unwmk. *Perf. 12½*

Designs: 15c, Mule-drawn hearse and Dr. King. 35c, Dr. King and Lincoln monument by Daniel Chester French, horiz.

480 A192	15c	brt bl & brn	18	15
481 A192	25c	ind & brn	26	18
482 A192	35c	ol & blk	40	22

Issued in memory of the Rev. Dr. Martin Luther King, Jr. (1929-1968). American civil rights leader. See No. C180.

Javelin and Diana Statue, Mexico City — A193

Designs: 25c, Discus, pyramid and serpent god Quetzalcoatl. 35c, Woman diver and Xochicalco from ruins near Cuernavaca.

1968, Aug. 22 Litho. *Perf. 12½*

483 A193	15c	dp vio & org brn	15	15
484 A193	25c	red & brt bl	22	18
485 A193	35c	brn & emer	32	24

19th Olympic Games, Mexico City, Oct. 12-27. See No. C181.

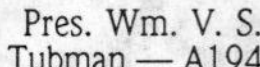

Pres. Wm. V. S. Tubman — A194

Unification Monument, Voinjama-Lofa County — A195

1968, Dec. 30 Unwmk. *Perf. 12½*

486 A194	25c	sil, blk & brn	70	32

Souvenir Sheet

Imperf

487 A195	80c	sil, ultra & red	1.65	1.25

25th anniv. of Pres. Tubman's administration.

"ILO" with Cogwheel and Wreath — A196

1969, Apr. 16 Litho. *Perf. 12½*

488 A196	25c	lt bl & gold	40	25

50th anniv. of the ILO. See No. C183.

Red Roofs, by Camille Pisarro — A197

Paintings: 3c, Prince Balthasar Carlos on Horseback, by Velazquez, vert. 10c, David and Goliath, by Caravaggio. 12c, Still Life, by Jean Baptiste Chardin. 15c, The Last Supper, by Leonardo da Vinci. 20c, Regatta at Argenteuil, by Claude Monet. 25c, Judgment of Solomon, by Giorgione. 35c, Sistine Madonna, by Raphael.

1969, June 26 Litho. *Perf. 11*

489 A197	3c	gray & multi	15	15
490 A197	5c	gray & multi	15	15
491 A197	10c	lt bl & multi	15	15
492 A197	12c	gray & multi	20	15
493 A197	15c	gray & multi	22	15
494 A197	20c	gray & multi	32	15
495 A197	25c	gray & multi	42	18
496 A197	35c	gray & multi	55	25
		Nos. 489-496 (8)	2.16	
		Set value		90

See Nos. 502-509.

African Development Bank Emblem — A198

1969, Aug. 12 Litho. *Perf. 12½*

497 A198	25c	bl & brn	35	30
498 A198	80c	yel grn & red	1.10	60

5th anniversary of the African Development Bank.

Moon Landing and Liberia No. C174 — A199

Designs: 15c, Memorial tablet left on moon, rocket, earth and moon, horiz. 35c, Take-off from moon.

1969, Oct. 15 Litho. *Perf. 12½*

499 A199	15c	bl & bis	32	15
500 A199	25c	dk vio bl & org	48	16
501 A199	35c	gray & red	70	22

Man's 1st landing on the moon, July 20, 1969. US astronauts Neil A. Armstrong and Col. Edwin E. Aldrin, Jr., with Lieut. Col. Michael Collins piloting Apollo 11. See No. C184.

Painting Type of 1969

1969, Nov. 18 Litho. *Perf. 11*

Paintings: 3c, The Gleaners, by Francois Millet. 5c, View of Toledo, by El Greco, vert. 10c, Heads of Negroes, by Rubens. 12c, The Last Supper, by El Greco. 15c, Dancing Peasants, by Brueghel. 20c, Hunters in the Snow, by Brueghel. 25c, Detail from Descent from the Cross, by Rogier van der Weyden, vert. 35c, The Ascension, by Murillo (inscribed "The Conception"), vert.

502 A197	3c	lt bl & multi	15	15
503 A197	5c	lt bl & multi	15	15
504 A197	10c	lt bl & multi	15	15
505 A197	12c	gray & multi	18	15
506 A197	15c	gray & multi	22	15
507 A197	20c	lt bl & multi	32	16
508 A197	25c	gray & multi	40	22
509 A197	35c	lt bl & multi	55	25
		Nos. 502-509 (8)	2.12	
		Set value		1.00

Peace Dove, UN Emblem and Atom — A200

1970, Apr. 16 Litho. *Perf. 12½*

510 A200	5c	grn & sil	15	15

25th anniv. of the UN. See No. C185.

Official Emblem A201

Designs: 10c, Statue of rain god Tlaloc, vert. 25c, Jules Rimet cup and sculptured wall, vert. 35c, Sombrero and soccer ball. 55c, Two soccer players.

1970, June 10 Litho. *Perf. 12½*

511 A201 5c pale bl & brn 15 15
512 A201 10c emer & ocher 15 15
513 A201 25c dp rose lil & gold 35 18
514 A201 35c ver & ultra 50 24
Set value 55

Souvenir Sheet

Perf. 11½

515 A201 55c brt bl, yel & grn 1.25 60

9th World Soccer Championships for the Jules Rimet Cup, Mexico City, May 30-June 21, 1970.

EXPO '70 Emblem, Japanese Singer and Festival Plaza — A202

Designs (EXPO '70 Emblem and): 3c, Male Japanese singer, EXPO Hall and floating stage. 5c, Tower of the Sun and view of exhibition. 7c, Tanabata Festival. 8c, Awa Dance Festival. 25c, Sado-Okesa Dance Festival. 50c, Ricoh Pavilion with "eye," and Mt. Fuji, vert.

1970, July Litho. *Perf. 11*

516 A202 2c multi 15 15
517 A202 3c multi 15 15
518 A202 5c multi 20 15
519 A202 7c multi 32 15
520 A202 8c multi 38 15
521 A202 25c multi 95 24
Nos. 516-521 (6) 2.15
Set value 60

Souvenir Sheet

522 A202 50c multi 2.00 65

Issued to publicize EXPO '70 International Exhibition, Osaka, Japan, Mar. 15-Sept. 13.

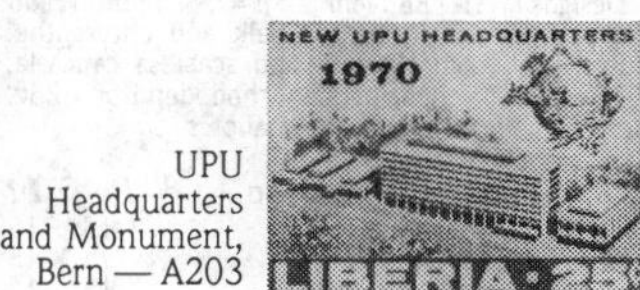

UPU Headquarters and Monument, Bern — A203

Design: 80c, Like 25c, vert.

1970, Aug. 25 *Perf. 12½*

523 A203 25c bl & multi 28 28
524 A203 80c multi 70 70

Inauguration of the new UPU Headquarters in Bern.

Napoleon as Consul, by Joseph Marie Vien, Sr. — A204

Paintings of Napoleon: 5c, Visit to a School, by unknown painter. 10c, Napoleon Bonaparte, by Franois Pascal Gerard. 12c, The French Campaign, by Ernest Meissonier. 20c, Napoleon Signing Abdication at Fontainebleau, by Franois Bouchot. 25c, Napoleon Meets Pope Pius VII, by Jean-Louis Demarne. 50c, Napoleon's Coronation, by Jacques Louis David.

1970, Oct. 20 Litho. *Perf. 11*

525 A204 3c bl & multi 15 15
526 A204 5c bl & multi 15 15
527 A204 10c bl & multi 24 15
528 A204 12c bl & multi 30 15
529 A204 20c bl & multi 48 15
530 A204 25c bl & multi 60 18
Nos. 525-530 (6) 1.92
Set value 62

Souvenir Sheet

Imperf

531 A204 50c bl & multi 1.25 48

200th anniv. of the birth of Napoleon Bonaparte (1769-1821). No. 531 contains one stamp with simulated perforations.

Pres. Tubman A205

1970, Nov. 20 Litho. *Perf. 13½*

532 A205 25c multi 70 35

Souvenir Sheet

Imperf

533 A205 50c multi 1.00 70

Pres. Tubman's 75th birthday. No. 533 contains one imperf. stamp with simulated perforations.

Adoration of the Kings, by Rogier van der Weyden — A206

Paintings (Adoration of the Kings, by): 5c, Hans Memling. 10c, Stefan Lochner. 12c, Albrecht Altdorfer, vert. 20c, Hugo van der Goes, Adoration of the Shepherds. 25c, Hieronymus Bosch, vert. 50c, Andrea Mantegna (triptych).

Perf. 13½x14, 14x13½

1970, Dec. 21 Litho.

534 A206 3c multi 15 15
535 A206 5c multi 15 15
536 A206 10c multi 18 15
537 A206 12c multi 24 15
538 A206 20c multi 35 15
539 A206 25c multi 48 15
Nos. 534-539 (6) 1.55
Set value 50

Souvenir Sheet

Imperf

540 A206 50c multi 1.65 40

Christmas 1970.
No. 540 contains one 60x40mm stamp.

Dogon Tribal Mask — A207

African Tribal Ceremonial Masks: 2c, Bapendé. 5c, Baoulé. 6c, Dédougou. 9c, Dan. 15c, Bamiléké. 20c, Bapendé mask and costume. 25c, Bamiléké mask and costume.

1971, Feb. 24 Litho. *Perf. 11*

541 A207 2c lt grn & multi 15 15
542 A207 3c pink & multi 15 15
543 A207 5c lt bl & multi 15 15
544 A207 6c lt grn & multi 15 15
545 A207 9c lt bl & multi 15 15
546 A207 15c pink & multi 22 15
547 A207 20c lt grn & multi 50 35
548 A207 25c pink & multi 26 18
Set value 1.35 90

Astronauts on Moon — A208

Designs: 5c, Astronaut and lunar transport vehicle. 10c, Astronaut with US flag on moon. 12c, Space capsule in Pacific Ocean. 20c, Astronaut leaving capsule. 25c, Astronauts Alan B. Shepard, Stuart A. Roosa and Edgar D. Mitchell.

1971, May 20 Litho. *Perf. 13½*

549 A208 3c vio bl & multi 15 15
550 A208 5c vio bl & multi 15 15
551 A208 10c vio bl & multi 24 15
552 A208 12c vio bl & multi 32 15
553 A208 20c vio bl & multi 45 20
554 A208 25c vio bl & multi 60 25
Nos. 549-554 (6) 1.91
Set value 70

Apollo 14 moon landing, Jan. 31-Feb. 9. See No. C186.

Map, Liberian Women and Pres. Tubman A209

Design: 3c, Pres. Tubman and women at ballot box, vert.

1971, May 27 *Perf. 12½*

555 A209 3c ultra & brn 15 15
556 A209 80c grn & brn 1.25 1.25

25th anniversary of women's suffrage.

Hall of Honor, Munich, and Olympic Flag — A210

Munich Views and Olympic Flag: 5c, General view. 10c, National Museum. 12c, Max Joseph's Square. 20c, Propylaeum on King's Square. 25c, Liesel-Karlstadt Fountain.

1971, June 28 Litho. *Perf. 11*

557 A210 3c multi 15 15
558 A210 5c multi 15 15
559 A210 10c multi 18 15
560 A210 12c multi 25 15
561 A210 20c multi 35 20
562 A210 25c multi 45 28
Nos. 557-562 (6) 1.53
Set value 80

Publicity for the 20th Summer Olympic Games, Munich, Germany, 1972. See No. C187.

Boy Scout, Emblem and US Flag — A211

Designs (Boy Scout, National Flag and Boy Scout Emblem of): 5c, German Federal Republic. 10c, Australia. 12c, Great Britain. 20c, Japan. 25c, Liberia.

1971, Aug. 6 Litho. *Perf. 13½*

563 A211 3c multi 15 15
564 A211 5c multi 15 15
565 A211 10c multi 18 15
566 A211 12c multi 25 15
567 A211 20c multi 38 15
568 A211 25c multi 50 20
Nos. 563-568 (6) 1.61
Set value 55

13th Boy Scout World Jamboree, Asagiri Plain, Japan, Aug. 2-10. See No. C188.

Pres. Tubman (1895-1971) A212

1971, Aug. 23 *Perf. 12½*

569 A212 3c blk, ultra & brn 15 15
570 A212 25c blk, brt rose lil & brn 42 42

Zebra and UNICEF Emblem — A213

Animals (UNICEF Emblem and Animals with their Young): 7c, Koala. 8c, Llama. 10c, Red fox. 20c, Monkey. 25c, Brown bear.

1971, Oct. 1 *Perf. 11*

571 A213 5c multi 20 15
572 A213 7c multi 28 15
573 A213 8c multi 32 15
574 A213 10c multi 38 15
575 A213 20c multi 80 28
576 A213 25c multi 1.00 38
Nos. 571-576 (6) 2.98
Set value 1.05

25th anniv. of UNICEF. See No. C189.

Sapporo 72 Emblem, Long-distance Skiing, Sika Deer — A214

Designs (Sapporo 72 Emblem and): 3c, Sledding and black woodpecker. 5c, Ski Jump and brown bear. 10c, Bobsledding and murres. 15c, Figure skating and pikas. 25c, Downhill skiing and Japanese cranes.

1971, Nov. 4 *Perf. 13x13½*

577 A214 2c multi 15 15
578 A214 3c multi 15 15
579 A214 5c multi 15 15
580 A214 10c multi 26 15
581 A214 15c multi 32 15
582 A214 25c multi 75 20
Set value 1.30 55

11th Winter Olympic Games, Sapporo, Japan, Feb. 3-13, 1972. See No. C190.

Dove Carrying Letter, APU Emblem A215

1971, Dec. 9 *Perf. 12½*

583 A215 25c ultra & dp org 38 32
584 A215 80c gray & dp brn 1.10 95

10th anniversary of African Postal Union.

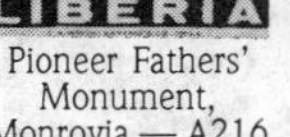

Pioneer Fathers' Monument, Monrovia — A216

Pres. William R. Tolbert, Jr. — A217

Designs: 3c, 25c, Sailing ship "Elizabeth," Providence Island, horiz. 35c, as 20c.

1972, Jan. 1

585 A216 3c bl & brt grn 15 15
586 A216 20c org & bl 60 42
587 A216 25c org & pur 65 55
588 A216 35c lil rose & brt grn 1.10 75

Sesquicentennial of founding of Liberia. See No. C191.

1972, Jan. 1

Design: 25c, Pres. Tolbert and map of Liberia, horiz.

589 A217 25c emer & brn 40 22
590 A217 80c bl & brn 1.40 45

Inauguration of William R. Tolbert, Jr. as 19th president of Liberia.

Soccer and Swedish Flag — A218

Designs (Olympic Rings, "Motion" Symbol and): 5c, Swimmers at start and Italian flag. 10c, Equestrian and British flag. 12c, Bicycling and French flag. 20c, Long jump and American flag. 25c, Running and Liberian flag.

1972, May 19 **Litho.** *Perf. 11*

591 A218 3c lem & multi 15 15
592 A218 5c lt lil & multi 15 15
593 A218 10c multi 30 15
594 A218 12c gray & multi 40 15
595 A218 20c lt bl & multi 55 24
596 A218 25c pink & multi 75 30
Nos. 591-596 (6) 2.30
Set value 90

20th Olympic Games, Munich, Aug. 26-Sept. 10. See No. C192.

Y's Men's Club Emblem, Map — A219

Design: 90c, Y's Men's Club emblem and globe; inscribed "fifty and forward."

1972, June 12 *Perf. 13½*

597 A219 15c pur & gold 22 18
598 A219 90c vio bl & emer 1.25 1.10

Intl. Y's Men's Club, 50th anniv.

Astronaut and Lunar Rover — A220

Designs: 5c, Moon scene reflected in astronaut's helmet. 10c, Astronauts with cameras. 12c, Astronauts placing scientific equipment on moon. 20c, Apollo 16 badge. 25c, Astronauts riding lunar rover.

1972, June 26

599 A220 3c lt bl & multi 15 15
600 A220 5c red org & multi 15 15
601 A220 10c pink & multi 18 15
602 A220 12c yel & multi 28 15
603 A220 20c lt vio & multi 42 15
604 A220 25c emer & multi 50 20
Nos. 599-604 (6) 1.68
Set value 60

Apollo 16 U.S. moon mission, Apr. 15-27, 1972. See No. C193.

Emperor Haile Selassie — A221

1972, July 21 *Perf. 14x14½*

605 A221 20c ol grn & yel 45 45
606 A221 25c mar & yel 55 55
607 A221 35c brn & yel 80 80

80th birthday of Emperor Haile Selassie of Ethiopia.

Ajax, 1809, and Figurehead — A222

1972, Sept. 6 *Perf. 11*

608 A222 3c *shown* 15 15
609 A222 5c *Hogue, 1811* 15 15
610 A222 7c *Ariadne, 1816* 20 15
611 A222 15c *Royal Adelaide, 1828* 40 15
612 A222 20c *Rinaldo, 1860* 55 16
613 A222 25c *Nymphe, 1888* 65 22
Nos. 608-613 (6) 2.10
Set value 65

Famous sailing ships and their figureheads. See No. C194.

Pres. Tolbert Taking Oath, Richard A. Henries A223

1972, Oct. 23 **Litho.** *Perf. 13½*

614 A223 15c grn & multi 55 55
615 A223 25c vio bl & multi 85 85

Pres. William R. Tolbert, Jr. sworn in as 19th President of Liberia, July 23, 1971. See No. C195.

Klaus Dibiasi, Italy, Diving — A224

Designs (Flag, Olympic Emblems and): 8c, Valery Borzov, USSR, running. 10c, Hideaki Yanagida, Japan, wrestling. 12c, Mark Spitz, US, swimming. 15c, Kipchoge Keino, Kenya, 3000-meter steeplechase. 25c, Richard Meade, Great Britain, equestrian. 55c, Hans Winkler, Germany, grand prix jumping.

1973, Jan. 5 **Litho.** *Perf. 11*

616 A224 5c lt bl & multi 15 15
617 A224 8c vio & multi 15 15
618 A224 10c multi 18 15
619 A224 12c grn & multi 22 15
620 A224 15c org & multi 30 20
621 A224 25c pale sal & multi 40 26
Nos. 616-621 (6) 1.40
Set value 90

Souvenir Sheet

622 A224 55c multi 1.25 65

Gold medal winners in 20th Olympic Games.

Astronaut on Moon and Apollo 17 Badge — A225

Designs (Apollo 17 Badge and): 3c, Astronauts on earth in lunar rover. 10c, Astronauts collecting yellow lunar dust. 15c, Astronauts in lunar rover exploring moon crater. 20c, Capt. Eugene A. Cernan, Dr. Harrison H. Schmitt and Comdr. Ronald E. Evans on launching pad. 25c, Astronauts on moon with scientific equipment.

1973, Mar. 28 **Litho.** *Perf. 11*

623 A225 2c bl & multi 15 15
624 A225 3c bl & multi 15 15
625 A225 10c bl & multi 15 15
626 A225 15c bl & multi 24 16
627 A225 20c bl & multi 35 24
628 A225 25c bl & multi 48 32
Set value 1.25 90

Apollo 17 US moon mission, Dec. 7-19, 1972. See No. C196.

Locomotive, England — A226

Designs: Locomotives, 1895-1905.

1973, May 4

629 A226 2c shown 15 15
630 A226 3c Netherlands 15 15
631 A226 10c France 24 15
632 A226 15c United States 32 15
633 A226 20c Japan 50 20
634 A226 25c Germany 65 26
Nos. 629-634 (6) 2.01
Set value 75

See No. C197.

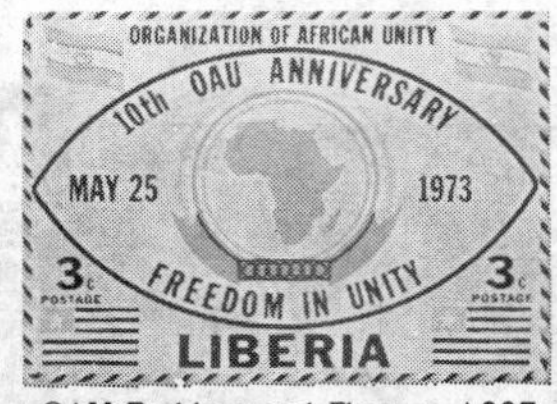

OAU Emblem and Flags — A227

1973, May 24 **Litho.** *Perf. 13½*

635 A227 3c multi 15 15
636 A227 5c multi 15 15
637 A227 10c multi 16 15
638 A227 15c multi 24 20
639 A227 25c multi 30 26
640 A227 50c multi 60 50
Nos. 635-640 (6) 1.60
Set value 1.20

10th anniv. of the Organization for African Unity.

WHO Emblem, Edward Jenner and Roses — A228

Designs (WHO Emblem and): 4c, Sigmund Freud and pansies. 10c, Jonas E. Salk and chrysanthemums. 15c, Louis Pasteur and scabiosa caucasia. 20c, Emil von Behring and rhododendron. 25c, Alexander Fleming and tree mallows.

1973, June 26 **Litho.** *Perf. 11*

641 A228 1c gray & multi 15 15
642 A228 4c org & multi 15 15
643 A228 10c lt bl & multi 15 15
644 A228 15c rose & multi 22 15
645 A228 20c bl & multi 30 18
646 A228 25c yel grn & multi 38 24
Set value 1.10 65

25th anniv. of WHO. See No. C198.

Stanley Steamer, 1910 — A229

Designs: Classic automobiles.

1973, Sept. 11 **Litho.** *Perf. 11*

647 A229 2c shown 15 15
648 A229 3c Cadillac, 1903 15 15
649 A229 10c Clement-Bayard, 1904 24 15
650 A229 15c Rolls Royce, 1907 35 15
651 A229 20c Maxwell, 1905 45 20
652 A229 25c Chadwick, 1907 60 28
Nos. 647-652 (6) 1.94
Set value 78

See No. C199.

Copernicus, Armillary Sphere, Satellite Communication — A230

Portraits of Copernicus and: 4c, Eudoxus solar system. 10c, Aristotle, Ptolemy, Copernicus and satellites. 15c, Saturn and Apollo spacecraft. 20c, Orbiting astronomical observatory. 25c, Satellite tracking station.

1973, Dec. 14 Litho. *Perf. 13½*

653	A230	1c	yel & multi	15	15
654	A230	4c	lt vio & multi	15	15
655	A230	10c	lt bl & multi	20	15
656	A230	15c	yel grn & multi	30	15
657	A230	20c	bis & multi	40	18
658	A230	25c	pink & multi	50	24
			Nos. 653-658 (6)	1.70	
			Set value		65

Nicolaus Copernicus (1473-1543), Polish astronomer. See No. C200.

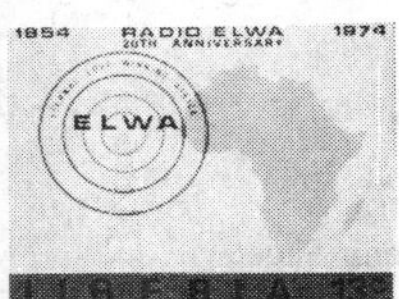

Radio Tower, Map of Africa — A231

Designs: 15c, 25c, Map of Liberia, Radio tower and man listening to broadcast. 17c, like 13c.

1974, Jan. 16 Litho. *Perf. 13½*

659	A231	13c	multi	35	35
660	A231	15c	yel & multi	35	28
661	A231	17c	lt gray & multi	42	32
662	A231	25c	brt grn & multi	55	42

20th anniv. of Radio ELWA, Monrovia.

Thomas Courts, 1817; Aureal, 1974; UPU Emblem — A232

Designs (UPU Emblem and): 3c, Jet, satellite, Post Office, Monrovia, ship. 10c, US and USSR telecommunication satellites. 15c, Mail runner and jet. 20c, Futuristic mail train and mail truck. 25c, American Pony Express rider.

1974, Mar. 4 Litho. *Perf. 13½*

663	A232	2c	ocher & multi	15	15
664	A232	3c	lt grn & multi	15	15
665	A232	10c	lt bl & multi	20	15
666	A232	15c	pink & multi	30	15
667	A232	20c	gray & multi	38	20
668	A232	25c	lt lil & multi	50	26
			Set value	1.20	75

Cent. of UPU. See No. C201.

Fox Terrier — A233

1974, Apr. 16 Litho. *Perf. 13½*

669	A233	5c	shown	15	15
670	A233	10c	Boxer	15	15
671	A233	16c	Chihuahua	30	15
672	A233	19c	Beagle	35	15
673	A233	25c	Golden retriever	42	15
674	A233	50c	Collie	90	24
			Nos. 669-674 (6)	2.27	
			Set value		62

See No. C202.

Soccer Game, West Germany and Chile — A234

Designs: Games between semi-finalists, and flags of competing nations.

1974, June 4 Litho. *Perf. 11*

675	A234	1c	shown	15	15
676	A234	2c	Australia and East Germany	15	15
677	A234	5c	Brazil and Yugoslavia	15	15
678	A234	10c	Zaire and Scotland	16	15
679	A234	12c	Netherlands and Uruguay	20	15
680	A234	15c	Sweden and Bulgaria	24	15
681	A234	20c	Italy and Haiti	32	18
682	A234	25c	Poland and Argentina	40	25
			Set value	1.45	80

World Cup Soccer Championship, Munich, June 13-July 7. See No. C203.

Chrysiridia Madagascariensis — A235

Tropical Butterflies: 2c, Catagramma sorana. 5c, Erasmia pulchella. 17c, Morpho cypris. 25c, Agrias amydon. 40c, Vanessa cardui.

1974, Sept. 11 Litho. *Perf. 13½*

683	A235	1c	gray & multi	15	15
684	A235	2c	gray & multi	15	15
685	A235	5c	gray & multi	15	15
686	A235	17c	gray & multi	40	15
687	A235	25c	gray & multi	55	22
688	A235	40c	gray & multi	90	38
			Set value	1.70	85

See No. C204.

Pres. Tolbert and Medal A236

Design: $1, Pres. Tolbert, medal and Liberian flag, vert.

1974, Dec. 10 Litho. *Perf. 13½*

689	A236	3c	multi	15	15
690	A236	$1	multi	1.65	1.25

Pres. William R. Tolbert, Jr., recipient of 1974 Family of Man Award.

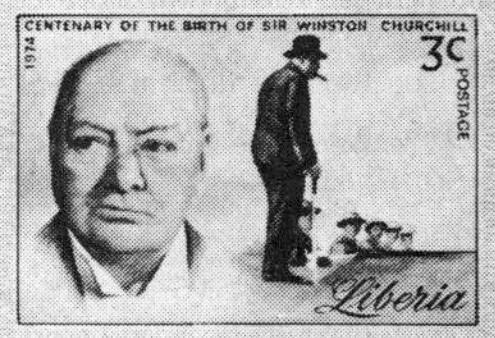

Winston Churchill, 1940 — A237

Designs (Churchill and): 10c, RAF planes in dog fight. 15c, In naval launch on way to Normandy. 17c, In staff car reviewing troops in desert. 20c, Aboard landing craft crossing Rhine. 25c, In conference with Pres. Roosevelt.

1975, Jan. 17 Litho. *Perf. 13½*

691	A237	3c	multi	15	15
692	A237	10c	multi	15	15
693	A237	15c	multi	18	15
694	A237	17c	multi	22	15
695	A237	20c	multi	24	15
696	A237	25c	multi	30	22
			Nos. 691-696 (6)	1.24	
			Set value		70

Sir Winston Churchill (1874-1965), birth centenary. See No. C205.

Women's Year Emblem and Marie Curie A238

Designs (Women's Year Emblem and): 3c, Mahalia Jackson with microphone. 5c, Joan of Arc. 10c, Eleanor Roosevelt and children. 25c, Matilda Newport firing cannon. 50c, Valentina Tereshkova in space suit.

1975, Mar. 14 Litho. *Perf. 14½*

697	A238	2c	cit & multi	15	15
698	A238	3c	dl org & multi	15	15
699	A238	5c	lil rose & multi	15	15
700	A238	10c	yel & multi	18	15
701	A238	25c	yel grn & multi	42	16
702	A238	50c	lil & multi	85	32
			Set value	1.60	65

Intl. Women's Year 1975. See No. C206.

Old State House, Boston, US No. 627 — A239

Designs: 10c, George Washington, US #644. 15c, Town Hall and Court House, Philadelphia, US #798. 20c, Benjamin Franklin, US #835. 25c, Paul Revere's Ride, US #618. 50c, Santa Maria, US #231.

1975, Apr. 25 Litho. *Perf. 13½*

703	A239	5c	multi	15	15
704	A239	10c	multi	24	15
705	A239	15c	multi	35	15
706	A239	20c	multi	45	15
707	A239	25c	multi	60	15
708	A239	50c	multi	1.25	24
			Nos. 703-708 (6)	3.04	
			Set value		70

American Revolution Bicentennial. See No. C207.

Dr. Schweitzer, Hospital and Baboon Mother — A240

Designs (Dr. Schweitzer and): 3c, Elephant, and tribesmen poling boat. 5c, Water buffalo, egret, man and woman paddling canoe. 6c, Antelope and dancer. 25c, Lioness, woman cooking outdoors. 50c, Zebra and colt, doctor's examination at clinic.

1975, June 26 Litho. *Perf. 13½*

709	A240	1c	multi	15	15
710	A240	3c	multi	15	15
711	A240	5c	multi	15	15
712	A240	6c	multi	15	15
713	A240	25c	multi	60	16
714	A240	50c	multi	1.25	38
			Set value	1.80	70

Dr. Albert Schweitzer (1875-1965), medical missionary, birth centenary. See No. C208.

American-Russian Handshake in Space — A241

Designs (Apollo-Soyuz Emblem and): 5c, Apollo. 10c, Soyuz. 20c, Flags and maps of US and USSR. 25c, A. A. Leonov, and V. N. Kubasov. 50c, D. K. Slayton, V. D. Brand, T. P. Stafford.

1975, Sept. 18 Litho. *Perf. 13½*

715	A241	5c	multi	15	15
716	A241	10c	multi	16	15
717	A241	15c	multi	24	15
718	A241	20c	multi	32	15
719	A241	25c	multi	40	15
720	A241	50c	multi	80	30
			Nos. 715-720 (6)	2.07	
			Set value		65

Apollo Soyuz space test project (Russo-American cooperation), launching July 15; link-up, July 17. See No. C209.

Presidents Tolbert, Siaka Stevens; Treaty Signing; Liberia and Sierra Leone Maps — A242

1975, Oct. 3 Litho. *Perf. 13½*

721	A242	2c	gray & multi	15	15
722	A242	3c	gray & multi	15	15
723	A242	5c	gray & multi	15	15
724	A242	10c	gray & multi	16	15
725	A242	25c	gray & multi	38	24
726	A242	50c	gray & multi	80	50
			Set value	1.50	1.00

Mano River Union Agreement between Liberia and Sierra Leone, signed Oct. 3, 1973.

Figure Skating A243

Designs (Winter Olympic Games Emblem and): 4c, Ski jump. 10c, Slalom. 25c, Ice hockey. 35c, Speed skating. 50c, Two-man bobsled.

1976, Jan. 23 Litho. *Perf. 13½*

727	A243	1c	lt bl & multi	15	15
728	A243	4c	lt bl & multi	15	15
729	A243	10c	lt bl & multi	16	15
730	A243	25c	lt bl & multi	42	15
731	A243	35c	lt bl & multi	55	18
732	A243	50c	lt bl & multi	80	28
			Nos. 727-732 (6)	2.23	
			Set value		72

12th Winter Olympic Games, Innsbruck, Austria, Feb. 4-15. See No. C210.

Pres. Tolbert Taking Oath of Office
A244

Designs: 25c, Pres. Tolbert at his desk, vert. $1, Seal and flag of Liberia, $400 commemorative gold coin.

1976, Apr. 5 Litho. *Perf. 13½*

733 A244 3c multi 15 15
734 A244 25c multi 26 26
735 A244 $1 multi 1.25 1.25

Inauguration of President William R. Tolbert, Jr., Jan. 5, 1976.

Weight Lifting and Olympic Rings — A245

Designs (Olympic Rings and): 3c, Pole vault. 10c, Hammer and shot put. 25c, Yachting. 35c, Women's gymnastics. 50c, Hurdles.

1976, May 4 Litho. *Perf. 13½*

736 A245 2c gray & multi 15 15
737 A245 3c org & multi 15 15
738 A245 10c lt vio & multi 16 15
739 A245 25c lt grn & multi 42 16
740 A245 35c yel & multi 60 25
741 A245 50c pink & multi 85 25
Nos. 736-741 (6) 2.33
Set value 80

21st Olympic Games, Montreal, Canada, July 17-Aug. 1. See No. C211.

A. G. Bell, Telephone and Receiver, 1876, UPU Emblem — A246

UPU Emblem and: 4c, Horsedrawn mail coach and ITU emblem. 5c, Intelsat IV satellite, radar and ITU emblem. 25c, A. G. Bell, ship laying underwater cable, 1976 telephone. 40c, A. G. Bell, futuristic train, telegraph and telephone wires. 50c, Wright brothers' plane, Zeppelin and Concorde.

1976, June 4 Litho. *Perf. 13½*

742 A246 1c grn & multi 15 15
743 A246 4c ocher & multi 15 15
744 A246 5c org & multi 15 15
745 A246 25c grn & multi 32 15
746 A246 40c lil & multi 50 18
747 A246 50c bl & multi 65 25
Set value 1.60 65

Cent. of 1st telephone call by Alexander Graham Bell, Mar. 10, 1876. See No. C212.

Gold Nugget on Chain, Gold Panner
A247

1976-81 Litho. *Perf. 14½*

749 A247 1c Mano River Bridge 15 15
750 A247 3c shown 15 15
751 A247 5c "V" ring 15 15
752 A247 7c like 5c ('81) 18 15
753 A247 10c Rubber tire, tree 24 15
754 A247 15c Harvesting 38 32
755 A247 17c like 55c ('81) 42 35
756 A247 20c Hydroelectric plant 50 42
757 A247 25c Mesurado shrimp 60 15
758 A247 27c Woman tie-dying cloth 65 55
759 A247 55c Lake Piso, barracuda 1.25 35
760 A247 $1 Train hauling iron ore 2.50 2.00
Nos. 749-760 (12) 7.17 4.89

See Nos. 945-953.

Rhinoceros — A249

African Animals: 3c, Zebra antelope. 5c, Chimpanzee, vert. 15c, Pigmy hippopotamus. 25c, Leopard. $1, Gorilla, vert.

1976, Sept. 1 Litho. *Perf. 13½*

763 A249 2c org & multi 15 15
764 A249 3c gray & multi 15 15
765 A249 5c bl & multi 15 15
766 A249 15c brt bl & multi 25 15
767 A249 25c ultra & multi 45 22
768 A249 $1 multi 1.65 75
Nos. 763-768 (6) 2.80
Set value 1.20

See No. C213.

Maps of US and Liberia; Statue of Liberty, Unification Monument, Voinjama and Liberty Bell — A250

Designs: $1, George Washington, Gerald R. Ford, Joseph J. Roberts (1st Pres. of Liberia), William R. Tolbert, Jr., Bicentennial emblem, US and Liberian flags.

1976, Sept. 21 Litho. *Perf. 13½*

769 A250 25c multi 45 25
770 A250 $1 multi 1.65 60

American Bicentennial and visit of Pres. William R. Tolbert, Jr. to the US, Sept. 21-30. See No. C214.

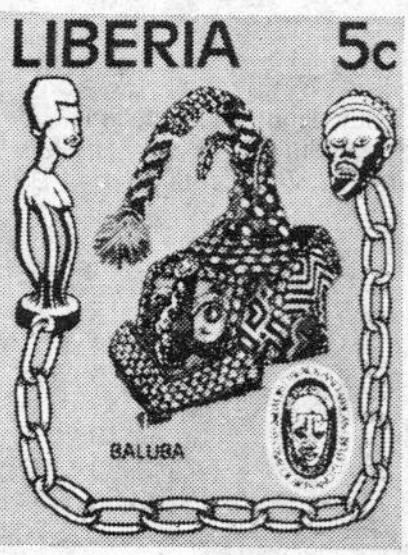

Baluba Masks and Festival Emblem
A251

Tribal Masks: 10c, Bateke. 15c, Basshilele. 20c, Igungun. 25c, Masai. 50c, Kifwebe.

1977, Jan. 20 Litho. *Perf. 13½*

771 A251 5c yel & multi 15 15
772 A251 10c grn & multi 16 15
773 A251 15c sal & multi 25 15
774 A251 20c lt bl & multi 32 15
775 A251 25c vio & multi 40 18
776 A251 50c lem & multi 80 28
Nos. 771-776 (6) 2.08
Set value 80

FESTAC '77, 2nd World Black and African Festival, Lagos, Nigeria, Jan. 15-Feb. 12. See No. C215.

Latham's Francolin — A252

Birds of Liberia: 10c, Narina trogon. 15c, Rufous-crowned roller. 20c, Brown-cheeked hornbill. 25c, Common bulbul. 50c, Fish eagle. 80c, Gold Coast touraco.

1977, Feb. 18 Litho. *Perf. 14*

777 A252 5c multi 15 15
778 A252 10c multi 20 15
779 A252 15c multi 30 15
780 A252 20c multi 40 15
781 A252 25c multi 50 18
782 A252 50c multi 1.00 28
Nos. 777-782 (6) 2.55
Set value 80

Souvenir Sheet

783 A252 80c multi 1.50 1.10

Edmund Coffin, Military Dressage, USA — A253

Designs: 15c, Alwin Schockemohle, single jump. Germany, vert. 20c, Christine Stuckelberger, Switzerland, single dressage. 25c, Prize of the Nations (team), France.

1977, Apr. 22 Litho. *Perf. 13½*

784 A253 5c ocher & multi 15 15
785 A253 15c ocher & multi 28 15
786 A253 20c ocher & multi 32 16
787 A253 25c ocher & multi 42 24
Nos. 784-787,C216 (5) 2.17 1.20

Equestrian gold medal winners in Montreal Olympic Games. See No. C217.

Elizabeth II Wearing Crown — A254

Designs: 25c, Elizabeth II Prince Philip, Pres. and Mrs. Tubman. 80c, Elizabeth II, Prince Philip, royal coat of arms.

1977, May 23 Litho. *Perf. 13½*

788 A254 15c sil & multi 28 15
789 A254 25c sil & multi 45 15
790 A254 80c sil & multi 1.40 45

25th anniversary of the reign of Queen Elizabeth II. See No. C218.

Jesus Blessing Children
A255

Christmas: 25c, The Good Shepherd. $1, Jesus and the Samaritan Woman. Designs after stained-glass windows, Providence Baptist Church, Monrovia.

1977, Nov. 3 Litho. *Perf. 13½*

791 A255 20c lt bl & multi 40 25
792 A255 25c lt bl & multi 52 28
793 A255 $1 lt bl & multi 1.75 95

Dornier DOX, 1928 — A256

Progress of Aviation: 3c, Piggyback space shuttle, 1977. 5c, Eddie Rickenbacker and Douglas DC 3. 25c, Charles A. Lindbergh and Spirit of St. Louis. 35c, Louis Bleriot and Bleriot XI. 50c, Orville and Wilbur Wright and flying machine, 1903. 80c, Concorde landing at night at Dulles Airport, Washington, DC.

1978, Jan. 6 Litho. *Perf. 13½*

794 A256 2c multi 15 15
795 A256 3c multi 15 15
796 A256 5c multi 15 15
797 A256 25c multi 45 24
798 A256 35c multi 65 30
799 A256 50c multi 95 42
Nos. 794-799 (6) 2.50
Set value 1.10

Souvenir Sheet

800 A256 80c multi 1.40 1.10

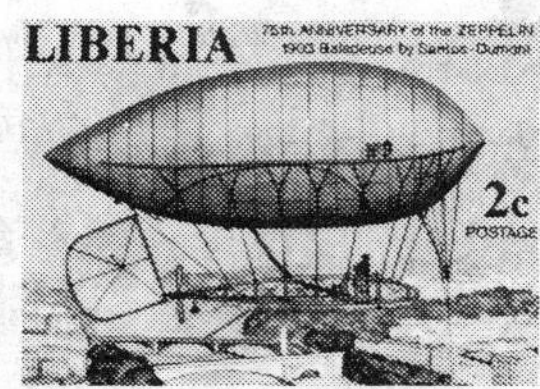

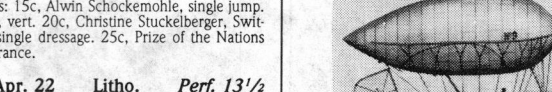

Baladeuse by Santos-Dumont, 1903 — A257

Airships: 3c, Baldwin's, 1908, and US flag. 5c, Tissandier brothers'. 1883. 25c, Parseval PL VII, 1912. 40c, Nulli Secundus II, 1908. 50c, R34 rigid airship, 1919.

1978, Mar. 9 Litho. *Perf. 13½*

801 A257 2c multi 15 15
802 A257 3c multi 15 15
803 A257 5c multi 15 15
804 A257 25c multi 35 15
805 A257 40c multi 55 16
806 A257 50c multi 75 20
Set value 1.75 55

75th anniv. of the Zeppelin. See No. C219.

Soccer, East Germany and Brazil — A258

Soccer Games: 2c, Poland and Argentina (vert.). 10c, West Germany and Netherlands. 25c, Yugoslavia and Brazil. 35c, Poland and Italy, vert. 50c, Netherlands and Uruguay.

1978, May 16 Litho. *Perf. 13½*

807 A258 2c multi 15 15
808 A258 3c multi 15 15
809 A258 10c multi 22 15
810 A258 25c multi 55 28
811 A258 35c multi 75 38
812 A258 50c multi 1.10 55
Nos. 807-812 (6) 2.92
Set value 1.40

11th World Cup Soccer Championships, Argentina, June 1-25. See No. C220.

Coronation Chair — A259

Designs: 25c, Imperial state crown. $1, Buckingham Palace, horiz.

1978, June 12

813	A259	5c multi	15	15
814	A259	25c multi	45	15
815	A259	$1 multi	1.65	65
		Set value		80

25th anniversary of coronation of Queen Elizabeth II. See No. C221.

Jinnah, Liberian and Pakistani Flags — A260

1978, June **Litho.** ***Perf. 13***

816	A260	30c multi	*25.00*	5.00

Mohammed Ali Jinnah (1876-1948), first Governor General of Pakistan.

Carter and Tolbert Families — A261

Designs: 25c, Pres. Tolbert, Rosalynn Carter and Pres. Carter at microphone, Robertsfield Airport. $1, Jimmy Carter and William R. Tolbert, Jr. in motorcade from airport.

1978, Oct. 26 **Litho.** ***Perf. 13½***

817	A261	5c multi	15	15
818	A261	25c multi	42	42
819	A261	$1 multi	1.75	1.75

Pres. Carter's visit to Liberia, Apr. 1978.

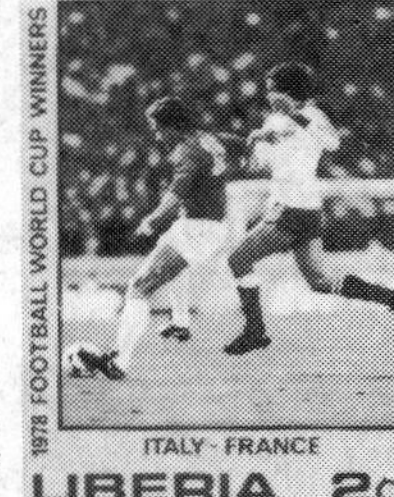

Soccer Game: Italy-France A262

Soccer Games: 1c, Brazil-Spain, horiz. 10c, Poland-West Germany, horiz. 27c, Peru-Scotland. 35c, Austria-West Germany. 50c, Argentina the victor.

1978, Dec. 8 **Litho.** ***Perf. 13½***

820	A262	1c multi	15	15
821	A262	2c multi	15	15
822	A262	10c multi	22	16
823	A262	27c multi	60	38
824	A262	35c multi	75	52
825	A262	50c multi	1.10	75
		Nos. 820-825 (6)	2.97	2.11

1978 World Cup Soccer winners. See No. C222.

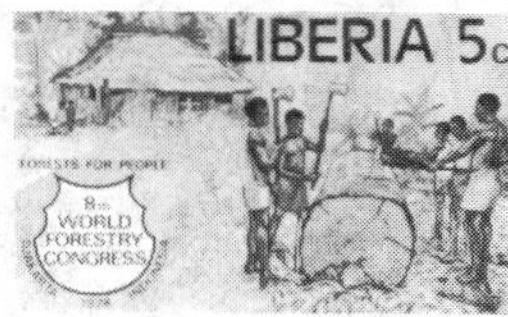

Liberian Lumbermen — A263

Designs: 10c, Hauling timber by truck, vert. 25c, Felling trees with chain saw. 50c, Moving logs.

1978, Dec. 15 **Litho.** ***Perf. 13½x14***

826	A263	5c multi	15	15
827	A263	10c multi	25	16
828	A263	25c multi	55	38
829	A263	50c multi	1.10	75

8th World Forestry Congress, Djakarta, Indonesia.

"25" and Waves — A264

Design: $1, Radio tower and waves.

1979, Apr. 6 **Litho.** ***Perf. 14x13½***

830	A264	35c multi	65	65
831	A264	$1 multi	1.90	1.90

25th anniversary of Radio ELWA.

Emblems of IYC, African Child's Decade and SOS Village — A265

Designs: 25c, $1, like 5c, with UNICEF emblem replacing SOS emblem. 35c, like 5c.

1979, Apr. 6 ***Perf. 13½x14***

832	A265	5c multi	15	15
833	A265	25c multi	38	38
834	A265	35c multi	52	52
835	A265	$1 multi	1.50	1.50

IYC and Decade of the African Child.

Presidents Gardner and Tolbert, and Post Office, Monrovia — A266

Design: 35c, Anthony W. Gardner, William R. Tolbert, Jr. and UPU emblem.

1979, Apr. 2 **Litho.** ***Perf. 13½x14***

836	A266	5c multi	15	15
837	A266	35c multi	80	80

Cent. of Liberia's joining UPU.

Unity Problem, Map of Africa, Torches — A267

Designs: 27c, Masks. 35c, Elephant, giraffe, lion, antelope, leopard and map of Africa. 50c, Huts, pepper birds and map of Africa.

1979, July 6 **Litho.** ***Perf. 14x13½***

838	A267	5c multi	15	15
839	A267	27c multi	52	52
840	A267	35c multi	65	65
841	A267	50c multi	95	95

Organization for African Unity, 16th anniversary, and OAU Summit Conference.

Liberia No. 666, Rowland Hill — A268

Rowland Hill and: 10c, Pony Express rider, 1860. 15c, British mail coach, 1800. 25c, Mail steamship John Penn, 1860. 27c, Stanier Pacific train, 1939. 50c, Concorde. $1, Curtiss Jenny, 1916.

1979, July 20

842	A268	3c multi	15	15
843	A268	10c multi	15	15
844	A268	15c multi	24	24
845	A268	25c multi	38	38
846	A268	27c multi	42	42
847	A268	50c multi	75	75
		Nos. 842-847 (6)	2.09	2.09

Souvenir Sheet

848	A268	$1 multi	1.50	1.25

Sir Rowland Hill (1795-1879), originator of penny postage.

Red Cross, Pres. Tolbert Donating Blood — A269

Design: 50c, Red Cross, Pres. Tolbert.

1979, Aug. 15 **Litho.** ***Perf. 13½***

849	A269	30c multi	55	55
850	A269	50c multi	95	95

National Red Cross, 30th anniversary and blood donation campaign.

M.S. World Peace A270

Design: $1, M.S. World Peace (diff.).

1979, Aug. 15

851	A270	5c multi	15	15
852	A270	$1 multi	1.90	1.90

2nd World Maritime Day, March 16; Liberia Maritime Program, 30th anniversary.

A Good Turn, by Norman Rockwell A271

Paintings: Scouting through the eyes of Norman Rockwell, 1925-1976. Each denomination in 10 different designs.

1979, Sept. 1 **Litho.** ***Perf. 11***

853	A271	5c any single	15	15
854	A271	10c any single	15	15
855	A271	15c any single	18	16
856	A271	25c any single	35	24
857	A271	35c any single	50	40
		Nos. 853-857 (50)	12.10	9.30

Mrs. Tolbert, Children, Children's Village Emblem — A272

Design: 40c, Mrs. Tolbert, children, emblem, vert.

1979, Nov. 14 **Litho.** ***Perf. 14***

858	A272	25c multi	50	50
859	A272	40c multi	80	80

SOS Children's Village in Monrovia, Liberia.

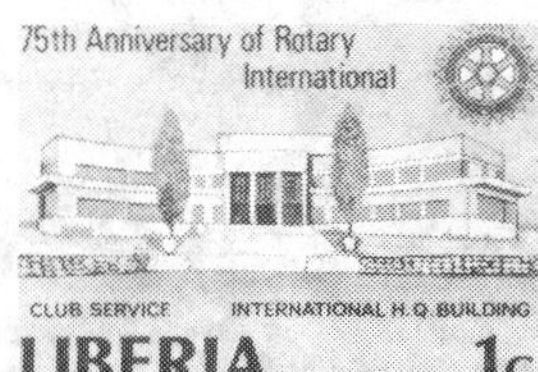

Rotary International Headquarters, Evanston, Ill., Emblem — A273

Rotary Emblem and: 5c, Vocational services. 17c, Man in wheelchair, nurse, vert. 27c, Flags of several nations. 35c, People of various races holding hands around globe. 50c, Pres. Tolbert, map of Africa, vert. $1, "Gift of Life."

1979, Dec. 28 ***Perf. 11***

860	A273	1c multi	15	15
861	A273	5c multi	15	15
862	A273	17c multi	22	22
863	A273	27c multi	45	45
864	A273	35c multi	55	55
865	A273	50c multi	85	85
		Nos. 860-865 (6)	2.37	2.37

Souvenir Sheet

866	A273	$1 multi	1.65	1.65

Rotary International, 75th anniversary.

The Scott Catalogue value is a retail price, what you could expect to pay for the stamp in a grade of Fine-Very Fine. The value listed is a reference which reflects recent actual dealer selling price.

Ski Jump, Lake Placid '80 Emblem — A274

Lake Placid '80 Emblem and: 5c, Figure skating. 17c, Bobsledding. 27c, Cross-country skiing. 35c, Women's speed skating. 50c, Ice hockey. $1, Slalom.

1980, Jan. 21

867 A274 1c multi 15 15
868 A274 5c multi 15 15
869 A274 17c multi 35 35
870 A274 27c multi 70 70
871 A274 35c multi 70 70
872 A274 50c multi 1.00 1.00
Nos. 867-872 (6) 3.05 3.05

Souvenir Sheet

873 A274 $1 multi 1.75 1.75

13th Winter Olympic Games, Lake Placid, NY, Feb. 12-24.

Pres. Tolbert, Pres. Stevens, Maps of Liberia and Sierra Leone, Mano River — A275

1980, Mar. 6 Litho. *Perf. 14x13½*

874 A275 8c multi 16 16
875 A275 27c multi 55 55
876 A275 35c multi 70 70
877 A275 80c multi 1.60 1.60

Mano River Agreement, 5th anniversary; Mano River Postal Union, 1st anniversary.

Sgt. Doe and Soldiers, Clenched Hands Angel — A276

1981 Litho. *Perf. 14*

878 A276 1c Redemption horn, vert. 15 15
879 A276 6c like 1c 15 15
880 A276 10c shown 15 15
881 A276 14c Citizens, map, Flag 20 20
882 A276 23c like 10c 32 32
883 A276 31c like 14c 45 45
884 A276 41c like $2 60 60
885 A276 $2 Sgt. Samuel Doe, vert. 3.00 3.00
Nos. 878-885 (8) 5.02 5.02

Establishment of new government under the People's Redemption Council, Apr. 12, 1980.

Soccer Players, World Cup, Flags of 1930 and 1934 Finalists — A277

Soccer Players, Cup, Flags of Finalists from: 5c, 1938, 1950. 20c, 1954, 1958. 27c, 1962, 1966. 40c, 1970, 1974. 55c. 1978. $1, Spanish team.

1981, Mar. 4 Litho. *Perf. 14*

886 A277 3c multi 15 15
887 A277 5c multi 15 15
888 A277 20c multi 32 32
889 A277 27c multi 45 45
890 A277 40c multi 65 65
891 A277 55c multi 95 95
Nos. 886-891 (6) 2.67 2.67

Souvenir Sheet

892 A277 $1 multi 1.65 1.65

ESPANA '82 World Cup Soccer Championship.

Sgt. Samuel Doe and Citizens — A278

1981, Apr. 7 Litho. *Perf. 14*

893 A278 22c shown 38 38
894 A278 27c Doe, Liberian flag 45 45
895 A278 30c Clasped arms 50 50
896 A278 $1 Doe, soldiers, Justice 1.65 1.65

People's Redemption Council government, first anniversary.

Royal Wedding — A279

1981, Aug. 12 Litho. *Perf. 14x13½*

897 A279 31c Couple 40 40
898 A279 41c Initials, roses 50 50
899 A279 62c St. Paul's Cathedral 1.00 1.00

Souvenir Sheet

900 A279 $1 Couple 1.50 1.50

John Adams, US President, 1797-1801 A280

Washington Crossing the Delaware A281

1981, July 4 *Perf. 11*

901 A280 4c shown *15 15*
902 A280 5c William H. Harrison *15 15*
903 A280 10c Martin Van Buren *16 15*
904 A280 17c James Monroe *30 24*
905 A280 20c John Q. Adams *35 28*
906 A280 22c James Madison *40 32*
907 A280 27c Thomas Jefferson *45 38*
908 A280 30c Andrew Jackson *50 40*
909 A280 40c John Tyler *70 55*
910 A280 80c George Washington *1.40 1.10*
Nos. 901-910 (10) *4.56 3.72*

Souvenir Sheet

911 A281 $1 multi *1.65 1.65*

1981, Nov. 26 Litho. *Perf. 11*

912 A280 6c Rutherford B. Hayes *15 15*
913 A280 12c Ulysses S. Grant *22 18*
914 A280 14c Millard Fillmore *22 18*
915 A280 15c Zachary Taylor *25 20*
916 A280 20c Abraham Lincoln *35 28*
917 A280 27c Andrew Johnson *45 38*
918 A280 31c James Buchanan *50 40*
919 A280 41c James A. Garfield *75 60*
920 A280 50c James K. Polk *90 70*
921 A280 55c Franklin Pierce *1.00 75*
Nos. 912-921 (10) *4.79 3.82*

Souvenir Sheet

922 A281 $1 Washington at Valley Forge *1.65 1.65*

1982, Apr. 7 Litho. *Perf. 11*

923 A280 4c William H. Taft *15 15*
924 A280 5c Calvin Coolidge *15 15*
925 A280 6c Benjamin Harrison *15 15*
926 A280 10c Warren G. Harding *16 15*
927 A280 22c Grover Cleveland *40 32*
928 A280 27c Chester Arthur *45 38*
929 A280 31c Woodrow Wilson *50 40*
930 A280 41c William McKinley *75 60*
931 A280 80c Theodore Roosevelt *1.40 1.10*
Nos. 923-931 (9) *4.11 3.40*

Souvenir Sheet

932 A281 $1 Signing Constitution, horiz. *1.65 1.65*

1982, July 15 Litho. *Perf. 11*

933 A280 4c Jimmy Carter *15 15*
934 A280 6c Gerald Ford *15 15*
935 A280 14c Harry Truman *22 18*
936 A280 17c Franklin D. Roosevelt *30 24*
937 A280 23c Lyndon B. Johnson *40 32*
938 A280 27c Richard Nixon *45 38*
939 A280 31c John F. Kennedy *50 40*
940 A280 35c Ronald Reagan *60 48*
941 A280 50c Herbert Hoover *90 70*
942 A280 55c Dwight D. Eisenhower *1.00 75*
Nos. 933-942 (10) *4.67 3.75*

Souvenir Sheet

Perf. 14x13½

943 A281 $1 Battle of Yorktown *1.65 1.65*

See No. 1113.

Type of 1976

1981-83 Litho. *Perf. 14½x13½*

Size: 34x20mm

945 A247 1c like #749 15 15
946 A247 3c like #750 15 15
947 A247 6c like #753 15 15
948 A247 15c like #754 32 32
949 A247 25c like #757 52 52
950 A247 31c like #756 65 65
951 A247 41c like #758 85 85
952 A247 80c like #759 1.75 1.75
953 A247 $1 like #760 2.00 2.00
Nos. 945-953 (9) 6.54 6.54

Issue dates: Nos. 946-947, 949, 950, Nov. 27, 1981; Nos. 945, 953, Oct. 12, 1982; Nos. 948, 951, Dec. 10, 1982. No. 952, Nov. 3, 1983.

Intl. Year of the Disabled (1981) A282

Designs: Various disabled people.

1982, Mar. 24 Litho. *Perf. 14*

954 A282 23c multi, vert. 38 38
955 A282 62c multi 1.00 1.00

30th Anniv. of West African Examinations Council — A283

1982, Mar. 24

956 A283 6c multi 15 15
957 A283 31c multi 50 50

21st Birthday of Princess Diana — A284

Designs: 31c, 41c, 62c, Diana portraits. $1, Wedding.

1982, July 1 *Perf. 14x13½*

958 A284 31c multi 50 50
959 A284 41c multi 65 65
960 A284 62c multi 1.00 1.00

Souvenir Sheet

961 A284 $1 multi 1.65 1.65

Nos. 958-961 Overprinted in Silver: "ROYAL BABY / 21-6-82 / PRINCE WILLIAM"

1982, Aug. 30 Litho. *Perf. 14x13½*

962 A284 31c multi 50 50
963 A284 41c multi 65 65
964 A284 62c multi 1.00 1.00

Souvenir Sheet

965 A284 $1 multi 1.65 1.65

Birth of Prince William of Wales, June 21.

3rd Natl. Redemption Day — A285

1983, Apr. 5 Litho. *Perf. 13½*

966 A285 3c Fallah Varney 15 15
967 A285 6c Samuel Doe 15 15
968 A285 10c Jlatoh N. Podier, Jr. 16 16
969 A285 15c Jeffry S. Gbatu 25 25
970 A285 31c Thomas G. Quiwonkpa 50 50
971 A285 41c Abraham D. Kollie 65 65
Nos. 966-971 (6) 1.86 1.86

Souvenir Sheet

972 A285 $1 like 6c 1.90 1.90

Natl. Archives Opening — A286

Building views.

1983, Apr. 5

973 A286 6c multi 15 15
974 A286 31c multi 50 50

Christmas 1983 — A287

Raphael Paintings: 6c, Circumcision of Christ. 15c, Adoration of the Magi. 25c, Announcement to Mary. 31c, Madonna with Baldachin. 41c, Holy Family. 62c, Detail of Madonna with Child Surrounded by Five Saints. $1.25 Madonna of Foligno.

1983, Dec. 14 Litho. *Perf. 13½*

975 A287 6c multi 15 15
976 A287 15c multi 25 25
977 A287 25c multi 40 40
978 A287 31c multi 50 50
979 A287 41c multi 65 65
980 A287 62c multi 1.00 1.00
Nos. 975-980 (6) 2.95 2.95

Souvenir Sheet

981 A287 $1.25 multi 2.00 2.00

Mano River Union, 10th Anniv. (1983) — A288

1984, Apr. 6 Litho. *Perf. 14x13½*

982 A288 6c Training school graduates 15 15
983 A288 25c Emblem 42 42
984 A288 31c Maps, leaders 50 50
985 A288 41c Guinea's accession 65 65

Souvenir Sheet

986 A288 75c Guinea's accession, diff. 1.25 1.25

4th Natl. Redemption Day — A289

1984, Apr. 12 *Perf. 14½*

987 A289 3c Hospital, New Kru Town 15 15
988 A289 10c Ganta-Harper Highway construction 16 16
989 A289 20c Constitution Assembly opening 32 32
990 A289 31c Doe at highway construction 50 50
991 A289 41c Draft Constitution presentation 65 65
Nos. 987-991 (5) 1.78 1.78

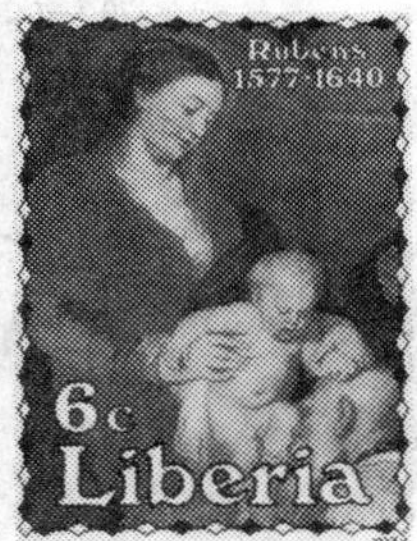

Adoration of the Wise Men, by Rubens (1577-1640) A290

1984, June 1 Litho. *Perf. 13½*

992 A290 6c shown 15 15
993 A290 15c Crowning of Katharina 25 25
994 A290 25c Mother and Child Adored by Wise Men 40 40
995 A290 31c Madonna and Child with Halo 50 50
996 A290 41c Adoration of the Shepherds 65 65
997 A290 62c Madonna and Child with Saints 1.00 1.00
Nos. 992-997 (6) 2.95 2.95

Souvenir Sheet

998 A290 $1.25 Madonna Adored by Saints 2.00 2.00

1984 Summer Olympics A291

1984, July 2 *Perf. 13½x14*

999 A291 3c Jesse Owens, 1936 15 15
1000 A291 4c Rafer Johnson, 1960 15 15
1001 A291 25c Miruts Yifter, 1980 50 50
1002 A291 41c Kipchoge Keino, 1968, 1972 80 80
1003 A291 62c Muhammad Ali, 1960 1.25 1.25
Nos. 999-1003 (5) 2.85 2.85

Souvenir Sheet

Perf. 14x13½

1004 A291 $1.25 Wilma Rudolph, 1960, horiz. 2.50 2.50

1984 Louisiana Expo A292

1984, July 24 *Perf. 14½*

1005 A292 6c Water birds 15 15
1006 A292 31c Ship, Buchanan Harbor 55 55
1007 A292 41c Fish 70 70
1008 A292 62c Train carrying iron ore 1.10 1.10

Pygmy Hippopotamus, World Wildlife Fund Emblem — A293

Various pygmy hippopotomi.

1984, Nov. 22 Litho. *Perf. 14½*

1009 A293 6c multi 15 15
1010 A293 10c multi 24 24
1011 A293 20c multi 48 48
1012 A293 31c multi 75 75

Indigent Children Home, Bensonville — A294

First Lady Mrs. Nancy Doe and various children.

1984, Dec. 14

1013 A294 6c multi 15 15
1014 A294 31c multi 50 50

Natl. Redemption Day, Apr. 12 — A295

1985, Apr. 5 Litho. *Perf. 14½*

1015 A295 6c Army barracks, Monrovia 15 15
1016 A295 31c Pan-African Plaza, Monrovia 50 50

Liberian Revolution, fifth anniv.

Audubon Birth Bicentenary — A296

Illustrations by artist/naturalist J. J. Audubon.

1985, Apr. 5

1017 A296 1c Bohemian waxwing 15 15
1018 A296 3c Bay-breasted warbler 15 15
1019 A296 6c White-winged crossbill 15 15
1020 A296 31c Red phalarope 62 62
1021 A296 41c Eastern bluebird 80 80
1022 A296 62c Northern cardinal 1.25 1.25
Nos. 1017-1022 (6) 3.12 3.12

Venus and Mirror — A297

Paintings (details) by Rubens: 15c, Adam & Eve in Paradise. 25c, Andromeda. 31c, The Three Graces. 41c, Venus & Adonis. 62c, The Daughters of Leucippus. $1.25, The Judgement of Paris.

1985, Nov. 14 Litho. *Perf. 14*

1023 A297 6c multi 15 15
1024 A297 15c multi 25 25
1025 A297 25c multi 40 40
1026 A297 31c multi 50 50
1027 A297 41c multi 60 60
1028 A297 62c multi 1.00 1.00
Nos. 1023-1028 (6) 2.90 2.90

Souvenir Sheet

1029 A297 $1.25 multi 2.00 2.00

1986 World Cup Soccer Championships, Mexico — A298

1985, Nov. 14

1030 A298 6c Germany-Morocco, 1970 15 15
1031 A298 15c Zaire-Brazil, 1974 25 25
1032 A298 25c Tunisia-Germany, 1978 40 40
1033 A298 31c Cameroun-Peru, 1982, vert. 50 50
1034 A298 41c Algeria-Germany, 1982 60 60
1035 A298 62c 1986 Senegal team 1.00 1.00
Nos. 1030-1035 (6) 2.90 2.90

Souvenir Sheet

1036 A298 $1.25 Liberia-Nigeria 2.00 2.00

Queen Mother, 85th Birthday — A299

World Food Day — A300

1985, Dec. 12 Litho. *Perf. 14½*

1037 A299 31c Elizabeth in garter robes 28 28
1038 A299 41c At the races 75 75
1039 A299 62c In garden, waving 1.10 1.10

Souvenir Sheet

1040 A299 $1.25 Wearing diadem 2.00 2.00

1985, Dec. 12

1041 A300 25c multi 40 40
1042 A300 31c multi 50 50

AMERIPEX '86 — A301

Statue of Liberty, Cent. — A302

1986, June 10 Litho. *Perf. 14½*

1043 A301 25c The Alamo 50 50
1044 A301 31c Liberty Bell 62 62
1045 A301 80c Nos. 344, 802, C102 1.60 1.60

1986, June 10

1046 A302 20c Unveiling, 1886 40 40
1047 A302 31c Frederic A. Bartholdi 62 62
1048 A302 $1 Statue close-up 2.00 2.00

1988 Winter Olympics, Calgary — A303

1984 Gold medalists: 3c, Max Julen, Switzerland, men's giant slalom. 6c, Debbie Armstrong, US, women's giant slalom. 31c, Peter Angerer, West Germany, biathlon. 60c, Bill Johnson, US, men's downhill. 80c, East Germany, 4-man bobsled. $1.25, H. Stangassinger, F. Wembacher, West Germany, 2-man luge.

1987, Aug. 21 Litho. *Perf. 14*

1049 A303 3c multi 15 15
1050 A303 6c multi 15 15
1051 A303 31c multi 62 62
1052 A303 60c multi 1.20 1.20
1053 A303 80c multi 1.60 1.60
Nos. 1049-1053 (5) 3.72 3.72

Souvenir Sheet

1054 A303 $1.25 multi 2.50 2.50

City of Berlin, 750th Anniv. — A304

Designs: 6c, State (Royal) Theater in the Gendarmenmarkt, c. 1820, architect Schinkel. 31c, Kaiser Friedrich Museum, Museum Is. on River Spree. 60c, Charlottenburg Castle, 17th cent. 80c, Modern church bell tower and Kaiser Wilhelm Gedachteinskirche. $1.50, MIRAK rocket development, Spaceship Society Airfield, Reinickendorf, 1930.

1987, Sept. 4

1055 A304	6c multi		15	15
1056 A304	31c multi		62	62
1057 A304	60c multi		1.20	1.20
1058 A304	80c multi		1.60	1.60

Souvenir sheet

Perf. 11½

1059 A304	$1.50 buff & dk brn	3.00	3.00

No. 1059 contains one 25x61mm stamp.

Shakespearean Plays — A305

1987, Nov. 6 Litho. *Perf. 14*

1060	Sheet of 8	8.10	8.10
a.	A305 3c Othello	15	15
b.	A305 6c Romeo & Juliet	15	15
c.	A305 10c The Merry Wives of Windsor	20	20
d.	A305 15c Henry IV	30	30
e.	A305 31c Hamlet	62	62
f.	A305 60c Macbeth	1.20	1.20
g.	A305 80c King Lear	1.60	1.60
h.	A305 $2 Shakespeare and the Globe Theater, 1598	4.00	4.00

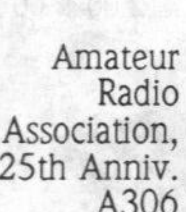

Amateur Radio Association, 25th Anniv. A306

1987, Nov. 23 Litho. *Perf. 14*

1061 A306	10c Emblem	25	25
1062 A306	10c Village	25	25
1063 A306	35c On-the-Air certificate	85	85
1064 A306	35c Globe, flags	85	85

Miniature Sheets

Statue of Liberty, Cent. (in 1986) A307

No. 1065a, Torch, southern view of NYC. b, Overhead view of crown and scaffold. c, 4 workmen repairing crown. d, 5 workmen, crown. e, Statue's right foot.

No. 1066a, Tall ship, statue. b, Bay Queen ferry. c, Statue on poster at a construction site, NYC. d, Tug boat, tall ship. e, Building frieze.

No. 1067a, Statue flanked by fireworks. b, Lighting of the statue. c, Crown observatory illuminated. d, Statue surrounded by fireworks. e, Crown and torch observatories illuminated.

No. 1068a, Liberty "Happy Birthday" poster at a construction site. b, Ships in NY Harbor. c, Woman renovating statue nose. d, Man and woman renovating nose. e, Man, nose. Nos. 1068a-1068e vert.

1987, Dec. 10 *Perf. 13½*

1065	Sheet of 5 + label	60	
a.-e.	A307 6c any single	15	15
1066	Sheet of 5 + label	1.50	
a.-e.	A307 15c any single	30	30
1067	Sheet of 5 + label	3.10	
a.-e.	A307 31c any single	62	62
1068	Sheet of 5 + label	6.00	
a.-e.	A307 60c any single	1.20	1.20

Nos. 1065-1068 contain label inscribed "CENTENARY OF THE STATUE OF LIBERTY" in two or five lines.

Second Republic, 2nd Anniv. — A308

Design: Natl. flag, coat of arms, hand grip, Pres. Doe and Vice Pres. Moniba.

1988, Jan. 6 *Perf. 14½*

1069 A308	10c multi	20	20
1070 A308	35c multi	70	70

UN Child Survival Campaign A309

Perf. 13x13½, 13½x13

1988, Jan. 15

1071 A309	3c Breast-feeding	15	15
1072 A309	6c Oral rehydration therapy, vert.	15	15
1073 A309	31c Immunization	62	62
1074 A309	$1 Growth monitoring, vert.	2.00	2.00

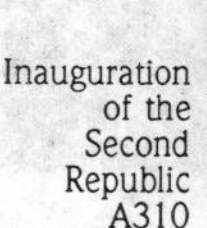

Inauguration of the Second Republic A310

Design: Pres. Doe greeting Chief Justice Emmanuel N. Gbalazeh.

1988, Jan. 15 *Perf. 13x13½*

1075 A310	6c multi	15	15

Samuel Kanyon Doe Sports Complex, Opened Apr. 12, 1986 A311

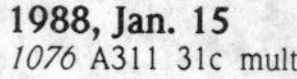

1988, Jan. 15

1076 A311	31c multi	62	62

Green (Agricultural) Revolution — A312

1988, Apr. 4 *Perf. 15*

1077 A312	10c multi	20	20
1078 A312	35c multi	70	70

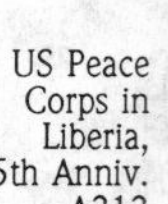

US Peace Corps in Liberia, 25th Anniv. A313

1988, Apr. 4

1079 A313	10c multi	20	20
1080 A313	35c multi	70	70

Souvenir Sheet

1988 Summer Olympics, Seoul — A314

1988, Apr. 14 *Perf. 14*

1081 A314	$3 multi	6.00	6.00

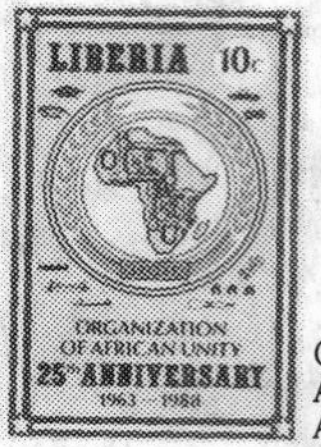

Organization of African Unity, 25th Anniv. — A315

1988, May 25

1082 A315	10c multi	20	20
1083 A315	35c multi	70	70
1084 A315	$1 multi	2.00	2.00

Rail Transport A316

1988, July 30 Litho. *Perf. 14½*

1085 A316	10c GP10 at Nimba	20	20
1086 A316	35c Triple-headed iron ore train	70	70

Souvenir Sheets

Perf. 11

1087 A316	$2 King Edward II, 1930	3.50	3.50
1088 A316	$2 GWR 57 No. 3697, 1941	3.50	3.50
1089 A316	$2 GWR 0-4-2T No. 1408, 1932	3.50	3.50
1090 A316	$2 GWR No. 7034 Ince Castle, 1950	3.50	3.50

#1087-1090 contain one 64x44mm stamp each.

1988 Summer Olympics, Seoul — A317

1988, Sept. 13 Litho.

1091 A317	10c Baseball	20	20
1092 A317	35c Hurdles	70	70
1093 A317	45c Fencing	90	90
1094 A317	80c Synchronized swimming	1.60	1.60
1095 A317	$1 Yachting	2.00	2.00
	Nos. 1091-1095 (5)	5.40	5.40

Souvenir Sheet

1096 A317	$1.50 Tennis	3.00	3.00

Intl. Tennis Federation, 75th anniv. ($1.50).

St. Joseph's Catholic Hospital, 25th Anniv. — A318

1988, Aug. 26 Litho. *Perf. 14½*

1097 A318	10c shown	20	20
1098 A318	10c Hospital, 4 staff members	20	20
1099 A318	35c St. John of God	70	70
1100 A318	$1 Doctor, nurse, map	2.00	2.00

Lloyds of London, 300th Anniv.

Common Design Type

CD341

Designs: 10c, Royal Exchange destroyed by fire, 1838, vert. 35c, Air Liberia BN2A aircraft. 45c, Supertanker *Chevron Antwerp*. $1, *Lakonia* on fire off Madeira, 1963, vert.

1988, Oct. 31 Litho. *Perf. 14*

1101 CD341	10c multi	20	20
1102 CD341	35c multi	70	70
1103 CD341	45c multi	90	90
1104 CD341	$1 multi	2.00	2.00

Sasa Players A319

Perf. 14x14½, 14½x14

1988, Sept. 30 Litho.

1105 A319	10c Monkey bridge, vert.	20	20
1106 A319	35c shown	70	70
1107 A319	45c Snake dancers, vert.	90	90

Intl. Fund for Agricultural Development, 10th Anniv. — A320

1988, Oct. 7 Litho. *Perf. 14x14½*

1108 A320	10c Crops	20	20
1109 A320	35c Spraying crops, livestock	70	70

3rd Anniv. of the 2nd Republic — A321

1989, Jan. 6 Litho. *Perf. 14*

1110 A321	10c Pres. Doe, officials	20	20
1111 A321	35c like 10c	70	70
1112 A321	50c Pres. Doe, doctor	1.00	1.00

US Presidents Type of 1981-82

1989, Jan. 20 *Perf. 13½x14*
1113 A280 $1 George Bush 2.00 2.00

Rissho Kosei-Kai Buddhist Assoc., Tokyo, 50th Anniv. — A322

Natl. flags and: No. 1114, "Harmony" in Japanese. No. 1115, Organization headquarters, Tokyo. No. 1116, Nikkyo Niwano, founder. 50c, Statue of Buddha in the Great Sacred Hall.

1989, Feb. 28 **Litho.** *Perf. 14x14½*
1114 A322 10c multi 25 25
1115 A322 10c multi 25 25
1116 A322 10c multi 25 25
1117 A322 50c multi 1.25 1.25

Liberian-Japanese friendship.

Souvenir Sheet

Emperor Hirohito of Japan (1901-1989) — A323

Commemorative coins: a, Silver. b, Gold.

1989, Feb. 28 **Unwmk.** *Perf. 14½*
1118 A323 Sheet of 2 3.00 3.00
a.-b. 75c any single 1.50 1.50

For overprint see No. 1147.

Mano River Union, 15th Anniv. A324

Natl. flag, crest and: 10c, Union Glass Factory, Gardnersville, Monrovia. 35c, Pres. Doe, Momoh of Sierra Leone and Conte of Guinea. 45c, Monrovia-Freetown Highway. 50c, Sierra Leone-Guinea land postal services. $1, Communique, 1988 summit.

Unwmk.

1989, May 8 **Litho.** *Perf. 14*
1119 A324 10c multi 20 20
1120 A324 35c multi 70 70
1121 A324 45c multi 90 90
1122 A324 50c multi 1.00 1.00
1123 A324 $1 multi 2.00 2.00
Nos. 1119-1123 (5) 4.80 4.80

World Telecommunications Day — A325

1989, May 17 **Litho.** *Perf. 12½*
1124 A325 50c multi 1.00 1.00

Moon Landing, 20th Anniv.
Common Design Type

CD342

Apollo 11: 10c, Recovery ship USS *Okinawa*. 35c, Buzz Aldrin, Neil Armstrong and Michael Collins. 45c, Mission emblem. $1, Aldrin steps on the Moon. $2, Aldrin preparing to conduct experiments on the Moon's surface.

Perf. 14x13½, 14 (35c, 45c)

1989, July 20 **Litho.** **Wmk. 384**
Size of Nos. 1126-1127: 29x29mm
1125 CD342 10c multi 20 20
1126 CD342 35c multi 70 70
1127 CD342 45c multi 90 90
1128 CD342 $1 multi 2.00 2.00

Souvenir Sheet

1129 CD342 $2 multi 4.00 4.00

Souvenir Sheet

The Women's March on Versailles — A326

1989, July 7 **Wmk. 384** *Perf. 14*
1130 A326 $1.50 multi 3.00 3.00

French revolution, bicent., PHILEXFRANCE '89.

Souvenir Sheet

Renovation and Re-dedication of the Statue of Liberty, 1986 — A327

Photographs: a, Workman. b, French dignitary, US flag. c, Dignitaries at ceremony, statue.

Perf. 14x13½

1989, Oct. 2 **Litho.** **Wmk. 373**
1131 Sheet of 3 1.50 1.50
a.-c. A327 25c any single 50 50

World Stamp Expo '89 and PHILEXFRANCE '89.

A328 A329

Souvenir Sheet

1989, Nov. 17 **Unwmk.** *Perf. 14½*
1132 A328 $2 black 4.00 4.00

World Stamp Expo '89, Washington, DC.

1989, Dec. 22 **Unwmk.** *Perf. 14*
1133 A329 45c Nehru, signature, flag 90 90
1134 A329 50c Nehru, signature 1.00 1.00

Jawaharlal Nehru, 1st Prime Minister of independent India.

New Standard-A Earth Satellite Station A330

1990, Jan. 5
1135 A330 10c shown 20 20
1136 A330 35c multi, diff. 70 70

US Educational & Cultural Foundation in Liberia, 25th Anniv. (in 1989) A331

1990, Jan. 5
1137 A331 10c multicolored 20 20
1138 A331 45c multicolored 90 90

Pan-African Postal Union, 10th Anniv. — A332

1990, Jan. 18 *Perf. 13x12½*
1139 A332 35c multicolored 70 70

Flags of Liberian Counties — A333

Designs: a, Bomi. b, Bong. c, Grand Bassa. d, Grand Cape Mount. e, Grand Gedeh. f, Grand Kru. g, Lofa. h, Margibi. i, Maryland. j, Montserrado. k, Nimba. l, Rivercess. m, Sinoe.

Perf. 14x13½

1990, Mar. 2 **Litho.** **Unwmk.**
1140 Strip of 13 2.60 2.60
a.-m. A333 10c any single 20 20
1141 Strip of 13 9.10 9.10
a.-m. A333 35c any single 70 70
1142 Strip of 13 11.70 11.70
a.-m. A333 45c any single 90 90
1143 Strip of 13 13.00 13.00
a.-m. A333 50c any single 1.00 1.00
1144 Strip of 13 26.00 26.00
a.-m. A333 $1 any single 2.00 2.00
Nos. 1140-1144 (5) 62.40 62.40

Queen Mother, 90th Birthday
Common Design Types

At Age 6 — CD343

At Age 22 — CD344

1991, Oct. 28 **Wmk. 384** *Perf. 14x15*
1145 CD343 10c multicolored 20 20

Perf. 14½

1146 CD344 $2 brn & blk 4.00 4.00

Souvenir Sheet

No. 1118 Overprinted

日本国際切手展'91

PHILA NIPPON'91

Perf. 14½

1991, Nov. 16 **Litho.** **Unwmk.**
1147 A323 Sheet of 2 3.00 3.00
a.-b. 75c any single 1.50 1.50

National Unity — A334

Designs: 35c, Hands clasp over map of Liberia. 45c, Liberian flag, hands, African map. 50c, All Liberia conference, March 1991, conferees, flag, map.

1991, Dec. 30 *Perf. 13½*
1148 A334 35c multicolored 70 70
1149 A334 45c multicolored 90 90
1150 A334 50c multicolored 1.00 1.00

1992 Summer Olympics, Barcelona A335

1992, Aug. 7 **Litho.** *Perf. 14*
1151 A335 45c Boxing 90 90
1152 A335 50c Soccer 1.00 1.00
1153 A335 $1 Weight lifting 2.00 2.00
1154 A335 $2 Water polo 4.00 4.00

Souvenir Sheet

1155 A335 $1.50 Running 3.00 3.00

Disarmament — A336

Designs: 50c, Disarm today. $1, Join your parents and build Liberia. $2, Peace must prevail in Liberia.

1993, Feb. 10 **Litho.** *Perf. 13½x14*
1156 A336 50c multicolored 1.00 1.00
1157 A336 $1 multicolored 2.00 2.00
1158 A336 $2 multicolored 4.00 4.00

SEMI-POSTAL STAMPS

No. 127 Surcharged in Red

+ 2c

1915 **Unwmk.** *Perf. 14*
B1 A49 2c + 3c on 10c 75 2.50
a. Double red surcharge
b. Double blue surcharge
c. Both surcharges double
d. Pair, one without "2c"

Same Surcharge On Official Stamp of 1912

B2	A49	2c + 3c on 10c blk & ultra	75	2.50
a.		Double surcharge		

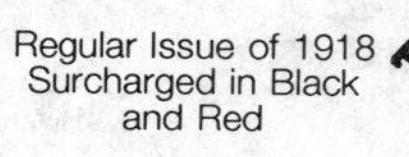

Regular Issue of 1918 Surcharged in Black and Red

1918 *Perf. 12½, 14*

B3	A59	1c + 2c dp grn & blk	35	35
B4	A60	2c + 2c rose & blk	35	35
a.		Double surch., one inverted		
b.		Invtd. surch., cross double		
c.		Invtd. surch., cross omitted	15.00	
B5	A61	5c + 2c gray bl & blk	15	15
a.		Imperf., pair	8.00	
B6	A62	10c + 2c dk grn	15	15
a.		Inverted surcharge	5.00	5.00
B7	A63	15c + 2c blk & dk grn	15	15
B8	A64	20c + 2c cl & blk	28	28
B9	A65	25c + 2c dk grn & grn	50	50
B10	A66	30c + 2c red vio & blk	35	35
B11	A67	50c + 2c ultra & blk	50	50
B12	A68	75c + 2c ol bis & blk	1.00	1.00
B13	A69	$1 + 2c yel brn & bl	1.65	1.65
B14	A70	$2 + 2c lt vio & blk	2.00	2.00
B15	A71	$5 + 2c dk brn	8.25	8.25
		Nos. B3-B15 (13)	15.68	15.68

Nos. 277-279 Surcharged in Red or Blue

1941 **Unwmk.** *Perf. 12*

B16	A107	3c + 2c dk bl (R)	1.10	1.25
B17	A108	5c + 2c dl red brn	1.10	1.25
B18	A109	10c + 2c dk grn (R)	1.10	1.25

Catalogue values for unused stamps in this section, from this point to the end of the section, are for Never Hinged items.

Research SP1

Lithographed and Engraved

1954 **Unwmk.** *Perf. 12½*

B19	SP1	5c + 5c rose lil & blk	15	15

The surtax was for the Liberian Government Hospital. No. B19 exists imperforate.

AIR POST STAMPS

Regular Issue of 1928 Surcharged in Black "AIR MAIL" and New Values

1936, Feb. 28 **Unwmk.** *Perf. 12*

C1	A102	6c on 2c vio	150.00	90.00
C2	A102	6c on 3c bis brn	150.00	90.00

Same Surcharge on Official Stamp of 1928

C3	A102	6c on 1c green	150.00	90.00
m.		On No. 230 (error)	*600.00*	

Many counterfeits exist.

Waco Plane AP1

1936, Sept. 30 **Engr.** *Perf. 14*

C3A	AP1	1c yel grn & blk	15	15
C3B	AP1	2c car & blk	15	15
C3C	AP1	3c pur & blk	15	15
C3D	AP1	4c org & blk	15	15
C3E	AP1	5c bl & blk	15	15
C3F	AP1	6c grn & blk	15	15
		Set value	74	36

Liberia's 1st air mail service of Feb. 28, 1936.

Nos. C3A-C3F exist in pairs imperf. between (value, $50 each) and in pairs imperf. (value $15 each).

Eagle in Flight — AP2

Sikorsky Amphibian — AP5

Trimotor Plane AP3

Egrets — AP4

Designs: 3c, 30c, Albatross.

1938, Sept. 12 **Photo.** *Perf. 12½*

C4	AP2	1c green	15	15
C5	AP3	2c red org	15	15
C6	AP3	3c ol grn	15	15
C7	AP4	4c orange	15	15
C8	AP4	5c brt bl grn	16	15
C9	AP3	10c violet	16	15
C10	AP5	20c magenta	22	15
C11	AP3	30c gray blk	32	15
C12	AP2	50c brown	45	15
C13	AP5	$1 blue	85	15
		Nos. C4-C13 (10)	2.76	
		Set value		75

For surcharges see Nos. C17-C36, C45-C46, C47-C48, C49-C50.

Nos. 280-282 Overprinted in Red or Dark Blue

1941, Feb. 25 *Perf. 12*

C14	A107	3c dk bl (R)	1.10	1.10
C15	A108	5c dl red brn (DB)	1.10	1.10
C16	A109	10c dk grn (R)	1.10	1.10

Nos. C4-C13 Surcharged in Black

First Flight
LIBERIA · U.S.
1941

—— 50c

1941 *Perf. 12½*

C17	AP2	50c on 1c grn	*1,650.*	190.00
C18	AP3	50c on 2c red org	110.00	70.00
C19	AP3	50c on 3c ol grn	110.00	70.00
C20	AP4	50c on 4c org	42.50	27.50
C21	AP4	50c on 5c brt bl grn	42.50	27.50
C22	AP3	50c on 10c vio	42.50	27.50
C23	AP5	50c on 20c mag	*1,350.*	45.00
C24	AP3	50c on 30c gray blk	37.50	21.00
C25	AP2	50c brown	37.50	21.00
C26	AP5	$1 blue	42.50	21.00

Nos. C17 to C26 with Additional Overprint of Two Bars, Obliterating "1941"

1942

C27	AP2	50c on 1c grn	4.74	4.75
C28	AP3	50c on 2c red org	4.75	4.00
C29	AP3	50c on 3c ol grn	4.25	4.00
C30	AP4	50c on 4c org	3.50	4.25
C31	AP4	50c on 5c brt bl grn	2.00	2.00
C32	AP3	50c on 10c vio	3.00	3.00
C33	AP5	50c on 20c mag	3.00	3.00
C34	AP3	50c on 30c gray blk	3.50	3.50
C35	AP2	50c brown	3.50	3.50
C36	AP5	$1 blue	3.00	3.00
		Nos. C27-C36 (10)	35.24	35.00

Plane and Air Route from United States to South America and Africa — AP6

Plane over House — AP7

1942-44 **Engr.** *Perf. 12*

C37	AP6	10c rose	15	15
C38	AP7	12c brt ultra ('44)	15	15
C39	AP7	24c turq grn ('44)	15	15
C40	AP6	30c brt grn	15	15
C41	AP6	35c red lil ('44)	15	15
C42	AP6	50c violet	15	15
C43	AP6	70c ol gray ('44)	25	15
C44	AP6	$1.40 scar ('44)	65	30
		Nos. C37-C44 (8)	1.80	
		Set value		86

No. C3A-C3C, C5-C8, C12 Surcharged with New Values and Large Dot, Bar or Diagonal Line in Violet, Blue, Black or Violet and Black

1944-45 *Perf. 12½*

C45	AP3	10c on 2c (V+Bk)	22.50	17.50
C46	AP4	10c on 5c (V+Bk) ('45)	8.00	8.00
C46A	AP1	30c on 1c (Bk)	85.00	42.50
C47	AP3	30c on 3c (V)	95.00	42.50
C48	AP4	30c on 4c (V+Bk)	8.00	8.00
C48A	AP1	50c on 3c (Bk)	19.00	19.00
C48B	AP1	70c on 2c (Bk)	37.50	37.50
C49	AP3	$1 on 3c (Bl)	15.00	15.00
C50	AP2	$1 on 50c (V)	22.50	17.50
		Nos. C45-C50 (9)	312.50	207.50

These surcharges were handstamped with the possible exception of the large "10 CTS." of No. C46 and the "30 CTS." of No. C48. On No. C47, the new value was created by handstamping a small, violet, broken "O" beside the large "3" of the basic stamp.

Surcharges on Nos. C46A, C48A, C48B are found inverted. Values same as normal.

Franklin D. Roosevelt Reviewing Troops AP8

1945, Nov. 26 **Engr.**

C51	AP8	70c brn & blk, *grysh*	1.10	1.25

In memory of Pres. Franklin D. Roosevelt (1882-1945).

Copies on thick white paper appeared later on the stamp market at reduced prices.

Opening Monrovia Harbor Project AP9

1947, Jan. 2

C52	AP9	24c brt bluish grn	1.10	1.20

Issued to commemorate the opening of the Monrovia Harbor Project, February 16, 1946.

Without Inscription at Top

1947, May 16

C53	AP9	25c dk car	35	40

1st US Postage Stamps and Arms of Liberia AP10

1947, June 6

C54	AP10	12c green	15	15
C55	AP10	25c brt red vio	15	15
C56	AP10	50c brt bl	15	15
a.		Souv. sheet of 4, #300, C54-C56	35.00	
		Set value	32	32

Cent. of US postage stamps and 87th anniv. of Liberian stamps.

No. C56a exists imperf., same value.

Matilda Newport Firing Cannon AP11

1947, Dec. 1 **Engr. & Photo.**

C57	AP11	25c scar & gray blk	1.10	28

See note after No. 304.

Monument to Joseph J. Roberts — AP12

Centenary Monument — AP14

Design: 25c, Flag of Liberia.

1947, Dec. 22 **Engr.**

C58	AP12	12c brick red	16	15
C59	AP12	25c carmine	26	15
C60	AP14	50c red brn	55	42

Centenary of independence.

L. I. A. Plane in Flight — AP15

1948, Aug. 17 *Perf. 11½*

C61	AP15	25c red	90	60
C62	AP15	50c deep blue	45	60

1st flight of Liberian Intl. Airways, Aug. 17, 1948.

Map and Citizens AP16

Farm Couple, Arms and Agricultural Products AP17

1949, Apr. 12 Litho. *Perf. 11½*

C63 AP16 25c multi 32 60
C64 AP17 50c multi 32 60

Nos. C63-C64 exist perf. 12½. Definite information concerning the status of the perf. 12½ set has not reached the editors. The set also exists imperf.

Type of Regular Issue of 1948-50

Design: William V. S. Tubman.

1949, July 21 Engr. *Perf. 12½*

C65 A128 25c blue & black 55 60

See No. C118.

Sun and Open Book — AP18

UPU Monument — AP19

1950, Feb. 14 Engr. *Perf. 12½*

C66 AP18 25c rose car 1.00 50
a. Souv. sheet of 2, #329, C66, imperf. 1.65 1.65

Campaign for National Literacy.

Catalogue values for unused stamps in this section, from this point to the end of the section, are for Never Hinged items.

1950, Apr. 21

C67 AP19 25c org & vio 1.75 1.75
a. Souv. sheet of 3, #330-331, C67, imperf. 4.50 4.50

UPU, 75th anniv. (in 1949).
No. C67 exists imperf.

Map of Monrovia, James Monroe and Ashmun AP20

Design: 50c, Jehudi Ashmun, President Tubman and map.

1952, Apr. 1 *Perf. 10½*

C68 AP20 25c lil rose & blk 20 20
C69 AP20 50c dk bl & car 40 40
a. Souvenir sheet of 8 12.50

Nos. C68-C69 exist imperf. Value about two and one half times that of the perf. set.
Nos. C68-C69 exist with center inverted. Value $50 each.
No. C69a contains one each of Nos. 332 and C68, and types of Nos. 333-337 and C69 with centers in black; imperf.
The 25c exists in colors of the 50c and vice versa. Value, each $3.50.

Flags of Five Nations AP21

1952, Dec. 10 *Perf. 12½*

C70 AP21 25c ultra & car 40 32
a. Souvenir sheet 1.65 1.65

Nos. C70 and C70a exist imperforate.

Road Building AP22

Designs: 25c, Ships in Monrovia harbor. 35c, Diesel locomotive. 50c, Free port, Monrovia. 70c, Roberts Field. $1, Wm. V. S. Tubman bridge.

1953, Aug. 3 Litho.

C71 AP22 12c org brn 15 15
C72 AP22 25c lil rose 25 15
C73 AP22 35c purple 35 15
C74 AP22 50c orange 40 18
C75 AP22 70c dl grn 68 20
C76 AP22 $1 blue 90 30
Nos. C71-C76 (6) 2.73 1.13

See Nos. C82-C87.

Flags, Emblem and Children — AP23

1954, Sept. 27

Size: 51x39mm

C77 AP23 $5 bl, red, vio bl & blk 20.00 20.00

A reproduction of No. C77, size 63x49mm, was prepared for presentation purposes. Value $20.
Half the proceeds from the sale of No. C77 was given to the UNICEF.

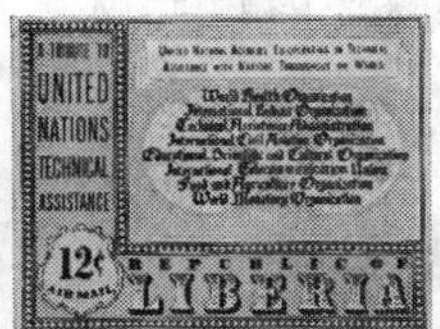

UN Technical Assistance Agencies AP24

Designs: 15c, Printing instruction. 20c, Sawmill maintenance. 25c, Geography class.

1954, Oct. 25

C78 AP24 12c blk & bl 15 15
C79 AP24 15c dk brn & yel 18 15
C80 AP24 20c blk & yel grn 25 15
C81 AP24 25c vio bl & red 32 20
Set value 50

UN Technical Assistance program.

Type of 1953 Inscribed: "Commemorating Presidential Visit U. S. A.-1954"

Designs as before.

1954, Nov. 19

C82 AP22 12c vermilion 15 15
C83 AP22 25c blue 20 15
C84 AP22 35c car rose 28 15
C85 AP22 50c rose vio 40 15
C86 AP22 70c org brn 55 26
C87 AP22 $1 dl grn 80 32
Nos. C82-C87 (6) 2.38
Set value 98

Visit of Pres. William V.S. Tubman to the US. Exist imperforate.

Baseball AP25

1955, Jan. 26 Litho. *Perf. 12½*

C88 AP25 10c shown 15 15
C89 AP25 12c Swimming 15 15
C90 AP25 25c Running 15 15
a. Souvenir sheet 12.00 12.00
Set value 28 28

No. C90a contains one each of Nos. 349 and C90 with colors transposed. Exists imperf.; same value.

Costus — AP26

Design: 25c, Barteria nigritiana.

1955, Sept. 28 Unwmk. *Perf. 12½*

C91 AP26 20c vio, grn & yel 15 15
C92 AP26 25c grn, red & yel 16 16
Set value 25 25

UN Emblem — AP27

UN Charter — AP28

Designs: 15c, General Assembly. 25c, Gabriel L. Dennis signing UN Charter for Liberia.

1955, Oct. 24 Unwmk. *Perf. 12*

C93 AP27 10c ultra & red 15 15
C94 AP27 15c vio & blk 20 15
C95 AP27 25c grn & red brn 32 15
C96 AP28 50c brick red & grn 70 18
Set value 38

10th anniv. of the UN, Oct. 24, 1955.

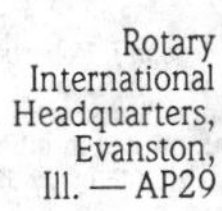

Rotary International Headquarters, Evanston, Ill. — AP29

Design: 15c, View of Monrovia.

1955, Dec. 5 Litho. *Perf. 12½*

C97 AP29 10c dp ultra & red 18 15
C98 AP29 15c redsh brn, red & bis 28 22

Souvenir Sheet

C99 AP29 50c dp ultra & red 95 95

No. C99 design as C97, but redrawn and with leaves omitted.
50th anniversary of Rotary International.
Nos. C97-C99 exist without Rotary emblem; No. C97 printed entirely in deep ultramarine; No. C98 with bister impression omitted.

New York Coliseum AP30

Statue of Liberty — AP31

Design: 12c, Globe inscribed FIPEX.

1956, Apr. 28 Unwmk. *Perf. 12*

C100 AP30 10c rose red & ultra 15 15
C101 AP30 12c org & pur 18 15
C102 AP31 15c aqua & red lil 22 15
Set value 21

Souvenir Sheet

C103 AP31 50c lt grn & brn 1.00 1.00

FIPEX, NYC, Apr. 28-May 6, 1956.

Olympic Park, Melbourne AP32

Designs: 20c, 40c, Map of Australia and Olympic torch.

1956, Nov. 15 Unwmk. *Perf. 12*

C104 AP32 12c emer & vio 15 15
C105 AP32 20c multi 18 15
Set value 15

Souvenir Sheet

C106 AP32 40c multi 1.00 1.00

Issued to commemorate the 16th Olympic Games, Melbourne, Nov. 22-Dec. 8.

Type of Regular Issue, 1957.

Designs: 12c, 25c, Idlewild airport, New York. 15c, 50c, Roberts Field, Liberia, plane and Pres. Tubman.

Lithographed and Engraved

1957, May 4 *Perf. 12*

C107 A146 12c brt grn & dk bl 15 15
C108 A146 15c red brn & blk 15 15
C109 A146 25c car & dk bl 24 15
C110 A146 50c lt ultra & blk 45 15
Set value 40

Type of Regular Issue, 1957

Orphanage and: 15c, Nurse inoculating boy. 35c, The Kamara triplets. 70c, Children and flag.

1957, Nov. 25 Litho. *Perf. 12*

C111 A147 15c lt bl & brn 15 15
C112 A147 35c mar & lt gray 22 15
Set value 21

Souvenir Sheet

C113 A147 70c ultra & rose car 95 85

Type of Regular Issue, 1958

Designs: 10c, Italian flag and Colosseum. No. C115, French flag and Arc de Triomphe. No. C116, Swiss flag and chalet. No. C117, Vatican flag and St. Peter's.

Engr. and Litho.

1958, Jan. 10 *Perf. 10½*

Flags in Original Colors

C114 A148 10c dk gray 15 15
C115 A148 15c dp yel grn 15 15
C116 A148 15c ultra 15 15
C117 A148 15c purple 15 15
Set value 44 25

Type of Regular Issue, 1948-50

Design: William V. S. Tubman.

1958 Engr. *Perf. 12*

C118 A128 25c lt grn & blk 38 28

Souvenir Sheet

Preamble to Declaration of Human Rights — AP33

1958, Dec. 10 Litho. *Perf. 12*

C119 AP33 20c bl & red 1.75 1.75

10th anniv. of the signing of the Universal Declaration of Human Rights.

Liberians Reading Proclamation — AP34

1959, Apr. 15 **Unwmk.**
C120 AP34 25c bl & brn 26 26

African Freedom Day, Apr. 15.

UNESCO Building, Paris — AP35

1959, May 1
C121 AP35 25c ultra & red 30 24
a. Souvenir sheet 1.40 1.40

Opening of UNESCO Headquarters in Paris, Nov. 3, 1958.

Lincoln Type of Regular Issue

1959, Nov. 20 **Engr.** ***Perf. 12***
C122 A152 25c emer & blk 38 38

For souvenir sheet see No. 386a.

Touré, Tubman and Nkrumah AP36

1960, Jan. 27 **Litho.** **Unwmk.**
C123 AP36 25c beige, vio bl & blk 30 30

See note after No. 387.

WRY Type of Regular Issue, 1960

1960, Apr. 7 ***Perf. 11½***
C124 A154 25c ultra & blk 42 35
a. Souv. sheet of 2, #388, C124, imperf. 2.00 2.00

Map of Africa — AP37

1960, May 11 ***Perf. 11½***
C125 AP37 25c ultra & brn 35 35

See note after No. 389.

Olympic Games Type of 1960

Designs: 25c, Javelin thrower and hunter, horiz. 50c, Runner and stadium, horiz.

1960, Sept. 6 ***Perf. 11½***
C126 A156 25c brn & brt ultra 50 38

Souvenir Sheet

Imperf

C127 A156 50c lil & brn 2.75 2.75

Stamp Centenary Type of 1960

1960, Dec. 1 **Litho.** ***Perf. 11½***
C128 A157 25c multi 32 32

Souvenir Sheet

C129 A157 50c multi 1.25 1.25

Globe, Dove and UN Emblem AP38

Design: 50c, Globe and dove.

1961, May 19 **Unwmk.** ***Perf. 11½***
C130 AP38 25c ind & red 22 22

Souvenir Sheet

C131 AP38 50c red brn & emer 1.25 1.25

Liberia's membership in the UN Security Council.
A second souvenir sheet contains one each of Nos. 395, C130 and the 50c from No. C131, imperf. Size: 133x83mm.
No. C130 exists imperf.

Science Class — AP39

Design: 50c, Science class, different design.

1961, Sept. 8 **Litho.**
C132 AP39 25c pur & brn 28 20

Souvenir Sheet

C133 AP39 50c bl & brn 1.00 1.00

15th anniv. of UNESCO.

Joseph J. Roberts and Providence Island AP40

1961, Oct. 25 **Litho.** ***Perf. 11½***
C134 AP40 25c emerald & sepia 30 30
a. Souv. sheet of 3 1.00 1.00

150th anniv. of the birth of Joseph J. Roberts, 1st pres. of Liberia.
No. C134a contains three imperf. stamps similar to Nos. 397-398 and C134, but printed in different colors; 5c, emerald & sepia. 10c, orange & sepia. 25c, ultramarine & sepia.

Scout Type of Regular Issue and

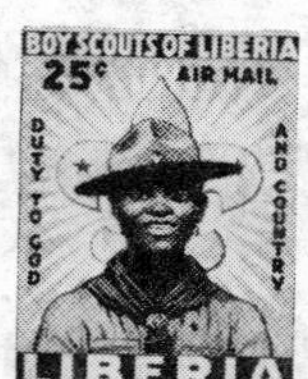

Boy Scout — AP41

1961, Dec. 4 **Unwmk.** ***Perf. 11½***
C135 AP41 25c emer & sepia 65 65

Souvenir Sheet

Design: Like No. 399.

C136 A161 35c dl bl & sepia 80 80

Dag Hammarskjold Type of 1962

1962, Feb. 1 **Unwmk.** ***Perf. 12***
C137 A162 25c blk & red lil 32 32

Souvenir Sheet

Imperf

C138 A162 50c blk & ultra 1.00 1.00

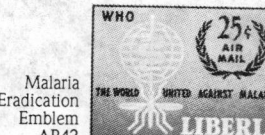

Malaria Eradication Emblem AP42

1962, Apr. 7 ***Perf. 12½***
C139 AP42 25c pur & org 32 20

Souvenir Sheet

Imperf

C140 AP42 50c dk red & ultra 80 80

Pres. Tubman, Statue of Liberty, New York Skyline and Flags of US and Liberia — AP43

1962, Sept. 17 **Litho.** ***Perf. 11½x12***
C141 AP43 12c multi 16 15
C142 AP43 25c multi 32 26
C143 AP43 50c multi 65 48

Pres. Tubman's visit to the US in 1961.

United Nations Emblem and Flags — AP44

Design: 50c, UN emblem.

1962, Oct. 22 ***Perf. 12x12½***
C144 AP44 25c lt ultra & dk bl 30 30

Souvenir Sheet

Imperf

C145 AP44 50c brt grnsh bl & blk 50 50

Observance of UN Day, Oct. 24, as a national holiday.

Building Type of Regular Issue

Buildings: 12c, 70c, Capitol. 50c, Information Service. $1, Treasury Department Building, Monrovia.

1962-63 ***Perf. 12x12½, 12 (70c)***
C146 A165 12c brt yel grn & mar 15 15
C147 A165 50c org & ultra 65 65
C147A A165 70c brt pink & dk bl ('63) 90 90
C148 A165 $1 sal & blk ('63) 1.25 35

"FAO" Emblem and Globe — AP45

Design: 50c, "FAO" and UN Emblems.

1963, Mar. 21 **Unwmk.** ***Perf. 12½***
C149 AP45 25c dk grn & yel 30 30

Souvenir Sheet

Perf. 12

C150 AP45 50c emer & ultra 1.00 1.00

FAO "Freedom from Hunger" campaign.

Type of Regular Issue, 1963

Designs: 25c, Telstar satellite, vert. 50c, Telstar and rocket, vert.

1963, May 27 **Litho.** ***Perf. 12½***
C151 A167 25c Prus bl & org 30 30

Souvenir Sheet

Perf. 12

C152 A167 50c dp vio & yel 1.00 52

Red Cross Type of Regular Issue

Design: 25c, Red Cross and globe. 50c, Centenary emblem and globe.

1963, Aug. 26 **Unwmk.** ***Perf. 12***
C153 A168 25c pur & red 22 22
C154 A168 50c dp ultra & red 42 42

Map of Africa — AP46

1963, Oct. 28 ***Perf. 12½***
C156 AP46 25c red org & grn 22 22

See note after No. 412.

Olympic Type of Regular Issue

Designs: 10c, Torch and mountains. 25c, Mountains, horiz. 50c, Torch, background like No. 413.

1963, Dec. 11 **Litho.** ***Perf. 12½***
C157 A170 10c vio bl & red 15 15
C158 A170 25c grn & org 32 32

Souvenir Sheet

Perf. 12

C159 A170 50c gray & red 1.00 1.00

Kennedy Type of Regular Issue, 1964

Designs: 25c, John F. Kennedy, vert. 50c, John F. Kennedy (like No. 414).

1964, Apr. 6 **Unwmk.** ***Perf. 12½***
C160 A171 25c blk & red lil 35 30

Souvenir Sheet

Perf. 12

C161 A171 50c blk & red lil 1.00 80

An imperf. miniature sheet containing one of No. C160 exists. No marginal inscription.

Satellite Type of Regular Issue
Souvenir Sheet

Design: Launching rocket separating from booster in space, vert.

1964, June 22 **Litho.**
C162 A172 50c vio bl & red 1.00 1.00

Olympic Type of Regular Issue
Souvenir Sheet

Design: 50c, Runner and Olympic rings.

1964, Sept. 15 **Unwmk.** ***Perf. 12***
C163 A173 50c grnsh bl & red 1.00 45

Scout Type of Regular Issue, 1965

Designs: 25c, Liberian flag and fleur-delis. 50c, Globe and Scout emblem.

1965, Mar. 8 **Litho.** ***Perf. 12½***
C164 A174 25c crim & ultra 45 45

Souvenir Sheet

Perf. 12

C165 A174 50c yel & lil 60 60

Lincoln Type of Regular Issue
Souvenir Sheet

Design: 50c, Lincoln and John F. Kennedy, horiz.

1965, May 3 **Unwmk.** ***Perf. 12***
C166 A175 50c dp plum & lt gray 1.25 1.25

ICY Type of Regular Issue, 1965
Souvenir Sheet

1965, June 21 **Litho.**
C167 A176 50c car rose & brn 1.25 1.25

ITU Type of Regular Issue, 1965

1965, Sept. 21 **Unwmk.** ***Perf. 12½***
C168 A177 50c red org & vio bl 50 45

Tubman Type of Regular Issue

Design: 25c, Pres. Tubman and coat of arms.

1965, Nov. 29 **Litho.** ***Perf. 12½***
C169 A178 25c ultra, red & brn 40 40
a. Souv. sheet of 2, #431, C169, imperf. 1.25 1.25

Churchill Type of Regular Issue

Designs: 25c, "Angry Lion" portrait by Karsh and Parliament, London. 50c, "Williamsburg Award Dinner" portrait by Karsh and map of Europe.

1966, Jan. 18 Litho. ***Perf. 12½***
C170 A179 25c blk & vio bl 30 24

Souvenir Sheet
Perf. 12

C171 A179 50c blk & red lil 1.25 1.25

Soccer Type of Regular Issue
Souvenir Sheet

Design: 50c, Soccer match in stadium.

1966, May 3 Litho. ***Perf. 11½***
C172 A181 50c ultra & red brn 1.25 1.25

Kennedy Type of Regular Issue

Designs: 25c, UN General Assembly and Pres. Kennedy. 35c, Pres. Kennedy and rocket on launching pad, Cape Kennedy. 40c, Flame on grave at Arlington.

1966, Aug. 16 Litho. ***Perf. 12½***
C173 A182 25c ultra, blk & ocher 28 15
C174 A182 35c dk vio bl & pink 35 20

Souvenir Sheet
Perf. 11½

C175 A182 40c dk vio bl & multi 1.25 1.25

Boy Scout Type of Regular Issue
Souvenir Sheet

Design: 50c, Scout at campfire and vision of moon landing.

1967, Mar. 23 Litho. ***Perf. 12½***
C176 A185 50c brt red lil & scar 1.25 1.25

Olympic Type of Regular Issue
Souvenir Sheet

Design: 50c, Pre-Hispanic sculpture, serape and Olympic rings, horiz.

1967, June 20 Litho. ***Perf. 12½***
C177 A186 50c vio & car 1.25 50

Winter Olympic Games Type of Regular Issue
Souvenir Sheet

Design: 50c, Woman skater.

1967, Nov. 20 Litho. ***Perf. 11½***
C178 A189 50c ver & blk 1.25 40

Human Rights Type of Regular Issue
Souvenir Sheet

1968, Apr. 26 Litho. ***Perf. 11½***
C179 A191 80c bl & red 1.50 55

M. L. King Type of Regular Issue
Souvenir Sheet

Design: 55c, Pres. Kennedy congratulating Dr. King.

1968, July 11 Litho. ***Perf. 11½***
C180 A192 55c brn & blk 1.25 40

Olympic Type of Regular Issue
Souvenir Sheet

Design: 50c, Steeplechase and ancient sculpture.

1968, Aug. 22 Litho. ***Perf. 11½***
C181 A193 50c brt bl & org brn 1.00 65

President Type of Regular Issue 1966-69

Design: 25c, Pres. William V. S. Tubman.

1969, Feb. 18 Litho. ***Perf. 11½x11***
C182 A180 25c blk & emer 40 30

ILO Type of Regular Issue

Design: 80c, "ILO" surrounded by cogwheel and wreath, vert.

1969, Apr. 16 Litho. ***Perf. 12½***
C183 A196 80c emer & gold 1.25 60

Apollo 11 Type of Regular Issue
Souvenir Sheet

Design: 65c, Astronauts Neil A. Armstrong, Col. Edwin E. Aldrin, Jr., and Lieut. Col. Michael Collins, horiz.

1969, Oct. 15 Litho. ***Perf. 11½***
C184 A199 65c dk vio bl & brt red 1.25 52

UN Type of 1970

Design: $1, UN emblem, olive branch and plane as symbols of peace and progress, vert.

1970, Apr. 16 Litho. ***Perf. 12½***
C185 A200 $1 ultra & sil 1.40 80

Apollo 14 Type of Regular Issue
Souvenir Sheet

Design: 50c, Moon, earth and star.

1971, May 20 Litho. ***Imperf.***
C186 A208 50c multi 1.60 1.60

Souvenir Sheet

Olympic Yachting Village, Kiel, and Yachting — AP47

Illustration reduced.

1971, June 28 Litho. ***Perf. 14½x14***
C187 AP47 Sheet of 2 1.25 1.25
a. 25c multi 50 50
b. 30c multi 60 60

Publicity for the 20th Summer Olympic Games, and the yachting races in Kiel, Germany, 1972.

Boy Scout Type of Regular Issue
Souvenir Sheet

Design: 50c, Boy Scouts of various nations cooking, horiz.

1971, Aug. 6 Litho. ***Perf. 15***
C188 A211 50c multi 1.00 40

UNICEF Type of Regular Issue
Souvenir Sheet

Design: 50c, UNICEF emblem and Bengal tigress with cubs.

1971, Oct. 1 ***Imperf.***
C189 A213 50c multi 1.25 1.25

Souvenir Sheet

Japanese Royal Family — AP48

1971, Nov. 4 ***Perf. 15***
C190 AP48 50c multi 2.00 80

11th Winter Olympic Games, Sapporo, Japan, Feb. 3-13, 1972.

Sesquicentennial Type of Regular Issue
Souvenir Sheet

Design: 50c, Sailing ship "Elizabeth" between maps of America and Africa, horiz.

1972, Jan. 1 Litho. ***Imperf.***
C191 A216 50c car & vio bl 1.50 1.50

Olympic Type of Regular Issue
Souvenir Sheet

Design: 55c, View of Olympic Stadium and symbol of "Motion."

1971, May 19 Litho. ***Perf. 15***
C192 A218 55c multi 1.50 65

Apollo 16 Type of Regular Issue
Souvenir Sheet

Design: 55c, Lt. Comdr. Thomas K. Mattingly, 2nd, Capt. John W. Young and Lt. Col. Charles M. Duke, Jr.

1972, June 26 Litho. ***Perf. 15***
C193 A220 55c pink & multi 1.00 1.00

Ship Type of 1972
Souvenir Sheet

Design: Lord Nelson's flagship Victory, and her figurehead (1765).

1972, Sept. 6 Litho. ***Perf. 15***
C194 A222 50c multi 1.50 1.50

Pres. Tolbert Type of 1972.
Souvenir Sheet

1972, Oct. 23 Litho. ***Perf. 15***
C195 A223 55c multi 1.10 1.10

Apollo 17 Type of Regular Issue
Souvenir Sheet

Design: 55c, Apollo 17 badge, moon and earth.

1973, Mar. 28 Litho. ***Perf. 11***
C196 A225 55c bl & multi 1.10 1.10

Locomotive Type of Regular Issue
Souvenir Sheet

Design: 55c, Swiss locomotive.

1973, May 4 Litho. ***Perf. 11***
C197 A226 55c multi 1.10 1.10

WHO Type of Regular Issue 1973
Souvenir Sheet

Design: 55c, WHO emblem, Paul Ehrlich and poppy anemones.

1973, June 26 Litho. ***Perf. 11***
C198 A228 55c lt vio & multi 1.00 1.00

Automobile Type of Regular Issue
Souvenir Sheet

Design: Franklin 10 HP cross-engined 1904-1905 models.

1973, Sept. 11 Litho. ***Perf. 11***
C199 A229 55c multi 1.50 1.50

Copernicus Type of Regular Issue
Souvenir Sheet

Design: 55c, Copernicus and concept of orbiting station around Mars.

1973, Dec. 14 Litho. ***Perf. 13½***
C200 A230 55c gray & multi 1.25 1.25

UPU Type of Regular Issue
Souvenir Sheet

Design: 55c, UPU emblem and English coach, 1784.

1974, Mar. 4 Litho. ***Perf. 13½***
C201 A232 55c multi 1.25 60

Dog Type of Regular Issue
Souvenir Sheet

Design: Hungarian sheepdog (kuvasz).

1974, Apr. 16 Litho. ***Perf. 13½***
C202 A233 75c multi 1.25 1.25

Soccer Type of Regular Issue
Souvenir Sheet

Design: 60c, World Soccer Championship Cup and Munich Stadium.

1974, June 4 Litho. ***Perf. 11***
C203 A234 60c multi 1.25 1.25

Butterfly Type of Regular Issue
Souvenir Sheet

Tropical butterfly: 60c, Pierella nereis.

1974, Sept. 11 Litho. ***Perf. 13½***
C204 A235 60c gray & multi 1.25 1.25

Churchill Type of 1974
Souvenir Sheet

Design: 60c, Churchill at easel painting landscape.

1975, Jan. 17 Litho. ***Perf. 13½***
C205 A237 60c multi 1.25 1.25

Women's Year Type of 1975
Souvenir Sheet

Design: 75c, Vijaya Lakshmi Pandit, Women's Year emblem and dais of UN General Assembly.

1975, Mar. 14 Litho. ***Perf. 13***
C206 A238 75c gray & multi 1.40 1.40

American Bicentennial Type
Souvenir Sheet

Design: 75c, Mayflower and US No. 548.

1975, Apr. 25 Litho. ***Perf. 13½***
C207 A239 75c multi 2.00 65

Dr. Schweitzer Type, 1975
Souvenir Sheet

Design: 60c, Dr. Schweitzer as surgeon in Lambarene Hospital.

1975, June 26 Litho. ***Perf. 13½***
C208 A240 60c multi 1.25 1.25

Apollo-Soyuz Type, 1975
Souvenir Sheet

Design: 75c, Apollo-Soyuz link-up and emblem.

1975, Sept. 18 Litho. ***Perf. 13½***
C209 A241 75c multi 1.40 1.40

Winter Olympic Games Type, 1976
Souvenir Sheet

Design: 75c, Downhill skiing and Olympic Games emblem.

1976, Jan. 23 Litho. ***Perf. 13½***
C210 A243 75c multi 1.40 1.40

Olympic Games Type, 1976
Souvenir Sheet

Design: 75c, Dressage and jumping.

1976, May 4 Litho. ***Perf. 13½***
C211 A245 75c multi 1.40 1.40

Bell Type
Souvenir Sheet

Design: 75c, A. G. Bell making telephone call, UPU and ITU emblems.

1976, June 4 Litho. ***Perf. 13½***
C212 A246 75c ocher & multi 1.40 1.40

Animal Type of 1976
Souvenir Sheet

Design: 50c, Elephant, vert.

1976, Sept. 1 Litho. ***Perf. 13½***
C213 A249 50c org & multi 1.50 1.50

Bicentennial Type of 1976
Souvenir Sheet

Design: 75c, Like No. 770.

1976, Sept. 21 Litho. ***Perf. 13½***
C214 A250 75c multi 1.50 1.50

Mask Type of 1977
Souvenir Sheet

Design: 75c, Ibo mask and Festival emblem.

1977, Jan. 20 Litho. ***Perf. 13½***
C215 A251 75c lil & multi 1.00 1.00

Equestrian Type of 1977

Designs: 55c, Military dressage (team), US. 80c, Winners receiving medals, vert.

1977, Apr. 22 Litho. ***Perf. 13½***
C216 A253 55c ocher & multi 1.00 50

Souvenir Sheet

C217 A253 80c ocher & multi 1.50 1.50

Elizabeth II Type of 1977
Souvenir Sheet

Design: 75c, Elizabeth II, laurel and crowns.

1977, May 23 Litho. ***Perf. 13½***
C218 A254 75c sil & multi 1.75 1.25

Zeppelin Type of 1978
Souvenir Sheet

Design: 75c, Futuristic Goodyear aerospace airship.

1978, Mar. 9 Litho. ***Perf. 13½***
C219 A257 75c multi 1.40 1.40

Soccer Type of 1978
Souvenir Sheet

Design: 75c, Soccer game Netherlands and Uruguay, vert.

1978, May 16 Litho. *Perf. 13½*
C220 A258 75c multi 1.40

Coronation Type of 1978
Souvenir Sheet

Design: 75c, Coronation coach, horiz.

1978, June 12
C221 A259 75c multi 1.40

Soccer Winners' Type of 1978
Souvenir Sheet

Design: 75c, Argentine team, horiz.

1978, Dec. 8 Litho. *Perf. 13½*
C222 A262 75c multi 1.40

AIR POST SEMI-POSTAL STAMPS

Nos. C14-C16 Overprinted in Red or Blue Like Nos. B16-B18

1941 Unwmk. *Perf. 12*
CB1 A107 3c +2c dk bl (R) 1.10 1.10
CB2 A108 5c +2c dl red brn (Bl) 1.10 1.10
CB3 A109 10c +2c dk grn (R) 1.10 1.10

Catalogue values for unused stamps in this section, from this point to the end of the section, are for Never Hinged items.

Nurses Taking Oath
SPAP1

Designs: 20c+5c, Liberian Government Hospital. 25c+5c, Medical examination.

1954, June 21 Litho. & Engr.
Size: 39½x28½mm
CB4 SPAP1 10c +5c car & blk 15 15
CB5 SPAP1 20c +5c emer & blk 18 15
Size: 45x34mm
CB6 SPAP1 25c +5c ultra, car & blk 20 15
Set value 26

Surtax for the Liberian Government Hospital. Nos. CB4-CB6 exist imperf. No. CB6 exists with carmine omitted.

AIR POST SPECIAL DELIVERY STAMP

No. C15 Overprinted in Dark Blue Like No. E1

1941 Unwmk. *Perf. 12*
CE1 A108 10c on 5c dl red brn 1.25 1.00

AIR POST REGISTRATION STAMP

No. C15 Overprinted in Dark Blue Like No. F35

1941 Unwmk. *Perf. 12*
CF1 A108 10c on 5c dl red brn 1.25 1.00

SPECIAL DELIVERY STAMP

No. 278 Surcharged in Dark Blue

SPECIAL DELIVERY
10 CENTS 10

1941 Unwmk. *Perf. 12*
E1 A108 10c on 5c dl red brn 1.25 1.00

REGISTRATION STAMPS

R1

1893 Unwmk. Litho. *Perf. 14, 15*
Without Value Surcharged
F1 R1 (10c) blk (Buchanan) 210.00 210.00
F2 R1 (10c) blk (Greenville) *1,750. 1,750.*
F3 R1 (10c) blk (Harper) *1,750. 1,750.*
F4 R1 (10c) blk (Monrovia) 25.00 25.00
F5 R1 (10c) blk (Robertsport) 800.00 800.00

Types of 1893 Surcharged in Black

10 CENTS 10

10 CENTS 10

1894 *Perf. 14*
F6 R1 10c bl, *pink* (Buchanan) 4.00 4.25
F7 R1 10c grn, *buff* (Harper) 4.00 4.25
F8 R1 10c red, *yel* (Monrovia) 4.00 4.25
F9 R1 10c rose, *bl* (Robertsport) 4.00 4.25

Exist imperf or missing one 10. Value, each $7.50.

President Garretson W. Gibson — R6

1903 Engr. *Perf. 14*
F10 R6 10c bl & blk (Buchanan) 1.00 15
 a. Center inverted 90.00
F11 R6 10c org red & blk ("Grenville") 1.00
 a. Center inverted 90.00
 b. 10c orange & black 1.60 15
F12 R6 10c grn & blk (Harper) 1.00 15
 a. Center inverted 90.00
F13 R6 10c vio & blk (Monrovia) 1.00 15
 a. Center inverted 90.00
 b. 10c lilac & black 1.60
F14 R6 10c mag & blk (Robertsport) 1.00 15
 a. Center inverted 90.00
Nos. F10-F14 (5) 5.00
Nos. F10, F11b, F12-F14 75

For surcharges see Nos. 178-182.

S.S. Quail on Patrol
R7

1919 Litho. *Serrate Roulette 12*
F15 R7 10c blk & bl (Buchanan) 50 1.00

Serrate Roulette 12, Perf. 14
F16 R7 10c ocher & blk ("Grenville") 50 1.00
F17 R7 10c grn & blk (Harper) 50 1.00
F18 R7 10c vio & bl (Monrovia) 50 1.00
F19 R7 10c rose & blk (Robertsport) 50 1.00
Nos. F15-F19 (5) 2.50 5.00

Gabon Viper
R8

Wmk. Crosses and Circles (116)
1921 Engr. *Perf. 13x14*
F20 R8 10c cl & blk (Buchanan) 22.50 1.25
F21 R8 10c red & blk (Greenville) 14.00 1.25
F22 R8 10c ultra & blk (Harper) 18.00 1.25
F23 R8 10c org & blk (Monrovia) 14.00 1.25
 a. Imperf., pair 120.00
F24 R8 10c grn & blk (Robertsport) 14.00 1.25
 a. Imperf., pair 120.00
Nos. F20-F24 (5) 82.50 6.25

Preceding Issue Overprinted "1921"
F25 R8 10c (Buchanan) 16.00 2.50
F26 R8 10c (Greenville) 17.00 2.50
F27 R8 10c (Harper) 16.00 2.50
F28 R8 10c (Monrovia) 15.00 2.50
F29 R8 10c (Robertsport) 16.00 2.50
Nos. F25-F29 (5) 80.00 12.50

Nos. F25-F29 exist with "1921" inverted. Value same as normal.

Passengers Going Ashore from Ship — R9

Designs: No. F31, Transporting merchandise, shore to ship (Greenville). No. F32, Sailing ship (Harper). No. F33, Ocean liner (Monrovia). No. F34, Canoe in surf (Robertsport).

1924 Litho. *Perf. 14*
F30 R9 10c gray & carmine 3.00 25
F31 R9 10c gray & blue grn 3.00 25
F32 R9 10c gray & orange 3.00 25
F33 R9 10c gray & blue 3.00 25
F34 R9 10c gray & violet 3.00 25
Nos. F30-F34 (5) 15.00 1.25

No. 278 Surcharged in Dark Blue

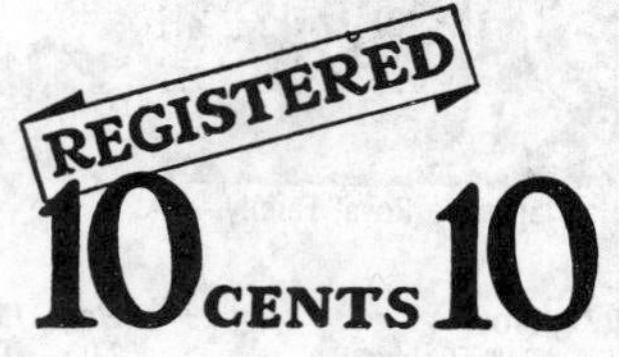

1941 Unwmk. *Perf. 12*
F35 A108 10c on 5c dl red brn 1.00 1.00

POSTAGE DUE STAMPS

Nos. 26, 28 Surcharged

POSTAGE DUE 3 CENTS.

1892 Unwmk. *Perf. 11*
J1 A5 3c on 3c violet 1.00 80
 a. Imperf., pair 10.00
 b. Inverted surcharge 30.00 30.00
 c. As "a," inverted surcharge 75.00

Perf. 12
J2 A5 6c on 6c olive gray 5.00 4.00
 a. Imperf., pair 15.00
 b. Inverted surcharge 35.00 35.00

D2

Engr.; Figures of Value Typographed in Black
1893 Wmk. 143 *Perf. 14, 15*
J3 D2 2c org, *yel* 1.00 52
J4 D2 4c rose, *rose* 1.00 52
J5 D2 6c brown, *buff* 1.00 70
J6 D2 8c blue, *blue* 1.00 70
J7 D2 10c grn, *lil rose* 1.35 90
J8 D2 20c vio, *gray* 1.35 90
 a. Center inverted 90.00 90.00
J9 D2 40c ol brn, *grnsh* 2.35 1.65
Nos. J3-J9 (7) 9.05 5.89

All values of the above set exist imperforate.

MILITARY STAMPS

"LFF" are the initials of "Liberian Frontier Force." Nos. M1-M7 were issued for the use of troops sent to guard the frontier.

Issues of 1905, 1906 and 1909 Surcharged

L F F
1c

1916 Wmk. 143
M1 A23 1c on 1c lt grn 135.00 135.00
 a. 2nd "F" inverted 175.00 175.00
 b. "FLF" 175.00 175.00
 c. Inverted surcharge 175.00 175.00
Unwmk.
M2 A33 1c on 1c grn & blk 425.00 425.00
 a. 2nd "F" inverted 450.00 450.00
 b. "FLF" 450.00 450.00
M3 A46 1c on 1c yel grn & blk 3.25 2.25
 a. 2nd "F" inverted 6.50 6.50
 b. "FLF" 6.50 6.50
M4 A47 1c on 2c lake & blk 3.25 2.25
 a. 2nd "F" inverted 6.50 6.50
 b. "FLF" 6.50 6.50

Surcharge exists sideways on Nos. M2, M5; double on Nos. M1-M4; inverted on Nos. M2-M4.

Nos. O46, O59-O60 Surcharged

L F F
1c

M5 A33 1c on 1c 325.00 325.00
 a. 2nd "F" inverted 450.00 450.00
 b. "FLF" 450.00 450.00
M6 A46 1c on 1c 3.25 2.25
 a. 2nd "F" inverted 6.50 6.50
 b. "FLF" 6.50 6.50
 c. "LFF 1c" inverted 8.50 8.50
 d. As "a" and "1c" inverted 12.00
 e. "FLF 1c" inverted 12.00
M7 A47 1c on 2c 2.50 1.90
 a. 2nd "F" inverted 5.00 5.00
 b. "FLF" 5.00 5.00
 c. Pair, one without "LFF 1c"

OFFICIAL STAMPS

Types of Regular Issues Overprinted "OFFICIAL" in Various Colors

Perf. 12½ to 15 and Compound
1892 Wmk. 143
O1 A9 1c vermilion 40 40
O2 A9 2c blue 40 40
O3 A10 4c grn & blk 40 40
O4 A11 6c bl grn 40 40
O5 A12 8c brn & blk 40 40
O6 A13 12c rose red 1.00 1.00
O7 A14 16c red lilac 1.00 1.00
 a. "OFFICSL"
O8 A15 24c ol grn, *yel* 1.00 1.00
O9 A16 32c grnsh bl 1.00 1.00
 a. "OFFICSL"
O10 A17 $1 bl & blk 20.00 7.75
O11 A18 $2 brn, *yel* 8.50 5.75
O12 A19 $5 car & blk 12.00 5.25
Nos. O1-O12 (12) 46.50 24.75

1893
O13 A11 (a) 5c on 6c bl grn (No. 50) 75 75
a. "5" with short flag 4.00 4.00
b. Both 5's with short flags 4.00 4.00
c. "i" dot omitted 15.00 15.00
d. Overprinted on #50d 37.50 37.50

1894
Overprinted "O S" in Various Colors
O15 A9 1c vermilion 40 20
O16 A9 2c blue 60 25
a. Imperf.
O17 A10 4c grn & blk 75 32
O18 A12 8c brn & blk 75 32
O19 A13 12c rose red 1.00 38
O20 A14 16c red lilac 1.00 38
O21 A15 24c ol grn, *yel* 1.00 42
O22 A16 32c grnsh bl 1.50 50
O23 A17 $1 bl & blk 12.00 12.00
a. $1 ultra & black 12.00 12.00
O24 A18 $2 brn, *yel* 12.00 12.00
O25 A19 $5 car & blk 75.00 50.00
Nos. O15-O25 (11) 106.00 76.77

Unwmk.
Imperf
O26 A22 5c vio & grn 2.50 1.50
Rouletted
O27 A22 5c vio & grn 2.50 1.50

Regular Issue of 1896-1905 Overprinted "O S" in Black or Red
1898-1905 Wmk. 143 *Perf. 14, 15*
O28 A23 1c lil rose 42 42
O29 A23 1c dp grn ('00) 42 42
O30 A23 1c lt grn (R) ('05) 42 42
O31 A24 2c bis & blk 75 25
a. Pair, one without overprint 50.00
O32 A24 2c org red & blk ('00) 1.25 60
O33 A24 2c rose & blk ('05) 1.90 1.25
O34 A25 5c lake & blk 1.25 60
O35 A25 5c gray bl & blk ('00) 1.65 60
O36 A25 5c ultra & blk (R) ('05) 1.65 70
O37 A12 10c chr yel & ind 75 75
O38 A13 15c slate 75 75
O39 A14 20c vermilion 1.25 90
O40 A15 25c yel grn 75 75
O41 A16 30c steel blue 1.90 1.25
O42 A26 50c red brn & blk 1.90 1.25
Nos. O28-O42 (15) 17.01 10.91

For surcharge see No. O92.

Official stamps overprinted "ORDINARY" or with a bar with an additional surcharge are listed as Nos. 64B-90, 92-93, 99.

Red Overprint — A29

1903 Unwmk. *Perf. 14*
O43 A29 3c green 16 15
a. Overprint omitted 5.00
b. Inverted overprint

Two overprint types: I - Thin, sharp, dark red. II - Thick, heavier, orange red. Same value.

ONE
O.S.

On No. 50

O3

1904 Black Surcharge Wmk. 143
O44 A11 1c on 5c on 6c bl grn 1.00 1.20
a. "5" with short flag 3.50
b. Both "5s" with straight flag 6.50 6.50
Red Surcharge
O45 O3 2c on 30c steel blue 6.50 6.00
a. Double surcharge, red and blk
b. Surcharge also on back

Types of Regular Issue Overprinted in Various Colors — a

1906 Unwmk.
O46 A33 1c grn & blk (R) 40 26
O47 A34 2c car & blk (Bl) 15 15
a. Center and overprint inverted 14.00 10.00
b. Inverted overprint 4.00
O48 A35 5c ultra & blk (Bk) 40 26
a. Inverted overprint 4.00 4.00
b. Center and overprint invtd. 25.00
O49 A36 10c dl vio & blk (R) 50 35
a. Inverted overprint
b. Center and overprint invtd. 27.50
O50 A37 15c brn & blk (Bk) 2.00 35
a. Inverted overprint 4.00
b. Overprint omitted
c. Center and overprint invtd. 35.00
O51 A38 20c dp grn & blk (R) 50 35
a. Overprint omitted
O52 A39 25c plum & gray (Bl) 30 15
a. With 2nd ovpt. in blue, invtd.
O53 A40 30c dk brn (Bk) 35 15
O54 A41 50c org brn & dp grn (G) 50 15
a. Inverted overprint 2.50
O55 A42 75c ultra & blk (Bk) 90 60
a. Inverted overprint 8.25 5.00
b. Overprint omitted 20.00
O56 A43 $1 dp grn & gray (R) 55 15
a. Inverted overprint
O57 A44 $2 plum & blk (Bl) 1.60 15
a. Overprint omitted 20.00
O58 A45 $5 org & blk (Bk) 3.50 15
a. Overprint omitted 10.00
b. Inverted overprint 5.50 3.50
Nos. O46-O58 (13) 11.65 3.22

Nos. O52, O54, O55, O56 and O58 are known with center inverted.
For surcharges see Nos. O72, O82-O85, O96.

1909-12
O59 A46 1c emer & blk (R) 22 16
O60 A47 2c car rose & brn (Bl) 22 16
a. Overprint omitted
O61 A48 5c turq & blk (Bk) 25 16
a. Double overprint, one inverted 6.50
O62 A49 10c blk & ultra (R) ('12) 35 16
O63 A50 15c cl & blk (Bl) 35 26
O64 A51 20c bis & grn (Bk) 65 30
O65 A52 25c ultra & grn (Bk) 65 32
a. Double overprint 4.25 4.25
O66 A53 30c dk bl (R) 50 16
O67 A54 50c brn & grn (Bk) 80 20
a. Center inverted 25.00
b. Inverted overprint 3.50 2.50
O68 A55 75c pur & blk (R) 90 18
Nos. O59-O68 (10) 4.89 2.06

Nos. O63, O64, O67 and O68 are known without overprint and with center inverted.
For surcharges see Nos. O74-O81, O86-O90, O97.

Rouletted
O69 A49 10c blk & ultra (R) 60 60

Nos. 126B and 127E Overprinted type "a" ("OS") in Red
1910-12 *Rouletted*
O70 A49 3c on 10c blk & ultra 60 1.00
Perf. 12¹/₂, 14, 12¹/₂x14
O71 A49 3c on 10c blk & ultra ('12) 60 30
a. Pair, one without surch., the other with dbl. surch., one invtd.
b. Double surcharge, one inverted 3.75

Stamps of Preceding Issues Surcharged with New Values like Regular Issue and

c

CENTS 20 OFFICIAL

1914
On Nos. O52 and 110
O72 A39 (a) 2c on 25c plum & gray 15.00 6.00
O73 A42 (c) 20c on 75c brn & blk 5.00 3.00
On Nos. O66 and O68
O74 A53 (b) 5c on 30c dk bl 5.00 3.00
O75 A55 (c) 20c on 75c pur & blk (R) 7.50 3.00

Official Stamps of 1906-09 Surcharged Like Regular Issues of Same Date
1915-16
O76 A50 (c) 2c on 15c (Bk) 65 45
O77 A52 (d) 2c on 25c (Bk) 3.75 3.75
O78 A51 (e) 5c on 20c (Bk) 65 45
O79 A53 (g) 5c on 30c (R) 5.00 5.00
O80 A54 (i) 10c on 50c (Bk) 4.00 2.50
O81 A55 (j) 20c on 75c (R) 2.00 2.00
O82 A43 (k) 25c on $1 (R) 12.50 12.50
a. "25" double 20.00
b. "OS" inverted 20.00
O83 A44 (l) 50c on $2 (Bk) 35.00 35.00
a. "Ceuts" 60.00 60.00
O84 A44 (m) 50c on $2 (Br) 15.00 15.00
O85 A45 (n) $1 on $5 (Bk) 13.00 13.00
Handstamped Surcharge
O86 A54 (i) 10c on 50c (Bk) 7.50 7.50
Nos. O60-O61 Surcharged like Nos. 153-154 in Black or Red
O87 A47 1c on 2c 2.00 2.00
Strip of 10 types 22.50
O88 A48 2c on 5c (R) 2.00 2.00
Strip of 10 types (R) 22.50
a. Black surcharge 7.50 7.50
Strip of 10 types (Bk) 110.00

See note following Nos. 153-154.

#O60-O61 Surcharged like #155-156
O90 A47 1c on 2c 35.00 35.00
O91 A48 2c on 5c 30.00 30.00

No. O42 Surcharged

10 10

O92 A26 10c on 50c (Bk) 10.00 10.00

No. O53 Surcharged like No. 161
1917
O96 A40 5c on 30c dk brn 13.00 15.00
a. "FIV" 25.00 25.00

The editors consider the 1915-17 issues unnecessary and speculative.

#O62 Surcharged in Red like #162
1918
O97 A49 3c on 10c blk & ultra 1.65 1.65

Types of Regular Issue of 1918 Overprinted Type "a" ("OS") in Black, Blue or Red
1918 Unwmk. *Perf. 12¹/₂, 14*
O98 A59 1c dp grn & red brn (Bk) 35 16
O99 A60 2c red & blk (Bl) 35 16
O100 A61 5c ultra & blk (R) 65 15
O101 A62 10c ultra (R) 35 15
O102 A63 15c choc & dk grn (Bl) 1.60 38
O103 A64 20c gray lil & blk (R) 50 15
O104 A65 25c choc & grn (Bk) 3.00 40
O105 A66 30c brt vio & blk (R) 3.75 40
O106 A67 50c mar & blk (Bl) 4.50 40
a. Overprint omitted 10.00
O107 A68 75c car brn & blk (Bl) 1.75 16
O108 A69 $1 ol bis & turq bl (Bk) 3.50 16
O109 A70 $2 ol bis & blk (R) 5.50 16
O110 A71 $5 yel grn (Bk) 7.00 20
Nos. O98-O110 (13) 32.80 3.03

For surcharges see Nos. 259-269, O111-O112, O155-O157. For overprint see No. 270.

Official Stamps of 1918 Surcharged like Regular Issue
1920
O111 A59 3c on 1c grn & red brn 75 50
a. "CEETS" 8.25
b. Double surcharge 2.50 2.50
c. Double surch., one invtd. 5.00 5.00
d. Triple surcharge 4.00 4.00
O112 A60 4c on 2c red & blk 50 50
a. Inverted surcharge 4.00 4.00
b. Double surcharge 4.00 4.00
c. Double surch., one invtd. 6.00 6.00
d. Triple surcharge 6.00 6.00

Types of Regular Issues of 1915-21 Overprinted OFFICIAL

1921 Wmk. 116 *Perf. 14*
O113 A57 2c rose red 4.50 15
O114 A58 3c brown 85 15
O115 A79 20c brn & ultra 1.25 22
Same, Overprinted "O S"
O116 A75 1c dp grn 85 15
O117 A76 5c dp bl & brn 85 15
O118 A77 10c red vio & blk 45 15
O119 A78 15c blk & grn 2.50 32
a. Double overprint
O120 A80 25c org & grn 3.50 32
O121 A81 30c brn & red 85 15
O122 A82 50c grn & blk 85 15
a. Overprinted "S" only
O123 A83 75c bl & vio 1.90 15
O124 A84 $1 bl & blk 12.00 35
O125 A85 $2 grn & org 6.50 55
O126 A86 $5 grn & bl 7.25 1.10
Nos. O113-O126 (14) 44.10
Set value 3.50

Preceding Issues Overprinted "1921"
1921
O127 A75 1c dp grn 3.50 15
O128 A57 2c rose red 3.50 15
O129 A58 3c brown 3.50 15
O130 A76 5c dp bl & brn 2.00 15
O131 A77 10c red vio & blk 3.50 15
O132 A78 15c blk & grn 4.00 15
O133 A79 20c brn & ultra 4.00 22
O134 A80 25c org & grn 4.50 42
O135 A81 30c brn & red 3.50 15
O136 A82 50c grn & blk 4.25 15
O137 A83 75c bl & vio 2.50 15
O138 A84 $1 bl & blk 7.00 1.00
O139 A85 $2 org & grn 9.00 1.10
O140 A86 $5 grn & bl 7.00 1.65
Nos. O127-O140 (14) 61.75 5.74

Types of Regular Issue of 1923 Overprinted "O S"
1923 *Perf. 13¹/₂x14¹/₂, 14¹/₂x13¹/₂*
White Paper
O141 A88 1c bl grn & blk 5.00 15
O142 A89 2c dl red & yel brn 5.00 15
O143 A90 3c gray bl & blk 5.00 15
O144 A91 5c org & dk grn 5.00 15
O145 A92 10c ol bis & dk vio 5.00 15
O146 A93 15c yel grn & bl 65 20
O147 A94 20c vio & ind 65 20
O148 A95 25c brn & red brn 20.00 20
White, Buff or Brownish Paper
O149 A96 30c dp ultra & brn 65 15
a. Overprint omitted
O150 A97 50c dl bis & red brn 65 20
O151 A98 75c gray & grn 65 15
O152 A99 $1 red org & grn 1.40 40
a. Overprint omitted 10.00
O153 A100 $2 red lil & ver 2.00 60
O154 A101 $5 bl & brn vio 3.50 50
Nos. O141-O154 (14) 55.15 3.35

No. O98 Surcharged in Red Brown

Two Cents

1926 Unwmk. *Perf. 14*
O155 A59 2c on 1c 2.00 2.00
a. "Gents" 6.25
b. Surcharged in black 5.00
c. As "b," "Gents" 8.25

No. O98 Surcharged in Black

Two Cents

1926
O156 A59 2c on 1c 75 75
a. Inverted surcharge
b. "Gents" 5.00

No. O98 Surcharged in Red

Two Cents

1927
O157 A59 2c on 1c 20.00 20.00
a. "Ceuts" 35.00
b. "Vwo" 35.00
c. "Twc" 35.00

Regular Issue of 1928 Overprinted in Red or Black

OFFICIAL SERVICE

1928 *Perf. 12*
O158 A102 1c grn (R) 75 35
O159 A102 2c gray vio (R) 1.40 55
O160 A102 3c bis brn (Bk) 1.40 35
O161 A103 5c ultra (R) 75 35
O162 A104 10c ol gray (R) 2.25 1.10
O163 A103 15c dl vio (R) 1.40 55
O164 A103 $1 red brn (Bk) 40.00 15.00
Nos. O158-O164 (7) 47.95 18.25

For surcharges see Nos. C3, O165.

No. O162 Surcharged with New Value and Bar in Black
1945 Unwmk. *Perf. 12*
O165 A104 4c on 10c (Bk) 6.00 6.00

LIBYA

(Libia)

LOCATION — North Africa, bordering on the Mediterranean Sea
GOVT. — Republic
AREA — 679,358 sq. mi.
POP. — 3,500,000 (est. 1982)
CAPITAL — Tripoli

In 1939, the four northern provinces of Libya, a former Italian colony, were incorporated in the Italian national territory. Included in the territory is the former Turkish Vilayet of Tripoli, annexed in 1912. Libya became a kingdom on Dec. 24, 1951. The Libyan Arab Republic was established Sept. 1, 1969. "People's Socialist . . ." was added to its name in 1977. See Cyrenaica and Tripolitania.

100 Centesimi = 1 Lira
Military Authority Lira (1951)
Franc (1951)
1,000 Milliemes = 1 Pound (1952)
1,000 Dirhams = 1 Dinar (1972)

Catalogue values for unused stamps in this country are for Never Hinged items, beginning with Scott 102 in the regular postage section, Scott C51 in the airpost section, Scott E13 in the special delivery section, Scott J25 in the postage due section, Scott O1 in the official section, Scott N1 in the Fezzan-Ghadames section, Scott 2N1 in the Fezzan section, Scott 2NB1 in the Fezzan semi-postal section, Scott 2NC1 in the Fezzan airpost section, Scott 2NJ1 in the Fezzan postage due section, Scott 3N1 in the Ghadames section, and Scott 3NC1 in the Ghadames airpost section.

Watermarks

Wmk. 195- Multiple Crown and Arabic F

Wmk. 310- Multiple Crescent and Star

Stamps of Italy Overprinted in Black **Libia**

1912-22 Wmk. 140 *Perf. 14*
1 A42 1c brown ('15) 15 50
a. Double overprint 70.00 110.00
2 A43 2c orange brn 15 25
3 A48 5c green 15 15
a. Double overprint 16.00 25.00
b. Imperf., pair 35.00 50.00
c. Inverted overprint *900.00*
d. Pair, one without overprint 45.00 65.00
4 A48 10c claret 15 15
a. Pair, one without overprint 60.00 90.00
b. Double overprint 30.00 45.00
5 A48 15c slate ('22) 80 *2.00*
6 A45 20c orange ('15) 25 25
a. Double overprint 45.00 65.00
b. Pair, one without overprint 125.00
7 A50 20c brn org ('18) 38 *1.00*
8 A49 25c blue 38 30
9 A49 40c brown 50 62
10 A45 45c ol grn ('17) 2.00 *5.50*
a. Inverted overprint 70.00
11 A49 50c violet 1.25 62
12 A49 60c brn car ('18) 2.00 *5.50*
13 A46 1 l brown & green ('15) 22.50 1.25
14 A46 5 l bl & rose ('15) 50.00 *80.00*
15 A51 10 l gray green & red ('15) 6.00 *18.00*
Nos. 1-15 (15) 86.66 *116.09*

For surcharges see Nos. 37-38.

Overprinted in Violet **LIBIA**

1912 Unwmk.
16 A58 15c slate 10.00 80
a. Blue black overprint *1,800.* 3.75

No. 16 Surcharged **CENT 20**

1916, Mar. Unwmk.
19 A58 20c on 15c slate 10.00 2.00

Roman Legionary — A1

Diana of Ephesus — A2

Ancient Galley Leaving Tripoli — A3

"Victory" — A4

1921 Engr. Wmk. 140 *Perf. 14*
20 A1 1c blk & gray brn 25 70
21 A1 2c blk & red brn 25 70
22 A1 5c black & green 38 38
a. 5c blk & red brn (error) 750.00
b. Center inverted 15.00 21.00
c. Imperf., pair 50.00 70.00
23 A2 10c blk & rose 38 25
a. Center inverted 15.00 21.00
24 A2 15c blk brn & brn orange 2.50 50
a. Center inverted 25.00 37.50
25 A2 25c dk bl & bl 38 20
a. Center inverted 3.75 6.00
b. Imperf., pair 100.00 150.00
26 A3 30c blk & blk brn 2.00 50
a. Center inverted 550.00 500.00
27 A3 50c blk & ol grn 1.50 15
a. 50c blk & brn (error) 125.00
b. Center inverted *1,300.* *825.00*
28 A3 55c black & vio 1.00 2.50
29 A4 1 l dk brn & brn 1.25 16
30 A4 5 l blk & dk blue 5.00 3.75
31 A4 10 l dk bl & ol grn 12.50 25.00
Nos. 20-31 (12) 27.39 34.79

Nos. 20-31 also exist perf. 14x13, with values somewhat higher.
See Nos. 47-61. For surcharges see Nos. 102-121.

Italy Nos. 136-139 Overprinted **LIBIA**

1921, Apr.
33 A64 5c olive green 38 *1.50*
a. Double overprint 70.00 90.00
34 A64 10c red 38 *1.50*
a. Double overprint 70.00 90.00
b. Inverted overprint 70.00 90.00
35 A64 15c slate green 50 *2.50*
36 A64 25c ultramarine 50 *2.00*

3rd anniv. of the victory of the Piave.

Nos. 11, 8 Surcharged **C. 40**

1922, June 1
37 A49 40c on 50c violet 62 70
38 A49 80c on 25c blue 80 *3.00*

Libyan Sibyl — A6

1924-31 Unwmk. *Perf. 14½x14*
39 A6 20c deep green 25 15
40 A6 40c brown 65 35
41 A6 60c deep blue 25 15
42 A6 1.75 l orange ('31) 15 15
43 A6 2 l carmine 80 60
44 A6 2.55 l violet ('31) 70 1.60
Nos. 39-44 (6) 2.80 3.00

1926-29 *Perf. 11*
39a A6 20c 10.00 20
40a A6 40c 6.00 1.25
41a A6 60c 2.00 15
43a A6 2 l ('29) 7.00 2.00

Type of 1921

1924-40 Unwmk. *Perf. 13½ to 14*
47 A1 1c blk & gray brown 25 1.00
48 A1 2c blk & red brn 38 1.00
49 A1 5c blk & green 50 38
50 A1 7½c blk & brown ('31) 30 1.00
51 A2 10c blk & dl red 15 15
b. Center inverted 25.00
52 A2 15c blk brn & org 80 42
b. Center inverted, perf. 11 550.00
53 A2 25c dk bl & bl 3.00 15
a. Center inverted 25.00 37.50
54 A3 30c blk & blk brn 22 30
55 A3 50c blk & ol grn 15 15
b. Center inverted 650.00 650.00
56 A3 55c black & vio 60.00 100.00
57 A4 75c violet & red ('31) 15 15
58 A4 1 l dk brn & brn 4.00 15
59 A3 1.25 l indigo & ultra ('31) 15 15
60 A4 5 l blk & dark blue ('40) 11.00 10.00
Nos. 47-60 (14) 81.05 115.00

Perf. 11
47a A1 1c 45.00
48a A1 2c 45.00
49a A1 5c 13.00 2.50
51a A2 10c 6.00 50
52a A2 15c 25.00 3.25
54a A3 30c 18.00 50
55a A3 50c 250.00 15
58a A4 1 l 2.50 20
60a A4 5 l ('37) *650.00* 45.00
61 A4 10 l dk bl & olive grn ('37) 150.00 80.00

Italy #197 and 88 Overprinted Like #1-15

1929 Wmk. 140 *Perf. 14*
62 A86 7½c light brown 5.25 *13.50*
63 A46 1.25 l blue & ultra 24.00 5.00

Italy #193 Overprinted Like #33-36

1929 Unwmk. *Perf. 11*
64 A85 1.75 l deep brown 30.00 1.50

Water Carriers — A7

Man of Tripoli — A8

Designs: 25c, Minaret. 30c, 1.25 l, Tomb of Holy Man near Tagiura. 50c, Statue of Emperor Claudius at Leptis. 75c, Ruins of gardens.

1934, Feb. 17 Photo. *Perf. 14*
64A A7 10c brown 2.00 *5.00*
64B A8 20c carmine rose 2.00 *5.00*
64C A8 25c green 2.00 *5.00*
64D A7 30c dark brown 2.00 *5.00*
64E A8 50c purple 2.00 *5.00*
64F A7 75c rose 2.00 *5.00*
64G A7 1.25 l blue 19.00 *32.50*
Nos. 64A-64G (7) 31.00 *62.50*

8th Sample Fair, Tripoli. See #C14-C18.

Bedouin Woman — A15

Highway Memorial Arch — A16

1936, May 11 Wmk. 140 *Perf. 14*
65 A15 50c purple 50 *75*
66 A15 1.25 l deep blue 65 *2.25*

10th Sample Fair, Tripoli.

1937, Mar. 15
67 A16 50c copper red 1.00 *2.50*
68 A16 1.25 l sapphire 1.00 *5.00*

Opening of a coastal road to the Egyptian frontier. See #C28-C29.

Nos. 67-68 Overprinted in Black **XI FIERA DI TRIPOLI**

1937, Apr. 24
69 A16 50c copper red 5.25 *7.00*
70 A16 1.25 l sapphire 5.25 *7.00*

11th Sample Fair, Tripoli. See #C30-C31.

Roman Wolf and Lion of St. Mark — A17

View of Fair Buildings A18

1938, Mar. 12
71 A17 5c brown 15 38
72 A18 10c olive brown 15 38
73 A17 25c green 25 38
74 A18 50c purple 25 25
75 A17 75c rose red 30 *1.00*
76 A18 1.25 l dark blue 38 *1.10*
Nos. 71-76,C32-C33 (8) 2.36 *6.01*

12th Sample Fair, Tripoli.

Augustus Caesar (Octavianus) A19

Goddess Abundantia A20

1938, Apr. 25
77 A19 5c olive brown 22 50
78 A20 10c brown red 22 50
79 A19 25c dk yel green 28 38
80 A20 50c dk violet 28 38
81 A19 75c orange red 59 *1.10*
82 A20 1.25 l dull blue 50 *1.10*
Nos. 77-82,C34-C35 (8) 2.89 *5.96*

Birth bimillenary of Augustus Caesar (Octavianus), first Roman emperor.

Desert City — A21

View of Ghadames A22

1939, Apr. 12 **Photo.**

No.	Type	Description	Unused	Used
83	A21	5c olive brown	15	38
84	A22	20c red brown	15	38
85	A21	50c rose violet	22	38
86	A22	75c scarlet	22	*62*
87	A21	1.25 l gray blue	25	*70*
		Nos. 83-87,C36-C38 (8)	1.74	*4.41*

13th Sample Fair, Tripoli.

Modern City — A23

Oxen and Plow — A24

Mosque — A25

1940, June 3 **Wmk. 140** ***Perf. 14***

No.	Type	Description	Unused	Used
88	A23	5c brown	15	38
89	A24	10c red orange	15	38
90	A25	25c dull green	35	*70*
91	A23	50c dark violet	35	*70*
92	A24	75c crimson	35	*1.10*
93	A25	1.25 l ultramarine	35	*1.10*
94	A24	2 l + 75c rose lake	35	*1.50*
		Nos. 88-94,C39-C42 (11)	3.31	*11.56*

Triennial Overseas Exposition, Naples.

"Two Peoples, One War," Hitler and Mussolini A26

1941, May 16

No.	Type	Description	Unused	Used
95	A26	5c orange	15	*2.50*
96	A26	10c brown	15	*2.50*
97	A26	20c dull violet	30	*2.50*
98	A26	25c green	30	*2.50*
99	A26	50c purple	38	*2.50*
100	A26	75c scarlet	38	*5.00*
101	A26	1.25 l sapphire	38	*5.00*
		Nos. 95-101,C43 (8)	2.29	*32.50*

The Rome-Berlin Axis.

Catalogue values for unused stamps in this section, from this point to the end of the section, are for Never Hinged items.

United Kingdom of Libya

Stamps of Cyrenaica 1950 Surcharged in Black

-- ليبيا --
٢ ليرة ع.

2 MAL.
LIBYA

For Use in Tripolitania

1951, Dec. 24 **Unwmk.** ***Perf. 12½***

No.	Type	Description	Unused	Used
102	A2	1mal on 2m rose car	15	20
103	A2	2mal on 4m dk grn	15	20
104	A2	4mal on 8m red org	15	25
105	A2	5mal on 10m pur	20	38
106	A2	6mal on 12m red	25	*65*
a.		Inverted surcharge	25.00	25.00
107	A2	10mal on 20m dp bl	35	*60*
a.		Arabic "20" for "10"	20.00	20.00
108	A3	24mal on 50m choc & ultra	1.10	*2.50*
109	A3	48mal on 100m bl blk & car rose	4.25	*8.00*
110	A3	96mal on 200m vio & pur	9.00	*19.00*
111	A3	240mal on 500m dk grn & org	20.00	*42.50*
		Nos. 102-111 (10)	35.60	*74.28*

The surcharge is larger on Nos. 108 to 111.

Same Surcharge in Francs

For Use in Fezzan

No.	Type	Description	Unused	Used
112	A2	2fr on 2m rose car	15	22
113	A2	4fr on 4m dk grn	15	22
114	A2	8fr on 8m red org	20	28
115	A2	10fr on 10m pur	20	28
116	A2	12fr on 12m red	70	1.10
117	A2	20fr on 20m dp bl	1.10	*1.60*
118	A3	48fr on 50m choc & ultra	11.00	*16.00*
119	A3	96fr on 100m bl blk & car rose	14.00	*21.00*
120	A3	192fr on 200m vio & pur	32.50	*50.00*
121	A3	480fr on 500m dk grn & org	25.00	*40.00*
		Nos. 112-121 (10)	85.00	*130.70*

The surcharge is larger on Nos. 118-121.

A second printing of Nos. 118-121 has an elongated first character in second line of Arabic surcharge.

ليبيا

Cyrenaica Nos. 65-77 Overprinted in Black

LIBYA

For Use in Cyrenaica

No.	Type	Description	Unused	Used
122	A2	1m dark brown	15	25
123	A2	2m rose carmine	15	25
124	A2	3m orange	15	38
125	A2	4m dark green	9.50	7.00
126	A2	5m gray	40	*70*
127	A2	8m red orange	40	*80*
128	A2	10m purple	45	*70*
129	A2	12m red	45	*1.00*
130	A2	20m deep blue	45	*70*
131	A3	50m choc & ultra	4.00	*7.00*
132	A3	100m bl blk & car rose	7.00	*12.00*
133	A3	200m violet & pur	19.00	*30.00*
134	A3	500m dk grn & org	50.00	*90.00*
		Nos. 122-134 (13)	92.10	*150.78*

Wider spacing between the two lines on Nos. 131-134.

King Idris
A27 A28

1952, Apr. 15 **Engr.** ***Perf. 11½***

No.	Type	Description	Unused	Used
135	A27	2m yellow brown	15	15
136	A27	4m gray	15	15
137	A27	5m blue green	10.00	16
138	A27	8m vermilion	16	15
139	A27	10m purple	9.25	15
140	A27	12m lilac rose	16	15
141	A27	20m deep blue	9.25	20
142	A27	25m chocolate	10.00	25
143	A28	50m brown & blue	90	35
144	A28	100m gray blk & car rose	1.40	40
145	A28	200m dk blue & pur	2.75	2.25
146	A28	500m dk grn & brn orange	13.00	7.50
		Nos. 135-146 (12)	57.17	11.86

For surcharge and overprints see Nos. 168, O1-O8.

Globe — A29

Perf. 13½x13

1955, Jan. 1 **Photo.** **Wmk. 195**

No.	Type	Description	Unused	Used
147	A29	5m yellow brown	40	38
148	A29	10m green	80	65
149	A29	30m violet	2.25	1.25

Arab Postal Union founding, July 1, 1954.

Nos. 147-149 Overprinted

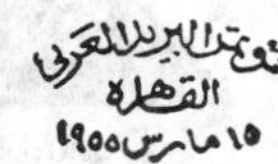
مؤتمر البريد العربي
القاهرة
١٥ مارس ١٩٥٥

1955, Aug. 1

No.	Type	Description	Unused	Used
150	A29	5m yellow brn	22	20
151	A29	10m green	32	32
152	A29	30m violet	1.10	65

Arab Postal Congress, Cairo, Mar. 15.

Emblems of Tripolitania, Cyrenaica and Fezzan with Royal Crown — A30

1955 **Engr.** **Wmk. 310** ***Perf. 11½***

No.	Type	Description	Unused	Used
153	A30	2m lemon	65	35
154	A30	3m slate blue	15	15
155	A30	4m gray green	65	60
156	A30	5m light blue grn	22	15
157	A30	10m violet	40	15
158	A30	18m crimson	15	15
159	A30	20m orange	20	15
160	A30	30m blue	45	15
161	A30	35m brown	25	15
162	A30	40m rose carmine	45	15
163	A30	50m olive	42	16

Size: 27½x32½mm

No.	Type	Description	Unused	Used
164	A30	100m dk green & pur	65	25
165	A30	200m ultra & rose car	6.50	2.50
166	A30	500m grn & orange	8.00	6.00

Size: 26½x32mm

No.	Type	Description	Unused	Used
167	A30	£1 ocher, brn & grn, *yel*	14.00	7.00
		Nos. 153-167 (15)	33.14	18.06

See Nos. 177-179, 192-206A.

No. 136 Surcharged 5 0

1955, Aug. 25 **Unwmk.**

No.	Type	Description	Unused	Used
168	A27	5m on 4m gray	80	80

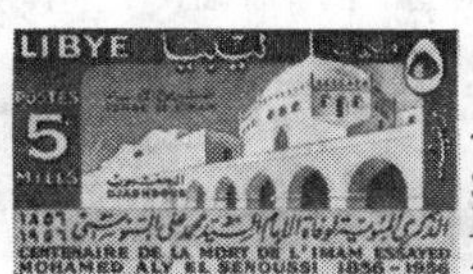
Tomb of El Senussi, Jagbub A31

Perf. 13x13½

1956, Sept. 14 **Photo.** **Wmk. 195**

No.	Type	Description	Unused	Used
169	A31	5m green	15	15
170	A31	10m bright violet	16	15
171	A31	15m rose carmine	25	25
172	A31	30m sapphire	70	50

Death centenary of the Imam Seyyid Mohammed Aly El Senussi (in 1859).

Map, Flags and UN Headquarters A32

Globe and Postal Emblems A33

1956, Dec. 14 **Litho.** ***Perf. 13½x13***

No.	Type	Description	Unused	Used
173	A32	15m bl, ocher & ol bis	25	15
174	A32	35m bl, ocher & vio brn	40	28

Libya's admission to the UN, 1st anniv.

1957 **Wmk. 195** ***Perf. 13½x13***

No.	Type	Description	Unused	Used
175	A33	15m blue	90	30
176	A33	500m yellow brown	4.50	3.50

Arab Postal Congress, Tripoli, Feb. 9.

Emblems Type of 1955

1957 **Wmk. 310** **Engr.** ***Perf. 11½***

No.	Type	Description	Unused	Used
177	A30	1m black, *yellow*	16	15
178	A30	2m bister brown	16	15
179	A30	4m brown carmine	16	15
		Set value		24

UN Emblem and Broken Chain — A34

Unwmk.

1958, Dec. 10 **Photo.** ***Perf. 14***

No.	Type	Description	Unused	Used
180	A34	10m bluish violet	15	15
181	A34	15m green	20	16
182	A34	30m ultramarine	50	40

Universal Declaration of Human Rights, 10th anniv.

Date Palms and FAO Emblem A35

1959, Dec. 5 **Unwmk.** ***Perf. 14***

No.	Type	Description	Unused	Used
183	A35	10m pale vio & black	15	15
184	A35	15m bluish grn & blk	20	16
185	A35	45m light blue & blk	50	45

1st Intl. Dates Conf., Tripoli, Dec. 5-11.

Arab League Center, Cairo, and Arms of Libya A36

Perf. 13x13½

1960, Mar. 22 **Wmk. 328**

No.	Type	Description	Unused	Used
186	A36	10m dull grn & blk	28	16

Opening of the Arab League Center and the Arab Postal Museum in Cairo.

Emblems of WRY and UN, Arms of Libya — A37

Palm Tree and Radio Mast — A38

1960, Apr. 7 Unwmk. *Perf. 14*

No.	Type	Description	Unused	Used
187	A37	10m violet & black	20	16
188	A37	45m blue & black	70	62

World Refugee Year, July 1, 1959-June 30, 1960.

1960, Aug. 4 Engr. *Perf. 13x13½*

No.	Type	Description	Unused	Used
189	A38	10m violet	15	15
190	A38	15m blue green	20	15
191	A38	45m dk carmine rose	65	28
		Set value		45

3rd Arab Telecommunications Conf., Tripoli, Aug. 4.

Emblems Type of 1955

1960 Wmk. 310 Engr. *Perf. 11½*

Size: 18x21½mm

No.	Type	Description	Unused	Used
192	A30	1m black, *gray*	15	15
193	A30	2m bis brn, *buff*	15	15
194	A30	3m blue, *bluish*	15	15
195	A30	4m brn car, *rose*	15	15
196	A30	5m grn, *greenish*	15	15
197	A30	10m vio, *pale vio*	15	15
198	A30	15m brown, *buff*	15	15
199	A30	20m orange, *buff*	15	15
200	A30	30m red, *pink*	15	15
201	A30	40m rose car, *rose*	15	15
202	A30	45m blue, *bluish*	15	16
203	A30	50m olive, *buff*	35	16

Size: 27½x32½mm

No.	Type	Description	Unused	Used
204	A30	100m dk grn & pur, *gray*	50	40
205	A30	200m bl & rose car, *bluish*	1.50	60
206	A30	500m green & org, *greenish*	8.25	2.50

Size: 26½x32mm

No.	Type	Description	Unused	Used
206A	A30	£1 ocher, brn & grn, *brn*	16.00	14.00
		Nos. 192-206A (16)	28.25	19.32

Watchtower and Broken Chain — A39

1961, Aug. 9 Photo. Unwmk.

No.	Type	Description	Unused	Used
207	A39	5m lt yel grn & brn	35	15
208	A39	15m light blue & brn	50	16

Issued for Army Day, Aug. 9, 1961.

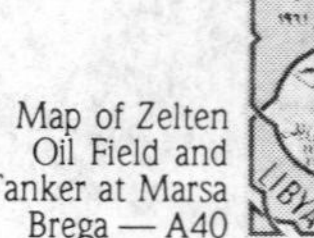

Map of Zelten Oil Field and Tanker at Marsa Brega — A40

1961, Oct. 25 *Perf. 11½*

No.	Type	Description	Unused	Used
209	A40	15m ol grn & buff	15	15
210	A40	50m red brn & pale vio	50	30
211	A40	100m ultra & blue	1.00	65

Opening of first oil pipe line in Libya.

Hands Breaking Chain, Tractor and Cows — A41

Designs: 50m, Modern highways and buildings. 100m, Machinery.

1961, Dec. 24 *Perf. 11½*

Granite Paper

No.	Type	Description	Unused	Used
212	A41	15m pale grn, grn & brown	15	15
213	A41	50m buff & brown	50	30
214	A41	100m sal, vio & brn	1.00	65

10th anniversary of independence.

Camel Riders — A42

Designs: 15m, Well. 50m, Oil installations in desert.

1962, Feb. 20 Photo. *Perf. 12*

No.	Type	Description	Unused	Used
215	A42	10m choc & org brn	15	15
216	A42	15m plum & yel grn	40	32
217	A42	50m emer & ultra	1.10	80
a.		Souv. sheet of 3, #215-217, imperf.	20.00	13.00

Intl. Fair, Tripoli, Feb. 20-Mar. 20.

Nos. 215-217 exist imperf. Value about twice that of perf.

Malaria Eradication Emblem and Palm — A43

Ahmed Rafik El Mehdawi (1989-1961), Poet — A44

1962, Apr. 7 Unwmk. *Perf. 11½*

No.	Type	Description	Unused	Used
218	A43	15m multicolored	35	16
219	A43	50m grn, yel & brn	45	45

WHO drive to eradicate malaria.

Exist imperf. Value about three times that of perf.

Two imperf. souvenir sheets exist, one containing the 15m, the other the 50m. Sold for 20m and 70m respectively. Value for both, $6.

1962, July 6 Engr. *Perf. 13x14*

No.	Type	Description	Unused	Used
220	A44	15m green	15	15
221	A44	20m brown	28	22

El Mehdawi, 1st death anniv.

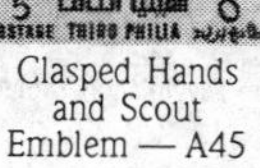

Clasped Hands and Scout Emblem — A45

Drop of Oil with New City, Desert, Oil Wells and Map of Coast Line — A46

Designs: 10m, 30m, Boy Scouts. 15m, 50m, Scout emblem and tents.

1962, July 13 Photo. *Perf. 12*

No.	Type	Description	Unused	Used
222	A45	5m yel, blk & red	15	15
223	A45	10m bl, blk & yel	22	15
224	A45	15m multicolored	28	20
		Set value		40

Souvenir Sheet

Imperf

No.	Type	Description	Unused	Used
225		Sheet of 3	3.75	3.50
a.	A45	20m yellow, black & red	65	65
b.	A45	30m blue, black & yellow	65	65
c.	A45	50m blue gray, yel, blk & grn	65	65

Third Libyan Scout meeting (Philia).

Nos. 222-224 exist imperf. Value for set, $1.50.

1962, Nov. 25 *Perf. 11x11½*

No.	Type	Description	Unused	Used
226	A46	15m grn & vio blk	15	15
227	A46	50m brn org & ol	45	35

Opening of the Essider Terminal Sidrah pipeline system.

Centenary Emblem — A47

Litho. & Photo.

1963, Jan. 1 *Perf. 11½*

No.	Type	Description	Unused	Used
228	A47	10m rose, blk, red & bl	15	15
229	A47	15m cit, blk, red & bl	20	15
230	A47	20m gray, blk, red & bl	45	35
		Set value		55

Centenary of the International Red Cross.

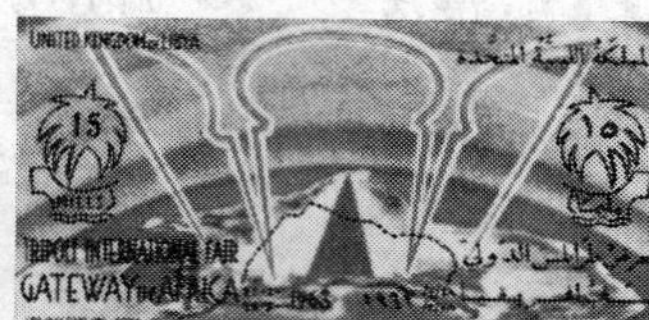

Rainbow and Arches over Map of Africa and Libya — A48

1963, Feb. 28 Litho. *Perf. 13½*

No.	Type	Description	Unused	Used
231	A48	15m multicolored	20	15
232	A48	30m multicolored	38	35
233	A48	50m multicolored	55	50

Tripoli Intl. Fair "Gateway of Africa," Feb. 28-Mar. 28. Every other horizontal row inverted in sheet of 50 (25 tête bêche pairs).

Date Palm and Well — A49

Designs: 15m, Camel and flock of sheep. 45m, Sower and tractor.

1963, Mar. 21 Photo. *Perf. 11½*

No.	Type	Description	Unused	Used
234	A49	10m green, lt bl & bis	15	15
235	A49	15m pur, lt grn & bis	15	15
236	A49	45m dk bl, sal & sep	55	28
		Set value		48

FAO "Freedom from Hunger" campaign.

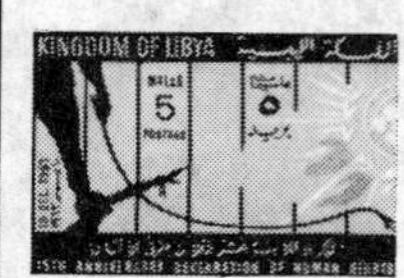

Man with Whip and Slave Reaching for UN Emblem — A50

1963, Dec. 10 Unwmk. *Perf. 11½*

No.	Type	Description	Unused	Used
237	A50	5m red brown & bl	15	15
238	A50	15m deep claret & bl	15	15
239	A50	50m green & blue	38	25
		Set value		40

Universal Declaration of Human Rights, 15th anniv.

Exhibition Hall and Finger Pointing to Libya — A51

1964, Feb. 28 Photo. *Perf. 11½*

No.	Type	Description	Unused	Used
240	A51	10m red brn, gray grn & brn	15	15
241	A51	15m pur, gray grn & brn	28	20
242	A51	30m dk bl, gray grn & brn	75	38

3rd Intl. Fair, Tripoli, Feb. 28-Mar. 20.

Child Playing with Blocks — A52

Design: 15m, Child in bird's nest.

1964, Mar. 22 *Perf. 11½*

No.	Type	Description	Unused	Used
243	A52	5m multicolored	15	15
244	A52	15m multicolored	15	15
245	A52	45m multicolored	42	28
a.		Souvenir sheet of 3, #243-245, imperf.	2.00	2.00
		Set value		48

Children's Day. Exist imperf. Value about 1½ times that of perf.

No. 245a sold for 100m.

Lungs and Stethoscope — A53

1964, Apr. 7 Photo. *Perf. 13½x14*

No.	Type	Description	Unused	Used
246	A53	20m deep purple	50	25

Campaign against tuberculosis.

Map of Libya — A54

1964, Apr. 27 Unwmk. *Perf. 11½*

No.	Type	Description	Unused	Used
247	A54	5m emerald & org	15	15
248	A54	50m blue & yellow	38	28
		Set value		32

First anniversary of Libyan union.

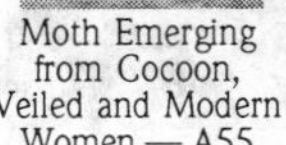

Moth Emerging from Cocoon, Veiled and Modern Women — A55

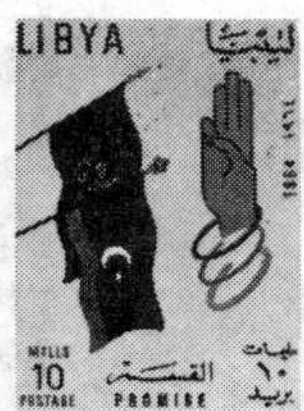

Hand Giving Scout Sign, Scout and Libyan Flags — A56

1964, June 15 — Litho. & Engraved

249 A55 10m vio bl & lt grn — 15 15
250 A55 20m vio blue & yel — 15 15
251 A55 35m vio bl & pink — 30 28
a. Souv. sheet of 3, #249-251 — 2.00 2.00
Set value — 40

To honor Libyan women in a new epoch. No. 251a sold for 100m.

1964, July 24 — Photo. — *Perf. 12x11½*

Design: 20m, Libyan Scout emblem and hands.

252 A56 10m lt bl & multi — 65 25
253 A56 20m multicolored — 1.10 40
a. Souvenir sheet of 2, #252-253, imperf. — 2.75 2.75

Opening of new Boy Scout headquarters; installation of Crown Prince Hassan al-Rida el Senussi as Chief Scout. No. 253a sold for 50m.

Nos. 252-253 exist imperf. Value about 1½ times that of perf.

Bayonet, Wreath and Map — A57

Ahmed Bahloul el-Sharef — A58

1964, Aug. 9 — Litho. — *Perf. 14x13½*

254 A57 10m yel grn & brn — 15 15
255 A57 20m org & blk — 25 15
Set value — 32 16

Founding of the Senussi Army.

1964, Aug. 11 — Engr. — *Perf. 11½*

256 A58 15m lilac — 15 15
257 A58 20m greenish blue — 35 16
Set value — 20

Poet Ahmed Bahloul el-Sharef, died 1953.

Soccer — A59

1964, Oct. 1 — Litho. — *Perf. 14*

Black Inscriptions and Gold Olympic Rings

258 A59 5m shown — 35 35
259 A59 10m Bicycling — 35 35
260 A59 20m Boxing — 35 35
261 A59 30m Sprinter — 35 35
262 A59 35m Woman diver — 35 35
263 A59 50m Hurdling — 35 35
a. Block of 6, #258-263 — 2.25 2.25
Nos. 258-263 (6) — 2.10 2.10

18th Olympic Games, Tokyo, Oct. 10-25. No. 263a printed in sheet of 48. The two blocks in each double row are inverted in relation to the two blocks in the next row, providing various tete beche and se-tenant arrangements.

#258-263 exist imperf. Value for set, $7.50.

Perf. and imperf. souvenir sheets exist containing six 15m stamps in the designs and colors of Nos. 258-263. Sheets sold for 100m. Value for both, $13.50.

Arab Postal Union Emblem — A59a

1964, Dec. 1 — Photo. — *Perf. 11x11½*

264 A59a 10m yellow & blue — 15 15
265 A59a 15m pale vio & org brn — 16 15
266 A59a 30m lt yel grn & brn — 55 40
Set value — 56

Permanent Office of the APU, 10th anniv.

International Cooperation Year Emblem — A60

1965, Jan. 1 — Litho. — *Perf. 14½x14*

267 A60 5m vio bl & gold — 15 15
268 A60 15m rose car & gold — 50 50

Imperfs. exist. Value about twice that of perfs.

See Nos. C51-C51a.

European Bee Eater — A61

Birds: 5m, Long-legged buzzard, vert. 15m, Chestnut-bellied sandgrouse. 20m, Houbara bustard. 30m, Spotted sandgrouse. 40m, Libyan Barbary partridge.

1965, Feb. 10 — Photo. — *Perf. 11½*

Granite Paper

Birds in Natural Colors

269 A61 5m gray & black — 15 15
270 A61 10m lt bl & org brn — 16 15
271 A61 15m lt green & blk — 35 15
272 A61 20m pale lil & blk — 42 16
273 A61 30m tan & dark brn — 55 22
274 A61 40m dull yel & blk — 65 40
Nos. 269-274 (6) — 2.28 1.23

Map of Africa with Libya — A62

1965, Feb. 28 — Photo. — *Perf. 11½*

Granite Paper

275 A62 50m multicolored — 35 20

4th Intl. Tripoli Fair, Feb. 28-Mar. 20.

Compass Rose, Rockets, Satellites and Stars — A63

1965, Mar. 23 — Litho.

276 A63 10m multicolored — 15 15
277 A63 15m multicolored — 15 15
278 A63 50m multicolored — 40 28
Set value — 56 30

Fifth World Meteorological Day.

ITU Emblem, Old and New Communication Equipment — A64

1965, May 17 — Unwmk.

279 A64 10m sepia — 15 15
280 A64 20m red lilac — 15 15
281 A64 50m lilac rose — 28 20
Set value — 48 32

ITU, centenary.

Library Aflame and Lamp — A65

1965, June — Litho. — *Perf. 11½*

282 A65 15m multicolored — 15 15
283 A65 50m multicolored — 40 20
Set value — 28

Burning of the Library of Algiers, June 7, 1962.

Rose — A66

Jet Plane and Globe — A67

1965, Aug. — Litho. — *Perf. 14*

284 A66 1m shown — 16 15
285 A66 2m Iris — 16 15
286 A66 3m Opuntia — 35 15
287 A66 4m Sunflower — 50 22
Set value — 52

1965, Oct. — Photo. — *Perf. 11½*

288 A67 5m multicolored — 15 15
289 A67 10m multicolored — 15 15
290 A67 15m multicolored — 28 15
Set value — 45 25

Issued to publicize Libyan Airlines.

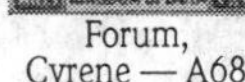

Forum, Cyrene — A68

Mausoleum at Germa — A69

Designs: 100m, Arch of Trajan. 200m, Temple of Apollo, Cyrene. 500m, Antonine Temple of Jupiter, Sabratha, horiz. £1, Theater, Sabratha.

Perf. 12x11½, 11½x12

1965, Dec. 24 — Engr. — Wmk. 310

291 A68 50m vio blue & ol — 32 15
292 A68 100m Prus bl & dp org — 65 22
293 A68 200m pur & Prus bl — 1.60 32
294 A68 500m car rose & grn — 2.50 1.40
295 A68 £1 grn & dp org — 7.50 2.75
Nos. 291-295 (5) — 12.57 4.84

Nos. 293-295 with "Kingdom of Libia" in both Arabic and English blocked out with a blue felt-tipped pen were issued June 21, 1970, by the Republic.

Perf. 11½

1966, Feb. 10 — Unwmk. — Litho.

296 A69 70m pur & salmon — 35 25

"POLIGRAFICA & CARTEVALORI-NAPLES" and Libyan Coat of Arms printed on back in yellow green. See No. E13.

Booklet pane containing 4 No. 296 and 4 No. E13 exists.

Globe in Space, Satellites — A70

1966, Feb. 28 — *Perf. 12*

297 A70 15m multicolored — 15 15
298 A70 45m multicolored — 20 20
299 A70 55m multicolored — 62 35
Set value — 60

5th Intl. Fair at Tripoli, Feb. 28-Mar. 20.

Arab League Center, Cairo, and Emblem — A71

Litho. & Photo.

1966, Mar. 22 — *Perf. 11*

300 A71 20m car, emer & blk — 15 15
301 A71 55m brt bl, ver & blk — 30 25

Issued to publicize the Arab League.

Souvenir Sheet

WHO Headquarters, Geneva, and Emblem — A72

1966, May 3 — Litho. — *Imperf.*

302 A72 50m multicolored — 1.90 1.90

Inauguration of the WHO headquarters. See Nos. C55-C57.

Tuareg and Camel — A73

Buying Sets

Frequently it is less expensive to purchase complete sets rather than the individual stamps that make up the set. "Set Values" are provided for many such sets.

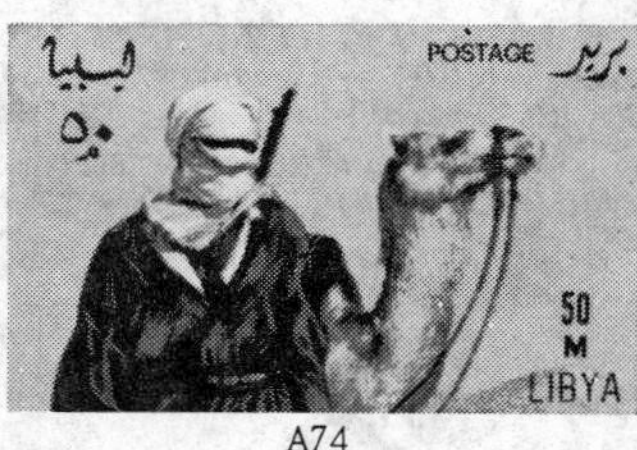

A74

Three Tuareg Riders — A75

Design: 20m, like 10m, facing left.

1966, June 20 Unwmk. *Perf. 10*

303 A73 10m bright red 25 20
304 A73 20m ultramarine 55 40
305 A74 50m multicolored 90 80
a. Strip of 3, Nos. 303-305 1.90 1.90

Souvenir Sheet

Imperf

306 A75 100m multicolored 2.50 2.00

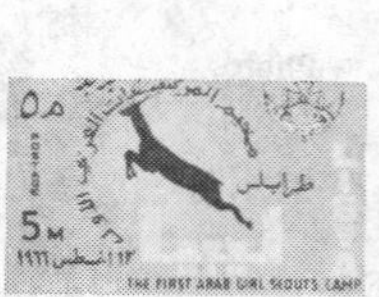

Gazelle — A76

Emblem — A77

Perf. 13x11, 11x13

1966, Aug. 12 Litho.

307 A76 5m lt grn, blk & red 16 15
308 A77 25m multicolored 35 20
309 A77 65m multicolored 65 35

1st Arab Girl Scout Camp (No. 307); 7th Arab Boy Scout Camp, Good Daim, Libya, Aug. 12 (Nos. 308-309).

UNESCO Emblem — A78

1967, Jan. Litho. *Perf. 10x10½*

310 A78 15m multicolored 15 15
311 A78 25m multicolored 20 16
Set value 24

UNESCO, 20th anniv. (in 1966).

Castle of Columns, Tolemaide A79

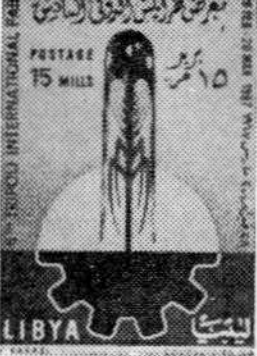

Fair Emblem A80

Design: 55m, Sebha Fort, horiz.

Perf. 13x13½, 13½x13

1966, Dec. 24 Engr.

312 A79 25m lil, red brn & blk 16 15
313 A79 55m blk, lil & red brn 35 28

1967, Feb. 28 Photo. *Perf. 11½*

314 A80 15m multicolored 16 15
315 A80 55m multicolored 35 20
Set value 25

6th Intl. Fair, Tripoli, Feb. 28-Mar. 20.

Oil Tanker, Marsa Al Hariga Terminal — A81

1967, Feb. 14 Litho. *Perf. 10*

316 A81 60m multicolored 40 22

Opening of Marsa Al Hariga oil terminal.

Tourist Year Emblem — A82

1967, May 1 Litho. *Perf. 10½x10*

317 A82 5m gray, blk & brt bl 15 15
318 A82 10m lt bl, blk & brt bl 15 15
319 A82 45m pink, blk & brt bl 28 16
Set value 40 25

International Tourist Year.

Map of Mediterranean and Runners A83

1967, Sept. 8 Litho. *Perf. 10½*

320 A83 5m shown 15 15
321 A83 10m Javelin 15 15
322 A83 15m Bicyling 15 15
323 A83 45m Soccer 20 16
324 A83 75m Boxing 50 25
Set value 90 55

5th Mediterranean Games, Tunis, Sept. 8-17.

Arab League Emblem and Hands Reaching for Knowledge — A84

1967, Oct. 1 Litho. *Perf. 12½x13*

325 A84 5m orange & dk pur 15 15
326 A84 10m brt grn & dk pur 15 15
327 A84 15m lilac & dk pur 15 15
328 A84 25m blue & dk pur 28 15
Set value 45 22

Literacy campaign.

Human Rights Flame — A85

1968, Jan. 15 Litho. *Perf. 13½x14*

329 A85 15m grn & vermilion 16 15
330 A85 60m org & vio bl 28 25
Set value 30

International Human Rights Year.

Map, Derrick, Plane and Camel Riders — A86

1968, Feb. 28 Photo. *Perf. 11½*

331 A86 55m car rose, brn & yel 45 35

7th Intl. Fair, Tripoli, Feb. 28-Mar. 20.

Arab League Emblem A87

1968, Mar. 22 Engr. *Perf. 13½*

332 A87 10m blue gray & car 15 15
333 A87 45m fawn & green 38 25

Issued for Arab League Week.

Children, Statuary Group — A88

Children's Day: 55m, Mother and children.

1968, Mar. 21 Litho. *Perf. 11*

334 A88 25m gray, blk & mag 16 15
335 A88 55m gray & multi 28 20
Set value 28

Hands Reaching for WHO Emblem — A89

Perf. 13½x14½

1968, Apr. 7 Photo.

336 A89 25m rose cl, dk bl & gray bl 20 15
337 A89 55m bl, blk & gray 45 20
Set value 28

WHO, 20th anniversary.

From Oil Field to Tanker — A90

1968, Apr. 23 Litho. *Perf. 11*

338 A90 10m multicolored 16 15
339 A90 60m multicolored 45 25

Opening of the Zueitina oil terminal.

Teacher and Crowd A91

1968, Sept. 8 Litho. *Perf. 13½*

340 A91 5m bright pink 15 15
341 A91 10m orange 15 15
342 A91 15m blue 15 15
343 A91 20m emerald 25 16
Set value 42 32

Literacy campaign.

Arab Labor Emblem A92

1968, Nov. 3 Photo. *Perf. 14x13½*

344 A92 10m multicolored 15 15
345 A92 15m multicolored 25 15
Set value 20

4th session of the Arab Labor Ministers' Conf., Tripoli, Nov. 3-10.

Wadi el Kuf Bridge and Road Sign — A93

1968, Dec. 25 Litho. *Perf. 11x11½*

346 A93 25m ultra & multi 16 15
347 A93 60m emer & multi 35 20

Opening of the Wadi el Kuf Bridge.

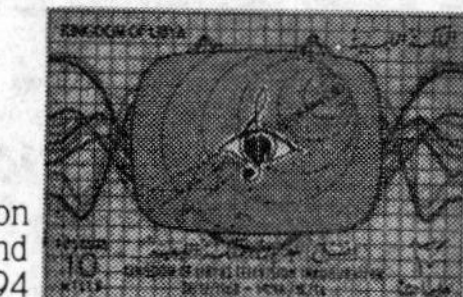

Television Screen and Chart — A94

1968, Dec. 25 Photo. *Perf. 14x13½*

348 A94 10m yellow & multi 15 15
349 A94 30m lilac & multi 25 16
Set value 20

Inauguration of television service, Dec. 24.

Melons — A95

1969, Jan. Photo. *Perf. 11½*
Granite Paper

350 A95	5m	shown	15	15
351 A95	10m	Peanuts	15	15
352 A95	15m	Lemons	15	15
353 A95	20m	Oranges	30	15
354 A95	25m	Peaches	38	15
355 A95	35m	Pears	50	30
		Set value	1.40	70

Nos. 350-355 with "Kingdom of Libya" in both English and Arabic blocked out with a blue felt-tipped pen were issued in December, 1971, by the Republic.

Tripoli Fair Emblem — A96

1969, Apr. 8
Granite Paper

356 A96	25m	silver & multi	15	15
357 A96	35m	bronze & multi	15	15
358 A96	40m	gold & multi	28	16
		Set value	48	32

8th Intl. Fair, Tripoli, Mar. 6-26.

Weather Balloon and Observer A97

1969, Mar. 21 Photo. *Perf. 14x13*

359 A97	60m	gray & multi	40	35

World Meteorological Day, Mar. 23.

Cogwheel and Workers A98

1969, Mar. 29 Litho. *Perf. 13½*

360 A98	15m	blue & multi	15	15
361 A98	55m	salmon & multi	35	20
		Set value		28

10th anniversary of Social Insurance.

ILO Emblem — A99

1969, June 1 Photo. *Perf. 14*

362 A99	10m	bl grn, blk & lt ol	15	15
363 A99	60m	car rose, blk & lt ol	38	20
		Set value		28

ILO, 50th anniversary.

African Tourist Year Emblem A100

1969, July *Perf. 11½*
Emblem in Emerald, Light Blue & Red

364 A100	15m	emer & silver	20	15
365 A100	30m	blk & gold	40	20
		Set value		28

Issued to publicize African Tourist Year.

Libyan Arab Republic

Soldiers, Tanks and Planes — A101

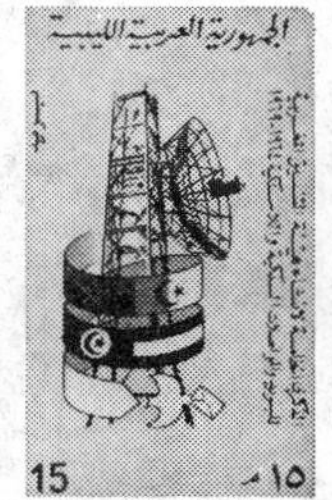

Radar, Flags and Carrier Pigeon — A102

1969, Dec. 7 Photo. *Perf. 12x12½*

366 A101	5m	org & multi	15	15
367 A101	10m	ultra & multi	15	15
368 A101	15m	multicolored	20	15
369 A101	25m	multicolored	30	15
370 A101	45m	brt bl & multi	45	25
371 A101	60m	multicolored	80	40
		Nos. 366-371 (6)	2.05	
		Set value		1.00

Establishment of the Libyan Arab Republic, Sept. 1, 1969. See Nos. 379-384.

1970, Mar. 1 Photo. *Perf. 11½*
Granite Paper

372 A102	15m	multicolored	22	15
373 A102	20m	multicolored	38	18
374 A102	25m	multicolored	45	22
375 A102	40m	multicolored	60	38

Map of Arab League Countries, Flag and Emblem A102a

1970, Mar. 22

376 A102a	10m	lt bl, brn & grn	15	15
377 A102a	15m	org, brn & grn	15	15
378 A102a	20m	ol, brn & grn	22	20
		Set value	42	35

25th anniversary of the Arab League.

Type A101 Redrawn — A103

1970, May 2 Photo. *Perf. 12x12½*

379 A103	5m	org & multi	15	15
380 A103	10m	ultra & multi	15	15
381 A103	15m	multicolored	16	15
382 A103	25m	multicolored	25	15
383 A103	45m	brt bl & multi	50	20
384 A103	60m	multicolored	60	25
		Nos. 379-384 (6)	1.81	
		Set value		70

On Nos. 379-384 the numerals are in black, the bottom inscription is in 2 lines and several other changes.

Inauguration of UPU Headquarters, Bern — A104

1970, May 20 Photo. *Perf. 11½x11*

385 A104	10m	multicolored	15	15
386 A104	25m	multicolored	20	15
387 A104	60m	multicolored	45	22
		Set value		38

Arms of Libyan Arab Republic A105

Flags, Soldiers and Tank A106

1970, June 20 Photo. *Perf. 11*

388 A105	15m	black & brt rose	15	15
389 A105	25m	vio bl, yel & brt rose	22	15
390 A105	45m	emer, yel & brt rose	55	20
		Set value		35

Evacuation of US military base in Libya.

1970, Sept. 1 Photo. *Perf. 11x11½*

391 A106	20m	multicolored	45	16
392 A106	25m	multicolored	55	22
393 A106	30m	blue & multi	90	45

Libyan Arab Republic, 1st anniv.

UN Emblem, Dove and Scales — A107

1970, Oct. 24 Photo. *Perf. 11x11½*

394 A107	5m	org & multi	38	15
395 A107	10m	olive & multi	45	22
396 A107	60m	multicolored	90	40

25th anniversary of the United Nations.

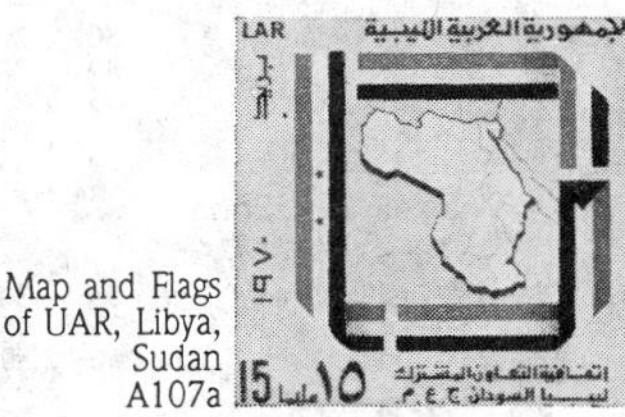

Map and Flags of UAR, Libya, Sudan A107a

1970, Dec. 27 Photo. *Perf. 11½*

397 A107a	15m	lt grn, car & blk	1.50	60

Signing of the Charter of Tripoli affirming the unity of UAR, Libya and the Sudan, Dec. 27, 1970.

UN Emblem, Dove and Globe — A108

1971, Jan. 10 Litho. *Perf. 12x11½*

398 A108	15m	multicolored	38	15
399 A108	20m	multicolored	45	16
400 A108	60m	lt vio & multi	90	30

UN declaration on granting of independence to colonial countries and peoples, 10th anniv.

Education Year Emblem — A109

Al Fatah Fighter — A110

1971, Jan. 16

401 A109	5m	red, blk & ocher	16	15
402 A109	10m	red, blk & emer	30	15
403 A109	20m	red, blk & vio bl	60	15
		Set value		28

International Education Year.

1971, Mar. 14 Photo. *Perf. 11*

404 A110	5m	ol & multi	50	15
405 A110	10m	yel & multi	80	15
406 A110	100m	multicolored	1.90	20

Fight for the liberation of Palestine.

Tripoli Fair Emblem A111

10th Anniv. of OPEC A112

1971, Mar. 18 Litho. *Perf. 14*

407 A111	15m	multicolored	20	15
408 A111	30m	org & multi	30	15
		Set value		22

9th International Fair at Tripoli.

1971, May 29 Litho. *Perf. 12*

409 A112	10m	yellow & brown	15	15
410 A112	70m	pink & vio bl	55	25
		Set value		30

Globe and Waves A113

1971, June 10 *Perf. 14½x13½*

411 A113	25m	brt grn, blk & vio bl	20	15
412 A113	35m	gray & multi	22	15
		Set value		24

3rd World Telecommunications Day, May 17, 1971.

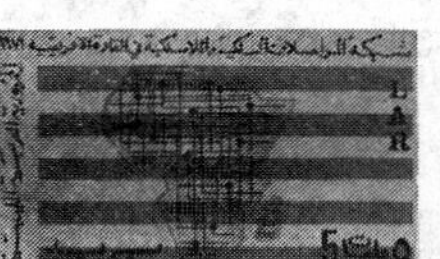

Map of Africa and Telecommunications Network — A114

1971, June 10

413 A114	5m	yel, blk & grn	15	15
414 A114	15m	dl bl, blk & grn	40	22
		Set value		28

Pan-African telecommunications system.

Torchbearer and Banner — A115

Ramadan Suehli — A116

1971, June 15 Photo. *Perf. 11½x12*

415 A115 5m yel & multi 20 15
416 A115 10m org & multi 35 15
417 A115 15m multicolored 50 15
Set value 16

Evacuation of US military base, 1st anniv.

1971, Aug. 24 *Perf. 14x14½*

418 A116 15m multicolored 15 15
419 A116 55m bl & multi 22 15
Set value 20

Ramadan Suehli (1879-1920), freedom fighter.
See #422-423, 426-427, 439-440, 479-480.

Date Palm — A117

Gamal Abdel Nasser (1918-1970), President of Egypt — A118

1971, Sept. 1

420 A117 5m multicolored 20 15
421 A117 15m multicolored 40 15
Set value 16

Sept. 1, 1969 Revolution, 2nd anniv.

Portrait Type of 1971

Portrait: Omar el Mukhtar (1858-1931), leader of the Martyrs.

1971, Sept. 16 *Perf. 14x14½*

422 A116 5m lt grn & multi 15 15
423 A116 100m multicolored 70 25
Set value 30

1971, Sept. 28 Photo. *Perf. 11x11½*

424 A118 5m lil, grn & blk 15 15
425 A118 15m grn, lil & blk 22 15
Set value 22

Portrait Type of 1971

Portrait: Ibrahim Usta Omar (1908-1950), patriotic poet.

1971, Oct. 8 Litho. *Perf. 14x14½*

426 A116 25m vio bl & multi 20 15
427 A116 30m multicolored 25 15

Racial Equality Emblem A119

Arab Postal Union Emblem A120

1971, Oct. 24 *Perf. 13½x14½*

428 A119 25m multicolored 22 15
429 A119 35m multicolored 30 15
Set value 22

Intl. Year Against Racial Discrimination.

1971, Nov. 6 Litho. *Perf. 14½*
Emblem in Black, Yellow and Blue

430 A120 5m red 15 15
431 A120 10m violet 15 15
432 A120 15m bright rose lil 20 15
Set value 36 20

Conference of Sofar, Lebanon, establishing Arab Postal Union, 25th anniv.

Postal Union Emblem and Letter A121

Design: 25m, 55m, APU emblem, letter and dove.

1971, Dec. Photo. *Perf. 11½x11*

433 A121 10m org brn, bl & blk 15 15
434 A121 15m org, lt bl & blk 15 15
435 A121 25m lt grn, org & blk 22 15
436 A121 55m lt brn, yel & blk 42 22
Set value 40

10th anniversary of African Postal Union.
Issue dates: 25m, 55m, Dec. 2; 10m, 15m, Dec. 12.

Book Year Emblem A122

Coat of Arms A123

1972, Jan. 1 Litho. *Perf. 12½x13*

437 A122 15d ultra, brn, gold & blk 20 15
438 A122 20d gold, brn, ultra & blk 22 15

International Book Year.

Portrait Type of 1971

Portrait: Ahmed Gnaba (1898-1968), poet of unity.

1972, Jan. 12 *Perf. 14x14½*

439 A116 20m red & multi 20 15
440 A116 35m olive & multi 22 15
Set value 20

1972, Feb. 10 Photo. *Perf. 14½*
Size: 19x23mm

441 A123 5m gray & multi 15 15
442 A123 10m lt ol & multi 16 15
443 A123 15d lilac & multi 15 15
445 A123 25m lt bl & multi 15 15
446 A123 30m rose & multi 22 15
447 A123 35m lt ol & multi 35 15
448 A123 40m dl yel & multi 25 15
449 A123 45m lt grn & multi 30 15
451 A123 55m multicolored 35 20
452 A123 60m bis & multi 50 20
453 A123 65d multicolored 40 22
454 A123 70d lt vio & multi 55 22
455 A123 80d ocher & multi 70 25
456 A123 90m bl & multi 1.10 35

Size: 27x32mm
Perf. 14x14½

457 A123 100d multicolored 1.50 38
458 A123 200d multicolored 2.25 45
459 A123 500d multicolored 4.50 2.50
460 A123 £1 multicolored 9.00 5.00
Nos. 441-460 (18) 22.58 10.97

A124

20m

50m

Coil Stamps

1972, July 27 Photo. *Perf. 14½x14*

461 A124 5m sl bl, ocher & black 70 15
462 A124 20m bl, lil & blk 2.75 30
463 A124 50m bl, ol & blk 6.00 1.10

See Nos. 496-498, 575-577.

Tombs at Ghirza — A125

Fair Emblem — A126

Designs: 10m, Kufic inscription, Agedabia, horiz. 15m, Marcus Aurelius Arch, Tripoli. 25m, Exchange of weapons, mural from Wan Amil Cave. 55m, Garamanthian (Berber) chariot, petroglyph, Wadi Zigza. 70m, Nymph Cyrene strangling a lion, bas-relief, Cyrene.

1972, Feb. 15 Litho. *Perf. 14*

464 A125 5m lilac & multi 15 15
465 A125 10m multicolored 15 15
466 A125 15m dp org & multi 16 15
467 A125 25m emer & multi 25 15
468 A125 55m scar & multi 70 22
469 A125 70m ultra & multi 1.00 38
Nos. 464-469 (6) 2.41
Set value 92

1972, Mar. 1

470 A126 25d gray & multi 22 15
471 A126 35d multicolored 30 18
472 A126 50d multicolored 55 25
473 A126 70d multicolored 70 38

10th International Fair at Tripoli.

Dissected Arm, and Heart — A127

"Arab Unity" — A128

1972, Apr. 7 *Perf. 14½*

474 A127 15d multicolored 80 30
475 A127 25d multicolored 1.50 60

"Your heart is your health," World Health Day.

Perf. 13½x13
1972, Apr. 17 Litho. & Engr.

476 A128 15d bl, yel & blk 15 15
477 A128 20d lt grn, yel & blk 20 15
478 A128 25d lt ver, yel & blk 55 20
Set value 40

Federation of Arab Republics Foundation, 1st anniv.

Portrait Type of 1971

Portrait: Suleiman el Baruni (1870-1940), patriotic writer.

1972, May 1 Litho. *Perf. 14x14½*

479 A116 10m yellow & multi 70 22
480 A116 70m dp org & multi 1.10 60

Environment Emblem A129

Olympic Emblems A130

1972, Aug. 15 Litho. *Perf. 14½*

481 A129 15m red & multi 38 15
482 A129 55m green & multi 80 22

UN Conference on Human Environment, Stockholm, June 5-16.

1972, Aug. 26

483 A130 25d brt bl & multi 70 30
484 A130 35d red & multi 1.10 60

20th Olympic Games, Munich, Aug. 26-Sept. 11.

Emblem and Broken Chain A131

Dome of the Rock, Jerusalem A132

1972, Oct. 1 Litho. *Perf. 14x13½*

485 A131 15d blue & multi 15 15
486 A131 25d yellow & multi 30 15
Set value 18

Libyan Arab Republic, 3rd anniv.

1972 *Perf. 12½x13*

487 A132 10d multicolored 35 15
488 A132 25d multicolored 50 15
Set value 16

Nicolaus Copernicus (1473-1543), Polish Astronomer A133

Blind Person, Books, Loom and Basket A135

Eagle and Fair Buildings A134

Design: 25d, Copernicus in Observatory, by Jan Matejko, horiz.

Perf. 14½x13½, 13½x14½
1973, Feb. 26

489 A133 15d yellow & multi 18 15
490 A133 25d blue & multi 22 15
Set value 22

1973, Mar. 1 *Perf. 13½x14½*

491 A134 5d dull red & multi 20 15
492 A134 10d blue grn & multi 22 15
493 A134 15d vio blue & multi 45 15
Set value 28

11th International Fair at Tripoli.

1973, Apr. 18 Photo. *Perf. 12x11½*

494 A135 20d gray & multi 2.25 45
495 A135 25d dull yel & multi 4.50 1.40

Role of the blind in society.

Coil Stamps
Numeral Type of 1972 Denominations in Dirhams

5d 20d 50d

1973, Apr. 26 Photo. *Perf. 14½x14*

496 A124 5d sl bl, ocher & blk 50 15
497 A124 20d blue, lilac & blk 65 16
498 A124 50d blue, olive & blk 1.50 22
Set value 42

Map of Africa — A136

1973, May 25 Photo. ***Perf. 11x11½***

499 A136 15d yel, green & brown 22 15
500 A136 25d lt yel grn, grn & blk 38 15
Set value 22

"Freedom in Unity" (Org. for African Unity).

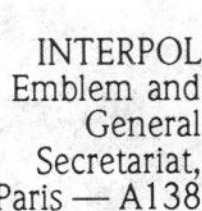

INTERPOL Emblem and General Secretariat, Paris — A138

Perf. 13½x14½

1973, June 30 Litho.

501 A138 10d lilac & multi 15 15
502 A138 15d ocher & multi 22 15
503 A138 25d lt grn & multi 38 15
Set value 24

50th anniv. of Intl. Criminal Police Org.

Map of Libya, Houses, People, Factories, Tractor A139

1973, July 15 Photo. ***Perf. 11½***

504 A139 10d rose red, black & ultra 90 25
505 A139 25d ultra, blk & grn 1.50 50
506 A139 35d grn, blk & org 2.50 75

General census.

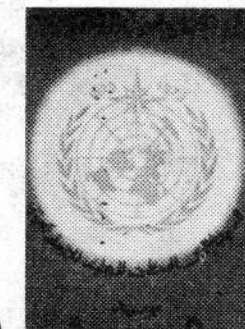

UN Emblem — A140

1973, Aug. 1 ***Perf. 12½x11***

507 A140 5d ver, blk & bl 15 15
508 A140 10d yel grn, blk & bl 22 15
Set value 15

Intl. meteorological cooperation, cent.

Soccer — A141

1973, Aug. 10 Photo. ***Perf. 11½***

509 A141 5d yel grn & dk brn 42 16
510 A141 25d orange & dk brn 80 15

2nd Palestinian Cup Soccer Tournament.

Torch and Grain — A142

Writing Hand, Lamp and Globe — A143

1973, Sept. 1 Litho. ***Perf. 14***

511 A142 15d brown & multi 18 15
512 A142 25d emer & multi 45 15
Set value 16

4th anniv. of Sept. 1 Revolution.

1973, Sept. 8

513 A143 25d multicolored 30 15

Literacy campaign.

Gate of First City Hall A144

Militia, Flag and Factories A145

1973, Sept. 18 ***Perf. 13***

514 A144 10d shown 20 15
515 A144 25d Khondok fountain 22 15
516 A144 35d Clock tower 38 15
Set value 24

Centenary of Tripoli as a municipality.

1973, Oct. 7 Photo. ***Perf. 11½x11***

517 A145 15d yel, blk & red 20 15
518 A145 25d green & multi 22 15
Set value 16

Libyan Militia.

Revolutionary Proclamation by Khadafy — A146

Design: 70d, as 25d, with English inscription.

1973, Oct. 15 Litho. ***Perf. 12½***

519 A146 25d orange & multi 20 15
520 A146 70d green & multi 45 22
Set value 28

Proclamation of People's Revolution by Pres. Muammar Khadafy.

FAO Emblem, Camel Pulling Plow A147

1973, Nov. 1 Photo. ***Perf. 11***

521 A147 10d ocher & multi 15 15
522 A147 25d dk brn & multi 20 15
523 A147 35d black & multi 22 15
Set value 22

World Food Org., 10th anniv.

Human Rights Flame — A148

1973, Dec. 20 Photo. ***Perf. 11x11½***

524 A148 25d pur, car & dk bl 20 15
525 A148 70d lt grn, car & dk bl 45 22
Set value 28

Universal Declaration of Human Rights, 25th anniv.

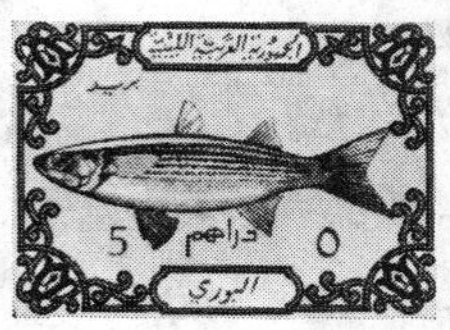

Fish — A149

Designs: Various fish from Libyan waters.

1973, Dec. 31 Photo. ***Perf. 14x13½***

526 A149 5d lt blue & multi 15 15
527 A149 10d lt blue & multi 20 15
528 A149 15d lt blue & multi 25 15
529 A149 20d lt blue & multi 42 15
530 A149 25d lt blue & multi 70 16
Nos. 526-530 (5) 1.72
Set value 45

1975, Jan. 5

526a A149 5d grnsh bl & multi 15 15
527a A149 10d grnsh bl & multi 15 15
528a A149 15d grnsh bl & multi 16 15
529a A149 20d grnsh bl & multi 35 15
530a A149 25d grnsh bl & multi 38 15
Nos. 526a-530a (5) 1.19
Set value 30

Scout, Sun and Scout Signs — A150

Fair Emblem, Flags of Participants — A151

1974, Feb. 1 Litho. ***Perf. 11½***

531 A150 5d blue & multi 28 15
532 A150 20d lt lil & multi 70 18
533 A150 25d lt grn & multi 1.50 30

Libyan Boy Scouts.

1974, Mar. 1 Litho. ***Perf. 12x11½***

534 A151 10d lt ultra & multi 22 15
535 A151 25d tan & multi 38 15
536 A151 35d lt green & multi 50 15
Set value 25

12th Tripoli International Fair.

Protected Family, WHO Emblem — A152

Minaret and Star — A153

1974, Apr. 7 Litho. ***Perf. 12½***

537 A152 5d lt green & multi 15 15
538 A152 25d red & multi 22 15
Set value 20

World Health Day.

1974, Apr. 16 ***Perf. 11½x11***

539 A153 10d pink & multi 16 15
540 A153 25d yellow & multi 30 15
541 A153 35d orange & multi 60 22
Set value 38

City University of Bengazi, inauguration.

UPU Emblem and Star — A154

Traffic Signs — A156

Perf. 13½x14½

1974, May 22 Litho.

542 A154 25d multicolored 2.25 38
543 A154 70d multicolored 5.00 80

Centenary of Universal Postal Union.

1974, June 8 Photo. ***Perf. 11***

547 A156 5d gold & multi 15 15
548 A156 10d gold & multi 15 15
549 A156 25d gold & multi 20 15
Set value 24

Automobile and Touring Club of Libya.

Tank, Oil Refinery, Book — A157

Symbolic "5" — A158

1974, Sept. 1 Litho. ***Perf. 14***

550 A157 5d red & multi 15 15
551 A157 20d violet & multi 15 15
552 A157 25d vio bl & multi 15 15
553 A157 35d green & multi 15 15
Set value 34 22

Souvenir Sheet

Perf. 13

554 A158 55d yel & maroon 2.00 1.75

Revolution of Sept. 1, 5th anniv. English inscription on No. 553.

WPY Emblem and Crowd — A159

Libyan Woman — A160

1974, Oct. 19 ***Perf. 14***

555 A159 25d multicolored 20 15
556 A159 35d lt brn & multi 22 15
Set value 22

World Population Year.

1975, Mar. 1 Litho. ***Perf. 13x12½***

Libyan Costumes: 10d, 15d, Women. 20d, Old man. 25d, Man riding camel. 50d, Man on horseback.

557 A160 5d org yel & multi 15 15
558 A160 10d org yel & multi 15 15
559 A160 15d org yel & multi 15 15
560 A160 20d org yel & multi 15 15
561 A160 25d org yel & multi 20 15
562 A160 50d org yel & multi 42 20
Set value 95 45

Congress Emblem — A161

1975, Mar. 4 Litho. *Perf. 12x12½*

563 A161 10d brown & multi 15 15
564 A161 25d vio & multi 15 15
565 A161 35d gray & multi 22 15
Set value 38 25

Arab Labor Congress.

Teacher Pointing to Blackboard A162

1975, Mar. 10 *Perf. 11½*

566 A162 10d gold & multi 15 15
567 A162 25d gold & multi 15 15
Set value 22 15

Teacher's Day.

Bodies, Globe, Proclamation A163

Woman and Man in Library A164

1975, Apr. 7 Litho. *Perf. 12½*

568 A163 20d lilac & multi 15 15
569 A163 25d emer & multi 18 15
Set value 15

World Health Day.

1975, May 25 Litho. *Perf. 12½*

570 A164 10d bl grn & multi 15 15
571 A164 25d olive & multi 15 15
572 A164 35d lt vio & multi 20 15
Set value 22

Libyan Arab Book Exhibition.

Festival Emblem — A165

Games Emblem and Arms — A166

1975, July 5 Litho. *Perf. 13x12½*

573 A165 20d lt bl & multi 15 15
574 A165 25d orange & multi 20 15
Set value 15

2nd Arab Youth Festival.

Coil Stamps

Redrawn Type of 1973 Without "LAR"

1975, Aug. 15 Photo. *Perf. 14½x14*

575 A124 5d blue, org & blk 25 15
576 A124 20d blue, yel & blk 50 15
577 A124 50d blue, grn & blk 65 15
Set value 22

1975, Aug. 23 *Perf. 13x12½*

578 A166 10d salmon & multi 15 15
579 A166 25d lilac & multi 15 15
580 A166 50d yellow & multi 30 16
Set value 28

7th Mediterranean Games, Algiers, Aug. 23-Sept. 6.

Peace Dove, Symbols of Agriculture and Industry — A167

Khadafy's Head Over Desert — A168

Design: 70d, Peace dove (different design).

1975, Sept. Litho. *Perf. 13x12½*

581 A167 25d multicolored 20 15
582 A167 70d multicolored 45 15

Souvenir Sheet

Imperf

Litho. & Embossed

583 A168 100d multicolored 1.90 1.90

6th anniversary of Sept. 1 revolution. No. 583 contains one stamp with simulated perforations.

Khalil Basha Mosque — A169

Al Kharruba Mosque — A170

Mosques: 10d, Sidi Abdulla El Shaab. 15d, Sidi Ali El Fergani. 25d, Katikhtha. 30d, Murad Agha. 35d, Maulai Mohammed.

1975, Dec. 13 Litho. *Perf. 12½*

584 A169 5d gray & multi 15 15
585 A169 10d purple & multi 15 15
586 A169 15d green & multi 16 15
587 A170 20d ocher & multi 20 15
588 A170 25d multicolored 22 15
589 A170 30d multicolored 25 15
590 A170 35d lilac & multi 35 15
Nos. 584-590 (7) 1.48
Set value 40

Mohammed's 1405th birthday.

Arms of Libya and People — A171

Islamic- Christian Dialogue Emblem — A172

1976, Jan. 15 Photo. *Perf. 13*

591 A171 35d blue & multi 20 15
592 A171 40d multicolored 22 15
Set value 18

General National (People's) Congress.

1976, Feb. 5 Litho. *Perf. 13x12½*

593 A172 40d gold & multi 20 15
594 A172 115d gold & multi 55 15
Set value 20

Seminar of Islamic-Christian Dialogue, Tripoli, Feb. 1-5.

Woman Blowing Horn — A173

National Costumes: 20d, Lancer. 30d, Drummer. 40d, Bagpiper. 100d, Woman carrying jug on head.

1976, Mar. 1 Litho. *Perf. 13x12½*

595 A173 10d multicolored 15 15
596 A173 20d multicolored 15 15
597 A173 30d pink & multi 20 15
598 A173 40d multicolored 22 15
599 A173 100d yel & multi 70 28
Nos. 595-599 (5) 1.42
Set value 64

14th Tripoli International Fair.

Telephones, 1876 and 1976, ITU and UPU Emblems A174

Design: 70d, Alexander Graham Bell, telephone, satellites, radar, ITU and UPU emblems.

1976, Mar. 10 Photo. *Perf. 13*

600 A174 40d multicolored 60 15
a. Souvenir sheet of 4 5.00 5.00
601 A174 70d multicolored 1.20 20
a. Souvenir sheet of 4 6.50 6.50

Centenary of first telephone call by Alexander Graham Bell, Mar. 10, 1876.

Mother and Child — A175

Hands, Eye and Head — A176

1976, Mar. 21 *Perf. 12*

602 A175 85d gray & multi 40 25
603 A175 110d pink & multi 60 30

International Children's Day.

1976, Apr. 7 Photo. *Perf. 13½x13*

604 A176 30d multicolored 15 15
605 A176 35d multicolored 16 15
606 A176 40d multicolored 20 15
Set value 30

"Foresight prevents blindness;" World Health Day.

Little Bittern A177

Birds of Libya: 10d, Great gray shrike. 15d, Songbird. 20d, European bee-eater, vert. 25d, Hoopoe.

Perf. 13x13½, 13½x13

1976, May 1 Litho.

607 A177 5d orange & multi *22* 15
608 A177 10d ultra & multi *42* 16
609 A177 15d rose & multi *80* 22
610 A177 20d yellow & multi *1.20* 30
611 A177 25d blue & multi *1.50* 45
Nos. 607-611 (5) *4.14* 1.28

Al Barambekh — A178

Bicycling — A179

Designs: 15d, Whale, horiz. 30d, Lizard (alwaral), horiz. 40d, Mastodon skull, horiz. 70d, Hawk. 115d, Wild mountain sheep.

1976, June 20 Litho. *Perf. 12½*

612 A178 10d multicolored 15 15
613 A178 15d multicolored 22 15
614 A178 30d multicolored 32 15
615 A178 40d multicolored 38 18
616 A178 70d multicolored 75 32
617 A178 115d multicolored 1.40 55
Nos. 612-617 (6) 3.22
Set value 1.25

Museum of Natural History.

1976, July 17 Litho. *Perf. 12x11½*

Granite Paper

618 A179 15d shown 15 15
619 A179 25d Boxing 15 15
620 A179 70d Soccer 35 20
Set value 32

Souvenir Sheet

621 A179 150d Symbolic of various sports *9.00 9.00*

21st Olympic Games, Montreal, Canada, July 17-Aug. 1.

Tree Growing from Globe — A180

Symbols of Agriculture and Industry — A181

Drummer and Pipeline — A182

1976, Aug. 9 *Perf. 13*

622 A180 115d multicolored 45 30

5th Conference of Non-Aligned Countries, Colombo, Sri Lanka, Aug. 9-19.

Beginning with No. 622 numerous issues are printed with multiple coats of arms in pale green on back of stamps.

1976, Sept. 1 *Perf. 14½x14*

623 A181 30d yel & multi 15 15
624 A181 40d multicolored 15 15
625 A181 100d multicolored 40 25
Set value 42

Souvenir Sheet

Perf. 13

626 A182 200d multicolored 1.90 1.90

Sept. 1 Revolution, 7th anniv.

Sports, Torch and Emblems A183

Chess Board, Rook, Knight, Emblem A184

Design: 145d, Symbolic wrestlers and various emblems, horiz.

1976, Oct. 6 Litho. *Perf. 13*

627 A183 15d multicolored 15 15
628 A183 30d multicolored 22 15
629 A183 100d multicolored 60 25
Set value 38

Souvenir Sheet

630 A183 145d multicolored 1.50 1.50

5th Arab Games, Damascus, Syria.

1976, Oct. 24 Photo. *Perf. 11½*

631 A184 15d pink & multi 55 15
632 A184 30d buff & multi 1.10 20
633 A184 100d multicolored 1.40 30

The "Against" (protest) Chess Olympiad, Tripoli, Oct. 24-Nov. 15.

A185

Designs: Various local flowers.

1976, Nov. 1 Photo. *Perf. 11½*

Granite Paper

634 A185 15d lilac & multi 15 15
635 A185 20d multicolored 15 15
636 A185 35d yellow & multi 20 15
637 A185 40d salmon & multi 25 15
638 A185 70d multicolored 60 22
Nos. 634-638 (5) 1.35
Set value 58

International Archives Council Emblem and Document — A186

1976, Nov. 10 Litho. *Perf. 13x13½*

639 A186 15d brown, org & buff 15 15
640 A186 35d brn, brt grn & buff 15 15
641 A186 70d brown, blue & buff 30 20
Set value 32

Arab Regional Branch of International Council on Archives, Baghdad.

Holy Ka'aba and Pilgrims A187

Numeral A188

1976, Dec. 12 Litho. *Perf. 14*

642 A187 15d multicolored 15 15
643 A187 30d multicolored 15 15
644 A187 70d multicolored 25 20
645 A187 100d multicolored 40 25
Set value 82 58

Pilgrimage to Mecca.

Coil Stamps

1977, Jan. 15 Photo. *Perf. 14½x14*

646 A188 5d multicolored 15 15
647 A188 20d multicolored 15 15
648 A188 50d multicolored 22 15
Set value 36 25

Covered Basket — A189

Designs: 20d, Leather bag. 30d, Vase. 40d, Embroidered slippers. 50d, Ornate saddle. 100d, Horse with saddle and harness.

1977, Mar. 1 Litho. *Perf. 12½x12*

649 A189 10d multicolored 15 15
650 A189 20d multicolored 15 15
651 A189 30d multicolored 16 15
652 A189 40d multicolored 20 15
653 A189 50d multicolored 25 15
Set value 75 45

Souvenir Sheet

Imperf

654 A189 100d multicolored 60 60

15th Tripoli International Fair. No. 654 contains one stamp 49x53mm with simulated perforations.

Girl and Flowers, UNICEF Emblem A190

Children's drawings, UNICEF Emblem and: 30d, Clothing store. 40d, Farm yard.

1977, Mar. 28 Litho. *Perf. 13x13½*

655 A190 10d multicolored 15 15
656 A190 30d multicolored 16 15
657 A190 40d multicolored 20 15
Set value 40 28

Children's Day.

Gun, Fighters, UN Headquarters A191

1977, Mar. 13 *Perf. 13½*

658 A191 15d multicolored 50 15
659 A191 25d multicolored 65 15
660 A191 70d multicolored 1.40 22
Set value 35

Battle of Al-Karamah, 9th anniversary.

Child, Raindrop, WHO Emblem — A192

Arab Postal Union, 25th Anniv. — A193

1977, Apr. 7 Litho. *Perf. 13x12½*

661 A192 15d multicolored 15 15
662 A192 30d multicolored 25 15
Set value 15

World Health Day.

1977, Apr. 12 *Perf. 13½*

663 A193 15d multicolored 15 15
664 A193 30d multicolored 25 15
665 A193 40d multicolored 40 16
Set value 28

Maps of Africa and Libya A194

1977, May 8 Litho. *Perf. 14x13½*

666 A194 40d multicolored 50 20
667 A194 70d multicolored 65 30

African Labor Day.

Map of Libya and Heart — A195

1977, May 10 *Perf. 14½x14*

668 A195 5d multicolored 15 15
669 A195 10d multicolored 22 15
670 A195 30d multicolored 42 15
Set value 24

Libyan Red Crescent Society.

Electronic Tree, ITU Emblem, Satellite and Radar A196

Electronic Tree, ITU Emblem and: 115d, Communications satellite, Montreal Olympics emblem, boxer on TV screen. 200d, Spacecraft over earth. 300d, Solar system.

1977, May 17 Litho. *Perf. 13½x13*

671 A196 60d multicolored 30 20
672 A196 115d multicolored 62 38
673 A196 200d multicolored 1.20 62

Souvenir Sheet

674 A196 300d multicolored *3.00 3.00*

9th World Telecommunications Day. No. 674 contains one stamp 52x35mm.

Plane over Tripoli, Messenger A197

UPU Emblem and: 25d, Concorde, messenger on horseback. 150d, Loading transport plane and messenger riding camel. 300d, Graf Zeppelin LZ127 over Tripoli.

1977, May 17 Litho. *Perf. 13½*

675 A197 20d multicolored 15 15
676 A197 25d multicolored 15 15
677 A197 150d multicolored 90 45
Set value 58

Souvenir Sheet

678 A197 300d multicolored *3.00 3.00*

UPU centenary (in 1974). No. 678 contains one stamp 52x35mm.

Mosque — A198

Various Mosques. 50d, 100d, vertical.

1977, June 1 Photo. *Perf. 14*

679 A198 40d multicolored 20 15
680 A198 50d multicolored 25 15
681 A198 70d multicolored 35 20
682 A198 90d multicolored 45 30
683 A198 100d multicolored 55 38
684 A198 115d multicolored 62 40
Nos. 679-684 (6) 2.42 1.58

Palestinian Archbishop Hilarion Capucci, Jailed by Israel in 1974, Map of Palestine — A199

1977, Aug. 18 Litho. *Perf. 13½*

687 A199 30d multicolored 35 15
688 A199 40d multicolored 50 15
689 A199 115d multicolored 70 38
Set value 58

Raised Hands, Pylons, Wheel, Buildings — A200

Star and Ornament — A201

1977, Sept. 1 Litho. *Perf. 13½x12½*

690 A200 15d multicolored 16 15
691 A200 30d multicolored 35 15
692 A200 85d multicolored 50 22
Set value 35

Souvenir Sheet

Perf. 12½

693 A201 100d gold & multi 70 70

8th anniversary of Sept. 1 Revolution.

Soccer A202

1977, Oct. 8 *Perf. 13½*

No.	Type	Value	Description	Unused	Used
694	A202	5d	Swimmers, vert.	15	15
695	A202	10d	shown	15	15
696	A202	15d	Soccer, vert.	15	15
697	A202	25d	Table tennis	22	20
698	A202	40d	Basketball, vert.	38	22
			Set value	85	60

7th Arab School Games.

Steeplechase — A203

Show Emblem and: 10d, Bedouin on horseback. 15d, Show emblem (Horse and "7"), vert. 45d, Steeplechase. 100d, Hurdles. 115d, Bedouins on horseback.

1977, Oct. 10 *Perf. 14½*

No.	Type	Value	Description	Unused	Used
699	A203	5d	multicolored	15	15
700	A203	10d	multicolored	15	15
701	A203	15d	multicolored	15	15
702	A203	45d	multicolored	30	15
703	A203	115d	multicolored	70	40
			Set value	1.25	70

Souvenir Sheet

No.	Type	Value	Description	Unused	Used
704	A203	100d	multicolored	70	70

7th Intl. Turf Championships, Tripoli, Oct. 1977.

Dome of the Rock, Jerusalem — A204

1977, Oct. 14 *Perf. 14½x14*

No.	Type	Value	Description	Unused	Used
705	A204	5d	multicolored	38	15
706	A204	10d	multicolored	50	15
			Set value		15

Palestinian fighters and their families.

"The Green Book" — A205

Designs: 35d, Hands with broken chain holding hook over citadel. 40d, Hands above chaos. 115d, Dove and Green Book rising from Africa, world map.

1977 **Litho.** *Perf. 14*

No.	Type	Description	Unused	Used
707	A205	Strip of 3	1.65	1.65
a.		35d multicolored	35	35
b.		40d multicolored	50	50
c.		115d multicolored	65	65

The Greek Book, by Khadafy outlines Libyan democracy. Green descriptive inscription on back beneath gum, in English on 35d, French on 40d, Arabic on 115d.

Emblems A206

1977 *Perf. 12½x13*

No.	Type	Value	Description	Unused	Used
708	A206	5d	multicolored	15	15
709	A206	15d	multicolored	15	15
710	A206	30d	multicolored	16	15
			Set value	28	20

Standardization Day.

Crocodile and Young A207

Rock Carvings, Wadi Mathendous, c. 8000 B.C.: 15d, Elephant hunt. 20d, Giraffe, vert. 30d, Antelope. 40d, Trumpeting elephant.

1978, Jan. 1 *Perf. 12½x13, 13x12½*

No.	Type	Value	Description	Unused	Used
711	A207	10d	multicolored	15	15
712	A207	15d	multicolored	15	15
713	A207	20d	multicolored	15	15
714	A207	30d	multicolored	20	15
715	A207	40d	multicolored	22	20
			Set value	70	50

Silver Pendant — A208

Emblem, Compass and Lightning — A209

Silver Jewelry: 10d, Ornamental plate. 20d, Necklace with pendants. 25d, Crescent-shaped brooch. 115d, Armband.

1978, Mar. 1 **Litho.** *Perf. 13x12½*

No.	Type	Value	Description	Unused	Used
716	A208	5d	multicolored	15	15
717	A208	10d	multicolored	15	15
718	A208	20d	multicolored	15	15
719	A208	25d	multicolored	15	15
720	A208	115d	multicolored	60	38
			Set value	90	55

Tripoli International Fair.

1978, Mar. 10 *Perf. 13½*

No.	Type	Value	Description	Unused	Used
721	A209	30d	multicolored	20	15
722	A209	115d	multicolored	70	38

Arab Cultural Education Organization.

Bride and Attendants A210

Children's drawings and UNESCO emblem.

1978, Mar. 21

No.	Type	Value	Description	Unused	Used
723	A210	40d	Dancing	20	15
724	A210	40d	Children with posters	20	15
725	A210	40d	Shopping street	20	15
726	A210	40d	Playground	20	15
727	A210	40d	shown	20	15
			Nos. 723-727 (5)	1.00	
			Set value		60

Children's Day. Nos. 723-727 printed se-tenant.

Clenched Fist, Made of Bricks A211

1978, Mar. 22

No.	Type	Value	Description	Unused	Used
728	A211	30d	multicolored	65	15
729	A211	115d	multicolored	1.20	38

Determination of Arab people.

Blood Pressure Gauge, WHO Emblem — A212

Games Emblem — A214

Antenna and ITU Emblem A213

1978, Apr. 7 *Perf. 13x12½*

No.	Type	Value	Description	Unused	Used
730	A212	30d	multicolored	16	15
731	A212	115d	multicolored	55	38

World Health Day, drive against hypertension.

1978, May 17 **Photo.** *Perf. 13½*

No.	Type	Value	Description	Unused	Used
732	A213	30d	silver & multi	16	15
733	A213	115d	gold & multi	55	38

10th World Telecommunications Day.

1978, July 13 **Litho.** *Perf. 12½*

No.	Type	Value	Description	Unused	Used
734	A214	15d	multicolored	15	15
735	A214	30d	multicolored	15	15
736	A214	115d	multicolored	60	38
			Set value		50

3rd African Games, Algiers, 1978.

Inauguration of Tripoli International Airport — A215

1978, Aug. 10 **Litho.** *Perf. 13½*

No.	Type	Value	Description	Unused	Used
737	A215	40d	shown	50	15
738	A215	115d	Terminal	1.50	38

View of Ankara — A216

Soldiers, Jet, Ship — A217

1978, Aug. 17

No.	Type	Value	Description	Unused	Used
739	A216	30d	multicolored	42	15
740	A216	35d	multicolored	45	15
741	A216	115d	multicolored	1.50	38
			Set value		55

Turkish-Libyan friendship.

1978, Sept. 1 *Perf. 14½*

Designs: 35d, Tower, Green Book, oil derrick. 100d, View of Tripoli with mosque and modern buildings. 115d, View of Tripoli within cogwheel.

No.	Type	Value	Description	Unused	Used
742	A217	30d	multicolored	42	15
743	A217	35d	org & multi	45	15
744	A217	115d	blue & multi	1.50	38
			Set value		55

Souvenir Sheet

No.	Type	Value	Description	Unused	Used
745	A217	100d	multicolored	2.50	50

9th anniversary of Sept. 1 Revolution. No. 745 contains one stamp 50x41mm.

Quarry and Symposium Emblem — A218

Designs: 40d, Oasis lake. 115d, Crater.

1978, Sept. 16 *Perf. 13½*

No.	Type	Value	Description	Unused	Used
746	A218	30d	multicolored	20	15
747	A218	40d	multicolored	38	15
748	A218	115d	multicolored	60	38
			Set value		56

2nd Symposium on Libyan Geology.

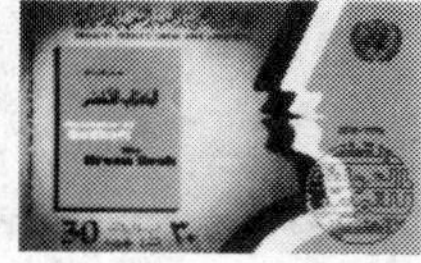
Green Book and Three Races A219

1978, Oct. 18 *Perf. 12½*

No.	Type	Value	Description	Unused	Used
749	A219	30d	multicolored	15	15
750	A219	40d	multicolored	20	15
751	A219	115d	multicolored	45	38
			Set value		56

International Anti-Apartheid Year.

Pilgrims, Minarets, Holy Kaaba A220

1978, Nov. 9 **Photo.** *Perf. 12*

No.	Type	Value	Description	Unused	Used
752	A220	5d	multicolored	15	15
753	A220	10d	multicolored	15	15
754	A220	15d	multicolored	15	15
755	A220	20d	multicolored	15	15
			Set value	30	22

Pilgrimage to Mecca.

Handclasp over Globe — A221

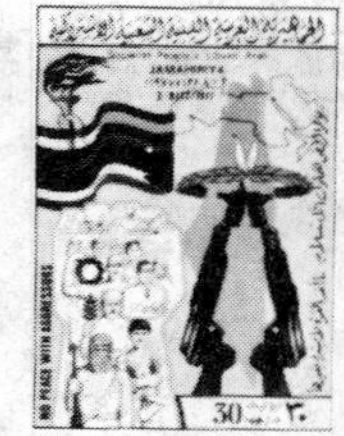

Fists, Guns, Map of Israel — A222

1978, Nov. 10 Litho. *Perf. 13½*
756 A221 30d multicolored *42* 15
757 A221 40d multicolored *50* 15
758 A221 115d multicolored *1.50* 38
Set value 56

Technical Cooperation Among Developing Countries Conference, Buenos Aires, Argentina, Sept. 1978.

1978, Dec. 5 Litho. *Perf. 13½*

Designs: 40d, 115d, Map of Arab countries and Israel, eagle and crowd, horiz. 145d, like 30d.

759 A222 30d multicolored 22 15
760 A222 40d multicolored 40 15
761 A222 115d multicolored 70 38
762 A222 145d multicolored 1.40 40

Anti-Israel Summit Conf., Baghdad, Dec. 2-8.

Scales, Globe and Human Rights Flame — A223

Libyan Fort and Horse Racing — A224

1978, Dec. 10
763 A223 15d multicolored *20* 15
764 A223 30d multicolored *30* 15
765 A223 115d multicolored *60* 38

Universal Declaration of Human Rights, 30th anniv.

1978, Dec. 11
766 A224 20d multicolored *38* 15
767 A224 40d multicolored *50* 15
768 A224 115d multicolored *1.50* 38
Set value 55

Libyan Study Center.

Lilienthal's Glider, 1896 — A225

Mounted Stag's Head — A226

Designs: 25d, Spirit of St. Louis, 1927. 30d, Adm. Byrd's Polar flight, 1929. 50d, Graf Zeppelin, 1934, hydroplane and storks. 115d, Wilbur and Orville Wright and Flyer A. No. 774, Icarus falling. No. 775, Eagle and Boeing 727.

1978, Dec. 26 Litho. *Perf. 14*
769 A225 20d multicolored 15 15
770 A225 25d multicolored 15 15
771 A225 30d multicolored 16 15
772 A225 50d multicolored 20 15
773 A225 115d multicolored 50 38
Nos. 769-773 (5) 1.16
Set value 72

Souvenir Sheets
774 A225 100d multicolored 55 55
775 A225 100d multicolored 55 55

75th anniversary of 1st powered flight. Nos. 769-773 issued also in sheets of 4.

Coil Stamps
1979, Jan. 15 Photo. *Perf. 14½x14*
776 A226 5d multicolored *35* 15
777 A226 20d multicolored *50* 15
778 A226 50d multicolored *65* 15
Set value 22

Carpobrotus Acinaciformis A227

Flora of Libya: 15d, Caralluma europaea. 20d, Arum cirenaicum. 35d, Lavatera arborea. 40d, Capparis spinosa. 50d, Ranunculus asiaticus.

1979, May 15 Litho. *Perf. 14*
779 A227 10d multicolored 15 15
780 A227 15d multicolored 15 15
781 A227 20d multicolored 15 15
782 A227 35d multicolored 28 18
783 A227 40d multicolored 28 18
784 A227 50d multicolored 35 22
Set value 1.12 75

People, Torch, Olive Branches — A228

1979 Litho. *Perf. 13x12½*
Size: 18x23mm
785 A228 5d multi *15* 15
786 A228 10d multi *15* 15
787 A228 15d multi *15* 15
788 A228 30d multi *30* 15
789 A228 50d multi *38* 15
790 A228 60d multi *42* 15
791 A228 70d multi *48* 15
792 A228 100d multi *75* 18
793 A228 115d multi *1.10* 20

Perf. 13½
Size: 26½x32mm
794 A228 200d multi *1.20* 35
795 A228 500d multi *2.25* 70
796 A228 1000d multi *5.00* 1.75
Nos. 785-796 (12) *12.33*
Set value 3.60

See Nos. 1053-1055.

Tortoise A229

Animals: 10d, Antelope. 15d, Hedgehog. 20d, Porcupine. 30d, Arabian camel. 35d, African wildcat. 45d, Gazelle. 115d, Cheetah. 10d, 30d, 35d, 45d, vert.

1979, Feb. 1 Litho. *Perf. 14½*
797 A229 5d multicolored 15 15
798 A229 10d multicolored 15 15
799 A229 15d multicolored 15 15
800 A229 20d multicolored 15 15
801 A229 30d multicolored 15 15
802 A229 35d multicolored 20 15
803 A229 45d multicolored 25 20
804 A229 115d multicolored 55 35
Set value 1.40 90

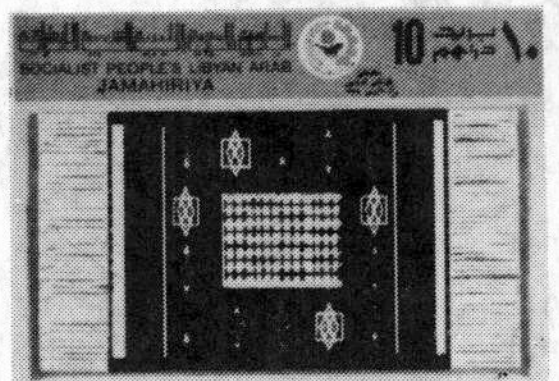
Rug and Tripoli Fair Emblem — A230

Tripoli Fair emblem and various rugs.

1979, Mar. 1 Litho. *Perf. 11*
805 A230 10d multicolored 15 15
806 A230 15d multicolored 15 15
807 A230 30d multicolored 15 15
808 A230 45d multicolored 15 15
809 A230 115d multicolored 50 38
Set value 90 60

17th Tripoli Fair.

Shepherd, Sheep and Dog A231

Children's drawings and IYC emblem.

1979, Mar. 20 *Perf. 13½*
810 A231 20d Families and planes 50 15
811 A231 20d shown 50 15
812 A231 20d Beach umbrellas 50 15
813 A231 20d Boat in storm 50 15
814 A231 20d Traffic policeman 50 15
Nos. 810-814 (5) 2.50
Set value 25

Intl. Year of the Child. Nos. 810-814 printed se-tenant.

Book, World Map, Arab Achievements A232

1979, Mar. 22 *Perf. 13*
815 A232 45d multicolored 20 15
816 A232 70d multicolored 30 20

WMO Emblem, Weather Map and Tower — A233

1979, Mar. 23
817 A233 15d multicolored 15 15
818 A233 30d multicolored 15 15
819 A233 50d multicolored 20 15
Set value 38 25

World Meteorological Day.

Medical Services, WHO Emblem A234

1979, Apr. 7
820 A234 40d multicolored 18 15

Farmer Plowing and Sheep — A235

1979, Sept. 1 Litho. *Perf. 14½*
821 Block of 4 30 20
a. A235 15d shown 15 15
b. A235 15d Men holding Green Book 15 15
c. A235 15d Oil field 15 15
d. A235 15d Oil refinery 15 15
822 Block of 4 60 38
a. A235 30d Dish antenna 15 15
b. A235 30d Hospital 15 15
c. A235 30d Doctor examining patient 15 15
d. A235 30d Surgery 15 15
823 Block of 4 75 42
a. A235 40d Street, Tripoli 18 15
b. A235 40d Steel mill 18 15
c. A235 40d Tanks 18 15
d. A235 40d Tuareg horsemen 18 15
824 Block of 4 1.50 80
a. A235 70d Revolutionaries, Green Book 35 20
b. A235 70d Crowd, map of Libya 35 20
c. A235 70d Mullah 35 20
d. A235 70d Student 35 20

Souvenir Sheets
Imperf
825 A235 50d Revolution symbols, Green Book 80 65
826 A235 50d Monument 80 65

Sept. 1st revolution, 10th anniversary.

Volleyball — A236

1979, Sept. 10
827 A236 45d shown 25 15
828 A236 115d Soccer 60 30

Universiade '79 World University Games, Mexico City, Sept.

Mediterranean Games, Split, Yugoslavia — A237

1979, Sept. 15 Litho. *Perf. 12x11½*
829 A237 15d multicolored 16 15
830 A237 30d multicolored 35 15
831 A237 70d multicolored 65 22
Set value 36

Exhibition Emblem — A238

1979, Sept. 25 Photo. *Perf. 11½x11*
832 A238 45d multicolored *28* 15
833 A238 115d multicolored *75* 30

TELECOM '79, 3rd World Telecommunications Exhibition, Geneva, Sept. 20-26.

Seminar Emblem, Green Book, Crowd — A239

1979, Oct. 1

834 A239	10d shown		*15*	15

Size: 67x43½mm

835 A239	35d Meeting hall		*28*	15

Size: 32x43½mm

836 A239	100d Col. Khadafy		*65*	30
a.	Miniature sheet, imperf.		*90*	60
	Set value			46

Intl. Seminar of the Green Book, Benghazi, Oct. 1-3. Nos. 834-836 se-tenant in continuous design. No. 836a contains an imperf. design similar to type A239.

Evacuation of Foreign Forces — A240

1979, Oct. 7

837 A240	30d shown	26	15
838 A240	40d Tuareg horsemen	38	15
	Set value		22

Souvenir Sheet

Imperf

839 A240	100d Vignettes	40	40

Cyclist, Championship Emblem — A241

1979, Nov. 21

840 A241	15d shown	15	15
841 A241	30d Cyclists, emblem, diff.	25	15
	Set value		15

Junior Cycling Championships, Tripoli, Nov. 21-23. Issued in sheetlets of 4.

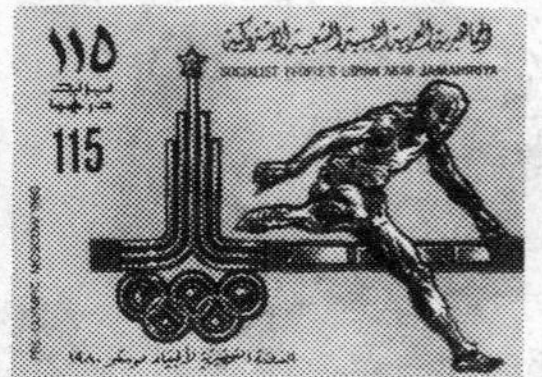
Hurdles, Olympic Rings, Moscow '80 Emblem — A242

1979, Nov. 21

842 A242	45d Equestrian	*18*	*15*
843 A242	60d Javelin	*28*	*15*
844 A242	115d shown	*60*	*20*
845 A242	160d Soccer	*75*	*28*

Souvenir Sheets

846 A242	150d like #844	*1.25*	*65*
847 A242	150d like #845	*2.50*	*65*

Pre-Olympics (Moscow '80 Olympic Games). Nos. 842-845 issued in sheetlets of 4 and sheets of 20 (4x5) with silver Moscow '80 Emblem covering background of every 20 stamps.

Intl. Day of Cooperation with Palestinian People — A242a

1979, Nov. 29 Photo. *Perf. 12*

847A A242a	30d multicolored	20	15
847B A242a	115d multicolored	70	40

Tug of War, Jumping A243

National Games: No. 848, Polo, leap frog. No. 849, Racing, ball game. No. 850, Wrestling, log rolling. No. 852, Horsemen.

1980, Feb. 15

848 A243	Block of 4	40	40
a.-d.	10d, single stamp	15	15
849 A243	Block of 4	50	40
a.-d.	15d, single stamp	15	15
850 A243	Block of 4	70	40
a.-d.	20d, single stamp	16	15
851 A243	Block of 4	1.00	65
a.-d.	30d, single stamp	25	16
852 A243	Block of 4	1.65	1.00
a.-d.	45d, single stamp	40	25
	Nos. 848-852 (5)	4.25	2.85

Battle of Gardabia, 1915 — A244

1980 Litho. *Perf. 14½*

853 A244	20d shown	*24*	*15*
854 A244	20d Shoghab, 1913	*24*	*15*
855 A244	20d Fundugh Al-Shibani, 1922	*24*	*15*
856 A244	20d Ghira	*24*	*15*
857 A244	35d Gardabia, diff.	*45*	*15*
858 A244	35d Shoghab, diff.	*45*	*15*
859 A244	35d Fundugh Al-Shibani, diff.	*45*	*15*
860 A244	35d Ghira, diff.	*45*	*15*
	Nos. 853-860 (8)	*2.76*	
	Set value		*88*

Issue dates: Gardabia, Apr. 28. Shoghab, May 25. Fundugh Al-Shibani, June 1. Ghira, Aug. 15. Stamps of same battle se-tenant in continuous design.

See Nos. 893-900, 921-944, 980-1003, 1059-1082.

Girl Guides Examining Plant — A245

1980, Aug. 22 *Perf. 13½*

861 A245	15d shown	15	15
862 A245	30d Guides cooking	30	15
863 A245	50d Scouts at campfire	48	30
864 A245	115d Scouts reading map	1.25	60

Souvenir Sheets

865 A245	100d like #861	1.00	50
866 A245	100d like #863	1.00	50

8th Pan Arab Girl Guide and 14th Pan Arab Scout Jamborees, Aug.

Men Holding OPEC Emblem — A246

1980, Sept. 15 *Perf. 14½*

867 A246	45d Emblem, globe	50	15
868 A246	115d shown	1.10	60

20th anniversary of OPEC.

Martyrdom of Omar Muktar, 1931 — A247

1980, Sept. 16

869 A247	20d multicolored	15	15
870 A247	35d multicolored	45	15
	Set value		20

Souvenir Sheet

870A A247	100d multicolored	1.90	1.90

UNESCO Emblem and Avicenna — A248

1980, Sept. 20

871 A248	45d Scientific symbols	70	15
872 A248	115d shown	1.65	60

School Scientific Exhibition, Sept. 20-24 and birth millenium of Arab physician Avicenna (115d).

18th Tripoli Fair — A249

Various musical instruments. 15d vert.

1980 Litho. *Perf. 13½*

873 A249	5d multicolored	15	15
874 A249	10d multicolored	15	15
875 A249	15d multicolored	18	15
876 A249	20d multicolored	25	15
877 A249	25d multicolored	32	18
	Set value		25

Souvenir Sheet

878 A249	100d Musicians	1.25	1.25

World Olive Oil Year A250

1980, Jan. 15 Litho. *Perf. 13½*

879 A250	15d multicolored	15	15
880 A250	30d multicolored	28	15
881 A250	45d multicolored	45	22
	Set value		42

Intl. Year of the Child (1979) A251

Children's drawings: a, Riding horses. b, water sports. c, Fish. d, Gift sale. e, Preparing feast.

1980, Mar. 21

882	Strip of 5	1.25	60
a.-e.	A251 20d any single	24	15

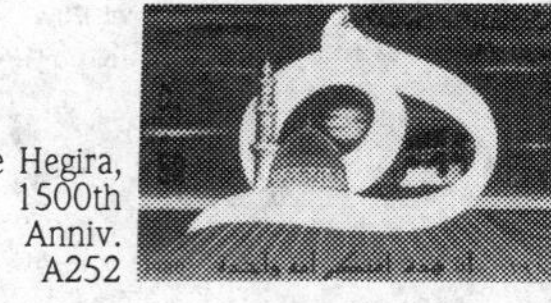
The Hegira, 1500th Anniv. A252

1980, Apr. 1

883 A252	50d multicolored	48	24
884 A252	115d multicolored	1.10	55

Operating Room, Hospital — A253

1980, Apr. 7 Litho. *Perf. 13½*

885 A253	20d multicolored	30	15
886 A253	50d multicolored	70	38

World Health Day.

Sheik Zarruq Festival, Misurata, June 16-20 A254

Arabian Towns Organization A255

1980, June 16

887 A254	40d multicolored	52	24
888 A254	115d multicolored	1.25	65

Souvenir Sheet

889 A254	100d multicolored	1.25	1.25

1980, July 1 *Perf. 11½x12*

890 A255	15d Ghadames	15	15
891 A255	30d Derna	38	15
892 A255	50d Tripoli	60	30

Battles Type of 1980

1980 *Perf. 13½*

893 A244 20d Yefren, 1915 25 15
894 A244 20d El Hani, 1911 25 15
895 A244 20d Sebha, 1914 25 15
896 A244 20d Sirt, 1912 25 15
897 A244 35d Yefren, diff. 45 30
898 A244 35d El Hani, diff. 45 30
899 A244 35d Sebha, diff. 45 30
900 A244 35d Sirt, diff. 45 30
Nos. 893-900 (8) 2.80 1.80

Issue dates: Yefren, July 16. El Hani, Oct. 23. Sebha, Nov. 27. Sirt, Dec. 31. Stamps of same battle printed se-tenant in a continuous design.

Sept. 1 Revolution, 11th Anniv. A256

Achievements of the Revolution.

1980, Sept. 1

901 A256 5d Oil industry 15 15
902 A256 10d Youth festival 15 15
903 A256 15d Agriculture 15 15
904 A256 25d Transportation 30 15
905 A256 40d Education 50 24
906 A256 115d Housing 1.40 65
Nos. 901-906 (6) 2.65
Set value 1.25

Souvenir Sheet

907 A256 100d Montage of achievements 1.25 1.25

No. 907 contains one stamp 30x50mm.

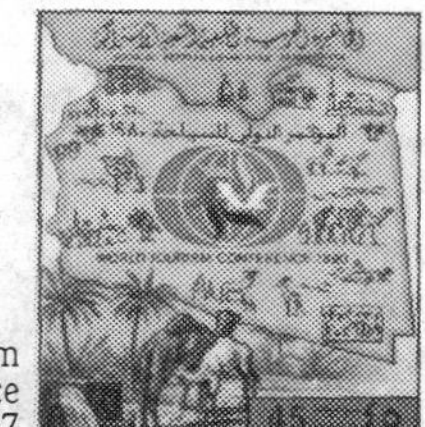

World Tourism Conference A257

1980, Sept. 10

908 A257 45d multicolored 50 30
909 A257 115d multicolored 1.40 65

Intl. Year of the Disabled — A258

1981, Jan. 1 *Perf. 15*

910 A258 20d multicolored 24 15
911 A258 45d multicolored 55 30
912 A258 115d multicolored 1.25 65

Redrawn

1981, Nov. 21 Litho. *Perf. 15*

913 A258 45d multicolored 55 30
914 A258 115d multicolored 1.25 65

UPA Disabled Persons Campaign. Design redrawn to include Arab League Emblem.

Mosaics A259

1981, Jan. 15 *Perf. 13½*

915 A259 10d Horse 15 15
916 A259 20d Sailing ship 20 15
917 A259 30d Peacocks 30 15
918 A259 40d Panther 45 15
919 A259 50d Musician 55 25
920 A259 115d Fish 1.25 60
Nos. 915-920 (6) 2.90 1.45

Battles Type of 1980

Perf. 13½, 14½ (#926, 932, 938, 944)

1981

921 A244 20d Dernah, 1912 50 16
922 A244 20d Bir Tagreft, 1928 50 16
923 A244 20d Tawargha, 1923 50 16
924 A244 20d Zuara, 1912 50 16
925 A244 20d Funduk El-Jamel Misurata, 1915 50 16
926 A244 20d Sidi El-Khemri, 1915 35 16
927 A244 20d El-Khoms, 1913 50 16
928 A244 20d Roghdalin, 1912 50 16
929 A244 20d Rughbat El-Naga, 1925 50 16
930 A244 20d Tobruk, 1911 50 16
931 A244 20d Bir Ikshadia, 1924 35 16
932 A244 20d Ain Zara, 1924 50 16
933 A244 35d Dernah, diff. 80 30
934 A244 35d Bir Tagreft, diff. 80 30
935 A244 35d Tawargha, diff. 80 30
936 A244 35d Zuara, diff. 80 30
937 A244 35d Funduk El-Jamel Misurata, diff. 80 30
938 A244 35d Sidi El-Khemri, diff. 80 30
939 A244 35d El-Khoms, diff. 80 30
940 A244 35d Roghdalin, diff. 80 30
941 A244 35d Rughbat El-Naga, diff. 80 30
942 A244 35d Tobruk, diff. 80 30
943 A244 35d Bir Ikshadia, diff. 80 30
944 A244 35d Ain Zara, diff. 80 30
Nos. 921-944 (24) 15.30 5.52

Issue dates: Dernah, Jan. 17. Bir Tagreft, Feb. 25. Tawargha, Mar. 20. Zuara, Apr. 13. Funduk El-Jamel Misurata, May 26. Sidi El-Khemri, June 4. El-Khoms, July 27. Roghdalin, Aug. 15. Rughbat El-Naga, Sept. 16. Tobruk, Oct. 27. Bir Ikshadia, Nov. 19. Ain Zara, Dec. 4. Stamps of the same battle printed se-tenant in a continuous design.

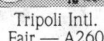

Tripoli Intl. Fair — A260

No. 707b, Crowd — A261

Ceramicware.

1981, Mar. 1 *Perf. 13½*

945 A260 5d Bowls, horiz. 15 15
946 A260 10d Lamp 15 15
947 A260 15d Vase 20 15
948 A260 45d Water jar, horiz. 65 25
949 A260 115d Spouted water jar, horiz. 1.50 85
Nos. 945-949 (5) 2.65 1.55

1981, Mar. 2 *Perf. 15*

950 A261 50d multicolored 50 15
951 A261 115d multicolored 1.10 55

People's Authority Declaration, The Green Book.

Children's Day, IYC — A262

Children's illustrations: a, Desert camp. b, Women doing chores. c, Village scene. d, Airplane over playground. e, Minaret, camel, man.

1981, Mar. 21 Litho. *Perf. 13½*

952 Strip of 5 1.25 60
a.-e. A262 20d any single 24 15

Bank of Libya, 25th Anniv. — A263

1981, Apr. 1 Litho. *Perf. 13½*

953 A263 45d multicolored 48 20
954 A263 115d multicolored 1.25 60

Souvenir Sheet

955 A263 50d multicolored 1.10 1.10

World Health Day — A264

1981, Apr. 7 *Perf. 14*

956 A264 45d multicolored 60 25
957 A264 115d multicolored 1.50 75

Intl. Year for Combating Racial Discrimination — A265

1981, July 1 *Perf. 15*

958 A265 45d multicolored 55 15
959 A265 50d multicolored 65 15

September 1 Revolution, 12th Anniv. — A266

Designs: #960a-960b, Helicopter and jets. #960c-960d, Paratroopers. #961a-961b, Tanks. #961c-961d, Frogman parade. #962a-962b, Twelve-barrel rocket launchers. #962c-962d, Trucks with rockets. #963a-963b, Sailor parade. #963c-963d, Jeep and trucks with twelve-barrel rocket launchers. #964a-964b, Wheeled tanks and jeeps. #964c-964d, Tank parade.

1981, Sept. 1 *Perf. 14½*

960 Block of 4 20 20
a.-d. A266 5d, any single 15 15
961 Block of 4 22 20
a.-d. A266 10d, any single 15 15
962 Block of 4 32 20
a.-d. A266 15d, any single 15 15
963 Block of 4 42 22
a.-d. A266 20d, any single 15 15
964 Block of 4 55 25
a.-d. A266 25d, any single 15 15
Nos. 961-964 (4) 1.51 87

Souvenir Sheet

Perf. 11

965 A266 50d Naval troop marching *1.25* 35

Horizontal pairs within 960-964 printed in continuous designs. Nos. 960-962 vert.

No. 965 contains one stamp 63x38mm.

Miniature Sheet

Butterflies — A267

1981, Oct. 1 *Perf. 14½*

966 Sheet of 16 *5.50*
a.-d. A267 5d, any single *15* 15
e.-h. A267 10d, any single *20* 15
i.-l. A267 15d, any single *30* 15
m.-p. A267 25d, any single *45* 15

Nos. 966a-966p printed se-tenant in a continuous design, stamps of same denomination in blocks of 4. Sheetlets exist containing blocks of 4 for each denomination.

World Food Day — A268

1981, Oct. 16 *Perf. 15*

967 A268 45d multicolored 45 15
968 A268 200d multicolored 2.25 1.10

Fruit — A269

1981, Nov. 17 *Perf. 13½*

969 A269 5d Grapes 15 15
970 A269 10d Dates 15 15
971 A269 15d Lemons 22 15
972 A269 20d Oranges 30 15
973 A269 35d Cactus fruit 45 15
974 A269 55d Pomegranates 60 15
Nos. 969-974 (6) 1.87
Set value 50

Miniature Sheet

Orpheus Playing Music to the Animals — A270

Mosaics: d, Fish. e, Fishermen. f, Fish in basket. g, Farm yard. h, Birds eating fruit. i, Milking a goat. Illustration reduced.

1982, Jan. 1 *Perf. 13½*

975 Sheet of 9 5.00
a.-i. A270 45d any single 50 22

Nos. 975a-975c, shown in illustration, printed in continuous design.

3rd Intl. Koran Reading Contest — A271

Designs: 10d, Stone tablets, Holy Ka'aba, Mecca. 35d, Open Koran, creation of the world. 115d, Scholar, students.

1982, Jan. 7

976 A271 10d multicolored 15 15
977 A271 35d multicolored 40 18
978 A271 115d multicolored 1.25 55

Souvenir Sheet

979 A271 100d like 115d 1.25 1.25

Battles Type of 1980

Perf. 13½, 14½ (#985-988, 997-1000)

1982

980 A244 20d Hun Gioffra, 1915 50 24
981 A244 20d Gedabia, 1914 50 24
982 A244 20d El-Asaba, 1913 50 24
983 A244 20d El-Habela, 1917 50 24
984 A244 20d Suk El-Ahad, 1915 50 24
985 A244 20d El-Tangi, 1913 50 24
986 A244 20d Sokna, 1913 50 24
987 A244 20d Wadi Smalus, 1925 50 24
988 A244 20d Sidi Abuagela, 1917 50 24
989 A244 20d Sidi Surur, 1914 50 24
990 A244 20d Kuefia, 1911 50 24
991 A244 20d Abunjeim, 1940 50 24
992 A244 35d Hun Gioffra, diff. 90 45
993 A244 35d Gedabia, diff. 90 45
994 A244 35d El-Asaba, diff. 90 45
995 A244 35d El-Habela, diff. 90 45
996 A244 35d Suk El-Ahad, diff. 90 45
997 A244 35d El-Tangi, diff. 90 45
998 A244 35d Sokna, diff. 90 45
999 A244 35d Wadi Smalus, diff. 90 45
1000 A244 35d Sidi Abuagela, diff. 90 45
1001 A244 35d Sidi Surur, diff. 90 45
1002 A244 35d Kuefia, diff. 90 45
1003 A244 35d Abunjeim, diff. 90 45
Nos. 980-1003 (24) 16.80 8.28

Issue dates: Nos. 980, 992, Jan. 26. Nos. 981, 993, Mar. 8. Nos. 982, 994, Mar. 23. Nos. 983, 995, Apr. 24. No. 984, 996, May 15. Nos. 985, 997, June 19. Nos. 986, 998, July 23. Nos. 987, 999, Aug. 11. Nos. 988, 1000, Sept. 4. Nos. 989, 1001, Oct. 14. Nos. 990, 1002, Nov. 28. Nos. 991, 1003, Dec. 13. Stamps of same battle printed se-tenant in a continuous design.

Tripoli Intl. Fair — A272

1982, Mar. 1 ***Perf. 13x12½***

1004 A272 5d Grinding stone 15 15
1005 A272 10d Ox-drawn plow 18 15
1006 A272 25d Pitching hay 30 15
1007 A272 35d Tapestry weaving 42 15
1008 A272 45d Traditional cooking 45 22
1009 A272 100d Grain harvest 1.10 55
Nos. 1004-1009 (6) 2.60
Set value 1.20

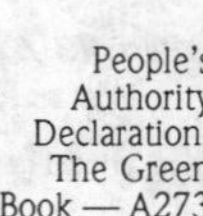

People's Authority Declaration, The Green Book — A273

1982, Mar. 2 ***Perf. 13½***

1010 Strip of 3 7.50 3.50
a. A273 100d Harvester combine 1.10 48
b. A273 200d Khadafy, scholar, rifles 2.50 1.10
c. A273 300d Govt. building, citizens 3.75 1.50

Scouting Movement, 75th Anniv. A274

13th African Soccer Cup Championships A275

1982, Mar. 2

1011 Strip of 4 10.00 5.00
a. A274 100d Cub scout, blimp 1.00 50
b. A274 200d Scouts, dog 2.00 1.00
c. A274 300d Scholar, scout 3.00 1.40
d. A274 400d Boy scout, rocket 4.00 2.00

Souvenir Sheets

1012 A274 500d Green Book 5.00 5.00
1013 A274 500d Khadafy, scouts 5.00 5.00

Nos. 1012-1013 each contain one stamp 39x42mm.

1982, Mar. 5

1014 A275 100d multi 1.00 50
1015 A275 200d multi 2.00 1.00

1982 World Cup Soccer Championships, Spain — A276

World Cup trophy and various soccer plays.

1982, Mar. 15 ***Perf. 14½***

1016 A276 45d multi 45 22
1017 A276 100d multi 1.00 50
1018 A276 200d multi 2.00 1.00
1019 A276 300d multi 3.00 1.65

Souvenir Sheets

1020 A276 500d like 45d 5.00 5.00
1021 A276 500d like 100d 5.00 5.00

Nos. 1016-1019 issued in sheets of 8 overprinted in silver with soccer ball in motion. Sheetlets of 4 in each denomination exist without overprint.

Nos. 1020-1021 have Arabic text in green on reverse.

Palestinian Children's Day — A277

Designs: a, Two children. b, Girl with bowl. c, Girl with kaffiyeh. d, Girl hiding. e, Boy.

1982, Mar. 7 ***Perf. 13½***

1022 Strip of 5 2.00 85
a.-e. A277 20d, any single 35 16

Birds — A278

Arab Postal Union, 30th — A280

Teaching Hospitals Anniv. A279

Miniature Sheet

1982, Apr. 1 ***Perf. 14½***

1023 Sheet of 16 9.00
a.-d. A278 15d, any single 15 15
e.-h. A278 25d, any single 35 15
i.-l. A278 45d, any single 60 22
m.-p. A278 95d, any single 95 45

No. 1023a-1023p printed se-tenant in a continuous design; stamps of same denomination in blocks of 4.

1982, Apr. 7 ***Perf. 13x12½***

1024 A279 95d multi 90 45
1025 A279 100d multi 1.00 50
1026 A279 205d multi 2.00 1.00

1982, Apr. 12 ***Perf. 13½***

1027 A280 100d multi 1.00 50
1028 A280 200d multi 2.00 1.00

1982 World Chess Championships — A281

Board positions and chessmen: a, Chinese piece. b, African piece. c, Modern piece. d, European piece.

1982, May 1

1029 Block of 4 4.00 1.75
a.-d. A281 100d, any single 1.00 40

Souvenir Sheet

1030 A281 500d Overhead view of chessboard 5.00 5.00

No. 1030 contains one stamp 39x42mm.

World Telecommunications Day — A282

1982, May 17

1031 A282 100d multi 1.00 50
1032 A282 200d multi 2.00 1.00

Map of Libya, Green Book — A283

1982, June 11

1033 A283 200d multi 2.00 75

Souvenir Sheet

1034 A283 300d multi 3.75 3.75

Post Day, FIP 51st anniv.

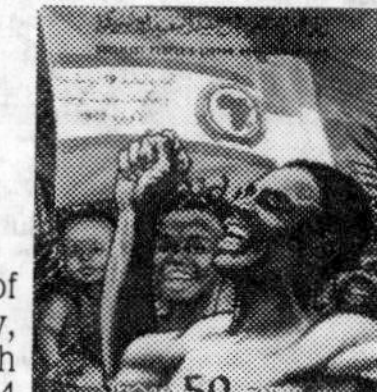
Organization of African Unity, 19th Summit — A284

1982, Aug. 5 ***Perf. 14***

1035 A284 50d OAU flag, Arab family 50 25
1036 A284 100d Map of Africa, emblem 1.00 50

Size: 69x40mm

1037 A284 200d Khadafy, Green Book 2.00 1.00

Souvenir Sheet

Perf. 13x13½

1038 A284 300d Fist, map 3.75 3.75

No. 1038 contains one stamp 29x42mm.

September 1 Revolution, 13th Anniv. — A285

Khadafy in uniforms and various armed forces' exercises.

1982, Sept. 1 ***Perf. 11½***

1039 A285 15d multi *24* 15
1040 A285 20d multi *30* 15
1041 A285 30d multi *32* 15
1042 A285 45d multi *50* 16
1043 A285 70d multi *65* 24
1044 A285 100d multi *90* 38
Nos. 1039-1044 (6) *2.91* 1.23

Souvenir Sheet

Imperf

1045 A285 200d multi *2.50 2.50*

Libyan Red Crescent, 25th Anniv. — A286

Intl. Day of Cooperation with Palestinian People — A287

1982, Oct. 5 *Perf. 13½*

1046 A286 100d Palm tree 1.00 50
1047 A286 200d "25," crescents 2.00 1.00

1982, Nov. 29

1048 A287 100d gray grn & blk 1.25 48
1049 A287 200d brt bl, gray grn & blk 2.75 90

Al-Fateh University Symposium on Khadafy's Green Book — A288

1982, Dec. 1 *Perf. 12*

1050 A288 100d Khadafy in uniform *1.00* 25
1051 A288 200d Khadafy, map, Green Book *2.00* 50

Flowers — A289

Customs Cooperation Council, 30th Anniv. — A290

Miniature Sheet

Designs: a, Philadelphus. b, Hypericum. c, Antinhinum. d, Lily. e, Capparis. f, Tropaeolum. g, Rose. h, Chrysanthemum. i, Nigella damascena. j, Guillardia lanceolata. k, Dahlia. l, Dianthus carophyllus. m, Notobasis syriaca. n, Nerium oleander. o, Iris histriodes. p, Scolymus hispanicus.

1983, Jan. 1 *Perf. 14½*

1052 Sheet of 16 5.00
a.-p. A289 25d, any single 30 20

Torch Type of 1979

1983, Jan. 2 *Perf. 13½*

Size: 26½x32mm

1053 A228 250d multi 3.50 1.10
1054 A228 1500d multi 15.00 6.50
1055 A228 2500d multi 27.50 10.00

1983, Jan. 15 *Perf. 14½x14*

1056 A290 25d Arab riding horse 25 15
1057 A290 50d Riding camel 50 25
1058 A290 100d Drawing sword 1.00 50

Battles Type of 1980

1983 *Perf. 13½*

1059 A244 50d Ghaser Ahmed, 1922 1.25 70
1060 A244 50d Same, right 1.25 70
1061 A244 50d Sidi Abuarghub, 1923 1.25 70
1062 A244 50d Same, right 1.25 70
1063 A244 50d Ghar Yunes, 1913 1.25 70
1064 A244 50d Same, right 1.25 70
1065 A244 50d Bir Otman, 1926 1.25 70
1066 A244 50d Same, right 1.25 70
1067 A244 50d Sidi Sajeh, 1922 1.25 70
1068 A244 50d Same, right 1.25 70
1069 A244 50d Ras El-Hamam, 1915 1.25 70
1070 A244 50d Same, right 1.25 70
1071 A244 50d Zawiet Ishghefa, 1913 1.25 70
1072 A244 50d Same, right 1.25 70
1073 A244 50d Wadi Essania, 1930 1.25 70
1074 A244 50d Same, right 1.25 70
1075 A244 50d El-Meshiashta, 1917 1.25 70
1076 A244 50d Same, right 1.25 70
1077 A244 50d Gharara, 1925 1.25 70
1078 A244 50d Same, right 1.25 70
1079 A244 50d Abughelan, 1922 1.25 70
1080 A244 50d Same, right 1.25 70
1081 A244 50d Mahruka, 1913 1.25 70
1082 A244 50d Same, right 1.25 70
Nos. 1059-1082 (24) 30.00 16.80

Issue dates: #1059-1060, Jan. 26. #1061-1062, Feb. 2. #1063-1064, Mar. 26. #1065-1066, Apr. 9. #1067-1068, May 2. #1069-1070, June 24. #1071-1072, July 13. #1073-1074, Aug. 8. #1075-1076, Sept. 9. #1077-1078, Oct. 22. #1079-1080, Nov. 17. #1081-1082, Dec. 24.

Miniature Sheet

Farm Animals — A291

Designs: a, Camel. b, Cow. c, Horse. d, Bull. e, Goat. f, Dog. g, Sheep. h, Ram. i, Goose. j, Turkey hen. k, Rabbit. l, Pigeon. m, Turkey. n, Rooster. o, Hen. p, Duck.

1983, Feb. 15 *Perf. 14½*

1083 Sheet of 16 5.00
a.-p. A291 25d any single 30 20

Tripoli Intl. Fair — A292

Libyans playing traditional instruments.

1983, Mar. 5 *Perf. 14½x14, 14x14½*

1084 A292 40d multi, vert. 40 15
1085 A292 45d multicolored 45 18
1086 A292 50d multi, vert. 50 22
1087 A292 55d multicolored 55 25
1088 A292 75d multi, vert. 75 40
1089 A292 100d multi, vert. 1.00 50
Nos. 1084-1089 (6) 3.65 1.70

Intl. Maritime Organization, 25th Anniv. — A293

Early sailing ships.

1983, Mar. 17 *Perf. 14½*

1090 A293 100d Phoenician 1.10 60
1091 A293 100d Viking 1.10 60
1092 A293 100d Greek 1.10 60
1093 A293 100d Roman 1.10 60
1094 A293 100d Libyan 1.10 60
1095 A293 100d Pharoah's ship 1.10 60
Nos. 1090-1095 (6) 6.60 3.60

Children's Day (1983) A294

Children's illustrations: a, Car. b, Tractor towing trailer. c, Children, dove. d, Boy Scouts. e, Dinosaur.

1983, Mar. 21 *Perf. 14x14½*

1096 Strip of 5 *3.00* 35
a.-e. A294 20d, any single *55* 15

1st Intl. Symposium on Khadafy's Green Book — A295

1983, Apr. 1 *Perf. 13½*

1097 A295 50d Khadafy, Green Book, map 42 15
1098 A295 70d Lecture hall, emblem 60 20
1099 A295 80d Khadafy, Green Book, emblem 90 25

Souvenir Sheet

Perf. 12½

1100 A295 100d Khadafy, Green Books *3.00* 1.25

No. 1100 contains one stamp 57x48mm.

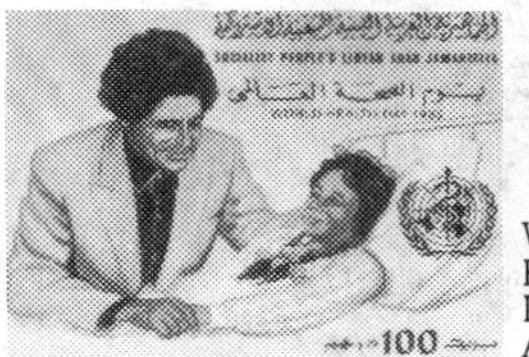

World Health Day A296

1983, Apr. 7 *Perf. 12½*

1101 A296 25d Healthy children, vert. *25* 15
1102 A296 50d Man in wheelchair, vert. *52* 16
1103 A296 100d Girl in hospital bed *85* 32

Pan-African Economic Committee, 25th Anniv. — A297

1983, Apr. 20 *Perf. 13½*

1104 A297 50d multi 48 15
1105 A297 100d multi 90 45
1106 A297 250d multi 2.75 1.25

Miniature Sheet

Fish A298

Designs: a, Labrus bimaculatus. b, Trigloporus lastoviza. c, Thalassoma pavo. d, Apogon imberbis. e, Scomber scombrus. f, Spondyliosoma cantharus. g, Trachinus draco. h, Blennius pavo. i, Scorpaena notata. j, Serranus scriba. k, Lophius piscatorius. l, Uranoscopus scaber. m, Auxis thazard. n, Zeus faber. o, Dactylopterus volitans. p, Umbrina cirrosa.

1983, May 15 *Perf. 14½*

1107 Sheet of 16 5.00
a.-p. A298 25d any single 30 20

Still-life by Gauguin (1848-1903) — A299

Paintings: No. 1108b, Abstract, unattributed. c, The Conquest of Tunis by Charles V, by Rubens. d, Arab Musicians in a Carriage, unattributed.

No. 1109a, Khadafy Glorified on Horseback, unattributed, vert. b, Triumph of David over the Syrians, by Raphael, vert. c, Laborers, unattributed, vert. d, Flower Vase, by van Gogh, vert.

1983, June 1 *Perf. 11*

1108 Strip of 4 2.00 90
a.-d. A299 50d, any single 50 20
1109 Strip of 4 2.00 90
a.-d. A299 50d, any single 50 20

Souvenir Sheet

Ali Siala — A300

Scientists: No. 1110b, Ali El-Najar.

1983, June 1

1110 Sheet of 2 *2.50* 1.50
a.-b. A300 100d, any single *1.10* 65

1984 Summer Olympic Games, Los Angeles — A301

1983, June 15 *Perf. 13½*

1111 A301 10d Basketball 15 15
1112 A301 15d High jump 15 15
1113 A301 25d Running 20 15
1114 A301 50d Gymnastics 40 20
1115 A301 100d Wind surfing 90 40
1116 A301 200d Shot put 1.90 90
Nos. 1111-1116 (6) 3.70 1.95

Souvenir Sheets

1117 A301 100d Equestrian *1.00 1.00*
1118 A301 100d Soccer *1.00 1.00*

Nos. 1111-1116 also exist in miniature sheets of 4.

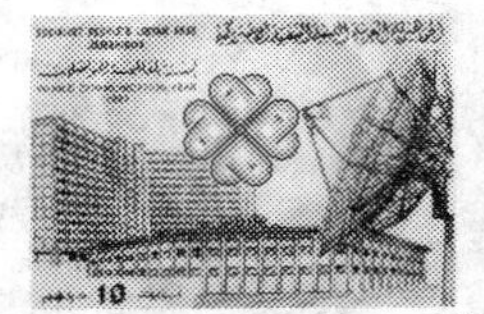

World Communications Year — A302

1983, July 1 *Perf. 13*

1119 A302 10d multicolored 15 15
1120 A302 50d multicolored 40 20
1121 A302 100d multicolored 90 40

The Green Book, by Khadafy A303

Ideologies: 10d, The House is to be served by its residents. 15d, Power, wealth and arms are in the hands of the people. 20d, Masters in their own castles, vert. 35d, No democracy without popular congress. 100d, The authority of the people, vert.

140d, The Green Book is the guide of humanity for final release.

1983, Aug. 1 *Perf. 13½*
1122 A303 10d multi 15 15
1123 A303 15d multi 20 15
1124 A303 20d multi 25 15
1125 A303 35d multi 38 15
1126 A303 100d multi 90 40
1127 A303 140d multi 1.40 75
Nos. 1122-1127 (6) 3.28 1.75

Souvenir Sheet
Litho. & Embossed

1128 A303 200d Khadafy in uniform 1.65 1.65

No. 1128 contains one gold embossed stamp 36x51mm.

2nd African Youth Sports Festival — A304

Designs: a, Team Handball. b, Basketball. c, Javelin. d, Running. e, Soccer.

1983, Aug. 22 **Litho.**
1129 Strip of 5 5.00 2.75
a.-e. A304 100d, any single 1.00 50

September 1 Revolution, 14th Anniv. — A305

Women in the Armed Forces.

1983, Sept. 1 *Perf. 11½*
1130 A305 65d multi 55 30
1131 A305 75d multi 75 40
1132 A305 90d multi 85 42
1133 A305 100d multi 90 45
1134 A305 150d multi 1.40 75
1135 A305 250d multi 2.75 1.25
Nos. 1130-1135 (6) 7.20 3.57

Souvenir Sheet
Perf. 11

1136 A305 200d multi 2.00 2.00

No. 1136 contains one stamp 63x38mm.

2nd Islamic Scout Jamboree — A306

1983, Sept. 2 *Perf. 12½*
1137 A306 50d Saluting 60 18
1138 A306 100d Camping 90 35

Souvenir Sheet

1139 Sheet of 2 1.25 90
a. A306 100d like 50d 60 40

No. 1139 contains Nos. 1138 and 1139a.

Traffic Day A307 Saadun (1893-1923) A308

1983, Oct. 1 *Perf. 14½x14*
1140 A307 30d Youth traffic monitors 30 15
1141 A307 70d Traffic officer 65 30
1142 A307 200d Motorcycle police 1.90 90

1983, Oct. 11 *Perf. 13½*
1143 A308 100d multicolored 1.00 50

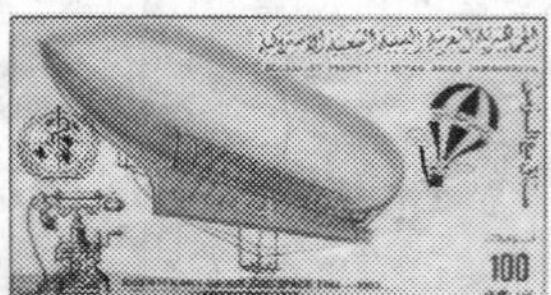

1st Manned Flight, Bicent. — A309

Early aircraft and historic flights: a, Americana, 1910. b, Nulli Secundus, 1907. c, J. B. Meusnier, 1785. d, Blanchard and Jeffries, 1785, vert. e, Pilatre de Rozier, 1784, vert. f, Montgolfiere, Oct. 19, 1783, vert.

1983, Nov. 1
1144 Strip of 6 7.50 3.50
a.-f. A309 100d, any single 1.25 55

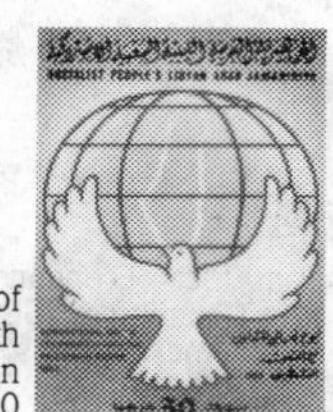

Intl. Day of Cooperation with Palestinian People — A310

1983, Nov. 29 *Perf. 14½x14*
1145 A310 30d pale vio & lt bl grn 30 15
1146 A310 70d lil & lt yel grn 90 30
1147 A310 200d lt ultra & grn 2.75 90

Miniature Sheet

Roman Mosaic — A311

Designs: Nos. 1148a-1148c, Gladiators. Nos. 1148d-1148f, Musicians, Nos. 1148g-1148i, Hunters. Illustration reduced.

1983, Dec. 1 *Perf. 12*
1148 Sheet of 9 5.50
a.-i. A311 50d. any single 60 25

Nos. 1148a-1148c, 1148d-1148f and 1148g-1148i se-tenant in a continuous design.

Achievements of the Sept. 1 Revolution — A312

1983, Dec. 15 *Perf. 13½*
1149 A312 10d Mosque 15 15
1150 A312 15d Agriculture 15 15
1151 A312 20d Industry 22 15
1152 A312 35d Office building 35 15
1153 A312 100d Health care 90 40
1154 A312 140d Airport 1.25 65
Nos. 1149-1154 (6) 3.02 1.65

Souvenir Sheet
Litho. & Embossed

1155 A312 200d Khadafy 2.50 2.50

No. 1155 contains one gold embossed stamp 36x51mm.

Khadafy, Irrigation Project Survey Map — A313

1983, Dec. 15
1156 A313 150d multicolored 1.50 75

A314

A315

Famous men: No. 1157a, Mahmud Burkis. No. 1157b, Ahmed El-Bakbak. No. 1157c, Mohamed El-Misurati. No. 1157d, Mahmud Ben Musa. No. 1157e, Abdulhamid Ben Ashiur. No. 1158a, Hosni Fauzi El-Amir. No. 1158b, Ali Haidar El-Saati. No. 1159, Mahmud Mustafa Dreza. No. 1160, Mehdi El-Sherif. No. 1161a, Ali El-Gariani. No. 1161b, Muktar Shakshuki. No. 1161c, Abdurrahman El-Busayri. No. 1161d, Ibbrahim Bakir. No. 1161e, Mahmud El-Janzuri. No. 1162a, Ahmed El-Feghi Hasan. No. 1162b, Bashir El Jawab.

1984 **Litho.** *Perf. 13½*
1157 Strip of 5 5.00 2.75
a.-e. A314 100d any single 1.00 55
1158 Pair 2.25 1.00
a.-b. A314 100d any single 1.10 50
1159 A314 100d multi 1.10 50
1160 A315 100d multi 1.10 50
1161 Strip of 5 10.00 5.00
a.-e. A314 200d any single 2.00 1.00
1162 Pair 4.00 2.25
a.-b. A315 200d any single 2.00 1.10
Nos. 1157-1162 (6) 23.45 12.00

Issue dates: Nos. 1158, 1161-1162, Jan. 1. Others, Feb. 20.

Miniature Sheet

Water Sports — A316

Designs: a, Two windsurfers. b, Two-man craft. c, Two-man craft, birds. d, Wind sailing, skis. e, Water skier facing front. f, Fisherman in boat. g, Power boating. h, Water skier facing right. i, Fisherman in surf. j, Kayaking. k, Surfing. l, Water skier wearing life jacket. m, Scuba diver sketching underwater. n, Diver. o, Snorkel diver removing fish from harpoon. p, Scuba diver surfacing.

1984, Jan. 10 *Perf. 14½*
1164 Sheet of 16 5.00 2.50
a.-p. A316 25d any single 30 15

African Children's Day — A317

Designs: a, Khadafy, girl scouts. b, Khadafy, children. c, Map, Khadafy, children (size: 63x44mm).

1984, Jan. 15 **Litho.** *Perf. 14½*
1165 Strip of 3 1.90 50
a.-b. A317 50d, any single 42 15
c. A317 100d multi 80 20

Women's Emancipation A318

Designs: 70d, Women, diff., vert. 100d, Soldiers, Khadafy.

1984, Jan. 20 *Perf. 12*
1166 A318 55d multicolored 55 25
1167 A318 70d multicolored 75 38
1168 A318 100d multicolored 1.00 45

Irrigation — A319

Designs: No. 1169a, Desert, water. No. 1169b, Produce, sheep grazing. No. 1169c, Khadafy, irrigation of desert (size: 63x44mm). Nos. 1170-1171, Khadafy, map.

1984, Feb. 1 *Perf. 14½*
1169 Strip of 3 2.00 1.00
a.-b. A319 50d any single 45 22
c. A319 100d multicolored 1.00 50

Size: 72x36mm
Perf. 13½

1170 A319 100d multicolored 1.00 50

Souvenir Sheet

1171 A319 300d multicolored *3.75 3.75*

World Heritage — A320

Architectural ruins. No. 1174 vert.

1984, Feb. 10 *Perf. 12*
1172 A320 50d Theater, Sabratha 48 15
1173 A320 60d Temple, Cyrene 60 30
1174 A320 70d Monument, Sabratha 75 35
1175 A320 100d Arena, Leptis Magna 1.00 45
1176 A320 150d Temple, Cyrene, diff. 1.50 75
1177 A320 200d Basilica, Leptis Magna 2.25 1.10
Nos. 1172-1177 (6) 6.58 3.10

Silver Dirhams Minted A.D. 671-757 — A321

Designs: a, Hegira 115. b, Hegira 93. c, Hegira 121. d, Hegira 49. e, Hegira 135.

Litho. & Embossed

1984, Feb. 15 *Perf. 13½*

1178 Strip of 5 10.00 5.00
a.-e. A321 200d, any single 2.00 1.00

Tripoli Intl. Fair A322

Tea served in various settings.

1984, Mar. 5 **Litho.** *Perf. 12½*

1179 A322 25d multicolored 20 15
1180 A322 35d multicolored 35 15
1181 A322 45d multicolored 45 16
1182 A322 55d multicolored 55 20
1183 A322 75d multicolored 75 35
1184 A322 100d multicolored 1.00 45
Nos. 1179-1184 (6) 3.30 1.46

Musicians — A323

Designs: a, Muktar Shiaker Murabet. b, El-Aref El-Jamal. c, Ali Shiaalia. d, Bashir Fehmi.

1984, Mar. 15 *Perf. 14½*

1185 Strip of 4 + label 4.00 2.00
a.-d. A323 100d, any single 95 45

No. 1185 has center label picturing musical instruments.

Children's Day, IYC A324

Children's drawings: a, Recreation. b, Rainy day. c, Military strength. d, Playground. e, Porch swing, children, motorcycle.

1984, Mar. 21 *Perf. 14*

1186 Strip of 5 2.00 90
a.-e. A324 20d, any single 40 18

Arab League Constitution, 39th Anniv. — A325

1984, Mar. 22 *Perf. 13½*

1187 A325 30d multicolored 32 15
1188 A325 40d multicolored 40 20
1189 A325 50d multicolored 50 25

Miniature Sheet

Automobiles, Locomotives — A326

1984, Apr. 1

1190 Sheet of 16 20.00 9.00
a.-h. A326 100d, Car, any single 1.25 55
i.-p. A326 100d, Locomotive, any single 1.25 55

No. 1190 pictures outline of two camels in gold. Size: 214x135mm.

World Health Day A327

1984, Apr. 7 *Perf. 14½*

1191 A327 20d Stop Polio 20 15
1192 A327 30d No. 910 32 15
1193 A327 40d Arabic text 40 20

Crafts — A328

Designs: a, Shoemaker. b, Saddler. c, Women, wool. d, Spinner. e, Weaver. f, Tapestry weavers.

1984, May 1 *Perf. 12½*

1194 Strip of 6 9.00 4.50
a.-f. A328 150d, any single 1.50 75

Postal and Telecommunications Union Congress — A329

Designs: a, Telephones, mail. b, Computer operators. c, Emblem.

1984, May 15 *Perf. 14½*

1195 Strip of 3 2.00 1.00
a.-b. A329 50d, any single 50 25
c. A329 100d multicolored 1.00 50

Armed Crowd — A330

Map, Fire, Military — A331

Designs: No. 1197b, Soldiers. No. 1197c, Khadafy. No. 1198, Khadafy giving speech.

1984, May 17 *Perf. 12, 14½ (#1197)*

1196 A330 50d multi 55 25
1197 Strip of 3 2.25 1.25
a.-b. A331 50d, any single 55 28
c. A331 100d multi 1.10 55
1198 A330 100d multi 1.25 55
Nos. 1196-1198 (3) 4.05 2.05

Abrogation of the May 17 Treaty. Size of No. 1197c: 63x45mm.

Youth War Casualties A332

1984, June 4 *Perf. 10*

1199 A332 70d Damaged flag 75 35
1200 A332 100d Children imprisoned 1.00 45

Miniature Sheet

Green Book Quotations A333

Designs: a, The Party System Aborts Democracy. b, Khadafy. c, Partners Not Wage-Workers. d, No Representation in Lieu of the People . . . e, Green Book. f, Committees Everywhere. g, Forming Parties Splits Societies. h, Party building, text on track. i, No Democracy without Popular Congresses.

1984, June 20 *Perf. 14*

1201 Sheet of 9 9.00 4.50
a.-i. A333 100d, any single 1.00 45

See No. 1270.

Folk Costumes — A334

1984, July 1 *Perf. 14½x14*

Background colors:
a, Green. b, Beige. c, Violet.
d, Pale greenish blue.
e, Salmon rose. f, Blue.

1202 Strip of 6 6.00 3.00
a.-f. A334 100d, any single 1.00 50

Miniature Sheet

Natl. Soccer Championships — A335

Stadium, star, world cup and various action scenes.

1984, July 15 *Perf. 13½*

1203 Sheet of 16 11.00 5.00
a.-p. A335 70d, any single 65 30

1984 Los Angeles Olympics — A336

World Food Day — A337

1984, July 28

1204 A336 100d Soccer 1.00 45
1205 A336 100d Basketball 1.00 45
1206 A336 100d Swimming 1.00 45
1207 A336 100d Sprinting 1.00 45
1208 A336 100d Windsurfing 1.00 45
1209 A336 100d Discus 1.00 45
Nos. 1204-1209 (6) 6.00 2.70

Souvenir Sheets

1210 A336 250d Equestrian 1.90 90
1211 A336 250d Arab equestrian 1.90 90

1984, Aug. 1 *Perf. 12*

1212 A337 100d Forest scenes 1.00 45
1213 A337 200d Men riding camels, oasis 2.00 1.00

Miniature Sheet

Sept. 1 Revolution, 15th Anniv. — A338

Designs: a, Green books, building at right angle. b, Green book, building, minaret. c, Minaret, party building and grounds. d, Revolution leader. e, Eight-story building. f, Construction, dome. g, Highway, bridge. h, Green book, building at left angle. i, Shepherd, sheep. j, Harvester. k, Tractors. l, Industry. m, Khadafy. n, Irrigation pipe, man drinking. o, Silos, factory. p, Shipping.

1984, Sept. 15 *Perf. 14½*

1214 Sheet of 16 5.00 5.00
a.-p. A338 25d any single 30 20

A339

Evacuation Day A340

Designs: No. 1215b, Warrior facing left. No. 1215c, Khadafy leading battle (size: 63x45mm). No. 1216, Female rider. No. 1217, Battle scene. No. 1218, Italian whipping Libyan.

1984, Oct. 7

1215 Strip of 3 2.00 1.00
a.-b. A339 50d, any single 50 22
c. A339 100d multi 1.00 45

Perf. 11½

1216 A340 100d multicolored 1.00 45
1217 A340 100d multicolored 1.00 45
1218 A340 100d multicolored 1.00 45
Nos. 1215-1218 (4) 5.00 2.35

Miniature Sheet

Equestrians A341

Various jumping, racing and dressage exercises printed in a continuous design.

1984, Oct. 15 ***Perf. 13½***

1219 Sheet of 16 5.00 5.00
a.-p. A341 25d any single 30 20

PHILAKOREA '84.

Agricultural Traditions — A342

Designs: a, Farmer. b, Well, man, ox. c, Basket weaver. d, Shepherd, ram. e, Tanning hide. f, Coconut picker.

1984, Nov. 1 ***Perf. 13½***

1220 Strip of 6 6.00 3.00
a.-f. A342 100d. any single 1.00 50

Union of Arab Pharmacists, 9th Congress A343

1984, Nov. 6 ***Perf. 12***

1221 A343 100d multicolored 1.00 45
1222 A343 200d multicolored 2.00 1.00

Arab-African Union — A344

1984, Nov. 15 ***Perf. 12***

1223 A344 100d Map, banner, crowd 1.00 45
1224 A344 100d Men, flags 1.00 45

Nos. 1046, 1147 A345

1984, Nov. 29 ***Perf. 12½***

1225 A345 100d pink & multi 1.25 60
1226 A345 150d brt yel grn & multi 1.75 90

Intl. Day of Cooperation with the Palestinian People.

Miniature Sheet

Intl. Civil Aviation Organization, 40th Anniv. — A346

Aircraft: a, Boeing 747 SP, 1975. b, Concorde, 1969. c, Lockheed L1011-500 Tristar, 1978. d, Airbus A310, 1982. e, Tupolev TU-134A, 1962. f, Shorts 360, 1981. g, Boeing 727, 1963. h, Caravelle 10, 1965. i, Fokker F27, 1955. j, Lockheed 749A Constellation, 1946. k, Martin 130, 1955. l, Douglas DC-3, 1936. m, Junkers JU-52, 1932. n, Lindbergh's Spirit of St. Louis, 1927 Ryan. o, De Havilland Moth, 1925. p, Wright Flyer, 1903.

1984, Dec. 7 ***Perf. 13½***

1227 Sheet of 16 14.00 7.50
a.-p. A346 70d any single 85 45

African Development Bank, 20th Anniv. — A347

UN Child Survival Campaign — A348

"20" in different configurations and: 70d, Map, symbols of industry, education and agriculture. 100d, Symbols of research and development.

1984, Dec. 15

1228 A347 50d multicolored 50 25
1229 A347 70d multicolored 75 40
1230 A347 100d multicolored 1.10 50

1985, Jan. 1 ***Perf. 12***

1231 A348 70d Mother, child 70 30
1232 A348 70d Children 70 30
1233 A348 70d Boys at military school 70 30
1234 A348 70d Khadafy, children 70 30

Irrigation — A349

Drop of Water, Map A350

1985, Jan. 15 ***Perf. 14½x14***

1235 A349 100d shown 1.00 45
1236 A349 100d Flowers 1.00 45
1237 A349 100d Map, water 1.00 45

Souvenir Sheet

Perf. 14x14½

1238 A350 200d shown 2.50 2.50

Musicians — A351

Designs: No. 1239a, Kamel El-Ghadi. No. 1239b, Lute. No. 1240a, Ahmed El-Khogia. No. 1240b, Violin. No. 1241a, Mustafa El-Fallah. No. 1241b, Zither. No. 1242a, Mohamed Hamdi. No. 1242b, Mask.

1985, Feb. 1 ***Perf. 14½***

1239 Pair 3.00 1.50
a.-b. A351 100d, any single 1.50 75
1240 Pair 3.00 1.50
a.-b. A351 100d, any single 1.50 75
1241 Pair 3.00 1.50
a.-b. A351 100d, any single 1.50 75
1242 Pair 3.00 1.50
a.-b. A351 100d, any single 1.50 75
Nos. 1239-1242 (4) 12.00 6.00

Nos. 1239-1242 printed in sheets of 20, four strips of 5 consisting of two pairs each musician flanking center stamps picturing instruments.

Gold Dinars Minted A.D. 699-727 — A352

Designs: No. 1243a, Hegira 105. No. 1243b, Hegira 91. No. 1243c, Hegira 77. No. 1244, Dinar from Zuela.

Litho. and Embossed

1985, Feb. 15 ***Perf. 13½***

1243 Strip of 3 6.00 3.00
a.-c. A352 200d, any single 2.00 1.00

Souvenir Sheet

1244 A352 300d multi 3.75 1.75

Fossils — A353

1985, Mar. 1 **Litho.** ***Perf. 13½***

1245 A353 150d Frog 1.40 65
1246 A353 150d Fish 1.40 65
1247 A353 150d Mammal 1.40 65

People's Authority Declaration — A354

Khadafy wearing: a, Folk costume. b, Academic robe. c, Khaki uniform. d, Black uniform. e, White uniform.

1985, Mar. 2 **Litho.** ***Perf. 14½***

1248 Strip of 5 6.50 3.25
a.-e. A354 100d, any single 1.25 65

Tripoli Intl. Fair — A355

Musicians playing: a, Cymbals. b, Double flute, bongo. c, Wind instrument, drum. d, Drum. e, Tambourine.

1985, Mar. 5 ***Perf. 14***

1249 Strip of 5 5.00 2.50
a.-e. A355 100d, any single 1.00 50

Children's Day, IYC — A356

Children's drawings, various soccer plays: a, Goalie and player. b, Four players. c, Players as letters of the alphabet. d, Goalie save. e, Player heading the ball.

1985, Mar. 21 ***Perf. 12***

1250 Strip of 5 2.00 75
a.-e. A356 20d, any single 40 15

Intl. Program for Development of Telecommunications A357

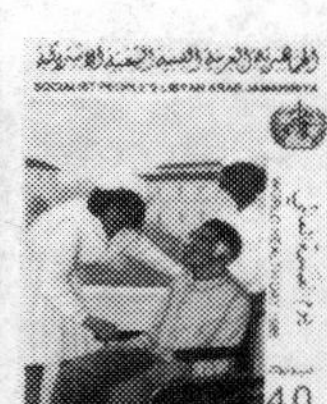

World Health Day A358

1985, Apr. 1

1251 A357 30d multicolored 35 16
1252 A357 70d multicolored 75 35
1253 A357 100d multicolored 1.10 50

1985, Apr. 7

1254 A358 40d Invalid, nurses 38 18
1255 A358 60d Nurse, surgery 60 30
1256 A358 100d Nurse, child 1.10 50

Miniature Sheet

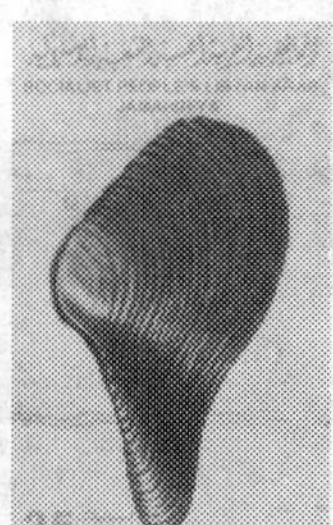

Sea Shells — A359

Designs: a, Mytilidae. b, Muricidae (white). c, Cardiidae. d, Corallophiliidae. e, Muricidae. f, Muricacea. g, Turridae. h, Argonautidae. i, Tonnidae. j, Aporrhaidae. k, Trochidae. l, Cancellariidae. m, Epitoniidae. n, Turbinidae. o, Mitridae. p, Pectinidae.

1985, Apr. 20

1257 Sheet of 16 5.00 2.75
a.-p. A359 25d, any single 30 15

Tripoli Intl. Book Fair — A360

Intl. Youth Year — A361

1985, Apr. 28 *Perf. 13½*

1258 A360 100d multi 1.00 50
1259 A360 200d multi 2.00 1.00

1985, May 1

Games: No. 1260a, Jump rope. No. 1260b, Board game. No. 1260c, Hopscotch. No. 1260d, Stickgame. No. 1260e, Tops. No. 1261a, Soccer. No. 1261b, Basketball.

1260 Strip of 5 1.90 90
a.-e. A361 20d, any single 55 18

Souvenir Sheet

1261 Sheet of 2 2.50 1.10
a.-b. A361 100d, any single 1.25 50

No. 1261 contains 2 stamps 30x42mm.

Miniature Sheet

Mosque Minarets and Towers — A362

Mosques: a, Abdussalam Lasmar. b, Zaoviat Kadria. c, Zaoviat Amura. d, Gurgi. e, Mizran. f, Salem. g, Ghat. h, Ahmed Karamanli. i, Atya. j, El Kettani. k, Benghazi. l, Derna. m, El Derug. n, Ben Moussa. o, Ghadames. p, Abdulwahab.

1985, May 15 *Perf. 12*

1262 Sheet of 16 11.00 5.00
a.-p. A362 50d, any single 60 30

A363

A364

1985, June 1 Litho. *Perf. 13½*

1263 A363 100d Hamida El-Anezi 1.00 40
1264 A363 100d Jamila Zemerli 1.00 40

Teachers' Day.

1985 June 12

Battle of the Philadelphia : a, Ship sinking. b, Militia. c, Hand-to-hand combat.

1265 Strip of 3 2.00 1.00
a.-b. A364 50d, any single 50 25
c. A364 100d multicolored 1.00 50

Size of No. 1265c: 60x48mm. Continuous design with No. 1265c in middle.

A365

Khadafy's Islamic Pilgrimage A366

"The Holy Koran is the Law of Society" and Khadafy: a, Writing. b, Kneeling. c, With Holy Kaaba. d, Looking in window. e, Praying at pilgrimage ceremony.

1985, June 16

1266 Strip of 5 10.00 4.50
a.-e. A365 200d, any single 2.00 90

Souvenir Sheet

1267 A366 300d multicolored 5.50 5.50

Miniature Sheet

Mushrooms A367

Designs: a, Leucopaxillus lepistoides. b, Amanita caesarea. c, Coriolus hirsutus. d, Cortinarius subfulgens. e, Dermocybe pratensis. f, Macrolepiota excoriata. g, Amanita curtipes. h, Trametes ljubarskyi. i, Pholiota aurivella. j, Boletus edulis. k, Geastrum sessile. l, Russula sanguinea. m, Cortinarius herculeus. n, Pholiota lenta. o, Amanita rubenscens. p, Scleroderma polyrhizum.

1985, July 15

1268 Sheet of 16 10.00 4.50
a.-p. A367 50d, any single 60 25

Women's Folk Costumes — A368

Designs: a, Woman in violet. b, In white. c, In brown and blue. d, In blue. e, In red.

1985, Aug. 1 *Perf. 14½x14*

1269 Strip of 5 5.00 2.25
a.-e. A368 100d, any single 1.00 45

Green Book Quotations Type of 1984

Miniature Sheet

Designs: a, In Need Freedom Is Latent. b, Khadafy reading. c, To Make A Party You Split Society. d, Public Sport Is for All the Masses. e, Green Books, doves. f, Wage-Workers Are a Type of Slave . . . g, People Are Only Harmonious with Their Own Arts and Heritages. h, Khadafy orating. i, Democracy Means Popular Rule Not Popular Expression.

1985, Aug. 15 *Perf. 14*

1270 Sheet of 9 9.00 4.50
a.-i. A333 100d, any single 1.00 50

A369

September 1 Revolution, 16th Anniv. — A370

Designs: a, Food. b, Oil pipeline, refinery. c, Capital, olive branch. d, Mosque, modern buildings. e, Flag, mountains. f, Telecommunications apparatus.

1985, Sept. 1 *Perf. 12½*

1271 Strip of 6 6.00 3.00
a.-f. A369 100d, any single 1.00 50
1272 A370 200d multi 2.50 1.25

Mosque Entrances — A371

Designs: a, Zauiet Amoura, Janzour. b, Shiaieb El-ain, Tripoli. c, Zauiet Abdussalam El-asmar, Zliten. d, Karamanli, Tripoli. e, Gurgi, Tripoli.

1985, Sept. 15 *Perf. 14*

1273 Strip of 5 5.00 2.25
a.-e. A371 100d, any single 1.00 45

Miniature Sheet

Basketball — A372

Various players in action.

1985, Oct. 1 Litho. *Perf. 13x12½*

1274 Sheet of 16 5.00 2.50
a. A372 25d any single 30 15

Evacuation A373

Designs: a, Man on crutches, web, tree. b, Man caught in web held by disembodied hands. c, Three men basking in light.

1985, Oct. 7 *Perf. 15*

1275 Strip of 3 3.00 1.50
a.-c. A373 100d any single 1.00 50

Stamp Day — A374

Italia 85: a, Man sitting at desk, Type A228, Earth. b, Magnifying glass, open stock book, Type A228. c, Stamps escaping envelope.

1985, Oct. 25 *Perf. 12*

1276 Strip of 3 1.50 75
a.-c. A374 50d, any single 50 25

1986 World Cup Soccer Championships A375

1985, Nov. 1 *Perf. 13½*

1277 A375 100d Block, heading the ball 1.00 50
1278 A375 100d Kick, goalie catching ball 1.00 50
1279 A375 100d Goalie, block, dribble 1.00 50
1280 A375 100d Goalie, dribble, sliding block 1.00 50
1281 A375 100d Goalie catching the ball 1.00 50
1282 A375 100d Block 1.00 50
Nos. 1277-1282 (6) 6.00 3.00

Souvenir Sheet

1283 A375 200d Four players 2.50 1.25

Intl. Day of Cooperation with the Palestinian People — A376

1985, Nov. 29 Litho. *Perf. 12½*

1284 A376 100d multi 1.25 60
1285 A376 150d multi 1.90 90

Importation Prohibited

Importation of the stamps of Libya was prohibited as of Jan. 7, 1986.

General Post and Telecommunications Co. — A378

1986, Jan. 15 *Perf. 12*

1298 A378 100d yel & multi
1299 A378 150d yel grn & multi

Peoples Authority Declaration — A379

Designs: b, Hand holding globe and paper. c, Dove, Khadafy's Green Book (size: 53x37mm).

1986, Mar. 2 *Perf. 12½x13*

1300 Strip of 3
a.-b. A379 50d, any single
c. A379 100d multicolored

Musical Instruments A380

Designs: a, Flute. b, Drums. c, Horn. d, Cymbals. e, Hand drum.

1986, Mar. 5

1301 Strip of 5
a.-e. A380 100d any single

Tripoli International Fair.

Intl. Children's Day — A381

Designs: a, Boy Scout fishing. b, Riding camel. c, Chasing butterflies. d, Beating drum. e, Soccer game.

1986, Mar. 21 *Perf. 13½*

1302 Strip of 5
a.-e. A381 50d any single

World Health Day — A382

1986, Apr. 7

1303 A382 250d sil & multi
1304 A382 250d gold & multi

Government Programs — A383

Designs: a, Medical examinations. b, Education. c, Farming (size: 63x42mm).

1986, May 1 *Perf. 14½*

1305 Strip of 3
a.-b. A383 50d any single
c. A383 100d multicolored

Miniature Sheet

World Cup Soccer Championships, Mexico — A384

Designs: No. 1306a, 2 players. No. 1306b, 3 players in red and white shirts, one in green. No. 1306c, 2 players, referee. No. 1306d, Shot at goal. No. 1306e, 2 players with striped shirts. No. 1306f, 2 players with blue shirts, one with red. No. 1307, 7 players. No. 1308, 1st Libyan team, 1931.

1986, May 31 *Perf. 13½*

1306 Sheet of 6
a.-f. A384 50d any single

Souvenir Sheets

1307 A384 200d multicolored
1308 A384 200d multicolored

Nos. 1307-1308 each contain one 52x37mm stamp.

Miniature Sheet

Vegetables — A385

Designs: a, Peas. b, Zucchini. c, Beans. d, Eggplant. e, Corn. f, Tomato. g, Red pepper. h, Cucumbers. i, Garlic. j, Cabbage. k, Cauliflower. l, Celery. m, Onions. n, Carrots. o, Potato. p, Radishes.

1986, June 1 *Perf. 13x12½*

1309 Sheet of 16
a.-p. A385 50d any single

No. 1309 has a continuous design.

Miniature Sheet

Khadafy and Irrigation Project A386

Khadafy and: a, Engineer reviewing plans, drill rig. b, Map. c, Well. d, Drought conditions. e, Water pipe. f, Pipes, pulleys, equipment. g, Lowering water pipe. h, Construction workers, trailer. i, Hands holding water. j, Opening water valve. k, Laying pipeline. l, Trucks hauling pipes. m, Khadafy holding green book, city. n, Giving vegetables to people. o, Boy drinking, man cultivating field. p, Men in prayer, irrigation. (Khadafy not shown on Nos. 1310h, 1310i, 1310k, 1310 l, 1310o.)

1986, July 1 *Perf. 13½*

1310 Sheet of 16
a.-p. A386 100d any single

A387

A388

American Attack on Libya, Apr. 15 — A389

Designs: Nos. 1311a-1311p, Various scenes in Tripoli during and after air raid. No. 1312a. F14 aircraft. No. 1312b, Aircraft carrier, people. No. 1312c, Sinking of USS *Philadelphia*, 1801.
Illustration A389 is reduced.

1986, July 13

1311 A387 Sheet of 16, #a.-p.
1312 Strip of 3
a.-b. A388 50d multicolored
c. A388 100d multicolored
1313 A389 100d multicolored

No. 1312 has a continuous design. Size of No. 1312b: 60x38mm.

Khadafy's Peace Methods A390

Khadafy: b, Reading Green Book. c, With old woman. d, Praying with children. e, Visiting sick. f, Driving tractor.

1986, July 13

1314 Sheet of 6
a.-f. A390 100d any single

Miniature Sheet

Green Book Quotations A391

Designs: a, The House Must be Served by its Own Tenant. b, Khadafy. c, The Child is Raised by His Mother. d, Democracy is the Supervision of the People by the People. e, Green Books. f, Representation is a Falsification of Democracy. g, The Recognition of Profit is an Acknowledgement of Exploitation. h, Flowers. i, Knowledge is a Natural Right of Every Human Being...

1986, Aug. 1 *Perf. 14*

1315 Sheet of 9
a.-i. A391 100d any single

Sept. 1st Revolution, 17th Anniv. — A392

Designs: a, Public health. b, Agriculture. c, Sunflowers by Vincent Van Gogh. d, Defense. e. Oil industry.

1986, Sept. 1

1316 Strip of 5
a.-e. A392 200d any single

A393

Arab-African Union, 1st Anniv. A394

1986, Sept. 15 *Perf. 12*

1317 A393 250d Libyan, Arab horsemen
1318 A394 250d Women in native dress

Evacuation Day — A395

Designs: a, Mounted warrior. b, Two horsemen, infantry. c, Cavalry charge.

1986, Oct. 7 *Perf. 13½*

1319 Strip of 3
a. A395 50d multicolored
b. A395 100d multicolored
c. A395 150d multicolored

Intl. Peace Year A396

1986, Oct. 24 *Perf. 14½*

1320 A396 200d bl & multi
1321 A396 200d grn & multi

Solidarity with the Palestinians — A397

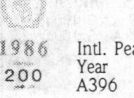

1986, Nov. 29 *Perf. 12½*
1322 A397 250d pink & multi
1323 A397 250d blue & multi

Music and Dance — A398

Designs: a, Man beating drum. b, Masked dancer. c, Woman dancing with jugs on her head. d, Man playing bagpipe. e, Man beating hand drum.

1986, Dec. 1 *Perf. 12*
1324 Strip of 5
a.-e. A398 70d any single

Gazella Leptoceros A399

1987, Mar. 2 *Perf. 13½*
1325 A399 100d Two adults
1326 A399 100d Fawn nursing
1327 A399 100d Adult sleeping
1328 A399 100d Adult drinking

World Wildlife Fund.

People's Authority Declaration — A400

Crowd of People and: a, Oilfields. b, Buildings. c, Khadafy, buildings, globe.

1987, Mar. 2 *Perf. 13½*
1329 Strip of 3
a.-b. A400 500d multicolored
c. A400 1000d multicolored

No. 1329 has a continuous design. Size of No. 1329c: 42x37mm.

Miniature Sheet

Sept. 1st Revolution, 18th Anniv. — A401

Designs: a, Shepherd, sheep. b, Khadafy. c, Mosque. d, Irrigation pipeline. e, Combine in field. f, Khadafy at microphones. g, Harvesting grain. h, Irrigation. i, Soldier. j, Militiaman. k, Fountain. l, Skyscrapers. m, House, women. n, Children. o, Assembly hall. p, Two girls.

1987, Sept. 1 *Perf. 13½*
1330 Sheet of 16
a.-p. A401 150d any single

No. 1330 has a continuous design.

Libyan Freedom Fighters — A402

No. 1331: a, Omer Abed Anabi Al Mansuri. b, Ahmed Ali Al Emrayd. c, Khalifa Said Ben Asker. d, Mohamed Ben Farhat Azawi. e, Mohamed Souf Al Lafi Al Marmori.

1988, Feb. 15
1331 Strip of 5
a. A402 100d multicolored
b. A402 200d multicolored
c. A402 300d multicolored
d. A402 400d multicolored
e. A402 500d multicolored

Freedom Festival Day — A403

1988, June 1
1332 A403 100d yel & multi
1333 A403 150d grn & multi
1334 A403 250d brn org & multi

Miniature Sheet

American Attack on Libya, 2nd Anniv. — A404

Khadafy: a, With woman and children. b, Playing chess. c, Fleeing from bombing with children. d, Praying in desert. e, Praying with children. f, Visiting wounded child. g, With infants and children, horiz. h, Delivering speech, horiz. i, With family, horiz.

#1336, In desert, vert. #1337, Making speech.

1988, July 13
1335 Sheet of 9
a.-i. A404 150d any single

Souvenir Sheets
Litho. & Embossed

1336 A404 500d gold & multi
1337 A404 500d gold & multi

No. 1335 exists imperf.

September 1st Revolution, 19th Anniv. A405

1988, Sept. 19 **Litho.**
1338 A405 100d brt bl & multi
1339 A405 250d gray & multi
1340 A405 300d cit & multi
1341 A405 500d bl grn & multi

1988 Summer Olympics, Seoul — A406

1988, Sept. 17
1342 A406 150d Tennis
1343 A406 150d Equestrian
1344 A406 150d Relay race
1345 A406 150d Soccer
1346 A406 150d Distance race
1347 A406 150d Cycling

Souvenir Sheet

1348 A406 750d Soccer, diff.

No. 1348 contains one 30x42mm stamp. Exists imperf. Nos. 1342-1347 exist in miniature sheets of 1.

Miniature Sheet

1988 Summer Olympics, Seoul — A407

1988, Sept 17
1350 Sheet of 3
a. A407 100d Bedouin rider
b. A407 200d shown
c. A407 200d Show jumping, diff.

Olymphilex '88, Seoul.

A408

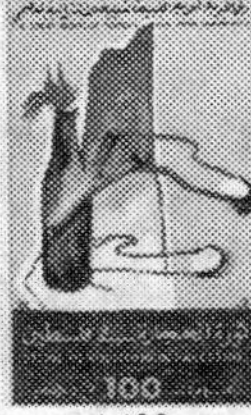
A409

Design: Libyan Palm Tree.

1988, Nov. 1
1351 A408 500d Fruit
1352 A408 1000d Palm tree

1988
1353 Strip of 3
a. A409 100d shown
b. A409 200d Boy with rocks
c. A409 300d Flag, map

Palestinian uprising. Size of No. 1353b: 45x39mm.

People's Authority Declaration A410

1989
1354 A410 260d dk grn & multi
1355 A410 500d gold & multi

Miniature Sheet

September 1 Revolution, 20th Anniv. — A411

Designs: a, Crowd, Green Books, emblem. b, Soldiers, Khadafy, irrigation pipeline. c, Military equipment, Khadafy, communication and transportation. d, Mounted warriors. e, Battle scenes.

1989 *Perf. 13½*
1356 Sheet of 5
a.-e. A411 150d any single
f. Bklt. pane of 5, perf. 13½ horiz.

Souvenir Sheet

1357 A411 250d Khadafy

No. 1357 contains one 36x51mm stamp. Stamps from No. 1356f have gold border at right.

Libyans Deported to Italy — A412

Designs: No. 1359, Libyans in boats. No. 1360, Khadafy, crescent moon. No. 1361, Khadafy at left, in desert. No. 1362, Khadafy at right, soldiers. No. 1363, Khadafy in center, Libyans.

1989
1358 A412 100d shown
1359 A412 100d multicolored
1360 A412 100d multicolored
1361 A412 100d multicolored
1362 A412 100d multicolored

Souvenir Sheet

1363 A412 150d multicolored

No. 1363 contains one 72x38mm stamp.

A413

A414

1989 *Perf. 12*
1364 A413 150d multicolored
1365 A413 200d multicolored

Demolition of Libyan-Tunisian border fortifications.

1989 *Perf. 12x11½*
1366 A414 100d shown
1367 A414 300d Man, flag, crowd
1368 A414 500d Emblem

Solidarity with the Palestinians.

Ibn Annafis, Physician A415

1989 *Perf. 12*
1369 A415 100d multicolored
1370 A415 150d multicolored

A416

A417

1990, Oct. 18 Litho. *Perf. 14*

Granite Paper

1371 A416 100d multicolored
1372 A416 300d multicolored

Intl. Literacy Year.

1990, Oct. 18

Granite Paper

1373 A417 100d multicolored
1374 A417 400d multicolored

Organization of Petroleum Exporting Countries (OPEC), 30th anniv.

A418

A419

1990, June 28 *Perf. 11½x12*

1375 A418 100d brt org & multi
1376 A418 400d grn & multi

Evacuation of US military base, 20th anniv.

1990, Apr. 24

1377 A419 300d bl & multi
1378 A419 500d vio & multi

People's authority declaration.

A420

A421

Plowing Season in Libya: 2000d, Man on tractor plowing field.

1990, Dec. 4 *Perf. 14*

Granite Paper

1379 A420 500d multicolored
1380 A420 2000d multicolored

1990, Nov. 5 *Perf. 14*

Granite Paper

1381 A421 100d grn & multi
1382 A421 400d vio & multi
1383 A421 500d bl & multi

Souvenir Sheet

Perf. 11½

1384 A421 500d Trophy, map, horiz.

World Cup Soccer Championships, Italy. No. 1384 contains one 38x33mm stamp.

Sept. 1st Revolution, 21st Anniv. — A422

1990, Sept. 3 *Perf. 14*

Granite Paper

1385 A422 100d multicolored
1386 A422 400d multicolored
1387 A422 1000d multicolored

Imperf

Size: 120x90mm

1388 A422 200d multi, diff.

Maghreb Arab Union, 2nd Anniv. — A423

1991, Mar. 10 Litho. *Perf. 13½*

1389 A423 100d multicolored
1390 A423 300d gold & multi

People's Authority Declaration — A424

1991, Mar. 10

1391 A424 300d multicolored
1392 A424 400d silver & multi

Children's Day — A425

World Health Day — A426

1991, Mar. 22

1393 A425 100d Butterflies, girl
1394 A425 400d Bird, boy

1991, Apr. 7

1395 A426 100d blue & multi
1396 A426 200d green & multi

Scenes from Libya A427

1991, June 20

1397 A427 100d Wadi el Hayat, vert.
1398 A427 250d Mourzuk
1399 A427 500d Ghadames

Irrigation Project A428

Designs: a, Laborers, heavy equipment. b, Khadafy, heavy equipment. c, Livestock, fruit and vegetables.

1991, Aug. 28 *Perf. 12*

1400 A428 50d Strip of 3, #a.-c.

No. 1400 has a continuous design. Size of No. 1400b: 60x36mm.

Sept. 1st Revolution, 22nd Anniv. A429

1991, Sept. 1 *Perf. 13½*

1401 A429 300d Chains, roses & "22"
1402 A429 400d Chains, "22"
a. Souv. sheet of 2, #1401-1402

Libyans Deported to Italy A431

1991, Oct. 26 Litho. *Perf. 13½*

1405 A431 100d Monument, soldier
1406 A431 400d Ship, refugees, soldiers
a. Souv. sheet of 2, #1405-1406

Arab Unity — A432

1991, Nov. 15 *Perf. 12*

1407 A432 50d tan & multi
1408 A432 100d blue & multi

Miniature Sheet

Trucks, Automobiles and Motorcycles A433

Designs: a-d, Various trucks. e-h, Various off-road race cars. i-p, Various motorcycles.

1991, Dec. 28 *Perf. 14*

1409 A433 50d Sheet of 16, #a.-p.

Eagle — A434

1992 *Perf. 11½*

Granite Paper

Background Colors

1412 A434 100d yellow
1413 A434 150d blue gray
1414 A434 200d bright blue
1415 A434 250d orange
1416 A434 300d purple
1418 A434 400d bright pink
1419 A434 450d bright green

Issue date: Nos. 1412-1416, 1418-1419, Jan. 1, 1992. This is an expanding set. Numbers may change.

People's Authority Declaration — A435

1992 Litho. *Perf. 12*

1425 A435 100d yellow & multi
1426 A435 150d blue & multi

African Tourism Year (in 1991) A436

1992 *Perf. 14½*

Granite Paper

1427 A436 50d purple & multi
1428 A436 100d pink & multi

1992 Summer Olympics, Barcelona — A437

1992 *Perf. 12*

1429 A437 50d Tennis
1430 A437 50d Long jump
1431 A437 50d Discus

Size: 106x82mm

Imperf

1432 A437 100d Olympic torch, rings

Revolutionary Achievements — A438

Designs: 100d, Palm trees. 150d, Steel mill. 250d, Cargo ship. 300d, Libyan Airlines. 400d, Natl. Assembly, Green Books. 500d, Irrigation pipeline, Khadafy.

1992 *Perf. 14*

Granite Paper

1433 A438 100d multicolored
1434 A438 150d multicolored
1435 A438 250d multicolored
1436 A438 300d multicolored
1437 A438 400d multicolored
1438 A438 500d multicolored

Tripoli Intl. Fair
A439

1992 *Perf. 12*

1439 A439 50d Horse & buggy
1440 A439 100d Horse & sulky

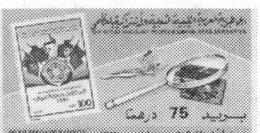

Mahgreb Arab Union Philatelic Exhibition — A440

1992 *Perf. 14½*

1441 A440 75d blue green & multi
1442 A440 80d blue & multi

Miniature Sheet

Fish — A441

Designs: a, Fish with spots near eye. b, Thin fish. d, Brown fish, currents. e, Fish, plants at LR. f, Fish, plants at LL.

1992 *Perf. 14*

1443 A441 100d Sheet of 6, #a.-f.

Miniature Sheet

Horsemanship — A442

Designs: a, Woman rider with gun. b, Man on white horse. c, Mongol rider. d, Roman officer. e, Cossack rider. f, Arab rider. 250d, Two Arab riders.

1992 *Perf. 13½x14*

1444 A442 100d Sheet of 6, #a.-f.

Souvenir Sheet

1445 A442 250d multicolored

Khadafy — A443

Designs: No. 1450a, like No. 1446. b, like No. 1447. c, like No. 1448. d, like No. 1449.

1992 *Perf. 14x13½*

1446 A443 100d blue green & multi
1447 A443 100d gray & multi
1448 A443 100d rose lake & multi
1449 A443 100d yellow & multi

Souvenir Sheet

1450 A443 150d Sheet of 4, #a.-d.

SEMI-POSTAL STAMPS

Many issues of Italy and Italian Colonies include one or more semipostal denominations. To avoid splitting sets, these issues are generally listed as regular postage, semipostals or airmails, etc.

Semi-Postal Stamps of Italy Overprinted **LIBIA**

1915-16 **Wmk. 140** *Perf. 14*

B1	SP1	10c + 5c rose	1.50	*2.25*
B2	SP2	15c + 5c slate	3.50	*6.00*
B3	SP2	20c + 5c org ('16)	2.00	*3.25*

No. B2 with Additional Surcharge **20**

1916, Mar.

B4	SP2	20c on 15c + 5c sl	3.50	*6.00*

View of Port, Tripoli — SP1

Designs: B5, B6, View of port, Tripoli. B7, B8, Arch of Marcus Aurelius. B9, B10, View of Tripoli.

1927, Feb. 15 **Litho.**

B5	SP1	20c + 5c brn vio & black	1.90	1.90
B6	SP1	25c + 5c bl grn & black	1.90	1.90
B7	SP1	40c + 10c blk brn & black	1.90	1.90
B8	SP1	60c + 10c org brn & black	1.90	1.90
B9	SP1	75c + 20c red & black	1.90	1.90
B10	SP1	1.25 l + 20c bl & blk	9.00	7.00
		Nos. B5-B10 (6)	18.50	16.50

First Sample Fair, Tripoli. Surtax aided fair. See Nos. EB1-EB2.

View of Tripoli — SP2

Knights of Malta Castle
SP3

Designs: 50c+20c, Date palm. 1.25 l+20c, Camel riders. 2.55 l+50c, View of Tripoli. 5 l+1 l, Traction well.

1928, Feb. 20 **Wmk. 140** *Perf. 14*

B11	SP2	30c + 20c mar & blk	1.25	*2.50*
B12	SP2	50c + 20c bl grn & blk	1.25	*2.50*
B13	SP2	1.25 l + 20c red & blk	1.25	*2.50*
B14	SP3	1.75 l + 20c bl & blk	1.25	*2.50*
B15	SP3	2.55 l + 50c brn & blk	1.75	*4.00*
B16	SP3	5 l + 1 l pur & blk	2.25	*6.00*
		Nos. B11-B16 (6)	9.00	*20.00*

2nd Sample Fair, Tripoli, 1928. The surtax was for the aid of the Fair.

Olive Tree — SP4

Herding
SP5

Designs: 50c+20c, Dorcas gazelle. 1.25 l+20c, Peach blossoms. 2.55 l+50c, Camel caravan. 5 l+1 l, Oasis with date palms.

1929, Apr. 7

B17	SP4	30c + 20c mar & blk	5.00	*7.00*
B18	SP4	50c + 20c bl grn & blk	5.00	*7.00*
B19	SP4	1.25 l + 20c scar & blk	5.00	*7.00*
B20	SP5	1.75 l + 20c bl & blk	5.00	*7.00*
B21	SP5	2.55 l + 50c yel brn & blk	5.00	*7.00*
B22	SP5	5 l + 1 l pur & blk	72.50	*100.00*
		Nos. B17-B22 (6)	97.50	*135.00*

3rd Sample Fair, Tripoli, 1929. The surtax was for the aid of the Fair.

Harvesting Bananas — SP6

Water Carriers — SP7

Designs: 50c, Tobacco plant. 1.25 l, Venus of Cyrene. 2.55 l+45c, Black bucks. 5 l+1 l, Motor and camel transportation. 10 l+2 l, Rome pavilion.

1930, Feb. 20 **Photo.**

B23	SP6	30c dark brown	1.10	*2.50*
B24	SP6	50c violet	1.10	*2.50*
B25	SP6	1.25 l deep blue	1.10	*2.50*
B26	SP7	1.75 l + 20c scar	1.75	*4.00*
B27	SP7	2.55 l + 45c dp grn	6.50	*7.00*
B28	SP7	5 l + 1 l dp org	4.75	*7.00*
B29	SP7	10 l + 2 l dk vio	8.25	*15.00*
		Nos. B23-B29 (7)	24.55	*40.50*

4th Sample Fair at Tripoli, 1930. The surtax was for the aid of the Fair.

Statue of Ephebus — SP8

Exhibition Pavilion
SP9

Designs: 25c, Arab musician. 50c, View of Zeughet. 1.25 l, Snake charmer. 1.75 l+25c, Windmill. 2.75 l+45c, "Zaptie." 5 l+1 l, Mounted Arab.

1931, Mar. 8

B30	SP8	10c black brown	2.50	*3.00*
B31	SP8	25c green	2.50	*3.00*
B32	SP8	50c purple	2.50	*3.00*
B33	SP8	1.25 l blue	2.50	*3.00*
B34	SP8	1.75 l + 25c car rose	3.00	*5.00*
B35	SP8	2.75 l + 45c org	3.00	*5.00*
B36	SP8	5 l + 1 l dl vio	8.25	*9.00*
B37	SP9	10 l + 2 l brn	17.00	*37.50*
		Nos. B30-B37 (8)	41.25	*68.50*

Fifth Sample Fair, Tripoli, 1931. Surtax aided fair. See Nos. C3, EB3.

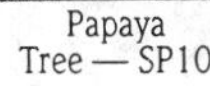

Papaya Tree — SP10

Dorcas Gazelle — SP12

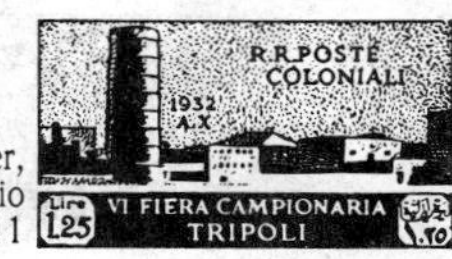

Ar Tower, Mogadiscio
SP11

Designs: 10c, 50c, Papaya tree. 20c, 30c, Euphorbia abyssinica. 25c, Fig cactus. 75c, Mausoleum, Ghirza. 1.75 l+25c, Lioness. 5 l+1 l, Bedouin with camel.

1932, Mar. 8

B38	SP10	10c olive brn	3.50	*5.00*
B39	SP10	20c brown red	3.50	*5.00*
B40	SP10	25c green	3.75	*5.00*
B41	SP10	30c olive blk	3.50	*5.00*
B42	SP10	50c dk violet	3.50	*5.00*
B43	SP10	75c carmine	5.25	*7.00*
B44	SP11	1.25 l dk blue	4.00	*7.00*
B45	SP11	1.75 l + 25c ol brown	14.00	*22.50*
B46	SP11	5 l + 1 l dp bl	14.00	*22.50*
B47	SP12	10 l + 2 l brn violet	47.50	*65.00*
		Nos. B38-B47 (10)	102.50	*149.00*

Sixth Sample Fair, Tripoli, 1932. Surtax aided fair. See Nos. C4-C7.

Ostrich
SP13

Arab Musician
SP14

Designs: 25c, Incense plant. 30c, Arab musician. 50c, Arch of Marcus Aurelius. 1.25 l, African eagle. 5 l+1 l, Leopard. 10 l+2.50 l, Tripoli skyline and fasces.

1933, Mar. 2 **Photo.** **Wmk. 140**

B48	SP13	10c dp violet	19.00	7.00
B49	SP13	25c dp green	5.75	*5.00*
B50	SP14	30c org brn	5.75	*7.00*
B51	SP13	50c purple	5.00	*5.00*
B52	SP13	1.25 l dk bl	26.00	*32.50*
B53	SP14	5 l + 1 l ol brn	30.00	*55.00*
B54	SP13	10 l + 2.50 l car	26.00	*62.50*
		Nos. B48-B54 (7)	117.50	*174.00*

Seventh Sample Fair, Tripoli, 1932. Surtax aided fair. See Nos. C8-C13.

Pomegranate Tree — SP15

Designs: 50c+10c, 2 l+50c, Musician. 75c+15c, 1.25 l+25c, Tribesman.

1935, Feb. 16

B55	SP15	10c + 10c brown	62	*2.25*
B56	SP15	20c + 10c rose red	62	*2.25*
B57	SP15	50c + 10c purple	62	*2.25*
B58	SP15	75c + 15c car	62	*2.25*
B59	SP15	1.25 l + 25c dl blue	62	*2.25*
B60	SP15	2 l + 50c ol grn	62	*2.25*
		Nos. B55-B60 (6)	3.72	*13.50*

Ninth Sample Fair, Tripoli, 1935. Surtax aided fair. See Nos. C19-C24.

AIR POST STAMPS

Italy Nos. C3 and C5 Overprinted **Libia**

1928-29 **Wmk. 140** *Perf. 14*

C1	AP2	50c rose red	3.00	1.50
C2	AP2	80c brn vio & brn ('29)	5.75	*11.00*

Airplane
AP1

1931, Mar. 8 Photo. Wmk. 140

C3 AP1 50c blue 1.00 *5.00*

See note after No. B37.

Seaplane over Bedouin Camp — AP2

Designs: 50c, 1 l, Seaplane over Bedouin camp. 2 l+1 l, 5 l+2 l, Seaplane over Tripoli.

1932, Mar. 1 ***Perf. 14***

C4 AP2 50c dark blue 4.50 *7.00*
C5 AP2 1 l org brown 4.50 *7.00*
C6 AP2 2 l + 1 l dk gray 12.50 *30.00*
C7 AP2 5 l + 2 l car 45.00 *80.00*

See note after No. B47.

Seaplane Arriving at Tripoli — AP3

Designs: 50c, 2 l+50c, Seaplane arriving at Tripoli. 75c, 10 l+2.50 l, Plane over Tagiura. 1 l, 4 l+1 l, Seaplane leaving Tripoli.

1933, Mar. 1

C8 AP3 50c dp green 3.50 *7.00*
C9 AP3 75c carmine 3.50 *7.00*
C10 AP3 1 l dk blue 3.50 *7.00*
C11 AP3 2 l + 50c pur 7.25 *10.00*
C12 AP3 5 l + 1 l org brn 16.00 *25.00*
C13 AP3 10 l + 2.50 l gray blk 16.00 *25.00*
Nos. C8-C13 (6) 49.75 *81.00*

See note after No. B54.

Seaplane over Tripoli Harbor
AP4

Airplane and Camel — AP5

Designs: 50c, 5 l+1 l, Seaplane over Tripoli harbor. 75c, 10 l+2 l, Plane and minaret.

1934, Feb. 17 Photo. Wmk. 140

C14 AP4 50c slate bl 3.75 *7.00*
C15 AP4 75c red org 3.75 *7.00*
C16 AP4 5 l + 1 l dp grn 37.50 *62.50*
C17 AP4 10 l + 2 l dl vio 37.50 *62.50*
C18 AP5 25 l + 3 l org brn 52.50 *80.00*
Nos. C14-C18 (5) 135.00 *219.00*

Eighth Sample Fair, Tripoli. Surtax aided fair. See Nos. CE1-CE2.

Values quoted in this catalogue are for stamps graded at Fine-Very Fine and with no faults. An illustrated guide to grade is provided in introductory material, beginning on Page 5A.

Plane and Ancient Tower — AP6

Camel Train — AP7

Designs: 25c+10c, 3 l+1.50 l, Plane and ancient tower. 50c+10c, 2 l+30c, Camel train. 1 l+25c, 10 l+5 l, Arab watching plane.

1935, Apr. 12

C19 AP6 25c + 10c green 75 *2.50*
C20 AP7 50c + 10c slate bl 75 *2.50*
C21 AP7 1 l + 25c blue 75 *2.50*
C22 AP7 2 l + 30c rose red 75 *2.50*
C23 AP6 3 l + 1.50 l brn 75 *2.50*
C24 AP7 10 l + 5 l dl vio 5.50 *12.50*
Nos. C19-C24 (6) 9.25 *25.00*

See note after No. B60.

Cyrenaica No. C6 Overprinted in Black **LIBIA**

1936, Oct.

C25 AP2 50c purple 38 15

Same on Tripolitania Nos. C8 and C12

1937

C26 AP1 50c rose carmine 20 15
C27 AP2 1 l deep blue 55 35
Set value 40

See Nos. C45-C50.

Ruins of Odeon Theater, Sabrata
AP8

1937, Mar. 15 Photo.

C28 AP8 50c dark violet 1.00 *3.25*
C29 AP8 1 l vio black 1.00 *4.25*

Opening of a coastal road to the Egyptian frontier.

Nos. C28-C29 Overprinted "XI FIERA DI TRIPOLI"

1937, Mar. 15

C30 AP8 50c dark violet 4.75 *7.00*
C31 AP8 1 l violet blk 4.75 *7.00*

11th Sample Fair, Tripoli.

View of Tripoli
AP9

Eagle Attacking Serpent
AP10

1938, Mar. 12 ***Perf. 14***

C32 AP9 50c dk olive grn 38 *62*
C33 AP9 1 l slate blue 50 *1.90*

12th Sample Fair, Tripoli.

1938, Apr. 25 Wmk. 140

C34 AP10 50c olive brown 30 *60*
C35 AP10 1 l brn violet 50 *1.40*

Birth bimillenary Augustus Caesar (Octavianus), first Roman emperor.

Arab and Camel
AP11

Design: 50c, Fair entrance.

1939, Apr. 12 Photo.

C36 AP11 25c green 20 *65*
C37 AP11 50c olive brown 25 *65*
C38 AP11 1 l rose violet 30 *65*

13th Sample Fair, Tripoli.

Plane Over Modern City — AP12

Design: 1 l, 5 l+2.50 l, Plane over oasis.

1940, June 3

C39 AP12 50c brn blk 25 *1.25*
C40 AP12 1 l brn vio 25 *1.25*
C41 AP12 2 l + 75c indigo 38 *1.60*
C42 AP12 5 l + 2.50 l cop brn 38 *1.60*

Triennial Overseas Exposition, Naples.

Hitler, Mussolini and Inscription "Two Peoples, One War"
AP13

1941, Apr. 24

C43 AP13 50c slate green 25 *10.00*

Rome-Berlin Axis.

Cyrenaica No. C9 Overprinted in Black Like No. C25

1941

C44 AP3 1 l black 1.60 *10.00*

Same Overprint on Tripolitania Nos. C9-C11, C13-C15

C45 AP1 60c red orange 25
C46 AP1 75c deep blue 25
C47 AP1 80c dull violet 25
C48 AP2 1.20 l dark brown 25
C49 AP2 1.50 l orange red 25
C50 AP2 5 l green 25
Nos. C44-C50 (7) 3.10

Catalogue values for unused stamps in this section, from this point to the end of the section, are for Never Hinged items.

United Kingdom of Libya

ICY Type of Regular Issue

Perf. 14½x14

1965, Jan. 1 Litho. Unwmk.

C51 A60 50m dp lil & gold 80 80
a. Souvenir sheet 2.00 2.00

No. C51a exists imperf.; same value.

Hands Holding Facade of Abu Simbel
AP14

1966, Jan. 1 Photo. ***Perf. 11½***

Granite Paper

C52 AP14 10m bis & dk brn 15 15
a. Souvenir sheet of 4 75 75
C53 AP14 15m gray grn & dk grn 15 15
a. Souvenir sheet of 4 75 75
C54 AP14 40m dl sal & dk brn 28 28
a. Souvenir sheet of 4 1.50 90
Set value 46 42

UNESCO world campaign to save historic monuments in Nubia.

Inauguration of WHO Headquarters, Geneva
AP15

Perf. 10x10½

1966, May 3 Litho. Unwmk.

C55 AP15 20m blk, yel & bl 15 15
C56 AP15 50m blk, yel grn & red 20 16
C57 AP15 65m blk, sal & brn red 35 25

Flag and Globe — AP16

1966, Oct. 1 Photo. ***Perf. 11½***

Granite Paper

C58 AP16 25m multicolored 15 15
C59 AP16 60m multicolored 28 20
C60 AP16 85m gray & multi 40 35

Inauguration of Kingdom of Libya Airlines, 1st anniv.

AIR POST SPECIAL DELIVERY STAMPS

APSD1

Wmk. 140

1934, Feb. 17 Photo. ***Perf. 14***

CE1 APSD1 2.25 l olive blk 17.50 *30.00*
CE2 APSD1 4.50 l + 1 l gray blk 17.50 *30.00*

8th Sample Fair at Tripoli. The surtax was for the aid of the Fair.

SPECIAL DELIVERY STAMPS

Special Delivery Stamps of Italy Overprinted **Libia**

1915, Nov. Wmk. 140 ***Perf. 14***

E1 SD1 25c rose red 6.00 3.00
E2 SD2 30c blue & rose 3.75 *7.00*

For surcharges see Nos. E7-E8.

"Italia"
SD3

1921-23 Engr. ***Perf. 13½***

E3 SD3 30c blue & rose 70 *1.50*
E4 SD3 50c rose red & brn 1.00 *2.00*
E5 SD3 60c dk red & brn ('23) 2.00 *4.00*
E6 SD3 2 l dk bl & red ('23) 4.50 *8.00*

30c, 2 l inscribed "EXPRES."
For surcharges see Nos. E9-E12.

Nos. E1-E2 Surcharged

Cent. 60 **1,60 LIRE 1,60**

1922, June 1

E7	SD1	60c on 25c rose red	4.25	*4.00*
E8	SD2	1.60 l on 30c bl & rose	5.75	*8.00*

Nos. E5-E6 Surcharged in Dark Blue or Red:

70 ٧٠

No. E9

2,50 ٢,٥٠

No. E10

1926, July

E9	SD3	70c on 60c	2.00	*4.00*
E10	SD3	2.50 l on 2 l (R)	4.75	*8.00*

Nos. E5-E6 Surcharged in Blue or Red:

LIRE 1,25

١,٢٥

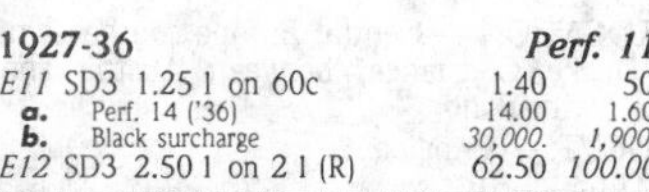

1927-36 *Perf. 11*

E11	SD3	1.25 l on 60c	1.40	50
a.		Perf. 14 ('36)	14.00	1.60
b.		Black surcharge	*30,000.*	*1,900.*
E12	SD3	2.50 l on 2 l (R)	62.50	*100.00*

Catalogue values for unused stamps in this section, from this point to the end of the section, are for Never Hinged items.

United Kingdom of Libya

Zuela Saracen Castle — SD4

Perf. 11½

1966, Feb. 10 Unwmk. Litho.

E13	SD4	90m car rose & lt grn	65	50

Coat of Arms of Libya and "POLIGRAFICA & CARTEVALORI - NAPLES" printed on back in yellow green.

SEMI-POSTAL SPECIAL DELIVERY STAMPS

Camel Caravan SPSD1

Wmk. 140

1927, Feb. 15 Litho. *Perf. 14*

EB1	SPSD1	1.25 l + 30c pur & blk	6.25	6.25
EB2	SPSD1	2.50 l + 1 l yel & blk	6.25	6.25

See note after No. B10.
No. EB2 is inscribed "EXPRES."

War Memorial SPSD2

1931, Mar. 8 Photo.

EB3	SPSD2	1.25 l + 20c car rose	2.25	*7.00*

See note after No. B37.

AUTHORIZED DELIVERY STAMPS

Italy No. EY1 Overprinted in Black **LIBIA**

1929, May 11 Wmk. 140 *Perf. 14*

EY1	AD1	10c dull blue	10.00	8.00
a.		Perf. 11	50.00	40.00

Italy No. EY2 Overprinted in Black **LIBIA**

1941, May *Perf. 14*

EY2	AD2	10c dark brown	4.00	3.25

A variety of No. EY2, with larger "LIBIA" and yellow gum, was prepared in 1942, but not issued. Value 35 cents.

AD1

1942 Litho. Wmk. 140

EY3	AD1	10c sepia	35

No. EY3 was not issued.

POSTAGE DUE STAMPS

Italian Postage Due Stamps, 1870-1903 Overprinted in Black **Libia**

1915, Nov. Wmk. 140 *Perf. 14*

J1	D3	5c buff & magenta	80	*1.25*
J2	D3	10c buff & magenta	1.00	*1.25*
J3	D3	20c buff & magenta	1.25	*2.50*
a.		Double overprint	50.00	50.00
b.		Inverted overprint	50.00	50.00
J4	D3	30c buff & magenta	1.25	*2.50*
J5	D3	40c buff & magenta	1.25	2.50
a.		"40" in black	*1,500.*	
J6	D3	50c buff & magenta	1.25	*2.50*
J7	D3	60c buff & magenta	2.50	*3.75*
J8	D3	1 l blue & magenta	1.25	60
a.		Double overprint	*2,000.*	*1,500.*
J9	D3	2 l blue & magenta	16.00	*12.50*
J10	D3	5 l blue & magenta	24.00	*16.00*
		Nos. J1-J10 (10)	50.55	*45.35*

1926

J11	D3	60c buff & brn	18.00	*37.50*

Postage Due Stamps of Italy, 1934, Overprinted in Black **LIBIA**

1934

J12	D6	5c brown	25	*60*
J13	D6	10c blue	25	*60*
J14	D6	20c rose red	62	50
J15	D6	25c green	70	50
J16	D6	30c red org	62	*80*
J17	D6	40c blk brn	70	*1.25*
J18	D6	50c violet	80	25
J19	D6	60c black	1.25	*3.00*
J20	D7	1 l red org	80	25
J21	D7	2 l green	15.00	3.75
J22	D7	5 l violet	35.00	9.00
J23	D7	10 l blue	7.50	*9.00*
J24	D7	20 l carmine	7.50	*11.00*
		Nos. J12-J24 (13)	70.99	*40.50*

In 1942 a set of 11 "Segnatasse" stamps, picturing a camel and rider and inscribed "LIBIA," was prepared but not issued. Value, $4.

Catalogue values for unused stamps in this section, from this point to the end of the section, are for Never Hinged items.

United Kingdom of Libya

Postage Due Stamps of Cyrenaica, 1950 Surcharged in Black

-- ليبيـا --
٢ ليرة ع.
2 MAL.
LIBYA

For Use in Tripolitania

1951 Unwmk. *Perf. 12½*

J25	D1	1mal on 2m dk brown	4.00	5.00
J26	D1	2mal on 4m dp grn	1.50	*5.00*
J27	D1	4mal on 8m scar	4.50	*10.00*
J28	D1	10mal on 20m org yel	10.00	*20.00*
a.		Arabic "20" for "10"	*200.00*	
J29	D1	20mal on 40m dp bl	14.00	*25.00*
		Nos. J25-J29 (5)	34.00	*65.00*

Cyrenaica Nos. J1-J7 Overprinted in Black

ليبيا
LIBYA

For Use in Cyrenaica

Overprint 13mm High

1952 Unwmk. *Perf. 12½*

J30	D1	2m dk brn	2.00	*3.75*
J31	D1	4m dp grn	2.00	*3.75*
J32	D1	8m scarlet	2.00	*3.75*
J33	D1	10m vermilion	4.50	*7.00*
J34	D1	20m org yel	6.00	*10.00*
J35	D1	40m dp bl	11.00	*20.00*
J36	D1	100m dk gray	15.00	*25.00*
		Nos. J30-J36 (7)	42.50	*73.25*

D1

Castle at Tripoli — D2

1952 Litho. *Perf. 11½*

J37	D1	2m chocolate	15	15
J38	D1	5m bl grn	60	30
J39	D1	10m carmine	1.10	65
J40	D1	50m vio blue	3.50	1.90

1964, Feb. 1 Photo. *Perf. 14*

J41	D2	2m red brn	16	20
J42	D2	6m Prus grn	16	20
J43	D2	10m rose red	16	20
J44	D2	50m brt bl	50	60

Men in Boat, Birds, Mosaic — D3

Ancient Mosaics: 10d, Head of Medusa. 20d, Peacock. 50d, Fish.

1976, Nov. 15 Litho. *Perf. 14*

J45	D3	5d bis & multi	15	15
J46	D3	10d org & multi	16	15
J47	D3	20d bl & multi	35	15
J48	D3	50d emer & multi	65	15
		Set value		26

Nos. J45-J48 have multiple coat of arms printed on back in pale green beneath gum.

OFFICIAL STAMPS

Catalogue values for unused stamps in this section are for Never Hinged items.

United Kingdom of Libya

Nos. 135-142 Overprinted in Black

رسمى
Official

1952 Unwmk. *Perf. 11½*

O1	A27	2m yel brn	1.10	1.10
O2	A27	4m gray	25	38
O3	A27	5m bl grn	2.50	3.75
O4	A27	8m vermilion	1.00	1.10
O5	A27	10m purple	2.25	2.25
O6	A27	12m lil rose	4.75	3.75
O7	A27	20m dp bl	5.75	7.50
O8	A27	25m chocolate	7.50	11.00
		Nos. O1-O8 (8)	25.10	30.83

PARCEL POST STAMPS

These stamps were used by affixing them to the way bill so that one half remained on it following the parcel, the other half staying on the receipt given the sender. Most used halves are right halves. Complete stamps were obtainable canceled, probably to order. Both unused and used values are for complete stamps.

Italian Parcel Post Stamps, 1914-22, Overprinted **LIBIA**

1915-24 Wmk. 140 *Perf. 13½*

Q1	PP2	5c brown	60	*2.00*
a.		Double overprint	50.00	
Q2	PP2	10c deep blue	60	*2.00*
Q3	PP2	20c blk ('18)	70	*2.00*
Q4	PP2	25c red	70	*2.00*
Q5	PP2	50c orange	1.00	*2.50*
Q6	PP2	1 l violet	1.00	*2.00*
Q7	PP2	2 l green	1.60	*3.00*
Q8	PP2	3 l bister	1.40	*3.00*
Q9	PP2	4 l slate	1.60	*3.00*
Q10	PP2	10 l rose lil ('24)	25.00	*30.00*
Q11	PP2	12 l red brn ('24)	37.50	*65.00*
Q12	PP2	15 l ol grn ('24)	37.50	*65.00*
Q13	PP2	20 l brn vio ('24)	37.50	*65.00*
		Nos. Q1-Q13 (13)	146.70	*246.50*

Same Overprint on Parcel Post Stamps of Italy, 1927-36

1927-38

Q14	PP3	10c dp bl ('36)	1.10	*3.00*
Q15	PP3	25c red ('36)	1.00	*3.00*
Q16	PP3	30c ultra ('29)	15	*1.00*
Q17	PP3	50c orange	120.00	150.00
a.		Overprint 8¾x2mm ('31)	70.00	*200.00*
Q18	PP3	60c red ('29)	15	*1.00*
Q19	PP3	1 l lilac ('36)	18.00	*30.00*
Q20	PP3	2 l grn ('38)	18.00	*30.00*
Q21	PP3	3 l bister	38	*1.50*
Q22	PP3	4 l gray	38	*1.50*
Q23	PP3	10 l rose lil ('36)	100.00	125.00
Q24	PP3	20 l brn vio ('36)	100.00	*150.00*
		Nos. Q14-Q24 (11)	359.16	*496.00*

The overprint measures 10x1½mm on No. Q17.

Same Overprint on Italy No. Q24

1939

Q25	PP3	5c brown	*5,000.*

The overprint was applied to the 5c in error. Few copies exist.

OCCUPATION STAMPS

Catalogue values for unused stamps in this section are for Never Hinged items.

Issued under French Occupation

Stamps of Italy and Libya were overprinted in 1943: "FEZZAN Occupation Franaise" and "R. F. FEZZAN" for use in this region when General Leclerc's forces 1st occupied it.

Fezzan-Ghadames

Sebha Fort — OS1

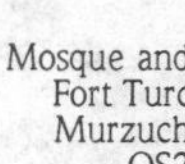

Mosque and Fort Turc Murzuch OS2

Map of Fezzan-Ghadames, Soldier and Camel — OS3

1946	Unwmk.	Engr.	*Perf. 13*	
1N1	OS1	10c black	15	15
1N2	OS1	50c rose	15	15
1N3	OS1	1fr brown	15	15
1N4	OS1	1.50fr green	15	15
1N5	OS1	2fr ultramarine	15	15
1N6	OS2	2.50fr violet	20	18
1N7	OS2	3fr rose carmine	30	30
1N8	OS2	5fr chocolate	35	38
1N9	OS2	6fr dark green	22	25
1N10	OS2	10fr blue	35	38
1N11	OS3	15fr violet	35	38
1N12	OS3	20fr red	50	65
1N13	OS3	25fr sepia	50	65
1N14	OS3	40fr dark green	70	80
1N15	OS3	50fr deep blue	70	80
		Nos. N1-N15 (15)	4.92	5.52

FEZZAN

Catalogue values for unused stamps in this section are for Never Hinged items.

Monument, Djerma Oasis — OS1

Tombs of the Beni-Khettab OS2

Well at Gorda — OS3

Col. Colonna d'Ornano and Fort at Murzuch OS4

Philippe F. M. de Hautecloque (Gen. Jacques Leclerc) OS5

1949	Unwmk.	Engr.	*Perf. 13*	
2N1	OS1	1fr black	20	20
2N2	OS1	2fr lil pink	20	20
2N3	OS2	4fr red brn	70	70
2N4	OS2	5fr emerald	70	70
2N5	OS3	8fr blue	42	42
2N6	OS3	10fr brown	1.40	1.40
2N7	OS3	12fr dk grn	2.50	2.50
2N8	OS4	15fr sal red	3.50	3.50
2N9	OS4	20fr brn blk	1.10	1.10
2N10	OS5	25fr dk bl	1.60	1.60
2N11	OS5	50fr cop red	2.25	2.25
		Nos. 2N1-2N11 (11)	14.57	14.57

Camel Raising — OS6

Agriculture OS7

Well Drilling — OS8

Ahmed Bey — OS9

1951				
2N12	OS6	30c brown	40	40
2N13	OS6	1fr dp bl	40	40
2N14	OS6	2fr rose car	40	40
2N15	OS7	4fr red	40	40
2N16	OS7	5fr green	42	42
2N17	OS7	8fr dp bl	42	42
2N18	OS8	10fr sepia	1.60	1.60
2N19	OS8	12fr dp grn	1.75	1.75
2N20	OS8	15fr brt red	2.00	2.00
2N21	OS9	20fr blk brn & vio brn	2.00	2.00
2N22	OS9	25fr dk bl & bl	2.50	2.50
2N23	OS9	50fr ind & brn org	2.50	2.50
		Nos. 2N12-2N23 (12)	14.79	14.79

OCCUPATION SEMI-POSTAL STAMPS

Catalogue values for unused stamps in this section are for Never Hinged items.

"The Unhappy Ones"
OSP1 OSP2

1950	Unwmk.	Engr.	*Perf. 13*	
2NB1	OSP1	15fr + 5fr red brn	1.00	1.00
2NB2	OSP2	25fr + 5fr blue	1.00	1.00

The surtax was for charitable works.

OCCUPATION AIR POST STAMPS

Catalogue values for unused stamps in this section are for Never Hinged items.

Airport in Fezzan OAP1

Plane over Fezzan — OAP2

1948	Unwmk.	Engr.	*Perf. 13*	
2NC1	OAP1	100fr red	2.50	2.50
2NC2	OAP2	200fr indigo	4.00	4.00

Oasis — OAP3

Murzuch OAP4

1951				
2NC3	OAP3	100fr dark blue	4.00	4.50
2NC4	OAP4	200fr vermilion	5.00	5.50

OCCUPATION POSTAGE DUE STAMPS

Catalogue values for unused stamps in this section are for Never Hinged items.

Oasis of Brak — D1

1950	Unwmk.	Engr.	*Perf. 13*	
2NJ1	D1	1fr brown black	30	30
2NJ2	D1	2fr deep green	40	40
2NJ3	D1	3fr red brown	50	50
2NJ4	D1	5fr purple	60	60
2NJ5	D1	10fr red	1.10	1.10
2NJ6	D1	20fr deep blue	1.75	1.75
		Nos. 2NJ1-2NJ6 (6)	4.65	4.65

GHADAMES

Catalogue values for unused stamps in this section are for Never Hinged items.

Cross of Agadem — OS1

1949	Unwmk.	Engr.	*Perf. 13*	
3N1	OS1	4fr sep & red brn	60	60
3N2	OS1	5fr pck bl & dk grn	60	60
3N3	OS1	8fr sep & org brn	1.50	1.50
3N4	OS1	10fr blk & dk ultra	1.50	1.50
3N5	OS1	12fr vio & red vio	4.50	4.50
3N6	OS1	15fr brn & red brn	2.50	2.50
3N7	OS1	20fr sep & emer	3.50	3.50
3N8	OS1	25fr sepia & blue	3.50	3.50
		Nos. 3N1-3N8 (8)	18.20	18.20

OCCUPATION AIR POST STAMPS

Catalogue values for unused stamps in this section are for Never Hinged items.

Cross of Agadem — OAP1

1949	Unwmk.	Engr.	*Perf. 13*	
3NC1	OAP1	50fr pur & rose	4.50	4.50
3NC2	OAP1	100fr sep & pur brn	5.50	5.50

LIECHTENSTEIN

LOCATION — Central Europe southeast of Lake Constance, between Austria and Switzerland

GOVT. — Principality

AREA — 61.8 sq. mi.

POP. — 4,896 (est. 1984)

CAPITAL — Vaduz

The Principality of Liechtenstein is a sovereign state consisting of the two counties of Schellenberg and Vaduz. Since 1921 the post office has been administered by Switzerland.

100 Heller = 1 Krone

100 Rappen = 1 Franc (1921)

Catalogue values for unused stamps in this country are for Never Hinged items, beginning with Scott 368 in the regular postage section, Scott B22 in the semi-postal section, and Scott O47 in the offical section.

Watermarks

Wmk. 183- Greek Cross

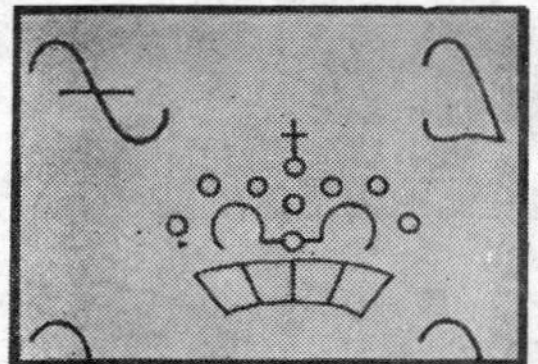

Wmk. 296- Crown and Initials

Austrian Administration of the Post Office

Prince Johann II — A1

1912 Unwmk. Typo. *Perf. 12½x13*
Thick Chalky Paper

1	A1	5h yellow green	10.50	4.50
2	A1	10h rose	32.50	4.50
3	A1	25h dark blue	40.00	22.50

1915

Thin Unsurfaced Paper

1a	A1	5h yellow green	3.50	6.75
2a	A1	10h rose	35.00	13.00
3a	A1	25h dark blue	375.00	90.00
b.		25h ultramarine	225.00	200.00

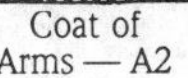
Coat of Arms — A2

Prince Johann II — A3

1917-18

4	A2	3h violet	75	60
5	A2	5h yellow green	75	60
6	A3	10h claret	75	60
7	A3	15h dull red	75	60
8	A3	20h dark green	75	60
9	A3	25h deep blue	75	60
		Nos. 4-9 (6)	4.50	3.60

Exist imperf.
For surcharges see Nos. 11-16.

Prince Johann II — A4

1918

Dates in Upper Corners

10	A4	20h dark green	42	65

Accession of Prince Johann II, 60th anniv. Exists imperf.

National Administration of the Post Office

Stamps of 1917-18 Overprinted or Surcharged

a

b 40

c 1 KRONE

1920

11	A2(a)	5h yel grn	1.40	4.00
a.		Inverted overprint	70.00	
b.		Double overprint	22.50	*45.00*
12	A3(a)	10h claret	1.40	4.00
a.		Inverted overprint	70.00	
b.		Double overprint	22.50	*45.00*
c.		Overprint type "c"	15.00	70.00
13	A3(a)	25h deep blue	1.40	4.00
a.		Inverted overprint	70.00	
14	A2(b)	40h on 3h violet	1.40	4.00
a.		Inverted surcharge	70.00	
15	A3(c)	1k on 15h dl red	1.40	4.00
a.		Inverted surcharge	70.00	
b.		Overprint type "a"	62.50	*150.00*
16	A3(c)	2½k on 20h dk grn	1.40	4.00
a.		Inverted surcharge	70.00	
		Nos. 11-16 (6)	8.40	24.00

Coat of Arms A5

Chapel of St. Mamertus A6

Coat of Arms with Supporters — A15

Designs: 40h, Gutenberg Castle. 50h, Courtyard, Vaduz Castle. 60h, Red Tower, Vaduz. 80h, Old Roman Tower, Schaan. 1k, Castle at Vaduz. 2k, View of Bendern. 5k, Prince Johann I. 7½k, Prince Johann II.

1920 Engr. *Imperf.*

18	A5	5h olive bister	15	15
19	A5	10h deep orange	15	15
20	A5	15h dark blue	15	15
21	A5	20h deep brown	15	15
22	A5	25h dark green	15	15
23	A5	30h gray black	15	15
24	A5	40h dark red	15	15
25	A6	1k blue	15	15

Perf. 12½

32	A5	5h olive bister	15	18
33	A5	10h deep orange	15	18
34	A5	15h deep blue	15	18
35	A5	20h red brown	15	18
36	A6	25h olive green	15	18
37	A5	30h dark gray	15	18
38	A6	40h claret	15	18
39	A6	50h yellow green	15	18
40	A6	60h red brown	15	18
41	A6	80h rose	15	18
42	A6	1k dull violet	15	18
43	A6	2k light blue	20	35
44	A6	5k black	28	35
45	A6	7½k slate	28	35
46	A15	10k ocher	28	35
		Nos. 18-46 (23)	3.89	4.58

Used values for Nos. 18-46 are for canceled to order stamps.

Many denominations of Nos. 32-46 are found imperforate, imperforate vertically and imperforate horizontally.

For surcharges see Nos. 51-52.

Madonna and Child — A16

1920, Oct. 5

47	A16	50h olive green	20	65
48	A16	80h brown red	20	65
49	A16	2k dark blue	20	65

80th birthday of Prince Johann II.

Imperf., Pairs

47a	A16	50h	4.25
48a	A16	80h	4.25
49a	A16	2k	4.25

Swiss Administration of the Post Office

No. 19 Surcharged

2 Rp. — No. 51

2 Rp. — No. 52

1921 Unwmk. Engr. *Imperf.*

51	A5	2rp on 10h dp org	30	*13.00*
a.		Double surcharge	30.00	*65.00*
b.		Inverted surcharge	30.00	*80.00*
c.		Double surch., one inverted	30.00	*65.00*
52	A5	2rp on 10h dp org	30	*13.00*
a.		Double surcharge	57.50	*150.00*
b.		Inverted surcharge	57.50	*150.00*
c.		Double surch., one inverted	57.50	*150.00*

Arms with Supporters A19

Chapel of St. Mamertus A20

View of Vaduz — A21

Designs: 25rp, Castle at Vaduz. 30rp, View of Bendern. 35rp, Prince Johann II. 40rp, Old Roman Tower at Schaan. 50rp, Gutenberg Castle. 80rp, Red Tower at Vaduz.

Perf. 12½ 9½ (2rp, 10rp, 15rp)

1921

Surface Tinted Paper (#54-61)

54	A19	2rp lemon	60	*6.75*
55	A19	2½rp black	75	*8.00*
a.		Perf. 9½	75	*40.00*
56	A19	3rp orange	75	*7.25*
a.		Perf. 9½	90.00	*3,000.*
57	A19	5rp ol grn	4.75	45
a.		Perf. 9½	32.50	*6.50*
58	A19	7½rp dk bl	3.50	*18.00*
a.		Perf. 9½	150.00	*825.00*
59	A19	10rp yel grn	27.50	1.65
a.		Perf. 12½	30.00	4.00
60	A19	13rp brown	5.50	*47.50*
a.		Perf. 9½	67.50	*2,000.*
61	A19	15rp dk vio	8.50	5.75
a.		Perf. 12½	12.00	12.00
62	A20	20rp dl vio & blk	30.00	75
63	A20	25rp rose red & blk	95	1.50
64	A20	30rp dp grn & blk	42.50	6.50
65	A20	35rp brn & blk, *straw*	1.65	4.75
66	A20	40rp dk bl & blk	1.65	1.40
67	A20	50rp dk grn & blk	1.90	1.50
68	A20	80rp gray & blk	11.00	*42.50*
69	A21	1fr dp cl & blk	21.00	20.00
		Nos. 54-69 (16)	162.50	*174.25*

Nos. 54-69 exist imperforate; Nos. 54-61, partly perforated. See Nos. 73, 81. For surcharges see Nos. 70-71.

Nos. 58, 60a Surcharged in Red **10**

1924 *Perf. 12½, 9½*

70	A19	5rp on 7½rp	70	1.50
a.		Perf. 9½	5.50	5.00
71	A19	10rp on 13rp	45	1.10
a.		Perf. 12½	10.50	25.00

Type of 1921

1924 Wmk. 183 *Perf. 11½*
Granite Paper

73	A19	10rp green	11.00	65

Peasant A28

Government Palace and Church at Vaduz A30

Design: 10rp, 20rp, Courtyard, Vaduz Castle.

1924-28 Typo. *Perf. 11½*

74	A28	2½rp ol grn & red vio ('28)	1.40	*4.00*
75	A28	5rp brn & blue	2.25	65
76	A28	7½rp bl grn & brn ('28)	1.40	*4.00*
77	A28	15rp red brn & bl grn ('28)	4.25	*21.00*

Engr.

No.	Type	Description	Unused	Used
78	A28	10rp yel grn	7.50	65
79	A28	20rp dp red	17.00	65
80	A30	1 1/2fr blue	52.50	65.00
		Nos. 74-80 (7)	86.30	95.95

Bendern Type of 1921

1925

No.	Type	Description	Unused	Used
81	A20	30rp bl & blk	10.50	65

Prince Johann II — A31

Prince Johann II as Boy and Man — A32

1928, Nov. 12 Typo. Wmk. 183

No.	Type	Description	Unused	Used
82	A31	10rp lt brn & ol grn	1.40	3.00
83	A31	20rp org red & ol grn	3.50	5.75
84	A31	30rp sl bl & ol grn	17.00	18.00
85	A31	60rp red vio & ol grn	45.00	*62.50*

Engr.

Unwmk.

No.	Type	Description	Unused	Used
86	A32	1.20fr ultra	40.00	*100.00*
87	A32	1.50fr blk brn	60.00	*145.00*
88	A32	2fr dp car	60.00	*145.00*
89	A32	5fr dk grn	60.00	*200.00*
		Nos. 82-89 (8)	286.90	*679.25*

70th year of the reign of Prince Johann II.

Prince Francis I, as a Child — A33

Prince Francis I as a Man — A34

Princess Elsa — A35

Prince Francis and Princess Elsa — A36

1929, Dec. 2 Photo.

No.	Type	Description	Unused	Used
90	A33	10rp ol grn	65	*2.00*
91	A34	20rp carmine	65	*3.25*
92	A35	30rp ultra	1.90	*13.00*
93	A36	70rp brown	14.00	*72.50*

Accession of Prince Francis I, Feb. 11, 1929.

Grape Girl — A37

Chamois Hunter — A38

Mountain Cattle — A39

Courtyard, Vaduz Castle — A40

Mt. Naafkopf — A41

Chapel at Steg — A42

Rofenberg Chapel — A43

Chapel of St. Mamertus — A44

Alpine Hotel, Malbun — A45

Gutenberg Castle — A46

Schellenberg Monastery — A47

Castle at Vaduz — A48

Mountain Cottage — A49

Prince Francis and Princess Elsa — A50

1930 ***Perf. 10 1/2, 11 1/2, 11 1/2x10 1/2***

No.	Type	Description	Unused	Used
94	A37	3rp brn lake	30	65
95	A38	5rp dp grn	60	45
96	A39	10rp dk vio	75	35
a.		Perf. 11 1/2x10 1/2	7.25	*19.00*
97	A40	20rp dp rose red	11.00	50
98	A41	25rp black	3.75	*21.00*
a.		Perf. 11 1/2	92.50	*165.00*
99	A42	30rp dp ultra	2.50	90
a.		Perf. 11 1/2x10 1/2	1,200.	1,200.
100	A43	35rp dk grn	3.50	*9.25*
a.		Perf. 11 1/2	*4,250.*	*4,250.*
101	A44	40rp lt brn	3.50	3.25
102	A45	50rp blk brn	42.50	11.50
a.		Perf. 11 1/2	160.00	105.00
103	A46	60rp ol blk	42.50	12.50
104	A47	90rp vio brn	42.50	80.00
105	A48	1.20fr ol brn	42.50	*125.00*
a.		Perf. 11 1/2x10 1/2	*2,400.*	*3,250.*
106	A49	1.50fr blk vio	25.00	40.00
107	A50	2fr gray grn & red brn	32.50	65.00
a.		Perf. 11 1/2x10 1/2	2,500.	*3,000.*
		Nos. 94-107 (14)	253.40	*370.35*

For overprints see Nos. O1-O8.

Mt. Naafkopf A51

Gutenberg Castle A52

Vaduz Castle — A53

1933, Jan. 23 ***Perf. 14 1/2***

No.	Type	Description	Unused	Used
108	A51	25rp red org	135.00	40.00
109	A52	90rp dk grn	8.50	*50.00*
110	A53	1.20fr red brn	75.00	*200.00*

For overprints see Nos. O9-O10.

Prince Francis I

A54 A55

1933, Aug. 28 ***Perf. 11***

No.	Type	Description	Unused	Used
111	A54	10rp purple	16.00	27.50
112	A54	20rp brn car	16.00	27.50
113	A54	30rp dk bl	16.00	27.50

80th birthday of Prince Francis I.

1933, Dec. 15 Engr. ***Perf. 12 1/2***

No.	Type	Description	Unused	Used
114	A55	3fr vio bl	100.00	150.00
		Never hinged	150.00	

See No. 152.

Agricultural Exhibition Issue

Souvenir Sheet

Arms of Liechtenstein — A56

1934, Sept. 29 ***Perf. 12***

Granite Paper

No.	Type	Description	Unused	Used
115	A56	5fr brown	*1,100.*	*2,000.*
		Never hinged	*1,800.*	

See No. 131.

Coat of Arms — A57

"Three Sisters" (Landmark) — A58

Church of Schaan — A59

Bendern — A60

Rathaus, Vaduz — A61

Samina Valley — A62

Samina Valley in Winter — A63

Ruin at Schellenberg A64

Government Palace — A65

Vaduz Castle — A66

Gutenberg Castle — A68

Alpine Hut — A69

Princess Elsa — A70

Coat of Arms — A71

Designs: 60rp, Vaduz castle, diff. 1.50fr, Valuna.

Perf. 11 1/2, 11x11 1/2, 12 1/2

1934-35 Photo.

No.	Type	Description	Unused	Used
116	A57	3rp cop red	20	52
117	A58	5rp emerald	2.75	45
118	A59	10rp dp vio	85	32
119	A60	15rp red org ('35)	40	1.00
120	A61	20rp red ('35)	70	45
121	A62	25rp brn ('35)	22.50	27.50
122	A63	30rp dk bl ('35)	3.75	1.25
123	A64	35rp gray grn ('35)	75	*4.00*
124	A65	40rp brn ('35)	85	2.50
125	A66	50rp lt brn	22.50	18.00
126	A66	60rp claret	1.25	*4.50*
127	A68	90rp dp grn	6.00	*18.00*
128	A69	1.20fr dp bl	1.65	*15.00*
129	A69	1.50fr brn car ('35)	2.50	*22.50*
		Nos. 116-129 (14)	66.65	*115.99*
		Set, never hinged	150.00	

Engr.

No.	Type	Description	Unused	Used
130	A70	2fr hn brn ('35)	57.50	*135.00*
		Never hinged	90.00	
131	A71	5fr dk vio ('35)	375.00	*725.00*
		Never hinged	525.00	

No. 131 has the same design as the 5fr in the souvenir sheet, No. 115. See #226, B14. For overprints see Nos. O11-O20.

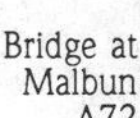

Bridge at Malbun A72

Labor: 20rp, Constructing Road to Triesenberg. 30rp, Binnen Canal. 50rp, Bridge near Planken.

1937, June 30 **Photo.**

132 A72	10rp brt vio		95	65
133 A72	20rp red		95	65
134 A72	30rp brt bl		95	1.00
135 A72	50rp yel brn		95	1.65
	Set, never hinged		8.50	

Ruin at Schalun — A76

Peasant in Rhine Valley — A77

Ruin at Schellenberg A78

Knight and Gutenberg Castle — A79

Baron von Brandis and Vaduz Castle — A80

Designs: 5rp, Chapel at Masescha. 10rp, Knight and Vaduz Castle. 15rp, Upper Valüna Valley. 20rp, Wooden Bridge over Rhine, Bendern. 25rp, Chapel at Steg. 90rp, "The Three Sisters". 1fr, Frontier stone. 1.20fr, Gutenberg Castle and Harpist. 1.50fr, Alpine View of Lawena and Schwartzhorn.

1937-38

136 A76	3rp yel brn	18	35
	Pale Buff Shading		
137 A76	5rp emerald	18	22
138 A76	10rp violet	18	15
139 A76	15rp dk sl grn	30	45
140 A76	20rp brn org	30	22
141 A76	25rp chestnut	55	1.50
142 A77	30rp bl & gray	3.50	52
144 A78	40rp dk grn	2.75	1.00
145 A79	50rp dk brn	1.00	2.00
146 A80	60rp dp cl ('38)	2.25	1.50
147 A80	90rp gray vio ('38)	10.50	8.00
148 A80	1fr red brn	1.75	*6.25*
149 A80	1.20fr dp brn ('38)	8.25	*16.00*
150 A80	1.50fr sl bl ('38)	7.50	*16.00*
	Nos. 136-150 (14)	39.19	*54.16*
	Set, never hinged	70.00	

For overprints see Nos. O21-O29.

Souvenir Sheet

Josef Rheinberger A91

1938, July 30 **Engr.** ***Perf. 12***

151	Sheet of 4	19.00	19.00
	Never hinged	45.00	
a.	A91 50rp slate gray	2.50	3.25
	Never hinged	5.50	

Third Philatelic Exhibition of Liechtenstein. Sheet size: 99¾x135mm.

See No. 153.

Francis Type of 1933

Thick Wove Paper

1938, Aug. 15 ***Perf. 12½***

152 A55	3fr blk, *buff*	11.00	*60.00*
	Never hinged	17.00	

Issued in memory of Prince Francis I, who died July 25, 1938. Sheets of 20.

Josef Gabriel Rheinberger (1839-1901), German Composer and Organist — A92

1939, Mar. 31

153 A92	50rp slate green	70	*3.50*
	Never hinged	1.00	

Issued in sheets of 20.

Scene of Homage, 1718 — A93

1939, May 29

154 A93	20rp grn lake	80	1.25
155 A93	30rp slate blue	80	1.25
156 A93	50rp gray grn	80	1.25
	Set, never hinged	5.50	

Issued to honor Prince Franz Joseph II. Sheets of 20.

Cantonal Coats of Arms — A94

Prince Franz Joseph II — A95

Design: 3fr, Arms of Principality.

1939

157 A94	2fr dk grn, *buff*	5.25	*27.50*
158 A94	3fr indigo, *buff*	4.50	*30.00*
159 A96	5fr brn, *buff*	10.50	*32.50*
a.	Sheet of 4	85.00	*130.00*
	Never hinged	120.00	
	Set, never hinged	47.50	

Nos. 157-158 issued in sheets of 12; No. 159 in sheets of 4.

Prince Johann as a Child — A100

Memorial Tablet — A101

Prince Johann II — A102

Designs: 30rp, Prince Johann and Tower at Vaduz. 50rp, Prince Johann and Gutenberg Castle. 1fr, Prince Johann in 1920 and Vaduz Castle.

1940 **Photo.** ***Perf. 11½.***

160 A100	20rp hn brn	45	*1.95*
161 A100	30rp indigo	60	*2.50*
162 A100	50rp dk sl grn	1.25	*5.75*
163 A100	1fr brn vio	6.50	*45.00*
164 A101	1.50fr vio blk	6.00	*45.00*
165 A102	3fr brown	3.00	*13.00*
	Nos. 160-165 (6)	17.80	*113.20*
	Set, never hinged	37.50	

Birth centenary of Prince Johann II.

Nos. 160-164 issued in sheets of 25; No. 165 in sheets of 12.

Issue dates: 3fr, Oct. 5; others Aug. 10.

Gathering Corn A103

Wine Press A104

Sharpening Scythe A105

Milkmaid and Cow — A106

Native Costume A107

1941, Apr. 7

166 A103	10rp dull red brn	20	40
167 A104	20rp lake	35	85
168 A105	30rp royal blue	42	*1.50*
169 A106	50rp myrtle green	1.65	*10.00*
170 A107	90rp deep claret	1.65	*13.00*
	Nos. 166-170 (5)	4.27	*25.75*
	Set, never hinged	12.50	

Madonna and Child — A108

1941, July 7 **Engr.**

171 A108	10fr brn car	55.00	100.00
	Never hinged	80.00	

Issued in sheets of 4.

Johann Adam Andreas — A109

Designs: 30rp, Wenzel. 100rp, Anton Florian. 150rp, Joseph Adam.

1941, Dec. 18 **Photo.**

172 A109	20rp brn car	40	55
173 A109	30rp royal bl	45	*1.40*
174 A109	100rp vio blk	1.50	*10.50*
175 A109	150rp slate grn	1.50	*10.50*
	Set, never hinged	8.50	

Saint Lucius A113

Designs: 30rp, Reconstruction of Vaduz Castle. 50rp, Signing the Treaty of May 3, 1342. 1fr, Battle of Gutenberg. 2fr, Scene of Homage, 1718.

1942, Apr. 22 **Engr.** ***Perf. 11½***

176 A113	20rp brn org, *buff*	1.00	52
177 A113	30rp steel bl, *buff*	80	1.50
178 A113	50rp dk ol grn, *buff*	2.00	*5.25*
179 A113	1fr dl brn, *buff*	2.00	*10.50*
180 A113	2fr vio blk, *buff*	1.75	*12.00*
	Nos. 176-180 (5)	7.55	*29.77*
	Set, never hinged	17.50	

600th anniversary of the separation of Liechtenstein from the House of Monfort.

Johann Karl — A118

Designs: 30rp, Franz Joseph I. 1fr, Alois I. 1.50fr, Johann I.

1942, Oct. 5 **Photo.**

181 A118	20rp rose	30	70
182 A118	30rp brt blue	45	*1.25*
183 A118	1fr rose lilac	1.25	*9.75*
184 A118	1.50fr deep brn	1.40	*9.75*
	Set, never hinged	8.00	

Prince Franz Joseph II — A122

Countess Georgina von Wilczek — A123

Prince and Princess A124

1943, Mar. 5

185 A122	10rp dp rose vio	45	70
186 A123	20rp henna brn	45	70
187 A124	30rp slate blue	45	70
	Set, never hinged	2.00	

Marriage of Prince Franz Joseph II and Countess Georgina von Wilczek.

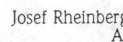

Prince Johann II — A126

Princes: 20rp, Alois II. 100rp, Franz Joseph I. 150rp, Franz Joseph II.

Perf. 11½

1943, July 5 Unwmk. Photo.

188 A126 20rp copper brn 20 40
189 A126 30rp deep ultra 40 80
190 A126 100rp olive gray 1.10 *5.75*
191 A126 150rp slate grn 1.10 *5.75*
Set, never hinged 6.00

Sheets of 20.

Terrain before Reclaiming A129

Designs: 30rp, Draining the Canal. 50rp, Plowing Reclaimed Land. 2fr, Harvesting Crops.

1943, Sept. 6

192 A129 10rp violet blk 16 40
193 A129 30rp deep blue 35 *2.25*
194 A129 50rp slate grn 75 *6.00*
195 A129 2fr olive brn 1.65 *9.25*
Set, never hinged 6.00

Vaduz A133

Gutenberg A134

1943, Dec. 27

196 A133 10rp dk gray 50 35
197 A134 20rp chestnut brn 65 90
Set, never hinged 2.25

Planken — A135

Bendern — A136

Designs: 10rp, Triesen. 15rp, Ruggell. 20rp, Vaduz. 25rp, Triesenberg. 30rp, Schaan. 40rp, Balzers. 50rp, Mauren. 60rp, Schellenberg. 90rp, Eschen. 1fr, Vaduz Castle. 120rp, Valuna Valley. 150rp, Lawena.

1944-45

198 A135 3rp dk brn & buff 15 22
199 A136 5rp sl grn & buff 15 15
200 A136 10rp gray & buff 18 15
201 A136 15rp bl gray & buff 28 *75*
202 A136 20rp org red & buff 24 18
203 A136 25rp dk rose vio & buff 28 *80*
204 A136 30rp bl & buff 35 45
205 A136 40rp brn & buff 55 95
206 A136 50rp bluish blk & pale gray 65 1.10
207 A136 60rp grn & buff 3.25 2.75
208 A136 90rp ol grn & buff 3.25 3.75
209 A136 1fr dp cl & buff 1.75 *3.50*
210 A136 120rp red brn 1.90 *3.75*
211 A136 150rp royal blue 1.90 *4.50*
Nos. 198-211 (14) 14.88 *23.00*
Set, never hinged 35.00

Issue years: 10rp, 15rp, 40rp-1fr, 1945; others, 1944. See No. 239. For surcharge and overprints see No. 236, O30-O36.

Crown and Rose — A149

1945, Apr. 9

212 A149 20rp multi 85 *52*
213 A149 30rp multi 85 *1.10*
214 A149 1fr multi 1.00 *3.75*
Set, never hinged 4.00

Birth of Prince Johann Adam Pius, Feb. 14, 1945. Sheets of 20.

Prince Franz Joseph II — A150

Arms of Liechtenstein and Vaduz Castle — A152

Design: 3fr, Princess Georgina.

1944-45 Photo.

215 A150 2fr brn, *buff* 5.25 *4.50*
216 A150 3fr dk grn 3.25 *4.25*

Engr.

217 A152 5fr bl gray, *cr* ('45) 9.50 *11.00*
Set, never hinged 37.50

Nos. 215-217 were issued in sheets of 8. See Nos. 222, 259-260.

Saint Lucius — A153

1946, Mar. 14 Unwmk. *Perf. 11½*

218 A153 10fr gray blk, *cr* 22.50 *24.00*
Never hinged 35.00
Sheet of 4 115.00 *115.00*
Never hinged 150.00

Issued in sheets measuring 105x130mm.

Red Deer — A154

Varying Hare — A155

Capercaillie — A156

1946, Dec. 10 Photo.

219 A154 20rp henna brn 1.25 1.25
220 A155 30rp grnsh bl 1.65 1.50
221 A156 150rp olive brn 2.75 *9.50*
Set, never hinged 10.50

Arms Type of 1945

1947, Mar. 20 Engr.

222 A152 5fr henna brn, *cr* 11.00 *27.50*
Never hinged 24.00

Issued in sheets of 8.

Chamois — A157

Alpine Marmot — A158

Golden Eagle — A159

1947, Oct. 15 Photo. Unwmk.

223 A157 20rp henna brn 1.65 2.75
224 A158 30rp grnsh bl 2.00 3.50
225 A159 150rp dark brn 3.00 *11.00*
Set, never hinged 14.00

Elsa Type of 1935

1947, Dec. 10 Engr. *Perf. 14½*

226 A70 2fr black, *yelsh* 2.25 *10.00*
Never hinged 3.50

Issued in memory of Princess Elsa, who died Sept. 28, 1947. Sheets of 20.

Portrait of Ginevra dei Benci by Leonardo da Vinci — A160

Designs: 20rp, Girl, Rubens. 30rp, Self-portrait, Rembrandt. 40rp, Canon, Massys. 50rp, Madonna, Memling. 60rp, French Painter, 1456, Fouquet. 80rp, Lute Player, Gentileschi. 90rp, Man, Strigel. 120rp, Man, Raphael.

1949, Mar. 15 Photo. *Perf. 11½*

227 A160 10rp dk grn 65 50
228 A160 20rp henna brn 85 50
229 A160 30rp sepia 1.65 2.00
230 A160 40rp blue 4.25 70
231 A160 50rp violet 3.75 5.50
232 A160 60rp grnsh gray 6.75 6.25
233 A160 80rp brn org 1.75 5.50
234 A160 90rp olive bis 6.75 5.50
235 A160 120rp claret 1.75 4.75
Nos. 227-235 (9) 28.15 31.20
Set, never hinged 45.00

Issued in sheets of 12.
See No. 238.

No. 198 Surcharged with New Value and Bars in Dark Brown

1949, Apr. 14

236 A135 5rp on 3rp dk brn & buff 25 30
Never hinged 50

Map, Post Horn and Crown A161

1949, May 23

237 A161 40rp blue & indigo 2.75 4.75
Never hinged 3.50

75th anniversary of the UPU.
For surcharge see No. 246.

Portrait Type of 1949
Souvenir Sheet

Unwmk.

1949, Aug. 6 Photo. *Imperf.*

238 Sheet of 3 60.00 *110.00*
a. A160 10rp dull green 10.50 14.00
b. A160 20rp lilac rose 10.50 14.00
c. A160 40rp blue 10.50 14.00
Never hinged 120.00

5th Philatelic Exhibition.
Sheet size: 121½x69½mm. Sold for 3fr.

Scenic Type of 1944

1949, Dec. 1 *Perf. 11½*

239 A136 5rp dk brn & buff 16.00 45
Never hinged 27.50

Rossauer Castle, Vienna — A163

Church at Bendern A164

Prince Johann Adam Andreas — A165

1949, Nov. 15 Engr. *Perf. 14½*

240 A163 20rp dk vio 75 1.65
241 A164 40rp blue 4.00 8.00
242 A165 150rp brn red 5.50 8.50
Set, never hinged 18.00

250th anniv. of the purchase of the former dukedom of Schellenberg. Sheets of 20.
For surcharge see No. 265.

Roe Deer — A166

Black Grouse — A167

Badger — A168

1950, Mar. 7 Photo. *Perf. 11½*

243 A166 20rp red brn 3.75 1.65
244 A167 30rp Prus grn 5.75 3.75
245 A168 80rp dk brn 21.00 40.00
Set, never hinged 62.50

Issued in sheets of 20.

No. 237 Surcharged with New Value and Bars Obliterating Commemorative Inscriptions

1950, Nov. 7

246 A161 1fr on 40rp bl & ind 15.00 *40.00*
Never hinged 25.00

Boy Cutting Bread — A169

Designs: 10rp, Laborer. 15rp, Cutting hay. 20rp, Harvesting corn. 25rp, Load of hay. 30rp, Wine grower. 40rp, Farmer and scythe. 50rp, Cattle raising. 60rp, Plowing. 80rp, Woman with potatoes. 90rp, Potato cultivation. 1fr, Tractor with potatoes.

Perf. 11½

1951, May 3 Unwmk. Photo.

247 A169 5rp claret 28 15
248 A169 10rp green 40 15
249 A169 15rp yel brn 2.75 4.50
250 A169 20rp ol brn 90 32

251 A169 25rp rose brn 2.75 4.50
252 A169 30rp grnsh gray 1.75 70
253 A169 40rp dp bl 5.25 5.50
254 A169 50rp vio brn 4.25 2.70
255 A169 60rp brown 4.00 2.75
256 A169 80rp hn brn 5.50 9.00
257 A169 90rp ol grn 9.00 4.25
258 A169 1fr indigo 32.50 6.00
Nos. 247-258 (12) 69.33 40.52
Set, never hinged 130.00

Types of 1944, Redrawn

Perf. 12½x12

1951, Nov. 20 Engr. Wmk. 296

259 A150 2fr dk bl 7.75 *35.00*
a. Perf. 14½ 575.00 165.00
260 A150 3fr dk red brn 100.00 80.00
a. Perf. 14½ 90.00 *225.00*
Set, never hinged 160.00
Set, never hinged 1,100.

Issued in sheets of 20.

Portrait, Savolodo A170

Madonna, Botticelli A171

Design: 40rp St. John, Del Sarto.

Perf. 11½

1952, May 27 Unwmk. Photo.

261 A170 20rp vio brn 21.00 3.75
262 A171 30rp brn olive 13.00 6.50
263 A170 40rp vio blue 8.00 5.25
Set, never hinged 75.00

Issued in sheets of 12.

Vaduz Castle — A172

Perf. 14½

1952, Sept. 25 Wmk. 296 Engr.

264 A172 5fr dp grn 115.00 140.00
Never hinged 200.00

Issued in sheets of 9.

No. 241 Surcharged with New Value and Wavy Lines in Red

1952, Sept. 25 Unwmk.

265 A164 1.20fr on 40rp blue 16.00 *45.00*
Never hinged 27.50

Portrait of a Young Man A173

St. Nicholas by Zeitblom A174

Designs: 30rp, St. Christopher by Cranach. 40rp, Leonhard, Duke of Hag, by Kulmbach.

Perf. 11½

1953, Feb. 5 Unwmk. Photo.

266 A173 10rp dk ol grn 42 1.00
267 A174 20rp olive brn 7.75 1.90
268 A174 30rp vio brn 17.00 7.50
269 A173 40rp slate bl 17.00 *45.00*
Set, never hinged 75.00

Issued in sheets of 12.

Lord Baden-Powell A175

1953, Aug. 4 Engr. *Perf. 13x13½*

270 A175 10rp dp grn 1.10 1.25
271 A175 20rp dk brn 7.50 2.75
272 A175 25rp red 7.50 16.00
273 A175 40rp dp bl 7.00 7.50
Set, never hinged 40.00

Intl. Scout Conf. Sheets of 20.

Alemannic Disc, 600 A. D. — A176

Prehistoric Settlement of Borscht — A177

Design: 1.20fr, Rössen jug.

1953, Nov. 26 *Perf. 11½*

274 A176 10rp org brn 5.00 *12.00*
275 A177 20rp dp gray grn 5.00 *9.00*
276 A176 1.20fr dk bl gray 27.50 *30.00*
Set, never hinged 60.00

Opening of National Museum, Vaduz.

Soccer Players — A178

Designs: 20rp, Player kicking ball. 25rp, Goalkeeper. 40rp, Two opposing players.

1954, May 18 Photo.

277 A178 10rp dl rose & brn 1.65 65
278 A178 20rp olive grn 2.50 65
279 A178 25rp org brn 9.25 *19.00*
280 A178 40rp lilac gray 6.25 5.00
Set, never hinged 37.50

See #289-292, 297-300, 308-311, 320-323.

Nos. B19-B21 Surcharged with New Value and Bars in Color of Stamp

1954, Sept. 28 Unwmk. *Perf. 11½*

281 SP15 35rp on 10rp+10rp 1.10 3.25
282 SP16 60rp on 20rp+10rp 11.50 10.00
283 SP15 65rp on 40rp+10rp 3.50 6.50
Set, never hinged 27.50

Madonna in Wood, 14th Century — A179

1954, Dec. 16 Engr.

284 A179 20rp henna brn 1.50 2.75
285 A179 40rp gray 8.50 18.00
286 A179 1fr dk brn 8.50 18.00
Set, never hinged 35.00

Prince Franz Joseph II — A180

Princess Georgina — A181

1955, Apr. 5 *Perf. 14½*

Cream Paper

287 A180 2fr dk brn 50.00 32.50
288 A181 3fr dk grn 50.00 32.50
Set, never hinged 165.00

Issued in sheets of 9.

Sports Type of 1954

Designs: 10rp, Slalom. 20rp, Mountain climbing. 25rp, Skiing. 40rp, Resting on summit.

1955, June 14 Photo. *Perf. 11½*

289 A178 10rp aqua & brn vio 1.00 85
290 A178 20rp grn & ol bis 2.50 85
291 A178 25rp lt ultra & sep 9.50 14.00
292 A178 40rp ol & pink 7.00 3.50
Set, never hinged 35.00

Prince Johann Adam — A183

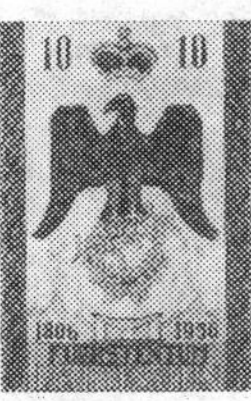

Eagle, Crown and Oak Leaves — A184

Portraits: 20rp, Prince Philipp. 40rp, Prince Nikolaus. 60rp, Princess Nora.

1955, Dec. 14

Granite Paper

Cross in Red

293 A183 10rp dull vio 60 42
294 A183 20rp slate grn 3.00 1.40
295 A183 40rp olive brn 4.50 7.00
296 A183 60rp rose brown 3.00 5.25
Set, never hinged 17.00

Liechtenstein Red Cross, 10th anniversary.

Sports Type of 1954

Designs: 10rp, Javelin thrower. 20rp, Hurdling. 40rp, Pole vaulting. 1fr, Sprinters.

Perf. 11½

1956, June 21 Unwmk. Photo.

Granite Paper

297 A178 10rp lt red brn & ol grn 65 30
298 A178 20rp lt ol grn & pur 1.65 55
299 A178 40rp bl & vio brn 2.50 3.25
300 A178 1fr org ver & ol brn 7.00 7.75
Set, never hinged 21.00

1956, Aug. 21

Granite Paper

301 A184 10rp dk brn & gold 1.10 1.00
302 A184 120rp sl blk & gold 5.75 3.50
Set, never hinged 14.00

150th anniversary of independence.

Prince Franz Joseph II — A185

Prince Johann Adam — A186

1956, Aug. 21

303 A185 10rp dk grn 90 40
304 A185 15rp brt ultra 2.00 2.75
305 A185 25rp purple 2.25 2.75
306 A185 60rp dk brn 4.00 2.75
Set, never hinged 15.00

50th birthday of Prince Franz Joseph II.

1956, Aug. 21

Granite Paper

307 A186 20rp olive green 1.75 48
Never hinged 2.75

Issued to publicize the 6th Philatelic Exhibition, Vaduz, Aug. 25-Sept. 2. Sheets of 9.

Sports Type of 1954

Designs: 10rp, Somersault on bar. 15rp, Jumping over vaulting horse. 25rp, Exercise on rings. 1.50fr, Somersault on parallel bars.

1957, May 14 Photo. *Perf. 11½*

308 A178 10rp pale rose & ol grn 80 52
309 A178 15rp pale grn & dl pur 2.75 4.50
310 A178 25rp ol bis & Prus grn 2.75 6.50
311 A178 1.50fr lemon & sepia 7.25 14.00
Set, never hinged 25.00

Pine A187

Lord Baden-Powell A188

Designs: 20rp, Wild roses. 1fr, Birches.

1957, Sept. 10 *Perf. 11½*

Granite Paper

312 A187 10rp dk vio 2.50 2.50
313 A187 20rp brn car 2.50 80
314 A187 1fr green 4.00 5.50
Set, never hinged 14.00

See Nos. 326-328, 332-334, 353-355.

1957, Sept. 10 Unwmk.

Design: 10rp, Symbolical torchlight parade.

315 A188 10rp bl blk 1.00 1.65
316 A188 20rp dk brn 1.00 1.65
a. Sheet of 12, 6 each #315-316 12.00 17.50
Never hinged 17.00
Set, never hinged 3.00

Cent. of the birth of Lord Baden-Powell and the 60th anniv. of the Boy Scout movement.

Chapel of St. Mamertus — A189

Designs: 40rp, Madonna and saints. 1.50fr, Pieta.

1957, Dec. 16 *Perf. 11½*

317 A189 10rp dk brn 40 32
318 A189 40rp dark blue 1.25 *5.00*
319 A189 1.50fr brn lake 7.00 8.75
Set, never hinged 15.00

Issued in sheets of 20. Sheet inscribed: "Furstentum Liechtenstein" and "Weihnacht 1957" (Christmas 1957).

Sports Type of 1954

Designs: 15rp, Girl swimmer. 30rp, Fencers. 40rp, Tennis. 90rp, Bicyclists.

1958, Mar. 18 Photo.

Granite Paper

320 A178 15rp lt bl & pur 70 95
321 A178 30rp pale rose lil & ol gray 3.50 5.75
322 A178 40rp sal pink & sl bl 3.50 5.75
323 A178 90rp lt ol grn & vio brn 1.75 3.75
Set, never hinged 12.50

Relief Map of Liechtenstein
A190

1958, Mar. 18
324 A190 25rp bis, vio & red 35 90
325 A190 40rp bl, vio & red 35 90
Set, never hinged 1.25

World's Fair, Brussels, Apr. 17-Oct. 19. Sheets of 25. For surcharges see Nos. B22-B23.

Tree-Bush Design of 1957

Designs: 20rp, Maples at Lawena. 50rp, Holly at Schellenberg. 90rp, Yew at Maurerberg.

1958, Aug. 12 *Perf. 11½*
Granite Paper
326 A187 20rp chocolate 1.75 75
327 A187 50rp olive green 7.00 4.50
328 A187 90rp vio blue 1.75 2.75
Set, never hinged 19.00

Sts. Moritz and Agatha
A191

"The Good Shepherd"
A192

Christmas: 35rp, St. Peter. 80rp, Chapel of St. Peter, Mals-Balzers.

1958, Dec. 4 Photo. Unwmk.
Granite Paper
329 A191 20rp dk slate grn 2.25 2.50
330 A191 35rp dk blue vio 2.25 2.50
331 A191 80rp dark brown 2.25 2.50
Set, never hinged 10.00

Issued in sheets of 20.

Tree-Bush Type of 1957

Designs: 20rp, Larch in Lawena. 50rp, Holly on Alpila. 90rp, Linden in Schaan.

1959, Apr. 15 *Perf. 11½*
332 A187 20rp dark vio 2.75 2.00
333 A187 50rp henna brn 2.75 2.00
334 A187 90rp dark green 2.75 2.00
Set, never hinged 14.00

1959, Apr. 15 Unwmk.
335 A192 30rp rose vio & gold 50 85
Never hinged 85

Issued in memory of Pope Pius XII.

Flags and Rhine Valley — A193

Man Carrying Hay — A194

Apple Harvest — A195

Designs: 5rp, Church at Bendern and sheaves. 20rp, Rhine embankment. 30rp, Gutenberg Castle. 40rp, View from Schellenberg. 50rp, Vaduz Castle. 60rp, Naafkopf, Falknis Range. 75rp, Woman gathering sheaves. 90rp, Woman in vineyard. 1fr, Woman in kitchen. 1.30fr, Return from the field. 1.50fr, Family saying grace.

1959-64
Granite Paper
336 A193 5rp gray ol ('61) 15 15
337 A193 10rp dl vio 15 15
338 A193 20rp lil rose 15 15
339 A193 30rp dk red 15 15
340 A193 40rp ol grn ('61) 1.25 55
341 A193 50rp deep blue 30 35
342 A193 60rp brt grnsh bl 45 55
343 A194 75rp dp ocher ('60) 1.25 1.00
344 A194 80rp ol grn ('61) 1.00 90
345 A194 90rp red lil ('61) 1.00 90
346 A194 1fr chnt ('61) 1.00 90
347 A195 1.20fr org ver ('60) 1.50 1.10
348 A195 1.30fr brt grn ('64) 1.25 90
349 A195 1.50fr brt bl ('60) 1.50 1.40
Nos. 336-349 (14) 11.10 9.15
Set, never hinged 13.00

Belfry, Bendern Church — A196

Christmas: 60rp, Sculpture, bell, St. Theodul's church. 1fr, Sculpture, tower of St. Lucius' church.

1959, Dec. 2 Unwmk. *Perf. 11½*
350 A196 5rp dk slate grn 55 22
351 A196 60rp olive 3.50 4.25
352 A196 1fr dp claret 2.75 2.50
Set, never hinged 11.00

Issued in sheets of 20.

Tree-Bush Type of 1957

Designs: 20rp, Beech tree on Gafadura. 30rp, Juniper on Alpila. 50rp, Pine on Sass.

1960, Sept. 19
353 A187 20rp brown 4.50 5.00
354 A187 30rp deep plum 4.50 5.00
355 A187 50rp Prus grn 15.00 5.00
Set, never hinged 40.00

Europa Issue, 1960

Honeycomb
A197

1960, Sept. 19 *Perf. 14*
356 A197 50rp multi 100.00 60.00
Never hinged 130.00

Issued to promote the idea of a united Europe. Sheets of 20.

Princess Gina
A198

Heinrich von Frauenberg
A199

Portraits: 1.70fr, Prince Johann Adam Pius. 3fr, Prince Franz Joseph II.

1960-64 Engr. *Perf. 14*
356A A198 1.70fr vio ('64) 1.00 1.50
b. Imperf., pair *1,750. 1,750.*
357 A198 2fr dk bl 2.50 2.25
a. Imperf., pair *1,750. 1,750.*
358 A198 3fr dp brn 2.50 2.25
Set, never hinged 7.50

Issued in sheets of 16.

1961-62 Photo. *Perf. 11½*

Minnesingers: 20rp, King Konradin. 25rp, Ulrich von Liechtenstein. 30rp, Kraft von Toggenburg. 35rp, Ulrich von Gutenberg. 40rp, Heinrich von Veldig. 1fr, Konrad von Alstetten. 1.50r, Walther von der Vogelweide. 2fr, Tannhäuser. (Designs from 14th century Manesse manuscript.)

359 A199 15rp multi 60 75
360 A199 20rp multi ('62) 30 30
361 A199 25rp multi 1.25 1.65
362 A199 30rp multi ('62) 40 40
363 A199 35rp multi 1.50 2.00
364 A199 40rp multi ('62) 65 65
365 A199 1fr multi 2.50 2.00
366 A199 1.50fr multi 9.25 15.00
367 A199 2fr multi ('62) 1.65 1.65
Nos. 359-367 (9) 18.10 24.40
Set, never hinged 22.50

Issued in sheets of 20. See #381-384, 471.

Catalogue values for unused stamps in this section, from this point to the end of the section, are for Never Hinged items.

Europa Issue, 1961

Cogwheels
A200

1961, Oct. 3 Unwmk. *Perf. 13½*
368 A200 50rp multi 25 25

Printed in sheets of 20.

Souvenir Sheet

Prince Johann II — A201

Portraits: 10rp, Francis I. 25rp, Franz Joseph II.

1962, Aug. 2 Photo. *Perf. 11½*
369 Sheet of 3 9.50 6.00
a. A201 5rp gray green 1.10 85
b. A201 10rp deep rose 3.50 2.75
c. A201 25rp blue 1.10 85

50th anniv. of Liechtenstein's postage stamps and in connection with the Anniv. Stamp Exhib., Vaduz, Aug. 4-12. No. 369 sold for 3fr.

Hands — A202

1962, Aug. 2
370 A202 50rp indigo & red 80 75

Europa. Issued in sheets of 20.

Malaria Eradication Emblem — A203

Pietà — A204

1962, Aug. 2 Engr.
371 A203 50rp turq blue 38 38

Issued for the World Health Organization drive to eradicate malaria. Sheets of 20.

1962, Dec. 6 Photo.

Designs: 50rp, Angel with harp, fresco. 1.20fr, View of Mauren.

372 A204 30rp magenta 60 60
373 A204 50rp dp org 85 85
374 A204 1.20fr deep blue 1.25 1.25

Issued in sheets of 20.

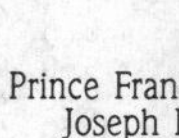

Prince Franz Joseph II
A205

1963, Apr. 3 Engr. *Perf. 13½x14*
375 A205 5fr dull green 4.00 2.50

25th anniversary of the accession of Prince Franz Joseph II. Sheets of 8.
Exists imperf. Value $1,500.

Angel of the Annunciation
A206

Greek Architectural Elements
A207

Designs: 80rp, Three Kings. 1fr, Family.

Perf. 11½
1963, Aug. 26 Unwmk. Photo.
376 A206 20rp multi 40 40
377 A206 80rp gray, pur & red 80 80
378 A206 1fr multi 80 80

Centenary of the International Red Cross.

Europa Issue, 1963
1963, Aug. 26
379 A207 50rp multi 2.00 1.50

Bread and Milk — A208

1963, Aug. 26
380 A208 50rp dk red pur & brn 40 40

FAO "Freedom from Hunger" campaign.

Minnesinger Type of 1961-62

Minnesingers: 25rp, Heinrich von Sax. 30rp, Kristan von Hamle. 75rp, Werner von Teufen. 1.70fr, Hartmann von Aue.

Perf. 11½
1963, Dec. 5 Unwmk. Photo.
381 A199 25rp multi 30 30
382 A199 30rp multi 30 30
383 A199 75rp multi 75 75
384 A199 1.70fr multi 1.25 1.25

Issued in sheets of 20.

Olympic Rings, Flags of Austria and Japan — A209

1964, Apr. 15 *Perf. 11½*
385 A209 50rp Prus bl, red & blk 40 40

Olympic Games 1964. Sheets of 20.

Arms of Counts of Werdenberg-Vaduz
A210

Coats of Arms: 30rp, Barons of Brandis. 80rp, Counts of Sulz. 1.50fr, Counts of Hohenems.

1964, Sept. 1 **Photo.**

386 A210 20rp multi 16 16
387 A210 30rp multi 25 25
388 A210 80rp multi 55 55
389 A210 1.50fr multi 80 80

See Nos. 396-399.

Europa Issue, 1964

Roman Castle, Schaan — A211

1964, Sept. 1 ***Perf. 13x14***

390 A211 50rp multi 3.75 95

Masescha Chapel — A212

Peter Kaiser — A213

Designs: 40rp, Mary Magdalene, altarpiece. 1.30fr, Madonna with Sts. Sebastian and Roch, altarpiece.

1964, Dec. 9 **Photo.** ***Perf. 11½***

391 A212 10rp vio blk 15 15
392 A212 40rp dk bl 40 40
393 A212 1.30fr dp cl 1.10 1.10

Issued in sheets of 20.

1964, Dec. 9 **Engr.**

394 A213 1fr dk grn, *buff* 60 60

Kaiser (1793-1864), historian. Sheets of 20.

Madonna, Wood Sculpture, 18th Century — A214

Perf. 11½

1965, Apr. 22 **Unwmk.** **Engr.**

395 A214 10fr org red 7.00 6.00

Issued in sheets of 4.

Arms Type of 1965

Coats of Arms (Lords of): 20rp, Schellenberg. 30rp, Gutenberg. 80rp, Frauenberg. 1fr, Ramschwag.

Perf. 11½

1965, Aug. 31 **Unwmk.** **Photo.**

396 A210 20rp multi 15 15
397 A210 30rp multi 15 15
398 A210 80rp multi 50 50
399 A210 1fr multi 55 55

Alemannic Ornament A215

Europa: The design is from a belt buckle, about 600 A.D., found in a man's tomb near Eschen.

1965, Aug. 31

400 A215 50rp vio bl, gray & brn 70 45

The Annunciation by Ferdinand Nigg — A216

Princess Gina and Prince Franz Josef Wenzel — A217

Paintings by Nigg: 30rp, The Three Kings. 1.20fr, Jesus in the Temple, horiz.

1965, Dec. 7 **Photo.** ***Perf. 11½***

401 A216 10rp yel grn & dk grn 15 15
402 A216 30rp org & red brn 28 28
403 A216 1.20fr ultra & grnsh bl 55 55

Ferdinand Nigg (1865-1949), painter.

1965, Dec. 7

404 A217 75rp gray, buff & gold 45 45

Communication Symbols — A218

1965, Dec. 7

405 A218 25rp multi 22 22

Centenary of the ITU.

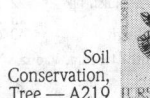

Soil Conservation, Tree — A219

Designs: 20rp, Clean air, bird. 30rp, Unpolluted water, fish. 1.50fr, Nature preservation, sun.

1966, Apr. 26 **Photo.** ***Perf. 11½***

406 A219 10rp brt yel & grn 15 15
407 A219 20rp bl & dk bl 15 15
408 A219 30rp brt grn & ultra 25 25
409 A219 1.50fr yel & red 70 70

Issued to publicize nature conservation.

Prince Franz Joseph II A220

Arms of Barons of Richenstein A221

1966, Apr. 26

410 A220 1fr gray, gold, buff & dk brn 60 60

60th birthday of Prince Franz Joseph II.

1966, Sept. 6 **Photo.** ***Perf. 11½***

Coats of Arms: 30rp, Vaistli knights. 60rp, Lords of Trisun. 1.20fr, von Schiel.

Light Gray Background

411 A221 20rp multi 15 15
412 A221 30rp multi 15 15
413 A221 60rp multi 25 25
414 A221 1.20fr multi 55 55

Europa Issue, 1966
Common Design Type

1966, Sept. 6 **Photo.** ***Perf. 14x13***
Size: 25x32mm

415 CD9 50rp ultra, dp org & lt grn 45 40

Vaduz Parish Church — A222

St. Florin — A223

Designs: 30rp, Madonna. 1.70fr, God the Father.

1966, Dec. 6 **Photo.** ***Perf. 11½***

416 A222 5rp org red & cit 15 15
417 A223 20rp lem & mag 15 15
418 A223 30rp dl rose & dp bl 20 20
419 A223 1.70fr gray & red brn 75 75

Restoration of the Vaduz Parish Church.

Europa Issue, 1967
Common Design Type

1967, Apr. 20 **Photo.** ***Perf. 11½***

420 CD10 50rp multi 42 42

The Man from Malans and his White Horse — A225

Fairy Tales of Liechtenstein: 30rp, The Treasure of Gutenberg. 1.20fr, The Giant of Guflina slaying the Dragon.

1967, Apr. 20

421 A225 20rp multi 15 15
422 A225 30rp multi 18 15
423 A225 1.20fr grn & multi 70 65

See Nos. 443-445, 458-460.

Souvenir Sheet

Prince Hans Adam and Countess Kinsky — A226

1967, June 26 **Engr.** ***Perf. 14x13½***

424 A226 Sheet of 2 2.25 2.25
a. 1.50fr slate blue (Prince) 1.10 1.10
b. 1.50fr red brown (Countess) 1.10 1.10

Wedding of Prince Hans Adam of Liechtenstein and Marie Aglae Countess Kinsky of Wichnitz and Tettau, July 30, 1967.

Common Design Types pictured in section at front of book.

EFTA Emblem — A227

1967, Sept. 28 **Photo.** ***Perf. 11½***

425 A227 50rp multi 55 55

European Free Trade Association. See note after Norway No. 501.

Trophaeum (The Victorious Cross) — A228

Christian Symbols: 20rp, Alpha and Omega. 70rp, Chrismon.

1967, Sept. 28

426 A228 20rp rose cl, blk, & gold 18 15
427 A228 30rp multi 25 18
428 A228 70rp dp ultra, blk & gold 60 48

Johann Baptist Büchel — A229

1967, Sept. 28 **Engr. & Litho.**

429 A229 1fr rose cl & pale grn 70 55

Issued in memory of Johann Baptist Büchel (1853-1927), priest, educator, historian and poet. Printed on fluorescent paper.

Peter and Paul, Patron Saints of Mauren — A230

Patron Saints: 5rp, St. Joseph, Planken. 10rp, St. Laurentius, Schaan. 30rp, St. Nicholas, Balzers. 40rp, St. Sebastian, Nendeln. 50rp, St. George, Schellenberg Chapel. 60rp, St. Martin, Eschen. 70rp, St. Fridolin, Ruggell. 80rp, St. Gallus, Triesen. 1fr, St. Theodul, Triesenberg. 1.20fr, St. Ann, Vaduz Castle. 1.50fr, St. Mary, Bendern-Gamprin. 2fr, St. Lucius, patron saint of the Principality.

1967-71 **Photo.** ***Perf. 11½***

430 A230 5rp multi ('68) 15 15
431 A230 10rp multi ('68) 15 15
432 A230 20rp bl & multi 15 15
433 A230 30rp dk red & multi 22 15
433A A230 40rp multi ('71) 45 35
434 A230 50rp multi ('68) 38 30
435 A230 60rp multi ('68) 45 35
436 A230 70rp multi 48 40
437 A230 80rp multi ('68) 55 50
438 A230 1fr multi ('68) 75 55
439 A230 1.20fr vio bl & multi 80 90
440 A230 1.50fr multi ('68) 1.10 95
441 A230 2fr multi ('68) 1.25 1.25
Nos. 430-441 (13) 6.88 6.15

Issue dates: 20rp, 30rp, 70rp, 1.20fr, Dec. 7, 1967; 5rp, 1.50fr, Aug. 29, 1968; 40rp, June 11, 1971. 2fr, Dec. 5, 1968. Others Apr. 25, 1968.

Europa Issue, 1968
Common Design Type

1968, Apr. 25
Size: 32½x23mm

442 CD11 50rp crim, gold & ultra 45 45

Fairy Tale Type of 1967

Fairy Tales of Liechtenstein: 30rp, The Treasure of St. Mamerten. 50rp, The Goblin from the Bergerwald. 80rp, The Three Sisters. (Denominations at right.)

1968, Aug. 29
443 A225 30rp Prus bl, yel & red 18 15
444 A225 50rp grn, yel & bl 32 32
445 A225 80rp brt bl, yel & lt bl 55 55

Arms of Liechtenstein and Wilczek — A231

1968, Aug. 29
446 A231 75rp multi 75 70

Silver wedding anniversary of Prince Franz Joseph II and Princess Gina.

Sir Rowland Hill — A232

Coat of Arms — A233

Portraits: 30rp, Count Philippe de Ferrari. 80rp, Carl Lindenberg. 1fr, Maurice Burrus. 1.20fr, Théodore Champion.

1968-69 Engr. ***Perf. 14x13½***
447 A232 20rp green 15 15
448 A232 30rp red brown 22 22
449 A232 80rp dark brown 55 45
450 A232 1fr black 70 65
451 A232 1.20fr dark blue 90 70
Nos. 447-451 (5) 2.52 2.17

Issued to honor "Pioneers of Philately."
Issue dates: 80rp, 1.20fr, Aug. 28, 1969. Others, Dec. 5, 1968.
See Nos. 509-511.

1969, Apr. 24 Engr. ***Perf. 14x13½***
452 A233 3.50fr dark brown 2.50 1.65

Sheets of 16.

Europa Issue, 1969
Common Design Type

1969, Apr. 24 Photo. ***Perf. 14***
Size: 33x23mm

453 CD12 50rp brn red, yel & grn 60 60

"Biology" (Man and DNA Molecule) A234

Designs: 30rp, "Physics" (man and magnetic field). 50rp, "Astronomy" (man and planets). 80rp, "Art" (artist and Prince Franz Joseph II and Princess Gina).

1969, Aug. 28 Photo. ***Perf. 11½***
454 A234 10rp grn, dk bl & dp cl 15 15
455 A234 30rp brn & multi 24 16
456 A234 50rp ultra & grn 42 30
457 A234 80rp brn, dk brn & yel 70 50

250th anniv. of the Duchy of Liechtenstein.

Fairy Tale Type of 1967

Fairy Tales of Liechtenstein: 20rp, The Cheated Devil. 50rp, The Fiery Red Goat. 60rp, The Grafenberg Treasure (toad). (Denominations at right.)

1969, Dec. 4 Photo. ***Perf. 11½***
458 A225 20rp multi 15 15
459 A225 50rp yel & multi 38 35
460 A225 60rp red & multi 52 45

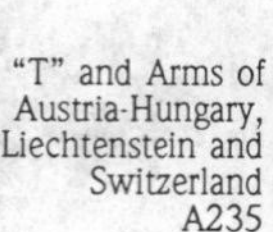

"T" and Arms of Austria-Hungary, Liechtenstein and Switzerland A235

1969, Dec. 4 ***Perf. 13½***
461 A235 30rp gold & multi 28 28

Cent. of the Liechtenstein telegraph system.

Arms of St. Lucius Monastery, Chur — A236

Prince Wenzel — A237

Arms of Ecclesiastic Patrons: 50rp, Pfäfers Abbey (dove). 1.50fr, Chur Bishopric (stag).

1969, Dec. 4 ***Perf. 11½***
462 A236 30rp multi 22 20
463 A236 50rp multi 38 35
464 A236 1.50fr multi 1.00 1.00

See Nos. 475-477, 486-488.

1970, Apr. 30 Photo. ***Perf. 11½***
465 A237 1fr sepia & multi 90 90

25th anniv. of the Liechtenstein Red Cross.

Orange Lily — A238

Native Flowers: 30rp, Bumblebee orchid. 50rp, Glacier crowfoot. 1.20fr, Buck bean.

1970, Apr. 30
466 A238 20rp multi 18 18
467 A238 30rp grn & multi 30 30
468 A238 50rp ol & multi 60 60
469 A238 1.20fr multi 1.25 1.25

Issued to publicize the European Conservation Year 1970. See Nos. 481-484, 500-503.

Europa Issue, 1970
Common Design Type

1970, Apr. 30 Litho. ***Perf. 14***
Size: 31½x20½mm

470 CD13 50rp emer, dk bl & yel 60 60

Minnesinger Type of 1961-62
Souvenir Sheet

Minnesingers: 30rp, Wolfram von Eschenbach. 50rp, Reinmar der Fiedler. 80rp, Hartmann von Starkenberg. 1.20fr, Friedrich von Hausen.

1970, Aug. 27 Photo. ***Perf. 11½***
471 Sheet of 4 2.25 2.25
a. A199 30rp multi 15 15
b. A199 50rp multi 28 28
c. A199 80rp multi 48 48
d. A199 1.20fr multi 65 65

Wolfram von Eschenbach (1170-1220), German minnesinger (poet). Sold for 3fr.

Prince Franz Joseph II — A239

Mother & Child, Sculpture by Rudolf Schädler — A240

Portrait: 2.50fr, Princess Gina.

1970-71 Engr. ***Perf. 14x13½***
472 A239 2.50fr violet blue 1.90 1.10
473 A239 3fr black 2.00 1.25

Issue dates: 2.50fr, June 11, 1971. 3fr, Dec. 3, 1970. Sheets of 16.

1970, Dec. 3 Photo. ***Perf. 11½***
474 A240 30rp dk red & multi 28 28

Christmas.

Ecclesiastic Arms Type of 1969

Arms of Ecclesiastic Patrons: 20rp, Abbey of St. John in Thur Valley (Lamb of God). 30rp, Ladies' Abbey, Schänis (crown). 75rp, Abbey of St. Gallen (bear rampant).

1970, Dec. 3
475 A236 20rp lt bl & multi 16 16
476 A236 30rp gray, red & gold 25 25
477 A236 75rp multi 60 60

Bronze Boar, La Tène Period — A241

Designs: 30rp, Peacock, Roman, 2nd century. 75rp, Decorated copper bowl, 13th century.

1971, Mar. 11 Photo. ***Perf. 11½***
478 A241 25rp dp ultra & bluish blk 22 22
479 A241 30rp dk brn & grn 25 25
480 A241 75rp grn, yel & brn 60 60

Opening of the National Museum, Vaduz.

Flower Type of 1970

Flowers: 10rp, Cyclamen. 20rp, Moonwort. 50rp, Superb pink. 1.50fr, Alpine columbine.

1971, Mar. 11
481 A238 10rp multi 15 15
482 A238 20rp multi 15 15
483 A238 50rp multi 45 45
484 A238 1.50fr multi 1.40 1.25

Europa Issue, 1971
Common Design Type

1971, June 11 Photo. ***Perf. 13½***
Size: 31x21mm

485 CD14 50rp grnsh bl, yel & blk 55 55

Ecclesiastic Arms Type of 1969

Arms of Ecclesiastic Patrons: 30rp, Knights of St. John, Feldkirch (Latin and moline crosses). 50rp, Weingarten Abbey (grapes). 1.20fr, Ottobeuren Abbey (eagle and cross).

1971, Sept. 2 Photo. ***Perf. 11½***
486 A236 30rp bis & multi 22 22
487 A236 50rp multi 35 35
488 A236 1.20fr gray & multi 90 90

Princely Crown — A242

Design: 70rp, Page from constitution.

1971, Sept. 2
489 A242 70rp grn, gold, blk & cop 52 52
490 A242 80rp dk bl, gold, red & plum 65 65

50th anniversary of the constitution.

Madonna, by Andrea della Robbia — A243

Long-distance Skiing — A244

1971, Dec. 9
491 A243 30rp multi 30 28

Christmas 1971.

1971, Dec. 9

Olympic Rings and: 40rp, Ice hockey. 65rp, Downhill skiing, women's. 1.50fr, Figure skating, women's.

492 A244 15rp lem & dk brn 15 15
493 A244 40rp multi 32 28
494 A244 65rp multi 52 52
495 A244 1.50fr multi 1.25 1.10

11th Winter Olympic Games, Sapporo, Japan, Feb. 3-13, 1972.

1972, Mar. 16 Photo. ***Perf. 11***

Olympic Rings and: 10rp, Gymnast. 20rp, High jump. 40rp, Running, women's. 60rp, Discus. All horiz.

496 A244 10rp cl, brn & gray 15 15
497 A244 20rp ol, brn & yel 20 20
498 A244 40rp red, brn & gray 35 35
499 A244 60rp brn, dk brn & bl 70 55

20th Olympic Games, Munich, Aug. 26-Sept. 10.

Flower Type of 1970

Flowers: 20rp, Anemone. 30rp, Turk's cap. 60rp, Alpine centaury. 1.20fr, Reed mace.

1972, Mar. 16
500 A238 20rp dk bl & multi 16 15
501 A238 30rp ol & multi 24 16
502 A238 60rp multi 52 52
503 A238 1.20fr multi 1.00 1.00

Europa Issue, 1972
Common Design Type

1972, Mar. 16
504 CD15 40rp dk ol, bl grn & rose red 60 50

Souvenir Sheet

Bendern and Vaduz Castle — A246

1972, June 8 Engr. ***Perf. 13½***
505 A246 Sheet of 2 2.75 2.75
a. 1fr violet blue 90 90
b. 2fr carmine 1.75 1.75

8th Liechtenstein Philatelic Exhibition, LIBA 1972, Vaduz, Aug. 18-27.

Liechtenstein stamps can be mounted in Scott's annual Liechtenstein Supplement.

Faun, by Rudolf Schädler
A247

Madonna with Angels, by Ferdinand Nigg
A248

1972, Sept. 7 Photo. *Perf. 11½*

506	A247	20rp shown	16	15
507	A247	30rp Dancer	25	22
508	A247	1.10fr Owl	95	80

Sculptures made of roots and branches by Rudolf Schädler.

Portrait Type of 1968-69

Portraits: 30rp, Emilio Diena. 40rp, André de Cock. 1.30fr, Theodore E. Steinway.

1972, Sept. 7 Engr. *Perf. 14x13½*

509	A232	30rp Prus grn	22	20
510	A232	40rp dk vio brn	35	30
511	A232	1.30fr vio bl	1.10	1.00

Pioneers of Philately.

1972, Dec. 7 Photo. *Perf. 11½*

512	A248	30rp blk & multi	30	28

Christmas 1972.

Lawena Springs — A249

Nautilus Cup — A250

Landscapes: 5rp, Silum. 15rp, Ruggell Marsh. 25rp, Steg, Kirchlispitz. 30rp, Fields, Schellenberg. 40rp, Rennhof, Mauren. 50rp, Tidrüfe Vaduz. 60rp, Eschner Riet. 70rp, Mittagspitz. 80rp, Three Sisters, Schaan Forest. 1fr, St. Peter's and Tower House, Mäls. 1.30fr, Road, Frommenhaus. 1.50fr, Ox Head Mountain. 1.80fr, Hehlawangspitz. 2fr, Saminaschlucht.

1972-73 Engr. & Litho. *Perf. 11½*

513	A249	5rp brn, yel & mag	15	15
514	A249	10rp sl grn & cit	15	15
515	A249	15rp red brn & cit	15	15
516	A249	25rp dk vio & pale grn	24	18
517	A249	30rp pur & buff	28	22
518	A249	40rp vio & pale sal	35	28
519	A249	50rp vio bl & rose	45	35
520	A249	60rp grn & yel	55	45
521	A249	70rp dk & lt bl	65	52
522	A249	80rp Prus grn & cit	70	55
523	A249	1fr red brn & lt grn	95	65
524	A249	1.30fr ultra & lt grn	1.25	1.00
525	A249	1.50fr brn & lt bl	1.40	1.00
526	A249	1.80fr brn & buff	1.65	1.25
527	A249	2fr sep & pale grn	1.75	1.40
		Nos. 513-527 (15)	10.67	8.30

Issue dates: 10rp, 15rp, 80rp, 1fr, 1.50fr, Dec. 7. 30rp, 1.30fr, 1.80fr, Mar. 8, 1973. 50rp, 60rp, 70rp, June 7, 1973. 5rp, 25rp, 40rp, 2fr, Dec. 6, 1973.

Europa Issue, 1973

Common Design Type

1973, Mar. 8 Photo. *Perf. 11½*
Size: 33x23mm

528	CD16	30rp pur & multi	30	30
529	CD16	40rp bl & multi	45	45

1973, June 7 Photo. *Perf. 11½*

Designs: 70rp, Ivory tankard. 1.10fr, Silver goblet.

530	A250	30rp gray & multi	24	24
531	A250	70rp multi	55	55
532	A250	1.10fr dk bl & multi	95	95

Drinking vessels from the Princely Treasury.

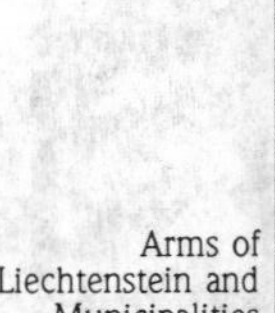

Arms of Liechtenstein and Municipalities
A251

Engraved & Photogravure

1973, Sept. 6 *Perf. 14x13½*

533	A251	5fr blk & multi	4.00	3.00

Coenonympha Oedippus
A252

Designs: 15rp, Alpine newt. 25rp, European viper (adder). 40rp, Common curlew. 60rp, Edible frog. 70rp, Dappled butterfly. 80rp, Grass snake. 1.10fr, Three-toed woodpecker.

1973-74 Photo. *Perf. 11½*

534	A252	15rp multi	15	15
535	A252	25rp multi	28	28
536	A252	30rp org & multi	25	25
537	A252	40rp brn & multi	35	35
538	A252	60rp multi	60	60
539	A252	70rp multi	65	60
540	A252	80rp multi	70	70
541	A252	1.10fr multi	1.00	1.00
		Nos. 534-541 (8)	3.98	3.93

Issue dates: 30rp, 40rp, 60rp, 80rp, Dec. 6. Others, June 6, 1974.

Virgin and Child, by Bartolomeo di Tommaso — A253

The Vociferant Horseman, by Andrea Riccio — A254

Engraved & Lithographed

1973, Dec. 6 *Perf. 13½*

542	A253	30rp gold & multi	38	30

Christmas 1973.

1974, Mar. 21 Photo. *Perf. 11½*

Europa: 40rp, Kneeling Venus, by Antonio Susini.

543	A254	30rp tan & multi	42	35
544	A254	40rp ultra & multi	60	50

Chinese Vase, 19th Century
A255

Soccer
A256

Designs: Chinese vases from Princely Treasury.

1974, Mar. 21

545	A255	30rp shown	32	32
546	A255	50rp from 1740	50	50
547	A255	60rp from 1830	65	65
548	A255	1fr circa 1700	1.10	1.10

1974, Mar. 21

549	A256	80rp lemon & multi	80	75

World Soccer Championships, Munich June 13-July 7.

Post Horn and UPU Emblem
A257

1974, June 6 *Perf. 13½*

550	A257	40rp gold, grn & blk	35	28
551	A257	60rp gold, red & blk	52	42

Centenary of Universal Postal Union.

Bishop F. A. Marxer — A258

Photogravure and Engraved

1974, June 6 *Perf. 14x13½*

552	A258	1fr multi	85	85

Bicentenary of the death of Bishop Franz Anton Marxer (1703-1775).

Prince Constantin
A259

Prince Hans Adam — A260

Princess Gina and Prince Franz Joseph II — A261

Designs: 80rp, Prince Maximilian. 1.20fr, Prince Alois.

1974-75 Photo. *Perf. 11½*

553	A259	70rp dk grn & gold	70	55
554	A259	80rp dp cl & gold	75	65
555	A259	1.20fr bluish blk & gold	1.10	1.00

Engr.

Perf. 14x13½

556	A260	1.70fr slate grn	1.40	1.25

Photogravure and Engraved

Perf. 13½x14

557	A261	10fr gold & choc	8.00	8.00

No. 557 printed in sheets of 4.

Issue dates: 1.70fr, Dec. 5, 1974; 10fr, Sept. 5, 1974; others, Mar. 13, 1975.

St. Florian — A262

Designs: 50rp, St. Wendelin. 60rp, Virgin Mary with Sts. Anna and Joachim. 70rp, Nativity.

1974, Dec. 5 Photo. *Perf. 12*

560	A262	30rp multi	28	22
561	A262	50rp multi	40	35
562	A262	60rp multi	55	50
563	A262	70rp multi	70	65

Designs are from 19th century devotional glass paintings. Christmas 1974.

"Cold Sun," by Martin Frommelt
A263

Europa: 60rp, "Village," by Louis Jaeger.

1975, Mar. 13 *Perf. 11½*

564	A263	30rp multi	28	28
565	A263	60rp multi	60	60

Red Cross Activities — A264

Imperial Crown — A266

Coronation Robe — A265

1975, June 5 Photo. *Perf. 11½*

566	A264	60rp dk bl & multi	55	55

30th anniv. of the Liechtenstein Red Cross.

1975 Engr. & Photo. *Perf. 14*

567	A266	30rp Imperial cross	55	45
568	A266	60rp Imperial sword	85	75
569	A266	1fr Orb	1.75	1.40
570	A265	1.30fr shown	21.00	18.00
571	A266	2fr shown	4.25	3.00
		Nos. 567-571 (5)	28.40	23.60

Treasures of the Holy Roman Empire from the Treasury of the Hofburg in Vienna, Austria.

Issue dates: 1.30fr, Sept. 4; others, June 5.

See Nos. 617-620.

St. Mamerten, Triesen — A267

Designs: 50rp, Red House, Vaduz, 14th century. 70rp, Prebendary House, Eschen, 14th century. 1fr, Gutenberg Castle.

1975, Sept. 4 Photo. *Perf. 11½*

572 A267 40rp multi 40 35
573 A267 50rp multi 42 35
574 A267 70rp plum & multi 85 85
575 A267 1fr dk bl & multi 1.10 1.10

European Architectural Heritage Year 1975.

Speed Skating — A268

Designs (Olympic Rings and): 25rp, Ice hockey. 70rp, Downhill skiing. 1.20fr, Slalom.

1975, Dec. 4 Photo. *Perf. 11½*

576 A268 20rp multi 18 15
577 A268 25rp multi 22 18
578 A268 70rp multi 60 50
579 A268 1.20fr yel & multi 1.10 95

12th Winter Olympic Games, Innsbruck, Austria, Feb. 4-15, 1976.

Daniel in the Lions' Den A269

River Crayfish A270

Designs: 60rp, Virgin and Child. 90rp, St. Peter. All designs are after Romanesque sculptured capitals in Chur Cathedral, c. 1208.

Photogravure and Engraved

1975, Dec. 4 *Perf. 14*

580 A269 30rp gold & pur 22 22
581 A269 60rp gold & grn 40 40
582 A269 90rp gold & claret 75 75

Christmas and Holy Year 1975.

1976, Mar. 11 Photo. *Perf. 11½*

World Wildlife Fund: 40rp, European pond turtle. 70rp, Old-world otter. 80rp, Lapwing.

583 A270 25rp multi 32 32
584 A270 40rp multi 50 50
585 A270 70rp multi 85 85
586 A270 80rp multi 1.25 1.25

Mouflon — A271

Europa: 80rp, Pheasant family. Ceramics by Prince Hans von Liechtenstein.

1976, Mar. 11

587 A271 40rp multi 48 42
588 A271 80rp vio & multi 1.00 85

Roman Fibula, 3rd Century — A272

1976, Mar. 11

589 A272 90rp vio bl, grn & gold 1.00 80

Historical Association of Liechtenstein, 75th anniversary.

Souvenir Sheet

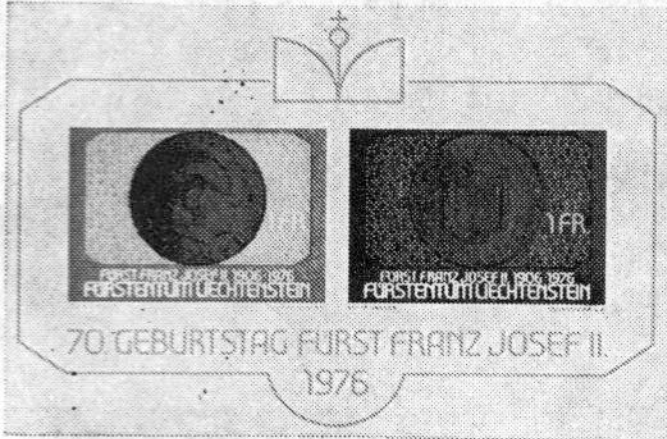

Franz Josef II 50fr-Memorial Coin — A273

1976, June 10 Photo. *Imperf.*

590 A273 Sheet of 2 1.75 1.75
a. 1fr blue & multi 85 85
b. 1fr red & multi 85 85

70th birthday of Prince Franz Joseph II of Liechtenstein.

Judo and Olympic Rings — A274

Rubens' Sons, Albrecht and Nikolas — A275

Designs (Olympic Rings and): 50rp, volleyball. 80rp, Relay race. 1.10fr, Long jump, women's.

1976, June 10 *Perf. 11½*

591 A274 35rp multi 30 30
592 A274 50rp multi 48 48
593 A274 80rp multi 70 70
594 A274 1.10fr multi 95 95

21st Olympic Games, Montreal, Canada, July 17-Aug. 1.

1976, Sept. 9 Engr. *Perf. 13½x14*

Rubens Paintings: 50rp, Singing Angels. 1fr, The Daughters of Cecrops, horiz. (from Collection of Prince of Liechtenstein).

Size: 24x38mm

595 A275 50rp gold & multi 1.40 1.40
596 A275 70rp gold & multi 2.00 2.00

Size: 48x38mm

597 A275 1fr gold & multi 5.25 5.25

400th anniversary of the birth of Peter Paul Rubens (1577-1640), Flemish painter. Sheets of 8 (2x4).

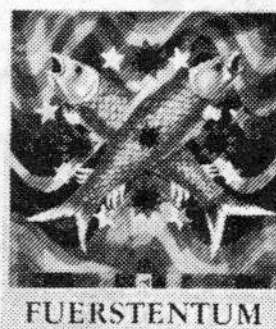

Zodiac Signs — A276

1976-78 Photo. *Perf. 11½*

598 A276 20rp Pisces 22 22
599 A276 40rp Aries 38 38
600 A276 40rp Cancer ('77) 45 42
601 A276 40rp Scorpio ('78) 50 45
602 A276 50rp Sagittarius ('78) 55 50
603 A276 70rp Leo ('77) 75 75
604 A276 80rp Taurus 85 80
605 A276 80rp Virgo ('77) 85 85
606 A276 80rp Capricorn ('78) 85 80
607 A276 90rp Gemini 1.10 85
608 A276 1.10fr Libra ('77) 1.25 1.25
609 A276 1.50fr Aquarius 1.50 1.50
Nos. 598-609 (12) 9.25 8.77

Flight into Egypt A277

Ortlieb von Brandis, Sarcophagus A278

Monastic Wax Works: 20rp, Holy Infant of Prague, horiz. 80rp, Holy Family and Trinity. 1.50fr, Holy Family, horiz.

1976, Dec. 9 Photo. *Perf. 11½*

610 A277 20rp multi 20 20
611 A277 50rp multi 40 40
612 A277 80rp multi 55 55
613 A277 1.50fr multi 1.25 1.25

Christmas 1976.

Photogravure and Engraved

1976, Dec. 9 *Perf. 13½x14*

614 A278 1.10fr gold & dk brn 90 70

Ortlieb von Brandis, Bishop of Chur (1458-1491).

Map of Liechtenstein, by J. J. Heber, 1721 — A279

Europa: 80rp, View of Vaduz, by Ferdinand Bachmann, 1815.

1977, Mar. 10 Photo. *Perf. 12½*

615 A279 40rp multi 45 45
616 A279 80rp multi 90 90

Treasure Type of 1975

Designs: 40rp, Holy Lance and Particle of the Cross. 50rp, Imperial Evangel of St. Matthew. 80rp, St. Stephen's Purse. 90rp, Tabard of Imperial Herald.

Engraved and Photogravure

1977, June 8 *Perf. 14*

617 A266 40rp gold & multi 40 32
618 A266 50rp gold & multi 48 45
619 A266 80rp gold & multi 75 65
620 A266 90rp gold & multi 1.10 1.00

Treasures of the Holy Roman Empire from the Treasury of the Hofburg in Vienna.

Emperor Constantius II Coin — A280

Coins: 70rp, Lindau bracteate, c. 1300. 80rp, Ortlieb von Brandis, 1458-1491.

1977, June 8 Photo. *Perf. 11½*

Granite Paper

621 A280 35rp gold & multi 35 28
622 A280 70rp sil & multi 60 52
623 A280 80rp sil & multi 80 65

Frauenthal Castle — A281

Castles: 50rp, Gross Ullersdorf. 80rp, Liechtenstein Castle near Mödling, Austria. 90rp, Liechtenstein Palace, Vienna.

Engraved and Photogravure

1977, Sept. 8 *Perf. 13½x14*

624 A281 20rp sl grn & gold 20 20
625 A281 50rp mag & gold 55 55
626 A281 80rp dk vio & gold 90 90
627 A281 90rp dk bl & gold 1.00 1.00

Children — A282

Traditional Costumes: 70rp, Two girls. 1fr, Woman in festival dress.

1977, Sept. 8 Photo. *Perf. 11½*

Granite Paper

628 A282 40rp multi 50 42
629 A282 70rp multi 75 70
630 A282 1fr multi 1.25 1.10

Princess Tatjana A283

1977, Dec. 7 Photo. *Perf. 11½*

631 A283 1.10fr brown & gold 90 85

Angel — A284

Liechtenstein Palace, Vienna — A285

Sculptures by Erasmus Kern: 50rp, St. Rochus. 80rp, Virgin and Child. 1.50fr, God the Father.

1977, Dec. 7

632 A284 20rp multi 18 18
633 A284 50rp multi 50 50
634 A284 80rp multi 80 80
635 A284 1.50fr multi 1.65 1.65

Christmas 1977.

Photogravure and Engraved

1978, Mar. 2 *Perf. 14*

Europa: 80rp, Feldsberg Castle.

636 A285 40rp gold & slate bl 42 42
637 A285 80rp gold & claret 85 85

Residential Tower, Balzers-Mäls — A286

Designs: 10rp, Farmhouse, Triesen. 20rp, Houses, Upper Village, Triesen. 35rp, Barns, Balzers. 40rp, Monastery, Bendern. 70rp, Parish house. 80rp, Farmhouse, Schellenberg. 90rp, Parish house, Balzers. 1fr, Rheinberger House, Music School, Vaduz. 1.10fr, Street, Mitteldorf, Vaduz. 1.50fr, Town Hall, Triesenberg. 2fr, National Museum and Administrator's Residence, Vaduz.

1978 Photo. *Perf. 11½*

638 A286 10rp multi 15 15
639 A286 20rp multi 16 16
640 A286 35rp multi 28 28
641 A286 40rp multi 30 30
642 A286 50rp multi 40 40
643 A286 70rp multi 55 55
644 A286 80rp multi 60 60
645 A286 90rp multi 70 70
646 A286 1fr multi 75 75
647 A286 1.10fr multi 90 90
648 A286 1.50fr multi 1.10 1.10
649 A286 2fr multi 1.50 1.50
Nos. 638-649 (12) 7.39 7.39

Vaduz Castle — A287

Vaduz Castle: 50rp, Courtyard. 70rp, Staircase. 80rp, Triptych from High Altar, Castle Chapel.

Engraved and Photogravure

1978, June 1 *Perf. 13½x14*

650 A287 40rp gold & multi 52 52
651 A287 50rp gold & multi 70 70
652 A287 70rp gold & multi 1.00 1.00
653 A287 80rp gold & multi 1.25 1.25

40th anniversary of reign of Prince Franz Joseph II. Sheet of 8.

Prince Karl I, Coin, 1614 A288

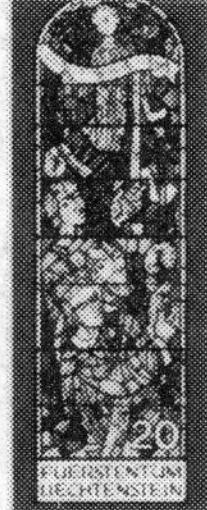

Adoration of the Shepherds A289

Designs: 50rp, Prince Johann Adam, medal, 1694. 80rp, Prince Josef Wenzel, medal, 1773.

1978, Sept. 7 Photo. *Perf. 11½*

654 A288 40rp multi 42 42
655 A288 50rp multi 60 60
656 A288 80rp multi 1.10 1.10

1978, Dec. 7 Photo. *Perf. 11½*

Stained-glass Windows, Triesenberg: 50rp, Holy Family. 80rp, Adoration of the Kings.

657 A289 20rp multi 22 22
658 A289 50rp multi 55 55
659 A289 80rp multi 85 85

Christmas 1978.

Piebald, by Hamilton and Faistenberger A290

Golden Carriage of Prince Joseph Wenzel, by Martin von Meytens — A291

Design: 80rp, Black stallion, by Johann Georg von Hamilton.

Photo. & Engr.

1978, Dec. 7 *Perf. 13½x14*

660 A290 70rp multi 60 60
661 A290 80rp multi 70 70

Perf. 12

662 A291 1.10fr multi 95 95

Sheets of 8.

Mail Plane over Schaan — A292

Europa: 80rp, Zeppelin over Vaduz Castle.

1979, Mar. 8 Photo. *Perf. 11½*

663 A292 40rp multi 80 80
664 A292 80rp multi 95 95

First airmail service, St. Gallen to Schaan, Aug. 31, 1930, and first Zeppelin flight to Liechtenstein, June 10, 1931.

Child Drinking — A293

Designs: 90rp, Child eating. 1.10fr, Child reading.

1979, Mar. 8

665 A293 80rp sil & multi 75 70
666 A293 90rp sil & multi 85 85
667 A293 1.10fr sil & multi 95 95

International Year of the Child.

Ordered Wave Fields A294

Sun over Continents A296

Council of Europe A295

1979, June 7 Litho. *Perf. 11½*

668 A294 50rp multi 38 38

Photo.

669 A295 80rp multi 75 75
670 A296 100rp multi 75 75

Intl. Radio Consultative Committee (CCIR) of the Intl. Telecommunications Union, 50th anniv. (50rp); Entry into Council of Europe (80rp); aid to developing countries (100rp).

Heraldic Panel of Carl Ludwig von Sulz — A297

Heraldic Panels of: 70rp, Barbara von Sulz, née zu Staufen. 1.10fr, Ulrich von Ramschwag and Barbara von Hallwil.

Photogravure and Engraved

1979, June 1 *Perf. 13½*

671 A297 40rp multi 30 30
672 A297 70rp multi 52 52
673 A297 1.10fr multi 95 95

Sts. Lucius and Florin, Fresco in Waltensburg-Vuorz Church — A298

Photogravure and Engraved

1979, Sept. 6 *Perf. 13½*

674 A298 20fr multi 14.00 14.00

Patron saints of Liechtenstein. Printed in sheets of 4.

Annunciation, Embroidery — A299

Christmas 1979 (Ferdnand Nigg Embroideries): 50rp, Christmas. 80rp, Blessed Are the Peacemakers.

1979, Dec. 6 Engr. *Perf. 13½*

675 A299 20rp multi 20 20
676 A299 50rp multi 45 45
677 A299 80rp multi 70 70

Cross-Country Skiing — A300

Olympic Rings and: 70rp, Oxhead Mountain. 1.50fr, Ski lift.

1979, Dec. 6 Photo. *Perf. 12*

678 A300 40rp multi 30 28
679 A300 70rp multi 55 52
680 A300 1.50fr multi 1.25 1.10

13th Winter Olympic Games, Lake Placid, NY, Feb. 12-24, 1980.

Arms of Bailiff Andreas Buchel, 1690 — A301

Designs: Various arms.

1980, Mar. 10 Photo. *Perf. 11½*

Granite Paper

681 A301 40rp shown 30 30
682 A301 70rp Georg Marxer, 1745 50 50
683 A301 80rp Luzius Frick, 1503 60 60
684 A301 1.10fr Adam Oehri, 1634 95 95

See Nos. 704-707, 729-732.

Princess Maria Leopoldine Esterhazy, by Antonio Canova — A302

Europa: 80rp, Maria Theresa, Duchess of Savoy, by Martin van Meytens.

1980, Mar. 10

685 A302 40rp multi 1.00 1.00
686 A302 80rp multi 1.00 1.00

Milking Pail A303

Liechtenstein A304

Old Alpine Farm Tools: 50rp, Wooden heart, ceremonial cattle decoration. 80rp, Butter churn.

1980, Sept. 8

687 A303 20rp multi 18 18
688 A303 50rp multi 42 42
689 A303 80rp multi 75 75

1980, Sept 8

690 A304 80rp multi 75 75

Postal Museum, 50th anniversary.

Crossbow with Spanning Device A305

1980, Sept. 8 Engr. *Perf. 13½x14*

691 A305 80rp shown 70 70
692 A305 90rp Spear, knife 75 75
693 A305 1.10fr Rifle, powderhorn 1.00 1.00

Triesenberg Family In Traditional Costumes A306

1980, Sept. 8 Photo. *Perf. 12*
Granite Paper

694 A306 40rp shown	35	35
695 A306 70rp Folk dancers, Schellenberg	55	55
696 A306 80rp Brass band, Mauren	65	65

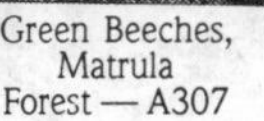

Green Beeches, Matrula Forest — A307

Glad Tidings — A308

Photogravure and Engraved
1980, Dec. 9 *Perf. 14*

697 A307 40rp shown	35	35
698 A307 50rp White firs, Valorsch Valley	45	45
699 A307 80rp Beech forest, Schaan	65	65
700 A307 1.50fr Forest, Oberplanken	1.25	1.25

1980, Dec. 9 Photo. *Perf. 11½*
Granite Paper

701 A308 20rp shown	18	18
702 A308 50rp Creche	45	45
703 A308 80rp Epiphany	70	70

Christmas 1980.

Bailiff Arms Type of 1980

1981, Mar. 9 Photo. *Perf. 11½*
Granite Paper

704 A301 40rp Anton Meier, 1748	32	32
705 A301 70rp Kaspar Kindle, 1534	55	55
706 A301 80rp Hans Adam Negele, 1600	65	65
707 A301 1.10fr Peter Matt, 1693	1.00	1.00

Fireworks at Vaduz Castle — A309

Europa: 80rp, National Day procession.

1981, Mar. 9 *Perf. 12½*
Granite Paper

708 A309 40rp multi	52	52
709 A309 80rp multi	1.00	1.00

Souvenir Sheet

Prince Alois, Princess Elisabeth and Prince Franz Joseph II — A310

1981, June 9 Photo. *Perf. 13*
Granite Paper

710 Sheet of 3	2.50	2.50
a. A310 70rp shown	50	50
b. A310 80rp Princes Alois and Franz Joseph II	55	55
c. A310 150rp Prince Franz Joseph II	1.00	1.00

75th birthday of Prince Franz Joseph II.

Scout Emblems A311

Man in Wheelchair A312

1981, June 9

711 A311 20rp multi	18	18

50th anniversary of Boy Scouts and Girl Guides.

1981, June 9

712 A312 40rp multi	28	28

International Year of the Disabled.

St. Theodul, 1600th Birth Anniv. — A313

Mosses and Lichens — A314

1981, June 9

713 A313 80rp multi	55	55

Photogravure and Engraved
1981, Sept. 7 *Perf. 13½*

714 A314 40rp Xanthoria parietina	30	30
715 A314 50rp Parmelia physodes	38	38
716 A314 70rp Sphagnum palustre	52	52
717 A314 80rp Amblystegium	60	60

Gutenberg Castle — A315

1981, Sept. 7

718 A315 20rp shown	15	15
719 A315 40rp Castle yard	30	30
720 A315 50rp Parlor	38	38
721 A315 1.10fr Great Hall	90	90

St. Charles Borromeo (1538-1584) — A316

St. Nicholas — A317

Famous Visitors to Liechtenstein (Paintings): 70rp, Goethe (1749-1832), by Angelica Kauffmann. 80rp, Alexander Dumas (1824-1895). 1fr, Hermann Hesse (1877-1962), by Cuno Amiet.

Lithographed and Engraved
1981, Dec. 7 *Perf. 14*

722 A316 40rp multi	35	35
723 A316 70rp multi	60	60
724 A316 80rp multi	70	70
725 A316 1fr multi	80	80

See Nos. 747-750.

1981, Dec. 7 Photo. *Perf. 11½*
Granite Paper

726 A317 20rp shown	18	18
727 A317 50rp Adoration of the Kings	45	45
728 A317 80rp Holy Family	70	70

Christmas 1981.

Bailiff Arms Type of 1980

1982, Mar. 8 Photo.
Granite Paper

729 A301 40rp Johann Kaiser, 1664	35	35
730 A301 70rp Joseph Anton Kaufmann, 1748	55	55
731 A301 80rp Christoph Walser, 1690	70	70
732 A301 1.10fr Stephan Banzer, 1658	1.00	1.00

Europa 1982 — A318

1982, Mar. 8
Granite Paper

733 A318 40rp Peasants' Uprising, 1525	35	35
734 A318 80rp Imperial Direct Rule, 1396	70	70

Hereditary Prince Hans Adam — A319

1982, June 7 Granite Paper

735 A319 1fr shown	75	75
736 A319 1fr Princess Marie Aglae	75	75

LIBA '82, 10th Liechtenstein Philatelic Exhibition, Vaduz, July 31-Aug. 8.

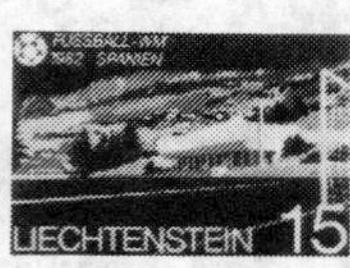

1982 World Cup — A320

Designs: Sports arenas.

1982, June 7 Granite Paper

737 A320 15rp Triesenberg	15	15
738 A320 25rp Mauren	18	18
739 A320 1.80fr Balzers	1.40	1.40

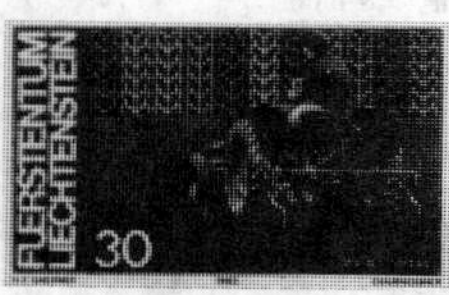

Farming A321

1982, Sept. 20 Photo. *Perf. 11½*
Granite Paper

740 A321 30rp shown	22	22
741 A321 50rp Horticulture	38	38
742 A321 70rp Forestry	52	52
743 A321 150rp Dairy farming	1.10	1.10

View of Neu-Schellenberg, 1861, by Moriz Menzinger (1832-1914) — A322

Photogravure and Engraved
1982, Sept. 20 *Perf. 13½x14*

744 A322 40rp shown	30	30
745 A322 50rp Vaduz, 1860	35	35
746 A322 100rp Bendern, 1868	85	85

Visitor Type of 1981

Paintings: 40rp, Emperor Maximilian I (1459-1519), by Bernhard Strigel. 70rp, Georg Jenatsch (1596-1639). 80rp, Angelika Kaufmann (1741-1807), self portrait. 1fr, Fidelis von Sigmaringen (1577-1622).

1982, Dec. 6 *Perf. 14*

747 A316 40rp multi	30	30
748 A316 70rp multi	52	52
749 A316 80rp multi	60	60
750 A316 1fr multi	75	75

Christmas 1982 — A323

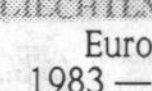

Europa 1983 — A324

Designs: Chur Cathedral sculptures.

1982, Dec. 6 Photo. *Perf. 11½*
Granite Paper

751 A323 20rp Angel playing lute	16	16
752 A323 50rp Virgin and Child	40	40
753 A323 80rp Angel playing organ	65	65

1983, Mar. 7 Photo.

Designs: 40rp, Notker Balbulus of St. Gall (840-912), Benedictine monk, poet and liturgical composer. 80rp, St. Hildegard of Bingen (1098-1179).

754 A324 40rp multi	32	32
755 A324 80rp multi	60	60

A325

A326

Shrovetide and Lenten customs: 40rp, Last Thursday before Lent. 70rp, Begging for eggs on Shrove Tuesday. 180fr, Bonfire, first Sunday in Lent.

Photogravure and Engraved
1983, Mar. 7 *Perf. 14*

756 A325 40rp multi	35	35
757 A325 70rp multi	60	60
758 A325 1.80fr multi	1.50	1.50

See Nos. 844-846, 915-917.

1983, June 6 Photo. *Perf. 12*

Designs: Landscapes by Anton Ender (b. 1898).

759 A326 40rp Schaan, on the Zollstrasse	35	35
760 A326 50rp Balzers with Gutenberg Castle	42	42
761 A326 2fr Stag by the Reservoir	1.75	1.75

Protection of Shores and Coasts — A327

1983, June 6

762 A327 20rp shown 80 80
763 A327 40rp Manned flight bicentenary 30 30
764 A327 50rp World communications year 38 38
765 A327 80rp Humanitarian aid 60 60

Pope John Paul II — A328

1983, Sept. 5 **Photo.**

766 A328 80rp multi 1.00 1.00

Princess Gina — A329

1983, Sept. 5 ***Perf. 12x11½***

767 A329 2.50fr shown 2.25 2.25
768 A329 3fr Prince Franz Joseph II 2.75 2.75

Christmas 1983 — A330

1983, Dec. 5 **Photo.** ***Perf. 12***
Granite Paper

769 A330 20rp Seeking shelter 16 16
770 A330 50rp Child Jesus 42 42
771 A330 80rp The Three Magi 70 70

1984 Winter Olympics, Sarajevo — A331

Snowflakes.

1983, Dec. 5 **Photo.** ***Perf. 11½x12***
Granite Paper

772 A331 40rp multi 40 40
773 A331 80rp multi 80 80
774 A331 1.80fr multi 1.65 1.65

Famous Visitors to Liechtenstein A332

Paintings: 40rp, Count Alexander Wassiljewitsch Suworow-Rimnikski (1730-1800), Austro-Russian Army general. 70rp, Karl Rudolf Count von Buol-Schauenstein (1760-1833). 80rp, Carl Zuckmayer (1896-1977), playwright. 1fr, Curt Goetz (1888-1960), actor and playwright.

Photogravure and Engraved
1984, Mar. 12 ***Perf. 14***

775 A332 40rp multi 40 40
776 A332 70rp multi 70 70
777 A332 80rp multi 80 80
778 A332 1fr multi 1.00 1.00

A333

A334

1984, Mar. 12 **Photo.** ***Perf. 12***
Granite Paper

779 A333 50rp multi 45 45
780 A333 80rp multi 70 70

Europa (1959-1984).

Photogravure and Engraved
1984, June 12 ***Perf. 14***

The Destruction of Trisona Fairy Tale Illustrations: Root Carvings by Beni Gassner.

781 A334 35rp Warning messenger 35 35
782 A334 50rp Buried town 50 50
783 A334 80rp Spared family 80 80

1984 Summer Olympics A335

1984, June 12 **Photo.** ***Perf. 11½***
Granite Paper

784 A335 70rp Pole vault 75 75
785 A335 80rp Discus 85 85
786 A335 1fr Shot put 1.10 1.10

Industries and Occupations A336

1984, Sept. 10 **Photo.** ***Perf. 11½***

787 A336 5rp Banking & trading 15 15
788 A336 10rp Construction, plumbing 15 15
789 A336 20rp Production, factory worker 22 22
790 A336 35rp Contracting, draftswoman 35 35
791 A336 45rp Manufacturing, sales rep 45 45
792 A336 50rp Catering 50 50
793 A336 60rp Carpentry 60 60
794 A336 70rp Public health 70 70
795 A336 80rp Industrial research 80 80
796 A336 1fr Masonry 1.00 1.00
797 A336 1.20fr Industrial management 1.25 1.25
798 A336 1.50fr Posta & communications 1.50 1.50
Nos. 787-798 (12) 7.67 7.67

Princess Marie Aglae — A337

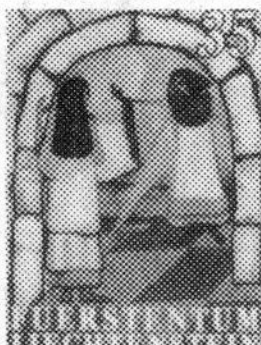

Christmas 1984 — A338

Photogravure and Engraved
1984, Dec. 10 ***Perf. 14x13½***

799 A337 1.70fr shown 1.65 1.65
800 A337 2fr Prince Hans Adam 2.00 2.00

1984, Dec. 10 **Photo.** ***Perf. 11***

801 A338 35rp Annunciation 35 35
802 A338 50rp Holy Family 52 52
803 A338 80rp Three Kings 80 75

Europa 1985 — A339

1985, Mar. 11 **Photo.** ***Perf. 11½***

804 A339 50rp Three Muses 48 48
805 A339 80rp Pan and Muses 75 75

Orders and Monestaries A340

Photogravure and Engraved
1985, Mar. 11 ***Perf. 13½x14***

806 A340 50rp St. Elisabeth 60 60
807 A340 1fr Schellenberg Convent 1.25 1.25
808 A340 1.70fr Gutenberg Mission 2.00 2.00

Cardinal Virtues — A341

1985, June 10 **Photo.** ***Perf. 11½x12***

809 A341 35rp Justice 40 40
810 A341 50rp Temperance 55 55
811 A341 70rp Prudence 75 75
812 A341 1fr Fortitude 1.10 1.10

Princess Gina, President of Natl. Red Cross, 40th Anniv. — A342

Portrait and: 20rp, Helping refugees, 1945. 50rp, Rescue service. 1.20fr, Child refugees, 1979.

1985, June 10 ***Perf. 12x11½***

813 A342 20rp multi 22 22
814 A342 50rp multi 55 55
815 A342 1.20fr multi 1.40 1.40

Souvenir Sheet

State Visit of Pope John Paul II — A343

Designs: 50rp, Papal coat of arms. 80rp, Chapel of St. Maria zum Trost, Dux, Schaan. 1.70fr, Our Lady of Liechtenstein, St. Mary the Comforter.

1985, Feb. 2 ***Perf. 11½***

816 Sheet of 3 4.25 4.25
a. A343 50rp multi 1.40 1.40
b. A343 80rp multi 1.40 1.40
c. A343 1.70fr multi 1.40 1.40

Paintings from the Princely Collections A344

Christmas 1985 A345

Designs: 50rp, Portrait of a Canon, by Quintin Massys (1466-1530). 1fr, Portrait of Clara Serena Rubens, by Peter Paul Rubens (1577-1640). 1.20fr, Portrait of the Duke of Urbino, by Raphael (1483-1520).

Photogravure and Engraved
1985, Sept. 2 ***Perf. 14***

817 A344 50rp multi 55 55
818 A344 1fr multi 1.10 1.10
819 A344 1.20fr multi 1.40 1.40

1985, Dec. 9 **Photo.** ***Perf. 11½x12***

820 A345 35rp Frankincense 40 40
821 A345 50rp Gold 55 55
822 A345 80rp Myrrh 90 90

Kirchplatz Theater, 15th Anniv. — A346

Photogravure and Engraved
1985, Dec. 9 ***Perf. 14***

823 A346 50rp Tragedy 40 40
824 A346 80rp Commedia dell'arte 55 55
825 A346 1.50rp Opera buffa 1.75 1.75

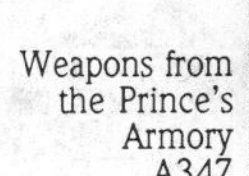

Weapons from the Prince's Armory A347

Designs: 35rp, Halberd, bodyguard of Prince Charles I. 50rp, German morion, 16th cent. 80rp, Halberd, bodyguard of Prince Carl Eusebius.

1985, Dec. 9 ***Perf. 13½x14½***

826 A347 35rp multi 40 40
827 A347 50rp multi 55 55
828 A347 80rp multi 90 90

A348

A349

1986, Mar. 10 **Photo.** ***Perf. 12***

829 A348 50rp Swallows 52 52
830 A348 90rp Robin 1.00 1.00

Europa 1986.

1986-89 **Photo.** ***Perf. 11½x12***

Views of Vaduz Castle.

Granite Paper

832 A349 20rp Outer courtyard 16 16
833 A349 25rp View from the south ('89) 35 35
835 A349 50rp Castle, mountains 40 40
838 A349 90rp Inner gate ('87) 1.20 1.20
840 A349 1.10fr Back view 90 90

841 A349 1.40fr Inner courtyard ('87) 1.85 1.85
Nos. 832-841 (6) 4.86 4.86

This is an expanding set. Numbers will change if necessary.

Fasting Sacrifice — A350

A352

1986, Mar. 10 Photo. *Perf. 12*
843 A350 1.40fr multi 1.40 1.40

Type of 1983
Photogravure and Engraved
1986, June 9 *Perf. 13½*
844 A325 35rp shown 45 45
845 A325 50rp Wedding 65 65
846 A325 70rp Rogation Day procession 90 90

1986, June 9 Photo. *Perf. 11½*

Karl Freiherr Haus von Hausen (1823-89), founder.

847 A352 50rp multi 58 58

Natl. Savings Bank, Vaduz, 125th anniv.

A353

Hunting — A354

Photogravure and Engraved
1986, June 9 *Perf. 13½*
848 A353 3.50fr multi 4.50 4.50

Prince Franz Joseph II, 80th birthday.

1986, Sept. 9 *Perf. 13x13½*
849 A354 35rp Roebuck, Ruggeller Riet 42 42
850 A354 50rp Chamois in winter, Rappenstein 60 60
851 A354 1.70fr Rutting stag, Lawena 2.05 2.05

Crops — A355

1986, Sept. 9 Photo. *Perf. 12x11½*
852 A355 50rp White cabbage, beets 65 65
853 A355 80rp Red cabbage 1.10 1.10
854 A355 90rp Potatoes, onions, garlic 1.25 1.25

Christmas A356

Trees A357

Archangels.

1986, Dec. 9 *Perf. 11½*
855 A356 35rp Michael 45 40
856 A356 50rp Gabriel 65 65
857 A356 90rp Raphael 1.20 1.20

1986, Dec. 9
858 A357 25rp Silver fir 32 32
859 A357 90rp Spruce 1.20 1.20
860 A357 1.40fr Oak 1.75 1.75

Europa 1987 — A358

Nicholas Among the Thorns — A359

Modern architecture: 50rp, Primary school, 1980, Gamprin. 90rp, Parish church, c. 1960, Schellenburg.

1987, Mar. 9 Photo. *Perf. 11½x12*
Granite Paper
861 A358 50rp multi 68 68
862 A358 90rp multi 1.20 1.20

1987, Mar. 9 *Perf. 11½*
Granite Paper
863 A359 1.10fr multi 1.50 1.50

Nicholas von der Flue (1417-1487), canonized in 1947.

Hereditary Prince Alois — A360

Fish — A361

Photo. & Engr.
1987, June 9 *Perf. 14*
864 A360 2fr multi 2.40 2.40

No. 864 printed in sheets of 8.

1987, June 9 Photo. *Perf. 11½*
865 A361 50rp Cottus gobio 60 60
866 A361 90rp Salmo trutta fario 1.10 1.10
867 A361 1.10fr Thymallus thymallus 1.40 1.40

A362

A363

Liechtenstein City Palace, Vienna.

1987, Sept. 7 Photo. *Perf. 11½*
Granite Paper
868 A362 35rp Arch 48 48
869 A362 50rp Entrance 68 68
870 A362 90rp Staircase 1.20 1.20

1987, Sept. 7 *Perf. 11½*
871 A363 1.40fr House of Liechtenstein coat of arms 1.90 1.90

Purchase of County of Vaduz, 275th anniv.

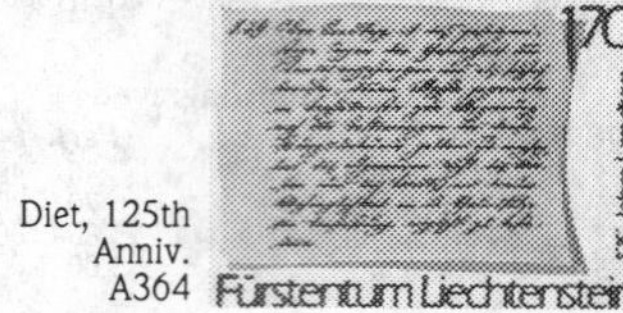
Diet, 125th Anniv. A364

1987, Sept. 7 *Perf. 11½*
872 A364 1.70fr Constitution of 1862 2.25 2.25

Christmas — A365

The Evangelists, illuminated codices from the Golden Book, c. 1100, Abbey of Pfafers, purportedly made under the direction of monks from Reichenau Is.

1987, Dec. 7 Photo. & Engr. *Perf. 14*
873 A365 35rp St. Matthew 30 30
874 A365 50rp St. Mark 42 42
875 A365 60rp St. Luke 50 50
876 A365 90rp St. John 75 75

1988 Winter Olympics, Calgary — A366

Humorous drawings by illustrator Paul Flora of Austria: 25rp, The Toil of the Cross-country Skier. 90rp, Courageous Pioneer of Skiing. 1.10fr, As Grandfather Used to Ride on a Bobsled.

1987, Dec. 7 *Perf. 14x13½*
877 A366 25rp multi 35 35
878 A366 90rp multi 1.25 1.25
879 A366 1.10fr multi 1.50 1.50

See Nos. 888-891.

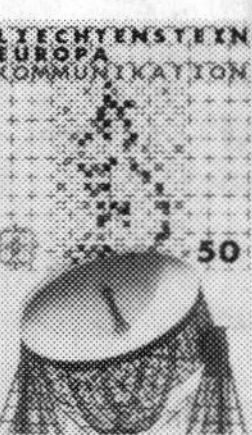
Europa 1988 — A367

Modern communication & transportation.

1988, Mar. 7 Photo. *Perf. 11½x12*
Granite Paper
880 A367 50rp Satellite dish 70 70
881 A367 90rp High-speed monorail 1.25 1.25

European Campaign to Protect Undeveloped and Developing Lands A368

1988, Mar. 7 *Perf. 12*
Granite Paper
882 A368 80rp Forest preservation 1.10 1.10
883 A368 90rp Layout for village development 1.25 1.25
884 A368 1.70rp Traffic planning 2.25 2.25

Balancing nature conservation with natl. development.

Souvenir Sheet

Succession to the Throne — A369

Portraits: a, Crown Prince Hans Adam. b, Prince Alois, successor to the crown prince. c, Prince Franz Josef II, ruler.

Perf. 14½x13½
1988, June 6 Photo. & Engr.
885 A369 Sheet of 3 4.25 4.25
a. 50rp blk, gold & bright blue 72 72
b. 50rp blk, gold & sage green 72 72
c. 2fr blk, gold & deep rose 2.80 2.80

North and South Campaign A370

Perf. 12x11½
1988, June 6 Photo. Granite Paper
886 A370 50rp Public radio 72 72
887 A370 1.40fr Adult education 2.00 2.00

Cultural cooperation with Costa Rica. See Costa Rica Nos. 401-402.

Olympics Type of 1988

Humorous drawings by illustrator Paul Flora of Austria: 50rp, Cycling. 80rp, Gymnastics. 90rp, Running. 1.40fr, Equestrian.

Photo. & Engr.
1988, Sept. 5 *Perf. 14x13½*
888 A366 50rp multi 68 68
889 A366 80rp multi 1.05 1.05
890 A366 90rp multi 1.20 1.20
891 A366 1.40fr multi 1.85 1.85

Roadside Shrines — A371

Christmas — A372

Perf. 11½x12
1988, Sept. 5 Photo. Granite Paper
892 A371 25rp Kaltweh Chapel, Balzers 35 35
893 A371 35rp Oberdorf, Vaduz, c. 1870 48 48
894 A371 50rp Bangstrasse, Ruggell 68 68

1988, Dec. 5 Photo. *Perf. 11½x12*
Granite Paper
895 A372 35rp Joseph, Mary 48 48
896 A372 50rp Christ child 68 68
897 A372 90rp Adoration of the Magi 1.20 1.20

A little time given to the study of the arrangement of the Scott Catalogue can make it easier to use effectively.

The Letter — A373

Europa 1989 — A374

Details of Portrait of Marie-Therese de Lamballe (The Letter), by Anton Hickel (1745-1798): 90rp, Handkerchief and writing materials in open desk. 2fr, Entire painting.

Photo. & Engr.

1988, Dec. 5 ***Perf. 13x13½***

898 A373 50rp shown 68 68
899 A373 90rp multi 1.20 1.20
900 A373 2fr multi 2.70 2.70

1989, Mar. 6 Photo. ***Perf. 11½x12***

Traditional children's games.

Granite Paper

901 A374 50rp Cat and Mouse 68 68
902 A374 90rp Stockleverband 1.20 1.20

Josef Gabriel Rheinberger (1839-1901), Composer, and Score A375

Photo. & Engr.

1989, Mar. 6 ***Perf. 14x13½***

903 A375 2.90fr multi 3.85 3.85

Fish — A376

1989, June 5 Photo. ***Perf. 12x11½***

Granite Paper

904 A376 50rp *Esox lucius* 65 65
905 A376 1.10fr *Salmo trutta lacustris* 1.45 1.45
906 A376 1.40fr *Noemacheilus barbatulus* 1.85 1.85

World Wildlife Fund — A377

1989, June 5 ***Perf. 12***

Granite Paper

907 A377 25rp *Charadrius dubuis* 32 32
908 A377 35rp *Hyla arborea* 45 45
909 A377 50rp *Libelloides coccajus* 65 65
910 A377 90rp *Putorius putorius* 1.15 1.15

Mountains — A378

1989, Sept. 4 Photo. ***Perf. 11½***

Granite Paper

911 A378 50rp Falknis 60 60
912 A378 75rp Plassteikopf 90 90
913 A378 80rp Naafkopf 95 95
914 A378 1.50fr Garselliturm 1.75 1.75

See Nos. 930-939.

Folklore Type of 1983

Autumn activities: 35rp, Alpine herdsman and flock return from pasture. 50rp, Shucking corn. 80rp, Cattle market.

1989, Sept. 4 Photo. & Engr. ***Perf. 14***

915 A325 35rp multi 42 42
916 A325 50rp multi 60 60
917 A325 80rp multi 95 95

Christmas — A379

Details of the triptych *Adoration of the Magi*, by Hugo van der Goes (50rp) and student (35rp, 90rp), late 15th cent.: 35rp, Melchior and Balthazar. 50rp, Caspar and holy family. 90rp, Donor with St. Stephen.

1989, Dec. 4 ***Perf. 13½***

Size of 35rp and 90rp: 23x41mm

918 A379 35rp multi 45 45
919 A379 50rp shown 62 62
920 A379 90rp multi 1.10 1.10

Minerals A380

1989, Dec. 4 ***Perf. 13½x13***

921 A380 50rp Scepter quartz 62 62
922 A380 1.10fr Pyrite ball 1.35 1.35
923 A380 1.50fr Calcite 1.85 1.85

Europa 1990 — A381

Postage Stamps, 150th Anniv. — A382

Post offices.

Perf. 11½x12

1990, Mar. 5 Photo. Granite Paper

924 A381 50rp shown 62 62
925 A381 90rp Modern p.o. 1.10 1.10

1990, Mar. 5 ***Perf. 11½***

Granite Paper

926 A382 1.50fr Penny Black 1.85 1.85

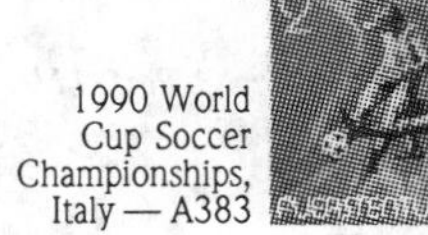
1990 World Cup Soccer Championships, Italy — A383

1990, Mar. 5 Granite Paper ***Perf. 12***

927 A383 2fr multicolored 2.50 2.50

Princess Gina A384

1990, June 5 Litho. ***Perf. 11½***

Granite Paper

928 A384 2fr shown 2.70 2.70
929 A384 3fr Prince Franz Joseph II 4.10 4.10

1st anniv of death.

Mountains Type of 1989

1990-93

Granite Paper

930 A378 5rp Augstenberg 15 15
931 A378 10rp Hahnenspiel 15 15
933 A378 35rp Nospitz 52 52
933A A378 40rp Ochsenkopf 52 52
934 A378 45rp Drei Schwestern 60 60
935 A378 60rp Kuhgrat 90 90
936 A378 70rp Galinakopf 95 95
938 A378 1fr Schonberg 1.35 1.35
939 A378 1.20fr Bleikaturm 1.80 1.80
940 A378 1.60fr Schwarzhorn 2.10 2.10
941 A378 2fr Scheienkopf 2.50 2.50
Nos. 930-941 (11) 11.54 11.54

Issue dates: 5, 45, 70rp, 1fr, June 5. 10, 35, 60rp, 1.20fr, Sept. 3. 40rp, June 3, 1991. 1.60fr, Mar. 2, 1992. 2fr, Mar. 1, 1993.

This is an expanding set. Numbers will change if neccessary.

A385

A386

Paintings by Benjamin Steck (1902-1981).

1990, June 5 Photo. & Engr. ***Perf. 14***

942 A385 50rp shown 70 70
943 A385 80rp Fruit, dish 1.10 1.10
944 A385 1.50fr Basket, fruit, stein 2.10 2.10

Photo. & Engr.

1990, Sept. 3 ***Perf. 13x13½***

Game birds.

945 A386 25rp Pheasant 35 35
946 A386 50rp Blackcock 70 70
947 A386 2fr Mallard duck 2.75 2.75

European Postal Communications, 500th Anniv. — A387

1990, Dec. 3 ***Perf. 13½x14***

948 A387 90rp multicolored 1.25 1.25

A388

A389

Christmas (Lenten Cloth of Bendern): 35rp, The Annunciation. 50rp, Birth of Christ. 90rp, Adoration of the Magi.

1990, Dec. 3 Photo. ***Perf. 12***

Granite Paper

949 A388 35rp multicolored 50 50
950 A388 50rp multicolored 72 72
951 A388 90rp multicolored 1.25 1.25

1990, Dec. 3 Photo. & Engr. ***Perf. 14***

Holiday Customs: 35rp, St. Nicholas Visiting Children on Feast of St. Nicholas. 50rp, Waking "sleepyheads" on New Year's Day. 1.50fr, Good wishes on New Year's Day.

952 A389 35rp multicolored 50 50
953 A389 50rp multicolored 72 72
954 A389 1.50fr multicolored 2.15 2.15

Europa — A390

Designs: 50rp, Telecommunications satellite, Olympus I. 90rp, Weather satellite, Meteosat.

1991, Mar. 4 Photo. ***Perf. 11½***

Granite Paper

955 A390 50rp multicolored 72 72
956 A390 90rp multicolored 1.25 1.25

St. Ignatius of Loyola (1491-1556), Founder of Jesuit Order — A391

Designs: 90rp, Wolfgang Amadeus Mozart (1756-1791), composer.

1991, Mar. 4 ***Perf. 11½***

Granite Paper

957 A391 80rp multicolored 1.15 1.15
958 A391 90rp multicolored 1.25 1.25

A392

A393

1991, Mar. 4 ***Perf. 11½***

Granite Paper

959 A392 2.50fr multicolored 3.50 3.50

UN membership, 1990.

1991, June 3 Photo. ***Perf. 11½***

Paintings: 50rp, Maloja, by Giovanni Giacometti. 80rp, Rheintal, by Ferdinand Gehr. 90rp, Bergell, by Augusto Giacometti. 1.10fr, Hoher Kasten, by Hedwig Scherrer.

Granite Paper

960 A393 50rp multicolored 65 65
961 A393 80rp multicolored 1.05 1.05
962 A393 90rp multicolored 1.15 1.15
963 A393 1.10fr multicolored 1.45 1.45

Swiss Confederation, 700th anniv.

Military Uniforms A394

Designs: 50rp, Non-commissioned officer, private. 70rp, Uniform tunic, trunk. 1fr, Sharpshooters, officer and private.

Photo. & Engr.

1991, June 3 *Perf. 13½x14*

964 A394 50rp multicolored 65 65
965 A394 70rp multicolored 90 90
966 A394 1fr multicolored 1.00 1.00

Last action of Liechtenstein's military, 1866 (70rp).

Princess Marie — A395

Photo. & Engr.

1991, Sept. 2 *Perf. 13x13½*

967 A395 3fr shown 3.90 3.90
968 A395 3.40fr Prince Hans Adam II 4.50 4.50

LIBA 92, Natl. Philatelic Exhibition A396

1991, Sept. 2 **Photo.** *Perf. 11½*

Granite Paper

969 A396 90rp multicolored 1.15 1.15

A397

A398

Christmas (Altar of St. Mamertus Chapel, Triesen): 50rp, Mary. 80rp, Madonna and Child. 90rp, Angel Gabriel.

Photo. & Engr.

1991, Dec. 2 *Perf. 13½x14*

970 A397 50rp multicolored 70 70
971 A397 80rp multicolored 1.10 1.10
972 A397 90rp multicolored 1.25 1.25

1991, Dec. 2 **Photo.** *Perf. 11½x12*

1992 Winter Olympics, Albertville: 70rp, Cross-country skiers, doping check. 80rp, Hockey players, good sportsmanship. 1.60rp, Downhill skier, safety precautions.

Granite Paper

973 A398 70rp multicolored 95 95
974 A398 80rp multicolored 1.10 1.10
975 A398 1.60fr multicolored 2.25 2.25

1992 Summer Olympics, Barcelona — A399

Designs: 50rp, Women's relay, drugs, broken medal. 70rp, Cycling, safety precautions. 2.50fr, Judo, good sportsmanship.

1992, Mar. 2 **Photo.** *Perf. 11½*

Granite Paper

976 A399 50rp multicolored 65 65
977 A399 70rp multicolored 90 90
978 A399 2.50fr multicolored 3.25 3.25

Discovery of America, 500th Anniv. A400

1992, Mar. 2

Granite Paper

979 A400 80rp shown 1.05 1.05
980 A400 90rp New York skyline 1.20 1.20

Europa.

A401

A402

Designs: No. 981, Postillion blowing horn. No. 982, Postillion delivering valentine. No. 983, Clown in envelope. No. 984, Wedding violinist.

Photo. & Engr.

1992, June 1 *Perf. 14x13½*

981 A401 50rp multicolored 65 65
982 A401 50rp multicolored 65 65

Photo.

Perf. 12½

Granite Paper

983 A402 50rp multicolored 65 65
984 A402 50rp multicolored 65 65

Souvenir Sheet

Prince Hans-Adam and Princess Marie, 25th Wedding Anniv. — A403

Designs: a, 2fr, Coat of Arms of Liechtenstein-Kinsky Alliance. b, 2.50fr, Prince Hans-Adam and Princess Marie.

1992, June 1 *Perf. 11½*

Granite Paper

985 A403 Sheet of 2, #a.-b. 5.85 5.85

Ferns — A404

Designs: 40rp, Blechnum spicant. 50rp, Asplenium trichomanes. 70rp, Phyllitis scolopendrium. 2.50fr, Asplenium ruta-muraria.

1992, Sept. 7 **Photo. & Engr.** *Perf. 14*

986 A404 40rp multicolored 65 65
987 A404 50rp multicolored 78 78
988 A404 70rp multicolored 1.10 1.10
989 A404 2.50fr multicolored 3.95 3.95

Creation of Vaduz County, 650th Anniv. — A405

1992, Sept. 7 *Perf. 13½x14*

990 A405 1.60fr multicolored 2.50 2.50

Christmas — A406

Hereditary Prince Alois — A407

Scenes in Triesen: 50rp, Chapel, St. Mamertus. 90rp, Nativity scene, St. Gallus Church. 1.60rp, St. Mary's Chapel.

1992, Dec. 7 **Photo.** *Perf. 11½*

Granite Paper

991 A406 50rp multicolored 68 68
992 A406 90rp multicolored 1.20 1.20
993 A406 1.60fr multicolored 2.15 2.15

Photo. & Engr.

1992, Dec. 7 *Perf. 13x13½*

994 A407 2.50fr multicolored 3.50 3.50

A408

A409

Europa (Contemporary paintings): 80rp, 910805, by Bruno Kaufmann. 1fr, The Little Blue, by Evi Kliemand.

1993, Mar. 1 **Photo.** *Perf. 11½x12*

Granite Paper

995 A408 80rp multicolored 1.00 1.00
996 A408 1fr multicolored 1.25 1.25

1993, Mar. 1 *Perf. 11½*

Paintings by Hans Gantner (1853-1914): 50rp, Chalets in Steg and Naafkopf. 60rp, Sass Mountain with Hunting Lodge. 1.80fr, Red House in Vaduz.

Granite Paper

997 A409 50rp multicolored 65 65
998 A409 60rp multicolored 75 75
999 A409 1.80fr multicolored 2.30 2.30

SEMI-POSTAL STAMPS

Prince Johann II — SP1

Coat of Arms — SP2

Perf. 11½

1925, Oct. 5 Engr. Wmk. 183

B1 SP1 10rp yel green 26.00 10.00
B2 SP1 20rp deep red 19.00 10.00
B3 SP1 30rp deep blue 5.50 3.50
Set, never hinged 150.00

85th birthday of the Prince Regent. Sold at a premium of 5rp each, the excess being devoted to charities.

1927, Oct. 5 Typo.

B4 SP2 10rp multi 7.50 *13.00*
B5 SP2 20rp multi 7.50 *13.00*
B6 SP2 30rp multi 7.50 *13.00*
Set, never hinged 47.50

87th birthday of Prince Johann II.
These stamps were sold at premiums of 5, 10 and 20rp respectively. The money thus obtained was devoted to charity.

Railroad Bridge Demolished by Flood — SP3

Designs: 10rp+10rp, Inundated Village of Ruggel. 20rp+10rp, Austrian soldiers rescuing refugees. 30rp+10rp, Swiss soldiers salvaging personal effects.

1928, Feb. 6 Litho. Unwmk.

B7 SP3 5rp + 5rp brn vio & brn 11.00 19.00
B8 SP3 10rp + 10rp bl grn & brn 14.00 19.00
B9 SP3 20rp + 10rp dl red & brn 14.00 19.00
B10 SP3 30rp + 10rp dp bl & brn 11.00 19.00
Set, never hinged 160.00

The surtax on these stamps was used to aid the sufferers from the Rhine floods.

Coat of Arms — SP7

Princess Elsa — SP8

Design: 30rp, Prince Francis I.

1932, Dec. 21 Photo.

B11 SP7 10rp (+ 5rp) ol grn 18.00 *24.00*
B12 SP8 20rp (+ 5rp) rose red 18.00 *24.00*
B13 SP8 30rp (+ 10rp) ultra 18.00 *24.00*
Set, never hinged 140.00

The surtax was for the Child Welfare Fund.

Postal Museum Issue

Souvenir Sheet

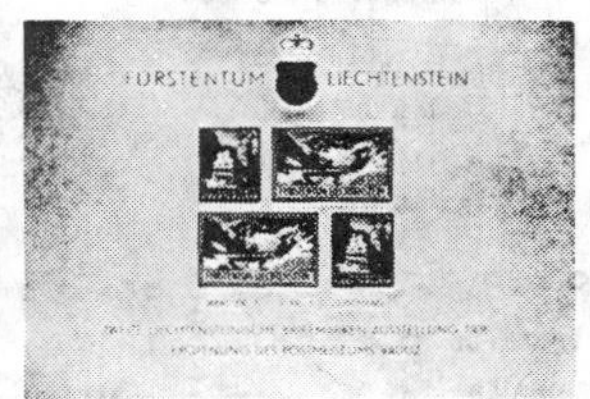

SP10

1936, Oct. 24 Litho. *Imperf.*

B14 SP10 Sheet of 4 15.00 *37.50*
Never hinged 35.00

Sheet contains 2 each, #120, 122. Sold for 2fr.

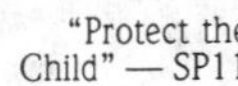

"Protect the Child" — SP11

Designs: No. B16, "Take Care of the Sick". No. B17, "Help the Aged".

Perf. 11½

1945, Nov. 27 Photo. Unwmk.

Cross in Red

B15 SP11 10rp + 10rp brn vio & buff 60 *1.75*
B16 SP11 20rp + 20rp hn brn & buff 70 *2.00*
B17 SP11 1fr + 1.40fr slate & buff 5.25 *16.00*
Set, never hinged 10.50

Souvenir Sheet

Post Coach SP14

1946, Aug. 10

B18 SP14 Sheet of 2 21.00 *30.00*
Never hinged 35.00
a. 10rp dark vio brn & buff 9.00 *13.00*
Never hinged 15.00

25th anniv. of the Swiss-Liechtenstein Postal Agreement. Sheet, size: 82x60½mm, sold for 3fr.

Canal by Albert Cuyp — SP15

Willem van Huythuysen by Frans Hals — SP16

Design: 40rp+10rp, Landscape by Jacob van Ruysdael.

1951, July 24 *Perf. 11½*

B19 SP15 10rp + 10rp ol grn 5.75 6.50
B20 SP16 20rp + 10rp dk vio brn 5.75 13.00
B21 SP15 40rp + 10rp bl 5.75 6.50
Set, never hinged 27.50

Issued in sheets of 12. For surcharges see Nos. 281-283.

Catalogue values for unused stamps in this section, from this point to the end of the section, are for Never Hinged items.

Nos. 324-325 Surcharged with New Value and Uprooted Oak Emblem

1960, Apr. 7

B22 A190 30rp + 10rp on 40rp bl, vio & red 90 90
B23 A190 50rp + 10rp on 25rp bis, vio & red 1.50 1.50

World Refugee Year, July 1, 1959-June 30, 1960. The surtax was for aid to refugees.

Growth Symbol — SP17

1967, Dec. 7 Photo. *Perf. 11½*

B24 SP17 50rp + 20rp multi 85 60

Surtax was for development assistance.

AIR POST STAMPS

Airplane over Snow-capped Mountain Peaks — AP1

Airplane above Vaduz Castle — AP2

Airplane over Rhine Valley — AP3

Perf. 10½, 10½x11½

1930, Aug. 12 Photo. Unwmk.

Gray Wavy Lines in Background

C1 AP1 15rp dk brn 6.00 6.25
C2 AP1 20rp slate 12.50 11.00
C3 AP2 25rp ol brn 9.00 9.50
C4 AP2 35rp sl bl 12.50 9.50
C5 AP3 45rp ol grn 22.50 37.50
C6 AP3 1fr lake 42.50 27.50
Nos. C1-C6 (6) 105.00 101.25
Set, never hinged 350.00

For surcharge see No. C14.

Zeppelin over Naafkopf, Falknis Range — AP4

Design: 2fr, Zeppelin over Valüna Valley.

1931, June 1 *Perf. 11½*

C7 AP4 1fr olive blk 52.50 95.00
C8 AP4 2fr blue blk 110.00 265.00
Set, never hinged 350.00

Golden Eagle — AP6

Designs: 15rp, Golden Eagle in flight, diff. 20rp, Golden Eagle in flight, diff. 30rp, Osprey. 50rp, Eagle.

1934-35

C9 AP6 10rp brt vio ('35) 4.50 13.00
C10 AP6 15rp red org ('35) 11.00 30.00
C11 AP6 20rp red ('35) 14.00 30.00
C12 AP6 30rp brt bl ('35) 12.50 30.00
C13 AP6 50rp emerald 8.00 21.00
Nos. C9-C13 (5) 50.00 124.00
Set, never hinged 150.00

No. C6 Surcharged with New Value

1935, June 24 *Perf. 10½x11½*

C14 AP3 60rp on 1fr lake 27.50 35.00
Never hinged 87.50

Airship "Hindenburg" — AP11

Design: 2fr, Airship "Graf Zeppelin."

1936, May 1 *Perf. 11½*

C15 AP11 1fr rose car 30.00 67.50
C16 AP11 2fr violet 27.50 55.00
Set, never hinged 130.00

AP13

AP20

Designs: 10rp, Barn swallows. 15rp, Black-headed Gulls. 20rp, Gulls. 30rp, Eagle. 50rp, Northern Goshawk. 1fr, Lammergeier. 2fr, Lammergeier.

1939, Apr. 3 Photo.

C17 AP13 10rp violet 28 20
C18 AP13 15rp red org 80 1.50
C19 AP13 20rp dark red 1.00 42
C20 AP13 30rp dull blue 1.00 70
C21 AP13 50rp brt grn 2.75 1.50
C22 AP13 1fr rose car 2.75 *10.50*
C23 AP13 2fr violet 2.00 *10.50*
Nos. C17-C23 (7) 10.58 *25.32*
Set, never hinged 20.00

1948

Designs: 10rp, Leonardo da Vinci. 15rp, Joseph Montgolfier. 20rp, Jacob Degen. 25rp, Wilhelm Kress. 40rp, E. G. Robertson. 50rp, W. S. Henson. 1fr, Otto Lilienthal. 2fr, S. A. Andrée. 5fr, Wilbur Wright. 10fr, Icarus.

C24 AP20 10rp dk grn 1.40 50
C25 AP20 15rp dk vio 1.10 1.10
C26 AP20 20rp brown 1.10 50
a. 20rp reddish brown 42.50 2.00
Never hinged 100.00
C27 AP20 25rp dark red 1.40 2.50
C28 AP20 40rp vio blue 2.00 1.25
C29 AP20 50rp Prus blue 2.75 2.25
C30 AP20 1fr chocolate 2.75 3.00
C31 AP20 2fr rose lake 4.00 4.00
C32 AP20 5fr olive grn 4.00 8.00
C33 AP20 10fr slate blk 25.00 13.00
Nos. C24-C33 (10) 45.50 36.10
Set, never hinged 62.50

Issued in sheets of 9.
Exist imperf. Value, set $6,500.

Helicopter, Bell 47-J — AP21

Planes: 40rp, Boeing 707 jet. 50rp, Convair 600 jet. 75rp, Douglas DC-8.

1960, Apr. 7 Unwmk. *Perf. 11½*

C34 AP21 30rp red orange 1.25 1.75
C35 AP21 40rp blue black 2.50 1.75
C36 AP21 50rp dp claret 4.75 3.75
C37 AP21 75rp olive grn 2.50 1.75
Set, never hinged 16.00

30th anniv. of Liechtenstein's air post stamps.

POSTAGE DUE STAMPS

National Administration of the Post Office

D1

1920 Unwmk. Engr. *Perf. 12½*

J1 D1 5h rose red 15 20
J2 D1 10h rose red 15 20
J3 D1 15h rose red 15 20
J4 D1 20h rose red 15 20
J5 D1 25h rose red 15 20
J6 D1 30h rose red 15 20
J7 D1 40h rose red 15 20
J8 D1 50h rose red 15 20
J9 D1 80h rose red 15 20
J10 D1 1k dull blue 15 20
J11 D1 2k dull blue 15 28

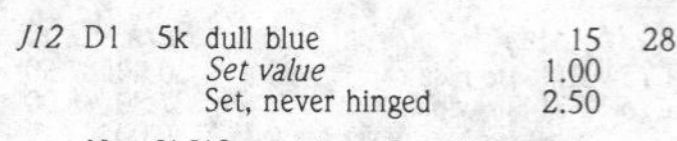

J12	D1	5k	dull blue	15	28
			Set value	1.00	
			Set, never hinged	2.50	

Nos. J1-J12 exist imperf. and part perf.

Swiss Administration of the Post Office

D2

Post Horn — D3

1928 Litho. Wmk. 183 *Perf. 11½*

Granite Paper

J13	D2	5rp	pur & orange	80	1.75
J14	D2	10rp	pur & orange	90	1.75
J15	D2	15rp	pur & orange	2.25	8.50
J16	D2	20rp	pur & orange	1.40	2.50
J17	D2	25rp	pur & orange	2.25	7.00
J18	D2	30rp	pur & orange	5.00	8.75
J19	D2	40rp	pur & orange	5.25	9.75
J20	D2	50rp	pur & orange	5.25	12.00
			Nos. J13-J20 (8)	23.10	52.00
			Set, never hinged	70.00	

Engraved; Value Typographed in Dark Red

1940 Unwmk. *Perf. 11½*

J21	D3	5rp	gray blue	1.50	5.50
J22	D3	10rp	gray blue	65	90
J23	D3	15rp	gray blue	60	3.50
J24	D3	20rp	gray blue	60	1.25
J25	D3	25rp	gray blue	1.25	3.25
J26	D3	30rp	gray blue	2.50	4.50
J27	D3	40rp	gray blue	2.50	4.00
J28	D3	50rp	gray blue	2.50	5.00
			Nos. J21-J28 (8)	12.10	27.90
			Set, never hinged	35.00	

OFFICIAL STAMPS

Regular Issue of 1930 Overprinted in Various Colors with Crown and:

REGIERUNGS DIENSTSACHE

Perf. 10½, 11½, 11½x10½

1932 Unwmk.

O1	A38	5rp	dk grn (Bk)	5.50	9.00
O2	A39	10rp	dk vio (R)	37.50	7.50
a.			Perf. 11½x10½	650.00	1,050.
O3	A40	20rp	dp rose red (Bl)	50.00	7.50
a.			Perf. 10½	175.00	40.00
O4	A42	30rp	ultra (R)	7.75	9.00
a.			Perf. 10½	22.50	13.00
O5	A43	35rp	dp grn (Bk)	5.50	14.00
a.			Perf. 11½	3,500.	5,500.
O6	A45	50rp	blk brn (Bl)	37.50	11.00
a.			Perf. 11½	130.00	130.00
O7	A46	60rp	ol blk (R)	5.50	30.00
O8	A48	1.20fr	ol brn (G)	77.50	265.00
			Nos. O1-O8 (8)	226.75	353.00

Nos. 108, 110 Overprinted in Black

1933 *Perf. 14½*

O9	A51	25rp	red org	37.50	40.00
O10	A53	1.20fr	red brn	60.00	175.00

Same Overprint in Various Colors on Regular Issue of 1934-35

1934-36 *Perf. 11½*

O11	A58	5rp	emer (R)	45	1.25
O12	A59	10rp	dp vio (Bk)	22	1.10
O13	A60	15rp	red org (V)	22	40
O14	A61	20rp	red (Bk)	35	1.10
O15	A62	25rp	brn (R)	27.50	80.00
O16	A62	25rp	brn (Bk)	1.50	8.75
O17	A63	30rp	dk bl (R)	1.90	3.50
O18	A66	50rp	lt brn (V)	85	2.00
O19	A68	90rp	dp grn (Bk)	5.00	24.00
O20	A70	1.50fr	brn car (Bl)	35.00	105.00
			Nos. O11-O20 (10)	72.99	227.10

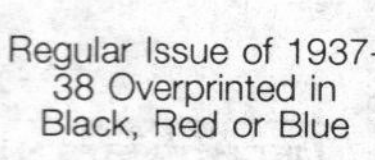
Regular Issue of 1937-38 Overprinted in Black, Red or Blue

1937-41

O21	A76	5rp	emer (Bk)	15	15
O22	A76	10rp	vio & buff (R)	15	22
O23	A76	20rp	brn org (Bl)	90	95
O24	A76	20rp	brn org (Bk) ('41)	90	95
O25	A76	25rp	chnt (Bk)	48	1.10
O26	A77	30rp	bl & gray (Bk)	70	48
O27	A79	50rp	dk brn & buff (R)	40	95
O28	A80	1fr	red brn (Bk)	80	4.00
O29	A80	1.50fr	sl bl (Bk) ('38)	2.75	6.50
			Nos. O21-O29 (9)	7.23	15.30
			Set, never hinged	15.00	

Stamps of 1944-45 Overprinted in Black

DIENSTMARKE

1947

O30	A136	5rp	sl grn & buff	55	75
O31	A136	10rp	gray & buff	75	75
O32	A136	20rp	org red & buff	75	75
O33	A136	30rp	bl & buff	1.50	1.40
O34	A136	50rp	bluish blk & pale gray	1.50	3.00
O35	A136	1fr	dp cl & buff	3.75	9.00
O36	A136	150rp	royal blue	4.75	9.00
			Nos. O30-O36 (7)	13.55	24.65
			Set, never hinged	30.00	

Crown — O1

Government Building, Vaduz — O2

Engr.; Value Typo.

1950-68 Unwmk. *Perf. 11½*

Buff Granite Paper

Narrow Gothic Numerals

O37	O1	5rp	red vio & gray	15	15
O38	O1	10rp	ol grn & mag	15	15
O39	O1	20rp	org brn & bl	15	20
O40	O1	30rp	dk red brn & org red	20	30
O41	O1	40rp	bl & hn brn	25	42
O42	O1	55rp	dk gray grn & red	1.10	1.50
a.			White paper ('68)	30.00	125.00
O43	O1	60rp	sl & mag	1.10	1.50
a.			White paper ('68)	4.75	32.50
O44	O1	80rp	red org & gray	52	75
O45	O1	90rp	choc & bl	70	1.10
O46	O1	1.20fr	grnsh bl & org	80	1.40
			Nos. O37-O46 (10)	5.12	7.47
			Set, never hinged	6.00	
			Set, #O42a, O43a, never hinged	62.50	

Catalogue values for unused stamps in this section, from this point to the end of the section, are for Never Hinged items.

1968-69 *Perf. 11½*

White Granite Paper

Broad Numerals, Varying Thickness

O47	O1	5rp	ol brn & org	15	15
O48	O1	10rp	vio & car	15	15
O49	O1	20rp	ver & emer	15	15
O50	O1	30rp	grn & red	16	16
O51	O1	50rp	ultra & red	20	20
O52	O1	60rp	org & ultra	24	24
O53	O1	70rp	mar & emer	30	30
O54	O1	80rp	bl grn & car	35	35
O55	O1	95rp	sl & red ('69)	60	60
O56	O1	1fr	rose cl & grn	42	42
O57	O1	1.20fr	lt red brn & grn	52	52
O58	O1	2fr	brn & org ('69)	1.00	1.00
			Nos. O47-O58 (12)	4.24	4.24

1976-89 Engr., Value Typo. *Perf. 14*

O59	O2	10rp	yel brn & vio	15	15
O60	O2	20rp	car lake & bl	15	16
O61	O2	35rp	bl & red	18	24
O62	O2	40rp	dl pur & grn	20	25
O63	O2	50rp	slate & mag	25	35
O64	O2	70rp	vio brn & bl grn	32	42
O65	O2	80rp	grn & mag	40	50
O66	O2	90rp	vio & bl grn	45	60
O67	O2	1fr	olive & mag	52	70
O68	O2	1.10fr	brn & ultra	60	75
O69	O2	1.50fr	dl grn & red	85	1.10
O70	O2	2fr	orange & blue	1.00	1.25
O75	O2	5fr	rose vio & brn org	6.00	6.00
			Nos. O59-O75 (13)	11.07	12.47

Issue dates: 5fr, Sept. 4, 1989. Others, Dec. 9, 1976.

This is an expanding set. Numbers will change if necessary.

LITHUANIA

(Lietuva)

LOCATION — Northern Europe bordering on the Baltic Sea
GOVT. — Independent republic
AREA — 22,959 sq. mi.
POP. — 2,879,070 (1940)
CAPITAL — Vilnius

Lithuania was under Russian rule when it declared its independence in 1918. The League of Nations recognized it in 1922. In 1940 it became a republic in the Union of Soviet Socialist Republics.

Lithuania declared its independence on March 11, 1990. Lithuanian independence was recognized by the Soviet Union on Sept. 6, 1991.

100 Skatiku = 1 Auksinas
100 Centai = 1 Litas (1922)
100 Kopecks = 1 Ruble (1991)

Catalogue values for unused stamps in this country are for Never Hinged items, beginning with Scott 400.

Nos. 1-26 were printed in sheets of 20 (5x4) which were imperf. at the outer sides, so that only 6 stamps in each sheet were fully perforated. Values are for the stamps partly imperf. The stamps fully perforated sell for at least double these values. There was also a printing of Nos. 19-26 in a sheet of 160, composed of blocks of 20 of each stamp. Pairs or blocks with different values se-tenant sell for considerably more than the values for the stamps singly.

Nos. 1-26 are without gum.

Watermarks

Wmk. 109- Webbing

Wmk. 144- Network

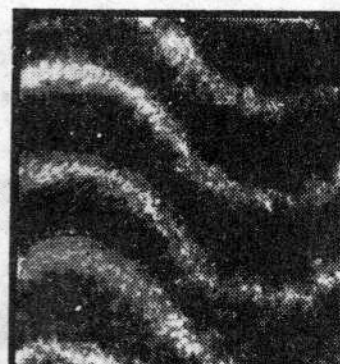
Wmk. 145- Wavy Lines

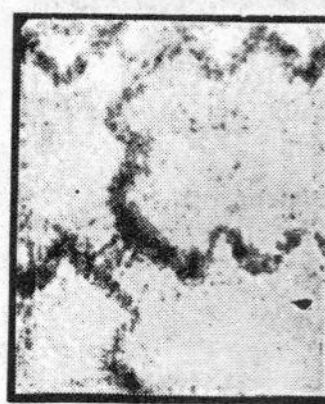
Wmk. 146- Zigzag Lines Forming Rectangles

Wmk. 147- Parquetry

Wmk. 198- Intersecting Diamonds

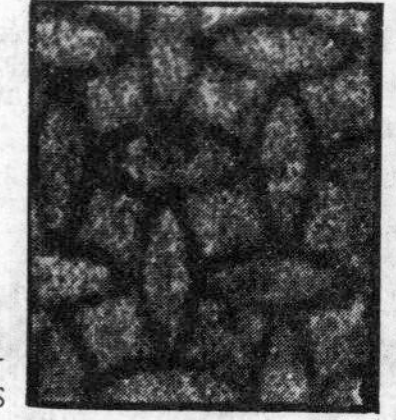
Wmk. 209- Multiple Ovals

Wmk. 238- Multiple Letters

A1

Lietuvos
10
skatikų
paštas

A2

Perf. 11½

1918, Dec. 27 Unwmk. Typeset

First Vilnius Printing

Thin Figures

1	A1	10sk	black	75.00	45.00
2	A1	15sk	black	75.00	45.00

1918, Dec. 31

Second Vilnius Printing

Thick Figures

3	A1	10sk	black	37.50	27.50
4	A1	15sk	black	37.50	25.00
5	A1	20sk	black	4.50	4.00
6	A1	30sk	black	4.50	4.00
7	A1	40sk	black	4.50	4.00
8	A1	50sk	black	4.50	4.00
			Nos. 3-8 (6)	93.00	68.50

First Kaunas Issue

1919

9	A2	10sk	black	6.00	3.50
10	A2	15sk	black	6.00	3.50
a.			"5" for "15"	50.00	50.00
11	A2	20sk	black	6.00	3.50
12	A2	30sk	black	6.00	3.50

Lietuvos
paštas
15

A3

Lietuvos
paštas
10

A4

Second Kaunas Issue

13	A3	10sk	black	2.50	1.25
14	A3	15sk	black	2.50	1.25
15	A3	20sk	black	2.50	1.25
a.			"astas" for "pastas"	60.00	55.00
16	A3	30sk	black	2.50	1.25
17	A3	40sk	black	2.50	1.50
18	A3	50sk	black	2.50	1.50
19	A3	60sk	black	2.50	1.50
			Nos. 13-19 (7)	17.50	9.50

Third Kaunas Issue

No.	Type	Description	Unused	Used
20	A4	10sk black	1.50	1.25
21	A4	15sk black	1.50	1.25
22	A4	20sk black	1.50	1.25
23	A4	30sk black	1.50	1.25
24	A4	40sk black	1.50	1.25
25	A4	50sk black	1.50	1.25
26	A4	60sk black	1.50	1.50
		Nos. 20-26 (7)	10.50	9.00

The White Knight "Vytis"
A5 A6

A7 A8

Perf. 10½ to 14 & Compound

1919 Litho. Wmk. 144

Gray Granite Paper

No.	Type	Description	Unused	Used
30	A5	10sk dp rose	22	22
a.		Wmk. vert.	12.50	6.75
31	A5	15sk violet	22	20
a.		Wmk. vert.	12.50	6.75
32	A5	20sk dk blue	22	20
33	A5	30sk dp orange	22	20
a.		Wmk. vert.	12.50	6.75
34	A5	40sk dk brown	22	20
35	A6	50sk blue green	38	28
36	A6	75sk org & dp rose	38	20
37	A7	1auk gray & rose	38	28
38	A7	3auk bis brn & rose	38	30
39	A7	5auk blue grn & rose	38	38
		Nos. 30-39 (10)	3.00	2.46
		Set, never hinged	3.75	
		Set, 30a, 31a, 33a, never hinged	42.50	

Nos. 30a, 31a and 33a are from the first printing with watermark vertical showing points to left; various perforations.

Nos. 30-39 exist imperf. Value in pairs, $40.

1919 Wmk. 145 Thick White Paper

No.	Type	Description	Unused	Used
40	A5	10sk dull rose	15	15
41	A5	15sk violet	15	15
42	A5	20sk dk blue	15	15
43	A5	30sk orange	15	15
44	A5	40sk red brn	15	15
45	A6	50sk green	15	15
46	A6	75sk yel & dp rose	15	15
47	A7	1auk gray & rose	30	20
48	A7	3auk yel brn & rose, perf. 12½	30	20
49	A7	5auk bl grn & rose	42	28
		Nos. 40-49 (10)	2.07	1.73
		Set, never hinged	2.25	

Nos. 40-49 exist imperf. Value in pairs, $40.

1919 *Perf. 10½ to 14 & Compound*

Thin White Paper

No.	Type	Description	Unused	Used
50	A5	10sk red	15	15
51	A5	15sk lilac	15	15
52	A5	20sk dull blue	15	15
53	A5	30sk buff	15	15
54	A5	40sk gray brn	15	15
55	A6	50sk lt green	15	15
56	A6	60sk vio & red	15	15
57	A6	75sk bis & red	15	15
58	A8	1auk gray & red	15	15
59	A8	3auk lt brn & red	15	15
60	A8	5auk bl grn & red	18	15
		Set value	1.00	95
		Set, never hinged	1.40	

Nos. 50-60 exist imperf. Value, pairs $50.

See Nos. 93-96. For surcharges see Nos. 114-115, 120-139, 149-150.

"Lithuania" Receiving Benediction
A9

The Spirit of Lithuania Rises
A10

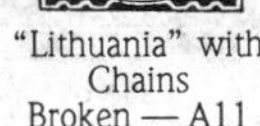

"Lithuania" with Chains Broken — A11

White Knight — A12

1920, Feb. 16 Wmk. 146 *Perf. 11½*

No.	Type	Description	Unused	Used
70	A9	10sk dp rose	1.50	1.25
71	A9	15sk lt violet	1.50	1.25
72	A9	20sk gray bl	1.50	1.25
73	A10	30sk yellow brn	1.50	1.25
74	A11	40sk brown & grn	1.50	1.25
75	A10	50sk dp rose	1.50	1.25
76	A10	60sk lt vio	1.50	1.25
77	A11	80sk purple & red	1.50	1.25
78	A11	1auk green & red	1.50	1.25
79	A12	3auk brown & red	1.50	1.25
80	A12	5auk green & red	1.50	1.25
a.		Right "5" dbl., grn and red	50.00	62.50
		Nos. 70-80 (11)	16.50	13.75
		Set, never hinged	22.50	

Anniv. of natl. independence. The stamps were on sale only 3 days. Only a limited number of stamps was sold at post offices but 40,000 sets were delivered to the bank of Kaunas.

All values exist imperforate.

White Knight
A13

Grand Duke Vytautas
A14

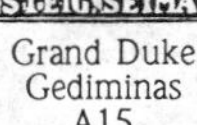

Grand Duke Gediminas
A15

Sacred Oak and Altar
A16

1920, Aug. 25

No.	Type	Description	Unused	Used
81	A13	10sk rose	38	38
a.		Imperf., pair	6.00	
82	A13	15sk dk violet	38	38
83	A14	20sk grn & lt grn	38	38
84	A13	30sk brown	38	38
a.		Pair, #82, 84	6.00	
85	A15	40sk gray grn & vio	38	50
86	A14	50sk brn & brn org	1.00	1.00
87	A14	60sk red & org	1.00	1.00
88	A15	80sk blk, db & red	1.00	1.00
89	A16	1auk orange & blk	1.00	1.00
90	A16	3auk green & blk	1.00	1.00
91	A16	5auk gray vio & blk	1.00	1.00
		Nos. 81-91 (11)	7.90	8.02
		Set, never hinged	10.50	

Opening of Lithuanian National Assembly. On sale for three days.

1920

No.	Type	Description	Unused	Used
92	A14	20sk green & lilac	40.00	
92A	A15	40sk gray grn, buff & vio	40.00	
92B	A14	50sk brn & gray lil	40.00	
92C	A14	60sk red & green	40.00	
92D	A15	80sk blk, grn & red	40.00	
		Nos. 92-92D (5)	200.00	
		Set, never hinged	250.00	

Nos. 92 to 92D were trial printings. By order of the Ministry of Posts, 2,000 copies of each were placed on sale at post offices.

Type of 1919 Issue

1920 Unwmk. *Perf. 11½*

No.	Type	Description	Unused	Used
93	A5	15sk lilac	2.50	1.50
94	A5	20sk dp blue	2.00	1.50
		Set, never hinged	7.75	

Wmk. 109

No.	Type	Description	Unused	Used
95	A5	20sk dp blue	1.25	75
96	A5	40sk gray brn	1.75	1.00
		Set, never hinged	4.75	

Watermark horizontal on Nos. 95-96.
No. 96 exists perf. 10½x11½.

Imperf., Pairs

No.	Type	Description	Unused	Used
93a	A5	15sk	3.00	2.00
94a	A5	20sk	3.00	2.00
95a	A5	20sk	3.25	2.50
96a	A5	40sk	3.25	3.75
		Set, never hinged	24.50	

Sower — A17

Peasant Sharpening Scythe — A18

Prince Kestutis
A19

Black Horseman
A20

Perf. 11, 11½ and Compound

1921-22

No.	Type	Description	Unused	Used
97	A17	10sk brt rose	15	55
98	A17	15sk violet	15	*70*
99	A17	20sk ultra	15	15
100	A18	30sk brown	38	*1.10*
101	A19	40sk red	15	15
102	A18	50sk olive	15	15
103	A18	60sk grn & vio	25	*1.65*
104	A19	80sk brn org & car	18	15
105	A19	1auk brown & grn	15	15
106	A19	2auk gray bl & red	15	15
107	A20	3auk yel brn & dk bl	30	42
108	A17	4auk yel & dk bl ('22)	25	15
109	A20	5auk gray blk & rose	38	*1.00*
110	A17	8auk grn & blk ('22)	38	15
111	A20	10auk rose & vio	75	55
112	A20	25auk bis brn & grn	90	85
113	A20	100auk dl red & gray blk	4.50	6.50
		Nos. 97-113 (17)	9.32	14.52
		Set, never hinged	12.50	

Imperf., Pairs

No.	Type	Description	Unused
97a	A17	10sk	12.50
98a	A17	15sk	10.00
99a	A17	20sk	12.50
100a	A18	30sk	17.50
102a	A18	50sk	1.25
103a	A18	60sk	12.50
104a	A19	80sk	12.50
105a	A19	1auk	12.50
106a	A19	2auk	12.50
107a	A20	3auk	12.50
109a	A20	5auk	15.00
110a	A17	8auk	10.00

For surcharges see Nos. 140-148, 151-160.

No. 57 Surcharged

Perf. 12½x11½

1922, May Wmk. 145

No.	Type	Description	Unused	Used
114	A6	4auk on 75sk bis & red	25	15
a.		Inverted surcharge	20.00	20.00

Same with Bars over Original Value

No.	Type	Description	Unused	Used
115	A6	4auk on 75sk bis & red	50	38
a.		Double surcharge	20.00	20.00
		Set, never hinged	2.75	

Povilas Luksis — A20a

Justinas Staugaitis, Antanas Smetona, Stasys Silingas
A20b

Portraits: 40s, Lt. Juozapavicius. 50s, Dr. Basanavicius. 60s, Mrs. Petkeviciute. 1auk, Prof. Voldemaras. 2auk, Pranas Dovidaitis. 3auk, Dr. Slezevicius. 4auk, Dr. Galvanauskas. 5auk, Kazys Grinius. 6auk, Dr. Stulginskis. 8auk, Pres. Smetona.

1922 Litho. Unwmk.

No.	Type	Description	Unused	Used
116	A20a	20s blk & car rose	42	42
116A	A20a	40s bl grn & vio	42	42
116B	A20a	50s plum & grnsh bl	42	42
117	A20a	60s pur & org	42	42
117A	A20a	1auk car & lt bl	42	42
117B	A20a	2auk dp bl & yel brn	42	42
c.		Center inverted	60.00	60.00
118	A20a	3auk mar & ultra	42	42
118A	A20a	4auk dk grn & red vio	42	42
118B	A20a	5auk blk brn & dp rose	42	42
119	A20a	6auk dk bl & grnsh bl	42	42
a.		Cliché of 8auk in sheet of 6auk	25.00	25.00
119B	A20a	8auk ultra & bis	55	55
119C	A20b	10auk dk vio & bl grn	1.10	1.10
		Nos. 116-119C (12)	5.85	5.85
		Set, never hinged	7.00	

League of Nations' recognition of Lithuania. Sold only on Oct. 1, 1922.

Forty sheets of the 6auk each included eight copies of the 8auk.

Stamps of 1919-22 Surcharged in Black, Carmine or Green

1 CENT **10 CENTU**

On Nos. 37-39

1922 Wmk. 144 *Perf. 11½x12*

Gray Granite Paper

No.	Type	Description	Unused	Used
120	A7	3c on 1auk	72.50	72.50
121	A7	3c on 3auk	57.50	57.50
122	A7	3c on 5auk	27.50	27.50
		Set, never hinged	225.00	

White Paper

Wmk. 145

Perf. 14, 11½, 12½x11½

No.	Type	Description	Unused	Used
123	A5	1c on 10sk red	52	70
124	A5	1c on 15sk lilac	52	70
125	A5	1c on 20sk dull bl	52	70
126	A5	1c on 30sk orange	70.00	70.00
127	A5	1c on 30sk buff	25	22
128	A5	1c on 40sk gray brn	52	70
129	A6	2c on 50sk green	52	70
130	A6	2c on 60sk vio & red	15	15
131	A6	2c on 75sk bis & red	35	70
132	A8	3c on 1auk gray & red	35	25
133	A8	3c on 3auk brn & red	18	18
134	A8	3c on 5auk bl grn & red	18	18
		Nos. 123-125,127-134 (11)	4.06	5.18

On Stamps of 1920

1922 Unwmk. *Perf. 11*

No.	Type	Description	Unused	Used
136	A5	1c on 20sk dp bl (C)	50	75

Wmk. Webbing. (109)

Perf. 11, 11½

No.	Type	Description	Unused	Used
138	A5	1c on 20sk dp bl (C)	50	65
139	A5	1c on 40sk gray brn (C)	1.25	1.25

On Stamps of 1921-22

No.	Type	Description	Unused	Used
140	A18	1c on 50sk ol (C)	15	15
a.		Imperf., pair	17.50	
b.		Inverted surcharge	15.00	
c.		Double surch., one invtd.		
141	A17	3c on 10sk	1.25	1.25
142	A17	3c on 15sk	15	15
143	A17	3c on 20sk	18	25
144	A18	3c on 30sk	90	1.00
145	A19	3c on 40sk	15	15
a.		Imperf., pair		
146	A18	5c on 50sk	15	15
147	A18	5c on 60sk	45	65
148	A19	5c on 80sk	15	15
a.		Imperf., pair	15.00	15.00

Wmk. Wavy Lines (145)

Perf. 12½x11½

No.	Type	Description	Unused	Used
149	A6	5c on 4auk on 75sk (No. 114) (G)	38	65
150	A6	5c on 4auk on 75sk (No. 115) (G)	1.25	1.50

Wmk. Webbing (109)

Perf. 11, 11½

No.	Type	Description	Unused	Used
151	A19	10c on 1auk	30	15
a.		Inverted surcharge	20.00	
152	A19	10c on 2auk	15	15
a.		Inverted surcharge	15.00	
b.		Imperf., pair	15.00	
153	A17	15c on 4auk	15	15
a.		Inverted surcharge	15.00	
154	A20	25c on 3auk	2.25	2.50
155	A20	25c on 5auk	1.90	1.50
156	A20	25c on 10auk	1.50	1.00
a.		Imperf., pair	15.00	

157	A17	30c on 8auk (C)	30	24
a.		Inverted surcharge	15.00	15.00
158	A20	50c on 25auk	1.75	1.75
160	A20	1 l on 100auk	2.50	2.00
		Nos. 136-160 (23)	18.21	18.14
		Set, never hinged	30.00	

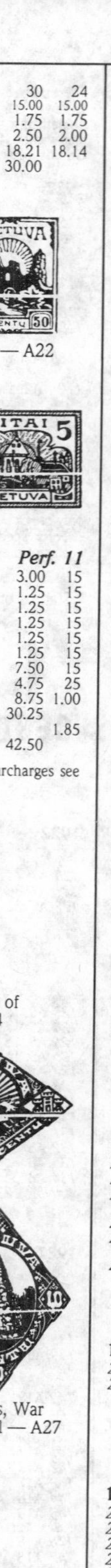

A21

Ruin — A22

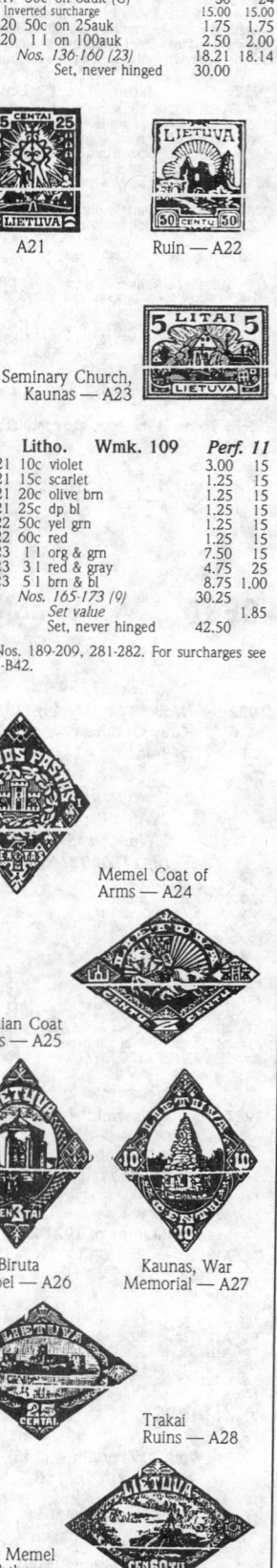

Seminary Church, Kaunas — A23

1923 Litho. Wmk. 109 *Perf. 11*

165	A21	10c violet	3.00	15
166	A21	15c scarlet	1.25	15
167	A21	20c olive brn	1.25	15
168	A21	25c dp bl	1.25	15
169	A22	50c yel grn	1.25	15
170	A22	60c red	1.25	15
171	A23	1 l org & grn	7.50	15
172	A23	3 l red & gray	4.75	25
173	A23	5 l brn & bl	8.75	1.00
		Nos. 165-173 (9)	30.25	
		Set value		1.85
		Set, never hinged	42.50	

See Nos. 189-209, 281-282. For surcharges see Nos. B1-B42.

Memel Coat of Arms — A24

Lithuanian Coat of Arms — A25

Biruta Chapel — A26

Kaunas, War Memorial — A27

Trakai Ruins — A28

Memel Lighthouse A29

Memel Harbor — A30

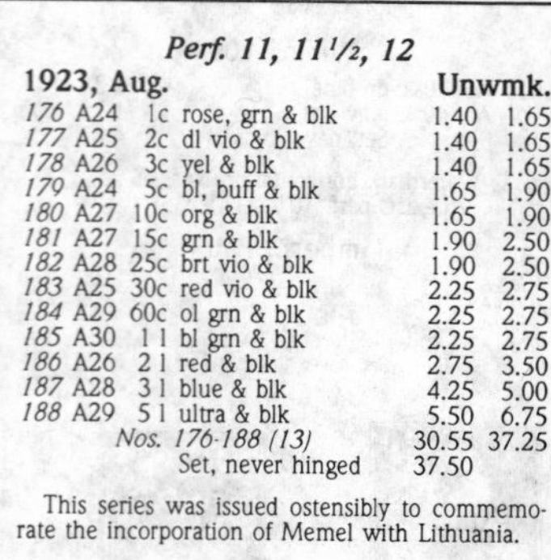

Perf. 11, 11½, 12

1923, Aug. Unwmk.

176	A24	1c rose, grn & blk	1.40	1.65
177	A25	2c dl vio & blk	1.40	1.65
178	A26	3c yel & blk	1.40	1.65
179	A24	5c bl, buff & blk	1.65	1.90
180	A27	10c org & blk	1.65	1.90
181	A27	15c grn & blk	1.90	2.50
182	A28	25c brt vio & blk	1.90	2.50
183	A25	30c red vio & blk	2.25	2.75
184	A29	60c ol grn & blk	2.25	2.75
185	A30	1 l bl grn & blk	2.25	2.75
186	A26	2 l red & blk	2.75	3.50
187	A28	3 l blue & blk	4.25	5.00
188	A29	5 l ultra & blk	5.50	6.75
		Nos. 176-188 (13)	30.55	37.25
		Set, never hinged	37.50	

This series was issued ostensibly to commemorate the incorporation of Memel with Lithuania.

Type of 1923 Issue

1923 Unwmk. *Perf. 11*

189	A21	5c pale green	1.75	15
190	A21	10c violet	2.50	15
a.		Imperf., pair	22.50	
191	A21	15c scarlet	3.00	15
a.		Imperf., pair	22.50	
193	A21	25c blue	4.75	15
		Set value		20
		Set, never hinged	17.50	

1923 Wmk. 147

196	A21	2c pale brown	90	25
197	A21	3c olive bis	1.00	18
198	A21	5c pale green	1.00	15
199	A21	10c violet	2.25	15
202	A21	25c deep blue	5.00	15
a.		Imperf., pair	24.00	
204	A21	36c orange brn	7.50	50
		Nos. 196-204 (6)	17.65	1.38
		Set, never hinged	25.00	

Perf. 11½, 14½, 11½x14½

1923-25 Wmk. 198

207	A21	25c deep blue	180.00	180.00
208	A22	50c dp grn ('25)	2.75	15
209	A22	60c car ('25)	3.25	15
		Set, never hinged	225.00	

Double- barred Cross — A31

Dr. Jonas Basanavicius — A32

1927, Jan. *Perf. 11½, 14½*

210	A31	2c orange	75	15
211	A31	3c dp brown	75	15
212	A31	5c green	1.25	15
a.		Imperf., pair	10.00	
213	A31	10c violet	2.00	15
214	A31	15c red	1.75	15
a.		Imperf., pair	10.00	
215	A31	25c blue	1.75	15
		Nos. 210-215 (6)	8.25	
		Set value		48
		Set, never hinged	13.00	

1927-29 Wmk. 147 *Perf. 14½*

216	A31	5c green	20.00	10.00
217	A31	30c blue ('29)	12.50	2.50
		Set, never hinged	37.50	

See Nos. 233-240, 278-280.

Perf. 11½, 14½x11½

1927 Unwmk.

219	A32	15c claret & blk	70	38
220	A32	25c dull bl & blk	70	38
221	A32	50c dk grn & blk	1.25	75
222	A32	60c dk vio & blk	1.75	1.00
		Set, never hinged	5.75	

Dr. Jonas Basanavicius (1851-1927), patriot and folklorist.

National Arms — A33

1927, Dec. 23 Wmk. 109 *Perf. 14½*

223	A33	1 l bl grn & gray	1.40	15
224	A33	3 l vio & pale grn	2.25	45
225	A33	5 l brown & gray	4.00	80
		Set, never hinged	12.00	

Pres. Antanas Smetona — A34

Decade of Independence — A35

Dawn of Peace — A36

1928, Feb. Wmk. 109

226	A34	5c org brn & grn	42	28
227	A34	10c vio & blk	55	28
228	A34	15c org & brn	55	28
229	A34	25c blue & indigo	55	28
230	A35	50c ultra & dl vio	55	28
231	A35	60c car & blk	85	55
232	A36	1 l blk brn & db	85	70
		Nos. 226-232 (7)	4.32	2.65
		Set, never hinged	5.50	

10th anniv. of Lithuanian independence.

Type of 1926 Issue

1929-31

233	A31	2c orange ('31)	1.25	15
234	A31	5c green	1.25	15
235	A31	10c violet ('31)	6.00	15
237	A31	15c red	1.75	15
a.		Tête bêche pair	10.00	10.00
239	A31	30c dk blue	3.00	15

Unwmk.

240	A31	15c red	6.25	15
		Nos. 233-240 (6)	19.50	
		Set value		52
		Set, never hinged	27.50	

Grand Duke Vytautas A37

Grand Duke, Mounted A38

1930, Feb. 16 *Perf. 14*

242	A37	2c yel brn & dk brn	25	15
243	A37	3c dk brn & vio	25	15
244	A37	5c yel grn & dp org	25	15
245	A37	10c vio & emer	25	15
246	A37	15c dp rose & vio	25	15
247	A37	30c dk bl & brn vio	38	15
248	A37	36c brn vio & ol blk	38	15
249	A37	50c dl grn & ultra	38	15
250	A37	60c dk bl & rose	38	15
251	A38	1 l bl grn, db & red brn	1.00	20
252	A38	3 l dk brn, sal & dk vio	1.25	1.00
253	A38	5 l ol brn, gray & red	2.50	1.00
254	A38	10 l multicolored	14.00	9.00
255	A38	25 l multicolored	27.50	20.00
		Nos. 242-255 (14)	49.02	32.55
		Set, never hinged	65.00	

5th cent. of the death of the Grand Duke Vytautas.

Kaunas, Railroad Station — A39

Cathedral at Vilnius — A39a

Designs: 15c, 25c, Landscape on the Neman River. 50c, Main Post Office, Kaunas.

Perf. 14, Imperf.

1932, July 21 Wmk. 238

256	A39	10c dk red brn & ocher	25	25
257	A39	15c dk brn & ol	38	38
258	A39	25c dk bl & ol	50	50
259	A39	50c gray blk & ol	75	90
260	A39a	1 l dk bl & ol	1.50	2.25
261	A39a	3 l red brn & gray grn	3.25	3.75

Wmk. 198

262	A39	5c vio bl & ocher	25	25
263	A39a	60c grnsh blk & lil	1.50	1.65
		Nos. 256-263 (8)	8.38	9.93
		Set, never hinged	9.50	

Issued for the benefit of Lithuanian orphans.

In September, 1935, a red overprint was applied to No. 259: "ORO PASTAS / LITUANICA II / 1935 / NEW YORK-KAUNAS". Value, $200; Never hinged, $250.

Vytautas Fleeing from Prison, 1382 A40

Designs: 15c, 25c, Conversion of Ladislas II Jagello and Vytautas (1386). 50c, 60c, Battle at Tannenberg (1410). 1 l, 3 l, Meeting of the Nobles (1429).

1932 Wmk. 209 *Perf. 14, Imperf.*

264	A40	5c red & rose lake	28	28
265	A40	10c ol bis & org brn	28	28
266	A40	15c rose lil & ol grn	35	35
267	A40	25c dk vio brn & ocher	85	1.10
268	A40	50c dp grn & bis brn	1.10	1.25
269	A40	60c ol grn & brn car	1.40	1.50
270	A40	1 l ultra & ol grn	1.65	1.90
271	A40	3 l dk brn & dk grn	2.50	2.75
		Nos. 264-271 (8)	8.41	9.41
		Set, never hinged	9.00	

15th anniversary of independence.

A. Visteliauskas A41

Mother and Child A42

Designs: 15c, 25c, Petras Vileisis. 50c, 60c, Dr. John Sliupas. 1 l, 3 l, Jonas Basanavicius.

1933 *Perf. 14, Imperf.*

272	A41	5c yel grn & car	15	15
273	A41	10c ultra & car	15	15
274	A41	15c org & red	18	22
275	A41	25c dk bl & blk brn	30	35
276	A41	50c ol gray & dk bl	75	1.10
277	A41	60c org brn & chnt	1.50	2.00
277A	A41	1 l red & vio brn	1.75	2.25
277B	A41	3 l turq grn & vio brn	3.00	4.50
		Nos. 272-277B (8)	7.78	10.72
		Set, never hinged	9.50	

50th anniv. of the 1st newspaper "Ausra" in Lithuanian language.

1933, Sept. *Perf. 14, Imperf.*

Designs: 15c, 25c, Boy reading. 50c, 60c, Boy playing with blocks. 1 l, 3 l, Woman and boy at the Spinning Wheel.

277C	A42	5c dp yel grn & org brn	15	15
277D	A42	10c rose brn & ultra	15	15
277E	A42	15c ol grn & plum	20	22
277F	A42	25c org & gray blk	30	32
277G	A42	50c ol grn & car	75	1.00
277H	A42	60c blk & yel org	1.50	1.90
277I	A42	1 l dk brn & ultra	1.75	2.00
277K	A42	3 l rose lil & ol grn	3.00	4.25
		Nos. 277C-277K (8)	7.80	9.99
		Set, never hinged	8.50	

Issued for the benefit of Lithuanian orphans.

Types of 1923-26 Issues

1933-34 Wmk. 238 *Perf. 14*

278 A31 2c orange 13.00 1.65
279 A31 10c dk violet 11.00 1.65
280 A31 15c red 17.50 80
281 A22 50c green 8.75 1.65
282 A22 60c red 11.00 80
Nos. 278-282 (5) 61.25 6.55
Set, never hinged 67.50

Pres. Antanas Smetona, 60th Birthday — A43

1934 Unwmk. Engr. *Perf. 11½*

283 A43 15c red 2.75 15
284 A43 30c green 4.50 15
285 A43 60c blue 6.75 20
Set value 36
Set, never hinged 21.00

A44

A47

Arms — A45

Knight — A48

Girl with Wheat — A46

Wmk. 198; Wmk. 209 (35c, 10 l)

1934-35 Litho. *Perf. 14*

286 A44 2c rose & dl org 60 15
287 A44 5c bl grn & grn 60 15
288 A45 10c chocolate 1.25 15
289 A46 25c dk brn & emer 2.25 15
290 A45 35c carmine 2.25 15
291 A46 50c dk bl & bl 2.75 15
292 A47 1 l sl & mar 12.00 15
293 A47 3 l grn & gray grn 18 15
294 A48 5 l mar & gray bl 24 45
295 A48 10 l choc & yel 1.50 1.50
Nos. 286-295 (10) 23.62
Set value 2.05
Set, never hinged 32.50

No. 290 exists imperf. Value, pair $25.
For overprint see No. 2N9.

1936-37 Wmk. 238 *Perf. 14*
Size: 17½x23mm

296 A44 2c orange ('37) 15 15
297 A44 5c green 18 15
Set value 18
Set, never hinged 55

Pres. Smetona — A49

Arms — A50

1936-37 Unwmk.

298 A49 15c carmine 4.00 15
299 A49 30c green ('37) 6.00 15
300 A49 60c ultra ('37) 6.00 15
Set value 30
Set, never hinged 20.00

1937-39 Wmk. 238 *Perf. 14*
Paper with Gray Network

301 A50 10c green 1.00 15
302 A50 25c magenta 15 15
303 A50 35c red 50 15
304 A50 50c brown 15 15
305 A50 1 l dp vio bl ('39) 15 15
Nos. 301-305 (5) 1.95
Set value 45
Set, never hinged 2.25

No. 304 exists in two types: I- "50" is fat and broad, with "0" leaning to right. II- "50" is thinner and narrower, with "0" straight.
For overprint see No. 2N10.

Jonas Basanavicius Reading Act of Independence A51

President Antanas Smetona — A52

Perf. 13x13½

1939, Jan. 15 Engr. Unwmk.

306 A51 15c dk red 32 30
307 A52 30c dp grn 32 30
308 A51 35c red lilac 70 45
309 A52 60c dark blue 70 45
a. Souvenir sheet of 2, #308-309 5.50 11.00
Souvenir sheet, never hinged 6.50
b. As "a," imperf. 15.00 19.00
Set, 309a-309b, never hinged 20.00
Set, 306-309, never hinged 2.75

20th anniv. of Independence.
Nos. 309a, 309b sold for 2 l.

Same Overprinted in Blue

VILNIUS 1939-X-10

1939

310 A51 15c dk red 50 80
311 A52 30c dp green 65 80
312 A51 35c red lilac 75 90
313 A52 60c dark blue 1.00 90
Set, never hinged 3.50

Recovery of Vilnius.

View of Vilnius — A53

Gediminas — A54

Trakai Ruins — A55

Lithuania stamps can be mounted in Scott's annual Baltic States Supplement.

Unwmk.

1940, May 6 Photo. *Perf. 14*

314 A53 15c brn & pale brn 30 20
315 A54 30c dk grn & lt grn 40 20
316 A55 60c dk bl & lt bl 80 40
a. Souv. sheet of 3, #314-316, imperf. 3.00 6.00
Souvenir sheet, never hinged 4.00
Set, never hinged 2.00

Return of Vilnius to Lithuania, Oct. 10, 1939. Exist imperf.
No. 316a has simulated perforations in gold. Sold for 2 l.

White Knight — A56

Angel — A57

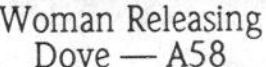

Woman Releasing Dove — A58

Mother and Children — A59

Liberty Bell — A60

Mythical Animal — A61

1940

317 A56 5c brown carmine 15 15
318 A57 10c green 15 15
319 A58 15c dull orange 15 15
320 A59 25c light brn 15 15
321 A60 30c Prussian grn 15 15
322 A61 35c red orange 15 25
Set value 42
Set, never hinged 50

Nos. 317-322 exist imperf.
For overprints see Nos. 2N11-2N16.

Catalogue values for unused stamps in this section, from this point to the end of the section, are for Never Hinged items.

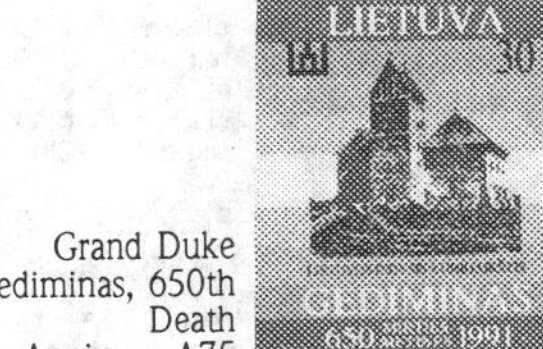

Grand Duke Gediminas, 650th Death Anniv. — A75

1991, Sept. 28 Litho. *Perf. 13x13½*

400 A75 30k Castle 1.40 70
401 A75 50k Grand Duke 2.40 1.20
402 A75 70k Early view of Vilnius 3.30 1.65

Ciconia Nigra — A76

Design: 50k, Grus grus.

1991, Nov. 21 Litho. *Perf. 14*

403 A76 30k +15k multi 2.35 1.15
404 A76 50k multicolored 2.60 1.30

A77

1991, Dec. 20 Photo. *Perf. 14*
Background Colors

411 A77 40k black 52 26
412 A77 50k purple 65 32
415 A77 100k dark green 1.30 65
418 A77 500k blue 6.50 3.25

Additional values of type A77 dated 1990 or 1991 were issued prior to Soviet recognition of Lithuanian independence. This is an expanding set, numbers may change.

A78

A79

1992, Mar. 15 Litho. *Perf. 13x13½*

421 A78 100k multicolored 1.25 62

Lithuanian admission to UN.

1992, Mar. 22

Emblems.

422 A79 50k +25k Olympic Committee 90 45
423 A79 130k Albertville 1.60 80
424 A79 280k Barcelona 3.40 1.70

Lithuanian Olympic participation. Surtax for Lithuanian Olympic Committee.

Flowers — A80

1992, July 11 *Perf. 12½x13*

425 A80 200k Cypripedium 2.65 1.30
426 A80 300k Eringium maritimum 4.00 2.00

New Currency - Talona

Birds of the Baltic Shores — A81

Designs: No. 427, Pandion haliaetus. No. 428, Limosa limosa. No. 429, Mergus merganser. No. 430, Tadorna tadorna.

Perf. 12½x13

1992, Oct. 3 Litho. & Engr.

427 A81 B (15t) grn & grnsh blk 78 40
428 A81 B (15t) grn & red brn 78 40
429 A81 B (15t) grn, red brn & brn 78 40
430 A81 B (15t) grn & red brn 78 40
a. Booklet pane of 4, #427-430 3.12

See Estonia Nos. 231-234a, Latvia Nos. 332-335a and Sweden Nos. 1975-1978a.

Coats of Arms — A82

19th Cent. Costumes — A83

1992, Oct. 11 **Litho.** ***Perf. 14***

431	A82	2t Kedainiai	25	15
432	A82	3t Vilnius	40	20
433	A82	10t National	1.35	65

1992, Oct. 18 ***Perf. 13x13½***

Couples in different traditional costumes of the Suwalki region.

434	A83	2t multicolored	25	15
435	A83	5t multicolored	65	32
436	A83	7t multicolored	95	48

SEMI-POSTAL STAMPS

Regular Issue of 1923-24 Surcharged in Blue, Violet or Black:

On A21

On A22

On A23

1924, Feb. **Wmk. 147** ***Perf. 11***

B1	A21	2c + 2c pale brn (Bl)	55	55
B2	A21	3c + 3c ol bis (Bl)	55	55
B3	A21	5c + 5c pale grn (V)	55	55
B4	A21	10c + 10c vio (Bk)	1.40	1.40
B5	A21	36c + 34c org brn (V)	4.75	4.75

Wmk. Webbing (109)

B6	A21	10c + 10c vio (Bk)	6.00	6.00
B7	A21	15c + 15c scar (V)	1.40	1.40
B8	A21	20c + 20c ol brn (Bl)	1.90	1.90
B9	A21	25c + 25c bl (Bk)	15.00	15.00
B10	A22	50c + 50c yel grn (V)	4.75	4.75
B11	A22	60c + 60c red (V)	6.00	6.00
B12	A23	1 l + 1 l org & grn (V)	6.00	6.00
B13	A23	3 l + 2 l red & gray (V)	7.75	7.75
B14	A23	5 l + 3 l brn & bl (V)	13.00	13.00

Unwmk.

B15	A21	25c + 25c dp bl (Bk)	3.75	3.75
		Nos. B1-B15 (15)	73.35	73.35

For War Invalids

Semi-Postal Stamps of 1924 Surcharged

Surcharged in Gold or Copper

1926, Dec. 3 **Wmk. 147**

B16	A21	1 + 1c on #B1	42	42
a.		Inverted surcharge	5.50	
B17	A21	2 + 2c on #B2 (C)	55	55
B19	A21	2 + 2c on #B3	55	55
a.		Double surch., one inverted	5.50	
B20	A21	5 + 5c on #B4	1.10	1.10
B21	A21	14 + 14c on #B5	3.50	3.50

Wmk. Webbing (109)

B22	A21	5 + 5c on #B6	10.00	10.00
B23	A21	5 + 5c on #B7	1.10	1.10
B24	A21	10 + 10c on #B8	1.10	1.10
B25	A21	10 + 10c on #B9	55.00	55.00

Unwmk.

B26	A21	10 + 10c on #B15	2.75	2.75

Surcharged in Copper or Silver:

On A22 On A23

Wmk. Webbing (109)

B27	A22	20 + 20c on #B10	2.75	2.75
B28	A22	25 + 25c on #B11	4.25	4.25
B29	A23	30 + 30c on #B12 (S)	5.50	5.50
		Nos. B16-B29 (13)	88.57	88.57

For War Orphans

Surcharged in Gold

1926, Dec. 3 **Wmk. 147**

B30	A21	1 + 1c on #B1	55	55
B31	A21	2 + 2c on #B2	55	55
a.		Inverted surcharge	6.00	
B32	A21	2 + 2c on #B3	55	55
a.		Inverted surcharge		
B33	A21	5 + 5c on #B4	1.10	1.10
B34	A21	19 + 19c on #B5	2.75	2.75

Wmk. Webbing (109)

B35	A21	5 + 5c on #B6	9.50	9.50
B36	A21	10 + 10c on #B7	1.10	1.10
B37	A21	15 + 15c on #B8	1.10	1.10
B38	A21	15 + 15c on #B9	55.00	55.00

Unwmk.

B39	A21	15 + 15c on #B15	2.75	2.75

Surcharged in Gold:

On A22

On A23

Wmk. 109

B40	A22	25c on #B10	3.25	3.25
B41	A22	30c on #B11	5.50	5.50
B42	A23	50c on #B12	5.50	5.50
		Nos. B30-B42 (13)	89.20	89.20

Archery — SP1

Natl. Olympiad, July 15-20: 15c+5c, Javelin throwing. 30c+10c, Diving. 60c+15c, Running.

Unwmk.

1938, July 13 **Photo.** ***Perf. 14***

B43	SP1	5c + 5c grn & dk grn	1.00	1.00
B44	SP1	15c + 5c org & red org	1.75	1.75
B45	SP1	30c + 10c bl & dk bl	3.00	3.00
B46	SP1	60c + 15c tan & brn	6.00	5.00
		Set, never hinged	13.00	

Same Overprinted in Red, Blue or Black:

Nos. B47, B50

Nos. B48-B49

1938, July 13

B47	SP1	5c + 5c (R)	4.75	4.75
B48	SP1	15c + 5c (Bl)	4.75	4.75
B49	SP1	30c + 10c (R)	6.00	6.00
B50	SP1	60c + 15c (Bk)	10.00	10.00
		Set, never hinged	30.00	

National Scout Jamboree, July 12-14.

Basketball Players
SP6 SP7

Flags of Competing Nations and Basketball — SP8

1939 **Photo.** ***Perf. 14***

B52	SP6	15c + 10c copper brn & brn	2.25	2.25
B53	SP7	30c + 15c myrtle grn & grn	3.50	2.25
B54	SP8	60c + 40c blue vio & gray vio	5.50	5.50
		Set, never hinged	13.00	

3rd European Basketball Championships held at Kaunas. The surtax was used for athletic equipment. Nos. B52-B54 exist imperf. Value, pair, $150.

AIR POST STAMPS

Winged Posthorn — AP1

Airplane over Neman River — AP2

Air Squadron — AP3

Plane over Gediminas Castle — AP4

1921 **Litho.** **Wmk. 109** ***Perf. 11½***

C1	AP1	20sk ultra	90	75
C2	AP1	40sk red orange	75	75
C3	AP1	60sk green	75	75
a.		Imperf., pair	22.50	
C4	AP1	80sk lt rose	75	75
a.		Horiz. pair, imperf. vert.	25.00	22.50
C5	AP2	1auk green & red	90	50
a.		Imperf., pair	12.50	12.50
C6	AP3	2auk brown & blue	1.00	75
C7	AP4	5auk slate & yel	1.50	1.25
		Nos. C1-C7 (7)	6.55	5.50
		Set, never hinged	7.50	

For surcharges see Nos. C21-C26, C29.

Lithuania German Occupation stamps can be mounted in Scott's Germany Part II Album.

Allegory of Flight — AP5

1921, Nov. 6

C8	AP5	20sk org & gray bl	70	1.10
C9	AP5	40sk dl bl & lake	70	1.10
C10	AP5	60sk vio bl & ol grn	70	1.10
C11	AP5	80sk ocher & dp grn	70	1.10
a.		Vertical pair, imperf. between	15.00	15.00
C12	AP5	1auk bl grn & bl	70	1.10
C13	AP5	2auk gray & brn org	85	1.10
C14	AP5	5auk dl lil & Prus bl	85	1.10
		Nos. C8-C14 (7)	5.20	7.70
		Set, never hinged	6.50	

Opening of airmail service.

Plane over Kaunas — AP6

Black Overprint

1922, July 16 ***Perf. 11, 11½***

C15	AP6	1auk ol brn & red	85	1.10
a.		Imperf., pair	40.00	
C16	AP6	3auk vio & grn	85	1.10
C17	AP6	5auk dp bl & yel	1.40	1.40
		Set, never hinged	3.75	

It was the intention to issue Nos. C15 to C17, without overprint, in commemoration of the founding of the Air Post service but they were not put in use at that time. Subsequently the word "ZENKLAS" (stamp) was overprinted over "ISTEIGIMAS" (founding) and the date "1921, VI, 25" was obliterated by short vertical lines.

For surcharge see No. C31.

Plane over Gediminas Castle — AP7

1922, July 22

C18	AP7	2auk blue & rose	85	85
C19	AP7	4auk brown & rose	85	85
C20	AP7	10auk black & gray bl	1.40	1.40
		Set, never hinged	3.75	

For surcharges see Nos. C27-C28, C30.

Nos. C1-C7, C17-C20 Surcharged like Regular Issues in Black or Carmine

1922

C21	AP1	10c on 20sk	1.00	1.25
C22	AP1	10c on 40sk	1.00	1.25
C23	AP1	10c on 60sk	75	90
a.		Inverted surcharge	17.50	
C24	AP1	10c on 80sk	1.00	1.25
C25	AP2	20c on 1auk	2.50	3.00
C26	AP3	20c on 2auk	4.00	4.50
a.		Without "CENT"	125.00	125.00
C27	AP7	25c on 2auk	75	50
a.		Inverted surcharge	17.50	17.50
C28	AP7	30c on 4auk (C)	75	65
a.		Double surcharge	20.00	20.00
C29	AP4	50c on 5auk	1.00	75
C30	AP7	50c on 10auk	65	65
a.		Inverted surcharge	20.00	20.00
C31	AP6	1 l on 5auk	7.50	8.75
a.		Double surcharge	27.50	
		Nos. C21-C31 (11)	20.90	23.45
		Set, never hinged	27.50	

Airplane and Carrier Pigeons AP8

"Flight" AP9

1924, Jan. 28 Wmk. 147 *Perf. 11*

C32	AP8	20c yellow	1.00	50
C33	AP8	40c emerald	1.00	50
a.		Horiz. or vert. pair, imperf. between	30.00	
C34	AP8	60c rose	1.25	50
a.		Imperf., pair	55.00	
C35	AP9	1 l dk brown	1.75	50
		Set, never hinged	6.75	

Most copies, if not all, of the "unwatermarked" varieties show faint traces of watermark, according to experts.

For surcharges see Nos. CB1-CB4.

Swallow — AP10

1926, June 17 Wmk. 198 *Perf. 14½*

C37	AP10	20c car rose	85	70
a.		Horiz. or vert. pair, imperf. between	25.00	
C38	AP10	40c vio & red org	85	70
a.		Horiz. or vert. pair, imperf. between	25.00	
C39	AP10	60c bl & blk	1.10	70
a.		Horiz. or vert. pair, imperf. between	25.00	
c.		Center inverted	125.00	125.00
		Set, never hinged	3.50	

Juozas Tubelis — AP11

Vytautas and Airplane over Kaunas — AP12

Vytautas and Antanas Smetona — AP13

1930, Feb. 16 Wmk. 109 *Perf. 14*

C40	AP11	5c blk, bis & brn	42	28
C41	AP11	10c dk bl, db & blk	42	28
C42	AP11	15c mar, gray & bl	42	28
C43	AP12	20c dk brn, org & dl red	42	35
C44	AP12	40c dk bl, lt bl & vio	70	42
C45	AP13	60c bl grn, lil & blk	85	55
C46	AP13	1 l dl red, lil & blk	1.15	70
		Nos. C40-C46 (7)	4.33	2.86
		Set, never hinged	5.50	

5th cent. of the death of the Grand Duke Vytautas.

Map of Lithuania, Klaipeda and Vilnius — AP14

Designs: 15c, 20c, Airplane over Neman. 40c, 60c, City Hall, Kaunas. 1 l, 2 l, Church of Vytautas, Kaunas.

Wmk. Multiple Letters (238)

1932, July 21 *Perf. 14, Imperf.*

C47	AP14	5c ver & ol grn	25	38
C48	AP14	10c dk red brn & ocher	25	38
C49	AP14	15c dk bl & org yel	25	38
C50	AP14	20c sl blk & org	38	50
C51	AP14	60c ultra & ocher	1.50	1.65
C52	AP14	2 l dk bl & yel	2.25	2.50

Wmk. 198

C53	AP14	40c vio brn & yel	1.10	1.40
C54	AP14	1 l vio brn & grn	1.75	2.00
		Nos. C47-C54 (8)	7.73	9.19
		Set, never hinged	9.50	

Issued for the benefit of Lithuanian orphans.

Mindaugas in the Battle of Shauyai, 1236 — AP15

Designs: 15c, 20c, Coronation of Mindaugas (1253). 40c, Grand Duke Gediminas and his followers. 60c, Founding of Vilnius by Gediminas (1332). 1 l, Gediminas capturing the Russian Fortifications. 2 l, Grand Duke Algirdas before Moscow (1368).

Perf. 14, Imperf.

1932, Nov. 28 Wmk. 209

C55	AP15	5c grn & red lil	45	60
C56	AP15	10c emer & rose	45	60
C57	AP15	15c rose vio & bis brn	45	60
C58	AP15	20c rose red & blk brn	45	40
C59	AP15	40c choc & dk gray	75	90
C60	AP15	60c org & gray blk	1.25	1.50
C61	AP15	1 l rose vio & grn	1.50	1.75
C62	AP15	2 l dp bl & brn	2.25	2.75
		Nos. C55-C62 (8)	7.55	9.10
		Set, never hinged	8.50	

Anniv. of independence.

Nos. C58-C62 exist with overprint "DARIUS-GIRENAS / NEW YORK-1933- KAUNAS" below small plane. The overprint was applied in New York with the approval of the Lithuanian consul general. Lithuanian postal authorities seem not to have been involved in the creation or release of these overprints.

Trakai Castle, Home of the Grand Duke Kestutis — AP16

Designs: 15c, 20c, Meeting of Kestutis and the Hermit Birute. 40c, 60c, Hermit Birute. 1 l, 2 l, Kestutis and his Brother Algirdas.

1933, May 6 *Perf. 14, Imperf.*

C63	AP16	5c ol gray & dp bl	25	38
C64	AP16	10c gray vio & org brn	25	38
C65	AP16	15c dp bl & lil	25	38
C66	AP16	20c org brn & lil	50	55
C67	AP16	40c lt ultra & lil	75	1.10
C68	AP16	60c brn & lt ultra	1.40	1.65
C69	AP16	1 l ol gray & dp bl	1.65	2.00
C70	AP16	2 l vio gray & yel grn	2.25	2.75
		Nos. C63-C70 (8)	7.30	9.19
		Set, never hinged	9.50	

Reopening of air service to Berlin-Kaunas-Moscow, and 550th anniv. of the death of Kestutis.

Joseph Maironis — AP17

Joseph Tumas-Vaizgantas — AP17a

Designs: 40c, 60c, Vincas Kudirka. 1 l, 2 l, Julia A. Zemaite.

1933, Sept. 15 *Perf. 14, Imperf.*

C71	AP17	5c crim & dp bl	42	55
C72	AP17	10c bl vio & grn	42	55
C73	AP17a	15c dk grn & choc	42	55
C74	AP17a	20c brn car & ultra	55	60
C75	AP17	40c red brn & ol grn	85	1.10
C76	AP17	60c dk bl & choc	1.10	1.40
C77	AP17	1 l cit & ind	1.25	1.50
C78	AP17	2 l dp grn & red brn	1.90	2.25
		Nos. C71-C78 (8)	6.91	8.50
		Set, never hinged	8.50	

Issued for the benefit of Lithuanian orphans.

Capts. Steponas Darius and Stas. Girenas AP18

Ill-Fated Plane "Lituanica" AP19

The Dark Angel of Death — AP20

"Lituanica" over Globe — AP21

"Lituanica" and White Knight — AP22

Perf. 11½

1934, May 18 Unwmk. Engr.

C79	AP18	20c scar & blk	15	15
C80	AP19	40c dp rose & bl	15	15
C81	AP18	60c dk vio & blk	15	15
C82	AP20	1 l blk & rose	28	15
C83	AP21	3 l gray grn & org	70	45
C84	AP22	5 l dk brn & bl	1.40	1.10
		Nos. C79-C84 (6)	2.83	
		Set value		1.75
		Set, never hinged	3.25	

Death of Capts. Steponas Darius and Stas. Girenas on their New York-Kaunas flight of 1933.

No. C80 exists with diagonal overprint: "F. VAITKUS / nugalejo Atlanta / 21-22-IX-1935." Value $275.

Felix Waitkus and Map of Transatlantic Flight — AP23

Wmk. 238

1936, Mar. 24 Litho. *Perf. 14*

C85	AP23	15c brown lake	65	55
C86	AP23	30c dark green	85	55
C87	AP23	60c blue	1.50	90
		Set, never hinged	3.50	

Transatlantic Flight of the Lituanica II, Sept. 21-22, 1935.

Lithuania Russian Occupation stamps can be mounted in Scott's Soviet Republics Part I Album.

AIR POST SEMI-POSTAL STAMPS

Nos. C32-C35 Surcharged like Nos. B1-B9 (No. CB1), Nos. B10-B11 (Nos. CB2-CB3), and Nos. B12-B14 (No. CB4) in Red, Violet or Black

1924 Wmk. 147 *Perf. 11*

CB1	AP8	20c + 20c yel (R)	5.00	6.75
CB2	AP8	40c + 40c emer (V)	5.00	6.75
CB3	AP8	60c + 60c rose (V)	5.00	6.75
CB4	AP9	1 l + 1 l dk brn	5.00	6.75
		Set, never hinged	27.50	

Surtax for the Red Cross. See note following No. C35.

SOUTH LITHUANIA

GRODNO DISTRICT

Russian Stamps of 1909-12 Surcharged in Black or Red

Lietuva
Літва.
50
skatikų
грашэй.

1919 Unwmk. *Perf. 14, 14½x15*

L1	A14	50sk on 3k red	42.50	24.00
a.		Double surcharge		
L2	A14	50sk on 5k claret	24.00	24.00
a.		Imperf., pair	200.00	200.00
L3	A15	50sk on 10k dk bl (R)	24.00	24.00
L4	A11	50sk on 15k red brn & bl	24.00	24.00
a.		Imperf., pair	225.00	225.00
L5	A11	50sk on 25k grn & gray vio (R)	24.00	24.00
L6	A11	50sk on 35k red brn & grn	24.00	24.00
L7	A8	50sk on 50k vio & grn	24.00	24.00
L8	A11	50sk on 70k brn & org	24.00	24.00
		Nos. L1-L8 (8)	210.50	192.00

Excellent counterfeits are plentiful.

This surcharge exists on Russia No. 119, the imperf. 1k orange of 1917. Value, unused $90, used $60.

OCCUPATION STAMPS

ISSUED UNDER GERMAN OCCUPATION

German Stamps Overprinted in Black

Postgebiet
Ob. Ost

On Stamps of 1905-17

1916-17 Wmk. 125 *Perf. 14, 14½*

1N1	A22	2½pf gray	15	15
1N2	A16	3pf brown	15	15
1N3	A16	5pf green	20	15
1N4	A22	7½pf orange	15	15
1N5	A16	10pf carmine	18	18
1N6	A22	15pf yel brn	3.50	3.00
1N7	A22	15pf dk vio ('17)	20	18
1N8	A16	20pf ultra	52	52
1N9	A16	25pf org & blk, *yel*	20	35
1N10	A16	40pf lake & blk	75	1.00
1N11	A16	50pf vio & blk, *buff*	75	65
1N12	A17	1m car rose	10.50	3.75
		Nos. 1N1-1N12 (12)	17.25	10.23
		Set, never hinged	27.50	

These stamps were used in the former Russian provinces of Suvalki, Vilnius, Kaunas, Kurland.

ISSUED UNDER RUSSIAN OCCUPATION

Lithuanian Stamps of 1937-40 Overprinted in Red or Blue

LTSR
1940 VII 21

1940 Wmk. 238 *Perf. 14*

2N9	A44	2c orange (Bl)	25	38
2N10	A50	50c brown (Bl)	50	50

Unwmk.

2N11	A56	5c brn car (Bl)	25	38
2N12	A57	10c grn (R)	1.75	1.75
2N13	A58	15c dl org (Bl)	25	38
2N14	A59	25c lt brn (R)	25	38

2N15 A60 30c Prus grn (R) 50 50
2N16 A61 35c red org (Bl) 75 1.00
Nos. 2N9-2N16 (8) 4.50 5.27
Set, never hinged 5.00

Values for used stamps are for CTOs. Postally used examples are considerably more.

The Lithuanian Soviet Socialist Republic was proclaimed July 21, 1940.

LOURENCO MARQUES

LOCATION — In the southern part of Mozambique in Southeast Africa
GOVT. — Part of Portuguese East Africa Colony
AREA — 28,800 sq. mi. (approx.)
POP. — 474,000 (approx.)
CAPITAL — Loureno Marques

Stamps of Mozambique replaced those of Loureno Marques in 1920. See Mozambique.

1000 Reis = 1 Milreis
100 Centavos = 1 Escudo (1913)

King Carlos — A1

Perf. 11½, 12½, 13½

1895 **Typo.** **Unwmk.**
1 A1 5r yellow 42 20
2 A1 10r redsh vio 42 35
3 A1 15r chocolate 60 48
4 A1 20r lavender 60 48
5 A1 25r bl grn 60 24
a. Perf. 11½ 2.50 70
6 A1 50r light blue 75 60
a. Perf. 13½ 7.25 3.75
b. Perf. 11½
7 A1 75r rose 1.40 1.25
8 A1 80r yel grn 4.50 2.75
9 A1 100r brn, *yel* 2.00 95
a. Perf. 12½ 3.75 2.50
10 A1 150r car, *rose* 3.00 2.50
11 A1 200r dk bl, *bl* 3.75 2.10
12 A1 300r dk bl, *sal* 3.75 2.10
Nos. 1-12 (12) 21.79 14.00

For surcharges and overprints see Nos. 29, 58-69, 132-137, 140-143, 156-157, 160.

Saint Anthony of Padua Issue

Regular Issues of Mozambique, 1886 and 1894, Overprinted in Black

L. MARQUES
CENTENARIO
DE
S. ANTONIO
MDCCCXCV

1895 **Without Gum** ***Perf. 12½***

On 1886 Issue

13 A2 5r black 11.00 8.00
14 A2 10r green 17.00 8.00
15 A2 20r rose 20.00 8.75
16 A2 25r lilac 21.00 14.00
17 A2 40r chocolate 19.00 11.00
18 A2 50r bl, perf. 13½ 16.00 8.75
a. Perf. 12½ 37.50 22.50
19 A2 100r yellow brn 40.00 22.50
20 A2 200r gray vio 27.50 19.00
21 A2 300r orange 37.50 30.00

On 1894 Issue

Perf. 11½

22 A3 5r yellow 16.00 7.50
23 A3 10r redsh vio 22.50 11.00
24 A3 50r light blue 27.50 14.00
a. Perf. 12½ 40.00 30.00
25 A3 75r rose, perf. 12½ 35.00 22.50
26 A3 80r yellow grn 47.50 25.00
27 A3 100r brown, *buff* 225.00 57.50
28 A3 150r car, *rose*, perf. 12½ 30.00 18.00
Nos. 13-28 (16) 612.50 285.50

No. 12 Surcharged in Black

50
réis

1897, Jan. 2
29 A1 50r on 300r 140.00 50.00

Most copies of No. 29 were issued without gum.

King Carlos — A2

1898-1903 ***Perf. 11½***

Name, Value in Black except 500r

30 A2 2½r gray 20 20
31 A2 5r orange 20 20
32 A2 10r lt green 20 20
33 A2 15r brown 1.00 85
34 A2 15r gray grn ('03) 40 35
a. Imperf.
35 A2 20r gray vio 40 20
a. Imperf.
36 A2 25r sea green 55 28
a. Perf. 13½ 30.00 6.75
b. 25r light green (error) *32.50 32.50*
c. Perf. 12½ *40.00* 50.00
37 A2 25r car ('03) 28 20
a. Imperf.
38 A2 50r blue 95 35
39 A2 50r brown ('03) 80 70
40 A2 65r dull bl ('03) 6.75 5.00
41 A2 75r rose 1.50 1.40
42 A2 75r lilac ('03) 1.10 95
a. Imperf.
43 A2 80r violet 1.50 1.25
44 A2 100r dk bl, *bl* 1.40 55
a. Perf. 13½ 14.00 4.75
45 A2 115r org brn, *pink* ('03) 5.25 5.00
46 A2 130r brn, *straw* ('03) 5.25 5.00
47 A2 150r brn, *straw* 1.75 1.40
48 A2 200r red lil, *pnksh* 2.50 1.25
49 A2 300r dk bl, *rose* 1.75 1.25
50 A2 400r dl bl, *straw* ('03) 7.00 5.00
51 A2 500r blk & red, *bl* ('01) 3.50 2.25
52 A2 700r vio, *yelsh* ('01) 6.75 5.75
Nos. 30-52 (23) 50.98 39.58

For surcharges and overprints see Nos. 57, 71-74, 76-91, 138, 144-155.

Coat of Arms — A3

Surcharged On Upper and Lower Halves of Stamp

1899 ***Imperf.***
53 A3 5r on 10r grn & brn 12.50 6.00
54 A3 25r on 10r grn & brn 12.50 6.00
55 A3 50r on 30r grn & brn 19.00 8.00
a. Inverted surcharge
56 A3 50r on 800r grn & brn 20.00 10.00

The lower half of No. 55 can be distinguished from that of No. 56 by the background of the label containing the word "REIS." The former is plain, while the latter is formed of white intersecting curved horizontal lines over vertical shading of violet brown.

Values are for undivided stamps. Halves sell for ¼ as much.

Most copies of Nos. 53-56 were issued without gum.

No. 41 Surcharged in Black

50 Réis

1899 ***Perf. 11½***
57 A2 50r on 75r rose 3.25 2.50

Most copies of No. 57 were issued without gum.

Surcharged in Black

On Issue of 1895

1902 ***Perf. 11½, 12½***
58 A1 65r on 5r yel 2.25 1.90
59 A1 65r on 15r choc 2.25 1.90
60 A1 65r on 20r lav 2.25 1.90
a. Perf. 12½ 22.50 12.00
61 A1 115r on 10r red vio 2.25 1.90
62 A1 115r on 200r bl, *bl* 2.25 1.90
63 A1 115r on 300r bl, *sal* 2.25 1.90
64 A1 130r on 25r grn, perf. 12½ 1.90 1.50
a. Perf. 11½ 24.00 19.00
65 A1 130r on 80r yel grn 2.00 1.90
66 A1 130r on 150r car, *rose* 2.00 1.90
67 A1 400r on 50r lt bl 6.00 4.00
68 A1 400r on 75r rose 6.00 4.00
69 A1 400r on 100r brn, *buff* 4.00 3.50

On Newspaper Stamp of 1893

70 N1 65r on 2½ brn 2.25 1.90
Nos. 58-70 (13) 37.65 30.10

Surcharge exists inverted on Nos. 61, 70.

Nos. 64, 67 and 68 have been reprinted on thin white paper with shiny white gum and clean-cut perforation 13½. Value $2 each.

For overprints see Nos. 132-137, 140-143, 156-157, 160.

Issue of 1898-1903 Overprinted in Black

PROVISORIO

1903 ***Perf. 11½***
71 A2 15r brown 1.25 85
72 A2 25r sea green 1.00 85
73 A2 50r blue 1.40 85
74 A2 75r rose 2.00 1.40
a. Inverted overprint 20.00 20.00

Surcharged in Black

50
RÉIS

1905
76 A2 50r on 65r dull blue 1.75 1.50

Regular Issues Overprinted in Carmine or Green

1911
77 A2 2½r gray 18 18
78 A2 5r orange 18 18
a. Double overprint 10.00 10.00
b. Inverted overprint 10.00 10.00
79 A2 10r lt grn 28 22
80 A2 15r gray grn 28 24
a. Inverted overprint 10.00 10.00
81 A2 20r dl vio 60 38
82 A2 25r car (G) 22 18
83 A2 50r brown 60 38
84 A2 75r lilac 60 38
85 A2 100r dk bl, *bl* 60 38
86 A2 115r org brn, *pink* 5.50 1.90
87 A2 130r brn, *straw* 60 40
88 A2 200r red lil, *pnksh* 60 40
89 A2 400r dl bl, *straw* 65 60
90 A2 500r blk & red, *bl* 90 75
91 A2 700r vio, *yelsh* 1.25 90
Nos. 77-91 (15) 13.04 7.47

Vasco da Gama Issue of Various Portuguese Colonies Common Design Types Surcharged

REPUBLICA
LOURENCO MARQUES
¼ C.

1913 ***Perf. 12½-16***

On Stamps of Macao

92 CD20 ¼c on ½a bl grn 2.25 2.25
93 CD21 ½c on 1a red 2.25 2.25
94 CD22 1c on 2a red vio 2.25 2.25
95 CD23 2½c on 4a yel grn 2.25 2.25
96 CD24 5c on 8a dk bl 2.25 2.25
97 CD25 7½c on 12a vio brn 4.25 4.25
98 CD26 10c on 16a bis brn 3.50 3.50
a. Inverted surcharge
99 CD27 15c on 24a bister 3.75 3.75
Nos. 92-99 (8) 22.75 22.75

On Stamps of Portuguese Africa

100 CD20 ¼c on 2½r bl grn 1.40 1.40
101 CD21 ½c on 5r red 1.40 1.40
102 CD22 1c on 10r red vio 1.40 1.40
103 CD23 2½c on 25r yel grn 1.40 1.40
104 CD24 5c on 50r dk bl 1.40 1.40
105 CD25 7½c on 75r vio brn 3.50 3.50
106 CD26 10c on 100r bis brn 2.50 2.50
107 CD27 15c on 150r bis 2.50 2.50
Nos. 100-107 (8) 15.50 15.50

On Stamps of Timor

108 CD20 ¼c on ½a bl grn 1.75 1.75
109 CD21 ½c on 1a red 1.75 1.75
110 CD22 1c on 2a red vio 1.75 1.75
111 CD23 2½c on 4a yel grn 1.75 1.75
112 CD24 5c on 8a dk bl 1.75 1.75
113 CD25 7½c on 12a vio brn 3.50 3.50
114 CD26 10c on 16a bis brn 2.75 2.75
115 CD27 15c on 24a bister 2.75 2.75
Nos. 108-115 (8) 17.75 17.75
Nos. 92-115 (24) 56.00 56.00

Ceres — A4

1914 **Typo.** ***Perf. 15x14***

Name and Value in Black

116 A4 ¼c olive brn 15 15
117 A4 ½c black 15 15
a. Value omitted
118 A4 1c blue grn 15 15
119 A4 1½c lilac brn 15 15
a. Imperf.
120 A4 2c carmine 15 15
121 A4 2½c lt vio 15 15
122 A4 5c dp blue 15 15
123 A4 7½c yellow brn 15 15
124 A4 8c slate 15 15
125 A4 10c orange brn 1.50 70
126 A4 15c plum 40 35
127 A4 20c yellow grn 1.75 50
128 A4 30c brown, *green* 1.90 1.00
129 A4 40c brown, *pink* 4.50 4.00
130 A4 50c orange, *sal* 2.25 2.25
131 A4 1e green, *blue* 2.50 1.75
Nos. 116-131 (16) 16.15 11.90

Values of Nos. 116-124 are for stamps on ordinary paper. Those on chalky paper sell for 8 to 12 times as much. Nos. 127-131 issued only on chalky paper.

For surcharges see Nos. 139, 159, 161-162, B1-B12.

In 1921 Nos. 117 and 119 were surcharged 10c and 30c respectively, for use in Mozambique as Nos. 230 and 231. These same values, surcharged 5c and 10c respectively, with the addition of the word "PORTEADO," were used in Mozambique as postage dues, Nos. J44 and J45.

Provisional Issue of 1902 Overprinted Locally in Carmine

REPUBLICA

1914 ***Perf. 11½, 12½***
132 A1 115r on 10r red vio 70 45
a. "Republica" inverted
133 A1 115r on 200r bl, *bl* 70 45
134 A1 115r on 300r bl, *sal* 70 45
a. Double overprint 27.50 27.50
135 A1 130r on 25r grn 1.10 70
a. Perf. 12½ 3.25 1.65
136 A1 130r on 80r yel grn 70 35
137 A1 130r on 150r car, *rose* 70 35
Nos. 132-137 (6) 4.60 2.75

No. 135a was issued without gum.

Nos. 78 and 117 Perforated Diagonally and Surcharged in Carmine

¼

¼

1915 *Perf. 11½*

138 A2	¼c on half of 5r org, pair	4.00	4.00
a.	Pair without dividing perfs.	12.00	12.00

Perf. 15x14

139 A4	¼c on half of ½c blk, pair	6.00	6.00

The added perforation on Nos. 138-139 runs from lower left to upper right corners, dividing the stamp in two. Values are for pairs, both halves of the stamp.

Provisional Issue of 1902 Overprinted in Carmine

1915 *Perf. 11½, 12½*

140 A1	115r on 10r red vio	55	40
141 A1	115r on 200r bl, *bl*	55	40
142 A1	115r on 300r bl, *sal*	55	40
143 A1	130r on 150r car, *rose*	55	40

Nos. 34 and 80 Surcharged

Dois

centavos

1915

On Issue of 1903

144 A2	2c on 15r gray grn	75	70

On Issue of 1911

145 A2	2c on 15r gray grn	75	70
a.	New value inverted	22.50	

Regular Issues of 1898-1903 Overprinted Locally in Carmine

1916

146 A2	15r gray grn	1.00	60
147 A2	50r brown	2.00	1.65
a.	Inverted overprint		
148 A2	75r lilac	2.25	1.40
149 A2	100r blue, *bl*	1.25	85
150 A2	115r org brn, *pink*	1.25	85
151 A2	130r brown, *straw*	8.00	5.00
152 A2	200r red lil, *pnksh*	2.00	1.50
153 A2	400r dull bl, *straw*	4.00	2.50
154 A2	500r blk & red, *bl*	3.00	2.00
155 A2	700r vio, *yelsh*	6.00	3.00
	Nos. 146-155 (10)	30.75	19.35

Same Overprint on Nos. 67-68

1917

156 A1	400r on 50r lt bl	1.25	65
a.	Perf. 13½	11.50	9.00
157 A1	400r on 75r rose	2.50	1.00

No. 69 exists with this overprint. It was not officially issued.

Type of 1914 Surcharged in Red

Quatro

centavos

1920 *Perf. 15x14*

159 A4	4c on 2½c violet	1.00	28

Stamps of 1914 Surcharged in Green or Black

Um quarto de centavo
a

1 Centavo
b

1921

160 A1(a)	¼c on 115r on 10r red vio (G)	80	80
161 A4(b)	1c on 2½c vio (Bk)	52	40
a.	Inverted surcharge	25.00	
162 A4(b)	1½c on 2½c vio (Bk)	80	60

Nos. 159-162 were postally valid throughout Mozambique.

SEMI-POSTAL STAMPS

Regular Issue of 1914 Overprinted or Surcharged:

= + 9-3-18
a

= $20 + 9-3-18
b

= 1$ + 9-3-18
c

1918 *Perf. 15x14½*

B1	A4(a)	¼c ol brn	2.00	2.00
B2	A4(a)	½c black	2.00	2.00
B3	A4(a)	1c bl grn	2.00	2.00
B4	A4(a)	2½c violet	4.00	4.00
B5	A4(a)	5c blue	4.00	4.00
B6	A4(a)	10c org brn	5.00	5.00
B7	A4(b)	20c on 1½c lil brn	5.00	5.00
B8	A4(a)	30c brn, *grn*	5.00	5.00
B9	A4(b)	40c on 2c car	5.00	5.00
B10	A4(b)	50c on 7½c bis	8.00	8.00
B11	A4(b)	70c on 8c slate	10.00	10.00
B12	A4(c)	$1 on 15c mag	10.00	10.00
		Nos. B1-B12 (12)	62.00	62.00

Nos. B1-B12 were used in place of ordinary postage stamps on Mar. 9, 1918.

NEWSPAPER STAMPS

Numeral of Value — N1

Perf. 11½

1893, July 28 **Typo.** **Unwmk.**

P1 N1	2½r brown	25	65
a.	Perf. 12½	20.00	17.50

For surcharge see No. 70.

Saint Anthony of Padua Issue

Mozambique No. P6 Overprinted

L. MARQUES
—
CENTENARIO
DE
S. ANTONIO
—
MDCCCXCV

1895, July 1 *Perf. 11½, 13½*

P2 N3	2½r brown	20.00	17.50
a.	Inverted overprint	30.00	30.00

LUXEMBOURG

LOCATION — Western Europe between southern Belgium, Germany and France
GOVT. — Grand Duchy
AREA — 998 sq. mi.
POP. — 365,800 (est. 1984)
CAPITAL — Luxembourg

12½ Centimes = 1 Silbergroschen 100 Centimes = 1 Franc

Catalogue values for unused stamps in this country are for Never Hinged items, beginning with Scott 357 in the regular postage section, Scott B216 in the semi-postal section.

Values of early Luxembourg stamps vary according to condition. Quotations for Nos. 1-12 are for fine copies. Very fine to superb specimens sell at much higher prices, and inferior or poor copies sell at reduced prices, depending on the condition of the individual specimen.

Watermarks

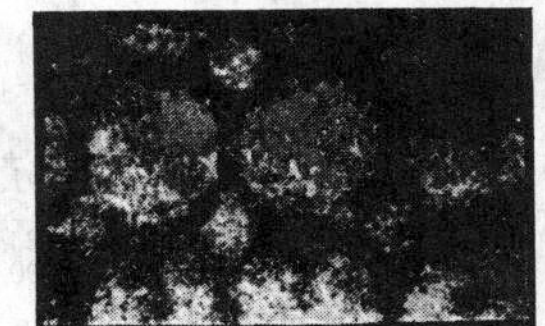

Wmk. 110- Octagons

Wmk. 149- W

Wmk. 213 - Double Wavy Lines

Wmk. 216- Multiple Airplanes

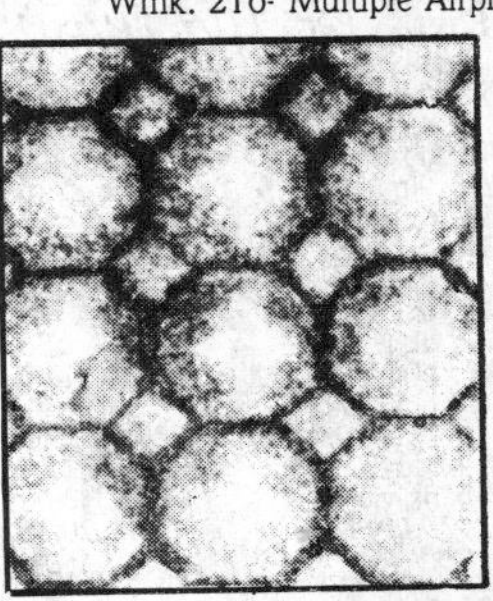

Wmk. 246- Multiple Cross Enclosed in Octagons

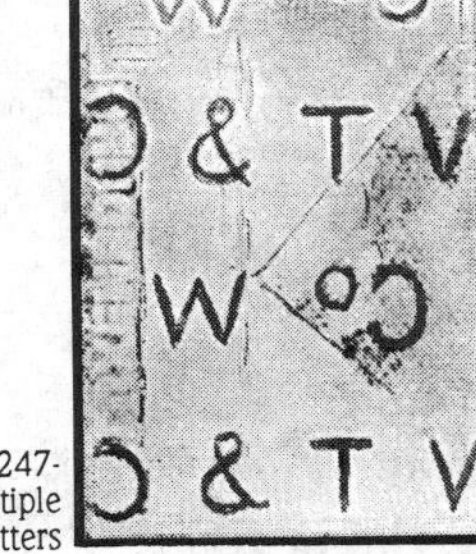

Wmk. 247- Multiple Letters

Grand Duke William III — A1

Luxembourg Print
Wmk. 149

1852, Sept. 15 **Engr.** *Imperf.*

1	A1	10c gray black	*925.00*	18.00
a.		10c black	*1,400.*	25.00
2	A1	1sg brick red	625.00	25.00
a.		1sg brown red	625.00	45.00
b.		1sg orange red	625.00	45.00
c.		1sg copper red	625.00	30.00
3	A1	1sg rose	575.00	60.00

Reprints of both values exist on watermarked paper. Some of the reprints show traces of lines cancelling the plates, but others can be distinguished only by an expert.

Coat of Arms
A2 A3

No. 26

Un Franc.

No. 39

Frankfort Print

1859-63 **Typo.** **Unwmk.**

4	A2	1c buff ('63)	75.00	*125.00*
5	A2	2c blk ('60)	60.00	*180.00*
6	A2	4c yel ('60)	100.00	75.00
a.		4c orange	125.00	100.00
7	A3	10c blue	125.00	7.00
8	A3	12½c rose	150.00	70.00
9	A3	25c brown	175.00	100.00
10	A3	30c rose lilac	190.00	85.00
11	A3	37½c green	190.00	80.00
12	A3	40c red org	500.00	110.00

Counterfeits of Nos. 1-12 exist.
See Nos. 13-25, 27-38, 40-47. For surcharges and overprints see Nos. 26, 39, O1-O51.

1865-71 *Rouletted*

13	A2	1c red brown	95.00	100.00
14	A2	2c black ('67)	12.00	8.50
15	A2	4c yellow ('67)	500.00	125.00
16	A2	4c green ('71)	25.00	15.00

1865-74 *Rouletted in Color*

17	A2	1c red brn ('72)	12.50	4.00
18	A2	1c org ('69)	18.00	3.50
a.		1c brown orange ('67)	75.00	22.50
19	A3	10c lilac	75.00	1.00
a.		10c rose lilac	75.00	1.00
b.		10c gray lilac	77.50	1.00
20	A3	12½c carmine	200.00	4.50
a.		12½c rose	250.00	6.00
21	A3	20c gray brn ('72)	80.00	2.50
a.		20c yellow brown ('69)	90.00	4.00
22	A3	25c bl ('72)	650.00	9.00
22A	A3	25c ultra ('65)	600.00	12.50
23	A3	30c lil rose	650.00	40.00
24	A3	37½c bis ('66)	600.00	150.00
25	A3	40c pale org ('74)	30.00	55.00
a.		40c orange red ('66)	800.00	40.00
26	A4	1fr on 37½c bis ('73)	750.00	45.00
a.		Surcharge inverted		*3,250.*

Luxembourg Print

1874 **Typo.** *Imperf.*

27	A2	4c green	75.00	75.00

1875-79 *Perf. 13*

Narrow Margins

29	A2	1c red brn ('78)	30.00	3.00
30	A2	2c black	125.00	15.00
31	A2	4c green	1.50	*5.00*
32	A2	5c yel ('76)	150.00	10.00
a.		5c orange yellow	600.00	100.00
b.		Imperf.	450.00	400.00
33	A3	10c gray lilac	400.00	1.00
b.		10c lilac	1,300.	15.00
c.		Imperf.	1,300.	*2,200.*
34	A3	12½c lil rose ('76)	500.00	15.00
35	A3	12½c car rose ('77)	300.00	12.50
36	A3	25c bl ('77)	700.00	10.00
37	A3	30c dl rose ('78)	650.00	400.00
38	A3	40c org ('79)	1.00	*8.00*

39	A5	1fr on 37½c bis ('79)	8.00	*15.00*
a.		"Pranc"	*5,000.*	*6,250.*
b.		Without surcharge	400.00	
c.		As "b," imperf.	400.00	

In the Luxembourg print the perforation is close to the border of the stamp. Excellent forgeries of No. 39a are plentiful, as well as faked cancellations on Nos. 31, 38 and 39.

Nos. 32b and 33c are said to be essays; Nos. 39b and 39c printer's waste.

Haarlem Print

Perf. 11½x12, 12½x12, 13½

1880-81

Wide Margins

40	A2	1c yel brn ('81)	8.00	5.00
41	A2	2c black	7.50	1.00
42	A2	5c yel ('81)	175.00	75.00
43	A3	10c gray lil	150.00	65
44	A3	12½c rose ('81)	175.00	160.00
45	A3	20c gray brn ('81)	40.00	11.00
46	A3	25c blue	200.00	3.50
47	A3	30c dl rose ('81)	3.00	13.00

Stamps on gray yellowish paper were not regularly issued.

Gray Yellowish Paper

Perf. 12½

42a	A2	5c	5.00
43a	A3	10c	1.50
44a	A3	12½c	7.50
46a	A3	25c	3.00

"Industry" and "Commerce" A6

Grand Duke Adolphe A7

Perf. 11½x12, 12½x12, 12½, 13½

1882, Dec. 1 **Typo.**

48	A6	1c gray lilac	20	25
49	A6	2c olive gray	20	20
a.		2c olive brown	25	40
50	A6	4c olive bis	40	60
51	A6	5c lt green	60	20
52	A6	10c rose	4.75	20
53	A6	12½c slate	3.00	6.00
54	A6	20c orange	4.50	1.40
55	A6	25c ultra	165.00	1.00
56	A6	30c gray grn	25.00	13.00
57	A6	50c bister brn	1.10	2.00
58	A6	1fr pale vio	1.10	6.00
59	A6	5fr brown org	30.00	70.00

For overprints see Nos. O52-O64.

Perf. 11, 11½, 11½x11 and 12½

1891-93 **Engr.**

60	A7	10c carmine	15	20
a.		Sheet of 25	60.00	
61	A7	12½c sl grn ('93)	28	30
62	A7	20c org ('93)	5.00	40
a.		20c brown (error)	*90.00*	165.00
63	A7	25c blue	38	25
a.		Sheet of 25	*725.00*	
64	A7	30c ol grn ('93)	90	80
65	A7	37½c green ('93)	1.90	2.00
66	A7	50c brown ('93)	3.75	2.00
67	A7	1fr dp vio ('93)	7.75	3.75
68	A7	2½fr black ('93)	75	*6.00*
69	A7	5fr lake ('93)	32.50	45.00

No. 62a was never on sale at any post office, but exists postally used.

Perf. 11½ stamps are from the sheets of 25.

For overprints see Nos. O65-O74.

Grand Duke Adolphe — A8

1895, May 4 **Typo.** ***Perf. 12½***

70	A8	1c pearl gray	3.00	20
71	A8	2c gray brown	25	18
72	A8	4c olive bister	25	45
73	A8	5c green	3.00	18
74	A8	10c carmine	13.00	18
		Nos. 70-74 (5)	19.50	1.19

For overprints see Nos. O75-O79.

Coat of Arms — A9

Grand Duke William IV — A10

1906-26 **Typo.** ***Perf. 12½***

75	A9	1c gray ('07)	15	15
76	A9	2c ol brn ('07)	15	15
77	A9	4c bister ('07)	15	15
78	A9	5c green ('07)	15	15
79	A9	5c lilac ('26)	15	15
80	A9	6c vio ('07)	15	32
81	A9	7½c org ('19)	15	65

Engr.

Perf. 11, 11½x11

82	A10	10c scarlet	1.40	15
a.		Souvenir sheet of 10	375.00	*725.00*
83	A10	12½c sl grn ('07)	1.65	15
84	A10	15c org brn ('07)	1.65	50
85	A10	20c org ('07)	2.00	40
86	A10	25c ultra ('07)	42.50	20
87	A10	30c ol grn ('08)	90	40
88	A10	37½c grn ('07)	90	40
a.		Perf. 12½	25.00	4.50
89	A10	50c brn ('07)	2.75	60
90	A10	87½c dk bl ('08)	1.65	5.75
91	A10	1fr vio ('08)	3.25	1.25
92	A10	2½fr ver ('08)	60.00	65.00
93	A10	5fr claret ('08)	8.00	24.00
		Nos. 75-93 (19)	127.70	100.52

No. 82a for accession of Grand Duke William IV to the throne.

For surcharges and overprints see Nos. 94-96, 112-117, O80-O98.

Nos. 90, 92-93 Surcharged in Red or Black **62½ cts.**

1912-15

94	A10	62½c on 87½c (R)	1.10	2.00
95	A10	62½c on 2½fr (Bk) ('15)	1.10	2.50
96	A10	62½c on 5fr (Bk) ('15)	38	1.50

Grand Duchess Marie Adelaide A11

Grand Duchess Charlotte A12

1914-17 **Engr.** ***Perf. 11½, 11½x11***

97	A11	10c lake	15	15
98	A11	12½c dull grn	15	15
99	A11	15c sepia	15	20
100	A11	17½c dp brn ('17)	15	25
101	A11	25c ultra	15	15
102	A11	30c bister	15	25
103	A11	35c dk blue	15	20
104	A11	37½c blk brn	15	20
105	A11	40c orange	15	20
106	A11	50c dk gray	20	33
107	A11	62½c bl grn	32	1.40
108	A11	87½c org ('17)	32	1.65
109	A11	1fr orange brn	2.00	60
110	A11	2½fr red	1.00	1.65
111	A11	5fr dk vio	5.25	13.00
		Nos. 97-111 (15)	10.44	20.38

For surcharges and overprints see Nos. 118-124, B7-B10, O99-O113.

Stamps of 1906-19 Surcharged with New Value and Bars in Black or Red

1916-24

112	A9	2½c on 5c ('18)	15	15
113	A9	3c on 2c ('21)	15	18
114	A9	5c on 1c ('23)	15	18
115	A9	5c on 4c ('23)	15	28
116	A9	5c on 7½c ('24)	15	18
117	A9	6c on 2c (R) ('22)	15	20
118	A11	7½c on 10c ('18)	15	15
119	A11	17½c on 30c	15	38
120	A11	20c on 17½c ('21)	15	20
121	A11	25c on 37½c ('23)	15	18
a.		Double surcharge	75.00	
122	A11	75c on 62½c (R) ('22)	15	20
123	A11	80c on 87½c ('22)	15	20
124	A11	87½c on 1fr	60	1.50
		Nos. 112-124 (13)	2.40	3.98

1921, Jan. 6 **Engr.** ***Perf. 11½***

125	A12	15c rose	15	15
a.		Sheet of 5, perf 11	125.00	125.00
b.		Sheet of 25, perf. 11½, 11x11½, 12x11½	4.50	14.00

Birth of Prince Jean, first son of Grand Duchess Charlotte, Jan. 5 (No. 125a). No. 125 was printed in sheets of 100.

See Nos. 131-150. For surcharges and overprints see Nos. 154-158, O114-O131, O136.

Vianden Castle — A13

Foundries at Esch — A14

Adolphe Bridge — A15

1921-34 ***Perf. 11, 11x11½, 11½***

126	A13	1fr carmine	15	30
127	A13	1fr dk bl ('26)	18	28

Perf. 11½x11; 11½ (#129)

128	A14	2fr indigo	15	50
129	A14	2fr dk brn ('26)	1.25	90
130	A15	5fr dk vio	7.50	4.50
a.		Perf. 12½ ('34)	16.00	9.50
		Nos. 126-130 (5)	9.23	6.48

For overprints see Nos. O132-O135, O137-138, O140.

Charlotte Type of 1921

1921-26 ***Perf. 11½***

131	A12	2c brown	15	15
132	A12	3c olive grn	15	15
a.		Sheet of 25	8.50	17.50
133	A12	6c violet	15	15
a.		Sheet of 25	8.50	17.50
134	A12	10c yel grn	18	15
135	A12	10c ol brn ('24)	15	15
136	A12	15c brown ol	18	15
137	A12	15c pale grn ('24)	15	15
138	A12	15c dp org ('26)	15	15
139	A12	20c dp orange	18	15
a.		Sheet of 25	50.00	80.00
140	A12	20c yel grn ('26)	15	15
141	A12	25c dk green	18	15
142	A12	30c car rose	18	15
143	A12	40c brown org	20	15
144	A12	50c dp blue	38	23
145	A12	50c red ('24)	25	35
146	A12	75c red	25	38
a.		Sheet of 25	350.00	
147	A12	75c dp bl ('24)	20	15
148	A12	80c black	38	30
a.		Sheet of 25	350.00	
		Nos. 131-148 (18)	3.61	3.36

For surcharges and overprints see Nos. 154-158, O114-O131, O136.

Philatelic Exhibition Issue

1922, Aug. 27 ***Imperf.***

Laid Paper

149	A12	25c dk green	1.65	2.75
150	A12	30c car rose	1.65	2.75

Nos. 149 and 150 were sold exclusively at the Luxembourg Phil. Exhib., Aug. 1922.

Souvenir Sheet

View of Luxembourg A16

1923, Jan. 3 ***Perf. 11***

151	A16	10fr dp grn, sheet	750.00	*2,200.*

Birth of Princess Elisabeth.

1923, Mar. ***Perf. 11½***

152	A16	10fr black	5.00	*14.00*
a.		Perf. 12½ ('34)	4.00	*8.50*

For overprint see No. O141.

The Wolfsschlucht near Echternach — A17

1923-34 ***Perf. 11½***

153	A17	3fr dk blue & blue	1.00	1.00
a.		Perf. 12½ ('34)	80	60

For overprint see No. O139.

Stamps of 1921-26 Surcharged with New Values and Bars

1925-28

154	A12	5c on 10c yel grn	20	20
155	A12	15c on 20c yel grn ('28)	15	20
a.		Bars omitted		
156	A12	35c on 40c brn org ('27)	15	20
157	A12	60c on 75c dp bl ('27)	15	20
158	A12	60c on 80c blk ('28)	35	32
		Nos. 154-158 (5)	1.00	1.12

Grand Duchess Charlotte — A18

1926-35 **Engr.** ***Perf. 12***

159	A18	5c dk violet	15	15
160	A18	10c olive grn	15	15
161	A18	15c blk ('30)	15	25
162	A18	20c orange	15	18
163	A18	25c yellow grn	15	18
164	A18	25c vio brn ('27)	15	20
165	A18	30c yel grn ('27)	20	38
166	A18	30c gray vio ('30)	16	30
167	A18	35c gray vio ('28)	1.00	22
168	A18	35c yel grn ('30)	15	15
169	A18	40c olive gray	15	18
170	A18	50c red brown	15	15
171	A18	60c bl grn ('28)	1.00	15
172	A18	65c black brn	15	50
173	A18	70c bl vio ('35)	15	15
174	A18	75c rose	15	25
175	A18	75c bis brn ('27)	15	15
176	A18	80c bister brn	18	50
177	A18	90c rose ('27)	45	75
178	A18	1fr black	35	50
179	A18	1fr rose ('30)	16	40
180	A18	1¼fr dk blue	15	35
181	A18	1¼fr yel ('30)	4.75	1.00
182	A18	1¼fr bl grn ('31)	28	18
183	A18	1¼fr rose car ('34)	20.00	1.40
184	A18	1½fr dp bl ('27)	80	1.00
185	A18	1¾fr dk bl ('30)	32	38
		Nos. 159-185 (27)	31.75	10.15

For surcharges and overprints see Nos. 186-193, O142-O178.

Stamps of 1926-35, Surcharged with New Values and Bars

1928-39

186	A18	10(c) on 30c yel grn ('29)	20	20
187	A18	15c on 25c yel grn	30	32
187A	A18	30c on 60c bl grn ('39)	15	32
188	A18	60c on 65c blk brn	30	32
189	A18	60c on 75c rose	30	28
190	A18	60c on 80c bis brn	35	40
191	A18	70(c) on 75c bis brn ('35)	8.00	20
192	A18	75(c) on 90c rose ('29)	1.00	20
193	A18	1¾(fr) on 1½fr dp bl ('29)	2.00	1.40
		Nos. 186-193 (9)	12.60	3.64

The surcharge on No. 187A has no bars.

View of Clervaux A19

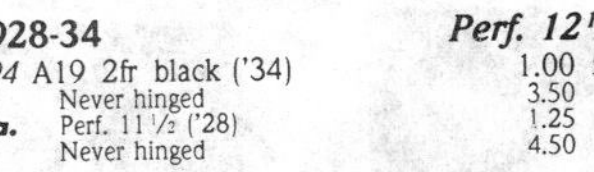

1928-34 *Perf. 12½*
194 A19 2fr black ('34) 1.00 50
Never hinged 3.50
a. Perf. 11½ ('28) 1.25 50
Never hinged 4.50

See No. B66. For overprint see No. O179.

Coat of Arms — A20

1930, Dec. 20 Typo. *Perf. 12½*
195 A20 5c claret 32 25
196 A20 10c olive green 55 15
Set value 32
Set, never hinged 2.75

View of the Lower City of Luxembourg
A21

Gate of "Three Towers"
A22

1931, June 20 **Engr.**
197 A21 20fr deep green 3.00 7.25
Never hinged 4.75

For overprint see No. O180.

1934, Aug. 30 *Perf. 14x13½*
198 A22 5fr blue green 1.25 2.75
Never hinged 2.75

For overprint see No. O181.

Castle From Our Valley
A23

1935, Nov. 15 *Perf. 12½x12*
199 A23 10fr green 2.00 4.75
Never hinged 4.00

For overprint see No. O182.

Municipal Palace — A24

1936, Aug. 26 Photo. *Perf. 11½*
Granite Paper
200 A24 10c brown 15 20
201 A24 35c green 15 40
202 A24 70c red orange 18 *60*
203 A24 1fr car rose 1.00 *4.00*
204 A24 1.25fr violet 1.75 *7.25*
205 A24 1.75fr brt ultra 1.00 *4.00*
Nos. 200-205 (6) 4.23 *16.45*
Set, never hinged 13.00

11th Cong. of Intl. Federation of Philately.

Arms of Luxembourg
A25

William I
A26

Designs: 70c, William II. 75c, William III. 1fr, Prince Henry. 1.25fr, Grand Duke Adolphe. 1.75fr, William IV. 3fr, Regent Marie Anne. 5fr, Grand Duchess Marie Adelaide. 10fr, Grand Duchess Charlotte.

1939, May 27 Engr. *Perf. 12½x12*
206 A25 35c brt green 25 20
207 A26 50c orange 25 25
208 A26 70c slate green 15 15
209 A26 75c sepia 55 *1.00*
210 A26 1fr red 1.40 *2.75*
211 A26 1.25fr brown vio 15 20
212 A26 1.75fr dark blue 15 20
213 A26 3fr lt brown 25 40
214 A26 5fr gray blk 40 *80*
215 A26 10fr copper red 65 *2.25*
Nos. 206-215 (10) 4.20 *8.20*
Set, never hinged 7.00

Centenary of Independence.

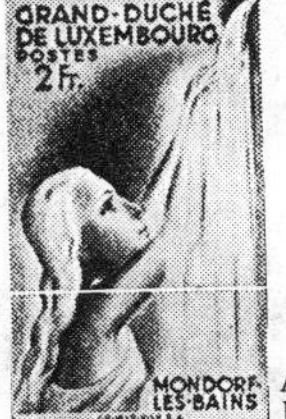

Allegory of Medicinal Baths — A35

1939, Sept. 18 Photo. *Perf. 11½*
216 A35 2fr brown rose 40 1.10
Never hinged 80

Elevation of Mondorf-les-Bains to town status.

Souvenir Sheet

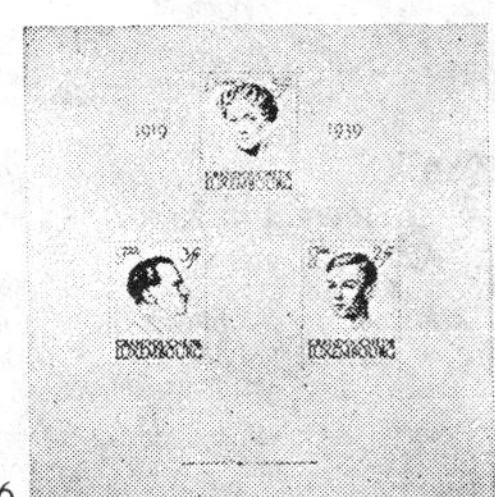

A36

1939, Dec. 20 Engr. *Perf. 14x13*
217 A36 Sheet of 3 27.50 *65.00*
Sheet, never hinged 40.00
a. 2fr vermilion, *buff* 7.50 *12.50*
b. 3fr dark green, *buff* 7.50 *12.50*
c. 5fr blue, *buff* 7.50 *12.50*

20th anniv. of the reign of Grand Duchess Charlotte (Jan. 15, 1919) and her marriage to Prince Felix (Nov. 6, 1919).
See Nos. B98-B103.

Grand Duchess Charlotte
A37

Lion from Duchy Arms
A38

1944-46 Unwmk. *Perf. 12*
218 A37 5c brown red 15 15
219 A37 10c black 15 15
219A A37 20c org ('46) 15 15
220 A37 25c sepia 15 15
220A A37 30c car ('46) 15 15
221 A37 35c green 15 15
221A A37 40c dk bl ('46) 15 15
222 A37 50c dk violet 15 15
222A A37 60c org ('46) 1.00 15
223 A37 70c rose pink 15 15
223A A37 70c dp green ('46) 30 55
223B A37 75c sepia ('46) 18 18
224 A37 1fr olive 15 15
225 A37 1¼fr red orange 15 15
226 A37 1½fr red org ('46) 15 15
227 A37 1¾fr blue 15 25
228 A37 2fr rose car ('46) 1.50 25
229 A37 2½fr dp vio ('46) 2.25 *4.00*
230 A37 3fr dp yel grn ('46) 30 45
231 A37 3½fr brt bl ('46) 38 *70*
232 A37 5fr dk bl grn 15 18
233 A37 10fr carmine 18 55
234 A37 20fr dp blue 30 *4.50*
Nos. 218-234 (23) 8.49 *13.56*
Set, never hinged 14.00

1945 Engr. *Perf. 14x13*
235 A38 20c black 15 15
236 A38 30c brt green 15 15
237 A38 60c dp violet 15 15
238 A38 75c brn red 15 15
239 A38 1.20fr red 15 15
240 A38 1.50fr rose lilac 15 15
241 A38 2.50fr lt blue 15 15
Set value 62 85
Set, never hinged 1.00

Patton's Grave, US Military Cemetery, Hamm
A39

Gen. Patton, Broken Chain and Advancing Tanks — A40

1947, Oct. 24 Photo. *Perf. 11½*
242 A39 1.50fr dk car 15 *20*
243 A40 3.50fr dull blue 65 *3.00*
244 A39 5fr dk slate grn 65 *2.00*
245 A40 10fr chocolate 3.00 *12.00*
Set, never hinged 7.50

George S. Patton, Jr. (1885-1945), American general.

Oesling Mountain Forts
A41

Luxembourg
A44

Moselle River — A42

Steel Mills — A43

Perf. 11½x11, 11x11½
1948, Aug. 5 Engr. Unwmk.
246 A41 7fr dk brown 5.00 60
247 A42 10fr dk green 38 20
248 A43 15fr carmine 38 60
249 A44 20fr dk blue 50 20
Set, never hinged 13.00

Grand Duchess Charlotte — A45

1948-49 *Perf. 11½*
250 A45 15c ol brn ('49) 15 15
251 A45 25c slate 15 15
252 A45 60c brown ('49) 25 15
253 A45 80c green ('49) 25 15
254 A45 1fr red lilac 65 15
255 A45 1.50fr grnsh bl 65 15
256 A45 1.60fr slate gray ('49) 65 80
257 A45 2fr dk vio brn 65 15
258 A45 4fr vio blue 1.25 28
259 A45 6fr brt red vio ('49) 2.00 28
260 A45 8fr dull grn ('49) 2.00 60
Nos. 250-260 (11) 8.65
Set value 2.50
Set, never hinged 16.00

See Nos. 265-271, 292, 337-340, B151.

Self-Inking Canceller
A46

1949, Oct. 6 **Photo.**
261 A46 80c blk, Prus grn & pale grn 20 55
262 A46 2.50fr dk brn, brn red & sal rose 1.00 2.75
263 A46 4fr blk, bl & pale bl 2.75 7.25
264 A46 8fr dk brn, brn & buff 8.75 25.00
Set, never hinged 25.00

UPU, 75th anniv.

Charlotte Type of 1948-49
1951, Mar. 15 Engr. Unwmk.
265 A45 5c red org 15 15
266 A45 10c ultra 15 15
267 A45 40c crimson 15 20
268 A45 1.25fr dk brown 65 28
269 A45 2.50fr red 65 15
270 A45 3fr blue 2.50 28
271 A45 3.50fr rose lake 1.75 40
Nos. 265-271 (7) 6.00 1.61
Set, never hinged 17.50

Agriculture and Industry
A47

Globe and Scales — A48

Design: 1fr, 3fr, People of Europe and Charter of Freedom.

1951, Oct. 25 Photo. *Perf. 11½*
272 A47 80c dp green 6.00 5.00
273 A47 1fr purple 3.00 42
274 A48 2fr black brn 15.00 42
275 A47 2.50fr dk car 19.00 13.00
276 A47 3fr orange brn 35.00 21.00
277 A48 4fr blue 42.50 30.00
Nos. 272-277 (6) 120.50 69.84
Set, never hinged 190.00

Issued to promote a united Europe.

Luxembourg stamps can be mounted in Scott's annually supplemented Luxembourg Album.

Grand Duke William III — A49

Perf. 13½x13

1952, May 24 Engr. Unwmk.

Dates, Ornaments in Olive Green

278 A49 2fr black 25.00 *50.00*
Never hinged 30.00
279 A49 4fr red brown 25.00 *50.00*
Never hinged 30.00

Printed in sheets containing two panes of eight stamps each, alternating the two denominations. Centenary of Luxembourg's postage stamps. Price per set, 26fr, which included admission to the CENTILUX exhibition.
See Nos. C16-C20.

Hurdle Race — A50

Designs: 2fr, Football. 2.50fr, Boxing. 3fr, Water polo. 4fr, Bicycle racing. 8fr, Fencing.

1952, Aug. 20 Photo. Perf. 11½

Designs in Black

280 A50 1fr pale green 20 30
281 A50 2fr brown buff 60 30
282 A50 2.50fr salmon pink 1.40 1.00
283 A50 3fr buff 1.70 1.65
284 A50 4fr lt blue 8.50 8.25
285 A50 8fr lilac 5.00 5.50
Nos. 280-285 (6) 17.40 17.00
Set, never hinged 35.00

15th Olympic Games, Helsinki; World Bicycling Championships of 1952.

Wedding of Princess Josephine-Charlotte of Belgium and Hereditary Grand Duke Jean — A51

1953, Apr. 1

286 A51 80c dull vio 22 20
287 A51 1.20fr lt brown 22 20
288 A51 2fr green 50 20
289 A51 3fr red lilac 80 60
290 A51 4fr brt blue 3.00 1.10
291 A51 9fr brown red 3.00 1.10
Nos. 286-291 (6) 7.74 3.40
Set, never hinged 12.00

Charlotte Type of 1948-49

1953, May 18 Engr.

292 A45 1.20fr gray 45 28
Never hinged 1.00

Radio Luxembourg A52

Victor Hugo's Home, Vianden A53

1953, May 18 Perf. 11½x11

293 A52 3fr purple 2.50 1.40
294 A53 4fr Prus blue 1.65 1.40
Set, never hinged 8.00

150th birth anniv. of Victor Hugo (No. 294).

St. Willibrord Basilica Restored — A54

Pierre d'Aspelt — A55

Design: 2.50fr, Interior view.

1953, Sept. 18 Perf. 13x13½

295 A54 2fr red 1.50 40
296 A54 2.50fr dk gray grn 2.50 6.50
Set, never hinged 8.00

Consecration of St. Willibrord Basilica at Echternach.

1953, Sept.

297 A55 4fr black 4.75 5.00
Never hinged 7.00

Pierre d'Aspelt (1250-1320), chancellor of the Holy Roman Empire and Archbishop of Mainz.

Fencing Swords, Mask and Glove — A56

Winged "L" Over Map — A57

1954, May 6 Perf. 13½x13

298 A56 2fr red brn & blk brn, *gray* 4.50 50
Never hinged 6.50

World Fencing Championship Matches, Luxembourg, June 10-22.

1954, May 6 Photo. Perf. 11½

299 A57 4fr dp bl, yel & red 6.00 3.50
Never hinged 13.00

6th Intl. Fair, Luxembourg, July 10-25.

Tulips — A58

Artisan, Wheel and Tools — A59

Flowers: 2fr, Daffodils. 3fr, Hyacinths. 4fr, Parrot tulips.

1955, Apr. 1

300 A58 80c dk brn, rose red & bl grn 15 15
301 A58 2fr cer, yel & grn 15 15
302 A58 3fr bl grn & lil rose 1.40 3.00
303 A58 4fr multicolored 1.65 3.50
Set, never hinged 6.25

Flower festival at Mondorf-les-Bains.
See Nos. 351-353.

1955, Sept. 1 Engr. Perf. 13

304 A59 2fr dk gray & blk brn 60 32
Never hinged 1.00

Natl. Handicraft Exposition at Luxembourg - Limpertsburg, Sept. 3-12.

Dudelange Television Station A60

1955, Sept. 1 Unwmk.

305 A60 2.50fr dk brn & redsh brn 60 32
Never hinged 1.00

Installation of the Tele-Luxembourg station at Dudelange.

United Nations Emblem and Children Playing A61

UN, 10th anniv.: 80c, "Charter". 4fr, "Justice" (Sword and Scales). 9fr, "Assistance" (Workers).

1955, Oct. 24 Perf. 11x11½

306 A61 80c blk & dk bl 22 42
307 A61 2fr red & brn 1.75 15
308 A61 4fr dk blue & red 1.40 3.75
309 A61 9fr dk brn & sl grn 55 1.40
Set, never hinged 7.75

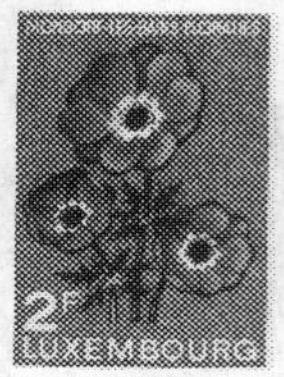

A62

A63

Designs: 2fr, Anemones. 2.50fr, 4fr, Roses. 3fr, Crocuses.

1956 Photo. Perf. 11½

Flowers in Natural Colors

310 A62 2fr gray vio 25 18
311 A62 2.50fr brt blue 2.25 4.50
312 A62 3fr red brown 95 1.50
313 A62 4fr purple 1.10 1.50
Set, never hinged 8.50

Flower Festival at Mondorfles-Bains (Nos. 310, 312). Nos. 311 and 313 are inscribed: "Luxembourg-Ville des Roses."
Issue dates: Nos. 310, 312, Apr. 27; Nos. 311, 313, May 30.

1956, May 30

Steel beam and city emblem.

314 A63 2fr brt grnsh bl, red & blk 75 40
Never hinged 1.65

50th anniversary of Esch-sur-Alzette.

Bessemer Converter and Blast Furnaces A64

Steel Beam and Model of City of Luxembourg A65

"Rebuilding Europe" A66

Design: 4fr, 6-link chain, miner's lamp.

Perf. 11x11½, 11½x11

1956, Aug. 10 Engr.

315 A64 2fr dull red 9.50 2.25
316 A65 3fr dk blue 9.50 19.00
317 A64 4fr green 1.90 3.25
Set, never hinged 37.50

4th anniv. of the establishment in Luxembourg of the headquarters of the European Coal and Steel Community.

1956, Sept. 15 Perf. 13

318 A66 2fr brown & blk 75.00 28
319 A66 3fr brick red & car 24.00 37.50
320 A66 4fr brt bl & dp bl 2.75 4.00
Set, never hinged 225.00

Cooperation among the six countries comprising the Coal and Steel Community.

Central Station from Train Window A67

1956, Sept. 29 Perf. 13x12½

321 A67 2fr black & sepia 75 45
Never hinged 2.00

Electrification of Luxembourg railways.

Ignace de la Fontaine — A68

Design: 7fr, Grand Duchess Charlotte.

1956, Nov. 7 Perf. 11½

322 A68 2fr gray brown 1.00 30
323 A68 7fr dull purple 2.00 65
Set, never hinged 4.75

Centenary of the Council of State.

Lord Baden-Powell and Luxembourg Scout Emblems — A69

Designs: 2.50fr, Lord Baden-Powell and Luxembourg Girl Scout emblems.

1957, June 17 Perf. 11½x11

324 A69 2fr ol grn & red brn 52 28
325 A69 2.50fr dk vio & claret 2.50 *4.25*
Set, never hinged 4.00

Birth centenary of Robert Baden-Powell and the 50th anniversary of the founding of the Scout movement.

Prince Henry — A70

Children's Clinic — A71

Design: 4fr, Princess Marie-Astrid.

1957, June 17 Photo. *Perf. 11½*

326	A70	2fr	brown	45	16
327	A71	3fr	bluish grn	1.75	*3.50*
328	A70	4fr	ultra	2.00	*3.75*
			Set, never hinged	5.75	

Children's Clinic of the Prince Jean-Princess Josephine-Charlotte Foundation.

"United Europe" — A72

Fair Building and Flags — A73

1957, Sept. 16 Engr. *Perf. 12½x12*

329	A72	2fr	reddish brn	60	32
330	A72	3fr	red	9.75	*18.00*
331	A72	4fr	rose lilac	9.75	11.00
			Set, never hinged	40.00	

A united Europe for peace and prosperity.

1958, Apr. 16 *Perf. 12x11½*

332	A73	2fr	ultra & multi	15	18
			Never hinged	25	

10th International Luxembourg Fair.

Luxembourg Pavilion, Brussels — A74

1958, Apr. 16 Unwmk.

333	A74	2.50fr	car & ultra	15	25
			Never hinged	20	

International Exposition at Brussels.

St. Willibrord — A75

Designs: 1fr, Sts. Willibrord and Irmina from "Liber Aureus." 5fr, St. Willibrord, young man and wine cask.

1958, May 23 Engr. *Perf. 13x13½*

334	A75	1fr	red	15	32
335	A75	2.50fr	olive brn	18	28
336	A75	5fr	blue	48	*1.00*
			Set, never hinged	1.50	

1300th birth anniv. of St. Willibrord, apostle of the Low Countries and founder of Echternach Abbey.

Charlotte Type of 1948-49

1958 Unwmk. *Perf. 11½*

337	A45	20c	dull claret	15	15
338	A45	30c	olive	15	15
339	A45	50c	dp org	18	15
340	A45	5fr	violet	4.75	55
			Set value		78
			Set, never hinged	9.00	

Europa Issue, 1958

Common Design Type

1958, Sept. 13 Litho. *Perf. 12½x13*

Size: 21x34mm

341	CD1	2.50fr	car & bl	15	15
342	CD1	3.50fr	green & org	15	22
343	CD1	5fr	blue & red	35	55
			Set, never hinged	95	

Wiltz Open-Air Theater A76

Vintage, Moselle A77

1958, Sept. 13 Engr. *Perf. 11x11½*

344	A76	2.50fr	slate & sepia	20	15
345	A77	2.50fr	lt grn & sep	20	15
			Set value		24
			Set, never hinged	75	

No. 345 issued to publicize 2,000 years of grape growing in Luxembourg region.

Grand Duchess Charlotte A78

NATO Emblem A79

1959, Jan. 15 Photo. *Perf. 11½*

346	A78	1.50fr	pale grn & dk grn	15	25
347	A78	2.50fr	pink & dk brn	15	15
348	A78	5fr	lt bl & dk bl	24	90
			Set, never hinged	1.00	

40th anniv. of the accession to the throne of the Grand Duchess Charlotte.

1959, Apr. 3 *Perf. 12½x12*

349	A79	2.50fr	brt ol & bl	15	15
350	A79	8.50fr	red brn & bl	24	45
			Set, never hinged	55	

NATO, 10th anniversary.

Flower Type of 1955, Inscribed "1959"

Flowers: 1fr, Iris. 2.50fr, Peonies. 3fr, Hydrangea.

1959, Apr. 3 *Perf. 11½*

Flowers in Natural Colors

351	A58	1fr	dk bl grn	18	40
352	A58	2.50fr	deep blue	24	50
353	A58	3fr	dp red lil	24	50
			Set, never hinged	1.00	

Flower festival, Mondorf-les-Bains.

Europa Issue, 1959

Common Design Type

Perf. 12½x13½

1959, Sept. 19 Litho.

Size: 22x33mm

354	CD2	2.50fr	olive	16	40
355	CD2	5fr	dk blue	35	80
			Set, never hinged	1.00	

Locomotive of 1859 and Hymn — A80

1959, Sept. 19 Engr. *Perf. 13½*

356	A80	2.50fr	red & ultra	42	18
			Never hinged	1.25	

Centenary of Luxembourg's railroads.

Catalogue values for unused stamps in this section, from this point to the end of the section, are for Never Hinged items.

Man and Child Knocking at Door — A81

Holy Family, Flight into Egypt — A82

Perf. 11½x11, 11x11½

1960, Apr. 7 Unwmk.

357	A81	2.50fr	org & slate	15	15
358	A82	5fr	pur & slate	30	30

World Refugee Year, July 1, 1959-June 30, 1960.

Steel Worker Drawing CECA Initials and Map of Member Countries A83

1960, May 9 *Perf. 11x11½*

359	A83	2.50fr	dk car rose	60	20

10th anniv. of the Schumann Plan for a European Steel and Coal Community.

European School and Children A84

1960, May 9

360	A84	5fr	bl & gray blk	90	90

Establishment of the first European school in Luxembourg.

Heraldic Lion and Tools — A85

1960, June 14 Photo. *Perf. 11½*

361	A85	2.50fr	gray, red, bl & blk	1.40	32

Natl. Exhibition of Craftsmanship, Luxembourg-Limpertsberg, July 9-18.

Grand Duchess Charlotte — A86

1960-64 Engr. Unwmk.

362	A86	10c	claret ('61)	15	15
363	A86	20c	rose red ('61)	20	15
363A	A86	25c	org ('64)	15	15
364	A86	30c	gray olive	20	15
365	A86	50c	dull grn	60	15
366	A86	1fr	vio blue	75	15
367	A86	1.50fr	rose lilac	75	20
368	A86	2fr	blue ('61)	80	15
369	A86	2.50fr	rose vio	1.40	20
370	A86	3fr	vio brn ('61)	1.60	15
371	A86	3.50fr	aqua ('64)	2.25	1.90
372	A86	5fr	lt red brn	2.25	25
373	A86	6fr	slate ('64)	2.75	20
			Nos. 362-373 (13)	13.85	3.95

The 50c, 1fr and 3fr were issued in sheets and in coils. Every fifth coil stamp has control number on back.

Europa Issue, 1960

Common Design Type

1960, Sept. 19 *Perf. 11x11½*

Size: 37x27mm

374	CD3	2.50fr	indigo & emer	25	20
375	CD3	5fr	maroon & blk	40	35

Great Spotted Woodpecker A87

Clervaux and Abbey of St. Maurice and St. Maur A88

Designs: 1.50fr, Cat, horiz. 3fr, Filly, horiz. 8.50fr, Dachshund.

1961, May 15 Photo. *Perf. 11½*

376	A87	1fr	multicolored	15	15
377	A87	1.50fr	multicolored	15	15
378	A87	3fr	gray, buff & red brn	40	40
379	A87	8.50fr	lt grn, blk & ocher	80	60

Issued to publicize animal protection.

1961, June 8 Engr. *Perf. 11½x11*

380	A88	2.50fr	green	25	15

General Patton Monument, Ettelbruck A89

1961, June 8 *Perf. 11x11½*

381	A89	2.50fr	dk bl & gray	25	15

The monument commemorates the American victory of the 3rd Army under Gen. George S. Patton, Jr., Battle of the Ardennes Bulge, 1944-45.

Europa Issue, 1961

Common Design Type

1961, Sept. 18 *Perf. 13x12½*

Size: 29½x27mm

382	CD4	2.50fr	red	15	15
383	CD4	5fr	blue	16	16
			Set value	24	24

Cyclist Carrying Bicycle — A90

St. Laurent's Church, Diekirch — A91

Design: 5fr, Emblem of 1962 championship.

1962, Jan. 22 Photo. *Perf. 11½*

384	A90	2.50fr lt ultra, crim & blk	18	17
385	A90	5fr multicolored	42	40

Intl. Cross-country Bicycle Race, Esch-sur-Alzette, Feb. 18.

Europa Issue, 1962

Common Design Type

1962, Sept. 17 Unwmk. *Perf. 11½*

Size: 32½x23mm

386	CD5	2.50fr ol bis, yel grn & brn blk	15	15
387	CD5	5fr rose lil, lt grn & brn blk	30	25

1962, Sept. 17 Engr. *Perf. 11½x11*

388	A91	2.50fr brown & blk	28	18

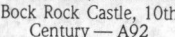

Bock Rock Castle, 10th Century — A92

Gate of Three Towers, 11th Century — A93

Designs (each stamp represents a different century): No. 391, Benedictine Abbey, Munster. No. 392, Great Seal of Luxembourg, 1237. No. 393, Rham Towers. No. 394, Black Virgin, Grund. No. 395, Grand Ducal Palace. No. 396, The Citadel of the Holy Ghost. No. 397, Castle Bridge. No. 398, Town Hall. No. 399, Municipal theater, bridge and European Community Center.

Perf. 14x13 (A92), 11½ (A93)

Engr. (A92), Photo. (A93)

1963, Apr. 13

389	A92	1fr slate blue	42	42
390	A93	1fr multicolored	15	15
391	A92	1.50fr dl red brn	42	42
392	A93	1.50fr multicolored	15	15
393	A92	2.50fr gray grn	42	42
394	A93	2.50fr multicolored	18	18
395	A92	3fr brown	42	42
396	A93	3fr multicolored	15	15
397	A92	5fr brt violet	60	60
398	A93	5fr multicolored	60	60
399	A92	11fr multicolored	90	90
		Nos. 389-399 (11)	4.41	4.41

Millennium of the city of Luxembourg; MELUSINA Intl. Phil. Exhib., Luxembourg, Apr. 13-21. Set sold only at exhibition. Value of 62fr included entrance ticket. Nos. 390, 392, 394 and 396 however were sold without restriction.

Blackboard Showing European School Buildings — A94

1963, Apr. 13 Photo. *Perf. 11½*

400	A94	2.50fr gray, grn & mag	20	20

10th anniv. of the European Schools in Luxembourg, Brussels, Varese, Mol and Karlsruhe.

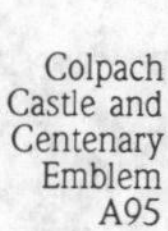

Colpach Castle and Centenary Emblem A95

1963, May 8 Engr. *Perf. 13*

401	A95	2.50fr hn brn, gray & red	20	20

Centenary of the Intl. Red Cross. Colpach Castle, home of Emile Mayrisch, was donated to the Luxembourg League of the Red Cross for a rest home.

Twelve Stars of Council of Europe — A96

Brown Trout Taking Bait — A97

1963, June 25 *Perf. 13x14*

402	A96	2.50fr dp ultra, *gold*	20	20

10th anniv. of the European Convention of Human Rights.

Europa Issue, 1963

Common Design Type

1963, Sept. 16 Photo. *Perf. 11½*

Size: 32½x23mm

403	CD6	3fr bl grn, lt grn & org	25	15
404	CD6	6fr red brn, org red & org	30	30

1963, Sept. 16 Engr. *Perf. 13*

405	A97	3fr indigo	25	15

World Fly-Fishing Championship, Wormeldange, Sept. 22.

Map of Luxembourg, Telephone Dial and Stars — A98

Power House — A99

1963, Sept. 16 Photo. *Perf. 11½*

406	A98	3fr ultra, brt grn & blk	25	15

Completion of telephone automation.

1964, Apr. 17 Engr. *Perf. 13*

Designs: 3fr, Upper reservoir, horiz. 6fr, Lohmuhle dam.

407	A99	2fr red brn & sl	15	15
408	A99	3fr red, sl grn & lt bl	20	15
409	A99	6fr choc, grn & bl	22	22

Inauguration of the Vianden hydroelectric station.

Barge Entering Lock at Grevenmacher Dam — A100

1964, May 26 Unwmk.

410	A100	3fr indigo & brt bl	35	18

Opening of Moselle River canal system.

Europa Issue, 1964

Common Design Type

1964, Sept. 14 Photo. *Perf. 11½*

Size: 22x38mm

411	CD7	3fr org brn, yel & dk bl	20	20
412	CD7	6fr yel grn, yel & dk brn	35	32

The first value column gives the catalogue value of an unused stamp, the second that of a used stamp.

New Atheneum Educational Center and Students — A101

1964, Sept. 14 Unwmk.

413	A101	3fr dk bl grn & blk	20	15

Benelux Issue

King Baudouin, Queen Juliana and Grand Duchess Charlotte — A101a

1964, Oct. 12

Size: 45x26mm

414	A101a	3fr dull bl, yel & brn	22	20

20th anniv. of the customs union of Belgium, Netherlands and Luxembourg.

Grand Duke Jean and Grand Duchess Josephine Charlotte — A102

1964, Nov. 11 Photo. *Perf. 11½*

415	A102	3fr indigo	35	16
416	A102	6fr dk brown	35	28

Grand Duke Jean's accession to throne.

Rotary Emblem and Cogwheels A103

Grand Duke Jean A104

1965, Apr. 5 Photo. *Perf. 11½*

417	A103	3fr gold, car, gray & ultra	40	20

Rotary International, 60th anniversary.

1965-71 Engr. Unwmk.

418	A104	25c ol bis ('66)	15	15
419	A104	50c rose red	24	15
420	A104	1fr ultra	24	15
421	A104	1.50fr dk vio brn ('66)	15	15
422	A104	2fr mag ('66)	18	15
423	A104	2.50fr org ('71)	35	15
424	A104	3fr gray	48	15
425	A104	3.50fr brn org ('66)	35	20
426	A104	4fr vio brn ('71)	30	15
427	A104	5fr green ('71)	35	15
428	A104	6fr purple	95	15
429	A104	8fr bl grn ('71)	80	15
		Nos. 418-429 (12)	4.54	
		Set value		1.05

The 50c, 1fr, 2fr, 3fr and 6fr were issued in sheets and in coils. Every fifth coil stamp has control number on back.

See Nos. 570-576.

ITU Emblem, Old and New Communication Equipment — A105

1965, May 17 Litho. *Perf. 13½*

431	A105	3fr dk pur, cl & blk	22	20

ITU, centenary.

Europa Issue, 1965

Common Design Type

Perf. 13x12½

1965, Sept. 27 Photo. Unwmk.

Size: 30x23½mm

432	CD8	3fr grn, mar & blk	25	18
433	CD8	6fr tan, dk bl & grn	40	40

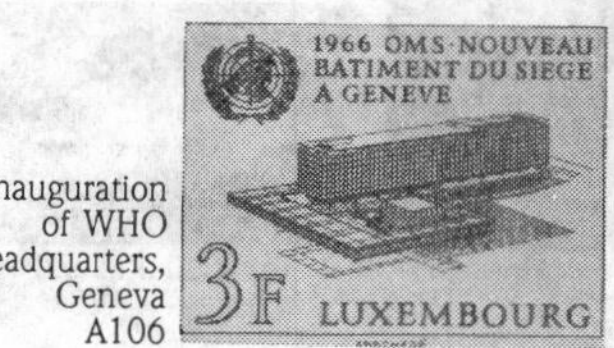

Inauguration of WHO Headquarters, Geneva A106

1966, Mar. 7 Engr. *Perf. 11x11½*

434	A106	3fr green	20	15

Torch and Banner — A107

Key and Arms of City of Luxembourg, and Arms of Prince of Chimay — A108

1966, Mar. 7 Photo. *Perf. 11½*

435	A107	3fr gray & brt red	20	15

50th anniversary of the Workers' Federation in Luxembourg.

1966, Apr. 28 Engr. *Perf. 13x14*

Designs: 2fr, Interior of Cathedral of Luxembourg, painting by Juan Martin. 3fr, Our Lady of Luxembourg, engraving by Richard Collin. 6fr, Column and spandrel with sculptured angels from Cathedral.

436	A108	1.50fr green	15	15
437	A108	2fr dull red	15	15
438	A108	3fr dk blue	15	15
439	A108	6fr red brown	25	25
		Set value	55	55

300th anniv. of the Votum Solemne (Solemn Promise) which made the Virgin Mary Patron Saint of the City of Luxembourg.

Europa Issue, 1966

Common Design Type

Perf. 13½x12½

1966, Sept. 26 Litho.

Size: 25x37mm

440	CD9	3fr gray & vio bl	20	15
441	CD9	6fr olive & dk grn	30	30

Diesel Locomotive A109

Design: 3fr, Electric locomotive.

1966, Sept. 26 Photo. *Perf. 11½*

442 A109 1.50fr multicolored 20 20
443 A109 3fr multicolored 25 20

5th Intl. Philatelic Exhibition of Luxembourg Railroad Men, Sept. 30-Oct. 3.

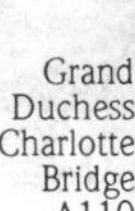

Grand Duchess Charlotte Bridge A110

1966, Sept. 26 Engr. *Perf. 13*

444 A110 3fr dk car rose 20 15

Tower Building, Kirchberg, Seat of European Community — A111

Design: 13fr, Design for Robert Schuman monument, Luxembourg.

1966, Sept. 26

445 A111 1.50fr dk green 16 16
446 A111 13fr dp blue 55 25

"Luxembourg, Center of Europe."

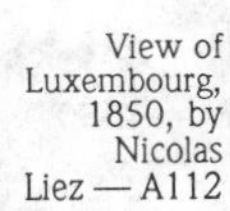

View of Luxembourg, 1850, by Nicolas Liez — A112

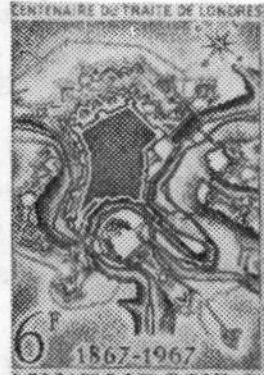

Map of Luxembourg Fortress, 1850, by Theodore de Cederstolpe — A113

1967, Mar. 6 Engr. *Perf. 13*

447 A112 3fr bl, vio brn & grn 20 15
448 A113 6fr bl, brn & red 25 20

Centenary of the Treaty of London, which guaranteed the country's neutrality after the dismantling of the Fortress of Luxembourg.

Europa Issue, 1967
Common Design Type

1967, May 2 Photo. *Perf. 11½*
Size: 33x22mm

449 CD10 3fr cl brn, gray & buff 30 20
450 CD10 6fr dk brn, vio gray & lt bl 35 35

Lion, Globe and Lions Emblem — A115

NATO Emblem and European Community Administration Building — A116

1967, May 2 Photo. *Perf. 11½*

451 A115 3fr multicolored 18 15

Lions International, 50th anniversary.

> Canceled to Order
> Luxembourg's Office des Timbres, Direction des Postes, was offering, at least as early as 1967, to sell commemorative issues canceled to order.

1967, June 13 Litho. *Perf. 13x12½*

452 A116 3fr lt grn & dk grn 25 15
453 A116 6fr dp rose & dk car 40 40

NATO Council meeting, Luxembourg, June 13-14.

Youth Hostel, Ettelbruck A117

Home Gardener A118

1967, Sept. 14 Photo. *Perf. 11½*

454 A117 1.50fr multicolored 20 15

Luxembourg youth hostels.

1967, Sept. 14

455 A118 1.50fr brt grn & org 18 15

16th Congress of the Intl. Assoc. of Home Gardeners.

Shaving Basin with Wedding Scene, 1819 — A119

Design: 3fr, Ornamental vase, 1820.

1967, Sept. 14

456 A119 1.50fr ol grn & multi 15 15
457 A119 3fr ultra & lt gray 25 20

Faience industry in Luxembourg, 200th anniv.

Wormeldingen on Mosel River — A120

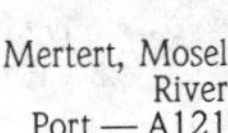

Mertert, Mosel River Port — A121

1967, Sept. 14 Engr. *Perf. 13*

458 A120 3fr dp bl, claret & ol 25 15
459 A121 3fr vio bl & slate 25 15

Swimming — A122

Sport: 1.50fr, Soccer. 2fr, Bicycling. 3fr, Running. 6fr, Walking. 13fr, Fencing.

1968, Feb. 22 Photo. *Perf. 11½*

460 A122 50c bl & grnsh bl 15 15
461 A122 1.50fr brt grn & emer 15 15
462 A122 2fr yel grn & lt yel grn 15 15
463 A122 3fr dp org & dl org 15 15
464 A122 6fr grnsh bl & pale grn 30 20
465 A122 13fr rose cl & rose 50 50
Nos. 460-465 (6) 1.40 1.30

Issued to publicize the 19th Olympic Games, Mexico City, Oct. 12-27.

Europa Issue, 1968
Common Design Type

1968, Apr. 29 Photo. *Perf. 11½*
Size: 32½x23mm

466 CD11 3fr ap grn, blk & org brn 20 15
467 CD11 6fr brn org, blk & ap grn 40 30

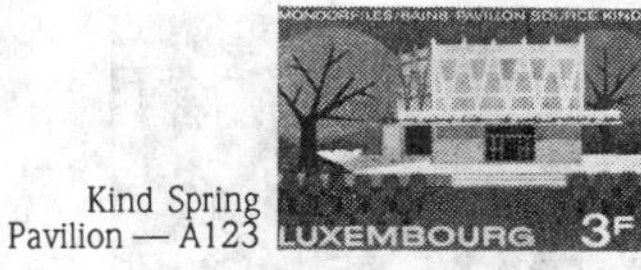

Kind Spring Pavilion — A123

1968, Apr. 29 Photo. *Perf. 11½*

468 A123 3fr multicolored 20 15

Issued to publicize Mondorf-les-Bains.

Fair Emblem A124

1968, Apr. 29

469 A124 3fr dp vio, dl bl gold & red 20 15

20th Intl. Fair, Luxembourg City, May 23-June 2.

Children's Village of Mersch A125

Orphan and Foster Mother — A126

1968, Sept. 18 Engr. *Perf. 13*

470 A125 3fr sl grn & dk red brn 15 15
471 A126 6fr sl bl, blk & brn 28 20

Mersch children's village. (Modeled after Austrian SOS villages for homeless children.)

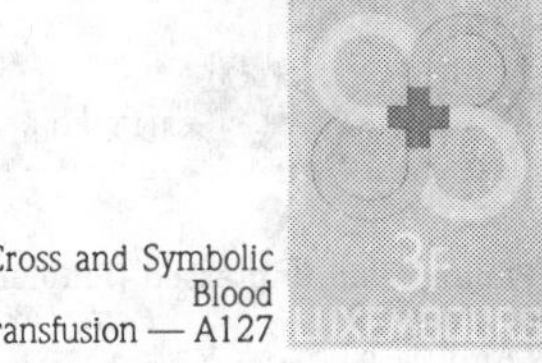

Red Cross and Symbolic Blood Transfusion — A127

1968, Sept. 18 Photo. *Perf. 11½*

472 A127 3fr lt blue & car 20 15

Voluntary Red Cross blood donors.

Luxair Plane over Luxembourg A128

1968, Sept. 18 Engr. *Perf. 13*

473 A128 50fr ol, bl & dk bl 1.65 70

Issued for tourist publicity.

Souvenir Sheet

"Youth and Leisure" — A129

Designs, 3fr, Doll. 6fr, Ballplayers. 13fr, Book, compass rose and ball.

1969, Apr. 3 Photo. *Perf. 11½*
Granite Paper

474 A129 Sheet of 3 3.25 3.25
a. 3fr ultra, black & orange 1.00 1.00
b. 6fr ultra, red & black 1.00 1.00
c. 13fr dull green, red & yel 1.00 1.00

1st Intl. Youth Phil. Exhib., JUVENTUS 1969, Luxembourg, Apr. 3-8.

No. 474 was on sale only at the exhibition. Sold only with entrance ticket for 40fr.

Europa Issue, 1969
Common Design Type

1969, May 19 Photo. *Perf. 11½*
Size: 32½x23mm

475 CD12 3fr gray, brn & org 25 15
476 CD12 6fr vio gray, blk & yel 38 35

Boy on Hobbyhorse, by Joseph Kutter (1894-1941) A130

Design: 6fr, View of Luxembourg, by Kutter.

1969, May 19 Engr. *Perf. 12x13*

477 A130 3fr multicolored 25 15
a. Green omitted *150.00 150.00*
478 A130 6fr multicolored 35 35

ILO, 50th Anniv. — A131

Photo.; Gold Impressed (Emblem)
1969, May 19 *Perf. 14x14½*
479 A131 3fr brt grn, vio & gold 20 15

Mobius Strip in Benelux Colors — A131a

1969, Sept. 8 Litho. *Perf. 12½x13½*
480 A131a 3fr multicolored 28 20

25th anniv. of the signing of the customs union of Belgium, Netherlands and Luxembourg.

NATO, 20th Anniv. — A132

Grain and Mersch Agricultural Center — A133

1969, Sept. 8 *Perf. 13½x12½*
481 A132 3fr org brn & dk brn 32 20

1969, Sept. 8 Photo. *Perf. 11½*
482 A133 3fr bl grn, gray & blk 20 15

Issued to publicize agricultural progress.

St. Willibrord's Basilica and Abbey, Echternach A134

Design: No. 484, Castle and open-air theater, Wiltz.

1969, Sept. 8 Engr. *Perf. 13*
483 A134 3fr dk bl & ind 22 15
484 A134 3fr sl grn & ind 22 15
Set value 24

Pasqueflower — A135

Design: 6fr, Hedgehog and 3 young.

1970, Mar. 9 Photo. *Perf. 11½*
485 A135 3fr multi 24 20
486 A135 6fr grn & multi 45 40

European Conservation Year.

Goldcrest A136

1970, Mar. 9 Engr. *Perf. 13*
487 A136 1.50fr org, grn & blk brn 20 15

Luxembourg Society for the protection and study of birds, 50th anniv.

Traffic Sign and Street Scene — A137

1970, May 4 Photo. *Perf. 11½*
488 A137 3fr rose mag, red & blk 22 15

The importance of traffic safety.

Europa Issue, 1970
Common Design Type
1970, May 4
Size: 32½x23mm
489 CD13 3fr brn & multi 24 15
490 CD13 6fr grn & multi 48 40

Empress Kunigunde and Emperor Henry II, Window, Luxembourg Cathedral — A138

1970, Sept. 14 Photo. *Perf. 12*
491 A138 3fr multi 20 20

Centenary of the Diocese of Luxembourg.

Census Symbol — A139

1970, Sept. 14 *Perf. 11½*
492 A139 3fr dk grn, grnsh bl & red 20 15

Census of Dec. 31, 1970.

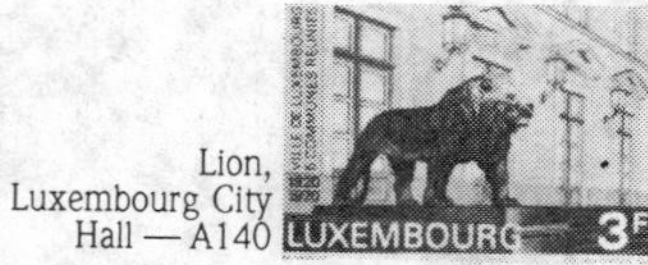

Lion, Luxembourg City Hall — A140

1970, Sept. 14
493 A140 3fr bis, lt bl & dk brn 18 15

50th anniversary of the City of Luxembourg through the union of 5 municipalities.

UN Emblem A141

Perf. 12½x13½
1970, Sept. 14 Litho.
494 A141 1.50fr bl & vio bl 18 15

25th anniversary of the United Nations.

Monks in Abbey Workshop A142

Olympic Rings, Arms of Luxembourg A143

Miniatures Painted at Echternach, about 1040: 3fr, Laborers going to the vineyard (Matthew 20:1-6). 6fr, Laborers toiling in vineyard. 13fr, Workers searching for graves of the saints.

1971, Mar. 15 Photo. *Perf. 12*
495 A142 1.50fr gold & multi 15 15
496 A142 3fr gold & multi 15 15
497 A142 6fr gold & multi 25 20
498 A142 13fr gold & multi 52 45
Set value 82

1971, May 3 Photo. *Perf. 12½*
499 A143 3fr ultra & multi 25 15

Intl. Olympic Committee, 71st session.

Europa Issue, 1971
Common Design Type
1971, May 3 *Perf. 12½x13*
Size: 34x25mm
500 CD14 3fr ver, brn & blk 32 15
501 CD14 6fr brt grn, brn & blk 45 35

A145

1971, May 3 Litho. *Perf. 13x13½*
502 A145 3fr org, dk brn & yel 20 20

Christian Workers Union, 50th anniv.

Artificial Lake, Upper Sure — A146

Designs: No. 504, Water treatment plant, Esch-sur-Sure. 15fr, ARBED Steel Corporation Headquarters, Luxembourg.

1971, Sept. 13 Engr. *Perf. 13*
503 A146 3fr ol, grnsh bl & ind 18 15
504 A146 3fr brn, sl grn & grnsh bl 24 15
505 A146 15fr ind & blk brn 70 40
Set value 60

School Girl with Coin — A147

1971, Sept. 13 Photo. *Perf. 11½*
506 A147 3fr vio & multi 22 15

School children's savings campaign.

Coins of Luxembourg and Belgium A148

Bronze Mask A149

1972, Mar. 6
507 A148 1.50fr lt grn, sil & blk 18 15

Economic Union of Luxembourg and Belgium, 50th anniversary.

1972, Mar. 6

Archaeological Objects, 4th to 1st centuries, B.C.: 1fr, Bronze bowl, horiz. 8fr, Limestone head. 15fr, Glass jug in shape of head.

508 A149 1fr lem & multi 15 15
509 A149 3fr multi 15 15
510 A149 8fr multi 60 60
511 A149 15fr multi 80 80

Europa Issue 1972
Common Design Type
1972, May 2 Photo. *Perf. 11½*
Size: 22x33mm
512 CD15 3fr rose vio & multi 25 15
513 CD15 8fr gray bl & multi 80 80

Archer — A150

1972, May 2
514 A150 3fr crim, blk & ol 38 22

3rd European Archery Championships.

Robert Schuman Medal — A151

The Fox Wearing Tails — A152

1972, May 2 Engr. *Perf. 13*
515 A151 3fr gray & slate grn 50 18

Establishment in Luxembourg of the European Coal and Steel Community, 20th anniv.

1972, Sept. 11 Photo. *Perf. 11½*
516 A152 3fr scar & multi 35 20

Centenary of the publication of "Renert," satirical poem by Michel Rodange.

National Monument A153

Court of Justice of European Communities, Kirchberg A154

1972, Sept. 11 Engr. *Perf. 13*

517 A153 3fr sl grn, ol & vio 22 15
518 A154 3fr brn, bl & sl grn 28 22

Epona on Horseback — A155

Archaeological Objects: 4fr, Panther killing swan, horiz. 8fr, Celtic gold stater inscribed Pottina. 15fr, Bronze boar, horiz.

1973, Mar. 14 Photo. *Perf. 11½*

519 A155 1fr sal & multi 15 15
520 A155 4fr beige & multi 20 15
521 A155 8fr multi 65 65
522 A155 15fr multi 65 65

Europa Issue 1973
Common Design Type

1973, Apr. 30 Photo. *Perf. 11½*
Size: 32x22mm

523 CD16 4fr org, dk vio & lt bl 38 15
524 CD16 8fr ol, vio blk & yel 1.10 75

Bee on Honeycomb A156

Nurse Holding Child A157

1973, Apr. 30 Photo. *Perf. 11½*

525 A156 4fr ocher & multi 35 15

Publicizing importance of beekeeping.

1973, Apr. 30

526 A157 4fr multi 28 20

Publicizing importance of day nurseries.

Laurel Branch — A158

1973, Sept. 10 Photo. *Perf. 11½*

527 A158 3fr vio bl & multi 22 18

50th anniv. of Luxembourg Board of Labor.

Jerome de Busleyden A159

National Strike Memorial, Wiltz A160

1973, Sept. 10 Engr. *Perf. 13*

528 A159 4fr blk, brn & pur 28 20

Council of Mechelen, 500th anniv.

1973, Sept. 10

529 A160 4fr ol bis, sl & sl grn 22 20

In memory of the Luxembourg resistance heroes who died during the great strike of 1942.

Capital, Byzantine Hall, Vianden — A161

St. Gregory the Great — A161a

Designs: No. 534, Sts. Cecilia and Valerian crowned by angel, Hollenfels Church. No. 535, Interior, Septfontaines Church. 8fr, Madonna and Child, St. Irmina's Chapel, Rosport. 12fr, St. Augustine Sculptures by Jean-Georges Scholtus from pulpit in Feulen parish church, c. 1734.

1973-77 *Perf. 13x12½, 14 (6fr, 12fr)*

533 A161 4fr grn & rose vio 22 15
534 A161 4fr red brn, grn & lil 35 20
535 A161 4fr gray, brn & dk vio 35 20
536 A161a 6fr maroon 28 28
537 A161 8fr sep & vio bl 60 60
538 A161a 12fr slate bl 65 65
Nos. 533-538 (6) 2.45 2.08

Architecture of Luxembourg: Romanesque, Gothic, Baroque.
Issue dates: No. 533, 8fr, Sept. 10, 1973; Nos. 534-535, Sept. 9, 1974; 6fr, 12fr, Sept. 16, 1977.

Princess Marie Astrid — A162

Torch — A163

1974, Mar. 14 Photo. *Perf. 11½*

540 A162 4fr bl & multi 65 18

Princess Marie-Astrid, president of the Luxembourg Red Cross Youth Section.

1974, Mar. 14

541 A163 4fr ultra & multi 20 15

50th anniversary of Luxembourg Mutual Insurance Federation.

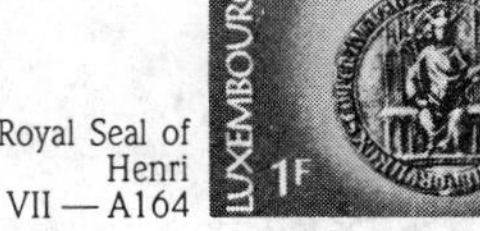

Royal Seal of Henri VII — A164

Seals from 13th-14th Centuries: 3fr, Equestrian, seal of Jean, King of Bohemia. 4fr, Seal of Town of Diekirch. 19fr, Virgin and Child, seal of Convent of Marienthal.

1974, Mar. 14

542 A164 1fr pur & multi 15 15
543 A164 3fr grn & multi 32 25
544 A164 4fr multi 45 15
545 A164 19fr multi 1.50 1.25

Hind, by Auguste Trémont A165

Winston Churchill, by Oscar Nemon A166

Europa: 8fr, "Growth," abstract sculpture, by Lucien Wercollier.

1974, Apr. 29 Photo. *Perf. 11½*

546 A165 4fr ocher & multi 38 24
547 A165 8fr brt bl & multi 1.25 1.00

1974, Apr. 29

548 A166 4fr lilac & multi 28 15

Sir Winston Churchill (1874-1965), statesman.

Fairground, Aerial View — A167

Theis, the Blind — A168

1974, Apr. 29

549 A167 4fr silver & multi 28 15

Publicity for New International Fairground, Luxembourg-Kirchberg.

1974, Apr. 29

550 A168 3fr multi 32 20

Mathias Schou, Theis the Blind (1747-1824), wandering minstrel.

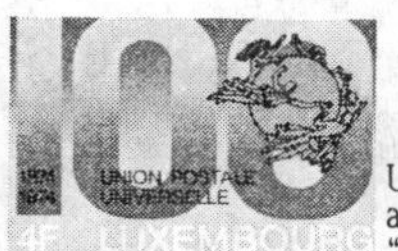

UPU Emblem and "100" — A169

1974, Sept. 9 Photo. *Perf. 11½*

551 A169 4fr multi 32 32
552 A169 8fr multi 80 80

Centenary of Universal Postal Union.

"BENELUX" A170

1974, Sept. 9

553 A170 4fr bl grn, dk grn & lt bl 80 20

30th anniversary of the signing of the customs union of Belgium, Netherlands and Luxembourg.

View of Differdange A171

1974, Sept. 9 Engr. *Perf. 13*

554 A171 4fr rose claret 22 15

Bourglinster A172

Designs: 1fr, Fish Market, Old Luxembourg, vert. 4fr, Market Square, Echternach. 19fr, St. Michael's Square, Mersch, vert.

Perf. 14x13½, 13½x14
1975, Mar. 10 Engr.

555 A172 1fr olive green 75 20
556 A172 3fr deep brown 1.40 40
557 A172 4fr dark purple 1.50 60
558 A172 19fr copper red 1.25 1.00

European Architectural Heritage Year.

Joseph Kutter, Self-portrait A173

Moselle Bridge, Remich, by Nico Klopp A174

Paintings: 8fr, Still Life, by Joseph Kutter. 20fr, The Dam, by Dominique Lang.

1975, Apr. 28 Photo. *Perf. 11½*

559 A173 1fr multi 28 18
560 A174 4fr multi 45 25
561 A174 8fr multi 2.20 75
562 A173 20fr multi 1.65 85

Cultural series. Nos. 560-561 are 1975 Europa Issue.

Robert Schuman, Gaetano Martino, Paul-Henri Spaak Medals — A175

1975, Apr. 28

563 A175 4fr yel grn, gold & brn 1.10 25

25th anniversary of Robert Schuman's declaration establishing European Coal and Steel Community.

Albert Schweitzer (1875-1965), Medical Missionary — A176

1975, Apr. 28 Engr. *Perf. 13*

564 A176 4fr brt bl 90 20

Civil Defense Emblem A177

Figure Skating A178

1975, Sept. 8 Photo. *Perf. 11½*

565 A177 4fr multi 65 25

Civil Defense Org. for protection and rescue.

1975, Sept. 8 Engr. *Perf. 13*

Designs: 4fr, Water skiing, horiz. 15fr, Mountain climbing.

566 A178 3fr grn, bl & lil 25 15
567 A178 4fr dk brn, grn & lt brn 40 30
568 A178 15fr brn, ind & grn 1.25 70

Grand Duke Type of 1965-71

1975-91 Engr. *Perf. 11½*

Granite Paper (14fr, 22fr)

570	A104	7fr orange	35	20
571	A104	9fr yellow green	55	35
572	A104	10fr black	45	15
573	A104	12fr brick red	50	45
573A	A104	14fr dark blue	85	85
574	A104	16fr green	70	60
574A	A104	18fr brown olive	65	58
575	A104	20fr blue	90	40
576	A104	22fr orange brown	1.35	1.35
		Nos. 570-576 (9)	6.30	4.93

Issue dates: 10fr, Jan. 9; 9fr, 12fr, 20fr, Dec. 23; 16fr, Feb. 25, 1982; 7fr, July 1, 1983; 18fr, Mar. 3, 1986; 14fr, Jan. 2, 1990. 22fr, Sept. 23, 1991.

This is an expanding set. Numbers will change if necessary.

Grand Duchess Charlotte — A179

Design: No. 580, Prince Henri.

1976, Mar. 8 Litho. *Perf. 14x13½*

579	A179	6fr grn & multi	38	22
580	A179	6fr dl bl & multi	90	25

80th birthday of Grand Duchess Charlotte and 21st birthday of Prince Henri, heir to the throne.

Gold Brooch — A180

Designs: 5fr, Footless beaker, horiz. 6fr, Decorated vessel, horiz. 12fr, Gold coin. All designs show excavated items of Franco-Merovingian period.

Perf. 13½x12½, 12½x13½

1976, Mar. 8

581	A180	2fr bl & multi	15	15
582	A180	5fr blk & multi	28	28
583	A180	6fr lil & multi	45	28
584	A180	12fr multi	1.00	1.10

Soup Tureen — A181

Europa: 12fr, Deep bowl. Tureen and bowl after pottery from Nospelt, 19th century.

1976, May 3 Photo. *Perf. 11½*

585	A181	6fr lt vio & multi	52	15
586	A181	12fr yel grn & multi	1.50	1.00

15-Cent Minimum Value

The minimum value for a single stamp is 15 cents. This value reflects the costs of the handlling of inexpensive stamps.

Independence Hall, Philadelphia A182

Boomerang A183

1976, May 3

587	A182	6fr lt bl & multi	32	25

American Bicentennial.

1976, May 3

588	A183	6fr brt rose lil & gold	35	20

21st Olympic Games, Montreal, Canada, July 17-Aug. 1.

"Vibrations of Sound" — A184

1976, May 3

589	A184	6fr red & multi	35	20

Jeunesses Musicales (Young Music Friends), association to foster interest in music and art.

Alexander Graham Bell — A185

Virgin and Child with St. Anne — A186

1976, Sept. 9 Engr. *Perf. 13*

590	A185	6fr slate green	35	25

Centenary of first telephone call by Alexander Graham Bell, Mar. 10, 1876.

1976, Sept. 9 Photo. *Perf. 11½*

Renaissance sculptures: 12fr, Grave of Bernard de Velbruck, Lord of Beaufort.

591	A186	6fr gold & multi	35	20
592	A186	12fr gold, gray & blk	70	70

Johann Wolfgang von Goethe A187

Old Luxembourg A188

Portraits: 5fr, J. M. William Turner. 6fr, Victor Hugo. 12fr, Franz Liszt.

1977, Mar. 14 Engr. *Perf. 13*

593	A187	2fr lake	15	15
594	A187	5fr purple	28	24
595	A187	6fr slate green	35	28
596	A187	12fr violet blue	70	65

Famous visitors to Luxembourg.

1977, May 3 Photo. *Perf. 11½*

Europa: 12fr, Adolphe Bridge and European Investment Bank headquarters.

597	A188	6fr multi	45	15
598	A188	12fr multi	1.25	65

Esch-sur-Sure A189

Marguerite de Busbach A190

Design: 6fr, View of Ehnen.

1977, May 3 Engr. *Perf. 13*

599	A189	5fr Prus bl	38	25
600	A189	6fr dp brn	32	25

1977, May 3 Photo. *Perf. 11½*

Design: No. 602, Louis Braille, by Lucienne Filippi.

601	A190	6fr multi	35	20
602	A190	6fr multi	35	20

Notre Dame Congregation, founded by Marguerite de Busbach, 350th anniversary; Louis Braille (1809-1852), inventor of the Braille system of writing for the blind.

Souvenir Sheet

Luxembourg Nos. 1-2 — A191

Engr. & Photo.

1977, Sept. 15 *Perf. 13½*

603	A191	40fr gray & red brn	4.50	4.50

125th anniv. of Luxembourg's stamps.

Head of Medusa, Roman Mosaic, Diekirch, 3rd Century A.D. — A192

1977, Sept. 15 Photo. *Perf. 11½*

604	A192	6fr multi	50	32

Orpheus and Eurydice, by C. W. Gluck A193

1977, Sept. 15 *Perf. 11½x12*

605	A193	6fr multi	60	25

Intl. Wiltz Festival, 25th anniv.

Europa Tamed, by R. Zilli, and Map of Europe A194

1977, Dec. 5 Photo. *Perf. 11½*

606	A194	6fr multi	60	30

20th anniversary of the Treaties of Rome, setting up the European Economic Community and the European Atomic Energy Commission.

Souvenir Sheet

Grand Duke and Grand Duchess of Luxembourg — A195

Photogravure and Engraved

1978, Apr. 3 *Perf. 13½x14*

607	A195	Sheet of 2	2.00	2.00
a.		6fr dark blue & multi	90	90
b.		12fr dark red & multi	90	90

Silver wedding anniversary of Grand Duke Jean and Grand Duchess Josephine Charlotte.

Souvenir Sheet

Youth Fountain, Streamer and Dancers — A196

1978, Apr. 3 Photo. *Perf. 11½*

608	A196	Sheet of 3	3.50	3.50
a.		5fr ultra & multi	1.10	1.10
b.		6fr orange & multi	1.10	1.10
c.		20fr yellow green & multi	1.10	1.10

Juphilux 78, 5th International Young Philatelists' Exhibition, Luxembourg, Apr. 6-10.

Charles IV, Statue, Charles Bridge, Prague A197

Emile Mayrish, by Theo Van Rysselberghe A198

Europa: 12fr, Pierre d'Aspelt, tomb, Mainz Cathedral.

1978, May 18 Engr. *Perf. 13½*

609	A197	6fr dk vio bl	30	20
610	A197	12fr dl rose lil	85	70

Charles IV (1316-1378), Count of Luxembourg, Holy Roman Emperor, 600th death anniversary. Pierre d'Aspelt (c. 1250-1320), Archbishop of Mainz and Prince-Elector.

1978, May 18 *Perf. 11½*

611	A198	6fr multi	85	30

Emile Mayrish (1862-1928), president of International Steel Cartel and promoter of United Europe, 50th death anniversary.

Our Lady of Luxembourg A199

Trumpeters and Old Luxembourg A200

1978, May 18 Photo. *Perf. 11½*

612 A199 6fr multi	25	25
613 A200 6fr multi	25	25

Our Lady of Luxembourg, patroness, 300th anniversary; 135th anniversary of Grand Ducal Military Band.

Starving Child, Helping Hand, Millet — A201

League Emblem, Lungs, Open Window — A202

Open Prison Door — A203

1978, Sept. 11 Photo. *Perf. 11½*

614 A201 2fr multi	15	15
615 A202 5fr multi	25	25
616 A203 6fr multi	40	30

"Terre des Hommes," an association to help underprivileged children; Luxembourg Anti-Tuberculosis League, 70th anniversary; Amnesty International and 30th anniversary of Universal Declaration of Human Rights.

Squared Stone Emerging from Rock, City of Luxembourg A204

1978, Sept. 11 Engr. *Perf. 13½x13*

617 A204 6fr vio bl	45	25

Masonic Grand Lodge of Luxembourg, 175th anniversary.

Julius Caesar on Denarius, c. 44 B.C. A205

St. Michael's Church, Mondorf-les-Bains A206

Roman Coins, Found in Luxembourg: 6fr, Empress Faustina I on Sestertius, 141 A.D. 9fr, Empress Helena on Follis, c. 324-330. 26fr, Emperor Valens on Solidus, c. 367-375.

1979, Mar. 5 Photo. *Perf. 11½*

618 A205 5fr multi	22	22
619 A205 6fr multi	22	22
620 A205 9fr multi	65	55
621 A205 26fr multi	1.25	1.00

1979, Mar. 5 Engr. *Perf. 13*

Design: 6fr, Luxembourg Central Station.

622 A206 5fr multi	30	20
623 A206 6fr rose claret	60	30

Troisvièrges Stagecoach A207

Europa: 12fr, Early wall telephone (vert.).

1979, Apr. 30 Photo. *Perf. 11½*

624 A207 6fr multi	1.10	40
625 A207 12fr multi	2.50	90

Michel Pintz Facing Jury — A208

1979, Apr. 30 Engr. *Perf. 13*

626 A208 2fr rose lil	30	15

180th anniversary of peasant uprising against French occupation.

Antoine Meyer — A209

Abundance Crowning Work and Thrift, by Auguste Vinet — A210

Design: 6fr, Sidney Gilchrist Thomas.

1979, Apr. 30

627 A209 5fr carmine	32	20
628 A209 6fr lt bl	32	25
629 A210 9fr black	50	35

Antoine Meyer (1801-1857), mathematician and first national poet; centenary of acquisition of Thomas process for production of high-quality steel; 50th anniversary of Luxembourg Stock Exchange.

European Parliament A211

1979, June 7 Photo. *Perf. 11½*

630 A211 6fr multi	5.00	90

European Parliament, first direct elections, June 7-10.

Angel with Chalice, by Barthelemy Namur — A212

Rococo Art: 12fr, Angel with anchor, by Namur, from High Altar, St. Michael's Church, Luxembourg.

Engraved and Photogravure

1979, Sept. 10 *Perf. 13½*

631 A212 6fr multi	35	25
632 A212 12fr multi	65	50

Road Safety for Children A213

1979, Sept. 10 Photo. *Perf. 11½*

633 A213 2fr multi	18	15

International Year of the Child.

Radio Tele-Luxembourg Emblem — A214

1979, Sept. 10

634 A214 6fr ultra, bl & red	45	25

50 years of broadcasting in Luxembourg.

John the Blind, Silver Coin, 1331 — A215

Ettelbruck Town Hall — A216

14th Century Coins: 2fr, Sts. Gervase and Protais, silver grosso. 6fr, Easter lamb, gold coin. 20fr, Crown and arms, silver grosso.

1980, Mar. 5 Photo. *Perf. 11½*

635 A215 2fr multi	15	15
636 A215 5fr multi	25	25
637 A215 6fr multi	35	35
638 A215 20fr multi	1.20	1.20

See Nos. 651-654.

1980, Mar. 5 Engr. *Perf. 13*

Design: No. 640, State Archives Building, horiz.

639 A216 6fr brn & dk red	35	25
640 A216 6fr multi	35	25

Jean Monnet — A217

Sports for All — A218

Europa: 12fr, St. Benedict of Nursia.

1980, Apr. 28 *Perf. 13½*

641 A217 6fr dk bl	52	25
642 A217 12fr ol grn	1.00	60

1980, Apr. 28 Photo. *Perf. 11½*

Granite Paper

643 A218 6fr multi	95	22

Worker Pouring Molten Iron — A219

Mercury by Jean Mich — A220

Design: 6fr, Man, hand, gears (horiz.).

1980, Apr. 28

644 A219 2fr multi	15	15
645 A219 6fr multi	42	22
Set value		30

9th World Congress on Prevention of Occupational Accidents and Diseases, Amsterdam, May 6-9.

1980, Sept. 10 Engr. *Perf. 14*

Art Nouveau Sculpture by Jean Mich.

646 A220 8fr shown	48	40
647 A220 12fr Ceres	70	55

Introduction of Postal Code — A221

1980, Sept. 10 Photo. *Perf. 11½*

648 A221 4fr multi	42	15

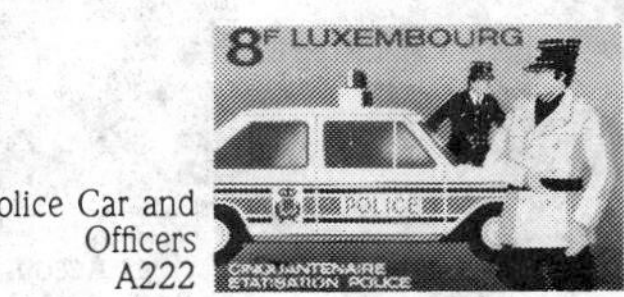
Police Car and Officers A222

1980, Sept. 10

649 A222 8fr multi	48	32

State control of police force, 50th anniv.

Grand Duke Jean — A223

Arms of Grand Duke Jean — A224

Photo. & Engr.

1981, Jan. 5 *Perf. 13½*

650 Sheet of 3	2.50	2.50
a. A223 8fr multi	65	65
b. A224 12fr multi	75	75
c. A223 30fr multi	1.00	1.00

Grand Duke Jean, 60th birthday.

Coin Type of 1980

Silver Coins: 4fr, Philip IV patagon, 1635. 6fr, Empress Maria Theresa 12 sol, 1775. 8fr, Emperor Joseph II 12 sol, 1789. 30fr, Emperor Francois II 72 sol, 1795.

1981, Mar. 5 **Photo.** *Perf. 11½*

651 A215 4fr multi	18	16
652 A215 6fr multi	25	20
653 A215 8fr multi	32	32
654 A215 30fr multi	1.25	1.10

National Library A225

1981, Mar. 5 **Engr.** *Perf. 13*

655 A225 8fr shown	35	20
656 A225 8fr European Hemicycle, Kirchberg	35	20

Hammelsmarsch (Sheep Procession) — A226

Europa: 12fr, Bird-shaped whistle, Eimaischen market.

1981, May 4 **Photo.** *Perf. 13½*

657 A226 8fr multi	38	30
658 A226 12fr multi	60	50

Knight on Chessboard A227

Savings Account Book, State Bank A228

First Bank Note, 1856 — A229

1981, May 4 *Perf. 11½*

Granite Paper

659 A227 4fr multi	25	22
660 A228 8fr multi	35	35
661 A229 8fr multi	35	35

Luxembourg Chess Federation, 50th anniv.; State Savings Bank, 125th anniv.; Intl. Bank of Luxembourg, 125th anniv. of issuing rights.

Wedding of Prince Henri and Maria Teresa Mestre, Feb. 14 A230

Photo. & Engr.

1981, June 22 *Perf. 13½*

662 A230 8fr multi	50	40

Sheets of 12.

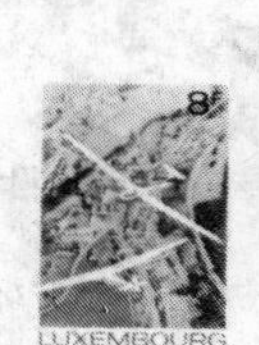

Single-seater Gliders A231

Energy Conservation A232

1981, Sept. 28 **Photo.** *Perf. 11½*

Granite Paper

663 A231 8fr shown	30	30
664 A231 16fr Propeller planes, horiz.	60	60
665 A231 35fr Jet, Luxembourg Airport, horiz.	1.50	1.40

1981, Sept. 28

Granite Paper

666 A232 8fr multi	35	35

Apple Trees in Blossom, by Frantz Seimetz (1858-1914) A233

World War II Resistance A234

Landscape Paintings: 6fr, Summer Landscape, by Pierre Blanc (1872-1946). 8fr, The Larger Hallerbach, by Guido Oppenheim (1862-1942). 16fr, Winter Evening, by Eugene Mousset (1877-1941).

1982, Feb. 25 **Engr.** *Perf. 11½*

667 A233 4fr multi	18	18
668 A233 6fr multi	28	28
669 A233 8fr multi	40	40
670 A233 16fr multi	80	80

1982, Feb. 25

Design: Cross of Hinzert (Natl. Monument of the Resistance and Deportation) and Political Prisoner, by Lucien Wercollier.

671 A234 8fr multi	38	35

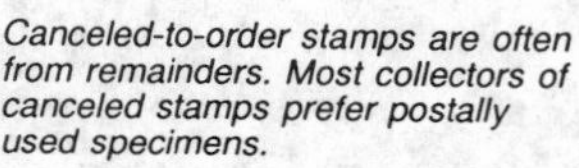
Canceled-to-order stamps are often from remainders. Most collectors of canceled stamps prefer postally used specimens.

Europa 1982 A235

St. Theresa of Avila (1515-1582) A236

1982, May 4 **Photo.**

Granite Paper

672 A235 8fr Treaty of London, 1867	50	35
673 A235 16fr Treaty of Paris, 1951	90	65

1982, May 4

Design: 8fr, Raoul Follereau (1903-1977), "Apostle of the Lepers."

Granite Paper

674 A236 4fr multi	20	18
675 A236 8fr multi	40	38

State Museums — A237

1982, May 4 **Photo. & Engr.**

676 A237 8fr shown	45	35
677 A237 8fr Synagogue of Luxembourg	45	35

Bourscheid Castle — A238

Intl. Youth Hostel Federation, 50th Anniv. — A239

Designs: Restored castles.

1982, Sept. 9 **Engr.** *Perf. 11½*

Granite Paper

678 A238 6fr shown	32	25
679 A238 8fr Vianden, horiz.	45	35

1982, Sept. 9 **Photo.**

680 A239 4fr shown	30	15
681 A239 8fr Scouting year, vert.	60	35

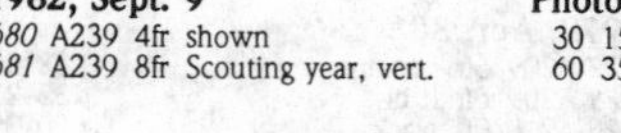

Civilian and Military Deportation Monument — A240

1982, Sept. 9

682 A240 8fr multi	50	35

Mercury, Sculpture by Auguste Tremond A241

NATO Emblem, Flags A242

1983, Mar. 7 **Photo.** *Perf. 11½*

Granite Paper

683 A241 4fr multi	20	15

FOREX '83, 25th Intl. Assoc. of Foreign Exchange Dealers' Congress, June 2-5.

1983, Mar. 7

Granite Paper

684 A242 6fr multi	25	25

25th anniv. of NAMSA (NATO Maintenance and Supply Agency).

Echternach Cross of Justice, 1236 — A243

Globe, CCC Emblem — A244

1983, Mar. 7

Granite Paper

685 A243 8fr multi	45	35

30th Congress of Intl. Union of Barristers, July 3-9.

1983, Mar. 7

Granite Paper

686 A244 8fr multi	45	35

30th anniv. of Council of Customs Cooperation.

Natl. Federation of Fire Brigades Centenary A245

1983, Mar. 7

Granite Paper

687 A245 8fr Fire engine, 1983	45	35
688 A245 16fr Hand pump, 1740	85	65

Europa 1983 — A246

The Good Samaritan, Codex Aureus Escorialensis Miniatures, 11th Cent., Echternach.

1983, May 3 **Photo.**

689 A246 8fr Highway robbers	52	35
690 A246 16fr Good Samaritan	1.00	65

Giant Bible, 11th Cent. — A247

World Communications Year — A248

Illuminated Letters.

1983, May 3 Photo. & Engr. *Perf. 14*

691	A247	8fr	"h," Book of Baruch	45	35
692	A247	35fr	"B," letter of St. Jerome	2.00	1.50

1983, May 3 Photo. *Perf. 11½*

693	A248	8fr	Post code	42	35
694	A248	8fr	Satellite relay, horiz.	42	35

Town Hall, Dudelange A249

Designs: 7fr, St. Lawrence Church, Diekirch, vert.

1983, Sept. 7 Photo. & Engr.

695	A249	7fr	multi	38	25
696	A249	10fr	multi	55	35

Basketball Fed., 50th Anniv. A250

European Working Dog Championship A251

Tourism — A252

1983, Sept. 7 Photo.

Granite Paper

697	A250	7fr	multi	38	25
698	A251	10fr	Alsatian sheepdog	55	35
699	A252	10fr	View of Luxembourg	55	35

Environment Protection A253

1984, Mar. 6 Photo. *Perf. 11½*

Granite Paper

700	A253	7fr	Pedestrian zoning	35	16
701	A253	10fr	Water purification	50	24

2nd European Parliament Election — A254

1984, Mar. 6

Granite Paper

702	A254	10fr	Hands holding emblem	60	40

A255

A256

1984, Mar. 6 Engr. *Perf. 12½x13*

703	A255	10fr	No. 1	50	35
704	A255	10fr	Union meeting	50	35
705	A255	10fr	Mail bag	50	35
706	A255	10fr	Train	50	35

Philatelic Federation (1934); Civil Service Trade Union (1909); Postal Workers' Union (1909); Railroad (1859).

1984, May 7 Photo. *Perf. 11½x12*

707	A256	10fr	The Race, by Jean Jacoby (1891-1936)	55	35

1984 Summer Olympics.

Europa (1959-84) A257

1984, May 7 *Perf. 11½*

Granite Paper

708	A257	10fr	green	55	30
709	A257	16fr	orange	80	60

Young Turk Caressing His Horse, by Delacroix A258

Paintings: 4fr, The Smoker, by David Teniers the Younger (1610-90). 10fr, Epiphany, by Han Steen (1626-79). 50fr, The Lacemaker, by Pieter van Slingelandt (1640-91). 4fr, 50fr vert.

1984, May 7 Photo. & Engr. *Perf. 14*

710	A258	4fr	multi	25	22
711	A258	7fr	multi	40	24
712	A258	10fr	multi	60	35
713	A258	50fr	multi	2.75	2.00

Marine Life Fossils A259

Restored Castles A260

1984, Sept. 10 Photo. *Perf. 11½*

714	A259	4fr	Pecten sp.	22	15
715	A259	7fr	Gryphaea arcuata	38	25
716	A259	10fr	Coeloceras raqyinianum	55	35
717	A259	16fr	Daildius	90	60

1984, Sept. 10 Engr.

718	A260	7fr	Hollenfels	38	25
719	A260	10fr	Larochette	55	40

A261

A262

1984, Sept. 10 *Perf. 12x12½*

720	A261	10fr	Soldier, US flag	75	35

40th Anniv. of D Day (June 6).

1985, Mar. 4 Photo. *Perf. 11½*

Portrait medals in the state museum: 4fr, Jean Bertels (1544-1607), Historian, Abbott of Echternach. 7fr, Emperor Charles V (1500-1558). 10fr, King Philip II of Spain (1527-1598). 30fr, Prince Maurice of Orange-Nassau, Count of Vianden (1567-1625).

Granite Paper

721	A262	4fr	multi	24	22
722	A262	7fr	multi	40	22
723	A262	10fr	multi	60	32
724	A262	30fr	multi	1.75	90

See Nos. 739-742.

Anniversaries A263

Designs: No. 725, Benz Velo, First automobile in Luxembourg, 1895. No. 726, Push-button telephone, sound waves. No. 727, Fencers.

1985, Mar. 4 *Perf. 12x11½*

Granite Paper

725	A263	10fr	multi	65	40
726	A263	10fr	multi	65	40
727	A263	10fr	multi	65	40

Centenary of the first automobile; Luxembourg Telephone Service, cent.; Luxembourg Fencing Federation, 50th anniv.

Visit of Pope John Paul II — A264

Europa 1985 — A265

1985, Mar. 4 *Perf. 11½x12*

Granite Paper

728	A264	10fr	Papal arms	75	40

1985, May 8 *Perf. 11½*

Designs: 10fr, Grand-Duke Adolphe Music Federation. 16fr, Luxembourg Music School.

729	A265	10fr	multi	80	40
730	A265	16fr	multi	1.25	60

Souvenir Sheet

End of World War II, 40th Anniv. — A266

Designs: a, Luxembourg resistance fighters, Wounded Fighters medal. b, Luxembourg War Cross. c, Badge of the Union of Luxembourg Resistance Movements. d, Liberation of the concentration camps.

1985, May 8 *Perf. 11½x12*

Granite Paper

731			Sheet of 4	2.75	2.75
a.-d.	A266	10fr,	any single	60	38

Endangered Wildlife — A267

1985, Sept. 23 Photo. *Perf. 12x11½*

732	A267	4fr	Athene nocturna	20	15
733	A267	7fr	Felis silvestris	38	22
734	A267	10fr	Vanessa atalantica, vert.	55	35
735	A267	50fr	Hyla arborea, vert.	2.75	1.65

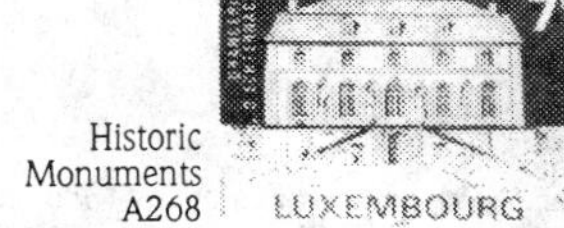

Historic Monuments A268

1985, Sept. 23 Engr. *Perf. 11½*

736	A268	7fr	Echternach Orangery, 1750	45	22
737	A268	10fr	Mohr de Waldt House, 17th cent.	65	45

Natl. Art Collection — A269

Photo. & Engr.

1985, Sept. 23 *Perf. 14*

738	A269	10fr	18th cent. book cover, Natl. Library	40	22

Portrait Medals Type of 1985

1986, Mar. 3 Photo. *Perf. 11½*

Granite Paper

739	A262	10fr	Count of Monterey, 1675	65	40
740	A262	12fr	Louis XIV, 1684	70	45
741	A262	18fr	Pierre de Weyms, c. 1700	1.10	70
742	A262	20fr	Duke of Marlborough, 1706	1.25	80

Federation of Luxembourg Beekeepers' Associations, Cent. — A270

Mondorf State Spa, Cent. — A271

Natl. Table Tennis Federation, 50th Anniv. — A272

1986, Mar. 3 *Perf. 11½*

743 A270 12fr Bee collecting pollen 75 50
744 A271 12fr Mosaic 75 50
745 A272 12fr Boy playing table tennis 75 50

Europa 1986 A273

Fortifications A274

1986, May 5 Photo. *Perf. 12*
Granite Paper

751 A273 12fr Polluted forest, city 75 50
752 A273 20fr Man, pollution sources 1.25 80

1986, May 5
Granite Paper

753 A274 15fr Ft. Thungen, horiz. 90 60
754 A274 18fr Invalid's Gate 1.10 72
755 A274 50fr Malakoff Tower 3.00 2.00

Robert Schuman (1886-1963), European Cooperation Promulgator — A275

1986, June 26 *Perf. 12 on 3 Sides*
Granite Paper

756 A275 2fr pink & blk 15 15
  a. Bklt. pane of 4 32
757 A275 10fr lt bl & blk 65 40
  a. Bklt. pane of 4 2.75
  b. Bklt. pane of 2, #756-757, + 2 labels 1.40

Nos. 756-757 issued in booklets only.

European Road Safety Year — A276

Countess Ermesinde (1186-1247), Ruler of Luxembourg — A278

Bas-relief, Town Hall, Esch-Sur-Alzette — A277

1986, Sept. 15 Photo. *Perf. 11½*

758 A276 10fr multi 55 40

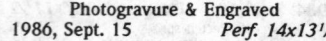

Photogravure & Engraved
1986, Sept. 15 *Perf. 14x13½*

Design: No. 760, Stairs to the Chapel of the Cross, Grevenmacher.

759 A277 12fr shown 75 50
760 A277 12fr multi 75 50

1986, Sept. 15 *Perf. 13½x14*

Designs: No. 761, Presentation of the letter of freedom to Echternach inhabitants, 1236, engraving (detail) by P.H. Witkamp, c. 1873. 30fr, Charter seal, Marienthal Convent, 1238.

761 A278 12fr multi 70 50
762 A278 30fr multi 1.65 1.20

Wildlife Conservation A279

Natl. Home Amateur Radio Operators Network, 50th Anniv. A280

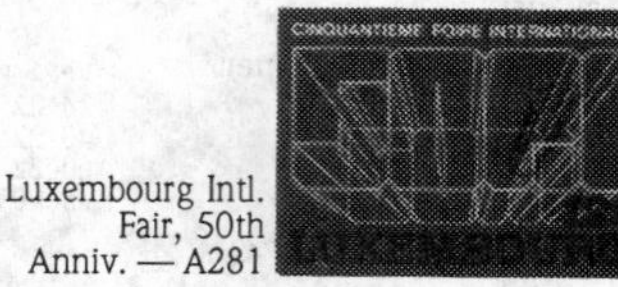

Luxembourg Intl. Fair, 50th Anniv. — A281

1987, Mar. 9 Photo. *Perf. 11½*

763 A279 6fr Eliomys quercinus 30 24
764 A279 10fr Calopteryx splendens, vert. 52 40
765 A279 12fr Cinclus cinclus, vert. 60 48
766 A279 25fr Salamandra salamandra terrestris 1.40 1.00

1987, Mar. 9

767 A280 12fr multi 62 48
768 A281 12fr multi 62 48

Europa 1987 — A282

Designs: 12fr, Aquatic Sports Center. 20fr, European Communities Court of Justice and abstract sculpture by Henry Moore (1898-1986).

1987, May 4 Photo. *Perf. 11½*

769 A282 12fr multi 75 48
770 A282 20fr multi 1.25 80

St. Michael's Church Millenary A283

Designs: 12fr, Consecration of the church by Archbishop Egbert of Trier, 987, stained glass window by Gustav Zanter. 20fr, Baroque organ-chest, 17th century.

Photogravure & Engraved
1987, May 4 *Perf. 14*

771 A283 12fr multi 75 48
772 A283 20fr multi 1.25 80

15th Century Paintings by Giovanni Ambrogio Bevilacqua — A284

Polyptych panels in the State Museum: 10fr, St. Bernard of Sienna and St. John the Baptist. 18fr, St. Jerome and St. Francis of Assisi.

1987, May 4 *Perf. 11½*

773 A284 10fr multi 55 40
774 A284 18fr multi 1.00 72

Rural Architecture A285

Photo. & Engr.
1987, Sept. 14 *Perf. 13½*

775 A285 10fr Hennesbau Bark Mill, 1826, Niederfeulen 50 40
776 A285 12fr Health Center, 18th cent., Mersch 60 48
777 A285 100fr Post Office, 18th cent., Bertrange 5.00 4.00

Chamber of Deputies (Parliament) 139th Anniv. — A286

Designs: 6fr, Charles Metz (1799-1853), first President. 12fr, Parliament, 1860, designed by Antoine Hartmann (1817-1891).

1987, Sept. 14 Engr. *Perf. 14*

778 A286 6fr violet brn 24 24
779 A286 12fr blue black 48 48

Flowers by Botanical Illustrator Pierre-Joseph Redoute (1759-1840) A287

1988, Feb. 8 Photo. *Perf. 11½x12*

780 A287 6fr Orange lily, water lily 35 35
781 A287 10fr Primula, double narcissus 60 60
782 A287 12fr Tulip 72 72
783 A287 50fr Iris, gorteria 3.00 3.00

European Conf. of Ministers of Transport A288

Eurocontrol, 25th Anniv. A289

1988, Feb. 8 *Perf. 12*

784 A288 12fr multi 72 72
785 A289 20fr multi 1.20 1.20

Souvenir Sheet

Family of Prince Henri — A290

1988, Mar. 29 Photo. *Perf. 12*

786 A290 Sheet of 3 4.75 4.75
  a. 12fr Maria Theresa 68 68
  b. 18fr Guillaume, Felix and Louis 1.00 1.00
  c. 50fr Prince Henri 2.75 2.75

JUVALUX '88, 9th intl. youth philatelic exhibition, Mar. 29-Apr. 4.

Europa 1988 — A291

Communication.

1988, June 6 Photo. *Perf. 11½*

787 A291 12fr Automatic mail handling 72 72
788 A291 20fr Electronic mail 1.20 1.20

Tourism — A292

Designs: 10fr, Wiltz town hall and Cross of Justice Monument, c. 1502. 12fr, Castle, Differdange, 16th cent., vert.

Photo. & Engr.
1988, June 6 *Perf. 13½*

789 A292 10fr multi 60 60
790 A292 12fr multi 72 72

See Nos. 824-825, 841-842.

League of Luxembourg Student Sports Associations (LASEL), 50th Anniv. A293

1988, June 6 Photo. *Perf. 11½*

791 A293 12fr multi 72 72

Doorways — A294

Architectural drawings by Joseph Wegener (1895-1980) and his students, 1949-1951: 12fr, Septfontaines Castle main entrance, 1785. 25fr, National Library regency north-wing entrance, c.

1720. 50fr, Holy Trinity Church baroque entrance, c. 1740.

Litho. & Engr.

1988, Sept. 12 *Perf. 14*

792 A294	12fr black & buff	65	65
793 A294	25fr blk & citron	1.30	1.30
794 A294	50fr blk & yel bis	2.60	2.60

Jean Monnet (1888-1979), French Economist — A295

1988, Sept. 12 **Engr.**

795 A295 12fr multi 65 65

European Investment Bank, 30th Anniv. A296

1988, Sept. 12 **Litho. & Engr.**

796 A296 12fr yel grn & blk 65 65

A297

A298

1988, Sept. 12 **Photo.** *Perf. 11½*

797 A297 12fr multi 65 65

1988 Summer Olympics, Seoul.

1989, Mar. 6 **Photo.** *Perf. 11½x12*

Design: 12fr, Portrait and excerpt from his speech to the Chamber of Deputies, 1896.

798 A298 12fr multi 62 62

C.M. Spoo (1837-1914), advocate of Luxembourgish as the natl. language.

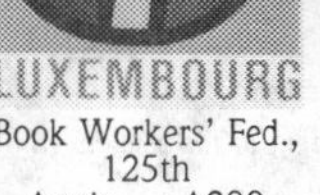

Book Workers' Fed., 125th Anniv. — A299

Natl. Red Cross, 75th Anniv. — A300

1989, Mar. 6

799 A299 18fr multi 95 95

1989, Mar. 6

800 A300 20fr Henri Dunant 1.05 1.05

Independence of the Grand Duchy, 150th Anniv. — A301

Design: 12fr, Lion, bronze sculpture by Auguste Tremont (1892-1980) guarding the grand ducal family vault, Cathedral of Luxembourg.

Photo. & Engr.

1989, Mar. 6 *Perf. 14*

801 A301 12fr multi 62 62

Astra Telecommunications Satellite — A302

1989, Mar. 6 **Photo.** *Perf. 11½*

802 A302 12fr multi 62 62

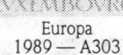

Europa 1989 — A303

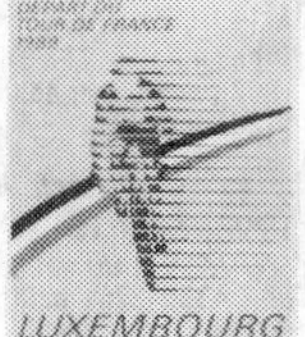

Tour de France — A304

Paintings (children at play): 12fr, *Three Children in a Park*, 19th cent., anonymous. 20fr, *Child with Drum*, 17th cent., anonymous.

1989, May 8 **Photo.** *Perf. 11½x12*

803 A303	12fr multi	62	62
804 A303	20fr multi	1.05	1.05

1989, May 8 *Perf. 11½*

805 A304 9fr multi 48 48

Start of the bicycle race in Luxembourg City.

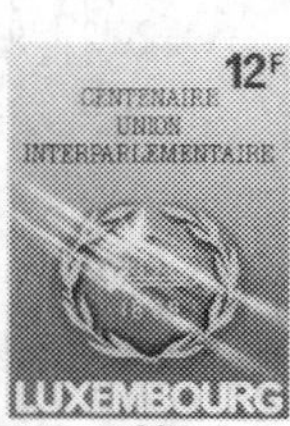

A305

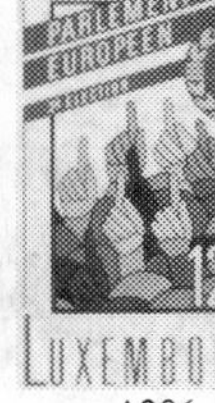

A306

1989, May 8 *Perf. 11½x12*

806 A305 12fr multi 62 62

Interparliamentary Union, cent.

1989, May 8

807 A306 12fr multi 62 62

European Parliament 3rd elections.

Council of Europe, 40th Anniv. A307

1989, May 8 *Perf. 12x11½*

808 A307 12fr multi 62 62

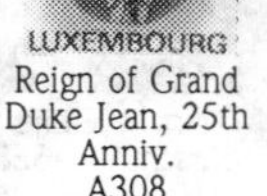

Reign of Grand Duke Jean, 25th Anniv. A308

Charles IV (1316-1378) A309

1989, Sept. 18 **Photo.** *Perf. 12x11½*

Booklet Stamps

810 A308	3fr	15	15
816 A308	9fr	42	42
a.	Bklt. pane, 5 each #810, 816	2.85	

This is an expanding set. Numbers will change if necessary.

Photo. & Engr.

1989, Sept. 18 *Perf. 13½x14*

Stained-glass windows by Joseph Oberberger in the Grand Ducal Loggia, Cathedral of Luxembourg: 20fr, John the Blind (1296-1346). 25fr, Wenceslas II (1361-1419).

821 A309	12fr shown	58	58
822 A309	20fr multi	95	95
823 A309	25fr multi	1.20	1.20

Independence of the Grand Duchy, 150th anniv.

Tourism Type of 1988

Designs: 12fr, Clervaux Castle interior courtyard, circa 12th cent. 18fr, Bronzed wild boar of Titelberg, 1st cent., vert.

Litho. & Engr.

1989, Sept. 18 *Perf. 13½*

824 A292	12fr multi	58	58
825 A292	18fr multi	88	88

Views of the Former Fortress of Luxembourg, 1814-1815, Engravings by Christoph Wilhelm Selig (1791-1837) — A310

1990, Mar. 5 **Photo.** *Perf. 12x11½*

826 A310	9fr shown	52	52
827 A310	12fr multi, diff.	70	70
828 A310	20fr multi, diff.	1.15	1.15
829 A310	25fr multi, diff.	1.40	1.40

Congress of Vienna, 1815, during which the Duchy of Luxembourg was elevated to the Grand Duchy of Luxembourg.

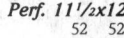

Schueberfouer Carnival, 650th Anniv. — A311

1990, Mar. 15 *Perf. 11½x12*

830 A311 9fr Carnival ride 52 52

Batty Weber (1860-1940), Writer — A312

ITU, 125th Anniv. — A313

1990, Mar. 15

831 A312 12fr multi 70 70

1990, Mar. 15

832 A313 18fr multicolored 1.05 1.05

Europa — A314

Post offices: 12fr, Luxembourg City. 20fr, Esch-Sur-Alzette, vert.

Litho. & Engr.

1990, May 28 *Perf. 13½*

833 A314	12fr buff & blk	72	72
834 A314	20fr lt bl & blk	1.20	1.20

Paul Eyschen (1841-1915) — A315

Prime Ministers: 12fr, Emmanuel Servais (1811-1890).

Photo. & Engr.

1990, May 28 *Perf. 14x13½*

835 A315	9fr multicolored	55	55
836 A315	12fr multicolored	72	72

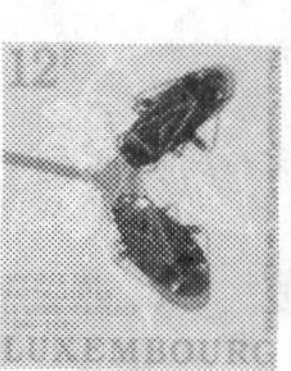

A316

A317

1990, May 28 **Photo.** *Perf. 11½*

837 A316 12fr Psallus Pseudoplatani 72 72

Luxembourg Naturalists' Society, cent.

Litho. & Engr.

1990, Sept. 24 *Perf. 14*

Fountains: 12fr, Sheep's march by Will Lofy. 25fr, Fountain of Doves. 50fr, "Maus Ketty" by Lofy.

838 A317 12fr 72 72
839 A317 25fr 1.50 1.50
840 A317 50fr 3.00 3.00

Tourism Type of 1988

1990, Sept. 24 *Perf. 13½*

841 A292 12fr Mondercange 72 72
842 A292 12fr Schifflange 72 72

Souvenir Sheet

Nassau-Weilbourg Dynasty, Cent. — A318

Designs: a, Grand Duke Adolphe. b, Grand Duchess Marie-Adelaide. c, Grand Ducal House arms. d, Grand Duchess Charlotte. e, Grand Duke Guillaume. f, Grand Duke Jean.
Illustration reduced.

Photo. & Engr.

1990, Nov. 26 *Perf. 14x13½*

843 A318 Sheet of 6 6.00 6.00
a.-b. 12fr multicolored 72 72
c.-d. 18fr multicolored 1.10 1.10
e.-f. 20fr multicolored 1.20 1.20

View From the Trier Road by Sosthene Weis (1872-1941) — A319

Paintings: 18fr, Vauban Street and the Viaduct. 25fr, St. Ulric Street.

Perf. 12x11½, 11½x12

1991, Mar. 4 **Photo.**

844 A319 14fr multicolored 85 85
845 A319 18fr multicolored 1.10 1.10
846 A319 25fr multi, vert. 1.50 1.50

Fungi — A320

1991, Mar. 4 *Perf. 11½*

847 A320 14fr Geastrum varians 85 85
848 A320 14fr Agaricus (Gymnopus) thiebautii 85 85
849 A320 18fr Agaricus (lepiota) lepidocephalus 1.10 1.10
850 A320 25fr Morchella favosa 1.50 1.50

Europa — A321

1991, May 13 Photo. *Perf. 12x11½*

851 A321 14fr Astra 1A, 1B satellites 85 85
852 A321 18fr Betzdorf ground station 1.10 1.10

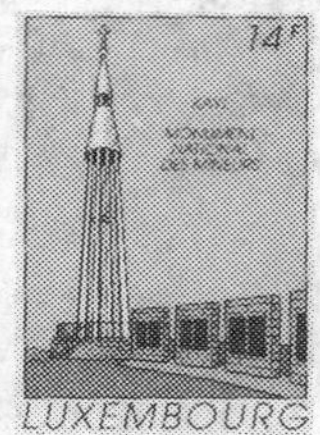

Natl. Miners' Monument, Kayl — A322

Art by Emile Kirscht — A323

Designs: No. 854, Magistrates' Court, Redange-Sur-Attert, horiz.

Perf. 11½x12, 12x11½

1991, May 23

853 A322 14fr multicolored 85 85
854 A322 14fr multicolored 85 85

1991, May 23 *Perf. 11½*

Design: No. 856, Edmund de la Fontaine (1823-1891), Poet.

855 A323 14fr multicolored 85 85
856 A323 14fr multicolored 85 85

Labor Unions, 75th anniv. (No. 855).

Post and Telecommunications Museum — A324

Perf. 11½ on 3 sides

1991, Sept. 23 **Photo.**

Booklet Stamps

857 A324 4fr Old telephone 24 24
a. Bklt. pane of 1 + 3 labels 24
858 A324 14fr Old postbox 85 85
a. Bklt. pane of 4 3.40

A325 A326

1991, Sept. 23 *Perf. 11½*

859 A325 14fr Stamp of Type A24 85 85

Stamp Day, 50th anniv.

Photo. & Engr.

1991, Sept. 23 *Perf. 14*

Designs: Gargoyles.

860 A326 14fr Young girl's head 85 85
861 A326 25fr Woman's head 1.50 1.50
862 A326 50fr Man's head 3.00 3.00

Jean-Pierre Pescatore Foundation, Cent. — A327

Buildings: No. 864, High Technology Institute. No. 865, New Fair and Congress Centre.

1992, Mar. 16 Photo. *Perf. 11½*

863 A327 14fr lil rose & multi 85 85
864 A327 14fr grn & multi 85 85
865 A327 14fr brt bl & multi 85 85

Bettembourg Castle — A328

1992, Mar. 16

866 A328 18fr shown 1.05 1.05
867 A328 25fr Walferdange station 1.50 1.50

Europa A329

Emigrants to US: 14fr, Nicholas Gonner (1835-1892), newspaper editor. 22fr, N. E. Becker (1842-1920), journalist.

Perf. 13½x14½

1992, May 18 **Photo. & Engr.**

868 A329 14fr multicolored 85 85
869 A329 22fr multicolored 1.35 1.35

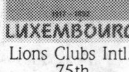

Lions Clubs Intl., 75th Anniv. — A330

General Strike, 50th Anniv. — A331

1992, May 18 Photo. *Perf. 11½*

870 A330 14fr multicolored 85 85
871 A331 18fr sepia & lake 1.10 1.10

1992 Summer Olympics, Barcelona A332

1992, May 18 *Perf. 12x11½*

872 A332 14fr multicolored 85 85

Expo '92, Seville — A333

1992, May 18 *Perf. 11½*

873 A333 14fr Luxembourg pavilion 85 85

Fountain of the Children with Grapes, Schwebsingen A336

Design: No. 882, Old Ironworks Cultural Center, Steinfort.

1993, Mar. 8 Photo. *Perf. 12x11½*

881 A336 14fr multicolored 85 85
882 A336 14fr multicolored 85 85

Grand Duke Jean — A337

Perf. 13½x13

1993, Mar. 8 **Litho. & Engr.**

Background Color

884 A337 5fr yellow green 30 30
885 A337 7fr brick red 42 42
888 A337 14fr pink 85 85
889 A337 18fr orange 1.10 1.10
891 A337 22fr dark green 1.30 1.30
892 A337 25fr gray blue 1.50 1.50
Nos. 884-892 (6) 5.47 5.47

This is an expanding set. Numbers may change.

SEMI-POSTAL STAMPS

Clervaux Monastery SP1

Designs: 15c+10c, View of Pfaffenthal. 25c+10c, View of Luxembourg.

Engr.; Surcharge Typo. in Red

1921, Aug. 2 Unwmk. *Perf. 11½*

B1 SP1 10c + 5c green 15 *90*
B2 SP1 15c + 10c org red 15 *1.10*
B3 SP1 25c + 10c dp grn 15 *90*
Set, never hinged 1.00

The amount received from the surtax on these stamps was added to a fund for the erection of a monument to the soldiers from Luxembourg who died in World War I.

Nos. B1-B3 with Additional Surcharge in Red or Black

+ 25

⨯ 27 mai 1923 ⨯

1923, May 27

B4 SP1 25c on #B1 (R) 1.00 *5.75*
B5 SP1 25c on #B2 1.25 *7.25*
B6 SP1 25c on #B3 1.00 *5.75*
Set, never hinged 7.00

Unveiling of the monument to the soldiers who died in World War I.

CARITAS

Regular Issue of 1914-15 Surcharged in Black or Red

+10c

1924, Apr. 17 *Perf. 11½x11*
B7 A11 12½c + 7½c grn 15 18
B8 A11 35c + 10c dk bl (R) 15 18
B9 A11 2½fr + 1fr red 60 4.50
B10 A11 5fr + 2fr dk vio 35 2.50
Set, never hinged 2.75

Nurse and Patient SP4

Prince Jean SP5

1925, Dec. 21 **Litho.** *Perf. 13*
B11 SP4 5c (+ 5c) dl vio 15 20
B12 SP4 30c (+ 5c) org 15 28
B13 SP4 50c (+ 5c) red brn 24 80
B14 SP4 1fr (+ 10c) dp bl 35 2.00
Set, never hinged 1.65

1926, Dec. 15 **Photo.** *Perf. 12½x12*
B15 SP5 5c (+ 5c) vio & blk 15 15
B16 SP5 40c (+ 10) grn & blk 15 20
B17 SP5 50c (+ 15c) lem & blk 15 20
B18 SP5 75c (+ 20c) lt red & blk 25 1.50
B19 SP5 1.50fr (+ 30c) gray bl & blk 30 2.50
Nos. B15-B19 (5) 1.00 4.55
Set, never hinged 1.65

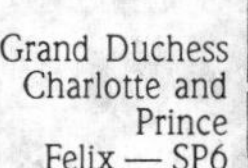

Grand Duchess Charlotte and Prince Felix — SP6

1927, Sept. 4 **Engr.** *Perf. 11½*
B20 SP6 25c dp vio 70 4.50
B21 SP6 50c green 1.10 7.50
B22 SP6 75c rose lake 70 4.50
B23 SP6 1fr gray blk 70 4.50
B24 SP6 1½fr dp bl 70 4.50
Nos. B20-B24 (5) 3.90 25.50
Set, never hinged 15.00

Introduction of postage stamps in Luxembourg, 75th anniv. These stamps were sold exclusively at the Luxembourg Philatelic Exhibition, September 4-8, 1927, at a premium of 3 francs per set, which was donated to the exhibition funds.

Princess Elisabeth SP7

Princess Marie Adelaide SP8

1927, Dec. 1 **Photo.** *Perf. 12½*
B25 SP7 10c (+ 5c) turq bl & blk 15 28
B26 SP7 50c (+ 10c) dk brn & blk 15 45
B27 SP7 75c (+ 20c) org & blk 15 75
B28 SP7 1fr (+ 30c) brn lake & blk 24 3.00
B29 SP7 1½fr (+ 50c) ultra & blk 18 3.00
Set value 66
Set, never hinged 1.65

The surtax was for Child Welfare societies.

1928, Dec. 12 *Perf. 12½x12*
B30 SP8 10c (+ 5c) ol grn & brn vio 15 80
B31 SP8 60c (+ 10c) brn & ol grn 25 1.65
B32 SP8 75c (+ 15c) vio rose & bl grn 40 3.00
B33 SP8 1fr (+ 25c) dk grn & brn 80 4.75
B34 SP8 1½fr (+ 50c) cit & bl 80 4.75
Nos. B30-B34 (5) 2.40 14.95
Set, never hinged 8.00

Princess Marie Gabrielle SP9

Prince Charles SP10

1929, Dec. 14 *Perf. 13*
B35 SP9 10c (+ 10c) mar & dp grn 15 90
B36 SP9 35c (+ 15c) dk grn & red brn 60 4.25
B37 SP9 75c (+ 30c) ver & blk 60 4.25
B38 SP9 1¼fr (+ 50c) mag & bl grn 1.10 7.75
B39 SP9 1¾fr (+ 75c) Prus bl & sl 1.10 7.75
Nos. B35-B39 (5) 3.55 24.90
Set, never hinged 16.00

The surtax was for Child Welfare societies.

1930, Dec. 10 *Perf. 12½*
B40 SP10 10c (+ 5c) bl grn & ol brn 15 35
B41 SP10 75c (+ 10c) vio brn & bl grn 60 2.25
B42 SP10 1fr (+ 25c) car rose & vio 1.75 6.75
B43 SP10 1¼fr (+ 75c) ol bis & dk brn 2.50 9.00
B44 SP10 1¾fr (+ 1.50fr) ultra & red brn 4.00 12.00
Nos. B40-B44 (5) 9.00 30.35
Set, never hinged 37.50

The surtax was for Child Welfare societies.

Princess Alix SP11

Countess Ermesinde SP12

1931, Dec. 10
B45 SP11 10c (+ 5c) brn org & gray 18 38
B46 SP11 75c (+ 10c) claret & bl grn 1.65 8.25
B47 SP11 1fr (+ 25c) dp grn & gray 3.50 16.00
B48 SP11 1¼fr (+ 75c) dk vio & bl grn 3.50 12.50
B49 SP11 1¾fr (+ 1.50fr) bl & gray 6.75 32.50
Nos. B45-B49 (5) 15.58 69.63
Set, never hinged 85.00

The surtax was for Child Welfare societies.

1932, Dec. 8
B50 SP12 10c (+ 5c) ol bis 28 48
B51 SP12 75c (+ 10c) dp vio 1.25 5.75
B52 SP12 1fr (+ 25c) scar 5.00 22.50
B53 SP12 1¼fr (+ 75c) red brn 6.00 24.00
B54 SP12 1¾fr (+ 1.50fr) dp bl 6.00 24.00
Nos. B50-B54 (5) 18.53 76.73
Set, never hinged 85.00

The surtax was for Child Welfare societies.

Count Henry VII — SP13

John the Blind — SP14

1933, Dec. 12
B55 SP13 10c (+ 5c) yel brn 35 35
B56 SP13 75c (+ 10c) dp vio 2.00 7.25
B57 SP13 1fr (+ 25c) car rose 7.50 22.50
B58 SP13 1¼fr (+ 75c) org brn 9.50 32.50
B59 SP13 1¾fr (+ 1.50fr) brt bl 9.50 32.50
Nos. B55-B59 (5) 28.85 95.10
Set, never hinged 100.00

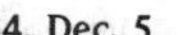

1934, Dec. 5
B60 SP14 10c (+ 5c) dk vio 18 28
B61 SP14 35c (+ 10c) dp grn 1.00 4.75
B62 SP14 75c (+ 15c) rose lake 1.00 4.75
B63 SP14 1fr (+ 25c) dp rose 7.50 30.00
B64 SP14 1¼fr (+ 75c) org 9.50 32.50
B65 SP14 1¾fr (+ 1.50fr) brt bl 9.50 32.50
Nos. B60-B65 (6) 28.68 104.78
Set, never hinged 120.00

Teacher SP15

Sculptor and Painter — SP16

Journalist SP17

Engineer SP18

Scientist SP19

Lawyer SP20

University SP21

Surgeon SP22

1935, May 1 **Unwmk.** *Perf. 12½*
B65A SP15 5c violet 15 24
B65B SP16 10c brown red 18 28
B65C SP17 15c olive 20 45
B65D SP18 20c orange 35 90
B65E SP19 35c yellow grn 45 1.25
B65F SP20 50c gray blk 50 1.25
B65G SP21 70c dk green 75 1.75
B65H SP22 1fr car red 1.00 2.50
B65J SP19 1.25fr turq 4.00 10.00
B65K SP18 1.75fr blue 5.00 20.00
B65L SP16 2fr lt brown 20.00 50.00
B65M SP17 3fr dk brown 24.00 57.50
B65N SP20 5fr lt blue 40.00 95.00
B65P SP15 10fr red vio 110.00 250.00
B65Q SP22 20fr dk green 150.00 300.00
Nos. B65A-B65Q (15) 356.58 791.12
Set, never hinged 850.00

Sold at double face, surtax going to intl. fund to aid professional people.

Philatelic Exhibition Issue

Type of Regular Issue of 1928

Wmk. 246

1935, Aug. 15 **Engr.** *Imperf.*
B66 A19 2fr (+ 50c) blk 4.00 12.00
Never hinged 12.00

Philatelic exhibition held at Esch-sur-Alzette.

Charles I — SP23

Perf. 11½

1935, Dec. 2 **Photo.** **Unwmk.**
B67 SP23 10c (+ 5c) vio 15 16
B68 SP23 35c (+ 10c) grn 18 70
B69 SP23 70c (+ 20c) dk brn 42 1.40
B70 SP23 1fr (+ 25c) rose lake 8.00 22.50
B71 SP23 1.25fr (+ 75c) org brn 8.00 22.50
B72 SP23 1.75fr (+ 1.50fr) bl 8.00 22.50
Nos. B67-B72 (6) 24.75 69.76
Set, never hinged 90.00

Wenceslas I, Duke of Luxembourg — SP24

1936, Dec. 1 *Perf. 11½x13*
B73 SP24 10c + 5(c) blk brn 15 20
B74 SP24 35c + 10(c) bl grn 15 40
B75 SP24 70c + 20(c) blk 25 80
B76 SP24 1fr + 25(c) rose car 1.00 4.00
B77 SP24 1.25fr + 75(c) vio 2.00 8.75
B78 SP24 1.75fr + 1.50(fr) saph 1.55 6.00
Nos. B73-B78 (6) 5.10 20.15
Set, never hinged 22.50

Wenceslas II — SP25

1937, Dec. 1 *Perf. 11½x12½*
B79 SP25 10c + 5c car & blk 15 18
B80 SP25 35c + 10c red vio & grn 15 20
B81 SP25 70c + 20c ultra & red brn 18 40
B82 SP25 1fr + 25c dk grn & scar 1.10 3.25
B83 SP25 1.25fr + 75c dk brn & vio 1.25 3.75
B84 SP25 1.75fr + 1.50fr blk & ultra 1.40 4.50
Nos. B79-B84 (6) 4.23 12.28
Set, never hinged 14.00

Souvenir Sheet

SP26

Wmk. 110

1937, July 25 **Engr.** *Perf. 13*
B85 SP26 Sheet of 2 2.25 7.00
Never hinged 7.00
a. 2fr red brown, single stamp 85 2.75

National Philatelic Exposition at Dudelange on July 25-26.

Sold for 5fr per sheet, of which 1fr was for the aid of the exposition.

Portrait of St. Willibrord — SP28

St. Willibrord, after a Miniature — SP29

Abbey at Echternach — SP30

Designs: No, B87, The Rathaus at Echternach. No. B88, Pavilion in Abbey Park, Echternach. No. B91, Dancing Procession in Honor of St. Willibrord.

Perf. 14x13, 13x14

1938, June 5 Engr. Unwmk.

B86	SP28	35c	+ 10c dk bl grn	15	*40*
B87	SP28	70c	+ 10c ol gray	40	*42*
B88	SP28	1.25fr	+ 25c brn car	85	*1.25*
B89	SP29	1.75fr	+ 50c sl bl	1.40	1.75
B90	SP30	3fr	+ 2fr vio brn	4.75	5.25
B91	SP30	5fr	+ 5fr dk vio	4.75	5.25
			Nos. B86-B91 (6)	12.30	14.32
			Set, never hinged	47.50	

12th centenary of the death of St. Willibrord. The surtax was used for the restoration of the ancient Abbey at Echternach.

Grand Duke Sigismond — SP32

Prince Jean — SP33

1938, Dec. 1 Photo. *Perf. 11½*

B92	SP32	10c	+ 5c lil & blk	15	15
B93	SP32	35c	+ 10c grn & blk	15	15
B94	SP32	70c	+ 20c buff & blk	18	*42*
B95	SP32	1fr	+ 25c red org & blk	1.50	*4.00*
B96	SP32	1.25fr	+ 75c gray bl & blk	1.50	*4.00*
B97	SP32	1.75fr	+ 1.50fr bl & blk	1.75	*5.75*
			Nos. B92-B97 (6)	5.23	*14.47*
			Set, never hinged	20.00	

1939, Dec. 1 Litho. *Perf. 14x13*

Designs: Nos. B99, B102, Prince Felix. Nos. B100, B103, Grand Duchess Charlotte.

B98	SP33	10c	+ 5c red brn, *buff*	15	20
B99	SP33	35c	+ 10c sl grn, *buff*	15	45
B100	SP33	70c	+ 20c blk, *buff*	18	*90*
B101	SP33	1fr	+ 25c red org, *buff*	1.75	*8.00*
B102	SP33	1.25fr	+ 75c vio brn, *buff*	2.25	*8.75*
B103	SP33	1.75fr	+ 1.50fr lt bl, *buff*	5.00	*20.00*
			Nos. B98-B103 (6)	9.48	*38.30*
			Set, never hinged	32.50	

See No. 217 (souvenir sheet).

Allegory of Medicinal Baths — SP36

1940, Mar. 1 Photo. *Perf. 11½*

B104	SP36	2fr	+ 50c gray, blk & slate grn	1.00	*6.00*
			Never hinged	2.50	

Stamps of 1944, type A37, surcharged "+50C," "+5F" or "+15F" in black, were sold only in canceled condition, affixed to numbered folders. The surtax was for the benefit of Luxembourg evacuees. Value for folder, $15.

Homage to France SP37

Thanks to: No. B118, Russia. No. B119, Britannia. No. B120, America.

1945, Mar. 1 Engr. *Perf. 13*

B117	SP37	60c	+ 1.40fr dp grn	15	15
B118	SP37	1.20fr	+ 1.80fr red	15	15
B119	SP37	2.50fr	+ 3.50fr dp bl	15	20
B120	SP37	4.20fr	+ 4.80fr dp vio	15	20
			Set value	38	60
			Set, never hinged	70	

Issued to honor the Allied Nations. Exist imperf. Value, set $60.

Statue Carried in Procession SP41

Statue of Our Lady "Patrona Civitatis" SP42

"Our Lady of Luxembourg" SP43

Cathedral Faade SP44

Altar with Statue of Madonna — SP45

1945, June 4

B121	SP41	60c	+ 40c grn	15	25
B122	SP42	1.20fr	+ 80c red	15	25
B123	SP43	2.50fr	+ 2.50fr dp bl	15	*1.10*

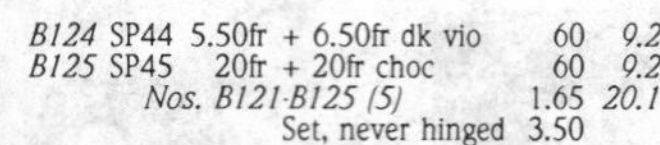

B124	SP44	5.50fr	+ 6.50fr dk vio	60	*9.25*
B125	SP45	20fr	+ 20fr choc	60	*9.25*
			Nos. B121-B125 (5)	1.65	*20.10*
			Set, never hinged	3.50	

Exist imperf. Value, set $52.50.

Souvenir Sheet

"Our Lady of Luxembourg" — SP46

1945, Sept. 30 Engr. *Imperf.*

B126	SP46	50fr	+ 50fr blk	1.10	*50.00*
			Never hinged	1.90	

Young Fighters SP47

Refugee Mother and Children SP48

Political Prisoner SP49

Executed Civilian SP50

1945, Dec. 20 Photo. *Perf. 11½*

B127	SP47	20c	+ 30c sl grn & buff	15	*80*
B128	SP48	1.50fr	+ 1fr brn red & buff	15	*80*
B129	SP49	3.50fr	+ 3.50fr bl, dp bl & buff	18	*5.75*
B130	SP50	5fr	+ 10fr brn, dk brn & buff	16	*5.75*
			Set value	48	
			Set, never hinged	1.25	

Souvenir Sheet

1946, Jan. 30 Unwmk. *Perf. 11½*

B131	Sheet of 4	8.00	*225.00*
	Never hinged	15.00	
a.	SP47 2.50fr + 2.50fr sl grn & buff	2.00	*45.00*
b.	SP48 3.50fr + 6.50fr brn red & buff	2.00	*45.00*
c.	SP49 5fr + 15fr bl, dp bl & buff	2.00	*45.00*
d.	SP50 20fr + 20fr brn, dk brn & buff	2.00	*45.00*

Tribute to Luxembourg's heroes and martyrs. The surtax was for the National Welfare Fund.

Souvenir Sheet

Old Rolling Mill, Dudelange — SP52

1946, July 28 Engr. & Typo.

B132	SP52	50fr	brn & dk bl, *buff*	5.00	*15.00*
			Never hinged	12.00	

National Postage Stamp Exhibition, Dudelange, July 28-29, 1946. The sheets sold for 55fr.

Jean l'Aveugle — SP53

1946, Dec. 5 Photo.

B133	SP53	60c	+ 40c dk grn	15	*40*
B134	SP53	1.50fr	+ 50c brn red	15	*55*
B135	SP53	3.50fr	+ 3.50fr dp bl	55	*4.50*
B136	SP53	5fr	+ 10fr sepia	28	*3.75*
			Set, never hinged	2.25	

600th anniv. of the death of Jean l'Aveugle (John the Blind), Count of Luxembourg.

Ruins of St. Willibrord Basilica — SP54

Twelfth Century Miniature of St. Willibrord SP59

Designs: #B138, Statue of Abbot Jean Bertels. #B139, Emblem of Echternach Abbey. #B140, Ruins of the Basilica's Interior. #B141, St. Irmine and Pepin of Hersta Holding Model of the Abbey.

Perf. 13x14, 14x13

1947, May 25 Engr.

B137	SP54	20c	+ 10c blk	20	25
B138	SP54	60c	+ 10c dk grn	35	45
B139	SP54	75c	+ 25c dk car	50	70
B140	SP54	1.50fr	+ 50c dk brn	65	70
B141	SP54	3.50fr	+ 2.50fr dk bl	1.25	*3.00*
B142	SP59	25fr	+ 25fr dk pur	14.00	*22.50*
			Nos. B137-B142 (6)	16.95	*27.60*
			Set, never hinged	37.50	

The surtax was to aid in restoring the Basilica of Saint Willibrord at Echternach.

Michel Lentz SP60

Edmond de La Fontaine (Dicks) SP61

1947, Dec. 4 Photo. *Perf. 11½*

B143	SP60	60c	+ 40c sep & buff	25	80
B144	SP60	1.50fr	+ 50c dp plum & buff	25	80
B145	SP60	3.50fr	+ 3.50fr dp bl & gray	2.25	*7.25*
B146	SP60	10fr	+ 5fr dk grn & gray	2.25	*7.25*
			Set, never hinged	11.00	

1948, Nov. 18

B147	SP61	60c	+ 40c brn & pale bis	20	55
B148	SP61	1.50fr	+ 50c brn car & buff	30	60
B149	SP61	3.50fr	+ 3.50fr dp bl & gray	3.75	*9.25*

B150 SP61 10fr + 5fr dk grn & gray 3.75 *9.25*
Set, never hinged 17.00

125th anniversary of the birth of Edmond de La Fontaine, poet and composer.

Type of Regular Issue of 1948
Souvenir Sheet

1949, Jan. 8 Unwmk. *Perf. 11½*
B151 Sheet of 3 55.00 70.00
Never hinged 82.50
a. A45 8fr + 3fr blue gray 15.00 24.00
b. A45 12fr + 5fr green 15.00 24.00
c. A45 15fr + 7fr brown 15.00 24.00

30th anniversary of Grand Duchess Charlotte's ascension to the throne. Border and dates "1919-1949" in gray.

Michel Rodange — SP62

1949, Dec. 5
B152 SP62 60c + 40c ol grn & gray 22 45
B153 SP62 2fr + 1fr dk vio & rose 2.00 *5.50*
B154 SP62 4fr + 2fr sl blk & gray 2.50 *6.75*
B155 SP62 10fr + 5fr brn & buff 3.25 *8.50*
Set, never hinged 20.00

Wards of the Nation
SP63 SP64

1950, June 24 Engr. *Perf. 12½x12*
B156 SP63 60c + 15c dk sl bl 30 40
B157 SP64 1fr + 20c dk car rose 70 90
B158 SP63 2fr + 30c red brn 70 90
B159 SP64 4fr + 75c dk bl 6.00 *12.00*
B160 SP63 8fr + 3fr blk 20.00 *40.00*
B161 SP64 10fr + 5fr lil rose 20.00 *40.00*
Nos. B156-B161 (6) 47.70 *94.20*
Set, never hinged 82.50

The surtax was for child welfare.

Jean A. Zinnen
SP65

Laurent Menager
SP66

1950, Dec. 5 Photo. *Perf. 11½*
B162 SP65 60c + 10c ind & gray 18 40
B163 SP65 2fr + 15c cer & buff 24 55
B164 SP65 4fr + 15c vio bl & bl gray 1.25 *5.00*
B165 SP65 8fr + 5fr dk brn & buff 8.00 *15.00*
Set, never hinged 25.00

1951, Dec. 5
Gray Background
B166 SP66 60c + 10c sepia 15 35
B167 SP66 2fr + 15c dl ol grn 24 55
B168 SP66 4fr + 15c blue 1.00 *3.00*
B169 SP66 8fr + 5fr vio brn 8.50 *24.00*
Set, never hinged 25.00

50th anniversary of the death of Laurent Menager, composer.

J. B. Fresez — SP67

Candlemas Singing — SP68

1952, Dec. 3
B170 SP67 60c + 15c dk bl grn & pale bl 15 35
B171 SP67 2fr + 25c chnt brn & buff 20 55
B172 SP67 4fr + 25c dk vio bl & gray 1.10 *3.50*
B173 SP67 8fr + 4.75fr dp plum & lil gray 8.25 *24.00*
Set, never hinged 30.00

1953, Dec. 3

Designs: 80c+20c, 4fr+50c, Procession with ratchets. 1.20fr+30c, 7fr+3.35fr, Breaking Easter eggs.

B174 SP68 25c + 15c red org & dp car 15 18
B175 SP68 80c + 20c vio brn & bl gray 15 18
B176 SP68 1.20fr + 30c bl grn & ol grn 25 70
B177 SP68 2fr + 25c brn car & brn 15 35
B178 SP68 4fr + 50c grnsh bl & vio bl 1.90 *4.25*
B179 SP68 7fr + 3.35fr vio & pur 4.75 *12.00*
Nos. B174-B179 (6) 7.35 *17.66*
Set, never hinged 19.00

The surtax was for the National Welfare Fund of Grand Duchess Charlotte.

Clay Censer and Whistle — SP69

Toys for St. Nicholas Day — SP70

Designs: 80c+20c, 4fr+50c, Sheep and bass drum. 1.20fr+30c, 7fr+3.45fr, Merry-go-round horses. 2fr+25c, As No. B180.

1954, Dec. 3
B180 SP69 25c + 5c car lake & cop brn 15 16
B181 SP69 80c + 20c dk gray 15 16
B182 SP69 1.20fr + 30c dk bl grn & cr 32 65
B183 SP69 2fr + 25c brn & ocher 15 32
B184 SP69 4fr + 50c brt bl 2.00 *3.25*
B185 SP69 7fr + 3.45fr pur 5.75 *12.00*
Nos. B180-B185 (6) 8.52 *16.54*
Set, never hinged 20.00

1955, Dec. 5 Unwmk. *Perf. 11½*

Designs: 80c+20c, 4fr+50c, Christ child and lamb (Christmas). 1.20fr+30c, 7fr+3.45fr, Star, crown and cake (Epiphany).

B186 SP70 25c + 5c sal & dk car 15 15
B187 SP70 80c + 20c gray & gray blk 15 15
B188 SP70 1.20fr + 30c ol grn & sl grn 35 60
B189 SP70 2fr + 25c buff & dk brn 25 20
B190 SP70 4fr + 50c lt bl & brt bl 1.40 *2.75*
B191 SP70 7fr + 3.45fr rose vio & cl 6.00 *12.00*
Nos. B186-B191 (6) 8.30 *15.85*
Set, never hinged 18.00

Arms of Echternach — SP71

Arms: 80c+20c, 4fr+50c, Esch-sur-Alzette. 1.20fr+30c, 7fr+3.45fr, Grevenmacher.

1956, Dec. 5 Photo.
Arms in Original Colors
B192 SP71 25c + 5c blk & sal pink 15 25
B193 SP71 80c + 20c ultra & yel 15 25
B194 SP71 1.20fr + 30c ultra & gray 22 40
B195 SP71 2fr + 25c blk & buff 15 25
B196 SP71 4fr + 50c ultra & lt bl 1.10 *3.25*
B197 SP71 7fr + 3.45fr ultra & pale vio 3.00 *8.75*
Nos. B192-B197 (6) 4.77 *13.15*
Set, never hinged 12.00

1957, Dec. 4 Unwmk. *Perf. 11½*

Arms: 25c+5c, 2fr+25c, Luxembourg. 80c+20c, 4fr+50c, Mersch. 1.20fr+30c, 7fr+3.45fr, Vianden.

Arms in Original Colors
B198 SP71 25c + 5c ultra & org 15 22
B199 SP71 80c + 20c blk & lem 15 22
B200 SP71 1.20fr + 30c ultra & lt bl grn 22 32
B201 SP71 2fr + 25c ultra & pale brn 15 22
B202 SP71 4fr + 50c blk & pale vio bl 45 70
B203 SP71 7fr + 3.45fr ultra & rose lil 3.00 4.50
Nos. B198-B203 (6) 4.12 6.18
Set, never hinged 6.50

1958, Dec. 3 *Perf. 11½*

Arms: 30c+10c, 2.50fr+50c, Capellen. 1fr+25c, 5fr+50c, Diekirch. 1.50fr+25c, 8.50fr+4.60fr, Redange.

Arms in Original Colors
B204 SP71 30c + 10c blk & pink 15 15
B205 SP71 1fr + 25c ultra & buff 15 15
B206 SP71 1.50fr + 25c ultra & pale grn 15 24
B207 SP71 2.50fr + 50c blk & gray 15 15
B208 SP71 5fr + 50c ultra 40 60
B209 SP71 8.50fr + 4.60fr ultra & lil 2.25 *4.75*
Nos. B204-B209 (6) 3.25 *6.04*
Set, never hinged 7.50

1959, Dec. 2

Arms: 30c+10c, 2.50fr+50c, Clervaux. 1fr+25c, 5fr+50c, Remich. 1.50fr+25c, 8.50fr+4.60fr, Wiltz.

Arms in Original Colors
B210 SP71 30c + 10c ultra & pink 15 15
B211 SP71 1fr + 25c ultra & pale lem 15 15
B212 SP71 1.50fr + 25c blk & pale grn 15 20
B213 SP71 2.50fr + 50c ultra & pale fawn 15 15
B214 SP71 5fr + 50c ultra & lt bl 40 75
B215 SP71 8.50fr + 4.60fr blk & pale vio 1.90 *3.75*
Nos. B210-B215 (6) 2.90 *5.15*
Set, never hinged 6.00

Catalogue values for unused stamps in this section, from this point to the end of the section, are for Never Hinged items.

Princess Marie-Astrid
SP72

Prince Jean
SP73

Designs: 1fr+25c, 5fr+50c, Princess in party dress. 1.50fr+25c, 8.50fr+4.60fr, Princess with book.

1960, Dec. 5 Photo. *Perf. 11½*
B216 SP72 30c + 10c brn & lt bl 15 15
B217 SP72 1fr + 25c brn & pink 15 15
B218 SP72 1.50fr + 25c brn & lt bl 20 20
B219 SP72 2.50fr + 50c brn & yel 15 15
B220 SP72 5fr + 50c brn & pale lil 1.25 1.25
B221 SP72 8.50fr + 4.60fr brn & pale ol 4.50 4.25
Nos. B216-B221 (6) 6.40 6.15

Type of 1960

Prince Henri: 30c+10c, 2.50fr+50c, Infant in long dress. 1fr+25c, 5fr+50c, Informal portrait. 1.50fr+25c, 8.50fr+ 4.60fr, In dress suit.

1961, Dec. 4 Unwmk. *Perf. 11½*
B222 SP72 30c + 10c brn & brt pink 15 15
B223 SP72 1fr + 25c brn & lt vio 15 15
B224 SP72 1.50fr + 25c brn & sal 15 15
B225 SP72 2.50fr + 50c brn & pale grn 15 15
B226 SP72 5fr + 50c brn & cit 32 32
B227 SP72 8.50fr + 4.60fr brn & gray 1.75 1.75
Nos. B222-B227 (6) 2.67 2.67

1962, Dec. 3 Photo. *Perf. 11½*

Designs: Different portraits of the twins Prince Jean and Princess Margaretha. Nos. B228 and B233 are horizontal.

Inscriptions and Portraits in Dark Brown
B228 SP73 30c + 10c org yel 15 15
B229 SP73 1fr + 25c lt bl 15 15
B230 SP73 1.50fr + 25c pale ol 15 15
B231 SP73 2.50fr + 50c rose 15 15
B232 SP73 5fr + 50c lt yel grn 24 24
B233 SP73 8.50fr + 4.60fr lil gray 2.00 2.00
Nos. B228-B233 (6) 2.84 2.84

St. Roch, Patron of Bakers — SP74

Three Towers — SP75

Patron Saints: 1fr+25c, St. Anne, tailors. 2fr+25c, St. Eloi, smiths. 3fr+50c, St. Michael, shopkeepers. 6fr+50c, St. Bartholomew, butchers. St. Theobald, seven crafts.

1963, Dec. 2 Unwmk. *Perf. 11½*
Multicolored Design
B234 SP74 50c + 10c pale lil 15 15
B235 SP74 1fr + 25c tan 15 15
B236 SP74 2fr + 25c lt grnsh bl 15 15
B237 SP74 3fr + 50c lt bl 15 22
B238 SP74 6fr + 50c buff 70 80
B239 SP74 10fr + 5.90fr pale yel grn 80 95
Nos. B234-B239 (6) 2.10 2.42

1964, Dec. 7 Photo. *Perf. 11½*

Children's paintings: 1fr+25c, 6fr+50c, Grand Duke Adolphe Bridge, horiz. 2fr+25c, 10fr+5.90fr, The Lower City.

B240 SP75 50c + 10c multi 15 15
B241 SP75 1fr + 25c multi 15 15
B242 SP75 2fr + 25c multi 15 30
a. Value omitted *300.00*
B243 SP75 3fr + 50c multi 15 30
B244 SP75 6fr + 50c multi 70 1.50
B245 SP75 10fr + 5.90fr multi 80 1.50
Nos. B240-B245 (6) 2.10 3.90

The Roman Lady of Titelberg — SP76

Fairy Tales of Luxembourg: 1fr+25c, Schäppchen, the Huntsman. 2fr+25c, The Witch of Koerich. 3fr+50c, The Gnomes of Schoenfels. 6fr+50c, Tollchen, Watchman of Hesperange. 10fr+5.90fr, The Old Spinster of Heispelt.

1965, Dec. 6 Photo. *Perf. 11½*
B246 SP76 50c + 10c multi 15 15
B247 SP76 1fr + 25c multi 15 15
B248 SP76 2fr + 25c multi 15 15
B249 SP76 3fr + 50c multi 15 20
B250 SP76 6fr + 50c multi 48 90
B251 SP76 10fr + 5.90fr multi 85 1.40
Nos. B246-B251 (6) 1.93 2.95

Fairy Tale Type of 1965

Fairy Tales of Luxembourg: 50c+10c, The Veiled Matron of Wormeldange. 1.50fr+25c, Jekel, Warden of the Wark. 2fr+25c, The Black Man of Vianden. 3fr+50c, The Gracious Fairy of Rosport. 6fr+1fr, The Friendly Shepherd of Donkolz. 13fr+6.90fr, The Little Sisters of Trois-Vièrges.

1966, Dec. 6 Photo. *Perf. 11½*

B252 SP76 50c + 10c multi 15 15
B253 SP76 1.50fr + 25c multi 15 15
B254 SP76 2fr + 25c multi 15 15
B255 SP76 3fr + 50c multi 15 30
B256 SP76 6fr + 1fr multi 28 60
B257 SP76 13fr + 6.90fr multi 85 1.90
Nos. B252-B257 (6) 1.73 3.25

Prince Guillaume SP77

Castle of Berg SP78

Portraits: 1.50fr+25c, Princess Margaretha. 2fr+25c, Prince Jean. 3fr+50c, Prince Henri as Boy Scout. 6fr+1fr, Princess Marie-Astrid.

1967, Dec. 6 Photo. *Perf. 11½*

B258 SP77 50c + 10c yel & brn 15 15
B259 SP77 1.50fr + 25c gray bl & brn 15 15
B260 SP77 2fr + 25c pale rose & brn 15 15
B261 SP77 3fr + 50c lt ol & brn 32 60
B262 SP77 6fr + 1fr lt vio & brn 45 60
B263 SP78 13fr + 6.90fr multi 60 1.40
Nos. B258-B263 (6) 1.82 3.05

Medico-professional Institute at Cap — SP79

Deaf-mute Child Imitating Bird — SP80

Handicapped Children: 2fr+25c, Blind child holding candle. 3fr+50c, Nurse supporting physically handicapped child. 6fr+1fr, Cerebral palsy victim. 13fr+6.90fr, Mentally disturbed child.

1968, Dec. 5 Photo. *Perf. 11½*

Designs and Inscriptions in Dark Brown

B264 SP79 50c + 10c lt bl 15 15
B265 SP80 1.50fr + 25c lt grn 15 15
B266 SP80 2fr + 25c yel 15 15
B267 SP80 3fr + 50c bl 16 24
B268 SP80 6fr + 1fr buff 50 1.10
B269 SP80 13fr + 6.90fr pink 75 1.50
Nos. B264-B269 (6) 1.86 3.29

Vianden Castle SP81

Children of Bethlehem SP82

Castles in Luxembourg: 1.50fr+25c, Lucilinburhuc. 2fr+25c, Bourglinster. 3fr+50c, Hollenfels. 6fr+1fr, Ansembourg. 13fr+6.90fr, Beaufort.

1969, Dec. 8 Photo. *Perf. 11½*

B270 SP81 50c + 10c multi 15 15
B271 SP81 1.50fr + 25c multi 15 15
B272 SP81 2fr + 25c multi 15 15
B273 SP81 3fr + 50c multi 15 30
B274 SP81 6fr + 1fr multi 60 1.00
B275 SP81 13fr + 6.90fr multi 85 1.50
Nos. B270-B275 (6) 2.05 3.25

1970, Dec. 7 Photo. *Perf. 11½*

Castles in Luxembourg: 50c+10c, Clervaux. 1.50fr+25c, Septfontaines. 2fr+25c, Bourscheid. 3fr+50c, Esch-sur-Sure. 6fr+1fr, Larochette. 13fr+6.90fr, Brandenbourg.

B276 SP81 50c + 10c multi 15 15
B277 SP81 1.50fr + 25c multi 15 15
B278 SP81 2fr + 25c multi 15 15
B279 SP81 3fr + 50c multi 15 30
B280 SP81 6fr + 1fr multi 60 1.00
B281 SP81 13fr + 6.90fr multi 85 1.75
Nos. B276-B281 (6) 2.05 3.50

The surtax on Nos. B180-B281 was for charitable purposes.

1971, Dec. 6 Photo. *Perf. 11½*

Wooden Statues from Crèche of Beaufort Church: 1.50fr+25c, Shepherds. 3fr+50c, Nativity. 8fr+1fr, Herdsmen. 18fr+6.50fr, King offering gift.

Sculptures in Shades of Brown

B282 SP82 1fr + 25c lilac 15 15
B283 SP82 1.50fr + 25c olive 15 15
B284 SP82 3fr + 50c gray 16 35
B285 SP82 8fr + 1fr lt ultra 1.10 1.50
B286 SP82 18fr + 6.50fr grn 1.90 4.00
Nos. B282-B286 (5) 3.46 6.15

The surtax was for various charitable organizations.

Angel — SP83

Sts. Anne and Joachim — SP84

Stained Glass Windows, Luxembourg Cathedral: 1.50fr+25c, St. Joseph. 3fr+50c, Virgin and Child. 8fr+1fr, People of Bethlehem. 18fr+6.50fr, Angel facing left.

1972, Dec. 4

B287 SP83 1fr + 25c multi 15 15
B288 SP83 1.50fr + 25c multi 15 15
B289 SP83 3fr + 50c multi 15 15
B290 SP83 8fr + 1fr multi 95 1.00
B291 SP83 18fr + 6.50fr multi 2.25 3.75
Nos. B287-B291 (5) 3.65 5.20

Surtax was for charitable purposes.

1973, Dec. 5 Photo. *Perf. 11½*

Sculptures: 3fr+25c, Mary meeting Elizabeth. 4fr+50c, Virgin and Child and a King. 8fr+1fr, Shepherds. 15fr+7fr, St. Joseph holding candle. Designs from 16th century reredos, Hermitage of Hachiville.

B292 SP84 1fr + 25c multi 15 15
B293 SP84 3fr + 25c multi 15 16
B294 SP84 4fr + 50c multi 24 70
B295 SP84 8fr + 1fr multi 1.10 2.00
B296 SP84 15fr + 7fr multi 1.90 3.75
Nos. B292-B296 (5) 3.54 6.76

Annunciation SP85

Crucifixion SP86

Designs: 3fr+25c, Visitation. 4fr+50c, Nativity. 8fr+1fr, Adoration of the King. 15fr+7fr, Presentation at the Temple. Designs of Nos. B297-B301 are from miniatures in the "Codex Aureus Epternacensis" (Gospel from Echternach Abbey). The Crucifixion is from the carved ivory cover of the Codex, by the Master of Echternach, c. 983-991.

1974, Dec. 5 Photo. *Perf. 11½*

B297 SP85 1fr + 25c multi 15 15
B298 SP85 3fr + 25c multi 15 18
B299 SP85 4fr + 50c multi 20 35
B300 SP85 8fr + 1fr multi 1.10 1.75
B301 SP85 15fr + 7fr multi 1.75 2.75
Nos. B297-B301 (5) 3.35 5.18

Souvenir Sheet

Photogravure & Engraved

Perf. 13½

B302 SP86 20fr + 10fr multi 3.50 5.00

50th anniversary of Caritas issues. No. B302 contains one 34x42mm stamp.

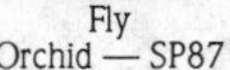

Fly Orchid — SP87

Lilies of the Valley — SP88

Flowers: 3fr+25c, Pyramidal orchid. 4fr+50c, Marsh hellebore. 8fr+1fr, Pasqueflower. 15fr+7fr, Bee orchid.

1975, Dec. 4 Photo. *Perf. 11½*

B303 SP87 1fr + 25c multi 15 15
B304 SP87 3fr + 25c multi 16 18
B305 SP87 4fr + 50c multi 24 35
B306 SP87 8fr + 1fr multi 1.00 1.40
B307 SP87 15fr + 7fr multi 2.25 3.00
Nos. B303-B307 (5) 3.80 5.08

The surtax on Nos. B303-B317 was for various charitable organizations.

1976, Dec. 6

Flowers: 2fr+25c, Gentian. 5fr+25c, Narcissus. 6fr+50c, Red hellebore. 12fr+1fr, Late spider orchid. 20fr+8fr, Two-leafed squill.

B308 SP87 2fr + 25c multi 15 15
B309 SP87 5fr + 25c multi 22 30
B310 SP87 6fr + 50c multi 30 60
B311 SP87 12fr + 1fr multi 65 1.10
B312 SP87 20fr + 8fr multi 2.00 2.75
Nos. B308-B312 (5) 3.32 4.90

1977, Dec. 5 Photo. *Perf. 11½*

Flowers: 5fr+25c, Columbine. 6fr+50c, Mezereon. 12fr+1fr, Early spider orchid. 20fr+8fr, Spotted orchid.

B313 SP88 2fr + 25c multi 15 15
B314 SP88 5fr + 25c multi 15 20
B315 SP88 6fr + 50c multi 22 40
B316 SP88 12fr + 1fr multi 95 1.75
B317 SP88 20fr + 8fr multi 1.90 2.75
Nos. B313-B317 (5) 3.37 5.25

St. Matthew — SP89

Spring — SP90

Behind-glass Paintings, 19th Century: 5fr+25c, St. Mark. 6fr+50c, Nativity. 12fr+1fr, St. Luke. 20fr+8fr, St. John.

1978, Dec. 5 Photo. *Perf. 11½*

B318 SP89 2fr + 25c multi 15 15
B319 SP89 5fr + 25c multi 24 32
B320 SP89 6fr + 50c multi 25 35
B321 SP89 12fr + 1fr multi 65 90
B322 SP89 20fr + 8fr multi 1.90 2.50
Nos. B318-B322 (5) 3.19 4.22

Surtax was for charitable organizations.

1979, Dec. 5 Photo. *Perf. 12*

Behind-glass Paintings, 19th Century: 5fr+25c, Summer. 6fr+50c, Charity. 12fr+1fr, Autumn. 20fr+8fr, Winter.

B323 SP90 2fr + 25c multi 15 15
B324 SP90 5fr + 25c multi 25 25
B325 SP90 6fr + 50c multi 30 30
B326 SP90 12fr + 1fr multi 85 85
B327 SP90 20fr + 8fr multi 1.75 1.75
Nos. B323-B327 (5) 3.30 3.30

St. Martin — SP91

Behind-glass Paintings, 19th Century: 6fr+50c, St. Nicholas. 8fr+1fr, Madonna and Child. 30fr+1fr, St. George the Martyr.

1980, Dec. 5 Photo. *Perf. 11½*

B328 SP91 4fr + 50c multi 20 20
B329 SP91 6fr + 50c multi 25 25
B330 SP91 8fr + 1fr multi 45 45
B331 SP91 30fr + 10fr multi 1.75 1.75

Surtax was for charitable organizations.

Arms of Petange SP92

Nativity, by Otto van Veen (1556-1629) SP93

1981, Dec. 4 Photo.

Granite Paper

B332 SP92 4fr + 50c shown 22 28
B333 SP92 6fr + 50c Larochette 30 35
B334 SP93 8fr + 1fr shown 50 60
B335 SP92 16fr + 2fr Stadtbredimus 90 1.10
B336 SP92 35fr + 12fr Weiswampach 2.25 2.75
Nos. B332-B336 (5) 4.17 5.08

Surtax was for charitable organizations.

1982, Dec. 6 Photo. *Perf. 11½*

Design: 8fr+1fr, Adoration of the Shepherds, stained-glass window, by Gust Zanter, Hoscheid Parish Church.

Granite Paper

B337 SP92 4fr + 50c Bettembourg 18 16
B338 SP92 6fr + 50c Frisange 35 30
B339 SP93 8fr + 1fr multi 45 40
B340 SP92 16fr + 2fr Mamer 90 80
B341 SP92 35fr + 12fr Heinerscheid 2.25 2.00
Nos. B337-B341 (5) 4.13 3.66

Surtax was for charitable organizations.

1983, Dec. 5 Photo.

B342 SP92 4fr + 1fr Winseler 20 20
B343 SP92 7fr + 1fr Beckerich 40 40
B344 SP93 10fr + 1fr Nativity 50 50
B345 SP92 16fr + 2fr Feulen 85 85
B346 SP92 40fr + 13fr Mertert 3.00 3.00
Nos. B342-B346 (5) 4.95 4.95

Surtax was for charitable organizations.

Inquisitive Child — SP94

Children Exhibiting Various Moods.

1984, Dec. 5 Photo.

B347 SP94 4fr + 1fr shown 20 18
B348 SP94 7fr + 1fr Daydreaming 45 40
B349 SP94 10fr + 1fr Nativity 55 50
B350 SP94 16fr + 2fr Sulking 95 85
B351 SP94 40fr + 13fr Admiring 3.25 3.00
Nos. B347-B351 (5) 5.40 4.93

Surtax was for charitable organizations.

1985, Dec. 5 Photo.

B352 SP94 4fr + 1fr Girl drawing 20 16
B353 SP94 7fr + 1fr Two boys 30 25
B354 SP94 10fr + 1fr Adoration of the Magi 40 32
B355 SP94 16fr + 2fr Fairy tale characters 1.00 85

B356	SP94	40fr + 13fr Embarrassed girl	2.75	2.25
		Nos. B352-B356 (5)	4.65	3.83

Surtax was for charitable organizations.

SP95

SP96

Book of Hours, France, c. 1550, Natl. Library — SP97

Christmas: illuminated text.

1986, Dec. 8 Photo. *Perf. 11½*

B357	SP95	6fr + 1fr Annunciation	38	30
B358	SP95	10fr + 1fr Angel appears to the Shepherds	55	45
B359	SP95	12fr + 2fr Nativity	70	58
B360	SP95	18fr + 2fr Adoration of the Magi	1.00	82
B361	SP95	20fr + 8fr Flight into Egypt	1.40	1.15
		Nos. B357-B361 (5)	4.03	3.30

Surtax for social work organizations.

1987, Dec. 1 Photo. *Perf. 12*

Christmas: illuminated text.

B362	SP96	6fr + 1fr Annunciation	40	40
B363	SP96	10fr + 1fr Visitation	62	62
B364	SP96	12fr + 2fr Adoration of the Magi	78	78
B365	SP96	18fr + 2fr Presentation in the Temple	1.15	1.15
B366	SP96	20fr + 8fr Flight into Egypt	1.60	1.60
		Nos. B362-B366 (5)	4.55	4.55

Surtax for charitable organizations.

1988, Dec. 5 Photo. *Perf. 11½*

Christmas: illuminated text.

B367	SP97	9fr +1fr Annunciation to the Shepherds	55	55
B368	SP97	12fr +2fr Adoration of the Magi	75	75
B369	SP97	18fr +2fr Virgin and Child	1.10	1.10
B370	SP97	20fr +8fr Pentecost	1.50	1.50

Surtax for charitable organizations.

Christmas SP98

Chapels: No. B371, St. Lambert and St. Blase, Fennange, vert. No. B372, St. Quirinus, Luxembourg. No. B373, St. Anthony the Hermit, Reisdorf, vert. No. B374, The Hermitage, Hachiville.

1989, Dec. 11 Photo. *Perf. 12x11½*

B371	SP98	9fr +1fr multi	50	50
B372	SP98	12fr +2fr multi	70	70
B373	SP98	18fr +3fr multi	1.10	1.10
B374	SP98	25fr +8fr multi	1.65	1.65

Surtax for social work.

1990, Nov. 26 Photo. *Perf. 11½*

Chapels: No. B375, Congregation of the Blessed Virgin Mary, Vianden, vert. No. B376, Our Lady, Echternach. No. B377, Our Lady, Consoler of the Afflicted, Grentzingen. B378, St. Pirmin, Kaundorf, vert.

B375	SP98	9fr +1fr multi	60	60
B376	SP98	12fr +2fr multi	85	85
B377	SP98	18fr +3fr multi	1.25	1.25
B378	SP98	25fr +8fr multi	2.00	2.00

Surtax for charitable organizations.

Chapels: No. B379, St. Donatus, Arsdorf, vert. No. B380, Our Lady of Sorrows, Brandenbourg. No. B381, Our Lady, Luxembourg. No. B382, The Hermitage, Wolwelange, vert.

1991, Dec. 9 Photo. *Perf. 11½*

B379	SP98	14fr +2fr multi	95	95
B380	SP98	14fr +2fr multi	95	95
B381	SP98	18fr +3fr multi	1.25	1.25
B382	SP98	22fr +7fr multi	1.75	1.75

Surtax used for philanthropic work.

Endangered Birds — SP99

Designs: No. B383, Hazel grouse. No. B384, Golden oriole, vert. 18fr+3fr, Black stork. 22fr+7fr, Red kite, vert.

1992, Dec. 7 Photo. *Perf. 11½*

B383	SP99	14fr +2fr multi	1.00	1.00
B384	SP99	14fr +2fr multi	1.00	1.00
B385	SP99	18fr +3fr multi	1.25	1.25
B386	SP99	22fr +7fr multi	1.75	1.75

Surtax for Luxembourg charitable organizations.

AIR POST STAMPS

Airplane over Luxembourg AP1

1931-33 Unwmk. Engr. *Perf. 12½*

C1	AP1	50c green ('33)	50	*1.10*
C2	AP1	75c dk brown	35	80
C3	AP1	1fr red	35	80
C4	AP1	1¼fr dk violet	35	80
C5	AP1	1¾fr dk blue	35	80
C6	AP1	3fr gray blk ('33)	50	*1.65*
		Nos. C1-C6 (6)	2.40	*5.95*
		Set, never hinged	6.00	

Air View of Mosel River AP2

Wing and View of Luxembourg AP3

Vianden Castle — AP4

1946, June 7 Photo. *Perf. 11½*

C7	AP2	1fr dk ol grn & gray	15	15
C8	AP3	2fr chnt brn & buff	15	15
C9	AP4	3fr sepia & brown	15	15
C10	AP2	4fr dp vio & gray vio	15	25
C11	AP3	5fr dp mag & buff	15	25
C12	AP4	6fr dk brown & gray	15	32
C13	AP2	10fr henna brn & buff	90	32
C14	AP3	20fr dk blue & cream	90	1.50
C15	AP4	50fr dk green & gray	1.75	1.50
		Nos. C7-C15 (9)	4.45	4.59
		Set, never hinged	8.00	

1852 and 1952 AP5

1952, May 24

Stamps in Gray and Dark Violet Brown

C16	AP5	80c olive grn	32	48
C17	AP5	2.50fr brt car	75	1.25
C18	AP5	4fr brt blue	1.50	2.75
C19	AP5	8fr brown red	27.50	*50.00*
C20	AP5	10fr dull brown	20.00	*42.50*
		Nos. C16-C20 (5)	50.07	*96.98*
		Set, never hinged	80.00	

Centenary of Luxembourg's postage stamps. Nos. C16-C18 were available at face, but complete sets sold for 45.30fr, which included admission to the CENTILUX exhibition.

POSTAGE DUE STAMPS

Coat of Arms — D1

1907 Unwmk. Typo. *Perf. 12½*

J1	D1	5c green & blk	15	15
J2	D1	10c green & blk	2.50	18
J3	D1	12½c green & blk	60	70
J4	D1	20c green & blk	60	45
J5	D1	25c green & blk	24.00	1.40
J6	D1	50c green & blk	60	1.40
J7	D1	1fr green & blk	30	*1.10*
		Nos. J1-J7 (7)	28.75	5.38

See Nos. J10-J22.

Nos. J3, J5 Surcharged

1920

J8	D1	15c on 12½c	2.75	2.25
J9	D1	30c on 25c	2.75	3.00

Arms Type of 1907

1921-35

J10	D1	5c green & red	30	30
J11	D1	10c green & red	30	30
J12	D1	20c green & red	45	30
J13	D1	25c green & red	45	30
J14	D1	30c green & red	50	55
J15	D1	35c green & red ('35)	1.10	30
J16	D1	50c green & red	50	55
J17	D1	60c green & red ('28)	85	30
J18	D1	70c green & red ('35)	1.10	30
J19	D1	75c green & red ('30)	85	25
J20	D1	1fr green & red	65	70
J21	D1	2fr green & red ('30)	1.50	2.00
J22	D1	3fr green & red ('30)	3.50	5.50
		Nos. J10-J22 (13)	12.05	11.65
		Set, never hinged	25.00	

D2

D3

1946-48 Photo. *Perf. 11½*

J23	D2	5c brt green	15	25
J24	D2	10c brt green	15	25
J25	D2	20c brt green	15	25
J26	D2	30c brt green	15	25
J27	D2	50c brt green	15	25
J28	D2	70c brt green	15	50
J29	D2	75c brt green ('48)	65	25
J30	D3	1fr carmine	15	25
J31	D3	1.50fr carmine	15	25
J32	D3	2fr carmine	15	25
J33	D3	3fr carmine	18	25
J34	D3	5fr carmine	50	40
J35	D3	10fr carmine	85	1.00
J36	D3	20fr carmine	2.50	5.00
		Nos. J23-J36 (14)	6.03	9.40
		Set, never hinged	12.00	

OFFICIAL STAMPS

Forged overprints on Nos. O1-O64 abound.

Regular Issues Overprinted Reading Diagonally Up or Down

Frankfort Print

Rouletted in Color except 2c

1875 Unwmk.

O1	A2	1c red brown	13.00	30.00
O2	A2	2c black	15.00	30.00
O3	A3	10c lilac	1,200.	900.00
O4	A3	12½c rose	350.00	450.00
O5	A3	20c gray brn	25.00	30.00
O6	A3	25c blue	150.00	100.00
O7	A3	25c ultra	900.00	800.00
O8	A3	30c lilac rose	26.00	*60.00*
O9	A3	40c pale org	135.00	160.00
a.		40c org red, thick paper	140.00	150.00
c.		As "a," thin paper	1,000.	825.00
O10	A4	1fr on 37½c bis	85.00	15.00

Double overprints exist on Nos. O1-O6, O8-O10.

Overprints reading diagonally down sell for more.

Inverted Overprint

O1a	A2	1c	100.00	160.00
O2a	A2	2c	110.00	175.00
O3a	A3	10c	1,600.	1,600.
O4a	A3	12½c	500.00	550.00
O5a	A3	20c	25.00	32.50
O6a	A3	25c	725.00	725.00
O7a	A3	25c	1,600.	1,350.
O8a	A3	30c	360.00	450.00
O9b	A3	40c pale orange	175.00	225.00
O10a	A4	1fr on 37½c	140.00	35.00

Luxembourg Print

1875-76 *Perf. 13*

O11	A2	1c red brown	10.00	20.00
O12	A2	2c black	12.50	20.00
O13	A2	4c green	90.00	175.00
O14	A2	5c yellow	50.00	90.00
a.		5c orange yellow	55.00	90.00
O15	A3	10c gray lilac	75.00	90.00
O16	A3	12½c rose	65.00	37.50
O17	A3	12½c lilac rose	140.00	125.00
O18	A3	25c blue	6.75	*35.00*
O19	A5	1fr on 37½c bis	37.50	60.00

Double overprints exist on Nos. O11-O15.

Inverted Overprint

O11a	A2	1c	40.00	*85.00*
O12a	A2	2c	135.00	175.00
O13a	A2	4c	150.00	200.00
O14b	A2	5c	450.00	600.00
O15a	A3	10c	140.00	175.00
O16a	A3	12½c	350.00	475.00
O17a	A3	12½c	350.00	475.00
O18a	A3	25c	110.00	150.00
O19a	A5	1fr on 37½c	175.00	250.00

Haarlem Print

1880 *Perf. 11½x12, 12½x12, 13½*

O22	A3	25c blue	3.00	4.00

Overprinted

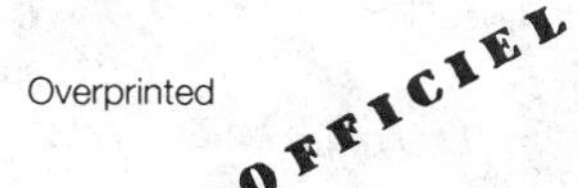

Frankfort Print

1878 *Rouletted in Color*

O23	A2	1c red brown	80.00	95.00
O25	A3	20c gray brn	125.00	125.00
O26	A3	30c lilac rose	525.00	500.00
O27	A3	40c orange	225.00	300.00
O28	A4	1fr on 37½c bis	400.00	90.00

Inverted Overprint

O23a	A2	1c	275.00	350.00
O25a	A3	20c	275.00	350.00
O26a	A3	30c	800.00	650.00
O27a	A3	40c	800.00	800.00
O28a	A4	1fr on 37½c	625.00	135.00

Luxembourg Print

1878-80 *Perf. 13*

O29	A2	1c red brown	575.00	675.00
O30	A2	2c black	150.00	200.00
O31	A2	4c green	165.00	165.00
O32	A2	5c yellow	350.00	350.00

O33	A3	10c gray lilac	350.00	375.00
O34	A3	12½c rose	65.00	75.00
O35	A3	25c blue	475.00	575.00

Inverted Overprint

O29a	A2	1c	90.00	140.00
O30a	A2	2c	13.00	20.00
O31a	A2	4c	100.00	125.00
O32a	A2	5c		
O33a	A3	10c	75.00	85.00
O34a	A3	12½c	425.00	500.00
O35a	A3	25c	650.00	750.00

Overprinted **S. P.**

Frankfort Print

1881 ***Rouletted in Color***

O39	A3	40c orange	30.00	57.50
a.		Inverted overprint	185.00	250.00

"S.P." are initials of "Service Public."

Luxembourg Print
Perf. 13

O40	A2	1c red brown	125.00	150.00
O41	A2	4c green	190.00	185.00
a.		Inverted overprint	225.00	
O42	A2	5c yellow	475.00	450.00
O43	A5	1fr on 37½c bis	24.00	35.00

Haarlem Print
Perf. 11½x12, 12½x12, 13½

O44	A2	1c yellow brn	6.75	8.00
O45	A2	2c black	8.00	8.00
O46	A2	5c yellow	110.00	140.00
a.		Inverted overprint	200.00	
O47	A3	10c gray lilac	110.00	140.00
O48	A3	12½c rose	200.00	225.00
O49	A3	20c gray brown	60.00	85.00
O50	A3	25c blue	65.00	85.00
O51	A3	30c dull rose	67.50	90.00

Stamps of the 1881 issue with overprint of type "d" were never issued.

Overprinted

S. P.
d

Perf. 11½x12, 12½x12, 12½, 13½

1882

O52	A6	1c gray lilac	40	45
a.		"S" omitted		
O53	A6	2c ol gray	40	45
O54	A6	4c ol bister	60	60
O55	A6	5c lt green	1.00	75
O56	A6	10c rose	20.00	18.00
O57	A6	12½c slate	3.50	2.75
O58	A6	20c orange	3.50	2.75
O59	A6	25c ultra	25.00	25.00
O60	A6	30c gray grn	7.50	9.00
O61	A6	50c bis brown	1.25	2.00
O62	A6	1fr pale vio	1.25	2.00
O63	A6	5fr brown org	19.00	22.50

Nos. O52-O63 exist without one or both periods, also with varying space between "S" and "P". Nine denominations exist with double overprint, six with inverted overprint.

Overprinted ***S. P.***

1883 ***Perf. 13½***

O64	A6	5fr brown org	*1,600.*	*1,200.*

Overprinted **S. P.**

Perf. 11, 11½, 11½x11, 12½

1891-93

O65	A7	10c carmine	32	30
a.		Sheet of 25	60.00	
O66	A7	12½c slate grn	8.00	5.50
O67	A7	20c orange	12.00	6.50
O68	A7	25c blue	40	35
a.		Sheet of 25	75.00	
O69	A7	30c olive grn	9.00	7.50
O70	A7	37½c green	9.00	9.00
O71	A7	50c brown	11.00	9.00
O72	A7	1fr dp vio	11.00	10.00
O73	A7	2½fr black	35.00	62.50
O74	A7	5fr lake	25.00	37.50

1895 ***Perf. 12½***

O75	A8	1c pearl gray	1.50	1.75
O76	A8	2c gray brn	1.50	1.75
O77	A8	4c olive bis	1.50	1.75
O78	A8	5c green	3.50	4.00
O79	A8	10c carmine	42.50	32.50

Nos. O66-O79 exist without overprint and perforated "OFFICIEL" through the stamp. Value for set, $25.

Nos. O65a and O68a were issued to commemorate the coronation of Duke Adolphe.

Regular Issue of 1906-26 Overprinted *Officiel*

1908-26 ***Perf. 11x11½, 12½***

O80	A9	1c gray	15	18
a.		Inverted overprint	110.00	
O81	A9	2c olive brn	15	16
O82	A9	4c bister	15	16
a.		Double overprint	125.00	
O83	A9	5c green	15	16
O84	A9	5c lilac ('26)	15	20
O85	A9	6c violet	15	16
O86	A9	7½c org ('19)	15	16
O87	A10	10c scarlet	24	32
O88	A10	12½c slate grn	24	32
O89	A10	15c orange brn	35	42
O90	A10	20c orange	35	60
O91	A10	25c ultra	35	32
O92	A10	30c olive grn	3.50	3.75
O93	A10	37½c green	60	60
O94	A10	50c brown	1.00	1.10
O95	A10	87½c dk blue	2.50	2.50
O96	A10	1fr violet	3.50	3.25
O97	A10	2½fr vermilion	42.50	42.50
O98	A10	5fr claret	42.50	42.50
		Nos. O80-O98 (19)	98.68	99.36

On Regular Issue of 1914-17

1915-17

O99	A11	10c lake	28	40
O100	A11	12½c dull grn	28	40
O101	A11	15c olive blk	28	40
O102	A11	17½c dp brn ('17)	28	40
O103	A11	25c ultra	28	40
O104	A11	30c bister	85	1.25
O105	A11	35c dk blue	28	40
O106	A11	37½c blk brn	28	40
O107	A11	40c orange	40	80
O108	A11	50c dk gray	40	80
O109	A11	62½c blue grn	40	80
O110	A11	87½c org ('17)	40	80
O111	A11	1fr orange brn	40	80
O112	A11	2½fr red	40	80
O113	A11	5fr dk violet	40	80
		Nos. O99-O113 (15)	5.61	9.65

On Regular Issues of 1921-26 in Black

1922-26 ***Perf. 11½, 11½x11, 12½***

O114	A12	2c brown	15	15
O115	A12	3c olive grn	15	15
O116	A12	6c violet	15	15
O117	A12	10c yellow grn	15	30
O118	A12	10c ol grn ('24)	15	28
O119	A12	15c brown ol	15	30
O120	A12	15c pale grn ('24)	15	28
O121	A12	15c dp org ('26)	15	25
O122	A12	20c dp orange	15	30
O123	A12	20c yel grn ('26)	15	25
O124	A12	25c dk green	15	30
O125	A12	30c car rose	15	30
O126	A12	40c brown org	15	30
O127	A12	50c dp blue	16	40
O128	A12	50c red ('24)	15	28
O129	A12	75c red	16	40
O130	A12	75c dp bl ('24)	16	40
O131	A12	80c black	4.25	10.00
O132	A13	1fr carmine	32	80
O133	A14	2fr indigo	2.75	6.00
O134	A14	2fr dk brn ('26)	1.65	4.50
O135	A15	5fr dk vio	16.00	37.50
		Nos. O114-O135 (22)	27.55	63.59

On Regular Issues of 1921-26 in Red
Perf. 11, 11½, 11½x11, 12½

1922-34

O136	A12	80c blk, perf. 11½	15	32
O137	A13	1fr dk bl, perf. 11½ ('26)	22	50
O138	A14	2fr ind, perf. 11½x11	40	1.10
O139	A17	3fr dk bl & bl, perf. 11	2.50	2.50
a.		Perf. 11½	80	1.25
b.		Perf. 12½	1.50	2.00
O140	A15	5fr dk vio, perf. 11½x11	3.50	6.75
a.		Perf. 12½ ('34)	25.00	25.00
O141	A16	10fr blk, perf. 11½	9.25	19.00
a.		Perf. 12½	25.00	25.00
		Nos. O136-O141 (6)	16.02	30.17

On Regular Issue of 1926-35

1926-27 ***Perf. 12***

O142	A18	5c dk violet	15	22
O143	A18	10c olive grn	15	22
O144	A18	20c orange	15	22
O145	A18	25c yellow grn	15	22
O146	A18	25c blk brn ('27)	30	48
O147	A18	30c yel grn ('27)	60	1.00
O148	A18	40c olive gray	15	22
O149	A18	50c red brown	15	22
O150	A18	65c black brn	15	22
O151	A18	75c rose	15	22
O152	A18	75c bis brn ('27)	38	65
O153	A18	80c bister brn	18	32
O154	A18	90c rose ('27)	30	48
O155	A18	1fr black	18	32
O156	A18	1¼fr dk bl	15	22
O157	A18	1½fr dp bl ('27)	48	80
		Nos. O142-O157 (16)	3.77	6.03

Type of Regular Issue, 1926-35, Overprinted *Officiel*

1928-35 **Wmk. 213**

O158	A18	5c dk vio	15	20
O159	A18	10c olive grn	15	20
O160	A18	15c blk ('30)	20	60
O161	A18	20c orange	40	60
O162	A18	25c violet brn	40	60
O163	A18	30c yellow grn	42	65
O164	A18	30c gray vio ('30)	20	60
O165	A18	35c yel grn ('30)	20	60
O166	A18	35c gray vio	42	65
O167	A18	40c ol gray	42	65
O168	A18	50c red brn	40	60
O169	A18	60c blue grn	40	60
O170	A18	70c bl vio ('35)	3.25	6.50
O171	A18	75c bister brn	40	60
O172	A18	90c rose	42	65
O173	A18	1fr black	42	65
O174	A18	1fr rose ('30)	20	60
O175	A18	1¼fr yel ('30)	1.65	4.00
O176	A18	1¼fr bl grn ('31)	1.65	4.00
O177	A18	1½fr dp blue	42	65
O178	A18	1¾fr dk bl ('30)	20	60
		Nos. O158-O178 (21)	12.37	24.80

Type of Regular Issues of 1928-31 Overprinted Like Nos. O80-O98

1928-31 **Wmk. 216** ***Perf. 11½***

O179	A19	2fr black	42	95

Wmk. 110 ***Perf. 12½***

O180	A21	20fr dp grn ('31)	2.00	4.50

No. 198 Overprinted Like Nos. O80-O98

1934 **Unwmk.** ***Perf. 14x13½***

O181	A22	5fr blue green	1.50	3.00

Type of Regular Issue of 1935 Overprinted Like Nos. O158-O178 in Red

1935 **Wmk. 247** ***Perf. 12½x12***

O182	A23	10fr green	1.50	3.50

OCCUPATION STAMPS

Issued under German Occupation

Stamps of Germany, 1933-36, Overprinted in Black

Luxemburg

1940 **Wmk. 237** ***Perf. 14***

N1	A64	3pf olive bis	18	*48*
N2	A64	4pf dull blue	18	*52*
N3	A64	5pf bright green	18	*48*
N4	A64	6pf dark green	18	*48*
N5	A64	8pf vermilion	18	*48*
N6	A64	10pf chocolate	18	*48*
N7	A64	12pf deep carmine	18	*48*
N8	A64	15pf maroon	25	*70*
a.		Inverted overprint	*450.00*	*1,300.*
N9	A64	20pf bright blue	25	*1.25*
N10	A64	25pf ultra	32	*1.75*
N11	A64	30pf olive green	32	*1.75*
N12	A64	40pf red violet	48	*1.90*
N13	A64	50pf dk green & blk	48	*2.00*
N14	A64	60pf claret & blk	48	*2.75*
N15	A64	80pf dk blue & blk	1.00	*3.75*
N16	A64	100pf orange & blk	1.25	*5.75*
		Nos. N1-N16 (16)	6.09	*25.00*
		Set, never hinged	16.00	

Nos. 159-162, 164, 168-171, 173, 175, 179, 182, 216, 198-199 Surcharged in Black

— 60 Rpf
b

80 Rpf

4 Rpf
a

c

100 Rpf
d

Perf. 12, 14x13½, 12½x12, 11½

1940 **Unwmk.**

N17	A18(a)	3rpf on 15c	15	*32*
N18	A18(a)	4rpf on 20c	15	*40*
N19	A18(a)	5rpf on 35c	15	*40*
N20	A18(a)	6rpf on 10c	15	*40*
N21	A18(a)	8rpf on 25c	15	*40*
N22	A18(a)	10rpf on 40c	15	*40*
N23	A18(a)	12rpf on 60c	15	*40*
N24	A18(a)	15rpf on 1fr rose	15	*40*
N25	A18(a)	20rpf on 50c	15	*75*
N26	A18(a)	25rpf on 5c	15	*1.25*
N27	A18(a)	30rpf on 70c	15	*60*
N28	A18(a)	40rpf on 75c	15	*1.00*
N29	A18(a)	50rpf on 1¼fr	15	*60*
N30	A35(b)	60rpf on 2fr	1.40	*12.50*
N31	A22(c)	80rpf on 5fr	40	*2.25*
N32	A23(d)	100rpf on 10fr	50	*3.00*
		Set value	3.00	
		Set, never hinged	7.00	

OCCUPATION SEMI-POSTAL STAMPS

Semi-Postal Stamps of Germany, 1940 Overprinted in Black **Luxemburg**

1941 **Unwmk.** ***Perf. 14***

NB1	SP153	3pf + 2pf dk brn	20	*85*
NB2	SP153	4pf + 3pf bluish blk	20	*85*
NB3	SP153	5pf + 3pf yel grn	20	*85*
NB4	SP153	6pf + 4pf dk grn	20	*85*
NB5	SP153	8pf + 4pf dp org	20	*85*
NB6	SP153	12pf + 6pf carmine	20	*85*
NB7	SP153	15pf + 10pf dk vio brn	28	*1.90*
NB8	SP153	25pf + 15pf dp ultra	85	*3.75*
NB9	SP153	40pf + 35pf red lil	1.50	*6.25*
		Nos. NB1-NB9 (9)	3.83	
		Set, never hinged	7.50	

MACAO

LOCATION — Off the Chinese coast at the mouth of the Canton River
GOVT. — Portuguese Overseas Territory
AREA — 6 sq. mi.
POP. — 261,680 (1981)
CAPITAL — Macao

The territory includes the two small adjacent islands of Coloane and Taipa.

1000 Reis = 1 Milreis
78 Avos = 1 Rupee (1894)
100 Avos = 1 Pataca (1913)

Catalogue values for unused stamps in this country are for Never Hinged items, beginning with Scott 339 in the regular postage section, Scott C16 in the air post section, Scott J50 in the semi-postal section, and Scott RA11 in the postal tax section.

Watermark

Wmk. 232- Maltese Cross

Portuguese Crown — A1

Perf. 12½, 13½

1884-85 Typo. Unwmk.

1 A1 5r black 7.25 1.90
2 A1 10r orange 10.00 2.50
3 A1 10r green ('85) 10.50 3.50
a. Perf. 13½ 35.00 12.00
4 A1 20r bister 10.50 4.50
5 A1 20r rose ('85) 10.00 3.50
6 A1 25r rose 3.50 3.50
7 A1 25r vio ('85) 3.50 1.90
a. Perf. 13½ 47.50 19.00
8 A1 40r blue 32.50 7.50
a. Perf. 12½ 47.50 10.00
9 A1 40r yel ('85) 10.25 4.50
a. Perf. 13½ 30.00 10.00
10 A1 50r green 35.00 8.00
a. Perf. 12½ 110.00 25.00
11 A1 50r blue ('85) 4.00 1.90
a. Perf. 13½ 35.00 14.00
12 A1 80r gray ('85) 37.50 8.00
13 A1 100r red lilac 5.25 2.25
a. 100r lilac 7.25 2.25
14 A1 200r orange 12.00 4.00
a. Perf. 12½ 35.00 14.00
15 A1 300r chocolate 10.25 4.50
a. Perf. 13½ 52.50 22.50

The reprints of the 1885 issue are printed on smooth, white chalky paper, ungummed and on thin white paper with shiny white gum and clean-cut perforation 13½.

For surcharges see Nos. 16-28, 108-109.

No. 13a Surcharged in Black

1884

16 A1 80r on 100r lilac 12.00 5.50
a. Inverted surcharge *16.00* *7.50*
b. Without accent on "e" of "reis" 12.00 5.50
c. Perf. 13½ 12.00 5.50

Nos. 16-23, 25 and 27 were issued without gum.

Nos. 6 and 10 Surcharged in Black, Blue or Red:

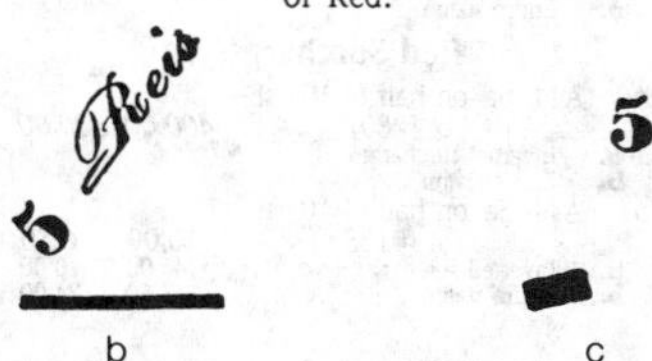

b c

1885

17 A1(b) 5r on 25r rose, perf. 12½ (Bk) 3.00 1.40
a. With accent on "e" of "Reis" 4.00 2.50
b. Double surcharge
c. Inverted surcharge 75.00 27.50
d. Perf. 13½ 55.00 15.00
18 A1(b) 10r on 25r rose (Bl) 5.00 2.75
a. Accent on "e" of "Reis"
b. Pair, one without surcharge 75.00
19 A1(b) 10r on 50r grn, perf. 13½ (Bl) 100.00 22.50
a. Perf. 12½ 110.00 22.50
20 A1(b) 20r on 50r grn (Bk) 4.00 1.40
a. Double surcharge 35.00
b. Accent on "e" of "Reis"
21 A1(b) 40r on 50r grn, perf. 13½ (R) 50.00 17.00
a. Perf. 12½ 35.00 19.00

1885

22 A1(c) 5r on 25r rose (Bk) 4.00 2.00
a. Original value not obliterated
23 A1(c) 10r on 50r grn (Bk) 4.00 2.00
a. Inverted surcharge
b. Perf. 12½ 7.00 2.75

Nos. 12, 13a and 14 Surcharged in Black

5
Reis

1887

24 A1 5r on 80r gray 7.25 2.00
a. "R" of "Reis" 4mm high 40.00 17.50
b. Perf. 12½ 22.50 8.75
25 A1 5r on 100r lilac 26.00 7.00
a. Perf. 12½ 24.00 8.50
26 A1 10r on 80r gray 9.25 3.50
a. "R" 4mm high 35.00 17.00
27 A1 10r on 200r org 32.50 11.50
a. "R" 4mm high 52.50 19.00
b. Perf. 13½ 30.00 7.75
28 A1 20r on 80r gray 14.00 4.25
a. "R" 4mm high 47.50 21.00
b. Perf. 12½

The surcharges with larger "R" (4mm) have accent on "e." Smaller "R" is 3mm high.

Coat of Arms — A6

Red Surcharge

1887, Oct. 20 *Perf. 12½*

Without Gum

32 A6 5r green & buff 6.00 1.90
a. With labels, 5r on 10r 50.00 20.00
b. With labels, 5r on 20r 50.00 20.00
c. With labels, 5r on 60r 50.00 20.00
33 A6 10r green & buff 6.00 1.90
a. With labels, 10r on 10r 50.00 20.00
b. With labels, 10r on 60r 50.00 24.00
34 A6 40r green & buff 6.00 2.75
a. With labels, 40r on 20r 50.00 25.00

The 10r also exists with 20r labels, and 40r with 10r labels.

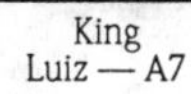

King Luiz — A7

King Carlos — A9

Typographed and Embossed

1888, Jan. *Perf. 12½, 13½*

Chalk-surfaced Paper

35 A7 5r black 4.00 1.25
36 A7 10r green 4.00 1.25
a. Perf. 13½ 15.00 6.50
37 A7 20r carmine 5.00 1.50
38 A7 25r violet 5.00 1.90
39 A7 40r chocolate 6.00 1.90
a. Perf. 13½ 9.00 3.50
40 A7 50r blue 6.00 2.25
41 A7 80r gray 8.00 2.75
a. Imperf., pair 50.00
42 A7 100r brown 8.00 2.75
43 A7 200r gray lilac 20.00 4.25
44 A7 300r orange 25.00 5.00

For surcharges and overprints see Nos. 45, 58-66B, 110-118, 164-170, 239.

No. 43 Surcharged in Red **30** **30**

1892

Without Gum

45 A7 30r on 200r gray lil 15.00 4.75
a. Inverted surcharge 60.00 20.00

1894, Nov. 15 Typo. *Perf. 11½*

46 A9 5r yellow 1.50 90
47 A9 10r redsh vio 1.50 90
48 A9 15r chocolate 1.90 1.10
49 A9 20r lavender 2.00 1.25
50 A9 25r green 4.75 1.90
51 A9 50r lt blue 5.00 1.90
a. Perf. 13½ 37.50 27.50
52 A9 75r carmine 5.00 1.90
53 A9 80r yellow grn 5.50 3.75
54 A9 100r brown, *buff* 4.75 3.50
55 A9 150r car, *rose* 8.25 4.25
56 A9 200r dk blue, *bl* 9.25 4.75
57 A9 300r dk blue, *sal* 10.50 6.00
Nos. 46-57 (12) 59.90 32.10

For surcharges and overprints see Nos. 119-130, 171-181, 183-186, 240, 251, 257-258.

Stamps of 1888 Surcharged in Red, Green or Black

1894 Without Gum *Perf. 12½*

58 A7 1a on 5r blk (R) 1.40 60
a. Short "1" 1.75 75
b. Inverted surcharge 12.00 6.00
c. Double surcharge
d. Surch. on back instead of face 35.00 15.00
59 A7 3a on 20r car (G) 3.75 1.25
a. Inverted surcharge
60 A7 4a on 25r vio (Bk) 4.25 1.25
a. Inverted surcharge 24.00 12.50
61 A7 6a on 40r choc (Bk) 4.00 1.25
a. Perf. 13½ 10.00 4.50
62 A7 8a on 50r bl (R) 8.75 3.25
a. Double surch., one inverted
b. Inverted surcharge 37.50 19.00
c. Perf. 13½ 27.50 10.50
63 A7 13a on 80r gray (Bk) 4.75 1.90
a. Double surcharge
64 A7 16a on 100r brn (Bk) 6.75 2.75
a. Inverted surcharge
b. Perf. 13½ 50.00 21.00
65 A7 31a on 200r gray lil (Bk) 14.00 5.00
a. Inverted surcharge 47.50 18.00
b. Perf. 13½ 15.00 5.50
66 A7 47a on 300r org (G) 12.50 5.00
a. Double surcharge

The style of type used for the word "PROVISORIO" on Nos. 58 to 66 differs for each value.

A 2a on 10r green was unofficially surcharged and denounced by the authorities.

On No. 45

66B A7 5a on 30r on 200r 40.00 5.00

Vasco da Gama Issue

Common Design Types

1898, Apr. 1 Engr. *Perf. 12½ to 16*

67 CD20 ½a blue grn 1.10 60
68 CD21 1a red 1.10 60
69 CD22 2a red violet 1.10 70
70 CD23 4a yellow grn 1.10 70
71 CD24 8a dk blue 2.50 1.10
72 CD25 12a violet brn 4.50 1.90
73 CD26 16a bister brn 3.00 1.25
74 CD27 24a bister 5.75 2.75
Nos. 67-74 (8) 20.15 9.60

For overprints and surcharges see Nos. 187-194.

King Carlos — A11

1898-1910 Typo. *Perf. 11½*

Name and Value in Black except #103

75 A11 ½a gray 42 20
a. Perf. 12½ 1.90 1.10
76 A11 1a orange 42 20
a. Perf. 12½ 1.90 1.10
77 A11 2a yellow grn 60 22
78 A11 2a gray grn ('03) 1.00 52
79 A11 2½a red brn 1.75 70
80 A11 3a gray vio 1.75 70
81 A11 3a slate ('03) 1.00 52
82 A11 4a sea green 1.75 95
83 A11 4a car ('03) 1.00 60
84 A11 5a gray brn ('00) 2.00 1.25
85 A11 5a pale yel brn ('03) 1.25 75
86 A11 6a red brn ('03) 1.90 1.40
87 A11 8a blue 2.50 95
88 A11 8a gray brn ('03) 3.00 1.25
89 A11 10a slate bl ('00) 2.75 1.25
90 A11 12a rose 3.00 1.90
91 A11 12a red lil ('03) 9.00 5.00
92 A11 13a violet 3.00 1.90
93 A11 13a gray lil ('03) 3.75 1.90
94 A11 15a pale ol grn ('00) 9.25 5.75
95 A11 16a dk blue, *bl* 3.75 1.90
96 A11 18a org brn, *pink* ('03) 5.75 3.50
97 A11 20a brn, *yelsh* ('00) 3.75 1.90
98 A11 24a brown, *buff* 3.75 1.90
99 A11 31a red lilac 4.75 2.25
100 A11 31a red lil, *pink* ('03) 5.75 3.75
101 A11 47a dk bl, *rose* 5.75 3.50
102 A11 47a dull bl, *straw* ('03) 8.00 5.00
103 A11 78a blk & red, *bl* ('00) 8.00 4.25
Nos. 75-103 (29) 100.34 55.86

Issued without gum: Nos. 76a, 77, 79-80, 82, 84, 89, 94, 97 and 103.

For surcharges and overprints see Nos. 104-107, 132-136, 141, 147-157D, 159-161, 182, 195-209, 253-255, 258A.

5

Nos. 92, 95, 98-99 Surcharged in Black

PROVISORIO

1900

104 A11 5a on 13a vio 2.50 90
105 A11 10a on 16a dk bl, *bl* 3.00 90
106 A11 15a on 24a brn, *buff* 3.00 1.00
107 A11 20a on 31a red lil 3.50 1.40

Regular Issues Surcharged

On Stamps of 1884-85

1902 *Perf. 11½*

Black Surcharge

108 A1 6a on 10r org 5.00 2.25
a. Double surcharge 50.00 25.00
109 A1 6a on 10r grn 2.50 1.25

On Stamps of 1888

Red Surcharge

Perf. 12½, 13½

110 A7 6a on 5r blk 1.50 75
a. Inverted surcharge 40.00 20.00

Black Surcharge

111 A7 6a on 10r grn 1.50 75
112 A7 6a on 40r choc 1.75 75
a. Double surcharge 40.00 19.00
b. Perf. 13½ 5.75 2.75
113 A7 18a on 20r rose 2.50 1.40
a. Double surcharge 50.00 25.00
114 A7 18a on 25r vio 24.00 9.00
115 A7 18a on 80r gray 27.50 13.00
a. Double surcharge 65.00 37.50
116 A7 18a on 100r brn 5.75 2.25
a. Perf. 13½ 20.00 10.50
117 A7 18a on 200r gray lil 21.00 12.00
a. Perf. 12½ 27.50 12.00
118 A7 18a on 300r org 7.00 2.75
a. Perf. 13½ 13.00 8.25

Issued without gum: Nos. 110-118.

Nos. 109 to 118 inclusive, except No. 111, have been reprinted. The reprints have white gum and clean-cut perforation 13½ and the colors are usually paler than those of the originals.

On Stamps of 1894

1902-10 *Perf. 11½, 13½*

119 A9 6a on 5r yel 1.10 60
a. Inverted surcharge 8.50 5.00
120 A9 6a on 10r red vio 1.10 60
121 A9 6a on 15r choc 1.10 60
122 A9 6a on 25r grn 1.10 60
123 A9 6a on 80r yel grn 1.10 60
124 A9 6a on 100r brn, *buff* 1.10 60
a. Perf. 11½ 7.00 3.25
125 A9 6a on 200r bl, *bl* 1.45 70
a. Vert. half used as 3a on cover ('10)
126 A9 18a on 20r lav 3.75 1.75
127 A9 18a on 50r lt bl 3.75 1.75
a. Perf. 13½ 12.50 6.50
128 A9 18a on 75r car 3.75 1.75
129 A9 18a on 150r car, *rose* 3.75 1.75
130 A9 18a on 300r bl, *salmon* 3.75 1.75

On Newspaper Stamp of 1893

Perf. 12½

131 N3 18a on 2½r brn 3.50 1.40
a. Perf. 13½ 6.50 2.10
b. Perf. 11½ 12.50 5.25
Nos. 108-131 (24) 130.30 60.60

Issued without gum: Nos. 122-130, 131b.

Stamps of 1898-1900 Overprinted in Black

PROVISORIO

1902 *Perf. 11½*

132 A11 2a yellow grn 4.50 1.75
133 A11 4a sea green 3.50 1.40
134 A11 8a blue 3.50 1.40
135 A11 10a slate blue 3.50 1.40
136 A11 12a rose 5.50 2.75
Nos. 132-136 (5) 20.50 8.70

Issued without gum: Nos. 133, 135.

Reprints of No. 133 have shiny white gum and clean-cut perforation 13½. Value $1.

No. 91 Surcharged

10 AVOS

1905

141 A11 10a on 12a red lilac 5.00 2.50

Nos. J1-J3 Overprinted

1910, Oct. *Perf. 11½x12*

144 D1 ½a gray grn 3.25 1.25
a. Inverted overprint 6.75 6.75
145 D1 1a yellow grn 3.25 1.25
a. Inverted overprint 6.75 6.75
146 D1 2a slate 3.25 1.50
a. Inverted overprint 16.00 16.00

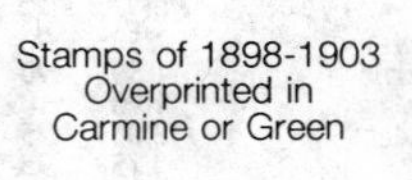

Stamps of 1898-1903 Overprinted in Carmine or Green

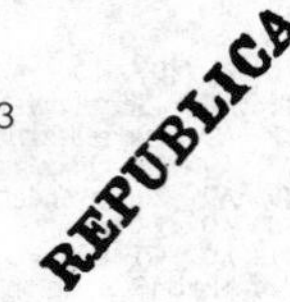

Lisbon Overprint

1911, Apr. 2 *Perf. 11½*

147 A11 ½a gray 22 15
a. Inverted overprint
147B A11 1a orange 22 15
c. Inverted overprint
148 A11 2a gray green 22 15
149 A11 3a slate 22 15
150 A11 4a car (G) 95 60
a. 4a pale yel brn (error) 32.50 20.00
151 A11 5a pale yel brn 95 60
152 A11 6a red brown 95 60
153 A11 8a gray brn 95 60
154 A11 10a slate blue 95 60
155 A11 13a gray lilac 1.10 75
156 A11 16a dk blue, *bl* 1.10 75
157 A11 18a org brn, *pink* 2.50 1.25
157A A11 20a brown, *straw* 2.50 1.25
157B A11 31a red lil, *pink* 2.50 1.25
157C A11 47a dull bl, *straw* 3.75 2.50
157D A11 78a blk & red, *bl* 5.00 3.00
Nos. 147-157D (16) 24.08 14.35

Issued without gum: Nos. 153-157D.

Coat of Arms — A14

1911 *Perf. 11½x12*

Red Surcharge

158 A14 1a on 5r brn & buff 1.90 1.10
a. "1" omitted 17.50 9.50
b. Inverted surcharge 10.00 5.75

Stamps of 1900-03 Surcharged

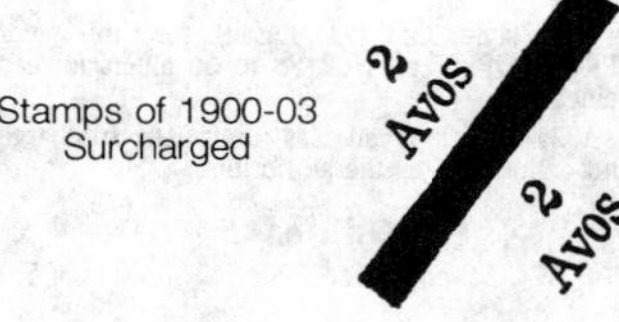

Diagonal Halves

1911 **Without Gum** *Perf. 11½*

Black Surcharge

159 A11 2a on half of 4a car 3.00 2.00
a. "2" omitted 22.50 22.50
b. Inverted surcharge 19.00 19.00
d. Entire stamp 22.50 22.50
159C A11 5a on half of 10a sl bl (#89) *600.00 600.00*
e. Entire stamp

Red Surcharge

160 A11 5a on half of 10a sl bl (#89) *400.00 300.00*
a. Inverted surcharge
b. Entire stamp
161 A11 5a on half of 10a sl bl (#135) 10.00 6.50
a. Inverted surcharge 40.00 18.00
b. Entire stamp 47.50 24.00

MACAU
N.° 5/63 1 avo
Director do Correio.

A15

1911 *Perf. 12x11½*

Laid or Wove Paper

162 A15 1a black 190.00 100.00
a. "Corrieo" 375.00 375.00
163 A15 2a black 225.00 115.00
a. "Corrieo" 375.00 375.00

Surcharged Stamps of 1902 Overprinted in Red or Green

Local Overprint

1913 **Without Gum** *Perf. 11½*

164 A1 6a on 10r grn (R) 10.50 3.00

Perf. 12½, 13½

165 A7 6a on 5r blk (G) 4.00 1.25
166 A7 6a on 10r grn (R) 10.50 3.00
167 A7 6a on 40r choc (R) 4.00 1.25
a. Perf. 13½ 8.50 4.75
168 A7 18a on 20r car (G) 7.25 1.90
169 A7 18a on 100r brn (R) 21.00 6.00
a. Perf. 13½ 20.00 10.00
170 A7 18a on 300r org (R) 13.00 4.00
a. Perf. 12½ 8.50 4.75
Nos. 164-170 (7) 70.25 20.40

"Republica" overprint exists inverted on Nos. 164-170.

"Republica" overprint exists double on No. 164.

1913 **Without Gum** *Perf. 11½, 13½*

171 A9 6a on 10r red vio (G) 1.90 85
172 A9 6a on 10r red vio (R) 42.50 3.50
173 A9 6a on 15r choc (R) 1.90 1.00
174 A9 6a on 25r grn (R) 2.50 1.40
175 A9 6a on 80r yel grn (R) 1.90 1.25
176 A9 6a on 100r brn, *buff*(R) 1.90 1.25
a. Perf. 11½ 5.00 1.75
177 A9 18a on 20r lav (R) 2.75 1.75
178 A9 18a on 50r lt bl (R) 2.75 1.75
a. Perf. 13½ 4.25 1.75
179 A9 18a on 75r car (G) 2.75 1.75
180 A9 18a on 150r car, *rose* (G) 4.25 2.00
181 A9 18a on 300r dk bl, *buff* (R) 3.50 2.00

On No. 141

182 A11 10a on 12a red lil (R) 2.50 1.75
Nos. 171-182 (12) 71.10 20.25

"Republica" overprint exists inverted on Nos. 171-181.

Stamps of Preceding Issue Surcharged

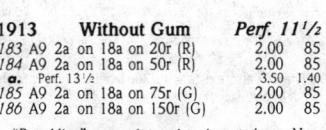

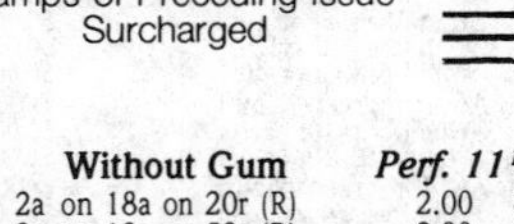

1913 **Without Gum** *Perf. 11½*

183 A9 2a on 18a on 20r (R) 2.00 85
184 A9 2a on 18a on 50r (R) 2.00 85
a. Perf. 13½ 3.50 1.40
185 A9 2a on 18a on 75r (G) 2.00 85
186 A9 2a on 18a on 150r (G) 2.00 85

"Republica" overprint exists inverted on Nos. 183-186. Value, each $3.50.

The 2a surcharge exists inverted or double on Nos. 183-186. Value, each $5.

Vasco da Gama Issue Overprinted or Surcharged:

REPUBLICA

REPUBLICA 10 A.
j k

187 CD20 (j) ½a blue green 1.25 60
188 CD21 (j) 1a red 1.25 60
189 CD22 (j) 2a red violet 1.25 80
a. Dbl. ovpt., one inverted 37.50
190 CD23 (j) 4a yellow grn 1.25 60
a. Half used as 2a on cover
191 CD24 (j) 8a dk blue 2.00 70
192 CD25 (k) 10a on 12a vio brn 3.75 1.65
193 CD26 (j) 16a bister brn 2.00 90
194 CD27 (j) 24a bister 3.25 1.40
Nos. 187-194 (8) 16.00 7.25

Stamps of 1898-1903 Overprinted in Red or Green

1913 **Without Gum** *Perf. 11½*

195 A11 4a car (G) 50.00 11.50
196 A11 5a yellow brn 15.00 2.75
a. Inverted overprint
197 A11 6a red brown 15.00 2.75
198 A11 8a gray brown 125.00 19.00
199 A11 13a violet 30.00 6.00
a. Inverted overprint 60.00
200 A11 13a gray lilac 15.00 2.75
201 A11 16a blue, *bl* 15.00 2.75
202 A11 18a org brn, *pink* 15.00 2.75
203 A11 20a brown, *yelsh* 15.00 2.75
204 A11 31a red lil, *pink* 15.00 2.75
205 A11 47a dull bl, *straw* 15.00 2.75
Nos. 195-205 (11) 325.00 58.50

½

Stamps of 1911-13 Surcharged

Avo

On Stamps of 1911 With Lisbon "Republica"

1913

206 A11 ½a on 5a yel brn (R) 2.00 90
a. "½ Avo" inverted 25.00
207 A11 4a on 8a gray brn (R) 2.50 1.10
a. "4 Avos" inverted 25.00

On Stamps of 1913 With Local "Republica"

208 A11 1a on 13a vio (R) 35.00 17.50
209 A11 1a on 13a gray lil (R) 2.00 70
a. "REPUBLICA" omitted

Issued without gum: Nos. 207-209.

"Ceres" — A16

1913-24 *Perf. 12x11½, 15x14*

Name and Value in Black

210 A16 ½a olive brn 24 15
a. Inscriptions inverted 12.00
211 A16 1a black 28 15
a. Inscriptions inverted 12.00
b. Inscriptions double 12.00
212 A16 1½a yel grn ('24) 24 15
213 A16 2a blue grn 24 15
a. Inscriptions inverted 6.00
214 A16 3a org ('23) 1.25 95
215 A16 4a carmine 90 28
216 A16 4a lem ('24) 1.75 95
217 A16 5a lilac brn 1.65 95
218 A16 6a lt violet 1.25 70
219 A16 6a gray ('23) 5.25 2.25
220 A16 8a lilac brn 1.10 60
221 A16 10a dp blue 1.10 60
222 A16 10a pale bl ('23) 3.50 1.75
223 A16 12a yellow brn 1.65 75
224 A16 14a lilac ('24) 7.25 3.50
225 A16 16a slate 2.25 1.40
226 A16 20a orange brn 4.25 1.50
227 A16 24a sl grn ('23) 3.25 1.90
228 A16 32a org brn ('24) 3.50 2.75
229 A16 40a plum 3.00 1.50

230 A16 56a dl rose ('24) 7.75 3.75
231 A16 58a brown, *grn* 5.25 3.00
232 A16 72a brown ('23) 9.00 5.25
233 A16 76a brown, *pink* 7.75 3.75
234 A16 1p orange, *sal* 9.00 4.50
235 A16 1p orange ('24) 27.50 7.50
236 A16 3p green, *bl* 35.00 14.00
237 A16 3p pale turq ('24) 65.00 22.50
238 A16 5p car rose ('24) 47.50 22.50
Nos. 210-238 (29) 257.65 109.68

For surcharges see Nos. 256, 259-267.

Preceding Issues and No. P4 Overprinted in Carmine

On Stamps of 1902

Perf. 11½, 12, 12½, 13½, 11½x12

1915

239 A7 6a on 10r green 1.25 60
240 A9 6a on 5r yel 1.25 65
241 A9 6a on 10r red vio 1.25 65
242 A9 6a on 15r choc 95 42
243 A9 6a on 25r grn 95 42
244 A9 6a on 80r yel grn 95 42
245 A9 6a on 100r brn, *buff* 1.75 70
246 A9 6a on 200r bl, *bl* 85 42
247 A9 18a on 20r lav 1.75 1.10
248 A9 18a on 50r lt bl 2.25 1.10
249 A9 18a on 75r car 2.00 1.25
250 A9 18a on 150r car, *rose* 2.25 1.25
251 A9 18a on 300r bl, *sal* 2.00 1.25
252 N3 18a on 2½r brn 1.50 60

With Additional Overprint PROVISORIO

253 A11 8a blue 95 52
254 A11 10a slate blue 95 52
a. "Provisorio" double 7.50

On Stamp of 1905

255 A11 10a on 12a red lil 95 52
Nos. 239-255 (17) 23.80 12.39

Issued without gum: Nos. 243-251 and 255.

No. 217 Surcharged ½ AVO

1919-20

Without Gum

256 A16 ½a on 5a lil brn 10.00 3.25

Nos. 243 and 244 Surcharged = 2

257 A9 2a on 6a on 25r grn 15.00 7.00
258 A9 2a on 6a on 80r yel grn 15.00 4.50

No. 152 Surcharged 2 avos

258A A11 2a on 6a red brn 20.00 6.00

Issued without gum: Nos. 256-258A.

Stamps of 1913-24 Surcharged

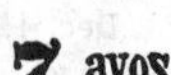

7 avos

1931-33

259 A16 1a on 24a sl grn 90 55
260 A16 2a on 32a org brn 90 55
261 A16 4a on 12a bis brn 90 55
262 A16 5a on 6a lt gray 3.50 1.40
263 A16 5a on 6a lt vio 2.50 1.40
264 A16 7a on 8a lil brn ('31) 1.75 80
265 A16 12a on 14a lil ('31) 1.65 80
266 A16 15a on 16a dk gray 1.65 80
267 A16 20a on 56a dl rose 2.25 1.10
Nos. 259-267 (9) 16.00 7.95

"Portugal" and Vasco da Gama's Flagship "San Gabriel" — A17

Perf. 11½

1934, Feb. 1 Typo. Wmk. 232

268 A17 ½a bister 15 15
269 A17 1a olive brn 15 15
270 A17 2a blue grn 15 15
271 A17 3a violet 15 15
272 A17 4a black 25 15
273 A17 5a gray 25 15
274 A17 6a brown 25 15
275 A17 7a brt rose 35 22
276 A17 8a brt blue 35 25
277 A17 10a red org 70 42
278 A17 12a dk blue 70 42
279 A17 14a olive grn 70 42
280 A17 15a maroon 70 42
281 A17 20a orange 70 42
282 A17 30a apple grn 1.50 70
283 A17 40a violet 1.50 70
284 A17 50a olive bis 3.25 90
285 A17 1p lt blue 13.00 1.75
286 A17 2p brown org 16.00 4.00
287 A17 3p emerald 32.50 5.25
288 A17 5p dk violet 67.50 10.50
Nos. 268-288 (21) 140.80 27.42

See Nos. 316-323. For overprints and surcharges see Nos. 306-315, C1-C6, J43-J49.

Common Design Types

Perf. 13½x13

1938, Aug. 1 Engr. Unwmk.

Name and Value in Black

289 CD34 1a gray grn 15 15
290 CD34 2a orange brn 28 15
291 CD34 3a dk vio brn 28 15
292 CD34 4a brt green 28 15
293 CD35 5a dk car 28 15
294 CD35 6a slate 28 15
295 CD35 8a rose vio 48 20
296 CD36 10a brt red vio 55 20
297 CD36 12a red 70 20
298 CD36 15a orange 70 20
299 CD37 20a blue 1.25 40
300 CD37 40a gray blk 2.75 55
301 CD37 50a brown 2.75 55
302 CD38 1p brn car 8.50 1.40
303 CD38 2p olive grn 20.00 2.00
304 CD38 3p blue vio 27.50 4.00
305 CD38 5p red brown 60.00 6.75
Nos. 289-305 (17) 126.73 17.35

For surcharge see No. 315A.

Stamps of 1934 Surcharged in Black:

5 avos (a) 5 avos (b)

1941 Wmk. 232 *Perf. 11½x12*

306 A17(a) 1a on 6a brn 1.75 85
307 A17(b) 2a on 6a brn 70 55
308 A17(b) 3a on 6a brn 70 55
309 A17(a) 5a on 7a brt rose 67.50 24.00
310 A17(b) 5a on 7a brt rose 70 55
311 A17(a) 5a on 8a brt bl 2.50 1.75
312 A17(b) 5a on 8a brt bl 70 55
313 A17(b) 8a on 30a ap grn 1.50 1.25
314 A17(b) 8a on 40a vio 1.50 1.25
315 A17(b) 8a on 50a ol bis 1.50 1.25
Nos. 306-315 (10) 79.05 32.55

No. 294 Surcharged in Black:

3 avos

1941 Unwmk. *Perf. 13½x13*

315A CD35 3a on 6a slate 22.50 13.00

Counterfeits exist.

"Portugal" Type of 1934

1942 Litho. *Rough Perf. 12*

Thin Paper Without Gum

316 A17 1a olive brown 60 35
317 A17 2a blue green 60 35
318 A17 3a vio, perf. 11 3.00 1.40
a. Perf. 12 5.50 1.50
319 A17 6a brown 4.25 1.25
a. Perf. 10 10.00 4.00
b. Perf. 11 8.25 3.00
320 A17 10a red org 2.75 1.25
321 A17 20a orange 2.75 1.25
a. Perf. 11 8.25 3.00
322 A17 30a apple grn 4.25 1.40
323 A17 40a violet 5.75 1.75
Nos. 316-323 (8) 23.95 9.00

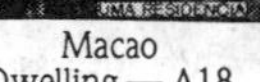

Macao Dwelling — A18

Gate of Cerco — A19

Designs: 2a, Mountain fort. 3a, View of Macao. 8a, Praia Grande Bay. 10a, Leal Senado Square. 20a, Sao Jeronimo Hill. 30a, Marginal Ave. 50a, Relief of Goddess Ma. 2p, Pagoda of Barra. 3p, Post Office. 5p, Solidao Walk.

1948, Dec. 20 Litho. *Perf. 10½*

324 A18 1a dk brn & org 35 15
325 A19 2a rose brn & rose 28 15
326 A18 3a brn vio & lil 60 15
327 A18 8a rose car & rose 35 15
328 A18 10a lil rose & rose 60 22
329 A18 20a dk bl & gray 70 22
330 A18 30a blk & gray 1.40 30
331 A18 50a brn & pale bis 2.00 38
332 A19 1p emer & pale grn 16.00 3.75
333 A19 2p scar & rose 14.00 3.75
334 A19 3p dl grn & gray grn 22.50 4.25
335 A18 5p vio bl & gray 32.50 6.75
Nos. 324-335 (12) 91.28 20.22

See Nos. 341-347A.

Lady of Fatima Issue

Common Design Type

1949, Feb. 1 Unwmk. *Perf. 14½*

336 CD40 8a scarlet 3.00 2.00

Symbols of the UPU — A20

Dragon — A21

1949, Dec. 24 Litho. Unwmk.

337 A20 32a claret & rose 20.00 6.00

75th anniv. of the formation of the UPU.

Catalogue values for unused stamps in this section, from this point to the end of the section, are for Never Hinged items.

Holy Year Issue

Common Design Types

1950, July 26 *Perf. 13x13½*

339 CD41 32a dk slate gray 5.00 90
340 CD42 50a carmine 5.00 90

Scenic Types of 1948

Designs as before.

1950-51 *Perf. 14*

341 A18 1a vio & rose 1.00 18
342 A19 2a ol bis & yel 1.00 18
343 A18 3a org red & buff 1.50 18
344 A18 8a sl & gray 1.50 18
345 A18 10a red brn & org 3.00 24
346 A18 30a vio bl & bl 4.00 42
347 A18 50a ol grn & yel grn 7.50 42
347A A19 1p dk org brn & org brn 20.00 60
Nos. 341-347A (8) 39.50 2.40

A 1p ultra & vio, perf. 11, was not sold in Macao. Value $22.50.

The 1p was issued in 1950, Nos. 341-347 in 1951.

1951 *Perf. 11½x12*

348 A21 1a org yel, *lem* 1.25 45
349 A21 2a dk grn, *bl* 1.25 45
350 A21 10a vio brn, *bl* 1.25 45
351 A21 10a brt pink, *bl* 1.25 45

For overprints see Nos. J50-J52.

Holy Year Extension Issue

Common Design Type

1951, Dec. 3 Litho. *Perf. 14*

352 CD43 60a mag & pink 10.00 1.25

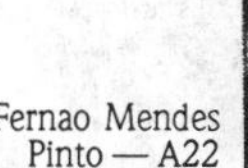

Fernao Mendes Pinto — A22

Portraits: 2a and 10a, St. Francis Xavier. 3a and 50a, Jorge Alvares. 6a and 30a, Luis de Camoens.

1951, Aug. 27 *Perf. 11½*

353 A22 1a steel bl & gray bl 25 15
354 A22 2a dk brown & ol grn 32 15
355 A22 3a deep grn & grn 25 15
356 A22 6a purple 1.20 18
357 A22 10a red brn & org 2.50 22
358 A22 20a brown car 3.75 42
359 A22 30a dk brn & ol grn 3.75 42
360 A22 50a red & orange 8.50 75
Nos. 353-360 (8) 20.52 2.44

Sampan — A23

Junk — A24

Design: 5p, Junk.

1951, Nov. 1 Unwmk.

361 A23 1p vio bl & bl 10.00 60
362 A24 3p blk & vio 25.00 1.75
363 A23 5p henna brn 75.00 5.50

Medical Congress Issue

Common Design Type

Design: Sao Rafael Hospital.

1952, June 16 Unwmk. *Perf. 13½*

364 CD44 6a black & purple 1.50 24

Statue of St. Francis Xavier — A25

Statue of Virgin Mary — A26

St. Francis Xavier Issue

Designs: 16a, Arm of St. Francis. 40a, Tomb of St. Francis.

1952, Nov. 28 Litho. *Perf. 14*

365 A25 3a blk, *grnsh gray* 1.00 15
366 A25 16a choc, *buff* 4.00 42
367 A25 40a blk, *blue* 7.50 1.10

400th anniversary of the death of St. Francis Xavier.

1953, Apr. 28 Unwmk. *Perf. 13½*

368 A26 8a choc & dull ol 1.50 18
369 A26 10a blue blk & buff 5.00 42
370 A26 50a slate grn & ol grn 8.00 1.25

Issued to commemorate the Exhibition of Sacred Missionary Art, held at Lisbon in 1951.

Stamp of Portugal and Arms of Colonies — A27

1954, Mar. 9 Photo. *Perf. 13*

371	A27	10a multicolored	2.00	60

Cent. of Portugal's first postage stamps.

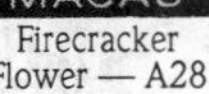

Firecracker Flower — A28

Map of Colony — A29

Flowers: 3a, Forget-me-not. 5a, Dragon claw. 10a, Nunflower. 16a, Narcissus. 30a, Peach flower. 39a, Lotus flower. 1p, Chrysanthemum. 3p, Cherry blossoms. 5p, Tangerine blossoms.

1953, Sept. 22 *Perf. 11½*

Flowers in Natural Colors

372	A28	1a dk red	15	15
373	A28	3a dk green	15	15
374	A28	5a dk brown	20	15
375	A28	10a dp grnsh bl	50	15
376	A28	16a yellow brn	75	15
377	A28	30a dk olive grn	75	15
378	A28	39a vio blue	1.00	15
379	A28	1p dp plum	4.00	75
380	A28	3p dk gray	7.00	1.25
381	A28	5p dp carmine	9.00	2.50
		Nos. 372-381 (10)	23.50	5.55

Sao Paulo Issue

Common Design Type

1954, Aug. 4 Litho. *Perf. 13½*

382	CD46	39a org, cream & blk	5.00	38

Sao Paulo founding, 400th anniversary.

Perf. 12½x13½

1956, May 10 Photo.

Inscriptions and design in brown, red, green, ultra & yellow (buff on 10a, 40a, 90a)

383	A29	1a gray	20	15
384	A29	3a pale gray	25	15
385	A29	5a pale pink	30	15
386	A29	10a buff	75	15
387	A29	30a lt blue	1.50	15
388	A29	40a pale green	3.00	18
389	A29	90a pale gray	5.00	30
390	A29	1.50p pink	8.00	40
		Nos. 383-390 (8)	19.00	
		Set value		1.25

Exhibition Emblems and View — A30

Armillary Sphere — A31

1958, Nov. 8 Litho. *Perf. 14½*

391	A30	70a multicolored	1.50	24

World's Fair, Brussels, Apr. 17-Oct. 19.

Macao stamps can be mounted in Scott's annual Portugal Supplement.

Tropical Medicine Congress Issue

Common Design Type

Design: Cinnamomum camphora.

1958, Nov. 15 *Perf. 13½*

392	CD47	20a multicolored	2.25	1.25

1960, June 25 Litho. *Perf. 13½*

393	A31	2p multicolored	6.00	60

500th anniversary of the death of Prince Henry the Navigator.

Sports Issue

Common Design Type

Sports: 10a, Field hockey. 16a, Wrestling. 20a, Table tennis. 50a, Motorcycling. 1.20p, Relay race. 2.50p, Badminton.

1962, Feb. 9 *Perf. 13½*

Multicolored Design

394	CD48	10a blue & yel grn	50	15
395	CD48	16a brt pink	2.00	40
396	CD48	20a orange	1.50	48
397	CD48	50a rose	1.50	48
398	CD48	1.20p blue & beige	5.00	1.00
399	CD48	2.50p gray & brown	12.50	2.00
		Nos. 394-399 (6)	23.00	4.51

Anti-Malaria Issue

Common Design Type

Design: Anopheles hyrcanus sinensis.

1962, Apr. 7 Litho. *Perf. 13½*

400	CD49	40a multicolored	3.00	55

Bank Building — A32

1964, May 16 Unwmk. *Perf. 13½*

401	A32	20a multicolored	3.50	48

Centenary of the National Overseas Bank of Portugal.

ITU Issue

Common Design Type

1965, May 17 Litho. *Perf. 14½*

402	CD52	10a pale grn & multi	2.00	60

National Revolution Issue

Common Design Type

Design: 10a, Infante D. Henrique School and Count de S. Januario Hospital.

1966, May 28 Litho. *Perf. 11½*

403	CD53	10a multicolored	2.00	35

Drummer, 1548 — A32a

Designs: 15a, Soldier with sword, 1548. 20a, Harquebusier, 1649. 40a, Infantry officer, 1783. 50a, Infantry soldier, 1783. 60a, Colonial infantry soldier (Indian), 1902. 1p, Colonial infantry soldier (Chinese), 1903. 3p, Colonial infantry soldier (Chinese) 1904.

1966, Aug. 8 Litho. *Perf. 13*

404	A32a	10a multicolored	75	28
405	A32a	15a multicolored	1.00	28
406	A32a	20a multicolored	1.00	28
407	A32a	40a multicolored	1.50	35
408	A32a	50a multicolored	1.50	35
409	A32a	60a multicolored	4.00	48
410	A32a	1p multicolored	6.00	55
411	A32a	3p multicolored	10.00	1.75
		Nos. 404-411 (8)	25.75	4.32

Navy Club Issue, 1967

Common Design Type

Designs: 10a, Capt. Oliveira E. Carmo and armed launch Vega. 20a, Capt. Silva Junior and frigate Dom Fernando.

1967, Jan. 31 Litho. *Perf. 13*

412	CD54	10a multicolored	40	20
413	CD54	20a multicolored	1.00	48

Arms of Pope Paul VI and Golden Rose — A33

Cabral Monument, Lisbon — A34

1967, May 13 *Perf. 12½x13*

414	A33	50a multicolored	1.50	35

50th anniversary of the apparition of the Virgin Mary to three shepherd children at Fatima.

Cabral Issue

Design: 70a, Cabral monument, Belmonte.

1968, Apr. 22 Litho. *Perf. 14*

415	A34	20a multicolored	80	40
416	A34	70a multicolored	1.50	48

500th anniversary of the birth of Pedro Alvares Cabral, navigator who took possession of Brazil for Portugal.

Admiral Coutinho Issue

Common Design Type

Design: 20a, Adm. Coutinho with sextant, vert.

1969, Feb. 17 Litho. *Perf. 14*

417	CD55	20a multicolored	2.00	28

Church of Our Lady of the Relics, Vidigueira — A35

Bishop D. Belchior Carneiro — A36

Vasco da Gama Issue

1969, Aug. 29 Litho. *Perf. 14*

418	A35	1p multicolored	3.50	28

Vasco da Gama (1469-1524), navigator.

Administration Reform Issue

Common Design Type

1969, Sept. 25 Litho. *Perf. 14*

419	CD56	90a multicolored	2.00	35

1969, Oct. 16 Litho. *Perf. 13*

420	A36	50a multicolored	1.50	28

4th centenary of the founding of the Santa Casa da Misericordia in Macao.

King Manuel I Issue

Portal of Mother Church, Golega — A37

1969, Dec. 1 Litho. *Perf. 14*

421	A37	30a multicolored	1.75	28

500th anniversary of the birth of King Manuel I.

Marshal Carmona Issue

Common Design Type

Design: 5a, Antonio Oscar Carmona in general's uniform.

1970, Nov. 15 Litho. *Perf. 14*

422	CD57	5a multicolored	1.00	28

Dragon Mask — A38

1971, Sept. 30 *Perf. 13½*

423	A38	5a lt blue & multi	50	15
424	A38	10a Lion mask	1.00	20

Lusiads Issue

Portuguese Delegation at Chinese Court — A39

1972, May 25 Litho. *Perf. 13*

425	A39	20a citron & multi	3.50	28

4th centenary of publication of The Lusiads by Luiz Camoens.

Olympic Games Issue

Common Design Type

Design: Hockey and Olympic emblem.

1972, June 20 *Perf. 14x13½*

426	CD59	50a multicolored	1.75	28

Lisbon-Rio de Janeiro Flight Issue

Common Design Type

Design: "Santa Cruz" landing in Rio de Janeiro.

1972, Sept. 20 Litho. *Perf. 13½*

427	CD60	5p multicolored	7.50	1.75

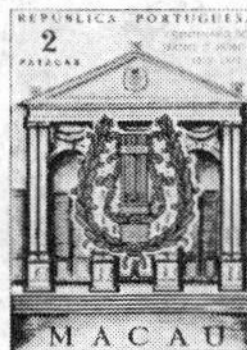

Pedro V Theater and Lyre — A42

1972, Dec. 25 Litho. *Perf. 13½*

428	A42	2p multicolored	3.00	55

Centenary of Pedro V Theater, Macao.

WMO Centenary Issue

Common Design Type

1973, Dec. 15 Litho. *Perf. 13*

429	CD61	20a bl grn & multi	1.75	28

Viscount St. Januario — A44

Design: 60a, Hospital, 1874 and 1974.

1974, Jan. 25 Litho. *Perf. 13½*
430 A44 15a multicolored 50 15
431 A44 60a multicolored 1.00 20
Set value 26

Centenary of Viscount St. Januario Hospital, Macao.
For surcharge see No. 457.

George Chinnery, Self-portrait — A45

1974, Sept. 23 Litho. *Perf. 14*
432 A45 30a multicolored 1.50 28

George Chinnery (1774-1852), English painter who lived in Macao.

Macao-Taipa Bridge A46

Design: 2.20p, Different view of bridge.

1974, Oct. 7 Litho. *Perf. 14x13½*
433 A46 20a multi 1.25 15
434 A46 2.20p multi 4.75 55

Inauguration of the Macao-Taipa Bridge.

Man Raising Banner A47

1975, Apr. 25 *Perf. 12*
435 A47 10a ocher & multi 1.10 20
436 A47 1p multicolored 4.75 70

Revolution of Apr. 25, 1974, 1st anniv.

Pou Chai Pagoda — A48

Design: 20p, Tin Hau Pagoda.

1976, Jan. 30 Litho. *Perf. 13½x13*
437 A48 10p multicolored 6.00 2.00
438 A48 20p multicolored 14.00 2.75

A 1p stamp for the 400th anniv. of the Macao Diocese was prepared but not issued. Some copies were sold in Lisbon.

"The Law" — A50

1978 Litho. *Perf. 13½*
440 A50 5a blk, dk & lt blue 1.00 15
441 A50 2p blk, org brn & buff 15.00 1.00
442 A50 5p blk, ol & yel grn 25.00 1.75

Legislative Assembly, Aug. 9, 1976.

Nos. 376, 378, 382, 434 Surcharged

1979, Nov.
443 A28 10a on 16a 2.00 70
444 A28 30a on 39a (#378) 2.00 70
445 CD46 30a on 39a (#382) 13.00 2.75
446 A46 2p on 2.20p 5.25 1.00

Luis de Camoens (1524-80), Poet — A51
Buddha, Macao Cathedral — A52

1981, June Litho. *Perf. 13½*
447 A51 10a multicolored 15 15
448 A51 30a multicolored 28 15
449 A51 1p multicolored 80 28
450 A51 3p multicolored 2.50 55

1981, Sept.
451 A52 15a multicolored 15 15
452 A52 40a multicolored 22 15
453 A52 50a multicolored 35 15
454 A52 60a multicolored 45 15
455 A52 1p multicolored 70 28
456 A52 2.20p multicolored 1.75 48
Nos. 451-456 (6) 3.62 1.36

Transcultural Psychiatry Symposium.

No. 431 Surcharged

1981 Litho. *Perf. 13½*
457 A44 30a on 60a multi 40 20

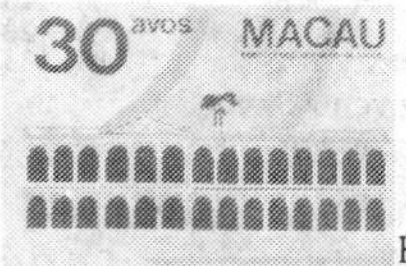
Health Services Building — A53

Designs: Public Buildings and Monuments.

1982, June 10 Litho. *Perf. 12x12½*
458 A53 30a shown 20 15
459 A53 40a Guia Lighthouse 25 15
460 A53 1p Portas do Cerco 70 24
461 A53 2p Luis de Camoes Museum 1.40 48
462 A53 10p School Welfare Service Building 7.00 2.50
Nos. 458-462 (5) 9.55 3.52

See Nos. 472-476, 489-493.

Autumn Festivals A54

Designs: Painted paper lanterns.

1982, Oct. 1 *Perf. 12x11½*
463 A54 40a multicolored 25 15
464 A54 1p multicolored 70 24
465 A54 2p multicolored 1.40 48
466 A54 5p multicolored 3.50 1.25

Geographical Position — A55

1982, Dec. 1 Litho. *Perf. 13*
467 A55 50a Aerial view 35 15
468 A55 3p Map 2.10 70

World Communications Year — A56

1983, Feb. 16 *Perf. 13½*
469 A56 60a Telephone operators 40 15
470 A56 3p Mailman, mailbox 2.10 70
471 A56 6p Globe, satellites 4.25 1.40

Architecture Type of 1982

1983, May 12 Litho. *Perf. 13*
472 A53 10a Social Welfare Institute 15 15
473 A53 80a St. Joseph's Seminary 50 18
474 A53 1.50p St. Dominic's Church 1.05 38
475 A53 2.50p St. Paul's Church ruins 1.75 60
476 A53 7.50p Senate House 5.25 1.75
Nos. 472-476 (5) 8.70 3.06

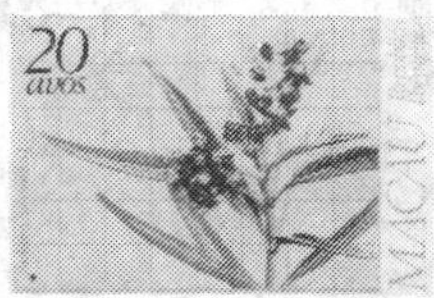
Medicinal Plants — A57

1983, July 14 Litho. *Perf. 13½x14*
477 A57 20a Asclepias curassavica 20 15
478 A57 40a Acanthus ilicifolius 30 20
479 A57 60a Melastoma sanguineum 50 20
480 A57 70a Nelumbo nucifera 60 20
481 A57 1.50p Bombax malabaricum 1.40 55
482 A57 2.50p Hibiscus mutabilis 2.00 70
a. Souvenir sheet of 6, #477-482 *32.50*
Nos. 477-482 (6) 5.00 2.00

No. 482a sold for 6.50p.

16th Century Discoveries
A58 A59

1983, Nov. 15 Litho. *Perf. 13½x14*
483 A58 4p multicolored 2.00 70
484 A59 4p multicolored 2.00 70
a. Pair, #483-484 4.00 1.50

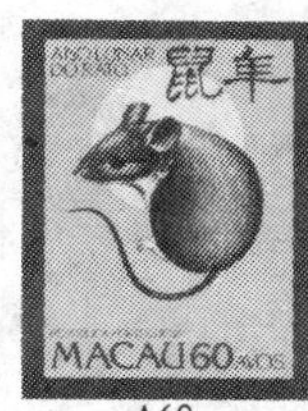
A60

A61

1984, Jan. 25 Litho. *Perf. 13½*
485 A60 60a multicolored 25 15
a. Booklet pane of 5 *9.00*

New Year 1984 (Year of the Rat). See Nos. 504, 522, 540, 560, 583, 611, 639, 662, 684.

1984, Mar. 1 Litho. *Perf. 12½*

Design of First Stamp Issue, 1884.

486 A61 40a orange & blk 15 15
487 A61 3p gray & blk 90 35
488 A61 5p sepia & blk 1.50 55
a. Souvenir sheet of 3, #486-488 *15.00*

Centenary of Macao postage stamps.

Architecture Type of 1982

1984, May 18 Litho. *Perf. 13½*
489 A53 20a Holy House of Mercy 15 15
490 A53 60a St. Lawrence Church 15 15
491 A53 90a King Peter V Theater 22 15
492 A53 3p Palace of St. Sancha 72 24
493 A53 15p Moorish barracks 3.50 1.25
Nos. 489-493 (5) 4.74
Set value 1.70

Birds, Ausipex '84 Emblem A62

1984, Sept. 21 Litho. *Perf. 13*
494 A62 30a Kingfishers 16 15
495 A62 40a European jay 30 15
496 A62 50a White eyes 40 15
497 A62 70a Hoopoe 48 15
498 A62 2.50p Peking nightingale 1.75 28
499 A62 6p Wild duck 3.50 55
Nos. 494-499 (6) 6.59
Set value 1.08

Philakorea '84 Emblem, Fishing Boats — A63

1984, Oct. 22 Litho.
500 A63 20a Hok lou t'eng 15 15
501 A63 60a Tai t'ong 28 15
502 A63 2p Tai mei chai 90 24
503 A63 5p Ch'at pong t'o 2.25 60
Set value 95

New Year Type of 1984

1985, Feb. 13 Litho. *Perf. 13½*
504 A60 1p Buffalo 1.25 15
a. Booklet pane of 5 6.25

Intl. Youth Year — A65

1985, Apr. 19 Litho. *Perf. 13½*
505 A65 2.50p shown 60 60
506 A65 3p Clasped hands 72 72

Visit of President Eanes of Portugal A66

1985, May 27 Litho.
507 A66 1.50p multicolored 50 50

Luis de Camoens Museum, 25th Anniv. — A67

Silk paintings by Chen Chi Yun.

1985, June 27 **Litho.**

508 A67 2.50p Two travelers, hermit 1.65 85
509 A67 2.50p Traveling merchant 1.65 85
510 A67 2.50p Conversation in a garden 1.65 85
511 A67 2.50p Veranda of a house 1.65 85
a. Strip of 4, #508-511 6.75 3.50

Butterflies, World Tourism Assoc. Emblem — A68

1985, Sept. 27 **Litho.**

512 A68 30a Euploea midamus 15 15
513 A68 50a Hebomoia glaucippe 20 15
514 A68 70a Lethe confusa 26 18
515 A68 2p Heliophorus epicles 70 50
516 A68 4p Euthalia phemius seitzi 1.75 1.25
517 A68 7.50p Troides helena 3.00 2.00
a. Sheet of 6, #512-517 *37.50*
Nos. 512-517 (6) 6.06 4.23

World Tourism Day.

Cargo Boats — A69

Designs: 50a, Tou. 70a, Veng Seng Lei motor junk. 1p, Tong Heng Long No. 2 motor junk. 6p, Fong Vong San cargo ship.

1985, Oct. 25 ***Perf. 14***

518 A69 50a multicolored 20 15
519 A69 70a multicolored 30 18
520 A69 1p multicolored 50 25
521 A69 6p multicolored 2.50 1.50

New Year Type of 1984

1986, Feb. 3 ***Perf. 13½***

522 A60 1.50p Tiger 90 38
a. Booklet pane of 5 4.50

City of Macau, 400th Anniv. — A71

1986, Apr. 10 **Litho.** ***Perf. 13½***

523 A71 2.20p multicolored 90 55

Musical Instruments — A72

1986, May 22

524 A72 20a Suo-na 15 15
525 A72 50a Sheng 18 15
526 A72 60a Er-hu 25 15
527 A72 70a Ruan 40 18
528 A72 5p Cheng 2.00 1.25
529 A72 8p Pi-pa 3.00 2.00
a. Souvenir sheet of 6, #524-529 *32.50*
Nos. 524-529 (6) 5.98 3.88

AMERIPEX '86.

Ferries — A73

1986, Aug. 28 **Litho.** ***Perf. 13***

530 A73 10a Hydrofoil 15 15
531 A73 40a Hovermarine 15 15
532 A73 3p Jetfoil 1.25 85
533 A73 7.5p High-speed ferry 3.00 2.00

Fortresses A74

1986, Oct. 3 **Litho.** ***Perf. 12½***

534 A74 2p Taipa 1.00 50
535 A74 2p Sao Paulo do Monte 1.00 50
536 A74 2p Our Lady of Guia 1.00 50
537 A74 2p Sao Francisco 1.00 50
a. Strip of 4, #534-537 4.25 3.50

Macao Security Forces, 10th anniv. No. 537a has continuous design.

Dr. Sun Yat-sen
A75 A76

1986, Nov. 12 **Litho.** ***Perf. 12½***

538 A75 70a multicolored *1.50 1.50*

Souvenir Sheet

539 A76 1.30p shown *14.00 14.00*

New Year Type of 1984

1987, Jan. 21 ***Perf. 13½***

540 A60 1.50p Hare 1.25 38
a. Booklet pane of 5 6.25

Shek Wan Ceramic Figures in the Luis de Camoens Museum — A78

1987, Apr. 10 **Litho.** ***Perf. 13½***

541 A78 2.20p Medicine man 1.25 55
542 A78 2.20p Choi San, god of good fortune 1.25 55
543 A78 2.20p Yi, sun god 1.25 55
544 A78 2.20p Chung Kuei, conqueror of demons 1.25 55

Printed se-tenant in blocks of four.

Dragon Boat Festival A79

1987, May 29 **Litho.** ***Perf. 13½***

545 A79 50a Dragon boat race 50 15
546 A79 5p Figurehead 2.25 1.25

Decorated Fans — A80

Casino Gambling — A81

1987, July 29 **Litho.** ***Perf. 12½***

547 A80 30a multicolored 25 15
548 A80 70a multi, diff. 50 20
549 A80 1p multi, diff. 70 28
550 A80 6p multi, diff. 4.50 1.75
a. Souvenir sheet of 4, #547-550 *37.50*

1987, Sept. 30 ***Perf. 13½***

551 A81 20a Fan-tan 15 15
552 A81 40a Cussec 18 15
553 A81 4p Baccarat 1.75 1.15
554 A81 7p Roulette 3.25 2.00

Traditional Transportation — A82

1987, Nov. 18 **Litho.** ***Perf. 13½***

555 A82 10a Market wagon 15 15
556 A82 70a Sedan chair 20 20
557 A82 90a Rickshaw 28 28
558 A82 10p Tricycle rickshaw 2.85 2.85

Souvenir Sheet

559 A82 7.50p Sedan chair, diff. *11.00*

New Year Type of 1984

1988, Feb. 10 **Litho.** ***Perf. 13½***

560 A60 2.50p Dragon 2.00 75
a. Booklet pane of 5 10.00

Wildlife Protection A84

1988, Apr. 14 **Litho.** ***Perf. 12½x12***

561 A84 3p Erinacens europaeus 80 80
562 A84 3p Meles meles 80 80
563 A84 3p Lutra lutra 80 80
564 A84 3p Manis pentadactyla 80 80
a. Strip of 4, #561-564 3.20 3.20

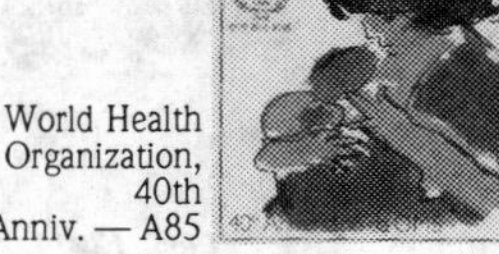

World Health Organization, 40th Anniv. — A85

1988, June 1 **Litho.** ***Perf. 13½***

565 A85 60a Breast-feeding 24 15
566 A85 80a Immunization 32 20
567 A85 2.40p Blood donation 95 60

Modes of Transportation — A86

1988, July 15 **Litho.**

568 A86 20a Bicycles 15 15
569 A86 50a Vespa, Lambretta 24 15
570 A86 3.30p 1907 Rover 20hp 1.40 82
571 A86 5p 1912 Renault delivery truck 2.00 1.25

Souvenir Sheet

572 A86 7.50p 1930s Sedan *12.50*

1988 Summer Olympics, Seoul — A87

1988, Sept. 19 **Litho.**

573 A87 40a Hurdles 16 15
574 A87 60a Basketball 25 15
575 A87 1p Soccer 42 25
576 A87 8p Table tennis 3.25 2.00
577 Sheet of 5, #573-576, 577a 22.50
a. A87 5p Tae kwon do *1.25* 1.25

World Post Day — A88

35th Macao Grand Prix — A89

1988, Oct. 10 **Litho.** ***Perf. 14***

578 A88 13.40p Electronic mail 3.35 3.35
579 A88 40p Express mail 10.00 10.00

1988, Nov. 24 **Litho.** ***Perf. 12½***

580 A89 80a Sedan 32 20
581 A89 2.80p Motorcycle 1.25 70
582 A89 7p Formula 3 3.00 1.75
a. Souvenir sheet of 3, #580-582 *25.00*

New Year Type of 1984

1989, Jan. 20 **Litho.** ***Perf. 13½***

583 A60 3p Snake 90 75
a. Booklet pane of 5 7.50

Occupations — A91

1989, Mar. 1 **Litho.** ***Perf. 12x12½***

584 A91 50a Water carrier 18 15
585 A91 1p Tan-kya woman 35 25
586 A91 4p Tin-tin (junk) man 1.40 1.00
587 A91 5p Tofu peddler 1.75 1.25

See Nos. 612-615, 640-643.

Watercolors by George Smirnoff in the Luis de Camoens Museum A92

1989, Apr. 10 **Litho.** ***Perf. 12½x12***

588 A92 2p multi (4-1) 80 50
589 A92 2p multi (4-2) 80 50
590 A92 2p multi (4-3) 80 50
591 A92 2p multi (4-4) 80 50
a. Strip of 4, #588-591 3.25 2.00

Snakes
A93

1989, July 7 **Litho.**
592 A93 2.50p *Naja naja* 85 62
593 A93 2.50p *Bungarus fasciatus* 85 62
594 A93 2.50p *Trimeresurus albolabris* 85 62
595 A93 2.50p *Elaphe radiata* 85 62
a. Strip of 4, #592-595 3.50 2.50

Traditional Games — A94

1989, July 31 **Litho.** ***Perf. 13½***
596 A94 10a Talu 15 15
597 A94 60a Triol 20 15
598 A94 3.30p Chiquia 1.10 82
599 A94 5p Xadrez Chines 1.75 1.25

Seaplanes — A95

1989, Oct. 9 **Litho.**
600 A95 50a Over church 18 15
601 A95 70a American over lighthouse 26 18
602 A95 2.80p shown 1.10 70
603 A95 4p Over junk 1.50 1.00

Souvenir Sheet

604 A95 7.50p Over harbor *7.00*

No. 604 contains one 40x30mm stamp.

World Stamp Expo '89, Washington, DC — A96

1989, Nov. 17 **Litho.** ***Perf. 12½***
605 A96 40a Malaca 15 15
606 A96 70a Thailand 18 18
607 A96 90a India 22 22
608 A96 2.50p Japan 62 62
609 A96 7.50p China 1.85 1.85
Nos. 605-609 (5) 3.02 3.02

Souvenir Sheet

610 Sheet of 6, #605-609, 610a *10.00*
a. A96 3p Macao 75 75

Influence of the Portuguese in the Far East.

New Year Type of 1984

1990, Jan. 19 **Litho.** ***Perf. 13½***
611 A60 4p Horse 1.00 1.00
a. Booklet pane of 5 5.00

Occupations Type of 1989

1990, Mar. 1 **Litho.** ***Perf. 12x12½***
612 A91 30a Long chau singer 15 15
613 A91 70a Cobbler 28 18
614 A91 1.50p Scribe 55 38
615 A91 7.50p Net fisherman 2.75 1.85

Souvenir Sheet

Penny Black, 150th Anniv. — A99

1990, May 3 **Litho.** ***Perf. 12***
616 A99 10p multicolored 6.00 2.50

Stamp World London 90.

Lutianus Malabaricus
A100

1990, June 8 ***Perf. 12x12½***
617 A100 2.40p shown 62 62
618 A100 2.40p Epinephelus megachir 62 62
619 A100 2.40p Macropodus opercularis 62 62
620 A100 2.40p Ophiocephalus maculatus 62 62
a. Strip of 4, #617-620 2.50 2.50

Decorative Porcelain
A101

1990, Aug. 24 **Litho.** ***Perf. 12½***
621 A101 3p shown 75 75
622 A101 3p Furniture 75 75
623 A101 3p Toys 75 75
624 A101 3p Artificial flowers 75 75
a. Souvenir sheet of 4, #621-624 6.00 3.00

Asian Games, Beijing — A102

1990, Sept. 22 **Litho.** ***Perf. 13½***
625 A102 80a Cycling 20 20
626 A102 1p Swimming 25 25
627 A102 3p Judo 75 75
628 A102 4.20p Shooting 1.05 1.05

Souvenir Sheet

629 Sheet of 5, #625-628, 629a 6.00 3.95
a. A102 6p Martial arts 1.50 1.50

Compass Roses from Portuguese Charts — A103

Charts by 16th century cartographers: Lazaro Luis, Diogo Homem, Fernao Vaz Dourado, and Luiz Teixeira.

1990, Oct. 9 **Litho.** ***Perf. 13½***
630 A103 50a shown 15 15
631 A103 1p multi, diff. 25 25
632 A103 3.50p multi, diff. 90 90
633 A103 6.50p multi, diff. 1.60 1.60

Souvenir Sheet

634 A103 5p multi, diff. 1.30 1.30

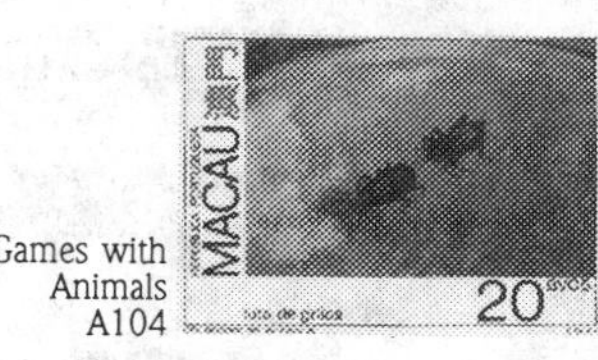
Games with Animals
A104

1990, Nov. 15 **Litho.** ***Perf. 14***
635 A104 20a Cricket fight 15 15
636 A104 80a Bird fight 20 20
637 A104 1p Greyhound race 25 25
638 A104 10p Horse race 2.50 2.50

New Year Type of 1984

1991, Feb. 8 **Litho.** ***Perf. 13½***
639 A60 4.50p Sheep 1.15 1.15
b. Booklet pane of 5 5.85 5.85

Occupations Type of 1987

1991, Mar. 1 ***Perf. 14***
640 A91 80a Knife grinder 20 20
641 A91 1.70p Flour puppet vender 45 45
642 A91 3.50p Street barber 90 90
643 A91 4.20p Fortune teller 1.05 1.05

Shells
A106

1991, Apr. 18 **Litho.** ***Perf. 14***
644 A106 3p Murex pecten 75 75
645 A106 3p Harpa harpa 75 75
646 A106 3p Chicoreus rosarius 75 75
647 A106 3p Tonna zonata 75 75
a. Strip of 4, #644-647 3.00 3.00

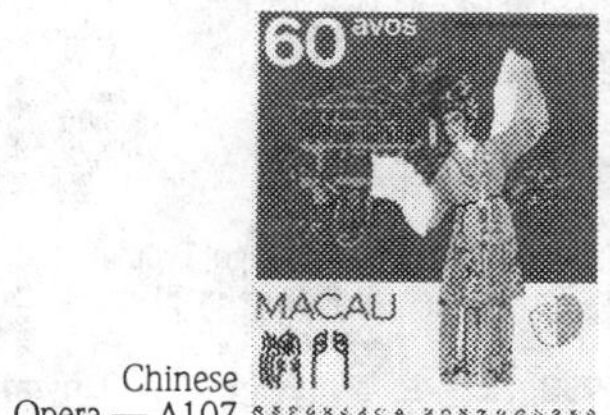
Chinese Opera — A107

Various performers in costume.

1991, June 5 **Litho.** ***Perf. 13½***
648 A107 60a multicolored 15 15
649 A107 80a multicolored 20 20
650 A107 1p multicolored 26 26
651 A107 10p multicolored 2.60 2.60

Flowers
A108

Designs: 1.70p, Delonix regia. 3p, Ipomoea cairica. 3.50p, Jasminum mesnyi. 4.20p, Bauhinia variegata.

1991, Oct. 9 **Litho.** ***Perf. 13½***
652 A108 1.70p multicolored 45 45
653 A108 3p multicolored 78 78
654 A108 3.50p multicolored 90 90
655 A108 4.20p multicolored 1.10 1.10
a. Souvenir sheet of 4, #652-655 3.25 3.25

Cultural Exchange — A109

Namban screen: No. 656, Unloading boat.

1991, Nov. 16 **Litho.** ***Perf. 12***
656 A109 4.20p multicolored 1.10 1.10
657 A109 4.20p shown 1.10 1.10
a. Souvenir sheet of 2, #656-657 2.20 2.20

Holiday Greetings A110

1991, Nov. 29 Litho. *Perf. 14½*
658 A110 1.70p Lunar New Year 44 44
659 A110 3p Santa Claus, Christmas 78 78
660 A110 3.50p Old man 90 90
661 A110 4.20p Girl at New Year party 1.10 1.10

New Year Type of 1984

1992, Jan. 28 Litho. *Perf. 13½*
662 A60 4.50p Monkey 1.15 1.15
a. Booklet pane of 5 12.00

Paintings of Doors and Windows A111

1992, Mar. 1 *Perf. 14*
663 A111 1.70p multicolored 45 45
664 A111 3p multi, diff. 78 78
665 A111 3.50p multi, diff. 90 90
666 A111 4.20p multi, diff. 1.10 1.10

Mythological Chinese Gods A112

1992, Apr. 3 Litho. *Perf. 14*
667 A112 3.50p T'it Kuai Lei (4-1) 90 90
668 A112 3.50p Chong Lei Kun (4-2) 90 90
669 A112 3.50p Cheong Kuo Lou (4-3) 90 90
670 A112 3.50p Loi Tong Pan (4-4) 90 90
a. Block or strip of 4, #667-670 3.60 3.60

Lion Dance Costume A113

Designs: 2.70p, Lion, diff. 6p, Dragon.

1992, May 18
671 A113 1p multicolored 25 25
672 A113 2.70p multicolored 70 70
673 A113 6p multicolored 1.55 1.55

World Columbian Stamp Expo '92, Chicago.

1992 Summer Olympics, Barcelona — A114

1992, July 1 Litho. *Perf. 13*
674 A114 80a High jump 25 25
675 A114 4.20p Badminton 1.30 1.30
676 A114 4.70p Roller hockey 1.45 1.45
677 A114 5p Yachting 1.50 1.50
a. Souvenir sheet of 4, #674-677 4.50 4.50

Temples A115

1992, Oct. 9 *Perf. 14*
678 A115 1p Na Cha 28 28
679 A115 1.50p Kun Iam 40 40
680 A115 1.70p Hong Kon 45 45
681 A115 6.50p A Ma 1.70 1.70

Portuguese-Chinese Friendship — A116

1992, Nov. 1 Litho. *Perf. 14*
682 A116 10p multicolored 2.65 2.65
a. Souv. sheet, perf. 13½ 2.65 2.65

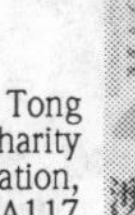
Tung Sin Tong Charity Organization, Cent. — A117

1992, Nov. 27 *Perf. 12x11½*
683 A117 1p multicolored 28 28

New Year Type of 1984

1993 Litho. *Perf. 13½*
684 A60 5p Rooster 1.35 1.35
a. Booklet pane of 5 6.75

AIR POST STAMPS

Stamps of 1934 Overprinted or Surcharged in Black

Avião — a

Avião 5 avos — b

1936 Wmk. 232 *Perf. 11½*
C1 A17 (a) 2a blue green 1.65 70
C2 A17 (a) 3a violet 1.65 70
C3 A17 (b) 5a on 6a brn 1.65 70
C4 A17 (a) 7a brt rose 1.65 70
C5 A17 (a) 8a brt blue 3.00 90
C6 A17 (a) 15a maroon 9.75 4.00
Nos. C1-C6 (6) 19.35 7.70

Common Design Type
Name and Value in Black
Perf. 13½x13

1938, Aug. 1 Engr. Unwmk.
C7 CD39 1a scarlet 40 15
C8 CD39 2a purple 40 15
C9 CD39 3a orange 50 28
C10 CD39 5a ultra 1.00 38
C11 CD39 10a lilac brn 2.00 38
C12 CD39 20a dk green 4.00 90
C13 CD39 50a red brown 5.00 1.10
C14 CD39 70a rose car 5.75 1.40
C15 CD39 1p magenta 10.00 5.00
Nos. C7-C15 (9) 29.05 9.74

No. C13 exists with overprint "Exposicao Internacional de Nova York, 1939-1940" and Trylon and Perisphere.

Catalogue values for unused stamps in this section, from this point to the end of the section, are for never hinged items.

Plane over Bay of Grand Beach — AP1

1960, Dec. 11 Litho. *Perf. 14*
C16 AP1 50a shown 1.00 18
C17 AP1 76a Penha Chapel 2.25 28
C18 AP1 3p Macao 4.00 60
C19 AP1 5p Bairro de Mong Ha 6.75 90
C20 AP1 10p Penha and Bay 10.00 1.25
Nos. C16-C20 (5) 24.00 3.21

No. C17 Surcharged

1979, Aug. 3 Litho. *Perf. 14*
C21 AP1 70a on 76a multi 6.00 1.50

POSTAGE DUE STAMPS

Numeral of Value — D1

Perf. 11½x12
1904, July Typo. Unwmk.
Name and Value in Black
J1 D1 ½a gray green 30 24
a. Name & value inverted 13.00 10.00
J2 D1 1a yellow grn 35 28
J3 D1 2a slate 35 28
J4 D1 4a pale brown 35 28
J5 D1 5a red orange 1.10 70
J6 D1 8a gray brown 1.10 70
J7 D1 12a red brown 1.25 70
J8 D1 20a dull blue 2.50 1.40
J9 D1 40a carmine 3.50 2.50
J10 D1 50a orange 6.00 4.00
J11 D1 1p gray vio 13.00 6.75
Nos. J1-J11 (11) 29.80 17.83

Issued without gum: Nos. J7-J11.
For overprints see Nos. 144-146, J12-J32.

Issue of 1904 Overprinted in Carmine or Green

1911
J12 D1 ½a gray grn 16 15
J13 D1 1a yellow grn 16 15
J14 D1 2a slate 16 15
J15 D1 4a pale brown 24 18
J16 D1 5a orange 24 18
J17 D1 8a gray brown 24 18
J18 D1 12a red brown 65 40
J19 D1 20a dull blue 1.25 85
J20 D1 40a car (G) 2.25 1.25
J21 D1 50a orange 4.50 2.50
J22 D1 1p gray violet 6.00 3.50
Nos. J12-J22 (11) 15.85 9.49

Issued without gum: Nos. J19-J22.

Issue of 1904 Overprinted in Red or Green

1914
J22A D1 ½a gray grn *475.00 425.00*
J23 D1 1a yellow grn 48 35
J24 D1 2a slate 48 35
J25 D1 4a pale brown 48 35
J26 D1 5a orange 55 35
J27 D1 8a gray brown 55 35
J28 D1 12a red brown 55 35
J29 D1 20a dull blue 2.00 1.40
J30 D1 40a car (G) 5.50 2.50
a. Double ovpt., red and grn 21.00 8.00
J31 D1 50a orange 5.50 2.50
J32 D1 1p gray violet 14.00 5.00
Nos. J23-J32 (10) *30.09 13.50*

Issued without gum: Nos. J28, J30-J32.

D2

Name and Value in Black
1947 Typo. *Perf. 11½x12*
J33 D2 1a red violet 1.50 85
J34 D2 2a purple 1.50 85
J35 D2 4a dark blue 1.50 85
J36 D2 5a chocolate 1.50 85
J37 D2 8a red violet 1.50 85
J38 D2 12a orange brn 4.75 85
J39 D2 20a yellow grn 2.75 2.00
J40 D2 40a brt carmine 4.75 2.25
J41 D2 50a orange yel 12.00 5.00
J42 D2 1p blue 12.00 3.50
Nos. J33-J42 (10) 43.75 17.85

Stamps of 1934 Surcharged "PORTEADO" and New Values in Carmine

1949, May 1 Wmk. 232
J43 A17 1a on 4a black 1.50 85
J44 A17 2a on 6a brown 1.50 85
J45 A17 4a on 8a brt bl 1.75 85
J46 A17 5a on 10a red org 2.00 85
J47 A17 8a on 12a dk bl 2.00 1.40
J48 A17 12a on 30a ap grn 2.50 1.50
J49 A17 20a on 40a violet 2.50 1.50
Nos. J43-J49 (7) 13.75 7.80

Catalogue values for unused stamps in this section, from this point to the end of the section, are for Never Hinged items.

Nos. 348, 349 and 351 Overprinted or Surcharged in Black or Carmine

PORTEADO

1951, June 6 Unwmk.
J50 A21 1a org yel, *lem* 75 18
J51 A21 2a dk grn, *bl* (C) 75 18
J52 A21 7a on 10a brt pink, *bl* 75 18

Common Design Type
1952 Photo. & Typo. *Perf. 14*
Numeral in Red; Frame Multicolored
J53 CD45 1a violet bl 15 15
J54 CD45 3a chocolate 15 15
J55 CD45 5a indigo 15 15
J56 CD45 10a dk red 60 24
J57 CD45 30a indigo 75 30
J58 CD45 1p chocolate 2.25 90
Nos. J53-J58 (6) 4.05
Set value 1.60

WAR TAX STAMPS

Victory WT1

1919, Aug. 11 Unwmk. *Perf. 15x14*
Overprinted in Black or Carmine
MR1 WT1 2a green 1.40 1.00
MR2 WT1 11a green (C) 2.00 1.40

Nos. MR1-MR2 were also for use in Timor. A 9a value was issued for revenue use.

NEWSPAPER STAMPS

JORNAES $2\frac{1}{2}$

JORNAES

$2\frac{1}{2}$ $2\frac{1}{2}$

Nos. P1-P2 No. P3

Typographed and Embossed

1892-93 Unwmk. *Perf. 12½, 13½*

Black Surcharge

P1 A7 2½r on 40r choc 2.50 70
a. Inverted surcharge 40.00 15.00
P2 A7 2½r on 80r gray 2.50 70
a. Inverted surcharge 40.00 15.00
b. Double surcharge
c. Perf. 13½ 40.00 11.00
P3 A7 2½r on 10r grn ('93) 2.50 70
a. Double surcharge

N3

N4

Perf. 11½, 12½, 13½

1893-94 Typo.

P4 N3 2½r brown 35 28
P5 N4 ½a on 2½r brn (Bk) ('94) 75 55
a. Double surcharge

For surcharges see Nos. 131, 252.

POSTAL TAX STAMPS

Pombal Commemorative Issue

Common Design Types

Perf. 12½

1925, Nov. 3 Engr. Unwmk.

RA1 CD28 2a red org & blk 1.00 70
RA2 CD29 2a red org & blk 1.00 70
RA3 CD30 2a red org & blk 1.00 70

Symbolical of Charity
PT1 PT2

1930, Dec. 25 Litho. *Perf. 11*

RA4 PT1 5a dk brown, *yel* 7.00 5.00

1945-47 *Perf. 11½, 12, 10*

RA5 PT2 5a blk brn, *yel* 10.50 7.50
RA6 PT2 5a bl, *bluish* ('47) 30.00 6.75
RA7 PT2 10a grn, *citron* 10.00 3.75
RA8 PT2 15a org, *buff* 1.50 3.75
RA9 PT2 20a rose red, *sal* 60.00 6.75
RA10 PT2 50a red vio, *pnksh* 3.00 3.00

Catalogue values for unused stamps in this section, from this point to the end of the section, are for Never Hinged items.

1953-56 *Perf. 10½x11½*

RA11 PT2 10a bl, *pale grn* ('56) 65 18
RA12 PT2 20a chocolate, *yel* 9.50 2.50
RA13 PT2 50a car, *pale rose* 8.75 2.75

1958 *Perf. 12x11½*

RA14 PT2 1a gray grn, *grnsh* 16 15
RA15 PT2 2a rose lilac, *grysh* 16 15
Set value 18

Type of 1945-47 Redrawn
Imprint: "Lito. Imp. Nac.-Macau"

1961-66 *Perf. 11*

RA16 PT2 1a gray grn, *grnsh* 16 15
RA17 PT2 2a rose lil, *grysh* 16 15
RA18 PT2 10a bl, *pale grn* ('62) 24 18
RA19 PT2 20a brn, *yel* ('66) 32 18
Set value 54

Nos. RA16-RA19 have accent added to "E" in "Assistencia."

Nos. RA4-RA19 were issued without gum.

POSTAL TAX DUE STAMPS

Pombal Commemorative Issue

Common Design Types

1925 Unwmk. *Perf. 12½*

RAJ1 CD31 4a red orange & blk 1.25 70
RAJ2 CD32 4a red orange & blk 1.25 70
RAJ3 CD33 4a red orange & blk 1.25 70

MADAGASCAR

Malagasy Republic

LOCATION — Large island off the coast of southeastern Africa
GOVT. — Republic
AREA — 226,658 sq. mi.
POP. — 9,735,000 (est. 1984)
CAPITAL — Antananarivo

Madagascar became a French protectorate in 1885 and a French colony in 1896 following several years of dispute among France, Great Britain, and the native government. The colony administered the former protectorates of Anjouan, Grand Comoro, Mayotte, Diego-Suarez, Nossi-Be and Sainte-Marie de Madagascar. Previous issues of postage stamps are found under these individual headings. The Malagasy Republic succeeded the colony in 1958 and became the Democratic Republic of Madagascar in 1975.

For Madagascar's British Consular Mail stamps of 1884-1886, see Vol. 1.

100 Centimes = 1 Franc
100 Centimes = 1 Ariary (1976)

Catalogue values for unused stamps in this country are for Never Hinged items, beginning with Scott 241 in the regular postage section, Scott B15 in the semi-postal section, Scott C37 in the airpost section, and Scott J31 in the postage due section.

French Offices in Madagascar

The general issues of French Colonies were used in these offices in addition to the stamps listed here.

Stamps of French Colonies Surcharged in Black:

25 05 5
a b c

1889 Unwmk. *Perf. 14x13½*

Overprint Type "a"

1 A9 05c on 10c blk, *lav* 200.00 80.00
a. Inverted surcharge 900.00 650.00
2 A9 05c on 25c blk, *rose* 200.00 80.00
a. Inverted surcharge 900.00 650.00
b. 25c on 10c lav (error) *4,500.* *3,500.*
3 A9 25c on 40c red, *straw* 190.00 65.00
a. Inverted surcharge 825.00 575.00

1891

Overprint Type "b"

4 A9 05c on 40c red, *straw* 100.00 42.50
5 A9 15c on 25c blk, *rose* 100.00 42.50
a. Surcharge vertical 100.00 62.50

Overprint Type "c"

6 A9 5c on 10c blk, *lav* 140.00 65.00
a. Double surcharge 400.00
7 A9 5c on 25c blk, *rose* 140.00 65.00

Forgeries of Nos. 1-7 exist.

A4

1891 Type-set *Imperf.*

Without Gum

8 A4 5c blk, *green* 65.00 14.00
9 A4 10c blk, *lt bl* 60.00 15.00
10 A4 15c ultra, *pale bl* 60.00 15.00
11 A4 25c brn, *buff* 10.00 6.00
12 A4 1fr blk, *yellow* 650.00 190.00
13 A4 5fr vio & blk, *lil* 1,200. 600.00

Ten varieties of each. Nos. 12-13 have been extensively forged.

Stamps of France 1876-90, Overprinted in Red or Black: POSTE FRANÇAISE Madagascar

1895 *Perf. 14x13½*

14 A15 5c grn, *grnsh* (R) 6.00 3.50
15 A15 10c blk, *lav* (R) 22.50 14.00
16 A15 15c bl (R) 30.00 8.25
17 A15 25c blk, *rose* (R) 49.00 10.00
18 A15 40c red, *straw* (Bk) 40.00 15.00
19 A15 50c rose, *rose* (Bk) 49.00 22.00
20 A15 75c dp vio, *org* (R) 49.00 22.00
21 A15 1fr brnz grn, *straw* (Bk) 50.00 27.50
22 A15 5fr vio, *lav* (Bk) 82.50 45.00

Majunga Issue

Stamps of France, 1876-86, Surcharged with New Value

1895

Manuscript Surcharge in Red

22A A15 0,15c on 25c blk, *rose* *4,500.*
22B A15 0,15c on 1fr brnz grn, *straw* *3,750.*

Handstamped in Black

22C A15 15c on 25c blk, *rose* *4,000.*
22D A15 15c on 1fr brnz grn, *straw* *9,000.* *4,250.*

Three types of "15" were used for No. 22C.

Stamps of France, 1876-84, Surcharged with New Value

1896

23 A15 5c on 1c blk, *bl* *4,000.* *1,500.*
24 A15 15c on 2c brn, *buff* *1,500.* *750.00*
25 A15 25c on 3c gray, *grysh* *1,750.* *750.00*
26 A15 25c on 4c cl, *lav* *4,000.* *750.00*
27 A15 25c on 40c red, *straw* *850.00* *575.00*

The oval of the 5c and 15c surcharges is smaller than that of the 25c, and it does not extend beyond the edges of the stamp as the 25c surcharge does.

Excellent counterfeits of the surcharges on Nos. 22A to 27 exist.

Issues of the Colony

Navigation and Commerce — A7

1896-1906 Typo. *Perf. 14x13½*

Colony Name in Blue or Carmine

28 A7 1c blk, *lil bl* 72 55
29 A7 2c brn, *buff* 72 55
a. Name in blue black 2.50 2.50
30 A7 4c claret, *lav* 80 55
31 A7 5c grn, *grnsh* 3.25 72
32 A7 5c yel grn ('01) 75 48
33 A7 10c blk, *lav* 3.50 80
34 A7 10c red ('00) 75 48
35 A7 15c blue, quadrille paper 4.75 55
36 A7 15c gray ('00) 80 70
37 A7 20c red, *grn* 2.50 70
38 A7 25c blk, *rose* 3.25 2.50
39 A7 25c blue ('00) 10.00 10.00
40 A7 30c brn, *bis* 4.00 2.00
41 A7 35c blk, *yel* ('06) 20.00 3.50
42 A7 40c red, *straw* 3.50 2.50
43 A7 50c car, *rose* 5.25 75
44 A7 50c brn, *az* ('00) 14.00 13.00
45 A7 75c dp vio, *org* 1.40 80
46 A7 1fr brnz grn, *straw* 5.25 1.75
a. Name in blue ('99) 14.00 7.00
47 A7 5fr red lil, *lav* ('99) 16.00 12.00
Nos. 28-47 (20) 101.19 54.88

Perf. 13½x14 stamps are counterfeits.

For surcharges see Nos. 48-55, 58-60, 115-118, 127-128.

Surcharged in Black **05**

1902

48 A7 05c on 50c car, *rose* 3.00 3.00
a. Inverted surcharge 52.50 52.50
49 A7 10c on 5fr red lil, *lav* 11.00 9.00
a. Inverted surcharge 57.50 57.50
50 A7 15c on 1fr ol grn, *straw* 3.00 3.00
a. Inverted surcharge 57.50 57.50
b. Double surcharge 175.00 175.00

Surcharged in Black **0,01**

51 A7 0,01 on 2c brn, *buff* 3.75 3.75
a. Inverted surcharge 32.50 32.50
b. "00,1" instead of "0.01" 45.00 45.00
c. As "b" inverted
d. Comma omitted 75.00 75.00
e. Name in blue black 4.25 4.25
52 A7 0,05 on 30c brn, *bis* 4.50 4.50
a. Inverted surcharge 32.50 32.50
b. "00,5" instead of "0,05" 45.00 45.00
c. As "b" inverted 175.00 175.00
d. Comma omitted 75.00 75.00
53 A7 0,10 on 50c car, *rose* 4.50 4.50
a. Inverted surcharge 32.50 32.50
b. Comma omitted 75.00 75.00
54 A7 0,15 on 75c vio, *org* 3.75 3.75
a. Inverted surcharge 40.00 40.00
b. Comma omitted 90.00 90.00
55 A7 0,15 on 1fr ol grn, *straw* 6.75 6.75
a. Inverted surcharge 50.00 50.00
b. Comma omitted 100.00 100.00

Surcharged On Stamps of Diego-Suarez

56 A11 0,05 on 30c brn, *bis* 62.50 62.50
a. "00,5" instead of "0,05" 425.00 425.00
b. Inverted surcharge 600.00 600.00
57 A11 0,10 on 50c car, *rose* *3,250.* *3,250.*

Counterfeits of Nos. 56-57 exist with surcharge both normal and inverted.

Surcharged in Black **0,01**

58 A7 0,01 on 2c brn, *buff* 3.25 3.25
a. Inverted surcharge 32.50 32.50
b. Comma omitted 75.00 75.00
59 A7 0,05 on 30c brn, *bis* 3.75 3.75
a. Inverted surcharge 32.50 32.50
b. Comma omitted 75.00 75.00
60 A7 0,10 on 50c car, *rose* 3.25 3.25
a. Inverted surcharge 32.50 32.50
b. Comma omitted 90.00 90.00

Surcharged On Stamps of Diego-Suarez

61 A11 0,05 on 30c brn, *bister* 85.00 85.00
a. Inverted surcharge 600.00 600.00
62 A11 0,10 on 50c car, *rose* *3,250.* *3,250.*

BISECTS

During alleged stamp shortages at several Madagascar towns in 1904, it is claimed that bisects were used. After being affixed to letters, these bisects were handstamped "Affranchissement - exceptionnel - (faute de timbres)" and other inscriptions of similar import. The stamps bisected were 10c, 20c, 30c and 50c denominations of Madagascar type A7 and Diego-Suarez type A11. The editors believe these provisionals were unnecessary and speculative.

Zebu, Traveler's Tree and Lemur — A8

Transportation by Sedan Chair — A9

1903 Engr. *Perf. 11½*

No.	Type	Description	Unused	Used
63	A8	1c dk vio	70	68
a.		On bluish paper	4.00	3.25
64	A8	2c ol brn	70	68
65	A8	4c brown	70	68
66	A8	5c yel grn	4.00	68
67	A8	10c red	4.00	70
68	A8	15c carmine	7.75	70
a.		On bluish paper	75.00	
69	A8	20c orange	3.00	90
70	A8	25c dl bl	16.00	2.50
71	A8	30c pale red	18.00	5.75
72	A8	40c gray vio	16.00	2.50
73	A8	50c brn org	32.50	10.50
74	A8	75c org yel	32.50	10.50
75	A8	1fr dp grn	32.50	15.00
76	A8	2fr slate	40.00	18.00
77	A8	5fr gray blk	52.50	20.00
		Nos. 63-77 (15)	260.85	89.77

Nos. 63-77 exist imperf. Value of set, $500.

For surcharges see Nos. 119-124, 129.

1908-28 Typo. *Perf. 13½x14*

No.	Type	Description	Unused	Used
79	A9	1c vio & ol	15	15
80	A9	2c red & ol	15	15
81	A9	4c ol brn & brn	15	15
82	A9	5c bl grn & ol	15	15
83	A9	5c blk & rose ('22)	15	15
84	A9	10c rose & brn	15	15
85	A9	10c bl grn & ol grn ('22)	15	15
86	A9	10c org brn & vio ('25)	15	15
87	A9	15c dl vio & rose ('16)	15	15
88	A9	15c dl grn & lt grn ('27)	15	15
89	A9	15c dk bl & rose red ('28)	65	50
90	A9	20c org & brn	15	15
91	A9	25c bl & blk	80	20
92	A9	25c vio & blk ('22)	15	15
93	A9	30c brn & blk	1.00	62
94	A9	30c rose red & brn ('22)	15	15
95	A9	30c grn & red vio ('25)	15	15
96	A9	30c dp grn & yel grn ('27)	60	55
97	A9	35c red & blk	60	25
98	A9	40c vio brn & blk	60	22
99	A9	45c bl grn & blk	42	22
100	A9	45c red & ver ('25)	15	15
101	A9	45c gray lil & mag ('27)	60	42
102	A9	50c vio & blk	42	20
103	A9	50c bl & blk ('22)	15	15
104	A9	50c blk & org ('25)	28	15
105	A9	60c vio, *pnksh* ('25)	28	25
106	A9	65c blk & bl ('25)	55	45
107	A9	75c rose red & blk	42	15
108	A9	85c grn & ver ('25)	55	50
109	A9	1fr brn & ol	35	15
110	A9	1fr dl bl ('25)	55	40
111	A9	1fr rose & grn ('28)	3.50	2.75
112	A9	1.10fr bis & bl grn ('28)	60	50
113	A9	2fr bl & ol	2.25	60
114	A9	5fr vio & vio brn	4.75	3.50
		Nos. 79-114 (36)	22.17	14.98

75c violet on pinkish stamps of type A9 are No. 138 without surcharge.

For surcharges and overprints see Nos. 125-126, 130-146, 178-179, B1, 212-214.

Preceding Issues Surcharged in Black or Carmine

05 10

1912, Nov. *Perf. 14x13½*

No.	Type	Description	Unused	Used
115	A7	5c on 15c gray (C)	35	35
116	A7	5c on 20c red, *grn*	42	42
a.		Inverted surcharge	60.00	60.00
117	A7	5c on 30c brn, *bis* (C)	50	50
118	A7	10c on 75c vio, *org*	5.00	5.00
a.		Double surcharge	100.00	100.00
119	A8	5c on 2c ol brn (C)	35	35
120	A8	5c on 20c org	40	40
121	A8	5c on 30c pale red	60	60
122	A8	10c on 40c gray vio (C)	65	65
123	A8	10c on 50c brn org	1.60	1.60
124	A8	10c on 75c org yel	3.50	3.50
a.		Inverted surcharge	110.00	110.00
		Nos. 115-124 (10)	13.37	13.37

Two spacings between the surcharged numerals are found on Nos. 115 to 118.

Stamps of Anjouan, Grand Comoro Island, Mayotte and Mohéli with similar surcharges were also available for use in Madagascar and the entire Comoro archipelago.

Preceding Issues Surcharged in Red or Black

0,30 g 1 FR. h

1921

On Nos. 98 & 107

No.	Type	Description	Unused	Used
125	A9 (g)	30c on 40c (R)	1.00	1.00
126	A9 (g)	60c on 75c	1.40	1.40

On Nos. 45 & 47

No.	Type	Description	Unused	Used
127	A7 (g)	60c on 75c (R)	3.25	3.25
a.		Inverted surcharge	120.00	120.00
128	A7 (h)	1fr on 5fr	48	48

On No. 77

No.	Type	Description	Unused	Used
129	A8 (h)	1fr on 5fr (R)	40.00	40.00

Stamps and Type of 1908-16 Surcharged in Black or Red

0,25

No.	Type	Description	Unused	Used
130	A9	1c on 15c dl vio & rose	48	48
131	A9	25c on 35c red & blk	2.25	2.25
132	A9	25c on 35c red & blk (R)	7.25	7.25
133	A9	25c on 40c brn & blk	2.25	2.25
134	A9	25c on 45c grn & blk	1.60	1.60
		Nos. 125-134 (10)	59.96	59.96

Stamps and Type of 1908-28 Surcharged with New Value and Bars

1922-27

No.	Type	Description	Unused	Used
135	A9	25c on 15c dl vio & rose ('25)	15	15
a.		Double surcharge	25.00	
136	A9	25c on 2fr bl & ol ('24)	15	15
137	A9	25c on 5fr vio & vio brn ('24)	15	15
138	A9	60c on 75c vio, *pnksh* ('22)	18	16
139	A9	65c on 75c rose red & blk ('25)	30	22
140	A9	85c on 45c bl grn & blk ('25)	30	22
141	A9	90c on 75c dl red & rose red ('27)	24	20
142	A9	1.25fr on 1fr lt bl (R) ('26)	18	15
143	A9	1.50fr on 1fr dp bl & dl bl ('27)	18	15
144	A9	3fr on 5fr grn & vio ('27)	50	40
145	A9	10fr on 5fr org & rose lil ('27)	3.00	2.00
146	A9	20fr on 5fr rose & sl bl ('27)	5.00	3.75
		Nos. 135-146 (12)	10.33	7.70

See Nos. 178-179.

Sakalava Chief — A10

Hova Woman — A12

Hova with Oxen — A11

Bétsiléo Woman A13

Perf. 13½x14, 14x13½

1930-44 Typo.

No.	Type	Description	Unused	Used
147	A11	1c dk bl & bl grn ('33)	15	15
148	A10	2c brn red & dk brn	15	15
149	A10	4c dk brn & vio	15	15
150	A11	5c lt grn & red	15	15
151	A12	10c ver & dp grn	15	15
152	A13	15c dp red	15	15
153	A11	20c yel brn & dk bl	15	15
154	A12	25c vio & dk brn	15	15
155	A13	30c Prus bl	25	15
156	A10	40c grn & red	30	30
157	A13	45c dl vio	55	40
158	A11	65c ol grn & vio	55	32
159	A13	75c dk brn	45	32
160	A11	90c brn red & dk red	58	45
161	A12	1fr yel brn & dk bl	75	60
162	A12	1fr dk red & car rose ('38)	40	32
163	A12	1.25fr dp bl & dk brn ('33)	60	45
164	A10	1.50fr dk & dp bl	3.25	85
165	A10	1.50fr brn & dk red ('38)	15	15
165A	A10	1.50fr dk red & brn ('44)	16	16
166	A10	1.75fr dk brn & dk red ('33)	1.75	65
167	A10	5fr vio & dk brn	68	32
168	A10	20fr yel brn & dk bl	1.10	90
		Nos. 147-168 (23)	12.72	
		Set value		6.60

For surcharges and overprints see Nos. 211, 215, 217-218, 222-223, 228-229, 233, 235, 239, 257.

Colonial Exposition Issue

Common Design Types

1931 Engr. *Perf. 12½*

Name of Country in Black

No.	Type	Description	Unused	Used
169	CD70	40c dp grn	42	35
170	CD71	50c violet	85	40
171	CD72	90c red org	70	50
172	CD73	1.50fr dl bl	1.00	60

General Joseph Simon Galliéni — A14

1931 Engr. *Perf. 14*

Size: 21½x34½mm

No.	Type	Description	Unused	Used
173	A14	1c ultra	28	15
174	A14	50c org brn	60	15
175	A14	2fr dp red	3.50	2.25
176	A14	3fr emerald	3.00	1.10
177	A14	10fr dp org	1.75	1.10
		Nos. 173-177 (5)	9.13	4.75

See Nos. 180-190. For overprints and surcharges see Nos. 216, 219, 221, 224, 232, 258.

25c

Nos. 113 and 109 Surcharged

1932 *Perf. 13½x14*

No.	Type	Description	Unused	Used
178	A9	25c on 2fr bl & ol	35	25
179	A9	50c on 1fr brn & ol	35	25

No. 178 has numerals in thick block letters. No. 136 has thin shaded numerals.

Galliéni Type of 1931

1936-40 Photo. *Perf. 13½, 13x13½*

Size: 21x34mm

No.	Type	Description	Unused	Used
180	A14	3c saph ('40)	15	15
181	A14	45c brt grn ('40)	15	15
182	A14	50c yel brn	15	15
183	A14	60c brt red lil ('40)	15	15
184	A14	70c brt rose ('40)	20	20
185	A14	90c cop brn ('39)	15	15
186	A14	1.40fr org yel ('40)	35	22
187	A14	1.60fr pur ('40)	35	28
188	A14	2fr dk car	15	15
189	A14	3fr green	2.00	1.00
190	A14	3fr ol blk ('39)	60	32
		Nos. 180-190 (11)	4.40	
		Set value		2.50

Paris International Exposition Issue

Common Design Types

1937, Apr. 15 Engr. *Perf. 13*

No.	Type	Description	Unused	Used
191	CD74	20c dp vio	60	60
192	CD75	30c dk grn	60	60
193	CD76	40c car rose	60	60
194	CD77	50c dk brn & blk	50	50
195	CD78	90c red	75	75
196	CD79	1.50fr ultra	75	75
		Nos. 191-196 (6)	3.80	3.80

Common Design Types pictured in section at front of book.

Colonial Arts Exhibition Issue

Common Design Type

Souvenir Sheet

1937 *Imperf.*

No.	Type	Description	Unused	Used
197	CD74	3fr org red	2.50	2.50

Jean Laborde A15

1938-40 *Perf. 13*

No.	Type	Description	Unused	Used
198	A15	35c green	35	20
199	A15	55c dp pur	35	20
200	A15	65c org red	53	20
201	A15	80c vio brn	35	20
202	A15	1fr rose car	35	20
203	A15	1.25fr rose car ('39)	15	15
204	A15	1.75fr dk ultra	65	20
205	A15	2.15fr yel brn	1.20	80
206	A15	2.25fr dk ultra ('39)	28	15
207	A15	2.50fr blk brn ('40)	20	20
208	A15	10fr dk grn ('40)	60	35
		Nos. 198-208 (11)	5.01	2.85

Nos. 198-202, 204, 205 commemorate the 60th anniv. of the death of Jean Laborde, explorer.

For overprints and surcharges see Nos. 220, 225-227, 230-231, 234, 236-237.

New York World's Fair Issue

Common Design Type

1939, May 10 Engr. *Perf. 12½x12*

No.	Type	Description	Unused	Used
209	CD82	1.25fr car lake	65	65
210	CD82	2.25fr ultra	65	65

For surcharge see No. 240.

Porters Carrying Man in Chair, and Marshal Petain — A15a

1941 Engr. *Perf. 12x12½*

No.	Type	Description	Unused	Used
210A	A15a	1fr bister brn	35	
210B	A15a	2.50fr blue	35	

Nos. 210A-210B were issued by the Vichy government and were not placed on sale in the colony.

An enhanced introduction to the Scott Catalogue begins on Page 5A. A thorough understanding of the material presented there will greatly aid your use of the catalogue itself.

Type of 1930-44 Surcharged in Black with New Value

1942 *Perf. 14x13½*
211 A11 50c on 65c dk brn & mag 65 15

V2

Stamps of the design shown above and types A10, A11, A12 and A14, without "RF," were issued in 1942-44 by the Vichy government, but were not placed on sale in the colony.

Nos. 143, 145-146 with Additional Overprint in Red or Black **FRANCE LIBRE**

1942 **Unwmk.** *Perf. 14x13½*
212 A9 1.50fr on 1fr (R) 55 55
213 A9 10fr on 5fr (Bk) 3.50 3.50
214 A9 20fr on 5fr (R) 5.00 5.00

Stamps of 1930-40 Overprinted Like Nos. 212-214 in Black or Red or:

FRANCE LIBRE

215 A10 2c brn red & dk brn 55 55
216 A14 3c saph (R) 65.00 65.00
217 A13 15c dp red 4.50 4.50
218 A11 65c dk brn & mag 45 45
219 A14 70c brt rose 40 40
220 A15 80c vio brn 1.10 1.10
221 A14 1.40fr org yel 40 40
222 A10 1.50fr dk bl & dp bl (R) 65 65
223 A10 1.50fr brn & dk red 65 65
224 A14 1.60fr purple 45 45
225 A15 2.25fr dk ultra (R) 35 35
226 A15 2.50fr blk brn (R) 1.60 1.60
227 A15 10fr dk grn 2.25 2.25
228 A10 20fr yel brn & dk bl (R) *450.00 450.00*

Stamps of 1930-40 Surcharged in Black or Red **FRANCE LIBRE 0,10 x**

229 A11 5c on 1c dk bl & bl grn 28 28
230 A15 10c on 55c dp pur 65 65
231 A15 30c on 65c org red 40 40
232 A14 50c on 90c cop brn 20 20
233 A12 1fr on 1.25fr dp bl & dk brn 1.00 1.00
234 A15 1fr on 1.25fr rose car 4.00 4.00
235 A10 1.50fr on 1.75fr dk brn & dk red 35 35
236 A15 1.50fr on 1.75fr ultra (R) 35 35
237 A15 2fr on 2.15fr yel brn 80 80

No. 211 with additional Overprint Like Nos. 217-218 in Black
239 A11 50c on 65c dk brn & mag 28 28

New York World's Fair Stamp Overprinted Like #217-218 in Red
Perf. 12½x12
240 CD82 2.25fr ultra 28 28
Nos. 212-227,229-240 (27) 95.99 95.99

Catalogue values for unused stamps in this section, from this point to the end of the section, are for Never Hinged items.

Traveler's Tree — A16

1943 Unwmk. Photo. *Perf. 14x14½*
241 A16 5c ol gray 15 15
242 A16 10c pale rose vio 15 15
243 A16 25c emerald 15 15
244 A16 30c dp org 15 15
245 A16 40c sl bl 15 15
246 A16 80c dk red brn 15 15
247 A16 1fr dl bl 15 15
248 A16 1.50fr crim rose 28 28
249 A16 2fr dl yel 15 15
250 A16 2.50fr brt ultra 15 15
251 A16 4fr aqua & red 20 20
252 A16 5fr grn & blk 35 22
253 A16 10fr sal pink & dk bl 45 38
254 A16 20fr dl vio & brn 60 60
Set value 2.50 2.30

For surcharges see Nos. 255-256, 261-268.

Nos. 241 and 242 Surcharged with New Values and Bars in Red or Blue

1944
255 A16 1.50fr on 5c (R) 32 32
256 A16 1.50fr on 10c (Bl) 42 42

Nos. 229 and 224 Surcharged with New Values and Bars in Red or Black
Perf. 14x13½, 14
257 A11 50c on 5c on 1c (R) 28 28
258 A14 1.50fr on 1.60fr (Bk) 35 35

Eboue Issue

Common Design Type

1945 **Engr.** *Perf. 13*
259 CD91 2fr black 28 28
260 CD91 25fr Prus grn 62 62

Nos. 241, 243 and 250 Surcharged with New Values and Bars in Carmine or Black

1945 *Perf. 14x14½*
261 A16 50c on 5c ol gray (C) 20 20
262 A16 60c on 5c ol gray (C) 35 35
263 A16 70c on 5c ol gray (C) 15 15
264 A16 1.20fr on 5c ol gray (C) 25 25
265 A16 2.40fr on 25c emer 20 20
266 A16 3fr on 25c emer 15 15
267 A16 4.50fr on 25c emer 38 38
268 A16 15fr on 2.50fr brt ultra (C) 28 28
Nos. 261-268 (8) 1.96 1.96

Southern Dancer — A17

Gen. J. S. Galliéni — A20

Herd of Zebus — A18

Sakalava Man and Woman A19

Betsimisaraka Mother and Child — A21

General Jacques C. R. A. Duchesne A22

Marshal Joseph J. C. Joffre A23

Perf. 13x13½, 13½x13
1946 **Photo.** **Unwmk.**
269 A17 10c green 15 15
270 A17 30c orange 15 15
271 A17 40c brn ol 15 15
272 A17 50c vio brn 15 15
273 A18 60c dp ultra 15 15
274 A18 80c bl grn 15 15
275 A19 1fr brown 15 15
276 A19 1.20fr green 15 15
276A A20 1.50fr dk red 15 15
277 A20 2fr slate blk 15 15
278 A20 3fr dp claret 15 15
278A A21 3.60fr dk car rose 55 50
279 A21 4fr dp ultra 15 15
280 A21 5fr red org 28 15
281 A22 6fr dk grnsh bl 15 15
282 A22 10fr red brn 28 15
283 A23 15fr vio brn 55 15
284 A23 20fr dk vio bl 62 38
285 A23 25fr brown 70 45
Set value 3.60 2.00

Military Medal Issue

Common Design Type

Engraved and Typographed

1952, Dec. 1 **Unwmk.** *Perf. 13*
286 CD101 15fr multi 1.00 75

Centenary of the creation of the French Military Medal.

Tropical Flowers — A24

Long-tailed Ground Roller — A25

1954 **Engr.**
287 A24 7.50fr ind & gray grn 80 15
288 A25 8fr brn car 60 20
289 A25 15fr dk grn & dp ultra 1.60 15
Set value 35

Colonel Lyautey and Royal Palace, Tananarive A26

1954-55
290 A26 10fr vio bl, ind & bl ('55) 65 15
291 A26 40fr dk sl bl & red brn 1.10 15
Set value 20

FIDES Issue

Common Design Type

Designs: 3fr, Tractor and modern settlement. 5fr, Gallieni school. 10fr, Pangalanes Canal. 15fr, Irrigation project.

1956, Oct. 22 **Engr.** *Perf. 13x12½*
292 CD103 3fr gray vio & vio brn 20 15
293 CD103 5fr org brn & dk vio brn 15 15
294 CD103 10fr ind & lil 35 15
295 CD103 15fr grn & bl grn 40 15
Set value 26

Coffee — A26a

1956, Oct. 22 *Perf. 13*
296 A26a 20r red brn & dk brn 40 15

Manioc — A27

Vanilla — A28

Design: 4fr, Cloves.

1957, Mar. 12 **Unwmk.** *Perf. 13*
297 A27 2fr bl, grn & sep 15 15
298 A28 4fr dp grn & red 22 15
299 A28 12fr dk vio, dl grn & sep 40 22
Set value 36

Malagasy Republic
Human Rights Issue

Common Design Type

1958, Dec. 10 **Engr.** *Perf. 13*
300 CD105 10fr brn & dk bl 22 15

Universal Declaration of Human Rights, 10th anniversary.
"CF" stands for "Communauté franaise."

Imperforates
Most Malagasy stamps from 1958 onward exist imperforate in issued and trial colors, and also in small presentation sheets in issued colors.

Flower Issue

Common Design Type

Perf. 12½x12, 12x12½
1959, Jan. 31 **Photo.**
301 CD104 6fr Datura, horiz. 15 15
302 CD104 25fr Poinsettia 22 15
Set value 28 15

Flag and Assembly Building A29

Flag and Map — A30

French and Malagasy Flags and Map — A31

1959, Feb. 28 **Engr.** *Perf. 13*
303 A29 20fr brn vio, car & emer 22 15
304 A30 25fr gray, red & emer 30 16

Proclamation of the Malagasy Republic.

1959, Feb. 28
305 A31 60fr multi 60 30

Issued to honor the French Community.

Chionaema Pauliani A32

Ylang-ylang — A33

Designs: 30c, 40c, 50c, 3fr, Various butterflies. 5fr, Sisal. 8fr, Pepper. 10fr, Rice. 15fr, Cotton.

1960 Unwmk. *Perf. 13*

306	A32	30c multi	15	15
307	A32	40c emer, sep & red brn	15	15
308	A32	50c vio brn, blk & stl bl	15	15
309	A32	1fr ind, red & dl pur	15	15
310	A32	3fr ol, vio blk & org	15	15
311	A32	5fr red, brn & emer	15	15
312	A33	6fr dk grn & brt yel	15	15
313	A32	8fr crim rose, emer & blk	15	15
314	A33	10fr dk grn, yel grn & lt brn	15	15
315	A32	15fr brn & grn	18	15
		Set value	75	60

Family Planting Trees — A34

1960, Feb. 1 Engr. *Perf. 13*

316	A34	20fr red brn, buff & grn	22	15

Issued for the "Week of the Tree," Feb. 1-7.

C.C.T.A. Issue
Common Design Type

1960, Feb. 22

317	CD106	25fr lt bl grn & plum	40	30

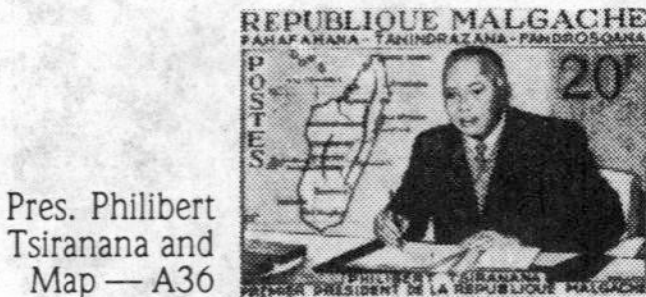
Pres. Philibert Tsiranana and Map — A36

1960, Mar. 25 Unwmk. *Perf. 13*

318	A36	20fr grn & brn	20	15

Athletes of Two Races — A37

Pres. Philibert Tsiranana — A38

1960 Engr. *Perf. 13*

319	A37	25fr choc, org brn & ultra	35	22

First Games of the French Community, Apr. 13-18, at Tananarive.

1960, July 29 Unwmk. *Perf. 13*

320	A38	20fr red, blk & brt grn	20	15

Issued to honor Pres. Tsiranana, "Father of Independence." For surcharge see No. B18.

Gray Lemur — A39

Designs: 4fr, Ruffed lemur, horiz. 12fr, Mongoose lemur.

1961, Dec. 9 *Perf. 13*

321	A39	2fr brn & grnsh bl	15	15
322	A39	4fr brn, grn & blk	15	15
323	A39	12fr grn & red brn	20	15
		Nos. 321-323,C67-C69 (6)	4.45	2.25

Pres. Tsiranana Bridge, Sofia River — A40

1962, Jan. 4 Unwmk. *Perf. 13*

324	A40	25fr brt bl	22	15

First Train Built at Tananarive A41

1962, Feb. 1

325	A41	20fr dk grn	20	15

UN and Malagasy Flags over Government Building, Tananarive — A42

1962, Mar. 14 *Perf. 13*

326	A42	25fr multi	22	16
327	A42	85fr multi	80	55

Malagasy Republic's admission to the UN.
For surcharge see No. 409.

Ranomafana Village — A43

Designs: 30fr, Tritriva crater lake. 50fr, Foulpointe shore. 60fr, Fort Dauphin.

1962, May 7 Engr. *Perf. 13*

328	A43	10fr sl grn, grnsh bl & cl	15	15
329	A43	30fr sl grn, cl & grnsh bl	22	15
330	A43	50fr ultra, cl & sl grn	40	25
331	A43	60fr cl, ultra & sl grn	50	35

See No. C70 and souvenir sheet No. C70a.

African and Malgache Union Issue
Common Design Type

1962, Sept. 8 Photo. *Perf. 12½x12*

332	CD110	30fr grn, bluish grn, red & gold	42	35

First anniversary of the African and Malgache Union.

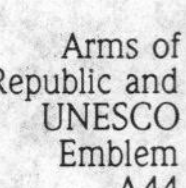

Arms of Republic and UNESCO Emblem A44

1962, Sept. 3 Unwmk.

333	A44	20fr rose, emer & blk	25	20

First Conference on Higher Education in Africa, Tananarive, Sept. 3-12.

Power Station — A45

Designs: 8fr, Atomic reactor and atom symbol, horiz. 10fr, Oil derrick. 15fr, Tanker, horiz.

Perf. 12x12½, 12½x12

1962, Oct. 18 Litho.

334	A45	5fr bl, yel & red	15	15
335	A45	8fr bl, red & yel	15	15
336	A45	10fr multi	15	15
337	A45	15fr bl, red brn & blk	15	15
		Set value	38	26

Industrialization of Madagascar.

Factory and Globe — A46

1963, Jan. 7 Typo. *Perf. 14x13½*

338	A46	25fr dp org & blk	22	15

International Fair at Tamatave.

Hertzian Cable, Tananarive-Fianarantsoa — A47

1963, Mar. 7 Photo. *Perf. 12½x12*

339	A47	20fr multi	20	15

Madagascar Blue Pigeon — A48

Gastrorchis Humblotii — A49

Birds: 2fr, Blue coua. 3fr, Red fody. 6fr, Madagascar pigmy kingfisher.
Orchids: 10fr, Eulophiella roempleriana. 12fr, Angraecum sesquipedale.

1963 Unwmk. *Perf. 13*

340	A48	1fr multi	20	20
341	A48	2fr multi	20	20
342	A48	3fr multi	20	20
343	A48	6fr multi	20	20
344	A49	8fr multi	16	15
345	A49	10fr multi	25	22
346	A49	12fr multi	25	22
		Nos. 340-346,C72-C74 (10)	4.81	2.86

Arms of Fianarantsoa — A50

Arms of: 1.50fr, Antsirabe. 5fr, Antalaha. 10fr, Tulear. 15fr, Majunga. 25fr, Tananarive. 50fr, Diégo-Suarez.

Imprint: "R. Louis del. So. Ge. Im."

1963-65 Litho. *Perf. 13*
Size: 23½x35½mm

347	A50	1.50fr multi ('64)	15	15
348	A50	5fr multi ('65)	15	15
349	A50	10fr multi ('64)	15	15
350	A50	15fr multi ('64)	15	15
351	A50	20fr multi	20	15
352	A50	25fr multi	22	15
353	A50	50fr multi ('65)	40	30
		Set value	1.10	70

See Nos. 388-390, 434-439.
For surcharge see No. 503.

Map and Centenary Emblem — A51

Globe and Hands Holding Torch — A52

1963, Sept. 2 *Perf. 12x12½*

354	A51	30fr multi	55	50

Centenary of the International Red Cross.

1963, Dec. 10 Engr. *Perf. 12½*

355	A52	60fr ol, ocher & car	50	35

15th anniversary of the Universal Declaration of Human Rights.

Scouts and Campfire A53

1964, June 6 Engr. *Perf. 13*

356	A53	20fr dk red, org & car	22	15

Issued to commemorate the 40th anniversary of the Boy Scouts of Madagascar.

Europafrica Issue, 1964

Dove and Globe — A54

1964, July 20 Engr.

357	A54	45fr ol grn, brn red & blk	40	25

First anniversary of economic agreement between the European Economic Community and the African and Malgache Union.

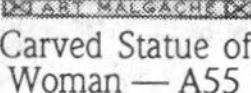
Carved Statue of Woman — A55

University Emblem — A56

Malagasy Art: 30fr, Statue of sitting man.

1964, Oct. 20 Unwmk. *Perf. 13*

358 A55 6fr dk bl, brt bl & sep 15 15
359 A55 30fr dp grn, ol bis & dk brn 30 20

See No. C79.

Cooperation Issue
Common Design Type

1964, Nov. 7 Engr. *Perf. 13*

360 CD119 25fr blk, dk brn & org brn 25 16

1964, Dec. 5 Litho. *Perf. 13x12½*

361 A56 65fr red, blk & grn 50 35

Issued to commemorate the founding of the University of Madagascar, Tananarive. The inscription reads: "Foolish is he who does not do better than his father."

Jejy — A57

Valiha Player — A58

Musical instruments: 3fr, Kabosa (lute). 8fr, Hazolahy (sacred drum).

1965 Engr. *Perf. 13*
Size: 22x36mm

362 A57 3fr mag, vio bl & dk brn 15 15
363 A57 6fr emer, rose lil & dk brn 15 15
364 A57 8fr brn, grn & blk 15 15

Photo. *Perf. 12½x13*

365 A58 25fr multi 25 16
Nos. 362-365,C80 (5) 2.60
Set value 1.35

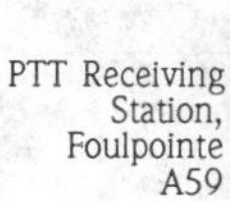

PTT Receiving Station, Foulpointe A59

1965, May 8 Engr. *Perf. 13*

366 A59 20fr red org, dk grn & ocher 16 15

Issued for Stamp Day, 1965.

ITU Emblem, Old and New Telecommunication Equipment — A60

1965, May 17

367 A60 50fr ultra, red & grn 65 40

ITU, centenary.

Jean Joseph Rabearivelo A61

Pres. Philibert Tsiranana A62

1965, June 22 Photo. *Perf. 13x12½*

368 A61 40fr dk brn & org 38 22

Issued to honor the poet Jean Joseph Rabearivelo, pen name of Joseph Casimir, (1901-37).

1965, Oct. 18 *Perf. 13x12½*

369 A62 20fr multi 15 15
a. Souv. sheet of 4 55 55
370 A62 25fr multi 15 15
a. Souv. sheet of 4 65 65
Set value 18

Issued to commemorate the 55th birthday of President Philibert Tsiranana.

Mail Coach — A63

History of the Post: 3fr, Early automobile. 4fr, Litter. 10fr, Mail runner, vert. 12fr, Mail boat. 25fr, Oxcart. 30fr, Old railroad mail car. 65fr, Hydrofoil.

1965-66 Engr. *Perf. 13*

371 A63 3fr vio, dp bis & sky bl ('66) 15 15
372 A63 4fr ultra, grn & dk brn ('66) 15 15
373 A63 10fr multi 15 15
374 A63 12fr multi 15 15
375 A63 20fr bis, grn & red brn 25 15
376 A63 25fr sl grn, dk brn & org 30 15
377 A63 30fr pck bl, red & sep ('66) 35 20
378 A63 65fr vio, brn & Prus bl ('66) 55 35
Nos. 371-378 (8) 2.05 1.45

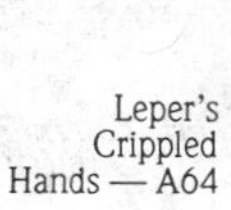

Leper's Crippled Hands — A64

1966, Jan. 30

379 A64 20fr dk grn, dk brn & red 25 20

Issued for the 13th World Leprosy Day.

Couple Planting Trees — A65

1966, Feb. 21

380 A65 20fr dk brn, pur & bl grn 20 15

Reforestation as a national duty.

Tiger Beetle — A66

Insects: 6fr, Mantis. 12fr, Long-horned beetle. 45fr, Weevil.

1966 Photo. *Perf. 12½x12*
Insects in Natural Colors

381 A66 1fr brick red 15 15
382 A66 6fr rose claret 15 15
383 A66 12fr Prus blue 15 15
384 A66 45fr lt yel grn 38 20
Set value 60 40

Stamp of 1903 — A67

1966, May 8 Engr. *Perf. 13*

385 A67 25fr red & sepia 25 20

Issued for Stamp Day 1966.

Betsileo Dancers A68

1966, June 13 Photo. *Perf. 12½x13*
Size: 36x23mm

386 A68 5fr multi 15 15

See No. C83.

Symbolic Tree and Emblems — A69

1966, June 26

387 A69 25fr multi 22 15

Issued to commemorate the conference of the Organisation Commune Africaine et Malgache (OCAM), Tananarive.

No. 387 dated "JUIN 1966," original date "Janvier 1966" obliterated with bar. Exists without overprint "JUIN 1966" and bar. Value $45.

Arms Type of 1963-65
Imprint: "S. Gauthier So. Ge. Im."

Arms: 20fr, Mananjary. 30fr, Nossi-Bé. 90fr, Antsohihy.

1966-68 Litho. *Perf. 13*
Size: 23½x35½mm

388 A50 20fr multi ('67) 15 15
389 A50 30fr multi 20 15
390 A50 90fr multi ('68) 55 35
Set value 50

For surcharge see No. 503.

Singers and Map of Madagascar — A70

1966, Oct. 14 Engr. *Perf. 13*

392 A70 20fr red brn, grn & dk car rose 15 15

Issued in honor of the National Anthem.

UNESCO Emblem A71

1966, Nov. 4

393 A71 30fr red, yel & slate 25 20

UNESCO, 20th anniv.

Lions Emblem — A72

1967, Jan. 14 Photo. *Perf. 13x12½*

394 A72 30fr multi 25 16

50th anniversary of Lions International.

Rice Harvest A73

1967, Jan. 27 *Perf. 12½x13*

395 A73 20fr multi 16 15

FAO International Rice Year.

Adventist Temple, Tanambao-Tamatave — A74

Designs: 5fr, Catholic Cathedral, Tananarive, vert. 10fr, Mosque, Tamatave.

1967, Feb. 20 Engr. *Perf. 13*

396 A74 3fr lt ultra, grn & bis 15 15
397 A74 5fr brt rose lil, grn & vio 15 15
398 A74 10fr dp bl, brn & grn 15 15
Set value 20 15

Norbert Raharisoa at Piano — A75

1967, Mar. 23 Photo. *Perf. 12½x12*

399 A75 40fr cit & multi 35 15

Issued in memory of Norbert Raharisoa (1914-1963), composer.

Jean Raoult Flying Blériot Plane, 1911 — A76

Design: 45fr, Barnard-Bougault and hydroplane, 1926.

1967, Apr. 28 Engr. *Perf. 13*
Size: 35½x22mm

400 A76 5fr gray bl, brn & grn 15 15
401 A76 45fr brn, stl bl & blk 40 22
Set value 26

History of aviation in Madagascar. See No. C84.

Ministry of Equipment and Communications — A77

1967, May 8 Engr. *Perf. 13*

402 A77 20fr ocher, ultra & grn 16 15

Issued for Stamp Day, 1967.

Lutheran Church, Tananarive, Madagascar Map — A78

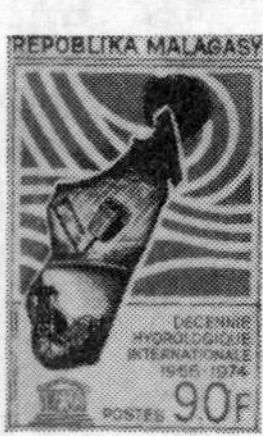

Map of Madagascar and Emblems — A79

1967, Sept. 24 Photo. *Perf. 12x12½*

403 A78 20fr multi 16 15

Issued to commemorate the centenary of the Lutheran Church in Madagascar.

1967, Oct. 16 Engr. *Perf. 13*

404 A79 90fr red brn, bl & dk red 65 40

Hydrological Decade (UNESCO), 1965-74.

Dance of the Bilo Sakalavas — A80

Design: 30fr, Atandroy dancers.

1967, Nov. 25 Photo. *Perf. 13x12½*
Size: 22x36mm

405 A80 2fr lt grn & multi 15 15
406 A80 30fr multi 25 15
Set value 30 18

See Nos. C86-C87.

Woman's Face, Scales and UN Emblem A81

1967, Dec. 16 *Perf. 12½x13*

407 A81 50fr emer, dk bl & brn 38 25

Issued to publicize the United Nations Commission on the Status of Women.

Human Rights Flame — A82

1968, Mar. 16 Litho. *Perf. 13x12½*

408 A82 50fr blk, ver & grn 38 22

International Human Rights Year.

No. 327 Surcharged with New Value and 3 Bars

1968, June 4 Engr. *Perf. 13*

409 A42 20fr on 85fr multi 16 15

"Industry" A83

Designs: 20fr, "Agriculture" (mother and child carrying fruit and grain, and cattle), vert. 40fr, "Communications and Investments," (train, highway, factory and buildings).

1968, July 15

410 A83 10fr rose car, grn & dk pur 15 15
411 A83 20fr dp car, grn & blk 16 15
412 A83 40fr brn, vio & sl bl 35 16
Set value 32

Completion of Five-year Plan, 1964-68.

Church, Translated Bible, Cross and Map of Madagascar A84

1968, Aug. 18 Photo. *Perf. 12½x12*

413 A84 20fr multi 16 15

Issued to commemorate the sesquicentennial of Christianity in Madagascar.

Isotry-Fitiavana Protestant Church — A85

Designs: 12fr, Catholic Cathedral, Fianarantsoa. 50fr, Aga Khan Mosque, Tananarive.

1968, Sept. 10 Engr. *Perf. 13*

414 A85 4fr red brn, brt grn & dk brn 15 15
415 A85 12fr plum, bl & hn brn 15 15
416 A85 50fr brt grn, bl & ind 35 20
Set value 52 32

President and Mrs. Tsiranana A86

1968, Oct. 14 Photo. *Perf. 12½x12*

417 A86 20fr car, org & blk 15 15
418 A86 30fr car, grnsh bl & blk 20 15
a. Souv. sheet of 4, 2 each #417-418 1.10 1.10
Set value 17

10th anniv. of the Republic.

Madagascar Map and Cornucopia with Coins — A87

Striving Mankind — A88

1968, Nov. 3 Photo. *Perf. 12x12½*

419 A87 20fr multi 16 15

Issued to commemorate the 50th anniversary of the Malagasy Savings Bank.

1968, Dec. 3 Photo. *Perf. 12½x12*

Design: 15fr, Mother, child and physician, horiz.

420 A88 15fr ultra, yel & crim 15 15
421 A88 45fr vio bl & multi 35 22
Set value 30

Completion of Five-Year Plan, 1964-68.

Queen Adelaide Receiving Malagasy Delegation, London, 1836 — A89

1969, Mar. 29 Photo. *Perf. 12x12½*

422 A89 250fr multi 2.25 1.40

Issued to commemorate the Malagasy delegation visiting London, 1836-1837.

Cogwheels, Wrench and ILO Emblem A90

1969, Apr. 11 *Perf. 12½x12*

423 A90 20fr grn & multi 16 15

ILO, 50th anniv.

Telecommunications and Postal Building, Tananarive — A91

1969, May 8 Engr. *Perf. 13*

424 A91 30fr bl, brt grn & car lake 22 15

Issued for Stamp Day 1969.

Steering Wheel, Map, Automobiles — A92

1969, June 1 Photo. *Perf. 12*

425 A92 65fr multi 50 25

Issued to commemorate the 20th anniversary of the Automobile Club of Madagascar.

Pres. Philibert Tsiranana — A93

Banana Plants — A94

1969, June 26 Photo. *Perf. 12x12½*

426 A93 20fr multi 15 15

10th anniversary of the inauguration of Pres. Philibert Tsiranana.

1969, July 7 Engr. *Perf. 13*

427 A94 5fr shown 15 15
428 A94 15fr Lichi tree 15 15
Set value 18 15

Runners A95

1969, Sept. 9 Engr. *Perf. 13*

429 A95 15fr yel grn, brn & red 16 15

Issued to commemorate the 19th Olympic Games, Mexico City, Oct. 12-27, 1968.

Malagasy House, Highlands — A96

Carnelian — A97

Designs (Malagasy Houses): No. 430, Betsileo house, Highlands. No. 431, Tsimihety house, West Coast, horiz. 60fr, Malagasy house, Highlands.

1969-70 Engr. *Perf. 13*

430 A96 20fr bl, ol & ver 15 15
431 A96 20fr sl, brt grn & red 15 15
432 A96 40fr blk, bl & dk red 30 15
433 A96 60fr vio bl, dp grn & brn 45 20
Set value 48

Issues dates: 40fr, 60fr, Nov. 25, 1969. Others, Nov. 25, 1970.

Arms Type of 1963-65

Arms: 1fr, Maintirano. 10fr, Ambalavao. No. 436, Morondava. No. 437, Ambatondrazaka. No. 438, Fenerive-Est. 80fr, Tamatave.

1970-72 Photo. *Perf. 13*

434 A50 1fr multi ('72) 15 15
435 A50 10fr multi ('72) 15 15
436 A50 25fr multi ('71) 22 15
437 A50 25fr multi ('71) 22 15

438 A50 25fr multi ('72) 20 15
439 A50 80fr pink & multi 55 30
Nos. 434-439 (6) 1.49
Set value 80

The 10fr and 80fr are dated "1970." No. 437 is dated "1971." Nos. 434, 438 are dated "1972."
Sizes: 22x37mm (#434, 438); 25½x36mm (others).
Imprints: "S. Gauthier" on Nos. 434, 438. "S. Gauthier Delrieu" on others.

Perf. 12x12½ (5, 20fr), 13 (12, 15fr)
1970-71 Photo.

Semi-precious Stones: 12fr, Yellow calcite. 15fr, Quartz. 20fr, Ammonite.

440 A97 5fr brn, dl rose & yel 15 15
441 A97 12fr multi ('71) 15 15
442 A97 15fr multi ('71) 16 15
443 A97 20fr grn & multi 20 15
Set value 42

UPU Headquarters Issue
Common Design Type
1970, May 20 Engr. *Perf. 13*
444 CD133 20fr lil rose, brn & ultra 20 15

UN Emblem and Symbols of Justice — A98

1970, June 26 Engr. *Perf. 13*
445 A98 50fr blk, ultra & org 38 20

25th anniversary of the United Nations.

Fruits of Madagascar — A99

1970, Aug. 18 Photo. *Perf. 13*
446 A99 20fr multi 15 15

Volute Delessertiana A100

Shells: 10fr, Murex tribulus. 20fr, Spondylus.

1970, Sept. 9 Photo. *Perf. 13*
447 A100 5fr Prus bl & multi 15 15
448 A100 10fr vio & multi 15 15
449 A100 20fr multi 20 15
Set value 36 18

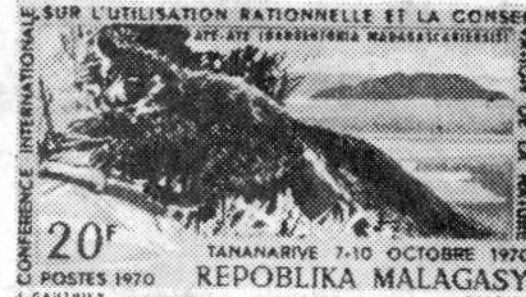

Aye-aye — A101

1970, Oct. 7 Photo. *Perf. 12½*
450 A101 20fr multi 35 25

Intl. Conference for Nature Conservation, Tananarive, Oct. 7-10.

Pres. Tsiranana — A102

1970, Dec. 30 Photo. *Perf. 12½*
451 A102 30fr grn & lt brn 20 15

60th birthday of Pres. Philibert Tsiranana.

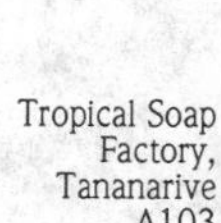

Tropical Soap Factory, Tananarive A103

Designs: 15fr, Comina chromium smelting plant, Andriamena. 50fr, Textile mill, Majunga.

1971, Apr. 14 Photo. *Perf. 12½x12*
452 A103 5fr multi 15 15

Engr. *Perf. 13*
453 A103 15fr vio bl, blk & ocher 15 15

Photo. *Perf. 13*
454 A103 50fr multi 38 20
Set value 55 32

Economic development.

Globe, Agriculture, Industry, Science A104

1971, Apr. 22 Photo. *Perf. 12½x12*
455 A104 5fr multi 15 15

Extraordinary meeting of the Council of the C.E.E.-E.A.M.A. (Communauté Economique Européen-Etats Africains et Malgache Associés).

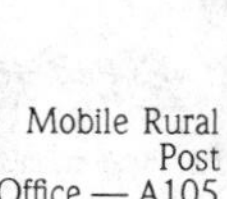

Mobile Rural Post Office — A105

1971, May 8 *Perf. 13*
456 A105 25fr multi 20 15

Stamp Day.

Gen. Charles de Gaulle — A106

Madagascar Hilton, Tananarive — A107

1971, June 26 Engr. *Perf. 13*
457 A106 30fr ultra, blk & rose 40 20

In memory of Charles de Gaulle (1890-1970), President of France.

For surcharge see No. B24.

1971, July 23 Photo.

Design: 25fr, Hotel Palm Beach, Nossi-Bé.

458 A107 25fr multi 20 15

Engr.
459 A107 65fr vio bl, brn & lt grn 45 25

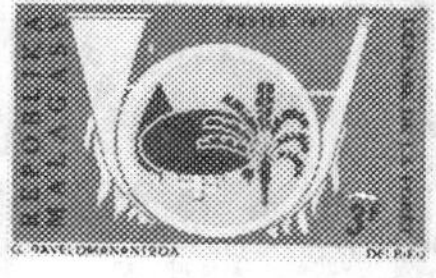
Trees and Post Horn — A108

1971, Aug. 6 Photo. *Perf. 12½x12*
460 A108 3fr red, yel & grn 15 15

Forest preservation campaign.

House, South West Madagascar A109

Design: 10fr, House from Southern Madagascar.

1971, Nov. 25 *Perf. 13x12½*
461 A109 5fr lt bl & multi 15 15
462 A109 10fr lt bl & multi 15 15
Set value 15 15

Children Playing, and Cattle A110

1971, Dec. 11 Litho. *Perf. 13*
463 A110 50fr grn & multi 40 22

UNICEF, 25th anniv.

Cable-laying Railroad Car, PTT Emblem A111

1972, Apr. 8 Engr. *Perf. 13*
464 A111 45fr sl grn, red & choc 35 22

Coaxial cable connection between Tananarive and Tamatave.

Philibert Tsiranana Radar Station — A112

1972, Apr. 8 Photo. *Perf. 13½*
465 A112 85fr bl & multi 65 38

A113

A114

Voters and Pres. Tsiranana.

1972, May 1 *Perf. 12½x13*
466 A113 25fr yel & multi 40 35

Presidential election, Jan. 30, 1972.

1972, May 30 Photo. *Perf. 12x12½*
467 A114 10fr Mail delivery 15 15

Stamp Day 1972.

Emblem and Stamps of Madagascar — A115

Design: Stamps shown are Madagascar Nos. 352, 410, 429, 449.

1972, June 26 *Perf. 13*
468 A115 25fr org & multi 15 15
469 A115 40fr org & multi 25 16
470 A115 100fr org & multi 65 35
a. Souv. sheet of 3, #468-470 1.40 1.40

2nd Malgache Philatelic Exhibition, Tananarive, June 26-July 9.

Andapa-Sambava Road and Monument — A116

1972, July 6 *Perf. 12½x12*
471 A116 50fr multi 30 20

Opening of the Andapa-Sambava road.

Diesel Locomotive A117

1972, July 6 Engr. *Perf. 13*
472 A117 100fr multi 65 40

Razafindrahety College A118

1972, Aug. 6
473 A118 10fr choc, bl & red brn 15 15

Sesquicentennial of Razafindrahety College, Tananarive.

Volleyball A119

1972, Aug. 6 Typo. *Perf. 12½x13*
474 A119 12fr org, blk & brn 15 15

African volleyball championship.

Oil Refinery, Tamatave
A120

1972, Sept. 18 Engr. *Perf. 13*
475 A120 2fr bl, bis & sl grn 15 15

Ravoahangy Andrianavalona Hospital — A121

1972, Oct. 14 Photo. *Perf. 13x12½*
476 A121 6fr multi 15 15

Plowing
A122

1972, Nov. 15 Photo. *Perf. 13½x14*
477 A122 25fr gold & multi 15 15

Betsimisaraka Costume
A123

Design: 15fr, Merina costume.

1972, Dec. 30 Photo. *Perf. 13x12½*
478 A123 10fr bl & multi 15 15
479 A123 15fr brn & multi 15 15
Set value 16 15

Farmer and Produce — A124

1973, Feb. 6 Photo. *Perf. 13*
480 A124 25fr lt bl & multi 16 15

10th anniversary of the Malagasy Committee of "Freedom from Hunger Campaign."
For surcharge see No. 499.

Volva Volva — A125

Shells: 10fr, 50fr, Lambis chiragra. 15fr, 40fr, Harpa major. 25fr, Like 3fr.

1973, Apr. 5 Litho. *Perf. 13*
481 A125 3fr ol & multi 15 15
482 A125 10fr bl grn & multi 15 15
483 A125 15fr brt bl & multi 15 15
484 A125 25fr lt bl & multi 16 15
485 A125 40fr multi 25 16
486 A125 50fr red lil & multi 40 22
Nos. 481-486 (6) 1.26 98

Tsimandoa Mail Carrier — A126
Builders and Map of Africa — A127

1973, May 13 Engr. *Perf. 13*
487 A126 50fr ind, ocher & sl grn 35 16

Stamp Day 1973.

1973, May 25 Photo. *Perf. 13*
488 A127 25fr multi 15 15

Organization for African Unity, 10th anniversary.

Campani Chameleon
A128

Various Chameleons: 5fr, 40fr, Male nasutus. 10fr, 85fr, Female nasutus. 60fr, Like 1fr.

1973, June 15 Photo. *Perf. 13x12½*
489 A128 1fr dp car & multi 15 15
490 A128 5fr brn & multi 15 15
491 A128 10fr grn & multi 15 15
492 A128 40fr red lil & multi 25 15
493 A128 60fr dk bl & multi 42 22
494 A128 85fr brn & multi 65 35
Set value 1.50 85

Lady's Slipper — A129

Orchids: 25fr, 40fr, Pitcher plant. 100fr, Like 10fr.

1973, Aug. 6 Photo. *Perf. 12½*
495 A129 10fr multi 15 15
496 A129 25fr rose & multi 16 15
497 A129 40fr lt bl & multi 22 15
498 A129 100fr multi 52 40
Set value 70

No. 480 Surcharged with New Value, 2 Bars, and Overprinted in Ultramarine: "SECHERESSE / SOLIDARITE AFRICAINE"

1973, Aug. 16 *Perf. 13*
499 A124 100fr on 25fr multi 52 35

African solidarity in drought emergency.

African Postal Union Issue
Common Design Type

1973, Sept. 12 Engr. *Perf. 13*
500 CD137 100fr vio, red & sl grn 55 35

Greater Dwarf Lemur
A131

Design: 25fr, Weasel lemur, vert.

1973, Oct. 9 Engr. *Perf. 13*
501 A131 5fr brt grn & multi 15 15
502 A131 25fr ocher & multi 15 15
Set value 18 15

Lemurs of Madagascar. See Nos. C117-C118.

25 Fmg

No. 389 Surcharged

1974, Feb. 9 Litho. *Perf. 13*
503 A50 25fr on 30fr multi 15 15

Scouts Helping to Raise Cattle — A132
Mother with Children and Clinic — A133

Design: 15fr, Scouts building house; African Scout emblem.

1974, Feb. 14 Engr. *Perf. 13*
504 A132 4fr bl, sl & emer 15 15
505 A132 15fr choc & multi 15 15
Set value 15 15

Malagasy Boy Scouts. See Nos. C122-C123.

1974, May 24 Photo. *Perf. 13*
506 A133 25fr multi 15 15

World Population Year.

Rainibetsimisaraka
A134

1974, July 26 Photo. *Perf. 13*
507 A134 25fr multi 15 15

In memory of Rainibetsimisaraka, independence leader.

Marble Blocks
A135

Design: 25fr, Marble quarry.

1974, Sept. 27 Photo. *Perf. 13*
508 A135 4fr multi 15 15
509 A135 25fr multi 15 15
Set value 18 15

Malagasy marble.

Europafrica Issue, 1974

Links, White and Black Faces, Map of Europe and Africa — A136

1974, Oct. 17 Engr. *Perf. 13*
510 A136 150fr dk brn & org 80 35

Grain and Hand — A137

1974, Oct. 29
511 A137 80fr lt bl & ocher 42 25

World Committee against Hunger.

Tuléar Dog — A138

Design: 100fr, Hunting dog.

1974, Nov. 26 Photo. *Perf. 13x13½*
512 A138 50fr multi 25 20
513 A138 100fr multi 55 42

Malagasy Citizens — A139

1974, Dec. 9 *Perf. 13½x13*
514 A139 5fr bl grn & multi 15 15
515 A139 10fr multi 15 15
516 A139 20fr yel grn & multi 15 15
517 A139 60fr org & multi 35 20
Set value 56 36

Introduction of "Fokonolona" community organization.

Symbols of Development
A140

1974, Dec. 16 Photo. *Perf. 13x13½*
518 A140 25fr ultra & multi 16 15
519 A140 35fr bl grn & multi 20 15
Set value 24

National Council for Development.

Woman, Rose, Dove and Emblem — A141

1975, Jan. 21 **Engr.** ***Perf. 13***
520 A141 100fr brn, emer & org 55 22

International Women's Year 1975.

Col. Richard Ratsimandrava A142

1975, Apr. 25 **Photo.** ***Perf. 13***
521 A142 15fr brn & sal 15 15
522 A142 25fr blk, bl & brn 15 15
523 A142 100fr blk, lt grn & brn 52 25
Set value 75 36

Col. Richard Ratsimandrava (1933-1975), head of state.

Sofia Bridge A143

1975, May 29 **Litho.** ***Perf. 12½***
524 A143 45fr multi 22 15

Count de Grasse and "Randolph" — A144

Design: 50fr, Marquis de Lafayette, "Lexington" and HMS "Edward."

1975, June 30 **Litho.** ***Perf. 11***
525 A144 40fr multi 30 15
526 A144 50fr multi 38 16
Nos. 525-526,C137-C139 (5) 4.38 1.91

American Bicentennial.
For overprints see Nos. 564-565, C164-C167.

Euphorbia Viguieri A145

Tropical Plants: 25fr, Hibiscus. 30fr, Plumieria rubra acutifolia. 40fr, Pachypodium rosulatum.

1975, Aug. 4 **Photo.** ***Perf. 12½***
527 A145 15fr lem & multi 15 15
528 A145 25fr blk & multi 15 15
529 A145 30fr org & multi 16 15
530 A145 40fr dk red & multi 22 20
Nos. 527-530,C141 (5) 1.13 1.00

Brown, White, Yellow and Black Hands Holding Globe — A146

1975, Aug. 26 **Litho.** ***Perf. 12***
531 A146 50fr multi 25 16

Namibia Day (independence for South-West Africa.)

Woodpecker — A147

Designs: 40fr, Rabbit. 50fr, Frog. 75fr, Tortoise.

1975, Sept. 16 **Litho.** ***Perf. 14x13½***
532 A147 25fr multi 20 15
533 A147 40fr multi 25 15
534 A147 50fr multi 35 20
535 A147 75fr multi 45 25
Nos. 532-535,C145 (5) 2.05 1.20

International Exposition, Okinawa.

Lily Waterfall A148

Design: 40fr, Lily Waterfall, different view.

1975, Sept. 17 **Litho.** ***Perf. 12½***
536 A148 25fr multi 15 15
537 A148 40fr multi 22 15
Set value 20

4-man Bob Sled A149

Designs: 100fr, Ski jump. 140fr, Speed skating.

1975, Nov. 19 **Litho.** ***Perf. 14***
538 A149 75fr multi 45 20
539 A149 100fr multi 60 22
540 A149 140fr multi 90 30
Nos. 538-540,C149-C150 (5) 4.70 1.92

12th Winter Olympic games, Innsbruck, 1976.
For overprints see Nos. 561-563, C161-C163.

Pirogue A150

Designs: 45fr, Boutre (Arabian coastal vessel).

1975, Nov. 20 **Photo.** ***Perf. 12½***
541 A150 8fr multi 15 15
542 A150 45fr ultra & multi 22 15
Set value 36 18

Canadian Canoe and Kayak — A151

Design: 50fr, Sprint and Hurdles.

1976, Jan. 21 **Litho.** ***Perf. 14x13½***
543 A151 40fr multi 25 15
544 A151 50fr multi 35 16
Nos. 543-544,C153-C155 (5) 4.35 2.01

21st Summer Olympic games, Montreal.
For overprints see Nos. 571-572, C168-C171.

Count Zeppelin and LZ-127 over Fujiyama, Japan — A152

Designs (Count Zeppelin and LZ-127 over): 50fr, Rio. 75fr, NYC. 100fr, Sphinx.

1976, Mar. 3 ***Perf. 11***
545 A152 40fr multi 28 15
546 A152 50fr multi 38 15
547 A152 75fr multi 55 20
548 A152 100fr multi 60 25
Nos. 545-548,C158-C159 (6) 4.81 2.25

75th anniversary of the Zeppelin.

Worker, Globe, Eye Chart and Eye — A153

1976, Apr. 7 **Photo.** ***Perf. 12½***
549 A153 100fr multi 55 35

World Health Day: "Foresight prevents blindness."

Aragonite A154

Designs: 50fr, Petrified wood. 150fr, Celestite.

1976, May 7 **Photo.** ***Perf. 12½***
550 A154 25fr bl & multi 15 15
551 A154 50fr bl grn & multi 25 15
552 A154 150fr org & multi 80 42

Alexander Graham Bell and First Telephone — A155

Designs: 50fr, Telephone lines, 1911. 100fr, Central office, 1895. 200fr, Cable ship, 1925. 300fr, Radio telephone. 500fr, Telstar satellite and globe.

1976, May 13 **Litho.** ***Perf. 14***
553 A155 25fr multi 16 15
554 A155 50fr multi 35 15
555 A155 100fr multi 62 30
556 A155 200fr multi 1.20 55
557 A155 300fr multi 1.90 75
Nos. 553-557 (5) 4.23 1.90

Souvenir Sheet

558 A155 500fr multi 3.25 1.40

Cent. of 1st telephone call by Alexander Graham Bell, Mar. 10, 1876.

Children with Books A156

Design: 25fr, Children with books (vert.).

1976, May 25 **Litho.**
559 A156 10fr multi 15 15
560 A156 25fr multi 15 15
Set value 18 15

Books for children.

Nos. 538-540 Overprinted

a. VAINQUEUR ALLEMAGNE FEDERALE
b. VAINQUEUR KARL SCHNABL AUTRICHE
c. VAINQUEUR SHEILA YOUNG ETATS-UNIS

1976, June 17
561 A149 (a) 75fr multi 40 20
562 A149 (b) 100fr multi 55 30
563 A149 (c) 140fr multi 70 42
Nos. 561-563,C161-C162 (5) 3.50 1.87

12th Winter Olympic games winners.

Nos. 525-526 Overprinted "4 Juillet / 1776-1976"

1976, July 4
564 A144 40fr multi 30 15
565 A144 50fr multi 35 16
Nos. 564-565,C164-C166 (5) 4.45 1.91

American Bicentennial.

Graph of Projected Landing Spots on Mars — A157

Viking project to Mars: 100fr, Viking probe in flight. 200fr, Viking probe on Mars. 300fr, Viking probe over projected landing spot. 500fr, Viking probe approaching Mars.

1976, July 17 Litho. *Perf. 14*

566 A157 75fr multi 35 20
567 A157 100fr multi 50 20
568 A157 200fr multi 1.00 40
569 A157 300fr multi 1.50 60

Souvenir Sheet

570 A157 500fr multi 2.50 1.00

Nos. 543-544 Overprinted

a. A. ROGOV / V. DIBA
b. H. CRAWFORD / J. SCHALLER

1977, Jan.

571 A151 (a) 40fr multi 30 15
572 A151 (b) 50fr multi 38 16
Nos. 571-572,C168-C170 (5) 4.25 1.91

21st Summer Olympic games winners.

Rainandriamampandry — A158

Portrait: No. 574, Rabezavana.

1976-77 Litho. *Perf. 12x12½*

573 A158 25fr multi 15 15
574 A158 25fr multi 15 15
Set value 20

Rainandriamampandry was Malagasy Foreign Minister who signed treaties in 1896.
Issue dates: No. 573, Oct. 15, 1976. No. 574, Mar. 29, 1977.

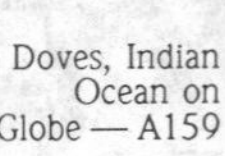

Doves, Indian Ocean on Globe — A159

Design: 12a, Globe with Africa and Indian Ocean, doves, vert.

Perf. 12½x12, 12x12½

1976, Nov. 18

575 A159 60fr multi 35 20
576 A159 160fr multi 90 50

"Indian Ocean - Zone of Peace."

Coat of Arms — A160

1976, Dec. 30 Litho. *Perf. 12*

577 A160 25fr multi 15 15

Democratic Republic of Malagasy, first anniversary.

> *Footnotes often refer to other stamps of the same design.*

Lt. Albert Randriamaromanana — A161

Portrait: #578, Avana Ramanantoanina.

1977, Mar. 29

578 A161 25fr multi 15 15
579 A161 25fr multi 15 15
Set value 20

National Mausoleum — A162

1977, Mar. 29 *Perf. 12½x12*

580 A162 100fr multi 50 35

Family — A163

1977, Apr. 7 *Perf. 12x12½*

581 A163 5fr yel & multi 15 15

World Health Day: Immunization protects the children.

Tananarive Medical School — A164

1977, June 30 Litho. *Perf. 12½x12*

582 A164 250fr multi 1.40 65

80th anniversary of Tananarive Medical School.

Mail Bus A165

1977, Aug. 18 Litho. *Perf. 12½x12*

583 A165 35fr multi 20 15

Rural mail delivery.

Telegraph Operator — A166

1977, Sept. 13 Litho. *Perf. 12½x12*

584 A166 15fr multi 15 15

90th anniversary of telegraph service Tananarive-Tamatave.

Malagasy Art — A167

1977, Sept. 29 *Perf. 12x12½*

585 A167 10fr multi 15 15

Malagasy Academy, 75th anniversary.

Lenin and Russian Flag — A168

1977, Nov. 7 Litho. *Perf. 12½x12*

586 A168 25fr multi 15 15

60th anniversary of Russian October Revolution.

Raoul Follereau, Map of Malagasy A169

1978, Jan. 28 Litho. *Perf. 12x12½*

587 A169 5fr multi 15 15

25th anniversary of Leprosy Day.

Antenna, ITU Emblem A170

1978, May 17 Litho. *Perf. 12x12½*

588 A170 20fr multi 41 15

10th World Telecommunications Day.

Black and White Men Breaking Chains of Africa — A171

1978, June 22 Photo. *Perf. 12½x12*

589 A171 60fr multi 40 16

Anti-Apartheid Year.

Boy and Girl, Arch: Pen, Gun and Hoe — A172

Farm Workers, Factory, Tractor — A173

1978, July 28 Litho. *Perf. 12½x12*

590 A172 125fr multi 80 35

Youth, the pillar of revolution.

1978, Aug. 24

591 A173 25fr multi 16 15

Socialist cooperation.

Women — A174

Children Bringing Gifts — A175

1979, Mar. 8 Litho. *Perf. 12½x12*

592 A174 40fr multi 25 15

Women, supporters of the revolution.

1979, June 1 Litho. *Perf. 12x12½*

593 A175 10fr multi 15 15

International Year of the Child.

Lemur Macaco A176

Fauna: 25fr, Lemur catta, vert. 1000fr, Foussa.

Perf. 12½x12, 12x12½

1979, July 6 Litho.

594 A176 25fr multi 16 15
595 A176 125fr multi 80 35
596 A176 1000fr multi 6.50 2.50
Nos. 594-596,C172-C173 (5) 8.23 3.37

Jean Verdi Salomon A177

1979, July 25 *Perf. 12x12½*
597 A177 25fr multi 16 15

Jean Verdi Salomon (1913-1978), poet.

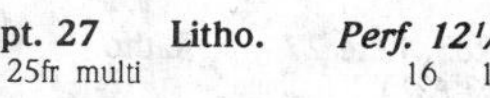

Talapetraka (Medicinal Plant) A178

1979, Sept. 27 **Litho.** *Perf. 12½*
598 A178 25fr multi 16 15

Map of Magagascar, Dish Antenna — A179

1979, Oct. 12
599 A179 25fr multi 16 15

Stamp Day 1979 A180

1979, Nov. 9
600 A180 500fr multi 3.50 1.40

Jet, Map of Africa A181

1979, Dec. 12 *Perf. 12½*
601 A181 50fr multi 35 15

ASECNA (Air Safety Board), 20th anniversary.

Lenin Addressing Workers in the Winter Palace — A182

1980, Apr. 22 **Litho.** *Perf. 12x12½*
602 A182 25fr multi 16 15

Lenin's 110th birth anniversary.

Bus and Road in Madagascar Colors — A183

Flag and Map under Sun — A184

1980, June 15 **Litho.** *Perf. 12x12½*
603 A183 30fr multi 20 15

Socialist Revolution, 5th anniversary.

1980, June 26 *Perf. 12½x12*
604 A184 75fr multi 50 22

Independence, 20th anniversary.

Armed Forces Day A185

1980, Aug. **Litho.** *Perf. 12½x12*
605 A185 50fr multi 35 15

Dr. Joseph Raseta (1886-1979) A186

1980, Oct. 15 **Litho.** *Perf. 12x12½*
606 A186 30fr multi 20 15

Anatirova Temple Centenary — A187

1980, Nov. 27 **Litho.** *Perf. 12½x12*
607 A187 30fr multi 20 15

Hurdles, Olympic Torch, Moscow '80 Emblem — A188

1980, Dec. 29
608 A188 30fr shown 20 15
609 A188 75fr Boxing 50 22
Set value 30

22nd Summer Olympic Games, Moscow, July 19-Aug. 3. See Nos. C175-C176.

Democratic Republic of Madagascar, 5th Anniversary A189

1980, Dec. 30 *Perf. 12x12½*
610 A189 30fr multi 20 15

Downhill Skiing — A190

1981, Jan. 26 **Litho.** *Perf. 12½x12*
611 A190 175fr multi 1.20 50

13th Winter Olympic Games, Lake Placid, Feb. 12-24, 1980.

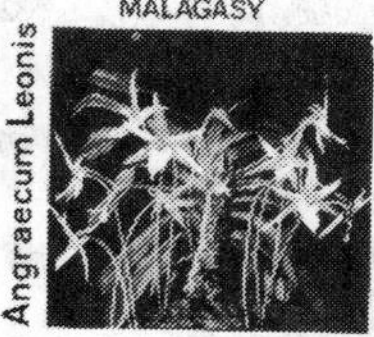

Angraecum Leonis — A191

1981, Mar. 23 **Litho.** *Perf. 11½*
612 A191 5fr shown 15 15
613 A191 80fr Angraecum ramosum 55 22
614 A191 170fr Angraecum sesquipedale 1.10 45

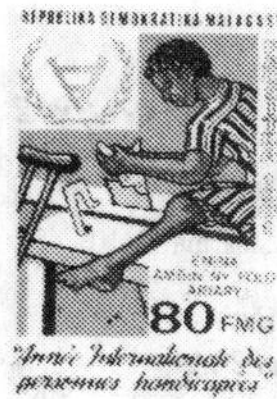

A192

A193

1981, June 12 **Litho.** *Perf. 12*
615 A192 25fr Student at desk 16 15
616 A192 80fr Carpenter 55 22
Set value 28

Intl. Year of the Disabled.

1981, July 10 **Litho.** *Perf. 12½x12*
617 A193 15fr multi 15 15
618 A193 45fr multi 30 15
Set value 15

13th World Telecommunications Day.

Neil Armstrong on Moon (Apollo 11) — A194

Space Anniversaries.

1981, July 23 *Perf. 11½*
619 A194 30fr Valentina Tereshkova 20 15
620 A194 80fr shown 55 22
621 A194 90fr Yuri Gagarin 60 25

Brother Raphael Louis Rafiringa (1854-1919) A195

1981, Aug. 10 **Litho.** *Perf. 12*
622 A195 30fr multi 20 15

World Literacy Day — A196

1981, Sept. 8
623 A196 30fr multi 20 15

World Food Day — A197

1981, Oct. 16 **Litho.** *Perf. 12x12½*
624 A197 200fr multi 1.40 55

See No. 635.

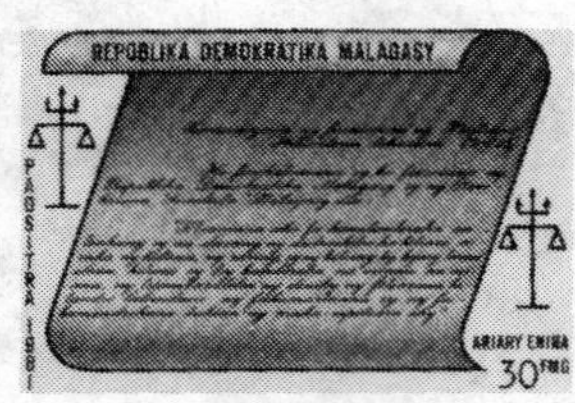

Oaths of Magistracy Renewal — A198

1981, Oct. 30 *Perf. 12½x12*
625 A198 30fr blk & lil rose 20 15

Dove, by Pablo Picasso (1881-1973) — A199

1981, Nov. 18 Photo. *Perf. 11½x12*
626 A199 80fr multi 55 20

20th Anniv. of UPU Membership A200

Design; Nos. C76, C77, emblem.

1981, Nov. 19 Litho. *Perf. 12*
627 A200 5fr multi 15 15
628 A200 30fr multi 20 15
Set value 25 15

TB Bacillus Centenary A201

1982, June 21 Litho. *Perf. 12*
629 A201 30fr multi 20 15

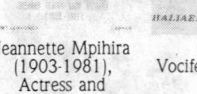

Jeannette Mpihira (1903-1981), Actress and Singer — A202

Haliaeetus Vociferoides — A203

1982, June 24 *Perf. 12½*
630 A202 30fr multi 20 15

1982, July
631 A203 25fr Vanga curvirostris, horiz. 16 15
632 A203 30fr Leptostomus discolor, horiz. 20 15
633 A203 200fr shown 1.40 55
Set value 70

Pierre Louis Boiteau (1911-1980), Educator A204

1982, Sept. 13
634 A204 30fr multi 20 15

World Food Day Type of 1981

1982, Oct. 16 *Perf. 12x12½*
635 A197 80fr multi 55 22

25th Anniv. of Launching of Sputnik I — A205

1982, Oct. 4 Litho. *Perf. 12*
636 A205 10fr Sputnik I 15 15
637 A205 80fr Yuri Gagarin, Vostok I 55 22
638 A205 100fr Soyuz-Salyut 65 25
Set value 50

1982 World Cup — A206

Designs: Various soccer players.

1982, Oct. 14 *Perf. 12x12½*
639 A206 30fr multi 15 15
640 A206 40fr multi 20 15
641 A206 80fr multi 40 18
Set value 32

Souvenir Sheet

Perf. 11½x12½

642 A206 450fr multi 2.25 90

Scene at a Bar, by Edouard Manet (1832-1883) — A207

1982, Nov. 25 *Perf. 12½x12*
643 A207 5fr shown 15 15
644 A207 30fr Lady in a White Dress 20 15
645 A207 170fr Portrait of Mallarme 1.10 50
Set value 62

Souvenir Sheet

Perf. 11½x12½

646 A207 400fr The Fifer, vert. 2.50 1.00

Local Fish — A208

1982, Dec. 14 *Perf. 11½*
647 A208 5fr Lutianus sebae 15 15
648 A208 20fr Istiophorus platypterus 15 15
649 A208 30fr Pterois volitans 20 15
650 A208 50fr Thunnus albacares 35 15
651 A208 200fr Epinephelus fasciatus 1.40 50
Nos. 647-651 (5) 2.25
Set value 80

Souvenir Sheet

Perf. 12½x12

652 A208 450fr Latimeria chalumnae 3.00 1.20

No. 652 contains one stamp 38x26mm.

Fort Mahavelona Ruins — A209

1982, Dec. 22 *Perf. 12½x12*
653 A209 10fr shown 15 15
654 A209 30fr Ramena Beach 20 15
655 A209 400fr Flowering jacaranda trees 2.50 1.00

60th Anniv. of USSR — A210

1982, Dec. 29
656 A210 10fr Tractors 15 15
657 A210 15fr Pylon 15 15
658 A210 30fr Kremlin, Lenin 20 15
659 A210 150fr Arms 1.00 40
Set value 55

World Communications Year — A211

Design: 80fr, Stylized figures holding wheel.

1983, May 17 Litho. *Perf. 12*
660 A211 30fr multi 20 15
661 A211 80fr multi 55 20

United African Organization, 20th Anniv. — A212

1983, May 25 Litho. *Perf. 12*
662 A212 30fr multi 20 15

Henri Douzon, Lawyer and Patriot — A213

1983, June 27 Litho. *Perf. 12*
663 A213 30fr multi 20 15

Souvenir Sheet

Manned Flight Bicentenary A214

1983, July 20 Litho. *Perf. 12*
664 A214 500fr Montgolfiere balloon 1.60 80

Souvenir Sheet

Raphael, 500th Birth Anniv. A215

1983, Aug. 10 Litho. *Perf. 12*
665 A215 500fr The Madonna Connestable 1.60 80

Lemur — A216

Various lemurs. Nos. 668-669, 671 vert.

Perf. 12½x12, 12x12½

1983, Dec. 6 Litho.

666 A216 30fr Daubentonia madagascariensis 15 15
667 A216 30fr Microcebus murinus 15 15
668 A216 30fr Lemur variegatus 15 15
669 A216 30fr Propithecus verreauxi 15 15
670 A216 200fr Indri indri 65 35
Set value 1.00 50

Souvenir Sheet

671 A216 500fr Perodicticus potto 1.60 80

1984 Winter Olympics A217

1984, Jan. 20 Litho. *Perf. 11½*

672 A217 20fr Ski jumping 15 15
673 A217 30fr Speed skating 15 15
674 A217 30fr Downhill skiing 15 15
675 A217 30fr Hockey 15 15
676 A217 200fr Figure skating 50 25
Set value 78 40

Souvenir Sheet

677 A217 500fr Cross-country skiing 1.25 65

No. 677 contains one stamp 48x32mm.

Vintage Cars — A218

1984, Jan. 27 *Perf. 12½x12*

678 A218 15fr Renault, 1907 15 15
679 A218 30fr Benz, 1896 15 15
680 A218 30fr Baker, 1901 15 15
681 A218 30fr Blake, 1901 15 15
682 A218 200fr FIAL, 1908 65 35
Set value 1.00 50

Souvenir Sheet

Perf. 12½x11½

683 A218 450fr Russo-Baltique, 1909 1.50 80

Pastor Ravelojaona (1879-1956), Encyclopedist A219

1984, Feb. 14 *Perf. 12x12½*

684 A219 30fr multi 15 15

Madonna and Child, by Correggio (1489-1534) A220

Various Correggio paintings.

1984, May 5 Litho. *Perf. 12x12½*

685 A220 5fr multi 15 15
686 A220 20fr multi 15 15
687 A220 30fr multi 15 15
688 A220 80fr multi 25 15
689 A220 200fr multi 65 35
Set value 1.10 60

Souvenir Sheet

690 A220 400fr multi 1.40 65

A221

A222

1984, July 27

691 A221 5fr Paris landmarks 15 15
692 A221 20fr Wilhelm Steinitz 15 15
693 A221 30fr Champion, cup 15 15
694 A221 30fr Vera Menchik 15 15
695 A221 215fr Champion, cup, diff. 70 38
Set value 1.00 55

Souvenir Sheet

696 A221 400fr Children playing chess 1.40 65

World Chess Federation, 60th anniv.

1984, Aug. 10

697 A222 100fr Soccer 35 16

1984 Summer Olympics.

Butterflies A223

1984, Aug. 30 Litho. *Perf. 11½*

698 A223 15fr Eudaphaenura splendens 15 15
699 A223 50fr Othreis boseae 15 15
700 A223 50fr Pharmacophagus antenor 15 15
701 A223 50fr Acraea hova 15 15
702 A223 200fr Epicausis smithii 55 25
Nos. 698-702 (5) 1.15
Set value 50

Miniature Sheet

Perf. 11½x12½

703 A223 400fr Papilio delandii 1.10 55

No. 703 contains one stamp 37x52mm.

Jean Ralaimongo (1884-1944), Birth Centenary — A224

1984, Oct. 4 *Perf. 12x12½*

704 A224 50fr Portrait 15 15

Children's Rights A225

1984, Nov. 20 Litho. *Perf. 12½x12*

705 A225 50fr Youths in school bag 15 15

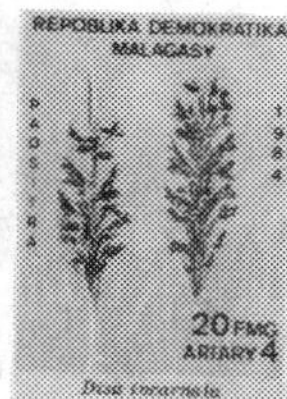

Malagasy Orchids — A226

Cotton Seminar, UN Trade and Development Conference — A227

1984, Nov. 20 Litho. *Perf. 12*

706 A226 20fr Disa incarnata 15 15
707 A226 235fr Eulophiella roempleriana 62 32
Nos. 706-707,C180-C182 (5) 1.22
Set value 56

Miniature Sheet

Perf. 12x12½

708 A226 400fr Gastrorchis tuberculosa 1.10 55

No. 708 contains one stamp 30x42mm.

1984, Dec. 15 Litho. *Perf. 13x12½*

709 A227 100fr UN emblem, cotton bolls 25 15

Malagasy Language Bible, 150th Anniv. A228

1985, Feb. 11 Litho. *Perf. 12½x12*

710 A228 50fr multi 16 15

1985 Agricultural Census — A229

1985, Feb. 21 Litho. *Perf. 12x12½*

711 A229 50fr Census taker, farmer 15 15

Allied Defeat of Nazi Germany, 40th Anniv. — A230

Designs: 20fr, Russian flag-raising, Berlin, 1945. 50fr, Normandy-Niemen squadron shooting down German fighter planes. No. 714, Soviet Victory Parade, Red Square, Moscow. No. 715, Victorious French troops marching through Arc de Triomphe, vert.

1985 *Perf. 12½x12, 12x12½*

712 A230 20fr multi 15 15
713 A230 50fr multi 15 15
714 A230 100fr multi 30 15
715 A230 100fr multi 30 15
Set value 42

Issue dates: #712-714, May 9. #715, Oct.

Cats and Dogs — A231

Perf. 12x12½, 12½x12

1985, Apr. 25

716 A231 20fr Siamese 15 15
717 A231 20fr Bichon 15 15
718 A231 50fr Abyssinian, vert. 15 15
719 A231 100fr Cocker spaniel, vert. 30 15
720 A231 235fr Poodle 65 35
Nos. 716-720 (5) 1.40
Set value 65

Souvenir Sheet

721 A231 400fr Kitten 1.20 1.20

No. 721 contains one stamp 42x30mm, perf. 12½x12.

Gymnastic Event, Natl. Stadium, Atananarivo A232

1985, July 9 *Perf. 12½x12*

722 A232 50fr multi 15 15

Natl. Socialist Revolution, 10th anniv.

Commemorative Medal, Memorial Stele — A233

1985, July 9

723 A233 50fr multi 15 15

Independence, 25th anniv.

Intl. Youth Year — A234

Natl. Red Cross, 70th Anniv. — A235

1985, Sept. 18 *Perf. 12*

724 A234 100fr Emblem, map 30 15

1985, Oct. 3 *Perf. 12x12½*

725 A235 50fr multi 15 15

15-Cent Minimum Value
The minimum catalogue value is 15 cents. Separating se-tenant pieces into individual stamps does not increase the "value" of the stamps... since demand for the separated stamps may be small.

Indira Gandhi — A236

22nd World Youth and Student's Festival, Moscow — A237

1985, Oct. 31 *Perf. 13½*
726 A236 100fr multi 30 15

1985, Nov. *Perf. 12*
727 A237 50fr multi 15 15

Rouen Cathedral at Night, by Monet — A238

UN, 40th Aniv. — A239

Impressionist paintings: No. 729, View of Sea at Sainte-Marie, by van Gogh, horiz. 45fr, Young Women in Black, by Renoir. 50fr, The Red Vineyard at Arles, by van Gogh, horiz. 100fr, Boulevard des Capucines in Paris, by Monet, horiz. 400fr, In the Garden, by Renoir.

1985, Oct. 25 **Litho.** *Perf. 12*
728 A238 20fr multi 15 15
729 A238 20fr multi 15 15
730 A238 45fr multi 15 15
731 A238 50fr multi 15 15
732 A238 100fr multi 30 15
Set value 65 38

Souvenir Sheet

Perf. 12x12½

733 A238 400fr multi 1.20 1.20

No. 733 contains one 30x42mm stamp.

1985, Oct. 31 *Perf. 12*
734 A239 100fr multi 30 15

Orchids A240

1985, Nov. 8
735 A240 20fr Aeranthes grandiflora 15 15
736 A240 45fr Angraecum magdalanae 15 15
737 A240 50fr Aerangis stylosa 15 15
738 A240 100fr Angraecum eburneum longicalcar 30 15
739 A240 100fr Angraecum sesquipedale 30 15
Nos. 735-739 (5) 1.05
Set value 50

Souvenir Sheet

Perf. 12x12½

740 A240 400fr Angraecum aburneum superbum 1.20 1.20

Nos. 735, 737-740 vert. No. 740 contains one 30x42mm stamp.

INTERCOSMOS — A241

Cosmonauts, natl. flags, rockets, satellites and probes.

1985, Nov. *Perf. 12x12½*
741 A241 20fr USSR, Czechoslovakia 15 15
742 A241 20fr Soyuz-Apollo emblem 15 15
743 A241 50fr USSR, India 15 15
744 A241 100fr USSR, Cuba 30 15
745 A241 200fr USSR, France 60 30
Nos. 741-745 (5) 1.35 90

Souvenir Sheet

746 A241 400fr Halley's Comet, probe 1.20 1.20

No. 746 contains one stamp 42x30mm.

Independence, 10th Anniv. — A242

1985, Dec. 30 **Litho.** *Perf. 12½x12*
747 A242 50fr Industrial symbols 16 15

Natl. Insurance and Securities Co. (ARO), 10th Anniv. — A243

1986, Jan. 20 *Perf. 12x12½*
748 A243 50fr dk brn, yel org & gray brn 16 15

Paintings in the Tretyakov Gallery, Moscow — A244

Designs: 20fr, Still-life with Flowers and Fruit, 1839, by I. Chroutzky. No. 750, Portrait of Alexander Pushkin, 1827, by O. Kiprenski, vert. No. 751, Portrait of an Unknown Woman, 1883, by I. Kramskoi. No. 752, The Crows Have Returned, 1872, by A. Sakrassov, vert. 100fr, March, 1895, by I. Levitan. 450fr, Portrait of Pavel Tretyakov, 1883, by I. Repin, vert.

Perf. 12½x12, 12x12½

1986, Apr. 26 **Litho.**
749 A244 20fr multi 15 15
750 A244 50fr multi 16 15
751 A244 50fr multi 16 15
752 A244 50fr multi 16 15
753 A244 100fr multi 35 16
Nos. 749-753 (5) 98
Set value 45

Souvenir Sheet

754 A244 450fr multi 1.50 70

1986 World Cup Soccer Championships, Mexico — A245

1986, May 31 *Perf. 13½*
755 A245 150fr multi 50 25

Paintings in Russian Museums — A246

Designs: No. 756, David and Urie, by Rembrandt, vert. No. 757, Danae, by Rembrandt. No. 758, Portrait of the Nurse of the Infant Isabella, by Rubens, vert. No. 759, The Alliance of Earth and Water, by Rubens, vert. No. 760, Portrait of an Old Man in Red, by Rembrandt. No. 761, The Holy Family, by Raphael.

Perf. 12x12½, 12½x12

1986, Mar. 24 **Litho.**
756 A246 20fr multi 15 15
757 A246 50fr multi 16 15
758 A246 50fr multi 16 15
759 A246 50fr multi 16 15
760 A246 50fr multi 16 15
Nos. 756-760 (5) 79
Set value 35

Souvenir Sheet

Perf. 11½x12½

761 A246 450fr multi 1.50 70

UN Child Survival Campaign — A247

A248

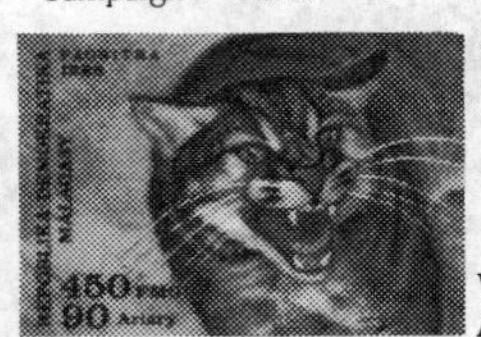

Wildcats A249

1986, June 1 **Litho.** *Perf. 12x12½*
762 A247 60fr multi 20 15

1986, July 17
763 A248 10fr Sable 15 15
764 A248 10fr Chaus 15 15
765 A248 60fr Serval 20 15
766 A248 60fr Caracal 20 15
767 A248 60fr Bengal 20 15
Set value 70 38

Souvenir Sheet

Perf. 12½x12

768 A249 450fr Golden 1.40 65

Intl. Peace Year A249a

1986, Sept. 12 *Perf. 12*
769 A249a 60fr shown 20 15
770 A249a 150fr Hemispheres, emblem, vert. 42 22

World Post Day — A250

1986, Oct. 9 **Litho.** *Perf. 13x12½*
771 A250 60fr multi 20 15
772 A250 150fr multi 42 22

No. 772 is airmail.

A251

Birds A252

Perf. 12x12½, 12½x12

1986, Dec. 23 **Litho.**
773 A251 60fr Xenopirostris daimi, vert. 20 15
774 A251 60fr Falculea palliata 20 15
775 A251 60fr Coua gigas 20 15
776 A251 60fr Coua cristata 20 15
777 A251 60fr Cianolanius madagascariensis, vert. 20 15
Nos. 773-777 (5) 1.00
Set value 50

Souvenir Sheet

778 A252 450fr Bubulcus ibis ibis 1.50 70

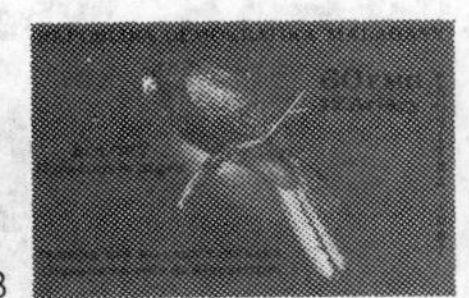

A253

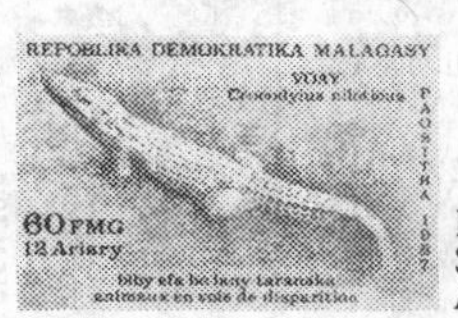

Endangered Species A254

Perf. 12x12½, 12½x12

1987, Mar. 13 **Litho.**
779 A253 60fr Lophotibis cristata, vert. 20 15
780 A253 60fr Coracopsis nigra 20 15
781 A254 60fr Crocodylus niloticus 20 15
782 A254 60fr Geochelone ynphora 20 15
Set value 40

Souvenir Sheet

783 A253 450fr Centropus toulou, vert. 1.50 70

Anti-Colonial Revolt, 40th Anniv.
A255 A256

1987, Mar. 29 *Perf. 12*
784 A255 60fr multi 20 15
785 A256 60fr multi 20 15
Set value 20

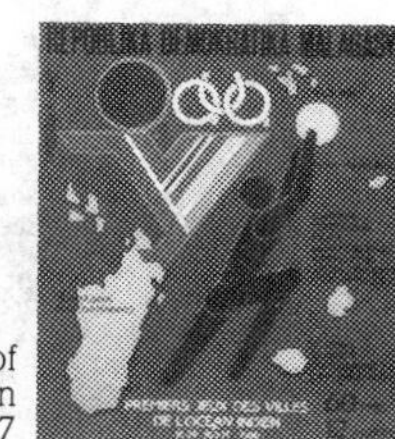

1st Games of Indian Ocean Towns — A257

1987, Apr. 15 *Perf. 13½*

786	A257	60fr multi	22	15
787	A257	150fr multi	60	30

Le Sarimanok A258

1987, Apr. 15

788	A258	60fr Port side	22	15
789	A258	150fr Starboard side	60	30

African and Madagascar Coffee Organization, 25th Anniv. A259

1987, Apr. 24 **Litho.** *Perf. 12*

790	A259	60fr Coffee plant	22	15
791	A259	150fr Map	60	30

Halley's Comet — A260

Space probes.

1987, May 13 *Perf. 13½*

792	A260	60fr Giotto, ESA	20	15
793	A260	150fr Vega 1, Russia	50	25
794	A260	250fr Vega 2, Russia	85	40
795	A260	350fr Planet-A1, Japan	1.10	60
796	A260	400fr Planet-A2, Japan	1.40	65
797	A260	450fr ICE, US	1.50	70
		Nos. 792-797 (6)	5.55	2.75

Souvenir Sheet

798	A260	600fr Halley, Giotto	2.00	1.00

Litho. & Embossed 'Gold Foil' Stamps
These stamps generally are of a different design format than the rest of the issue. Since there is a commemorative inscription tying them to the issue a separate illustration is not being shown.

1988 Calgary Winter Olympics — A261

Jean-Joseph Rabearivelo (d. 1937), Poet — A263

Men's Downhill A262

1987, May 13

799	A261	60fr Biathlon	20	15
800	A261	150fr shown	50	25
801	A261	250fr Luge	85	40
802	A261	350fr Speed skating	1.10	60
803	A261	400fr Hockey	1.40	65
804	A261	450fr Pairs figure skating	1.50	70
		Nos. 799-804 (6)	5.55	2.75

Litho. & Embossed

804A	A261	1500fr Speed skating		

Souvenir Sheets

Litho.

805	A262	600fr shown	2.00	1.00

Litho. & Embossed

805A	A262	1500fr Slalom skiing		

No. 804A exists in souvenir sheet of 1.

1987, June 22 *Perf. 13½*

806	A263	60fr multi	20	15

1992 Summer Olympics, Barcelona — A264

Athletes, emblem and art or architecture: 60fr, Equestrian, and the Harlequin, by Picasso. 150fr, Weight lifting, church. 250fr, Hurdles, Canaletas Fountain. 350fr, High jump, amusement park. 400fr, Men's gymnastics, abbey. 450fr, Rhythmic gymnastics, Arc de Triomphe. 600fr, Equestrian, Columbus monument.

1987, Oct. 7 **Litho.** *Perf. 13½*

807	A264	60fr multi	20	15
808	A264	150fr multi	50	25
809	A264	250fr multi	85	42
810	A264	350fr multi	1.10	60
811	A264	400fr multi	1.40	65
812	A264	450fr multi	1.50	70
		Nos. 807-812 (6)	5.55	2.77

Souvenir Sheet

813	A264	600fr multi	2.00	1.00

Nos. 811-813 are airmail.

A265

Discovery of America, 500th Anniv. (in 1992) A266

Anniv. emblem and: 60fr, Bartolomeu Dias (c. 1450-1500), Portuguese navigator, departure from De Palos, 1492. 150fr, Henry the Navigator (1394-1460), prince of Portugal, Samana Cay. 250fr, A. De Marchena landing, 1492. 350fr, Paolo Toscanelli dal Pozzo (1397-1482), Italian physician and cosmographer, La Navidad Fort. 400fr, Queen Isabella I, Barcelona, 1493. 450fr, Christopher Columbus, the Nina. 600fr, Landing in New World, 1492.

1987, Sept. 24 **Litho.** *Perf. 13½*

814	A265	60fr multi	28	15
815	A265	150fr multi	70	35
816	A265	250fr multi	1.10	55
817	A265	350fr multi	1.65	85
818	A265	400fr multi	1.90	1.00
819	A265	450fr multi	2.25	1.10
		Nos. 814-819 (6)	7.88	4.00

Souvenir Sheet

820	A266	600fr multi	3.00	1.50

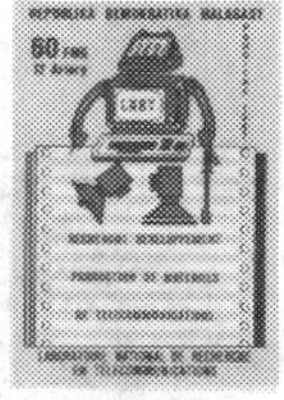
A267

A268

1987, July 27 *Perf. 12½x12*

821	A267	60fr multi	22	15

Natl. telecommunications research laboratory.

1987, Aug. 14

822	A268	60fr lt blue, blk & brt ultra	22	15

Rafaravavy Rasalama (d. 1837), Christian martyr.

Antananarivo-Tamatave Telegraph Link, Cent. — A269

1987, Sept. 15 *Perf. 12x12½*

823	A269	60fr multi	22	15

Pasteur Institute, Paris, Cent. — A270

1987, Oct. 26 *Perf. 13½*

824	A270	250fr multi	1.00	45

City of Berlin, 750th Anniv. — A271

Design: Anniv. emblem, television tower and the Interhotel in East Berlin.

1987, Oct. 18 **Litho.** *Perf. 12½x12*

825	A271	150fr multi	22	15

Schools Festival A272

1987, Oct. 23 *Perf. 12x12½*

826	A272	60fr multi	15	15

Paintings in the Pushkin Museum, Moscow — A273

Designs: 10fr, After the Shipwreck (1847), by Eugene Delacroix (1798-1863). No. 828, Still-life with Swan (c. 1620), by Frans Snyders (1579-1647). No. 829, Jupiter and Callisto (1744), by Francois Boucher (1703-1770), vert. No. 830, Chalet in the Mountains (1874), by Jean Desire Gustav Courbet (1819-1877). 150fr, At the Market (1564), by Joachim Bueckelaer. 1000fr, Minerva (1560), by Paolo Veronese (1528-1588), vert.

Perf. 12½x12, 12x12½

1987, Nov. 10

827	A273	10fr multi	15	15
828	A273	60fr multi	15	15
829	A273	60fr multi	15	15
830	A273	60fr multi	15	15
831	A273	150fr multi	22	15
		Set value	55	35

Souvenir Sheet

832	A273	1000fr multi	1.50	1.50

Pan-African Telecommunications Union, 10th Anniv. — A274

1987, Dec. 28 *Perf. 13x12½*

833	A274	250fr multi	1.00	45

Intl. Year of Shelter for the Homeless A275

1988, Feb. 15 **Litho.** *Perf. 12*

834	A275	80fr shown	16	15
835	A275	250fr Family in shelter, rain, vert.	52	25

Fauna A276

1988, Apr. 18 **Litho.** *Perf. 13½*

836	A276	60fr Hapalemur simus	15	15
837	A276	150fr Propithecus diadema diadema	32	16
838	A276	250fr Indri indri	55	28
839	A276	350fr Varecia variegata variegata	75	38
840	A276	550fr Madagascar young heron	1.20	60
841	A276	1500fr Nosy-be chameleon	3.15	1.60
		Nos. 836-841 (6)	6.12	3.17

Souvenir Sheet

842	A276	1500fr Uratelornis (bird)	3.25	3.25

Conservation and service organization emblems: World Wildlife Fund (60fr, 150fr, 250fr and 350fr); Rotary Intl. (550fr and No. 842); and Scouting trefoil (No. 841).

October Revolution, Russia, 70th Anniv. — A277

1988, Mar. 7 Litho. *Perf. 12x12½*

843 A277	60fr	Lenin	15	15
844 A277	60fr	Revolutionaries	15	15
845 A277	150fr	Lenin, revolutionaries	32	16
		Set value		32

1988 Winter Olympics, Calgary — A278

1988, May 11 *Perf. 11½*

846 A278	20fr	Pairs figure skating	15	15
847 A278	60fr	Slalom	15	15
848 A278	60fr	Speed skating	15	15
849 A278	100fr	Cross-country skiing	22	15
850 A278	250fr	Ice hockey	55	28
		Nos. 846-850 (5)	1.22	
		Set value		58

Souvenir Sheet

851 A278	800fr	Ski jumping	1.75	1.75

Discovery of Radium by Pierre and Marie Curie, 90th Anniv. A279

1988, July 14 Litho. *Perf. 12*

852 A279	150fr	blk & rose lil	35	18

OAU, 25th Anniv. A280

1988, May 25 Litho. *Perf. 13*

853 A280	80fr	multi	20	15

Natl. Telecommunications and Posts Institute, 20th Anniv. — A281

1988, June 22 *Perf. 13½*

854 A281	80fr	multi	20	15

Saint-Michel College, Cent. — A282

1988, July 9

855 A282	250fr	multi	55	28

Alma-Ata Declaration, 10th Anniv. — A283

WHO, 40th Anniv. — A284

1988, Aug. 11 Litho. *Perf. 12*

856 A283	60fr	multi	15	15

1988, Aug. 11

857 A284	150fr	multi	32	16

Tsimbazaza Botanical and Zoological Park, 150th Anniv. — A285

Perf. 12x12½, 12½x12

1988, Aug. 22

858 A285	20fr	Lemur habitat	15	15
859 A285	80fr	Lemur and young	20	15
860 A285	250fr	shown	55	28
		Set value		42

Souvenir Sheet

861 A285	1000fr	Lemur and mate	2.25	2.25

Size of No. 859: 25x37mm.

Boy Scouts Studying Birds and Butterflies — A286

Designs: 80fr, Upupa epops maginata, Coua caerulea and scout photographing bird. 250fr, Chrysiridia croesus and comparing butterfly to a sketch. 270fr, Nelicurvius nelicourvi, Foudia omissa and constructing bird feeder. 350fr, Papilio dardanus and studying butterflies with magnifying glass. 550fr, Coua critata and tagging bird. No. 867, Argema mittrei and writing observations. No. 868, Merops superciliosus and recording bird calls.

1988, Sept. 29

862 A286	80fr	multi	20	15
863 A286	250fr	multi	55	28
864 A286	270fr	multi	60	30
865 A286	350fr	multi	78	40
866 A286	550fr	multi	1.20	60
867 A286	1500fr	multi	3.25	1.65
		Nos. 862-867 (6)	6.58	3.38

Souvenir Sheet

868 A286	1500fr	multi	3.25	3.25

No. 868 contains one stamp 36x51mm.

Composers and Entertainers A287

Designs: 80fr, German-made clavier and Carl Philipp Emanuel Bach (1714-1788), organist and composer. 250fr, Piano and Franz Peter Schubert (1797-1828), Austrian composer. 270fr, Scene from opera Carmen, 1875, and Georges Bizet (1838-1875), French composer. 350fr, Scene from opera Pelleas et Melisande, 1902, and Claude Debussy (1862-1918), French composer. 550fr, George Gershwin (1898-1937), American composer. No. 874, Elvis Presley (1935-1977), American entertainer. No. 875, Rimsky-Korsakov (1844-1908), Russian composer, and Le Coq d'Or from the opera of the same name.

1988, Oct. 28

869 A287	80fr	multi	20	15
870 A287	250fr	multi	55	28
871 A287	270fr	multi	60	30
872 A287	350fr	multi	78	40
873 A287	550fr	multi	1.20	60
874 A287	1500fr	multi	3.25	1.65
		Nos. 869-874 (6)	6.58	3.38

Souvenir Sheet

875 A287	1500fr	multi	3.25	3.25

Intl. Fund for Agricultural Development (IFAD), 10th Anniv. A288

1988, Sept. 4 Litho. *Perf. 12*

876 A288	250fr	multi	48	25

School Feast — A289

1988, Nov. 22

877 A289	80fr	multi	16	15

A290

Ships — A291

Paintings: 20fr, The Squadron of the Sea, Black Feodossia, by Ivan Aivazovski, vert. No. 879, Seascape with Sailing Ships, by Simon de Vlieger, vert. No. 880, The Ship Lesnoie, by N. Semenov, vert. 100fr, The Merchantman, Orel, by N. Golitsine. 250fr, Naval Exercises, by Adam Silo, vert. 550fr, On the River, by Abraham Beerstraten.

1988, Dec. 5 *Perf. 12x12½, 12½x12*

878 A290	20fr	multi	15	15
879 A290	80fr	multi	16	15
880 A290	80fr	multi	16	15
881 A290	100fr	shown	20	15
882 A290	250fr	multi	48	25
		Nos. 878-882 (5)	1.15	
		Set value		55

Souvenir Sheet

Perf. 11½x12½

883 A291	550fr	shown	1.05	1.05

World Wildlife Fund — A292

Insect species in danger of extinction: 20fr, Tragocephala crassicornis. 80fr, Polybothris symptuosa-gema. 250fr, Euchroea auripigmenta. 350fr, Stellognata maculata.

1988, Dec. 13 *Perf. 12*

884 A292	20fr	multi	15	15
885 A292	80fr	multi	16	15
886 A292	250fr	multi	48	25
887 A292	350fr	multi	68	35
		Set value		72

Intl. Red Cross and Red Crescent Organizations, 125th Annivs. A293

1988, Dec. 27 Litho. *Perf. 12*

888 A293	80fr	Globe, stretcher-bearers, vert.	16	15
889 A293	250fr	Emblems, Dunant	48	24
		Set value		32

UN Declaration of Human Rights, 40th Anniv. (in 1988) — A294

1989, Jan. 10

890 A294	80fr	shown	16	15
891 A294	250fr	Hands, "4" and "0"	48	24
		Set value		32

Dated 1988.

Transportation — A295

Designs: 80fr, 1909 Mercedes-Benz Blitzen Benz. 250fr, Micheline ZM 517 Tsikirity, Tananarive-Moramanga line. 270fr, Bugatti Coupe Binder 41. 350fr, Electric locomotive 1020-DES OBB, Germany. 1500fr, Souleze Autorail 701 DU CFN, Madagascar. No. 897, 1913 Opel race car. No. 898, Bugatti Presidential Autorail locomotive and Bugatti Type 57 Atalante automobile.

1989, Jan. 24 *Perf. 13½*

892 A295 80fr multi 16 15
893 A295 250fr multi 48 24
894 A295 270fr multi 52 25
895 A295 350fr multi 70 35
896 A295 1500fr multi 2.85 1.45
897 A295 2500fr multi 4.75 2.40
Nos. 892-897 (6) 9.46 4.84

Souvenir Sheet

898 A295 2500fr multi 4.75 4.75

Dinosaurs — A296

1989, Feb. 1 Litho. *Perf. 12½x12*

899 A296 20fr Tyrannosaurus 15 15
900 A296 80fr Stegosaurus 16 15
901 A296 250fr Arsinoitherium 48 24
902 A296 450fr Triceratops 90 45
Set value 80

Souvenir Sheet

Perf. 11½x12½

903 A296 600fr Sauralophus, vert. 1.20 1.20

Women as the Subject of Paintings — A297

Designs: 20fr, *Tahitian Pastorales*, by Gauguin. No 905, *Portrait of a Young Woman*, by Titian, vert. No. 906, *Portrait of a Little Girl*, by Jean-Baptiste Greuze (1725-1805), vert. 100fr, *Woman in Black*, by Renoir, vert. 250fr, *Lacemaker*, by Vassili Tropinine, vert. 550fr, *The Annunciation*, by Cima Da Conegliano (c. 1459-1517), vert.

Perf. 12½x12, 12x12½

1989, Feb. 10

904 A297 20fr multi 15 15
905 A297 80fr multi 16 15
906 A297 80fr multi 16 15
907 A297 100fr multi 20 15
908 A297 250fr multi 48 24
Nos. 904-908 (5) 1.15
Set value 55

Souvenir Sheet

Perf. 11½x12½

909 A297 550fr multi 1.05 1.05

Orchids A298

1989, Feb. 28 Litho. *Perf. 12*

910 A298 5fr *Sobennikoffia robusta*, vert. 15 15
911 A298 10fr *Grammangis fallax* 15 15
912 A298 80fr *Cymbidiella humblotii*, vert. 15 15
913 A298 80fr *Angraecum sororium*, vert. 15 15
914 A298 250fr *Oenia oncidiiflora*, vert. 38 18
Set value 70 40

Souvenir Sheet

915 A298 1000fr *Aerangis curnowiana* 1.40 1.40

Jawaharlal Nehru (1889-1964), 1st Prime Minister of Independent India — A299

1989, Mar. 7 Litho. *Perf. 13*

916 A299 250fr multi 48 24

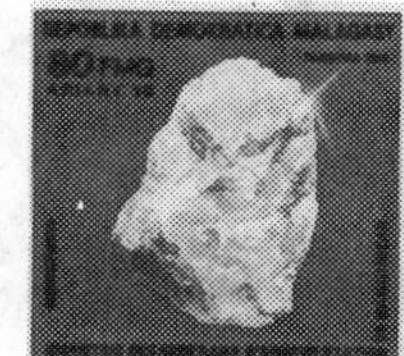

Ornamental Mineral Industry A300

1989, Apr. 12 Litho. *Perf. 13½*

917 A300 80fr Rose quartz 16 15
918 A300 250fr Petrified wood 48 24
Set value 32

Views of Antananarivo A301

Designs: 5fr, Mahamasina Sports Complex, Ampefiloha Quarter. 20fr, Andravoahangy and Anjanahary Quarters. No. 921, Zoma Market and Faravohitra Quarter. No. 922, Andohan'Analakely Quarter and March 29th monument. 250fr, Independence Avenue and Jean Ralaimongo monument. 550fr, Queen's Palace and Andohalo School on Lake Anosy.

1989, Mar. 31 Litho. *Perf. 13½*

919 A301 5fr multi 15 15
920 A301 20fr multi 15 15
921 A301 80fr multi 48 24
922 A301 80fr multi 48 24
923 A301 250fr multi 1.50 75
924 A301 550fr multi 3.25 1.65
Nos. 919-924 (6) 6.01 3.18

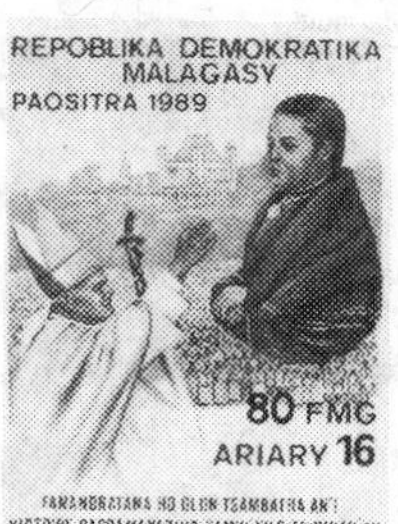

Visit of Pope John Paul II — A302

1989, Apr. 28 *Perf. 12x12½*

925 A302 80fr shown 48 24
926 A302 250fr Pope, map 1.50 75

French Revolution, Bicent. A303

1989, July 7 Litho. *Perf. 12½*

927 A303 250fr Storming of the Bastille 48 24

Phobos Space Program for the Exploration of Mars A304

1989, Aug. 29 Litho. *Perf. 12½x12*

928 A304 20fr Mars 1 15 15
929 A304 80fr Mars 3 15 15
930 A304 80fr Sond 2 15 15
931 A304 250fr Mariner 9 32 16
932 A304 270fr Viking 2 35 18
Set value 90 45

Souvenir Sheet

933 A304 550fr Phobos 70 70

PHILEXFRANCE '89 and French Revolution Bicent. — A305

Exhibition emblems, key people and scenes from the revolution: 250fr, Honore-Gabriel Riqueti (1749-1791), Count of Mirabeau, at the meeting of Estates-General, June 23, 1789. 350fr, Camille Desmoulins (1760-1794), call to arms, July 12, 1789. 1000fr, Lafayette (1757-1834), women's march on Versailles, Oct. 5, 1789. 1500fr, King tried by the National Convention, Dec. 26, 1792. 2500fr, Charlotte Corday (1768-1793), assassination of Marat, July 13, 1793. 3000fr, Bertrand Barere de Vieuzac, Robespierre, Jean-Marie Collot D'Herbois, Lazare Nicolas Carnot, George Jacques Danton, Georges Auguste Couthon, Pierre-Louis Prieur, Antoine Saint-Just and Marc Guillaume Vadiez, Committee of Public Safety, July, 1793.

1989, July 14 Litho. *Perf. 13½*

934 A305 250fr multicolored 32 16
935 A305 350fr multicolored 45 22
936 A305 1000fr multicolored 1.30 65
937 A305 1500fr multicolored 1.95 98
938 A305 2500fr multicolored 3.25 1.65
Nos. 934-938 (5) 7.27 3.66

Souvenir Sheet

939 A305 3000fr multicolored 4.00 4.00

French Revolution, Bicent. — A306

Paintings and sculpture: 5fr, *Liberty Guiding the People*, by Eugene Delacroix. 80fr, "La Marseillaise" from *Departure of the Volunteers in 1792*, high relief on the Arc de Triomphe, 1833-35, by Francois Rude. 250fr, *The Tennis Court Oath*, by David.

1989, Oct. 25 *Perf. 12½x12*

940 A306 5fr multicolored 15 15
941 A306 80fr multicolored 15 15
942 A306 250fr multicolored 32 16
Set value 46 20

No. 942 is airmail.

Rene Cassin (1887-1976), Nobel Peace Prize Winner and Institute Founder — A307

1989, Nov. 21 *Perf. 12*

943 A307 250fr multicolored 35 18

Intl. Law Institute of the French-Speaking Nations, 25th anniv.

Hapalemur aureus A308

1989, Dec. 5 Litho. *Perf. 12*

944 A308 250fr multicolored 38 20

A309

A310

Various athletes, cup and: 350fr, Cavour Monument, Turin. 1000fr, Christopher Columbus Monument, Genoa, 1903. 1500fr, Michelangelo's *David*. 2500fr, *Abduction of Prosperina*, by Bernini, Rome. 3000fr, Statue of Leonardo da Vinci, 1903.

1989, Dec. 12 Litho. *Perf. 13½*

945 A309 350fr multicolored 45 22
946 A309 1000fr multicolored 1.30 65
947 A309 1500fr multicolored 2.00 1.00
948 A309 2500fr multicolored 3.25 1.65

Souvenir Sheet

949 A309 3000fr multicolored 4.00 2.00

1990 World Cup Soccer Championships, Italy.

1989, Oct. 7 Litho. *Perf. 13½*

950 A310 80fr Long jump 15 15
951 A310 250fr Pole vault 35 18
952 A310 550fr Hurdles 78 40
953 A310 1500fr Cycling 2.15 1.10
954 A310 2000fr Baseball 2.85 1.45
955 A310 2500fr Tennis 3.50 1.75
Nos. 950-955 (6) 9.78 5.03

Souvenir Sheet

956 A310 3000fr Soccer 4.25 2.15

1992 Summer Olympics, Barcelona.

Scenic Views and Artifacts A311

1990, May 29

Size: 47x33mm (#958, 960)

957 A311 70fr Queen Isalo Rock 15 15
958 A311 70fr Sakalava pipe 15 15
959 A311 150fr Sakalava combs 22 15
960 A311 150fr Lonjy Is., Diego Suarez Bay 22 15
Set value 64 32

Fish — A312

1990, Apr. 26 **Litho.** ***Perf. 12***

961 A312 5fr Heniochus acuminatus 15 15
962 A312 20fr Simenhelys dofleinl 15 15
963 A312 80fr Phinobatos perceli 15 15
964 A312 250fr Epinephelus fasciatus 40 20
965 A312 320fr Sphurna zygaena 50 25
Set value 1.10 60

Souvenir Sheet

966 A312 550fr Latimeria chalumnae 90 90

Nos. 962-963 vert. Nos. 961-966 inscribed 1989.

Moon Landing, 20th Anniv. — A314

Designs: 80fr, Voyager 2, Neptune. 250fr, Hydro 2000 flying boat. 550fr, NOAA satellite. 1500fr, Magellan probe, Venus. 2000fr, Concorde. 2500fr, Armstrong, Aldrin, Collins, lunar module. 3000fr, Apollo 11 astronauts, first step on moon.

1990, June 19 **Litho.** ***Perf. 13½***

967 A314 80fr multicolored 15 15
968 A314 250fr multicolored 35 18
969 A314 550fr multicolored 82 40
970 A314 1500fr multicolored 2.25 1.10
971 A314 2000fr multicolored 3.00 1.50
972 A314 2500fr multicolored 3.75 1.90
Nos. 967-972 (6) 10.32 5.23

Souvenir Sheet

973 A314 3000fr multicolored 4.50 2.25

A315

A316

1990, July 17

974 A315 350fr Bobsled 52 25
975 A315 1000fr Speed skating 1.50 75
976 A315 1500fr Nordic skiing 2.25 1.10
977 A315 2500fr Super giant slalom 3.75 1.90

Souvenir Sheet

978 A315 3000fr Giant slalom 4.50 2.25

1992 Winter Olympics, Albertville.

1990, June 19 **Litho.** ***Perf. 12***

979 A316 250fr blk, ultra & bl 40 20

Intl. Maritime Organization, 30th anniv.

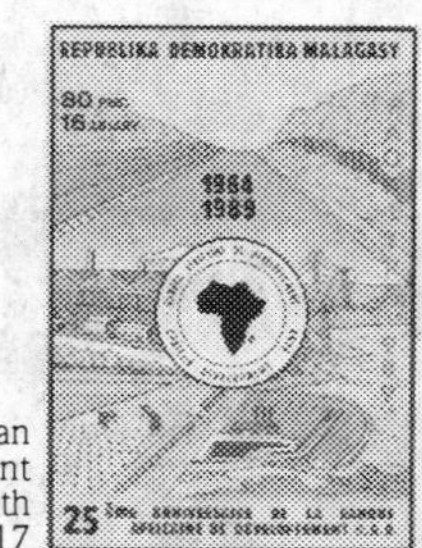

African Development Bank, 25th Anniv. — A317

1990, June 19

980 A317 80fr multicolored 15 15

A318

A319

1990, June 28

981 A318 150fr multicolored 22 15

Campaign against polio.

1990, Aug. 22

982 A319 100fr multicolored 16 15

Independence, 30th anniv.

A320

A322

1990, Aug. 24 ***Perf. 12½x12***

983 A320 100fr yellow & multi 16 15
984 A320 350fr lil rose & multi 52 25
Set value 32

3rd Indian Ocean Games.

1990, Oct. 19 **Litho.** ***Perf. 12***

986 A322 350fr multicolored 60 30

Ho Chi Minh (1890-1969), Vietnamese leader.

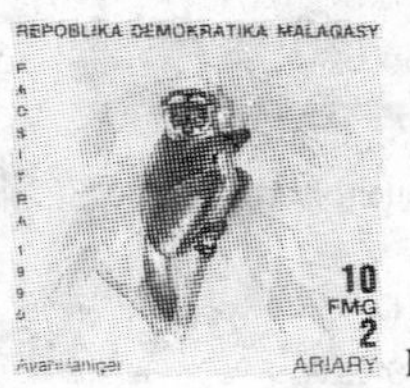

Lemurs — A323

1990, Nov. 23 **Litho.** ***Perf. 11½***

987 A323 10fr Avahi laniger 15 15
988 A323 20fr Lemur fulvus sanfordi 15 15
989 A323 20fr Lemur fulvus albifrons 15 15
990 A323 100fr Lemur fulvus collaris 18 15
991 A323 100fr Lepulemur ruficaudatus 18 15
Set value 46 23

Souvenir Sheet

992 A323 350fr Lemur fulvus fulvus 60 30

Shells A324

1990, Dec. 21 ***Perf. 12½***

993 A324 40fr Tridacna squamosa 15 15
994 A324 50fr Terebra demidiata, Terebra subulata 15 15
Set value 18 15

Anniversaries and Events — A325

Charles de Gaulle A325a

Designs: 100fr, Charles de Gaulle, liberation of Paris, 1944. 350fr, Galileo probe orbiting Jupiter. 800fr, Apollo 11 crew and Columbia command module, first Moon landing, 1969. 900fr, De Gaulle, 1942. 1250fr, Concorde jet, TGV high-speed train. 2500fr, De Gaulle as head of provisional government, 1944. 3000fr, Apollo 11 crew, Eagle lunar module. No. 1001A, De Gaulle with Roosevelt and Churchill.

1990, Dec. 28 **Litho.** ***Perf. 13½***

995 A325 100fr multi 18 15
996 A325 350fr multi 60 30
997 A325 800fr multi 1.40 70
998 A325 900fr multi 1.60 80
999 A325 1250fr multi 2.20 1.10
1000 A325 2500fr multi 4.40 2.20
Nos. 995-1000 (6) 10.38 5.25

Souvenir Sheet

1001 A325 3000fr multi 5.30 2.65

Litho. & Embossed

1001A A325a 5000fr gold & multi

Souvenir Sheet

1001B A325a 5000fr gold & multi

#995-1000, 1001A exist in souvenir sheets of 1.

Mushrooms — A325b

Designs: 25fr, Boletus edulis. 100fr, Suillus luteus. 350fr, Amanita muscaria. 450fr, Boletus calopus. 680fr, Boletus erythropus. 800fr, Leccinum scabrum. 900fr, Leccinum testaceoscabrum.

1990, Dec. 28 **Litho.** ***Perf. 12***

1001C A325b 25fr multicolored 15 15
1001D A325b 100fr multicolored 15 15
1001E A325b 350fr multicolored 45 22
1001F A325b 450fr multicolored 58 30
1001G A325b 680fr multicolored 90 45
1001H A325b 800fr multicolored 1.05 52
1001I A325b 900fr multicolored 1.20 60
Nos. 1001C-1001I (7) 4.48 2.39

A number has been reserved for a souvenir sheet with this set.

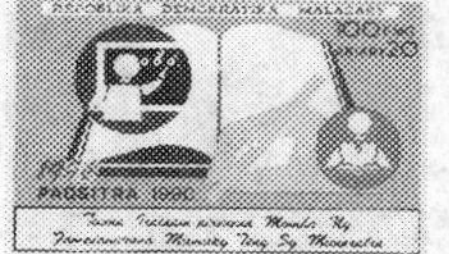

Intl. Literacy Year — A326

1990, Dec. 30 ***Perf. 12***

1002 A326 20fr Book, guiding hands, vert. 15 15
1003 A326 100fr shown 18 15
Set value 22 15

Dogs — A326a

1991, Mar. 20 **Litho.** ***Perf. 12***

1003A A326a 30fr Greyhound 15 15
1003B A326a 50fr Japanese spaniel 15 15
1003C A326a 140fr Toy terrier 18 15
1003D A326a 350fr Chow 45 22
1003E A326a 500fr Miniature pinscher 65 32
1003F A326a 800fr Afghan 1.05 52
1003G A326a 1140fr Papillon 1.50 75
Nos. 1003A-1003G (7) 4.13 2.26

Imperf

Size: 70x90mm

1003H A326a 1500fr Shih tzu 2.00 1.00

Nos. 1003D-1003H are airmail.

Democratic Republic of Madagascar, 15th Anniv. (in 1990) A327

1991, Apr. 8 **Litho.** ***Perf. 12***

1004 A327 100fr multicolored 18 15

Dated 1990.

Trees — A328

1991, June 20 **Litho.** ***Perf. 13½***

1005 A328 140fr Adansonia fony 22 15
1006 A328 500fr Didierea madagascariensis 75 40

Scouts, Insects and Mushrooms A329

Insects: 140fr, Helictopleurus splendidicollis. 640fr, Cocles contemplator. 1140fr, Euchroea oberthurii.
Mushrooms: 500fr, Russula radicans. 1025fr, Russula singeri. 3500fr, Lactariopsis pandani.
4500fr, Euchroea spinnasuta fairmaire and Russula aureotacta.

1991, Aug. 2 Litho. *Perf. 13½*

No.	Type	Value	Color	Unused	Used
1007	A329	140fr	multicolored	18	15
1008	A329	500fr	multicolored	65	32
1009	A329	640fr	multicolored	82	40
1010	A329	1025fr	multicolored	1.30	65
1011	A329	1140fr	multicolored	1.45	72
1012	A329	3500fr	multicolored	4.50	2.25
		Nos. 1007-1012 (6)		8.90	4.49

Souvenir Sheet

No.	Type	Value	Color	Unused	Used
1013	A329	4500fr	multicolored	5.85	5.85

Nos. 1007-1012 exist in souvenir sheets of 1.

Discovery of America, 500th Anniv. A330

Designs: 15fr, Ship, 9th cent.. 65fr, Clipper ship, 1878. 140fr, Golden Hind. 500fr, Galley, 18th cent. 640fr, Galleon Ostrust, 1721, vert. 800fr, Caravel Amsterdam, 1539, vert. 1025fr, Santa Maria, 1492. 1500fr, Map.

1991, Sept. 10 Litho. *Perf. 12*

No.	Type	Value	Color	Unused	Used
1014	A330	15fr	multicolored	15	15
1015	A330	65fr	multicolored	15	15
1016	A330	140fr	multicolored	18	15
1017	A330	500fr	multicolored	65	32
1018	A330	640fr	multicolored	85	42
1019	A330	800fr	multicolored	1.05	52
1020	A330	1025fr	multicolored	1.35	65
		Nos. 1014-1020 (7)		4.38	2.36

Size: 90x70mm

No.	Type	Value	Color	Unused	Used
1021	A330	1500fr	multicolored	2.00	1.00

No. 1021 contains one 40x27mm perf. 12 label in center of stamp picturing ships and Columbus.

Domesticated Animals — A331

Designs: 140fr, Dog. 500fr, Arabian horse. 640fr, House cats. 1025fr, Himalayan cats. 1140fr, Draft horse. 5000fr, German shepherd. 10,000fr, Horse, cat & dog.

1991, Sept. 27 Litho. *Perf. 13½*

No.	Type	Value	Color	Unused	Used
1022	A331	140fr	multicolored	18	15
1023	A331	500fr	multicolored	65	32
1024	A331	640fr	multicolored	82	40
1025	A331	1025fr	multicolored	1.30	65
1026	A331	1140fr	multicolored	1.45	72
1027	A331	5000fr	multicolored	6.50	3.25
		Nos. 1022-1027 (6)		10.90	5.49

Souvenir Sheet

No.	Type	Value	Color	Unused	Used
1028	A331	10,000fr	multicolored	13.00	6.50

Nos. 1022-1028 exist imperf. and in souvenir sheets of 1.

1992 Winter Olympics, Albertville — A333

1991, Dec. 30 Litho. *Perf. 12x12½*

No.	Type	Value	Description	Unused	Used
1037	A333	5fr	Cross-country skiing	15	15
1038	A333	15fr	Biathlon	15	15
1039	A333	60fr	Ice hockey	15	15
1040	A333	140fr	Downhill skiing	18	15
1041	A333	640fr	Figure skating	85	42
1042	A333	1000fr	Ski jumping	1.30	65
1043	A333	1140fr	Speed skating	1.50	75
		Nos. 1037-1043 (7)		4.28	2.42

Imperf

Size: 90x70mm

No.	Type	Value	Description	Unused	Used
1044	A333	1500fr	Three hockey players	2.00	1.00

Space Program A334

Designs: 140fr, Astronaunts repairing space telescope. 500fr, Soho solar observation probe. 640fr, Topex-Poseidon, observing oceans. 1025fr, Hipparcos probe, Galaxy 3C75. 1140fr, Voyager II surveying Neptune. 5000fr, Adeos, ETS VI, earth observation and communications satellites. 7500fr, Crew of Apollo 11.

1992, Apr. 22 *Perf. 13½*

No.	Type	Value	Color	Unused	Used
1045	A334	140fr	multi	18	15
1046	A334	500fr	multi	65	32
1047	A334	640fr	multi	82	40
1048	A334	1025fr	multi	1.30	65
1049	A334	1140fr	multi	1.45	72
1050	A334	5000fr	multi	6.50	3.20
		Nos. 1045-1050 (6)		10.90	5.44

Souvenir Sheet

No.	Type	Value	Color	Unused	Used
1051	A334	7500fr	multi	9.75	9.75

#1045-1050 exist in souvenir sheets of one.

Entertainers A335

1992, Apr. 29

No.	Type	Value	Description	Unused	Used
1052	A335	100fr	Ryuichi Sakamoto	15	15
1053	A335	350fr	John Lennon	45	22
1054	A335	800fr	Bruce Lee	1.05	52
1055	A335	900fr	Sammy Davis, Jr.	1.18	58
1056	A335	1250fr	John Wayne	1.65	80
1057	A335	2500fr	James Dean	3.25	1.65
		Nos. 1052-1057 (6)		7.73	3.92

Souvenir Sheet

No.	Type	Value	Description	Unused	Used
1058	A335	3000fr	Clark Gable & Vivien Leigh	3.90	1.95

#1021-1026 exist in souvenir sheets of one.

Fight Against AIDS — A336

1990 Sports Festival — A338

Reforestation A337

1992, July 29 Litho. *Perf. 12*

No.	Type	Value	Color	Unused	Used
1059	A336	140fr	lil rose & black	24	15

Dated 1991.

1992, July 29 Litho. *Perf. 12*

No.	Type	Value	Color	Unused	Used
1060	A337	140fr	black & green	24	15

Dated 1991.

1992, Aug. 20

No.	Type	Value	Color	Unused	Used
1061	A338	140fr	multicolored	24	15

Dated 1991.

Meteorology in Madgascar, Cent. — A339

1992, Nov. 10 Litho. *Perf. 12x12½*

No.	Type	Value	Color	Unused	Used
1062	A339	140fr	multicolored	22	15

SEMI-POSTAL STAMPS

No. 84 Surcharged in Red 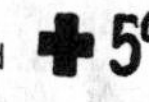

1915, Feb. Unwmk. *Perf. 13½x14*

No.	Type	Value	Color	Unused	Used
B1	A9	10c + 5c	rose & brn	45	45

Curie Issue
Common Design Type

1938, Oct. 24 *Perf. 13*

No.	Type	Value	Color	Unused	Used
B2	CD80	1.75fr + 50c	brt ultra	5.75	5.75

French Revolution Issue
Common Design Type
Name and Value Typographed in Black

1939, July 5 Photo.

No.	Type	Value	Color	Unused	Used
B3	CD83	45c + 25c	grn	3.75	3.75
B4	CD83	70c + 30c	brn	3.75	3.75
B5	CD83	90c + 35c	red org	3.75	3.75
B6	CD83	1.25fr + 1fr	rose pink	3.75	3.75
B7	CD83	2.25fr + 2fr	blue	3.75	3.75
		Nos. B3-B7 (5)		18.75	18.75

Common Design Type and

Malgache Sharpshooter — SP1

Tank Corpsman SP2

1941 Photo. *Perf. 13½*

No.	Type	Value	Color	Unused	Used
B8	SP1	1fr + 1fr	red	80	
B9	CD86	1.50fr + 3fr	maroon	80	
B10	SP2	2.50fr + 1fr	blue	1.00	

Nos. B8-B10 were issued by the Vichy government, and were not placed on sale in the colony.
Nos. 162 and 190 surcharged "SECOURS +50c NATIONAL," and Nos. 210A-210B surcharged "OEUVRES COLONIALES" and surtax (including change of denomination of the 2.50fr to 50c) were issued in 1942-44 by the Vichy government, and not placed on sale in the colony.

Catalogue values for unused stamps in this section, from this point to the end of the section, are for Never Hinged items.

Red Cross Issue
Common Design Type

1944 Unwmk. *Perf. 14½x14*

No.	Type	Value	Color	Unused	Used
B15	CD90	5fr + 20fr	dk grn	38	38

The surtax was for the French Red Cross and national relief.

Gen. J. S. Galliéni and Malagasy Plowing — SP3

1946, Nov. Engr. *Perf. 13*

No.	Type	Value	Color	Unused	Used
B16	SP3	10fr + 5fr	dk vio brn	28	28

Issued to commemorate the 50th anniversary of Madagascar's existence as a French Colony.

Tropical Medicine Issue
Common Design Type

1950, May 15

No.	Type	Value	Color	Unused	Used
B17	CD100	10fr + 2fr	dk Prus grn & brn vio	2.75	2.75

The surtax was for charitable work.

Malagasy Republic
No. 320 Surcharged in Ultramarine with New Value and: "FETES DE L'INDEPENDANCE"

1960, July 29 Engr. *Perf. 13*

No.	Type	Value	Color	Unused	Used
B18	A38	20fr + 10fr	red, blk & brt grn	40	35

Anti-Malaria Issue
Common Design Type

1962, Apr. 7 *Perf. 12½x12*

No.	Type	Value	Color	Unused	Used
B19	CD108	25fr + 5fr	yel grn	50	50

Post Office, Tamatave SP4

1962, May 8 Engr. *Perf. 13*

No.	Type	Value	Color	Unused	Used
B20	SP4	25fr + 5fr	sl grn, bl & lt red brn	25	25

Issued for Stamp Day, 1962.

Freedom from Hunger Issue
Common Design Type

1963, Mar. 21 *Perf. 13*

No.	Type	Value	Color	Unused	Used
B21	CD112	25fr + 5fr	red org, plum & brn	45	45

FAO "Freedom from Hunger" campaign.

Type of 1962

Design: 20fr+5fr, Central Parcel Post Office, Tananarive.

1963, May 8 **Engr.**
B22 SP4 20fr + 5fr bl grn & red brn 30 30

Issued for Stamp Day, 1963.

Postal Savings and Checking Accounts Building, Tananarive — SP5

1964, May 8 **Unwmk.** ***Perf. 13***
B23 SP5 25fr + 5fr bl, bis & dk grn 40 40

Issued for Stamp Day, 1964.

No. 457 Surcharged in Violet Blue

+ 20F
MEMORIAL

1972, June 26 **Engr.** ***Perf. 13***
B24 A106 30fr + 20fr multi 40 40

Charles de Gaulle memorial.

SP6

SP7

1989, June 15 **Litho.**
B25 SP6 80fr +20fr Torch bearer 20 15

Village games.

1990, Aug. 7 **Litho.** ***Perf. 12***
B26 SP7 100fr+20fr on 80fr+20fr 20 15
B27 SP7 350fr+20fr on 250fr+20fr 60 30

3rd Indian Ocean Games. Nos. B26-B27 were not issued without surcharge.

AIR POST STAMPS

Airplane and Map of Madagascar — AP1

Perf. 13x13½

1935-41 **Photo.** **Unwmk.**
C1 AP1 50c yel grn & red 48 32
C2 AP1 90c yel grn & red ('41) 28
C3 AP1 1.25fr claret & red 35 32
C4 AP1 1.50fr brt bl & red 35 32
C5 AP1 1.60fr brt bl & red ('41) 15 15
C6 AP1 1.75fr org & red 4.50 2.75
C7 AP1 2fr Prus bl & red 48 32
C8 AP1 3fr dp org & red ('41) 15 15
C9 AP1 3.65fr ol blk & red ('38) 35 32
C10 AP1 3.90fr pck grn & red ('41) 15 15
C11 AP1 4fr rose & red 30.00 2.00
C12 AP1 4.50fr blk & red 15.00 1.25
C13 AP1 5.50fr ol blk & red ('41) 18 15
C14 AP1 6fr rose lil & red ('41) 18 18
C15 AP1 6.90fr dl vio & red ('41) 15 15
C16 AP1 8fr rose lil & red 60 52
C17 AP1 8.50fr grn & red 70 70
C18 AP1 9fr ol grn & red ('41) 32 35
C19 AP1 12fr vio brn & red 52 40
C20 AP1 12.50fr dl vio & red 1.00 60
C21 AP1 15fr org yel & red ('41) 68 48
C22 AP1 16fr ol grn & red 90 70
C23 AP1 20fr dk brn & red 1.40 70
C24 AP1 50fr brt ultra & red ('38) 2.50 2.00
Nos. C1,C3-C24 (23) 61.09 14.98

According to some authorities the 90c was not placed on sale in Madagascar.

V5

Stamps of type AP1, without "RF" monogram, and stamp of design shown above were issued in 1942 to 1944 by the Vichy Government, but were not placed on sale in the colony.

Air Post Stamps of 1935-38 Overprinted in Black

FRANCE
LIBRE

1942 ***Perf. 13x13½***
C27 AP1 1.50fr brt bl & red 2.75 2.75
C28 AP1 1.75fr org & red 42.50 42.50
C29 AP1 8fr rose lil & red 75 75
C30 AP1 12fr vio brn & red 1.10 1.10
C31 AP1 12.50fr dl vio & red 80 80
C32 AP1 16fr ol grn & red 2.75 2.75
C33 AP1 50fr brt ultra & red 1.75 1.75

Nos. C3, C9, C17 Surcharged in Black

FRANCE
LIBRE

1,00 ×

C34 AP1 1fr on 1.25fr 2.00 2.00
C35 AP1 3fr on 3.65fr 65 65
C36 AP1 8fr on 8.50fr 65 65
Nos. C27-C36 (10) 55.70 55.70

Catalogue values for unused stamps in this section, from this point to the end of the section, are for Never Hinged items.

Common Design Type

1943 **Photo.** ***Perf. 14½x14***
C37 CD87 1fr dk org 15 15
C38 CD87 1.50fr brt red 15 15
C39 CD87 5fr brn red 15 15
C40 CD87 10fr black 20 20
C41 CD87 25fr ultra 35 25
C42 CD87 50fr dk grn 50 38
C43 CD87 100fr plum 80 50
Nos. C37-C43 (7) 2.30
Set value 1.50

Victory Issue

Common Design Type

Perf. 12½

1946, May 8 **Unwmk.** **Engr.**
C44 CD92 8fr brn red 30 20

Issued to commemorate the European victory of the Allied Nations in World War II.

Chad to Rhine Issue

Common Design Types

1946, June 6
C45 CD93 5fr brt bl 50 50
C46 CD94 10fr dk car rose 50 50
C47 CD95 15fr gray grn 50 50
C48 CD96 20fr brn ol 60 60
C49 CD97 25fr dk vio 65 65
C50 CD98 50fr brn org 65 65
Nos. C45-C50 (6) 3.40 3.40

Tamatave — AP2

Allegory of Air Mail — AP3

Plane over Map of Madagascar — AP4

Perf. 13½x12½, 12½x13½

1946 **Photo.** **Unwmk.**
C51 AP2 50fr bl vio & car 65 25
C52 AP3 100fr brn & car 1.65 40
C53 AP4 200fr bl grn & brn 3.25 1.00

No. C52 Overprinted in Carmine

TERRE ADÉLIE
DUMONT D'URVILLE
1840

1948, Oct. 26 ***Perf. 12½x13½***
C54 AP3 100fr brn & car 22.50 24.00

Issued to publicize the French claim to Antarctic Adelie Land, discovered by Jules S. C. Dumont d'Urville in 1840.

UPU Issue

Common Design Type

1949, July 4 **Engr.** ***Perf. 13***
C55 CD99 25fr multi 1.90 1.50

Scene Near Bemananga — AP5

1952, June 30 **Unwmk.** ***Perf. 13***
C56 AP5 500fr brn, blk brn & dk grn 10.50 3.25

Liberation Issue

Common Design Type

1954, June 6
C57 CD102 15fr vio & vio brn 80 65

Pachypodes — AP6

Designs: 100fr, Antsirabé viaduct. 200fr, Ring-tailed lemurs.

1954, Sept. 20
C58 AP6 50fr dk bl grn & dk grn 1.00 15
C59 AP6 100fr dp ultra, blk & choc 1.60 65
C60 AP6 200fr dk grn & sep 4.00 1.20

Malagasy Republic

Sugar Cane Harvest — AP7

Charaxes Antamboulou — AP8

Designs: 40fr, Tobacco field. 100fr, Chrysiridia Madagascariensis. 200fr, Argema mittrel, vert. 500fr, Mandrare bridge.

1960 **Unwmk.** **Engr.** ***Perf. 13***
C61 AP7 30fr grn, vio brn & pale brn 42 15
C62 AP7 40fr Prus grn & ol gray 65 20
C63 AP8 50fr multi 70 16
C64 AP8 100fr sl grn, emer & org 1.50 22
C65 AP8 200fr pur & yel 2.25 60
C66 AP7 500fr Prus grn, bis & ultra 5.50 1.50
Nos. C61-C66 (6) 11.02 2.83

Diademed Sifakas — AP9

Lemurs: 85fr, Indri. 250fr, Verreaux's sifaka.

1961, Dec. 9 **Unwmk.** ***Perf. 13***
C67 AP9 65fr sl grn & red brn 65 25
C68 AP9 85fr ol, blk & brn 80 35
C69 AP9 250fr Prus grn, blk & mar 2.50 1.20

For surcharge see No. C90.

Plane over Nossi-Bé — AP10

1962, May 7 **Engr.** ***Perf. 13***
C70 AP10 100fr red brn, bl & dk grn 70 40
a. Souv. sheet of 5, #328-331, C70 1.50 1.50

1st Malagasy Philatelic Exhibition, Tananarive, May 5-13.

Turbojet Airliner, Emblem — AP11

1963, Apr. 18 Unwmk. *Perf. 13*
C71 AP11 500fr dk bl, red & grn 3.50 1.25

Madagascar commercial aviation.

Helmet Bird — AP12

Birds: 100fr, Pitta-like ground roller. 200fr, Crested wood ibis.

1963, Aug. 12 Photo. *Perf. 13x12½*
C72 AP12 40fr multi 35 25
C73 AP12 100fr multi 1.00 42
C74 AP12 200fr multi 2.00 80

African Postal Union Issue
Common Design Type

1963, Sept. 8 *Perf. 12½*
C75 CD114 85fr grn, ocher & red 1.00 70

Map of Madagascar, Jet Plane and UPU Emblem — AP13

1963, Nov. 2 Engr. *Perf. 13*
C76 AP13 45fr dk car, grnsh bl & ultra 40 20
C77 AP13 85fr dk car, vio & bl 70 40

Malagasy Republic's admission to the UPU, Nov. 2, 1961.

Meteorological Center, Tananarive and Tiros Satellite — AP14

1964, Mar. 23 Unwmk.
C78 AP14 90fr org brn, ultra & grn 1.20 50

UN 4th World Meteorological Day, Mar. 23.

Zebu, Wood Sculpture — AP15

1964, Oct. 20 Engr. *Perf. 13*
C79 AP15 100fr lil rose, dk vio & brn 90 62

Musical Instrument Type of Regular Issue

Design: 200fr, Lokanga bara (stringed instrument).

1965, Feb. 16 Unwmk. *Perf. 13*
Size: 26x47mm
C80 A57 200fr grn, org & choc 1.90 1.00

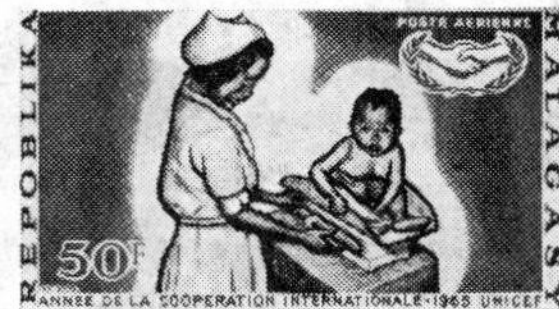
Nurse Weighing Infant, and ICY Emblem — AP16

Design: 100fr, Small boy and girl, child care scenes and ICY emblem.

1965, Sept. 20 Engr. *Perf. 13*
C81 AP16 50fr multi 42 25
C82 AP16 100fr multi 80 50

International Cooperation Year.

Dance Type of Regular Issue

Design: 250fr, Dance of a young girl, Sakalava, vert.

1966, June 13 Photo. *Perf. 13*
Size: 27x49mm
C83 A68 250fr multi 2.00 80

Aviation Type of Regular Issue

Design: 500fr, Dagnaux-Dufert and his Bréguet biplane, 1927.

1967, Apr. 28 Engr. *Perf. 13*
Size: 48x27mm
C84 A76 500fr Prus bl, blk & brn 4.00 1.40

No. C84 for the 40th anniv. of the 1st Majunga-Tananarive flight.

African Postal Union Issue, 1967
Common Design Type

1967, Sept. 9 Engr. *Perf. 13*
C85 CD124 100fr ol bis, red brn & brt pink 80 35

Dancer Type of Regular Issue

Designs: 100fr, Tourbillon dance, horiz. 200fr, Male dancer from the South.

1967-68 Photo. *Perf. 11½*
Size: 38x23mm
C86 A80 100fr multi ('68) 65 38

Perf. 13
Size: 27x48mm
C87 A80 200fr multi 1.60 70

Issue dates: 100fr, Nov. 25. 200fr, Nov. 25.

WHO Emblem, Bull's Head Totem and Palm Fan — AP17

1968, Apr. 7 Photo. *Perf. 12½x13*
C88 AP17 200fr bl, yel brn & red 1.50 80

WHO, 20th anniv.; Intl. Congress of Medical Science, Apr. 2-12.

Tananarive-Ivato International Airport — AP18

1968, May 8 Engr. *Perf. 13*
C89 AP18 500fr lt red brn, dl bl & dl grn 3.75 2.00

Issued for Stamp Day.

No. C68 Surcharged in Vermilion with New Value and 2 Bars

1968, June 24 Engr. *Perf. 13*
C90 AP9 20fr on 85fr multi 16 15

PHILEXAFRIQUE Issue

Lady Sealing Letter, by Jean Baptiste Santerre AP19

1968, Dec. 30 Photo. *Perf. 12½x12*
C91 AP19 100fr lil & multi 1.10 60

Issued to publicize PHILEXAFRIQUE Philatelic Exhibition in Abidjan, Feb. 14-23. Printed with alternating lilac label.

2nd PHILEXAFRIQUE Issue
Common Design Type

Design: 50fr, Madagascar No. 274, map of Madagascar and Malagasy emblem.

1969, Feb. 14 Engr. *Perf. 13*
C92 CD128 50fr gray, brn red & sl grn 60 35

Sunset over Madagascar Highlands, by Henri Ratovo — AP20

Painting: 100fr, On the Seashore of the East Coast of Madagascar, by Alfred Razafinjohany.

1969, Nov. 5 Photo. *Perf. 12x12½*
C93 AP20 100fr brn & multi 80 50
C94 AP20 150fr multi 1.20 80

Lunar Landing Module and Man on the Moon — AP21

1970, July 20 Engr. *Perf. 13*
C95 AP21 75fr ultra, dk gray & sl grn 45 38

Issued to commemorate the first anniversary of man's first landing on the moon.

Boeing 737 — AP22

1970, Dec. 18 Engr. *Perf. 13*
C96 AP22 200fr bl, red brn & grn 1.20 65

Jean Ralaimongo (1884-1944) — AP23

Portraits: 40fr, René Rakotobe (1918-71). 65fr, Albert Sylla (1909-67). 100fr, Joseph Ravoahangy Andrianavalona (1893-1970).

1971-72 Photo. *Perf. 12½; 13 (40fr)*
C97 AP23 25fr red brn, org & blk 16 15
C98 AP23 40fr dp cl, ocher & blk 22 16
C99 AP23 65fr grn, lt grn & blk 35 25
C100 AP23 100fr vio bl, lt bl & blk 60 35

Famous Malagasy men.
Issue dates: No. C98, July 25, 1972; others, Oct. 14, 1971.

African Postal Union Issue, 1971

"Mpisikidy" by G. Rakotovao and UAMPT Building, Brazzaville, Congo — AP24

1971, Nov. 13 Photo. *Perf. 13x13½*
C105 AP24 100fr bl & multi 65 42

10th anniv. of African and Malagasy Posts and Telecommunications Union (UAMPT).

Scott's editorial staff cannot undertake to identify, authenticate or appraise stamps and postal markings.

Running, Olympic Village
REPOBLIKA MALAGASY AP25

Design: 200fr, Judo, Olympic Stadium.

1972, Sept. 11 Photo. *Perf. 13½*
C106 AP25 100fr multi 65 35
C107 AP25 200fr multi 1.10 55

20th Olympic Games, Munich, Aug. 26-Sept. 11.

Mohair Goat AP26

1972, Nov. 15
C108 AP26 250fr multi 1.90 1.00

Adoration of the Kings, by Andrea Mantegna — AP27

Christmas: 85fr, Virgin and Child, Florentine School, 15th century, vert.

1972, Dec. 15 Photo. *Perf. 13*
C109 AP27 85fr gold & multi 50 25
C110 AP27 150fr gold & multi 90 42

Landing Module, Astronauts and Lunar Rover — AP28

1973, Jan. 25 Engr. *Perf. 13*
C111 AP28 300fr dp cl, gray & brn 1.50 1.25

Apollo 17 moon mission, Dec. 7-19, 1972.

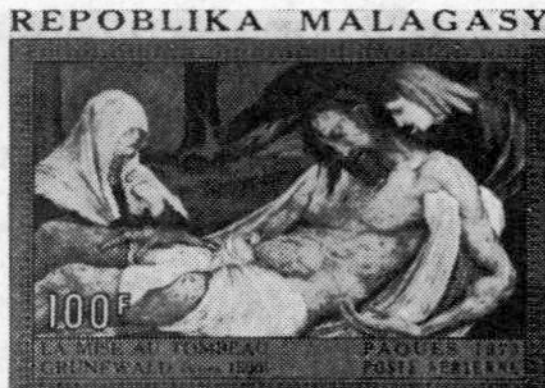

The Burial of Christ, by Grunewald — AP29

Easter: 200fr, Resurrection, by Mattias Grunewald, horiz. Both paintings from panels of Issenheim altar.

1973, Mar. 22 Photo. *Perf. 13*
C112 AP29 100fr gold & multi 45 25
C113 AP29 200fr gold & multi 1.00 50

Early Excursion Car — AP30

Design: 150fr, Early steam locomotive.

1973, July 25 Photo. *Perf. 13x12½*
C114 AP30 100fr multi 45 25
C115 AP30 150fr multi 70 40

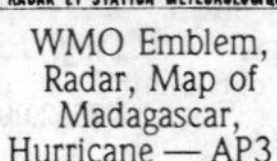

WMO Emblem, Radar, Map of Madagascar, Hurricane — AP31

Pres. John F. Kennedy, US Flag — AP32

1973, Sept. 3 Engr. *Perf. 13*
C116 AP31 100fr blk, ultra & org 60 30

Cent. of intl. meteorological cooperation.

Lemur Type of Regular Issue

Designs: 150fr, Lepilemur mustelinus, vert. 200fr, Cheirogaleus major.

1973, Oct. 9 Engr. *Perf. 13*
C117 A131 150fr multi 90 55
C118 A131 200fr multi 1.20 80

1973, Nov. 22 Photo. *Perf. 13*
C119 AP32 300fr multi 1.60 1.00

10th anniv. of the death of John F. Kennedy.

Soccer — AP33

1973, Dec. 20 Engr. *Perf. 13*
C120 AP33 500fr lil rose, dk brn & org brn 3.00 2.00

World Soccer Cup, Munich, 1974.
For overprint see No. C130.

Copernicus, Skylab and Heliocentric System — AP34

1974, Jan. 22
C121 AP34 250fr multi 1.20 45

500th anniversary of the birth of Nicolaus Copernicus (1473-1543), Polish astronomer.

Scout Type of Regular Issue

Designs (African Scout Emblem and): 100fr, Scouts bringing sick people to Red Cross tent, horiz. 300fr, Scouts fishing and fish, horiz.

1974, Feb. 14 Engr. *Perf. 13*
C122 A132 100fr multi 55 22
C123 A132 300fr multi 1.60 70

Camellia, Hummingbird, Table Tennis Player — AP35

Design: 100fr, Girl player, flower and bird design.

1974, Mar. 19 Engr. *Perf. 13*
C124 AP35 50fr bl & multi 25 15
C125 AP35 100fr multi 55 25

Table Tennis Tournament, Peking.

Autorail Micheline — AP36

Designs (Malagasy Locomotives): 85fr, Track inspection trolley. 200fr, Garratt (steam).

1974, June 7 Engr. *Perf. 13*
C126 AP36 50fr multi 25 16
C127 AP36 85fr multi 42 22
C128 AP36 200fr multi 1.10 80

Letters and UPU Emblem — AP37

1974, July 9 Engr. *Perf. 13*
C129 AP37 250fr multi 1.40 65

Centenary of Universal Postal Union.
For overprint see No. C133.

No. C120 Overprinted: "R.F.A. 2 / HOLLANDE 1"

1974, Aug. 20 Engr. *Perf. 13*
C130 AP33 500fr multi 2.50 1.50

World Cup Soccer Championship, 1974, victory of German Federal Republic.

Link-up in Space, Globe, Emblem — AP38

Design: 250fr, Link-up, globe and emblem (different).

1974, Sept. 12
C131 AP38 150fr org, bl & sl grn 80 65
C132 AP38 250fr bl, brn & sl grn 1.40 90

Russo-American space cooperation.
For overprints see Nos. C142-C143.

No. C129 Overprinted

100 ANS DE COLLABORATION INTERNATIONALE

1974, Oct. 9 Engr. *Perf. 13*
C133 AP37 250fr multi 1.40 65

100 years of international collaboration.

Adoration of the Kings, by J. L. David — AP39

Christmas: 300fr, Virgin of the Cherries and Child, by Quentin Massys.

1974, Dec. 20 Photo. *Perf. 13*
C134 AP39 200fr gold & multi 90 40
C135 AP39 300fr gold & multi 1.40 60

UN Emblem and Globe — AP40

1975, June 24 Litho. *Perf. 12½*
C136 AP40 300fr grn, bl & blk 1.60 80

United Nations Charter, 30th anniversary.

American Bicentennial Type, 1975

Designs: 100fr, Count d'Estaing and "Languedoc." 200fr, John Paul Jones, "Bonhomme Richard" and "Serapis." 300fr, Benjamin Franklin, "Millern" and "Montgomery." 500fr, George Washington and "Hanna."

1975, June 30 Litho. *Perf. 11*
C137 A144 100fr multi 60 25
C138 A144 200fr multi 1.20 55
C139 A144 300fr multi 1.90 80

Souvenir Sheet

C140 A144 500fr multi 3.25 1.50

For overprints see Nos. C164-C167.

Flower Type of 1975

Design: 85fr, Turraea sericea.

1975, Aug. 4 Photo. *Perf. 12½*
C141 A145 85fr dp grn, yel & org 45 35

Nos. C131-C132 Overprinted

JONCTION 17 JUILLET 1975

1975, Aug. 5 Engr. *Perf. 13*
C142 AP38 150fr multi 80 40
C143 AP38 250fr multi 1.40 65

Apollo Soyuz link-up in space, July 17, 1975.

Bas-relief and Stupas — AP41

1975, Aug. 10 Engr. *Perf. 13*

C144 AP41 50fr bl, car & bis 25 16

UNESCO campaign to save Borobudur Temple, Java.

Exposition Type, 1975

Designs: 125fr, Deer. 300fr, Jay.

1975, Sept. 16 Litho. *Perf. 14x13 1/2*

C145 A147 125fr multi 80 45

Souvenir Sheet

C146 A147 300fr multi 2.00 1.00

Hurdling and Olympic Rings — AP42

Design: 200fr, Weight lifting and Olympic rings, vert.

1975, Oct. 9 Litho. *Perf. 12 1/2*

C147 AP42 75fr multi 40 20
C148 AP42 200fr multi 1.10 55

Pre-Olympic Year 1975.

12th Winter Olympics Type, 1975

Designs: 200fr, Cross-country skiing. 245fr, Down-hill skiing. 450fr, Figure skating, pairs.

1975, Nov. 19 *Perf. 14*

C149 A149 200fr multi 1.25 55
C150 A149 245fr multi 1.50 65

Souvenir Sheet

C151 A149 450fr multi 3.00 1.50

For overprints see Nos. C161-C163.

Landing Module, Apollo 14 Emblem — AP43

1976, Jan. 18 Engr. *Perf. 13*

C152 AP43 150fr red, grn & ind 80 40

Apollo 14 moon landing, 5th anniversary.
For overprint see No. C157.

21st Summer Olympics Type, 1976

Designs: 100fr, Shot-put and long jump. 200fr, Gymnastics, horse and balance bar. 300fr, Diving, 3-meter and platform. 500fr, Swimming, free-style and breast stroke.

1976, Jan. 21 Litho. *Perf. 13 1/2*

C153 A151 100fr multi 60 28
C154 A151 200fr multi 1.25 62
C155 A151 300fr multi 1.90 80

Souvenir Sheet

C156 A151 500fr multi 3.25 1.50

For overprints see Nos. C168-C171.

No. C152 Overprinted: "5e Anniversaire / de la mission / APOLLO XIV"

1976, Feb. 5 Engr. *Perf. 13*

C157 AP43 150fr red, grn & ind 80 40

Apollo 14 moon landing, 5th anniversary.

Zeppelin Type of 1976

Designs (Count Zeppelin and LZ-127 over): 200fr, Brandenburg Gate, Berlin 300fr, Parliament, London. 450fr, St. Peter's Cathedral, Rome.

1976, Mar. 3 Litho. *Perf. 11*

C158 A152 200fr multi 1.40 60
C159 A152 300fr multi 1.60 90

Souvenir Sheet

C160 A152 450fr multi 3.00 1.40

Nos. C149-C151 Overprinted

a. VAINQUEUR IVAR FORMO NORVEGE
b. VAINQUEUR ROSI MITTERMAIER ALLEMAGNE DE L'OUEST
c. VAINQUEUR IRINA RODNINA ALEXANDER ZAITSEV URSS

1976, June 17

C161 A149 (a) 200fr multi 85 45
C162 A149 (b) 245fr multi 1.00 50

Souvenir Sheet

C163 A149 (c) 450fr multi 1.75 1.20

12th Winter Olympic games winners.

Nos. C137-C140 Overprinted "4 Juillet / 1776-1976"

1976, July 4

C164 A144 100fr multi 65 25
C165 A144 200fr multi 1.25 55
C166 A144 300fr multi 1.90 80

Souvenir Sheet

C167 A144 500fr multi 3.25 1.60

American Bicentennial.

Nos. C153-C156 Overprinted

a. U. BEYER / A. ROBINSON
b. N. ANDRIANOV / N. COMANECI
c. K. DIBIASI / E. VAYTSEKHOVSKAIA,
d. J. MONTGOMERY / H. ANKE

1977, Jan.

C168 A151 (a) 100fr multi 62 25
C169 A151 (b) 200fr multi 1.20 55
C170 A151 (c) 300fr multi 1.75 80

Souvenir Sheet

C171 A151 (d) 500fr multi 3.25 1.60

21st Summer Olympic Games winners.

Fauna Type of 1979

1979, July 6

C172 A176 20fr Tortoises 15 15
C173 A176 95fr Macaco lemurs 62 22
Set value 36

International Palestinian Solidarity Day — AP44

1979, Nov. 29 Litho. *Perf. 12x12 1/2*

C174 AP44 60fr multi 40 16

Olympic Type of 1980

1980, Dec. 29 Litho. *Perf. 12 1/2x12*

C175 A188 250fr Judo 1.60 70
C176 A188 500fr Swimming 3.50 1.50

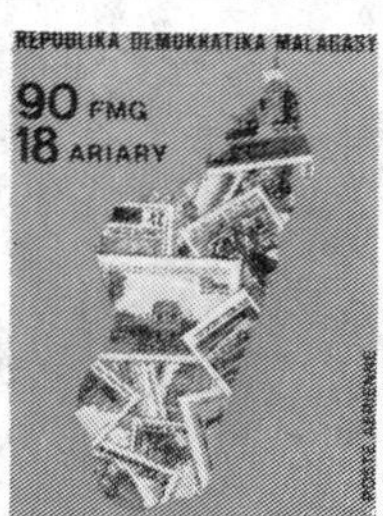

Stamp Day — AP45

1981, Dec. 17 Litho. *Perf. 12x12 1/2*

C177 AP45 90fr multi 60 22

20th Anniv. of Pan-African Women's Org. — AP46

1982, Aug. 6 Litho. *Perf. 12*

C178 AP46 80fr dk brn & lt brn 55 22

Hydroelectric Plant, Andekaleka — AP47

1982, Sept. 13 *Perf. 12 1/2x12*

C179 AP47 80fr multi 55 22

Orchid Type of 1984

1984, Nov. 20 Litho. *Perf. 12*

C180 A226 50fr Eulophiella elisabethae, horiz. 15 15
C181 A226 50fr Grammangis ellisii, horiz. 15 15
C182 A226 50fr Grammangis spectabilis 15 15
Set value 20

Solar Princess, by Sadiou Diouf AP48

1984, Dec. 22 Litho. *Perf. 12*

C183 AP48 100fr multi 30 15

Intl. Civil Aviation Org., 40th anniv.

Halley's Comet AP49

1986, Apr. 5 Litho. *Perf. 12 1/2x13*

C184 AP49 150fr multi 50 25

Admission of Madagascar into the UPU, 25th Anniv. — AP50

1986, Dec. 23 Litho. *Perf. 11 1/2*

C185 AP50 150fr multi 50 25

Air Madagascar, 25th Anniv. AP51

1987, June 17 Litho. *Perf. 12x12 1/2*

C186 AP51 60fr Piper Aztec 22 15
C187 AP51 60fr Twin Otter 22 15
C188 AP51 150fr Boeing 747 60 28
Set value 48

Socialist Revolution, 15th Anniv. — AP52

1990, June 16 Litho. *Perf. 13 1/2*

C189 AP52 100fr Map 16 15
C190 AP52 350fr Architecture 58 30
Set value 38

Madagascan Bible Society, 25th Anniv. AP53

1990, Sept. 17 *Perf. 12 1/2*

C191 AP53 25fr lt bl & multi 15 15
C192 AP53 100fr bl, blk & grn, vert. 16 15
Set value 20 15

Stamp Day — AP54

1990, Oct. 9 Litho. *Perf. 13x12 1/2*

C193 AP54 350fr multicolored 60 30

World Environment Day — AP55

1992, June 5 Litho. *Perf. 12 1/2*

C194 AP55 140fr multicolored 24 15

AIR POST SEMI-POSTAL STAMPS

French Revolution Issue
Common Design Type
Unwmk.
1939, July 5 Photo. *Perf. 13*
Name and Value in Orange

CB1 CD83 4.50fr + 4fr brn blk 8.00 8.00

V6

V7

V8

Stamps of the designs shown above, and type of Cameroun V10 inscribed "Madagascar", were issued in 1942 by the Vichy Government, but were not placed on sale in the colony.

POSTAGE DUE STAMPS

D1

Governor's Palace — D2

Postage Due Stamps of French Colonies Overprinted in Red or Blue

1896 Unwmk. *Imperf.*
J1 D1 5c blue (R) 4.00 3.75
J2 D1 10c brn (R) 4.00 3.25
J3 D1 20c yel (Bl) 4.50 4.00
J4 D1 30c rose red (Bl) 4.50 4.00
J5 D1 40c lilac (R) 35.00 22.50
J6 D1 50c gray vio (Bl) 6.00 4.75
J7 D1 1fr dk grn (R) 37.50 35.00
Nos. J1-J7 (7) 95.50 77.25

1908-24 Typo. *Perf. 13½x14*
J8 D2 2c vio brn 15 15
J9 D2 4c violet 15 15
J10 D2 5c green 15 15
J11 D2 10c deep rose 15 15
J12 D2 20c olive green 15 15
J13 D2 40c brn, *straw* 15 15
J14 D2 50c brn, *bl* 15 15
J15 D2 60c orange ('24) 35 35
J16 D2 1fr dark blue 42 42
Set value 1.25 1.25

Type of 1908 Issue Surcharged **60c**

1924-27
J17 D2 60c on 1fr org 1.00 1.00

Surcharged **2f**

J18 D2 2fr on 1fr lil rose ('27) 42 42
J19 D2 3fr on 1fr ultra ('27) 42 42

Postage Due Stamps of 1908-27 Overprinted or Surcharged in Black

FRANCE LIBRE

1943 *Perf. 13½x14*
J20 D2 10c dp rose 52 52
J21 D2 20c olive grn 52 52
J22 D2 30c on 5c green 52 52
J23 D2 40c brn, *straw* 52 52
J24 D2 50c brn, *blue* 52 52
J25 D2 60c orange 52 52
J26 D2 1fr dark blue 52 52
J27 D2 1fr on 2c vio brn 2.25 2.25
J28 D2 2fr on 1fr lil rose 52 52
J29 D2 2fr on 4c vio 90 90
J30 D2 3fr on 1fr ultra 52 52
Nos. J20-J30 (11) 7.83 7.83

Catalogue values for unused stamps in this section, from this point to the end of the section, are for Never Hinged items.

D3

Independence Monument — D4

1947 Photo. *Perf. 13*
J31 D3 10c dk vio 15 15
J32 D3 30c brown 15 15
J33 D3 50c dk bl grn 15 15
J34 D3 1fr dp org 15 15
J35 D3 2fr red vio 15 15
J36 D3 3fr red brn 15 15
J37 D3 4fr blue 25 25
J38 D3 5fr henna brown 30 30
J39 D3 10fr slate green 42 42
J40 D3 20fr vio blue 80 80
Set value 2.30 2.30

Malagasy Republic
Engraved; Denomination Typographed
1962, May 7 Unwmk. *Perf. 13*
J41 D4 1fr brt grn 15 15
J42 D4 2fr copper brn 15 15
J43 D4 3fr brt vio 15 15
J44 D4 4fr slate 15 15
J45 D4 5fr red 15 15
J46 D4 10fr yel grn 15 15
J47 D4 20fr dull claret 20 15
J48 D4 40fr blue 45 38
J49 D4 50fr rose red 70 65
J50 D4 100fr black 1.40 1.20
Set value 3.00 2.65

MADEIRA

LOCATION — A group of islands in the Atlantic Ocean northwest of Africa
GOVT. — Part of the Republic of Portugal
AREA — 314 sq. mi.
POP. — 150,574 (1900)
CAPITAL — Funchal

These islands are considered an integral part of Portugal and since 1898 postage stamps of Portugal have been in use. See Portugal for issues also inscribed Madeira, starting in 1980.

1000 Reis = 1 Milreis
100 Centavos = 1 Escudo (1925)

King Luiz
A1 A2

Stamps of Portugal Overprinted

1868, Jan. 1 Unwmk. *Imperf.*
Black Overprint
2 A1 20r bister 150.00 50.00
a. Inverted overprint
b. Rouletted
3 A1 50r green 150.00 50.00
4 A1 80r orange 165.00 60.00
a. Double overprint
5 A1 100r lilac 165.00 50.00

The 5r black does not exist as a genuinely imperforate original.

Reprints of 1885 are on stout white paper, ungummed. (Also, 5r, 10r and 25r values were overprinted.) Reprints of 1905 are on ordinary white paper with shiny gum and have a wide "D" and "R." Value, $12 each.

Lozenge Perf.

2c A1 20r
3a A1 50r
4b A1 80r
5a A1 100r

Overprinted in Red or Black

1868-70 *Perf. 12½*
6 A1 5r black (R) 22.50 10.00
8 A1 10r yellow 50.00 18.00
9 A1 20r bister 40.00 18.00
10 A1 25r rose 25.00 4.00
a. Inverted overprint
11 A1 50r green 100.00 30.00
a. Inverted overprint
12 A1 80r orange 150.00 35.00
13 A1 100r lilac 135.00 25.00
a. Inverted overprint
14 A1 120r blue 50.00 20.00
15 A1 240r violet ('70) 300.00 75.00

Two types of 5r differ in the position of the "5" at upper right.

The reprints are on stout white paper, ungummed, with rough perforation 13½, and on thin white paper with shiny white gum and clean-cut perforation 13½. The overprint has the wide "D" and "R" and the first reprints included the 5r with both black and red overprint. Value $10 each.

Common Design Types pictured in section at front of book.

Overprinted in Red or Black

1871-80 *Perf. 12½, 13½*
16 A2 5r black (R) 3.00 2.00
a. Inverted overprint
b. Double overprint
c. Perf. 14 80.00 40.00
18 A2 10r yellow 15.00 6.00
19 A2 10r bl grn ('79) 50.00 25.00
a. Perf. 13½ 60.00 50.00
20 A2 10r yel grn ('80) 20.00 15.00
21 A2 15r brn ('75) 6.00 3.50
22 A2 20r bister 12.00 7.00
23 A2 25r rose 6.00 1.00
a. Inverted overprint
24 A2 50r green ('72) 25.00 8.00
a. Double overprint
b. Inverted overprint
25 A2 50r blue ('80) 50.00 15.00
26 A2 80r orange ('72) 50.00 18.00
27 A2 100r pale lil ('73) 25.00 12.00
a. Perf. 14 225.00 175.00
b. Perf. 13½ 27.50 20.00
28 A2 120r blue 45.00 18.00
29 A2 150r blue ('76) 125.00 40.00
a. Perf. 13½ 150.00 100.00
30 A2 150r yel ('79) 195.00 175.00
31 A2 240r vio ('74) 450.00 150.00
32 A2 300r vio ('76) 55.00 20.00

There are two types of the overprint, the second one having a broad "D."

The reprints have the same characteristics as those of the 1868-70 issues.

King Luiz
A4 A5

1880-81
33 A4 5r black 11.00 6.00
34 A5 25r pearl gray 13.00 7.00
a. Inverted overprint
35 A4 25r lilac 15.00 3.00

No. 35 is overprinted on Portugal type A18.

Nos. 33, 34 and 35 have been reprinted on stout white paper, ungummed, and the last three on thin white paper with shiny white gum. The perforations are as previously described.

Vasco da Gama Issue
Common Design Types
1898, Apr. 1 Engr. *Perf. 14-15*
37 CD20 2½r blue grn 1.50 55
38 CD21 5r red 1.50 55
39 CD22 10r red violet 2.75 1.25
40 CD23 25r yel green 1.50 60
41 CD24 50r dk blue 4.50 2.25
42 CD25 75r vio brown 6.50 4.50
43 CD26 100r bister brn 4.50 3.75
44 CD27 150r bister 9.25 5.75
Nos. 37-44 (8) 32.00 19.20

Nos. 37-44 with "REPUBLICA" overprint and surcharges are listed as Portugal Nos. 199-206.

Ceres — A6

1928, May 1 Engr. *Perf. 13½*
Value Typographed in Black
45 A6 3c deep violet 22 *50*
46 A6 4c orange 22 *50*
47 A6 5c light blue 22 *50*
48 A6 6c brown 22 *50*
49 A6 10c red 22 *50*
50 A6 15c yel green 22 *50*
51 A6 16c red brown 25 *50*
52 A6 25c violet rose 30 *50*
53 A6 32c blue grn 30 *50*
54 A6 40c yel brown 65 *1.50*
55 A6 50c slate 65 *1.50*
56 A6 64c Prus blue 85 *2.50*
57 A6 80c dk brown 85 *2.50*
58 A6 96c carmine rose 85 *2.50*
59 A6 1e black 85 *2.50*
a. Value omitted
60 A6 1.20e light rose 85 *2.50*
61 A6 1.60e ultra 85 *2.50*
62 A6 2.40e yellow 1.10 *3.00*
63 A6 3.36e dull green 2.50 *5.00*
64 A6 4.50e brown red 3.00 *8.00*
65 A6 7e dk blue 4.00 *15.00*
Nos. 45-65 (21) 19.17 *53.50*

It was obligatory to use these stamps in place of those in regular use on May 1, June 5, July 1 and Dec. 31, 1928, Jan. 1 and 31, May 1 and June 5, 1929. The amount obtained from this sale was donated to a fund for building a museum.

NEWSPAPER STAMP

Numeral of Value — N1

Newspaper Stamp of Portugal Overprinted in Black

Perf. 12½, 13½
1876, July 1 Unwmk.
P1 N1 2½r olive 3.50 1.00
a. Inverted overprint 22.50

The reprints have the same papers, gum, perforations and overprint as the reprints of the regular issues.

POSTAL TAX STAMPS

Pombal Commemorative Issue
Common Design Types
1925 Unwmk. Engr. *Perf. 12½*
RA1 CD28 15c gray & black 55 60
RA2 CD29 15c gray & black 55 60
RA3 CD30 15c gray & black 55 60

POSTAL TAX DUE STAMPS

Pombal Commemorative Issue
Common Design Types

1925 Unwmk. *Perf. 12½*

RA1	CD31	30c gray & black	75	1.10
RA2	CD32	30c gray & black	75	1.10
RA3	CD33	30c gray & black	75	1.10

MALI

Federation of Mali

LOCATION — West Africa
GOVT. — Republic within French Community
AREA — 531,000 sq. mi.
POP. — 5,862,000 (est.)
CAPITAL — Dakar and Bamako

The Federation of Mali, founded Jan. 17, 1959, consisted of the Republic of Senegal and the Sudanese Republic. It broke up in June, 1960. See Senegal.

100 Centimes = 1 Franc

Catalogue values for all unused stamps in this country are for Never Hinged items.

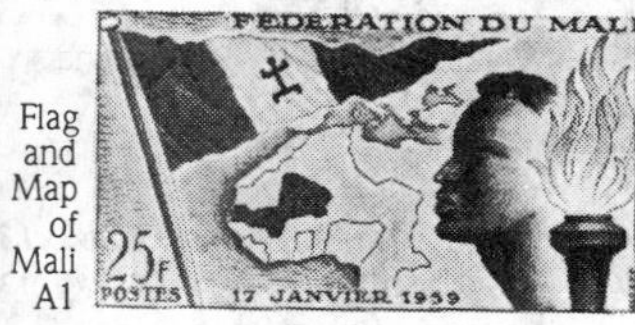

Flag and Map of Mali A1

Unwmk.
1959, Nov. 7 Engr. *Perf. 13*

1	A1	25fr grn, car & dp claret	35	35

Founding of the Federation of Mali.

Imperforates
Most Mali stamps exist imperforate in issued and trial colors, and also in small presentation sheets in issued colors.

Parrotfish A2

Fish: 10fr, Triggerfish. 15fr, Psetta. 20fr, Blepharis crinitus. 25fr, Butterflyfish. 30fr, Surgeonfish. 85fr, Dentex.

1960, Mar. 5
Fish in Natural Colors

2	A2	5fr olive	18	15
3	A2	10fr brt grnsh bl	20	15
4	A2	15fr dk bl	25	16
5	A2	20fr gray grn	38	20
6	A2	25fr slate grn	42	25
7	A2	30fr dk bl	60	40
8	A2	85fr dk grn	1.40	1.00
		Nos. 2-8 (7)	3.43	2.31

For overprints see Nos. 10-12.

C.C.T.A. Issue
Common Design Type

1960, May 21 *Perf. 13*

9	CD106	25fr lt vio & magenta	70	55

REPUBLIC OF MALI

GOVT. — Republic
AREA — 463,500 sq. mi.
POP. — 5,990,000 (est. 1977)
CAPITAL — Bamako

The Republic of Mali, formerly the Sudanese Republic, proclaimed its independence on June 20, 1960, when the Federation of Mali ceased to exist. See French Sudan.

Nos. 5, 6 and 8 Overprinted "REPUBLIQUE DU MALI" and Bar

Unwmk.
1961, Jan. 15 Engr. *Perf. 13*
Fish in Natural Colors

10	A2	20fr gray green	32	25
11	A2	25fr slate green	40	25
12	A2	85fr dark green	90	55

Pres. Mamadou Konate — A3

Design: 25fr, Pres. Modibo Keita.

1961, Mar. 18

13	A3	20fr green & blk	15	15
14	A3	25fr maroon & blk	18	15
		Set value		15

For miniature sheet see No. C11a.

Reading Class, Bullock Team and Factory — A4

1961, Sept. 22 Unwmk. *Perf. 13*

15	A4	25fr multi	35	20

First anniversary of Independence.

Common Design Types pictured in section at front of book.

Shepherd and Sheep — A5

Designs: 1fr, 10fr, 40fr, Cattle. 2fr, 15fr, 50fr, Mali Arts Museum. 3fr, 20fr, 60fr, Plowing. 4fr, 25fr, 85fr, Harvester.

Unwmk.
1961, Dec. 24 Engr. *Perf. 13*

16	A5	50c car rose, blk & dk grn	15	15
17	A5	1fr grn, bl & bis	15	15
18	A5	2fr ultra, grn & org red	15	15
19	A5	3fr bl, grn & brn	15	15
20	A5	4fr bl grn, ind & bis	15	15
21	A5	5fr bl, ol & mar	15	15
22	A5	10fr ol blk, bl & sep	15	15
23	A5	15fr ultra, grn & bis brn	15	15
24	A5	20fr bl, grn & org red	16	15
25	A5	25fr dk bl & yel grn	20	15
26	A5	30fr vio, grn & dk brn	24	16
27	A5	40fr sl grn, bl & org red	32	15
28	A5	50fr ultra, grn & rose car	30	15
29	A5	60fr bl, grn & brn	40	16
30	A5	85fr bl, bis & dk red brn	60	20
		Set value	2.65	1.20

King Mohammed V of Morocco and Map of Africa — A6

1962, Jan. 4 Photo. *Perf. 12*

31	A6	25fr multi	20	15
32	A6	50fr multi	38	15
		Set value		24

1st anniv. of the conference of African heads of state at Casablanca.

Patrice Lumumba A7

1962, Feb. 12 Unwmk. *Perf. 12*

33	A7	25fr choc & brn org	16	15
34	A7	100fr choc & emer	65	38

Issued in memory of Patrice Lumumba, Premier of the Congo (Democratic) Republic.

Pegasus and UPU Monument, Bern — A8

1962, Apr. 21 *Perf. 12½x12*

35	A8	85fr red brn, yel & brt grn	65	50

1st anniv. of Mali's admission to the UPU.

Map of Africa and Post Horn — A8a

1962, Apr. 23 *Perf. 13½x13*

36	A8a	25fr dk red brn & dp grn	18	15
37	A8a	85fr dp grn & org	60	35

Establishment of African Postal Union.

Sansanding Dam — A9

Cotton Plant — A10

1962, Oct. 27 Photo. *Perf. 12*

38	A9	25fr dk gray, ultra & grn	18	15
39	A10	45fr multi	42	20

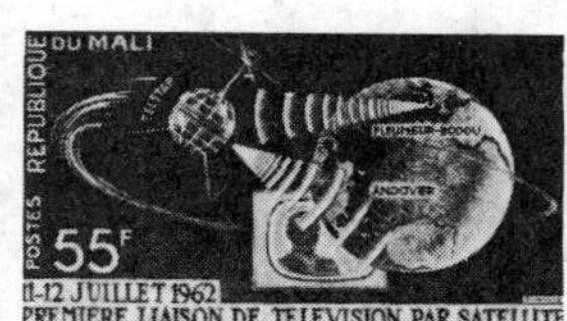

Telstar, Earth and Television Set — A10a

1962, Nov. 24 Engr. *Perf. 13*

40	A10a	45fr dk car, vio & brn	50	40
41	A10a	55fr grn, vio & ol	70	50

1st television connection of the US and Europe through the Telstar satellite, July 11-12.

Bull, Chemical Equipment, Chicks — A11

1963, Feb. 23 Unwmk. *Perf. 13*

42	A11	25fr red brn & grnsh bl	22	15

Issued to publicize the Sotuba Zootechnical Institute. See No. C15.

Tractor A12

1963, Mar. 21 Engr.

43	A12	25fr vio bl, dk brn & blk	18	15
44	A12	45fr bl grn, red brn & grn	40	25

FAO "Freedom from Hunger" campaign.

High Altitude Balloon and WMO Emblem — A13

Winners, 800-meter Race — A14

1963, June 12 Photo. *Perf. 12½*
Green Emblem; Yellow and Black Balloon

45	A13	25fr ultra	20	15
46	A13	45fr car rose	38	25
47	A13	60fr red brn	50	40

Studies of the atmosphere.

1963, Aug. 10 Unwmk. *Perf. 12*

Designs: 20fr, Acrobatic dancers, horiz. 85fr, Soccer, horiz.

48	A14	5fr multi	15	15
49	A14	10fr multi	15	15
50	A14	20fr multi	18	15
51	A14	85fr multi	60	35
		Set value	92	62

Issued to publicize Youth Week.

Centenary Emblem — A15

Kaempferia Aethiopica — A16

1963, Sept. 1 *Perf. 13½x13*

Emblem in Gray, Yellow and Red

52	A15	5fr lt ol grn & blk	15	15
53	A15	10fr yel & blk	15	15
54	A15	85fr red & blk	60	40
		Set value		58

Centenary of the International Red Cross.

1963, Dec. 23 Unwmk. *Perf. 13*

Tropical plants: 70fr, Bombax costatum. 100fr, Adenium Honghel.

55	A16	30fr multi	22	15
56	A16	70fr multi	55	22
57	A16	100fr multi	70	25

Plane Spraying, Locust and Village — A17

Designs (each inscribed "O.I.C.M.A."): 5fr, Head of locust and map of Africa, vert. 10fr, Locust in flight over map of Mali, vert.

1964, June 15 Engr. *Perf. 13*

58	A17	5fr org brn, dl cl & grn	15	15
59	A17	10fr org brn, ol & bl grn	15	15
60	A17	20fr bis, org brn & yel grn	20	15
		Set value		26

Anti-locust campaign.

Soccer Player and Tokyo Stadium — A18

Designs (stadium in background): 10fr, Boxer, vert. 15fr, Runner, vert. 85fr, Hurdler.

1964, June 27 Unwmk.

61	A18	5fr red, brt grn & dk pur	15	15
62	A18	10fr blk, dl bl & org brn	15	15
63	A18	15fr vio & dk red	16	15
64	A18	85fr vio, dk brn & sl grn	65	45
a.		Min. sheet of 4, #61-64	1.40	1.40
		Set value		70

18th Olympic Games, Tokyo, Oct. 10-25.

IQSY Emblem and Eclipse of Sun — A19

1964, July 27 Engr. *Perf. 13*

65	A19	45fr multi	45	20

International Quiet Sun Year, 1964-65.

For unused stamps, more recent issues are valued as never hinged, with the beginning point determined on a country-by-country basis. Notes to show the beginning points are prominently placed in the text.

Map of Viet Nam A20

Defassa Waterbuck A21

1964, Nov. 2 Photo. *Perf. 12x12½*

66	A20	30fr multi	22	15

Issued to publicize the solidarity of the workers of Mali and those of South Viet Nam.

1965, Apr. 5 Engr.

Designs: 5fr, Cape buffalo, horiz. 10fr, Scimitar-horned oryx. 30fr, Leopard, horiz. 90fr, Giraffe.

67	A21	1fr choc, brt bl & grn	15	15
68	A21	5fr grn, ocher & choc	15	15
69	A21	10fr grn, brt pink & bis brn	15	15
70	A21	30fr dk red, grn & choc	22	15
71	A21	90fr bis brn, sl & yel grn	60	42
		Set value	1.00	72

Abraham Lincoln — A22

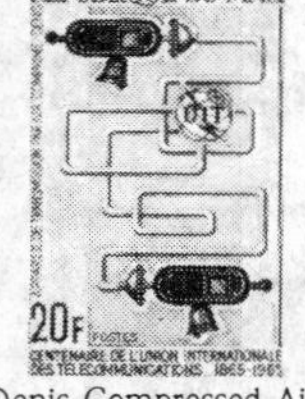

Denis Compressed Air Transmitter — A23

1965, Apr. 15 Photo. *Perf. 13x12½*

72	A22	45fr blk & multi	40	30
73	A22	55fr dp grn & multi	45	40

Centenary of the death of Lincoln.

1965, May 17 Engr. *Perf. 13*

Designs: 30fr, Hughes telegraph system, horiz. 50fr, Lescurre heliograph.

74	A23	20fr org, blk & bl	18	15
75	A23	30fr org, ocher & sl grn	22	16
76	A23	50fr org, dk brn & sl grn	38	25

Centenary of the ITU.

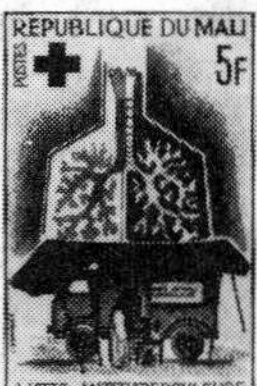

Mobile X-ray Unit and Lungs — A24

Designs: 10fr, Mother and infants. 25fr, Examination of patient at Marchoux Institute and slide. 45fr, Biology laboratory.

1965, July 5 Unwmk. *Perf. 13*

77	A24	5fr lake, red & vio	15	15
78	A24	10fr brn ol, red & sl grn	15	15
79	A24	25fr dk brn, red & grn	18	15
80	A24	45fr dk brn, red & sl grn	35	22
		Set value	68	48

Issued to publicize the Health Service.

Swimmer A25

1965, July 19 Engr.

81	A25	5fr shown	15	15
82	A25	15fr Judo	16	15
		Set value	24	16

1st African Games, Brazzaville, July 18-25.

Globe, Vase, Quill, Trumpet A26

Designs: 55fr, Mask, palette and microphones. 90fr, Dancers, mask and printed cloth.

1966, Apr. 4 Engr. *Perf. 13*

83	A26	30fr blk, red & ocher	22	15
84	A26	55fr car rose, emer & blk	38	25
85	A26	90fr ultra, org & dk brn	60	38

International Negro Arts Festival, Dakar, Senegal, Apr. 1-24.

WHO Headquarters, Geneva A27

1966, May 3 Photo. *Perf. 12½x13*

86	A27	30fr org yel, bl & ol grn	22	15
87	A27	45fr org yel, bl & dl red	30	20

Inauguration of the WHO Headquarters.

Fishermen with Nets — A28

River Fishing: 4fr, 60fr, Group fishing with large net. 20fr, 85fr, Commercial fishing boats.

1966, May 30 Engr. *Perf. 13*

88	A28	3fr ultra & brn	15	15
89	A28	4fr Prus bl & org brn	15	15
90	A28	20fr dk brn, ultra & grn	15	15
91	A28	25fr dk brn, bl & brt grn	18	15
92	A28	60fr mag, brn & brt grn	38	16
93	A28	85fr dk pur, dl bl & grn	50	25
		Set value	1.30	65

Initiation of Pioneers A29

Design: 25fr, Dance and Pioneer emblem.

1966, July 25 Engr. *Perf. 13*

94	A29	5fr multi	15	15
95	A29	25fr multi	18	15
		Set value	22	15

Issued to honor the pioneers of Mali.

Inoculation of Zebu — A30

1967, Jan. 16 Photo. *Perf. 12½x13*

96	A30	10fr dp grn, yel grn & brn	15	15
97	A30	30fr Prus bl, bl & brn	20	15
		Set value	26	20

Campaign against cattle plague.

View of Timbuktu and Tourist Year Emblem A31

1967, May 15 Engr. *Perf. 13*

98	A31	25fr Prus bl, red lil & org	18	15

International Tourist Year, 1967.

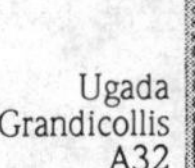

Ugada Grandicollis A32

Insects: 5fr, Chelorrhina polyphemus, vert. 50fr, Phymateus cinctus.

1967, Aug. 14 Engr. *Perf. 13*

99	A32	5fr brt bl, sl grn & brn	15	15
100	A32	15fr sl grn, dk brn & red	16	15
101	A32	50fr sl grn, dk brn & dp org	35	20
		Set value		32

Teacher and Adult Class — A33

1967, Sept. 8 Photo. *Perf. 12½x13*

102	A33	50fr blk, grn & car	35	15

International Literacy Day, Sept. 8.

Europafrica Issue

Birds, New Buildings and Map — A34

1967, Sept. 18 *Perf. 12½x12*

103	A34	45fr multi	38	16

Lions Emblem and Crocodile — A35

1967, Oct. 16 Photo. *Perf. 13x12½*

104	A35	90fr yel & multi	45	25

50th anniversary of Lions International.

Water Cycle and UNESCO Emblem A36

1967, Nov. 15 Photo. *Perf. 13*

105	A36	25fr multi	16	15

Hydrological Decade (UNESCO), 1965-74.

WHO Emblem
A37

1968, Apr. 8 Engr. *Perf. 13*
106 A37 90fr sl grn, dk car rose & bl 38 15

20th anniv. of the World Health Organization.

Linked Hearts and People — A38

1968, Apr. 28 Engr. *Perf. 13*
107 A38 50fr sl grn, red & vio bl 22 18

International Day of Sister Communities.

Books, Student, Chart, and Map of Africa — A39

1968, Aug. 12 Engr. *Perf. 13*
108 A39 100fr car, ol & blk 40 20

10th anniv. of the Intl. Assoc. for the Development of Libraries and Archives in Africa.

Draisienne, 1809 — A40

Designs: 5fr, De Dion-Bouton automobile, 1894, horiz. 10fr, Michaux bicycle, 1861. 45fr, Panhard & Levassor automobile, 1914, horiz.

1968, Aug. 12
109 A40 2fr grn, ol & mag 15 15
110 A40 5fr lem, ind & red 15 15
111 A40 10fr brt grn, ind & brn 15 15
112 A40 45fr ocher, gray grn & blk 18 15
Set value 38 25

See Nos. C60-C61.

Tourist Emblem with Map of Africa and Dove — A41

1969, May 12 Photo. *Perf. 12½x13*
113 A41 50fr lt ultra, grn & red 18 15

Year of African Tourism.

ILO Emblem and "OIT" — A42

1969, May 12 Engr. *Perf. 13*
114 A42 50fr vio, sl grn & brt bl 22 15
115 A42 60fr sl, red & ol brn 25 15
Set value 20

Issued to commemorate the 50th anniversary of the International Labor Organization.

Panhard, 1897, and Citroen 24, 1969 — A43

Design: 30fr, Citroen, 1923, and Citroen DS 21, 1969.

1969, May 30 Engr. *Perf. 13*
116 A43 25fr blk, mar & lem 15 15
117 A43 30fr blk, brt grn & dk grn 16 15
Set value 16

See Nos. C71-C72.

Play Blocks A44

Toys: 10fr, Mule on wheels. 15fr, Ducks. 20fr, Racing car and track.

1969 Photo. *Perf. 12½x13*
118 A44 5fr red, gray & yel 15 15
119 A44 10fr red, yel & ol 15 15
120 A44 15fr red, sal & yel grn 15 15
121 A44 20fr red, ind & org 15 15
Set value 38 22

Issued to publicize the International Toy Fair in Nuremberg, Germany.

Ram — A45

1969, Aug. 18 Engr. *Perf. 13*
122 A45 1fr shown 15 15
123 A45 2fr Goat 15 15
124 A45 10fr Donkey 15 15
125 A45 35fr Horse 22 16
126 A45 90fr Dromedaries 55 35
Set value 90 68

Development Bank Issue
Common Design Type

1969, Sept. 10
127 CD130 50fr brt lil, grn & ocher 20 15
128 CD130 90fr ol brn, grn & ocher 38 15

Boy Being Vaccinated A46

1969, Nov. 10 Engr. *Perf. 13*
129 A46 50fr brn, ind & brt grn 22 15

Campaign against smallbox and measles.

ASECNA Issue
Common Design Type

1969, Dec. 12 Engr. *Perf. 13*
130 CD132 100fr dk sl grn 40 20

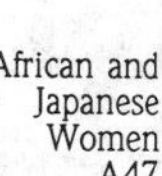

African and Japanese Women A47

Design: 150fr, Flags and maps of Mali and Japan.

1970, Apr. 13 Engr. *Perf. 13*
131 A47 100fr brn, bl & ocher 42 16
132 A47 150fr dk red, yel grn & org 60 20

Issued to publicize EXPO '70 International Exhibition, Osaka, Japan, Mar. 15-Sept. 13.

Satellite Telecommunications, Map of Africa and ITU Emblem — A48

1970, May 17 Engr. *Perf. 13*
133 A48 90fr car rose & brn 40 20

World Telecommunications Day.

UPU Headquarters Issue
Common Design Type

1970, May 20 Engr. *Perf. 13*
134 CD133 50fr dk red, bl grn & ol 20 15
135 CD133 60fr red lil, ultra & red brn 25 16

Post Office, Bamako A49

Public Buildings: 40fr, Chamber of Commerce, Bamako. 60fr, Public Works Ministry, Bamako. 80fr, City Hall, Segou.

1970, Nov. 23 Engr. *Perf. 13*
136 A49 30fr brn, brt grn & ol 15 15
137 A49 40fr brn, sl grn & dp cl 15 15
138 A49 60fr brn red, sl grn & gray 20 15
139 A49 80fr brn, brt grn & emer 25 16
Set value 45

Gallet 030T, 1882 — A50

Old Steam Locomotives: 40fr, Felou 030T, 1882. 50fr, Bechevel 230T, 1882. 80fr, Type 231, 1930. 100fr, Type 141, 1930.

1970, Dec. 14 Engr. *Perf. 13*
140 A50 20fr brt grn, dk car & blk 15 15
141 A50 40fr blk, dk grn & ocher 18 15
142 A50 50fr bis brn, bl grn & blk 20 15
143 A50 80fr car rose, blk & bl grn 25 20
144 A50 100fr ocher, bl grn & blk 40 22
Nos. 140-144 (5) 1.18 87

Scout Sounding Retreat — A51

Bambara Mask, San — A52

Designs (Boy Scouts): 5fr, Crossing river, horiz. 100fr, Canoeing, horiz.

Perf. 13x12½, 12½x13

1970, Dec. 28 Litho.
145 A51 5fr multi 15 15
146 A51 30fr multi 15 15
147 A51 100fr multi 38 18
Set value 56 30

1971, Jan. 25 Photo. *Perf. 12x12½*

Designs: 25fr, Dogon mask, Bandiagara. 50fr, Kanaga ideogram. 80fr, Bambara ideogram.

148 A52 20fr org & multi 15 15
149 A52 25fr brt grn & multi 15 15
150 A52 50fr dk pur & multi 20 15
151 A52 80fr bl & multi 30 15
Set value 68 36

Boy, Medical and Scientific Symbols A53

1971, Mar. 22 Engr. *Perf. 13*
152 A53 100fr dp car, ocher & grn 42 22

B.C.G. inoculation (Bacillus-Calmette-Guerin) against tuberculosis, 50th anniv.

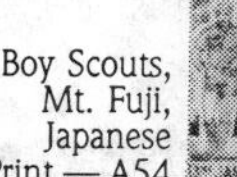

Boy Scouts, Mt. Fuji, Japanese Print — A54

1971, Apr. 19
153 A54 80fr lt ultra, dp plum & brt grn 22 15

13th Boy Scout World Jamboree, Asagiri Plain, Japan, Aug. 2-10.

UNICEF Emblem, Hands and Rose — A55

Design: 60fr, UNICEF emblem, women and children, vert.

1971, May 24 Engr. *Perf. 13*
154 A55 50fr brn org, car & dk brn 16 15
155 A55 60fr vio bl, grn & red brn 18 15
Set value 22

25th anniv. of UNICEF.

Mali Farmer — A56

Map of Africa with Communications Network — A57

Costumes of Mali: 10fr, Mali farm woman. 15fr, Tuareg. 60fr, Embroidered robe, Grand Boubou. 80fr, Ceremonial robe, woman.

1971, June 14 Photo. *Perf. 13*
156 A56 5fr gray & multi 15 15
157 A56 10fr vio bl & multi 15 15
158 A56 15fr yel & multi 15 15
159 A56 60fr gray & multi 18 15
160 A56 80fr tan & multi 22 16
Set value 60 40

1971, Aug. 16 Photo. *Perf. 13*
161 A57 50fr bl, vio bl & org 20 15

Pan-African telecommunications system.

Hibiscus
A58

Flowers: 50fr, Poinsettia. 60fr, Adenium obesum. 80fr, Dogbane. 100fr, Satanocrater berhautii.

1971, Oct. 4 Litho. *Perf. 14x13½*

162 A58 20fr multi 15 15
163 A58 50fr multi 16 15
164 A58 60fr multi 22 15
165 A58 80fr multi 25 15
166 A58 100fr multi 35 15
Nos. 162-166 (5) 1.13
Set value 42

For surcharge see No. 204.

Mother, Child and Bird (Sculpture)
A59

1971, Dec. 27 Engr. *Perf. 13x12½*

167 A59 70fr mag, sep & bl grn 22 15

National Institute of Social Security, 15th anniversary.

ITU Emblem
A60

1972, May 17 Photo. *Perf. 13x13½*

168 A60 70fr bl, mar & blk 22 15

4th World Telecommunications Day.

Clay Funerary Statuette — A61

Mali Art: 40fr, Female torso, wood. 50fr, Masked figure, painted stone. 100fr, Animals and men, wrought iron.

1972, May 29 *Perf. 12½x13*

169 A61 30fr org red & multi 15 15
170 A61 40fr yel & multi 15 15
171 A61 50fr red & multi 16 15
172 A61 100fr lt grn & multi 30 15
Set value 42

Morse and Telegraph
A62

1972, June 5 Engr. *Perf. 13*

173 A62 80fr red, emer & choc 22 15

Centenary of the death of Samuel F. B. Morse (1791-1872), inventor of the telegraph.

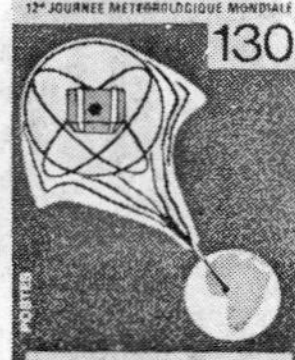

Weather Balloon over Africa — A63

1972, July 10 Photo. *Perf. 12½x13*

174 A63 130fr multi 40 22

12th World Meteorology Day.

Sarakolé Dance, Kayes — A64

People, Book, Pencil — A65

Designs: Folk dances.

1972, Aug. 21 Photo. *Perf. 13*

175 A64 10fr shown 15 15
176 A64 20fr LaGomba, Bamako 15 15
177 A64 50fr Hunters' dance, Bougouni 15 15
178 A64 70fr Koré Duga, Ségou 18 15
179 A64 80fr Kanaga, Sanga 20 15
180 A64 120fr Targui, Timbuktu 25 16
Set value 90 65

1972, Sept. 8 Typo. *Perf. 12½x13*

181 A65 80fr blk & yel grn 20 15

World Literacy Day, Sept. 8.

"Edison Classique," Mali Instruments — A66

1972, Sept. 18 Engr. *Perf. 13*

182 A66 100fr multi 30 15

First Anthology of Music of Mali.

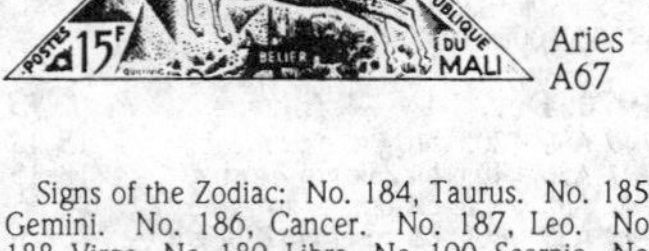

Aries
A67

Signs of the Zodiac: No. 184, Taurus. No. 185, Gemini. No. 186, Cancer. No. 187, Leo. No. 188, Virgo. No. 189, Libra. No. 190, Scorpio. No. 191, Sagittarius. No. 192, Capricorn. No. 193, Aquarius. No. 194, Pisces.

1972, Oct. 23 Engr. *Perf. 11*

183 A67 15fr lil & bis brn 15 15
184 A67 15fr bis brn & blk 15 15
185 A67 35fr mar & ind 15 15
186 A67 35fr emer & mar 15 15
187 A67 40fr bl & red brn 15 15
188 A67 40fr dk pur & red brn 15 15
189 A67 45fr dk bl & mar 16 15
190 A67 45fr mar & brt grn 16 15
191 A67 65fr dk vio & ind 20 15
192 A67 65fr dk vio & gray ol 20 15
193 A67 90fr brt pink & ind 22 16
194 A67 90fr brt pink & grn 22 16
Set value 1.75 1.20

Arrival of First Locomotive in Bamako, 1906 — A68

Designs (Locomotives): 30fr, Thies-Bamako, 1920. 60fr, Thies-Bamako, 1927. 120fr, Two Alsthom BB, 1947.

1972, Dec. 11 Engr. *Perf. 13*

195 A68 10fr ind, brn & sl grn 15 15
196 A68 30fr sl grn, ind & brn 15 15
197 A68 60fr sl grn, ind & brn 20 15
198 A68 120fr sl grn & choc 35 20
Set value 72 45

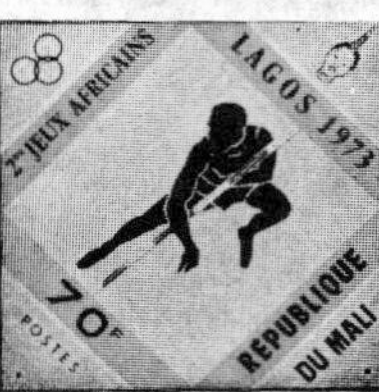

2nd African Games, Lagos, Nigeria, Jan. 7-18 — A69

1973, Jan. 15 Photo. *Perf. 12½*

199 A69 70fr High jump 22 15
200 A69 270fr Discus 80 40
201 A69 280fr Soccer 85 40

INTERPOL Emblem and Headquarters
A70

1973, Feb. 28 Photo. *Perf. 13*

202 A70 80fr multi 22 15

50th anniversary of International Criminal Police Organization (INTERPOL).

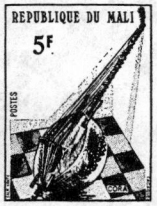

Blind Man and Disabled Boy — A71

Cora — A72

1973, Apr. 24 Engr. *Perf. 12½x13*

203 A71 70fr dk car, brick red & blk 22 15

Help for the handicapped.

No. 166 Surcharged with New Value, 2 Bars, and Overprinted: "SECHERESSE / SOLIDARITE AFRICAINE"

1973, Aug. 16 Litho. *Perf. 13½*

204 A58 200fr on 100fr multi 55 35

African solidarity in drought emergency.

Perf. 12½x13, 13x12½

1973, Dec. 10 Engr.

Musical Instruments: 10fr, Balafon, horiz. 15fr, Djembe. 20fr, Guitar. 25fr, N'Djarka. 30fr, M'Bolon. 35fr, Dozo N'Goni. 40fr, N'Tamani.

205 A72 5fr mar, dk grn & brn 15 15
206 A72 10fr bl & choc 15 15
207 A72 15fr brn, dk red & yel 15 15
208 A72 20fr mar & brn ol 15 15
209 A72 25fr org, yel & blk 15 15
210 A72 30fr vio bl & blk 15 15
211 A72 35fr dk red & brn 15 15
212 A72 40fr dk red & choc 15 15
Set value 65 45

Farmer with Newspaper, Corn — A73

Soccer, Goalkeeper, Symbolic Globe and Net — A74

1974, Mar. 11 Engr. *Perf. 12½x13*

213 A73 70fr multi 20 15

2nd anniversary of "Kibaru," rural newspaper.

1974, May 6 Engr. *Perf. 13*

Design: 280fr, Games' emblem, soccer and ball.

214 A74 270fr multi 80 42
215 A74 280fr multi 85 42

World Cup Soccer Championships, Munich, June 13-July 7.

For surcharges see Nos. 219-220.

Old and New Ships, UPU Emblem — A75

Artisans of Mali — A76

Designs: 90fr, Old and new planes, UPU emblem. 270fr, Old and new trains, UPU emblem.

1974, June 2 Engr. *Perf. 12½x13*

216 A75 80fr brn & multir 22 16
217 A75 90fr ultra & multi 30 20
218 A75 270fr lt grn & multi 80 42

Centenary of Universal Postal Union.

For surcharges see Nos. 229-230.

Nos. 214-215 Surcharged and Overprinted in Black or Red: "R.F.A. 2 / HOLLANDE 1"

1974, Aug. 28 Engr. *Perf. 13*

219 A74 300fr on 270fr multi 90 45
220 A74 330fr on 280fr multi (R) 90 45

World Cup Soccer Championship, 1974, victory of German Federal Republic.

1974, Sept. 16 Photo. *Perf. 12½x13*

221 A76 50fr Weaver 15 15
222 A76 60fr Potter 16 15
223 A76 70fr Smiths 20 15
224 A76 80fr Sculptor 22 15
Set value 44

Niger River near Gao — A77

Landscapes: 20fr, The Hand of Fatma (rock formation), vert. 40fr, Gouina Waterfall. 70fr, Dogon houses, vert.

Perf. 13x12½, 12½x13

1974, Sept. 23

225 A77 10fr multi 15 15
226 A77 20fr multi 15 15
227 A77 40fr multi 15 15
228 A77 70fr multi 20 15
Set value 40 40

Nos. 216 and 218 Surcharged and Overprinted in Black or Red: "9 OCTOBRE 1974"

1974, Oct. 9 Engr. *Perf. 13*

229 A75 250fr on 80fr multi 90 45
230 A75 300fr on 270fr multi (R) 90 45

UPU Day.

Mao Tse-tung, Flags, Great Wall — A78

1974, Oct. 21 Engr. *Perf. 13*

231 A78 100fr multi 25 16

People's Republic of China, 25th anniversary.

Artisans and Lions Emblem — A79

Design: 100fr, View of Samanko and Lions emblem.

1975, Feb. 3 Photo. *Perf. 13*

232 A79 90fr red & multi 25 16
233 A79 110fr bl & multi 30 20

5th anniversary of lepers' rehabilitation village, Samanko, sponsored by Lions International.

For surcharges see Nos. 303-304.

Tetrodon Fahaka A80

Designs: Fish.

1975, May 12 Engr. *Perf. 13*

234 A80 60fr *shown* 16 15
235 A80 70fr *Malopterurus electricus* 20 15
236 A80 80fr *Citharinus latus* 20 15
237 A80 90fr *Hydrocyon forskali* 22 15
238 A80 110fr *Lates niloticus* 25 15
Nos. 234-238 (5) 1.03
Set value 62

See Nos. 256-260.

Woman and IWY Emblem — A81

1975, June 9 Engr. *Perf. 13*

239 A81 150fr red & grn 40 20

International Women's Year 1975.

Morris "Oxford," 1913 — A82

Automobiles: 130fr, Franklin "E," 1907. 190fr, Daimler, 1900. 230fr, Panhard & Levassor, 1895.

1975, June 16

240 A82 90fr blk, ol & lil 22 15
241 A82 130fr vio bl, gray & red 35 20
242 A82 190fr bl, grn & ind 50 30
243 A82 230fr red, ultra & brn ol 60 38

Carthaginian Tristater, 500 B.C. — A83

Ancient Coins: 170fr, Decadrachma, Syracuse, 413 B.C. 190fr, Acanthe tetradrachma, 400 B.C. 260fr, Didrachma, Eritrea, 480-445 B.C.

1975, Oct. 13 Engr. *Perf. 13*

244 A83 130fr bl, cl & blk 35 18
245 A83 170fr emer, brn & blk 42 22
246 A83 190fr grn, red & blk 50 30
247 A83 260fr dp bl, org & blk 65 42

UN Emblem and "ONU" — A84

1975, Nov. 10 Engr. *Perf. 13*

248 A84 200fr emer & brt bl 55 35

30th anniversary of UN.

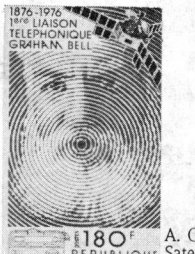

A. G. Bell, Waves, Satellite, Telephone — A85

1976, Mar. 8 Litho. *Perf. 12x12½*

249 A85 180fr brn, ultra & ocher 50 25

Centenary of first telephone call by Alexander Graham Bell, Mar. 10, 1876.

Chameleon A86

1976, Mar. 31 Litho. *Perf. 12½*

250 A86 20fr shown 15 15
251 A86 30fr Lizard 15 15
252 A86 40fr Tortoise 15 15
253 A86 90fr Python 22 15
254 A86 120fr Crocodile 35 20
Set value 80 45

Konrad Adenauer and Cologne Cathedral — A87

1976, Apr. 26 Engr. *Perf. 13*

255 A87 180fr mag & dk brn 45 25

Konrad Adenauer (1876-1967), German Chancellor, birth centenary.

Fish Type of 1975

1976, June 28 Engr. *Perf. 13*

256 A80 100fr *Heterotis niloticus* 25 16
257 A80 120fr *Synodontis budgetti* 35 18
258 A80 130fr *Heterobranchus bidorsalis* 38 18
259 A80 150fr *Tilapia monodi* 40 20
260 A80 220fr *Alestes macrolepidotus* 55 35
Nos. 256-260 (5) 1.93 1.07

Page from Children's Book — A88

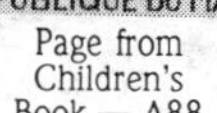

"Le Roi de l'Air" — A89

1976, July 19

261 A88 130fr red & multi 35 20

Books for children.

1976, July 26 Litho. *Perf. 12½x13*

262 A89 120fr multi 30 16

First lottery, sponsored by L'Essor newspaper.

"Do not overload scaffold" — A90

1976, Aug. 16 Litho. *Perf. 13*

263 A90 120fr multi 30 16

National Insurance Institute, 20th anniv.

Letters, UPU and UN Emblems — A91

1976, Oct. 4 Engr. *Perf. 13*

264 A91 120fr lil, org & grn 30 16

UN Postal Administration, 25th anniv.

Moto-Guzzi 254, Italy — A92

Motorcycles: 120fr, BMW 900, Germany. 130fr, Honda-Egli, Japan. 140fr, Motobecane LT-3, France.

1976, Oct. 18 Engr. *Perf. 13*

265 A92 90fr multi 22 15
266 A92 120fr multi 32 20
267 A92 130fr multi 35 20
268 A92 140fr multi 38 22

Fishing Boat, Masgat — A93

Designs: 180fr, Coaster, Cochin China. 190fr, Fireboat, Dunkirk, 1878. 200fr, Nile river boat.

1976, Dec. 6 Engr. *Perf. 13*

269 A93 160fr multi 42 18
270 A93 180fr multi 45 22
271 A93 190fr multi 50 25
272 A93 200fr multi 55 25

Indigo Finch — A94

Birds: 25fr, Yellow-breasted barbet. 30fr, Vitelline masked weaver. 40fr, Bee-eater. 50fr, Senegal parrot.

1977, Apr. 18 Photo. *Perf. 13*

273 A94 15fr multi 15 15
274 A94 25fr multi 15 15
275 A94 30fr multi 15 15
276 A94 40fr multi 16 15
277 A94 50fr multi 20 15
Set value 62 40

See Nos. 298-302.

Braille Statue, Script and Reading Hands — A95

1977, Apr. 25 Engr. *Perf. 13*

278 A95 200fr multi 55 30

Louis Braille (1809-1852), inventor of the reading and writing system for the blind.

Foreign postal stationery (stamped envelopes, postal cards and air letter sheets) lies beyond the scope of this Catalogue, which is limited to adhesive postage stamps.

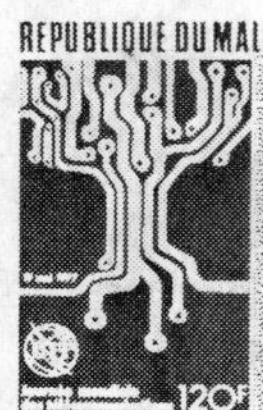

Electronic Tree, ITU Emblem — A96

1977, May 17 **Photo.**
279 A96 120fr dk brn & org 32 18

World Telecommunications Day.

Dragonfly A97

Insects: 10fr, Praying mantis. 20fr, Tropical wasp. 35fr, Cockchafer. 60fr, Flying stag beetle.

1977, June 15 **Photo.** ***Perf. 13x12½***
280 A97 5fr multi 15 15
281 A97 10fr multi 15 15
282 A97 20fr multi 15 15
283 A97 35fr multi 15 15
284 A97 60fr multi 22 16
Set value 52 40

Knight and Rook — A98

Chess Pieces: 130fr, Bishop and pawn, vert. 300fr, Queen and King.

1977, June 27 **Engr.** ***Perf. 13***
285 A98 120fr multi 50 25
286 A98 130fr multi 50 25
287 A98 300fr multi 1.20 65

Europafrica Issue

Symbolic Ship, White and Brown Persons — A99

1977, July 18 **Litho.** ***Perf. 13***
288 A99 400fr multi 1.10 65

Horse, by Leonardo da Vinci — A100

Drawings by Leonardo da Vinci: 300fr, Head of Young Woman. 500fr, Self-portrait.

1977, Sept. 5 **Engr.** ***Perf. 13***
289 A100 200fr dk brn & blk 55 35
290 A100 300fr dk brn & ol 80 42
291 A100 500fr dk brn & red 1.40 62

Hotel de l'Amitié, Bamako — A101

1977, Oct. 15 **Litho.** ***Perf. 13x12½***
292 A101 120fr multi 35 18

Opening of the Hotel de l'Amitié, Oct. 15.

Dome of the Rock Jerusalem — A102

1977, Oct. 17 ***Perf. 12½***
293 A102 120fr multi 35 18
294 A102 180fr multi 45 25

Palestinian fighters and their families.

Black Man, Chains and UN Emblem A103

Design: 130fr, Statue of Liberty, people and UN emblem. 180fr, Black children and horse behind fence.

1978, Mar. 13 **Engr.** ***Perf. 13***
295 A103 120fr multi 35 18
296 A103 130fr multi 35 18
297 A103 180fr multi 45 25

International Year against Apartheid.

Bird Type of 1977

Birds: 20fr, Granatine bengala. 30fr, Lagonosticta vinacea. 50fr, Lagonosticta. 70fr, Turtle dove. 80fr, Buffalo weaver.

1978, Apr. 10 **Litho.** ***Perf. 13***
298 A94 20fr multi 15 15
299 A94 30fr multi 15 15
300 A94 50fr multi 15 15
301 A94 70fr multi 18 15
302 A94 80fr multi 20 15
Set value 65 40

Nos. 232-233 Surcharged with New Value, Bar and: "XXe ANNIVERSAIRE DU LIONS CLUB DE BAMAKO 1958-1978"

1978, May 8 **Photo.**
303 A79 120fr on 90fr multi 32 16
304 A79 130fr on 100fr multi 35 18

20th anniversary of Bamako Lions Club.

Wall and Desert — A105

1978, May 18 **Litho.** ***Perf. 13***
306 A105 200fr multi 55 25

Hammamet Conference for reclamation of the desert.

Mahatma Gandhi and Roses — A106

1978, May 29 **Engr.**
307 A106 140fr blk, brn & red 38 18

Mohandas K. Gandhi (1869-1948), Hindu spiritual leader, 30th death anniversary.

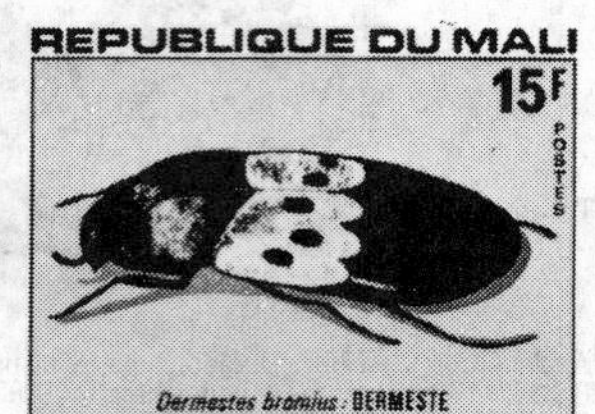

Dermestes — A107

Insects: 25fr, Ground beetle. 90fr, Cricket. 120fr, Ladybird. 140fr, Goliath beetle.

1978, June 12 **Photo.** ***Perf. 13***
308 A107 15fr multi 15 15
309 A107 25fr multi 15 15
310 A107 90fr multi 22 15
311 A107 120fr multi 35 18
312 A107 140fr multi 38 20
Set value 1.05 60

Bridge — A108

Design: 100fr, Dominoes, vert.

1978, June 26 **Engr.**
313 A108 100fr multi 25 15
314 A108 130fr multi 35 18

Aristotle — A109

1978, Oct. 16 **Engr.** ***Perf. 13***
315 A109 200fr multi 55 25

Aristotle (384-322 B.C.), Greek philosopher.

Human Rights and UN Emblems — A110

1978, Dec. 11 **Engr.** ***Perf. 13***
316 A110 180fr red, bl & brn 48 22

Universal Declaration of Human Rights, 30th anniversary.

Manatee — A111

Endangered Wildlife: 120fr, Chimpanzee. 130fr, Damaliscus antelope. 180fr, Oryx. 200fr, Derby's eland.

1979, Apr. 23 **Litho.** ***Perf. 12½***
317 A111 100fr multi 25 15
318 A111 120fr multi 32 16
319 A111 130fr multi 35 18
320 A111 180fr multi 48 25
321 A111 200fr multi 55 30
Nos. 317-321 (5) 1.95 1.04

Boy Praying and IYC Emblem — A112

Designs (IYC emblem and): 200fr, Girl and Boy Scout holding bird. 300fr, IYC emblem, boys with calf.

1979, May 7 **Engr.** ***Perf. 13***
322 A112 120fr multi 32 20
323 A112 200fr multi 55 30
324 A112 300fr multi 80 40

International Year of the Child.

Judo and Notre Dame, Paris — A113

1979, May 14 **Engr.** ***Perf. 13***
325 A113 200fr multi 55 30

World Judo Championship, Paris.

Telecommunications A114

Wood Carving A115

1979, May 17 **Litho.**

326 A114 120fr multi 32 16

11th Telecommunications Day.

1979, May 18 ***Perf. 13x12½***

Sculptures from National Museum: 120fr, Ancestral figures. 130fr, Animal heads, and kneeling woman.

327 A115 90fr multi 25 16
328 A115 120fr multi 32 16
329 A115 130fr multi 35 18

International Museums Day.

Rowland Hill and Mali No. 15 — A116

Designs: 130fr, Zeppelin and Saxony No. 1. 180fr, Concorde and France No. 3. 200fr, Stagecoach and US No. 2. 300fr, UPU emblem and Penny Black.

1979, May 21 **Engr.** ***Perf. 13***

330 A116 120fr multi 32 16
331 A116 130fr multi 35 18
332 A116 180fr multi 50 25
333 A116 200fr multi 55 30
334 A116 300fr multi 80 45
Nos. 330-334 (5) 2.52 1.34

Sir Rowland Hill (1795-1879), originator of penny postage.

Cora Players — A117

1979, June 4 **Litho.** ***Perf. 13***

335 A117 200fr multi 55 30

Adenium Obesum and Sankore Mosque — A118

Design: 300fr, Satellite, mounted messenger, globe and letter, vert.

1979, June 8 **Photo.**

336 A118 120fr multi 32 16

Engr.

337 A118 300fr multi 80 45

Philexafrique II, Libreville, Gabon, June 8-17. Nos. 336, 337 printed in sheets of 10 and 5 labels showing exhibition emblem.

Map of Mali — A119

Design: 300fr, Men planting trees.

1979, June 18 **Litho.** ***Perf. 13x12½***

338 A119 200fr multi 55 30
339 A119 300fr multi 80 45

Operation Green Sahel.

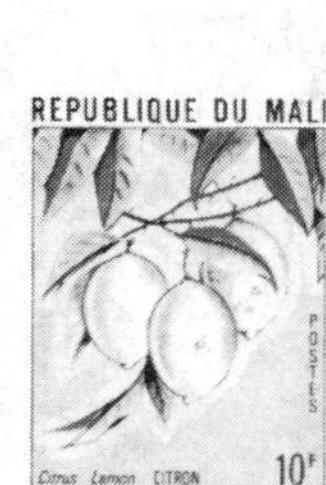
Lemons — A120

Sigmund Freud — A121

1979, June 25 ***Perf. 12½x13***

340 A120 10fr shown 15 15
341 A120 60fr Pineapple 16 15
342 A120 100fr Papayas 25 15
343 A120 120fr Soursops 32 16
344 A120 130fr Mangoes 35 18
Nos. 340-344 (5) 1.23
Set value 60

1979, Sept. 17 **Engr.** ***Perf. 13***

345 A121 300fr vio bl & sep 80 45

Sigmund Freud (1856-1939), founder of psychoanalysis.

Timbuktu, Man and Camel A122

Design: 130fr, Caillié, Map of Sahara.

1979, Sept. 27 ***Perf. 13x12½***

346 A122 120fr multi 32 16
347 A122 130fr multi 35 18

René Caillié (1799-1838), French explorer, 180th birth anniversary.

Eurema Brigitta A123

1979, Oct. 15 **Litho.** ***Perf. 13***

348 A123 100fr *shown* 25 15
349 A123 120fr *Papilio pylades* 32 16
350 A123 130fr *Melanitis leda satyridae* 35 18
351 A123 180fr *Gonimbrasia belina occidentalis* 48 25
352 A123 200fr *Bunaea alcinoe* 55 30
Nos. 348-352 (5) 1.95 1.04

Greyhound A124

Designs: Dogs.

1979, Nov. 12 **Litho.** ***Perf. 12½***

353 A124 20fr multi 15 15
354 A124 50fr multi 15 15
355 A124 70fr multi 18 15
356 A124 80fr multi 20 15
357 A124 90fr multi 25 15
Nos. 353-357 (5) 93
Set value 35

Wild Donkey — A125

1980, Feb. 4 **Litho.** ***Perf. 13x13½***

358 A125 90fr shown 25 15
359 A125 120fr Addax 32 15
360 A125 130fr Leopards 35 15
361 A125 140fr Mouflon 35 15
362 A125 180fr Buffalo 50 20
Nos. 358-362 (5) 1.77 80

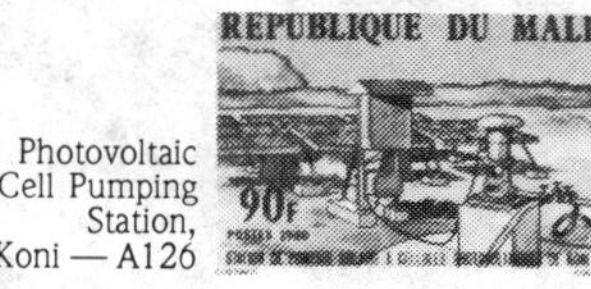
Photovoltaic Cell Pumping Station, Koni — A126

Solar Energy Utilization: 100fr, Sun shields, Dire. 120fr, Solar stove, Bamako. 130fr, Heliodynamic solar energy generating station, Dire.

1980, Mar. 10 **Litho.** ***Perf. 13***

363 A126 90fr multi 25 15
364 A126 100fr multi 25 15
365 A126 120fr multi 32 15
366 A126 130fr multi 35 15
Set value 45

For surcharge see No. 511.

Horse Breeding, Mopti — A127

1980, Mar. 17

367 A127 100fr shown 25 15
368 A127 120fr Nioro 32 15
369 A127 130fr Koro 35 15
370 A127 180fr Coastal zone 50 20
371 A127 200fr Banamba 55 22
Nos. 367-371 (5) 1.97 87

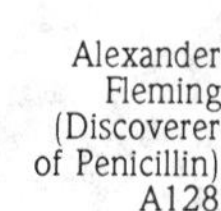

Alexander Fleming (Discoverer of Penicillin) A128

1980, May 5 **Engr.** ***Perf. 13***

372 A128 200fr multi 55 20

Avicenna and Medical Instruments A129

Design: 180fr, Avicenna as teacher (12th century manuscript illustration)

1980, May 12 ***Perf. 13x12½***

373 A129 120fr multi 32 15
374 A129 180fr multi 50 20

Avicenna (980-1037), Arab physician and philosopher, 1000th birth anniversary.

Pilgrim at Mecca — A130

Guavas — A131

1980, May 26 **Litho.** ***Perf. 13***

375 A130 120fr shown 32 15
376 A130 130fr Praying hands, stars, Mecca 35 15
377 A130 180fr Pilgrims, camels, horiz. 50 20

Hegira, 1500th Anniversary.

1980, June 9

378 A131 90fr shown 22 15
379 A131 120fr Cashews 32 15
380 A131 130fr Oranges 35 15
381 A131 140fr Bananas 38 15
382 A131 180fr Grapefruit 50 20
Nos. 378-382 (5) 1.77 80

League of Nations, 60th Anniversary A132

1980, June 23 **Engr.** ***Perf. 13***

383 A132 200fr multi 55 20

Festival Emblem, Mask, Xylophone A133

1980, July 5 **Litho.** ***Perf. 12½***

384 A133 120fr multi 32 15

6th Biennial Arts and Cultural Festival, Bamako, July 5-15.

Set Values

A 15-cent minimum now applies to individual stamps and sets. Where the 15-cent minimum per stamp would increase the "value" of a set beyond retail, there is a "Set Value" notation giving the retail value of the set.

Sun Rising over Map of Africa — A134

1980, July 7 **Engr.** ***Perf. 13***
385 A134 300fr multi 80 38

Afro-Asian Bandung Conference, 25th anniversary.

Market Place, Conference Emblem A135

1980, Sept. 15 **Litho.** ***Perf. 13***
386 A135 120fr View of Mali, vert. 32 15
387 A135 180fr shown 50 20

World Tourism Conf., Manila, Sept. 27.

Hydro-electric Dam and Power Station — A136

20th Anniversary of Independence: 120fr, Pres. Traore, flag of Mali, National Assembly building. 130fr, Independence monument, Bamako, Political Party badge, vert.

1980, Sept. 15 ***Perf. 13x12½***
388 A136 100fr multi 25 15
389 A136 120fr multi 32 15
390 A136 130fr multi 35 15
Set value 35

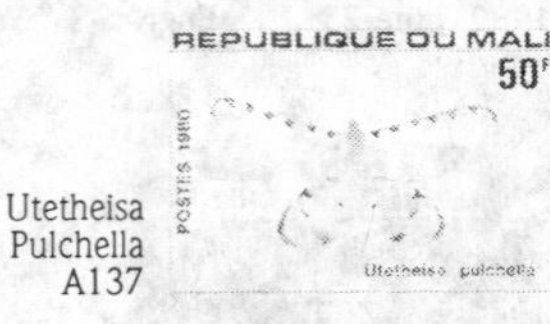
Utetheisa Pulchella A137

1980, Oct. 6 ***Perf. 13½***
391 A137 50fr *shown* 15 15
392 A137 60fr *Mylothis chloris pieridae* 16 15
393 A137 70fr *Hypolimnas misippus* 18 15
394 A137 80fr *Papilio demodocus* 20 15
Nos. 391-394,C402 (5) 1.89
Set value 75

Fight Against Cigarette Smoking — A138

1980, Oct. 13 **Litho.** ***Perf. 12½x12***
395 A138 200fr multi 55 20

European-African Economic Convention — A139

1980, Oct. 20 ***Perf. 12½***
396 A139 300fr multi 80 38

Agricultural Map of West Africa A140

West African Economic Council, 5th anniversary (Economic Maps): 120fr, Transportation. 130fr, Industry. 140fr, Communications.

1980, Nov. 5 ***Perf. 13½x13***
397 A140 100fr multi 25 15
398 A140 120fr multi 32 15
399 A140 130fr multi 35 15
400 A140 140fr multi 38 16
Set value 52

African Postal Union, 5th Anniv. — A141

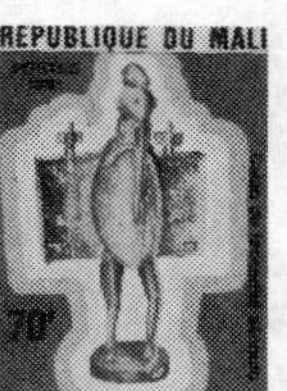
Senuofo Fertility Statue — A142

1980, Dec. 24 **Photo.** ***Perf. 13½***
401 A141 130fr multi 35 15

1981, Jan. 12 **Litho.** ***Perf. 13***

Designs: Fertility statues.

402 A142 60fr Nomo dogon 16 15
403 A142 70fr shown 18 15
404 A142 90fr Bamanan 25 15
405 A142 100fr Spirit 25 15
406 A142 120fr Dogon 32 15
Nos. 402-406 (5) 1.16
Set value 46

Mambi Sidibe — A143

Hegira (Pilgrimage Year) — A144

Designs: Philosophers.

1981, Feb. 16 ***Perf. 12½x13***
407 A143 120fr shown 32 15
408 A143 130fr Amadou Hampate 35 15

1981, Feb. 23 ***Perf. 13***
409 A144 120fr multi 32 15
410 A144 180fr multi 50 20

Maure Zebu A145

Designs: Cattle breeds.

1981, Mar. 9 ***Perf. 12½***
411 A145 20fr Kaarta zebu 15 15
412 A145 30fr Peul du Macina zebu 15 15
413 A145 40fr Maure zebu 15 15
414 A145 80fr Touareg zebu 20 15
415 A145 100fr N'Dama cow 25 15
Set value 65 35

See Nos. 433-437.

Hibiscus Double Rose — A146

Designs: Flowers.

1981, Mar. 16
416 A146 50fr Crinum de Moore 15 15
417 A146 100fr Double Rose Hibiscus 25 15
418 A146 120fr Pervenche 32 15
419 A146 130fr Frangipani 35 15
420 A146 180fr Orgueil de Chine 50 20
Nos. 416-420 (5) 1.57
Set value 60

See Nos. 442-446.

Wrench Operated by Artificial Hand — A147

Perf. 13x12½, 12x13
1981, May 4 **Engr.**
421 A147 100fr Heads, vert. 25 15
422 A147 120fr shown 32 15
Set value 22

Intl. Year of the Disabled.

13th World Telecommunications Day — A148

1981, May 17 **Litho.** ***Perf. 13x12½***
423 A148 130fr multi 35 15

Pierre Curie, Lab Equipment A149

1981, May 25 **Engr.**
424 A149 180fr multi 50 20

Curie (1859-1906), discoverer of radium.

Scouts at Water Hole — A150

1981, June 8 **Litho.** ***Perf. 13***
425 A150 110fr shown 30 15
426 A150 160fr Sending signals 42 20
427 A150 300fr Salute, vert. 80 35

Souvenir Sheet

428 A150 500fr Lord Baden-Powell 1.40 65

4th African Scouting Conf., Abidjan, June.

Nos. 425-428 Overprinted in Red in 2 or 3 Lines: "DAKAR 8 AOUT 1981/28e CONFERENCE MONDIALE DU SCOUTISME"

1981, June 29
429 A150 110fr multi 30 15
430 A150 160fr multi 42 20
431 A150 300fr multi 80 35

Souvenir Sheet

432 A150 500fr multi 1.40 65

28th World Scouting Conf., Dakar, Aug. 8.

Cattle Type of 1981

Various goats.

1981, Sept. 14 **Litho.** ***Perf. 13x13½***
433 A145 10fr Maure 15 15
434 A145 25fr Peul 15 15
435 A145 140fr Sahel 40 16
436 A145 180fr Tuareg 50 20
437 A145 200fr Djallonke 55 20
Nos. 433-437 (5) 1.75
Set value 65

World UPU Day — A151

1981, Oct. 9 **Engr.** ***Perf. 13***
438 A151 400fr multi 1.10 42

World Food Day — A152

1981, Oct. 16
439 A152 200fr multi 55 20

Europafrica Economic Convention — A153

1981, Nov. 23 **Engr.** ***Perf. 13***
440 A153 700fr multi 1.90 1.20

60th Anniv. of Tuberculosis Inoculation
A154

1981, Dec. 7 *Perf. 13x12½*
441 A154 200fr multi 55 20

Flower Type of 1981

1982, Jan. 18 Litho. *Perf. 13*
442 A146 170fr White water lilies 45 20
443 A146 180fr Red kapok bush 50 20
444 A146 200fr Purple mimosa 55 22
445 A146 220fr Pobego lilies 60 22
446 A146 270fr Satan's chalices 70 30
Nos. 442-446 (5) 2.80 1.14

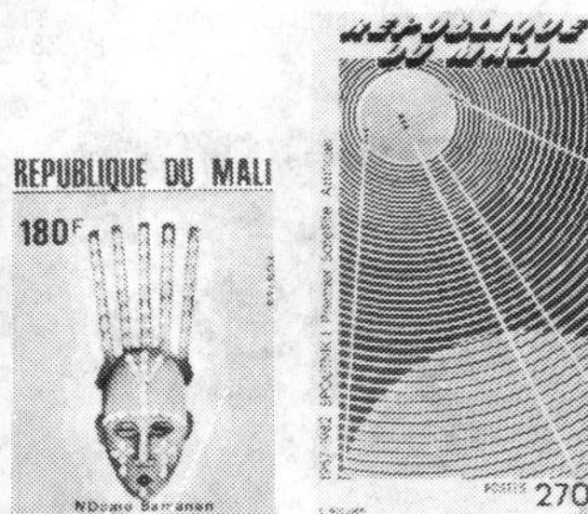

Ceremonial Mask — A155
25th Anniv. of Sputnik I Flight — A156

Designs: Various masks.

1982, Feb. 22 Litho. *Perf. 12½*
447 A155 5fr multi 15 15
448 A155 35fr multi 15 15
449 A155 180fr multi 50 20
450 A155 200fr multi 55 22
451 A155 250fr multi 65 25
Nos. 447-451 (5) 2.00
Set value 75

1982, Mar. 29 Litho. *Perf. 13*
452 A156 270fr multi 70 28

Fight Against Polio — A157

1982, May 3
453 A157 180fr multi 50 20

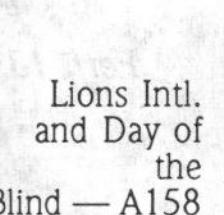

Lions Intl. and Day of the Blind — A158

1982, May 10 **Engr.**
454 A158 260fr multi 65 25

"Good Friends" Hairstyle — A159

Designs: Various hairstyles.

1982, May 24 Litho.
455 A159 140fr multi 40 16
456 A159 150fr multi 42 18
457 A159 160fr multi 45 20
458 A159 180fr multi 50 20
459 A159 270fr multi 70 30
Nos. 455-459 (5) 2.47 1.04

Zebu
A160

Designs: Various breeds of zebu.

1982, July 5 *Perf. 12½*
460 A160 10fr multi 15 15
461 A160 60fr multi 16 15
462 A160 110fr multi 30 15
463 A160 180fr multi 50 20
464 A160 200fr multi 55 22
Nos. 460-464 (5) 1.66
Set value 62

Wind Surfing (New Olympic Class) — A161
Pres. John F. Kennedy — A162

Designs: Various wind surfers.

1982, Nov. 22 Litho. *Perf. 12½x13*
465 A161 200fr multi 55 20
466 A161 270fr multi 70 30
467 A161 300fr multi 90 38

1983, Apr. 4 Engr. *Perf. 13*
468 A162 800fr shown 2.25 90
469 A162 800fr Martin Luther King 2.50 90

Oua Traditional Hairstyle — A163

1983, Apr. 25 Litho.
470 A163 180fr shown 50 20
471 A163 200fr Nation 60 22
472 A163 270fr Rond point 70 28
473 A163 300fr Naamu-Naamu 80 35
474 A163 500fr Bamba-Bamba 1.40 55
Nos. 470-474 (5) 4.00 1.60

World Communications Year — A164

1983, May 17 Litho. *Perf. 13*
475 A164 180fr multi 50 20

Bicent. of Lavoisier's Water Analysis — A165
Musicians — A166

1983, May 27 Engr. *Perf. 13*
476 A165 300fr multi 90 38

1983, June 13 Litho. *Perf. 13x13½*
477 A166 200fr Banzoumana Sissoko 60 22
478 A166 300fr Batourou Sekou Kouyate 90 38

Nicephore Niepce, Photography Pioneer, (1765-1833)
A167

1983, July 4 Engr. *Perf. 13*
479 A167 400fr Portrait, early camera 1.20 45

2nd Pan African Youth Festival — A168

Palestinian Solidarity — A169
14th World UPU Day — A170

1983, Aug. 22 Litho. *Perf. 12½*
480 A168 240fr multi 70 30
481 A169 270fr multi 80 32

1983, Oct. 10 Engr. *Perf. 12½*
482 A170 240fr multi 70 30

For surcharge see No. 500.

Sahel Goat — A171

1984, Jan. 30 Litho. *Perf. 13*
483 A171 20fr shown 15 15
484 A171 30fr Billy goat 15 15
485 A171 50fr Billy goat, diff. 15 15
486 A171 240fr Kaarta goat 70 18
487 A171 350fr Southern goats 1.10 32
Nos. 483-487 (5) 2.25
Set value 68

For surcharges see Nos. 497-499, 501-502.

Rural Development
A172
Fragrant Trees
A173

1984, June 1 Litho. *Perf. 13*
488 A172 5fr Crop disease prevention 15 15
489 A172 90fr Carpenters, horiz. 28 15
490 A172 100fr Tapestry weaving, horiz. 32 16
491 A172 135fr Metal workers, horiz. 42 20
Set value 55

1984, June 1
492 A173 515fr Borassus flabelifer 1.60 80
493 A173 1225fr Vitelaria paradoxa 4.00 1.90

For surcharge see No. 583.

UN Infant Survival Campaign — A174

1984, June 12 Engr.
494 A174 120fr Child, hearts 40 20
495 A174 135fr Children 42 20

1984 UPU Congress — A175

1984, June 18
496 A175 135fr Anchor, UPU emblem, view of Hamburg 42 20

Nos. 482-487 Overprinted and Surcharged

1984
497 A171 10fr on 20fr #483 15 15
498 A171 15fr on 30fr #484 15 15
499 A171 25fr on 50fr #485 15 15
500 A170 120fr on 240fr #482 35 16
501 A171 120fr on 240fr #486 35 16
502 A171 175fr on 350fr #487 45 22
Set value 1.35 65

West African Economic Community, CEAO, 10th Anniv.
A176

1984, Oct. 22 Litho. *Perf. 13½*
503 A176 350fr multi 1.00 35

For surcharge see No. 588.

Prehistoric Animals A177

1984, Nov. 5 Litho. *Perf. 12½*

504 A177 10fr Dimetrodon 15 15
505 A177 25fr Iguanodon, vert. 15 15
506 A177 30fr Archaeopteryx, vert. 15 15
507 A177 120fr Like 10fr 35 15
508 A177 175fr Like 25fr 50 15
509 A177 350fr Like 30fr 1.00 30
510 A177 470fr Triceratops 1.40 40
Nos. 504-510 (7) 3.70
Set value 1.00

For surcharges see Nos. 579, 593.

No. 366 Overprinted "Aide au Sahel 84" and Surcharged

1984 Litho. *Perf. 13*

511 A126 470fr on 130fr 1.40 40

Issued to publicize drought relief efforts.

Mali Horses A178

1985, Jan. 21 Litho. *Perf. 13½*

512 A178 90fr Modern horse 25 15
513 A178 135fr Horse from Beledougou 38 15
514 A178 190fr Horse from Nara 50 16
515 A178 530fr Horse from Trait 1.50 45

For surcharges see Nos. 586, 591.

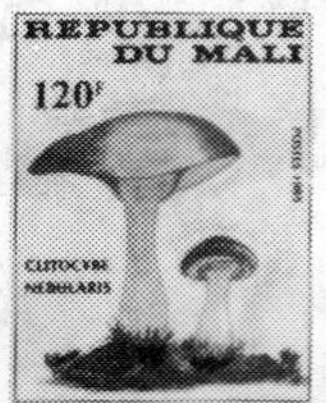

Fungi — A179

1985, Jan. 28 Litho. *Perf. 12½*

516 A179 120fr Clitocybe nebularis 35 15
517 A179 200fr Lepiota cortinarius 55 18
518 A179 485fr Agavicus semotus 1.40 42
519 A179 525fr Lepiota procera 1.50 45

For surcharges see Nos. 589-590.

Health — A180

Designs: 120fr, 32nd World Leprosy Day, Emile Marchoux (1862-1943), Marchoux Institute, 150th anniv. 135fr, Lions Intl., Samanko Convalescence Village, 15th anniv. 470fr, Anti-polio campaign, research facility, victim.

1985, Feb. 18 Litho. *Perf. 13*

520 A180 120fr multi 35 15
521 A180 135fr multi 38 15
522 A180 470fr multi 1.40 40

For surcharges see Nos. 580, 584. No. 522 is airmail.

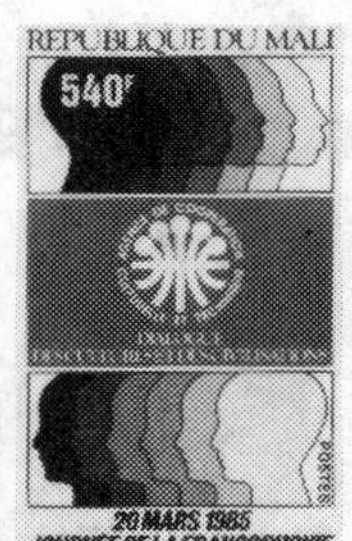

Cultural and Technical Cooperation Agency, 15th Anniv. — A181

1985, Mar. 20

523 A181 540fr brn & brt bl grn 1.50 45

Intl. Youth Year — A182

Youth activities.

1985, May 13 *Perf. 12½x13*

524 A182 120fr Natl. Pioneers Movement emblem 35 15
525 A182 190fr Agricultural production 50 16
526 A182 500fr Sports 1.40 42

For surcharge see No. 587.

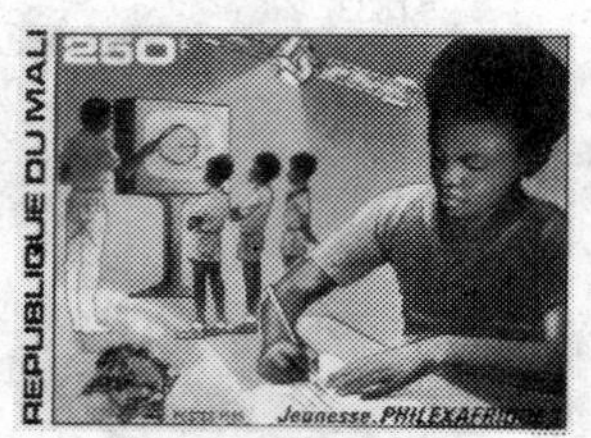

PHILEXAFRICA '85, Lome, Togo — A183

1985, June 24 *Perf. 13*

527 A183 250fr Education, telecommunications 65 20
528 A183 250fr Road, dam, computers 65 20

Nos. 527-528 show the UPU emblem and are printed se-tenant with center label picturing map of Africa or UAPT emblem. See Nos. C517-C518.

Cats — A184

1986, Feb. 15 Litho. *Perf. 13½*

529 A184 150fr Gray 60 20
530 A184 200fr White 70 25
531 A184 300fr Tabby 1.25 40

For surcharge see No. 582.

Fight Against Apartheid — A185

1986, Feb. 24 *Perf. 13*

532 A185 100fr shown 38 15
533 A185 120fr Map, broken chain 42 15

Telecommunications and Agriculture — A186

1986, May 17 Litho. *Perf. 13*

534 A186 200fr multi 75 25

1986 World Cup Soccer Championships, Mexico — A187

Various soccer plays.

1986, May 24 Litho. *Perf. 12½*

535 A187 160fr multi 60 20
536 A187 225fr multi 80 25

Souvenir Sheet

537 A187 500fr multi 2.00 60

For overprints surcharges see #539-541, 585.

James Watt (1736-1819), Inventor, and Steam Engine — A188

1986, May 26 *Perf. 12½x12*

538 A188 110fr multi 40 15

For surcharge see No. 581.

Nos. 535-537 Ovptd. "ARGENTINE 3 / R.F.A. 2" in Red

1986, July 30 Litho. *Perf. 12½*

539 A187 160fr multi 60 20
540 A187 225fr multi 80 28

Souvenir Sheet

541 A187 500fr multi 2.00 60

World Wildlife Fund — A189

Derby's Eland, Taurotragus derbianus.

1986, Aug. 11 Litho. *Perf. 13*

542 A189 5fr Adult head 15 15
543 A189 20fr Adult in brush 15 15
544 A189 25fr Adult walking 15 15
545 A189 200fr Calf suckling 75 25
Set value 98 40

Henry Ford (1863-1947), Auto Manufacturer, Inventor of Mass Production — A190

1987, Feb. 16 Litho. *Perf. 13*

546 A190 150fr Model A, 1903 60 20
547 A190 200fr Model T, 1923 70 25
548 A190 225fr Thunderbird, 1968 80 28
549 A190 300fr Lincoln Continental, 1963 1.10 38

Bees — A191

1987, May 11 Litho. *Perf. 13½*

550 A191 100fr Apis florea, Asia 38 20
551 A191 150fr Apis dorsata, Asia 55 25
552 A191 175fr Apis adansonii, Africa 65 35
553 A191 200fr Apis mellifica, worldwide 70 38

Lions Club Activities — A192

1988, Jan. 13 Litho. *Perf. 12½*

554 A192 200fr multi 1.00 50

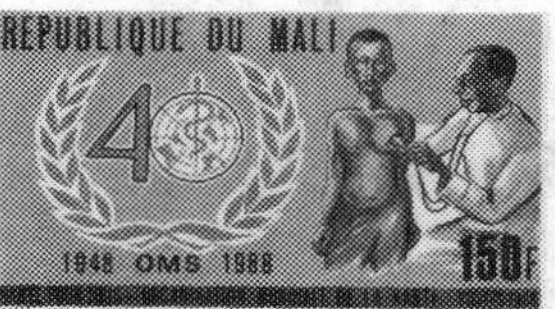

World Health Organization, 40th Anniv. — A193

1988, Feb. 22 Litho. *Perf. 12½x12*

555 A193 150fr multi 70 38

For surcharge see No. 557.

John F. Kennedy (1917-1963), 35th US President — A194

1988, June 6 Litho. *Perf. 13*

556 A194 640fr multi 4.25 2.15

For surcharge see No. 592.

No. 555 Surcharged in Dark Red

MISSION MALI
HOPITAL de MOPTI
300F

1988, June 13 *Perf. 12½x12*

557 A193 300fr on 150fr multi 2.00 1.00

Mali Mission Hospital in Mopti and World Medicine organization.

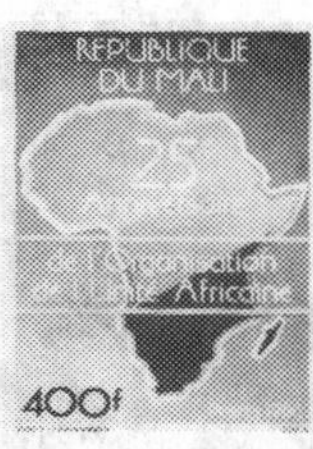

Organization of African Unity, 25th Anniv. — A194a

1988, June 27 Litho. *Perf. 12½*
558 A194a 400fr multi 2.65 1.35

Universal Immunization Campaign A195

1989, May 2 Litho. *Perf. 13½*
559 A195 20fr shown 15 15
560 A195 30fr Inoculating woman 18 15
561 A195 50fr Emblem, needles, diff. 30 15
562 A195 175fr Inoculating boy 1.05 52
Set value 82

Intl. Law Institute of the French-Speaking Nations — A196

1989, May 15 *Perf. 12½*
563 A196 150fr multi 90 45
564 A196 200fr multi 1.20 60

World Post Day — A197

1989, Oct. 9 Litho. *Perf. 13*
565 A197 625fr multicolored 4.00 2.00

For surcharge see No. 594.

Visit of Pope John Paul II — A198

1990, Jan. 28 Litho. *Perf. 13x12½*
566 A198 200fr multicolored 1.45 72

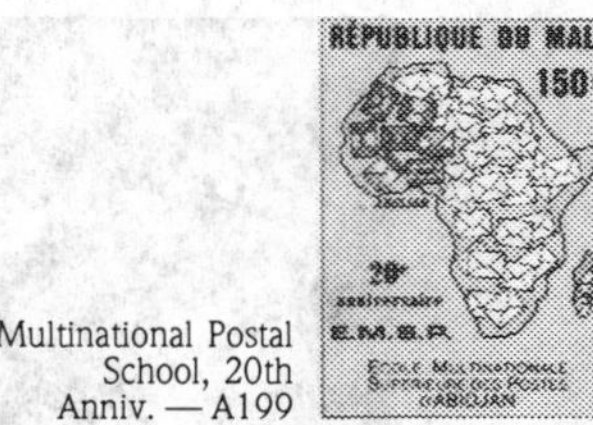

Multinational Postal School, 20th Anniv. — A199

1990, May 31 Litho. *Perf. 12½*
567 A199 150fr multicolored 1.10 55

Independence, 30th Anniv. — A200

1990, Sept. 20 Litho. *Perf. 13x12½*
568 A200 400fr multicolored 3.00 1.50

Intl. Literacy Year — A201

1990, Sept. 24 Litho. *Perf. 13½*
569 A201 150fr grn & multi 1.30 65
570 A201 200fr org & multi 1.75 90

A202 A203

Lions Intl. Water Project, 6th anniv.: No. 572, Rotary Club fight against polio, 30th anniv.

1991, Feb. 25 Litho. *Perf. 13x12½*
571 A202 200fr multicolored 1.75 90
572 A202 200fr multicolored 1.75 90

1991, Apr. 29 Litho. *Perf. 12½*

Designs: Tribal dances of Mali.

573 A203 50fr Takamba 45 22
574 A203 100fr Mandiani 90 45
575 A203 150fr Kono 1.40 70
576 A203 200fr Songho 1.75 90

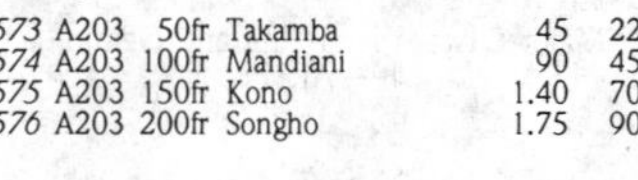

A204 A205

1991, Dec. 2 Litho. *Perf. 12½*
577 A204 200fr multicolored 1.75 90

Central Fund for Economic Cooperation, 50th anniv.

1992, Mar. 26 Litho. *Perf. 12½*
578 A205 150fr multicolored 1.20 60

National Women's Movement.

Various Stamps of 1984-89 Surcharged in Black or Black and Silver

25F

1992, June Litho. *Perfs. as Before*
579 A177 25fr on 470fr #510 20 15
580 A180 25fr on 470fr #522 20 15
581 A188 30fr on 110fr #538 24 15
582 A184 50fr on 300fr #531 40 20
583 A173 50fr on 1225fr #493 40 20
584 A180 150fr on 135fr #521 (Bk & S) 1.20 60
585 A187 150fr on 160fr #535 1.20 60
586 A178 150fr on 190fr #514 1.20 60
587 A182 150fr on 190fr #525 1.20 60
588 A176 150fr on 350fr #503 1.20 60
589 A179 150fr on 485fr #518 1.20 60
590 A179 150fr on 525fr #519 1.20 60
591 A178 150fr on 530fr #515 1.20 60
592 A194 200fr on 640fr #556 1.60 80
593 A177 240fr on 350fr #509 1.95 1.00
594 A197 240fr on 625fr #565 1.95 1.00
Nos. 579-594 (16) 16.54 8.45

No. 580 is airmail. Size and location of surcharge varies. No. 585 also overprinted "Euro '92."

SEMI-POSTAL STAMPS

Anti-Malaria Issue
Common Design Type
Perf. 12½x12

1962, Apr. 7 Engr. Unwmk.
B1 CD108 25fr + 5fr pale vio bl 50 50

Algerian Family — SP1

1962, Dec. 24 Photo. *Perf. 12x12½*
B2 SP1 25fr + 5fr multi 22 22

Issued for the national campaign to show the solidarity of the peoples of Mali and Algeria.

AIR POST STAMPS

Federation

Composite View of St. Louis, Senegal — AP1

Unwmk.
1959, Dec. 11 Engr. *Perf. 13*
C1 AP1 85fr multi 1.00 80

Issued to commemorate the tercentenary of the founding of St. Louis, Senegal, and to honor the opening of the 6th meeting of the executive council of the French Community.

AP2 AP3

Birds: 100fr, Amethyst starling. 200fr, Bateleur eagle, horiz. 500fr, Barbary shrike.

Perf. 12½x13, 13x12½
1960, Feb. 13 Photo.
Birds in Natural Colors
C2 AP2 100fr multi 1.00 55
C3 AP2 200fr multi 1.65 1.00
C4 AP2 500fr blk & bl 6.50 4.50

Republic

Nos. C2-C4 Overprinted or Surcharged "REPUBLIQUE DU MALI" and Bars

1960, Dec. 18
C5 AP2 100fr multi 1.40 90
C6 AP2 200fr multi 2.25 1.50
C7 AP2 300fr on 500fr multi 3.50 3.00
C8 AP2 500fr multi 6.25 4.75

1961, Mar. 18 Engr. *Perf. 13*

Designs: 200fr, Mamadou Konate. 300fr, Pres. Modibo Keita.

C9 AP3 200fr cl & gray brn 1.60 65
C10 AP3 300fr grn & blk 2.25 90

Flag, Map, UN Emblem — AP4

1961, Mar. 18
C11 AP4 100fr multi 75 60
a. Min. sheet of 3, #13, 14, C11 1.40 1.40

Proclamation of independence and admission to UN.

Sankore Mosque, Timbuktu — AP5

Designs: 200fr, View of Timbuktu. 500fr, Bamako and arms.

1961, Apr. 15 Unwmk. *Perf. 13*

C12 AP5 100fr Prus bl, red brn & gray 65 20
C13 AP5 200fr grn, brn & red 1.25 65
C14 AP5 500fr red brn, Prus bl & dk grn 3.50 1.25

Issued for the inauguration of Timbuktu airport and Air Mali.

Bull, Chemical Equipment and Chicks — AP6

1963, Feb. 23 Engr.

C15 AP6 200fr bis, mar & grnsh bl 1.50 70

Sotuba Zootechnical Institute.

Air Ambulance — AP7

Designs: 55fr, National Line plane loading. 100fr, Intl. Line Vickers Viscount in flight.

1963, Nov. 2 Unwmk. *Perf. 13*

C16 AP7 25fr dk bl, emer & red brn 22 15
C17 AP7 55fr bis, bl & red brn 50 25
C18 AP7 100fr dk bl, red brn & yel grn 80 42

Issued to publicize Air Mali.

Crowned Crane and Giant Tortoise — AP8

1963, Nov. 23 Unwmk. *Perf. 13*

C19 AP8 25fr sep, org & ver 40 25
C20 AP8 200fr multi 1.90 1.25

Animal protection.

The Scott Catalogue value is a retail price, what you could expect to pay for the stamp in a grade of Fine-Very Fine. The value listed is a reference which reflects recent actual dealer selling price.

UN Emblem, Flag, Doves — AP9

1963, Dec. 10 Engr.

C21 AP9 50fr lt grn, yel & red 40 20

15th anniversary of the Universal Declaration of Human Rights.

Cleopatra and Ptolemy at Kôm Ombo — AP10

1964, Mar. 9 Unwmk. *Perf. 12*

C22 AP10 25fr dp cl & bis 35 15
C23 AP10 55fr dp cl & lt ol grn 60 30

UNESCO world campaign to save historic monuments in Nubia.

Pres. John F. Kennedy — AP11

1964, Oct. 26 Photo. *Perf. 12½*

C24 AP11 100fr sl, red brn & blk 65 65
a. Souv. sheet of 4 3.00 3.00

Touracos — AP12

Birds: 200fr, Abyssinian ground hornbills, vert. 300fr, Egyptian vultures, vert. 500fr, Goliath herons.

1965, Feb. 15 Engr. *Perf. 13*

C25 AP12 100fr grn, dk bl & red 65 38
C26 AP12 200fr blk, red & brt bl 1.10 55
C27 AP12 300fr blk, sl grn & yel 1.65 1.00
C28 AP12 500fr sl grn, dk brn & claret 3.50 1.50

UN Headquarters, New York, and ICY Emblem — AP13

1965, Mar. 15 Unwmk. *Perf. 13*

C29 AP13 55fr bis, dk bl & vio brn 45 30

International Cooperation Year.

Pope John XXIII — AP14

Perf. 12½x13

1965, Sept. 14 Photo. Unwmk.

C30 AP14 100fr multi 90 60

Winston Churchill — AP15

1965, Oct. 11 Engr. *Perf. 13*

C31 AP15 100fr brn & ind 90 60

Dr. Albert Schweitzer and Sick Child — AP16

1965, Dec. 20 Photo. *Perf. 12½*

C32 AP16 100fr multi 1.00 60
a. Souv. sheet of 4 4.00 3.25

Major Edward H. White and Gemini 4 — AP17

Designs: No. C34, Lt. Col. Alexei A. Leonov. 300fr, Gordon Cooper, Charles Conrad, Alexei Leonov and Pavel Belyayev, Parthenon, Athens, and vase, vert.

1966, Jan. 10

C33 AP17 100fr vio, yel, lt bl & blk 90 40
C34 AP17 100fr bl, red, yel & blk 90 40
C35 AP17 300fr multi 2.75 1.75

Achievements in space research and 16th Intl. Astronautical Congress, Athens, Sept. 12-18, 1965.

Papal Arms and UN Emblem — AP18

1966, July 11 Engr. *Perf. 13*

C36 AP18 200fr brt bl, grnsh bl & grn 1.60 55

Visit of Pope Paul VI to the UN, NYC, Oct. 4, 1965.

People and UNESCO Emblem — AP19

1966, Sept. 5 Engr. *Perf. 13*

C37 AP19 100fr dk car rose, sl grn & ultra 70 42

20th anniv. of UNESCO.

Soccer Players, Ball, Globe, and Jules Rimet Cup — AP20

1966, Oct. 31 Photo. *Perf. 13*

C38 AP20 100fr multi 70 42

8th International Soccer Championship Games, Wembley, England, July 11-30.

Crab and Mt. Fuji — AP21

UNICEF Emblem and Children — AP22

1966, Nov. 30 Photo. *Perf. 13*

C39 AP21 100fr multi 70 35

9th Intl. Anticancer Cong., Tokyo, Oct. 23-29.

1966, Dec. 10 Engr.

C40 AP22 45fr dp bl, bis brn & red lil 38 16

20th anniv. of UNICEF.

Land Cruisers in Hoggar Mountain Pass — AP23

1967, Mar. 20 Engr. *Perf. 13*

C41 AP23 200fr multi 1.25 65

"Black Cruise 1924," which crossed Africa from Beni-Abbes, Algeria to the Indian Ocean and on to Tananarive, Madagascar, Oct. 28, 1924-June 26, 1925.

Diamant Rocket and Francesco de Lana's 1650 Flying Boat — AP24

Designs: 100fr, A-1 satellite and rocket launching adapted from Jules Verne. 200fr, D-1 satellite and Leonardo da Vinci's bird-borne flying machine.

1967, Apr. 17 Engr. *Perf. 13*

C42 AP24 50fr brt bl, pur & grn 60 35
C43 AP24 100fr dk Prus bl, dk car & lil 1.40 65
C44 AP24 200fr sl bl, ol & pur 2.25 1.00

Honoring French achievements in space.

Amelia Earhart and Map of Mali — AP25

1967, May 29 Photo. *Perf. 13*

C45 AP25 500fr bl & multi 2.75 1.25

30th anniversary of Amelia Earhart's stop at Gao, West Africa.

Paul as Harlequin, by Picasso AP26

Picasso Paintings: 50fr, Bird Cage. 250fr, The Flutes of Pan.

1967, June 16 *Perf. 12½*

C46 AP26 50fr multi 30 16
C47 AP26 100fr multi 60 32
C48 AP26 250fr multi 1.40 75

See No. C82.

Jamboree Emblem, Scout Knots and Badges — AP27

Design: 100fr, Scout with portable radio transmitter, tents and Jamboree badge.

1967, July 10 Engr. *Perf. 13*

C49 AP27 70fr dk car, emer & bl grn 42 22
C50 AP27 100fr dk car lake, sl grn & blk 65 30
a. Strip of 2, #C49-C50 + label 1.40 1.20

12th Boy Scout World Jamboree, Farragut State Park, Idaho, Aug. 1-9.

Head of Horse, by Toulouse-Lautrec — AP28

Design: 300fr, Cob-drawn gig, by Toulouse-Lautrec, vert.

Perf. 12x12½, 12½x12

1967, Dec. 11 Photo.

C51 AP28 100fr multi 60 40
C52 AP28 300fr multi 1.75 75

See Nos. C66-C67.

Grenoble — AP29

Design: 150fr, Bobsled course on Huez Alp.

1968, Jan. 8 Engr. *Perf. 13*

C53 AP29 50fr bl, yel brn & grn 25 15
C54 AP29 150fr brn, vio bl & stl bl 65 30

10th Winter Olympic Games, Grenoble, France, Feb. 6-18.

Roses and Anemones, by Van Gogh — AP30

Paintings: 150fr, Peonies in Vase, by Edouard Manet (36x49mm). 300fr, Bouquet, by Delarcroix (41x42mm). 500fr, Daisies in Vase, by Jean Francois Millet (49x37mm).

Perf. 13, 12½x12, 12x12½

1968, June 24 Photo.

C55 AP30 50fr multi 25 15
C56 AP30 150fr grn & multi 65 30
C57 AP30 300fr grn & multi 1.20 65
C58 AP30 500fr car & multi 2.25 90

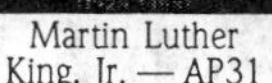
Martin Luther King, Jr. — AP31

Long Jumper and Satellite — AP32

1968, July 22 *Perf. 12½*

C59 AP31 100fr rose lil, sal pink & blk 38 16

Bicycle Type of Regular Issue

Designs: 50fr, Bicyclette, 1918. 100fr, Mercedes Benz, 1927, horiz.

1968, Aug. 12 Engr. *Perf. 13*

C60 A40 50fr gray, dk grn & brick red 22 20
C61 A40 100fr lem, ind & car 45 22

1968, Nov. 25 Photo. *Perf. 12½*

Design: 100fr, Soccer goalkeeper and satellite, horiz.

C62 AP32 100fr multi 42 25
C63 AP32 150fr multi 65 35

Issued to commemorate the 19th Olympic Games, Mexico City, Oct. 12-27.

PHILEXAFRIQUE Issue

Editorial Department, by Franois Marius Granet AP33

1968, Dec. 23 Photo. *Perf. 12½x12*

C64 AP33 200fr multi 90 65

Issued to publicize PHILEXAFRIQUE Philatelic Exhibition in Abidjan, Feb. 14-23. Printed with alternating light green label.
See Nos. C85-C87, C110-C112, C205-C207, C216-C217.

2nd PHILEXAFRIQUE Issue

Common Design Type

Design: 100fr, French Sudan #64, sculpture.

1969, Feb. 14 Engr. *Perf. 13*

C65 CD128 100fr pur & multi 50 50

Painting Type of 1967

Paintings: 150fr, Napoleon as First Consul, by Antoine Jean Gros, vert. 250fr, Bivouac at Austerlitz, by Louis Franois Lejeune.

Perf. 12½x12, 12x12½

1969, Feb. 25 Photo.

C66 AP28 150fr multi 1.20 70
C67 AP28 250fr multi 1.60 1.20

Napoleon Bonaparte (1769-1821).

Concorde — AP34

Designs: 50fr, Montgolfier's balloon. 150fr, Ferber 5, experimental biplane.

1969, Mar. 10 Photo. *Perf. 13*

C68 AP34 50fr multi 25 15
C69 AP34 150fr multi 65 25
C70 AP34 300fr multi 1.40 70
a. Strip of 3, #C68-C70 2.50 2.00

1st flight of the prototype Concorde plane at Toulouse, France, Mar. 1, 1969.
For overprints see Nos. C78-C80.

Auto Type of Regular Issue

Designs: 55fr, Renault, 1898, Renault 16, 1969. 90fr, Peugeot, 1893, Peugeot 404, 1969.

1969, May 30 Engr. *Perf. 13*

C71 A43 55fr rose car, blk & brt pink 25 20
C72 A43 90fr blk, dp car & ind 40 20

Ronald Clark, Australia, 10,000-meter Run, 1965 — AP35

World Records: 90fr, Yanis Lusis, USSR, Javelin, 1968. 120fr, Yoshinobu Miyake, Japan, weight lifting, 1967. 140fr, Randy Matson, US, shot put, 1968. 150fr, Kipchoge Keino, Kenya, 3,000-meter run, 1965.

1969, June 23 Engr. *Perf. 13*

C73 AP35 60fr bl & ol brn 18 15
C74 AP35 90fr car rose & red brn 28 16
C75 AP35 120fr emer & gray ol 35 16
C76 AP35 140fr gray & brn 45 20
C77 AP35 150fr red org & blk 50 25
Nos. C73-C77 (5) 1.76 92

Issued to honor sports world records.

Nos. C68-C70 Overprinted in Red with Lunar Landing Module and: "L'HOMME SUR LA LUNE / JUILLET 1969 / APOLLO 11"

1969, July 25 Photo. *Perf. 13*

C78 AP34 50fr multi 42 30
C79 AP34 150fr multi 1.10 80
C80 AP34 300fr multi 2.25 1.60
a. Strip of 3, #C78-C80 4.00 3.50

Man's 1st landing on moon, July 20, 1969. US astronauts Neil A. Armstrong and Col. Edwin E. Aldrin, Jr., with Lieut. Col. Michael Collins piloting Apollo 11.

Apollo 8, Moon and Earth AP35a

Embossed on Gold Foil

1969, July 24 *Die-cut perf 10½*

C81 AP35a 2000fr gold 9.00 9.00

US Apollo 8 mission, the 1st men in orbit around the moon, Dec. 21-27, 1968.

Painting Type of 1967

Design: 500fr, Mona Lisa, by Leonardo da Vinci.

1969, Oct. 20 Photo. *Perf. 12½*

C82 AP26 500fr multi 2.25 1.65

Values quoted in this catalogue are for stamps graded at Fine-Very Fine and with no faults. An illustrated guide to grade is provided in introductory material, beginning on Page 5A.

Mahatma Gandhi — AP36

1969, Nov. 24 **Engr.** ***Perf. 13***

C83 AP36 150fr brt bl, ol brn & red brn 65 35

Map of West Africa, Post Horns and Lightning Bolts — AP37

1970, Feb. 23 **Photo.** ***Perf. 12½***

C84 AP37 100fr multi 42 25

11th anniversary of the West African Postal Union (CAPTEAO).

Painting Type of 1968

Paintings: 100fr, Madonna and Child, from Rogier van der Weyden school. 150fr, Nativity, by the master of Flemalle. 250fr, Madonna and Child with St. John, from the Dutch School.

1970, Mar. 2

C85 AP33 100fr multi 38 22

C86 AP33 150fr multi 55 35

C87 AP33 250fr multi 90 55

Roosevelt — AP38

Lenin — AP39

1970, Mar. 30 **Photo.** ***Perf. 12½***

C88 AP38 500fr red, lt ultra & blk 2.75 1.35

Pres. Franklin D. Roosevelt (1882-1945).

1970, Apr. 22

C89 AP39 300fr pink, grn & blk 1.25 55

Jules Verne and Firing of Moon Rockets — AP40

Designs: 150fr, Jules Verne, rockets, landing modules and moon. 300fr, Jules Verne and splashdown.

1970, May 4

C90 AP40 50fr multi 35 16

C91 AP40 150fr multi 1.20 42

C92 AP40 300fr multi 2.00 80

Nos. C90-C92 Overprinted in Red or Blue: "APOLLO XIII / EPOPEE SPATIALE / 11-17 AVRIL 1970"

1970, June **Photo.** ***Perf. 12½***

C93 AP40 50fr multi (Bl) 40 25

C94 AP40 150fr multi (R) 1.00 42

C95 AP40 300fr multi (Bl) 2.25 1.40

Flight and safe return of Apollo 13, Apr. 11-13, 1970.

Intelsat III — AP41

Telecommunications Through Space: 200fr, Molniya I satellite. 300fr, Radar. 500fr, "Project Symphony" (various satellites).

1970, July 13 **Engr.** ***Perf. 13***

C96 AP41 100fr gray, brt bl & org 65 35

C97 AP41 200fr bl, gray & red lil 1.40 60

C98 AP41 300fr org, dk brn & gray 1.90 80

C99 AP41 500fr dk brn, sl & grnsh bl 3.00 1.40

For surcharges see Nos. C108-C109.

Auguste and Louis Lumière, Jean Harlow and Marilyn Monroe AP42

1970, July 27 **Photo.** ***Perf. 12½x12***

C100 AP42 250fr multi 90 55

Issued to honor Auguste Lumière (1862-1954), and his brother Louis Jean Lumière (1864-1948), inventors of the Lumière process of color photography and of a motion picture camera.

Soccer — AP43

1970, Sept. 7 **Engr.** ***Perf. 13***

C101 AP43 80fr bl, dp car & brn ol 35 16

C102 AP43 200fr dp car, bl grn & ol brn 70 42

Issued to commemorate the 9th World Soccer Championships for the Jules Rimet Cup, Mexico City, May 30-June 21, 1970.

Rotary Emblem, Map of Mali and Ceremonial Antelope Heads — AP44

Men Holding UN Emblem, and Doves — AP45

1970, Sept. 21 **Photo.** ***Perf. 12½***

C103 AP44 200fr multi 70 42

Issued to honor Rotary International.

1970, Oct. 5 **Engr.** ***Perf. 13***

C104 AP45 100fr dk pur, red brn & dk bl 38 22

25th anniversary of the United Nations.

Koran Page, Baghdad, 11th Century AP46

Moslem Art: 200fr, Tree, and lion killing deer, mosaic, Jordan, c. 730, horiz. 250fr, Scribe, miniature, Baghdad, 1287.

1970, Oct. 26 **Photo.** ***Perf. 12½x12***

C105 AP46 50fr multi 22 15

C106 AP46 200fr multi 60 30

C107 AP46 250fr multi 70 38

Nos. C97-C98 Surcharged and Overprinted: "LUNA 16 / PREMIERS PRELEVEMENTS AUTOMATIQUES / SUR LA LUNE / SEPTEMBRE 1970"

1970, Nov. 9 **Engr.** ***Perf. 13***

C108 AP41 150fr on 200fr multi 1.10 55

C109 AP41 250fr on 300fr multi 2.00 85

Unmanned moon probe of the Russian space ship Luna 16, Sept. 12-24.

Painting Type of 1968

Paintings: 100fr, Nativity, Antwerp School, c. 1530. 250fr, St. John the Baptist, by Hans Memling. 300fr, Adoration of the Kings, Flemish School, 17th century.

1970, Dec. 1 **Photo.** ***Perf. 12½x12***

C110 AP33 100fr brn & multi 32 16

C111 AP33 250fr brn & multi 65 32

C112 AP33 300fr brn & multi 90 40

Christmas 1970.

Gamal Abdel Nasser — AP47

Embossed on Gold Foil

1970, Nov. 25 ***Perf. 12½***

C113 AP47 1000fr gold 5.00 5.00

In memory of Gamal Abdel Nasser (1918-1970), President of Egypt.

Charles de Gaulle AP48

Embossed on Gold Foil

1971, Feb. 8 ***Die-cut Perf. 10***

C114 AP48 2000fr gold, red & dp ultra 12.00 12.00

In memory of Gen. Charles de Gaulle (1890-1970), President of France.

Alfred Nobel — AP49

Tennis, Davis Cup — AP50

1971, Feb. 22 **Engr.** ***Perf. 13***

C115 AP49 300fr multi 90 60

Alfred Nobel (1833-1896), inventor of dynamite, sponsor of Nobel Prize.

1971, Mar. 8

Designs: 150fr, Derby at Epsom, horiz. 200fr, Racing yacht, America's Cup.

C116 AP50 100fr bl, lil & sl 25 15

C117 AP50 150fr brn, brt grn & ol 38 16

C118 AP50 200fr brt bl, ol & brn 65 22

The Arabian Nights — AP51

Designs: 180fr, Ali Baba and the 40 Thieves. 200fr, Aladdin's Lamp.

1971, Apr. 5 **Photo.** ***Perf. 13***

C119 AP51 120fr gold & multi 35 22

C120 AP51 180fr gold & multi 42 25

C121 AP51 200fr gold & multi 65 38

Olympic Rings and Sports — AP52

1971, June 28 **Photo.** ***Perf. 12½***

C122 AP52 80fr ultra, yel grn & brt mag 22 15

Pre-Olympic Year.

Mariner 4 — AP53

Design: 300fr, Venera 5 in space.

1971, Sept. 13 Engr. *Perf. 13*

C123 AP53 200fr multi 55 30

C124 AP53 300fr multi 80 42

Space explorations of US Mariner 4 (200fr); and USSR Venera 5 (300fr).

Santa Maria, 1492 — AP54

Famous Ships: 150fr, Mayflower, 1620. 200fr, Potemkin, 1905. 250fr, Normandie, 1935.

1971, Sept. 27

C125 AP54 100fr brn, bluish grn & pur 22 15

C126 AP54 150fr sl grn, brn & pur 38 20

C127 AP54 200fr car, bl & dk ol 60 35

C128 AP54 250fr blk, bl & red 70 42

Symbols of Justice and Maps — AP55

1971, Oct. 18

C129 AP55 160fr mar, ocher & dk brn 50 22

25th anniversary of the International Court of Justice in The Hague, Netherlands.

Statue of Zeus, by Phidias — AP56

Nat "King" Cole — AP57

The Seven Wonders of the Ancient World: 80fr, Cheops Pyramid and Sphinx. 100fr, Temple of Artemis, Ephesus, horiz. 130fr, Lighthouse at Alexandria. 150fr, Hanging Gardens of Babylon, horiz. 270fr, Mausoleum of Halicarnassus. 280fr, Colossus of Rhodes.

1971, Dec. 13

C130 AP56 70fr ind, dk red & pink 22 15

C131 AP56 80fr brn, bl & blk 22 15

C132 AP56 100fr org, ind & pur 30 16

C133 AP56 130fr rose lil, blk & grnsh bl 40 16

C134 AP56 150fr brn, brt grn & bl 42 16

C135 AP56 270fr sl, brn & plum 80 20

C136 AP56 280fr sl lil & ol 80 20

Nos. C130-C136 (7) 3.16 1.18

1971, Dec. 6 Photo. *Perf. 13x12½*

Famous American Black Musicians: 150fr, Erroll Garner. 270fr, Louis Armstrong.

C137 AP57 130fr blk, brn & yel 40 16

C138 AP57 150fr blk, bl & yel 42 18

C139 AP57 270fr blk, rose car & yel 80 35

Slalom and Japanese Child — AP58

Design: 200fr, Ice hockey and character from Noh play.

1972, Jan. 10 Engr. *Perf. 13*

C140 AP58 150fr sl grn, dk brn & red 42 20

C141 AP58 200fr red, sl grn & dk brn 60 35

a. Souv. sheet of 2, #C140-C141 1.40 1.40

11th Winter Olympic Games, Sapporo, Japan, Feb. 3-13.

Santa Maria della Salute, by Ippolito Caffi — AP59

Paintings of Venice, by Ippolito Caffi: 270fr, Rialto Bridge. 280fr, St. Mark's Square, vert.

1972, Feb. 21 Photo. *Perf. 13*

C142 AP59 130fr gold & multi 45 22

C143 AP59 270fr gold & multi 80 42

C144 AP59 280fr gold & multi 90 55

UNESCO campaign to save Venice.

Hands of 4 Races Holding Scout Flag — AP60

1972, Mar. 27 Engr. *Perf. 13*

C145 AP60 200fr dk red, ocher & ol gray 55 28

World Boy Scout Seminar, Cotonou, Dahomey, March, 1972.

"Your Heart is your Health" — AP61

1972, Apr. 7 Engr. *Perf. 13*

C146 AP61 150fr brt bl & red 42 25

World Health Day.

Soccer Player and Frauenkirche, Munich — AP62

Designs (Sport and Munich Landmarks): 150fr, Judo and TV Tower, vert. 200fr, Steeplechase and Propylaeum, vert. 300fr, Runner and Church of the Theatines.

1972, Apr. 17

C147 AP62 50fr ocher, dk bl & grn 20 15

C148 AP62 150fr dk bl, ocher & grn 45 20

C149 AP62 200fr grn, dk bl & ocher 60 28

C150 AP62 300fr dk bl, grn & ocher 90 40

a. Min. sheet of 4, #C147-C150 3.00 3.00

20th Olympic Games, Munich, Aug. 26-Sept. 10. For overprints see Nos. C165-C166, C168.

Apollo 15, Lunar Rover, Landing Module — AP63

Design: 250fr, Cugnot's steam wagon and Montgolfier's Balloon.

1972, Apr. 27

C151 AP63 150fr ver, sl grn & rose mag 55 25

C152 AP63 250fr ultra, grn & rose red 80 38

Development of transportation.

Cinderella AP64

Fairy Tales: 80fr, Puss in Boots. 150fr, Sleeping Beauty.

1972, June 19 Engr. *Perf. 13x12½*

C153 AP64 70fr car rose, sl grn & ol 25 15

C154 AP64 80fr choc, brt grn & dp org 35 18

C155 AP64 150fr vio, bl & lil 55 25

Charles Perrault (1628-1703), French writer.

Astronauts and Lunar Rover on Moon — AP65

1972, July 24 Engr. *Perf. 13*

C156 AP65 500fr ol bis, vio & brt grn 1.60 75

US Apollo 16 moon mission, Apr. 15-27.

Book Year Emblem — AP66

1972, Aug. 7 Litho. *Perf. 12½*

C157 AP66 80fr bl, gold & grn 25 16

International Book Year 1972.

Bamako Rotary Emblem with Crocodiles — AP67

1972, Oct. 9 Engr. *Perf. 13*

C158 AP67 170fr dk brn, red & ultra 55 20

10th anniv. of the Bamako Rotary Club.

Hurdler, Olympic Rings, Melbourne Cathedral, Kangaroo — AP68

Designs (Olympic Rings and): 70fr, Boxing, Helsinki Railroad Station, arms of Finland, vert. 140fr, Running, Colosseum, Roman wolf. 150fr, Weight lifting, Tokyo stadium, phoenix, vert. 170fr, Swimming, University Library, Mexico City; Aztec sculpture. 210fr, Javelin, Munich Stadium, Arms of Munich. Stamps inscribed with name of gold medal winner of event shown.

1972, Nov. 13 Engr. *Perf. 13*

C159 AP68 70fr red, ocher & ind 20 15

C160 AP68 90fr red brn, bl & sl 25 16

C161 AP68 140fr brn, brt grn & ol gray 40 16

C162 AP68 150fr dk car, emer & gray ol 42 18

C163 AP68 170fr red lil, brn & Prus bl 45 20

C164 AP68 210fr ultra, emer & brick red 65 35

Nos. C159-C164 (6) 2.37 1.20

Retrospective of Olympic Games 1952-1972. For overprint see No. C167.

Nos. C148-C150 and C164 Overprinted:

a. JUDO / RUSKA / 2 MEDAILLES D'OR
b. STEEPLE / KEINO / MEDAILLE D'OR
c. MEDAILLE D'OR / 90m. 48
d. 100m.-200m. / BORZOV / 2 MEDAILLES D'OR

1972, Nov. 27 Engr. *Perf. 13*

C165 AP62 150fr multi (a) 42 22

C166 AP62 200fr multi (b) 55 25

C167 AP68 210fr multi (c) 60 30

C168 AP62 300fr multi (d) 90 42

Gold medal winners in 20th Olympic Games: Wim Ruska, Netherlands, heavy-weight judo (#C165); Kipchoge Keino, Kenya, 3000m. steeplechase (#C166); Klaus Wolfermann, Germany, javelin (#C167); Valery Borzov, USSR, 100m., 200m. race (#C168).

Emperor Haile Selassie — AP69

1972, Dec. 26 Photo. *Perf. 12½*

C169 AP69 70fr grn & multi 22 15

80th birthday of Emperor Haile Selassie of Ethiopia.

The lack of a value for a listed item does not necessarily indicate rarity.

Plane, Balloon, Route Timbuktu to Bamako — AP70

Design: 300fr, Balloon, jet and route Timbuktu to Bamako.

1972, Dec. 29 *Perf. 13½*

C170 AP70 200fr multi	65	30
C171 AP70 300fr bl & multi	90	42

First postal balloon flight in Mali.

Bishop of 14th Century European Chess Set — AP71

Design: 200fr, Knight (elephant), from 18th century Indian set.

1973, Feb. 19 **Engr.** *Perf. 13*

C172 AP71 100fr dk car, bl & ind	40	20
C173 AP71 200fr blk, red & brn	65	30

World Chess Championship, Reykjavik, Iceland, July-Sept., 1972.

Postal Union Emblem, Letter and Dove AP72

1973, Mar. 9 **Photo.** *Perf. 11½x11*

C174 AP72 70fr bl, blk & org	22	16

10th anniv. (in 1971) of African Postal Union. This stamp was to be issued Dec. 8, 1971. It was offered by the agency on Mar. 9, 1973. Copies were sold in Mali as early as July or August, 1972.

No. C20, Collector's Hand and Philatelic Background — AP73

1973, Mar. 12 **Engr.** *Perf. 13*

C175 AP73 70fr multi	30	16

Stamp Day, 1973.

Astronauts and Lunar Rover on Moon — AP74

1973, Mar. 26

C176 AP74 250fr bl, ind & bis	70	42

Souvenir Sheet

C177 AP74 350fr choc, vio bl & ultra	1.10	1.10

Apollo 17 US moon mission, Dec. 7-19, 1972.

Nicolaus Copernicus — AP75

1973, Apr. 9 **Engr.** *Perf. 13*

C178 AP75 300fr brt bl & mag	1.00	50

500th anniversary of the birth of Nicolaus Copernicus (1473-1543), Polish astronomer.

Dr. Armauer G. Hansen and Leprosy Bacillus — AP76

1973, May 7 **Engr.** *Perf. 13*

C179 AP76 200fr blk, yel grn & red	65	40

Centenary of the discovery of the Hansen bacillus, the cause of leprosy.

Bentley and Alfa Romeo, 1930 — AP77

Designs: 100fr, Jaguar and Talbot, 1953. 200fr, Matra and Porsche, 1972.

1973, May 21 **Engr.** *Perf. 13*

C180 AP77 50fr bl, org & grn	16	15
C181 AP77 100fr grn, ultra & car	35	15
C182 AP77 200fr ind, grn & car	65	25
Set value		46

50th anniversary of the 24-hour automobile race at Le Mans, France.

Camp Fire, Fleur-de-Lis AP78

Designs (Fleur-de-Lis and): 70fr, Scouts saluting flag, vert. 80fr, Scouts with flags. 130fr, Lord Baden-Powell, vert. 270fr, Round dance and map of Africa.

1973, June 4

C183 AP78 50fr dk red, ultra & choc	16	15
C184 AP78 70fr sl grn, dk brn & red	22	15
C185 AP78 80fr mag, sl grn & ol	25	15
C186 AP78 130fr brn, ultra & sl grn	45	20
C187 AP78 270fr mag, gray & vio bl	90	45
Nos. C183-C187 (5)	1.98	1.10

Mali Boy and Girl Scouts and International Scouts Congress.

For surcharges see Nos. C222-C223.

Swimming, US and "Africa" Flags — AP79

Designs (US, Africa Flags and): 80fr, Discus and javelin, vert. 330fr, Runners.

1973, July 30 **Engr.** *Perf. 13*

C188 AP79 70fr red, sl grn & bl	22	15
C189 AP79 80fr vio bl, dk ol & red	30	16
C190 AP79 330fr red & vio bl	1.00	42

First African-United States Sports Meet.

Head and City Hall, Brussels — AP80

Perseus, by Benvenuto Cellini — AP81

1973, Sept. 17 **Engr.** *Perf. 13*

C191 AP80 70fr brt ultra, ol & vio	22	15

Africa Weeks, Brussels, Sept. 15-30, 1973.

1973, Sept. 24

Famous Sculptures: 150fr, Pietá, by Michelangelo. 250fr, Victory of Samothrace, Greek 1st century B.C.

C192 AP81 100fr dk car & sl grn	35	20
C193 AP81 150fr dk car & dp cl	45	25
C194 AP81 250fr dk car & dk ol	80	42

Stephenson's Rocket and Buddicom Engine — AP82

Locomotives: 150fr, Union Pacific, 1890, and Santa Fe, 1940. 200fr, Mistral and Tokaido, 1970.

1973, Oct. 8 **Engr.** *Perf. 13*

C195 AP82 100fr brn, bl & blk	30	15
C196 AP82 150fr red, brt ultra & dk car	45	20
C197 AP82 200fr ocher, bl & ind	65	30

Apollo XI on Moon — AP83

Designs: 75fr, Landing capsule, Apollo XIII. 100fr, Astronauts and equipment on moon, Apollo XIV. 280fr, Rover, landing module and astronauts on moon, Apollo XV. 300fr, Lift-off from moon, Apollo XVII.

1973, Oct. 25

C198 AP83 50fr vio, org & sl grn	16	15
C199 AP83 75fr sl, red & bl	22	15
C200 AP83 100fr sl, bl & ol brn	35	16
C201 AP83 280fr vio bl, red & sl grn	80	38
C202 AP83 300fr sl, red & sl grn	1.00	45
Nos. C198-C202 (5)	2.53	1.29

Apollo US moon missions.

For surcharges see Nos. C224-C225.

Pablo Picasso — AP84

John F. Kennedy — AP85

1973, Nov. 7 **Litho.** *Perf. 12½*

C203 AP84 500fr multi	1.60	80

Pablo Picasso (1881-1973), painter.

1973, Nov. 12

C204 AP85 500fr gold, brt rose lil & blk	1.60	80

10th anniversary of the death of President John F. Kennedy (1917-1963).

Painting Type of 1968

Paintings: 100fr, Annunciation, by Vittore Carpaccio, horiz. 200fr, Virgin of St. Simon, by Federigo Baroccio. 250fr, Flight into Egypt, by Andrea Solario.

Perf. 13x12½, 12½x12, 12½x13

1973, Nov. 30 **Litho.**

C205 AP33 100fr blk & multi	30	20
C206 AP33 200fr blk & multi	65	30
C207 AP33 250fr blk & multi	80	40

Christmas 1973.

Soccer Player and Ball — AP86

Designs: 250fr, Goalkeeper and ball. 500fr, Frauenkirche, Munich, Arms of Munich and soccer ball, horiz.

1973, Dec. 3 **Engr.** *Perf. 13*

C208 AP86 150fr emer, ol brn & red	50	25
C209 AP86 250fr emer, vio bl & ol brn	80	38

Souvenir Sheet

C210 AP86 500fr bl & multi	1.60	1.60

World Soccer Cup, Munich.

Musicians, Mosaic from Pompeii — AP87

Designs (Mosaics from Pompeii): 250fr, Alexander the Great in battle, vert. 350fr, Bacchants, vert.

1974, Jan. 21 Engr. *Perf. 13*

C211 AP87 150fr sl bl, ol & rose 45 25
C212 AP87 250fr mag, ol & ocher 80 42
C213 AP87 350fr ol, dp brn & ocher 1.25 60

Winston Churchill — AP88

1974, Mar. 18 Engr. *Perf. 13*

C214 AP88 500fr black 1.25 85

Centenary of the birth of Sir Winston Churchill (1874-1965), statesman.

Chess Game AP89

1974, Mar. 25 Engr. *Perf. 13*

C215 AP89 250fr multi 90 42

21st Chess Olympic Games, Nice 1974.

Painting Type of 1968

Paintings: 400fr, Crucifixion, Alsatian School, c. 1380, vert. 500fr, Burial of Christ, by Titian.

Perf. 12½x13, 13x12½

1974, Apr. 12 Photo.

C216 AP33 400fr multi 90 50
C217 AP33 500fr multi 1.10 55

Easter 1974.

Lenin AP90

1974, Apr. 22 Engr. *Perf. 13*

C218 AP90 150fr vio bl & lake 40 20

50th anniversary of the death of Lenin.

Women's Steeplechase — AP91

1974, May 20 Engr. *Perf. 13*

C219 AP91 130fr bl, lil & brn 40 22

World Horsewomen's Championship, La Baule, France, June 30-July 7.

Skylab Docking in Space — AP92

Design: 250fr, Skylab over globe with Africa.

1974, July 1 Engr. *Perf. 13*

C220 AP92 200fr bl, sl & org 55 30
C221 AP92 250fr lil, sl & org 65 38

Skylab's flight over Africa, 1974.

Nos. C184-C185 Surcharged in Violet Blue with New Value, Two Bars and:

a. 11e JAMBOREE ARABE / AOUT 1974 LIBAN
b. CONGRES PANARABE LIBAN / AOUT 1974

1974, July 8 Engr. *Perf. 13*

C222 AP78 130fr on 70fr (a) 40 25
C223 AP78 170fr on 80fr (b) 55 40

11th Pan-Arab Jamboree and Pan-Arab Congress, Batrun, Lebanon, Aug. 1974.

Nos. C200-C201 Surcharged in Red with New Value, Two Bars and:

c. 1er DEBARQUEMENT / SUR LA LUNE / 20-VII-69
d. 1er PAS SUR LA / LUNE 21-VII-69

1974, July 15

C224 AP83 130fr on 100fr (c) 38 25
C225 AP83 300fr on 280fr (d) 80 42

First manned moon landing, July 20, 1969, and first step on moon, July 21, 1969.

1906 and 1939 Locomotives — AP93

Locomotives: 120fr, Baldwin, 1870, and Pacific, 1920. 210fr, Al., 1925, and Buddicom, 1847. 330fr, Hudson, 1938, and La Gironde, 1839.

1974, Oct. 7 Engr. *Perf. 13*

C226 AP93 90fr dk car & multi 25 16
C227 AP93 120fr ocher & multi 35 20
C228 AP93 210fr org & multi 55 30
C229 AP93 330fr grn & multi 90 42

Skier, Winter Sports and Olympic Rings — AP94

1974, Oct. 7

C230 AP94 300fr multi 80 42

Holy Family, by Hans Memling AP95

Designs: 310fr, Virgin and Child, Bourgogne School. 400fr, Adoration of the Kings, by Martin Schongauer.

1974, Nov. 4 Photo. *Perf. 12½*

C231 AP95 290fr multi 80 38
C232 AP95 310fr multi 80 42
C233 AP95 400fr multi 1.10 55

Christmas 1974.

See Nos. C238-C240, C267-C269.

Raoul Follereau — AP96

1974, Nov. 18 Engr. *Perf. 13*

C234 AP96 200fr brt bl 55 35

Raoul Follereau (1903-1977), apostle to the lepers and educator of the blind. See No. C468.

Europafrica Issue

Train, Jet, Cogwheel, Grain, Maps of Africa and Europe — AP97

1974, Dec. 27 Engr. *Perf. 13*

C235 AP97 100fr brn, grn & indigo 25 16
C236 AP97 110fr ocher, vio bl & pur 30 20

Painting Type of 1974

Designs: 200fr, Christ at Emmaus, by Phillipe de Champaigne, horiz. 300fr, Christ at Emmaus, by Paolo Veronese, horiz. 500fr, Christ in Majesty, Limoges, 13th century.

Perf. 13x12½, 12½x13

1975, Mar. 24 Litho.

C238 AP95 200fr multi 55 35
C239 AP95 300fr multi 80 42
C240 AP95 500fr multi 1.40 70

Easter 1975.

"Voyage to the Center of the Earth" — AP99

Jules Verne's Stories: 170fr, "From Earth to Moon" and Verne's portrait. 190fr, "20,000 Leagues under the Sea." 220fr, "A Floating City."

1975, Apr. 7 Engr. *Perf. 13*

C241 AP99 100fr multi 25 18
C242 AP99 170fr multi 45 25
C243 AP99 190fr multi 55 30
C244 AP99 220fr multi 60 38

Dawn, by Michelangelo AP100

Design: 500fr, Moses, by Michelangelo.

1975, Apr. 28 Photo. *Perf. 13*

C245 AP100 400fr multi 1.10 65
C246 AP100 500fr multi 1.40 80

500th birth anniversary of Michelangelo Buonarroti (1475-1564), Italian sculptor, painter and architect.

Astronaut on Moon — AP101

Designs: 300fr, Constellations Virgo and Capricorn. 370fr, Statue of Liberty, Kremlin, Soyuz and Apollo spacecraft.

1975, May 19 Engr. *Perf. 13*

C247 AP101 290fr multi 1.20 50
C248 AP101 300fr multi 1.20 65
C249 AP101 370fr multi 1.50 80

Russo-American space cooperation.

For overprints see Nos. C264-C266.

Boy Scout, Globe, Nordjamb 75 Emblem AP103

Designs (Globe, Nordjamb 75 Emblem and): 150fr, Boy Scout giving Scout sign. 290fr, Scouts around campfire.

1975, June 23 Engr. *Perf. 13*

C251 AP103 100fr cl, brn & bl 25 16
C252 AP103 150fr red, brn & grn 40 20
C253 AP103 290fr bl, grn & claret 80 42

Nordjamb 75, 14th Boy Scout Jamboree, Lillehammer, Norway, July 29-Aug. 7.

Battle Scene and Marquis de Lafayette — AP104

Designs: 300fr, Battle scene and George Washington. 370fr, Battle of Chesapeake Bay and Count de Grasse.

1975, July 7 Engr. *Perf. 13*

C254 AP104 290fr lt bl & indigo 80 42
C255 AP104 300fr lt bl & indigo 80 42
C256 AP104 370fr lt bl & indigo 90 55
a. Strip of 3, #C254-C256 2.50 1.90

Bicentenary of the American Revolution. No. C256a has continuous design.

Schweitzer, Bach and Score AP105

Designs: No. C257, Albert Einstein (1879-1955), theoretical physicist. No. No. C258, André-Marie Ampère (1775-1836), French physicist. 100fr, Clément Ader (1841-1925), French aviation pioneer. No. C260, Dr. Albert Schweitzer (1875-1965), Medical missionary and musician. No. C261, Sir Alexander Fleming (1881-1955), British bacteriologist, discoverer of penicillin.

1975 Engr. *Perf. 13*

C257 AP105	90fr multi		22	16
C258 AP105	90fr pur, org & bis		22	15
C259 AP105	100fr bl, red & lil		25	16
C260 AP105	150fr grn, bl & dk grn		40	20
C261 AP105	150fr lil, bl & brick red		40	20
	Nos. C257-C261 (5)		1.49	87

Issue dates: No. C257, May 26. No. C258, Sept. 23. 100fr, Dec. 8. No. C260, Jan. 14. No. C261, July 21.

For surcharge see No. C358.

Olympic Rings and Globe — AP106

Design: 400fr, Montreal Olympic Games' emblem.

1975, Oct.

C262 AP106	350fr pur & bl	70	40
C263 AP106	400fr blue	80	45

Pre-Olympic Year 1975.

Nos. C247-C249 Overprinted: "ARRIMAGE / 17 Juil. 1975"

1975, Oct. 20 Engr. *Perf. 13*

C264 AP101	290fr multi	80	38
C265 AP101	300fr multi	80	38
C266 AP101	370fr multi	1.00	55

Apollo-Soyuz link-up in space, July 17, 1975.

Painting Type of 1974

Designs: 290fr, Visitation, by Ghirlandaio. 300fr, Nativity, Fra Filippo Lippi school. 370fr, Adoration of the Kings, by Velazquez.

1975, Nov. 24 Litho. *Perf. 12½x13*

C267 AP95	290fr multi	80	38
C268 AP95	300fr multi	80	42
C269 AP95	370fr multi	1.00	55

Christmas 1975.

Concorde — AP107

1976, Jan. 12 Litho. *Perf. 13*

C270 AP107	500fr multi	1.40	90

Concorde supersonic jet, first commercial flight, Jan. 21, 1976.

For overprint see No. C315.

AP108

AP109

1976, Feb. 16 Litho. *Perf. 13*

C271 AP108	120fr Figure skating	35	16
C272 AP108	420fr Ski jump		
C273 AP108	430fr Slalom		

12th Winter Olympic Games, Innsbruck, Austria, Feb. 4-15.

1976, Apr. 5 Litho. *Perf. 12½*

Eye examination, WHO emblem.

C274 AP109	130fr multi	35	18

World Health Day: "Foresight prevents blindness."

Space Ship with Solar Batteries — AP110

Design: 300fr, Astronaut working on orbital space station, vert.

1976, May 10 Engr. *Perf. 13*

C275 AP110	300fr org, dk & lt bl	65	32
C276 AP110	400fr mag, dk bl & org	80	45

Futuristic space achievements.

American Eagle, Flag and Liberty Bell — AP111

Designs: 400fr, Revolutionary War naval battle and American eagle. 440fr, Indians on horseback and American eagle, vert.

1976, May 24 Litho. *Perf. 12½*

C277 AP111	100fr multi	25	16
C278 AP111	400fr multi	1.10	65
C279 AP111	440fr multi	1.25	70

American Bicentennial. Nos. C278-C279 also for Interphil 76, International Philatelic Exhibition, Philadelphia, Pa, May 29-June 6.

Running AP112

Designs (Olympic Rings and): 250fr, Swimming. 300fr, Field ball. 440fr, Soccer.

1976, June 7 Engr. *Perf. 13*

C280 AP112	200fr red brn & blk	55	25
C281 AP112	250fr multi	65	38
C282 AP112	300fr multi	80	42
C283 AP112	440fr multi	1.25	60

21st Olympic Games, Montreal, Canada, July 17-Aug. 1.

Cub Scout and Leader — AP113

Designs: 180fr, Scouts tending sick animal, horiz. 200fr, Night hike.

1976, June 14 Engr. *Perf. 13*

C284 AP113	140fr ultra & red brn	38	30
C285 AP113	180fr dk brn & multi	45	35
C286 AP113	200fr brn org & vio bl	55	38

First African Boy Scout Jamboree, Nigeria.

Mohenjo-Daro, Bull from Wall Relief — AP114

Design: 500fr, Man's head, animals, wall and UNESCO emblem.

1976, Sept. 6 Engr. *Perf. 13*

C287 AP114	400fr blk, bl & pur	1.10	55
C288 AP114	500fr dk red, bl & grn	1.40	80

UNESCO campaign to save Mohenjo-Daro excavations.

Europafrica Issue

Freighter, Plane, Map of Europe and Africa — AP115

1976, Sept. 20

C289 AP115	200fr vio brn & bl	55	35

Nativity, by Taddeo Gaddi — AP116

Paintings: 300fr, Adoration of the Kings, by Hans Memling. 320fr, Nativity, by Carlo Crivelli.

1976, Nov. 8 Litho. *Perf. 13x12½*

C290 AP116	280fr multi	70	38
C291 AP116	300fr multi	80	42
C292 AP116	320fr multi	90	45

Christmas 1976.

Viking Flying to Mars — AP117

Design: 1000fr, Viking landing craft on Mars.

1976, Dec. 8 Engr. *Perf. 13*

C293 AP117	500fr red, brn & bl	1.25	55
C294 AP117	1000fr multi	2.50	1.25
a.	Miniature sheet of 2	4.50	2.50

Operation Viking, US Mars mission, No. C294a contains 2 stamps similar to Nos. C293-C294 in changed colors.

Pres. Giscard d'Estaing, Village and Bambara Antelope — AP118

1977, Feb. 13 Photo. *Perf. 13*

C295 AP118	430fr multi	1.00	42

Visit of Pres. Valéry Giscard d'Estaing of France, Feb. 13-15.

Elizabeth II and Prince Philip — AP119

Designs: 200fr, Charles de Gaulle, vert. 250fr, Queen Wilhelmina, vert. 300fr, King Baudouin and Queen Fabiola. 480fr, Coronation of Queen Elizabeth II, vert.

1977, Mar. 21 Litho. *Perf. 12*

C296 AP119	180fr multi	45	25
C297 AP119	200fr multi	55	35
C298 AP119	250fr multi	65	38
C299 AP119	300fr multi	80	45
C300 AP119	480fr multi	1.40	65
	Nos. C296-C300 (5)	3.85	2.08

Personalities involved in de-colonization.

Newton, Rocket and Apple — AP120

1977, May 7 Engr. *Perf. 13*

C301 AP120	400fr grn, brn & red	1.20	55

Isaac Newton (1643-1727), natural philosopher and mathematician, 250th death anniversary.

Charles Lindbergh and Spirit of St. Louis — AP121

Design: 430fr, Spirit of St. Louis flying over clouds.

1977, Apr. 4 Litho. *Perf. 12*

C302 AP121	420fr org & pur	80	40
C303 AP121	430fr multi	85	40

Charles A. Lindbergh's solo transatlantic flight from New York to Paris, 50th anniversary.

Sassenage Castle, Grenoble — AP122

1977, May 21 Litho. *Perf. 12½*
C304 AP122 300fr multi 80 42

10th anniversary of International French Language Council.

Zeppelin No. 1, 1900 — AP123

Designs: 130fr, Graf Zeppelin, 1924. 350fr, Hindenburg aflame at Lakehurst, NJ, 1937. 500fr, Ferdinand von Zeppelin and Graf Zeppelin.

1977, May 30 Engr. *Perf. 13*
C305 AP123 120fr multi 35 18
C306 AP123 130fr multi 35 18
C307 AP123 350fr multi 90 55
C308 AP123 500fr multi 1.40 65

History of the Zeppelin.

Martin Luther King, American and Swedish Flags — AP124

Design: 600fr, Henri Dunant, Red Cross, Swiss and Swedish flags.

1977, July 4 Engr. *Perf. 13*
C309 AP124 600fr multi 1.20 65
C310 AP124 700fr multi 1.40 70

Nobel Peace Prize recipients.

Soccer — AP125

Designs: 200fr, 3 soccer players, vert. 420fr, 3 soccer players.

1977, Oct. 3 Engr. *Perf. 13*
C311 AP125 180fr multi 35 20
C312 AP125 200fr multi 40 25
C313 AP125 420fr multi 90 45

World Soccer Cup Elimination Games.

Mao Tse-tung and COMATEX Hall, Bamako — AP126

1977, Nov. 7 Engr. *Perf. 13*
C314 AP126 300fr dl red 80 42

Chairman Mao Tse-tung (1893-1976), first death anniversary.

No. C270 Overprinted in Violet Blue: "PARIS NEW-YORK 22.11.77"

1977, Nov. 22 Litho. *Perf. 13*
C315 AP107 500fr multi 3.50 1.90

Concorde, first commerical transatlantic flight, Paris to New York.

Virgin and Child, by Rubens AP127

Rubens Paintings: 400fr, Adoration of the Kings. 600fr, Detail from Adoration of the Kings, horiz.

1977, Dec. 5 *Perf. 12½x12, 12x12½*
C316 AP127 400fr gold & multi 1.10 60
C317 AP127 500fr gold & multi 1.40 80
C318 AP127 600fr gold & multi 1.60 90

Christmas 1977, and 400th birth anniversary of Peter Paul Rubens (1577-1640).

Battle of the Amazons, by Rubens — AP128

Rubens Paintings: 300fr, Return from the fields. 500fr, Hercules fighting the Nemean Lion, vert.

Perf. 12x12½, 12½x12

1978, Jan. 16 Litho.
C319 AP128 200fr multi 55 35
C320 AP128 300fr multi 80 50
C321 AP128 500fr multi 1.40 80

Peter Paul Rubens, 400th birth anniversary.

Schubert Composing "Winterreise" — AP129

Design: 300fr, Schubert and score, vert.

1978, Feb. 13
C322 AP129 300fr multi 80 50
C323 AP129 420fr multi 1.20 60

Franz Schubert (1797-1828), Austrian composer, death sesquicentennial.

Capt. Cook Receiving Hawaiian Delegation — AP130

Design: 300fr, Cook landing on Hawaii. Designs after sketches by John Weber.

1978, Feb. 27 Engr. *Perf. 13*
C324 AP130 200fr multi 55 35
C325 AP130 300fr multi 80 42

Capt. James Cook (1728-1779), bicentenary of his arrival in Hawaii.

Soccer — AP131

Designs: 250fr, One player. 300fr, Two players, horiz.

1978, Mar. 20
C326 AP131 150fr multi 40 22
C327 AP131 250fr multi 65 40
  a. "REPUPLIQUE" 65 40
C328 AP131 300fr multi 80 42
  a. Min. sheet of 3, #C326-C328 + label 1.90 1.50
  b. As "a," #C326, C327a, C328

World Soccer Cup Championships, Argentina, 1978, June 1-25.

Nos. C327 and C328a were issued in July to correct the spelling error.

For overprints see Nos. C338-C340.

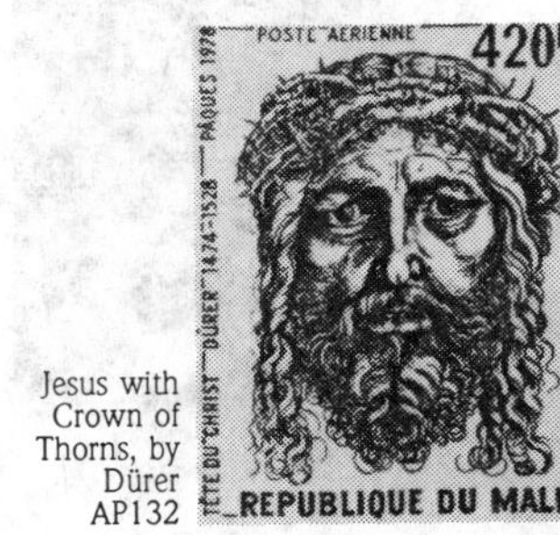

Jesus with Crown of Thorns, by Dürer AP132

Design: 430fr, Resurrection, by Albrecht Dürer.

1978, Mar. 28
C329 AP132 420fr multi 1.10 65
C330 AP132 430fr multi 1.20 65

Easter 1978. See Nos. C359-C361.

Citroen, C3-Trefle, 1922 — AP133

Citroen Cars: 130fr, Croisiere Noire, 1924, tractor. 180fr, B14G, 1927. 200fr, "11" Tractor Avant, 1934.

1978, Apr. 24 Engr. *Perf. 13*
C331 AP133 120fr multi 30 20
C332 AP133 130fr multi 35 20
C333 AP133 180fr multi 50 25
C334 AP133 200fr multi 55 30

Andre Citroen (1878-1935), automobile designer and manufacturer.

UPU Emblem, World Map, Country Names — AP133a

Design: 130fr, UPU emblem, globe and names of member countries.

1978, May 15
C334A AP133a 120fr multi 32 16
C335 AP133a 130fr red, grn & emer 35 20

Centenary of Congress of Paris where General Postal Union became the Universal Postal Union.

Europafrica Issue

Ostrich Incubating Eggs, Syrian Manuscript, 14th Century — AP134

Design: 110fr, Zebra, Miniature by Mansur, Jehangir School, 1620.

1978, July 24 Litho. *Perf. 13x12½*
C336 AP134 100fr multi 25 16
C337 AP134 110fr multi 30 18

Nos. C326-C328a Overprinted in Black:

a. CHAMPION / 1978 / ARGENTINE
b. 2e HOLLANDE
c. 3e BRESIL / 4e ITALIE

1978, Aug. 7 Engr. *Perf. 13*
C338 AP131 150fr multi (a) 40 22
C339 AP131 250fr multi (b) 65 40
C340 AP131 300fr multi (c) 80 42
  a. Souvenir sheet of 3 1.50 1.50

Winners, World Soccer Cup Championship, Argentina. Overprints on No. C340a are green including label overprint: FINALE / ARGENTINA 3 HOLLANDE 1.

Elizabeth II in Coronation Robes AP135

Design: 500fr, Coronation coach.

1978, Sept. 18 Litho. *Perf. 12½x12*
C341 AP135 500fr multi 1.00 65
C342 AP135 1000fr multi 2.00 1.50

25th anniversary of coronation of Queen Elizabeth II.

US No. C3a and Douglas DC-3
AP136

History of Aviation: 100fr, Belgium No. 252 and Stampe SV-4. 120fr, France No. C48 and Ader's plane No. 3. 130fr, Germany No. C2 and Junker Ju-52. 320fr, Japan No. C25 and Mitsubishi A-6M "Zero."

1978, Oct. 16 Engr. *Perf. 13*

C343 AP136	80fr multi	20	15
C344 AP136	100fr multi	25	18
C345 AP136	120fr multi	32	20
C346 AP136	130fr multi	35	22
C347 AP136	320fr multi	90	55
	Nos. C343-C347 (5)	2.02	1.30

Annunciation, by Dürer — AP137

Etchings by Dürer: 430fr, Virgin and Child. 500fr, Adoration of the Kings.

1978, Nov. 6

C348 AP137	420fr blk & rose car	85	45
C349 AP137	430fr ol grn & brn	90	50
C350 AP137	500fr blk & red	1.00	65

Christmas 1978 and 450th death anniversary of Albrecht Dürer (1471-1528), German painter.

Rocket and Trajectory Around Moon — AP138

Design: 300fr, Spaceship circling moon.

1978, Nov. 20 Engr. *Perf. 13*

C351 AP138	200fr multi	80	55
C352 AP138	300fr multi	1.20	70

10th anniversary of 1st flight around moon. Nos. C351-C352 printed se-tenant with label between showing earth, moon and US astronauts' names.

Ader's Plane and Concorde — AP139

Designs: 130fr, Wright Flyer A and Concorde. 200fr, Spirit of St. Louis and Concorde.

1979, Jan. 25 Litho. *Perf. 13*

C353 AP139	120fr multi	35	20
C354 AP139	130fr multi	35	22
C355 AP139	200fr multi	55	38

1st supersonic commercial flight, 3rd anniv.
For surcharges see Nos. C529-C531.

Philexafrique II-Essen Issue
Common Design Types

Designs: No. C356, Dromedary and Mali No. C26. No. C357, Bird and Lubeck No. 1.

1979, Jan. 29 Litho. *Perf. 13x12½*

C356 CD138	200fr multi	55	38
C357 CD139	200fr multi	55	38

Nos. C356-C357 printed se-tenant.

No. C257 Surcharged

"1879-1979"
130 F

1979, Mar. 26 Engr. *Perf. 13*

C358 AP105	130fr on 90fr multi	35	22

Centenary of the birth of Albert Einstein (1879-1955).

Easter Type of 1978

Dürer Etchings: 400fr, Jesus Carrying Cross. 430fr, Crucified Christ. 480fr, Pietà.

1979, Apr. 9

C359 AP132	400fr bl & blk	1.10	70
C360 AP132	430fr red & blk	1.20	80
C361 AP132	480fr ultra & blk	1.25	90

Easter 1979.

Basketball and St. Basil's Cathedral, Moscow — AP140

Design: 430fr, Soccer and Kremlin.

1979, Apr. 17 Litho. *Perf. 13*

C362 AP140	420fr multi	1.10	75
C363 AP140	430fr multi	1.20	80

Pre-Olympic Year.

Mali #C92, Apollo Spacecraft
AP141

Design: 500fr, Mali No. C176, lift-off.

1979, Oct. 22 Litho. *Perf. 12½x13*

C364 AP141	430fr multi	1.20	60
C365 AP141	500fr multi	1.40	70

Apollo 11 moon landing, 10th anniversary.

Capt. Cook, Ship, Kerguelen Island — AP142

Design: 480fr, Capt. Cook, Ship, Hawaii.

1979, Oct. 29 *Perf. 13x12½*

C366 AP142	300fr multi	1.20	65
C367 AP142	480fr multi	1.40	1.00

Capt. James Cook (1728-1779), explorer, death bicentenary.

David Janowski (1868-1927), Chess Pieces
AP143

Chess Pieces and Grand Masters: 140fr, Alexander Alekhine (1892-1946). 200fr, W. Schlage. 300fr, Effim D. Bogoljubow (1889-1952).

1979, Nov. 30 Engr. *Perf. 13*

C368 AP143	100fr red & brn	35	16
C369 AP143	140fr multi	42	20
C370 AP143	200fr multi	65	35
C371 AP143	300fr multi	1.00	50

For overprints see Nos. C441-C442.

Adoration of the Kings, by Dürer
AP144

Christmas 1979: 400fr, 500fr, Adoration of the Kings by Dürer, diff.

1979, Dec. 10 *Perf. 13x13½*

C372 AP144	300fr brn org & brn	80	35
C373 AP144	400fr bl & brn	1.10	42
C374 AP144	500fr dk grn & brn	1.40	55

Jet, Map of Africa
AP145

1979, Dec. 27 Litho. *Perf. 12½*

C375 AP145	120fr multi	32	15

ASECNA (Air Safety Board), 20th anniv.

Train, Globe, Rotary Emblem
AP146

Rotary International, 75th Anniversary: 250fr, Jet. 430fr, Bamako Club emblem, meeting hall.

1980, Jan. 28 Litho. *Perf. 12½*

C376 AP146	220fr multi	70	35
C377 AP146	250fr multi	90	40
C378 AP146	430fr multi	1.50	60

Speed Skating, Lake Placid '80 Emblem, Snowflake — AP147

1980, Feb. 11 *Perf. 13*

C379 AP147	200fr shown	55	22
C380 AP147	300fr Ski jump	80	35
a.	Souvenir sheet of 2	1.40	65

13th Winter Olympic Games, Lake Placid, NY, Feb. 12-24. No. C380a contains Nos. C379-C380 in changed colors.

Stephenson's Rocket, Mali No. 196 — AP148

Liverpool-Manchester Railroad, 150th Anniversary: 300fr, Stephenson's Rocket, Mali No. 142.

1980, Feb. 25 Engr.

C381 AP148	200fr multi	55	22
C382 AP148	300fr multi	80	35

Equestrian, Moscow '80 Emblem — AP149

1980, Mar. 10 Engr. *Perf. 13*

C383 AP149	200fr shown	55	20
C384 AP149	300fr Yachting	80	35
C385 AP149	400fr Soccer	1.10	42
a.	Souvenir sheet of 3, #C383-C385	3.00	3.00

22nd Summer Olympic Games, Moscow, July 19-Aug. 3.
For overprints see Nos. C399-C401.

Jesus Carrying Cross, by Maurice Denis
AP150

Easter 1980: 500fr, Jesus before Pilate, by Dürer.

1980, Mar. 31

C386 AP150	480fr brn & org red	1.25	50
C387 AP150	500fr org red & brn	1.40	55

Kepler, Copernicus and Solar System Diagram — AP151

Design: 200fr, Kepler and diagram of earth's orbit, vert.

1980, Apr. 7 Engr. *Perf. 13*

C388 AP151 200fr multi	55	20
C389 AP151 300fr multi	80	35

Discovery of Pluto, 50th Anniversary — AP152

1980, Apr. 21

C390 AP152 420fr multi	1.10	70

Lunokhod I, Russian Flag — AP153

Design: 500fr, Apollo and Soyuz spacecraft, flags of US and Russia.

1980, Apr. 28

C391 AP153 480fr multi	1.25	50
C392 AP153 500fr multi	1.40	55

Lunokhod I, 10th anniversary; Apollo-Soyuz space test program, 5th anniversary.

Rochambeau, French Fleet Landing at Newport, R.I. — AP154

French Cooperation in American Revolution: 430fr, Rochambeau and George Washington, eagle.

1980, June 16 Engr. *Perf. 13*

C393 AP154 420fr multi	1.10	70
C394 AP154 430fr multi	1.20	70

Jet Flying Around Earth — AP155

Designs: No. C396, Ship, people, attack. No. C397, Astronaut on moon. No. C398, Space craft, scientists, moon. Nos. C395-C396 from "Around the World in 80 Days;" Nos. C397-C398 from "From Earth to Moon."

1980, June 30 Engr. *Perf. 11*

C395 AP155 100fr multi	25	15
C396 AP155 100fr multi	25	15
C397 AP155 150fr multi	40	15
C398 AP155 150fr multi	40	15
Set value		50

Jules Verne (1828-1905), French science fiction writer. Nos. C395-C398 each printed se-tenant with label showing various space scenes.

Nos. C383-C385a Overprinted:
200fr- CONCOURS COMPLET/ INDIVIDUEL/ROMAN (It.)/ BLINOV (Urss) /SALNIKOV (Urss)
300fr- FINN/RECHARDT (Fin.)/ MAYRHOFER (Autr.)/ BALACHOV (Urss)
400fr- TCHECOSLOVAQUIE/ ALLEMAGNE DE L'EST/URSS

1980, Sept. 8 Engr. *Perf. 13*

C399 AP149 200fr multi	55	20
C400 AP149 300fr multi	80	35
C401 AP149 400fr multi	1.10	42
a. Souvenir sheet of 3	2.50	2.50

Butterfly Type of 1980

1980, Oct. 6 Litho. *Perf. 13x12½*
Size: 48x36mm

C402 A137 420fr *Denaus chrysippus*	1.20	45

Charles De Gaulle, Map and Colors of France — AP156

1980, Nov. 9 Litho. *Perf. 13½x13*

C403 AP156 420fr shown	1.40	65
C404 AP156 430fr De Gaulle, cross	1.40	70

Charles De Gaulle, 10th anniv. of death.

Mali No. 140, Amtrak Train — AP157

Mali Stamps and Trains: 120fr, No. 195, Tokaido, Japan, vert. 200fr, No. 144, Rembrandt, Germany. 480fr, No. 143, TGV-001 France, vert.

1980, Nov. 17 Engr. *Perf. 13*

C405 AP157 120fr multi	32	15
C406 AP157 130fr multi	35	15
C407 AP157 200fr multi	55	20
C408 AP157 480fr multi	1.25	50

For overprint see No. C425.

Holy Family, by Lorenzo Lotto — AP158

Christmas 1980 (Paintings): 400fr, Flight to Egypt, by Rembrandt, vert. 500fr, Christmas Night, by Gauguin.

1980, Dec. 1 Litho. *Perf. 13x12½*

C409 AP158 300fr multi	80	38
C410 AP158 400fr multi	1.10	42
C411 AP158 500fr multi	1.40	60

Self-portrait, by Picasso AP159

1981, Jan. 26 Litho. *Perf. 12½x13*

C412 AP159 1000fr multi	2.50	1.10

Pablo Picasso (1881-1973), birth centenary.

Soccer Players — AP160

Designs: Soccer players.

1981, Feb. 28 *Perf. 13*

C413 AP160 100fr multi	25	15
C414 AP160 200fr multi	55	20
C415 AP160 300fr multi	80	35

Souvenir Sheet

C416 AP160 600fr multi	1.60	65

World Cup Soccer preliminary games.

Mozart and Instruments — AP161

225th Birth Anniversary of Wolfgang Amadeus Mozart: 430fr, Mozart and instruments, diff.

1981, Mar. 30 Litho. *Perf. 13*

C417 AP161 420fr multi	1.10	45
C418 AP161 430fr multi	1.20	50

Jesus Falls on the Way to Calvary, by Raphael AP162

Easter 1981: 600fr, Ecce Homo, by Rembrandt.

1981, Apr. 6 *Perf. 12½x13*

C419 AP162 500fr multi	1.40	60
C420 AP162 600fr multi	1.60	65

Alan B. Shepard — AP163 Exploration of Saturn — AP164

Space Anniversaries: No. C422, Yuri Gagarin's flight, 1961. 430fr, Uranus discovery bicentennial, horiz.

1981, Apr. 21 Litho. *Perf. 13*

C421 AP163 200fr multi	55	20
C422 AP163 200fr multi	55	20
C423 AP164 380fr multi	1.00	40
C424 AP163 430fr multi	1.20	50

No. C408 Overprinted: "26 fevrier 1981/Record du monde de/vitesse- 380 km/h."

1981, June 15 Engr.

C425 AP157 480fr multi	1.25	50

New railroad speed record.

US No. 233, Columbus and His Fleet — AP165

475th Death Anniversary of Christopher Columbus (Santa Maria and): 200fr, Spain No. 418, vert. 260fr, Spain No. 421, vert. 300fr, US No. 232.

1981, June 22

C426 AP165 180fr multi	50	20
C427 AP165 200fr multi	55	20
C428 AP165 260fr multi	70	30
C429 AP165 300fr multi	80	35

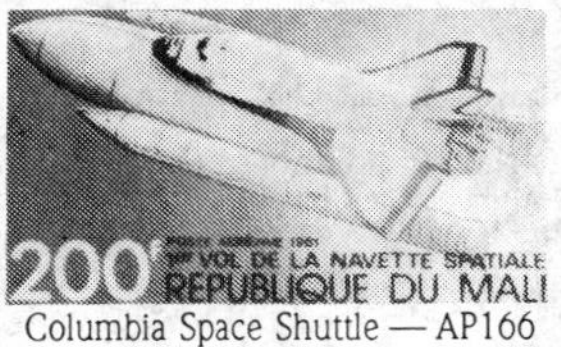

Columbia Space Shuttle — AP166

Designs: Space shuttle.

1981, July 6 Litho. *Perf. 13*

C430 AP166 200fr multi	55	20
C431 AP166 500fr multi	1.40	50
C432 AP166 600fr multi	1.60	65

Souvenir Sheet
Perf. 12

C433 AP166 700fr multi	2.00	80

For overprint see No. C440.

Buying Sets
Frequently it is less expensive to purchase complete sets rather than the individual stamps that make up the set. "Set Values" are provided for many such sets.

Harlequin on Horseback AP167

Picasso Birth Centenary: 750fr, Child Holding a Dove.

1981, July 15 *Perf. 12½x13*
C434 AP167 600fr multi 1.60 65
C435 AP167 750fr multi 2.25 1.00

Prince Charles and Lady Diana, St. Paul's Cathedral AP168

1981, July 20 *Perf. 12½*
C436 AP168 500fr shown 1.40 50
C437 AP168 700fr Couple, coach 2.00 80

Royal wedding.

Christmas 1981 AP169

Designs: Virgin and Child paintings.

1981, Nov. 9 **Litho.** *Perf. 12½x13*
C438 AP169 500fr Grunewald 1.40 50
C439 AP169 700fr Correggio 2.00 80

See Nos. C451-C452, C464-C466, C475-C477, C488-C489, C511.

No. C433 Overprinted In Blue: "JOE ENGLE / RICHARD TRULY / 2 eme VOL SPATIAL"

1981, Nov. 12 **Litho.** *Perf. 12*
C440 AP166 700fr multi 2.00 80

Nos. C369, C371 Overprinted with Winners' Names and Dates

1981, Dec. **Engr.** *Perf. 13*
C441 AP143 140fr multi 38 15
C442 AP143 300fr multi 80 35

Lewis Carroll (1832-1908) — AP170

Designs: Scenes from Alice in Wonderland.

1982, Jan. 30 **Litho.** *Perf. 12½*
C443 AP170 110fr multi 30 15
C444 AP170 130fr multi 35 15
C445 AP170 140fr multi 38 15

AP171 AP172

1982, Feb. 8 *Perf. 13*
C446 AP171 700fr Portrait, by Gilbert Stuart 2.00 80

George Washington's Birth, 250th anniv. Incorrectly inscribed "Stuart Gilbert."

1982, Mar. 15 **Litho.** *Perf. 13*

1982 World Cup: Various soccer players.

C447 AP172 220fr multi 60 22
C448 AP172 420fr multi 1.20 45
C449 AP172 500fr multi 1.40 50

Souvenir Sheet
Perf. 12½
C450 AP172 680fr multi 1.90 65

For overprints see Nos. C458-C461.

Art Type of 1981

Paintings: 680fr, Transfiguration, by Fra Angelico. 1000fr, Pieta, by Bellini, horiz.

Perf. 12½x13, 13x12½
1982, Apr. 19 **Litho.**
C451 AP169 680fr multi 1.90 65
C452 AP169 1000fr multi 2.50 1.00

Mali No. O30, France No. 1985 — AP174

1982, June 1 *Perf. 13*
C453 AP174 180fr shown 50 20
C454 AP174 200fr No. C356 55 20

PHILEXFRANCE '82 Intl. Stamp Exhibition, Paris, June 11-21. Nos. C453-C454 se-tenant with label showing show emblem and dates.

Fire Engine, France, 1850 — AP175

Designs: French fire engines.

1982, June 14
C455 AP175 180fr shown 50 20
C456 AP175 200fr 1921 55 22
C457 AP175 270fr 1982 70 28

Nos. C447-C450 Overprinted with Finalists' and Scores in Brown, Black, Blue or Red

1982, Aug. 16 **Litho.** *Perf. 13*
C458 AP172 220fr multi (Brn) 60 22
C459 AP172 420fr multi 1.20 45
C460 AP172 500fr multi (Bl) 1.40 50

Souvenir Sheet
Perf. 12½
C461 AP172 680fr multi (R) 1.90 65

Italy's victory in 1982 World Cup.

Scouting Year — AP176

1982 *Perf. 12½*
C462 AP176 300fr Tent, Baden-Powell 80 35
C463 AP176 500fr Salute, emblem 1.40 50

Art Type of 1981

Design: Boy with Cherries, by Edouard Manet (1832-83).

1982, Oct. 28 **Litho.** *Perf. 12½x13*
C464 AP169 680fr multi 1.90 65

Art Type of 1981

Madonna and Child Paintings.

1982, Nov. 10
C465 AP169 500fr Titian 1.40 50
C466 AP169 1000fr Bellini 2.50 1.00

Johann von Goethe (1749-1832), Poet — AP179

1982, Dec. 13 **Engr.** *Perf. 13*
C467 AP179 500fr multi 1.40 50

Follereau Type of 1974

1983, Jan. 24
C468 AP96 200fr dk brn 55 16

Vostok VI, 20th Anniv. — AP180 Manned Flight, 200th Anniv. — AP181

1983, Feb. 14 **Litho.** *Perf. 12½*
C469 AP180 400fr Valentina Tereshkova 1.10 35

1983, Feb. 28 *Perf. 13*
C470 AP181 500fr Eagle transatlantic balloon 1.40 50
C471 AP181 700fr Montgolfiere 2.00 90

Pre-Olympic Year — AP182

1983, Mar. 14 **Litho.** *Perf. 13*
C472 AP182 180fr Soccer 50 20
C473 AP182 270fr Hurdles 70 28
C474 AP182 300fr Wind surfing 80 35

Art Type of 1981

Raphael paintings.

1983, Mar. 28 *Perf. 12½x13*
C475 AP169 400fr Deposition 1.20 40
C476 AP169 600fr Transfiguration 1.60 55

Art Type of 1981

Design: Family of Acrobats with Monkey, by Picasso (1881-1973).

1983, Apr. 30 **Litho.** *Perf. 12½x13*
C477 AP169 680fr multi 1.60 80

Lions Intl. — AP185

1983, May 9 *Perf. 12½*
C478 Pair 4.00 1.90
a. AP185 700fr shown 2.00 90
b. AP185 700fr Rotary Intl. 2.00 90

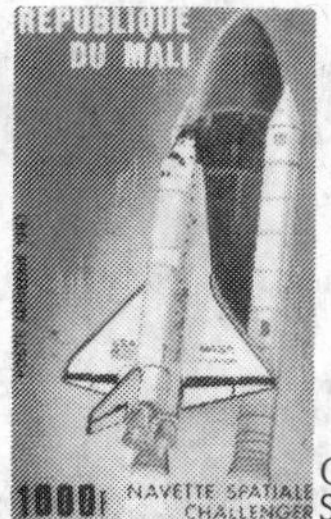

Challenger Spacecraft — AP186

1983, July 29 **Litho.** *Perf. 13*
C479 AP186 1000fr multi 2.50 90

Printed se-tenant with orange red label showing astronaut Sally Ride.

Paris-Dakar Auto Race — AP187

1983, Sept. 5 **Litho.** *Perf. 12½*
C480 AP187 240fr Mercedes, 1914 55 20
C481 AP187 270fr SSK, 1929 60 22
C482 AP187 500fr W196, 1954 1.20 42

Souvenir Sheet
C483 AP187 1000fr Mercedes van 2.50 1.00

For surcharge see No. C506.

Chess Game — AP188

1983, Oct. 24 Engr. *Perf. 13*
C484 AP188 300fr Pawn, bishop 90 35
C485 AP188 420fr Knight, castle 1.40 60
C486 AP188 500fr King, Queen 1.60 60

Souvenir Sheet
C487 AP188 700fr Various chess pieces 2.00 80

Art Type of 1981

Raphael Paintings.

1983, Nov. 7 Litho. *Perf. 12½x13*
C488 AP169 700fr Canigiani Madonna 2.00 80
C489 AP169 800fr Madonna with Lamb 2.50 90

Portrait of Leopold Zborowski, by Amedeo Modigliani (1884-1920) AP190

1984, Feb. 13 Litho. *Perf. 12½x13*
C490 AP190 700fr multi 2.00 60

Abraham Lincoln — AP191

Duke Ellington — AP192

1984, Feb. 27 *Perf. 12½*
C491 AP191 400fr Henri Dunant 1.20 35
C492 AP191 540fr shown 1.60 50

1984, Mar. 12 *Perf. 13½x13*
C493 AP192 470fr Sidney Bechet 1.50 40
C494 AP192 500fr shown 1.50 40

Glider — AP193

1984, Mar. 26
C495 AP193 270fr shown 80 25
C496 AP193 350fr Hang glider 1.10 40

1984 Summer Olympics — AP194

1984, Apr. 9 *Perf. 13*
C497 AP194 265fr Weight lifting 80 22
C498 AP194 440fr Equestrian 1.40 40
C499 AP194 500fr Hurdles 1.60 45

Souvenir Sheet
Perf. 12½
C500 AP194 700fr Wind surfing 2.00 90

For surcharges see Nos. C507-C510.

Easter 1984 — AP195

Paintings; 940fr, Crucifixion, by Rubens, vert. 970fr, Resurrection, by Mantegna.

1984, Apr. 24 Engr.
C501 AP195 940fr multi 3.00 80
C502 AP195 970fr multi 3.25 90

Gottlieb Daimler Birth Sesquicentenary — AP196

1984, June 1 Engr. *Perf. 13*
C503 AP196 350fr Mercedes Simplex 1.10 55
C504 AP196 470fr Mercedes-Benz 370-S 1.50 70
C505 AP196 485fr 500-SEC 1.60 80

No. C480 Overprinted and Surcharged

1984 Litho. *Perf. 12½*
C506 AP187 120fr on 240fr #C480 32 16

Nos. C497-C500 Overprinted and Surcharged

1984, Oct. Litho. *Perf. 13*
C507 AP194 135fr on 265fr 40 15
C508 AP194 220fr on 440fr 60 20
C509 AP194 250fr on 500fr 70 20

Souvenir Sheet
C510 AP194 350fr on 700fr 90 40

Overprints refer to the winners of the events depicted.

Art Type of 1981

Painting: Virgin and Child, by Lorenzo Lotto.

1984, Nov. 20 Litho. *Perf. 12½x13*
C511 AP169 500fr multi 1.40 42

Audubon Birth Bicentenary — AP198

1985, Apr. 15 Litho. *Perf. 13*
C512 AP198 180fr Kingfisher 45 16
C513 AP198 300fr Bustard, vert. 70 25
C514 AP198 470fr Ostrich, vert. 1.20 40
C515 AP198 540fr Buzzard 1.40 45

For surcharge see No. C560, C562, C567.

ASECNA Airlines, 25th Anniv. — AP199

1985, June 10 *Perf. 12½*
C516 AP199 700fr multi 1.90 60

For surcharge see No. C559.

PHILEXAFRICA Type of 1985

1985, June 24 *Perf. 13*
C517 A183 200fr Boy Scouts, lion 50 16
C518 A183 200fr Satellite communications 50 16

Nos. C517-C518 are printed se-tenant with center label picturing map of Africa or UAPT emblem.

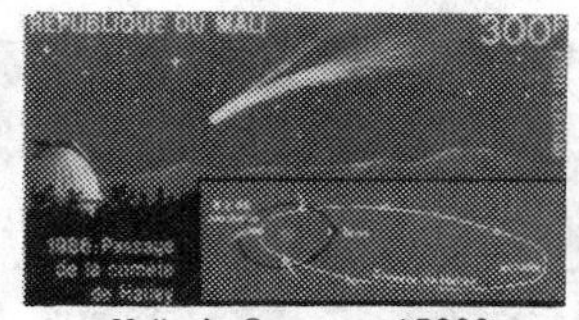

Halley's Comet — AP200

1986, Mar. 24 Litho. *Perf. 12½*
C519 AP200 300fr multi 1.10 38

For surcharge see No. C558.

Statue of Liberty, Cent. — AP201

1986, Apr. 7 *Perf. 13*
C520 AP201 600fr multi 2.25 70

Gottlieb Daimler Motorcycle — AP202

1986, Apr. 14
C521 AP202 400fr multi 1.50 50

1st Internal combustion automotive engine, cent.

Paul Robeson (1898-1976), American Actor, Singer — AP203

1986, May 10
C522 AP203 500fr Portrait, Show Boat 2.00 65

Karl Eberth (1835-1926), Bacteriologist, and Typhoid Bacilli AP204

World Chess Championships AP205

1986, June 7 Litho. *Perf. 12x12½*
C523 AP204 550fr multi 2.00 65

1986, June 16 *Perf. 12½*
C524 AP205 400fr Chessmen 1.50 50
C525 AP205 500fr Knight 2.00 60

Disappearance of Jean Mermoz, 50th Anniv. — AP206

Mermoz and: 150fr, Latecoere-300 seaplane. 600fr, Cams 53 Oiseau Tango, seaplane. 625fr, Flight map, Le Comte de La Vaulx aircraft.

1986, Aug. 18 Litho. *Perf. 13*
C526 AP206 150fr multi 60 22
C527 AP206 600fr multi 2.50 85
C528 AP206 625fr multi 2.50 85

Nos. C353-C355 Surcharged "1986-10e Anniversaire du 1er Vol/Commercial Supersonique" and New Value

1986, Sept. 29
C529 AP139 175fr on 120fr 70 38
C530 AP139 225fr on 130fr 1.00 50
C531 AP139 300fr on 200fr 1.10 60

Hansen, Leprosy Bacillus, Follereau and Lepers — AP207

1987, Jan. 26 Litho. *Perf. 13*
C532 AP207 500fr multi 2.00 1.00

Gerhard Hansen (1841-1912), Norwegian physician who discovered the leprosy bacillus (1869); Raoul Follereau (1903-1977), philanthropist.

Konrad Adenauer (1876-1967), West German Chancellor — AP208

1987, Mar. 9 Litho. *Perf. 13*
C533 AP208 625fr org, buff & blk 2.25 1.10

Pre-Olympics Year — AP209

Buddha and: 400fr, Runners. 500fr, Soccer players.

1987, Apr. 6 **Engr.**

C534 AP209 400fr blk & red brn 1.50 70
C535 AP209 500fr lil rose, ol grn & ol 2.00 1.00

25th Summer Olympics, Seoul, 1988.

Al Jolson in The Jazz Singer — AP210

1987, Apr. 20

C536 AP210 550fr dk red brn & car rose 2.00 1.00

Sound films, 60th anniv.

Albert John Luthuli (1899-1967), 1960 Nobel Peace Prize Winner — AP211

1987, May 26 **Engr.** ***Perf. 13***

C537 AP211 400fr multi 1.50 75

Service Organizations AP212

1987, June 8 **Litho.** ***Perf. 13***

C538 AP212 500fr Rotary Int'l. 2.00 1.00
C539 AP212 500fr Lions Int'l. 2.00 1.00

Coubertin, Ancient Greek Runners, Contemporary Athletes — AP213

1988, Feb. 14 **Litho.** ***Perf. 13***

C540 AP213 240fr shown 1.10 60
C541 AP213 400fr 5-ring emblem, stadium 2.00 1.00

125th birth anniv. of Baron Pierre de Coubertin (1863-1937), French educator and sportsman who promulgated revival of the Olympic Games; 1988 Summer Olympics, Seoul.

For surcharge see No. C.565

Harlequin, by Pablo Picasso (1881-1973), Spanish Painter and Sculptor AP214

1988, Apr. 4 **Litho.** ***Perf. 13***

C542 AP214 600fr multi 4.25 1.15

For surcharge see No. C563.

1st Scheduled Transatlantic Flight of the Concorde (London-New York), 15th Anniv. — AP215

1988, May 2 ***Perf. 13***

C543 AP215 500fr multi 3.50 1.75

Home Improvement for a Verdant Mali — AP216

1989, Feb. 6 **Litho.** ***Perf. 12½***

C544 AP216 5fr shown 15 15
C545 AP216 10fr Furnace, tree, field 15 15
C546 AP216 25fr like 5fr 18 15
C547 AP216 100fr like 10fr 70 35
Set value 1.00 50

1st Man on the Moon, 20th Anniv. — AP217

1989, Mar. 13 **Engr.** ***Perf. 13***

C548 AP217 300fr multi. 2.10 1.05
C549 AP217 500fr multi, vert. 3.50 1.75

For surcharges see Nos. C561, C564.

French Revolution, Bicent. AP218

1989, July 3 **Engr.** ***Perf. 13***

C550 AP218 400fr Women's march on Versailles 2.35 1.20
C551 AP218 600fr Storming of the Bastille 3.50 1.75

For surcharges see Nos. C566, C568.

World Cup Soccer Championships, Italy — AP219

1990, June 4 **Litho.** ***Perf. 13***

C552 AP219 200fr multi 1.20 60
C553 AP219 225fr multi, diff. 1.35 68

Souvenir Sheet

C554 AP219 500fr like #C552 3.00 1.50

No. C552 overprinted in red "ITALIE : 2 / ANGLETERRE : 1"

No. C553 overprinted in red "R.F.A. : 1 / ARGENTINE : 0"

No. C554 overprinted in red in margin "1er : R.F.A. 2eme : ARGENTINE 3eme : ITALIE"

1990

C555 AP219 200fr on #C552 1.20 60
C556 AP219 225fr on #C553 1.35 68

Souvenir Sheet

C557 AP219 500fr on #C554 3.00 1.50

Various Stamps of 1985-89 Surcharged Like #579-594

1992, June ***Perfs. as Before***

Printing Methods as Before

C558 AP200 20fr on 300fr #C519 16 15
C559 AP199 20fr on 700fr #C516 16 15
C560 AP198 30fr on 180fr #C512 24 15
C561 AP217 30fr on 500fr #C549 24 15
C562 AP198 100fr on 540fr #C515 80 40
C563 AP214 100fr on 600fr #C542 80 40
C564 AP217 150fr on 300fr #C548 1.20 60
C565 AP213 150fr on 400fr #C541 1.20 60
C566 AP218 150fr on 400fr #C550 1.20 60
C567 AP198 200fr on 300fr #C513 1.60 80
C568 AP218 240fr on 600fr #C551 1.95 1.00
Nos. C558-C568 (11) 9.55 5.00

Size and location of surcharge varies. No. C565 also overprinted "BARCELONE 92."

POSTAGE DUE STAMPS

Bambara Headpiece — D1

Perf. 14x13½

1961, Mar. 18 **Engr.** **Unwmk.**

J1	D1	1fr	black	15	15
J2	D1	2fr	bright ultra	15	15
J3	D1	5fr	red lilac	15	15
J4	D1	10fr	orange	16	15
J5	D1	20fr	bright green	20	15
J6	D1	25fr	red brown	22	18
			Set value	80	65

Polyptychus Roseus — D2

Designs: No. J8, Deilephila Nerii. No. J9, Gynanisa maja. No. J10, Bunaea alcinoe. No. J11, Teracolus eris. No. J12, Colotis antevippe. No. J13, Charaxes epijasius. No. J14, Manatha microcera. No. J15, Hypokopelates otraeda. No. J16, Lipaphnaeus leonina. No. J17, Gonimbrasia hecate. No. J18, Lobounaea christyi. No. J19, Hypolimnas misippus. No. J20, Catopsilia florella.

1964, June 1 **Photo.** ***Perf. 11***

Butterflies and Moths in Natural Colors

J7	D2	1fr	olive green	15	15
J8	D2	1fr	org & brn	15	15
J9	D2	2fr	emer & brn	15	15
J10	D2	2fr	emer & brn	15	15
J11	D2	3fr	rose lil & brn	15	15
J12	D2	3fr	rose lil & brn	15	15
J13	D2	5fr	blk & rose	15	15
J14	D2	5fr	green	15	15
J15	D2	10fr	yel, org & blk	15	15
J16	D2	10fr	blue	15	15
J17	D2	20fr	lt bl & brn	22	22
J18	D2	20fr	lt bl & brn	22	22
J19	D2	25fr	grn & yel	30	30
J20	D2	25fr	dp grn & blk	30	30
			Set value	1.80	1.80

The two stamps of the same denomination are printed together in the sheet, se-tenant at the base.

Nos. J7-J20 Surcharged

1984 **Photo.** ***Perf. 11***

J21	D2	5fr	on 1fr #J7	15	15
J22	D2	5fr	on 1fr #J8	15	15
J23	D2	10fr	on 2fr #J9	15	15
J24	D2	10fr	on 2fr #J10	15	15
J25	D2	15fr	on 3fr #J11	15	15
J26	D2	15fr	on 3fr #J12	15	15
J27	D2	25fr	on 5fr #J13	15	15
J28	D2	25fr	on 5fr #J14	15	15
J29	D2	50fr	on 10fr #J15	15	15
J30	D2	50fr	on 10fr #J16	15	15
J31	D2	100fr	on 20fr #J17	25	25
J32	D2	100fr	on 20fr #J18	25	25
J33	D2	125fr	on 25fr #J19	35	35
J34	D2	125fr	on 25fr #J20	35	35
			Set value	1.85	1.85

OFFICIAL STAMPS

Dogon Mask — O1

Mali Coat of Arms — O2

Perf. 14x13½

1961, Mar. 18 **Engr.** **Unwmk.**

O1	O1	1fr	gray	15	15
O2	O1	2fr	red orange	15	15
O3	O1	3fr	black	15	15
O4	O1	5fr	light blue	15	15
O5	O1	10fr	bister brown	15	15
O6	O1	25fr	brt ultra	15	15
O7	O1	30fr	car rose	20	15
O8	O1	50fr	Prus green	35	15
O9	O1	85fr	red brown	50	30
O10	O1	100fr	emerald	65	35
O11	O1	200fr	red lilac	1.20	75
			Set value	3.25	1.85

1964, June 1 Photo. *Perf. 12½*

National Colors and Arms in Multicolor, Background in Light Green

O12 O2	1fr	green	15	15
O13 O2	2fr	light vio	15	15
O14 O2	3fr	gray	15	15
O15 O2	5fr	lilac rose	15	15
O16 O2	10fr	bright blue	15	15
O17 O2	25fr	ocher	16	16
O18 O2	30fr	dark green	18	18
O19 O2	50fr	orange	25	25
O20 O2	85fr	dark brown	40	40
O21 O2	100fr	red	50	40
O22 O2	200fr	dk vio bl	1.10	40
		Set value	2.80	2.00

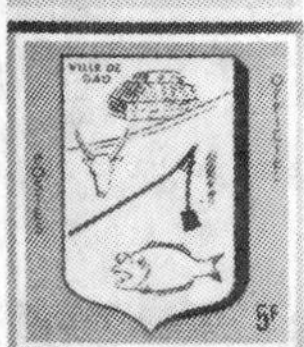

City Coats of Arms — O3

1981, Sept. Photo. *Perf. 12½x13*

O23 O3	5fr	Gao	15	15
O24 O3	15fr	Timbuktu	15	15
O25 O3	50fr	Mopti	15	15
O26 O3	180fr	Segou	30	16
O27 O3	200fr	Sikasso	40	20
O28 O3	680fr	Koulikoro	1.20	60
O29 O3	700fr	Kayes	1.40	65
O30 O3	1000fr	Bamako	2.00	1.00
		Nos. O23-O30 (8)	5.75	3.06

Nos. O23-O30 Surcharged

1984 Photo. *Perf. 12½x13*

O31 O3	15fr	on 5fr	15	15
O32 O3	50fr	on 15fr	15	15
O33 O3	120fr	on 50fr	35	15
O34 O3	295fr	on 180fr	80	40
O35 O3	470fr	on 200fr	1.25	60
O36 O3	515fr	on 680fr	1.40	65
O37 O3	845fr	on 700fr	2.25	1.10
O38 O3	1225fr	on 1000fr	3.50	1.40
		Nos. O31-O38 (8)	9.85	4.60

MANCHUKUO

LOCATION — Covering Manchuria, or China's three northeastern provinces--Fengtien, Kirin and Heilungkiang--plus Jehol province.

GOVT. — A former independent state under Japanese influence

AREA — 503,013 sq. mi. (estimated)

POP. — 43,233,954 (est. 1940)

CAPITAL — Hsinking (Changchun)

Manchukuo was formed in 1932 with the assistance of Japan. In 1934 Henry Pu-yi, Chief Executive, was enthroned as Emperor Kang Teh. In 1945, when Japan surrendered to the Allies, the terms included the return of Manchukuo to China. The puppet state was dissolved.

100 Fen = 1 Yuan

Watermarks

Wmk. 141- Horizontal Zigzag Lines

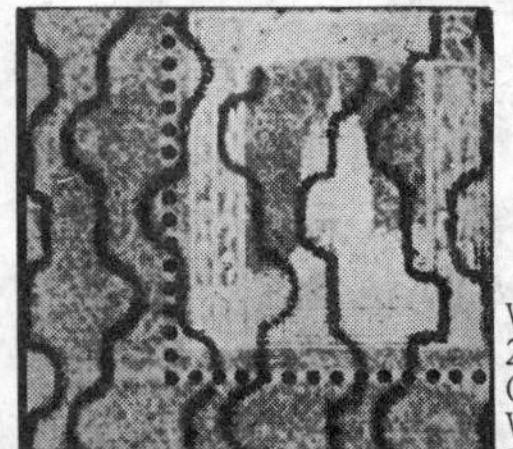

Wmk. 239- Curved Wavy Lines

Wmk. 242- Characters

Pagoda at Liaoyang A1

Chief Executive Henry Pu-yi A2

Five characters in top label.

Inscription reads "Manchu State Postal Administration."

Perf. 13x13½

Lithographed

1932, July 26 Unwmk.

White Paper

1	A1	½f	gray brown	1.00	65
2	A1	1f	dull red	1.40	30
3	A1	1½f	lilac	3.50	2.00
4	A1	2f	slate	2.75	80
5	A1	3f	dull brown	6.25	3.00
6	A1	4f	olive green	2.00	40
7	A1	5f	green	2.50	50
8	A1	6f	rose	7.25	1.50
9	A1	7f	gray	2.50	80
10	A1	8f	ocher	11.00	6.00
11	A1	10f	orange	3.25	40
12	A2	13f	dull brown	8.75	4.50
13	A2	15f	rose	8.75	2.00
14	A2	16f	turquoise grn	19.00	7.50
15	A2	20f	gray brown	6.25	1.50
16	A2	30f	orange	6.25	1.75
17	A2	50f	olive green	14.00	3.00
18	A2	1y	violet	30.00	7.50
			Nos. 1-18 (18)	136.40	44.10

A local provisional overprint of a horizontal line of four characters in red or black, reading "Chinese Postal Administration," was applied to Nos. 1-18 by followers of Gen. Su Ping-wen, who rebelled against the Manchukuo government in September, 1932. Many counterfeits exist.

See Nos. 23-31. For surcharges see Nos. 36, 59-61.

Flags, Map and Wreath — A3

Old State Council Building — A4

1933, Mar. 1 *Perf. 12½*

19	A3	1f	orange	4.00	3.00
20	A4	2f	dull green	10.50	7.00
21	A3	4f	light red	4.00	3.00
22	A4	10f	deep blue	27.50	18.00

1st anniv. of the establishing of the State. Nos. 19-22 were printed in sheets of 100 with a special printing in sheets of 20.

Type of 1932

Perf. 13x13½

1934, Feb. Engr. Wmk. 239

Granite Paper

23	A1	½f	dk brn	1.50	1.00
24	A1	1f	red brn	1.50	75
25	A1	1½f	dk vio	2.50	1.25
26	A1	2f	slate	3.50	1.00
27	A1	3f	brown	2.25	40
28	A1	4f	ol brn	20.00	2.50
29	A1	10f	dp org	6.00	70
30	A2	15f	rose	375.00	150.00
31	A2	1y	violet	17.00	7.50
			Nos. 23-31 (9)	429.25	165.10

For surcharge see No. 60.

Emperor's Palace — A5

Phoenix — A6

1934, Mar. 1 *Perf. 12½*

32	A5	1½f	org brn	3.50	1.75
33	A6	3f	carmine	3.50	1.50
34	A5	6f	green	6.50	6.00
35	A6	10f	dk bl	17.50	7.00

Enthronement of Emperor Kang Teh. Nos. 32-35 were printed in sheets of 100, with a special printing in sheets of 20.

No. 6 Surcharged in Black

壹 暫
分 作

Perf. 13x13½

1934 Unwmk. White Paper

36	A1	1f	on 4f ol grn	3.50	2.00
a.			Brown surcharge	24.00	15.00
b.			Upper left character of surcharge omitted		
c.			Inverted surcharge	80.00	80.00

Pagoda at Liaoyang A7

Emperor Kang Teh A8

Six characters in top label instead of five as in 1932-34 issues.

Inscription reads "Manchu Empire Postal Administration."

Perf. 13x13½

1934-36 Wmk. 239 Engr.

Granite Paper

37	A7	½f	brown	40	25
38	A7	1f	red brn	50	25
39	A7	1½f	dk vio	85	40
a.			Booklet pane of 6	40.00	
41	A7	3f	brn ('35)	50	30
a.			Booklet pane of 6	45.00	
42	A7	5f	dk bl ('35)	5.00	90
43	A7	5f	gray ('36)	2.25	75
44	A7	6f	rose ('35)	2.25	40
45	A7	7f	dk gray ('36)	2.00	1.50
47	A7	9f	red org ('35)	2.25	50
50	A8	15f	ver ('35)	1.75	60
51	A8	18f	Prus grn ('35)	20.00	3.00
52	A8	20f	dk brn ('35)	2.75	60
53	A8	30f	org brn ('35)	3.50	60
54	A8	50f	ol grn ('35)	4.50	1.25
55	A8	1y	dk vio ('35)	14.00	4.50
a.			1y violet	14.00	6.75
			Nos. 37-55 (15)	62.50	15.80

4f and 8f, type A7, were prepared but not issued.

1935 Wmk. 242 *Perf. 13x13½*

57	A7	10f	deep blue	7.00	85
58	A8	13f	light brown	7.50	3.25

Nos. 6 and 28 Surcharged in Black

三 暫
分 作

1935 White Paper Unwmk.

59	A1	3f	on 4f ol grn	47.50	40.00

1935 Granite Paper Wmk. 239

60	A1	3f	on 4f ol brn	4.75	2.75

Similar Surcharge on No. 14

1935 White Paper Unwmk.

61	A2	3f	on 16f turq grn	11.00	7.25

Orchid Crest of Manchukuo A9

Sacred White Mountains and Black Waters A10

1935, Jan. 1 Litho. Wmk. 141

Granite Paper

62	A9	2f	green	3.00	1.25
63	A10	4f	dl ol grn	1.10	90
64	A9	8f	ocher	2.50	1.00
65	A10	12f	brn red	8.50	2.50

Nos. 62-65 exist imperforate.

1935 Wmk. 242

66	A9	2f	yel grn	3.00	45
68	A9	8f	ocher	5.25	1.40
70	A10	12f	brown red	9.00	3.25

Nos. 62-70 issued primarily to pay postage to China, but valid for any postal use.

See Nos. 75-78, 113, 115, 158. For surcharges see Nos. 101, 103-104, 106-109, People's Republic of China No. 2L19.

Mt. Fuji — A11

Phoenix — A12

Perf. 11, 12½ and Compound

1935, Apr. 1 Engr. Wmk. 242

71	A11	1½f	dl grn	1.90	1.10
72	A12	3f	orange	2.00	1.75
a.			3f red orange	5.00	4.00
73	A11	6f	dk car	4.50	3.75
a.			Horiz. pair, imperf. btwn.	175.00	
b.			Perf. 11x12½	25.00	25.00
74	A12	10f	dk bl	5.00	5.25
a.			Perf. 12½x11	20.00	17.50
b.			Perf. 12½	20.00	

Visit of the Emperor of Manchukuo to Tokyo.

Orchid Crest — A13

Types of A9 & A10

Redrawn and Engraved

1936 Wmk. 242 *Perf. 13x13½*

75	A13	2f	lt grn	50	22
76	A10	4f	ol grn	2.25	50
77	A13	8f	ocher	1.25	50
78	A10	12f	org brn	30.00	17.50

Unbroken lines of shading in the background of Nos. 76 and 78. Shading has been removed from right and left of the mountains. Nearly all lines have been removed from the lake. There are numerous other alterations in the design.

Issued primarily to pay postage to China, but valid for any postal use.

See #112. For surcharges see #102-106.

Wild Goose over Sea of Japan — A14

Communications Building at Hsinking — A15

Perf. 12x12½, 12½x12

1936, Jan. 26 **Wmk. 242**

79 A14 1½f blk brn 1.90 1.75
80 A15 3f rose lilac 1.90 50
81 A14 6f car rose 5.00 4.00
82 A15 10f blue 6.25 5.00

Postal convention with Japan.

New State Council Building A16

Carting Soybeans A17

North Mausoleum at Mukden A18

Summer Palace at Chengteh A19

1936-37 **Wmk. 242** ***Perf. 13x13½***

83 A16 ½f brown 35 15
84 A16 1f red brn 35 15
85 A16 1½f violet 3.00 2.25
a. Booklet pane of 6 55.00
86 A17 2f lt grn ('37) 35 15
a. Booklet pane of 6 12.00
87 A16 3f chocolate 35 15
a. Booklet pane of 6 100.00
88 A18 4f lt ol grn ('37) 35 15
a. Booklet pane of 6 12.00
89 A16 5f gray blk 15.00 6.00
90 A17 6f carmine 40 15
91 A18 7f brn blk 50 15
92 A18 9f red org 60 20
93 A19 10f blue 60 15
94 A18 12f dp org ('37) 50 15
95 A18 13f brown 27.50 19.00
96 A18 15f carmine 1.00 30
97 A17 20f dk brn 1.00 30
98 A19 30f chestnut brn 1.00 30
99 A17 50f olive grn 1.25 40
100 A19 1y violet 2.50 50
Nos. 83-100 (18) 56.60 30.60

Nos. 83, 84, 86, 88 and 93 are known imperforate but were not regularly issued.

See Nos. 159-163. For overprints see Nos. 140-141, 148-151. For surcharges see People's Republic of China Nos. 2L1-2L2, 2L11-2L18, 2L20-2L37, 2L40-2L52.

暫作 貳分五厘
a

暫作 五分
b

暫作 壹角參分
c

暫作 二分五厘
d

1937

Surcharged on No. 66

101 A9 (a) 2½f on 2f 1.50 1.25

Surcharged on Nos. 75, 76 and 78

102 A13 (a) 2½f on 2f 1.50 1.25
103 A10 (b) 5f on 4f 2.00 1.75
104 A10 (c) 13f on 12f 8.00 7.50

Surcharged in Black on Nos. 75, 76 and 70

Space between bottom characters of surcharge 4½mm

105 A13 (d) 2½f on 2f 1.50 1.25
a. Inverted surcharge 100.00 75.00
b. Vert. pair, one without surch. 85.00
106 A10 (b) 5f on 4f 2.25 1.50
107 A10 (c) 13f on 12f 7.00 4.50

Surcharged on No. 70

Space between characters 6½mm

108 A10 (c) 13f on 12f 150.00 105.00

Same Surcharge on No. 63

Space between characters 4½mm

Wmk. 141

109 A10 (b) 5f on 4f 4.75 3.00
Nos. 101-109 (9) 178.50 127.00

Nos. 101-109 were issued primarily to pay postage to China, but were valid for any postal use.

Rising Sun over Manchurian Plain — A20

Composite Picture of Manchurian City — A21

Perf. 12½

1937, Mar. 1 **Litho.** **Unwmk.**

110 A20 1½f car rose 2.25 1.65
111 A21 3f bl grn 2.00 1.65

5th anniv. of the founding of the State of Manchukuo.

Types of 1936

Perf. 13x13½

1937 **Wmk. 242** **Engr.**

112 A13 2½f dk vio 60 25
113 A10 5f black 20 15
115 A10 13f dk red brn 40 25

Issued primarily to pay postage to China, but were valid for any postal use.

Pouter Pigeon A22

National Flag and Buildings A23

Perf. 12x12½

1937, Sept. 16 **Unwmk.**

116 A22 2f dk vio 1.25 1.25
117 A23 4f rose car 1.25 85
118 A22 10f dk grn 2.75 1.65
119 A23 20f dk bl 3.75 3.50

Completion of the national capital, Hsinking, under the first Five-Year Construction Plan.

Map — A24

Dept. of Justice Building — A27

Japanese Residents' Association Building A25

Postal Administration Building — A26

Perf. 12x12½, 13

1937, Dec. 1 **Litho.** **Unwmk.**

121 A24 2f dk car 80 65
122 A25 4f green 1.40 90
123 A25 8f orange 3.25 2.50
124 A26 10f blue 3.25 3.00
125 A27 12f lt vio 4.00 3.75
126 A26 20f lil brn 4.50 4.00
Nos. 121-126 (6) 17.20 14.80

Issued in commemoration of the abolition of extraterritorial rights within Manchukuo.

New Year Greetings — A28

Map and Cross — A29

1937, Dec. 15 **Engr.** ***Perf. 12x12½***

127 A28 2f dk bl & red 1.65 50
a. Double impression of border

Issued to pay postage on New Year's greeting cards.

Wmk. 242

1938, Oct. 15 **Litho.** ***Perf. 13***

128 A29 2f lake & scar 55 50
129 A29 4f slate grn & scar 55 50

Founding of the Red Cross Society in Manchukuo.

Network of State Railroads in Manchukuo A30

Express Train "Asia" A31

1939, Oct. 21

130 A30 2f dk org, blk & dp bl 75 65
131 A31 4f dp bl & indigo 75 65

Attainment of 10,000 kilometers in the railway mileage in Manchuria.

Stork Flying above Mast of Imperial Flagship — A32

1940 **Photo.** **Unwmk.**

132 A32 2f brt red vio 16 16
133 A32 4f brt grn 20 20

Second visit of Emperor Kang Teh to Emperor Hirohito of Japan.

Census Taker and Map of Manchukuo — A33

Census Form — A34

1940, Sept. 10 **Litho.** **Wmk. 242**

134 A33 2f vio brn & org 16 16
135 A34 4f blk & grn 25 20
a. Double impression of green 27.50

National census starting Oct. 1.

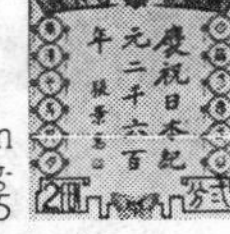

Message of Congratulation from Premier Chang Ching-hui — A35

Dragon Dance A36

1940, Sept. 18 **Engr.**

136 A35 2f carmine 16 20
137 A36 4f indigo 25 30
a. Imperf., pair 80.00

2600th anniversary of the birth of the Japanese Empire.

Soldier — A37

1941, May 25 **Photo.** **Unwmk.**

138 A37 2f dp car 18 18
139 A37 4f brt ultra 25 25

Conscription Law, effective June 1, 1941.

Nos. 86 and 88 Overprinted in Red or Blue

紀念新嘉坡
復歸我東亞
年九德康

Perf. 13x13½

1942, Feb. 16 **Wmk. 242**

140 A17 2f lt grn (R) 16 16
141 A18 4f lt ol grn (Bl) 20 20

"Return of Singapore to East Asia, 9th year of Kang Teh."

Kengoku Shrine A38

Map of Manchukuo A39

Flag of Manchukuo — A40

Perf. 12x12½, 12½x12

1942, Mar. 1 **Engr.**

142 A38 2f carmine 25 25
143 A38 4f lilac 25 25
144 A39 10f red, *yel* 70 70
145 A40 20f indigo, *yel* 90 90

"10th anniv. of Manchukuo, Mar. 1, 1942".

Allegory of National Harmony — A41

Women of Five Races, Dancing — A42

1942, Sept. 15

No.	Type	Description	Unused	Used
146	A41	3f orange	25	25
147	A42	6f light green	35	35

"10th anniv. of the founding of Manchukuo, Sept. 15, 1942."

Nos. 87 and 90 Overprinted in Green or Blue

1942, Dec. 8 *Perf. 13x13½*

No.	Type	Description	Unused	Used
148	A16	3f chocolate (G)	20	20
149	A17	6f carmine (Bl)	20	20

1st anniv. of the "Greater East Asia War."
The overprint reads "Asiatic Prosperity Began This Day December 8, 1941."

Nos. 87 and 90 Overprinted in Red or Blue

1943, May 1

No.	Type	Description	Unused	Used
150	A16	3f chocolate (R)	20	20
151	A17	6f carmine (Bl)	20	20

Proclamation of the labor service law.

Red Cross Nurse Carrying Stretcher
A43

Smelting Furnace
A44

1943, Oct. 1 **Photo.**

No.	Type	Description	Unused	Used
152	A43	6f green	20	20

5th anniv. of the founding of the Red Cross Society of Manchukuo, Oct. 1, 1938.

1943, Dec. 8 **Unwmk.** *Perf. 13*

No.	Type	Description	Unused	Used
153	A44	6f red brown	20	20

2nd anniv. of the "Greater East Asia War."

Chinese Characters
A45

Japanese Characters
A46

Perf. 13x13½

1944 **Wmk. 242** **Litho.**

No.	Type	Description	Unused	Used
154	A45	10f rose	60	60
a.		Imperf., vert. pair #154, 155	4.00	4.00
b.		Vert. pair #154, 155	1.25	1.25
155	A46	10f rose	60	60
156	A45	40f gray green	1.50	1.50
a.		Imperf., vert. pair #156, 157	7.50	7.50
b.		40f with 10f vignette, perf.	45.00	40.00
c.		40f with 10f vignette, imperf.	90.00	
d.		Vert. pair #156, 157	3.00	3.00
157	A46	40f gray green	1.50	1.50

"Japan's Progress Is Manchukuo's Progress." Issued as propaganda for the close relationship of Japan and Manchukuo.
Frames of the 10f vignettes have rounded corners, those of the 40f vignettes have indented corners.

Types of 1935 and 1936-37

1944-45 **Litho.**

No.	Type	Description	Unused	Used
158	A10	5f gray black	50	60
a.		Imperf., pair	3.50	
159	A17	6f crimson rose	1.25	1.25
160	A19	10f light blue	90	1.50
161	A17	20f brown	1.00	1.50
162	A19	30f buff ('45)	1.25	1.50
163	A19	1y dull lilac	1.50	2.25
		Nos. 158-163 (6)	6.40	8.60

For surcharges see People's Republic of China Nos. 2L1, 2L14, 2L19, 2L24, 2L27, 2L30-2L31, 2L35, 2L37, 2L49, 2L52.

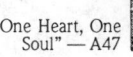

"One Heart, One Soul" — A47

1945, May 2

No.	Type	Description	Unused	Used
164	A47	10f red	25	25
a.		Imperf., pair	2.00	2.00

10th anniv. of the emperor's edict issued May 2, 1935.

AIR POST STAMPS

Sheep Grazing
AP1

Railroad Bridge
AP2

Wmk. Characters (242)
Perf. 13x13½

1936-37 **Engr.** **Granite Paper**

No.	Type	Description	Unused	Used
C1	AP1	18f green	10.00	5.50
C2	AP1	19f bl grn ('37)	2.50	1.75
C3	AP2	38f blue	10.00	10.00
C4	AP2	39f dp bl ('37)	1.10	1.00

MARIANA ISLANDS

LOCATION — A group of 14 islands in the West Pacific Ocean, about 1500 miles east of the Philippines.
GOVT. — Former possession of Spain, then of Germany
AREA — 246 sq. mi.
POP. — 44,025 (1935)
CAPITAL — Saipan

Until 1899 this group belonged to Spain but in that year all except Guam were ceded to Germany.

100 Centavos = 1 Peso
100 Pfennig = 1 Mark (1899)

Issued under Spanish Dominion

King Alfonso XIII — A1

Stamps of the Philippines Handstamped Vertically in Blackish Violet Reading Up or Down

1899, Sept. **Unwmk.** *Perf. 14*

No.	Type	Description	Unused	Used
1	A1	2c dk bl grn	350.00	70.00
2	A1	3c dk brn	250.00	67.50
3	A1	5c car rose	350.00	70.00
4	A1	6c dark blue	1,500.	425.00
5	A1	8c gray brn	225.00	70.00
6	A1	15c slate grn	850.00	425.00

Overprint forgeries of Nos. 1-6 exist.

Issued under German Dominion

Stamps of Germany, 1889-90, Overprinted in Black at 56 degree Angle

Perf. 13½x14½

1900, May **Unwmk.**

No.	Type	Description	Unused	Used
11	A9	3pf dk brn	15.00	30.00
12	A9	5pf green	18.00	30.00
13	A10	10pf carmine	22.50	30.00
14	A10	20pf ultra	27.50	115.00
15	A10	25pf orange	60.00	125.00
b.		Inverted overprint	2,000.	
16	A10	50pf red brn	60.00	125.00
		Nos. 11-16 (6)	203.00	455.00

Forged cancellations exist on Nos. 11-16, 17-29.

Overprinted at 48 degree Angle

1899, Nov. 18

No.	Type	Description	Unused	Used
11a	A9	3pf light brown	1,500.	1,100.
12a	A9	5pf green	2,000.	1,050.
13a	A10	10pf carmine	225.00	225.00
14a	A10	20pf ultra	250.00	275.00
15a	A10	25pf orange	2,500.	1,750.
16a	A10	50pf red brown	2,500.	1,750.

Kaiser's Yacht "Hohenzollern"
A4 A5

1901, Jan. **Typo.** *Perf. 14*

No.	Type	Description	Unused	Used
17	A4	3pf brown	90	90
18	A4	5pf green	90	90
19	A4	10pf carmine	90	2.75
20	A4	20pf ultra	1.00	6.25
21	A4	25pf org & blk, *yel*	1.75	12.00
22	A4	30pf org & blk, *sal*	1.75	12.00
23	A4	40pf lake & blk	1.90	12.00
24	A4	50pf pur & blk, *sal*	1.90	14.00
25	A4	80pf lake & blk, *rose*	3.00	27.50

Engr.
Perf. 14½x14

No.	Type	Description	Unused	Used
26	A5	1m carmine	3.50	70.00
27	A5	2m blue	6.25	85.00
28	A5	3m blk vio	9.00	130.00
29	A5	5m slate & car	150.00	450.00
		Nos. 17-29 (13)	182.75	

Wmk. Lozenges (125)

1916-19 **Typo.** *Perf. 14*

No.	Type	Description	Unused	Used
30	A4	3pf brown ('19)	1.00	

Engr.
Perf. 14½x14

No.	Type	Description	Unused	Used
31	A5	5m slate & car	22.50	

Nos. 30 and 31 were never placed in use.

MARIENWERDER

LOCATION — Northeastern Germany, bordering on Poland
GOVT. — A former district of West Prussia

By the Versailles Treaty the greater portion of West Prussia was ceded to Poland but the district of Marienwerder was allowed a plebiscite which was held in 1920 and resulted in favor of Germany.

100 Pfennig = 1 Mark

Plebiscite Issues

Symbolical of Allied Supervision of the Plebiscite — A1

1920 **Unwmk.** **Litho.** *Perf. 11½*

No.	Type	Description	Unused	Used
1	A1	5pf green	42	35
2	A1	10pf rose red	32	28
3	A1	15pf gray	45	40
4	A1	20pf brn org	28	22
5	A1	25pf deep blue	65	55
6	A1	30pf orange	1.00	85
7	A1	40pf brown	65	55
8	A1	50pf violet	65	45
9	A1	60pf red brown	4.00	2.75
10	A1	75pf chocolate	1.00	90
11	A1	1m brn & grn	80	70
12	A1	2m dk vio	4.00	3.25
13	A1	3m red	4.75	3.75
14	A1	5m blue & rose	20.00	16.00
		Nos. 1-14 (14)	38.97	31.00

These stamps occasionally show parts of two papermakers" watermarks, consisting of the letters "O. B. M." with two stars before and after, or "P. & C. M."
Nos. 1-14 exist imperf.; value for set, $700. Nearly all exist part perf.

Stamps of Germany, 1905-19, Overprinted

Commission
Interalliée
Marienwerder

1920 **Wmk. 125** *Perf. 14, 14½*

No.	Type	Description	Unused	Used
24	A16	5pf green	15.00	25.00
a.		Inverted overprint	130.00	210.00
26	A16	20pf bl vio	6.00	10.00
a.		Inverted overprint	80.00	130.00
b.		Double overprint	165.00	150.00
28	A16	50pf vio & blk, *buff*	225.00	600.00
29	A16	75pf grn & blk	4.25	6.00
a.		Inverted overprint	80.00	100.00
30	A16	80pf lake & blk, *rose*	85.00	150.00
31	A17	1m car rose	90.00	175.00
a.		Inverted overprint	250.00	425.00
		Nos. 24-31 (6)	425.25	966.00

Trial impressions were made in red, green and lilac, and with 2½mm instead of 3mm space between the lines of the overprint. These were printed on the 75pf and 80pf. The 1 mark was overprinted with the same words in 3 lines of large sans-serif capitals. All these are essays. Some were passed through the post, apparently with speculative intent.

Stamps of Germany, 1905-18, Surcharged

1 Mark 1
Commission
Interalliée
Marienwerder

No.	Type	Description	Unused	Used
32	A22	1m on 2pf gray	18.00	30.00
33	A22	2m on 2½pf gray	9.00	17.50
a.		Inverted surcharge	55.00	110.00
34	A16	3m on 3pf brn	9.00	15.00
a.		Double surcharge	55.00	110.00
b.		Inverted surcharge	55.00	110.00
35	A22	5m on 7½pf org	9.00	12.00
a.		Inverted surcharge	55.00	110.00
b.		Double surcharge	55.00	110.00

There are two types of the letters "M", "C", "i" and "e" and of the numerals "2" and "5" in these surcharges.
Counterfeits exist of Nos. 24-35.

Stamps of Germany, 1920, Overprinted

Commission
Interalliée
Marienwerder

1920, July *Perf. 15x14½*

No.	Type	Description	Unused	Used
36	A17	1m red	2.50	4.25
37	A17	1.25m green	2.75	5.25
38	A17	1.50m yel brown	2.75	6.75
39	A21	2.50m lilac rose	2.50	4.25

A2

1920 **Unwmk.** *Perf. 11½*

No.	Type	Description	Unused	Used
40	A2	5pf green	2.25	1.90
41	A2	10pf rose red	2.25	1.90
42	A2	15pf gray	11.00	10.50
43	A2	20pf brn org	1.50	1.50
44	A2	25pf dp bl	13.00	12.00
45	A2	30pf orange	1.25	95
46	A2	40pf brown	90	55
47	A2	50pf violet	1.50	1.10
48	A2	60pf red brn	4.50	3.50
49	A2	75pf chocolate	5.50	5.00
50	A2	1m brn & grn	90	75
51	A2	2m dk vio	1.25	1.00
52	A2	3m lt red	1.75	1.10
53	A2	5m blue & rose	2.25	1.40
		Nos. 40-53 (14)	49.80	43.15

Mariana Islands stamps can be mounted in Scott's Germany Part II Album.

MARSHALL ISLANDS

LOCATION — Two chains of islands in the West Pacific Ocean, northwest of the Gilbert and Ellice group
GOVT. — Former German possession
AREA — 176 sq. mi.
POP. — 15,179 (1913)
CAPITAL — Jaluit

100 Pfennig = 1 Mark

Watermark

Wmk. 125-Lozenges

Issued under German Dominion

A1

A2

Stamps of Germany Overprinted "Marschall-Inseln" in Black

1897 Unwmk. *Perf. 13½x14½*

1 A1 3pf dk brn 140.00 *550.00*
a. 3pf light brown *3,500. 1,500.*
2 A1 5pf green 100.00 *500.00*
3 A2 10pf carmine 37.50 *80.00*
4 A2 20pf ultra 37.50 *95.00*
5 A2 25pf orange 110.00
6 A2 50pf red brown 110.00

Nos. 5 and 6 were not placed in use, but canceled copies exist.

A small quantity of the 3pf, 5pf, 10pf and 20pf were issued at Jaluit. These have yellowish, dull gum. Later overprintings of Nos. 1-6 were sold only at Berlin, and have white, smooth, shiny gum. No. 1a belongs to the Jaluit issue.

Forged cancellations are found on almost all Marshall Islands stamps.

Overprinted "Marshall-Inseln"

1899-1900

7 A1 3pf dk brn ('00) 4.00 4.75
a. 3pf light brown *130.00 310.00*
8 A1 5pf green 9.00 6.75
9 A2 10pf car ('00) 11.00 17.00
10 A2 20pf ultra ('00) 18.00 *25.00*
11 A2 25pf orange 20.00 *40.00*
12 A2 50pf red brown 30.00 *55.00*
Nos. 7-12 (6) 92.00 *148.50*

Kaiser's Yacht "Hohenzollern"
A3 A4

1901 Unwmk. Typo. *Perf. 14*

13 A3 3pf brown 70 1.00
14 A3 5pf green 70 1.00
15 A3 10pf carmine 70 *4.25*
16 A3 20pf ultra 85 *8.25*
17 A3 25pf org & blk, *yel* 95 *14.00*
18 A3 30pf org & blk, *sal* 95 *14.00*
19 A3 40pf lake & blk 95 *14.00*
20 A3 50pf pur & blk, *sal* 1.90 *20.00*
21 A3 80pf lake & blk, *rose* 2.75 *45.00*

Engr.
Perf. 14½x14

22 A4 1m carmine 3.75 *65.00*
23 A4 2m blue 5.75 *110.00*
24 A4 3m blk vio 8.75 *165.00*
25 A4 5m slate & car 125.00 *375.00*
Nos. 13-25 (13) 153.70

Wmk. Lozenges (125)

1916 Typo. *Perf. 14*

26 A3 3pf brown 65

Engr.
Perf. 14½x14

27 A4 5m slate & carmine 22.50

Nos. 26 and 27 were never placed in use.

The stamps of Marshall Islands overprinted "G. R. I." and new values in British currency were all used in New Britain and are listed among the issues for that country, in Vol. 1 of the Standard Postage Stamp Catalogue.

See Vol. 1 for issues beginning in 1984 for the Marshall Islands as a US Trust Territory.

MARTINIQUE

LOCATION — Island in the West Indies, southeast of Puerto Rico
GOVT. — Former French Colony
AREA — 385 sq. mi.
POP. — 261,595 (1946)
CAPITAL — Fort-de-France

Formerly a French colony, Martinique became an integral part of the Republic, acquiring the same status as the departments in metropolitan France, under a law effective Jan. 1, 1947.

100 Centimes = 1 Franc

Catalogue values for unused stamps in this country are for Never Hinged items, beginning with Scott 196 in the regular postage section, Scott C1 in the airpost section, and Scott J37 in the postage due section.

See France Nos. 70, 1278, 1508 for French stamps inscribed "Martinique."

Stamps of French Colonies 1881-86 Surcharged in Black

MARTINIQUE 5 — Nos. 1, 7
MARTINIQUE 5c — No. 2
MQE 15 c. — No. 3
MQE 15 c. — No. 4
MARTINIQUE 01 — Nos. 5-6, 8
MARTINIQUE 01c. — Nos. 9-20

1886-91 Unwmk. *Perf. 14x13½*

1 A9 5 on 20c 24.00 19.00
a. Double surcharge *325.00 325.00*
2 A9 5c on 20c *9,000. 9,000.*
3 A9 15c on 20c ('87) 110.00 100.00
a. Inverted surcharge *1,200. 1,200.*
4 A9 15c on 20c ('87) 42.50 37.50
a. Inverted surcharge *575.00 575.00*
5 A9 01 on 20c ('88) 5.50 4.00
a. Inverted surcharge *150.00 125.00*
6 A9 05 on 20c 5.00 3.00
7 A9 15 on 20c ('88) 90.00 60.00
c. Inverted surcharge *325.00 325.00*
8 A9 015 on 20c ('87) 24.00 22.50
a. Inverted surcharge *400.00 400.00*
9 A9 01c on 2c ('88) 1.25 90
a. Double surcharge *175.00 140.00*
10 A9 01c on 4c ('88) 5.00 1.25
11 A9 05c on 4c ('88) 825.00 600.00
12 A9 05c on 10c ('90) 42.50 17.50
a. Slanting "5" *125.00 75.00*
13 A9 05c on 20c ('88) 9.00 6.00
a. Slanting "5" *50.00 35.00*
b. Inverted surcharge *175.00 140.00*
14 A9 05c on 30c ('91) 12.50 9.00
a. Slanting "5" *60.00 37.50*
15 A9 05c on 35c ('91) 7.50 5.00
a. Slanting "5" *45.00 37.50*
b. Inverted surcharge *150.00 90.00*
16 A9 05c on 40c ('91) 25.00 16.00
a. Slanting "5" *90.00 60.00*
17 A9 15c on 4c ('88) *7,000. 5,500.*
18 A9 15c on 20c ('87) 62.50 37.50
a. Slanting "5" *225.00 140.00*
b. Double surcharge *275.00 225.00*
19 A9 15c on 25c ('90) 7.00 5.25
a. Slanting "5" *45.00 35.00*
b. Inverted surcharge *175.00 125.00*
20 A9 15c on 75c ('91) 80.00 50.00
a. Slanting "5" *250.00 190.00*

French Colonies No. 47 Surcharged — TIMBRE-POSTE 01c. MARTINIQUE

1891

21 A9 01c on 2c brn, *buff* 4.25 3.25

French Colonies Nos. J5-J9 Surcharged — TIMBRE-POSTE 05c. MARTINIQUE

1891-92 Black Surcharge *Imperf.*

22 D1 05c on 5c blk ('92) 5.50 4.50
a. Slanting "5" *32.50 22.50*
23 D1 05c on 15c blk 4.00 2.75
b. Slanting "5" *32.50 22.50*
24 D1 15c on 20c blk 5.50 5.00
a. Inverted surcharge *125.00 125.00*
b. Double surcharge *125.00 125.00*
25 D1 15c on 30c blk 5.50 5.00
a. Inverted surcharge *125.00 125.00*
b. Slanting "5" *32.50 27.50*

Red Surcharge

26 D1 05c on 10c blk 4.00 4.00
a. Inverted surcharge *125.00 110.00*
27 D1 05c on 15c blk 5.25 4.50
28 D1 15c on 20c blk 19.00 12.50
a. Inverted surcharge *180.00 140.00*

French Colonies No. 54 Surcharged in Black

1892 MARTINIQUE 05c. — j
1892 05c. MARTINIQUE — k

1892 *Perf. 14x13½*

29 A9 (j) 05c on 25c 25.00 19.00
a. Slanting "5" *125.00 100.00*
30 A9 (j) 15c on 25c 10.00 8.00
a. Slanting "5" *125.00 100.00*
31 A9 (k) 05c on 25c 25.00 19.00
a. "1882" instead of "1892" *250.00 190.00*
b. "95" instead of "05" *325.00 225.00*
c. Slanting "5" *125.00 100.00*
32 A9 (k) 15c on 25c 10.00 8.00
a. "1882" instead of "1892" *225.00 175.00*
b. Slanting "5" *75.00 60.00*

Navigation and Commerce — A15

1892-1906 Typo. *Perf. 14x13½*
"MARTINIQUE" Colony in Carmine or Blue

33 A15 1c blk, *lil bl* 65 62
a. "MARTINIQUE" in blue 325.00 325.00
34 A15 2c brn, *buff* 65 62
35 A15 4c claret, *lav* 65 62
36 A15 5c grn, *grnsh* 90 40
37 A15 5c yel grn ('99) 90 40
38 A15 10c blk, *lav* 4.00 62
39 A15 10c red ('99) 1.10 40
40 A15 15c blue, quadrille paper 15.00 3.50
41 A15 15c gray ('99) 4.00 60
42 A15 20c red, *grn* 6.50 2.75
43 A15 25c blk, *rose* 8.00 80
44 A15 25c blue ('99) 5.50 5.00
45 A15 30c brn, *bis* 15.00 5.00
46 A15 35c blk, *yel* ('06) 5.75 3.75
47 A15 40c red, *straw* 15.00 5.00
48 A15 50c car, *rose* 12.50 6.50
49 A15 50c brn, *az* ('99) 13.50 10.00
50 A15 75c dp vio, *org* 12.50 7.00
51 A15 1fr brnz grn, *straw* 10.00 5.50
52 A15 2fr vio, *rose* ('04) 42.50 37.50
53 A15 5fr lil, *lav* ('03) 50.00 42.50
Nos. 33-53 (21) 224.60 139.08

Perf. 13½x14 stamps are counterfeits.
For surcharges see Nos. 54-61, 101-104.

Stamps of 1892-1903 Surcharged in Black — 10c

1904

54 A15 10c on 30c brn, *bis* 3.50 3.50
a. Double surcharge
55 A15 10c on 5fr lil, *lav* 4.25 4.25

Surcharged — 1904 0f10

56 A15 10c on 30c brn, *bis* 7.00 7.00
57 A15 10c on 40c red, *straw* 7.00 7.00
a. Double surcharge 225.00 225.00
58 A15 10c on 50c car, *rose* 7.00 7.00
59 A15 10c on 75c dp vio, *org* 5.75 5.75
60 A15 10c on 1fr brnz grn, *straw* 7.00 7.00
a. Double surcharge 125.00 125.00
61 A15 10c on 5fr lil, *lav* 100.00 100.00
Nos. 54-61 (8) 141.50 141.50

Martinique Woman — A16

Girl Bearing Pineapple in Cane Field — A18

View of Fort-de-France A17

1908-30 **Typo.**

62 A16 1c red brn & brn 15 15
63 A16 2c ol grn & brn 15 15
64 A16 4c vio brn & brn 15 15
65 A16 5c grn & brn 15 15
66 A16 5c org & brn ('22) 15 15
67 A16 10c car & brn 28 15
68 A16 10c bl grn & grn ('22) 15 15
69 A16 10c brn vio & rose ('25) 15 15
70 A16 15c brn vio & rose ('17) 15 15
71 A16 15c bl grn & gray grn ('25) 15 15
72 A16 15c dp bl & red org ('27) 60 60
73 A16 20c vio & brn 60 38
74 A17 25c bl & brn 60 15
75 A17 25c org & brn ('22) 15 15
76 A17 30c brn org & brn 60 32
77 A17 30c dl red & brn ('22) 15 15
78 A17 30c rose & ver ('24) 15 15
79 A17 30c ol brn & brn ('25) 15 15
80 A17 30c sl bl & bl grn ('27) 60 60
81 A17 35c vio & brn 28 20
82 A17 40c gray grn & brn 28 15
83 A17 45c dk brn & brn 28 20
84 A17 50c rose & brn 60 28
85 A17 50c bl & brn ('22) 60 55
86 A17 50c org & grn ('25) 15 15
87 A17 60c dk bl & lil rose ('25) 15 15
88 A17 65c vio & ol brn ('27) 65 65
89 A17 75c slATE & brn 60 28
90 A17 75c ind & dk bl ('25) 15 15
91 A17 75c org brn & lt bl ('27) 1.10 1.10
92 A17 90c brn red & brt red ('30) 2.25 2.25
93 A18 1fr dl bl & brn 28 15
94 A18 1fr dk bl ('25) 28 15
95 A18 1fr ver & ol grn ('27) 80 80
96 A18 1.10fr vio & dk brn ('28) 1.50 1.50
97 A18 1.50fr ind & ultra ('30) 2.50 2.50
98 A18 2fr gray & brn 1.40 50
99 A18 3fr red vio ('30) 3.50 3.50
100 A18 5fr org red & brn 4.00 3.50
Nos. 62-100 (39) 26.58 22.86

For surcharges see Nos. 105-128, B1.

Nos. 41, 43, 47 and 53 Surcharged in Carmine or Black

05 10

1912, Aug.

No.	Type	Description	Unused	Used
101	A15	5c on 15c gray (C)	42	42
102	A15	5c on 25c blk, *rose* (C)	65	65
103	A15	10c on 40c red, *straw*	65	65
104	A15	10c on 5fr lil, *lav*	1.00	1.00

Two spacings between the surcharged numerals are found on Nos. 101 to 104.

Nos. 62, 63, 70 Surcharged

1920, June 15

No.	Type	Description	Unused	Used
105	A16	5c on 1c	70	70
a.		Double surcharge	12.50	12.50
b.		Inverted surcharge	12.50	12.50
106	A16	10c on 2c	65	65
a.		Inverted surcharge	12.50	12.50
107	A16	25c on 15c	50	50
a.		Double surcharge	21.00	21.00
b.		Inverted surcharge	21.00	21.00

No. 70 Surcharged in Various Colors ≡ 0,01 ≡

1922, Dec.

No.	Type	Description	Unused	Used
108	A16	1c on 15c (Bk)	15	15
109	A16	2c on 15c (Bl)	15	15
110	A16	5c on 15c (R)	15	15
a.		Imperf., pair	40.00	
		Set value	34	34

Types of 1908-30 Surcharged 60

1923-25

No.	Type	Description	Unused	Used
111	A17	60c on 75c bl & rose	22	22
112	A17	65c on 45c ol brn & brn ('25)	50	50
113	A17	85c on 75c blk & brn (R) ('25)	60	60

Nos. 63, 73, 76-77, 84-85 Surcharged in Brown 0,01

Surcharge is horiz. on #114-115, vert. reading up on #116, 119 and down on #117-118.

1924, Feb. 14

No.	Type	Description	Unused	Used
114	A16	1c on 2c	70	70
a.		Double surcharge	150.00	150.00
b.		Inverted surcharge	27.50	27.50
115	A16	5c on 20c	80	80
a.		Inverted surcharge	27.50	27.50
116	A17	15c on 30c	4.50	4.50
a.		Surcharge reading down	15.00	15.00
117	A17	15c on 30c	6.25	6.25
a.		Surcharge reading up	20.00	20.00
118	A17	25c on 50c	140.00	140.00
119	A17	25c on 50c	1.90	1.90
a.		Surcharge reading down	15.00	15.00
		Nos. 114-119 (6)	154.15	154.15

Stamps and Types of 1908-30 Surcharged with New Value and Bars

1924-27

No.	Type	Description	Unused	Used
120	A16	25c on 15c brn vio & rose ('25)	20	20
121	A18	25c on 2fr gray & brn	15	15
122	A18	25c on 5fr org red & brn (Bl)	40	35
123	A17	90c on 75c brn red & red ('27)	1.40	1.10
124	A18	1.25fr on 1fr dk bl ('26)	15	15
125	A18	1.50fr on 1fr dk bl & ultra ('27)	52	40
126	A18	3fr on 5fr dl red & grn ('27)	90	70
127	A18	10fr on 5fr dl grn & dp red ('27)	4.25	4.25
128	A18	20fr on 5fr org brn & red vio ('27)	6.50	6.00
		Nos. 120-128 (9)	14.47	13.30

Colonial Exposition Issue
Common Design Types

1931, Apr. 13 Engr. *Perf. 12½*
Name of Country in Black

No.	Type	Description	Unused	Used
129	CD70	40c dp grn	1.60	1.60
130	CD71	50c violet	1.60	1.60
131	CD72	90c red org	1.60	1.60
132	CD73	1.50fr dull blue	1.60	1.60

Village of Basse-Pointe A19

Government Palace, Fort-de-France A20

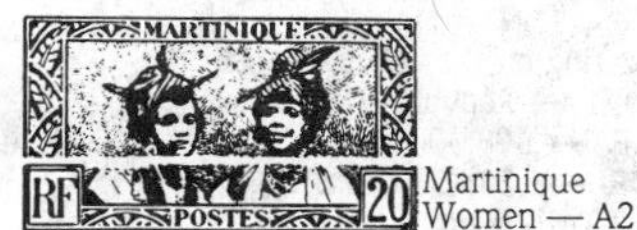
Martinique Women — A21

1933-40 Photo. *Perf. 13½*

No.	Type	Description	Unused	Used
133	A19	1c red, *pink*	15	15
134	A20	2c dull blue	15	15
135	A20	3c sepia ('40)	15	15
136	A19	4c olive grn	15	15
137	A20	5c dp rose	15	15
138	A19	10c blk, *pink*	15	15
139	A20	15c blk, *org*	15	15
140	A21	20c org brn	15	15
141	A19	25c brn vio	15	15
142	A20	30c green	15	15
143	A20	30c lt ultra ('40)	15	15
144	A21	35c dl grn ('38)	15	15
145	A21	40c olive brn	15	15
146	A20	45c dk brn	65	65
147	A20	45c grn ('40)	15	15
148	A20	50c red	15	15
149	A19	55c brn red ('38)	28	28
150	A19	60c lt bl ('40)	15	15
151	A21	65c red, *grn*	20	20
152	A21	70c brt red vio ('40)	15	15
153	A19	75c dk brn	40	40
154	A20	80c vio ('38)	15	15
155	A19	90c carmine	65	65
156	A19	90c brt red vio ('39)	28	28
157	A20	1fr blk, *grn*	65	55
158	A20	1fr rose red ('38)	28	15
159	A21	1.25fr dk vio	28	15
160	A21	1.25fr dp rose ('39)	28	28
161	A19	1.40fr lt ultra ('40)	28	28
162	A20	1.50fr dp bl	28	15
163	A20	1.60fr chnt ('40)	28	28
164	A21	1.75fr ol grn	3.75	2.00
165	A21	1.75fr dp bl ('38)	15	15
166	A19	2fr dk bl,*grn*	15	15
167	A21	2.25fr blue ('39)	35	35
168	A19	2.50fr sepia ('40)	40	40
169	A21	3fr brn vio	15	15
170	A21	5fr red, *pink*	58	28
171	A19	10fr dk bl, *bl*	28	20
172	A20	20fr red, *yel*	60	40
		Nos. 133-172 (40)	13.90	
		Set value		9.50

For surcharges see Nos. 190-195.

Landing of Bélain d'Esnambuc — A22

Freed Slaves Paying Homage to Victor Schoelcher A23

1935, Oct. 22 Engr. *Perf. 13*

No.	Type	Description	Unused	Used
173	A22	40c blk brn	1.50	90
174	A22	50c dl red	1.50	90
175	A22	1.50fr ultra	12.00	7.50
176	A23	1.75fr lil rose	10.00	7.00
177	A23	5fr brown	10.00	7.00
178	A23	10fr bl grn	8.25	5.25
		Nos. 173-178 (6)	43.25	28.55

Tercentenary of French possessions in the West Indies.

Colonial Arts Exhibition Issue
Common Design Type
Souvenir Sheet

1937 *Imperf.*

No.	Type	Description	Unused	Used
179	CD74	3fr brt grn	2.25	2.25

Paris International Exposition Issue
Common Design Types

1937, Apr. 15 *Perf. 13*

No.	Type	Description	Unused	Used
180	CD74	20c dp vio	60	60
181	CD75	30c dk grn	60	60
182	CD76	40c car rose	60	60
183	CD77	50c dk brn & blk	80	80
184	CD78	90c red	80	80
185	CD79	1.50fr ultra	80	80
		Nos. 180-185 (6)	4.20	4.20

New York World's Fair Issue
Common Design Type

1939, May 10 *Perf. 12½x12*

No.	Type	Description	Unused	Used
186	CD82	1.25fr car lake	60	60
187	CD82	2.25fr ultra	60	60

View of Fort-de-France and Marshal Pétain — A23a

1941 Engr. *Perf. 12½x12*

No.	Type	Description	Unused	Used
188	A23a	1fr dull lilac	22	
189	A23a	2.50fr blue	22	

Nos. 188-189 were issued by the Vichy government, and were not placed on sale in Martinique.

Nos. 134, 135, 136 and 151 Surcharged with New Values and Bars or Wavy Lines in Red, Black or Blue

1945 *Perf. 13½, 13x13½*

No.	Type	Description	Unused	Used
190	A20	1fr on 2c dl bl (R)	15	15
191	A19	2fr on 4c ol grn	20	20
192	A20	3fr on 2c dl bl (R)	22	22
193	A21	5fr on 65c red, *grn*	42	42
194	A21	10fr on 65c red, *grn*	42	42
195	A20	20fr on 3c sepia (Bl)	55	55
		Nos. 190-195 (6)	1.96	1.96

Catalogue values for unused stamps in this section, from this point to the end of the section, are for Never Hinged items.

Eboue Issue
Common Design Type

1945 Engr. *Perf. 13*

No.	Type	Description	Unused	Used
196	CD91	2fr black	15	15
197	CD91	25fr Prussian green	42	42

Victor Schoelcher and View of Town of Schoelcher A24

1945 Unwmk. Litho. *Perf. 11½*

No.	Type	Description	Unused	Used
198	A24	10c dp bl vio & ultra	15	15
199	A24	30c dk org brn & lt org brn	15	15
200	A24	40c grnsh bl & pale bl	15	15
201	A24	50c car brn & rose lil	15	15
202	A24	60c org yel & yel	15	15
203	A24	70c brn & pale brn	15	15
204	A24	80c lt bl grn & pale grn	15	15
205	A24	1fr bl & lt bl	15	15
206	A24	1.20fr rose vio & rose lil	15	15
207	A24	1.50fr red org & org	15	15
208	A24	2fr blk & gray	15	15
209	A24	2.40fr red & pink	65	60
210	A24	3fr pink & pale pink	15	15
211	A24	4fr ultra & lt ultra	20	15
212	A24	4.50fr yel grn & lt grn	38	15
213	A24	5fr org brn & lt org brn	15	15
214	A24	10fr dk vio & lil	38	22
215	A24	15fr rose car & lil rose	45	22
216	A24	20fr ol grn & lt ol grn	65	60
		Set value	3.75	2.85

Martinique Girl — A25

Mountains — A30

Cliffs — A26

Gathering Sugar Cane — A27

Mount Pelée — A28

Tropical Fruit — A29

1947, June 2 Engr. *Perf. 13*

No.	Type	Description	Unused	Used
217	A25	10c red brown	15	15
218	A25	30c deep blue	15	15
219	A25	50c olive brown	15	15
220	A26	60c dark green	15	15
221	A26	1fr red brown	15	15
222	A26	1.50fr purple	20	20
223	A27	2fr blue green	50	35
224	A27	2.50fr blk brn	40	30
225	A27	3fr deep blue	38	22
226	A28	4fr dk brown	38	28
227	A28	5fr dark green	35	30
228	A28	6fr lilac rose	38	28
229	A29	10fr indigo	62	38
230	A29	15fr red brown	70	62
231	A29	20fr blk brown	1.00	62
232	A30	25fr violet	1.00	70
233	A30	40fr blue grren	1.25	80
		Nos. 217-233 (17)	7.91	5.80

SEMI-POSTAL STAMPS

Regular Issue of 1908 Surcharged in Red

Perf. 13½x14

1915, May 15 Unwmk.

No.	Type	Description	Unused	Used
B1	A16	10c + 5c car & brn	80	62

Curie Issue
Common Design Type

1938, Oct. 24 *Perf. 13*

No.	Type	Description	Unused	Used
B2	CD80	1.75fr + 50c brt ultra	5.00	5.00

French Revolution Issue
Common Design Type
Photo.; Name & Value Typo. in Black

1939, July 5

No.	Type	Description	Unused	Used
B3	CD83	45c + 25c grn	3.50	3.50
B4	CD83	70c + 30c brn	3.50	3.50
B5	CD83	90c + 35c red org	3.50	3.50
B6	CD83	1.25fr + 1fr rose pink	3.50	3.50
B7	CD83	2.25fr + 2fr blue	3.50	3.50
		Nos. B3-B7 (5)	17.50	17.50

Common Design Type and

Colonial Infantry with Machine Gun — SP1

Naval Rifleman SP2

1941 Photo. *Perf. 13½*

B8	SP1	1fr + 1fr red	40
B9	CD86	1.50fr + 3fr maroon	40
B10	SP2	2.50fr + 1fr blue	40

Nos. B8-B10 were issued by the Vichy government, and were not placed on sale in Martinique.

Nos. 188-189 were surcharged "OEUVRES COLONIALES" and surtax (including change of denomination of the 2.50fr to 50c). These were issued in 1944 by the Vichy government, and were not placed on sale in Martinique.

Red Cross Issue
Common Design Type

1944 *Perf. 14½x14*

B11	CD90	5fr + 20fr dark purpler	40	40

The surtax was for the French Red Cross and national relief.

AIR POST STAMPS

Catalogue values for unused stamps in this section are for Never Hinged items.

Common Design Type

1945 Unwmk. Photo. *Perf. 14½x14*

C1	CD87	50fr dark green	40	22
C2	CD87	100fr plum	45	35

Two other values, 8.50fr orange and 18fr red brown, were prepared but not issued. Value, $50 each.

Victory Issue
Common Design Type

1946, May 8 Engr. *Perf. 12½*

C3	CD92	8fr indigo	60	60

Issued to commemorate the European victory of the Allied Nations in World War II.

Chad to Rhine Issue
Common Design Types

1946, June 6

C4	CD93	5fr orange	35	35
C5	CD94	10fr slate grn	35	35
C6	CD95	15fr carmine	40	40
C7	CD96	20fr chocolate	40	40
C8	CD97	25fr deep blue	55	55
C9	CD98	50fr gray blk	70	70
		Nos. C4-C9 (6)	2.75	2.75

Seaplane and Beach Scene — AP1

Plane over Tropic Shore — AP2

Albatross — AP3

1947, June 2 *Perf. 13*

C10	AP1	50fr dk brn vio	1.50	1.25
C11	AP2	100fr dk bl grn	2.25	1.75
C12	AP3	200fr violet	14.00	10.00

AIR POST SEMI-POSTAL STAMPS
Stamps similar to French Guiana type V6 inscribed "Martinique" and stamp of Cameroun type V10 inscribed "Martinique" were issued in 1942 by the Vichy Government, but were not placed on sale in Martinique.

POSTAGE DUE STAMPS

The set of 14 French Colonies postage due stamps (Nos. J1-J14) overprinted "MARTINIQUE" diagonally in red in 1887 was not an official issue.

Postage Due Stamps of France, 1893-1926 Overprinted **MARTINIQUE**

1927, Oct. 10 *Perf. 14x13½*

J15	D2	5c light blue	62	62
J16	D2	10c brown	70	70
J17	D2	20c olive green	70	70
J18	D2	25c rose	1.10	1.10
J19	D2	30c red	1.20	1.20
J20	D2	45c green	1.20	1.20
J21	D2	50c brn violet	2.50	2.50
J22	D2	60c blue green	2.75	2.75
J23	D2	1fr red brown	3.75	3.75
J24	D2	2fr bright vio	4.50	4.50
J25	D2	3fr magenta	5.75	5.75
		Nos. J15-J25 (11)	24.77	24.77

Tropical Fruit — D3

Map — D4

1933, Feb. 15 Photo. *Perf. 13½*

J26	D3	5c dk bl, *green*	22	22
J27	D3	10c orange brown	22	22
J28	D3	20c dk blue	55	55
J29	D3	25c red, *pink*	55	55
J30	D3	30c dk vio	35	35
J31	D3	45c red, *yel*	22	22
J32	D3	50c dk brn	55	55
J33	D3	60c dl grn	55	55
J34	D3	1fr blk, *org*	65	65
J35	D3	2fr dp rose	55	55
J36	D3	3fr dk blue, *bl*	55	55
		Nos. J26-J36 (11)	4.96	4.96

Stamps of type D3 without the "RF" monogram were issued in 1943 by the Vichy Government, but were not placed on sale in Martinique.

1947, June 2 Engr. *Perf. 14x13*

J37	D4	10c ultra	15	15
J38	D4	30c brt bl grn	15	15
J39	D4	50c slate gray	15	15
J40	D4	1fr org red	15	15
J41	D4	2fr dk vio brn	30	30
J42	D4	3fr lilac rose	30	30
J43	D4	4fr dk brn	42	42
J44	D4	5fr red	45	45
J45	D4	10fr black	70	70
J46	D4	20fr olive grn	70	70
		Nos. J37-J46 (10)	3.47	3.47

PARCEL POST STAMP

Postage Due Stamp of French Colonies Surcharged in Black

TIMBRE POSTE
5 F.
MARTINIQUE
COLIS POSTAUX

1903, Oct. Unwmk. *Imperf.*

Q1	D1	5fr on 60c brn, *buff*	375.00	400.00
a.		Inverted surcharge	*425.00*	*500.00*

MAURITANIA

LOCATION — Northwestern Africa, bordering on the Atlantic Ocean
GOVT. — Republic
AREA — 398,000 sq. mi.
POP. — 1,834,500 (est. 1984)
CAPITAL — Nouakchott

The Islamic Republic of Mauritania was proclaimed Nov. 28, 1958.

Stamps of French West Africa were used in the period between the issues of the colony and the republic.

100 Centimes = 1 Franc
Ouguiya ("um") (1973)

Catalogue values for unused stamps in this country are for Never Hinged items, beginning with Scott 116 in the regular postage section, Scott B16 in the semi-postal section, Scott C14 in the airpost section, Scott J19 in the postage due section, and Scott O1 in the official section.

General Louis Faidherbe — A1

Oil Palms — A2

Dr. Noel Eugène Ballay — A3

Perf. 14x13½
1906-07 Typo. Unwmk.
"Mauritanie" in Red or Blue

1	A1	1c slate	20	20
2	A1	2c chocolate	38	32
3	A1	4c choc, *gray bl*	50	40
4	A1	5c green	38	25
5	A1	10c car (B)	3.25	2.00
7	A2	20c blk, *azure*	10.00	6.25
8	A2	25c bl, *pnksh*	3.25	2.25
9	A2	30c choc, *pnksh*	45.00	32.50
10	A2	35c blk, *yellow*	3.25	2.25
11	A2	40c car, *az* (B)	3.50	2.25
12	A2	45c choc, *grnsh* ('07)	3.25	2.50
13	A2	50c dp vio	3.25	2.50
14	A2	75c bl, *org*	3.25	2.50
15	A3	1fr blk, *azure*	6.50	5.50
16	A3	2fr bl, *pink*	22.50	21.50
17	A3	5fr car, *straw* (B)	70.00	60.00
		Nos. 1-17 (16)	178.46	143.17

Crossing Desert — A4

1913-38

18	A4	1c brn vio & brn	15	15
19	A4	2c blk & bl	15	15
20	A4	4c vio & blk	15	15
21	A4	5c yel grn & bl grn	20	20
22	A4	5c brn vio & rose ('22)	15	15
23	A4	10c rose & red org	40	40
24	A4	10c yel grn & bl grn ('22)	15	15
25	A4	10c lil rose, *bluish* ('25)	20	20
26	A4	15c dk brn & blk ('17)	20	20
27	A4	20c bis brn & org	15	15
28	A4	25c bl & vio	42	42
29	A4	25c grn & rose ('22)	15	15
30	A4	30c bl grn & rose	35	35
31	A4	30c rose & red org ('22)	40	40
32	A4	30c blk & yel ('26)	15	15
33	A4	30c bl grn & yel grn ('28)	58	58
34	A4	35c brn & vio	28	28
35	A4	35c dp grn & lt grn ('38)	40	40
36	A4	40c gray & bl grn	90	90
37	A4	45c org & bis brn	38	38
38	A4	50c brn vio & rose	28	28
39	A4	50c dk bl & ultra ('22)	15	15
40	A4	50c gray grn & dp bl ('26)	35	35
41	A4	60c vio, *pnksh* ('26)	15	15
42	A4	65c yel brn & lt bl ('26)	42	42
43	A4	75c ultra & brn	35	35
44	A4	85c myr grn & lt brn ('26)	55	55
45	A4	90c brn red & rose ('30)	65	65
46	A4	1fr rose & blk	35	35
47	A4	1.10fr vio & ver ('28)	5.50	5.50
48	A4	1.25fr dk bl & blk brn ('33)	90	90
49	A4	1.50fr lt bl & dp bl ('30)	35	35
50	A4	1.75fr bl grn & brn red ('33)	40	40
51	A4	1.75fr dk bl & ultra ('38)	40	40
52	A4	2fr red org & vio	80	62
53	A4	3fr red vio ('30)	80	80
54	A4	5fr vio & bl	1.20	1.00
		Nos. 18-54 (37)	19.51	19.13

For surcharges see Nos. 55-64, B1-B2.

Stamp and Type of 1913-38 Surcharged

60 **60**

1922-25

55	A4	60c on 75c vio, *pnksh*	40	40
56	A4	65c on 15c dk brn & blk ('25)	70	70
57	A4	85c on 75c ultra & brn ('25)	70	70

Stamp and Type of 1913-38 Surcharged with New Value and Bars

1924-27

58	A4	25c on 2fr red org & vio	50	50
59	A4	90c on 75c brn red & cer ('27)	1.00	1.00
60	A4	1.25fr on 1fr dk bl & ultra ('26)	20	20
61	A4	1.50fr on 1fr bl & dp bl ('27)	60	60
62	A4	3fr on 5fr ol brn & red vio ('27)	4.00	4.00
63	A4	10fr on 5fr mag & bl grn ('27)	3.25	3.25
64	A4	20fr on 5fr bl vio & dp org ('27)	3.25	3.25
		Nos. 58-64 (7)	12.80	12.80

Colonial Exposition Issue
Common Design Types

Engr.; Name of Country Typo. in Black
1931, Apr. 13 *Perf. 12½*

65	CD70	40c dp grn	2.25	2.25
66	CD71	50c violet	1.60	1.60
67	CD72	90c red org	1.60	1.60
68	CD73	1.50fr dull blue	1.60	1.60

Paris International Exposition Issue
Common Design Types

1937, Apr. 15 *Perf. 13*

69	CD74	20c dp vio	55	55
70	CD75	30c dk grn	55	55
71	CD76	40c car rose	50	50
72	CD77	50c dk brn & blk	50	50
73	CD78	90c red	58	58
74	CD79	1.50fr ultra	58	58
		Nos. 69-74 (6)	3.26	3.26

Colonial Arts Exhibition Issue
Common Design Type
Souvenir Sheet

1937 *Imperf.*

75	CD76	3fr dark blue	2.25	2.25

Camel Rider — A5

Mauri Couple — A8

Mauris on Camels — A6

Family before Tent — A7

1938-40 *Perf. 13*

76	A5	2c	vio blk	15	15
77	A5	3c	dp ultra	15	15
78	A5	4c	rose vio	15	15
79	A5	5c	org red	15	15
80	A5	10c	brn car	15	15
81	A5	15c	dk vio	15	15
82	A6	20c	red	15	15
83	A6	25c	dp ultra	15	15
84	A6	30c	dp brn	15	15
85	A6	35c	Prus grn	20	20
86	A6	40c	rose car ('40)	15	15
87	A6	45c	Prus grn ('40)	15	15
88	A6	50c	purple	15	15
89	A7	55c	rose vio	28	28
90	A7	60c	vio ('40)	20	20
91	A7	65c	dp grn	38	38
92	A7	70c	red ('40)	40	40
93	A7	80c	dp bl	70	70
94	A7	90c	rose vio ('39)	30	30
95	A7	1fr	red	70	70
96	A7	1fr	dp grn ('40)	30	30
97	A7	1.25fr	rose car ('39)	65	65
98	A7	1.40fr	dp bl ('40)	30	30
99	A7	1.50fr	violet	30	30
99A	A7	1.50fr	red brn ('40)	50.00	50.00
100	A7	1.60fr	blk brn ('40)	65	65
101	A8	1.75fr	dp ultra	42	42
102	A8	2fr	rose vio	42	42
103	A8	2.25fr	dl ultra ('39)	38	38
104	A8	2.50fr	blk brn ('40)	50	50
105	A8	3fr	dp grn	30	30
106	A8	5fr	scarlet	60	60
107	A8	10fr	dp brn	80	80
108	A8	20fr	brn car	80	80
			Nos. 76-108 (34)	61.38	61.38

Nos. 91 and 109 surcharged with new values are listed under French West Africa.

For surcharges see Nos. B9-B12.

Caillie Issue

Common Design Type

1939, Apr. 5 **Engr.** *Perf. 12½x12*

109	CD81	90c	org brn & org	50	50
110	CD81	2fr	brt vio	50	50
111	CD81	2.25fr	ultra & dk bl	50	50

New York World's Fair Issue

Common Design Type

1939, May 10

112	CD82	1.25fr	car lake	35	35
113	CD82	2.25fr	ultra	35	35

Caravan and Marshal Pétain — A9

1941

114	A9	1fr	green	20
115	A9	2.50fr	deep blue	20

Nos. 114-115 were issued by the Vichy government, and were not placed on sale in the colony. This also holds true for six stamps of types A5-A7 without "RF," issued in 1943-44.

Catalogue values for unused stamps in this section, from this point to the end of the section, are for Never Hinged items.

Islamic Republic

Camel and Hands Raising Flag — A10

Unwmk.

1960, Jan. 20 **Engr.** *Perf. 13*

116	A10	25fr	multi, *pink*	35	20

Issued to commemorate the proclamation of the Islamic Republic of Mauritania.

Imperforates

Most Mauritania stamps from 1960 onward exist imperforate in issued and trial colors, and also in small presentation sheets in issued colors.

C.C.T.A. Issue

Common Design Type

1960, May 16

117	CD106	25fr	bluish grn & ultra	38	22

Flag and Map — A11

1960, Dec. 15 **Engr.** *Perf. 13*

118	A11	25fr	org brn, emer & sep	22	16

Proclamation of independence, Nov. 28, 1960.

Pastoral Well — A12

Scimitar- horned Oryx — A15

Spotted Hyena — A13

Ore Train and Camel Riders — A14

Designs: 50c, 1fr, Well. 2fr, Date harvesting. 3fr, Aoudad. 4fr, Fennecs. 5fr, Millet harvesting. 10fr, Shoemaker. 15fr, Fishing boats. 20fr, Nomad school. 25fr, 30fr, Seated dance. No. 130, Religious student. 60fr, Metalworker.

1960-62 **Unwmk.** *Perf. 13*

119	A12	50c	mag, yel & brn ('61)	15	15
120	A12	1fr	brn, yel brn & grn	15	15
121	A12	2fr	dk brn, bl & grn	15	15
122	A13	3fr	bl grn, red brn & gray ('61)	15	15
123	A13	4fr	yel grn & ocher ('61)	15	15
124	A12	5fr	red, dk brn & yel brn	15	15
125	A14	10fr	dk bl & org	15	15
126	A14	15fr	ver, dk brn, grn & bl	15	15
127	A14	20fr	grn, sl grn & red brn	22	15
128	A12	25fr	ultra & gray grn ('61)	25	15
129	A12	30fr	lil, bis & indigo	30	15
130	A12	50fr	org brn & grn	60	20
131	A14	50fr	red brn, bl & ol ('62)	55	38
132	A12	60fr	grn, cl & pur	65	20
133	A15	85fr	bl, brn & blk ('61)	1.00	50
			Set value	4.00	1.75

An overprint, "Jeux Olympiques / Rome 1960 / Tokyo 1964," the 5-ring Olympic emblem and a 75fr surcharge were applied to Nos. 126-127 in 1962.

An overprint, "Aide aux Rèfugiès" with uprooted oak emblem, was applied in 1962 to No. 132 and to pink-paper printings of Nos. 129-130.

Other overprints, applied to airmail stamps, are noted after No. C16.

1963, July 6

Designs: 50c, Striped hyena. 1.50fr, Cheetah. 2fr, Guinea baboons. 5fr, Dromedaries. 10fr, Leopard. 15fr, Bongo antelopes. 20fr, Aardvark. 25fr, Patas monkeys. 30fr, Crested porcupine. 50fr, Dorcas gazelle. 60fr, Common chameleon.

134	A15	50c	sl grn, blk & org brn	15	15
135	A13	1fr	ultra, blk & yel	15	15
136	A15	1.50fr	ol grn, brn & bis	15	15
137	A13	2fr	dk brn, grn & dp org	15	15
138	A15	5fr	brn, ultra & bis	15	15
139	A13	10fr	blk & bis	15	15
140	A13	15fr	vio bl & red brn	16	15
141	A13	20fr	dk red brn, dk bl & bis	18	15
142	A15	25fr	brt grn, red brn & ol bis	30	15
143	A13	30fr	dk brn, dk bl & ol bis	40	15
144	A15	50fr	grn, ocher & brn	55	25
145	A13	60fr	dk bl, emer & ocher	80	45
			Set value	2.80	1.30

UN Headquarters, New York, and View of Nouakchott — A15a

1962, June 1 **Engr.** *Perf. 13*

167	A15a	15fr	blk, ultra & cop red	16	15
168	A15a	25fr	cop red, sl grn & ultra	25	22
169	A15a	85fr	dk bl, dl pur & cop red	80	65

Mauritania's admission to the UN.

African-Malagasy Union Issue

Common Design Type

1962, Sept. 8 **Photo.** *Perf. 12½x12*

170	CD110	30fr	multi	35	30

Organization Emblem and View of Nouakchott A16

1962, Oct. 15 *Perf. 12½*

171	A16	30fr	dk red brn, ultra & brt grn	25	22

8th Conf. of the Organization to Fight Endemic Diseases, Nouakchott, Oct. 15-18.

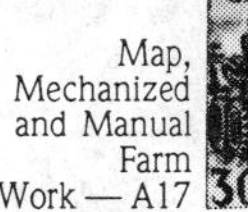

Map, Mechanized and Manual Farm Work — A17

1962, Nov. 28 **Engr.** *Perf. 13*

172	A17	30fr	blk, grn & vio brn	30	22

2nd anniversary of independence.

People in European and Mauritanian Clothes A18

1962, Dec. 24 **Unwmk.**

173	A18	25fr	multi	22	16

First anniversary of Congress for Unity.

Since 1863 American stamp collectors have been using the Scott Catalogue to identify their stamps and Scott Albums to house their collections.

Weather and WMO Symbols — A20

1964, Mar. 23 **Unwmk.** *Perf. 13*

175	A20	85fr	dk brn, dk bl & org	1.25	80

UN 4th World Meteorological Day, Mar. 23.

IQSY Emblem A21

1964, July 3 **Engr.**

176	A21	25fr	dk bl, red & grn	22	16

International Quiet Sun Year, 1964-65.

Striped Mullet A22

Designs: 5fr, Mauritanian lobster, vert. 10fr, Royal lobster, vert. 60fr, Maigre fish.

1964, Oct. 5 **Engr.** *Perf. 13*

177	A22	1fr	org brn, dk bl & grn	15	15
178	A22	5fr	org brn, sl grn & choc	15	15
179	A22	10fr	dk bl, bis & sl grn	20	15
180	A22	60fr	dk brn, dp grn & dl bl	60	45
			Set value	94	70

Cooperation Issue

Common Design Type

1964, Nov. 7 **Unwmk.** *Perf. 13*

181	CD119	25fr	mag, sl grn & dk brn	25	20

Water Lilies — A23

Tropical Plants: 10fr, Acacia, vert. 20fr, Adenium obesum. 45fr, Caralluma retrospiciens, vert.

1965, Jan. 11 **Engr.** *Perf. 13*

182	A23	5fr	grn, dk bl & pink	15	15
183	A23	10fr	grn, dl pur & bis	15	15
184	A23	20fr	dk car, dk brn & pale brn	15	15
185	A23	45fr	plum, dk sl grn & Prus bl	35	25
			Set value	68	54

Hardine A24

Musical Instruments: 8fr, Tobol (drums). 25fr, Tidinit (stringed instruments). 40fr, Musicians.

1965, Mar. 8 *Perf. 13*

186	A24	2fr	red brn, brt bl & sep	15	15
187	A24	8fr	red brn, red & brn	15	15
188	A24	25fr	red brn, emer & blk	20	15
189	A24	40fr	vio bl, plum & blk	30	18
			Set value	65	40

Abraham Lincoln (1809-1865) — A25

1965, Apr. 23 Photo. *Perf. 13x12½*

190 A25 50fr lt ultra & multi	50	25

Palms at Adrar — A26

Designs: 4fr, Chinguetti mosque, vert. 15fr, Clay pit and donkeys. 60fr, Decorated door, Oualata.

1965, June 14 Engr. *Perf. 13*

191 A26 1fr brn, bl & grn	15	15
192 A26 4fr dk red, bl & brn	15	15
193 A26 15fr multi	15	15
194 A26 60fr grn, dk brn & red brn	55	35
Set value	75	50

Issued for tourist publicity.

Tea Service in Inlaid Box — A27

Designs: 7fr, Tobacco pouch and pipe, vert. 25fr, Dagger, vert. 50fr, Mederdra ornamental chest.

1965, Sept. 13 Unwmk. *Perf. 13*

195 A27 3fr gray, choc & ocher	15	15
196 A27 7fr red lil, Prus bl & org	15	15
197 A27 25fr blk, org red & brn	16	15
198 A27 50fr brt grn, brn org & mar	35	20
Set value	60	40

Choum Railroad Tunnel — A28

Designs: 10fr, Nouakchott wharf, ships and anchor, horiz. 85fr, Nouakchott hospital and caduceus, horiz.

1965, Oct. 18 Engr. *Perf. 13*

199 A28 5fr dk brn & brt grn	15	15
200 A28 10fr dk vio bl, brn red & Prus bl	15	15
201 A28 30fr brn red, red & red brn	25	15
202 A28 85fr dp bl, rose cl & lil	65	40
Set value	1.00	55

Sculptured Heads — A29

Designs: 30fr, "Music and Dance." 60fr, Movie camera and huts.

1966, Apr. Engr. *Perf. 13*

203 A29 10fr brt grn, blk & brn	15	15
204 A29 30fr brt bl, red lil & blk	25	16
205 A29 60fr red, org & dk brn	55	35

Intl. Negro Arts Festival, Dakar, Senegal, Apr. 1-24.

Mimosa — A30

Myrina Silenus — A31

Flowers: 15fr, Schouwia purpurea. 20fr, Ipomea asarifolia. 25fr, Grewia bicolor. 30fr, Pancratium trianthum. 60fr, Blepharis linariifolia.

1966, Aug. 8 Photo. *Perf. 13x12½*
Flowers in Natural Colors

206 A30 10fr dl bl & dk bl	15	15
207 A30 15fr dk brn & buff	15	15
208 A30 20fr grnsh bl & lt bl	20	15
209 A30 25fr brn & buff	22	15
210 A30 30fr lil & vio	30	15
211 A30 60fr grn & pale grn	50	25
Nos. 206-211 (6)	1.52	
Set value		65

1966, Oct. 3 Photo. *Perf. 12x12½*
Various Butterflies

212 A31 5fr buff & multi	15	15
213 A31 30fr bl grn & multi	35	15
214 A31 45fr yel grn & multi	50	16
215 A31 60fr dl bl & multi	65	30
Set value		62

Hunter, Petroglyph from Adrar — A32

Designs: 3fr, Two men fighting, petroglyph from Tenses (Adrar). 30fr, Copper jug, Le Mreyer (Adrar). 50fr, Camel caravan.

1966, Oct. 24 Engr. *Perf. 13*

216 A32 2fr dk brn & brn org	15	15
217 A32 3fr bl & brn org	15	15
218 A32 30fr sl grn & dk red	30	15
219 A32 50fr mag, sl grn & brn	50	35
Set value	90	55

Issued for tourist publicity.

UNESCO, 20th Anniv. — A33

1966, Dec. 5 Litho. *Perf. 12½x13*

220 A33 30fr multi	30	15

Plaza of Three Cultures, Mexico City — A34

Olympic Village, Grenoble A35

Designs: 40fr, Olympic torch and skating rink. 100fr, Olympic Stadium, Mexico City.

1967, Mar. 11 Engr. *Perf. 13*

221 A34 20fr dl bl, brn & sl grn	20	15
222 A35 30fr dl bl, brn & grn	30	15
223 A34 40fr brt bl, dk brn & sep	38	16
224 A35 100fr brn, emer & blk	70	42

Nos. 221 and 223 publicize the 19th Olympic Games, Mexico City; Nos. 222 and 224 the 10th Winter Olympic Games, Grenoble.

Trees — A36

1967 Jamboree Emblem and Campsite — A37

1967, May 15 Engr. *Perf. 13*

225 A36 10fr Prosopis	15	15
226 A36 15fr Jujube	15	15
227 A36 20fr Date palm	16	15
228 A36 25fr Peltophorum	22	15
229 A36 30fr Baobob	25	15
Nos. 225-229 (5)	93	
Set value		45

1967, June 5

Design: 90fr, 1967 Jamboree emblem and Mauritanian Boy Scouts, horiz.

230 A37 60fr brn, ultra & sl grn	55	25
231 A37 90fr dl red, bl & sl grn	80	38

12th Boy Scout World Jamboree, Farragut State Park, Idaho, Aug. 1-9.

Weavers A38

Design: 10fr, Embroiderer, vert. 20fr, Nurse, mother and infant. 30fr, Laundress, vert. 50fr, Seamstresses.

1967, July 3 Engr. *Perf. 13*

232 A38 5fr plum, blk & cl	15	15
233 A38 10fr plum, brt grn & blk	15	15
234 A38 20fr brt bl, plum & blk	15	15
235 A38 30fr dk bl, brn & blk	20	15
236 A38 50fr plum, sl & blk	35	16
Set value	80	45

Progress made by working women.

Cattle and Hypodermic Syringe — A39

1967, Aug. 21 Engr. *Perf. 13*

237 A39 30fr sl grn, brt bl & rose cl	20	15

Campaign against cattle plague.

Monetary Union Issue
Common Design Type

1967, Nov. 4 Engr. *Perf. 13*

238 CD125 30fr gray & org	30	15

Fruit — A40

Human Rights Flame — A41

1967, Dec. 4 Engr. *Perf. 13*

239 A40 1fr Doom palm	15	15
240 A40 2fr Bito, horiz.	15	15
241 A40 3fr Baobob	15	15
242 A40 4fr Jujube, horiz.	15	15
243 A40 5fr Daye	15	15
Set value	26	24

For surcharges see Nos. 323-327.

1968, Jan. 8 Photo. *Perf. 13x12½*

244 A41 30fr brt grn, blk & yel	25	15
245 A41 50fr brn org, blk & yel	40	18

International Human Rights Year.

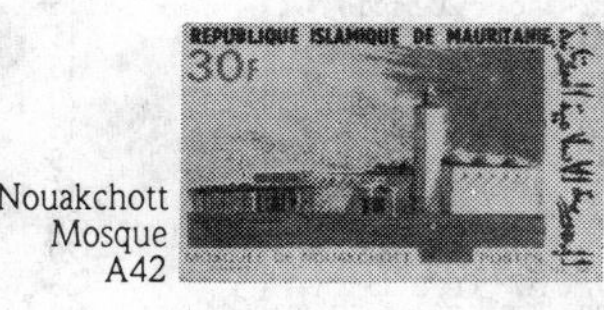

Nouakchott Mosque A42

Designs: 45fr, Amogjar Pass. 90fr, Cavaliers' Towers.

1968, Apr. 1 Photo. *Perf. 12½x13*

246 A42 30fr multi	20	15
247 A42 45fr multi	25	15
248 A42 90fr multi	55	25

For surcharges see Nos. 332-333.

UPU Building, Bern, Globe and Map of Africa — A43

1968, June 3 Engr. *Perf. 13*

249 A43 30fr ver, ultra & ol	20	15

Mauritania's admission to the UPU.

Symbolic Water Cycle — A44

1968, June 24

250 A44 90fr car, lake, grn & sl grn	55	30

Hydrological Decade (UNESCO), 1965-74.

Land Yacht Racing — A45

Donkey and Foal — A46

Designs: 40fr, Three land yachts racing, horiz. 60fr, Crew changing wheel of land yacht.

1968, Oct. 7 Engr. *Perf. 13*

251 A45 30fr ultra, org & ocher	20	15
252 A45 40fr ultra, dp org & plum	25	15
253 A45 60fr brt grn, dp org & ocher	40	18

1968, Dec. 16 Photo. *Perf. 13*

Domestic Animals: 10fr, Ewe and lamb. 15fr, Camel and calf. 30fr, Mare and foal. 50fr, Cow and calf. 90fr, Goat and kid.

254 A46 5fr ocher & multi	15	15
255 A46 10fr multi	15	15
256 A46 15fr multi	15	15
257 A46 30fr multi	20	15
258 A46 50fr pur & multi	30	15
259 A46 90fr multi	55	30
Set value	1.25	70

For surcharge see No. 303.

ILO Emblem and Map — A47

Desert Monitor — A48

1969, Apr. 14 Photo. *Perf. 13x12½*
260 A47 50fr dk & lt bl, pur & org 42 16

ILO, 50th anniversary.

1969, May 5 Photo. *Perf. 13x12½*

Reptiles: 10fr, Horned viper. 30fr, Common spitting cobra. 60fr, Rock python. 85fr, African crocodile.

261 A48 5fr brn, pink & yel 15 15
262 A48 10fr brn, lt grn & yel 16 15
263 A48 30fr dk brn, pink & yel 25 15
264 A48 60fr dk brn, lt bl & yel 45 25
265 A48 85fr dk brn, yel & red 65 45
Nos. 261-265 (5) 1.66 1.15

Lady Beetle Eating Noxious Insects A49

1969, May 26 Engr. *Perf. 13*
266 A49 30fr ind, grn & mar 25 15

Natural protection of date palms.

Development Bank Issue
Common Design Type

1969, Sept. 10 Engr. *Perf. 13*
267 CD130 30fr Prus bl, grn & ocher 22 15

Pendant — A50

Design: 20fr, Rahla headdress, horiz.

1969, Oct. 13 Engr. *Perf. 13*
268 A50 10fr dk brn, lil & brn 15 15
269 A50 20fr blk, Prus bl & mag 16 15
Set value 24 15

For surcharges see Nos. 309-310.

Desalination Plant — A51

Designs: 15fr, Fishing harbor, Nouadhibou. 30fr, Meat refrigeration plant, Kaedi.

1969, Dec. 1 Engr. *Perf. 13*
270 A51 10fr brt rose lil, dk bl & red brn 15 15
271 A51 15fr dk car, blk & dp bl 15 15
272 A51 30fr blk, dk bl & rose brn 20 15
Set value 36 25

Issued to publicize economic progress.

Lenin (1870-1924) A52

Sternocera Interrupta A53

1970, Feb. 16 Photo. *Perf. 12x12½*
273 A52 30fr car, lt bl & blk 22 15

1970, Mar. 16 Engr. *Perf. 13*

Insects: 10fr, Anoplocnemis curvipes. 20fr, Julodis aequinoctialis. 30fr, Thermophilum sexmaculatum marginatum. 40fr, Plocaederus denticornis.

274 A53 5fr red brn, buff & blk 15 15
275 A53 10fr red brn, yel & brn 15 15
276 A53 20fr red brn, lil & dk ol 15 15
277 A53 30fr red brn, grn & vio 20 15
278 A53 40fr red brn, lt bl & brn 25 16
Set value 70 42

For surcharges see Nos. 311-315.

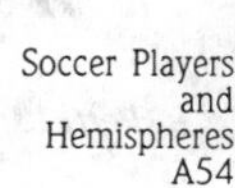

Soccer Players and Hemispheres A54

Designs: Hemispheres and various views of soccer play.

1970, May 11 Engr. *Perf. 13*
279 A54 25fr bl, vio bl & dk brn 16 15
280 A54 30fr vio bl, brn & ol brn 20 15
281 A54 70fr brt pink, mar & dk brn 40 22
282 A54 150fr brn red, grn & dk brn 90 50

Issued to publicize the 9th World Soccer Championships for the Jules Rimet Cup, Mexico City, May 29-June 21.

UPU Headquarters Issue
Common Design Type

1970, May 20 Engr. *Perf. 13*
283 CD133 30fr grn, dk brn & red brn 20 15

Woman Wearing "Boubou" — A55

Various Traditional Costumes: 30fr, 70fr, Men. 40fr, 50fr, Women.

1970, Sept. 21 Engr. *Perf. 12½x13*
284 A55 10fr red brn & org 15 15
285 A55 30fr ol, red brn & ind 16 15
286 A55 40fr red brn, plum & dk brn 25 15
287 A55 50fr dk brn & brt bl 30 16
288 A55 70fr bl, brn & dk brn 40 20
Nos. 284-288 (5) 1.26
Set value 65

People of Various Races — A55a

Design: 40fr, Outstretched hands, vert.

1971, Mar. 22 Engr. *Perf. 13*
288A A55a 30fr brn vio, ol & brt bl 20 15
288B A55a 40fr brn red, bl & blk 22 15
Set value 24

Intl. year against racial discrimination.

Gen. Charles de Gaulle (1890-1970), President of France — A56

Design: 100fr, De Gaulle as President.

1971, June 18 Photo. *Perf. 13*
289 A56 40fr gold, blk & grnsh bl 40 40
290 A56 100fr lt bl, gold & blk 1.10 1.10
a. Souvenir sheet of 2, #289-290 1.90 1.90

Iron Ore Freight Train of Miferma Mines A57 A58

1971, Nov. 8 Photo. *Perf. 12½x12*
291 A57 35fr bl & multi 25 15
292 A58 100fr bl & multi 70 40
a. Pair, #291-292 1.00 90

UNICEF Emblem and Child A59

1971, Dec. 11 Litho. *Perf. 13½*
293 A59 35fr lt ultra, blk & brn 22 15

UNICEF, 25th anniv.

Samuel F. B. Morse and Telegraph — A60

Designs: 40fr, Relay satellite over globes. 75fr, Alexander Graham Bell.

1972, May 17 Engr. *Perf. 13*
294 A60 35fr lilac, indigo & vio 25 15
295 A60 40fr bl, ocher & choc 28 16
296 A60 75fr grn, ol grn & Prus bl 45 25

4th World Telecommunications Day.
For surcharge see No. 343.

Fossil Spirifer Shell A61

1972, July 31 Litho. *Perf. 12½*
297 A61 25fr shown 16 15
298 A61 75fr Phacops rana 42 30

Fossil shells.
For surcharges see Nos. 306, 308.

West African Monetary Union Issue
Common Design Type

1972, Nov. 2 Engr. *Perf. 13*
299 CD136 35fr brn, yel grn & gray 22 15

Mediterranean Monk Seal and Pup — A63

1973, Feb. 28 Litho. *Perf. 13*
300 A63 40fr multi 30 16

See #C130. For surcharges see #307, C145.

Food Program Symbols and Emblem A64

1973, Apr. 30 Photo. *Perf. 12x12½*
301 A64 35fr gray bl & multi 22 15

World Food Program, 10th anniversary.

UPU Monument and Globe — A65

1973, May 28 Engr. *Perf. 13*
302 A65 100fr grn, ocher & bl 65 50

Universal Postal Union Day.

Currency Change to Ouguiya ("um")
No. 258 Surcharged with New Value, 2 Bars, and Overprinted: "SECHERESSE / SOLIDARITE / AFRICAINE"

1973, Aug. 16 Photo. *Perf. 13*
303 A46 20um on 50fr multi 60 38

African solidarity in drought emergency.

African Postal Union Issue
Common Design Type

1973, Sept. 12 Engr. *Perf. 13*
304 CD137 20um org, brn & ocher 60 38

INTERPOL Emblem, Detective, Criminal, Fingerprint A66

1973, Sept. 24
305 A66 15um brn, ver & vio 50 30

50th anniv. of Intl. Criminal Police Org.

Nos. 297-298, 300 and 268-269 Surcharged with New Value and Two Bars in Ultramarine, Red or Black

1973-74 Litho. *Perf. 12½*
306 A61 5um on 25fr (U) ('74) 16 15
307 A63 8um on 40fr (R) 25 15
308 A61 15um on 75fr (U) ('74) 45 25

Engr.
Perf. 13
309 A50 27um on 10fr (B) ('74) 70 38
310 A50 28um on 20fr (R) ('74) 80 42
Nos. 306-310 (5) 2.36 1.35

Nos. 274-278 Surcharged with New Value and Two bars in Violet Blue or Red

1974, July 29 Engr. *Perf. 13*
311 A53 5um on 5fr 16 15
312 A53 7um on 10fr 22 15
313 A53 8um on 20fr 22 16

314 A53 10um on 30fr (R) 35 20
315 A53 20um on 40fr 65 40
Nos. 311-315 (5) 1.60 1.06

UPU Emblem and Globes — A67

1974, Aug. 5 Photo. *Perf. 13*
316 A67 30um multi 90 65
317 A67 50um multi 1.50 90

Centenary of Universal Postal Union.
For overprints see Nos. 321-322.

5-Ouguiya Coin and Bank Note — A68

Designs: 8um, 10-ouguiya coin. 20um, 20-ouguiya coin. Each design includes picture of different bank note.

1974, Aug. 12 Engr.
318 A68 7um blk, ultra & grn 20 15
319 A68 8um blk, sl grn & mag 22 15
320 A68 20um blk, red & bl 60 35
Set value 52

First anniversary of currency reform.

Nos. 316-317 Overprinted in Red: "9 OCTOBRE / 100 ANS D'UNION POSTALE / INTERNATIONALE"

1974, Oct. 9 Photo. *Perf. 13*
321 A67 30um multi 90 50
322 A67 50um multi 1.50 65

Centenary of Universal Postal Union.

Nos. 239-243 Surcharged with New Value and Two Bars in Black or Violet Blue

1975, Feb. 14 Engr. *Perf. 13*
323 A40 1um on 5fr multi (B) 15 15
324 A40 2um on 4fr multi (VB) 15 15
325 A40 3um on 2fr multi (B) 15 15
326 A40 10um on 1fr multi (B) 30 15
327 A40 12um on 3fr multi (VB) 35 15
Set value 85 40

Hunters, Rock Carvings — A69

White and Black Men, Map of Europe and Africa — A70

Rock Carvings from Zemmour Cave: 5um, Ostrich. 10um, Elephant, horiz.

1975, May 26 Engr. *Perf. 13*
328 A69 4um lt brn & car 15 15
329 A69 5um red lil 16 15
330 A69 10um blue 30 16
Set value 28

Europafrica Issue

1975, July 7 Engr. *Perf. 13*
331 A70 40um dk brn & red 1.20 70

Nos. 247-248 Surcharged in Red or Black

15UM

SECHERESSE SOLIDARITE
AFRICAINE

1975, Aug. 25 Photo. *Perf. 12½x13*
332 A42 15um on 45fr (R) 42 30
333 A42 25um on 90fr 70 50

African solidarity in drought emergency.

Map of Africa with Mauritania, Akjoujt Blast Furnace, Camel — A71

Fair Emblem — A72

Design: 12um, Snim emblem, furnace, dump truck, excavator.

1975, Sept. 22 Engr. *Perf. 13*
334 A71 10um brt bl, choc & org 30 16
335 A71 12um brt bl & multi 38 20

Mining and industry: Somima (Société Minière de Mauritanie) and Snim (Société Nationale Industrielle et Minière).

1975, Oct. 5 Litho. *Perf. 12*
336 A72 10um multi 30 15

National Nouakchott Fair, Nov. 28-Dec. 7.

Commemorative Medal — A73

Design: 12um, Map of Mauritania, vert.

1975, Nov. 28 Litho. *Perf. 12*
337 A73 10um sil & multi 30 15
338 A73 12um grn, yel & grn 38 20

15th anniversary of independence.

Docked Space Ships and Astronauts — A74

Docked Space Ships and: 10um, Soyuz rocket launch.

1975, Dec. 29 Litho. *Perf. 14*
339 A74 8um multi 30 16
340 A74 10um multi 38 20
Nos. 339-340,C156-C158 (5) 3.68 1.88

Apollo Soyuz space test project, Russo-American cooperation, launched July 15, link-up July 17, 1975.

French Legion Infantryman A75

Uniform: 10um, Green Mountain Boy.

1976, Jan. 26 *Perf. 13½x14*
341 A75 8um multi 25 15
342 A75 10um multi 30 15
Nos. 341-342,C160-C162 (5) 3.80 1.60

American Bicentennial.

No. 296 Surcharged

10e ANNIVERSAIRE DE LA
CHARTE ARABE DU TRAVAIL

12UM

1976, Mar. 1 Engr. *Perf. 13*
343 A60 12um on 75fr multi 35 16

Arab Labor Charter, 10th anniversary.

Map of Mauritania with Spanish Sahara Incorporated — A76

1976, Mar. 15 Litho. *Perf. 13x12½*
344 A76 10um grn & multi 30 16

Reunified Mauritania, Feb. 29, 1976.

LZ-4 over Hangar — A77

75th anniv. of the Zeppelin: 10um, Dr. Hugo Eckener and "Schwaben" (LZ-10). 12um, "Hansa" (LZ-13) over Heligoland. 20um, "Bodensee" (LZ-120) and Dr. Ludwig Dürr.

1976, June 28 Litho. *Perf. 11*
345 A77 5um multi 18 15
346 A77 10um multi 38 18
347 A77 12um multi 42 22
348 A77 20um multi 70 30
Nos. 345-348,C167-C168 (6) 5.08 2.30

Mohenjo-Daro — A78

1976, Sept. 6 Litho. *Perf. 12*
349 A78 15um multi 42 20

UNESCO campaign to save Mohenjo-Daro excavations, Pakistan.

A. G. Bell, Telephone and Satellite — A79

1976, Oct. 11 Engr. *Perf. 13*
350 A79 10um bl, car & red 30 16

Centenary of first telephone call by Alexander Graham Bell, Mar. 10, 1876.

Mohammed Ali Jinnah (1876-1948), Governor General of Pakistan — A80

1976, Dec. 25 Litho. *Perf. 13*
351 A80 10um multi 30 16

NASA Control Room, Houston — A81

Design: 12um, Viking components, vert.

1977, Feb. 28 *Perf. 14*
352 A81 10um multi 35 15
353 A81 12um multi 42 20
Nos. 352-353,C173-C175 (5) 3.97 1.77

Viking Mars project.
For surcharge and overprints see Nos. 425-426, C192-C195.

Jackals — A82

Designs: 5um, Wild rabbits. 12um, Warthogs. 14um, Lions. 15um, Elephants.

1977, Mar. 14 Litho. *Perf. 12½*

354 A82	5um multi	15	15
355 A82	10um multi	30	16
356 A82	12um multi	38	20
357 A82	14um multi	40	20
358 A82	15um multi	45	20
	Nos. 354-358 (5)	1.68	91

Irene and Frederic Joliot-Curie, Chemistry — A83

Nobel prize winners: 15um, Emil A. von Bering, medicine.

1977, Apr. 29 Litho. *Perf. 14*

359 A83	12um multi	40	20
360 A83	15um multi	45	25
	Nos. 359-360,C177-C179 (5)	3.92	1.90

APU Emblem, Member's Flags — A84

1977, May 30 Photo. *Perf. 13*

361 A84	12um multi	38	20

Arab Postal Union, 25th anniversary.

Oil Lamp — A85

Tegdaoust Pottery: 2um, 4-handled pot. 5um, Large jar. 12um, Jug with filter.

1977, June 13 Engr. *Perf. 13*

362 A85	1um multi	15	15
363 A85	2um multi	15	15
364 A85	5um multi	15	15
365 A85	12um multi	38	18
	Set value	64	32

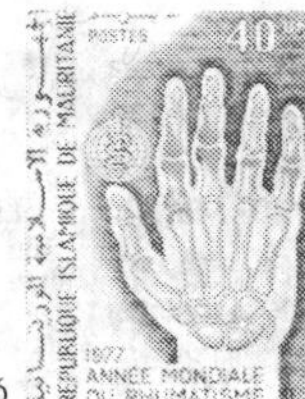

X-ray of Hand — A86

1977, June 27 Engr. *Perf. 12½x13*

366 A86	40um multi	1.20	65

World Rheumatism Year.

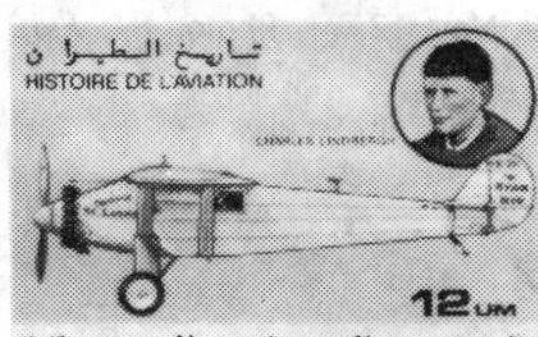

Charles Lindbergh and "Spirit of St. Louis" — A87

History of aviation: 14um, Clement Ader and "Eole!" 15um, Louis Bleriot over channel. 55um, Italo Balbo and seaplanes. 60um, Concorde. 100um, Charles Lindbergh and "Spirit of St. Louis."

1977, Sept. 19

367 A87	12um multi	40	20
368 A87	14um multi	42	20
369 A87	15um multi	45	25
370 A87	55um multi	1.75	80
371 A87	60um multi	1.90	90
	Nos. 367-371 (5)	4.92	2.35

Souvenir Sheet

372 A87	100um multi	3.00	1.75

Dome of the Rock, Jerusalem — A88

1977, Oct. 31 Litho. *Perf. 12½*

373 A88	12um multi	38	20
374 A88	14um multi	40	22

Palestinian fighters and their families.

Soccer and Emblems — A89

Emblems and: 14um, Alf Ramsey and stadium. 15um, Players and goalkeeper.

1977, Dec. 19 Litho. *Perf. 13½*

375 A89	12um multi	40	18
376 A89	14um multi	45	22
377 A89	15um multi	50	22
	Nos. 375-377,C182-C183 (5)	4.05	1.77

Elimination Games for World Cup Soccer Championship, Argentina, 1978.
For overprints see Nos. 399-401, C187-C189.

Helen Fourment and her Children, by Rubens — A90

Paintings by Peter Paul Rubens (1577-1640): 14um, Knight in armor. 67um, Three Burghers. 69um, Landscape, horiz. 100um, Rubens with wife and son.

1977, Dec. 26

378 A90	12um multi	40	18
379 A90	14um multi	45	25
380 A90	67um multi	2.25	80
381 A90	69um multi	2.25	80

Souvenir Sheet

382 A90	100um gold & multi	3.75	1.60

Sable Antelope and Wildlife Fund Emblem — A91

Endangered Animals: 12um, Gazelles, vert. 14um, Manatee. 55um, Aoudad, vert. 60um, Elephant. 100um, Ostrich, vert.

1978, Feb. 28 Litho. *Perf. 13½x14*

383 A91	5um multi	18	15
384 A91	12um multi	40	16
385 A91	14um multi	42	20
386 A91	55um multi	1.75	62
387 A91	60um multi	1.90	65
388 A91	100um multi	3.25	1.10
	Nos. 383-388 (6)	7.90	2.88

Soccer and Games' Emblem — A92

Designs: 14um, Rimet Cup. 20um, Soccer ball and F.I.F.A. flag. 50um, Soccer ball and Rimet Cup, horiz.

1978, June 26 Photo. *Perf. 13*

389 A92	12um multi	40	16
390 A92	14um multi	45	20
391 A92	20um multi	65	25

Souvenir Sheet

392 A92	50um multi	1.75	1.00

11th World Cup Soccer Championship, Argentina, June 1-25.

Raoul Follereau and St. George Slaying Dragon — A93

1978, Sept. 4 Engr. *Perf. 13*

393 A93	12um brn & dp grn	40	16

25th anniversary of the Raoul Follereau Anti-Leprosy Foundation.

Anti-Apartheid Emblem, Fenced-in People — A94

Design: 30um, Anti-Apartheid emblem and free people, vert.

1978, Oct. 9

394 A94	25um bl, red & brn	80	38
395 A94	30um grn, bl & brn	1.00	42

Anti-Apartheid Year.

Charles de Gaulle A95

Portraits: 14um, King Baudouin. 55um, Queen Elizabeth II.

1978, Oct. 16 Litho. *Perf. 12½x12*

396 A95	12um multi	40	16
397 A95	14um multi	45	20
398 A95	55um multi	1.90	80

Rulers who helped in de-colonization. No. 398 also commemorates 25th anniversary of coronation of Queen Elizabeth II.

Nos. 375-377 Overprinted in Arabic and French in Silver: "ARGENTINE- / PAYS BAS 3-1"

1978, Dec. 11 Litho. *Perf. 13½*

399 A89	12um multi	40	16
400 A89	14um multi	45	20
401 A89	15um multi	50	20
	Nos. 399-401,C187-C188 (5)	4.10	1.71

Argentina's victory in World Cup Soccer Championship 1978.

View of Nouakchott — A96

1978, Dec. 18 Litho. *Perf. 12*

402 A96	12um multi	40	16

20th anniversary of Nouakchott.

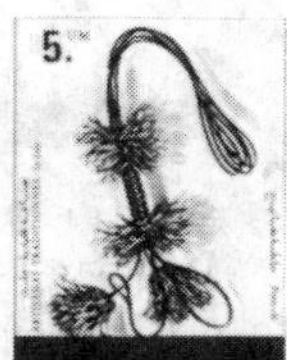

Flame Emblem — A97

Leather Key Holder — A98

1978, Dec. 26 *Perf. 12½*

403 A97	55um ultra & red	1.90	80

Universal Declaration of Human Rights, 30th anniv.

1979, Feb. 5 Litho. *Perf. 13½x14*

Leather Craft: 7um, Toothbrush case. 10um, Knife holder.

404 A98	5um multi	16	15
405 A98	7um multi	22	15
406 A98	10um multi	35	16
	Set value		35

Farmers at Market, by Dürer — A99

Engravings by Albrecht Durer (1471-1528): 14um, Young Peasant and Wife. 55um, Mercenary with flag. 60um, St. George Slaying Dragon. 100um, Mercenaries, horiz.

Litho.; Red Foil Embossed

1979, May 3 *Perf. 13½x14*
407 A99 12um blk, *buff* 40 20
408 A99 14um blk, *buff* 45 22
409 A99 55um blk, *buff* 1.90 90
410 A99 60um blk, *buff* 2.00 1.10

Souvenir Sheet
Perf. 14x13½
411 A99 100um blk, *buff* 3.50 1.60

Buddha, Borobudur Temple and UNESCO Emblem — A100

UNESCO Emblem and: 14um, Hunter on horseback, Carthage. 55um, Caryatid, Acropolis.

1979, May 14 **Photo.** *Perf. 12½*
412 A100 12um multi 40 20
413 A100 14um multi 45 22
414 A100 55um multi 1.90 90

Preservation of art treasures with help from UNESCO.

Paddle Steamer Sirius, Rowland Hill — A101

Sir Rowland Hill (1795-1879), originator of penny postage, and: 14um, Paddle steamer Great Republic. 55um, S.S. Mauritania. 60um, M.S. Stirling Castle. 100um, Mauritania No. 8.

1979, June 4 **Litho.** *Perf. 13½x14*
415 A101 12um multi 50 22
416 A101 14um multi 65 30
417 A101 55um multi 2.25 1.20
418 A101 60um multi 2.50 1.40

Souvenir Sheet
419 A101 100um multi 3.50 2.00

Embossed Leather Cushion — A102

Design: 30um, Satellite, jet, ship, globe and UPU emblem, vert.

1979, June 8 **Litho.** *Perf. 12½*
420 A102 12um multi 40 22

Engr.
Perf. 13
421 A102 30um multi 1.00 55

Philexafrique II, Libreville, Gabon, June 8-17. Nos. 420, 421 each printed in sheets of 10 and 5 labels showing exhibition emblem.

Mother and Children, IYC Emblem — A103

1979, Oct. 2 **Litho.** *Perf. 12½*
422 A103 12um multi 40 20
423 A103 14um multi 45 22
424 A103 40um multi 1.40 65

International Year of the Child

Nos. 352-353 Overprinted in Silver: "ALUNISSAGE / APOLLO XI / JUILLET 1969" and Emblem

1979, Oct. 24 **Litho.** *Perf. 14*
425 A81 10um multi 35 16
426 A81 12um multi 40 20
Nos. 425-426,C192-C194 (5) 3.85 1.94

Apollo 11 moon landing, 10th anniversary.

Runner, Moscow '80 Emblem A104

Moscow '80 Emblem and: 14um, 55um, 100um, Running, diff. 60um, Hurdles.

1979, Oct. 26 **Litho.** *Perf. 13½*
427 A104 12um multi 40 20
428 A104 14um multi 45 22
429 A104 55um multi 1.90 90
430 A104 60um multi 2.00 1.00

Souvenir Sheet
431 A104 100um multi 3.50 3.50

Pre-Olympic Year.

Scomberesox Saurus Walbaum — A104a

1979, Nov. 12 **Photo.** *Perf. 14*
431A A104a 1um shown 15 15
431B A104a 5um Trigla lucerna 16 15
Set value 20 15

Ice Hockey, Lake Placid '80 Emblem A105

Lake Placid '80 Emblem and various ice hockey plays.

1979, Dec. 6 **Litho.** *Perf. 14½*
432 A105 10um multi 35 15
433 A105 12um multi 40 20
434 A105 14um multi 45 25
435 A105 55um multi 1.90 90
436 A105 60um multi 2.00 1.10
437 A105 100um multi 3.50 1.60
Nos. 432-437 (6) 8.60 4.20

13th Winter Olympic Games. Lake Placid, NY, Feb. 12-24, 1980.
For overprints see Nos. 440-445.

Arab Achievements A106

1980, Mar. 22 **Litho.** *Perf. 13*
438 A106 12um multi 40 20
439 A106 15um multi 50 25

Nos. 432-437 Overprinted:

a. Médaille / de bronze / SUÈDE
b. MÉDAILLE / DE BRONZE / SUÈDE
c. Médaille / d'argent / U.R.S.S.
d. MÉDAILLE / D'ARGENT/ U.R.S.S.
e. MÉDAILLE / D'OR / ÉTATS-UNIS
f. Médaille / d'or / ÉTATS-UNIS

1980, June 14 **Litho.** *Perf. 14½*
440 A105(a) 10um multi 35 15
441 A105(b) 12um multi 40 20
442 A105(c) 14um multi 45 25
443 A105(d) 55um multi 1.90 90
444 A105(e) 60um multi 2.00 1.10
445 A105(f) 100um multi 3.50 1.75
Nos. 440-445 (6) 8.60 4.35

Equestrian, Olympic Rings — A107

Designs: Equestrian scenes. 10um, 20um, 70um, 100um, vert.

1980, June **Litho.** *Perf. 14*
446 A107 10um multi 35 15
447 A107 20um multi 65 30
448 A107 50um multi 1.60 70
449 A107 70um multi 2.25 1.00

Souvenir Sheet
450 A107 100um multi 3.50 1.50

22nd Summer Olympic Games, Moscow, July 19-Aug. 3.

Armed Forces Day — A108

1980, July 9 *Perf. 13x12½*
451 A108 12um multi 40 20
452 A108 14um multi 45 25

World Red Cross Day — A109

1980, June 14 *Perf. 13*
453 A109 20um multi 65 30

Pilgrimage to Mecca — A110

Design: 50um, Mosque, outside view.

1980
454 A110 10um multi 35 15
455 A110 50um multi 1.60 70

Man with Turban, by Rembrandt A111

Rembrandt Paintings: 10um, Self-portrait. 20um, His mother. 70um, His son Titus reading. 100um, Polish knight, horiz.

1980, July **Litho.** *Perf. 12½*
456 A111 10um multi 35 15
457 A111 20um multi 65 30
458 A111 50um multi 1.60 70
459 A111 70um multi 2.25 1.00

Souvenir Sheet
460 A111 100um multi 3.50 3.50

Tea Time — A112

1980, Mar. 11 **Litho.** *Perf. 12½*
460A A112 1um multi 15 15
461 A112 5um multi 16 15
462 A112 12um multi 40 20
Set value 60 32

Arbor Day — A113

1980, Aug. 29
463 A113 12um multi 40 20

Nos. 446-450 Overprinted with Winner and Country

1980, Oct. Litho. *Perf. 14*
464 A107 10um multi 35 15
465 A107 20um multi 65 30
466 A107 50um multi 1.60 70
467 A107 70um multi 2.25 1.00

Souvenir Sheet
468 A107 100um multi 3.50 1.50

Mastodont Locomotive, 1850 — A114

Designs: Various locomotives.

1980, Nov. *Perf. 12½*
469 A114 10um shown 35 15
470 A114 12um Iron ore train 40 20
471 A114 14um Chicago-Milwaukee line, 1900 45 25
472 A114 20um Bury, 1837 65 30
473 A114 67um Reseau North line, 1870 2.25 1.00
474 A114 100um Potsdam, 1840 3.50 1.40
Nos. 469-474 (6) 7.60 3.30

20th Anniversary of Independence — A115

1980, Nov. 27 *Perf. 13*
475 A115 12um multi 40 20
476 A115 15um multi 50 22

El Haram Mosque — A116

1981, Apr. 13 Litho. *Perf. 12½*
477 A116 2um shown 15 15
478 A116 12um Medina Mosque 40 20
479 A116 14um Chinguetti Mosque 45 25
Set value 50

Hegira, 1500th anniversary.

Prince Charles and Lady Diana, Coach A117

Designs: Coaches.

1981, July 8 Litho. *Perf. 14½*
480 A117 14um multi 35 35
481 A117 18um multi 45 45
482 A117 77um multi 1.90 1.10

Souvenir Sheet
483 A117 100um multi 5.00 2.50

Royal wedding.
For overprints see Nos. 518-521.

Intl. Year of the Disabled A119

1981, June 29 Litho. *Perf. 13x13½*
486 A119 12um multi 40 20

Battle of Yorktown Bicentenary (American Revolution) — A120

1981, Oct. 5 *Perf. 12½*
487 A120 14um George Washington, vert. 45 22
488 A120 18um Admiral de Grasse, vert. 60 30
489 A120 63um Surrender of Cornwallis 2.00 1.10
490 A120 81um Battle of Chesapeake Bay 2.50 1.40

450th Death Anniv. of Christopher Columbus (1451-1506) — A121

1981, Oct. 5
491 A121 19um Pinta 62 32
492 A121 55um Santa Maria 1.90 90

World Food Day — A122

Kemal Ataturk Birth Cent. — A123

1981, Oct. 16 *Perf. 13*
493 A122 19um multi 62 32

1981, Oct. 29 *Perf. 12½*
494 A123 63um multi 2.00 1.10

Scouting Year — A124

Designs: Boating scenes. 92um vert.

1982, Jan. 20 Litho. *Perf. 12½*
495 A124 14um multi 45 22
496 A124 19um multi 62 32
497 A124 22um multi 70 40
498 A124 92um multi 3.00 1.25

Souvenir Sheet
Perf. 13
499 A124 100um Baden-Powell, scout 3.50 1.60

75th Anniv. of Grand Prix — A125

Designs: Winners and their Cars.

1982, Jan. 23 *Perf. 13½*
500 A125 7um Deusenberg, 1921 22 15
501 A125 12um Alfa Romeo, 1932 40 20
502 A125 14um Juan Fangio, 1949 45 22
503 A125 18um Renault, 1979 60 30
504 A125 19um Niki Lauda, 1974 62 32
Nos. 500-504 (5) 2.29 1.19

Souvenir Sheet
505 A125 100um Race 3.50 1.60

Birds of the Arguin Bank A126

1981, Dec. 17 Photo. *Perf. 13*
506 A126 2um White pelicans 15 15
507 A126 18um Pink flamingoes 60 30
Set value 35

Battle of Karameh — A127

1982, Dec. 19 Litho.
508 A127 14um Hand holding tattered flag 45 22

Deluth Turtle — A128

APU, 30th Anniv. — A129

Designs: Sea turtles.

1981, Dec. 21 Photo. *Perf. 14x13½*
509 A128 1um shown 15 15
510 A128 3um Green turtle 15 15
511 A128 4um Shell turtle 15 15
Set value 28 16

1982, May 14 Litho. *Perf. 13*
512 A129 14um org & brn 45 22

A130

A131

1982, May 17 Photo. *Perf. 13½x13*
513 A130 21um multi 70 35

14th World Telecommunications Day.

1982, June 7 Litho. *Perf. 12½*
514 A131 14um grnsh bl 45 22

UN Conference on Human Environment, 10th anniv.

21st Birthday of Princess Diana of Wales — A132

Portraits.

1982, July *Perf. 14x13½*
515 A132 21um multi 70 35
516 A132 77um multi 2.50 1.10

Souvenir Sheet
517 A132 100um multi 3.50 1.60

Nos. 480-483 Overprinted in Blue: "NAISSANCE ROYALE 1982"

1982, Aug. 2 *Perf. 14½*
518 A117 14um multi 45 22
519 A117 18um multi 60 30
520 A117 77um multi 2.50 1.20

Souvenir Sheet
521 A117 100um multi 3.50 1.60

Birth of Prince William of Wales, June 21.

An enhanced introduction to the Scott Catalogue begins on Page 5A. A thorough understanding of the material presented there will greatly aid your use of the catalogue itself.

Manned Flight Bicentenary A133

1982, Dec. 29 Litho. *Perf. 14*

522 A133	14um	Montgolfiere balloon, 1783, vert.	45	22
523 A133	18um	Hydrogen balloon, 1783	60	30
524 A133	19um	Zeppelin, vert.	62	32
525 A133	55um	Nieuport plane	1.90	90
526 A133	63um	Concorde	2.25	1.10
527 A133	77um	Apollo II, vert.	2.50	1.10
		Nos. 522-527 (6)	8.32	3.94

Preservation of Ancient Cities — A134

1983, Feb. 16 Litho. *Perf. 14x14½*

528 A134	14um	City Wall, Ouadane	45	22
529 A134	18um	Chinguetti	60	30
530 A134	24um	Staircase, panels, Qualata	80	42
531 A134	30um	Ruins, Tichitt	1.00	50

World Communications Year — A135

1983, June 21 Litho. *Perf. 13*

532 A135 14um multi 45 22

30th Anniv. of Customs Cooperation Council — A136

1983, June 25

533 A136 14um multi 45 22

Traditional Houses — A137

Ancient Manuscript Page — A138

1983, June 14 Photo. *Perf. 13½*

534 A137	14um	Peule	38	18
535 A137	18um	Toucouleur	50	25
536 A137	19um	Tent	52	28

1983, June 15 Photo. *Perf. 12½x13*

537 A138	2um	shown	15	15
538 A138	5um	Ornamental scrollwork	15	15
539 A138	7um	Sheath	18	15
		Set value	36	22

Manned Flight Bicentenary — A139

Early Fliers and their Balloons or Dirigibles. 10um, 14um vert.

1983, Oct. 17 Litho. *Perf. 13½*

540 A139	10um	F. Pilatre de Rozier	25	15
541 A139	14um	John Wise	38	18
542 A139	25um	Charles Renard	65	35
543 A139	100um	Henri Julliot	2.50	1.40

Souvenir Sheet

544 A139 100um Joseph Montgolfier 2.50 1.40

No. 544 contains one stamp 47x37mm. Nos. 543-544 airmail.

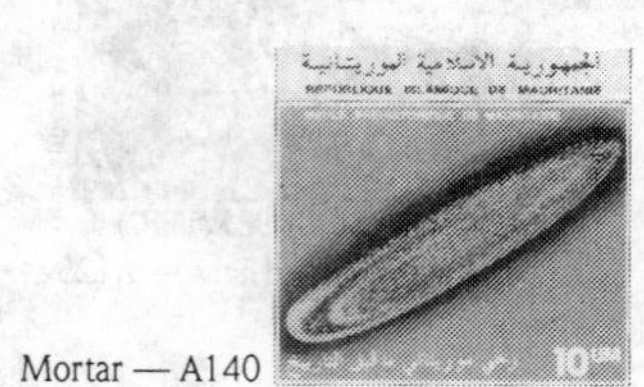
Mortar — A140

Various prehistoric grinding implements.

1983, Dec. 28 Litho. *Perf. 13*

545 A140	10um	multi	25	15
546 A140	14um	multi	38	18
547 A140	18um	multi	50	25

Pre-Olympics — A141

1983, Dec. 31 Litho. *Perf. 13½*

548 A141	1um	Basketball	15	15
549 A141	20um	Wrestling	25	15
550 A141	50um	Equestrian	65	35
551 A141	77um	Running	1.00	50

Souvenir Sheet

552 A141 100um Soccer 1.40 65

No. 552 contains one stamp 41x36mm. Nos. 551-552 airmail.

Scouting Year — A142

Artemis, by Rembrandt — A142a

Events & Annivs.: 14um, Johann Wolfgang von Goethe. 25um, Virgin and Child, by Peter Paul Rubens.

No. 553C illustration reduced.

1984, Jan. 24

553 A142	5um	Flag, Baden-Powell	15	15
553A A142	14um	multicolored	22	15
553B A142	25um	multicolored	35	16

Souvenir Sheet

553C A142a 100um multicolored 1.40 65

No. 553C is airmail and contains one 42x51mm stamp.

Sand Rose — A143

1984, Mar. Litho. *Perf. 14*

554 A143 21um multi 28 15

Inscribed 1982.

Anniversaries and Events A145

1984, Apr. 26

555 A145	10um	Albrecht Durer (1471-1528)	15	15
556 A145	12um	Apollo XI, 15th anniv.	16	15
557 A145	50um	Chess	65	35
		Set value		50

1984, Apr. 16 Litho. *Perf. 13½*

Designs: 77um, Prince Charles, Princess Diana. 100um, Prince Charles, Princess Diana, vert.

557A A145 77um multi 1.50 70

Miniature Sheet

557B A145 100um multi 2.00 1.00

Nos. 557A-557B airmail.

Fishing Industry A146

1984

558 A146	1um	Tuna	15	15
559 A146	2um	Mackerel	15	15
560 A146	5um	Haddock	15	15
561 A146	14um	Black chinchard	18	15
562 A146	18um	Boat building	25	15
		Set value	55	35

Nouakchott Olympic Complex A148

1984, Sept. 26 Litho. *Perf. 13½*

569 A148 14um multi 28 15

Infant Survival Campaign — A149

1984, Sept. 26 Litho. *Perf. 12½*

570 A149	1um	Feeding by glass	15	15
571 A149	4um	Breastfeeding	15	15
572 A149	10um	Vaccinating	20	15
573 A149	14um	Weighing	28	15
		Set value	60	35

Pilgrimage to Mecca — A150

1984, Oct. 3 Litho. *Perf. 13*

574 A150	14um	Tents, mosque	28	15
575 A150	18um	Tents, courtyard	38	18

10th Anniv., West African Union — A151

1984, Nov. Litho. *Perf. 13*

576 A151 14um Map of member nations 28 15

No. 355 Overprinted "Aide au Sahel 84" and Surcharged

1984 Litho. *Perf. 12½*

577 A82 18um on 10um 38 18

Issued to publicize drought relief efforts.

Technical & Cultural Cooperation Agency, 15th Anniv. — A152

1985, Mar. 20 Litho. *Perf. 12½*

578 A152 18um Profiles, emblem 35 16

League of Arab States, 40th Anniv. — A153

1985, May 7 *Perf. 13*

579 A153 14um brt yel grn & blk 28 15

German Railways 150th Anniv. — A154

Anniversaries and events: 12um, Adler, 1st German locomotive, 1835. 18um, Series 10, 1956, last Fed. German Railways locomotive. 44um, European Music Year, Johann Sebastian Bach, composer, and Angels Making Music, unattributed painting. 77um, George Frideric Handel. 90um, Statue of Liberty, cent., vert. 100um, Queen Mother, 85th birthday, vert.

1985, Sept.

580	A154	12um multi	22	15
581	A154	18um multi	35	16
582	A154	44um multi	80	40
583	A154	77um multi	1.50	80
584	A154	90um multi	1.60	80
		Nos. 580-584 (5)	4.47	2.31

Souvenir Sheet

585 A154 100um multi 2.00 1.00

World Food Day — A155

1985, Oct. 16 *Perf. 13x12½*

586 A155 18um multi 35 16

UN Food and Agriculture Org., 40th anniv.

Fight Against Drought — A156

1985 **Litho.** *Perf. 13*

587	A156	14um Antelope	28	15
588	A156	18um Oasis	35	16

Fight Against Desert Encroachment — A157

1985

589	A157	10um Grain harvest, vert.	20	15
590	A157	14um Brush fire	28	15
591	A157	18um Planting brush	35	16
		Set value		40

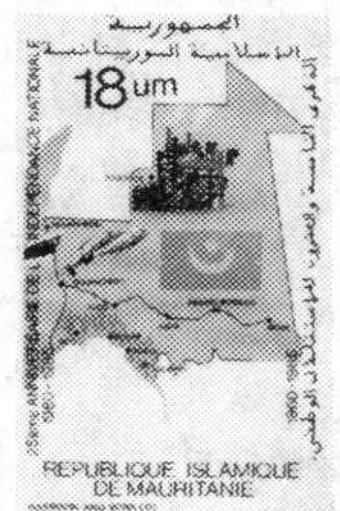

Natl. Independence, 25th Anniv. — A158

1985 *Perf. 15x14½*

592 A158 18um multi 35 16

Intl. Youth Year A159

1986, Feb. 13 **Litho.** *Perf. 13*

593	A159	18um Development	15	15
594	A159	22um Participation	15	15
595	A159	25um Peace, vert.	15	15
		Set value	35	18

Toujounine Satellite Station — A160

1986, May 22 **Litho.** *Perf. 12½*

596 A160 25um multi 15 15

World Wildlife Fund — A161

Monk seal (Monachus monachus).

1986, June 12 *Perf. 13*

597	A161	2um multi	15	15
598	A161	5um multi	15	15
599	A161	10um multi	15	15
600	A161	18um multi	15	15
		Set value	25	25

Souvenir Sheet

601 A161 50um multi 28 15

Weaving — A162

1986, July 20 **Litho.** *Perf. 12½*

602 A162 18um multi 35 18

Sabra and Chatila Massacre, 4th Anniv. — A163

1986, Oct. 18

603 A163 22um multi 45 22

A164

Christopher Columbus — A165

Indians, maps on globe and: 2um, Santa Maria. 22um, Nina. 35um, Pinta. 150um, Columbus.

1986, Oct. 14 **Litho.** *Perf. 13½*

604	A164	2um multi	15	15
605	A164	22um multi	65	32
606	A164	35um multi	1.05	52
607	A164	150um multi	4.50	2.25

Souvenir Sheet

608 A165 100um Columbus, Earth 3.00 1.50

Nos. 607-608 are airmail.

US Space Shuttle Challenger Explosion, Jan. 28, 1986 — A166

Crew members and: 7um, Space shuttle. 22um, Canadarm. 32um, Sky, moon. 43um, Memorial emblem.

1986, Oct. 14

609	A166	7um multi	22	15
610	A166	22um multi	65	32
611	A166	32um multi	95	48
612	A166	43um multi	1.30	65

Souvenir Sheet

613 A166 100um Crew, lift-off 3.00 1.50

Nos. 612-613 are airmail.

Fish A167

1986, Oct. 16 *Perf. 13*

614	A167	4um Dorade	15	15
615	A167	98um Truite de mer	3.00	1.50

See Nos. 631-633.

Birds A168

1986, Oct. 16

616	A168	22um Spatule blanche	65	32
617	A168	32um Sterne bridee	95	48

See Nos. 634-635.

World Food Day — A169

1986, Nov. 6 *Perf. 12½*

618 A169 22um multi 65 32

A170

Halley's Comet — A171

Space probes and portraits: 5um, J.H. Dort, Giotto probe. 18um, Sir William Huggins (1824-1910), English astronomer, and launch of Giotto on Ariane rocket. 26um, E.J. Opik, Giotto and Vega. 80um, F.L. Whipple, Planet-A. 100um, Edmond Halley, Giotto.

1986, Oct. 14 **Litho.** *Perf. 13½*

619	A170	5um multi	15	15
620	A170	18um multi	30	15
621	A170	26um multi	40	20
622	A170	80um multi	1.25	60

Souvenir Sheet

623 A171 100um multi 2.00 1.00

Nos. 622-623 are airmail.

Jerusalem Day — A172

1987, May 21 **Litho.** *Perf. 13½*

624 A172 22um Dome of the Rock 65 32

Cordoue Mosque, 1200th Anniv. A173

1987, Sept. 5 Litho. *Perf. 13½*
625 A173 30um multi 1.10 55

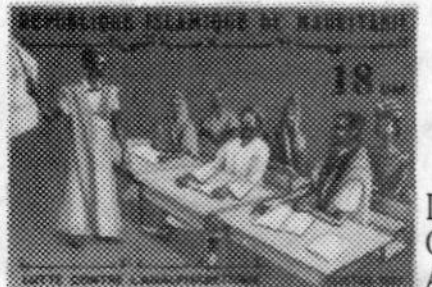

Literacy Campaign A174

1987, Sept. 12
626 A174 18um Classroom 65 32
627 A174 22um Family reading, vert. 80 40

World Health Day — A175

1987, Oct. 1 *Perf. 13*
628 A175 18um multi 65 32

Natl. Population Census A176

1988, Aug. 21 Litho. *Perf. 13½*
629 A176 20um multi 60 30

WHO, 40th Anniv. — A177

Arab Scouting Movement, 75th Anniv. — A178

1988, Sept. 19 *Perf. 13*
630 A177 30um multi 90 45

Fish Type of 1986

1988, Sept. 10 Litho. *Perf. 13*
631 A167 1um Rascasse blanche 15 15
632 A167 7um Baliste 48 25
633 A167 15um Bonite a ventre raye 1.00 50

Bird Type of 1986

1988, Sept. 15
634 A168 18um Grand cormorant 1.20 60
635 A168 80um Royal tern 5.40 2.70

1988, Sept. 29 Litho. *Perf. 13*
636 A178 35um multi 1.15 58

1st Municipal Elections — A179

1988, Nov. 22 *Perf. 13½*
637 A179 20um Men casting ballots 65 32
638 A179 24um Woman casting ballot 78 40

Organization of African Unity, 25th Anniv. (in 1988) — A180

Intl. Fund for Agricultural Development, 10th Anniv. (in 1988) — A181

1988, Dec. 7 Litho. *Perf. 13*
639 A180 40um multi 1.30 65

1988, Dec. 15
640 A181 35um multi 1.15 58

Autonomy of Nouakchott (Amitie) Port, 1st Anniv. — A182

1988, Dec. 20 Litho. *Perf. 13*
641 A182 24um multi 78 40

A183

A184

1989, July 7 Litho. *Perf. 13*
642 A183 35um multi 1.10 55

French Revolution bicent., PHILEXFRANCE '89.

1989, July 17
643 A184 20um multi 60 30

1990 World Cup Soccer Championships, Italy.

Pilgrimage to Mecca A185

1989, Aug. 26 Litho. *Perf. 13½*
644 A185 20um Mosque 65 32

African Development Bank, 25th Anniv. — A186

1989, Sept. 2
645 A186 37um lt vio & blk 1.20 60

Tapestry — A187

1989, Oct. 1 *Perf. 13*
646 A187 50um multicolored 1.60 80

Locusts, Moths and Ladybugs — A188

1989, Dec. 29
647 A188 2um *Heliothis armigera* 15 15
648 A188 5um Locust 16 15
649 A188 6um *Aphis gossypii* 20 15
650 A188 10um *Agrotis ypsilon* 35 17
651 A188 20um *Chilo* 68 35
652 A188 20um Two locusts, egg case 68 35
653 A188 24um Locusts emerging 80 40
654 A188 24um *Plitella xylostella* 80 40
655 A188 30um *Henosepilachna elaterii* 1.00 50
656 A188 40um Locust flying 1.35 68
657 A188 42um *Trichoplusia ni* 1.40 70
658 A188 88um Locust, diff. 2.85 1.45
Nos. 647-658 (12) 10.42 5.45

Revolt — A189

1989, Dec. 8 Litho. *Perf. 13*
659 A189 35um multicolored 1.10 55

2nd Anniv. of the Palestinian Uprising and 1st anniv. of the declaration of a Palestinian State.

Maghreb Arab Union, 1st Anniv. — A190

Illustration reduced.

1990, Feb. 17 Litho. *Perf. 13½*
660 A190 50um multicolored 1.35 65

Mineral Resources A191

1990, July 27 *Perf. 11½*
661 A191 60um multicolored 1.65 85

Intl. Literacy Year — A192

1990, July 27
662 A192 60um multicolored 1.65 85

1992 Summer Olympics, Barcelona A193

Litho. & Typo.

1990, Sept. 2 *Perf. 13½*
663 A193 5um Equestrian 15 15
664 A193 50um Archery 1.35 65
665 A193 60um Hammer throw 1.65 85
666 A193 75um Field hockey 2.00 1.00
667 A193 90um Handball 2.50 1.25
668 A193 220um Table tennis 6.00 3.00
Nos. 663-668 (6) 13.65 6.90

Souvenir Sheet

669 A193 150um Runner 4.00 2.00

Nos. 668-669 airmail.

A194

A195

1990, July 27 *Perf. 11½*
670 A194 50um multicolored 1.35 65

Multinational Postal School, 20th anniv.

1990, Nov. 21 Litho. *Perf. 11½*
671 A195 85um multicolored 3.20 1.60

Declaration of the Palestinian State, 2nd anniv.

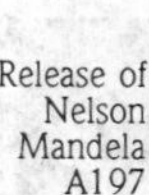

Release of Nelson Mandela A197

1990, Dec. 10
677 A197 85um multicolored 3.20 1.60

Return of Senegalese Refugees A198

1990, Dec. 10
678 A198 50um Cooking at encampment 1.90 95
679 A198 75um Women sewing 2.80 1.40
680 A198 85um Drawing water 3.40 1.70

Boy Scouts Observing Nature — A199

Scout: 5um, Picking mushrooms. 50um, Holding mushroom. 60um, Drawing butterfly. 75um, Feeding butterfly. 90um, Photographing butterfly. 220um, Drying mushrooms. No. 687, Using microscope.

1991, Jan. 16 Litho. *Perf. 13½*
681 A199 5um multicolored 20 15
682 A199 50um multicolored 1.90 95
683 A199 60um multicolored 2.25 1.15
684 A199 75um multicolored 2.80 1.40
685 A199 90um multicolored 3.40 1.70
686 A199 220um multicolored 8.25 4.15
Nos. 681-686 (6) 18.80 9.50

Souvenir Sheet

687 A199 150um multicolored 5.85 2.95

Nos. 684 and 687 are airmail. Nos. 683-685 exist in souvenir sheets of 1.

Independence, 30th Anniv. — A200

1991, Mar. 5
688 A200 50um Satellite dish antennae 1.90 95
689 A200 60um Container ship 2.25 1.15
690 A200 100um Harvesting rice 3.80 1.90

World Meteorology Day — A201

1991, Mar. 23 *Perf. 14x15*
691 A201 100um multicolored 3.80 1.90

World Population Day — A202

1991, July 27 Litho. *Perf. 13½*
692 A202 90um multicolored 3.60 1.80

Campaign Against Blindness A204

1991, Nov. 10 Litho. *Perf. 13½*
694 A204 50um multicolored 2.00 1.00

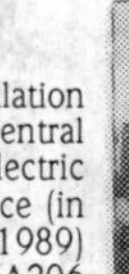

Installation of Central Electric Service (in 1989) A206

1991, Dec. 29 Litho. *Perf. 13½*
696 A206 50um multicolored 2.00 1.00

SEMI-POSTAL STAMPS

Nos. 23 and 26 Surcharged in Red

1915-18 Unwmk. *Perf. 14x13½*
B1 A4 10c + 5c rose & red org 38 38
B2 A4 15c + 5c dk brn & blk ('18) 25 25

Curie Issue
Common Design Type

1938, Oct. 24 *Perf. 13*
B3 CD80 1.75fr + 50c brt ultra 3.75 3.75

French Revolution Issue
Common Design Type
Photo.; Name and Value Typographed in Black

1939, July 5 Unwmk.
B4 CD83 45c + 25c grn 3.75 3.75
B5 CD83 70c + 30c brn 3.75 3.75
B6 CD83 90c + 35c red org 3.75 3.75
B7 CD83 1.25fr + 1fr rose pink 3.75 3.75
B8 CD83 2.25fr + 2fr bl 3.75 3.75
Nos. B4-B8 (5) 18.75 18.75

Stamps of 1938 Surcharge in Red or Black

SECOURS
+ 1 fr.
NATIONAL

1941
B9 A6 50c + 1fr pur (R) 80 80
B10 A7 80c + 2fr dp bl (R) 3.50 3.50
B11 A7 1.50fr + 2fr vio (R) 3.50 3.50
B12 A8 2fr + 3fr rose vio (Bk) 3.50 3.50

Common Design Type and

Moorish Goumier SP1

White Goumier SP2

1941 Photo. *Perf. 13½*
B13 SP1 1fr + 1fr red 40
B14 CD86 1.50fr + 3fr claret 40
B15 SP2 2.50fr + 1fr blue 40

Nos. B13-B15 were issued by the Vichy government, and were not placed on sale in the colony.

Nos. 114-115 were surcharged "OEUVRES COLONIALES" and surtax (including change of denomination of the 2.50fr to 50c). These were issued in 1944 by the Vichy government and were not placed on sale in the colony.

Catalogue values for unused stamps in this section, from this point to the end of the section, are for Never Hinged items.

Islamic Republic
Anti-Malaria Issue
Common Design Type

1962, Apr. 7 Engr. *Perf. 12½x12*
B16 CD108 25fr + 5f lt ol grn 40 40

Freedom from Hunger Issue
Common Design Type

1963, Mar. 21 Unwmk. *Perf. 13*
B17 CD112 25fr + 5fr multi 35 35

Nurse Tending Infant — SP3

1972, May 8 Photo. *Perf. 12½x13*
B18 SP3 35fr + 5fr grn, red & brn 25 25

Surtax was for Mauritania Red Crescent Society.

AIR POST STAMPS

Common Design Type
Perf. 12½x12

1940, Feb. 8 Engr. Unwmk.
C1 CD85 1.90fr ultra 20 20
C2 CD85 2.90fr dk red 20 20
C3 CD85 4.50fr dk gray grn 28 28
C4 CD85 4.90fr yel bister 60 60
C5 CD85 6.90fr deep org 60 60
Nos. C1-C5 (5) 1.88 1.88

Common Design Types

1942
C6 CD88 50c car & bl 15
C7 CD88 1fr brn & blk 16
C8 CD88 2fr dk grn & red brn 20
C9 CD88 3fr dk bl & scar 22
C10 CD88 5fr vio & brn red 30

Frame Engraved, Center Typo.

C11 CD89 10fr ultra, ind & hn 32
a. Center inverted *600.00*
C12 CD89 20fr rose car, mag & buff 35
C13 CD89 50fr yel grn, dl grn & org 45 1.00
Nos. C6-C13 (8) 2.15

There is doubt whether Nos. C6-C12 were officially placed in use.

Catalogue values for unused stamps in this section, from this point to the end of the section, are for Never Hinged items.

Islamic Republic

Flamingoes — AP1

Designs: 200fr, African spoonbills. 500fr, Slender-billed gull, horiz.

Unwmk.

1961, June 30 Engr. *Perf. 13*
C14 AP1 100fr red org, brn & ultra 1.40 90
C15 AP1 200fr red org, sep & sl grn 2.75 1.90
C16 AP1 500fr red org, gray & bl 6.50 3.75

An overprint, "Europa / CECA / MIFERMA," was applied in carmine to No. C16 in 1962.

The anti-malaria emblem, including slogan "Le Monde contre le Paludisme," was overprinted on Nos. C14-C15 in 1962.

Air Afrique Issue
Common Design Type

1962, Feb. 17
C17 CD107 100fr sl grn, choc & bis 1.00 65

UN Headquarters, New York; View of Nouakchott — AP2

1962, Oct. 27 Engr. *Perf. 13*
C18 AP2 100fr bluish grn, dk bl & org brn 1.00 70

Mauritania's admission to the UN.

Plane, Nouakchott Airport — AP3

1963, May 3 Unwmk. *Perf. 13*
C19 AP3 500fr dp bl, gldn brn & slate grn 3.75 2.25

Miferma Open-pit Mine at Zouerate — AP4

Design: 200fr, Ore transport at Port Etienne.

1963, June Photo. *Perf. 13x12*

C20 AP4 100fr multi 65 35
C21 AP4 200fr multi 1.50 75

African Postal Union Issue
Common Design Type

1963, Sept. 8 Unwmk. *Perf. 12½*

C22 CD114 85fr blk brn, ocher & red 70 40

Globe and Telstar — AP5

Design: 150fr, Relay satellite and stars.

1963, Oct. 7 Engr. *Perf. 13*

C23 AP5 50fr yel grn, pur & red brn 50 32
C24 AP5 150fr red brn & sl grn 1.40 1.00

Communication through space.

Tiros Satellite and Emblem of WMO — AP6

UN Emblem, Doves and Sun — AP7

1963, Nov. 4

C25 AP6 200fr ultra, brn & grn 1.50 90

Space research for meteorology and navigation.

1963 Air Afrique Issue
Common Design Type

1963, Nov. 19 Photo. *Perf. 13x12*

C26 CD115 25fr multi 30 18

1963, Dec. 10 Engr. *Perf. 13*

C27 AP7 100fr vio, brn, & dk bl 1.00 55

Universal Declaration of Human Rights, 15th anniv.

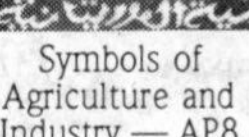

Symbols of Agriculture and Industry — AP8

Lichtenstein's Sand Grouse — AP9

Europafrica Issue

1964, Jan. 6 Photo.

C28 AP8 50fr multi 80 50

Signing of economic agreement between the European Economic Community and the African and Malgache Union at Yaoundé, Cameroun, July 20, 1963.

1964, Feb. 3 Engr. *Perf. 13*

Birds: 200fr, Long-tailed cormorant. 500fr, Chanting goshawk.

C29 AP9 100fr ocher, ol & dk brn 1.00 40
C30 AP9 200fr blk, dk bl & brn 1.90 80
C31 AP9 500fr rose red, grn & sl 4.50 2.00

Isis, Temple at Philae and Trajan's Kiosk — AP10

1964, Mar. 8 Unwmk. *Perf. 13*

C32 AP10 10fr red brn, Prus bl & blk 25 18
C33 AP10 25fr red brn, ind & Prus bl 40 30
C34 AP10 60fr blk brn, Prus bl & red brn 80 60

UNESCO world campaign to save historic monuments in Nubia.

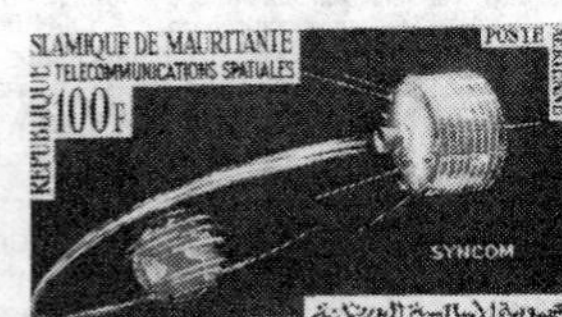

Syncom Satellite, Globe — AP11

1964, May 4 Engr.

C35 AP11 100fr red, red brn & ultra 1.00 60

Issued to publicize space communications.

Horse Race on Bowl — AP12

Sport Designs from Ancient Pottery: 50fr, Runner, vert. 85fr, Wrestlers, vert. 100fr, Charioteer.

1964, Sept. 27 Unwmk. *Perf. 13*

C36 AP12 15fr ol bis & choc 15 15
C37 AP12 50fr bl & org brn 38 22
C38 AP12 85fr crim & brn 65 38
C39 AP12 100fr emer & dk red brn 75 45
a. Min. sheet of 4, #C36-C39 2.25 2.25

18th Olympic Games, Tokyo, Oct. 10-25.

Pres. John F. Kennedy (1917-1963) — AP13

1964, Dec. 7 Photo. *Perf. 12½*

C40 AP13 100fr red brn, bl grn & dk brn 75 65
a. Souv. sheet of 4 3.25 3.25

ITU Emblem, Induction Telegraph and Relay Satellite — AP14

1965, May 17 Engr. *Perf. 13*

C41 AP14 250fr multi 1.90 1.25

ITU, centenary.

Fight Against Cancer — AP15

Winston Churchill — AP16

1965, July 19 Unwmk. *Perf. 13*

C42 AP15 100fr bis, Prus bl & red 1.00 42

Issued to publicize the fight against cancer.

1965, Dec. 6 Photo. *Perf. 13*

C43 AP16 200fr multi 1.50 60

Sir Winston Spencer Churchill (1874-1965), statesman and WWII leader.

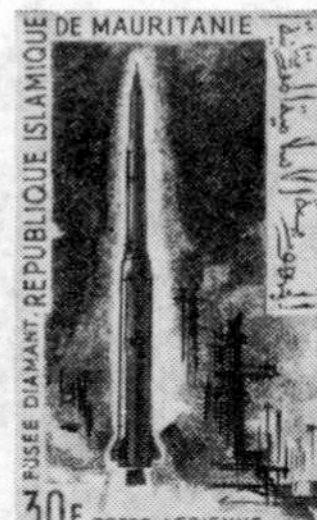

Diamant Rocket Ascending — AP17

French achievements in space: 60fr, Satellite A-1 and earth, horiz. 90fr, Scout rocket and satellite FR-1, horiz.

1966, Feb. 7 Engr. *Perf. 13*

C44 AP17 30fr dp bl, red & grn 60 22
C45 AP17 60fr mar, Prus grn & bl 1.10 40
C46 AP17 90fr dp bl, rose cl & vio 1.40 65

Dr. Albert Schweitzer and Clinic — AP18

1966, Feb. 21 Photo. *Perf. 12½*

C47 AP18 50fr multi 50 22

Schweitzer (1875-1965), medical missionary to Gabon, theologian and musician.

Thomas P. Stafford, Walter M. Schirra and Gemini 6 — AP19

Designs: 100fr, Frank A. Borman, James A. Lovell, Jr., and Gemini 7. 200fr, Pavel Belyayev, Alexei Leonov, Voskhod 2.

1966, Mar. 7 Photo. *Perf. 12½*

C48 AP19 50fr multi 40 18
C49 AP19 100fr multi 70 35
C50 AP19 200fr multi 1.50 60

Issued to honor achievements in space.

Map of Africa and Dove — AP20

D-1 Satellite over Earth — AP21

1966, May 9 Photo. *Perf. 13*

C51 AP20 100fr red brn, sl & yel grn 90 38

Organization for African Unity.

1966, June 6 Engr.

C52 AP21 100fr bl, dk pur & ocher 1.90 42

Launching of the D-1 satellite at Hammaguir, Algeria, Feb. 17, 1966.

Bréguet 14 — AP22

Planes: 100fr, Goliath Farman, and camel caravan. 150fr, Couzinet "Arc-en-Ciel." 200fr, Latécoère 28 hydroplane.

1966, July 4 Engr. *Perf. 13*

C53 AP22 50fr sl bl, dl grn & ol bis 50 18
C54 AP22 100fr brt bl, dk grn & dk red brn 90 30
C55 AP22 150fr dl brn, Prus bl & saph 1.40 45
C56 AP22 200fr dk red brn, bl & ind 2.00 70

Air Afrique Issue, 1966
Common Design Type

1966, Aug. 31 Photo. *Perf. 13*

C57 CD123 30fr red, blk & gray 30 15

"The Raft of the Medusa," by Théodore Géricault — AP23

1966, Sept. 5 Photo. *Perf. 12½*

C58 AP23 500fr multi 3.75 2.00

Sinking of the frigate "Medusa" off Mauritania, July 2, 1816.

Symbols of Agriculture and Industry — AP24

1966, Nov. 7 Photo. *Perf. 13x12*

C59 AP24 50fr multi 42 16

Third anniversary, economic agreement between the European Economic Community and the African and Malgache Union.

Crowned Crane — AP25

Eye, Globe and Rockets — AP26

1967, Apr. 3 *Perf. 12½x13*

C60 AP25 100fr shown		65	40
C61 AP25 200fr Common egret		1.40	60
C62 AP25 500fr Ostrich		3.50	1.60

For surcharge see No. C129.

1967, May 2 Engr. *Perf. 13*

C63 AP26 250fr brn, Prus bl & blk 1.90 1.00

EXPO '67 Intl. Exhibition, Montreal, Apr. 28-Oct. 27.

Emblem of Atomic Energy Commission AP27

1967, Aug. 7 Engr. *Perf. 13*

C64 AP27 200fr dk red, brt grn & ultra 2.25 1.00

International Atomic Energy Commission.

African Postal Union Issue, 1967

Common Design Type

1967, Sept. 9 Engr. *Perf. 13*

C65 CD124 100fr brn org, vio brn & brt grn 90 40

Francesca da Rimini, by Ingres AP28

Paintings by and of Ingres: 100fr, Young man's torso. 150fr, "The Iliad" (seated woman). 200fr, Ingres in his Studio, by Alaux. 250fr, "The Odyssey" (seated woman).

1967-68 Photo. *Perf. 12½*

C66 AP28 90fr multi	90	42
C67 AP28 100fr multi ('68)	80	45
C68 AP28 150fr multi ('68)	1.40	65
C69 AP28 200fr multi	2.00	90
C70 AP28 250fr multi ('68)	2.25	1.20
Nos. C66-C70 (5)	7.35	3.62

Jean Dominique Ingres (1780-1867), French painter.

Issue dates: Oct. 2, 1967, 90fr, 200fr. Sept. 2, 1968, others.

See No. C79.

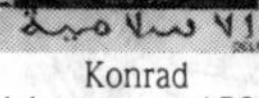

Konrad Adenauer — AP29

Gymnast — AP30

1968, Feb. 5 Photo. *Perf. 12½*

C71 AP29 100fr org brn, lt bl & blk 75 35

a. Souv. sheet of 4 3.00 2.50

Adenauer (1876-1967), chancellor of West Germany (1949-63).

1968, Mar. 4 Engr. *Perf. 13*

Sports: 20fr, Slalom, horiz. 50fr, Ski jump. 100fr, Hurdling, horiz.

C72 AP30 20fr plum, blk & bl	16	15
C73 AP30 30fr dl pur, brt grn & brn	22	15
C74 AP30 50fr Prus bl, bis & bl grn	40	18
C75 AP30 100fr brn, grn & ver	80	35
Set value		70

1968 Olympic Games.

WHO Emblem, Man and Insects — AP31

1968, May 2 Engr. *Perf. 13*

C76 AP31 150fr red lil, dp bl & org red 1.20 60

WHO, 20th anniversary.

Martin Luther King — AP32

Design: No. C78, Mahatma Gandhi.

1968, Nov. 4 Photo. *Perf. 12½*

C77 AP32 50fr sl bl, cit & blk	35	18
C78 AP32 50fr sl bl, lt bl & blk	35	18
a. Souv. sheet of 4, 2 each #C77-C78	1.60	1.60

Issued to honor two apostles of peace.

PHILEXAFRIQUE Issue

Painting Type of 1967

Design: 100fr, The Surprise Letter, by Charles Antoine Coypel.

1968, Dec. 9 Photo. *Perf. 12½*

C79 AP28 100fr multi 1.00 1.00

PHILEXAFRIQUE, Phil. Exhib., Abidjan, Feb. 14-23. Printed with alternating brown red label.

2nd PHILEXAFRIQUE Issue

Common Design Type

Design: 50fr, Mauritania No. 89 and family on jungle trail.

1969, Feb. 14 Engr. *Perf. 13*

C80 CD128 50fr sl grn, vio brn & red brn 55 55

Napoleon Installed in Council of State, by Louis Charles Couder AP33

Paintings: 50fr, Napoleon at Council of the 500, by F. Bouchot. 250fr, Farewell at Fontainebleau, by Horace Vernet.

1969, Feb. 24 Photo. *Perf. 12½*

C81 AP33 50fr pur & multi	80	65
C82 AP33 90fr multi	1.20	1.00
C83 AP33 250fr multi	3.50	2.25

Napoleon Bonaparte (1769-1821).

Camel, Gazelles, and Tourist Year Emblem — AP34

1969, June 9 Engr. *Perf. 13*

C84 AP34 50fr org, dk brn & lt bl 42 22

Year of African Tourism.

Dancers and Temple Ruins, Baalbek — AP35

1969, June 16

C85 AP35 100fr Prus bl, ol brn & rose car 65 35

International Baalbek Festival, Lebanon.

Apollo 8 and Moon Surface — AP36

Embossed on Gold Foil

1969 *Die-cut Perf. 10*

C86 AP36 1000fr gold 9.00 9.00

Man's first flight around the moon, Dec. 21-28, 1968 (US astronauts Col. Frank Borman, Capt. James Lovell and Maj. William Anders).

Mamo Wolde, Ethiopia, Marathon — AP37

Designs: 70fr, Bob Beamon, US, broad jump. 150fr, Vera Caslavska, Czechoslovakia, gymnastics.

1969, July 7 Engr. *Perf. 13*

C87 AP37 30fr multi	20	15
C88 AP37 70fr multi	42	20
C89 AP37 150fr multi	90	55

Issued to honor gold medal winners in the 19th Olympic Games, Mexico City.

Map of London-Istanbul Route — AP38

London to Sydney automobile rally: 20fr, Map showing Ankara to Teheran route, and compass rose. 50fr, Map showing Kandahar to Bombay route, arms of Afghanistan and elephant. 70fr, Map of Australia with Perth to Sydney route, and kangaroo.

1969, Aug. 14 Engr. *Perf. 13*

C90 AP38 10fr multicolored	15	15
C91 AP38 20fr multicolored	15	15
C92 AP38 50fr multicolored	35	15
C93 AP38 70fr multicolored	40	18
a. Min. sheet of 4, #C90-C93	1.40	1.40
Set value		45

Palette with World Map, Geisha and EXPO '70 Emblem — AP39

Designs (EXPO '70 Emblem and): 75fr, Fan and fireworks. 150fr, Stylized bird, map of Japan and boat.

1970, June 15 Photo. *Perf. 12½*

C94 AP39 50fr multi 38 16
C95 AP39 75fr multi 50 25
C96 AP39 150fr multi 1.10 45

Issued to publicize EXPO '70 International Exhibition, Osaka, Japan, Mar. 15-Sept. 13.

UN Emblem, Balloon, Rocket, Farm Woman, Tractor, Old and New Record Players — AP40

1970, June 22 Engr. *Perf. 13*

C97 AP40 100fr ultra, dk brn & grn 70 42

25th anniversary of the United Nations.

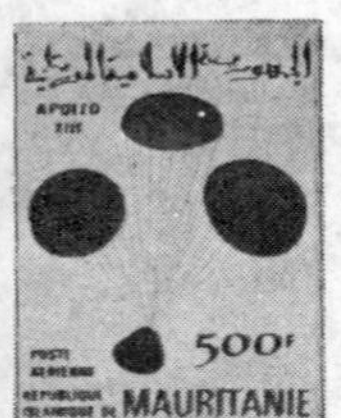

Elliott See (1927-1966), American Astronaut — AP41

Apollo 13 Capsule with Parachutes — AP42

Portraits: No. C99, Vladimir Komarov (1927-1967). C100, Yuri Gagarin (1934-1968). No. C101, Virgil Grissom (1926-1967). No. C102, Edward White (1930-1967). No. C103, Roger Chaffee (1935-1967).

1970 Engr. *Perf. 13*

Portrait in Brown

C98 AP41 150fr gray & brt bl 1.00 42
C99 AP41 150fr gray & org 1.00 42
C100 AP41 150fr gray & org 1.00 42
a. Souv. sheet of 3, #C98-C100 4.00 4.00
C101 AP41 150fr ultra & grnsh bl 1.00 42
C102 AP41 150fr ultra & org 1.00 42
C103 AP41 150fr ultra & grnsh bl 1.00 42
a. Souv. sheet of 3, #C101-C103 6.00 6.00
Nos. C98-C103 (6) 6.00 2.52

American and Russian astronauts who died in space explorations.

Gold Embossed

1970, Aug. 17 *Perf. 12½*

C104 AP42 500fr gold, crim & bl 4.00 4.00

Safe return of Apollo 13 crew.

Parliament, Nouakchott, and Coat of Arms — AP43

1970, Nov. 28 Photo. *Perf. 12½*

C105 AP43 100fr multi 65 35

10th anniversary of Independence.

Hercules Wrestling Antaeus — AP44

1971, Mar. 8 Engr. *Perf. 13*

C106 AP44 100fr red lil, brn & ultra 80 50

Pre-Olympic Year. Design from a vase decoration by Euphronius.

Gamal Abdel Nasser (1918-1970), President of U.A.R. — AP46

1971, May 10 Photo. *Perf. 12½*

C109 AP46 100fr gold & multi 60 30

Boy Scout, Emblem and Map of Mauritania — AP47

1971, Aug. 16 Photo. *Perf. 12½*

C110 AP47 35fr yel & multi 20 15
C111 AP47 40fr pink & multi 22 16
C112 AP47 100fr multi 60 35

13th Boy Scout World Jamboree, Asagiri Plain, Japan, Aug. 2-10.

African Postal Union Issue, 1971

Common Design Type

Design: 100fr, Women musicians and UAMPT building, Brazzaville, Congo.

1971, Nov. 13 Photo. *Perf. 13x13½*

C113 CD135 100fr bl & multi 65 42

Letter and Postal Emblem AP48

1971, Dec. 2 *Perf. 13*

C114 AP48 35fr bis & multi 22 15

10th anniversary of African Postal Union.

Mosul Monarch, from Book of Songs, c. 1218 — AP49

Designs from Mohammedan Miniatures: 40fr, Prince holding audience, Egypt, 1334. 100fr, Pilgrim caravan, from "Maquamat," Baghdad, 1237.

1972, Jan. 10 Photo. *Perf. 13*

C115 AP49 35fr gold & multi 22 16
C116 AP49 40fr gray & multi 25 20
C117 AP49 100fr buff & multi 65 42

For surcharges see Nos. C140, C143-C144.

Grand Canal, by Canaletto — AP50

Designs: 45fr, Venice Harbor, by Carlevaris, vert. 250fr, Santa Maria della Salute, by Canaletto.

1972, Feb. 14

C118 AP50 45fr gold & multi 20 15
C119 AP50 100fr gold & multi 45 25
C120 AP50 250fr gold & multi 1.25 60

UNESCO campaign to save Venice.

Hurdles and Olympic Rings — AP51

1972, Apr. 27 Engr. *Perf. 13*

C121 AP51 75fr org, vio brn & blk 35 16
C122 AP51 100fr Prus bl, vio brn & brn 50 25
C123 AP51 200fr lake, vio brn & blk 1.00 40
a. Min. sheet of 3, #C121-C123 1.90 1.90

20th Olympic Games, Munich, Aug. 26-Sept. 11.
For overprints see Nos. C126-C128.

Luna 17 on Moon AP52

Design: 75fr, Luna 16 take-off from moon, vert.

1972, Oct. 9

C124 AP52 75fr vio bl, bis & grn 45 20
C125 AP52 100fr dl pur, sl & ol bis 65 35

Russian moon missions, Luna 16, Sept. 12-14, 1970; and Luna 17, Nov. 10-17, 1970.

Nos. C121-C123 Overprinted in Violet Blue or Red:

a. 110m HAIES / MILBURN MEDAILLE D'OR
b. 400m HAIES / AKII-BUA MEDAILLE D'OR
c. 3.000m STEEPLE / KEINO MEDAILLE D'OR

1972, Oct. 16

C126 AP51(a) 75fr multi (VB) 45 20
C127 AP51(b) 100fr multi (R) 65 35
C128 AP51(c) 200fr multi (VB) 1.40 55

Gold medal winners in 20th Olympic Games: Rod Milburn, US, John Akii-Bua, Uganda, and Kipchoge Keino, Kenya.

No. C62 Surcharged with New Value, Two Bars and: "Apollo XVII / December 1972"

1973, Jan. 29 Photo. *Perf. 12½x13*

C129 AP25 250fr on 500fr multi 1.50 65

Apollo 17 moon mission, Dec. 7-19, 1972.

Seal Type of Regular Issue

1973, Feb. 28 Litho. *Perf. 13*

C130 A63 135fr Seal's head 1.20 70

For surcharge see No. C145.

Lion Eating Caiman, by Delacroix — AP53

Painting: 250fr, Lion Eating Boar, by Delacroix.

1973, Mar. 26 Photo. *Perf. 13x12½*

C131 AP53 100fr blk & multi 80 42
C132 AP53 250fr blk & multi 2.00 1.10

For surcharges see Nos. C148-C149.

Villagers Observing Solar Eclipse — AP54

Designs: 40fr, Rocket take-off and Concord, vert. 140fr, Scientists with telescopes observing eclipse.

1973, June 20 Engr. *Perf. 13*

C133 AP54 35fr grn & pur 22 15
C134 AP54 40fr ultra, pur & scar 25 15
C135 AP54 140fr scar & pur 90 55
a. Souvenir sheet of 3 2.00 2.00

Solar eclipse, June 30, 1973. No. C135a contains 3 stamps similar to Nos. C133-C135 in changed colors (35fr, 140fr in magenta and violet blue; 40fr in magenta, violet blue and orange).
For surcharges see Nos. C141-C142, C146.

Soccer AP55

1973, Dec. 24 Photo. *Perf. 13*

C136 AP55 7um multi 22 15
C137 AP55 8um multi 22 15
C138 AP55 20um multi 65 42

Souvenir Sheet

C139 AP55 30um multi 1.10 1.10

World Soccer Cup, Munich, 1974.

Nos. C115-C117, C130 and C133-C135 Surcharged with New Value and Two Bars in Red, Black or Ultramarine

1973-74 Photo., Litho. or Engr.

C140 AP49 7um on 35fr (R) ('74) 22 15
C141 AP54 7um on 35fr (B) 25 15
C142 AP54 8um on 40fr (B) 25 16
C143 AP49 8um on 40fr (U) ('74) 25 16
C144 AP49 20um on 100fr (R) ('74) 70 42
C145 A63 27um on 135fr (R) 80 50
C146 AP54 28um on 140fr (B) 95 55
Nos. C140-C146 (7) 3.42 2.09

Winston Churchill (1874-1965) AP56

Lenin (1870-1924) AP57

1974, June 3 Engr. *Perf. 13*

C147 AP56 40um blk, brn & hn brn 1.00 60

Nos. C131-C132 Surcharged with New Value and Two Bars in Red

1974, July 15 Photo. *Perf. 13x12½*

C148 AP53 20um on 100fr multi 45 28
C149 AP53 50um on 250fr multi 1.20 70

1974, Sept. 16 Engr. *Perf. 13*

C150 AP57 40um sl grn & red 1.00 60

Women, IWY Emblem AP58

Design: 40um, Woman's head and IWY emblems.

1975, June 16 Engr. *Perf. 13*

C151 AP58 12um multi 38 20
C152 AP58 40um dk brn, lt brn & bl 1.25 65

International Women's Year.

Albert Schweitzer and Patients Arriving — AP59

1975, Aug. 4 Engr. *Perf. 13*

C153 AP59 60um multi 1.60 1.00

Schweitzer (1875-1965), medical missionary.

Javelin and Olympic Emblem — AP60

Design: 52um, Running and Olympic emblem.

1975, Nov. 17 Engr. *Perf. 13*

C154 AP60 50um sl grn, red & ol 1.50 80
C155 AP60 52um car, ocher & ultra 1.40 80

Pre-Olympic Year 1975.

Apollo Soyuz Type, 1975

Docked Space Ships and: 20um, Apollo rocket launch. 50um, Handshake in linked-up cabin. 60um, Apollo splash-down. 100um, Astronauts and Cosmonauts.

1975, Dec. 29 Litho. *Perf. 14*

C156 A74 20um multi 50 22
C157 A74 50um multi 1.10 60
C158 A74 60um multi 1.40 70

Souvenir Sheet

C159 A74 100um multi 2.40 1.25

American Bicentennial Type, 1976

Uniforms: 20um, French Hussar officer. 50um, 3rd Continental Artillery officer. 60um, French infantry regiment grenadier. 100um, American infantryman.

1976, Jan. 26

C160 A75 20um multi 50 20
C161 A75 50um multi 1.25 50
C162 A75 60um multi 1.50 60

Souvenir Sheet

C163 A75 100um multi 2.50 1.25

Running and Olympic Rings — AP61

Olympic Rings and: 12um, High jump. 52um, Fencing.

1976, June 14 Engr. *Perf. 13*

C164 AP61 10um pur, grn & brn 30 16
C165 AP61 12um pur, grn & brn 38 20
C166 AP61 52um pur, grn & brn 1.50 80

21st Olympic Games, Montreal, Canada, July 17-Aug. 1.

Zeppelin Type, 1976

Designs: 50um, "Graf Zeppelin" (LZ-127) over US Capitol. 60um, "Hindenburg" (LZ-130) over Swiss Alps. 100um, "Führersland" (LZ-129) over 1936 Olympic stadium.

1976, June 28 Litho. *Perf. 11*

C167 A77 50um multi 1.50 65
C168 A77 60um multi 1.90 80

Souvenir Sheet

C169 A77 100um multi 3.25 1.40

Marabou Storks — AP62

African Birds: 50um, Sacred ibis, vert. 200um, Long-crested eagles, vert.

1976, Sept. 20 Litho. *Perf. 13½*

C170 AP62 50um multi 1.50 62
C171 AP62 100um multi 3.00 1.40
C172 AP62 200um multi 5.75 2.25

Viking Type, 1977

Designs: 20um, Viking orbiter in flight to Mars. 50um, Viking "B" in descent to Mars. 60um, Various phases of descent. 100um, Viking lander using probe.

1977, Feb. 28 *Perf. 14*

C173 A81 20um multi 50 22
C174 A81 50um multi 1.20 55
C175 A81 60um multi 1.50 65

Souvenir Sheet

C176 A81 100um multi 2.50 1.00

For surcharge and overprints see Nos. C192-C195.

Nobel Prize Type, 1977

Designs: 14um, George Bernard Shaw, literature. 55um, Thomas Mann, literature. 60um, International Red Cross Society, peace. 100um, George C. Marshall, peace.

1977, Apr. 29 Litho. *Perf. 14*

C177 A83 14um multi 32 20
C178 A83 55um multi 1.25 60
C179 A83 60um multi 1.50 65

Souvenir Sheet

C180 A83 100um multi 2.50 1.00

Holy Kaaba AP63

1977, July 25 Litho. *Perf. 12½*

C181 AP63 12um multi 38 20

Pilgrimage to Mecca.

Soccer Type of 1977

Designs (Emblems and): 50um, Soccer ball. 60um, Eusebio Ferreira. 100um, Players holding pennants.

1977, Dec. 19 Litho. *Perf. 13½*

C182 A89 50um multi 1.20 50
C183 A89 60um multi 1.50 65

Souvenir Sheet

C184 A89 100um multi 2.40 1.00

For overprints see Nos. C187-C189.

Franco-African Co-operation — AP63a

1978, June 7 Embossed *Perf. 10½*

C184A AP63a 250um silver
C184B AP63a 500um gold

Philexafrique II - Essen Issue

Common Design Types

Designs: No. C185, Hyena and Mauritania No. C60. No. C186, Wading bird and Hamburg No. 1.

1978, Nov. 1 Litho. *Perf. 12½*

C185 CD138 20um multi 65 35
C186 CD139 20um multi 65 35
a. Pair, #C185-C186 1.30 75

Nos. C182-C184 Overprinted in Arabic and French in Silver: "ARGENTINE- / PAYS BAS 3-1"

1978, Dec. 11 Litho. *Perf. 13½*

C187 A89 50um multi 1.25 50
C188 A89 60um multi 1.50 65

Souvenir Sheet

C189 A89 100um multi 2.75 1.25

Argentina's victory in World Cup Soccer Championship 1978.

Flyer A and Prototype Plane — AP64

Design: 40um, Flyer A and supersonic jet.

1979, Jan. 29 Engr. *Perf. 13*

C190 AP64 15um multi 42 20
C191 AP64 40um multi 1.10 55

75th anniversary of first powered flight.

Nos. C173-C176 Overprinted and Surcharged in Silver: "ALUNISSAGE / APOLLO XI / JUILLET 1969" and Emblem

1979, Oct. 24 Litho. *Perf. 14*

C192 A81 14um on 20um multi 35 18
C193 A81 50um multi 1.25 65
C194 A81 60um multi 1.50 75

Souvenir Sheet

C195 A81 100um multi 2.75 2.75

Apollo 11 moon landing, 10th anniversary.

Soccer Players — AP65

Designs: Various soccer scenes.

1980, Sept. 29 Litho. *Perf. 12½*

C196 AP65 10um multi 35 15
C197 AP65 12um multi 40 18
C198 AP65 14um multi 45 20
C199 AP65 20um multi 65 30
C200 AP65 67um multi 2.25 1.10
Nos. C196-C200 (5) 4.10 1.93

Souvenir Sheet

C201 AP65 100um multi 3.50 1.50

World Soccer Cup 1982.
For overprints see Nos. C212-C217.

Flight of Columbia Space Shuttle — AP66

Designs: Views of Columbia space shuttle.

1981, Apr. 27 Litho. *Perf. 12½*

C202 AP66 12um multi 40 20
C203 AP66 20um multi 65 30
C204 AP66 50um multi 1.60 80
C205 AP66 70um multi 2.25 1.20

Souvenir Sheet

C206 AP66 100um multi 3.50 1.60

The Catalogue editors cannot undertake to appraise, identify or judge the genuineness or condition of stamps.

Dinard Landscape, by Pablo Picasso — AP67

Picasso Birth Centenary: 12um, Harlequin, vert. 20um, Vase of Flowers, vert. 50um, Three Women at the Well. 100um, Picnic.

1981, June 29 Litho. *Perf. 12½*

C207 AP67 12um multi 40 20
C208 AP67 20um multi 65 35
C209 AP67 50um multi 1.60 80
C210 AP67 70um multi 2.25 1.10
C211 AP67 100um multi 3.50 1.60
Nos. C207-C211 (5) 8.40 4.05

Nos. C196-C201 Overprinted in Red with Finalists and Score on 1 or 2 Lines

1982, Sept. 18 Litho. *Perf. 12½*

C212 AP65 10um multi 35 15
C213 AP65 12um multi 40 18
C214 AP65 14um multi 45 20
C215 AP65 20um multi 65 30
C216 AP65 67um multi 2.25 1.10
Nos. C212-C216 (5) 4.10 1.93

Souvenir Sheet

C217 AP65 100um multi 3.50 1.50

Italy's victory in 1982 World Cup.

25th Anniv. of Intl. Maritime Org. — AP68

1983, June 18 Litho. *Perf. 12½x13*

C218 AP68 18um multi 60 28

Paul Harris, Rotary Founder — AP69

1984, Jan. 20 Litho. *Perf. 13½*

C219 AP69 100um multi 1.40 65

1984 Summer Olympics — AP70

1984, July 15 Litho. *Perf. 14*

C223 AP70 14um Running, horiz. 18 15
C224 AP70 18um Shot put 25 15
C225 AP70 19um Hurdles 25 15
C226 AP70 44um Javelin 60 30
C227 AP70 77um High jump 1.00 50
Nos. C223-C227 (5) 2.28 1.25

Souvenir Sheet

C228 AP70 100um Hurdles, diff. 1.40 65

Olympics Winners — AP71

1984, Dec. 20 Litho. *Perf. 13*

C229 AP71 14um Van den Berg, sailboard, Netherlands 28 15
C230 AP71 18um Coutts, Finn sailing, N.Z. 38 18
C231 AP71 19um 470 class, Spain 40 20
C232 AP71 44um Soling, US 90 45

Souvenir Sheet

C233 AP71 100um Sailing, US 2.00 1.00

PHILEXAFRICA '85, Lome, Togo — AP72

1985, May 23 Litho. *Perf. 13*

C234 AP72 40um Youths, map, IYY emblem 70 40
C235 AP72 40um Oil refinery, Nouadhibou 70 40

1985, Nov. 12 *Perf. 13x12½*

C236 AP72 50um Iron mine, train 1.00 50
C237 AP72 50um Boy reading, herding sheep 1.00 50

Nos. C234-C237 printed se-tenant with center labels picturing map of Africa or UAPT emblem.

Audubon Birth Bicentenary AP73

1985, Aug. 14

C238 AP73 14um Passeriformes thraupidae 28 15
C239 AP73 18um Larus philadelphia 35 16
C240 AP73 19um Cyanocitta cristata 38 18
C241 AP73 44um Rhyncops nigra 80 40

Souvenir Sheet

C242 AP73 100um Anhinga anhinga 2.00 1.00

1st South Atlantic Crossing, 55th Anniv. — AP74

1986, May 19 Litho. *Perf. 13*

C243 AP74 18um Comte de Vaux, 1930 55 28
C244 AP74 50um Flight reenactment, 1985 1.50 75

Nos. C243-C244 printed se-tenant with center label.

1986 World Cup Soccer Championships, Mexico — AP75

Various soccer plays.

1986, June 19 Litho. *Perf. 13*

C245 AP75 8um No. 279 24 15
C246 AP75 18um No. 280 55 28
C247 AP75 22um No. 281 65 32
C248 AP75 25um No. 282 75 38
C249 AP75 40um Soccer cup 1.20 60
Nos. C245-C249 (5) 3.39 1.73

Souvenir Sheet

C250 AP75 100um multi 3.00 1.50

Air Africa, 25th Anniv. — AP76

1986, Oct. 6 Litho. *Perf. 13*

C251 AP76 26um multi 80 40

1988 Summer Olympics, Seoul — AP77

1987, Aug. 13 Litho. *Perf. 13*

C252 AP77 30um Boxing 90 45
C253 AP77 40um Judo 1.20 60
C254 AP77 50um Fencing 1.50 75
C255 AP77 75um Wrestling 2.25 1.10

Souvenir Sheet

C256 AP77 150um Judo, diff. 4.50 2.25

1988 Winter Olympics, Calgary — AP78

1987, Sept.

C257 AP78 30um Women's slalom 90 45
C258 AP78 40um Speed skating 1.20 60
C259 AP78 50um Ice hockey 1.50 75
C260 AP78 75um Women's down-hill skiing 2.25 1.10

Souvenir Sheet

C261 AP78 150um Men's cross-country skiing 4.50 2.25

For overprints see Nos. C267-C271.

1988 Summer Olympics, Seoul — AP79

1988, Sept. 17 Litho. *Perf. 13*

C262 AP79 20um Hammer throw 60 30
C263 AP79 24um Discus 72 35
C264 AP79 30um Shot put 90 45
C265 AP79 150um Javelin 4.50 4.50

Souvenir Sheet

C266 AP79 170um Javelin, diff. 5.00 2.50

Nos. C257-C261 Overprinted "Medaille d'or" in Red or Bright Blue and:
a. "Vreni Schneider (Suisse)"
b. "1500 m / Andre Hoffman (R.D.A.)"
c. "U.R.S.S."
d. "Marina Kiehl (R.F.A.)"
e. "15 km / Mikhail Deviatiarov (U.R.S.S.)"

1988, Sept. 18

C267 AP78(a) 30um multi 90 45
C268 AP78(b) 40um multi (BB) 1.20 60
C269 AP78(c) 50um multi 1.50 75
C270 AP78(d) 75um multi 2.25 1.10

Souvenir Sheet

C271 AP78(e) 150um multi 4.50 2.25

World Cup Soccer Championships, Italy — AP80

Map of Italy and various soccer plays.

1990 Litho. *Perf. 13*

C272 AP80 50um multicolored 1.35 65
C273 AP80 60um multicolored 1.65 85
C274 AP80 70um multicolored 1.90 95
C275 AP80 90um multicolored 2.50 1.25
C276 AP80 150um multicolored 4.00 2.00
Nos. C272-C276 (5) 11.40 5.70

POSTAGE DUE STAMPS

D1 D2

Perf. 14x13½

1906-07 Unwmk. Typo.

J1 D1 5c grn, *grnsh* 1.40 1.40
J2 D1 10c red brn 2.25 2.25
J3 D1 15c dk bl 5.00 3.75
J4 D1 20c blk, *yellow* 5.25 4.75
J5 D1 30c red, *straw* 5.25 5.25
J6 D1 50c violet 7.25 7.25
J7 D1 60c blk, *buff* 5.50 5.00
J8 D1 1fr blk, *pinkish* 9.25 8.00
Nos. J1-J8 (8) 41.15 37.65

Issue dates: 20c, 1906; others 1907.

Regular postage stamps canceled "T" in a triangle were used for postage due.

1914

J9 D2 5c green 15 15
J10 D2 10c rose 15 15
J11 D2 15c gray 15 15
J12 D2 20c brown 15 15
J13 D2 30c blue 15 15
J14 D2 50c black 80 80
J15 D2 60c orange 38 38
J16 D2 1fr violet 60 60
Nos. J9-J16 (8) 2.53 2.53

Type of 1914 Issue Surcharged **2F.**

1927, Oct. 10

J17 D2 2fr on 1fr lil rose 1.25 1.25
J18 D2 3fr on 1fr org brn 1.60 1.60

Catalogue values for unused stamps in this section, from this point to the end of the section, are for Never Hinged items.

Islamic Republic

Oualata Motif — D3

Perf. 14x13½

1961, July 1 Typo. Unwmk.

Denominations in Black

J19 D3 1fr plum & org yel 15 15
J20 D3 2fr red & gray 15 15
J21 D3 5fr mar & pink 15 15
J22 D3 10fr dk grn & grn 25 15
J23 D3 15fr ol & brn org 30 16
J24 D3 20fr red brn & lt bl 40 20
J25 D3 25fr grn & vermilion 60 38
Nos. J19-J25 (7) 2.00
Set value 1.10

Vulture (Ruppell's Griffon) — D4

Birds: No. J27, Eurasian crane. No. J28, Pink-backed pelican. No. J29, Garganey teal. No. J30, European golden oriole. No. J31, Variable sunbird. No. J32, Shoveler ducks. No. J33, Great snipe. No. J34, Vulturine guinea fowl. No. J35, Black stork. No. J36, Gray heron. No. J37, White stork. No. J38, Red-legged partridge. No. J39, Paradise whydah. No. J40, Sandpiper (little stint). No. J41, Sudan bustard.

1963, Sept. 7 Engr. *Perf. 11*

J26 D4 50c blk, yel org & red 15 15
J27 D4 50c blk, yel org & red 15 15
J28 D4 1fr blk, red & yel 15 15
J29 D4 1fr blk, red & yel 15 15
J30 D4 2fr blk, bl grn & yel 15 15
J31 D4 2fr blk, bl grn & yel 15 15
J32 D4 5fr blk, grn & red brn 15 15
J33 D4 5fr blk, grn & red brn 15 15
J34 D4 10fr blk, red & tan 38 38
J35 D4 10fr blk, red & tan 38 38
J36 D4 15fr blk, emer & red 45 45
J37 D4 15fr blk, emer & red 45 45
J38 D4 20fr blk, yel grn & red 70 70
J39 D4 20fr blk, yel grn & red 70 70
J40 D4 25fr blk, yel grn & brn 1.00 1.00
J41 D4 25fr blk, yel grn & brn 1.00 1.00
Nos. J26-J41 (16) 6.26 6.26

Ornament D5

1976, May 10 Litho. *Perf. 12½x13*

J42 D5 1um buff & multi 15 15
J43 D5 3um buff & multi 15 15
J44 D5 10um buff & multi 38 38
J45 D5 12um buff & multi 42 42
J46 D5 20um buff & multi 70 70
Nos. J42-J46 (5) 1.80 1.80

OFFICIAL STAMPS

Catalogue values for unused stamps in this section are for Never Hinged items.

Islamic Republic

Cross of Trarza — O1

Perf. 14x13½

1961, July 1 Typo. Unwmk.

O1 O1 1fr vio & lilac 15 15
O2 O1 3fr red & slate 15 15
O3 O1 5fr grn & brown 15 15
O4 O1 10fr grn & vio bl 18 15
O5 O1 15fr blue & org 26 15
O6 O1 20fr sl grn & emer 30 15
O7 O1 25fr red org & mar 35 26
O8 O1 30fr maroon & grn 42 30
O9 O1 50fr dk red & dk brn 85 42
O10 O1 100fr orange & blue 1.50 80
O11 O1 200fr grn & red org 3.00 1.50
Nos. O1-O11 (11) 7.31 4.18

Ornament O2

1976, May 3 Litho. *Perf. 12½x13*

O12 O2 1um black & multi 15 15
O13 O2 2um black & multi 15 15
O14 O2 5um black & multi 20 15
O15 O2 10um black & multi 40 16
O16 O2 12um black & multi 55 22
O17 O2 40um black & multi 1.50 70
O18 O2 50um black & multi 2.00 1.00
Nos. O12-O18 (7) 4.95
Set value 2.20

AIR POST SEMI-POSTAL STAMPS

Stamps of Dahomey types V1, V2, V3 and V4 inscribed "Mauritanie" were issued in 1942 by the Vichy Government, but were not placed on sale in the colony.

MAYOTTE

LOCATION — One of the Comoro Islands situated in the Mozambique Channel midway between Madagascar and Mozambique (Africa)
GOVT. — Former French Colony
AREA — 140 sq. mi.
POP. — 13,783 (1914)
CAPITAL — Dzaoudzi

See Comoro Islands

100 Centimes = 1 Franc

See France No. 2271 for French stamp inscribed "Mayotte."

Navigation and Commerce — A1

Perf. 14x13½

1892-1907 Typo. Unwmk.

Name of Colony in Blue or Carmine

1 A1 1c blk, *lil bl* 35 35
2 A1 2c brn, *buff* 40 40
a. Name double 200.00 200.00
3 A1 4c claret, *lav* 62 55
4 A1 5c grn, *grnsh* 1.25 1.00
5 A1 10c blk, *lavender* 1.50 1.25
6 A1 10c red ('00) 20.00 14.00
7 A1 15c blue, quadrille paper 5.00 3.25
8 A1 15c gray ('00) 40.00 32.50
9 A1 20c red, *grn* 4.00 3.25
10 A1 25c blk, *rose* 3.00 2.25
11 A1 25c blue ('00) 3.50 2.25
12 A1 30c brn, *bis* 5.75 4.25
13 A1 35c blk, *yel* *2.50* 2.25
14 A1 40c red, *straw* 5.00 4.25
15 A1 45c blk, *gray grn* ('07) 5.75 4.50
16 A1 50c carmine, *rose* 8.00 6.00
17 A1 50c brn, *az* ('00) 6.00 6.00
18 A1 75c dp vio, *org* 9.00 6.00
19 A1 1fr brnz grn, *straw* 7.00 6.00
20 A1 5fr red lil, *lav* ('99) 45.00 40.00
Nos. 1-20 (20) 173.62 140.30

Perf. 13½x14 stamps are counterfeits.

Issues of 1892-1907 Surcharged in Black or Carmine

05 **10**

1912

22 A1 5c on 2c brn, *buff* 65 65
23 A1 5c on 4c cl, *lav* (C) 60 60
24 A1 5c on 15c bl (C) 45 45
25 A1 5c on 20c red, *grn* 60 60
26 A1 5c on 25c blk, *rose* (C) 60 60
a. Double surcharge 150.00
27 A1 5c on 30c brn, *bis* (C) 60 60
28 A1 10c on 40c red, *straw* 60 60
a. Double surcharge 100.00
29 A1 10c on 45c blk, *gray grn* (C) 60 60
a. Double surcharge 100.00
30 A1 10c on 50c car, *rose* 1.10 1.10
31 A1 10c on 75c dp vio, *org* 75 75
32 A1 10c on 1fr brnz grn, *straw* 75 75
Nos. 22-32 (11) 7.30 7.30

Two spacings between the surcharged numerals are found on Nos. 22-32.

Nos. 22-32 were available for use in Madagascar and the entire Comoro archipelago.

Stamps of Mayotte were replaced successively by those of Madagascar, Comoro Islands and France.

MEMEL

LOCATION — In northern Europe, bordering on the Baltic Sea
GOVT. — Special commission (see below)
AREA — 1099 sq. mi.
POP. — 151,960

Following World War I this territory was detached from Germany and by Treaty of Versailles assigned to the government of a commission of the Allied and Associated Powers (not the League of Nations), which administered it until January, 1923, when it was forcibly occupied by Lithuania. In 1924 Memel became incorporated as a semi-autonomous district of Lithuania with the approval of the Allied Powers and the League of Nations.

100 Pfennig = 1 Mark
100 Centu = 1 Litas (1923)

Stamps of Germany, 1905-20, Overprinted **Memel-gebiet**

Wmk. Lozenges (125)

1920, Aug. 1 *Perf. 14, 14½*

1 A16 5pf green 22 35
2 A16 10pf car rose 2.00 4.50
3 A16 10pf orange 15 32
4 A22 15pf vio brn 2.00 5.00
5 A16 20pf bl vio 20 15
6 A16 30pf org & blk, *buff* 1.00 1.25
7 A16 30pf dl bl 15 32
8 A16 40pf lake & blk 15 15
9 A16 50pf pur & blk, *buff* 15 15
10 A16 60pf ol grn 45 1.45
11 A16 75pf grn & blk 1.75 4.00
12 A16 80pf bl vio 85 1.75

Overprinted **Memelgebiet**

13 A17 1m car rose 24 45
14 A17 1.25m green 8.25 18.00
15 A17 1.50m yel brn 3.00 6.00
16 A21 2m blue 1.25 2.50
17 A21 2.50m red lilac 8.25 14.00
Nos. 1-17 (17) 30.06 60.34

Stamps of France, Surcharged in Black

On A22 **MEMEL 5 pfennig**

On A18 **MEMEL 60 pfennig**

1920 Unwmk. *Perf. 14x13½*

18 A22 5pf on 5c green 15 15
19 A22 10pf on 10c red 15 15
20 A22 20pf on 25c blue 15 15
21 A22 30pf on 30c org 15 15
22 A22 40pf on 20c red brn 15 15
23 A22 50pf on 35c vio 15 30
24 A18 60pf on 40c red & pale bl 18 40
25 A18 80pf on 45c grn & bl 15 18
26 A18 1m on 50c brn & lav 15 16
27 A18 1m 25pf on 60c vio & ultra 75 1.65
28 A18 2m on 1fr cl & ol grn 15 20
29 A18 3m on 5fr bl & buff 9.00 12.00
Nos. 18-29 (12) 11.28 15.64

For stamps with additional surcharges and overprints see Nos. 43-49, C1-C4.

French Stamps of 1900-20 Surcharged like Nos. 24 to 29 in Red or Black

4 **4**
Four Marks
Type I Type II

1920-21 Unwmk. *Perf. 14x13½*

30 A18 3m on 2fr org & pale bl 8.50 14.00
31 A18 4m on 2fr org & pale bl (I) (Bk) 15 28
a. Type II 50.00 *125.00*
32 A18 10m on 5fr bl & buff 1.50 2.75
33 A18 20m on 5fr bl & buff 27.50 40.00

For stamps with additional overprints see Nos. C5, C19.

New Value with Initial Capital

1921

39 A18 60Pf on 40c red & pale bl 2.00 3.75
40 A18 3M on 60c vio & ultra 50 70
41 A18 10M on 5fr bl & buff 60 95
42 A18 20M on 45c grn & bl 2.25 5.00

The surcharged value on No. 40 is in italics.

For stamps with additional overprints see Nos. C6-C7, C18.

Stamps of 1920 Surcharged with Large Numerals in Dark Blue or Red

1921-22

43 A22 15pf on 10pf on 10c 15 25
a. Inverted surcharge 52.50 67.50
44 A22 15pf on 20pf on 25c 18 32
a. Inverted surcharge 60.00 67.50
45 A22 15pf on 50pf on 35c (R) 15 28
a. Inverted surcharge 60.00 67.50
46 A22 60pf on 40pf on 20c 15 18
a. Inverted surcharge 52.50 67.50
47 A18 75pf on 60pf on 40c 40 55
48 A18 1.25m on 1m on 50c 15 20
49 A18 5.00m on 2m on 1fr 55 60
a. Inverted surcharge 240.00 280.00
Nos. 43-49 (7) 1.73 2.38

Stamps of France Surcharged in Black or Red

On A22 ***MEMEL* 5 Pfennig**

MEMEL
On A18 40 Pfennig

1922

50 A22 5pf on 5c org 15 15
51 A22 10pf on 10c red 50 1.10
52 A22 10pf on 10c grn 15 15
53 A22 15pf on 10c grn 20 35
54 A22 20pf on 20c red brn 2.25 5.50
55 A22 20pf on 25c bl 2.25 5.50
56 A22 25pf on 5c org 15 15
57 A22 30pf on 30c red 35 1.40
58 A22 35pf on 35c vio 15 15
59 A22 50pf on 50c dl bl 15 18
60 A22 75pf on 15c grn 15 15
61 A22 75pf on 35c vio 15 18
62 A22 1m on 25c blue 15 15
63 A22 1 1/4m on 30c red 15 30
64 A22 3m on 5c org 15 40
65 A22 6m on 15c grn (R) 22 40
66 A22 8m on 30c red 20 80

Type A18

67 40pf on 40c red & pale bl 15 18
68 80pf on 45c grn & bl 15 18
69 1m on 40c red & pale bl 15 18
70 1.25m on 60c vio & ultra (R) 15 18
71 1.50m on 45c grn & bl (R) 15 18
72 2m on 45c grn & bl 15 15
73 2m on 1fr cl & ol grn 15 18
74 2 1/4m on 40c red & pale bl 15 15
75 2 1/2m on 60c vio & ultra 20 32
76 3m on 60c vio & ultra (R) 40 60
77 4m on 45c grn & bl 15 15
78 5m on 1fr cl & ol grn 18 30
79 6m on 60c vio & ultra 15 15
80 6m on 2fr org & pale bl 18 30
81 9m on 1fr cl & ol grn 22 22
82 9m on 5fr bl & buff (R) 24 40
83 10m on 45c grn & bl (R) 18 35
84 12m on 40c red & pale bl 22 22
85 20m on 40c red & pale bl 18 35
86 20m on 2fr org & pale bl 22 22
87 30m on 60c vio & ultra 18 35
88 30m on 5fr dk bl & buff 1.90 4.75
89 40m on 1fr cl & ol grn 18 35
90 50m on 2fr org & pale bl 5.50 12.50
91 80m on 2fr org & pale bl (R) 18 40
92 100m on 5fr bl & buff 25 48
Nos. 50-92 (43) 19.38 40.65

Nos. 59, 60 and 65 are on France type A20.
A 500m on 5fr dark blue and buff was prepared, but not officially issued. Value, $750.
For stamps with additional surcharges and overprints see Nos. 93-99, C8-C17, C20-29C.

Nos. 52, 54, 67, 59 Surcharged "Mark"

1922-23

93 A22 10m on 10pf on 10c 55 1.50
a. Double surcharge 125.00 140.00
94 A22 20m on 20pf on 20c 40 40
95 A18 40m on 40pf on 40c ('23) 40 70
96 A20 50m on 50pf on 50c 1.10 1.90

Nos. 72, 61, 70 Surcharged with New Values in Red or Black

1922-23

97 A18 10m on 2m on 45c 75 95
98 A22 25m on 1m on 25c 75 95
99 A18 80m on 1.25m on 60c (Bk) ('23) 40 70

For No. 99 with additional surcharges see Nos. N28-N30.

AIR POST STAMPS

Nos. 24-26, 28, 31, 39-40 Overprinted in Dark Blue

1921, July 6 Unwmk. *Perf. 14x13 1/2*

C1 A18 60pf on 40c 27.50 45.00
C2 A18 80pf on 45c 1.40 3.50
C3 A18 1m on 50c 1.25 2.75
C4 A18 2m on 1fr 1.40 4.00
a. "Flugpost" inverted 200.00 240.00
C5 A18 4m on 2fr (I) 1.90 6.25
a. Type II 200.00 240.00

New Value with Initial Capital

C6 A18 60Pf on 40c 1.75 4.25
a. "Flugpost" inverted 200.00 240.00
C7 A18 3M on 60c 1.75 4.25
a. "Flugpost" inverted 200.00 225.00
Nos. C1-C7 (7) 36.95 70.00

The surcharged value on No. C7 is in italics.

Nos. 67-71, 73, 76, 78, 80, 82 Overprinted in Dark Blue

1922, May 12

C8 A18 40pf on 40c 30 75
C9 A18 80pf on 45c 30 75
C10 A18 1m on 40c 30 75
C11 A18 1.25m on 60c 45 1.25
C12 A18 1.50m on 45c 45 1.25
C13 A18 2m on 1fr 45 1.25
C14 A18 3m on 60c 45 1.25
C15 A18 5m on 1fr 55 1.40
C16 A18 6m on 2fr 55 1.40
C17 A18 9m on 5fr 55 1.40

Same Overprint On Nos. 40, 31

C18 A18 3M on 60c 80.00 *400.00*
C19 A18 4m on 2fr 45 1.25
Nos. C8-C17,C19 (11) 4.80 12.70

Nos. 67, 69-71, 73, 76, 78, 80, 82 Overprinted in Black or Red FLUGPOST

1922, Oct. 17

C20 A18 40pf on 40c 55 *2.50*
C21 A18 1m on 40c 55 *2.50*
C22 A18 1.25m on 60c (R) 55 *2.50*
C23 A18 1.50m on 45c (R) 55 *2.50*
C24 A18 2m on 1fr 55 *2.50*
C25 A18 3m on 60c (R) 55 *2.50*
C26 A18 4m on 2fr 55 *2.50*
C27 A18 5m on 1fr 55 *2.50*
C28 A18 6m on 2fr 55 *2.50*
C29 A18 9m on 5fr (R) 55 *2.50*
Nos. C20-C29 (10) 5.50 *25.00*

No. C26 is not known without the "FLUGPOST" overprint.

OCCUPATION STAMPS

Issued under Lithuanian Occupation

Surcharged in Various Colors on Unissued Official Stamps of Lithuania Similar to Type O4

Klaipėda (Memel) 10 Markių — On Nos. N1-N6
KLAIPĖDA (MEMEL) 25 MARKĖS — On Nos. N7-N11

Memel Printing

1923 Unwmk. Litho. *Perf. 11*

N1 O4 10m on 5c bl (Bk) 65 1.25
a. "Memel" and bars omitted 5.00 *12.50*
N2 O4 25m on 5c bl (R) 65 1.25
N3 O4 50m on 25c red (Bk) 65 1.25
N4 O4 100m on 25c red (G) 65 1.25
N5 O4 400m on 1 l brn (R) 75 1.50
N6 O4 500m on 1 l brn (Bl) 75 1.50
Nos. N1-N6 (6) 4.10 8.00

Nos. N1 and N3-N6 exist with double surcharge. Value $50 each.

Kaunas Printing

Black Surcharge

N7 O4 10m on 5c blue 30 55
N8 O4 25m on 5c blue 30 55
N9 O4 50m on 25c red 30 55
N10 O4 100m on 25c red 45 80
N11 O4 400m on 1 l brn 75 1.40
Nos. N7-N11 (5) 2.10 3.85

No. N8 has the value in "Markes," others of the group have it in "Markiu."
For additional surcharge see No. N87.

Memel stamps can be mounted in Scott's Germany Part II Album.

Surcharged in Various Colors on Unissued Official Stamps of Lithuania Similar to Type O4

KLAIPĖDA (Memel) 25 MARKĖS

1923

N12 O4 10m on 5c bl (R) 50 1.10
a. "Markes" instead of "Markiu" 22.50 50.00
N13 O4 20m on 5c bl (R) 50 1.10
N14 O4 25m on 25c red (Bl) 50 1.10
N15 O4 50m on 25c red (Bl) 55 1.40
a. Inverted surcharge 40.00
N16 O4 100m on 1 l brn (Bk) 70 1.65
a. Inverted surcharge 40.00
N17 O4 200m on 1 l brn (Bk) 70 1.65
Nos. N12-N17 (6) 3.45 8.00

No. N14 has the value in "Markes," others of the group have it in "Markiu."

"Vytis"
O4 O5

1923, Mar.

N18 O4 10m lt brn 22 28
N19 O4 20m yellow 22 28
N20 O4 25m orange 22 28
N21 O4 40m violet 22 28
N22 O4 50m yel grn 50 55
N23 O5 100m carmine 28 32
N24 O5 300m olive grn 2.50 *22.50*
N25 O5 400m olive brn 35 40
N26 O5 500m lilac 2.50 *22.50*
N27 O5 1000m blue 50 55
Nos. N18-N27 (10) 7.51 *47.94*

No. N20 has the value in "Markes."
For surcharges see Nos. N44-N69, N88-N114.

No. 99 Surcharged in Green

Klaipėda 400 M

1923, Apr. 13

N28 A18 100m on No. 99 3.00 5.00
N29 A18 400m on No. 99 3.00 5.00
N30 A18 500m on No. 99 3.00 5.00

The normal position of the green surcharge is sideways, with the top at the left. It exists reversed on the three stamps.

Ship — O7

Seal — O8

Lighthouse — O9

1923, Apr. 12 Litho.

N31 O7 40m olive grn 2.00 6.00
N32 O7 50m brown 2.00 6.00
N33 O7 80m green 2.00 6.00
N34 O7 100m red 2.00 6.00
N35 O8 200m deep blue 2.00 6.00
N36 O8 300m brown 2.00 6.00
N37 O8 400m lilac 2.00 6.00
N38 O8 500m orange 2.00 6.00
N39 O8 600m olive grn 2.00 6.00
N40 O9 800m deep blue 2.00 6.00
N41 O9 1000m lilac 2.00 6.00
N42 O9 2000m red 2.00 6.00
N43 O9 3000m green 2.00 6.00
Nos. N31-N43 (13) 26.00 78.00

Union of Memel with Lithuania. Forgeries exist.
For surcharges see Nos. N70-N86.

Nos. N20, N24, N26 Surcharged in Various Colors

3 CENTŲ

1923

Thin Figures

N44 O5 2c on 300m (R) 2.50 3.75
N45 O5 3c on 300m (R) 2.50 3.75
N46 O4 10c on 25m (Bk) 2.50 3.75
a. Double surcharge 65.00
N47 O4 15c on 25m (Bk) 2.50 3.75
N48 O5 20c on 500m (Bl) 3.00 6.25
N49 O5 30c on 500m (Bk) 2.50 3.75
N50 O5 50c on 500m (G) 5.00 9.50
a. Inverted surcharge 125.00
Nos. N44-N50 (7) 20.50 34.50

Nos. N19, N21-N27 Surcharged:

2 CENT. — 1 LITAS

N51 O4 2c on 20m yel 1.65 2.50
N52 O4 2c on 50c yel grn 1.65 2.75
N53 O4 3c on 40m vio 2.00 2.50
a. Double surcharge 65.00
N54 O5 3c on 300m ol grn 1.65 2.00
a. Double surcharge 65.00
N55 O5 5c on 100m car 2.00 2.00
N56 O5 5c on 300m ol grn (R) 2.75 3.75
N57 O5 10c on 400m ol brn 4.00 4.00
N58 O5 30c on 500m lilac 2.25 6.25
N59 O5 1 l on 1000m bl 8.00 12.50
Nos. N51-N59 (9) 25.95 38.25

There are several types of the numerals in these surcharges. Nos. N56 and N58 have "CENT" in short, thick letters, as on Nos. N44 to N50.

Nos. N18-N23, N25, N27 Surcharged

2 CENT.

Thick Figures

N60 O4 2c on 10m lt brn 75 *3.75*
N61 O4 2c on 20m yel 6.25 *37.50*
N62 O4 2c on 50m yel grn 1.50 *4.50*
N63 O4 3c on 10m lt brn 1.50 *4.50*
a. Double surcharge 60.00
N64 O4 3c on 40m vio 10.00 *50.00*
N65 O5 5c on 100m car 1.50 *4.50*
a. Double surcharge 60.00
N66 O5 10c on 400m ol brn 50.00 *250.00*
N67 O4 15c on 25m org 50.00 *250.00*
N68 O5 50c on 1000m bl 1.50 *4.50*
a. Double surcharge 60.00
N69 O5 1 l on 1000m bl 3.00 *7.50*
a. Double surcharge 90.00
Nos. N60-N69 (10) 126.00 *616.75*

No. N69 is surcharged like type "b" in the following group.

Nos. N31-N43 Surcharged:

30 CENT. — a
1 LITAS — b

N70 O7(a) 15c on 40m ol grn 3.25 *6.25*
N71 O7(a) 30c on 50m brn 2.75 *5.00*
N72 O7(a) 30c on 80m grn 3.25 *6.25*
N73 O7(a) 30c on 100m red 2.75 *5.00*

N74 O8(a) 50c on 200m dp bl 3.25 *6.25*
N75 O8(a) 50c on 300m brn 2.75 *5.00*
N76 O8(a) 50c on 400m lil 3.25 *6.25*
N77 O8(a) 50c on 500m org 2.75 *5.00*
N78 O8(b) 1 l on 600m ol grn 3.25 *6.25*
N79 O9(b) 1 l on 800m dp bl 3.25 *6.25*
N80 O9(b) 1 l on 1000m lil 3.25 *6.25*
N81 O9(b) 1 l on 2000m red 3.25 *6.25*
N82 O9(b) 1 l on 3000m grn 3.25 *6.25*
Nos. N70-N82 (13) 40.25 *76.25*

These stamps are said to have been issued to commemorate the institution of autonomous government.

Double or inverted surcharges exist on Nos. N71, N75-N77. Value, each $60.

Nos. N32, N34, N36, N38 Surcharged in Green

25 CENT.

1923

N83 O7 15c on 50m brn 87.50 *1,200.*
N84 O7 25c on 100m red 57.50 *800.00*
N85 O8 30c on 300m brn 87.50 *1,000.*
N86 O8 60c on 500m org 52.50 *800.00*

Surcharges on Nos. N83-N86 are of two types, differing in width of numerals. Values are for stamps with narrow numerals, as illustrated. Stamps with wide numerals sell for two to four times as much.

Nos. N8, N10-N11, N3 Surcharged in Red or Green

15 Centų

N87 O4 10c on 25m on 5c bl (R) 12.50 *22.50*
N88 O4 15c on 100m on 25c red (G) 15.00 *50.00*
a. Inverted surcharge 125.00 75.00
N89 O4 30c on 400m on 1 l brn (R) 3.75 *7.50*
N90 O4 60c on 50m on 25c red (G) 16.00 *50.00*

Nos. N18-N22 Surcharged in Green or Red

15 Centų

N91 O4 15c on 10m 3.75 *15.00*
N92 O4 15c on 20m 2.00 *8.75*
N93 O4 15c on 25m 2.50 *9.00*
N94 O4 15c on 40m 2.00 *8.75*
N95 O4 15c on 50m (R) 1.50 *6.50*
N96 O4 25c on 10m 2.75 *12.50*
N97 O4 25c on 20m 2.00 *8.75*
N98 O4 25c on 25m 2.50 *9.00*
N99 O4 25c on 40m 2.00 *8.75*
N100 O4 25c on 50m (R) 1.50 *6.50*
N101 O4 30c on 10m 3.75 *15.00*
N102 O4 30c on 20m 2.00 *8.75*
N103 O4 30c on 25m 2.50 *9.00*
N104 O4 30c on 40m 2.00 *8.75*
N105 O4 30c on 50m (R) 1.50 *6.50*
Nos. N91-N105 (15) 34.25 *141.50*

Nine stamps between Nos. N95 and N114 exist with inverted surcharge. No. 102 exists with double surcharge.

Nos. N23, N25, N27 Surcharged in Green or Red

15 Centų

N106 O5 15c on 100m 1.40 *6.50*
N107 O5 15c on 400m 1.25 *6.00*
N108 O5 15c on 1000m (R) 27.50 *200.00*
N109 O5 25c on 100m 1.40 *6.50*
N110 O5 25c on 400m 1.25 *6.00*
N111 O5 25c on 1000m (R) 30.00 *225.00*
N112 O5 30c on 100m 1.40 *6.50*
N113 O5 30c on 400m 1.25 *6.00*
N114 O5 30c on 1000m (R) 27.50 *200.00*
Nos. N106-N114 (9) 92.95 *662.50*

Nos. N96 to N100 and N109 to N111 are surcharged "Centai," the others "Centu."

Excellent counterfeits of all Memel issues exist.

MEXICO

LOCATION — Extreme southern part of the North American continent, south of the United States
GOVT. — Republic
AREA — 756,198 sq. mi.
POP. — 76,791,819 (est. 1984)
CAPITAL — Mexico, D.F

8 Reales = 1 Peso
100 Centavos = 1 Peso

Catalogue values for unused stamps in this country are for Never Hinged items, beginning with Scott 960 in the regular postage section, Scott C302 in the airpost section, Scott E22 in the special delivery section, and Scott G21 in the insured letter section.

Values of early Mexico stamps vary according to condition. Quotations for Nos. 1-104 are for fine copies. Very fine to superb specimens sell at much higher prices, and inferior or poor copies sell at reduced prices, depending on the condition of the individual specimen.

District Overprints

Nos. 1-149 are overprinted with names of various districts, and sometimes also with district numbers and year dates. Some of the district overprints are rare and command high prices. Values given for Nos. 1-149 are for the more common district overprints.

Watermarks

Wmk. 150- PAPEL SELLADO in Sheet

Wmk. 151- R. P. S. in the Sheet (R.P.S. stands for "Renta Papel Sellado")

Wmk. 152- "CORREOS E U M" on Every Horizontal Line of Ten Stamps

Wmk. 153- "R M" Interlaced

Wmk. 154- Eagle and R M

Wmk. 155- SERVICIO POSTAL DE LOS ESTADOS UNIDOS MEXICANOS

Wmk. 156- CORREOS MEXICO

Wmk. 248- SECRETARIA DE HACIENDA MEXICO

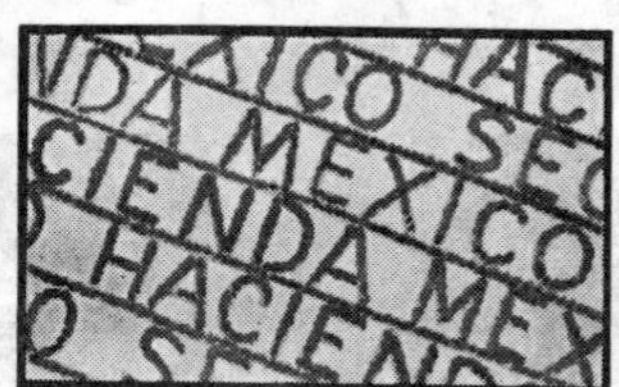
Wmk. 260- Lines and SECRETARIA DE HACIENDA MEXICO

Wmk. 272- "S. H. C. P. MEXICO" and Eagle in Circle

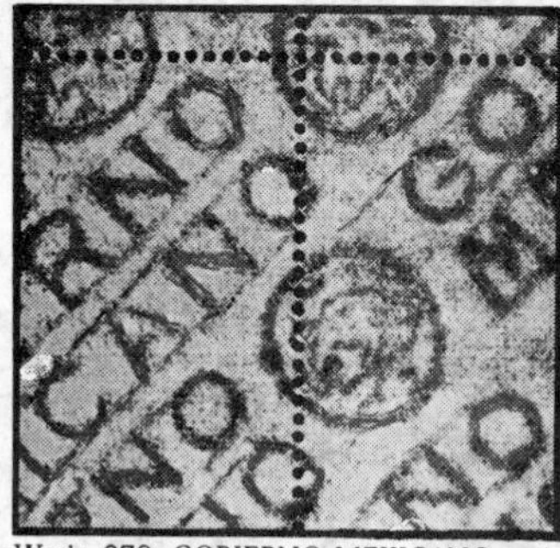
Wmk. 279- GOBIERNO MEXICANO and Eagle in Circle

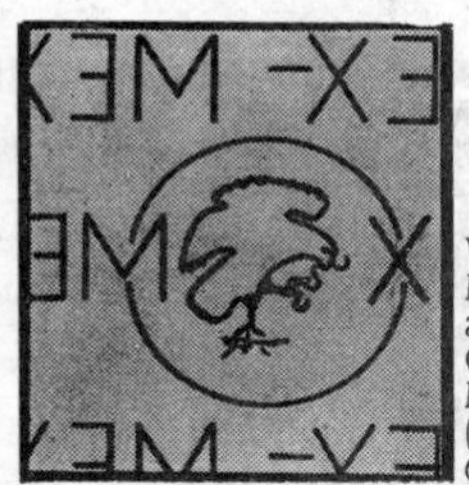
Wmk. 300- MEX-MEX and Eagle in Circle, Multiple (Letters 6mm)

Wmk. 350- MEX and Eagle in Circle, Multiple. Letters 8-9mm

Miguel Hidalgo y Costilla — A1

Handstamped with District Name

1856 Unwmk. Engr. ***Imperf.***

1 A1 ½r blue 35.00 17.50
a. ½r dark blue 35.00 17.50
b. Without overprint 20.00 22.00
c. Double impression 150.00
2 A1 1r yellow 17.50 2.50
a. 1r deep yellow 17.50 2.50
b. Half used as ½r on cover *5,000*
c. Without overprint 10.00 12.00
d. 1r green (error)
3 A1 2r yel grn 17.50 2.50
a. 2r blue green 140.00 25.00
b. 2r emerald 175.00 40.00
c. Half used as 1r on cover 400.00

d. Without overprint 25.00 15.00
e. Printed on both sides (yel green) 150.00 175.00
4 A1 4r red 110.00 60.00
a. Half used as 2r on cover 140.00
b. Quarter used as 1r on cover 250.00
c. Without overprint 90.00 120.00
d. Three quarters used as 3r on cover 7,000.
5 A1 8r red lilac 225.00 140.00
a. 8r violet 200.00 130.00
b. Without overprint 120.00 150.00
c. Eighth used as 1r on cover 2,500.
d. Quarter used as 2r on cover 160.00
e. Half used as 4r on cover 250.00

The 1r and 2r were printed in sheets of 60 with wide spacing between stamps, and in sheets of 190 or 200 with narrow spacing.

All values have been reprinted, some of them several times. The reprints usually show signs of wear and the impressions are often smudgy. The paper is usually thicker than that of the originals. Reprints are usually on very white paper. Reprints are found with and without overprints and with cancellations made both from the original handstamps and from forged ones.

Counterfeits exist.

See Nos. 6-12. For overprints see Nos. 35-45.

1861

6 A1 ½r blk, *buff* 35.00 20.00
a. Without overprint 20.00 27.50
7 A1 1r blk, *green* 13.00 3.50
a. Impression of 2r on back 400.00
b. Without overprint 4.00 4.50
c. Printed on both sides 300.00
d. As "b," blk, *pink* (error)
f. Double impression 150.00
8 A1 2r blk, *pink* 10.00 2.00
a. Impression of 1r on back 450.00
b. Half used as 1r on cover 325.00
c. Without overprint 2.25 5.00
d. Printed on both sides 2,250.
e. Double impression 100.00
9 A1 4r blk, *yellow* 125.00 40.00
a. Half used as 2r on cover 175.00
b. Without overprint 35.00 55.00
c. Quarter used as 1r on cover 275.00
d. Three-quarters used as 3r on cover 3,000.
10 A1 4r dl rose, *yel* 140.00 50.00
a. Half used as 2r on cover 450.00
b. Without overprint 80.00 100.00
c. Printed on both sides 1,500.
d. Quarter used as 1r on cover 500.00
11 A1 8r blk, *red brn* 250.00 150.00
b. Quarter used as 2r on cover 150.00
c. Half used as 4r on cover 275.00
d. Without overprint 75.00 150.00
e. Three quarters used as 6r on cover 3,500.
12 A1 8r grn, *red brn* 350.00 140.00
a. Half used as 4r on cover
b. Without overprint 100.00 125.00
c. Quarter used as 2r on cover
d. Printed on both sides *1,250.* *1,250.*

Nos. 6, 9, 10, 11 and 12 have been reprinted. Most reprints of the ½r, 4r and 8r are on vertically grained paper. Originals are on horizontally grained paper. The original ½r stamps are much worn but the reprints are unworn. The paper of the 4r is too deep and rich in color and No. 10 is printed in too bright red.

Reprints of the 8r can only be told by experts. All these reprints are found in fancy colors and with overprints and cancellations as in the 1856 issue.

Counterfeits exist.

Hidalgo — A3

Coat of Arms — A4

With District Name

1864 *Perf. 12*

14 A3 1r red *500.00* *1,000.*
a. Without District Name 50
15 A3 2r blue *450.00* *800.00*
a. Without District Name 50
16 A3 4r brown *1,000.* *2,000.*
a. Without District Name 75
b. Vert. pair, imperf. between
17 A3 1p black *2,500.* *22,500.*
a. Without District Name 1.50

Nos. 14 to 17 were issued with district overprints of Saltillo or Monterrey on the toned paper of 1864. Overprints on the 1867 white paper are fraudulant. Counterfeit cancellations are plentiful. The 1r red with "½" surcharge is bogus.

Overprint of District Name, etc.

1864-66 *Imperf.*

Five types of overprints:
I- District name only.
II- District name, consignment number and "1864" in large figures.
III- District name, number and "1864" in small figures.
IV- District name, number and "1865."
V- District name, number and "1866."

18 A4 3c brn (IV, V) 1,000. *1,900.*
a. Without overprint 550.00
b. Laid paper *3,500.* *5,500.*
19 A4 ½r brown (I) 300.00 210.00
a. Type II 1,500. 1,000.
b. Without overprint 140.00 350.00
20 A4 ½r lilac (IV) 55.00 45.00
a. Type III 60.00 55.00
b. Type II 110.00 100.00
c. Type V 3,000.
d. ½r gray (V) 65.00 65.00
e. Without overprint 4.00
21 A4 1r blue (IV, V) 13.00 8.00
a. Type III 20.00 12.00
b. Without overprint 2.00
c. Half used as ½r on cover 3,000.
22 A4 1r ultra (I, II) 100.00 27.50
a. Type III 75.00 35.00
b. Without overprint 130.00 120.00
c. Half used as ½r on cover 3,000.
23 A4 2r org (III, IV, V) 4.00 2.50
a. Type II 15.00 3.00
b. Type I 40.00 4.50
c. 2r dp org, without ovpt., early plate 150.00 50.00
d. Without ovpt., late plate 1.25
e. Half used as 1r on cover 1,000.
24 A4 4r grn (III, IV, V) 85.00 50.00
a. Types I, II 120.00 60.00
b. 4r dk grn, without ovpt. 3.50 *125.00*
d. Half used as 2r on cover 675.00
25 A4 8r red (IV, V) 125.00 75.00
a. Types II, III 150.00 70.00
b. Type I 300.00 115.00
c. 8r dk red, without ovpt. 5.25 *250.00*
f. Quarter used as 2r on cover 3,000.
g. Three-quarters used as 6r on cover

The 2r printings from the early plates are 25½mm high; those from the late plate, 24½mm.

Varieties listed as "Without overprint" in unused condition are remainders.

Besides the overprints of district name, number and date, Nos. 18-34 often received, in the district offices, additional overprints of numbers and sometimes year dates. Copies with these "sub-consignment numbers" sell for more than stamps without them.

Faked quarterlings and bisects of 1856-64 are plentiful.

The 3c has been reprinted from a die on which the words "TRES CENTAVOS," the outlines of the serpent and some of the background lines have been retouched.

Emperor Maximilian — A5

Overprinted with District Name, Number and Date 1866 or 866; also with Number and Date only, or with Name only

1866 **Litho.**

26 A5 7c lilac gray 50.00 95.00
a. 7c deep gray 70.00 95.00
27 A5 13c blue 18.00 18.00
a. Half used as 7c on cover *5,000.*
b. 13c cobalt blue 22.50 22.50
c. Without overprint
28 A5 25c buff 8.00 5.00
a. Half used as 13c on cover
29 A5 25c orange 8.00 7.00
a. 25c red orange 15.00 11.00
b. 25c red brown 35.00 25.00
c. 25c brown 50.00 30.00
30 A5 50c green 18.00 18.00

Litho. printings have round period after value numerals.

Overprinted with District Name, Number and Date 866 or 867; also with Number and Date only

Engr.

31 A5 7c lilac 350.00 *4,000.*
a. Without overprint 2.75
32 A5 13c blue 6.00 9.00
a. Without overprint 1.00
33 A5 25c org brn 5.00 8.00
a. Without overprint 1.00
34 A5 50c green 550.00 55.00
a. Without overprint 2.00

See "sub-consignment" note after No. 25.

Engraved printings have square period after value numerals.

Varieties listed as "Without overprint" in unused condition are remainders.

Stamps of 1856-61 Overprinted *Mexico*

1867

35 A1 ½r blk, *buff* 1,400. 1,750.
36 A1 1r blk, *green* 40.00 6.00
37 A1 2r blk, *pink* 17.50 3.00
a. Printed on both sides 125.00
38 A1 4r red, *yel* 250.00 14.00
a. Printed on both sides 175.00
39 A1 4r red 4,000. 1,200.
40 A1 8r blk, *red brn* 1,100. 250.00
41 A1 8r grn, *red brn* 1,800.

Dangerous counterfeits exist of the "Mexico" overprint.

Same Overprint
Thin Gray Blue Paper
Wmk. 151

42 A1 ½r gray 225.00 175.00
a. Without overprint 175.00 175.00
43 A1 1r blue 375.00 60.00
b. Without overprint 300.00 75.00
44 A1 2r green 70.00 7.00
a. Printed on both sides 900.00
b. Without overprint 75.00 20.00
45 A1 4r rose 1,400. 55.00
a. Without overprint 60.00

Reprints of the ½r and 4r exist on watermarked paper. Reprints of ½r and 8r also exist in gray on thick grayish wove paper, unwatermarked.

Hidalgo — A6

Thin Figures of Value, without Period after Numerals

6 CENT. 12 CENT.
25 CENT. 50 CENT.
100 CENT.

Overprinted with District Name, Number and Abbreviated Date

1868 **Unwmk.** **Litho.** ***Imperf.***

46 A6 6c blk, *buff* 27.50 14.00
47 A6 12c blk, *green* 25.00 12.00
a. Period after "12" 40.00
48 A6 25c bl, *pink* 45.00 10.00
a. Without overprint 100.00
49 A6 50c blk, *yellow* 400.00 40.00
50 A6 100c blk, *brown* 500.00 90.00
51 A6 100c brn, *brn* 1,200. 400.00

Perf.

52 A6 6c blk, *buff* 16.00 12.00
a. Without overprint 100.00
b. Period after "6" 50.00
53 A6 12c blk, *green* 16.00 6.00
a. Period after "12" 60.00 20.00
b. Very thick paper 22.50 15.00
c. Without overprint 85.00
54 A6 25c bl, *pink* 35.00 4.00
b. Without overprint 125.00
55 A6 50c blk, *yellow* 200.00 20.00
56 A6 100c blk, *brown* 275.00 65.00
c. Without overprint 250.00
57 A6 100c brn, *brn* 650.00 200.00
a. Printed on both sides 850.00 700.00

Four kinds of perforation are found in the 1868 issue: serrate, square, pin and regular.

Thick Figures of Value, with Period after Numerals

6. CENT. 12. CENT
25. CENT. 50. CENT.
100. CENT

Overprinted with District Name, Number and Abbreviated Date

Imperf

58 A6 6c blk, *buff* 7.00 4.00
59 A6 12c blk, *green* 3.00 1.00
a. Very thick paper 7.50
c. 12c black, *buff* (error) 425.00 425.00
61 A6 25c blue, *pink* 5.50 75
a. No period after "25" 85.00
c. Very thick paper 20.00 5.00
d. "85" for "25" 50.00 25.00
e. "35" for "25" 40.00
62 A6 50c blk, *yellow* 100.00 12.00
a. No period after "50" 150.00 20.00
b. 50c blue, *lt pink* (error) *2,500.* *1,750.*
c. Half used as 25c on cover 600.00
d. Very thick paper 40.00
64 A6 100c blk, *brown* 100.00 35.00
a. No period after "100" 110.00 40.00
b. Very thick paper 50.00
c. Quarter used as 25c on cover *1,000.*

Perf.

65 A6 6c blk, *buff* 30.00 15.00
a. Very thick paper 40.00 25.00
66 A6 12c blk, *green* 4.00 4.00
a. Very thick paper 14.00 10.00
b. 12c black, *buff* (error) 450.00 450.00

No.	Type	Description	Unused	Used
68	A6	25c blue, *pink*	15.00	1.50
a.		No period after "25"		60.00
c.		Thick paper		10.00
d.		"85" for "25"	50.00	30.00
69	A6	50c blk, *yellow*	150.00	20.00
a.		No period after "50"	170.00	24.00
b.		50c blue, *lt pink* (error)	*2,000.*	*1,500.*
c.		Thick paper		40.00
70	A6	100c blk, *brown*	150.00	45.00
a.		No period after "100"	160.00	50.00
b.		Very thick paper		60.00

Postal forgeries of Nos. 58-70 were printed from original plates with district name overprints forged. These include the pelure paper varieties and some thick paper varieties. The "Anotado" handstamp was applied to some of the confiscated forgeries and they were issued, including Nos. 73a and 78a.

Stamps of 1868
Handstamped

Overprinted with District Name, Number and Abbreviated Date
Thick Figures with Period

1872 *Imperf.*

No.	Type	Description	Unused	Used
71	A6	6c blk, *buff*	500.00	550.00
72	A6	12c blk, *green*	50.00	55.00
73	A6	25c bl, *pink*	30.00	35.00
a.		Pelure paper	40.00	50.00
b.		"85" for "25"		100.00
74	A6	50c blk, *yellow*	650.00	350.00
a.		No period after "50"	700.00	375.00
75	A6	100c blk, *brown*	1,200.	1,000.
a.		No period after "100"		1,050.

Perf.

No.	Type	Description	Unused	Used
76	A6	6c blk, *buff*		
77	A6	12c blk, *green*	70.00	70.00
78	A6	25c blue, *pink*	25.00	30.00
a.		Pelure paper	65.00	70.00
79	A6	50c blk, *yellow*	700.00	400.00
a.		No period after "50"		425.00
80	A6	100c blk, *brown*		1,200.

Counterfeit "Anotado" overprints abound. Genuine cancellations other than Mexico City are unknown.

The stamps of the 1872 issue are found perforated with square holes, pin-perf. 13, 14 or 15, and with serrate perforation.

Counterfeits of the 1868 6c, 12c buff, 50c and 100c (both colors) from new plates have clear, sharp impressions and more facial shading lines than the originals. These counterfeits are found perf. and imperf., with thick and thin numerals, and with the "Anotado" overprint.

Hidalgo — A8

Moiré on White Back
Overprinted with District Name, Number and Abbreviated Date
White Wove Paper

1872 Litho. Wmk. 150 *Imperf.*

No.	Type	Description	Unused	Used
81	A8	6c green	60.00	45.00
82	A8	12c blue	35.00	25.00
a.		Laid paper		
83	A8	25c red	90.00	20.00
a.		Laid paper		
84	A8	50c yellow	400.00	200.00
a.		50c blue (error)		800.00
b.		Laid paper		
c.		As "a," without ovpt.	55.00	
86	A8	100c gray lilac	265.00	150.00

Wmk. "LA + F"

No.	Type	Description	Unused	Used
81a	A8	6c green	175.00	100.00
82b	A8	12c blue	125.00	45.00
83b	A8	25c red	160.00	35.00
c.		Without overprint	200.00	
84d	A8	50c yellow	1,000.	750.00
86a	A8	100c gray lilac	700.00	500.00

1872 Wmk. 150 *Pin-perf.*

No.	Type	Description	Unused	Used
87	A8	6c green	250.00	250.00
88	A8	12c blue	40.00	35.00
89	A8	25c red	95.00	30.00
b.		Laid paper		
90	A8	50c yellow	450.00	225.00
a.		50c blue (error)	*500.00*	*625.00*
b.		As "a," without overprint	75.00	
92	A8	100c gray lilac	250.00	200.00

Wmk. "LA + F"

No.	Type	Description	Unused	Used
87a	A8	6c green	325.00	265.00
88a	A8	12c blue	100.00	100.00
89a	A8	25c red	300.00	60.00
90c	A8	50c yellow	900.00	650.00
92a	A8	100c gray lilac	650.00	425.00

The watermark "LA+F" stands for La Croix Frères, the paper manufacturers, and is in double-lined block capitals 13mm high. A single stamp will show only part of this watermark.

1872 Unwmk. *Imperf.*

No.	Type	Description	Unused	Used
93	A8	6c green	10.00	10.00
a.		Without moiré on back	50.00	55.00
b.		Vertically laid paper		1,300.
c.		Bottom label retouched	80.00	75.00
d.		Very thick paper		20.00
94	A8	12c blue	1.60	1.40
a.		Without moiré on back	20.00	30.00
b.		Vertically laid paper	300.00	175.00
c.		Thin gray bl paper of 1867 (Wmk 151)		
95	A8	25c red	5.50	1.50
a.		Without moiré on back	20.00	30.00
b.		Vertically laid paper	400.00	175.00
c.		Thin gray bl paper of 1867 (Wmk 151)		
96	A8	50c yellow	110.00	25.00
a.		50c orange	110.00	25.00
b.		Without moiré on back	40.00	55.00
c.		Vertically laid paper		1,500.
d.		50c blue (error)		550.00
e.		As "d," without overprint	35.00	
f.		As "e," without moiré on back	55.00	
98	A8	100c gray lilac	75.00	40.00
a.		100c lilac	80.00	35.00
b.		Without moiré on back	40.00	90.00
c.		Vertically laid paper		800.00

Counterfeits of these stamps are 24½mm high instead of 24mm. The printing is sharper and more uniform than the genuine. Forged district names and consignment numbers exist.

Pin-perf. and Serrate Perf.

No.	Type	Description	Unused	Used
99	A8	6c green	60.00	50.00
100	A8	12c blue	2.25	1.90
a.		Vertically laid paper		225.00
b.		Horiz. pair, imperf. vert.	75.00	75.00
c.		Vert. pair, imperf. between		
101	A8	25c red	2.50	1.00
a.		Vertically laid paper		300.00
b.		Horiz. pair, imperf. vert.	75.00	75.00
102	A8	50c yellow	110.00	40.00
a.		50c orange	110.00	40.00
b.		50c blue (error)	325.00	
c.		As "b," without overprint	30.00	
104	A8	100c lilac	100.00	55.00
a.		100c gray lilac	85.00	55.00

Hidalgo
A9 A10

A11

A12

A13

A14

Overprinted with District Name and Number and Date; also with Number and Date only
Thick Wove Paper, Some Showing Vertical Ribbing

1874-80 Unwmk. Engr. *Perf. 12*

No.	Type	Description	Unused	Used
105	A9	4c org ('80)	10.00	9.00
a.		Vert. pair, imperf. btwn.	50.00	
b.		Without overprint	5.50	10.00
c.		Half used as 2c on cover		1,000.
106	A10	5c brown	3.50	2.25
a.		Horizontally laid paper	75.00	45.00
b.		Imperf., pair	50.00	
c.		Horiz. pair, imperf. btwn.	40.00	
d.		Vert. pair, imperf. btwn.	90.00	90.00
e.		Without overprint	30.00	
f.		As "a," wmkd. "LACROIX"	250.00	175.00
107	A11	10c black	1.75	1.00
a.		Horizontally laid paper	2.00	2.00
b.		Horiz. pair, imperf. btwn.	50.00	50.00
c.		Without overprint	22.50	22.50

d. Half used as 5c on cover		600.00
e. Imperf., pair		
f. As "a," wmkd. "LACROIX"	50.00	37.50
108 A11 10c org ('78)	1.75	1.00
a. 10c yellow bister	5.00	3.50
b. Imperf., pair		
c. Without overprint	45.00	45.00
d. Half used as 5c on cover		100.00
109 A12 25c blue	70	60
b. Horizontally laid paper	1.80	
c. Imperf., pair	35.00	25.00
d. Without overprint	30.00	17.50
e. Horiz. pair, imperf. btwn.	100.00	
f. As "b," horiz. pair, imperf. vert.	100.00	
g. As "b," wmkd. "LACROIX"	40.00	30.00
h. Printed on both sides		
i. Half used as 10c on cover		
110 A13 50c green	11.00	10.00
a. Without overprint	40.00	
b. Half used as 25c on cover		
111 A14 100c carmine	15.00	13.00
a. Imperf., pair	150.00	
b. Without overprint	40.00	
c. Quarterf used as 25c on cover		
Nos. 105-111 (7)	43.70	36.85

The "LACROIX" watermark is spelled out "LACROIX FRERES" in 2 lines of block capitals without serifs once to a sheet of horiz. laid paper. 6-12 stamps may have a portion of the wmk.

1875-77 **Wmk. 150**

112 A10 5c brown	30.00	30.00
113 A11 10c black	30.00	30.00
114 A12 25c blue	27.50	27.50
115 A13 50c green	175.00	175.00
116 A14 100c carmine	140.00	140.00

1881 Unwmk. Thin Wove Paper

117 A9 4c orange	37.50	37.50
a. Without overprint	11.00	11.00
118 A10 5c brown	6.00	4.00
a. Without overprint	32	11.00
b. As "a," vert. pair, imperf. horiz.	87.50	
119 A11 10c orange	3.25	1.90
a. Imperf., pair		
b. Vert. pair, imperf. horiz.	37.50	37.50
c. Without overprint	45	2.25
d. Vert. pair, imperf. btwn.	37.50	37.50
e. Half used as 5c on cover		
120 A12 25c blue	2.25	1.40
a. Imperf., pair		
b. Without overprint	32	
c. Double impression		37.50
121 A13 50c green	26.00	21.00
a. Without overprint	2.25	16.00
122 A14 100c carmine	35.00	27.50
a. Without overprint	3.25	
Nos. 117-122 (6)	110.00	93.30

The stamps of 1874-81 are found with number and date wide apart, close together or omitted, and in various colors.

The thin paper is fragile and easily damaged. Values for Nos. 117-122 are for undamaged, 4 margined copies.

Benito Juárez — A15

Overprinted with District Name and Number and Date; also with Number and Date only

1879 ***Perf. 12***

Thick Wove Paper, Some Showing Vertical Ribbing

123 A15 1c brown	3.00	2.75
a. Without overprint	60.00	110.00
b. 1c gray	14.00	12.00
124 A15 2c dk vio	2.75	2.40
a. Without overprint	60.00	75.00
b. Printed on both sides		
c. 2c dark gray	15.00	12.00
125 A15 5c orange	2.10	1.25
a. Without overprint	40.00	60.00
126 A15 10c blue	2.50	1.90
a. Without overprint	45.00	70.00
b. 10c ultra	150.00	150.00
127 A15 25c rose	6.50	7.50
a. Without overprint	1.50	
128 A15 50c green	10.00	9.50
a. Without overprint	1.00	
b. Printed on both sides		150.00
129 A15 85c violet	17.50	15.00
a. Without overprint	2.00	
130 A15 100c black	20.00	17.50
a. Without overprint	2.25	
Nos. 123-130 (8)	64.35	57.80

1882

Thin Wove Paper

131 A15 1c brown	24.00	20.00
a. Without overprint	82.50	
132 A15 2c dk vio	18.00	14.00
a. 2c slate	25.00	20.00
b. Without overprint	65.00	
c. Half used as 1c on cover		
133 A15 5c orange	6.00	3.00
a. Without overprint	80	
b. Half used as 2c on cover		
c. As "a," vert. pair, imperf. btwn.		
134 A15 10c blue	6.00	3.00
a. Without overprint	80	
b. Half used as 5c on cover		
135 A15 10c brown	6.00	
a. Imperf., pair	2.00	
136 A15 12c brown	5.00	5.00
a. Without overprint	1.65	
b. Imperf., pair	5.00	5.00
c. Half used as 6c on cover		
137 A15 18c org brn	6.00	5.00
a. Horiz. pair, imperf. btwn.	60.00	60.00
b. Without overprint	1.40	8.25
138 A15 24c violet	6.00	5.00
a. Without overprint	1.40	11.00
139 A15 25c rose	30.00	30.00
a. Without overprint	2.75	
140 A15 25c org brn	3.50	
141 A15 50c green	27.50	30.00
a. Without overprint	4.25	
142 A15 50c yellow	55.00	60.00
a. Without overprint	90.00	
143 A15 85c red vio	35.00	
144 A15 100c black	40.00	*60.00*
a. Without overprint	3.25	
b. Vert. pair, imperf. btwn.	110.00	110.00
145 A15 100c orange	65.00	75.00
a. Without overprint	100.00	
Nos. 131-145 (15)	333.00	

No. 135, 140 and 143 exist only without overprint. They were never placed in use.

Used values for 50c, 85c and 100c of type A15 are for privately canceled copies. Postally used examples sell for several times as much.

See note on thin paper after No. 122.

A16

Hidalgo — A17

Overprinted with District Name, Number and Abbreviated Date

1882-83

146 A16 2c green	5.00	4.00
a. Without overprint	12.00	9.00
147 A16 3c car lake	5.00	4.00
a. Without overprint	2.50	3.00
148 A16 6c blue ('83)	18.00	15.00
a. Without overprint	12.50	17.00
149 A16 6c ultra	4.00	3.00
a. Without overprint	1.50	3.00
b. Imperf., pair	40.00	

See note on thin paper after No. 122.

1884 Wove or Laid Paper ***Perf. 12***

150 A17 1c green	2.00	50
a. Imperf., pair	17.50	
b. 1c blue (error)	325.00	325.00
151 A17 2c green	3.00	75
a. Imperf., pair	30.00	30.00
b. Half used as 1c on cover		
152 A17 3c green	6.00	1.25
a. Imperf., pair	60.00	60.00
b. Horiz. pair, imperf. vert.		50.00
153 A17 4c green	8.00	1.25
a. Imperf., pair	45.00	45.00
b. Half used as 2c on cover		100.00
154 A17 5c green	8.00	1.00
a. Imperf., pair	60.00	60.00
155 A17 6c green	7.25	90
a. Imperf., pair	45.00	45.00
156 A17 10c green	7.50	50
a. Imperf., pair	20.00	20.00
157 A17 12c green	14.00	2.00
a. Vert. pair, imperf. between	45.00	45.00
b. Half used as 6c on cover		90.00
158 A17 20c green	40.00	1.50
a. Diagonal half used as 10c on cover		100.00
b. Imperf., pair	85.00	85.00
159 A17 25c green	70.00	3.00
a. Imperf., pair	150.00	150.00
160 A17 50c green	50	*2.00*
a. Imperf., pair	14.00	14.00
161 A17 1p blue	50	*7.50*
a. Imperf., pair	30.00	30.00
b. Vert. pair, imperf. between		
162 A17 2p blue	50	*14.00*
a. Imperf., pair	40.00	40.00
163 A17 5p blue	165.00	125.00
164 A17 10p blue	250.00	150.00
Nos. 150-162 (13)	167.25	*36.15*

Imperforate varieties should be purchased in pairs or larger. Single imperforates are usually trimmed perforated stamps.

Beware of copies of No. 150 that have been chemically changed to resemble No. 150b.

Some values exist perf. 11.

Values for unused stamps are for copies without gum.

See Nos. 165-173, 230-231.

1885

165 A17 1c pale grn	15.00	5.00
166 A17 2c carmine	10.00	2.25
a. Diagonal half used as 1c on cover		75.00
167 A17 3c org brn	14.00	4.00
a. Imperf., pair	60.00	60.00
168 A17 4c red org	20.00	12.00
169 A17 5c ultra	14.00	2.50
170 A17 6c dk brn	16.00	4.00
a. Half used as 3c on cover		75.00
171 A17 10c orange	12.00	90
a. 10c yellow	12.00	90
b. Horiz. pair, imperf. btwn.	60.00	60.00
172 A17 12c olive brn	25.00	6.00
173 A17 25c grnsh blue	90.00	14.00
Nos. 165-173 (9)	216.00	50.65

Numeral of Value — A18

1886 ***Perf. 12***

174 A18 1c blue grn	75	25
a. 1c yellow green	75	25
b. Horiz. pair, imperf. btwn.	20.00	15.00
c. Perf. 11	10.00	10.00
175 A18 2c carmine	1.00	35
a. Horiz. pair, imperf. btwn.		20.00
b. Vert. pair, imperf. between	20.00	20.00
c. Perf. 11	10.00	10.00
d. Half used as 1c on cover		75.00
176 A18 3c lilac	4.00	2.00
177 A18 4c lilac	7.00	1.50
a. Perf. 11	12.00	12.00
178 A18 5c ultra	75	25
a. 5c blue	80	30
179 A18 6c lilac	8.00	1.00
180 A18 10c lilac	8.00	30
a. Perf. 11	10.00	10.00
181 A18 12c lilac	8.00	5.00
182 A18 20c lilac	65.00	35.00
183 A18 25c lilac	25.00	6.00
Nos. 174-183 (10)	127.50	51.65

Nos. 175, 191, 194B, 196, 202 with blue or black surcharge "Vale 1 Cvo." These were made by the Colima postmaster.

1887

184 A18 3c scarlet	60	20
a. Imperf., pair		
185 A18 4c scarlet	2.50	60
186 A18 6c scarlet	4.00	75
a. Horiz. pair, imperf. btwn.	20.00	
187 A18 10c scarlet	1.10	20
a. Imperf., pair		
b. Horiz. pair, imperf. btwn.	15.00	
188 A18 20c scarlet	6.00	50
a. Horiz. pair, imperf. btwn.	25.00	
189 A18 25c scarlet	5.00	1.25
Nos. 184-189 (6)	19.20	3.50

Perf. 6

190 A18 1c blue grn	6.00	4.00
191 A18 2c brn car	8.00	4.00
191A A18 3c scarlet	*150.00*	60.00
192 A18 5c ultra	4.50	1.50
a. 5c blue	4.50	1.50
193 A18 10c lilac	5.00	1.50
193A A18 10c brn lil	4.00	1.00
194 A18 10c scarlet	10.00	5.00

Perf. 6x12

194A A18 1c blue grn	20.00	15.00
194B A18 2c brn car	25.00	20.00
194C A18 3c scarlet		100.00
194D A18 5c ultra	20.00	15.00
194E A18 10c lilac	20.00	18.00
194F A18 10c scarlet	25.00	20.00
194G A18 10c brn lil	25.00	15.00

Many shades exist.

Paper ruled with blue lines on face or reverse of stamp

1887 ***Perf. 12***

195 A18 1c green	25.00	14.00
196 A18 2c brn car	40.00	15.00
196A A18 3c scarlet		
198 A18 5c ultra	40.00	8.00
199 A18 10c scarlet	40.00	7.00

Perf. 6

201 A18 1c green	20.00	6.00
202 A18 2c brn car	20.00	7.50
204 A18 5c ultra	16.00	4.00
205 A18 10c brn lil	14.00	3.00
206 A18 10c scarlet	85.00	12.00

Perf. 6x12

207 A18 1c green	80.00	50.00
208 A18 2c brn car	80.00	50.00
209 A18 5c ultra	80.00	50.00
210 A18 10c brn lil	100.00	40.00
211 A18 10c scarlet	110.00	70.00

1890-95 Wmk. 152 ***Perf. 11 & 12***

Wove or Laid Paper

212 A18 1c yel grn	20	15
a. 1c blue green	20	15
b. Horiz. pair, imperf. btwn.	14.00	14.00
c. Laid paper	1.00	1.00
d. Horiz. pair, imperf. vert.	14.00	14.00
213 A18 2c brn car	50	30
a. 2c carmine	50	25
b. Vert. pair, imperf. btwn.	60.00	
c. Imperf., pair	80.00	
214 A18 3c vermilion	30	20
b. Horiz. pair, imperf. between	12.00	
215 A18 4c vermilion	1.25	80
a. Horiz. pair, imperf. between	30.00	
216 A18 5c ultra	20	15
a. 5c dull blue	30	20
217 A18 6c vermilion	1.25	1.00
a. Horiz. pair, imperf. btwn.	15.00	
218 A18 10c vermilion	15	15
b. Horiz. or vert. pair, imperf. btwn.	15.00	
c. Vert. pair, imperf. horiz.	15.00	15.00
d. Imperf., pair	20.00	
219 A18 12c ver ('95)	5.00	6.00
220 A18 20c vermilion	1.00	40
220A A18 20c dk violet	50.00	60.00
221 A18 25c vermilion	1.50	75
Nos. 212-220,221 (10)	11.35	9.90

No. 219 has been reprinted in slightly darker shade than the original.

1892

222 A18 3c orange	1.50	75
223 A18 4c orange	1.75	1.00
224 A18 6c orange	2.25	75
225 A18 10c orange	12.00	75
226 A18 20c orange	20.00	2.50
227 A18 25c orange	6.50	1.75
Nos. 222-227 (6)	44.00	7.50

1892

228 A18 5p carmine	550.00	375.00
229 A18 10p carmine	900.00	550.00
230 A17 5p bl grn	1,600.	550.00
231 A17 10p bl grn	*4,000.*	*1,250.*

1894 ***Perf. 5½, 6***

232 A18 1c yel grn	85	85
233 A18 3c vermilion	2.75	2.75
234 A18 4c vermilion	14.00	10.00
235 A18 5c ultra	4.00	1.50
236 A18 10c vermilion	2.50	1.00
236A A18 20c vermilion	40.00	40.00
237 A18 25c vermilion	20.00	20.00

Perf. 5½x11, 11x5½, Compound and Irregular

238 A18 1c yel grn	1.75	1.75
238A A18 2c brn car	5.00	5.00
238B A18 3c vermilion	10.00	10.00
238C A18 4c vermilion	15.00	15.00
239 A18 5c ultra	4.00	4.00
a. 5c blue	4.00	4.00
239C A18 6c vermilion	20.00	20.00
240 A18 10c vermilion	7.00	2.00
240A A18 20c vermilion	75.00	50.00
241 A18 25c vermilion	20.00	15.00

The stamps of the 1890 to 1895 issues are also to be found unwatermarked, as part of the sheet frequently escaped the watermark.

Letter Carrier — A20

Mounted Courier with Pack Mule — A21

Statue of Cuauhtémoc A22

Mail Coach A23

Mail Train — A24

Regular or Pin Perf. 12

1895 **Wmk. 152**

Wove or Laid Paper

242 A20 1c green	45	20
a. Vert. pair, imperf. horiz.	50.00	
243 A20 2c carmine	65	25
a. Half used as 1c on cover		30.00
244 A20 3c org brn	65	25
a. Vert. pair, imperf. horiz.		50.00
246 A21 4c orange	2.40	55
a. 4c org red	2.40	55

No.	Design	Description	Unused	Used
247	A22	5c ultra	1.20	15
a.		Imperf., pair	25.00	25.00
b.		Horiz. or vert. pair, imperf. between	25.00	25.00
e.		Half used as 2c on cover		60.00
248	A23	10c lil rose	1.00	25
a.		Horiz. or vert. pair, imperf. between		40.00
b.		Half used as 5c on cover		40.00
249	A21	12c olive brn	13.00	6.00
251	A23	15c brt blue	6.50	1.25
252	A23	20c brn rose	6.50	1.00
b.		Half used as 10c on cover		50.00
253	A23	50c purple	19.00	7.50
a.		Half used as 25c on cover		75.00
254	A24	1p brown	37.50	18.00
255	A24	5p scarlet	125.00	75.00
256	A24	10p deep blue	200.00	140.00
		Nos. 242-256 (13)	413.85	250.40

No. 248 exists in perf. 11.

Perf. 6

No.	Design	Description
242b	A20	1c green
243b	A20	2c carmine
244b	A20	3c orange brown
247c	A22	5c ultra
248c	A23	10c lilac rose
249a	A21	12c olive brown

Perf. 6x12, 12x6 & Compound or Irregular

No.	Design	Description
242c	A20	1c green
244c	A20	3c orange brown
246b	A21	4c orange
247d	A22	5c ultra
248d	A23	10c lilac rose
249b	A21	12c olive brown
251a	A23	15c brt blue
252a	A23	20c brown rose
253b	A23	50c purple

See Nos. 257-291. For overprints see Nos. O10-O48A.

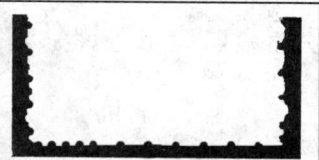

"Irregular" Perfs.
Some copies perf. 6x12, 12x6, 5½x11 and 11x5½ have both perf. 6 and 12 or perf. 5½ and 11 on one or more sides of the stamp. These are known as irregular perfs.

1896-97 Wmk. 153 *Perf. 12*

No.	Design	Description	Unused	Used
257	A20	1c green	2.00	35
c.		Imperf., pair		
258	A20	2c carmine	2.50	40
a.		Horiz. pair, imperf. vert.		
259	A20	3c org brn	2.75	45
260	A21	4c orange	5.00	55
c.		4c deep orange	8.00	2.00
261	A22	5c ultra	2.00	20
a.		Imperf., pair	24.00	
b.		Vert. pair, imperf. btwn.	40.00	
262	A21	12c ol brn	35.00	24.00
263	A23	15c brt bl	35.00	4.00
264	A23	20c brn rose	250.00	125.00
265	A23	50c purple	40.00	35.00
266	A24	1p brown	110.00	50.00
267	A24	5p scarlet	325.00	200.00
268	A24	10p dp bl	500.00	240.00
		Nos. 257-268 (12)	1,309.	679.95

Perf. 6

No.	Design	Description
257a	A20	1c green
259a	A20	3c orange brown
260a	A21	4c orange
261c	A22	5c ultra
263a	A23	15c bright blue

Perf. 6x12, 12x6 and Compound or Irregular

No.	Design	Description
257b	A20	1c green
258b	A20	2c carmine
259b	A20	3c orange brown
260b	A21	4c orange
261d	A22	5c ultra
262a	A21	12c olive brown
263b	A23	15c bright blue
264a	A23	20c brown rose
265a	A23	50c purple

1897-98 Wmk. 154 *Perf. 12*

No.	Design	Description	Unused	Used
269	A20	1c green	3.00	70
270	A20	2c scarlet	5.00	1.00
271	A21	4c orange	12.00	80
a.		Horizontal pair, imperf. vertical		
272	A22	5c ultra	7.00	45
a.		Imperf., pair	40.00	
273	A21	12c ol brn	36.00	10.00
275	A23	15c brt bl	55.00	30.00
276	A23	20c brn rose	40.00	4.00
277	A23	50c purple	60.00	20.00
278	A24	1p brown	110.00	45.00
278A	A24	5p scarlet	*10,000.*	*10,000.*
		Nos. 269-278 (9)	328.00	111.95

Perf. 6

No.	Design	Description
269a	A20	1c green
270a	A20	2c scarlet
272b	A22	5c ultra
273a	A21	12c olive brown
276a	A23	20c brown rose

Perf. 6x12, 12x6 and Compound or Irregular

No.	Design	Description
269b	A20	1c green
270b	A20	2c scarlet
271b	A21	4c orange
272c	A22	5c ultra
273b	A21	12c olive brown
275a	A23	15c bright blue
276b	A23	20c brown rose
277a	A23	50c purple

1898 Unwmk. *Perf. 12*

No.	Design	Description	Unused	Used
279	A20	1c green	45	15
a.		Horiz. pair, imperf. vert		
b.		Imperf., pair	45.00	
280	A20	2c scarlet	1.10	25
a.		2c green (error)	*210.00*	
281	A20	3c org brn	1.00	25
a.		Imperf., pair	55.00	
b.		Pair, imperf. between	30.00	
282	A21	4c orange	6.00	1.20
b.		4c deep orange	15.00	5.00
283	A22	5c ultra	60	15
a.		Imperf., pair	25.00	25.00
b.		Pair, imperf. between	45.00	
284	A23	10c lil rose	165.00	85.00
285	A21	12c ol brn	17.50	7.00
a.		Imperf., pair	110.00	
286	A23	15c brt bl	47.50	3.00
287	A23	20c brn rose	15.00	2.00
a.		Imperf., pair	110.00	
288	A23	50c purple	37.50	16.00
289	A24	1p brown	55.00	24.00
290	A24	5p car rose	400.00	225.00
291	A24	10p deep blue	500.00	300.00
		Nos. 279-291 (13)	1,246.	664.00

Perf. 6

No.	Design	Description
279c	A20	1c green
280b	A20	2c scarlet
281c	A20	3c orange brown
283c	A22	5c ultra
287b	A23	20c brown rose
291a	A24	10p deep blue

Perf. 6x12, 12x6 and Compound or Irregular

No.	Design	Description
279d	A20	1c green
280c	A20	2c scarlet
281d	A20	3c orange brown
282a	A21	4c orange
283d	A22	5c ultra
284a	A23	10c lilac rose
285b	A21	12c olive brown
286a	A23	15c bright blue
287c	A23	20c brown rose
288a	A23	50c purple

Forgeries of the 6 and 6x12 perforations of 1895-98 are plentiful.

Coat of Arms
A25 A26

A27

A28

A29

A30

A31

Juanacatlán Falls — A32

View of Mt. Popocatépetl A33

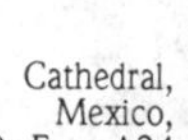

Cathedral, Mexico, D. F. — A34

1899 Wmk. 155 *Perf. 14, 15*

No.	Design	Description	Unused	Used
294	A25	1c green	1.65	15
295	A26	2c vermilion	3.75	20
296	A27	3c org brn	2.50	15
297	A28	5c dark blue	4.00	15
298	A29	10c vio & org	5.25	30
299	A30	15c lav & claret	6.75	25
300	A31	20c rose & dk bl	7.75	35
301	A32	50c red lil & blk	30.00	2.00
a.		50c lilac & black	35.00	2.00
302	A33	1p bl & blk	67.50	3.00
303	A34	5p car & blk	200.00	10.00
		Nos. 294-303 (10)	329.15	16.55

See Nos. 304-305, 307-309. For overprints see Nos. 420-422, 439-450, 452-454, 482-483, 515-516, 539, 550, O49-O60, O62-O66, O68-O74, O101.

A35

1903

No.	Design	Description	Unused	Used
304	A25	1c violet	1.25	15
a.		Booklet pane of 6	50.00	
305	A26	2c green	1.65	15
a.		Booklet pane of 6	75.00	
306	A35	4c carmine	4.00	40
307	A28	5c orange	95	15
a.		Booklet pane of 6	75.00	
308	A29	10c blue & org	4.00	30
309	A32	50c car & blk	65.00	5.50
		Nos. 304-309 (6)	76.85	6.65

For overprints see Nos. 451, O61, O67.

Independence Issue

Josefa Ortiz — A36

Leona Vicario — A37

López Rayón — A38

Juan Aldama — A39

Miguel Hidalgo — A40

Ignacio Allende — A41

Epigmenio González — A42

Mariano Abasolo — A43

Declaration of Independence A44

Mass on the Mount of Crosses — A45

Capture of Granaditas A46

1910 *Perf. 14*

No.	Design	Description	Unused	Used
310	A36	1c dull vio	15	20
a.		Booklet pane of 4	35.00	
311	A37	2c green	15	15
a.		Booklet pane of 8	35.00	
312	A38	3c org brn	55	25
313	A39	4c carmine	2.00	40
314	A40	5c orange	15	15
a.		Booklet pane of 8	25.00	
315	A41	10c blue & org	1.25	20
316	A42	15c gray bl & cl	7.00	45
317	A43	20c red & bl	4.00	35
318	A44	50c red brn & blk	10.00	1.50
319	A45	1p blue & blk	12.00	1.75
320	A46	5p car & blk	45.00	4.50
		Nos. 310-320 (11)	82.25	9.90

Centenary of the independence of Mexico from Spain.

For overprints and surcharges see Nos. 370-380, 423-433, 455-465, 484-494, 517-538, 540-549, 551-558, 577-590, O75-O85, O102-O112, O191-O192, O195, RA13, Merida 1.

CIVIL WAR ISSUES

During the 1913-16 Civil War, provisional issues with various handstamped overprints were circulated in limited areas.

Sonora

A47

Seal

Typeset in a row of five varieties. Two impressions placed tête bêche (foot to foot) constitute a sheet. The settings show various wrong font and defective letters, "!" for "1" in "1913," etc. The paper occasionally has a manufacturer's watermark.

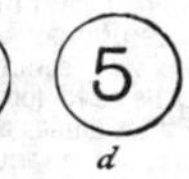

a *b* *c* *d*

Four Types of the Numerals.
- *a*- Wide, heavy-faced numerals.
- *b*- Narrow Roman numerals.
- *c*- Wide Roman numerals.
- *d*- Gothic or sans-serif numerals.

Embossed "CONSTITUCIONAL"

1913 Typeset Unwmk. *Perf. 12*

No.	Design	Description	Unused	Used
321	A47 (a)	5c blk & red	2,500.	650.00
a.		"CENTAVOB"	*2,750.*	*700.00*

Colorless Roulette

No.	Design	Description	Unused	Used
322	A47(b)	1c blk & red	10.00	12.00
a.		With green seal	*750.00*	*650.00*
323	A47(a)	2c blk & red	7.00	7.00
a.		With green seal	*950.00*	*950.00*
324	A47(c)	2c blk & red	35.00	35.00
a.		With green seal	*2,000.*	*2,000.*
325	A47(a)	3c blk & red	45.00	37.50
a.		With green seal	*400.00*	*400.00*
326	A47(a)	5c blk & red	150.00	37.50
a.		"CENTAVOB"	175.00	42.50
327	A47(d)	5c blk & red	400.00	200.00
a.		With green seal		650.00
328	A47(b)	10c blk & red	12.50	15.00

Black Roulette

329 A47(d) 5c blk & red 75.00 45.00
a. "MARO" 85.00 50.00

Stamps are known with the embossing double or omitted.

The varieties with green seal are from a few sheets embossed "Constitucional" which were in stock at the time the green seal control was adopted.

Without Embossing
With Green Seal
Colorless Roulette

336 A47(b) 1c blk & red 5.00 5.00
337 A47(a) 3c blk & red 4.50 4.50
a. Imperf. 250.00
338 A47(a) 5c blk & red 700.00 200.00
a. "CENTAVOB" *750.00* 225.00
339 A47(b) 10c blk & red 3.00 3.00

Colored Roulette

340 A47(d) 5c brnsh blk & red 6.00 3.00
a. 5c lilac brown & red 45.00 11.00
b. Double seal *1,000. 750.00*
c. Red printing omitted *1,000.*

1913-14 ***Black Roulette***

With Green Seal

341 A47(a) 1c blk & red 1.20 1.00
b. "erano" ('14) 60.00 60.00
342 A47(d) 2c blk & red 1.20 90
a. "erano" ('14) 30.00 35.00
343 A47(a) 3c blk & red 1.75 1.50
a. "CENTAVO" 25.00 25.00
b. "erano" ('14) 35.00 35.00
344 A47(d) 5c blk & red 1.75 1.00
b. Heavy black penetrating roulette 2.75 1.75
c. As "b," "MARO" 7.50 5.00

Stamps without seal are unfinished remainders.

On Nos. 341-344 the rouletting cuts the paper slightly or not at all. On Nos. 344b-344c the rouletting is heavy, cutting deeply into the paper.

1914

345 A47(a) 5c blk & red 2.00 1.75
346 A47(b) 10c blk & red 1.20 1.20

Coat of Arms — A49

Revenue Stamps Used for Postage

1913 **Litho.** ***Rouletted 14, 14x7***

347 A49 1c yel grn 1.50 1.50
a. With coupon 5.00 5.00
348 A49 2c violet 3.00 3.00
a. With coupon 12.00 12.00
349 A49 5c brown 45 45
a. With coupon 1.25 1.25
350 A49 10c claret 2.00 2.00
a. With coupon 10.00 10.00
351 A49 20c gray grn 2.25 2.75
a. With coupon 15.00 15.00
352 A49 50c ultra 8.00 10.00
a. With coupon 50.00 40.00
353 A49 1p orange 35.00 40.00
a. With coupon 125.00 100.00
Nos. 347-353 (7) 52.20 59.70

For a short time these stamps (called "Ejercitos") were used for postage with coupon attached. Later this was required to be removed unless they were to be used for revenue. Stamps overprinted with district names are revenues. Values above 1p were used for revenue. Imperfs exist of all values, but were not issued.

Many copies do not have gum because of a flood.

Use of typeset Sonora revenue stamps for postage was not authorized or allowed.

Coat of Arms
A50 A51

5c (A50): "CINCO CENTAVOS" 14x2mm

1914 ***Rouletted 9½x14***

354 A50 1c dp bl 45 45
355 A50 2c yel grn 60 35
a. 2c green 3.00 1.75
356 A50 4c bl vio 11.00 2.50
a. Horiz. pair, imperf. btwn. 225.00
357 A50 5c gray grn 11.00 3.00
a. Horiz. pair imperf. btwn. 65.00
358 A50 10c red 45 45
359 A50 20c yel brn 60 60
a. 20c deep brown 2.25 2.25
b. Horiz. pair, imperf. btwn. 225.00
360 A50 50c claret 2.50 3.50
a. Horiz. pair, imperf. btwn. 225.00
361 A50 1p brt vio 14.00 16.00
a. Horiz. pair, imperf. btwn. 200.00
Nos. 354-361 (8) 40.60 26.85

Nos. 354-361 (called "Transitorios") exist imperf. but were not regularly issued.

Many copies do not have gum because of a flood.

See Note after No. 465.

See No. 369. For overprints see Nos. 362-368, 559-565.

Overprinted in Black

Victoria de
TORREON
ABRIL 2-1914

1914

362 A50 1c dp bl 150.00 125.00
363 A50 2c yel grn 175.00 150.00
364 A50 4c bl vio 200.00 250.00
365 A50 5c gray grn 18.00 20.00
a. Horiz. pair, imperf. btwn. 425.00
366 A50 10c red 100.00 100.00
367 A50 20c yel brn *1,750. 1,750.*
368 A50 50c claret *2,000. 2,000.*

Values are for copies with design close to, or just touching, the perfs.

Excellent counterfeits of this overprint exist.

Redrawn
"CINCO CENTAVOS" 16x2½mm

1914 ***Perf. 12***

369 A51 5c gray green 15 15

Imperfs are printers' waste.

Regular Issue of 1910 Overprinted in Violet, Magenta, Black or Green

1914 **Wmk. 155** ***Perf. 14***

370 A36 1c dl vio 70 60
a. Booklet pane of 4 75.00
371 A37 2c green 1.50 1.25
a. Booklet pane of 8 75.00
372 A38 3c org brn 1.50 1.25
373 A39 4c carmine 2.50 2.00
374 A40 5c orange 50 30
a. Booklet pane of 8 60.00
375 A41 10c bl & org 3.00 2.00
376 A42 15c gray bl & cl 5.00 3.00
377 A43 20c red & blue 10.00 6.00
378 A44 50c red brn & blk 12.00 8.00
379 A45 1p bl & blk 25.00 10.00
380 A46 5p car & blk 165.00 150.00
Nos. 370-380 (11) 226.70 184.40

Overprinted On Postage Due Stamps of 1908

381 D1 1c blue 14.00 16.00
382 D1 2c blue 14.00 16.00
383 D1 4c blue 14.00 16.00
384 D1 5c blue 14.00 16.00
385 D1 10c blue 14.00 16.00
Nos. 381-385 (5) 70.00 80.00

This overprint is found double, inverted, sideways and in pairs with and without the overprint. There are two or more types of this overprint.

The Postage Due Stamps and similar groups of them which follow were issued and used as regular postage stamps.

Values are for copies where the overprint is clear enough to be expertised.

Counterfeits abound.

A52

A53

1914 **Unwmk.** **Litho.** ***Perf. 12***

386 A52 1c pale blue 35 50
387 A52 2c light green 30 45
388 A52 3c orange 50 50
389 A52 5c deep rose 50 30
390 A52 10c rose 70 85
391 A52 15c rose lilac 1.20 1.75
392 A52 50c yellow 2.00 2.50
a. 50c ocher 1.75
393 A52 1p violet 8.50 12.00
Nos. 386-393 (8) 14.05 18.85

Nos. 386-393, are known imperforate.

This set is usually called the Denver Issue because it was printed there.

See Note after No. 465.

For overprints and surcharges see Nos. 566-573, 591-592.

Revenue Stamps Used for Postage

1914, July ***Perf. 12***

393A A53 1c rose 20.00
393B A53 2c lt grn 18.00
393C A53 3c lt org 20.00
393D A53 5c red 8.00
393E A53 10c gray grn 35.00

Nos. 393A-393E were used in the northeast. Values are for examples with postal cancellations.

Unused copies are to be considered as revenues.

Background as
A55 — A54

A55

1914 ***Imperf.***

Values and Inscriptions in Black
Inscribed "SONORA"

394 A54 1c bl & red 25 25
a. Double seal
b. Without seal 20.00
395 A54 2c grn & org 30 30
a. Without seal 100.00
396 A54 5c yel & grn 30 30
a. 5c orange & green 1.50 1.25
b. Without seal 200.00
397 A54 10c lt bl & red 3.50 1.75
a. 10c blue & red 40.00 15.00
398 A54 20c yel & grn 1.75 2.00
399 A54 20c org & bl 15.00 17.50
400 A54 50c grn & org 1.25 1.25
Nos. 394-400 (7) 22.35 23.35

Shades. Stamps of type A54 are usually termed the "Coach Seal Issue."

Inscribed "DISTRITO SUR DE LA BAJA CAL"

401 A54 1c yel & bl 2.00 *30.00*
a. Without seal 50.00
402 A54 2c gray & ol grn 2.50 *25.00*
403 A54 5c olive & rose 2.00 *20.00*
a. Without seal 50.00
404 A54 10c pale red & dl vio 2.00 *20.00*
a. Without seal 50.00

Counterfeit cancellations exist.

Inscribed "SONORA"

405 A55 1c blue & red 6.00
a. Without seal 50.00
406 A55 2c grn & org 50
407 A55 5c yel & grn 50 *2.50*
a. Without seal 75.00
408 A55 10c blue & red 50 *2.50*
409 A55 20c yel & grn 30.00 *15.00*
a. Without seal 50.00
b. Double seal *80.00*
Nos. 405-409 (5) 37.50

With "PLATA" added to the inscription

410 A55 1c bl & red 1.00
a. "PLATA" inverted 60.00
b. Pair, one without "PLATA" 15.00
411 A55 10c blue & red 1.00
412 A55 20c yel & grn 2.50
a. "PLATA" double 50.00
413 A55 50c gray grn & org 1.75
a. Without seal 1.00
b. As "a," "P" of "PLATA" missing 150.00

Stamps of type A55 are termed the "Anvil Seal Issue".

Nos. 394-413 were issued without gum.

Nos. 410-413 were not placed in use.

Oaxaca

Coat of Arms — A56

5c:
Type I- Thick numerals, 2mm wide.
Type II- Thin numerals, 1½mm wide.

Perf. 8½ to 14

1915 **Typo.** **Unwmk.**

414 A56 1c dull vio 85 1.25
415 A56 2c emerald 1.50 2.25
a. Inverted numeral 30.00
e. Numeral omitted 35.00
416 A56 3c red brn 2.25 3.50
b. Inverted numeral 24.00
417 A56 5c org (type I) 20.00 25.00
a. Tête bêche pair 60.00 60.00
418 A56 5c org (type II) 50 75
a. Types I and II in pair 70.00
419 A56 10c bl & car 1.75
Nos. 414-419 (6) 26.85

Many printing errors, imperfs and part perfs exist. Mostly these are printers' waste, private reprints or counterfeits.

Nos. 414-419 printed on backs of post office receipt forms.

Regular Issues of 1899-1910 Overprinted in Black

GOBIERNO
$
CONSTITUCIONALISTA

1914 **Wmk. 155** ***Perf. 14***

On Issues of 1899-1903

420 A28 5c orange
421 A30 15c lav & claret 150.00 150.00
422 A31 20c rose & dk bl 500.00 400.00

Counterfeits exist.

On Issue of 1910

423 A36 1c dl vio 20 20
424 A37 2c green 25 25
425 A38 3c org brn 40 40
426 A39 4c carmine 50 50
427 A40 5c orange 15 15
428 A41 10c bl & org 25 25
429 A42 15c gray bl & claret 70 60
430 A43 20c red & bl 75 70

Overprinted

GOBIERNO
y
CONSTITUCIONALISTA

431 A44 50c red brn & blk 1.75 1.50
432 A45 1p bl & blk 7.50 5.00
433 A46 5p car & blk 40.00 30.00
Nos. 423-433 (11) 52.45 39.55

In the first setting of the overprint on 1c to 20c, the variety "GONSTITUCIONALISTA" occurs 4 times in each sheet of 100. In the second setting it occurs on the last stamp in each row of 10.

The overprint exists reading downward on Nos. 423-430; inverted on Nos. 431-433; double on Nos. 423-425, 427.

See Note after No. 465.

Postage Due Stamps of 1908 Overprinted

434 D1 1c blue 1.75 1.75
435 D1 2c blue 2.00 2.00
436 D1 4c blue 15.00 15.00
437 D1 5c blue 15.00 15.00
438 D1 10c blue 2.50 2.50
a. Double overprint
Nos. 434-438 (5) 36.25 36.25

Preceding Issues Overprinted

This is usually called the "Villa" monogram. Counterfeits abound.

1915

On Issue of 1899

439 A25 1c green 100.00
440 A26 2c vermilion 100.00
441 A27 3c org brn 50.00
442 A28 5c dark blue 100.00
443 A29 10c vio & org 100.00
444 A30 15c lav & claret 100.00
445 A31 20c rose & bl 100.00
446 A32 50c red lil & blk 250.00
447 A33 1p blue & blk 250.00
448 A34 5p car & blk 500.00

On Issue of 1903

449 A25 1c violet 100.00
450 A26 2c green 100.00
451 A35 4c carmine 100.00
452 A28 5c orange 12.50
a. Inverted overprint 20.00
453 A29 10c blue & org 75.00
454 A32 50c car & blk 200.00

In Sept. 1915 Postmaster Hinojosa ordered a special printing of Nos. 439-454 (as valued) for sale to collectors. Earlier a small quantity of Nos. 444-445, 448 and 452-454 was regularly issued. They are hard to distinguish and sell for much more. Counterfeits abound.

On Issue of 1910

455 A36 1c dl vio 85 1.00
456 A37 2c green 40 60
457 A38 3c org brn 60 75
458 A39 4c carmine 4.00 4.50
459 A40 5c orange 18 18
460 A41 10c bl & org 7.00 7.50
461 A42 15c gray bl & cl 3.00 4.00
462 A43 20c red & bl 5.50 7.00
463 A44 50c red brn & blk 13.00 14.00
464 A45 1p bl & blk 17.00 20.00
465 A46 5p car & blk 150.00
Nos. 455-464 (10) 51.53 59.53

Nos. 455-465 are known with overprint inverted, double and other variations. Most were ordered by Postmaster General Hinojosa for philtelic purposes. They were sold at a premium. This applies to Nos. 354-361, 386-393, 431-433 with this monogram as well.

Overprinted On Postage Due Stamps of 1908

466 D1 1c blue 9.50 10.00
467 D1 2c blue 9.50 10.00
468 D1 4c blue 9.50 10.00
469 D1 5c blue 9.50 10.00
470 D1 10c blue 9.50 10.00
Nos. 466-470 (5) 47.50 50.00

Nos. 466 to 470 are known with inverted overprint. All other values of the 1899 and 1903 issues exist with this overprint. See note after No. 465.

Issues of 1899-1910 Overprinted

This is called the "Carranza" or small monogram. Counterfeits abound.

On Issues of 1899-1903

482 A28 5c orange 20.00 20.00
483 A30 15c lav & claret 80.00 80.00

On Issue of 1910

484 A36 1c dl vio 70 70
485 A37 2c green 70 60
486 A38 3c org brn 75 75
487 A39 4c carmine 2.00 2.00
488 A40 5c orange 25 25
489 A41 10c bl & org 1.50 1.50
a. Double ovpt., one invtd. 25.00
490 A42 15c gray bl & cl 1.50 1.50
491 A43 20c red & blue 1.50 1.50
492 A44 50c red brn & blk 10.00 10.00
493 A45 1p bl & blk 15.00 15.00
494 A46 5p car & blk 150.00 150.00
Nos. 484-494 (11) 183.90 183.80

All values exist with inverted overprint; all but 5p with double overprint.

Overprinted On Postage Due Stamps of 1908

495 D1 1c blue 11.00 12.00
496 D1 2c blue 11.00 12.00
497 D1 4c blue 11.00 12.00
498 D1 5c blue 11.00 12.00
499 D1 10c blue 11.00 12.00
Nos. 495-499 (5) 55.00 60.00

Nos. 495-499 exist with inverted overprint.

It is stated that, in parts of Mexico occupied by the revolutionary forces, instructions were given to apply a distinguishing overprint to all stamps found in the post offices. This overprint was usually some arrangement or abbreviation of "Gobierno Constitucionalista". Such overprints as were specially authorized or were in general use in large sections of the country are listed. Numerous other handstamped overprints were used in one town or locality. They were essentially military faction control marks necessitated in most instances by the chaotic situation following the split between Villa and Carranza. The fact that some were often struck in a variety of colors and positions suggests the influence of philatelists.

Coat of Arms
A57

Statue of Cuauhtémoc
A58

Ignacio Zaragoza
A59

José María Morelos
A60

Francisco Madero
A61

Benito Juárez
A62

1915 Unwmk. Litho. *Rouletted 14*

500 A57 1c violet 15 15
501 A58 2c green 25 20
502 A59 3c brown 25 25
503 A60 4c carmine 30 25
504 A61 5c orange 30 25
505 A62 10c ultra 25 20
Nos. 500-505 (6) 1.50 1.30

Nos. 500-505 exists imperf.; some exist imperf. vertically or horizontally; some with rouletting and perforation combined. These probably were not regularly issued in these forms.

See Nos. 506-511. For overprints see Nos. O86-O97.

Map of Mexico — A63

Veracruz Lighthouse
A64

Post Office, Mexico, D.F. — A65

TEN CENTAVOS:
Type I- Size 19½x24mm. Crossed lines on coat.
Type II- Size 19x23½mm. Diagonal lines only on coat.

1915-16 *Perf. 12*

506 A57 1c violet 20 30
507 A58 2c green 20 30
508 A59 3c brown 30 30
509 A60 4c carmine 30 35
a. "CEATRO" 5.00 7.00
510 A61 5c orange 35 35
511 A62 10c ultra, type I 35 35
a. 10c ultra, II 20 25

Engr.

512 A63 40c slate 50 45
513 A64 1p brn & blk 70 1.00
a. Inverted center 200.00
514 A65 5p cl & ultra ('16) 8.00 9.00
a. Inverted center 400.00
Nos. 506-514 (9) 10.90 12.40

Nos. 507-508, 510-514, exist imperf; Nos. 513-514 imperf with inverted center. These varieties were not regularly issued.

See Nos. 626-628, 647. For overprints see Nos. O92-O100, O121-O123, O132-O133, O142-O144, O153-O154, O162-O164, O174, O188, O193, O207, O222.

Issues of 1899-1910 Overprinted in Blue, Red or Black

1916 Wmk. 155 *Perf. 14*

On Issues of 1899-1903

515 A28 5c org (Bl) 85.00
516 A30 15c lav & cl (Bl) 425.00 425.00

On Issue of 1910

517 A36 1c dl vio (R) 3.50 5.00
518 A37 2c grn (R) 50 35
519 A38 3c org brn (Bl) 55 35
a. Double overprint 500.00
520 A39 4c car (Bl) 6.00 8.00
521 A40 5c org (Bl) 25 25
a. Double overprint 75.00
522 A41 10c bl & org (R) 1.25 1.50
523 A42 15c gray bl & cl (Bk) 1.75 3.00
524 A43 20c red & bl (Bk) 1.75 3.00
525 A44 50c red brn & blk (R) 8.50 5.00
526 A45 1p bl & blk (R) 15.00 6.50
527 A46 5p car & blk (R) 150.00 125.00
Nos. 517-527 (11) 189.05 157.95

Nos. 519-524 exist with this overprint (called the "Corbata") reading downward and Nos. 525-527 with it inverted. Of these varieties only Nos. 519-521 were regularly issued.

On Nos. 423-430

528 A36 1c dl vio (R) 2.50 4.00
529 A37 2c grn (R) 75 60
530 A38 3c org brn (Bl) 60 60
531 A39 4c car (Bl) 60 60
532 A40 5c org (Bl) 1.00 30
533 A41 10c bl & org (R) 75 60
534 A42 15c gray bl & cl (Bk) 80 80
535 A43 20c red & bl (Bk) 80 80

On Nos. 431-433 in Red

536 A44 50c red brn & blk 7.50 6.00
537 A45 1p bl & blk 16.00 16.00
538 A46 5p car & blk 150.00 140.00
a. Tablet inverted 200.00
Nos. 528-538 (11) 181.30 170.30

Nos. 529 to 535 are known with the overprint reading downward and Nos. 536 to 538 with it inverted.

On No. 482

539 A28 5c org (Bl) 60.00 60.00

On Nos. 484-494

540 A36 1c dl vio (R) 2.50 3.50
541 A37 2c grn (R) 60 60
a. Monogram inverted 40.00
542 A38 3c org brn (Bl) 50 60
543 A39 4c car (Bl) 5.00 6.00
544 A40 5c org (Bl) 85 25
545 A41 10c bl & org (R) 1.50 2.00
546 A42 15c gray bl & cl (Bk) 1.25 60
a. Tablet double 500.00 500.00
b. Monogram double 500.00
547 A43 20c red & bl (Bk) 1.20 1.10
548 A44 50c red brn & blk (R) 7.50 9.00
a. Monogram inverted 65.00
b. Tablet inverted 75.00
549 A45 1p bl & blk (R) 11.00 12.00
a. Tablet double 175.00
b. Monogram inverted 60.00
Nos. 539-549 (11) 91.90 95.65

Nos. 541-547 exist with overprint reading downward. A few 5p were overprinted for the Post Office collection.

On No. 453

550 A28 5c org (Bl) 90.00 90.00

On Nos. 455-462

551 A36 1c dl vio (R) 11.00 15.00
552 A37 2c grn (R) 1.50 90
553 A38 3c org brn (Bl) 3.25 4.50
554 A39 4c car (Bl) 13.00 15.00
555 A40 5c org (Bl) 4.50 6.00
556 A41 10c bl & org (R) 12.00 14.00
a. Monogram inverted 125.00
557 A42 15c gray bl & cl (Bk) 12.00 14.00
a. Monogram inverted 90.00
558 A43 20c red & bl (Bk) 12.00 14.00
a. Monogram inverted 82.50
Nos. 550-558 (9) 159.25 173.40

Stamps of 50c, 1p and 5p were overprinted for the Post Office collection but were not regularly issued.

Issues of 1914 Overprinted

On "Transitorio" Issue

Rouletted 9½x14

Unwmk.

559 A50 1c dp bl (R) 24.00 24.00
560 A50 2c yel grn (R) 12.00 18.00
561 A50 4c bl vio (R) 250.00 200.00
562 A50 10c red (Bl) 2.00 6.00
a. Vertical overprint 125.00
563 A50 20c yel brn (Bl) 3.00 6.00
564 A50 50c claret (Bl) 15.00 20.00
565 A50 1p vio (Bl) 24.00 24.00
a. Horiz. pair, imperf. btwn.

Overprinted in Blue
On "Denver" Issue
Perf. 12

566 A52 1c pale bl 3.75
567 A52 2c lt grn 3.75
568 A52 3c orange 45
569 A52 5c dp rose 45
570 A52 10c rose 45
571 A52 15c rose lilac 45
572 A52 50c yellow 1.10
573 A52 1p violet 9.50
Nos. 566-573 (8) 19.90

Many of the foregoing stamps exist with the "G. P. DE M." overprint printed in other colors than those listed. These "trial color" stamps were not regularly on sale at post offices but were available for postage and used copies are known.

There appears to have been speculation in Nos. 516, 517, 520, 528, 539, 540, 543, 566, and 567. A small quantity of each of these stamps was sold at post offices but subsequently they could be obtained only from officials or their agents at advanced prices.

Venustiano Carranza
A66

Coat of Arms
A67

1916, June 1 Engr. *Perf. 12*

574 A66 10c blue 1.25 65
a. Imperf., pair 22.50
575 A66 10c lilac brown 12.00 13.00
a. Imperf., pair 45.00

Entry of Carranza into Mexico, D.F.

Stamps of type A66 with only horizontal lines in the background of the oval are essays.

1916

576 A67 1c lilac 20 20

Issue of 1910 Surcharged in Various Colors

This overprint is called the "Barril."

1916 Wmk. 155 *Perf. 14*

577 A36 5c on 1c dl vio (Br) 25 30
a. Vertical surcharge 1.25 1.25
b. Double surcharge 150.00
578 A36 10c on 1c dl vio (Bl) 35 40
a. Double surcharge 100.00
579 A40 20c on 5c org (Br) 20 30
a. Double surcharge 90.00
580 A40 25c on 5c org (G) 40 50
581 A37 60c on 2c grn (R) 17.00 20.00
Nos. 577-581 (5) 18.20 21.50

On Nos. 423-424, 427

582 A36 5c on 1c (Br) 25 35
a. Double tablet, one vertical 100.00
b. Inverted tablet 250.00 250.00
583 A36 10c on 1c (Bl) 90 90
584 A40 25c on 5c (G) 35 45
a. Inverted tablet 225.00 225.00
585 A37 60c on 2c (R) 200.00 275.00

No. 585 was not regularly issued.

The variety "GONSTITUCIONALISTA" is found on Nos. 582 to 585.

On No. 459

586 A40 25c on 5c org (G) 20 15

On Nos. 484-485, 488

587 A36 5c on 1c (Br) 15.00 20.00
a. Vertical tablet 100.00 125.00

588	A36	10c on 1c (Bl)	5.00	7.50
589	A40	25c on 5c (G)	1.00	1.50
a.		Inverted tablet	225.00	
590	A37	60c on 2c (R)	225.00	

No. 590 was not regularly issued.

Surcharged on "Denver" Issue of 1914

1916 **Unwmk.** ***Perf. 12***

591	A52	60c on 1c pale bl (Br)	3.00	6.00
592	A52	60c on 2c lt grn (Br)	3.00	6.00
a.		Inverted surcharge	500.00	

Postage Due Stamps Surcharged Like Nos. 577-581

1916 **Wmk. 155** ***Perf. 14***

593	D1	5c on 1c blue (Br)	2.50	
594	D1	10c on 2c blue (V)	2.50	
595	D1	20c on 4c blue (Br)	2.50	
596	D1	25c on 5c blue (G)	2.50	
597	D1	60c on 10c blue (R)	1.50	
598	D1	1p on 1c blue (C)	1.50	
599	D1	1p on 2c blue (C)	1.50	
600	D1	1p on 4c blue (C)	80	80
601	D1	1p on 5c blue (C)	2.50	
602	D1	1p on 10c blue (C)	2.50	
		Nos. 593-602 (10)	20.30	

There are numerous "trial colors" and "essays" of the overprints and surcharges on Nos. 577 to 602. They were available for postage though not regularly issued.

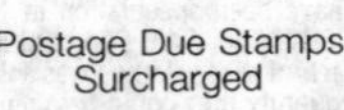
Postage Due Stamps Surcharged

1916

603	D1	2.50p on 1c blue	1.25	1.25
604	D1	2.50p on 2c blue	10.00	
605	D1	2.50p on 4c blue	10.00	
606	D1	2.50p on 5c blue	10.00	
607	D1	2.50p on 10c blue	10.00	
		Nos. 603-607 (5)	41.25	

Regular Issue

Ignacio Zaragoza A68

Ildefonso Vázquez A69

M. J. Pino Suárez A70

Jesús Carranza A71

Maclovio Herrera A72

F. I. Madero A73

Belisario Domínguez A74

Aquiles Serdán A75

Roulетted 14½

1917-20 **Engr.** **Unwmk.**

Thick Paper

608	A68	1c dl vio	40	20
609	A68	1c gray ('20)	2.00	1.50
a.		1c lilac gray ('20)	1.00	25
610	A69	2c gray grn	50	15
611	A70	3c bis brn	50	15
612	A71	4c carmine	1.00	40
613	A72	5c ultra	1.50	25
a.		Horiz. pair, imperf. btwn.	50.00	
b.		Imperf., pair		50.00
614	A73	10c blue	2.00	15
a.		Without imprint	3.00	25
615	A74	20c rose	22.50	60
a.		20c brown rose	25.00	60
616	A75	30c gray brn	60.00	1.00
617	A75	30c gray blk ('20)	70.00	1.00
		Nos. 608-617 (10)	160.40	5.40

Perf. 12

Thick or Medium Paper

618	A68	1c dl vio	20.00	20.00
619	A69	2c gray grn	5.00	5.00
620	A70	3c bis brn ('17)	100.00	100.00
621	A71	4c carmine	*300.00*	*300.00*
622	A72	5c ultra	2.00	20
623	A73	10c bl ('17)	4.50	20
a.		Without imprint ('17)	12.00	12.00
624	A74	20c rose ('20)	95.00	2.00
625	A75	30c gray blk ('20)	80.00	1.65

Thin or Medium Paper

626	A63	40c violet	40.00	50
627	A64	1p bl & blk	35.00	1.00
a.		With center of 5p	450.00	
b.		1p bl & dark blue (error)	500.00	20.00
c.		Vert. pair, imperf. btwn.		250.00
628	A65	5p grn & blk	1.00	1.00
a.		With violet or red control number		7.50
b.		With center of 1p	425.00	

The 1, 2, 3, 5 and 10c are known on thin paper perforated. It is stated they were printed for Postal Union and "specimen" purposes.

All values exist imperf; these are not known to have been regularly issued. Nos. 627a and 628b were not regularly issued.

All values except 3c have an imprint.

For overprints and surcharges see Nos. B1-B2, O113-O165.

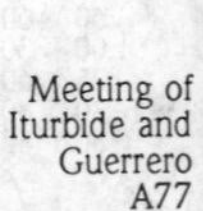
Meeting of Iturbide and Guerrero A77

Entering City of Mexico — A78

1921

632	A77	10c bl & brn	15.00	3.00
a.		Center inverted		*6,000.*
633	A78	10p blk brn & blk	15.00	35.00

Commemorating the meeting of Augustin de Iturbide and Vincente Guerrero and the entry into City of Mexico in 1821.

For overprint see No. O194.

"El Salto de Agua," Public Fountain A79

Pyramid of the Sun at Teotihuacán A80

Chapultepec Castle A81

Columbus Monument A82

Juárez Colonnade, Mexico, D. F. — A83

Monument to Josefa Ortiz de Dominguez A84

Cuauhtémoc Monument A85

1923 **Unwmk.** ***Rouletted 14½***

634	A79	2c scarlet	1.75	20
635	A80	3c bis brn	1.75	25
636	A81	4c green	2.50	75
637	A82	5c orange	4.25	20
638	A83	10c brown	3.75	15
639	A85	10c claret	3.00	15
640	A84	20c dk bl	40.00	1.75
641	A85	30c dk grn	27.50	2.00
		Nos. 634-641 (8)	84.50	5.45

See Nos. 642-646, 650-657, 688-692, 727A, 735A-736. For overprints see Nos. O166-O173, O178-O181, O183-O187, O196-O197, O199-O206, O210, O212-O214, O217-O222.

Communications Building — A87

Palace of Fine Arts (National Theater) — A88

Two types of 1p:
I- Eagle on palace dome.
II- Without eagle.

1923 **Wmk. 156** ***Perf. 12***

642	A79	2c scarlet	9.00	9.00
643	A81	4c green	1.40	35
644	A82	5c orange	8.00	7.00
645	A85	10c brn lake	11.00	6.00
646	A83	30c dk grn	95	20
647	A63	40c violet	1.00	25
648	A87	50c ol brn	60	25
649	A88	1p red brn & bl (I)	1.00	55
a.		Type II	3.00	*10.00*
		Nos. 642-649 (8)	32.95	23.60

Most of Nos. 642-649 are known imperforate or part perforate but probably were not regularly issued.

For overprints see Nos. O175-O176, O189-O190, O208-O209, O223.

1923-34 ***Rouletted 14½***

650	A79	2c scarlet	25	15
651	A80	3c bis brn ('27)	25	15
652	A81	4c green	20.00	8.00
653	A82	4c grn ('27)	25	15
654	A82	5c orange	25	15
655	A85	10c lake	25	15
656	A84	20c dp bl	75	30
657	A83	30c dk grn ('34)	75	30
		Nos. 650-657 (8)	22.75	9.35

Nos. 650 to 657 inclusive exist imperforate.

Medallion A90

Map of Americas A91

Francisco García y Santos — A92

Post Office, Mexico, D. F. — A93

1926 ***Perf. 12***

658	A90	2c red	2.00	75
659	A91	4c green	2.00	85
660	A90	5c orange	2.00	60
661	A91	10c brn red	3.00	60
662	A92	20c dk bl	3.00	1.00
663	A92	30c dk grn	5.00	3.00
664	A92	40c violet	10.00	2.50
665	A93	1p brn & blue	20.00	6.00
a.		1p red & blue	30.00	12.00
		Nos. 658-665 (8)	47.00	15.30

Pan-American Postal Congress.

Nos. 658-665 were also printed in black, on unwatermarked paper, for presentation to delegates to the Universal Postal Congress at London in 1929. Remainders were overprinted in 1929 for use as airmail official stamps, and are listed as Nos. CO3-CO10.

For overprints see Nos. 667-674, 675A-682, CO3-CO10.

Benito Juárez — A94

1926 ***Rouletted 14½***

666	A94	8c orange	30	15

For overprint see No. O182.

Nos. 658-665 Overprinted

HABILITADO 1930

1930 ***Perf. 12***

667	A90	2c red	3.50	2.25
a.		Reading down	12.50	14.00
668	A91	4c green	3.50	2.00
a.		Reading down	12.50	14.00
669	A90	5c orange	3.50	1.75
a.		Reading down	12.50	
b.		Double overprint	60.00	*60.00*
670	A91	10c brn red	6.00	2.00
671	A92	20c dk bl	8.00	3.00
672	A92	30c dk grn	7.00	3.50
a.		Reading down	8.50	12.00
673	A92	40c violet	10.00	7.00
a.		Reading down	40.00	
674	A93	1p red brn & bl	9.00	6.00
a.		Double overprint	125.00	
b.		Triple overprint	175.00	
		Nos. 667-674 (8)	50.50	27.50

Overprint horizontal on 1p.

Arms of Puebla — A95

1931, May 1 **Engr.**

675	A95	10c dk bl & dk brn	2.50	50

400th anniversary of Puebla.

Nos. 658-665a Overprinted HABILITADO 1931

1931

675A	A90	2c red	750.00	
676	A91	4c green	55.00	60.00
677	A90	5c orange	10.00	14.00
678	A91	10c brn red	10.00	12.00
679	A92	20c dk bl	10.00	15.00
680	A92	30c dk grn	17.50	20.50
681	A92	40c violet	25.00	30.00
682	A93	1p brn & bl	22.50	30.00
a.		1p red & blue	35.00	40.00
		Nos. 676-682 (7)	150.00	181.50

Overprint horizontal on 1p.

Nos. 676 and 682 are not known to have been sold to the public through post offices.

Forgeries of overprint exist.

Bartolomé de las Casas — A96

Emblem of Mexican Society of Geography and Statistics — A97

1933, Mar. 3 Engr. *Rouletted 14½*

683	A96	15c dark blue	20	15

For overprint see No. O215.

1933, Oct. *Rouletted 14½*

684	A97	2c dp grn	1.50	60
685	A97	5c dk brn	1.75	50
686	A97	10c dk bl	75	15
687	A97	1p dk vio	50.00	60.00

XXI International Congress of Statistics and the first centenary of the Mexican Society of Geography and Statistics.

Types of 1923 and PT1

1934 *Perf. 10½, 11 (4c)*

687A	PT1	1c brown	1.00	30
688	A79	2c scarlet	35	15
689	A82	4c green	35	15
690	A85	10c brn lake	35	15
691	A84	20c dk bl	75	75
692	A83	30c dk bl grn	1.00	1.25
		Nos. 687A-692 (6)	3.80	2.75

See 2nd note after Postal Tax stamp No. RA3.

Indian Archer A99

Indian A100

Woman Decorating Pottery A101

Peon A102

Potter A103

Sculptor A104

Craftsman A105

Offering to the Gods A106

Worshiper — A107

1934, Sept. 1 Wmk. 156 *Perf. 10½*

698	A99	5c dk grn	1.65	35
699	A100	10c brn lake	2.00	60
700	A101	20c ultra	8.00	5.00
701	A102	30c black	14.00	12.00
702	A103	40c blk brn	24.00	16.00
703	A104	50c dl bl	45.00	50.00
704	A105	1p brn lake & blk	50.00	47.50
705	A106	5p brn blk & red brn	190.00	250.00
706	A107	10p brn & vio	800.00	1,050.
a.		Unwatermarked	*3,250.*	
		Nos. 698-706 (9)	1,134.	1,431.

National University.

The design of the 1p is wider than the rest of the set. Values are for copies with perfs just touching the design.

See Nos. C54-C61, RA13B.

Yalalteca Indian — A108

Tehuana Indian — A109

Arch of the Revolution — A110

Tower of Los Remedios — A111

Cross of Palenque — A112

Independence Monument — A113

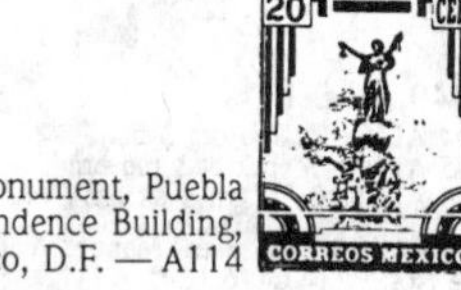
Monument, Puebla Independence Building, Mexico, D.F. — A114

Monument to the Heroic Cadets — A115

Stone of Tizoc — A116

Ruins of Mitla — A117

Coat of Arms — A118

Cowboy — A119

Imprint: "Oficina Impresora de Hacienda-Mexico"

1934-40 Wmk. 156 *Perf. 10½*

Size: 20x26mm

707	A108	1c orange	65	15
a.		Unwmkd.		350.00
708	A109	2c green	65	15
a.		Unwmkd.	3.75	3.75
709	A110	4c carmine	90	20
710	A111	5c ol brn	65	15
a.		Unwmkd.	400.00	350.00
711	A112	10c dk bl	80	15
712	A112	10c vio ('35)	1.25	15
a.		Unwmkd.	200.00	40.00
713	A113	15c lt bl	4.00	30
714	A114	20c gray grn	1.90	20
a.		20c olive green	2.00	20
715	A114	20c ultra ('35)	1.40	15
a.		Unwmkd.		150.00
716	A115	30c lake	90	15
a.		Unwmkd.	350.00	
716B	A115	30c lt ultra ('40)	1.00	15
717	A116	40c red brn	1.00	15
718	A117	50c grnsh blk	90	15
a.		Imperf., pair	110.00	
b.		Unwmkd.		375.00
719	A118	1p dk brn & org	2.50	15
a.		Imperf., pair	350.00	
720	A119	5p org & vio	7.75	75
		Nos. 707-720 (15)	26.25	
		Set value		2.60

No. 718a was not regularly issued.

See Nos. 729-733, 733B, 735, 784-788, 795A-800A, 837-838, 840-841, 844, 846-851. For overprints see Nos. 728, O224-O232.

Tractor — A120

1935, Apr. 1 Wmk. 156 *Perf. 10½*

721	A120	10c violet	4.00	50

Industrial census of Apr. 10, 1935.

Arms of Chiapas A121

Emiliano Zapata A122

1935, Sept. 14

722	A121	10c dark blue	50	20
a.		Unwmkd.	125.00	100.00

The 111th anniversary of the joining of the state of Chiapas with the federal republic of Mexico. See No. 734.

1935, Nov. 20 Wmk. 156

723	A122	10c violet	75	20

25th anniversary of the Plan of Ayala.

US and Mexico Joined by Highways A123

Matalote Bridge A124

View of Nuevo Laredo Highway — A125

1936 Wmk. 248 *Perf. 14*

725	A123	5c bl grn & rose	30	15
726	A124	10c sl bl & blk	50	15
727	A125	20c brn & dk grn	1.50	1.00

Issued to commemorate the opening of the Nuevo Laredo Highway. See Nos. C77-C79.

Monument Type of 1923

1936 Wmk. 248 Engr. *Perf. 10½*

727A	A85	10c brn lake	*1,150.*	650.00

No. 712 Overprinted in Green PRIMER CONGRESO NAL. DE HIGIENE Y MED. DEL TRABAJO

1936, Dec. 15 Wmk. 156

728	A112	10c violet	60	50

1st National Congress of Industrial Hygiene and Medicine.

Type of 1934

Redrawn size: 17½x21mm

Imprint: "Talleres de Imp. de Est. y Valores-Mexico"

1937 Photo. Wmk. 156 *Perf. 14*

729	A108	1c orange	60	15
a.		Imperf., pair	12.50	
730	A109	2c dl grn	60	15
a.		Imperf., pair	12.50	
731	A110	4c carmine	90	15
a.		Imperf., pair	12.50	
732	A111	5c ol brn	80	15
a.		Unwmkd.		*150.00*
733	A112	10c violet	70	15
a.		Imperf., pair	10.00	
		Nos. 729-733 (5)	3.60	75

The imperfs were not regularly issued.

Types of 1934-35

1937 Wmk. 260

Size: 17½x21mm

733B	A111	5c ol brn	650.00	185.00

1937 Engr. *Perf. 10½*

734	A121	10c dark blue	15.00	12.00

1937

Size: 20x26mm

735	A112	10c violet	275.00	35.00

Types of 1923

1934-37 Wmk. 260 *Perf. 10½*

735A	A79	2c scarlet		*4,000.*
735B	A85	10c brn lake		

Forged perforations exist.

Rouletted 14½

736	A85	10c claret	*1,800.*	*125.00*

Blacksmith A126

Revolutionary Soldier A127

Revolutionary Envoy — A128

Wmk. 156

1938, Mar. 26 Photo. *Perf. 14*

737 A126	5c blk & brn	80	20
738 A127	10c red brn	35	15
739 A128	20c maroon & org	5.00	1.00

25th anniv. of the Plan of Guadalupe. See Nos. C82-C84.

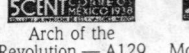

Arch of the Revolution — A129

Liberty Monument — A131

Design: 10c, National Theater.

1938, July 1

740 A129 5c bis brn	1.25	60
741 A129 5c red brn	2.50	2.25
742 A130 10c orange	14.00	11.00
743 A130 10c chocolate	60	18
744 A131 20c brn lake	3.50	4.00
745 A131 20c black	18.00	15.00
Nos. 740-745 (6)	39.85	33.03

16th International Congress of Planning and Housing. See Nos. C85-C90.

Arch of the Revolution A132

1939, May 1

746 A132 10c Prus blue 65 20

New York World's Fair. See Nos. C91-C93.

Indian — A133

1939, May 17

747 A133 10c red orange 45 15

Tulsa World Philatelic Convention. See Nos. C94-C96.

> ***15-Cent Minimum Value***
> *The minimum value for a single stamp is 15 cents. This value reflects the costs of the handling of inexpensive stamps.*

Juan Zumárraga A134

First Printing Shop in Mexico, 1539 A135

Design: 10c, Antonio de Mendoza.

1939, Sept. 1 Engr. *Perf. 10½*

748 A134 2c brn blk	75	25
749 A135 5c green	75	20
750 A134 10c red brn	25	15

400th anniversary of printing in Mexico. See Nos. C97-C99.

View of Taxco A137

Allegory of Agriculture A138

Design: 10c, Two hands holding symbols of commerce.

1939, Oct. 1 Photo. *Perf. 12x13*

751 A137 2c dk car	1.25	20
752 A138 5c sl grn & gray grn	15	15
753 A138 10c org brn & buff	15	15
Set value		40

Census Taking. See Nos. C100-C102.

"Penny Black" of 1840 A140

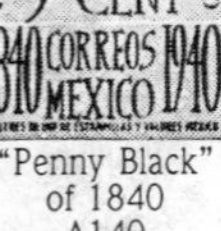

Roadside Monument A141

1940, May *Perf. 14*

754 A140 5c blk & lem	90	50
755 A140 10c dk vio	25	15
756 A140 20c lt bl & car	32	15
757 A140 1p gray & red org	7.00	4.00
758 A140 5p blk & Prus bl	37.50	30.00
Nos. 754-758 (5)	45.97	34.80

Issued to commemorate the centenary of the postage stamp. See Nos. C103-C107.

1940 Wmk. 156

759 A141 6c dp grn 50 15

Opening of the highway between Mexico, D. F., and Guadalajara. See Nos. 789, 842.

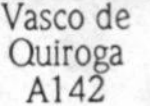
Vasco de Quiroga A142

Melchor Ocampo A143

College Seal — A144

1940, July 15 Engr. *Perf. 10½*

760 A142 2c violet	1.30	50
761 A143 5c copper red	80	20
762 A144 10c olive bister	80	30
a. Imperf., pair	150.00	

400th anniv. of the founding of the National College of San Nicolas de Hidalgo. See Nos. C108-C110.

Coat of Arms of Campeche A145

1940, Aug. 7 Photo. *Perf. 12x13*

763 A145 10c bis brn & dk car 3.00 1.25

400th anniversary of the founding of Campeche. See Nos. C111-C113.

Man at Helm A146

1940, Dec. 1

764 A146 2c red org & blk	1.65	60
765 A146 5c pck bl & red brn	6.25	3.50
766 A146 10c sl grn & dk brn	2.25	85

Inauguration of Pres. Manuel Avila Camacho. See Nos. C114-C116.

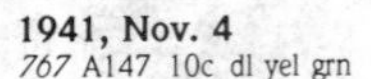

Javelin Thrower — A147

1941, Nov. 4 *Perf. 14*

767 A147 10c dl yel grn 3.50 50

National Athletic Games of the Revolution, Nov. 4-20, 1941.

Serpent Columns, Chichén Itzá A148

Mayan Sculpture A149

Coat of Arms of Merída — A150

1942, June 30

768 A148 2c dk ol bis	1.40	75
769 A149 5c dp org	2.25	60
770 A150 10c dk vio	1.65	25

400th anniversary of the founding of Merida. See Nos. C117-C119.

Independence Monument to Hidalgo — A151

Government Palace — A152

View of Guadalajara — A153

1942, Feb. 11 Engr. *Perf. 10x10½*

771 A151 2c bl vio & vio brn	35	30
772 A152 5c blk & cop red	1.25	50
773 A153 10c red org & ultra	1.25	40

Founding of Guadalajara, 400th anniv. See Nos. C120-C122.

No. 773 exists imperf. on unwatermarked paper.

Black Cloud in Orion A154

Designs: 5c, Total solar eclipse. 10c, Spiral galaxy in the "Hunting Dogs."

1942, Feb. 17 Photo. *Perf. 12x13*

774 A154 2c lt vio & ind	1.65	1.00
775 A154 5c bl & ind	8.75	2.00
776 A154 10c red org & ind	8.75	75

Astrophysics Congress and the inauguration of an observatory at Tonanzintla, Feb. 17, 1942. See Nos. C123-C125.

"Mother Earth" A157

Sowing Wheat A158

Western Hemisphere Carrying Torch A159

1942, July 1

777 A157	2c	chestnut	85	40
778 A158	5c	turq bl	3.00	1.10
779 A159	10c	red org	1.25	55

2nd Inter-American Agricultural Conference. See Nos. C126-C128.

Fuente Academy A160

1942, Nov. 16 *Perf. 14*

780 A160 10c grnsh blk 1.75 75

75th anniversary of Fuente Academy.

Las Monjas Church A161

Generalissimo Ignacio José de Allende A163

Design: 5c, San Miguel Church.

1943, May 11

781 A161	2c	intense blue	1.00	35
782 A161	5c	deep brown	1.10	30
783 A163	10c	dull black	3.50	1.00

400th anniv. of the founding of San Miguel de Allende. See Nos. C129-C131.

Types of 1937

1944 Photo. Wmk. 272

784 A108	1c	orange	1.10	15
785 A109	2c	dl grn	1.10	15
786 A110	4c	carmine	2.00	20
787 A111	5c	ol brn	1.75	15
788 A112	10c	violet	90	15

Type of 1940

789 A141	6c	green	90	15
		Nos. 784-789 (6)	7.75	95

"Liberty" — A164

Juan M. de Castorena — A165

1944 Photo.

790 A164 12c vio brn 35 15

See No. 845.

1945, Oct. 12 Engr. *Perf. 10*

791 A165 12c dk brn 60 15

Third Book Fair. See No. C142.

Hands Holding Globe Showing Western Hemisphere A166

1945, Feb. 27 Photo. *Perf. 12x13*

792 A166	12c	dk car	60	15
793 A166	1p	slate grn	1.00	25
794 A166	5p	olive brn	5.75	4.50
795 A166	10p	black	10.00	8.00

Inter-American Conf. held at Chapultepec, Feb. 1945. See Nos. C143-C147.

Types of 1934-40

Perf. 10½

1945-46 Wmk. 272 Engr.

795A A113	15c	lt grnsh bl ('46)	190.00	40.00
796 A114	20c	gray grn	2.50	15
797 A115	30c	lt ultra	3.25	15
798 A116	40c	brown	2.50	20
799 A117	50c	grnsh blk	1.65	20
800 A118	1p	dk brn & org	2.50	20
b.		Imperf., pair		
800A A119	5p	org & vio ('46)	9.00	6.00
		Nos. 795A-800A (7)	211.40	46.90

Theater of Peace, San Luis Potosi A167

Fountain of Diana, the Huntress A168

1945, July 27 Photo. *Perf. 12x13*

801 A167	12c	blk & vio brn	45	15
802 A167	1p	blk & bl gray	60	40
803 A167	5p	blk & brn lake	5.50	5.00
804 A167	10p	blk & grnsh bl	12.50	12.00

Reconstruction of the Peace Theater (Teatro de la Paz), San Luis Potosi. See Nos. C148-C152.

1945 *Perf. 14*

805 A168 3c vio blue 55 15

See No. 839.

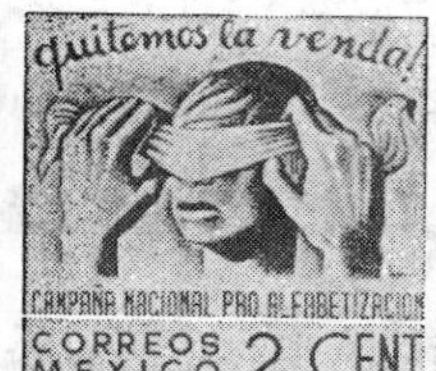

Removing Blindfold A169

1945, Nov. 2 *Perf. 12x13*

806 A169	2c	bluish grn	40	20
807 A169	6c	orange	40	20
808 A169	12c	ultra	40	20
809 A169	1p	olive	60	25
810 A169	5p	gray & pale rose	3.50	3.00
811 A169	10p	bl & yel grn	20.00	20.00
		Nos. 806-811 (6)	25.30	23.85

Issued to publicize the national literacy campaign. See Nos. C153-C157.

M. E. de Almanza — A170

1946 *Perf. 14*

812 A170 8c black 1.25 25

Martines Enriquez de Almanza, founder of the Mexican posts. See No. 843.

Allegory of World Peace — A171

1946, Apr. 10 *Perf. 12x13*

813 A171	2c	dk ol bis	35	20
814 A171	6c	red brn	30	20
815 A171	12c	Prus grn	25	15
816 A171	1p	lt grn	60	40
817 A171	5p	dl red vio	5.00	5.00
818 A171	10p	lt ultra	22.50	20.00
		Nos. 813-818 (6)	29.00	25.95

United Nations. See Nos. C158-C162.

Arms of Zacatecas A173

Monument to Gen. Gonzalez Ortega A174

Ramón Lopez Velarde A175

Francisco Garcia Salinas A176

Wmk. 279

1946, Sept. 1 Photo. *Perf. 14*

820 A173	2c	org brn	55	15
821 A173	12c	Prus blue	25	15

Engr.

Perf. 10x10½

822 A174	1p	lilac rose	70	20
823 A175	5p	red	5.50	3.00
824 A176	10p	dk bl & blk	30.00	10.00
		Nos. 820-824 (5)	37.00	13.50

400th anniversary of the founding of the city of Zacatecas. See Nos. C163-C166.

A177

A178

1947 Photo. *Perf. 14*

825 A177 15c Postman 25 15
a. Imperf., pair 110.00

1947, May 16

Design: 10c, Franklin D. Roosevelt and Stamp of 1st Mexican Issue. 15c, Arms of Mexico and Stamp of 1st US Issue.

826 A178	10c	yel brn	1.65	1.00
827 A178	15c	green	25	15

Cent. Intl. Phil. Exhib., NYC, May 17-25, 1947. See Nos. C167-C169.

Justo Sierra — A180

Communications Building — A181

Perf. 10x10½, 10½x10

1947, Engr. Wmk. 279

828 A180	10p	brn & dl grn	85.00	15.00
829 A181	20p	dk grn & lil	1.65	2.00

Cadet Francisco Márquez A182

Gen. Manuel Rincón A186

Flag of San Blas Battalion — A188

Designs: 5c, Cadet Fernando Montes de Oca. 10c, Cadet Juan Escutia. 15c, Cadet Agustin Melgar. 1p, Gen. Lucas Balderas.

1947, Sept. 8 Photo. *Perf. 14*

830	A182	2c brn blk	42	15
831	A182	5c red org	30	15
832	A182	10c dk brn	25	15
833	A182	15c dk Prus grn	25	15
834	A182	30c dl ol grn	35	15

Engr.

Perf. 10x10½

835	A186	1p aqua	45	45
836	A188	5p dk bl & claret	1.90	1.90
		Nos. 830-836 (7)	3.92	3.10

Centenary of the battles of Chapultepec, Churubusco and Molino del Rey. See Nos. C180-C184.

Types of 1934-46

1947-50 Wmk. 279 Photo. *Perf. 14*

837	A108	1c orange	1.00	30
a.		Imperf., pair	90.00	
838	A109	2c dk grn	60	15
839	A168	3c vio bl	60	15
840	A110	4c dl red	1.90	15
841	A111	5c ol brn	2.50	15
842	A141	6c dp grn	45	15
a.		Imperf., pair	90.00	
843	A170	8c black	35	15
844	A112	10c violet	1.90	25
845	A164	12c vio brn	9.00	75

Types A108 to A112 are in the redrawn size of 1937.

Size: 19x25mm

Engr. *Perf. 10½*

846	A114	20c ol grn	1.25	20
a.		20c green	3.00	30
847	A115	30c lt ultra	8.75	40
848	A116	40c red brn	1.40	25
849	A117	50c green	1.90	20
a.		Imperf., pair	110.00	
850	A118	1p dk brn & org	25.00	9.00
851	A119	5p org & vio ('50)	16.00	11.00
		Nos. 837-851 (15)	72.60	23.25

Puebla Cathedral — A189

Designs: 3c, Modernistic church, Nuevo Leon. 5c, Modern building, Mexico City. 10c, Convent, Morelos. 15c, Benito Juarez. 30c, Indian dancer, Michoacan. 40c, Stone head, Tabasco. 50c, Carved head, Veracruz. 1p, Convent and carved head, Hidalgo. 5p, Galleon, arms of Campeche. 10p, Francisco I. Madero. 20p, Modern building, Mexico City.

1950-52 Wmk. 279 Photo. *Perf. 14*

856	A189	3c bl vio ('51)	50	15
857	A189	5c dk red brn	75	15
858	A189	10c dk grn	3.50	15
859	A189	15c dk grn ('51)	1.75	15
860	A189	20c bl vio	14.00	15
861	A189	30c red	50	15
862	A189	40c red org ('51)	1.00	15
863	A189	50c blue	1.25	15

Engr.

864	A189	1p dl brn	4.50	15
865	A189	5p ultra & bl grn	7.00	4.00
866	A189	10p blk & dp ultra ('52)	7.00	7.00
867	A189	20p pur & grn ('52)	10.00	10.00
		Nos. 856-867 (12)	51.75	22.35

See Nos. 875-885, 909, 928-931, 943-952, 1003-1004, 1054-1055, 1072, 1076, 1081, 1090-1091, 1094-1102.

Highway Bridge A190

Symbolical of Construction in 1950 A191

Railroad Laborer A192

Perf. 10½x10, 10x10½

1950, May 5 Photo.

868	A190	15c purple	60	15
869	A191	20c deep blue	40	20

Completion of the International Highway between Ciudad Juarez and the Guatemala border. See Nos. C199-C200.

Inscribed: "Ferrocarril del Sureste 1950"

Design: 20c, Map and locomotive.

1950, May 24 *Perf. 10x10½*

870	A192	15c chocolate	1.25	15
871	A192	20c dp car	45	15
		Set value		20

Opening of the Southeastern Railroad between Veracruz, Coatzocoalcos and Yucatan, 1950. See Nos. C201-C202.

Postal Service — A193

Miguel Hidalgo y Costilla — A194

1950, June 25 *Perf. 10x10½*

872	A193	50c purple	40	15

75th anniv. (in 1949) of the UPU. See Nos. C203-C204.

1953, May 8 Wmk. 300 *Perf. 14*

873	A194	20c grnsh bl & dk brn	1.75	25

Bicentenary of birth of Miguel Hidalgo y Costilla. See Nos. C206-C207.

Type of 1950-52
Designs as before.

Two types of 5p:
I- Imprint ½mm high and blurred.
II- Imprint ¾mm high and clear.

1954-67 Photo. *Perf. 14*

875	A189	5c red brn	50	15
876	A189	10c dk grn	2.50	15
a.		10c green, redrawn	65	15
877	A189	15c dk grn	40	15
878	A189	20c dk bl	3.50	15
a.		20c bluish blk, white paper, colorless gum ('67)	60	15
879	A189	30c brn red	75	15
a.		30c redsh brn	75	15
880	A189	40c red org	1.50	15
881	A189	50c lt bl	1.00	15

Engr.

882	A189	1p ol brn	12.00	20
a.		1p olive green	7.00	20
b.		As "a.", perf. 11, vert. wmk. ('58)	4.00	25
883	A189	5p ultra & bl grn, I	7.00	1.00
a.		Type II	500.00	8.00
884	A189	10p sl & dp ultra ('56)	9.00	5.00
a.		10p slate green & ultra	35.00	5.00
885	A189	20p pur & grn	11.00	9.00
a.		20p brn vio & yel grn	75.00	20.00
		Nos. 875-885 (11)	49.15	16.25

Nos. 875-881 comes only with watermark vertical, and in various shades. Watermark inverted on Nos. 884, 885.

On No. 876a, imprint extends full width of stamp.

Vert. pairs, imperf. horiz. of Nos. 878, 880 are noted after No. 1004.

Aztec Messenger of the Sun A195

Symbolizing Adoption of National Anthem A196

1954, Mar. 6

886	A195	20c rose & bl gray	1.10	15

7th Central American and Caribbean Games. See Nos. C222-C223.

1954, Sept. 16 Photo.

887	A196	5c rose lil & dk bl	75	20
888	A196	20c yel brn & brn vio	90	20
889	A196	1p gray grn & cer	65	40

Centenary of the adoption of Mexico's National Anthem. See Nos. C224-C226.

Torch-Bearer and Stadium A197

Aztec Designs A198

1955, Mar. 12 Wmk. 300 *Perf. 14*

890	A197	20c dk grn & red brn	85	20

Issued to publicize the second Pan American Games, 1955. See Nos. C227-C228.

1956, Aug. 1

891	A198	5c "Motion"	50	15
892	A198	10c Bird	50	15
893	A198	30c Flowers	40	15
894	A198	50c Corn	50	15
895	A198	1p Deer	60	20
896	A198	5p Man	2.25	2.25
a.		Souv. sheet, #891-896, imperf.	30.00	30.00
		Nos. 891-896 (6)	4.75	3.05

Centenary of Mexico's 1st postage stamps. No. 896a sold for 15p. See Nos. C229-C234.

Stamp of 1856 A199

Francisco Zarco A200

1956, Aug. 1

897	A199	30c brn & intense bl	75	25

Centenary International Philatelic Exhibition, Mexico City, Aug. 16, 1956.

1956-63

Portraits: 25c, 45c, Guillermo Prieto. 60c, Ponciano Arriaga.

897A	A200	25c dk brn ('63)	75	50
898	A200	45c dk bl grn	35	25
899	A200	60c red lil	35	35
900	A200	70c vio bl	40	20

Centenary of the constitution (in 1957). See Nos. C236-C237A, C289, 1075, 1092-1093.

"Mexico" A201

Mexican Eagle and Oil Derrick A202

Design: 1p, National Assembly.

1957, Aug. 31 Photo. *Perf. 14*

901	A201	30c mar & gold	50	15
902	A201	1p pale brn & metallic grn	35	25

Centenary of the constitution. See Nos. C239-C240.

1958, Aug. 30 Wmk. 300 *Perf. 14*

Design: 5p, Map of Mexico and refinery.

903	A202	30c lt bl & blk	50	15
904	A202	5p hn brn & Prus grn	4.00	4.00

20th anniv. of the nationalization of Mexico's oil industry. See Nos. C243-C244.

UNESCO Building and Eiffel Tower — A203

UN Headquarters, New York — A204

1959, Jan. 20

905	A203	30c dl lil & blk	50	15

Opening of UNESCO Headquarters in Paris, Nov. 9.

1959, Sept. 7 Litho. *Perf. 14*

906	A204	30c org yel & bl	50	15

Meeting of UNESCO.

Carranza A205

Humboldt Statue A206

1960, Jan. 15 Photo. Wmk. 300

907	A205	30c pale grn & plum	35	15

Birth centenary of Pres. Venustiano Carranza. See No. C246.

1960, Mar. 16 Wmk. 300 *Perf. 14*

908	A206	40c bis brn & grn	35	15

Cent. of the death (in 1859) of Alexander von Humboldt, German naturalist and geographer.

Type of 1950-52 Inscribed: "HOMENAJE AL COLECCIONISTA DEL TIMBRE DE MEXICO-JUNIO 1960"

1960, June 8 Engr. Wmk. 300

909	A189	10p lil, brn & grn	35.00	42.50

25th anniversary visit of the Elmhurst (Ill.) Philatelic Society of Mexico Specialists to Mexico. See No. C249.

Independence Bell & Monument
A207 A208

Designs: 5p, Bell of Dolores and Miguel Hidalgo.

Wmk. 300

1960, Sept. 15 Photo. *Perf. 14*

910	A207	30c grn & rose red	1.00	15
911	A208	1p dl grn & dk brn	50	20
912	A208	5p mar & dk bl	5.00	5.00

150th anniv. of Mexican independence. See US No. 1157, Mexico Nos. C250-C252.

Agricultural Reform A209

Symbols of Health Education — A210

Designs: 20c, Sailor and Soldier, 1960, and Fighter of 1910. 30c, Electrification. 1p, Political development (schools). 5p, Currency stability (Bank and money).

1960-61 Photo. *Perf. 14*

913 A209 10c sl grn, blk & red org 75 20
914 A210 15c grn & org brn 2.75 50
915 A210 20c brt bl & lt brn ('61) 1.00 15
916 A210 30c vio brn & sep 40 15
917 A210 1p redsh brn & sl 50 15
918 A210 5p mar & gray 3.50 3.50
Nos. 913-918 (6) 8.90 4.65

50th anniversary (in 1960) of the Mexican Revolution. See Nos. C253-C256.

Tunnel A211

Microscope, Mosquito and Globe A212

1961, Dec. Wmk. 300 *Perf. 14*

919 A211 40c blk & brt grn 40 15

Opening of the railroad from Chihuahua to the Pacific Ocean. See Nos. C258-C259.

1962, Apr. 6

920 A212 40c dl bl & maroon 40 15

WHO drive to eradicate malaria.

President Joao Goulart of Brazil — A213

Mexican Indian at Marker for Battle of Puebla — A214

Wmk. 300

1962, Apr. 11 Photo. *Perf. 14*

921 A213 40c brn olive 1.00 25

Issued to commemorate the visit of Joao Goulart, president of Brazil, to Mexico.

1962, May 5

922 A214 40c sepiaz & dk grn 35 15

Centenary of the Battle of May 5 at Puebla and the defeat of French forces by Gen. Ignacio Zaragoza. See No. C260.

Draftsman and Surveyor A215

Plumbline A216

1962, June 11

923 A215 40c sl grn & dk bl 90 20

25th anniversary of the National Polytechnic Institute. See No. C261.

1962, June 21

924 A216 20c dp bl & blk 1.40 20

Issued to publicize the importance of mental health.

"Space Needle" and Gear Wheels A217

Globe A218

1962, July 6

925 A217 40c dk grn & gray 35 15

"Century 21" International Exposition, Seattle, Wash., Apr. 21-Oct. 12.

1962, Oct. 1 *Perf. 14*

926 A218 40c gray & brn 35 15

1962 meeting of the Inter-American Economic and Social Council. See No. C263.

Pres. Alessandri of Chile A219

Pres. Betancourt of Venezuela A220

1962, Dec. 20 Wmk. 300 *Perf. 14*

927 A219 20c olive black 75 20

Visit of President Jorge Alessandri Rodriguez of Chile to Mexico, Dec. 17-20.

Type of 1950-52

Designs as before.

Wmk. 300, Vertical

1962-74 Photo. *Perf. 14*

928 A189 1p ol gray ('67) 1.25 15
a. 1p green 4.00 20
929 A189 5p dl bl & dk grn 3.50 75
a. 5p bluish gray & dark green, white paper ('67) 3.50 50
930 A189 10p gray & bl ('63) 8.50 5.00
a. 10p green & deep blue ('74) 7.50 5.50
931 A189 20p lil & blk ('63) 9.00 7.50
a. Redrawn, white paper 10.00 10.00

No. 928 is on thick, luminescent paper. No. 929 is 20½mm high; No. 929a, 20¾mm. Nos. 931a and 1102 (unwmkd.) have more shading in sky and spots on first floor windows.

1963, Feb. 28 Wmk. 300

932 A220 20c slate 70 20

Visit of President Romulo Betancourt of Venezuela to Mexico.

Congress Emblem A221

Wheat Emblem A222

1963, Apr. 22 Wmk. 300 *Perf. 14*

933 A221 49c fawn & blk 60 20

19th International Chamber of Commerce Congress. See No. C271.

1963, June 17 Wmk. 300 *Perf. 14*

934 A222 40c crim & dk bl 60 20

FAO "Freedom from Hunger" campaign.

Mercado Mountains and Arms of Durango A223

Belisario Dominguez A224

1963, July 13 Photo.

935 A223 20c dk bl & choc 60 20

400th anniv. of the founding of Durango.

1963, July 13 Photo.

936 A224 20c dk grn & ol gray 60 20

Centenary of the birth of Belisario Dominguez, revolutionary leader.

Stamp of 1956 — A225

1963, Oct. 9 Wmk. 350 *Perf. 14*

937 A225 1p int bl & brn 1.25 75

77th Annual Convention of the American Philatelic Society, Mexico City, Oct. 7-13. See No. C274.

Tree of Life A226

José Morelos A227

1963, Oct. 26 Wmk. 350 *Perf. 14*

938 A226 20c dl bl grn & car 40 20

Centenary of the International Red Cross. See No. C277.

1963, Nov. 9

939 A227 40c grn & dk sl grn 55 20

150th anniv. of the 1st congress of Anahuac.

Pres. Victor Paz Estenssoro A228

Arms of Sinaloa University A229

1963, Nov. 9 Wmk. 350 *Perf. 14*

940 A228 40c dk brn & dk red brn 60 20

Issued to commemorate the visit of President Victor Paz Estenssoro of Bolivia.

1963 Photo.

941 A229 40c sl grn & ol bis 60 20

90th anniversary of the founding of the University of Sinaloa.

Diesel Train, Rail Cross Section and Globe A230

1963, Nov. 29 Photo.

942 A230 20c blk & dk brn 90 50

Issued to commemorate the 11th Pan-American Railroad Congress. See No. C279.

Type of 1950-52

Designs as before.

1963-66 Wmk. 350 Photo. *Perf. 14*

943 A189 5c red brn ('65) 60 15
944 A189 10c dk grn ('64) 65 15
945 A189 15c dk grn ('66) 60 15
946 A189 20c dark blue 60 15
948 A189 40c red org 70 15
949 A189 50c bl ('64) 1.25 15
950 A189 1p ol grn ('64) 3.00 15
951 A189 5p dl bl & dk grn ('66) 100.00 30.00
952 A189 10p gray & Prus bl ('65) 35.00 25.00
Nos. 943-952 (9) 142.40 56.05

The 20c is redrawn; clouds almost eliminated and other slight variations.

15-Cent Minimum Value
The minimum catalogue value is 15 cents. Separating se-tenant pieces into individual stamps does not increase the "value" of the stamps... since demand for the separated stamps may be small.

"F.S.T.S.E." Emblem A231

Academy of Medicine Emblem A232

1964, Feb. 15

954 A231 20c red org & dk brn 40 15

25th anniv. (in 1963) of the Civil Service Statute affecting federal employees.

1964, May 18 Wmk. 350 *Perf. 14*

955 A232 20c gold & blk 40 15

National Academy of Medicine, cent.

José Rizal A233

View of Zacatecas A234

Design: 40c, Miguel Lopez de Legaspi, Spanish navigator.

1964, Nov. 10 Photo. *Perf. 14*

956 A233 20c dk bl & dp grn 50 20
957 A233 40c dk bl & brt vio 60 20

Issued to honor 400 years of Mexican-Philippine friendship. See Nos. C300-C301.

1964, Nov. 10 Wmk. 350

958 A234 40c slate grn & red 55 20

50th anniv. of the capture of Zacatecas.

Col. Gregorio Mendez A235

Morelos Theater, Aguascalientes A236

1964, Nov. 10

959 A235 40c grysh blk & dk brn 50 20

Cent. of the Battle of Jahuactal, Tabasco.

Catalogue values for unused stamps in this section, from this point to the end of the section, are for Never Hinged items.

1965, Jan. 9 Photo. *Perf. 14*

960 A236 20c dl cl & dk gray 35 15

50th anniversary of the Aguascalientes Convention, Oct. 1-Nov. 9, 1914.

Andrés Manuel del Río — A237

1965, Feb. 19 Wmk. 350 *Perf. 14*

961 A237 30c gray 40 20

Bicentenary of the birth of Andrés Manuel del Rio, founder of the National School of Mining and discoverer of vanadium.

José Morelos and Constitution — A238

Trees — A239

1965, Apr. 24 Photo. *Perf. 14*

962 A238 40c brt grn & dk red brn 45 20

Sesquicentennial (in 1964) of the 1st Mexican constitution.

1965, July 14 Wmk. 350 *Perf. 14*

963 A239 20c bl & grn 30 15

Issued to commemorate Tree Day, July 8.

ICY Emblem A240

1965, Sept. 13 Photo.

964 A240 40c ol gray & sl grn 30 15

International Cooperation Year, 1965.

Athlete with Sling, Clay Figure A241

Design: 40c, Batter. Clay figures on 20c and 40c found in Colima, period 300-650 A.D.

1965, Dec. 17 Wmk. 350 *Perf. 14*

965 A241 20c ol & vio bl 90 20
966 A241 40c pink & blk 30 15

Issued to publicize the 19th Olympic Games, Mexico, 1968. For souvenir sheet see No. C310a. See Nos. C309-C311.

José Morelos by Diego Rivera A242

Emiliano Zapata A243

1965, Dec. 22

967 A242 20c lt vio bl & blk 40 20

José Maria Morelos y Pavon (1765-1815), priest and patriot in 1810 revolution against Spain.

1966, Jan. 10 Photo.

Design: 20c, Corn, cotton, bamboo, wheat and cow.

968 A243 20c car rose 35 15
969 A243 40c black 45 20

50th anniv. of the Agrarian Reform Law.

Mexican Postal Service Emblem A244

Bartolomé de Las Casas A245

1966, June 24 Wmk. 300 *Perf. 14*

970 A244 40c brt grn & blk 40 15

Congress of the Postal Union of the Americas and Spain, UPAE, Mexico City, June 24-July 23. See Nos. C314-C315.

1966, Aug. 1 Photo. Wmk. 300

971 A245 20c blk & buff 40 15

400th anniv. of the death of Bartolomé de Las Casas (1474-1566), "Apostle of the Indies."

Mechanical Drawings and Cogwheels A246

1966, Aug. 15 Photo. *Perf. 14*

972 A246 20c gray & grn 30 15

50th anniversary of the founding of the School of Mechanical and Electrical Engineering (ESIME).

FAO Emblem — A247

1966, Sept. 30 Wmk. 300 *Perf. 14*

973 A247 40c green 30 15

FAO International Rice Year.

Running and Jumping, by Diego Rivera A248

1966, Oct. 15

Size: 35x21mm

974 A248 20c shown 70 20
975 A248 40c Wrestling 35 15
a. Souvenir sheet 1.40 1.40

Issued to publicize the 19th Olympic Games, Mexico City, D.F., 1968. No. 975a contains 2 imperf. stamps similar to Nos. 974-975 with simulated perforations. Sold for 90c.

See Nos. C318-C320.

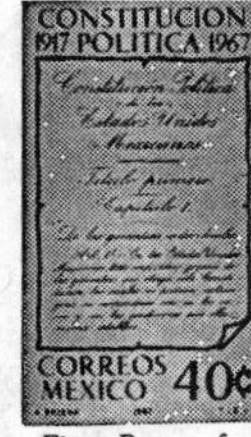

First Page of Constitution A249

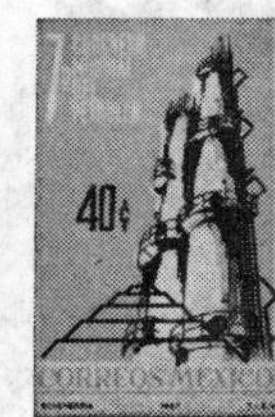

Oil Refinery and Pyramid of the Sun A250

Wmk. 300

1967, Feb. 5 Photo. *Perf. 14*

976 A249 40c black 50 20

50th anniversary of the Constitution. See No. C322.

1967, Apr. 2 Wmk. 300 *Perf. 14*

977 A250 40c lt bl & blk 35 15

Issued to publicize the 7th International Oil Congress, Mexico City, September, 1967.

Nayarit Indian — A251

Wmk. 300

1967, May 1 Photo. *Perf. 14*

978 A251 20c pale grn & blk 30 15

50th anniversary of Nayarit State.

Degollado Theater, Guadalajara A252

Wmk. 300

1967, June 12 Photo. *Perf. 14*

979 A252 40c pink & blk 20 20

Centenary of the founding of the Degollado Theater, Guadalajara.

Mexican Eagle over Imperial Crown — A253

Perf. 10x10½

1967, June 19 Litho. Wmk. 350

980 A253 20c blk & ocher 30 15

Centenary of the victory of the Mexican republican forces and of the execution of Emperor Maximilian I.

Canoeing A254

Designs: 40c, Basketball. 50c, Hockey. 80c, Bicycling. 2p, Fencing.

Wmk. 300

1967, Oct. 12 Photo. *Perf. 14*

981 A254 20c bl & blk 35 15
982 A254 40c brick red & blk 30 15
983 A254 50c brt yel grn & blk 30 15
a. Souvenir sheet of 3, #981-983, imperf. 1.10 1.10
984 A254 80c brt pur & blk 42 15
985 A254 2p org & blk 70 30
a. Souvenir sheet of 2, #984-985, imperf. 2.00 2.00
Nos. 981-985 (5) 2.07 90

Issued to publicize the 19th Olympic Games, Mexico City, Oct. 12-27, 1968.

No. 983a sold for 1.50p; No. 985a sold for 3.50p. Both sheets are watermark 350.

See Nos. 990-995, C328-C331, C335-C338.

Artemio de Valle-Arizpe A255

Pedro Moreno A256

1967, Nov. 1 Photo.

986 A255 20c brn & slate 35 30

Centenary of the Ateneo Fuente, a college at Saltillo, Coahuila.

1967, Nov. 18 Wmk. 300 *Perf. 14*

987 A256 40c blk & lt bl 35 15

Moreno (1775-1817), revolutionary leader.

Gabino Barreda A257

Staircase, Palace of Mining A258

1968, Jan. 27 Photo. *Perf. 14*

988 A257 40c dk bl & rose cl 40 15
989 A258 40c blk & bl gray 40 15

Centenary of the founding of the National Preparatory and Engineering Schools.

Type of Olympic Issue, 1967

Designs: 20c, Wrestling. 40c, Pentathlon. 50c, Water polo. 80c, Gymnastics. 1p, Boxing. 2p, Pistol shoot.

1968, Mar. 21 Wmk. 300 *Perf. 14*

990 A254 20c ol & blk 40 15
991 A254 40c red lil & blk 40 20
992 A254 50c brt grn & blk 40 20
a. Souvenir sheet of 3, #990-992, imperf. 1.25 1.25
993 A254 80c brt pink & blk 45 25
994 A254 1p org brn & blk 2.25 50
995 A254 2p gray & blk 2.50 1.50
a. Souvenir sheet of 3, #993-995, imperf. 3.00 3.00
Nos. 990-995 (6) 6.40 2.80

19th Olympic Games, Mexico City, Oct. 12-27. No. 992a sold for 1.50p; No. 995a sold for 5p. Both sheets are watermark 350.

See Nos. C335-C338.

Map of Mexico, Peace Dove — A259

Arms of Veracruz — A261

Symbols of Cultural Events A260

Designs: 40c, University City Olympic stadium. 50c, Telecommunications tower. 2p, Sports Palace. 10p, Pyramid of the Sun, Teotihuacan, and Olympic torch.

Wmk. 350

1968, Oct. Photo. *Perf. 14*

996 A259 20c bl, yel & grn 25 15
997 A259 40c multi 35 20
998 A259 50c multi 35 20
a. Souv. sheet of 3, #996-998, imperf. 6.50 7.00
999 A260 2p multi 55 50
1000 A260 5p sil & blk 2.25 1.25
a. Souv. sheet of 2, #999-1000, imperf. 6.00 6.50
1001 A259 10p multi 3.00 2.00
Nos. 996-1001 (6) 6.75 4.30

19th Olympic Games, Mexico City, Oct. 12-27 (Nos. 996-1000). Arrival of the Olympic torch in Veracruz (No. 1001).

No. 998a sold for 1.50p. No. 1000a sold for 9p.

See Nos. C340-C344a.

1969, May 20 Wmk. 350 *Perf. 14*

1002 A261 40c multi 35 15

450th anniv. of the founding of Veracruz.

Type of 1950-52
Coil Stamps
Perf. 11 Vert.

1969 Wmk. 300 Photo.

1003 A189 20c dk bl 1.00 75
1004 A189 40c red org 1.50 1.60

Vert. pairs, imperf. horiz. may be from uncut rolls of coils.

Subway Train — A262

1969, Sept. 4 Wmk. 350 *Perf. 14*

1005 A262 40c multi 35 15

Inauguration of Mexico City subway.

Honeycomb, Bee and ILO Emblem A263

Gen. Allende, by Diego Rivera A264

1969, Oct. 18 Photo. *Perf. 14*

1006 A263 40c multi 25 15

50th anniversary of the ILO.

1969, Nov. 15 Wmk. 350 *Perf. 14*

1007 A264 40c multi 25 15

Gen. Ignacio Allende Unzaga (1769-1811), father of Mexican independence.

Tourist Issue

Pyramid of Niches at El Tajin, Veracruz, and Dancers Swinging from Pole A265

Anthropology Museum, Mexico City — A266

Deer Dance, Sonora — A267

Designs: No. 1010, View of Puerto Vallarta. No. 1011, Puebla Cathedral. No. 1012, Calle Belaunzaran. No. 1014, Ocotlan Cathedral, horiz.

1969-73 Photo. Wmk. 350

1008 A265 40c shown 45 15
1009 A266 40c shown ('70) 45 15
1010 A266 40c Jalisco ('70) 45 15
1011 A266 40c Puebla ('70) 45 15
1012 A266 40c Guanajuato ('70) 45 15

Wmk. 300

1013 A267 40c shown ('73) 25 15
1014 A267 40c Tlaxcala ('73) 25 15
Nos. 1008-1014 (7) 2.75 1.05

No. 1010 is inscribed "1970" below the design. Copies inscribed "1969" are from an earlier, unissued printing.

See Nos. C357-C358.

Luminescence

Fluorescent stamps include Nos. 1013-1014, 1035, 1038, 1041, 1043-1045, 1047-1050, 1054-1059. (See Luminescence note over No. C527.)

"How Many, Who and What are We?" — A268

Design: 40c, "What, How and How Much do we produce?" (horse's head and symbols of agriculture).

1970, Jan. 26 Wmk. 350 *Perf. 14*

1024 A268 20c multi 30 15
1025 A268 40c bl & multi 25 15

Issued to publicize the 1970 census.

Human Eye and Spectrum A269

1970, Mar. 8 Photo. Wmk. 350

1026 A269 40c multi 25 15

21st International Congress of Ophthalmology, Mexico City, Mar. 8-14.

Helmets of 1920 and 1970 — A270

1970, Apr. 11 Wmk. 350 *Perf. 14*

1027 A270 40c dk car rose, blk & lt brn 20 15

50th anniversary of the Military College.

José Maria Pino Suarez A271

Coat of Arms of Celaya A272

1970, Apr. 25 Photo.

1028 A271 40c blk & multi 20 15

Centenary of the birth of José Maria Pino Suarez (1869-1913), lawyer, poet and Vice President of Mexico.

1970, Oct. 12 Photo. *Perf. 14*

1029 A272 40c blk & multi 20 15

City of Celaya, 400th anniversary.

Eclipse of Sun — A273

1970, Nov. 11 Wmk. 350 *Perf. 14*

1030 A273 40c black & gray 25 15

Total eclipse of the sun, Mar. 7, 1970.

Spheres with Dates 1970-1770 A274

1971, June 26 Photo. *Perf. 14*

1031 A274 40c emer & blk 25 15

Bicentenary of National Lottery.

Vasco de Quiroga, Mural by O'Gorman A275

1971, July 10 **Photo.**
1032 A275 40c multi 20 15

500th anniversary of the birth of Vasco de Quiroga (1470-1565), Archbishop of Michoacan, founder of hospitals and schools.

Amado Nervo (1870-1919), Poet — A276

1971, Aug. 7 **Wmk. 350** ***Perf. 14***
1033 A276 40c multi 20 15

Waves and Transformer A277

1971, Oct. 9
1034 A277 40c blk, lt bl & lt grn 30 15

50th anniversary of Mexican radio.

Pres. Lazaro Cardenas (1895-1970) — A278

1971, Oct. 19 **Wmk. 300**
1035 A278 40c blk & pale lil 30 15

Keyboard and Lara's Signature A279

1971, Nov. 6 **Wmk. 350**
1036 A279 40c blk, buff & pale bl 30 15

Agustin Lara (1900-70), composer.

Arms of Monterrey A280

Cardiology Institute and WHO Emblems A281

1971, Dec. 18
1037 A280 40c blk & multi 30 15

375th anniv. of the founding of Monterrey.

1972, Apr. 8 **Wmk. 300**
1038 A281 40c multi 25 15

"Your heart is your health," World Health Day 1972. See No. C395.

Gaceta de Mexico, Jan. 1, 1722 — A282

1972, June 24 **Wmk. 350**
1039 A282 40c multi 25 15

250th anniv. of 1st Mexican newspaper.

Lions Intl. Emblem — A283

Sailing Ship Zaragoza — A284

1972, June 28
1040 A283 40c blk & multi 25 15

55th Lions International Convention.

1972, July 1
1041 A284 40c bl & multi 25 15

75th anniv. of the Naval School of Veracruz.

A285

A286

Olive tree and branch.

1972, July 18 **Wmk. 350** ***Perf. 14***
1042 A285 40c lt grn, ocher & blk 25 15
a. 40c light green, yellow & black 50 35

Centenary of Chilpancingo as capital of Guerrero State.

1972, Sept. 15 **Photo.** **Wmk. 300**

Design: 20c, Margarita Maza de Juárez. 40c, Benito Juárez, by Diego Rivera.

1043 A286 20c pink & multi 40 15
1044 A286 40c dp yel & multi 40 15
Nos. 1043-1044,C403-C405 (5) 1.57
Set value 66

Benito Juárez (1806-1872), revolutionary leader and president of Mexico.

Emperor Justinian I, Mosaic A287

1972, Sept. 30 **Wmk. 300**
1045 A287 40c multi 65 15

Mexican Bar Association, 50th anniv.

Caravel — A288

Library, Book Year Emblem — A290

Olympic Emblems A289

1972, Oct. 12 **Wmk. 350**
1046 A288 80c buff, pur & ocher 40 15

Stamp Day of The Americas.

1972, Dec. 9 **Wmk. 300**
1047 A289 40c multi 35 15

20th Olympic Games, Munich, Aug. 26-Sept. 11. See Nos. C410-C411.

1972, Dec. 16
1048 A290 40c blk & multi 25 15

International Book Year 1972.

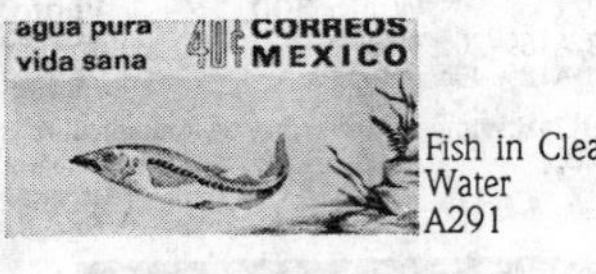

Fish in Clean Water A291

1972, Dec. 16
1049 A291 40c blk & lt bl 40 15

Anti-pollution campaign. See No. C412.

Metlac Railroad Bridge A292

1973, Feb. 2 ***Perf. 14***
1050 A292 40c multi 85 15

Centenary of Mexican railroads.

Cadet — A293

1973, Oct. 11 **Photo.** **Wmk. 300**
1051 A293 40c blk & multi 45 15

Sesquicentennial of Military College.

Madero, by Diego Rivera — A294

Antonio Narro — A295

1973, Nov. 9 **Wmk. 350** ***Perf. 14***
1052 A294 40c multi 20 15

Pres. Francisco I. Madero (1873-1913).

1973, Nov. 9 **Photo.**
1053 A295 40c stl gray 35 15

50th anniversary of the Antonio Narro Agriculture School in Saltillo.

Type of 1950-52

Designs as before

1973 **Unwmk.** ***Perf. 14***
1054 A189 20c bl vio 2.00 1.50
1055 A189 40c red org 2.00 1.50

Fluorescent printing on back (or on front of 40c) consisting of beehive pattern and diagonal inscription.

Hydrocarbon Molecule A296

Wmk. 300

1973, Dec. 7 **Photo.** ***Perf. 14***
1056 A296 40c blk, dk car & yel 20 15

Pointing Hand Emblem of Foreign Trade Institute — A297

1974, Jan. 11 Photo. Wmk. 300
1057 A297 40c dk grn & blk 20 15

Export promotion.

A298

1974, Jan. 18 Litho. Wmk. 300
1058 A298 40c black 20 15

EXMEX 73 Philatelic Exhibition, Cuernavaca, Apr. 7-15. See No. C424.

Manuel M. Ponce at Keyboard A299

1974, Jan. 18 Photo. Wmk. 300
1059 A299 40c gold & multi 20 15

Manuel M. Ponce (1882-1948), composer.

Silver Statuette of Mexican Woman — A300

1974, Mar. 23 Photo. *Perf. 14*
1060 A300 40c red & multi 20 15

First World Silver Fair.

Mariano Azuela A301

1974, Apr. 10 Wmk. 300 *Perf. 14*
1061 A301 40c multi 20 15

Mariano Azuela (1873-1952), writer.

Dancing Dogs, Pre-Columbian — A302

1974, Apr. 10
1062 A302 40c multi 20 15

6th Traveling Dog Exhibition, Mexico City, Nov. 23-Dec. 1.

Aqueduct, Tepotzotlan — A303

1974, July 10 Photo. Wmk. 300
1063 A303 40c brt bl & blk 45 15

National Engineers' Day, July 1.

Dr. Rodolfo Robles A304

1974, July 19 *Perf. 14*
1064 A304 40c bis & grn 20 15

25th anniv. of WHO (in 1973).

EXFILMEX 74 Emblem — A305

1974, July 26 *Perf. 13x12*
1065 A305 40c buff, grn & blk 20 15

EXFILMEX 74, Fifth Inter-American Philatelic Exhibition honoring centenary of Universal Postal Union, Mexico City, Oct. 26-Nov. 3. See No. C429.

Demosthenes — A306

1974, Aug. 2 Photo. *Perf. 14*
1066 A306 20c grn & brn 35 15

2nd Spanish-American Cong. for Reading and Writing Studies, Mexico City, May 7-14.

Map of Chiapas and Head A307

1974, Sept. 14 Wmk. 300 *Perf. 14*
1067 A307 20c blk & grn 20 15

Centenary of Chiapas statehood.

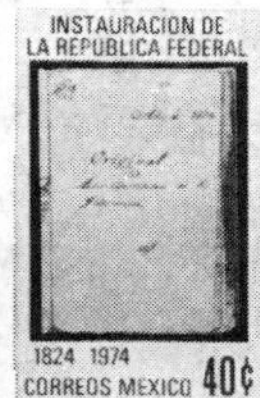
Law of 1824 — A308

Sebastian Lerdo de Tejada — A309

1974, Oct. 11 Wmk. 300
1068 A308 40c gray & grn 20 15

Sesquicentennial of the establishment of the Federal Republic of Mexico.

1974, Oct. 11 Photo.
1069 A309 40c blk & lt bl 20 15

Centenary of restoration of the Senate.

UPU Monument, Bern A310

1974, Dec. 13 Wmk. 300 *Perf. 14*
1070 A310 40c ultra & org brn 20 15

Cent. of UPU. See Nos. C437-C438.

Types of 1950-56

Designs (as 1951-56 issues): 2.30p, Guillermo Prieto. 3p, Modernistic church, Nuevo Leon. 50p, Benito Juarez.

1975 Photo. Wmk. 300 *Perf. 14*

1072 A189	80c	green	55	25
1075 A200	2.30p	dp vio bl	85	35
1076 A189	3p	brick red	85	35
1081 A189	50p	org & grn	10.00	7.50

See No. 1097 for unwmkd. 3p with no shading under "Leon."

Gov. José Maria Mora — A312

1975, Feb. 21 Photo. Wmk. 300
1084 A312 20c yel & multi 20 15

Sesquicentennial (in 1974) of establishment of the State of Mexico.

Merchants with Pre-Columbian Goods — A313

1975, Apr. 18 Photo. Unwmk.
1085 A313 80c multi 20 15

Centenary (in 1974) of the National Chamber of Commerce in Mexico City. Design from Florentine Codex.

Juan Aldama, by Diego Rivera A314

1975, June 6 *Perf. 14*
1086 A314 80c multi 20 15

Juan Aldama (1774-1811), officer and patriot, birth bicentenary.

Indians and Eagle on Cactus Destroying Serpent, from Duran Codex A315

1975, Aug. 1 Photo. Unwmk.
1087 A315 80c multi 20 15

650th anniv. of Tenochtitlan (Mexico City).

Julián Carrillo A316

Academy Emblem A317

1975, Sept. 12 Photo. Unwmk.
1088 A316 80c brt grn & red brn 20 15

Julián Carrillo (1875-1965), violinist and composer, birth centenary.

1975, Sept. 13 *Perf. 14*
1089 A317 80c brn & ocher 20 15

Cent. of Mexican Academy of Languages.

Types of 1950-56

Designs (as 1950-56 issues): 80c, Indian dancer, Michoacan. 2p, Convent, Morelos.

1975-76 Photo. Unwmk.

1090	A189	40c orange	30	15
1091	A189	50c blue	35	15
1092	A200	60c red lil	45	15
1093	A200	70c vio bl	40	15
1094	A189	80c green	40	15
1095	A189	1p ol grn	40	15
1096	A189	2p scarlet	80	50
1097	A189	3p brick red	80	50
1099	A189	5p gray bl & grn	1.75	1.00
1101	A189	10p grn & dp ultra ('76)	4.00	2.00
1102	A189	20p lil & blk ('76)	8.25	4.00
		Nos. 1090-1102 (11)	17.90	8.90

University of Guadalajara A318

1975, Oct. 1 Photo. *Perf. 14*

1107	A318	80c multi	20	15

University of Guadalajara, 50th anniversary.

Road Workers — A319

1975, Oct. 17 Photo. Unwmk.

1108	A319	80c gray grn, grn & blk	20	15

50 years of road building for progress.

Pistons A320

Designs: Export Emblem and 5c, 6p, Steel pipes. 20c, Chemistry flasks. 40c, Cup of coffee. 80c, Meat cuts marked on steer. 1p, Electrical conductor. 2p, Abalone. 3p, Men's shoes. 4p, Tiles. 5p, Minerals. 7p, 8p, 9p, Overalls. 10p, Tequila. 15p, Honey. 20p, Wrought iron. 25p, Copper vase. 35p, 40p, No. 1132, 80p, Jewelry. No. 1133, Books. 100p, Strawberry. 200p, Citrus fruit. 300p, Motor vehicles. 400p, Circuit board. 500p, Cotton.

Some stamps have a gray burelage;

Type I- Burelage lines run lower left to upper right with arch towards lower right.

Type II- Burelage lines run lower left to upper right with arch towards upper left.

1975-87 Photo. Unwmk. *Perf. 14*

1109	A320	5c sl bl ('77)	15	15
1110	A320	20c blk ('76)	15	15
1111	A320	40c dk brn ('76)	50	20
a.		40c claret brown ('81)	1.00	25
1112	A320	50c dl bl	60	15
a.		50c slate blue ('76)	20	15
b.		50c black ('83)	15	15
c.		50c slate, thin paper ('81)	30	15
1113	A320	80c brt car ('76)	20	15
a.		Perf. 11	40	15
b.		Perf. 11½x11	20	15
c.		As "a," thin paper ('81)	30	25
d.		As "b," thin paper ('81)	15	15
1114	A320	1p vio bl & org ('78)	15	15
1115	A320	1p lt vio & org ('83)	15	15
1116	A320	1p blk & org ('84)	15	15
1117	A320	2p bl grn & dk bl ('76)	75	15
a.		2p green & brt blue ('81)	15	15
1118	A320	3p red brn	15	15
a.		3p brn, perf 11½x11 ('82)	30	15
b.		Golden brn, thin paper ('81)	30	15
1119	A320	4p tan & dk brn ('80)	20	15
1120	A320	5p gray ol ('78)	20	15
a.		Perf 11½x11 ('84)	15	15
1121	A320	6p brt org ('83)	30	15
a.		Perf 11½x11 ('83)	30	15
b.		Perf 11 ('84)	1.00	15
1121C	A320	6p gray, perf. 11½x11 ('84)	15	15
1122	A320	7p Prus bl ('84)	15	15
a.		7p blue gray ('84)	5.00	15
1123	A320	8p bis brn, perf 11 ('84)	1.25	15
a.		Perf 11½x11 ('84)	15	15
1124	A320	9p dk bl ('84)	15	15
1125	A320	10p dk & lt grn ('78)	15	15
a.		Thin paper ('81)	30	30
b.		Dk ol grn & yel grn ('86)	15	15
c.		Dk ol grn & brt ol grn ('87)	15	15
1126	A320	15p yel org & red brn ('84)	15	15
1127	A320	20p blk ('78)	60	15
1128	A320	20p dk gray ('84)	15	15
1129	A320	25p org brn ('84)	15	15
1130	A320	35p brt cer & yel ('84)	20	20
1131	A320	40p org brn & lt yel ('84)	20	20
1132	A320	50p gray, sil, brt vio & pur ('80)	2.00	75
1133	A320	50p brt bl & lt yel ('83)	35	15
1133A	A320	80p pink & gold ('85)	35	35
1134	A320	100p scar & brt grn, I ('83)	1.00	25
1135	A320	200p emer & yel grn, II ('83)	3.00	50
a.		Emer & lemon, I ('87)	2.00	1.00
b.		Emer & yel grn, I ('83)	1.00	25
1136	A320	300p brt bl & red, I ('83)	1.00	1.00
a.		Type II ('87)	80	60
1137	A320	400p lem & red brn, I ('84)	1.50	60
1138	A320	500p lt ol grn & yel org, I ('84)	3.00	50
		Nos. 1109-1138 (32)	19.15	
		Set value		6.40

No. 1125b is 2mm wider than No. 1125. Size of No. 1125b: 37x21mm.

Nos. 1117, 1119, 1126, 1135 exist with one or more colors missing. These were not regularly issued.

See Nos. 1166-1176, 1465-1470A, 1491-1505, 1583-1603, 1763-1776, C486-C508, C594-C603.

Aguascalientes Cathedral A323

JAIME TORRES BODET 1902-1974
CORREOS 80¢ MEXICO
Jaime Torres Bodet A324

1975, Nov. 28

1140	A323	50c bl grn & blk	75	20

400th anniversary of Aguascalientes.

1975, Nov. 28

1141	A324	80c blue & brn	20	15

Jaime Torres Bodet (1920-1974), writer, director general of UNESCO (1958-1962).

Allegory, by José Clemente Orozco — A325

1975, Dec. 9 *Perf. 14*

1142	A325	80c multi	20	15

Sesquicentennial of Supreme Court.

Set Values

A 15-cent minimum now applies to individual stamps and sets. Where the 15-cent minimum per stamp would increase the "value" of a set beyond retail, there is a "Set Value" notation giving the retail value of the set.

The Death of Cuauhtemoc, by Chavez Morado — A326

1975, Dec. 12 Photo.

1143	A326	80c multi	20	15

450th anniv. of the death of Cuauhtemoc (1495?-1525), last Aztec emperor.

Netzahualcoyotl (Water God) — A327

1976, Jan. 9 Unwmk. *Perf. 14*

1144	A327	80c bl & vio bl	20	15

50th anniv. of Mexican irrigation projects.

Arch, Léon A328

1976, Jan. 20

1145	A328	80c dk brn & ocher	20	15

400th anniversary of Léon, Guanajuato.

Forest Fire A329

1976, July 8 Photo. *Perf. 14*

1146	A329	80c blk, grn & red	20	15

Prevent fires!

Hat and Scout Emblem A330

Exhibition Emblem A331

1976, Aug. 24 Photo. Unwmk.

1147	A330	80c ol & red brn	20	15

Mexican Boy Scout Assoc., 50th anniv.

1976, Sept. 2

1148	A331	80c blk, red & grn	20	15

Mexico Today and Tomorrow Exhibition.

New Building, Military College A332

1976, Sept. 13 *Perf. 14*

1149	A332	50c red brn & ocher	20	15

Military College, new installations.

Dr. Ricardo Vertiz — A333

1976, Sept. 24 Photo. *Perf. 14*

1150	A333	80c blk & redsh brn	20	15

Our Lady of Light Ophthalmological Hospital, centenary.

National Basilica of Guadeloupe A334

1976, Oct. 12

1151	A334	50c blk & ocher	20	15

Inauguration of the new National Basilica of Our Lady of Guadeloupe.

"40" and Emblem A335

1976, Oct. 28 Photo. *Perf. 14*

1152	A335	80c blk, lt grn & car	20	15

Natl. Polytechnic Institute, 40th anniv.

Blast Furnace A336

1976, Nov. 4

1153	A336	50c multi	20	15

Inauguration of the Lazaro Cardenas Steel Mill, Las Truchas.

Saltillo Cathedral
A337

Electrification
A338

1977, July 25 Photo. *Perf. 14*
1154 A337 80c yel & dk brn 20 15

400th anniversary of the founding of Saltillo.

1977, Aug. 14 Photo. *Perf. 14*
1155 A338 80c multi 20 15

40 years of Mexican development program.

Flags of Spain and Mexico
A339

1977, Oct. 8 Photo. Wmk. 300
1156 A339 50c multi 20 15
1157 A339 80c multi 20 15
Nos. 1156-1157,C537-C539 (5) 1.02
Set value 58

Resumption of diplomatic relations with Spain.

Aquiles Serdan (1877-1910), Martyr of the Revolution — A340

1977, Nov. 18 Photo. *Perf. 14*
1158 A340 80c lt & dk grn & blk 20 15

Poinsettia
A341

1977, Dec. 2 Wmk. 300 *Perf. 14*
1159 A341 50c multi 15 15

Christmas 1977.

Old and New Telephones — A342

1978, Mar. 15 Photo. *Perf. 14*
1160 A342 80c sal & mar 20 15

Centenary of first telephone in Mexico.

Oil Derrick
A343

1978, Mar. 18
1161 A343 80c dp org & mar 20 15

40th anniversary of nationalization of oil industry. See Nos. C556-C557.

Institute Emblem
A344

1978, July 21 Photo. *Perf. 14*
1162 A344 80c bl & blk 20 15

Pan-American Institute for Geography and History, 50th anniv. See Nos. C574-C575.

Dahlias
A345

Decorations and Candles
A346

1978, Sept. 29 Photo. Wmk. 300
1163 A345 50c shown 20 15
1164 A345 80c Frangipani 20 15

1978, Nov. 22 Photo. *Perf. 14*
1165 A346 50c multi 15 15

Christmas 1978.

Export Type of 1975

Designs as before. 50p, Jewelry.

1979-81 Photo. Wmk. 300 *Perf. 14*
1166 A320 20c blk ('81) 40 20
1167 A320 50c slate bl 20 20
 a. 50c bluish black 30 20
1168 A320 80c brt car 75 20
 a. Perf. 11 30 20
1169 A320 1p ultra & org 30 15
1170 A320 2p brt grn & bl 30 20
1171 A320 3p dk brn 30 15
1172 A320 4p tan & dk brn ('80) 30 20
1173 A320 5p gray olive 40 35
1174 A320 10p dk & lt grn 1.50 75
1175 A320 20p black 2.00 75
1176 A320 50p gray, sil, brt vio & pur 4.00 2.50
Nos. 1166-1176 (11) 10.45 5.65

A347

Soccer Ball — A348

1979, Apr. 26 Wmk. 300 *Perf. 14*
1177 A347 80c multi 15 15

Centenary of Hermosillo, Sonora.

1979, June 15 Photo. Wmk. 300

Designs: 80c, Aztec ball player. 1p, Wall painting showing athletes. 5p, Runners, horiz.

1178 A348 50c bl & blk 15 15
1179 A348 80c multi 15 15
1180 A348 1p multi 15 15
Nos. 1178-1180,C606-C607 (5) 91
Set value 56

Souvenir Sheet
Imperf

1181 A348 5p multi 80 80

Universiada '79, World Games, Mexico City, Sept. 1979. No. 1181 has simulated perforations.

Josefa Ortiz de Dominguez, Mayor of Queretaro, 150th Death Anniv. — A349

1979, July 6 *Perf. 14*
1182 A349 80c multi 15 15

Allegory of National Culture, by Alfaro Siqueiros — A350

Design: 3p, Conquest of Energy, by Chavez Morado.

1979, July 10
1183 A350 80c multi 16 15
1184 A350 3p multi 24 15

National University, 50th anniversary of autonomy. See Nos. C609-C610.

Emiliano Zapata, by Diego Rivera — A351

1979, Aug. 8 Photo. *Perf. 14*
1185 A351 80c multi 20 15

Emiliano Zapata (1879-1919), revolutionist.

Soccer
A352

Designs: 80c, Women's volleyball. 1p, Basketball. 5p, Fencing.

1979, Sept. 2
1186 A352 50c multi 15 15
1187 A352 80c multi 15 15
1188 A352 1p multi 15 15
Nos. 1186-1188,C612-C613 (5) 88
Set value 56

Souvenir Sheet
Imperf

1189 A352 5p multi 80 80

Universiada '79 World University Games, Mexico City. No. 1189 has simulated perforations.

Tepoztlan, Morelos — A353

Tourism: No. 1191, Mexcaltitan, Nayarit.

1979, Sept. 28 Photo. *Perf. 14*
1190 A353 80c multi 15 15
1191 A353 80c multi 15 15
Set value 15

See Nos. C615-C616, 1274-1277, 1318-1321, 1513-1516.

Postmaster Martin de Olivares — A354

Shepherd and Sheep — A355

1979 Wmk. 300 *Perf. 14*
1192 A354 80c multi 15 15

Royal proclamation of mail service in the New World (New Spain), 400th anniversary. See Nos. C618-C620.

1979, Nov. 15
1193 A355 50c multi 15 15

Christmas 1979. See No. C623.

Serpent, Mayan Temple
A356

1980, Feb. 16 Photo. *Perf. 14x14½*
1194 A356 80c multi 15 15

Pre-Hispanic monuments. See Nos. C625-C626.

North American Turkey — A357

Tajetes Erecta — A358

Wmk. 300

1980, Mar. 8 **Photo.** ***Perf. 14***

1195 A357 80c multi 15 15
1196 A358 80c multi 15 15
Set value 15

See Nos. C632-C633, 1234-1237.

A359

A360

Designs: 50c, China Poblana (woman's costume), Puebla. 80c, Jarocha, Veracruz.

Wmk. 300

1980, Apr. 26 **Photo.** ***Perf. 14***

1197 A359 50c multi 15 15
1198 A359 80c multi 15 15
Set value 15

See No. C636, 1231-1233.

1980, June 4 **Unwmk.**

1200 A360 3p silver & blk 20 15

10th national census.

Cuauhtemoc (Last Aztec Emperor), 1520, Matritense Codex A361

Pre-Hispanic Art (Leaders): 1.60p, Nezahualcoyotl (1402-1472), governor of Tetzcoco, poet, Azcatitlan Codex. 5.50p, Eight Deer Tiger's Claw (1011-1063), 11th king of Mixtec, Nuttall Codex.

1980, June 21

1201 A361 80c multi 15 15
1202 A361 1.60p multi 16 15
1203 A361 5.50p multi 42 20
Set value 40

See Nos. 1285-1287, 1510-1512.

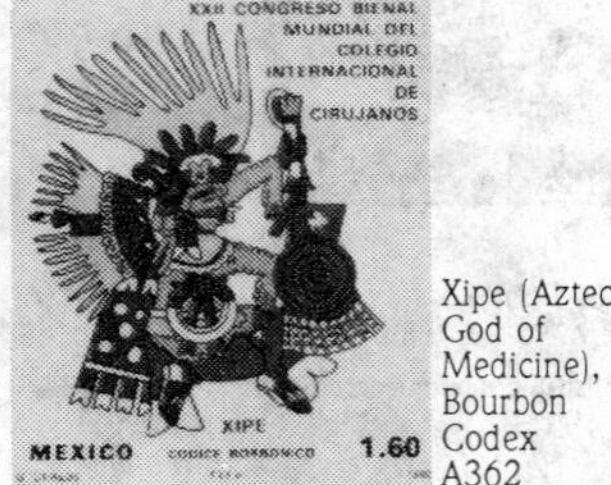

Xipe (Aztec God of Medicine), Bourbon Codex A362

1980, June 29

1204 A362 1.60p multi 15 15

22nd International Biennial Congress of the International College of Surgeons, Mexico City, June 29-July 4.

Moscow '80 Bronze Medal, Emblem, Misha, Olympic Rings — A363

1980, July 19 **Photo.** ***Perf. 14***

1205 A363 1.60p shown 15 15
1206 A363 3p Silver medal 26 15
1207 A363 5.50p Gold medal 38 25

22nd Summer Olympic Games, Moscow, July 19-Aug. 3.

Ceremonial Vessel, Tenochtitlan Temple A364

Wmk. 300

1980, Aug. 23 **Photo.** ***Perf. 14***

1208 A364 80c shown 15 15
1209 A364 1.60p Caracol 15 15
1210 A364 5.50p Chacmool 28 15
Set value 30

Pre-Columbian Art.

Sacromonte Sanctuary, Amecameca — A365

Colonial Monuments: No. 1212, St. Catherine's Convent, Patzcuaro. No. 1213, Basilica, Cuilapan, vert. No. 1214, Calvary Hermitage, Cuernavaca.

1980, Sept. 26 **Photo.** ***Perf. 14***

1211 A365 2.50p black 20 15
1212 A365 2.50p black 20 15
1213 A365 3p black 25 15
1214 A365 3p black 25 15
Set value 40

See Nos. 1260-1263, 1303-1306, 1338-1341.

Quetzalcoatl (God) — A366

Sinaloa Coat of Arms — A367

1980, Sept. 27

1215 A366 2.50p multi 20 15

World Tourism Conf., Manila, Sept. 27.

1980, Oct. 13

1216 A367 1.60p multi 20 15

Sinaloa state sesquicentennial.

Straw Angel — A368

Christmas 1980: 1.60p, Poinsettias.

1980, Nov. 17 **Photo.** ***Perf. 14***

1217 A368 50c multi 15 15
1218 A368 1.60p multi 15 15
Set value 20

Congress Emblem A369

1980, Dec. 10

1219 A369 1.60p multi 15 15

4th International Civil Justice Congress.

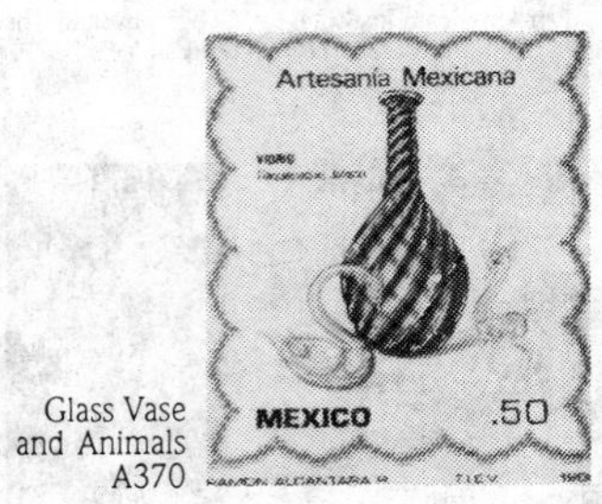

Glass Vase and Animals A370

1980, Dec. 13 **Wmk. 300**

1220 A370 50c shown 15 15
1221 A370 1p Poncho 15 15
1222 A370 3p Wooden mask, 17th century 30 15
Set value 35

See Nos. 1267-1269.

Simon Bolivar, by Paulin Guerin A371

Vicente Guerrero A372

1980, Dec. 17

1223 A371 4p multi 40 25

Simon Bolivar death sesquicentennial.

1981, Feb. 14

1224 A372 80c multi 15 15

Vicente Guerrero (1783-1831), statesman.

Valentin Gomez Farias — A373

1981, Feb. 14

1225 A373 80c brt grn & gray 15 15

First Latin-American Table Tennis Cup — A374

Wmk. 300

1981, Feb. 27 **Photo.** ***Perf. 14***

1226 A374 4p multi 40 25

Jesus Gonzalez Ortega, Politician, Birth Cent. A375

Gabino Barreda (1818-1881), Physician A376

Wmk. 300

1981, Mar. 10 **Photo.** ***Perf. 14***

1227 A375 80c brn & yel org 15 15

1981, Feb. 28

1228 A376 80c multi 15 15

Benito Juarez, 175th Death Anniv. A377

1981, Mar. 21

1229 A377 1.60p multi 15 15

450th Anniv. of Puebla City — A378

1981, Apr. 16 **Unwmk.**

1230 A378 80c multi 15 15
a. Wmk. 300 40 20

Costume Type of 1980

1981, Apr. 25 **Unwmk.**

1231 A359 50c Purepecha, Michoacan 15 15
1232 A359 80c Charra, Jalisco 15 15
1233 A359 1.60p Mestiza, Yucatan 15 15
Set value 30 15

Flora and Fauna Types of 1980

Wmk. 300 (#1235), Unwmkd.

1981, May 30

1234 A357 80c Mimus polyglottos 15 15
1235 A358 80c Persea americana 15 15
1236 A357 1.60p Trogon mexicanus 15 15
1237 A358 1.60p Theobromo cacao 15 15
Set value 40 20

Workers' Strike, by David Altaro Siqueiros A379

1981, June 10 Photo. *Perf. 14*
1238 A379 1.60p multi 15 15

Labor strike martyrs of Cananea, 75th anniversary.

Intl. Year of the Disabled A380

1981, July 4 Unwmk. *Perf. 14*
1239 A380 4p multi 40 25

450th Anniv. of Queretaro City — A381

1981, July 25 Unwmk.
1240 A381 80c multi 15 15
a. Wmk. 300 40 15

Alexander Fleming (1881-1955), Discoverer of Penicillin A382

1981, Aug. 1 Unwmk.
1241 A382 5p bl & org 40 15

No. 1 A383

1981, Aug. 6
1242 A383 4p multi 32 15
a. Wmk. 300 40 15

125th anniv. of Mexican stamps.

St. Francis Xavier Clavijero, 250th Birth Anniv. — A384

1981, Sept. 9 Unwmk. *Perf. 14*
1243 A384 80c multi 15 15

Union Congress Building Opening — A385

1981, Sept. 10
1244 A385 1.60p red & brt grn 15 15

1300th Anniv. of Bulgarian State A386

1981, Sept. 19 Photo. *Perf. 14*
1245 A386 1.60p Desislava, mural, 1259 15 15
1246 A386 4p Thracian gold cup 30 15
1247 A386 7p Horseman 45 15
Set value 35

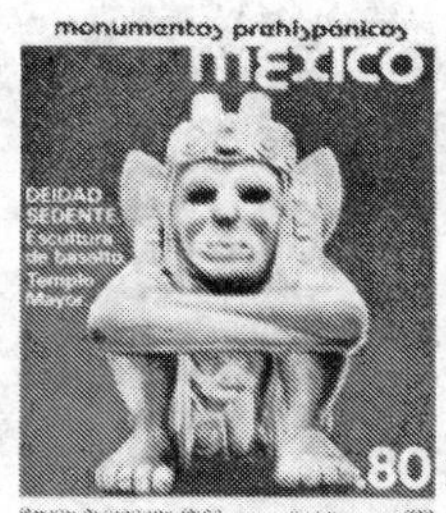

Pre-Hispanic Art — A387

1981, Sept. 26
1248 A387 80c Squatting diety 20 15
1249 A387 1.60p Animal head 30 15
1250 A387 4p Fish 40 25
Set value 45

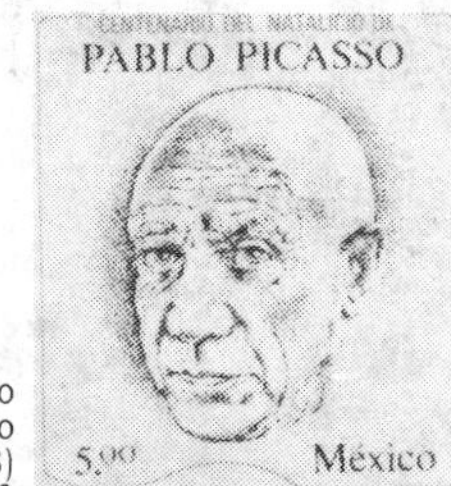

Pablo Picasso (1881-1973) A388

1981, Oct. 5
1251 A388 5p lt ol grn & grn 40 24

Christmas 1981 — A389

1981, Oct. 15
1252 A389 50c Shepherd 15 15
1253 A389 1.60p Girl 20 15
Set value 20

World Food Day — A390

1981, Oct. 16
1254 A390 4p multi 30 18

50th Death Anniv. of Thomas Edison A391

1981, Oct. 18
1255 A391 4p multi 30 18

Intl. Meeting on Cooperation and Development — A392

1981, Oct. 22
1256 A392 4p multi 30 15

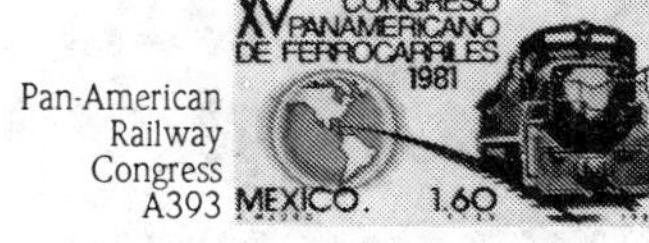

Pan-American Railway Congress A393

1981, Oct. 25 Unwmk.
1257 A393 1.60p multi 15 15

50th Anniv. of Mexican Sound Movies A394

1981, Nov. 3 Photo. *Perf. 14*
1258 A394 4p multi 30 15

Inauguration of Zip Codes A395

1981, Nov. 12
1259 A395 80c multi 15 15

Colonial Monument Type of 1980

Design: No. 1260, Mascarones House. No. 1261, La Merced Order Convent. No. 1262, Third Order Chapel, Texoco. No. 1263, Friar Tembleque Aqueduct, Otumba.

1981, Nov. 28
1260 A365 4p black 18 15
1261 A365 4p black 18 15
1262 A365 5p black 20 15
1263 A365 5p black 20 15
Set value 40

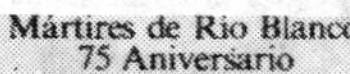

Martyrs of Rio Blanco, 75th Anniv. A396

1982, Jan. 7 Photo. *Perf. 14*
1264 A396 80c multi 15 15

Death Sesquicentennial of Ignacio Lopez Rayon — A397

1982, Feb. 2
1265 A397 1.60p multi 15 15

75th Anniv. of Postal Headquarters — A398

1982, Feb. 17
1266 A398 4p grn & ocher 20 15

Crafts Type of 1980

1982, Mar. 6 Photo. *Perf. 14*
1267 A370 50c Huichole art 15 15
1268 A370 1p Ceramic snail 20 15
1269 A370 3p Tiger mask, Madera 20 15
Set value 15

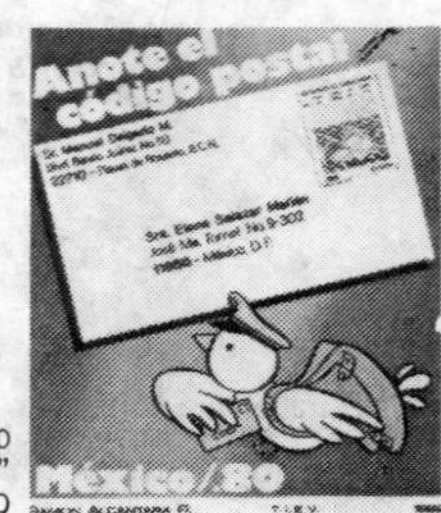

"Use Zip Codes" A399

1982, Mar. 20

1270 A399 80c multi 15 15

TB Bacillus Centenary and World Health Day — A400

1982, Apr. 7 Photo. *Perf. 14*

1271 A400 4p multi 20 15

50th Anniv. of Military Academy A401

1982, Apr. 15

1272 A401 80c multi 15 15

City Oaxaca, 450th Anniv. — A402

1982, Apr. 25

1273 A402 1.60p multi 15 15

Tourism Type of 1979

Designs: No. 1274, Basaseachic Cascade, Chihuahua. No. 1275, Silence Zone, Durango. No. 1276, Ruins, Maya city of Edzna, Campeche. No. 1277, Olmec sculpture, Tabasco.

1982, May 29 Photo. *Perf. 14*

1274 A353	80c multi		15	15
1275 A353	80c multi		15	15
1276 A353	1.60p multi		15	15
1277 A353	1.60p multi		15	15
	Set value			20

1982 World Cup A403

Designs: Various soccer players.

1982, June 13

1278 A403	1.60p	multi	16	15
1279 A403	4p	multi	20	15
1280 A403	7p	multi	24	15
		Set value		15

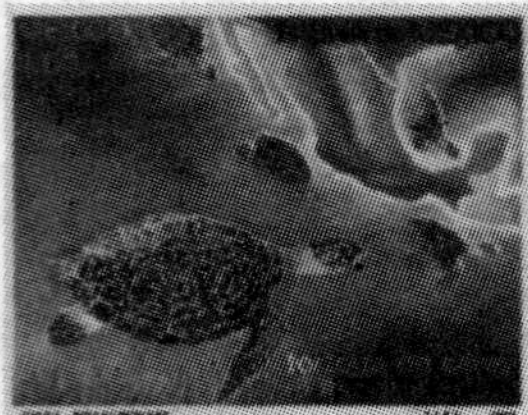
Turtles and Map A404

1982, July 3

1281 A404	1.60p	shown	20	15
1282 A404	4p	Gray whales	25	15
		Set value		15

Gen. Vicente Guerrero (1782-1831) — A405

1982, Aug. 10 Photo. *Perf. 14*

1283 A405 80c multi 15 15

2nd UN Conference on Peaceful Uses of Outer Space, Vienna, Aug. 9-21 A406

1982, Aug. 14

1284 A406 4p multi 20 15

Pre-Hispanic Art Type of 1980

Designs: 80c, Tariacuri, founder of Tarasco Kingdom, Chronicle of Michoacan, 16th cent. 1.60p, Acamapichtli, Aztec emperor, 1376-1396, Azcatitlan Codex. 4p, 10-Deer Tiger's Breastplate, wife of Lord 13-Eagle Tlaloc Copal Ball, 12th cent., Nuttal Mixtec Codex.

1982, Sept. 4

1285 A361	80c	multi	15	15
1286 A361	1.60p	multi	20	15
1287 A361	4p	multi	25	15
		Set value		15

Papaya A407

Perf. 14x14½

1982, Sept. 18 Unwmk.

1288 A407	80c	shown	15	15
1289 A407	1.60p	Corn	20	15
		Set value		15

The indexes in each volume of the Scott Catalogue contain many listings which help to identify stamps.

Florentine Codex Illustrations A408

1982, Oct. 2

1290 A408	80c	Astrologer	15	15
1291 A408	1.60p	School	15	15
1292 A408	4p	Musicians	18	15
		Set value		15

See Nos. 1520-1522.

Manuel Gamio (1883-1960) Anthropologist — A409

Scientists: No. 1294, Isaac Ochoterena (1855-1950), biologist. No. 1295, Angel Maria Garibay K. (1892-1976), philologist. No. 1296, Manuel Sandoval Vallarta (1899-), nuclear physicist. No. 1297, Guillermo Gonzalez Camarena (b. 1917), electronic engineer.

1982, Oct. 16 Photo. *Perf. 14x14½*

1293 A409	1.60p	multi	20	15
1294 A409	1.60p	multi	20	15
1295 A409	1.60p	multi	20	15
1296 A409	1.60p	multi	20	15
1297 A409	1.60p	multi	20	15
a.	Strip of 5, #1293-1297		1.25	75
	Nos. 1293-1297 (5)		1.00	
	Set value			25

Natl. Archives Opening, Aug. 27 — A410

1982, Oct. 23 *Perf. 14½x14*

1298 A410 1.60p brt grn & blk 20 15

Christmas 1982 A411

1982, Oct. 30 *Perf. 14*

1299 A411	50c	Dove	15	15
1300 A411	1.60p	Dove, diff.	20	15
		Set value		15

Mexican Food System A412

1982, Nov. 13 Photo. *Perf. 14x14½*

1301 A412 1.60p multi 20 15

Opening of Revolutionary Museum, Chihuahua — A413

1982, Nov. 17 *Perf. 14½x14*

1302 A413 1.60p No. C232 20 15

Colonial Monument Type of 1980

Designs: 1.60p, College of Sts. Peter and Paul, Mexico City, 1576. 8p, Convent of Jesus Maria, Mexico City, 1603. 10p, Open Chapel, Tlalmanalco, 1585. 14p, Convent at Actopan, Hidalgo State, 1548.

1982, Nov. 27

1303 A365	1.60p	blk & gray	20	15
1304 A365	8p	blk & gray	30	15
1305 A365	10p	blk & gray	30	15
1306 A365	14p	blk & gray	40	15
		Set value		34

Alfonso Garcia Robles, 1982 Nobel Peace Prize Winner A414

Perf. 14x14½

1982, Nov. 30 Unwmk.

1307 A414	1.60p	multi	15	15
1308 A414	14p	multi	30	15
		Set value		18

Jose Vasconcelos, Philosopher — A415

1982, Dec. 11 *Perf. 14*

1309 A415 1.60p bl & blk 20 15

World Communications Year — A416

1983, Feb. 12 Photo. *Perf. 14*
1310 A416 16p multi 30 16

I EXPOSICION FILATELICA DE LA REVOLUCION MEXICANA
HERFILEX 83

First Philatelic Exposition of the Mexican Revolution
A417

1983, Mar. 13 Photo. *Perf. 14*
1311 A417 6p No. 326 20 15

25th Anniv. of Intl. Maritime Org. — A418

1983, Mar. 17
1312 A418 16p multi 32 18

Year of Constitutional Right to Health Protection — A419

1983, Apr. 7
1313 A419 6p red & ol 20 15

Society of Geography and Statistics Sesquicentennial — A420

1983, Apr. 18
1314 A420 6p Founder Gomez Farias 20 15

2nd World Youth Soccer Championships — A421

1983, June 2 Photo. *Perf. 14*
1315 A421 6p grn & blk 20 15
1316 A421 13p red & blk 32 15
1317 A421 14p bl & blk 32 15
Set value 32

Tourism Type of 1979

Designs: No. 1318, Federal Palace Building, Queretaro. No. 1319, Fountain, San Luis Potosi. 13p, Cable car, Zacatecas. 14p, Mayan stone head, Quintana Roo.

1983, June 24 Photo. *Perf. 14*
1318 A353 6p multi 20 15
1319 A353 6p multi 20 15
1320 A353 13p multi 32 15
1321 A353 14p multi 32 15
a. Vert. strip of 4, #1318-1321 + label 1.25 1.00
Set value 38

Simon Bolivar (1783-1830) — A422

1983, July 14
1322 A422 21p multi 38 20

Angela Peralta, Opera Singer (1845-1883) — A423

1983, Photo. *Perf. 14*
1323 A423 9p multi 25 15

Mexican Flora — A424

1983, Sept. 23 Photo. *Perf. 14*
1324 A424 9p Achras zapota 25 15
1325 A424 9p Agave atrovirens 25 15
Set value 20

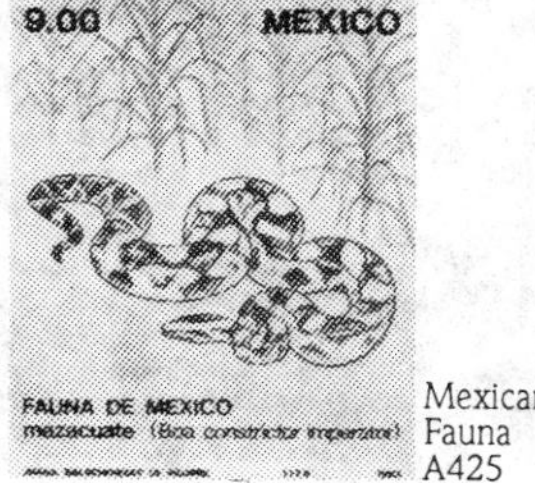

Mexican Fauna A425

1983, Sept. 23 Photo. *Perf. 14*
1326 A425 9p Boa constrictor imperator 25 15
1327 A425 9p Papilio machaon 25 15
Set value 20

Christmas 1983 — A426

1983, Oct. 15 Photo. *Perf. 14*
1328 A426 9p multi 20 15
1329 A426 20p multi 30 18

Integral Communications and Transportation Systems — A427

1983, Oct. 17 Photo. *Perf. 14*
1330 A427 13p brt bl & blk 30 15

Carlos Chavez (1899-1978), Musician, Composer A428

Contemporary Artists: No. 1332, Francisco Goitia (1882-1960), Painter. No. 1333, Salvador Diaz Miron (1853-1927), Lyrical Poet. No. 1334, Carlos Bracho (1899-1966), Sculptor. No. 1335, Fanny Anitua (1887-1968), Singer.

1983, Nov. 7 Photo. *Perf. 14*
1331 A428 9p brn & multi 24 15
1332 A428 9p brn & multi 24 15
1333 A428 9p brn & multi 24 15
1334 A428 9p brn & multi 24 15
1335 A428 9p brn & multi 24 15
a. Horiz. strip of 5, #1331-1335 1.40 1.00
Nos. 1331-1335 (5) 1.20
Set value 50

Jose Clemente Orozco (1883-1949), Painter A429

1983, Nov. 23 Photo. *Perf. 14*
1336 A429 9p multi 25 15

35th Anniv. of Human Rights Declaration A430

1983, Dec. 10 *Perf. 14*
1337 A430 20p multi 30 18

Colonial Monument Type of 1980

Designs: 9p, Convent Garden, Malinalco, 16th cent. 20p, Open Chapel, Cuernavaca Cathedral, Morelos. 21p, Tepeji del Rio Convent, Hidalgo. 24p, Atlatlahuacan Convent, Morelos.

1983, Dec. 16 Photo. *Perf. 14½x14*
1338 A365 9p blk & gray 28 15
1339 A365 20p blk & gray 40 18
1340 A365 21p blk & gray 40 20
1341 A365 24p blk & gray 40 22

Antonio Caso (1883-1946), Philosopher A431

1983, Dec. 19
Granite Paper
1342 A431 9p multi 25 15

Royal Mining Decree Bicentenary A432

1983, Dec. 21
1343 A432 9p Joaquin Velazquez Leon, reform author 25 15

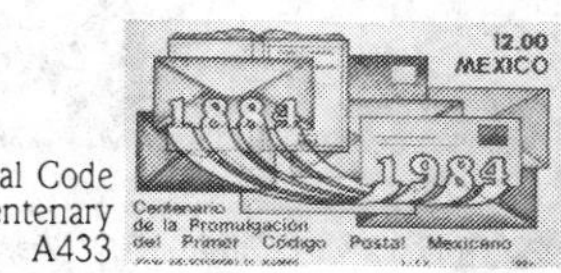

Postal Code Centenary A433

1984, Jan. 2 Photo. *Perf. 14*
1344 A433 12p Envelopes 32 15

Fight Against Polio — A434

1984, Apr. 7 Photo. *Perf. 14*
1345 A434 12p Children dancing 32 15

Aquatic Birds A435

1984, May 4 **Photo.** ***Perf. 14***

1346 A435 12p Muscovy duck 40 15
1347 A435 20p Black-bellied whistling tree duck 45 15
Set value 20

World Dog Exposition, Mexico City — A436

1984, May 27

1348 A436 12p multi 32 15

Natl. Bank of Mexico Centenary — A437

1984, June 2

1349 A437 12p multi 32 15

Forest Protection and Conservation — A438

1984, July 12 **Photo.** ***Perf. 14***

1350 A438 20p Hands holding trees 38 15

1984 Summer Olympics A439

1984, July 28

1351 A439 14p Shot put 25 15
1352 A439 20p Equestrian 28 15
1353 A439 23p Gymnastics 28 16
1354 A439 24p Diving 28 16
1355 A439 25p Boxing 30 16
1356 A439 26p Fencing 30 16

Size: 56x62mm

Imperf

1357 A439 40p Rings 52 30
Nos. 1351-1357 (7) 2.21 1.24

Mexico-Russian Diplomatic Relations, 60th Anniv. — A440

1984, Aug. 4

1358 A440 23p Flags 38 16

Intl. Population Conference, Aug. 5-14 — A441

1984, Aug. 6

1359 A441 20p UN emblem, hand 38 15

Economic Culture Fund, 50th Anniv. — A442

1984, Sept. 3

1360 A442 14p multi 30 15

Gen Francisco J. Mugica A443

1984,

1361 A443 14p blk & brn 18 15

Red Cactus, by Sebastian A444

Airline Emblem A445

1984, Sept. 14 **Photo.** ***Perf. 14x14½***

1362 A444 14p multi 15 15
1363 A445 20p blk & org 20 15

Aeromexico (airline), 50th anniv.

Palace of Fine Arts, 50th Anniv. A446

1984, Sept. 29

1364 A446 14p multi 15 15

275th Anniv. of Chihuahua City — A447

1984, Oct. 12

1365 A447 14p Cathedral exterior detail 15 15

Coatzacoalcos Bridge Inauguration — A448

1984, Oct. 17 ***Perf. 14½x14***

1366 A448 14p Aerial view 15 15

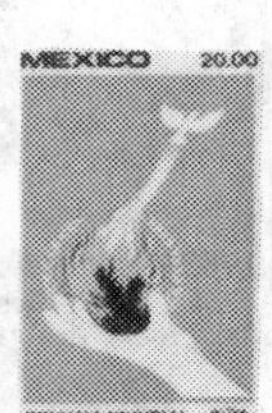

UN Disarmament Week — A449

1984, Oct. 14 **Photo.** ***Perf. 14***

1367 A449 20p multi 20 15

Christmas 1984 A450

1984, Oct. 31 **Photo.** ***Perf. 14***

1368 A450 14p Toy train & tree 15 15
1369 A450 20p Pinata breaking 20 15

Politician-Journalist Ignacio M. Altamirano (1834-1893) — A451

1984, Nov. 13 **Photo.** ***Perf. 14***

1370 A451 14p blk & lt red brn 15 15

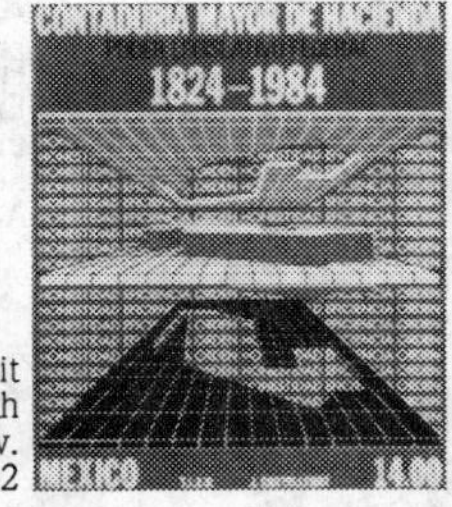

State Audit Office, 160th Anniv. A452

1984, Nov. 16

1371 A452 14p multi 15 15

1986 World Cup Soccer Championships, Mexico — A453

1984, Nov. 19

1372 A453 20p multi *16 15*
1373 A453 24p multi *20 15*
a. Pair, #1372-1373 + label *40 40*

Romulo Gallegos (1884-1969), Author and Former Pres. of Venezuela — A454

1984, Dec. 6

1374 A454 20p bl & gray 20 15

State Registry Office, 125th Anniv. A455

1984, Dec. 13

1375 A455 24p slate blue 24 18

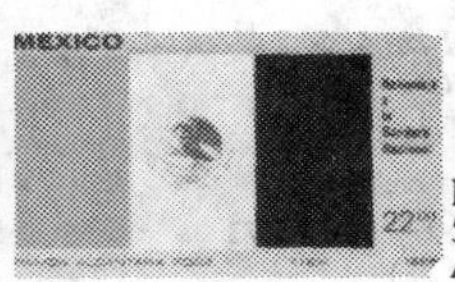

Natl. Flag, 50th Anniv. A456

1985, Feb. 24
1376 A456 22p multi 22 16

Johann Sebastian Bach — A457

Intl. Youth Year — A458

1985, Mar. 21 **Photo.** ***Perf. 14***
1377 A457 35p dl red brn, gold & blk 24 18

1985, Mar. 28 **Photo.** ***Perf. 14***
1378 A458 35p rose vio, gold & blk 24 18

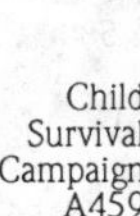

Child Survival Campaign A459

1985, Mar. 28 **Photo.** ***Perf. 14***
1379 A459 36p multi 24 18

Mexican Mint, 450th Anniv. A460

1985, May 11 **Photo.** ***Perf. 14***
1380 A460 35p 1st gold & copper coins 24 18

Victor Hugo A461

1985, May 22 **Photo.** ***Perf. 14***
1381 A461 35p slate 24 18

MEXFIL '85 — A462

1985, June 9 **Photo.** ***Perf. 14***
1382 A462 22p No. 5 15 15
1383 A462 35p No. 574 22 18
1384 A462 36p No. 1081 24 18

Souvenir Sheet

1985, June 27 ***Imperf.***
1385 A462 90p No. 111 on cover 50 35

Morelos Telecommunications Satellite Launch — A463

1985, June 17 ***Perf. 14x14½***
1386 A463 22p Shuttle launch 15 15
1387 A463 36p Ground receiver 20 18
1388 A463 90p Modes of communication 50 38
a. Strip of 3, #1386-1388 + 2 labels 1.25 1.00

Souvenir Sheet
Imperf

1389 A463 100p multi 60 45

Nos. 1386-1388 has continuous design. No. 1389 pictures uninscribed continuous design of Nos. 1386-1388.

9th World Forestry Congress, Mexico City, July 1-9 — A464

1985, July 1 ***Perf. 14x14½***
1390 A464 22p Conifer 15 15
1391 A464 35p Silk-cotton tree 18 15
1392 A464 36p Mahogany 20 16
a. Strip of 3, #1390-1392 + 2 labels 1.25 1.00
Set value 38

Martin Luis Guzman (1887-1977), Journalist, Politician A465

Contemporary writers: No. 1394, Agustin Yanez (1904-1980), politician. No. 1395, Alfonso Reyes (1889-1959), diplomat. No. 1396, Jose Ruben Romero (1890-1952), diplomat. No. 1397, Artemio de Valle Arizpe (1888-1961), historian.

1985, July 19 ***Perf. 14***
1393 A465 22p multi 15 15
1394 A465 22p multi 15 15
1395 A465 22p multi 15 15
1396 A465 22p multi 15 15
1397 A465 22p multi 15 15
a. Strip of 5, #1393-1397 75 75
Set value 50 50

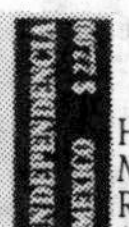

Heroes of the Mexican Revolution, 1810 — A466

1985, Sept. 15
1398 A466 22p Miguel Hidalgo 15 15
1399 A466 35p Jose Morelos 15 15
1400 A466 35p Ignacio Allende 15 15
1401 A466 36p Leona Vicario 18 18
1402 A466 110p Vicente Guerrero 50 50
Nos. 1398-1402 (5) 1.13 1.13

Souvenir Sheet
Imperf

1403 A466 90p Bell, church 40 30

175th anniv. of independence from Spanish rule. #1403 contains one 56x49mm stamp.

University of Mexico, 75th Anniv. A467

1985, Sept. 22 **Photo.** ***Perf. 14x14½***
1404 A467 26p San Ildefonso, 1910 15 15
1405 A467 26p University emblem 15 15
1406 A467 40p Rectory, 1985 22 18
1407 A467 45p 1st Rector Justo Sierra, crest, 1910 25 20
1408 A467 90p Crest, 1985 50 38
a. Strip of 5, #1404-1407 1.50 1.00
Nos. 1404-1408 (5) 1.27 1.06

Interamerican Development Bank, 25th Anniv. — A468

1985, Oct. 23 **Photo.** ***Perf. 14½x14***
1409 A468 26p multi 15 15

UN Disarmament Week A469

1985, Oct. 24 ***Perf. 14x14½***
1410 A469 36p Guns, doves 20 15

UN, 40th Anniv. — A470

1985, Oct. 25 ***Perf. 14½x14***
1411 A470 26p Hand, dove 15 15

Christmas 1985 A471

Children's drawings.

1985, Nov. 15 **Photo.** ***Perf. 14x14½***
1412 A471 26p multi 15 15
1413 A471 35p multi 15 15
Set value 22

1910 Revolution, 75th Anniv. A472

1985, Nov. 18 ***Perf. 14***
1414 A472 26p Soldadera 15 15
1415 A472 35p Francisco Villa 15 15
1416 A472 40p Emiliano Zapata 16 15
1417 A472 45p Venustiano Carranza 18 15
1418 A472 110p Francisco Madero 32 25
Nos. 1414-1418 (5) 96 85

Souvenir Sheet
Imperf

1419 A472 90p Liberty bell 35 28

No. 1419 contains one 48x40mm stamp.

Astronaut, by Sebastian A473

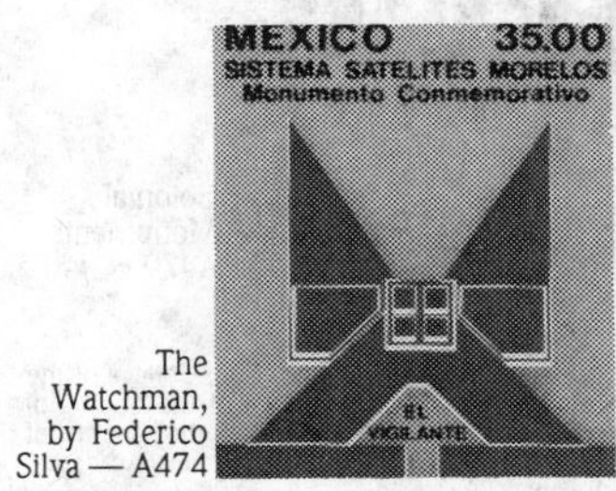

The Watchman, by Federico Silva — A474

Mexican Astronaut, Rodolfo Neri, by Cauduro — A475

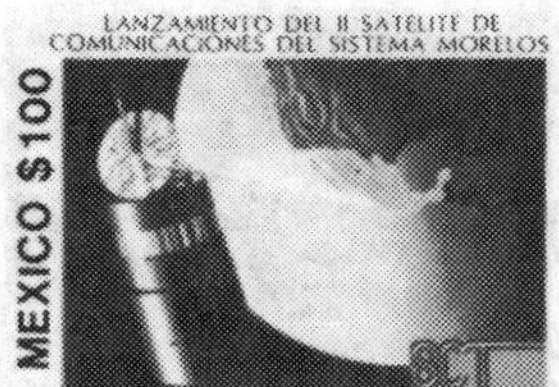

Morelos and Telecommunications Satellite Launch — A476

1985, Nov. 26 *Perf. 14x14½*

1420 A473 26p multi 15 15
1421 A474 35p multi 15 15
1422 A475 45p multi 18 15
Set value 36

Miniature Sheet

Imperf

1423 A476 100p multi 35 28

1986 World Cup Soccer Championships, Mexico — A477

1985, Dec. 15 Photo. *Perf. 14½x14*

1424 A477 26p Olympic Stadium 15 15
1425 A477 45p Aztec Stadium 20 15

1st Free Textbook for Primary Education, 25th Anniv. — A478

1985, Dec. 16

1426 A478 26p Book cover 15 15

Colonial Monuments A479

Landmarks in Mexico City: 26p, College of the Vizcainas, c. 1735. 35p, Palace of the Counts of Heras and Soto. 40p, Palace of the Counts of Calimaya, 16th cent. 45p, San Carlos Academy, 16th cent.

1985, Dec. 27 *Perf. 14x14½*

1427 A479 26p grnsh blk & fawn 15 15
1428 A479 35p grnsh blk & fawn 16 15
1429 A479 40p grnsh blk & fawn 18 15
1430 A479 45p grnsh blk & fawn 20 15
a. Strip of 4, #1427-1430 + label 1.00 75
Set value 50

Natl. Polytechnic Institute, 50th Anniv. A480

1986, Feb. 7 *Perf. 14*

1431 A480 40p Luis Enrique Erro Planetarium 15 15
1432 A480 65p School of Arts & Communications 24 20
1433 A480 75p Emblem, founders 28 24
a. Strip of 3, #1431-1433 + 2 labels 90 75

Fruit — A481

1986, Feb. 21 *Perf. 14½x14*

1434 A481 40p Cucurbita pepo 18 15
1435 A481 65p Nopalea coccinelifera 30 24

World Health Day — A482

1986, Apr. 7 Photo. *Perf. 14*

1436 A482 65p Doll 20 16

Halley's Comet A483

1986, Apr. 25

1437 A483 90p multi 25 20

Natl. Geology Institute, Cent. A484

1986, May 26

1438 A484 40p multi 16 15

1986 World Cup Soccer Championships — A485

Paintings by Angel Zarraga (1886-1946) and Sergio Guerrero Morales: 30p, Three Soccer Players with Cap. 40p, Portrait of Ramon Novaro. 65p, Dimanche. 70p, Portrait of Ernest Charles Gimpel. 90p, Three Soccer Players. 110p, Poster for 1986 championships, by Morales.

1986, May 31

1439 A485 30p multi 15 15
1440 A485 40p multi 16 15
1441 A485 65p multi 25 18
1442 A485 70p multi 28 22
1443 A485 90p multi 35 28

Size: 120x91mm

Imperf

1444 A485 110p multi 35 25
Nos. 1439-1444 (6) 1.54 1.23

Independence War Heroes A486

175th Death anniv. of: 40p, Ignacio Allende (1769-1811). 65p, Juan Aldama (1774-1811). 75p, Mariano Jimenez (1781-1811).

1986, June 26 Photo. *Perf. 14*

1445 A486 40p multi 15 15
1446 A486 65p multi 22 16
1447 A486 75p multi 25 18

Miguel Hidalgo y Costilla (1753-1811), Mural by Jose Clemente Orozco A487

1986, July 30 Photo. *Perf. 14*

1448 A487 40p multi 15 15

Federal Tax Court, 50th Anniv. — A488

Gen. Nicolas Bravo (1786-1854) — A489

1986, Aug. 27 *Perf. 14½x14*

1449 A488 40p gray, bl & blk 15 15

1986, Sept. 10 *Perf. 14*

1450 A489 40p multi 15 15

Paintings by Diego Rivera — A490

Designs: 50p, Paisaje Zapatista, 1915, vert. 80p, Desnudo con Alcatraces, 1944, vert. 110p, Sueno de una Tarde Dominical en la Alameda Central, 1947-48.

Perf. 14x14½, 14½x14

1986, Sept. 26

1451 A490 50p multi 15 15
1452 A490 80p multi 22 18
1453 A490 110p multi 32 25

See Nos. 1571-1573.

Guadalupe Victoria (1786-1843), 1st President — A491

1986, Sept. 29 *Perf. 14½x14*

1454 A491 50p multi 15 15

Natl. Storage Warehouse, 50th Anniv. — A492

1986, Oct. 3

1455 A492 40p multi 15 15

Intl. Post Day — A493

1986, Oct. 9 *Perf. 14x14½*

1456 A493 120p multi 25 20

Natl. Committee Commemorating the 500th Anniv. (1992) of the Meeting of Two Worlds — A494

1986, Oct. 12 *Perf. 14½x14*

1457 A494 50p blk & lake 15 15

15th Pan American Highways Congress, Mexico City — A495

1986, Oct. 17 Photo. *Perf. 14x14½*

1458 A495 80p Palacio de Mineria 18 16

Franz Liszt, Composer, 175th Birth Anniv. — A496

1986, Oct. 22 *Perf. 14½x14*

1459 A496 100p blk & brn 22 18

Intl. Peace Year A497

1986, Oct. 24

1460 A497 80p blk, bl & dk red 18 16

Interment of Pino Suarez in the Rotunda of Illustrious Men — A498

1986, Nov. 6

1461 A498 50p multi 15 15

Jose Maria Pino Suarez, vice-president of 1st revolutionary government, 1911.

See Nos. 1472, 1475, 1487, 1563.

Christmas — A499

Clay figurines from Tonala, Jalisco.

1986, Nov. 28

1462 A499 50p King 15 15
1463 A499 80p Angel 15 15

Diego Rivera (1886-1957), Painter A500

1986, Dec. 4 **Photo.** *Perf. 14x14½*

1464 A500 80p Self-portrait 18 15

Export Type of 1975

Designs as before and: 60p, Men's shoes. 70p, Copperware. 80p, Denim overalls. 90p, Abalone. 100p, Cup of coffee.

1986-87 **Unwmk.** *Perf. 11½x11*

1465 A320 20p gray 15 15

Perf. 14

1466 A320 40p pale grn & gold 15 15

Perf. 11½x11

1467 A320 60p brown 15 15

Perf. 14

1468 A320 70p org brn 20 20
a. Perf. 11½x11 20 20
1469 A320 80p blue 20 20
1470 A320 90p grn & bl 22 22
1470A A320 100p brown ('88) 40 20
b. 100p dark brown, perf. 11½x11 ('87) 40 30
Nos. 1465-1470A (7) 1.47 1.27

Natl. Polio Vaccination Program, Jan. 24-Mar. 28 — A501

1987, Jan. 20 **Photo.** *Perf. 14½x14*

1471 A501 50p Oral vaccine 15 15

Rotunda of Illustrious Men Type of 1986

1987, Feb. 4

1472 A498 100p multi 28 22

Jose Maria Iglesias (1823-1891), president in 1876.

Natl. Teachers' College, 100th Anniv. A503

1987, Feb. 24 *Perf. 14x14½*

1473 A503 100p multi 28 22

Exploration of Pima Indian Territory by Eusebio Francisco Kino, 300th Anniv. — A504

1987, Feb. 27 *Perf. 14½x14*

1474 A504 100p multi 28 22

Rotunda of Illustrious Men Type of 1986

1987, Mar. 20 **Photo.** *Perf. 14*

1475 A498 100p Pedro Sainz de Baranda 28 22

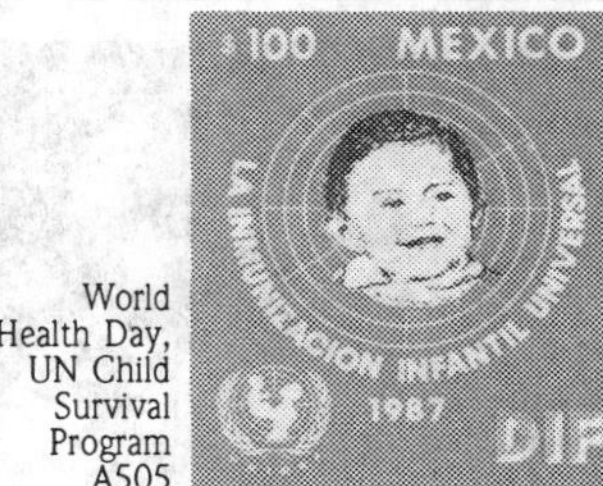

World Health Day, UN Child Survival Program A505

1987, Apr. 7

1476 A505 100p blue & slate blue 28 22

Autonomous University of Puebla, 50th Anniv. A506

1987, Apr. 23

1477 A506 200p multi 48 35

Battle of Puebla, 125th Anniv. — A507

1987, May 5 **Photo.** *Perf. 14½x14*

1478 A507 100p multi 24 18

METROPOLIS '87 — A508

1987, May 19

1479 A508 310p gray blk, grn & red 65 45

Cong. of metropolitan areas, Mexico City.

Handicrafts A509

Designs: 100p, Lacquerware tray, Uruapan, Michoacan. 200p, Blanket, Santa Ana Chiautempan, Tlaxcala. 230p, Lidded jar, Puebla, Pue.

1987, May 29 **Photo.** *Perf. 14*

1480 A509 100p multi 22 15
1481 A509 200p multi 45 32
1482 A509 230p multi 50 38

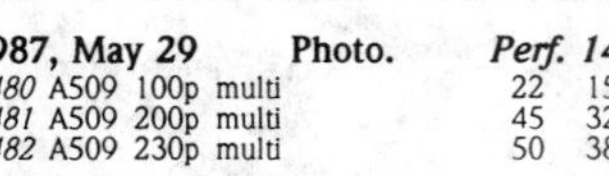

Genaro Estrada, (1887-1937) Political Reformer — A510

1987, June 2

1483 A510 100p pale pink, blk & pale rose 22 16

See Nos. 1509, 1568-1569.

Native Traders, 1961, Mural by P. O'Higgins A511

1987, June 8

1484 A511 100p multi 22 16

Nat'l. Bank of Int'l. Commerce, 50th anniv.

Publication of the 1st Shipbuilding Manual in the Americas, by Diego Garcia Palacio, 400th Anniv. A512

1987, June 15

1485 A512 100p multi 22 16

Nat'l. Food Program, 50th Anniv. A513

1987, June 22

1486 A513 100p multi 22 16

Rotunda of Illustrious Men Type of 1986

1987, June 22

1487 A498 100p multi 22 16

Leandro Valle (1833-1861), revolution leader.

A particular stamp may be scarce, but if few collectors want it, its market value may remain relatively low.

Paintings by Saturnino Herran (1887-1918) A514

1917 paintings: No. 1488, Self-portrait with Skull. No. 1489, The Offering. No. 1490, Creole Woman with Mantilla.

1987, July 9
1488 A514 100p blk & red brn 24 18
1489 A514 100p multi 24 18
1490 A514 400p multi 95 75

Export Type of 1975

Designs: 10p, Meat cuts marked on steer. 20p, Bicycle. 50p, Tomatoes. 300p, Motor vehicle. 500p, Petroleum valves. 600p, Jewelry. 700p, Film. 800p, Construction materials. 900p, Pistons. 1,000p, Agricultural machinery. 2,000p, Wrought iron. 3,000p, Electric wiring. 4,000p, Honey. 5,000p, Cotton.

1987-88 Photo. *Perf. 14*
1491 A320 10p brt car 15 15
1492 A320 20p blk & org 15 15
1493 A320 50p verm & yel grn 15 15
1494 A320 300p chalky blue & scar, type I ('88) 30 15
1495 A320 300p Prus blue & brt rose ('88) 30 15
1496 A320 500p dark gray & Prus blue ('88) 48 25
1497 A320 600p multi ('88) 58 30
1498 A320 700p brt yel grn, dark red & blk ('88) 68 35
a. Brt yel grn, lil rose & blk ('88) 68 35
1499 A320 800p dark red brn & golden brn ('88) 78 40
1500 A320 900p blk ('88) 88 45

Wmk. 300
Granite Paper
Type I Burelage in Gray

1501 A320 1000p dark red & blk ('88) 98 50
1502 A320 2000p blk ('88) 1.95 1.00
1503 A320 3000p gray blk & org ('88) 2.90 1.45
1504 A320 4000p yel org & red brn ('88) 3.85 1.90
1505 A320 5000p apple grn & org ('88) 4.75 2.40
Nos. 1491-1505 (15) 18.88 9.75

See No. 1590 for No. 1501 without burelage.

A515

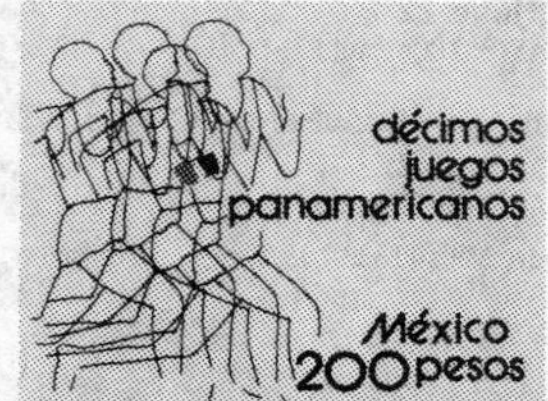

10th Pan American Games, Indianapolis — A516

Perf. 14¹/₂x14
1987, Aug. 7 Photo. Unwmk.
1506 A515 100p multi 15 15
1507 A516 200p blk, brt grn & dark red 24 20

Federal Power Commission, 50th Anniv. A517

1987, Aug. 14 Photo. *Perf. 14x14¹/₂*
1508 A517 200p multi 28 22

Art and Science Type of 1987

Design: J.E. Hernandez y Davalos (1827-1893), historian.

1987, Aug. 25 *Perf. 14¹/₂x14*
1509 A510 100p buff, blk & dull red brn 15 15

Pre-Hispanic Art Type of 1980

Designs: 100p, Xolotl (d. 1232), king of Amaquemecan. 200p, Nezahualpilli (1460-1516), king of Texcoco, conqueror. 400p, Motecuhzoma Ilhuicamina (Montezuma I d. 1469), emperor of Tenochtitlan (1440-1469).

1987, Aug. 31 *Perf. 14x14¹/₂*
1510 A361 100p multi 18 15
1511 A361 200p multi 35 28
1512 A361 400p multi 72 35

Tourism Type of 1979

Designs: 100p, Central Public Library, Mexico State. No. 1514, Patzcuaro Harbor, Michoacan. No. 1515, Garcia Caverns, Nuevo Leon. No. 1516, Beach resort, Mazatlan, Sinaloa.

1987 *Perf. 14¹/₂x14*
1513 A353 100p multi 15 15
1514 A353 150p multi 18 15
1515 A353 150p multi 18 15
1516 A353 150p multi 18 15
Set value 52

Issue dates: 100p, Sept. 11. Others, Oct. 19.

Formula 1 Grand Prix Race, Oct. 18 A518

1987, Sept. 11
1517 A518 100p multi 15 15

13th Intl. Cartography Conference — A519

1987, Oct. 12
1518 A519 150p Map, 16th cent. 18 15

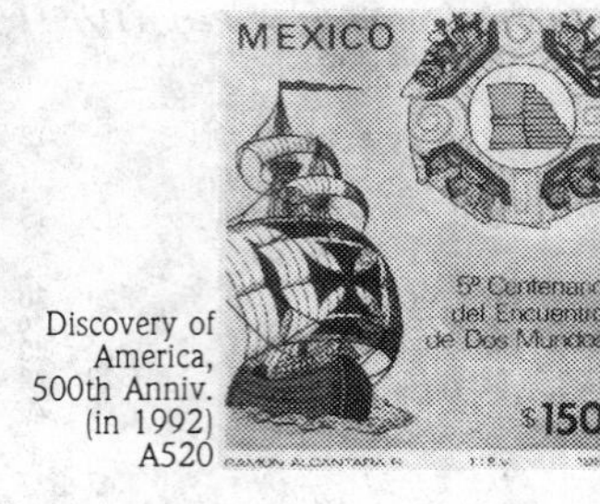

Discovery of America, 500th Anniv. (in 1992) A520

Design: Santa Maria, emblem of the Discovery of America Festival to be held in 1992.

1987, Oct. 12 *Perf. 14x14¹/₂*
1519 A520 150p multi 18 15

For overprint see No. 1698.

Illuminated Codices Type of 1982

Mendocino Codex (c. 1541): No. 1520, Founding of Tenochtitlan by the Aztecs, 1324. No. 1521, Pre-Hispanic wedding. No. 1522, Montezuma's Council.

1987, Nov. 3
1520 A408 150p multi 18 15
1521 A408 150p multi 18 15
1522 A408 150p multi 18 15

Christmas 1987 — A521

1987, Nov. 6
1523 A521 150p brt pink 18 15
1524 A521 150p dull blue 18 15

World Post Day — A522

Documents: 150p, Ordinance for expediting mail by sea, 1777. 600p, Roster of correspondence transported by coach, 1857.

1987, Nov. 12
1525 A522 150p pale gray & slate gray 18 15

Size: 129x102mm

Imperf

1526 A522 600p rose lake & yel bis 75 55

Meeting of Eight Latin American Presidents, 1st Anniv. — A523

1987, Nov. 26 *Perf. 14¹/₂x14*
1527 A523 250p shown 25 18
1528 A523 500p Flags, peace doves 50 38

Dualidad 1964, by Rufino Tamayo (b. 1899) — A524

1987, Dec. 9
1529 A524 150p multi 18 15

Nationalization of Mexican Railroads, 50th Anniv. — A525

1987, Dec. 15
1530 A525 150p Metlac Bridge 18 15

Antonio Stradivarius (c. 1644-1737), Italian Violin Maker A526

1987, Dec. 18 *Perf. 14x14¹/₂*
1531 A526 150p bluish lil 18 15

Constitutional Tribunal of the Supreme Court, Plenum Hall, Jan. 15 — A527

Design: Statue of Manuel Rejon, author of the Mexican constitution.

1988, Jan. 15 Photo. *Perf. 14x14¹/₂*
1532 A527 300p multi 35 28

Fauna A528

1988, Feb. 29 Photo. *Perf. 14*
1533 A528 300p *Ambystoma mexicanum* 30 22
1534 A528 300p *Trichechus manatus* 30 22

A529

Nationalization of the Petroleum Industry, 50th Anniv. — A530

1988, Mar. 18

1535 A529 300p blue & blk 30 22
1536 A530 300p PEMEX emblem, vert. 30 22
1537 A530 500p shown 45 35

Vaccination, Detroit, 1932, Mural (detail) by Diego Rivera — A531

1988, Apr. 7

1538 A531 300p olive grn & henna brn 35 25

World Health Day: child immunization.

The People in Pursuit of Health, 1953, by Diego Rivera A532

1988, Apr. 7

1539 A532 300p multi 35 25

World Health Organization, 40th anniv.

Vallejo in Repose (Large) A533

Vallejo in Repose (Small) A534

1988, Apr. 15

1540 A533 300p shown 32 22
1541 A533 300p Portrait, diff. (large) 32 22
b. Bklt. pane of 4 (2 each #1540-1541) + label
1542 A534 300p shown 32 22
1543 A534 300p As #1541 (small) 32 22

Cesar Vallejo (1892-1938), Peruvian poet. Stamps of the same type printed se-tenant in sheets of 20 stamps containing 10 pairs plus 5 labels between inscribed with various Vallejo quotes or commemorative text.

Issue date: No. 1541b, Nov. 9, 1990. Label in No. 1541b is overprinted in red with Mexican Chicagopex '90 souvenir cancel.

Sketch of Carlos Pellicer Camara (1897-1977), Poet, by Fontanelly — A535

1988, Apr. 23

1544 A535 300p pale vio, blk & sal 35 25

MEPSIRREY '88 Philatelic Exhibition, Monterrey, May 27-29 — A536

1988, May 27

1545 A536 300p Youth collectors 35 25
1546 A536 300p Handstamped cover 35 25
1547 A536 500p Emblem 55 42

Mexico-Elmhurst Philatelic Society Intl. (MEPSI).

1988 Formula I Championships, Mexico — A537

Design: Layout of Hermanos Rodriguez race track, Mexico City, and car.

1988, May 28 Photo. *Perf. 14*

1548 A537 500p multi 48 35

A538

Ramon Lopez Velarde (1888-1921), Poet A539

1988, June 15

1549 A538 300p multi 30 22
1550 A539 300p multi 30 22
a. Bklt. pane of 4 + label

Issue date: No. 1550a, Nov. 9, 1990. Label in No. 1550a is overprinted in red with Mexican Chicagopex '90 souvenir cancel.

University Military Pentathlon, 50th Anniv. — A540

1988, July 9 Photo. *Perf. 14*

1551 A540 300p multi 30 22

1st Mexico-Japan Friendship, Commerce and Navigation Treaty, Cent. — A541

1988, Aug. 16

1552 A541 500p multi 48 35

Joint Oceanographic Assembly, Acapulco, Aug. 23-31 — A542

1988, Aug. 23

1553 A542 500p multi 48 35

1988 Summer Olympics, Seoul — A543

1988, Aug. 31 Photo. *Perf. 14½x14*

1554 A543 500p multi 48 35

Size: 71x55mm

Imperf

1555 A543 700p Emblems, torch 68 52

World Boxing Council, 25th Anniv. A544

1988, Sept. 9

1556 A544 500p multi 48 35

Intl. Red Cross and Red Crescent Organizations, 125th Annivs. A545

1988, Sept. 23 Photo. *Perf. 14x14½*

1557 A545 300p blk, gray & scar 30 22

Jose Guadalupe Posada (1852-1913), Painter, Illustrator — A546

1988, Sept. 29

1558 A546 300p sil & blk 30 22

World Wildlife Fund — A547

Various monarch butterflies, *Danaus plexippus.*

1988, Sept. 30 *Perf. 14½x14*

1559 A547 300p shown 30 22
1560 A547 300p Three adults 30 22
1561 A547 300p Larva, adult, pupa 30 22
1562 A547 300p Five adults 30 22

Rotunda of Illustrious Men Type of 1986

Portrait and eternal flame: Manuel Sandoval Vallarta (1899-1977), physicist.

1988, Oct. 5

1563 A498 300p multi 30 22

World Post Day A548

1988, Oct. 9 *Perf. 14x14½*

1564 A548 500p World map 48 35

Size: 75x44mm

Imperf

1565 A548 700p Envelope, doves, Earth 68 52

Discovery of America, 500th Anniv. (in 1992) — A549

Illuminations: Aztec painter Tlacuilo from the Mendocine Codex, 1541, and Dominican scribe from the Yanhuitlan Codex, 1541-50.

1988, Oct. 12 ***Perf. 14½x14***
1566 A549 500p multi 48 35

World Food Day — A550

1988, Oct. 15 ***Perf. 14x14½***
1567 A550 500p multi 48 35

Art and Science Type of 1987

Designs: No. 1568, Alfonso Caso (1896-1970), educator, founder of the Natl. Museum of Anthropology. No. 1569, Vito Alessio Robles (1879-1957), historian.

1988, Oct. 24 ***Perf. 14½x14***
1568 A510 300p gray & blk 30 22
1569 A510 300p pale yel, blk & red brn 30 22

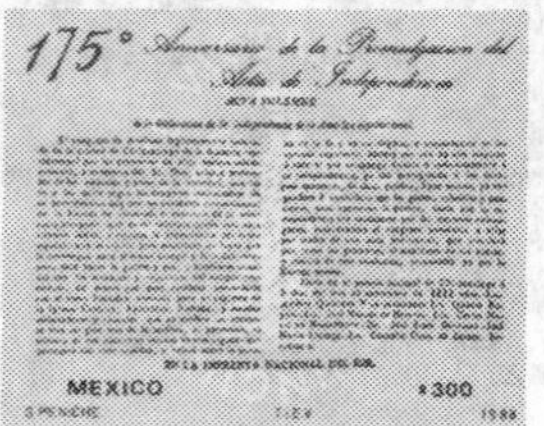

Act of Independence, 175th Anniv. — A551

1988, Nov. 9
1570 A551 300p claret brn & fawn 30 22

Art Type of 1986

Paintings by Antonio M. Ruiz (1895-1964): No. 1571, *Parade*, 1936. No. 1572, *La Malinche*, 1939. No. 1573, *Self-portrait*, 1925, vert.

Perf. 14½x14, 14x14½
1988, Nov. 21
1571 A490 300p multi 30 22
1572 A490 300p multi 30 22
1573 A490 300p multi 30 22

Tempera and Oil Paintings by Jose Reyes (b. 1924) A552

Perf. 14x14½, 14½x14
1988, Nov. 25
1574 A552 300p Feast 30 22
1575 A552 300p Pinata, vert. 30 22

Christmas.

For unused stamps, more recent issues are valued as never hinged, with the beginning point determined on a country-by-country basis. Notes to show the beginning points are prominently placed in the text.

Municipal Workers' Trade Union, 50th Anniv. A553

1988, Dec. 5 ***Perf. 14x14½***
1576 A553 300p pale bister & blk 30 22

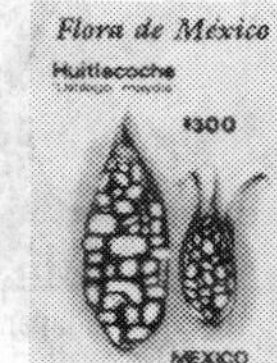

Flora — A554

1988, Dec. 20 ***Perf. 14½x14***
1577 A554 300p *Ustilago maydis* 30 22
1578 A554 300p *Mimosa tenuiflora* 30 22

Exporta Type of 1975

Designs: 40p, 1400p, Chemistry flasks. 200p, Citrus fruit. 450p, Circuit board. 750p, Film. 950p, Pistons. 1000p, Agricultural machinery. 1100p, Minerals. 1300p, Strawberries. 1500p, Copper vase. 1600p, Steel pipes. 1700p, Tequila. 1900p, Abalone. 2000p, Wrought iron. 2100p, Bicycles. 2500p, Overalls. 5000p, Cotton.
#1600, 1602-1603 have gray burelage Type I.

1988-92 Photo. Unwmk. ***Perf. 14***

No.	Type	Value	Color	Unused	Used
1583	A320	40p	black	15	15
1584	A320	200p	emer & brt yel	20	15
a.			Thin paper	20	15
1585	A320	450p	yel bister & lil rose	45	22
a.			Thin paper	45	22
1586	A320	750p	brt yel grn, dark red & dark gray	75	38
1587	A320	950p	indigo	95	42
a.			Thin paper	95	42
1588	A320	1000p	dark red & blk	70	40
1589	A320	1100p	dark gray, type I	1.10	55
1590	A320	1100p	dark gray, type II	1.10	55
1591	A320	1300p	red & grn	90	62
1592	A320	1300p	red & grn, type I	90	62
1593	A320	1400p	black	95	66
1594	A320	1500p	tan	1.00	70
a.			1500p orange brown	1.00	70
1595	A320	1600p	red orange	1.05	72
1596	A320	1700p	dk grn & yel grn	1.15	80
1597	A320	1900p	bl grn & bl	1.30	90
1598	A320	2000p	black	1.50	1.10
1599	A320	2100p	black & orange	1.65	82
1600	A320	2100p	black & ver	1.55	1.15
1601	A320	2500p	dark blue	2.00	1.40
1602	A320	2500p	slate blue, no burelage	1.85	1.35
1603	A320	5000p	apple grn & org, type I	3.60	2.70
			Nos. 1583-1603 (21)	24.80	16.36

Issue dates: 40p, Jan. 5. 200p, Feb. 27, 1989. 450p, Feb. 10, 1989. No. 1585a, 950p, Nos. 1587a, 1589, Mar. 30, 1989. 1,000p, 1989. Nos. 1590, 1599, 1601, 1991. Nos. 1600, 1602, 5000p, 1992. Others, 1990.

Graphic Arts Workshop, 50th Anniv. A555

1989, Feb. 9 Photo. ***Perf. 14***
1604 A555 450p yel bis, red & blk 45 35

Coat of Arms and *E Santo Domingo*, the Natl. Hymn — A556

1989, Feb. 27
1605 A556 450p multi 45 35

Dominican Republic independence, 145th anniv.

Intl. Border and Territorial Waters Commission of Mexico and the US, Cent. — A557

1989, Mar. 1
1606 A557 1100p multi 1.10 80

10th Intl. Book Fair — A558

1989, Mar. 4
1607 A558 450p UNAM School of Engineering 45 35

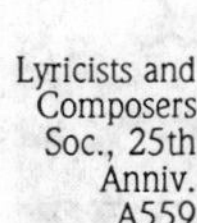

Lyricists and Composers Soc., 25th Anniv. A559

1989, Mar. 17
1608 A559 450p multi 45 35

World Day for the Fight Against AIDS A560

1989, Apr. 7
1609 A560 450p multi 45 35

Leona Vicario (1779-1842), Heroine of the Independence Movement A561

Alfonso Reyes (1879-1959), Author, Educator A562

1989, Apr. 20 Photo. ***Perf. 14***
1610 A561 450p blk, sepia & golden brn 45 35

1989, May 17
1611 A562 450p multi 45 35

Formula 1 Grand Prix of Mexico — A563

1989, May 28 ***Perf. 14***
1612 A563 450p multi 45 35

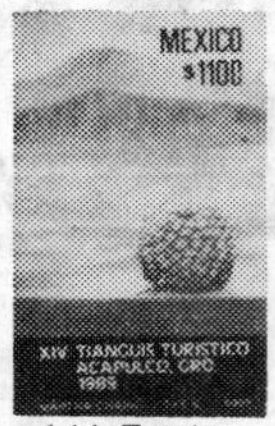

14th Tourism Congress, Acapulco — A564

14th Intl. Gerontology Congress, Mexico — A565

1989, June 11 ***Perf. 14***
1613 A564 1100p multi 1.10 80

1989, June 18

Statue: The god Huehueteotl as an old man bearing the weight of the world on his shoulders.

1614 A565 450p multi 45 35

Battle of Zacatecas, 75th Anniv. — A566

1989, June 23
1615 A566 450p black 45 35

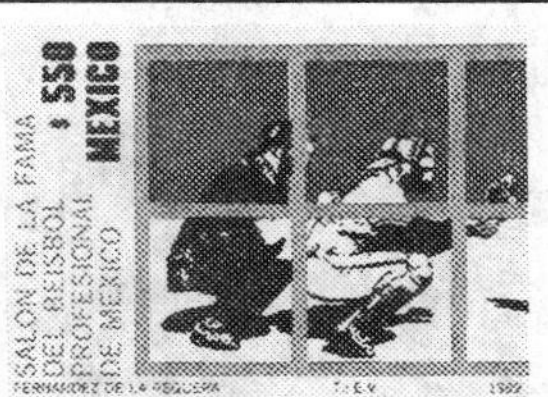
Baseball Hall of Fame of Mexico — A567

1989, June 25

1616 A567 550p Umpire, catcher	55	42
1617 A567 550p Batter	55	42
a. Pair, #1616-1617 + label	1.25	1.25

No. 1617a has continuous design.

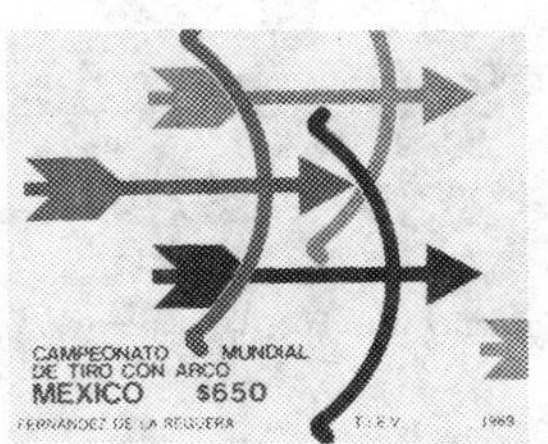
35th World Archery Championships, Lausanne, Switzerland, July 4-8 — A568

1989, July 2

1618 A568 650p Bows and arrows	65	50
1619 A568 650p Arrows, target	65	50
a. Pair, #1618-1619 + label	1.50	1.50

No. 1619a has continuous design.

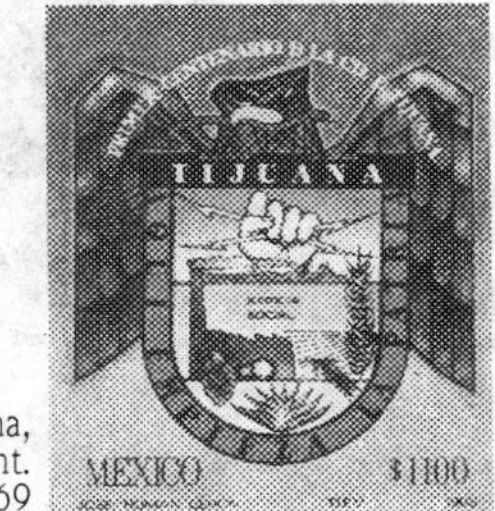
Tijuana, Cent. A569

1989, July 11 Photo. *Perf. 14x14½*

1620 A569 1100p Municipal arms 90 68

French Revolution, Bicent. A570

1989, July 14

1621 A570 1300p blue, blk & dark red 1.10 80

Gen. Francisco Xavier Mina (1789-1817), Revolution Martyr A571

1989, Sept. 7

1622 A571 450p green, blk & dark red 38 28

Natl. Museum of Anthropology, Chapultepec, 25th Anniv. — A572

1989, Sept. 17 *Perf. 14½x14*

1623 A572 450p multicolored 38 28

7th Mexico City Marathon — A573

1989, Sept. 24

1624 A573 450p multicolored 38 28

Printing in America, 450th Anniv. — A574

1989, Sept. 28

1625 A574 450p multicolored 38 28

World Post Day A575

1989, Oct. 9 Photo. *Perf. 14*

1626 A575 1100p multicolored 82 62

Sovereign Revolutionary Convention of Aguascalientes, 75th Anniv. — A576

1989, Oct. 10

1627 A576 450p multicolored 35 25

Exploration and Colonization of the Americas by Europeans A577

1989, Oct. 12

1628 A577 1300p multicolored 98 72

America Issue — A578

UPAE emblem and symbols like those produced on art by pre-Columbian peoples.

1989, Oct. 12

1629 A578 450p shown	35	25
1630 A578 450p multi, diff., vert.	35	25

Natl. Tuberculosis Foundation, 50th Anniv. — A579

1989, Nov. 10

1631 A579 450p multicolored 35 25

Mask of the Bat God, Zapoteca Culture, c. 200-300 A580

1989, Nov. 28

1632 A580 450p multicolored 35 25

Serfin Commercial Bank of Mexico, 125th Anniv. A581

1989, Nov. 29

1633 A581 450p deep blue, gold & blk 35 25

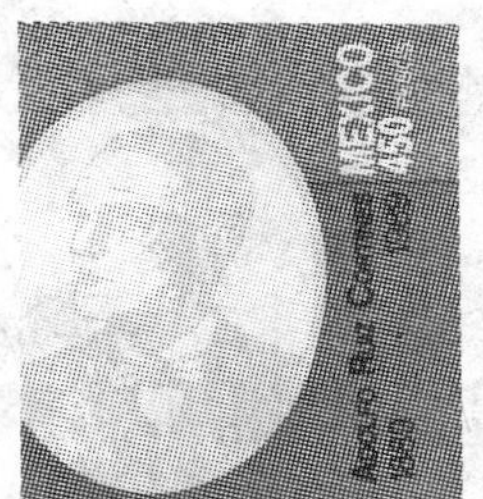
Pres. Adolfo Ruiz Cortines (1889-1973) — A582

1989, Dec. 3

1634 A582 450p multicolored 35 25

Christmas A583

1989, Dec. 11

1635 A583 450p Candlelight vigil	35	25
1636 A583 450p Man sees star, vert.	35	25

Natl. Institute of Anthropology and Natural History, 50th Anniv. — A584

1989, Dec. 13

1637 A584 450p dark red, gold & black 35 25

Nationalization of the Railway System in Mexico, 80th Anniv. — A585

1989

1638 A585 450p multicolored 35 25

Issue dates for some 1990-1991 issues are based on First Day cancels. Original printings were small. Later printings, made in 1991, were distributed to the stamp trade and seem to be the ones used for "First Day Covers."

Tampico Bridge — A586

1990, Jan. 11 Photo. *Perf. 14*

1639 A586 600p gold, blk & red 42 30

Eradication of Polio — A587

1990, Feb. 1
1640 A587 700p multicolored 50 35

Natl. Census A588

1990, Mar. 12
1641 A588 700p lt grn & yel 50 35

Mexican Philatelic Assoc., 10th Anniv. — A589

1990, Apr. 19
1642 A589 700p multicolored 50 35

Natl. Archives, Bicentennial — A590

1990, Apr. 24
1643 A590 700p pale violet 50 35

Intl. Conf. of Advertising Agencies — A591

1990, Apr. 27
1644 A591 700p multicolored 50 35

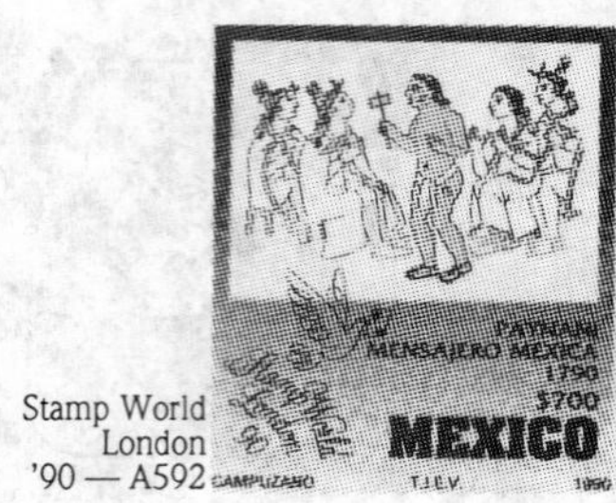

Stamp World London '90 — A592

1990, May 3
1645 A592 700p multicolored 50 35

First Postage Stamps, 150th Anniv. — A593

1990, May 6
1646 A593 700p lake, gold & blk 50 35

15th Tourism Exposition — A594

1990, May 6
1647 A594 700p multicolored 50 35

Visit of Pope John Paul II A595

1990, May 6
1648 A595 700p multicolored 50 35

Health of Young Mothers A596

1990, May 10
1649 A596 700p multicolored 50 35

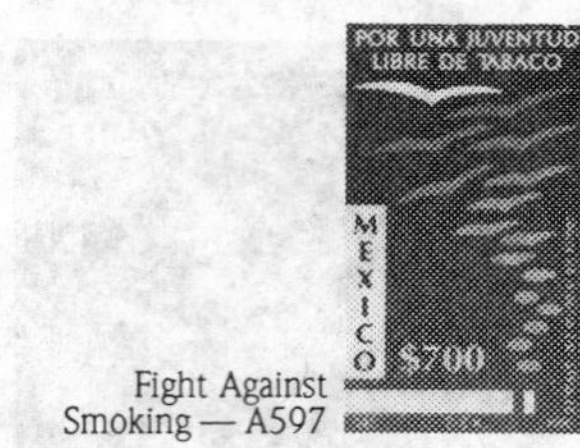

Fight Against Smoking — A597

1990, May 31
1650 A597 700p multicolored 50 35

World Environment Day — A598

1990, June 5
1651 A598 700p multicolored 50 35

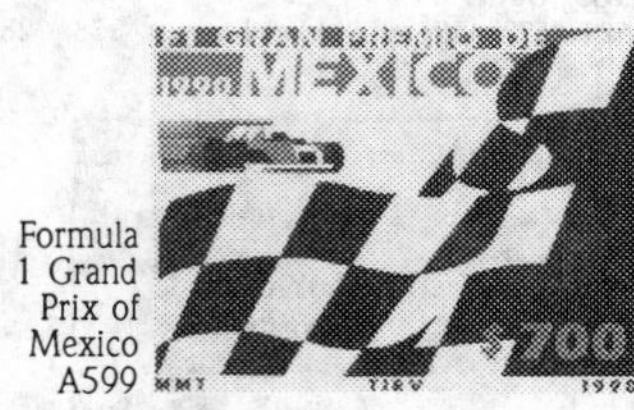

Formula 1 Grand Prix of Mexico A599

1990, June 24
1652 A599 700p grn, red & blk 50 35

Airport & Auxiliary Services, 25th Anniv. — A600

1990, June 25 Photo. *Perf. 14*
1653 A600 700p multicolored 50 35

Fight Against Drugs A601

1990, June 26
1654 A601 700p multicolored 50 35

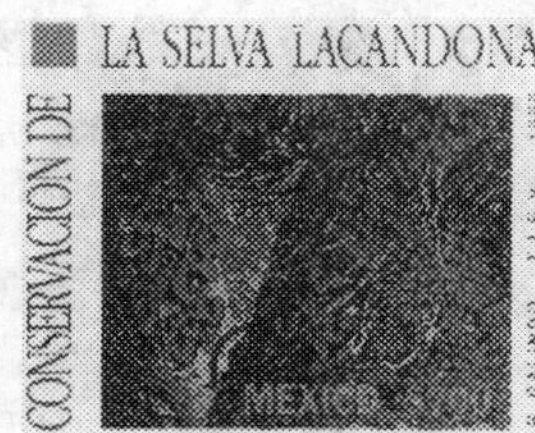

Protection of Rain Forests — A602

1990, July 6
1655 A602 700p multicolored 50 35

Solidarity with Poor People — A603

1990, Aug. 8
1656 A603 700p multicolored 50 35

Solidarity is a governmental social program of Pres. Salinas de Gortari. See No. 1704.

Oaxaca Cultural Heritage — A604

1990, Aug. 10
1657 A604 700p multicolored 50 35

Nature Conservation A605

1990, Aug. 21
1658 A605 700p blk, gray & org 50 35

Mexican Institute of Petroleum, 25th Anniv. A606

1990, Aug. 23
1659 A606 700p black & blue 50 35

8th Mexico City Marathon — A607

1990, Aug. 24
1660 A607 700p blk, red & grn 50 35

University of Colima, 50th Anniv. A608

1990, Sept. 16
1661 A608 700p gray, bister, red & grn 50 35

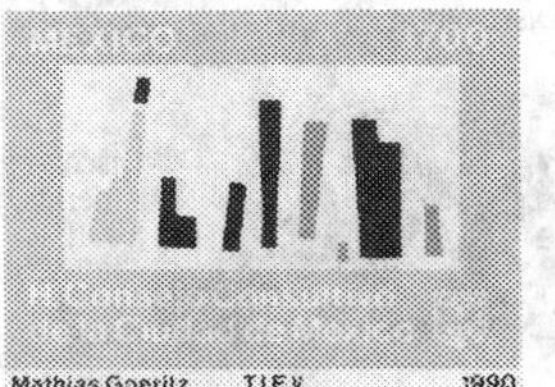

Mexico City Advisory Council, 61st Anniv. — A609

1990, Sept. 17
1662 A609 700p sil, yel, blk & org 50 35

Nationalization of Electric Industry, 30th Anniv. — A610

1990, Sept. 27
1663 A610 700p gray, grn, red & blk 50 35

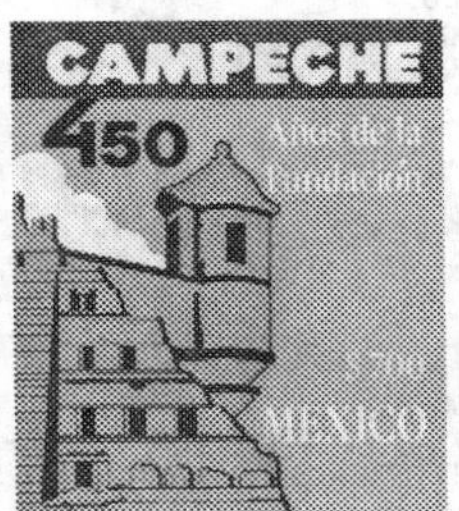

City of Campeche, 450th Anniv. A611

1990, Oct. 4
1664 A611 700p multicolored 50 35

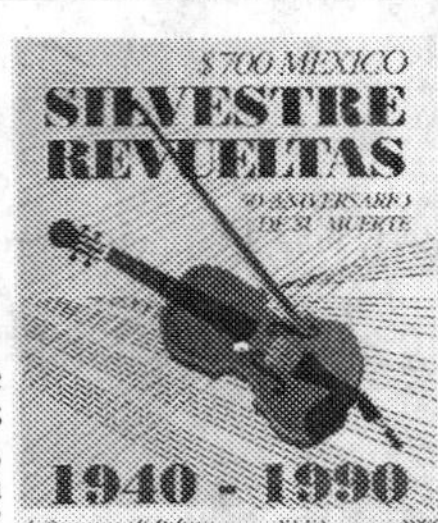

Silvestre Revueltas (1899-1940), Musician A612

1990, Oct. 4
1665 A612 700p multicolored 50 35

Plan of San Luis, 80th Anniv. A613

1990, Oct. 5
1666 A613 700p multicolored 50 35

14th World Conference of Supreme Counselors — A614

1990, Oct. 8
1667 A614 1500p vio, sil, gold & grn 1.10 78

Discovery of America, 498th Anniv. — A615

1990, Oct. 12
1668 A615 700p multicolored 50 35

Mexican Archaeology, Bicentennial A616

1990, Nov. 18
1669 A616 1500p multicolored 1.10 78

16th Central American and Caribbean Games — A617

1990, Nov. 20
1670 A617 750p shown 55 40
1671 A617 750p Mayan ball player 55 40
1672 A617 750p Mayan ball player, vert. 55 40
1673 A617 750p Ball court, stone ring, vert. 55 40
a. Strip of 4, #1670-1673 2.20 1.60

Christmas

A618 A619

1990, Dec. 3
1674 A618 700p Poinsettias 50 35
1675 A619 700p Candles 50 35

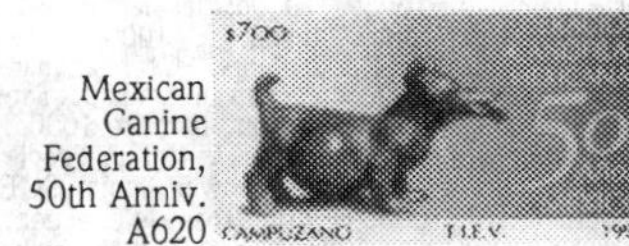

Mexican Canine Federation, 50th Anniv. A620

1990, Dec. 9
1676 A620 700p multicolored 50 35

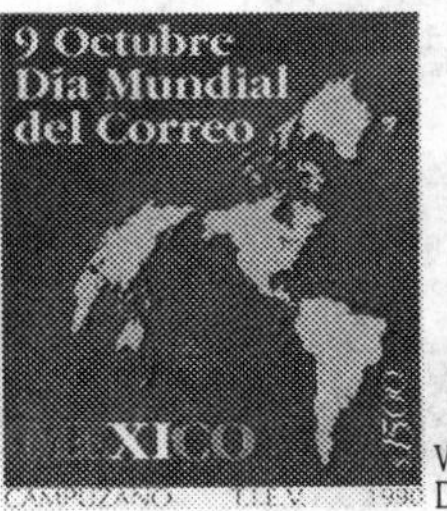

World Post Day — A621

1990, Oct. 9 Photo. ***Perf. 14x14½***
1677 A621 1500p multicolored 1.10 78

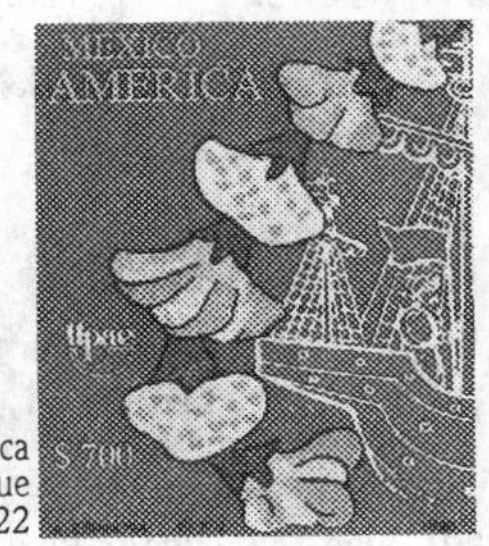

America Issue A622

Designs: No. 1678, Flowers, galleon. No. 1679, Galleon, parrot.

1990, Oct. 12
1678 A622 700p multicolored 50 35
1679 A622 700p multicolored 50 35
a. Pair, #1678-1679 + blank label 1.00 70

No. 1679a has continuous design.

Mexican Brewing Industry, Cent. — A623

1990, Nov. 8 ***Perf. 14½x14***
1680 A623 700p multicolored 50 35

National Chamber of Industrial Development, 50th Anniv. — A624

1990, Dec. 5 ***Perf. 14½x14***
1681 A624 1500p multicolored 1.10 78

Naval Secretariat, 50th Anniv. A625

1991 Photo. ***Perf. 14***
1682 A625 1000p bl, blk & gold 70 50

Prevent Transportation Accidents — A626

1991, Jan. 11 Photo. ***Perf. 14½x14***
1683 A626 700p multicolored 55 38

Natl. Consumers Institute, 15th Anniv. — A627

1991, Feb. 11
1684 A627 1000p multicolored 78 55

Voter Registration A628

1991, Feb. 13 ***Perf. 14x14½***
1685 A628 1000p org, blk & grn 78 55

Olympic Basketball — A629

1991, Feb. 25 *Perf. 14½x14*
1686 A629 1000p black & yellow 78 55

Campaign Against Polio — A630

1991, Mar. 8
1687 A630 1000p multicolored 78 55

Childrens' Day for Peace and Development — A631

Health and Family Life — A632

1991, Apr. 16 *Perf. 14½x14*
1688 A631 1000p multicolored 78 55
Perf. 14x14½
1689 A632 1000p multicolored 78 55

Mining in Mexico, 500th Anniv. — A633

1991, Apr. 25 *Perf. 14½x14*
1690 A633 1000p multicolored 78 55

Promotion of Breastfeeding A634

1991, May 10 *Perf. 14x14½*
1691 A634 1000p multicolored 78 55

16th Tourism Exposition — A635

1991, May 12 *Perf. 14½x14*
1692 A635 1000p brt grn & dk grn 85 60

Rotary Intl. Convention A636

1991, June 2 *Rouletted 6½*
1693 A636 1000p blue & gold 85 60

Integrated Communications and Transportation Systems (SCT), Cent. — A637

Designs: No. 1695a, 1000p, Jet landing. b, 1500p, Airport control tower. c, 1000p, FAX machine. d, 1500p, Upper floors, SCT headquarters. e, 1000p, Communications van. f, 1500p, Satellite. g, 1000p, Satellite in orbit, earth. h, 1000p, Boxcars. i, 1500p, Locomotives. j, 1000p, People using telephones. k, 1500p, Lower floors, SCT headquarters. l, 1000p, Hillside road, left section, highway bridge. m, 1500p, Center section, highway bridge. n, 1000p, Right section of bridge. o, 1000p, Cranes loading cargo ship. p, 1500p, Bow of cargo ship. q, 1000p, Television camera. r, 1500p, Bus. s, 1000p, Truck. t, 1500p, Trailers passing through toll plaza. u, 1000p, Bridge construction. Continuous design.

1991, June 11 *Rouletted 6½*
1694 A637 1000p gray & multi 85 60
1695 A637 Block of 21, #a.-u. 22.00 15.00

Jaguar A638

1991, June 12 *Perf. 14½x14*
1696 A638 1000p black & orange 85 60

Conservation of the rain forests.

Formula 1 Grand Prix of Mexico A639

1991, June 16 **Litho.** *Rouletted 6½*
1697 A639 1000p multicolored 65 48

No. 1519 Ovptd. in Red 

1991, June 14 **Photo.** *Perf. 14x14½*
1698 A520 150p multicolored

No. 1698 was available in strips of 5 only in booklets with limited distribution.

Total Solar Eclipse — A640

Designs: No. 1699a, 1000p, Denomination at lower right. b, Globe showing Mexico. c, 1000p, Denomination at lower left. Continuous design.

1991, July 5 *Rouletted 6½*
1699 A640 Strip of 3, #a.-c. 3.50 2.50

A641 A642

1991, July 18
1700 A641 1500p blk, org & yel 1.10 78

First Latin American Presidential Summit, Guadalajara.

1991, July 31
1701 A642 2000p Solidarity bridge 1.70 1.20

A643

A644

1991, Aug. 22
1702 A643 1000p multicolored 85 60

Ninth Mexico City marathon.

1991, Aug. 27
1703 A644 1000p blue & silver 85 60

Federal tax court, 55th anniv.

Solidarity Type of 1990 and

A645

1991 *Perf. 14½x14*
1704 A603 1000p multicolored 85 60
Rouletted 6½
1705 A645 1000p multicolored 85 60

Issue dates: No. 1704, Dec. 17; No. 1705, Sept. 9.

World Post Day — A646

1991, Oct. 9 *Rouletted 6½*
1706 A646 1000p multicolored 85 60

Voyages of Discovery A647

Discovery of America, 500th Anniv. (in 1992) A648

Design: No. 1708, Sailing ship, storm.

1991, Oct. 12
1707 A647 1000p multicolored 85 60
1708 A647 1000p multicolored 85 60
a. Pair, #1707-1708 1.70 1.20
1709 A648 1000p multicolored 85 60

No. 1708a has continuous design. Printed in sheets of 20+5 labels.

A649

Christmas A650

1991, Nov. 26
1710 A649 1000p multicolored 85 60
1711 A650 1000p multicolored 85 60

Carlos Merida, Birth Cent. A651

1991, Dec. 2 **Photo.** *Rouletted 6½*
1712 A651 1000p multicolored 85 60

Wolfgang Amadeus Mozart, Death Bicent. A652

1991, Dec. 5
1713 A652 1000p multicolored 85 60

Self-sufficiency in Corn and Bean Production — A653

1991, Dec. 11 Photo. *Rouletted 6½*
1714 A653 1000p multicolored 78 55

City of Morelia, 450th Anniv. A654

1991, Dec. 13
1715 A654 1000p multicolored 78 55

Merida, 450th Anniv. A655

1992, Jan. 6 Photo. *Rouletted 6½*
1716 A655 1300p multicolored 1.00 70

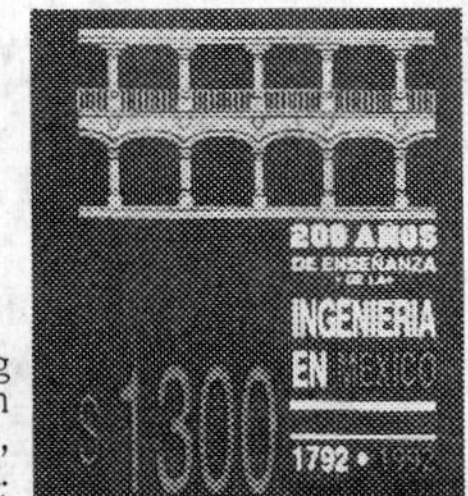
Engineering Education in Mexico, Bicent. A656

1992, Jan. 15
1717 A656 1300p blue & red 1.00 70

1992 Summer Olympics, Barcelona A657

Design: No. 1719, Stylized Olympic Rings.

1992 Photo. *Rouletted 6½*
1718 A657 2000p multicolored 1.50 1.05
1719 A657 2000p multicolored 1.35 95

Issued: No. 1718, Feb. 10. No. 1719, Mar. 1.

Guadalajara, 450th Anniv. — A658

Designs: No. 1720a, 1300p, Coat of arms. b, 1300p, Municipal buildings. c, 1300p, Guadalajara Cathedral. d, 1900p, Allegory of the city's founding. e, 1900p, Anniversary emblem.

1992, Feb. 14
1720 A658 Strip of 5, #a.-e. 5.25 3.65

Healthy Child Development — A659

1992, Feb. 26
1721 A659 2000p multicolored 1.35 95

Formula 1 Grand Prix of Mexico A660

1992, Mar. 22
1722 A660 1300p multicolored 90 65

Introduction of the wheel and domesticated horses to America, 500th anniv.

Telecom '92 — A661

1992, Apr. 6
1723 A661 1300p multicolored 90 65

World Health Day — A662

1992, Apr. 7
1724 A662 1300p blk, red & bl 90 65

War College, 60th Anniv. A663

1992, Apr. 15
1725 A663 1300p multicolored 90 65

Discovery of America, 500th Anniv. A664

Paintings: No. 1726, Inspiration of Christopher Columbus, by Jose Maria Obregon. No. 1727, Meeting of the Races, by Jorge Gonzalez Camarena. No. 1728, Spanish, Indian and Mestizo, from the Natl. Historical Museum. No. 1729, Origin of the Sky, from Selden Codex. No. 1730, Quetzalcoatl and Tezcatlipoca, from Borbonico Codex. No. 1731, Human Culture by Camarena.

1992, Apr. 24 Litho. *Perf. 14x14½*
1726 A664 1300p multicolored 90 65
1727 A664 1300p multicolored 90 65
1728 A664 2000p multicolored 1.35 95
1729 A664 2000p multicolored 1.35 95
1730 A664 2000p multicolored 1.35 95
Nos. 1726-1730 (5) 5.85 4.15

Size: 107x84mm
Imperf
1731 A664 7000p multicolored 4.65 3.25

Granada '92. For overprints see Nos. 1752-1757.

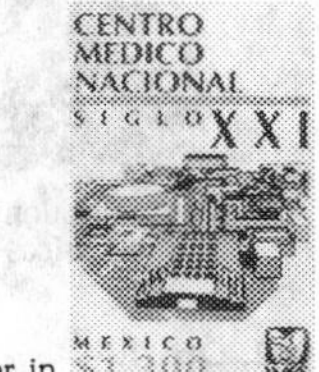
Natl. Medical Center in the 21st Cent. — A665

1992, Apr. 27 Photo. *Rouletted 6½*
1732 A665 1300p multicolored 90 65

Rights of the Child A666

1992, Apr. 30
1733 A666 1300p multicolored 90 65

Midwives in Mexico — A667

1992, May 10
1734 A667 1300p multicolored 90 65

Discovery of America, 500th Anniv. — A668

Illustration reduced.

1992, May 22 Litho. *Imperf.*
1735 A668 7000p multicolored 5.25 3.65

World Columbian Stamp Expo, Chicago.

Notary College of Mexico, Mexico City, Bicent. A669

1992, June 18 Litho. *Rouletted 6½*
1736 A669 1300p multicolored 90 68

Arbor Day — A670

1992, July 9 *Rouletted 5*
1737 A670 1300p multicolored 90 68

1992 Summer Olympics, Barcelona A671

1992, July 30 *Perf. 14*
1738 A671 1300p Boxing 90 68
1739 A671 1300p Fencing 90 68
1740 A671 1300p High jump 90 68
1741 A671 1300p Gymnastics 90 68
1742 A671 1300p Shooting 90 68
1743 A671 1900p Swimming 1.30 98
1744 A671 1900p Running 1.30 98
1745 A671 1900p Rowing 1.30 98
1746 A671 1900p Soccer 1.30 98
1747 A671 2000p Equestrian 1.35 1.00
Nos. 1738-1747 (10) 11.05 8.32

Souvenir Sheet
Perf. 10
1748 A671 7000p Torch bearer 4.75 4.75

10th Intl. Marathon of Mexico City — A672

1992, Aug. 26 Litho. *Rouletted 5*
1749 A672 1300p multicolored 85 65

Solidarity, United for Progress — A673

1992, Sept. 8 *Perf. 10*
1750 A673 1300p multicolored 85 65

Demand, as well as supply, determines a stamp's market value. One is as important as the other.

Souvenir Sheet

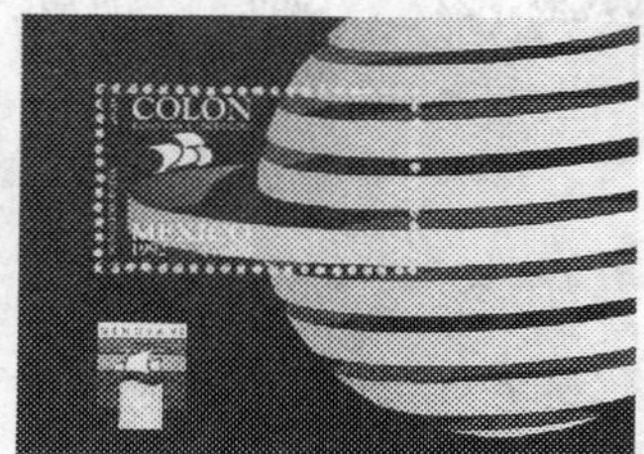

Discovery of America, 500th Anniv. — A674

1992, Sept. 18 *Perf. 10*

1751 A674 7000p multicolored	4.50	3.25

Genoa '92.

Nos. 1726-1731 Ovptd. with emblem of World Columbian Stamp Expo '92, Chicago

1992 Litho. *Perf. 14x14½*

1752 A664 1300p on #1726		
1753 A664 1300p on #1727		
1754 A664 2000p on #1728		
1755 A664 2000p on #1729		
1756 A664 2000p on #1730		

Size: 107x84mm

Imperf

1757 A664 7000p on #1731

Nos. 1752-1757 were produced in limited quantities and had limited distribution with no advance release information available.

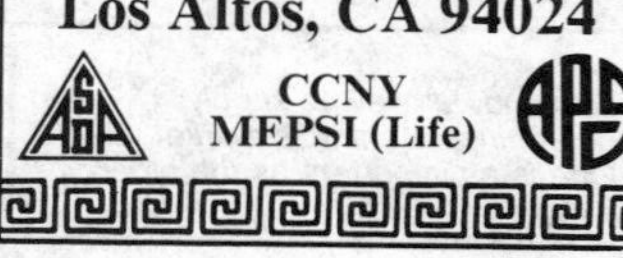

Natl. Council of Radio and Television, 50th Anniv. A675

1992, Oct. 5 Litho. *Perf. 10*

1758 A675 1300p multicolored	85	65

World Post Day A676

1992, Oct. 9 Litho. *Perf. 10*

1759 A676 1300p multicolored	85	65

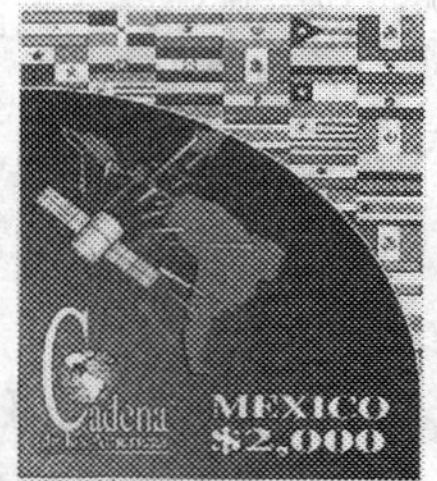

Communications System of the Americas — A677

1992, Oct. 12

1760 A677 2000p multicolored	1.30	1.00

Discovery of America, 500th Anniv. A678

Designs: No. 1761, Aztec calendar stone. No. 1762, Snake, fish, compass.

1992, Oct. 12

1761 A678 2000p shown	1.30	1.00
1762 A678 2000p multicolored	1.30	1.00
a. Pair, #1761-1762	2.60	2.00

Exporta Type of 1975

Designs: 2200p, Cuts of meat marked on steer. 2800p, Chemistry flasks. 3600p, Pistons. 3900p, Petroleum valves. 4000p, Honey. 4800p, Tomatoes. 6000p, Citrus fruit. 7200p, Film.

1992 Photo. *Perf. 14x14½*

1763 A320 2200p red	1.60	1.25
1764 A320 2800p black	2.00	1.50
With Gray Burelage		
1765 A320 3600p blk, Type I	2.65	2.00
1766 A320 3900p gray & bl, Type II	2.90	2.20
1767 A320 4000p yel org & red brn, Type I	2.85	2.15
1768 A320 4800p red & grn, Type I	3.50	2.65
1769 A320 6000p yel & grn, Type I	4.50	3.40
1770 A320 7200p grn, red & blk, Type I	5.30	4.00
Nos. 1763-1770 (8)	25.30	19.15

San Luis Potosi, 400th Anniv. — A679

1992, Nov. 3 Litho. *Perf. 10*

1777 A679 1300p multicolored	85	65

United for Conservation — A680

1992, Nov. 17

1778 A680 1300p multicolored	85	65

Navy Day — A681

1992, Nov. 23

1779 A681 1300p multicolored	85	65

Christmas A682

Design: 1300p, Christmas tree, children, pinata, vert.

1992, Nov. 26

1780 A682 1300p multicolored	85	65
1781 A682 2000p multicolored	1.30	1.00

Mexican Social Security Institute, 50th Anniv. — A683

1993, Jan. 19 Litho. *Perf. 10*

1807 A683 1.50p multicolored	1.10	82

Mexican Society of Ophthomolgists, Cent. — A687

1993, Feb. 18 Litho. *Perf. 10*

1811 A687 1.30p multicolored	95	70

Children's Month — A688

1993, Feb.

1812 A688 1.30p multicolored	95	70

SEMI-POSTAL STAMPS

Regular Issue of 1916 Surcharged in Red **+ 3 ¢**

1918, Dec. 25 Unwmk. *Perf. 12*

B1 A72 5c + 3c ultra	14.00	15.00
Rouletted		
B2 A73 10c + 5c blue	17.50	15.00

AIR POST STAMPS

Eagle — AP1

Unwmk.

1922, Apr. 2 Engr. *Perf. 12*

C1 AP1 50c bl & red brn	60.00	40.00
a. 50c dark blue & claret ('29)	90.00	90.00

See Nos. C2-C3. For overprints and surcharges see Nos. C47-C48, CO1-CO2B, CO18-CO19, CO29.

1927, Oct. 13 Wmk. 156

C2 AP1 50c dk bl & red brn	75	25
a. 50c dark blue & claret ('29)	75	25
b. Vert. strip of 3, imperf. btwn.	*10,000.*	

The vignettes of Nos. C1a and C2a fluoresce a bright rose red under UV light.

1928

C3 AP1 25c brn car & gray brn	45	15
C4 AP1 25c dk grn & gray brn	45	20

On May 3, 1929, certain proofs or essays were sold at the post office in Mexico, D. F. They were printed in different colors from those of the regularly issued stamps. There were 7 varieties perf. and 2 imperf. and a total of 225 copies. They were sold with the understanding that they were for collections but the majority of them were used on air mail sent out that day.

Capt. Emilio Carranza and his Airplane "México Excelsior" AP2

1929, June 19

C5 AP2 5c ol grn & sepia	1.15	65
C6 AP2 10c sep & brn red	1.30	70
C7 AP2 15c vio & dk grn	3.00	1.25
C8 AP2 20c brn & blk	1.20	75
C9 AP2 50c brn red & blk	6.00	2.00
C10 AP2 1p blk & brn	12.50	2.75
Nos. C5-C10 (6)	25.15	8.10

1st anniv. of death of Carranza (1905-28). For overprints see Nos. C29-C36, C40-C44.

Coat of Arms and Airplane AP3

1929-34 *Perf. 11½, 12*
C11 AP3 10c violet 35 15
C12 AP3 15c carmine 1.35 20
C13 AP3 20c brn ol 27.50 1.25
C14 AP3 30c gray blk 20 20
C15 AP3 35c blue grn 35 25
a. Imperf., pair 1,200.
C16 AP3 50c red brn ('34) 1.25 65
C17 AP3 1p blk & dk bl 1.25 65
C18 AP3 5p claret & dp bl 4.00 3.50
C19 AP3 10p vio & ol brn 6.00 7.00
Nos. C11-C19 (9) 42.25 13.85

1930-32 *Rouletted 13, 13½*
C20 AP3 5c lt bl ('32) 25 15
C21 AP3 10c violet 25 15
C22 AP3 15c carmine 35 15
a. 15c rose carmine 40 15
C23 AP3 20c brown olive 1.50 15
a. 20c brown 50 15
b. 20c yellow brown 50 15
c. Horiz. pair, imperf. btwn.
C24 AP3 25c violet 95 80
C25 AP3 50c red brown 90 75
Nos. C20-C25 (6) 4.20 2.15

Trial impressions of No. C20 were printed in orange but were never sold at post offices.
See Nos. C62-C64, C75. For overprints and surcharges see Nos. C28, C38-C39, C46, C49-C50, CO17, CO20-CO28, CO30.

Plane over Plaza, Mexico City — AP4

1929, Dec. 10 **Wmk. 156** *Perf. 12*
C26 AP4 20c blk vio 1.25 1.00
C27 AP4 40c slate grn 85.00 75.00

Aviation Week, Dec. 10-16.
For overprint see No. CO11.

No. C21 Overprinted in Red

Primer Congreso Nacional de Turismo. México. Abril 20-27 de 1930.

1930, Apr. 20 *Rouletted 13, 13½*
C28 AP3 10c violet 2.00 1.25

National Tourism Congress at Mexico, D. F., Apr. 20-27, 1930.

Nos. C5 and C7 Overprinted **HABILITADO 1930**

1930, Sept. 1 *Perf. 12*
C29 AP2 5c ol grn & sepia 5.50 4.50
a. Double overprint 220.00
C30 AP2 15c vio & dk grn 9.00 7.75

Nos. C5-C10 Overprinted **HABILITADO Aéreo 1930-1931**

1930, Dec. 18
C31 AP2 5c ol grn & sepia 6.00 6.50
C32 AP2 10c sep & brn red 3.50 4.00
a. Double overprint 50.00 50.00
C33 AP2 15c vio & dk grn 6.50 7.00
C34 AP2 20c brn & blk 7.00 5.50
C35 AP2 50c brn red & blk 14.00 10.00
C36 AP2 1p blk & brn 4.00 2.75
Nos. C31-C36 (6) 41.00 35.75

Plane over Flying Field AP5

1931, May 15 **Engr.** *Perf. 12*
C37 AP5 25c lake 4.00 4.50
a. Imperf., pair 80.00 72.50

Aeronautic Exhibition of the Aero Club of Mexico. Of the 25c, 15c paid air mail postage and 10c went to a fund to improve the Mexico City airport.
For surcharge see No. C45.

Nos. C13 and C23 Surcharged in Red

HABILITADO Quince centavos

1931
C38 AP3 15c on 20c brn ol 32.50 35.00

Rouletted 13, 13½
C39 AP3 15c on 20c brn ol 30 15
a. Inverted surcharge 150.00
b. Double surcharge 150.00
c. Pair, one without surcharge 350.00

Nos. C5 to C9 Overprinted **HABILITADO AEREO-1932**

1932, July 13 *Perf. 12*
C40 AP2 5c ol grn & sep 6.00 5.00
a. Imperf., pair 60.00 60.00
C41 AP2 10c sep & brn red 5.00 3.00
a. Imperf., pair 60.00 60.00
C42 AP2 15c vio & bk grn 6.00 4.00
a. Imperf., pair 60.00 60.00
C43 AP2 20c brn & blk 5.00 2.75
a. Imperf., pair 60.00 60.00
C44 AP2 50c brn red & blk 35.00 35.00
a. Imperf., pair 60.00 60.00
Nos. C40-C44 (5) 57.00 49.75

Issued to commemorate the fourth anniversary of the death of Capt. Emilio Carranza.

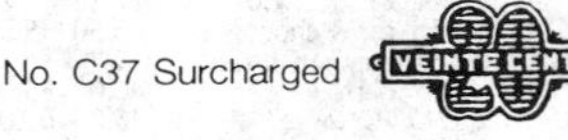
No. C37 Surcharged

1932
C45 AP5 20c on 25c lake 70 30
a. Imperf., pair 72.50 72.50

No. C13 Surcharged

C46 AP3 30c on 20c brn ol 30.00 30.00

Similar Surcharge on Nos. C3 and C4
C47 AP1 40c on 25c (#C3) 90 90
a. Inverted surcharge 1,000.
C48 AP1 40c on 25c (#C4) 40.00 40.00

Surcharged on Nos. C23 and C24
Rouletted 13, 13½
C49 AP3 30c on 20c brn ol 35 18
a. Inverted surcharge 2,750.
C50 AP3 80c on 25c dl vio 1.80 1.20

Palace of Fine Arts — AP6

1933, Oct. 1 **Engr.** *Perf. 12*
C51 AP6 20c dk red & dl vio 3.50 1.40
C52 AP6 30c dk brn & dl vio 6.75 6.00
C53 AP6 1p grnsh blk & dl vio 67.50 70.00

21st Intl. Cong. of Statistics and the cent. of the Mexican Soc. of Geography and Statistics.

National University Issue

Nevado de Toluca — AP7

Pyramids of the Sun and Moon — AP8

View of Ajusco AP9

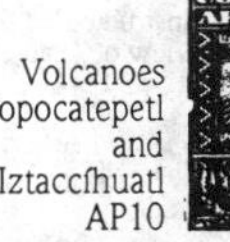

Volcanoes Popocatepetl and Iztaccíhuatl AP10

Bridge over Tepecayo AP11

Chapultepec Fortress AP12

Orizaba Volcano (Citlaltépetl) AP13

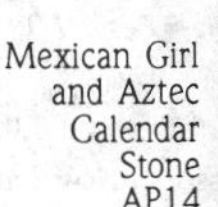

Mexican Girl and Aztec Calendar Stone AP14

1934, Sept. 1 **Wmk. 156** *Perf. 10½*
C54 AP7 20c orange 2.75 2.50
C55 AP8 30c red lil & vio 5.75 6.75
C56 AP9 50c ol grn & bis brn 6.50 10.00
C57 AP10 75c blk & yel grn 7.50 14.00
C58 AP11 1p blk & pck bl 8.00 10.00
C59 AP12 5p bis brn & dk bl 42.50 95.00
C60 AP13 10p ind & mar 125.00 200.00
C61 AP14 20p brn & brn lake 750.00 1,200.
Nos. C54-C61 (8) 948.00 1,538.

Type of 1929-34

1934-35 *Perf. 10½, 10½x10*
C62 AP3 20c olive green 35 15
a. 20c slate 500.00 500.00
C63 AP3 30c slate 40 40
C64 AP3 50c red brn ('35) 2.00 2.00

Symbols of Air Service AP15

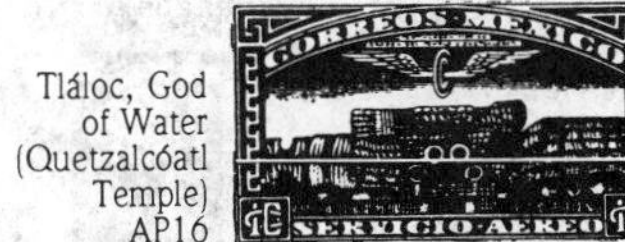

Tláloc, God of Water (Quetzalcóatl Temple) AP16

Orizaba Volcano (Citlaltépetl) AP17

"Eagle Man" AP18

Symbolical of Flight AP19

Aztec Bird-Man — AP20

Allegory of Flight and Pyramid of the Sun — AP21

"Eagle Man" and Airplanes AP22

Natives Looking at Airplane and Orizaba Volcano — AP23

Imprint: "Oficina Impresora de Hacienda-Mexico"

Perf. 10½x10, 10x10½

1934-35 **Wmk. 156**
C65 AP15 5c black 42 15
a. Imperf., pair
C66 AP16 10c red brn 90 15
C67 AP17 15c gray grn 1.25 15
a. Imperf., pair 300.00
C68 AP18 20c brn car 3.00 15
a. 20c lake 4.00 15
b. Imperf. pair
C69 AP19 30c brn ol 70 15
C70 AP20 40c blue ('35) 1.25 15
C71 AP21 50c green 2.50 15
a. Imperf., pair 275.00
C72 AP22 1p gray grn & red brn 3.50 15
C73 AP23 5p dk car & blk 7.25 70
Nos. C65-C73 (9) 20.77
Set value 1.55

See Nos. C76A, C80, C81, C132-C140, C170-C177A. For overprint see No. C74.

No. C68 Overprinted in Violet

AMELIA EARHART VUELO DE BUENA VOLUNTAD MEXICO 1935

1935, Apr. 16
C74 AP18 20c lake *3,000. 4,000.*

Amelia Earhart's goodwill flight to Mexico.

Arms-Plane Type of 1929-34

1935 **Wmk. 248** *Perf. 10½x10*
C75 AP3 30c slate 3.00 5.00

Francisco I. Madero AP24

1935, Nov. 20 Wmk. 156

C76 AP24 20c scarlet 30 15

25th anniversary of the Plan of San Luis. See No. C76B.

Eagle Man Type of 1934-35

1936 Wmk. 260

C76A AP18 20c lake *5,500.* 52.50

Madero Type of 1935

C76B AP24 20c scarlet *15,000.*

Tasquillo Bridge AP25

Corona River Bridge AP26

Bridge on Nuevo Laredo Highway AP27

Wmk. 248

1936, July 1 Photo. *Perf. 14*

C77 AP25 10c slate bl & lt bl 20 15
C78 AP26 20c dl vio & org 28 15
C79 AP27 40c dk bl & dk grn 55 50

Opening of Nuevo Laredo Highway.

Eagle Man Type of 1934-35

Perf. 10½x10

1936, June 18 Engr. Unwmk.

C80 AP18 20c brn car 6.50 7.00

Imprint: "Talleres de Imp. de Est. y Valores-Mexico"

1937 Wmk. 156 Photo. *Perf. 14*

C81 AP18 20c rose red 1.25 15
a. 20c brown carmine 1.50 15
b. 20c dark carmine 2.00 15
c. Imperf., pair 37.50 42.50

There are two sizes of watermark 156. No. C81c was not regularly issued.

Cavalryman AP28

Early Biplane over Mountains AP29

Venustiano Carranza on Horseback AP30

1938, Mar. 26

C82 AP28 20c org red & bl 50 20
C83 AP29 40c bl & org red 75 30
C84 AP30 1p bl & bis brn 4.75 2.25

Plan of Guadalupe, 25th anniversary.

The Zócalo and Cathedral, Mexico City — AP31

Designs: Nos. C87, C88, Reconstructed edifices of Chichén Itzá. Nos. C89, C90, View of Acapulco.

1938, July 1

C85 AP31 20c car rose 35 25
C86 AP31 20c purple 14.00 10.00
C87 AP31 40c brt grn 7.75 5.00
C88 AP31 40c dk grn 7.00 5.00
C89 AP31 1p light blue 7.00 5.00
C90 AP31 1p slate blue 7.00 5.00
Nos. C85-C90 (6) 43.10 30.25

16th Intl. Cong. of Planning & Housing.

Statue of José María Morelos AP34

Statue of Pioneer Woman, Ponca City, OK AP35

1939 Engr. *Perf. 10½*

C91 AP34 20c green 70 50
C92 AP34 40c red vio 2.00 1.25
C93 AP34 1p vio brn & car 1.40 1.00

New York World's Fair. Released in New York May 2, in Mexico May 24.

Type of 1939 Overprinted in Cerise

1939, May 23

C93A AP34 20c bl & red 250.00 500.00

Issued for the flight of Francisco Sarabia from Mexico City to New York on May 25.

1939, May 17

C94 AP35 20c gray brown 1.00 40
C95 AP35 40c slate grn 2.50 1.25
C96 AP35 1p violet 1.65 90

Tulsa World Philatelic Convention.

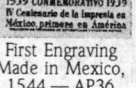

First Engraving Made in Mexico, 1544 — AP36

First Work of Legislation Printed in America, 1563 — AP37

Designs: 1p, Reproduction of oldest preserved Mexican printing.

1939, Sept. 7 Wmk. 156

C97 AP36 20c slate blue 25 15
a. Unwmkd.
C98 AP37 40c slate green 65 15
a. Imperf., pair *700.00*
C99 AP37 1p dk brn & car 1.10 70

400th anniversary of printing in Mexico.

Transportation — AP39

Designs: 40c, Finger counting and factory. 1p, "Seven Censuses."

Perf. 12x13, 13x12

1939, Oct. 2 Photo.

C100 AP39 20c dk bl & bl 1.00 20
C101 AP39 40c red org & org 75 25
C102 AP39 1p ind & vio bl 2.75 75

National Census of 1939-40.

Penny Black Type of Regular Issue, 1940

1940, May *Perf. 14*

C103 A140 5c blk & dk grn 65 60
C104 A140 10c bis brn & dp bl 52 25
C105 A140 20c car & bl vio 38 20
C106 A140 1p car & choc 3.50 5.00
C107 A140 5p gray grn & red brn 40.00 55.00
Nos. C103-C107 (5) 45.05 61.05

Issue dates: 5c-1p, May 2; 5p, May 15.

Part of Original College at Pátzcuaro AP43

College at Morelia (18th Century) — AP44

College at Morelia (1940) AP45

1940, July 15 Engr. *Perf. 10½*

C108 AP43 20c brt grn 45 20
C109 AP44 40c orange 50 30
C110 AP45 1p dp pur, red brn & org 1.25 1.00

400th anniv. of the founding of the National College of San Nicolas de Hidalgo.

Pirate Ship — AP46

Designs: 40c, Castle of San Miguel. 1p, Temple of San Francisco.

Perf. 12x13, 13x12

1940, Aug. 7 Photo.

C111 AP46 20c red brn & bis brn 1.15 70
C112 AP46 40c blk & sl grn 1.50 75
C113 AP46 1p vio bl & blk 5.00 3.00

400th anniversary of Campeche.

Inauguration Type of Regular Issue, 1940

1940, Dec. 1 *Perf. 12x13*

C114 A146 20c gray blk & red org 1.90 1.00
C115 A146 40c chnt brn & dk sl 2.00 1.50
C116 A146 1p brt vio bl & rose 3.50 2.00

Tower of the Convent of the Nuns — AP50

Casa de Montejo — AP51

Design: 1p, Campanile of Cathedral at Merída.

1942, Jan. 2 *Perf. 14*

C117 AP50 20c Prus bl 1.50 75
C118 AP51 40c grnsh blk (C) 2.25 2.00
a. Without overprint 7.50 7.50
C119 AP50 1p carmine 2.50 2.00

400th anniversary of Merída.
No. C118 bears the overprint "Servicio Aereo" in carmine.

Church of Zapopán AP53

Our Lady of Guadalupe Church AP54

Guadalajara Arms — AP55

1942, Feb. 11 Engr. *Perf. 10½x10*

C120 AP53 20c grn & blk 1.65 75
C121 AP54 40c ol & yel grn 1.75 1.00
C122 AP55 1p pur & sepia 1.65 1.25

400th anniversary of Guadalajara.

Astrophysics Type of Regular Issue, 1942

Designs: 20c, Spiral Galaxy NGC 4594. 40c, Planetary Nebula in Lyra. 1p, Russell Diagrams.

1942, Feb. 17 Photo. *Perf. 12x13*

C123 A154 20c dk grn & ind 12.50 3.00
C124 A154 40c car lake & ind 11.00 4.00
C125 A154 1p org & blk 11.00 4.50

Corn AP59

1942, July 1

No.	Type	Description	Unused	Used
C126	AP59	20c shown	1.90	70
C127	AP59	40c Coffee	1.50	75
C128	AP59	1p Bananas	2.50	2.00

2nd Inter-American Agricultural Conf.

View of San Miguel de Allende AP62

Designs: 40c, Birthplace of Allende. 1p, Church of Our Lady of Health.

1943, May 18 *Perf. 14*

No.	Type	Description	Unused	Used
C129	AP62	20c dk slate grn	95	60
C130	AP62	40c purple	1.25	60
C131	AP62	1p dp car	2.75	2.50

400th anniversary of the founding of San Miguel de Allende.

Types of 1934-35

1944 Photo. Wmk. 272

No.	Type	Description	Unused	Used
C132	AP18	20c brn car	75	15

Perf. 10½x10

1944-46 Engr. Wmk. 272

No.	Type	Description	Unused	Used
C133	AP15	5c black	50	15
C134	AP16	10c red brn ('45)	1.25	15
C135	AP17	15c gray grn ('45)	85	15
C136	AP19	30c brn ol ('45)	12.50	75
C137	AP20	40c gray bl ('45)	1.10	20
C138	AP21	50c green	85	15
C139	AP22	1p gray grn & red brn ('45)	6.00	1.50
C140	AP23	5p dk car & blk ('46)	4.75	2.00
		Nos. C133-C140 (8)	27.80	5.05

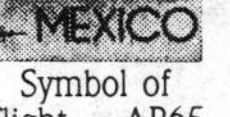

Symbol of Flight — AP65 Microphone, Book and Camera — AP66

1944 Photo. *Perf. 14*

No.	Type	Description	Unused	Used
C141	AP65	25c chestnut brown	35	15

See No. C185.

1944, Nov. 8 Wmk. 272

No.	Type	Description	Unused	Used
C142	AP66	25c dl slate grn	65	15

Issued to commemorate the third Book Fair.

Globe-in-Hands Type of Regular Issue, 1945

1945, Feb. 27 *Perf. 12x13*

No.	Type	Description	Unused	Used
C143	A166	25c red org	28	15
C144	A166	1p brt grn	35	25
C145	A166	5p indigo	2.00	1.75
C146	A166	10p brt rose	5.50	4.50
C147	A166	20p brt vio bl	11.50	11.00
		Nos. C143-C147 (5)	19.63	17.65

Theater Type of Regular Issue, 1945

1945, July 27

No.	Type	Description	Unused	Used
C148	A167	30c sl & ol	20	15
C149	A167	1p sl & lil	30	30
C150	A167	5p sl & blk	2.25	2.00
C151	A167	10p sl & lt ultra	4.25	3.50
C152	A167	20p blk & gray grn	9.75	8.50
		Nos. C148-C152 (5)	16.75	14.45

Blindfold Type of Regular Issue, 1945

1945, Nov. 21

No.	Type	Description	Unused	Used
C153	A169	30c sl grn	16	16
C154	A169	1p brn red	30	20
C155	A169	5p red brn & pale bl	2.50	2.25
C156	A169	10p sl blk & pale lil	4.25	4.25
C157	A169	20p grn & lt brn	21.00	20.00
		Nos. C153-C157 (5)	28.21	26.86

Torch, Laurel and Flag-decorated ONU — AP70

1946, Apr. 10

No.	Type	Description	Unused	Used
C158	AP70	30c chocolate	16	15
C159	AP70	1p sl grn	28	24
C160	AP70	5p chnt & dk grn	1.40	1.00
C161	AP70	10p dk brn & chnt	4.25	3.25
C162	AP70	20p sl grn & org red	9.75	7.75
		Nos. C158-C162 (5)	15.84	12.39

Issued to honor the United Nations.

Father Margil de Jesus and Plane over Zacatecas AP71

Designs (Zacatecas scene and): 1p, Genaro Codina. 5p, Gen. Enrique Estrada. 10p, Fernando Villalpando.

Perf. 10½x10

1946, Sept. 13 Engr. Wmk. 279

No.	Type	Description	Unused	Used
C163	AP71	30c gray	16	15
C164	AP71	1p brn & Prus grn	35	30
C165	AP71	5p red & ol	2.50	2.50
C166	AP71	10p Prus grn & dk brn	8.75	4.25

400th anniversary of Zacatecas.

Franklin D. Roosevelt and Stamp of 1st Mexican Issue AP72

Design: 30c, Arms of Mexico and Stamp of 1st US Issue.

1947, May 16 Photo. *Perf. 14*

No.	Type	Description	Unused	Used
C167	AP72	25c lt vio bl	75	40
C168	AP72	30c gray blk	50	20
a.		Imperf., pair	325.00	
C169	AP72	1p blue & car	1.00	35

Centenary International Philatelic Exhibition, New York, May 17-25, 1947.

Type of 1934-35

Perf. 10½x10, 10x10½

1947 Engr. Wmk. 279

No.	Type	Description	Unused	Used
C170	AP15	5c black	90	15
C171	AP16	10c red brn	1.50	25
C172	AP17	15c ol grn	1.50	25
C173	AP19	30c brn ol	1.00	15
C174	AP20	40c bl gray	1.00	15
C175	AP21	50c green	9.00	25
a.		Imperf., pair	450.00	
C176	AP22	1p gray grn & red brn	2.25	20
a.		Imperf., pair	500.00	
C177	AP23	5p red & blk	6.00	1.00
c.		5p dark car & black	200.00	3.00

Perf. 14

No.	Type	Description	Unused	Used
C177A	AP18	20c brn car	2.00	40
b.		Imperf., pair	250.00	
		Nos. C170-C177A (9)	25.15	2.80

Emilio Carranza AP74

Douglas DC-4 — AP75

1947, June 25 Engr. *Perf. 10½x10*

No.	Type	Description	Unused	Used
C178	AP74	10p red & dk brn	1.40	1.25
a.		10p dark carmine & brown		6.50
C179	AP75	20p bl & red brn	2.00	2.00

Cadet Vincente Suárez AP76

Chapultepec Castle — AP78

Designs: 30c, Lieut. Juan de la Barrera. 1p, Gen. Pedro M. Anaya. 5p, Gen. Antonio de Leon.

1947, Sept. 8 Photo. *Perf. 14*

No.	Type	Description	Unused	Used
C180	AP76	25c dl vio	20	15
C181	AP76	30c blue	20	15

Engr.

Perf. 10x10½

No.	Type	Description	Unused	Used
C182	AP78	50c dp grn	30	15
C183	AP78	1p violet	40	15
C184	AP78	5p aqua & brn	1.65	1.65
a.		Imperf. pair	600.00	
		Nos. C180-C184 (5)	2.75	2.25

Centenary of the battles of Chapultepec, Churubusco and Molino del Rey.

Flight Symbol Type of 1944

1947 Wmk. 279 Photo. *Perf. 14*

No.	Type	Description	Unused	Used
C185	AP65	25c chnt brn	35	15
a.		Imperf., pair	250.00	

Puebla, Dance of the Half Moon AP81

Designs: 5c, Guerrero, Acapulco water-front. 10c, Oaxaca, dance. 20c, Chiapas, musicians (Mayan). 25c, Michoacan, masks. 30c, Cuauhtemoc. 35c, Guerrero, view of Taxco. 40c, San Luis Potosi, head. 50c, Chiapas, bas-relief profile, Mayan culture. 80c, Mexico City University Stadium. 5p, Queretaro, architecture. 10p, Miguel Hidalgo. 20p, Modern building.

Two types of 20p:

I- Blue gray part 21¼mm wide. Child's figure touching left edge.

II- Blue gray part 21¾mm wide; "LQ" at lower left corner. Child's figure 1mm from left edge.

Imprint: "Talleres de Impresion de Estampillas y Valores-Mexico"

Perf. 10½x10

1950-52 Wmk. 279 Engr.

No.	Type	Description	Unused	Used
C186	AP81	5c aqua ('51)	40	15
C187	AP81	10c brn org ('51)	2.00	40
C188	AP81	20c carmine	90	15
C189	AP81	25c redsh brn	90	15
C190	AP81	30c ol bister	40	15
C191	AP81	35c violet	2.00	15
a.		Retouched die	16.00	25
b.		As "a," imperf., pair	400.00	
C192	AP81	40c dk gray bl ('51)	1.75	15
a.		Imperf., pair	400.00	
C193	AP81	50c green	3.00	15
C194	AP81	80c cl ('52)	1.75	40
a.		Imperf., pair	400.00	
C195	AP81	1p bl gray	1.00	15
C196	AP81	5p dk brn & org ('51)	4.25	75
a.		Imperf., pair		*1,800.*
C197	AP81	10p blk & aqua ('52)	55.00	17.50
C198	AP81	20p car & bl gray, I ('52)	7.00	7.75
a.		Type II	400.00	75.00
		Nos. C186-C198 (13)	80.35	28.00

No. C191a: A patch of heavy shading has been added at right of "MEXICO;" lines in sky increased and strengthened. On Nos. C191, C191a, the top of the highest tower is even with the top of the "o" in "Guerrero," and has no frame line at right. No. C220C has frame line at right and tower top is even with "Arquitectura."

Many shades exist of Nos. C186-C198.

See Nos. C208-C221, C249, C265-C268, C285-C288, C290-C298, C347-C349, C422, C444, C446-C450, C471-C480.

Pres. Aleman and Highway Bridging Map of Mexico AP82

Design: 35c, Pres. Juarez and map.

1950, May 21 Engr.

No.	Type	Description	Unused	Used
C199	AP82	25c lilac rose	2.50	20
C200	AP82	35c deep green	20	15

Completion of the Intl. Highway between Ciudad Juarez and the Guatemala border.

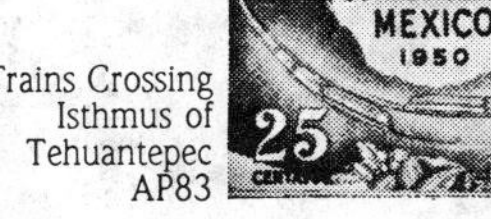

Trains Crossing Isthmus of Tehuantepec AP83

Design: 35c, Pres. Aleman and bridge.

1950, May 24

No.	Type	Description	Unused	Used
C201	AP83	25c green	40	20
C202	AP83	35c ultra	30	20

Issued to commemorate the opening of the Southeastern Railroad between Veracruz, Coatzocoalcos and Yucatan, 1950.

Aztec Courier, Plane, Train — AP84

Design: 80c, Symbols of universal postal service.

1950, June 15

No.	Type	Description	Unused	Used
C203	AP84	25c red org	30	15
C204	AP84	80c blue	40	25

75th anniv. (in 1949) of the UPU.

Miguel Hidalgo — AP86

Design: 35c, Hidalgo and Mexican Flag.

Wmk. 300

1953, May 8 Photo. *Perf. 14*

No.	Type	Description	Unused	Used
C206	AP86	25c gray bl & dk red brn	70	15
C207	AP86	35c slate grn	70	20

Bicentenary of birth of Miguel Hidalgo y Costilla (1753-1811), priest and revolutionist.

Type of 1950-52

Designs as before.

Imprint: "Talleres de Impresion de Estampillas y Valores-Mexico"

Wmk. 300, Horizontal

1953-56 Engr. *Perf. 10½x10*

No.	Type	Description	Unused	Used
C208	AP81	5c aqua	38	15
C209	AP81	10c org brn	4.50	70
a.		10c orange	9.00	2.00
C210	AP81	30c gray ol	15.00	1.00
C211	AP81	40c gray bl ('56)	15.00	1.50
C212	AP81	50c green	225.00	115.00
C213	AP81	80c claret	85.00	6.00
C214	AP81	1p bl gray	2.50	25
C215	AP81	5p dk brn & org	2.25	50
C216	AP81	10p blk & aqua	4.75	1.00
C217	AP81	20p car & bl gray (II) ('56)	45.00	8.00
		Nos. C208-C211,C213-C217 (9)	174.38	19.10

Printed in sheets of 30.

Type of 1950-52

Designs as in 1950-52. 2p, Guerrero, view of Taxco. 2.25p, Michoacan, masks.

Two types of 2p:

I- No dots after "Colonial". Frame line at right broken near top.

II- Three dots in a line after "Colonial". Right frame line unbroken.

Wmk. 300, Vertical

1955-65 ***Perf. 11½x11***

C218	AP81	5c bluish grn ('56)	15	15
		Perf. 11		
C219	AP81	10c org brn ('60)	28	15
a.		Perf. 11½x11	90	35
C220	AP81	20c car ('60)	28	15
k.		Perf. 11½x11 ('57)	1.40	15
C220A	AP81	25c vio brn, perf. 11½x11	1.50	15
C220B	AP81	30c ol gray ('60)	15	15
l.		Perf. 11½x11	70	15
C220C	AP81	35c dk vio, perf. 11½x11	70	15
C220D	AP81	40c sl bl ('60)	28	15
m.		Perf. 11½x11	8.50	15
C220E	AP81	50c green, perf. 11½x11	70	15
n.		Perf. 11 ('60)	90	15
q.		50c yellow green	90	18
C220F	AP81	80c cl ('60)	4.25	50
o.		Perf. 11½x11	4.25	50
C220G	AP81	1p grn gray ('60)	90	25
p.		Perf. 11½x11	10.50	25
C220H	AP81	2p dk org brn, II ('63)	90	50
i.		2p lt org brn, perf. 11½x11 ('65)	110.00	35.00
j.		2p org brn, I, perf. 11	7.00	1.00
C221	AP81	2.25p mar ('63)	55	60
		Nos. C218-C221 (12)	10.64	3.05

Printed in sheets of 50. Nos. C218-C221 have been re-engraved.

No. C218 has been redrawn and there are many differences. "CTS" measures 7mm; it is 5½mm on No. C208.

Nos. C208-C221 exist in various shades.

For No. C220C, see note after No. C198.

No. C220n was privately overprinted in red: "25vo Aniversario / Primer Cohete Internacional / Reynosa, Mexico-McAllen, U.S.A. / 1936-1961".

Mayan Ball Court and Player — AP87

Design: 35c, Modern Stadium, Mexico.

1954, Mar. 6 **Photo.** ***Perf. 14***

C222	AP87	25c brn & dk bl grn	75	30
C223	AP87	35c dl sl grn & lil rose	60	20

7th Central American & Caribbean Games.

Allegory AP88

1954, Sept. 15

C224	AP88	25c red brn & dp bl	42	20
C225	AP88	35c dk bl & vio brn	18	15
C226	AP88	80c blk & bl grn	20	20

Centenary of national anthem.

Aztec God Tezcatlipoca and Map — AP89

Design: 35c, Stadium and map.

1955, Mar. 12

C227	AP89	25c dk Prus grn & red brn	60	25
C228	AP89	35c car & brn	60	25

2nd Pan American Games, 1955.

Ornaments and Mask, Archeological Era — AP90

Designs: 10c, Virrey Enriquez de Almanza, bell tower and coach, colonial era. 50c, Jose Maria Morelos and cannon, heroic Mexico. 1p, Woman and child and horse back rider, revolutionary Mexico. 1.20p, Sombrero and Spurs, popular Mexico. 5p, Pointing hand and school, modern Mexico.

Perf. 11½x11

1956, Aug. 1 **Engr.** **Wmk. 300**

C229	AP90	5c black	35	15
C230	AP90	10c lt bl	35	15
C231	AP90	50c vio brn	25	15
C232	AP90	1p bl gray	35	15
C233	AP90	1.20p magenta	35	20
C234	AP90	5p bl grn	1.00	1.00
a.		Souv. sheet of 6, #C229-C234, perf. 10½x10	30.00	30.00
		Nos. C229-C234 (6)	2.65	1.80

Centenary of Mexico's 1st postage stamps. No. C234a sold for 15 pesos.

Paricutin Volcano AP91

1956, Sept. 5 **Photo.** ***Perf. 14***

C235	AP91	50c dk vio bl	40	15

20th Intl. Geological Cong., Mexico City.

Valentin Gomez Farias and Melchor Ocampo AP92

Design: 1.20p, Leon Guzman and Ignacio Ramirez.

1956-63 **Wmk. 300** ***Perf. 14***

C236	AP92	15c intense bl	40	15
C237	AP92	1.20p dk grn & pur	70	30
b.		Dark green omitted	90.00	
c.		Purple omitted	100.00	
C237A	AP92	2.75p pur ('63)	1.00	65

Centenary of the constitution (in 1957). See Nos. C289, C445, C451, C471A.

Map — AP93

1956, Dec. 1

C238	AP93	25c gray & dk bl	30	15

Issued to publicize the 4th Inter-American Regional Tourism Congress of the Gulf of Mexico and the Caribbean (in 1955).

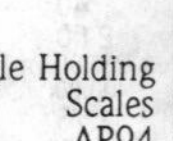

Eagle Holding Scales AP94

Design: 1p, Allegorical figure writing the law.

1957, Aug. 31 **Photo.** ***Perf. 14***

C239	AP94	50c metallic red brn & green	30	15
C240	AP94	1p metallic lilac & ultra	40	20

Centenary of 1857 Constitution.

Globe, Weights and Measure AP95

1957, Sept. 21

C241	AP95	50c metallic bl & blk	40	15

Issued to commemorate the centenary of the adoption of the metric system in Mexico.

Death of Jesus Garcia AP96

1957, Nov. 7 **Wmk. 300** ***Perf. 14***

C242	AP96	50c car rose & dk vio	35	15

50th anniversary of the death of Jesus Garcia, hero of Nacozari.

Oil Industry Symbols AP97

Design: 1p, Derricks at night.

1958, Aug. 30

C243	AP97	50c emer & blk	25	15
C244	AP97	1p car & bluish blk	40	15
		Set value		20

20th anniversary of the nationalization of Mexico's oil industry.

Independence Monument Figure AP98

1958, Dec. 15 **Engr.** ***Perf. 11***

C245	AP98	50c gray blue	25	15

10th anniversary of the signing of the Universal Declaration of Human Rights.

Pres. Venustiano Carranza AP99

1960, Jan. 15 **Photo.** ***Perf. 14***

C246	AP99	50c salmon & dk bl	25	15

Centenary of the birth of President Venustiano Carranza.

Alberto Braniff's 1910 Plane, Douglas DC-7 and Mexican Airlines Map AP100

1960, May 15 **Wmk. 300** ***Perf. 14***

C247	AP100	50c lt brn & vio	50	15
C248	AP100	1p lt brn & bl grn	40	20

50th anniversary of Mexican aviation.

Type of 1950-52 inscribed: "HOMENAJE AL COLECCIONISTA DEL TIMBRE DEL MEXICO-JUNIO 1960"

1960, June 8 **Engr.** ***Perf. 10½x10***

C249	AP81	20p lil, brn & lt grn	42.50	80.00

See note below No. 909.

Flag — AP101

Designs: 1.20p, Bell of Dolores and eagle. 5p, Dolores Church.

Wmk. 300

1960, Sept. 16 **Photo.** ***Perf. 14***

C250	AP101	50c dp grn & brt red	35	15
C251	AP101	1.20p grnsh bl & dk brn	45	20
C252	AP101	5p sep & grn	4.50	1.75

150th anniversary of independence.

Aviation (Douglas DC-8 Airliner) AP102

Designs: 1p, Oil industry. 1.20p, Road development. 5p, Water power (dam).

1960, Nov. 20 **Photo.** ***Perf. 14***

C253	AP102	50c gray bl & blk	35	15
C254	AP102	1p dk grn & rose car	40	20
C255	AP102	1.20p dk grn & sep	40	25
C256	AP102	5p bl & lil	2.00	90

50th anniversary of Mexican Revolution.

Count de Revilla Gigedo — AP103

1960, Dec. 23

C257	AP103	60c dk car & blk	50	15

80th census and to honor Juan Vicente Güémez Pacheco de Padilla Horcasitas, Count de Revilla Gigedo, was conducted the 1st census in America, 1793.

Railroad Tracks and Map AP104

Design: 70c, Railroad bridge.

1961, Nov. **Wmk. 300** ***Perf. 14***

C258	AP104	60c chlky bl & dk grn	35	15
C259	AP104	70c dk bl & gray	35	15

Opening of the railroad from Chihuahua to the Pacific Ocean.

Gen. Ignacio Zaragoza and View of Puebla
AP105

1962, May 5
C260 AP105 1p gray grn & sl grn 50 15

Centenary of the Battle of May 5 at Puebla and the defeat of French forces by Gen. Ignacio Zaragoza.

Laboratory
AP106

1962, June 11
C261 AP106 1p ol & vio bl 50 15

25th anniversary of the National Polytechnic Institute.

Pres. John F. Kennedy
AP107

1962, June 29
C262 AP107 80c brt bl & car 1.50 35

Issued to commemorate the visit of President John F. Kennedy to Mexico, June 29-30.

Globe
AP108

1962, Oct. 20
C263 AP108 1.20p vio & dk brn 50 20

Inter-American Economic and Social Council meeting.

Balloon over Mexico City, 1862 — AP109

1962, Dec. 21 Wmk. 300 *Perf. 14*
C264 AP109 80c lt bl & blk 1.40 50

Cent. of the 1st Mexican balloon ascension by Joaquin de la Cantolla y Rico.

Type of 1950-52
Imprint: "Talleres de Imp. de Est. y Valores-Mexico"

Designs as before.

Wmk. 300, Vertical
1962-72 Photo. *Perf. 14*

Two sizes of 80c:
I- 35½x20mm.
II- 37x20½mm.

C265 AP81	80c cl, I ('63)		1.25	25
a.	Perf. 11½x11, size II ('63)		3.50	30
b.	Perf. 11, size II ('63)		3.00	25
c.	Perf. 11, size I ('72)		2.00	15
C266 AP81	5p dk brn & yel org		3.50	85
C267 AP81	10p blk & lt grn ('63)		6.00	3.00
C268 AP81	20p car & bl gray		14.00	3.00
a.	2p carmine & aqua		14.00	4.00

Vert. pairs, imperf. horiz. of No. C265, perf. 11, may be from uncut rolls of No. C348.

ALALC Emblem
AP110

1963, Feb. 15 Wmk. 300
C269 AP110 80c org & dl pur 90 25

2nd general session of the Latin American Free Trade Assoc. (ALALC), held in 1962.

Mexican Eagle and Refinery
AP111

1963, Mar. 23
C270 AP111 80c red org & slate 50 15

25th anniversary of the nationalization of the oil industry.

Polyconic Map — AP112

1963, Apr. 22 Photo. *Perf. 14*
C271 AP112 80c bl & blk 75 25

19th Intl. Chamber of Commerce Congress.

EXMEX Emblem and Postmark
AP113

1963, Oct. 9 Wmk. 350 *Perf. 14*
C274 AP113 5p rose red 2.25 1.50

77th Annual Convention of the American Philatelic Society, Mexico City, Oct. 7-13.

Marshal Tito — AP114

1963, Oct. 15 Wmk. 350 *Perf. 14*
C275 AP114 2p dk grn & vio 1.75 60

Visit of Marshal Tito of Yugoslavia.

Modern Architecture — AP115

1963, Oct. 19
C276 AP115 80c dk bl & gray 60 20

Issued to publicize the International Architects' Convention, Mexico City.

Dove — AP116

1963, Oct. 26
C277 AP116 80c dl bl grn & car 1.00 30

Centenary of the International Red Cross.

Don Quixote by José Guadalupe Posada
AP117

1963, Nov. 9 Engr. *Perf. 10½x10*
C278 AP117 1.20p black 1.50 40

50th anniversary of the death of José Guadalupe Posada, satirical artist and Mexican independence hero.

Horse-drawn Rail Coach, Old and New Trains
AP118

Wmk. 350
1963, Nov. 29 Photo. *Perf. 14*
C279 AP118 1.20p vio bl & bl 80 30

11th Pan-American Railroad Congress.

Eleanor Roosevelt, Flame and UN Emblem
AP119

1964, Feb. 22 Wmk. 350 *Perf. 14*
C280 AP119 80c lt ultra & red 70 20

15th anniversary (in 1963) of the Universal Declaration of Human Rights and to honor Eleanor Roosevelt.

Gen. Charles de Gaulle
AP120

1964, Mar. 16 Photo.
C281 AP120 2p dl vio bl & brn 2.00 70

Visit of President Charles de Gaulle of France to Mexico, Mar. 16-18.

Pres. John F. Kennedy and Pres. Adolfo López Mateos and Map — AP121

1964, Apr. 11 Photo.
C282 AP121 80c vio bl & gray 75 20

Ratification of the Chamizal Treaty, returning the Chamizal area of El Paso, Texas, to Mexico, July 18, 1963.

Queen Juliana
AP122

1964, May 8 Wmk. 350 *Perf. 14*
C283 AP122 80c bis & vio bl 1.00 20

Visit of Queen Juliana of the Netherlands.

Lt. José Azueta and Cadet Virgilio Uribe
AP123

1964, June 18 Wmk. 350 *Perf. 14*
C284 AP123 40c dk brn & blk 45 15

50th anniversary of the defense of Veracruz (against US Navy).

Types of 1950-62

Designs as before.

Engraved; Photogravure (C296-C298)
Perf. 11 (20c, 40c, 50c, 80c, 2p); 14
1964-73 Wmk. 350

C285 AP81	20c car ('71)		70	1.00
C286 AP81	40c gray bl ('71)		125.00	*125.00*
C287 AP81	50c grn ('71)		45	45
C288 AP81	80c cl, I ('73)		45	45
C289 AP92	1.20p dk grn & pur		5.50	2.00
C290 AP81	2p red brn, II ('71)		1.40	1.25
C296 AP81	5p brn & org ('66)		9.00	7.50
C297 AP81	10p blk & aqua		20.00	15.00
C298 AP81	20p car & bl gray		32.50	22.50
Nos. C285-C290,C296-C298 (9)			195.00	*175.15*

National Emblem, Cahill's Butterfly World Map, Sword and Scales of Justice
AP124

1964, July 29 Photo.
C299 AP124 40c sepia & dp bl 60 15

10th conference of the International Bar Association, Mexico City, July 27-31.

Galleon
AP125

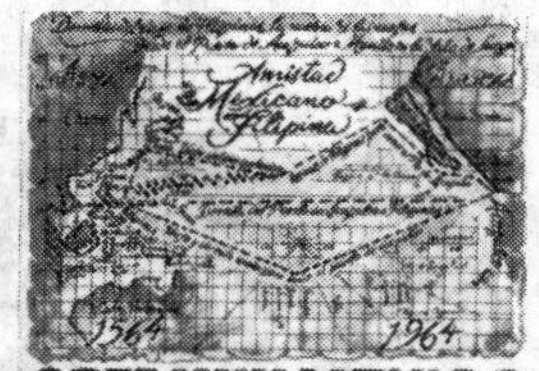

Map Showing 16th Century Voyages Between Mexico and Philippines — AP126

1964, Nov. 10 Wmk. 350 *Perf. 14*
C300 AP125 80c ultra & ind 2.25 35
C301 AP126 2.75p brt yel & blk 2.75 1.00

400 years of Mexican-Philippine friendship.

Catalogue values for unused stamps in this section, from this point to the end of the section, are for Never Hinged items.

Netzahualcoyotl Dam, Grijalva River — AP127

1965, Feb. 19 Photo. *Perf. 14*
C302 AP127 80c vio gray & dk brn 50 15

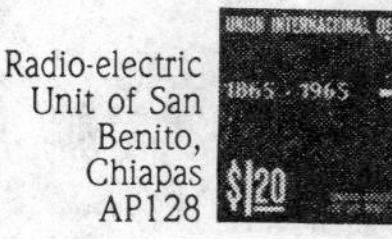
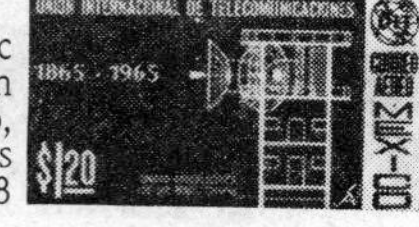

Radio-electric Unit of San Benito, Chiapas AP128

Design: 80c, Microwave tower, Villahermosa, Tabasco.

1965, June 19 Wmk. 350 *Perf. 14*
C303 AP128 80c lt bl & dk bl 65 30
C304 AP128 1.20p dk grn & blk 70 30

Centenary of the ITU.

Campfire, Tent and Scout Emblem AP129

1965, Sept. 27 Photo. *Perf. 14*
C305 AP129 80c lt ultra & vio bl 65 30

Issued to publicize the 20th World Scout Conference, Mexico City, Sept. 27-Oct. 3.

King Baudouin, Queen Fabiola and Arms of Belgium AP130

1965, Oct. 18 Wmk. 350 *Perf. 14*
C306 AP130 2p sl grn & dl bl 1.00 40

Visit of the King and Queen of Belgium.

Mayan Antiquities and Unisphere AP131

1965, Nov. 9 Photo.
C307 AP131 80c lem & emer 50 20

Issued for the NY World's Fair, 1964-65.

Dante by Raphael — AP132

Perf. 10x10½
1965, Nov. 23 Wmk. 350 Engr.
C308 AP132 2p hn brn 1.25 65

700th anniv. of the birth of Dante Alighieri.

Runner in Starting Position, Terra Cotta Found in Colima, 300-650 A.D. AP133

Designs: 1.20p, Chin cultic disk, ball game scoring stone with ball player in center, Mayan culture, c. 500 A.D., found in Chiapas. 2p, Clay sculpture of ball court, players, spectators and temple. Pieces on 80c and 2p from 300-650 A.D.

1965, Dec. 17 Photo. *Perf. 14*
Size: 35x21mm
C309 AP133 80c org & sl 65 25
C310 AP133 1.20p bl & vio bl 80 30
a. Souv. sheet of 4, #965-966, C309-C310, imperf. 1.50 1.50

Size: 43x36mm
C311 AP133 2p brt bl & dk brn 65 25
a. Souv. sheet, imperf. 1.50 1.50

19th Olympic Games, Mexico, 1968. No. C310a sold for 3.90p. No. C311a sold for 3p.

Nos. C310a and C311a have large watermark of national arms (diameter 54mm) and "SECRETARIA DE HACIENDA Y CREDITO PUBLICO." Issued without gum.

Ruben Dario — AP134

1966, Mar. 17 Wmk. 350 *Perf. 14*
C312 AP134 1.20p sepia 60 32

Ruben Dario (pen name of Felix Ruben Garcia Sarmiento, 1867-1916), Nicaraguan poet, newspaper correspondent and diplomat.

Father Andres de Urdaneta and Compass Rose AP135

Perf. 10½x10
1966, June 4 Engr. Wmk. 350
C313 AP135 2.75p bluish blk 1.25 60

4th centenary of Father Urdaneta's return trip from the Philippines.

UPAE Type of Regular Issue

Designs: 80c, Pennant and post horn. 1.20p, Pennant and UPAE emblem, horiz.

Wmk. 300
1966, June 24 Photo. *Perf. 14*
C314 A244 80c mag & blk 25 15
C315 A244 1.20p lt ultra & blk 32 15
Set value 24

U Thant and UN Emblem AP136

1966, Aug. 24 Photo. Wmk. 300
C316 AP136 80c blk & ultra 50 20

Visit of U Thant, Secretary General of the UN.

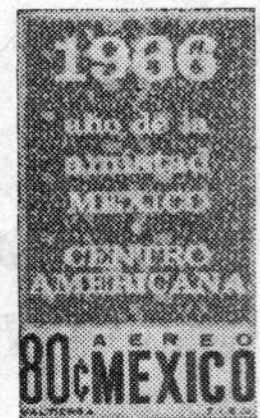

AP137

1966, Aug. 26 *Perf. 14*
C317 AP137 80c grn & red 22 15

Issued to publicize the year of friendship between Mexico and Central America.

Olympic Type of Regular Issue

Designs by Diego Rivera: 80c, Obstacle race. 2.25p, Football. 2.75p, Lighting Olympic torch.

1966, Oct. 15 Wmk. 300 *Perf. 14*
Size: 57x21mm
C318 A248 80c org brn & blk 40 15
C319 A248 2.25p grn & blk 60 35
C320 A248 2.75p dp pur & blk 1.00 50
a. Souv. sheet of 3 3.00 3.00

Issued to publicize the 19th Olympic Games, Mexico City, D.F., 1968. No. C320a contains 3 imperf. stamps similar to Nos. C318-C320 with simulated perforations. Sold for 8.70p.

UNESCO Emblem AP138

Litho. & Engr.
1966, Nov. 4 *Perf. 11*
C321 AP138 80c blk, car, brt grn & org 50 15
a. Perf. 10½ 5.00 2.00
b. Perf. 10½x11 25.00
c. Perf. 11x10½ 12.50 5.00

UNESCO 20th anniv.

Venustiano Carranza AP139

Tiros Satellite over Earth AP140

1967, Feb. 5 Photo. *Perf. 14*
C322 AP139 80c dk red brn & ocher 35 15

50th anniversary of the constitution. Venustiano Carranza (1859-1920), was president of Mexico 1917-20.

1967, Mar. 23 Photo. Wmk. 300
C323 AP140 80c blk & dk bl 50 20

World Meteorological Day, Mar. 23.

Medical School Emblem AP141

Captain Horacio Ruiz Gaviño AP142

1967, July 10 Wmk. 300 *Perf. 14*
C324 AP141 80c blk & ocher 32 15

Issued to commemorate the 50th anniversary of the Mexican Military Medical School.

1967, July 17 Photo.

Design: 2p, Biplane, horiz.

C325 AP142 80c blk & brn 24 15
C326 AP142 2p blk & brn 42 25

50th anniv. of the 1st Mexican airmail flight, from Pachuca to Mexico City, July 6, 1917.

Marco Polo and ITY Emblem — AP143

1967, Sept. 9 Wmk. 300 *Perf. 14*
C327 AP143 80c rose cl & blk 22 15

Issued for International Tourist Year, 1967.

Olympic Games Type of Regular Issue, 1967

Designs: 80c, Diving. 1.20p, Runners. 2p, Weight lifters. 5p, Soccer.

1967, Oct. 12 Photo. *Perf. 14*
C328 A254 80c dp lil rose & blk 24 15
C329 A254 1.20p brt grn & blk 28 20
a. Souv. sheet of 2, #C328-C329, imperf. 1.75 1.75
C330 A254 2p yel & blk 1.00 40
C331 A254 5p ol & blk 1.65 75
a. Souv. sheet of 2, #C330-C331, imperf. 4.25 3.75

No. C329a sold for 2.50p; No. C331a sold for 9p. Both sheets are watermark 350.

Heinrich Hertz and James Clerk Maxwell AP144

1967, Nov. 15 Photo. Wmk. 300
C332 AP144 80c brt grn & blk 28 15

2nd Intl. Telecommunications Plan Conf., Mexico City, Oct. 30-Nov. 15.

EFIMEX Emblem, Showing Official Stamp of 1884 — AP145

1968, Feb. 24 Wmk. 300 *Perf. 14*
C333 AP145 80c blk & grn 45 24
C334 AP145 2p blk & ver 45 24

EFIMEX '68, International Philatelic Exhibition, Mexico City, Nov. 1-9, 1968.

Olympic Games Type of Regular Issue, 1967

Designs: 80c, Sailing. 1p, Rowing. 2p, Volleyball. 5p, Equestrian.

1968, Mar. 21 Photo. *Perf. 14*

C335 A254 80c ultra & blk		22	15
C336 A254 1p brt bl grn & blk		28	20
a. Souv. sheet of 2, #C335-C336, imperf.		1.50	1.50
C337 A254 2p yel & blk		60	30
C338 A254 5p red brn & blk		1.25	1.10
a. Souv. sheet of 2, #C337-C338, imperf.		2.75	2.75

No. C336a sold for 2.40p; No. C338a sold for 9p. Both sheets are watermark 350.

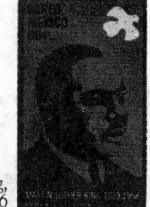

Martin Luther King, Jr. — AP146

1968, June 8 Photo. Wmk. 300

C339 AP146 80c blk & gray	35	15

Rev. Dr. Martin Luther King, Jr. (1929-1968), American civil rights leader.

Olympic Types of Regular Issue, 1968

Designs: 80c, Peace dove and Olympic rings. 1p, Discobolus. 2p, Olympic medals. 5p, Symbols of Olympic sports events. 10p, Symbolic design for Mexican Olympic Games.

1968, Oct. 12 Wmk. 350 *Perf. 14*

C340 A259 80c grn, lil & org	24	15
C341 A259 1p grn, bl & blk	28	15
C342 A259 2p multi	75	50
a. Souvenir sheet of 3, #C340-C342, imperf.	4.50	4.50
C343 A260 5p multi	3.00	1.40
C344 A260 10p blk & multi	2.50	1.50
a. Souvenir sheet of 2, #C343-C344, imperf.	7.50	7.50
Nos. C340-C344 (5)	6.77	3.70

19th Olympic Games, Mexico City, Oct. 12-27. No. C342a sold for 5p. No. C344a sold for 20p.

Souvenir Sheet

EFIMEX Emblem — AP147

1968, Nov. 1 Photo. *Imperf.*

C345 AP147 5p blk & ultra	2.10	2.10

EFIMEX '68 International philatelic exhibition, Mexico City, Nov. 1-9. No. C345 contains one stamp with simulated perforations.

Father Francisco Palóu (See footnote) AP148

1969, July 16 Wmk. 350 *Perf. 14*

C346 AP148 80c multi	38	15

Issued to honor Father Junipero Serra (1713-1784), Franciscan missionary, founder of San Diego, Calif. The portrait was intended to be that of Father Serra. By error the head of Father Palóu, his coworker, was taken from a painting (c. 1785) by Mariano Guerrero which also contains a Serra portrait.

Type of 1950-52 Redrawn

Coil Stamps

Wmk. 300 Vert.

1969 Photo. *Perf. 11 Vert.*

Imprint: "T.I.E.V."

C347 AP81 20c carmine	90	90

Imprint: "Talleres de Est. y Valores-Mexico"

C348 AP81 80c claret	1.10	1.10

Imprint: "T.I.E.V."

C349 AP81 1p gray grn	1.25	1.25

Soccer Ball — AP149

Design: 2p, Foot and soccer ball.

1969, Aug. 16 Wmk. 350 *Perf. 14*

C350 AP149 80c red & multi	32	15
C351 AP149 2p grn & multi	50	15

9th World Soccer Championships for the Jules Rimet Cup, Mexico City, May 30-June 21, 1970.

Mahatma Gandhi AP150

Astronaut's Footprint AP151

1969, Sept. 27 Photo. *Perf. 14*

C352 AP150 80c multi	28	15

of Mohandas K. Gandhi (1869-1948), leader in India's fight for independence.

1969, Oct. 29 Photo.

C353 AP151 2p black	50	22

Man's 1st landing on the moon, July 20, 1969. See note after US No. C76.

Tourist Issue

Type of Regular Issue, 1969-73 and

"Sound and Light" at Pyramid, Teotihuacan AP152

Designs: No. C355, Acapulco Bay. No. C356, El Caracol Observatory, Yucatan. No. C357, Dancer with fruit basket, Oaxaca. No. C358, Sports fishing, Lower California, horiz.

1969-73 Wmk. 350 *Perf. 14*

C354 AP152 80c shown	90	30
C355 AP152 80c multi	90	30
C356 AP152 80c multi	90	30

Wmk. 300

C357 A267 80c multi	35	25
C358 A267 80c multi	35	20
Nos. C354-C358 (5)	3.40	1.35

Issue dates: Nos. C354-C356, Nov. 1, 1969. Nos. C357-C358, Mar. 16, 1973.

Red Crosses AP154

1969, Nov. 8 Photo. Wmk. 350

C370 AP154 80c blk & multi	28	15
a. Red omitted	150.00	

50th anniv. of the League of Red Cross Societies.

AP155

AP156

1969, Dec. 6 Wmk. 350 *Perf. 14*

C371 AP155 80c multi	32	15

Installation of the ground station for communications by satellite at Tulancingo, Hidalgo.

1970, May 31 Wmk. 350 *Perf. 14*

Design: 80c, Soccer Ball, and Mexican Masks. 2p, Pre-Columbian sculptured heads and soccer ball.

C372 AP156 80c bl & multi	24	15
C373 AP156 2p multi	42	18

World Soccer Championships for the Jules Rimet Cup, Mexico City, May 30-June 21, 1970. The design of Nos. C372-C373 is continuous.

SPORTMEX '70 Emblem — AP157

1970, June 19 *Rouletted 13*

C374 AP157 2p gray & car	3.75	3.00

SPORTMEX '70 philatelic exposition devoted to sports, especially soccer, on stamps. Mexico City, June 19-28. The 2p stamp of No. C374 is imperf.

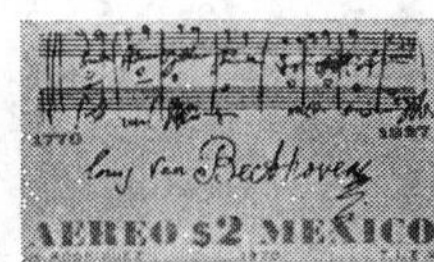

Ode to Joy and Beethoven's Signature AP158

1970, Sept. 26 Wmk. 350 *Perf. 14*

C375 AP158 2p multi	48	22

200th anniversary of the birth of Ludwig van Beethoven (1770-1827), composer.

UN General Assembly Floor Plan AP159

1970, Oct. 24 Photo. *Perf. 14*

C376 AP159 80c multi	30	15

25th anniversary of United Nations.

Isaac Newton AP160

1971, Feb. 27 Wmk. 350 *Perf. 14*

C377 AP160 2p shown	45	20
C378 AP160 2p Galileo	45	20
C379 AP160 2p Johannes Kepler	45	20

Mayan Warriors, Dresden Codex AP161

Designs: No. C381, Sister Juana, by Miguel Cabrera (1695-1768). No. C382, José Maria Velasco (1840-1912), self-portrait. No. C383, El Paricutin (volcano), by Gerardo Murillo ("Dr. Atl," 1875-1964). No. C384, Detail of mural, Man in Flames, by José Clemente Orozco (1883-1949).

Imprint includes "1971"

1971, Apr. 24 Photo. Wmk. 350

C380 AP161 80c multi	30	18
C381 AP161 80c multi	30	18
C382 AP161 80c multi	30	18
C383 AP161 80c multi	30	18
C384 AP161 80c multi	30	18
Nos. C380-C384 (5)	1.50	90

Mexican art and science through the centuries. See Nos. C396-C400, C417-C421, C439-C443, C513-C517, C527-C531.

Stamps of Venezuela, Mexico and Colombia AP162

1971, May 22 Photo. Wmk. 350

C385 AP162 80c multi	35	20

EXFILCA 70, 2nd Interamerican Philatelic Exhibition, Caracas, Venezuela, Nov. 27-Dec. 6, 1970.

Francisco Javier Clavijero AP163

1971, July 10 Wmk. 350 *Perf. 14*

C386 AP163 2p lt ol bis & dk brn	50	22

Francisco Javier Clavijero (1731-1786), Jesuit and historian, whose remains were returned from Italy to Mexico in 1970.

Buying Sets
Frequently it is less expensive to purchase complete sets rather than the individual stamps that make up the set. "Set Values" are provided for many such sets.

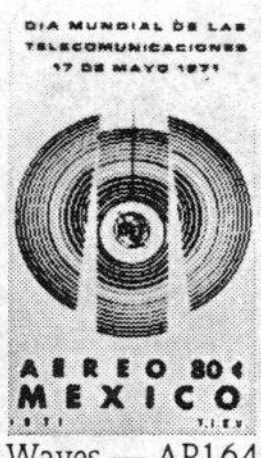

Waves — AP164

Mariano Matamoros, by Diego Rivera — AP165

1971, Aug. 7 Wmk. 350 *Perf. 14*
C387 AP164 80c multi 22 15

3rd World Telecommunications Day, May 17.

1971, Aug. 28 Photo.
C388 AP165 2p multi 42 20

Bicentenary of the birth of Mariano Matamoros (1770-1814), priest and patriot.

Vicente Guerrero AP166

Circles AP167

1971, Sept. 27
C389 AP166 2p multi 38 18

Vicente Guerrero (1783-1831), independence leader, president of Mexico. Painting by Juan O'Gorman.

1971, Nov. 4 Wmk. 300
C390 AP167 80c grnsh bl, dk bl & blk 30 15

25th anniv. of UNESCO.

Stamps of Venezuela, Mexico, Colombia and Peru AP168

1971, Nov. 4
C391 AP168 80c multi 42 15

EXFILIMA '71, 3rd Interamerican Philatelic Exhibition, Lima, Peru, Nov. 6-14.

Faces and Hand AP169

1971, Nov. 29
C392 AP169 2p blk, dk bl & pink 45 18

5th Congress of Psychiatry, Mexico City, Nov. 28-Dec. 4.

Ex Libris by Albrecht Dürer AP170

1971, Dec. 18
C393 AP170 2p blk & buff 65 18

Albrecht Dürer (1471-1528), German painter and engraver.

Retort, Pulley and Burner AP171

Scientists and WHO Emblem AP172

1972, Feb. 26 Wmk. 300 *Perf. 14*
C394 AP171 2p lil, blk & yel 35 15

Anniversary of the National Council on Science and Technology.

1972, Apr. 8
C395 AP172 80c multi 24 15

World Health Day 1972. Stamp shows Willem Einthoven and Frank Wilson.

Art and Science Type of 1971

Designs: No. C396, King Netzahuacoyotl (1402-1472) of Texcoco, art patron. No. C397, Juan Ruiz de Alarcon (c. 1580-1639), lawyer. No. C398, José Joaquin Fernandez de Lizardi (1776-1827), author. No. C399, Ramon Lopez Velarde (1888-1921), writer. No. C400, Enrique Gonzalez Martinez (1871-1952), poet.

Imprint includes "1972"

1972, Apr. 15 Wmk. 350
Black Inscriptions

C396 AP161 80c ocher 1.25 25
C397 AP161 80c green 1.25 25
C398 AP161 80c brown 1.25 25
C399 AP161 80c carmine 1.25 25
C400 AP161 80c gray bl 1.25 25
Nos. C396-C400 (5) 6.25 1.25

Mexican art and science through the centuries.

Rotary Emblem AP173

1972, Apr. 5
C401 AP173 80c multi 28 15

Rotary Intl. in Mexico, 50th anniv.

Tire Treads AP174

1972, May 11 Wmk. 300
C402 AP174 80c gray & blk 28 15

74th Assembly of the International Tourism Alliance, Mexico City, May 8-11.

Benito Juárez AP175

Design: 80c, Page of Civil Register. 1.20p, Juárez, by Pelegrin Clavé.

1972 Photo. *Perf. 14*
C403 AP175 80c gray bl & blk 20 15
C404 AP175 1.20p multi 25 15
C405 AP175 2p yel & multi 32 20

Centenary of the death of Benito Juárez (1806-1872), revolutionary leader and president of Mexico.
Issue dates: 80c, 2p, July 18; 1.20p, Sept. 15.

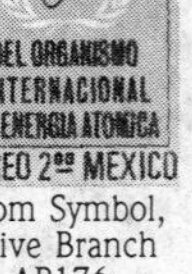

Atom Symbol, Olive Branch AP176

"Over the Waves," by Juventina Rosas AP177

1972, Oct. 3 Photo. Wmk. 300
C406 AP176 2p gray, bl & blk 40 15

16th Conference of the Atomic Energy Commission, Mexico City, Sept. 26.

1972, Oct. 16 *Perf. 14*
C407 AP177 80c olive bister 25 15

28th Intl. Cong. of the Societies of Authors and Composers, Mexico City, Oct. 16-21.

Child with Doll, by Guerrero Galvan, UNICEF Emblem AP178

1972, Nov. 4
C408 AP178 80c multi 75 20

25th anniv. (in 1971) of UNICEF.

Pedro de Gante, by Rodriguez y Arangorti AP179

Map of Americas with Tourists' Footprints AP180

1972, Nov. 22 *Perf. 14*
C409 AP179 2p multi 28 15

Brother Pedro de Gante (Pedro Moor or van der Moere; 1480?-1572), Franciscan brother who founded first school in Mexico, and writer.

Olympic Games Type of Regular Issue, 1972

Designs: 80c, Olympic emblems and stylized soccer game. 2p, Olympic emblems, vert.

1972, Dec. 9 Photo. Wmk. 300
C410 A289 80c grn & multi 20 15
C411 A289 2p yel grn, blk & bl 32 15
Set value 24

20th Olympic Games, Munich, Aug. 26-Sept. 11.

Anti-pollution Type of Regular Issue

Design: 80c, Bird sitting on ornamental capital, vert.

1972, Dec. 16
C412 A291 80c lt bl & blk 24 16

Anti-pollution campaign.

1972, Dec. 23
C413 AP180 80c blk, yel & grn 24 15

Tourism Year of the Americas.

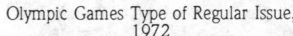

Mexico #O1, Brazil #992, Colombia #130, Venezuela #22, Peru #C320 AP181

1973, Jan. 19 *Perf. 14*
C414 AP181 80c multi 24 15

4th Interamerican Philatelic Exhibition, EXFILBRA 72, Rio de Janeiro, Brazil, Aug. 26-Sept. 2, 1972.

Aeolus, God of Winds AP182

1973, Sept. 14 Photo. Wmk. 300
C415 AP182 80c brt pink, blk & bl 60 20

Cent. of intl. meteorological cooperation.

Nicolaus Copernicus AP183

San Martin Monument AP184

Wmk. 300
1973, Oct. 10 Photo. *Perf. 14*
C416 AP183 80c slate green 30 15

500th anniversary of the birth of Nicolaus Copernicus (1473-1543), Polish astronomer.

Art and Science Type of 1971

Designs: No. C417, Aztec calendar stone. No. C418, Carlos de Sigüenza y Gongora (1645-1700), mathematician, astronomer. No. C419, Francisco Diaz Covarrubias (1833-1889), topographer. No. C420, Joaquin Gallo (1882-1965), geographer, astronomer. No. C421, Luis Enrique Erro (1897-1955), founder of Tonanzintla Observatory.

Imprint includes "1973"

1973, Nov. 21 Wmk. 350

C417 AP161 80c car & sl grn			15	15
C418 AP161 80c multi			15	15
C419 AP161 80c multi			15	15
C420 AP161 80c multi			15	15
C421 AP161 80c multi			15	15
Nos. C417-C421 (5)			75	
Set value				60

Type of 1950-52

Design: Mexico City University Stadium.

Imprint: "Talleres de. Imp. de Est. y Vallores-Mexico"

1973 Unwmk. *Perf. 11*

C422 AP81 80c claret, I — 1.25 95

Fluorescent printing on front or back of stamps consisting of beehive pattern and diagonal inscription.

Wmk. 350

1973, Nov. 9 Photo. *Perf. 14*

C423 AP184 80c org, ind & yel — 18 15

Erection of a monument to San Martin in Mexico City, a gift of Argentina.

Palace of Cortes, Cuernavaca AP185

Wmk. 300

1974, Jan. 18 Litho. *Perf. 14*

C424 AP185 80c blk & multi — 18 15

EXMEX 73 Philatelic Exhibition, Cuernavaca, Apr. 7-15.

Gold Brooch, Mochica Culture AP186

1974, Mar. 6 Photo. Wmk. 300

C425 AP186 80c gold & multi — 18 15

Exhibition of Peruvian gold treasures, Mexico City, 1973-74.

Luggage — AP187

1974, Mar. 22 *Perf. 14*

C426 AP187 80c multi — 20 15

16th Convention of the Federation of Latin American Tourist Organizations (COTAL), Acapulco, May 1974.

CEPAL Emblem AP188

1974, Mar. 22

C427 AP188 80c blk & multi	18	15
a. Red omitted	100.00	

25th anniversary (in 1973) of the Economic Commission for Latin America (CEPAL).

"The Enameled Casserole," by Picasso — AP189

1974, Mar. 29 Wmk. 300

C428 AP189 80c multi — 30 15

Pablo Ruiz Picasso (1881-1973), painter and sculptor.

EXFILMEX Type of 1974

1974, July 26 *Perf. 13x12*

C429 A305 80c buff, red brn & blk — 18 15

See note after No. 1065.

Biplane — AP190

Perf. 13x12

1974, Aug. 20 Photo. Wmk. 300

C430 AP190 80c shown	15	15
C431 AP190 2p Jet plane	22	15
Set value		20

50th anniversary of Mexican Airlines (MEXICANA).

Transmitter and Waves Circling Globe — AP191

1974, Oct. 4 Wmk. 300 *Perf. 14*

C432 AP191 2p multi — 20 15

First International Congress of Electric and Electronic Communications, Sept. 17-21.

Volleyball AP192

1974, Oct. 12 *Perf. 13x12*

C433 AP192 2p org, bis & blk — 20 15

8th World Volleyball Championship. Perforation holes are of two sizes.

Souvenir Sheet

Mexico #O1, Colombia #130, Venezuela #22, Peru #C320, Brazil #992, Mexico #123 — AP193

Wmk. 300

1974, Oct. 28 Photo. *Imperf.*

C434 AP193 10p multi — 1.50 1.50

EXFILMEX 74, 5th Inter-American Philatelic Exhibition, Mexico City, Oct. 26-Nov. 3.
Exists with red omitted.

Felipe Carrillo Puerto AP194

1974, Nov. 8 *Perf. 14*

C435 AP194 80c grn & gldn brn — 20 15

Birth centenary of Felipe Carrillo Puerto (1874-1924), politician and journalist.

Mask, Bat and Catcher's Mitt — AP195

1974, Nov. 29 Wmk. 350 *Perf. 14*

C436 AP195 80c multi — 20 15

Mexican Baseball League, 50th anniversary.

Man's Face, Mailbox, Colonial Period AP196

Design: 2p, Heinrich von Stephan, contemporary engraving.

1974, Dec. 13 Photo. Wmk. 300

C437 AP196 80c multi	18	15
C438 AP196 2p grn & ocher	18	15
Set value		24

Centenary of Universal Postal Union.

Art and Science Type of 1971

Designs: No. C439, Mayan mural (8th century), Bonampak, Chiapas. No. C440, First musical score printed in Mexico, 1556. No. C441, Miguel Lerdo de Tejada (1869-1941), composer. No. C442, Silvestre Revueltas (1899-1940), composer (bronze bust). No. C443, Angela Peralta (1845-1883), singer.

Imprint includes "1974"

1974, Dec. 20 Wmk. 300

C439 AP161 80c multi	15	15
C440 AP161 80c multi	15	15
C441 AP161 80c multi	15	15
C442 AP161 80c multi	15	15
C443 AP161 80c multi	15	15
Nos. C439-C443 (5)	75	
Set value		60

Types of 1950-56

Designs (as 1950-56 issues): 40c, San Luis Potosi, head. 60c, Leon Guzman and Ignacio Ramirez. 1.60p, Chiapas, Mayan bas-relief. 1.90p, Guerrero, Acapulco waterfront. 4.30p, Oaxaca, dance. 5.20p, Guerrero, view of Taxco. 5.60p, Michoacan, masks. 50p, Valentin Gomez Farias and Melchor Ocampo.

Engraved (40c), Photogravure
Perf. 11 (40c, 1.60p), 14

1975 Wmk. 300

C444 AP81 40c bluish gray	22	15
C445 AP92 60c yel grn	22	15
C446 AP81 1.60p red	90	15
C447 AP81 1.90p rose red	60	15
C448 AP81 4.30p ultra	75	15
C449 AP81 5.20p purple	1.10	40
C450 AP81 5.60p bl grn	2.25	50
C451 AP92 50p dk bl & brick red	13.00	2.50
Nos. C444-C451 (8)	19.04	4.15

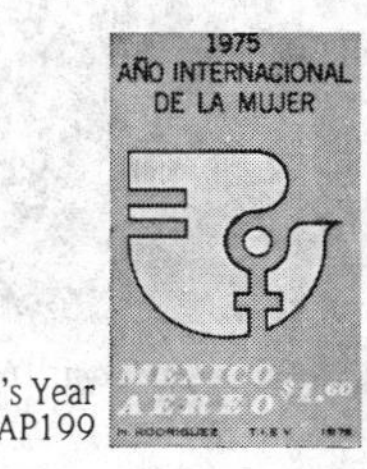

Women's Year Emblem — AP199

1975, Jan. 3 Wmk. 300 *Perf. 14*

C456 AP199 1.60p brt pink & blk — 20 15

International Women's Year 1975.

Declaration, UN Emblem, Mexican Flag AP200

1975, Feb. 7 Photo. Wmk. 300

C457 AP200 1.60p multi — 15 15

Declaration of Economic Rights and Duties of Nations.

Balsa Raft "Acali" AP201

1975, Mar. 7 Wmk. 300 *Perf. 14*

C458 AP201 80c multi — 20 15

Trans-Atlantic voyage of the "Acali" from Canary Islands to Yucatan, May-Aug. 1973.

The Scott Catalogue value is a retail price, what you could expect to pay for the stamp in a grade of Fine-Very Fine. The value listed is a reference which reflects recent actual dealer selling price.

Dr. Miguel Jimenez, by I. Ramirez
AP202

Miguel de Cervantes
AP203

1975, Mar. 24 Unwmk. *Perf. 14*

C459	AP202	2p multi	20	15

Fifth World Gastroenterology Congress.

1975, Apr. 26 Photo. Unwmk.

C460	AP203	1.60p bl blk & dk car	20	15

Third International Cervantes Festival, Guanajuato, Apr. 26-May 11.

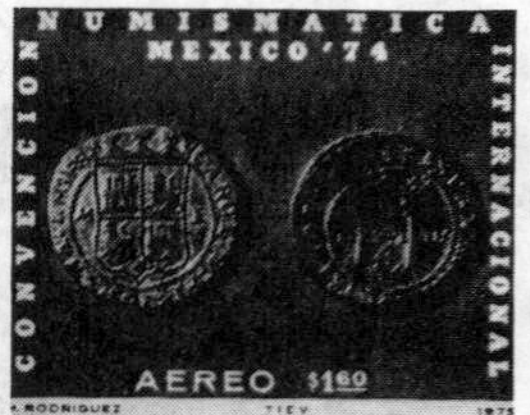

Four-reales Coin, 1675 — AP204

1975, May 2

C461	AP204	1.60p bl, gold & blk	20	15

Intl. Numismatic Convention, Mexico City, Mar. 28-30, 1974, and 300th anniv. of 1st coin struck by Mexico City Mint.

Salvador Novo, by Roberto Montenegro
AP205

1975, May 9

C462	AP205	1.60p multi	20	15

Salvador Novo (1904-1974), author.

Mural, Siqueiros — AP206

1975, May 16

C463	AP206	1.60p multi	20	15

David Alfaro Siqueiros (1896-1974), painter.

UN and IWY Emblems
AP207

1975, June 19

C464	AP207	1.60p ultra & pink	20	15

International Women's Year World Conference, Mexico City, June 19-July 2.

Mexico City Coat of Arms
AP208

Unwmk.

1975, Aug. 1 Photo. *Perf. 14*

C465	AP208	1.60p multi	20	15

650th anniv. of Tenochtitlan (Mexico City).

Domingo F. Sarmiento
AP209

Teachers' Monument
AP210

Unwmk.

1975, Aug. 9 Photo. *Perf. 14*

C466	AP209	1.60p brn & sl grn	20	15

1st International Congress of Third World Educators, Acapulco, Aug. 5-9. Domingo Faustino Sarmiento (1811-1888), Argentinian statesman, writer and educator.

1975, Aug. 9

C467	AP210	4.30p grn & ocher	30	15

Mexican-Lebanese friendship. The monument in Mexico City, by I Naffa al Rozzi, shows Cadmus, a mythical Phoenician, teaching the alphabet.

7th Pan American Games' Emblem
AP211

1975, Aug. 29

C468	AP211	1.60p multi	20	15

Pan American Games, Mexico City, Oct. 13-26.

Dr. Atl, Self-portrait
AP212

Unwmk.

1975, Oct. 3 Photo. *Perf. 14*

C469	AP212	4.30p multi	30	15

Geraldo Murillo ("Dr. Atl," 1875-1924), painter and writer, birth centenary.

Globe and Traffic Circle — AP213

1975, Oct. 12

C470	AP213	1.60p bl, blk & gray	20	15

15th World Road Congress, Mexico City, Oct. 12-26.

Type of 1950-52

Designs: 40c, San Luis Potosi, head. 80c, Mexico City University stadium. 1p, Puebla, Half Moon dance. 1.60p, Chiapas, Mayan bas-relief. 5p, Queretaro, architecture. 5.60p, Michoacan, masks. 10p, Miguel Hidalgo. 20p, Modern building.

Perf. 11 (40c, 80c, 1p, 1.60p), 14
Engraved (40c, 1p), Photogravure

1975-76 Unwmk.

C471	AP81	40c	bluish gray	32	32
C471A	AP92	60c	yel grn		
C472	AP81	80c	claret, II	60	48
C473	AP81	1p	grysh grn	1.00	80
C474	AP81	1.60p	red	1.40	1.00
C476	AP81	5p	dk brn & org ('76)	1.25	1.00
a.			5p dark brown & red org	2.00	2.00
C477	AP81	5.60p	bluish grn ('76)	4.75	3.25
C479	AP81	10p	blk & grn	3.50	2.50
C480	AP81	20p	red & dl grn ('76)	6.25	4.00
			Nos. C471,C472-C480 (8)	19.07	13.35

Bicycle and Export Emblem
AP214

Designs: Export Emblem and 30c, Copper vase. 80c, Overalls. 1.90p, Oil valves. 2p, Books. 4p, Honey. 4.30p, Strawberry. 5p, Motor vehicles. 5.20p, Farm machinery. 5.60p, Cotton. 20p, Film. 50p, Cotton thread.

1975-82 Unwmk. Photo. *Perf. 14*

C486	AP214	30c	cop ('76)	15	15
C489	AP214	80c	dl bl ('76)	20	15
C491	AP214	1.60p	blk & org	15	15
a.			Thin paper ('81)	40	15
C492	AP214	1.90p	ver & dk grn	35	15
C493	AP214	2p	ultra & gold ('76)	40	15
C495	AP214	4p	yel bis & brn ('82)	1.00	20
C496	AP214	4.30p	brt pink & ol	15	15
C497	AP214	5p	dk bl & ocher ('76)	20	20
C498	AP214	5.20p	red & blk ('76)	40	40
C499	AP214	5.60p	yel grn & org ('76)	20	20
C503	AP214	20p	multi, thin paper ('81)	60	20
C508	AP214	50p	multi ('82)	2.00	2.00
			Nos. C486-C508 (12)	5.80	4.10

See Nos. C594-C603.

Art and Science Type of 1971

Designs: No. C513, Title page of "Medical History of New Spain," by Francisco Hernandez, 1628. No. C514, Alfonso L. Herrera (1868-1942), biologist. No. C515, Title page, Aztec Herbal, 1552. No. C516, Arturo S. Rosenblueth (1900-1970). No. C517, Alfredo Augusto Duges (1826-1910) French-born naturalist.

Imprint includes "1975"

1975, Nov. 21 Unwmk. *Perf. 14*

C513	AP161	1.60p buff, red & blk	15	15
C514	AP161	1.60p vio bl & multi	15	15
C515	AP161	1.60p blk & multi	15	15
C516	AP161	1.60p gray & multi	15	15
C517	AP161	1.60p grn & multi	15	15
		Nos. C513-C517 (5)	75	
		Set value		25

Telephone
AP216

60-peso Gold Coin, Oaxaca, 1917
AP217

1976, Mar. 10 Photo.

C518	AP216	1.60p gray & blk	20	15

Centenary of first telephone call by Alexander Graham Bell, Mar. 10, 1876.

1976, Mar. 25 Photo. Unwmk.

C519	AP217	1.60p blk, ocher & yel	20	15

4th International Numismatic Convention, Mexico City, March 1976.

Rain God Tlaloc and Calles Dam
AP218

1976, Mar. 29 *Perf. 14*

C520	AP218	1.60p vio brn & dk grn	20	15

12th International Great Dams Congress, Mar. 29-Apr. 2.

Perforation Gauge
AP219

1976, May 7 Photo. Unwmk.

C521	AP219	1.60p blk, red & bl	20	15

Interphil 76 International Philatelic Exhibition, Philadelphia, Pa., May 29-June 6.

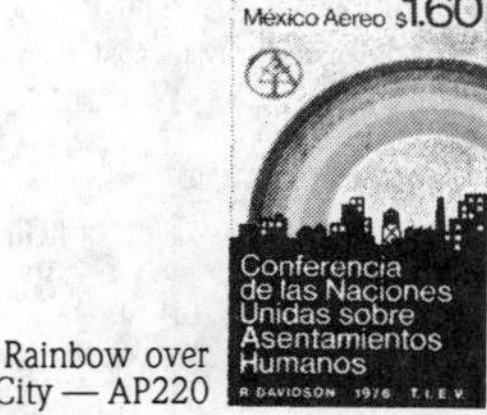

Rainbow over City — AP220

1976, May 31 Unwmk. *Perf. 14*

C522	AP220	1.60p blk & multi	20	15

Habitat, UN Conf. on Human Settlements, Vancouver, Canada, May 31-June 11.

Liberty Bell
AP221

"Peace"
AP222

1976, July 4 Photo. *Perf. 14*

C523	AP221	1.60p ultra & red	20	15

American Bicentennial.

1976, Aug. 3 Photo. *Perf. 14*

Design: "Peace" written in Chinese, Japanese, Hebrew, Hindi and Arabic.

C524 AP222 1.60p multi 20 15

30th Intl. Cong. of Science and Humanities of Asia and North Africa, Mexico, Aug. 3-8.

Television Screen AP223

1976, Aug. 24 Photo. Unwmk.

C525 AP223 1.60p multi 20 15

1st Latin-American Forum on Children's Television.

Luminescence

Fluorescent airmail stamps include Nos. C265, C265c, C288, C357-C358, C390-C415, C422-C423.

Airmail stamps issued on both ordinary and fluorescent paper include Nos. C220, C220D-C220E, C220G-C220H, C265b, C266-C268, C286.

Sky, Sun, Water and Earth AP224

1976, Nov. 8 Photo. *Perf. 14*

C526 AP224 1.60p multi 20 15

World Conservation Day.

Art and Science Type of 1971

Designs: No. C527, Coatlicue, Mother of Earth, Aztec sculpture. No. C528, El Caballito, statue of Charles IV of Spain, by Manuel Tolsá. No. C529, Chief Tlahuicole, bronze statue by Manuel Vilar. No. C530, Today's God, Money, seated ceramic figure, by L. Ortiz Monasterio. No. C531, Signal, abstract sculpture by Angela Gurria.

Imprint includes "1976"

1976, Dec. 10 Photo. *Perf. 14*

C527	AP161	1.60p blk & yel	15	15
C528	AP161	1.60p blk & red brn	15	15
C529	AP161	1.60p blk & multi	15	15
C530	AP161	1.60p car & multi	15	15
C531	AP161	1.60p car & blk	15	15
		Nos. C527-C531 (5)	75	
		Set value		25

Score for El Pesebre by Casals AP225

1976, Dec. 29

C532 AP225 4.30p lt bl, blk & brn 35 15

Pablo Casals (1876-1973), cellist and composer, birth centenary.

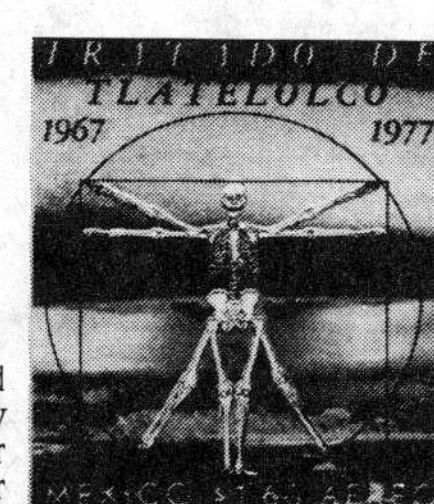

Mankind Destroyed by Nuclear Power AP226

1977, Feb. 14 Photo. *Perf. 14*

C533 AP226 1.60p multi 20 15
a. Wmk. 300 40.00 40.00

10th anniv. of the Agreement of Tlatelolco, banning nuclear arms in Latin America.

Soccer AP227

Anniversary Emblem AP228

1977, Aug. 23 Wmk. 300 *Perf. 14*

C534 AP227 1.60p multi 18 15
C535 AP228 4.30p blk, bl & yel 28 15

Mexican Soccer Fed., 50th anniv.

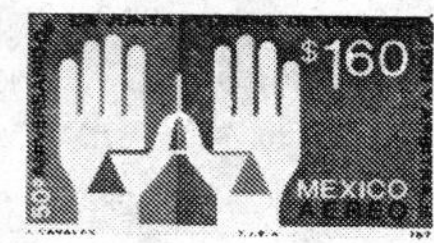

Hands and Scales AP229

1977, Sept. 28 Photo. *Perf. 14*

C536 AP229 1.60p org, brn & blk 18 15

Federal Council of Reconciliation and Arbitration, 50th anniversary.

Arms of Mexico and Spain AP230

Designs: 1.90p, Maps of Mexico and Spain. 4.30p, Pres. José Lopez Portillo and King Juan Carlos.

1977, Oct. 8 *Perf. 14*

C537 AP230 1.60p dl bl & blk 18 15
C538 AP230 1.90p lt grn & mar 22 15
C539 AP230 4.30p tan, grn & brn 22 15

Resumption of diplomatic relations with Spain.

Tlaloc, the Rain God AP231

Ludwig van Beethoven AP232

Wmk. 300

1977, Nov. 4 Photo. *Perf. 14*

C540 AP231 1.60p multi 18 15

National Central Observatory, centenary.

1977, Nov. 12 Photo.

C541 AP232 1.60p brt grn & brn 15 15
C542 AP232 4.30p lil rose & bl 25 15

Tractor and Dam AP233

1977, Nov. 25 Photo. *Perf. 14*

C543 AP233 1.60p multi 18 15

United Nations Desertification Conference.

Mexico City-Cuernavaca Highway — AP234

1977, Nov. 30

C544 AP234 1.60p multi 18 15

25th anniversary of first national highway.

Arms of Campeche — AP235

1977, Dec. 3

C545 AP235 1.60p multi 18 15

200th anniv. of the naming of Campeche.

Congress Emblem AP236

1977, Dec. 9

C546 AP236 1.60p multi 18 15

20th World Congress for Education, Hygiene and Recreation, July 18-24, 1977.

Freighter Navimex AP237

1977, Dec. 16

C547 AP237 1.60p multi 18 15

60th anniv. of National Merchant Marine.

Mayan Dancer, Jaina — AP238

Pre-Columbian Sculptures: No. C549, Aztec dance god. No. C550, Snake dancer, bas-relief. No. C551, Monte Alban, bas-relief. No. C552, Totonaca figurine.

1977, Dec. 26 *Perf. 14*

C548	AP238	1.60p sal, blk & car	15	15
C549	AP238	1.60p lt & dk bl & blk	15	15
C550	AP238	1.60p yel, blk & gray	15	15
C551	AP238	1.60p bl grn, blk & grn	15	15
C552	AP238	1.60p gray, blk & red brn	15	15
		Nos. C548-C552 (5)	75	
		Set value		25

Mexican art.

Tumor Clinic, by David A. Siqueiros — AP239

Design: 4.30p, La Raza Medical Center, by Diego Rivera.

1978, Jan. 19 Photo. Wmk. 300

C553 AP239 1.60p multi 18 15
C554 AP239 4.30p multi 28 15

35th anniversary of Mexican Social Security Institute.

Moorish Fountain — AP240

1978, Mar. 1 Photo. *Perf. 14*

C555 AP240 1.60p multi 18 15

450th anniversary of the founding of Chiapa de Corzo, Chiapas.

Oil Industry Type of 1978

Designs: 1.60p, Gen. Lazaro Cardenas. 4.30p, Offshore oil rig.

Wmk. 300

1978, Mar. 18 Photo. *Perf. 14*

C556 A343 1.60p brt bl & lil rose 18 15
C557 A343 4.30p bl, brt bl & blk 28 15

Oil industry nationalization, 40th anniv.

Arms of Diego de Mazariegos AP241

Wmk. 300

1978, Apr. 3 Photo. *Perf. 14*

C558 AP241 1.60p pink, blk & pur 18 15

400th anniversary of the founding of San Cristobal de las Casas, Chiapas, by Diego de Mazariegos.

Blood Pressure Gauge, Map of Mexico AP242

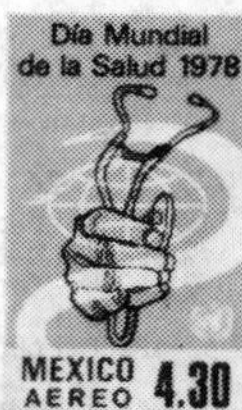

Globe, Snake, Hand Holding Stethoscope AP243

1978, Apr. 30

C559 AP242	1.60p	dk bl & car	18	15
C560 AP243	4.30p	org & dk bl	28	15

Drive against hypertension and World Health Day.

X-ABC1 Plane AP244

1978, Mar. 15

C561 AP244	1.60p	ultra & multi	18	15
C562 AP244	4.30p	ultra & multi	28	15

1st Mexican airmail route, 50th anniv.

Globe, Cogwheel, UN Emblem — AP245

Design: 4.30p, Globe, flags, cogwheel, UN emblem.

1978, Apr. 21

C563 AP245	1.60p	multi	18	15
C564 AP245	4.30p	multi	28	15

World Conference on Technical Cooperation of Underdeveloped Countries.

Soccer — AP246

Designs: 1.90p, Goalkeeper catching ball. 4.30p, Soccer player.

Wmk. 300

1978, June 1 Photo. *Perf. 14*

C565 AP246	1.60p	multi	15	15
C566 AP246	1.90p	multi	15	15
C567 AP246	4.30p	multi	28	15

11th World Cup Soccer Championship, Argentina, June 1-25.

Francisco (Pancho) Villa AP247

1978, June 5

C568 AP247	1.60p	multi	18	15

Pancho Villa (1878-1923), revolutionary leader, birth centenary.

Mexico No. C6, Independence Monument, Washington Monument — A248

1978, June 11

C569 AP248	1.60p	ol gray & red	18	15

50th anniversary of flight Mexico to Washington by Emilio Carranza (1905-1928).

Woman and Calendar Stone — AP249

Wmk. 300

1978, July 15 Photo. *Perf. 14*

C570 AP249	1.60p	rose, blk & brn	18	15
C571 AP249	1.90p	brt grn, blk & brn	18	15
C572 AP249	4.30p	org, blk & brn	28	15

Miss Universe contest, Acapulco, July 1978.

Alvaro Obregón AP250

1978, July 17

C573 AP250	1.60p	multi	18	15

Obregón (1880-1928), president of Mexico.

Geographical Institute Type of 1978

Designs: Institute emblem in different arrangements.

1978, July 21 Photo. Wmk. 300

C574 A344	1.60p	emer & blk	18	15
C575 A344	4.30p	ocher & blk	28	15

Pan-American Institute for Geography and History, 50th anniversary.

Sun Rising over Obregón AP251

1978, Aug. 4 *Perf. 14*

C576 AP251	1.60p	multi	18	15

50th anniv. of the founding of Obregón.

Mayan Figure, Castle and Pawn — AP252

Aristotle (384-322 B.C.), Philosopher — AP253

1978, Aug. 19 Photo. *Perf. 14*

C577 AP252	1.60p	multi	18	15
C578 AP252	4.30p	multi	28	15

World Youth Team Chess Championship, Ajedrez, Aug. 19-Sept. 7.

1978, Aug. 25

Design: 4.30p, Statue of Aristotle.

C579 AP253	1.60p	multi	18	15
C580 AP253	4.30p	multi	28	15

Mule Deer AP254

Man's Head, Dove, UN Emblem AP255

1978, Sept. 8 Photo. Wmk. 300

C581 AP254	1.60p	shown	18	15
C582 AP254	1.60p	Ocelot	18	15
		Set value		24

Protected animals.

1978, Sept. 22 *Perf. 14*

Design: 4.30p, Woman's head, dove, UN emblem.

C583 AP255	1.60p	ver, gray & blk	18	15
C584 AP255	4.30p	lil, gray & blk	28	15

Anti-Apartheid Year.

Emblem — AP256

Wmk. 300

1978, Oct. 23 Photo. *Perf. 14*

C585 AP256	1.60p	multi	18	15

13th Congress of International Union of Architects, Mexico City, Oct. 23-27.

Dr. Rafael Lucio (1819-1886) AP257

Franz Schubert, "Death and the Maiden" AP258

1978, Nov. 13 Wmk. 350

C586 AP257	1.60p	yel grn	18	15

11th International Anti-Leprosy Congress.

1978, Nov. 19 Photo. *Perf. 14*

C587 AP258	4.30p	brn, grn & blk	28	15

Schubert (1797-1828), Austrian composer.

Children, Christmas Decorations AP259

Antonio Vivaldi AP260

Wmk. 350

1978, Nov. 22 Photo. *Perf. 14*

C588 AP259	1.60p	multi	18	15

Christmas 1978.

1978, Dec. 1

C589 AP260	4.30p	multi	28	15

Antonio Vivaldi (1675-1741), Italian violinist and composer.

Wright Brothers' Flyer AP261

Design: 4.30p, Flyer, different view.

1978, Dec. 17

C590 AP261	1.60p	multi	18	15
C591 AP261	4.30p	multi	28	15

75th anniversary of 1st powered flight.

Einstein and his Equation AP262

Wmk. 300

1979, Apr. 20 Photo. *Perf. 14*

C592 AP262	1.60p	multi	18	15

Albert Einstein (1879-1955), theoretical physicist.

Rowland Hill — AP263

1979, Apr. 27
C593 AP263 1.60p multi 18 15

Sir Rowland Hill (1795-1879), originator of penny postage.

Export Type of 1975

Designs: Export Emblem and 50c, Circuit board. 1.60p, Bicycle. 1.90p, Oil valves. 2.50p, Tomato. 4p, Honey. 5p, Motor vehicles. 10p, Citrus fruit. 50p, Cotton thread.

1979-81 Photo. Wmk. 300

C594 AP214	50c ocher & red brn		15	15
C596 AP214	1.60p blk & org		20	15
C597 AP214	1.90p ver & dk grn ('81)		45	40
C599 AP214	2.50p ver & grn		15	15
C600 AP214	4p yel bis & brn ('81)		35	25
C601 AP214	5p dk bl & dl org		1.50	50
C602 AP214	10p grn & yel grn ('81)		90	75
C603 AP214	50p multi		2.50	1.50
	Nos. C594-C603 (8)		6.20	3.85

No. C600 exists with brown omitted.

Children, Child's Drawing — AP264

1979, May 16
C604 AP264 1.60p multi 15 15

International Year of the Child.

Registered Letter from Mexico to Rome, 1860 — AP265

Wmk. 300
1979, June 7 Photo. *Perf. 14*
C605 AP265 1.60p multi 15 15

MEPSIPEX '79, 3rd International Exhibition of Elmhurst Philatelic Society, Mexico City, June 7-10.

Sports Type of 1979

Designs: 1.60p, Games emblem. 4.30p, Symbolic flame and birds. 10p, Women gymnasts, horiz.

1979, June 15
C606 A348 1.60p multi 18 15
C607 A348 4.30p multi 28 15

Souvenir Sheet
Imperf

C608 A348 10p multi 1.00

No. C608 has simulated perforations.

University Type of 1979

Paintings: 1.60p, The Return of Quetzalcoatl, by Chavez Morado. 4.30p, Students Reaching for Culture, by Alfaro Siqueiros.

1979, July 10 *Perf. 14*
C609 A350 1.60p multi 15 15
C610 A350 4.30p multi 28 15

Messenger and UPU Emblem AP266

1979, July 27 Photo. Wmk. 300
C611 AP266 1.60p multi 18 15

Cent. of Mexico's membership in UPU.

Sports Type of 1979

Designs: 1.60p, Tennis. 5.50p, Swimming. 10p, Various sports.

1979, Sept. 2 Wmk. 300 *Perf. 14*
C612 A352 1.60p multi 15 15
C613 A352 5.50p multi 28 15

Souvenir Sheet
Imperf

C614 A352 10p multi 1.10

Tourism Type of 1979

Designs: No. C615, Agua Azul Waterfall, Chiapas. No. C616, King Coliman statue, Colima.

Wmk. 300
1979, Sept. 28 Photo. *Perf. 14*
C615 A353 1.60p multi 18 15
C616 A353 1.60p multi 18 15
Set value 24

Graphic Design AP267

1979, Oct. 14 Photo. Wmk. 300
C617 AP267 1.60p multi 18 15

ICSID, 11th Congress and Assembly of the Intl. Industrial Design Council, Oct. 1979.

Mail Service Type of 1979

Designs: 1.60p, Martin Enriquez de Almanza, Viceroy of New Spain. 5.50p, King Philip II of Spain. 10p, Sailing ship, horiz.

1979
C618 A354 1.60p multi 15 15
C619 A354 5.50p multi 30 20

Souvenir Sheet
Imperf

C620 A354 10p multi 90 90

No. C620 contains stamp with simulated perforations.

Early Lamp — AP268

1979, Oct. 21 Wmk. 300
C621 AP268 1.60p multi 18 15

Centenary of invention of electric light.

Union Emblem AP269

Wmk. 300
1979, Nov. 12 Photo. *Perf. 14*
C622 AP269 1.60p multi 18 15

Latin American Universities Union, 8th general assembly.

Christmas Type of 1979

Design: 1.60p, Girl and Christmas tree.

1979, Nov. 15
C623 A355 1.60p multi 18 15

Moon Symbol from Mexican Codex AP270

1979, Nov. 30
C624 AP270 2.50p multi 18 15

Apollo 11 moon landing, 10th anniversary.

Monument Type of 1980

Stone Sculptures: 1.60p, Tlaloc, water god. 5.50p, Coyolxauqui, goddess.

1980, Feb. 16 Photo. *Perf. 14x14½*
C625 A356 1.60p multi 18 15
C626 A356 5.50p multi 28 20

16th Century Church, Acolman AP271

16th Century Churches in: No. C628, Actopan Convent. No. C629, Tlayacapan. No. C630, Yanhuitlan. No. C631, Yuriria. No. C628 actually shows Tlayacapan; No. C629, Actopan convent (inscriptions reversed).

1980
C627 AP271 1.60p multi 15 15
C628 AP271 1.60p multi 15 15
C629 AP271 1.60p multi 15 15
C630 AP271 1.60p multi 15 15
C631 AP271 1.60p multi 15 15
Nos. C627-C631 (5) 75
Set value 60

Flora and Fauna Types of 1980

Designs: No. C632, Flamingo. No. C633, Vanilla plant.

1980, Mar. 8 *Perf. 14*
C632 A357 1.60p multi 15 15
C633 A358 1.60p multi 15 15
Set value 24

Jules Verne AP272

Perf. 14x14½
1980, Mar. 24 Photo. Wmk. 300
C634 AP272 5.50p blk & red brn 30 15

Jules Verne (1828-1905) French science fiction writer.

Skeleton Smoking Cigar, UN Emblem AP273

1980, Apr. 7 *Perf. 14x14½*
C635 AP273 1.60p multi 18 15

World Health Day/Fight against cigarette smoking.

Costume Type

1980, Apr. 26 *Perf. 14*
C636 A359 1.60p Chiapaneca, Chiapas 18 15

AIR POST OFFICIAL STAMPS

Nos. C4 and C3 Overprinted in Black or Red **OFICIAL.**

1929 Wmk. 156 *Perf. 12*

CO1 AP1	25c dk grn & gray brn	2.50	3.00
a.	Without period	10.00	10.00
CO2 AP1	25c dk grn & gray brn (R)	2.50	3.50
a.	Without period	12.00	14.00
CO2B AP1	25c brn car & gray brn	7.00	8.50
c.	Without period	15.00	17.50

Types of Regular Issue of 1926 Overprinted in Red **HABILITADO Servicio Oficial Aereo**

1929, Oct. 15 Unwmk.

CO3 A90	2c black	42.50	42.50
CO4 A91	4c black	42.50	42.50
CO5 A90	5c black	42.50	42.50
CO6 A91	10c black	42.50	42.50
CO7 A92	20c black	42.50	42.50
CO8 A92	30c black	42.50	42.50
CO9 A92	40c black	42.50	42.50
	Nos. CO3-CO9 (7)	297.50	297.50

Horizontal Overprint

CO10 A93 1p black *1,500. 1,500.*

Nos. CO3-CO9 also exist with overprint reading up.

No. C26 Overprinted in Black **OFICIAL.**

1930 **Wmk. 156**
CO11 AP4 20c blk vio 75 *1.25*
a. Without period 12.00 *14.00*
b. Inverted overprint 10.00 *14.00*
c. As "a," inverted overprint 125.00

No. CO11 with red overprint is believed not to have been issued for postal purposes.

Plane over Mexico City OA1

1930 **Engr.**
CO12 OA1 20c gray blk 4.50 4.50
CO13 OA1 35c lt vio 85 *1.50*
CO14 OA1 40c ol brn & dp bl 1.00 *1.40*
CO15 OA1 70c vio & ol gray 1.00 *1.50*

No. CO12 Surcharged in Red

HABILITADO
Quince centavos

1931
CO16 OA1 15c on 20c 65 *1.00*
a. Inverted surcharge 125.00
b. Double surcharge 125.00

No. C20 Overprinted **OFICIAL.**

1932 ***Rouletted 13, 13½***
CO17 AP3 5c light blue 65 *75*

Air Post Stamps of 1927-32 Overprinted

SERVICIO OFICIAL

On No. C1a
1932 **Unwmk.** ***Perf. 12***
CO18 AP1 50c dk bl & cl 850.00 850.00

On Nos. C2, C2a
Wmk. 156
CO19 AP1 50c dk bl & red brn 1.00 *1.25*
a. 50c dark blue & claret 1.25 *1.50*

See note after No. C2.

On Nos. C11 and C12
1932 ***Perf. 12***
CO20 AP3 10c violet 15.00 18.00
CO21 AP3 15c carmine 225.00 250.00

On Nos. C21 to C23
Rouletted 13, 13½
CO22 AP3 10c violet 25 *40*
CO23 AP3 15c carmine 1.00 *1.40*
CO24 AP3 20c brn olive 1.00 *1.40*

Nos. C20, C21 C23 and C25 Overprinted **SERVICIO OFICIAL**

1933-34 ***Rouletted 13½***
CO25 AP3 5c light blue 25 *40*
CO26 AP3 10c vio ('34) 25 *60*
CO27 AP3 20c brn olive 50 *75*
CO28 AP3 50c red brn ('34) 65 *1.50*

On No. C2
Perf. 12
CO29 AP1 50c dk bl & red brn 1.00 *1.40*
a. 50c dark blue & claret 1.50 *2.00*

On No. C11
Perf. 12
CO30 AP3 10c vio ('34) 100.00 *125.00*
a. Double overprint *300.00*

SPECIAL DELIVERY STAMPS

Motorcycle Postman SD1

1919 **Unwmk.** **Engr.** ***Perf. 12***
E1 SD1 20c red & black 50.00 2.25

1923 **Wmk. 156**
E2 SD1 20c blk car & blk 25 20

For overprint see No. E7

Toltec Messenger with Quipu — SD2

1934
E3 SD2 10c brn red & blue 25 40

Indian Archer — SD3

Imprint: "Oficina Impresora de Hacienda Mexico."

1934 ***Perf. 10x10½***
E4 SD3 10c blk vio 1.25 40

See Nos. E5-E6, E8-E9.

Redrawn
Imprint: "Talleres de Imp. de Est. y Valores-Mexico."

1938-41 **Photo.** ***Perf. 14***
E5 SD3 10c slate violet 60 20
E6 SD3 20c orange red ('41) 40 15

Imperforate copies of No. E6 were not regularly issued.

No. E2 Overprinted "1940" in Violet
1940 **Engr.** ***Perf. 12***
E7 SD1 20c red & black 32 16

Redrawn Archer Type of 1941
1944-47 **Wmk. 272** **Photo.** ***Perf. 14***
E8 SD3 20c org red 1.10 20
Wmk. 279
E9 SD3 20c org red ('47) 1.40 20

Special Delivery Messenger SD4

Messengers' Hands Transferring Letter — SD5

1950-51 **Photo.** **Wmk. 279**
E10 SD4 25c bright red 30 15
E11 SD5 60c dk bl grn ('51) 1.75 75

Redrawn
1951
E12 SD4 25c bright red 24.00 3.00

Sharper impression, heavier shading; motorcycle sidecar ½mm from "s" of "centavos;" imprint wider, beginning under "n" of "inmediata."

Second Redrawing
1952
E13 SD4 25c bright red 7.00 1.00

Design 35½mm wide (33mm on Nos. E10 and E12); finer lettering at left, and height of letters in imprint reduced 50 per cent; three distinct lines in tires.

Redrawn Type of 1951
1954 **Wmk. 300**
E14 SD4 25c red orange 40 15

Type of 1951
1954
E15 SD5 60c dk bl grn 50 *1.00*

Hands and Pigeon — SD6

Plane Circling Globe — SD7

1956 **Wmk. 300** **Photo.** ***Perf. 14***
E16 SD6 35c red lilac 20 15
E17 SD7 80c henna brown 30 *1.25*

1962
E18 SD6 50c green 70 15
E19 SD7 1.20p dark purple 1.10 *1.25*

1964 **Wmk. 350**
E20 SD6 50c green 60 15
E21 SD7 1.20p dk pur 1.25 90

Catalogue values for unused stamps in this section, from this point to the end of the section, are for Never Hinged items.

1973 **Unwmk.**
E22 SD6 50c green 3.50 3.25

Fluorescent printing on front or back consists of beehive pattern and diagonal inscription.

1975 **Wmk. 300**
E23 SD6 2p orange 20 *1.00*
E24 SP7 5p vio bl 1.25 90

1976 **Unwmk.**
E25 SD6 2p red org 25 40
E26 SD7 5p dk vio bl 35 1.00

Watch — SD8

1976 **Unwmk.** **Photo.** ***Perf. 14***
E27 SD8 2p org & blk 15 *1.00*

INSURED LETTER STAMPS

Insured Letters — IL1

Registered Mailbag — IL2

Safe — IL3

1935 **Engr.** **Wmk. 156** ***Perf. 10½***
G1 IL1 10c vermilion 1.75 75
a. Perf. 10x10½
G2 IL2 50c dk bl 1.25 60
G3 IL3 1p turq grn 1.25 85

Nos. G1 and G4 were issued both with and without imprint.

1944-45 **Wmk. 272** ***Perf. 10x10½***
G4 IL1 10c ver ('45) 9.50 1.50
G5 IL2 50c dk bl 1.40 50
G6 IL3 1p turq grn 2.50 65

1947 **Wmk. 279** ***Perf. 10x10½***
G7 IL1 10c vermilion 8.00 85
G8 IL2 50c dark blue 10.00 1.50
G9 IL3 1p turq grn 3.50 1.00

Vault — IL4

1950-51 **Photo.** ***Perf. 14***
G10 IL4 20c blue 2.00 45
G11 IL4 40c purple 30 20
G12 IL4 1p yel grn ('51) 65 50
G13 IL4 5p dk bl & gray grn ('51) 1.00 1.00
G14 IL4 10p car & ultra ('51) 4.00 4.00
Nos. G10-G14 (5) 7.95 6.15

1954-71 **Wmk. 300**
G15 IL4 20c blue ('56) 20 15
G16 IL4 40c lt pur ('56) 20 15
G17 IL4 1p yel grn 30 20
a. Size: 37x20½mm ('71) 1.10 1.10
G18 IL4 5p bl & grn ('59) 1.00 1.00
G19 IL4 10p car & ultra ('63) 4.75 2.50
Nos. G15-G19 (5) 6.45 4.00

No. G17 measures 35x19½mm. Vertical measurement excludes imprint.

Catalogue values for unused stamps in this section, from this point to the end of the section, are for Never Hinged items.

1967 **Wmk. 350** ***Perf. 14***
G21 IL4 40c light purple 1.25 1.50
G22 IL4 1p yellow green 1.25 1.50

1975 **Photo.** **Wmk. 300**
G23 IL4 2p lilac rose 30 30
G24 IL4 20p orange & gray 1.80 3.00

Padlock — IL5

1976-81 **Unwmk.** **Photo.** ***Perf. 14***
G25 IL5 40c black & blue 15 15
G26 IL5 1p black & blue 15 15
G26A IL5 2p blk & bl ('81) 15 15
G27 IL5 5p black & blue 15 15
G28 IL5 10p black & blue 15 15
G28A IL5 20p black & blue 30 30
Set value 65 65

1979 **Photo.** **Wmk. 300**
G29 IL5 40c black & blue 15 40
G30 IL5 1p black & blue 15 20
G31 IL5 5p black & blue 15 40

G32 IL5 10p black & blue 15 20
G33 IL5 20p black & blue 50 65
Nos. G29-G33 (5) 1.10 1.85

Perf. 14½x14
1983-86 Photo. Unwmk.
Size of Lock: 20x31mm

G36 IL5 5p black & blue 45 40
G37 IL5 10p black & blue 45 40
G38 IL5 20p black & blue 80 80
G39 IL5 50p black & blue 1.50 1.50
G40 IL5 100p blk & bl ('86) 1.00 1.00
Nos. G36-G40 (5) 4.20 4.10

This is an expanding set. Numbers will change if necessary.

POSTAGE DUE STAMPS

D1

1908 Engr. Wmk. 155 *Perf. 14*

J1 D1 1c blue 1.00 1.00
J2 D1 2c blue 1.00 1.00
J3 D1 4c blue 1.00 1.00
J4 D1 5c blue 1.00 1.00
J5 D1 10c blue 1.00 1.00
Nos. J1-J5 (5) 5.00 5.00

For overprints and surcharges see Nos. 381-385, 434-438, 466-470, 495-499, 593-607.

PORTE DE MAR STAMPS

These stamps were used to indicate the amount of cash to be paid to the captains of the mail steamers taking outgoing foreign mail.

PM2

PM3

1875 Unwmk. Litho. *Imperf.*

JX9 PM2 2c black 60 50.00
a. "5" added to make 25c 12.00 100.00
JX10 PM2 10c black 80 30.00
JX11 PM2 12c black 80 50.00
JX12 PM2 20c black 1.00 50.00
JX13 PM2 25c black 3.25 50.00
JX14 PM2 35c black 3.25 60.00
JX15 PM2 50c black 3.00 60.00
JX16 PM2 60c black 3.00 75.00
JX17 PM2 75c black 3.50 75.00
JX18 PM2 85c black 3.25 100.00
JX19 PM2 100c black 4.00 100.00
Nos. JX9-JX19 (11) 26.45

Same, Numerals Larger

JX20 PM2 5c black 1.00 50.00
JX21 PM2 25c black 1.65 50.00
JX22 PM2 35c black 175.00
JX23 PM2 50c black 1.00 50.00
JX24 PM2 60c black 65.00
JX25 PM2 100c black 60 100.00
Nos. JX20-JX25 (6) 244.25

In Nos. JX9-JX19 the figures of value are 7mm high and "CENTAVOS" is 7½mm long. On Nos. JX20-JX25 the figures of value are 8mm high and "CENTAVOS" is 9½mm long.

Nos. JX9-JX25 exist with overprints of district names.

Counterfeits exist of Nos. JX9-JX31.

1879

JX26 PM3 2c brown 50
JX27 PM3 5c yellow 50
JX28 PM3 10c red 50
JX29 PM3 25c blue 50
JX30 PM3 50c green 50
JX31 PM3 100c violet 50
Nos. JX26-JX31 (6) 3.00

Nos. JX26-JX31 were never put in use.

Stamps of this design were never issued. Copies appeared on the market in 1884. Value, set, $22.

All were printed in same sheet of 49 (7x7). Sheet consists of 14 of 10c; 7 each of 25c, 35c, 50c; 4 each of 60c, 85c; 3 each of 75c, 100c. There are four varieties of 10c, two of 25c, 35c and 50c.

OFFICIAL STAMPS

Hidalgo — O1

Wove or Laid Paper

1884-93 Unwmk. Engr. *Perf. 12*

O1 O1 red 70 50
a. Vert. pair, imperf. betwn. 90.00
O2 O1 olive brn ('87) 45 30
a. Blue ruled lines on paper
O3 O1 orange 1.25 45
a. Vert. pair, imperf. betwn. 80.00
b. Perf. 11 10.00 8.00
O4 O1 blue grn ('93) 70 40
a. Imperf., pair 10.00 8.00
b. Perf. 11 10.00 8.00

Pin-perf. 6

O5 O1 olive brown 40.00 16.00

Wmk. "Correos E U M" on every Vertical Line of Ten Stamps (152)

1894 *Perf. 5½*

O6 O1 ultra 1.50 1.40
a. Vert. pair, imperf. horiz. 30.00
b. Imperf., pair 40.00

Perf. 11, 12

O7 O1 ultra 90 80

Perf. 5½x11, 11x5½

O9 O1 ultra 6.00 4.00

Regular Issues with Handstamped Overprint in Black **OFICIAL**

1895 *Perf. 12*

O10 A20 1c green 6.00 2.00
O11 A20 2c carmine 7.00 2.00
O12 A20 3c org brn 6.00 2.00
O13 A21 4c red org 9.00 4.00
a. 4c orange 14.00 5.00
O14 A22 5c ultra 12.00 4.00
O15 A23 10c lil rose 11.00 1.00
O16 A21 12c ol brn 24.00 10.00
O17 A23 15c brt bl 14.00 6.00
O18 A23 20c brn rose 14.00 6.00
O19 A23 50c purple 30.00 15.00
O20 A24 1p brown 75.00 30.00
O21 A24 5p scarlet 175.00 90.00
O22 A24 10p deep blue 300.00 165.00

Similar stamps with red overprint were not officially placed in use.

Black Overprint

1896-97 Wmk. 153

O23 A20 1c green 20.00 3.50
O24 A20 2c carmine 20.00 4.00
O25 A20 3c org brn 20.00 4.00
O26 A21 4c red org 20.00 4.00
a. 4c orange 25.00 7.50
O27 A22 5c ultra 20.00 4.00
O28 A21 12c ol brn 30.00 10.00
O29 A23 15c brt bl 35.00 15.00
O29A A23 50c purple 275.00 275.00
Nos. O23-O29A (8) 440.00 319.50

Black Overprint

1897 Wmk. 154

O30 A20 1c green 35.00 10.00
O31 A20 2c scarlet 30.00 12.00
O33 A21 4c orange 45.00 20.00
O34 A22 5c ultra 35.00 12.00
O35 A21 12c ol brn 45.00 15.00
O36 A23 15c brt bl 60.00 15.00
O37 A23 20c brn rose 40.00 6.00
O38 A23 50c purple 50.00 10.00
O39 A24 1p brown 125.00 40.00
Nos. O30-O39 (9) 465.00 140.00

Black Overprint

1898 Unwmk.

O40 A20 1c green 12.00 3.00
O41 A20 2c scarlet 12.00 3.00
O42 A20 3c org brn 12.00 3.00
O43 A21 4c orange 20.00 4.00
O44 A22 5c ultra 20.00 7.00
O45 A23 10c lil rose 260.00 175.00
O46 A21 12c ol brn 45.00 10.00
O47 A23 15c brt bl 45.00 10.00
O48 A23 20c brn rose 75.00 25.00
O48A A23 50c purple 125.00 50.00
Nos. O40-O48A (10) 626.00 290.00

The 10p unwatermarked exists.

Black Overprint

1900 Wmk. 155 *Perf. 14, 15*

O49 A25 1c green 15.00 1.00
O50 A26 2c vermilion 20.00 1.50
O51 A27 3c yel brn 20.00 1.00
O52 A28 5c dk bl 20.00 1.75
O53 A29 10c vio & org 25.00 2.25
O54 A30 15c lav & cl 25.00 2.25
O55 A31 20c rose & dk bl 30.00 1.00
O56 A32 50c red lil & blk 60.00 10.00
O57 A33 1p bl & blk 125.00 10.00
O58 A34 5p car & blk 250.00 30.00
Nos. O49-O58 (10) 590.00 60.75

Black Overprint

1903

O59 A25 1c violet 14.00 1.50
O60 A26 2c green 14.00 1.50
O61 A35 4c carmine 25.00 1.00
O62 A28 5c orange 25.00 5.00
O63 A29 10c bl & org 30.00 1.50
O64 A32 50c car & blk 75.00 10.00
Nos. O59-O64 (6) 183.00 20.50

Regular Issues Overprinted **OFICIAL**

On Issues of 1899-1903

1910

O65 A26 2c green 70.00 2.50
O66 A27 3c org brn 70.00 1.75
O67 A35 4c carmine 85.00 4.00
O68 A28 5c orange 90.00 20.00
O69 A29 10c bl & org 80.00 1.50
O70 A30 15c lav & claret 90.00 2.50
O71 A31 20c rose & dk bl 110.00 1.20
O72 A32 50c car & blk 150.00 14.00
O73 A33 1p bl & blk 275.00 50.00
O74 A34 5p car & blk 80.00 50.00
Nos. O65-O74 (10) 1,100. 147.45

On Issue of 1910

1911

O75 A36 1c violet 2.00 2.00
O76 A37 2c green 1.50 90
O77 A38 3c org brn 2.00 1.00
O78 A39 4c carmine 3.00 90
O79 A40 5c orange 5.00 2.75
O80 A41 10c bl & org 3.00 1.00
O81 A42 15c gray bl & cl 5.00 3.25
O82 A43 20c red & blue 4.00 1.00
O83 A44 50c red brn & blk 14.00 6.00
O84 A45 1p blue & blk 24.00 10.00
O85 A46 5p car & blk 90.00 50.00
Nos. O75-O85 (11) 153.50 78.80

Nos. 500 to 505 Overprinted **OFICIAL**

1915 Unwmk. *Rouletted 14½*

O86 A57 1c violet 50 1.00
O87 A58 2c green 50 1.00
O88 A59 3c brown 60 1.00
O89 A60 4c carmine 50 1.00
O90 A61 5c orange 50 1.00
O91 A62 10c ultra 60 1.00
Nos. O86-O91 (6) 3.20 6.00

All values are known with inverted overprint. All values exist imperforate and part perforate but were not regularly issued in these forms.

On Nos. 506 to 514

1915-16 *Perf. 12*

O92 A57 1c violet 50 1.00
O93 A58 2c green 50 1.00
O94 A59 3c brown 50 1.00
O95 A60 4c carmine 50 1.00
a. "CEATRO" 7.00 15.00
O96 A61 5c orange 50 1.00
O97 A62 10c ultra, type II 50 1.00
a. Double overprint 12.00
O98 A63 40c slate 4.00 6.00
a. Inverted overprint 12.00 10.00
b. Double overprint 20.00
O99 A64 1p brn & blk 5.00 6.00
a. Inverted overprint 14.00 14.00
O100 A65 5p cl & ultra 30.00 25.00
a. Inverted overprint 40.00
Nos. O92-O100 (9) 42.00 43.00

Nos. O98 and O99 exist imperforate but probably were not issued in that form.

Preceding Issues Overprinted in Red, Blue or Black

On No. O74

1916 Wmk. 155

O101 A34 5p car & blk 650.00

On Nos. O75 to O85

O102 A36 1c violet 3.00
O103 A37 2c green 60
O104 A38 3c org brn (Bl) 75
O105 A39 4c car (Bl) 3.25
O106 A40 5c org (Bl) 75
O107 A41 10c bl & org 75
O108 A42 15c gray bl & cl (Bk) 75
O109 A43 20c red & bl (Bk) 85
O110 A44 50c red brn & blk 90.00
O111 A45 1p bl & blk 5.00
O112 A46 5p car & blk 2,500.
Nos. O102-O111 (10) 105.70

No. O102 with blue overprint is a trial color. Counterfeits exist of Nos. O110, O112.

Nos. 608, 610 to 612, 615 and 616 Overprinted Vertically in Red or Black **OFICIAL**

Thick Paper

1918 Unwmk. *Rouletted 14½*

O113 A68 1c vio (R) 25.00 14.00
O114 A69 2c gray grn (R) 27.50 15.00
O115 A70 3c bis brn (R) 25.00 14.00
O116 A71 4c car (Bk) 25.00 15.00
O117 A74 20c rose (Bk) 50.00 40.00
O118 A75 30c gray brn (R) 80.00 70.00

On Nos. 622-623
Medium Paper
Perf. 12

O119 A72 5c ultra (R) 17.50 17.50
O120 A73 10c blue (R) 15.00 10.00
a. Double overprint 200.00
Nos. O113-O120 (8) 265.00 195.50

Overprinted Horizontally in Red **OFICIAL**

On Nos. 626-628
Thin Paper

O121 A63 40c vio (R) 14.00 12.00
O122 A64 1p bl & blk (R) 35.00 30.00
O123 A65 5p grn & blk (R) 225.00 250.00

Nos. 608 and 610 to 615 Overprinted Vertically Up in Red or Black **OFICIAL**

Thick Paper

1919 *Rouletted 14½*

O124 A68 1c dl vio (R) 2.50 2.50
a. "OFICIAN" 30.00 30.00
O125 A69 2c gray grn (R) 4.00 1.50
a. "OFICIAN" 30.00 30.00
O126 A70 3c bis brn (R) 6.00 2.50
a. "OFICIAN" 40.00 40.00
O127 A71 4c car (Bk) 12.00 5.50
O127A A72 5c ultra 70.00 50.00
b. "OFICIAN"
O128 A73 10c bl (R) 4.00 1.00
a. "OFICIAN" 35.00 20.00
O129 A74 20c rose (Bk) 25.00 20.00
a. "OFICIAN" 60.00

On Nos. 618, 622
Perf. 12

O130 A68 1c dl vio (R) 20.00 20.00
a. "OFICIAN" 60.00 40.00
O131 A72 5c ultra (R) 20.00 9.00
a. "OFICIAN" 60.00 40.00

Overprinted Horizontally
On Nos. 626-627
Thin Paper

O132 A63 40c vio (R) 20.00 14.00
O133 A64 1p bl & blk (R) 12.00 10.00
Nos. O124-O133 (11) 195.50 136.00

Nos. 608 to 615 and 617 Overprinted Vertically down in Black, Red or Blue

OFICIAL

Size: 17½x3mm

1921 ***Rouletted 14½***

O134 A68 1c gray (Bk) 12.00 5.00
a. 1c dull violet (Bk) 7.00 3.00
O135 A69 2c gray grn (R) 2.00 1.20
O136 A70 3c bis brn (R) 3.50 1.25
O137 A71 4c car (Bk) 8.00 6.00
O138 A72 5c ultra (R) 10.00 5.00
O139 A73 10c bl, reading down (R) 12.50 5.00
a. Overprint reading up 25.00 25.00
O140 A74 20c rose (Bl) 20.00 12.00
O141 A75 30c gray blk (R) 10.00 10.00

Overprinted Horizontally
On Nos. 626-628
Perf. 12

O142 A63 40c vio (R) 12.50 12.50
O143 A64 1p bl & blk (R) 10.00 10.00
O144 A65 5p grn & blk (Bk) *200.00 200.00*
Nos. O134-O144 (11) *300.50 267.95*

Nos. 609 to 615 Overprinted Vertically in Black **OFICIAL.**

1921-30 ***Rouletted 14½***

O145 A68 1c gray 2.00 1.00
a. 1c lilac gray 40 30
O146 A69 2c gray grn 75 25
O147 A70 3c bis brn 35 25
a. "OFICAL" 20.00 10.00
b. "OIFCIAL" 20.00 10.00
c. Double overprint 60.00
O148 A71 4c carmine 6.00 1.00
O149 A72 5c ultra 40 25
O150 A73 10c blue 40 20
a. "OIFCIAL" 20.00
O151 A74 20c brn rose 4.00 4.00
a. 20c rose 2.00 1.00

On No. 625
Perf. 12

O152 A75 30c gray blk 6.00 2.00

Overprinted Horizontally
On Nos. 626, 628

O153 A63 40c violet 3.00 2.00
a. "OFICAL" 25.00 25.00
b. "OICIFAL" 25.00 25.00
c. Inverted overprint 35.00
O154 A65 5p grn & blk ('30) 100.00 *125.00*
Nos. O145-O154 (10) 122.90 *135.95*

Overprinted Vertically in Red On Nos. 609, 610, 611, 613 and 614

1921-24 ***Rouletted 14½***

O155 A68 1c lilac 65 40
O156 A69 2c gray grn 60 35
O157 A70 3c bis brn 1.65 40
O158 A72 5c ultra 65 35
O159 A73 10c blue 15.00 1.50
a. Double overprint

On Nos. 624-625
Perf. 12

O160 A74 20c rose 3.00 65
O161 A75 30c gray blk 8.00 2.00

Overprinted Horizontally
On Nos. 626-628

O162 A63 40c violet 6.00 3.00
a. Vert. pair, imperf. betwn.
O163 A64 1p bl & blk 15.00 10.00
O164 A65 5p grn & blk 90.00 *150.00*

Overprinted Vertically in Blue on No. 612
Rouletted 14½

O165 A71 4c carmine 3.00 1.50
Nos. O155-O165 (11) 143.55 *170.15*

Same Overprint Vertically in Red or Blue
On Nos. 635 and 637

1926-27 ***Rouletted 14½***

O166 A80 3c bis brn, ovpt. horiz. (R) 6.00 6.00
a. Period omitted 15.00 15.00
O167 A82 5c org (R) 14.00 15.00

Same Overprint Vertically Down On Nos. 650, 651, 655 and 656
Wmk. 156

O168 A79 2c scar (Bl) 10.00 10.00
a. Overprint reading up 15.00 15.00
O169 A80 3c bis brn, ovpt. horiz. (R) 2.50 2.50
a. Inverted overprint 30.00
O170 A85 10c claret (Bl) 17.50 8.00
O171 A84 20c dp bl (R) 7.00 6.00
a. Overprint reading up 7.00 6.00

Overprinted Horizontally
On Nos. 643, 646 to 649
Perf. 12

O172 A81 4c grn (R) 3.00 3.00
O173 A83 30c dk grn (R) 3.00 3.00
O174 A63 40c vio (R) 8.00 8.00
a. Inverted overprint 40.00
O175 A87 50c ol brn (R) 75 75
a. 50c yellow brown (R) 9.00 9.00
O176 A88 1p red brn & bl (R) 7.50 7.50
Nos. O168-O176 (9) 59.25 48.75

Same Overprint Horizontally on No. RA3, Vertically Up on Nos. 650-651, 653-656, 666

1927-31 ***Rouletted 14½***

O177 PT1 1c brn ('31) 30 50
O178 A79 2c scarlet 30 50
a. "OFICAIL" 15.00 15.00
b. Overprint reading down 75 1.00
O179 A80 3c bis brn, ovpt. horiz. 1.00 75
a. "OFICAIL" 20.00 15.00
O180 A82 4c green 75 55
a. "OFICAIL" 20.00 20.00
b. Overprint reading down 5.00 1.00
O181 A82 5c orange 2.00 1.50
a. Overprint reading down 2.00 1.25
O182 A94 8c orange 6.00 4.00
a. Overprint reading down 3.50 3.00
O183 A85 10c lake 1.00 1.00
a. Overprint reading down 1.00 1.00
O184 A84 20c dk bl 5.00 4.00
a. "OFICAIL" 20.00 20.00
b. Overprint reading down 10.00 10.00
Nos. O177-O184 (8) 16.35 12.80

Overprinted Horizontally
On Nos. 643 and 645 to 649

1927-33 ***Perf. 12***

O185 A81 4c green 3.00 2.50
a. Inverted overprint 15.00 15.00
O186 A85 10c brn lake 27.50 27.50
O187 A83 30c dk grn 70 50
a. Inverted overprint 15.00 15.00
b. Pair, tête bêche overprints 17.50 17.50
c. "OFICAIL" 17.50 17.50
O188 A63 40c violet 6.00 4.00
O189 A87 50c ol brn ('33) 1.75 2.00
O190 A88 1p red brn & bl 12.00 10.00
Nos. O185-O190 (6) 50.95 46.50

The overprint on No. O186 is vertical.

Nos. 320, 628, 633 Overprinted Horizontally **OFICIAL**

On Stamp No. 320

1927-28 **Wmk. 155** ***Perf. 14, 15***

O191 A46 5p car & blk (R) 90.00 *125.00*
O192 A46 5p car & blk (Bl) 90.00 *125.00*

Unwmk. ***Perf. 12***

O193 A65 5p grn & blk (Bk) 85.00 *125.00*
a. Inverted overprint 120.00 *120.00*
O194 A78 10p blk brn & blk (Bl) 100.00 *150.00*

No. 320 Overprinted Horizontally **OFICIAL.**

Wmk. 155 ***Perf. 14***

O195 A46 5p car & blk 150.00

Nos. 650 and 655 Overprinted Horizontally **OFICIAL**

1928-29 **Wmk. 156** ***Rouletted 14½***
Size: 16x2½mm

O196 A79 2c dull red 9.00 6.00
O197 A85 10c rose lake 14.00 6.00

Nos. RA1, 650-651, 653-656 Overprinted **SERVICIO OFICIAL**

1932-33

O198 PT1 1c brown 30 50
O199 A79 2c dl red 40 40
O200 A80 3c bis brn 1.50 1.50
O201 A82 4c green 5.00 4.00
O202 A82 5c orange 6.00 4.00
O203 A85 10c rose lake 1.75 1.50
O204 A84 20c dark blue 7.50 5.00
a. Double overprint 75.00 *45.00*
Nos. O198-O204 (7) 22.45 16.90

Nos. 651, 646-649 Overprinted Horizontally **SERVICIO OFICIAL**

1933 ***Rouletted 14½***

O205 A80 3c bis brn 1.50 1.50

Perf. 12

O206 A83 30c dk grn 4.00 1.50
O207 A63 40c violet 7.50 3.00
O208 A87 50c ol brn 1.25 1.50
a. "OFICIAL OFICIAL" 25.00 25.00
O209 A88 1p red brn & bl, type I 1.50 1.50
a. Type II 1.40 1.75

Overprinted Vertically On No. 656
Rouletted 14½

O210 A84 20c dk bl 9.00 5.00
Nos. O205-O210 (6) 24.75 14.00

Nos. RA1, 651, 653, 654, 683 Overprinted Horizontally **OFICIAL**

1934-37 ***Rouletted 14½***
Size: 13x2mm

O211 PT1 1c brown 2.50 3.00
O212 A80 3c bis brn 30 30
O213 A82 4c green 6.00 5.00
O214 A82 5c orange 30 30
O215 A96 15c dk bl ('37) 50 50
Nos. O211-O215 (5) 9.60 9.10

See No. O217a.

Same Overprint on Nos. 687A-692

1934-37 ***Perf. 10½***

O216 PT1 1c brn ('37) 50 60
O217 A79 2c scarlet 50 75
a. On No. 650 (error) 175.00
b. Double overprint 75.00
O218 A82 4c grn ('35) 70 80
O219 A85 10c brn lake 50 50
O220 A84 20c dk bl ('37) 60 60
O221 A83 30c dk bl grn ('37) 1.00 1.00

On Nos. 647 and 649
Perf. 12, 11½x12

O222 A63 40c violet 1.50 1.75
O223 A88 1p red brn & bl (I) 2.50 3.00
a. Type II 2.00 2.00
Nos. O216-O223 (8) 7.80 9.00

On Nos. 707 to 709, 712, 715, 716, 717, 718 and 719

O224 A108 1c orange 1.00 *2.00*
O225 A109 2c green 60 *1.00*
O226 A110 4c carmine 60 *70*
O227 A112 10c violet 60 *1.25*
O228 A114 20c ultra 80 *1.25*
O229 A115 30c lake 1.00 *2.00*
O230 A116 40c red brn 1.25 *2.00*
O231 A117 50c black 1.40 *1.40*
O232 A118 1p dk brn & org 4.00 *6.00*
Nos. O224-O232 (9) 11.25 *17.60*

PARCEL POST STAMPS

Railroad Train — PP1

1941 **Photo.** **Wmk. 156** ***Perf. 14***

Q1 PP1 10c brt rose 2.75 35
Q2 PP1 20c dk vio bl 1.75 35

1944-46 **Wmk. 272**

Q3 PP1 10c brt rose 1.75 1.00
Q4 PP1 20c dk vio bl ('46) 5.00 2.50

1947-49 **Wmk. 279**

Q5 PP1 10c brt rose 1.25 60
Q6 PP1 20c dk vio bl ('49) 1.60 60

Streamlined Locomotive PP2

1951

Q7 PP2 10c rose pink 2.00 40
Q8 PP2 20c blue violet 1.75 70

1954 **Wmk. 300**

Q9 PP2 10c rose pink 1.25 60
Q10 PP2 20c blue violet 1.25 1.50

POSTAL TAX STAMPS

Morelos Monument — PT1

Rouletted 14½

1925 **Engr.** **Wmk. 156**

RA1 PT1 1c brown 35 15
a. Imperf. 30.00

1926 ***Perf. 12***

RA2 PT1 1c brown 75 *5.00*
a. Booklet pane of 2 12.00

1925 **Unwmk.** ***Rouletted 14½***

RA3 PT1 1c brown 25.00 9.00

It was obligatory to add a stamp of type PT1 to the regular postage on every article of domestic mail matter. The money obtained from this source formed a fund to combat a plague of locusts.

In 1931, 1c stamps of type PT1 were discontinued as Postal Tax stamps. It was subsequently used for the payment of postage on drop letters (announcement cards and unsealed circulars) to be delivered in the city of cancellation. See No. 687A.

For overprints see Nos. O177, O198, O211, O216, RA4.

Protección a la Infancia

Mother and Child — PT3

Red Overprint

1929 **Wmk. 156**

RA4 PT1 1c brown 35 15
a. Overprint reading down 40.00 40.00

There were two settings of this overprint. They may be distinguished by the two lines being spaced 4mm or 6mm apart.

The money from sales of this stamp was devoted to child welfare work.

1929 **Litho.** ***Rouletted 13, 13½***

RA5 PT3 1c violet 25 15

PT4 PT5

1929 **Unwmk.**
Size: 18x24½mm

RA6 PT4 2c dp grn 40 15
RA7 PT4 5c brown 40 15
a. Imperf., pair 40.00 40.00
Set value 20

For surcharges see Nos. RA10-RA11.

1929 **Size: 19x25¼mm**

Two types of 1c:

Type I- Background lines continue through lettering of top inscription. Denomination circle hangs below second background line. Paper and gum white.

Type II- Background lines cut away behind some letters. Circle rests on second background line. Paper and gum yellowish.

RA8 PT5 1c vio, type I		15	15
a. Booklet pane of 4		10.00	
b. Booklet pane of 2		18.00	
c. Type II		40	15
d. Imperf., pair		35.00	35.00
RA9 PT5 2c deep green		40	15
a. Imperf., pair		12.00	

The use of these stamps, in addition to the regular postage, was compulsory. The money obtained from their sale was used for child welfare work.

For surcharge see No. RA12.

Nos. RA6, RA7, RA9 Surcharged

1930

RA10 PT4 1c on 2c dp grn	75	40
RA11 PT4 1c on 5c brn	1.00	60
RA12 PT5 1c on 2c dp grn	2.00	1.00

Used stamps exist with surcharge double or reading down.

No. 423 Overprinted

1931, Jan. 30 **Wmk. 155** ***Perf. 14***

RA13 A36 1c dull vio	30	40
a. "PRO INFANCIA" double	50.00	

Indian Mother and Child — PT6

Mosquito Attacking Man — PT7

Perf. 10½

1934, Sept. 1 **Engr.** **Wmk. 156**

RA13B PT6 1c dull orange	20	15

1939 **Photo.** **Wmk. 156** ***Perf. 14***

RA14 PT7 1c Prus blue	1.50	15
a. Imperf.	3.00	3.00

This stamp was obligatory on all mail, the money being used to aid in a drive against malaria.

See Nos. RA16, RA19.

Miguel Hidalgo y Costilla — PT8

Learning Vowels — PT9

1941

RA15 PT8 1c brt car	45	15

Type of 1939

1944 **Wmk. 272** ***Perf. 14***

RA16 PT7 1c Prus blue	1.00	15

1946 **Photo.** **Wmk. 279**

RA17 PT9 1c blk brn	45	15
a. 1c green black	1.00	1.00

1947 **Wmk. 272**

RA18 PT9 1c blk brn	40.00	4.00

Type of 1939
Wmk. 279

RA19 PT7 1c Prus blue	3.50	30

PROVISIONAL ISSUES

During the struggle led by Juarez to expel the Emperor Maximilian, installed June, 1864 by Napoleon III and French troops, a number of towns when free of Imperial forces issued provisional postage stamps. Maximilian was captured and executed June 19, 1867, but provisional issues continued current for a time pending re-establishment of Republican Government.

Campeche

A southern state in Mexico, comprising the western part of the Yucatan peninsula.

A1

White Paper
Numerals in Black

1876 **Handstamped** ***Imperf.***

1 A1 5c gray bl & bl		*2,000.*
2 A1 25c gray bl & bl		*1,100.*
3 A1 50c gray bl & bl		*4,500.*

The stamps printed in blue-black and blue on yellowish paper, formerly listed as issued in 1867, are now known to be an unofficial production of later years. They are reprints, but produced without official sanction.

Chiapas

A southern state in Mexico, bordering on Guatemala and the Pacific Ocean.

A1

1866 **Typeset**

1 A1 ½r blk, *gray bl*	*2,000.*	*1,300.*
2 A1 1r blk, *lt grn*		*850.00*
3 A1 2r blk, *rose*		*900.00*
4 A1 4r blk, *lt buff*		*2,000.*
a. Vertical half used as 2r on cover		*3,000.*
5 A1 8r blk, *rose*		*15,000.*
a. Quarter used as 2r on cover		*4,000.*
b. Half used as 4r on cover		*5,000.*

Chihuahua

A city of northern Mexico and capital of the State of Chihuahua.

A1

1872 **Handstamped**

1 A1 12(c) black	*1,200.*
2 A1 25(c) black	*1,000.*

Cuautla

A town in the state of Morelos.

A1

1867 **Handstamped**

1 A1 (2r) black	*7,000.*

Cuernavaca

A city of Mexico, just south of the capital, and the capital of the State of Morelos.

A1

1867 **Handstamped**

1 A1 (2r) black	*1,500.*	*1,750.*

The CUERNAVACA district name handstamp was used to cancel the stamp.

Counterfeits exist.

Guadalajara

A city of Mexico and capital of the State of Jalisco.

A1

Dated "1867"
1st Printing
Medium Wove Paper

1867 **Handstamped** ***Imperf.***

1 A1 Medio r blk, *white*	125.00	90.00
2 A1 un r blk, *gray bl*		90.00
3 A1 un r blk, *dk bl*		80.00
4 A1 un r blk, *white*		70.00
5 A1 2r blk, *dk grn*	40.00	18.00
6 A1 2r blk, *white*		70.00
7 A1 4r blk, *rose*	110.00	70.00
a. Half used as 2r on cover		250.00
8 A1 4r blk, *white*		100.00
9 A1 un p blk, *lilac*	120.00	125.00

Serrate Perf.

10 A1 un r blk, *gray bl*		125.00
11 A1 2r blk, *dk grn*		70.00
12 A1 4r blk, *rose*		80.00

2nd Printing
No Period after "2" or "4"
Thin Quadrille Paper
Imperf

13 A1 2r blk, *green*	25.00	17.50
a. Half used as 1r on cover		250.00

Serrate Perf.

14 A1 2r blk, *green*		50.00

Thin Laid Batonné Paper
Imperf

15 A1 2r blk, *green*	37.50	20.00

Serrate Perf.

16 A1 2r blk, *green*		42.50

3rd Printing
Capital "U" in "Un" on 1r, 1p
Period after "2" and "4"
Thin Wove Paper
Imperf

16A A1 Un r blk, *white*		75.00
17 A1 Un r blk, *blue*		50.00
17A A1 Un r blk, *lilac*	70.00	
18 A1 2r blk, *rose*		42.50
18A A1 4r blk, *blue*		

Serrate Perf.

19 A1 Un r blk, *blue*		85.00

Thin Quadrille Paper
Imperf

20 A1 2r blk, *rose*	35.00	35.00
21 A1 4r blk, *blue*	12.50	25.00
22 A1 4r blk, *white*	55.00	
23 A1 Un p blk, *lilac*	12.50	50.00
24 A1 Un p blk, *rose*	55.00	

Serrate Perf.

25 A1 Un p blk, *lilac*		125.00
25A A1 Un p blk, *rose*		125.00

Thin Laid Batonné Paper
Imperf

26 A1 Un r blk, *green*	18.00	14.00
27 A1 2r blk, *rose*	22.50	19.00
27A A1 2r blk, *green*		40.00
28 A1 4r blk, *blue*	14.00	35.00
29 A1 4r blk, *white*	55.00	
30 A1 Un p blk, *lilac*	25.00	45.00
31 A1 Un p blk, *rose*	55.00	

Serrate Perf.

32 A1 Un r blk, *green*	55.00	
33 A1 2r blk, *rose*	60.00	*70.00*
34 A1 4r blk, *blue*		85.00

Thin Oblong Quadrille Paper
Imperf

35 A1 Un r blk, *blue*		19.00
36 A1 4r blk, *blue*		150.00

Serrate Perf.

37 A1 Un r blk, *blue*		65.00

4th Printing
Dated "1868"
Wove Paper

1868 ***Imperf.***

38 A1 2r blk, *lilac*	25.00	12.00
a. Half used as 1r on cover		275.00
39 A1 2r blk, *rose*	45.00	55.00

Serrate Perf.

40 A1 2r blk, *lilac*		45.00
41 A1 2r blk, *rose*		80.00

Laid Batonné Paper
Imperf

42 A1 un r blk, *green*	10.00	10.00
a. "nu" instead of "un"		70.00
43 A1 2r blk, *lilac*	10.00	10.00

Serrate Perf.

44 A1 un r blk, *green*	60.00	45.00

Quadrille Paper.
Imperf

45 A1 2r blk, *lilac*	20.00	12.00

Serrate Perf.

46 A1 2r blk, *lilac*	55.00	55.00

Laid Paper
Imperf

47 A1 un r blk, *green*	11.00	14.00
a. "nu" instead of "un"		60.00
48 A1 2r blk, *lilac*	27.50	27.50
49 A1 2r blk, *rose*	32.50	32.50

Serrate Perf.

50 A1 un r blk, *green*		47.50
51 A1 2r blk, *rose*	90.00	

Counterfeits of Nos. 1-51 abound.

Merida

A city of southeastern Mexico, capital of the State of Yucatan.

Mexico No. 521 Surcharged **25**

1916 **Wmk. 155** ***Perf. 14***

1 A40 25(c) on 5c org, on cover	*500.00*

The G.P.DE.M. overprint reads down.

Authorities consider the Monterey, Morelia and Patzcuaro stamps to be bogus.

Tlacotalpan

A village in the state of Veracruz.

A1

1856, Oct. **Handstamped**

No.	Type	Description	Unused	Used
1	A1	½(r) black		*10,000.*

REVOLUTIONARY ISSUES

SINALOA

A northern state in Mexico, bordering on the Pacific Ocean. Stamps were issued by a provisional government.

Coat of Arms — A1

1929 **Unwmk.** **Litho.** ***Perf. 12***

No.	Type	Description	Unused	Used
1	A1	10c blk, red & bl	2.50	
a.		Tête bêche pair	30.00	
2	A1	20c blk, red & gray	2.50	

Just as Nos. 1 and 2 were ready to be placed on sale the state was occupied by the Federal forces and the stamps could not be used. At a later date a few copies were canceled by favor.

A recent find included a number of errors or printers waste.

YUCATAN

A southeastern state of Mexico.

Mayan Altar Support — A1

"Casa de Monjas" — A2

Temple of the Tigers — A3

1924 **Unwmk.** **Litho.** ***Imperf.***

No.	Type	Description	Unused	Used
1	A1	5c violet	10.00	10.00
2	A2	10c carmine	35.00	35.00
3	A3	50c olive green	175.00	
		Perf. 12		
4	A1	5c violet	20.00	20.00
5	A2	10c carmine	60.00	60.00
6	A3	50c olive green	250.00	

Nos. 3 and 6 were not regularly issued.

MIDDLE CONGO

LOCATION — Western Africa at the Equator, bordering on the Atlantic Ocean

GOVT. — Former French Colony

AREA — 166,069

POP. — 746,805 (1936)

CAPITAL — Brazzaville

In 1910 Middle Congo, formerly a part of French Congo, was declared a separate colony. It was grouped with Gabon and the Ubangi-Shari and Chad Territories and officially designated French Equatorial Africa. This group became a single administrative unit in 1934. See Gabon.

See Congo Republic (ex-French) for issues of 1959 onward.

100 Centimes = 1 Franc

Leopard — A1

Bakalois Woman — A2

Coconut Grove — A3

Perf. 14x13½

1907-22 **Typo.** **Unwmk.**

No.	Type	Description	Unused	Used
1	A1	1c ol gray & brn	15	15
2	A1	2c vio & brn	15	15
3	A1	4c bl & brn	15	15
4	A1	5c dk grn & bl	20	15
5	A1	5c yel & bl ('22)	38	38
6	A1	10c car & bl	22	15
7	A1	10c dp grn & bl grn ('22)	90	90
8	A1	15c brn vio & rose	65	42
9	A1	20c brn & bl	1.00	70
10	A2	25c bl & grn	30	28
11	A2	25c bl grn & gray ('22)	38	38
12	A2	30c scar & grn	60	40
13	A2	30c dp rose & rose ('22)	60	60
14	A2	35c vio brn & bl	45	45
15	A2	40c dl grn & brn	45	45
16	A2	45c vio & red	2.25	1.50
17	A2	50c bl grn & red	60	50
18	A2	50c bl & grn ('22)	60	60
19	A2	75c brn & bl	2.50	2.25
20	A3	1fr dp grn & vio	4.50	3.50
21	A3	2fr vio & gray grn	4.00	2.50
22	A3	5fr bl & rose	12.00	10.00
		Nos. 1-22 (22)	33.03	26.56

For stamps of types A1-A3 in changed colors, see Chad, French Congo and Ubangi-Shari.

For overprints and surcharges see Nos. 23-60, B1-B2.

Stamps and Types of 1907-22 Overprinted in Black, Blue or Red

AFRIQUE EQUATORIALE FRANÇAISE

1924-30

No.	Type	Description	Unused	Used
23	A1	1c ol gray & brn	15	15
24	A1	2c vio & brn	15	15
25	A1	4c bl & brn	15	15
26	A1	5c yel & bl	15	15
27	A1	10c grn & bl grn (R)	15	15
28	A1	10c car & gray ('25)	15	15
29	A1	15c brn vio & rose (Bl)	15	15
a.		Double surcharge	50.00	
30	A1	20c brn & bl	15	15
31	A1	20c bl grn & yel grn ('26)	15	15
32	A1	20c dp brn & rose lil ('27)	35	15

Overprinted **AFRIQUE EQUATORIALE FRANÇAISE**

No.	Type	Description	Unused	Used
33	A2	25c bl grn & gray	20	20
34	A2	30c rose & pale rose (Bl)	30	20
35	A2	30c gray & bl vio (R) ('25)	28	20
36	A2	30c dk grn & grn ('27)	55	42
37	A2	35c choc & bl	25	20
38	A2	40c ol grn & brn	30	20
39	A2	45c vio & pale red (Bl)	58	35
a.		Inverted overprint	50.00	50.00
40	A2	50c bl & grn (R)	30	22
41	A2	50c org & blk ('25)	28	20
a.		Without overprint	82.50	
42	A2	65c org brn & bl ('27)	1.20	80
43	A2	75c brn & bl	32	22
44	A2	90c brn red & pink ('30)	1.60	1.40
45	A3	1fr grn & vio	58	45
a.		Double overprint	90.00	85.00
46	A3	1.10fr vio & brn ('28)	1.60	1.00
47	A3	1.50fr ultra & bl ('30)	2.50	2.25
48	A3	2fr vio & gray grn	62	55
49	A3	3fr red vio ('30)	3.25	2.50
50	A3	5fr bl & rose	2.00	1.10
		Nos. 23-50 (28)	18.41	13.96

Nos. 48 and 50 Surcharged with New Values

1924

No.	Type	Description	Unused	Used
51	A3	25c on 2fr vio & gray grn	28	28
52	A3	25c on 5fr bl & rose (Bl)	28	28

Types of 1924-27 Surcharged with New Values in Black or Red

1925-27

No.	Type	Description	Unused	Used
53	A3	65c on 1fr red org & ol brn	40	40
54	A3	85c on 1fr red org & ol brn	40	40
55	A2	90c on 75c brn red & rose red ('27)	55	55
56	A3	1.25fr on 1fr dl bl & ultra (R)	20	16
57	A3	1.50fr on 1fr ultra & bl ('27)	70	55
a.		New value omitted	60.00	
58	A3	3fr on 5fr org brn & dl red ('27)	80	65
a.		New value omitted	110.00	
59	A3	10fr on 5fr ver & bl grn ('27)	4.00	3.50
60	A3	20fr on 5fr org brn & vio ('27)	6.00	4.50
		Nos. 53-60 (8)	13.05	10.71

Bars cover old values on Nos. 56-60.

Colonial Exposition Issue

Common Design Types

1931 **Engr.** ***Perf. 12½***

Name of Country in Black

No.	Type	Description	Unused	Used
61	CD70	40c dp grn	1.60	1.50
62	CD71	50c violet	90	80
63	CD72	90c red org	1.20	1.00
64	CD73	1.50fr dl bl	1.60	1.00

Viaduct at Mindouli A4

Pasteur Institute at Brazzaville A5

Government Building, Brazzaville A6

1933 **Photo.** ***Perf. 13½***

No.	Type	Description	Unused	Used
65	A4	1c lt brn	15	15
66	A4	2c dl bl	15	15
67	A4	4c ol grn	15	15
68	A4	5c red vio	15	15
69	A4	10c slate	15	15
70	A4	15c dk vio	20	20
71	A4	20c red, *pink*	2.75	2.00
72	A4	25c orange	28	20
73	A4	30c yel grn	80	65
74	A5	40c org brn	65	45
75	A5	45c blk, *green*	80	60
76	A5	50c blk vio	50	30
77	A5	65c brn red, *grn*	50	40
78	A5	75c blk, *pink*	4.00	2.50
79	A5	90c carmine	50	45
80	A5	1fr dk red	50	40
81	A5	1.25fr Prus bl	80	60
82	A5	1.50fr dk bl	2.50	1.10
83	A6	1.75fr dk vio	80	62
84	A6	2fr grnsh blk	65	62
85	A6	3fr orange	1.25	1.25
86	A6	5fr slate bl	5.75	4.50
87	A6	10fr black	25.00	12.00
88	A6	20fr dark brown	16.00	10.00
		Nos. 65-88 (24)	64.98	39.59

SEMI-POSTAL STAMPS

No. 6 Surcharged in Black

1916 **Unwmk.** ***Perf. 14x13½***

No.	Type	Description	Unused	Used
B1	A1	10c + 5c car & blue	60	40
a.		Double surcharge	45.00	45.00
b.		Inverted surcharge	40.00	40.00

A printing with the surcharge placed lower and more to the left was made and used in Ubangi.

No. 6 Surcharged in Red

No.	Type	Description	Unused	Used
B2	A1	10c + 5c car & blue	40	40

POSTAGE DUE STAMPS

MOYEN-CONGO

Postage Due Stamps of France Overprinted

A. E. F.

1928 **Unwmk.** ***Perf. 14x13½***

No.	Type	Description	Unused	Used
J1	D2	5c light blue	28	28
J2	D2	10c gray brn	28	28
J3	D2	20c ol grn	42	42
J4	D2	25c brt rose	42	42
J5	D2	30c lt red	42	42
J6	D2	45c bl grn	50	50
J7	D2	50c brn vio	60	60
J8	D2	60c yel brn	70	70
J9	D2	1fr red brn	70	70
J10	D2	2fr org red	1.25	1.25
J11	D2	3fr brt vio	2.25	2.25
		Nos. J1-J11 (11)	7.82	7.82

Village on Ubangi, Dance Mask — D3

Steamer on Ubangi River — D4

1930 **Typo.**

No.	Type	Description	Unused	Used
J12	D3	5c dp bl & ol	35	35
J13	D3	10c dp red & brn	45	45
J14	D3	20c grn & brn	1.20	1.20
J15	D3	25c lt bl & brn	1.40	1.40
J16	D3	30c bis brn & Prus bl	2.25	2.25
J17	D3	45c Prus bl & ol	2.25	2.25
J18	D3	50c red vio & brn	2.25	2.25
J19	D3	60c gray lil & bl blk	2.50	2.50
J20	D4	1fr bis brn & bl blk	4.25	4.25
J21	D4	2fr vio & brn	5.25	5.25
J22	D4	3fr dk red & brn	5.25	5.25
		Nos. J12-J22 (11)	27.40	27.40

Rubber Trees and Djoué River — D5

1933 **Photo.** ***Perf. 13½***

No.	Type	Description	Unused	Used
J23	D5	5c apple grn	32	32
J24	D5	10c dk bl, *bl*	32	32
J25	D5	20c red, *yel*	45	45
J26	D5	25c chocolate	45	45
J27	D5	30c org red	52	52
J28	D5	45c dk vio	52	52
J29	D5	50c gray blk	90	90
J30	D5	60c blk, *orange*	1.25	1.25
J31	D5	1fr brn rose	2.00	2.00
J32	D5	2fr org yel	2.75	2.75
J33	D5	3fr Prus bl	4.50	4.50
		Nos. J23-J33 (11)	13.98	13.98

MOHELI

LOCATION — One of the Comoro Islands, situated in the Mozambique Channel midway between Madagascar and Mozambique (Africa)
GOVT. — Former French Colony
AREA — 89 sq. mi.
POP. — 4,000
CAPITAL — Fomboni
See Comoro Islands

100 Centimes = 1 Franc

Navigation and Commerce — A1

Perf. 14x13½

1906-07 Typo. Unwmk.

Name of Colony in Blue or Carmine

No.	Type	Description	Unused	Used
1	A1	1c blk, *lil bl*	65	65
2	A1	2c brn, *buff*	65	60
3	A1	4c claret, *lav*	1.00	90
4	A1	5c yel grn	1.00	90
5	A1	10c carmine	1.25	1.00
6	A1	20c red, *green*	4.50	2.25
7	A1	25c blue	4.50	2.50
8	A1	30c brn, *bister*	7.00	5.00
9	A1	35c blk, *yellow*	3.50	1.75
10	A1	40c red, *straw*	6.00	3.75
11	A1	45c blk, *gray grn* ('07)	35.00	22.50
12	A1	50c brn, *az*	10.00	6.50
13	A1	75c dp vio, *org*	10.00	9.00
14	A1	1fr brnz grn, *straw*	10.00	6.50
15	A1	2fr vio, *rose*	16.00	14.00
16	A1	5fr lil, *lavender*	65.00	55.00
		Nos. 1-16 (16)	176.05	132.80

Perf. 13½x14 stamps are counterfeits.

Issue of 1906-07 Surcharged in Carmine or Black

05 **10**

1912

No.	Type	Description	Unused	Used
17	A1	5c on 4c cl, *lav* (C)	60	60
18	A1	5c on 20c red, *grn*	1.50	1.50
19	A1	5c on 30c brn, *bis* (C)	65	65
20	A1	10c on 40c red, *straw*	65	65
21	A1	10c on 45c blk, *gray grn* (C)	65	65
a.		"Moheli" double	150.00	
b.		"Moheli" triple	150.00	
22	A1	10c on 50c brn, *az* (C)	1.00	1.00
		Nos. 17-22 (6)	5.05	5.05

Two spacings between the surcharged numerals are found on Nos. 17 to 22.

The stamps of Mohéli were supposed to have been superseded by those of Madagascar, January, 1908. However, Nos. 17-22 were surcharged in 1912 to use up remainders. These were available for use in Madagascar and the entire Comoro archipelago. In 1950 stamps of Comoro Islands came into use.

MOLDOVA

(Moldavia)

LOCATION — Southeastern Europe, bounded by Romania and the Ukraine
GOVT. — Independent republic, member of the Commonwealth of Independent States
AREA — 13,012 sq. mi.
POP. — 4,300,000 (1989)
CAPITAL — Kishinev

With the breakup of the Soviet Union on Dec. 26, 1991, Moldova and ten former Soviet republics established the Commonwealth of Independent States.

100 Kopecks = 1 Ruble

Catalogue values for all unused stamps in this country are for Never Hinged items.

Codrii Nature Preserve A6

1992, Feb. 8 Litho. *Perf. 12*

No.	Type	Description	Value
25	A6	25k multicolored	*38*

Natl. Arms — A7

1992, May 24 Photo. *Perf. 13½*

No.	Type	Description	Value
26	A7	35k green	*20*
27	A7	50k red	*28*
28	A7	65k brown	*38*
29	A7	1r purple	*58*
30	A7	1.50r blue	*85*
		Nos. 26-30 (5)	*2.29*

Birds — A8

She-Wolf Suckling Romulus and Remus — A10

Church of St. Panteleimon, Cent. — A9

Designs: 50k, Merops apiaster. 65k, Oriolus oriolus. 2.50r, Picus viridis. 6r, Coracias garrulus. 7.50r, Upupa epops. 15r, Cuculus canorus.

1992, Aug. 5 Litho. *Perf. 13½x14*

No.	Type	Description	Value
31	A8	50k multicolored	*15*
32	A8	65k multicolored	*15*
33	A8	2.50r multicolored	*45*
34	A8	6r multicolored	*1.10*
35	A8	7.50r multicolored	*1.40*
36	A8	15r multicolored	*2.80*
		Nos. 31-36 (6)	*6.05*

No. 31 incorrectly inscribed "ariaster."

1992, Aug. 10 Photo. *Perf. 11½*

No.	Type	Description	Value
37	A9	1.50r multicolored	*30*

1992, Aug. 10 *Perf. 12x11½*

No.	Type	Description	Value
38	A10	5r multicolored	*70*

Russia Nos. 4598-4599, 5839 Surcharged "MOLDOVA" and New Value in Black or Red

1992, Aug. 31 Litho. *Perf. 12x12½*

No.	Type	Description	Value
39	A2138	2.50r on 4k #4599	*15*
40	A2139	6r on 3k #4598	*25*
41	A2138	8.50r on 4k #4599	*35*
42	A2765	10r on 3k #5839 (R)	*42*

AIR POST STAMPS

Catalogue values for unused stamps in this section are for Never Hinged items.

TU-144 — AP1

1992, July 20 Litho. *Perf. 12*

No.	Type	Description	Value
C1	AP1	1.75r maroon	*1.00*
C2	AP1	2.50r red vio	*1.45*
C3	AP1	7.75r blue	*4.50*
C4	AP1	8.50r blue green	*5.00*

MONACO

LOCATION — Southern coast of France, bordering on the Mediterranean Sea
GOVT. — Principality
AREA — 481 acres
POP. — 27,063 (1982)
CAPITAL — Monaco

100 Centimes = 1 Franc

Catalogue values for unused stamps in this country are for Never Hinged items, beginning with Scott 182 in the regular postage section, Scott B51 in the semi-postal section, Scott C2 in the airpost section, Scott CB1 in the airpost semi-postal section, and Scott J28 in the postage due section.

Prince Charles III — A1

Prince Albert I — A2

1885 Unwmk. Typo. *Perf. 14x13½*

No.	Type	Description	Unused	Used
1	A1	1c olive grn	6.50	3.75
2	A1	2c dull lilac	20.00	8.50
3	A1	5c blue	27.50	10.00
4	A1	10c brn, *straw*	35.00	11.00
5	A1	15c rose	110.00	4.00
6	A1	25c green	275.00	17.00
7	A1	40c slate, *rose*	32.50	13.00
8	A1	75c blk, *rose*	85.00	25.00
9	A1	1fr blk, *yellow*	700.00	130.00
10	A1	5fr rose, *grn*	1,500.	875.00

1891-1921

No.	Type	Description	Unused	Used
11	A2	1c ol grn	40	38
12	A2	2c dl vio	40	38
13	A2	5c blue	20.00	85
14	A2	5c yel grn ('01)	38	25
15	A2	10c brn, *straw*	52.50	4.25
16	A2	10c car ('01)	1.50	35
17	A2	15c rose	70.00	85
18	A2	15c vio brn, *straw* ('01)	1.40	60
19	A2	15c gray grn ('21)	1.50	1.25
20	A2	25c green	190.00	9.00
21	A2	25c dp bl ('01)	5.00	90
22	A2	40c sl, *rose* ('94)	1.75	70
23	A2	50c vio, *org*	3.00	1.65
24	A2	75c vio brn, *buff* ('94)	7.50	4.25
a.		75c lilac brown, *buff*	14.00	6.00
25	A2	75c ol brn, *buff* ('21)	9.50	8.00
26	A2	1fr blk, *yellow*	6.25	3.25
27	A2	5fr rose, *grn*	52.50	18.00
28	A2	5fr dl vio ('21)	140.00	80.00
29	A2	5fr dk grn ('21)	16.00	15.00
		Nos. 11-29 (19)	579.58	149.91

The handstamp "OL" in a circle of dots is a cancellation, not an overprint.

See No. 1782. For overprints and surcharges see Nos. 30-35, 57-59, B1.

Stamps of 1901-21 Overprinted or Surcharged:

28 DÉCEMBRE 1920

28 DÉCEMBRE 1920 2f

1921, Mar. 5

No.	Type	Description	Unused	Used
30	A2	5c lt grn	70	60
31	A2	75c brn, *buff*	4.50	4.50
32	A2	2fr on 5fr dl vio	35.00	35.00

Issued to commemorate the birth of Princess Antoinette, daughter of Princess Charlotte and Prince Pierre, Comte de Polignac.

Stamps and Type of 1891-1921 Surcharged

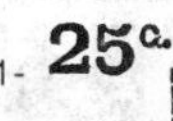

1922

No.	Type	Description	Unused	Used
33	A2	20c on 15c gray grn	1.00	90
34	A2	25c on 10c rose	60	60
35	A2	50c on 1fr blk, *yel*	5.50	4.50

Prince Albert I — A5

Oceanographic Museum — A6

"The Rock" of Monaco — A7

Royal Palace — A8

1922-24 Engr. *Perf. 11*

No.	Type	Description	Unused	Used
40	A5	25c olive brn	5.00	4.00
41	A6	30c dk grn	80	80
42	A6	30c scar ('23)	32	32
43	A6	50c ultra	3.25	3.25
44	A7	60c blk brn	25	25
45	A7	1fr blk, *yellow*	16	16
46	A7	2fr scarlet	32	32
47	A8	5fr red brn	32.50	25.00
48	A8	5fr dk grn, *lil* ('24)	6.00	6.00
49	A8	10fr carmine	11.00	11.00
		Nos. 40-49 (10)	59.60	51.10

Nos. 40-49 exist imperf.

Prince Louis II
A9 A10

St. Dévote Viaduct ("Bridge of Suicides") — A11

1923-24 Engr.

No.	Type	Description	Unused	Used
50	A9	10c deep green	28	28
51	A9	15c car rose ('24)	42	42
52	A9	20c red brn	26	26
53	A9	25c violet	26	26
a.		Without engraver's name	4.00	4.00
54	A11	40c org brn ('24)	38	38
55	A10	50c ultra	26	26
		Nos. 50-55 (6)	1.86	1.86

The 25c comes in 2 types, one with larger "5" and "c" touching frame of numeral tablet.

Stamps of the 1922-24 issues sometimes show parts of the letters of a papermaker's watermark.

The engraved stamps of type A11 measure 31x21½mm. The typographed stamps of that design measure 36x21½mm.

See #86-88. For surcharges see #95-96.

Stamps and Type of 1891-1921 Surcharged

45

1924, Aug. 5 *Perf. 14x13½*

No.	Type	Description	Unused	Used
57	A2	45c on 50c brn ol, *buff*	52	52
a.		Double surcharge	600.00	600.00
58	A2	75c on 1fr blk, *yel*	30	30
a.		Double surcharge	475.00	475.00
59	A2	85c on 5fr dk grn	30	30
a.		Double surcharge	530.00	530.00

Grimaldi Family Coat of Arms — A12

Prince Louis II — A13

Louis II — A14

View of Monaco — A15

1924-33 **Typo.**

No.	Design	Description	Unused	Used
60	A12	1c gray black	15	15
61	A12	2c red brown	15	15
62	A12	3c brt vio ('33)	1.25	28
63	A12	5c org ('26)	22	22
64	A12	10c blue	15	15
65	A13	15c apple grn	15	15
66	A13	15c dl vio ('29)	1.25	60
67	A13	20c violet	16	15
68	A13	20c rose	22	15
69	A13	25c rose	15	15
70	A13	25c red, *yel*	16	16
71	A13	30c orange	15	15
72	A13	40c blk brn	16	15
73	A13	40c lt bl, *bluish*	22	22
74	A13	45c gray blk ('26)	52	32
75	A14	50c myr grn ('25)	16	16
76	A13	50c brn, *org*	15	15
77	A14	60c yel brn ('25)	16	16
78	A13	60c ol grn, *grnsh*	16	15
79	A13	75c ol grn, *grnsh* ('26)	32	22
80	A13	75c car, *straw* ('26)	16	15
81	A13	75c slate	42	22
82	A13	80c red, *yel* ('26)	26	22
83	A13	90c rose, *straw* ('27)	80	80
84	A13	1.25fr bl, *bluish* ('26)	15	15
85	A13	1.50fr bl, *bluish* ('27)	1.40	90

Size: 36x21½mm

No.	Design	Description	Unused	Used
86	A11	1fr blk, *orange*	16	16
87	A11	1.05fr red vio ('26)	16	16
88	A11	1.10fr bl grn ('27)	5.75	3.25
89	A15	2fr vio & ol brn ('25)	65	50
90	A15	3fr rose & ultra, *yel* ('27)	10.00	6.00
91	A15	5fr grn & rose ('25)	4.50	3.00
92	A15	10fr yel brn & bl ('25)	11.00	8.75
		Nos. 60-92 (33)	41.42	28.25

Nos. 60 to 74 and 76 exist imperforate.
For surcharges see Nos. 93-94, 97-99, C1.

Type of 1924-33 Surcharged with New Value and Bars

1926-31

No.	Design	Description	Unused	Used
93	A13	30c on 25c rose	22	20
94	A13	50c on 60c ol grn, *grnsh* ('28)	75	22
95	A11	50c on 1.05fr red vio ('28)	45	30
a.		Double surcharge		
96	A11	50c on 1.10fr bl grn ('31)	5.25	3.25
97	A13	50c on 1.25fr bl, *bluish* (R) ('28)	66	32
98	A13	1.25fr on 1fr bl, *bluish*	38	22
99	A15	1.50fr on 2fr vio & ol brn ('28)	2.75	2.25
		Nos. 93-99 (7)	10.46	6.76

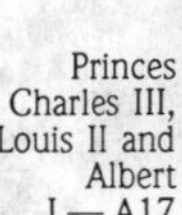

Princes Charles III, Louis II and Albert I — A17

1928, Feb. 18 **Engr.** ***Perf. 11***

No.	Design	Description	Unused	Used
100	A17	50c dl car	75	75
101	A17	1.50fr dk bl	75	75
102	A17	3fr dk vio	75	75

Nos. 100-102 were sold exclusively at the Intl. Phil. Exhib. at Monte Carlo, Feb., 1928. One set was sold to each purchaser of a ticket of admission to the exhibition which cost 5fr.

Exist imperf. Value, set $20.

Old Watchtower A20

Royal Palace — A21

Church of St. Dévote — A22

Prince Louis II — A23

"The Rock" of Monaco A24

Gardens of Monaco A25

Fortifications and Harbor — A26

1932-37 ***Perf. 13, 14x13½***

No.	Design	Description	Unused	Used
110	A20	15c lil rose	52	15
111	A20	20c org brn	52	15
112	A21	25c ol blk	60	30
113	A22	30c yel grn	48	30
114	A23	40c dk brn	1.25	75
115	A24	45c brn red	1.40	52
a.		45c red	250.00	250.00
116	A23	50c purple	1.25	55
117	A25	65c bl grn	1.40	40
118	A26	75c dp bl	1.75	85
119	A23	90c red	3.25	1.75
120	A22	1fr red brn ('33)	7.50	4.00
121	A26	1.25fr rose lil	2.50	1.90
122	A23	1.50fr ultra	12.00	6.00
123	A21	1.75fr rose lil	16.00	4.00
124	A21	1.75fr car rose ('37)	14.00	5.00
125	A24	2fr dk bl	3.00	1.90
126	A20	3fr purple	4.25	2.75
127	A21	3.50fr org ('35)	27.50	20.00
128	A22	5fr violet	9.00	8.50
129	A21	10fr dp bl	65.00	30.00
130	A25	20fr black	85.00	50.00
		Nos. 110-130 (21)	258.17	139.77

Postage Due Stamps of 1925-32 Surcharged or Overprinted in Black:

POSTES
=5

POSTES

1937-38 ***Perf. 14x13***

No.	Design	Description	Unused	Used
131	D3	5c on 10c vio	52	52
132	D3	10c violet	52	52
133	D3	15c on 30c bis	52	52
134	D3	20c on 30c bis	52	52
135	D3	25c on 60c red	85	85
136	D3	30c bister	1.50	1.40
137	D3	40c on 60c red	1.40	1.40
138	D3	50c on 60c red	1.90	1.75
139	D3	65c on 1fr lt bl	1.50	1.40
140	D3	85c on 1fr lt bl	3.25	3.00
141	D3	1fr light blue	3.75	3.50
142	D3	2.15fr on 2fr dl red	3.75	3.75
143	D3	2.25fr on 2fr dl red ('38)	9.25	9.25
144	D3	2.50fr on 2fr dl red ('38)	12.00	11.00
		Nos. 131-144 (14)	41.23	39.38

Grimaldi Arms — A27

Prince Louis II — A28

1937-43 **Engr.**

No.	Design	Description	Unused	Used
145	A27	1c dk vio brn ('38)	15	15
146	A27	2c emerald	15	15
147	A27	3c brt red vio	15	15
148	A27	5c red	15	15
149	A27	10c ultra	15	15
149A	A27	10c blk ('43)	15	15
150	A27	15c vio ('39)	85	75
150A	A27	30c dl grn ('43)	15	15
150B	A27	40c rose car ('43)	15	15
150C	A27	50c brt vio ('43)	15	15
151	A28	55c red brn ('38)	1.90	75
151A	A27	60c Prus bl ('43)	15	15
152	A28	65c vio ('38)	17.00	6.00
153	A28	70c red brn ('39)	15	15
153A	A27	70c red brn ('43)	15	15
154	A28	90c vio ('39)	16	16
155	A28	1fr rose red ('38)	3.00	1.75
156	A28	1.25fr rose red ('39)	16	15
157	A28	1.75fr ultra ('38)	7.25	3.25
158	A28	2.25fr ultra ('39)	16	15
		Nos. 145-158 (20)	32.28	14.76
		Set, never hinged	60.00	

Nos. 151, 152, 155 and 157 exist imperforate.

Souvenir Sheet

Prince Louis II — A29

1938, Jan. 17 **Unwmk.** ***Imperf.***

No.	Design	Description	Unused	Used
159	A29	10fr magenta	25.00	25.00
		Never hinged	37.50	

"Fête Nationale" Jan. 17, 1938. Size: 99x120mm.

Cathedral of Monaco — A30

St. Nicholas Square — A31

Palace Gate — A32

Palace of Monaco — A34

Panorama of Monaco A33

Harbor of Monte Carlo — A35

1939-46 ***Perf. 13***

No.	Design	Description	Unused	Used
160	A30	20c rose lil	20	20
161	A31	25c gldn brn	40	22
162	A32	30c dk bl grn	28	22
162A	A32	30c brn red ('40)	26	20
163	A31	40c hn brn	60	35
164	A33	45c brt red vio	26	22
165	A34	50c dk bl grn	28	20
166	A32	60c rose car	35	22
166A	A32	60c dk grn ('40)	28	22
166B	A35	70c brt red vio ('41)	26	16
167	A35	75c dk grn	26	16
167A	A30	80c dl grn ('43)	20	20
168	A34	1fr brn blk	26	16
168A	A33	1fr cl ('43)	15	15
168B	A35	1.20fr ultra ('46)	16	16
168C	A34	1.30fr brn blk ('41)	26	16
168D	A31	1.50fr ultra ('46)	26	26
169	A31	2fr rose vio	35	22
169A	A35	2fr lt ultra ('43)	15	15
169B	A34	2fr grn ('46)	15	15
170	A33	2.50fr red	20.00	11.00
171	A33	2.50fr dp bl ('40)	1.00	40
172	A35	3fr brn red	40	20
172A	A31	3fr blk ('43)	15	15
172B	A30	4fr rose lil ('46)	28	28
172C	A34	4.50fr brt vio ('43)	15	15
173	A30	5fr Prus bl	2.00	40
173A	A32	5fr dp grn ('43)	15	15
173B	A34	6fr lt vio ('46)	45	45
174	A33	10fr green	1.40	35
174A	A30	10fr dp bl ('43)	20	20
174B	A35	15fr rose pink ('43)	26	20
175	A32	20fr brt ultra	1.40	35
175A	A33	20fr sepia ('43)	26	20
175B	A35	25fr bl grn ('46)	1.25	85
		Nos. 160-175B (35)	34.72	19.31
		Set, never hinged	50.00	

See Nos. 214-221, 228-232, 274-275, 319-320, 407-408, 423, 426, 428-429, B36-B50.

Louis II Stadium A36

1939, Apr. 23 **Engr.**

No.	Design	Description	Unused	Used
176	A36	10fr dk grn	85.00	85.00
		Never hinged	150.00	

Inauguration of Louis II Stadium.

Louis II Stadium A37

1939, Aug. 15

No.	Design	Description	Unused	Used
177	A37	40c dl grn	80	80
178	A37	70c brn blk	90	90
179	A37	90c dk vio	1.25	1.25
180	A37	1.25fr cop red	1.50	1.50
181	A37	2.25fr dk bl	2.25	2.25
		Nos. 177-181 (5)	6.70	6.70
		Set, never hinged	10.00	

8th International University Games.

Imperforates

Nearly all Monaco stamps from 1940 onward exist imperforate. Officially 20 sheets, ranging from 25 to 100 subjects, were left imperforate.

Catalogue values for unused stamps in this section, from this point to the end of the section, are for Never Hinged items.

A38

Prince Louis II A39

1941-46 ***Perf. 14x13***

No.	Design	Description	Unused	Used
182	A38	40c brn car	30	30
183	A38	80c dp grn	30	30
184	A38	1fr rose vio	15	15
185	A38	1.20fr grn ('42)	15	15
186	A38	1.50fr rose	15	15
187	A38	1.50fr vio ('42)	15	15
187A	A38	2fr lt grn ('46)	22	18
188	A38	2.40fr red ('42)	15	15
189	A38	2.50fr dp ultra	55	55
190	A38	4fr blue ('42)	15	15
		Set value	1.70	1.65

1943 ***Perf. 13***

No.	Design	Description	Unused	Used
191	A39	50fr purple	70	70

Prince Louis II
A40 A41

1946 Unwmk. Engr. Perf. 14x13

192	A40	2.50fr dk bl grn	25	20
193	A40	3fr brt red vio	25	20
194	A40	6fr brt red	30	30
195	A40	10fr brt ultra	38	40

Perf. 13

196	A41	50fr dp Prus grn	1.65	1.50
197	A41	100fr red	2.50	2.25
		Nos. 192-197 (6)	5.33	4.85

Nos. 196-197 exist imperforate.

See Nos. 222-227, 233-236. For overprints see Nos. C8-C9.

Franklin D. Roosevelt A42

Harbor of Monte Carlo — A43

Palace of Monaco A44

Map of Monaco — A45

Prince Louis II — A46

1946, Dec. 13 Unwmk. Perf. 13

198	A42	10c red vio	15	15
199	A43	30c dp bl	15	15
200	A44	60c bl blk	15	15
201	A45	1fr sepia	35	35
202	A45	3fr lt vio	65	65
		Nos. 198-202,B93,C14-C15,CB6 (9)	3.43	3.33

Issued in tribute to the memory of Franklin D. Roosevelt.

1947, May 15

203	A46	10fr dk bl grn	1.40	1.40

See No. C20a.

Hurdler A47

Runner — A48

Designs: 2fr, Discus thrower. 2.50fr, Basketball. 4fr, Swimmer.

1948, July 1 Perf. 13

204	A47	50c bl grn	22	22
205	A48	1fr rose brn	25	25
206	A48	2fr grnsh bl	50	50
207	A48	2.50fr vermilion	80	80
208	A48	4fr slate gray	1.00	1.00
		Nos. 204-208,CB7-CB10 (9)	62.27	62.27

Issued to publicize Monaco's participation in the 1948 Olympic Games held at Wembley, England, during July and August.

Nymph Salmacis A49

Hercules — A50

Aristaeus — A51

Hyacinthus A52

Franois J. Bosio and Louis XIV Statue — A53

1948, July 12

209	A49	50c dk grn	15	15
210	A50	1fr red	18	18
211	A51	2fr dp ultra	20	20
212	A52	2.50fr dp vio	35	35
213	A53	4fr purple	60	60
		Nos. 209-213,CB11-CB14 (9)	39.98	39.98

Issued to honor Franois J. Bosio (1768-1845), sculptor. No. 213 inscribed "J F Bosio."

Scenic Types of 1939

1948 Engr.

214	A30	50c sepia	30	22
215	A31	60c rose pink	30	22
216	A32	3fr vio rose	50	30
217	A31	4fr emerald	50	30
218	A34	8fr red brn	1.75	75
219	A34	10fr brn red	3.00	60
220	A33	20fr car rose	1.25	45
221	A35	25fr gray blk	25.00	11.00
		Nos. 214-221 (8)	32.60	13.84

Louis II Type of 1946

1948, July Perf. 14x13

222	A40	30c black	28	15
223	A40	5fr org brn	42	28
224	A40	6fr purple	1.50	45
225	A40	10fr orange	42	28
226	A40	12fr dp car	2.25	70
227	A40	18fr dk bl	4.75	4.25
		Nos. 222-227 (6)	9.62	6.11

Scenic Types of 1939

1949 Perf. 13

228	A33	5fr bl grn	45	15
229	A35	10fr orange	72	26
230	A32	25fr blue	14.00	5.50
231	A30	40fr brn red	5.25	2.50
232	A30	50fr purple	3.50	65
		Nos. 228-232 (5)	23.92	9.06

Louis II Type of 1946

1949, Mar. 10 Perf. 14x13

233	A40	50c olive	28	15
234	A40	1fr dk vio bl	20	20
235	A40	12fr dk sl grn	4.50	2.50
236	A40	15fr brn car	4.50	3.00

Hirondelle I — A54

Cactus Plants — A55

Designs: 4fr, Oceanographic Museum. 5fr, Princess Alice II at Spitzbergen. 6fr, Albert I Monument. 10fr, Hirondelle II. 12fr, Albert I whaling. 18fr, Bison.

1949, Mar. 5 Perf. 13

237	A54	2fr brt bl	15	15
238	A55	3fr dk grn	18	18
239	A54	4fr blk brn & bl	28	28
240	A54	5fr crimson	32	32
241	A55	6fr dk vio	55	55
242	A54	10fr blk brn	65	65
243	A54	12fr brt red vio	85	85
244	A54	18fr dk brn & org brn	2.25	2.25
		Nos. 237-244 (8)	5.23	5.23

See Nos. C21-C26.

Palace, Globe and Pigeon — A56

1949-50 Engr. Unwmk.

245	A56	5fr blue green	26	26
245A	A56	10fr orange	2.25	2.25
246	A56	15fr carmine	32	32
		Nos. 245-246,C30-C33 (7)	8.23	8.23

75th anniversary of the UPU.

Nos. 245, 245A and 246 exist imperf.

Issued: 5fr, 15fr, Dec. 27; 10fr, Sept. 12, 1950.

Prince Rainier III
A57 A58

1950, Apr. 11

247	A57	10c red & blk brn	15	15
248	A57	50c dp yel & dk brn	15	15
249	A57	1fr purple	18	18
250	A57	5fr dk grn	65	65
251	A57	15fr carmine	1.25	1.25
252	A57	25fr ultra, ol grn & ind	1.90	1.90
		Nos. 247-252,C34-C35 (8)	11.53	11.53

Enthronement of Prince Rainier III.

1950, Apr. Engr. Perf. 14x13

253	A58	50c purple	15	15
254	A58	1fr org brn	24	20
255	A58	8fr bl grn	3.25	1.25
256	A58	12fr blue	1.10	45
257	A58	15fr crimson	1.50	48
		Nos. 253-257 (5)	6.24	2.53

1951, Apr. 31 Typo.

258	A58	5fr emerald	4.75	3.00
259	A58	10fr orange	8.25	4.25

See Nos. 276-279.

Statue of Prince Albert I — A59

1951, Apr. 11 Engr. Perf. 13

260	A59	15fr deep blue	6.25	5.25

Edmond and Jules de Goncourt A60

1951, Apr. 11

261	A60	15fr vio brn	7.00	5.75

Issued to commemorate the 50th anniversary of the foundation of Goncourt Academy.

St. Vincent de Paul A61

Judgment of St. Dévote — A62

Symbolizing Monaco's Adoption of Catholicism — A63

Mosaic of the Immaculate Conception A64

Blessed Rainier of Westphalia — A65

Holy Year, 1951: 50c, Pope Pius XII. 12fr, Prince Rainier III at Prayer. 15fr, St. Nicholas de Patare. 20fr, St. Roman. 25fr, St. Charles Borromée. 40fr, Cross, arms and Roman Coliseum. 50fr, Chapel of St. Dévote.

Inscribed: "Anno Santo"

1951, June 4 Unwmk. *Perf. 13*

No.	Type	Description	Unused	Used
262	A61	10c ultra & red	18	18
263	A61	50c dk rose lake & pur	18	18
264	A62	1fr brn & dk grn	24	24
265	A63	2fr vio brn & ver	30	30
266	A64	5fr bl grn	35	35
267	A63	12fr rose vio	48	48
268	A63	15fr vermilion	2.50	2.50
269	A63	20fr red brn	3.75	3.75
270	A63	25fr ultra	4.00	4.00
271	A63	40fr dk car rose & pur	5.00	5.00
272	A63	50fr ol grn & dk vio brn	6.25	6.25
273	A65	100fr dk vio brn	17.00	17.00
		Nos. 262-273 (12)	40.23	40.23

Scenic Types of 1939-46

1951, Dec. 22 *Perf. 13*

No.	Type	Description	Unused	Used
274	A31	3fr dp turq grn	85	40
275	A32	30fr slate blk	4.75	2.75

Rainier Type of 1950

1951, Dec. 22 *Perf. 14x13*

No.	Type	Description	Unused	Used
276	A58	6fr bl grn	65	45
277	A58	8fr orange	70	45
278	A58	15fr indigo	85	28
279	A58	18fr crimson	2.50	1.25

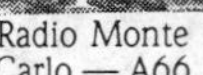

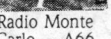

Radio Monte Carlo — A66

Knight in Armor — A67

1951, Dec. 22 *Perf. 13*

No.	Type	Description	Unused	Used
280	A66	1fr bl, car & org	24	18
281	A66	15fr pur, car & rose vio	90	32
282	A66	30fr ind & red brn	1.90	1.00

1951, Dec. 22

No.	Type	Description	Unused	Used
283	A67	1fr purple	1.00	48
284	A67	5fr gray blk	2.50	1.00
285	A67	8fr dp car	4.75	2.75
286	A67	15fr emerald	6.50	5.50
287	A67	30fr sl blk	9.25	5.50
		Nos. 283-287 (5)	24.00	15.23

See Nos. 328-332.

Nos. B96-B99a Surcharged with New Values and Bars in Black

1951, Dec. *Perf. 13½x13, Imperf.*

No.	Type	Description	Unused	Used
288	SP51	1fr on 10fr + 5fr	5.50	5.50
289	SP52	3fr on 15fr + 5fr	5.50	5.50
290	SP52	5fr on 25fr + 5fr	5.50	5.50
291	SP51	6fr on 40fr + 5fr	5.50	5.50
b.		Block of 4, #288-291	27.50	27.50

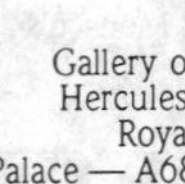

Gallery of Hercules, Royal Palace — A68

1952, Apr. 26 Engr. *Perf. 13*

No.	Type	Description	Unused	Used
292	A68	5fr red brn & brn	38	35
293	A68	15fr pur & lil rose	55	35
294	A68	30fr indigo & ultra	70	55

Opening of a philatelic museum at the royal palace, Apr. 26, 1952.

Basketball — A69

Designs: 2fr, Soccer. 3fr, Sailing. 5fr, Cyclist. 8fr, Gymnastics. 15fr, Louis II Stadium.

1953, Feb. 23 Unwmk. *Perf. 11*

No.	Type	Description	Unused	Used
295	A69	1fr dk pur & mag	22	20
296	A69	2fr dk grn & sl bl	28	22
297	A69	3fr bl & lt bl	30	28
298	A69	5fr dk brn & grnsh blk	70	35
299	A69	8fr brn lake & red	1.40	85
300	A69	15fr bl, brn blk & dk grn	85	60
		Nos. 295-300,C36-C39 (10)	43.25	37.50

Issued to publicize Monaco's participation in the Helsinki Olympic Games.

Books, Pens and Proof Pages — A70

1953, June 29 *Perf. 13*

No.	Type	Description	Unused	Used
301	A70	5fr dk grn	42	38
302	A70	15fr red brn	80	62

Issued to publicize the publication of a first edition of the unexpurgated diary of Edmond and Jules Goncourt.

Physalia and Laboratory Ship Hirondelle II — A71

1953, June 29

No.	Type	Description	Unused	Used
303	A71	2fr Prus grn, pur & choc	20	15
304	A71	5fr dp mag, red & Prus grn	32	32
305	A71	15fr ultra, vio brn & Prus grn	1.40	1.40

Issued to commemorate the 50th anniversary of the discovery of anaphylaxis by Charles Richet and Paul Portier.

Frederic Ozanam — A72

Nun — A73

1954, Apr. 12 Engr. *Perf. 13*

No.	Type	Description	Unused	Used
306	A72	1fr brt red	15	15
307	A73	5fr dk bl	35	35
308	A72	15fr black	80	80

Issued to commemorate the centenary of the death of Frederic Ozanam, founder of the Society of Saint Vincent de Paul.

Jean Baptiste de la Salle
A74 A75

1954, Apr. 12

No.	Type	Description	Unused	Used
309	A74	1fr dk car	15	15
310	A75	5fr blk brn	35	35
311	A74	15fr brt ultra	80	80

Issued to honor Jean Baptiste de la Salle, founder of the Christian Brothers Institute and saint.

A76 A77

Grimaldi Arms — A78

Knight in Armor — A79

Perf. 13½x14, 14x13½

1954, Apr. 12 Typo.

Various Forms of Grimaldi Arms in Black and Red or Black, Red and Deep Plum (5fr)

No.	Type	Description	Unused	Used
312	A76	50c blk & mag	15	15
313	A77	70c blk & aqua	15	15
314	A76	80c blk, red & dk grn	15	15
315	A77	1fr vio bl	15	15
316	A77	2fr blk & dp org	15	15
317	A77	3fr blk & grn	15	15
318	A78	5fr blk & lt grn	20	20
		Set value	72	72

Scenic Types of 1939-46

1954, Apr. 12 Engr. *Perf. 13*

No.	Type	Description	Unused	Used
319	A34	25fr brt red	1.50	85
320	A31	75fr dk grn	12.50	7.25

1954, Apr. 12 Unwmk. *Perf. 13*

No.	Type	Description	Unused	Used
321	A79	4fr dk red	85	38
322	A79	8fr dk grn	70	70
323	A79	12fr dk pur	3.00	1.25
324	A79	24fr dk mar	6.50	3.50

Nos. 321-324 were issued precanceled only. Values for precanceled stamps in first column are for those which have not been through the post and have original gum. Values in the second column are for postally used, gumless stamps.

See Nos. 400-404, 430-433, 466-469.

Lambarene Landing, Gabon — A80

Dr. Albert Schweitzer — A81

Design: 15fr, Lambarene hospital.

1955, Jan. 14 *Perf. 11x11½*

No.	Type	Description	Unused	Used
325	A80	2fr ol grn, bl grn & ind	15	15
326	A81	5fr dk grnsh bl & grn	80	80
327	A81	15fr dk bl grn, dp cl & brn blk	1.50	1.50

Issued to honor Dr. Albert Schweitzer, medical missionary. See No. C40.

Knight Type of 1951

1955, Jan. 14 *Perf. 13*

No.	Type	Description	Unused	Used
328	A67	5fr purple	1.90	85
329	A67	6fr red	2.25	1.25
330	A67	8fr red brn	2.50	1.65
331	A67	15fr ultra	6.60	3.75
332	A67	30fr dk grn	7.50	4.75
		Nos. 328-332 (5)	20.75	12.25

Automobile and Representation of Eight European Cities — A82

Prince Rainier III — A83

1955, Jan. 14 Unwmk.

No.	Type	Description	Unused	Used
333	A82	100fr dk brn & red	50.00	50.00

25th Monte Carlo Automobile Rally.

1955, June 7 Engr. *Perf. 13*

No.	Type	Description	Unused	Used
334	A83	6fr grn & vio brn	24	38
335	A83	8fr red & vio	24	38
336	A83	12fr car & grn	24	38
337	A83	15fr pur & bl	60	22
338	A83	18fr org & bl	60	40
339	A83	30fr ultra & gray	8.25	5.50
		Nos. 334-339 (6)	10.17	7.26

See Nos. 405-406, 424-425, 427, 462-465, 586, 603-604A, 725-728, 730, 789, 791.

"Five Weeks in a Balloon" — A84

"A Floating City" and Jules Verne — A85

"Michael Strogoff" A86

"Around the World in 80 Days" — A87

USS Nautilus and Verne A88

Designs (Scenes from Jules Verne's Books): 3fr, The House of Vapors. 6fr, The 500 Millions of the Begum. 8fr, The Magnificent Orinoco. 10fr, A

Journey to the Center of the Earth. 25fr, Twenty Thousand Leagues under the Sea.

1955, June 7

340 A84 1fr red brn & bl gray 15 15
341 A85 2fr bl, ind & brn 15 15
342 A85 3fr red brn, gray & sl 15 15
343 A86 5fr car & blk brn 26 26
344 A84 6fr blk brn & bluish gray 30 30
345 A86 8fr ol grn & aqua 38 38
346 A85 10fr ind, turq & brn 1.00 90
347 A87 15fr rose brn & ver 75 70
348 A85 25fr bl grn, grn & gray 1.50 1.25
349 A88 30fr vio, turq & blk 3.75 3.75
Nos. 340-349,C45 (11) 28.39 27.99

50th anniv. of the death of Jules Verne.

Virgin by Francois Brea — A89

Blessed Rainier A90

Design: 10fr, Pieta by Louis Brea.

1955, June 7

350 A89 5fr vio brn, gray & dk grn 25 25
351 A89 10fr vio brn, gray & dk grn 35 35
352 A90 15fr blk brn & org brn 50 50

Issued to commemorate the Marian Year.

Rotary Emblem, World Map — A91

1955, June 7

353 A91 30fr bl & org 75 75

Issued to commemorate the 50th anniversary of the founding of Rotary International.

George Washington — A92

Franklin D. Roosevelt — A93

Dwight D. Eisenhower — A94

Palace of Monaco, c. 1790 — A95

Palace of Monaco, c. 1750 — A96

Designs: 3fr, Abraham Lincoln. 30fr, Columbus landing in America. 40fr, Prince Rainier III. 100fr, Early Louisiana scene.

1956, Apr. 3 Engr. *Perf. 13*

354 A92 1fr dk pur 15 15
355 A93 2fr claret & dk pur 15 15
356 A93 3fr vio & dp ultra 18 18
357 A94 5fr brn lake 30 30
358 A95 15fr brn blk & vio brn 55 55
359 A95 30fr ind, blk & ultra 1.00 1.00
360 A94 40fr dk brn & vio brn 1.10 80
361 A96 50fr vermilion 1.25 1.10
362 A96 100fr Prus grn 1.50 1.50
a. Strip of 3, #360-362 4.25 4.00
Nos. 354-362 (9) 6.18 5.73

5th Intl. Phil. Exhib. (FIPEX), NYC, Apr. 28-May 6, 1956.

Ski Jump, Cortina d'Ampezzo — A97

Design: 30fr, Olympic Scenes.

1956, Apr. 3

363 A97 15fr brn vio, brn & dk grn 85 52
364 A97 30fr red org 1.40 1.25

Issued to publicize Monaco's participation in the 1956 Olympic Games.

"Glasgow to Monte Carlo" — A98

1956, Apr. 3 Unwmk.

365 A98 100fr red brn & red 19.00 19.00

The 26th Monte Carlo Automobile Rally.
See Nos. 411, 437, 460, 483, 500, 539, 549, 600, 629.

Princess Grace and Prince Rainier III — A99

1956, Apr. 19 Engr. *Perf. 13*

Portraits in Black

366 A99 1fr dk grn 15 15
367 A99 2fr dk car 15 15
368 A99 3fr ultra 28 20
369 A99 5fr brt yel grn 35 22
370 A99 15fr redsh brn 35 28
Nos. 366-370,C46-C48 (8) 4.98 4.70

Wedding of Prince Rainier III to Grace Kelly, Apr. 19, 1956.

Nos. J41-J47, J50-J56 Overprinted with Bars and Surcharged in Indigo, Red or Black

Unwmk.

1956, Apr. 3 Engr. *Perf. 11*

Designs: Early Transportation.

371 D6 2fr on 4fr (I) 38 38
372 D6 3fr (R) 38 38
373 D6 5fr on 4fr 60 60
374 D6 10fr on 4fr (R) 75 75
375 D6 15fr on 5fr (I) 1.50 1.50
376 D6 20fr (R) 2.50 2.50
377 D6 25fr on 20fr 3.25 3.25
378 D6 30fr on 10fr (I) 5.25 5.25
379 D6 40fr on 50fr (R) 6.00 6.00
380 D6 50fr on 100fr 8.50 8.50

Designs: Modern Transportation.

381 D7 2fr on 4fr (I) 38 38
382 D7 3fr (R) 38 38
383 D7 5fr on 4fr 60 60
384 D7 10fr on 4fr (R) 75 75
385 D7 15fr on 5fr (I) 1.50 1.50
386 D7 20fr (R) 2.50 2.50
387 D7 25fr on 20fr 3.25 3.25
388 D7 30fr on 10fr (I) 5.25 5.25
389 D7 40fr on 50fr (R) 6.00 6.00
390 D7 50fr on 100fr 8.50 8.50
Nos. 371-390,C49-C50 (22) 76.72 76.72

The two types of each value in Nos. 371-390 were printed tête bêche, se-tenant at the base.

Princess Grace — A100

1957, May 11 Engr. *Perf. 13*

391 A100 1fr bl vio 15 15
392 A100 2fr lt ol grn 15 15
393 A100 3fr yel brn 15 15
394 A100 5fr magenta 18 18
395 A100 15fr pink 18 18
396 A100 25fr Prus bl 35 22
397 A100 30fr purple 35 26
398 A100 50fr scarlet 52 26
399 A100 75fr orange 70 60
Nos. 391-399 (9) 2.73 2.15

Birth of Princess Caroline of Monaco.

Knight Type of 1954

1957 Unwmk. *Perf. 13*

400 A79 5fr dk bl 24 18
401 A79 10fr yel grn 24 15
402 A79 15fr brt org 80 60
403 A79 30fr brt bl 1.00 70
404 A79 45fr crimson 1.50 1.00
Nos. 400-404 (5) 3.78 2.63

Nos. 400-404 were issued precanceled only. See note after No. 324.

Types of 1955 and 1939-46

1957

405 A83 20fr grnsh bl 70 45
406 A83 35fr red brn 2.25 1.25
407 A33 65fr brt vio 7.00 5.50
408 A30 70fr org yel 8.00 7.25

Princesses Grace and Caroline A101

1958, May 15 Engr. *Perf. 13*

409 A101 100fr bluish blk 3.75 3.75

Birth of Prince Albert Alexander Louis, Mar. 14.

Order of St. Charles — A102

1958, May 15

410 A102 100fr car, grn & bis 1.65 1.65

Centenary of the National Order of St. Charles.

Rally Type of 1956

Design: 100fr, "Munich to Monte Carlo."

1958, May 15

411 A98 100fr red, grn & sepia 6.50 6.00

27th Monte Carlo Automobile Rally.

Virgin Mary, Popes Pius IX and XII — A103

Bernadette Soubirous — A104

Tomb of Bernadette, Nevers A105

Designs: 3fr, Shepherdess Bernadette at Bartres. 5fr, Bouriette kneeling (first miracle). 8fr, Stained glass window showing apparition. 10fr, Empty grotto at Lourdes. 12fr, Grotto with statue and altar. 20fr, Bernadette praying. 35fr, High Altar at St. Peter's during canonization of Bernadette. 50fr, Bernadette, Pope Pius XI, Mgr. Laurence and Abbe Peyramale.

1958, May 15 **Unwmk.**

412	A103	1fr lil gray & vio brn	15	15
413	A104	2fr bl & vio	15	15
414	A104	3fr grn & sep	15	15
415	A104	5fr gray brn & vio bl	15	15
416	A104	8fr blk, ol bis & ind	30	25
417	A105	10fr multi	28	25
418	A105	12fr ind, ol bis & ol grn	30	25
a.		Strip of 3, #416-418	1.00	90
419	A104	20fr dk sl grn & rose	35	30
420	A104	35fr ol, gray ol & dk sl grn	45	35
421	A103	50fr lake, ol grn & ind	60	50
422	A105	65fr ind & grnsh bl	1.00	65
		Nos. 412-422,C51-C52 (13)	7.38	6.15

Centenary of the apparition of the Virgin Mary at Lourdes.

Sizes: Nos. 413-415, 419-420 26x36mm. No. 416 22x36mm. Nos. 417-418 48x36mm. No. 422 36x26mm.

Types of 1939-46 and 1955

1959 **Engr.** ***Perf. 13***

423	A32	5fr cop red	90	80
424	A83	25fr org & blk	1.10	80
425	A83	30fr dk vio	1.75	1.50
426	A34	35fr dk bl	5.50	2.00
427	A83	50fr bl grn & rose cl	2.50	1.50
428	A31	85fr dk car rose	9.00	4.50
429	A33	100fr brt grnsh bl	8.00	6.25
		Nos. 423-429 (7)	28.75	17.35

Knight Type of 1954

1959

430	A79	8fr deep magenta	60	24
431	A79	20fr bright green	80	75
432	A79	40fr chocolate	1.65	80
433	A79	55fr ultra	3.50	1.65

Nos. 430-433 were issued precanceled only. See note after No. 324.

Princess Grace Polyclinic — A106

1959, May 16

434	A106	100fr gray, brn & grn	1.25	1.25

Opening of Princess Grace Hospital.

UNESCO Building, Paris, and Cultural Emblems — A107

Design: 50fr, UNESCO Building and children of various races.

1959, May 16

435	A107	25fr multi	28	20
436	A107	50fr ol, bl grn & blk brn	55	48

Opening of UNESCO Headquarters in Paris, Nov. 3, 1958.

Rally Type of 1956

Design: 100fr, "Athens to Monaco."

1959, May 16

437	A98	100fr vio bl, red & sl grn, *bl*	4.75	4.75

28th Monte Carlo Automobile Rally.

Carnations — A108

Bougainvillea A109

Flowers: 10fr on 3fr, Princess Grace Carnations. 15fr on 1fr, Mimosa, vert. 25fr on 6fr, Geranium, vert. 35fr, Oleander. 50fr, Jasmine. 85fr on 65fr, Lavender. 100fr, Grace de Monaco Rose.

1959, May 16

438	A108	5fr brn, Prus grn & rose car	22	15
439	A108	10fr on 3fr brn, grn & rose	22	15
440	A109	15fr on 1fr dk grn & cit	30	15
441	A109	20fr ol grn & mag	40	32
442	A109	25fr on 6fr yel grn & red	55	38
443	A109	35fr dk grn & pink	75	70
444	A109	50fr dk brn & dk grn	1.10	90
445	A109	85fr on 65fr ol grn & gray vio	1.50	1.50
446	A108	100fr grn & pink	1.90	1.75
		Nos. 438-446 (9)	6.94	6.00

Nos. 439-440, 442 and 445 were not issued without surcharge.

View of Monaco and Uprooted Oak Emblem — A110

1960, June 1 **Unwmk.** ***Perf. 13***

447	A110	25c bl, ol grn & sep	20	20

Issued to publicize World Refugee Year, July 1, 1959-June 30, 1960.

Entrance to Oceanographic Museum — A111

Museum and Aquarium — A112

Designs: 15c, Museum conference room. 20c, Arrival of equipment, designed by Prince Albert I. 25c, Research on electrical qualities of cephalopodes. 50c, Albert I and vessels Hirondelle I and Princesse Alice.

1960, June 1 **Engr.** ***Perf. 13***

448	A111	5c bl, sep & cl	22	15
449	A112	10c multi	40	28
450	A112	15c sep, ultra & bis	25	15
451	A112	20c rose lil, blk & bl	48	22
452	A112	25c grnsh bl	1.00	75
453	A112	50c lt ultra & brn	1.10	90
		Nos. 448-453 (6)	3.45	2.45

50th anniv. of the inauguration of the Oceanographic Museum of Monaco. See No. 475.

Horse Jumping — A113

Sports: 10c, Women swimmers. 15c, Broad jumper. 20c, Javelin thrower. 25c, Girl figure skater. 50c, Skier.

1960, June 1

454	A113	5c dk brn, car & emer	15	15
455	A113	10c red brn, bl & grn	18	18
456	A113	15c dl red brn, ol & mag	18	18
457	A113	20c blk, bl & grn	2.25	2.25
458	A113	25c dk grn & dl pur	60	60
459	A113	50c dk bl, grnsh bl & dl pur	90	90
		Nos. 454-459 (6)	4.26	4.26

Nos. 454-457 for the 17th Olympic Games, Rome, Aug. 25-Sept. 11; Nos. 458-459 for the 8th Winter Olympic Games, Squaw Valley, Feb. 18-29.

Rally Type of 1956

Design: 25c, "Lisbon to Monte Carlo."

1960, June 1

460	A98	25c bl, brn & car, *bluish*	1.90	1.90

29th Monte Carlo Automobile Rally.

Stamps of Sardinia and France, 1860, and Stamp of Monaco, 1885 — A114

1960, June 1 **Engr. & Embossed**

461	A114	25c vio, bl & ol	80	70

Issued to commemorate the 75th anniversary of postage stamps of Monaco.

Prince Rainier Type of 1955

1960 **Engr.** ***Perf. 13***

462	A83	25c org & blk	15	15
463	A83	30c dk vio	22	15
464	A83	50c bl grn & rose lil	42	15
465	A83	65c yel brn & slate	3.25	60
		Set value		85

Knight Type of 1954

1960

466	A79	8c dp mag	1.40	42
467	A79	20c brt grn	1.90	42
468	A79	40c chocolate	2.25	80
469	A79	55c ultra	4.00	1.25

Nos. 466-469 were issued precanceled only. See note after No. 324.

Sea Horse — A115

Designs: Nos. 471 Cactus (Cereanee). No. 472, Cactus (Nopalea dejecta). No. 473, Scorpion fish, horiz.

1960, June 1

470	A115	15c org brn & sl grn	50	20
471	A115	15c ol grn, yel & brn	60	15
472	A115	20c mar & ol grn	40	15
473	A115	20c brn, red brn, red & ol	60	15
		Set value		54

See Nos. 581-584.

Type of 1960 and

Palace of Monaco A116

Designs: 10c, Type A111 without inscription. 45c, Aerial view of Palace. 85c, Honor court. 1fr, Palace at night.

1960, June 1 **Engr.**

474	A116	5c grn & sepia	15	15
475	A111	10c dk bl & vio brn	48	24
476	A116	45c dk bl, sep & grn	75	24
477	A116	85c sl, gray & bis	3.50	24
478	A116	1fr dk bl, red brn & sl grn	1.40	35
		Nos. 474-478 (5)	6.28	1.22

See Nos. 585, 602, 729, 731, 731A, 790, 792.

Sphinx of Wadi-es-Sebua — A117

1961, June 3 **Unwmk.** ***Perf. 13***

479	A117	50c choc, dk bl & ocher	80	80

Issued as publicity to save historic monuments in Nubia.

The only foreign revenue stamps listed in this Catalogue are those authorized for prepayment of postage.

Murena, Starfish, Sea Urchin, Sea Cucumber and Coral — A118

Medieval Town and Leper — A119

1961, June 3

480 A118 25c vio buff & dk red 22 20

Issued to commemorate the World Congress of Aquariology, Monaco, Nov. 1960.

1961, June 3

481 A119 25c ol gray, ocher & car 22 18

Issued to honor the Sovereign Order of the Knights of Malta.

Hand and Ant — A120

1961, June 3

482 A120 25c mag & dp car 22 16

Issued to publicize "Respect for Life."

Rally Type of 1956

Design: 1fr, "Stockholm to Monte Carlo."

1961, June 3

483 A98 1fr multi 1.50 1.50

30th Monte Carlo Automobile Rally.

Turcat-Mery, 1911 Winner, and 1961 Car — A121

1961, June 3

484 A121 1fr org brn, vio & rose red 1.50 1.25

50th anniv. of the founding of the Monte Carlo Automobile Rally.

Chevrolet, 1912 — A122

Automobiles (pre-1912): 2c, Peugeot. 3c, Fiat. 4c, Mercedes. 5c, Rolls Royce. 10c, Panhard-Levassor. 15c, Renault. 20c, Ford. 25c, Rochet-Schneider. 30c, FN-Herstal. 45c, De Dion Bouton. 50c, Buick. 65c, Delahaye. 1fr, Cadillac.

1961, June 13 **Engr.**

485 A122 1c org brn, dk brn & grn 15 15
486 A122 2c org red, dk bl & brn 15 15
487 A122 3c multi 15 15
488 A122 4c multi 15 15
489 A122 5c ol bis, sl grn & car 15 15
490 A122 10c brn, sl & red 18 18

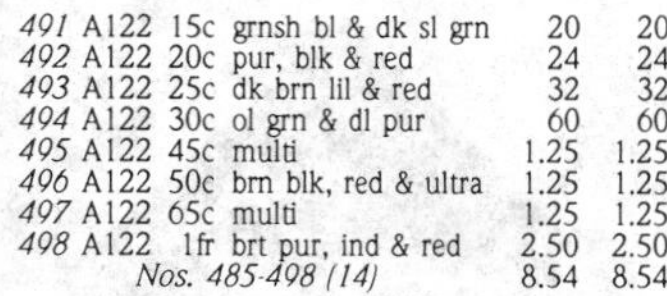

491 A122 15c grnsh bl & dk sl grn 20 20
492 A122 20c pur, blk & red 24 24
493 A122 25c dk brn lil & red 32 32
494 A122 30c ol grn & dl pur 60 60
495 A122 45c multi 1.25 1.25
496 A122 50c brn blk, red & ultra 1.25 1.25
497 A122 65c multi 1.25 1.25
498 A122 1fr brt pur, ind & red 2.50 2.50
Nos. 485-498 (14) 8.54 8.54

See Nos. 648-661.

Bugatti, First Winner, and Course — A123

1962, June 6 **Unwmk.** ***Perf. 13***

499 A123 1fr lilac rose 1.50 1.25

20th Automobile Grand Prix of Monaco.

Rally Type of 1956

Design: 1fr, "Oslo to Monte Carlo."

1962, June 6

500 A98 1fr multi 1.40 1.25

31st Monte Carlo Automobile Rally.

Louis XII and Lucien Grimaldi A124

Designs: 50c, Document granting sovereignty. 1fr, Seals of Louis XII and Lucien Grimaldi.

1962, June 6 **Engr.**

501 A124 25c ver, blk & vio bl 26 20
502 A124 50c dk bl, brn & mag 26 20
503 A124 1fr dk brn, grn & car 70 60

450th anniversary of Monaco's reception of sovereignty from Louis XII.

Mosquito and Swamp A125

1962, June 6

504 A125 1fr brn ol & lt grn 60 55

WHO drive to eradicate malaria.

Aquatic Stadium at Night A126

1962, June 6

505 A126 10c dk bl, ind & grn 16 15

Sun, Flowers and Hope Chest A127

1962, June 6

506 A127 20c multi 20 16

Issued to publicize the National Multiple Sclerosis Society of New York.

Wheat Harvest A128

1962, June 6

507 A128 25c dk bl, red brn & brn 15 15
508 A128 50c ind, ol bis & dk bl grn 25 25
509 A128 1fr red lil & ol bis 60 60

Europa. See No. C61.

Blood Donor's Arm and Globe A129

1962, Nov. 15 **Engr.** ***Perf. 13***

510 A129 1fr dk red, blk & org 50 45

3rd International Blood Donors' Congress, Nov. 15-18 at Monaco.

Yellow Wagtails — A130

Birds: 10c, European robins. 15c, European goldfinches. 20c, Blackcaps. 25c, Great spotted woodpeckers. 30c, Nightingale. 45c, Barn owls. 50c, Common starlings. 85c, Red crossbills. 1fr, White storks.

1962, Dec. 12 **Unwmk.**

511 A130 5c grn, sep & yel 15 15
512 A130 10c bis, dk pur & red 18 18
513 A130 15c multi 24 24
514 A130 20c mag, grn & blk 28 24
515 A130 25c multi 35 22
516 A130 30c brn, sl grn & bl 42 30
517 A130 45c vio & gldn brn 60 48
518 A130 50c bl grn, blk & yel 85 65
519 A130 85c multi 1.10 85
520 A130 1fr blk, grn & red 1.25 1.10
Nos. 511-520 (10) 5.42 4.41

Protection of useful birds.

Divers A131

Designs: 10c, Galeazzi's turret, vert. 25c, Williamson's photosphere, 1914 and bathyscape "Trieste," 1962. 45c, Diving suits. 50c, Diving chamber. 85c, Fulton's "Nautilus," 1800 and modern submarine. 1fr, Alexander the Great's underwater chamber and bathysphere of the New York Zoological Society.

1962, Dec. 12

521 A131 5c bluish grn, vio & blk 15 15
522 A131 10c multi 15 15
523 A131 25c bis, bluish grn & sl grn 20 20
524 A131 45c grn, ind & blk 30 30
525 A131 50c cit & dk bl 45 45
526 A131 85c Prus grn & dk vio bl 60 60
527 A131 1fr dk bl, dk brn & dk grn 1.00 1.00
Nos. 521-527 (7) 2.85 2.85

Issued in connection with an exhibition at the Oceanographic Museum "Man Under Water," showing ancient and modern methods of underwater exploration.

Dancing Children and UN Emblem — A132

Children on Scales A133

Designs: 10c, Bird feeding nestlings, vert. 20c, Sun shining on children of different races, vert. 25c, Mother and child, vert. 50c, House and child. 95c, African mother and child, vert. 1fr, Prince Albert and Princess Caroline.

1963, May 3 **Unwmk.** ***Perf. 13***

528 A132 5c ocher, dk red & ultra 15 15
529 A133 10c vio bl, emer & ol gray 16 15
530 A133 15c ultra, red & grn 20 15
531 A133 20c multi 20 15
532 A133 25c bl, brn & pink 20 20
533 A133 50c multi 45 40
534 A133 95c multi 60 55
535 A132 1fr grnsh bl, dl pur & rose red 1.10 1.00
Nos. 528-535 (8) 3.06 2.75

Publicizing the UN Children's Charter.

Figurehead with Red Cross, Red Crescent and Red Lion and Sun — A134

Design: 1fr, Centenary emblem, Gustave Moynier, Henri Dunant and Gen. Henri Dufour (horiz.).

1963, May 3 **Engr.**

536 A134 50c bluish grn, red & red brn 38 38
537 A134 1fr bl, sl grn & red 60 60

Centenary of International Red Cross.

Racing Cars on Monte Carlo Course and Map of Europe A135

1963, May 3

538 A135 50c multi 45 38

European Automobile Grand Prix.

Rally Type of 1956

Design: 1fr, "Warsaw to Monte Carlo."

1963, May 3

539 A98 1fr multi 1.40 1.25

32nd Monte Carlo Auto Race.

Lions International Emblem A136

1963, May 3

540 A136 50c bis, lt vio & bl 75 75

Issued to commemorate the founding of the Lions Club of Monaco, Mar. 24, 1962.

Hôtel des Postes, Paris, and UPU Allegory — A137

1963, May 3

541 A137 50c multi 60 60

Centenary of the first International Postal Conference, Paris, 1863.

Globe and Telstar A138

1963, May 3

542 A138 50c grn, dk pur & mar 75 75

1st television connection of the US and Europe through the Telstar satellite, July 11-12, 1962.

Holy Spirit over St. Peter's and World — A139

1963, May 3

543 A139 1fr grn, red brn & bl 75 75

Vatican II, the 21st Ecumenical Council of the Roman Catholic Church.

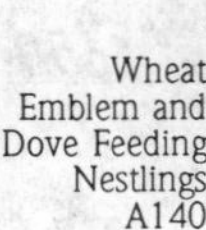

Wheat Emblem and Dove Feeding Nestlings A140

1963, May 3 **Engr.**

544 A140 1fr multi 85 85

FAO "Freedom from Hunger" campaign.

Henry Ford and 1903 Model A — A141

1963, Dec. 12 **Unwmk.** ***Perf. 13***

545 A141 20c sl grn & lil rose 38 32

Centenary of the birth of Henry Ford, American automobile manufacturer.

Bicyle Racer in Town — A142

Design: 50c, Bicyclist on country road.

1963, Dec. 12

546 A142 25c bl, sl grn & red brn 30 25
547 A142 50c bl, gray grn, & blk brn 38 38

50th anniv. of the Bicycle Tour de France.

Pierre de Coubertin and Myron's Discobolus A143

1963, Dec. 12

548 A143 1fr dp cl, car & ocher 1.00 90

Centenary of the birth of Baron Pierre de Coubertin, organizer of the modern Olympic Games.

Rally Type of 1956

Design: 1fr, "Paris to Monte Carlo."

1963, Dec. 12

549 A98 1fr multi 1.40 1.40

33rd Monte Carlo Automobile Rally.

Children with Stamp Album and UNESCO Emblem A144

1963, Dec. 12

550 A144 50c dp ultra, red & vio 45 42

International Philatelic and Educational Exposition, Monaco, Nov.-Dec., 1963.

Europa Issue, 1963

Woman, Dove and Lyre — A145

1963, Dec. 12

551 A145 25c brn, grn & car 30 25
552 A145 50c dk brn, bl & car 60 48

Wembley Stadium and British Football Association Emblem — A146

Overhead Kick — A147

Soccer Game, Florence, 16th Century A148

Tackle A149

Designs: 3c, Goalkeeper. 4c, Louis II Stadium and emblem of Sports Association of Monaco, with black overprint: "Championnat /1962-1963/Coupe de France." 15c, Soule Game, Brittany, 19th century. 20c, Soccer, England, 1827. 25c, Soccer, England, 1890. 50c, Clearing goal area. 95c, Heading the ball. 1fr, Kicking the ball.

1963, Dec. 12

553 A146 1c grn, vio & dk red 15 15
554 A147 2c blk, red & grn 15 15
555 A147 3c gray ol, org & red 15 15
556 A146 4c bl, red, grn, pur & blk 15 15
557 A148 10c dk bl, car & sep 15 15
558 A148 15c sepia & car 15 15
559 A148 20c sepia & dk bl 22 22
560 A148 25c sepia & lilac 22 22
a. Block of 4 70 70
561 A149 30c grn, sep & red 45 45
562 A149 50c sep, grn & red 52 52
563 A149 95c sep, grn & red 1.00 1.00
564 A149 1fr sep, grn & red 1.25 1.25
a. Block of 4 3.50 3.50
Nos. 553-564 (12) 4.56 4.56

Cent. of British Football Assoc. (organized soccer). No. 556 also for the successes of the soccer team of Monaco, 1962-63 (overprint typographed). No. 556 was not regularly issued without overprint. Value $525.

The 4 stamps of No. 560a are connected by an 1863 soccer ball in red brown; the stamps of No. 564a by a modern soccer ball.

Design from 1914 Rally Post Card — A150

Farman Biplane over Monaco — A151

Designs: 3c, Nieuport monoplane. 4c, Breguet biplane. 5c, Morane-Saulnier monoplane. 10c, Albatros biplane. 15c, Deperdussin monoplane. 20c, Vickers-Vimy biplane and map (Ross Smith's flight London-Port Darwin, 1919). 25c, Douglas Liberty biplane (first American around-the-world flight. 4 planes, 1924). 30c, Savoia S-16 hydroplane (De Pinedo's Rome-Australia-Japan-Rome flight, 1925). 45c, Trimotor Fokker F-7 monoplane (first aerial survey of North Pole, Richard E. Byrd and James Gordon Bennett, 1925). 50c, Spirit of St. Louis (first crossing of Atlantic, New York-Paris, Charles Lindbergh, 1927). 65c, Breguet 19 (Paris-New York, Coste and Bellonte, 1930). 95c, Laté 28 hydroplane (first South Atlantic airmail route, Dakar-Natal, 1930). 1fr, Dornier DO-X, (Germany-Rio de Janeiro, 1930).

1964, May 22 **Engr.** ***Perf. 13***

565 A150 1c grn, bl & ol 15 15
566 A151 2c bl, bis & red brn 15 15
567 A151 3c ol, grn & bl 15 15
568 A151 4c red brn, bl & Prus grn 15 15
569 A151 5c gray ol, vio & mag 15 15
570 A151 10c vio, bl & ol 15 15
571 A151 15c bl, org & brn 15 15
572 A151 20c brt grn, blk & bl 16 15
573 A151 25c red, bl & ol 20 15
574 A151 30c bl, sl grn & dp cl 28 20
575 A151 45c red brn, grnsh bl & blk 48 32
576 A151 50c pur, ol & bis 60 45
577 A151 65c stl bl, blk & red 70 48
578 A151 95c ocher, sl grn & red 96 65
579 A151 1fr sl grn, bl & vio brn 1.10 80
Nos. 565-579,C64 (16) 9.03 7.25

50th anniv. of the 1st airplane rally of Monte Carlo. Nos. 565-571 show planes which took part in the 1914 rally, Nos. 572-579 and C64 show important flights from 1919 to 1961.

Ancient Egyptian Message Transmitters and Rocket — A152

1964, May 22 **Unwmk.**

580 A152 1fr dk bl, ind & org brn 80 80

Issued to publicize "PHILATEC", International Philatelic and Postal Techniques Exhibition, Paris, June 5-21, 1964.

Types of 1955-60

Designs: 1c, Crab (Macrocheira Kampferi) (horiz.). 2c, Flowering cactus (Selenicereus Gr.). 12c, Shell (Fasciolaria trapezium). 18c, Aloe ciliaris. 70c, Honor court of palace (like No. 477). 95c, Prince Rainier III.

1964, May 19 ***Perf. 13***

581 A115 1c bl grn & dk red 15 15
582 A115 2c dk grn & multi 15 15
583 A115 12c vio & brn red 42 18
584 A115 18c grn, yel & car 55 15
585 A116 70c lt grn, choc & red org 55 32
586 A83 95c ultra 1.50 38
Nos. 581-586 (6) 3.32
Set value 1.05

Rainier III Aquatic Stadium A153

1964-67 **Engr.** ***Perf. 13***

587 A153 10c dk car, rose, bl & blk 1.50 18
587A A153 15c dk car, rose, brt bl & blk ('67) 65 18
588 A153 25c dl grn, dk bl & blk 65 18
589 A153 50c lil, bl grn & blk 1.50 65

Nos. 587-589 were issued precanceled only. See note after No. 324. The "1962" date has been obliterated with 2 bars. See Nos. 732-734, 793-796, 976-979.

Europa Issue, 1964

Common Design Type

1964, Sept. 12

Size: 22x34½mm

590 CD7 25c brt red, brt grn & dk grn 18 18
591 CD7 50c ultra, ol bis & dk red brn 45 45

Weight Lifter — A154

1964, Dec. 3 Unwmk. *Perf. 13*

592 A154 1c shown 15 15
593 A154 2c Judo 15 15
594 A154 3c Pole vault 15 15
595 A154 4c Archery 15 15
Set value 20 20

Issued to commemorate the 18th Olympic Games, Tokyo, Oct. 10-25. See No. C65.

Pres. John F. Kennedy and Mercury Capsule — A155

1964, Dec. 3

596 A155 50c brt bl & indigo 65 65

Pres. John F. Kennedy (1917-63).

Television Set and View of Monte Carlo — A156

1964, Dec. 3

597 A156 50c dk car rose, dk bl & brn 38 38

Fifth International Television Festival.

Frédéric Mistral, (1830-1914), Provenal Pet — A157

1964, Dec. 3 Engr.

598 A157 1fr gray ol & brn red 45 45

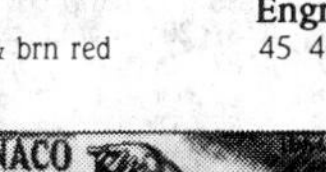

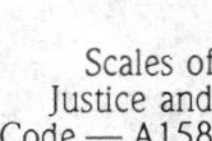

Scales of Justice and Code — A158

1964, Dec. 3

599 A158 1fr gldn brn & sl grn 60 60

Universal Declaration of Human Rights.

Rally Type of 1956

Design: 1fr, "Minsk to Monte Carlo."

1964, Dec. 3

600 A98 1fr bl grn, ocher & brn 65 60

34th Monte Carlo Automobile Rally.

International Football Association Emblem — A159

1964, Dec. 3

601 A159 1fr red, bl & ol bis 70 70

60th anniv. of FIFA, the Federation Internationale de Football (soccer).

Types of 1955 and 1960

Designs: 40c, Aerial view of palace. 60c, 1.30fr, 2.30fr, Prince Rainier III.

1965-66 Engr. *Perf. 13*

602 A116 40c sl grn, dl cl & brt grn 30 15
603 A83 60c sl grn & blk 38 20
604 A83 1.30fr dk red & blk 2.75 65
604A A83 2.30fr org & rose lil ('66) 90 40

Telstar and Pleumeur-Bodou Relay Station — A160

Alexander Graham Bell and Telephone A161

Designs (ITU Emblem and): 5c, Syncom II and Earth. 10c, Echo II and Earth. 12c, Relay satellite and Earth, vert. 18c, Lunik III and Moon. 50c, Samuel Morse and telegraph. 60c, Edouard Belin, belinograph and newspaper. 70c, Roman signal towers and Chappe telegraph. 95c, Cable laying ships; "The Great Eastern" (British, 1858) and "Alsace" (French, modern). 1fr, Edouard Branly, Guglielmo Marconi and map of English Channel.

1965, May 17

605 A161 5c vio bl & sl grn 15 15
606 A161 10c dk bl & sep 15 15
607 A161 12c gray, brn & dk car 15 15
608 A161 18c ind, dk car & plum 15 15
609 A160 25c vio, ol & rose brn 15 15
610 A161 30c dk brn, ol & bis brn 18 18
611 A161 50c grn & ind 24 24
612 A161 60c dl red brn & brt bl 26 26
613 A160 70c brn blk, org & dk bl 45 45
614 A160 95c ind, blk & bl 55 55
615 A160 1fr brn, blk & ultra 80 80
Nos. 605-615,C66 (12) 7.48 7.48

Issued to commemorate the centenary of the International Telecommunication Union.

Europa Issue, 1965

Common Design Type

1965, Sept. 25 Engr. *Perf. 13*

Size: 36x22mm

616 CD8 30c red brn & grn 18 18
617 CD8 60c vio & dk car 40 40

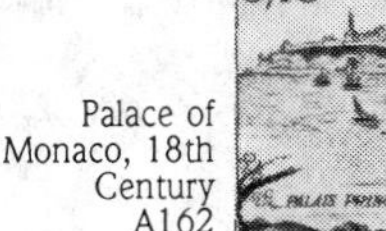

Palace of Monaco, 18th Century A162

Views of Palace: 12c, From the Bay, 17th century. 18c, Bay with sailboats, 18th century. 30c, From distance, 19th century. 60c, Close-up, 19th century. 1.30fr, Aerial view, 20th century.

1966, Feb. 1 Engr. *Perf. 13*

618 A162 10c vio, dl grn & ind 15 15
619 A162 12c bl, bis brn & dk brn 15 15
620 A162 18c blk, grn & bl 15 15
621 A162 30c vio bl, sep & red brn 24 24
622 A162 60c bl, grn & brn 38 38
623 A162 1.30fr dk grn & red brn 75 75
Nos. 618-623 (6) 1.82 1.82

750th anniversary of Palace of Monaco.

Dante Alighieri — A163

Designs: 60c, Dante facing Panther of Envy. 70c, Dante and Virgil boating across muddy swamp of 5th Circle. 95c, Dante watching the arrogant and Cross of Salvation. 1fr, Invocation of St. Bernard; Dante and Beatrice.

1966, Feb. 1

624 A163 30c crim & dp grn 38 38
625 A163 60c dl grn, Prus bl & ind 65 65
626 A163 70c blk, sep & car 85 85
627 A163 95c red lil & bl 1.25 1.25
628 A163 1fr ultra & bluish grn 1.40 1.40
Nos. 624-628 (5) 4.53 4.53

700th anniv. (in 1965) of the birth of Dante (1265-1321), poet.

Rally Type of 1956

Design: 1fr, "London to Monte Carlo."

1966, Feb. 1

629 A98 1fr pur, red & ind 95 95

The 35th Monte Carlo Automobile Rally.

Nativity by Gerard van Honthorst A164

1966, Feb. 1

630 A164 30c brown 22 22

Issued to honor the World Association for the Protection of Children.

Casino, Monte Carlo — A165

View of La Condamine, 1860, and Francois Blanc — A166

Designs: 12c, Prince Charles III, vert. 40c, Charles III monument, Bowling Green Gardens. 60c, Seaside Promenade and Rainier III. 70c, René Blum, Sergei Diaghilev and "Petroushka." 95c, Jules Massenet and Camille Saint-Saens. 1.30fr, Gabriel Fauré and Maurice Ravel.

1966, June 1 Engr. *Perf. 13*

631 A165 12c dp bl, blk & mag 15 15
632 A165 25c multi 15 15
633 A166 30c bl, plum, grn & org 15 15
634 A165 40c multi 16 16
635 A166 60c multi 40 40
636 A166 70c rose cl & ind 40 40
637 A165 95c pur & blk 60 60
638 A165 1.30fr brn org, ol bis & brn 1.00 1.00
Nos. 631-638,C68 (9) 5.51 5.51

Centenary of founding of Monte Carlo.

Europa Issue, 1966

Common Design Type

1966, Sept. 26 Engr. *Perf. 13*

Size: 21½x35½mm

639 CD9 30c orange 16 16
640 CD9 60c lt grn 32 32

Prince Albert I, Yachts Hirondelle I and Princesse Alice — A167

1966, Dec. 12 Engr. *Perf. 13*

641 A167 1fr ultra & dk vio brn 70 60

1st Intl. Congress of the History of Oceanography, Monaco, Dec. 12-17. Issued in sheets of 10.

Red Chalk Drawing by Domenico Zampieri — A168

Television Screen and Cross over Monaco — A169

1966, Dec. 12

642 A168 30c brt rose & dk brn 16 16
643 A168 60c brt bl & yel brn 26 26

20th anniv. of UNESCO.

1966, Dec. 12

644 A169 60c dk car rose, lil & red 28 18

10th meeting of "UNDA," the International Catholic Association for Radio and Television.

Precontinent III and Divers on Ocean Floor — A170

1966, Dec. 12

645 A170 1fr Prus bl, yel & dk brn 45 38

First anniversary of the submarine research station Precontinent III.

WHO Headquarters, Geneva A171

1966, Dec. 12

646 A171 30c dp bl, ol brn & dp bl grn 15 15
647 A171 60c dk grn, crim & dk brn 22 20

Opening of WHO Headquarters, Geneva.

Automobile Type of 1961

Automobiles (Previous Winners): 1c, Bugatti, 1931. 2c, Alfa Romeo, 1932. 5c, Mercedes, 1936. 10c, Maserati, 1948. 18c, Ferrari, 1955. 20c, Alfa Romeo, 1950. 25c, Maserati, 1957. 30c, Cooper-Climax, 1958. 40c, Lotus-Climax, 1960. 50c, Lotus-Climax, 1961. 60c, Cooper-Climax, 1962. 70c, B.R.M., 1963-66. 1fr, Walter Christie, 1907. 2.30fr, Peugeot, 1910.

1967, Apr. 28 Engr. ***Perf. 13x12½***

648 A122	1c	ind, red & brt bl	15	15
649 A122	2c	grn, red & blk	15	15
650 A122	5c	red, ind & gray	15	15
651 A122	10c	vio, red & ind	15	15
652 A122	18c	ind & red	15	15
653 A122	20c	dk grn, red & ind	15	15
654 A122	25c	ultra, red & ind	15	15
655 A122	30c	brn, ind & grn	20	15
656 A122	40c	car rose, ind & grn	28	20
657 A122	50c	lil, ind & grn	40	25
658 A122	60c	car, ind & grn	55	35
659 A122	70c	dl yel, bl grn & ind	65	45
660 A122	1fr	brn red, blk & gray	80	60
661 A122	2.30fr	multi	1.75	1.25
		Nos. 648-661,C73 (15)	7.93	6.30

25th Grand Prix of Monaco, May 7.

Dog, Egyptian Statue — A172

1967, Apr. 28 ***Perf. 12½x13***

662 A172 30c dk grn, brn & blk 45 38

Congress of the International Dog Fanciers Federation, Monaco, Apr. 5-9.

View of Monte Carlo — A173

1967, Apr. 28 ***Perf. 13***

663 A173 30c sl grn, brt bl & brn 25 18

International Tourist Year, 1967.

Chessboard and Monte Carlo Harbor — A174

1967, Apr. 28

664 A174 60c brt bl, dk pur & blk 65 60

International Chess Championships, Monaco, Mar. 19-Apr. 1.

Melvin Jones, View of Monte Carlo and Lions Emblem — A175

1967, Apr. 28

665 A175 60c ultra, sl bl & choc 42 32

50th anniversary of Lions International.

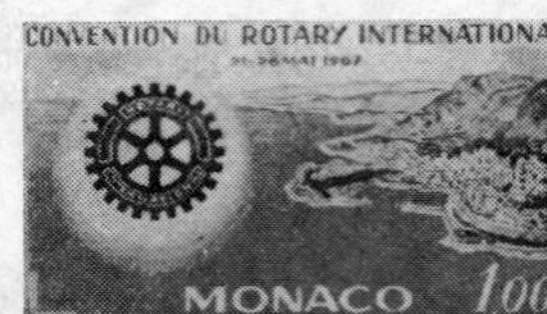

Rotary Emblem and View of Monte Carlo — A176

1967, Apr. 28

666 A176 1fr brt bl & lt ol grn 50 40

Issued to publicize the Rotary International Convention, Monaco, May 21-26.

EXPO '67 Monaco Pavilion — A177

1967, Apr. 28

667 A177 1fr multi 38 32

EXPO '67, International Exhibition, Montreal, Apr. 28-Oct. 27, 1967.

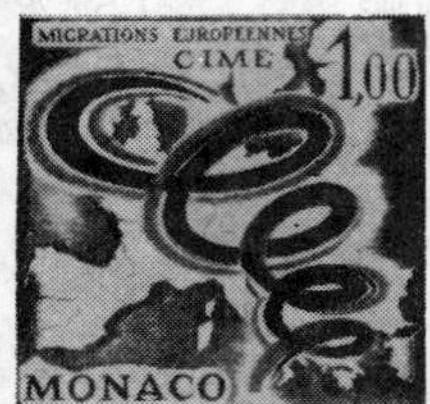

Map of Europe A178

1967, Apr. 28

668 A178 1fr choc, lem & Prus bl 38 30

Issued to publicize the International Committee for European Migration, CIME.

Europa Issue, 1967

Common Design Type

1967, Apr. 28 ***Perf. 12½x13***

669 CD10 30c brt car, rose lil & brt vio 18 18
670 CD10 60c grn ol & bl grn 35 32

Skier and Olympic Emblem — A179

1967, Dec. 7 Engr. ***Perf. 13***

671 A179 2.30fr red brn, gray & brt bl 1.10 95

10th Winter Olympic Games, Grenoble, France, Feb. 6-18, 1968.

Sounding Line and Map — A180

1967, Dec. 7

672 A180 1fr dk bl, grn & ol 50 40

9th International Hydrographic Conference, Monte Carlo, April-May, 1967.

Marie Curie, Chemical Apparatus and Atom Symbol — A181

1967, Dec. 7

673 A181 1fr brn, ultra & ol 52 40

Marie Curie (1867-1934), discoverer of radium and polonium.

Princes of Monaco Issue

Rainier I, by Eugene Charpentier A182

Design: No. 675, Lucien Grimaldi, by Ambrogio di Predis.

1967, Dec. 7 ***Perf. 12x13***

674 A182 1fr multi 95 70
675 A182 1fr multi 95 70

See Nos. 710-711, 735-736, 774-775, 813-814, 860-861, 892-893, 991-992, 1035-1036, 1093, 1135-1136, 1187-1188, 1246-1247, 1302-1303.

Shot Put — A183

Sport: 30c, High jump. 60c, Gymnast on rings. 70c, Water polo. 1fr, Wrestling. 2.30fr, Gymnast.

1968, Apr. 29 Engr. ***Perf. 13***

676 A183	20c	brt bl, grn & brn	15	15
677 A183	30c	vio bl, sep & brn vio	15	15
678 A183	60c	car, brt rose lil & dp bl	24	24
679 A183	70c	ocher, brn org & Prus bl	30	30
680 A183	1fr	brn org, brn & ind	48	48
681 A183	2.30fr	dk car, vio bl & ol	1.00	1.00
		Nos. 676-681,C74 (7)	4.32	4.07

Issued to publicize the 19th Olympic Games, Mexico City, Oct. 12-27.

St. Martin and the Beggar A184

1968, Apr. 29

682 A184 2.30fr brn red, Prus bl & blk brn 1.00 90

Red Cross of Monaco, 20th anniversary.

Anemones, by Raoul Dufy A185

1968, Apr. 29 Photo. ***Perf. 12x13***

683 A185 1fr lt bl & multi 60 48

International Flower Show in Monte Carlo. See Nos. 766, 776, 815-816, 829, 865.

Arms of Pope Pius IX and Prince Charles III — A186

St. Nicholas — A187

Designs: 30c, St. Benedict. 60c, Benedictine Monastery, Subiaco (Italy). 1fr, Church of St. Nicholas, Monaco, 13th century, horiz.

Perf. 12½x13, 13x12½

1968, Apr. 29 Engr.

684 A186	10c	red & brn	15	15
685 A187	20c	sl grn, ocher & car	15	15
686 A187	30c	ultra & ol grn	22	16
687 A187	60c	lt bl, brn & dk grn	30	30
688 A187	1fr	ind, bl & ol bis	55	45
		Nos. 684-688 (5)	1.37	1.21

Centenary of the elevation of St. Nicholas Church to an Abbey *Nullius*, directly subject to the Holy See.

Europa Issue, 1968

Common Design Type

1968, Apr. 29 ***Perf. 13***

Size: 36x22mm

689 CD11 30c dp org & car 20 15
690 CD11 60c car & ultra 30 18
691 CD11 1fr grn & red brn 65 42

Locomotive 030, 1868 — A188

Locomotives and Views: 30c, Type "C"-220, 1898. 60c, Type 230-"C", 1910. 70c, Type 231-"F," 1925. 1fr, Type 241-"A," 1932. 2.30fr, Type "BB," 1968.

1968, Dec. 12 Engr. *Perf. 13*

692 A188 20c vio bl, brn & blk 22 16
693 A188 30c dk ol grn, bl & blk 32 18
694 A188 60c bl, bis & blk 50 24
695 A188 70c vio, red brn & blk 60 38
696 A188 1fr bl, brn red & blk 1.10 65
697 A188 2.30fr sal pink, brt bl & blk 2.25 1.65
Nos. 692-697 (6) 4.99 3.26

Centenary of the Nice-Monaco Railroad.

Chateaubriand and Combourg Castle — A189

Scenes from Chateaubriand Novels: 20c, The Genius of Christianity. 25c, René. 30c, The Last Abencerage. 60c, The Martyrs. 2.30fr, Atala.

1968, Dec. 12

698 A189 10c dk grn, grn & pur 15 15
699 A189 20c brt bl, vio & mag 15 15
700 A189 25c sl, pur & brn 16 15
701 A189 30c dp brn, brn & pur 25 16
702 A189 60c brn red, bl grn & dk brn 32 30
703 A189 2.30fr dk bl, ol & mag 1.10 95
Nos. 698-703 (6) 2.13 1.86

Vicomte Franois René de Chateaubriand (1768-1848), novelist and statesman.

"France" and "Fidelity" by Bosio — A190

Franois Joseph Bosio (1768-1845), Sculptor — A191

Designs: 25c, Henri IV as a boy. 60c, Louis XIV on horseback, Place des Victoires. 2.30fr, Busts of Louis XVIII, Napoleon I and Charles X.

1968, Dec. 12

704 A190 20c brown 15 15
705 A191 25c sal pink & dk brn 15 15
706 A191 30c sl & vio bl 16 15
707 A191 60c dk ol grn & gray grn 28 20
708 A190 2.30fr blk & sl 90 70
Nos. 704-708 (5) 1.64 1.35

WHO Emblem — A192

1968, Dec. 12 Photo.

709 A192 60c multi 30 25

Issued to commemorate the 20th anniversary of the World Health Organization.

Princes of Monaco Type of 1967

Designs: 1fr, Charles II (1581-89). 2.30fr, Jeanne Grimaldi (1596-1620).

1968, Dec. 12 Engr. *Perf. 12x13*

710 A182 1fr multi 42 42
711 A182 2.30fr multi 1.10 1.10

Faust and Mephistopheles — A193

Scenes from "Damnation of Faust" by Berlioz: 10c, Rakoczy March. 25c, Auerbach's Cellar. 30c, Dance of the Sylphs. 40c, Dance of the Sprites. 50c, Faust and Marguerite. 70c, Woods and Meadows. 1fr, The Ride to the Abyss. 1.15fr, Heaven.

1969, Apr. 26 Engr. *Perf. 13*

712 A193 10c bl grn, pur & org brn 15 15
713 A193 20c mag, dk ol & lt brn 15 15
714 A193 25c ind, brn & mag 15 15
715 A193 30c yel grn, sl & blk 15 15
716 A193 40c org red, sl & blk 18 15
717 A193 50c ol, plum & sl 22 20
718 A193 70c dp grn, sl & lt brn 35 28
719 A193 1fr mag, blk & ol bis 48 40
720 A193 1.15fr Prus bl, blk & ultra 60 60
Nos. 712-720,C75 (10) 3.68 3.33

Issued to commemorate the centenary of the death of Hector Berlioz (1803-1869), French composer.

St. Elizabeth and Husband, Louis IV, Landgrave of Thuringia A194

1969, Apr. 26

721 A194 3fr dk red, sl & gray 1.65 1.40

Issued for the Red Cross.

See Nos. 767, 812, 830, 905, 963, 1037, 1094, 1189.

Europa Issue, 1969

Common Design Type

1969, Apr. 26

Size: 36x26mm

722 CD12 40c scar & pur 18 15
723 CD12 70c brt bl & blk 42 26
724 CD12 1fr yel bis, brn & bl 55 38

Prince Rainier Type of 1955 and Palace Type of 1960

Designs: 80c, Aerial view of Palace. 1.15fr, 1.30fr, Honor Court.

1969-70 Engr. *Perf. 13*

725 A83 40c ol & rose red 24 18
726 A83 45c slate & ocher 28 18
727 A83 50c ocher & mar 45 18
728 A83 70c dk pur & brt vio bl 65 35
729 A116 80c bl, red brn & grn 70 35
730 A83 85c dk vio & brt grn 75 50
731 A116 1.15fr blk, bl & mar 1.10 70
731A A116 1.30fr ol brn, lt bl & dl grn ('70) 85 45
Nos. 725-731A (8) 5.02 2.89

Aquatic Stadium Type of 1964-67, "1962" Omitted

1969 Engr. *Perf. 13*

732 A153 22c choc, brt bl & blk 35 15
733 A153 35c Prus bl, brt bl & blk 35 28
734 A153 70c blk & vio bl 60 24

Nos. 732-734 were issued precanceled only. See note after No. 324.

Princes of Monaco Type of 1967

Designs: 1fr, Honoré II (1604-1662), by Philippe de Champaigne. 3fr, Louise-Hippolyte (1697-1731), by Pierre Gobert.

1969, Nov. 25 Engr. *Perf. 12x13*

735 A182 1fr multi 38 38
736 A182 3fr multi 1.10 1.10

Woman's Head, by Leonardo da Vinci — A195

Drawings by Leonardo da Vinci: 40c, Self-portrait. 70c, Head of old man. 80c, Study for head of St. Magdalene. 1.15fr, Man's head. 3fr, Professional soldier.

1969, Nov. 25 *Perf. 13*

737 A195 30c dl brn 20 15
738 A195 40c brn & rose red 22 16
739 A195 70c gray grn 30 22
740 A195 80c dk brn 35 30
741 A195 1.15fr org brn 60 55
742 A195 3fr ol brn 1.50 1.10
Nos. 737-742 (6) 3.17 2.48

Leonardo da Vinci (1452-1519), Florentine painter, sculptor and scientist.

Alphonse Daudet and Scenes from "Letters from My Windmill" — A196

Various Scenes from "Letters from My Windmill" (Lettres de Mon Moulin).

1969, Nov. 25

743 A196 30c bl grn & multi 16 15
744 A196 40c brn, vio bl & ol 28 24
745 A196 70c pur, brn & ol gray 32 30
746 A196 80c sl grn, vio bl & mar 38 35
747 A196 1.15fr ocher, sep & blk 50 48
Nos. 743-747 (5) 1.64 1.52

Centenary of publication of "Letters from My Windmill," by Alphonse Daudet (1840-1897).

ILO Emblem A197

1969, Nov. 25 *Perf. 13x12½*

748 A197 40c dk bl & dk pur 35 28

50th anniv. of the ILO.

World Map and JCI Emblem A198

1969, Nov. 25

749 A198 40c ol, dk bl & bl 24 20

25th anniversary of the Junior Chamber of Commerce in Monaco.

Television Camera and View of Monte Carlo — A199

1969, Nov. 25

750 A199 40c red brn, lil & bl 24 20

10th International Television Festival in 1970.

King Alfonso XIII, Prince Albert I and Underwater Scene — A200

1969, Nov. 25 *Perf. 12½x13*

751 A200 40c dk brn, blk & grnsh bl 28 28

50th anniv. of the International Commission for the Scientific Exploration of the Mediterranean.

Congress Building, Princes Albert I and Rainier III — A201

1970, Feb. 21 Engr. *Perf. 13*

752 A201 40c gray & car 22 16

Meeting of the Interparliamentary Union, Monaco, Mar. 30-Apr. 5.

EXPO '70 Emblem, Japanese Scroll — A202

Designs (EXPO '70 Emblem and): 30c, Ibis. 40c, Torii. 70c, Cherry blossoms, horiz. 1.15fr, Palace and arms of Monaco, Osaka Castle and arms, horiz.

1970, Mar. 16

753 A202 20c brn, yel grn & car 15 15
754 A202 30c brn, yel grn & buff 15 20
755 A202 40c ol bis & pur 22 22
756 A202 70c lt gray & red 55 55
757 A202 1.15fr red & multi 60 60
Nos. 753-757 (5) 1.67 1.72

Issued to publicize EXPO '70 International Exposition, Osaka, Japan, Mar. 15-Sept. 13.

Harbor Seal Pup — A203

1970, Mar. 16

758 A203 40c red lil, bl & gray 50 42

Protection of seal pups.

Doberman Pinscher A204

1970, Apr. 25

759 A204 40c ocher & blk 1.65 60

International Dog Show, Monte Carlo, Apr. 25. See No. 996.

Basque Ponies A205

Designs: 30c, Parnassius Apollo butterfly. 50c, Harbor seal in Somme Bay. 80c, Pyrenean chamois, vert. 1fr, Whitetailed sea eagles, vert. 1.15fr, European otter, vert.

1970, May 4

760 A205 30c Prus bl & multi 22 15
761 A205 40c bl & multi 28 16
762 A205 50c grnsh bl, bis & brn 40 16
763 A205 80c gray grn, sl bl & brn 58 28
764 A205 1fr gray, brn & bis 95 38
765 A205 1.15fr dk brn, lt bl & yel grn 1.10 45
Nos. 760-765 (6) 3.53 1.58

20th anniversary of the International Federation of Animal Protection.

Flower Type of 1968

Design: 3fr, Roses and Anemones, by Vincent van Gogh.

1970, May 4 Photo. *Perf. 12x13*

766 A185 3fr blk & multi 1.50 1.50

International Flower Show, Monte Carlo.

Red Cross Type of 1969

Design: 3fr, St. Louis giving alms to the poor.

1970, May 4 Engr. *Perf. 13*

767 A194 3fr dk gray, ol gray & slate grn 1.50 1.50

Issued for the Red Cross.

Europa Issue, 1970

Common Design Type

1970, May 4

Size: 26x36mm

768 CD13 40c deep rose lilac 22 15
769 CD13 80c bright green 45 28
770 CD13 1fr deep blue 55 35

UPU Headquarters and Monument, Bern — A206

1970, May 4

771 A206 40c brn ol, gray & bl grn 22 16

New UPU Headquarters in Bern opening.

Plaque and Flag on the Moon, Presidents Kennedy and Nixon — A207

Design: 80c, Astronauts and landing module on moon, and Apollo 11 emblem.

1970, May 4 Photo.

772 A207 40c multi 28 24
773 A207 80c multi 55 42

Man's first landing on moon, July 20, 1969. US astronauts Neil A. Armstrong and Col. Edwin E. Aldrin, Jr., with Lt. Col. Michael Collins piloting Apollo 11.

Princes of Monaco Type of 1967

Designs: 1fr, Louis I (1662-1701), by Jean Francois de Troy. 3fr, Charlotte de Gramont (1639-1678), by Sebastian Bourdon.

1970, Dec. 15 Engr. *Perf. 12x13*

774 A182 1fr multi 45 45
775 A182 3fr multi 1.25 1.40

Painting Type of 1968

Design: 3fr, Portrait of Dédie, by Amedeo Modigliani (1884-1920).

1970, Dec. 15

776 A185 3fr multi 1.00 70

Beethoven and "Ode to Joy" — A208

1970, Dec. 15

777 A208 1.30fr brn & mar 1.00 70

Bicentenary of the birth of Ludwig van Beethoven (1770-1827), composer.

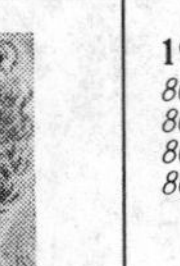

Dumas and Scene from "Three Musketeers" — A209

Designs: 40c, Henri Rougier and biplane over Monaco. 80c, Alphonse de Lamartine and scenes from his works.

1970, Dec. 15

778 A209 30c bl, brn & gray 15 15
779 A209 40c bl, sep & gray 26 18
780 A209 80c multi 35 22

Nos. 778-780 commemorate: Centenary of the death of Alexandre Dumas, père (1802-1870), novelist; 60th anniversary of first flight over the Mediterranean by Henri Rougier; 150th anniversary of the publication of "Méditations Poétiques" by Alphonse de Lamartine (1790-1869), poet.

Camargue Horse A210

Horses: 20c, Anglo-Arabian thoroughbred. 30c, French saddle horse. 40c, Lippizaner. 50c, Trotter. 70c, English thoroughbred. 85c, Arabian. 1.15fr, Barbary.

1970, Dec. 15 Engr. *Perf. 13*

781 A210 10c bl, ol bis & dk bl 15 15
782 A210 20c vio bl, brn & ol 15 15
783 A210 30c bl, brn & grn 22 15
784 A210 40c gray, ind & ol bis 32 18
785 A210 50c bl, dk brn & ol 45 22
786 A210 70c dk grn, ol brn & red brn 55 28
787 A210 85c dk grn, ol & sl 70 45
788 A210 1.15fr bl, emer & blk 95 55
Nos. 781-788,C77 (9) 5.74 4.13

Prince Rainier Type of 1955 and Palace Type of 1960

Designs: 90c, Honor Court. 1.40fr, Aerial view of Palace.

1971 Engr. *Perf. 13*

789 A83 60c plum & blk 65 32
790 A116 90c dk car, ultra & blk 90 42
791 A83 1.10fr gray & ultra 1.10 65
792 A116 1.40fr pur, org & grn 1.25 1.00

Aquatic Stadium Type of 1964-67, "1962" Omitted

1971

793 A153 26c pur, ultra & blk 35 18
794 A153 30c cop red, bl, lil & blk 45 18
795 A153 45c sl grn, vio bl & blk 70 24
796 A153 90c ol, Prus bl & blk 1.25 40

Nos. 793-796 were issued precanceled only. See note after No. 324.

Europa Issue, 1971

Common Design Type

1971, Sept. 6

797 CD14 50c car rose 25 15
798 CD14 80c brt bl 38 22
799 CD14 1.30fr slate grn 90 32

Old Bridge at Sospel — A211

Designs: 80c, Roquebrune Castle. 1.30fr, Grimaldi Castle. 3fr, Roman Monument, La Turbie, vert. All views in Alpes-Maritimes Department, France.

1971, Sept. 6

800 A211 50c sl grn, bl & ol brn 20 15
801 A211 80c sl grn, sl & brn 35 16
802 A211 1.30fr brn, sl grn & red 50 35
803 A211 3fr brt bl, sl & ol 1.25 85

Protection of historic monuments.

Theodolite, Underwater Scene and Coast Line — A212

1971, Sept. 6

804 A212 80c bl grn & multi 42 35

50th anniversary of International Hydrographical Bureau.

Sea Bird Covered with Oil — A213

1971, Sept. 6

805 A213 50c dp bl & indigo 45 35

Against pollution of the seas.

"Arts" (Organ Pipes and Michelangelo's Creation of Adam) A214

"Science" (Alchemist, Radar and Rocket) — A215

Prince Pierre of Monaco — A216

Design: 80c, "Culture" (medieval scholar, book, film and television).

1971, Sept. 6 Engr. *Perf. 13*

806 A214 30c brt bl, pur & brn 15 15
807 A215 50c slate & brn org 18 15
808 A214 80c emer & brn 28 18

Photo. *Perf. 12½x13*

809 A216 1.30fr gray grn 42 32
Set value 66

25th anniv. of UNESCO.

Cocker Spaniel A217

1971, Sept. 6 ***Perf. 13x12½***
810 A217 50c multi 1.25 1.00

Intl. Dog Show. See Nos. 826, 879, 910.

Hand Holding Blood Donor Emblem A218

1971, Sept. 6 **Engr.** ***Perf. 13***
811 A218 80c red, vio & gray 45 32

7th International Blood Donors Congress, Monaco, Oct. 21-24.

Red Cross Type of 1969

Design: 3fr, St. Vincent de Paul appearing to prisoners.

1971, Sept. 6
812 A194 3fr bl grn, ol grn & dp grn 1.40 1.10

For the Red Cross

Princes of Monaco Type of 1967

Designs: 1fr, Antoine I (1701-1731), by Hyacinthe Rigaud. 3fr, Marie de Lorraine (1674-1724), French School.

1972, Jan. 18 ***Perf. 12x13***
813 A182 1fr multi 45 45
814 A182 3fr multi 1.40 1.25

Painting Type of 1968

Designs: 2fr, The Cradle, by Berthe Morisot. 3fr, Clown, by Jean Antoine Watteau.

1972, Jan. 18
815 A185 2fr grn & multi 1.10 95
816 A185 3fr multi 1.50 1.25

No. 815 issued for 25th anniv. (in 1971) of UNICEF.

Christ Before Pilate, by Dürer A219

1972, Jan. 18 ***Perf. 13***
817 A219 2fr lt brn & blk 1.25 1.00

500th anniv. of the birth of Albrecht Dürer (1471-1528), German painter and engraver.

La Fontaine and Animals — A220

Saint-Saens and "Samson et Dalila" — A221

Design: 1.30fr, Charles Baudelaire, nudes and cats.

1972, Jan. 18
818 A220 50c brn, grn & sl grn 35 24
819 A221 90c dk brn & yel brn 52 38
820 A220 1.30fr blk, red & vio brn 65 52

350th anniversary of the birth of Jean de La Fontaine (1621-1695), fabulist (50c); 50th anniversary of the death of Camille Saint-Saens (1835-1921), composer (90c); 150th anniversary of the birth of Charles Baudelaire (1821-1867), poet (1.30fr).

Father Christmas — A222

1972, Jan. 18
821 A222 30c bis, sl bl & red 15 15
822 A222 50c vio brn, grn & red 24 15
823 A222 90c ocher, ind & red 40 22

Christmas 1971.

Battle of Lepanto — A223

1972, Jan. 18
824 A223 1fr dl bl, red & brn 50 40

400th anniversary of the Battle of Lepanto against the Turks.

Steam and Diesel Locomotives, UIC Emblem — A224

1972, Apr. 27 **Engr.** ***Perf. 13***
825 A224 50c dk car, lil & choc 42 32

50th anniversary of the founding of the International Railroad Union (UIC).

Dog Type of 1971

1972, Apr. 27 **Photo.** ***Perf. 13x12½***
826 A217 60c Great Dane 80 70

International Dog Show.

Serene Landscape, Pollution, Destruction — A225

1972, Apr. 27 **Engr.** ***Perf. 13***
827 A225 90c grn, brn & blk 48 30

Anti-pollution fight.

Ski Jump, Sapporo '72 Emblem — A226

1972, Apr. 27
828 A226 90c bl grn, dk red & blk 50 40

11th Winter Olympic Games, Sapporo, Japan, Feb. 3-13.

Flower Type of 1968

Design: 3fr, Flowers in Vase, by Paul Cezanne.

1972, Apr. 27 **Photo.** ***Perf. 12x13***
829 A185 3fr multi 1.65 1.10

International Flower Show, Monte Carlo.

Red Cross Type of 1969

Design: 3fr, St. Francis of Assisi comforting poor man.

1972, Apr. 27 **Engr.** ***Perf. 13***
830 A194 3fr dk pur & brn 1.65 1.40

For the Red Cross.

Europa Issue 1972

Common Design Type

1972, Apr. 27 ***Perf. 12½x13***
Size: 26x36mm
831 CD15 50c vio bl & org 68 35
832 CD15 90c vio bl & emer 1.25 80

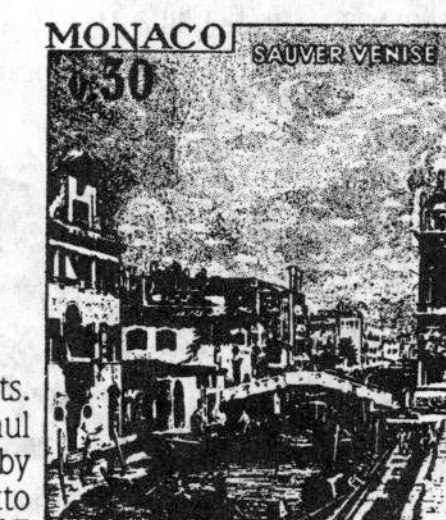

Church of Sts. John and Paul (detail), by Canaletto A227

Designs: 60c, Church of St. Peter of Castello, by Francesco Guardi. 2fr, St. Mark's Square, by Bernardo Bellotto.

1972, Apr. 27 ***Perf. 13***
Sizes: 36x48mm (30c, 2fr); 26½x48mm (60c)
833 A227 30c rose red 24 20
834 A227 60c brt pur 32 24
835 A227 2fr Prus bl 1.75 1.25

UNESCO campaign to save Venice.

Dressage A228

Designs (Equestrian Events): 90c, Jump over fences. 1.10fr, Jump over wall. 1.40fr, Jump over gates.

1972, Apr. 27
836 A228 60c rose car, vio bl & brn 70 70
837 A228 90c vio bl, rose car & brn 1.10 1.10
838 A228 1.10fr brn, rose car & vio bl 1.75 1.75
839 A228 1.40fr vio bl, rose car & brn 2.50 2.50
a. Block of 4 + 2 labels 8.00 8.00

20th Olympic Games, Munich, Aug. 26-Sept. 10. Nos. 836-839 printed se-tenant in sheets of 24 stamps and 6 labels.

Auguste Escoffier and his Birthplace A229

1972, May 6 **Engr.** ***Perf. 13***
840 A229 45c blk & olive 32 24

125th anniversary of the birth of Georges Auguste Escoffier (1846-1935), French chef.

Young Drug Addict — A230

Congress Emblem, Birds and Animals — A231

1972, July 3
841 A230 50c car, sep & org 40 22
842 A230 90c sl grn, sep & ind 60 38

Fight against drug abuse.

1972, Sept. 25

Designs: 50c, Congress emblem, Neptune, sea, earth and land creatures, horiz. 90c, Globe, land, sea and air creatures.

843 A231 30c ol, brt grn & car 15 15
844 A231 50c ocher, brn & org brn 25 15
845 A231 90c org brn, bl & ol 38 24

17th International Zoology Congress, Monaco, Sept. 24-30.

Arrangement of Lilies and Palm — A232

Designs: Floral arrangements.

1972, Nov. 13 **Photo.** ***Perf. 13***

846 A232 30c org red & multi 24 15
847 A232 50c multi 35 24
848 A232 90c blk & multi 60 32

International Flower Show, Monte Carlo, May, 1973. See Nos. 894-896.

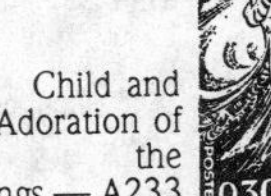

Child and Adoration of the Kings — A233

1972, Nov. 13 **Engr.**

849 A233 30c gray, vio bl & brt pink 15 15
850 A233 50c dp car, lil & brn 22 15
851 A233 90c vio bl & pur 45 24

Christmas 1972.

Louis Bleriot and his Monoplane — A234

Designs: 50c, Roald Amundsen and Antarctic landscape. 90c, Louis Pasteur and laboratory.

1972, Dec. 4

852 A234 30c choc & brt bl 22 15
853 A234 50c Prus bl & ind 35 28
854 A234 90c choc & ocher 60 50

Louis Bleriot (1872-1936), French aviation pioneer (30c); Roald Amundsen (1872-1928), Norwegian polar explorer (50c); Louis Pasteur (1822-1895), French chemist and bacteriologist (90c).

Gethsemane, by Giovanni Canavesio A235

Frescoes by Canavesio, 15th century, Chapel of Our Lady of Fountains at La Brique: 50c, Christ Stripped of His Garments. 90c, Christ Carrying the Cross. 1.40fr, Resurrection. 2fr, Crucifixion.

1972, Dec. 4

855 A235 30c brt rose 16 15
856 A235 50c indigo 28 22
857 A235 90c sl grn 50 32
858 A235 1.40fr brt red 60 45
859 A235 2fr purple 1.10 70
Nos. 855-859 (5) 2.64 1.84

Protection of historic monuments.

Princes of Monaco Type of 1967

Designs: 1fr, Jacques I, by Nicolas de Largillière. 3fr, Louise Hippolyte (1697-1731), by Jean Baptiste Vanloo.

1972, Dec. 4 ***Perf. 12x13***

860 A182 1fr multi 60 35
861 A182 3fr multi 1.50 1.25

Girl, Syringe, Addicts A236

1973, Jan. 5 **Engr.** ***Perf. 13***

862 A236 50c brt bl, cl & sl grn 24 15
863 A236 90c org, lil & emer 52 38

Fight against drug abuse.

Souvenir Sheet

Sts. Barbara, Dévote and Agatha, by Louis Brea — A237

1973, Apr. 30

864 A237 5fr dull red 10.50 10.50

Red Cross of Monaco, 25th anniv.

Flower Type of 1968

Design: 3.50fr, Flowers in Vase, by Ambrosius Bosschaert.

1973, Apr. 30 **Photo.** ***Perf. 12x13***

865 A185 3.50fr multi 2.00 1.65

International Flower Show, Monte Carlo.

Europa Issue 1973

Common Design Type

1973, Apr. 30 **Engr.** ***Perf. 13***

Size: 36x26mm

866 CD16 50c orange 65 52
867 CD16 90c bl grn 1.20 75

Molière, Scene from "Le Malade Imaginaire" — A238

Costumed Players and Mask — A239

1973, Apr. 30

868 A238 20c red, vio bl & brn 38 18

Tricentenary of the death of Molière (1622-1673), French actor and writer.

1973, Apr. 30

869 A239 60c red, lil & bl 48 28

5th International Amateur Theater Festival.

Virgin Mary, St. Teresa, Lisieux Basilica — A240

1973, Apr. 30

870 A240 1.40fr ind, ultra & brn 65 45

Centenary of the birth of St. Teresa of Lisieux (Thérèse Martin, 1873-1897), Carmelite nun.

Charles Peguy and Cathedral of Chartres — A241

1973, Apr. 30

871 A241 50c dp cl, ol brn & sl 38 24

Centenary of the birth of Charles Pierre Peguy (1873-1914), French writer.

Colette, Books and Cat — A242

Designs: No. 873, Eugene Ducretet and transmission from Eiffel Tower to Pantheon. 45c, Jean Henri Fabre and insects. 50c, Blaise Pascal, vert. 60c, Radar installation and telegraph wire insulators. No. 877, William Webb Ellis and rugby. No. 878, Sir George Cayley and early model plane.

1973, Apr. 30

872 A242 30c dp org, bl & dk bl 48 24
873 A242 30c brn & multi 30 24
874 A242 45c dp bl & multi 48 30
875 A242 50c vio bl, lil & dk pur 30 24
876 A242 60c brn, bl blk & brt bl 38 30
877 A242 90c brn & car rose 60 40
878 A242 90c red & multi 60 48
Nos. 872-878 (7) 3.14 2.20

Anniversaries: Colette (1873-1954), French writer (#872); 75th anniv. of 1st Hertzian wave transmission (#873); Fabre (1823-1915), entomologist (45c); Pascal (1623-1662), scientist and philosopher (50c); 5th Intl. Telecommunications Day (60c); Sesquicentennial of the invention of rugby (#877); Cayley (1821-95), aviation pioneer (#878).

Dog Type of 1971

Design: German shepherd.

1973, Apr. 30 **Photo.** ***Perf. 13x12½***

879 A217 45c multi 3.75 1.90

International Dog Show.

The First Crèche, by Giotto — A243

Paintings of the Nativity by: 45c, School of Filippo Lippi. 50c, Giotto. 1fr, 15th century miniature, vert. 2fr, Fra Angelico, vert.

Perf. 13x12, 12x13

1973, Nov. 12 **Engr.**

880 A243 30c purple 38 25
881 A243 45c rose mag 60 45
882 A243 50c brn org 75 50
883 A243 1fr sl grn 1.25 85
884 A243 2fr ol grn 2.00 1.65
Nos. 880-884,C78 (6) 7.73 5.70

750th anniversary of the first crèche assembled by St. Francis of Assisi.

Picnic and View of Monte Carlo — A244

Designs: 20c, Dance around maypole, vert. 30c, "U Brandi" folk dance. 45c, Dance around St. John's fire. 50c, Blessing of the Christmas bread. 60c, Blessing of the sea. 1fr, Good Friday procession.

1973, Nov. 12 ***Perf. 13***

885 A244 10c sl grn, dk bl & sep 15 15
886 A244 20c bl, ol & lil 15 15
887 A244 30c lt grn, bl & brn 22 22
888 A244 45c dk brn, vio & red brn 28 28
889 A244 50c blk, brn & ver 28 28
890 A244 60c bl, mag & vio bl 42 42
891 A244 1fr ind, vio & ol bis 70 70
Nos. 885-891 (7) 2.20 2.20

Monegasque customs.

Princes of Monaco Type of 1967

Paintings of Charlotte Grimaldi, by Pierre Gobert, 1733: No. 892, in court dress, No. 893, in nun's habit.

1973, Nov. 12 ***Perf. 12x13***

892 A182 2fr multi 1.25 1.10
893 A182 2fr multi 1.25 1.10

Flower Type of 1972

Designs: Floral arrangements.

1973, Nov. 12 **Photo.** ***Perf. 13***

894 A232 45c vio bl & multi 42 28
895 A232 60c dk brn & multi 55 42
896 A232 1fr brn org & multi 90 70

Intl. Flower Show, Monte Carlo, May 1974.

Children, Syringes, Drug Addicts A245

1973, Nov. 12 **Engr.**

897 A245 50c bl, grn & brn 28 22
898 A245 90c red, brn & ind 70 42

Fight against drug abuse.

Souvenir Sheet

1949 1974

Prince Rainier III — A246

1974, May 8 **Engr.** ***Imperf.***

899 A246 10fr black 6.00 6.00

25th anniv. of the accession of Prince Rainier III.

Art from Around the World — A247

King of Rome (Napoleon's Son), by Bosio — A248

Designs (UPU Emblem and): 70c, Hands holding letters. 1.10fr, Famous buildings, Statue of Liberty and Sphinx.

1974, May 8 ***Perf. 13***

900 A247 50c choc & org brn 22 18
901 A247 70c aqua & multi 35 30
902 A247 1.10fr indigo & multi 90 65

Centenary of the Universal Postal Union.

1974, May 8

Europa: 1.10fr, Madame Elisabeth (sister of Louis XVI), by Francois Joseph Bosio.

903	A248	45c sl grn & sep	85	65
904	A248	1.10fr brn & ol brn	1.50	1.00
a.		Souv. sheet, 5 #903, 5 #904	20.00	20.00

Red Cross Type of 1969

Design: St. Bernard of Menthon rescuing mountain traveler.

1974, May 8

905	A194	3fr Prus bl & vio brn	1.65	1.25

For the Red Cross.

Henri Farman and Farman Planes A249

Designs: 40c, Guglielmo Marconi, circuit diagram and ships which conducted first tests. 45c, Ernest Duchesne and penicillin. 50c, Fernand Forest and 4-cylinder motor.

1974, May 8

906	A249	30c multi	18	15
907	A249	40c multi	20	15
908	A249	45c multi	25	18
909	A249	50c multi	24	18

Farman (1874-1934), French aviation pioneer; Marconi (1874-1937), Italian inventor; Duchesne (1874-1912), French biologist; Forest (1851-1914), inventor.

Dog Type of 1971

1974, May 8 Photo. *Perf. 13x12½*

910	A217	60c Schnauzer	1.25	85

Intl. Dog Show, Monte Carlo, Apr. 6-7.

Ronsard and Scenes from his Sonnet à Hélène — A250

1974, May 8 Engr. *Perf. 13*

911	A250	70c choc & dk car	42	32

450th anniversary of the birth of Pierre de Ronsard (1524-1585), French poet.

Winston Churchill — A251

1974, May 8

912	A251	1fr gray & brn	52	32

Centenary of the birth of Sir Winston Churchill (1874-1965), statesman.

Palaces of Monaco and Vienna — A252

1974, May 8

913	A252	2fr multi	1.00	85

60th anniversary of the first International Police Congress, Monaco, Apr. 1914.

The Box, by Auguste Renoir A253

Rising Sun, by Claude Monet — A254

Impressionist Paintings: No. 915, Dancing Class, by Edgar Degas. No. 917, Entrance to Voisins Village, by Camille Pissarro. No. 918, House of the Hanged Man, by Paul Cezanne. No. 919, The Flooding of Port Marly, by Alfred Sisley.

Perf. 12x13, 13x12

1974, Nov. 12 Engr.

914	A253	1fr multi	1.25	95
915	A253	1fr multi	1.25	95
916	A254	2fr multi	1.90	1.25
917	A254	2fr multi	1.90	1.25
918	A254	2fr multi	1.90	1.25
919	A254	2fr multi	1.90	1.25
		Nos. 914-919 (6)	10.10	6.90

Trainer and Tigers A255

Prancing Horses — A256

Perf. 13x12½, 12½x13

1974, Nov. 12

920	A255	2c shown	15	15
921	A256	3c shown	15	15
922	A255	5c Elephants	15	15
923	A256	45c Equestrian act	40	18
924	A255	70c Clowns	52	32
925	A256	1.10fr Jugglers	90	65
926	A256	5fr Trapeze act	3.75	2.50
		Nos. 920-926 (7)	6.02	4.10

International Circus Festival.

Honoré II Coin — A257

1974, Nov. 12 ***Perf. 13***

927	A257	60c rose red & blk	45	32

350th anniversary of coins of Monaco.

Underwater Fauna and Flora — A258

Designs: 45c, Fish, and marine life. 1.10fr, Coral.

1974, Nov. 12 Photo. *Perf. 13x12½*

Size: 35x25mm

928	A258	45c multi	48	35

Size: 48x27mm

Perf. 13

929	A258	70c multi	60	35
930	A258	1.10fr multi	80	60

Congress of the International Commission for the Scientific Exploration of the Mediterranean, Monaco, Dec. 6-14.

Floral Arrangements

A259 A260

1974, Nov. 12 ***Perf. 13x12½***

931	A259	70c multi	60	35
932	A260	1.10fr multi	85	48

International Flower Show, Monte Carlo, May 1975. See Nos. 1003-1004, 1084-1085.

Prince Rainier III — A261

1974-78 Engr. ***Perf. 13***

933	A261	60c slate grn	42	15
934	A261	80c red	70	15
935	A261	80c brt grn	48	15
936	A261	1fr brown	85	42
937	A261	1fr scarlet	75	15
938	A261	1fr slate grn	60	15
939	A261	1.20fr vio bl	1.25	80
940	A261	1.20fr red	70	15
941	A261	1.25fr blue	1.00	48
942	A261	1.50fr black	80	24
943	A261	1.70fr dp bl	80	30
944	A261	2fr dk pur	2.25	80
945	A261	2.10fr olive bister	1.00	65
946	A261	2.50fr indigo	1.75	70
947	A261	9fr brt vio	4.25	2.00
		Nos. 933-947 (15)	17.60	7.29

Issue dates: 60c, Nos. 934, 936, 939, 2fr, Dec. 23. Nos. 935, 937, 1.25fr, 2.50fr, Jan. 10, 1977. Nos. 938, 940, 1.50fr, 1.70fr, 2.10fr, 9fr, Aug. 18, 1978.

See Nos. 1200-1204, 1255-1256.

Monte Carlo Beach A262

Clock Tower — A263

Prince Albert I Statue and Museum — A264

1974-77

948	A262	25c shown	30	20
949	A263	50c shown	42	26
950	A262	1.10fr shown ('77)	95	40
951	A264	1.40fr shown	1.25	52
952	A262	1.70fr All Saints' Tower	1.65	1.10
953	A263	3fr Fort Antoine	3.50	1.50
954	A262	5.50fr La Condamine (view)	5.00	2.25
		Nos. 948-954 (7)	13.07	6.23

Issue dates: 1.10fr, Jan. 10. Others, Dec. 23.

See Nos. 1005-1008, 1030-1033, 1069-1072, 1138-1152.

Haageocereus A265

1974, Dec. 23 Photo. ***Perf. 12½x13***

955	A265	10c *shown*	15	15
956	A265	20c *Matucana*	15	15
957	A265	30c *Parodia*	26	20
958	A265	85c *Mediolobivia*	55	40
959	A265	1.90fr *Matucana*	1.50	1.10
960	A265	4fr *Echinocereus*	3.00	1.65
		Nos. 955-960 (6)	5.61	3.65

Plants from Monaco Botanical Gardens.

Europa Issue 1975

Sailor, by Philibert Florence — A266

St. Dévote, by Ludovic Brea — A267

1975, May 13 Engr. ***Perf. 13***

961	A266	80c brt red lil	95	80
962	A267	1.20fr brt bl	1.25	90
a.		Souv. sheet, 5 each #961-962	18.00	18.00

Red Cross Type of 1969

Design: St. Bernardino of Siena (1380-1444) burying the dead.

1975, May 13

963	A194	4fr pur & Prus bl	2.75	1.75

For the Red Cross.

Carmen, at the Tavern A268

Scenes from Carmen: 30c, Prologue, vert. 80c, The smugglers' hide-out. 1.40fr, Entrance to bull ring.

1975, May 13

964 A268	30c multi		16	15
965 A268	60c multi		28	16
966 A268	80c multi		55	35
967 A268	1.40fr multi		1.00	75

Centenary of first performance of opera Carmen by George Bizet (1838-1875).

Louis de Saint-Simon A269

Albert Schweitzer A270

1975, May 13

968 A269	40c bluish blk	40	32
969 A270	60c blk & dl red	48	40

300th birth anniversary of Louis de Saint-Simon (1675-1755), statesman and writer, and birth centenary of Albert Schweitzer (1875-1965), medical missionary.

ARPHILA 75 Emblem, G Clef — A271

1975, May 13

970 A271	80c sepia & org brn	65	45

ARPHILA 75 International Philatelic Exhibition, Paris, June 6-16.

Seagull and Rising Sun — A272

1975, May 13 **Photo.**

971 A272	85c multi	55	45

Oceanexpo 75, International Exhibition, Okinawa, July 20, 1975-Jan. 1976.

Charity Label and "1f" Destroying Cancer A273

1975, May 13 **Engr.**

972 A273	1fr multi	80	60

Fight against cancer.

Jesus with Crown of Thorns, Holy Year Emblem — A274

1975, May 13

973 A274	1.15fr lil, bis & ind	85	60

Holy Year 1975.

Villa Sauber, by Charles Garnier A275

1975, May 13

974 A275	1.20fr multi	90	65

European Architectural Heritage Year 1975.

Woman, Globe, IWY Emblem A276

1975, May 13

975 A276	1.20fr multi	85	65

International Women's Year.

Nos. 793-796 Surcharged

1975, Apr. 1 **Engr.** ***Perf. 13***

976 A153	42c on 26c multi	1.10	65
977 A153	48c on 30c multi	1.75	80
978 A153	70c on 45c multi	3.75	1.10
979 A153	1.35fr on 90c multi	4.75	1.40

Nos. 976-979 were issued precanceled only. See note after No. 324.

Rolls Royce "Silver Ghost" 1907 — A277

1975, Nov. **Engr.** ***Perf. 13***

980 A277	5c shown	15	15
981 A277	10c Hispano Suiza, 1926	15	15
982 A277	20c Isotta Fraschini, 1928	15	15
983 A277	30c Cord L. 29	26	16
984 A277	50c Voisin, 1930	45	26
985 A277	60c Duesenberg, 1933	52	32
986 A277	80c Bugatti, 1938	80	45
987 A277	85c Delahaye, 1940	1.25	65
988 A277	1.20fr Cisitalia, 1946	2.00	85
989 A277	1.40fr Mercedes Benz, 1955	2.25	1.25
990 A277	5.50fr Lamborghini, 1974	5.25	2.75
	Nos. 980-990 (11)	13.23	7.14

Development of the automobile.

Princes of Monaco Type of 1967

Paintings (Unknown Artists): 2fr, Prince Honoré III (1733-1795). 4fr, Princess Catherine de Brignole (1759-1813).

1975, Nov.

991 A182	2fr multi	1.25	90
992 A182	4fr multi	2.50	1.50

Caged Dog — A278

Designs: 80c, Cat chased up a tree, vert. 1.20fr, Horses pulling heavy load.

1975, Nov.

993 A278	60c blk & brn	60	42
994 A278	80c blk, gray & brn	75	48
995 A278	1.20fr mag & sl grn	1.00	60

125th anniversary of the Grammont (J. P. Delmas Grammont) Law against cruelty to animals.

Dog Type of 1970

1975, Nov.

996 A204	60c Poodle	1.40	1.00

International Dog Show, Monte Carlo.

Maurice Ravel — A279

Clown — A280

Design: 1.20fr, Johann Strauss and dancers.

1975, Nov.

997 A279	60c mar & sep	48	35
998 A279	1.20fr mar & ind	90	70

Maurice Ravel (1875-1937), birth centenary, and Johann Strauss (1804-1849), sesquicentennial of birth, composers.

1975, Nov. **Photo.** ***Perf. 12½x13***

999 A280	80c multi	55	38

2nd International Circus Festival, Monte Carlo, Dec. 1975.

Honoré II Florin, 1640 — A281

1975, Nov. **Engr.** ***Perf. 13***

1000 A281	80c slate & gray	55	38

See Nos. 1040, 1088, 1234.

Ampère and Ampère Balance A282

1975, Nov.

1001 A282	85c ultra & ind	52	38

André Marie Ampère (1775-1836), physicist, birth bicentennial.

Lamentation for the Dead Christ, by Michelangelo A283

1975, Nov.

1002 A283	1.40fr blk & ol gray	95	65

Michelangelo Buonarroti (1475-1564), Italian sculptor, painter and architect, 500th anniversary of birth.

Flower Types of 1974

Designs: Floral arrangements.

1975, Nov. **Photo.** ***Perf. 13x12½***

1003 A259	60c multi	48	25
1004 A260	80c multi	60	35

International Flower Show, Monte Carlo, May 1976.

Clock Tower Type, 1974

1976, Jan. 26 **Engr.** ***Perf. 13***

1005 A263	50c brn lake	55	38
1006 A263	60c ol grn	65	52
1007 A263	90c purple	1.00	75
1008 A263	1.60fr brt bl	1.50	1.40

Nos. 1005-1008 were issued precanceled only. See note after No. 324.

Prince Pierre — A284

André Maurois and Colette — A285

Portraits: 25c, Jean and Jerome Tharaud. 30c, Emile Henriot, Marcel Pagnol, Georges Duhamel. 50c, Philippe Heriat, Jules Supervielle, L. Pierard. 60c, Roland Dorgeles, M. Achard, G. Bauer. 80c, Franz Hellens, A. Billy, Msgr. Grente. 1.20fr, Jean Giono, L. Pasteur-Vallery-Radot, M. Garcon.

1976, May 3 **Engr.** ***Perf. 13***

1009 A284	10c black	15	15
1010 A285	20c red & sl	15	15
1011 A285	25c red, dk bl & blk	20	15
1012 A285	30c brown	30	20
1013 A285	50c brn, red & vio bl	38	24
1014 A285	60c grn, brn & lt brn	52	30
1015 A285	80c blk & mag	70	35
1016 A285	1.20fr blk, vio & cl	1.25	70
	Nos. 1009-1016 (8)	3.65	2.24

Literary Council of Monaco, 25th anniv.

Dachshunds — A286

1976, May 3 **Photo.**

1017 A286	60c multi	1.00	65

International Dog Show, Monte Carlo.

Bridge Table, Coast — A287

1976, May 3 **Engr.**
1018 A287 60c multi 52 35

Fifth Bridge Olympiade, Monte Carlo.

A. G. Bell, Telephone, 1876, Satellite Dish — A288

1976, May 3
1019 A288 80c multi 50 35

Centenary of first telephone call by Alexander Graham Bell, Mar. 10, 1876.

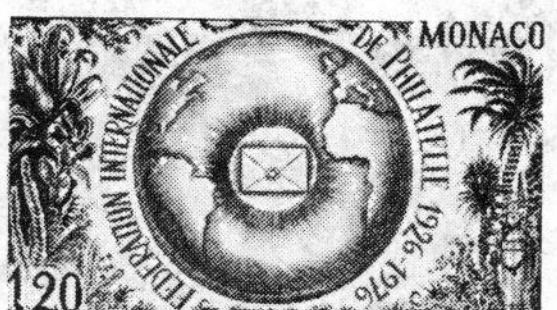

Federation Emblem — A289

1976, May 3
1020 A289 1.20fr multi 80 55

International Federation of Philately (F.I.P.), 50th anniversary.

US Liberty Bell Type of 1926 — A290

1976, May 3
1021 A290 1.70fr car & blk 1.25 95

American Bicentennial.

Fritillaria, by Vincent van Gogh — A291

1976, May 3 **Photo.** ***Perf. 12x13***
1022 A291 3fr multi 3.50 2.75

International Flower Show, Monte Carlo, May 1976.

Plate with Lemon Branch — A292 Diving — A293

Europa: 1.20fr, The Peddler, 19th century figurine, and CEPT emblem.

1976, May 3 ***Perf. 12½x13***
1023 A292 80c sal & multi 85 55
1024 A292 1.20fr ultra & multi 1.25 70
a. Souv. sheet of 10, 5 each #1023-1024 16.00 16.00

1976, May 3 **Engr.** ***Perf. 13***

Designs (Olympic Rings and): 80c, Athlete on parallel bars. 85c, Hammer throw. 1.20fr, Rowing, horiz. 1.70fr, Boxing, horiz.

1025 A293 60c multi 32 26
1026 A293 80c multi 42 32
1027 A293 85c multi 52 42
1028 A293 1.20fr multi 70 60
1029 A293 1.70fr multi 1.10 1.00
a. Souv. sheet of 5, #1025-1029, perf. 14 3.50 3.50
Nos. 1025-1029 (5) 3.06 2.60

21st Olympic Games, Montreal, Canada, July 17-Aug. 1.

Clock Tower Type, 1974

1976, Sept. 1 **Engr.** ***Perf. 13***
1030 A263 52c bister 35 24
1031 A263 62c red lilac 48 30
1032 A263 95c scarlet 70 50
1033 A263 1.70fr blue green 1.25 85

Nos. 1030-1033 were issued precanceled only. See note after No. 324.

Princes of Monaco Type of 1967

Paintings: 2fr, Honoré IV (1815-1819), by Francois Lemoyne. 4fr, Louise d'Aumont-Mazarin (1750-1826), by Marie Verroust.

1976, Nov. 9 ***Perf. 12½x13***
1035 A182 2fr vio brn 1.25 1.00
1036 A182 4fr multi 2.50 1.65

Red Cross Type of 1969

Design: St. Louise de Marillac and children.

1976, Nov. 9 ***Perf. 13***
1037 A194 4fr grn, gray & plum 2.25 1.40

St. Vincent de Paul, View of Monaco A294

1976, Nov. 9
1038 A294 60c multi 55 45

St. Vincent de Paul Conference, Monaco, July 31, 1876, centenary.

Marquise de Sevigné — A295

1976, Nov. 9
1039 A295 80c multi 42 28

Marie de Rabutin-Chantal, Marquise de Sevigné (1626-1696), writer.

Coin Type of 1975

Design: 80c, Honoré II 2-gros coin.

1976, Nov. 9
1040 A281 80c grn & stl bl 60 38

Richard E. Byrd, Roald Amundsen, North Pole — A296

1976, Nov. 9
1041 A296 85c ol, blk & bl 75 55

1st flights over the North Pole, 50th anniv.

Gulliver Holding King, Queen and Enemy Fleet — A297

1976, Nov. 9
1042 A297 1.20fr ind, bl & brn 70 55

250th anniversary of the publication of Gulliver's Travels, by Jonathan Swift.

Child and Christmas Decorations A298

1976, Nov. 9 ***Perf. 13x12½***
1043 A298 60c multi 38 24
1044 A298 1.20fr multi 75 42

Christmas 1976.

"Trapped by Drugs" A299

1976, Nov. 9
1045 A299 80c grn, ultra & org 60 35
1046 A299 1.20fr red brn, vio & car 85 48

Fight against drug abuse.

Floral Arrangement A300

Clown and Circus Acts A301

Design: 1fr, Floral arrangement. Designs by Princess Grace.

1976, Nov. 9 **Photo.** ***Perf. 13½x13***
1047 A300 80c yel grn & multi 60 30
1048 A300 1fr lt bl & multi 85 40

International Flower Show, Monte Carlo, May 1977. See Nos. 1124-1125, 1191.

1976, Nov. 9
1049 A301 1fr multi 85 70

3rd Intl. Circus Festival, Dec. 26-30.

L'Hirondelle I — A302

Prince Albert I — A303

Designs (Gouaches by Louis Tinayre): 30c, Crew of L'Hirondelle. 80c, L'Hirondelle in Storm. 1fr, The Helmsman, vert. 1.25fr, L'Hirondelle in Storm. 1.40fr, Shrimp Fishermen in Boat. 1.90fr, Hauling in the Net, vert. 2.50fr, Catching Opah Fish.

1977, May 3 **Engr.** ***Perf. 13***
1050 A302 10c multi 15 15
1051 A303 20c multi 18 15
1052 A302 30c multi 25 18
1053 A302 80c multi 42 30
1054 A302 1fr multi 65 35
1055 A302 1.25fr multi 75 50
1056 A302 1.40fr multi 1.10 75
1057 A302 1.90fr multi 1.50 1.00
1058 A302 2.50fr multi 2.00 1.50
Nos. 1050-1058 (9) 7.00 4.88

75th anniversary of publication of "The Career of a Sailor," by Prince Albert I.
See Nos. 1073-1081.

Pyreneean Mountain Dogs — A304

1977, May 3 **Photo.**
1059 A304 80c multi 1.40 1.00

International Dog Show, Monte Carlo.
See No. 1199.

Motherhood, by Mary Cassatt — A305

1977, May 3 **Engr.**
1060 A305 80c multi 55 40

World Association of the Friends of Children.

Archers, Target and Monte Carlo — A306

1977, May 3

1061 A306 1.10fr multi 65 48

10th International Rainier III Archery Championships.

Spirit of St. Louis and Lindbergh — A307

1977, May 3

1062 A307 1.90fr multi 1.10 85

50th anniversary of first transatlantic flight by Charles Lindbergh.

The Dock at Deauville, by Dufy — A308

1977, May 3 **Photo.**

1063 A308 2fr multi 1.90 1.40

Raoul Dufy (1877-1953), painter, birth centenary.

Young Girl, by Rubens — A309

Helmet Tower, Monaco — A310

Rubens Paintings: 1fr, Duke of Buckingham. 1.40fr, Rubens' son Nicolas, 2 years old.

1977, May 3 **Engr.**

1064 A309	80c	multi	40	35
1065 A309	1fr	multi	55	35
1066 A309	1.40fr	multi	95	70

Peter Paul Rubens (1577-1640).

1977, May 3

Europa: 1.40fr, St. Michael's Church, Menton.

1067 A310	1fr	multi	60	48
1068 A310	1.40fr	multi	1.25	70
a.	Souv. sheet, 5 each #1067-1068		15.00	15.00

Clock Tower Type of 1974

1977, Apr. 1 **Engr.** ***Perf. 13***

1069 A263	54c	brt grn	38	32
1070 A263	68c	orange	52	45
1071 A263	1.05fr	olive	75	52
1072 A263	1.85fr	brown	1.40	1.00

Nos. 1069-1072 were issued precanceled only. See note after No. 324.

Career of a Sailor Types of 1977

Designs (Gouaches by Louis Tinayre): 10c, Yacht Princess Alice II, Kiel harbor. 20c, Laboratory on board ship. 30c, Yacht amidst ice floes. 80c, Crew in arctic outfits. 1fr, Yacht in polar region. 1.25fr, Yacht in snow storm. 1.40fr, Building camp on ice. 1.90fr, Yacht under steam amidst ice floes. 3fr, Yacht passing iceberg.

1977, Nov. **Engr.** ***Perf. 13***

1073 A302	10c	blk & brt bl	15	15
1074 A302	20c	Prus bl	18	15
1075 A302	30c	blk & brt bl	25	18
1076 A303	80c	multi	42	30
1077 A302	1fr	brt grn & blk	62	35
1078 A302	1.25fr	vio, sep & blk	70	48
1079 A302	1.40fr	ol, bl & pur	1.10	70
1080 A302	1.90fr	blk & brt bl	1.50	1.00
1081 A302	3fr	dk grn, ol & brt bl	2.00	1.50
	Nos. 1073-1081 (9)		6.92	4.81

75th anniversary of publication of "The Career of a Sailor," by Prince Albert I.

Santa Claus — A311

1977, Nov.

1082 A311	80c	multi	40	24
1083 A311	1.40fr	multi	65	40

Christmas 1977.

Flowers Types of 1974

Designs: 80c, Snapdragons and bellflowers. 1fr, Ikebana arrangement.

1977, Nov. **Photo.** ***Perf. 13½x13***

1084 A259	80c	multi	60	32
1085 A260	1fr	multi	75	45

Intl. Flower Show, Monte Carlo, May 1978.

Face (Van Gogh), Syringe, Hallucination Pattern A312

Clown, Flags of Participants A313

1977, Nov. **Engr.** ***Perf. 13***

1086 A312 1fr multi 75 45

Fight against drug abuse.

1977, Nov. **Photo.** ***Perf. 13½x13***

1087 A313 1fr multi 75 55

Fourth International Circus Festival. Monte Carlo, December 1977.

Coin Type of 1975

Design: 80c, Doubloon of Honoré II, 1648.

1977, Nov. **Engr.** ***Perf. 13***

1088 A281 80c lil & brn 60 45

Mediterranean Landscape and Industrial Pollution — A314

1977, Nov.

1089 A314 1fr multi 85 52

Protection of the Mediterranean. Meeting of the UN Mediterranean Environmental Protection Group, Monte Carlo, Nov. 28-Dec. 6.

Men Spreading Tar, Dr. Guglielminetti, 1903 Car — A315

1977, Nov.

1090 A315 1.10fr multi 60 42

75th anniversary of first tarred roads, invented by Swiss Dr. Guglielminetti.

View of Monaco and Tennis Emblem — A316

First Match at Wimbledon and Stadium — A317

1977, Nov.

1091 A316	1fr	multi	65	48
1092 A317	1.40fr	multi	90	70

50th anniversary of the Lawn Tennis Federation of Monaco and centenary of first international tennis match at Wimbledon.

Prince of Monaco Type of 1967

Painting: 6fr, Honoré V (1819-1841), by Marie Verroust.

1977, Nov. ***Perf. 12½x13***

1093 A182 6fr multi 3.00 2.00

Red Cross Type of 1969

Design: 4fr, St. John Bosco and boys.

1977, Nov. ***Perf. 13***

1094 A194 4fr multi 2.00 1.40

Nos. 1069-1072 Surcharged

1978, Jan. 17

1095 A263	58c on 54c	brt grn	45	35
1096 A263	73c on 68c	org	65	45
1097 A263	1.15fr on 1.05fr	olive	85	55
1098 A263	2fr on 1.85fr	brn	1.50	1.10

See note after No. 324.

The Abandoned Ship, from "Mysterious Island" — A318

Illustrations, Novels by Jules Verne: 5c, Shipwreck. 30c, Secret of the Island. 80c, Robur, the Conqueror. 1fr, Master Zacharius. 1.40fr, The Castle in the Carpathians. 1.70fr, The Children of Capt. Grant. 5.50fr, Jules Verne and allegories.

1978, May 2 **Engr.** ***Perf. 13***

1099 A318	5c	multi	15	15
1100 A318	25c	multi	15	15
1101 A318	30c	multi	18	15
1102 A318	80c	multi	40	28
1103 A318	1fr	multi	60	35
1104 A318	1.40fr	multi	80	52
1105 A318	1.70fr	multi	1.10	70
1106 A318	5.50fr	multi	3.25	1.65
	Nos. 1099-1106 (8)		6.63	3.95

Jules Verne (1828-1905), science fiction writer, birth sesquicentennial.

Congress Center and Monte Carlo — A319

Design: 1.40fr, Congress Center, view from the sea.

1978, May 2

1107 A319	1fr	multi	52	42
1108 A319	1.40fr	multi	65	52

Inauguration of Monaco Congress Center.

Soccer Players and Globe — A320

1978, May 2

1109 A320 1fr multi 52 42

11th World Soccer Cup Championship, Argentina, June 1-25.

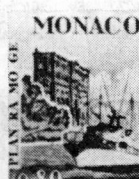

Vivaldi and St. Mark's Place, Venice — A321

Control Ship and Grimaldi Palace — A322

1978, May 2

1110 A321 1fr dk brn & red 60 52

Antonio Vivaldi (1675?-1741), Italian violinist and composer.

1978, May 2

Design: 1fr, Map of coastal area and city emblems, horiz.

Size: 26x36mm

1111 A322 80c multi 48 30

Size: 48x27mm

1112 A322 1fr multi 60 40

Protection of the environment, signing of "Ra Mo Ge" agreement for the protection of the Mediterranean Coast between Saint-Raphael, France, and Genoa, Italy (including Monaco).

Monaco Cathedral — A323

Europa: 1.40fr, View of Principality from East.

1978, May 2 ***Perf. 12½x13***

1113 A323	1fr	multi	70	42
1114 A323	1.40fr	multi	1.00	55
a.	Souv. sheet, 5 each #1113-1114		12.00	12.00

Cinderella — A324

Mother Goose Tales: 25c, Puss in Boots. 30c, Sleeping Beauty. 80c, Fairy tale princess. 1fr, Little Red Riding Hood. 1.40fr, Bluebeard. 1.70fr, Tom Thumb. 1.90fr, Riquet with the Tuft of Hair. 2.50fr, The Fairies.

1978, Nov. 8 Engr. *Perf. 13*

1115	A324	5c	multi	15	15
1116	A324	25c	multi	15	15
1117	A324	30c	multi	15	15
1118	A324	80c	multi	35	22
1119	A324	1fr	multi	45	32
1120	A324	1.40fr	multi	90	42
1121	A324	1.70fr	multi	1.10	52
1122	A324	1.90fr	multi	1.10	65
1123	A324	2.50fr	multi	1.25	75
	Nos. 1115-1123 (9)			5.60	3.33

Charles Perrault (1628-1703), compiler of Mother Goose Tales.

Flower Type of 1976

Van Gogh Paintings: 1fr, Sunflowers. 1.70fr, Iris.

1978, Nov. 8 Photo. *Perf. 12½x13*

1124	A300	1fr	multi	75	55
1125	A300	1.70fr	multi	1.00	80

Intl. Flower show, Monte Carlo, May 1979, and 125th birth anniv. of Vincent van Gogh (1853-1890), Dutch painter.

Afghan Hound A325

Design: 1.20fr, Russian wolfhound.

1978, Nov. 8 *Perf. 13x12½*

1126	A325	1fr	multi	1.25	90
1127	A325	1.20fr	multi	1.65	1.10

International Dog Show, Monte Carlo.

Child Holding Gift of Shoes — A326

1978, Nov. 8 Engr. *Perf. 12½x13*

1128	A326	1fr	multi	52	40

Christmas 1978.

Catherine and William Booth, Salvation Army Band — A327

1978, Nov. 8 Engr. *Perf. 13*

1129	A327	1.70fr	multi	80	70

Centenary of founding of Salvation Army.

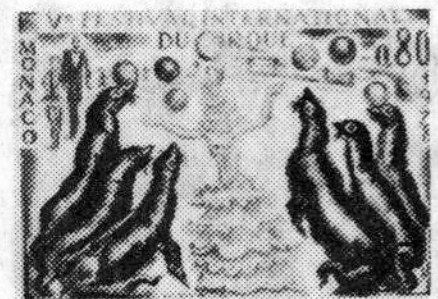

Trained Seals A328

Designs: 1fr, Lions, vert. 1.40fr, Equestrian act. 1.90fr, Monkey music band. 2.40fr, Trapeze act.

1978, Nov. 8 *Perf. 13x12½*

1130	A328	80c	multi	40	30
1131	A328	1fr	multi	55	40
1132	A328	1.40fr	multi	95	60
1133	A328	1.90fr	multi	1.10	85
1134	A328	2.40fr	multi	1.50	1.10
	Nos. 1130-1134 (5)			4.50	3.25

5th Intl. Circus Festival, Monte Carlo.

Princes of Monaco Type of 1967

Paintings: 2fr, Florestan I (1841-1856), by G. Dauphin. 4fr, Caroline Gilbert de Lametz (1793-1879), by Marie Verroust.

1978, Nov. 8 Engr. *Perf. 12½x13*

1135	A182	2fr	multi	95	65
1136	A182	4fr	multi	2.00	1.25

Souvenir Sheet

Henri Dunant and Battle Scene — A329

1978, Nov. 8 Engr. *Perf. 13*

1137	A329	5fr	multi	3.25	3.25

Henri Dunant (1828-1910), founder of Red Cross.

View Types of 1974

1978-80

1138	A262	25c	All Saints' Tower	15	15
1139	A262	65c	Monte Carlo Beach	32	32
1140	A263	70c	Exotic Garden, cacti ('80)	35	20
1142	A262	1.10fr	Palais de Justice ('80)	48	20
1144	A263	1.30fr	Cathedral	65	26
1145	A264	1.50fr	Prince Albert Statue and Museum ('80)	80	42
1146	A262	1.80fr	La Condamine	1.00	60
1148	A262	2.30fr	Palace ('80)	1.10	60
1152	A262	6.50fr	Monte Carlo Auditorium	3.00	1.65
	Nos. 1138-1152 (9)			7.85	4.40

Convention Center, Monte Carlo — A330

1978-79

1154	A330	61c	vermilion	42	20
1155	A330	64c	green	38	24
1156	A330	68c	brt bl	30	20
1157	A330	78c	dp rose lil	55	26
1158	A330	83c	vio bl	42	26
1159	A330	88c	orange	38	26
1160	A330	1.25fr	brown	90	42
1161	A330	1.30fr	purple	75	45
1162	A330	1.40fr	brt yel grn	70	42
1163	A330	2.10fr	vio bl	1.40	80
1164	A330	2.25fr	brn org	1.25	75
1165	A330	2.35fr	lil rose	1.10	60
	Nos. 1154-1165 (12)			8.55	4.86

Issued precanceled only. See note after No. 324.

Issue dates: 61c, 78c, 1.25fr, 2.10fr, July 10, 1978. Others, 1979.

Souvenir Sheet

Prince Albert — A331

1979, Apr. 30 Engr. *Perf. 12½x13*

1166	A331	10fr	multi	6.25	6.25

21st birthday of Hereditary Prince Albert.

The Juggler of Notre Dame, by Jules Massenet A332

Designs: 1.20fr, Hans, the Flute Player, by Gaston L. Ganne. 1.50fr, Don Quichotte, by Massenet. 1.70fr, L'Aiglon, by Jacques Ibert and Arthur Honegger, vert. 2.10fr, The Child and the Sorcerer, by Maurice Ravel. 3fr, Monte Carlo Opera and Charles Garnier, architect.

1979, Apr. 30 *Perf. 13*

1167	A332	1fr	multi	52	24
1168	A332	1.20fr	multi	65	30
1169	A332	1.50fr	multi	85	55
1170	A332	1.70fr	multi	1.25	70
1171	A332	2.10fr	multi	1.50	1.10
1172	A332	3fr	multi	2.00	1.25
	Nos. 1167-1172 (6)			6.77	4.14

Centenary of the Salle Garnier, Monte Carlo Opera.

Flower, Bird, Butterfly, IYC Emblem A333

Children's Drawings (IYC Emblem and): 1fr, Horse and child. 1.20fr, Children shaking hands, and heart. 1.50fr, Children of the world for peace. 1.70fr, Children against pollution.

1979, Apr. 30

1173	A333	50c	multi	24	15
1174	A333	1fr	multi	45	32
1175	A333	1.20fr	multi	65	42
1176	A333	1.50fr	multi	75	52
1177	A333	1.70fr	multi	1.10	65
	Nos. 1173-1177 (5)			3.19	2.06

International Year of the Child.

Armed Messenger, 15th-16th Centuries A334

Europa (designs similar to 1960 postage dues); 1.50fr, Felucca, 18th cent. 1.70fr, Arrival of 1st train, Dec. 12, 1868.

1979, Apr. 30

1178	A334	1.20fr	multi	55	40
1179	A334	1.50fr	multi	75	45
1180	A334	1.70fr	multi	90	60
a.	Souv. sheet of 6, 2 each #1178-1180, perf. 13x12½			7.50	7.50

Les Biches, by Francis Poulenc A335

Ballets: 1.20fr, Les Matelots, by George Auric. 1.50fr, Le Spectre de la Rose, by Carl Maria Weber, vert. 1.70fr, GaietéParisienne, by Jacques Offenbach. 2.10fr, Dance of Salomé, by Richard Strauss, vert. 3fr, Instrumental Music, ceiling decoration of Salle Garnier.

1979, Nov. 12

Size: 26x36mm, 36x26mm

1181	A335	1fr	multi	55	22
1182	A335	1.20fr	multi	70	35
1183	A335	1.50fr	multi	95	55
1184	A335	1.70fr	multi	1.10	75
1185	A335	2.10fr	multi	1.40	1.10

Size: 48x27mm

1186	A335	3fr	multi	2.00	1.40
	Nos. 1181-1186 (6)			6.70	4.37

Centenary of the Salle Garnier, Monte Carlo Opera.

Princes of Monaco Type of 1967

Paintings: 3fr, Charles III (1856-1889). 4fr, Antoinette de Merode (1828-1864).

1979, Nov. 12 *Perf. 12½x13*

1187	A182	3fr	multi	1.24	95
1188	A182	4fr	multi	1.75	1.25

Red Cross Type of 1969

Design: 5fr, St. Peter Claver preaching to slaves.

1979, Nov. 12 *Perf. 13*

1189	A194	5fr	multi	2.00	1.65

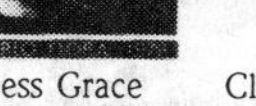

Princess Grace Orchid — A336

Clown Balancing on Globe — A337

1979, Nov. 12 Photo.

1190	A336	1fr	multi	65	60

International Orchid Exhibition, Monte Carlo, April 1980.

Flower Type of 1976

Design: 1.20fr, Princess Grace rose.

1979, Nov. 12

1191	A300	1.20fr	multi	65	55

International Flower Show, Monte Carlo, May 1980.

1979, Nov. 12

1192	A337	1.20fr	multi	65	52

6th International Circus Festival, Monte Carlo, Dec. 6-10.

Rowland Hill, Penny Black — A338

1979, Nov. 12 Engr. *Perf. 13*

1193	A338	1.70fr	multi	70	52

Sir Rowland Hill (1795-1879), originator of penny postage.

Albert Einstein, Equations — A339

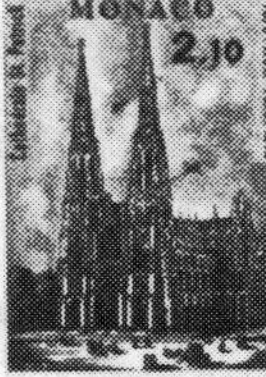

St. Patrick's Cathedral — A340

1979, Nov. 12

1194	A339	1.70fr multi	75	55

Albert Einstein (1879-1955), theoretical physicist.

1979, Nov. 12

1195	A340	2.10fr multi	1.00	75

St. Patrick's Cathedral, New York City, centenary.

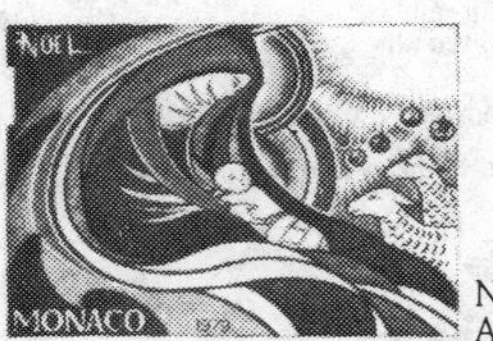

Nativity A341

1979, Nov. 12

1196	A341	1.20fr multi	60	26

Christmas 1979.

Bugatti, Monte Carlo, 1929 Winner — A342

1979, Nov. 12

1197	A342	1fr multi	60	40

50th anniversary of Grand Prix auto race, Monte Carlo.

Arms of Charles V and Monaco, View of Monaco — A343

1979, Nov. 12

1198	A343	1.50fr multi	65	45

Emperor Charles V visit to Monaco, 450th anniversary.

Dog Type of 1977

Design: 1.20fr, Setter and pointer.

1979, Nov. 12 **Photo.**

1199	A304	1.20fr multi	1.40	80

International Dog Show, Monte Carlo.

Prince Rainier Type of 1974

1980, Jan. 17 **Engr.** ***Perf. 13***

1200	A261	1.10fr emerald	55	15
1201	A261	1.30fr rose red	60	15
1202	A261	1.60fr dk bl gray	75	18
1203	A261	1.80fr grnsh bl	90	26
1204	A261	2.30fr red lilac	1.00	30
		Nos. 1200-1204 (5)	3.80	1.04

Chestnut Branch in Spring A344

Designs of 1980, 1981 stamps show chestnut branch. 1982 stamps show peach branch. 1983 stamps show apple branch.

1980-83 **Engr.** ***Perf. 13x12½***

1205	A344	76c shown	40	28
1206	A344	88c Spring ('81)	40	28
1207	A344	97c Spring ('82)	45	28
1208	A344	99c Summer	55	35
1209	A344	1.05fr Spring ('83)	40	25
1210	A344	1.14fr Summer ('81)	55	35
1211	A344	1.25fr Summer ('82)	60	35
1212	A344	1.35fr Summer ('83)	48	32
1213	A344	1.60fr Autumn	85	65
1214	A344	1.84fr Autumn ('81)	85	65
1215	A344	2.03fr Autumn ('82)	1.10	60
1216	A344	2.19fr Autumn ('83)	85	52
1217	A344	2.65fr Winter	1.50	1.10
1218	A344	3.05fr Winter ('81)	1.50	1.10
1219	A344	3.36fr Winter ('82)	1.65	1.10
1220	A344	3.63fr Winter ('83)	1.40	1.10
		Nos. 1205-1220 (16)	13.53	9.28

Issued precanceled only. See note after No. 324. See Nos. 1406-1409, 1457-1460.

Gymnast — A345

1980, Apr. 28

1221	A345	1.10fr shown	32	22
1222	A345	1.30fr Handball	35	28
1223	A345	1.60fr Shooting	55	40
1224	A345	1.80fr Volleyball	70	52
1225	A345	2.30fr Ice hockey	95	60
1226	A345	4fr Slalom	1.40	1.00
		Nos. 1221-1226 (6)	4.27	3.02

22nd Summer Olympic Games, Moscow, July 19-Aug. 3; 13th Winter Olympic Games, Lake Placid, NY, Feb. 12-24.

Colette, Novelist — A346

Europa: 1.80fr, Marcel Pagnol (1895-1974), French playwright.

1980, Apr. 28 ***Perf. 12½x13***

1227	A346	1.30fr multi	45	42
1228	A346	1.80fr multi	65	45
a.		Souv. sheet, 5 each #1227-1228	5.00	5.00

The Source, by Ingres A347

1980, Apr. 28

1229	A347	4fr multi	2.75	1.90

Jean Auguste Dominique Ingres (1780-1867).

Michel Eyquem de Montaigne A348

Guillaume Apollinaire A349

1980, Apr. 28 ***Perf. 13***

1230	A348	1.30fr multi	52	35

Essays of Montaigne (1533-1592), 400th anniversary of publication.

1980, Apr. 28

1231	A349	1.10fr multi	42	30

Guillaume Apollinaire (1880-1918), French writer.

Paul P. Harris, Chicago Skyline, Rotary Emblem — A350

1980, Apr. 28

1232	A350	1.80fr multi	75	42

Rotary International, 75th anniversary.

Convention Center, Map of Europe, Kiwanis Emblem — A351

1980, Apr. 28

1233	A351	1.30fr multi	55	48

Kiwanis International, European Convention, Monte Carlo, June.

Coin Type of 1975

Design: 1.50fr, Honoré II silver ecu, 1649.

1980, Apr. 28

1234	A281	1.50fr multi	65	52

Lhasa Apso and Shih-Tzu — A352

1980, Apr. 28 **Photo.**

1235	A352	1.30fr multi	1.25	75

International Dog Show, Monte Carlo.

The Princess and the Pea — A353

Hans Christian Andersen (1805-1875) Fairy Tales: 1.30fr, The Little Mermaid. 1.50fr, The Chimneysweep and the Shepherdess. 1.60fr, The Brave Little Tin Soldier. 1.80fr, The Little Match Girl. 2.30fr, The Nightingale.

1980, Nov. 6 **Engr.** ***Perf. 13***

1236	A353	70c multi	25	18
1237	A353	1.30fr multi	38	24
1238	A353	1.50fr multi	60	20
1239	A353	1.60fr multi	75	55
1240	A353	1.80fr multi	1.00	60
1241	A353	2.30fr multi	1.10	75
		Nos. 1236-1241 (6)	4.08	2.52

Women on Balcony, by Van Dongen — A354

Paintings from 1905 Paris Fall Salon: 2fr, The Road, by de Vlaminck. 4fr, Woman Reading, by Matisse. 5fr, Three Women in a Meadow, by André Derain.

1980, Nov. 6 ***Perf. 13x12***

1242	A354	2fr multi	1.25	95
1243	A354	3fr multi	1.75	1.50
1244	A354	4fr multi	2.50	1.90
1245	A354	5fr multi	3.25	2.50

Princes of Monaco Type of 1967

Paintings: No. 1246, Prince Albert I (1848-1922), by Leon Bonnat. No. 1247, Princess Alice (1857-1925), by L. Maeterlinck.

1980, Nov. 6 ***Perf. 12½x13***

1246	A182	4fr multi	1.75	1.40
1247	A182	4fr multi	1.75	1.40

Sun and Birds, by Perrette Lambert — A355

1980, Nov. 6 ***Perf. 13***

1248	A355	6fr multi	2.50	2.25

Red Cross.

7th International Circus Festival — A356

1980, Nov. 6 ***Perf. 13x12½***

1249	A356	1.30fr multi	70	50

Christmas 1980 A357

1980, Nov. 6

1250	A357	1.10fr multi	38	26
1251	A357	2.30fr multi	85	65

Princess Stephanie of Monaco Rose — A358

1980, Nov. 6 Photo. *Perf. 12½x13*

1252 A358	1.30fr shown	60	48
1253 A358	1.80fr Ikebana	80	60

International Flower Show, Monte Carlo, May 1981.

Prince Rainier Type of 1974

1980 Engr. *Perf. 13*

1255 A261 1.20fr brt grn	52	20
1256 A261 1.40fr red	75	15

Issue dates: 1.20fr, Aug. 19; 1.40fr, Aug. 11.

Paramuricea Clavata A359

5c-20c, 40c, 50c, vert.

1980, Nov. 6 *Perf. 13x12½*

1259 A359 5c Spirographis spallanzanii	15	15
1260 A359 10c Anemonia sulcata	15	15
1261 A359 15c Leptosammia pruvoti	15	15
1262 A359 20c Pteroides	15	15
1263 A359 30c shown	16	15
1264 A359 40c Alcyonium	20	15
1265 A359 50c Corallium rubrum	24	16
1266 A359 60c Caliactis parisitica	45	16
1267 A359 70c Cerianthus membranaceus	55	20
1268 A359 1fr Actinia equina	60	20
1269 A359 2fr Protula	1.10	35
Nos. 1259-1269 (11)	3.90	
Set value		1.50

See Nos. 1316-1321, 1380.

25th Wedding Anniversary of Prince Rainier and Princess Grace — A360

1981, May 4 *Perf. 13*

1270 A360 1.20fr grn & blk	55	25
1271 A360 1.40fr car & blk	70	25
1272 A360 1.70fr ol grn & blk	85	38
1273 A360 1.80fr brn & blk	90	42
1274 A360 2fr brt bl & blk	1.10	60
Nos. 1270-1274 (5)	4.10	1.90

Mozart with his Father and Sister, by Carmontelle — A361

Wolfgang Amadeus Mozart (1756-1791), 225th Birth Anniversary (Paintings): 2fr, Portrait, by Lorenz Vogel (26x36mm). 3.50fr, Conducting his Requiem Two Days Before his Death, by F.C. Baude.

1981, May 4 Engr. *Perf. 13½x13*

1275 A361 2fr multi	1.25	1.10
1276 A361 2.50fr multi	1.75	1.50
1277 A361 3.50fr multi	2.25	1.90
a. Strip of 3, #1275-1277	5.25	4.50

Cross of Palms — A362

Europa (Palm Sunday Traditions): 2fr, Children with palms at benediction.

1981, May 4 *Perf. 12½x13*

1278 A362 1.40fr multi	40	25
1279 A362 2fr multi	60	40
a. Souv. sheet, 5 each #1278-1279	6.00	6.00

European Soccer Cup, 25th Anniversary A363

1981, May 4 *Perf. 13*

1280 A363 2fr black & blue	75	65

International Year of the Disabled A364

1981, May 4

1281 A364 1.40fr brt grn & bl	52	38

Monegasque National Pavilion Centenary — A365

1981, May 4

1282 A365 2fr multi	85	70

Oceanographic Institute, Monaco and Museum, Paris — A366

1981, May 4

1283 A366 1.20fr multi	52	38

75th anniversary of the Oceanographic Institute (Monaco-France).

50th Anniversary of the International Hydrographic Bureau — A367

1981, May 4

1284 A367 2.50fr multi	90	80

Rough Collies and Shetland Sheepdogs — A368

1981, May 4 Photo.

1285 A368 1.40fr multi	1.65	1.40

International Dog Show, Monte Carlo.

Marine Life Preservation A369

Prince Rainier and Hereditary Prince Albert A370

1981, Mar. 21 Photo.

1286 A369 1.20fr multi	85	52

1981-84 Engr. *Perf. 13*

1287 A370 1.40fr dk grn	80	15
1288 A370 1.60fr carmine	95	15
1289 A370 1.60fr ol grn ('82)	70	15
1290 A370 1.70fr bluish grn ('84)	70	15
1291 A370 1.80fr mag ('82)	95	15
1292 A370 2fr red ('83)	1.00	15
1293 A370 2.10fr red ('84)	95	15
1294 A370 2.30fr blue	1.65	70
1295 A370 2.60fr vio bl ('82)	1.25	48
1296 A370 2.80fr stl bl ('83)	1.25	60
1297 A370 3fr sky bl ('84)	1.25	48
1298 A370 4fr brown	1.50	40
1299 A370 5.50fr black	1.90	1.10
Nos. 1287-1299 (13)	14.85	4.81

See Nos. 1505-1515.

Hauling Ice Floes, 17th Cent. Map Antarctic A371

1981, Oct. 5

1301 A371 1.50fr multi	75	38

First Intl. Arctic Committee Congress, Rome, Oct. 5-9.

Princes of Monaco Type of 1967

Paintings by P.A. de Laszlo, 1929: 3fr, Prince Louis II. 5fr, Princess Charlotte.

1981, Nov. 5 Engr. *Perf. 12½x13*

1302 A182 3fr multi	1.25	85
1303 A182 5fr multi	2.00	1.40

Ettore Bugatti, Auto Designer and Racer, Birth Centenary A372

George Bernard Shaw (1856-1950) A373

1981, Nov. 5 *Perf. 13*

1304 A372 1fr multi	42	35

1981, Nov. 5

Design: 2.50fr, Fernand Leger, painter, birth centenary.

1305 A373 2fr multi	90	65
1306 A373 2.50fr multi	1.10	80

Self-portrait, by Pablo Picasso (1881-1973) A374

Design: No. 1308, Self-portrait, by Rembrandt (1606-1669).

1981, Nov. 5 *Perf. 12½x13*

1307 A374 4fr multi	2.00	1.65
1308 A374 4fr multi	2.00	1.65

Ikebana, Painting by Ikenobo, 1673 — A375

Intl. Flower Show, Monte Carlo, 1982: 1.40fr, Elegantines, morning glories.

1981, Nov. 5 Photo. *Perf. 12½*

1309 A375 1.40fr multi	50	38
1310 A375 2fr multi	75	58

Catherine Deneuve Rose — A376

1981, Nov. 5 *Perf. 13x12½*

1311 A376 1.80fr multi	85	70

First Intl. Rose Competition, Monte Carlo, June 12-14.

15-Cent Minimum Value
The minimum value for a single stamp is 15 cents. This value reflects the costs of the handlling of inexpensive stamps.

8th Intl. Circus Festival, Monte Carlo, Dec. 10-14 — A377

1981, Nov. 5 Engr. *Perf. 13*
1312 A377 1.40fr multi 65 50

Christmas 1981 — A378

1981, Nov. 5
1313 A378 1.20fr multi 50 42

50th Monte Carlo Auto Race — A379

1981, Nov. 5
1314 A379 1fr Lancia-Stratos 42 30

Souvenir Sheet

Persimmon Branch in Spring A380

1981, Nov. 5 *Perf. 13x12½*

1315	Sheet of 4	4.25 4.25
a.	A380 1fr shown	42 42
b.	A380 2fr Summer	80 80
c.	A380 3fr Autumn	1.10 1.10
d.	A380 4fr Winter	1.65 1.65

Coral Type of 1980

Exotic Plants. 1.40fr, 1.60fr, 2.30fr vert.

Perf. 12½x13, 13x12½

1981-82 Photo.

1316	A359	1.40fr	Hoya bella	1.10 30
1317	A359	1.60fr	Bolivicereus samaipatanus	75 30
1317A	A359	1.80fr	Trichocereus grandiflorus	1.00 60
1318	A359	2.30fr	Euphorbia milii	90 52
1319	A359	2.60fr	Echinocereus fitchii	1.00 75
1320	A359	2.90fr	Rebutia heliosa	1.25 1.00
1321	A359	4.10fr	Echinopsis multiplex	1.65 1.25
			Nos. 1316-1321 (7)	7.65 4.72

Issue dates: 1.80fr, June 7, others Dec. 10.

Miniature Sheet

1982 World Cup A381

Designs: Various soccer players.

1982, May 3 *Perf. 13*

1322	Sheet of 4	4.50 4.50
a.	A381 1fr multi	48 48
b.	A381 2fr multi	80 80
c.	A381 3fr multi	1.25 1.25
d.	A381 4fr multi	1.75 1.75

Mercantour Natl. Park Birds — A382

Europa — A383

1982, May 3 *Perf. 12½x13, 13x12½*

1323	A382	60c	Nutcracker	30 22
1324	A382	70c	Black grouse	38 22
1325	A382	80c	Rock partridge	38 30
1326	A382	90c	Wall creeper, horiz.	52 30
1327	A382	1.40fr	Ptarmigan, horiz.	95 38
1328	A382	1.60fr	Golden eagle	1.25 38
			Nos. 1323-1328 (6)	3.78 1.80

1982, May 3 *Perf. 12½x13*

1329	A383	1.60fr	Guelph attacking Fortress of Monaco, 1297	52 25
1330	A383	2.30fr	Treaty of Peronne, 1641	80 38
a.			Souv. sheet, 5 each #1329-1330	6.25 6.25

Fontvielle Landfill Project A384

1982, May 3 *Perf. 13x12½*

1331	A384	1.40fr	Old coastline	48 24
1332	A384	1.60fr	Landfill site	55 24
1333	A384	2.30fr	Completed site	90 55

Fontvielle Stadium — A385

1982, May 3 *Perf. 13*
1334 A385 2.30fr multi 85 70

PHILEXFRANCE '82 Stamp Exhibition, Paris, June 11-21 — A386

1982, May 3
1335 A386 1.40fr multi 52 42

Intl. Dog Show, Monte Carlo A387

1982, May 3 Photo. *Perf. 13x12½*
1336 A387 60c Old English sheepdog 52 35
1337 A387 1fr Briard terrier 70 45

See No. 1366, 1431, 1479, 1539, 1676, 1704, 1756, 1806.

Monaco Cathedral, Arms of Pope John Paul II and Monaco A388

1982, May 3 Engr.
1338 A388 1.60fr multi 55 40

Creation of archbishopric of Monaco, July 25, 1981.

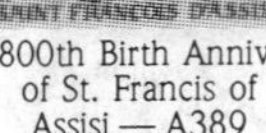
800th Birth Anniv. of St. Francis of Assisi — A389

TB Bacillus Cent. — A390

1982, May 3 *Perf. 12½x13*
1339 A389 1.40fr multi 55 45

1982, May 3
1340 A390 1.40fr multi 45 35

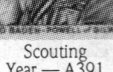

Scouting Year — A391

Intl. Hunting Council, 29th Meeting — A392

1982, May 3
1341 A391 1.60fr dk brn & blk 60 42

1982, June 11 Photo. *Perf. 12½*
1342 A392 1.60fr St. Hubert 60 45

Intl. Bibliophile Assoc. General Assembly — A393

1982, Sept. 30 Engr. *Perf. 13*
1343 A393 1.60fr multi 50 35

Monte Carlo and Monaco During the Belle Epoch (1870-1925), by Hubert Clerissi — A394

Photogravure and Engraved

1982, Nov. 8 *Perf. 13x12½*
1344 A394 3fr Casino, 1870 1.25 80
1345 A394 5fr Palace, 1893 2.25 1.25

See Nos. 1385-1386, 1436-1437, 1488-1489, 1546-1547, 1605-1606, 1638-1639, 1695-1696.

Nicolo Paganini (1782-1840), Composer and Violinist — A395

Designs: 1.80fr, Anna Pavlova (1881-1931), ballerina. 2.60fr, Igor Stravinsky (1882-1971), composer.

1982, Nov. 8 Engr. *Perf. 12½x13*
1346 A395 1.60fr multi 70 45
1347 A395 1.80fr multi 1.00 45
1348 A395 2.60fr multi 1.25 60

In a Boat, by Manet (1832-1883) — A396

Design: No. 1348, Les Poissons Noir, by Georges Braque (1882-1963).

Photogravure and Engraved

1982, Nov. 8 *Perf. 13x12½*
1349 A396 4fr multi 2.00 1.10
1350 A396 4fr multi 2.00 1.10

Intl. Flower Show, Monte Carlo — A397

Designs: Various floral arrangements.

1982, Nov. 8 Photo. *Perf. 12½x13*

1351	A397	1.60fr	multi	60	38
1352	A397	2.60fr	multi	85	65

Bouquet — A398

Christmas 1982 — A399

1982 *Perf. 13*

1353	A398	1.60fr	multi	70	45

1982, Nov. 8 Engr. *Perf. 12½x13*

1354	A399	1.60fr	Three Kings	48	35
1355	A399	1.80fr	Holy Family	70	35
1356	A399	2.60fr	Shepherds	90	48
a.			Souv. sheet of 3, #1354-1356	2.50	2.50

Intl. Polar Year Centenary — A400

1982, Nov. 8 Engr. *Perf. 13*

1358	A400	1.60fr	Prince Louis, Discovery	75	55

Discovery of Greenland Millenium — A401

1982, Nov. 8

1359	A401	1.60fr	Erik the Red's longship	70	52

Death Bimillenium of Virgil — A402

1982, Nov. 8

1360	A402	1.80fr	Scene from Aeneid, Book 6	75	60

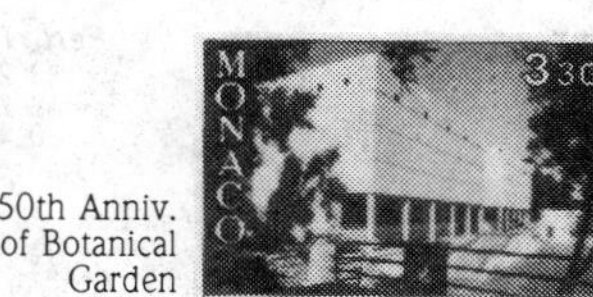

50th Anniv. of Botanical Garden A403

1983, Feb. 11 Photo. *Perf. 12½x13*

1361	A403	1.80fr	Cacti, vert.	65	35
1362	A403	2fr	Exotic plants, vert.	80	35
1363	A403	2.30fr	Intl. exhibits, vert.	80	65
1364	A403	2.60fr	Cave	90	70
1365	A403	3.30fr	Prehistoric Anthropology Museum	1.40	1.00
			Nos. 1361-1365 (5)	4.55	3.05

Monte Carlo Dog Show Type

1983, Apr. 13 *Perf. 13x12½*

1366	A387	1.80fr	Alaskan malamute	1.25	85

Souvenir Sheet

Princess Grace (1929-1982) — A405

1983, Apr. 19 Engr. *Perf. 13*

1367	A405	10fr	black	7.50	7.50

A406

A407

1983, Apr. 27 *Perf. 12½x13*

1368	A406	1.80fr	Montgolfiere balloon flight, 1783	60	42
1369	A406	2.60fr	Columbia space shuttle	90	65
a.			Souv. sheet, 5 each #1368-1369	7.25	7.25

Europa.

1983, Apr. 27 Engr.

1370	A407	2.60fr	St. Charles Borromeo	80	48

Centenary of St. Charles' Church, Monte Carlo.

Franciscan College Centenary A408

1983, Apr. 27 *Perf. 13x12½*

1371	A408	2fr	Church, medallion	70	45

Fontvielle Stadium Interior — A409

1983, Apr. 28 *Perf. 13*

1372	A409	2fr	multi	70	50

Automobile Centenary — A410

1983, Apr. 27

1373	A410	2.90fr	Benz, 1883, Formula One racer	95	65

Save the Whales Campaign — A411

1983, Apr. 27

1374	A411	3.30fr	Blue whale	1.65	95

World Communications Year — A412

1983, Apr. 27

1375	A412	4fr	lil rose & brn vio	1.25	90

Souvenir Sheet

Fig Branch in Spring A413

1983, Nov. 9 Engr. *Perf. 13x12½*

1376			Sheet of 4	4.00	4.00
a.	A413		1fr shown	38	38
b.	A413		2fr Summer	75	75
c.	A413		3fr Autumn	1.10	1.10
d.	A413		4fr Winter	1.40	1.40

Exotic Plant Type of 1980

1983, Nov. 9 Photo. *Perf. 13*

1380	A359	2fr	Argyroderma roseum	95	40

Belle Epoch Type of 1982

Paintings by Hubert Clerissi: 3fr, Thermes Valentia from the Beach, 1902. 5fr, Cafe de Paris and Place du Casino, 1905.

Photogravure and Engraved

1983, Nov. 9 *Perf. 13x12½*

1385	A394	3fr	multi	1.10	70
1386	A394	5fr	multi	1.50	1.10

Portrait of a Young Man, by Raphael (1483-1520) A414

Passage Cottin, by Maurice Utrillo (1883-1955) A415

Photogravure and Engraved

1983, Nov. 9 *Perf. 13*

1387	A414	4fr	multi	1.25	75
1388	A415	4fr	multi	1.25	75

Johannes Brahms (1833-1897), Composer — A416

Design: No. 1390, Giacomo Puccini (1858-1924), composer, scene from Madame Butterfly.

1983, Nov. 9 Engr. *Perf. 13½x13*

1389	A416	3fr	multi	95	48
1390	A416	3fr	multi	95	48

9th Intl. Circus Festival, Monte Carlo, Dec. 8-12 — A417

Intl. Flower Show, Monte Carlo — A418

1983, Nov. 9 *Perf. 13*

1391	A417	2fr	multi	80	65

1983, Nov. 9 Photo.

1392	A418	1.60fr	Pansies, convolvulus, carnations	60	35
1393	A418	2.60fr	Oriental poppies	85	65

Christmas 1983 — A419

1983, Nov. 9 Photo.

1394	A419	2fr	Provencal creche figures	65	42

Alfred Nobel (1833-1896), Literature Medal A420

1983, Nov. 9 Engr.

1395	A420	2fr	multi	65	42

Sesquicentenary of Society of St. Vincent de Paul — A421

1983, Nov. 9 Engr.

1396	A421	1.80fr	F. Ozanam, founder, Paris headquarters	60	48

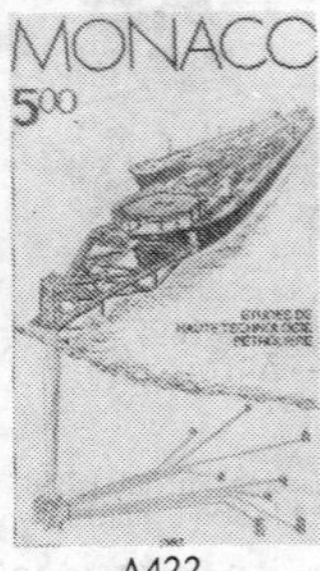
A422

A423

1983, Nov. 9

1397 A422 5fr Offshore petroleum plant 1.50 95

1983, Nov. 9 Photo. *Perf. 12½x13*

19th cent. figurines, Galea toy collection.

1398	A423	50c	Water pipe smoker	16	15
1399	A423	60c	Clown with yo-yo	20	15
1400	A423	70c	Smoking monkey	20	16
1401	A423	80c	Farmer and pig	24	16
1402	A423	90c	Buffalo Bill	30	20
1403	A423	1fr	Snake charmer	35	15
1404	A423	1.50fr	Piano and harp player	45	30
1405	A423	2fr	Girl powdering her face	65	30
	Nos. 1398-1405 (8)			2.55	1.57

Quince Branch in Spring A424

1984, May 10 Photo. *Perf. 13x12½*

1406	A424	1.14fr	shown	35	25
1407	A424	1.47fr	Summer	45	32
1408	A424	2.38fr	Autumn	70	42
1409	A424	3.95fr	Winter	1.40	85

Issued precanceled only. See note after No. 324.

Place de la Visitation, by Hubert Clerissi — A425

Drawings by Hubert Clerissi: 10c, Town Hall. 15c, Rue Basse. 20c, Place Saint-Nicolas. 30c, Quai du Commerce. 40c, Rue des Iris. 3fr, Bandstand. 6fr, Opera House.

1984, May 10 Engr. *Perf. 12½x13*

1410	A425	5c	brown	15	15
1411	A425	10c	claret	15	15
1412	A425	15c	violet	15	15
1413	A425	20c	dark blue	15	15
1414	A425	30c	deep blue	15	15
1415	A425	40c	dark green	15	15
1416	A425	3fr	red brown	1.10	55
1417	A425	6fr	yellow green	2.00	1.25
			Set value	3.40	2.10

See Nos. 1516-1524, 1750-1755, 1821-1825.

Souvenir Sheet

1984 Los Angeles Olympics — A426

Rhythmic Gymnastics.

1984, May 10 *Perf. 13*

1418	Sheet of 4	5.25	5.25
a.	A426 2fr Ball	70	70
b.	A426 3fr Clubs	1.10	1.10
c.	A426 4fr Ribbon	1.40	1.40
d.	A426 5fr Hoop	1.75	1.75

1984 Winter Olympics — A427

1984, May 10

1422 A427 2fr Rink, speed skater 65 48
1423 A427 4fr Skater, snowflake 1.25 95

Europa (1959-84) A428

1984, May 10 *Perf. 13x12½*

1424 A428 2fr blue 70 38
1425 A428 3fr yel grn 95 70
a. Souv. sheet, 4 each #1424-1425 8.00 8.00

Butterflies and Rare Flowers, Mercantour Natl. Park A429

1.60fr, Boloria graeca tendensis, ranunculus montanus. 2fr, Zygaena vesubiana, saxifraga aizoides. 2.80fr, Erebia aethiopella, myosotis alpestris. 3fr, Parnassius phoebus gazeli, rhododendron ferrugineum. 3.60fr, Papilio alexanor, myrrhis odorata. Nos. 1426-1428 vert.

Perf. 12½x13, 13x12½

1984, May 10 Photo.

1426	A429	1.60fr	multi	52	20
1427	A429	2fr	multi	70	20
1428	A429	2.80fr	multi	90	35
1429	A429	3fr	multi	1.00	48
1430	A429	3.60fr	multi	1.40	70
	Nos. 1426-1430 (5)			4.52	1.93

Monte Carlo Dog Show Type

1984, May 10 *Perf. 13x12½*

1431 A387 1.60fr Auvergne pointer 75 52

A431

A432

1984, May 10 Engr. *Perf. 12½x13*

1432 A431 2fr Statue, rosary, pilgrimage sanctuary 65 40

Sanctuary of Our Lady of Laghet.

1984, May 10

1433 A432 2.80fr Stratosphere balloon 1.00 60
1434 A432 4fr Bathyscaphe 1.50 85

Auguste Piccard birth centenary.

25th Anniv. of Princely Palace Concerts A433

1984, May 10 *Perf. 13x12½*

1435 A433 3.60fr Orchestra 1.00 60

Belle Epoch Type of 1982

Paintings by Hubert Clerissi: 4fr, Rue Grimaldi, 1908. 5fr, Train Entering Monte Carlo Station, 1910.

Photo. & Engr.

1984, Nov. 8 *Perf. 12½x13*

1436 A394 4fr multi 1.10 1.00
1437 A394 5fr multi 1.65 1.40

25th Intl. Television Festival, Monte Carlo, Feb. 1985 — A434

1984, Nov. 8 Engr. *Perf. 13*

1438 A434 2.10fr Lights 60 35
1439 A434 3fr Golden nymph (prize) 75 55

Intl. Flower Show, Monte Carlo — A435

Pharmaceuticals, Cosmetics Industry — A436

1984, Nov. 8 Photo. *Perf. 12½x13*

1440 A435 2.10fr Mixed bouquet 60 32
1441 A435 3fr Ikebana 80 60

See Nos. 1491-1492, 1552-1553.

1984, Nov. 8 Engr. *Perf. 13*

1442 A436 2.40fr multi 1.10 85

Illustration from Gargantua, by Rabelais — A437

Francois Rabelais (1490-1553), 17th Cent. Drawing A438

1984, Nov. 8 *Perf. 13x12½, 12½x13*

1443 A437 2fr With animals 70 52
1444 A437 2fr With sheep of Panurge 70 52
1445 A438 4fr multi 1.40 1.10

Souvenir Sheet

10th Intl. Circus Festival, Dec. 6-10 — A439

1984, Nov. 8 Photo. *Perf. 13*

1446 A439 5fr Poster 1.65 1.65

La Femme a la Potiche, by Degas A440

1984, Nov. 8 Engr. *Perf. 12x13*

1447 A440 6fr multi 2.00 1.75

Christmas 1984 — A441

Figurines from Provence.

1984, Nov. 8 *Perf. 12½x13*

1448	A441	70c	Shepherd	26	20
1449	A441	1fr	Blind man	32	26
1450	A441	1.70fr	Happy man	52	45
1451	A441	2fr	Woman spinning	60	52
1452	A441	2.10fr	Angel	65	55
1453	A441	2.40fr	Garlic seller	80	60
1454	A441	3fr	Drummer	90	75
1455	A441	3.70fr	Knife grinder	1.25	85
1456	A441	4fr	Elderly couple	1.25	95
	Nos. 1448-1456 (9)			6.55	5.13

See Nos. 1737-1739, 1766-1768, 1838-1840.

Cherry Tree — A442

1985, Mar. 1 Engr. *Perf. 13*

1457	A442	1.22fr	Spring	40	20
1458	A442	1.57fr	Summer	48	28
1459	A442	2.55fr	Fall	80	42
1460	A442	4.23fr	Winter	1.40	85

Issued precanceled only. See note after No. 324.

No. 1 in Green
A443

1985, Mar. 25

1461 A443 1.70fr shown 60 42
1462 A443 2.10fr #1 in scarlet 70 22
1463 A443 3fr #1 in lt peacock bl 90 42

Stamp centenary, Natl. Stamp Exhibition, Dec. 5-8, Monte Carlo.

Europa 1985 — A444

Portraits: 2.10fr Prince Antoine I (1661-1731), Founder of Monaco Palace, music library. 3fr, Jean-Baptiste Lully (1632-1687), composer, violinist, superintendent of music to King Louis XIV.

1985, May 23 ***Perf. 12½x13***

1464 A444 2.10fr brt bl 70 52
1465 A444 3fr dk car 1.00 85
a. Souv. sheet, 5 #1464, 5 #1465 10.50 10.50

Flowers in Mercantour Park
A444a

Perf. 13x12½, 12½x13

1985, May 23 **Photo.**

1466 A444a 1.70fr Berardia subacaulis 60 38
1467 A444a 2.10fr Saxifraga florulenta, vert. 70 38
1468 A444a 2.40fr Fritillaria moggridgei, vert. 75 70
1469 A444a 3fr Sempervivum allionii, vert. 1.00 90
1470 A444a 3.60fr Silene cordifolia, vert. 1.25 1.00
1471 A444a 4fr Primula allionii 1.40 1.10
Nos. 1466-1471 (6) 5.70 4.46

Japanese Medlar
A445

1985, May 23 **Engr.** ***Perf. 13x12½***

1472 Sheet of 4 3.25 3.25
a. A445 1fr Spring 32 32
b. A445 2fr Summer 65 65
c. A445 3fr Autumn 85 85
d. A445 4fr Winter 1.25 1.25

Nadia Boulanger (1887-1979), Musician, Composer, Conductor — A446

Portraits, manuscripts and music: 2.10fr, Georges Auric (1899-1983), composer of film, ballet music, Music Foundation council president.

1985, May 23 ***Perf. 13***

1473 A446 1.70fr brown 55 48
1474 A446 2.10fr brt ultra 77 55

Prince Pierre de Monaco Music Foundation composition prize, 25th anniv.

Natl. Oceanographic Museum, 75th Anniv. — A447

1985, May 23

1475 A447 2.10fr brt bl, grn & blk 70 45

Graphs, Fish, Molecular Structures, Lab Apparatus — A448

1985, May 23

1476 A448 3fr dk bl grn, blk & dk rose lil 90 60

Prince Rainier III Scientific Research Center, 25th anniv.

Intl. Athletic Championships, May 25-26 — A449

1985, May 23

1477 A449 1.70fr Running 52 30
1478 A449 2.10fr Swimming 70 35

Opening of Louis II Stadium, May 25.

Monte Carlo Dog Show Type

1985, May 3 **Photo.** ***Perf. 13x12½***

1479 A387 2.10fr Boxer 1.65 90

Intl. Youth Year — A450

1985, May 23 **Engr.** ***Perf. 13***

1480 A450 3fr fawn, sep & dp grn 95 55

Fish, Natl. Oceanographic Museum Aquarium — A451

1985, Aug. 13 **Photo.** ***Perf. 12½x13***

1481 A451 1.80fr Pygoplites diacanthus 60 35
1482 A451 2.20fr Acanthurus leucosternon 70 32
1483 A451 3.20fr Chaetodon collare 1.10 70
1484 A451 3.90fr Balistoides conspicillum 1.25 75

Size: 40x52mm

Perf. 13

1485 A451 7fr Aquarium 2.25 1.65
Nos. 1481-1485 (5) 5.90 3.77

See Nos. 1560-1561, 1610-1615.

Souvenir Sheet

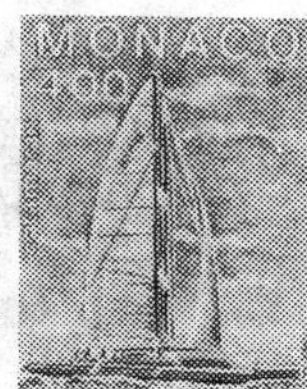

Transatlantic Yachting Race, Oct. 13 — A452

Yacht classes: No. 1486a, Catamaran. No. 1486b, Monocoque. No. 1486c, Trimaran.

1985, Oct. **Engr.** ***Perf. 13***

1486 Sheet of 3 4.25 4.25
a.-c. A452 4fr, any single 1.25 1.25

Monaco-New York competition.

ITALIA '85, Rome, Oct. 25-Nov. 3 — A453

Design: Exhibition emblem, St. Peter's Cathedral and Temple of Castor ruins.

1985, Oct. 25 ***Perf. 13½x13***

1487 A453 4fr int blk, brt grn & red rose 1.40 80

Belle Epoch Type of 1982

Illustrations by Hubert Clerissi.

Photo. & Engr.

1985, Nov. 7 ***Perf. 13x12½***

1488 A394 4fr Port of Monaco, 1912 1.40 1.40
1489 A394 6fr La Gare Vers Avenue, 1920 2.00 2.00

11th Intl. Circus Festival, Dec. 5-9 — A454

1985, Nov. 7 **Photo.** ***Perf. 13***

1490 A454 1.80fr multi 55 22

Intl. Flower Show Type of 1984

1985, Nov. 7

1491 A435 2.20fr Roses, tulips, jonquils 75 26
1492 A435 3.20fr Ikebana of chrysanthemums, bryony 1.10 52

Dated 1986.

Factory, Ship, Fish, Crustaceans — A455

Christmas 1985 — A456

1985, Nov. 7 **Engr.** ***Perf. 13x13½***

1493 A455 2.20fr brt bl, dp brn & dk grnsh bl 75 38

Monagasque fishing industry, Fontvieille District. See No. 1555.

1985, Nov. 7 **Photo.** ***Perf. 12½x13***

1494 A456 2.20fr multi 75 25

EUTELSAT Orbiting Earth — A457

1985, Nov. 7 **Engr.** ***Perf. 13***

1495 A457 3fr int blk, dp rose lil & dk bl 1.00 60

European Telecommunications Satellite Org.

Sacha Guitry (1885-1957), Actor, Dramatist — A458

Authors, composers: 4fr, Brothers Grimm. 5fr, Frederic Chopin and Robert Schumann, composers. 6fr, Johann Sebastian Bach and George Frideric Handel, composers.

1985, Nov. 7

1496 A458 3fr brn blk & gldn brn 1.10 75
1497 A458 4fr dp rose lil, sep & turq bl 1.50 95
1498 A458 5fr stl bl, dp bl & grnsh bl 1.65 1.25
1499 A458 6fr blk, brn & stl bl 1.90 1.50

Souvenir Sheet

Natl. Postage Stamp Cent. — A459

Altered designs: a, Type A1. b, Type A2. c, Type A13. d, Type A83.

1985, Dec. 5

1500 Sheet of 4 7.75 7.75
a.-d. A459 5fr, any single 1.90 1.90

Rainier and Albert Type of 1981-84

1985-88 **Engr.** ***Perf. 13***

1505 A370 1.80fr brt grn 55 15
1506 A370 1.90fr ol grn ('86) 58 30
1507 A370 2fr emer grn ('87) 68 35
1508 A370 2.20fr red rose 60 15
1509 A370 2.50fr dk brn 65 30
1510 A370 3.20fr brt bl 95 22
1511 A370 3.40fr ind ('86) 1.05 52
1512 A370 3.60fr dp ultra ('87) 1.20 60
1513 A370 10fr cl ('86) 2.50 1.50

1514 A370 15fr dk bl grn ('86) 4.75 2.40
1515 A370 20fr brt blue ('88) 7.20 3.60
Nos. 1505-1515 (11) 20.71 10.09

This is an expanding set. Numbers will change if necessary.

Views of Old Monaco Type of 1984

Illustrations by Hubert Clerissi: 50c, Port of Monaco. 60c, St. Charles Church. 70c, Promenade. 80c, Harbor, olive trees. 90c, Quay. 1fr, Palace Square. 2fr, Ships, harbor mouth. 4fr, Monaco Tram Station. 5fr, Mail coach.

1986, Jan. 23

1516 A425 50c red 15 15
1517 A425 60c Prus blue 15 15
1518 A425 70c orange 18 15
1519 A425 80c brt yel grn 20 18
1520 A425 90c rose violet 32 20
1521 A425 1fr brt blue 32 15
1522 A425 2fr black 65 28
1523 A425 4fr ultramarine 1.40 55
1524 A425 5fr olive green 1.50 70
Nos. 1516-1524 (9) 4.87 2.51

Hazel Nut Tree — A460

1986, Feb. 24 Engr. ***Perf. 13x12½***

1525 A460 1.28fr Spring 42 25
1526 A460 1.65fr Summer 52 38
1527 A460 2.67fr Fall 85 50
1528 A460 4.44fr Winter 1.50 85

Nos. 1525-1528 known only precanceled. See note after No. 324.

See Nos. 1580-1583, 1616-1619, 1685-1688, 1719-1722, 1809-1812.

Port of Monaco, 18th Cent. — A461

1986, Feb. 24

1529 A461 2.20fr ultra, gray & brown 75 38

Publication of Annales Monegasques, 10th anniv.

Europa 1986 — A462

1986 World Cup Soccer Championships, Mexico — A463

1986, May 22 Engr. ***Perf. 12½x13***

1530 A462 2.20fr Ramoge Nature Protection Treaty 85 42
1531 A462 3.20fr Natl. marine reserve 95 65
a. Souv. sheet, 5 each #1530-1531 9.00 9.00

Souvenir Sheet

1986, May 22

1532 Sheet of 2 3.75 3.75
a. A463 5fr Player 1.50 1.50
b. A463 7fr Goalie 2.00 2.00

Ovis Musimon A464

1986, May 22 Photo. ***Perf. 13x12½***

1533 A464 2.20fr shown 65 24
1534 A464 2.50fr Capra ibex 70 35
1535 A464 3.20fr Rupicapra rupicapra 1.00 35
1536 A464 3.90fr Marmota marmota 1.10 48
1537 A464 5fr Lepus timidus varronis 1.40 80
1538 A464 7.20fr Mustela erminea 2.25 1.25
Nos. 1533-1538 (6) 7.10 3.47

Nos. 1536-1538 vert.

Monte Carlo Dog Show Type

1986, May 22 Photo. ***Perf. 13x12½***

1539 A387 1.80fr Terriers 90 42

Prince Albert I, Parliament — A465

1986, May 22 ***Perf. 13***

1540 A465 2.50fr brn & ol grn 70 52

First Constitution, 75th anniv.

Serge Diaghilev, Founder — A466

1986, May 22 ***Perf. 13***

1541 A466 3.20fr brn blk, carm rose & blk 90 75

Diaghilev's first permanent ballet company, 75th anniv., and creation of Monte Carlo Ballet Company, 1986.

1st Monte Carlo Auto Rally, 75 Anniv. — A467

Design: Winner Henri Rougier and Turcat-Mery, 1911.

1986, May 22

1542 A467 3.90fr rose mag & car 1.10 90

Statue of Liberty, Cent. — A468

1986, May 22

1543 A468 5fr multi 1.40 1.10

Halley's Comet — A469

1986, May 22

1544 A469 10fr Sightings, 1986, 1352 2.75 2.25

AMERIPEX '86, Chicago, May 22-June 1 — A470

1986, May 22

1545 A470 5fr US flag, skyline 1.40 1.10

Belle Epoch Type of 1982

Illustrations by Hubert Clerissi.

Photo. & Engr.

1986, Oct. 28 ***Perf. 12½x13***

1546 A394 6fr Pavilion, 1920, vert. 1.80 90
1547 A394 7fr Beau Rivage Avenue, 1925, vert. 2.10 1.05

Premiere of El Cid, by Pierre Corneille, 350th Anniv. — A471

1986, Oct. 28 Engr. ***Perf. 13***

1548 A471 4fr Scenes 1.20 60

Franz Liszt, Composer — A472

1986, Oct. 28

1549 A472 5fr dk red brn & brt ultra 1.50 75

The Olympic Swimmer, 1961, by Emma de Sigaldi A473

1986, Oct. 28 ***Perf. 12½x13***

1550 A473 6fr multi 1.80 90

Intl. Insurers Congress, Monte Carlo, Sept. 30 — A474

1986, Oct. 28 ***Perf. 13½x13***

1551 A474 3.20fr brn, dp grn & brt bl 95 48

Intl. Flower Show Type of 1984

Designs: 2.20fr, Bouquet of roses, acidenthera. 3.90fr, Ikebana of lilies, beech branches.

1986, Oct. 28 Photo. ***Perf. 12½x13***

1552 A435 2.20fr multi 65 32
1553 A435 3.90fr multi 1.15 58

Dated 1987.

A475

A476

1986, Oct. 28 ***Perf. 13***

1554 A475 2.20fr multi 65 32

12th Intl. Circus Festival, Dec. 4-8.

Industries Type of 1985

Design: 3.90fr, Plastics industry.

1986, Oct. 28 **Engr.**

1555 A455 3.90fr dk red, dk gray & bl grn 1.15 58

1986, Oct. 28 Photo. ***Perf. 12½x13***

1556 A476 1.80fr Holly 55 28
1557 A476 2.50fr Poinsettia 75 38

Christmas.

Ascent of Mt. Blanc by J. Balmat and M.G. Paccard, Bicent. — A477

1986, Oct. 28 Engr. ***Perf. 13***

1558 A477 5.80fr red, brt bl & slate bl 1.75 90

Miniature Sheet

Arbutus Tree — A478

1986, Oct. 28 ***Perf. 13x12½***

1559 Sheet of 4 5.40 2.70
a. A478 3fr Spring 90 45
b. A478 4fr Summer 1.20 60
c. A478 5fr Fall 1.50 75
d. A478 6fr Winter 1.80 90

See Nos. 1645, 1680, 1736, 1775, 1804, 1852.

Aquarium Type of 1985

1986, Sept. 25 Photo. ***Perf. 12½x13***

1560 A451 1.90fr like No. 1481 58 30
1561 A451 3.40fr like No. 1483 1.05 52

Prince Rainier III — A479

Villa Miraflores, Seat of the Philatelic Bureau — A480

Design: No. 1562b, Prince Louis II, founder of the bureau.

1987, Apr. 23 Engr. *Perf. 12½x13*

1562	Strip of 3	5.50	2.75
a.	A479 4fr bright blue	1.35	68
b.	A479 4fr dark red	1.35	68
c.	A480 8fr multi	2.70	1.35

Philatelic Bureau, 50th anniv.
See No. 1607.

Louis II Stadium A481

1987, Apr. 23 *Perf. 13x12½*

1563	A481 2.20fr Exterior	75	38
1564	A481 3.40fr Interior	1.15	58
a.	Min. sheet, 5 each #1563-1564	9.50	4.80

Europa 1987.

Insects — A482

St. Devote Parish, Cent. — A483

1987, Apr. 23 Photo.

1565	A482	1fr Carabe de solier	35	18
1566	A482	1.90fr Guepe dorec	65	32
1567	A482	2fr Cicindele	68	35
1568	A482	2.20fr Grande aeschne	75	38
1569	A482	3fr Chrysomele	1.00	50
1570	A482	3.40fr Grande sauterelle verte	1.15	58
		Nos. 1565-1570 (6)	4.58	2.31

Nos. 1565, 1567 and 1569 horiz.

1987, Apr. 23 Engr. *Perf. 12½x13*

1571 A483 1.90fr black 65 32

Monaco Diocese, Cent. — A484

1987, Apr. 23

1572 A484 2.50fr dk yel grn 85 42

50th Intl. Dog Show, Monte Carlo A485

1987, Apr. 23 *Perf. 13x12½*

1573	A485 1.90fr Dog breeds	65	32
1574	A485 2.70fr Poodle	90	45

Stamp Day — A486

1987, Apr. 23 *Perf. 13*

1575 A486 2.20fr multi 75 38

Red Curley Tail, Mobile by Alexander Calder (1898-1976), Sculptor — A487

1987, Apr. 23 Photo.

1576 A487 3.70fr multi 1.25 62

Sculpture Exhibition, Monte Carlo.

2nd Small European Countries Games, May 14-17 — A488

1987, Apr. 23 Engr.

1577	A488 3fr Tennis	1.00	50
1578	A488 5fr Windsurfing	1.70	85

Miniature Sheet

Grape Vines A489

1987, Apr. 23 *Perf. 13x12½*

1579	Sheet of 4	6.00	3.00
a.	A489 3fr Spring	1.00	50
b.	A489 4fr Summer	1.30	65
c.	A489 5fr Autumn	1.70	85
d.	A489 6fr Winter	2.00	1.00

Four Seasons Type of 1986

Life cycle of the chestnut tree.

1987, Mar. 17 Engr. *Perf. 13x12½*

1580	A460 1.31fr Spring	45	22
1581	A460 1.69fr Summer	55	28
1582	A460 2.74fr Fall	90	45
1583	A460 4.56fr Winter	1.50	75

Nos. 1580-1583 known only precanceled. See note after No. 324.

The Life of St. Devote, Patron Saint of Monaco A490

Text: 4fr, Born in 283, in Quercio, Devote was martyred in Mariana, Corsica. 5fr, Devote's nurse teaches the saint about Christianity.

1987, Nov. 13 Photo. *Perf. 13x12½*

1584	A490 4fr multi	1.30	65
1585	A490 5fr multi	1.65	82

Red Cross of Monaco.
See Nos. 1643-1644, 1692-1693, 1714-1715, 1776-1777, 1836-1837.

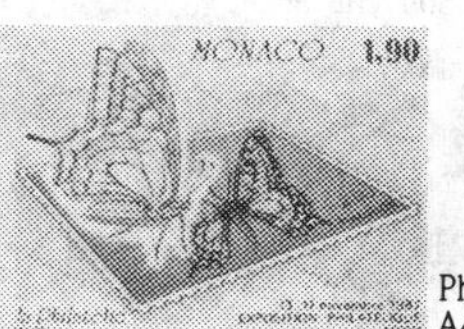
Philately A491

Butterflies and butterflies on simulated stamps.

1987, July 28 Engr.

1586	A491 1.90fr brt grn & dk gray	62	30
1587	A491 2.20fr rose red & rose lake	72	35
1588	A491 2.50fr red lil & vio	82	40
1589	A491 3.40fr brt bl & bluish blk	1.15	58

A492

A493

1987, Nov. 13 Photo. *Perf. 12½x13*

1590 A492 2.20fr multi 72 35

13th Int'l. Circus Festival, Monte Carlo, Jan. 28-Feb. 1.

1987, Nov. 13

1591	A493 2.20fr Ikebanas	72	35
1592	A493 3.40fr multi, horiz.	1.15	58

1988 Int'l Flower Show.
Dated 1988. See Nos. 1651, 1749.

Christmas A494

1987, Nov. 13 Engr. *Perf. 13x12½*

1593 A494 2.20fr crimson 72 35

5-Franc Prince Honoré V Coin — A495

1987, Nov. 13 *Perf. 13*

1594 A495 2.50fr scar & dk gray 82 40

Recapture of the Mint, 150th anniv.

Electronics Industry — A496

1987, Nov. 13

1595 A496 2.50fr henna brn, vio bl & grn 82 40

Int'l. Marine Radioactivity Laboratory, 25th Anniv. — A497

Design: Monaco Oceanographic Museum and Int'l. Agency of Atomic Energy, Vienna.

1987, Nov. 13

1596 A497 5fr brt bl, red brn & blk 1.65 82

Louis Jouvet (b.1887), French Actor — A498

1987, Nov. 16 *Perf. 13x12½*

1597 A498 3fr black 1.00 50

A499

1987, Nov. 16

1598 A499 3fr The River Crossing 1.00 50

Paul and Virginia, by Bernardin de Saint-Pierre, first edition bcent. (in 1988).

Marc Chagall (1887-1985), Painter — A500

1987, Nov. 16 *Perf. 13*

1599 A500 4fr terra cotta & bl gray 1.30 65

Jean Jenneret (Le Corbusier, 1887-1965), French Architect — A501

1987, Nov. 16
1600 A501 4fr Architect, Ronchamp Chapel 1.30 65

Newton's Theory of Gravity, 300th Anniv. — A502

Invention of the Telegraph by Samuel Morse, 150th Anniv. — A503

1987, Nov. 16
1601 A502 4fr mag & dk bl 1.30 65
1602 A503 4fr brt vio, turq bl & brn 1.30 65

Don Juan, Opera by Mozart, Bicent. — A504

Mass of the Dead, by Berlioz — A505

1987, Nov. 16
1603 A504 5fr ind, vio brn & sage grn 1.65 82
1604 A505 5fr sl grn, vio brn & bl 1.65 82

Belle Epoch Type of 1982

Illustrations by Hubert Clerissi. Nos. 1605-1606 vert.

Photo. & Engr.
1987, Nov. 16 *Perf. 12½x13*
1605 A394 6fr Rampe Major 2.00 1.00
1606 A394 7fr Old Monte Carlo Station 2.35 1.20

Philatelic Bureau Type of 1987

1987, Nov. 13 Engr. *Perf. 12½x13*
1607 Sheet of 3 5.50 5.50
a. A479 4fr blk vio, like #1562a 1.35 1.35
b. A479 4fr blk vio, like #1562b 1.35 1.35
c. A480 8fr blk vio, like #1562c 2.70 2.70

Postage Due Arms Type of 1985
Booklet Stamps

1987-88 Photo. *Perf. 13 on 3 Sides*
1608 D10 2fr multi ('88) 72 35
a. Bklt. pane of 10 7.25
1609 D10 2.20fr multi 72 35
a. Bklt. pane of 10 7.25

Issued: 2fr, Jan. 15; 2.20fr, Nov. 13.

Aquarium Type of 1985
Perf. 13x12½, 12½x13

1988, Jan. 15 Photo.
1610 A451 2fr Bodianus rufus 72 35
1611 A451 2.20fr Chelmon rostratus 80 40
1612 A451 2.50fr Oxymonacanthus longirostris 90 45
1613 A451 3fr Ostracion lentiginosum 1.10 55
1614 A451 3.70fr Pterois volitans 1.30 65
1615 A451 7fr Thalassoma lunare, horiz. 2.50 1.25
Nos. 1610-1615 (6) 7.32 3.65

Four Seasons Type of 1986

Life cycle of the pear tree.

1988, Feb. 15 *Perf. 13x12½*
1616 A460 1.36fr Spring 50 25
1617 A460 1.75fr Summer 65 32
1618 A460 2.83fr Fall 1.00 50
1619 A460 4.72fr Winter 1.70 85

Nos. 1616-1619 known only precanceled. See note after No. 324.

Souvenir Sheet

Biathlon, 1988 Winter Olympics, Calgary — A506

1988, Feb. 15 Litho. & Engr. *Perf. 13*
1620 Sheet of 2 3.60 3.60
a. A506 4fr Skiing 1.45 1.45
b. A506 6fr Shooting 2.15 2.15

51st Intl. Dog Show, Monte Carlo — A507

1988, Mar. 30 Photo. *Perf. 12½x13*
1621 A507 3fr Dachshunds 1.50 75

World Assoc. of the Friends of Children (AMADE), 25th Anniv. A508

1988, Mar. 30 Engr. *Perf. 13*
1622 A508 5fr dark vio blue, dark brn & brt olive grn 1.80 90

Europa 1988 — A509

Transport and communication: 2.20fr, Globe picturing hemispheres, man, brain, telecommunications satellite. 3.60fr, Plane propeller and high-speed locomotive.

1988, Apr. 21 *Perf. 12½x13*
1623 A509 2.20fr multi 80 40
1624 A509 3.60fr multi 1.30 65
a. Souv. sheet, 5 each #1623-1624 10.50 10.50

Mushrooms of Mercantour Natl. Park — A510

Perf. 13x12½, 12½x13

1988, May 26 Photo.
1625 A510 2fr Leccinum rotundifoliae 70 35
1626 A510 2.20fr Hygrocybe punicea 78 40
1627 A510 2.50fr Pholiota flammans 90 45
1628 A510 2.70fr Lactarius lignyotus 95 42
1629 A510 3fr Cortinarius traganus 1.05 52
1630 A510 7fr Russula olivacea 2.50 1.25
Nos. 1625-1630 (6) 6.88 3.39

Nos. 1629-1630 vert.

Nautical Soc., Cent. — A511

1988, May 26 Engr. *Perf. 13*
1631 A511 2fr dark red, lt blue & dark grn 70 35

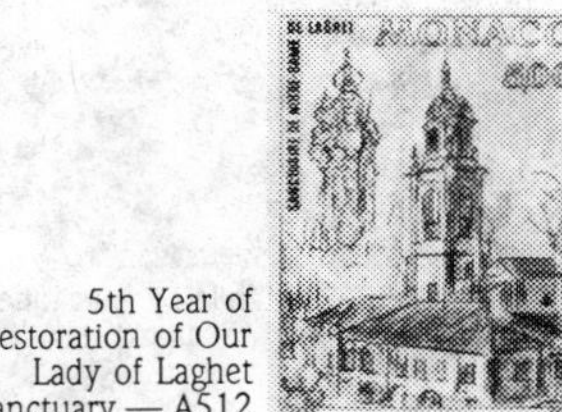

5th Year of Restoration of Our Lady of Laghet Sanctuary — A512

1988, May 26 *Perf. 12½*
1632 A512 5fr multi 1.75 88

World Health Organization, 40th Anniv. A513

1988, May 26 *Perf. 13*
1633 A513 6fr brt blue & lake 2.15 1.10

Intl. Red Cross and Red Crescent Organizations, 125th Annivs. A514

1988, May 26 Photo. *Perf. 13x12½*
1634 A514 6fr dull red, blk & gray 2.15 1.10

Jean Monnet (1888-1979), Nobel Peace Prize Winner in 1922 — A515

Maurice Chevalier (1888-1972), Actor — A516

1988, May 26 Engr. *Perf. 12½x13*
1635 A515 2fr brt blue, dark olive bister & blk 70 35
1636 A516 2fr blk & dark blue 70 35

1st Crossing of Greenland by Fridtjof Nansen (1861-1930), Cent. — A517

1988, May 26 *Perf. 13*
1637 A517 4fr brt vio 1.40 70

Belle Epoch Type of 1982

Illustrations by Hubert Clerissi.

Photo. & Engr.
1988, Sept. 8 *Perf. 13x12½*
1638 A394 6fr Packet in Monte Carlo Harbor, 1910 1.90 95
1639 A394 7fr Monte Carlo Station, c. 1910 2.25 1.15

Souvenir Sheet

1988 Summer Olympics, Seoul A518

Woman wearing Korean regional costume, Games emblem and event: 2fr, Women's tennis. 3fr, Women's table tennis. 5fr, Women's yachting. 7fr, Women's cycling.

1988, Sept. 8 Engr.
1640 Sheet of 4 5.50 5.50
a. A518 2fr blk, lt ultra & brn 65 65
b. A518 3fr blk, lt ultra & brn 95 95
c. A518 5fr blk, lt ultra & brn 1.60 1.60
d. A518 7fr blk, lt ultra & brn 2.25 2.25

A519

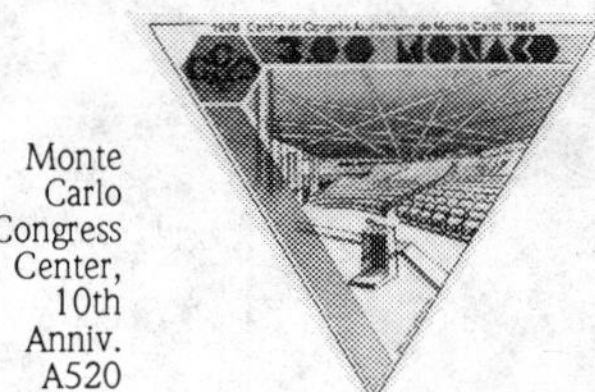

Monte Carlo Congress Center, 10th Anniv. A520

1988, Sept. 8 *Perf. 13*

1641 A519 2fr dark blue grn 68 35
1642 A520 3fr henna brn 1.00 50
a. Pair, #1641-1642 1.75 1.00

Monegasque Red Cross Type of 1987

The Life of St. Devote, patron saint of Monaco: 4fr, Devote witnessing the arrival of the governor of Rome. 5fr, Devote and the governor.

1988, Oct. 20 Photo. *Perf. 13x12½*

1643 A490 4fr multi 1.30 65
1644 A490 5fr multi 1.60 80

Tree Type of 1986

Life cycle of the olive tree.

1988, Oct. 20 Engr. *Perf. 13x12½*

1645 Sheet of 4 5.75 5.75
a. A478 3fr Spring 95 95
b. A478 4fr Summer 1.30 1.30
c. A478 5fr Fall 1.60 1.60
d. A478 6fr Winter 1.90 1.90

Le Nain and Brothers, Detail of a Painting in the Louvre, by Antoine Le Nain (c. 1588-1648) A521

1988, Oct. 20 *Perf. 12½x13*

1646 A521 5fr ol brn, dull brn & car rose 1.60 80

Les Grands Archeologues, Bronze Sculpture by Giorgio De Chirico (1888-1978), Italian Painter and Sculptor A522

1988, Oct. 20 *Perf. 13*

1647 A522 5fr ol bis, blk brn & dark bl 1.60 80

Pierre Carlet de Chamblain de Marivaux (1688-1763), French Playwright and Novelist — A523

Lord Byron (1788-1824), English Poet — A524

1988, Oct. 20

1648 A523 3fr dull ol & ultra 95 48

1988, Oct. 20

1649 A524 3fr grnsh bl, brn & blk 95 48

14th Intl. Circus Festival, Monte Carlo, Feb. 2-6, 1989 — A525

1988, Oct. 20 Photo. *Perf. 12½x13*

1650 A525 2fr multi 65 32

Intl. Flower Show Type of 1987

1988, Oct. 20

1651 A493 3fr Ikebana 95 48

22nd Intl. Flower Show and Flower Arranging Contest, Monte Carlo.

Textile Industry (Ready-to-Wear Clothes by Bettina and Le Squadra) — A526

1988, Oct. 20 Engr. *Perf. 13*

1652 A526 3fr blk, yel org & dk ol grn 95 48

Christmas — A527

1988, Oct. 20 Litho. *Perf. 12½x13*

1653 A527 2fr blk & lem 65 32

Petroglyphs, Mercantour Natl. Park — A528

Perf. 13x12½, 12½x13

1989, Feb. 8 Litho.

1654 A528 2fr multi 65 32
1655 A528 2.20fr multi, diff. 72 35
1656 A528 3fr multi, diff. 98 50
1657 A528 3.60fr multi, diff. 1.20 60
1658 A528 4fr multi, diff., vert. 1.30 65
1659 A528 5fr multi, diff., vert. 1.65 82
Nos. 1654-1659 (6) 6.50 3.24

Rue des Spelugues — A528a

1989, Feb. 8 Litho. *Perf. 13½x13*

Booklet Stamps

1660 A528a 2fr shown 65 32
b. Bklt. pane of 10 6.50
1660A A528a 2.20fr St. Nicolas Place 72 35
c. Bklt. pane of 10 7.25

See Nos. 1702-1703, 1826-1827.

Prince Rainier III — A529

1989-91 Photo. & Engr. *Perf. 13*

1661 2fr pale blue grn & Prus grn 65 16
1662 2.10fr lt blue & Prus blue 75 18
1663 2.20fr pink & rose brn 72 18
1664 2.20fr pale greenish bl & greenish bl 80 40
1665 2.30fr pale pink & car lake 82 20
1666 2.50fr pale rose & rose lake 90 45
1667 3.20fr pale blue & brt blue 1.15 28
1668 3.40fr lt bl & dk bl 1.25 62
1669 3.60fr lt blue & sapphire 1.20 30
1670 3.80fr pale pink & dk lil rose 1.35 32
1671 4fr pale vio & rose vio 1.40 70
1672 5fr buff & dark vio brn 1.65 55
1673 15fr pale vio & indigo 4.75 2.40
1673A 20fr pink & rose car 6.80 3.40
1674 25fr pale gray & blk 9.00 4.50
Nos. 1661-1674 (15) 33.19 14.64

Issue dates: 2fr, No. 1663, 3.60fr, 5fr, 15fr, Mar. 14. 2.10fr, 2.30fr, 25fr, Jan. 11, 1990. 3.20fr, 3.80fr, Mar. 15, 1990. 20fr, Apr. 26, 1991. No. 1664, 2.50fr, 3.40fr, 4fr, Sept. 24, 1991.

See No. 1797.

5th Magic Grand Prix, Monte Carlo, Mar. 17-19 A530

1989, Mar. 14 Engr. *Perf. 13x12½*

1675 A530 2.20fr multi 72 35

Dog Show Type of 1982

1989, Mar. 14 Photo.

1676 A387 2.20fr Yorkshire terrier 72 35

Our Lady of Mercy Soc., 350th Anniv. A531

1989, Mar. 14 Engr. *Perf. 13*

1677 A531 3fr choc, dark red & blk 98 50

Theater & Film — A532

Designs: 3fr, Jean Cocteau (1889-1963), French writer, artist. 4fr, Charlie Chaplin (1889-1977), English actor, film producer.

1989, Mar. 14

1678 A532 3fr Prus grn, olive grn & deep rose lil 98 50
1679 A532 4fr dark grn, dark vio & dark red 1.30 65

Tree Type of 1986

Life cycle of the pomegranate tree.

1989, Mar. 14 *Perf. 13x12½*

Miniature Sheet

1680 Sheet of 4 5.90 5.90
a. A478 3fr Spring 98 98
b. A478 4fr Summer 1.30 1.30
c. A478 5fr Fall 1.65 1.65
d. A478 6fr Winter 1.95 1.95

Souvenir Sheet

Reign of Prince Rainier III, 40th Anniv. A533

1989, May 9 Engr. *Perf. 13*

1681 A533 20fr rose vio 6.00 6.00

Europa 1989 — A534

Children's games.

1989, May 9 *Perf. 12½x13*

1682 A534 2.20fr Marbles 68 35
1683 A534 3.60fr Jumping rope 1.10 55
a. Souv. sheet, 5 each #1682-1683 9.00 9.00

Souvenir Sheet

French Revolution, Bicent., PHILEXFRANCE '89 — A535

Designs: a, Liberty. b, Equality. c, Fraternity.

1989, July 7 Engr. *Perf. 12½x13*

1684 A535 Sheet of 3 4.35 4.35
a. 5fr sapphire 1.45 1.45
b. 5fr black 1.45 1.45
c. 5fr dark red 1.45 1.45

Four Seasons Type of 1986

Life cycle of the pear tree.

1989, July 27 Photo. *Perf. 13x12½*

1685 A460 1.39fr like No. 1616 45 22
1686 A460 1.79fr like No. 1617 58 30
1687 A460 2.90fr like No. 1618 92 45
1688 A460 4.84fr like No. 1619 1.55 78

Nos. 1685-1688 known only precanceled. See note after No. 324.

Portrait of the Artist's Mother, by Philibert Florence
A536

Regatta at Molesey, by Alfred Sisley (1839-1899) — A537

Paintings: 8fr, *Enclosed Courtyard, Auvers*, by Paul Cezanne (1839-1906), vert.

Perf. 13, 13x12½ (6fr), 12½x13 (8fr)

1989, Sept. 7 **Engr.**

1689 A536 4fr olive black 1.20 60
1690 A537 6fr multi 1.80 90
1691 A537 8fr multi 2.40 1.20

Birth sesquicentennials of painters.

Monegasque Red Cross Type of 1987

The life of St. Devote, patron saint of Monaco: 4fr, Eutychius refuses to betray Devote to Barbarus and is poisoned. 5fr, Devote is condemned to torture by Barbarus when she refuses to make sacrifices to the Gods.

1989, Sept. 7 **Photo.** ***Perf. 13x12½***

1692 A490 4fr multi 1.20 60
1693 A490 5fr multi 1.50 75

Interparliamentary Union, Cent. — A538

1989, Oct. 26 **Engr.** ***Perf. 13***

1694 A538 4fr multi 1.20 60

Belle Epoch Type of 1982

Illustrations by Hubert Clerissi.

1989, Oct. 26 ***Perf. 12½x13***

1695 A394 7fr Ship in Monaco Port 2.10 1.05
1696 A394 8fr Gaming hall, Monte Carlo Casino 2.40 1.20

Souvenir Sheet

Princess Grace Foundation, 25th Anniv. — A539

Designs: a, Princess Grace. b, Princess Caroline.

1989, Oct. 26

1697 Sheet of 2 3.00 3.00
a.-b. A539 5fr any single 1.50 1.50

20th UPU Congress — A540

Design: Views of the Prince of Monaco's palace and the White House.

1989, Oct. 26 ***Perf. 13***

1698 A540 6fr multi 1.80 90

A541

Monaco Aid and Presence, 10th Anniv.
A543

A542

1989, Oct. 26 **Litho.** ***Perf. 12½x13***

1699 A541 2fr Poinsettia 65 32

Christmas.

1989, Dec. 7 **Photo.** ***Perf. 12½x13***

1700 A542 2.20fr multicolored 78 40

15th Intl. Circus Festival, Monte Carlo, Feb. 1-5, 1990.

1989, Dec. 7 **Engr.** ***Perf. 13x12½***

1701 A543 2.20fr brown & red 78 40

Avenues Type of 1989

1990, Feb. 8 **Litho.** ***Perf. 13½x13***

1702 A528a 2.10fr The Great Stairs 75 38
a. Bklt. pane of 10 + 2 labels 7.50
1703 A528a 2.30fr Mayoral Court of Honor 82 40
a. Bklt. pane of 10 + 2 labels 8.25

Dog Show Type of 1982

1990, Mar. 15 ***Perf. 13x12½***

1704 A387 2.30fr Bearded collie 90 42

Sir Rowland Hill, Great Britain No. 1 — A544

1990, Mar. 15 **Engr.** ***Perf. 13***

1705 A544 5fr royal blue & black 1.80 90

Penny Black, 150th anniv.

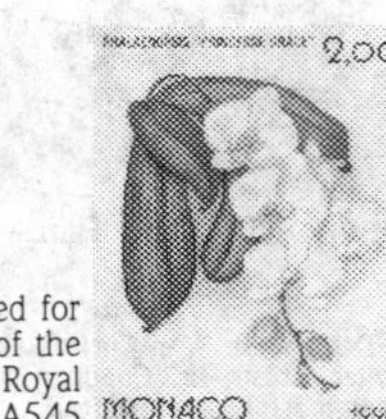

Flowers Named for Members of the Royal Family — A545

1990, Mar. 15 **Litho.** ***Perf. 12½x13***

1706 A545 2fr Princess Grace 72 35
1707 A545 3fr Prince Rainier III 1.05 52
1708 A545 3fr Grace Patricia 1.05 52
1709 A545 4fr Principessa Grace 1.45 72
1710 A545 5fr Caroline of Monaco 1.75 90
Nos. 1706-1710 (5) 6.02 3.01

Intl. Telecommunications Union, 125th Anniv. — A546

1990, Mar. 15 **Engr.** ***Perf. 13***

1711 A546 4fr pink, deep vio & dull blue grn 1.45 72

Antony Noghes (1890-1978), Creator of the Monaco Grand Prix and Monte Carlo Rally — A547

1990, Mar. 15

1712 A547 3fr deep vio, blk & dark red 1.10 55

A548

A549

1990, Mar. 15

1713 A548 4fr brt pur, sepia & brt blue 1.45 72

Automobile Club, centenary.

Monegasque Red Cross Type of 1987

The life of St. Devote, patron saint of Monaco: 4fr, Devote tortured to death (whipped). 5fr, Body layed out in a small boat.

1990, Mar. 15 **Litho.** ***Perf. 13x12½***

1714 A490 4fr multicolored 1.45 72
1715 A490 5fr multicolored 1.75 88

1990, May 3 **Engr.** ***Perf. 12½x12***

1716 A549 2.30fr multicolored 80 40
1717 A549 3.70fr multicolored 1.30 60
a. Souv. sheet of 8, 4 each #1716, 1717, perf. 12½x13 8.75 8.75

Europa.

Souvenir Sheet

World Cup Soccer Championships, Italy — A550

1990, May 3 ***Perf. 13x12½***

1718 A550 Sheet of 4 7.00 7.00
a. 5fr Players, trophy 1.75 1.75
b. 5fr Player dribbling ball 1.75 1.75
c. 5fr Ball 1.75 1.75
d. 5fr Players, stadium 1.75 1.75

Four Seasons Type of 1986

Life cycle of the plum tree.

1990, Sept. 17 ***Perf. 13***

1719 A460 1.46fr Spring 52 26
1720 A460 1.89fr Summer 65 32
1721 A460 3.06fr Fall 1.10 55
1722 A460 5.10fr Winter 1.80 90

Nos. 1719-1722 known only precanceled. See note after No. 324.

Minerals, Mercantour Natl. Park — A551

Perf. 13x12½, 12½x13

1990, Sept. 4 **Litho.**

1723 A551 2.10fr Anatase 75 38
1724 A551 2.30fr Albite 80 40
1725 A551 3.20fr Rutile 1.15 58
1726 A551 3.80fr Chlorite 1.35 68
1727 A551 4fr Brookite 1.40 70
1728 A551 6fr Quartz 2.10 1.05
Nos. 1723-1728 (6) 7.55 3.79

Nos. 1727-1728 vert.

Pierrot Ecrivain — A552

1990, Sept. 4 **Engr.** ***Perf. 12½x13***

1729 A552 3fr dark blue 1.10 55

Helicopter, Monaco Heliport
A553

Design: 5fr, Helicopters, Monte Carlo skyline.

1990, Sept. 4 ***Perf. 13***

1730 A553 3fr red, brn & blk 1.10 55
1731 A553 5fr blk, gray bl & brn 1.80 90

30th World Congress of Civilian Airports, Monte Carlo.

C. Samuel Hahnemann (1755-1843), Physician — A554

1990, Sept. 4

1732 A554 3fr multicolored 1.10 55

Homeopathic medicine, bicentennial.

Jean-Francois Champollion (1790-1832), Egyptologist — A555

1990, Sept. 4
1733 A555 5fr blue & brown 1.80 90

A556

A558

Design: 6fr, Petanque World Championships.

1990, Sept. 4
1734 A556 2.30fr brt ultra, brn & red 90 45
1735 A556 6fr brn org, brn & bl 2.25 1.10

Offshore Power Boating World Championships.

Tree Type of 1986
Miniature Sheet

Life cycle of the lemon tree.

1990, Oct. 17 Litho. ***Perf. 13x12½***
1736 Sheet of 4 6.75 6.75
a. A478 3fr Spring 1.15 1.15
b. A478 4fr Summer 1.50 1.50
c. A478 5fr Fall 1.90 1.90
e. A478 6fr Winter 2.25 2.25

Type of 1984

1990, Oct. 17 Litho. ***Perf. 12½x13***
1737 A441 2.30fr Miller riding donkey 90 45
1738 A441 3.20fr Woman carrying firewood 1.25 65
1739 A441 3.80fr Baker 1.50 75

1990, Oct. 17 Engr. ***Perf. 12½***

The Cathedral, by Auguste Rodin (1840-1917).

1740 A558 5fr bl & cream 1.90 95

La Pie by Claude Monet (1840-1926) — A559

1990, Oct. 17 ***Perf. 13x12***
1741 A559 7fr multicolored 2.60 1.30

A560

A561

1990, Oct. 17 ***Perf. 12½x13***
1742 A560 5fr dark grn & bl 1.90 95

Peter Ilich Tchaikovsky, composer (1840-1893).

1991, Jan. 2 Photo. ***Perf. 13***
1743 A561 2.30fr multicolored 90 45

16th Intl. Circus Festival, Monte Carlo. See No. 1801.

A562

A563

Migratory birds and their continents: 2fr, Ciconia abdimii, Africa. 3fr, Selasphorus platycercus, America. 4fr, Anas querquedula, Asia. 5fr, Eurystomus orientalis, Australia. 6fr, Merops apiaster, Europe.

1991, Feb. 22 Litho. ***Perf. 12½x13***
1744 A562 2fr multicolored 80 40
1745 A562 3fr multicolored 1.20 60
1746 A562 4fr multicolored 1.60 80
1747 A562 5fr multicolored 2.00 1.00
1748 A562 6fr multicolored 2.40 1.20
Nos. 1744-1748 (5) 8.00 4.00

Intl. Symposium on Migratory Birds.

Intl. Flower Show Type of 1987

1991, Feb. 22
1749 A493 3fr Cyclamen 1.20 60

Views of Old Monaco Type of 1984

Designs: 20c, Cliffs of Monaco, Port de Fontvieille. 40c, Place du Casino. 50c, Place de la Cremaillere. 70c, Prince's Palace. 80c, Avenue du Beau Rivage. 1fr, Place d'Armes.

1991, Feb. 22 **Engr.**
1750 A425 20c rose violet 15 15
1751 A425 40c dk green 15 15
1752 A425 50c claret 20 15
1753 A425 70c ol green 25 15
1754 A425 80c ultramarine 30 15
1755 A425 1fr dk blue 40 20
Nos. 1750-1755 (6) 1.45
Set value 78

Dog Show Type of 1982

1991, Feb. 22 Litho. ***Perf. 12***
1756 A387 2.50fr Schnauzer 1.00 50

1991, Feb. 22
1757 A563 2.10fr Phytoplankton 85 42

Oceanographic Museum.

1992 Olympics A564

Design: No. 1758b, Cross country skiers, diff. No. 1759a, Relay runner receiving baton. No. 1759b, Runner passing baton.

1991, Apr. 26 Engr. ***Perf. 13x12½***
1758 Pair 2.80 1.40
a. A564 3fr dk grn, bl & olive 1.20 60
b. A564 4fr dk grn, bl & olive 1.60 80
1759 Pair 3.20 1.60
a. A564 3fr brown & Prussian blue 1.20 60
b. A564 5fr brown & Prussian blue 2.00 1.00

Nos. 1758 and 1759 have continuous designs.

Europa A565

1991, Apr. 26
1760 A565 2.30fr Eutelsat 90 45
1761 A565 3.20fr Inmarsat 1.25 65
a. Min. sheet, 5 ea. #1760-1761 10.75 5.35

25th Intl. Contemporary Art Competition A566

Prince Pierre Foundation, 25th Anniv. A567

1991, Apr. 26 Engr. ***Perf. 12½x13***
1762 A566 4fr multicolored 1.40 70

1991, Apr. 26
1763 A567 5fr multicolored 1.75 88

Coral — A568

1991, Apr. 26 Photo. ***Perf. 12***
1764 A568 2.20fr shown 75 38
1765 A568 2.40fr Coral necklace 85 42

Christmas Type of 1984

1991, Nov. 7 Litho. ***Perf. 12***
1766 A441 2.50fr Consul 90 45
1767 A441 3.50fr Woman from Arles 1.30 65
1768 A441 4fr Mayor 1.45 75

Conifers, Mercantour Natl. Park — A569

1991, Nov. 7
1769 A569 2.50fr Epicea 90 45
1770 A569 3.50fr Sapin 1.30 65
1771 A569 4fr Pin a crochets 1.45 75
1772 A569 5fr Pin sylvestre, vert. 1.85 90
1773 A569 6fr Pin cembro 2.20 1.10
1774 A569 7fr Meleze, vert. 2.55 1.30
Nos. 1769-1774 (6) 10.25 5.15

Tree Type of 1986
Miniature Sheet

Life cycle of an orange tree.

1991, Nov. 7 Engr. ***Perf. 13x12½***
1775 Sheet of 4 6.60 3.30
a. A478 3fr Spring 1.10 55
b. A478 4fr Summer 1.45 75
c. A478 5fr Fall 1.85 90
d. A478 6fr Winter 2.20 1.10

Monagasque Red Cross Type of 1987

Life of St. Devote, Monaco's Patron Saint: 4.50fr, The Storm is Rising. 5.50fr, Arrival of the Rock of Monaco.

1991, Nov. 7 **Photo.**
1776 A490 4.50fr multicolored 1.65 85
1777 A490 5.50fr multicolored 2.00 1.00

Testudo Hermanni A570

1991, Nov. 7 Litho. ***Perf. 12***
1778 A570 1.25fr Two crawling right 45 22
1779 A570 1.25fr Peering from shell 45 22
1780 A570 1.25fr Walking in grass 45 22
1781 A570 1.25fr Walking amid plants 45 22
a. Block or strip of 4, #1778-1781 1.80 90

Prince Albert I Type of 1891
Miniature Sheet

1991, Nov. 7 Engr. ***Perf. 13***
Stamp size: 22½x28mm
1782 Sheet of 3 11.10 5.55
a. A2 10fr dark red 3.70 1.85
b. A2 10fr dark blue green 3.70 1.85
c. A2 10fr deep violet 3.70 1.85

Portrait of Claude Monet by Auguste Renoir A571

1991, Nov. 7 Engr. ***Perf. 12½x13***
1783 A571 5fr multicolored 1.80 90

Treaty of Peronne, 350th Anniv. A572

Portraits by Philippe de Champaigne (1602-1674): 6fr, Honore II (1604-1662), Monaco. 7fr, Louis XIII (1610-1643), France.

1991, Nov. 7
1784 A572 6fr multicolored 2.20 1.10
1785 A572 7fr multicolored 2.55 1.30

Values quoted in this catalogue are for stamps graded at Fine-Very Fine and with no faults. An illustrated guide to grade is provided in introductory material, beginning on Page 5A.

Princess Grace Theatre, 10th Anniv. A573

1991, Nov. 7 **Litho.**
1786 A573 8fr Princess Grace 3.00 1.50

Prince Rainier III Type of 1989

1991, Nov. 7 **Photo. & Engr.** ***Perf. 13***
1797 A529 10fr lt bl grn & deep bl grn 3.70 1.85

This is an expanding set. Numbers will change if necessary.

16th Intl. Circus Festival Type

1992, Jan. 6 **Photo.** ***Perf. 12½x13***
1801 A561 2.50fr multicolored 90 45

1992 Winter and Summer Olympics, Albertville and Barcelona A574

Designs: 7fr, Two-man bobsled. 8fr, Soccer.

1992, Feb. 7 **Engr.** ***Perf. 13***
1802 A574 7fr multicolored 2.50 1.25
1803 A574 8fr multicolored 2.90 1.45

Tree Type of 1986
Miniature Sheet

Life cycle of a cactus plant.

1992, Apr. 24 **Photo.** ***Perf. 13x12½***
1804 Sheet of 4 7.25 7.25
a. A478 3fr Spring 1.20 1.20
b. A478 4fr Summer 1.60 1.60
c. A478 5fr Fall 2.00 2.00
d. A478 6fr Winter 2.40 2.40

60th Monte Carlo Rally — A575

1992, Mar. 13 **Engr.** ***Perf. 13x12½***
1805 A575 4fr dk bl grn, blk & red 1.45 75

Intl. Dog Show Type of 1982

1992, Mar. 13 **Litho.** ***Perf. 13x12½***
1806 A387 2.20fr Labrador retriever 80 40

50th Grand Prix of Monaco A576

1992, Mar. 13 **Engr.**
1807 A576 2.50fr vio brn, blk & brt bl 90 45

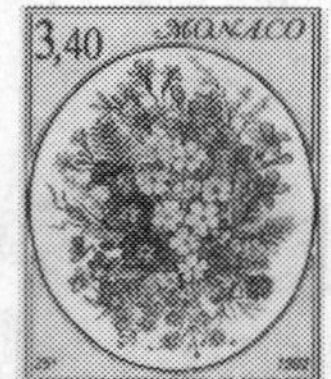

25th Intl. Flower Show, Monte Carlo — A577

1992, Mar. 13 **Photo.** ***Perf. 12½x13***
1808 A577 3.40fr multicolored 1.25 60

See No. 1848.

Four Seasons Type of 1986

Life cycle of a walnut tree.

1992, Mar. 13 **Photo.**
1809 A460 1.60fr Spring 58 28
1810 A460 2.08fr Summer 75 38
1811 A460 2.98fr Fall 1.10 55
1812 A460 5.28fr Winter 1.90 95

Nos. 1809-1812 known only precanceled. See the note after No. 324.

Souvenir Sheet

Dolphins A578

1992, Mar. 13
1813 A578 Sheet of 4 8.00 8.00
a. 4fr Steno bredanensis 1.50 1.50
b. 5fr Delphinus delphis 1.80 1.80
c. 6fr Tursiops truncatus 2.20 2.20
d. 7fr Stenella coeruleoalba 2.50 2.50

See No. 1853.

Discovery of America, 500th Anniv. A579

1992, Apr. 24
1814 A579 2.50fr Pinta 90 45
1815 A579 3.40fr Santa Maria 1.25 65
1816 A579 4fr Nina 1.45 75
a. Sheet, 2 each #1814-1816 7.25 7.25

Europa.

Ameriflora Intl. Flower Show, Columbus, Ohio — A580

1992, Apr. 24 **Litho.** ***Perf. 12½x13***
1817 A580 4fr Fruits & vegetables 1.45 75
1818 A580 5fr Vase of flowers 1.80 90

Columbus Exposition, Genoa '92 — A581

1992, Apr. 24 **Engr.** ***Perf. 13***
1819 A581 6fr multicolored 2.20 1.10

Expo '92, Seville — A582

1992, Apr. 24
1820 A582 7fr multicolored 2.50 1.25

Views of Old Monaco Type of 1984

Illustrations by Hubert Clerissi: 60c, National Council. 90c, Port of Fontvieille. 2fr, Condamine Market. 3fr, Sailing ship. 7fr, Oceanographic Museum.

1992, May 25 **Engr.** ***Perf. 12½x13***
1821 A425 60c dark blue 22 15
1822 A425 90c violet brown 35 16
1823 A425 2fr vermilion 75 38
1824 A425 3fr black 1.15 58
1825 A425 7fr gray blue & blk 2.70 1.35
Nos. 1821-1825 (5) 5.17 2.62

Avenues Type of 1989

1992, May 25 **Litho.** ***Perf. 13x13½***
Booklet Stamps
1826 A528a 2.20fr Porte Nueve, horiz. 82 42
a. Bklt. pane of 10 + 2 labels 8.25
1827 A528a 2.50fr Placette Bosio, horiz. 92 46
a. Bklt. pane of 10 + 2 labels 9.25

Genoa '92 — A583

Roses: 3fr, Christopher Columbus. 4fr, Prince of Monaco.

1992, Sept. 18 **Litho.** ***Perf. 12***
1828 A583 3fr multicolored 1.20 60
1829 A583 4fr multicolored 1.60 80

Gypaetus Barbatus, Mercantour Natl. Park — A584

1992, Oct. 20 **Engr.** ***Perf. 13x12½***
1830 A584 2.20fr grn, org & blk 85 42

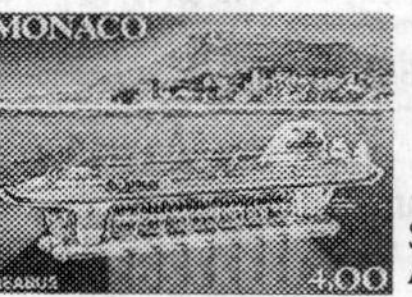

Seabus A585

1992, Oct. 20
1831 A585 4fr multicolored 1.55 78

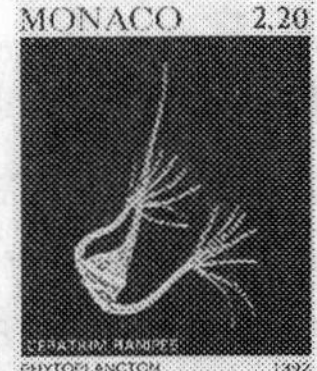

Phytoplankton A586

Designs: 2.20fr, Ceratium ranipes. 2.50fr, Ceratium hexacanthum.

1992, Oct. 20 **Litho.** ***Perf. 12***
1832 A586 2.20fr multicolored 85 42
1833 A586 2.50fr multicolored 95 48

Baron de Coubertin's Call for Modern Olympics, Cent. — A587

1992, Oct. 20 **Engr.** ***Perf. 13***
1834 A587 10fr blue 3.85 1.90

Chapel of St. Catherine — A588

Prince of Monaco, the Marquisat of Baux-de-Provence.

1992, Oct. 20 **Litho. & Engr.**

1835	A588	15fr multicolored	5.75	2.85

Monagasque Red Cross Type of 1987

The life of St. Devote, patron saint of Monaco: 6fr, Fire aboard ship. 8fr, Procession of the reliquary.

1992, Oct. 20 **Engr.**

Size: 48x36mm

1836	A490	6fr multicolored	2.30	1.15
1837	A490	8fr multicolored	3.10	1.55

Christmas Type of 1984

1992, Oct. 20 **Litho.** ***Perf. 12***

1838	A441	2.50fr Basket maker	95	48
1839	A441	3.40fr Fishmonger	1.30	65
1840	A441	5fr Drummer	1.95	98

Miniature Sheet

Postal Museum — A589

1992, Oct. 20 **Litho. & Engr.** ***Perf. 13***

1841		Sheet of 2	8.30	8.30
a.	A589	10fr Sardinia Type A4	4.15	4.15
b.	A589	10fr France Type A3	4.15	4.15

17th Intl. Circus Festival, Monte Carlo — A590

Birds, Mercantour Natl. Park — A591

1993, Jan. 5 **Litho.** ***Perf. 13¹/₂x13***

1842	A590	2.50fr multicolored	90	45

Perf. 13x12¹/₂, 12¹/₂x13

1993, Feb. 15 **Engr.**

Designs: 2fr, Circaetus gallicus, horiz. 3fr, Falco peregrinus, horiz. 4fr, Bubo bubo. 5fr, Pernis apivorus. 6fr, Aegolius funereus.

1843	A591	2fr multicolored	72	36
1844	A591	3fr multicolored	78	40
1845	A591	4fr multicolored	1.45	72
1846	A591	5fr multicolored	1.80	90
1847	A591	6fr multicolored	2.20	1.10
		Nos. 1843-1847 (5)	6.95	3.48

Intl. Flower Show Type of 1992

1993, Mar. 1 **Photo.** ***Perf. 12¹/₂x13***

1848	A577	3.40fr multicolored	1.25	62

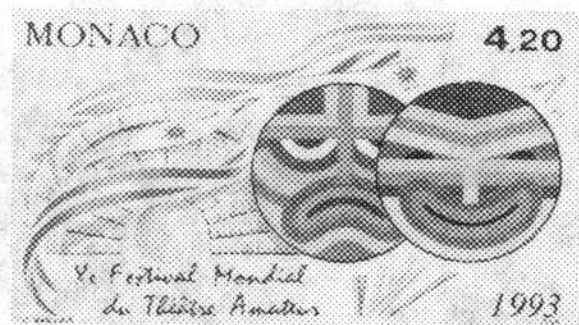

10th World Amateur Theater Festival — A592

1993, Mar. 1 **Litho.** ***Perf. 13***

1849	A592	4.20fr multicolored	1.50	75

A593

A594

1993, Mar. 1 **Engr.** ***Perf. 12¹/₂x13***

1850	A593	6fr multicolored	2.20	1.10

Intl. Civil Protection Day

1993, Mar. 24 **Engr.** ***Perf. 13***

1851	A594	5fr Princess Grace	1.80	90

See US No. 2749.

Tree Type of 1986
Miniature Sheet

Life cycle of an almond tree: a, Spring. b, Summer. c, Autumn. d, Winter.

1993 **Photo.** ***Perf. 13x12¹/₂***

1852		Sheet of 4	7.40	7.40
a.-d.	A478	5fr any single	1.85	1.85

Marine Mammals Type of 1992
Miniature Sheet

1993

1853		Sheet of 4	8.00	8.00
a.	A578	4fr Balaenoptera physalus	1.45	1.45
b.	A578	5fr Balaenoptera acutorostrata	1.80	1.80
c.	A578	6fr Physeter catodon	2.25	2.25
d.	A578	7fr Ziphius cavirostris	2.50	2.50

SEMI-POSTAL STAMPS

No. 16 Surcharged in Red **✚ 5c**

1914, Oct. **Unwmk.** ***Perf. 14x13¹/₂***

B1	A2	10c + 5c carmine	4.25	3.25

View of Monaco — SP2

1919, Sept. 20 **Typo.**

B2	SP2	2c + 3c lilac	10.00	10.00
B3	SP2	5c + 5c green	7.25	7.25
B4	SP2	15c + 10c rose	7.25	7.25
B5	SP2	25c + 15c blue	17.00	17.00
B6	SP2	50c + 50c brn, *buff*	70.00	70.00
B7	SP2	1fr + 1fr blk, *yel*	235.00	235.00
B8	SP2	5fr + 5fr dl red	750.00	750.00
		Nos. B2-B8 (7)	1,096.	1,096.

Nos. B4-B8 Surcharged

20 mars
1920
2c + 3c

1920, Mar. 20

B9	SP2	2c + 3c on #B4	24.00	24.00
a.		"c" of "3c" inverted	*1,250.*	*1,250.*
B10	SP2	2c + 3c on #B5	24.00	24.00
a.		"c" of "3c" inverted	*1,250.*	*1,250.*
B11	SP2	2c + 3c on #B6	24.00	24.00
a.		"c" of "3c" inverted	*1,250.*	*1,250.*
B12	SP2	5c + 5c on #B7	24.00	24.00
B13	SP2	5c + 5c on #B8	24.00	24.00

Overprinted

20 mars
1920

B14	SP2	15c + 10c rose	16.00	16.00
B15	SP2	25c + 15c blue	6.50	6.50
B16	SP2	50c + 50c brn, *buff*	27.50	27.50
B17	SP2	1fr + 1fr blk, *yel*	37.50	37.50
B18	SP2	5fr + 5fr red	*4,000.*	*4,000.*
		Nos. B9-B17 (9)	207.50	207.50

Marriage of Princess Charlotte to Prince Pierre, Comte de Polignac.

Palace Gardens SP3

"The Rock" of Monaco SP4

Bay of Monaco SP5

Prince Louis II — SP6

1937, Apr. **Engr.** ***Perf. 13***

B19	SP3	50c + 50c grn	1.90	1.90
B20	SP4	90c + 90c car	1.90	1.90
B21	SP5	1.50fr + 1.50fr bl	4.00	4.00
B22	SP6	2fr + 2fr vio	5.25	5.25
B23	SP6	5fr + 5fr brn red	52.50	52.50
		Nos. B19-B23 (5)	65.55	65.55

The surtax was used for welfare work.

Pierre and Marie Curie — SP7

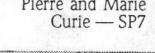

Monaco Hospital, Date Palms — SP8

1938, Nov. 15 ***Perf. 13***

B24	SP7	65c + 25c dp bl grn	4.25	4.25
B25	SP8	1.75fr + 50c dp ultra	5.00	5.00

B24 and B25 exist imperforate.

The surtax was for the International Union for the Control of Cancer.

Lucien — SP9

Honoré II — SP10

Louis I SP11

Charlotte de Gramont SP12

Antoine I — SP13

Marie de Lorraine — SP14

Jacques I SP15

Louise-Hippolyte SP16

Honoré III — SP17

"The Rock," 18th Century SP18

1939, June 26

B26	SP9	5c + 5c brn blk	60	60
B27	SP10	10c + 10c rose vio	60	60
B28	SP11	45c + 15c brt grn	1.10	1.10
B29	SP12	70c + 30c brt red vio	2.75	2.75
B30	SP13	90c + 35c vio	2.75	2.75
B31	SP14	1fr + 1fr ultra	11.00	11.00
B32	SP15	2fr + 2fr brn org	12.00	12.00
B33	SP16	2.25fr + 1.25fr Prus bl	20.00	20.00
B34	SP17	3fr + 3fr dp rose	27.50	27.50
B35	SP18	5fr + 5fr red	55.00	55.00
		Nos. B26-B35 (10)	133.30	133.30
		Set, never hinged	325.00	

Types of Regular Issue, 1939 Surcharged in Red

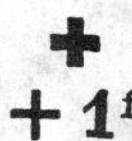

+ 1f

1940, Feb. 10 **Engr.** ***Perf. 13***

B36	A30	20c + 1fr vio	1.65	1.65
B37	A31	25c + 1fr dk grn	1.65	1.65
B38	A32	30c + 1fr brn red	1.65	1.65
B39	A31	40c + 1fr dk bl	1.65	1.65
B40	A33	45c + 1fr rose car	1.65	1.65
B41	A34	50c + 1fr brn	1.65	1.65
B42	A32	60c + 1fr dk grn	1.65	1.65
B43	A35	75c + 1fr brn blk	1.65	1.65
B44	A34	1fr + 1fr scar	1.90	1.90
B45	A31	2fr + 1fr ind	1.90	1.90
B46	A33	2.50fr + 1fr dk grn	5.50	5.50
B47	A35	3fr + 1fr dk bl	6.00	6.00
B48	A30	5fr + 1fr brn blk	7.00	7.00

B49	A33	10fr + 5fr lt bl	11.00	11.00
B50	A32	20fr + 5fr brn vio	12.00	12.00
		Nos. B36-B50 (15)	58.50	58.50
		Set, never hinged	150.00	

The surtax was used to purchase ambulances for the French government.

Catalogue values for unused stamps in this section, from this point to the end of the section, are for Never Hinged items.

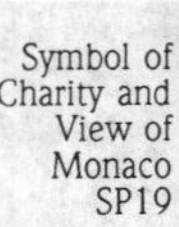

Symbol of Charity and View of Monaco SP19

Symbol of Charity and View of Monaco — SP20

1941, May 15

B51	SP19	25c + 25c brt red vio	1.65	1.65
B52	SP20	50c + 25c dk brn	1.65	1.65
B53	SP20	75c + 50c rose vio	2.00	2.00
B54	SP19	1fr + 1fr dk bl	2.00	2.00
B55	SP20	1.50fr + 1.50fr rose red	3.00	3.00
B56	SP19	2fr + 2fr Prus grn	3.00	3.00
B57	SP20	2.50fr + 2fr brt ultra	3.50	3.50
B58	SP19	3fr + 3fr dl red brn	3.50	3.50
B59	SP20	5fr + 5fr dk bl grn	6.75	6.75
B60	SP19	10fr + 8fr brn blk	12.50	12.50
		Nos. B51-B60 (10)	39.55	39.55

The surtax was for various charities.

Rainier Grimaldi SP21

Charles II SP22

Jeanne Grimaldi SP23

Charles-August Goyon de Matignon SP24

Jacques I SP25

Louise-Hippolyte SP26

Charlotte Grimaldi SP27

Marie-Charles Grimaldi SP28

Honoré III — SP29

Honoré IV — SP30

Honoré V — SP31

Florestan I — SP32

Charles III — SP33

Albert I — SP34

Marie-Victoire — SP35

1942, Dec. 10

B61	SP21	2c + 3c ultra	18	18
B62	SP22	5c + 5c org ver	18	18
B63	SP23	10c + 5c blk	18	18
B64	SP24	20c + 10c brt grn	18	18
B65	SP25	30c + 30c brn vio	18	18
B66	SP26	40c + 40c rose red	18	18
B67	SP27	50c + 50c vio	18	18
B68	SP28	75c + 75c brt red vio	18	18
B69	SP29	1fr + 1fr dk grn	18	18
B70	SP30	1.50fr + 1fr car brn	18	18
B71	SP31	2.50fr + 2.50fr pur	2.25	2.25
B72	SP32	3fr + 3fr turq bl	2.50	2.50
B73	SP33	5fr + 5fr sepia	2.50	2.50
B74	SP34	10fr + 5fr rose lil	2.50	2.50
B75	SP35	20fr + 5fr ultra	2.50	2.50
		Nos. B61-B75 (15)	14.05	14.05

Saint Dévote SP36

Procession SP37

Procession SP38

Church of St. Dévote — SP39

Burning of Symbolic Boat — SP40

Blessing of the Sea — SP41

Church of St. Dévote SP42

Trial of St. Barbara — SP43

Arrival of St. Dévote at Monaco — SP44

1944, Jan. 27 Unwmk. *Perf. 13*

B76	SP36	50c + 50c sepia	22	22
B77	SP37	70c + 80c dp ultra	22	22
B78	SP38	80c + 70c green	18	18
B79	SP39	1fr + 1fr rose vio	18	18
B80	SP40	1.50fr + 1.50fr red	35	35
B81	SP41	2fr + 2fr brn vio	40	40
B82	SP42	5fr + 2fr violet	45	45
B83	SP43	10fr + 40fr royal bl	45	45
B84	SP44	20fr + 60fr chlky bl	4.25	4.25
		Nos. B76-B84 (9)	6.70	6.70

Issued in honor of St. Dévote.

Type SP43 is inscribed "Jugement de Sainte Dévote," but actually shows the trial of St. Barbara in 235 A.D.

Needy Child — SP45

Nurse and Child — SP46

1946, Feb. 18 Engr.

B85	SP45	1fr + 3fr dp bl grn	18	18
B86	SP45	2fr + 4fr rose pink	18	18
B87	SP45	4fr + 6fr dk bl	18	18
B88	SP45	5fr + 40fr dk vio	40	40
B89	SP45	10fr + 60fr brn red	48	48
B90	SP45	15fr + 100fr indigo	65	65
		Nos. B85-B90 (6)	2.07	2.07

The surtax was for child welfare.

1946, Feb. 18

B91	SP46	2fr + 8fr brt bl	15	15

The surtax was used for prevention of tuberculosis.

19th Century Steamer and Map — SP47

1946

B92	SP47	3fr + 2fr deep blue	16	16

Stamp Day, June 23, 1946.

Harbor of Monte Carlo — SP48

1946, Dec. 13

B93	SP48	2fr + 3fr dk bluish grn	38	38

Issued in tribute to the memory of Franklin D. Roosevelt. The surtax was for a fund to erect a monument in his honor.

Souvenir Sheet

SP49

Unwmk.

1947, May 15 Engr. *Imperf.*

B94	SP49	200fr + 300fr dk red & choc	8.75	8.75

25th anniv. of the reign of Prince Louis II.

Prince Charles III — SP50

1948, Mar. 6 *Perf. 14x13*

B95	SP50	6fr + 4fr dk bl grn, *lt bl*	24	24

Issued for Stamp Day, Mar. 6.

Princess Charlotte SP51

Prince Rainier III SP52

Perf. 13½x13, Imperf.

1949, Dec. 27 Engr.

Cross Typo. in Red

B96	SP51	10fr + 5fr red brn	7.25	7.25
B97	SP52	15fr + 5fr brt red	7.25	7.25
B98	SP52	25fr + 5fr dk vio bl	7.25	7.25
B99	SP51	40fr + 5fr dl grn	7.25	7.25
a.		Block of 4, #B96-B99	30.00	30.00

Printed in sheets measuring 151x173mm, perf. and imperf., containing 4 of No. B99a.

The surtax was for the Red Cross.

For surcharges see Nos. 288-291.

Hercules Strangling the Lion of Nemea — SP53

Twelve Labors of Hercules: No. B101, Capturing the Erymanthean boar. No. B102, Killing the Hydra of Lerna. No. B103, Killing Stymphalian birds. No. B104, Hercules and the Ceryneian Hind. No. B105, The Augean Stables. No. B106, Hercules and the Cretan Bull. No. B107, Wild horses of Diomedes. No. B108, Hercules and the Oxen of Geryon. No. B109, Hercules and the Belt of Hippolytus. No. B110, Winning the golden apple of Hesperides. No. B111, Battling Cerberus.

1981-82 Engr. *Perf. 13*

B100	SP53	2.50fr + 50c multi	1.25	1.25
B101	SP53	2.50fr + 50c multi	1.10	1.10
B102	SP53	3.50fr + 50c multi	1.40	1.40
B103	SP53	3.50fr + 50c multi	1.25	1.25

Issue dates: Nos. B100, B102 Nov. 5. Nos. B101, B103 Nov. 8, 1982.

1983, Nov. 9

B104	SP53	2.50fr + 50c multi	1.10	1.10
B105	SP53	3.50fr + 50c multi	1.25	1.25

1984, Nov. 8

B106	SP53	3fr + 50c multi	1.25	1.25
B107	SP53	4fr + 50c multi	1.65	1.65

1985, Nov. 7

B108	SP53	3fr + 70c multi	1.25	48
B109	SP53	4fr + 80c multi	1.65	62

1986, Oct. 28

B110	SP53	3fr + 70c multi	1.25	42
B111	SP53	4fr + 80c multi	1.50	55
		Nos. B100-B111 (12)	15.90	12.32

Surtax on #B100-B111 for the Red Cross.

AIR POST STAMPS

No. 91 Surcharged in Black

1F50

Perf. 14x13½

1933, Aug. 22 Unwmk.

C1	A15	1.50fr on 5fr	20.00	15.00
a.		Imperf., pair	275.00	

Catalogue values for unused stamps in this section, from this point to the end of the section, are for Never Hinged items.

Plane over Monaco — AP1

Plane Propeller and Buildings — AP2

Pegasus — AP3

Sea Gull — AP4

Plane, Globe and Arms of Monaco AP5

1942, Apr. 15 Engr. *Perf. 13*

C2	AP1	5fr bl grn	22	22
C3	AP1	10fr ultra	22	22
C4	AP2	15fr sepia	35	35
C5	AP3	20fr hn brn	55	55
C6	AP4	50fr red vio	2.50	1.40
C7	AP5	100fr red & vio brn	2.25	1.40
		Nos. C2-C7 (6)	6.09	4.14

For surcharges see Nos. CB1-CB5.

Nos. 196-197 Overprinted in Blue

POSTE AÉRIENNE

1946, May 20

C8	A41	50fr dp Prus grn	1.65	1.65
C9	A41	100fr red	2.50	2.55
a.		Inverted overprint	*17,000.*	
b.		Double overprint	*13,000.*	

Douglas DC-3 and Arms — AP6

1946, May 20

C10	AP6	40fr red	80	50
C11	AP6	50fr red brn	90	70
C12	AP6	100fr dp bl grn	1.40	1.25
C13	AP6	200fr violet	2.25	2.00

Exist imperforate. See Nos. C27-C29.

Harbor of Monte Carlo — AP7

Map of Monaco — AP8

1946, Dec. 13

C14	AP7	5fr car rose	38	38
C15	AP8	10fr vio blk	42	42

Issued in tribute to the memory of Franklin D. Roosevelt.

Franklin D. Roosevelt Examining his Stamp Collection AP9

Main Post Office, New York City — AP10

Oceanographic Museum, Monaco — AP11

Harbor of Monte Carlo — AP12

Statue of Liberty and New York City Skyline — AP13

1947, May 15 Unwmk.

C16	AP9	50c violet	32	32
C17	AP10	1.50fr rose vio	42	42
C18	AP11	3fr hn brn	50	50
C19	AP12	10fr dp bl	1.75	1.75
C20	AP13	15fr rose car	2.25	2.25
a.		Strip of 3, #C20, 203, C19	5.50	5.50
		Nos. C16-C20 (5)	5.24	5.24

Issued to commemorate the principality's participation in the Centenary International Philatelic Exhibition, New York, May, 1947.

Crowd Acclaiming Constitution of 1911 — AP14

Anthropological Museum — AP15

Designs: 25fr, Institute of Human Paleontology, Paris. 50fr, Albert I. 100fr, Oceanographic Institute, Paris. 200fr, Albert I medal.

1949, Mar. 5 Engr. *Perf. 13*

C21	AP14	20fr brn red	70	70
C22	AP14	25fr indigo	80	80
C23	AP15	40fr bl grn	1.25	1.25
C24	AP15	50fr blk, brn & grn	1.50	1.50
C25	AP15	100fr cerise	5.50	5.50
C26	AP14	200fr dp org	8.25	8.25
		Nos. C21-C26 (6)	18.00	18.00

Plane-Arms Type of 1946

1949, Mar. 10

C27	AP6	300fr dp ultra & ind	47.50	35.50
C28	AP6	500fr grnsh blk & bl grn	32.50	32.50
C29	AP6	1000fr blk & red vio	52.50	42.50

UPU Type of Regular Issue

1949-50

C30	A56	25fr deep blue	55	55
C31	A56	40fr red brn & sep	85	85
C32	A56	50fr dk grn & ultra	1.25	1.25
C33	A56	100fr dk car & dk grn	2.75	2.75

75th anniv. of the UPU.

Nos. C30 to C33 exist imperforate, also No. C30 in deep plum and violet, imperforate.

Issued: 25fr, Dec. 27; others, Sept. 12, 1950.

Rainier Type of Regular Issue

1950, Apr. 11 Unwmk.

C34	A57	50fr blk & red brn	2.75	2.75
C35	A57	100fr red brn, sep & ind	4.50	4.50

Enthronement of Prince Rainier III.

Runner — AP18

Designs: 50fr, Fencing. 100fr, Target Shooting. 200fr, Olympic Torch.

1953, Feb. 23 *Perf. 11*

C36 AP18 40fr black 8.25 7.00
C37 AP18 50fr brt pur 8.25 7.00
C38 AP18 100fr dk sl grn 11.00 10.00
C39 AP18 200fr dp car 12.00 11.00

Issued to publicize Monaco's participation in the Helsinki Olympic Games.

Dr. Albert Schweitzer and Ogowe River Scene, Gabon — AP19

1955, Jan. 14 *Perf. 13*

C40 AP19 200fr sl blk, dk bl grn & bl 19.00 19.00

Issued to honor Dr. Albert Schweitzer, medical missionary.

Mediterranean Sea Swallows — AP20

Birds: 200fr, Sea gulls. 500fr, Albatross. 1000fr, Great cormorants.

1955-57 *Perf. 11*

C41 AP20 100fr dp bl & ind 21.00 8.00
a. Perf. 13 17.00 8.00
C42 AP20 200fr bl & blk 21.00 8.00
a. Perf. 13 250.00 25.00
C43 AP20 500fr gray & dk grn 30.00 14.00

Perf. 13

C44 AP20 1000fr dk bl grn & blk brn 80.00 32.50
a. Perf. 11 175.00 80.00

Issue dates: Perf. 11, Jan. 14, 1955. Perf. 13, 1957.

"From the Earth to the Moon" and Jules Verne — AP21

1955, June 7 **Unwmk.**

C45 AP21 200fr dp bl & sl 20.00 20.00

50th anniv. of the death of Jules Verne.

Wedding Type of Regular Issue

1956, Apr. 19 **Engr.**

Portraits in Brown

C46 A99 100fr purple 55 55
C47 A99 200fr carmine 90 90
C48 A99 500fr gray vio 2.25 2.25

Wedding of Prince Rainier III to Grace Kelly, Apr. 19, 1956.

Nos. J45 and J54 Surcharged and Overprinted "Poste Aerienne" and bars

1956, Apr. *Perf. 11*

C49 D6 100fr on 20fr 9.25 9.25
a. Double surcharge 425.00 425.00
C50 D7 100fr on 20fr 9.25 9.25
a. Double surcharge 425.00 425.00

See footnote after No. 390.

Basilica of Lourdes — AP23

Design: 200fr, Pope Pius X and underground basilica.

1958, May 15 **Unwmk.** *Perf. 13*

C51 AP23 100fr dk bl, grn & gray 1.50 1.10
C52 AP23 200fr red brn & sep 2.00 1.90

Issued to commemorate the centenary of the apparition of the Virgin Mary at Lourdes.

Prince Rainier III and Princess Grace — AP24

1959, May 16

C53 AP24 300fr dk pur 5.25 4.25
C54 AP24 500fr blue 9.50 6.25

St. Dévote AP25

1960, June 1 **Engr.** *Perf. 13*

C55 AP25 2fr grn, bl & vio 1.40 85
C56 AP24 3fr dk pur 32.50 12.00
C57 AP24 5fr blue 32.50 13.00
C58 AP25 10fr grn & brn 6.50 3.00

1961, June 3

C59 AP25 3fr ultra, grn & gray ol 1.75 1.00
C60 AP25 5fr rose car 3.50 50

Europa Issue, 1962

Mercury over Map of Europe AP26

1962, June 6 **Unwmk.** *Perf. 13*

C61 AP26 2fr dk grn, sl grn & brn 1.25 1.00

Oceanographic Museum, Atom Symbol and Princes Albert I and Rainier III — AP27

1962, June 6

C62 AP27 10fr vio, bl & bis 8.50 7.75

Issued to commemorate the establishment of a scientific research center by agreement with the International Atomic Energy Commission.

Roland Garros AP28

1963, Dec. 12 **Engr.** *Perf. 13*

C63 AP28 2fr dk bl & dk brn 1.25 95

Issued to commemorate the 50th anniversary of the first airplane crossing of the Mediterranean by Roland Garros (1888-1918).

Type of Regular Issue, 1964

Design: 5fr, Convair B-58 Hustler (New York-Paris in 3 hours, 19 minutes, 41 seconds, Maj. William R. Payne, USAF, 1961).

1964, May 22 **Unwmk.** *Perf. 13*

C64 A151 5fr brn, blk & bl 3.50 3.00

Issued to commemorate the 50th anniversary of the first airplane rally of Monte Carlo.

Bobsledding — AP29

1964, Dec. 3 **Engr.** *Perf. 13*

C65 AP29 5fr multi 2.75 2.75

Issued to commemorate the 9th Winter Olympic Games, Innsbruck, Austria, Jan. 29-Feb. 9, 1964.

ITU Type of Regular Issue

Design: 10fr, ITU Emblem and Monte Carlo television station on Mount Agel, vert.

1965, May 17 **Engr.** *Perf. 13*

C66 A161 10fr bis brn, sl grn & bl 4.25 4.25

Princess Grace with Albert Alexander Louis, Caroline and Stephanie — AP30

1966, Feb. 1 **Engr.** *Perf. 13*

C67 AP30 3fr pur, red brn & Prus bl 2.25 1.75

Issued to commemorate the birth of Princess Stephanie, Feb. 1, 1965.

Opera House Interior AP31

1966, June 1 **Engr.** *Perf. 13*

C68 AP31 5fr Prus bl, bis & dk car rose 2.50 2.50

Centenary of founding of Monte Carlo.

Prince Rainier III and Princess Grace — AP32

1966-71 **Engr.** *Perf. 13*

C69 AP32 2fr pink & sl 1.00 40
C70 AP32 3fr emer & sl 2.00 65
C71 AP32 5fr lt bl & sl 2.50 1.10
C72 AP32 10fr lem & sl ('67) 4.00 2.75
C72A AP32 20fr org & brn ('71) 30.00 15.00
Nos. C69-C72A (5) 39.50 19.90

Issue dates: 10fr, Dec. 7, 1967; 20fr, Sept. 6, 1971. Others, Dec. 12, 1966.

Panhard-Phenix, 1895 — AP33

1967, Apr. 28 **Engr.** *Perf. 13*

C73 AP33 3fr Prus bl & blk 2.25 2.00

25th Grand Prix of Monaco.

Olympic Games Type of Regular Issue

1968, Apr. 29 **Engr.** *Perf. 13*

C74 A183 3fr Field hockey 2.00 1.75

Berlioz Monument, Monte Carlo — AP34

1969, Apr. 26 Engr. *Perf. 13*

C75	AP34	2fr grn, blk & ultra	1.25	1.10

Hector Berlioz (1803-69), French composer.

Napoleon, by Paul Delaroche AP35

1969, Apr. 26 Photo. *Perf. 12x13*

C76	AP35	3fr multi	1.50	1.25

Bicentenary of birth of Napoleon I.

Horses, Prehistoric Drawing from Lascaux Cave — AP36

1970, Dec. 15 Engr. *Perf. 13*

C77	AP36	3fr multi	2.25	2.00

Nativity Type of Regular Issue

Design: 3fr, Nativity, Flemish School, 15th century, vert.

1973, Nov. 12 Engr. *Perf. 12x13*

C78	A243	3fr Prus grn	2.75	2.00

Prince Rainier III — AP37

1974, Dec. 23 Engr. *Perf. 12½x13*

C81	AP37	10fr dk pur	3.00	2.25
C82	AP37	15fr hn brn	4.75	3.50
C83	AP37	20fr ultra	6.75	4.50

Prince Rainier and Hereditary Prince Albert — AP38

1982-84 Engr. *Perf. 13x13½*

C84	AP38	5fr dp vio	1.40	75
C85	AP38	10fr red	2.75	1.50
C86	AP38	15fr dk bl grn	4.00	2.25
C87	AP38	20fr brt bl	5.00	3.00
C88	AP38	30fr brn ('84)	7.75	4.25
		Nos. C84-C88 (5)	20.90	11.75

AIR POST SEMI-POSTAL STAMPS

Catalogue values for unused stamps in this section are for Never Hinged items.

Types of 1942 Air Post Stamps Surcharged with New Values and Bars

Unwmk.

1945, Mar. 27 Engr. *Perf. 13*

CB1	AP1	1fr + 4fr on 10fr rose red	25	25
CB2	AP2	1fr + 4fr on 15fr red brown	25	25
CB3	AP3	1fr + 4fr on 20fr sep	25	25
CB4	AP4	1fr + 4fr on 50fr ultra	25	25
CB5	AP5	1fr + 4fr on 100fr brt red violet	25	25
		Nos. CB1-CB5 (5)	1.25	1.25

Surtax for the benefit of prisoners of war.

Franklin D. Roosevelt SPAP1

1946, Dec. 13

CB6	SPAP1	15fr + 10fr red	80	70

Issued in tribute to the memory of Franklin D. Roosevelt. The surtax was for a fund to erect a monument in his honor.

Rowing SPAP2

Sailboat Race SPAP3

1948, July

CB7	SPAP2	5fr +5fr shown	8.00	8.00
CB8	SPAP2	6fr +9fr Skiing	11.50	11.50
CB9	SPAP2	10fr +15fr Tennis	16.00	16.00
CB10	SPAP3	15fr +25fr shown	24.00	24.00

Issued to publicize Monaco's participation in the 1948 Olympic Games held at Wembley, England, during July and August.

Salmacis Nymph SPAP4

Designs similar to regular issue.

1948, July

CB11	A50	5fr + 5fr blk bl	8.00	8.00
CB12	A51	6fr + 9fr dk grn	9.50	9.50
CB13	A52	10fr + 15fr crim	10.00	10.00
CB14	SPAP4	15fr + 25fr red brn	11.00	11.00

Franois J. Bosio (1769-1845), sculptor.

POSTAGE DUE STAMPS

D1

Prince Albert I — D2

Perf. 14x13½

1905-43 Unwmk. Typo.

J1	D1	1c olive green	52	52
J2	D1	5c green	65	52
J3	D1	10c rose	52	52
J4	D1	10c brn ('09)	250.00	72.50
J5	D1	15c vio brn, *straw*	1.90	1.10
J6	D1	20c bis brn, *buff* ('26)	18	18
J7	D1	30c blue	52	52
J8	D1	40c red vio ('26)	18	18
J9	D1	50c brn, *org*	4.00	2.25
J10	D1	50c bl grn ('27)	18	18
J11	D1	60c gray blk ('26)	55	55
J12	D1	60c brt vio ('34)	8.50	8.50
J13	D1	1fr red brn, *straw* ('26)	15	15
J14	D1	2fr red org ('27)	38	38
J15	D1	3fr mag ('27)	38	38
J15A	D1	5fr ultra ('43)	52	52
		Nos. J1-J15A (16)	269.13	88.95

For surcharge see No. J27.

1910

J16	D2	1c olive green	22	22
J17	D2	10c light violet	32	32
J18	D2	30c bister	140.00	110.00

In January, 1917, regular postage stamps overprinted "T" in a triangle were used as postage due stamps.

Nos. J17 and J18 Surcharged **20c.**

1918

J19	D2	20c on 10c lt vio	2.00	2.00
a.		Double surcharge	*725.00*	
J20	D2	40c on 30c bister	2.00	2.00

D3

1925-32

J21	D3	1c gray green	20	20
J22	D3	10c violet	20	20
J23	D3	30c bister	30	30
J24	D3	60c red	40	40
J25	D3	1fr lt bl ('32)	47.50	32.50
J26	D3	2fr dull red ('32)	72.50	47.50
		Nos. J21-J26 (6)	121.10	81.10

Nos. J25 and J26 have the numerals of value double-lined.

"Recouvrements" stamps were used to recover charges due on undelivered or refused mail which was returned to the sender.

No. J9 Surcharged **1 franc à percevoir**

1925

J27	D1	1fr on 50c brn, *org*	50	40
a.		Double surcharge	*650.00*	

Catalogue values for unused stamps in this section, from this point to the end of the section, are for Never Hinged items.

D4

D5

1946-57 Engr. *Perf. 14x13, 13*

J28	D4	10c sepia	18	18
J29	D4	30c dk vio	18	18
J30	D4	50c dp bl	18	18
J31	D4	1fr dk grn	18	18
J32	D4	2fr yel brn	18	18
J33	D4	3fr brt red vio	25	25
J34	D4	4fr carmine	38	38
J35	D5	5fr chocolate	30	30
J36	D5	10fr dp ultra	55	55
J37	D5	20fr grnsh bl	60	60
J38	D5	50fr red vio & red ('50)	50.00	50.00
J38A	D5	100fr dk grn & red ('57)	8.75	8.75
		Nos. J28-J38A (12)	61.73	61.73

Sailing Vessel — D6

Early Postal Transport: 1fr, Carrier pigeons. 3fr, Old railroad engine. 4fr, Old monoplane. 5fr, Steam automobile. 10fr, daVinci's flying machine. 20fr, Balloon. 50fr, Post rider. 100fr, Old mail coach.

1953-54 *Perf. 11*

J39	D6	1fr dk grn & brt red ('54)	15	15
J40	D6	2fr dp ultra & bl grn	15	15
J41	D6	3fr Prus grn & brn lake	16	16
J42	D6	4fr dk brn & Prus grn	26	26
J43	D6	5fr ultra & pur	65	65
J44	D6	10fr dp ultra & dk bl	6.75	6.75
J45	D6	20fr ind & pur	2.25	2.25
J46	D6	50fr red & dk brn	6.00	6.00
J47	D6	100fr vio brn & dp grn	12.00	12.00

The two types of each value in Nos. J39-J56 (early and modern transportation) were printed tête bêche, se-tenant at the base.

S. S. United States D7

Modern Postal Transport: 1fr, Sikorsky S-51 helicopter. 3fr, Modern locomotive. 4fr, Comet airliner. 5fr, Sabre sports car. 10fr, Rocket. 20fr, Graf Zeppelin. 50fr, Motorcyclist. 100fr, Railroad mail car.

J48	D7	1fr brt red & dk grn ('54)	15	15
J49	D7	2fr bl grn & dp ultra	15	15
J50	D7	3fr brn lake & Prus grn	16	16
J51	D7	4fr Prus grn & dk brn	26	26
J52	D7	5fr pur & ultra	65	65
J53	D7	10fr dk bl & dp ultra	6.75	6.75
J54	D7	20fr pur & ind	2.25	2.25
J55	D7	50fr dk brn & red	6.00	6.00
J56	D7	100fr dp grn & vio brn	12.00	12.00
		Nos. J39-J56 (18)	56.74	56.74

See note following No. J47.

For overprints see Nos. 371-390.

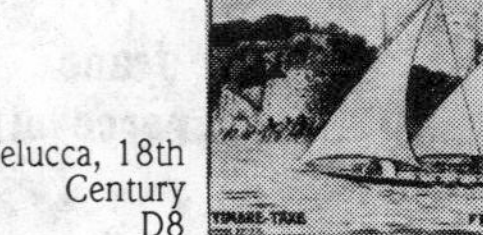

Felucca, 18th Century
D8

Designs: 2c, Paddle steamer La Palmaria, 19th century. 5c, Arrival of first train. 10c, Armed messenger, 15th-16th century. 20c, Monaco-Nice courier, 18th century. 30c, "Charles III," 1866. 50c, Courier on horseback, 17th century. 1fr, Diligence, 19th century.

1960-69 Engr. *Perf. 13*

J57	D8	1c	bl grn, bis brn & bl	40	40
J58	D8	2c	sl grn, sep & ultra	15	15
J59	D8	5c	grnsh bl, gray & red brn	15	15
J60	D8	10c	vio bl, blk & grn	25	25
J61	D8	20c	bl, brn & grn	90	90
J62	D8	30c	brn, brt grn & brt bl ('69)	50	50
J63	D8	50c	dk bl, brn & sl grn	90	90
J64	D8	1fr	sl grn, bl & brn	1.25	1.25
			Nos. J57-J64 (8)	4.50	4.50

Knight in Armor
D9

1980-83 Engr. *Perf. 13*

J65	D9	5c	red & gray	15	15
J66	D9	10c	salmon & red	15	15
J67	D9	15c	vio & red	15	15
J68	D9	20c	lt grn & red	15	15
J69	D9	30c	bl & red	15	15
J70	D9	40c	lt brn & red	16	16
J71	D9	50c	lilac & red	16	16
J72	D9	1fr	black & blue	38	38
J73	D9	2fr	dk brn & org ('82)	70	70
J74	D9	3fr	sl bl & rose car ('83)	1.10	1.10
J75	D9	4fr	red & dk grn ('82)	1.25	1.25
J76	D9	5fr	mag & brn ('83)	2.00	2.00
			Nos. J65-J76 (12)	6.50	6.50

Nos. J65-J76 printed in horizontal rows with princely coat of arms between stamps. Sold in strips of 3 only.

Issue dates: Nos. J65-J72, Feb. 8; Nos. J73, J75, Feb. 15; Nos. J74, J76, Jan. 3.

Natl. Coat of Arms — D10

1985-86 Photo. *Perf. 13x12½*

J77	D10	5c	multi	15	15
J78	D10	10c	multi	15	15
J79	D10	15c	multi	15	15
J80	D10	20c	multi	15	15
J81	D10	30c	multi	15	15
J82	D10	40c	multi	15	15
J83	D10	50c	multi ('86)	15	15
J84	D10	1fr	multi ('86)	30	15
J85	D10	2fr	multi ('86)	60	30
J86	D10	3fr	multi	70	35
J87	D10	4fr	multi ('86)	1.25	60
J88	D10	5fr	multi	1.25	60
			Set value	4.40	2.30

See Nos. 1608-1609.

MONGOLIA

Mongolian People's Republic
(Outer Mongolia)

LOCATION — Central Asia, bounded on the north by Siberia, on the west by Sinkiang, on the south and east by China proper and Manchuria
GOVT. — Republic
AREA — 604,250 sq. mi.
POP. — 1,820,000 (est. 1984)
CAPITAL — Ulan Bator

Outer Mongolia, which had long been under Russian influence although nominally a dependency of China, voted at a plebescite on October 20, 1945, to sever all ties with China and become an independent nation. See Tannu Tuva.

100 Cents = 1 Dollar
100 Mung = 1 Tugrik (1926)

Catalogue values for unused stamps in this country are for Never Hinged items, beginning with Scott 149 in the regular postage section, Scott B1 in the semi-postal section, Scott C1 in the airpost section, and Scott CB1 in the airpost semi-postal section.

Watermark

Wmk. 170- Greek Border and Rosettes

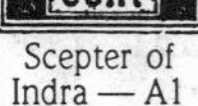

Scepter of Indra — A1

A2

1924 Litho. Unwmk. *Perf. 10, 13½*
Surface Tinted Paper

1	A1	1c	multi, *bister*	2.75	2.50
2	A1	2c	multi, *brnsh*	2.50	2.50
a.			Perf. 13½	15.00	13.00
3	A1	5c	multi	19.00	13.00
a.			Perf. 10	19.00	17.00
4	A1	10c	multi, *gray bl*	4.50	3.75
a.			Perf. 10	5.50	4.00
5	A1	20c	multi, *gray*	6.50	5.50
6	A1	50c	multi, *salmon*	19.00	12.00
7	A1	$1	multi, *yellow*	25.00	25.00
b.			Perf. 10	30.00	30.00
			Nos. 1-7 (7)	79.25	64.25

These stamps vary in size from 19x25mm (1c) to 30x39mm ($1). They also differ in details of the design.

Errors of perforating and printing exist.

Some quantities of Nos. 1-2, 4-7 were defaced with horizontal perforation across the center.

The 5c exists perf 11½.

Revenue Stamps Handstamp Overprinted "POSTAGE" in Violet

Sizes: 1c to 20c: 22x36mm
50c, $1: 26x43½mm
$5: 30x45½mm

1926 *Perf. 11*

16	A2	1c	blue	5.00	5.00
17	A2	2c	orange	5.00	5.00
18	A2	5c	plum	5.00	5.00
19	A2	10c	green	5.00	5.00
20	A2	20c	yel brn	5.00	5.00
21	A2	50c	brn & ol grn	*85.00*	*85.00*
22	A2	$1	brn & salmon	*275.00*	*275.00*
23	A2	$5	red, yel & gray	*175.00*	*175.00*

Black Overprint

16a	A2	1c	blue	8.75	8.75
17a	A2	2c	orange	8.75	8.75
18a	A2	5c	plum	8.75	8.75
19a	A2	10c	green	8.75	8.75
20a	A2	20c	yellow brown	8.75	8.75
21a	A2	50c	brn & olive grn	*125.00*	*125.00*
22a	A2	$1	brown & salmon	*300.00*	*300.00*
23a	A2	$5	red, yellow & gray		
			Nos. 16a-22a (7)	*468.75*	*468.75*

Red Overprint

16b	A2	1c	blue
17b	A2	2c	orange
18b	A2	5c	plum
19b	A2	10c	green
20b	A2	20c	yellow brown

The preceding handstamped overprints may be found inverted, double, etc. Counterfeits abound.

For overprints and surcharges see #48-61.

Yin Yang and other Symbols
A3 A4

TYPE I - The pearl above the crescent is solid. The devices in the middle of the stamp are not outlined.

TYPE II - The pearl is open. The devices and panels are all outlined in black.

1926-29 *Perf. 11*

Type I

Size: 22x28mm

32	A3	5m	lil & blk	2.50	2.50
33	A3	20m	bl & blk	2.00	2.00

Type II

Size: 22x29mm

34	A3	1m	yel & blk	60	60
35	A3	2m	brn org & blk	75	75
36	A3	5m	lil & blk	1.25	1.25
37	A3	10m	lt bl & blk	75	60
a.			Imperf.		
38	A3	20m	dp bl & blk ('29)	5.50	4.75
a.			Imperf.		
39	A3	25m	yel grn & blk	2.50	2.50
a.			Imperf.		

Size: 26x34mm

40	A3	40m	lem & blk	2.50	2.50
41	A3	50m	buff & blk	3.00	2.75

Size: 28x37mm

42	A4	1t	brn, grn & blk	11.00	11.00
43	A4	3t	red, yel & blk	25.00	25.00
44	A4	5t	brn vio, rose & blk	50.00	45.00
			Nos. 32-44 (13)	107.35	101.20

In 1929 a change was made in the perforating machine. Every fourth pin was removed, which left the perforation holes in groups of three with blank spaces between the groups. Nos. 38 and 44A have only this interrupted perforation. Nos. 37 and 39 are found with both perforations.

For overprints and surcharges see #45-47.

Yin Yang and other Symbols — A5

1929

44A	A5	5m	lil & blk	6.00	6.00

See note after No. 44.

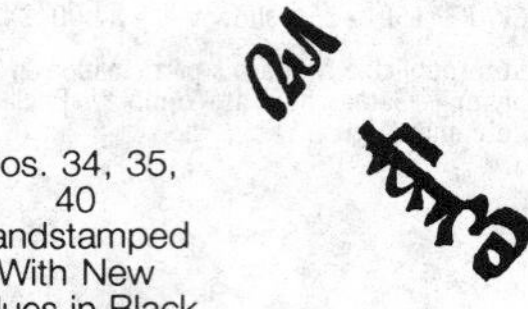

Nos. 34, 35, 40 Handstamped With New Values in Black

1930

45	A3	10m	on 1m	12.50	10.00
46	A3	20m	on 2m	12.50	10.00
47	A3	25m	on 40m	17.50	14.00

Symbols of Government
A6 A7

Violet Overprint, Handstamped

1931

48	A6	1c	blue	5.50	5.50
a.			Blue overprint	8.00	5.50
49	A6	2c	orange	8.00	5.50
50	A6	5c	brn vio	8.00	6.50
a.			Blue overprint	8.50	6.00
51	A6	10c	green	8.50	6.00
a.			Blue overprint	11.00	9.50
52	A6	20c	bis brn	11.00	6.00
53	A6	50c	brn & ol yel	65.00	50.00
54	A6	$1	brn & salmon	85.00	67.50
			Nos. 48-54 (7)	191.00	147.00

Revenue Stamps Surcharged in Black, Red or Blue

1931

59	A7	5m	on 5c brn vio (Bk)	12.50	6.00
a.			Inverted surcharge		17.50
b.			Imperf., pair	22.00	22.00
60	A7	10m	on 10c grn (R)	25.00	12.50
a.			Inverted surcharge	15.00	12.50
b.			Imperf., pair	35.00	35.00
61	A7	20m	on 20c bis brn (Bl)	32.50	19.00
a.			Inverted surcharge		18.00
b.			Imperf., pair	55.00	55.00

On Nos. 59-61, "Postage" is always diagonal, and may read up or down.

Weaver at Loom — A8

Telegrapher
A9

Sukhe Bator
A10

Lake and Mountains — A11

Designs: 5m, Mongol at lathe. 10m, Government building, Ulan Bator. 15m, Young Mongolian revolutionary. 20m, Studying Latin alphabet. 25m, Mongolian soldier. 50m, Monument to Sukhe Bator. 3t, Sheep shearing. 5t, Camel caravan. 10t, Chasing wild horses.

Perf. 12½x12

1932 Photo. Wmk. 170

62	A8	1m	brown	40	35
63	A9	2m	red vio	40	35
64	A8	5m	indigo	35	28
65	A8	10m	dull green	35	28
66	A9	15m	dp brn	35	28
67	A9	20m	rose red	35	28
68	A9	25m	dull vio	35	28
69	A10	40m	gray blk	38	35
70	A10	50m	dull blue	38	38

Perf. 11x12

71	A11	1t	dull grn	40	40
72	A11	3t	dull vio	1.25	1.25
73	A11	5t	brown	3.50	3.50
74	A11	10t	ultra	7.00	7.00
			Nos. 62-74 (13)	15.46	14.98

Used values are for c-t-o's.

Marshal Kharloin Choibalsan — A21

1945 Unwmk. Perf. 12½

83	A21	1t blk brn	2.75	2.75

Choibalsan — A22

Victory Medal — A24

Sukhe Bator and Choibalsan A23

Designs: #86, Choibalsan as young man. #87, Choibalsan University, Ulan Bator. 1t, Anniversary medal. 2t, Sukhe Bator.

1946, July Photo. Perf. 12½

84	A22	30m olive bister	1.40	1.40
85	A23	50m dl pur	2.00	2.00
86	A24	60m black	2.00	2.00
87	A23	60m org brn	2.50	2.50
88	A24	80m dk org brn	2.75	2.75
89	A24	1t indigo	5.75	5.75
90	A24	2t dp brn	7.50	7.50
		Nos. 84-90 (7)	23.90	23.90

25th anniversary of independence.

New Housing — A25

School Children — A26

Mongolian Arms and Flag — A27

Sukhe Bator — A28

Flags of Communist Countries — A29

Lenin — A30

Designs: 15m, Altai Hotel. No. 94, State Store. No. 95, Like 30m. 25m, University. 40m, National Theater. 50m, Pedagogical Institute. 60m, Sukhe Bator monument. Sizes of type A25: Nos. 91, 93-94, 98-99, 32½x22mm. 25m, 55x26mm.

1951

91	A25	5m brn, *pink*	80	80
92	A26	10m dp bl, *pink*	1.00	1.00
93	A25	15m grn, *grnsh*	1.00	1.00
94	A25	20m red org	1.40	1.40
95	A27	20m dk bl & multi	1.40	1.40
96	A25	25m bl, *bluish*	1.50	1.50
97	A27	30m red & multi	1.50	1.50
98	A25	40m pur, *pink*	1.50	1.50
99	A25	50m brn, *grysh*	5.50	5.50
100	A28	60m brn blk	5.50	5.50
101	A29	1t multi	5.50	5.50
102	A28	2t dk brn & org brn	6.75	6.75
103	A30	3t multi	14.00	14.00
		Nos. 91-103 (13)	47.35	47.35

30th anniversary of independence.

Choibalsan A31

Choibalsan and Farmer A32

Choibalsan and Sukhe Bator — A33

Designs: No. 108, 30m, Choibalsan and factory worker (47x33mm). 50m, Choibalsan and Young Pioneer. No. 112, 2t, Choibalsan in uniform.

1953, Dec. Photo. Perf. 12½

104	A31	15m dl bl	1.00	1.00
105	A32	15m dl grn	1.00	1.00
106	A31	20m dl grn	1.40	1.40
107	A32	20m sepia	1.50	1.50
108	A32	20m vio bl	1.50	1.50
109	A32	30m dk brn	1.75	1.75
110	A33	50m org brn	2.00	2.00
111	A33	1t car rose	2.00	2.00
112	A31	1t sepia	2.00	2.00
113	A31	2t red	2.00	2.00
114	A33	3t sepia	2.75	2.75
115	A33	5t red	4.00	4.00
		Nos. 104-115 (12)	22.90	22.90

First anniversary of death of Marshal Karloin Choibalsan (1895-1952).

Arms of Mongolia — A34

1954, Mar. Litho. Perf. 12½

116	A34	10m carmine	2.00	1.75
117	A34	20m carmine	4.00	2.75
118	A34	30m carmine	2.50	1.90
119	A34	40m carmine	3.50	1.75
120	A34	60m carmine	3.00	1.75
		Nos. 116-120 (5)	15.00	9.90

Sukhe Bator and Choibalsan — A35

Lake Hubsugul — A36

Guard with Dog — A37

Designs: No. 122, Lenin Statue, Ulan Bator. 50m, Choibalsan University. 1t, Arms and flag of Mongolia.

1955, June Photo. Perf. 12½

121	A35	30m green	20	15
122	A35	30m org ver	28	15
123	A36	30m brt bl	20	15
124	A37	40m dp red lil	35	15
125	A36	50m ocher	70	30
126	A37	1t red & multi	1.50	1.00
		Nos. 121-126 (6)	3.23	
		Set value		1.65

35th anniversary of independence.

1955

Design: 2t, Lenin.

127	A35	2t brt bl	2.50	1.25

85th anniversary of birth of Lenin.

Flags of Communist Countries A38

Arms of Mongolia A39

1955

128	A38	60m blue & multi	1.00	55

Fight for peace.

1956 Photo. Perf. 12½

129	A39	20m dark brown	18	15
130	A39	30m dark olive	20	15
131	A39	40m bright blue	28	20
132	A39	60m blue green	40	28
133	A39	1t deep carmine	70	28
		Nos. 129-133 (5)	1.76	1.06

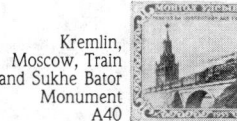

Kremlin, Moscow, Train and Sukhe Bator Monument A40

Design: 2t, Flags of Mongolia and USSR.

1956

134	A40	1t dk bl & multi	1.40	70
135	A40	2t red & multi	2.75	1.00

Establishment of railroad connection between Moscow and Ulan Bator.

Mongolian Arms and Flag — A41

Hunter with Golden Eagle — A42

Wrestlers — A43

Designs: No. 138, 3 children (33x26½mm).

1956, July Typo. Perf. 9

136	A41	30m blue	2.00	2.00
137	A42	30m pale brn	8.00	8.00
138	A42	60m orange	9.00	8.00
139	A43	60m yel grn	9.00	8.00

35th anniversary of independence.

Types A41 and A43 without "XXXV"

1958

140	A41	20m red	50	50
141	A43	50m brn, *pink*	2.75	2.75

Nos. 140-143 were issued both with and without gum.

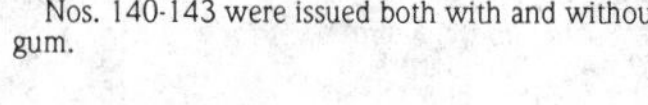

Poster — A44

Globe and Dove — A45

1958, Mar. Litho. Perf. 9

142	A44	30m maroon & sal	2.25	1.40

13th Congress of Mongolian People's Party.

1958, May

143	A45	60m deep blue	2.00	85

4th Congress of International Democratic Women's Federation, Vienna, June, 1958. Nos. 142-143 exist imperf.

Yak — A46

Designs: No. 144, Pelicans, vert. No. 145, Siberian ibex, vert. No. 147, Yak. No. 148, Camels.

1958, July Typo. Perf. 9

144	A46	30m lt bl	70	35
145	A46	30m brt grn	70	35
146	A46	60m orange	1.00	50

Mongolia stamps through 1932 can be mounted in Scott's Soviet Republics Part I Album.

147 A46	1t blue		2.50	1.00
148 A46	1t rose		2.50	1.00
	Nos. 144-148 (5)		7.40	3.20

Shades exist.

Canceled to Order

Some quantity of all issues not printed by the State Printing Works, Ulan Bator, except Nos. 296-303, were canceled to order.

Used values are for c-t-o. Postally used specimens sell for considerably more.

Catalogue values for unused stamps in this section, from this point to the end of the section, are for Never Hinged items.

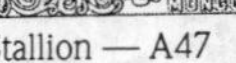

Stallion — A47

Holy Flame (Tulaga) — A48

Designs: 5m, 40m, Goat. 10m, 30m, Ram. 15m, 60m, Stallion. 20m, 50m, Bull. 25m, 1t, Bactrian camel.

Perf. 10½x11½

1958, Nov. 11 **Litho.**

149 A47	5m	yel & brn	15	15
150 A47	10m	lt grn & brn	15	15
151 A47	15m	lil & brn	15	15
152 A47	20m	lt bl & brn	15	15
153 A47	25m	rose & brn	15	15
154 A47	30m	lil & pur	15	15
155 A47	40m	lt & dk grn	15	15
156 A47	50m	sal & brn	18	15
157 A47	60m	lt bl & ind	20	15
158 A47	1t	yel & brn	50	20
		Set value	1.40	75

1959, May 1 **Litho.** ***Perf. 9***

159 A48	1t	multi	1.75	70

See No. C36.

Archer — A49

Mongol Sports: 5m, Taming wild horse. 10m, Wrestlers. 15m, Horseback riding. 25m, Horse race. 30m, Archers. 70m, Hunting wild horse. 80m, Proclaiming a champion.

1959, June 6 **Photo.** ***Perf. 11***

160 A49	5m	multi	15	15
161 A49	10m	multi	15	15
162 A49	15m	multi	15	15
163 A49	20m	multi	15	15
164 A49	25m	multi	18	15
165 A49	30m	multi	18	15
166 A49	70m	multi	35	15
167 A49	80m	multi	55	24
		Set value	1.55	75

Young Wrestlers — A50

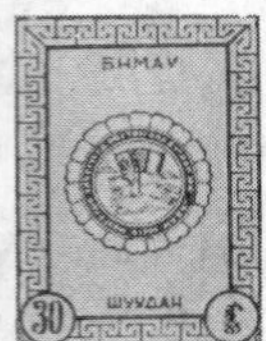

Youth Festival Emblem — A51

Designs: 5m, Young musician, horiz. 20m, Boy on horseback. 25m, Two opera singers. 40m, Young Pioneers with flags, horiz.

Photo.; Litho. (30m)

1959, July ***Perf. 12, 11 (30m)***

168 A50	5m	vio bl & rose car	15	15
169 A50	10m	bl grn & brn	15	15
170 A50	20m	claret & grn	15	15
171 A50	25m	grn & vio bl	18	15
172 A51	30m	lil & lt bl	18	15
173 A50	40m	grn & pur	35	20
		Set value	1.00	62

Mongolian Youth Festival.

The 30m was printed by State Printing Works, Ulan Bator.

Issue dates: 30m, July 11; others July 10.

"Mongol" in Stylized Uighur Script — A52

"Mongol" in Various Scripts: 40m, Soyombo. 50m, Kalmuck. 60m, Square (Pagspa). 1t, Cyrillic. Printed by State Printing Works, Ulan Bator.

1959, Sept. 1 **Litho.** ***Perf. 11***

Size: 29x42½mm

174 A52	30m	blk & multi	2.00	2.00
175 A52	40m	blk & multi	2.00	2.00
176 A52	50m	blk & multi	2.75	2.75
177 A52	60m	blk & multi	4.00	4.00

Size: 21x31mm

Perf. 9

178 A52	1t	blk & multi	8.50	8.50
		Nos. 174-178 (5)	19.25	19.25

1st Intl. Mongolian Language Congress.

Battle Emblem A53

Battle Monument A54

1959, Sept. 15 **Photo.** ***Perf. 12½x12***

179 A53	40m	yel, brn & car	24	15
180 A54	50m	multi	28	15
		Set value		20

Battle of Ha-lo-hsin (Khalka) River, 20th anniversary.

Congress Emblem — A55

Printed by State Printing Works, Ulan Bator.

1959, Dec. **Litho.** ***Perf. 11***

181 A55	30m	green	1.40	1.40

2nd meeting of rural economy cooperatives of Mongolia.

Sable — A56

Pheasants — A57

1959, Dec. 21 **Photo.** ***Perf. 15, 11x13***

182 A56	5m	shown	15	15
183 A57	10m	shown	15	15
184 A56	15m	Muskrat	15	15
185 A57	20m	Otter	15	15
186 A56	30m	Argali	16	15
187 A57	50m	Saigas	35	20
188 A57	1t	Musk deer	70	38
		Set value	1.50	90

Lunik 3 — A58

Design: 50m, Lunik 3 with path around moon, horiz.

1959, Dec. 30 **Photo.** ***Perf. 12***

189 A58	30m	vio & yel grn	40	18
190 A58	50m	red, dk bl & grn	60	20

Lunik 3 Russian moon mission, Oct. 7, 1959.

Motherhood Badge — A59

Flower Emblem — A60

1960, Mar. 8 ***Perf. 11, 12½x11½***

191 A59	40m	bl & bis	40	15
192 A60	50m	bl, grn & yel	55	20

International Women's Day.

Lenin — A61

Jacob's-ladder — A62

1960, Apr. 22 **Photo.** ***Perf. 11½x12***

193 A61	40m	dk rose car	35	15
194 A61	50m	rose vio	48	15
		Set value		24

90th anniversary, birth of Lenin.

1960, May 31 ***Perf. 11½x12***

195 A62	5m	Larkspur	15	15
196 A62	10m	Tulips	15	15
197 A62	15m	shown	15	15
198 A62	20m	Globeflowers	15	15
199 A62	30m	Bellflowers	15	15
200 A62	40m	Parnassia	15	15
201 A62	50m	Geranium	20	18
202 A62	1t	Begonia	40	30
		Set value	1.05	85

For overprints see Nos. 296-303.

Equestrian — A63

Running — A64

1960, Aug. 1 ***Perf. 15, 11***

203 A63	5m	shown	15	15
204 A64	10m	shown	15	15
205 A63	15m	Diving	15	15
206 A64	20m	Wrestling	15	15
207 A63	30m	Hurdling	18	15
208 A64	50m	Gymnastics, women's	28	15
209 A63	70m	High jump	35	15
210 A64	1t	Discus, women's	70	28
		Nos. 203-210 (8)	2.11	
		Set value		80

17th Olympic Games, Rome, Aug. 25-Sept. 11.

Red Cross A65

1960, Aug. 29 *Perf. 11*
211 A65 20m bl, red & yel 24 15

Newspaper "Unen" (Truth) A66

1960, Dec. 19 *Perf. 12x11½*
212 A66 20m red, yel & sl grn 15 82
213 A66 30m grn, yel & red 20 15

40th anniversary of Mongolian press.

Golden Orioles — A67

Songbirds: 5m, Rose-colored starling. 10m, Hoopoe. 20m, Black-billed capercaillie. 50m, Oriental broad-billed roller. 70m, Tibetan sandgrouse. 1t, Mandarin duck. (Triangle points down on 5m, 50m, 70m, 1t.)

1961, Jan. 3 *Perf. 11*
214 A67 5m multi 15 15
215 A67 10m multi 15 15
216 A67 15m multi 15 15
217 A67 20m multi 15 15
218 A67 50m multi 28 15
219 A67 70m multi 40 18
220 A67 1t multi 60 24
Nos. 214-220 (7) 1.88
Set value 80

Federation Emblem A68

Design: 30m, Worker and emblem, vert.

Perf. 11½x12, 12x11½
1961, Jan. 29 **Photo.**
221 A68 30m dk gray & rose 15 15
222 A68 50m ultra & red 20 15
Set value 18

World Federation of Trade Unions, 15th anniv.

Patrice Lumumba (1925-1961), Premier of Congo — A69

1961, Apr. 8 *Perf. 11½x12*
223 A69 30m brown 85 28
224 A69 50m vio gray 1.75 40

Bridge — A70

Designs: 10m, Shoemaker. 15m, Department Store, Ulan Bator. 20m, Government building. 30m, State Theater, Ulan Bator. 50m, Machinist. 1t, Modern and old buildings.

1961, Apr. 30 *Perf. 11½x12, 15*
Sizes: 31½x21mm, 59x20mm (20m)
225 A70 5m emerald 15 15
226 A70 10m blue 15 15
227 A70 15m rose red 15 15
228 A70 20m brown 18 15
229 A70 30m blue 28 18
230 A70 50m ol grn 35 24
231 A70 1t violet 50 35
Nos. 225-231 (7) 1.76
Set value 1.05

40th anniversary of independence; modernization of Mongolia.

Yuri Gagarin and Globe — A71

Designs: 20m, Gagarin with rocket, vert. 50m, Gagarin making parachute descent, vert. 1t, Gagarin wearing helmet, globe.

1961, May 31 *Perf. 15*
232 A71 20m multi 20 15
233 A71 30m multi 28 15
234 A71 50m multi 50 18
235 A71 1t multi 70 45

Yuri A. Gagarin, first man in space, Apr. 12, 1961.

Postman on Reindeer A72

Designs: 15m, No. 241a, Postman on camel. 10m, 20m, Postman with yaks. 25m, No. 241c, Postman with ship. 30m, 50m, Diesel train.

1961, June 5 *Perf. 15*
236 A72 5m multi 15 15
237 A72 15m multi 15 15
238 A72 20m multi 15 15
239 A72 25m multi 18 15
240 A72 30m multi 24 18
Nos. 236-240,C1-C3 (8) 2.02
Set value 95

Souvenir Sheet
Perf. 11
241 Sheet of 4 1.25 1.25
a. A72 5m light blue & brn 28 28
b. A72 10m green, brown & blue 28 28
c. A72 15m green, violet & brown 28 28
d. A72 50m violet, green & black 28 28

40th anniv. of independence; postal modernization. See No. C4b for 25m, perf. 11.

Souvenir Sheet

Ornamental Column — A73

1961, June 20 *Perf. 12*
242 A73 Sheet of 2 + label 2.00 1.75
a. 2t blue, red & gold 85 85

40th anniversary of the Mongolian People's Revolution. No. 242 contains two No. 242a and label, imperf. between.

Herdsman and Oxen — A74

Designs: Herdsmen and domestic animals (except 1t and No. 252a).

1961, July 10 *Perf. 13*
243 A74 5m Rams 15 15
244 A74 10m shown 15 15
245 A74 15m Camels 15 15
246 A74 20m Pigs and geese 15 15
247 A74 25m Angora goats 15 15
248 A74 30m Horses 18 15
249 A74 40m Sheep 20 15
250 A74 50m Cows 28 20
251 A74 1t Combine harvester 48 35
Set value 1.60 1.15

Souvenir Sheets
Perf. 12
252 Sheet of 3 1.00 1.00
a. A74 5m Combine harvester 28 28
b. A74 15m Angora goats 28 28
c. A74 40m Oxen 28 28
253 Sheet of 3 1.00 1.00
a. A74 10m Pigs and geese 28 28
b. A74 20m Horses 28 28
c. A74 30m Cows 28 28
254 Sheet of 3 1.00 1.00
a. A74 25m Camels 28 28
b. A74 50m Rams 28 28
c. A74 1t Sheep 28 28

40th anniversary of independence. Nos. 252-254 each contain 3 stamps imperf. between.

Horseback Riders — A75

Designs: 5m, Young wrestlers and instructor. 15m, Camel and pony riders. 20m, Falconers. 30m, Skier. 50m, Archers. 1t, Male dancers.

1961, Aug. 10 *Perf. 11*
255 A75 5m multi 15 15
256 A75 10m multi 15 15
257 A75 15m multi 15 15
258 A75 20m multi 15 15
259 A75 30m multi 18 15
260 A75 50m multi 35 15
261 A75 1t multi 50 24
Set value 1.30 70

40th anniversary of independence; Mongolian youth sports.

Statue of Sukhe Bator A76

Arms of Mongolia A77

Designs: 5m, Mongol youth. 10m, Mongol chieftain. 20m, Singer. 30m, Dancer. 50m, Dombra player. 70m, Musicians. 1t, Gymnast. 5m, 10m, 70m, 1t, horiz.

Perf. 12x11½, 11½x12
1961, Sept. 16
262 A76 5m brt grn & red lil 15 15
263 A76 10m red & dk bl 15 15
264 A76 15m bl & lt brn 15 15
265 A76 20m pur & brt grn 15 15
266 A76 30m vio bl & car 15 15
267 A76 50m ol & vio 28 28
268 A76 70m brt lil rose & ol 38 38
269 A76 1t dk bl & ver 50 45
Nos. 262-269 (8) 1.91 1.86

40th anniversary of independence; Mongolian culture.

1961, Nov. 17 *Perf. 11½x12*
270 A77 5m multi 15 15
271 A77 10m multi 15 15
272 A77 15m multi 15 15
273 A77 20m multi 15 15
274 A77 30m multi 18 15
275 A77 50m multi 20 15
276 A77 70m multi 28 18
277 A77 1t multi 50 28
Set value 1.50 88

Congress Emblem A78

1961, Dec. 4 **Litho.** *Perf. 11½*
278 A78 30m vio bl, yel & red 18 15
279 A78 50m brn, yel & red 24 18
Set value 28

5th World Congress of Trade Unions, Moscow, Dec. 4-16.

UN Emblem and Arms of Mongolia — A79

Designs: 10m, Globe, map of Mongolia and dove. 50m, Flags of UN and Mongolia. 60m, UN Headquarters, New York and Parliament, Ulan Bator. 70m, UN assembly, UN and Mongolian flags.

1962, Mar. 15 **Photo.** *Perf. 11*
280 A79 10m gold & multi 15 15
281 A79 30m gold & multi 15 15
282 A79 50m gold & multi 20 15
283 A79 60m gold & multi 40 18
284 A79 70m gold & multi 60 35
Nos. 280-284 (5) 1.50
Set value 75

Mongolia's admission to UN.

Soccer — A80

Designs: 10m, Soccer ball, globe and flags. 50m, Soccer players, globe and ball. 60m, Goalkeeper. 70m, Stadium.

1962, May 15 Litho. *Perf. 10½*

285 A80 10m multi	15	15
286 A80 30m multi	15	15
287 A80 50m multi	18	15
288 A80 60m multi	35	18
289 A80 70m multi	50	20
Nos. 285-289 (5)	1.33	
Set value		55

World Soccer Championship, Chile, May 30-June 17.

D. Natsagdorji A81

Solidarity Emblem A82

1962, May 15 Photo. *Perf. 15x14½*

290 A81 30m brown	18	15
291 A81 50m bluish grn	24	15
Set value		20

Mongolian writers' congress.
For overprints see Nos. 430-431.

Perf. 11½x10½

1962, May 22 Litho.

292 A82 20m yel grn & multi	18	15
293 A82 30m bl & multi	24	15
Set value		20

Afro-Asian Peoples' solidarity.

Flags of USSR and Mongolia — A83

Perf. 11½x10½

1962, June 25 Litho.

294 A83 30m brn & multi	15	15
295 A83 50m vio bl & multi	20	15
Set value		20

Mongol-Soviet friendship.

Nos. 195-202 Overprinted

1962, July 20 Photo. *Perf. 11½x12*

296 A62 5m multi	15	15
297 A62 10m multi	15	15
298 A62 15m multi	20	20
299 A62 20m multi	20	20
300 A62 30m multi	24	24
301 A62 40m multi	30	30
302 A62 50m multi	48	48
303 A62 1t multi	75	75
Nos. 296-303 (8)	2.47	2.47

WHO drive to eradicate malaria.

Military Field Emblem — A84

Designs: 30m, Tablets with inscriptions. 50m, Stone column. 60m, Genghis Khan.

1962, July 20 *Perf. 11½x12*

304 A84 20m blue & multi	70	70
305 A84 30m red & multi	70	70
306 A84 50m pink, brn & blk	1.50	1.50
307 A84 60m blue & multi	2.25	2.25

Genghis Khan (1162-1227), Mongol conqueror.
For overprints see Nos. 1846-1849.

River Perch — A85

1962, Dec. 28 *Perf. 11*

308 A85 5m shown	15	15
309 A85 10m Burbot	15	15
310 A85 15m Arctic grayling	15	15
311 A85 20m Shorthorn sculpin	15	15
312 A85 30m Marine zander	18	15
313 A85 50m Siberian sturgeon	20	15
314 A85 70m Waleck's chub minnow	35	18
315 A85 1.50t Cottocomephorid	55	30
Set value	1.60	85

Sukhe Bator (1893-1923), National Hero — A86

1963, Feb. 2 Photo. *Perf. 11½x12*

316 A86 30m blue	15	15
317 A86 60m rose car	20	15
Set value		20

Laika and Rocket A87

Designs: 15m, Rocket launching, vert. 25m, Lunik 2, vert. 70m, Andrian G. Nikolayev and Pavel R. Popovich. 1t, Mars rocket.

1963, Apr. 1 Litho. *Perf. 12½x12*

Size: 46x32mm

318 A87 5m multicolored	15	15

Size: 20x68mm

319 A87 15m multicolored	15	15
320 A87 25m multicolored	24	15

Size: 46x32mm

321 A87 70m multicolored	38	20
322 A87 1t multicolored	60	35
Nos. 318-322 (5)	1.52	
Set value		78

Soviet space explorations.

Blood Transfusion — A88

1963, Aug. 15 *Perf. 10½*

323 A88 20m Packing Red Cross parcels	15	15
324 A88 30m shown	15	15
325 A88 50m Vaccination	18	15
326 A88 60m Ambulance service	24	18
327 A88 1.30t Centenary emblem	50	40
Nos. 323-327 (5)	1.22	
Set value		80

Red Cross centenary.

Karl Marx — A89

Mongolian Woman — A90

1963, Sept. 16 Photo. *Perf. 11½x12*

328 A89 30m blue	15	15
329 A89 60m dk car rose	20	15
Set value		20

145th anniversary of birth of Karl Marx.

1963, Sept. 26

330 A90 30m blue & multi	18	15

5th International Women's Congress, Moscow, June 24-29.

Inachis A91

Designs: Mongolian butterflies.

1963, Nov. 7 Litho. *Perf. 11½*

331 A91 5m shown	15	15
332 A91 10m Gonepteryxrhamni	15	15
333 A91 15m Aglais urticae	15	15
334 A91 20m Parnassius apollo	15	15
335 A91 30m Papilio machaon	20	15
336 A91 60m Agrodiaetus damon	35	20
337 A91 1t Limenitis populi	48	28
Set value	1.38	85

UNESCO Emblem, Globe and Scales — A92

1963, Dec. 10 Photo. *Perf. 12*

338 A92 30m multicolored	18	15
339 A92 60m multicolored	28	15
Set value		18

Universal Declaration of Human Rights, 15th anniversary.

Coprinus Comatus — A93

Designs: Mushrooms.

1964, Jan. 1 Litho. *Perf. 10½*

340 A93 5m shown	15	15
341 A93 10m Lactarius torminosus	15	15
342 A93 15m Psalliota campestris	15	15
343 A93 20m Russula delica	15	15
344 A93 30m Ixocomus granulatus	20	15
345 A93 50m Lactarius scrobiculatus	24	18
346 A93 70m Lactarius deliciosus	35	20
347 A93 1t Ixocomus variegatus	50	28
Set value	1.60	95

Souvenir Sheet

Skier — A94

1964, Feb. 12 Photo. *Perf. 12x11½*

348 A94 4t gray	2.00	2.00

9th Winter Olympic Games, Innsbruck, Jan. 29-Feb. 9.

Lenin — A95

1964 Photo. *Perf. 11½x12*

349 A95 30m salmon & multi	48	15
350 A95 50m blue & multi	55	15
Set value		20

60th anniversary of Communist Party. Nos. 349-350 printed with alternating label showing Lenin quotation.

Javelin — A96

1964, Apr. 30 Litho. *Perf. 10½*

351	A96	5m	Gymnastics, women's	15	15
352	A96	10m	shown	15	15
353	A96	15m	Wrestling	15	15
354	A96	20m	Running, women's	15	15
355	A96	30m	Equestrian	20	15
356	A96	50m	Diving, women's	28	15
357	A96	60m	Bicycling	35	20
358	A96	1t	Olympic Games emblem	60	28
			Set value	1.70	95

Souvenir Sheet

Perf. 12x11½

359	A96	4t	Wrestling	2.50	2.50

18th Olympic Games, Toyko, Oct. 10-25. No. 359 contains one horizontal stamp, 37x27½mm. Issued Sept. 1.

Congress Emblem — A97

1964, Sept. 30 Photo. *Perf. 11*

360	A97	30m	multicolored	24	15

4th Mongolian Women's Congress.

Lunik 1 — A98

Russian Space Research: 10m, Vostok 1 and 2. 15m, Tiros weather satellite, vert. 20m, Cosmos circling earth, vert. 30m, Mars probe, vert. 60m, Luna 4, vert. 80m, Echo 2. 1t, Radar and rockets.

1964, Oct. 30

361	A98	5m	multicolored	15	15
362	A98	10m	multicolored	15	15
363	A98	15m	multicolored	15	15
364	A98	20m	multicolored	15	15
365	A98	30m	multicolored	20	15
366	A98	60m	multicolored	24	15
367	A98	80m	multicolored	24	15
368	A98	1t	multicolored	45	24
			Set value	1.50	70

Rider Carrying Flag — A99

1964, Nov. 26 Photo. *Perf. 11½x12*

369	A99	25m	multicolored	20	15
370	A99	50m	multicolored	30	15
			Set value		20

40th anniversary of Mongolian constitution.

Weather Balloon A100

Designs: 5m, Oceanographic exploration. 60m, Northern lights and polar bears. 80m, Gemagnetism. 1t, I.Q.S.Y. emblem and Mercator map.

1965, May 15 Photo. *Perf. 13½*

371	A100	5m	gray & multi	15	15
372	A100	10m	grn & multi	15	15
373	A100	60m	blue, blk & pink	20	15
374	A100	80m	citron & multi	40	20
375	A100	1t	brt green & multi	70	38
			Nos. 371-375,C6-C8 (8)	2.10	
			Set value		1.10

International Quiet Sun Year.

Horses — A101

Designs: Mongolian horses.

1965, Aug. 25 *Perf. 11*

376	A101	5m	shown	15	15
377	A101	10m	Falconers	15	15
378	A101	15m	Taming wild horse	15	15
379	A101	20m	Horse race	15	15
380	A101	30m	Hurdles	18	15
381	A101	60m	Wolf hunt	20	15
382	A101	80m	Milking a mare	28	20
383	A101	1t	Mare and foal	45	30
			Set value	1.40	95

Girl Holding Lambs — A102

1965, Oct. 10 Photo. *Perf. 11*

384	A102	5m	shown	15	15
385	A102	10m	Boy and girl drummers	15	15
386	A102	20m	Camp fire	15	15
387	A102	30m	Wrestlers	24	15
388	A102	50m	Emblem	35	28
			Set value	82	58
			Nos. 384-388 (5)	1.04	88

40th anniv. of Mongolian Youth Org.

Chinese Perch — A103

1965, Nov. 25

389	A103	5m	shown	15	15
390	A103	10m	Lenok trout	15	15
391	A103	15m	Siberian sturgeon	15	15
392	A103	20m	Amur salmon	15	15
393	A103	30m	Bagrid catfish	18	15
394	A103	60m	Siluri catfish	24	15
395	A103	80m	Northern pike	35	18
396	A103	1t	River perch	50	28
			Nos. 389-396 (8)	1.87	
			Set value		90

Marx and Lenin — A104

1965, Dec. 15 *Perf. 11½x12*

397	A104	10m	red & blk	15	15

6th Conference of Postal Ministers of Communist Countries, Peking, June 21-July 15.

Sable — A105

1966, Feb. 15 Photo. *Perf. 12½*

398	A105	5m	shown	15	15
399	A105	10m	Fox	15	15
400	A105	15m	Otter, vert.	15	15
401	A105	20m	Cheetah, vert.	15	15
402	A105	30m	Pallas's cat	18	15
403	A105	60m	Stone marten	24	15
404	A105	80m	Ermine, vert.	30	20
405	A105	1t	Woman in mink coat, vert.	50	28
			Set value	1.50	90

Opening of WHO Headquarters, Geneva A106

1966, May 3 Photo. *Perf. 12x11½*

406	A106	30m	bl grn, bl & gold	15	15
407	A106	50m	red, bl & gold	28	15
			Set value		16

For overprints see Nos. 483-484.

Soccer — A107

Designs: 30m, 60m, 80m, Various soccer plays. 1t, British flag and World Soccer Cup emblem. 4t, Wembley Stadium, horiz.

1966, May 31 Photo. *Perf. 11*

408	A107	10m	multicolored	15	15
409	A107	30m	multicolored	15	15
410	A107	60m	multicolored	18	15
411	A107	80m	multicolored	30	18
412	A107	1t	multicolored	50	30
			Nos. 408-412 (5)	1.28	
			Set value		70

Souvenir Sheet

Perf. 12½, Imperf.

413	A107	4t	gray & brown	2.00	2.00

World Soccer Championship for Jules Rimet Cup, Wembley, England, July 11-30. No. 413 contains one stamp 61x83mm.

Sukhe Bator, Parliament Building, Ulan Bator A108

1966, June 7 Litho. *Perf. 12x12½*

414	A108	30m	red, bl & brn	20	15

15th Congress of Mongolian Communist Party.

Wrestling — A109

Designs: Various wrestling holds.

1966, June 15 Photo. *Perf. 11½x12*

415	A109	10m	multicolored	15	15
416	A109	30m	multicolored	15	15
417	A109	60m	multicolored	24	15
418	A109	80m	multicolored	28	18
419	A109	1t	multicolored	35	28
			Set value	1.00	68

World Wrestling Championship, Toledo, Spain.

Emblem and Map of Mongolia — A110

Sukhe Bator, Grain and Factories A111

Perf. 11½x12, 12x11½

1966, July 11 Litho.

420	A110	30m	red & multi	20	15
421	A111	50m	red & multi	30	18

45th anniversary of independence.
For overprints see Nos. 552-553.

Lilium Tenuifolium A112

1966, Oct. 15 Photo. *Perf. 12x11½*

422	A112	5m	Physochlaena physaloides	15	15
423	A112	10m	Allium polyrrhizum	15	15
424	A112	15m	shown	15	15
425	A112	20m	Thermopsis lanceolata	15	15
426	A112	30m	Amygdalus mongolica	18	15
427	A112	60m	Caryopteris mongolica	24	15

428 A112 80m Piptanthus mongolicus 30 20
429 A112 1t Iris bungei 45 30
Set value 1.55 90

Nos. 290-291 Overprinted: "1906/1966"

1966, Oct. 26 Photo. *Perf. 15x14½*
430 A81 30m brown 28 15
431 A81 50m bluish grn 35 15
Set value 22

60th anniv. of birth of D. Natsagdorji, writer. 50m exists double, one inverted.

Child with Dove — A113

1966, Dec. 2 *Perf. 11½x12, 12x11½*
432 A113 10m shown 15 15
433 A113 15m Children with reindeer 15 15
434 A113 20m Boys wrestling, vert. 15 15
435 A113 30m Horseback riding 20 15
436 A113 60m Children riding camel, vert. 24 15
437 A113 80m Child with sheep 35 15
438 A113 1t Boy archer, vert. 50 28
Nos. 432-438 (7) 1.74
Set value 80

Children's Day.

Proton 1 — A114

Perf. 11½x12½, 12½x11½
1966, Dec. 28 Photo.
439 A114 5m Vostok 2, vert. 15 15
440 A114 10m shown 15 15
441 A114 15m Telstar 1, vert. 15 15
442 A114 20m Molnija 1, vert. 15 15
443 A114 30m Syncom 3, vert. 18 15
444 A114 60m Luna 9 24 15
445 A114 80m Luna 12, vert. 30 18
446 A114 1t Mariner 4 45 20
Set value 1.55 90

Space exploration.

Tarbosaurus A115

1967, Mar. 31 *Perf. 12x11½*
447 A115 5m shown 15 15
448 A115 10m Talarurus 15 15
449 A115 15m Proceratops 15 15
450 A115 20m Indricotherium 15 15
451 A115 30m Saurolophus 18 15
452 A115 60m Mastodon 20 15
453 A115 80m Mongolotherium 30 18
454 A115 1t Mammoth 45 20
Set value 1.50 90

Prehistoric animals.

A116

A117

Congress emblem.

1967, June 9 Litho. *Perf. 12*
455 A116 30m lt blue & multi 18 15
456 A116 50m pink & multi 24 20

9th Youth Festival for Peace and Friendship, Sofia.

1967, Oct. 25 Litho. *Perf. 11½x12*

Design: 40m, Sukhe Bator and soldiers. 60m, Lenin and soldiers.

457 A117 40m red & multi 28 24
458 A117 60m red & multi 35 28

Russian October Revolution, 50th anniv.

Ice Hockey and Olympic Rings A118

1967, Dec. 29 *Perf. 12x12½*
459 A118 5m Figure skating 15 15
460 A118 10m Speed skating 15 15
461 A118 15m shown 15 15
462 A118 20m Ski jump 18 15
463 A118 30m Bobsledding 20 15
464 A118 60m Figure skating, pair 40 15
465 A118 80m Slalom 55 24
Nos. 459-465 (7) 1.78
Set value 72

Souvenir Sheet
Perf. 12
466 A118 4t Women's figure skating 2.00 2.00

10th Winter Olympic Games, Grenoble, France, Feb. 6-18.

Bactrian Camels A119

1968, Jan. 15 Photo. *Perf. 12*
467 A119 5m shown 15 15
468 A119 10m Yak 15 15
469 A119 15m Lamb 18 15
470 A119 20m Foal 20 15
471 A119 30m Calf 24 15
472 A119 60m Bison 30 15
473 A119 80m Roe deer 38 18
474 A119 1t Reindeer 55 28
Nos. 467-474 (8) 2.15
Set value 90

Young animals.

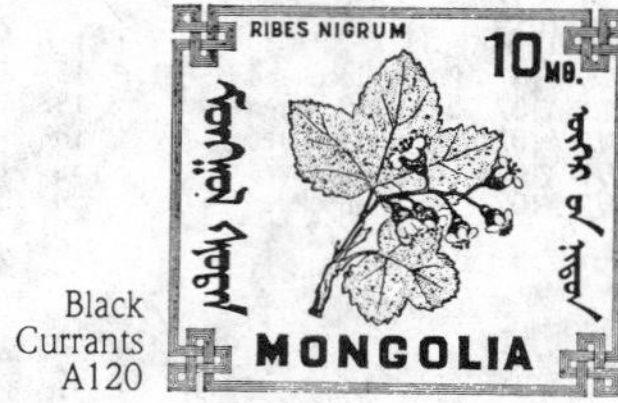

Black Currants A120

Berries: 5m, Rosa acicularis. 15m, Gooseberries. 20m, Malus. 30m, Strawberries. 60m, Ribes altissimum. 80m, Blueberries. 1t, Hippophae rhamnoides.

Lithographed & Engraved
1968, Feb. 15
475 A120 5m blue & ultra 15 15
476 A120 10m buff & brn 15 15
477 A120 15m lt grn & grn 15 15
478 A120 20m yel & red 18 15
479 A120 30m pink & car 28 15
480 A120 60m sal & org brn 35 15
481 A120 80m pale & dl bl 45 18
482 A120 1t lt yel & red 60 24
Nos. 475-482 (8) 2.31
Set value 85

Nos. 406-407 Overprinted ДЭХБ 20 ЖИЛ WHO

1968, Apr. 16 Photo. *Perf. 12x11½*
483 A106 30m bl grn, bl & gold 18 15
484 A106 50m red, blue & gold 24 15
Set value 22

WHO, 20th anniversary.

Human Rights Flame — A121

1968, June 20 Litho. *Perf. 12*
485 A121 30m turq & vio bl 15 15

International Human Rights Year.

"Das Kapital," by Karl Marx A122

Design: 50m, Karl Marx.

1968, July 1 Litho. *Perf. 12*
486 A122 30m blue & multi 18 15
487 A122 50m red & multi 24 15
Set value 20

Karl Marx (1818-1883).

Artist, by A. Sangatzohyo A123

Paintings: 10m, On Remote Roads, by Sangatzohyo. 15m, Camel calf, by B. Avarzad. 20m, Milk, by Avarzad. 30m, The Bowman, by B. Gombosuren. 80m, Girl Sitting on Yak, by Sangatzohyo. 1.40t, Cagan Dara Eke, by Janaivajara. 4t, Meeting, by Sangatzohyo, horiz.

1968, July 11 Litho. *Perf. 12*
488 A123 5m brown & multi 15 15
489 A123 10m brown & multi 15 15
490 A123 15m brown & multi 15 15
491 A123 20m brown & multi 24 15
492 A123 30m brown & multi 35 15
493 A123 80m brown & multi 48 18
494 A123 1.40t brown & multi 70 35
Nos. 488-494 (7) 2.22
Set value 90

Miniature Sheets
Perf. 11½, Imperf.
495 A123 4t brown & multi 2.25 2.25

Paintings from national museum, Ulan Bator. #495 contains one 54x84mm stamp.

Volleyball A124

Sports (Olympic Rings and): 10m, Wrestling. 15m, Bicycling. 20m, Javelin, women's. 30m, Soccer. 60m, Running. 80m, Gymnastics, women's. 1t, Weight lifting. 4t, Equestrian.

1968, Sept. 1 Litho. *Perf. 12*
496 A124 5m multicolored 15 15
497 A124 10m multicolored 15 15
498 A124 15m multicolored 15 15
499 A124 20m multicolored 15 15
500 A124 30m multicolored 20 15
501 A124 60m multicolored 28 15
502 A124 80m multicolored 30 18
503 A124 1t multicolored 60 20
Set value 1.75 78

Souvenir Sheets
Perf. 11½, Imperf.
504 A124 4t orange & multi 2.75 2.75

19th Olympic Games, Mexico City, Oct. 12-27. #504 contains one 52x44mm stamp.

A125

A126

Hammer, spade & cogwheel.

1968, Sept. 17 Litho. *Perf. 11½*
505 A125 50m blue & vermilion 15 15

Industrial development in town of Darhan.

1968, Nov. 6 Litho. *Perf. 12*
506 A126 60m turquoise & sep 18 15

Maxim Gorki (1868-1936), Russian writer.

Madonna and Child, by Boltraffio A127

Paintings: 10m, St. Roch Healed by an Angel, by Brescia. 15m, Madonna and Child with St. Anne, by Macchietti. 20m, St. John on Patmos, by Cano. 30m, Lady with Viola da Gamba, by Kupetzky. 80m, Boy, by Amerling. 1.40t, Death of Adonis, by Furini. 4t, Portrait of a Lady, by Renoir.

1968, Nov. 20 Litho. *Perf. 12*
507 A127 5m gray & multi 15 15
508 A127 10m gray & multi 15 15
509 A127 15m gray & multi 15 15
510 A127 20m gray & multi 20 15

511	A127	30m	gray & multi	30	15
512	A127	80m	gray & multi	45	20
513	A127	1.40t	gray & multi	60	28
			Nos. 507-513 (7)	2.00	
			Set value		94

Miniature Sheet

514	A127	4t	gray & multi	2.25	2.25

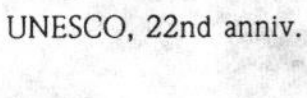

UNESCO, 22nd anniv.

Jesse Owens, USA A128

Olympic Gold Medal Winners: 5m, Paavo Nurmi, Finland. 15m, Fanny Blankers-Koen, Netherlands. 20m, Laszlo Papp, Hungary. 30m, Wilma Rudolph, US. 60m, Boris Sahlin, USSR. 80m, Donald Schollander, US. 1t Akinori Nakayama, Japan. 4t, Jigjidin Munhbat, Mongolia.

1969, Mar. 25 Litho. *Perf. 12*

515	A128	5m	multicolored	15	15
516	A128	10m	multicolored	15	15
517	A128	15m	multicolored	15	15
518	A128	20m	multicolored	15	15
519	A128	30m	multicolored	15	15
520	A128	60m	multicolored	15	15
521	A128	80m	multicolored	28	24
522	A128	1t	multicolored	60	28
			Set value	1.30	85

Souvenir Sheet

523	A128	4t	green & multi	2.75	2.75

Bayit Woman A129

Regional Costumes: 10m, Torgut man. 15m, Dzakhachin woman. 20m, Khalkha woman. 30m, Dariganga woman. 60m, Mingat woman. 80m, Khalkha man. 1t, Bargut woman.

1969, Apr. 20 Litho. *Perf. 12*

524	A129	5m	multicolored	15	15
525	A129	10m	multicolored	15	15
526	A129	15m	multicolored	15	15
527	A129	20m	multicolored	15	15
528	A129	30m	multicolored	18	15
529	A129	60m	multicolored	24	15
530	A129	80m	multicolored	30	15
531	A129	1t	multicolored	48	20
			Set value	1.55	75

Red Cross Emblem and Helicopter — A130

Design: 50m, Emblem, Red Cross car and shepherd.

1969, May 15 Litho. *Perf. 12*

532	A130	30m	multicolored	15	15
533	A130	50m	multicolored	20	15
			Set value		22

30th anniversary of Mongolian Red Cross.

Landscape and Edelweiss — A131

Designs: Mongolian landscapes and flowers.

1969, May 20

534	A131	5m	shown	15	15
535	A131	10m	Pinks	15	15
536	A131	15m	Dianthus superbus	15	15
537	A131	20m	Geranium	15	15
538	A131	30m	Dianthus ramosissimus	18	15
539	A131	60m	Globeflowers	24	15
540	A131	80m	Delphinium	28	20
541	A131	1t	Haloxylon	45	28
			Set value	1.50	90

See No. 1105.

Bull Fight, by Tsewegdjaw — A132

Paintings from National Museum: 10m, Fighting Colts, by O. Tsewegdjaw. 15m, Horseman and Herd, by A. Sangatzohyo. 20m, Camel Caravan, by D. Damdinsuren. 30m, On the Steppe, by N. Tsultem. 60m, Milking Mares, by Tsewegdjaw. 80m, Going to School, by B. Avarzad. 1t, After Work, by G. Odon. 4t, Horses, by Damdinsuren.

1969, July 11 Litho. *Perf. 12*

542	A132	5m	multicolored	15	15
543	A132	10m	multicolored	15	15
544	A132	15m	multicolored	15	15
545	A132	20m	multicolored	15	15
546	A132	30m	multicolored	18	15
547	A132	60m	multicolored	24	15
548	A132	80m	multicolored	28	18
549	A132	1t	multicolored	45	20
			Set value	1.45	80

Souvenir Sheet

550	A132	4t	multicolored	1.75	1.75

10th anniversary of cooperative movement. No. 550 contains one stamp 65x42mm.

Mongolian Flag and Emblem — A133

1969, Sept. 20 Litho. *Perf. 12*

551	A133	50m	multicolored	18	15

Battle of Ha-lo-hsin (Khalka) River, 30th anniversary.

Nos. 420-421 Overprinted

ВНМАУ-ыг тунхагласны 45 жилийн ой 1969—XI—26

Perf. 11½x12, 12x11½

1969, Nov. 26 Photo.

552	A110	30m	red & multi	20	15
553	A111	50m	red & multi	28	20

45th anniv. of Mongolian People's Republic.

Mercury 7 — A134

Designs: 5m, Sputnik 3. 10m, Vostok 1. 20m, Voskhod 2. 30m, Apollo 8. 60m, Soyuz 5. 80m, Apollo 12.

1969, Dec. 6 Photo. *Perf. 12x11½*

554	A134	5m	multicolored	15	15
555	A134	10m	multicolored	15	15
556	A134	15m	multicolored	15	15
557	A134	20m	multicolored	18	15
558	A134	30m	multicolored	28	15
559	A134	60m	multicolored	38	18
560	A134	80m	multicolored	55	20
			Nos. 554-560 (7)	1.84	
			Set value		65

Souvenir Sheet

561	A134	4t	multicolored	2.25	2.25

Space achievements of US and USSR.

Wolf — A135

Designs: 10m, Brown bear. 15m, Lynx. 20m, Wild boar. 30m, Moose. 60m, Bobac marmot. 80m, Argali. 1t, Old wall carpet showing hunter and dog.

1970, Mar. 25 Photo. *Perf. 12*

562	A135	5m	multicolored	15	15
563	A135	10m	multicolored	15	15
564	A135	15m	multicolored	15	15
565	A135	20m	multicolored	15	15
566	A135	30m	multicolored	15	15
567	A135	60m	multicolored	24	15
568	A135	80m	multicolored	35	18
569	A135	1t	multicolored	45	28
			Set value	1.55	90

Lenin and Mongolian Delegation, by Sangatzohyo — A136

Designs: 20m, Lenin, embroidered panel, by Cerenhuu, vert. 1t, Lenin, by Mazhig, vert.

1970, Apr. 22 Photo. & Litho.

570	A136	20m	multicolored	15	15
571	A136	50m	multicolored	18	15
572	A136	1t	lt bl, blk & red	35	18
			Set value	56	32

Centenary of the birth of Lenin.

Souvenir Sheet

EXPO '70 Pavilion of Matsushita Electric Co. and Time Capsule — A137

1970, May 26 Photo. *Perf. 12½*

573	A137	4t	gold & multi	2.25	2.25

EXPO '70 International Exposition, Osaka, Japan, Mar. 15-Sept. 13.

Sumitomo Fairy Tale Pavilion A138

1970, June 5 Photo. *Perf. 12x11½*

574	A138	1.50t	multicolored	50	40

EXPO '70 International Exposition, Osaka. No. 574 printed in sheets of 20 (5x4) with alternating horizontal rows of tabs showing various fairy tales and EXPO '70 emblem.

Soccer, Rimet Cup — A139

Designs: Soccer players of various teams in action.

1970, June 20 *Perf. 12½x11½*

575	A139	10m	multi	15	15
576	A139	20m	multi	15	15
577	A139	30m	multi	15	15
578	A139	50m	multi	15	15
579	A139	60m	multi	20	15
580	A139	1t	multi	40	20
581	A139	1.30t	multi	50	30
			Nos. 575-581 (7)	1.70	
			Set value		85

Souvenir Sheet

Perf. 12½

582	A139	4t	multi	2.00	2.00

World Soccer Championship for Jules Rimet Cup, Mexico City, May 30-June 21. No. 582 contains one stamp 51x37mm.

Old World Buzzard A140

Birds of Prey: 20m, Tawny owls. 30m, Northern goshawk. 50m, White-tailed sea eagle. 60m, Peregrine falcon. 1t, Old world kestrel. 1.30t, Black kite.

1970, June 30 Litho. *Perf. 12*

583 A140	10m bl & multi		15	15
584 A140	20m pink & multi		15	15
585 A140	30m yel grn & multi		15	15
586 A140	50m bl & multi		18	15
587 A140	60m yel & multi		20	15
588 A140	1t grn & multi		35	24
589 A140	1.30t bl & multi		50	28
	Nos. 583-589 (7)		1.68	
	Set value			90

Russian War Memorial, Berlin — A141

1970, July 11 Litho. *Perf. 12*

590 A141 60m bl & multi 18 15

25th anniversary of end of World War II.

Bogdo-Gegen Palace — A142

Designs: 10m, Archer. 30m, Horseman. 40m, "White Mother" Goddess. 50m, Girl in national costume. 60m, Lion statue. 70m, Dancer's mask. 80m, Detail from Bogdo-Gegen Palace, Ulan Bator.

1970, Sept. 20 Litho. *Perf. 12*

591 A142	10m multi	15	15
592 A142	20m multi	15	15
593 A142	30m multi	18	15
594 A142	40m multi	20	15
595 A142	50m multi	28	20
596 A142	60m multi	35	28
597 A142	70m multi	40	35
598 A142	80m multi	50	40
	Nos. 591-598 (8)	2.21	1.83

Nos. 595-598 printed se-tenant in blocks of 4, in sheets of 40.

Souvenir Sheet

Recovery of Apollo 13 Capsule A143

1970, Nov. 1 Litho. *Perf. 12*

599 A143 4t bl & multi 2.00 2.00

Space missions of Apollo 13, Apr. 11-17, and Soyuz 9, June 1-10, 1970.

Mongolian Flag, UN and Education Year Emblems A144

1970, Nov. 7

600 A144 60m multi 40 18

International Education Year.

Mounted Herald A145

1970, Nov. 7 Litho. *Perf. 12*

601 A145 30m gold & multi 15 15

50th anniv. of newspaper Unen (Truth).

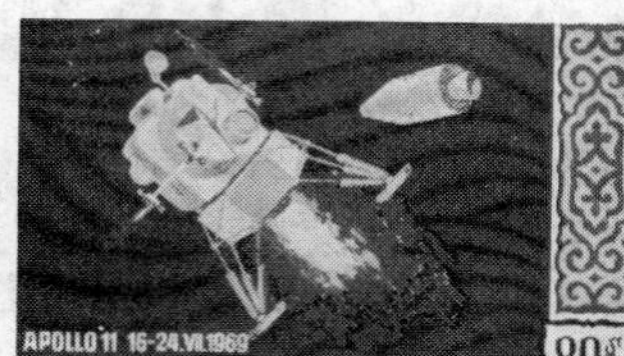

Apollo 11 Lunar Landing Module — A146

Designs: 10m, Vostok 2 and 3. 20m, Voskhod 2 and space walk. 30m, Gemini 6 and 7 capsules. 50m, Soyuz 4 and 5 docking in space. 60m, Soyuz 6, 7 and 8 group flight. 1t, Apollo 13 with damaged capsule. 1.30t, Luna 16 unmanned moon landing. 4t, Radar ground tracking station.

1971, Feb. 25 Litho. *Perf. 12*

602 A146	10m multi	15	15
603 A146	20m multi	15	15
604 A146	30m multi	15	15
605 A146	50m multi	20	15
606 A146	60m multi	26	15
607 A146	80m multi	26	15
608 A146	1t multi	45	15
609 A146	1.30t multi	55	15
	Nos. 602-609 (8)	2.17	
	Set value		65

Souvenir Sheet

610 A146 4t vio bl & multi 2.25 2.25

US and USSR space explorations.

Rider with Mongolian Flag — A147

Designs: 30m, Party meeting. 90m, Lenin with Mongolian leader. 1.20t, Marchers, pictures of Lenin and Marx.

1971, Mar. 1 Photo. *Perf. 12½*

611 A147	30m gold & multi	15	15
612 A147	60m gold & multi	15	15
613 A147	90m gold & multi	18	15
614 A147	1.30t gold & multi	35	28
	Set value		54

50th anniversary of Mongolian Revolutionary Party.

A little time given to the study of the arrangement of the Scott Catalogue can make it easier to use effectively.

Souvenir Sheet

Lunokhod 1 on Moon — A148

Design: No. 615b, Apollo 14 on moon.

1971, Apr. 15 Photo. *Perf. 14*

615 A148	Sheet of 2	2.00	2.00
a.-b.	2t any single	80	80

Luna 17 unmanned automated moon mission, Nov. 10-17, 1970, and Apollo 14 moon landing, Jan. 31-Feb. 9, 1971.

Dancer's Mask — A149

Designs: Various masks for dancers.

1971, Apr. 25 Litho. *Perf. 12*

616 A149	10m gold & multi	15	15
617 A149	20m gold & multi	15	15
618 A149	30m gold & multi	20	15
619 A149	50m gold & multi	24	15
620 A149	60m gold & multi	28	15
621 A149	1t gold & multi	55	20
622 A149	1.30t gold & multi	75	24
	Nos. 616-622 (7)	2.32	
	Set value		75

Red Flag and Emblems A150

1971, May 31 Photo. *Perf. 12x11½*

623 A150 60m bl, red & gold 18 15

16th Congress of Mongolian Revolutionary Party.

Steam Locomotive — A151

1971, July 11 Litho. *Perf. 12*

624 A151	20m shown	15	15
625 A151	30m Diesel locomotive	15	15
626 A151	40m Truck	15	15
627 A151	50m Automobile	20	15
628 A151	60m Biplane PO-2	24	15
629 A151	80m AN-24 plane	32	18
630 A151	1t Fishing boat	40	20
	Nos. 624-630 (7)	1.61	
	Set value		72

50th anniversary of modern transportation.
For overprints see Nos. 850A-850G.

Arms of Mongolia and Soldier — A152

Design: 1.50t, Arms, policeman and child.

1971, July 11 Litho. *Perf. 12*

631 A152	60m multi	15	15
632 A152	1.50t multi	40	18
	Set value		26

50th anniversary of the people's army and police.

Mongolian Flag and Emblem A153

1971, Aug. 25 Photo. *Perf. 12x11½*

633 A153 60m lt bl & multi 18 15

International Year Against Racial discrimination.

Flag of Youth Organization — A154

1971, Aug. 25 Litho. *Perf. 12*

634 A154 60m org & multi 20 15

50th anniversary of Mongolian revolutionary youth organization.

The Woodsman and the Tiger — A155

Designs: Various Mongolian fairy tales.

1971, Sept. 15 Litho. *Perf. 12*

635 A155	10m gold & multi	15	15
636 A155	20m gold & multi	15	15
637 A155	30m gold & multi	15	15
638 A155	50m gold & multi	18	15
639 A155	60m gold & multi	25	15
640 A155	80m gold & multi	30	15
641 A155	1t gold & multi	38	18
642 A155	1.30t gold & multi	55	24
	Nos. 635-642 (8)	2.11	
	Set value		88

Bactrian Camel A156

1971, Nov. 1 Litho. *Perf. 12½*

No.	Type	Value	Design	Unused	Used
643	A156	20m	Yaks	15	15
644	A156	30m	shown	15	15
645	A156	40m	Sheep	15	15
646	A156	50m	Goats	18	15
647	A156	60m	Cattle	28	18
648	A156	80m	Horses	35	20
649	A156	1t	White horse	45	24
			Nos. 643-649 (7)	1.71	
			Set value		90

Mongolian livestock breeding.

Cross-country Skiing — A157

Designs (Sapporo Olympic Emblem and): 20m, Bobsledding. 30m, Women's figure skating. 50m, Slalom. 60m, Speed skating. 80m, Downhill skiing. 1t, Ice hockey. 1.30t, Figure skating, pairs. 4t, Ski jump.

Perf. 12½x11½

1972, Jan. 20 Photo.

No.	Type	Value	Color	Unused	Used
650	A157	10m	multi	15	15
651	A157	20m	ol & multi	15	15
652	A157	30m	ultra & multi	15	15
653	A157	50m	brt bl & multi	15	15
654	A157	60m	multi	20	15
655	A157	80m	grn & multi	24	15
656	A157	1t	bl & multi	30	18
657	A157	1.30t	vio & multi	38	24
			Set value	1.50	90

Souvenir Sheet

Perf. 12½

No.	Type	Value	Color	Unused	Used
658	A157	4t	lt bl & multi	2.00	2.00

11th Winter Olympic Games, Sapporo, Japan, Feb. 3-13.

Taming Wild Horse — A158

Paintings: 20m, Mythological animal in winter. 30m, Lancer on horseback. 50m, Athletes. 60m, Waterfall and horses. 80m, The Wise Musician, by Sarav. 1t, Young musician. 1.30t, Old sage with animals.

1972, Apr. 15 Litho. *Perf. 12*

No.	Type	Value	Color	Unused	Used
659	A158	10m	multi	15	15
660	A158	20m	multi	15	15
661	A158	30m	multi	15	15
662	A158	50m	multi	15	15
663	A158	60m	multi	20	15
664	A158	80m	multi	24	15
665	A158	1t	multi	30	20
666	A158	1.30t	multi	38	24
			Set value	1.50	90

Paintings by contemporary artists in Ulan Bator Museum.

Calosoma Fischeri A159

Designs: Various insects.

1972, Apr. 30 Litho. *Perf. 12*

No.	Type	Value	Color	Unused	Used
667	A159	10m	multi	15	15
668	A159	20m	multi	15	15
669	A159	30m	multi	15	15
670	A159	50m	multi	15	15
671	A159	60m	multi	24	15
672	A159	80m	multi	28	15
673	A159	1t	multi	35	20
674	A159	1.30t	multi	40	24
			Nos. 667-674 (8)	1.87	
			Set value		90

UN Emblem — A160

1972, Aug. 30 Photo. *Perf. 12*

No.	Type	Value	Color	Unused	Used
675	A160	60m	multi	20	15

ECAFE (UN Economic Commission for Asia and the Far East), 25th anniv.

Slow Lizard — A161

Designs: 15m, Radd's toad. 20m, Pallas's viper. 25m, Toad-headed agamid. 30m, Siberian wood frog. 60m, Przewalski's lizard. 80m, Taphrometopon lineolatum (snake). 1t, Stoliczka's agamid.

1972, Sept. 5 Litho. *Perf. 12*

No.	Type	Value	Color	Unused	Used
676	A161	10m	multi	15	15
677	A161	15m	multi	15	15
678	A161	20m	multi	15	15
679	A161	25m	multi	15	15
680	A161	30m	multi	18	15
681	A161	60m	multi	28	15
682	A161	80m	multi	35	20
683	A161	1t	multi	40	24
			Nos. 676-683 (8)	1.81	
			Set value		90

Symbols of Technical Knowledge A162

Design: 60m, University of Mongolia.

1972, Sept. 25

No.	Type	Value	Color	Unused	Used
684	A162	50m	org & multi	18	15
685	A162	60m	lil & multi	20	15
			Set value		15

30th anniversary of Mongolian State University.

Virgin and Child with St. John, by Bellini — A163

Paintings by Venetian Masters: 20m, Transfiguration, by Bellini, vert. 30m, Virgin and Child, by Bellini, vert. 50m, Presentation in the Temple, by Bellini. 60m, St. George, by Mantegna, vert. 80m, Departure of St. Ursula, by Carpaccio, vert. 1t, Departure of St. Ursula, by Carpaccio.

1972, Oct. 1

No.	Type	Value	Color	Unused	Used
686	A163	10m	multi	15	15
687	A163	20m	multi	15	15
688	A163	30m	multi	15	15
689	A163	50m	multi	20	15
690	A163	60m	multi	35	18
691	A163	80m	multi	40	20
692	A163	1t	multi	55	24
			Nos. 686-692 (7)	1.95	
			Set value		95

Save Venice campaign. See No. B3.

Manlay Bator Ramdinsuren A164

Designs: 20m, Ard Ayus, horiz. 50m, Hatan Bator Magsarzhav. 60m, Has Bator, horiz. 1t, Sukhe Bator.

1972, Oct. 20 Litho. *Perf. 12*

No.	Type	Value	Color	Unused	Used
693	A164	10m	gold & multi	15	15
694	A164	20m	gold & multi	15	15
695	A164	50m	gold & multi	20	15
696	A164	60m	gold & multi	30	18
697	A164	1t	gold & multi	40	28
			Nos. 693-697 (5)	1.20	
			Set value		68

Paintings of national heroes.

Spasski Tower, Moscow — A165

1972, Nov. 7 Photo. *Perf. 11*

No.	Type	Value	Color	Unused	Used
698	A165	60m	multi	20	15

50th anniversary of USSR. Printed with small label showing arms of USSR.

Mark Spitz, US, Gold Medal — A166

Designs (Medal and): 10m, Ulrike Meyfarth, Germany. 20m, Sawao Kato, Japan. 30m, András Balczó, Hungary. 60m, Lasse Viren, Finland. 80m, Shane Gould, Australia. 1t, Anatoli Bondarchuk, USSR. 4t, Khorloo Baianmunk, Mongolia.

1972, Dec. 15 Photo. *Perf. 12½*

No.	Type	Value	Color	Unused	Used
699	A166	5m	grn & multi	15	15
700	A166	10m	ver & multi	15	15
701	A166	20m	bl & multi	15	15
702	A166	30m	multi	20	15
703	A166	60m	lt vio & multi	28	15
704	A166	80m	ol & multi	35	18
705	A166	1t	lem & multi	50	28
			Nos. 699-705 (7)	1.78	
			Set value		85

Souvenir Sheet

No.	Type	Value	Color	Unused	Used
706	A166	4t	red & multi	2.00	2.00

Winners in 20th Olympic Games, Munich.

Chimpanzee on Bicycle A167

Circus Scenes: 10m, Seal playing ball. 15m, Bear riding wheel. 20m, Woman acrobat on camel. 30m, Woman equestrian. 50m, Clown playing flute. 60m, Woman gymnast. 1t, Circus building, Ulan Bator, horiz.

1973, Jan. 29 Litho. *Perf. 12*

No.	Type	Value	Color	Unused	Used
707	A167	5m	multi	15	15
708	A167	10m	multi	15	15
709	A167	15m	multi	15	15
710	A167	20m	multi	15	15
711	A167	30m	multi	18	15
712	A167	50m	multi	20	15
713	A167	60m	multi	28	15
714	A167	1t	multi	38	24
			Set value	1.40	80

Postrider — A168

Designs: 60m, Diesel locomotive. 1t, Truck.

1973, Jan. 31 Photo. *Perf. 12*

No.	Type	Value	Color	Unused	Used
715	A168	50m	brown	24	15
716	A168	60m	green	30	15
717	A168	1t	rose claret	50	20
			Set value		36

See No. C34.

Sukhe Bator and Merchants A169

Paintings of Sukhe Bator: 20m, With elders. 50m, Leading partisans. 60m, With revolutionary council. 1t, Receiving deputation, horiz.

1973, Feb. 2 Photo. *Perf. $11^1/_2$x12*

No.	Type	Value	Description	Unused	Used
718	A169	10m	gold & multi	15	15
719	A169	20m	gold & multi	15	15
720	A169	50m	gold & multi	18	15
721	A169	60m	gold & multi	20	18
722	A169	1t	gold & multi	35	28
			Nos. 718-722 (5)	1.03	
			Set value		66

Sukhe Bator (1893-1923).

Nicolaus Copernicus A170

Marx and Lenin A171

Designs: 60m, 2t, Copernicus in laboratory, by Jan Matejko (horiz.; 55x35mm.). 1t (No. 725, 726b), Portrait. 1t (No. 726a), like 50m.

1973, Mar. Litho. *Perf. 12*

No.	Type	Value	Description	Unused	Used
723	A170	50m	gold & multi	18	15
724	A170	60m	gold & multi	24	15
725	A170	1t	gold & multi	38	20

Souvenir Sheet

No.	Description	Unused	Used
726	Sheet of 3	2.00	2.00
a.	A170 1t multi	35	35
b.	A170 1t multi	35	35
c.	A170 2t multi	70	70

500th anniversary of the birth of Nicolaus Copernicus (1473-1543), Polish astronomer.

1973, July 15 Photo. *Perf. $11^1/_2$x12*

No.	Type	Value	Description	Unused	Used
727	A171	60m	gold, car & ultra	28	15

9th meeting of postal administrations of socialist countries, Ulan Bator.

Common Shelducks — A172

Designs: Aquatic birds.

1973, Aug. 10 Litho. *Perf. 12x11*

No.	Type	Value	Description	Unused	Used
728	A172	5m	shown	15	15
729	A172	10m	Arctic loons	15	15
730	A172	15m	Bar-headed geese	15	15
731	A172	30m	Great crested grebe	18	15
732	A172	50m	Mallards	24	15
733	A172	60m	Mute swans	30	20
734	A172	1t	Greater scaups	55	28
			Nos. 728-734 (7)	1.72	
			Set value		88

1973, Aug. 25 Litho. *Perf. 12x11*

Designs: Fur-bearing animals.

No.	Type	Value	Description	Unused	Used
735	A172	5m	Siberian weasel	15	15
736	A172	10m	Siberian chipmunk	15	15
737	A172	15m	Flying squirrel	15	15
738	A172	20m	Eurasian badger	15	15
739	A172	30m	Eurasian red squirrel	15	15
740	A172	60m	Wolverine	20	15
741	A172	80m	Mink	24	20
742	A172	1t	White hare	30	24
			Set value	1.15	90

1973, Dec. 15 Litho. *Perf. 12x11*

Designs: Flowers.

No.	Type	Value	Description	Unused	Used
743	A172	5m	Alpine aster	15	15
744	A172	10m	Mongolian silene	15	15
745	A172	15m	Rosa davurica	15	15
746	A172	20m	Mongolian dandelion	15	15
747	A172	30m	Rhododendron dahuricum	15	15
748	A172	50m	Clematis tangutica	18	15
749	A172	60m	Siberian primula	24	18
750	A172	1t	Pasqueflower	35	24
			Set value	1.20	90

Globe and Red Flag Emblem — A173

1973, Dec. 10 Photo. *Perf. 12x$12^1/_2$*

No.	Type	Value	Description	Unused	Used
751	A173	60m	gold, red & bl	28	15

15th anniversary of the review "Problems of Peace and Socialism," published in Prague.

Limenitis Populi A174

Butterflies: 10m, Arctia hebe. 15m, Rhyparia purpurata. 20m, Catocala pacta. 30m, Isoceras kaszabi. 50m, Celerio costata. 60m, Arctia caja. 1t, Diacrisia sannio.

1974, Jan. 15 Litho. *Perf. 11*

No.	Type	Value	Description	Unused	Used
752	A174	5m	lil & multi	15	15
753	A174	10m	brn & multi	15	15
754	A174	15m	bl & multi	15	15
755	A174	20m	brn org & multi	15	15
756	A174	30m	lt vio & multi	15	15
757	A174	50m	dl red & multi	20	16
758	A174	60m	yel grn & multi	28	24
759	A174	1t	ultra & multi	40	30
			Set value	1.35	1.00

"Hehe Namshil" by L. Merdorsh A175

Designs (Various Scenes from): 20m, "Sive Hiagt," by D. Luvsansharav. 25m, 80m, 1t, "Edre," by D. Namdag. 30m, "The 3 Khans of Sara-Gol" (legend). 60m, "Amarsana," by B. Damdinsuren. 20m and 30m horizontal.

1974, Feb. 20 Litho. *Perf. 12*

No.	Type	Value	Description	Unused	Used
760	A175	15m	sil & multi	15	15
761	A175	20m	sil & multi	15	15
762	A175	25m	sil & multi	15	15
763	A175	30m	sil & multi	18	15
764	A175	60m	sil & multi	24	15
765	A175	80m	sil & multi	35	18
766	A175	1t	sil & multi	38	20
			Nos. 760-766 (7)	1.60	
			Set value		80

Mongolian operas and dramas.

Government Building and Sukhe Bator — A176

1974, Mar. 1 Photo. *Perf. 11*

No.	Type	Value	Description	Unused	Used
767	A176	60m	gold & multi	20	15

50th anniv. of renaming capital Ulan Bator.

Juggler A177

Designs: 10m, Dressage, horiz. 30m, Trained elephant. 40m, Yak pushing ball, horiz. 60m, Acrobats with ring. 80m, Woman acrobat on unicycle.

1974, May 4 Litho. *Perf. 12*

No.	Type	Value	Description	Unused	Used
768	A177	10m	multi	15	15
769	A177	20m	multi	15	15
770	A177	30m	multi	15	15
771	A177	40m	multi	16	15
772	A177	60m	multi	28	20
773	A177	80m	multi	35	24
			Nos. 768-773,C65 (7)	1.72	
			Set value		1.00

Mongolian Circus. No. 773 has se-tenant label, with similar design.

Girl on Bronco A178

Children's Activities: 20m, Boy roping calf. 30m, 40m, Boy taming horse (different designs). 60m, Girl with doves. 80m, Wrestling. 1t, Dancing.

1974, June 2 Litho. *Perf. 12*

No.	Type	Value	Description	Unused	Used
774	A178	10m	dl yel & multi	15	15
775	A178	20m	lt bl & multi	15	15
776	A178	30m	grn & multi	15	15
777	A178	40m	yel & multi	18	15
778	A178	60m	pink & multi	24	15
779	A178	80m	bl & multi	35	18
780	A178	1t	dl bl & multi	38	20
			Set value	1.35	72

Children's Day.

Archer — A179

National Sports: 20m, Two horsemen fighting for goatskin. 30m, Archer on horseback. 40m, Horse race. 60m, Riding wild horse. 80m, Rider chasing riderless horse. 1t, Boys wrestling.

1974, July 11 Photo. *Perf. 11*

No.	Type	Value	Description	Unused	Used
781	A179	10m	vio bl & multi	15	15
782	A179	20m	yel & multi	15	15
783	A179	30m	lil & multi	15	15
784	A179	40m	multi	15	15
785	A179	60m	multi	20	15
786	A179	80m	multi	30	18
787	A179	1t	multi	45	24
			Set value	1.30	76

Nadam, Mongolian national festival.

Grizzly Bear — A180

1974, July Litho. *Perf. 12*

No.	Type	Value	Description	Unused	Used
788	A180	10m	shown	15	15
789	A180	20m	Common panda	15	15
790	A180	30m	Giant panda	15	15
791	A180	40m	Two brown bears	18	15
792	A180	60m	Sloth bear	28	15
793	A180	80m	Asiatic black bears	40	18
794	A180	1t	Giant brown bear	55	20
			Nos. 788-794 (7)	1.86	
			Set value		80

Stag in Zuun Araat Wildlife Preserve — A181

1974, Sept. Litho. *Perf. 12*

No.	Type	Value	Description	Unused	Used
795	A181	10m	shown	15	15
796	A181	20m	Beaver	15	15
797	A181	30m	Leopard	15	15
798	A181	40m	Great black-backed gull	15	15
799	A181	60m	Deer	20	15
800	A181	80m	Mouflon	30	20
801	A181	1t	Deer and entrance to Bogd-uul Preserve	45	28
			Set value	1.30	90

Protected fauna in Mongolian wildlife preserves.

Buddhist Temple, Bogdo Gegen Palace — A182

Mongolian Architecture: 15m, Buddhist Temple, now Museum. 30m, Entrance to Charity Temple, Ulan Bator. 50m, Mongolian yurta. 80m, Gazebo in convent yard.

1974, Oct. 15 Litho. *Perf. 12*

No.	Type	Description	Unused	Used
802	A182	10m bl & multi	15	15
803	A182	15m multi	15	15
804	A182	30m grn & multi	15	15
805	A182	50m multi	24	15
806	A182	80m yel & multi	40	24
		Set value	88	56

Spasski Tower, Sukhe Bator Statue — A183

1974, Nov. 26 Photo. *Perf. 11½x12*

No.	Type	Description	Unused	Used
807	A183	60m multi	28	15

Visit of General Secretary Brezhnev and a delegation from the USSR to participate in celebration of 50th anniversary of People's Republic of Mongolia.

Sukhe Bator Proclaiming Republic — A184

Designs: No. 808, "First Constitution," symbolic embroidery. No. 809, Flag over landscape, lane and communications tower.

1974, Nov. 28 Litho.

No.	Type	Description	Unused	Used
808	A184	60m multi	28	15
809	A184	60m multi	28	15
810	A184	60m multi	28	15
		Set value		30

50th anniversary of People's Republic of Mongolia.

Decanter — A185

Designs: 20m, Silver jar. 30m, Night lamp. 40m, Tea jug. 60m, Candelabra. 80m, Teapot. 1t, Silver bowl on 3-legged stand.

1974, Dec. 1 Photo.

No.	Type	Description	Unused	Used
811	A185	10m bl & multi	15	15
812	A185	20m cl & multi	15	15
813	A185	30m multi	15	15
814	A185	40m dp bl & multi	15	15
815	A185	60m multi	20	15
816	A185	80m grn & multi	35	18
817	A185	1t lil & multi	45	24
		Set value	1.35	75

Mongolian 19th century goldsmiths' work.

Lapwing (plover) — A186

1974, Dec. Litho. *Perf. 11*

No.	Type	Description	Unused	Used
818	A186	10m shown	15	15
819	A186	20m Fish	15	15
820	A186	30m Marsh marigolds	16	15
821	A186	40m White pelican	25	15
822	A186	60m Perch	32	20
823	A186	80m Mink	50	28
		Nos. 818-823,C66 (7)	2.08	
		Set value		1.10

Water and nature protection.

American Mail Coach, UPU Emblem — A187

Designs (UPU Emblem and): 20m, French two-wheeled coach. 30m, Changing horses, Russian coach. 40m, Swedish caterpillar mail truck. 50m, First Hungarian mail truck. 60m, German Daimler-Benz mail truck. 1t, Mongolian dispatch rider.

1974, Dec. Litho. *Perf. 12*

No.	Type	Description	Unused	Used
824	A187	10m multi	15	15
825	A187	20m multi	15	15
826	A187	30m multi	15	15
827	A187	40m multi	18	15
828	A187	50m multi	20	15
829	A187	60m multi	28	15
830	A187	1t multi	45	24
		Nos. 824-830 (7)	1.56	
		Set value		80

Cent. of the UPU and Stockholmia 74.

Mongolian Flag, Broken Swastika — A188

1975, May 9 Photo. *Perf. 11½x12*

No.	Type	Description	Unused	Used
832	A188	60m multi	28	15

30th anniversary of the end of World War II and victory over fascism.

Mongolian Woman — A189

1975, May

No.	Type	Description	Unused	Used
833	A189	60m multi	28	15

International Women's Year 1975.

Zygophyllum Xanthoxylon — A190

Medicinal Plants: 20m, Ingarvillea potaninii. 30m, Lancea tibetica. 40m, Jurinea mongolica. 50m, Saussurea involucrata. 60m, Allium mongolicum. 1t, Adonis mongolica.

1975, May 24 Photo. *Perf. 11x11½*

No.	Type	Description	Unused	Used
834	A190	10m dp org & multi	15	15
835	A190	20m grn & multi	15	15
836	A190	30m yel & multi	15	15
837	A190	40m vio & multi	15	15
838	A190	50m brn & multi	24	15
839	A190	60m bl & multi	28	18
840	A190	1t multi	48	28
		Set value	1.35	88

12th International Botanists' Conference.

Shepherd — A191

Puppet Theater: 20m, Boy on horseback. 30m, Boy and disobedient bull calf. 40m, Little orphan camel's tale. 50m, Boy and obedient little yak. 60m, Boy riding swan. 1t, Children's choir.

1975, June 30 Litho. *Perf. 12*

No.	Type	Description	Unused	Used
841	A191	10m multi	15	15
842	A191	20m multi	15	15
843	A191	30m multi	15	15
844	A191	40m multi	15	15
845	A191	50m multi	24	15
846	A191	60m multi	28	18
847	A191	1t multi	48	28
		Set value	1.35	88

Pioneers Tending Fruit Tree — A192

Designs: 60m, Pioneers studying, and flying model plane. 1t, New emblem of Mongolian Pioneers.

1975, July 15 *Perf. 12x11½*

No.	Type	Description	Unused	Used
848	A192	50m multi	20	15
849	A192	60m multi	24	15
850	A192	1t multi	35	24
		Set value		44

Mongolian Pioneers, 50th anniversary.

Nos. 624-630 Overprinted

Тээвэр—50
1975—7—15

1975, July 15 Litho. *Perf. 12*

No.	Type	Description	Unused	Used
850A	A151	20m multi	85	85
850B	A151	30m multi	85	85
850C	A151	40m multi	1.25	1.25
850D	A151	50m multi	1.25	1.25
850E	A151	60m multi	1.40	1.40
850F	A151	80m multi	2.00	2.00
850G	A151	1t multi	2.50	2.50
		Nos. 850A-850G (7)	10.10	10.10

Fifty years of communication.

Golden Eagle Hunting Fox — A193

Hunting Scenes: 20m, Dogs treeing lynx, vert. 30m, Hunter stalking marmots. 40m, Hunter riding reindeer, vert. 50m, Boar hunt. 60m, Trapped wolf, vert. 1t, Bear hunt.

1975, Aug. 25 Litho. *Perf. 12*

No.	Type	Description	Unused	Used
851	A193	10m multi	15	15
852	A193	20m multi	20	15
853	A193	30m multi	30	15
854	A193	40m multi	35	15
855	A193	50m multi	45	18
856	A193	60m multi	60	20
857	A193	1t multi	1.00	35
		Nos. 851-857 (7)	3.05	
		Set value		1.00

Hunting in Mongolia.

Mesocottus Haitej — A194

Various Fish: 20m, Pseudaspius lepto cephalus. 30m, Oreoleuciscus potanini. 40m, Tinca tinca. 50m, Coregonus lavaretus pidschian. 60m, Erythroculter mongolicus. 1t, Carassius auratus.

1975, Sept. 15 Photo. *Perf. 11*

No.	Type	Description	Unused	Used
858	A194	10m multi	15	15
859	A194	20m multi	15	15
860	A194	30m multi	15	15
861	A194	40m bl & multi	18	15
862	A194	50m grn & multi	28	18
863	A194	60m lil & multi	35	20
864	A194	1t vio bl & multi	55	35
		Nos. 858-864 (7)	1.81	
		Set value		1.00

Neck and Bow of Musical Instrument (Morin Hur) — A195

National Handicraft: 20m, Saddle. 30m, Silver headgear. 40m, Boots. 50m, Tasseled Woman's cap. 60m, Pipe and tobacco pouch. 1t, Sable cap.

Perf. 11½x12½

1975, Oct. 10 **Litho.**

865 A195 10m multi 15 15
866 A195 20m multi 15 15
867 A195 30m multi 15 15
868 A195 40m multi 18 15
869 A195 50m multi 28 18
870 A195 60m multi 35 20
871 A195 1t multi 55 35
Nos. 865-871 (7) 1.81
Set value 1.00

Revolutionists with Flags — A196

1975, Nov. 15 **Litho.** *Perf. 11½x12*

872 A196 60m multi 28 15

70th anniversary of Russian Revolution.

Ski Jump, Olympic Games Emblem — A197

Designs (Winter Olympic Games Emblem and): 20m, Ice hockey. 30m, Skiing. 40m, Bobsled. 50m, Biathlon. 60m, Speed skating. 1t, Figure skating, women's. 4t, Skier carrying torch.

Perf. 11½x12½

1975, Dec. 20 **Litho.**

873 A197 10m multi 15 15
874 A197 20m multi 15 15
875 A197 30m brn & multi 15 15
876 A197 40m grn & multi 18 15
877 A197 50m multi 28 18
878 A197 60m ol & multi 35 20
879 A197 1t multi 55 35
Nos. 873-879 (7) 1.81
Set value 1.00

Souvenir Sheet

880 A197 4t multi 3.00 3.00

12th Winter Olympic Games, Innsbruck, Austria, Feb. 4-15, 1976.

Taming Wild Horse — A198

Mongolian Paintings: 20m, Camel caravan, horiz. 30m, Man playing lute. 40m, Woman adjusting headdress, horiz. 50m, Woman wearing ceremonial costume. 60m, Women fetching water. 1t, Woman musician. 4t, Warrior on horseback.

1975, Nov. 30 *Perf. 12*

881 A198 10m brn & multi 15 15
882 A198 20m bl & multi 15 15
883 A198 30m ol & multi 15 15
884 A198 40m lil & multi 15 15
885 A198 50m bl & multi 24 18
886 A198 60m lil & multi 28 18
887 A198 1t sil & multi 48 30
Set value 1.40 95

Souvenir Sheet

888 A198 4t bl & multi 1.75 1.75

House of Young Technicians — A199

Designs: 60m, Hotel Ulan Bator. 1t, Museum of the Revolution.

1975, Dec. 30 **Photo.** *Perf. 12x11½*

893 A199 50m ultra 20 15
894 A199 60m bl grn 40 15
895 A199 1t brick red 60 20
Set value 40

Camels in Gobi Desert A200

Designs: 20m, Horse taming. 30m, Horseback riding. 40m, Pioneers' camp. 60m, Young musician. 80m, Children's festival. 1t, Mongolian wrestling.

1976, June 1 **Litho.** *Perf. 12*

896 A200 10m multi 15 15
897 A200 20m multi 15 15
898 A200 30m multi 15 15
899 A200 40m multi 20 15
900 A200 60m multi 35 15
901 A200 80m multi 48 24
902 A200 1t multi 60 28
Nos. 896-902 (7) 2.08
Set value 90

International Children's Day.

Red Star — A201

1976, May 1 **Photo.** *Perf. 11x12½*

903 A201 60m red, mar & sil 30 15

17th Congress of the Mongolian People's Revolutionary Party, June 14.

Archery, Montreal Games' Emblem, Canadian Flag — A202

Designs (Montreal Olympic Games' Emblem, Canadian Flag and): 20m, Judo. 30m, Boxing. 40m, Vaulting. 60m, Weight lifting. 80m, High Jump. 1t, Target shooting.

Perf. 12½x11½

1976, May 20 **Litho.**

904 A202 10m yel & multi 15 15
905 A202 20m yel & multi 15 15
906 A202 30m yel & multi 15 15
907 A202 40m yel & multi 18 15
908 A202 60m yel & multi 28 15
909 A202 80m yel & multi 35 24
910 A202 1t yel & multi 45 28
Set value 1.45 90

21st Olympic Games, Montreal, Canada, July 17-Aug. 1. See No. C81.

Partisans A203

Fighter and Sojombo Independence Symbol — A204

Perf. 12x11½, 11½x12

1976, June 15 **Litho.**

911 A203 60m multi 35 15
912 A204 60m multi 40 15

55th anniversary of Mongolia's independence. See No. C82.

Souvenir Sheet

Sukhe Bator Medal — A205

1976, July 11 *Perf. 11½*

913 A205 4t multi 1.75 1.75

Mongolian honors medals.

Osprey A206

Protected Birds: 20m, Griffon vulture. 30m, Bearded lammergeier. 40m, Marsh harrier. 60m, Black vulture. 80m, Golden eagle. 1t, Tawny eagle.

1976, Aug. 16 **Litho.** *Perf. 12*

914 A206 10m multi 15 15
915 A206 20m multi 15 15
916 A206 30m multi 15 15
917 A206 40m multi 20 15
918 A206 60m multi 35 18
919 A206 80m multi 40 28
920 A206 1t multi 55 35
Nos. 914-920 (7) 1.95
Set value 1.05

"Nadom" Military Game — A207

Paintings by O. Cevegshava: 10m, Taming Wild Horse, vert. 30m, Hubsugul Lake Harbor. 40m, The Steppe Awakening. 80m, Wrestlers. 1.60t, Yak Descending in Snow, vert.

1976, Sept. **Litho.** *Perf. 12*

921 A207 10m multi 15 15
922 A207 20m multi 15 15
923 A207 30m multi 15 15
924 A207 40m multi 20 15
925 A207 80m multi 40 24
926 A207 1.60t multi 55 28
Nos. 921-926 (6) 1.60
Set value 78

Interlocking Circles, Industry and Transport — A208

1976, Oct. 15 **Photo.** *Perf. 12x11½*

927 A208 60m brn, bl & red 35 18

Soviet-Mongolian friendship.

John Naber, US Flag, Gold Medals — A209

Designs: 20m, Nadia Comaneci, Romanian flag. 30m, Kornelia Ender, East German flag. 40m, Mitsuo Tsukahara, Japanese flag. 60m, Gregor Braun, German flag. 80m, Lasse Viren, Finnish flag. 1t, Nikolai Andrianov, Russian flag.

1976, Nov. 30 **Litho.** *Perf. 12*

928 A209 10m multi 15 15
929 A209 20m multi 15 15
930 A209 30m multi 15 15
931 A209 40m multi 20 15
932 A209 60m multi 35 15
933 A209 80m multi 40 24
934 A209 1t multi 55 28
Nos. 928-934 (7) 1.95
Set value 90

Gold medal winners, 21st Olympic Games, Montreal. See No. C83.

Stone Tablet on Tortoise A210

Carved Tablet, 6th-8th Centuries A211

1976, Dec. 15 Litho. *Perf. 11½x12*
935 A210 50m brn & lt bl 85 15
936 A211 60m gray & brt grn 1.25 15
Set value 24

International Archaeological Conference, Ulan Bator.

R-1 Plane — A212

Designs: Various Mongolian planes.

1976, Dec. 22 *Perf. 12*
937 A212 10m multi 15 15
938 A212 20m multi 15 15
939 A212 30m multi 15 15
940 A212 40m multi 18 15
941 A212 60m multi 35 18
942 A212 80m multi 40 24
943 A212 1t multi 48 30
Nos. 937-943 (7) 1.86
Set value 95

Dancers — A213

Folk Dances: 20m, 13th century costumes. 30m, West Mongolian dance. 40m, "Ekachi," or horse-dance. 60m, "Bielge," West Mongolian trunk dance. 80m, "Hodak," or friendship dance. 1t, "Dojarka."

1977, Mar. 20 Litho. *Perf. 12½*
944 A213 10m multi 15 15
945 A213 20m multi 15 15
946 A213 30m multi 15 15
947 A213 40m multi 18 15
948 A213 60m multi 35 18
949 A213 80m multi 40 28
950 A213 1t multi 48 35
Nos. 944-950 (7) 1.86
Set value 1.10

Miniature Sheet

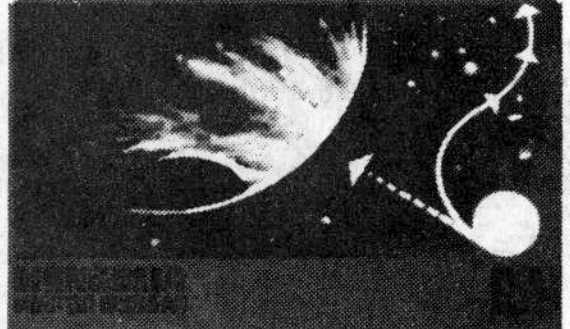

Path of Pioneer from Earth to Jupiter, deflected by Mars — A214

Isaac Newton — A215

1977, Mar. 31 Litho. *Perf. 11½x12*
951 Sheet of 9 2.00 85
a. A214 60m shown 20 15
b. A215 60m Apple tree 20 15
c. A214 60m Sextant and planets 20 15
d. A214 60m Astronauts in space 20 15
e. A215 60m shown 20 15
f. A214 60m Prism and spectrum 20 15
g. A214 60m Rain falling on earth 20 15
h. A215 60m Motion of celestial bodies 20 15
i. A214 60m Pioneer 10 over Jupiter 20 15

Sir Isaac Newton (1642-1727), English natural philosopher and mathematician.

Nos. 951a-951i arranged in 3 rows of 3. Nos. 951d and 951i inscribed AIR MAIL.

D. Natsagdorji, Writer, and Quotation — A216

Design: No. 953, Grazing horses, landscape, ornament and quotation.

1977 *Perf. 11½x12*
952 A216 60m multi 35 18
953 A216 60m multi 40 18

D. Natsagdorji, founder of modern Mongolian literature. Label and vignette separated by simulated perforations.

Primitive Tortoises — A217

Prehistoric Animals: 20m, Ungulate (titanothere). 30m, Flying lizard. 40m, Entelodon (swine). 60m, Antelope. 80m, Hipparion. 1t, Aurochs.

1977, May 7 Photo. *Perf. 12½*
954 A217 10m multi 15 15
955 A217 20m multi 15 15
956 A217 30m multi 15 15
957 A217 40m multi 18 15
958 A217 60m multi 35 18
959 A217 80m multi 40 28
960 A217 1t multi 48 35
Nos. 954-960 (7) 1.86
Set value 1.10

Souvenir Sheet

Mongolia, Type A2 and Netherlands No. 1 — A218

1977, May 20
961 A218 4t multi 2.00 2.00

AMPHILEX '77 International Philatelic Exhibition, Amsterdam, May 27-June 5. No. 961 contains one 37x52mm stamp.

Boys on Horseback — A219

Designs: 20m, Girl on horseback. 30m, Hunter on horseback. 40m, Grazing horses. 60m, Mare and foal. 80m, Grazing horse and student. 1t, White stallion.

1977, June 15 Litho. *Perf. 12*
962 A219 10m multi 15 15
963 A219 20m multi 18 15
964 A219 30m multi 24 15
965 A219 40m multi 38 15
966 A219 60m multi 65 15
967 A219 80m multi 75 24
968 A219 1t multi 1.00 28
Nos. 962-968 (7) 3.35
Set value 90

Copper and Molybdenum Plant, Vehicles — A220

1977, June 15 Litho. *Perf. 12*
969 A220 60m multi 35 18

Erdenet, a new industrial town.

Bucket Brigade Fighting Fire — A221

Fire Fighting: 20m, Horse-drawn fire pump. 30m, Horse-drawn steam pump. 40m, Men in protective suits fighting forest fire. 60m, Modern foam extinguisher. 80m, Truck and ladder. 1t, Helicopter fighting fire on steppe.

1977, Aug. Litho. *Perf. 12*
970 A221 10m multi 15 15
971 A221 20m multi 15 15
972 A221 30m multi 15 15
973 A221 40m multi 20 15
974 A221 60m multi 35 18
975 A221 80m multi 40 28
976 A221 1t multi 55 35
Nos. 970-976 (7) 1.95
Set value 1.05

Radar and Molnya Satellite on TV Screen — A222

1977, Sept. 12 Photo. *Perf. 12x11½*
977 A222 60m gray, bl & blk 35 18

40th anniversary of Technical Institute.

Lenin Museum, Ulan Bator A223

1977, Oct. 1 Litho. *Perf. 12*
978 A223 60m multi 40 18

Inauguration of Lenin Museum in connection with the 60th anniversary of the Russian October Revolution.

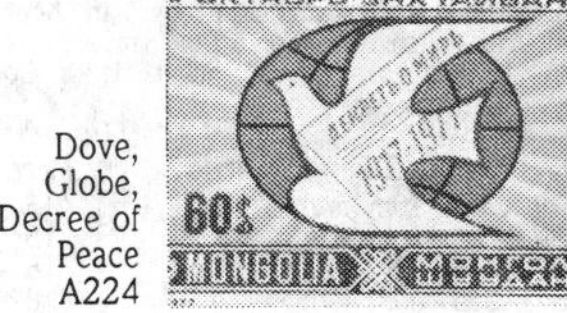

Dove, Globe, Decree of Peace A224

Designs: 50m, Cruiser Aurora and Russian flag, vert. 1.50t, Globe and "Freedom."

Perf. 11½x12, 12x11½
1977, Oct. 1 Photo.
979 A224 50m gold & multi 28 15
980 A224 60m gold & multi 35 18
981 A224 1.50t gold & multi 80 48

60th anniversary of the Russian Revolution.

Aporia Crataegi A225

Moths: 20m, Gastropacha quercifolia. 30m, Colias chrysoteme. 40m, Dasychira fascelina. 60m, Malocosoma neustria. 80m, Diacrisia sanno. 1t, Heodes virgaureae.

1977, Sept. 25 Photo. *Perf. 12½*
982 A225 10m multi 15 15
983 A225 20m multi 15 15
984 A225 30m multi 18 15
985 A225 40m multi 24 15
986 A225 60m multi 38 18
987 A225 80m multi 48 28
988 A225 1t multi 60 35
Nos. 982-988 (7) 2.18
Set value 1.05

Giant Pandas — A226

Pandas: 10m, Eating bamboo, vert. 30m, Female and cub in washtub, vert. 40m, Male and cub playing with bamboo. 60m, Female and cub, vert. 80m, Family. 1t, Male, vert.

1977, Nov. 25 Litho. *Perf. 12*
989 A226 10m multi 15 15
990 A226 20m multi 15 15
991 A226 30m multi 15 15
992 A226 40m multi 20 15
993 A226 60m multi 35 18
994 A226 80m multi 40 28
995 A226 1t multi 55 35
Nos. 989-995 (7) 1.95
Set value 1.05

Souvenir Sheet

Helen Fourment and her Children, by Rubens — A227

1977, Dec. 5 *Perf. 11½x10½*
996 A227 4t multi 2.25 2.25

Peter Paul Rubens (1577-1640).

Ferrari Racing Car — A228

Experimental Racing Cars: 30m, Ford McLaren. 40m, Madi, USSR. 50m, Mazda. 60m, Porsche. 80m, Russian model car. 1.20t, The Blue Flame, US speed car.

1978, Jan. 28 Litho. *Perf. 12*

997	A228	20m multi	15	15
998	A228	30m multi	15	15
999	A228	40m multi	18	15
1000	A228	50m multi	24	18
1001	A228	60m multi	28	20
1002	A228	80m multi	35	28
1003	A228	1.20t multi	55	38
		Nos. 997-1003 (7)	1.90	
		Set value		1.25

Boletus Variegatus — A229

Mushrooms: 30m, Russula cyanoxantha. 40m, Boletus aurantiacus. 50m, Boletus scaber. 60m, Russula flava. 80m, Lactarius resimus. 1.20t, Flammula spumosa.

1978, Feb. 28 Photo. *Perf. 11x11½*

1004	A229	20m yel & multi	15	15
1005	A229	30m yel & multi	15	15
1006	A229	40m yel & multi	18	15
1007	A229	50m yel & multi	24	18
1008	A229	60m yel & multi	30	20
1009	A229	80m yel & multi	38	28
1010	A229	1.20t yel & multi	60	38
		Nos. 1004-1010 (7)	2.00	
		Set value		1.25

Young Couple with Youth Flag — A230

1978, Apr. Litho. *Perf. 11½x12*

1011	A230	60m multi	35	18

17th Congress of Mongolian Youth Organization, Ulan Bator, Apr. 1978.

Soccer, Sugar Loaf Mountain, Rio de Janeiro, Brazil 1950 Emblem — A231

Designs (Various Soccer Scenes and): 30m, Old Town Tower, Bern, Switzerland, 1954. 40m, Town Hall, Stockholm, Sweden, 1958. 50m, University of Chile, Chile, 1962. 60m, Parliament and Big Ben, London, 1966. 80m, Degolladeo Theater, Guadalajara, Mexico, 1970. 1.20t, Town Hall and TV Tower, Munich, Germany.

1978, Apr. 15 *Perf. 12*

1012	A231	20m multi	15	15
1013	A231	30m multi	15	15
1014	A231	40m multi	20	15
1015	A231	50m multi	28	15
1016	A231	60m multi	35	18
1017	A231	80m multi	40	20
1018	A231	1.20t multi	70	28
		Nos. 1012-1018 (7)	2.23	
		Set value		1.00

11th World Cup Soccer Championship, Argentina, June 1-25. See No. C109.

Capex Emblem, Eurasian Beaver and Canada #336 — A232

Designs: 30m, Tibetan sand grouse and Canada #478. 40m, Red-throated loon and Canada #369. 50m, Argali and Canada #324. 60m, Eurasian brown bear and Canada #322. 80m, Moose and Canada #323. 1.20t, Great black-backed gull and Canada #343.

1978, June Litho. *Perf. 12*

1019	A232	20m multi	15	15
1020	A232	30m multi	15	15
1021	A232	40m multi	18	15
1022	A232	50m multi	20	18
1023	A232	60m multi	28	20
1024	A232	80m multi	40	30
1025	A232	1.20t multi	60	40
		Nos. 1019-1025 (7)	1.96	
		Set value		1.30

CAPEX '78 International Philatelic Exhibition, Toronto, June 9-18. See No. C110.

Marx, Engels and Lenin A233

1978, July 11 Photo. *Perf. 12x11½*

1026	A233	60m gold, blk & red	35	18

50th anniversary of publication in Prague of "Problems of Peace and Socialism."

Souvenir Sheet

Outdoor Rest, by Amgalan — A234

Paintings by D. Amgalan: No. 1027b, Winter Night (dromedary and people in snow). No. 1027c, Saddling up.

1978, Aug. 10 Litho. *Perf. 12*

1027		Sheet of 3	2.75	2.75
a.-c.		A234 1.50t any single	80	

Philatelic cooperation between Hungary and Mongolia, 20th anniversary. No. 1027 contains 3 stamps and 3 labels.

Papillon — A235

Dogs: 20m, Black Mongolian sheepdog. 30m, Puli. 40m, St. Bernard. 50m, German shepherd. 60m, Mongolian watchdog. 70m, Samoyed. 80m, Laika (1st dog in space) and rocket. 1.20t, Cocker spaniels and poodle.

1978, Sept. 25 Litho. *Perf. 12*

1028	A235	10m multi	15	15
1029	A235	20m multi	15	15
1030	A235	30m multi	15	15
1031	A235	40m multi	18	15
1032	A235	50m multi	20	15
1033	A235	60m multi	24	15
1034	A235	70m multi	28	18
1035	A235	80m multi	30	20
1036	A235	1.20t multi	50	24
		Nos. 1028-1036 (9)	2.15	
		Set value		1.10

Open Book and Pen — A236

1978, Oct. 20 Photo. *Perf. 12x11½*

1037	A236	60m car & ultra	35	18

Mongolian Writers' Association, 50th anniversary.

Souvenir Sheets

Clothed Maya, by Goya — A237

Melancholy, by Dürer — A238

Paintings: No. 1038b, "Ta Matete," by Gauguin. No. 1038c, Bridge at Arles, by Van Gogh.

1978, Oct. 30 Litho. *Perf. 12*

1038		Sheet of 3 + 3 labels	2.75	2.75
a.-c.		A237 1.50t any single	80	80

Perf. 11½

1039	A238	4t black	2.25	2.25

Anniversaries of European painters: Francisco Goya; Paul Gauguin; Vincent van Gogh; Albrecht Dürer.

Camel and Calf — A239

Bactrian Camels: 30m, Young camel. 40m, Two camels. 50m, Woman leading pack camel. 60m, Old camel. 80m, Camel pulling cart. 1.20t, Race.

1978, Nov. 30 Litho. *Perf. 12*

1040	A239	20m multi	15	15
1041	A239	30m multi	15	15
1042	A239	40m multi	20	15
1043	A239	50m multi	24	15
1044	A239	60m multi	35	15
1045	A239	80m multi	40	15
1046	A239	1.20t multi	60	20
		Nos. 1040-1046 (7)	2.09	
		Set value		75

Flags of Comecon Members, Globe A240

1979, Jan. 2 Litho. *Perf. 12*

1047	A240	60m multi	28	15

30th anniversary of the Council of Mutual Assistance (Comecon).

Silver Tabby — A241

Domestic Cats: 30m, White Persian. 50m, Red Persian. 60m, Cream Persian. 70m, Siamese. 80m, Smoky Persian. 1t, Burmese.

1979, Feb. 10

1048	A241	10m multi	15	15
1049	A241	30m multi	15	15
1050	A241	50m multi	20	15
1051	A241	60m multi	24	15
1052	A241	70m multi	28	15
1053	A241	80m multi	35	18
1054	A241	1t multi	40	28
		Nos. 1048-1054 (7)	1.77	
		Set value		98

Potaninia Mongolica — A242

Flowers: 30m, Sophora alopecuroides. 50m, Halimodendron halodendron. 60m, Forget-me-nots. 70m, Pincushion flower. 80m, Leucanthemum Sibiricum. 1t, Edelweiss.

1979, Mar. 10 Litho. *Perf. 12*

1055	A242	10m multi	15	15
1056	A242	30m multi	15	15
1057	A242	50m multi	22	15
1058	A242	60m multi	28	15
1059	A242	70m multi	30	15
1060	A242	80m multi	38	15
1061	A242	1t multi	45	18
		Nos. 1055-1061 (7)	1.93	
		Set value		75

Finland-Czechoslovakia, Finnish Flag — A243

Ice Hockey Games and 1980 Olympic Emblems: 30m, German Fed. Rep.-Sweden, German flag. 50m, US-Canada, US flag. 60m, USSR-Sweden, Russian flag. 70m, Canada-USSR, Canadian flag. 80m, Swedish goalie and flag. 1t, Czechoslovakia-USSR, Czechoslovak flag.

1979, Apr. 10 Litho. *Perf. 12*

1062 A243 10m multi 15 15
1063 A243 30m multi 15 15
1064 A243 50m multi 22 15
1065 A243 60m multi 28 15
1066 A243 70m multi 35 15
1067 A243 80m multi 40 18
1068 A243 1t multi 50 20
Nos. 1062-1068 (7) 2.05
Set value 82

Ice Hockey World Championship, Moscow, Apr. 14-27.

Lambs — A244

Paintings: 30m, Milking, camels. 50m, Plane bringing supplies in winter. 60m, Herdsmen and horses. 70m, Milkmaids, vert. 80m, Summer Evening (camels). 1t, Landscape with herd. 4t, After the Storm.

Perf. 12x11½, 11½x12

1979, May 3 Litho.

1069 A244 10m multi 15 15
1070 A244 30m multi 15 15
1071 A244 50m multi 18 15
1072 A244 60m multi 24 15
1073 A244 70m multi 32 15
1074 A244 80m multi 40 18
1075 A244 1t multi 48 20
Nos. 1069-1075 (7) 1.92
Set value 82

Souvenir Sheet

1076 A244 4t multi 2.25 2.25

20th anniv. of 1st agricultural cooperative.

Souvenir Sheet

Mongolia No. 4, Bulgaria No. 1, Philaserdica Emblem — A245

Designs (Rowland Hill and): No. 1077b, American mail coach. No. 1077c, Mail car, London-Birmingham railroad, 1838. 1077d, Packet leaving Southampton, Sept. 24, 1842, opening Indian mail service.

1979, May 15 Litho. *Perf. 12*

1077 Sheet of 4, multi 1.75 1.75
a.-d. A245 1t any single 38 38

Philaserdica '79, Sofia, May 18-27, and Rowland Hill (1795-1879), originator of penny postage.

Rocket, Manchester, 1829 — A246

Locomotives: 20m, "Adler" Nuremberg-Furth, 1835. 30m, American engine, 1860. 40m, Ulan Bator-Nalajh run, 1931. 50m, Moscow-Ulan Bator run, 1936. 60m, Moscow-Ulan Bator, 1970. 70m, Tokyo-Osaka run, 1963. 80m, Orleans Aerotrain, 1967. 1.20t, Soviet Rapidity, experimental train.

1979, June 8 Litho. *Perf. 12*

1078 A246 10m multi 15 15
1079 A246 20m multi 15 15
1080 A246 30m multi 15 15
1081 A246 40m multi 18 15
1082 A246 50m multi 20 15
1083 A246 60m multi 28 15
1084 A246 70m multi 30 15
1085 A246 80m multi 35 15
1086 A246 1.20t multi 48 20
Nos. 1078-1086 (9) 2.24
Set value 85

Intl. Transportation Exhibition, Hamburg.

Mongolian and Russian Flags — A247

Battle Scene and Emblem — A248

1979, Aug. 10 Photo. *Perf. 11½x12*

1087 A247 60m multi 28 15
1088 A248 60m multi 28 15
Set value 24

Battle of Ha-lo-hsin River, 40th anniversary.

Manuls A249

Wild Cats: 30m, Lynx. 50m, Tigers. 60m, Snow leopards. 70m, Black panthers. 80m, Leopards. 1t, Lions.

1979, Sept. 10 Litho. *Perf. 12*

1089 A249 10m multi 15 15
1090 A249 30m multi 15 15
1091 A249 50m multi 20 15
1092 A249 60m multi 24 15
1093 A249 70m multi 28 15
1094 A249 80m multi 35 15
1095 A249 1t multi 40 18
Nos. 1089-1095 (7) 1.77
Set value 72

Souvenir Sheet

Brazil No. 1582 A250

Designs: b, Brazil #1144 (Pele). c, Mongolia #C1.

1979, Sept. 15 Litho. *Perf. 11*

1096 Sheet of 3 + 3 labels 2.50 2.50
a.-c. A250 1.50t any single 75 75

Brasiliana '79, 3rd World Thematic Stamp Exhibition, Rio de Janeiro, Sept. 15-23.

Cross-Country Skiing, Lake Placid '80 Emblem — A251

Lake Placid '80 Emblem and: 30m, Biathlon. 40m, Ice hockey. 50m, Ski jump. 60m, Downhill skiing. 80m, Speed skating. 1.20t, Bobsledding. 4t, Figure skating.

Perf. 11½x12½

1980, Jan. 20 Litho.

1097 A251 20m multi 15 15
1098 A251 30m multi 16 15
1099 A251 40m multi 22 15
1100 A251 50m multi 25 15
1101 A251 60m multi 35 15
1102 A251 80m multi 42 15
1103 A251 1.20t multi 65 22
Nos. 1097-1103 (7) 2.20
Set value 75

Souvenir Sheet

1104 A251 4t multi 2.75 2.75

13th Winter Olympic Games, Lake Placid, NY, Feb. 12-24.

Flower Type of 1969
Souvenir Sheet

Design: Landscape and edelweiss.

1980, May 5 Litho. *Perf. 11*

1105 A131 4t multi 3.00 3.00

London 1980 Intl. Stamp Exhib., May 6-14. No. 1105 contains one stamp 43x26mm.

Weightlifting, Moscow '80 Emblem — A252

1980, June 2 Litho. *Perf. 12*

1106 A252 20m shown 15 15
1107 A252 30m Archery 15 15
1108 A252 40m Gymnast 18 15
1109 A252 50m Running 20 15
1110 A252 60m Boxing 24 15
1111 A252 80m Judo 35 15
1112 A252 1.20t Bicycling 50 18
Nos. 1106-1112 (7) 1.77
Set value 66

Souvenir Sheet

1113 A252 4t Wrestling 2.75 2.75

22nd Summer Olympic Games, Moscow, July 19-Aug. 3.

Gold Medal, Swimmer, Moscow '80 Emblem — A253

Gold Medal, Moscow '80 Emblem and Number of Medals won by Top Countries: 30m, Fencing. 50m, Judo. 60m, Track. 80m, Boxing. 1t, Weight lifting. 1.20t, Kayak.

1980, Sept. 15 Litho. *Perf. 12½*

1114 A253 20m multi 15 15
1115 A253 30m multi 16 15
1116 A253 50m multi 28 15
1117 A253 60m multi 32 15
1118 A253 80m multi 45 15
1119 A253 1t multi 55 15
1120 A253 1.20t multi 65 18
Nos. 1114-1120 (7) 2.56
Set value 75

See No. C144.

A254

A255

1980, Sept. 17 *Perf. 11½x12*

1121 A254 60m Jumdshaigiin Zedenbal 32 15
1122 A254 60m Zedenbal, 1941, grn 32 15
1123 A254 60m Zedenbal, 1979, gray grn 32 15
1124 A254 60m with Brezhnev, horiz. 32 15
1125 A254 60m with children 32 15
1126 A254 60m Sukhe Bator, dk brn 32 15
1127 A254 60m Choibalsan, ultra 32 15
Nos. 1121-1127 (7) 2.24
Set value 84

Miniature Sheet

Cosmonauts from various Intercosmos flights: a, A. Gubarjev. b, Czechoslovakia #2222. c, P. Klimuk. d, Poland #2270. e, V. Bykovsky. f, DDR #1947. g, N. Rukavishnikov. h, Bulgaria #2576. i, V. Kubasov. j, Hungary #C417.

1980, Oct. 10 Litho. *Perf. 12*

1128 Sheet of 12 2.50 2.50
a.-j. A255 40m any single 22 22

Intercosmos cooperative space program.
See No. 1232.

Benz, Germany, 1885 — A256

Antique Cars: 30m, President, Austria-Hungary, 1897. 40m, Armstrong Siddley, 1904. 50m, Russo-Balt, 1909. 60m, Packard, United States, 1909. 80m, Lancia, Italy, 1911. 1.60t, Marne taxi, France, 1914. 4t, Nami-1, Russia, 1927.

1980, Nov. 20 Litho. *Perf. 12½*

1129 A256 20m multi 15 15
1130 A256 30m multi 16 15
1131 A256 40m multi 22 15
1132 A256 50m multi 28 15
1133 A256 60m multi 32 15
1134 A256 80m multi 45 15
1135 A256 1.60t multi 90 28
Nos. 1129-1135 (7) 2.48
Set value 82

Souvenir Sheet

1136 A256 4t multi 2.50 2.50

Penguins A257

1980, Dec. 1 *Perf. 12*

1137 A257 20m shown 15 15
1138 A257 30m Giant blue whale 16 15
1139 A257 40m Albatross 22 15
1140 A257 50m Weddell seals 28 15
1141 A257 60m Emperor penguins 32 15
1142 A257 70m Skua 38 15
1143 A257 80m Grampus 45 15
1144 A257 1.20t Penguins, Soviet plane 65 18
Nos. 1137-1144 (8) 2.61
Set value 78

Souvenir Sheet

1145 A257 4t World map showing continental drift 2.50 2.50

Antarctic animals and exploration. No. 1145 contains one 44mm circular stamp.

Souvenir Sheet

A258

1980, Dec. 20 Litho. *Perf. 11*

1146 Sheet of 2 2.50 85
a. A258 2t shown 1.25 40
b. A258 2t Old Marketplace 1.25 40

The Shepherd Speaking the Truth, IYC Emblem — A259

IYC Emblem and Nursery Tales: 30m, Above Them the Sky is Always Clear. 40m, Winter's Joys. 50m, Little Musicians. 60m, Happy Birthday. 80m, The First Day of School. 1.20t, May Day. 4t, The Wonder-working Squirrels.

1980, Dec. 29 *Perf. 12*

1147 A259 20m multi 15 15
1148 A259 30m multi 16 15
1149 A259 40m multi 22 15
1150 A259 50m multi 35 15
1151 A259 60m multi 40 15
1152 A259 80m multi 55 16
1153 A259 1.20t multi 75 22
Nos. 1147-1153 (7) 2.58
Set value 75

Souvenir Sheet

1154 A259 4t multi 2.50 2.50

Intl. Year of the Child (1979).

60th Anniversary of People's Army — A260

1981, Jan. 31 Litho. *Perf. 12*

1155 A260 60m multi 32 15

60th Anniversary of People's Revolutionary Party — A261

1981, Feb. 2

1156 A261 60m multi 32 15

Ice Racing — A262

Designs: Various racing motorcycles.

1981, Feb. 28 *Perf. 12½*

1157 A262 10m multi 15 15
1158 A262 20m multi 15 15
1159 A262 30m multi 16 15
1160 A262 40m multi 22 15
1161 A262 50m multi 28 15
1162 A262 60m multi 32 15
1163 A262 70m multi 35 15
1164 A262 80m multi 45 15
1165 A262 1.20t multi 65 18
Nos. 1157-1165 (9) 2.73
Set value 82

Cosmonauts Boarding Soyuz 39 — A263

Designs: 30m, Rocket designer Koroljov. 40m, Vostok I, Yuri Gagarin. 50m, Salyut space station. 60m, Satellite photographing earth. 80m, Light crystallization from Salyut spacecraft. 1.20t, Salyut, Kremlin, Sukhe Bator statue. 4t, Soviet and Mongolian cosmonauts.

1981, Mar. 22 Litho. *Perf. 12*

1166 A263 20m multi 15 15
1167 A263 30m multi 16 15
1168 A263 40m multi 22 15
1169 A263 50m multi 28 15
1170 A263 60m multi 35 15
1171 A263 80m multi 45 15
1172 A263 1.20t multi 65 22
Nos. 1166-1172 (7) 2.26
Set value 75

Souvenir Sheet

Perf. 11½

1173 A263 4t multi 2.50 2.50

Intercosmos cooperative space program (Mongolia-USSR). No. 1173 contains one 29x39mm stamp.

No. 240, Ulan Bator A264

1981, Apr. 28 Litho. *Perf. 12*

1174 Sheet of 4 2.50 2.50
a. A264 1t shown 55 20
b. A264 1t Germany #8N4, 8N34 55 20
c. A264 1t Austria #B110 55 20
d. A264 1t Japan #827 55 20

1981 Stamp Exhibitions: Mongolian Natl., Ulan Bator; Naposta, Stuttgart; WIPA, Vienna; Japex, Tokyo. Nos. 1174a-1174d se-tenant with labels showing show emblems.

Star Shining on Factories and Sheep — A265

1981, May 5

1175 A265 60m multi 32 15

18th Congress of Revolutionary People's Party, May.

Souvenir Sheet

Statue of Sukhe Bator, Mongolian Flag A266

1981, May 20 *Perf. 12½*

1176 A266 4t multi 2.50 2.50

Mongolian Revolutionary People's Party, 60th anniv.

Sheep Farming (Economic Development) — A267

1981, June 1 *Perf. 12½x11½*

1177 A267 20m shown 15 15
1178 A267 30m Transportation 16 15
1179 A267 40m Telecommunications 22 15
1180 A267 50m Public health service 28 15
1181 A267 60m Agriculture 35 15
1182 A267 80m Power plant 45 15
1183 A267 1.20t Public housing 65 22
Nos. 1177-1183 (7) 2.26
Set value 75

A268

A269

Souvenir Sheet

Perf. 12½x11½

1981, July 11 Litho.

1184 A268 4t multi 2.50 2.50

20th anniv. of UN membership.

1981, Aug. 1 *Perf. 12*

Designs: Sailing ships. 10m, 20m, horiz.

1185 A269 10m Egyptian, 15th cent. BC 15 15
1186 A269 20m Mediterranean, 9th cent. 15 15
1187 A269 40m Hansa Cog, 12th cent. 22 15
1188 A269 50m Venitian, 13th cent. 28 15
1189 A269 60m Santa Maria 35 15
1190 A269 80m Endeavor 45 15
1191 A269 1t Poltava, 18th cent. 55 20
1192 A269 1.20t US schooner, 19th cent. 65 22
Nos. 1185-1192 (8) 2.80
Set value 95

Mongolian-USSR Friendship Pact — A270

1981, Sept. 1 *Perf. 11½x12*

1193 A270 60m multi 35 15

Flora, by Rembrandt A271

1981, Sept. 1 *Perf. 11½x12½*

1194 A271 20m shown 15 15
1195 A271 30m Hendrickje in the Bed 16 15
1196 A271 40m Young Woman with Earrings 22 15
1197 A271 50m Young Girl in the Window 28 15
1198 A271 60m Hendrickje like Flora 35 15
1199 A271 80m Saskia with Red Flower 45 15
1200 A271 1.20t Holy Family with Drape 65 22
Nos. 1194-1200 (7) 2.26
Set value 75

Souvenir Sheet

1201 A271 4t Self-portrait with Saskia 2.50 2.50

375th birth anniv. of Rembrandt.

Goat (Pawn) A272

Designs: Wood chess pieces.

1981, Sept. 30 Litho. *Perf. 12½*

1202 A272 20m shown 15 15
1203 A272 40m Cart (castle) 22 15
1204 A272 50m Camel (bishop) 28 15
1205 A272 60m Horse (knight) 35 15
1206 A272 80m Lion (queen) 45 15
1207 A272 1.20t Man and dog (king) 65 15
Nos. 1202-1207 (6) 2.10
Set value 58

Souvenir Sheet

1208 A272 4t Men playing 2.50 2.50

Camel and Circus Tent A273

1981, Oct. 30 Litho. *Perf. 12*

1209 A273 10m shown 15 15
1210 A273 20m Horsemen 15 15
1211 A273 40m Wrestlers 22 15
1212 A273 50m Archers 28 15
1213 A273 60m Folksinger 35 15
1214 A273 80m Girl playing jatga 45 15
1215 A273 1t Ballet dancers 55 18
1216 A273 1.20t Statue 65 20
Nos. 1209-1216 (8) 2.80
Set value 85

Wolfgang Amadeus Mozart and Scene from his Magic Flute A274

Designs: Composers and Scenes from their Works.

1981, Nov. 16

1217 A274 20m shown 15 15
1218 A274 30m Beethoven, Fidelio 16 15
1219 A274 40m Bartok, Miraculous Mandarin 22 15
1220 A274 50m Verdi, Aida 28 15
1221 A274 60m Tchaikovsky, Sleeping Beauty 35 15
1222 A274 80m Dvorak, New World Symphony score 45 15
1223 A274 1.20t Chopin, piano 65 20
Nos. 1217-1223 (7) 2.26
Set value 70

Ribbon Weaver A275

Designs: Mongolian women.

Perf. 11½x12½

1981, Dec. 10 Litho.

1224 A275 20m multi 15 15
1225 A275 30m multi 16 15
1226 A275 40m multi 22 15
1227 A275 50m multi 28 15
1228 A275 60m multi 35 15
1229 A275 80m multi 45 15
1230 A275 1.20t multi 65 22
Nos. 1224-1230 (7) 2.26
Set value 75

Souvenir Sheet

1231 A275 4t multi 2.75 2.75

Intercosmos Type of 1980

Designs: a, V. Gorbatko. b, Y. Romanenko. c, V. Dzhanibekov. d, L. Popov. e, Vietnamese stamp. f, Cuban stamp. g, No. 1173. h, Romania No. C241.

1981, Dec. 28 *Perf. 12*

1232 Sheet of 8, multi 2.50 2.50
a.-h. A255 50m, any single 30 30

Historic Bicycles A276

1982, Mar. 25 Litho. *Perf. 11*

1233 A276 10m Germany, 1816 15 15
1234 A276 20m Scotland, 1838 15 15
1235 A276 40m US, 1866 22 15
1236 A276 50m France, 1863 28 15
1237 A276 60m "Kangaroo", 1877 35 15
1238 A276 80m England, 1870 45 15
1239 A276 1t 1878 55 20
1240 A276 1.20t Modern bike 65 22
Nos. 1233-1240 (8) 2.80
Set value 95

Souvenir Sheet

Perf. 12½

1241 A276 4t Racing 2.75 2.75

No. 1241 contains one stamp 47x47mm.

1982 World Cup — A277

1982, Apr. 20 *Perf. 12*

1242 A277 10m Brazil, 1950 15 15
1243 A277 20m Switzerland, 1954 15 15
1244 A277 40m Sweden, 1958 22 15
1245 A277 50m Chile, 1962 28 15
1246 A277 60m England, 1966 35 15
1247 A277 80m Mexico, 1970 45 15
1248 A277 1t Germany, 1974 55 20
1249 A277 1.20t Argentina, 1978 65 22
Nos. 1242-1249 (8) 2.80
Set value 95

Souvenir Sheet

Perf. 11

1250 A277 4t Spain, 1982 2.50 2.50

No. 1250 contains one stamp 48x48mm.

12th Trade Union Congress, Ulan Bator — A278

Perf. 11½x12½

1982, May 20 Litho.

1251 A278 60m multi 35 15

Souvenir Sheet

PHILEXFRANCE Intl. Stamp Exhibition, Paris, June 11-21 — A279

1982, June 11 *Perf. 10½*

1252 A279 4t No. B13 design 2.50 2.50

George Dimitrov (1882-1949), First Prime Minister of Bulgaria — A280

1982, June 18 *Perf. 12*

1253 A280 60m gold & blk 35 15

Chicks — A281

1982, June 25 *Perf. 11*

1254 A281 10m shown 15 15
1255 A281 20m Colt 15 15
1256 A281 30m Lamb 16 15
1257 A281 40m Fawn 22 15
1258 A281 50m Camel calf 28 15
1259 A281 60m Kid 35 15
1260 A281 70m Calf 38 15
1261 A281 1.20t Young boar 65 22
Nos. 1254-1261 (8) 2.34
Set value 75

Coal Mining Industry — A282

1982, July 5 *Perf. 12*

1262 A282 60m Mine, truck 35 15

18th Mongolian Youth Org. Congress — A283

1982, Aug. 14 *Perf. 11½x12*

1263 A283 60m multi 35 15

Siberian Pine A284

1982, Aug. 16

1264 A284 20m shown 15 15
1265 A284 30m Abies sibirica 15 15
1266 A284 40m Populus diversifolia 18 15
1267 A284 50m Larix sibirica 20 15
1268 A284 60m Pinus silvestris 28 15
1269 A284 80m Betula platyphylla 35 15
1270 A284 1.20t Picea obovata 50 22
Nos. 1264-1270 (7) 1.81
Set value 75

60th Anniv. of Mongolian Youth Org. — A285

1982, Aug. 30

1271 A285 60m multi 35 15

Iseki-6500 Tractor, Japan — A286

1982, Oct. 1 Litho. *Perf. 12½*

1272 A286 10m shown 15 15
1273 A286 20m Deutz-DX-230, Germany 15 15
1274 A286 40m Bonser, Gt. Britain 18 15
1275 A286 50m Intl.-884, US 22 15
1276 A286 60m Renault TX-145-14, France 28 15
1277 A286 80m Belarus-611, USSR 35 15
1278 A286 1t K-7100, USSR 45 15
1279 A286 1.20t DT-75, USSR 55 18
Nos. 1272-1279 (8) 2.33
Set value 70

Scenes from The Foal and The Hare Folktale
A287

1983, Jan. 1 Litho. *Perf. 14*

1280 A287 10m multi 15
1281 A287 20m multi 15
1282 A287 30m multi 15
1283 A287 40m multi 22
1284 A287 50m multi 26
1285 A287 60m multi 35
1286 A287 70m multi 38
1287 A287 80m multi 42
1288 A287 1.20t multi 70
Nos. 1280-1288 (9) 2.78

Souvenir Sheet

Imperf

1289 A287 7t multi 4.00

No. 1289 contains one stamp 58x58mm.

Scenes from Walt Disney's The Sorcerer's Apprentice — A288

1983, Jan. 1

1290 A288 25m multi 15
1291 A288 35m multi 16
1292 A288 45m multi 24
1293 A288 55m multi 28
1294 A288 65m multi 32
1295 A288 75m multi 35
1296 A288 85m multi 42
1297 A288 1.40t multi 70
1298 A288 2t multi 95
Nos. 1290-1298 (9) 3.57

Souvenir Sheet

1299 A288 7t multi 4.00

Fish, Lake Hevsgel — A289

1982, Nov. 30 *Perf. 12*

1300 A289 20m shown 15
1301 A289 30m Sheep, Zavhan Highlands 15
1302 A289 40m Beaver, Lake Hovd 18
1303 A289 50m Horses, Lake Uvs 22
1304 A289 60m Chamois, Bajanhongor Steppe 28
1305 A289 80m Mounted hunter, eagle, Bajan-Elgij Highlands 35
1306 A289 1.20t Camels, Gobi Desert 55
Nos. 1300-1306 (7) 1.88

Mongolian Skin Tent (Yurt) — A290

1983, Mar. 30 Litho. *Perf. 14*

1307 A290 20m Antonov AN-24B plane 15
1308 A290 30m shown 15
1309 A290 40m Deer 18
1310 A290 50m Bighorn sheep 22
1311 A290 60m Eagle 28
1312 A290 80m Museum of the Khans, Ulan Bator 35
1313 A290 1.20t Sukhe Bator monument, Ulan Bator 55
Nos. 1307-1313 (7) 1.88

Souvenir Sheet

90th Birth Anniv. of Sukhe Bator — A291

1983 *Perf. 13x14*

1314 A291 4t multi 2.50

Local Flowers — A292

1983, Feb. 4 Photo. *Perf. 13*

1315 A292 20m Rose 15
1316 A292 30m Dahlias 16
1317 A292 40m Tagetes faula 22
1318 A292 50m Narcissus 28
1319 A292 60m Violets 35
1320 A292 80m Tulips 40
1321 A292 1.20t Heliopsis helianthoides 70
Nos. 1315-1321 (7) 2.26

50th Anniv. of Border Forces — A293

1983, Feb. 9 Litho. *Perf. 14*

1322 A293 60m multi 35

Souvenir Sheet

BRASILIANA, Philatelic Exhibition — A294

1983, July 10 Litho. *Perf. 14*

1323 A294 4t multi 2.50

Karl Marx — A295

1983, Oct. 1 Litho. *Perf. 14*

1324 A295 60m gold, dp car & bl 40

18th Party Congress, Ulan Bator — A296

1983, Nov. 1 Litho. *Perf. 14*

1325 A296 10m Cattle 15
1326 A296 20m Coal 15
1327 A296 30m Garment 20
1328 A296 40m Agricultural 28
1329 A296 60m Communications 40
1330 A296 80m Transportation 55
1331 A296 1t Educational System 70
Nos. 1325-1331 (7) 2.43

Souvenir Sheet

Sistine Madonna, by Raphael (1483-1520)
A297

1983, Dec. 15 Litho. *Perf. 14x13½*

1332 A297 4t multi 2.75

A298

Children in Various Activities.

1984, Jan. 1 Photo. *Perf. 13*

1333 A298 10m multi 15
1334 A298 20m multi 15
1335 A298 30m multi 20
1336 A298 40m multi 28
1337 A298 50m multi 35
1338 A298 70m multi 48
1339 A298 1.20t multi 80
Nos. 1333-1339 (7) 2.41

Rodents — A299

Various rodents.

1984, Jan. 15 Litho. *Perf. 13½x13*

1340 A299 20m multi 15
1341 A299 30m multi 20
1342 A299 40m multi 28
1343 A299 50m multi 35
1344 A299 60m multi 40
1345 A299 80m multi 55
1346 A299 1.20t multi 80
Nos. 1340-1346 (7) 2.73

1984 Winter Olympics — A300

1984, Feb. 15 Litho. *Perf. 14*

1347 A300 20m Bobsledding 15
1348 A300 30m Cross-country skiing 20
1349 A300 40m Hockey 28
1350 A300 50m Speed skating 35
1351 A300 60m Downhill skiing 40
1352 A300 80m Figure skating 55
1353 A300 1.20t Biathlon 80
Nos. 1347-1353 (7) 2.73

Souvenir Sheet

1354 A300 4t Ski jumping 2.75

Size of No. 1354: 134x106mm. Nos. 1347-1352 vert.

Children Feeding Lambs — A301

1984, Mar. 1 Litho. *Perf. 12*

1355 A301 20m Ice skating 15
1356 A301 30m shown 20
1357 A301 40m Planting tree 28
1358 A301 50m Playing on beach 35
1359 A301 60m Carrying pail 40
1360 A301 80m Dancing 55
1361 A301 1.20t Dancing, diff. 80
Nos. 1355-1361 (7) 2.73

Souvenir Sheet

1362 A301 4t Boy, girl 2.75

No. 1362 contains one stamp 48x46mm.

Mail Car, Communications Emblems — A302

1984, Apr. 15 *Perf. 13½x14*

1363 A302 10m shown 15
1364 A302 20m Earth satellite receiving station 15
1365 A302 40m Airplane 28
1366 A302 50m Central PO 35
1367 A302 1t Radar station 70
1368 A302 1.20t Train 80
Nos. 1363-1368 (6) 2.43

Souvenir Sheet

Imperf

1369 A302 4t Dish antenna 2.75

1984 Summer Olympics — A303

1984, June 1 Photo. *Perf. 14*

1370	A303	20m	Gymnastics	15
1371	A303	30m	Bicycling	20
1372	A303	40m	Weight lifting	28
1373	A303	50m	Judo	35
1374	A303	60m	Archery	40
1375	A303	80m	Boxing	55
1376	A303	1.20t	High jump	80
			Nos. 1370-1376 (7)	2.73

Souvenir Sheet

1377 A303 4t Wrestling 2.75

Souvenir Sheet

AUSIPEX '84 and ESPANA '84 — A304

1984, May Litho. *Perf. 14*

1378 A304 4t Jet 2.75

Cuban Revolution, 25th Anniv. — A304a

1984, June 2 Litho. *Perf. 14*

1378A A304a 60m multi 24

State Bank, 60th Anniv. — A304b

1984, Sept. 25 *Perf. 13½x13*

1378B A304b 60m Commemorative coins, 1981 24

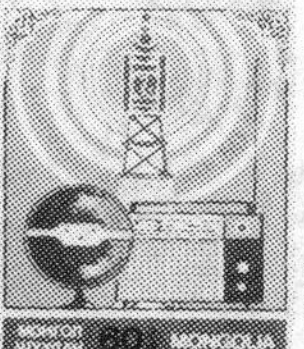

Radio Broadcasting in Mongolia, 50th Anniv. — A304c

1984, Sept. 1 Litho. *Perf. 13x13½*

1378C A304c 60m multicolored 75

Scenes from Walt Disney's Mickey and the Beanstalk — A305

1984, Dec. 20 Litho. *Perf. 11*

1379	A305	25m	multi	15
1380	A305	35m	multi	15
1381	A305	45m	multi	20
1382	A305	55m	multi	24
1383	A305	65m	multi	28
1384	A305	75m	multi	30
1385	A305	85m	multi	35
1386	A305	1.40t	multi	60
1387	A305	2t	multi	80
			Nos. 1379-1387 (9)	3.07

Miniature Sheet

Perf. 14

1388 A305 7t multi 3.75

Fairy Tales — A306

1984, Dec. 20 Litho. *Perf. 13½*

1389	A306	10m	multi	15
1390	A306	20m	multi	15
1391	A306	30m	multi	16
1392	A306	40m	multi	20
1393	A306	50m	multi	28
1394	A306	60m	multi	35
1395	A306	70m	multi	40
1396	A306	80m	multi	45
1397	A306	1.20t	multi	65
			Nos. 1389-1397 (9)	2.79

Miniature Sheet

1398 A306 4t multi 3.00

Souvenir Sheet

60th Anniv. of Mongolian Stamps — A308

1984, Dec. 20 Litho. *Perf. 14*

1400 A308 4t No. 1 2.75

Ulan Bator, 60th Anniv. — A309

Mongolian People's Republic, 60th Anniv. — A310

1984, Nov. 26 Litho. *Perf. 13x13½*

1401 A309 60m multicolored 75

Perf. 14

1402 A310 60m multicolored 75

Mongolian People's Party, 60th Anniv. — A311

1984, Nov. 26 Litho. *Perf. 14*

1403 A311 60m multi 35

Native Masks — A312

1984, Dec. 31 Litho. *Perf. 14*

1404	A312	20m	multi	15
1405	A312	30m	multi	20
1406	A312	40m	multi	25
1407	A312	50m	multi	35
1408	A312	60m	multi	40
1409	A312	80m	multi	60
1410	A312	1.20t	multi	85
			Nos. 1404-1410 (7)	2.80

Souvenir Sheet

1411 A312 4t multi 2.75

Dogs A313

1984, Dec. 31 Litho. *Perf. 13*

1412	A313	20m	Collie	15
1413	A313	30m	German Sheepdog	20
1414	A313	40m	Papillon	25
1415	A313	50m	Cocker Spaniel	35
1416	A313	60m	Puppy	40
1417	A313	80m	Dalmatians	60
1418	A313	1.20t	Mongolian Sheep-dog	85
			Nos. 1412-1418 (7)	2.80

Cattle — A314

1985, Jan. *Perf. 14*

1419	A314	20m	Shar tarlan	15
1420	A314	30m	Bor khaliun	18
1421	A314	40m	Sarlag	25
1422	A314	50m	Dornod taliin bukh	32
1423	A314	60m	Char tarlan	38
1424	A314	80m	Nutgiin uulderiin unee	50
1425	A314	1.20t	Tsagaan tolgoit	75
			Nos. 1419-1425 (7)	2.53

1984 Olympic Winners — A315

Gold medalists: 20m, Gaetan Boucher, Canada, 1500-meter speed skating. 30m, Eirik Kvalfoss, Norway, 10-kilometer biathlon. 40m, Marja-Lissa Haemaelainen, Finland, 5-kilometer Nordic skiing. 50m, Max Julen, Switzerland, men's giant slalom. 60m, Jens Weissflag, German Democratic Republic, 70-meter ski jump. 80m, W. Hoppe and D. Schauerhammer, German Democratic Republic, 2-man bobsled. 1.20t, Elena Valova and Oleg Vassiliev, USSR, pairs figure skating. 4t, USSR, ice hockey. Nos. 1430-1432 vert.

1985, Apr. 25

1426	A315	20m	multi	15
1427	A315	30m	multi	15
1428	A315	40m	multi	20
1429	A315	50m	multi	25
1430	A315	60m	multi	30
1431	A315	80m	multi	40
1432	A315	1.20t	multi	60
			Nos. 1426-1432 (7)	2.05

Souvenir Sheet

1433 A315 4t multi 2.00

Souvenir Sheet

Girl, Fawn — A316

1985, Apr. 25

1434 A316 4m multi 2.00

Birds — A317

World Youth Festival, Moscow — A318

1985, May 1 *Perf. 12½x13*

1435	A317	20m	Ciconia nigra	15
1436	A317	30m	Haliaetus albicilla	15
1437	A317	40m	Grus leucogeranus	20
1438	A317	50m	Paradoxornis heudei	25
1439	A317	60m	Grus monahas	30
1440	A317	80m	Grus vipio	40
1441	A317	1.20t	Buteo lagopus	60
			Nos. 1435-1441 (7)	2.05

National Wildlife Preservation Association.

1985, June *Perf. 14*

1442 A318 60m Girls in folk costumes 30

Camelus Bactrianus — A319

Panthera Unicias — A320

Cervus Elaphus — A321

Camels, leopards and deer.

1985

1443 A319 50m Adults, young 25
1444 A319 50m Facing right 25
1445 A319 50m Facing left 25
1446 A319 50m Trotting 25
1447 A320 50m Hunting 25
1448 A320 50m Standing in snow 25
1449 A320 50m Female, young 25
1450 A320 50m Adults 25
1451 A321 50m Fawn 25
1452 A321 50m Doe in woods 25
1453 A321 50m Adult male 25
1454 A321 50m Adults, fawn 25
Nos. 1443-1454 (12) 3.00

#1443-1446 show the World Wildlife Fund emblem, #1447-1454 the Natl. Wildlife Preservation emblem. Issue dates: #1443-1446, July 1; #1447-1454, Aug. 1.

UN, 40th Anniv. — A322

1985, Aug. 1 ***Perf. 13½x13***

1455 A322 60m Flags, UN building 30

Indigenous Flowering Plants — A323

1985, Aug. 1 ***Perf. 14***

1456 A323 20m Rosa dahurica 15
1457 A323 30m Matricaria chamomilla 15
1458 A323 40m Taraxacum officinale 20
1459 A323 50m Saxzitraga nirculus 25
1460 A323 60m Vaccinium vitis idaea 30
1461 A323 80m Sanguisorba officinalis 40
1462 A323 1.20t Plantago major 60
Nos. 1456-1462 (7) 2.05

Souvenir Sheet

1463 A323 4t Hyppopae thamnoides 2.00

A324 A325

1985, Sept. 15 ***Perf. 13x13½***

1464 A324 60m Monument 30

Defeat of Nazi Germany, 40th anniv.

1985, Oct. 1 ***Perf. 14***

Various soccer plays. No. 1472 horiz.

1465 A325 20m multi 15
1466 A325 30m multi 15
1467 A325 40m multi 20
1468 A325 50m multi 25
1469 A325 60m multi 30
1470 A325 80m multi 40
1471 A325 1.20t multi 60
Nos. 1465-1471 (7) 2.05

Souvenir Sheet

1472 A325 4t multi 2.00

1985 Junior World Soccer Championships, Moscow.

Souvenir Sheet

ITALIA '85 — A326

1985, Oct. 1

1473 A326 4t Horseman 2.00

Conquest of Space — A327

Russian spacecraft.

1985, Nov. 1

1474 A327 20m Soyuz 15
1475 A327 30m Cosmos 15
1476 A327 40m Venera 9 20
1477 A327 50m Salyut 25
1478 A327 60m Luna 9 30
1479 A327 80m Train 40
1480 A327 1.20t Dish receiver 60
Nos. 1474-1480 (7) 2.05

Souvenir Sheet

1985, Dec. 15

1481 A327 4t Cosmonaut on space walk 2.00

> ***15-Cent Minimum Value***
> *The minimum catalogue value is 15 cents. Separating se-tenant pieces into individual stamps does not increase the "value" of the stamps... since demand for the separated stamps may be small.*

Mushrooms — A328

1985, Dec. 1 ***Perf. 13½***

1482 A328 20m Tricholoma mongolica 15
1483 A328 30m Cantharellus cibarius 15
1484 A328 40m Armillariella mellea 20
1485 A328 50m Amanita caesarea 25
1486 A328 70m Xerocomus badius 35
1487 A328 80m Agaricus silvaticus 40
1488 A328 1.20t Boletus edulis 60
Nos. 1482-1488 (7) 2.10

Souvenir Sheet

Phalacrocorax Penicillatus — A329

1986, Jan. 15 ***Perf. 12½x13***

1489 A329 4t multi 3.00

No. 1489 contains one stamp plus 2 labels picturing various bird species.

Young Pioneers A330

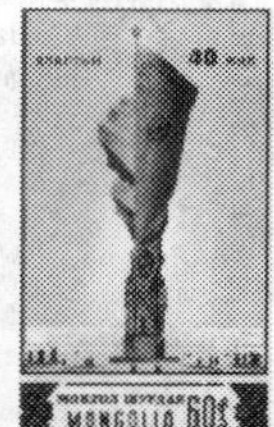

Victory Monument A331

1985, Dec. 31 Litho. ***Perf. 13x13½***

1490 A330 60m multi 38

1985, Dec. 31 ***Perf. 12½x13***

1491 A331 60m multi 38

Victory over Japan ending WWII, 40th anniv.

Natl. Costumes — A332

1986, Mar. 1 Litho. ***Perf. 14***

Background Color

1492 A332 60m yel grn, shown 20
1493 A332 60m red 20
1494 A332 60m pale yel grn 20
1495 A332 60m violet 20
1496 A332 60m ultra 20
1497 A332 60m bluish grn 20
1498 A332 60m pale org brn 20
Nos. 1492-1498 (7) 1.40

Ernst Thalmann (1886-1944) A333

1986, May 15 Litho. ***Perf. 14***

1499 A333 60m gold, redsh brn & dk brn 28

Natl. Revolution, 65th Anniv. — A334

1986, May 15

1500 A334 60m Statue of Sukhe Bator 28

19th Socialist Party Congress — A335

1986, May 15

1501 A335 60m multi 28

1986 World Cup Soccer Championships, Mexico — A336

FIFA emblem and various soccer plays. Nos. 1502-1503, 1505-1508 vert.

1986, May 31

1502 A336 20m multi 15
1503 A336 30m multi 15
1504 A336 40m multi 20
1505 A336 50m multi 24
1506 A336 60m multi 28

1507	A336	80m	multi	38
1508	A336	1.20t	multi	55
			Nos. 1502-1508 (7)	1.95

Souvenir Sheet

1509	A336	4t	multi	1.90

Mink, Wildlife Conservation — A337

1986, June 15

1510	A337	60m	Spring	35
1511	A337	60m	Summer	35
1512	A337	60m	Autumn	35
1513	A337	60m	Winter	35

Flowers — A338 Butterflies — A339

1986, June 1 Litho. *Perf. 14*

1514	A338	20m	Valeriana officinalis	15
1515	A338	30m	Hyoscymus niger	16
1516	A338	40m	Ephedra sinica	20
1517	A338	50m	Thymus gobica	25
1518	A338	60m	Paeonia anomala	30
1519	A338	80m	Achilea millefolium	40
1520	A338	1.20t	Rhododendron adamsii	60
			Nos. 1514-1520 (7)	2.06

1986, Aug. 1 *Perf. $13^1/_2$*

1521	A339	20m	Neptis coenobita	15
1522	A339	30m	Colias tycha	20
1523	A339	40m	Leptidea amurensis	28
1524	A339	50m	Oeneis tarpenledevi	32
1525	A339	60m	Mesoacidalia charlotta	40
1526	A339	80m	Smerinthus ocellatus	50
1527	A339	1.20t	Pericalia matronula	80
			Nos. 1521-1527 (7)	2.65

Circus — A340

Animal trainers and acrobats. Nos. 1531-1534 vert.

1986, Aug. 1 *Perf. 14*

1528	A340	20m	multi	15
1529	A340	30m	multi	16
1530	A340	40m	multi	20
1531	A340	50m	multi	25
1532	A340	60m	multi	30
1533	A340	80m	multi	40
1534	A340	1.20t	multi	60
			Nos. 1528-1534 (7)	2.06

Przewalski's Horses — A341

1986, Aug. 1 Litho. *Perf. 14*

1535	A341	50m	Two horses, foal	35
1536	A341	50m	One facing left, two facing right	35
1537	A341	50m	Three facing right	35
1538	A341	50m	Four in storm	35

Pelicans *(Pelecanus)* — A341a

1986, Sept. 1 Litho. *Perf. 14*

1538A	A341a	60m	*crispus* feeding	58
1538B	A341a	60m	*crispus* wading	58
1538C	A341a	60m	*onocrotalus* flying	58
1538D	A341a	60m	*onocrotalus* on land	58

Saiga tatarica mongolica — A341b

1986, Sept. 15

1538E	A341b	60m	Spring (doe, fawn)	58
1538F	A341b	60m	Summer (buck, doe)	58
1538G	A341b	60m	Fall (buck)	58
1538H	A341b	60m	Winter (buck, doe)	58

Musical Instruments — A342

1986, Sept. 4

1539	A342	20m	Morin khuur	15
1540	A342	30m	Bishguur	20
1541	A342	40m	Ever buree	28
1542	A342	50m	Shudarga	35
1543	A342	60m	Khiil	40
1544	A342	80m	Janchir	55
1545	A342	1.20t	Jatga	80
			Nos. 1539-1545 (7)	2.73

Souvenir Sheet

1546	A342	4t	like 20m, vert.	2.75

STOCKHOLMIA '86. Nos. 1539-1543 vert.

Intl. Peace Year — A342a

1986, Sept. 20 Litho. *Perf. 13x$13^1/_2$*

1546A	A342a	10m	multicolored	75

North American Bird Species — A343

1986, Oct. 1

1547	A343	60m	Anthus spinoletta	35
1548	A343	60m	Aythya americana	35
1549	A343	60m	Bonasa umbellus	35
1550	A343	60m	Olor columbianus	35

Eastern Architecture — A343a

Various two-story buildings.

1986, Oct. 1

Color of Border

1551	A343a	60m	dark grn & blk	70
1552	A343a	60m	beige & blk	70
1553	A343a	60m	apple grn & blk	70
1554	A343a	60m	red brn & blk	70

Classic Automobiles — A344

1986, Oct. 1 Litho. *Perf. 14*

1554A	A344	20m	1922 Alfa Romeo RL Sport, Italy	15
1554B	A344	30m	1912 Stutz Bearcat, US	24
1554C	A344	40m	1902 Mercedes Simplex, Germany	30
1554D	A344	50m	1923 Tatra 11, Czechoslovakia	38
1554E	A344	60m	1908 Ford Model T, US	45
1554F	A344	80m	1905 Vauxhall, England	60
1554G	A344	1.20t	1913 Russo-Baltik, Russia	90
			Nos. 1554A-1554G (7)	3.02

Souvenir Sheet

1554H	A344	4t	like 1.20t	3.00

Woodpeckers A344a

1986, Nov. 1

1555	A344a	20m	Picus canus	16
1556	A344a	30m	Jynx torquilla	24
1557	A344a	40m	Dryobates major	32
1558	A344a	50m	Dryobates leucotos	40
1559	A344a	60m	Dryobates minor	48
1560	A344a	80m	Dryocopus martius	65
1561	A344a	1.20t	Picoides tridactylus	90
			Nos. 1555-1561 (7)	3.15

Souvenir Sheet

1562	A344a	4t	Saphopipo noguchi	3.25

Chess Champions — A345

Portraits and chessmen on boards in match-winning configurations. No. 1562H, Chess champions Gary Kasparov, Jose R. Capablanca, Max Euwe, Vassily Smyslow, Mikhail Tal, Tigran Petrosian, Boris Spasski and Bobby Fischer; W. Menchik, L. Rudenko, E. Bykowa and O. Rubzowa.

1986, Nov. 1 *Perf. 14*

1562A	A345	20m	Steinitz, Austria	15
1562B	A345	30m	Lasker, Germany	24
1562C	A345	40m	Alekhine, France	30
1562D	A345	50m	Botvinnik, USSR	38
1562E	A345	60m	Karpov, USSR	45
1562F	A345	80m	N. Gaprindashvili	60
1562G	A345	1.20t	M. Chiburdanidze	90

Size: 110x100mm

Imperf

1562H	A345	4t	multi	3.00
			Nos. 1562A-1562H (8)	6.02

Souvenir Sheet

Halley's Comet — A346

1986, Nov. 30 Litho. *Perf. 14*

1563	A346	4t	multicolored	5.50

Ovis Ammon Ammon — A347

1987, Jan. 1

1564	A347	60m	shown	42
1565	A347	60m	In the mountains	42
1566	A347	60m	Close-up of head	42
1567	A347	60m	Male, female, lamb	42

Children's Activities — A348

1987, Feb. 1

1568	A348	20m	Backpacking, hunting butterflies	15
1569	A348	30m	Playing with calves	24
1570	A348	40m	Chalk-writing on cement	30
1571	A348	50m	Playing soccer	38
1572	A348	60m	Go-cart, model rocket, boat	45
1573	A348	80m	Agriculture	60

1574 A348 1.20t Playing the morin khuur, dancing 90
Nos. 1568-1574 (7) 3.02

Int'l. Peace Year (40m); Child Survival Campaign (50m).

13th Trade Unions Congress — A349

1987, Feb. 15 *Perf. 13½x13*
1575 A349 60m multi 45

Equestrian Sports — A350

1987, Mar. 1

1576	A350	20m	Lassoer	15
1577	A350	30m	Breaking horse	24
1578	A350	40m	Shooting bow	30
1579	A350	50m	Race	38
1580	A350	60m	Retrieving flags	45
1581	A350	80m	Tug-of-war	60
1582	A350	1.20t	Racing wolf	90
			Nos. 1576-1582 (7)	3.02

Admission into Comecon, 25th Anniv. — A351

1987, Apr. 15 *Perf. 13x13½*
1583 A351 60m multi 45

Fruit — A352 A353

1987, June 1 *Perf. 13½*

1584	A352	20m	Hippophae rhamnoides	15
1585	A352	30m	Ribes nigrum	24
1586	A352	40m	Ribes rubrus	30
1587	A352	50m	Ribes altissimum	38
1588	A352	60m	Rubus sachalinensis	45
1589	A352	80m	Padus asiatica	60
1590	A352	1.20t	Fragaria orientalis	90
			Nos. 1584-1590 (7)	3.02

Souvenir Sheet

Perf. 14

1591 A353 4t Malus domestica 3.00

Soviet-Mongolian Diplomatic Relations, 50th Anniv. — A354

Russian Revolution, 70th Anniv. — A355

1987, July 1 *Perf. 13x13½*
1592 A354 60m multi 55

1987, July 1
1593 A355 60m multi 55

Folk Dances — A356

1987, Aug. 1 *Perf. 14*

1594	A356	20m	multi	15
1595	A356	30m	multi, diff.	24
1596	A356	40m	multi, diff.	30
1597	A356	50m	multi, diff.	38
1598	A356	60m	multi, diff.	45
1599	A356	80m	multi, diff.	60
1600	A356	1.20t	multi, diff.	90
			Nos. 1594-1600 (7)	3.02

Antiques — A357

Full costume and accessories.

1987, Aug. 10

1601	A357	20m	Folk costumes	15
1602	A357	30m	Gilded nunchaku	24
1603	A357	40m	Brooches	30
1604	A357	50m	Draw-string pouch, rice bowl	38
1605	A357	60m	Headdress	45
1606	A357	80m	Pouches, bottle, pipe	60
1607	A357	1.20t	Sash, brooch	90
			Nos. 1601-1607 (7)	3.02

The first value column gives the catalogue value of an unused stamp, the second that of a used stamp.

Souvenir Sheet

HAFNIA '87 — A358

1987, Aug. 10
1608 A358 4t multi 3.00

Swans — A359

1987, Aug. 15

1609	A359	60m	Cygnus olor on land	35
1610	A359	60m	Cygnus olor in water	35
1611	A359	60m	Cygnus beruickii	35
1612	A359	60m	Cygnus beruickii, gunus and olor	35

Domestic and Wild Cats — A360

1987, Oct. 1 **Litho.** *Perf. 14*

1613	A360	20m	multi, vert.	15
1614	A360	30m	multi, vert.	24
1615	A360	40m	multi, vert.	30
1616	A360	50m	shown	38
1617	A360	60m	multi	45
1618	A360	80m	multi	60
1619	A360	1.20t	multi	90
			Nos. 1613-1619 (7)	3.02

Miniature Sheet

1620 A360 4t multi, vert. 3.00

Helicopter — A361

1987, Oct. 3 *Perf. 12½x11½*

1621	A361	20m	B-12	15
1622	A361	30m	Westland-WG-30	24
1623	A361	40m	Bell-S-206L	30
1624	A361	50m	Kawasaki-369HS	38
1625	A361	60m	KA-32	45
1626	A361	80m	MI-17	60
1627	A361	1.20t	MI-10K	90
			Nos. 1621-1627 (7)	3.02

Disney Cartoons — A362

The Brave Little Tailor (25m-55m, 2t, No. 1637), and The Celebrated Jumping Frog of Calaveras County (65m-1.40t, No. 1638).

1987, Nov. 23 *Perf. 14*

1628	A362	25m	multi	15
1629	A362	35m	multi	18
1630	A362	45m	multi	22
1631	A362	55m	multi	28
1632	A362	65m	multi	32
1633	A362	75m	multi	38
1634	A362	85m	multi	40
1635	A362	1.40t	multi	70
1636	A362	2t	multi	1.00
			Nos. 1628-1636 (9)	3.63

Souvenir Sheets

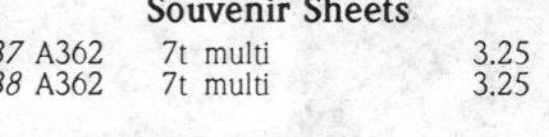

1637 A362 7t multi 3.25
1638 A362 7t multi 3.25

A363

Tropical Fish — A364

1987, Oct. *Perf. 13x12½, 12½x13*

1639	A363	20m	Betta splendens	15
1640	A363	30m	Carassius auratus	24
1641	A363	40m	Rasbora hengeli	30
1642	A363	50m	Aequidens	38
1643	A363	60m	Xiphophorus macalatus	45
1644	A363	80m	Xiphophorus helleri	60
1645	A363	1.20t	Pterophyllum scalare, vert.	90
			Nos. 1639-1645 (7)	3.02

Miniature Sheet

Perf. 14

1646 A364 4t Crenuchus spilurus 3.00

19th Communist Party Congress — A365

1987, Dec. *Perf. 14*

1647	A365	60m	Family	45
1648	A365	60m	Construction	45
1649	A365	60m	Jet, harvesting, produce	45
1650	A365	60m	Education	45
1651	A365	60m	Transportation	45
1652	A365	60m	Heavy industry	45
1653	A365	60m	Science and technology	45
			Nos. 1647-1653 (7)	3.15

Vulpes Vulpes (Fox) — A366

1987, Dec.

1654	A366	60m	Adult in snow	45
1655	A366	60m	Adult, young	45
1656	A366	60m	Adult in field	45
1657	A366	60m	Close-up of head	45

Souvenir Sheet

INTERCOSMOS — A367

1987, Dec. 15 **Litho.** ***Perf. 14***

1658	A367	4t	multi	3.00

Souvenir Sheet

PRAGA '88 — A368

1988, Jan. 30

1659	A368	4t	1923 Tatra 11	3.00

Sukhe Bator — A369

1988, Feb. 2 ***Perf. 13x13½***

1660	A369	60m	multi	60

A370

A371

Roses.

1988, Feb. 20 ***Perf. 14***

1661	A370	20m	Invitation	15
1662	A370	30m	Meilland	24
1663	A370	40m	Pascali	30
1664	A370	50m	Tropicana	40
1665	A370	60m	Wendy cussons	45
1666	A370	80m	Blue moon	60
1667	A370	1.20t	Diorama	90
			Nos. 1661-1667 (7)	3.04

Souvenir Sheet

1668	A370	4t	shown	3.00

1988, Apr. 15 ***Perf. 12½x13***

1669	A371	60m	multi	60

19th Communist Youth Congress.

Puppets — A372

Folk tales.

1988, Apr. 1 **Litho.** ***Perf. 14***

1670	A372	20m	Ukhaant Ekhner	20
1671	A372	30m	Altan Everte Mungun Turuut	30
1672	A372	40m	Aduuchyn Khuu	40
1673	A372	50m	Suulenkhuu	48
1674	A372	60m	Khonchyn Khuu	60
1675	A372	80m	Argat Byatskhan Baatar	80
1676	A372	1.20t	Botgochyn Khuu	1.25
			Nos. 1670-1676 (7)	4.03

1988 Summer Olympics, Seoul A373

Soviet Space Achievements A374

1988, Feb. 15

1677	A373	20m	Judo	15
1678	A373	30m	Women's archery	24
1679	A373	40m	Weight lifting	30
1680	A373	50m	Women's gymnastics	40
1681	A373	60m	Cycling	45
1682	A373	80m	Running	60
1683	A373	1.20t	Wrestling	90
			Nos. 1677-1683 (7)	3.04

Souvenir Sheet

1684	A373	4t	Boxing	3.00

1988, May 15

1685	A374	20m	Cosmos	15
1686	A374	30m	Meteor	24
1687	A374	40m	Salyut-Soyuz	30
1688	A374	50m	Prognoz-6	40
1689	A374	60m	Molniya-1	45
1690	A374	80m	Soyuz	60
1691	A374	1.20t	Vostok	90
			Nos. 1685-1691 (7)	3.04

Effigies of Buddhist Deities — A375

Various statues.

1988, June 15 **Litho.** ***Perf. 14***

1692	A375	20m	multi	15
1693	A375	30m	multi, diff.	20
1694	A375	40m	multi, diff.	28
1695	A375	50m	multi, diff.	35
1696	A375	60m	multi, diff.	40
1697	A375	70m	multi, diff.	48
1698	A375	80m	multi, diff.	55
1699	A375	1.20t	multi, diff.	80
			Nos. 1692-1699 (8)	3.21

Wildlife Conservation — A376

Eagles, Haliaeetus albicilla. Nos. 1700-1702 vert.

1988, Aug. 1 **Litho.** ***Perf. 14***

1700	A376	60m	Eagle facing left, diff.	40
1701	A376	60m	Landing on branch	40
1702	A376	60m	Facing right	40
1703	A376	60m	shown	40

Souvenir Sheet

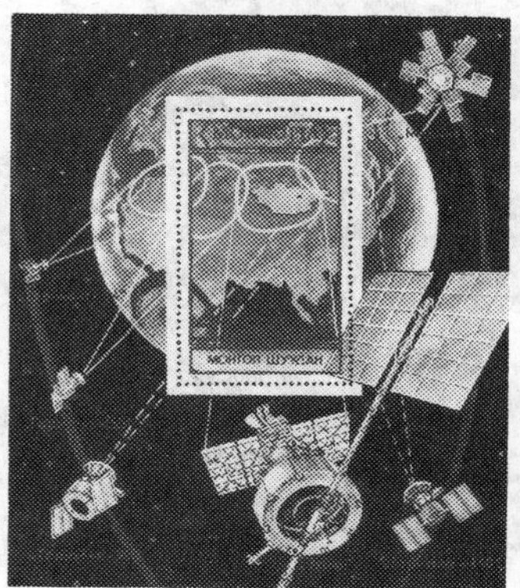

Cosmos — A377

1988, Sept. 15 **Litho.** ***Perf. 14***

1704	A377	4t	Satellite links	3.25

Opera A378

1988, Oct. 1 **Litho.** ***Perf. 13x12½***

1705	A378	60m	multi	90

No. 1705 printed se-tenant with label picturing composer.

Equus hemionus — A380

1988, May 3

1713	A380	60m	Mare, foal	58
1714	A380	60m	Horse's head	58
1715	A380	60m	Horse galloping	58
1716	A380	60m	Horses cantering	58

Winners of the 1988 Winter Olympics, Calgary — A381

1988, July 1

1717	A381	1.50t	Matti Nykaenen, Finland	58
1718	A381	1.50t	Bonnie Blair, US	58
1719	A381	1.50t	Alberto Tomba, Italy	58
1720	A381	1.50t	USSR hockey team	58

Souvenir Sheet

1721	A381	4t	Katarina Witt, DDR	2.35

Nos. 1718-1720 vert.

A382

A383

1988, Sept. 1

1722	A382	10m	shown	15
1723	A382	20m	Horsemanship	20
1724	A382	30m	Archery	30
1725	A382	40m	Wrestling	40
1726	A382	50m	Archery, diff.	50
1727	A382	70m	Horsemanship, diff.	70
1728	A382	1.20t	Horsemanship, wrestling, archery	1.20
			Nos. 1722-1728 (7)	3.45

1988, Dec. 1 ***Perf. 13x13½***

1729	A383	60m	multicolored	80

Socialism and Peace.

Goats — A384

Various species.

1989, Jan. 15 ***Perf. 14***

1730	A384	20m	multi	25
1731	A384	30m	multi	38
1732	A384	40m	multi	50
1733	A384	50m	multi	62
1734	A384	60m	multi	75
1735	A384	80m	multi	1.00
1736	A384	1.20t	multi	1.50
			Nos. 1717-1723 (7)	5.02

Souvenir Sheet

1737	A384	4t	multi, vert.	5.00

An enhanced introduction to the Scott Catalogue begins on Page 5A. A thorough understanding of the material presented there will greatly aid your use of the catalogue itself.

Souvenir Sheet

Child Survival — A385

1989, Jan. 28 **Litho.** ***Perf. 14***
1738 A385 4t Drawing by H. Jargalsuren 5.00

Karl Marx — A386

1989, Feb. 25 **Litho.** ***Perf. 13x13½***
1739 A386 60m multicolored 80

Miniature Sheet

Statue of Sukhe Bator — A387

Mongolian Airline Jet — A388

1989, July 1 ***Perf. 14***
1740 Sheet of 3 2.60
a. A387 20m Concorde jet 25
b. A387 60m TGV high-speed train 78
c. A387 1.20t shown 1.55

Souvenir Sheet

1741 A388 4t shown 4.25

PHILEXFRANCE '89, BULGARIA '89.
For overprint see No. 1756.

World War II Memorial — A389

1989, Sept. 2
1742 A389 60m multicolored 80

Cacti — A390

1989, Sept. 7
1743 A390 20m *O. microdasys* 22
1744 A390 30m *E. multiplex* 32
1745 A390 40m *R. tephracanthus* 42
1746 A390 50m *B. haselbergii* 55
1747 A390 60m *G. mihanovichii* 65
1748 A390 80m *C. strausii* 85
1749 A390 1.20t *Horridocactus tuberisvicatus* 1.25
Nos. 1743-1749 (7) 4.26

Souvenir Sheet

1750 A390 4t *Astrophytum ornatum* 4.25

A391 A392

Winners at the 1988 Summer Olympics, Seoul.

1989, Oct. 1
1751 A391 60m Kristin Otto, East Germany 58
1752 A391 60m Florence Griffith-Joyner, US 58
1753 A391 60m Gintaoutas Umaras, USSR 58
1754 A391 60m Stefano Cerioni, Italy 58

Souvenir Sheet

1755 A391 4t N. Enkhbat, Mongolia 4.25

No. 1740 Overprinted for WORLD STAMP EXPO '89

1989, Nov. 17 **Miniature Sheet**
1756 Sheet of 3 2.60
a. A387 20m multicolored 25
b. A387 60m multicolored 78
c. A387 1.20t multicolored 1.55

1989, Dec. 1
1757 A392 60m Books, fountain pen 58

Beavers *(Castor fiber birulai)* — A393

1989, Dec. 10
1758 A393 60m Cutting down saplings 58
1759 A393 60m Rolling wood across ground 58
1760 A393 60m Beaver on land, in water 58
1761 A393 60m Beaver and young 58

Medals and Military Decorations — A394

1989, Dec. 31 ***Perf. 13x13½***
1762 A394 60m pink & multi 58
1763 A394 60m lt blue grn & multi 58
1764 A394 60m vio & multi 58
1765 A394 60m org & multi 58
1766 A394 60m brt blue & multi 58
1767 A394 60m ver & multi 58
1768 A394 60m vio blue & multi 58
Nos. 1762-1768 (7) 4.06

Bears and Giant Pandas — A395

1990, Jan. 1 ***Perf. 14***
1769 A395 20m *Ursus pruinosis* 22
1770 A395 30m *Ursus arctos syriacus* 32
1771 A395 40m *Ursus thibetanus* 42
1772 A395 50m *Ursus maritimus* 55
1773 A395 60m *Ursus arctos bruinosus* 65
1774 A395 80m *Ailuropus melanoleucus* 85
1775 A395 1.20t *Ursus arctos isabellinus* 1.25
Nos. 1771-1775 (5) 3.72

Souvenir Sheet

1776 A395 4t *Ailuropus melanoleucus,* diff. 4.25

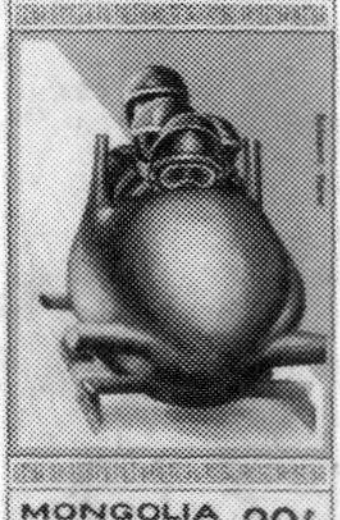

Winter Sports — A396

1990, Jan. 6
1777 A396 20m 4-man bobsled 22
1778 A396 30m Luge 32
1779 A396 40m Women's figure skating 42
1780 A396 50m 1-man bobsled 55
1781 A396 60m Pairs figure skating 65
1782 A396 80m Speed skating 85
1783 A396 1.20t Ice speedway 1.25
Nos. 1777-1783 (7) 4.26

Souvenir Sheet

1784 A396 4t Ice hockey 4.25

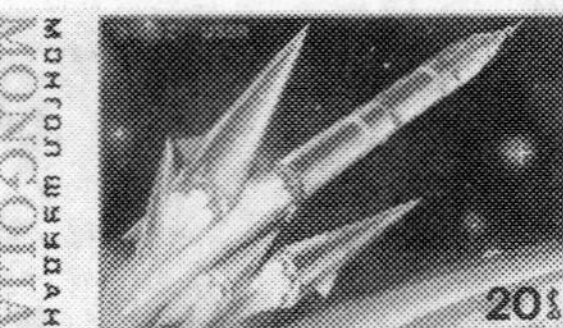

Space Exploration — A397

Rockets and spacecraft: 20m, Soyuz, USSR. 30m, Apollo-Soyuz, US-USSR. 40m, *Columbia* space shuttle, US, vert. 50m, *Hermes,* France. 60m, *Nippon,* Japan, vert. 80m, *Energy,* USSR, vert. 1.20t, *Buran,* USSR, vert. 4t, *Sanger,* West Germany.

1990, Jan. 30
1785 A397 20m shown 22
1786 A397 30m multicolored 32
1787 A397 40m multicolored 42
1788 A397 50m multicolored 55
1789 A397 60m multicolored 65
1790 A397 80m multicolored 85
1791 A397 1.20t multicolored 1.25
Nos. 1785-1791 (7) 4.26

Souvenir Sheet

1792 A397 4t multicolored 4.25

Jawaharlal Nehru, 1st Prime Minister of Independent India — A398

1990, Feb. 10
1793 A398 10m gold, blk & dark red brn 80

Statue of Sukhe Bator — A399

1990, Feb. 27
1794 A399 10m multicolored 80

Mongolian Ballet — A400

Dancers in scenes from various ballets. 40m, 80m, 1.20t vert.

1990, Feb. 28
1795 A400 20m shown 22
1796 A400 30m multi 32
1797 A400 40m multi 42
1798 A400 50m multi 55
1799 A400 60m multi 65
1800 A400 80m multi 85
1801 A400 1.20t multi 1.20
Nos. 1795-1801 (7) 4.21

Automobiles — A401

1990, Mar. 26

1802	A401	20m	Citroen, France	22
1803	A401	30m	Volvo 760 GLF, Sweden	32
1804	A401	40m	Honda, Japan	42
1805	A401	50m	Volga, USSR	55
1806	A401	60m	Ford Granada, US	65
1807	A401	80m	BAZ 21099, USSR	85
1808	A401	1.20t	Mercedes Class 190, West Germany	1.25
			Nos. 1802-1808 (7)	4.26

Souvenir Sheet

1809	A401	4t	like 50m	4.25

Lenin — A402

1990, Mar. 27 *Perf. 13x13½*

1810	A402	60m	gold, black & ver	80

Unen Newspaper, 70th Anniv. — A403

1990, Apr. 1 *Perf. 14*

1811	A403	60m	multicolored	80

End of World War II, 45th Anniv. — A404

1990, Apr. 1

1812	A404	60m	multicolored	80

Buddhist Deities (18th-20th Cent. Paintings) — A405

1990, Apr. 1

1813	A405	20m	Damdin Sandub	22
1814	A405	30m	Pagwa Lama	32
1815	A405	40m	Chu Lha	42
1816	A405	50m	Agwanglobsan	55
1817	A405	60m	Dorje Dags Dan	65
1818	A405	80m	Wangchikdorje	85
1819	A405	1.20t	Buddha	1.25
			Nos. 1813-1819 (7)	4.26

Souvenir Sheet

1820	A405	4t	Migjed Jang-Rasek	4.25

A406

Aspects of a Cooperative Settlement — A407

Paintings: 20m, Animals on plain, rainbow. 30m, Workers, reindeer, dog, vert. 40m, Two men, mountains, Bactrian camels. 50m, Man, Bactrian camels. 60m, Huts, animal shelter, corral. 60m, Breaking horses, vert. 1.20t, Sheep, shepherd girl on horse. 4t, Wrestling match.

1990, Apr. 1

1821	A406	20m	shown	22
1822	A406	30m	multicolored	32
1823	A406	40m	multicolored	42
1824	A406	50m	multicolored	55
1825	A406	60m	multicolored	65
1826	A406	80m	multicolored	85
1827	A406	1.20t	multicolored	1.25
			Nos. 1821-1827 (7)	4.26

Souvenir Sheet

1828	A407	4t	shown	4.25

Scenes from Various Mongolian-made Films — A408

1990, Apr. 1

1829	A408	20m	shown	22
1830	A408	30m	multi, diff.	32
1831	A408	40m	multi, diff.	42
1832	A408	50m	multi, diff.	55
1833	A408	60m	multi, diff.	65
1834	A408	80m	multi, diff.	85
1835	A408	1.20t	multi, diff.	1.25
			Nos. 1829-1835 (7)	4.26

Souvenir Sheet

1836	A408	4t	multi, diff., vert.	4.25

Souvenir Sheet

Stamp World London '90 — A409

1990, Apr. 1

1837	A409	4t	multicolored	4.25

1990 World Cup Soccer Championships, Italy — A410

Trophy and various athletes.

1990, Apr. 30

1838	A410	20m	multicolored	22
1839	A410	30m	multicolored	32
1840	A410	40m	multicolored	42
1841	A410	50m	multicolored	55
1842	A410	60m	multicolored	65
1843	A410	80m	multicolored	85
1844	A410	1.20t	multicolored	1.25
			Nos. 1838-1844 (7)	4.26

Souvenir Sheet

1845	A410	4t	Trophy, vert.	4.25

Nos. 304-307 Ovptd. CHINGGIS KHAN CROWNATION 1189

1990, May 1 Photo. *Perf. 11½x12*

1846	A84	20m	multicolored	*2.50*
1847	A84	30m	multicolored	*3.75*
1848	A84	50m	multicolored	*6.25*
1849	A84	60m	multicolored	*7.50*

Coronation of Genghis Khan, 800th anniv. (in 1989).

Souvenir Sheet

Genghis Khan — A411

1990, May 8 Litho. *Perf. 13½*

1850	A411	7t	multicolored	4.90

Stamp World London '90. Exists imperf. Exists without "Stamp World London '90" and Great Britain No. 1.

Cranes *(Grus vipio pallas)* — A412

1990, May 23 *Perf. 14*

1851	A412	60m	brt blue & multi	58
1852	A412	60m	brt rose lil & multi	58
1853	A412	60m	red lil & multi	58
1854	A412	60m	car rose & multi	58

Nos. 1853-1854 are vert.

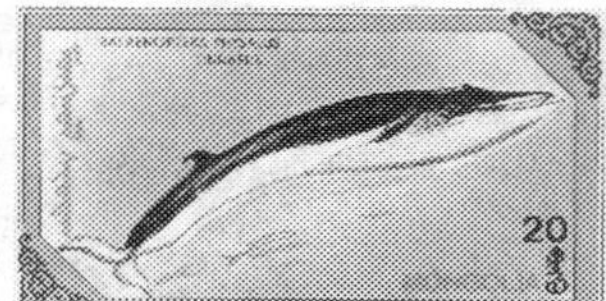
Marine Mammals — A413

1990 Litho. *Perf. 14*

1855	A413	20m	Balaenoptera physalus	24
1856	A413	30m	Megaptera novaeangliae	35
1857	A413	40m	Monodon monoceros	48
1858	A413	50m	Grampus griseus	60
1859	A413	60m	Tursiops truncatus	70
1860	A413	80m	Lagenorhynchus acutius	95
1861	A413	1.20t	Balaena mysticetus	1.40
			Nos. 1855-1861 (7)	4.72

Souvenir Sheet

1861A	A413	4t	Killer whale	4.65

Cultural Heritage
A414 A415

1990 *Perf. 13x12½*

1862	A414	10m	shown	15
1863	A414	10m	Like No. 1862, arrows at left	15
1864	A415	40m	Fire ring	48
1865	A415	60m	Genghis Khan	70
1866	A414	60m	Tent	70
1867	A414	60m	Horses	70
1868	A414	80m	Royal family (green panel)	95
1869	A414	80m	Royal court (dk bl panel)	95
a.			Souv. sheet, #1862-1869 + label	5.00
			Nos. 1862-1869 (8)	4.78

20th Party Congress — A416

1990 Litho. *Perf. 14*

1870	A416	60m	multicolored	90

Dinosaurs — A417

1990

1871 A417	20m shown		25
1872 A417	30m multi, diff.		35
1873 A417	40m multi, diff.		50
1874 A417	50m multi, diff		60
1875 A417	60m multi, vert.		70
1876 A417	80m multi, diff.		1.00

Size: 60x21mm

Perf. 13

1877 A417	1.20t multi, diff.		1.40
	Nos. 1871-1877 (7)		4.80

Souvenir Sheet

1878 A417	4t multi, diff.		4.75

Giant Pandas — A418

1990 Litho. *Perf. 14*

1879 A418	10m Adult on rock, vert.		15
1880 A418	20m Adult, eating, vert.		25
1881 A418	30m Adult and cub, vert.		35
1882 A418	40m shown		50
1883 A418	50m Adult and cub, resting		60
1884 A418	60m Adult, mountains		70
1885 A418	80m Adult and cub, playing		1.00
1886 A418	1.20t Adult, in winter		1.40
	Nos. 1879-1886 (8)		4.95

Souvenir Sheet

1887 A418	4t Family		4.70

Pyramids of Egypt — A419

Seven wonders of the ancient world: 20m, Lighthouse of Alexander, vert. 40m, Statue of Zeus, vert. 50m, Colossus of Rhodes, vert. 60m, Mausoleum of Halicarnassus, vert. 80m, Temple of Artemis. 1.20t, Hanging gardens of Babylon, vert. 4t, Pyramids of Egypt, vert.

1990

1888 A419	20m multicolored		25
1889 A419	30m shown		35
1890 A419	40m multicolored		50
1891 A419	50m multicolored		62
1892 A419	60m multicolored		70
1893 A419	80m multicolored		1.00
1894 A419	1.20t multicolored		1.40
	Nos. 1888-1894 (7)		4.82

Souvenir Sheet

1895 A419	4t multicolored		4.65

Moschus Moschiferus — A419a

1990, Sept. 26 Litho. *Perf. 14*

1895A A419a	60m shown		70
1895B A419a	60m In snow		70
1895C A419a	60m Facing left		70
1895D A419a	60m Two, one on ground		70

Parrots — A420

1990 Litho. *Perf. 14*

1896 A420	20m shown		25
1897 A420	30m multi, diff.		35
1898 A420	40m multi, diff.		50
1899 A420	50m multi, diff.		60
1900 A420	60m multi, diff.		70
1901 A420	80m multi, diff.		1.00
1902 A420	1.20t multi, diff.		1.50
	Nos. 1896-1902 (7)		4.90

Souvenir Sheet

1903 A420	4t multi, diff.		4.65

Butterflies — A421

Designs: 20m, Purpurbar. 30m, Grosses nachtpfauenauge. 40m, Grosser C-Falter. 50m, Stachelbeerspanner. 60m, Damenbrett. 80m, Schwalbenschwanz. 1.20t, Aurorafalter. 4t, Linienschwarmer, vert.

1990 Litho. *Perf. 14*

1904 A421	20m multicolored		25
1905 A421	30m multicolored		35
1906 A421	40m multicolored		50
1907 A421	50m multicolored		60
1908 A421	60m multicolored		70
1909 A421	80m multicolored		1.00
1910 A421	1.20t multicolored		1.50
	Nos. 1904-1910 (7)		4.90

Souvenir Sheet

1911 A421	4t multicolored		4.65

Flintstones Visit Mongolia — A422

Designs: 25m, Dino, Bamm-Bamm. 35m, Dino, Bamm-Bamm, diff., vert. 45m, Betty, Wilma, Bamm-Bamm, Pebbles. 55m, Fred, Barney, Dino. 65m, Flintstones & Rubbles. 75m, Bamm-Bamm riding Dino. 85m, Fred, Barney, Bamm-Bamm. 1.40t, Flintstones, Rubbles in car. 2t, Fred, Barney. No. 1921, Wilma, Betty & Bamm-Bamm. No. 1922, Bamm-Bamm, Pebbles riding Dino.

1991, Feb. 10 Litho. *Perf. 14*

1912 A422	25m multicolored		30
1913 A422	35m multicolored		42
1914 A422	45m multicolored		55
1915 A422	55m multicolored		65
1916 A422	65m multicolored		78
1917 A422	75m multicolored		90
1918 A422	85m multicolored		1.00
1919 A422	1.40t multicolored		1.70
1920 A422	2t multicolored		2.40
	Nos. 1912-1920 (9)		8.70

Souvenir Sheets

1921 A422	7t multicolored		3.50
1922 A422	7t multicolored		3.50

The Jetsons A423

Designs: 20m, Jetsons blasting off in spaceship. 25m, Jetsons on planet, horiz. 30m, George, Jane, Elroy & Astro. 40m, George, Judy, Elroy & Astro. 50m, Jetsons in spaceship, horiz. 60m, George, Jane, Elroy & Mr. Spacely, horiz. 70m, George, Elroy wearing jet packs. 80m, Elroy. 1.20t, Elroy, Judy & Astro. No. 1932, Elroy, red flowers. No. 1933, Elroy, blue flowers.

1991, Feb. 10

1923 A423	20m multicolored		25
1924 A423	25m multicolored		30
1925 A423	30m multicolored		35
1926 A423	40m multicolored		50
1927 A423	50m multicolored		60
1928 A423	60m multicolored		70
1929 A423	70m multicolored		85
1930 A423	80m multicolored		1.00
1931 A423	1.20t multicolored		1.50
	Nos. 1923-1931 (9)		6.05

Souvenir Sheets

1932 A423	7t multicolored		3.50
1933 A423	7t multicolored		3.50

Stamp World London '90
A424 A425

Various birds.

1991, Mar. 3 Litho. *Perf. 14½*

1934 A424	25m multicolored		30
1935 A424	35m multicolored		42
1936 A424	45m multicolored		55
1937 A424	55m multicolored		65
1938 A424	65m multicolored		78
1939 A424	75m multi, horiz.		90
1940 A424	85m multicolored		1.00
1941 A424	1.40t multicolored		1.70
1942 A424	2t multicolored		2.40
	Nos. 1934-1942 (9)		8.70

Souvenir Sheets

1943 A424	7t multicolored		3.50
1944 A425	7t multicolored		3.50

Butterflies and Flowers of Mongolia — A426

Designs: 20m, 30m-60m, various butterflies. Others, various flowers.

1991, Mar. 3 Litho. *Perf. 14½*

1945 A426	20m multicolored		25
1946 A426	25m multicolored		30
1947 A426	30m multicolored		35
1948 A426	40m multicolored		48
1949 A426	50m multicolored		60
1950 A426	60m multicolored		70
1951 A426	70m multicolored		80
1952 A426	80m multicolored		95
1953 A426	1.20t multicolored		1.40
	Nos. 1945-1953 (9)		5.83

Nos. 1945-1953 and Types Overprinted

EXPO'90

1991, Mar. 3

1954 A426	20m multicolored		25
1955 A426	25m multicolored		30
1956 A426	30m multicolored		35
1957 A426	40m multicolored		48
1958 A426	50m multicolored		60
1959 A426	60m multicolored		70
1960 A426	70m multicolored		80
1961 A426	80m multicolored		95
1962 A426	1.20t multicolored		1.40
	Nos. 1954-1962 (9)		5.83

Souvenir Sheets

1963 A426	7t Butterfly		5.35
1964 A426	7t Flower		5.35

Nos. 1963-1964 were not issued without overprint which appears in sheet margin only.

Birds — A427

1991, Apr. 1 *Perf. 14*

1965 A427	20m Lururus tetrix		25
1966 A427	30m Tadorna tadorna		35
1967 A427	40m Phasianus colchicus		48
1968 A427	50m Clangula byemalis		60
1969 A427	60m Tetrastes bonasia		70
1970 A427	80m Mergus serrator		95
1971 A427	1.20t Bucephaia clangula		1.40
	Nos. 1965-1971 (7)		4.73

Souvenir Sheet

1972 A427	4t Anas crecca, vert.		4.65

Flowers — A428

1991, Apr. 15

1973 A428	20m Dianthus superbus		25
1974 A428	30m Gentiana puenmonanthe		35
1975 A428	40m Taraxacum officinale		48
1976 A428	50m Iris sibrica		60
1977 A428	60m Lilium martagon		70
1978 A428	80m Aster amellus		95
1979 A428	1.20t Cizsium rivulare		1.40
	Nos. 1973-1979 (7)		4.73

Souvenir Sheet

1980 A428	4t Campanula persicifolia		4.65

Buddhist Effigies — A429

1991, May 1

1981 A429	20m Defend		25
1982 A429	30m Badmasanhava		35
1983 A429	40m Avalokitecvara		48
1984 A429	50m Buddha		60
1985 A429	60m Mintugwa		70

1986 A429 80m Shyamatara 95
1987 A429 1.20t Samvara 1.40
Nos. 1981-1987 (7) 4.73

Souvenir Sheet

1988 A429 4t Lamidhatara 4.65

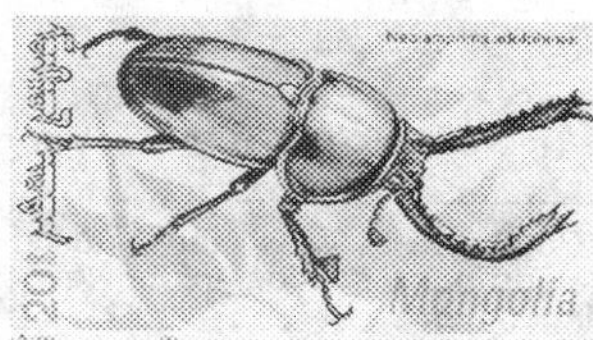

Insects — A430

1991, May 22

1989 A430 20m Neolamprima adolphinae 25
1990 A430 30m Chelorrhina polyphemus 35
1991 A430 40m Coptolabrus coelestis 48
1992 A430 50m Epepeotes togatus 60
1993 A430 60m Cicindela chinensis 70
1994 A430 80m Macrodontia cervicornis 95
1995 A430 1.20t Dynastes hercules 1.40
Nos. 1989-1995 (7) 4.73

African Animals — A431

1991, May 23

1996 A431 20m Zebras 25
1997 A431 30m Cheetah 35
1998 A431 40m Black rhinos 48
1999 A431 50m Giraffe, vert. 60
2000 A431 60m Gorilla 70
2001 A431 80m Elephants 95
2002 A431 1.20t Lion, vert. 1.40
Nos. 1996-2002 (7) 4.73

Souvenir Sheet

2003 A431 4t Gazelle 4.65

No. 1997 is incorrectly spelled "Cheetan."

Exhibition of Meiso Mizuhara's Mongolian Stamp Collection — A432

1991, June Litho. *Perf. 13½*

2004 A432 1.20t multicolored 1.10

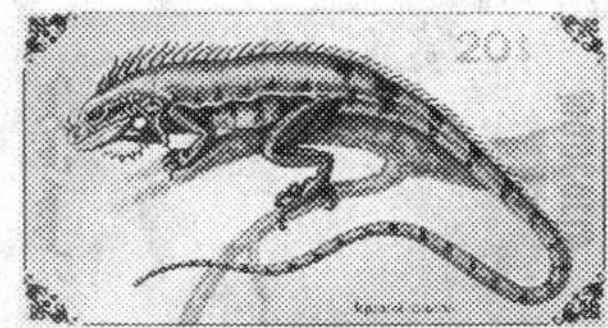

Lizards — A433

1991, Oct. 29 *Perf. 14*

2005 A433 20m Iguana iguana 30
2006 A433 30m Ptychozoon kihli 45
2007 A433 40m Chlamydo- saurus kingii 62
2008 A433 50m Cordylus cordylus 78
2009 A433 60m Basiliscus basilisus 90
2010 A433 80m Tupinambis teguixin 1.25
2011 A433 1.20t Amblyrhynchus cristatus 1.85
Nos. 2005-2011 (7) 6.15

Souvenir Sheet

2012 A433 4t Varanus bengalensis, vert. 4.75

Masks and Costumes — A434

Various masks and costumes.

1991, Oct. 1

2013 A434 35m multicolored 40
2014 A434 45m multicolored 52
2015 A434 55m multicolored 65
2016 A434 65m multicolored 75
2017 A434 85m multicolored 1.00
2018 A434 1.40t multicolored 1.65
2019 A434 2t multicolored 2.35
Nos. 2013-2019 (7) 7.32

Souvenir Sheet

2020 A434 4t multicolored 4.75

Phila Nippon '91 — A435

1991, Oct. 29

2021 A435 1t Pagoda
2022 A435 2t Japanese beauty
2023 A435 3t Mongolian woman
2024 A435 4t Mongolian building

Fantasia, 50th Anniv. A436

Designs: 1.70t, Poster, 1985. 2t, Poster, 1940. 2.30t, Poster, 1982. 2.60t, Poster, 1981. 4.20t, Poster, 1969. 10t, Poster, 1941. 15t, Drawing of Mlle. Upanova, 1940. 16t, Sketch of Mickey as Sorcerer's Apprentice.

No. 2033, Mickey as Sorcerer's Apprentice. No. 2034, Dinosaurs from "The Rite of Spring," horiz. No. 2035, Thistles and orchids from "Russian Dance," horiz. No. 2036, Dancing mushrooms from "Chinese Dance," horiz.

Perf. 13½x14, 14x13½

1991, Dec. 31

2025 A436 1.70t multicolored 28
2026 A436 2t multicolored 32
2027 A436 2.30t multicolored 38
2028 A436 2.60t multicolored 42
2029 A436 4.20t multicolored 68
2030 A436 10t multicolored 1.60
2031 A436 15t multicolored 2.40
2032 A436 16t multicolored 2.60
Nos. 2025-2032 (8) 8.68

Souvenir Sheets

2033 A436 30t multicolored 4.80
2034 A436 30t multicolored 4.80
2035 A436 30t multicolored 4.80
2036 A436 30t multicolored 4.80

1992 Winter Olympics, Albertville — A437

1992, Feb. 1 *Perf. 14*

2037 A437 60m Speed skating, vert. 90
2038 A437 80m Ski jumping, vert. 1.20
2039 A437 1t Hockey, vert. 1.50
2040 A437 1.20t Figure skating, vert. 1.80
2041 A437 1.50t Biathlon 2.25
2042 A437 2t Downhill skiing 3.00
2043 A437 2.40t Two-man bobsled 3.60
Nos. 2037-2043 (7) 14.25

Souvenir Sheet

2044 A437 8t Four-man bobsled, vert. 4.75

Dogs — A438

Various breeds of dogs.

1991, Dec. 1 Litho. *Perf. 14*

2045 A438 20m multi 25
2046 A438 30m multi, vert. 35
2047 A438 40m multi, vert. 48
2048 A438 50m multi 58
2049 A438 60m multi 70
2050 A438 80m multi 95
2051 A438 1.20t multi 1.40
Nos. 2045-2051 (7) 4.71

Souvenir Sheet

2052 A438 4t multi 4.70

Cats — A439

Various breeds of cats.

1991, Dec. 27

2053 A439 20m multi 25
2054 A439 30m multi, vert. 35
2055 A439 40m multi 48
2056 A439 50m multi, vert. 58
2057 A439 60m multi, vert. 70
2058 A439 80m multi, vert. 95
2059 A439 1.20t multi, vert. 1.40
Nos. 2053-2059 (7) 4.71

Souvenir Sheet

2060 A439 4t multi 4.70

Alces Alces — A440

1992, May 1 Litho. *Perf. 14*

2061 A440 3t Male 65
2062 A440 3t Two females 65
2063 A440 3t One female, vert. 65
2064 A440 3t Male's head, vert. 65

Souvenir Sheet

Ferdinand von Zeppelin (1838-1917), Airship Designer — A441

1992, May 1

2065 A441 16t multicolored 4.75

Souvenir Sheets

People and Events — A442

Designs: No. 2066, Pres. Punsalmaagiyn Orchirbat visiting Pres. George Bush at White House. No. 2067, Mother Teresa helping poor in Calcutta. No. 2068, Pope John Paul II at mass. Nos. 2069-2070, Boy Scout blowing bugle.

1992, May 22 *Perf. 14x13½*

2066 A442 30t silver & multi 4.75

Perf. 14

2067 A442 30t silver & multi 4.75
2068 A442 30t silver & multi 4.75
2069 A442 30t silver & multi 4.75
2070 A442 30t silver & multi 4.75

Nos. 2067-2070 each contain one 43x28mm stamp. Nos. 2069-2070 exist with gold inscription and border. No. 2069, 17th World Boy Scout Jamboree, Korea. No. 2070, 18th World Boy Scout Jamboree, Netherlands, 1995.

Souvenir Sheet

Discovery of America, 500th Anniv. — A443

Designs: a, Columbus. b, Sailing ship.

1992, May

2071 A443 30t Sheet of 2, #a.-b. 9.25

World Columbian Stamp Expo '92, Chicago, Genoa '92.

Miniature Sheets

Railways of the World A444

Designs: No. 2072a, 3t, Tank locomotive, Darjeeling-Himalaya Railway, India. b, 3t, Royal Scot, Great Britain. c, 6t, Bridge on the River Kwai, Burma-Siam Railway. d, 6t, Baltic tank engine, Burma. e, 8t, Baldwin locomotive, Thailand. f, 8t, Western Railway locomotive, Pakistan. g, 16t, P.36 class locomotive, USSR. h, 16t, Shanghai-Beijing Express, China.

Orient Express: No. 2073a, 3t, 1931 Advertising poster. b, 3t, 1928 poster. c, 6t, Dawn departure. d, 6t, Golden Arrow departing Victoria Station. e, 8t, Waiting at station in Yugoslavia. f, 8t, Turn of the century picture of train. g, 16t, Fleche d'Or locomotive approaching Etaples, France. h, 16t, Arrival in Istanbul, Turkey.

No. 2074, New Tokaido line, Japan. No. 2076a, Emblem of Pullman Car Company. b, Emblem of Intl. Wagons-lits Company. No. 2075, TGV, France. No. 2077, Passengers waiting to board Orient Express.

1992, May 24

2072 A444 Sheet of 8, #a.-h. 12.00
2073 A444 Sheet of 8, #a.-h. 12.00

Souvenir Sheets

2074 A444 30t multicolored 4.75
2075 A444 30t multicolored 4.75
2076 A444 30t Sheet of 2, #a.-b. 9.50
2077 A444 30t black & gold 4.75

Nos. 2074-2075 contain one 58x42mm stamp.

Miniature Sheet

Birds — A445

Various birds: a, 3t. b, 3t, Owl. c, 6t, Gull, horiz. d, 6t, horiz. e, 8t. f, 8t, horiz. g, 16t. h, 16t, horiz.

1992, May 24

2078 A445 Sheet of 8, #a.-h. 12.00

Souvenir Sheet

Perf. 14x13½

2079 A445 30t Ducks, 30t in UR 4.75
2080 A445 30t Duck, 30t in LR 4.75

Nos. 2079-2080 contain one 50x38mm stamp.

Miniature Sheet

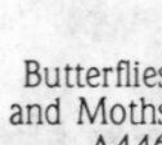

Butterflies and Moths A446

Various butterflies or moths and: a, 3t, Mountains. b, 3t, Desert. c, 6t, Grass. d, 6t, Lake. e, 8t, Mountain, diff. f, 8t, Flowers. g, 16t, Rocks. h, 16t, Lake, diff.

1992, May 24 ***Perf. 14***

2081 A446 Sheet of 8, #a.-h. 12.00

Souvenir Sheet

Perf. 14x13½

2082 A446 30t pink & multi 4.75
2083 A446 30t blue & multi 4.75

Nos. 2082-2083 contain one 50x38mm stamp.

1992 Summer Olympics, Barcelona — A447

Designs: a, Gold medal. b, Torch.

1992 **Litho.** ***Perf. 14***

2084 A447 30t Sheet of 2, #a.-b. 9.50

Souvenir Sheet

Genghis Khan — A448

1992 **Litho.** ***Perf. 14***

2085 A448 16t multicolored

Mushrooms — A449

Designs: 20m, Marasmius oreades. 30m, Boletus luridus. 40m, Hygrophorus marzuelus. 50m, Cantharellus cibarius. 60m, Agaricus campester. 80m, Boletus aereus. 1.20t, Amanita caesarea. 2t, Tricholoma terreum. 4t, Mitrophora hybrida.

1992 **Litho.** ***Perf. 13***

2086 A449 20m multicolored 18
2087 A449 30m multicolored 28
2088 A449 40m multicolored 35
2089 A449 50m multicolored 45
2090 A449 60m multicolored 55
2091 A449 80m multicolored 70
2092 A449 1.20t multicolored 1.10
2093 A449 2t multicolored 1.80
Nos. 2086-2093 (8) 5.41

Souvenir Sheet

2094 A449 4t multicolored 4.75

Dated 1990. No. 2094 contains one 32x40mm stamp.

Discovery of America, 500th Anniv. — A450

Columbus and: 3t, Two sailing ships. 7t, Natives approaching Santa Maria. 10t, Pinta. 16t, Santa Maria, vert. 30t, Santa Maria, diff. 40t, Santa Maria, dolphins. 50t, Nina.

No. 2103, Ship, vert. No. 2104, Portrait, vert.

1992, Aug. **Litho.** ***Perf. 14***

2095 A450 3t multicolored 16
2096 A450 7t multicolored 40
2097 A450 10t multicolored 55
2098 A450 16t multicolored 90
2099 A450 30t multicolored 1.70
2100 A450 40t multicolored 2.25
2101 A450 50t multicolored 2.75
Nos. 2095-2101 (7) 8.71

Souvenir Sheets

Perf. 13½x14

2102 A450 80t multicolored 4.50
2103 A450 80t multicolored 4.50

Nos. 2102-2103 each contain one 38x52mm stamp.

Miniature Sheet

Butterflies A451

Designs: No. 2104a, 3t, Anthocharis cardamines. b. 8t, Inachis io. c, 10t, Fabriciana adippe. d, 16t, Limenitis reducta. e, 30t, Agrumaenia carniolica. f, 40t, Polyommatus icarus. g, 50t, Parnassius apollo. h, 60t, Saturnia pyri.

No. 2105, Limenitis populi. No. 2106, Heodes virgaureae.

1992, Dec. **Litho.** ***Perf. 14***

2104 A451 Sheet of 8, #a.-h. 10.80

Souvenir Sheets

Perf. 14x13½

2105 A451 80t multicolored 4.00
2106 A451 80t multicolored 4.00

Nos. 2105-2106 each contain one 51x38mm stamp.

1992 Summer Olympics, Barcelona A452

1993, Jan. **Litho.** ***Perf. 13½***

2107 A452 3t Long jump 15
2108 A452 6t Pommel horse 28
2109 A452 8t Boxing 38
2110 A452 16t Wrestling 80
2111 A452 20t Archery, vert. 1.00
2112 A452 30t Cycling 1.50
2113 A452 40t Equestrian 2.15
2114 A452 50t High jump 2.50
2115 A452 60t Weight lifting 3.25
Nos. 2107-2115 (9) 12.01

Souvenir Sheet

Perf. 15x14

2116 A452 80t Judo 4.35
2117 A452 80t Javelin 4.00

Nos. 2116-2117 contain one 40x30mm stamp.

Miniature Sheet

Birds A453

Designs: No. 2118a, 3t, Tetrae tetrix. b, 8t, Gallinula chloropus. c, 10t, Regulus satrapa. d, 16t, Alcede atthis. e, 30t, Gavia stellata. f, 40t, Ardes cinerea. g, 50t, Upupa epops. h, 60t, Niltava rubeculoides. No. 2119, Gyps fulvus. No. 2120, Podiceps cristatus.

1993, Feb. **Litho.** ***Perf. 14***

2118 A453 Sheet of 8, #a.-h. 12.00

Souvenir Sheets

Perf. 14x13½

2119 A453 80t multicolored 4.35
2120 A453 80t multicolored 4.35

Nos. 2119-2120 each contain one 51x38mm stamp.

SEMI-POSTAL STAMPS

Catalogue values for unused stamps in this section are for Never Hinged items.

Vietnamese Mother and Child — SP1

1967, Dec. 22 **Photo.** ***Perf. 12x11½***

B1 SP1 30m + 20m multi 20 15
B2 SP1 50m + 30m multi 30 20

Solidarity with Vietnam.

Save Venice Type of Regular Issue
Souvenir Sheet

Design: 3t+1t, Departure of St. Ursula, by Carpaccio.

1972, Oct. 1 **Litho.** ***Perf. 12***

B3 A163 3t + 1t multi 3.25 3.25

Save Venice Campaign. No. B3 contains one horizontal stamp.

Girl Feeding Lambs — SP2

Designs (UNICEF Emblem and): 20m+5m, Boy playing flute and dancing girl. 30m+5m, Girl chasing butterflies. 40m+5m, Girl with ribbon. 60m+5m, Girl with flowers. 80m+5m, Girl carrying bucket. 1t+5m, Boy going to school.

1977, June 1 **Litho.** ***Perf. 12***

B4 SP2 10m + 5m multi 15 15
B5 SP2 20m + 5m multi 18 15
B6 SP2 30m + 5m multi 30 18
B7 SP2 40m + 5m multi 40 25
B8 SP2 60m + 5m multi 60 30
B9 SP2 80m + 5m multi 70 40
B10 SP2 1t + 5m multi 90 55
Nos. B4-B10 (7) 3.23 1.98

Surtax was for Mongolian Children's Village. See No. CB1.

Boys on Horseback — SP3

Mongolian Children and IYC Emblem: 30m+5m, Raising chickens. 50m+5m, With deer. 60m+5m, With flowers. 70m+5m, Planting tree. 80m+5m, Studying space project. 1t+5m, Dancing. 4t+50m, Girl on horseback.

1979, Jan. 10

B11	SP3	10m + 5m multi	15	15
B12	SP3	30m + 5m multi	18	15
B13	SP3	50m + 5m multi	32	15
B14	SP3	60m + 5m multi	35	15
B15	SP3	70m + 5m multi	45	22
B16	SP3	80m + 5m multi	55	32
B17	SP3	1t + 5m multi	70	40
		Nos. B11-B17 (7)	2.70	
		Set value		1.25

Souvenir Sheet

B18	SP3	4t + 50m multi	3.00	3.00

International Year of the Child.

AIR POST STAMPS

Catalogue values for unused stamps in this section are for Never Hinged items.

Postal Modernization Type of Regular Issue

Designs: 10m, 20m, Postman with horses. 25m, Postman with reindeer. 30m, 50m, Plane over map of Mongolia. 1t, Post horn and flag of Mongolia.

1961, June 5 **Photo.** ***Perf. 15***

C1	A72	10m multi	15	15
C2	A72	50m multi	30	15
C3	A72	1t multi	70	40
		Set value		58

Souvenir Sheet

Perf. 11

C4		Sheet of 4	1.00	1.00
a.	A72	20m lt blue grn & multi	24	24
b.	A72	25m light blue & multi	24	24
c.	A72	30m light green & multi	24	24
d.	A72	1t rose carmine & multi	24	24

40th anniversary of independence; postal modernization. No. C4b is not inscribed Airmail.

Souvenir Sheet

Austria Type SP55, Austrian and Mongolian Stamps Circling Globe — AP1

1965, May 1 **Engr.** ***Perf. 11½***

C5	AP1	4t brn car	2.50	2.50

Vienna Intl. Philatelic Exhibition, WIPA, June 4-13. #C5 contains one 61x38mm stamp.

Weather Satellite AP2

Designs: 20m, Antarctic exploration. 30m, Space exploration.

1965, May 15 **Photo.** ***Perf. 13½***

C6	AP2	15m lil, gold & blk	15	15
C7	AP2	20m bl & multi	15	15
C8	AP2	30m rose & multi	20	15
		Set value		28

International Quiet Sun Year, 1964-65.

ITU Emblem — AP3

Design: 4t, Communications satellite.

1965, Dec. 20 ***Perf. 11½x12***

C9	AP3	30m bl & bis	15	15
C10	AP3	50m red & bis	20	15
		Set value		16

Souvenir Sheet

Perf. 11, Imperf.

C11	AP3	4t gold, bl & blk	2.25	2.25

ITU, centenary. No. C11 contains one stamp, 38x51mm.

Souvenir Sheet

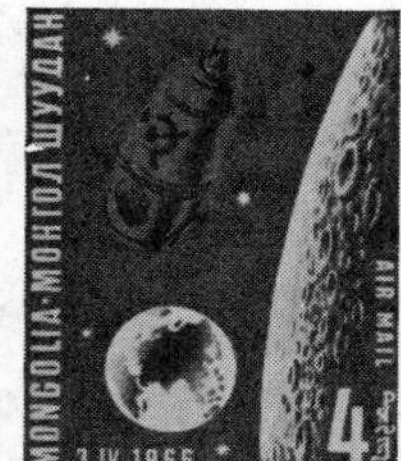

Luna 10, Moon and Earth — AP4

1966, July 10 **Photo.** ***Imperf.***

C12	AP4	4t multi	2.50	2.50

Luna 10 Russian moon mission, Apr. 3, 1966.

Souvenir Sheet

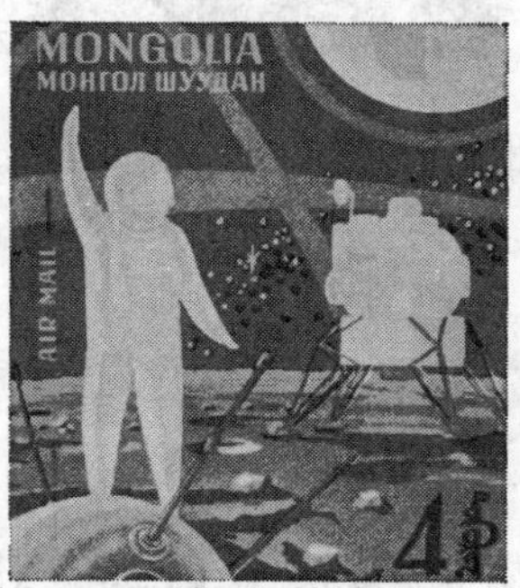

Astronaut and Landing Module — AP5

1969, Aug. 20 **Litho.** ***Perf. 11½***

C13	AP5	4t ultra & multi	2.50	2.50

Apollo 11 US moon mission, first man landing on moon.

Souvenir Sheet

Apollo 16 — AP6

Perf. 12½x11½

1972, Apr. 16 **Photo.**

C14	AP6	4t multi	2.50	2.50

Apollo 16 moon mission, Apr. 15-27.

Souvenir Sheet

Mongolian Horse — AP7

1972, May 10 **Photo.** ***Perf. 12½***

C15	AP7	4t multi	2.50	2.50

Centenary of the discovery of the Przewalski wild horse, bred in captivity in Berlin Zoo.

Telecommunication — AP8

Designs: 30m, Horse breeding. 40m, Train and plane. 50m, Corn and farm machinery. 60m, Red Cross ambulance and hospital. 80m, Actors. 1t, Factories.

1972, July 11 **Litho.** ***Perf. 12***

C16	AP8	20m ol & multi	15	15
C17	AP8	30m vio & multi	15	15
C18	AP8	40m rose & multi	15	15
C19	AP8	50m red & multi	20	15
C20	AP8	60m multi	35	15
C21	AP8	80m lt bl & multi	35	18
C22	AP8	1t grn & multi	40	28
		Nos. C16-C22 (7)	1.75	
		Set value		88

Mongolian Achievements.

Mongolian Flag, Globe and Radar — AP9

Perf. 12½x11½

1972, July 20 **Photo.**

C23	AP9	60m ol & multi	28	18

Intl. Telecommunications Day, May 17, 1972.

Running and Olympic Rings — AP10

Olympic Rings and: 15m, Boxing. 20m, Judo. 25m, High jump. 30m, Rifle shooting. 60m, Wrestling. 80m, Weight lifting. 1t, Mongolian flag and sport emblem. 4t, Woman archer, vert.

Perf. 12½x11½

1972, July 30 **Photo.**

C24	AP10	10m multi	15	15
C25	AP10	15m multi	15	15
C26	AP10	20m multi	15	15
C27	AP10	25m multi	18	15
C28	AP10	30m multi	20	15
C29	AP10	60m multi	30	20
C30	AP10	80m multi	38	24
C31	AP10	1t multi	55	32
		Nos. C24-C31 (8)	2.06	
		Set value		1.10

Souvenir Sheet

Perf. 11½x12½

C32	AP10	4t org & multi	2.00	2.00

20th Olympic Games, Munich, Aug. 26-Sept. 11.

Dragon and Mariner 2 — AP11

Designs: a, Snake, Mars 1. c, Hare, Soyuz 5. d, Monkey, Explorer 6. e, Cock, Venus 1. f, Rat, Apollo 15. g, Horse, Apollo 8. h, Boar, Cosmos 110. i, Tiger, Gemini 7. j, Sheep, Electron 2. k, Dog, Ariel 2. l, Ram, Venus 4.

1972, Dec. 4 **Photo.** ***Perf. 12***

C33	AP11	Sheet of 12	4.00	1.50
a.-f.		60m any single, size: 55x35mm	30	15
g.-l.		60m any single, size: 35x35mm	30	15

Space achievements of US and USSR, and signs of Eastern Calendar.

Airliner — AP12

1973, Jan. **Photo.** ***Perf. 12***

C34	AP12	1.50t blue	70	20

Weather Satellite, Earth Station, WMO Emblem — AP13

1973, Feb. **Photo.** ***Perf. 12x11½***

C35	AP13	60m multi	28	15

Intl. meteorological cooperation, cent.

Holy Flame Type of 1959

Souvenir Sheet

1973, Apr. 15 **Photo.** ***Perf. 12½***

C36	A48	4t gold & multi	1.75	1.75

IBRA München 1973 Intl. Stamp Exhibition, Munich, May 11-20. No. C36 contains one 40x63mm stamp in redrawn design of A48 with simulated perforations and wide gold margin.

Russia No. 3100 — AP14

Designs: Stamps (with mail-connected designs) of participating countries.

1973, July 31 Litho. *Perf. 12½*

C37	AP14	30m shown	20	15
C38	AP14	30m Mongolia #236	20	15
C39	AP14	30m Bulgaria #1047	20	15
C40	AP14	30m Hungary #B202	20	15
C41	AP14	30m Czechoslavia #C72	20	15
C42	AP14	30m German Dem. Rep. #369	20	15
C43	AP14	30m Cuba #C31	20	15
C44	AP14	30m Romania #2280	20	15
C45	AP14	30m Poland #802	20	15
		Nos. C37-C45 (9)	1.80	1.35

Conference of Permanent Committee for Posts and Telecommunications of Council for Economic Aid (COMECON), Ulan Bator, Aug. 1973.

Launching of Soyuz Spacecraft — AP15

1973, Oct. 26 Litho. *Perf. 12½*

C46	AP15	5m shown	15	15
C47	AP15	10m Apollo 8	15	15
C48	AP15	15m Soyuz 4 & 5 docking	15	15
C49	AP15	20m Apollo 11 lunar module	15	15
C50	AP15	30m Apollo 14 splashdown	28	15
C51	AP15	50m Soyuz 6, 7 & 8	35	16
C52	AP15	60m Apollo 16 moon rover	40	28
C53	AP15	1t Lunokhod 1 on moon	60	38
		Nos. C46-C53 (8)	2.23	
		Set value		1.20

Souvenir Sheet

C54	AP15	4t Soyuz and Apollo	2.25	2.25

US and Russian achievements in space.

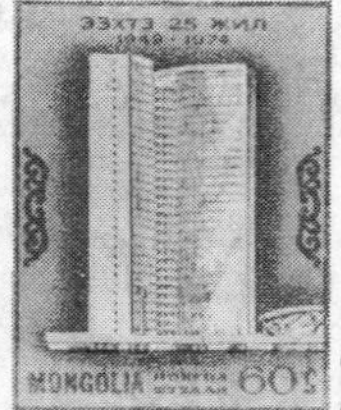

Comecon Building, Moscow — AP16

1974, Feb. 28 Photo. *Perf. 11½x12*

C55	AP16	60m bl & multi	28	15

25th anniversary of the Council of Mutual Economic Assistance.

Souvenir Sheet

Mongolia No. 4 — AP17

1974, Mar. 15 Photo. *Perf. 12½*

C56	AP17	4t multi	1.90	1.90

50th anniv. of 1st stamps of Mongolia.

Postrider and UPU Emblem AP18

Designs: UPU emblem and means of transportation.

1974, Apr. Litho. *Perf. 12*

C57	AP18	50m shown	35	18
C58	AP18	50m Reindeer post	35	18
C59	AP18	50m Mail coach	35	18
C60	AP18	50m Balloon post	35	18
C61	AP18	50m Steamship and AN-2 plane	35	18
C62	AP18	50m Train, truck and city	35	18
C63	AP18	50m Rocket over North Pole	35	18
		Nos. C57-C63 (7)	2.45	1.26

Souvenir Sheet

C64	AP18	4t Globe and post horn, vert.	2.50	2.50

Centenary of Universal Postal Union.

Circus Type of 1974

Design: 1t, Two women contortionists.

1974, May 4 Litho. *Perf. 12*

C65	A177	1t multi	48	30

No. C65 has se-tenant label, with similar design.

Nature Type of Regular Issue

Designs: 1t, Scientist checking water, globe. 4t, Wild rose.

1974, Dec. Litho. *Perf. 11*

C66	A186	1t multi	55	30

Souvenir Sheet

Perf. 12½

C67	A186	4t multi	2.25	2.25

UPU Type of 1974
Souvenir Sheet

Design: UPU Emblem, vert.

1974, Dec. *Perf. 11½x12*

C68	A187	4t multi	4.00	4.00

Soyuz on Launching Pad, Project Emblem — AP19

Project Emblem and: 20m, Radar and Apollo. 30m, Apollo, Soyuz and earth. 40m, Spacecraft before docking. 50m, Spacecraft after docking. 60m, Soyuz circling earth. 1t, Spacecraft, space station and earth. 4t, Russian and American astronauts.

1975, June 14 Litho. *Perf. 12*

C69	AP19	10m bl & multi	15	15
C70	AP19	20m multi	15	15
C71	AP19	30m sep & multi	20	15
C72	AP19	40m sil & multi	24	15
C73	AP19	50m multi	35	15
C74	AP19	60m multi	48	20
C75	AP19	1t multi	60	30
		Nos. C69-C75 (7)	2.17	
		Set value		90

Souvenir Sheet

C76	AP19	4t blk & multi	3.00	3.00

Apollo Soyuz space test project (Russo-American space cooperation), launching July 15; link-up July 17.

Mongolian Mountain Sheep — AP20

1975, Aug. 4 Litho. *Perf. 12*

C77	AP20	1.50t multi	80	30

South Asia Tourism Year. No. C77 printed se-tenant with label showing modern hotel, map and stone turtle.

Satellite over Weather Map of Mongolia AP21

1976, Mar. 20 *Perf. 12x11½*

C78	AP21	60m bl & yel	35	15

40th anniversary of meteorological service.

Souvenir Sheet

Girl with Books and Flowers — AP22

1976, Mar. 30 *Perf. 12*

C79	AP22	4t multi	2.25	2.25

30th anniversary of UNESCO.

Souvenir Sheet

The Wise Musician, by Sarav — AP23

1976, May 3 Litho. *Perf. 11½x12½*

C80	AP23	4t multi	2.25	2.25

Interphil 76 Phil. Exhib., Philadelphia, Pa., May 29-June 6.

Olympic Games Type of 1976
Souvenir Sheet

1976, May 20 *Perf. 12½x11½*

C81	A202	4t Wrestling	2.25	2.25

Independence Type of 1976

Design: 60m, Progress in agriculture and industry.

1976, June 20 Litho. *Perf. 12x11½*

C82	A203	60m multi	35	18

Olympic Medalists Type, 1976
Souvenir Sheet

Design: 4t, Oidov Zeveg, Mongolian flag.

1976, Nov. 30 Litho. *Perf. 11x11½*

C83	A209	4t multi	2.00	2.00

Mounting Carrier Rocket with Bell-shaped Gear — AP24

Designs: 20m, Launching of Intercosmos 3. 30m, Marine Observatory Gagarin (ship). 40m, Satellite observation of lunar eclipse. 60m, Observatory with multiple antenna system. 80m, Examination of Van Allen Zone, magnetosphere. 1t, Meteorological earth satellite. 4t, Intercosmos satellite with lines showing participating countries on globe.

1977, June 20 Litho. *Perf. 12*

C84	AP24	10m multi	15	15
C85	AP24	20m multi	15	15
C86	AP24	30m multi	18	15
C87	AP24	40m multi	28	15
C88	AP24	60m multi	48	20
C89	AP24	80m multi	60	28
C90	AP24	1t multi	75	38
		Nos. C84-C90 (7)	2.59	
		Set value		1.15

Souvenir Sheet

Perf. 12½

C91	AP24	4t multi	2.50	2.50

11th anniv. of Intercosmos program, cooperation of 9 socialist countries for space research. No. C91 contains one stamp 58x37mm.

Trade Union Emblem, Factory and Sheep AP25

1977, June *Perf. 12x11½*

C92	AP25	60m multi	40	18

11th Congress of Mongolian Trade Unions, May 12.

Montgolfier's Balloon — AP26

Dirigibles: 30m, Zeppelin over North Pole, 1931. 40m, Osoaviahim, Russian Arctic cargo. 50m, North, Russian heavy duty cargo. 60m, Aeron-340, Russian planned. 80m, Machinery transport, Russian planned. 1.20t, Flying crane, French planned. 4t, Russia No. C26 (stamp) and Sukhe Bator statue.

1977, Dec. Litho. *Perf. 12*

C93	AP26	20m multi	15	15
C94	AP26	30m multi	15	15
C95	AP26	40m multi	20	15
C96	AP26	50m multi	28	15
C97	AP26	60m multi	35	18
C98	AP26	80m multi	40	24
C99	AP26	1.20t multi	60	38
		Nos. C93-C99 (7)	2.13	
		Set value		1.20

Souvenir Sheet

Perf. 12½x11½

C100	AP26	4t multi	2.00	2.00

History of airships.

A. F. Mozhaiski and his Plane, 1884 — AP27

Designs: 30m, Henry Farman and his plane, 1909. 40m, Geoffrey de Havilland and D. H. 66 Hercules, 1920's. 50m, Charles A. Lindbergh, Spirit of St. Louis and route New York to Paris, 1927. 60m, Mongolian pilots Shagdarsuren and Demberel and plane over Altai Mountains, 1935. 80m, Soviet aviators Chkalov, Baidukov, Beliakov, plane and route Moscow to Vancouver, 1937. 1.20t, A. N. Tupolev, supersonic plane TU 154, route Moscow to Alma-Ata, 1968. 4t, Wilbur and Orville Wright and their plane.

1978, Mar. 25 Litho. *Perf. 12½x11*

C101 AP27 20m multi 15 15
C102 AP27 30m multi 15 15
C103 AP27 40m multi 20 15
C104 AP27 50m multi 28 15
C105 AP27 60m multi 35 18
C106 AP27 80m multi 40 24
C107 AP27 1.20t multi 70 38
Nos. C101-C107 (7) 2.23
Set value 1.20

Souvenir Sheet

C108 AP27 4t multi 3.00 3.00

75th anniversary of first powered flight, Wright brothers, 1903.

Soccer Type of 1978
Souvenir Sheet

Design: 4t, Two soccer players.

1978, Apr. 15 *Perf. 11½*

C109 A231 4t multi 2.50 2.50

World Soccer Championships, Argentina 78, June 1-25. No. C109 contains one stamp 45x38mm.

Souvenir Sheet

Canada No. 553 and Mongolia No. 549 — AP28

1978, June Litho. *Perf. 12½*

C110 AP28 4t multi 3.00 3.00

CAPEX '78, Intl. Phil. Exhibition, Toronto, June 9-18.

Map of Cuba, Ship, Plane and Festival Emblem — AP29

1978, July 28 Litho. *Perf. 12*

C111 AP29 1t multi 60 24

11th World Youth Festival, Havana, July 28-Aug. 5.

Souvenir Sheet

Aleksei Gubarev and Vladimir Remek, PRAGA '78 Emblem — AP30

1978, Sept. 5 Litho. *Perf. 12*

C112 AP30 4t multi 3.00 3.00

PRAGA '78 Intl. Phil. Exhib., Prague, Sept. 8-17, and Russian-Czechoslovak space cooperation, Intercosmos.

DDR Flag, TV Tower, Berlin, Satellite — AP31

1979, Oct. 9 Litho. *Perf. 11½x12*

C113 AP31 60m multi 35 15

German Democratic Republic, 30th anniv.

Demoiselle Crane — AP32

Protected Birds: 30m, Hawk warbler. 50m, Ruddy shelduck. 60m, Blue magpie. 70m, Goldfinch. 80m, Titmouse. 1t, Golden oriole.

1979, Oct. 25

C114 AP32 10m multi 15 15
C115 AP32 30m multi 15 15
C116 AP32 50m multi 28 15
C117 AP32 60m multi 30 15
C118 AP32 70m multi 30 15
C119 AP32 80m multi 35 15
C120 AP32 1t multi 45 18
Nos. C114-C120 (7) 1.98
Set value 72

Venera 5 and 6 — AP33

American and Russian Space Missions: 30m, Mariner 5. 50m, Mars 3. 60m, Viking 1 and 2. 70m, Luna 1, 2 and 3. 80m, Lunokhod 2. 1t, Apollo 15. 4t, Apollo 11, astronauts on moon.

Perf. 12½x11½

1979, Nov. 24 Litho.

C121 AP33 10m multi 15 15
C122 AP33 30m multi 16 15
C123 AP33 50m multi 28 15
C124 AP33 60m multi 32 15
C125 AP33 70m multi 38 15
C126 AP33 80m multi 45 15
C127 AP33 1t multi 55 18
Nos. C121-C127 (7) 2.29
Set value 75

Souvenir Sheet

C128 AP33 4t multi 2.50 2.50

Apollo 11 moon landing, 10th anniversary.

Andrena Scita — AP34

Insects: 30m, Paravespula germanica. 40m, Perilampus ruficornis. 50m, Bumblebee. 60m, Honey bee. 80m, Stilbum cyanurum. 1.20t, Ruby tail.

1980, Feb. 25 Litho. *Perf. 11x12*

C129 AP34 20m multi 15 15
C130 AP34 30m multi 16 15
C131 AP34 40m multi 25 15
C132 AP34 50m multi 40 15
C133 AP34 60m multi 45 15
C134 AP34 80m multi 60 25
C135 AP34 1.20t multi 80 30
Nos. C129-C135 (7) 2.81
Set value 1.05

Z-526 AFS Stunt Planes, Czechoslovakia — AP35

1980, Aug. 4 Litho. *Perf. 12*

C136 AP35 20m shown 15 15
C137 AP35 30m RS-180 "Sportsman," Germany 20 15
C138 AP35 40m Yanki-Anu, US 28 15
C139 AP35 50m MJ-2 "Tempete," France 35 15
C140 AP35 60m "Pits," Canada 40 15
C141 AP35 80m "Acrostar," Switzerland 55 18
C142 AP35 1.20t JAK-50, USSR 85 20
Nos. C136-C142 (7) 2.78
Set value 78

Souvenir Sheet

C143 AP35 4t JAK-52, USSR 2.00 1.75

10th World Aerobatic Championship, Oshkosh, Wisconsin, Aug. 17-30. Nos. C143 contains one stamp 50x43mm.

Olympic Type of 1980
Souvenir Sheet

1980, Sept. 15 Litho. *Perf. 12½*

C144 A253 4t Wrestlers 2.00 1.75

J. Davaajav, Mongolian silver medalist, 22nd Summer Olympic Games, Moscow. Inscribed "Los Angeles '84".

AP36 AP37

1980, Dec. 10 Litho. *Perf. 11½x11*

C145 AP36 4t multi 3.00 2.75

Johannes Kepler (1571-1630), German astronomer.

1981, Oct. 5 Litho. *Perf. 12x11½*

Graf Zeppelin and: 20m, Germany #C40, sea eagle. 30m, Germany #C41, polar fox. 40m, Germany #C42, sea ox. 50m, Russia #C26, polar bear. 60m, Russia #C27, snowy owl. 80m, Russia #C28, puffin. 1.20t, Russia #C29, seal. 4t, Icebreaker Maligin.

C146 AP37 20m multi 15 15
C147 AP37 30m multi 18 15
C148 AP37 40m multi 28 15
C149 AP37 50m multi 35 15
C150 AP37 60m multi 40 15
C151 AP37 80m multi 50 15
C152 AP37 1.20t multi 70 22
Nos. C146-C152 (7) 2.56
Set value 75

Souvenir Sheet

C153 AP37 4t multi 2.50 2.50

Graf Zeppelin polar flight, 50th anniv. No. C153 contains one stamp 36x51mm.

ITU Plenipotentiaries Conference, Nairobi, Sept. — AP38

1982, Sept. 27 Litho. *Perf. 12*

C154 AP38 60m Map 28 15

2nd UN Conference on Peaceful Uses of Outer Space, Vienna, Aug. 9-21 — AP39

1982, Dec. 15 Litho. *Perf. 12*

C155 AP39 60m Sputnik 1 28 15
C156 AP39 60m Sputnik 2 28 15
C157 AP39 60m Vostok 1 28 15
C158 AP39 60m Venera 8 28 15
C159 AP39 60m Vostok 6 28 15
C160 AP39 60m Voskhod 2 28 15
C161 AP39 60m Apollo II 28 15
C162 AP39 60m Soyuz 6 28 15
Nos. C155-C162 (8) 2.24
Set value 65

Souvenir Sheet

Perf. 12½x12

C163 AP39 4t Soyuz 39, Salyut 6 3.00 3.00

Balloon Flight Bicentenary AP40

1982, Dec. 31 *Perf. 11½x12½*

C164 AP40 20m Montgolfiere, 1783 15 15
C165 AP40 30m Blanchard, 1785 15 15
C166 AP40 40m Royal-Vauzhall, 1836 20 15
C167 AP40 50m Oernen, 1897 24 15
C168 AP40 60m Gordon Bennett Race, 1906 35 15
C169 AP40 80m Paris, 1931 40 15
C170 AP40 1.20t USSR-VR-62, 1933 70 18
Nos. C164-C170 (7) 2.19
Set value 60

Souvenir Sheet

C171 AP40 4t Mongolia, 1977 3.00 2.50

Souvenir Sheet

Revolutionary Mongolia Monument — AP41

1983 **Litho.** *Imperf.*

C172 AP41 4t multi	2.50	

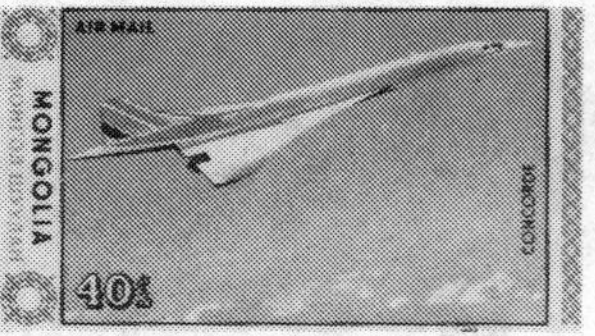

Concorde — AP42

1984, Aug. 15 **Litho.** *Perf. 14*

C173 AP42 20m DC-10, vert.	15	
C174 AP42 30m Airbus A-300 B-2	20	
C175 AP42 40m shown	28	
C176 AP42 50m Boeing 747	35	
C177 AP42 60m IL-62	40	
C178 AP42 80m TU-154	55	
C179 AP42 1.20t IL-86	80	
Nos. C173-C179 (7)	2.73	

Souvenir Sheet

C180 AP42 4t Yak-42	2.75	

1988 Winter Olympics, Calgary — AP43

1988, Jan. 20 **Litho.** *Perf. 14*

C181 AP43 20m Bobsled	15	
C182 AP43 30m Ski jumping	22	
C183 AP43 40m Downhill skiing	30	
C184 AP43 50m Biathlon	40	
C185 AP43 60m Speed skating	45	
C186 AP43 80m Women's figure skating	60	
C187 AP43 1.20t Ice hockey	90	
Nos. C181-C187 (7)	3.02	

Souvenir sheet

C188 AP43 4t Cross-country skiing	3.00	

AIR POST SEMI-POSTAL STAMP

Catalogue values for unused stamps in this section are for Never Hinged items.

UNICEF Type of 1977
Souvenir Sheet

Design: 4t+50m, Balloon with Mongolian flag, children and UNICEF emblem.

1977, June 1 **Litho.** *Perf. 12*

CB1 SP2 4t + 50m multi	2.50	2.50

First balloon flight in Mongolia. Surtax was for Children's Village.

MONTENEGRO

LOCATION — Southern Europe, bordering on the Adriatic Sea
GOVT. — A former Kingdom
AREA — 5,603 sq. mi.
POP. — 516,000 (estimated)
CAPITAL — Cetinje

This kingdom, formerly a Turkish Protectorate, later became independent. On December 1, 1918, Montenegro united with Serbia, Bosnia and Herzegovina, Croatia, Dalmatia and Slovenia to form the Kingdom of the Serbs, Croats and Slovenes which became Yugoslavia in 1929.

100 Novcic = 1 Florin
100 Helera = 1 Kruna (1902)
100 Para = 1 Kruna (1907)
100 Para = 1 Perper (1910)

Canceled to Order
Used values for Nos. 1-110, H1-H5, J1-J26, are for canceled to order stamps. Postally used specimens sell for considerably more.

Watermarks

Wmk. 91- "BRIEF-MARKEN" (#1-14) or "ZEITUNGS-MARKEN" (#15-21) in Double-lined Capitals once across sheet

Prince Nicholas I — A1

1874 **Typo.** **Wmk. 91**

Early Printings

Perf. 10½ Large Holes, pointed teeth

Narrow Spacing (2-2½mm)

1	A1	2n	yellow	30.00	30.00
2	A1	3n	green	45.00	40.00
3	A1	5n	rose red	32.50	30.00
4	A1	7n	lt lil	40.00	32.50
5	A1	10n	blue	95.00	60.00
6	A1	15n	yel bis	100.00	82.50
7	A1	25n	lil gray	200.00	165.00

Middle Printings (1879)

Perf. 12, 12½, 13 and Compound

Narrow spacing

8	A1	2n	yellow	8.00	5.50
a.			Perf. 12-13x10½	*65.00*	*65.00*
9	A1	3n	green	6.50	4.00
10	A1	5n	red	6.50	4.00
11	A1	7n	rose lilac	6.50	3.75
a.			7n lilac	16.00	13.00
12	A1	10n	blue	8.50	5.50
a.			Perf. 12-13x10½	65.50	52.50
13	A1	15n	bis brn	17.00	10.00
14	A1	25n	gray lilac	17.00	13.00

Late Printings (1893?)

Perf. 10½, 11½ Small holes, broad teeth
(Perf. 11½ also with pointed teeth)

Narrow and wide spacing
(2¾-3½mm)

15	A1	2n	yellow	2.25	1.50
a.			Perf. 11 ('94)	*20.00*	*16.00*
16	A1	3n	green	1.50	1.00
17	A1	5n	red	1.50	70
18	A1	7n	rose	1.50	70
a.			Perf. 11 ('94)	*5.25*	*5.00*
19	A1	10n	blue	1.75	1.50
20	A1	15n	brown	1.75	1.50
21	A1	25n	brn vio	1.65	1.50
			Nos. 15-21 (7)	11.90	8.40

Dates of issue of the late printings are still being researched.

Прослава
1493 1893
Штампарије

Types of 1874-93 Overprinted in Black or Red

1893 ***Perf. 10½, 11½***

22	A1	2n	yellow	27.50	5.00
a.			Perf. 11	*40.00*	*35.00*
23	A1	3n	green	1.75	1.50
24	A1	5n	red	1.10	85
25	A1	7n	rose	2.75	1.50
a.			Perf. 12	50.00	42.50
b.			7n rose lilac	3.00	1.75
c.			7n lilac, perf. 12	*125.00*	
d.			Perf. 11	*22.50*	*20.00*
26	A1	10n	blue	1.65	1.65
27	A1	10n	blue (R)	2.25	2.25
28	A1	15n	brown	1.10	1.10
a.			Perf. 12	50.00	42.50
29	A1	15n	brn (R)	*1,500.*	*1,500.*
30	A1	25n	brn vio	2.00	2.00
31	A1	25n	brn vio (R)	2.00	2.00
a.			Perf. 12½		*225.00*

Introduction of printing to Montenegro, 400th anniversary.

This overprint had many settings. Several values exist with "1494" or "1495" instead of "1493", or with missing letters or numerals due to wearing of the clichés. Double and inverted overprints exist. Some printings were made after 1893 to supply a philatelic demand, but were available for postage.

The 7n with red overprint was not issued.

1894-98 **Wmk. 91** ***Perf. 10½, 11½***

32	A1	1n	gray blue	15	15
33	A1	2n	emer ('98)	20	15
34	A1	3n	car rose ('98)	15	15
35	A1	5n	orange ('98)	50	22
36	A1	7n	gray lilac ('98)	20	15
37	A1	10n	magenta ('98)	18	15
38	A1	15n	red brn ('98)	22	20
39	A1	20n	brn org	15	15
40	A1	25n	dull blue ('98)	22	20
41	A1	30n	maroon	15	15
42	A1	50n	ultra	24	22
43	A1	1fl	deep green	40	35
44	A1	2fl	red brown	70	70
			Nos. 32-44 (13)	3.46	2.94

Monastery at Cetinje (Royal Mausoleum) A3

Perf. 10½, 11½

1896, Sept. 1 **Litho.** **Unwmk.**

45	A3	1n	dk bl & bis	15	15
46	A3	2n	mag & yel	22	22
47	A3	3n	org brn & yel grn	22	22
48	A3	5n	bl grn & bis	22	22
49	A3	10n	yel & ultra	22	22
50	A3	15n	dk bl & grn	22	22
a.			Perf. 11½	27.50	27.50
51	A3	20n	bl grn & ultra	22	22
a.			Perf. 11½	27.50	27.50
52	A3	25n	dk bl & yel	22	22
53	A3	30n	mag & bis	22	22
54	A3	50n	red brn & gray bl	22	22
55	A3	1fl	rose & gray bl	42	42
56	A3	2fl	brn & blk	42	42
			Nos. 45-56 (12)	2.97	2.97

Bicentenary of the ruling dynasty, founded by the Vladika, Danilo Petrovich of Nyegosh.

Inverted centers and other errors exist, but experts believe these to be printer's waste.

Perf. 11½ counterfeits are common.

Prince Nicholas I
A4 A5

Perf. 13x13½, 13x12½ (2h, 5h, 50h, 2k, 5k), 12½ (1h, 25h)

1902, July 12

57	A4	1h	ultra	15	15
58	A4	2h	rose lilac	15	15
59	A4	5h	green	15	15
60	A4	10h	rose	25	25
61	A4	25h	dull blue	15	15
62	A4	50h	gray grn	25	25
63	A4	1k	chocolate	25	25
64	A4	2k	pale brn	40	40
65	A4	5k	buff	65	65
			Nos. 57-65 (9)	2.40	2.40

The 2h black brown and 25h indigo were not issued. The 25h, perf. 12½, probably was never issued.

Constitution Issue

УСТАВ
Constitution Никољдан
1905

Same Overprinted in Red or Black "Constitution" 15mm

1905, Dec. 5

66	A4	1h	ultra (R)	15	15
67	A4	2h	rose lil	15	15
68	A4	5h	green (R)	20	20
69	A4	10h	rose	20	20
70	A4	25h	dl bl (R)	20	20
71	A4	50h	gray grn (R)	20	20
72	A4	1k	choc (R)	22	22
73	A4	2k	pale brn (R)	40	40
74	A4	5k	buff	50	50
			Nos. 66-74 (9)	2.22	2.22

Overprints in other colors are proofs.

1906

"Constitution" 16½mm

66a	A4	1h	ultra (R)	15	15
67a	A4	2h	rose lilac	15	15
68a	A4	5h	green (R)	15	15
69a	A4	10h	rose	15	15
70a	A4	25h	dull blue (R)	15	15
71a	A4	50h	gray green (R)	15	15
72a	A4	1k	chocolate (R)	15	15
73a	A4	2k	pale brown (R)	25	25
74a	A4	5k	buff	50	50
			Nos. 66a-74a (9)	1.80	1.80

Three settings of Nos. 66a-74a containing four types of "YCTAB": I, 9¾mm, II, 11¼mm, III, 10¼mm, IV, 8½mm. Type IV occurs only in one setting, at two positions. Nos. 67a, 69a-74a, H3a exist in type IV.

Two errors occur: "Constitutton" and "Coustitution." Many other varieties including reversed color overprints exist.

Values are for types I and II.

1907, June 1 **Engr.** ***Perf. 12½***

75	A5	1pa	ocher	15	15
76	A5	2pa	black	15	15
77	A5	5pa	yel grn	15	15
78	A5	10pa	rose red	15	15
79	A5	15pa	ultra	15	15
80	A5	20pa	red org	15	15
81	A5	25pa	indigo	15	15
82	A5	35pa	bis brn	15	15
83	A5	50pa	dl vio	20	20
84	A5	1kr	car rose	28	28
85	A5	2kr	green	32	32
86	A5	5kr	red brn	35	35
			Nos. 75-86 (12)	2.35	2.35

Many Montenegro stamps exist imperforate or part perforate. Experts believe these to be printer's waste.

King Nicholas I as a Youth — A6

King Nicholas I and Queen Milena — A7

King Nicholas I — A11

Prince Nicholas — A12

Designs: 5pa, 10pa, 35pa, Nicholas in 1910. 15pa, Nicholas in 1878. 20pa, King and Queen, diff.

1910, Aug. 28 — **Engr.**

87	A6	1pa black	15	15
88	A7	2pa pur brn	15	15
89	A6	5pa dk grn	15	15
90	A6	10pa carmine	15	15
91	A6	15pa slate blue	15	15
92	A7	20pa olive green	15	15
93	A6	25pa deep blue	15	15
94	A6	35pa chestnut	22	22
95	A11	50pa violet	25	25
96	A11	1per lake	25	25
97	A11	2per yel grn	42	42
98	A12	5per pale bl	65	65
		Nos. 87-98 (12)	2.84	2.84

Proclamation of Montenegro as a kingdom, the 50th anniv. of the reign of King Nicholas and the golden wedding celebration of the King and Queen.

King Nicholas I — A13

1913, Apr. 1 — **Typo.**

99	A13	1pa orange	15	15
100	A13	2pa plum	15	15
101	A13	5pa dp grn	15	15
102	A13	10pa dp rose	15	15
103	A13	15pa bl gray	15	15
104	A13	20pa dk brn	15	15
105	A13	25pa deep blue	15	15
106	A13	35pa vermilion	25	25
107	A13	50pa pale blue	15	15
108	A13	1per yel brn	15	15
109	A13	2per gray vio	22	22
110	A13	5per yel grn	22	22
		Nos. 99-110 (12)	2.04	2.04

ACKNOWLEDGMENT OF RECEIPT STAMPS

Prince Nicholas I
AR1 AR2

Perf. 10½, 11½

1895 — **Litho.** — **Wmk. 91**

H1	AR1	10n ultra & rose	40	40

1902 — **Unwmk.** — ***Perf. 12½***

H2	AR2	25h org & car	40	40

Constitution Issue

No. H2 Overprinted in Black Like Nos. 66-74

1905

H3	AR2	25h org & car	40	40
a.		"Constitution" 16½mm ('06)	40	40

See note after 74a.

Nicholas I
AR3 AR4

1907 — **Engr.**

H4	AR3	25pa olive	25	25

1913 — **Typo.**

H5	AR4	25pa olive green	25	25

Montenegro under German Occupation stamps can be mounted in Scott's Germany Part II Album.

POSTAGE DUE STAMPS

D1 D2

Perf. 10½, 11, 11½

1894 — **Litho.** — **Wmk. 91**

J1	D1	1n red	1.75	1.75
J2	D1	2n yel grn	32	32
J3	D1	3n orange	32	32
J4	D1	5n ol grn	20	20
J5	D1	10n violet	20	20
J6	D1	20n ultra	20	20
J7	D1	30n emerald	20	20
J8	D1	50n pale gray grn	20	20
		Nos. J1-J8 (8)	3.39	3.39

1902 — **Unwmk.** — ***Perf. 12½***

J9	D2	5h orange	15	15
J10	D2	10h ol grn	15	15
J11	D2	25h dl lil	15	15
J12	D2	50h emerald	15	15
J13	D2	1k pale gray grn	15	15
		Set value	50	50

Constitution Issue

Postage Due Stamps of 1902 Overprinted in Black or Red Like Nos. 66-74

1905

J14	D2	5h orange	15	15
J15	D2	10h ol grn (R)	15	15
J16	D2	25h dl lil	15	15
J17	D2	50h emerald	15	15
J18	D2	1k pale gray grn	15	15
		Set value	52	52

The 10h with "Constitution" 16½mm is not known used. It probably is an essay or fake.

D3 D4

1907 — **Typo.** — ***Perf. 13x13½***

J19	D3	5pa red brn	15	15
J20	D3	10pa violet	15	15
J21	D3	25pa rose	15	15
J22	D3	50pa green	15	15
		Set value	40	40

1913 — ***Perf. 12½***

J23	D4	5pa gray	22	22
J24	D4	10pa violet	20	20
J25	D4	25pa bl gray	20	20
J26	D4	50pa lil rose	22	22

ISSUED UNDER AUSTRIAN OCCUPATION

Austrian Military Stamps of 1917 Overprinted

K.U.K. MILIT.- VERWALTUNG

MONTENEGRO

1917 — **Unwmk.** — ***Perf. 12½***

1N1	M1	10h blue	5.75	3.50
1N2	M1	15h car rose	5.75	3.50

Austrian Military Stamps of 1917 Overprinted in Black

Montenegro

1918

1N3	M1	10h blue	25.00
1N4	M1	15h car rose	1.65

Nos. 1N3-1N4 were never placed in use.

This overprint exists on other stamps of Austria and Bosnia and Herzegovina, and in blue or red.

ISSUED UNDER ITALIAN OCCUPATION

Yugoslavia Nos. 142, 144-154 Overprinted

Montenegro
Црна Гора
17-IV-41-XIX

1941 — **Unwmk.** — **Typo.** — ***Perf. 12½***

2N1	A16	25p black	15	20
2N2	A16	1d yel grn	15	20
2N3	A16	1.50d red	15	20
2N4	A16	2d dp mag	15	20
2N5	A16	3d dl red brn	15	20
2N6	A16	4d ultra	15	20
2N7	A16	5d dk bl	1.00	1.50
2N8	A16	5.50d dk vio brn	1.00	1.50
2N9	A16	6d slate bl	1.00	1.50
2N10	A16	8d sepia	1.00	1.50
2N11	A16	12d brt vio	1.00	1.50
2N12	A16	16d dl vio	1.00	1.50
2N13	A16	20d blue	110.00	125.00
2N14	A16	30d brt pink	65.00	85.00
		Nos. 2N1-2N14 (14)	181.90	220.20

The 25p, 1d, 3d, 6d and 8d exist with inverted overprint.

Stamps of Italy, 1929, Overprinted in Red or Black

ЦРНА ГОРА

1941 — **Wmk. 140** — ***Perf. 14***

2N15	A90	5c ol brn (R)	15	*35*
2N16	A92	10c dk brn	15	*35*
2N17	A93	15c sl grn (R)	15	*35*
2N18	A91	20c rose red	15	*35*
2N19	A94	25c dp grn	15	*35*
2N20	A95	30c ol brn (R)	15	*35*
2N21	A95	50c pur (R)	15	*35*
2N22	A94	75c rose red	15	*35*
2N23	A94	1.25 l dp bl (R)	15	*35*
		Set value	90	

Yugoslavia Nos. 144-145, 147-148, 148B, 149-152 Overprinted in Black

Governatorato del Montenegro

Valore LIRE

1942 — **Unwmk.** — **Typo.** — ***Perf. 12½***

2N24	A16	1d yel grn	65	85
2N25	A16	1.50d red	20.00	22.50
2N26	A16	3d dl red brn	65	85
2N27	A16	4d ultra	65	85
2N28	A16	5.50d dk vio brn	65	85
2N29	A16	6d slate bl	65	85
2N30	A16	8d sepia	65	85
2N31	A16	12d brt vio	65	85
2N32	A16	16d dl vio	65	85
		Nos. 2N24-2N32 (9)	25.20	29.30

Yugoslavia Nos. 142 and 146 with this overprint in red were not officially issued.

Red Overprint

2N24a	A16	1d	65	*1.65*
2N25a	A16	1.50d	20.00	*22.50*
2N26a	A16	3d	65	*1.65*
2N27a	A16	4d	65	*1.65*
2N28a	A16	5.50d	65	*1.65*
2N29a	A16	6d	65	*1.65*
2N30a	A16	8d	65	*1.65*
2N31a	A16	12d	65	*1.65*
2N32a	A16	16d	65	*1.65*
		Nos. 2N24a-2N32a (9)	25.20	*35.70*

Peter Nyegosh and Mt. Lovchen View — OS1

Mt. Lovchen Scene — OS2

Peter Petrovich Nyegosh — OS3

Designs: 15c, Mountain Church, Eve of Trinity Feast. 20c, Chiefs at Cetinje Monastery. 25c, Folk Dancing at Cetinje Monastery. 50c, Eagle dance. 1.25 l, Chiefs taking loyalty oath. 2 l, Moslem wedding procession. 5 l, Group sitting up with injured standard bearer.

Unwmk.

1943, May 9 — **Photo.** — ***Perf. 14.***

2N33	OS1	5c dp vio	15	*60*
2N34	OS2	10c dl ol grn	15	*60*
2N35	OS1	15c brown	15	*60*
2N36	OS1	20c dl org	15	*60*
2N37	OS1	25c dl grn	15	*60*
2N38	OS1	50c rose pink	15	*60*
2N39	OS1	1.25 l sapphire	24	*1.00*
2N40	OS1	2 l bl grn	35	*1.50*
2N41	OS2	5 l dk red, *sal*	1.75	*5.00*
2N42	OS3	20 l dk vio, *gray*	5.25	*10.50*
		Nos. 2N33-2N42 (10)	8.49	*21.60*

Quotations from national poem on backs of stamps.

For overprints and surcharges see Nos. 3N10-3N14, 3NB3-3NB8.

OCCUPATION AIR POST STAMPS

Yugoslavia Nos. C7-C14 Overprinted Like Nos. 2N1-2N14

Perf. 12½, 11½x12½, 12½x11½

1941 — **Photo.** — **Unwmk.**

2NC1	AP6	50p brown	3.25	4.00
2NC2	AP7	1d yel grn	1.50	2.00
2NC3	AP8	2d bl gray	1.50	2.00
2NC4	AP9	2.50d rose red	3.25	4.00
2NC5	AP6	5d brn vio	30.00	30.00
2NC6	AP7	10d brn lake	30.00	30.00
2NC7	AP8	20d dk grn	45.00	45.00
2NC8	AP9	30d ultra	30.00	30.00
		Nos. 2NC1-2NC8 (8)	144.50	147.00

Italy No. C13 Overprinted in Red Like Nos. 2N15-2N23

1941 — **Wmk. 140** — ***Perf. 14***

2NC9	AP3	50c olive brn	15	50

Yugoslavia Nos. C7-C14 Overprinted in Black

Governatorato del Montenegro Valore in Lire
a

Governatorato del Montenegro Valore in Lire
b

Perf. 12½, 11½x12½, 12½x11½

1942, Jan. 9 — **Unwmk.**

2NC10	AP6(a)	50p brown	1.10	*2.00*
2NC11	AP7(a)	1d yel grn	1.10	*2.00*
2NC12	AP8(b)	2d bl gray	1.10	*2.00*
2NC13	AP9(b)	2.50d rose red	1.10	*2.00*
2NC14	AP6(a)	5d brn vio	1.10	*2.00*
2NC15	AP7(a)	10d brn lake	1.10	*2.00*
2NC16	AP8(b)	20d dk grn	100.00	100.00
2NC17	AP9(b)	30d ultra	32.50	32.50
		Nos. 2NC10-2NC17 (8)	139.10	144.50

Nos. 2NC10-2NC17 exist with red overprints. Value, each $80 unused, $90 used.

Governatorato del Montenegro
c

Overprints *a*, *b* or *c* were applied in 1941-42 to the following Yugoslavia stamps under Italian occupation:

a. or *b.* Nos. B120-B123 (4 values) in black and in red.

c. Nos. B116-B119 (4 values) in black and in red.

Cetinje AP1

Mt. Durmitor — AP6

Designs: 1 l, Seacoast. 2 l, Budus. 5 l, Mt. Lovchen. 10 l, Rieka River.

1943 Unwmk. Photo. *Perf. 14*

2NC18	AP1	50c brown	15	*60*
2NC19	AP1	1 l ultra	15	*60*
2NC20	AP1	2 l rose pink	24	*1.00*
2NC21	AP1	5 l green	35	*1.50*
2NC22	AP1	10 l lake, *rose buff*	2.00	*6.00*
2NC23	AP6	20 l ind, *rose*	7.25	*10.50*
		Nos. 2NC18-2NC23 (6)	10.14	*20.20*

For overprints and surcharges see Nos. 3NC1-3NC5, 3NCB1-3NCB6.

OCCUPATION POSTAGE DUE STAMPS

Yugoslavia Nos. J28-J32 Overprinted Like Nos. 2N1-2N14

1941 Unwmk. Typo. *Perf. 12½*

2NJ1	D4	50p violet	24	50
2NJ2	D4	1d dp mag	24	50
2NJ3	D4	2d dp bl	24	50
2NJ4	D4	5d orange	16.00	20.00
2NJ5	D4	10d chocolate	1.65	3.50
		Nos. 2NJ1-2NJ5 (5)	18.37	25.00

Postage Due Stamps of Italy, 1934, Overprinted in Black Like Nos. 2N15-2N23

1942 Wmk. 140 *Perf. 14*

2NJ6	D6	10c blue	15	*70*
2NJ7	D6	20c rose red	15	*70*
2NJ8	D6	30c red org	15	*70*
2NJ9	D6	50c violet	15	*70*
2NJ10	D7	1 l red org	15	*70*
		Set value		60

ISSUED UNDER GERMAN OCCUPATION

Yugoslavia Nos. 147-148 Surcharged

Deutsche Militaer-Verwaltung Montenegro

0.50 LIRE

1943 Unwmk. Typo. *Perf. 12½*

3N1	A16	50c on 3d	2.25	*10.00*
3N2	A16	1 l on 3d	2.25	*10.00*
3N3	A16	1.50 l on 3d	2.25	*10.00*
3N4	A16	2 l on 3d	4.50	*20.00*
3N5	A16	4 l on 3d	4.00	*20.00*
3N6	A16	5 l on 4d	4.50	*20.00*
3N7	A16	8 l on 4d	5.50	*50.00*
3N8	A16	10 l on 4d	11.50	*65.00*
3N9	A16	20 l on 4d	16.00	*130.00*
		Nos. 3N1-3N9 (9)	52.75	*335.00*

Montenegro Nos. 2N37-2N41 Ovptd.

Nationaler Verwaltungsausschuss 10.XI.1943

1943 Photo. *Perf. 14*

3N10	OS1	25c dl grn	6.50	*65.00*
3N11	OS1	50c rose pink	6.50	*65.00*
3N12	OS1	1.25 l sapphire	6.50	*65.00*
3N13	OS1	2 l bl grn	6.50	*65.00*
3N14	OS2	5 l dk red, *sal*	230.00	*1,600.*
		Nos. 3N10-3N14 (5)	256.00	*1,860.*

Counterfeits exist.

SEMI-POSTAL STAMPS

Yugoslavia Nos. 147-148 Surcharged

Flüchtlingshilfe Montenegro

0.15+0.85 RM.

1944 Unwmk. Typo. *Perf. 12½*

3NB1	A16	15pf + 85pf on 3d	6.50	*55.00*
3NB2	A16	15pf + 85pf on 4d	6.50	*85.00*

Montenegro Nos. 2N37-2N40 Surcharged

Flüchtlingshilfe Montenegro

0,15 + 0,85 RM.

d

1944 Photo. *Perf. 14*

3NB3	OS1	15pf +85pf on 25c	6.00	*85.00*
3NB4	OS1	15pf +1.35m on 50c	6.50	*85.00*
3NB5	OS1	25pf +1.75m on 1.25 l	6.50	*85.00*
3NB6	OS1	25pf +1.75m on2 l	6.50	*85.00*
		Nos. 3NB1-3NB6 (6)	38.50	*480.00*

Surtax on Nos. 3NB1-3NB6 aided refugees.

Montenegro Nos. 2N37-2N38 Surcharged

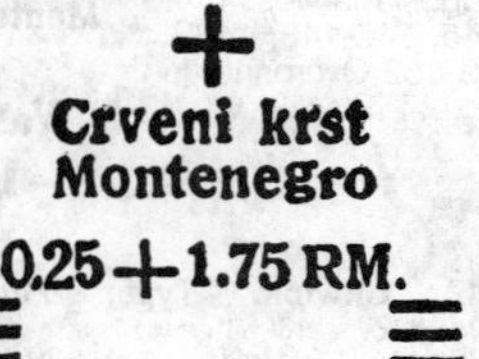

Crveni krst Montenegro

0.25+1.75 RM.

e

1944

3NB7	OS1	15pf + 85pf on 25c	6.00	*65.00*
3NB8	OS1	15pf + 1.35m on 50c	6.00	*65.00*

Yugoslavia Nos. 147-148 Surcharged

Crveni krst Montenegro

0.50+2.50 RM.

Typo. *Perf. 12½*

3NB9	A16	50pf + 2.50m on 3d	6.00	*65.00*
3NB10	A16	50pf + 2.50m on 4d	6.00	*65.00*

The surtax on Nos. 3NB7-3NB10 aided the Montenegro Red Cross.

AIR POST STAMPS

Montenegro Nos. 2NC18-2NC22 Overprinted Like Nos. 3N10-3N14

1943 Unwmk. Photo. *Perf. 14*

3NC1	AP1	50c brown	8.00	*85.00*
3NC2	AP1	1 l ultra	8.00	*85.00*
3NC3	AP1	2 l rose pink	8.00	*85.00*
3NC4	AP1	5 l green	8.00	*85.00*
3NC5	AP1	10 l lake, *rose buff*	1,400.	*15,000.*

Counterfeits exist.

AIR POST SEMI-POSTAL STAMPS

Montenegro Nos. 2NC18-2NC20 Surcharged Type "d"

1944 Unwmk. Photo. *Perf. 14*

3NCB1	AP1	15pf +85pf on 50c	6.50	*65.00*
3NCB2	AP1	25pf +1.25m on1 l	6.50	*65.00*
3NCB3	AP1	50pf +1.50m on2 l	6.50	*65.00*

The surtax aided refugees.

Same Surcharged Type "e"

1944

3NCB4	AP1	25pf +1.75m on 50c	6.00	*65.00*
3NCB5	AP1	25pf +2.75m on1 l	6.00	*65.00*
3NCB6	AP1	50pf +2m on 2 l	6.00	*65.00*

The surtax aided the Montenegro Red Cross.

MOROCCO

LOCATION — Northwest coast of Africa
GOVT. — Kingdom
AREA — 171,953 sq. mi.
POP. — 21,160,000 (est. 1984)
CAPITAL — Rabat

In 1956 the three zones of Morocco, French, Spanish and Tangier, were united to form an independent nation. Nos. 1-24 and C1-C3 were intended for use only in the southern (French currency) zone. Issues of the northern zone (Spanish currency) are listed after Postage Due stamps.

For earlier issues see French Morocco and Spanish Morocco.

100 Centimes = 1 Franc
100 Centimes = 1 Dirham (1962)

Catalogue values for all unused stamps in this country are for Never Hinged items.

Sultan Mohammed V — A1

Men Reading — A2

1956-57 Unwmk. Engr. *Perf. 13*

1	A1	5fr brt bl & indigo	15	15
2	A1	10fr bis brn & choc	15	15
3	A1	15fr dp grn & mag	16	15
4	A1	25fr purple ('57)	50	15
5	A1	30fr green ('57)	90	15
6	A1	50fr rose red ('57)	1.40	15
7	A1	70fr dk brn & brn red ('57)	2.00	40
		Nos. 1-7 (7)	5.26	
		Set value		78

For surcharges, see Nos. B1-B5, B8-B9.

1956, Nov. 5

Campaign against illiteracy: 15fr, Girls reading. 20fr, Instructor and pupils. 30fr, Old man and child reading. 50fr, Girl pointing out poster.

8	A2	10fr pur & vio	85	65
9	A2	15fr car & rose lake	1.10	70
10	A2	20fr bl grn & grn	1.25	1.25
11	A2	30fr rose lake & brt red	2.00	1.40
12	A2	50fr dp bl & bl	3.50	2.25
		Nos. 8-12 (5)	8.70	6.25

Sultan Mohammed V — A3

Prince Moulay el Hassan — A4

1957, Mar. 2 Photo. *Perf. 13½x13*

13	A3	15fr blue green	75	65
14	A3	25fr gray olive	1.00	65
15	A3	30fr deep rose	1.40	90

Anniversary of independence.

1957, July 9 *Perf. 13*

16	A4	15fr blue	70	50
17	A4	25fr green	85	65
18	A4	30fr car rose	1.40	90

Designation of Prince Moulay el Hassan as heir to the throne.

King Mohammed V — A5

1957, Nov. *Perf. 12½*

19	A5	15fr blk & brt grn	45	40
20	A5	25fr blk & rose red	70	50
21	A5	30fr blk & vio	75	65

Enthronement of Mohammed V, 30th anniv.

Morocco Pavilion, Brussels World's Fair — A6

1958, Apr. 20 Engr. *Perf. 13*

22	A6	15fr brt grnsh bl	20	15
23	A6	25fr carmine	20	15
24	A6	30fr indigo	25	20

World's Fair, Brussels.

UNESCO Building, Paris, and Mohammed V — A7

1958, Nov. 23

25	A7	15fr green	20	15
26	A7	25fr lake	20	15
27	A7	30fr blue	25	20

Opening of UNESCO Headquarters in Paris, Nov. 3.

Ben Smin Sanatorium A8

1959, Jan. 18 Unwmk. *Perf. 13*

28	A8	50fr dk brn, car & sl grn	38	25

Red Cross-Red Crescent Society.

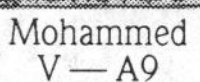
Mohammed V — A9

Princess Lalla Amina — A10

1959, Aug. 18 Engr. *Perf. 13*

29 A9 15fr dk car rose 30 20
30 A9 25fr brt bl 40 22
31 A9 45fr dk grn 45 30

50th birthday of King Mohammed V.

1959, Nov. 17

32 A10 15fr blue 20 15
33 A10 25fr green 22 15
34 A10 45fr rose lil 25 20

Issued for International Children's Week.

Map of Africa and Symbols of Agriculture, Industry and Commerce — A11

1960, Jan. 31 *Perf. 13*

35 A11 45fr vio, ocher & emer 45 30

Issued to publicize the meeting of the Economic Commission for Africa, Tangier.

Refugees and Uprooted Oak Emblem A12

Design: 45fr, Refugee family and uprooted oak emblem.

1960, Apr. 7 Unwmk. *Perf. 13*

36 A12 15fr ocher, blk & grn 16 15
37 A12 45fr blk & grn 28 20

World Refugee Year, July 1, 1959-June 30, 1960.

Marrakesh A13

1960, Apr. 25 Engr. *Perf. 13*

38 A13 100fr grn, bl & red brn 55 40

900th anniversary of Marrakesh.

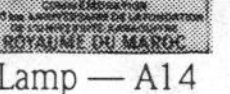
Lamp — A14

Wrestlers — A16

Arab League Center, Cairo and Mohammed V — A15

Designs: 25fr, Fountain and arched door. 30fr, Minaret. 35fr, Ornamented wall. 45fr, Moorish architecture.

1960, May 12 *Perf. 13½*

39 A14 15fr rose lil 25 22
40 A14 25fr dk bl 30 25
41 A14 30fr org red 55 40
42 A14 35fr black 70 50
43 A14 45fr yel grn 1.00 70
Nos. 39-43 (5) 2.80 2.07

1,100th anniversary of Karaouiyne University, Fez.

1960, June 28 Photo. *Perf. 12½*

44 A15 15fr grn & blk 15 15

Opening of the Arab League Center and the Arab Postal Museum, Cairo.

1960, Sept. 26 Engr. *Perf. 13*

Sports: 10fr, Gymnast. 15fr, Bicyclist. 20fr, Weight lifter. 30fr, Runner. 40fr, Boxers. 45fr, Sailboat. 70fr, Fencers.

45 A16 5fr ol, vio bl & plum 15 15
46 A16 10fr org brn, bl & brn 15 15
47 A16 15fr emer, bl & org brn 15 15
48 A16 20fr ultra, ol & brn 20 16
49 A16 30fr vio bl, mar & sep 25 20
50 A16 40fr grnsh bl, dk pur & red brn 40 20
51 A16 45fr grn, plum & ultra 45 25
52 A16 70fr dk brn, bl & gray 70 30
Nos. 45-52 (8) 2.45 1.56

17th Olympic Games, Rome, Aug. 25-Sept. 11.

Runner A17

1961, Aug. 30 Unwmk. *Perf. 13*

53 A17 20fr dk grn 15 15
54 A17 30fr dk car rose 25 15
55 A17 50fr brt bl 32 25

3rd Pan-Arabic Games, Casablanca.

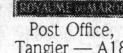

Post Office, Tangier — A18

View of Tangier and Gibraltar — A19

Design: 30fr, Telephone operator.

1961, Dec. 8 Litho. *Perf. 12½*

56 A18 20fr red vio 20 16
57 A18 30fr green 25 20
57A A19 90fr lt bl & vio bl 50 32

Conference of the African Postal and Telecommunications Union, Tangier.

Mohammed V and Map of Africa — A20

Patrice Lumumba and Map of Congo — A21

1962, Jan. 4 Unwmk. *Perf. 11½*

58 A20 20c buff & vio brn 15 15
59 A20 30c lt & dk bl 20 15
Set value 22

1st anniv. of the conference of African heads of state at Casablanca.

1962, Feb. 12 *Perf. 12½*

60 A21 20c bis & blk 15 15
61 A21 30c dl red brn & blk 20 16
Set value 25

1st death anniv. of Patrice Lumumba, Premier of Congo Democratic Republic.

Moroccan Students — A22

Arab League Building, Cairo — A23

1962, Mar. 5 Engr.

62 A22 20fr multi 20 15
63 A22 30fr multi 25 20
64 A22 90fr gray grn, ind & brn 45 32

Issued to honor the nation's students.

1962, Mar. 22 Photo. *Perf. 13½x13*

65 A23 20c red brn 38 15

Arab Propaganda Week, Mar. 22-28. See No. 146.

Malaria Eradication Emblem and Swamp — A24

Design: 50c, Dagger stabbing mosquito, vert.

1962, Sept. 3 Engr. *Perf. 13*

66 A24 20c dk grn & grnsh blk 15 15
67 A24 50c dk grn & mag 25 15
Set value 22

WHO drive to eradicate malaria.

Fish and Aquarium — A25

1962, Nov. 5 Unwmk. *Perf. 13*

68 A25 20c shown 25 16
69 A25 30c Moray eel 25 16

Casablanca Aquarium.

Courier and Sherifian Stamp of 1912 — A26

Designs: 30c, Courier on foot and round Sherifian cancellation. 50c, Sultan Hassan I and octagonal cancellation.

1962, Dec. 15 Unwmk.

70 A26 20c Prus grn & redsh brn 30 20
71 A26 30c dk car rose & blk 40 22
72 A26 50c bl & bister 65 30

Stamp Day; 1st National Stamp Exhibition, Dec. 15-23; 75th anniv. of the Sherifian Post and the 50th anniv. of its reorganization.

Boy Scout — A27

King Hassan II — A28

1962, Aug. 8 Litho. *Perf. 11½*

73 A27 20c vio brn & lt bl 15 15

5th Arab Boy Scout Jamboree, Rabat.

1962 Engr. *Perf. 13½x13*

75 A28 1c gray olive 15 15
76 A28 2c violet 15 15
77 A28 5c black 15 15
78 A28 10c brn org 15 15
79 A28 15c Prus grn 15 15
80 A28 20c purple 16 15
81 A28 30c dp yel grn 20 15
82 A28 50c vio brn 40 15
83 A28 70c deep blue 65 15
84 A28 80c magenta 1.00 16
Set value 2.70 60

See Nos. 110-114. "Mazelin" (designer-engraver) reads down on Nos. 75-84.

King Moulay Ismail — A29

Al Idrissi, Geographer — A30

1963, Mar. 3 *Perf. 12½*

85 A29 20c sepia 25 16

Tercentenary of Meknes as Ismaili capital.

1963-66 Engr.

Portraits: Nos. 87, 88A, Ibn Batota, explorer. No. 88, Ibn Khaldoun, historian and sociologist.

86 A30 20c dk sl grn 25 15
87 A30 20c dk car rose 25 15
88 A30 20c black 25 15
88A A30 40c dk vio bl ('66) 25 15

Famous medieval men of Morocco (Maghreb). No. 88A also marks the inauguration of the ferryboat "Ibn Batota" connecting Tangier and Malaga.

Issue dates: Nos. 86-88, May 7, 1963. No. 88A, July 15, 1966.

Sugar Beet and Sugar Refinery, Sidi Slimane A31

1963, June 10 Unwmk. *Perf. 13*

89 A31 20c shown 20 15

90 A31 50c Tuna fisherman, vert. 32 22

FAO "Freedom from Hunger" campaign.

Heads of Ramses II, Abu Simbel — A32

Designs: 30c, Isis, Kalabsha Temple, vert. 50c, Temple of Philae.

1963, July 15 Engr. *Perf. 11½*

91 A32 20c black 15 15

92 A32 30c vio, *grysh* 20 16

93 A32 50c maroon, *buff* 30 22

Campaign to save historic monuments in Nubia.

Agadir Before Earthquake A33

Designs: 30c, Like 20c, with "29 Février 1960" and crossed bars added. 50c, Agadir rebuilt.

Engr.; Engr. & Photo. (No. 95)

1963, Oct. 10 *Perf. 13½x13*

94 A33 20c bl & brn red 22 20

95 A33 30c bl, brn red & red 30 22

96 A33 50c bl & brn red 80 32

Issued to publicize the rebuilding of Agadir.

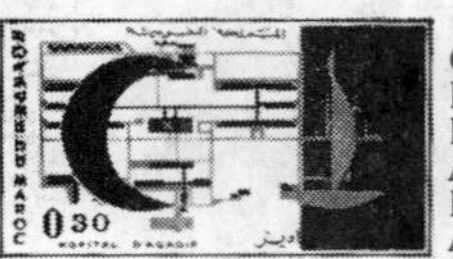

Centenary Emblem and Plan of Agadir Hospital A34

1963, Oct. 28 Photo. *Perf. 12½x13*

97 A34 30c blk, dp car & sil 20 16

Centenary of the International Red Cross.

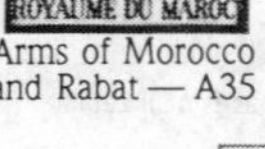

Arms of Morocco and Rabat — A35

Flag — A37

Hands Breaking Chain — A36

1963, Nov. 18 *Perf. 13x12½*

98 A35 20c gold, red, blk & emer 16 16

Installation of Parliament.

1963, Dec. 10 Engr. *Perf. 13*

99 A36 20c dk brn, grn & org 20 16

15th anniversary of the Universal Declaration of Human Rights.

1963, Dec. 25 Photo. *Perf. 13x12½*

100 A37 20c blk, dp car & grn 20 16

Evacuation of all foreign military forces from Moroccan territory.

Moulay Abd-er-Rahman, by Delacroix — A38

1964, Mar. 3 Engr. *Perf. 12x13*

101 A38 1d multi 1.50 1.00

Coronation of King Hassan II, 3rd anniv.

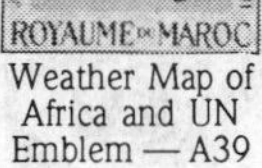

Weather Map of Africa and UN Emblem — A39

Children on Vacation — A40

Designs: 30c, World map and barometer trace, horiz.

1964, Mar. 23 Photo. *Perf. 11½*

Granite Paper

102 A39 20c multi 20 16

103 A39 30c multi 25 20

UN 4th World Meteorological Day. See No. C10.

1964, July 6 Litho. *Perf. 12½*

Design: 30c, Heads of boy and girl, buildings.

104 A40 20c multi 20 16

105 A40 30c multi 25 22

Issued for vacation camps for children of P.T.T. employees.

Olympic Torch A41

Cape Spartel Lighthouse, Sultan Mohammed ben Abd-er-Rahman A42

1964, Sept. 22 Engr. *Perf. 13*

106 A41 20c car lake, dk pur & grn 25 16

107 A41 30c bl, dk grn & red brn 38 20

108 A41 50c grn, red & brn 50 25

18th Olympic Games, Tokyo, Oct. 10-25.

Perf. 12½x11½

1964, Oct. 15 Photo.

109 A42 25c multi 20 16

Centenary of the Cape Spartel lighthouse.

King Type of 1962

1964-65 Engr. *Perf. 12½x13*

Size: 17x23mm

110 A28 20c purple (redrawn) 38 25

Perf. 13½x13

Size: 18x22mm

111 A28 25c rose red ('65) 22 15

112 A28 35c slate ('65) 35 15

113 A28 40c ultra ('65) 38 15

114 A28 60c red lilac ('65) 55 15

Nos. 110-114 (5) 1.88

Set value 45

The Arabic inscription touches the frame on No. 110. "Mazelin" (designer-engraver) reads up on No. 110, down on Nos. 111-114. No. 110 is a coil stamp with red control numbers on the back of some copies.

Iris — A43

Mohammed V Arriving by Plane — A44

1965 Photo. *Perf. 11½*

Granite Paper

115 A43 25c shown 45 30

116 A43 40c Gladiolus segetum 50 38

117 A43 60c Capparis spinosa, horiz. 85 65

Printed in sheets of 10. Five tête-bêche pairs in every sheet; vertical stamps arranged 5x2, horizontal stamps 2x5.

See Nos. 129-131.

1965, Mar. 15 Litho. *Perf. 12½*

118 A44 25c lt bl & dk grn 20 15

10th anniv. of the return of King Mohammed V from exile and the restoration of the monarchy.

ITU Emblem, Punched-Tape Writer and Telegraph Wires — A45

Design: 40c, ITU emblem, Syncom satellite, radio waves and "ITU" in Morse code.

Perf. 13x14

1965, May 17 Unwmk. Typo.

119 A45 25c multi 16 16

120 A45 40c lt bl, dp bl & bis 25 20

ITU, centenary.

ICY Emblem A46

1965, June 14 Engr. *Perf. 13*

121 A46 25c slate grn 16 15

122 A46 60c dk car rose 25 15

Set value 22

International Cooperation Year.

Triton Shell — A47

Designs: No. 124, Varnish shell (pitaria chione). No. 125, Great voluted shell (cymbium neptuni). No. 126, Helmet crab, vert. 40c, Mantis shrimp, vert. 1d, Royal prawn.

1965 Photo. *Perf. 11½*

Granite Paper

123 A47 25c vio & multi 38 15

124 A47 25c lt bl & multi 38 15

125 A47 25c org & multi 38 16

126 A47 25c lt grn & multi 38 25

127 A47 40c bl & multi 75 45

128 A47 1d yel & multi 1.00 65

Nos. 123-128 (6) 3.27 1.81

Printed in sheets of 10. Nos. 126-127 (5x2); others (2x5). Five tête bêche pairs in every sheet.

Flower Type of 1965

Orchids: 25c, Ophrys speculum. 40c, Ophrys fusca. 60c, Ophrys tenthredinifera (front and side view), horiz.

1965, Dec. 13 Photo. *Perf. 11½*

Granite Paper

129 A43 25c yel & multi 25 22

130 A43 40c dl rose & multi 38 22

131 A43 60c lt bl & multi 75 55

Note on tête bêche pairs after No. 117 also applies to Nos. 129-131.

Grain — A48

Designs: 40c, Various citrus fruit. 60c, Olives, horiz.

1966 Photo. *Perf. 11½*

Granite Paper

133 A48 25c blk & bis 15 15

136 A48 40c multi 20 16

137 A48 60c gray & multi 25 15

Set value 35

For surcharge see No. 231.

Flag, Map and Dove — A49

1966, Mar. 2 Typo. *Perf. 14x13*

139 A49 25c brt grn & red 15 15

Tenth anniversary of Independence.

King Hassan II — A50

1966, Mar. 2 Engr. *Perf. 13*

140 A50 25c red, brt grn & ind 15 15

Coronation of King Hassan II, 5th anniv.

Cross-country Runner A51

1966, Mar. 20 Engr. *Perf. 13*

141 A51 25c blue green 16 15

53rd International Cross-country Race.

WHO Headquarters from West — A52

Design: 40c, WHO Headquarters from the East.

1966, May 3 Engr. *Perf. 13*

142 A52 25c rose lil & blk 15 15
143 A52 40c dp bl & blk 20 15

Inauguration of the WHO Headquarters, Geneva.

Crown Prince Hassan Kissing Hand of King Mohammed V — A53

Design: 25c, King Hassan II and parachutist.

Perf. 12½x12

1966, May 14 Photo. Unwmk.

144 A53 25c gold & blk 30 22
145 A53 40c gold & blk 30 22
a. Strip of 2, #144-145 + label 65 50

10th anniv. of the Royal Armed Forces.

Type of 1962 Inscribed: "SEMAINE DE LA PALESTINE"

1966, May 16 *Perf. 11x11½*

146 A23 25c slate blue 15 15

Issued for Palestine Week.

Train — A54

1966, Dec. 19 Photo. *Perf. 13½*

147 A54 25c shown 22 16
148 A54 40c Ship 30 20
149 A54 1d Autobus 38 25

Twaite Shad — A55

Fish: 40c, Plain bonito. 1d, Bluefish, vert.

1967, Feb. 1 Photo. *Perf. 11½*

Granite Paper

150 A55 25c yel & multi 38 15
151 A55 40c yel & multi 50 22
152 A55 1d lt grn & multi 1.00 55

Printed tête bêche in sheets of 10. Nos. 150-151 (2x5); No. 152 (5x2).

Ait Aadel Dam A56

1967, Mar. 3 Engr. *Perf. 13*

153 A56 25c sl grn, Prus bl & gray 20 16
154 A56 40c Prus bl & lt brn 28 16

Inauguration of Ait Aadel Dam.

Rabat Hilton Hotel, Map of Morocco and Roman Arch — A57

1967, Mar. 3

155 A57 25c brt bl & blk 20 16
156 A57 1d brt bl & pur 38 16

Opening of the Rabat Hilton Hotel.

Torch, Globe, Town and Lions Emblem — A58

1967, Apr. 22 Photo. *Perf. 12½*

157 A58 40c gold & saph bl 22 16
158 A58 1d gold & slate grn 45 25

Lions International, 50th anniversary.

Three Hands Holding Pickax — A59

1967, July 9 Engr. *Perf. 13*

159 A59 25c slate green 15 15

Community Development Campaign.

Intl. Tourism Year Emblem A60

1967, Aug. 9 Photo. *Perf. 12½*

160 A60 1d lt ultra & dk bl 38 25

Arrow and Map of Mediterranean — A61

1967, Sept. 8 *Perf. 13x12*

161 A61 25c dk bl, ultra, red & tan 16 15
162 A61 40c blk, bl grn, red & tan 20 15
Set value 24

Mediterranean Games, Tunis, Sept. 8-17.

Steeplechase A62

1967, Oct. 14 Photo. *Perf. 12½*

163 A62 40c yel grn, blk & brt rose lilac 22 15
164 A62 1d lt ultra, blk & brt rose lilac 32 22

International Horseshow.

Cotton — A63

Human Rights Flame — A64

1967, Nov. 15 Photo. *Perf. 12½*

165 A63 40c lt bl, grn & yel 22 15

1968, Jan. 10 Engr. *Perf. 13*

166 A64 25c gray 15 15
167 A64 1d rose claret 22 20

International Human Rights Year.

King Hassan II — A65

1968-74 Litho. *Perf. 13*

Portrait in Magenta, Brown and Black

Size: 23x30mm

169 A65 1c cream & blk 15 15
170 A65 2c lt grnsh bl & blk 15 15
171 A65 5c lt ol grn & blk 15 15
172 A65 10c pale rose & blk 15 15
173 A65 15c gray bl & blk 15 15
174 A65 20c pink & blk 15 15
175 A65 25c black 18 15
176 A65 30c pale rose & blk 20 15
177 A65 35c bl & blk 22 25
178 A65 40c gray & blk 22 15
179 A65 50c lt bl & blk 32 15
180 A65 60c sal & blk 85 15
181 A65 70c gray & blk 2.00 50
182 A65 75c pale yel ('74) 50 25
183 A65 80c ocher & blk 1.00 15

Perf. 13½x14

Size: 26x40mm

184 A65 90c lt bl grn & blk 65 35
185 A65 1d tan & blk 85 15
186 A65 2d lt ultra & blk 1.90 25
187 A65 3d bluish lil & blk 2.75 45
188 A65 5d apple grn & blk 3.75 1.50
Nos. 169-188 (20) 16.29
Set value 4.40

For overprints & surcharges see #224, B17-B18.

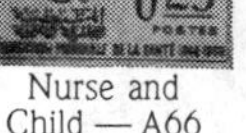
Nurse and Child — A66

Pendant — A67

1968, Apr. 8 Engr. *Perf. 13*

189 A66 25c ultra, red & olive 15 15
190 A66 40c slate, red & olive 16 15
Set value 18

WHO, 20th anniv.

1968, May 15 Photo. *Perf. 11½*

Design: 40c, Bracelet.

191 A67 25c dk ol bis & multi 38 20
192 A67 40c ultra & multi 50 25

Moroccan Red Crescent Society.

Nos. 191-192 were printed se-tenant in sheets of 10 (5x2) arranged vertically tête bêche.

See Nos. 373-374.

Map of Morocco and Rotary Emblem — A68

1968, May 23 *Perf. 13*

193 A68 40c multi 30 15
194 A68 1d ultra & multi 45 22

Rotary Intl. District Conference, Casablanca, May 24-25.

Ornamental Design — A69

Designs: Various patterns used for sashes.

1968, July 12 Photo. *Perf. 11½*

195 A69 25c multi 90 40
196 A69 40c multi 1.10 50
197 A69 60c multi 1.75 85
198 A69 1d multi 3.00 1.65

Berber (Riff), North Morocco — A70

Princess Lalla Meryem — A71

Regional Costumes: 10c, Man from Ait Moussa ou Ali. 15c, Woman from Ait Mouhad. No. 200, Bargeman from Rabat Salé. No. 201, Citadin man. 40c, Citadin woman. 60c, Royal Mokhazni. No. 204, Zemmours man. No. 204A, Man from Meknassa. No. 206, Msouffa woman, Sahara.

1968-74 Litho. *Perf. 13x12½*

198A A70 10c multi ('69) 45 32
199 A70 15c yel & multi ('69) 75 40
200 A70 25c bis & multi 75 45
201 A70 25c tan & multi ('69) 85 45
202 A70 40c lt bl & multi 90 65
203 A70 60c emer & multi 1.25 85
204 A70 1d lt bl & multi 1.65 1.10
204A A70 1d gray & multi ('69) 1.50 75

Perf. 15

205 A70 1d bis & multi 1.40 90
206 A70 1d grn & multi 1.40 90
a. Souvenir sheet of 10, #198A-206, perf. 13 13.75 12.50

b. As "a," with red overprint & surcharge 15.00 15.00
Nos. 198A-206 (10) 10.90 6.77

No. 206a issued June 30, 1970, for the opening of the National P.T.T. Museum, Rabat. Sold for 10d.

No. 206b issued Nov. 22, 1974, for the 8th Cong. of the Intl. Fed. of Blood Donors. Each stamp overprinted vertically "8eme Congres de la F.I.O.D.S." and blood container emblem. Black marginal inscription partially obliterated with lines, new Arabic inscription and price added. Sold for 20d.

1968, Oct. 7 Litho. *Perf. 13½*

Children's Week: 40c, Princess Lalla Asmaa. 1d, Crown Prince Sidi Mohammed.

207 A71 25c red & multi 30 15
208 A71 40c yel & multi 38 22
209 A71 1d lt bl & multi 50 38

Wrestling, Aztec Calendar Stone and Olympic Rings — A72

1968, Oct. 25 Photo. *Perf. 12x11½*

210 A72 15c shown 15 15
211 A72 20c Basketball 15 15
212 A72 25c Cycling 22 20
213 A72 40c Boxing 25 16
214 A72 60c Running 32 20
215 A72 1d Soccer 50 30
Nos. 210-215 (6) 1.59 1.16

19th Olympic Games, Mexico City, Oct. 12-27.

10 Dirham Coin of Tetuan, 1780 — A73

Women from Zagora — A74

Coins: 25c, Dirham, Agmat, c. 1138 A.D. 40c, Dirham, El Alya (Fes), c. 840 A.D. 60c, Dirham, Marrakesh, c. 1248 A.D.

1968, Dec. 17 Photo. *Perf. 11½*
Granite Paper

216 A73 20c dp plum, sil & blk 22 15
217 A73 25c dk rose brn, gold & blk 32 22
218 A73 40c dk grn, sil & blk 55 30
219 A73 60c dk red, gold & blk 75 45

See Nos. C16-C17.

1969, Jan. 21 Litho. *Perf. 12*

Design: 25c, Women from Ait Adidou.

220 A74 15c multi 55 30
221 A74 25c multi 75 45

See No. C15.

For unused stamps, more recent issues are valued as never hinged, with the beginning point determined on a country-by-country basis. Notes to show the beginning points are prominently placed in the text.

Painting by Belkahya — A75

King Hassan II — A76

1969, Mar. 27 Litho. *Perf. 11½x12*

222 A75 1d lt grnsh bl, blk & brn 32 16

International Day of the Theater.

1969, July 9 Photo. *Perf. 11½*

223 A76 1d gold & multi 55 22

40th birthday of King Hassan II. A souvenir sheet contains one of No. 223. Size: 75x105mm. Sold for 2.50d.

No. 185 Overprinted

مؤتمر القمة الاسلامي
الرباط ١٠ رجب 1389

1969, Sept. 22 Litho. *Perf. 13*

224 A65 1d tan & multi 2.25 1.90

First Arab Summit Conference, Rabat.

Mahatma Gandhi — A77

1969, Oct. 16 Photo. *Perf. 11½*

225 A77 40c pale vio, blk & gray 50 25

Mohandas K. Gandhi (1869-1948), leader in India's struggle for independence.

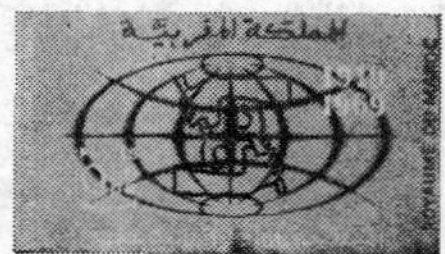
ILO Emblem A78

1969, Oct. 29

226 A78 50c multi 38 20

ILO, 50th anniv.

King Hassan II on Way to Prayer — A79

1969, Nov. 20 Photo. *Perf. 11½*

227 A79 1d multi 50 25

1st Arab Summit Conference, Rabat, Sept. 1969. For overprint, see No. 311.

Spahi Horsemen, by Haram al Glaoui A80

1970, Jan. 23 Engr. *Perf. 12x13*

228 A80 1d multi 50 25

Main Sewer, Fez — A81

Guedra Dance, by P. C. Beaubrun — A82

1970, Mar. 23 Litho. *Perf. 12*

229 A81 60c multi 28 15

50th Congress of Municipal Engineers, Rabat, Mar. 1970.

1970, Apr. 15

230 A82 40c multi 38 20

Folklore Festival, Marrakesh, May 1970.

No. 137 Overprinted "1970", "Census" in Arabic in Red and Surcharged in Black

1970 احصاء

0,25

1970, July 9 Photo. *Perf. 11½*

231 A48 25c on 60c multi 50 30

Issued to publicize the 1970 census.

Radar Station at Souk El Arba des Sehoul, and Satellite — A83

Ruddy Shelduck — A84

1970, Aug. 20

232 A83 1d lt ultra & multi 50 30

Revolution of King and People, 17th anniv.

1970, Sept. 25 Photo. *Perf. 11½*

233 A84 25c shown 42 22
234 A84 40c Houbara bustard 55 30

Campaign to save Moroccan wildlife.

Man Reading Book, Intl. Education Year Emblem — A85

1970, Oct. 20 Litho. *Perf. 12x11½*

235 A85 60c dl yel & multi 50 25

Symbols of Peace, Justice and Progress — A86

1970, Oct. 27 *Perf. 13½*

236 A86 50c multi 38 25

United Nations, 25th anniversary.

Arab League Countries and Emblem — A87

1970, Nov. 13 Photo. *Perf. 11½*

237 A87 50c multi 38 25

Arab League, 25th anniversary.

Olive Grove, Tree and Branch — A88

1970, Dec. 3 Litho. *Perf. 12*

238 A88 50c red brn & grn 45 28

International Olive Year.

Es Sounna Mosque, Rabat — A89

1971, Jan. 5 Engr. *Perf. 13*

239 A89 60c ol bis, bl & sl grn 40 22

Restoration of Es Sounna Mosque, Rabat, built in 1785.

Heart and Horse — A90

1971, Feb. 23 Photo. *Perf. 12x12½*

240 A90 50c blk & multi 35 18

European heart research week, Feb. 21-28.

Dam and Hassan II — A91

1971, Mar. 3 *Perf. 11½*

241 A91 25c multi 35 15
a. Souv. sheet of 4 1.50 1.50

Accession of King Hassan II, 10th anniv. No. 241a issued Mar. 24. Sold for 2.50d.

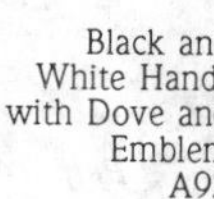

Black and White Hands with Dove and Emblem A92

1971, June 16 **Photo.** *Perf. 13*

242 A92 50c brn & multi 35 20

Intl. Year against Racial Discrimination.

Children Around the World — A93

Shah Mohammed Riza Pahlavi of Iran — A94

1971, Oct. 4 **Litho.** *Perf. 13x14*

243 A93 40c emer & multi 32 15

International Children's Day.

1971, Oct. 11 **Photo.** *Perf. 11½*

244 A94 1d bl & multi 30 22

2500th anniv. of the founding of the Persian empire by Cyrus the Great.

Mausoleum of Mohammed V — A95

Designs: 50c, Mausoleum, close-up view, and Mohammed V. 1d, Decorated interior wall, vert.

1971, Nov. 10 **Litho.** *Perf. 14*

245 A95 25c multi 15 15
246 A95 50c multi 20 15
247 A95 1d multi 40 25

Soccer Ball and Games Emblem A96

1971, Nov. 30 **Photo.** *Perf. 13x13½*

248 A96 40c shown 22 20
249 A96 60c Runner 30 20

Mediterranean Games, Izmir, Turkey, Oct. 6-17.

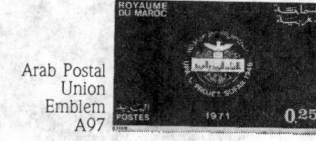

Arab Postal Union Emblem A97

1971, Dec. 23 **Litho.** *Perf. 13x12½*

250 A97 25c dk & lt bl & org 15 15

25th anniv. of the Conference of Sofar, Lebanon, establishing APU.

Sun over Cultivated Sand Dunes — A98

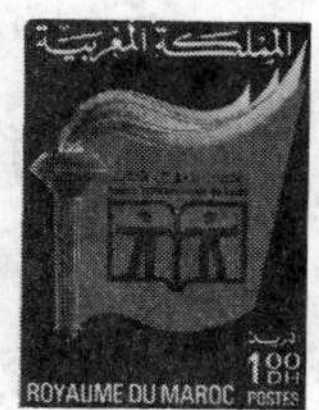

Torch and Book Year Emblem — A99

1971, Dec. 30 **Photo.** *Perf. 12½*

251 A98 70c blk, bl & yel 22 15

Sherifian Phosphate Office (fertilizer production and export), 50th anniversary.

1972, Jan. 12 *Perf. 11½*

252 A99 1d sil & multi 25 15

International Book Year.

National Lottery — A100

Bridge of Sighs — A101

1972, Feb. 7 **Photo.** *Perf. 13*

253 A100 25c tan, blk & gold 15 15

Creation of a national lottery.

1972, Feb. 25

Designs: 50c, St. Mark's Basilica and waves, horiz. 1d, Lion of St. Mark.

254 A101 25c multi 15 15
255 A101 50c red, blk & buff 15 15
256 A101 1d lt bl & multi 30 15
Set value 35

UNESCO campaign to save Venice.

Bridge, Road, Map of Africa A102

1972, Apr. 21 *Perf. 13*

257 A102 75c blue & multi 22 15

2nd African Road Conf., Rabat, Apr. 17-22.

Morocco No. 223 — A103

1972, Apr. 27 *Perf. 11½*

258 A103 1d lt ultra & multi 30 20

Stamp Day.

The Engagement of Imilchil, by Tayeb Lahlou — A104

1972, May 26 **Litho.** *Perf. 13x13½*

259 A104 60c blk & multi 38 22

Folklore Festival, Marrakesh, May 26-June 4.

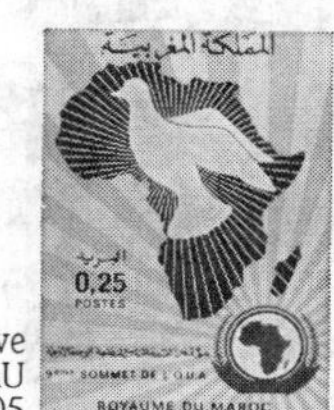

Map of Africa, Dove and OAU Emblem — A105

1972, June 12 **Photo.** *Perf. 11½*

260 A105 25c multi 15 15

9th Summit Conference of Organization for African Unity, Rabat, June 12-15.

Landscape, Environment Emblem A106

1972, July 20 **Photo.** *Perf. 12½x12*

261 A106 50c bl & multi 20 15

UN Conference on Human Environment, Stockholm, June 5-16

Olympic Emblems, Running A107

1972, Aug. 29 **Photo.** *Perf. 13x13½*

262 A107 25c shown 15 15
263 A107 50c Wrestling 15 15
264 A107 75c Soccer 25 20
265 A107 1d Cycling 32 22
Set value 60

20th Olympic Games, Munich, Aug. 26-Sept. 11.

Sow Thistle — A108

Mountain Gazelle — A109

1972, Sept. 15 **Litho.** *Perf. 14*

266 A108 25c shown 20 15
267 A108 40c Amberboa crupinoides 25 20
Set value 28

See No. 305-306.

1972, Sept. 29 **Photo.** *Perf. 11½*

268 A109 25c shown 22 20
269 A109 40c Barbary sheep 32 25

Nos. 266-269 issued for nature protection.

Rabat Rug — A110

Child and UNICEF Emblem — A111

Designs: 25c, High Atlas rug. 70c, Tazenakht rug. 75c, Rabat rug, different pattern.

Perf. 13½ (25fr, 70fr), 11½

1972-73 **Photo.**

270 A110 25c multi 50 15
270A A110 50c multi 75 22
271 A110 70c multi 90 30
271A A110 75c multi 1.00 30

Issue dates: 50c, 75c, Oct. 27, 1972; 25c, 70c, Dec. 28, 1973.

See Nos. 326-327.

1972, Dec. 20 **Photo.** *Perf. 13½x13*

272 A111 75c brt grn & bl 22 15

International Children's Day.

Symbolic Letter Carrier and Stamp — A112

1973, Jan. 30 **Photo.** *Perf. 13x13½*

273 A112 25c brn & multi 15 15

Stamp Day.

Weather Map, Northern Hemisphere — A113

1973, Feb. 23 **Photo.** *Perf. 13*

274 A113 70c sil & multi 25 16

Intl. meteorological cooperation, cent.

King Hassan II, Coat of Arms — A114

1973-76 Photo. *Perf. 14*

No.	Type	Value	Color	Unused	Used
275	A114	1c	pale yel & multi	15	15
276	A114	2c	pale bl & multi	15	15
277	A114	5c	pale ol & multi	15	15
278	A114	10c	brn org & multi	15	15
279	A114	15c	vio gray & multi	15	15
280	A114	20c	pink & multi	22	15
281	A114	25c	pale bl & multi	15	15
282	A114	30c	rose & multi	22	15
283	A114	35c	org yel & multi	15	15
284	A114	40c	lt gray & multi	1.50	25
285	A114	50c	ultra & multi	22	15
286	A114	60c	sal & multi	25	15
287	A114	70c	yel grn & multi	20	15
288	A114	75c	lem & multi	38	15
289	A114	80c	multi	25	20
290	A114	90c	brt grn & multi	50	15
291	A114	1d	beige & multi	65	15
292	A114	2d	gray & multi	2.00	38
293	A114	3d	lt lil & multi	2.25	50
294	A114	5d	lt brn & multi ('75)	2.00	55
294A	A114	5d	pink & multi ('76)	2.00	70
			Nos. 275-294A (21)	13.69	
			Set value		3.50

Nos. B26-B27 Surcharged to Obliterate Surtax

مناظرة
السساحة
1973

1973, Mar. 13 *Perf. 11½*
295 SP1 25c multi 1.10 1.10
296 SP1 70c multi 1.10 1.10

Tourism Conference 1973. Arabic overprint and date on one line on No. 296.
See se-tenant note below No. B11.
See Nos. 351-352.

Holy Ka'aba, Mecca, Mosque and Minaret, Rabat A115

1973, May 3 Photo. *Perf. 13½x14*
297 A115 25c lt bl & multi 15 15

Mohammed's 1,403rd birthday.

Roses and M'Gouna A116

1973, May 14 *Perf. 13*
298 A116 25c bl & multi 15 15

Rose Festival of M'Gouna.

Hands, Torch, OAU Emblem — A117

1973, May 25 Photo. *Perf. 14x13*
299 A117 70c dp cl & multi 20 15

OAU, 10th anniversary.

Dancers with Tambourines A118

Design: 1d, Dancer with handbells, Marrakesh Minaret, Atlas Mountain.

1973, May 30 *Perf. 12½x13*
300 A118 50c multi 20 15
301 A118 1d multi 25 20

Folklore Festival, Marrakesh.

Heliocentric System A119

1973, June 29 *Perf. 13x13½*
302 A119 70c dk bl & multi 30 15

Nicolaus Copernicus (1473-1543), Polish astronomer.

Microscope, WHO Emblem, World Map — A120

1973, July 16 Photo. *Perf. 13x12½*
303 A120 70c multi 22 15

WHO, 25th anniversary.

INTERPOL Emblem, Fingerprint A121

1973, Sept. 12 Photo. *Perf. 13x13½*
304 A121 70c brn, sil & bl 20 15

50th anniv. of Intl. Criminal Police Org.

Flower Type of 1972

1973, Oct. 12 Litho. *Perf. 14*
305 A108 25c Daisies, horiz. 38 15
306 A108 1d Thistle 75 25

Nature protection.

Berber Hyena A122

Design: 50c, Eleonora's falcon, vert.

1973, Nov. 23 Photo. *Perf. 14*
307 A122 25c multi 38 15
308 A122 50c multi 50 20

Nature protection.

Map and Colors of Morocco, Algeria and Tunisia A123

1973, Dec. 7 *Perf. 13x13½*
309 A123 25c gold & multi 15 15

Maghreb Committee for Coordination of Posts and Telecommunications.

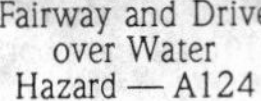

Fairway and Drive over Water Hazard — A124

Map of Africa, Scales, Human Rights Flame — A125

1974, Feb. 8 Photo. *Perf. 14x13*
310 A124 70c multi 30 20

International Golf Grand Prix for the Hassan II Morocco trophy.

No. 227 Overprinted in Red

المؤتمر الاسلامي - لاهور
1394

1974, Feb. 25 *Perf. 11½*
311 A79 1d multi 1.40 75

Islamic Conference, Lahore, India, 1974.

1974, Mar. 15 Photo. *Perf. 14x13½*
312 A125 70c gold & multi 40 25

25th anniversary of the Universal Declaration of Human Rights.

Vanadinite — A126

Minaret, Marrakesh Mosque, Rotary Emblem — A127

1974-75 Photo. *Perf. 13*
313 A126 25c shown 15 15
313A A126 50c Aragonite 38 15
314 A126 70c Erythrine 38 22
314A A126 1d Agate 75 16

Issue dates: 25c, 70c, Apr. 30, 1974; 50c, 1d, Feb. 14, 1975.

1974, May 11 Photo. *Perf. 14*
315 A127 70c multi 25 15

District 173 Rotary International annual meeting, Marrakesh, May 10-12.

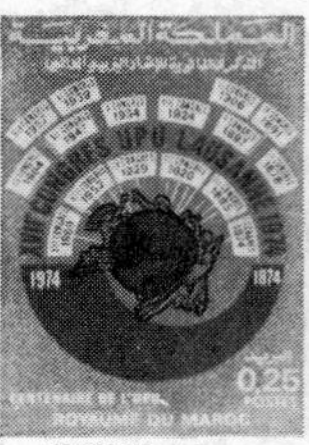

UPU Emblem, Congress Dates — A128

Drummer and Dancers — A129

Design: 1d, Scroll with UPU emblem, Lausanne coat of arms and 17th UPU Congress emblem, horiz.

1974, May 30 Photo.
316 A128 25c lt grn, org & blk 15 15
317 A128 1d dk grn & multi 32 20

Centenary of Universal Postal Union.

1974, June 7 Photo. *Perf. 14*

Design: 70c, Knife juggler and women.

318 A129 25c multi 22 15
319 A129 70c multi 50 22

National folklore festival, Marrakesh.

Environment Emblem, Polution, Clean Water and Air — A130

1974, June 25 *Perf. 13*
320 A130 25c multi 15 15

World Environment Day.

Simulated Stamps, Cancel and Magnifier A131

1974, Aug. 2 Photo. *Perf. 13*
321 A131 70c sil & multi 22 15

Stamp Day.

No. J5 Surcharged الاحصاء الفلاحي

1،00

1974, Sept. 25 Photo. *Perf. 14*
322 D2 1d on 5c multi 85 65

Agricultural census.

Canceled-to-order stamps are often from remainders. Most collectors of canceled stamps prefer postally used specimens.

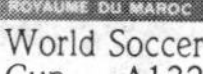

World Soccer Cup — A132

Double-spurred Francolin — A133

1974, Oct. 11

323 A132 1d brt bl & multi 50 30

World Cup Soccer Championship, Munich, June 13-July 7.

A stamp similar to No. 323, also issued Oct. 11, has gold inscription: "CHAMPION: R.F.A." in French and Arabic, honoring the German Federal Republic as championship winner. Value $32.50

Perf. 14x13½, 13½x14

1974, Dec. 5 **Photo.**

324 A133 25c shown 38 15

325 A133 70c Leopard, horiz. 70 22

Nature protection.

Zemmour Rug A134

Columbine A135

Design: 1d, Beni Mguilo rug.

1974, Dec 20 ***Perf. 13***

326 A134 25c multi 38 15

327 A134 1d multi 75 22

See Nos. 349-350, 398-400.

1975 **Photo.** ***Perf. 13½***

328	A135	10c Daisies	15	15
329	A135	25c Columbine	20	15
330	A135	35c Orange lilies	22	15
331	A135	50c Anemones	22	15
332	A135	60c White starflower	30	20
333	A135	70c Poppies	32	22
334	A135	90c Carnations	45	32
335	A135	1d Pansies	50	38
		Nos. 328-335 (8)	2.36	
		Set value		1.50

Issue dates: 25c, 35c, 70c, 90c, Jan. 10; others, Apr. 29.

Water Carrier, by Feu Tayeb Lahlou — A136

1975, Apr. 3 ***Perf. 13***

338 A136 1d multicolored 65 30

Stamp Collector, Carrier Pigeon, Globe — A137

Musicians and Dancers — A138

1975, May 21 **Photo.** ***Perf. 13***

339 A137 40c gold & multi 15 15

Stamp Day.

1975, June 12 **Photo.** ***Perf. 14x13½***

340 A138 1d multicolored 40 22

16th Folklore Festival, Marrakesh, May 30-June 15.

Guitar and Association for the Blind Emblem A139

1975, July 8 ***Perf. 13x13½***

341 A139 1d purple & multi 38 15

Week of the Blind.

Animals in Forest — A140

1975, July 25 **Photo.** ***Perf. 13x13½***

342 A140 25c multicolored 15 15

Children's Week.

Games' Emblem, Runner, Weight Lifter — A141

1975, Sept. 4 **Photo.** ***Perf. 13***

343 A141 40c gold, mar & buff 15 15

7th Mediterranean Games, Algiers, Aug. 23-Sept. 6.

Bald Ibis A142

1975, Oct. 21 **Photo.** ***Perf. 13***

344 A142 40c shown 38 15

345 A142 1d Persian lynx, vert. 55 30

Nature protection.

King Mohammed V Greeting Crowd, Prince Moulay Hassan at Left — A143

King Hassan II — A144

Design: #348, King Mohammed V wearing fez.

1975, Nov. 21 **Photo.** ***Perf. 13½***

346 A143 40c blk, sil & dk bl 20 15

347 A144 1d blk, gold & dk bl 32 20

348 A144 1d blk, gold & dk bl 32 20

a. Sheet of 3, #346-348 9.00 9.00

20th anniversary of independence.

Rug Type of 1974

Designs: 25c, Ouled Besseba rug. 1d, Ait Ouaouzguid rug.

1975, Dec. 11

349 A134 25c red & multi 38 25

350 A134 1d orange & multi 55 32

المسيرة الخضراء
1975

Nos. B29-B30 Surcharged in Green to Obliterate Surtax

1975 ***Perf. 11½***

351 SP1 25c blue & multi 1.50 1.50

352 SP1 70c orange & multi 1.50 1.50

March of Moroccan people into Spanish Sahara, Dec. 1975.

See se-tenant note after No. B11.

"Green March of the People" — A145

Copper Coin, Fez, 1883-84 — A146

1975, Dec. 30 **Photo.** ***Perf. 13½x13***

353 A145 40c multicolored 15 15

March of Moroccan people into Spanish Sahara, Dec. 1975.

1976 **Photo.** ***Perf. 14x13½***

Coins: 15c, 50c, silver coin, Rabat, 1774-75. 35c, 65c, Gold coin, Sabta, 13th-14th centuries. 1d, Square coin, Sabta, 12th-13th centuries.

354	A146	5c dull rose & multi	15	15
355	A146	15c brown & multi	15	15
356	A146	35c gray & multi	38	15
357	A146	40c ocher & multi	16	15
358	A146	50c ultra & blk	25	15
359	A146	65c yellow & multi	30	22
360	A146	1d multicolored	40	25
		Nos. 354-360 (7)	1.79	
		Set value		98

Issue dates: Nos. 354-356, Apr. 26. Nos. 357-360, Jan. 20.

1976, Sept. 9

Designs: Various Moroccan coins.

361	A146	5c green & multi	15	15
362	A146	15c dp rose & multi	15	15
363	A146	20c lt bl & multi	18	15
364	A146	30c lil rose & multi	20	15
365	A146	35c green & multi	38	15
366	A146	70c orange & multi	50	18
		Nos. 361-366 (6)	1.56	
		Set value		64

See Nos. 403-406A, 524B-524C.

Family — A147

Arch, Ibn Zaidoun Mosque — A148

1976, Feb. 12 ***Perf. 14x13½***

367 A147 40c multicolored 25 20

Family planning.

Perf. 13½x14, 14x13½

1976, Feb. 12 **Photo.**

Design: 40c, Hall, Ibn Zaidoun Mosque, horiz.

368 A148 40c multicolored 15 15

369 A148 65c multicolored 25 20

Set value 28

Ibn Zaidoun Mosque, millennium.

Medersa bou Anania, Fez A149

1976, Feb. 26 ***Perf. 13x14½***

370 A149 1d multicolored 25 20

Borobudur Temple A150

Design: 40c, Bas-relief, Borobudur.

1976, Mar. 11 **Photo.** ***Perf. 13***

371 A150 40c multicolored 15 15

372 A150 1d multicolored 25 15

Set value 24

UNESCO campaign to save Borobudur Temple, Java.

Islamic Conference, 6th Anniv. A151

1976 Litho. *Perf. 13½x13*

372A A151 1d Dome of the Rock 3.50 1.25

Jewelry Type of 1968

Designs: 40c, Pendant. 1d, Breastplate.

1976, June 29 Photo. *Perf. 14x13½*

373 A67 40c blue & multi 25 15
374 A67 1d olive & multi 38 20

Moroccan Red Crescent Society.
Nos. 373-374 were printed se-tenant in sheets of 10 (5x2) arranged vertically tête-bêche.

Bicentennial Emblem, Flags and Map of US and Morocco — A152

Design: 1d, George Washington, King Hassan, Statue of Liberty and Royal Palace, Rabat, vert.

1976, July 27 Photo. *Perf. 14*

375 A152 40c multicolored 20 15
376 A152 1d multicolored 32 22

American Bicentennial.

Wrestling A153

1976, Aug. 11 *Perf. 13x13½*

377 A153 35c shown 15 15
378 A153 40c Cycling 22 15
379 A153 50c Boxing 35 22
380 A153 1d Running 50 38

21st Olympic Games, Montreal, Canada, July 17-Aug. 1.

Old and New Telephones, Radar A154

1976, Sept. 29 Photo. *Perf. 14*

381 A154 1d gold & multi 30 15

Centenary of first telephone call by Alexander Graham Bell, Mar. 10, 1876.

Blind Person's Identification A155

1976, Oct. 12 Photo. *Perf. 13½x14*

382 A155 50c multicolored 16 15

Week of the Blind.

Chanting Goshawk — A156

1976, Oct. 29 *Perf. 13x13½*

383 A156 40c shown 45 15
384 A156 1d Purple gallinule 75 30

Nature protection.

King Hassan, Star, Torch, Map of Morocco — A157

Africa Cup — A159

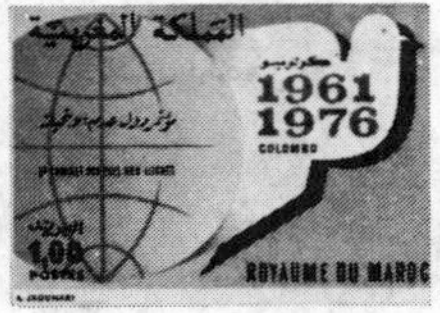

Globe and Dove — A158

1976, Nov. 19 Photo. *Perf. 12½x13*

385 A157 40c multicolored 15 15

First anniversary of Green March into Spanish Sahara.

Nos. B34-B35 Overprinted with 2 Bars over Surcharge and 4-line Arabic Inscription

1976, Nov. 29 Photo. *Perf. 13½*

386 SP1 25c ultra, blk & org 75 75
387 SP1 70c red, blk & org 90 90

5th African Tuberculosis Conference, Rabat.

1976, Dec. 16 *Perf. 13*

388 A158 1d blue, blk & red 22 15

5th Summit Meeting of Non-aligned Countries, Colombo, Aug. 9-19, and 25th anniv. of Org. of Non-aligned Countries.

1976, Dec. 29 Photo. *Perf. 14*

389 A159 1d multicolored 25 16

African Soccer Cup.

Letters Circling Globe, Postmark A160

1977, Jan. 24 Photo. *Perf. 13½*

390 A160 40c multicolored 16 15

Stamp Day.

Aeonium Arboreum — A161

Malope Trifida — A162

Design: 1d, Hesperolaburnum platyclarpum.

Perf. 13x13½, 14 (A162)

1977, Feb. 22

391 A161 40c multicolored 32 15
392 A162 50c multicolored 45 22
393 A161 1d multicolored 55 22

Ornamental Lamps, View of Salé A163

1977, Mar. 24 Photo. *Perf. 14*

394 A163 40c multicolored 20 15

Candle procession of Salé.

No. J6 Surcharged in Orange

موسم حب الملوك
1977
0,40

1977, May 11 Photo. *Perf. 14*

395 D2 40c on 10c multi 32 20

Cherry Festival.

Map of Arab Countries, Emblem A164

1977, June 2 Photo. *Perf. 14*

396 A164 50c multicolored 20 15

5th Congress of Organization of Arab Cities.

APU Emblem, Members' Flags A165

1977, June 20

397 A165 1d multicolored 35 20

Arab Postal Union, 25th anniversary.

Rug Type of 1974

Designs: 35c, No. 399A, Marmoucha rug, diff. No. 399, Ait Haddou rug. 1d, Salé rug.

Perf. 11½x12, 13½ (#399A)

1977-79 Photo.

398 A134 35c multicolored 25 15
399 A134 40c multicolored 32 15
399A A134 40c multicolored 32 15
400 A134 1d multicolored 45 22
Set value 56

Issue dates: No. 399A, Mar. 8, 1979, others, July 21, 1977.

Cithara — A166

Ali Jinnah and Map of Pakistan — A167

1977, Aug. 18 Photo. *Perf. 14*

401 A166 1d multi 25 15

Week of the Blind.

1977, Oct. 10 Photo. *Perf. 13½x13*

402 A167 70c multi 20 15

Mohammed Ali Jinnah (1876-1948), first Governor General of Pakistan.

Coin Type of 1976

Designs: Various Moroccan coins.

1977-81 *Perf. 14x13½*

403 A146 10c gray & multi 15 15
403A A146 25c ap grn & multi ('81) 15 15
404 A146 60c dk red & multi ('78) 22 15
405 A146 75c citron & multi 25 15
405A A146 80c pale vio & mult ('81) 20 15
406 A146 2d yel grn & multi 75 25
406A A146 3d beige & multi ('81) 75 40
Nos. 403-406A (7) 2.47
Set value 1.00

Marcher with Flag, Map of Morocco and Spanish Sahara — A168

1977, Nov. 6 Photo. *Perf. 14*

407 A168 1d multi 28 15

Green March into Spanish Sahara, 2nd anniv.

Chamber of Representatives — A169

1977, Nov. 6 *Perf. 13½*

408 A169 1d multi 25 15
a. Souvenir sheet 1.40 1.40

Opening of Chamber of Representatives. No. 408a sold for 3d.

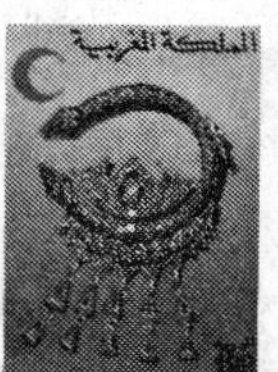

Enameled Silver Brooch — A170

Copper Vessel — A171

1977, Dec. 14 **Photo.** *Perf. 11½*

409 A170 1d multi 30 16

Moroccan Red Crescent Society.

1978, Jan. 5 **Photo.** *Perf. 13*

Design: 1d, Standing filigree copper bowl with cover.

410 A171 40c gold & multi 25 15
411 A171 1d gold & multi 45 20
Set value 28

Printed se-tenant in sheets of 10 (5x2) arranged vertically tête bêche.

Map of Sahara, Cogwheel Emblem — A172

Covered Jar — A173

Design: 1d, Map of North Africa, fish in net, camels, horiz.

1978, Feb. 27 **Photo.** *Perf. 14*

412 A172 40c multi 15 15
413 A172 1d multi 30 15

Promotion of the Sahara. See Nos. 441-442 for similar stamps overprinted.

1978, Mar. 27 *Perf. 13½x13*

414 A173 1d shown 38 22
415 A173 1d Vase 38 22

Week of the Blind.

Red Crescent, Red Cross, Arab Countries A174

1978, Apr. 14 *Perf. 13x13½*

416 A174 1d multi 25 15

10th Conference of Arab Red Crescent and Red Cross Societies, Apr. 10-15.

View of Fez, Rotary Emblem — A175

1978, Apr. 22 **Photo.** *Perf. 14*

417 A175 1d multi 25 15

Rotary Intl. Meeting, Fez, District 173.

Dome of the Rock, Jerusalem — A176

Folk Dancers and Flutist — A177

1978, May 29 *Perf. 14½*

418 A176 5c multi 15 15
419 A176 10c multi 15 15
Set value 24 18

Palestinian fighters and their families. For overprints, see Nos. 502-502A.

1978, June 15 *Perf. 13½x13*

420 A177 1d multi 50 25

National Folklore Festival, Marrakesh.

Sugar Cane Field, and Conveyor Belt A178

1978, July 24 **Photo.** *Perf. 13*

421 A178 40c multi 15 15

Sugar industry.

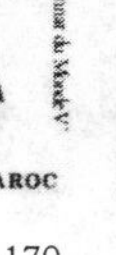

Games Emblem — A179

Bird, Tree, Tent, Scout Emblem — A180

1978, Aug. 25

422 A179 1d multi 30 20

World sailing championships.

1978, Sept. 26 **Photo.** *Perf. 13*

423 A180 40c multi 1.75 50

Pan-Arab Scout Jamboree, Rabat.

View of Fez A181

1978, Oct. 10

424 A181 40c multi 15 15

Moulay Idriss the Great, Festival, Fez.

Flame Emblem — A182

Houses, Agadir — A183

1978, Dec. 21 **Photo.** *Perf. 14*

425 A182 1d multi 38 20

30th anniversary of Universal Declaration of Human Rights.

1979, Jan. 25 **Photo.** *Perf. 12*

426 A183 40c shown 15 15
427 A183 1d Old Fort, Marrakesh 30 15

Soccer and Cup A184

1979, Mar. 2 *Perf. 13*

428 A184 40c multi 15 15

Mohammed V Soccer Cup.

Vase — A185

Procession — A186

1979, Mar. 29 **Photo.** *Perf. 14*

429 A185 1d multi 25 20

Week of the Blind.

Perf. 13x13½, 13½x13

1979, Apr. 18

Design: 1d, Festival, by Mohamed Ben Ali Rbati, horiz.

430 A186 40c multi 15 15
431 A186 1d multi 30 20

Brass Containers, Red Crescent A187

Perf. 13x13½, 13½x13

1979, May 16 **Photo.**

432 A187 40c shown 25 15
433 A187 1d Heated coffee urn, vert. 50 20

Red Crescent Society.

Dancers — A188

Silver Dagger — A189

1979, June 1 **Photo.** *Perf. 13*

434 A188 40c multi 15 15

National Festival of Marrakech.

1979, June 20 *Perf. 14*

435 A189 1d multi 30 15

King Hassan II, 50th Birthday — A190

1979, July 9 **Photo.** *Perf. 14*

436 A190 1d multi 25 15

4th Arab Youth Festival, Rabat A191

1979, July 30 **Photo.** *Perf. 13½x14*

437 A191 1d multi 25 15

King Hassan II and Crowd — A192

1979, Aug. 20 *Perf. 14x13½*

438 A192 1d multi 22 15

Revolution of the King and the People, 25th anniv.

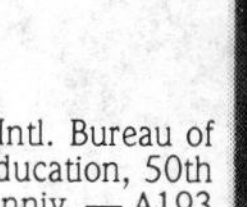

Intl. Bureau of Education, 50th Anniv. — A193

1979, Sept. 28 **Photo.** *Perf. 13x13½*

439 A193 1d multi 38 20

Pilgrimage to Mecca, Mt. Arafat, Holy Ka'aba
A194

1979, Oct. 25 *Perf. 13½*
440 A194 1d multi 25 15

No. 413 Redrawn in Smaller Size and Overprinted in Red

استرجاع اقليم وادي الذهب
1979-8-14

1979, Nov. 7 Litho. *Perf. 14*
Size: 33x23mm
441 A172 40c multi 25 15
442 A172 1d multi 38 25

Return of Oued Eddahab province, Aug. 14.

Leucanthemum Catanance
A195

Children, Globe, IYC Emblem
A196

1979, Nov. 21 Photo. *Perf. 14½*
443 A195 40c Centaurium 15 15
444 A195 1d shown 32 15
Set value 22

1979, Dec. 3 *Perf. 14*
445 A196 40c multi 65 25

International Year of the Child.

Otter — A197

Traffic Signs and Road — A198

1979, Dec. 18 *Perf. 13½x13*
446 A197 40c shown 25 15
447 A197 1d Redstart 40 22
Set value 30

1980, Jan. 3 Photo. *Perf. 14*
448 A198 40c shown 15 15
449 A198 1d Children at curb 20 15
Set value 16

Fortress
A199

1980, Jan. 29 *Perf. 13x13½*
450 A199 1d multi 25 15

Copper Bowl and Lid, Red Crescent — A200

Week of the Blind — A201

Red Crescent Society: 70c, Copper kettle and brazier. Nos. 451-452 tete-beche.

1980, Feb. 28 Photo. *Perf. 14*
451 A200 50c multi 20 15
452 A200 70c multi 28 15

1980, Mar. 19 Photo. *Perf. 14*
453 A201 40c multi 15 15

Rabat Mechanical Sorting Office
A202

1980, Apr. 17
454 A202 40c multi 15 15

Stamp Day.

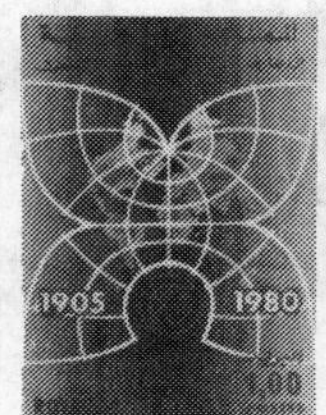

Rotary Intl., 75th Anniv. — A203

Cloth and Leather Goods — A204

1980, May 14 Photo. *Perf. 14*
455 A203 1d multi 22 15

1980, May 31 Photo. *Perf. 13½x13*
456 A204 1d multi 22 15

4th Textile and Leather Exhibition, Casablanca, May 2-9.

Gypsum — A205

Falcon — A206

1980, June 19 Photo. *Perf. 13½x13*
457 A205 40c multi 20 15

See Nos. 477-478.

1980, July 26 *Perf. 11½*
458 A206 40c multi 20 15

Hunting with falcons.

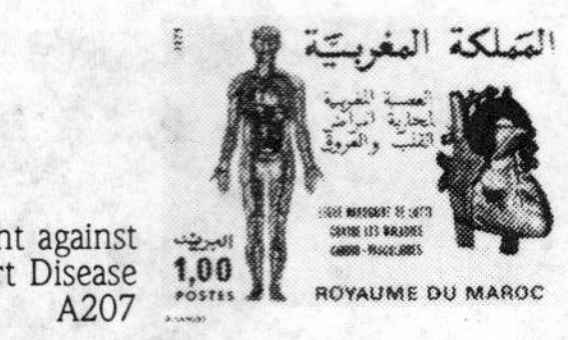

Fight against Heart Disease
A207

1980, Aug. 7 Photo. *Perf. 13x13½*
459 A207 1d multi 30 15

A208

A210

Ornamental Saddle and Harness — A209

1980, Aug. 18 *Perf. 14*
460 A208 40c shown 15 15
461 A208 1d Emblems, diff. 25 15
Set value 16

United Nations Decade for Women.

1980, Sept. 3 *Perf. 14½*
462 A209 40c Saddle, harness, diff. 15 15
463 A209 1d shown 30 15
Set value 22

1980, Sept. 18
464 A210 40c multi 15 15

World Meteorological Day.

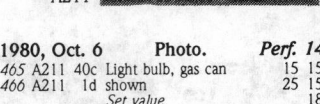

Hand Holding Dry Gas Pump
A211

1980, Oct. 6 Photo. *Perf. 14*
465 A211 40c Light bulb, gas can 15 15
466 A211 1d shown 25 15
Set value 18

Energy conservation.

World Tourism Conference, Manila, Sept. 27 — A212

1980, Oct. 22 *Perf. 11½x12*
467 A212 40c multi 15 15

Symbolic Tree Rooted in Europe and Africa
A213

1980, Oct. 30 *Perf. 14*
468 A213 1d multi 25 15

Straits of Gibraltar linking Europe and Africa.

5th Anniversary of the Green March
A214

1980, Nov. 6
469 A214 1d multi 22 15

Holy Ka'aba
A215

Senecio Antheuphorbium
A216

1980, Nov. 9
470 A215 40c shown 15 15
471 A215 1d Mecca Mosque 25 15
a. Souv. sheet of 2, #480-471 1.25
Set value 22

No. 471a sold for 3d.

1980, Dec. 4 *Perf. 13*
472 A216 50c shown 15 15
473 A216 1d Periploca laevigata 30 16
Set value 25

Leaves, by Mahjoubi Aherdan — A217

Nejjarine Fountain, Fes — A218

Design: 40c. Untitled painting by Mahjoubi Aherdan (23x38mm).

1980, Dec. 18 *Perf. 12*
474 A217 40c multi 15 15
475 A217 1d multi 25 15
Set value 22

1981, Jan. 22 *Perf. 14x13½*
476 A218 40c multi 15 15

Mineral Type of 1980

1981, Feb. 19 Photo. *Perf. 13½x13*
477 A205 40c Onyx 16 15
478 A205 1d Malachite-azurite 35 20
Set value 28

Inscribed 1980.

King Hassan II — A219

1981, Mar. 2 *Perf. 14*
479 A219 60c shown 15 15
480 A219 60c Map of Morocco 15 15
481 A219 60c King Mohammed V 15 15
Set value 26

25th anniv. of independence. Nos. 479-481 se-tenant.

25th Anniv. of King Hassan II Coronation A220

1981, Mar. 3
482 A220 1.30d multi 30 20

The Source, by Jillali Gharbaoui — A221

1981, Apr. 8 *Perf. 13x12½*
483 A221 1.30d multi 30 20

Anagalis Monelli — A222

Army Badge — A223

1981, Apr. 23 *Perf. 13*
484 A222 40c shown 15 15
485 A222 70c Bubonium intricatum 22 15
Set value 20

1981, May 14 Photo. *Perf. 14x13½*

Moroccan Armed Forces, 25th Anniv: Nos. 486, 488, King Hassan as army major general.

486 A223 60c multi 15 15
487 A223 60c multi 15 15
488 A223 60c multi 15 15
a. Strip of 3, #486-488 45 30
Set value 26

13th World Telecommunications Day — A224

1981, May 18 *Perf. 14x13*
489 A224 1.30d multi 25 16

Hand-painted Plate — A225

22nd Marrakesh Arts Festival — A226

1981, June 5 *Perf. 14*
490 A225 50c shown 15 15
491 A225 1.30d Plate, diff. 25 15
Set value 22

Week of the Blind.

1981, June 18 *Perf. 13½x13*
492 A226 1.30d multi 30 20

For overprint, see No. 579.

Seboula Dagger, Oujda — A227

Copper Mortar and Pestle, Red Crescent — A228

1981, Sept. 7 Photo. *Perf. 13½*
493 A227 1.30d multi 25 16

1981, Sept. 24 *Perf. 14*
494 A228 60c shown 25 15
495 A228 1.30d Tripod 40 16
Set value 25

Intl. Year of the Disabled A229

Iphiclides Feisthamelii A230

1981, Oct. 15 *Perf. 13½*
496 A229 60c multi 22 15

1981, Oct. 29 *Perf. 13½x13*
497 A230 60c shown 20 15
498 A230 1.30d Zerynthia rumina 40 22

See Nos. 528-529.

6th Anniv. of Green March — A231

Intl. Palestinian Solidarity Day — A232

1981, Nov. 6 *Perf. 13x13½*
499 A231 1.30d multi 50 25

1981, Nov. 22 *Perf. 13½x13*
500 A232 60c multi 38 25

Congress Emblem — A233

1981, Nov. 22 *Perf. 13½*
501 A233 1.30d multi 38 25

World Federation of Twin Cities, 10th Congress, Casablanca, Nov. 15-18.

مؤتمر القمة العربي
الثاني عشر
فاس 1981

Nos. 418-419 Overprinted

0,40

ROYAUME DU MAROC

1981, Nov. 25 Photo. *Perf. 14½*
502 A176 40c on 5c multi 3.00 3.00
502A A176 40c on 10c multi 2.25 2.25

First Anniv. of Mohammed V Airport — A234

King Hassan II — A236

Al Massirah Dam Opening A235

1981, Dec. 8 Photo. *Perf. 14x13*
503 A234 1.30d multi 25 20

1981, Dec. 17 *Perf. 11½*
504 A235 60c multi 15 15

1981, Dec. 28 *Perf. 13x12½*
505 A236 5c multi 15 15
506 A236 10c multi 15 15
507 A236 15c multi 15 15
508 A236 20c multi 15 15
509 A236 25c multi 15 15
510 A236 30c multi 15 15
511 A236 35c multi 15 15
512 A236 40c multi 38 15
513 A236 50c multi 15 15
514 A236 60c multi 18 15
515 A236 65c multi 18 15
516 A236 70c multi 20 15
517 A236 75c multi 20 15
518 A236 80c multi 22 15
519 A236 90c multi 28 15

1983, Mar. 1 Photo. *Perf. 14½*
Size: 25x32mm
520 A236 1d multi 32 15
521 A236 1.40d multi 38 15
522 A236 2d multi 45 15
523 A236 3d multi 65 20
524 A236 5d multi 85 40
524A A236 10d multi 1.65 70
Nos. 505-524A (21) 7.14
Set value 2.40

See Nos. 566-575, 715.

Type of 1976

1979-81 Photo. *Perf. 12½*
Size: 18x23mm
524B A146 40c ocher & multi 15 15
524C A146 50c brt bl, blk & dk brn ('81) 15 15
d. Bklt. pane of 10 1.25
Set value 20 15

Equestrian Sports A237

1981, Dec. 29 *Perf. 13x13½*
525 A237 1.30d multi 30 20

Traditional Carpet Design — A238

1982, Jan. 21
526 A238 50c Glaoua pattern 15 15
527 A238 1.30d Ouled Besseba pattern 30 20
Set value 28

Butterfly Type of 1981

1982, Feb. 25 *Perf. 13½x13*
528 A230 60c Celerio oken lineata 15 15
529 A230 1.30d Mesoacidalia aglaja lyauteyi 32 22

World Forest Day — A240

Blind Week — A241

1982, Apr. 8 *Perf. 14*
531 A240 40c multi 15 15

1982, May 10
532 A241 1d Jug 20 15

> ***Set Values***
> *A 15-cent minimum now applies to individual stamps and sets. Where the 15-cent minimum per stamp would increase the "value" of a set beyond retail, there is a "Set Value" notation giving the retail value of the set.*

Folk Dancers, Rabat — A242

Copper Candlestick, Red Crescent — A243

1982, June 3
533 A242 1.40d multi 25 16

1982, July 1
534 A243 1.40d multi 25 16

Women in Traditional Clothing, by M. Mezian — A244

ITU Conf., Nairobi, Sept. — A246

Natl. Census A245

1982, Aug. 16 Photo. *Perf. 14*
535 A244 1.40d multi 25 16

1982, Sept. 6 Photo. *Perf. 11½*
536 A245 60c multi 15 15

1982 *Perf. 13½x13*
537 A246 1.40d multi 25 15

TB Bacillus Centenary — A247

World Food Day — A248

1982, Sept. 30
538 A247 1.40d multi 25 15

1982, Oct. 16 *Perf. 14*
539 A248 60c multi 15 15

Unity Railroad A249

1982, Nov. 6 *Perf. 13x13½*
540 A249 1.40d multi 25 16

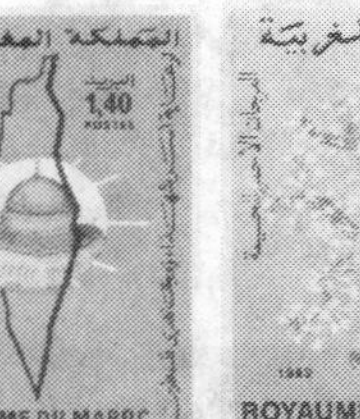
30th Anniv. of Arab Postal Union A250

1982, Nov. 17 *Perf. 14*
541 A250 1.40d multi 25 15

Intl. Palestinian Solidarity Day — A251

Red Coral, Al-Hoceima — A252

1982, Nov. 29 *Perf. 14*
542 A251 1.40d sil & multi 38 18

1982, Dec. 20 *Perf. 13½*
543 A252 1.40d multi 25 15

Stamp Day — A253

Week of the Blind — A254

1983, Jan. 26 *Perf. 13½x13*
544 A253 1.40d Nos. 3, 178 25 15

1983, Apr. 20 Photo. *Perf. 14*
545 A254 1.40d multi 25 15

Popular Arts A255

1983, June 27 Photo. *Perf. 14*
546 A255 1.40d multi 25 15

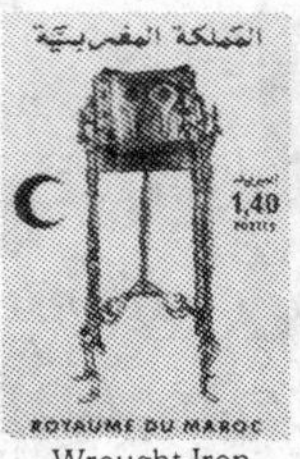
Wrought-Iron Lectern — A256

Moroccan Flora — A258

Economic Commission for Africa, 25th Anniv. A257

1983, July 7 Litho. *Perf. 13½*
547 A256 1.40d multi 25 16

1983, July 18 Photo. *Perf. 14*
548 A257 1.40d multi 25 15

1983, Aug. 1 Litho. *Perf. 14*
549 A258 60c Tecoma 15 15
550 A258 1.40d Strelitzia 25 15
Set value 34 22

Kings Mohammed V and Hassan II — A259

1983, Aug. 20 Litho. *Perf. 14*
551 A259 80c multi 15 15
a. Souvenir sheet of 1 90 90

King and People's Revolution, 30th Anniv. No. 551a sold for 5 dinars.

Mediterranean Games — A260

Palestinian Solidarity — A262

Touiza A261

1983, Sept. 3 Photo. *Perf. 14*
552 A260 80c Stylized sportsmen 15 15
553 A260 1d Emblem 16 15
554 A260 2d Stylized runner, horiz. 32 22
a. Souv. sheet of 3, #552-554, imperf. 90 90

No. 554a sold for 5d.

1983, Sept. 30 Photo. *Perf. 13*
555 A261 80c Tractors 15 15

1983, Nov. 10 Photo. *Perf. 13½x13*
556 A262 80c multi 25 15

8th Anniv. of the Green March into Spanish Sahara A263

1983, Nov. 17 *Perf. 13x13½*
557 A263 80c multi 15 15

Ouzoud Waterfall — A264

1983, Nov. 28 *Perf. 14*
558 A264 80c multi 15 15

Children's Day — A265

Zemmouri Carpet — A266

1983, Dec. 5 Photo. *Perf. 13½x13*
559 A265 2d multi 32 15

1983, Dec. 15 *Perf. 13½*

Various carpets.

560 A266 60c multi 15 15
561 A266 1.40d multi 25 15
Set value 34 22

World Communications Year — A267

1983, Dec. 20 *Perf. 14*
562 A267 2d multi 32 15

Union of Cities Al-Qods and Fez — A268

1984, Jan. 16 Photo. *Perf. 13x13½*
563 A268 2d multi 32 15

Desert Fox — A269

Perf. 11½x12, 12x11½
1984, Feb. 13
564 A269 80c shown 15 15
565 A269 2d Jumping mouse, vert. 32 20
Set value 28

King Hassan II Type of 1981

1984-88 Photo. *Perf. 14½*
Size: 25x32mm

566 A236 1.20d multi ('88) 32 15
567 A236 1.25d multi 20 15
568 A236 1.60d multi ('87) 18 15

569 A236 2.50d multi ('87) 28 15
570 A236 3.60d multi ('88) 1.00 40
571 A236 4d multi 65 25
572 A236 5.20d multi ('88) 1.45 58
573 A236 6.50d multi ('87) 70 28
574 A236 7d multi ('87) 75 30
575 A236 8.50d multi ('87) 90 35
Nos. 566-575 (10) 6.43 2.76

Dated 1986: 1.60d, 2.50d, 6.50d, 7d and 8.50d. Issue date: 1.20d, 3.60d, 5.20d, Dec. 26, 1988.

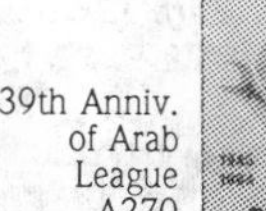

39th Anniv. of Arab League A270

1984, May 24 *Perf. 14½x14*
578 A270 2d Emblem 32 15

No. 492 Overprinted المهرجان 25

1984, June 12 *Perf. 13½x13*
579 A226 1.30d multi 30 20

25th Anniv. of Marrakesh Arts Festival.

Local Plants — A271

Red Crescent — A273

Week of the Blind — A272

1984, June 13 *Perf. 14*
580 A271 80c Mentha viridis 15 15
581 A271 2d Aloe 32 20
Set value 28

See Nos. 602-603.

1984, July 10 *Perf. 13x13½*
582 A272 80c Painted bowl 15 15

1984, July 16 *Perf. 14*
583 A273 2d Octagonal brass container 32 20

1984 Summer Olympics — A274

Intl. Child Victims' Day — A275

1984, Aug. 8 *Perf. 13½x13*
584 A274 2d Sports 32 20

1984, Aug. 22 *Perf. 14*
585 A275 2d Children held by dove 32 15

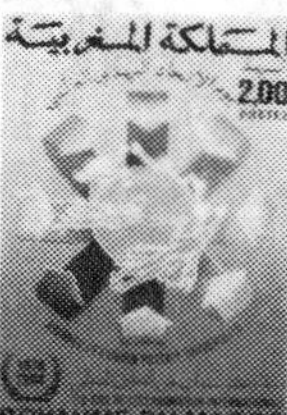
UPU Day — A276

World Food Day — A277

1984, Oct. 9 **Photo.** *Perf. 13½*
586 A276 2d multi 50 25

1984, Oct. 16 *Perf. 14*
587 A277 80c multi 20 15

Intl. Civil Aviation Org., 40th Anniv. — A278

Green March, 9th Anniv. — A279

1984, Oct. 20 *Perf. 13½*
588 A278 2d multi 1.00 50

1984, Nov. 6 *Perf. 14*
589 A279 80c Scroll, text 40 20

Palestinian Solidarity — A281

UN Human Rights Declaration, 36th Anniv. — A282

1984, Nov. 29 *Perf. 13½*
591 A281 2d Arab Revolt flag, 1918-19 1.00 50

1984, Dec. 10 *Perf. 14*
592 A282 2d multi 65 35

Native Dogs — A283

UN Child Survival Campaign — A284

1984, Dec. 21 **Photo.** *Perf. 14*
593 A283 80c Aidi 15 15
594 A283 2d Sloughi 32 15
Set value 22

1985, Mar. 5 **Photo.** *Perf. 14*
595 A284 80c Growth monitoring 20 15

1st SOS Children's Village in Morocco — A285

1985, Mar. 11 *Perf. 13x13½*
596 A285 2d multi 50 25

Sherifian Hand Stamp, 1892 — A287

World Environment Day — A288

1985, Mar. 25 **Photo.** *Perf. 14*
597 A287 2d dl pink, blk & gray 50 25

Souvenir Sheet

Perf. 13½

598 Sheet of 6 1.25 1.25
a. A287 80c green, black & gray 20 15
b. A287 80c yellow, black & gray 20 15
c. A287 80c blue, black & gray 20 15
d. A287 80c red, black & gray 20 15
e. A287 80c purple, black & gray 20 15
f. A287 80c brown, black & gray 20 15

Stamp Day. #598 sold for 5d. See #615-616, 633-634, 668-669, 684-685, 701-702, 733-734.

1985, June 5 *Perf. 13*
599 A288 80c Emblem, ecosystem 20 15

Susi Dancers from Marrakesh and Kutabia, Minaret — A289

1985, June 7 *Perf. 13x13½*
600 A289 2d multi 50 25

Folk Arts Festival.

Week of the Blind — A290

Berber Woman — A291

1985, June 24 *Perf. 14*
601 A290 80c Ceramic bowl 20 15

See type A316.

Flower Type of 1984

1985, July 1
602 A271 80c Bougainvillea 20 15
603 A271 2d Red hibiscus 50 25

1985, July 15 *Perf. 14*
604 A291 2d multi 50 25

Red Crescent Society.

6th Pan-Arab Games — A292

UN, 40th Anniv. — A293

1985 *Perf. 14½x13½*
605 A292 2d Torch, emblem, map 50 25

1985, Oct. 7 *Perf. 13*
606 A293 2d multi 50 25

Intl. Youth Year — A294

Green March, 10th Anniv. — A295

1985, Oct. 21
607 A294 2d multi 50 25

1985, Nov. 6 *Perf. 14½x13½*
608 A295 2d Commemorative medal 50 25

Palestinian Solidarity — A296

Butterflies — A297

1985, Nov. 29 *Perf. 13½*
609 A296 2d multi 50 25

1985, Dec. 16 **Photo.** *Perf. 14*
610 A297 80c Euphydryas desfontainii 15 15
611 A297 2d Colotis evagore 20 15
Set value 18

Accession of King Hassan II, 25th Anniv. — A298

Perf. 13x13½, 13½x13

1986, Mar. 3 **Litho.**
612 A298 80c Natl. arms, vert. 25 16
613 A298 2d shown 65 40
a. Souvenir sheet of 2, #612-613, imperf. 1.00 1.00

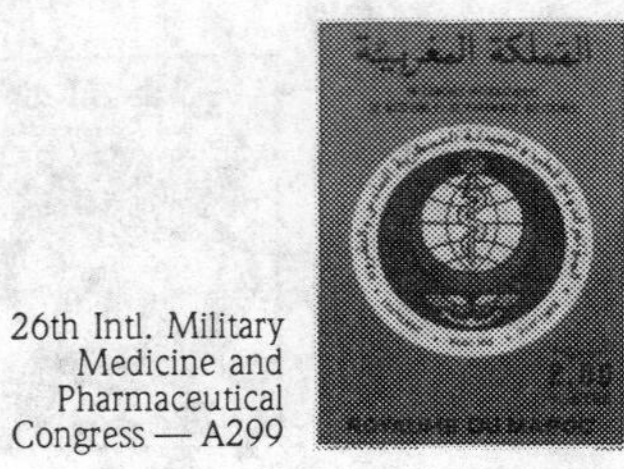

26th Intl. Military Medicine and Pharmaceutical Congress — A299

1986, Mar. 24 **Photo.** ***Perf. 14***
614 A299 2d multi 42 25

Hand Stamp Type of 1985

Sherifian postal seals of Maghzen-Safi, 1892.

1986, Apr. 7
615 A287 80c orange & blk 18 15
616 A287 2d green & blk 42 25

Week of the Blind — A300

1986 World Cup Soccer Championships, Mexico — A301

1986, Apr. 21
617 A300 1d multi 22 15

1986, May 31 ***Perf. 13½***
618 A301 1d Emblems, horiz. 22 15
619 A301 2d Soccer cup, emblems 42 25

Red Crescent Soc. — A302

Flowers — A304

Popular Arts A303

1986, June ***Perf. 14***
620 A302 2d multi 42 25

1986, June
621 A303 2d Folk band, dancers 42 25

1986, July 21 **Photo.** ***Perf. 14***
622 A304 1d Warionia saharae 22 15
623 A304 2d Mandragora autumnalis 42 25

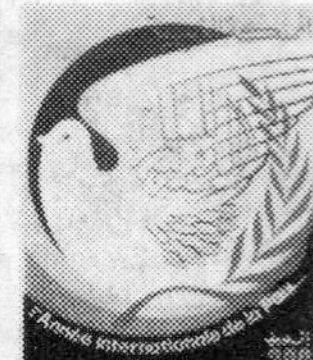

Intl. Peace Year A305

18th Skydiving Championships A306

1986, Aug. 4 ***Perf. 13***
624 A305 2d multi 42 25

1986, Aug. 18 ***Perf. 13½x13***
625 A306 2d multi 42 25

Horse Week A307

1986, Oct. 10 ***Perf. 13***
626 A307 1d multicolored 22 15

Green March, 11th Anniv. — A308

World Food Day — A309

1986, Nov. 6 **Photo.** ***Perf. 14***
627 A308 1d multicolored 22 15

1986, Nov. 12
628 A309 2d multicolored 42 25

Aga Khan Architecture Prize — A310

1986, Nov. 24 **Litho.** ***Perf. 13***
629 A310 2d multicolored 42 25

Operation Grain: One Million Hectares — A311

Butterflies — A312

1986, Dec. 8
630 A311 1d multicolored 22 15

1986, Dec. 22 ***Perf. 14***
631 A312 1d Elphinstonia charlonia 22 15
632 A312 2d Anthocharis belia 42 25

Hand Stamp Type of 1985

Stamp Day: Sherifian postal seals of Maghzen-Tetouan, 1892.

1987, Jan. 26 **Photo.**
633 A287 1d blue & blk 22 15
634 A287 2d red & black 42 25

King Mohammed V, Flag, 1947 A313

1987, Apr. 9 **Photo.** ***Perf. 13½x13***
635 A313 1d shown 22 15
636 A313 1d King Hassan II, 1987 22 15
a. Souvenir sheet of 2, Nos. 635-636 75 75

Tangiers Conf., 40th anniv. #636a sold for 3d.

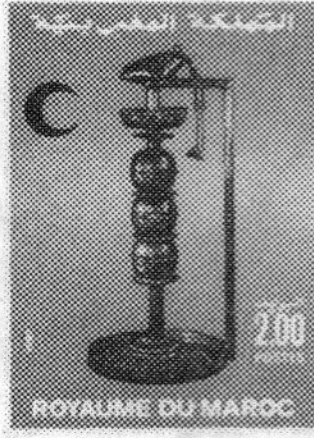

Red Crescent Society — A314

UN Child Survival Campaign — A315

1987, May 1 **Photo.** ***Perf. 14***
637 A314 2d Brass lamp 50 35

1987, May 25 ***Perf. 12½x13***
638 A315 1d Oral rehydration 25 18

See Nos. 647, 687.

Week of the Blind — A316

1987, June 8 ***Perf. 14***
639 A316 1d Porcelain cup 25 18

Flowering Plants — A317

US-Morocco Diplomatic Relations, 200th Anniv. — A318

1987, July 6 **Photo.**
640 A317 1d Zygophyllum fontanesii 25 18
641 A317 2d Otanthus maritimus 50 35

See Nos. 661-662.

1987, July 22 **Litho & Engr.**
642 A318 1d lt bl, blk & scar 25 18

See United States No. 2349.

Give Blood — A319

1987, Aug. 20 **Photo.** ***Perf. 13x13½***
643 A319 2d King Hassan II, map 60 45

Desert Costumes, the Sahara — A320

13th Intl. Cong. on Irrigation and Drainage — A321

1987, Sept. 14 ***Perf. 13***
644 A320 1d Woman from Melhfa 32 24
645 A320 2d Man from Derraa 65 48

See Nos. 711-712, 740-741.

1987, Sept. 21
646 A321 1d multi 35 28

UN Child Survival Type of 1987

1987, Sept. 28
647 A315 1d Universal immunization 35 28

Congress on Mineral Industries, Marrakesh — A322

Green March, 12th Anniv. — A323

1987, Oct.
648 A322 1d Azurite 32 24
649 A322 2d Wulfenite 65 48

1987, Nov. 6 **Photo.** ***Perf. 14***
650 A323 1d multi 30 22

See Nos. 667, 683, 695, 727, 750.

Royal Armed Forces Social Services Month A324

1987, Nov. 13 ***Perf. 13x12½***
651 A324 1d multicolored 30 22

Birds — A325

1987, Dec. 1 Litho. *Perf. 14*
652 A325 1d Passer simplex saharae 30 22
653 A325 2d Alectoris barbara 60 45

Natl. Postage Stamp 75th Anniv. — A326

Design: Postmark and Sherifian postage stamp (French Morocco) of 1912.

1987, Dec. 31 Photo. *Perf. 14x13½*
654 A326 3d pale lil rose, blk & blue grn 92 70

Cetiosaurus Mogrebiensis — A327

1988, Jan. 18 Photo. *Perf. 13½*
655 A327 2d multicolored 62 48

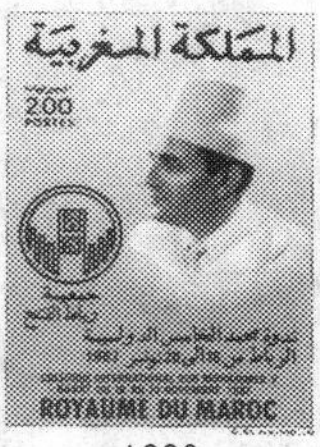

A328 A329

1988, Feb. 16 Litho. *Perf. 14*
656 A328 2d multicolored 62 45

Intl. Symposium on Mohammed V, Aug. 16-Nov. 20, 1987.

Perf. 14½x13½
1988, Mar. 13 Photo.
657 A329 3d multi 85 75

16th Africa Cup Soccer Championships.

Horse Week A330

1988, Mar. 20 Litho. *Perf. 14*
658 A330 3d multi 85 75

Intl. Red Cross and Red Crescent Orgs., 125th Annivs. — A331

1988, Apr. 30 Photo. *Perf. 12½x13*
659 A331 3d pink, blk & dark red 85 65

Week of the Blind — A332

UN Child Survival Campaign — A333

1988, May 25 Litho. *Perf. 14*
660 A332 3d Pottery bottle 85 65

Flower Type of 1987

1988, June 27 Litho. *Perf. 14*
661 A317 3.60d Citrullus colocynthis 95 75
662 A317 3.60d Calotropis procera 95 75

1988, July 18 Litho. *Perf. 12½x13*
663 A333 3d multi 82 62

1988 Summer Olympics, Seoul — A334

Birds — A335

Perf. 14½x13½
1988, Sept. 19 Litho.
664 A334 2d multi 62 48

1988, Oct. 26 Litho. *Perf. 14*
665 A335 3.60d Grande outarde 1.00 75
666 A335 3.60d Flamant rose 1.00 75

Green March Anniv. Type of 1987

1988, Nov. 6
667 A323 2d multi 55 42

Green March, 13th anniv.

Hand Stamp Type of 1985

Sherifian postal seals of Maghzen-El Jadida, 1892: No. 668, Octagonal. No. 669, Circular.

1988, Nov. 22 Photo. *Perf. 14*
668 A287 3d olive bister & blk 82 62
669 A287 3d violet & blk 82 62

Stamp Day.

Housing of the Ksours and Casbahs A336

1989, Jan. 23 *Perf. 13x13½*
670 A336 2d multi 55 42

Royal Chess Federation, 25th Anniv. A337

1989, Apr. 17 Litho. *Perf. 14*
671 A337 2d multi 52 38

Red Crescent Society — A338

Week of the Blind — A339

1989, May 29 Litho. *Perf. 14x13½*
672 A338 2d multi 55 42

1989, June 12 *Perf. 14*
673 A339 2d multi 55 42

King Hassan II, 60th Birthday — A340

1989, July 9 Litho. *Perf. 13x13½*
674 A340 2d multi 52 40
675 A340 2d King Hassan II, diff. 52 40
a. Souvenir sheet of 2, #674-675, imperf. & embossed 1.30 1.30

No. 675a sold for 5d.

Flowering Plants — A341

1989, Sept. 11 Litho. *Perf. 14*
676 A341 2d *Narcissus papyraceus* 60 45
677 A341 2d *Cerinthe major* 60 45

See Nos. 709-710, 742-743.

World Telecommunications Day — A342

1989, Sept. 25 *Perf. 13x12½*
678 A342 2d multicolored 60 45

13th World Congress on Fertility and Sterility — A343

1989, Oct. 6 *Perf. 14*
679 A343 2d multicolored 60 45

Birds A344

1989, Oct. 16 *Perf. 14*
680 A344 2d Desert beater 60 45
681 A344 3d Gorget lark 90 68

Interparliamentary Union, Cent. — A345

1989, Oct. 27
682 A345 2d multicolored 60 45

Green March Anniv. Type of 1987

1989, Nov. 6
683 A323 3d multicolored 90 68

Green March, 14th anniv.

Hand Stamp Type of 1985

Sherifian postal seals of Maghzen-Casablanca, 1892: 2d, Circular. 3d, Octagonal.

1990, Jan. 15 Photo. *Perf. 14*
684 A287 2d orange & blk 62 45
685 A287 3d green & blk 95 72

Maghreb Union, 1st Anniv. A346

1990, Feb. 17 *Perf. 13½x14*
686 A346 2d multicolored 62 45
a. Souv. sheet of one, perf. 13½ 95 95

No. 686a sold for 3d.

Child Survival Type of 1987

1990 *Perf. 12½x13*
687 A315 3d Breast feeding 95 72

3rd World Olive Day A347

1990, May 14 Litho. *Perf. 14*
688 A347 2d Olive press 50 36
689 A347 3d King Hassan II 75 55

Week of the Blind A348

1990, May 28 Litho. *Perf. 14*
690 A348 2d multicolored 70 52

Red Crescent Society A349

1990, June 11
691 A349 2d multicolored 50 36

Intl. Literacy Year — A350

1990, Sept. 17 **Litho.** ***Perf. 14***
692 A350 3d blk, yel grn & grn 1.10 82

Birds A351

1990, Oct. 26
693 A351 2d Tourterelle, vert. 70 52
694 A351 3d Huppe fasciee 1.10 82

Green March Type of 1987

1990, Nov. 5
695 A323 3d multicolored 1.10 82

Green March, 15th anniv.

Independence, 35th Anniv. — A353

1990, Nov. 18
696 A353 3d multicolored 1.10 82

Dam A354

1990, Nov. 26
697 A354 3d multicolored 1.10 82

Footnotes often refer to other stamps of the same design.

Royal Academy of Morocco, 10th Anniv. — A355

1990, Dec. 28 **Litho.** ***Perf. 14***
698 A355 3d multicolored 1.00 75

Opening of Postal Museum, 20th Anniv. A356

Designs: No. 699, Telegraph machine. No. 700, Horse-drawn mail carriage fording river.

1990, Dec. 31 **Litho.** ***Perf. 13½x13***
699 A356 2d multicolored 65 50
700 A356 3d multicolored 1.00 75
a. Souv. sheet of 2, #699-700, imperf. 2.15 2.15

No. 700a sold for 6d, has simulated perforations.

Hand Stamp Type of 1985

Sherifian postal seals of Maghzen-Rabat, 1892: 2d, Circular. 3d, Octagonal.

1991, Jan. 25 ***Perf. 14***
701 A287 2d ver & blk 65 50
702 A287 3d blue & blk 1.00 75

UN Development Program, 40th Anniv. — A357

1991, Feb. 18
703 A357 3d multicolored 1.00 75

A358 A359

1991, Mar. 3 **Litho.** ***Perf. 14½x13***
704 A358 3d shown 1.00 75
705 A358 3d Wearing business suit 1.00 75
a. Souv. sheet of 2, #704-705, imperf. 3.00 2.35

Coronation of King Hassan II, 30th anniv. Nos. 704-705 exist tete beche. No. 705a has simulated perforations and sold for 10d.

1991, Mar. 28 **Litho.** ***Perf. 14***
706 A359 3d multicolored 1.00 75

Phosphate Mining, 70th anniv.

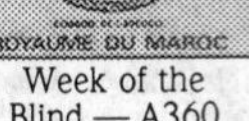

Week of the Blind — A360   Red Crescent Society — A361

1991, May 15 **Photo.** ***Perf. 14***
707 A360 3d multicolored 1.00 75

1991, May 27 **Litho.** ***Perf. 14***
708 A361 3d multicolored 95 70

Flowering Plants Type of 1989

1991, June 27 **Litho.** ***Perf. 14***
709 A341 3d Pyrus mamorensis 95 70
710 A341 3d Cynara humilis 95 70

Desert Costumes Type of 1987

Costumes of Ouarzazate.

1991, July 31 **Photo.**
711 A320 3d Woman 95 70
712 A320 3d Man 95 70

King Hassan II Type of 1981

1991 **Photo.** ***Perf. 14½***
Size: 25x32mm
715 A236 1.35d multicolored 42 16

Issue date: 1.35d, Sept. 2.
This is an expanding set. Numbers will change if necessary.

A362 A363

1991, Sept. 23 **Litho.** ***Perf. 14***
725 A362 3d multicolored 95 70

19th World Congress on Roads, Marrakesh.

1991, Oct. 30 **Litho.**
726 A363 3d multicolored 95 70

4th Session of the Council of Presidents of the Maghreb Arab Union.

Green March Anniv. Type of 1987

1991, Nov. 6 **Photo.** ***Perf. 14***
727 A323 3d multicolored 95 70

Green March, 16th anniv.

Birds — A364   Fight Against AIDS — A365

1991, Nov. 20 **Litho.** ***Perf. 14***
728 A364 3d Merops apiaster 1.00 80
729 A364 3d Ciconia ciconia 1.00 80

1991, Dec. 16
730 A365 3d multicolored 1.00 80

Organization of the Islamic Conference, 20th Anniv. — A366

1991, Dec. 16
731 A366 3d multicolored 1.00 80

A367 A368

1991 **Litho.** ***Perf. 14***
732 A367 3d multicolored 1.00 80

African Tourism Year.

Handstamp Type of 1985

Sherifian postal seals of Maghzen-Essaouira, 1892: No. 733, Circular. No. 734, Octagonal.

1992, Jan. 13
733 A287 3d olive & blk 1.00 80
734 A287 3d purple & blk 1.00 80

1992, Feb. 17
735 A368 3d multicolored 1.00 80

Intl. Space Year.

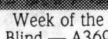

Week of the Blind — A369   Red Crescent Society — A370

1992, Mar. 19 **Photo.** ***Perf. 14***
736 A369 3d multicolored 1.00 80

1992, Mar. 30
737 A370 3d multicolored 1.00 80

Minerals — A371   A372

1992, May 11 **Litho.** ***Perf. 14***
738 A371 1.35d Quartz 48 38
739 A371 3.40d Calcite 1.25 1.00

Desert Costumes Type of 1987

Costumes of Tata.

1992, May 25 **Photo.** ***Perf. 14***
740 A320 1.35d Woman 50 38
741 A320 3.40d Man 1.25 1.00

Flowering Plants Type of 1989

1992, July 13

742 A341 1.35d Campanula afra 50 38
743 A341 3.40d Thymus broussonetii 1.25 1.00

1992, July 24

744 A372 3.40d multicolored 1.25 1.00

1992 Summer Olympics, Barcelona.

Modes of Transportion and Communications, Map of Africa — A373

1992, Sept. 14 Litho. *Perf. 14*

745 A373 3.40d multicolored 95 75

Expo '92, Seville — A374

1992, Oct. 12

746 A374 3.40d multicolored 95 75

Discovery of America, 500th Anniv. A375

1992, Oct. 12

747 A375 3.40d multicolored 95 75

Green March Anniv. Type of 1987

1992, Nov. 6 Litho. *Perf. 14*

750 A323 3.40d multicolored 95 75

Green March, 17th anniv.

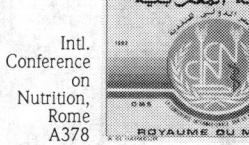

Intl. Conference on Nutrition, Rome A378

1992, Dec. 7 Litho. *Perf. 14*

754 A378 3.40d multicolored 95 75

SEMI-POSTAL STAMPS

+10f

Nos. 1-5 Surcharged

اعانة ضحايا
الزيوت المسممة
اكتوبر 1959

1960, Mar. Unwmk. Engr. *Perf. 13*

B1 A1 5fr + 10fr brt bl & ind 22 20
B2 A1 10fr + 10fr bis brn & choc 30 28
B3 A1 15fr + 10fr dp grn & mag 55 45
B4 A1 25fr + 15fr purple 65 55
B5 A1 30fr + 20fr green 1.00 1.00
Nos. B1-B5 (5) 2.72 2.48

The surtax aided families whose members consumed adulterated cooking oil with crippling or fatal results.

French Morocco Nos. 321 and 322 Surcharged

اسبوعا
التضامن
1380
1960
15+3

1960, Sept. 12

B6 A71 15fr + 3fr on 18fr dk grn 32 32
B7 A71 20fr + 5fr brown lake 50 50

Nos. 1 and 6 Surcharged in Red or Black

فيضانات
1
9
6
3
20+5

1963, Jan. 28 Engr. *Perf. 13*

B8 A1 20c + 5c on 5fr brt bl & ind (R) 38 38
B9 A1 30c + 10c on 50fr rose red 45 38

The surtax was for flood victims.

Moroccan Brooch — SP1

Design: 40c+10c, Brooch with pendants.

1966, May 23 Photo. *Perf. 11½*
Granite Paper

B10 SP1 25c + 5c ultra, sil, blk & red 38 30
B11 SP1 40c + 10c mag, sil, blk, ultra & bl 55 38

Meeting in Morocco of the Middle East and North African Red Cross-Red Crescent Seminar. The surtax was for the Moroccan Red Crescent Society.

Nos. B10-B11 were printed se-tenant in sheets of 10 (5x2) arranged vertically tête bêche.

See Nos. B12-B13, B15-B16, B19-B22, B26-B27, B29-B30, B34-B35.

1967, May 15 Granite Paper

Designs: 60c+5c, Two brooches linked by silver drapery. 1d+10c, Two bracelets.

B12 SP1 60c + 5c yel bis & multi 40 40
B13 SP1 1d + 10c emer & multi 85 85

The surtax was for the Moroccan Red Crescent Society. Each value printed tête bêche in sheets of 10 (5x2).

Hands Reading Braille and Map of Morocco — SP2

1969, Mar. 21 Photo. *Perf. 12½*

B14 SP2 25c + 10c multi 15 15

Week of the Blind, Mar. 21-29.

Jewelry Type of 1966

Designs: 25c+5c, Silver earrings. 40c+10c, Gold ear pendant.

1969, May 9 Photo. *Perf. 11½*
Granite Paper

B15 SP1 25c + 5c gray grn & multi 38 30
B16 SP1 40c + 10c tan & multi 55 38

50th anniversary of the League of Red Cross Societies. Surtax was for Moroccan Red Crescent Society.

See se-tenant note after No. B11.

Nos. 173-174 Surcharged

+ 0²⁵
فيضانات 1970

1970, Feb. 26 Litho. *Perf. 13*

B17 A65 10c + 25c multi 1.50 1.50
B18 A65 15c + 25c multi 1.50 1.50

The surtax was for flood victims.

Jewelry Type of 1966

Designs: 25c+5c, Necklace with pendants. 50c+10c, Earring with 5 pendants.

1970, May 25 Photo. *Perf. 11½*
Granite Paper

B19 SP1 25c + 5c gray & multi 40 38
B20 SP1 50c + 10c brt vio & multi 65 65

Surtax for Moroccan Red Crescent Society.
See se-tenant note after No. B11.

1971, May 10

Designs: 25c+5c, Brooch. 40c+10c, Stomacher.

Granite Paper

B21 SP1 25c + 5c gray & multi 30 30
B22 SP1 40c + 10c yel & multi 45 38

See se-tenant note after No. B11.

Globe and Map of Palestine SP3

1971, Apr. 30 *Perf. 13*

B23 SP3 25c + 10c multi 50 25

Palestine Week, May 3-8.

String Instrument and Bow — SP4

1971, June 28 Photo. *Perf. 12*

B24 SP4 40c + 10c multi 20 15

Week of the Blind.

Mizmar (Double Flute) — SP5

1972, Mar. 31 Photo. *Perf. 13x13½*

B25 SP5 25c + 10c multi 22 22

Week of the Blind.

Jewelry Type of 1966

Designs: 25c+5c, Jeweled bracelets. 70c+10c, Rectangular pendant with ball drop.

1972, May 8 Photo. *Perf. 11½*
Granite Paper

B26 SP1 25c + 5c brn & multi 30 30
B27 SP1 70c + 10c dp grn & multi 45 38

See se-tenant note after No. B11. For overprints, see Nos. 295-296.

Drums SP6

1973, Mar. 30 Photo. *Perf. 13x14*

B28 SP6 70c + 10c multi 30 25

Week of the Blind.

Jewelry Type of 1966

Designs: 25c+5c, Silver box pendant. 70c+10c, Bracelet.

1973, June 15 Photo. *Perf. 11½*

B29 SP1 25c + 5c bl & multi 40 30
B30 SP1 70c + 10c org & multi 50 38

Moroccan Red Crescent Society. See 2nd note after No. B11. For overprints, see Nos. 351-352.

Pistol — SP7

Erbab (Fiddle) — SP8

Design: 70c+10c, Decorated antique powder box.

1974, July 8 Photo. *Perf. 14x13½*

B31 SP7 25c + 5c multi 30 30
B32 SP7 70c + 10c multi 45 38

Moroccan Red Crescent Society. See se-tenant note after B11.

1975, Jan. 10 Photo. *Perf. 13*

B33 SP8 70c + 10c multi 38 22

Week of the Blind.

Jewelry Type of 1966

Designs: 25c+5c, Silver pendant. 70c+10c, Earring.

1975, Mar. 13 Photo. *Perf. 13½*

B34 SP1 25c + 5c multi 30 30
B35 SP1 70c + 10c multi 45 38

Moroccan Red Crescent Society. See se-tenant note after No. B11. For overprints, see Nos. 386-387.

AIR POST STAMPS

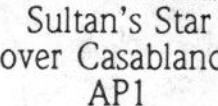
Sultan's Star over Casablanca AP1

King Hassan II AP2

Unwmk.

1957, May 4 Engr. *Perf. 13*

C1 AP1 15fr car & brt grn 55 50
C2 AP1 25fr brt grnsh bl 1.00 70
C3 AP1 30fr red brn 1.40 90

Intl. Fair, Casablanca, May 4-19.

1962

C5 AP2 90c black 32 15
C6 AP2 1d rose red 50 15
C7 AP2 2d deep blue 65 32
C8 AP2 3d dl bl grn 1.10 65
C9 AP2 5d purple 2.25 90
Nos. C5-C9 (5) 4.82 2.17

Meteorological Day Type of Regular Issue

Design: 90c, Anemometer and globe.

1964, Mar. 23 Photo. *Perf. 11½*
Granite Paper

C10 A39 90c multi 40 30

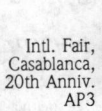

Intl. Fair, Casablanca, 20th Anniv. AP3

1964, Apr. 30 Photo. *Perf. 12½*

C11 AP3 1d bl, bis & org 50 38

Moroccan Pavilion and Unisphere AP4

1964, May 25 Unwmk. *Perf. 12½*

C12 AP4 1d dk grn, red & bl 55 40

New York World's Fair, 1964-65.

Ramses II and UNESCO Emblem — AP5

Perf. 12x11½

1966, Oct. 3 Litho. & Engr.

C13 AP5 1d magenta, *yel* 55 38

UNESCO, 20th anniv.

Jet Plane AP6

Perf. 12½x13½

1966, Dec. 19 Photo.

C14 AP6 3d multi 2.25 1.25

Costume Type of Regular Issue

Design: 1d, Women from Ait Ouaouzguit.

1969, Jan. 21 Litho. *Perf. 12*

C15 A74 1d multi 1.20 55

Coin Type of Regular Issue, 1968

Coins: 1d, King Mohammed V, 1960. 5d, King Hassan II, 1965.

1969, Mar. 3 Photo. *Perf. 11½*
Granite Paper

C16 A73 1d brt bl, sil & blk 2.25 1.50
C17 A73 5d vio blk, sil & blk 6.00 3.75

King Hassan II — AP7

1983, Mar. 1 Photo. *Perf. 12*
Granite Paper

C18 AP7 1.40d multi 38 15
C19 AP7 2d multi 45 15
C20 AP7 3d multi 65 20
C21 AP7 5d multi 1.00 30
C22 AP7 10d multi 2.00 65
Nos. C18-C22 (5) 4.48 1.45

No. C19 Overprinted

الملتقى العالمي الاول
لخطباء الجمعة

1987, Mar. 23 Photo. *Perf. 12*
Granite Paper

C23 AP7 2d multi 42 25

1st World Congress of Friday Preachers, Al Joumouaa.

No. C18 Overprinted

اتحاد المغرب العربي

مراكش ـ فبراير 89

1989, Mar. 27 Photo. *Perf. 12*
Granite Paper

C24 AP7 1.40d multi 38 20

Maghreb Union, agreement between Morocco, Algeria and Tunisia.

POSTAGE DUE STAMPS

D1

Oranges — D2

1965 Unwmk. Typo. *Perf. 14x13½*

J1 D1 5c green 75 20
J2 D1 10c bister brown 30 15
J3 D1 20c red 45 15
J4 D1 30c brown black 75 20

1974-86 Photo. *Perf. 14*

J5 D2 5c shown 15 15
J6 D2 10c Cherries 15 15
J7 D2 20c Grapes 18 15
J8 D2 30c Peaches, horiz. 22 15
J9 D2 40c Grapes ('78) 15 15
J10 D2 60c Peaches, horiz. ('78) 20 15
J11 D2 80c Oranges ('78) 28 15
J12 D2 1d Apples ('86) 22 15
J13 D2 1.20d Cherries ('84) 25 15
J14 D2 1.60d Peaches ('85) 48 25
J15 D2 2d Strawberries ('86) 42 25
Nos. J5-J15 (11) 2.70
Set value 1.45

For surcharges, see Nos. 322, 395.

Type D2 is an expanding set. Numbers will change again if more stamps are added.

NORTHERN ZONE

100 Centimos = 1 Peseta

Sultan Mohammed V — A1

Villa Sanjurjo Harbor A2

Designs: 25c, Polytechnic school. 50c, 10p, Institute of Culture, Tetuan.

Perf. 13x12½, 12½x13

1956, Aug. 23 Photo. Unwmk.

1 A1 10c deep rose 15 15
2 A2 15c yellow brn 15 15
3 A2 25c dk bl gray 15 15
4 A1 50c dark olive 15 15
5 A1 80c brt green 15 15
6 A2 2p brt red lil 1.40 1.00
7 A2 3p brt blue 3.00 1.65
8 A1 10p green 10.50 7.00
Nos. 1-8 (8) 15.65 10.40

Sultan Mohammed V
A3 A4

1957, Mar. 2 *Perf. 13½x13*

9 A3 80c blue green 22 15
10 A3 1.50p gray olive 85 55
11 A3 3p deep rose 2.75 1.75

1st anniversary of independence. See Morocco Nos. 13-15.

1957 Engr. *Perf. 13*

12 A4 30c brt bl & indigo 15 15
13 A4 70c bis, brn & choc 15 15
14 A4 80c brt violet 50 15
15 A4 1.50p dp grn & mag 15 15
16 A4 3p green 20 15
17 A4 7p rose red 1.00 25
Nos. 12-17 (6) 2.15
Set value 55

Prince Moulay el Hassan — A5

King Mohammed V — A6

1957, July 15 Photo. *Perf. 13*

18 A5 80c blue 18 15
19 A5 1.50p green 75 50
20 A5 3p carmine rose 2.25 1.65

Nos. 13 and 15 Surcharged in Carmine or Black

سنتيما
15 Cts.

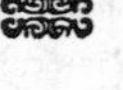

بسيطة
1'20
Pesetas

1957 Engr.

21 A4 15c on 70c (C) 18 15
22 A4 1.20p on 1.50p (Bk) 42 18

1957, Nov. Photo. *Perf. 12½*

23 A6 1.20p blk & brt grn 20 20
24 A6 1.80p blk & rose red 22 22
25 A6 3p black & violet 65 42

Enthronement of Mohammed V, 30th anniv.

AIR POST STAMPS

Plane over Lau Dam — AP1

Design: 1.40p, 4.80p, Plane over Nekor bridge.

Perf. 12½x13

1956, Dec. 17 Photo. Unwmk.

C1 AP1 25c rose violet 15 15
C2 AP1 1.40p lilac rose 15 15
C3 AP1 3.40p org vermilion 75 65
C4 AP1 4.80p dull violet 1.25 1.00

MOZAMBIQUE

LOCATION — Southeastern Africa, bordering on the Mozambique Channel
GOVT. — Republic
AREA — 308,642 sq. mi.
POP. — 14,140,000 (est. 1983)
CAPITAL — Maputo

Formerly a Portuguese colony, Mozambique, or Portuguese East Africa, was divided into eight districts: Lourenco Marques, Inhambane, Quelimane, Tete, Mozambique, Zambezia, Nyassa and the Manica and Sofala region formerly administered by the Mozambique Company. At various times the districts issued their own stamps which were eventually replaced by those inscribed "Mocambique."

Mozambique achieved independence June 25, 1975, taking the name People's Republic of Mozambique.

1000 Reis = 1 Milreis
100 Centavos = 1 Escudo (1913)
100 Centavos = 1 Metical (1980)

Catalogue values for unused stamps in this country are for Never Hinged items, beginning with Scott 330 in the regular postage section, Scott C29 in the airpost section, Scott J51 in the postage due section, and Scott RA55 in the postal tax section.

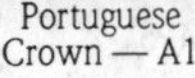

Portuguese Crown — A1

King Luiz — A2

Perf. 12½, 13½

1877-85 Typo. Unwmk.

1 A1 5r black 70 50
 a. Perf. 13½ 1.50 1.40
2 A1 10r yellow 5.00 4.00
3 A1 10r green ('81) 85 60
4 A1 20r bister 1.00 60
 a. Perf. 13½ 2.00 1.25
5 A1 20r rose ('85) 250.00 135.00
6 A1 25r rose 50 35
 a. Perf. 13½ 5.50 1.35
7 A1 25r vio ('85) 2.50 1.35
8 A1 40r blue 14.00 8.00
9 A1 40r yel buff ('81) 1.75 1.35
 a. Perf. 12½ 2.50 2.00
10 A1 50r green 50.00 11.00
 a. Perf. 13½ 75.00 50.00
11 A1 50r blue ('81) 50 40
12 A1 100r lilac 70 48

13 A1 200r orange 1.90 1.40
a. Perf. 12½ 3.75 3.00
14 A1 300r chocolate 1.90 1.50

The reprints of the 1877-85 issues are printed on a smooth white chalky paper, ungummed, with rough perforation 13½, also on thin white paper, with shiny white gum and clean-cut perforation 13½.

Typographed and Embossed

1886 ***Perf. 12½***

15 A2 5r black 1.00 60
16 A2 10r green 1.00 60
17 A2 20r rose 1.10 85
18 A2 25r dull lilac 9.00 1.75
19 A2 40r chocolate 1.40 85
20 A2 50r blue 1.50 50
21 A2 100r yel brn 1.75 50
22 A2 200r gray violet 2.50 1.75
23 A2 300r orange 2.75 2.00

Perf. 13½

15a A2 5r 3.00 2.25
16a A2 10r 3.75 2.50
17a A2 20r 10.00 4.50
18a A2 25r 10.00 4.00
19a A2 40r 10.00 7.00
20a A2 50r 12.50 3.00
22a A2 200r 12.50 10.00
Nos. 15a-22a (7) 61.75 33.25

Nos. 15, 18, 19, 20, 21 and 23 have been reprinted. The reprints have shiny white gum and clean-cut perforation 13½. Many of the colors are paler than those of the originals.

For surcharges and overprints see Nos. 23A, 36-44, 46-48, 72-80, 192, P1-P5.

No. 19 Surcharged in Black

PROVISORIO
5 5

1893, Jan. ***Perf. 12½***

Without Gum

23A A2 5r on 40r choc 95.00 45.00

There are three varieties of No. 23A:
I- "PROVISORIO" 19mm long, numerals 4½mm high.
II- "PROVISORIO" 19½mm long, numerals 5mm high.
III- "PROVISORIO" 19½mm long, numerals of both sizes.

King Carlos I — A3

1894 **Typo.** ***Perf. 11½, 12½***

24 A3 5r yellow 50 35
25 A3 10r red lilac 50 35
26 A3 15r red brown 70 50
27 A3 20r gray lil 85 50
28 A3 25r blue green 70 20
29 A3 50r lt blue 5.00 1.00
a. Perf. 12½ 7.50 2.00
30 A3 75r rose 1.40 1.25
31 A3 80r yellow grn 2.75 1.40
32 A3 100r brown, *buff* 1.75 1.50
33 A3 150r car, *rose* 13.00 6.75
a. Perf. 11½
34 A3 200r dk blue, *bl* 2.75 2.00
35 A3 300r dk blue, *sal* 3.50 2.50

Nos. 28 and 31-33 have been reprinted with shiny white gum and clean-cut perf. 13½.

For surcharges and overprints see Nos. 45, 81-92, 193-199, 201-206, 226-228, 238-239.

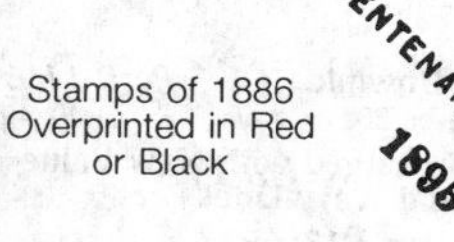

Stamps of 1886 Overprinted in Red or Black

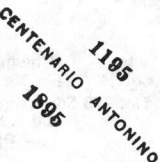

CENTENARIO ANTONINO
1195
1895

1895, July 1 ***Perf. 12½***

Without Gum

36 A2 5r black (R) 6.00 5.50
37 A2 10r green 6.75 6.00
38 A2 20r rose 8.00 6.00
39 A2 25r violet 8.00 6.00
a. Double overprint
40 A2 40r chocolate 9.00 7.50
41 A2 50r blue 9.00 7.50
a. Perf. 13½ 67.50 55.00
42 A2 100r yellow brn 9.00 7.50
43 A2 200r gray vio 19.00 11.00
a. Perf. 13½ 67.50 55.00
44 A2 300r orange 20.00 14.00

7th centenary of the birth of Saint Anthony of Padua.

No. 35 Surcharged in Black

50
réis

1897, Jan. 2 ***Perf. 12½***

Without Gum

45 A3 50r on 300r dk bl, *sal* 150.00 40.00

Nos. 17, 19 Surcharged

a
MOCAMBIQUE
2 ½
REIS

b
MOCAMBIQUE
2½
RÉIS

c
MOÇAMBIQUE
5
RÉIS

1898

Without Gum

46 A2 (a) 2½r on 20r rose 37.50 11.00
47 A2 (b) 2½r on 20r rose 27.50 10.00
a. Inverted surcharge 55.00 30.00
48 A2 (c) 5r on 40r choc 35.00 10.00
a. Inverted surcharge 90.00 45.00

King Carlos I — A4

1898-1903 **Typo.** ***Perf. 11½***

Name and Value in Black except 500r

49 A4 2½r gray 18 15
50 A4 5r orange 18 15
51 A4 10r lt grn 20 18
52 A4 15r brown 3.50 1.50
53 A4 15r gray grn ('03) 70 55
54 A4 20r gray vio 85 40
55 A4 25r sea grn 85 40
56 A4 25r car ('03) 70 28
57 A4 50r dk bl 1.00 48
58 A4 50r brn ('03) 1.90 1.50
59 A4 65r dl bl ('03) 7.50 6.00
60 A4 75r rose 4.75 2.75
61 A4 75r red lil ('03) 1.90 1.75
62 A4 80r violet 4.75 2.75
63 A4 100r dk bl, *bl* 1.90 1.00
64 A4 115r org brn, *pink* ('03) 5.50 4.00
65 A4 130r brn, *straw* ('03) 5.50 4.00
66 A4 150r brn, *straw* 4.75 2.75
67 A4 200r red lil, *pnksh* 1.90 1.40
68 A4 300r dk bl, *rose* 4.75 2.75
69 A4 400r dl bl, *straw* ('03) 9.00 6.00
70 A4 500r blk & red, *bl* ('01) 12.00 6.75
71 A4 700r vio, *yelsh* ('01) 12.00 8.00
Nos. 49-71 (23) 86.26 55.49

For overprints and surcharges see Nos. 94-113, 200, 207-220.

Stamps of 1886-94 Surcharged

1902 ***Perf. 12½, 13½***

On Stamps of 1886

Red Surcharge

72 A2 115r on 5r blk 1.75 1.25

Black Surcharge

73 A2 65r on 20r rose 3.00 2.00
a. Double surcharge 30.00 30.00
74 A2 65r on 40r choc 4.00 3.75
75 A2 65r on 200r vio 3.00 1.50
76 A2 115r on 50r bl 1.25 1.00
77 A2 130r on 25r red vio 1.65 85
78 A2 130r on 300r org 1.40 85
79 A2 400r on 10r grn 4.50 3.00
80 A2 400r on 100r yel brn 27.50 20.00

The reprints of Nos. 74, 75, 76, 77, 79 and 80 have shiny white gum and clean-cut perforation 13½.

On Stamps of 1894

Perf. 11½

81 A3 65r on 10r red lil 2.00 1.90
82 A3 65r on 15r red brn 2.25 1.90
a. Pair, one without surcharge
83 A3 65r on 20r gray lil 2.25 1.90
84 A3 115r on 5r yel 2.25 1.90
a. Inverted surcharge
85 A3 115r on 25r bl grn 2.25 1.90
86 A3 130r on 75r rose 2.25 1.90
87 A3 130r on 100r brn, *buff* 4.00 4.00
88 A3 130r on 150r car, *rose* 2.25 1.90
89 A3 130r on 200r bl, *bl* 3.75 3.50
90 A3 400r on 50r lt bl 1.00 85
91 A3 400r on 80r yel grn 1.00 85
92 A3 400r on 300r bl, *sal* 1.00 85

On Newspaper Stamp of 1893

Perf. 13½

93 N3 115r on 2½r brn 2.00 1.90

Reprints of No. 87 have shiny white gum and clean-cut perforation 13½.

Overprinted in Black PROVISORIO

On Stamps of 1898

Perf. 11½

94 A4 15r brown 1.40 85
95 A4 25r sea green 1.40 85
96 A4 50r blue 2.00 1.75
97 A4 75r rose 3.75 2.00

No. 59 Surcharged in Black

50
RÉIS

1905

98 A4 50r on 65r dull blue 1.90 1.75

Stamps of 1898-1903 Overprinted in Carmine or Green

1911

99 A4 2½r gray 20 18
a. Inverted overprint 8.00 8.00
100 A4 5r orange 20 18
101 A4 10r lt green 1.00 50
102 A4 15r gray grn 20 18
103 A4 20r gray vio 85 40
104 A4 25r carmine (G) 18 15
a. 25r gray violet (error)
105 A4 50r brown 28 20
106 A4 75r red lilac 60 48
107 A4 100r dk blue, *bl* 60 48
108 A4 115r org brn, *pink* 85 75
109 A4 130r brown, *straw* 85 75
a. Double overprint
110 A4 200r red lil, *pnksh* 1.25 70
111 A4 400r dull bl, *straw* 1.25 85
112 A4 500r blk & red, *bl* 1.25 85
113 A4 700r vio, *straw* 1.25 85
Nos. 99-113 (15) 10.81 7.50

King Manoel — A5

Overprinted in Carmine or Green

1912 ***Perf. 11½x12***

114 A5 2½r violet 15 15
115 A5 5r black 15 15
116 A5 10r gray grn 20 18
117 A5 20r carmine (G) 55 40
118 A5 25r vio brn 15 15
119 A5 50r dp blue 40 35
120 A5 75r bis brn 40 35
121 A5 100r brn, *lt grn* 40 35
122 A5 200r dk grn, *sal* 85 70
123 A5 300r black, *azure* 85 70

Perf. 14x15

124 A5 500r ol grn & vio brn 1.25 1.00
Nos. 114-124 (11) 5.35 4.48

Vasco da Gama Issue of Various Portuguese Colonies Common Design Types Surcharged

REPUBLICA
MOCAMBIQUE
¼ C.

1913

On Stamps of Macao

125 CD20 ¼c on ½a bl grn 1.50 1.50
126 CD21 ½c on 1a red 1.50 1.50
127 CD22 1c on 2a red vio 1.50 1.50
128 CD23 2½c on 4a yel grn 1.50 1.50
a. Double surcharge 35.00 35.00
129 CD24 5c on 8a dk bl 3.50 3.50
130 CD25 7½c on 12a vio brn 2.50 2.50
131 CD26 10c on 16a bis brn 2.00 2.00
132 CD27 15c on 24a bis 2.00 2.00
Nos. 125-132 (8) 16.00 16.00

On Stamps of Portuguese Africa

133 CD20 ¼c on 2½r bl grn 1.25 1.25
134 CD21 ½c on 5r red 1.25 1.25
135 CD22 1c on 10r red vio 1.25 1.25
a. Inverted surcharge 30.00 30.00
136 CD23 2½c on 25r yel grn 1.25 1.25
137 CD24 5c on 50r dk bl 1.25 1.25
138 CD25 7½c on 75r vio brn 1.75 1.75
139 CD26 10c on 100r bis brn 1.50 1.50
140 CD27 15c on 150r bis 1.50 1.50
Nos. 133-140 (8) 11.00 11.00

On Stamps of Timor

141 CD20 ¼c on ½a bl grn 1.50 1.50
142 CD21 ½c on 1a red 1.50 1.50
143 CD22 1c on 2a red vio 1.50 1.50
144 CD23 2½c on 4a yel grn 1.50 1.50
145 CD24 5c on 8a dk bl 1.50 1.50
146 CD25 7½c on 12a vio brn 3.00 3.00
147 CD26 10c on 16a bis brn 1.50 1.50
148 CD27 15c on 24a bis 2.00 2.00
Nos. 141-148 (8) 14.00 14.00
Nos. 125-148 (24) 41.00 41.00

Ceres — A6

1914-26 **Typo.** ***Perf. 15x14, 12x11½***

Name and Value in Black

149 A6 ¼c olive brown 15 15
150 A6 ½c black 15 15
151 A6 1c blue green 15 15
152 A6 1½c lilac brown 15 15
153 A6 2c carmine 15 15
154 A6 2c gray ('26) 18 18
155 A6 2½c lt vio 15 15
156 A6 3c org ('21) 15 15
157 A6 4c pale rose ('21) 15 15
158 A6 4½c gray ('21) 15 15
159 A6 5c deep blue 15 15
160 A6 6c lilac ('21) 15 15
a. Name and value printed twice
161 A6 7c ultra ('21) 15 15
162 A6 7½c yel brn 15 15
163 A6 8c slate 15 15
164 A6 10c org brn 15 15
165 A6 12c gray brn ('21) 18 15
166 A6 12c bl grn ('22) 18 15
167 A6 15c plum 1.40 1.00
a. Perf. 12x11½ ('30) 35 18
168 A6 15c brn rose ('22) 15 15
169 A6 20c yel grn 15 15
170 A6 24c ultra ('26) 4.50 95

171 A6 25c choc ('26) 70 50
172 A6 30c brn, *grn* 1.00 70
173 A6 30c dp grn ('21) 28 15
174 A6 30c gray bl, *pink* ('21) 1.00 85
175 A6 40c brn, *pink* 1.25 85
176 A6 40c turq bl ('22) 60 20
177 A6 50c org, *salmon* 2.50 2.00
178 A6 50c lt vio ('26) 28 15
179 A6 60c red brn, *pink* ('21) 1.00 70
180 A6 60c dk bl ('22) 70 30
181 A6 60c rose ('26) 70 24
182 A6 80c dk brn, *bl* ('21) 1.00 70
183 A6 80c brt rose ('22) 70 24
184 A6 1e grn, *bl*, perf. 12x11½ ('21) 1.40 60
a. Perf. 15x14 6.00 2.00
185 A6 1e rose ('21) 1.10 48
186 A6 1e blue ('26) 1.00 50
187 A6 2e brt vio, *pink* ('21) 1.40 60
188 A6 2e dk vio ('22) 70 35
189 A6 5e buff ('26) 6.75 2.50
190 A6 10e pink ('26) 12.00 4.75
191 A6 20e pale turq ('26) 35.00 15.00
Nos. 149-191 (43) 80.05 37.34

For surcharges see Nos. 232-234, 236-237, 249-250, J46-50.

Stamps of 1902 Overprinted Locally in Carmine

REPUBLICA

1915

On Provisional Stamps of 1902

192 A2 115r on 5r blk 40.00 30.00
193 A3 115r on 5r yel 85 75
194 A3 115r on 25r bl grn 85 75
195 A3 130r on 75r rose 85 75
196 A3 130r on 100r brn, *buff* 85 75
197 A3 130r on 150r car, *rose* 85 75
198 A3 130r on 200r bl, *bl* 85 75
199 A3 115r on 2½r brn 60 40

On No. 97

200 A4 75r rose 1.25 70
Nos. 192-200 (9) 46.95 35.60

Stamps of 1902-05 Overprinted in Carmine

1915

On Provisional Stamps of 1902

201 A3 115r on 5r yellow 55 48
202 A3 115r on 25r bl grn 55 48
203 A3 130r on 75r rose 55 48
204 A3 130r on 150r car, *rose* 70 50
205 A3 130r on 200r bl, *bl* 70 50
206 A3 115r on 2½r brn 55 48

On No. 96

207 A4 50r blue 70 50

On No. 98

208 A4 50r on 65r dull blue 70 50
Nos. 201-208 (8) 5.00 3.92

Stamps of 1898-1903 Overprinted Locally in Carmine Like Nos. 192-200

1917

209 A4 2½r gray 16.00 10.00
210 A4 15r gray grn 12.50 6.00
211 A4 20r gray vio 12.50 7.50
212 A4 50r brown 11.00 6.75
213 A4 75r red lilac 25.00 17.00
214 A4 100r blue, *bl* 3.50 1.90
215 A4 115r org brn, *pink* 3.50 1.90
216 A4 130r brown, *straw* 3.50 1.90
217 A4 200r red lil, *pnksh* 3.50 1.90
218 A4 400r dull bl, *straw* 3.50 1.90
219 A4 500r blk & red, *bl* 3.50 1.90
220 A4 700r vio, *yelsh* 4.75 3.00
Nos. 209-220 (12) 102.75 61.65

War Tax Stamps of 1916-18 Surcharged

2 ½
CENTAVOS

1918 *Rouletted 7*

221 WT2 2½c on 5c rose 95 70

Perf. 11, 12

222 WT2 2½c on 5c red 95 70
a. "PETRIA" 2.00 1.75
b. "PEPUBLICA" 2.00 1.75
c. "1910" for "1916" 5.00 2.50

War Tax Stamps of 1916-18 Surcharged

"CORREIOS" 1 c.

1919 *Perf. 11*

224 WT1 1c on 1c gray grn 55 40
a. "PEPUBLICA" 4.75 4.00
b. Rouletted 7 200.00 85.00

Perf. 12

225 WT2 1½c on 5c red 40 35
a. "PETRIA" 2.50 2.00
b. "PEPUBLICA" 2.50 2.00
c. "1910" for "1916" 3.50 2.75

Stamps of 1902 Overprinted Locally in Carmine Like Nos. 192-200

1920

226 A3 400r on 50r lt bl 1.00 85
227 A3 400r on 80r yel grn 1.00 85
228 A3 400r on 300r bl, *sal* 1.00 85

War Tax Stamp of 1918 Surcharged in Green

SEIS
CENTAVOS

229 WT2 6c on 5c red 60 48
a. "1910" for "1916" 6.00 3.50
b. "PETRIA" 2.00 1.40
c. "PEPUBLICA" 2.00 1.40

Lourenco Marques Nos. 117, 119 Surcharged in Red or Bue

10 c.

1921 *Perf. 15x14*

230 A4 10c on ½c blk (R) 55 40
231 A4 30c on 1½c brn (Bl) 55 40

Same Surcharge on Mozambique Nos. 150, 152, 155 in Red, Blue or Green

232 A6 10c on ½c blk (R) 1.25 85
233 A6 30c on 1½c brn (Bl) 1.25 85
234 A6 60c on 2½c vio (G) 1.75 1.00
Nos. 230-234 (5) 5.35 3.50

War Tax Stamp of 1918 Surcharged in Green

2$00

1921 *Perf. 12*

235 WT2 2e on 5c red 1.00 50
a. "PETRIA" 1.75 1.40
b. "PEPUBLICA" 3.50 2.00
c. "1910" for "1916" 6.00 5.00

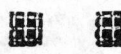

No. 157 Surcharged

50 c.

1923 *Perf. 12x11½*

236 A6 50c on 4c pale rose 85 55

No. 183 Overprinted in Green

Vasco da Gama
1924

1924

237 A6 80c bright rose 85 60

4th centenary of the death of Vasco da Gama.

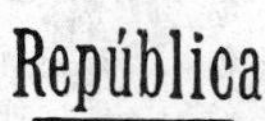

Nos. 90 and 91 Surcharged

40 C.

1925 *Perf. 11½*

238 A3 40c on 400r on 50r 70 48
239 A3 40c on 400r on 80r 60 48
a. "a" omitted 42.50 42.50

Postage Due Stamp of 1917 Overprinted in Black and Bars in Red

CORREIOS

1929, Jan. *Perf. 12*

247 D1 50c gray 85 55

No. 188 Surcharged

70 C.

1931 *Perf. 11½*

249 A6 70c on 2e dk vio 70 50
250 A6 1.40e on 2e dk vio 1.00 50

"Portugal" Holding Volume of the "Lusiads" — A7

Wmk. Maltese Cross (232)

1933, July 13 **Typo.** *Perf. 14*

Value in Red or Black

251 A7 1c bis brn (R) 15 15
252 A7 5c black brn 15 15
253 A7 10c dp violet 15 15
254 A7 15c black (R) 15 15
255 A7 20c light gray 15 15
256 A7 30c blue green 15 15
257 A7 40c org red 15 15
258 A7 45c brt blue 20 15
259 A7 50c dk brown 15 15
260 A7 60c olive grn 20 15
261 A7 70c org brown 20 15
262 A7 80c emerald 20 15
263 A7 85c dp rose 85 50
264 A7 1e red brn 50 15
265 A7 1.40e dk bl (R) 8.00 1.40
266 A7 2e dk vio 1.25 35
267 A7 5e apple grn 2.00 50
268 A7 10e olive bister 4.75 1.00
269 A7 20e orange 25.00 1.75
Nos. 251-269 (19) 44.35
Set value 6.40

See Nos. 298-299.

Common Design Types

Perf. 13½x13

1938, Aug. **Engr.** **Unwmk.**

Name and Value in Black

270 CD34 1c gray grn 15 15
271 CD34 5c org brn 15 15
272 CD34 10c dk car 15 15
273 CD34 15c dk vio brn 15 15
274 CD34 20c slate 15 15
275 CD35 30c rose vio 15 15
276 CD35 35c brt grn 18 15
277 CD35 40c brown 28 15
278 CD35 50c brt red vio 28 15
279 CD36 60c gray blk 28 15
280 CD36 70c brn vio 28 15
281 CD36 80c orange 50 15
282 CD36 1e red 40 20
283 CD37 1.75e blue 1.50 30
284 CD37 2e brn car 1.50 30
285 CD37 5e olive green 3.50 50
286 CD38 10e bl vio 9.00 1.00
287 CD38 20e red brn 25.00 1.40
Nos. 270-287 (18) 43.60
Set value 4.80

For surcharges see Nos. 297, 301.

Common Design Types pictured in section at front of Catalogue.

No. 258 Surcharged in Black

40
centavos

1938, Jan. 16 **Wmk. 232** *Perf. 14*

288 A7 40c on 45c brt bl 2.50 1.00

Map of Africa — A7a

Perf. 11½x12

1939, July 17 **Litho.** **Unwmk.**

289 A7a 80c vio, *pale rose* 1.50 1.25
290 A7a 1.75e bl, *pale bl* 4.00 2.75
291 A7a 3e grn, *yel grn* 6.00 4.00
292 A7a 20e brn, *buff* 30.00 50.00

Presidential visit.

New Cathedral, Loureno Marques — A8

Railroad Station — A9

Municipal Hall — A10

1944, Dec. **Litho.** *Perf. 11½*

293 A8 50c dk brown 70 40
294 A8 50c dk green 70 40
295 A9 1.75e ultra 3.75 85
296 A10 20e dk gray 8.50 85

4th cent. of the founding of Loureno Marques. See No. 302. For surcharge see No. 300.

No. 283 Surcharged in Carmine

60
CENTAVOS

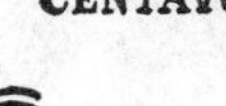

1946 **Engr.** *Perf. 13½x13*

297 CD37 60c on 1.75e blue 85 40

Lusiads Type of 1933

1947 **Wmk. 232** **Typo.** *Perf. 14*

Value in Black

298 A7 35c yellow grn 4.00 1.40
299 A7 1.75e deep blue 4.00 1.40

No. 296 Surcharged in Pink

2$00

1946 **Unwmk.** *Perf. 11½*

300 A10 2e on 20e dk gray 1.40 40

No. 273 Surcharged with New Value and Wavy Lines

Perf. 13½x13

301 CD34 10c on 15c dk vio brn 70 40
a. Inverted surcharge 15.00

Cathedral Type of 1944
Commemorative Inscription Omitted

1948 Litho. *Perf. 11½*

302 A8	4.50e	brt vermilion	1.40	38

Antonio Enes — A11

1948, Oct. 4 *Perf. 14*

303 A11	50c	black & cream	1.00	35
304 A11	5e	vio brn & cream	3.00	85

Birth centenary of Antonio Enes.

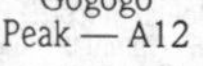

Gogogo Peak — A12

Zambezi River Bridge — A13

Zumbo River A14

Waterfall at Nhanhangare A15

Loureno Marques — A16

Plantation, Baixa — A17

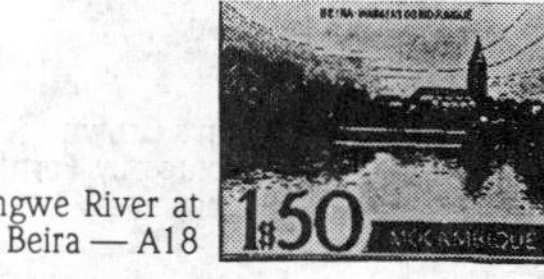

Pungwe River at Beira — A18

Polana Beach — A19

Loureno Marques — A20

Malema River — A21

Perf. 13½x13, 13x13½

1948-49 Typo. Unwmk.

305 A12	5c	org brn	18	15
306 A13	10c	vio brn	18	15
307 A14	20c	dk brn	18	15
308 A12	30c	plum	18	15
309 A14	40c	dl grn	18	15
310 A16	50c	slate	18	15
311 A15	60c	brn car	18	15
312 A16	80c	vio blk	18	15
313 A17	1e	carmine	35	18
314 A13	1.20e	slate gray	35	18
315 A18	1.50e	dk pur	35	18
316 A19	1.75e	dk bl ('49)	75	24
317 A18	2e	brown	50	18
318 A20	2.50e	dk sl ('49)	1.50	20
319 A19	3e	gray ol ('49)	1.00	20
320 A15	3.50e	olive gray	1.10	20
321 A17	5e	bl grn	1.10	20
322 A20	10e	choc ('49)	2.50	35
323 A21	15e	dp car ('49)	6.00	1.75
324 A21	20e	org ('49)	10.00	1.75
		Nos. 305-324 (20)	26.94	6.81

On No. 320 the "$" is reversed.

Lady of Fatima Issue
Common Design Type

1948, Oct. Litho. *Perf. 14½*

325 CD40	50c	blue	1.00	50
326 CD40	1.20e	red vio	3.00	1.00
327 CD40	4.50e	emerald	8.00	2.00
328 CD40	20e	chocolate	16.00	2.50

Symbols of the UPU — A21a

1949, Apr. 11 *Perf. 14*

329 A21a	4.50e	ultra & pale gray	1.00	50

75th anniversary of UPU.

Catalogue values for unused stamps in this section, from this point to the end of the section, are for Never Hinged items.

Holy Year Issue
Common Design Types

1950, May *Perf. 13x13½*

330 CD41	1.50e	red org	70	24
331 CD42	3e	brt blue	1.00	28

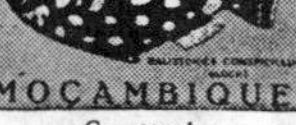

Spotted Triggerfish — A22

Pennant Coral Fish — A22a

Fish: 10c, Golden butterflyfish. 15c, Orange butterflyfish. 20c, Lionfish. 30c, Sharpnose puffer. 40c, Porky filefish. 50c, Dark brown surgeonfish. 1.50e Rainbow wrasse. 2e, Orange-spotted gray-skin. 2.50e, Kasmir snapper. 3e, Convict fish. 3.50e, Stellar triggerfish. 4e, Cornetfish. 4.50e, Vagabond butterflyfish. 5e, Mail-cheeked fish. 6e, Pinnate batfish. 8e, Moorish idol. 9e, Triangulate boxfish. 10e, Flying gurnard. 15e, Redtooth triggerfish. 20e, Striped triggerfish. 30e, Horned cowfish. 50e, Spotted cowfish.

Photogravure and Lithographed

1951 Unwmk. *Perf. 14x14½*

Fish in Natural Colors

332 A22	5c	dp yellow	24	*50*
333 A22	10c	lt blue	15	*50*
334 A22	15c	yellow	60	*1.00*
335 A22	20c	pale olive	28	18
336 A22	30c	gray	24	18
337 A22	40c	pale green	18	15
338 A22	50c	pale buff	18	15
339 A22a	1e	aqua	18	15
340 A22	1.50e	olive	15	15
341 A22	2e	blue	20	18
342 A22	2.50e	brnsh lil	50	18
343 A22	3e	aqua	50	18
344 A22	3.50e	ol grn	40	18
345 A22	4e	bl gray	85	70
346 A22	4.50e	green	85	70
347 A22	5e	buff	85	18
348 A22a	6e	sal pink	85	20
349 A22a	8e	gray bl	85	24
350 A22	9e	lil rose	1.50	30
351 A22	10e	gray lil	15.00	2.00
352 A22	15e	gray	35.00	6.50
353 A22	20e	lemon	20.00	3.50
354 A22	30e	yel grn	15.00	4.00
355 A22	50e	gray vio	35.00	6.50
		Nos. 332-355 (24)	129.55	28.50

Holy Year Extension Issue
Common Design Type

1951, Oct. Litho. *Perf. 14*

356 CD43	5e	car & rose	1.75	1.00

Victor Cordon A23

Plane and Ship A24

1951, Oct. *Perf. 11½*

357 A23	1e	dk brown	1.25	35
358 A23	5e	black & slate	6.00	1.00

Centenary of the birth of Victor Cordon, explorer.

Medical Congress Issue
Common Design Type

Design: Miguel Bombarda Hospital.

1952, June 19 Litho. *Perf. 13½*

359 CD44	3e	dk bl & brn buff	85	35

1952, Sept. 15 Unwmk.

360 A24	1.50e	multi	48	35

4th African Tourism Congress.

Missionary A25

Papilio Demodocus A26

1953

361 A25	10c	red brn & pale vio	15	15
362 A25	1e	red brn & pale yel grn	50	20
363 A25	5e	blk & lt bl	1.40	35
		Set value		60

Exhibition of Sacred Missionary Art, held at Lisbon in 1951.

Canceled to Order
Certain issues, including Nos. 364-383, were canceled to order under Republican administration.

Photogravure and Lithographed

1953, May 28 *Perf. 13x14*

Various Butterflies and Moths in Natural Colors

364 A26	10c	lt blue	15	15
365 A26	15c	cream	15	15
366 A26	20c	yellow grn	15	15
367 A26	30c	lt violet	15	15
368 A26	40c	brown	15	15
369 A26	50c	bluish gray	15	15
370 A26	80c	brt blue	15	15
371 A26	1e	gray bl	15	15
372 A26	1.50e	ocher	18	15
373 A26	2e	orange brn	4.50	50
374 A26	2.30e	blue	3.50	35
375 A26	2.50e	citron	6.00	35
376 A26	3e	lilac rose	1.75	15
377 A26	4e	light blue	24	15
378 A26	4.50e	orange	28	15
379 A26	5e	green	28	15
380 A26	6e	pale vio	35	15
381 A26	7.50e	buff	3.25	30
382 A26	10e	pink	6.25	75
383 A26	20e	grnsh gray	8.00	70
		Nos. 364-383 (20)	35.78	
		Set value		4.00
		Set value, CTO		50

For overprints see Nos. 517, 527.

Stamps of Portugal and Mozambique A27

Stamp of Portugal and Arms of Colonies A27a

1953, July 23 Litho. *Perf. 14*

384 A27	1e	multicolored	85	40
385 A27	3e	multicolored	2.50	70

Issued in connection with the Loureno Marques philatelic exhibition, July 1953.

Stamp Centenary Issue

1953 Photo. *Perf. 13*

386 A27a	50c	multicolored	55	40

Map — A28

1954, Oct. 15 Litho.

Colors (except Colony) on map: Gray, Light Blue, Blue, Carmine and Black

387 A28	10c	pale rose lil	15	15
388 A28	20c	pale yel	15	15
389 A28	50c	lilac	15	15
390 A28	1e	org yel	18	15
391 A28	2.30e	white	45	18
392 A28	4e	pale salmon	60	20
393 A28	10e	lt green	1.90	20
394 A28	20e	brn buff	2.50	35
		Nos. 387-394 (8)	6.08	
		Set value		1.10

For overprints see Nos. 516, 530.

Sao Paulo Issue
Common Design Type

1954, July 2

395 CD46	3.50e	dk gray, cr & ol	35	28

Arms of Beira A29

Mousinho de Albuquerque A30

Paper with network as in parenthesis

1954, Dec. 1 *Perf. 13x13½*

Arms in Silver, Gold, Red and Pale Green

396 A29	1.50e	dk bl *(bl)*	35	28
397 A29	3.50e	brn *(buff)*	75	35

Issued to publicize the first philatelic exhibition of Manica and Sofala.

1955, Feb. 1 Litho. *Perf. 11½x12*

Design: 2.50e, Statue of Mousinho de Albuquerque.

398 A30	1e	gray, blk & buff	60	35
399 A30	2.50e	ol bis, blk & bl	1.00	60

100th anniversary of the birth of Mousinho de Albuquerque, statesman.

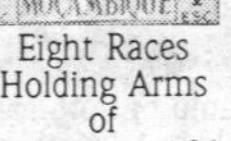

Eight Races Holding Arms of Portugal — A31

View of Beira — A32

1956, Aug. 4 Unwmk. *Perf. 14½*
Central Design in Multicolored

400 A31	1e pale yel		28	20
401 A31	2.50e lt blue		70	28

Issued to commemorate the visit of President Antonio Oscar de Fragoso Carmona.

1957, Aug. 15 Litho.

402 A32 2.50e multicolored		48	28

50th anniversary of the city of Beira.

Brussels Fair Issue

Exhibition Emblems and View — A32a

1958, Oct. 8 Unwmk. *Perf. 14½*

403 A32a 3.50c blk, grn, yel, red & bl	20	15

Tropical Medicine Congress Issue
Common Design Type

Design: Strophanthus grandiflorus.

1958, Sept. 14 *Perf. 13½*

404 CD47 1.50e sal brn, grn & red	1.25	70

Caravel — A33

Technical Instruction — A34

1960, June 25 Litho. *Perf. 13½*

405 A33 5e multicolored	28	15

500th anniversary of the death of Prince Henry the Navigator.

1960, Nov. 21 Unwmk. *Perf. 14½*

406 A34 3e multicolored	40	28

10th anniversary of the Commission for Technical Co-operation in Africa South of the Sahara (C.C.T.A.).

Arms of Loureno Marques — A35

Arms of various cities of Mozambique.

1961, Jan. 30 Litho. *Perf. 13½*
Arms in Original Colors; Black, Ultramarine and Red Inscriptions

407 A35	5c salmon	15	15
408 A35	15c pale green	15	15
409 A35	20c lt vio gray	15	15
410 A35	30c buff	15	15
411 A35	50c bluish gray	15	15
412 A35	1e pale ol	30	15
413 A35	1.50e lt blue	30	15
414 A35	2e pale pink	45	15
415 A35	2.50e lt bl grn	1.00	15
416 A35	3e beige	60	20
417 A35	4e yellow	38	15
418 A35	4.50e pale gray	38	15
419 A35	5e pale bluish grn	85	15
420 A35	7.50e rose	1.00	24
a.	"CORREIOS 7$50" omitted		
421 A35	10e lt yel grn	1.50	24
422 A35	20e beige	4.00	50
423 A35	50e gray	4.75	1.00
	Nos. 407-423 (17)	16.26	
	Set value		3.00

Sports Issue
Common Design Type

Sports: 50c, Water skiing. 1e, Wrestling. 1.50e, Woman gymnast. 2.50e, Field hockey. 4.50e, Women's basketball. 15e, Speedboat racing.

1962, Feb. 10 Unwmk. *Perf. 13½*
Multicolored Designs

424 CD48	50c gray green	15	15
425 CD48	1e dk gray	70	35
426 CD48	1.50e pink	28	15
427 CD48	2.50e buff	35	15
428 CD48	4.50e gray	70	40
429 CD48	15e gray green	1.75	1.00
	Nos. 424-429 (6)	3.93	2.20

For overprints see Nos. 522, 526, 529.

Anti-Malaria Issue
Common Design Type

Design: Anopheles funestus.

1962, Apr. 5 *Perf. 13½*

430 CD49 2.50e multicolored	60	35

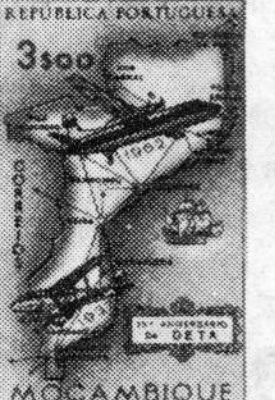

Planes over Mozambique A36

Loureno Marques 1887 and 1962 A37

1962, Oct. 15 Litho. *Perf. 14½*

431 A36 3e multicolored	35	20

25th anniversary of DETA airlines.

1962, Nov. 1 *Perf. 13*

432 A37 1e multicolored	28	15

75th anniversary of Loureno Marques.

Vasco da Gama Statue and Arms — A38

1963, Apr. 25 Unwmk. *Perf. 14½*

433 A38 3e multicolored	28	15

200th anniversary of the founding of Mozambique City.

Airline Anniversary Issue
Common Design Type

1963, Oct. 21 Litho. *Perf. 14½*

434 CD50 2.50e brt pink & multi	28	15

Barque, 1430 — A39

Caravel, 1436 — A40

Development of Sailing Ships: 30c, Lateen-rigged caravel, 1460. 50c, "Sao Gabriel," 1497. 1e, Dom Manuel's ship, 1498. 1.50e, Warship, 1500. 2e, "Flor de la Mar," 1511. 2.50e, Redonda caravel, 1519. 3.50e, 800-ton ship, 1520. 4e, Portuguese India galley, 1521. 4.50e, "Santa Tereza," 1639. 5e, "Nostra Senhora da Conceiao," 1716. 6e, "Nostra Senhora do Bom Sucesso," 1764. 7.50e, Launch with mortar, 1788. 8e, Brigantine, 1793. 10e, Corvette, 1799. 12.50e, Schooner "Maria Teresa," 1820. 15e, "Vasco da Gama," 1841. 20e, Frigate "Dom Fernando II," 1843. 30e, Training Ship "Sagres," 1924.

1963, Dec. 1 Litho. *Perf. 14½*

435 A39	10c multicolored	15	15
436 A40	20c multicolored	15	15
437 A40	30c multicolored	15	15
438 A40	50c multicolored	15	15
439 A40	1e multicolored	35	15
440 A40	1.50e multicolored	18	15
441 A40	2e multicolored	24	15
442 A39	2.50e multicolored	50	15
443 A40	3.50e multicolored	38	28
444 A39	4e multicolored	45	15
445 A40	4.50e multicolored	70	18
446 A40	5e multicolored	7.50	18
447 A39	6e multicolored	70	20
448 A39	7.50e multicolored	90	24
449 A39	8e multicolored	90	28
450 A39	10e multicolored	1.25	40
451 A39	12.50e multicolored	1.40	50
452 A39	15e multicolored	1.40	50
453 A40	20e multicolored	2.00	70
454 A40	30e multicolored	2.75	1.25
	Nos. 435-454 (20)	22.20	
	Set value		5.35

National Overseas Bank Issue

Modern Bank Building, Luanda — A40a

1964, May 16 *Perf. 13½*

455 A40a 1.50e bl, yel gray & grn	35	20

Centenary of the National Overseas Bank of Portugal.

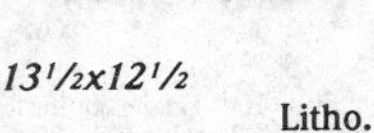

Pres. Americo Rodrigues Thomaz — A41

Perf. 13½x12½
1964, July 23 Litho.

456 A41 2.50e multicolored	20	15

Visit of Pres. Americo Rodrigues Thomaz of Portugal to Mozambique, in July.

Royal Barge of King John V, 1728 — A42

Designs: 35c, Barge of Dom Jose I, 1753. 1e, Customs barge, 1768. 1.50e, Sailor, 1780, vert. 2.50e, Royal barge, 1780. 5e, Barge of Dona Carlota Joaquina, 1790. 9e, Barge of Dom Miguel, 1831.

1964, Dec. 18 Litho. *Perf. 14½*

457 A42	15c multicolored	15	15
458 A42	35c lt bl & multi	15	15
459 A42	1e gray & multi	40	15
460 A42	1.50e gray & multi	28	15
461 A42	2.50e multicolored	20	15
462 A42	5e multicolored	28	15
463 A42	9e multicolored	48	40
	Nos. 457-463 (7)	1.94	
	Set value		90

ITU Issue
Common Design Type

1965, May 17 Unwmk. *Perf. 14½*

464 CD52 1e yellow & multi	40	28

National Revolution Issue
Common Design Type

Design: 1e, Beira Railroad Station, and Antonio Enes School.

1966, May 28 Litho. *Perf. 11½*

465 CD53 1e multicolored	20	20

Harquebusier, 1560 — A42a

Designs: 30c, Harquebusier, 1640. 40c, Infantry soldier, 1777. 50c, Infantry officer, 1777. 80c, Drummer, 1777. 1e, Infantry sergeant, 1777. 2e, Infantry major, 1784. 2.50e, Colonial officer, 1788. 3e, Infantry soldier, 1789. 5e, Colonial bugler, 1801. 10e, Colonial officer, 1807. 15e, Colonial infantry soldier, 1817.

1967, Jan. 12 Photo. *Perf. 14*

466 A42a	20c multicolored	15	15
467 A42a	30c multicolored	15	15
468 A42a	40c multicolored	15	15
469 A42a	50c multicolored	15	15
470 A42a	80c multicolored	40	28
471 A42a	1e multicolored	28	15
472 A42a	2e multicolored	28	20
473 A42a	2.50e multicolored	48	28
474 A42a	3e multicolored	35	20
475 A42a	5e multicolored	48	28
476 A42a	10e multicolored	60	35
477 A42a	15e multicolored	75	55
	Nos. 466-477 (12)	4.22	2.89

Navy Club Issue
Common Design Type

Designs: 3e, Capt. Azevedo Coutinho and gunboat (stern-wheeler) Tete. 10e, Capt. Joao Roby and gunboat (paddle steamer) Granada.

1967, Jan. 31 Litho. *Perf. 13*

478 CD54	3e multicolored	35	15
479 CD54	10e multicolored	85	40

Virgin's Crown, Presented by Portuguese Women — A43

1967, May 13 Litho. *Perf. 12½x13*

480 A43 50c multicolored	15	15

50th anniversary of the appearance of the Virgin Mary to 3 shepherd children at Fatima.

Cabral Issue

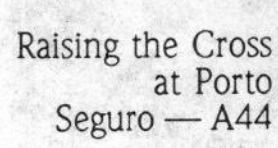

Raising the Cross at Porto Seguro — A44

Designs: 1.50e, First mission to Brazil. 3e, Grace Church, Santarem, vert.

1968, Apr. 22 Litho. *Perf. 14*

No.	Type	Denom.	Color	Unused	Used
481	A44	1e	multicolored	15	15
482	A44	1.50e	multicolored	20	15
483	A44	3e	multicolored	40	20
			Set value		30

500th anniversary of the birth of Pedro Alvares Cabral, navigator who took possession of Brazil for Portugal.

Admiral Coutinho Issue
Common Design Type

Design: 70c, Adm. Coutinho and Adm. Gago Coutinho Airport.

1969, Feb. 17 Litho. *Perf. 14*

No.	Type	Denom.	Color	Unused	Used
484	CD55	70c	multicolored	15	15

Luiz Vaz de Camoens — A45

Sailing Ship, 1553 — A46

Designs: 1.50e, Map of Mozambique, 1554. 2.50e, Chapel of Our Lady of Baluarte, 1552. 5e, Excerpt from Lusiads about Mozambique (1st Song, 14th Stanza).

Perf. 12½x13, 13x12½
1969, June 10 Litho.

No.	Type	Denom.	Color	Unused	Used
485	A45	15c	multicolored	15	15
486	A46	50c	multicolored	15	15
487	A45	1.50e	multicolored	15	15
488	A46	2.50e	multicolored	15	15
489	A45	5e	multicolored	28	15
			Set value	75	40

400th anniversary of the visit to Mozambique of Luiz Vaz de Camoens (1524-1580), poet.

Vasco da Gama Issue

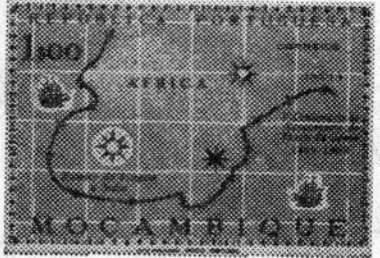

Map Showing Voyage to Mozambique and India — A47

1969, Aug. 29 Litho. *Perf. 14*

No.	Type	Denom.	Color	Unused	Used
490	A47	1e	multicolored	15	15

Vasco da Gama (1469-1524), navigator.

Administration Reform Issue
Common Design Type

1969, Sept. 25 Litho. *Perf. 14*

No.	Type	Denom.	Color	Unused	Used
491	CD56	1.50e	multicolored	15	15

King Manuel I Issue

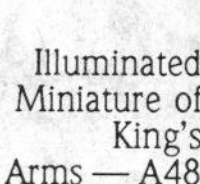

Illuminated Miniature of King's Arms — A48

1969, Dec. 1 Litho. *Perf. 14*

No.	Type	Denom.	Color	Unused	Used
492	A48	80c	multicolored	15	15

500th anniversary of the birth of King Manuel I.

Marshal Carmona Issue
Common Design Type

Design: 5e, Antonio Oscar Carmona in marshal's uniform.

1970, Nov. 15 Litho. *Perf. 14*

No.	Type	Denom.	Color	Unused	Used
493	CD57	5e	multicolored	20	15

Fossil Fern A49

Fossils and Minerals: 50c, Fossil snail. 1e, Stibnite. 1.50e, Pink beryl. 2e, Dinosaur. 3e, Tantalocolumbite. 3.50e, Verdelite. 4e, Zircon. 10e, Petrified wood.

1971, Jan. 15 Litho. *Perf. 13*

No.	Type	Denom.	Color	Unused	Used
494	A49	15c	gray & multi	15	15
495	A49	50c	lt ultra & multi	15	15
496	A49	1e	green & multi	15	15
497	A49	1.50e	multicolored	15	15
498	A49	2e	multicolored	35	15
499	A49	3e	lt bl & multi	35	15
500	A49	3.50e	lilac & multi	70	20
501	A49	4e	multicolored	70	20
502	A49	10e	dl red & multi	2.75	48
			Nos. 494-502 (9)	5.45	
			Set value		1.25

For overprints see Nos. 525, 528.

Mozambique Island — A49a

1972, May 25 Litho. *Perf. 13*

No.	Type	Denom.	Color	Unused	Used
503	A49a	4e	ultra & multi	28	15

4th centenary of publication of The Lusiads by Luiz Camoens.

Olympic Games Issue
Common Design Type

Design: 3e, Hurdles and swimming, Olympic emblem.

1972, June 20 *Perf. 14x13½*

No.	Type	Denom.	Color	Unused	Used
504	CD59	3e	multi	20	15

For overprint see No. 523.

Lisbon-Rio de Janeiro Flight Issue
Common Design Type

Design: 1e, "Santa Cruz" over Recife harbor.

1972, Sept. 20 Litho. *Perf. 13½*

No.	Type	Denom.	Color	Unused	Used
505	CD60	1e	multi	15	15

Sailboats A50

Designs: Various sailboats.

1973, Aug. 21 Litho. *Perf. 12x11½*

No.	Type	Denom.	Color	Unused	Used
506	A50	1e	multi	15	15
507	A50	1.50e	multi	15	15
508	A50	3e	multi	28	15
			Set value		25

World Sailing Championships, Vauriens Class, Loureno Marques, Aug. 21-30.
For overprints see Nos. 519-520, 524.

WMO Centenary Issue
Common Design Type

1973, Dec. 15 Litho. *Perf. 13*

No.	Type	Denom.	Color	Unused	Used
509	CD61	2e	rose red & multi	20	15

For overprint see No. 521.

Radar Station A51

1974, June 25 Litho. *Perf. 13*

No.	Type	Denom.	Color	Unused	Used
510	A51	50c	multi	15	15

Establishment of satellite communications network via Intelsat among Portugal, Angola and Mozambique.
For overprint see No. 518.

"Bird" Made of Flags of Portugal and Mozambique A52

1975, Jan. Litho. *Perf. 14½*

No.	Type	Denom.	Color	Unused	Used
511	A52	1e	pink & multi	15	15
512	A52	1.50e	yel & multi	15	15
513	A52	2e	gray & multi	20	15
514	A52	3.50e	lem & multi	28	15
515	A52	6e	lt bl & multi	75	28
a.			Souv. sheet of 5, #511-515 + label	3.50	
			Nos. 511-515 (5)	1.53	
			Set value		70

Lusaka Agreement, Sept. 7, 1974, which gave Mozambique independence from Portugal, effective June 25, 1975.
No. 515a sold for 25e.
For overprints see Nos. 543-545.

Republic
Issues of 1953-74 Overprinted in Red or Black:

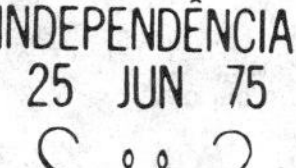

a

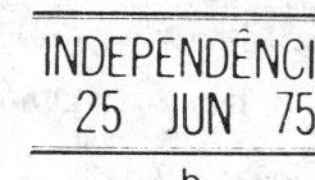

b

1975, June 25

No.	Type	Denom.	Overprint	Unused	Used
516	A28 (a)	10c	(R; #387)	15	15
517	A26 (a)	40c	(R; #368)	15	15
518	A51 (b)	50c	(B; #510)	15	15
519	A50 (b)	1e	(B; #506)	15	15
520	A50 (b)	1.50e	(B; #507)	20	15
521	CD61 (a)	2e	(B; #509)	20	15
522	CD48 (b)	2.50e	(B; #427)	40	20
523	CD59 (a)	3e	(B; #504)	40	20
524	A50 (b)	3e	(B; #508)	40	40
525	A49 (b)	3.50e	(B; #500)	40	40
526	CD48 (b)	4.50e	(B; #428)	2.50	1.75
527	A26 (a)	7.50e	(R; #381)	85	40
528	A49 (b)	10e	(B; #502)	1.75	60
529	CD48 (b)	15e	(B; #429)	1.75	85
530	A28 (a)	20e	(R; #394)	1.00	60
			Nos. 516-530,C35-C38 (19)	13.60	7.26

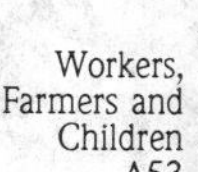

Workers, Farmers and Children A53

Designs: 30c, 50c, 2.50e, like 20c. 4.50e, 5e, 10e, 50e, Dancers, workers, armed family.

1975 Litho. *Perf. 12x11½*

No.	Type	Denom.	Color	Unused	Used
531	A53	20c	pink & multi	15	15
532	A53	30c	bis & multi	15	15
533	A53	50c	bl & multi	15	15
534	A53	2.50e	grn & multi	15	15
535	A53	4.50e	brn & multi	18	15
536	A53	5e	bis & multi	18	15
537	A53	10e	bl & multi	35	20
538	A53	50e	yel & multi	1.65	80
a.			Souvenir sheet of 8	3.25	3.25
			Set value	2.60	1.35

No. 538a contains 8 stamps similar to Nos. 531-538 with simulated perforation. Sold for 75e.
For overprint see No. 554.

Farm Woman — A54

Designs: 1.50e, Teacher. 2.50e, Nurse. 10e, Mother.

1976, Apr. 7 Litho. *Perf. 14½*

No.	Type	Denom.	Color	Unused	Used
539	A54	1e	yel grn & blk	15	15
540	A54	1.50e	tan & multi	16	16
541	A54	2.50e	lt ultra & multi	25	25
542	A54	10e	red & multi	50	35

Day of the Mozambique Woman, Apr. 7.

Nos. 513-515 Overprinted in Red: "PRESIDENTE KENNETH KAUNDA / PRIMEIRA VISITA 20/4/1976"

1976, Apr. 20 Litho. *Perf. 14½*

No.	Type	Denom.	Color	Unused	Used
543	A52	2e	gray & multi	18	18
544	A52	3.50e	lem & multi	30	30
545	A52	6e	lt bl & multi	50	50

Visit of President Kaunda of Zambia.

Pres. Machel's Arrival at Maputo — A55

Mozambique No. 1 — A56

Designs: 1e, Independence proclamation ceremony. 2.50e, Pres. Samora Moises Machel taking office. 7.50e, Military parade. 20e, Flame of Unity and festival.

1976, June 25

No.	Type	Denom.	Color	Unused	Used
546	A55	50c	multi	15	15
547	A55	1e	multi	15	15
548	A55	2.50e	multi	24	20
549	A55	7.50e	multi	40	24
550	A55	20e	multi	1.00	50
			Nos. 546-550 (5)	1.94	1.24

First anniversary of independence.

1976, July *Perf. 11½x12*

No.	Type	Denom.	Color	Unused	Used
551	A56	1.50e	ocher & multi	18	18
552	A56	6e	red & multi	35	28

Centenary of Mozambique postage stamps.

Flag and Weapons — A57

1976, Sept. 25 Litho. *Perf. 14½*

No.	Type	Denom.	Color	Unused	Used
553	A57	3e	multi	24	15

Army Day 1976.

No. 534 Overprinted in Silver: "FACIM"

1976 Litho. *Perf. 12x11½*

No.	Type	Denom.	Color	Unused	Used
554	A53	2.50e	multi	28	15

FACIM, Industrial Fair.

Mozambique stamps can be mounted in Scott's annual Portugal Supplement.

Bush Baby — A58

Animals: 1e, Honey badger. 1.50e, Pangolin. 2e, Steinbok. 2.50e, Guenon (monkey). 3e, Cape hunting dog. 4e, Cheetah. 5e, Spotted hyena. 7.50e, Wart hog. 8e, Hippopotamus. 10e, Rhinoceros. 15e, Sable antelope. 1e, 2e, 3e, 4e, 7.50e, 8e, 10e horiz.

1977, Jan. Litho. *Perf. 14½*

No.	Design	Value	Color	Unused	Used
555	A58	50c	multi	15	15
556	A58	1e	multi	15	15
557	A58	1.50e	multi	15	15
558	A58	2e	multi	15	15
559	A58	2.50e	multi	18	15
560	A58	3e	multi	20	15
561	A58	4e	multi	28	15
562	A58	5e	multi	35	15
563	A58	7.50e	multi	50	20
564	A58	8e	multi	55	28
565	A58	10e	multi	70	28
566	A58	15e	multi	1.00	40
	Nos. 555-566 (12)			4.36	
	Set value				2.00

Congress Emblem — A59

Monument in Maputo — A60

Design: 3.50e, Monument in Macheje, site of 2nd Frelimo Congress, horiz.

1977, Feb. 7 *Perf. 14½*

No.	Design	Value	Color	Unused	Used
567	A59	3e	multi	20	20

Perf. 12x11½, 11½x12

No.	Design	Value	Color	Unused	Used
568	A60	3.50e	multi	28	28
569	A60	20e	multi	1.00	35

3rd FRELIMO Party Congress, Maputo, Feb. 3-7.

Women, Child's Design — A61

Worker and Farmer — A62

1977, Apr. 7 Litho. *Perf. 14½*

No.	Design	Value	Color	Unused	Used
570	A61	5e	dp org & multi	28	18
571	A61	15e	lt grn & multi	70	20

Mozambique Women's Day 1977.

1977, May 1 Litho. *Perf. 14½*

No.	Design	Value	Color	Unused	Used
572	A62	5e	red, blk & yel	38	28

Labor Day.

People, Flags and Rising Sun — A63

1977, June 25 Litho. *Perf. 11½x12*

No.	Design	Value	Color	Unused	Used
573	A63	50c	multi	15	15
574	A63	1.50e	multi	15	15
575	A63	3e	multi	20	15
576	A63	15e	multi	70	20
	Set value				48

2nd anniversary of independence.

Bread Palm — A64

1977, Dec. 21 Litho. *Perf. 12x11½*

No.	Design	Value	Color	Unused	Used
577	A64	1e	shown	15	15
578	A64	10e	Nyala	50	24
	Set value				30

Nature protection and Stamp Day.

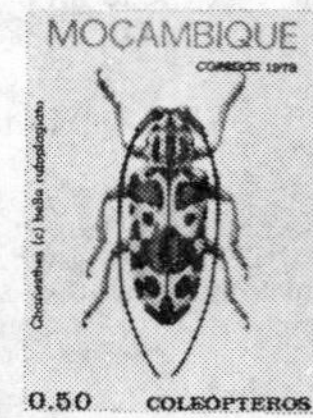

Chariesthes Bella Rufoplagiata — A65

Violet-crested Touraco — A66

Beetles: 1e, Tragocephalus variegata. 1.50e, Monochamus leuconotus. 3e, Prospocera lactator meridionalis. 5e, Dinocephalus ornatus. 10e, Tragiscoschema nigroscriptum maculata.

1978, Jan. 20 Litho. *Perf. 11½x12*

No.	Design	Value	Color	Unused	Used
579	A65	50c	multi	15	15
580	A65	1e	multi	15	15
581	A65	1.50e	multi	15	15
582	A65	3e	multi	20	20
583	A65	5e	multi	35	35
584	A65	10e	multi	50	35
	Set value			1.25	1.10

1978, Mar. 20 Litho. *Perf. 11½*

Birds of Mozambique: 1e, Lilac-breasted roller. 1.50e, Weaver. 2.50e, Violet-backed starling. 3e, Peter's twinspot. 15e, European bee-eater.

No.	Design	Value	Color	Unused	Used
585	A66	50c	multi	15	15
586	A66	1e	multi	15	15
587	A66	1.50e	multi	15	15
588	A66	2.50e	multi	18	18
589	A66	3e	multi	20	20
590	A66	15e	multi	70	35
	Set value			1.30	92

Mother and Child, WHO Emblem A67

1978, Apr. 17 *Perf. 12*

No.	Design	Value	Color	Unused	Used
591	A67	15e	multi	50	28

Smallpox eradication campaign.

Crinum Delagoense — A68

No. 1, Canada No. 1 — A69

Flowers of Mozambique: 1e, Gloriosa superba. 1.50e, Eulophia speciosa. 3e, Erithrina humeana. 5e, Astripomoea malvacea. 10e, Kigelia africana.

1978, May 16 *Perf. 11½x12*

No.	Design	Value	Color	Unused	Used
592	A68	50c	multi	15	15
593	A68	1e	multi	15	15
594	A68	1.50e	multi	15	15
595	A68	3e	multi	20	20
596	A68	5e	multi	24	24
597	A68	10e	multi	48	28
	Set value			1.12	92

1978, June 9

No.	Design	Value	Color	Unused	Used
598	A69	15e	multi	50	28

CAPEX Canadian International Philatelic Exhibition, Toronto, Ont., June 9-18.

National Flag — A70

Soldiers, Festival Emblem — A71

Designs: 1.50e, Coat of arms. 7.50e, Page of Constitution and people. 10e, Music band and national anthem.

1978, June 25 *Perf. 11½x12*

No.	Design	Value	Color	Unused	Used
599	A70	1e	multi	15	15
600	A70	1.50e	multi	15	15
601	A70	7.50e	multi	28	18
602	A70	10e	multi	50	24
a.	Souvenir sheet of 4			1.75	1.75
	Set value				58

3rd anniversary of proclamation of independence. No. 602a contains 4 stamps similar to Nos. 599-602 with simulated perforations. Sold for 30e.

1978, July 28

Designs (Festival Emblem and): 2.50e, Student. 7.50e, Farmworkers.

No.	Design	Value	Color	Unused	Used
603	A71	2.50e	multi	18	15
604	A71	3e	multi	20	15
605	A71	7.50e	multi	25	18

11th World Youth Festival, Havana, July 28-Aug. 5.

Czechoslovakia No. B126 and PRAGA '78 Emblem — A72

1978, Sept. 8 Litho. *Perf. 12x11½*

No.	Design	Value	Color	Unused	Used
606	A72	15e	multi	50	24
a.	Souvenir sheet			2.50	2.50

PRAGA '78 International Philatelic Exhibition, Prague, Sept. 8-17.

No. 606a contains one stamp with simulated perforations. Sold for 30e.

Soccer — A73

Stamp Day: 1.50e, Shotput. 3e, Hurdling. 7.50e, Fieldball. 12.50e, Swimming. 25e, Roller skate hockey.

1978, Dec. 21 Litho. *Perf. 12x11½*

No.	Design	Value	Color	Unused	Used
607	A73	50c	multi	15	15
608	A73	1.50e	multi	15	15
609	A73	3e	multi	15	15
610	A73	7.50e	multi	28	15
611	A73	12.50e	multi	35	20
612	A73	25e	multi	70	35
	Nos. 607-612 (6)			1.78	
	Set value				92

Carrier Pigeon, UPU Emblem A74

1979, Jan. 1 Litho. *Perf. 11x11½*

No.	Design	Value	Color	Unused	Used
613	A74	20e	multi	55	40

Membership in Universal Postal Union.

Soldier Giving Gourd to Woman — A75

Edward Chivambo Mondlane A76

Designs: 3e, Frelimo soldiers. 7.50e, Mozambique children in school.

1979, Feb. 3 *Perf. 11½x11, 11x11½*

No.	Design	Value	Color	Unused	Used
614	A75	1e	multi	15	15
615	A75	3e	multi	20	15
616	A75	7.50e	multi	28	15
617	A76	12.50e	multi	55	20
	Set value				55

10th anniversary of death of Dr. Edward Chivambo Mondlane (1920-1969), educator, founder of Frelimo Party.

Shaded Silver Cat — A77

Cats: 1.50e, Manx. 2.50e, English blue. 3e, Turkish. 12.50e, Long-haired Mid-East tabby. 20e, African wild cat.

1979, Mar. 27 Litho. *Perf. 11*

No.	Design	Value	Color	Unused	Used
618	A77	50c	multi	15	15
619	A77	1.50e	multi	15	15
620	A77	2.50e	multi	15	15
621	A77	3e	multi	18	15
622	A77	12.50e	multi	50	20
623	A77	20e	multi	70	28
	Nos. 618-623 (6)			1.83	
	Set value				85

Wrestling and Moscow '80 Emblem — A78

Sport and Moscow '80 Emblem: 2e, Running. 3e, Equestrian. 5e, Canoeing. 10e, High jump. 15e, Archery.

1979, Apr. 24 Litho. *Perf. 11*

624 A78 1e gray grn & blk 15 15
625 A78 2e brt bl & blk 15 15
626 A78 3e lt brn & blk 15 15
627 A78 5e multi 18 15
628 A78 10e grn & blk 30 15
629 A78 15e lil rose & blk 50 18
Nos. 624-629 (6) 1.43
Set value 58

Souvenir Sheet

Imperf

630 A78 30e rose & dk brn 1.75 1.75

22nd Olympic Games, Moscow, July 10-Aug. 3, 1980. No. 630 contains one 47x37mm stamp.

Garden and IYC Emblem A79

Children's Drawings and IYC Emblem: 1.50e, Dancers. 3e, City. 5e, Farmers. 7.50e, Village. 12.50e, Automobiles, train and flowers.

1979, June 1 Litho. *Perf. 11*

631 A79 50c multi 15 15
632 A79 1.50e multi 15 15
633 A79 3e multi 15 15
634 A79 5e multi 15 15
635 A79 7.50e multi 20 15
636 A79 12.50e multi 40 15
Set value 1.00 55

International Year of the Child.

Flight from Colonialism — A80

Designs: 2e, Founding of FRELIMO and Pres. Eduardo Chivambo Mondlane. 3e, Advance of armed strruggle and death of Mondlane. 7.50e, Final fight for liberation. 15e, Proclamation of victory, Pres. Samora Moises Machel, flag and torch. Designs after mural in Heroes' Square, Maputo. 30e, Building up the country. Nos. 637-641 printed se-tenant.

1979, June 25

637 A80 50c multi 15 15
638 A80 2e multi 15 15
639 A80 3e multi 15 15
640 A80 7.50e multi 20 15
641 A80 15e multi 50 20
Nos. 637-641 (5) 1.15
Set value 48

Souvenir Sheet

1979 *Imperf.*

641A A80 30e multi 3.25 3.25

4th anniversary of independence. No. 641A contains one stamp with simulated perforations.

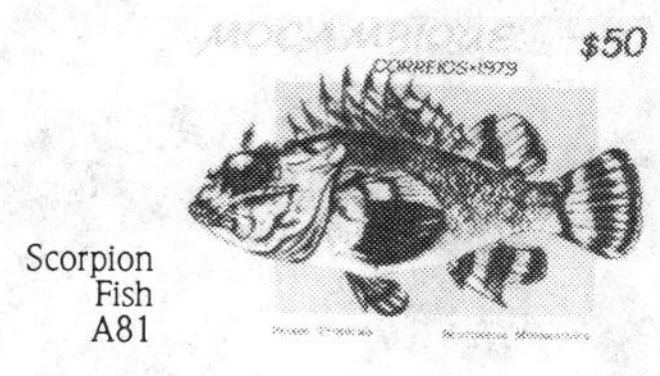

Scorpion Fish A81

Tropical Fish: 1.50e, King fish. 2.50e, Gobius inhaca. 3e, Acanthurus lineatus. 10e, Gobuchthys lemayi. 12.50e, Variola louti.

1979, Aug. 7 Litho. *Perf. 11*

642 A81 50c multi 15 15
643 A81 1.50e multi 15 15
644 A81 2.50e multi 18 15
645 A81 3e multi 20 15
646 A81 10e multi 50 15
647 A81 12.50e multi 60 20
Nos. 642-647 (6) 1.78
Set value 65

Quartz A82

Mozambique Minerals: 1.50e, Beryl. 2.50e, Magnetite. 5e, Tourmaline. 10e, Euxenite. 20e, Fluorite.

1979, Sept. 10

648 A82 1e multi 15 15
649 A82 1.50e multi 15 15
650 A82 2.50e multi 18 15
651 A82 5e multi 20 15
652 A82 10e multi 35 15
653 A82 20e multi 70 35
Nos. 648-653 (6) 1.73
Set value 82

Citizens Gathering Arms A83

1979, Sept. 25

654 A83 5e multi 28 15

15th anniversary of independence.

Locomotive — A85

Designs: Historic Locomotives.

1979, Nov. 11 Litho. *Perf. 11*

656 A85 50c multi 15 15
657 A85 1.50e multi 15 15
658 A85 3e multi 15 15
659 A85 7.50e multi 24 15
660 A85 12.50e multi 35 18
661 A85 15e multi 50 20
Nos. 656-661 (6) 1.54
Set value 72

Dalmatian — A86

Perf. 11½x11, 11x11½

1979, Dec. 17 Litho.

662 A86 50c Basenji, vert. 15 15
663 A86 1.50e shown 15 15
664 A86 3e Boxer 15 15
665 A86 7.50e Blue gasconha braco 25 15
666 A86 12.50e Cocker spaniel 35 15
667 A86 15e Pointer 50 18
Nos. 662-667 (6) 1.55
Set value 60

Nireus Lyaeus A87

Butterflies: 1.50e, Amauris ochlea. 2.50e, Pinacopterix eriphia. 5e, Junonia hierta cebrene. 10e, Nephronia argia. 20e, Catacroptera cloanthe.

1979, Dec. 21

668 A87 1e multi 15 15
669 A87 1.50e multi 15 15
670 A87 2.50e multi 15 15
671 A87 5e multi 20 15
672 A87 10e multi 45 24
673 A87 20e multi 1.00 50
Nos. 668-673 (6) 2.10
Set value 1.00

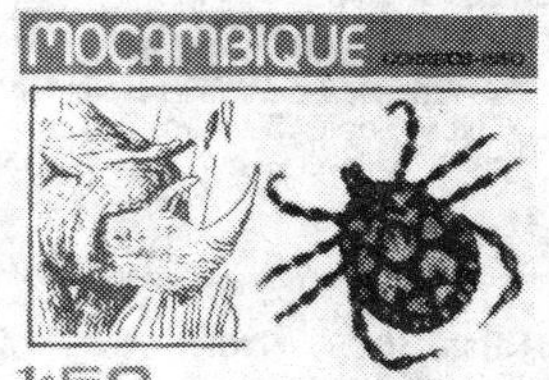

Dermacentor Rhinocerinus, Rhinoceros — A88

Ticks and Animals: 50c, Dermacentor circumguttatus cunhasilvai, elephant. 2.50e, Green tick, giraffe. 3e, Red tick, antelope. 5e, Amblyomma theilerae, cattle. 7.50e, Buffalo tick, buffalo.

1980, Jan. 29 Litho. *Perf. 11½x11*

674 A88 50c multi 15 15
675 A88 1.50e multi 15 15
676 A88 2.50e multi 15 15
677 A88 3e multi 15 15
678 A88 5e multi 18 15
679 A88 7.50e multi 24 15
Set value 85 58

Ford Hercules, 1950 A89

Public Transportation: 1.50e, Scania Marcopolo, 1978. 3e, Bussing Nag, 1936. 5e, Articulated Ikarus, 1978. 7.50e, Ford taxi, 1929. 12.50e, Fiat 131 taxi, 1978.

1980, Feb. 29 Litho. *Perf. 11*

680 A89 50c multi 15 15
681 A89 1.50e multi 15 15
682 A89 3e multi 15 15
683 A89 5e multi 20 15
684 A89 7.50e multi 35 15
685 A89 12.50e multi 50 15
Nos. 680-685 (6) 1.50
Set value 58

Marx, Engels, and Lenin A90

1980, May 1 Litho. *Perf. 11*

686 A90 10e multi 28 15

Workers' Day.

"Heads," by Malangatana, London 1980 Emblem — A91

Paintings by Mozambique Artists: 1.50e, Crowded Market, by Moises Simbine. 3e, Heads with Helmets, by Malangatana. 5e, Women with Goods, by Machiana. 7.50e, Crowd with Masks, by Malangatana. 12.50e, Man and Woman with Spear, by Mankeu.

1980, May 6

687 A91 50c multi 15 15
688 A91 1.50e multi 15 15
689 A91 3e multi 15 15
690 A91 5e multi 18 15
691 A91 7.50e multi 28 15
692 A91 12.50e multi 50 15
Nos. 687-692 (6) 1.41
Set value 58

London 1980 International Stamp Exhibition, May 6-14.

World Telecommunications Day — A92

1980, May 17 Litho. *Perf. 12*

693 A92 15e multi 50 28

Mueda Massacre, 20th Anniv. — A93

People with Weapons and Flag — A94

1980, June 16 Litho. *Perf. 11*

694 A93 15e multi 50 28

1980, June 25

695 A94 1e Development projects, 1975 15 15
696 A94 2e shown 15 15
697 A94 3e Arms, flags, 1977 15 15
698 A94 4e Raised fists, 1978 20 15
699 A94 5e Hand holding grain, flags, 1979 24 15
700 A94 10e Year banners, 1980 38 15
Nos. 695-700 (6) 1.27
Set value 60

Souvenir Sheet

Litho. ***Imperf.***

700A	A94	30e	Soldiers	3.00	

5th anniv. of independence. No. 700A contains one stamp with simulated perforations.

Gymnast, Moscow '80 Emblem A95

1980, July 19

701	A95	50c	shown	15	15
702	A95	1.50e	Soccer	15	15
703	A95	2.50e	Running	15	15
704	A95	3e	Volleyball	15	15
705	A95	10e	Bicycling	40	18
706	A95	12.50e	Boxing	50	28
			Set value	1.25	80

22nd Summer Olympic Games, Moscow, July 19-Aug. 3.

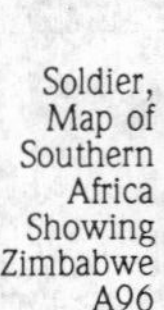

Soldier, Map of Southern Africa Showing Zimbabwe A96

1980, Apr. 18

707	A96	10e	multi	28	15

Establishment of independent Zimbabwe, Apr. 18.

Narina Trogon — A97

1980, July 30 **Litho.** ***Perf. 11***

708	A97	1m	shown	15	15
709	A97	1.50m	Crowned crane	15	15
710	A97	2.50m	Red-necked francolin	15	15
711	A97	5m	Ostrich	18	15
712	A97	7.50m	Spur-winged goose	30	15
713	A97	12.50m	Fish eagle	50	24
			Set value	1.20	75

First Census, Aug. 1-15 A98

1980, Aug. 12 ***Perf. 11***

714	A98	3.5m	multi	15	15

Brush Fire Control Campaign A99

1980, Sept. 7

715	A99	3.5m	multi	15	15

Harpa Major A100

1980, Dec. 12 **Litho.** ***Perf. 11***

716	A100	1m	*shown*	15	15
717	A100	1.50m	*Lambis chiragra*	15	15
718	A100	2.50m	*Murex pecten*	15	15
719	A100	5m	*Architectonia perspectiva*	15	15
720	A100	7.50m	*Murex ramosus*	28	15
721	A100	12.50m	*Strombus aurisdinae*	50	24
			Set value	1.12	68

Pres. Machel and Symbols of Industry and Transportation — A101

Decade of Development, 1981-1990 (Pres. Machel and): 7.50m, Soldiers. 12.50m, Symbols of education.

1981, Jan. 1 **Litho.** ***Perf. 11x11½***

722	A101	3.50m	red & bl	15	15
723	A101	7.50m	grn & red brn	30	15
724	A101	12.50m	dk bl & lil rose	48	15

Bilbao Soccer Stadium, Soccer Player — A102

Designs: Soccer players and various stadiums.

1981, Jan. 30 **Litho.** ***Perf. 11***

725	A102	1m	multi	15	15
726	A102	1.50m	multi	15	15
727	A102	2.50m	multi	15	15
728	A102	5m	multi	15	15
729	A102	7.50m	multi	28	15
730	A102	12.50m	multi	50	20
c.			Souvenir sheet of 6	1.25	1.25
			Set value	1.12	65

Souvenir Sheets

Imperf

730A	A102	20m	multi	85	85
730B	A102	20m	multi	85	85

ESPANA '82 World Cup Soccer Championship. No. 730c contains Nos. 725-730 with simulated perforations. Sizes: No. 730A, 105x85mm; 730B, 141x111mm.

Giraffe — A103

1981, Mar. 3 ***Perf. 11***

731	A103	50c	shown	15	15
732	A103	1.50m	Tsessebe	15	15
733	A103	2.50m	Aardvark	15	15
734	A103	3m	African python	15	15
735	A103	5m	Loggerhead turtle	18	15
736	A103	10m	Marabou	40	15
737	A103	12.50m	Saddlebill stork	50	20
738	A103	15m	Kori bustard	60	28
			Nos. 731-738 (8)	2.28	
			Set value		1.12

Pankwe A104

1981, Apr. 8 **Litho.** ***Perf. 11***

739	A104	50c	Chitende, vert.	15	15
740	A104	2m	shown	15	15
741	A104	2.50m	Kanyembe, vert.	15	15
742	A104	7m	Nyanga	28	28
743	A104	10m	Likuti and m'petheni	40	40
			Set value	90	90

International Year of the Disabled — A105

1981, Apr. 18

744	A105	5m	multi	20	15

African Buffalo and Helicopter, Exhibition Emblem — A106

1981, June 14 ***Perf. 11***

745	A106	2m	shown	15	15
746	A106	5m	Hunters, blue kids	15	15
747	A106	6m	Hunter, impala	18	15
748	A106	7.5m	Hunters shooting	30	15
749	A106	12.5m	Elephants	50	15
750	A106	20m	Trap	80	30
a.			Souv. sheet of 6, #745-750, imperf.	2.50	2.50
			Nos. 745-750 (6)	2.08	
			Set value		80

World Hunting Exhibition, Plovdiv, Bulgaria.

50-centavo Coin, Obverse and Reverse A107

Sunflower A108

First Anniversary of New Currency (Coins on stamps of matching denomination).

1981, June 16

751	A107	50c	multi	15	15
752	A107	1m	multi	15	15
753	A107	2.50m	multi	15	15
754	A107	5m	multi	20	15
755	A107	10m	multi	40	20
756	A107	20m	multi	80	28
a.			Souv. sheet of 6, #751-756, imperf.	1.75	1.75
			Set value	1.55	75

1981, July 24 **Litho.** ***Perf. 14½***

757	A108	50c	shown	15	15
758	A108	1m	Cotton	15	15
759	A108	1.50m	Sisal	15	15
760	A108	2.50m	Cashews	15	15
761	A108	3.50m	Tea leaves	15	15
762	A108	4.50m	Sugar cane	20	15
763	A108	10m	Castor-oil plant	40	15
764	A108	12.50m	Coconut	50	18
765	A108	15m	Tobacco leaves	60	20
766	A108	25m	Rice	1.00	40
767	A108	40m	Corn	1.65	60
768	A108	60m	Peanut	2.50	85
			Nos. 757-768 (12)	7.60	
			Set value		2.75

For surcharge see No. 1185.

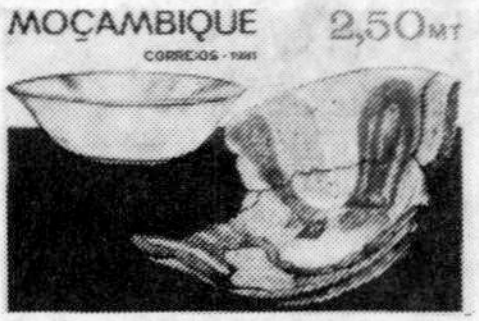

9th Cent. Persian Bowl, Chibuene Excavation Site — A109

1981, Aug. 30 ***Perf. 11***

769	A109	1m	Manyikeni Museum	15	15
770	A109	1.50m	Hand ax, Massingir Dam	15	15
771	A109	2.50m	shown	15	15
772	A109	7.50m	Pot, Chibuene, 9th cent.	30	15
773	A109	12.50m	Gold beads, Manyikeni	50	20
774	A109	20m	Iron, Manyikeni, 15th cent.	80	30
			Nos. 769-774 (6)	2.05	
			Set value		80

Sculptures — A110

1981, Sept. 25 **Litho.** ***Perf. 11***

775	A110	50c	Mapiko mask	15	15
776	A110	1m	Suffering woman	15	15
777	A110	2.50m	Mother and child	15	15
778	A110	3.50m	Man making fire	20	15
779	A110	5m	Chietane	50	28
780	A110	12.50m	Chietane, diff.	50	50
			Set value	1.40	1.00

World Food Day A111

1981, Oct. 16 **Litho.** ***Perf. 11***

781	A111	10m	multi	40	15

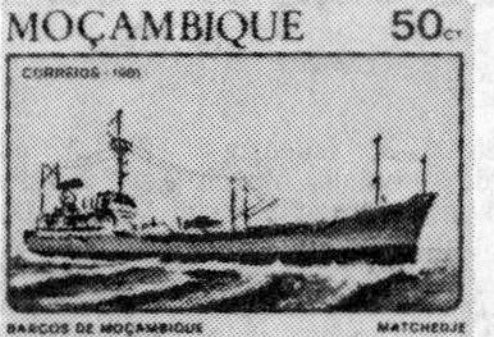

Ocean Tanker Matchedje — A112

1981, Nov. 22 **Litho.** ***Perf. 11***

782	A112	50c	shown	15	15
783	A112	1.50m	Tugboat Macuti	15	15
784	A112	3m	Prawn trawler Vega 7	15	15
785	A112	5m	Freighter Linde	20	15
786	A112	7.50m	Ocean freighter Pemba	30	20
787	A112	12.50m	Dredger Rovuma	50	25
			Set value	1.22	75

Chinaman Crab
A113

1981, Dec. 6

788 A113 50c shown 15 15
789 A113 1.50m Scylla serrata 15 15
790 A113 3m White prawn 15 15
791 A113 7.50m Palinurus delagoae 30 15
792 A113 12.50m Mantis shrimp 50 18
793 A113 15m Panulirus ornatus 60 28
Nos. 788-793 (6) 1.85
Set value 80

Hypoxis Multiceps — A114

1981, Dec. 21 **Litho.** ***Perf. 11***

794 A114 1m shown 15 15
795 A114 1.50m Pelargonium luridum 15 15
796 A114 2.50m Caralluma melananthera 15 15
797 A114 7.50m Ansellia gigantea 30 15
798 A114 12.50m Stapelia leendertsiae 50 18
799 A114 25m Adenium multiflorium 1.00 28
Nos. 794-799 (6) 2.25
Set value 75

First Anniv. of Posts and Telecommunications Dept. — A115

1982, Jan. 1 **Litho.** ***Perf. 11***

800 A115 6m Phone, globe 25 15
801 A115 15m Envelope 60 20

Gasoline Conservation
A116

1982, Jan. 25

802 A116 5m Piston 20 15
803 A116 7.50m Car 30 15
804 A116 10m Truck 40 15
Set value 30

Sea Snake
A117

1982, Feb. 27 **Litho.** ***Perf. 11***

805 A117 50c shown 15 15
806 A117 1.50m Mozambique spitting cobra 15 15
807 A117 3m Savanna vine snake 15 15
808 A117 6m Black mamba 25 15
809 A117 15m Boomslang 60 20
810 A117 20m Bitis arietans 80 28
Nos. 805-810 (6) 2.10
Set value 78

TB Bacillus Centenary
A118

1982, Mar. 15 **Litho.** ***Perf. 11***

811 A118 20m multi 80 28

ITU Plenipotentiary Conference, Nairobi, Sept. 28-Nov. 5 — A119

1982, Mar. 31 ***Perf. 13½***

812 A119 20m multi 80 35

1982 World Cup — A120

Designs: Various soccer players.

1982, Apr. 19 **Litho.** ***Perf. 13½***

813 A120 1.5m multi 15 15
814 A120 3.5m multi 15 15
815 A120 7m multi 30 15
816 A120 10m multi 40 15
817 A120 20m multi 80 28
Nos. 813-817 (5) 1.80
Set value 65

Souvenir Sheet

Imperf

818 A120 50m multi 2.00 2.00

Souvenir Sheet

Two Tahitian Women, by Gauguin — A121

1982, June 11 **Litho.** ***Imperf.***

819 A121 35m multi 1.75 1.75

PHILEXFRANCE '82 Intl. Stamp Exhibition, Paris, June 11-21.

Natl. Liberation Front, 20th Anniv. — A122

Vangueria Infausta — A123

1982, June 25 ***Perf. 13***

820 A122 4m Pres. Mondland addressing crowd 16 15
821 A122 8m Guarded fields 35 15
822 A122 12m Procession 50 18
Set value 38

1982, Sept. 13 ***Perf. 11***

Designs: Fruits.

823 A123 1m shown 15 15
824 A123 2m Mimusops caffra 15 15
825 A123 4m Sclerocarya caffra 16 15
826 A123 8m Strychnos spinosa 35 15
827 A123 12m Salacia kraussi 50 18
828 A123 32m Trichilia emetica 1.40 40
Nos. 823-828 (6) 2.71
Set value 90

25th Anniv. of Sputnik 1 Flight
A124

1982, Oct. 4 **Litho.** ***Perf. 11***

829 A124 1m Sputnik, 1957 15 15
830 A124 2m Yuri Gagarin's flight, 1961 15 15
831 A124 4m A. Leonov's spacewalk, 1965 18 15
832 A124 8m Apollo 11, 1969 35 15
833 A124 16m Apollo-Soyuz, 1975 70 24
834 A124 20m Salyut-6, 1978 85 30
a. Min. sheet of 6, #829-834 2.50 2.50
Nos. 829-834 (6) 2.38
Set value 85

People's Vigilance Day — A125

Caique — A126

1982, Oct. 11 ***Perf. 13½***

835 A125 4m multi 18 15

1982, Nov. 29

Traditional boats. 4m, 8m, 12m, 16m horiz.

836 A126 1m shown 15 15
837 A126 2m Machua 15 15
838 A126 4m Calaua 18 15
839 A126 8m Chitatarro 35 15
840 A126 12m Cangaia 50 18
841 A126 16m Chata (flatboat) 70 24
Nos. 836-841 (6) 2.03
Set value 72

Marine Life — A127

1982, Dec. 21 **Litho.** ***Perf. 11***

842 A127 1m Ophiomastix venosa 15 15
843 A127 2m Protoreaster lincki 15 15
844 A127 4m Tropiometra carinata 18 15
845 A127 8m Holothuria scabra 35 18
846 A127 12m Prionocidaris baculosa 50 18
847 A127 16m Colobocentrotus atnatus 70 24
Nos. 842-847 (6) 2.03
Set value 80

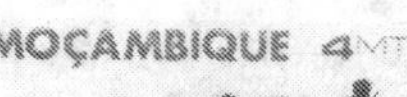

Frelimo Party 4th Congress
A128

1983, Jan. 17

848 A128 4m Map, soldier 18 15
849 A128 8m Voters 35 15
850 A128 16m Farm workers 70 18
Set value 38

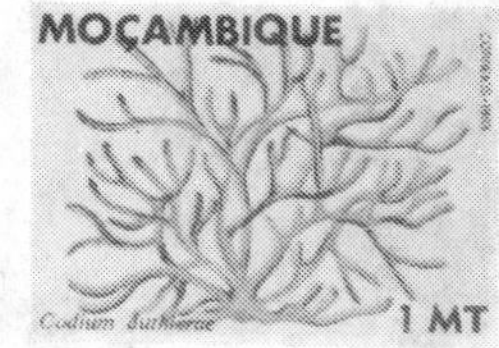

Seaweed
A129

1983, Feb. 28 **Litho.** ***Perf. 11***

851 A129 1m Codium duthierae 15 15
852 A129 2m Halimeda cuncata 15 15
853 A129 4m Dictyota liturata 18 15
854 A129 8m Encorachne binghamiae 35 15
855 A129 12m Laurencia flexuosa 50 18
856 A129 20m Acrosorium sp. 85 35
Nos. 851-856 (6) 2.18
Set value 85

1984 Olympic Games, Los Angeles — A130

1983, Mar. 31 **Litho.** ***Perf. 11***

857 A130 1m Diving 15 15
858 A130 2m Boxing 15 15
859 A130 4m Basketball 18 15
860 A130 8m Handball 35 15
861 A130 12m Volleyball 50 18
862 A130 16m Running 70 24
863 A130 20m Sailing 85 35
Nos. 857-863 (7) 2.88
Set value 1.12

Souvenir Sheet

Imperf

864 A130 50m Discus 2.00 2.00

Steam Locomotives — A131

1983, Apr. 29 **Litho.** ***Perf. 11***

865 A131 1m 1912 15 15
866 A131 2m 1947 15 15
867 A131 4m 1923 18 15
868 A131 8m 1924 35 18
869 A131 16m 1924, diff. 70 28
870 A131 32m 1950 1.40 40
Nos. 865-870 (6) 2.93
Set value 1.05

The Scott Catalogue value is a retail price, what you could expect to pay for the stamp in a grade of Fine-Very Fine. The value listed is a reference which reflects recent actual dealer selling price.

20th Anniv. of Org. of African Unity A132

1983, May 25 **Litho.** ***Perf. 11***

871 A132 4m multi 18 15

Mammals — A133

1983, May 30

872 A133 1m Petrodromus tetradactylus 15 15
873 A133 2m Rhabdomys pumilio 15 15
874 A133 4m Paraxerus vincenti 18 15
875 A133 8m Cryptomys hottentotus 35 15
876 A133 12m Pronolagus crassicaudatus 50 18
877 A133 16m Eidolon helvum 70 28
Nos. 872-877 (6) 2.03
Set value 78

Souvenir Sheet

Marimba Players — A134

1983, July 29 **Litho.** ***Perf. 11***

878 A134 30m multi 1.50 1.50

BRASILIANA '83 Intl. Stamp Show, Rio de Janeiro, July 29-Aug. 7.

World Communications Year — A135

1983, Aug. 26 **Litho.** ***Perf. 11***

879 A135 8m multi 35 15

Fishing Techniques A136

1983, Oct. 29 **Litho.** ***Perf. 11***

880 A136 50c Line fishing 15 15
881 A136 2m Chifonho 15 15
882 A136 4m Momba 15 15
883 A136 8m Gamboa 28 15
884 A136 16m Mono 55 18
885 A136 20m Lema 70 28
Nos. 880-885 (6) 1.98
Set value 75

World Communications Year, Stamp Day — A137

1983, Dec. 21 **Litho.**

886 A137 50c Horn 15 15
887 A137 1m Drum 15 15
888 A137 4m Native mail carriers 15 15
889 A137 8m Boat 28 15
890 A137 16m Truck 55 20
891 A137 20m Train 70 28
Nos. 886-891 (6) 1.98
Set value 75

2nd Anniv. of Mozambique Red Cross (July 10) — A138

1983, Oct. 29 **Litho.** ***Perf. 11***

892 A138 4m Flood relief 15 15
893 A138 8m Rescue truck 28 15
894 A138 16m First aid 55 20
895 A138 32m Field first aid 1.10 40
Set value 75

Olympic Games 1984, Los Angeles — A139

1984, Jan. 2 **Litho.** ***Perf. 11***

896 A139 50c Swimming 15 15
897 A139 4m Soccer 15 15
898 A139 8m Hurdles 28 20
899 A139 16m Basketball 55 25
900 A139 32m Handball 1.10 30
901 A139 60m Boxing 2.00 50
Nos. 896-901 (6) 4.23 1.55

Indigenous Trees — A140

1984, Mar. 30 **Litho.** ***Perf. 11***

902 A140 50c Trichilia emetica 15 15
903 A140 2m Brachystegia spiciformis 15 15
904 A140 4m Androstachys johnsonii 15 15
905 A140 8m Pterocarpus angolensis 16 15
906 A140 16m Milletia stuhlmannii 32 20
907 A140 50m Dalbergia melanoxylon 1.00 40
Set value 1.65 85

Nkomati Accord, Mar. 16 — A141

1984, Mar. 16

908 A141 4m Dove 15 15

Natl. Arms A142

909 A142 4m shown 15 15
910 A142 8m Natl. flag 16 15
Set value 24 15

Traditional Dances — A143

1984, May 9

911 A143 4m Makway 15 15
912 A143 8m Mapiko 16 15
913 A143 16m Wadjaba 32 15
Set value 30

LUBRAPEX '84, May 9-17.

Museums and Artifacts A144

Designs: 50c, Nampula Museum, African carrying water jar, wooden statue. 4m, Museum of Natural History, preserved bird. 8m, Revolution Museum, guerrilla fighter statue. 16m, Colonial Occupation Museum, fort and cannon. 20m, Numismatic Museum, coins. 30m, Palace of St. Paul, char, 19th cent.

1984, June 25

914 A144 50c multi 15 15
915 A144 4m multi 15 15
916 A144 8m multi 16 15
917 A144 16m multi 32 20
918 A144 20m multi 40 25
919 A144 30m multi 60 30
Nos. 914-919 (6) 1.78
Set value 1.00

Freshwater Fish A145

1984, Aug. 24

920 A145 50c Alestes imberi 15 15
921 A145 4m Labeo congoro 15 15
922 A145 12m Syndontis zambezensis 40 20
923 A145 16m Noto branchius zachovii 55 30
924 A145 40m Barbus paludinosus 1.40 40
925 A145 60m Barilius zambezensis 2.00 60
Nos. 920-925 (6) 4.65 1.80

Traditional Weapons — A146

1984, Sept. 25

926 A146 50c Knife, cudgel *18* *15*
927 A146 4m Axes *25* *15*
928 A146 8m Shield, assagai *45* *20*
929 A146 16m Bow and arrow *75* *30*
930 A146 32m Muzzleloader *2.00* *40*
931 A146 50m Assagai, arrow *3.00* *50*
Nos. 926-931 (6) *6.63* *1.70*

Natl. Revolution, 20th anniv.

Natl. Trade Unions, 1st Anniv. — A147

1984, Oct. 13 ***Perf. 13½***

932 A147 4m Workers, emblem 15 15

Stamp Day — A149

Cancellations on altered stamps and stationery: 4m, Barue cancel on 1885 20r postal card. 8m, Zumbo cancel on design similar to No. 52. 12m, Mozambique Co. cancel on design similar to Mozambique Company Type API. 16m, Macequece cancel on design similar to Mozambique Company No. 190.

1984, Dec. 21 ***Perf. 11½x11***

936 A149 4m multi 15 15
937 A149 8m multi 28 15
938 A149 12m multi 40 20
939 A149 16m multi 55 25

African Development Bank, 20th Anniv. — A150

1984, Sept. 16 **Photo.** ***Perf. 11½x11***

940 A150 4m multi 15 15

Apiculture — A151

1985, Feb. 3

941	A151	4m	Beekeeper	15	15
942	A151	8m	Bee gathering pollen	15	15
943	A151	16m	Entering nest	22	15
944	A151	20m	Building honeycomb	28	20
			Set value		50

OLYMPHILEX '85, Lausanne — A152

1985, Mar. 18 *Perf. 11*

945	A152	16m	Shot putter	22	15

World Meteorology Day — A153

1985, Mar. 23 **Litho.** *Perf. 11*

946	A153	4m	multi	15	15

Southern African Development Coordination Conference, 5th Anniv. — A154

1985, Apr. 1

947	A154	4m	Map	15	15
948	A154	8m	Map, transmission tower	15	15
949	A154	16m	Industry	22	15
950	A154	32m	Flags	45	20
			Set value		50

Independence, 10th Anniv. — A155

Colonial resistance battles: 1m, Mujenga, 1896. 4m, Mungari, 1917. 8m, Massangano, 1868. 16m, Marracuene, 1895, and Gungunhana (c. 1840-1906), resistance leader.

1985, June 25 **Litho.** *Perf. 11*

951	A155	1m	multi	15	15
952	A155	4m	multi	15	15
953	A155	8m	multi	15	15
954	A155	16m	multi	22	15
			Set value	45	35

UN, 40th Anniv. — A156

1985, June 26

955	A156	16m	multi	*1.10*	*15*

Traditional Games A157

1985, Aug. 28 **Litho.** *Perf. 11*

956	A157	50c	Mathacuzana	15	15
957	A157	4m	Mudzobo	18	18
958	A157	8m	Muravarava	35	35
959	A157	16m	N'Tshuwa	70	70

Frogs and Toads A158

1985, Oct. 25 **Litho.** *Perf. 11*

960	A158	50c	Rana angolensis	15	15
961	A158	1m	Hyperolius pictus	15	15
962	A158	4m	Ptychadena porosissima	15	15
963	A158	8m	Afrixalus formasinii	15	15
964	A158	16m	Bufo regularis	22	15
965	A158	32m	Hyperolius marmoratus	45	25
			Set value	90	62

Medicinal Plants — A159

1985, Nov. 28 **Litho.** *Perf. 11*

966	A159	50c	Aloe ferox	15	15
967	A159	1m	Boophone disticha	15	15
968	A159	3.50m	Gloriosa superba	15	15
969	A159	4m	Cotyledon orbiculata	15	15
970	A159	8m	Homeria breyniana	15	15
970A	A159	50m	Haemanthus coccineus	70	25
			Set value	1.00	54

Stamp Day A160

Stamps: 1m, Mozambique Company No. 126. 4m, Nyassa Type A6. 8m, Mozambique Company No. 110. 16m, Nyassa No. J2.

1985, Dec. 21

971	A160	1m	multi	15	15
972	A160	4m	multi	15	15
973	A160	8m	multi	15	15
974	A160	16m	multi	22	15
			Set value	45	35

Halley's Comet — A161

Comet and: 4m, Space probe. 8m, Trajectory diagram. 16m, Newton's telescope, observatory, probe. 30m, Earth.

1986, Jan. 2

975	A161	4m	multi	15	15
976	A161	8m	multi	15	15
977	A161	16m	multi	22	15
978	A161	30m	multi	45	25
			Set value		55

1986 World Cup Soccer Championships, Mexico — A162

Players.

1986, Feb. 28 **Litho.** *Perf. 11½x11*

979	A162	3m	Vicente	15	15
980	A162	4m	Coluna	15	15
981	A162	8m	Costa Pereira	15	15
982	A162	12m	Hilario	16	15
983	A162	16m	Matateu	22	20
984	A162	50m	Eusebio	70	40
			Set value	1.30	95

Intl. Peace Year — A163

1986, Mar. 18 *Perf. 11*

985	A163	16m	multi	22	15

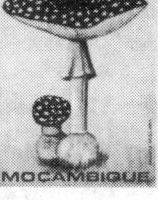

Mushrooms A164

1986, Apr. 8

986	A164	4m	Amanita muscaria	15	15
987	A164	8m	Lactarius deliciosus	15	15
988	A164	16m	Amanita phaloides	22	15
989	A164	30m	Tricholoma nudum	40	20
			Set value	78	50

Souvenir Sheet

Statue of Liberty, Cent. — A165

1986, May 22 *Imperf.*

990	A165	100m	multi	1.40	1.40

AMERIPEX '86. No. 990 has simulated perforations.

Traditional Women's Hair Styles — A166

1986, June **Litho.** *Perf. 11½x11*

991	A166	1m	Tanzanian	15	15
992	A166	4m	Miriam	15	15
993	A166	8m	Estrelinhas	15	15
994	A166	16m	Toto	22	20
			Set value	45	42

Marine Mammals A167

1986, Aug. *Perf. 11*

995	A167	1m	Dugongo dugon	15	15
996	A167	8m	Delphinus delphis	15	15
997	A167	16m	Neobalena marginata	22	15
998	A167	50m	Balaenoptera physalus	70	25
			Set value		50

Continuing Youth Education Organization, 1st Anniv. — A168

1986, Sept. 16 **Litho.** *Perf. 11½x11*

999	A168	4m	multi	15	15

Natl. Savings Campaign — A169

Bank notes, front and back.

1986, Oct. 22 Litho. *Perf. 11½x11*

1000	A169	4m	50m note	15	15
1001	A169	8m	100m note	15	15
1002	A169	16m	500m note	22	15
1003	A169	30m	1000m note	40	20
			Set value	80	50

Stamp Day A170

Post offices.

1986, Dec. 21 Litho. *Perf. 11*

1004	A170	3m	Quelimane	15	15
1005	A170	4m	Maputo	15	15
1006	A170	8m	Beira	15	15
1007	A170	16m	Nampula	22	20
			Set value	45	50

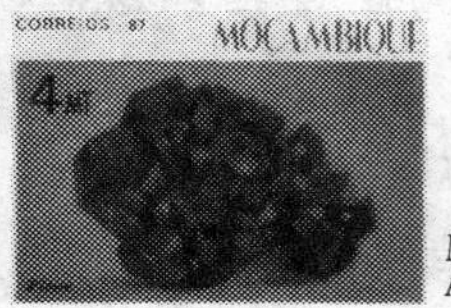

Minerals A171

1987, Jan. 2 *Perf. 11x11½*

1008	A171	4m	Pyrite	15	15
1009	A171	8m	Emerald	15	15
1010	A171	12m	Agate	16	15
1011	A171	16m	Malachite	22	20
1012	A171	30m	Garnet	40	25
1013	A171	50m	Amethyst	70	40
			Nos. 1008-1013 (6)	1.78	1.30

Frelimo Party, 10th Anniv. — A172

1987, Feb. 3 *Perf. 11*

1014 A172 4m multi 15 15

Pequenos Libombos Dam — A173

1987, Feb. 17 *Perf. 11½x11*

1015 A173 16m multi 22 15

World Health Day — A174

1987, Apr. 7 Litho. *Perf. 11x11½*

1016 A174 50m multi 70 25

Birds — A175

1987, Apr. 27 Litho. *Perf. 11½x11*

1017	A175	3m	Granatina granatina	15	15
1018	A175	4m	Halcyon senegalensis	15	15
1019	A175	8m	Mellittophagus bullockoides	15	15
1020	A175	12m	Perinestes minor	16	20
1021	A175	16m	Coracias naevia mosambica	22	25
1022	A175	30m	Cimmyris neergardi	40	30
			Set value	1.00	1.00

Souvenir Sheet

CAPEX '87, Toronto, June 13-21 — A176

1987, June *Imperf.*

1023 A176 200m multi 2.00 2.00

No. 1023 contains one stamp having simulated perforations.

1988 Summer Olympics, Seoul — A177

1987, May Litho. *Perf. 11½x11*

1024	A177	12.50m	Soccer players and ball	15	15
1025	A177	25m	Runner's legs	25	20
1026	A177	50m	Volleyball	50	30
1027	A177	75m	Chess	75	40
1028	A177	100m	Basketball	1.00	50
1029	A177	200m	Swimming	2.00	75
			Nos. 1024-1029 (6)	4.65	2.30

Tapestries A178

1987, Aug. *Perf. 11*

1030	A178	20m	Incomplete pattern on loom	15	15
1031	A178	40m	Diamond-shaped pattern	16	15
1032	A178	80m	Landscape pattern	32	25
1033	A178	200m	Oriental pattern	80	40

Maputo City A179

Early Portuguese map of Lourenco Marques.

1987, Nov. 10 Litho. *Perf. 11*

1034 A179 20m multi 15 15

No. 762 Surcharged in Silver and Dark Red **4,00 MT**

1987 Litho. *Perf. 14½*

1034A A108 4m on 4.50m multi 25 25

1988 Summer Olympics, Seoul — A180

Flowering Plants — A181

1988, Feb. 10 Litho. *Perf. 11*

1035	A180	10m	Javelin	15	15
1036	A180	20m	Baseball	28	15
1037	A180	40m	Boxing	58	25
1038	A180	80m	Field hockey	1.15	40
1039	A180	100m	Gymnastic rings	1.40	50
1040	A180	400m	Cycling	5.65	1.90
			Nos. 1035-1040 (6)	9.21	3.35

Nos. 1036-1040 horiz.

1988, Mar. 18 *Perf. 11½x11*

1041	A181	10m	Heamanthus nelsonii	15	15
1042	A181	20m	Crinum polyphyllum	28	15
1043	A181	40m	Boophane disticha	58	25
1044	A181	80m	Cyrtanthus contractus	1.15	40
1045	A181	100m	Nerine angustifolia	1.40	50
1046	A181	400m	Cyrtanthus galpinnii	5.65	1.90
			Nos. 1041-1046 (6)	9.21	3.35

World Health Organization, 40th Anniv. — A182

1988, Apr. 7

1047 A182 20m multi 28 28

Anti-smoking campaign.

Wickerwork — A183

1988, June 16 Litho. *Perf. 11*

1048	A183	20m	Mat	16	15
1049	A183	25m	Lidded container	20	15
1050	A183	80m	Market basket	62	20
1051	A183	100m	Fan	78	25
1052	A183	400m	Flat basket	3.15	1.00
1053	A183	500m	Funnel basket	3.90	1.25
			Nos. 1048-1053 (6)	8.81	3.00

Souvenir Sheet

FINLANDIA '88 — A184

1988, June 12 Litho. *Imperf.*

1054 A184 500m multi 2.50 1.00

Stamp in No. 1054 has simulated perfs.

Souvenir Sheet

State Visit of Pope John Paul II, Sept. 16-19 — A185

1988 Litho. *Perf. 13½*

1055 A185 500m multi 1.50 1.50

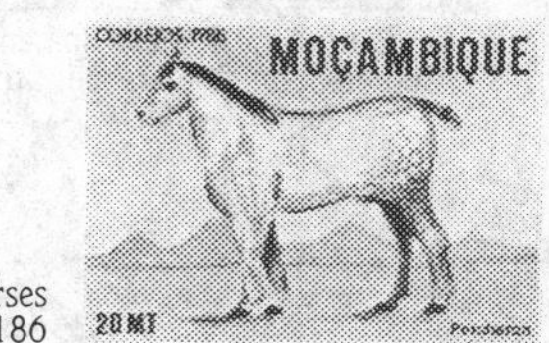

Horses A186

1988, Sept. 20 Litho. *Perf. 11*

1056	A186	20m	Percheron	20	15
1057	A186	40m	Arab	38	15
1058	A186	80m	Purebred	75	25
1059	A186	100m	Pony	92	30

Pres. Samora Machel (1933-1986) A187

1988, Oct. 19 Litho. *Perf. 11*

1060 A187 20m multi 15 15

Stamp Day — A188

Perf. 11x11½, 11½x11

1988, Dec. 21

1061 A188 20m P.O. trailer 15 15
1062 A188 40m Mailbox, vert. 20 15

Ports A189

1988, Nov. 30 *Perf. 11*

1063 A189 25m Inhambane 15 15
1064 A189 50m Quelimane, vert. 20 15
1065 A189 75m Pemba 30 15
1066 A189 100m Beira 42 15
1067 A189 250m Nacala, vert. 1.05 25
1068 A189 500m Maputo 2.05 50
Nos. 1063-1068 (6) 4.17
Set value 1.00

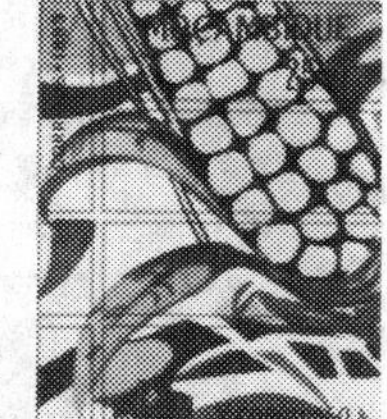
5th Frelimo Party Congress — A190

1989, Jan. 19

1069 Strip of 5 2.40 1.25
a. A190 25m Corn 15 15
b. A190 50m Axe 24 15
c. A190 75m Abstract shapes 35 18
d. A190 100m 2½ Gearwheels 48 24
e. A190 250m ½ Gearwheel 1.20 60

Printed se-tenant in a continuous design.

French Revolution Bicent. A191

Designs: 100m, *Storming of the Bastille,* by Thevenin. 250m, *Liberty Guiding the People,* by Delacroix. 500m, *Declaration of the Rights of Man and the Citizen,* a print by Blanchard.

1989, Feb. 16 *Perf. 11*

1070 A191 100m multi 30 15
1071 A191 250m multi 75 25

Souvenir Sheet

1072 A191 500m multi 1.50 75

Eduardo Chivambo Mondlane (1920-1969), Frelimo Party Founder, 20th Death Anniv. — 192

1989, Feb. 3 **Litho.** *Perf. 11*

1073 A192 25m blk, gold & dark red 15 15

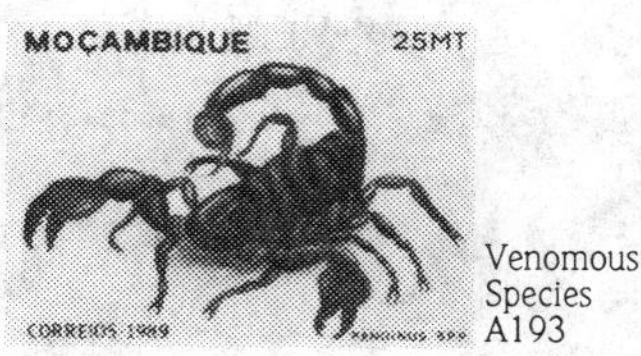

Venomous Species A193

1989, Mar. 23

1074 A193 25m *Pandinus* 15 15
1075 A193 50m *Naja haje* 20 15
1076 A193 75m *Bombus* 30 15
1077 A193 100m *Paraphysa* 42 15
1078 A193 250m *Conus marmoreus* 1.05 25
1079 A193 500m *Pterois volitans* 2.05 50
Nos. 1074-1079 (6) 4.17
Set value 1.00

Coral A194

1989, May 2 **Litho.** *Perf. 11*

1080 A194 25m *Acropora pulchra* 15 15
1081 A194 50m *Eunicella papilosa* 15 15
1082 A194 100m *Dendrophyla migrantus* 28 15
1083 A194 250m *Favia fragum* 68 25
Set value 40

1990 World Cup Soccer Championships, Italy — A195

Athletes executing various plays.

1989, June 22 **Litho.** *Perf. 11½x11*

1084 A195 30m multi 15 15
1085 A195 60m multi 16 15
1086 A195 125m multi 32 15
1087 A195 200m multi 55 18
1088 A195 250m multi 68 22
1089 A195 500m multi 1.35 45
Nos. 1084-1089 (6) 3.21
Set value 1.00

Lighthouses A196

1989, July 24 **Litho.** *Perf. 11*

1090 A196 30m Macuti 15 15
1091 A196 60m Pinda 16 15
1092 A196 125m Cape Delgado 35 15
1093 A196 200m Isle of Goa 55 18
1094 A196 250m Caldeira Point 68 22
1095 A196 500m Vilhena 1.35 45
Nos. 1090-1095 (6) 3.24
Set value 1.00

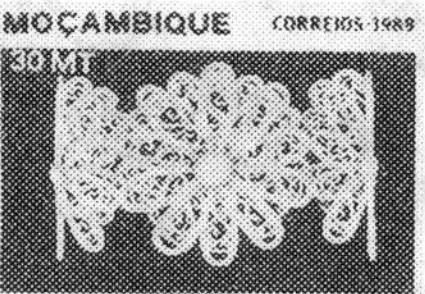

Filigree Workmanship in Silver A197

1989, Aug. 30 **Litho.** *Perf. 11x11½*

1096 A197 30m shown 15 15
1097 A197 60m Flower on band 15 15
1098 A197 125m Necklace 32 15
1099 A197 200m Decorative box 50 15
1100 A197 250m Utensils 62 22
1101 A197 500m Butterfly 1.25 45
Nos. 1096-1101 (6) 2.99
Set value 1.00

Natl. Liberation War, 25th Anniv. A198

1989, Sept. 25

1102 A198 30m multicolored 15 15

Meteorological Instruments — A199

Designs: 30m, Rain gauge. 60m, Weather system on radar. 125m, Instrument shelter. 200m, Computer monitor and keyboard.

1989, Oct. 12 *Perf. 11½x11*

1103 A199 30m multicolored 15 15
1104 A199 60m multicolored 15 15
1105 A199 125m multicolored 32 16
1106 A199 200m multicolored 50 25

Souvenir Sheet

World Stamp Expo '89, Washington, DC — A200

1989, Nov. 17 *Perf. 13½*

1107 A200 500m Washington Monument 1.25 75

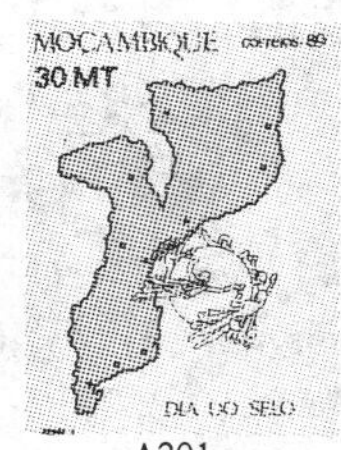

A201 A201a

Stamp Day: Maps and emblems.

1989, Dec. 21 **Litho.** *Perf. 11½x11*

1108 A201 30m UPU emblem 15 15
1109 A201 60m P.O. emblem 16 16
Set value 24 24

1990, Jan. 31 *Perf. 11½x11*

1109A A201a 35m multicolored 15 15

Southern African Development Coordination Conf. (SADCC), 10th anniv.

Textile Designs A202

1990, Feb. 28 **Litho.** *Perf. 11x11½*

1110 A202 42m multi, diff. 15 15
1111 A202 90m multi, diff. 28 16
1112 A202 150m multi, diff. 45 22
1113 A202 200m multi, diff. 60 30
1114 A202 400m multi, diff. 1.20 60
1115 A202 500m multi, diff. 1.50 75
Nos. 1110-1115 (6) 4.18 2.18

Forts — A203

1990, Mar. 20 *Perf. 11x11½*

1116 A203 45m Sena 15 15
1117 A203 90m Santo Antonio 28 16
1118 A203 150m Santo Sebastiao 45 22
1119 A203 200m Santo Caetano 60 30
1120 A203 400m Our Lady of Conceicao 1.20 60
1121 A203 500m Santo Luis 1.50 75
Nos. 1116-1121 (6) 4.18 2.18

Souvenir Sheet

Penny Black, Mozambique No. 1 — A204

1990, May 3 **Litho.** *Perf. 11½x11*

1122 A204 1000m red, blk & bl 2.85 1.50

Penny Black, 150th anniversary. Stamp World London '90.

Bank of Mozambique, 15th Anniv. A205

1990, May 17 **Litho.** *Perf. 11x11½*

1123 A205 100m multicolored 30 16

Natl. Independence, 15th Anniv. — A206

1990, June 25 *Perf. 11*

1124	A206	42.50m	Eduardo Mondlane	15	15
1125	A206	150m	Samora Machel	45	22

Endangered Species A207

1990, Aug. 20 Litho. *Perf. 11x11½*

1126	A207	42.50m	Ceratotherium simum	15	15
1127	A207	100m	Dugong dugong	30	16
1128	A207	150m	Loxodonta africana	45	22
1129	A207	200m	Acinonix jubatus	60	30
1130	A207	400m	Lutra maculicollis	1.20	60
1131	A207	500m	Eretmochelys imbricata	1.45	70
			Nos. 1126-1131 (6)	4.15	2.13

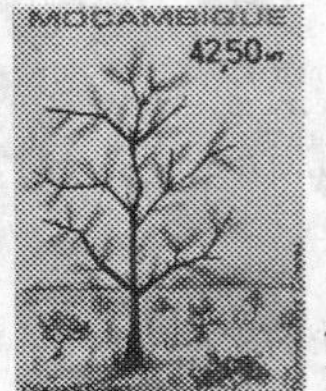

Trees and Plants — A208

1990, Oct. 15 Litho. *Perf. 11½x11*

1132	A208	42.50m	Dichrostachys cinerea	15	15
1133	A208	100m	Queimadas	30	16
1134	A208	150m	Casuariana equisetifolia	45	22
1135	A208	200m	Rhizophora muronata	60	30
1136	A208	400m	Estrato herbaceo	1.20	60
1137	A208	500m	Atzelia cuanzensis	1.45	70
			Nos. 1132-1137 (6)	4.15	2.13

A209

A210

Stamp Day: a, Pick-up at letter box. b, Canceling letters. c, Letter carrier. d, Delivery to recipient.

1990 Litho. *Perf. 11½x11*

1138		Strip of 4	60	40
a.-d.	A209	42.50m any single	15	15

1991, Jan. 2

Post Office Dept., 10th Anniv.: #1140, Telecommunications Dept.

1139	A210	50m	dk bl, red & blk	20	15
1140	A210	50m	grn, blk & brn	20	15
			Set value		20

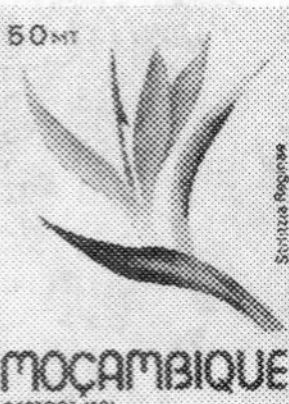

Flowers A211

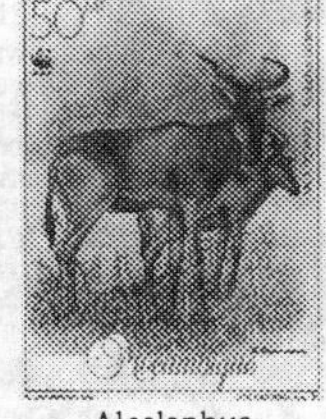

Alcelaphus Lichtensteini A212

1991, Feb. 25 Litho. *Perf. 11½x11*

1141	A211	50m	Strilitzia reginae	20	15
1142	A211	125m	Anthurium andraeanum	50	25
1143	A211	250m	Zantedeschia pentlandii	1.00	50
1144	A211	300m	Canna indica	1.20	60

1991, Mar. 27 *Perf. 14*

1145		Strip of 4	3.60	1.85
a.	A212	50m Two adults	20	15
b.	A212	100m Adult	40	20
c.	A212	250m Adult grazing	1.00	50
d.	A212	500m Nursing calf	2.00	1.00

A213

A214

Fountains of Maputo: 50m, Mpompine. 125m, Chinhambanine. 250m, Sao Pedro-Zaza. 300m, Xipamanine.

1991 Litho. *Perf. 11½x11*

1146	A213	50m	multicolored	15	15
1147	A213	125m	multicolored	28	15
1148	A213	250m	multicolored	55	28
1149	A213	300m	multicolored	65	32
			Set value		80

1991, May 18 Litho. *Perf. 11½x11*

1150	A214	180m	Samale	40	20
1151	A214	250m	Malangatana	55	30
1152	A214	560m	Malangatana, diff.	1.25	60

Paintings by Mozambican artists.

A215

A216

1991, June 25 Litho. *Perf. 11½x11*

1153	A215	10m	Swimming	15	15
1154	A215	50m	Roller hockey	15	15
1155	A215	100m	Tennis	22	15
1156	A215	200m	Table tennis	45	22
1157	A215	500m	Running	1.10	55
1158	A215	1000m	Badminton	2.20	1.10
			Nos. 1153-1158 (6)	4.27	2.32

1992 Summer Olympics, Barcelona.

1991, Oct. 9 Litho. *Perf. 11½x11*

1159	A216	600m	Map of 1890	85	42
1160	A216	800m	Map of 1891	1.15	58

British-Portuguese agreement on Mozambique borders, cent.

Souvenir Sheet

Phila Nippon '91 — A217

1991, Nov. 15 Litho. *Perf. 11½x11*

1161	A217	1500m	Map of Japan	1.40	1.40

Children's Games — A218

Stained Glass Windows — A219

1991, Dec. 21

1162	A218	40m	Jumping rope	15	15
1163	A218	150m	Spinning top	15	15
1164	A218	400m	Marbles	36	18
1165	A218	900m	Hopscotch	82	40
			Set value		68

1992, Jan. 22

Various designs: a, 40m. b, 150m. c, 400m. d, 900m.

1166	A219	Block of 4, #a.-d.	1.36	68

A220 A221

Designs: Plants.

1992, Mar. 23 Litho. *Perf. 11½x11*

1167	A220	300m	Rhisophora mucronata	52	28
1168	A220	600m	Cymodocea ciliata	1.10	52
1169	A220	1000m	Sophora inhambanensis	1.75	90

1992, May 9

Designs: Traditional tools.

1170	A221	100m	Spear, spear-thrower	18	15
1171	A221	300m	Pitch forks	52	25
1172	A221	500m	Hatchet	90	45
1173	A221	1000m	Dagger	1.75	90

Lubrapex '92, Lisbon.

A222

A223

Birds: 150m, Chalcomitra amethystina. 200m, Cercopis senegalensis. 300m, Cossypha natalensis. 400m, Lamprocolius chloropterus. 500m, Malaconotus poliocephalus. 800m, Oriolus auratus.

1992, July 24 Litho. *Perf. 11½x11*

1174	A222	150m	multicolored	28	15
1175	A222	200m	multicolored	35	18
1176	A222	300m	multicolored	52	25
1177	A222	400m	multicolored	68	35
1178	A222	500m	multicolored	85	42
1179	A222	800m	multicolored	1.40	70
			Nos. 1174-1179 (6)	4.08	2.05

1992, Aug. 21

1180	A223	150m	grn, brn & blk	28	15

Eduardo Mondlane University, 30th anniv.

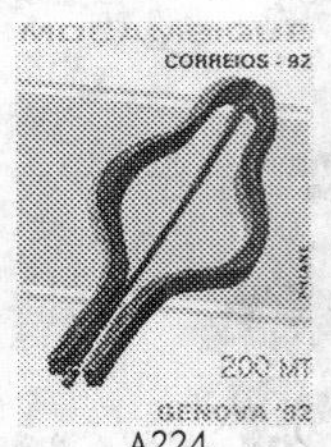

A224

A225

Designs: Traditional musical instruments.

1992, Sept. 18

1181	A224	200m	Phiane	35	18
1182	A224	300m	Xirupe	52	25
1183	A224	500m	Ngulula	85	42
1184	A224	1500m	Malimba	2.50	1.25
a.			Souvenir sheet of 4, #1181-1184, imperf.	4.25	2.10

Genoa '92. No. 1184a has simulated perforations.

No. 757 Surcharged

1992 Litho. *Perf. 14½*

1185	A108	50m	on 50c #757	78	40

1992 *Perf. 11½x11*

1186	A225	450m	multicolored	75	38

Intl. Conference on Nutrition.

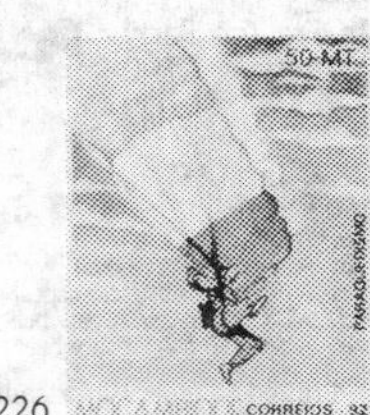

Parachuting — A226

Various parchutists descending from sky.

1992 Litho. *Perf. 11½x11*

1187	A226	50m	multicolored	15	15
1188	A226	400m	multicolored	65	32
1189	A226	500m	multicolored	78	38
1190	A226	1500m	multicolored	2.35	1.15

SEMI-POSTAL STAMPS

"History" Pointing out to "the Republic" Need for Charity SP1

Nurse Leading Wounded Soldiers SP2

Veteran Relating Experiences SP3

Perf. 11½

1920, Dec. 1 Litho. Unwmk.

B1 SP1 ¼c olive 2.75 2.75
B2 SP1 ½c olive blk 2.75 2.75
B3 SP1 1c dp bister 2.75 2.75
B4 SP1 2c lilac brn 2.75 2.75
B5 SP1 3c lilac 2.75 2.75
B6 SP1 4c green 2.75 2.75
B7 SP2 5c grnsh blue 2.75 2.75
B8 SP2 6c light blue 2.75 2.75
B9 SP2 7½c red brown 2.75 2.75
B10 SP2 8c lemon 2.75 2.75
B11 SP2 10c gray lilac 2.75 2.75
B12 SP2 12c pink 2.75 2.75
B13 SP3 18c rose 2.75 2.75
B14 SP3 24c vio brn 2.75 2.75
B15 SP3 30c pale ol grn 2.75 2.75
B16 SP3 40c dull red 2.75 2.75
B17 SP3 50c yellow 2.75 2.75
B18 SP3 1e ultra 2.75 2.75
Nos. B1-B18 (18) 49.50 49.50

Nos. B1-B18 were used Dec. 1, 1920, in place of ordinary stamps. The proceeds were for war victims.

AIR POST STAMPS

Common Design Type
Perf. 13½x13

1938, Aug. Engr. Unwmk.
Name and Value in Black

C1 CD39 10c scarlet 28 22
C2 CD39 20c purple 28 22
C3 CD39 50c orange 28 20
C4 CD39 1e ultra 38 28
C5 CD39 2e lilac brn 85 30
C6 CD39 3e dk green 1.25 38
C7 CD39 5e red brown 2.00 70
C8 CD39 9e rose car 3.75 75
C9 CD39 10e magenta 4.75 1.10
Nos. C1-C9 (9) 13.82 4.15

No. C7 exists with overprint "Exposicao Internacional de Nova York, 1939-1940" and Trylon and Perisphere.

No. C7 Surcharged in Black

3$00

1946, Nov. 2 *Perf. 13½x13*

C10 CD39 3e on 5e red brn 4.50 1.75
a. Inverted surcharge

Plane AP1

1946, Nov. 2 Typo. *Perf. 11½*
Denomination in Black

C11 AP1 1.20e carmine 1.10 85
C12 AP1 1.60e blue 1.40 90
C13 AP1 1.70e plum 3.50 1.40
C14 AP1 2.90e brown 3.50 1.90
C15 AP1 3e green 3.00 1.75
Nos. C11-C15 (5) 12.50 6.80

Inscribed "Taxe perue" and Denomination in Brown Carmine or Black

1947, May 20

C16 AP1 50c blk (BrC) 50 25
C17 AP1 1e pink 50 25
C18 AP1 3e green 1.00 40
C19 AP1 4.50e yel grn 2.50 75
C20 AP1 5e red brown 2.00 90
C21 AP1 10e ultra 6.00 1.25
C22 AP1 20e violet 10.00 4.00
C23 AP1 50e orange 15.00 6.00
Nos. C16-C23 (8) 37.50 13.80

Dangerous counterfeits exist.

Planes Circling Globe — AP2

Oil Refinery, Sonarep — AP3

1949, Mar.

C24 AP2 50c sepia 28 15
C25 AP2 1.20e violet 50 28
C26 AP2 4.50e dull blue 1.25 50
C27 AP2 5e blue green 1.75 50
C28 AP2 20e chocolate 4.00 85
Nos. C24-C28 (5) 7.78 2.28

Catalogue values for unused stamps in this section, from this point to the end of the section, are for Never Hinged items.

1963, Mar. 5 Litho. *Perf. 13*

Designs: 2e, Salazar High School, Loureno Marques. 3.50e, Loureno Marques harbor. 4.50e, Salazar dam. 5e, Trigo de Morais bridge. 20e, Marcelo Caetano bridge.

C29 AP3 1.50e multi 60 15
C30 AP3 2e multi 30 15
C31 AP3 3.50e multi 60 15
C32 AP3 4.50e multi 38 20
C33 AP3 5e multi 38 20
C34 AP3 20e multi 1.10 50
Nos. C29-C34 (6) 3.36 1.35

Republic

Nos. C31-C34 Overprinted in Red

INDEPENDÊNCIA
25 JUN 75

1975, June 25 Litho. *Perf. 13*

C35 AP3 3.50e multi 20 18
C36 AP3 4.50e multi 35 18
C37 AP3 5e multi 85 20
C38 AP3 20e multi 1.75 40

DeHavilland Dragonfly, 1937 AP4

Designs: 1.50m, Junker JU-52-3M, 1938. 3m, Lockheed Lodestar L-18-08, 1940. 7.50m, DeHavilland Dove DH-104, 1948. 10m, Douglas Dakota DC-3, 1956. 12.5m, Fokker Friendship F-27, 1962.

1981, May 14 Litho. *Perf. 11*

C39 AP4 50c multi 15 15
C40 AP4 1.50m multi 15 15
C41 AP4 3m multi 14 15
C42 AP4 7.50m multi 30 15
C43 AP4 10m multi 40 18
C44 AP4 12.5m multi 50 35
Nos. C39-C44 (6) 1.64
Set value 92

Piper Navajo Over Hydroelectric Dam — AP5

Designs: 40m, De Havilland Hornet trainer, 1936. 80m, Boeing 737, Maputo Airport, 1973. 120m, Beechcraft King-Air. 160m, Piper Aztec. 320m, Douglas DC-10, 1982.

1987, Oct. 28 Litho. *Perf. 11*

C45 AP5 20m multi 15 15
C46 AP5 40m multi 16 15
C47 AP5 80m multi 30 20
C48 AP5 120m multi 48 25
C49 AP5 160m multi 60 30
C50 AP5 320m multi 1.25 40
Nos. C45-C50 (6) 2.94 1.45

POSTAGE DUE STAMPS

D1

1904 Unwmk. Typo. *Perf. 11½x12*
Name and Value in Black

J1 D1 5r yel grn 28 20
J2 D1 10r slate 28 20
J3 D1 20r yel brn 28 20
J4 D1 30r orange 50 40
J5 D1 50r gray brn 70 40
J6 D1 60r red brn 2.50 1.25
J7 D1 100r red lil 2.50 1.25
J8 D1 130r dl bl 1.00 85
J9 D1 200r carmine 1.75 1.00
J10 D1 500r violet 1.75 1.00
Nos. J1-J10 (10) 11.54 6.75

See J34-J43. For overprints see Nos. 247, J11-J30.

Same Overprinted in Carmine or Green

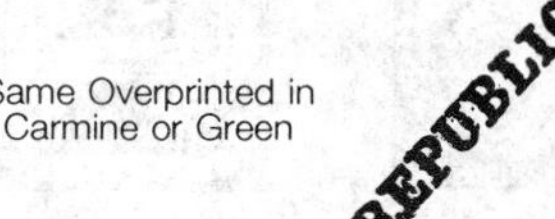

1911

J11 D1 5r yel grn 20 20
J12 D1 10r slate 20 20
J13 D1 20r yel brn 28 20
J14 D1 30r orange 28 20
J15 D1 50r gray brn 28 20
J16 D1 60r red brn 50 35
J17 D1 100r red lil 40 35
J18 D1 130r dl bl 85 60
J19 D1 200r car (G) 1.00 85
J20 D1 500r violet 1.00 85
Nos. J11-J20 (10) 4.99 4.00

Nos. J1-J10 Overprinted Locally in Carmine

REPUBLICA

1916

J21 D1 5r yel grn 2.50 2.00
J22 D1 10r slate 3.50 1.25
J23 D1 20r yel brn 57.50 35.00
J24 D1 30r orange 10.00 7.50
J25 D1 50r gray brn 45.00 35.00
J26 D1 60r red brn 40.00 27.50
J27 D1 100r red lil 57.50 40.00
J28 D1 130r dl bl 1.75 1.40
J29 D1 200r carmine 1.75 1.90
J30 D1 500r violet 3.50 3.00
Nos. J21-J30 (10) 223.00 154.55

War Tax Stamps of 1916 Overprinted Diagonally

PORTEADO

1918 *Rouletted 7*

J31 WT1 1c gray grn 85 70
J32 WT2 5c rose 85 70
a. Inverted overprint 6.50 5.00

Perf. 11

J33 WT1 1c gray grn 85 70
a. "PEPUBLICA" 3.75 2.75

Type of 1904 Issue With Value in Centavos

1917 *Perf. 12*

J34 D1 ½c yel grn 15 15
J35 D1 1c slate 15 15
J36 D1 2c org brn 15 15
J37 D1 3c orange 15 15
J38 D1 5c gray brn 15 15
J39 D1 6c pale brn 15 15
J40 D1 10c red vio 15 15
J41 D1 13c dp bl 15 15
J42 D1 20c rose 15 15
J43 D1 50c gray 18 18
Set value 90 90

Lourenco Marques Nos. 117, 119 Surcharged in Red

10 C.
PORTEADO

1921

J44 A4 5c on ½c blk 1.00 70
J45 A4 10c on 1½c brn 1.00 70

Same Surcharge on Mozambique Nos. 151, 155, 157 in Red or Green

J46 A6 6c on 1c bl grn (R) 85 70
J47 A6 20c on 2½c vio (R) 85 70
J48 A6 50c on 4c rose (G) 85 70
Nos. J44-J48 (5) 4.55 3.50

Regular Issues of 1921-22 Surcharged in Black or Red

Porteado
50 C.

1924 *Perf. 12x11½*

J49 A6 20c on 30c ol grn (Bk) 55 40
a. Perf. 15x14 17.50 4.00
J50 A6 50c on 60c dk bl (R) 85 55

Catalogue values for unused stamps in this section, from this point to the end of the section, are for Never Hinged items.

Common Design Type
Photo. and Typo.

1952 Unwmk. *Perf. 14*
Numeral in Red Orange or Red; Frame Multicolored

J51 CD45 10c car (RO) 15 15
J52 CD45 30c blk brn 15 15
J53 CD45 50c black 15 15
J54 CD45 1e vio bl 15 15
J55 CD45 2e olive green 20 15
J56 CD45 5e org brn 50 28
Set value 1.00 72

WAR TAX STAMPS

Coats of Arms of Portugal and Mozambique on Columns, Allegorical Figures of History of Portugal and the Republic Holding Scroll with Date of Declaration of War — WT1

Prow of Galley of Discoveries. Left, "Republic" Teaching History of Portugal; Right "History" with Laurels (Victory) and Sword (Symbolical of Declaration of War) — WT2

1916 Unwmk. Litho. *Rouletted 7*

MR1 WT1 1c gray grn 2.00 48
a. Imperf., pair
MR2 WT2 5c rose 2.00 48
a. Imperf., pair

1918 *Perf. 11, 12*

MR3 WT1 1c gray grn 50 48
a. "PEPUBLICA" 3.75 3.50

MR4 WT2 5c red 70 60
a. "PETRIA" 1.75 1.75
b. "PEPUBLICA" 2.00 1.75
c. "1910" for "1916" 3.75 2.75
d. Imperf., pair

For surcharges and overprints see Nos. 221-225, 229, 235, J31-J33.

NEWSPAPER STAMPS

No. 19 Surcharged in Black, Red or Blue:

JORNAES JORNAES

2 ½ REIS 2½ 2½
a b

Perf. 11½, 12½, 13½
1893 Unwmk.
P1 A2 (a) 2½r on 40r 165.00 60.00
P2 A2 (a) 5r on 40r 110.00 60.00
P3 A2 (a) 5r on 40r (R) 100.00 47.50
P4 A2 (a) 5r on 40r (Bl) 140.00 57.50
P5 A2 (b) 2½r on 40r 24.00 17.50

Nos. P1-P5 exist with double surcharge, Nos. P2-P4 with inverted surcharge.

N3

1893 Typo. *Perf. 11½, 13½*
P6 N3 2½r brown 35 28

For surcharge see No. 93.

No. P6 has been reprinted on chalk-surfaced paper with clean-cut perforation 13½. Value, 50 cents.

POSTAL TAX STAMPS

Pombal Commemorative Issue
Common Design Types
1925 Engr. *Perf. 12½*
RA1 CD28 15c brown & black 30 24
RA2 CD29 15c brown & black 30 24
RA3 CD30 15c brown & black 30 24

Seal of Local Red Cross Society
PT7 PT8

Surcharged in Various Colors
1925 Typo. *Perf. 11½*
RA4 PT7 50c slate & yel (Bk) 1.40 1.40

1926
RA5 PT8 40c slate & yel (Bk) 1.90 1.90
RA6 PT8 50c slate & yel (R) 1.90 1.90
RA7 PT8 60c slate & yel (V) 1.90 1.90
RA8 PT8 80c slate & yel (Br) 1.90 1.90
RA9 PT8 1e slate & yel (Bl) 1.90 1.90
RA10 PT8 2e slate & yel (G) 1.90 1.90
Nos. RA5-RA10 (6) 11.40 11.40

Obligatory on mail certain days of the year. The tax benefited the Cross of the Orient Society.

Type of 1926 Issue
1927
Black Surcharge
RA11 PT8 5c red & yel 1.75 1.75
RA12 PT8 10c green & yel 1.75 1.75
RA13 PT8 20c gray & yel 1.75 1.75
RA14 PT8 30c lt bl & yel 1.75 1.75
RA15 PT8 40c vio & yel 1.75 1.75
RA16 PT8 50c car & yel 1.75 1.75
RA17 PT8 60c brown & yel 1.75 1.75
RA18 PT8 80c blue & yel 1.75 1.75
RA19 PT8 1e olive & yel 1.75 1.75
RA20 PT8 2e yel brn & yel 1.75 1.75
Nos. RA11-RA20 (10) 17.50 17.50

See note after No. RA10.

PT9

1928 Litho.
RA21 PT9 5c grn, yel & blk 2.50 2.50
RA22 PT9 10c sl bl, yel & blk 2.50 2.50
RA23 PT9 20c gray blk, yel & blk 2.50 2.50
RA24 PT9 30c brn rose, yel & blk 2.50 2.50
RA25 PT9 40c cl brn, yel & blk 2.50 2.50
RA26 PT9 50c red org, yel & blk 2.50 2.50
RA27 PT9 60c brn, yel & blk 2.50 2.50
RA28 PT9 80c dk brn, yel & blk 2.50 2.50
RA29 PT9 1e gray, yel & blk 2.50 2.50
RA30 PT9 2e red, yel & blk 2.50 2.50
Nos. RA21-RA30 (10) 25.00 25.00

See note after RA10.

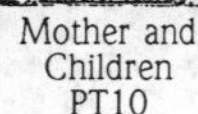
Mother and Children
PT10

Mousinho de Albuquerque
PT11

1929 Photo. *Perf. 14*
RA31 PT10 40c ultra, cl & blk 1.75 1.75

The use of this stamp was compulsory on all correspondence to Portugal and Portuguese Colonies for eight days beginning July 24th, 1929.

See Nos.RA39-RA47.

1930-31 *Perf. 14½x14*
Inscribed: "MACONTENE"
RA32 PT11 50c lake, red & gray 4.00 4.00
Inscribed: "COOLELA"
RA33 PT11 50c red vio, red brn & gray 4.00 4.00
Inscribed: "MUJENGA"
RA34 PT11 50c org red, red & gray 4.00 4.00
Inscribed: "CHAIMITE"
RA35 PT11 50c dp grn, bl grn & gray 4.00 4.00
Inscribed: "IBRAHIMO"
RA36 PT11 50c dk bl, blk & gray 4.00 4.00
Inscribed: "MUCUTO-MUNO"
RA37 PT11 50c ultra, blk & gray 4.00 4.00
Inscribed: "NAGUEMA"
RA38 PT11 50c dk vio, lt vio & gray 4.00 4.00
Nos. RA32-RA38 (7) 28.00 28.00

The portrait is that of Mousinho de Albuquerque, the celebrated Portuguese warrior, and the names of seven battles in which he took part appear at the foot of the stamps. The stamps were issued for the memorial fund bearing his name and their use was obligatory on all correspondence posted on eight specific days in the year.

Type of 1929 Issue
Denominations in Black
1931 *Perf. 14*
RA39 PT10 40c rose & vio 3.50 2.75

1932
RA40 PT10 40c ol grn & vio 3.50 2.75

1933
RA41 PT10 40c bis brn & rose 3.50 2.75

Without Denomination
1934
RA42 PT10 bl grn & rose 3.50 2.75

Denominations in Black
1936-40
RA43 PT10 40c org & ultra 3.50 2.75
RA44 PT10 40c choc & ultra ('37) 3.50 2.75
RA45 PT10 40c grn & brn car ('38) 5.00 4.00
RA46 PT10 40c yel & blk ('39) 5.00 4.00
RA47 PT10 40c gray brn ('40) 5.00 4.00

Allegory of Charity — PT12

White Pelican — PT13

1942 Unwmk. Litho. *Perf. 11½*
Denomination in Black
RA48 PT12 50c rose car 8.25 1.40

1943-51 *Perf. 11½, 14*
Denomination in Black
RA49 PT13 50c rose car 12.50 30
RA50 PT13 50c emerald 8.25 30
RA51 PT13 50c purple 10.00 30
RA52 PT13 50c blue 8.25 30
RA53 PT13 50c red brown 14.00 30
RA54 PT13 50c olive bister 10.00 30
Nos. RA49-RA54 (6) 63.00 1.80

There are two sizes of the numeral on No. RA49.

Catalogue values for unused stamps in this section, from this point to the end of the section, are for Never Hinged items.

Inscribed: "Provincia de Mocambique"
1954-56 *Perf. 14½x14*
RA55 PT13 50c orange 1.40 28
RA56 PT13 50c ol grn ('56) 1.40 28
RA57 PT13 50c brown ('56) 1.40 28

No. RA57 Surcharged with New Value and Wavy Lines
1956
RA58 PT13 30c on 50c brown 70 35

Pelican Type of 1954-56
1958 Litho. *Perf. 14*
Denomination in Black
RA59 PT13 30c yellow 70 35
RA60 PT13 50c salmon 70 35

Imprint: "Imprensa Nacional de Mocambique"
1963-64
Denomination Typographed in Black
RA61 PT13 30c yellow ('64) 48 20
RA62 PT13 50c salmon 35 20

Women and Children
PT14

Lineman on Pole and Map of Mozambique
PT15

1963-65 Litho. *Perf. 14*
RA63 PT14 50c blk, bis & red 28 15
RA64 PT14 50c blk, pink & red ('65) 28 15

See Nos. RA68-RA76.

1965, Apr. 1 Unwmk. *Perf. 14*
Design: 30c, Telegraph poles and map of Mozambique.

Size: 23x30mm
RA65 PT15 30c blk, sal & lil 15 15
Size: 19x36mm
RA66 PT15 50c blk, bl & sep 18 15
RA67 PT15 1e blk, yel & org 18 15
Set value 42 24

The tax was for improvement of the telecommunications system. Obligatory on inland mail. A 2.50e in the design of the 30c was issued for use on telegrams.

Type of 1963
1967, June 29 Litho. *Perf. 14*
RA68 PT14 50c blk, lt yel grn & red 28 18

1969
RA69 PT14 50c blk, lt bl & red 40 18

1970
RA70 PT14 50c blk, buff & brt red 40 18

1972-73
RA71 PT14 30c blk, lt grn & red 15 15
RA72 PT14 50c blk, gray & red ('73) 1.00 18
RA73 PT14 1e blk, bis & red ('73) 18 15
Set value 30

1974-75
RA74 PT14 50c blue, yel & red 15 15
RA75 PT14 1e blk, gray & ver 70 15
RA76 PT14 1e blk, lil rose & red ('75) 28 15
Set value 35

POSTAL TAX DUE STAMPS

Pombal Commemorative Issue
Common Design Types
1925 Unwmk. *Perf. 12½*
RAJ1 CD31 30c brown & black 50 60
RAJ2 CD32 30c brown & black 50 60
RAJ3 CD33 30c brown & black 50 60

MOZAMBIQUE COMPANY

LOCATION — Comprises the territory of Manica and Sofala of the Mozambique Colony in southeastern Africa
GOVT. — A part of the Portuguese Colony of Mozambique
AREA — 51,881 sq. mi.
POP. — 368,447 (1939)
CAPITAL — Beira

The Mozambique Company was chartered by Portugal in 1891 for 50 years. The territory was under direct administration of the Company until July 18, 1941

1000 Reis = 1 Milreis
100 Centavos = 1 Escudo (1916)

Mozambique Nos. 15-23 Overprinted in Carmine or Black

COMPª DE
MOÇAMBIQUE

1892 Unwmk. *Perf. 12½, 13½*
1 A2 5r black (C) 70 24
a. Pair, one without overprint 22.50 22.50
2 A2 10r green 70 24
3 A2 20r rose 70 24
a. Perf. 13½ 45.00 30.00
4 A2 25r violet 85 35
a. Double overprint 27.50
5 A2 40r chocolate 70 30
a. Double overprint 20.00
6 A2 50r blue 75 24
7 A2 100r yel brown 75 35
8 A2 200r gray violet 1.00 45
9 A2 300r orange 1.00 70
Nos. 1-9 (9) 7.15 3.11

Nos. 1 to 6, 8-9 were reprinted in 1905. These reprints have white gum and clean-cut perf. 13½ and the colors are usually paler than those of the originals.

Company Coat of Arms — A2

Perf. 11½, 12½, 13½

1895-1907 **Typo.**

Black or Red Numerals

10 A2 2½r olive yel 18 18
11 A2 2½r gray ('07) 80 35
12 A2 5r orange 18 18
a. Value omitted 10.00
b. Perf. 13½ 1.40 70
13 A2 10r red lilac 30 30
14 A2 10r yel grn ('07) 1.50 40
a. Value inverted at top of stamp 14.00 10.00
15 A2 15r red brown 50 28
16 A2 15r dk grn ('07) 1.50 40
17 A2 20r gray lilac 70 28
18 A2 25r green 50 28
a. Perf. 13½ 1.75 1.00
19 A2 25r car ('07) 1.50 60
a. Value omitted 11.00 8.00
20 A2 50r blue 70 28
21 A2 50r brown ('07) 1.50 60
a. Value omitted 6.00
22 A2 65r slate bl ('02) 70 35
23 A2 75r rose 38 28
24 A2 75r red lilac ('07) 2.75 1.00
25 A2 80r yellow grn 35 28
26 A2 100r brown, *buff* 40 30
27 A2 100r dk bl, *bl* ('07) 2.75 1.00
28 A2 115r car, *pink* ('04) 1.00 70
29 A2 115r org brn, *pink* ('07) 3.50 1.40
30 A2 130r grn, *pink* ('04) 1.50 70
31 A2 130r brn, *yel* ('07) 3.50 1.40
32 A2 150r org brn, *pink* 35 35
33 A2 200r dk bl, *bl* 35 35
a. Perf. 13½ 1.75 1.25
34 A2 200r red lil, *pink* ('07) 3.50 1.40
35 A2 300r dk bl, *salmon* 48 30
a. Perf. 13½ 2.50 1.40
36 A2 400r brn, *bl* ('04) 1.25 70
37 A2 400r dl bl, *yel* ('07) 4.25 1.90
38 A2 500r blk & red 55 40
39 A2 500r blk & red, *bl* ('07) 4.25 1.90
a. 500r pur & red, *yel* (error)
40 A2 700r sl, *buff* ('04) 4.75 2.00
41 A2 700r pur, *yel* ('07) 3.75 2.00
42 A2 1000r vio & red 85 40
Nos. 10-42 (33) 51.02 23.24

Nos. 12b, 18a, 33a and 35a were issued without gum.

For overprints & surcharges see #43-107, B1-B7.

Nos. 25 and 6 Surcharged or Overprinted in Red:

PROVISORIO

25

b

PROVISORIO

c

1895 *Perf. 12½, 13½*

43 A2(b) 25r on 80r yel grn 18.00 15.00
44 A2(c) 50r blue 2.75 2.00

Overprint "c" on No. 44 also exists reading from upper left to lower right.

Stamps of 1895 Overprinted in Bister, Orange, Violet, Green, Black or Brown

1498

Centenario da India

1898

1898 *Perf. 12½, 13½*

Without Gum

45 A2 2½r ol yel (Bi) 1.50 70
a. Double overprint *18.00 18.00*
b. Red overprint *25.00 25.00*
46 A2 5r orange (O) 1.75 85
47 A2 10r red lil (V) 1.75 85
48 A2 15r red brn (V) 2.75 1.25
a. Red overprint
49 A2 20r gray lil (V) 2.25 1.25
50 A2 25r green (G) 3.25 1.40
a. Inverted overprint 27.50 16.00
51 A2 50r blue (Bk) 3.00 1.40
a. Inverted overprint 27.50 20.00
52 A2 75r rose (V) 3.25 2.25
a. Inverted overprint 30.00 25.00
b. Red overprint
53 A2 80r yel grn (G) 4.50 1.90
a. Inverted overprint
54 A2 100r brn, *buff* (Br) 4.50 2.50
55 A2 150r org brn, *pink* (O) 4.50 2.50
a. Inverted overprint 19.00 16.00
b. Double overprint
56 A2 200r dk bl, *bl* (Bk) 6.50 3.00
57 A2 300r dk bl, *sal* (Bk) 7.50 4.00
a. Inverted overprint 27.50 25.00
b. Green overprint
Nos. 45-57 (13) 47.00 23.85

Vasco da Gama's discovery of route to India, 400th anniversary.

No. 57b was prepared but not issued.

Nos. 45 and 49 were also issued with gum.

The "Centenario" overprint on stamps perf. 11½ is forged.

Nos. 23, 12, 17 Surcharged in Black, Carmine or Violet

25

PROVISORIO

e

25 Réis

f

50 RÉIS

g

1899 *Perf. 12½*

59 A2(e) 25r on 75r rose (Bk) 2.50 1.40

1900 *Perf. 12½, 12½x11½*

60 A2(f) 25r on 5r org (C) 1.75 1.00
61 A2(g) 50r on half of 20r gray lil (V) 85 70
b. Entire stamp 7.50 5.00

No. 61b is perf. 11½ vertically through center.

Stamps of 1895-1907 Overprinted Locally in Carmine or Green

REPUBLICA

1911 *Perf. 11½, 13½*

61A A2 2½r gray (C) 60 40
62 A2 5r orange (G) 90 60
63 A2 10r yel grn (C) 70 50
64 A2 15r dk grn (C) 70 50
a. Double overprint 17.00 9.50
65 A2 20r gray lil (G) 85 50
a. Perf. 13½ 85 60
66 A2 25r carmine (G) 85 60
67 A2 50r brown (G) 70 45
68 A2 75r red lil (G) 85 45
69 A2 100r dk bl, *bl* (C) 90 50
70 A2 115r org brn, *pink* (G) 1.25 60
71 A2 130r brn, *yel* (G) 1.75 60
72 A2 200r red lil, *pink* (G) 1.75 60
73 A2 400r dl bl, *yel* (C) 1.75 60
74 A2 500r blk & red, *bl* (C) 2.25 95
75 A2 700r pur, *yel* (G) 2.25 95
Nos. 61A-75 (15) 18.05 8.80

Nos. 63, 67 and 71 exist with inverted overprint; Nos. 63, 72 and 75 with double overprint.

Overprinted in Lisbon in Carmine or Green

1911 *Perf. 11½, 12½*

75B A2 2½r gray 28 18
76 A2 5r orange 28 15
77 A2 10r yel grn 24 15
78 A2 15r dk grn 35 15
79 A2 20r gray lilac 28 15
80 A2 25r car (G) 35 15
a. Value inverted at top of stamp 18.00
81 A2 50r brown 35 15
82 A2 75r red lil 35 15
a. Value omitted 15.00
83 A2 100r dk bl, *bl* 60 20
84 A2 115r org brn, *pink* 85 30
85 A2 130r brn, *yel* 90 35
a. Double overprint 18.00
86 A2 200r red lil, *pink* 50 24
87 A2 400r dl bl, *yel* 70 28
88 A2 500r blk & red, *bl* 70 28
89 A2 700r pur, *yel* 85 48
Nos. 75B-89 (15) 7.58 3.36

Nos. 75B-89 Surcharged ¼ C

1916 *Perf. 11½*

90 A2 ¼c on 2½r gray 18 18
91 A2 ½c on 5r org 18 18
a. "½c" double 11.00
92 A2 1c on 10r yel grn 40 18
93 A2 1½c on 15r dk grn 40 18
a. Imperf., pair 17.50
94 A2 2c on 20r gray lil 50 18
95 A2 2½c on 25r car 70 18
96 A2 5c on 50r brn 40 20
a. Imperf., pair 17.50
97 A2 7½c on 75r red lil 50 20
98 A2 10c on 100r dk bl, *bl* 65 30
a. Inverted surcharge 20.00 20.00
99 A2 11½c on 115r org brn, *pink* 2.25 35
a. Inverted surcharge 30.00 30.00
100 A2 13c on 130r brn, *yel* 3.50 30
101 A2 20c on 200r red lil, *pink* 2.75 30
102 A2 40c on 400r dl bl, *yel* 3.50 35
103 A2 50c on 500r blk & red, *bl* (R) 4.25 70
104 A2 70c on 700r pur, *yel* 4.50 75
Nos. 90-104 (15) 24.66 4.53

Nos. 87 to 89 Surcharged

½ Cent.

1918 *Perf. 11½*

105 A2 ½c on 700r pur, *yel* 1.25 95
106 A2 2½c on 500r blk & red, *bl* (Bl) 1.25 95
107 A2 5c on 400r dl bl, *yel* 1.25 95

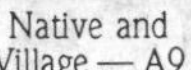

Native and Village — A9

Man and Ivory Tusks — A10

Corn — A11

Tapping Rubber Tree — A12

Sugar Refinery — A13

Buzi River Scene — A14

Tobacco Field — A15

View of Beira — A16

Coffee Plantation A17

Orange Tree A18

Cotton Field A19

Sisal Plantation A20

Scene on Beira R. R. — A21

Court House at Beira — A22

Coconut Palm — A23

Mangroves — A24

Cattle — A25

Company Arms — A26

1918-31 **Engr.** *Perf. 14, 15, 12½*

108 A9 ¼c brn & yel grn 15 15
109 A9 ¼c ol grn & blk ('25) 15 15
110 A10 ½c black 15 15
111 A11 1c grn & blk 15 15
112 A12 1½c blk & grn 15 15
113 A13 2c car & blk 15 15
114 A13 2c ol blk & blk ('25) 15 15
115 A14 2½c lil & blk 15 15
116 A11 3c ocher & blk ('23) 20 15
117 A15 4c grn & brn ('21) 20 15
118 A15 4c red & blk ('25) 18 15
119 A9 4½c gray & blk ('23) 20 18
120 A16 5c bl & blk 18 18
121 A17 6c cl & bl ('21) 45 28
122 A17 6c lil & blk ('25) 18 15
123 A21 7c ultra & blk ('23) 70 45
124 A18 7½c org & grn 40 24
125 A19 8c vio & blk 20 18
126 A20 10c red org & blk 20 15
128 A19 12c brn & blk ('23) 70 35
129 A19 12c bl grn & blk ('25) 40 24
130 A21 15c car & blk 40 28
131 A22 20c dp grn & blk 35 20
132 A23 30c red brn & blk 2.50 70
133 A23 30c gray grn & blk ('25) 85 20
134 A23 30c bl grn & blk ('31) 2.50 28
135 A24 40c yel grn & blk 85 45
136 A24 40c grnsh bl & blk ('25) 70 28
137 A25 50c org & blk 1.75 75
138 A25 50c lt vio & blk ('25) 1.75 35
139 A25 60c rose & brn ('23) 1.00 48
140 A20 80c ultra & brn ('23) 1.75 70
141 A20 80c car & blk ('25) 70 35
142 A26 1e dk grn & blk 1.75 45
143 A26 1e bl & blk ('25) 1.75 35
144 A16 2e rose & vio ('23) 2.50 70
145 A16 2e lil & blk ('25) 2.00 35
Nos. 108-145 (37) 28.49 10.92

Shades exist of several denominations.

For surcharges see Nos. 146-154, RA1.

Nos. 132, 142, 115, 120, 131, 135, 125, 137 Surcharged with New Values in Red, Blue, Violet or Black:

Um e meio Centavo

h

4 Cent.

i

Seis Centavos

j

1920 *Perf. 14, 15*

146 A23(h) ½c on 30c (Bk) 5.25 4.50
147 A26(h) ½c on 1e (R) 5.25 4.50
148 A14(h) 1½c on 2½c (Bl) 2.75 2.25
149 A16(h) 1½c on 5c (V) 3.75 3.50
150 A14(h) 2c on 2½c (R) 1.75 1.75
151 A22(i) 4c on 20c (V) 6.00 4.50
152 A24(i) 4c on 40c (V) 6.25 5.00
153 A19(j) 6c on 8c (R) 7.00 5.50
154 A25(j) 6c on 50c (Bk) 7.50 5.50
Nos. 146-154 (9) 45.50 37.00

The surcharge on No. 148 is placed vertically between two bars. On No. 154 the two words of the surcharge are 13mm apart.

Native — A27

View of Beira — A28

Tapping Rubber Tree — A29

Picking Tea — A30

Zambezi River — A31

1925-31 Engr. Perf. 12

No.	Type	Description	Unused	Used
155	A27	24c ultra & blk	1.00	50
156	A28	25c choc & ultra	1.00	50
157	A27	85c brn red & blk ('31)	85	45
158	A28	1.40e dl bl & blk ('31)	85	45
159	A29	5e yel brn & ultra	1.25	30
160	A30	10e rose & blk	1.75	75
161	A31	20e green & blk	1.75	75
		Nos. 155-161 (7)	8.45	3.70

Ivory Tusks — A32

Panning Gold — A33

1931 Litho. Perf. 14

No.	Type	Description	Unused	Used
162	A32	45c lt blue	2.00	85
163	A33	70c yellow brn	1.40	35

Zambezi Railroad Bridge A34

1935 Engr. Perf. 12½

No.	Type	Description	Unused	Used
164	A34	1e dk bl & blk	2.00	1.40

Opening of a new bridge over the Zambezi River.

Airplane over Beira — A35

1935

No.	Type	Description	Unused	Used
165	A35	5c blue & blk	45	35
166	A35	10c red org & blk	45	35
a.		Square pair, imperf. between	35.00	
167	A35	15c red & blk	45	35
a.		Square pair, imperf. between	35.00	
168	A35	20c yel grn & blk	45	35
169	A35	30c grn & blk	45	35
170	A35	40c gray bl & blk	45	35
171	A35	45c bl & blk	45	35
172	A35	50c vio & blk	45	35
a.		Square pair, imperf. between	40.00	
173	A35	60c car & brn	60	35
174	A35	80c car & blk	60	35
		Nos. 165-174 (10)	4.80	3.50

Issued to commemorate the opening of the Blantyre-Beira Salisbury air service.

Giraffe — A36

Thatched Huts — A37

Rock Python A41

Coconut Palms A50

Zambezi Railroad Bridge A52

Sena Gate — A53

Company Arms — A54

Designs: 10c, Dhow. 15c, St. Caetano Fortress, Sofala. 20c, Zebra. 40c, Black rhinoceros. 45c, Lion. 50c, Crocodile. 60c, Leopard. 70c, Mozambique woman. 80c, Hippopotami. 85c, Vasco da Gama's flagship. 1e, Man in canoe. 2e, Greater kudu.

1937, May 16 Perf. 12½

No.	Type	Description	Unused	Used
175	A36	1c yel grn & vio	15	20
176	A37	5c bl & yel grn	15	15
177	A36	10c ver & ultra	15	15
178	A37	15c car & blk	15	15
179	A36	20c grn & ultra	15	15
180	A41	30c dk grn & ind	15	28
181	A41	40c gray bl & blk	15	28
182	A41	45c bl & brn	15	28
183	A41	50c dk vio & emer	15	28
184	A37	60c car & bl	15	15
185	A36	70c yel brn & pale grn	15	15
186	A37	80c car & pale grn	24	30
187	A41	85c org red & blk	24	40
188	A41	1e dp bl & blk	20	15
189	A50	1.40e dk bl & pale grn	18	15
190	A41	2e pale lil & brn	40	15
191	A52	5e yel brn & bl	50	70
192	A53	10e car & blk	1.25	1.40
193	A54	20e grn & brn vio	1.75	2.75
		Set value	5.65	

Stamps of 1937 Overprinted in Red or Black

28-VII-1939

Visita Presidencial

1939, Aug. 28

No.	Type	Description	Unused	Used
194	A41	30c dk grn & ind (R)	85	70
195	A41	40c gray bl & blk (R)	85	70
196	A41	45c bl & brn (Bk)	85	70
197	A41	50c dk vio & emer (R)	85	70
198	A41	85c org red & blk (Bk)	85	70
199	A41	1e dp bl & blk (R)	1.25	1.00
200	A41	2e pale lil & brn (Bk)	1.25	1.40
		Nos. 194-200 (7)	6.75	5.90

Visit of the President of Portugal to Beira in 1939.

King Alfonso Henriques A55

King John IV A56

1940, Feb. 16 Typo. Perf. 11½x12

No.	Type	Description	Unused	Used
201	A55	1.75e bl & lt bl	70	55

800th anniv. of Portuguese independence.

1941 Engr. Perf. 12½

No.	Type	Description	Unused	Used
202	A56	40c gray grn & blk	30	20
203	A56	50c dk vio & brt grn	30	20
204	A56	60c brt car & dp bl	30	20
205	A56	70c brn org & dk grn	30	20
206	A56	80c car & dp grn	30	20
207	A56	1e dk bl & blk	30	20
		Nos. 202-207 (6)	1.80	1.20

300th anniv. of the restoration of the Portuguese Monarchy.

Mozambique Company's charter terminated July 18th, 1941 after which date its stamps were superseded by those of the territory of Mozambique.

SEMI-POSTAL STAMPS

Lisbon Issue of 1911 Overprinted in Red

31. 7. 17.

1917 Unwmk. Perf. 11½

No.	Type	Description	Unused	Used
B1	A2	2½r gray	7.50	10.50
a.		Double overprint	40.00	40.00
B2	A2	10r yel grn	7.50	15.00
B3	A2	20r gray lilac	9.00	20.00
B4	A2	50r brown	20.00	25.00
B5	A2	75r red lilac	55.00	70.00
B6	A2	100r dk bl, *bl*	55.00	70.00
B7	A2	700r purple, *yel*	165.00	225.00
		Nos. B1-B7 (7)	319.00	435.50

Nos. B1-B7 were used on July 31, 1917, in place of ordinary stamps. The proceeds were given to the Red Cross.

AIR POST STAMPS

Airplane over Beira — AP1

1935 Unwmk. Engr. Perf. 12½

No.	Type	Description	Unused	Used
C1	AP1	5c blue & blk	15	15
C2	AP1	10c org red & blk	15	15
C3	AP1	15c red & blk	15	15
C4	AP1	20c yel grn & blk	15	15
C5	AP1	30c green & blk	15	15
C6	AP1	40c gray bl & blk	15	15
C7	AP1	45c blue & blk	15	15
C8	AP1	50c dk vio & blk	15	15
C9	AP1	60c car & brn	15	15
C10	AP1	80c car & blk	15	15
C11	AP1	1e blue & blk	15	15
C12	AP1	2e mauve & blk	1.00	24
C13	AP1	5e bis brn & bl	1.00	40
C14	AP1	10e car & blk	1.25	60
C15	AP1	20e bl grn & blk	2.50	85
		Set value	6.50	2.75

POSTAGE DUE STAMPS

D1

1906 Unwmk. Typo. Perf. 11½x12

Denominations in Black

No.	Type	Description	Unused	Used
J1	D1	5r yellow grn	70	18
J2	D1	10r slate	70	18
J3	D1	20r yellow brn	70	18
J4	D1	30r orange	85	24
J5	D1	50r gray brn	85	24
J6	D1	60r red brown	20.00	3.50
J7	D1	100r red lilac	2.50	70
J8	D1	130r dull blue	27.50	4.00
J9	D1	200r carmine	10.00	1.75
J10	D1	500r violet	13.00	2.00
		Nos. J1-J10 (10)	76.80	12.97

Nos. J1-J10 Overprinted in Carmine or Green

1911

No.	Type	Description	Unused	Used
J11	D1	5r yel grn	15	15
J12	D1	10r slate	15	15
J13	D1	20r yel brn	15	15
J14	D1	30r orange	20	15
J15	D1	50r gray brn	30	20
J16	D1	60r red brn	40	28
J17	D1	100r red lilac	40	28
J18	D1	130r dull blue	2.00	1.00
J19	D1	200r carmine (G)	1.25	85
J20	D1	500r violet	2.50	1.00
		Nos. J11-J20 (10)	7.50	4.21

D2

Company Arms — D3

1916 Typo.

With Value in Centavos in Black

No.	Type	Description	Unused	Used
J21	D2	½c yel grn	15	15
J22	D2	1c slate	15	15
J23	D2	2c org brn	15	15
J24	D2	3c orange	28	15
J25	D2	5c gray brn	35	15
J26	D2	6c pale brn	28	15
J27	D2	10c red lilac	35	18
J28	D2	13c gray blue	80	35
J29	D2	20c rose	1.00	35
J30	D2	50c gray	1.50	50
		Nos. J21-J30 (10)	5.01	2.28

Perf. 11½, 13½, 14 to 15½

1919 Engr.

No.	Type	Description	Unused	Used
J31	D3	½c green	15	15
J32	D3	1c slate	15	15
J33	D3	2c red brown	15	15
J34	D3	3c orange	15	15
J35	D3	5c gray brown	20	20
J36	D3	6c lt brn	45	45
J37	D3	10c lilac rose	45	45
J38	D3	13c dull blue	45	45
J39	D3	20c rose	45	45
J40	D3	50c gray	45	45
		Nos. J31-J40 (10)	3.05	3.05

NEWSPAPER STAMP

Newspaper Stamp of Mozambique Overprinted Like Nos. 1-9

1894 Unwmk. Perf. 11½

No.	Type	Description	Unused	Used
P1	N3	2½r brown	48	40
a.		Inverted overprint	12.00	12.00
b.		Perf. 12½	85	50

Reprints are on stout white paper with clean-cut perf. 13½. Value $1.

POSTAL TAX STAMPS

Assistencia
Publica

2 Ctvos. 2

No. 116 Surcharged in Black

1932 *Perf. 12½*

RA1 A11 2c on 3c org & blk 1.40 *2.00*

Charity — PT2

1933 **Litho.** *Perf. 11*

RA2 PT2 2c magenta & blk 1.00 *2.00*

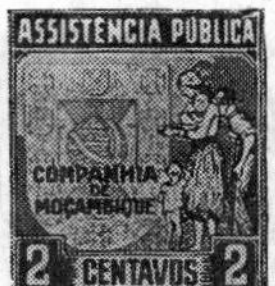
PT3

PT4

1940 **Unwmk.** *Perf. 10½*

RA3 PT3 2c black & ultra 12.00 *15.00*

1941

RA4 PT4 2c blk & brt red 12.00 *15.00*

NETHERLANDS

(Holland)

LOCATION — Northwestern Europe, bordering on the North Sea
GOVT. — Kingdom
AREA — 13,203 sq. mi.
POP. — 14,394,589 (1984)
CAPITAL — Amsterdam

100 Cents = 1 Gulden
(Guilder or Florin)

Catalogue values for unused stamps in this country are for Never Hinged items, beginning with Scott 216 in the regular postage section, Scott B123 in the semi-postal section, Scott C15 in the airpost section, Scott J80 in the postage due section, and Scott O44 in the official section.

Values of early Netherlands stamps vary according to condition. Quotations for Nos. 4-12 are for copies with perforations cutting into the design (with original gum if unused).

Watermarks

Wmk. 158

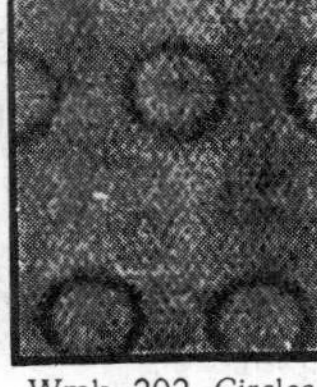
Wmk. 202- Circles

King William III
A1 A2

Wmk. 158

1852, Jan. 1 **Engr.** *Imperf.*

1 A1 5c blue 350.00 20.00
a. 5c light blue 375.00 15.00
b. 5c steel blue 1,500. 50.00
c. 5c dark blue 350.00 22.50
2 A1 10c lake 400.00 14.00
3 A1 15c orange 575.00 75.00

In 1895 the 10c was privately reprinted in several colors on unwatermarked paper by Joh. A. Moesman, whose name appears on the back.

1864 **Unwmk.** *Perf. 12½x12*

4 A2 5c blue 225.00 10.00
5 A2 10c lake 350.00 4.00
6 A2 15c orange 850.00 65.00
a. 15c yellow 975.00 70.00

The paper varies considerably in thickness. It is sometimes slightly bluish, also vertically ribbed.

William III — A3

Coat of Arms — A4

Perf. 12½x12, 13, 13½, 14 and Compound

1867

7 A3 5c ultra 60.00 90
8 A3 10c lake 110.00 1.75
9 A3 15c orange brn 500.00 22.50
10 A3 20c dk green 450.00 15.00
11 A3 25c dk violet 1,700. 60.00
12 A3 50c gold 1,900. 110.00

The paper of Nos. 7-22 sometimes has an accidental bluish tinge of varying strength. During its manufacture a chemical whitener (bluing agent) was added in varying quantities. No particular printing was made on bluish paper.

Two varieties of numerals in each value, differing chiefly in the thickness.

Oxidized copies of the 50c are worth much less.

Imperforate varieties of Nos. 7-12 are proofs.

1869 *Perf. 10½x10*

7c A3 5c ultra 110.00 6.50
8c A3 10c lake 160.00 3.25
9c A3 15c orange brn *2,000.* 375.00
10c A3 20c dk green *850.00* 100.00

1869-71 **Typo.** *Perf. 13½, 14*

17 A4 ½c red brn ('71) 22.50 1.75
c. Perf. 14 *2,000.* 550.00
18 A4 1c black 190.00 57.50
19 A4 1c green 9.00 1.25
c. Perf. 14 22.50 5.00
20 A4 1½c rose 125.00 65.00
b. Perf. 14 100.00 65.00
21 A4 2c buff 47.50 8.50
c. Perf. 14 50.00 8.50
22 A4 2½c vio ('71) 450.00 40.00
c. Perf. 14 575.00 300.00

Imperforate varieties are proofs.

A5

A6

Perf. 12½, 13, 13½, 14, 12½x12 and 11½x12

1872-88

23 A5 5c ultra 10.00 24
a. 5c blue 10.00 40
24 A5 7½c red brn ('88) 37.50 15.00
25 A5 10c rose 57.50 70
26 A5 12½c gray ('75) 65.00 1.10
27 A5 15c brn org 375.00 4.00
28 A5 20c green 450.00 4.00
29 A5 22½c dk grn ('88) 75.00 35.00
30 A5 25c dull vio 575.00 3.00
31 A5 50c bister 700.00 7.50
32 A5 1g gray vio ('88) 500.00 22.50
33 A6 2g50c rose & ultra 950.00 75.00

Imperforate varieties are proofs.

Numeral of Value — A7

HALF CENT:
Type I- Fraction bar 8 to 8½mm long.
Type II- Fraction bar 9mm long and thinner.

1876-94 *Perf. 12½*

34 A7 ½c rose, II 2.75 18
a. ½c rose, I 11.00 18
c. Laid paper 42.50
d. Perf. 14, I 1,100. 500.00
35 A7 1c emer grn ('94) 1.90 18
b. Laid paper 55.00 4.50
c. 1c green 8.50 18
36 A7 2c ol yel ('94) 30.00 2.50
a. 2c yellow 60.00 2.50
37 A7 2½c vio ('94) 13.00 20
b. 2½c dark violet ('94) 17.00 65
c. 2½c lilac 90.00 70

Imperforate varieties are proofs.

Queen Wilhelmina
A8 A9

1891-94 *Perf. 12½*

40 A8 3c org ('94) 5.75 1.00
a. 3c orange yellow ('92) 10.50 1.00
41 A8 5c lt ultra ('94) 2.75 15
a. 5c dull blue 3.75 15
42 A8 7½c brn ('94) 16.00 4.50
a. 7½c red brn 24.00 4.50
43 A8 10c brt rose ('94) 22.50 65
a. 10c brick red 55.00 2.75
44 A8 12½c bluish gray ('94) 22.50 75
a. 12½c gray 50.00 1.50
45 A8 15c yel brn ('94) 52.50 4.00
a. 15c orange brown 70.00 4.00
46 A8 20c grn ('94) 57.50 2.00
a. 20c yellow green 70.00 2.50
47 A8 22½c dk grn ('94) 30.00 10.50
a. 22½c dp blue grn 47.50 10.50
48 A8 25c dl vio ('94) 100.00 4.00
a. 25c dark violet 110.00 4.00
49 A8 50c yel brn ('94) 500.00 14.00
a. 50c bister 675.00 25.00
50 A8 1g gray vio 675.00 52.50

The paper used in 1891-93 was white, rough and somewhat opaque. In 1894, a thinner, smooth and sometimes transparent paper was introduced.

The 5c orange was privately produced.

1891-96 *Perf. 11½x11*

51 A9 50c emer & yel brn ('96) 75.00 8.00
a. Perf. 11 *2,750.* 225.00
52 A9 1g brn & ol grn ('96) 190.00 21.00
a. Perf. 11 240.00 57.50
53 A9 2g 50c brt rose & ultra 475.00 125.00
a. 2g 50c lil rose & ultra, perf. 11 475.00 130.00
b. Perf. 11½ 500.00 150.00

Perf. 11

54 A9 5g brnz grn & red brn ('96) 650.00 300.00

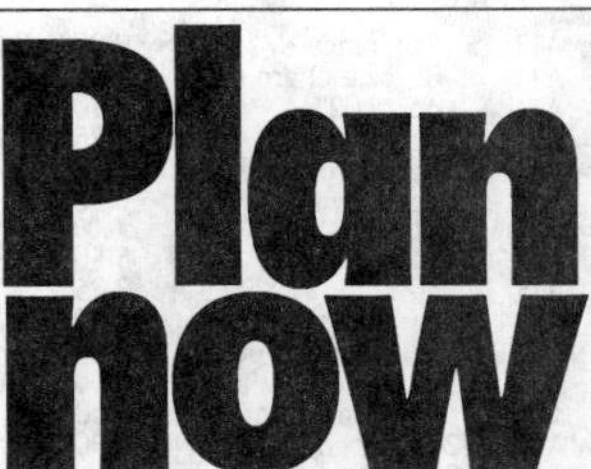

A10

Wilhelmina — A11

Perf. 12½, 11½, 11½x11

1898-1924

55 A10 ½c violet 40 15
56 A10 1c red 85 15
b. Imperf., pair *4,000.* *5,000.*
57 A10 1½c ultra ('08) 2.25 50
58 A10 1½c dp bl ('13) 3.25 15
59 A10 2c yel brn 3.25 15
60 A10 2½c dp grn 3.25 15
b. Imperf., pair *8,000.*

61 A11 3c orange 9.00 3.00
62 A11 3c pale ol grn ('01) 90 15
63 A11 4c cl ('21) 1.10 80
64 A11 4½c vio ('19) 3.25 3.00
65 A11 5c car rose 1.25 15
66 A11 7½c brown 50 15
a. Tête bêche pair ('24) 60.00 70.00
67 A11 10c gray lil 5.50 15
68 A11 12½c blue 3.25 15
69 A11 15c yel brn 70.00 2.25
70 A11 15c bl & car ('08) 3.75 15
71 A11 17½c vio ('06) 40.00 9.00
73 A11 17½c ultra & brn ('10) 14.00 45
74 A11 20c yel grn 75.00 65
75 A11 20c ol grn & gray ('08) 8.00 22
76 A11 22½c brn & ol grn 6.00 18
77 A11 25c car & bl 6.00 15
78 A11 30c lil & vio brn ('17) 18.00 15
79 A11 40c grn & org ('20) 35.00 50
80 A11 50c brnz grn & red brn 37.50 70
81 A11 50c gray & vio ('14) 40.00 50
a. Perf. 11½x11 80.00 7.50
82 A11 60c ol grn & grn ('20) 30.00 80
a. Perf. 11½ 175.00 20.00
Nos. 55-82 (27) 421.25 24.50

See Nos. 107-112. For overprints and surcharges see Nos. 102-102, 106, 117-123, 135-136, O1-O8.

A12 Type I Type II

Type I- The figure "1" is 3¾mm high and 2¾mm wide.
Type II- The figure "1" is 3½mm high and 2½mm wide, it is also thinner than in type I.

Perf. 11, 11x11½, 11½, 11½x11

1898-1905 **Engr.**

83 A12 1g dk grn, II ('99) 45.00 30
a. 1g dark green, I ('98) 95.00 47.50
84 A12 2½g brn lil ('99) 65.00 3.25
85 A12 5g claret ('99) 150.00 5.25
86 A12 10g org ('05) 450.00 450.00

For surcharge see No. 104.

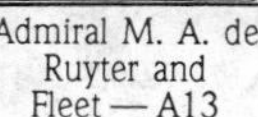

Admiral M. A. de Ruyter and Fleet — A13

King William I — A14

1907, Mar. 23 **Typo.** ***Perf. 12x12½***

87 A13 ½c blue 60 75
88 A13 1c claret 2.25 2.85
89 A13 2½c vermilion 7.25 2.25

De Ruyter (1607-1676), naval hero.
For surcharges see Nos. J29-J41.

Perf. 11½, 11½x11

1913, Nov. 29 **Engr.**

Designs: 2½c, 12½c, 1g, King William I. 3c, 20c, 2½g, King William II. 5c, 25c, 5g, King William III. 10c, 50c, 10g, Queen Wilhelmina.

90 A14 2½c green, *grn* 65 60
91 A14 3c buff, *straw* 90 75
92 A14 5c rose red, *sal* 80 40
93 A14 10c gray blk 2.25 1.00
94 A14 12½c dp blue, *bl* 1.50 1.00
95 A14 20c org brn 8.00 4.00
96 A14 25c pale blue 8.25 4.00
97 A14 50c yellow grn 20.00 14.00
98 A14 1g claret 30.00 8.25
a. Perf. 11½ 40.00 10.50
99 A14 2½g dull vio 85.00 32.50
100 A14 5g yel, *straw* 175.00 30.00
101 A14 10g red, *straw* 525.00 500.00
Nos. 90-101 (12) 857.35 596.50
Set, never hinged 2,250.

Centenary of Dutch independence.
For surcharge see No. 105.

No. 78 Surcharged in Red or Black

Veertig Cent
a

Zestig Cent
b

1919, Dec. 1 ***Perf. 12½***

102 A11 (a) 40c on 30c (R) 20.00 3.25
103 A11 (b) 60c on 30c (Bk) 18.00 3.00
Set, never hinged 150.00

Nos. 86 and 101 Surcharged in Black

2.50

1920, Aug. 17 ***Perf. 11, 11½***

104 A12 2.50g on 10g 85.00 95.00
Never hinged 375.00
105 A14 2.50g on 10g 95.00 60.00
Never hinged 350.00

No. 64 Surcharged in Red

—4C—

1921, Mar. 1 ***Perf. 12½***

106 A11 4c on 4½c vio 3.75 1.40
Never hinged 8.50

A17

1921, Aug. 5 **Typo.** ***Perf. 12½***

107 A17 5c green 8.00 15
108 A17 12½c vermilion 11.00 1.75
109 A17 20c blue 17.00 18
Set, never hinged 190.00

Queen Type of 1898-99, 10c Redrawn

1922 ***Perf. 12½***

110 A11 10c gray 25.00 15
Never hinged 65.00

Imperf

111 A11 5c car rose 5.75 5.75
Never hinged 12.00
112 A11 10c gray 6.75 6.25
Never hinged 13.00

In redrawn 10c the horizontal lines behind the Queen's head are wider apart.

Orange Tree and Lion of Brabant A18

Post Horn and Lion A19

Numeral of Value — A20

1923, Mar. ***Perf. 12½***

113 A18 1c dark violet 50 55
114 A18 2c orange 6.75 15
115 A19 2½c bluish green 1.75 75
116 A20 4c deep blue 1.40 55
Set, never hinged 17.00

Nos. 56, 58, 62, 65, 68, 73, 76 Surcharged in Various Colors

c

d

Perf. 12½, 11½x11, 11½

1923, Aug.

117 A10(c) 2c on 1c (Bl) 45 15
118 A10(c) 2c on 1½c (Bk) 45 15
119 A11(d) 10c on 3c (Br) 4.75 15
120 A11(d) 10c on 5c (Bk) 9.00 35
121 A11(d) 10c on 12½c (R) 8.00 60
122 A11(d) 10c on 17½c (R) 2.75 3.75
a. Perf. 11½ 1,600. 900.00
b. Perf. 11½x11 2.75 3.75
123 A11(d) 10c on 22½c (R) 2.75 3.75
a. Perf. 11½ 2.75 3.75
b. Perf. 11½x11 2.75 3.75
Nos. 117-123 (7) 28.15 8.90
Set, never hinged 60.00

Queen Wilhelmina
A21 A22

Perf. 11, 11½, 12, 12½ and Compound

1923, Aug. 31 **Engr.**

124 A22 2c myrtle grn 15 15
a. Vert. pair, imperf. between 2,250.
125 A21 5c green 15 15
a. Vert. pair, imperf. between 2,400.
126 A22 7½ carmine 20 15
127 A22 10c vermilion 24 15
a. Vert. pair, imperf. between 750.00 800.00
128 A22 20c ultra 2.25 32
129 A22 25c yellow 3.00 52
130 A22 35c orange 3.75 1.75
131 A22 50c black 11.00 20
132 A21 1g red 20.00 4.00
133 A21 2½g black 140.00 125.00
134 A21 5g dark blue 125.00 100.00
Nos. 124-134 (11) 305.74 232.39
Set, never hinged 800.00

25th anniv. of the assumption of the Government of the Netherlands by Queen Wilhelmina at the age of 18.

Nos. 119, 73 Overprinted in Red "DIENSTZEGEL PORTEN AANTEEKENRECHT; No. 73 with New Value in Blue

1923 ***Perf. 12½***

135 A11 10c on 3c 1.10 1.10
Never hinged 3.00
136 A11 1g on 17½c 60.00 14.00
Never hinged 175.00
a. Perf. 11½ 60.00 22.50
b. Perf. 11½x11 52.50 18.00

Stamps with red surcharge were prepared for use as Officials but were not issued.

Queen Wilhelmina — A23

1924, Sept. 6 **Photo.** ***Perf. 12½***

137 A23 10c slate green 30.00 30.00
Never hinged 57.50
138 A23 15c gray black 35.00 35.00
Never hinged 65.00
139 A23 35c brown orange 30.00 30.00
Never hinged 57.50

These stamps were available solely to visitors to the International Philatelic Exhibition at The Hague and were not obtainable at regular post offices.
See Nos. 147-160, 172-193. For overprints and surcharge see Nos. 194, O11, O13-O15.

Ship in Distress A23a

Lifeboat A23b

1924, Sept. 15 **Litho.** ***Perf. 11½***

140 A23a 2c black brn 1.65 1.40
Never hinged 4.25
141 A23b 10c orange brn 5.75 1.40
Never hinged 16.00

Centenary of Royal Dutch Lifeboat Society.

Type A23 and

Gull — A24

1924-26 ***Perf. 12½***

142 A24 1c deep red 40 48
143 A24 2c red org 1.90 15
144 A24 2½c deep green 2.25 65
145 A24 3c yel grn ('25) 10.00 90
146 A24 4c dp ultra 2.25 48

Photo.

147 A23 5c dull green 4.50 60
148 A23 6c org brn ('25) 55 42
149 A23 7½c org ('25) 25 15
150 A23 9c org red & blk ('26) 1.25 1.00
151 A23 10c red 1.10 15
152 A23 12½c dp rose 1.40 32
153 A23 15c ultra 5.00 35
154 A23 20c dp blue ('25) 9.00 48
155 A23 25c ol bis ('25) 20.00 65
156 A23 30c violet 11.00 55
157 A23 35c ol brn ('25) 27.50 5.00
158 A23 40c dp brown 25.00 55
159 A23 50c blue grn ('25) 50.00 48
160 A23 60c dk vio ('25) 22.50 70
Nos. 142-160 (19) 195.85 14.06
Set, never hinged 675.00

See Nos. 164-171. For overprints and surcharges see Nos. 226-243, O9-O10.

Syncopated Perforations

Type A

Type C

Type B

These special "syncopated" or "interrupted" perforations, devised for coil stamps, are found on Nos. 142-156, 158-160, 164-166, 168-185, 187-193 and certain semipostals of 1925-33, between Nos. B9 and B69. There are four types:
A. On two shorter sides, groups of four holes separated by blank spaces equal in width to two or three holes.
B. As "A," but on all four sides.
C. On two shorter sides, end holes are omitted.
D. Four-hole sequence on horiz. sides, three-hole on vert. sides.

1925-26 ***Syncopated, Type A (2 Sides)***

142a A24 1c deep red 52 45
143a A24 2c red orange 2.00 1.50
144a A24 2½c deep green 2.00 60
145a A24 3c yellow green 14.00 20.00
146a A24 4c deep ultra 1.90 1.25
147a A23 5c dull green 4.25 1.25
148a A23 6c orange brown 100.00 95.00
149a A23 7½c orange 70 75

150a	A23	9c	org red & blk	1.40	75
151a	A23	10c	red	9.00	2.75
152a	A23	12½c	deep rose	1.40	75
153a	A23	15c	ultra	55.00	7.50
154a	A23	20c	deep blue	8.25	3.25
155a	A23	25c	olive bister	37.50	45.00
156a	A23	30c	violet	11.00	6.75
158a	A23	40c	deep brown	42.50	30.00
159a	A23	50c	blue green	55.00	12.00
160a	A23	60c	dark violet	22.50	7.50
			Nos. 142a-160a (18)	368.92	237.05
			Set, never hinged	950.00	

A25

1925-27 Engr. *Perf. 11½, 12½*

161	A25	1g	ultra	7.50	25
			Never hinged	15.00	
162	A25	2½g	car ('27)	75.00	3.50
			Never hinged	150.00	
163	A25	5g	gray blk	140.00	2.25
			Never hinged	275.00	

Types of 1924-26 Issue

Perf. 12½, 13½x12½, 12½x13½

1926-39 Wmk. 202 Litho.

164	A24	½c	gray ('28)	90	1.00
165	A24	1c	dp red ('27)	15	15
166	A24	1½c	red vio ('28)	1.25	15
c.			"CEN" for "CENT"	165.00	325.00
c.			Never hinged	300.00	
167	A24	1½c	gray ('35)	15	15
a.			1½c dark gray	15	15
168	A24	2c	dp org	15	15
a.			2c red orange	15	15
169	A24	2½c	green ('27)	2.25	15
170	A24	3c	yel grn ('27)	15	15
171	A24	4c	dp ultra ('27)	15	15
			Photo.		
172	A23	5c	dp green	15	15
173	A23	6c	org brn ('27)	15	15
174	A23	7½c	dk vio ('27)	3.50	15
175	A23	7½c	red ('28)	15	15
176	A23	9c	org red & blk ('28)	10.00	11.00
b.			Value omitted	*12,500.*	
177	A23	10c	red	1.00	15
178	A23	10c	dl vio ('29)	2.25	15
179	A23	12½c	dp rose ('27)	40.00	4.25
180	A23	12½c	ultra ('28)	30	15
181	A23	15c	ultra	6.00	25
182	A23	15c	orange ('29)	70	15
183	A23	20c	dp blue ('28)	6.00	15
184	A23	21c	ol brn ('31)	22.50	1.00
185	A23	22½c	ol brn ('27)	5.75	2.75
186	A23	22½c	dp org ('39)	14.00	17.00
187	A23	25c	ol bis ('27)	3.50	15
188	A23	27½c	gray ('28)	3.50	80
189	A23	30c	violet	4.25	15
190	A23	35c	ol brn	55.00	15.00
191	A23	40c	dp brown	9.00	25
192	A23	50c	blue grn	4.50	25
193	A23	60c	black ('29)	24.00	1.00
			Nos. 164-193 (30)	221.35	57.25
			Set, never hinged	650.00	

See Nos. 243A-243Q.

Syncopated, Type A (2 Sides), 12½

1926-27

168b	A24	2c	deep orange	40	40
170a	A24	3c	yellow green	60	60
171a	A24	4c	deep ultra	60	60
172a	A23	5c	deep green	80	75
173a	A23	6c	orange brown	40	50
174a	A23	7½c	dark violet	4.00	2.00
177a	A23	10c	red	1.00	80
181a	A23	15c	ultra	6.00	2.50
185a	A23	22½c	olive brown	7.00	2.50
187a	A23	25c	olive bister	18.00	16.00
189a	A23	30c	violet	16.00	10.00
190a	A23	35c	olive brown	70.00	20.00
191a	A23	40c	deep brown	40.00	37.50
			Nos. 168b-191a (13)	164.80	94.15
			Set, never hinged	360.00	

1928 *Syncopated, Type B (4 Sides)*

164a	A24	½c	gray	48	32
165a	A24	1c	deep red	22	22
166a	A24	1½c	red violet	22	15
168c	A24	2c	deep orange	65	1.00
169a	A24	2½c	green	2.00	18
170b	A24	3c	yellow green	45	35
171b	A24	4c	deep ultra	45	35
172b	A23	5c	deep green	65	52
173b	A23	6c	orange brown	45	35
174b	A23	7½c	dark violet	3.00	1.75
175a	A23	7½c	red	22	18
176a	A23	9c	org red & blk	9.00	8.00
178a	A23	10c	dull violet	4.00	3.50
179a	A23	12½c	deep rose	75.00	75.00
180a	A23	12½c	ultra	1.10	26
181b	A23	15c	ultra	5.25	1.75
182a	A23	15c	orange	52	26
183a	A23	20c	deep blue	5.25	2.75
187b	A23	25c	olive bister	14.00	9.00
188a	A23	27½c	gray	3.50	1.40
189b	A23	30c	violet	12.50	7.25
191b	A23	40c	deep brown	27.50	22.50

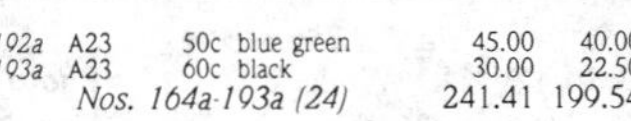

192a	A23	50c	blue green	45.00	40.00
193a	A23	60c	black	30.00	22.50
			Nos. 164a-193a (24)	241.41	199.54

Syncopated, Type C (2 Sides, Corners Only)

1930

164b	A24	½c	gray	42	35
165b	A24	1c	deep red	60	35
166b	A24	1½c	red violet	18	15
168d	A24	2c	deep orange	48	38
169b	A24	2½c	green	2.25	26
170c	A24	3c	yellow green	70	42
171c	A24	4c	deep ultra	35	18
172c	A23	5c	deep green	52	35
173c	A23	6c	orange brown	45	35
178b	A23	10c	dull violet	7.00	6.75
183b	A23	20c	deep blue	5.25	3.50
184a	A23	21c	olive brown	22.50	6.00
189c	A23	30c	violet	10.50	6.75
192b	A23	50c	blue green	35.00	35.00
			Nos. 164b-192b (14)	86.20	60.79
			Set, never hinged	225.00	

1927

Syncopated, Type D (3 Holes Vert., 4 Holes Horiz.)

174c	A23	7½c	dark violet	*2,000.*	*2,000.*
			Never hinged	2,100.	

No. 185 Surcharged in Red

21

1929, Nov. 11 *Perf. 12½*

194	A23	21c on 22½c	ol brn	15.00	1.25
			Never hinged	50.00	

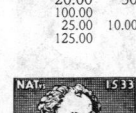

Queen Wilhelmina — A26

1931, Oct. Photo. *Perf. 12½*

195	A26	70c	dk bl & red	20.00	50
			Never hinged	100.00	
a.			Perf. 14½x13½ ('39)	25.00	10.00
			Never hinged	125.00	

Arms of the House of Orange — A27

William I, Portrait by Goltzius — A28

Designs: 6c, Portrait of William I by Van Key. 12½c, Portrait attributed to Moro.

Perf. 12½

1933, Apr. 1 Unwmk. Engr.

196	A27	1½c	black	50	15
197	A28	5c	dark green	1.40	28
198	A28	6c	dull violet	3.50	15
199	A28	12½c	deep blue	15.00	3.25
			Set, never hinged	65.00	

400th anniv. of the birth of William I, Count of Nassau and Prince of Orange, frequently referred to as William the Silent.

Star, Dove and Sword — A31

Queen Wilhelmina and Ships — A32

1933, May 18 Photo. Wmk. 202

200	A31	12½c	dp ultra	8.00	35
			Never hinged	32.50	

For overprint see No. O12.

Perf. 14½x13½

1933, July 26 Unwmk.

201	A32	80c	Prus bl & red	90.00	3.25
			Never hinged	400.00	

Willemstad Harbor — A33

Van Walbeeck's Ship — A34

1934, July 2 Engr. *Perf. 14x12½*

202	A33	6c	violet blk	3.00	15
203	A34	12½c	dull blue	17.00	3.25
			Set, never hinged	80.00	

Tercentenary of Curacao.

Minerva — A35

Design: 12½c, Gisbertius Voetius.

Perf. 12½

1936, May 15 Photo. Wmk. 202

204	A35	6c	brown lake	1.90	22
205	A35	12½c	indigo	3.25	3.25
			Set, never hinged	15.00	

300th anniversary of the founding of the University at Utrecht.

Boy Scout Emblem A37

"Assembly" A38

Mercury — A39

1937, Apr. 1 *Perf. 14½x13½*

206	A37	1½c	green & blk	20	15
207	A38	6c	red brn & blk	1.00	15
208	A39	12½c	blue & blk	2.75	1.00
			Set, never hinged	12.00	

Fifth Boy Scout World Jamboree, Vogelenzang, Netherlands, July 31-Aug. 13, 1937.

Wilhelmina A40

St. Willibrord A41

1938, Aug. 27 *Perf. 12½x12*

209	A40	1½c	black	15	15
210	A40	5c	red orange	20	15
211	A40	12½c	royal blue	3.00	1.25
			Set, never hinged	13.00	

40th anniversary of the reign of Queen Wilhelmina.

Perf. 12½x13½

1939, June 15 Engr. Unwmk.

Design: 12½c, St. Willibrord as older man.

212	A41	5c	dk slate grn	75	15
213	A41	12½c	slate blue	4.00	2.50
			Set, never hinged	16.00	

12th centenary of the death of St. Willibrord.

Woodburning Engine — A43

Queen Wilhelmina — A45

Design: 12½c, Streamlined electric car.

Perf. 14½x13½

1939, Sept. 1 Photo. Wmk. 202

214	A43	5c	dk slate grn	1.00	15
215	A43	12½c	dark blue	8.00	3.50
			Set, never hinged	22.00	

Centenary of Dutch Railroads.

Catalogue values for unused stamps in this section, from this point to the end of the section, are for Never Hinged items.

1940-47 *Perf. 13½x12½*

216	A45	5c	dk green	15	15
216B	A45	6c	hn brn ('47)	52	18
217	A45	7½c	brt red	15	15
218	A45	10c	brt red vio	15	15
219	A45	12½c	sapphire	15	15
220	A45	15c	light blue	15	15
220B	A45	17½c	slate bl ('46)	1.25	80
221	A45	20c	purple	15	15
222	A45	22½c	olive grn	85	60
223	A45	25c	rose brn	20	15
224	A45	30c	bister	60	40
225	A45	40c	brt green	1.00	60
225A	A45	50c	orange ('46)	8.75	75
225B	A45	60c	pur brn ('46)	7.00	2.75
			Nos. 216-225B (14)	21.07	7.13

Imperf. copies of Nos. 216, 218-220 were released through philatelic channels during the German occupation, but were never issued at any post office. Value, set, $1.

For overprints see Nos. O16-O24.

Type of 1924-26 Surcharged in Black or Blue

Perf. 12½x13½

1940, Oct. Photo. Wmk. 202

226	A24	2½c	on 3c ver	1.50	15
227	A24	5c	on 3c lt grn	15	15
228	A24	7½c	on 3c ver	15	15
a.			Pair, #226, 228		
229	A24	10c	on 3c lt grn	15	15
230	A24	12½c	on 3c lt bl (Bl)	22	20
231	A24	17½c	on 3c lt grn	52	65
232	A24	20c	on 3c lt grn	32	15

233 A24 22½c on 3c lt grn 1.00 85
234 A24 25c on 3c lt grn 35 20
235 A24 30c on 3c lt grn 45 32
236 A24 40c on 3c lt grn 60 60
237 A24 50c on 3c lt grn 70 42
238 A24 60c on 3c lt grn 1.25 85
239 A24 70c on 3c lt grn 2.25 1.65
240 A24 80c on 3c lt grn 4.50 3.50
241 A24 1g on 3c lt grn 35.00 30.00
242 A24 2.50g on 3c lt grn 40.00 35.00
243 A24 5g on 3c lt grn 35.00 32.50
Nos. 226-243 (18) 124.11 107.49

No. 228a is from coils.

Gull Type of 1924-26

1941
243A A24 2½c dk green 1.25 35
b. Booklet pane of 6 10.00
243C A24 5c brt green 15 15
243E A24 7½c henna 15 15
r. Pair, #243A, 243E 1.00
243G A24 10c brt violet 15 15
243H A24 12½c ultra 15 15
243J A24 15c lt blue 15 15
243K A24 17½c red org 15 15
243L A24 20c lt violet 18 20
243M A24 22½c dk ol grn 15 15
243N A24 25c lake 15 20
243O A24 30c olive 3.50 20
243P A24 40c emerald 15 20
243Q A24 50c orange brn 15 20
Nos. 243A-243Q (13) 6.43 2.40

No. 243r is from coils.

Post Horn and Lion — A46

Gold Surcharge

1943, Jan. 15 Photo. *Perf. 12½x12*
244 A46 10c on 2½c yel 15 25
a. Surcharge omitted 6,000. 6,500.

Founding of the European Union of Posts and Telegraphs at Vienna, Oct. 19, 1942. Surcharge reads: "Europeesche P T T Vereeniging 19 October 1942 10 Cent."

Sea Horse — A47

Triple-crown Tree — A48

Admiral M. A. de Ruyter — A54

Designs: 2c, Swans. 2½c, Tree of Life. 3c, Tree with snake roots. 4c, Man on horseback. 5c, Prancing white horses. 10c, Johan Evertsen. 12½c, Martin Tromp. 15c, Piet Hein. 17½c, Willem van Ghent. 20c, Witte de With. 22½c, Cornelis Evertsen. 25c, Tjerk de Vries. 30c, Cornelis Tromp. 40c, Cornelis Evertsen De Jongste.

Perf. 12x12½, 12½x12
1943-44 Photo. Wmk. 202
245 A47 1c black 15 15
246 A48 1½c rose lake 15 15
247 A47 2c dk blue 15 15
248 A48 2½c dk blue grn 15 15
249 A47 3c copper red 15 15
250 A48 4c black brown 15 15
251 A47 5c dull yel grn 15 15

Unwmk.
252 A54 7½c henna brn 15 15
a. Thinner numerals and letters ('44) 15 15
253 A54 10c dk green 15 15
254 A54 12½c blue 15 18
255 A54 15c dull lilac 15 15
256 A54 17½c slate ('44) 15 15
257 A54 20c dull brown 15 15
258 A54 22½c org red 15 25
259 A54 25c vio rose ('44) 35 55
260 A54 30c cobalt bl ('44) 15 18

Engr.
261 A54 40c bluish blk 15 20
Nos. 245-261 (17) 2.75 3.16

In 1944, 200,000 copies of No. 247 were privately punched with a cross and printed on the back with a number and the words "Prijs 15 Cent toeslag ten bate Ned. Roode Kruis." These were sold at an exhibition, the surtax going to the Red Cross. The Dutch post office tolerated these stamps.

Soldier — A64

S. S. "Nieuw Amsterdam" — A65

Pilot — A66

Cruiser "De Ruyter" — A67

Queen Wilhelmina — A68

Perf. 12, 12½
1944-46 Unwmk. Engr.
262 A64 1½c black 15 15
263 A65 2½c yellow grn 15 15
264 A66 3c dull red brn 15 15
265 A67 5c dk blue 15 15
266 A68 7½c vermilion 15 15
267 A68 10c yellow org 15 20
268 A68 12½c ultra 15 18
269 A68 15c dl red brn ('46) 1.40 4.50
270 A68 17½c gray grn ('46) 1.00 2.50
271 A68 20c violet 15 28
272 A68 22½c rose red ('46) 55 1.00
273 A68 25c brn org ('46) 2.00 2.75
274 A68 30c blue grn 15 20
275 A68 40c dk vio brn ('46) 2.00 4.50
276 A68 50c red vio ('46) 1.10 2.00
Nos. 262-276 (15) 9.40 18.86

These stamps were used on board Dutch war and merchant ships until Netherlands' liberation.

Lion and Dragon — A69

Queen Wilhelmina — A70

1945, July 15 *Perf. 12½x14*
277 A69 7½c red orange 15 15

Issued to commemorate Netherlands' liberation or "rising again."

1946 Engr. *Perf. 13½x14*
278 A70 1g dk blue 45 28
279 A70 2½g brick red 125.00 3.25
280 A70 5g dk olive grn 125.00 12.50
281 A70 10g dk purple 125.00 11.00

A71

Perf. 12½x13½
1946-47 Wmk. 202 Photo.
282 A71 1c dk red 15 15
283 A71 2c ultra 15 15
284 A71 2½c dp org ('47) 8.75 1.65
285 A71 4c olive grn 28 15

The 1c was reissued in 1969 on phosphorescent paper in booklet pane No. 345b. The 4c was reissued on fluorescent paper in 1962.

The 2c was issued in coils in 1972. Every fifth stamp has black control number on back.

See Nos. 340-343A, 404-406.

Queen Wilhelmina
A72 A73

1947-48 *Perf. 13½x12½*
286 A72 5c ol grn ('48) 52 15
287 A72 6c brown blk 15 15
288 A72 7½c dp red brn ('48) 15 15
289 A72 10c brt red vio 30 15
290 A72 12½c scar ('48) 30 38
291 A72 15c purple 1.90 15
292 A72 20c dp blue 3.50 15
293 A72 22½c ol brn ('48) 45 55
294 A72 25c ultra 11.00 15
295 A72 30c dp orange 6.00 22
296 A72 35c dk bl grn 5.25 45
297 A72 40c henna brn 17.00 45

Engr.
298 A73 45c dp bl ('48) 22.50 10.00
299 A73 50c brown ('48) 18.00 30
300 A73 60c red ('48) 19.00 2.00
Nos. 286-300 (15) 106.02 15.40

For surcharge see No. 330.

Type of 1947

1948 Photo.
301 A72 6c gray blue 25 15

Queen Wilhelmina A74

Queen Juliana A75

Perf. 12½x14
1948, Aug. 30 Engr. Unwmk.
302 A74 10c vermilion 15 15
303 A74 20c dp blue 1.65 1.50

50th anniv. of the reign of Queen Wilhelmina.

Perf. 14x13
1948, Sept. 7 Photo. Wmk. 202
304 A75 10c dark brown 90 15
305 A75 20c ultra 1.75 60

Investiture of Queen Juliana, Sept. 6, 1948.

Queen Juliana
A76 A77

1949 *Perf. 13½x12½*
306 A76 5c olive grn 55 15
307 A76 6c gray blue 28 15
308 A76 10c deep orange 28 15
309 A76 12c org red 1.50 1.00
310 A76 15c olive brn 3.25 15
311 A76 20c brt blue 3.00 15
312 A76 25c org brn 9.50 15
313 A76 30c violet 7.50 15
314 A76 35c gray 13.00 20
315 A76 40c red vio 27.50 20
316 A76 45c red org 1.40 1.00
317 A76 50c blue green 7.50 20
318 A76 60c red brown 11.00 20
Nos. 306-318 (13) 86.26 3.85

See No. 325-327. For surcharge see No. B248.

1949 Unwmk. Engr. *Perf. 12½x12*
319 A77 1g rose red 2.50 15
320 A77 2½g black brn 165.00 1.00
321 A77 5g orange brn 375.00 2.50
322 A77 10g dk vio brn 300.00 12.00

Two types exist of No. 321.

Post Horns Entwined — A78

Janus Dousa — A79

Perf. 11½x12½
1949, Oct. 1 Photo. Wmk. 202
323 A78 10c brown red 15 15
324 A78 20c dull blue 6.00 2.75

75th anniversary of the UPU.

Juliana Type of 1949

1950-51 *Perf. 13½x12½*
325 A76 12c scar ('51) 5.75 60
326 A76 45c vio brn 35.00 30
327 A76 75c car rose ('51) 85.00 1.25

1950, Oct. 3 *Perf. 11½x13*

Design: 20c, Jan van Hout.

328 A79 10c olive brn 3.50 20
329 A79 20c deep blue 4.00 1.65

375th anniversary of the founding of the University of Leyden.

No. 288 Surcharged with New Value

1950 *Perf. 13½x12½*
330 A72 6c on 7½c dp red brn 2.00 15

Miner — A80

Perf. 12x12½
1952, Apr. 16 Engr. Unwmk.
331 A80 10c dark blue 2.50 15

50th anniversary of the founding of Netherlands' mining and chemical industry.

Telegraph Poles and Train of 1852 — A81

Designs: 6c, Radio towers. 10c, Mail Delivery 1852. 20c, Modern postman.

1952, June 28 *Perf. 13x14*
332 A81 2c gray violet 35 20
333 A81 6c vermilion 42 35
334 A81 10c green 60 20
335 A81 20c gray blue 5.00 2.75

Centenary of Dutch postage stamps and of the telegraph service.

1952, June 28
336 A81 2c chocolate 12.00 17.00
337 A81 6c dk bluish grn 12.00 17.00
338 A81 10c brn car 12.00 17.00
339 A81 20c vio blue 12.00 17.00

Nos. 336 to 339 sold for 1.38g, which included the price of admission to the International Postage Stamp Centenary Exhibition, Utrecht.

Numeral Type of 1946-47

Perf. 12½x13½

1953-57 Wmk. 202 Photo.

340 A71 3c dp org brn 15 15
341 A71 5c orange 15 15
342 A71 6c gray ('54) 25 15
343 A71 7c red org 15 15
343A A71 8c brt lil ('57) 15 15
Set value 65 40

The 5c and 7c perf. on 3 sides, and with watermark vertical, are from booklet panes Nos. 346a-346b. The 5c perf. on 3 sides, with wmk. horiz., is from No. 349a.

In 1972 the 5c was printed on phosphorescent paper.

Queen Juliana
A82 A83

1953-71 Wmk. 202 *Perf. 13½x12½*

344 A82 10c dk red brn 15 15
a. Bklt. pane of 6 (1 #344 + 5 #346C)('65) 5.00
345 A82 12c dk Prus grn ('54) 15 15
a. Bklt. pane of 7 + label (5 #345 + 2 #347)('67) 5.50
b. Bklt. pane, 4 #282 + 8 #345 ('69) 12.50
346 A82 15c dp carmine 15 15
a. Bklt. pane of 8 (2 #341 in vert. pair + 6 #346)('64) 17.00
b. Bklt. pane of 12 (10 #343 + 2 #346)('64) 12.50
e. Bklt. pane of 8 (2 #341 in horiz. pair + 6 #346)('70) 9.00
346C A82 18c dull bl ('65) 30 15
d. Bklt. pane of 10 (8 #343A + 2 #346C)('65) 4.50
347 A82 20c dk gray 15 15
b. Bklt. pane of 5 + label ('66) 4.00
347A A82 24c olive ('63) 32 15
348 A82 25c dp blue 15 15
349 A82 30c dp org 38 15
a. Bklt. pane of 5 + label (2 #341 + 3 #349)('71) 22.50
350 A82 35c dk ol brn ('54) 95 15
351 A82 37c aqua ('58) 55 15
352 A82 40c dk slate 26 15
353 A82 45c scarlet 42 15
354 A82 50c dk bl grn 32 15
355 A82 60c brown bis 32 15
356 A82 62c dl red lil ('58) 4.50 4.00
357 A82 70c blue ('57) 45 15
358 A82 75c deep plum 45 15
359 A82 80c brt vio ('58) 52 15
360 A82 85c brt bl grn ('56) 70 15
360A A82 95c org brn ('67) 1.40 26
Nos. 344-360A (20) 12.59
Set value 5.65

Coils of the 12, 15, 20, 25, 30, 40, 45, 50, 60, 70, 75 and 80c were issued in 1972. Black control number on back of every fifth stamp.

Watermark is vertical on some stamps from booklet panes.

Some booklet panes, Nos. 344a, 347b, 349a, etc., have a large selvage the size of four or six stamps, with printed inscription and sometimes illustration.

Phosphorescent paper was introduced in 1967 for the 12, 15, 20 and 45c; in 1969 for the 25c, and in 1971 for the 30, 40, 50, 60, 70, 75 and 80c.

Of the booklet panes, Nos. 345a, 345b, 346d, 346e and 347b were issued on both ordinary and phosphorescent paper, and No. 349a only on phosphorescent paper.

See No. 407. For surcharge see No. 374.

Perf. 12½x12

1954-57 Unwmk. Engr.

361 A83 1g vermilion 2.75 15
362 A83 2½g dk green ('55) 9.00 15
363 A83 5g black ('55) 2.25 30
364 A83 10g vio bl ('57) 16.00 1.25

St. Boniface — A84

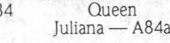

Queen Juliana — A84a

1954, June 16

365 A84 10c blue 2.00 15

1200th anniversary of the death of St. Boniface.

Perf. 13½

1954, Dec. 15 Photo. Wmk. 202

366 A84a 10c scarlet 80 15

Issued to publicize the Charter of the Kingdom, adopted December 15, 1954.

Flaming Sword — A85

"Rebuilding Europe" — A86

1955, May 4 *Perf. 12½x12*

367 A85 10c crimson 1.10 15

10th anniv. of Netherlands' liberation.

1956, Sept. 15 Unwmk. *Perf. 13x14*

368 A86 10c rose brn & blk 75 15
369 A86 25c brt bl & blk 37.50 2.25

Europa. Issued to symbolize the cooperation among the six countries comprising the Coal and Steel Community.

Admiral M. A. de Ruyter — A87

"United Europe" — A88

Design: 30c, Flagship "De Zeven Provincien."

1957, July 2 Engr. *Perf. 12½x12*

370 A87 10c orange 35 15
371 A87 30c dk blue 3.50 1.75

350th anniversary of the birth of Adm. M. A. de Ruyter (1607-1676).

1957, Sept. 16 Photo. *Perf. 13x14*

372 A88 10c blk, gray & ultra 65 15
373 A88 30c dull grn & ultra 6.50 1.50

United Europe for peace and prosperity.

No. 344 Surcharged in Silver with New Value and Bars

Perf. 13½x12½

1958, May 16 Photo. Wmk. 202

374 A82 12c on 10c 1.10 15
a. Double surcharge 450.00 450.00
b. Inverted surcharge 450.00 450.00

Europa Issue, 1958

Common Design Type

Perf. 13x14

1958, Sept. 13 Litho. Unwmk.

Size: 22x33mm

375 CD1 12c org ver & blue 25 15
376 CD1 30c blue & red 1.00 1.10

NATO Emblem — A89

1959, Apr. 3 *Perf. 12½x12*

377 A89 12c yel org & blue 15 15
378 A89 30c red & blue 65 80

10th anniversary of NATO.

Europa Issue, 1959.

Common Design Type

1959, Sept. 19 *Perf. 13x14*

Size: 22x33mm

379 CD2 12c crimson 38 15
380 CD2 30c yellow grn 2.00 1.75

Douglas DC-8 and World Map — A90

J. C. Schroeder van der Kolk — A91

Design: 30c, Douglas DC-8 in flight.

1959, Oct. 5 Engr. *Perf. 14x13*

381 A90 12c carmine & ultra 22 15
382 A90 30c dp blue & dp grn 1.00 1.40

40th anniversary of the founding of KLM, Royal Dutch Airlines.

Perf. 12½x12

1960, July 18 Unwmk.

Design: 30c, Johannes Wier.

383 A91 12c red 16 15
384 A91 30c dark blue 3.75 2.25

Issued to publicize Mental Health Year and to honor Schroeder van der Kolk and Johannes Wier, pioneers of mental health.

Europa Issue, 1960

Common Design Type

1960, Sept. 19 Photo. *Perf. 12x12½*

Size: 27x21mm

385 CD3 12c car rose & org 24 20
386 CD3 30c dk blue & yel 2.50 1.90

1st anniv. of CEPT. Spokes symbolize 19 founding members of Conference.

Europa Issue, 1961

Common Design Type

1961, Sept. 18 *Perf. 14x13*

Size: 32½x21½mm

387 CD4 12c golden brown 15 15
388 CD4 30c Prus blue 24 20
Set value 28

Queen Juliana and Prince Bernhard — A92

Telephone Dial — A93

Perf. 14x13

1962, Jan. 5 Unwmk. Photo.

389 A92 12c dk red 20 15
390 A92 30c dk green 1.75 1.00

Silver wedding anniversary of Queen Juliana and Prince Bernhard.

1962, May 22 *Perf. 13x14, 14x13*

Designs: 12c, Map showing telephone network. 30c, Arch and dial, horiz.

391 A93 4c brown red & blk 20 15
392 A93 12c brown ol & blk 32 15
393 A93 30c black, bis & Prus bl 2.00 1.50

Completion of the automation of the Netherlands telephone network.

Europa Issue, 1962

Common Design Type

1962, Sept. 17 *Perf. 14x13*

Size: 33x22mm

394 CD5 12c lemon, yel & blk 20 15
395 CD5 30c blue, yel & blk 95 75

Polder with Canals and Windmills — A94

Design: 4c, Cooling towers, Limburg State Coal Mines. 10c, Dredging in Delta.

Perf. 12½x13½

1962-66 Wmk. 202 Photo.

399 A94 4c dk blue ('63) 20 15
401 A94 6c grn & dk grn 70 15
403 A94 10c dp claret ('63) 20 15
a. Booklet pane of 10 ('66) 4.00
Set value 24

The 10c was issued in coils in 1972. Every fifth stamp has black control number on back.

See No. 461b.

Types of 1946 and 1953

1962-73 Unwmk.

Phosphorescent Paper

404 A71 4c olive green 40 20
405 A71 5c orange ('73) 40 15
406 A71 8c bright lilac 15.00 12.00
407 A82 12c dk Prus green 60 40

The 5c is from booklets and has the phosphor on the front only.

Issue dates: 5c, Jan. 12; others Aug. 27.

See Nos. 460d, 461c, 461d and 463a.

Wheat Emblem and Globe — A95

Inscription in Circle — A96

1963, Mar. 21 Photo. *Perf. 14x13*

413 A95 12c dl bl, dk bl & yel 15 15
414 A95 30c dl car, rose & yel 1.10 95

FAO "Freedom from Hunger" campaign.

Perf. 13x14

1963, May 7 Unwmk. Litho.

415 A96 30c brt blue, blk & grn 1.40 1.00

1st Intl. Postal Conf., Paris, cent.

Europa Issue, 1963

Common Design Type

1963, Sept. 16 Photo. *Perf. 14x13*

Size: 33x22mm

416 CD6 12c red brown & yel 15 15
417 CD6 30c Prus green & yel 1.40 1.40

Prince William of Orange Landing at Scheveningen — A97

Designs: 12c, G. K. van Hogendorp, A. F. J. A. Graaf van der Duyn van Maasdam and L. Graaf van Limburg Stirum, Dutch leaders, 1813. 30c, Prince William taking oath of allegiance.

1963, Nov. 18 Photo. *Perf. 12x12½*

Size: 27½x27½mm

418 A97 4c dull bl, blk & brn 15 15
419 A97 5c dk grn, blk & red 15 15
420 A97 12c olive & blk 15 15
421 A97 30c maroon & blk 60 55
Set value 84 78

150th anniversary of the founding of the Kingdom of the Netherlands.

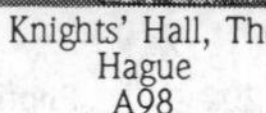

Knights' Hall, The Hague
A98

Arms of Groningen University
A99

1964, Jan. 9 ***Perf. 14x13***

422 A98 12c olive & blk 15 15

500th anniversary of the meeting of the States-General (Parliament).

1964, June 16 **Engr.** ***Perf. 12½x12***

Design: 30c, Initials "AG" and crown.

423 A99 12c slate 15 15
424 A99 30c yellow brown 20 20

350th anniv. of the University of Groningen.

Railroad Light Signal — A100

Design: 40c, Electric locomotive.

1964, July 28 **Photo.** ***Perf. 14x13***

425 A100 15c black & brt grn 15 15
426 A100 40c black & yellow 90 55

125th anniv. of the Netherlands railroads.

Bible, Chrismon and Dove — A101

1964, Aug. 25 **Unwmk.**

427 A101 15c brown red 15 15

150th anniversary of the founding of the Netherlands Bible Society.

Europa Issue, 1964
Common Design Type

1964, Sept. 14 **Photo.** ***Perf. 13x14***
Size: 22x33mm

428 CD7 15c dp olive grn 15 15
429 CD7 20c yellow brown 32 32

Benelux Issue

King Baudouin, Queen Juliana and Grand Duchess Charlotte
A101a

1964, Oct. 12 ***Perf. 14x13***
Size: 33x22mm

430 A101a 15c purple & buff 15 15

20th anniversary of the signing of the customs union of Belgium, Netherlands and Luxembourg.

Scott's editorial staff cannot undertake to identify, authenticate or appraise stamps and postal markings.

Queen Juliana — A102

"Killed in Action" and "Destroyed Town" — A103

1964, Dec. 15 **Photo.** ***Perf. 13x14***

431 A102 15c green 15 15

10th anniversary of the Charter of the Kingdom of the Netherlands.

1965, Apr. 6 **Photo.** ***Perf. 12x12½***

Statues: 15c, "Docker" Amsterdam, and "Killed in Action" Waalwijk. 40c, "Destroyed Town" Rotterdam, and "Docker" Amsterdam.

432 A103 7c black & dk red 15 15
433 A103 15c black & dk olive 15 15
434 A103 40c black & dk red 85 60
Set value 1.00 75

Resistance movement of World War II.

Knight Class IV, Order of William
A104

ITU Emblem
A105

1965, Apr. 29 ***Perf. 13x14***

435 A104 1g gray 90 75

150th anniversary of the establishment of the Military Order of William.

1965, May 17 **Litho.** ***Perf. 14x13***

436 A105 20c dull bl & tan 18 15
437 A105 40c tan & dull bl 40 32

Centenary of the International Telecommunication Union.

Europa Issue, 1965
Common Design Type

1965, Sept. 27 **Photo.**
Size: 33x22mm

438 CD8 18c org brn, dk red & blk 15 15
439 CD8 20c sapphire, brn & blk 28 16
Set value 24

Marines of 1665 and 1965 — A106

1965, Dec. 10 **Engr.** ***Perf. 13x14***

440 A106 18c dk vio bl & car 15 15

300th anniversary of the Netherlands Marine Corps.

Europa Issue, 1966
Common Design Type

1966, Sept. 26 **Photo.** ***Perf. 13x14***
Size: 22x33mm

441 CD9 20c citron 15 15
442 CD9 40c dull blue 25 16
Set value 24

Assembly Hall, Delft University
A107

1967, Jan. 5 **Litho.** ***Perf. 14x13***

443 A107 20c lemon & sepia 15 15

125th anniversary of the founding of the Delft University of Technology.

Europa Issue, 1967
Common Design Type
Perf. 13x14

1967, May 2 **Unwmk.** **Photo.**
Ordinary Paper
Size: 22x32½mm

444 CD10 20c dull blue 50 20
445 CD10 45c dull vio brn 1.50 80

Wmk. 202

446 CD10 20c dull blue 1.00 25
447 CD10 45c dull vio brn 1.50 95

Nos. 446-447 are on phosphorescent paper.

Stamp of 1852, #1 — A108

1967, May 8 **Engr.** **Unwmk.**

448 A108 20c shown 2.00 2.00
449 A108 25c No. 5 2.00 2.00
450 A108 75c No. 10 2.00 2.00

AMPHILEX 67, Amsterdam, May 11-21. Sold only in complete sets together with a 2.50g admission ticket to Amsterdam Philatelic Exhibition. Issued in sheets of 10 (5x2).

Coins and Punched Card — A109

1968, Jan. 16 **Photo.** ***Perf. 14x13***

451 A109 20c ver, blk & dl yel 20 15

50th anniversary of the postal checking service.

Luminescence

All commemorative issues from No. 451 to No. 511 are printed on phosphorescent paper except No. 478 which is printed with phosphorescent ink, and Nos. 490-492. Some later issues are tagged.

Europa Issue, 1968
Common Design Type

1968, Apr. 29 **Photo.** ***Perf. 14x13***
Size: 32½x22mm

452 CD11 20c deep blue 35 15
453 CD11 45c crimson 1.10 85

National Anthem — A110

Fokker F.2, 1919, and Friendship F.29 — A111

1968, Aug. 27 **Litho.** ***Perf. 13x14***

454 A110 20c gray, org, car & dk bl 25 15

400th anniversary of the national anthem "Wilhelmus van Nassouwe."

1968, Oct. 1 **Photo.** ***Perf. 14x13***

Planes: 12c, Wright A, 1909, and Cessna sports plane. 45c, De Havilland DH-9, 1919, and Douglas DC-9.

455 A111 12c crim, pink & blk 15 15
456 A111 20c brt grn, bl grn & blk 15 15
457 A111 45c brt bl, lt grn & blk 1.40 1.10

50th anniversaries of the founding in 1919 of Royal Dutch Airlines and the Royal Netherlands Aircraft Factories Fokker, and the 60th anniversary in 1967 of the Royal Netherlands Aeronautical Association.

"iao" — A112

Design is made up of 28 minute lines, each reading "1919 internationale arbeids-organisatie 1969".

1969, Feb. 25 **Engr.** ***Perf. 14x13***

458 A112 25c brick red & blk 45 15
459 A112 45c ultra & blue 1.00 65

International Labor Organization, 50th anniversary.

Queen Juliana
A113 A114

Perf. 13½ horiz. x 12½ on one vert. side

1969-75 **Photo.**

460 A113 25c orange ver 3.00 32
a. Bklt. pane of 4 + 2 labels 12.50
460B A113 25c dull red ('73) 2.00 15
c. Booklet pane of 6 (#460B + 5 #461A) 27.50
d. Booklet pane of 12 (5 #405 + 7 #460B) 16.00

Perf. 13x12½

461 A113 30c choc ('72) 48 15
d. Bklt. pane of 10 (4 #405 + 6 #461 + 2 labels)('74) 6.50
461A A113 35c grnsh bl ('72) 48 15
b. Bklt. pane of 5 (3 #403, 2 #461A + label)('72) 20.00
c. Bklt. pane of 10 (5 #405 + 5 #461A + 2 labels)('75) 4.50
462 A113 40c car rose ('72) 48 15
a. Bklt. pane of 5 + label ('73) 7.50
463 A113 45c ultra ('72) 48 15
a. Bklt. pane of 8 (4 #405 + 4 #463) ('74) 4.00
464 A113 50c lilac ('72) 48 15
a. Bklt. pane of 4 + 2 labels ('75) 3.00
465 A113 60c slate bl ('72) 55 15
a. Bklt. pane of 5 + label ('80) 3.00
466 A113 70c bister ('72) 65 15
467 A113 75c green ('72) 65 15
468 A113 80c red org ('72) 70 15
468A A113 90c gray ('75) 80 18

Perf. 13x14

469 A114 1g yel green 90 15
470 A114 1.25g maroon 1.10 15
471 A114 1.50g yel bis ('71) 1.25 15
471A A114 2g dp rose lil ('72) 1.75 15
472 A114 2.50g grnsh bl 2.00 15

473 A114 5g gray ('70) 4.25 20
474 A114 10g vio bl ('70) 8.50 1.50
Nos. 460-474 (19) 30.50
Set value 3.75

Both 25c stamps issued only in booklets.
Printings were both ordinary and phosphorescent paper for Nos. 460, 460a, 469, 471-474.
Coil printings were issued later for Nos. 461, 462-471. Black control number on back of every fifth stamp.
Booklet panes have a large selvage the size of 4 or 6 stamps, with printed inscription.
See No. 542.

Europa Issue, 1969
Common Design Type

1969, Apr. 28 Photo. *Perf. 14x13*
Size: 33 ½x22mm

475 CD12 25c dark blue 1.25 15
476 CD12 45c red 2.00 1.90

A114a

A115

Möbius strip in Benelux colors.

1969, Sept. 8 Photo. *Perf. 13x14*
477 A114a 25c multicolored 40 15

25th anniversary of the signing of the customs union of Belgium, Netherlands and Luxembourg.

Photo. & Engr.
1969, Sept. 30 *Perf. 13x14*
478 A115 25c yellow grn & mar 40 15

Desiderius Erasmus (1469-1536), scholar.

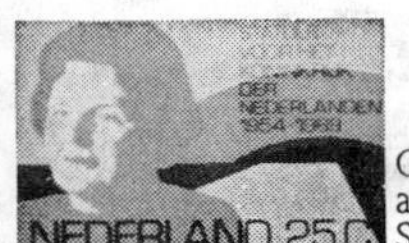

Queen Juliana and Rising Sun — A116

1969, Dec. 15 Photo. *Perf. 14x13*
479 A116 25c blue & multi 32 15

15th anniversary of the Charter of the Kingdom of the Netherlands.

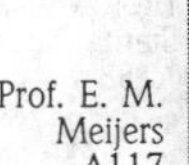

Prof. E. M. Meijers A117

1970, Jan. 13 Photo. *Perf. 14x13*
480 A117 25c blue, vio bl & grn 38 15

Issued to publicize the new Civil Code and to honor Prof. Meijers, who prepared it.

Dutch Pavilion, EXPO '70 — A118

1970, Mar. 16 Photo. *Perf. 14x13*
481 A118 25c multicolored 32 15

EXPO '70 International Exposition, Osaka, Japan, Mar. 15-Sept. 13.

"V" for Victory — A119

1970, Apr. 21 Photo. *Perf. 13x14*
482 A119 12c red, ultra, brn ol & lt bl 1.10 15

25th anniv. of liberation from the Germans.

Europa Issue, 1970
Common Design Type

1970, May 4 Photo. *Perf. 14x13*
Size: 32 ½x21 ½mm

483 CD13 25c carmine 45 15
484 CD13 45c dk blue 2.00 2.00

Panels — A120

Globe — A121

1970, June 23 Photo. *Perf. 13x14*
485 A120 25c gray, blk & brt yel grn 45 15
486 A121 45c ultra, blk & pur 1.00 85

No. 485 publicizes the meeting of the interparliamentary Union; No. 486 for the 25th anniv. of the UN.

Punch Cards — A122

1971, Feb. 16 Photo. *Perf. 14x13*
487 A122 15c dp rose lilac 22 15

14th national census, 1971.

Europa Issue, 1971
Common Design Type

1971, May 3 Photo. *Perf. 14x13*
Size: 33x22mm

488 CD14 25c lil rose, yel & blk 30 15
489 CD14 45c ultra, yel & blk 2.25 1.25

No. 488 was issued in coils and sheets. In the coils every fifth stamp has a black control number on the back.

Prince Bernhard, Fokker F27, Boeing 747 B — A123

Designs: 15c, Stylized carnation (Prince Bernhard Fund). 20c, Giant Panda (World Wildlife Fund). 15c, 20c horiz.

Photo., Litho. (20c)
1971, June 29 *Perf. 13x14*
490 A123 15c black & yellow 30 15
491 A123 20c multicolored 50 20
492 A123 25c multicolored 65 15
Set value 40

60th birthday of Prince Bernhard. See No. B475.

Map of Delta — A124

1972, Feb. 15 Photo. *Perf. 14x13*
493 A124 20c bl, grn, blk & red 42 15

Publicity for the Delta plan, a project to shorten the coastline and to build roads.

Europa Issue 1972
Common Design Type

1972, May 52 Photo. *Perf. 13x14*
Size: 22x33mm

494 CD15 30c blue & bis 1.00 15
495 CD15 45c orange & bis 1.75 1.50

No. 494 was issued in coils and sheets. In the coils every fifth stamp has a black control number on the back.

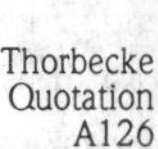
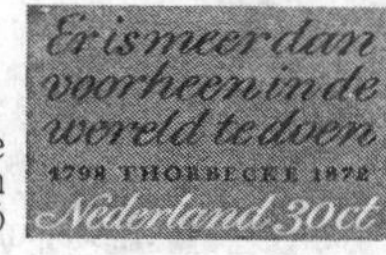

Thorbecke Quotation A126

1972, June 2 Photo. *Perf. 14x13*
496 A126 30c lt ultra & blk 45 15

Jan Rudolf Thorbecke (1798-1872), statesman, who said: "There is more to be done in the world than ever before."

Dutch Flag — A127

1972 *Perf. 13x14*
497 A127 20c blue & multi 75 15
498 A127 25c blue & multi 2.50 15

400th anniversary of the Dutch flag.
Issue dates: 20c, July 4; 25c, Nov. 1.

Woman Hurdler A128

Designs: 30c, Woman swimmer. 45c, Bicycling.

1972, July 11 *Perf. 14x13*
499 A128 20c multicolored 30 15
500 A128 30c crimson & multi 35 15
501 A128 45c violet & multi 1.40 1.10

20th Olympic Games, Munich, Aug. 26-Sept. 11.

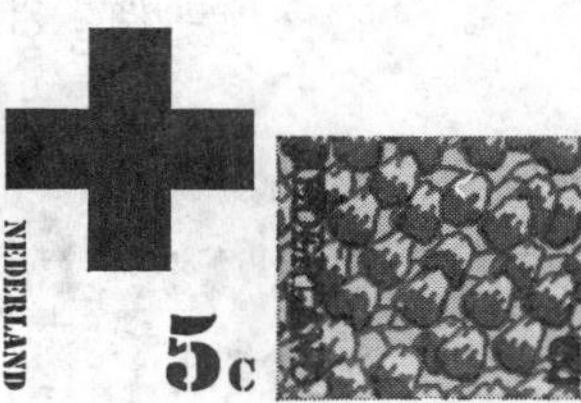

Red Cross — A129

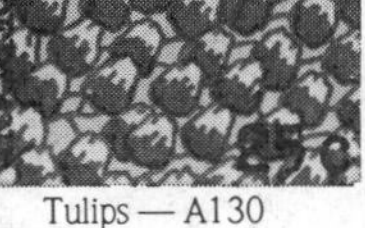
Tulips — A130

1972, Aug. 15 Photo. *Perf. 13x14*
502 A129 5c red 15 15
Nos. 502,B485-B488 (5) 3.95 2.95

Netherlands Red Cross.

1973, Mar. 20 Photo. *Perf. 14x13*
503 A130 25c rose, brt grn & blk 1.50 15

Dutch flower and bulb exports.

Europa Issue 1973
Common Design Type

1973, May 1 Photo. *Perf. 14x13*
Size: 32 ½x22mm

504 CD16 35c bright blue 50 15
505 CD16 50c purple 1.50 90

Hockey A132

Woman Gymnast A133

Antenna, Burum — A134

Rainbow, Measures A135

Photo. (25c, 35c); Litho. (30c, 50c)
1973, July 31 *Perf. 13x14, 14x13*
506 A132 25c black & green 25 15
507 A133 30c gray & multi 2.50 55
508 A134 35c blue & multi 30 15
509 A135 50c blue & multi 70 65

Netherlands Hockey Assoc., 75th anniv. (25c); Rhythmical Gymnastics World Championship, Rotterdam (30c); inauguration of satellite ground station at Burum (35c); cent. of intl. meteorological cooperation (50c).

Queen Juliana, Dutch and House of Orange Colors — A136

Engr. & Photo.
1973, Sept. 4 *Perf. 13x12*
510 A136 40c silver & multi 60 15

25th anniversary of reign of Queen Juliana.

Chain with Open Link — A137

1973, Oct. 16 Photo. *Perf. 13x14*
511 A137 40c grn, blk, gold & sil 2.75 15

Development Corporation.

Nature and Environment — A138

1974, Feb. 19 Photo. *Perf. 13x14*

512 A138 Strip of 3 6.00 5.25
a. 25c Bird of prey 1.65 52
b. 25c Tree 1.65 52
c. 25c Fisherman in boat and frog 1.65 52

75th anniv. of the Netherlands Assoc. for the Protection of Birds and of the State Forestry Service.

Soccer Ball — A139

Tennis Ball — A140

Perf. 14x13, 13x14

1974, June 5 Photo.

513 A139 25c multicolored 35 15
514 A140 40c multicolored 40 15

World Cup Soccer Championship, Munich, June 13-July 7 (25c) and 75th anniversary of the Royal Dutch Lawn Tennis Association (40c).

Cattle — A141

Pierced Crab under Lens — A142

Shipwreck Seen Through Binoculars — A143

1974, July 30 *Perf. 13x14*

515 A141 25c multicolored 11.00 1.75
516 A142 25c salmon pink & multi 16 16
517 A143 40c dk violet & multi 24 15

Cent. of the Netherlands Cattle Herdbook Soc. (#515); 25th anniv. of Queen Wilhelmina Fund (for cancer research) (#516); sesquicentennial of Royal Dutch Lifeboat Soc. (#517).

BENELUX Issue

"BENELUX" A143a

1974, Sept. 10 Photo. *Perf. 14x13*

518 A143a 30c bl grn, dk grn & lt bl 45 15

30th anniv. of the signing of the customs union of Belgium, Netherlands and Luxembourg.

Council of Europe Emblem A144

NATO Emblem and Sea Gull A145

1974, Sept. 10 *Perf. 13x14*

519 A144 45c black, bl & yel 45 15
520 A145 45c dk blue & silver 70 15

25th anniv. of Council of Europe (No. 519) and of North Atlantic Treaty Organization (No. 520).

Letters and Hands, Papier-maché Sculpture — A146

1974, Oct. 9

521 A146 60c purple & multi 80 50

Centenary of Universal Postal Union.

People and Map of Dam Square — A147

Brain with Window Symbolizing Free Thought — A148

Design: No. 523, Portuguese Synagogue and map of Mr. Visser Square. 35c, No. 526, like No. 522.

1975 Photo. *Perf. 13x14*

522 A147 30c multicolored 35 15
523 A147 30c multicolored 30 20
524 A147 35c multicolored 45 15
525 A148 45c dp blue & multi 38 20

Coil Stamps

Perf. 13 Horiz.

526 A147 30c multicolored 42 20
527 A147 35c multicolored 60 20

700th anniv. of Amsterdam (No. 522); 300th anniv. of the Portuguese Synagogue in Amsterdam (No. 523) and 400th anniv. of the founding of the University of Leyden and the beginning of higher education in the Netherlands (No. 525).

Issue dates: Nos. 522-523, 525-526, Feb. 26; Nos. 524, 527, Apr. 1.

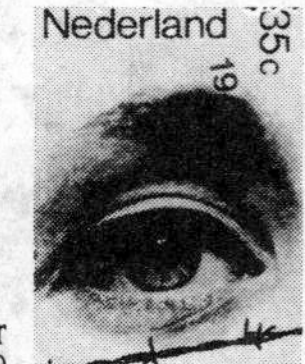

Eye Looking over Barbed Wire — A149

1975, Apr. 29 Photo. *Perf. 13x14*

528 A149 35c black & carmine 45 15

Liberation of the Netherlands from Nazi occupation, 30th anniversary.

Company Emblem and "Stad Middelburg" A150

1975, May 21 Photo. *Perf. 14x13*

529 A150 35c multicolored 30 15

Zeeland Steamship Company, centenary.

Albert Schweitzer in Boat — A151

1975, May 21

530 A151 50c multicolored 40 15

Albert Schweitzer (1875-1965), medical missionary.

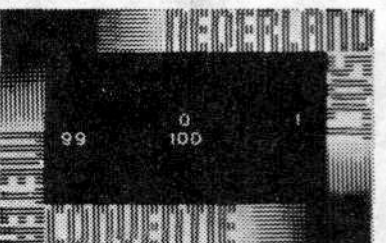

Symbolic Metric Scale — A152

1975, July 29 Litho. *Perf. 14x13*

531 A152 50c multicolored 40 15

Centenary of International Meter Convention, Paris, 1875.

Playing Card with Woman, Man, Pigeons, Pens — A153

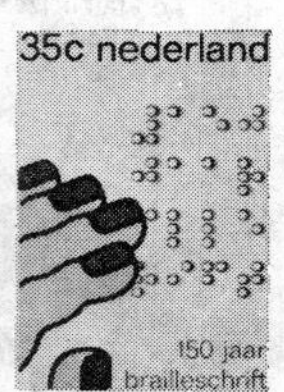

Fingers Reading Braille — A154

1975, July 29 *Perf. 13x14*

532 A153 35c multicolored 30 15

International Women's Year 1975.

1975, Oct. 7 Photo. *Perf. 13x14*

533 A154 35c multicolored 30 15

Sesquicentennial of the invention of Braille system of writing for the blind by Louis Braille (1809-1852).

Rubbings of 25¢ Coins — A155

1975, Oct. 7 *Perf. 14x13*

534 A155 50c green, blk & bl 40 15

To publicize the importance of saving.

Lottery Ticket, 18th Century A156

1976, Feb. 3 Photo. *Perf. 14x13*

535 A156 35c multicolored 25 15

250th anniversary of National Lottery.

Queen Type of 1969 and

A157

1976-86 Photo. *Perf. 12½x13½*

536 A157 5c gray 15 15
Booklet Panes
a. (3 #536, 2 #537, 3 #542) 3.00
b. (4 #536, 2 #537, 4 #539 + 2 labels) 3.25
c. (#536, 2 #537, 5 #542) 3.00
d. (4 #536, 7 #539 + label) 3.00
e. (2 #536, 2 #540, 4 #541) 3.00
f. (5 #536, 2 #537, 2 #540, 3 #542) + 2 labels 4.00
g. (1 #536, 2 #537, 5 #543) ('86) 3.00
537 A157 10c ultra 15 15
538 A157 25c violet 18 15
539 A157 40c sepia 28 15
540 A157 45c brt blue 35 15
541 A157 50c lil rose ('80) 42 15
a. Bklt. pane, 5 each #537, 541 + 2 labels 2.50
542 A113 55c carmine 50 15
543 A157 55c brt grn ('81) 45 20
544 A157 60c apple grn ('81) 45 20
545 A157 65c dk red brn ('86) 60 60
Nos. 536-545 (10) 3.53
Set value 1.50

Compare No. 544 with No. 790. No. 542 also issued in coils with control number on the back of every 5th stamp.

Coil Stamps

1976-86 *Perf. 13½ Vert.*

546 A157 5c slate gray 15 15
547 A157 10c ultra 15 15
548 A157 25c violet 18 15
549 A157 40c sepia ('77) 38 15
550 A157 45c brt blue 40 15
551 A157 50c brt rose ('79) 50 20
552 A157 55c brt grn ('81) 50 20
553 A157 60c apple grn ('81) 50 20
554 A157 65c dk red brn ('86) 60 60
Nos. 546-554 (9) 3.36
Set value 1.60

See Nos. 773, 776, 785, 787, 790.

De Ruyter Statue, Flushing A158

1976, Apr. 22 Photo. *Perf. 14x13*

555 A158 55c multicolored 55 15

Adm. Michiel Adriaenszon de Ruyter (1607-1676), Dutch naval hero, 300th death anniversary.

Van Prinsterer and Page — A159

1976, May 19 Photo. *Perf. 14x13*

556 A159 55c multicolored 55 15

Guillaume Groen van Prinsterer (1801-1876), statesman and historian.

Women Waving American Flags — A160

Design is from a 220-year old permanent wooden calendar from Ameland Island.

1976, May 25 **Litho.**
557 A160 75c multicolored 70 55

American Bicentennial.

Marchers A161

1976, June 15 **Photo.** ***Perf. 14x13***
558 A161 40c multicolored 35 15

Nijmegen 4-day march, 60th anniversary.

A number of stamps issued from 1970 on appear to have parts of the designs misregistered, blurry, or look off-center. These stamps are deliberately designed that way. Most prominent examples are Nos. 559, 582, 602, 656, 711-712, 721, B638-B640, B662-B667.

Runners A162

1976, June 15 **Litho.**
Tagged
559 A162 55c multicolored 90 15

Royal Dutch Athletic Soc., 75th anniv.

Printing: One Communicating with Many — A163

1976, Sept. 2 **Photo.** ***Perf. 13x14***
560 A163 45c blue & red 35 15

Netherlands Printers Organization, 75th anniversary.

Sailing Ship and City — A164

Design: 75c, Sea gull over coast.

1976, Sept. 2 **Litho.** ***Perf. 14x13***
Tagged
561 A164 40c bister, red & bl 35 15
562 A164 75c ultra, yel & red 65 40

Zuider Zee Project, the conversion of water areas into land.

Radiation of Heat and Light — A165

Ballot and Pencil — A166

Perf. 13x14, 14x13

1977, Jan. 25 **Photo.**
563 A165 40c multicolored 28 15
564 A166 45c black, red & ocher 48 15
Set value 24

Coil Stamps
Perf. 13 Horiz.
565 A165 40c multicolored 28 15
Perf. 13 Vert.
566 A166 45c multicolored 35 15

Publicity for wise use of energy (40c) and forthcoming elections (45c). Nos. 565-566 have black control number on back of every 5th stamp.

For overprint see No. 569.

Spinoza — A167

1977, Feb. 21 **Photo.** ***Perf. 13x14***
567 A167 75c multicolored 60 40

Baruch Spinoza (1632-1677), philosopher, 300th death anniversary.

Delft Bible Text, Old Type, Electronic "a" — A168

1977, Mar. 8 ***Perf. 14x13***
568 A168 55c ocher & black 45 20

Delft Bible (Old Testament), oldest book printed in Dutch, 500th anniversary. Printed in sheets of 50 se-tenant with label inscribed with description of stamp design and purpose.

No. 564 Overprinted in Blue

25 MEI'77

1977, Apr. 15 **Photo.** ***Perf. 14x13***
569 A166 45c multicolored 50 15

Elections of May 25.

Kaleidoscope of Activities — A169

1977, June 9 **Litho.** ***Perf. 13x14***
570 A169 55c multicolored 40 15

Netherlands Society for Industry and Commerce, bicentenary.

Man in Wheelchair Looking at Obstacles A170

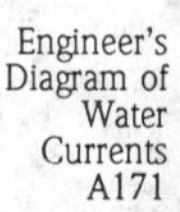
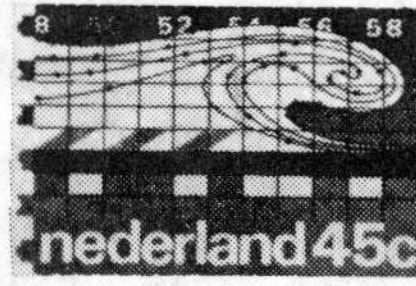

Engineer's Diagram of Water Currents A171

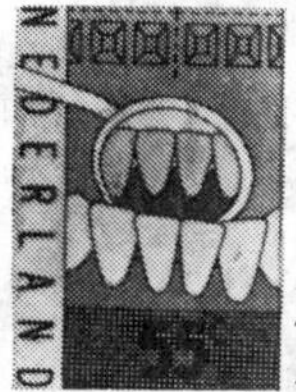

Teeth, Dentist's Mirror — A172

1977, Sept. 6 **Photo.** ***Perf. 14x13***
571 A170 40c multicolored 30 15
Litho.
572 A171 45c multicolored 30 15
Perf. 13x14
573 A172 55c multicolored 40 15

50th anniversaries of AVO (Actio vincit omnia), an organization to help the handicapped (40c), and of Delft Hydraulic Laboratory (45c); centenary of Dentists' Training in the Netherlands (55c).

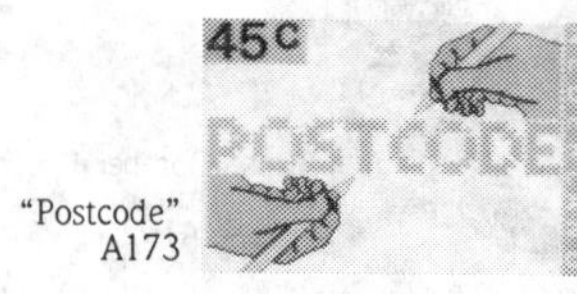

"Postcode" A173

1978, Mar. 14 **Photo.** ***Perf. 14x13***
574 A173 40c dk blue & red 30 15
575 A173 45c red, dk & lt bl 30 15
Set value 24

Introduction of new postal code.

European Human Rights Treaty — A174

Haarlem City Hall — A175

1978, May 2 **Photo.** ***Perf. 13x14***
576 A174 45c gray, blue & blk 32 15

European Treaty of Human Rights, 25th anniversary.

Europa Issue

1978, May 2
577 A175 55c multicolored 60 15

Chess Board and Move Diagram — A176

Korfball — A177

1978, June 1 **Photo.** ***Perf. 13x14***
578 A176 40c multicolored 30 15
Litho.
579 A177 45c red & vio bl 30 15

18th IBM Chess Tournament, Amsterdam, July 12, and 75th anniversary of korfball in the Netherlands.

Man Pointing to his Kidney — A178

Heart, Torch, Gauge and Clouds — A179

1978, Aug. 22 **Photo.** ***Perf. 13x13½***
580 A178 40c multicolored 30 15
Perf. 13x14
581 A179 45c multicolored 30 15

Importance of kidney transplants and drive against hypertension.

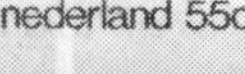

Epaulettes, Military Academy — A180

1978, Sept. 12 **Photo.** ***Perf. 13x14***
582 A180 55c multicolored 40 15

Royal Military Academy, sesquicentennial. Printed in continuous design in sheets of 100 (10x10).

Verkade as Hamlet A181

1978, Oct. 17 **Photo.** ***Perf. 14x13***
583 A181 45c multicolored 30 15

Eduard Rutger Verkade (1878-1961), actor and producer.

Clasped Hands and Arrows — A182

1979, Jan. 23 **Engr.** ***Perf. 13x14***
584 A182 55c blue 40 15

Union of Utrecht, 400th anniversary.

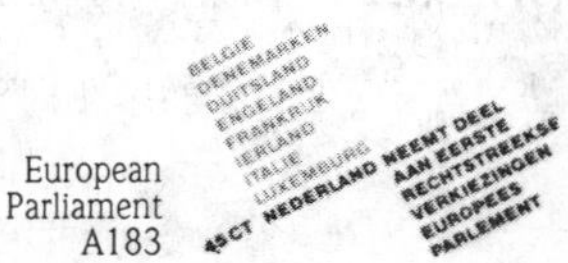

European Parliament A183

1979, Feb. 20 **Litho.** ***Perf. 13½x13***
585 A183 45c blue, blk & red 35 15

European Parliament, first direct elections, June 7-10.

Queen Juliana A184

1979, Mar. 13 Photo. *Perf. 13½x14*
586 A184 55c multicolored 48 20

70th birthday of Queen Juliana.

A185

A186

Europa: 55c, Dutch Stamps and magnifying glass. 75c, Hand on Morse key, and ship at sea.

1979, May 2 Litho. *Perf. 13x13½*
587 A185 55c multicolored 45 20
588 A185 75c multicolored 60 40

1979, June 5 Litho. *Perf. 13x14*

Map of Netherlands with chamber locations.

589 A186 45c multicolored 35 15

Netherlands Chambers of Commerce and 175th anniversary of Maastricht Chamber.

Soccer — A187

1979, Aug. 28 Litho. *Perf. 14x13*
590 A187 45c multicolored 30 15

Centenary of soccer in the Netherlands.

Suffragettes — A188

1979, Aug. 28 Photo. *Perf. 13x14*
591 A188 55c multicolored 40 15

Voting right for women, 60th anniversary.

Inscribed Tympanum and Architrave A189

1979, Oct. 2 Photo. *Perf. 14x13*
592 A189 40c multicolored 30 15

Joost van den Vondel (1587-1679), Dutch poet and dramatist.

"Gay Company," Tile Floor — A190

1979, Oct. 2
593 A190 45c multicolored 30 15

Jan Steen (1626-1679), Dutch painter.

Alexander de Savorin Lohman (1837-1924) — A191

Politicians: 50c, Pieter Jelles Troelstra (1860-1930), Social Democratic Workmen's Party leader. 60c, Pieter Jacobus Oud (1886-1968), mayor of Rotterdam.

1980, Mar. 4 Photo. *Perf. 13x13½*
594 A191 45c multicolored 24 15
595 A191 50c multicolored 32 15
596 A191 60c multicolored 50 15
Set value 36

British Bomber Dropping Food, Dutch Flag — A192

Anne Frank — A193

Perf. 13x14, 14x13
1980, Apr. 25 Photo.
597 A192 45c multicolored 30 15
598 A193 60c multicolored 40 15
Set value 22

35th anniv. of liberation from the Germans.

Queen Beatrix, Palace — A194

1980, Apr. 30 *Perf. 13x14, 13x13½*
599 A194 60c multicolored 42 20

Installation of Queen Beatrix.
See No. 608.

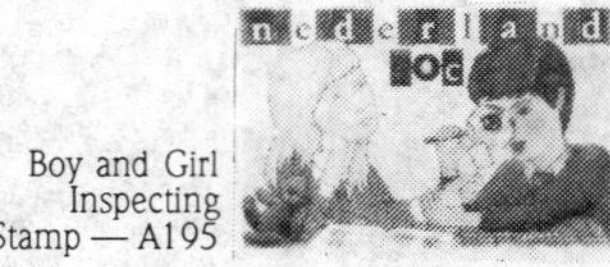

Boy and Girl Inspecting Stamp — A195

1980, May 1 *Perf. 14x13*
600 A195 50c multicolored 32 25

Youth philately; NVPH Stamp Show, s'Gravenhagen, May 1-3 and JUPOSTEX Stamp Exhibition, Eindhoven, May 23-27. No. 600 printed se-tenant with label.

Bridge Players, "Netherlands" Hand — A196

1980, June 3 Litho. *Perf. 13x14*
601 A196 50c multicolored 32 15

6th Bridge Olympiad, Valkenburg, Sept. 27-Oct. 11.

Truck Transport A197

1980, Aug. 26 Photo. *Perf. 13½x13*
602 A197 50c shown 32 15
603 A197 60c Two-axle railway hopper truck 42 15
604 A197 80c Inland navigation barge 60 32

Queen Wilhelmina, Excerpt from Speech, Netherlands Flag — A198

1980, Sept. 23 Litho. *Perf. 13½x13*
605 A198 60c shown 42 15
606 A198 80c Winston Churchill, British flag 60 32

Europa.

Abraham Kupyer, University Emblem, "100" — A199

1980, Oct. 14 Litho. *Perf. 13½x13*
607 A199 50c multicolored 35 15

Free University centennial (founded by Kupyer).

Queen Beatrix Type of 1980
Perf. 13x13½, 13x14
1981, Jan. 6 Photo.
608 A194 65c multicolored 50 15

Parcel — A200

Designs: 55c, Dish antenna and telephone. 65c, Bank books.

1981, May 19 Litho. *Perf. 13½x13*
609 A200 45c multicolored 30 18
610 A200 55c multicolored 38 18
611 A200 65c multicolored 50 18
a. Souvenir sheet of 3, #609-611 1.25 1.25

Centenaries: Parcel Post Service (45c); Public telephone service (55c); National Savings Bank (65c).

Huis ten Bosch (Royal Palace), The Hague — A201

1981, June 16 Litho. *Perf. 13½x13*
612 A201 55c multicolored 38 15

Europa Issue 1981

Carillon A202

1981, Sept. 1 Litho. *Perf. 13½x13*
613 A202 45c shown 30 18
614 A202 65c Barrel organ 50 18

450th Anniv. of Council of State — A203

1981, Oct. 1 Photo. *Perf. 13½x13*
615 A203 65c multi 50 15

Excavator and Ship's Screw (Exports) A204

1981, Oct. 20 Photo. *Perf. 13½x13*
616 A204 45c shown 30 15
617 A204 55c Cast iron component, scale 35 15
618 A204 60c Tomato, lettuce 42 15
619 A204 65c Egg, cheese 45 15
Set value 48

Queen Beatrix — A205

1981-86 Photo. *Perf. 13½x12½*

620	65c	tan & blk	52	15
621	70c	lt vio & blk ('82)	55	15
a.		Bklt. pane (4 #536, 4 #621) ('85)	2.50	
622	75c	pale pink & blk ('82)	60	15
a.		Bklt. pane of 4 ('86)	2.20	
623	90c	lt grn & blk ('82)	70	15
624	1g	lt vio & blk ('82)	75	15
625	1.40g	pale grn & blk ('82)	1.10	15
626	2g	lem & blk ('82)	1.50	15
627	3g	pale vio & blk ('82)	2.25	70
628	4g	brt yel grn & blk ('82)	3.00	1.00
629	5g	lt grnsh bl & blk ('82)	4.00	1.50
630	6.50g	lt lil rose & blk ('82)	5.00	2.50
631	7g	pale bl & blk ('86)	5.75	5.25
		Nos. 620-631 (12)	25.72	12.00

Coil Stamps
Perf. 13½ Horiz.

632	70c	lt vio & blk ('82)	55	50
633	75c	pale pink & blk ('86)	60	58
634	1g	lt vio & blk ('82)	75	70
635	2g	lem & blk ('82)	1.50	1.40
636	6.50g	lt lil rose & blk ('82)	5.00	2.50
637	7g	pale bl & blk ('86)	5.75	5.25
		Nos. 632-637 (6)	14.15	10.93

See Nos. 685-699.

University of Amsterdam, 350th Anniv. — A206

1982, Jan. 14 Litho. *Perf. 13½x13*
638 A206 65c multi 45 15

Royal Dutch Skating Assoc. Centenary — A207

1982, Feb. 26 Litho. *Perf. 13x13½*
639 A207 45c multi 32 22

Bicentenary of US-Netherlands Diplomatic Relations A208

1982, Apr. 20 Photo. *Perf. 13½x13*
640 A208 50c multi 32 22
641 A208 65c multi 45 22

See US No. 2003.

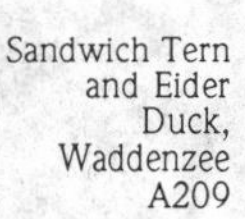
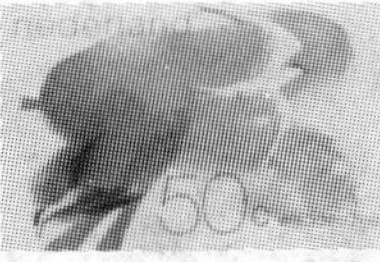

Sandwich Tern and Eider Duck, Waddenzee A209

1982, June 8 Litho. *Perf. 13½x13*
642 A209 50c shown 32 22
643 A209 70c Barnacle geese 45 22

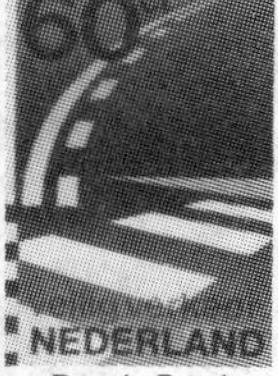

Dutch Road Safety Assoc, 50th Anniv. — A210

Europa 1982 — A211

1982, Aug. 24 Photo. *Perf. 13x14*
644 A210 60c multi 45 25

1982, Sept. 16 Litho. *Perf. 13x13½*
Fortification Layouts.

645 A211 50c Enkhuizen, 1590 38 15
646 A211 70c Coevorden, 1680 50 15
Set value 24

Royal Palace, Dam Square, Amsterdam — A212

1982, Oct. 5 Litho. *Perf. 13x13½*
647 A212 50c Facade, cross-section 38 20
648 A212 60c Aerial view 45 25

Royal Dutch Touring Club Centenary A213

1983, Mar. 1 Litho. *Perf. 13½x13*
649 A213 70c multi 50 25

A214

A215

Europa: 50c, Netherlands Newspaper Publishers Assoc., 75th anniv. 70c, Launching of European Telecommunication Satellite Org. ECS F-1 rocket, June 3.

1983, May 17 Litho. *Perf. 13x13½*
650 A214 50c multi 38 18
651 A214 70c multi 50 20

1983, June 21 Litho. *Perf. 13x13½*
De Stijl ("The Style") Modern Art Movement, 1917-31: 50c, Composition 1922, by P. Mondriaan. 65c, Maison Particuliere contra Construction, by C. van Eesteren and T. van Doesburg.

652 A215 50c multi 38 20
653 A215 65c multi 45 25

Symbolic Separation of Church — A216

1983, Oct. 11 Litho. *Perf. 13x13½*
654 A216 70c multi 50 25

Martin Luther (1483-1546).

2nd European Parliament Election, June 14 — A217

1984, Mar. 13 Litho. *Perf. 13½x13*
655 A217 70c multi 45 18

St. Servatius (d. 384) — A218

1984, May 8 Photo. *Perf. 13x14*
656 A218 60c Statue, 1732 60 15

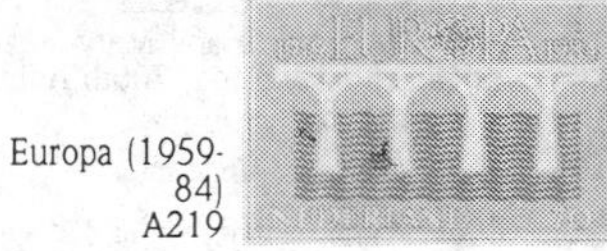

Europa (1959-84) A219

1984, May 22 *Perf. 13½x13*
657 A219 50c blue 45 15
  a. Perf. 14x13 *10.00 1.00*
658 A219 70c yel grn 70 18
  a. Perf. 14x13 *10.00 1.00*

Perf. 14x13 stamps are coils. Every fifth stamp has a control number on the back.

William of Orange (1533-84) A220

1984, July 10 Photo. *Perf. 14x13*
659 A220 70c multi 70 18

World Wildlife Fund — A221

1984, Sept. 18 Litho. *Perf. 14x13*
660 A221 70c Pandas, globe 65 18

11th Intl. Small Business Congress, Amsterdam, Oct. 24-26 — A222

1984, Oct. 23 Litho. *Perf. 13x13½*
661 A222 60c Graph, leaf 60 15

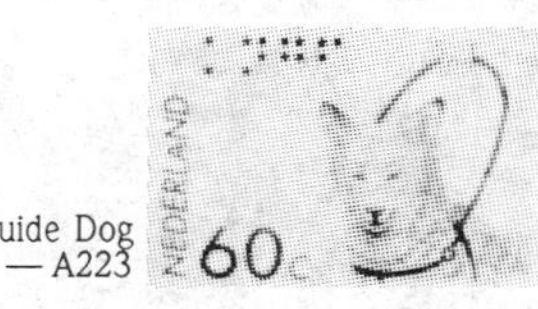

Guide Dog Fund — A223

Photogravure and Engraved

1985, Jan. 21 *Perf. 14x13*
662 A223 60c Sunny, first guide dog 60 15

A224

Tourism A224a

1985, Feb. 26 Photo.
663 A224 50c multicolored 50 15
664 A224a 70c multicolored 75 15

Cent. of the Tourist office "Geuldal," and 50th anniv. of the Natl. Park "De Hoge Veluwe."

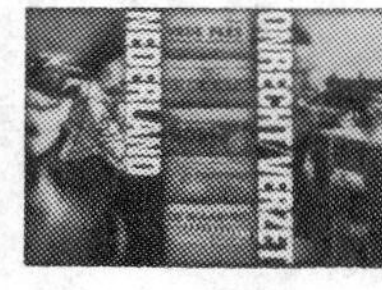

Liberation from German Forces, 40th Anniv. — A225

Designs: 50c, Jewish star, mastheads of underground newspapers, resistance fighter. 60c, Allied supply air drop, masthead of The Flying Dutchman, Polish soldier at Arnhem. 65c, Liberation Day in Amsterdam, masthead, first edition of Het Parool (underground newspaper), American cemetary at Margraten. 70c, Dutch women in Japanese prison camp, Japanese occupation currency, building of the Burma Railway.

1985, May 5 Photo. *Perf. 14x13*
665 A225 50c blk, buff & red 50 15
666 A225 60c blk, buff & brt bl 60 15
667 A225 65c blk, buff & org 60 15
668 A225 70c blk, buff & brt grn 70 18

WWII resistance effort (1940-1945) and liberation of Europe, 1945.

Europa '85 — A226

1984, June 4 Litho. *Perf. 13x13½*
669 A226 50c Piano keyboard 75 15
670 A226 70c Stylized organ pipes 1.00 18

Natl. Museum of Fine Arts, Amsterdam, Cent. — A227

Anniversaries and events: 60c, Nautical College, Amsterdam, bicent. 70c, SAIL-85, Amsterdam.

1985, July 2 Photo. *Perf. 13½x13*
671 A227 50c Museum in 1885, 1985 50 15
672 A227 60c Students training 60 15
Perf. 14x13
673 A227 70c Sailboat rigging 70 18

Wildlife Conservation A228

Designs: 50c, Porpoise, statistical graph. 70c, Seal, molecular structure models.

1985, Sept. 10 Litho. *Perf. 13½x13*
674 A228 50c multi 50 15
675 A228 70c multi 70 18

Penal Code, Cent. — A229

Amsterdam Datum Ordinance, 300th Anniv. — A230

Lithographed, Photogravure (60c)

1986, Jan. 21 *Perf. 14x13*
676 A229 50c Text 52 15
677 A230 60c Elevation gauge 60 15

Sexbierum Windmill Test Station Inauguration A231

1986, Mar. 4 Litho. *Perf. 14x13*
678 A231 70c multi 70 18

Het Loo Palace Gardens, Apeldorn — A232

1986, May 13 Litho. *Perf. 13x14*
679 A232 50c shown 55 15
Photo.
680 A232 70c Air and soil pollution 70 18

Europa 1986.

Utrecht Cathedral A233

Willem Drees (1886-), Statesman A234

1986, June 10 Photo. *Perf. 13x14*
681 A233 50c shown 48 15
682 A233 60c German House, c.1350 55 15
Perf. 14x13
683 A233 70c Utrecht University charter, horiz. 65 18

Cathedral restoration, 1986. Heemschut Conservation. Soc., 75th anniv. Utrecht University, 350th anniv.

1986, July 1 Litho. *Perf. 13x13¹/₂*
684 A234 55c multi 52 15

Queen Type of 1981

1986-90 Photo. *Perf. 13¹/₂x12¹/₂*
685 A205 1.20g citron & blk 1.10 15
686 A205 1.50g lt rose vio & blk 1.40 15
688 A205 2.50g tan & blk 2.25 15
694 A205 7.50g lt grn & blk 8.00 8.00

Coil Stamps
Perf. 13¹/₂ Horiz.
697 A205 1.50g lt rose vio & blk 1.40 15
699 A205 2.50g tan & blk 2.25 15

Issue dates: Nos. 685, 688, 699, Sept. 23. Nos. 686, 697, Aug. 19. 7.50g, May 29, 1990.
This is an expanding set. Numbers will change if necessary.

Billiards — A235

Perf. 14x13, 13x14
1986, Sept. 9 Photo.
705 A235 75c shown 70 58
706 A235 75c Checkers, vert. 70 58

Royal Dutch Billiards Assoc., Checkers Association, 75th annivs.

Delta Project Completion A236

1986, Oct. 7 Photo. *Perf. 14x13*
708 A236 65c Storm-surge barrier 70 15
709 A236 75c Barrier withstanding flood 75 15

Princess Juliana and Prince Bernhard, 50th Wedding Anniv. — A237

1987, Jan. 6 Photo. *Perf. 13x14*
710 A237 75c multi 75 15

Intl. Year of Shelter for the Homeless A238

Designs: 75c, Salvation Army, cent.

1987, Feb. 10 Photo. *Perf. 14x13*
711 A238 65c multi 60 15
712 A238 75c multi 70 15

Dutch Literature A239

Authors: 55c, Eduard Douwes Dekker (1820-1887) and De Harmonie Club, Batavia. 75c, Constantijn Huygens (1596-1687) and Scheveningseweg, The Hague.

1987, Mar. 10 Litho. *Perf. 13¹/₂x13*
713 A239 55c multi 52 15
714 A239 75c multi 70 15
Set value 24

Europa 1987 — A240

Modern architecture: 55c, Scheveningen Dance Theater, designed by Rem Koolhaas. 75c, Montessori School, Amsterdam, designed by Herman Hertzberger.

1987, May 12 Litho. *Perf. 14x13*
715 A240 55c multi 55 15
716 A240 75c multi 80 15

Produce Auction at Broeck op Langedijk, 1887 — A241

Designs: 65c, Field in Groningen Province, signatures of society founders. 75c, Auction, bidding, clock, 1987.

1987, June 16 Photo. *Perf. 14x13*
717 A241 55c shown 55 15
718 A241 65c multi 65 15
719 A241 75c multi 80 15
Set value 36

Sale of produce by auction in the Netherlands, cent., and Groningen Agricultural Society, 150th anniv. (No. 718).

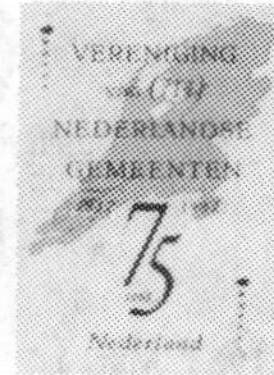

Union of the Netherlands Municipalities, 75th Anniv. — A242

1987, Oct. 6 Litho. *Perf. 13x14*
720 A242 75c multi 80 15

Noordeinde Palace, The Hague — A243

1987, Oct. 27 Photo. *Perf. 14x13*
721 A243 65c multicolored 65 15

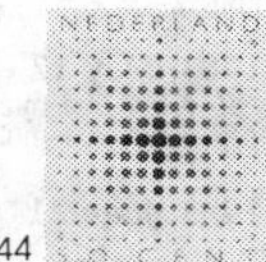

A244

Booklet Stamps
Perf. 13¹/₂x13 on 3 Sides
1987, Dec. 1 Photo.
722 A244 50c dark ultra, emer & dark red 50 15
723 A244 50c dark red, dark ultra & yel 50 15
724 A244 50c dark ultra, yel & dark red 50 15
725 A244 50c dark red, emer & yel 50 15
726 A244 50c emer, dark red & dark ultra 50 15
a. Bklt. pane of 20, 4 each #722-726 10.50
Nos. 722-726 (5) 2.50 75

Netherlands Cancer Institute, 75th Anniv. — A246

1988, Apr. 19 Litho. *Perf. 13¹/₂x13*
728 A246 75c multi 80 16

Europa 1988 — A247

Modern transportation meeting ecological requirements: 55c, Cyclist, rural scenery, chemical formulas, vert. 75c, Cyclists seen through car-door mirror.

1988, May 17 Litho. *Perf. 13x13¹/₂*
729 A247 55c multi 60 15
Perf. 13¹/₂x13
730 A247 75c multi 80 20

Coronation of William III and Mary Stuart, King and Queen of England, 300th Anniv. (in 1989) — A248

Designs: 65c, Prism splitting light as discovered by Sir Isaac Newton, planet Saturn as observed by Christian Huygens, and pendulum clock, c. 1688. 75c, William of Orange (1650-1702) and Mary II (1662-1694).

1988, June 14 *Perf. 14x13*
731 A248 65c multi 70 18
732 A248 75c multi 80 20

Arrival of Dutch William in England, 300th anniv.

Modern Art — A249

Paintings by artists belonging to Cobra: 55c, *Cobra Cat*, 1950, by Appel. 65c, *Stag Beetle*, 1948, by Corneille. 75c, *Fallen Horse*, 1950, by Constant.

1988, July 5 Litho. *Perf. 13¹/₂x13*
733 A249 55c multi 55 15
734 A249 65c multi 65 16
735 A249 75c multi 75 18

Each stamp printed se-tenant with label picturing the featured artist's signature.
Cobra, an intl. organization established in 1948 by expressionist artists from Copenhagen, Brussels and Amsterdam.

Australia Bicentennial — A250

1988, Aug. 30 Photo. *Perf. 13x14*
736 A250 75c multi 72 18

Erasmus University, Rotterdam, 75th Anniv. — A251

Amsterdam Concertgebouw and Orchestra, Cent. — A252

1988, Sept. 27 Litho. *Perf. 13x13¹/₂*
737 A251 75c dark grn & grn 72 18
738 A252 75c brt vio 72 18

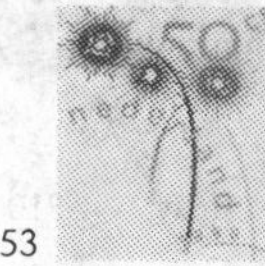

Holiday Greetings — A253

Perf. 13¹/₂x12¹/₂
1988, Dec. 1 Photo.
739 A253 50c multi 52 15

"Holland," etc.
Stamps inscribed "Holland," "Stadspost," etc., are private issues. In some cases overprints or surcharges on Netherlands stamps may be created.

Privatization of the Netherlands Postal Service — A254

Design: Mailbox, sorting machine, mailbag, mailman, telephone key pad, fiber optics cable, microwave transmitter and telephone handset.

Perf. 13x13½

1989, Jan. 3 **Litho. & Engr.**

740 A254 75c multi 78 20

Dutch Trade Unions — A255

1989, Feb. 7 **Litho.** ***Perf. 13x13½***

741 A255 55c shown 55 15

Photo.

Perf. 13x14

742 A255 75c Hands, mouths 72 15

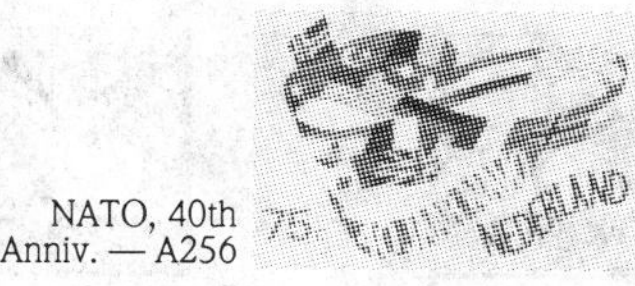

NATO, 40th Anniv. — A256

1989, Mar. 14 **Litho.** ***Perf. 14x13***

743 A256 75c multi 75 20

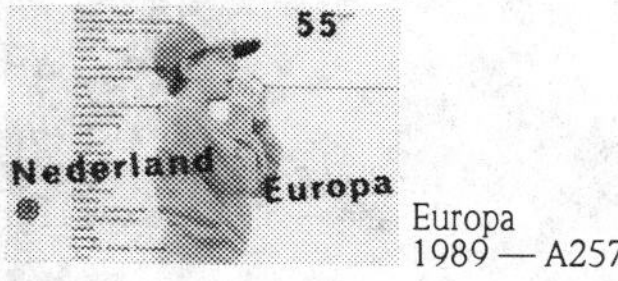

Europa 1989 — A257

Children's games (string telephone): 55c, Boy. 75c Girl.

1989, May 9 **Litho.** ***Perf. 13½x13***

744 A257 55c multi 55 15

745 A257 75c multi 75 20

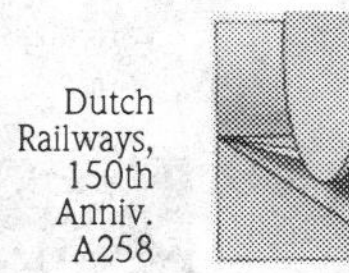

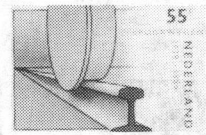

Dutch Railways, 150th Anniv. A258

1989, June 20 **Litho.** ***Perf. 13½x13***

746 A258 55c Rails 55 15

747 A258 65c Trains 65 16

Perf. 14x13

748 A258 75c Passengers 75 20

Royal Dutch Soccer Assoc., Cent. — A259

Treaty of London, 150th Anniv. — A260

1989, Sept. 5 **Photo.** ***Perf. 13x14***

749 A259 75c multi 72 18

1989, Oct. 2 **Litho.** ***Perf. 13x14***

750 A260 75c Map of Limburg Provinces 72 18

See Belgium No. 1327.

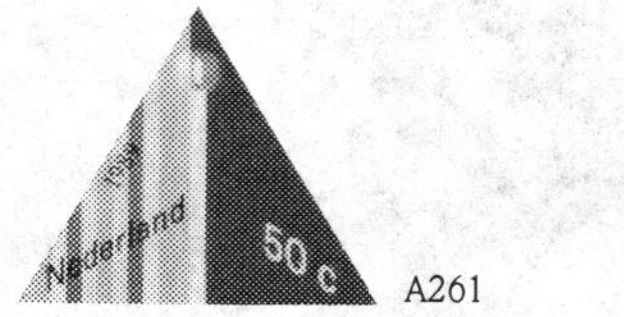

A261

Perf. 13x13x13½

1989, Nov. 30 **Photo.**

751 A261 50c multicolored 48 15

Sold only in sheets of 20.

Anniversaries A262

Vincent van Gogh (1853-1890) A263

Designs: 65c, Leiden coat of arms (tulip), and layout of the Hortus Botanicus in 1601. 75c, Assessing work conditions (clock, sky, wooden floor), horiz.

Perf. 13x13½,13½x13

1990, Feb. 6 **Litho.**

752 A262 65c multicolored 70 18

753 A262 75c multicolored 80 22

Hortus Botanicus, Leiden, 400th anniv. (65c); Labor Inspectorate, cent. (75c).

1990, Mar. 6 ***Perf. 13x13½***

Details of works by van Gogh: 55c, *Self-portrait*, pencil sketch, 1886-87. 75c, *The Green Vineyard*, painting, 1888.

754 A263 55c multicolored 58 16

755 A263 75c multicolored 80 22

Rotterdam Reconstruction A264

1990, May 8 **Litho.** ***Perf. 13½x13***

756 A264 55c shown 58 16

757 A264 65c Diagram 70 18

758 A264 75c Modern bldgs. 80 22

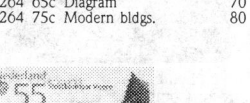

Europa A264a

Post offices.

1990, June 12

759 A264a 55c Veere 58 16

760 A264a 75c Groningen 80 22

Dutch East India Co. Ships — A265

Sail '90 — A266

1990, July 3 ***Perf. 13x13½***

761 A265 65c multi 70 18

762 A266 75c multi 80 22

Queens of the House of Orange A267

1990, Sept. 5 **Litho.** ***Perf. 13½***

763 A267 150c multi 1.60 60

Century of rule by Queens Emma, Wilhelmina, Juliana and Beatrix.

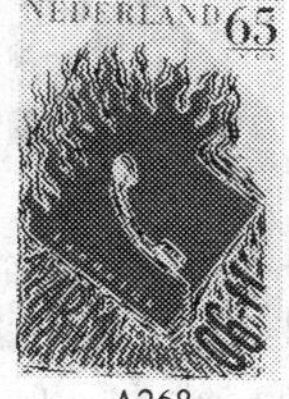

A268

A269

1990, Oct. 9 **Photo.** ***Perf. 13x14***

764 A268 65c multicolored 70 18

Natl. emergency phone number.

1990, Nov. 29 **Photo.** ***Perf. 14***

765 A269 50c multicolored 55 15

Threats to the Environment A270

1991, Jan. 30 **Litho.** ***Perf. 13½x13***

766 A270 55c Air pollution 60 15

767 A270 65c Water pollution 70 15

768 A270 75c Soil pollution 80 16

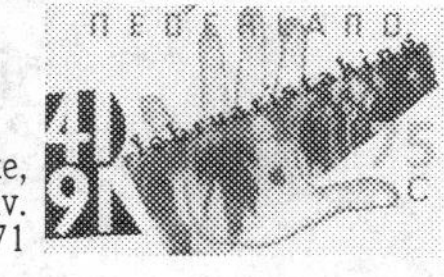

General Strike, 50th Anniv. A271

1991, Feb. 25 **Photo.** ***Perf. 14x13***

769 A271 75c multicolored 80 16

Queen Beatrix and Prince Claus, 25th Wedding Anniv. A272

1991, Mar. 11 **Litho.** ***Perf. 13½x13***

770 A272 75c shown 82 20

771 A272 75c Riding horses 82 20

a. Pair, #770-771 1.64 40

Numeral Type of 1976 and

Queen Beatrix — A273

Perf. 12½x13½, 13½x12½

1991 **Photo.**

773 A157 70c gray violet 75 18

774 A273 75c green 78 15

a. Bklt. pane of 4 + 2 labels 3.25

776 A157 80c red lilac 85 20

779 A273 1.30g gray blue 1.50 38

780 A273 1.40g gray olive 1.60 40

781 A273 1.60g magenta 1.70 40

Nos. 773-781 (6) 7.18 1.71

Coil Stamps

Perf. 13½ Vert. (A157), Horiz. (A273)

785 A157 70c gray violet 75 18

786 A273 75c green 80 15

787 A157 80c red lilac 85 20

788 A273 1.60g magenta 1.70 40

Booklet Stamps

790 A157 60c lemon 62 15

a. Bklt. pane of 2 #790, 4 #773 4.25

791 A273 80c red brown 85 20

a. Booklet pane of 5 + label 4.25

Issue dates: 75c, Mar. 14; 60c, 70c, 80c, 1.60g, June 25. 1.30g, 1.40g, Sept. 3.

This is an expanding set. Numbers will change if neccesary.

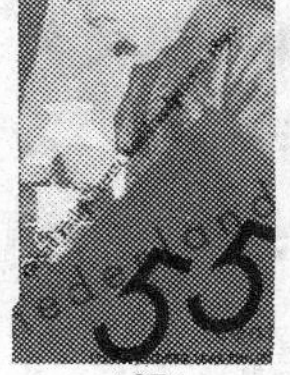

A274

A276

A275

Designs: 55c, Gerard Philips, carbon filament experiments, 1890. 65c, Electrical wiring. 75c, Laser video disk experiment.

Perf. 13x14, 14x13

1991, May 15 **Photo.**

792 A274 55c multicolored 60 15

793 A275 65c multicolored 72 18

794 A274 75c multicolored 82 20

Philips Electronics, cent. (Nos. 792, 794). Netherlands Normalization Institute, 75th anniv. (No. 793).

1991, June 11 **Litho.** ***Perf. 13x13½***

Europa: 75c, Ladders to another world.

795 A276 55c multicolored 60 15

796 A276 75c multicolored 82 20

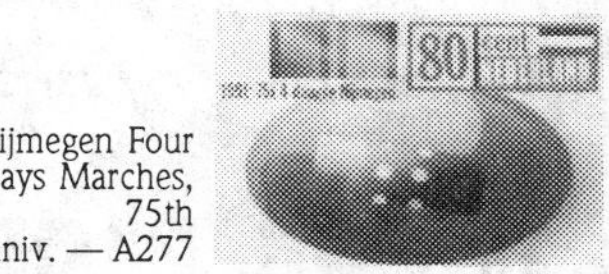

Nijmegen Four Days Marches, 75th Anniv. — A277

1991, July 9 **Photo.** ***Perf. 14x13***

797 A277 80c multicolored 85 20

Dutch Nobel Prize Winners A278

Designs: 60c, Jacobus H. Van't Hoff, chemistry, 1901. 70c, Pieter Zeeman, physics, 1902. 80c, Tobias M. C. Asser, peace, 1911.

1991, Sept. 3 ***Perf. 14x13***

798 A278 60c multicolored 62 15

799 A278 70c multicolored 75 18

800 A278 80c multicolored 85 20

Public Libraries, Cent. — A279

1991, Oct. 1 Litho. *Perf. 13½x13*

801 A279 70c Children reading	80	16
802 A279 80c Books	90	18

A280

1991, Nov. 28 Photo. *Perf. 14*

803 A280 55c multicolored 65 16

Delft University of Technology, Sesquicent. A281

New Civil Code — A282

1992, Jan. 7 Litho. *Perf. 13½x13*

804 A281 60c multicolored	70	18
805 A282 80c multicolored	95	25

A283 A284

1992 Olympics, Albertville and Barcelona: No. 806a, Volleyball, rowing. b, Shotput, rowing. c, Speedskating, rowing. d, Field hockey.

1992, Feb. 4 Litho. *Perf. 13x14*

Souvenir Sheet

806 A283 80c Sheet of 4, #a.-d. 3.60 3.60

1992, Feb. 25 Litho. *Perf. 13x12½*

807 A284 70c Tulips 85 22

Photo.

Perf. 13x14

808 A284 80c Map 1.00 25

Expo '92, Seville.

Discovery of New Zealand and Tasmania by Abel Tasman, 350th Anniv. — A285

1992, Mar. 12 Photo. *Perf. 14x13*

809 A285 70c multicolored 85 22

A286

A287

1992, Apr. 28 Litho. *Perf. 13x13½*

810 A286 60c multicolored	75	18
811 A287 80c multicolored	1.00	25

Royal Assoc. of Netherlands Architects, 150th Anniv. (#810). Opening of Building for Lower House of States General (#811).

Discovery of America, 500th Anniv. — A288

Perf. 13½x13, 13x13½

1992, May 12 Litho.

812 A288 60c Globe, Columbus	68	18
813 A288 80c Sailing ship, vert.	95	22

Europa. On normally centered stamps the white border appears at the left side of No. 813.

Royal Netherlands Numismatics Society, Cent. — A289

1992, May 19 Photo. *Perf. 13x14*

814 A289 70c multicolored 85 22

Netherlands Pediatrics Society, Cent. — A290

1992, June 16 Litho. *Perf. 13½x13*

815 A290 80c multicolored 1.00 25

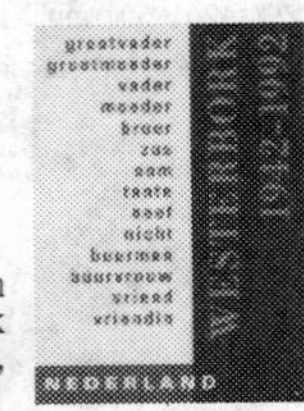
First Deportation Train from Westerbork Concentration Camp, 50th Anniv. — A291

1992, Aug. 25 *Perf. 13x13½*

816 A291 70c multicolored 85 22

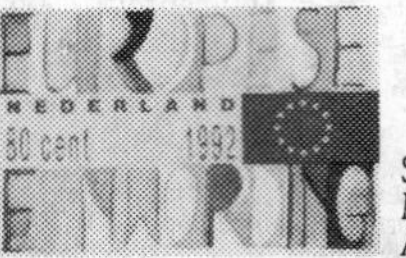
Single European Market A292

1992, Oct. 6 *Perf. 13½x13*

817 A292 80c multicolored 1.00 25

Queen Beatrix, 12½ Years Since Investiture — A293

1992, Oct. 30 *Perf. 13x13½*

818 A293 80c multicolored 1.00 25

SEMI-POSTAL STAMPS

Design Symbolical of the Four Chief Means for Combating Tuberculosis: Light, Water, Air and Food — SP1

Perf. 12½

1906, Dec. 21 Typo. Unwmk.

B1 SP1 1c (+1c) rose red	2.50	1.90
B2 SP1 3c (+3c) pale ol grn	27.50	19.00
B3 SP1 5c (+5c) gray	27.50	6.50
Set, never hinged	275.00	

Surtax aided the Society for the Prevention of Tuberculosis.

Nos. B1-B3 canceled-to-order "AMSTERDAM 31.07 10-12 N," sell at $2 a set.

Symbolical of Charity — SP2

SP3

1923, Dec. 15 *Perf. 11½*

B4 SP2 2c (+5c) vio bl	12.50	12.50
B5 SP3 10c (+5c) org red	12.50	12.50
Set, never hinged	87.50	

The surtax was for the benefit of charity.

Allegory, Charity Protecting Child — SP6

1924, Dec. 15 Photo. *Perf. 12½*

B6 SP6 2c (+2c) emer	70	1.40
B7 SP6 7½c (+3½c) dk brn	4.00	5.00
B8 SP6 10c (+2½c) ver	3.75	85
Set, never hinged	20.00	

These stamps were sold at a premium over face value for the benefit of Child Welfare Societies.

Arms of North Brabant SP7

Arms of Gelderland SP8

Arms of South Holland — SP9

1925, Dec. 17 *Perf. 12½ Syncopated*

B9 SP7 2c (+2c) grn & org	85	1.00
B10 SP8 7½c (+3½c) vio & bl	2.75	3.50
B11 SP9 10c (+2½c) red & org	2.25	45
Set, never hinged	20.00	

Surtax went to Child Welfare Societies.
See note after No. 141.

Syncopated Perfs., Type A

B9a SP7 2c (+2c)	6.75	6.75
B10a SP8 7½c (+3½c)	20.00	22.50
B11a SP9 10c (+2½c)	55.00	47.50
Set, never hinged	260.00	

Arms of Utrecht SP10

Arms of Zeeland SP11

Arms of North Holland SP12

Arms of Friesland SP13

1926, Dec. 1 Wmk. 202 *Perf. 12½*

B12 SP10 2c (+2c) sil & red	40	25
B13 SP11 5c (+3c) grn & gray bl	95	50
B14 SP12 10c (+3c) red & gold	1.90	18
B15 SP13 15c (+3c) ultra & yel	4.75	2.50
Set, never hinged	27.50	

The surtax on these stamps was devoted to Child Welfare Societies.

Syncopated Perfs., Type A

B12a SP10 2c (+2c)	3.00	3.00
B13a SP11 5c (+3c)	6.00	6.50
B14a SP12 10c (+3c)	12.00	6.50
B15a SP13 15c (+3c)	14.00	16.00
Set, never hinged	90.00	

King William III — SP14

Red Cross and Doves — SP18

Designs: 3c, Queen Emma. 5c, Prince Consort Henry. 7½c, Queen Wilhelmina.

Perf. 11½, 11½x12

1927, June Photo. Unwmk.

B16	SP14	2c (+2c) scar	1.00	1.50

Engr.

B17	SP14	3c (+2c) dp grn	3.50	5.75
B18	SP14	5c (+3c) slate bl	40	42

Photo.

B19	SP14	7½c (+3½c) ultra	2.50	1.25
B20	SP18	15c (+5c) ultra & red	7.25	9.00
		Nos. B16-B20 (5)	14.65	17.92
		Set, never hinged	55.00	

60th anniversary of the Netherlands Red Cross Society. The surtaxes in parentheses were for the benefit of the Society.

Arms of Drenthe SP19

Arms of Groningen SP20

Arms of Limburg SP21

Arms of Overijssel SP22

1927, Dec. 15 Wmk. 202 *Perf. 12½*

B21	SP19	2c (+2c) dp rose & vio	32	32
B22	SP20	5c (+3c) ol grn & yel	1.00	1.25
B23	SP21	7½c (+3½c) red & blk	2.50	32
B24	SP22	15c (+3c) ultra & org brn	3.50	4.25
		Set, never hinged	27.50	

The surtax on these stamps was for the benefit of Child Welfare Societies.

Syncopated Perfs., Type A

B21a	SP19	2c (+2c)	1.65	1.65
B22a	SP20	5c (+3c)	3.00	2.75
B23a	SP21	7½c (+3½c)	3.75	1.75
B24a	SP22	15c (+3c)	10.00	6.50
		Set, never hinged	55.00	

Rowing — SP23

Fencing — SP24

Soccer SP25

Yachting SP26

Putting the Shot SP27

Riding — SP29

Boxing — SP30

Running SP28

Perf. 11½, 12, 11½x12, 12x11½

1928, Mar. 27 Litho.

B25	SP23	1½c (+1c) dk grn	85	65
B26	SP24	2c (+1c) red vio	1.25	95
B27	SP25	3c (+1c) green	1.25	75
B28	SP26	5c (+1c) lt bl	1.40	65
B29	SP27	7½c (+2½c) org	1.65	95
B30	SP28	10c (+2c) scarlet	5.00	4.25
B31	SP29	15c (+2c) dk bl	4.25	2.75
B32	SP30	30c (+3c) dk brn	17.00	19.00
		Nos. B25-B32 (8)	32.65	29.95
		Set, never hinged	150.00	

The surtax on these stamps was used to help defray the expenses of the Olympic Games of 1928.

Jean Pierre Minckelers SP31

Child on Dolphin SP35

Designs: 5c, Hermann Boerhaave. 7½c, Hendrik Antoon Lorentz. 12½c, Christian Huygens.

1928, Dec. 10 Photo. *Perf. 12x12½*

B33	SP31	1½c (+1½c) vio	40	35
B34	SP31	5c (+3c) grn	65	60

Perf. 12

B35	SP31	7½c (+3½c) ver	2.00	22
a.		Perf. 12x12½	4.75	70
		Never hinged	11.00	
B36	SP31	12½c (+3½c) ultra	7.50	6.50
a.		Perf. 12x12½	77.50	7.75
		Never hinged	175.00	
		Set, never hinged	37.50	

The surtax on these stamps was for the benefit of Child Welfare Societies.

1929, Dec. 10 Litho. *Perf. 12½*

B37	SP35	1½c (+1½c) gray	1.00	45
B38	SP35	5c (+3c) bl grn	2.00	55
B39	SP35	6c (+4c) scar	1.25	32
B40	SP35	12½c (+3½c) dk bl	11.00	11.00
		Set, never hinged	60.00	

Surtax for child welfare.

Syncopated Perfs., Type B

B37a	SP35	1½c (+1½c)	1.65	32
B38a	SP35	5c (+3c)	3.50	32
B39a	SP35	6c (+4c)	3.00	32
B40a	SP35	12½c (+3½c)	13.00	10.50
		Set, never hinged	57.50	

Rembrandt and His "Cloth Merchants of Amsterdam" SP36

"Spring" SP37

Perf. 11½

1930, Feb. 15 Engr. Unwmk.

B41	SP36	5c (+5c) bl grn	5.00	5.50
B42	SP36	6c (+5c) gray blk	2.00	1.10
B43	SP36	12½c (+5c) dp bl	8.00	8.25
		Set, never hinged	55.00	

The surtax on these stamps was for the benefit of the Rembrandt Society.

1930, Dec. 10 *Perf. 12½*

Designs: 5c, Summer. 6c, Autumn. 12½c, Winter.

B44	SP37	1½c (+1½c) lt red	95	45
B45	SP37	5c (+3c) gray grn	1.50	70
B46	SP37	6c (+4c) claret	1.40	25
B47	SP37	12½c (+3½c) lt ultra	11.00	8.00
		Set, never hinged	55.00	

Surtax was for Child Welfare work.

Syncopated Perfs., Type C

B44a	SP37	1½c (+1½c)	1.25	1.10
B45a	SP37	5c (+3c)	1.25	1.10
B46a	SP37	6c (+4c)	1.25	1.10
B47a	SP37	12½c (+3½c)	19.00	12.00
		Set, never hinged	60.00	

Stained Glass Window and Detail of Repair Method SP41

Deaf Mute Learning Lip Reading SP43

Design: 6c, Gouda Church and repair of window frame.

Perf. 12½

1931, Oct. 1 Photo. Wmk. 202

B48	SP41	1½c (+1½c) bl grn	9.50	10.00
B49	SP41	6c (+4c) car rose	21.00	20.00
		Set, never hinged	90.00	

1931, Dec. 10 *Perf. 12½*

Designs: 5c, Imbecile child. 6c, Blind girl learning to read Braille. 12½c, Child victim of malnutrition.

B50	SP43	1½c (+1½c) ver & ultra	95	55
B51	SP43	5c (+3c) Prus bl & vio	1.50	50
B52	SP43	6c (+4c) vio & grn	1.25	42
B53	SP43	12½c (+3½c) ultra & dp org	20.00	20.00
		Set, never hinged	95.00	

The surtax was for Child Welfare work.

Syncopated Perfs., Type C

B50a	SP43	1½c (+1½c)	1.75	1.10
B51a	SP43	5c (+3c)	4.75	1.40
B52a	SP43	6c (+4c)	4.75	1.40
B53a	SP43	12½c (+3½c)	26.00	17.50
		Set, never hinged	87.50	

Windmill and Dikes — SP47

Furze and Boy — SP51

Designs: 6c, Council House, Zierikzee. 7½c, Drawbridge. 12½c, Flower fields.

1932, May 23 *Perf. 12½*

B54	SP47	2½c (+1½c) turq grn & blk	2.25	2.00
B55	SP47	6c (+4c) gray blk & blk	4.50	2.00
B56	SP47	7½c (+3½c) brt red & blk	26.00	15.00
B57	SP47	12½c (+2½c) ultra & blk	30.00	17.00
		Set, never hinged	250.00	

The surtax was for the benefit of the National Tourist Association.

1932, Dec. 10 *Perf. 12½*

Designs (Heads of children and flowers typifying the seasons): 5c, Cornflower. 6c, Sunflower. 12½c, Christmas rose.

B58	SP51	1½c (+1½c) brn & yel	1.25	45
B59	SP51	5c (+3c) red org & ultra	1.25	70
B60	SP51	6c (+4c) dk grn & ocher	1.25	45
B61	SP51	12½c (+3½c) ocher & ultra	19.00	18.00
		Set, never hinged	95.00	

The surtax aided Child Welfare Societies.

Syncopated Perfs., Type C

B58a	SP51	1½c (+1½c)	2.50	1.25
B59a	SP51	5c (+3c)	3.00	1.25
B60a	SP51	6c (+4c)	3.00	1.25
B61a	SP51	12½c (+3½c)	25.00	21.00
		Set, never hinged	82.50	

Monument at Den Helder SP55

The "Hope," A Church and Hospital Ship SP56

Lifeboat in a Storm SP57

Dutch Sailor and Sailors' Home SP58

1933, June 10 *Perf. 14½x13½*

B62	SP55	1½c (+1½c) dp red	1.25	1.50
B63	SP56	5c (+5c) bl grn & red org	7.25	2.75
B64	SP57	6c (+4c) dp grn	12.50	2.75
B65	SP58	12½c (+3½c) ultra	16.00	13.00
		Set, never hinged	120.00	

The surtax was for the aid of Sailors' Homes.

Child Carrying the Star of Hope, Symbolical of Christmas Cheer — SP59

1933, Dec. 11 *Perf. 12½*

B66	SP59	1½c (+1½c) sl & org brn	1.10	38
B67	SP59	5c (+3c) dk brn & ocher	1.40	55
B68	SP59	6c (+4c) bl grn & gold	1.50	55
B69	SP59	12½c (+3½c) dk bl & sil	16.00	15.00
		Set, never hinged	80.00	

The surtax aided Child Welfare Societies.

Syncopated Perfs., Type C

B66a	SP59	1½c (+1½c)	1.50	75
B67a	SP59	5c (+3c)	2.25	75
B68a	SP59	6c (+4c)	3.00	75
B69a	SP59	12½c (+3½c)	22.50	19.00
		Set, never hinged	70.00	

Queen Wilhelmina SP60

Princess Juliana SP61

Perf. 12½

1934, Apr. 28 Engr. Unwmk.

B70	SP60	5c (+4c) dk vio	6.75	2.00
B71	SP61	6c (+5c) blue	8.25	4.00
		Set, never hinged	60.00	

The surtax was for the benefit of the Anti-Depression Committee.

Dowager Queen Emma SP62

Poor Child SP63

1934, Oct. 1 *Perf. 13x14*

B72 SP62	6c (+2c) blue	7.75	1.10
Never hinged		35.00	

Surtax for the Fight Tuberculosis Society.

Perf. 13 1/2x13

1934, Dec. 10 Photo. Wmk. 202

B73 SP63	1 1/2c (+1 1/2c) olive	80	35
B74 SP63	5c (+3c) rose red	1.25	90
B75 SP63	6c (+4c) bl grn	1.25	20
B76 SP63	12 1/2c (+3 1/2c) ultra	14.00	13.00
	Set, never hinged	60.00	

The surtax aided child welfare.

Henri D. Guyot SP64

A. J. M. Diepenbrock SP65

F. C. Donders SP66

J. P. Sweelinck SP67

Perf. 12 1/2 x 12, 12

1935, June Engr. Unwmk.

B77 SP64	1 1/2c (+1 1/2c) dk car	90	1.25
B78 SP65	5c (+3c) blk brn	2.50	3.50
B79 SP66	6c (+4c) myr grn	2.75	24
B80 SP67	12 1/2c (+3 1/2c) dp bl	17.50	3.75
	Set, never hinged	100.00	

Surtax for social and cultural projects.

Netherlands Map, DC-3 Planes' Shadows SP68

Girl Picking Apple SP69

Perf. 14x13

1935, Oct. 16 Photo. Wmk. 202

B81 SP68	6c (+4c) brn	20.00	2.25
Never hinged		70.00	

Surtax for Natl. Aviation.

1935, Dec. 4 *Perf. 14 1/2x13 1/2*

B82 SP69	1 1/2c (+1 1/2c) crim	38	30
B83 SP69	5c (+3c) dk yel grn	1.10	1.10
B84 SP69	6c (+4c) blk brn	1.10	30
B85 SP69	12 1/2c (+3 1/2c) ultra	16.00	6.75
	Set, never hinged	65.00	

The surtax aided child welfare.

H. Kamerlingh Onnes — SP70

Dr. A. S. Talma — SP71

Msgr. Hjam Schaepman SP72

Desiderius Erasmus SP73

Perf. 12 1/2x12

1936, May 1 Engr. Unwmk.

B86 SP70	1 1/2c (+1 1/2c) brn blk	80	75
B87 SP71	5c (+3c) dl grn	3.25	3.25
B88 SP72	6c (+4c) dk red	1.10	35
B89 SP73	12 1/2c (+3 1/2c) dl bl	10.00	2.50
	Set, never hinged	65.00	

Surtax for social and cultural projects.

Cherub — SP74

Perf. 14 1/2x13 1/2

1936, Dec. 1 Photo. Wmk. 202

B90 SP74	1 1/2c (+1 1/2c) lil gray	52	26
B91 SP74	5c (+3c) turq grn	1.50	85
B92 SP74	6c (+4c) dp red brn	1.50	26
B93 SP74	12 1/2c (+3 1/2c) ind	10.50	3.25
	Set, never hinged	50.00	

The surtax aided child welfare.

Jacob Maris — SP75

Franciscus de la Boe Sylvius — SP76

Joost van den Vondel SP77

Anthony van Leeuwenhoek SP78

Perf. 12 1/2x12

1937, June 1 Engr. Unwmk.

B94 SP75	1 1/2c (+1 1/2c) blk brn	38	30
B95 SP76	5c (+3c) dl grn	3.00	2.50
B96 SP77	6c (+4c) brn vio	65	15
B97 SP78	12 1/2c (+3 1/2c) dl bl	6.00	1.00
	Set, never hinged	37.50	

Surtax for social and cultural projects.

"The Laughing Child" after Frans Hals — SP79

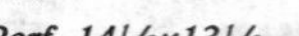

Perf. 14 1/2x13 1/2

1937, Dec. 1 Photo. Wmk. 202

B98 SP79	1 1/2c (+1 1/2c) blk	15	15
B99 SP79	3c (+2c) grn	1.00	1.00
B100 SP79	4c (+2c) hn brn	45	30
B101 SP79	5c (+3c) bl grn	40	15
B102 SP79	12 1/2c (+3 1/2c) dk bl	5.00	1.40
	Nos. B98-B102 (5)	7.00	3.00
	Set, never hinged	32.50	

The surtax aided child welfare.

Marnix de Sint Aldegonde — SP80

Otto Gerhard Heldring — SP81

Maria Tesselschade SP82

Hermann Boerhaave SP84

Harmenszoon Rembrandt van Rijn — SP83

Perf. 12 1/2x12

1938, May 16 Engr. Unwmk.

B103 SP80	1 1/2c (+1 1/2c) sep	32	60
B104 SP81	3c (+2c) dk grn	38	32
B105 SP82	4c (+2c) rose lake	1.10	1.65
B106 SP83	5c (+3c) dk sl grn	1.50	24
B107 SP84	12 1/2c (+3 1/2c) dl bl	6.25	90
	Nos. B103-B107 (5)	9.55	3.71
	Set, never hinged	35.00	

The surtax was for the benefit of cultural and social relief.

Child with Flowers, Bird and Fish — SP85

Perf. 14 1/2x13 1/2

1938, Dec. 1 Photo. Wmk. 202

B108 SP85	1 1/2c (+1 1/2c) blk	15	15
B109 SP85	3c (+2c) mar	30	15
B110 SP85	4c (+2c) dk bl grn	60	80
B111 SP85	5c (+3c) hn brn	28	15
B112 SP85	12 1/2c (+3 1/2c) dp bl	5.50	1.75
	Nos. B108-B112 (5)	6.83	3.00
	Set, never hinged	30.00	

The surtax aided child welfare.

Mathijs Maris — SP86

Anton Mauve — SP87

Gerard van Swieten SP88

Nikolaas Beets SP89

Peter Stuyvesant — SP90

Perf. 12 1/2x12

1939, May 1 Engr. Unwmk.

B113 SP86	1 1/2c (+1 1/2c) sep	32	38
B114 SP87	2 1/2c (+2 1/2c) gray grn	2.50	2.50
B115 SP88	3c (+3c) ver	60	75
B116 SP89	5c (+3c) dk sl grn	1.25	22
B117 SP90	12 1/2c (+3 1/2c) ind	4.50	75
	Nos. B113-B117 (5)	9.17	4.60
	Set, never hinged	37.50	

The surtax was for the benefit of cultural and social relief.

Child Carrying Cornucopia — SP91

Perf. 14 1/2x13 1/2

1939, Dec. 1 Photo. Wmk. 202

B118 SP91	1 1/2c (+1 1/2c) blk	15	15
B119 SP91	2 1/2c (+2 1/2c) dk ol grn	2.75	1.90
B120 SP91	3c (+3c) hn brn	40	15
B121 SP91	5c (+3c) dk grn	68	15
B122 SP91	12 1/2c (+3 1/2c) dk bl	3.00	1.00
	Nos. B118-B122 (5)	6.98	3.35
	Set, never hinged	32.50	

The surtax was used for destitute children.

Catalogue values for unused stamps in this section, from this point to the end of the section, are for Never Hinged items.

Vincent van Gogh SP92

E. J. Potgieter SP93

Petrus Camper SP94

Jan Steen SP95

Joseph Scaliger — SP96

Perf. 12 1/2x12

1940, May 11 Engr. Unwmk.

No.	Type	Description	Unused	Used
B123	SP92	1 1/2c +1 1/2c brn blk	1.75	16
B124	SP93	2 1/2c +2 1/2c dk grn	5.75	70
B125	SP94	3c +3c car	3.50	65
B126	SP95	5c +3c dp grn	7.50	15
a.		Booklet pane of 4	250.00	
B127	SP96	12 1/2c +3 1/2c dp bl	6.50	40

Surtax for social and cultural projects.

Type of 1940 Surcharged in Black **7½+2½**

1940, Sept. 7

No.	Type	Description	Unused	Used
B128	SP95	7 1/2c +2 1/2c on 5c +3c dk red	45	20
		Nos. B123-B128 (6)	25.45	2.26

Child with Flowers and Doll — SP97

Perf. 14 1/2x13 1/2

1940, Dec. 2 Photo. Wmk. 202

No.	Type	Description	Unused	Used
B129	SP97	1 1/2c +1 1/2c dl bl gray	60	15
B130	SP97	2 1/2c +2 1/2c dp ol	2.25	50
B131	SP97	4c +3c royal bl	2.25	65
B132	SP97	5c +3c dk bl grn	2.25	15
B133	SP97	7 1/2c +3 1/2c hn	60	15
		Nos. B129-B133 (5)	7.95	1.60

The surtax was used for destitute children.

Dr. Antonius Mathijsen SP98

Dr. Jan Ingenhousz SP99

Aagje Deken SP100

Johannes Bosboom SP101

A. C. W. Staring — SP102

Perf. 12 1/2x12

1941, May 29 Engr. Unwmk.

No.	Type	Description	Unused	Used
B134	SP98	1 1/2c +1 1/2c blk brn	60	15
B135	SP99	2 1/2c +2 1/2c dk sl grn	60	15
B136	SP100	4c +3c red	60	15
B137	SP101	5c +3c slate grn	60	15
B138	SP102	7 1/2c +3 1/2c rose vio	60	15
		Nos. B134-B138 (5)	3.00	
		Set value		60

The surtax was for cultural and social relief.

Rembrandt's Painting of Titus, His Son — SP103

Perf. 14 1/2x13 1/2

1941, Dec. 1 Photo. Wmk. 202

No.	Type	Description	Unused	Used
B139	SP103	1 1/2c +1 1/2c vio blk	20	15
B140	SP103	2 1/2c +2 1/2c dk ol	20	15
B141	SP103	4c +3c royal blue	20	15
B142	SP103	5c +3c dp grn	20	15
B143	SP103	7 1/2c +3 1/2c dp hn brn	20	15
		Nos. B139-B143 (5)	1.00	
		Set value		50

The surtax aided child welfare.

Legionary

SP104 SP105

1942, Nov. 1 *Perf. 12 1/2x12, 12x12 1/2*

No.	Type	Description	Unused	Used
B144	SP104	7 1/2c +2 1/2c dk red	35	15
a.		Sheet of 10	65.00	80.00
B145	SP106	12 1/2c +87 1/2c ultra	4.50	3.50
a.		Sheet of 4	60.00	90.00

The surtax aided the Netherlands Legion.

#B144a, B145a measure 155x111mm and 94x94mm respectively.

19th Century Mail Cart — SP108

1943, Oct. 9 Unwmk. *Perf. 12x12 1/2*

No.	Type	Description	Unused	Used
B148	SP108	7 1/2c +7 1/2c henna brn	15	15

Issued to commemorate Stamp Day.

Child and House — SP109

Designs: No. B150, Mother and Child. No. B151, Mother and Children. No. B152, Child Carrying Sheaf of Wheat. No. B153, Mother and Children, diff.

Perf. 12 1/2x12

1944, Mar. 6 Wmk. 202

No.	Type	Description	Unused	Used
B149	SP109	1 1/2c +3 1/2c dl blk	15	15
B150	SP109	4c +3 1/2 rose lake	15	15
B151	SP109	5c +5c dk bl grn	15	15
B152	SP109	7 1/2c +7 1/2c dp hn brn	15	15
B153	SP109	10c +40c royal blue	15	15
		Set value	50	

The surtax aided National Social Service and winter relief.

Child SP114

Fortuna SP115

Perf. 14 1/2x13 1/2

1945, Dec. 1 Photo.

No.	Type	Description	Unused	Used
B154	SP114	1 1/2c +2 1/2c gray	18	15
B155	SP114	2 1/2c +3 1/2c dk bl grn	18	15
B156	SP114	5c +5c brn red	18	15
B157	SP114	7 1/2c +4 1/2c red	18	15
B158	SP114	12 1/2c +5 1/2c brt bl	18	15
		Nos. B154-B158 (5)	90	
		Set value		60

The surtax was for Child Welfare.

Perf. 12 1/2x12

1946, May 1 Engr. Unwmk.

No.	Type	Description	Unused	Used
B159	SP115	1 1/2c +3 1/2c brn blk	45	15
B160	SP115	2 1/2c +5c dl grn	60	32
B161	SP115	5c +10c dk vio	65	40
B162	SP115	7 1/2c +15c car lake	45	15
B163	SP115	12 1/2c +37 1/2c dk bl	75	30
		Nos. B159-B163 (5)	2.90	1.32

The surtax was for victims of World War II.

Princess Irene SP116

Child on Merry-go-round SP119

Designs: Nos. B165, B167, Princess Margriet. Nos. B168-B169, Princess Beatrix.

1946, Sept. 16

No.	Type	Description	Unused	Used
B164	SP116	1 1/2c +1 1/2c blk brn	50	42
B165	SP116	2 1/2c +1 1/2c bl grn	50	42
B166	SP116	4c +2c magenta	52	42
B167	SP116	5c +2c brown	52	42
B168	SP116	7 1/2c +2 1/2c red	50	15
B169	SP116	12 1/2c +7 1/2c dk bl	50	42
		Nos. B164-B169 (6)	3.04	2.25

The surtax was for child welfare and anti-tuberculosis work.

1946, Dec. 2 Photo. Wmk. 202

No.	Type	Description	Unused	Used
B170	SP119	2c +2c lil gray	42	20
B171	SP119	4c +2c dk grn	42	20
B172	SP119	7 1/2c +2 1/2c brt red	42	20
B173	SP119	10c +5c dp plum	42	15
B174	SP119	20c +5c dp bl	42	28
		Nos. B170-B174 (5)	2.10	1.03

The surtax was for child welfare.

Dr. Hendrik van Deventer SP120

Peter Cornelisz Hooft SP121

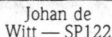

Johan de Witt — SP122

Jean F. van Royen — SP123

Hugo de Groot — SP124

1947, Aug. 1 Engr. Unwmk.

No.	Type	Description	Unused	Used
B175	SP120	2c +2c dk red	60	25
B176	SP121	4c +2c dk grn	1.25	42
B177	SP122	7 1/2c +2 1/2c dk pur brn	1.90	42
B178	SP123	10c +5c brn	1.40	15
B179	SP124	20c +5c dk bl	1.10	42
		Nos. B175-B179 (5)	6.25	1.66

The surtax was for social and cultural purposes.

Children SP125

Infant SP126

1947, Dec. 1 Photo. *Perf. 13x14*

No.	Type	Description	Unused	Used
B180	SP125	2c +2c red brn	15	15
B181	SP126	4c +2c bl grn	1.25	40
B182	SP126	7 1/2c +2 1/2c sepia	1.25	55
B183	SP126	10c +5c dk red	75	15
B184	SP125	20c +5c blue	1.25	65
		Nos. B180-B184 (5)	4.65	1.90

The surtax was for child welfare.

Hall of Knights, The Hague — SP127

Boy in Kayak — SP128

Designs: 6c+4c, Royal Palace, Amsterdam. 10c+5c, Kneuterdyk Palace, The Hague. 20c+5c, New Church, Amsterdam.

1948, June 17 Engr. *Perf. 13 1/2x14*

No.	Type	Description	Unused	Used
B185	SP127	2c +2c dk brn	1.50	25
B186	SP127	6c +4c grn	1.50	25
B187	SP127	10c +5c brt red	1.25	15
B188	SP127	20c +5c dp bl	1.50	65

The surtax was for cultural and social purposes.

1948, Nov. 15 Photo. *Perf. 13x14*

Designs: 5c+3c, Swimming. 6c+4c, Sledding. 10c+5c, Swinging. 20c+8c, Figure skating.

No.	Type	Description	Unused	Used
B189	SP128	2c +2c yel grn	15	15
B190	SP128	5c +3c dk bl grn	2.00	65
B191	SP128	6c +4c gray	85	15
B192	SP128	10c +5c red	15	15
B193	SP128	20c +8c blue	2.25	65
		Nos. B189-B193 (5)	5.40	1.75

The surtax was for child welfare.

Beach Terrace — SP129

Boy and Girl Hikers — SP130

Campers SP131

Reaping — SP132

Sailboats SP133

1949, May 2 Wmk. 202 *Perf. 14x13*

No.	Type	Denomination	Color	Unused	Used
B194	SP129	2c +2c	bl & org yel	90	15
B195	SP130	5c +3c	bl & yel	1.50	1.00
B196	SP131	6c +4c	dk bl grn	1.50	30
B197	SP132	10c +5c	bl & org yel	2.50	15
B198	SP133	20c +5c	blue	1.75	1.25
		Nos. B194-B198 (5)		8.15	2.85

The surtax was for cultural and social purposes.

Hands Reaching for Sunflower SP134

"Autumn" SP135

Perf. 14½x13½

1949, Aug. 1 Photo. Unwmk.

Flower in Yellow

No.	Type	Denomination	Color	Unused	Used
B199	SP134	2c +3c	gray	1.10	20
B200	SP134	6c +4c	red brn	70	32
B201	SP134	10c +5c	brt bl	2.25	20
B202	SP134	30c +10c	dk brn	6.25	2.00

The surtax was for the Red Cross and for Indonesia Relief work.

1949, Nov. 14 Engr. *Perf. 13x14*

Designs: 5c+3c, "Summer." 6c+4c, "Spring." 10c+5c, "Winter." 20c+7c, "New Year."

No.	Type	Denomination	Color	Unused	Used
B203	SP135	2c +3c	brn	15	15
B204	SP135	5c +3c	red	3.25	95
B205	SP135	6c +4c	dl grn	1.10	20
B206	SP135	10c +5c	gray	22	15
B207	SP135	20c +7c	blue	3.50	85
		Nos. B203-B207 (5)		8.22	2.30

The surtax was for child welfare.

Figure from PTT Monument, The Hague SP136

Grain Binder SP137

Designs: 4c+2c, Dike repairs. 5c+3c, Apartment House, Rotterdam. 10c+5c, Bridge section being towed. 20c+5c, Canal freighter.

1950, May 2 *Perf. 12½x12, 12x12½*

No.	Type	Denomination	Color	Unused	Used
B208	SP136	2c +2c	dk brn	1.25	65
B209	SP136	4c +2c	dk grn	11.00	6.00
B210	SP136	5c +3c	sepia	5.75	2.00
B211	SP137	6c +4c	purple	2.50	60
B212	SP137	10c +5c	bl gray	2.50	20
B213	SP137	20c +5c	dp bl	11.00	7.00
		Nos. B208-B213 (6)		34.00	16.45

The surtax was for social and cultural works.

Church Ruins and Good Samaritan SP138

Baby and Bees SP139

1950, July 17 Photo. *Perf. 12½x12*

No.	Type	Denomination	Color	Unused	Used
B214	SP138	2c +2c	ol brn	2.50	85
B215	SP138	5c +3c	brn red	13.00	*9.00*
B216	SP138	6c +4c	dp grn	7.50	1.00
B217	SP138	10c +5c	brt lil rose	8.00	20
B218	SP138	20c +5c	ultra	19.00	*16.00*
		Nos. B214-B218 (5)		50.00	27.05

The surtax was for the restoration of ruined churches.

1950, Nov. 13 *Perf. 13x12*

Designs: 5c+3c, Boy and rooster. 6c+4c, Girl feeding birds. 10c+5c, Boy and fish. 20c+7c, Girl, butterfly and toad.

No.	Type	Denomination	Color	Unused	Used
B219	SP139	2c +3c	car	15	15
B220	SP139	5c +3c	ol grn	5.00	1.90
B221	SP139	6c +4c	dk bl grn	1.50	40
B222	SP139	10c +5c	lilac	15	15
B223	SP139	20c +7c	blue	9.00	5.00
		Nos. B219-B223 (5)		15.80	7.60

The surtax was to aid needy children.

Hillenraad Castle — SP140

Bergh Castle — SP141

Castles: 6c+4c, Hernen. 10c+5c, Rechteren. 20c+5c, Moermond.

Perf. 12x12½, 12½x12

1951, May 15 Engr. Unwmk.

No.	Type	Denomination	Color	Unused	Used
B224	SP140	2c +2c	pur	2.00	1.00
B225	SP141	5c +3c	dk red	6.00	5.00
B226	SP140	6c +4c	dk brn	1.00	80
B227	SP141	10c +5c	dk grn	2.00	35
B228	SP141	20c +5c	dp bl	5.00	*5.00*
		Nos. B224-B228 (5)		16.00	*12.15*

The surtax was for cultural, medical and social purposes.

Girl and Windmill SP142

Jan van Riebeeck SP143

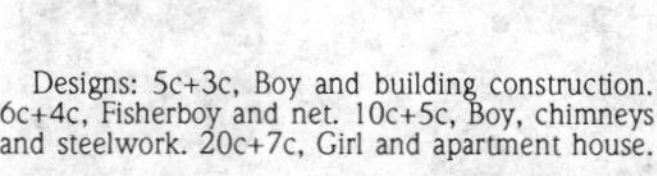

Designs: 5c+3c, Boy and building construction. 6c+4c, Fisherboy and net. 10c+5c, Boy, chimneys and steelwork. 20c+7c, Girl and apartment house.

1951, Nov. 12 Photo. *Perf. 13x14*

No.	Type	Denomination	Color	Unused	Used
B229	SP142	2c +3c	dp grn	25	15
B230	SP142	5c +3c	sl vio	4.75	2.75
B231	SP142	6c +4c	dk brn	4.75	15
B232	SP142	10c +5c	red brn	18	15
B233	SP142	20c +7c	dp bl	6.25	*4.50*
		Nos. B229-B233 (5)		16.18	*7.70*

The surtax was for child welfare.

1952, Mar. *Perf. 12½x12*

No.	Type	Denomination	Color	Unused	Used
B234	SP143	2c +3c	dk gray	2.50	1.65
B235	SP143	6c +4c	dk bl grn	5.75	4.00
B236	SP143	10c +5c	brt red	6.00	3.00
B237	SP143	20c +5c	brt bl	2.50	1.65

Tercentenary of Van Riebeeck's landing in South Africa. Surtax was for Van Riebeeck monument fund.

Scotch Rose — SP144

Girl and Dog — SP145

Designs: 5c+3c, Marsh marigold. 6c+4c, Tulip. 10c+5c, Ox-eye daisy. 20c+5c, Cornflower.

1952, May 1

No.	Type	Denomination	Color	Unused	Used
B238	SP144	2c +2c	cer & dl grn	60	40
B239	SP144	5c +3c	dp grn & yel	85	65
B240	SP144	6c +4c	red & dl grn	1.10	30
B241	SP144	10c +5c	org yel & dl grn	1.25	15
B242	SP144	20c +5c	bl & dl grn	11.00	7.50
		Nos. B238-B242 (5)		14.80	9.00

The surtax was for social, cultural and medical purposes.

Perf. 12x12½

1952, Nov. 17 Unwmk.

Designs: 2c+3c, Boy and goat. 5c+3c, Girl on donkey. 10c+5c, Boy and kitten. 20c+7c, Boy and rabbit.

Design in Black

No.	Type	Denomination	Color	Unused	Used
B243	SP145	2c +3c	olive	15	15
B244	SP145	5c +3c	dp rose	90	45
B245	SP145	6c +4c	aqua	1.90	28
B246	SP145	10c +5c	org yel	15	15
B247	SP145	20c +7c	blue	6.75	4.75
		Nos. B243-B247 (5)		9.85	5.78

The surtax was for child welfare.

No. 308 Surcharged in Black

19 53
10c +10
WATERSNOOD

Perf. 13½x13

1953, Feb. 10 Wmk. 202

No.	Type	Denomination	Color	Unused	Used
B248	A76	10c +10c	org yel	38	15

The surtax was for flood relief.

Hyacinth SP146

Red Cross on Shield SP147

Designs: 5c+3c, African Marigold. 6c+4c, Daffodil. 10c+5c, Anemone. 20c+5c, Iris.

1953, May 1 Unwmk. *Perf. 12½x12*

No.	Type	Denomination	Color	Unused	Used
B249	SP146	2c +2c	vio & grn	50	20
B250	SP146	5c +3c	dp org & grn	75	65
B251	SP146	6c +4c	grn & yel	1.00	30
B252	SP146	10c +5c	dk red & grn	1.90	15
B253	SP146	20c +5c	dp ultra & grn	10.50	*9.00*
		Nos. B249-B253 (5)		14.65	*10.30*

The surtax was for social, cultural and medical purposes.

1953, Aug. 24 Engr.

Designs: 6c+4c, Man holding lantern. 7c+5c, Worker and ambulance at flood. 10c+5c, Nurse giving blood transfusion. 25c+8c, Red Cross flags.

Cross in Red

No.	Type	Denomination	Color	Unused	Used
B254	SP147	2c +3c	dk ol	50	20
B255	SP147	6c +4c	dk vio brn	2.00	1.65
B256	SP147	7c +5c	dk gray grn	1.00	25
B257	SP147	10c +5c	red	75	15
B258	SP147	25c +8c	dp bl	5.25	3.50
		Nos. B254-B258 (5)		9.50	5.75

The surtax was for the Red Cross.

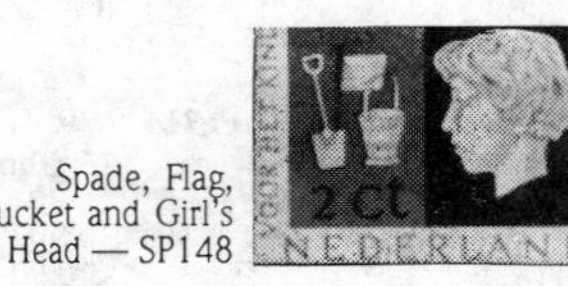

Spade, Flag, Bucket and Girl's Head — SP148

Designs: Head of child and: 5c+3c, Apple. 7c+5c, Pigeon. 10c+5c, Sailboat. 25c+8c, Tulip.

1953, Nov. 16 Litho. *Perf. 12x12½*

No.	Type	Denomination	Color	Unused	Used
B259	SP148	2c +3c	yel & bl gray	20	15
B260	SP148	5c +3c	ap grn & brn car	1.50	60
B261	SP148	7c +5c	lt bl & sep	3.25	70
B262	SP148	10c +5c	ol bis & lil	20	15
B263	SP148	25c +8c	pink & bl grn	12.00	7.75
		Nos. B259-B263 (5)		17.15	9.35

The surtax was for child welfare.

Martinus Nijhoff, Poet — SP149

Boy Flying Model Plane — SP150

Portraits: 5c+3c, Willem Pijper, composer. 7c+5c, H. P. Berlage, architect. 10c+5c, Johan Huizinga, historian. 25c+ 8c, Vincent van Gogh, painter.

1954, May 1 Photo. *Perf. 12½x12*

No.	Type	Denomination	Color	Unused	Used
B264	SP149	2c +3c	dp bl	1.40	1.00
B265	SP149	5c +3c	ol brn	70	40
B266	SP149	7c +5c	dk red	2.25	85
B267	SP149	10c +5c	dl grn	5.00	15
B268	SP149	25c +8c	plum	9.00	*8.75*
		Nos. B264-B268 (5)		18.35	*11.15*

The surtax was for social and cultural purposes.

1954, Aug. 23 *Perf. 12½x12*

Portrait: 10c+4c, Albert E. Plesman.

No.	Type	Denomination	Color	Unused	Used
B269	SP150	2c +2c	ol grn	55	48
B270	SP150	10c +4c	dk gray bl	1.90	48

The surtax was for the Netherlands Aviation Foundation.

Children Making Paper Chains SP151

Girl Brushing Teeth SP152

Designs: 7c+5c, Boy sailing toy boat. 10c+5c, Nurse drying child. 25c+8c, Young convalescent, drawing.

Perf. 12x12½, 12½x12

1954, Nov. 15

No.	Type	Denomination	Color	Unused	Used
B271	SP151	2c +3c	brn	15	15
B272	SP152	5c +3c	ol grn	70	35
B273	SP152	7c +5c	gray bl	1.00	30
B274	SP152	10c +5c	brn red	15	15
B275	SP151	25c +8c	dp bl	7.50	5.00
		Nos. B271-B275 (5)		9.50	5.95

The surtax was for child welfare.

Factory, Rotterdam SP153

Amsterdam Stock Exchange SP154

Designs: 5c+3c, Post office, The Hague. 10c+5c, Town hall, Hilversum. 25c+8c, Office building, The Hague.

1955, Apr. 25 Engr.

No.	Type	Denomination	Color	Unused	Used
B276	SP153	2c +3c	brnsh bis	85	95
B277	SP153	5c +3c	bl grn	28	20
B278	SP154	7c +5c	rose brn	85	95
B279	SP153	10c +5c	steel bl	1.25	15
B280	SP153	25c +8c	choc	10.00	*7.00*
		Nos. B276-B280 (5)		13.23	*9.25*

The surtax was for social and cultural purposes.

Microscope and Crab — SP155

Willem van Loon by Dirck Santvoort — SP156

1955, Aug. 15 Photo. *Perf. 12½x12*
Crab in Red

B281	SP155	2c +3c dk gray	70	40
B282	SP155	5c +3c dk grn	42	25
B283	SP155	7c +5c dk vio	90	50
B284	SP155	10c +5c dk bl	90	15
B285	SP155	25c +8c olive	6.00	4.75
		Nos. B281-B285 (5)	8.92	6.05

The surtax was for cancer research.

1955, Nov. 14 Unwmk.

Portraits: 5+3c, Boy by Jacob Adriaanszoon Backer. 7+5c, Girl by unknown artist. 10+5c, Philips Huygens by Adriaan Hanneman. 25+8c, Constantijn Huygens by Adriaan Hanneman.

B286	SP156	2c +3c dk grn	15	15
B287	SP156	5c +3c dp car	38	38
B288	SP156	7c +5c dl red brn	1.75	45
B289	SP156	10c +5c dp bl	15	15
B290	SP156	25c +8c purple	8.00	5.75
		Nos. B286-B290 (5)	10.43	6.88

The surtax was for child welfare.

Farmer Wearing High Cap SP157

Sailboat SP158

Rembrandt Etchings: 5c+3c, Young Tobias with Angel. 7c+5c, Persian Wearing Fur Cap. 10c+5c, Old Blind Tobias. 25c+ 8c, Self-portrait of 1639.

1956, Apr. 23 Engr. *Perf. 13½x14*

B291	SP157	2c +3c bluish blk	1.90	*3.25*
B292	SP157	5c +3c ol grn	1.00	1.10
B293	SP157	7c +5c brown	3.25	*3.25*
B294	SP157	10c +5c dk grn	12.00	20
B295	SP157	25c +8c redsh brn	14.00	*14.00*
		Nos. B291-B295 (5)	32.15	*21.80*

Issued to commemorate the 350th anniversary of the birth of Rembrandt van Rijn.
Surtax for social and cultural purposes.

1956, Aug. 27 Litho. *Perf. 12½x12*

Designs: 5c+3c, Woman runner. 7c+5c, Amphora depicting runners. 10c+5c, Field hockey. 25c+8c, Waterpolo player.

B296	SP158	2c +3c brt bl & blk	22	20
B297	SP158	5c +3c dl yel & blk	22	20
B298	SP158	7c +5c red brn & blk	85	65
B299	SP158	10c +5c gray & blk	1.10	65
B300	SP158	25c +8c brt grn & blk	4.75	*4.75*
		Nos. B296-B300 (5)	7.14	*6.45*

Issued to publicize the forthcoming 16th Olympic Games at Melbourne, Nov. 22-Dec. 8, 1956.
The surtax was for the benefit of the Netherlands Olympic Committee.

Boy by Jan van Scorel — SP159

Motor Freighter — SP160

Children's Portraits: 5c+3c, Boy, 1563. 7c+5c, Girl, 1563. 10c+5c, Girl, 1590. 25c+8c, Eechie Pieters, 1592.

Perf. 12½x12
1956, Nov. 12 Photo. Unwmk.

B301	SP159	2c +3c blk vio	15	15
B302	SP159	5c +3c ol grn	42	30
B303	SP159	7c +5c brn vio	1.65	50
B304	SP159	10c +5c dp red	15	15
B305	SP159	25c +8c dk bl	4.75	2.75
		Nos. B301-B305 (5)	7.12	3.85

The surtax was for child welfare.

1957, May 13 Photo. *Perf. 14x13*

Ships: 6+4c, Coaster. 7+5c, "Willem Barendsz." 10+8c, Trawler. 30+8c, S. S. "Nieuw Amsterdam."

B306	SP160	4c +3c brt bl	90	95
B307	SP160	6c +4c brt vio	55	40
B308	SP160	7c +5c dk car rose	1.10	85
B309	SP160	10c +8c grn	1.50	15
B310	SP160	30c +8c choc	5.00	*4.00*
		Nos. B306-B310 (5)	9.05	*6.35*

The surtax was for social and cultural purposes.

White Pelican Feeding Young SP161

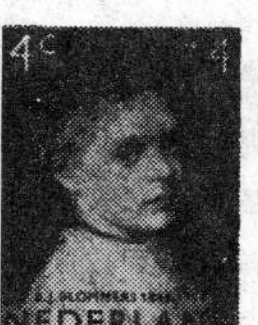

Girl by B. J. Blommers SP162

Designs: 6c+4c, Vacation ship, "Castle of Staverden." 7c+5c, Cross and dates: 1867-1957. 10c+8c, Cross and laurel wreath. 30c+8c, Globe and Cross.

1957, Aug. 19 Litho. *Perf. 12x12½*
Cross in Red

B311	SP161	4c +3c bl & red	55	65
B312	SP161	6c +4c dk grn	45	30
B313	SP161	7c +5c dk grn & pink	60	40
B314	SP161	10c +8c yel org	60	15
B315	SP161	30c +8c vio bl	2.50	*2.75*
		Nos. B311-B315 (5)	4.70	*4.25*

Issued for the 90th anniversary of the founding of the Netherlands Red Cross.

1957, Nov. 18 Photo. *Perf. 12½x12*

Girls' Portraits by: 6c+4c, William B. Tholen. 8c+4c, Jan Sluyters. 12c+9c, Matthijs Maris. 30c+9c, Cornelis Kruseman.

B316	SP162	4c +4c dp car	15	15
B317	SP162	6c +4c ol grn	1.45	50
B318	SP162	8c +4c gray	1.75	1.00
B319	SP162	12c +9c dp claret	15	15
B320	SP162	30c +9c dk bl	5.25	5.00
		Nos. B316-B320 (5)	8.75	6.80

The surtax was for child welfare.

Woman from Walcheren, Zeeland SP163

Girl on Stilts and Boy on Tricycle SP164

Regional Costumes: 6c+4c, Marken. 8c+4c, Scheveningen. 12c+9c, Friesland. 30c+9c, Volendam.

Perf. 12½x12
1958, Apr. 28 Photo. Unwmk.

B321	SP163	4c +4c blue	50	40
B322	SP163	6c +4c bister	75	60
B323	SP163	8c +4c dk car rose	2.25	1.25
B324	SP163	12c +9c org brn	80	20
B325	SP163	30c +9c vio	4.75	*5.00*
		Nos. B321-B325 (5)	9.05	*7.45*

The surtax was for social and cultural purposes.

1958, Nov. 17 Litho.

Children's Games: 6c+4c, Boy and girl on scooters. 8c+4c, Leapfrog. 12c+9c, Roller skating. 30c+9c, Boy in toy car and girl jumping rope.

B326	SP164	4c +4c lt bl	15	15
B327	SP164	6c +4c dp red	1.10	65
B328	SP164	8c +4c brt bl grn	1.10	65
B329	SP164	12c +9c red org	15	15
B330	SP164	30c +9c dk bl	3.50	3.25
		Nos. B326-B330 (5)	6.00	4.85

The surtax was for child welfare.

Tugs and Caisson SP165

Designs: 6c+4c, Dredger. 8c +4c, Laborers making fascine mattresses. 12c+9c, Grab cranes. 30c+9c, Sand spouter.

1959, May 11 *Perf. 14x13*

B331	SP165	4c +4c dk bl, *bl grn*	70	80
B332	SP165	6c +4c red org, *gray*	80	60
B333	SP165	8c +4c bl vio, *lt bl*	1.25	90
B334	SP165	12c +9c bl grn, *brt yel*	2.50	15
B335	SP165	30c +9c dk brn, *brick red*	4.50	*5.00*
		Nos. B331-B335 (5)	9.75	*7.45*

Issued to publicize the endless struggle to keep the sea out and the land dry.
The surtax was for social and cultural purposes.

Child in Playpen SP166

Refugee Woman SP167

Designs: 6c+4c, Playing Indian. 8c+4c, Child feeding geese. 12c+9c, Children crossing street. 30c+9c, Doing homework.

Perf. 12½x12
1959, Nov. 16 Unwmk.

B336	SP166	4c +4c dp rose & dk bl	15	15
B337	SP166	6c +4c red brn & emer	1.25	85
B338	SP166	8c +4c red & bl	1.25	1.00
B339	SP166	12c +9c grnsh bl, org & gray	15	15
B340	SP166	30c +9c yel & bl	2.50	2.50
		Nos. B336-B340 (5)	5.30	4.65

The surtax was for child welfare.

1960, Apr. 7 Photo. *Perf. 13x14*

B341	SP167	12c +8c dp claret	48	15
B342	SP167	30c +10c dk ol grn	2.50	1.25

Issued to publicize World Refugee Year, July 1, 1959-June 30, 1960. The surtax was for aid to refugees.

Tulip SP168

Girl from Marken SP169

Flowers: 6c+4c, Gorse. 8c+4c, White waterlily, horiz. 12c+8c, Red poppy. 30c+10c, Blue sea holly.

Perf. 12½x12, 12x12½
1960, May 23 Unwmk.

B343	SP168	4c +4c gray, grn & red	80	40
B344	SP168	6c +4c sal, grn & yel	60	30
B345	SP168	8c +4c multi	1.75	85
B346	SP168	12c +8c dl org, red & grn	1.75	30
B347	SP168	30c +10c yel, grn & ultra	6.25	4.50
		Nos. B343-B347 (5)	11.15	6.35

The surtax was for social and cultural purposes.

1960, Nov. 14 *Perf. 12½x12*

Regional Costumes: 6c+4c, Volendam. 8c+4c, Bunschoten. 12c+9c, Hindeloopen. 30c+9c, Huizen.

B348	SP169	4c +4c multi	16	15
B349	SP169	6c +4c multi	1.10	80
B350	SP169	8c +4c multi	3.50	1.10
B351	SP169	12c +9c multi	16	15
B352	SP169	30c +9c multi	6.00	3.50
		Nos. B348-B352 (5)	10.92	5.70

The surtax was for child welfare.

Herring Gull SP170

St. Nicholas on his Horse SP171

Birds: 6c+4c, Oystercatcher, horiz. 8c+4c, Curlew. 12c+8c, Avocet, horiz. 30c+10c, Lapwing.

Perf. 12½x12, 12x12½
1961, Apr. 24 Litho. Unwmk.

B353	SP170	4c +4c yel & grnsh gray	85	85
B354	SP170	6c +4c fawn & blk	40	20
B355	SP170	8c +4c ol & red brn	85	70
B356	SP170	12c +8c lt bl & gray	1.75	20
B357	SP170	30c +10c grn & blk	3.50	2.75
		Nos. B353-B357 (5)	7.35	4.70

The surtax was for social and cultural purposes.

1961, Nov. 13 *Perf. 12½x12*

Holiday folklore: 6c+4c, Epiphany. 8c+4c, Palm Sunday. 12c+9c, Whitsun bride, Pentecost. 30c+9c, Martinmas.

B358	SP171	4c +4c brt red	15	15
B359	SP171	6c +4c brt bl	1.10	85
B360	SP171	8c +4c olive	1.10	85
B361	SP171	12c +9c dp grn	15	15
B362	SP171	30c +9c dp org	3.00	2.00
		Nos. B358-B362 (5)	5.50	4.00

The surtax was for child welfare.

Christian Huygens' Pendulum Clock by van Ceulen SP172

Children Cooking SP173

Designs: 4c+4c, Cat, Roman sculpture, horiz. 6c+4c, Fossil Ammonite. 12c+ 8c, Figurehead from admiralty ship model. 30c+10c, Guardsmen Hendrick van Berckenrode and Jacob van Lourensz, by Frans Hals, horiz.

Perf. 14x13, 13x14
1962, Apr. 27 Photo.

B363	SP172	4c +4c ol grn	1.00	85
B364	SP172	6c +4c gray	50	40
B365	SP172	8c +4c dp claret	1.10	85
B366	SP172	12c +8c olive bis	1.10	20
B367	SP172	30c +10c bl blk	1.25	1.25
		Nos. B363-B367 (5)	4.95	3.55

The surtax was for social and cultural purposes. Issued to publicize the International Congress of Museum Experts, July 4-11.

1962, Nov. 12 *Perf. 12½x12*

Children's Activities: 6c+4c, Bicycling. 8c+4c, Watering flowers. 12c+9c, Feeding chickens. 30c+9c, Music making.

B368 SP173 4c +4c red 15 15
B369 SP173 6c +4c yel bis 1.25 30
B370 SP173 8c +4c ultra 1.50 85
B371 SP173 12c +9c dp grn 15 15
B372 SP173 30c +9c dk car rose 2.50 1.90
Nos. B368-B372 (5) 5.55 3.35

The surtax was for child welfare.

Gallery Windmill SP174

Roadside First Aid Station SP175

Windmills: 6c+4c, North Holland polder mill. 8c+4c, South Holland polder mill, horiz. 12c+8c, Post mill. 30c+10c, Wip mill.

Perf. 13x14, 14x13
1963, Apr. 24 Litho. Unwmk.

B373 SP174 4c +4c dk bl 1.00 75
B374 SP174 6c +4c dk pur 1.00 75
B375 SP174 8c +4c dk grn 1.25 90
B376 SP174 12c +8c blk 2.00 25
B377 SP174 30c +10c dk car 2.00 1.75
Nos. B373-B377 (5) 7.25 4.40

The surtax was for social and cultural purposes.

1963, Aug. 20 *Perf. 14x13*

Designs: 6c+4c, Book collection box. 8c+4c, Crosses. 12c+9c, International aid to Africans. 30c+9c, First aid team.

B378 SP175 4c +4c dk bl & red 35 20
B379 SP175 6c +4c dl pur & red 24 20
B380 SP175 8c +4c blk & red 85 50
B381 SP175 12c +9c red brn & red 50 15
B382 SP175 30c +9c yel grn & red 1.50 1.00
Nos. B378-B382 (5) 3.44 2.05

Centenary of the International Red Cross. The surtax went to the Netherlands Red Cross.

"Aunt Lucy Sat on a Goosey" SP176

Seeing-Eye Dog SP177

Nursery Rhymes: 6c+4c, "In the Hague there lives a count." 8c+4c, "One day I passed a puppet's fair." 12c+9c, "Storky, storky, Billy Spoon." 30c+9c, "Ride on in a little buggy."

1963, Nov. 12 Litho. *Perf. 13x14*

B383 SP176 4c +4c grnsh bl & dk bl 15 15
B384 SP176 6c +4c org red & sl grn 70 45
B385 SP176 8c +4c dl grn & dk brn 1.00 45
B386 SP176 12c +9c yel & dk pur 15 15
B387 SP176 30c +9c rose & dk bl 1.75 1.25
Nos. B383-B387 (5) 3.75 2.45

The surtax was for mentally and physically handicapped children.

1964, Apr. 21 *Perf. 12x12½*

Designs: 8c+5c, Three red deer. 12c+9c, Three kittens. 30c+9c, European bison and young.

B388 SP177 5c +5c gray ol, red & blk 35 20
B389 SP177 8c +5c dk red, pale brn & blk 35 15
B390 SP177 12c +9c dl yel, blk & gray 35 15
B391 SP177 30c +9c bl, gray & blk 55 38

The surtax was for social and cultural purposes.

Child Painting SP178

View of Veere SP179

"Artistic and Creative Activities of Children": 10c+5c, Ballet dancing. 15c+10c, Girl playing the flute. 20c+10c, Little Red Riding Hood (masquerading children). 40c+15c, Boy with hammer at work bench.

Perf. 13x14
1964, Nov. 17 Photo. Unwmk.

B392 SP178 7c +3c lt ol grn & bl 45 32
B393 SP178 10c +5c red, brt pink & grn 35 25
B394 SP178 15c +10c yel bis, blk & yel 15 15
B395 SP178 20c +10c brt pink, brn & red 45 25
B396 SP178 40c +15c bl & yel grn 75 48
Nos. B392-B396 (5) 2.15 1.45

The surtax was for child welfare.

1965, June 1 Litho. *Perf. 14x13*

Views: 10c+6c, Thorn. 18c+12c, Dordrecht. 20c+10c, Staveren. 40c+10c, Medemblik.

B397 SP179 8c +6c yel & blk 24 15
B398 SP179 10c +6c grnsh bl & blk 25 20
B399 SP179 18c +12c sal & blk 24 15
B400 SP179 20c +10c bl & blk 25 20
B401 SP179 40c +10c ap grn & blk 50 30
Nos. B397-B401 (5) 1.48 1.00

The surtax was for social and cultural purposes.

Child — SP180

Designs by Children: 10c+6c, Ship. 18c+12c, Woman, vert. 20c+10c, Child, lake and swan. 40c+10c, Tractor.

Perf. 14x13, 13x14
1965, Nov. 16 Photo.

B402 SP180 8c +6c multi 15 15
B403 SP180 10c +6c multi 45 38
B404 SP180 18c +12c multi 15 15
a. Min. sheet of 11, 5 #B402, 6 #B404 + label 18.00 8.00
B405 SP180 20c +10c multi 48 38
B406 SP180 40c +10c multi 80 45
Nos. B402-B406 (5) 2.03 1.51

The surtax was for child welfare.

"Help them to a safe haven" — SP181

1966, Jan. 31 Photo. *Perf. 14x13*

B407 SP181 18c +7c blk & org yel 40 18
B408 SP181 40c +20c blk & red 40 15
a. Min. sheet of 3, #B407, 2 #B408 4.00 3.00

The surtax was for the Intergovernmental Committee for European Migration (ICEM). The message on the stamps was given and signed by Queen Juliana.

Inkwell, Goose Quill and Book — SP182

Designs: 12c+8c, Fragment of Gysbert Japicx manuscript. 20c+10c, Knight on horseback, miniature from "Roman van Walewein" manuscript, 1350. 25c+10c, Initial "D" from "Ferguut" manuscript, 1350. 40c+20c, Print shop, 16th century woodcut.

1966, May 3 *Perf. 13x14*

B409 SP182 10c +5c multi 32 30
B410 SP182 12c +8c multi 35 32
B411 SP182 20c +10c multi 45 40
B412 SP182 25c +10c multi 48 42
B413 SP182 40c +20c multi 55 50
Nos. B409-B413 (5) 2.15 1.94

Gysbert Japicx (1603-1666), Friesian poet, and the 200th anniversary of the founding of the Netherlands Literary Society.

The surtax was for social and cultural purposes.

Infant — SP183

Designs: 12c+8c, Daughter of the painter S. C. Lixenberg. 20c+10c, Boy swimming. 25c+10c, Dominga Blazer, daughter of Carel Blazer, photographer of this set. 40c+20c, Boy and horse.

1966, Nov. 15 Photo. *Perf. 14x13*

B414 SP183 10c +5c dp org & bl 15 15
B415 SP183 12c +8c ap grn & red 15 15
B416 SP183 20c +10c brt bl & red 15 15
a. Min. sheet of 12, 4 #B414, 5 #B415, 3 #B416 3.00 3.00
B417 SP183 25c +10c brt rose lil & dk bl 80 75
B418 SP183 40c +20c dp car & dk grn 70 65
Nos. B414-B418 (5) 1.95 1.85

The surtax was for child welfare.

Whelk Eggs — SP184

Designs: 15c+10c, Whelk. 20c+10c, Mussel with acorn shells. 25c+10c, Jellyfish. 45c+20c, Crab.

1967, Apr. 11 Unwmk. Litho.

B419 SP184 12c +8c ol grn & tan 28 25
B420 SP184 15c +10c lt bl, ultra & blk 28 25
B421 SP184 20c +10c gray, blk & red 28 15
B422 SP184 25c +10c brn car, plum & ol brn 55 52
B423 SP184 45c +20c multi 70 65
Nos. B419-B423 (5) 2.09 1.82

Red Cross and Dates Forming Cross SP185

"Lullaby for the Little Porcupine" SP186

Designs (Red Cross and): 15c+10c, Crosses. 20c+10c, Initials "NRK" forming cross. 25c+10c, Maltese cross and crosses. 45c+20c, "100" forming cross.

1967, Aug. 8 *Perf. 14x13*

B424 SP185 12c +8c dl bl & red 30 24
B425 SP185 15c +10c red 38 35
B426 SP185 20c +10c ol & red 28 15
B427 SP185 25c +10c ol grn & red 38 35
B428 SP185 45c +20c gray & red 70 48
Nos. B424-B428 (5) 2.04 1.57

Centenary of the Dutch Red Cross.

1967, Nov. 7 Litho. *Perf. 13x14*

Nursery Rhymes: 15c+10c, "Little Whistling Kettle." 20c+10c, "Dikkertje Dap and the Giraffe." 25c+10c, "The Nicest Flowers." 45c+20c, "Pippeljoentje, the Little Bear."

B429 SP186 12c +8c multi 15 15
B430 SP186 15c +10c multi 15 15
B431 SP186 20c +10c multi 15 15
a. Min. sheet of 10, 3 #B429, 4 #B430, 3 #B431 4.25 4.25
B432 SP186 25c +10c multi 85 75
B433 SP186 45c +20c multi 1.00 75
Nos. B429-B433 (5) 2.30 1.95

The surtax was for child welfare.

St. Servatius Bridge, Maastricht SP187

Bridges: 15c+10c, Narrow Bridge, Amsterdam. 20c+10c, Railroad Bridge, Culenborg. 25c+10c, Van Brienenoord Bridge, Rotterdam. 45c+20c, Zeeland Bridge, Schelde Estuary.

1968, Apr. 9 Photo. *Perf. 14x13*

B434 SP187 12c +8c grn 65 85
B435 SP187 15c +10c ol brn 75 90
B436 SP187 20c +10c rose red 65 25
B437 SP187 25c +10c gray 65 85
B438 SP187 45c +20c ultra 1.00 1.25
Nos. B434-B438 (5) 3.70 4.10

Goblin — SP188

Fairy Tale Characters: 15c+10c, Giant. 20c+10c, Witch. 25c+10c, Dragon. 45c+ 20c, Magician.

1968, Nov. 12 Photo. *Perf. 14x13*

B439 SP188 12c +8c grn, pink & blk 15 15
B440 SP188 15c +10c bl, pink & blk 15 15
B441 SP188 20c +10c bl, emer & blk 15 15
a. Min. sheet of 10, 3 #B439, 4 #B440, 3 #B441 8.00 6.25
B442 SP188 25c +10c org red, org & blk 2.00 1.90
B443 SP188 45c +20c yel, org & blk 1.90 1.90
Nos. B439-B443 (5) 4.35 4.25

The surtax was for child welfare.

Villa Huis ter Heide, 1915 — SP189

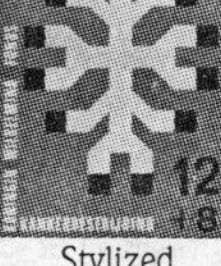

Stylized Crab — SP190

Contemporary Architecture: 15c+10c, House, Utrecht, 1924. 20c+10c, First open-air school, Amsterdam, 1960. 25c+ 10c, Burgweeshuis (orphanage), Amsterdam, 1960. 45c+20c, Netherlands Congress Building, The Hague, 1969.

1969, Apr. 15 Photo. *Perf. 14x13*

B444 SP189 12c +8c lt brn & sl 85 85
B445 SP189 15c +10c bl, gray & red 85 1.10
B446 SP189 20c +10c vio & blk 85 1.10
B447 SP189 25c +10c grn & gray 1.00 52
B448 SP189 45c +20c gray, bl & yel 1.10 1.25
Nos. B444-B448 (5) 4.65 4.82

Surtax for social and cultural purposes.

1969, Aug. 12 Photo. *Perf. 13x14*

B449 SP190 12c +8c vio 1.00 1.10
B450 SP190 25c +10c org 1.40 55
B451 SP190 45c +20c bl grn 1.75 2.50

20th anniv. of the Queen Wilhelmina Fund. The surtax was for cancer research.

Child with Violin — SP191

Isometric Projection from Circle to Square — SP192

Designs: 12c+8c, Child with flute. 20c+10c, Child with drum. 25c+10c, Three children singing, horiz. 45c+20c, Two girls dancing, horiz.

1969, Nov. 11 *Perf. 13x14, 14x13*

No.	Type	Description	Unused	Used
B452	SP191	12c +8c ultra, blk & yel	25	15
B453	SP191	15c +10c blk & red	25	15
B454	SP191	20c +10c red, blk & yel	2.00	1.75
B455	SP191	25c +10c yel, blk & red	32	15
a.		Min. sheet of 10, 4 #B452, 4 #B453, 2 #B455	8.75	7.25
B456	SP191	45c +20c grn, blk & red	2.75	2.75
		Nos. B452-B456 (5)	5.57	4.95

The surtax was for child welfare.

Lithographed and Engraved

1970, Apr. 7 *Perf. 13x14*

Designs made by Computer: 15c+10c, Parallel planes in a cube. 20c+10c, Two overlapping scales. 25c+10c, Transition phases of concentric circles with increasing diameters. 45c+20c, Four spirals.

No.	Type	Description	Unused	Used
B457	SP192	12c +8c yel & blk	1.25	1.75
B458	SP192	15c +10c sil & blk	1.25	1.50
B459	SP192	20c +10c blk	1.25	1.40
B460	SP192	25c +10c brt bl & blk	1.25	70
B461	SP192	45c +20c sil & white	1.25	1.75
		Nos. B457-B461 (5)	6.25	7.10

Surtax for social and cultural purposes.

Bleeding Heart — SP193

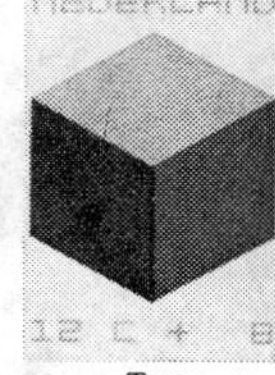

Toy Block — SP194

1970, July 28 **Photo.** *Perf. 13x14*

No.	Type	Description	Unused	Used
B462	SP193	12c +8c org yel, red & blk	90	1.10
B463	SP193	25c +10c pink, red & blk	90	55
B464	SP193	45c +20c brt grn, red & blk	90	1.10

The surtax was for the Netherlands Heart Foundation.

1970, Nov. 10 **Photo.** *Perf. 13x14*

No.	Type	Description	Unused	Used
B465	SP194	12c +8c bl, vio bl & grn	15	15
B466	SP194	15c +10c grn, bl & yel	1.75	2.00
B467	SP194	20c +10c lil rose, red & vio bl	1.75	2.00
B468	SP194	25c +10c red, yel & lil rose	25	15
a.		Min. sheet of 11, 9 #B465, 2 #B468 + label	13.00	13.00
B469	SP194	45c +20c gray & blk	2.25	2.50
		Nos. B465-B469 (5)	6.15	6.80

The surtax was for child welfare.

St. Paul SP195

Detail from Borobudur SP196

Designs: 15c+10c, "50" and people. 25c+10c, Joachim and Ann. 30c+15c, John the Baptist and the Scribes. 45c+ 20c, St. Anne. The sculptures are wood, 15th century, and in Dutch museums.

1971, Apr. 20 **Litho.** *Perf. 13x14*

No.	Type	Description	Unused	Used
B470	SP195	15c +10c multi	1.75	1.40

Lithographed and Photogravure

No.	Type	Description	Unused	Used
B471	SP195	20c +10c gray, grn & blk	1.40	1.40
B472	SP195	25c +10c buff, org & blk	1.40	55
B473	SP195	30c +15c gray, bl & blk	1.75	1.50
B474	SP195	45c +20c pink, ver & blk	1.75	1.50
		Nos. B470-B474 (5)	8.05	6.35

50th anniversary of the Federation of Netherlands Universities for Adult Education.

1971, June 29 **Litho.** *Perf. 13x14*

No.	Type	Description	Unused	Used
B475	SP196	45c +20c pur, yel & blk	2.50	2.50

60th birthday of Prince Bernhard. Surtax for Save Borobudur Temple Fund.

"Earth" SP197

Stylized Fruits SP198

Designs: 20c+10c, "Air" (butterfly). 25c+10c, "Sun," horiz. 30c+15c, "Moon," horiz. 45c+20c, "Water" (child looking at reflection).

Perf. 13x14, 14x13

1971, Nov. 9 **Photo.**

No.	Type	Description	Unused	Used
B476	SP197	15c +10c blk, lil & org	15	15
B477	SP197	20c +10c yel, blk & rose lil	55	42
B478	SP197	25c +10c multi	42	15
a.		Min. sheet of 9, 6 #B476, #B477, 2 #B478	10.00	7.25
B479	SP197	30c +15c bl, blk & pur	1.50	55
B480	SP197	45c +20c grn, blk & bl	2.50	2.50
		Nos. B476-B480 (5)	5.12	3.77

The surtax was for child welfare.

Luminescence

Some semipostal issues from Nos. B481-B484 onward are on phosphorescent paper.

1972, Apr. 11 **Litho.** *Perf. 13x14*

No.	Type	Description	Unused	Used
B481	SP198	20c +10c shown	1.25	1.50
B482	SP198	25c +10c Flower	1.25	1.50
B483	SP198	30c +15c "Sunlit Landscape"	1.25	75
B484	SP198	45c +25c "Music"	1.25	1.50

Summer festivals: Nos. B481-B482 publicize the Floriade, flower festival; Nos. B483-B484 the Holland Festival of Arts.

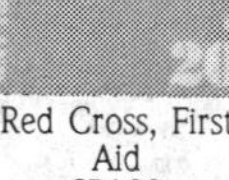

Red Cross, First Aid SP199

Prince Willem-Alexander SP200

Designs (Red Cross and): 25c+10c, Blood bank. 30c+15c, Disaster relief. 45c+25c, Child care.

1972, Aug. 15 *Perf. 13x14*

No.	Type	Description	Unused	Used
B485	SP199	20c +10c brt pink & red	80	45
B486	SP199	25c +10c org & red	95	80
B487	SP199	30c +15c blk & red	95	30
B488	SP199	45c +25c ultra & red	1.10	1.25

Surtax for the Netherlands Red Cross.

Perf. 13x14, 14x13

1972, Nov. 7 **Photo.**

Photographs of Dutch Princes: 30c+10c, Johan Friso. 35c+15c, Constantijn. 50c+20c, Johan Friso, Constantijn and Willem-Alexander. All are horizontal.

No.	Type	Description	Unused	Used
B489	SP200	25c +15c multi	28	15
B490	SP200	30c +10c multi	1.10	90
B491	SP200	35c +15c multi	1.10	15
a.		Min. sheet of 7, 4 #B489, #B490, 2 #B491 + label	7.75	6.50
B492	SP200	50c +20c multi	2.50	2.50

Surtax was for child welfare.

"W. A. Scholten," 1874 — SP201

Ships: 25c+15c, Flagship "De Seven Provincien," 1673, vert. 35c+15c, "Veendam," 1923. 50c+20c, Zuider Zee fish well boat, 17th century, vert.

1973, Apr. 10 **Litho.**

No.	Type	Description	Unused	Used
B493	SP201	25c +15c multi	1.50	1.40
B494	SP201	30c +10c multi	1.50	1.40
B495	SP201	35c +15c multi	1.50	90
B496	SP201	50c +20c multi	1.50	1.40

Tercentenary of the Battle of Kijkduin and centenary of the Holland-America Line.
Surtax for social and cultural purposes.

Chessboard — SP202

Games: 30c+10c, Tick-tack-toe. 40c+ 20c, Labyrinth. 50c+20c, Dominoes.

1973, Nov. 13 **Photo.** *Perf. 13x14*

No.	Type	Description	Unused	Used
B497	SP202	25c +15c multi	60	28
B498	SP202	30c +10c multi	1.10	70
B499	SP202	40c +20c multi	1.10	15
a.		Min. sheet of 6, 2 #B497, #B498, 3 #B499	8.75	6.75
B500	SP202	50c +20c multi	2.00	2.00

Surtax was for child welfare.

Netherlands stamps can be mounted in Scott's annual Netherlands Supplement.

Music Bands SP203

Herman Heijermans SP204

Designs: 30c+10c, Ballet dancers and traffic lights. 50c+20c, Kniertje, the fisher woman, from play by Heijermans.

1974, Apr. 23 **Litho.** *Perf. 13x14*

No.	Type	Description	Unused	Used
B501	SP203	25c +15c multi	95	95
B502	SP203	30c +10c multi	95	95

Photo.

No.	Type	Description	Unused	Used
B503	SP204	40c +20c multi	95	45
B504	SP204	50c +20c multi	95	95

Surtax was for various social and cultural institutions.

Boy with Hoop — SP205

Designs: 35c+20c, Girl and infant. 45c+20c, Two girls. 60c+20c, Girl sitting on balustrade. Designs are from turn-of-the-century photographs.

1974, Nov. 12 **Photo.** *Perf. 13x14*

No.	Type	Description	Unused	Used
B505	SP205	30c +15c blk & grn	38	30
B506	SP205	35c +20c mar	50	45
B507	SP205	45c +20c blk brn	60	18
a.		Min. sheet of 6, 4 #B505, #B506, #B507	4.25	3.75
B508	SP205	60c +20c ind	1.25	1.40

Surtax was for child welfare.

Beguinage, Amsterdam SP206

Cooper's Gate, Middelburg SP207

Designs: 35c+20c, St. Hubertus Hunting Lodge, horiz. 60c+20c, Orvelte Village, horiz.

Perf. 14x13, 13x14

1975, Apr. 4 **Litho.**

No.	Type	Description	Unused	Used
B509	SP206	35c +20c multi	65	55
B510	SP206	40c +15c multi	65	70
B511	SP207	50c +20c multi	80	55
B512	SP207	60c +20c multi	1.10	70

European Architectural Heritage Year 1975. Surtax was for various social and cultural institutions.

Orphans, Sculpture, 1785 — SP208

Designs: 40c+15c, Milkmaid, 17th century. 50c+25c, Aymon's 4 sons on steed Bayard, 17th century. 60c+25c, Life at orphanage, 1557. All designs are after ornamental stones from various buildings.

1975, Nov. 11 Photo. *Perf. 14x13*

B513 SP208 35c +15c multi 28 15
B514 SP208 40c +15c multi 55 55
B515 SP208 50c +25c multi 42 15
  a. Min. sheet of 5, 3 #B513, 2 #B515 + label 2.75 2.75
B516 SP208 60c +25c multi 90 90

Surtax was for child welfare.

Hedgehog
SP209

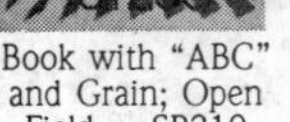

Book with "ABC" and Grain; Open Field — SP210

Green Frog and Spawn — SP212

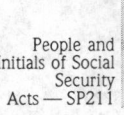

People and Initials of Social Security Acts — SP211

Perf. 14x13, 13x14

1976, Apr. 6 Litho.

B517 SP209 40c +20c multi 50 50
B518 SP210 45c +20c multi 50 38

Photo.

B519 SP211 55c +20c multi 80 38
B520 SP212 75c +25c multi 80 65

Surtax for various social and cultural institutions. #B517, B520 for wildlife protection; #B518 cent. of agricultural education and 175th anniv. of elementary education legislation; #B519 75th anniv. of social legislation and the Social Insurance Bank.

Patient Surrounded by Caring Hands — SP213

Netherlands No. 41 — SP214

1976, Sept. 2 Litho. *Perf. 13x14*

B521 SP213 55c +25c multi 60 60

Dutch Anti-Rheumatism Association, 50th anniversary.

1976, Oct. 8 Litho. *Perf. 13x14*

Designs: No. B523, #64. No. B524, #155. No. B525, #294. No. B526, #220.

B522 SP214 55c +55c multi 85 1.00
B523 SP214 55c +55c multi 85 1.00
B524 SP214 55c +55c multi 85 1.00
  a. Strip of 3, #B522-B524 2.75 3.00

Photo.

B525 SP214 75c +75c multi 85 1.00
B526 SP214 75c +75c multi 85 1.00
  a. Pair, #B525-B526 1.75 2.00
  Nos. B522-B526 (5) 4.25 5.00

Amphilex 77 Philatelic Exhibition, Amsterdam, May 26-June 5, 1977. No. B526a printed checkerwise.

See Nos. B535-B538.

Soccer — SP215

Designs (Children's Drawings): 45c+20c, Sailboat. 55c+20c, Elephant. 75c+25c, Mobile home.

1976, Nov. 16 Photo. *Perf. 14x13*

B527 SP215 40c +20c multi 32 15
B528 SP215 45c +20c multi 32 18
B529 SP215 55c +20c multi 32 15
  a. Min. sheet of 6, 2 each #B527-B529 2.75 2.75
B530 SP215 75c +25c multi 85 85

Surtax was for child welfare.

Hot Room, Thermal Bath, Heerlen
SP216

Designs: 45c+20c, Altar of Goddess Nehalennia, 200 A.D., Eastern Scheldt. 55c+20c, Part of oaken ship, Zwammerdam. 75c+25c, Helmet with face, Waal River at Nijmegen.

1977, Apr. 19 Photo. *Perf. 14x13*

B531 SP216 40c +20c multi 32 32
B532 SP216 45c +20c multi 32 32
B533 SP216 55c +20c multi 32 32
B534 SP216 75c +25c multi 48 48

Archaeological finds of Roman period.

Type of 1976

Designs: No. B535, Netherlands No. 83. No. B536, Netherlands No. 128. No. B537, Netherlands No. 211. No. B538, Netherlands No. 302.

1977, May 26 Litho. *Perf. 13x14*

B535 SP214 55c +45c multi 55 52
B536 SP214 55c +45c multi 55 52
  a. Pair, #B535-B536 1.10 1.10
B537 SP214 55c +45c multi 55 52
B538 SP214 55c +45c multi 55 52
  a. Souv. sheet of 2, #B535, B538 1.25 1.25
  b. Pair, #B537-B538 1.10 1.10

Amphilex 77 International Philatelic Exhibition, Amsterdam May 26-June 5. No. B538a sold at Exhibition only.

Risk of Drowning — SP217

Childhood Dangers: 45c+20c, Poisoning. 55c+20c, Following ball into street. 75c+ 25c, Playing with matches.

1977, Nov. 15 Photo. *Perf. 13x14*

B539 SP217 40c +20c multi 24 16
B540 SP217 45c +20c multi 24 16
B541 SP217 55c +20c multi 30 16
  a. Min. sheet of 6, 2 each #B539-B541 2.50 2.50
B542 SP217 75c +25c multi 75 75

Surtax was for child welfare.

Anna Maria van Schuurman
SP218

Delft Plate
SP219

Designs: 45c+20c, Part of letter written by author Belle van Zuylen (1740-1805). 75c+25c, Makkum dish with dog.

1978, Apr. 11 Litho. *Perf. 13x14*

B543 SP218 40c +20c multi 32 32
B544 SP218 45c +20c multi 32 32

Photo.

B545 SP219 55c +20c multi 35 24
B546 SP219 75c +25c multi 48 48

Dutch authors and pottery products.

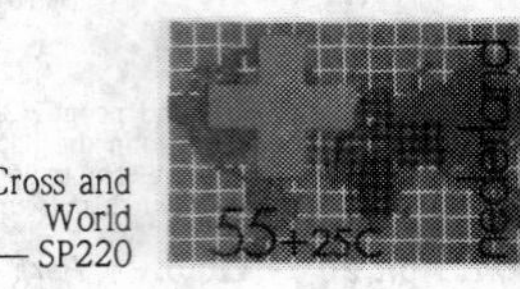

Red Cross and World Map — SP220

1978, Aug. 22 Photo. *Perf. 14x13*

B547 SP220 55c +25c multi 45 32
  a. Souvenir sheet of 3 1.75 1.50

Surtax was for Dutch Red Cross.

Boy Ringing Doorbell
SP221

Designs: 45c+20c, Child reading book. 55c+20c, Boy writing "30x Children for Children," vert. 75c+25c, Girl at blackboard, arithmetic lesson.

Perf. 14x13, 13x14

1978, Nov. 14 Photo.

B548 SP221 40c +20c multi 28 15
B549 SP221 45c +20c multi 30 15
B550 SP221 55c +20c multi 32 15
  a. Min. sheet of 6, 2 each #B548-B550 2.25 2.25
B551 SP221 75c +25c multi 60 60

Surtax was for child welfare.

Psalm Trilogy, by Jurriaan Andriessen
SP222

Birth of Christ (detail) Stained-glass Window
SP223

Designs: 45c+20c, Amsterdam Toonkunst Choir. 75c+25c, William of Orange, stained-glass window, 1603. Windows from St. John's Church, Gouda.

1979, Apr. 5 Photo. *Perf. 13x14*

B552 SP222 40c +20c multi 30 25
B553 SP222 45c +20c multi 30 25
B554 SP223 55c +20c multi 35 25
B555 SP223 75c +25c multi 50 48

Surtax for social and cultural purposes.

Child Sleeping Under Blanket
SP224

Designs: 45c+20c, Infant. 55c+20c, African boy, vert. 75c+25c, Children, vert.

1979, Nov. 13 *Perf. 14x13, 13x14*

B556 SP224 40c +20c blk, red & yel 30 15
B557 SP224 45c +20c blk & red 30 15
B558 SP224 55c +20c blk & yel 38 15
  a. Min. sheet, 2 each #B556-B558 2.00 2.00
B559 SP224 75c +25c blk, ultra & red 60 60

Surtax was for child welfare (in conjuction with International Year of the Child).

Roads Through Sand Dunes — SP225

Designs: 50c+20c, Park mansion vert. 60c+25c, Sailing. 80c+35c, Bicycling, moorlands.

Perf. 14x13, 13x14

1980, Apr. 15 Litho.

B560 SP225 45c +20c multi 28 28
B561 SP225 50c +20c multi 35 28
B562 SP225 60c +25c multi 42 22
B563 SP225 80c +35c multi 52 52

Society for the Promotion of Nature Preserves, 75th anniv. Surtax for social and cultural purposes.

Wheelchair Basketball — SP226

1980, June 3 Litho. *Perf. 13x14*

B564 SP226 60c +25c multi 48 20

Olympics for the Disabled, Arnhem and Veenendaal, June 21-July 5. Surtax was for National Sports for the Handicapped Fund.

Harlequin and Girl Standing in Open Book — SP227

Designs: 50c+20c, Boy on flying book, vert. 60c+30c, Boy reading King of Frogs, vert. 80c+30c, Boy "engrossed" in book.

Perf. 14x13, 13x14

1980, Nov. 11 Photo.

B565 SP227 45c +20c multi 30 22
B566 SP227 50c +20c multi 35 35
B567 SP227 60c +30c multi 42 22
  a. Min. sheet of 5, 2 #B565, 3 #B567 + label 2.00 2.00
B568 SP227 80c +30c multi 52 52

Surtax was for child welfare.

Salt Marsh with Outlet Ditch at Low Tide — SP228

Designs: 55c+25c, Dike. 60c+25c, Land drainage. 65c+30c, Cultivated land.

1981, Apr. 7 Photo. *Perf. 13x14*

B569 SP228 45c +20c multi 30 30
B570 SP228 55c +25c multi 38 38
B571 SP228 60c +25c multi 42 42
B572 SP228 65c +30c multi 55 55

Intl. Year of the Disabled SP229

Perf. 14x13, 13x14

1981, Nov. 10 **Photo.**
B573 SP229 45c +25c multi 32 25
B574 SP229 55c +20c multi, vert 35 32
B575 SP229 60c +25c multi, vert. 38 38
B576 SP229 65c +30c multi 45 38
a. Min. sheet of 5, 3 #B573, 2 #B576 + label 2.00 1.50

Surtax was for child welfare.

Floriade '82, Amsterdam, Apr. — SP230

1982, Apr. 7 **Litho.** ***Perf.*** ***$13^1/_2$x13***
B577 SP230 50c +20c shown 40 40
B578 SP230 60c +25c Anemones 45 45
B579 SP230 65c +25c Roses 52 52
B580 SP230 70c +30c African violets 55 55

Surtax was for culture and social welfare institutions.

Birds on Child's Head — SP231

Children and Animals: 60c+20c, Boy and cat. 65c+20c, Boy and rabbit. 70c+30c, Boy and bird.

1982, Nov. 16 **Photo.** ***Perf. 13x14***
B581 SP231 50c +30c multi 45 45
B582 SP231 60c +20c multi 45 45
a. Min. sheet of 5, 4 #B581, #B582 2.75 2.75
B583 SP231 65c +20c multi 50 50
B584 SP231 70c +30c multi 55 55

Surtax was for child welfare.

Johan van Oldenbarneveldt (1547-1619), Statesman, by J. Houbraken SP232

Paintings: 60c+25c, Willem Jansz Blaeu (1571-1638), cartographer, by Thomas de Keijser. 65c+25c, Hugo de Groot (1583-1645), statesman, by J. van Ravesteyn. 70c+30c, Portrait of Saskia van Uylenburch, by Rembrandt (1606-1669).

1983, Apr. 19 **Photo.** ***Perf. 14x13***
B585 SP232 50c +20c multi 42 42
B586 SP232 60c +25c multi 48 48
B587 SP232 65c +25c multi 55 55
B588 SP232 70c +30c multi 60 60

Surtax was for cultural and social welfare institutions.

Red Cross Workers — SP233

Designs: 60c+20c, Principles. 65c+25c, Sociomedical work. 70c+30c, Peace.

1983, Aug. 30 **Photo.** ***Perf. 13x14***
B589 SP233 50c +25c multi 42 42
B590 SP233 60c +20c multi 48 48
B591 SP233 65c +25c multi 55 55
B592 SP233 70c +30c multi 60 60
a. Bklt. pane, 4 #B589, 2 #B592 6.00

Surtax was for Red Cross.

Children's Christmas SP235

1983, Nov. 16 **Photo.** ***Perf. 14x13***
B596 SP235 50c +10c Ox & donkey 42 42
B597 SP235 50c +25c Snowman 50 50
B598 SP235 60c +30c Stars 60 60
B599 SP235 70c +30c Epiphany 70 70
a. Min. sheet, 4 #B597, 2 #B599 3.25 3.25

Surtax was for Child Welfare.

Eurasian Lapwings SP236

Birds: 60c+25c, Ruffs. 65c+25c, Redshanks, vert. 70c+30c, Black-tailed godwits, vert.

1984, Apr. 3 ***Perf. 14x13, 13x14***
B600 SP236 50c +20c multi 55 55
B601 SP236 60c +25c multi 70 70
B602 SP236 65c +25c multi 75 75
B603 SP236 70c +30c multi 85 85
a. Bklt. pane, 2 #B600, 2 #B603 3.25

Surtax for cultural and social welfare institutions.

FILACENTO '84 — SP237

Centenary of Organized Philately: 50c+20c, Eye, magnifying glass (36x25mm). 60c+25c, Cover, 1909 ($34^1/_2$x25mm). 70c+30c, Stamp club meeting, 1949 ($34^1/_2$x24mm).

1984, June 13 **Litho.** ***Perf. 14x13***
B604 SP237 50c +20c multi 60 60
B605 SP237 60c +25c multi 70 70
B606 SP237 70c +30c multi 90 90
a. Souv. sheet of 3, #B604-B606 2.00 2.00

No. B606a issued Sept. 5, 1984.

Comic Strips — SP238

1984, Nov. 14 **Litho.** ***Perf. 13x$13^1/_2$***
B607 SP238 50c +25c Music lesson 60 60
B608 SP238 60c +20c Dentist 65 65
B609 SP238 65c +25c Plumber 70 70
B610 SP238 70c +30c King 80 80
a. Min. sheet, 4 #B607, 2 #B610 4.00 4.00

Surtax was for child welfare.

Winterswijk Synagogue, Holy Arc — SP239

Religious architecture: 50+20c, St. Martin's Church, Zaltbommel, vert. 65+25c, Village Congregational Church, Bolsward, vert. 70+30c, St. John's Cathedral, 'S-Hertogenbosch, detail of buttress.

Perf. 13x14, 14x13

1985, Mar. 26 **Photo.**
B611 SP239 50c +20c gray & brt bl 65 65
B612 SP239 60c +25c dk red brn, Prus bl & pck bl 75 75
B613 SP239 65c +25c sl bl, red brn & gray ol 80 80
B614 SP239 70c +30c gray, brt bl & bis 90 90
a. Bklt. pane, 2 #B611, 2 #B614 3.75

Surtax for social and cultural purposes.

Traffic Safety — SP240

1985, Nov. 13 **Photo.** ***Perf. 13x14***
B615 SP240 50c +25c Photograph, lock, key 75 75
B616 SP240 60c +20c Boy, target 80 80
B617 SP240 65c +20c Girl, hazard triangle 90 90
B618 SP240 70c +30c Boy, traffic sign 1.00 1.00
a. Souv. sheet, 4 #B615, 2 #B618 5.00 5.00

Surtax was for child welfare organizations.

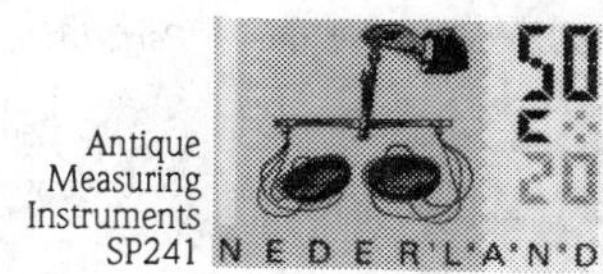

Antique Measuring Instruments SP241

Perf. $13^1/_2$x13, 13x$13^1/_2$

1986, Apr. 8 **Litho.**
B619 SP241 50c +20c Balance 65 65
B620 SP241 60c +25c Clock mechanism 85 85
B621 SP241 65c +25c Barometer 90 90
B622 SP241 70c +30c Jacob's staff 95 95
a. Bklt. pane, 2 each #B619, B622 4.75

Nos. B620-B621 vert.

Youth and Culture SP242

1986, Nov. 12 **Litho.** ***Perf. 14x13***
B623 SP242 55c +25c Music 80 80

Perf. $13^1/_2$x13

B624 SP242 65c +35c Visual arts 95 95
B625 SP242 75c +35c Theater 1.00 1.00
a. Min. sheet of 5, #B623, 2 each #B624-B625, perf. 14x13 4.75

Surtax for child welfare organizations.

Traditional Industries SP243

Designs: 55c+30c, Steam pumping station, Nijkerk. 65c+35c, Water tower, Deventer. 75c+35c, Brass foundry, Joure.

1987, Apr. 7 **Photo.** ***Perf. 14x13***
B626 SP243 55c +30c multi 70 70
B627 SP243 65c +35c multi 80 80
B628 SP243 75c +35c multi 90 90
a. Bklt. pane, 2 #B626, 2 #B628 3.50

Surtax for social and cultural welfare organizations.

Red Cross — SP244

1987, Sept. 1 **Photo.** ***Perf. 14x13***
B629 SP244 55c +30c multi 70 70
B630 SP244 65c +35c multi, diff. 80 80
B631 SP244 75c +35c multi, diff. 90 90
a. Bklt. pane, 2 #B629, 2 #B631 3.75

Surtax for nat'l. Red Cross.

Youth and Professions SP245

Perf. 13x14, 14x13

1987, Nov. 11 **Photo.**
B632 SP245 55c +25c Woodcutter, vert. 80 80
B633 SP245 65c +35c Sailor 95 95
B634 SP245 75c +35c Pilot 1.00 1.00
a. Miniature sheet of 5, #B632, 2 #B633, 2 #B634 4.75 4.75

Surtax for child welfare organizations.

FILACEPT '88, October 18, The Hague SP246

Designs: 55c +55c, Narcissus cyclamineus and poem "I call you flowers," by Jan Hanlo. No. B636, Rosa gallica versicolor. No. B637, Eryngium maritimum and map of The Hague from 1270.

1988, Feb. 23 **Litho.** ***Perf. $13^1/_2$x13***
B635 SP246 55c +55c multi 1.10 1.10
B636 SP246 75c +70c multi 1.40 1.40
B637 SP246 75c +70c multi 1.40 1.40
a. Souv. sheet of 3 + 3 labels, #B635-B637 4.00 4.00

Surtax helped finance exhibition.
No. B637a issued Oct. 18, 1988.

Man and the Zoo — SP247

Perf. 14x13, 13x14

1988, Mar. 22 **Photo.**
B638 SP247 55c +30c Equus quagga quagga 80 80
B639 SP247 65c +35c Carribean sea cow 95 95
B640 SP247 75c +35c Sam the orangutan, vert. 1.10 1.10
a. Bklt. pane, 2 #B638, 2 #B640 3.75

Natural Artis Magistra zoological soc., 150th anniv. Surtax for social and cultural welfare organizations.

Royal Dutch Swimming Federation, Cent. SP248

Children's drawings on the theme "Children and Water."

1988, Nov. 16 **Photo.** ***Perf. 14x13***
B641 SP248 55c +25c Rain 82 82
B642 SP248 65c +35c Getting Ready for the Race 1.00 1.00

B643 SP248 75c +35c Swimming Test 1.15 1.15
a. Souv. sheet of 5, #B641, 2 each #B642-B643 5.15 5.15

Surtax to benefit child welfare organizations.

Ships — SP249

Designs: No. B644, Pleasure yacht (boyer), vert. No. B645, Zuiderzee fishing boat (smack). No. B646, Clipper.

Perf. 13x14, 14x13

1989, Apr. 11 **Photo.**
B644 SP249 55c +30c multi 85 85
B645 SP249 65c +35c multi 98 98
B646 SP249 75c +35c multi 1.05 1.05
a. Bklt. pane of 4 (Nos. B644-B645, 2 No. B646) 4.00

Surtax for social and cultural organizations.

Children's Rights — SP250

1989, Nov. 8 **Litho.** ***Perf. 13½x13***
B647 SP250 55c +25c Housing 75 75
B648 SP250 65c +35c Food 95 95
B649 SP250 75c +35c Education 1.05 1.05
a. Min. sheet of 5, #B647, 2 each #B648-B649 4.75 4.75

UN Declaration of Children's Rights, 30th anniv. Surtax for child welfare.

Summer Weather SP251

Perf. 14x13, 13x14

1990, Apr. 3 **Photo.**
B650 SP251 55c +30c Girl, flowers 90 90
B651 SP251 65c +35c Clouds, isobars, vert. 1.05 1.05
B652 SP251 75c +35c Weather map, vert. 1.15 1.15
a. Bklt. pane of 4, #B650-B651, 2 #B652 4.25

Surtax for social and culture welfare organizations.

Children's Hobbies SP252

1990, Nov. 7 **Litho.** ***Perf. 13½x13***
B653 SP252 55c +25c Riding 85 85
B654 SP252 65c +35c Computers 1.05 1.05
B655 SP252 75c +35c Philately 1.20 1.20
a. Souv. sheet of 5, #B653, 2 each #B654-B655 5.35

Surtax for child welfare.

Dutch Farms SP253

Designs: 55c+30c, Frisian farm, Wartena. 65c+35c, Guelders T-style farm, Kesteren. 75c+35c, Closed construction farm, Nuth (Limburg).

1991, Apr. 16 **Litho.** ***Perf. 13½x13***
B656 SP253 55c +30c multi 95 25
a. Photo. 95 25
B657 SP253 65c +35c multi 1.10 28
B658 SP253 75c +35c multi 1.20 30
a. Photo. 1.20 30
b. Bklt. pane, 2 #B656a, 3 #B658a 5.50

Surtax for social and cultural welfare organizations.

Children Playing SP254

1991, Nov. 6 **Litho.** ***Perf. 13½x13***
B659 SP254 60c +30c Doll, robot 1.05 26
a. Photo., perf. 14x13½ 1.05 26
B660 SP254 70c +35c Cycle race 1.20 30
B661 SP254 80c +40c Hide and seek 1.40 35
a. Photo., perf. 14x13½ 1.40 35
b. Min. sheet, 4 #B659a, 2 #B661a 7.00

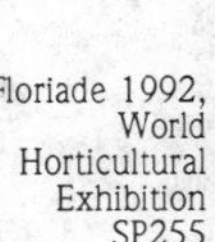

Floriade 1992, World Horticultural Exhibition SP255

Various plants and flowers.

1992, Apr. 7 **Litho.** ***Perf. 13½x13***
B662 SP255 60c +30c multi 1.10 28
B663 SP255 70c +35c multi 1.30 32
B664 SP255 80c +40c multi 1.50 38

Surtax for social and cultural welfare organizations.

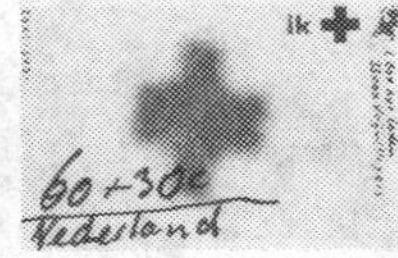

Netherlands Red Cross, 125th Anniv. SP256

1992, Sept. 8 **Litho.** ***Perf. 13½x13***
B665 SP256 60c +30c Shadow of cross 1.10 28
a. Photo., perf. 14 on 3 sides 1.10 28
B666 SP256 70c +35c Aiding victim 1.25 30
a. Photo., perf. 14 on 3 sides 1.25 30
B667 SP256 80c +40c Red cross on bandage 1.35 35
a. Photo., perf. 14 on 3 sides 1.35 35
b. Bklt. pane, 3 #B665a, 2 #B666a, 1 #B667a 7.25

On normally centered stamps, the white border appears on the top, bottom and right sides only.

Children Making Music — SP257

1992, Nov. 11 **Litho.** ***Perf. 13x13½***
B668 SP257 60c +30c Saxophone player 1.05 28
a. Photo., perf. 13½x14 1.05 28
B669 SP257 70c +35c Piano player 1.20 30
a. Photo., perf. 13½x14 1.20 30
B670 SP257 80c +40c Bass player 1.40 35
a. Photo., perf. 13½x14 1.40 35
b. Souvenir sheet, 3 #B668a, 2 #B669a, #B670a 7.00

AIR POST STAMPS

Stylized Seagull — AP1

Perf. 12½

1921, May 1 **Unwmk.** **Typo.**
C1 AP1 10c red 1.10 95
C2 AP1 15c yellow grn 5.75 1.90
C3 AP1 60c dp blue 17.00 18
Set, never hinged 170.00

Nos. C1-C3 were used to pay airmail fee charged by the carrier, KLM.

Lt. G. A. Koppen — AP2

Capt. Jan van der Hoop — AP3

Wmk. Circles (202)

1928, Aug. 20 **Litho.** ***Perf. 12***
C4 AP2 40c orange red 25 25
C5 AP3 75c blue green 25 25
Set, never hinged 85

Mercury AP4

Queen Wilhelmina AP5

Perf. 11½

1929, July 16 **Unwmk.** **Engr.**
C6 AP4 1½g gray 2.25 1.40
C7 AP4 4½g carmine 1.75 2.50
C8 AP4 7½g blue green 21.00 3.75
Set, never hinged 60.00

Perf. 12½, 14x13

1931, Sept. 24 **Photo.** **Wmk. 202**
C9 AP5 36c org red & dk bl 8.00 45
Never hinged 65.00

Fokker Pander — AP6

1933, Oct. 9 ***Perf. 12½***
C10 AP6 30c dark green 35 35
Never hinged 50

Nos. C10-C12 were issued for use on special flights.

Crow in Flight — AP7

1938-53 ***Perf. 13x14***
C11 AP7 12½c dk blue & gray 15 18
C12 AP7 25c dk bl & gray ('53) 90 1.10
Set, never hinged 3.25

Seagull — AP8

Airplane — AP9

Perf. 13x14

1951, Nov. 12 **Engr.** **Unwmk.**
C13 AP8 15g gray 125.00 67.50
C14 AP8 25g blue gray 125.00 67.50
Set, never hinged 350.00

Catalogue values for unused stamps in this section, from this point to the end of the section, are for Never Hinged items.

1966, Sept. 2 **Litho.** ***Perf. 14x13***
C15 AP9 25c gray, blk & bl 32 32

Issued for use on special flights.

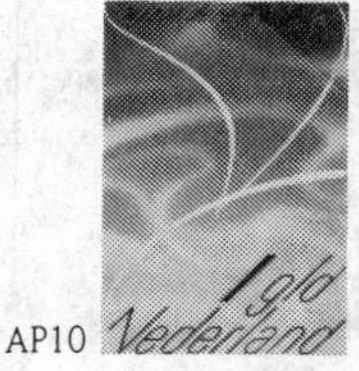

AP10

1980, May 13 **Photo.** ***Perf. 13x14***
C16 AP10 1g multi 70 70

MARINE INSURANCE STAMPS

Floating Safe Attracting Gulls — MI1

Floating Safe with Night Flare — MI2

Fantasy of Floating Safe — MI3

Perf. 11½

1921, Feb. 2 **Unwmk.** **Engr.**
GY1 MI1 15c slate grn 3.50 *27.50*
GY2 MI1 60c car rose 3.50 *32.50*
GY3 MI1 75c gray brn 5.50 *37.50*
GY4 MI2 1.50g dk bl 60.00 *310.00*
GY5 MI2 2.25g org brn 150.00 *400.00*
GY6 MI3 4½g black 150.00 *500.00*
GY7 MI3 7½g red 180.00 *700.00*
Nos. GY1-GY7 (7) 552.50 *2,007.*
Set, never hinged 1,400.

POSTAGE DUE STAMPS

Postage due types of Netherlands were also used for Curacao, Netherlands Indies and Surinam in different colors.

D1

D2

Perf. 12½x12, 13
1870, May 15 Typo. Unwmk.
J1 D1 5c brn, *org* 45.00 8.00
a. Imperf., pair 450.00
J2 D1 10c vio, *bl* 100.00 8.75
a. Imperf., pair 300.00

Type I - 34 loops. "T" of "BETALEN" over center of loop; top branch of "E" of "TE" shorter than lower branch.
Type II - 33 loops. "T" of "BETALEN" between two loops.
Type III - 32 loops. "T" of "BETALEN" slightly to the left of loop; top branch of first "E" of "BETALEN" shorter than lower branch.
Type IV - 37 loops. Letters of "PORT" larger than in the other three types.

Perf. 11½x12, 12½x12, 12½, 13½
1881-87
Value in Black
J3 D2 1c lt blue (III) 8.75 8.75
a. Type I 10.50 13.00
b. Type II 14.00 14.00
c. Type IV 35.00 40.00
J4 D2 1½c lt blue (III) 12.50 11.00
a. Type I 14.00 15.00
b. Type II 19.00 18.00
c. Type IV 55.00 55.00
J5 D2 2½c lt blue (III) 27.50 3.50
a. Type I 32.50 4.00
b. Type II 40.00 4.75
c. Type IV 150.00 90.00
J6 D2 5c lt blue (III) ('87) 100.00 2.75
a. Type I 125.00 3.50
b. Type II 140.00 4.00
c. Type IV 1,500. 250.00
J7 D2 10c lt blue (III) ('87) 100.00 3.00
a. Type I 125.00 3.50
b. Type II 140.00 4.00
c. Type IV 2,100. 275.00
J8 D2 12½c lt blue (III) 100.00 25.00
a. Type I 125.00 30.00
b. Type II 140.00 32.50
c. Type IV 350.00 95.00
J9 D2 15c lt blue (III) 90.00 2.75
a. Type I 110.00 3.50
b. Type II 125.00 4.00
c. Type IV 140.00 19.00
J10 D2 20c lt blue (III) 27.50 2.75
a. Type I 35.00 3.50
b. Type II 37.50 4.00
c. Type IV 140.00 19.00
J11 D2 25c lt blue (III) 230.00 2.50
a. Type I 240.00 2.75
b. Type II 300.00 3.75
c. Type IV 450.00 140.00

Value in Red
J12 D2 1g lt blue (III) 85.00 22.50
a. Type I 87.50 27.50
b. Type II 110.00 30.00
c. Type IV 175.00 55.00

See Nos. J13-J26, J44-J60. For surcharges see Nos. J27-J28, J42-J43, J72-J75.

1896-1910 *Perf. 12½*
Value in Black
J13 D2 ½c dk bl (I) ('01) 15 15
J14 D2 1c dk blue (I) 1.10 15
a. Type III 2.00 2.50
J15 D2 1½c dk blue (I) 48 30
a. Type III 2.00 2.00
J16 D2 2½c dk blue (I) 1.25 24
a. Type III 2.50 40
J17 D2 3c dk bl (I) ('10) 1.40 1.00
J18 D2 4c dk bl (I) ('09) 1.40 1.50
J19 D2 5c dk blue (I) 9.00 20
a. Type III 12.50 30
J20 D2 6½c dk bl (I) ('07) 30.00 27.50
J21 D2 7½c dk bl (I) ('04) 1.10 42
J22 D2 10c dk blue (I) 25.00 30
a. Type III 35.00 1.25
J23 D2 12½c dk blue (I) 22.50 75
a. Type III 32.50 2.50
J24 D2 15c dk blue (I) 25.00 65
a. Type III 40.00 75
J25 D2 20c dk blue (I) 14.00 5.75
a. Type III 14.00 6.25
J26 D2 25c dk blue (I) 30.00 60
a. Type III 35.00 75
Nos. J13-J26 (14) 162.38 39.51

Surcharged in Black **50 CENT**

1906, Jan. 10 *Perf. 12½*
J27 D2 50c on 1g lt bl (III) 125.00 110.00
a. 50c on 1g light blue (I) 140.00 140.00
b. 50c on 1g light blue (II) 150.00 140.00

Surcharged in Red

1906, Oct. 6
J28 D2 6½c on 20c dk bl (I) 4.00 4.50

Nos. 87-89 Surcharged **PORTZEGEL 1 CENT**

1907, Nov. 1
J29 A13 ½c on 1c claret 1.25 1.25
J30 A13 1c on 1c claret 48 40
J31 A13 1½c on 1c claret 48 40
J32 A13 2½c on 1c claret 1.10 1.10
J33 A13 5c on 2½c ver 1.25 32
J34 A13 6½c on 2½c ver 3.00 3.00
J35 A13 7½c on ½c blue 1.50 1.10
J36 A13 10c on ½c blue 1.65 60
J37 A13 12½c on ½c blue 4.50 4.00
J38 A13 15c on 2½c ver 5.75 3.25
J39 A13 25c on ½c blue 8.25 7.25
J40 A13 50c on ½c blue 37.50 32.50
J41 A13 1g on ½c blue 55.00 47.50
Nos. J29-J41 (13) 121.71 102.67

Two printings of the above surcharges were made. Some values show differences in the setting of the fractions; others are practically impossible to distinguish.

No. J20 Surcharged in Red

1909, June
J42 D2 4c on 6½c dark blue 5.00 5.00
Never hinged 15.00

No. J12 Surcharged in Black **3 CENT**

1910, July 11
J43 D2 3c on 1g lt bl, type III 25.00 25.00
Never hinged 67.50
a. Type I 32.50 32.50
Never hinged 85.00
b. Type II 35.00 35.00
Never hinged 92.50

Type I
1912-21 *Perf. 12½, 13½x13*
Value in Color of Stamp
J44 D2 ½c pale ultra 15 15
J45 D2 1c pale ultra ('13) 15 15
J46 D2 1½c pale ultra ('15) 1.10 90
J47 D2 2½c pale ultra 15 15
J48 D2 3c pale ultra 38 20
J49 D2 4c pale ultra ('13) 15 15
J50 D2 4½c pale ultra ('16) 5.25 3.50
J51 D2 5c pale ultra 15 15
J52 D2 5½c pale ultra ('16) 5.00 3.50
J53 D2 7c pale ultra ('21) 2.25 1.50
J54 D2 7½c pale ultra ('13) 2.50 60
J55 D2 10c pale ultra ('13) 15 15
J56 D2 12½c pale ultra ('13) 15 15
J57 D2 15c pale ultra ('13) 15 15
J58 D2 20c pale ultra ('20) 15 15
J59 D2 25c pale ultra ('17) 65.00 50
J60 D2 50c pale ultra ('20) 38 15
Nos. J44-J60 (17) 83.21 12.20
Set, never hinged 210.00

D3

Perf. 12½, 13½x12½
1921-38 Typo.
J61 D3 3c pale ultra ('28) 15 15
J62 D3 6c pale ultra ('27) 15 15
J63 D3 7c pale ultra ('28) 15 15
J64 D3 7½c pale ultra ('26) 24 15
J65 D3 8c pale ultra ('38) 15 15
J66 D3 9c pale ultra ('30) 15 15
J67 D3 11c ultra ('21) 11.00 2.50
J68 D3 12c pale ultra ('28) 15 15
J69 D3 25c pale ultra ('25) 15 15
J70 D3 30c pale ultra ('35) 24 15
J71 D3 1g ver ('21) 70 15
Nos. J61-J71 (11) 13.23
Set value 3.45
Set, never hinged 30.00

Stamps of 1912-21 Surcharged

1923, Dec. *Perf. 12½*
J72 D2 1c on 3c ultra 40 40
J73 D2 2½c on 7c ultra 40 32
J74 D2 25c on 1½c ultra 8.00 40
J75 D2 25c on 7½c ultra 8.00 32
Set, never hinged 35.00

Nos. 55-56, 62, 65 Surcharged

TE BETALEN

PORT

1924, Aug.
J76 A11 4c on 3c ol grn 1.10 1.10
J77 A11 5c on 1c red 38 15
a. Surcharge reading down 450.00 450.00
J78 A11 10c on ½c bl 95 15
a. Tête bêche pair 8.50 8.50
J79 A11 12½c on 5c car 95 15
a. Tête bêche pair 12.00 12.00

The basic stamps of Nos. J76 and J79 are type A11; those of J77-J78 are type A10.
Stamps of type D4 of denominations of 11c on 22½c and 15c on 17½c exist. These were used by the postal service for accounting of parcel post fees.

Catalogue values for unused stamps in this section, from this point to the end of the section, are for Never Hinged items.

D5

Perf. 13½x12½
1947-58 Wmk. 202 Photo.
J80 D5 1c light blue ('48) 16 15
J81 D5 3c light blue ('48) 35 15
J82 D5 4c light blue 11.00 80
J83 D5 5c light blue ('48) 42 15
J84 D5 6c light blue ('50) 25 32
J85 D5 7c light blue 16 20
J86 D5 8c light blue ('48) 16 20
J87 D5 10c light blue 16 15
J88 D5 11c light blue 30 40
J89 D5 12c light blue ('48) 50 1.00
J90 D5 14c light blue ('53) 85 80
J91 D5 15c light blue 30 15
J92 D5 16c light blue 75 1.10
J93 D5 20c light blue 30 15
J94 D5 24c light blue ('57) 1.10 1.25
J95 D5 25c light blue ('48) 42 15
J96 D5 26c light blue ('58) 1.75 1.75
J97 D5 30c light blue ('48) 52 15
J98 D5 35c light blue 60 15
J99 D5 40c light blue 70 15
J100 D5 50c light blue ('48) 75 15
J101 D5 60c light blue ('58) 95 40
J102 D5 85c light blue ('50) 15.00 40
J103 D5 90c light blue ('56) 2.50 40
J104 D5 95c light blue ('57) 2.50 52
J105 D5 1g carmine ('48) 2.25 15
J106 D5 1.75g carmine ('57) 5.25 32
Nos. J80-J106 (27) 49.95 11.66

OFFICIAL STAMPS

Regular Issues of 1898-1908 Overprinted **ARMENWET**

1913 Typo. Unwmk. *Perf. 12½*
O1 A10 1c red 3.25 1.65
O2 A10 1½c ultra 80 1.25
O3 A10 2c yel brn 5.75 5.75
O4 A10 2½c dp grn 13.00 10.00
O5 A11 3c ol grn 3.25 65
O6 A11 5c car rose 3.25 3.50
O7 A11 10c gray lil 30.00 35.00
Nos. O1-O7 (7) 59.30 57.80

Same Overprint in Red on No. 58
1919
O8 A10 1½c dp bl (R) 85.00 92.50

Nos. O1 to O8 were used to defray the postage on matter relating to the Poor Laws.
Counterfeit overprints exist.

For the International Court of Justice

Regular Issue of 1926-33 Overprinted in Gold **COUR PERMANENTE DE JUSTICE INTERNATIONALE**

1934 Wmk. 202 *Perf. 12½*
O9 A24 1½c red vio 60
O10 A24 2½c dp grn 60
O11 A23 7½c red 1.10
O12 A31 12½c dp ultra 32.50
O13 A23 15c orange 1.25
O14 A23 30c violet 2.00
a. Perf. 13½x12½ 2.00
Nos. O9-O14 (6) 38.05

Same Overprint on No. 180 in Gold
1937 *Perf. 13½x12½*
O15 A23 12½c ultra 16.00

"Mint" Officials
Nos. O9-O15, O20-O43 were sold to the public only canceled. Uncanceled, they were obtainable only by favor of an official or from UPU specimen copies.

Same on Regular Issue of 1940 Overprinted in Gold
1940 *Perf. 13½x12½*
O16 A45 7½c brt red 14.00 8.00
O17 A45 12½c sapphire 14.00 8.00
O18 A45 15c lt blue 14.00 8.00
O19 A45 30c bister 14.00 8.00

Nos. 217 to 219, 221 and 223 Overprinted in Gold **COUR INTERNATIONALE DE JUSTICE**

1947
O20 A45 7½c brt red 1.00
O21 A45 10c brt red vio 1.00
O22 A45 12½c sapphire 1.00
O23 A45 20c purple 1.00
O24 A45 25c rose brn 1.00
Nos. O20-O24 (5) 5.00

O1

Perf. 14½x13½
1950 Unwmk. Photo.
O25 O1 2c ultra 8.00
O26 O1 4c olive green 8.00

Palace of Peace, The Hague — O2

Queen Juliana — O3

1951-58 *Perf. 12½x12*
O27 O2 2c red brown 35
O28 O2 3c ultra ('53) 35
O29 O2 4c dp green 35
O30 O2 5c ol brn ('53) 35
O31 O2 6c ol grn ('53) 70
O32 O2 7c red ('53) 55

Engr.

O33 O3 6c brown vio 5.50
O34 O3 10c dull green 15
O35 O3 12c rose red 65
O36 O3 15c rose brn ('53) 15
O37 O3 20c dull blue 15
O38 O3 25c violet brn 15
O39 O3 30c rose lil ('58) 28
O40 O3 1g slate gray 70
Nos. O27-O40 (14) 10.38

1977, May Photo. *Perf. 12½x12*

O41 O2 40c brt grnsh blue 32
O42 O2 45c brick red 32
O43 O2 50c brt rose lilac 32

Catalogue values for unused stamps in this section, from this point to the end of the section, are for Never Hinged items.

Peace Palace, The Hague — O4

Design: 5g, 7g, Palm, sun, column.

1989, Oct. 24 Litho. *Perf. 13x14*

O44 O4 55c black & pink 52 55
O45 O4 75c black & yellow 70 70

Litho. & Engr.

O46 O4 7g multicolored 6.50 6.50

1990, Oct. 23 Litho.

O47 O4 65c blk & bl grn 75 75
O48 O4 1g blk & org 1.10 1.10
O49 O4 1.50g blk & bl 1.60 1.60

Litho. & Engr.

O50 O4 5g multicolored 5.50 5.50

1991, Oct. 22 Litho.

O51 O4 5c black & org yel 15 15
O52 O4 10c black & blue 15 15
O53 O4 25c black & red 30 30
O54 O4 50c black & yel grn 60 60
O55 O4 60c black & bister 75 75
O56 O4 70c black & gray blue 88 88
O57 O4 80c black & gray grn 1.00 1.00
Nos. O44-O57 (14) 20.50 20.53

This is an expanding set. Numbers will change when complete.

NETHERLANDS ANTILLES

(Curacao)

LOCATION — Two groups of islands about 500 miles apart in the West Indies, north of Venezuela
AREA — 383 sq. mi.
POP. — 260,000 (est. 1983)
CAPITAL — Willemstad

Formerly a colony, Curacao, Netherlands Antilles became an integral part of the Kingdom of the Netherlands under the Constitution of 1954. On Jan. 1, 1986, the island of Aruba achieved a separate status within the Kingdom and began issuing its own stamps.

100 Cents = 1 Gulden

Catalogue values for unused stamps in this country are for Never Hinged items, beginning with Scott 164 in the regular postage section, Scott B1 in the semi-postal section, Scott C18 in the airpost section, Scott CB9 in the airpost semi-postal section, and Scott J41 in the postage due section.

King William III
A1

Numeral
A2

Regular Perf. 11½, 12½, 11½x12, 12½x12, 13½x13, 14

1873-79 Typo. Unwmk.

1 A1 2½c green 3.00 6.50
2 A1 3c bister 45.00 *110.00*
3 A1 5c rose 6.00 6.00
4 A1 10c ultra 42.50 12.00
5 A1 25c brown org 35.00 6.00
6 A1 50c violet 1.40 2.50
7 A1 2.50g bis & pur ('79) 25.00 21.00

See bluish paper note with Netherlands #7-22.
The gulden denominations, Nos. 7 and 12, are of larger size.
See 8-12. For surcharges see #18, 25-26.

Perf. 14, Small Holes

1b A1 2½c 9.00 13.00
2b A1 3c 50.00 *100.00*
3b A1 5c 9.00 15.00
4b A1 10c 50.00 60.00
5b A1 25c 50.00 40.00
6b A1 50c 24.00 26.00

"Small hole" varieties have the spaces between the holes wider than the diameter of the holes.

1886-89 *Perf. 11½, 12½, 12½x12*

8 A1 12½c yellow 70.00 32.50
9 A1 15c olive ('89) 19.00 11.00
10 A1 30c pearl gray ('89) 25.00 35.00
11 A1 60c olive bis ('89) 30.00 12.50
12 A1 1.50g lt & dk bl ('89) 80.00 65.00

Nos. 1-12 were issued without gum until 1890. Imperfs. are proofs.

1889 *Perf. 12½*

13 A2 1c gray 65 85
14 A2 2c violet 48 1.00
15 A2 2½c green 3.25 2.00
16 A2 3c bister 3.75 4.50
17 A2 5c rose 16.00 1.10
Nos. 13-17 (5) 24.13 9.45

King William III
A3

Queen Wilhelmina
A4

Black Surcharge, Handstamped

1891 *Perf. 12½x12*

Without Gum

18 A3 25c on 30c pearl gray 13.00 13.00

No. 18 exists with dbl. surch., value $225, and with invtd. surch., value $275.

1892-96 *Perf. 12½*

19 A4 10c ultra ('95) 70 95
20 A4 12½c green 26.00 7.00
21 A4 15c rose ('93) 2.25 2.50
22 A4 25c brown org 82.50 6.50
23 A4 30c gray ('96) 2.25 *6.50*
Nos. 19-23 (5) 113.70 23.45

King William III
A5 A6

Magenta Surcharge, Handstamped

1895 *Perf. 12½, 13½x13*

25 A5 2½c on 10c ultra 10.00 6.75

Perf. 12½x12

Black Surcharge, Handstamped

26 A6 2½c on 30c gray 125.00 5.00

Nos. 25-26 exist with surcharge double or inverted. Values: No. 25, double $275 and $200; inverted $350 and $250. No. 26, double $275, inverted $550.
No. 26 and No. 25, perf. 13½x13, were issued without gum.

25 Cᵗ

CURAÇAO

Nos. 27, 29

Queen Wilhelmina — A8

1902, Jan. 1 *Perf. 12½*

Netherlands Nos. 77, 84, 68 Surcharged in Black

27 A7 25c on 25c car & bl 90 90

1901, May 1 Engr. *Perf. 11½x11*

28 A8 1.50g on 2.50g brn lil 14.00 19.00

1902, Mar. 1 Typo. *Perf. 12½*

29 A7 12½c on 12½c blue 25.00 6.75

A9

A10

1904-08

30 A9 1c ol grn 1.10 60
31 A9 2c yel brn 11.00 3.50
32 A9 2½c bl grn 3.50 28
33 A9 3c orange 6.50 3.50
34 A9 5c rose red 5.75 28
35 A9 7½c gray ('08) 27.50 5.75
36 A10 10c slate 9.75 3.50
37 A10 12½c dp bl 1.10 18
38 A10 15c brown 14.00 9.25
39 A10 22½c brn & ol ('08) 14.00 7.50
40 A10 25c violet 14.00 1.90
41 A10 30c brn org 32.50 13.00
42 A10 50c red brn 27.50 8.25
Nos. 30-42 (13) 168.20 57.49

Queen Wilhelmina — A11

1906, Nov. 1 Engr. *Perf. 11½*

Without Gum

43 A11 1½g red brown 35.00 24.00
44 A11 2½g slate blue 35.00 24.00

A12

Queen Wilhelmina
A13 A14

Perf. 12½, 11, 11½, 11x11½

1915-33 Typo.

45 A12 ½c lilac ('20) 40 85
46 A12 1c olive grn 18 15
47 A12 1½c blue ('20) 15 15
48 A12 2c yel brn 1.25 1.40
49 A12 2½c green 1.10 16
50 A12 3c yellow 1.25 1.50
51 A12 3c green ('26) 2.25 2.50
52 A12 5c rose 1.40 15
53 A12 5c green ('22) 2.50 2.75
54 A12 5c lilac ('26) 1.10 15
55 A12 7½c drab 1.50 32
56 A12 7½c bister ('20) 1.10 15
57 A12 10c lilac ('22) 4.25 4.50
58 A12 10c rose ('26) 4.25 1.25
59 A13 10c car rose 13.00 3.00
60 A13 12½c blue 1.50 50
61 A13 12½c red ('22) 1.40 1.65
62 A13 15c ol grn 45 65
63 A13 15c lt bl ('26) 3.00 2.50
64 A13 20c blue ('22) 6.00 3.00
65 A13 20c ol grn ('26) 1.65 2.25
66 A13 22½c orange 1.40 2.25
67 A13 25c red vio 3.00 90
68 A13 30c slate 3.00 65
69 A13 35c sl & red ('22) 3.00 4.25

Perf. 11½x11, 11½, 12½, 11

Engr.

70 A14 50c green 2.50 16
71 A14 1½g violet 12.00 10.00
72 A14 2½g carmine 20.00 19.00
a. Perf. 12½ ('33) 140.00 *300.00*
Nos. 45-72 (28) 94.58 66.74

Some stamps of 1915 were also issued without gum.
For surcharges see #74, 107-108, C1-C3.

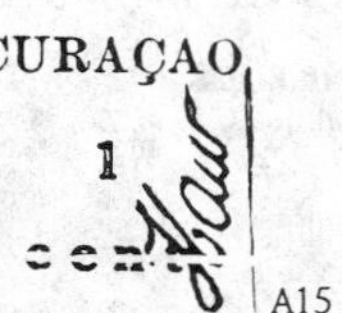

A15

Laid Paper, without Gum

1918, July 16 Typo. *Perf. 12*

73 A15 1c black, *buff* 6.75 3.75

"HAW" are the initials of Postmaster H. A. Willemsen.

No. 60 Surcharged in Black

5
CENT

1918, Sept. 1 *Perf. 12½*

74 A13 5c on 12½c blue 3.75 2.00
a. "5" 2½mm wide 55.00 30.00
b. Double surcharge 450.00

The "5" of No. 74 is 3mm wide. Illustration shows No. 74a surcharge.

Queen Wilhelmina
A16 A17

1923 Engr. *Perf. 11½, 11x11½*

75 A16 5c green 60 2.00
76 A16 7½c ol grn 1.10 1.65
77 A16 10c car rose 1.10 2.00
78 A16 20c indigo 1.90 3.50
a. Perf. 11x11½ 2.50 4.00
79 A16 1g brn vio 25.00 19.00
80 A16 2½g gray blk 60.00 *45.00*
81 A16 5g brown 80.00 *55.00*
a. Perf. 11x11½ 750.00
Nos. 75-81 (7) 169.70 *128.15*

25th anniv. of the assumption of the government of the Netherlands by Queen Wilhelmina, at the age of 18.
Nos. 80-81 with clear cancel between Aug. 1, 1923 and Apr. 30, 1924, sell for considerably more.

Types of Netherlands Marine Insurance Stamps, Inscribed "CURACAO" Surcharged in Black

FRANKEER
= ZEGEL =
10
CENT

1927, Oct. 3

87	MI1	3c on 15c dk grn	18	24
88	MI1	10c on 60c car rose	22	30
89	MI1	12½c on 75c gray brn	24	30
90	MI2	15c on 1.50g dk bl	3.00	2.50
a.		Double surcharge	475.00	
91	MI2	25c on 2.25g org brn	6.50	6.25
92	MI3	30c on 4½g blk	14.00	11.00
93	MI3	50c on 7½g red	7.50	7.25
		Nos. 87-93 (7)	31.64	27.84

Nos. 90, 91 and 92 have "FRANKEERZEGEL" in one line of small capitals. Nos. 90 and 91 have a heavy bar across the top of the stamp.

1928-30 Engr. *Perf. 11½, 12½*

95	A17	6c org red ('30)	1.50	18
a.		Booklet pane of 6		
96	A17	7½c org red	60	42
97	A17	10c carmine	1.50	35
98	A17	12½c red brn	1.50	1.00
a.		Booklet pane of 6		
99	A17	15c dk bl	1.50	28
a.		Booklet pane of 6		
100	A17	20c bl blk	5.75	55
101	A17	21c yel grn ('30)	9.25	14.00
102	A17	25c brn vio	3.50	1.40
103	A17	27½c blk ('30)	12.00	14.00
104	A17	30c dp grn	5.75	55
105	A17	35c brnsh blk	2.00	1.75
		Nos. 95-105 (11)	44.85	34.48

No. 96 Surcharged in Black with Bars over Original Value **6 ct.**

1929, Nov. 1

106	A17	6c on 7½c org red	1.40	1.00
a.		Inverted surcharge	300.00	260.00

No. 51 Surcharged in Red **2 ½**

1931, Mar. 1 Typo. *Perf. 12½*

107	A12	2½c on 3c grn	1.10	1.10

No. 49 Surcharged in Red **1½**

1932, Oct. 29

108	A12	1½c on 2½c grn	3.50	3.50

Prince William I, Portrait by Van Key — A18

1933 Photo. *Perf. 12½*

109	A18	6c deep orange	1.75	1.40

400th birth anniv. of Prince William I, Count of Nassau and Prince of Orange, frequently referred to as William the Silent.

Willem Usselinx — A19

Van Walbeeck's Ship — A22

Designs: 2½c, 5c, 6c, Frederik Hendrik, 10c, 12½c, 15c, Jacob Binckes. 27½c, 30c, 50c, Cornelis Evertsen the Younger. 1.50g, 2.50g, Louis Brion.

1934, Jan. 1 Engr. *Perf. 12½*

110	A19	1c black	1.00	1.25
111	A19	1½c dl vio	75	30
112	A19	2c orange	1.00	1.25
113	A19	2½c dl grn	85	1.25
114	A19	5c blk brn	85	85
115	A19	6c vio bl	75	25
116	A19	10c lake	2.00	1.00
117	A19	12½c bis brn	6.50	7.00
118	A19	15c blue	1.65	1.00
119	A22	20c black	3.00	2.00
120	A22	21c brown	10.00	13.00
121	A22	25c dl grn	10.00	10.50
122	A19	27½c brn vio	13.00	16.00
123	A19	30c scarlet	10.00	4.50
124	A19	50c orange	10.00	7.50
125	A19	1.50g indigo	45.00	47.50
126	A19	2.50g yel grn	52.50	47.50
		Nos. 110-126 (17)	168.85	162.65

3rd centenary of the founding of the colony.

Numeral A25

Queen Wilhelmina A26

1936, Aug. 1 Litho. *Perf. 13½x13*

Size: 18x22mm

127	A25	1c brn blk	15	15
128	A25	1½c dp ultra	18	15
129	A25	2c orange	22	22
130	A25	2½c green	20	20
131	A25	5c scarlet	18	15

Engr.

Perf. 12½

Size: 20¼x30½mm

132	A26	6c brn vio	45	15
133	A26	10c org red	85	15
134	A26	12½c dk bl grn	1.25	95
135	A26	15c dk bl	1.00	38
136	A26	20c org yel	1.00	45
137	A26	21c dk gray	1.90	2.25
138	A26	25c brn lake	1.25	75
139	A26	27½c vio brn	2.25	2.75
140	A26	30c ol brn	50	15

Perf. 13x14

Size: 22x33mm

141	A26	50c dl yel grn	2.50	15
a.		Perf. 14	30.00	25
142	A26	1.50g blk brn	18.00	15.00
a.		Perf. 14	30.00	22.50
143	A26	2.50g rose lake	10.50	8.50
a.		Perf. 14	10.00	8.50
		Nos. 127-143 (17)	42.38	32.50

See Nos. 147-151. For surcharges see Nos. B1-B3.

Queen Wilhelmina — A27

Perf. 12½x12

1938, Aug. 27 Photo. Wmk. 202

144	A27	1½c dl pur	15	22
145	A27	6c red org	80	75
146	A27	15c royal blue	1.50	1.25

Reign of Queen Wilhelmina, 40th anniv.

Numeral Type of 1936 and

Queen Wilhelmina — A28

1941-42 Unwmk. Litho. *Perf. 12½*

Thick Paper

Size: 17¾x22mm

147	A25	1c gray brn ('42)	55	75
148	A25	1½c dl bl ('42)	6.50	15
149	A25	2c lt org ('42)	3.75	3.50
150	A25	2½c grn ('42)	32	15
151	A25	5c crim ('42)	32	15

Photo.

Perf. 12½, 13

Size: 18½x23mm

152	A28	6c rose vio	1.75	4.25
153	A28	10c red org	1.10	75
154	A28	12½c lt grn	1.50	50
155	A28	15c brt ultra	3.00	1.75
156	A28	20c orange	22	35
157	A28	21c gray	1.40	1.10
158	A28	25c brn lake	1.65	1.40
159	A28	27½c dp brn	1.90	2.50
160	A28	30c ol bis	8.25	2.50

Size: 21x26½mm

161	A28	50c ol grn ('42)	9.00	15
162	A28	1½g gray ol ('42)	11.00	75
163	A28	2½g rose lake ('42)	10.00	90
		Nos. 147-163 (17)	62.21	21.60

Imperfs. are proofs.

See Nos. 174-187.

Catalogue values for unused stamps in this section, from this point to the end of the section, are for Never Hinged items.

Bonaire — A29

St. Eustatius — A30

Designs: 2c, View of Saba. 2½c, St. Maarten. 5c, Aruba. 6c, Curacao.

Perf. 13x13½, 13½x13

1943, Feb. 1 Engr. Unwmk.

164	A29	1c rose vio & org brn	15	15
165	A30	1½c dp bl & yel grn	15	15
166	A29	2c sl blk & org brn	42	25
167	A29	2½c grn & org	18	18
168	A29	5c red & slate blk	80	15
169	A29	6c rose lil & lt bl	50	45
		Nos. 164-169 (6)	2.20	1.33

Royal Family — A35

1943, Nov. 8 *Perf. 13½x13*

170	A35	1½c deep org	15	15
171	A35	2½c red	15	15
172	A35	6c black	75	45
173	A35	10c deep blue	75	60

Issued in honor of Princess Margriet Francisca of the Netherlands.

Wilhelmina Type of 1941

1947 Photo. *Perf. 13½x13*

Size: 18x22mm

174	A28	6c brn vio	1.25	1.65
175	A28	10c org red	1.25	1.65
176	A28	12½c dk bl grn	1.25	1.65
177	A28	15c dk bl	1.25	1.65
178	A28	20c org yel	1.25	2.50
179	A28	21c dk gray	1.50	1.65
180	A28	25c brn lake	15	15
181	A28	27½c chocolate	1.25	1.10
182	A28	30c ol bis	1.40	65
183	A28	50c dl yel grn	1.65	15

Perf. 13½x14

Engr.

Size: 25x31¼mm

184	A28	1½g dk brn	80	45
185	A28	2½g rose lake	15.00	3.75
186	A28	5g ol grn	80.00	105.00
187	A28	10g red org	110.00	175.00
		Nos. 174-187 (14)	218.00	297.00

Used values for Nos. 186-187 are for genuinely canceled copies clearly dated before the end of 1949.

Queen Wilhelmina
A36 A37

1948 Unwmk. Photo. *Perf. 13½x13*

188	A36	6c dk vio brn	95	90
189	A36	10c scarlet	95	1.25
190	A36	12½c dk bl grn	95	75
191	A36	15c dp bl	95	90
192	A36	20c red org	95	1.50
193	A36	21c black	95	1.50
194	A36	25c brt red vio	30	15
195	A36	27½c hn brn	16.00	13.00
196	A36	30c ol brn	13.00	75
197	A36	50c ol grn	13.00	18

Perf. 12½x12

Engr.

198	A37	1.50g chocolate	21.00	3.50
		Nos. 188-198 (11)	69.00	24.38

Queen Wilhelmina A38

Queen Juliana A39

1948, Aug. 30 *Perf. 13x14*

199	A38	6c vermilion	45	45
200	A38	12½c deep blue	45	45

Reign of Queen Wilhelmina, 50th anniv.

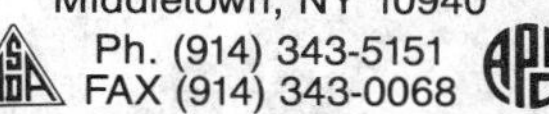

Perf. 14x13½

1948, Oct. 18 Photo. Wmk. 202

201 A39 6c red brn 35 35
202 A39 12½c dk grn 35 35

Investiture of Queen Juliana, Sept. 6, 1948. Nos. 201-202 were issued in Netherlands Sept. 6.

Ship of Ojeda — A40

Alonso de Ojeda — A41

Perf. 14x13, 13x14

1949, July 26 Photo. Unwmk.

203 A40 6c ol grn 2.50 1.75
204 A41 12½c brn red 3.25 3.00
205 A40 15c ultra 3.25 2.00

450th anniversary of the discovery of Curacao by Alonso de Ojeda, 1499.

Post Horns Entwined — A42

1949, Oct. 3 ***Perf. 12x12½***

206 A42 6c brown red 3.00 2.00
207 A42 25c dull blue 3.00 95

UPU, 75th anniversary.

A43

Queen Juliana
A44 A45

1950-79 Photo. ***Perf. 13x13½***

208 A43 1c red brn 15 15
209 A43 1½c blue 15 15
210 A43 2c orange 15 15
211 A43 2½c green 60 15
212 A43 3c purple 15 15
212A A43 4c yel grn ('59) 32 30
213 A43 5c dk red 15 15

Perf. 13½x13

214 A44 6c dp plum 65 15
215 A44 7½c red brn ('54) 3.50 15
216 A44 10c red 1.10 15
a. Redrawn ('79) 15 15
217 A44 12½c dk grn 1.40 15
218 A44 15c dp bl 1.40 15
a. Redrawn ('79) 15 15
219 A44 20c orange 1.65 15
a. Redrawn ('79) 18 15
220 A44 21c black 1.65 1.25
221 A44 22½c bl grn ('54) 4.50 15
222 A44 25c violet 2.00 15
a. Redrawn ('79) 22 15
223 A44 27½c henna brn 3.75 1.50
224 A44 30c ol brn 4.50 15
225 A44 50c ol grn 4.50 15

Perf. 12½x12

Engr.

226 A45 1½g slate grn 7.50 20
227 A45 2½g blk brn 12.00 75
228 A45 5g rose red 35.00 7.75
229 A45 10g dk vio brn 135.00 40.00
Nos. 208-229 (23) 221.77 54.15

Nos. 216a, 218a, 219a and 222a are from booklets Nos. 427a and 428a. Background design is sharper and stamps have one or two straight edges.

See Nos. 427-429. For surcharge see No. B20.

Fort Beekenburg — A46

Perf. 13½x12½

1953, June 16 Photo.

230 A46 22½c olive brown 3.00 32

250th anniversary of the founding of Fort Beekenburg.

Beach at Aruba — A47

1954, May 1 ***Perf. 11x11½***

231 A47 15c dk bl, sal & dp bl 3.25 2.00

3rd congress of the Caribbean Tourist Assoc., Aruba, May 3-6.

Queen Juliana — A48

1954, Dec. 15 ***Perf. 13½***

232 A48 7½c ol grn 70 60

Charter of the Kingdom, adopted Dec. 15, 1954. See Netherlands #366 & Surinam #264.

Beach — A49

Petroleum Refinery, Aruba — A50

1955, Dec. 5 Litho. ***Perf. 12***

233 A49 15c chnt, bl & emer 2.25 1.75
234 A50 25c chnt, bl & emer 2.50 2.00

Caribbean Commission, 21st meeting, Aruba.

St. Annabaai Harbor and Flags — A51

1956, Dec. 6 Unwmk. ***Perf. 14x13***

235 A51 15c lt bl, blk & red 28 28

Caribbean Commission, 10th anniversary.

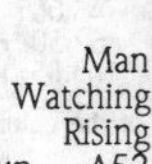

Man Watching Rising Sun — A52

1957, Mar. 14 Photo. ***Perf. 11x11½***

236 A52 15c brn, blk & yel 28 28

1st Caribbean Mental Health Conference, Aruba, Mar. 14-19.

Saba — A53

Views: 15c, St. Maarten. 25c, St. Eustatius.

1957, July 1 Litho. ***Perf. 14x13***

237 A53 7½c multi 32 32
238 A53 15c multi 32 32
239 A53 25c multi 32 32

Issued to publicize these islands as tourist attractions.

Curacao Intercontinental Hotel — A54

1957, Oct. 12 ***Perf. 14x13***

240 A54 15c lt ultra 28 28

Opening of the Intercontinental Hotel, Willemstad.

Map of Curacao — A55

1957, Dec. 10 ***Perf. 14x13½***

241 A55 15c indigo & lt bl 60 55

International Geophysical Year.

Flamingoes, Bonaire — A56

Designs: 7½c, 8c, 25c, 1½g, Old buildings, Curacao. 10c, 5g, Extinct volcano and palms, Saba. 15c, 30c, 1g, Fort Willem III, Aruba. 20c, 35c, De Ruyter obelisk, St. Eustatius. 12c, 40c, 2½g, Town Hall, St. Maarten.

1958-59 Litho. ***Perf. 14x13***

Size: 33x22mm

242 A56 6c lt ol grn & pink 2.00 15
243 A56 7½c red brn & org 15 15
244 A56 8c dk bl & org ('59) 15 15
245 A56 10c gray & org yel 15 15
246 A56 12c bluish grn & gray ('59) 15 15
247 A56 15c grn & lt ultra 15 15
a. 15c green & lilac 15 15
248 A56 20c crim & gray 16 15
249 A56 25c Prus bl & yel grn 20 15
250 A56 30c brn & bl grn 22 15
251 A56 35c gray & rose ('59) 28 15
252 A56 40c mag & grn 30 15
253 A56 50c grysh brn & pink 35 15
254 A56 1g brt red & gray 75 15
255 A56 1½g rose vio & pale brn 1.10 18
256 A56 2½g blue & citron 1.25 38
257 A56 5g lt red brn & rose lil 3.75 75
Nos. 242-257 (16) 11.11
Set value 2.50

See Nos. 340-348, 400-403. For surcharge see No. B58.

Globe — A57

1958, Oct. 16 ***Perf. 11x11½***

258 A57 7½c bl & lake 15 15
259 A57 15c red & ultra 28 28

50th anniv. of the Netherlands Antilles Radio and Telegraph Administration.

Hotel Aruba Caribbean A58

1959, July 18 ***Perf. 14x13***

260 A58 15c multi 28 28

Opening of the Hotel Aruba Caribbean, Aruba.

Sea Water Distillation Plant — A59

1959, Oct. 16 Photo. ***Perf. 14x13***

261 A59 20c bright blue 32 32

Opening of sea water distillation plant at Balashi, Aruba.

Netherlands Antilles Flag — A60

1959, Dec. 14 Litho. ***Perf. 13½***

262 A60 10c ultra & red 28 28
263 A60 20c ultra, yel & red 28 28
264 A60 25c ultra, grn & red 28 28

5th anniv. of the new constitution (Charter of the Kingdom).

Fokker "Snip" and Map of Caribbean — A61

Designs: 20c, Globe showing route flown, and plane. 25c, Map of Atlantic ocean and view of Willemstad. 35c, Map of Atlantic ocean and plane on Aruba airfield.

1959, Dec. 22 Unwmk. ***Perf. 14x13***

265 A61 10c yel, lt & dk bl 32 28
266 A61 20c yel, lt & dk bl 32 28
267 A61 25c yel, lt & dk bl 32 15
268 A61 35c yel, lt & dk bl 32 40

25th anniv. of Netherlands-Curacao air service.

Msgr. Martinus J. Niewindt — A62

1960, Jan. 12 **Photo.** ***Perf. 13½***

269	A62	10c	deep claret	32	32
270	A62	20c	deep violet	48	48
271	A62	25c	olive green	32	32

Death centenary of Monsignor Niewindt, first apostolic vicar for Curacao.

Worker, Flag and Factories — A63

1960, Apr. 29 ***Perf. 12½x13½***

272	A63	20c	multi	32	32

Issued for Labor Day, May 1, 1960.

US Brig "Andrea Doria" and Gun at Fort Orange, St. Eustatius A64

1961, Nov. 16 **Litho.** ***Perf. 14x13½***

273	A64	20c	bl, red, grn & blk	50	50

185th anniversary of first salute by a foreign power to the US flag flown by an American ship.

Queen Juliana and Prince Bernhard A64a

1962, Jan. 31 **Photo.** ***Perf. 14x13***

274	A64a	10c	dp org	15	15
275	A64a	25c	dp bl	20	20

Silver wedding anniversary of Queen Juliana and Prince Bernhard.

Benta Player — A65

Designs: 6c, Corn masher. 20c, Petji kerchief. 25c, "Jaja" (nurse) with child, sculpture.

Perf. 12½x13½

1962, Mar. 14 **Photo.**

276	A65	6c	red brn & yel	15	15
277	A65	10c	multi	18	15
278	A65	20c	crim, ind & brt grn	30	28
279	A65	25c	brt grn, brn & gray	32	28
a.			Souv. sheet of 4, #276-279	1.25	1.25

Emblem of Family Relationship A66

Design: 25c, Emblem of mental health (cross).

1963, Apr. 17 **Litho.** ***Perf. 14x13½***

280	A66	20c	dk bl & ocher	28	28
281	A66	25c	bl & red	28	28

Fourth Caribbean Conference for Mental Health, Curacao, Apr. 17-23.

Dove with Olive Branch — A67

1963, July 1 **Unwmk.** ***Perf. 14x13***

282	A67	25c	org yel & dk brn	22	22

Centenary of emancipation of the slaves.

Hotel Bonaire — A68

1963, Aug. 31 ***Perf. 14x13***

283	A68	20c	dk red brn	22	22

Opening of Hotel Bonaire on Bonaire.

Prince William of Orange Taking Oath of Allegiance — A69

1963, Nov. 21 **Photo.** ***Perf. 13½x14***

284	A69	25c	grn, blk & rose	22	22

150th anniversary of the founding of the Kingdom of the Netherlands.

Chemical Equipment A70

1963, Dec. 10 **Litho.** ***Perf. 14x13½***

285	A70	20c	bl grn, brt yel grn & red	32	32

Opening of chemical factories on Aruba.

Airmail Letter and Wings — A71

Design: 25c, Map of Caribbean, Miami-Curacao route and planes of 1929 and 1964.

1964, June 22 **Photo.** ***Perf. 11x11½***

286	A71	20c	lt bl, red & ultra	28	28
287	A71	25c	lt grn, bl, red & blk	28	28

35th anniversary of the first regular Curacao airmail service.

Map of the Caribbean A72

1964, Nov. 30 **Litho.** **Unwmk.**

288	A72	20c	ultra, org & dk red	22	22

5th meeting of the Caribbean Council, Curacao, Nov. 30-Dec. 4.

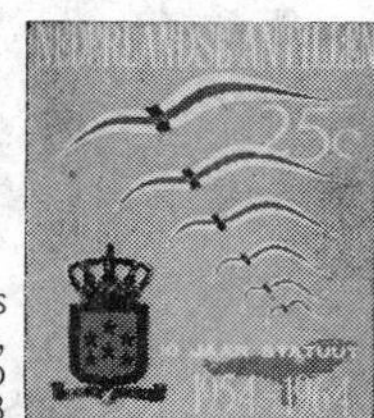

Netherlands Antilles Flags, Map of Curacao and Crest — A73

1964, Dec. 14 **Litho.** ***Perf. 11½x11***

289	A73	25c	lt bl & multi	22	22

10th anniversary of the Charter of the Kingdom of the Netherlands. The flags, shaped like seagulls, represent the six islands comprising the Netherlands Antilles.

Princess Beatrix — A74

1965, Feb. 22 **Photo.** ***Perf. 13½x14***

290	A74	25c	brick red	28	28

Visit of Princess Beatrix of Netherlands.

ITU Emblem, Old and New Communication Equipment — A75

1965, May 17 **Litho.** ***Perf. 13½***

291	A75	10c	brt bl & dk bl	15	15

ITU, centenary.

Shell Refinery, Curacao A76

Designs: 10c, Catalytic cracking installation, vert. 25c, Workers operating manifold, primary distillation plant, vert.

Perf. 13½x14, 14x13½

1965, June 22 **Photo.**

292	A76	10c	blk, red & yel	15	15
293	A76	20c	multi	15	15
294	A76	25c	multi	22	22

50th anniv. of the oil industry in Curacao.

Floating Market, Curacao — A77

Designs (flag and): 2c, Divi-divi tree and Haystack Mountain, Aruba. 3c, Lace, Saba. 4c, Flamingoes, Bonaire. 5c, Church ruins, St. Eustatius. 6c, Lobster, St. Maarten.

1965, Aug. 25 **Litho.** ***Perf. 14x13***

295	A77	1c	lt grn, ultra & red	15	15
296	A77	2c	yel, ultra & red	15	15
297	A77	3c	chlky bl, ultra & red	15	15
298	A77	4c	org, ultra & red	15	15
299	A77	5c	lt bl, ultra & red	15	15
300	A77	6c	pink, ultra & red	15	15
			Set value	36	36

Marine Guarding Beach — A78

1965, Dec. 10 **Photo.** ***Perf. 13x10½***

301	A78	25c	multi	15	15

Issued to commemorate the 300th anniversary of the Netherlands Marine Corps.

Budgerigars, Wedding Rings and Initials — A79

1966, Mar. 10 **Photo.** ***Perf. 13½x14***

302	A79	25c	gray & multi	15	15

Issued to commemorate the marriage of Princess Beatrix and Claus van Amsberg.

M. A. de Ruyter and Map of St. Eustatius A80

1966, June 19 **Photo.** ***Perf. 13½***

303	A80	25c	vio, ocher & lt bl	15	15

Visit of Adm. Michiel Adriaanszoon de Ruyter (1607-1676) to St. Eustatius, 1666.

Liberal Arts and Grammar — A81

Designs: 10c, Rhetoric and dialectic. 20c, Arithmetic and geometry. 25c, Astronomy and music.

Perf. 13½x12½

1966, Sept. 19 **Litho.** **Unwmk.**

304	A81	6c	yel, bl & blk	15	15
305	A81	10c	yel grn, red & blk	15	15
306	A81	20c	bl, yel & blk	15	15
307	A81	25c	red, yel grn & blk	15	15
			Set value	38	38

25th anniversary of secondary education.

Cruiser — A82

Ships: 10c, Sailing ship. 20c, Tanker. 25c, Passenger ship.

Perf. 13½x14

1967, Mar. 29 Litho. Unwmk.

308 A82	6c lt & dk grn	15	15
309 A82	10c org & brn	15	15
310 A82	20c sep & brn	15	15
311 A82	25c chlky bl & dk bl	16	15
	Set value	44	44

60th anniv. of *Onze Vloot* (Our Fleet), an organization which publicizes the Dutch navy and merchant marine and helps seamen.

Manuel Carlos Piar (1777-1817), Independence Hero — A83

Discobolus after Myron — A84

1967, Apr. 26 Photo. *Perf. 14x13*

312 A83	20c red & blk	15	15

1968, Feb. 19 Litho. *Perf. 13x14*

Designs: 10c, Hand holding torch, and Olympic rings. 25c, Stadium, doves and Olympic rings.

313 A84	10c multi	20	20
314 A84	20c dk brn, ol & yel	20	20
315 A84	25c bl, dk bl & brt yel grn	20	20

19th Olympic Games, Mexico City, Oct. 12-27.

Friendship 500 — A84a

Designs: 20c, Beechcraft Queen Air. 25c, Friendship and DC-9.

1968, Dec. 3 Litho. *Perf. 14x13*

315A A84a	10c dl yel, blk & brt bl	22	22
315B A84a	20c tan, blk & brt bl	22	22
315C A84a	25c sal pink, blk & brt bl	22	22

Issued to publicize Dutch Antillean Airlines (ALM).

Map of Bonaire, Radio Mast and Waves — A85

Code of Law — A86

1969, Mar. 6 *Perf. 14x13½*

316 A85	25c bl, emer & blk	22	22

Opening of the relay station of the Dutch World Broadcasting System on Bonaire.

Perf. 12½x13½

1969, May 19 Photo.

Designs: 25c, Scales of Justice.

317 A86	20c dk grn, yel grn & gold	22	22
318 A86	25c vio bl, bl & gold	22	22

Court of Justice, centenary.

ILO Emblem, Cactus and House — A87

1969, Aug. 25 Litho. *Perf. 14x13*

319 A87	10c bl & blk	15	15
320 A87	25c dk red & blk	15	16

ILO, 50th anniversary.

Queen Juliana and Rising Sun — A87a

1969, Dec. 12 Photo. *Perf. 14x13*

321 A87a	25c bl & multi	22	22

15th anniv. of the Charter of the Kingdom of the Netherlands. Phosphorescent paper.

Radio Bonaire Studio and Transmitter A88

Design: 15c, Radio waves and cross set against land, sea and air.

1970, Feb. 5 Photo. *Perf. 12½x13½*

322 A88	10c multi	15	15
323 A88	15c multi	15	16

5th anniv. of the opening of the Trans World Missionary Radio Station, Bonaire.

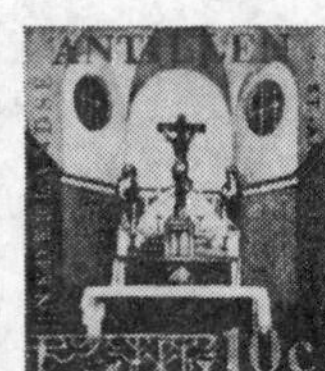

Altar, St. Anna's Church, Otraband 1752 — A89

Designs: 20c, Interior, Synagogue at Punda, 1732, horiz. 25c, Pulpit, Fort Church, Fort Amsterdam, 1769.

Perf. 13½x14, 14x13½

1970, May 12 Photo.

324 A89	10c gold & multi	20	20
325 A89	20c gold & multi	20	20
326 A89	25c gold & multi	20	20

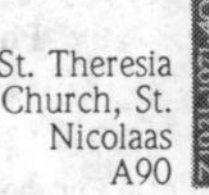

St. Theresia Church, St. Nicolaas A90

1971, Feb. 9 Litho. *Perf. 14x13½*

327 A90	20c dl bl, gray & rose	22	22

40th anniversary of the Parish of St. Theresia at St. Nicolaas, Aruba.

A91

A91a

1971, Feb. 24 *Perf. 13½x14*

328 A91	25c Lions emblem	28	28

Lions Club in the Netherlands Antilles, 25th anniversary.

1971, June 29 Photo. *Perf. 13x14*

Prince Bernhard, Fokker F27, Boeing 747B.

329 A91a	45c multi	40	40

60th birthday of Prince Bernhard.

Pedro Luis Brion (1782-1821), Naval Commander in Fight for South American Independence A92

1971, Sept. 27 Photo. *Perf. 13x12½*

330 A92	40c multi	28	28

Flamingoes, Bonaire — A93

Ship in Dry Dock — A94

Designs: 1c, Queen Emma Bridge, Curaao. 2c, The Bottom, Saba. 4c, Water tower, Aruba. 5c, Fort Amsterdam, St. Maarten. 6c, Fort Orange, St. Eustatius.

1972, Jan. 17 Litho. *Perf. 13½x14*

331 A93	1c yel & multi	15	15
332 A93	2c yel grn & multi	15	15
333 A93	3c dp org & multi	15	15
334 A93	4c brt bl & multi	15	15
335 A93	5c red org & multi	15	15
336 A93	6c lil rose & multi	15	15
	Set value	36	36

1972, Apr. 7 *Perf. 14x13½*

337 A94	30c bl gray & multi	28	28

Inauguration of large dry dock facilities in Willemstad.

Netherlands Antilles stamps can be mounted in Scott's annual Netherlands Supplement.

Juan Enrique Irausquin A95

Costa Gomez A96

1972, June 20 Photo. *Perf. 13x14*

338 A95	30c dp org	28	28

Irausquin (1904-1962), financier and patriot.

1972, Oct. 27 Litho.

339 A96	30c yel grn & blk	28	28

Moises Frumencio da Costa Gomez (1907-1966), lawyer, legislator, patriot.

Island Series Type of 1958-59

Designs: 45c, 85c, Extinct volcano and palms, Saba. 55c, 90c, De Ruyter obelisk, St. Eustatius. 65c, 75c, 10g, Flamingoes, Bonaire. 70c, Fort Willem III, Aruba. 95c, Town Hall, St. Maarten.

1973, Feb. 12 Litho. *Perf. 14x13*

Size: 33x22mm

340 A56	45c vio bl & lt bl	32	15
341 A56	55c dk car rose & emer	42	18
342 A56	65c grn & pink	48	22
343 A56	70c gray vio & org	50	25
344 A56	75c brt lil & sal	55	28
345 A56	85c brn ol & ap grn	60	30
346 A56	90c bl & ocher	70	35
347 A56	95c org & yel	70	38
348 A56	10g brt ultra & sal	7.00	3.75
	Nos. 340-348 (9)	11.27	5.86

Mailman — A97

Designs: 15c, King William III from 1873 issue. 30c, Emblem of Netherlands Antilles postal service.

1973, May 23 Photo. *Perf. 13x14*

349 A97	15c lil, gold & vio	28	22
350 A97	20c dk grn & multi	32	28
351 A97	30c org & multi	32	28

Centenary of first stamps of Netherlands Antilles.

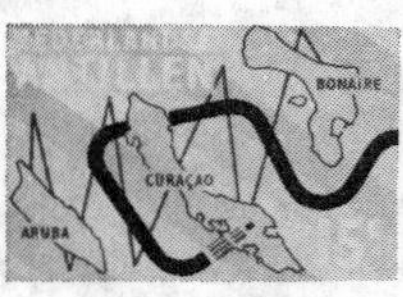

Cable Linking Aruba, Curacao and Bonaire — A98

Designs: 30c, 6 stars symbolizing the islands, and cable. 45c, Saba, St. Maarten and St. Eustatius linked by cable.

1973, June 20 Litho. *Perf. 14x13*

352 A98	15c multi	32	32
353 A98	30c multi	32	32
354 A98	45c multi	32	23
a.	Souvenir sheet of 3, #352-354	2.00	1.50

Inauguration of the inter-island submarine cable.

Queen Juliana, Netherlands Antilles and House of Orange Colors — A99a

Engr. & Photo.

1973, Sept. 4 *Perf. 12½x12*
355 A99a 15c silver & multi 40 40

25th anniversary of reign of Queen Juliana.

Jan Hendrik Albert Eman — A99

Lionel Bernard Scott — A100

1973, Oct. 17 **Litho.** *Perf. 13x14*
356 A99 30c lt yel grn & blk 28 28

Eman (1888-1957), founder of the People's Party in Aruba, member of Antillean Parliament.

1974, Jan. 28
357 A100 30c lt bl & multi 28 28

Scott (1897-1966), architect and statesman.

Family at Supper — A101

Designs: 12c, Parents watching children at play. 15c, Mother and daughter sewing, father and son gardening.

1974, Feb. 18 **Litho.** *Perf. 13x14*
358 A101 6c bl & multi 15 15
359 A101 12c bis & multi 22 20
360 A101 15c grn & multi 28 22
Set value 56 48

Planned parenthood and World Population Year.

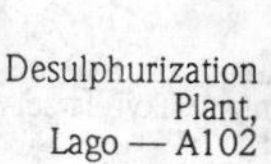

Desulphurization Plant, Lago — A102

Designs: 30c, Distillation plant. 45c, Lago refinery at night.

1974, Aug. 12 **Litho.** *Perf. 14x13*
361 A102 15c lt bl, blk & yel 28 28
362 A102 30c lt bl, blk & yel 28 28
363 A102 45c dk brn & multi 28 28

Oil industry in Aruba, 50th anniversary.

UPU Emblem — A103

1974, Oct. 9 **Litho.** *Perf. 13x14*
364 A103 15c yel grn, blk & gold 32 32
365 A103 30c bl, blk & gold 32 32

Centenary of Universal Postal Union.

Queen Emma Bridge — A104

Willemstad Bridges: 30c, Queen Juliana Bridge. 40c, Queen Wilhelmina Bridge.

1975, Feb. 5 **Litho.** *Perf. 14x13*
366 A104 20c ultra & multi 32 32
367 A104 30c ultra & multi 32 32
368 A104 40c ultra & multi 40 40

Dedication of new Queen Juliana Bridge spanning Caracao Harbor.

Salt Crystals A105

Designs: 20c, Solar salt pond. 40c, Map of Bonaire and location of solar salt pond, vert.

Perf. 14x13, 13x14

1975, Apr. 24 **Litho.**
369 A105 15c multi 32 32
370 A105 20c multi 32 32
371 A105 40c multi 40 32

Bonaire's salt industry.

Aruba Airport, 1935 and Fokker F-18 — A106

Designs: 30c, Aruba Airport, 1950, and Douglas DC-9. 40c, New Princess Beatrix Airport and Boeing 727.

1975, June 19 **Litho.** *Perf. 14x13*
372 A106 15c vio & multi 28 22
373 A106 30c blk & multi 32 28
374 A106 40c yel & multi 32 32

40th anniversary of Aruba Airport.

International Women's Year Emblem A107

Designs: 12c, "Women's role in social development." 20c, Embryos within female and male symbols.

1975, Aug. 1 **Photo.** *Perf. 14x13*
375 A107 6c multi 15 15
376 A107 12c multi 28 22
377 A107 20c multi 32 28

International Women's Year 1975.

Beach, Aruba — A108

Tourist Publicity: No. 379, Beach pavilion and boat, Bonaire. No. 380, Table Mountain and Spanish Water, Curacao.

1976, June 21 **Litho.** *Perf. 14x13*
378 A108 40c blue & multi 40 40
379 A108 40c blue & multi 40 40
380 A108 40c blue & multi 40 40

Julio Antonio Abraham A109

Dike and Produce A110

1976, Aug. 10 **Photo.** *Perf. 13x14*
381 A109 30c tan & claret 32 32

Julio Antonio Abraham (1909-1960), founder of Democratic Party of Bonaire.

1976, Sept. 21 **Litho.**
382 A110 15c shown 28 22
383 A110 35c Cattle 40 32
384 A110 45c Fish 40 40

Agriculture, husbandry and fishing in Netherlands Antilles.

Plaque, Fort Oranje Memorial A111

Designs: 40c, Andrea Doria in St. Eustatius harbor receiving salute. 55c, Johannes de Graaff, Governor of St. Eustatius, holding Declaration of Independence.

1976, Nov. 16 **Litho.** *Perf. 14x13*
385 A111 25c multi 55 32
386 A111 40c multi 90 32
387 A111 55c multi 60 55

First gun salute to US flag, St. Eustatius, Nov. 16, 1776.

Dancer with Cactus Headdress A112

Bird Petroglyph, Aruba A113

Carnival: 35c, Woman in feather costume. 40c, Woman in pompadour costume.

1977, Jan. 20 **Litho.** *Perf. 13x14*
388 A112 25c multi 40 32
389 A112 35c multi 40 32
390 A112 40c multi 40 32

1977, Mar. 29

Indian Petroglyphs: 35c, Loops and spiral, Savonet Plantation, Curacao. 40c, Tortoise, Onima, Bonaire.

391 A113 25c red & multi 32 28
392 A113 35c brn & multi 32 32
393 A113 40c yel & multi 40 32

Cordia Sebestena A114

Chimes, Spritzer & Fuhrmann Building A115

Tropical Trees: 40c, East Indian walnut, vert. 55c, Tamarind.

1977, July 20 *Perf. 14x13, 13x14*
394 A114 25c blk & multi 32 28
395 A114 40c blk & multi 40 32
396 A114 55c blk & multi 48 48

1977, Sept. 27 **Litho.** *Perf. 13x14*

Designs: 40c, Globe with Western Hemisphere and sun over Curacao. 55c, Diamond ring and flag of Netherlands Antilles.

397 A115 20c brt grn & multi 32 28
398 A115 40c yel & multi 40 40
399 A115 55c bl & multi 48 48

Spritzer & Fuhrmann, jewelers of Netherlands Antilles, 50th anniversary.

Type of 1958-59

Designs: 20c, 35c, 55c, De Ruyter obelisk, St. Eustatius. 40c, Town Hall, St. Maarten.

Perf. 13½ Horiz.

1977, Nov. 30 **Photo.**

Size: 39x22mm

400 A56 20c crim & gray 70 50
a. Bklt. pane of 6 (2 #400, 4 #402) 5.25
401 A56 35c gray & rose 1.10 80
a. Bklt. pane of 4 (1 #401, 3 #403) 6.00
402 A56 40c magenta & grn 70 50
403 A56 55c dk car rose & emer 1.10 1.10

Nos. 400-403 issued in booklets only. No. 400a has label with red inscription in size of 3 stamps; No. 401a has label with dark carmine rose inscription in size of 2 stamps.

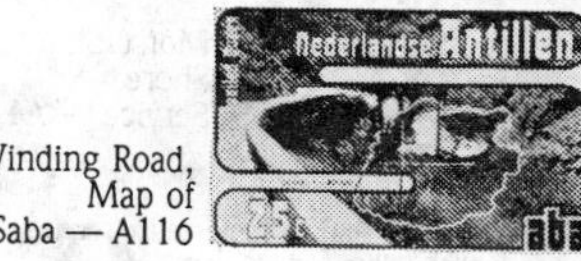

Winding Road, Map of Saba — A116

Tourist Publicity: 35c, Ruins of Synagogue, map of St. Eustatius. 40c, Greatbay, Map of St. Maarten.

1977, Nov. 30 **Litho.** *Perf. 14x13*
404 A116 25c multi 15 15
405 A116 35c multi 15 15
406 A116 40c multi 22 22
Set value 42 42

Tete-beche gutter pairs exist.

Treasure Chest — A117

Designs: 20c, Logo of Netherlands Antilles Bank. 40c, Safe deposit door.

1978, Feb. 7 **Litho.** *Perf. 14x13*
407 A117 15c brt & dk bl 15 15
408 A117 20c org & gold 15 15
409 A117 40c brt & dk grn 15 15
Set value 28 28

Bank of Netherlands Antilles, 150th anniv. Tete-beche gutter pairs exist.

Flamboyant A118

Polythysana Rubrescens A119

Flowers: 25c, Erythrina velutina. 40c, Guaiacum officinale, horiz. 55c, Gliricidia sepium, horiz.

Perf. 13x14, 14x13

1978, May 31 **Litho.**

410 A118 15c multi 15 15
411 A118 25c multi 22 20
412 A118 40c multi 28 25
413 A118 55c multi 32 32

1978, June 20 *Perf. 13x14*

Butterflies: 25c, Caligo eurilochus. 35c, Prepona omphale amesis. 40c, Morpho aega.

414 A119 15c multi 15 15
415 A119 25c multi 22 20
416 A119 35c multi 28 25
417 A119 40c multi 32 32

"Conserve Energy" — A120

1978, Aug. 31 **Litho.** *Perf. 13x14*

418 A120 15c org & blk 15 15
419 A120 20c dp grn & blk 18 15
420 A120 40c dk red & blk 30 30

Morse Ship-to-Shore Service — A121

Designs: 40c, Ship-to-shore telex service. 55c, Future radar-satellite service, vert.

Perf. 14x13, 13x14

1978, Oct. 16 **Litho.**

421 A121 20c multi 22 22
422 A121 40c multi 28 28
423 A121 55c multi 40 40

70th anniversary of ship-to-shore communications.

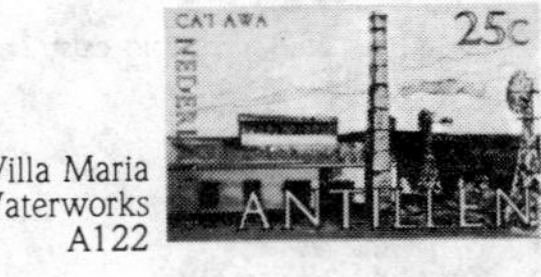

Villa Maria Waterworks A122

Designs: 35c, Leonard B. Smith, vert. 40c, Opening of Queen Emma Bridge, Willemstadt, 1888.

1978, Dec. 13

424 A122 25c multi 18 16
425 A122 35c multi 22 20
426 A122 40c multi 30 25

Leonard B. Smith, engineer, 80th death anniversary.

Queen Juliana Type of 1950

1979, Jan. 11 **Photo.** *Perf. 13½x13*

427 A44 5c dp yel 15 15
a. Bklt. pane of 10 (4 #427, 1 #216a, 2 #222a, 3 #429) 3.00
428 A44 30c brown 25 15
a. Bklt. pane of 10 (1 #428, 4 #218a, 3 #219a, 2 #222a) 3.00
429 A44 40c brt bl 32 15
Set value 20

Nos. 427-429 issued in booklets only. Nos. 427a-428a have 2 labels and selvages the size of 6 stamps. Background design of booklet stamps sharper than 1950 issue. All stamps have 1 or 2 straight edges.

Goat and Conference Emblem A123

Designs: 75c, Horse and map of Curacao. 150c, Cattle, Netherlands Antilles flag, UN and Conference emblems.

1979, Apr. 18 **Litho.** *Perf. 14x13*

437 A123 50c multi 28 28
438 A123 75c multi 40 40
439 A123 150c multi 75 75
a. Souv. sheet of 3, perf. 13½x13 1.50 1.50

12th Inter-American Meeting at Ministerial Level on Foot and Mouth Disease and Zoonosis Control, Curacao, Apr. 17-20. No. 439a contains Nos. 437-439 in changed colors.

Dutch Colonial Soldier, Emblem — A124

1979, July 4 **Litho.** *Perf. 13x14*

440 A124 1g multi 55 52

50th anniversary of Netherlands Antilles Volunteer Corps. See Nos. B166-B167.

A125

A126

Flowering Trees: 25c, Casearia Tremula. 40c, Cordia cylindro-stachya. 1.50g, Melochia tomentosa.

1979, Sept. 3 **Litho.** *Perf. 13x14*

441 A125 25c multi 18 18
442 A125 40c multi 28 28
443 A125 1.50g multi 75 75

1979, Dec. 6 **Litho.** *Perf. 13x14*

Designs: 65c, Dove and Netherlands flag. 1.50g, Dove and Netherlands Antilles flag.

444 A126 65c multi 48 40
445 A126 1.50g multi 80 80

Constitution, 25th anniversary.

Map of Aruba, Foundation Emblem A127

Design: 1g, Foundation headquarters, Aruba.

1979, Dec. 18 *Perf. 14x13*

446 A127 95c multi 60 60
447 A127 1g multi 70 70

Cultural Foundation Center, Aruba, 30th anniv.

Cupola, 1910, Fort Church — A128

1980, Jan. 9 *Perf. 13x14*

448 A128 100c multi 60 60

Fort Church, Curacao, 210th anniversary (1979). See Nos. B172-B173.

Rotary Emblem A129

Designs: 50c, Globe and cogwheels. 85c, Cogwheel and Rotary emblem.

1980, Feb. 22 **Litho.** *Perf. 14x13*

449 A129 45c multi 25 25
450 A129 50c multi 30 30
451 A129 85c multi 48 48
a. Souvenir sheet of 3, #449-451, perf. 13½x13 1.10 1.10
b. Strip of 3, #449-451 1.05 1.05

Rotary Intl., 75th anniv. No. 451a has continuous design.

Coin Box, 1905 — A130

Post Office Savings Bank of Netherlands Antilles, 75th Anniversary: 150c, Coin box, 1980.

1980, Apr. 2 **Litho.** *Perf. 14x13*

452 A130 25c multi 18 18
453 A130 150c multi 90 90

Netherlands Antilles No. 200, Arms — A131

1980, Apr. 29 **Photo.**

454 A131 25c shown 15 15
455 A131 60c No. 290, royal crown 32 32
a. Bklt. pane of 5 + 3 labels (#428, 2 #454, 2 #455) 3.00

Abdication of Queen Juliana of the Netherlands. Tete-beche gutter pairs exist.

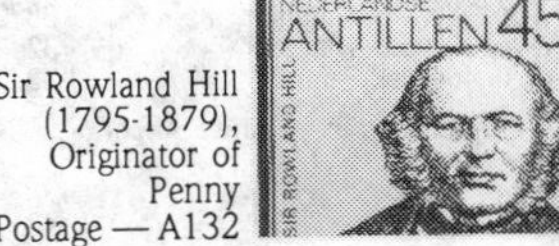

Sir Rowland Hill (1795-1879), Originator of Penny Postage — A132

1980, May 6 **Litho.**

456 A132 45c shown 28 28
457 A132 60c London 1980 emblem 32 32
458 A132 1g Airmail label 70 70
a. Souv. sheet of 3, perf. 13½x14 1.40 1.40

London 1980 Intl. Stamp Exhibition, May 6-14. No. 458a contains Nos. 456-458 in changed colors.

Leptotila Verreauxi A133

1980, Sept. 3 **Litho.** *Perf. 14x13*

459 A133 25c shown 28 25
460 A133 60c Mockingbird 55 55
461 A133 85c Coereba flaveola 75 75

Rudolf Theodorus Palm — A134

Alliance Mission Emblem, Map of Aruba — A135

1981, Jan. 27 **Litho.** *Perf. 13x14*

462 A134 60c shown 40 38
463 A134 1g Score, hand playing piano 75 70

Palm, composer, birth centenary.

1981, Mar. 24 *Perf. 14x13*

464 A135 30c shown 22 22
465 A135 50c Curacao map 40 32
466 A135 1g Bonaire map 75 70

Evangelical Alliance Mission anniversaries: 35th in Aruba, 50th in Curacao, 30th in Bonaire.

St. Elisabeth's Hospital, 125th Anniv. — A136

1981, June 24 **Litho.** *Perf. 14x13*

467 A136 60c Gateway 40 40
468 A136 1.50g shown 1.00 1.00

Oregano Blossom A137

Ship Pilot Service Cent. A138

1981, Nov. 24 **Litho.** *Perf. 13x14*

469 A137 45c shown 30 30
470 A137 70c Flaira 52 52
471 A137 100c Welisali 70 70

1982, Jan. 13 **Litho.** *Perf. 13x14*

Designs: Various ships.

472 A138 70c multi 55 55
473 A138 85c multi 60 60
474 A138 1g multi 70 70

250th Anniv. of Community Mikve Israel-Emanuel Synagogue — A139

1982, Mar. 15 **Litho.** *Perf. 13x14*

475 A139 75c Altar 60 60
476 A139 85c Building 60 60
477 A139 150c Pulpit 1.00 1.00

US-Netherlands Diplomatic Relations Bicentenary A140

Intl. Air Traffic Controllers' Year A141

1982, Apr. 21 **Litho.** *Perf. 13x14*

478 A140 75c Flags, Peter Stuyvesant 70 70
a. Souvenir sheet 75 75

1982, May 5

479 A141 35c Radar screen 28 28
480 A141 75c Control tower 60 60
481 A141 150c Antenna 1.00 1.00

PHILEXFRANCE '82 Stamp Exhibition, Paris, June 11-21 — A142

1982, June 9 Litho. *Perf. 13x14*

482 A142 45c Emblem 32 32
483 A142 85c Mail bag 60 60
484 A142 150c Flags of France, Neth. Ant. 1.10 1.00
a. Souvenir sheet of 3, #482-484 2.25 2.25

Brown Chromis A143

1982, Sept. 15 Litho. *Perf. 14x13*

485 A143 35c shown 48 48
486 A143 75c Spotted trunkfish 1.00 1.00
487 A143 85c Blue tang 1.10 1.10
488 A143 100c French angelfish 1.40 1.40

Natural Bridge, Aruba — A144

1983, Apr. 12 Litho. *Perf. 14x13*

489 A144 35c shown 32 32
490 A144 45c Lac-Bay, Bonaire 40 40
491 A144 100c Willemstad, Curacao 90 90

World Communications Year — A145

1983, May 17 Litho. *Perf. 13x14*

492 A145 1g multi 90 90
a. Souvenir sheet 95 95

BRASILIANA '83 — A146

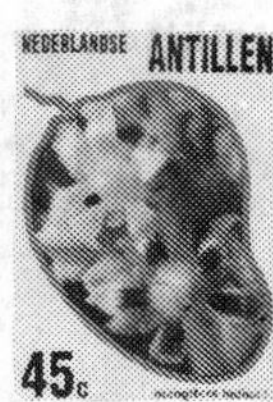

Fruit Tree — A147

1983, June 29 Litho. *Perf. 13x14*

493 A146 45c Ship, postal building, Waaigat 48 48
494 A146 55c Flags, emblem 55 55
495 A146 100c Governor's Palace, Sugar Loaf Mt. 95 95
a. Souvenir sheet of 3, #493-495 2.25 2.25

1983, Sept. 13 Litho. *Perf. 13x14*

496 A147 45c Mangifera indica 70 70
497 A147 55c Malpighia punicifolia 80 80
498 A147 100c Citrus aurantifolia 1.40 1.40

Local Government Buildings A148

1983, Dec. 20 Litho. *Perf. 14x13*

499 A148 20c Saba 20 20
500 A148 25c St. Eustatius 22 22
501 A148 30c St. Maarten 28 28
502 A148 35c Aruba *30 30*
503 A148 45c Bonaire 38 38
a. Perf. 13½ horiz. ('86) 20 20
504 A148 55c Curacao 48 48
a. Perf. 13½ horiz. ('86) 25 25
b. Bklt. pane of 4 + label (2 #503a, 504a) ('86) 1.75
Nos. 499-504 (6) 1.86 1.86

See Nos. 515-520, 543A-555.

Amigoe di Curacao Newspaper Centenary A149

1984, Jan. 5 Litho.

505 A149 45c Copy programming 40 40
506 A149 55c Printing press 48 48
507 A149 85c Man reading newspaper 90 90

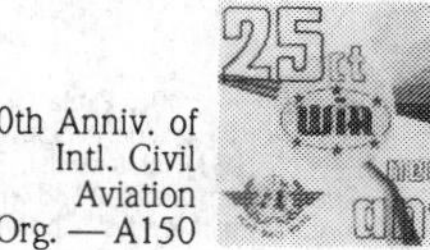

40th Anniv. of Intl. Civil Aviation Org. — A150

Various emblems.

1984, Feb. 28 Litho. *Perf. 14x13*

508 A150 25c Winair 20 20
509 A150 45c ICAO 40 40
510 A150 55c ALM 50 50
511 A150 100c Plane 90 90

Chamber of Commerce and Industry Centenary — A151

1984, May 29 Litho. *Perf. 13½*

512 A151 45c Bonnet maker 60 60
513 A151 55c Emblem 60 60
514 A151 100c River, bridge, boat 95 95
a. Strip of 3, #512-514 2.25 2.25

Govt. Building Type of 1983

1984, June 26 Litho. *Perf. 14x13*

515 A148 60c like 20c 55 55
516 A148 65c like 25c 60 60
517 A148 75c like 30c 75 75
518 A148 85c like 35c 85 85
519 A148 90c like 45c 90 90
520 A148 95c like 55c 1.00 1.00
Nos. 515-520 (6) 4.65 4.65

Local Birds — A152

1984, Sept. 18 Litho. *Perf. 14x13*

521 A152 45c Tiaris bicolor 85 85
522 A152 55c Zonotrichia capensis 1.10 1.10
523 A152 150c Chlorostilbon mellisugus 2.25 2.25

Eleanor Roosevelt (1884-1962) — A153

1984, Oct. 11 Litho. *Perf. 13x14*

524 A153 45c At Hyde Park 48 48
525 A153 85c Portrait 80 80
526 A153 100c Reading to children 90 90

Tete-beche gutter pairs exist.

Flamingos — A154

Curacao Masonic Lodge Bicent. — A155

1985, Jan. 9 Litho. *Perf. 14x13*

527 A154 25c Adult pullets 55 55
528 A154 45c Juveniles 90 90
529 A154 55c Adults wading 1.10 1.10
530 A154 100c Adults flying 1.65 1.65

1985, Feb. 21 Litho. *Perf. 13x14*

531 A155 45c Compass, sun, moon and stars 50 50
532 A155 55c Doorway, columns and 5 steps 70 70
533 A155 100c Star, 7 steps 1.10 1.10

UN, 40th Anniv. — A156

1985, June 5 Litho. *Perf. 14x13*

534 A156 55c multi 60 60
535 A156 1g multi 1.00 1.00

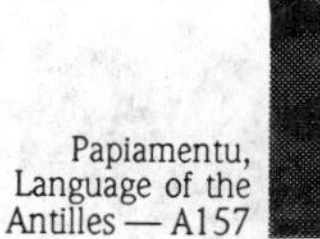

Papiamentu, Language of the Antilles — A157

Designs: 45c, Pierre Lauffer (1920-1981), author and poem Patria. 55c, Waves of Papiamentu.

1985, Sept. 4 Litho. *Perf. 14x13*

536 A157 45c multi 45 45
537 A157 55c multi 60 60

Tete-beche gutter pairs exist.

Flora — A158

1985, Nov. 6 *Perf. 13x14*

538 A158 5c Calotropis procera 15 15
539 A158 10c Capparis flexuosa 22 22
540 A158 20c Mimosa distachya 28 28
541 A158 45c Ipomoea nil 60 60
542 A158 55c Heliotropium ternatum 70 70
543 A158 1.50g Ipomoea incarnata 2.00 2.00
Set value 1.35 1.35

Govt. Building Type of 1983

1985-89 *Perf. 14x13*

543A A148 70c like 20c ('88) 52 52
543B A148 85c like 45c ('88) 60 60
544 A148 1g like 20c 85 85
545 A148 1.50g like 25c 1.10 1.10
546 A148 2.50g like 30c ('86) 2.00 2.00
551 A148 5g like 45c ('86) 3.50 3.50
554 A148 10g like 55c ('87) 7.25 7.25
555 A148 15g like 20c ('89) 14.50 14.50
Nos. 543A-555 (8) 30.32 30.32

Issue dates: 70c, 85c, Mar. 16. 1g, 1.50g, Dec. 4. 2.50g, Jan. 8. 5g, Dec. 3. 10g, May 20. 15g, Feb. 8.

This is an expanding set. Numbers will change if necessary.

Curacao Town Hall, 125th Anniv. A159

1986, Jan. 8 *Perf. 14x13, 13x14*

561 A159 5c Town Hall 15 15
562 A159 15c State room, vert. 18 18
563 A159 25c Court room 25 25
564 A159 55c Entrance, vert. 52 52
Set value 50 50

Amnesty Intl., 25th Anniv. — A160

1986, May 28 Litho. *Perf. 14x13*

565 A160 45c Prisoner chained 40 40
566 A160 55c Peace bird imprisoned 50 50
567 A160 100c Prisoner behind bars 90 90

Mailboxes A161

Perf. 14x13, 13x14

1986, Sept. 3 Litho.

568 A161 10c PO mailbox 15 15
569 A161 25c Steel mailbox 22 22
570 A161 45c Mailbox on brick wall 35 35
571 A161 55c Pillar box 42 42

Nos. 569-571 vert.

Friars of Tilburg in the Antilles, Cent. — A162

Designs: 10c, Brother Mauritius Vliegendehond, residence, 1886. 45c, Monsignor Ferdinand Kieckens, St. Thomas College, Roodeweg. 55c, Father F.S. de Beer, 1st general-superior, and college courtyard.

1986, Nov. 13 Litho. *Perf. 13x14*

572 A162 10c multi 15 15
573 A162 45c multi 35 35
574 A162 55c multi 42 42

Princess Juliana & Prince Bernhard, 50th Wedding Anniv. — A163

Maduro Holding, Inc., Sesquicent. — A164

1987, Jan. 7 Litho. *Perf. 13x14*

575 A163 1.35g multi 1.10 1.10
a. Souvenir sheet 1.25 1.25

1987, Jan. 26

576 A164 70c Expansion map 48 48
577 A164 85c Corporate divisions 60 60
578 A164 1.55g S.E.L. Maduro, founder 1.10 1.10

Curacao Rotary Club, 50th Anniv. — A165

1987, Apr. 2 **Litho.** ***Perf. 14x13***

579 A165 15c Map of the Antilles 20 20
580 A165 50c Rotary headquarters 42 42
581 A165 65c Map of Curacao 52 52

Bolivar-Curacao Friendship, 175th Anniv. — A166

Designs: 60c, Octagon, residence of Simon Bolivar in Curacao. 70c, Bolivarian Society Headquarters, 1949, Willemstad. 80c, Octagon interior (bedroom). 90c, Manual Carlos Piar, Simon Bolivar (1783-1830) and Pedro Luis Brion.

1987, July 24 **Litho.** ***Perf. 14x13***

582 A166 60c multi 42 42
583 A166 70c multi 52 52
584 A166 80c multi 55 55
585 A166 90c multi 65 65

Bolivarian Society, 50th anniv. (70c, 90c).

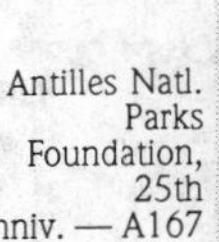

Antilles Natl. Parks Foundation, 25th Anniv. — A167

1987, Dec. 1 **Litho.** ***Perf. 14x13***

586 A167 70c Phaethon lepturus 65 65
587 A167 85c Odocoileus virginianus curassavicus 80 80
588 A167 1.55g Iguana iguana 1.50 1.50

The Curacao Courant, 175th Anniv. A168

Designs: 55c, 19th Cent. printing press, lead type. 70c, Keyboard, modern press.

1987, Dec. 11

589 A168 55c multi 48 48
590 A168 70c multi 60 60

Mijnmaatschappij Phosphate Mining Co., Curacao, 75th Anniv. — A169

1988, Jan. 21

591 A169 40c William Godden, founder 30 30
592 A169 105c Processing plant 80 80
593 A169 155c Tafelberg 1.25 1.25

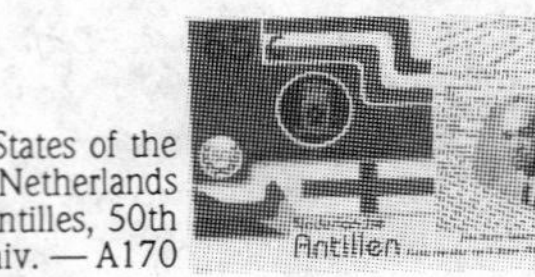

States of the Netherlands Antilles, 50th Anniv. — A170

Designs: 65c, John Horris Sprockel, 1st president, and natl. colors, crest. 70c, Development of state elections, women's suffrage. 155c, Natl. colors, crest, constellation representing the 5 islands and separation of Aruba.

1988, Apr. 5 **Litho.**

594 A170 65c multi 50 50
595 A170 70c multi 52 52
596 A170 155c multi 1.10 1.10

Abolition of Slavery, 125th Anniv. — A171

1988, July 1 **Litho.** ***Perf. 14x13***

597 A171 155c shown 1.25 1.25
598 A171 190c Slave Wall, Curacao 1.40 1.40

3rd Conference for Great Cities of the Americas, Curacao, Aug. 24-27 — A172

1988, Aug. 24 **Litho.**

599 A172 80c shown 60 60
600 A172 155c Bridge, globe 1.25 1.25

Interamerican Foundation of Cities conference on building bridges between peoples.

Charles Ernst Barend Hellmund (1896-1952) A173

Cacti A174

Men and women who initiated community development: 65c, Atthelo Maud Edwards Jackson (1901-1970). 90c, Nicolaas Debrot (1902-1981). 120c, William Charles De La Try Ellis (1881-1977).

1988, Sept. 20 ***Perf. 13x14***

601 A173 55c multi 42 42
602 A173 65c multi 50 50
603 A173 90c multi 65 65
604 A173 120c multi 85 85

Tete-beche gutter pairs exist.

1988, Dec. 13 **Litho.** ***Perf. 13x14***

605 A174 55c Cereus hexagonus 58 58
606 A174 115c Melocactus 1.20 1.20
607 A174 125c Opuntia wentiana 1.30 1.30

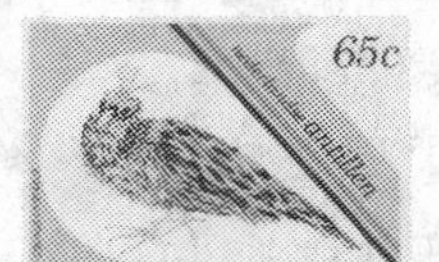

Wildlife Protection and Curacao Foundation for the Prevention of Cruelty to Animals A175

1989, Mar. 9 **Litho.** ***Perf. 14x13***

608 A175 65c Crested quail 65 65
609 A175 115c Dogs, cats 1.15 1.15

Cruise Ships at St. Maarten and Curacao A176

1989, May 8 **Litho.**

610 A176 70c Great Bay Harbor 55 55
611 A176 155c St. Annabay 1.25 1.25

Tourism.

A177

A178

Social and Political Figures: 40c, Paula Clementina Dorner (1901-1969), teacher. 55c, John Aniceto de Jongh (1885-1951), pharmacist, Parliament member. 90c, Jacobo Palm (1887-1982), composer. 120c, Abraham Mendes Chumaceiro (1841-1902), political reformer.

1989, Sept. 20 **Litho.** ***Perf. 13x14***

612 A177 40c multi 35 35
613 A177 55c multi 45 45
614 A177 90c multi 80 80
615 A177 120c multi 1.10 1.10

1989, Nov. 7 **Litho.**

616 A178 30c 7 Symptoms of cancer 30 30
617 A178 60c Radiation treatment 58 58
618 A178 80c Fund emblem, healthy person 75 75

Queen Wilhelmina Fund, 40th anniv. Nos. 616-618 printed se-tenant with inscribed labels.

Souvenir Sheet

World Stamp Expo '89 and 20th UPU Congress, Washington, DC — A179

Designs: 70c, Monument, St. Eustatius, where the sovereignty of the US was 1st recognized by a foreign officer, Nov. 16, 1776. 155c, Peter Stuyvesant, flags representing bicent. of US-Antilles diplomatic relations, vert. 250c, 9-Gun salute of the *Andrea Doria.*

1989, Nov. 17 **Litho.** ***Perf. 13***

619 Sheet of 3 3.75 3.75
a. A179 70c multicolored 55 55
b. A179 155c multicolored 1.25 1.25
c. A179 250c multicolored 1.75 1.75

A180

A181

1989, Dec. 1 ***Perf. 13½x14***

620 A180 30c Fireworks 22 22
621 A180 100c Ornaments on tree 75 75

Christmas 1989 and New Year 1990. Nos. 620-621 printed se-tenant with labels inscribed "Merry X-mas and Happy New Year" in four languages.

1990, Jan. 31 **Litho.** ***Perf. 13x14***

Flowering plants.

622 A181 30c *Tephrosia cinerea* 22 22
623 A181 55c *Erithalis fruticosa* 40 40
624 A181 65c *Evolvulus antillanus* 50 50
625 A181 70c *Jacquinia arborea* 55 55
626 A181 125c *Tournefortia gnaphalodes* 1.00 1.00
627 A181 155c *Sesuvium portulacastrum* 1.10 1.10
Nos. 622-627 (6) 3.77 3.77

Dominican Nuns in the Netherlands Antilles, Cent. — A182

Designs: 10c, Nurse, flag, map. 55c, St. Rose Hospital and St. Martin's Home. 60c, St. Joseph School.

1990, May 7 **Litho.** ***Perf. 14x13***

628 A182 10c multicolored 16 16
629 A182 55c multicolored 62 62
630 A182 60c multicolored 70 70

A183

A184

Poets: 40c, Carlos Alberto Nicolaas-Perez (1915-1989). 60c, Evert Stephanus Jordanus Kruythoff (1893-1967). 80c, John De Pool (1873-1947). 150c, Joseph Sickman Corsen (1853-1911).

1990, Aug. 8 **Litho.** ***Perf. 13x14***

631 A183 40c multicolored 46 46
632 A183 60c multicolored 70 70
633 A183 80c multicolored 95 95
634 A183 150c multicolored 1.75 1.75

1990, Sept. 5 ***Perf. 13x14***

Netherlands queens.

635 A184 100c Emma 1.15 1.15
636 A184 100c Wilhelmina 1.15 1.15
637 A184 100c Juliana 1.15 1.15
638 A184 100c Beatrix 1.15 1.15

Souvenir Sheet

Perf. 14x13

639 A184 250c Four Queens, horiz. 2.85 2.85

Oil Refining in Curacao, 75th Anniv. — A185

1990, Oct. 1 **Litho.** ***Perf. 14x13***

640 A185 100c multicolored 1.15 1.15

Christmas — A186

1990, Dec. 5 **Litho.** ***Perf. 13½x14***

641 A186 30c Gifts 35 35
642 A186 100c shown 1.15 1.15

Nos. 641-642 printed with se-tenant label showing holiday greetings. 25th anniv. of Bon Bisina Project (No. 641).

Express Mail Service, 5th Anniv. — A187

1991, Jan. 16 Litho. *Perf. 14x13*
643 A187 20g multicolored 24.00 24.00

Fish — A188

Designs: 10c, Scuba diver, French grunt. 40c, Spotted trunkfish. 55c, Coppersweeper. 75c, Skindiver, yellow goatfish. 100c, Blackbar soldierfish.

1991, Mar. 13 *Perf. 13x14*
644 A188 10c multicolored 15 15
645 A188 40c multicolored 50 50
646 A188 55c multicolored 65 65
647 A188 75c multicolored 90 90
648 A188 100c multicolored 1.20 1.20
Nos. 644-648 (5) 3.40 3.40

Greetings A189

1991, May 8 *Perf. 14x13*
649 A189 30c Good luck 35 35
650 A189 30c Thank you 35 35
651 A189 30c Love you 35 35
652 A189 30c Happy day 35 35
653 A189 30c Get well soon 35 35
654 A189 30c Happy birthday 35 35
Nos. 649-654 (6) 2.10 2.10

Lighthouses — A190

1991, June 19 Litho. *Perf. 13x14*
655 A190 30c Westpoint, Curacao 35 35
656 A190 70c Willem's Tower, Bonaire 85 85
657 A190 115c Little Curacao, Curacao 1.40 1.40

Peter Stuyvesant College, 50th Anniv. — A191

Espamer '91 — A192

1991, July 5 *Perf. 14x13, 13x14*
658 A191 65c multicolored 78 78
659 A192 125c multicolored 1.50 1.50

Christmas — A193

A194

1991, Dec. 2 Litho. *Perf. 13½x14*
660 A193 30c shown 35 35
661 A193 100c Angel, shepherds 1.10 1.10

Nos. 660-661 printed with se-tenant labels.

Litho. & Typo.

1991, Dec. 16 *Perf. 13x14*
662 A194 30c J. A. Correa 35 35
663 A194 70c "75," coat of arms 85 85
664 A194 155c I. H. Capriles 1.85 1.85
a. Strip of 3, #662-664 3.05 3.05

Maduro and Curiel's Bank NV, 75th anniv.

Odocoileus Virginianus A195

1992, Jan. 29 Litho. *Perf. 14x13*
666 A195 5c Fawn 15 15
667 A195 10c Two does 15 15
668 A195 30c Buck 35 35
669 A195 40c Buck & doe in water 45 45
670 A195 200c Buck drinking 2.20 2.20
671 A195 355c Buck, diff. 4.00 4.00
Nos. 666-671 (6) 7.30 7.30

World Wildlife Fund. Nos. 670-671 are airmail and do not have the WWF emblem.

Souvenir Sheet

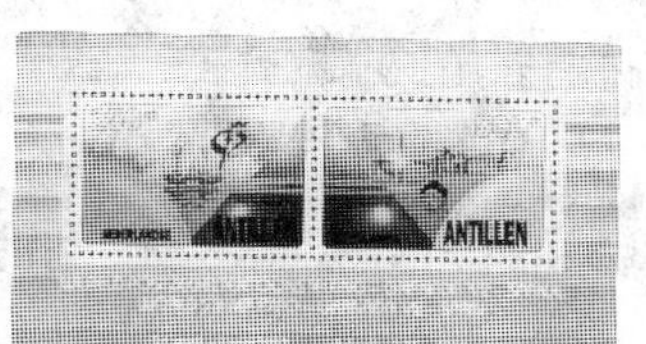

Discovery of America, 500th Anniv. — A196

Designs: a, 250c, Alhambra, Granada, Spain. b, 500c, Carthusian Monastery, Seville, Spain.

1992, Apr. 1 Litho. *Perf. 14x13*
672 A196 Sheet of 2, #a.-b. 9.00 9.00

No. 672a, Granada '92. No. 672b, Expo '92, Seville.

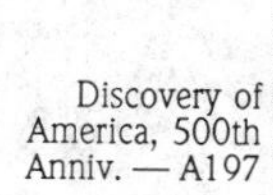

Discovery of America, 500th Anniv. — A197

Designs: 250c, Sailing ship. 500c, Map, Columbus.

1992, May 13 Litho. *Perf. 14x13*
673 A197 250c multicolored 3.00 3.00
674 A197 500c multicolored 6.00 6.00

World Columbian Stamp Expo '92, Chicago.

Container Terminal, Curacao A198

1992, June 26
675 A198 80c multi 95 95
676 A198 125c multi, diff. 1.50 1.50

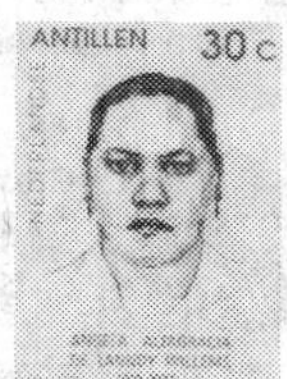

Famous People — A199

Designs: 30c, Angela Altagracia de Lannoy-Willems (1913-1983), politician and social activist. 40c, Lodewijk Daniel Gerharts (1901-1983), politician and promoter of tourism for Bonaire. 55c, Cyrus Wilberforce Wathey (1901-1969), businessman and philanthropist. 70c, Christiaan Winkel (1899-1962), deputy governor of Netherlands Antilles. 100c, Franciscan Nuns of Roosendaal, educational and charitable group, 150th anniversary of arrival in Curacao.

1992, Sept. 1 Litho. *Perf. 13x14*
677 A199 30c tan, grn & blk 38 38
678 A199 40c tan, blue & blk 48 48
679 A199 55c tan, yel org & blk 65 65
680 A199 70c tan, lake & blk 85 85
681 A199 100c tan, blue & blk 1.25 1.25
Nos. 677-681 (5) 3.61 3.61

Queen Beatrix's 1992 Visit — A200

Designs: 70c, Queen in white hat, Prince Claus. 100c, Queen signing jubilee register. 175c, Queen in black hat, Prince Claus, native girl.

1992, Nov. 9 Litho. *Perf. 14x13*
682 A200 70c multicolored 90 90
683 A200 100c multicolored 1.25 1.25
684 A200 175c multicolored 2.20 2.20

Queen Beatrix's accession to the throne, 12½ year anniv. (#683).

Christmas A201

Perf. 14x13½, 13½x14

1992, Dec. 1 Litho.
685 A201 30c Nativity scene 35 35
686 A201 100c Mary, Joseph, vert. 1.20 1.20

No. 686 printed with se-tenant label.

SEMI-POSTAL STAMPS

Catalogue values for unused stamps in this section are for Never Hinged items.

NIWIN

Nos. 132, 133 and 135 Surcharged in Black

1½ ct.
+ 2½ ct.

1947, Dec. 1 Unwmk. *Perf. 12½*
B1 A26 1½c + 2½c on 6c 85 75
B2 A26 2½c + 5c on 10c 85 75
B3 A26 5c + 7½c on 15c 85 75

The surtax was for the National Inspanning Welzijnszorg in Nederlandsch Indie, relief organization for Netherlands Indies.

Curaao Children
SP1 SP2

Design: Nos. B6, B9, Girl.

1948, Nov. 3 Photo. *Perf. 12½x12*
B4 SP1 6c + 10c ol brn 2.25 1.75
B5 SP2 10c + 15c brt red 2.25 1.75
B6 SP2 12½c + 20c Prus grn 2.25 1.75
B7 SP1 15c + 25c brt bl 2.25 1.75
B8 SP2 20c + 30c red brn 2.25 1.75
B9 SP2 25c + 35c pur 2.25 1.75
Nos. B4-B9 (6) 13.50 10.50

The surtax was for crippled children.

Leapfrog — SP4

Ship and Gull — SP5

Designs: 5c+2½c, Flying kite. 6c+2½c, Girls swinging. 12½c+5c, "London Bridge." 25c+10c, Rolling hoops.

Perf. 14½x13½

1951, Aug. 16 Unwmk.
B10 SP4 1½c + 1c pur 1.65 2.00
B11 SP4 5c + 2½c brn 8.50 4.00
B12 SP4 6c + 2½c blue 8.50 4.00
B13 SP4 12½c + 5c red 8.50 4.00
B14 SP4 25c + 10c dl grn 8.50 3.50
Nos. B10-B14 (5) 35.65 17.50

The surtax was for child welfare.

1952, July 16 *Perf. 13x14*

Designs: 6c+4c, Sailor and lighthouse. 12½c+7c, Prow of sailboat. 15c+10c, Ships. 25c+15c, Ship, compass and anchor.

B15 SP5 1½c + 1c dk grn 90 1.00
B16 SP5 6c + 4c choc 6.25 3.00
B17 SP5 12½c + 7c red vio 6.25 3.25
B18 SP5 15c + 10c dp bl 8.00 4.00
B19 SP5 25c + 15c red 8.00 3.00
Nos. B15-B19 (5) 29.40 14.25

The surtax was for the seamen's welfare fund.

22½ Ct. **+7½ Ct.**

No. 226 Surcharged in Black

WATERSNOOD
NEDERLAND
1953

1953, Feb. 21
B20 A45 22½c + 7½c on 1½g 90 1.00

The surtax was for flood relief in the Netherlands.

Tribulus Cistoides — SP6

Flowers: 7½c+5c, Yellow hibiscus. 15c+5c, Oleander. 22½c+7½c, Cactus. 25c+10c, Red hibiscus.

1955, May 17 Photo. *Perf. 14x13*
Flowers in Natural Colors

B21 SP6 1½c + 1c bl grn & dk bl 30 35
B22 SP6 7½c + 5c dp ultra 2.50 1.75
B23 SP6 15c + 5c ol grn 2.50 1.90
B24 SP6 22½c + 7½c dk bl 2.50 1.75
B25 SP6 25c + 10c ind & gray 2.50 1.90
Nos. B21-B25 (5) 10.30 7.65

The surtax was for child welfare.

Prince Bernhard and Queen Juliana — SP7

1955 *Perf. 11x12*

B26 SP7 7½c + 2½c rose brn 15 15
B27 SP7 22½c + 7½c dp bl 80 80

Royal visit to the Netherlands Antilles, Oct. 1955. Surtax paid for a gift.

Lord Baden-Powell SP8

1957, Feb. 22 *Perf. 14x13½*

B28 SP8 6c + 1½c org yel 40 40
B29 SP8 7½c + 2½c dp grn 40 40
B30 SP8 15c + 5c red 40 40

50th anniv. of the Boy Scout movement.

Soccer Player — SP9

Map of Central America and the Caribbean SP10

Designs: 15c+5c, Goalkeeper catching ball. 22½c+7½c, Men playing soccer.

1957, Aug. 6 *Perf. 12x11, 11x12*

B31 SP9 6c + 2½c org 40 55
B32 SP10 7½c + 5c dk red 80 90
B33 SP9 15c + 5c brt bl grn 90 90
B34 SP9 22½c + 7½c brt bl 90 70

8th Central American and Caribbean Soccer Championships, Aug. 11-25.
Surtax was for organizing costs.

American Kestrel — SP11

Flag and Map — SP12

Birds: 7½+1½c, Yellow oriole. 15+2½c, Common ground doves. 22½+2½c, Brown-throated parakeet.

1958, Apr. 15 Photo. *Perf. 13½x14*

B35 SP11 2½c + 1c multi 22 22
B36 SP11 7½c + 1½c multi 70 60
B37 SP11 15c + 2½c multi 80 80
B38 SP11 22½c + 2½c multi 90 70

The surtax was for child welfare.

1958, Dec. 1 Litho. *Perf. 13½*
Cross in Red

B39 SP12 6c + 2c red brn 28 28
B40 SP12 7½c + 2½c bl grn 40 40
B41 SP12 15c + 5c org yel 40 40
B42 SP12 22½c + 7½c blue 40 40

The surtax was for the Red Cross.

Community House, Zeeland SP13

Designs (historic buildings): 7½c+2½c, Molenplein. 15c+5c, Saba, vert. 22½c+7½c, Scharlooburg. 25c+7½c, Community House, Brievengat.

Perf. 14x13½, 13½x14
1959, Sept. 16 Litho.

B43 SP13 6c + 1½c multi 80 70
B44 SP13 7½c + 2½c multi 80 80
B45 SP13 15c + 5c multi 80 80
B46 SP13 22½c + 7½c multi 80 80
B47 SP13 25c + 7½c multi 80 80
Nos. B43-B47 (5) 4.00 3.90

The surtax went to the Foundation for the Preservation of Historical Monuments.

Fish — SP14

Designs. 10c+2c, SCUBA diver with spear gun, vert. 25c+5c, Two fish.

1960, Aug. 24 Photo. *Perf. 13½*

B48 SP14 10c + 2c saph 80 80
B49 SP14 20c + 3c multi 1.10 1.10
B50 SP14 25c + 5c blk, brt pink & dk bl 1.10 1.10

The surtax was for the fight against cancer.

Infant — SP15

Designs: 10c+3c, Girl and doll. 20c+6c, Boy on beach. 25c+8c, Children in school.

1961, July 24 Litho. *Perf. 13½x14*
Designs in Black

B51 SP15 6c + 2c lt yel grn 20 20
B52 SP15 10c + 3c rose red 20 20
B53 SP15 20c + 6c yellow 20 20
B54 SP15 25c + 8c organe 20 20

The surtax was for child welfare.

Globe and Knight — SP16

1962, May 2 *Perf. 13½x14½*

B55 SP16 10c + 5c green 60 55
B56 SP16 20c + 10c carmine 60 55
B57 SP16 25c + 10c dk bl 60 55

Intl. Candidates Chess Tournament, Willemstad, May-June.

TEGEN DE HONGER
+10c

No. 248 Surcharged

1963, Mar. 21

B58 A56 20c + 10c crim & gray 40 40

FAO "Freedom from Hunger" campaign.

Child and Flowers SP17

Bougainvillea SP18

Designs: 6c+3c, Three girls and flowers, horiz. 10c+5c, Girl with ball and trees, horiz. 20c+10c, Three boys with flags, horiz. 25c+12c, Singing boy.

Perf. 14½x13½, 13½x14½
1963, Oct. 23 Photo. Unwmk.

B59 SP17 5c + 2c multi 22 22
B60 SP17 6c + 3c multi 22 22
B61 SP17 10c + 5c multi 22 22
B62 SP17 20c + 10c multi 22 22
B63 SP17 25c + 12c multi 22 22
Nos. B59-B63 (5) 1.10 1.10

The surtax was for the Antillean Youth Federation.

1964, Oct. 21 *Perf. 14x13*

Designs: 10c+5c, Wild rose. 20c+10c, Chalice flower. 25c+11c, Bellisima.

Flowers in Natural Colors

B64 SP18 6c + 3c bl vio & blk 15 15
B65 SP18 10c + 5c yel brn, yel & blk 15 15
B66 SP18 20c + 10c dl red & blk 15 15
B67 SP18 25c + 11c cit & brn 15 15

The surtax was for child welfare.

Sea Anemones and Star Coral — SP19

Corals: 6c+3c, Blue cup sponges. 10c+5c, Green cup sponges. 25c+11c, Basket sponge, knobbed brain coral and reef fish.

1965, Nov. 10 Photo. *Perf. 14x13½*

B68 SP19 6c + 3c multi 15 15
B69 SP19 10c + 5c multi 15 15
B70 SP19 20c + 10c multi 15 15
B71 SP19 25c + 11c multi 20 20
Set value 55 55

The surtax was for child welfare.

ICEM Type of Netherlands

1966, Jan. 31 Photo. *Perf. 14x13*

B72 SP181 35c + 15c brn & dl yel 20 20

The surtax was for the Intergovernmental Committee for European Migration (ICEM). The message on the stamps was given and signed by Queen Juliana.

Girl Cooking SP20

Helping Hands Supporting Women SP21

Youth at Work: 10c+5c, Nurse's aide with infant. 20c+10c, Young metalworker. 25c+11c, Girl ironing.

1966, Nov. 15 *Perf. 13½*

B73 SP20 6c + 3c multi 15 15
B74 SP20 10c + 5c multi 15 15
B75 SP20 20c + 10c multi 15 15
B76 SP20 25c + 11c multi 20 20
Set value 46 46

The surtax was for child welfare.

1967, July 4 Litho. *Perf. 13x14*

B77 SP21 6c + 3c bl & blk 15 15
B78 SP21 10c + 5c brt pink & blk 15 15
B79 SP21 20c + 19c lilac 15 15
B80 SP21 25c + 11c dk bl 15 15
Set value 44 44

The surtax was for various social and cultural institutions.

Nanzi the Spider and the Tiger — SP22

Nanzi Stories (Folklore): 6c+3c, Princess Longnose, vert. 10c+5c, The Turtle and the Monkey. 25c+11c, Adventure of Shon Arey.

Perf. 14x13, 13x14
1967, Nov. 15 Photo.

B81 SP22 6c + 3c dk red, pink & org 15 15
B82 SP22 10c + 5c vio bl & org 15 15
B83 SP22 20c + 10c grn & org 18 18
B84 SP22 25c + 11c brt bl & org 18 18

The surtax was for child welfare.

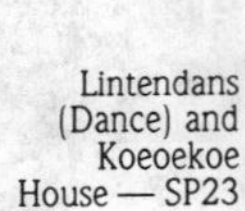
Lintendans (Dance) and Koeoekoe House — SP23

1968, May 29 Litho. *Perf. 14x13*

B85 SP23 10c + 5c multi 15 15
B86 SP23 15c + 5c multi 15 15
B87 SP23 20c + 10c multi 15 15
B88 SP23 25c + 10c multi 15 15

The surtax was for various social and cultural institutions.

Boy and Pet Cat — SP24

Designs: 6c+3c, Boy and goat. 10c+5c, Girl and poodle. 25c+11c, Girl and duckling.

1968, Nov. 13 Photo. *Perf. 13½*

B89 SP24 6c + 3c multi 15 15
B90 SP24 10c + 5c multi 15 15
B91 SP24 20c + 10c multi 18 18
B92 SP24 25c + 11c multi 18 18

The surtax was for child welfare.

Carnival Headpiece — SP25

Designs (Folklore): 15c+5c, Harvest-home festival. 20c+10c, Feast of St. John (dancers and cock). 25c+10c, "Dande" New Year's celebration.

1969, July 23 Litho. *Perf. 13½x14*

B93 SP25 10c + 5c multi	22	22
B94 SP25 15c + 5c multi	22	22
B95 SP25 20c + 10c multi	32	32
B96 SP25 25c + 10c multi	32	32

The surtax was for various social and cultural institutions.

Boy Playing Guitar — SP26

Designs: 10c+5c, Girl with English flute. 20c+10c, Boy playing the marimula. 25c+11c, Girl playing the piano.

1969, Nov. 3 Litho. *Perf. 14x13*

B97 SP26 6c + 3c org & vio	20	20
B98 SP26 10c + 5c yel & brt grn	28	28
B99 SP26 20c + 10c bl & car	28	28
B100 SP26 25c + 11c pink & brn	32	32

The surtax was for child welfare.

Printing Press and Quill — SP27

Mother and Child — SP28

Mass Media: 15c+5c, Filmstrip and reels. 20c+10c, Horn and radio mast. 25c+10c, Television antenna and eye focused on globe.

1970, July 14 Litho. *Perf. 13½x14*

B101 SP27 10c + 5c multi	32	32
B102 SP27 15c + 5c multi	32	32
B103 SP27 20c + 10c multi	32	32
B104 SP27 25c + 10c multi	32	32

The surtax was for various social and cultural institutions.

1970, Nov. 16

Designs: 10c+5c, Girl holding piggy bank. 20c+10c, Boys wrestling (Judokas). 25c+11c, Youth carrying small boy on his shoulders.

B105 SP28 6c + 3c multi	50	50
B106 SP28 10c + 5c multi	50	50
B107 SP28 20c + 10c multi	50	50
B108 SP28 25c + 11c multi	50	50

The surtax was for child welfare.

Charcoal Burner — SP29

Kitchen Utensils: 15c+5c, Earthenware vessel for water. 20c+10c, Baking oven. 25c+10c, Soup plate, stirrer and kneading stick.

1971, May 12 *Perf. 14x13½*

B109 SP29 10c + 5c multi	40	40
B110 SP29 15c + 5c multi	40	40
B111 SP29 20c + 10c multi	40	40
B112 SP29 25c + 10c multi	40	40

Surtax was for various social and cultural institutions.

Homemade Dolls and Comb — SP30

Homemade Toys: 20c+10c, Cars. 30c+15c, Musical top made from calabash.

1971, Nov. 16 *Perf. 13½x14*

B113 SP30 15c + 5c multi	48	48
B114 SP30 20c + 10c multi	48	48
B115 SP30 30c + 15c multi	48	48

Surtax was for child welfare.

Steel Band — SP31

Designs: 20c+10c, Harvest festival (Seu). 30c+15c, Tambu dancers.

1972, May 16

B116 SP31 15c + 5c multi	60	60
B117 SP31 20c + 10c multi	60	60
B118 SP31 30c + 15c multi	60	60

Surtax was for various social and cultural institutions.

Child at Play on Ground SP32

Designs: 20c+10c, Child playing in water. 30c+15c, Child throwing ball into air.

1972, Nov. 14 Litho. *Perf. 14x13*

B119 SP32 15c + 5c multi	70	70
B120 SP32 20c + 10c multi	70	70
B121 SP32 30c + 15c multi	70	70

Surtax was for child welfare.

Pedestrian Crossing, Traffic Sign — SP33

Designs: 15c+7c, School crossing. 40c+20c, Traffic light, road and car.

1973, Apr. 9 Litho. *Perf. 13x14*

B122 SP33 12c + 6c multi	60	60
B123 SP33 15c + 7c multi	60	60
B124 SP33 40c + 20c multi	60	60

Surtax was for various social and cultural institutions.

"1948-73" SP34

Designs: 20c+10c, Children. 30c+15c, Mother and child.

1973, Nov. 19 Litho. *Perf. 14x13*

B125 SP34 15c + 5c multi	70	70
B126 SP34 20c + 10c multi	70	70
a. Min. sheet, 2 each #B125-B126	3.00	3.00
B127 SP34 30c + 15c multi	1.10	1.10

25th anniversary of first Child Welfare semi-postal stamps.

Girl Combing her Hair — SP35

Designs: 15c+7c, Young people listening to rock music. 40c+20c, Drummer, symbolizing rock music.

1974, Apr. 9 Litho. *Perf. 14x13*

B128 SP35 12c + 6c multi	80	80
B129 SP35 15c + 7c multi	80	80
B130 SP35 40c + 20c multi	80	80

Surtax was for various social and cultural institutions.

Child, Saw and Score — SP36

Designs: 20c+10c, Footprints in circle. 30c+15c, Moon and sun. Each design includes score of a children's song.

1974, Nov. 12 Litho. *Perf. 13x14*

B131 SP36 15c + 5c multi	60	60
B132 SP36 20c + 10c multi	60	60
B133 SP36 30c + 15c multi	60	60

Surtax was for child welfare.

Carved Stone Grid, Flower Pot SP37

Jewish Tombstone, Mordecai's Procession SP38

Design: 40c+20c, Ornamental stone from facade of Jewish House, 1728.

1975, Mar. 21 Litho. *Perf. 13x14*

B134 SP37 12c + 6c multi	60	60
B135 SP38 15c + 7c multi	60	60
B136 SP37 40c + 20c multi	60	60

Surtax was for various social and cultural institutions.

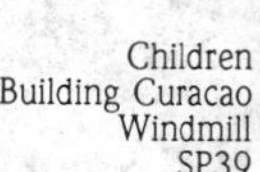

Children Building Curacao Windmill SP39

Designs: 20c+10c, Girl molding clay animal. 30c+15c, Children drawing picture.

1975, Nov. 12 Litho. *Perf. 14x13*

B137 SP39 15c + 5c multi	55	55
B138 SP39 20c + 10c multi	55	55
B139 SP39 30c + 15c multi	55	55

Surtax was for child welfare.

Carrying a Child — SP40

Designs: Different ways of carrying a child. 40c+18c is vertical.

Perf. 14x13, 13x14

1976, Oct. 4 Litho.

B140 SP40 20c + 10c multi	45	45
B141 SP40 25c + 12c multi	45	45
B142 SP40 40c + 18c multi	45	45

Surtax was for child welfare.

Composite: Aces of Hearts, Clubs, Diamonds and Spades — SP41

Designs: 25c+12c, "King" and inscription. 40c+18c, Hand holding cards; map of Aruba as ace of hearts, horiz.

Perf. 13x14, 14x13

1977, May 6 Litho.

B143 SP41 20c + 10c red & blk	32	28
B144 SP41 25c + 12c multi	32	32
a. Min. sheet, 2 each #B143-B144	1.40	1.10
B145 SP41 40c + 18c multi	48	48

Central American and Caribbean Bridge Championships, Aruba.

Souvenir Sheet

1977, May 26 *Perf. 13½x14*

B146 SP41 Sheet of 3	2.75	2.50

Amphilex 77 International Philatelic Exhibition, Amsterdam, May 26-June 5. No. B146 contains 3 stamps similar to Nos. B143-B145 with bright green background.

Children and Toys — SP42

Designs: Children playing with fantasy animals.

1977, Oct. 25 Litho. *Perf. 14x13*

B147 SP42 15c + 5c multi	28	22
B148 SP42 20c + 10c multi	32	32
B149 SP42 25c + 12c multi	38	38
B150 SP42 40c + 18c multi	48	42
a. Min. sheet, 2 each #B148, B150	1.75	1.65

Surtax was for child welfare.

Water Skiing — SP43

Roller Skating — SP45

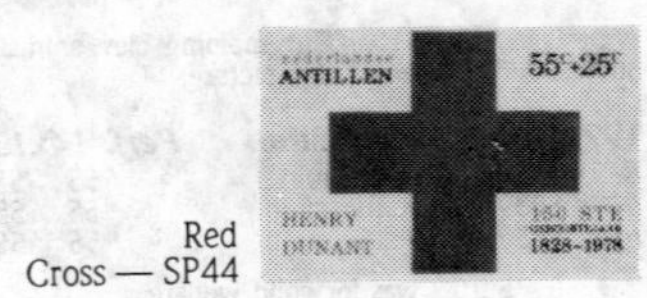

Red Cross — SP44

Designs: 20c+10c, Sailing. 25c+12c, Soccer. 40c+18c, Baseball.

1978, Mar. 31 Litho. *Perf. 13x14*

B151	SP43 15c + 5c multi	15	15
B152	SP43 20c + 10c multi	15	15
B153	SP43 25c + 12c multi	15	15
B154	SP43 40c + 18c multi	22	22
	Set value	56	56

Surtax was for sports. Tete-beche gutter pairs exist.

1978, Sept. 19 Litho. *Perf. 14x13*

B155	SP44 55c + 25c red & blk	22	22
a.	Souv. sheet of 3, perf. 13½x13	1.65	1.65

Henri Dunant (1828-1910), founder of Red Cross. Surtax for the Red Cross. Tete-beche gutter pairs exist.

1978, Nov. 7 Litho. *Perf. 13x14*

Children's Activities: 20c+10c, Kite flying. 25c+12c, Playing marbles. 40c+ 18c, Bicycling.

B156	SP45 15c + 5c multi	32	28
B157	SP45 20c + 10c multi	40	32
a.	Min. sheet, 2 each #B156-B157	1.75	1.50
B158	SP45 25c + 12c multi	40	38
B159	SP45 40c + 18c multi	48	45

Surtax was for child welfare.

Carnival King — SP46

Regatta Emblem — SP47

25th Aruba Carnival: 75c+20c, Carnival Queen and coat of arms.

1979, Feb. 20 Litho. *Perf. 13x14*

B160	SP46 40c + 10c multi	38	30
B161	SP46 75c + 20c multi	55	52

Perf. 13x14, 14x13

1979, May 16 Litho.

Designs: 35c+10c, Race. 40c+15c, Globe and yacht, horiz. 55c+25c, Yacht, birds and sun.

B162	SP47 15c + 5c multi	15	15
B163	SP47 35c + 10c multi	25	25
B164	SP47 40c + 15c multi	32	32
B165	SP47 55c + 25c multi	40	40
a.	Souv. sheet of 4, #B162-B165	1.10	1.10

12th International Sailing Regatta, Bonaire. #B164 in souvenir sheet is perf 13x14.

Volunteer Corps Type, 1979

Designs: 15c+10c, Soldiers, 1929 and 1979. 40c+20c, Soldier guarding oil refinery, Guard emblem.

1979, July 4 Litho. *Perf. 13x14*

B166	A124 15c + 10c multi	18	16
B167	A124 40c + 20c multi	38	35

Girls Reading Book, IYC Emblem SP48

Volleyball, Olympic Rings SP49

IYC Emblem and Children's Drawings: 25c+12c, Infant and cat. 35c+15c, Girls walking under palm trees. 50c+20c, Children wearing adult clothing.

1979, Oct. 24 Litho. *Perf. 13x14*

B168	SP48 20c + 10c multi	20	20
B169	SP48 25c + 12c multi	30	28
B170	SP48 35c + 15c multi	38	32
a.	Souv. sheet, 2 #B168, 2 #B170	1.25	1.20
B171	SP48 50c + 20c multi	48	48

International Year of the Child.

Fort Church Type of 1980

Designs: 20c+10c, Brass chandelier, 1909, horiz. 50c+25c, Pipe organ.

Perf. 14x13, 13x14

1980, Jan. 9 Litho.

B172	A128 20c + 10c multi	18	18
B173	A128 50c + 15c multi	45	45

1980, June 25 Litho. *Perf. 13x14*

Designs: 25c+10c, Woman gymnast. 30c+15c, Male gymnast. 60c+25c, Basketball.

B174	SP49 25c + 10c multi	18	18
B175	SP49 30c + 15c multi	30	30
B176	SP49 45c + 20c multi	38	35
B177	SP49 60c + 25c multi	50	45
a.	Souvenir sheet of 6, 3 each #B174, B177, perf. 14x13½	2.25	1.90

22nd Summer Olympic Games, Moscow, July 19-Aug. 3.

St. Maarten Landscape SP50

Children's Drawings: 30c+15c, House in Bonaire. 40c+20c, Child at blackboard. 60c+25c, Cancers, vert.

Perf. 14x13, 13x14

1980, Oct. 22 Litho.

B178	SP50 25c + 10c multi	28	24
B179	SP50 30c + 15c multi	35	32
B180	SP50 40c + 20c multi	40	38
B181	SP50 60c + 25c multi	50	48
a.	Souvenir sheet of 6+ 4 labels, 3 each #B178, B181	2.50	2.25

Surtax was for Federation of Antillean Youth Care.
#B178 in souvenir sheet is perf 13x14.

Girl Using Sign Language SP51

Tennis Player SP52

Designs: 25c+10c, Blind woman. 30c+15c, Man in wheelchair. 45c+20c, Infant in walker.

1981, Apr. 7 Litho. *Perf. 13x14*

B182	SP51 25c + 10c multi	25	25
B183	SP51 30c + 15c multi	32	32
B184	SP51 45c + 20c multi	55	55
B185	SP51 60c + 25c multi	60	60

International Year of the Disabled. Surtax was for handicapped children.

1981, May 27 Litho. *Perf. 13x14*

B186	SP52 30c + 15c shown	35	35
B187	SP52 50c + 20c Diving	55	55
B188	SP52 70c + 25c Boxing	75	75
a.	Min. sheet of 3, #B186-B188	1.75	1.75

Surtax was for sporting events.

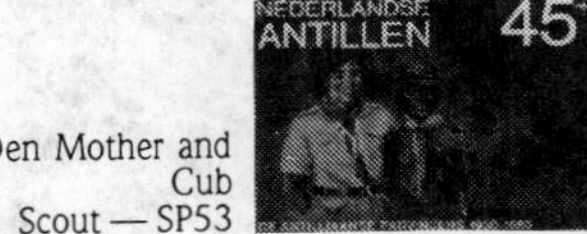

Den Mother and Cub Scout — SP53

Scouting in Netherlands Antilles, 50th Anniv.: 70c+25c, van der Maarel, national founder. 1g+50c, Ronde Klip (headquarters).

1981, Sept. 16 Litho. *Perf. 14x13*

B189	SP53 45c + 20c multi	60	60
B190	SP53 70c + 25c multi	80	80
B191	SP53 1g + 50c multi	1.25	1.25
a.	Min. sheet of 3, #B189-B191, perf. 13½x13	2.75	2.50

Surtax was for various social and cultural institutions.

Girl and Teddy Bear — SP54

Designs: 35c+15c, Mother and child. 45c+20c, Two children. 55c+25c, Boy and cat.

1981, Oct. 21 Litho. *Perf. 13x14*

B192	SP54 35c + 15c multi	32	32
B193	SP54 45c + 20c multi	48	48
B194	SP54 55c + 25c multi	60	60
B195	SP54 85c + 40c multi	90	90
a.	Min. sheet of 4, #B192-B195	2.50	2.50

Surtax was for Federation of Antillean Youth Care.

Fencing — SP55

1982, Feb. 17 Litho. *Perf. 14x13*

B196	SP55 35c + 15c shown	32	32
B197	SP55 45c + 20c Judo	50	50
B198	SP55 70c + 35c Soccer	80	80
a.	Miniature sheet of 2 + label	1.75	1.75
B199	SP55 85c + 40c Bicycling	90	90

Surtax was for sporting events.

Girl Playing Accordion SP56

1982, Oct. 20 Litho.

B200	SP56 35c + 15c shown	40	40
B201	SP56 75c + 35c Guitar	90	90
B202	SP56 85c + 40c Violin	1.00	1.00
a.	Min. sheet of 3, #B200-B202	2.50	2.50

Traditional House, Saba — SP57

1982, Nov. 17 Litho.

B203	SP57 35c + 15c shown	40	40
B204	SP57 75c + 35c Aruba	90	90
B205	SP57 85c + 40c Curacao	1.00	1.00
a.	Souv. sheet of 3, #B203-B205	2.50	2.50

Surtax was for various social and cultural institutions.

High Jump SP58

1983, Feb. 22 Litho.

B206	SP58 35c + 15c shown	32	32
B207	SP58 45c + 20c Weight lifting	60	60
B208	SP58 85c + 40c Wind surfing	1.00	1.00

Surtax was for sporting events.

Child with Lizard — SP59

Pre-Columbian Artifacts — SP60

1983, Oct. 18 Litho. *Perf. 13x14*

B209	SP59 45c + 20c shown	60	60
B210	SP59 55c + 25c Child with insects	75	75
B211	SP59 100c + 50c Child with animal	1.40	1.40
a.	Souv. sheet of 3, #B209-B211	2.75	2.75

Surtax was for Childrens' Charity.

1983, Nov. 22 Litho. *Perf. 13x14*

B212	SP60 45c + 20c multi	70	70
B213	SP60 55c + 25c multi	80	80
B214	SP60 85c + 40c multi	1.00	1.00
B215	SP60 100c + 50c multi	1.40	1.40

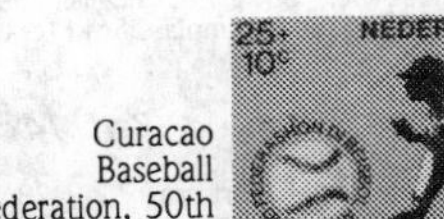

Curacao Baseball Federation, 50th Anniv. — SP61

1984, Mar. 27 Litho. *Perf. 14x13*

B216	SP61 25c + 10c Catching	40	40
B217	SP61 45c + 20c Batting	75	75
B218	SP61 55c + 25c Pitching	95	95
B219	SP61 85c + 40c Running	1.10	1.10
a.	Min. sheet of 3, #B217-B219	3.25	3.25

Surtax was for baseball fed., 1984 Olympics.

Microphones, Radio — SP62

Designs: 55c+25c, Radio, record player. 100c+50c, Record players.

1984, Apr. 24 Litho. *Perf. 14x13*

B220	SP62 45c + 20c multi	75	75
B221	SP62 55c + 25c multi	1.00	1.00
B222	SP62 100c + 50c multi	1.25	1.25

Surtax was for social and cultural institutions.

Boy Reading — SP63

Designs: 55c+25c, Parents reading to children. 100c+50c, Family worship.

1984, Nov. 7 Litho. *Perf. 13x14*

B223	SP63 45c + 20c multi	70	70
B224	SP63 55c + 25c multi	1.00	1.00
B225	SP63 100c + 50c multi	1.25	1.25
a.	Souv. sheet of 3, #B223-B225	3.25	3.25

Surtax was for children's charity.

Soccer Players — SP64

1985, Mar. 27 Litho. *Perf. 14x13*

B226	SP64	10c + 5c multi	22	22
B227	SP64	15c + 5c multi	25	25
B228	SP64	45c + 20c multi	70	70
B229	SP64	55c + 25c multi	90	90
B230	SP64	85c + 40c multi	1.25	1.25
		Nos. B226-B230 (5)	3.32	3.32

The surtax was for sporting events.

Intl. Youth Year — SP65

1985, Apr. 29 Litho.

B231	SP65	45c + 20c Youth, computer keyboard	75	75
B232	SP65	55c + 25c Girl listening to music	1.00	1.00
B233	SP65	100c + 50c Youth breakdancing	1.50	1.50

Surtax for youth, social and cultural organizations.

Children — SP66

1985, Oct. 16 Litho. *Perf. 13x14*

B234	SP66	5c + 5c Eskimo	18	18
B235	SP66	10c + 5c African	20	20
B236	SP66	25c + 10c Asian	42	42
B237	SP66	45c + 20c Dutch	70	70
B238	SP66	55c + 25c American Indian	80	80
a.		Souv. sheet of 3, #B236-B238	2.00	2.00
		Nos. B234-B238 (5)	2.30	2.30

Surtax for Youth Care Federation.

Sports SP67

Handicrafts SP68

1986, Feb. 19 Litho. *Perf. 13x14*

B239	SP67	15c + 5c Running	18	18
B240	SP67	25c + 10c Horse racing	38	38
B241	SP67	45c + 20c Car racing	65	65
B242	SP67	55c + 25c Soccer	75	75

Surtax for the natl. Sports Federation.

1986, Apr. 29

B243	SP68	30c + 15c Painting	40	40
B244	SP68	45c + 20c Sculpting	55	55
B245	SP68	55c + 25c Ceramics	70	70

Surtax for Curacao Youth Care Federation.

Sports SP69

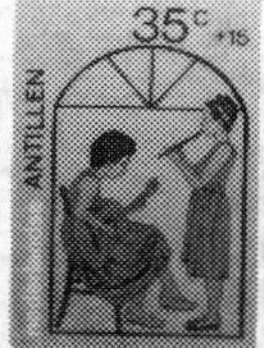

Social and Cultural Programs SP70

1986, Oct. 15 Litho. *Perf. 13x14*

B246	SP69	20c + 10c Soccer	26	26
B247	SP69	25c + 15c Tennis	35	35
B248	SP69	45c + 20c Judo	52	52
B249	SP69	55c + 25c Baseball	65	65
a.		Min. sheet of 2, #B248-B249	1.25	1.25

Surtax for the natl. Sports Foundation.

1987, Mar. 11 Litho.

B250	SP70	35c + 15c Musicians	38	38
B251	SP70	45c + 25c Handicapped	50	50
B252	SP70	85c + 40c Pavilion	95	95

Surtax for the Jong Wacht (Youth Guard) and the natl. Red Cross.

Boy in Various Stages of Growth — SP71

1987, Oct. 21 Litho. *Perf. 14x13*

B253	SP71	40c +15c Infant	45	45
B254	SP71	55c +25c Toddler	60	60
B255	SP71	115c +50c Boy	1.25	1.25
a.		Souv. sheet of 3, #B253-B255	2.50	2.50

Surtax benefited Youth Care programs.

Queen Emma Bridge, Cent. — SP72

Designs: 55c+25c, Bridge, vert. 115c+55c, View of Willemstad Harbor and quay. 190c+60c, Flags of the Netherlands, Antilles and United States, Leonard B. Smith, engineer.

1988, May 9 *Perf. 13x14, 14x13*

B256	SP72	55c +25c multi	60	60
B257	SP72	115c +55c multi	1.25	1.25
B258	SP72	190c +60c multi	1.75	1.75

Surtax for social and cultural purposes.

Youth Care Campaign SP73

1988, Oct. 26 Litho. *Perf. 14x13*

B259	SP73	55c +25c Girl, television	60	60
B260	SP73	65c +30c Boy, portable stereo	70	70
B261	SP73	115c +55c Girl, computer	1.25	1.25
a.		Souv. sheet of 3, #B259-B261	2.50	2.50

Surtax for the Antillean Youth Care Federation.

Curacao Stamp Assoc., 50th Anniv. — SP75

Designs: 30c+10c, Type A25 and No. 461 under magnifying glass. 55c+20c, Simulated stamp (learning to use tongs). 80c+30c, Barn owl, album, magnifying glass, tongs.

1989, Jan. 18 Litho. *Perf. 13x14*

B264	SP75	30c +10c multi	30	30
B265	SP75	55c +20c multi	55	55
B266	SP75	80c +30c multi	75	75

Nos. B264-B266 printed se-tenant in a continuous design. Surtaxed for welfare organizations.

SP76

1989, Oct. 25 Litho. *Perf. 14x13*

B267	SP76	40c +15c Girl, boy, tree	35	35
B268	SP76	65c +30c Playing on beach	70	70
B269	SP76	115c +55c Father and child	1.25	1.25

Souvenir Sheet

B270	SP76	155c +75c At the beach, diff.	1.65	1.65

Surtax for child welfare.

Natl. Girl Scout Movement, 60th Anniv. — SP77

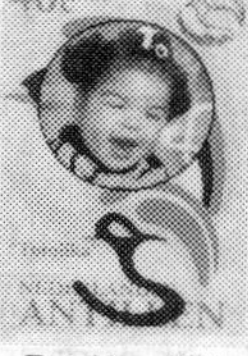

Totolika, 60th Anniv. — SP78

Natl. Boy Scout Movement, 60th Anniv. — SP79

1990, Mar. 7 Litho. *Perf. 13x14*

B271	SP77	30c +10c multi	35	35
B272	SP78	40c +15c multi	45	45
B273	SP79	155c +65c multi	1.75	1.75

Parents' and Friends Association of Persons with a Mental Handicap (Totolika).

SP80

SP81

1990, June 13 Litho. *Perf. 13x14*

B274	SP80	65c +30c multi	90	90

Sport Unie Brion Trappers Soccer Club. Exists in tete-beche gutter pairs.

1990, June 13

B275	SP81	115c +55c multi	1.60	1.60

Anti-drug campaign. Exists in tete-beche gutter pairs.

Youth Care Campaign SP82

1990, Oct. 31 Litho. *Perf. 14x13*

B276	SP82	30c +5c Bees, flowers	40	40
B277	SP82	55c +10c Dolphins	72	72
B278	SP82	65c +15c Donkey, bicycle	90	90
B279	SP82	100c +20c Goat, house	1.35	1.35
B280	SP82	115c +25c Rabbit	1.60	1.60
B281	SP82	155c +55c Lizard, moon	2.35	2.35
		Nos. B276-B281 (6)	7.32	7.32

Surtax for the benefit of the Antillean Youth Care Federation.

See Nos. B285-B288.

Social and Cultural Care — SP83

Designs: 30c+10c, Youth philately. 65c+25c, St. Vincentius Brass Band, 50th anniv. 155c+55c, Curacao Community Center Federation.

1991, Apr. 3 Litho. *Perf. 14x13*

B282	SP83	30c +10c multi	50	50
B283	SP83	65c +25c multi	1.10	1.10
B284	SP83	155c +55c multi	2.55	2.55

Youth Care Campaign Type of 1990

Fight illiteracy: 40c+15c, Octopus holding numbers and letters. 65c+30c, Birds, blackboard. 155c+65c, Turtle telling time. No. B288a, Owl, flag. b, Books, bookworms. c, Seahorse.

1991, Oct. 31 Litho. *Perf. 14x13*

B285	SP82	40c +15c multi	60	60
B286	SP82	65c +30c multi	1.00	1.00
B287	SP82	155c +65c multi	2.35	2.35

Souvenir Sheet

Imperf

B288		Sheet of 3	4.25	4.25
a.		SP82 55c +25c multi	90	90
b.		SP82 100c +35c multi	1.50	1.50
c.		SP82 115c +50c multi	1.85	1.85

Surtax for the benefit of the Antillean Yorth Care Federation.

SP84

SP85

1992 Summer Olympics, Barcelona: a, 30c + 10c, Triangle and oval. b, 55c + 25c, Globe showing location of Netherland Antilles, flag. c, 115c + 55c, Emblem of Netherlands Antilles Olympic Committee.

1992, Mar. 4 Litho. *Perf. 13x14*

B289	SP84	Strip of 3, #a.-c.	3.50	3.50

Netherlands Antilles Olympic Committee, 60th Anniv.

1992, Oct. 28 Litho. *Perf. 13x14*

B290	SP85	30c +10c Spaceship	48	48
B291	SP85	70c +30c Robot	1.20	1.20
B292	SP85	100c +40c Extraterrestrial	1.70	1.70

Souvenir Sheet

B293	SP85	155c +70c Extraterrestrial, diff.	2.75	2.75

Surtax for benefit of the Antillean Youth Care Federation.

AIR POST STAMPS

Regular Issues of 1915-22 Surcharged in Black

LUCHTPOST

1 gld.

Perf. 12½

1929, July 6 Typo. Unwmk.

C1 A13 50c on 12½c red 9.75 12.00
C2 A13 1g on 20c blue 9.75 12.00
C3 A13 2g on 15c ol grn 40.00 50.00

Excellent forgeries exist.

Allegory, "Flight" — AP1

1931-39 Engr.

C4 AP1 10c Prus grn ('34) 15 15
C5 AP1 15c dl bl ('38) 15 15
C6 AP1 20c red 60 15
C7 AP1 25c gray ('38) 32 28
C8 AP1 30c yellow ('39) 22 15
C9 AP1 35c dull blue 65 55
C10 AP1 40c green 48 15
C11 AP1 45c orange 1.90 2.25
C12 AP1 50c lake ('38) 32 42
C13 AP1 60c brn vio 50 28
C14 AP1 70c black 5.75 2.25
C15 AP1 1.40g brown 3.75 4.75
C16 AP1 2.80g bister 4.50 5.00
Nos. C4-C16 (13) 19.29 16.53

No. C6 Surcharged in Black **10 CT**

1934, Aug. 25

C17 AP1 10c on 20c red 18.00 17.00

Catalogue values for unused stamps in this section, from this point to the end of the section, are for Never Hinged items.

Map of the Atlantic — AP2

Plane over Islands — AP3

Map of Curaao, Aruba and Bonaire — AP4

Planes — AP5

Plane — AP6

1942, Oct. 20 *Perf. 13x13½*

C18 AP2 10c grn & bl 15 15
C19 AP3 15c rose car & yel grn 20 15
C20 AP4 20c red brn & grn 24 35
C21 AP5 25c dp ultra & org brn 15 15
C22 AP6 30c red & lt vio 30 18
C23 AP2 35c dk vio & ol grn 45 18
C24 AP3 40c gray ol & chnt 50 28
C25 AP4 45c dk red & blk 35 42
C26 AP5 50c vio & blk 85 15
C27 AP6 60c lt yel brn & dl bl 85 45
C28 AP2 70c red brn & Prus bl 1.10 45
C29 AP3 1.40g bl vio & sl grn 4.50 1.10
C30 AP4 2.80g int bl & lt bl 5.50 2.25
C31 AP5 5g rose lake & sl grn 12.00 9.50
C32 AP6 10g grn & red brn 18.00 14.00
Nos. C18-C32 (15) 45.14 29.76

For surcharges see Nos. CB9-CB12.

Plane and Post Horn — AP7

DC-4 above Waves — AP8

1947 Photo. *Perf. 12½x12*

C32A AP7 6c gray blk 15 15
C33 AP7 10c dp red 15 15
C33A AP7 12½c plum 18 15
C34 AP7 15c dp bl 18 16
C35 AP7 20c dl yel grn 25 20
C36 AP7 25c org yel 25 15
C37 AP7 30c lil gray 25 22
C38 AP7 35c org red 32 45
C39 AP7 40c bl grn 38 45
C40 AP7 45c brt vio 45 60
C41 AP7 50c carmine 38 15
C42 AP7 60c brt bl 60 45
C43 AP7 70c brown 1.25 90

Engr.

Perf. 12x12½

C44 AP8 1.50g black 90 45
C45 AP8 2.50g dk car 7.75 2.50
C46 AP8 5g green 16.00 5.50
C47 AP8 7.50g dk bl 47.50 42.50
C48 AP8 10g dk red vio 35.00 10.50
C49 AP8 15g red org 55.00 50.00
C50 AP8 25g chocolate 55.00 42.50
Nos. C32A-C50 (20) 221.94 158.13

AIR POST SEMI-POSTAL STAMPS

Flags of the Netherlands and the House of Orange with Inscription "Netherlands Shall Rise Again"
SPAP1

Engr. & Photo.

1941, Dec. 11 Unwmk. *Perf. 12*

CB1 SPAP1 10c + 10c multi 2.50 1.90
CB2 SPAP1 15c + 25c multi 12.50 8.00
CB3 SPAP1 20c + 25c multi 12.50 10.00
CB4 SPAP1 25c + 25c multi 12.50 10.00
CB5 SPAP1 30c + 50c multi 12.50 10.00
CB6 SPAP1 35c + 50c multi 12.50 10.00
CB7 SPAP1 40c + 50c multi 12.50 10.00
CB8 SPAP1 50c +100c multi 12.50 10.00
Nos. CB1-CB8 (8) 90.00 69.90

The surtax was used by the Prince Bernhard Committee to purchase war material for the Netherlands' fighting forces in Great Britain.

Catalogue values for unused stamps in this section, from this point to the end of the section, are for Never Hinged items.

Nos. C29-C32 Surcharged in Black

**Voor Krijgs-
gevangenen**

50 ct. + 75 ct

1943, Dec. 1 *Perf. 13x13½*

CB9 AP3 40c + 50c on 1.40g 4.50 3.50
CB10 AP4 45c + 50c on 2.80g 4.50 3.25
CB11 AP5 50c + 75c on 5g 4.50 3.25
CB12 AP6 60c + 100c on 10g 4.50 3.25

The surtax was for the benefit of prisoners of war. These stamps were not sold to the public in the normal manner. All were sold in sets by advance subscription, the majority to philatelic speculators.

On No. CB9 overprint reads: "Voor / Krijgsgevangenen."

Princess Juliana — SPAP2

Engr. & Photo.

1944, Aug. 16 *Perf. 12*

Frame in carmine & deep blue, cross in carmine

CB13 SPAP2 10c + 10c lt brn 1.50 1.25
CB14 SPAP2 15c + 25c turq grn 1.40 1.25
CB15 SPAP2 20c + 25c dk ol gray 1.40 1.25
CB16 SPAP2 25c + 25c slate 1.40 1.25
CB17 SPAP2 30c + 50c sepia 1.40 1.25
CB18 SPAP2 35c + 50c chnt 1.40 1.25
CB19 SPAP2 40c + 50c grn 1.40 1.25
CB20 SPAP2 50c + 100c dk vio 1.50 1.40
Nos. CB13-CB20 (8) 11.40 10.15

The surtax was for the Red Cross.

Map of Netherlands Indies
SPAP3

Map of Netherlands SPAP4

Photo. & Typo.

1946, July 1 *Perf. 11x11½*

CB21 SPAP3 10c + 10c 75 75
CB22 SPAP3 15c + 25c 85 75
CB23 SPAP3 20c + 25c 85 75
CB24 SPAP3 25c + 25c 85 75
CB25 SPAP3 30c + 50c 85 1.00
a. Double impression of denomination 325.00 325.00
CB26 SPAP3 35c + 50c 85 1.00
CB27 SPAP3 40c + 75c 85 1.10
CB28 SPAP3 50c + 100c 85 1.10
CB29 SPAP4 10c + 10c 75 75
CB30 SPAP4 15c + 25c 85 75
CB31 SPAP4 20c + 25c 85 75
CB32 SPAP4 25c + 25c 85 75
CB33 SPAP4 30c + 50c 85 1.00
CB34 SPAP4 35c + 50c 85 1.00
CB35 SPAP4 40c + 75c 85 1.10
CB36 SPAP4 50c + 100c 85 1.10
Nos. CB21-CB36 (16) 13.40 14.40

The surtax on Nos. CB21 to CB36 was for the National Relief Fund.

POSTAGE DUE STAMPS

D1

D2

Type I - 34 loops. "T" of *"BETALEN"* over center of loop, top branch of "E" of *"TE"* shorter than lower branch.

Type II - 33 loops. "T" of *"BETALEN"* over center of two loops.

Type III - 32 loops. "T" of *"BETALEN"* slightly to the left of loop, top of first "E" of *"BETALEN"* shorter than lower branch.

Value in Black

1889 Unwmk. Typo. *Perf. 12½*

Type III

J1 D1 2½c green 2.00 3.25
J2 D1 5c green 1.50 1.75
J3 D1 10c green 30.00 27.50
J4 D1 12½c green 275.00 140.00
J5 D1 15c green 20.00 18.00
J6 D1 20c green 9.00 9.00
J7 D1 25c green 140.00 90.00
J8 D1 30c green 9.00 9.00
J9 D1 40c green 9.00 9.00
J10 D1 50c green 40.00 37.50

Nos. J1-J10 were issued without gum.

Type I

J1a D1 2½c 3.00 4.00
J2a D1 5c 40.00 35.00
J3a D1 10c 35.00 35.00
J4a D1 12½c 300.00 150.00
J5a D1 15c 21.00 19.00
J6a D1 20c 55.00 55.00
J7a D1 25c 375.00 250.00
J8a D1 30c 60.00 60.00
J9a D1 40c 60.00 60.00
J10a D1 50c 45.00 40.00

Type II

J1b D1 2½c 5.00 4.75
J2b D1 5c 175.00 125.00
J3b D1 10c 40.00 37.50
J4b D1 12½c 300.00 175.00
J5b D1 15c 22.50 20.00
J6b D1 20c 300.00 300.00
J7b D1 25c *1,000.* *1,000.*
J8b D1 30c 300.00 300.00
J9b D1 40c 300.00 27.50
J10b D1 50c 47.50 47.50

Value in Black

1892-98 *Perf. 12½*

J11 D2 2½c grn (III) 22 18
J12 D2 5c grn (III) 55 42
J13 D2 10c grn (III) 90 40
J14 D2 12½c grn (III) 1.00 45
J15 D2 15c grn (III) ('95) 1.40 95
J17 D2 25c grn (III) 1.10 95

Type I

J11a D2 2½c 45 45
J12a D2 5c 1.40 1.40
J13a D2 10c 1.90 1.90
J14a D2 12½c 1.40 1.40
J16 D2 20c grn ('95) 1.75 1.10
J17a D2 25c 1.50 1.50
J18 D2 30c grn ('95) 14.00 9.25
J19 D2 40c grn ('95) 14.00 12.50
J20 D2 50c grn ('95) 17.00 12.50

Type II

J11b D2 2½c 16.00 16.00
J12b D2 5c 90 90
J13b D2 10c 1.10 1.10
J14b D2 12½c 6.75 6.75
J17b D2 25c *9.50* *9.50*

Type I
On Yellowish or White Paper
Value in Color of Stamp

1915 *Perf. 12½, 13½x12½*

J21 D2 2½c green 1.00 95
J22 D2 5c green 1.00 95
J23 D2 10c green 90 80
J24 D2 12½c green 1.25 1.10
J25 D2 15c green 1.90 2.00
J26 D2 20c green 1.00 1.75
J27 D2 25c green 35 16
J28 D2 30c green 4.25 4.00
J29 D2 40c green 4.25 4.00
J30 D2 50c green 3.50 3.50
Nos. J21-J30 (10) 19.40 19.21

1944 *Perf. 11½*

J23a D2 10c yellow green 15.00 16.00
J24a D2 12½c yellow green 13.00 9.00
J27a D2 25c yellow green 32.50 1.10

Type of 1915
Type I
Value in Color of Stamp

Perf. 13½x13

1948-49 Unwmk. Photo.

J31 D2 2½c bl grn ('48) 38 1.00
J32 D2 5c bl grn ('48) 38 1.00
J33 D2 10c bl grn 9.25 8.50
J34 D2 12½c bl grn 9.25 1.50
J35 D2 15c bl grn 15.00 15.00
J36 D2 20c bl grn 13.00 15.00
J37 D2 25c bl grn 1.10 26
J38 D2 30c bl grn 15.00 19.00
J39 D2 40c bl grn 15.00 19.00
J40 D2 50c bl grn 15.00 15.00
Nos. J31-J40 (10) 93.36 95.26

Catalogue values for unused stamps in this section, from this point to the end of the section, are for Never Hinged items.

D3

1953-59 Photo.

J41 D3 1c dk bl grn ('59) 15 15
J42 D3 2½c dk bl grn 50 45
J43 D3 5c dk bl grn 15 15
J44 D3 6c dk bl grn ('59) 45 30
J45 D3 7c dk bl grn ('59) 45 30

J46	D3	8c dk bl grn ('59)	45	30
J47	D3	9c dk bl grn ('59)	45	30
J48	D3	10c dk bl grn	22	15
J49	D3	12½c dk bl grn	22	15
J50	D3	15c dk bl grn	30	18
J51	D3	20c dk bl grn	30	30
J52	D3	25c dk bl grn	45	15
J53	D3	30c dk bl grn	1.10	90
J54	D3	35c dk bl grn ('59)	1.25	90
J55	D3	40c dk bl grn	1.10	90
J56	D3	45c dk bl grn ('59)	1.25	90
J57	D3	50c dk bl grn	1.10	65
		Nos. J41-J57 (17)	9.89	7.13

NETHERLANDS INDIES

(Dutch Indies, Indonesia)

LOCATION — East Indies
GOVT. — Former Dutch colony
AREA — 735,268 sq. mi.
POP. — 76,000,000 (estimated 1949)
CAPITAL — Jakarta (formerly Batavia)

Netherlands Indies consisted of the islands of Sumatra, Java, the Lesser Sundas, Madura, two thirds of Borneo, Celebes, the Moluccas, western New Guinea and many small islands.

Netherlands Indies changed its name to Indonesia in 1948. Holland transferred sovereignty on Dec. 28, 1949, to the Republic of the United States of Indonesia (see "Indonesia"), except for the western part of New Guinea (see "Netherlands New Guinea"). The Republic of Indonesia was proclaimed Aug. 15, 1950.

100 Cents = 1 Gulden
100 Sen = 1 Rupiah (1949)

Catalogue values for unused stamps in this country are for Never Hinged items, beginning with Scott 250 in the regular postage section, Scott B57 in the semi-postal section, and Scott J43 in the postage due section.

Watermarks

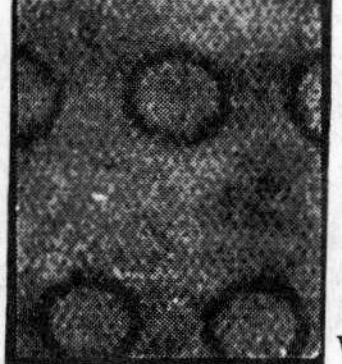

Wmk. 202- Circles

Wmk. 228- Small Crown and C of A Multiple

King William III
A1 A2

1864, Apr. 1 Unwmk. Engr. ***Imperf.***

1	A1	10c lake	165.00	75.00

1868 ***Perf. 12½x12***

2	A1	10c lake	600.00	115.00

Privately perforated examples of No. 1 sometimes are mistaken for No. 2.

Perf. 11½x12, 12½, 12½x12, 13x14, 13½, 14, 13½x14

1870-88 **Typo.**

ONE CENT:
Type I - "CENT" 6mm long.
Type II - "CENT" 7½mm long.

3	A2	1c sl grn, type I	5.25	4.25
4	A2	1c sl grn, type II	2.00	1.25
5	A2	2c red brn	4.75	2.75
a.		2c fawn	4.75	3.25
6	A2	2c vio brn	90.00	75.00
7	A2	2½c orange	27.50	19.00
8	A2	5c pale grn	47.50	3.00
a.		Perf. 14, small holes	45.00	3.25
b.		Perf. 13x14, small holes	40.00	4.25
9	A2	10c org brn	11.00	15
a.		Perf. 14, small holes	20.00	55
b.		Perf. 13x14, small holes	27.50	75
10	A2	12½c gray	2.25	95
a.		Perf. 12½x12		725.00
11	A2	15c bister	15.00	70
a.		Perf. 13x14, small holes	22.50	1.50
12	A2	20c ultra	85.00	1.70
a.		Perf. 14, small holes	85.00	1.75
b.		Perf. 13x14, small holes	85.00	1.90
13	A2	25c dk vio	14.00	55
b.		Perf. 13x14, small holes	20.00	1.50
c.		Perf. 14, large holes	325.00	72.50
14	A2	30c green	24.00	2.25
15	A2	50c carmine	13.00	65
a.		Perf. 14, small holes	16.00	65
b.		Perf. 13x14, small holes	13.00	85
c.		Perf. 14, large holes	18.00	1.25
16	A2	2.50g grn & vio	72.50	11.00
b.		Perf. 14, small holes	72.50	11.00
c.		Perf. 14, large holes	72.50	11.00

Imperforate examples of Nos. 3-16 are proofs. The 1c red brown and 2c yellow are believed to be bogus.

"Small hole" varieties have the spaces between the holes wider than the diameter of the holes.

Numeral of Value
A3

Queen Wilhelmina
A4

1883-90 ***Perf. 12½***

17	A3	1c slate grn ('88)	55	15
a.		Perf. 12½x12	1.10	65
18	A3	2c brown ('84)	55	15
a.		Perf. 12½x12	75	30
b.		Perf. 11½x12	65.00	22.50
19	A3	2½c yellow	65	65
a.		Perf. 12½x12	1.25	75
b.		Perf. 11½x12	12.00	4.75
20	A3	3c lilac ('90)	75	15
21	A3	5c green ('87)	24.00	15.00
22	A3	5c ultra ('90)	8.00	15

For surcharges and overprintsee Nos. 46-47, O4.

1892-97 ***Perf. 12½***

23	A4	10c org brn	3.75	15
24	A4	12½c gray	6.75	12.50
25	A4	15c bister	11.00	70
26	A4	20c ultra	27.50	80
27	A4	25c violet	27.50	1.10
28	A4	30c green	35.00	1.50
29	A4	50c carmine	25.00	60
30	A4	2.50g org brn & ultra	110.00	27.50

For overprints see Nos. O21-O27.

Queen Wilhelmina — A5

Stamps of Netherlands, 1898-99 Surcharged in Black

1900, July 1

31	A5	10c on 10c gray lil	1.25	15
32	A5	12½c on 12½c blue	1.90	55
33	A5	15c on 15c yel brn	2.25	18
34	A5	20c on 20c yel grn	13.00	45
35	A5	25c on 25c car & bl	13.00	55
36	A5	50c on 50c brnz grn & red brn	22.50	75

Netherlands No. 84, Surcharged in Black

Perf. 11½x11

37	A12	2.50g on 2½g brn lil	42.50	7.50
a.		Perf. 11	47.50	8.25
		Nos. 31-37 (7)	96.40	10.13

A6

1902-09 ***Perf. 12½***

38	A6	½c violet	30	15
39	A6	1c ol grn	30	15
a.		Booklet pane of 6		
40	A6	2c yel brn	2.25	18
41	A6	2½c green	1.50	15
a.		Booklet pane of 6		
42	A6	3c orange	1.50	1.10
43	A6	4c ultra ('09)	9.25	8.75
44	A6	5c rose red	4.00	15
a.		Booklet pane of 6		
45	A6	7½c gray ('09)	2.00	28
		Nos. 38-45 (8)	21.10	10.91

For overprints see Nos. 63-69, 81-87, O1-O9.

Nos. 18, 20 Surcharged

1902

46	A3	½c on 2c yel brn	20	20
a.		Double surcharge	175.00	150.00
47	A3	2½c on 3c vio	25	25

Queen Wilhelmina
A9 A10

1902-08

48	A9	10c slate	85	15
a.		Booklet pane of 6		
49	A9	12½c dp bl	1.40	15
a.		Booklet pane of 6		
50	A9	15c chocolate	7.25	2.00
a.		Ovptd. with 2 horiz. bars	1.50	75
51	A9	17½c bister ('08)	2.50	15
52	A9	20c grnsh slate	1.50	1.75
53	A9	20c ol grn	20.00	15
54	A9	22½c brn & ol grn ('08)	3.75	15
55	A9	25c violet	7.75	15
56	A9	30c org brn	25.00	15
57	A9	50c red brn	17.50	15
		Nos. 48-57 (10)	87.50	4.95

For overprints and surcharges see Nos. 58, 70-78, 88-96, 139, O10-O18.

No. 52 Surcharged in Black

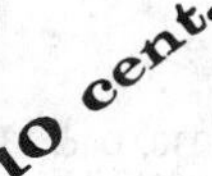

1905, July 6

58	A9	10c on 20c grnsh slate	1.90	1.25

1905-12 Engr. ***Perf. 11x11½***

59	A10	1g dl lil ('05)	42.50	20
a.		Perf. 11½x11	42.50	35
b.		Perf. 11	52.50	3.50
60	A10	1g dl lil, *bl* ('12)	45.00	6.50
a.		Perf. 11	55.00	57.50
61	A10	2½g slate bl ('05)	52.50	1.50
a.		Perf. 11½	52.50	1.65
b.		Perf. 11½x11	60.00	1.65
c.		Perf. 11	675.00	
62	A10	2½g sl bl, *bl* ('12)	65.00	32.50
a.		Perf. 11	75.00	75.00

Sheets of Nos. 60 & 62 were soaked in an indigo solution.

For overprints and surcharge see Nos. 79-80, 97-98, 140, O19-O20.

Previous Issues Overprinted BUITEN BEZIT.

1908, July 1

63	A6	½c violet	20	18
64	A6	1c ol grn	30	18
65	A6	2c yel brn	1.40	2.00
66	A6	2½c green	60	18
67	A6	3c orange	50	95
68	A6	5c rose red	2.00	38
69	A6	7½c gray	2.25	2.25
70	A9	10c slate	50	15
71	A9	12½c dp blue	8.25	2.00
72	A9	15c choc (#50a)	3.75	1.90
73	A9	17½c bister	1.40	95
74	A9	20c ol grn	7.00	1.25
75	A9	22½c brn & ol grn	5.75	3.50
76	A9	25c violet	4.50	28
77	A9	30c org brn	16.00	1.90
78	A9	50c red brn	7.00	60
79	A10	1g dl lil	52.50	3.50
80	A10	2½g slate blue	80.00	57.50
		Nos. 63-80 (18)	193.90	79.65

The above stamps were overprinted for use in the territory outside of Java and Madura, stamps overprinted "Java" being used in these latter places.

The 15c is overprinted, in addition, with two horizontal lines, 2½mm apart.

Overprint Reading Down

63a	A6	½c	50	*3.25*
64a	A6	1c	42	*2.25*
65a	A6	2c	2.00	*4.25*
66a	A6	2½c	85	*2.75*
67a	A6	3c	14.00	*37.50*
68a	A6	5c	1.00	*2.50*
70a	A9	10c	50	*1.90*
71a	A9	12½c	4.50	*8.00*
72a	A9	15c	22.50	*57.50*
74a	A9	20c	4.25	8.00
75a	A9	22½c	*1,300*	*1,300.*
76a	A9	25c	4.25	6.50
77a	A9	30c	11.00	15.00
78a	A9	50c	7.50	9.00
79a	A10	1g	175.00	200.00
80a	A10	2½g	*1,900.*	*2,400.*

Overprinted **JAVA.**

1908, July 1

81	A6	½c violet	15	18
a.		Inverted overprint	48	*2.25*
b.		Double overprint	350.00	
82	A6	1c ol grn	16	16
a.		Inverted overprint	38	*2.75*
83	A6	2c yel brn	1.50	1.50
a.		Inverted overprint	1.40	*6.00*
84	A6	2½c green	75	15
a.		Inverted overprint	1.90	*3.25*
85	A6	3c orange	55	75
a.		Inverted overprint	16.00	22.50
86	A6	5c rose red	2.00	15
a.		Inverted overprint	1.40	2.50
87	A6	7½c gray	1.90	1.65
88	A9	10c slate	45	15
a.		Inverted overprint	45	*2.00*
89	A9	12½c dp bl	2.75	55
a.		Inverted overprint	2.75	5.00
b.		Dbl. ovpt., one inverted	95.00	95.00
90	A9	15c choc (on No. 50a)	3.00	2.25
a.		Inverted overprint	2.75	*9.00*
91	A9	17½c bister	1.50	60
92	A9	20c ol grn	8.50	55
a.		Inverted overprint	8.25	10.00
93	A9	22½c brn & ol grn	4.00	2.00
94	A9	25c violet	3.50	18
a.		Inverted overprint	4.50	*9.00*
95	A9	30c org brn	24.00	2.00
a.		Inverted overprint	18.00	26.00
96	A9	50c red brn	15.00	55
a.		Inverted overprint	12.00	19.00
97	A10	1g dl lil	37.50	2.25
a.		Inverted overprint	150.00	150.00
b.		Perf. 11	47.50	4.00
98	A10	2½g slate blue	57.50	40.00
a.		Inverted overprint	*1,900.*	*2,400.*
		Nos. 81-98 (18)	164.71	55.62

A11

Queen Wilhelmina
A12 A13

Typo., Litho. (#114A)

1912-40 *Perf. 12½*

No.	Type	Description	Unused	Used
101	A11	½c lt vio	15	15
102	A11	1c ol grn	15	15
103	A11	2c yel brn	30	15
104	A11	2c gray blk ('30)	32	15
105	A11	2½c green	1.25	15
106	A11	2½c lt red ('22)	22	15
107	A11	3c yellow	32	15
108	A11	3c grn ('29)	60	15
109	A11	4c ultra	55	25
110	A11	4c dp grn ('28)	1.25	20
111	A11	4c yel ('30)	8.50	4.00
112	A11	5c rose	75	15
113	A11	5c grn ('22)	90	15
114	A11	5c chlky bl ('28)	38	15
114A	A11	5c ultra ('40)	80	15
115	A11	7½c bister	35	15
116	A11	10c lil ('22)	95	15
117	A12	10c car rose ('14)	55	15
118	A12	12½c dl bl ('14)	85	15
119	A12	12½c red ('22)	85	15
120	A12	15c bl ('29)	7.50	15
121	A12	17½c red brn ('15)	85	15
122	A12	20c grn ('15)	1.40	15
123	A12	20c blue ('22)	1.40	15
124	A12	20c org ('32)	13.00	15
125	A12	22½c org ('15)	1.40	45
126	A12	25c red vio ('15)	1.40	15
127	A12	30c slate ('15)	1.65	15
128	A12	32½c vio & red ('22)	1.65	15
129	A12	35c org brn ('29)	8.50	52
130	A12	40c grn ('22)	1.65	15

Perf. 11½

Engr.

No.	Type	Description	Unused	Used
131	A13	50c grn ('13)	2.75	15
a.		Perf. 11x11½	3.50	15
b.		Perf. 12½	4.25	22
132	A13	60c dp bl ('22)	3.50	15
133	A13	80c org ('22)	3.75	15
134	A13	1g brn ('13)	2.75	15
a.		Perf. 11x11½	3.50	15
135	A13	1.75g dk vio, p. 12½ ('31)	14.00	1.90
136	A13	2½g car ('13)	11.00	38
a.		Perf. 11x11½	13.00	60
b.		Perf. 12½	14.00	48
		Nos. 101-136 (37)	98.14	12.20

For surcharges and overprints see Nos. 137-138, 144-150, 102a-123a, 158, 194-195, B1-B3, C1-C5.

Water Soluble Ink

Some values of types A11 and A12 and late printings of types A6 and A9 are in soluble ink and the design disappears when immersed in water.

Nos. 105, 109, 54, 59 Surcharged

½ 1 17½

30 CENT

1917-18 **Typo.** *Perf. 12½*

No.	Type	Description	Unused	Used
137	A11	½c on 2½c	22	18
138	A11	1c on 4c ('18)	55	45
139	A9	17½c on 22½c ('18)	90	38
a.		Inverted surcharge	350.00	425.00

Perf. 11x11½

No.	Type	Description	Unused	Used
140	A10	30c on 1g ('18)	7.00	1.40
a.		Perf. 11½x11	110.00	42.50

Nos. 121, 125, 131, 134 Surcharged in Red or Blue

12½ CENT
On A12

40 CENT
On A13

Two types of 32½c on 50c:
I- Surcharge bars spaced as in illustration.
II- Bars more closely spaced.

1922, Jan. *Perf. 12½*

No.	Type	Description	Unused	Used
144	A12	12½c on 17½c (R)	28	15
145	A12	12½c on 22½c (R)	38	15
146	A12	20c on 22½c (Bl)	38	15

Perf. 11½, 11x11½

No.	Type	Description	Unused	Used
147	A13	32½c on 50c (Bl) (I, perf. 11½)	1.25	15
a.		Type II, perf. 11½	10.00	15
b.		Type I, perf. 11x11½	275.00	7.00
c.		Type II, perf. 11x11½	22.50	1.25
148	A13	40c on 50c (R)	3.75	45
149	A13	60c on 1g (Bl)	6.00	38
150	A13	80c on 1g (R)	6.75	80
		Nos. 144-150 (7)	18.79	2.23

Stamps of 1912-22 Overprinted in Red, Blue, Green or Black

3de N.I. JAARBEURS BANDOENG 1922
a

3de N. I. JAARBEURS
BANDOENG 1922
b

1922, Sept. 18 **Typo.** *Perf. 12½*

No.	Type	Description	Unused	Used
102a	A11(a)	1c ol grn (R)	5.75	4.75
103a	A11(a)	2c yel brn (Bl)	5.75	4.75
106a	A11(a)	2½c lt red (G)	47.50	52.50
107a	A11(a)	3c yel (R)	5.75	5.75
109a	A11(a)	4c ultra (R)	32.50	30.00
113a	A11(a)	5c grn (R)	11.00	8.25
115a	A11(a)	7½c db (Bl)	7.50	4.75
116a	A11(a)	10c lil (Bk)	57.50	67.50
145a	A12(b)	12½c on 22½c org (Bl)	5.75	5.75
121a	A12(b)	17½c red brn (Bk)	3.75	4.75
123a	A12(b)	20c bl (Bk)	5.75	4.75
		Nos. 102a-123a (11)	188.50	193.50

Issued to publicize the 3rd Netherlands Indies Industrial Fair at Bandoeng, Java. On No. 145a the overprint is vertical.

Nos. 102a-123a were sold at a premium for 3, 4, 5, 6, 8, 9, 10, 12½, 15, 20 and 22½ cents respectively.

Queen Wilhelmina
A15

Prince William I, Portrait by Van Key
A16

1923, Aug. 31 **Engr.** *Perf. 11½*

No.	Type	Description	Unused	Used
151	A15	5c myr grn	15	15
a.		Perf. 11½x11	350.00	110.00
b.		Perf. 11x11½	4.50	55
152	A15	12½c rose	18	15
a.		Perf. 11x11½	1.25	18
b.		Perf. 11½x11	1.75	25
153	A15	20c dk bl	35	15
a.		Perf. 11½x11	3.25	40
154	A15	50c red org	1.40	60
a.		Perf. 11x11½	6.50	1.25
b.		Perf. 11½x11	2.00	90
c.		Perf. 11	4.50	85
155	A15	1g brn vio	2.75	38
a.		Perf. 11½x11	7.50	80
156	A15	2½g gray blk	22.50	8.75
157	A15	5g org brn	90.00	87.50
		Nos. 151-157 (7)	117.33	97.68

25th anniversary of the assumption of the government of the Netherlands by Queen Wilhelmina, at the age of 18.

No. 123 Surcharged

12½

1930, Dec. 13 **Typo.** *Perf. 12½*

No.	Type	Description	Unused	Used
158	A12	12½c on 20c bl (R)	32	15
a.		Inverted surcharge	375.00	475.00

1933, Apr. 18 **Photo.**

No.	Type	Description	Unused	Used
163	A16	12½c dp org	1.25	18

400th anniv. of the birth of Prince William I, Count of Nassau and Prince of Orange, frequently referred to as William the Silent.

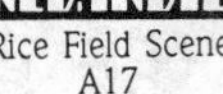

Rice Field Scene
A17

Queen Wilhelmina
A18

Queen Wilhelmina — A19

1933-37 **Unwmk.** *Perf. 12x12½*

No.	Type	Description	Unused	Used
164	A17	1c lil gray ('34)	20	15
165	A17	2c plum ('34)	20	15
166	A17	2½c bister ('34)	20	15
167	A17	3c yel grn ('34)	20	15
168	A17	3½c dk gray ('37)	15	15
169	A17	4c dk ol ('34)	85	15
170	A17	5c ultra ('34)	15	15
171	A17	7½c vio ('34)	1.25	15
172	A17	10c ver ('34)	1.75	15
173	A18	10c ver ('37)	25	15
174	A18	12½c dp org ('34)	25	15
a.		12½c lt org, perf. 12½	6.25	35
175	A18	15c ultra ('34)	25	15
176	A18	20c plum ('34)	38	15
177	A18	25c bl grn ('34)	1.75	15
178	A18	30c lil gray ('34)	2.75	15
179	A18	32½c bis ('34)	7.50	6.50
180	A18	35c vio ('34)	4.25	95
181	A18	40c yel grn ('34)	2.50	15
182	A18	42½c yel ('34)	2.50	18

1934, Jan 16 *Perf. 12½*

No.	Type	Description	Unused	Used
183	A19	50c lilac gray	3.25	18
184	A19	60c ultra	4.00	45
185	A19	80c vermilion	4.00	55
186	A19	1g violet	6.25	38
187	A19	1.75g yel grn	16.00	11.00
188	A19	2.50g plum	19.00	1.25
		Nos. 164-188 (25)	79.83	23.84

See Nos. 200-225. For overprints and surcharges see Nos. 271-276, B48, B57.

Water Soluble Ink

Nos. 164-188 and the first printing of No. 163 have soluble ink and the design disappears when immersed in water.

Nos. C6-C7, C14, C9-C10 Surcharged in Black:

1934 **Typo.** *Perf. 12½x11½, 12½*

No.	Type	Description	Unused	Used
189	AP1(a)	2c on 10c	28	45
190	AP1(a)	2c on 20c	18	18
191	AP3(b)	2c on 30c	38	60
192	AP1(a)	42½c on 75c	4.25	28
193	AP1(a)	42½c on 1.50g	4.25	38
		Nos. 189-193 (5)	9.34	1.89

Nos. 127-128 Surcharged with New Value in Red or Black

1937, Sept. *Perf. 12½*

No.	Type	Description	Unused	Used
194	A12	10c on 30c (R)	2.50	25
a.		Double surcharge	*675.00*	
195	A12	10c on 32½c (Bk)	2.75	28

Wilhelmina — A20

Perf. 12½x12

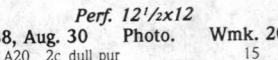

1938, Aug. 30 **Photo.** **Wmk. 202**

No.	Type	Description	Unused	Used
196	A20	2c dull pur	15	15
197	A20	10c car lake	15	15
198	A20	15c royal blue	1.25	75
199	A20	20c red orange	48	28

40th anniv. of the reign of Queen Wilhelmina.

Types of 1933-37

1938-40 **Photo.** *Perf. 12½x12*

No.	Type	Description	Unused	Used
200	A17	1c lil gray ('39)	28	*80*
201	A17	2c plum ('39)	15	15
202	A17	2½c bister ('39)	48	48
203	A17	3c yel grn ('39)	1.50	1.25
205	A17	4c gray ol ('39)	1.50	1.25
206	A17	5c ultra ('39)	15	15
a.		Perf. 12x12½	1.25	15
207	A17	7½c vio ('39)	2.50	1.00
208	A18	10c ver ('39)	15	15
210	A18	15c ultra ('39)	15	15
211	A18	20c plum ('39)	18	15
a.		Perf. 12x12½	1.25	18
212	A18	25c bl grn ('39)	25.00	24.00
213	A18	30c lil gray ('39)	6.50	80
215	A18	35c vio ('39)	2.75	65
216	A18	40c dp yel grn ('40)	5.00	20

Perf. 12½

No.	Type	Description	Unused	Used
218	A19	50c lil gray ('40)	275.00	
219	A19	60c ultra ('39)	10.50	1.25
220	A19	80c ver ('39)	62.50	26.00
221	A19	1g vio ('39)	27.50	85
223	A19	2g Prus grn	27.50	14.00
225	A19	5g yel brn	25.00	6.00
		Nos. 200-216,219-225 (19)	199.29	79.28

The note following No. 188 applies also to this issue.

The 50c was sold only at the philatelic window in Amsterdam.

War Dance of Nias Island — A23

Legong Dancer of Bali — A24

Wayang Wong Dancer of Java — A25

Padjogé Dancer, Southern Celebes — A26

Dyak Dancer of Borneo — A27

1941 **Unwmk.** *Perf. 12½*

No.	Type	Description	Unused	Used
228	A23	2½c rose vio	15	20
229	A24	3c green	16	48
230	A25	4c ol grn	15	45
231	A26	5c blue	15	15
232	A27	7½c dk vio	50	15
		Nos. 228-232 (5)	1.11	1.43

See Nos. 279-280, 293, N38.

Imperfs. are printers waste.

Queen Wilhelmina
A28 A28a

1941 *Perf. 12½*

Size: 18x22¾mm

No.	Type	Description	Unused	Used
234	A28	10c red org	15	15
235	A28	15c ultra	1.50	1.25
236	A28	17½c orange	40	60
237	A28	20c plum	21.00	35.00
238	A28	25c Prus grn	30.00	47.50
239	A28	30c ol bis	1.90	1.10

No.	Type	Description	Unused	Used
240	A28	35c pur	95.00	325.00
241	A28	40c yel grn	8.00	2.50

Perf. 13½

Size: 20½x26mm

No.	Type	Description	Unused	Used
242	A28	50c car lake	2.00	68
243	A28	60c ultra	1.65	58
244	A28	80c red org	1.90	95
245	A28	1g purple	2.00	28
246	A28	2g Prus grn	10.00	1.10
247	A28	5g bis, perf. 12½	250.00	675.00
248	A28	10g green	30.00	15.00

Size: 26x32mm

No.	Type	Description	Unused	Used
249	A28a	25g orange	175.00	125.00
		Nos. 234-249 (16)	630.50	1,231.

Nos. 242-246 come with pin-perf. 13½.

For overprints and surcharge see Nos. 276-278, J43-J46.

Catalogue values for unused stamps in this section, from this point to the end of the section, are for Never Hinged items.

Rice Fields — A29

Barge on Java Lake — A30

University of Medicine, Batavia — A31

Palms on Shore — A32

Plane over Bromo Volcano — A33

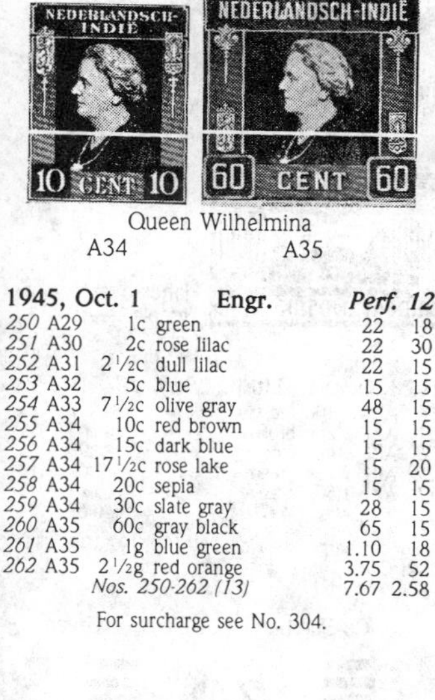

Queen Wilhelmina
A34 A35

1945, Oct. 1 **Engr.** *Perf. 12*

No.	Type	Description	Unused	Used
250	A29	1c green	22	18
251	A30	2c rose lilac	22	30
252	A31	2½c dull lilac	22	15
253	A32	5c blue	15	15
254	A33	7½c olive gray	48	15
255	A34	10c red brown	15	15
256	A34	15c dark blue	15	15
257	A34	17½c rose lake	15	20
258	A34	20c sepia	15	15
259	A34	30c slate gray	28	15
260	A35	60c gray black	65	15
261	A35	1g blue green	1.10	18
262	A35	2½g red orange	3.75	52
		Nos. 250-262 (13)	7.67	2.58

For surcharge see No. 304.

Railway Viaduct Near Soekaboemi — A36

Dam and Power Station — A37

Palm Tree and Menangkabau House — A38

Huts on Piles — A39

Buddhist Stupas — A40

Perf. 14½x14

1946 **Typo.** **Wmk. 228**

No.	Type	Description	Unused	Used
263	A36	1c dk grn	15	15
264	A37	2c blk brn	15	15
265	A38	2½c scarlet	18	15
266	A39	5c indigo	15	15
267	A40	7½c ultra	18	15
		Set value	65	52

Nos. 265, 267, 263 Surcharged

1947, Sept. 25

No.	Type	Description	Unused	Used
268	A38	3c on 2½c scar	15	15
269	A40	3c on 7½c ultra	15	15
a.		Double surcharge	150.00	150.00
270	A36	4c on 1c dk grn	15	18
		Set value		32

No. 219 Surcharged with New Value and Bars in Red

1947, Sept. 25 **Wmk. 202** *Perf. 12½*

No.	Type	Description	Unused	Used
271	A19	45c on 60c ultra	1.25	1.25

Nos. 212, 218 and 220 Overprinted "1947" in Red or Black

1947, Sept. 25 *Perf. 12½x12, 12½*

No.	Type	Description	Unused	Used
272	A18	25c bl grn (R)	18	15
a.		Unwmkd.		125.00
273	A19	50c lil gray (R)	75	25
274	A19	80c vermilion	1.10	75
a.		Unwmkd.	500.00	140.00

Bar above "1947" on No. 274.

Nos. 174, 241, 247 and Type of 1941 Overprinted "1947" in Black

Perf. 12½, 12½x12 (2g)

1947, Sept. 25 **Unwmk.**

No.	Type	Description	Unused	Used
275	A18	12½c dp org	15	15
276	A28	40c yel grn	38	15
277	A28	2g Prus grn	3.75	50
278	A28	5g bister	11.00	7.50

The overprint is vertical on #276-278.

Dancer Types of 1941, 1945

1948, May 13 **Litho.** *Perf. 12½*

No.	Type	Description	Unused	Used
279	OS21	3c rose red	15	15
280	A24	4c dl ol grn	15	15
		Set value	24	24

Queen Wilhelmina — A41

1948 **Photo.** *Perf. 12½*

Size: 18x22mm

No.	Type	Description	Unused	Used
281	A41	15c red org	60	80
282	A41	20c brt bl	15	15
283	A41	25c dk grn	18	15
284	A41	40c dp yel grn	18	15
285	A41	45c plum	38	60
286	A41	50c red brn	22	15
287	A41	80c brt red	30	15

Perf. 13

Size: 20½x26mm

No.	Type	Description	Unused	Used
288	A41	1g dp vio	22	15
a.		Perf. 12½ x 12	75	38
289	A41	10g green	30.00	8.25
290	A41	25g orange	62.50	45.00
		Nos. 281-290 (10)	94.73	55.55

See Nos. 201-202. For overprints see Nos. 294-303.

Wilhelmina Type of 1948 Inscribed: "1898 1948"

1948, Aug. 31 *Perf. 12½x12*

Size: 21x26½mm

No.	Type	Description	Unused	Used
291	A41	15c orange	28	20
292	A41	20c ultra	28	16

Reign of Queen Wilhelmina, 50th anniv.

Dancer Type of 1941

1948, Sept. **Photo.** *Perf. 12½*

No.	Type	Description	Unused	Used
293	A27	7½c olive bister	70	80

Juliana Type of Netherlands 1948

Perf. 14½x13½

1948, Sept. 25 **Wmk. 202**

No.	Type	Description	Unused	Used
293A	A75	15c red org	30	20
293B	A75	20c dp ultra	30	16

Investiture of Queen Juliana, Sept. 6, 1948.

Indonesia

Nos. 281 to 287 Overprinted in Black

INDONESIA

Two types of overprint:
I- Shiny ink, bar 1.8mm wide. By G. C. T. van Dorp & Co.
II- Dull ink, bar 2.2mm. By G. Kolff & Co.

1948 *Perf. 12½*

No.	Type	Description	Unused	Used
294	A41	15c red orange (I)	60	15
a.		Type II	55	15
295	A41	20c bright bl (I)	16	15
a.		Type II	16	15
296	A41	25c dark grn (I)	22	15
a.		Type II	15	15
297	A41	40c dp yel grn (I)	22	15
298	A41	45c plum ('49) (II)	80	70
299	A41	50c red brn ('49) (II)	18	15
300	A41	80c bright red (I)	65	15
a.		Type II	65	15

Nos. 288-290 Overprinted in Black

INDONESIA

Two or Three Bars
Perf. 12½x12

No.	Type	Description	Unused	Used
301	A41	1g dp vio	55	15
a.		Perf. 13	95	15

Perf. 13

No.	Type	Description	Unused	Used
302	A41	10g green	50.00	6.25
303	A41	25g orange	60.00	47.50
		Nos. 294-303 (10)	113.38	55.50

Same Overprint in Black on No. 262

1949 **Engr.** *Perf. 12*

Bars 28½mm long

No.	Type	Description	Unused	Used
304	A35	2½g red orange	14.00	5.50

A42

Tjandi Puntadewa Temple Entrance, East Java — A43

Detail, Temple of the Dead, Bedjuning, Bali A44

Menangkabau House, Sumatra A45

Toradja House, Celebes — A46

Globe and Arms of Bern — A48

Designs: 5r, 10r, 25r, Temple entrance.

Perf. 12½, 11½

1949 **Unwmk.** **Photo.**

No.	Type	Description	Unused	Used
307	A42	1s gray	20	15
308	A42	2s claret	25	15
a.		Perf. 11½	5.00	14.00
309	A42	2½s ol brn	20	15
310	A42	3s rose pink	25	15
a.		Perf. 11½	1.10	75
311	A42	4s green	32	50
312	A42	5s blue	15	15
a.		Perf. 11½	1.00	20
313	A42	7½s dk grn	38	15
a.		Perf. 11½	1.00	75
314	A42	10s violet	16	15
a.		Perf. 11½		375.00
315	A42	12½s brt red	32	15
a.		Perf. 11½	4.00	4.00
316	A43	15s rose red	30	15
317	A43	20s gray blk	30	15
318	A43	25s ultra	30	15
319	A44	30s brt red	30	15
320	A44	40s gray grn	32	15
321	A44	45s claret	32	25
a.		Perf. 12½	2.75	50
322	A45	50s org brn	32	15
323	A45	60s brown	38	15
324	A45	80s scarlet	32	15
a.		Perf. 12½	4.00	25

Perf. 12½

No.	Type	Description	Unused	Used
325	A46	1r purple	22	15
326	A46	2r gray grn	2.00	15
327	A46	3r red vio	21.00	15
328	A46	5r dk brn	21.00	15
329	A46	10r gray	42.50	22
330	A46	25r org brn	22	25
		Nos. 307-330 (24)	92.03	
		Set value		3.25

The 4s, 1r-25r are perf. 12½. Others come both 12½ and 11½.

1949 *Perf. 12½*

No.	Type	Description	Unused	Used
331	A48	15s brt red	70	35
332	A48	25s ultra	70	25

75th anniv. of UPU.

See Indonesia (republic) for subsequent listings.

SEMI-POSTAL STAMPS

Regular Issue of 1912-14 Surcharged in Carmine

+

+ 5 cts

1915, June 10 **Unwmk.** *Perf. 12½*

No.	Type	Description	Unused	Used
B1	A11	1c + 5c ol grn	3.25	3.25
B2	A11	5c + 5c rose	4.00	4.00
B3	A12	10c + 5c rose	6.25	6.25

Surtax for the Red Cross.

Buying Sets
Frequently it is less expensive to purchase complete sets rather than the individual stamps that make up the set. "Set Values" are provided for many such sets.

Bali Temple
SP1

Watchtower
SP2

Menangkabau Compound
SP3

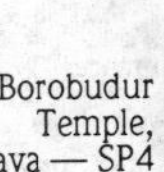

Borobudur Temple, Java — SP4

Perf. 11½x11, 11x11½

1930, Dec. 1 **Photo.**

No.	Type	Description	Unused	Used
B4	SP1	2c (+ 1c) vio & brn	80	75
B5	SP2	5c (+ 2½c) dk grn & brn	3.25	2.25
B6	SP3	12½c (+ 2½c) dp red & brn	2.25	45
B7	SP4	15c (+ 5c) ultra & brn	4.25	5.00

Surtax for youth care.

Farmer and Carabao — SP5

Designs: 5c, Fishermen. 12½c, Dancers. 15c, Musicians.

1931, Dec. 1 **Engr.** ***Perf. 12½***

No.	Type	Description	Unused	Used
B8	SP5	2c (+ 1c) olive bis	2.00	1.65
B9	SP5	5c (+ 2½c) bl grn	3.25	3.00
B10	SP5	12½c (+ 2½c) dp red	2.00	45
B11	SP5	15c (+ 5c) dl bl	8.00	6.75

The surtax was for the aid of the Leper Colony at Salatiga.

Weaving — SP9

Designs: 5c, Plaiting rattan. 12½c, Woman batik dyer. 15c, Coppersmith.

1932, Dec. 1 **Photo.** ***Perf. 12½***

No.	Type	Description	Unused	Used
B12	SP9	2c (+ 1c) dp vio & bis	40	38
B13	SP9	5c (+ 2½c) dp grn & bis	2.50	2.00
B14	SP9	12½c (+ 2½c) brt rose & bis	80	28
B15	SP9	15c (+ 5c) bl & bis	3.25	3.00

The surtax was donated to the Salvation Army.

Woman and Lotus — SP13

Designs: 5c, "The Light that Shows the Way." 12½c, YMCA emblem. 15c, Jobless man.

1933, Dec. 1 ***Perf. 12½***

No.	Type	Description	Unused	Used
B16	SP13	2c (+ 1c) red vio & ol bis	65	28
B17	SP13	5c (+ 2½c) grn & ol bis	2.25	1.90
B18	SP13	12½c (+ 2½c) ver & ol bis	2.50	28
B19	SP13	15c (+ 5c) bl & ol bis	2.75	2.00

The surtax was for the Amsterdam Young Men's Society for Relief of the Poor in Netherlands Indies.

Dowager Queen Emma — SP17

A Pioneer at Work — SP18

1934, Sept. 20 ***Perf. 13x14***

No.	Type	Description	Unused	Used
B20	SP17	12½c (+ 2½c) blk brn	1.25	45

Issued in memory of the late Dowager Queen Emma of Netherlands. The surtax was for the Anti-Tuberculosis Society.

1935 ***Perf. 12½***

Designs: 5c, Cavalryman rescuing wounded native. 12½c, Artilleryman under fire. 15c, Bugler.

No.	Type	Description	Unused	Used
B21	SP18	2c (+ 1c) plum & ol bis	1.25	1.00
B22	SP18	5c (+ 2½c) grn & ol bis	3.25	2.25
B23	SP18	12½c (+ 2½c) red org & ol bis	3.25	22
B24	SP18	15c (+ 5c) brt bl & ol bis	4.50	4.50

The surtax was for the Indian Committee of the Christian Military Association for the East and West Indies.

Child Welfare Work — SP22

Boy Scouts — SP23

1936, Dec. 1 **Size: 23x20mm**

No.	Type	Description	Unused	Used
B25	SP22	2c (+ 1c) plum	1.00	60
		Size: 30x26½mm		
B26	SP22	5c (+ 2½c) gray vio	1.25	1.10
B27	SP22	7½c (+ 2½c) dk vio	1.25	1.25
B28	SP22	12½c (+ 2½c) red org	1.25	28
B29	SP22	15c (+5c) brt bl	2.00	1.75
		Nos. B25-B29 (5)	6.75	4.98

Surtax for Salvation Army.

1937, May 1

No.	Type	Description	Unused	Used
B30	SP23	7½c + 2½c dk ol brn	1.25	1.00
B31	SP23	12½c + 2½c rose car	1.25	50

Fifth Boy Scout World Jamboree, Vogelenzang, Netherlands, July 31-Aug. 13, 1937. Surtax for Netherlands Indies Scout association.

Sifting Rice — SP24

Designs: 3½c, Mother and children. 7½c, Plowing with carabao team. 10c, Carabao team and cart. 20c, Native couple.

1937, Dec. 1

No.	Type	Description	Unused	Used
B32	SP24	2c (+ 1c) dk brn & org	1.10	80
B33	SP24	3½c (+ 1½c) gray	1.10	80
B34	SP24	7½c (+ 2½c) Prus grn & org	1.25	95
B35	SP24	10c (+ 2½c) car & org	1.25	18
B36	SP24	20c (+ 5c) brt bl	1.25	1.10
		Nos. B32-B36 (5)	5.95	3.83

Surtax for the Public Relief Fund for indigenous poor.

Modern Plane — SP28

Design: 20c, Plane nose facing left.

Perf. 12½

1938, Oct. 15 **Photo.** **Wmk. 202**

No.	Type	Description	Unused	Used
B36A	SP28	17½c (+5c) ol brn	85	85
B36B	SP28	20c (+5c) slate	85	55

10th anniversary of the Dutch East Indies Royal Air Lines. (K. N. I. L. M.)

Surtax for the Aviation Fund in the Netherlands Indies.

Nun and Child
SP29 SP30

Designs: 7½c, Nurse examining child's arm. 10c, Nurse bathing baby. 20c, Nun bandaging child's head.

1938, Dec. 1 **Wmk. 202** ***Perf. 12½***

No.	Type	Description	Unused	Used
B37	SP29	2c (+ 1c) vio	60	45
		Perf. 11½x12		
B38	SP30	3½c (+ 1½c) brt grn	1.00	90
		Perf. 12x11½		
B39	SP30	7½c (+ 2½c) cop red	80	85
B40	SP30	10c (+ 2½c) ver	90	18
B41	SP30	20c (+ 5c) brt ultra	1.00	95
		Nos. B37-B41 (5)	4.30	3.33

The surtax was for the Central Mission Bureau in Batavia.

Social Workers
SP34

Indonesian Nurse Tending Patient
SP35

European Nurse Tending Patient — SP36

Perf. 13x11½, 11½x13

1939, Dec. 1 **Photo.**

No.	Type	Description	Unused	Used
B42	SP34	2c (+ 1c) purple	22	16
B43	SP35	3½c (+ 1½c) bl grn & pale bl grn	32	22
B44	SP34	7½c (+ 2½c) cop brn	22	18
B45	SP35	10c (+ 2½c) scar & pink	1.40	80
B46	SP36	10c (+ 2½c) scar	1.40	80
B47	SP36	20c (+ 5c) dk bl	40	35
		Nos. B42-B47 (6)	3.96	2.51

No. B44 shows native social workers.

Nos. B45 and B46 were issued se-tenant vertically and horizontally. The surtax was used for the Bureau of Social Service.

No. 174 Surcharged in Brown

10+5 ct

1940, Dec. 2 **Unwmk.** ***Perf. 12x12½***

No.	Type	Description	Unused	Used
B48	A18	10c + 5c on 12½c dp org	1.10	40

SP37

SP38

Netherlands coat of arms and inscription "Netherlands Shall Rise Again"

1941, May 10 **Typo.** ***Perf. 12½***

No.	Type	Description	Unused	Used
B49	SP37	5c + 5c multi	15	15
B50	SP37	10c + 10c multi	22	15
B51	SP37	1g + 1g multi	9.00	6.75

The surtax was used to purchase fighter planes for Dutch pilots fighting with the Royal Air Force in Great Britain.

1941, Sept. 22 **Photo.**

Designs: 2c, Doctor and child, 3½c, Rice eater. 7½c, Nurse and patient. 10c, Nurse and children. 15c, Basket weaver.

No.	Type	Description	Unused	Used
B52	SP38	2c (+ 1c) yel grn	60	55
B53	SP38	3½c (+ 1½c) vio brn	4.00	3.50
B54	SP38	7½c (+ 2½c) vio	3.25	2.75
B55	SP38	10c (+ 2½c) dk red	90	18
B56	SP38	15c (+ 5c) saph	9.50	6.00
		Nos. B52-B56 (5)	18.25	12.98

The surtax was used for various charities.

Catalogue values for unused stamps in this section, from this point to the end of the section, are for Never Hinged items.

Indonesia

No. 208 Surcharged in Black

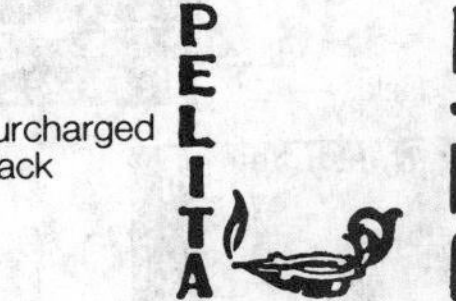

Perf. 12½x12

1948, Feb. 2 **Wmk. 202**

No.	Type	Description	Unused	Used
B57	A18	15c + 10c on 10c	15	15
a.		Inverted surcharge	210.00	210.00

The surtax was for war victims and other charitable purposes.

AIR POST STAMPS

LUCHTPOST

Regular Issues of 1913-1923 Surcharged and New Values in Black or Blue

Perf. 12½, 11½

1928, Sept. 20 **Unwmk.**

No.	Type	Description	Unused	Used
C1	A12	10c on 12½c red	90	85
C2	A12	20c on 25c red vio	1.90	1.90
C3	A13	40c on 80c org	1.50	1.10
C4	A13	75c on 1g brn (Bl)	80	35
C5	A13	1½g on 2½g car	5.25	4.25
		Nos. C1-C5 (5)	10.35	8.45

On Nos. C4 and C5 there are stars over the original values and the airplane is of different shape. On No. C3 there are no bars under "OST."

Planes over Temple — AP1

1928, Dec. 1 **Litho.** ***Perf. 12½x11½***

No.	Type	Description	Unused	Used
C6	AP1	10c red vio	22	15
C7	AP1	20c brown	65	55
C8	AP1	40c rose	90	55
C9	AP1	75c green	1.65	14
C10	AP1	1.50g orange	3.25	45
		Nos. C6-C10 (5)	6.67	1.84

For surcharges see Nos. 189-190, 192-193, C11-C12, C17.

No. C8 Surcharged in Black or Green

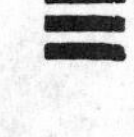

1930-32
C11 AP1 30c on 40c rose 75 15
C12 AP1 30c on 40c rose (G) ('32) 90 15

Pilot at Controls of Plane — AP2

1931, Apr. 1 Photo. *Perf. 12½*
C13 AP2 1g blue & brown 10.00 12.00

Issued for the first air mail flight from Java to Australia.

Landscape and Garudas — AP3

1931, May
C14 AP3 30c red violet 1.75 15
C15 AP3 4½g bright blue 7.25 2.75
C16 AP3 7½g yellow green 8.00 3.00

For surcharge see No. 191.

No. C10 Surcharged in Blue

1932, July 21 *Perf. 12½x11½*
C17 AP1 50c on 1.50g org 2.50 38
a. Inverted surcharge *1,400.* *1,600.*

Airplane AP4

1933, Oct. 18 Photo. *Perf. 12½*
C18 AP4 30c deep blue 1.10 1.50

MARINE INSURANCE STAMPS

Floating Safe Attracting Gulls — MI1

Floating Safe with Night Flare — MI2

Artistic Fantasy of Floating Safe — MI3

Perf. 11½
1921, Nov. 1 Unwmk. Engr.
GY1 MI1 15c slate grn 1.90 *30.00*
GY2 MI1 60c rose 3.75 *45.00*
GY3 MI1 75c gray brn 3.75 *50.00*
GY4 MI2 1.50g dk bl 22.50 *225.00*
GY5 MI2 2.25g org brn 30.00 *300.00*
GY6 MI3 4½g black 57.50 *500.00*
GY7 MI3 7½g red 67.50 *575.00*
Nos. GY1-GY7 (7) 186.90 *1,725.*

POSTAGE DUE STAMPS

Aangebragt per Land-Mail.
Te betalen port duiten.
Batavia,

D1

Aangebragt per Land-Mail.
Te betalen port *f* koper.
Batavia,

D2

1845-46 Unwmk. Typeset *Imperf.*
Bluish Paper
J1 D1 black ('46) *1,400.*
J2 D2 black *1,400.*
a. "Maill" instead of "Mail" *3,200.*

D3

Perf. 12½x12, 13x14, 10½x12
1874 Typo.
J3 D3 5c ocher 210.00 225.00
J4 D3 10c green, *yel* 95.00 75.00
J5 D3 15c ocher, *org* 18.00 12.00
a. Perf. 11½x12 35.00 30.00
J6 D3 20c green, *blue* 30.00 7.50
a. Perf. 11½x12 60.00 15.00

D4

D5

Type I - 34 loops. "T" of "Betalen" over center of loop, top branch of "E" of "Te" shorter than lower branch.

Type II - 33 loops. "T" of "Betalen" over center of two loops.

Type III - 32 loops. "T" of "Betalen" slightly to the left of loop, top branch of first "E" of "Betalen" shorter than lower branch.

Type IV - 37 loops and letters of "PORT" larger than in the other three types.

Value in Black

Perf. 11½x12, 12½, 12½x12, 13½
1882-88

Type III
J7 D4 2½c carmine 40 1.10
J8 D4 5c carmine 22 40
J9 D4 10c carmine 2.50 3.00
J10 D4 15c carmine 3.00 3.00
J11 D4 20c carmine 82.50 50
J12 D4 30c carmine 1.75 2.50
J13 D4 40c carmine 1.25 2.00
J14 D4 50c deep salmon 55 60
J15 D4 75c carmine 45 50

Type I
J7a D4 2½c carmine 42 1.10
J8a D4 5c carmine 25 45
J9a D4 10c carmine 3.25 4.00
J10a D4 15c carmine 3.25 3.50
J11a D4 20c carmine 95.00 50
J12a D4 30c carmine 3.25 4.00
J13a D4 40c carmine 1.40 2.00
J14a D4 50c deep salmon 65 60
J15a D4 75c carmine 45 60

Type II
J7b D4 2½c carmine 50 1.40
J8b D4 5c carmine 28 50
J9b D4 10c carmine 3.50 4.50
J10b D4 15c carmine 3.75 4.00
J11b D4 20c carmine 110.00 65
J12b D4 30c carmine 7.00 7.50
J13b D4 40c carmine 1.50 2.50
J14b D4 50c deep salmon 75 75
J15b D4 75c carmine 65 85

Type IV
J7c D4 2½c carmine 2.25 3.00
J8c D4 5c carmine 1.00 1.50
J9c D4 10c carmine 20.00 24.00
J10c D4 15c carmine 13.00 14.00
J11c D4 20c carmine 200.00 5.00
J13c D4 40c carmine 2.50 3.50
J14c D4 50c deep salmon 9.00 14.00
J15c D4 75c carmine 1.25 2.50

1892-95 *Perf. 12½*

Type I
J16 D5 10c carmine 1.65 30
J17 D5 15c carmine ('95) 9.50 1.75
J18 D5 20c carmine 2.00 20

Type III
J16a D5 10c dull red 2.75 1.75
J18a D5 20c dull red 3.75 1.40

Type II
J16b D5 10c dull red 13.00 13.00
J18b D5 20c dull red 18.00 6.50

1906-09

Type I
J19 D5 2½c carmine ('08) 48 30
J20 D5 5c carmine ('09) 2.00 15
J21 D5 30c carmine 17.50 5.75
J22 D5 40c carmine ('09) 12.50 1.50
J23 D5 50c carmine ('09) 8.50 90
J24 D5 75c carmine ('09) 16.00 4.00

Value in Color of Stamp

1913-39 *Perf. 12½*
J25 D5 1c salmon ('39) 15 *1.25*
J26 D5 2½c salmon 15 15
J27 D5 3½c salmon ('39) 15 *1.25*
J28 D5 5c salmon 15 15
J29 D5 7½c salmon ('22) 15 15
J30 D5 10c salmon 15 15
J31 D5 12½c salmon ('22) 2.75 15
J32 D5 15c salmon 2.75 15
J33 D5 20c salmon 16 15
J34 D5 25c salmon ('22) 18 15
J35 D5 30c salmon 20 20
J36 D5 37½c salmon ('30) 18.00 19.00
J37 D5 40c salmon 20 15
J38 D5 50c salmon 1.40 15
J39 D5 75c salmon 2.50 18
Nos. J25-J39 (15) 29.04 23.38

Thick White Paper
Invisible Gum
Numerals Slightly Larger

1941 Litho. *Perf. 12½*
J25a D5 1c light red 60 *2.00*
J28a D5 5c light red 65 1.00
J30a D5 10c light red 10.50 10.00
J32a D5 15c light red 1.00 1.00
J33a D5 20c light red 80 80
J35a D5 30c light red 1.25 1.00
J37a D5 40c light red 1.00 80
Nos. J25a-J37a (7) 15.80 16.60

No. J36 Surcharged with New Value

1937, Oct. 1 Unwmk. *Perf. 12½*
J40 D5 20c on 37½c salmon 24 30

D6

D7

1939-40
J41 D6 1g salmon 4.50 6.50
J42 D6 1g blue ('40) 20 *3.00*
a. 1g light blue, thick paper, invisible gum 65 80

Catalogue values for unused stamps in this section, from this point to the end of the section, are for Never Hinged items.

TE BETALEN

Nos. 233, 237 and 241 Surcharged or Overprinted in Black

PORT

1946, Mar. 11 Unwmk. *Perf. 12½*
J43 A28 2½c on 10c red org 60 55
J44 A28 10c red org 1.25 1.10
J45 A28 20c plum 6.25 3.50
J46 A28 40c yel grn 60.00 45.00

Perf. 14½x14
1946, Aug. 14 Wmk. 228 Typo.
J47 D7 1c purple 1.00 1.40
J48 D7 2½c brn org 3.50 2.00
J49 D7 3½c ultra 1.00 1.40
J50 D7 5c red org 1.00 1.40
J51 D7 7½c Prus grn 1.00 1.40
J52 D7 10c dp mag 1.00 1.40
J53 D7 20c lt ultra 1.00 1.40
J54 D7 25c olive 1.50 2.00
J55 D7 30c red brn 1.50 2.00
J56 D7 40c yel grn 2.25 1.50
J57 D7 50c yellow 2.25 1.50
J58 D7 75c aqua 2.25 1.50
J59 D7 100c apple green 2.25 1.50
Nos. J47-J59 (13) 21.50 20.40

1948 Unwmk. *Perf. 12½*
J59A D7 2½c brn org 75 1.50

OFFICIAL STAMPS

Regular Issues of 1883-1909 Overprinted

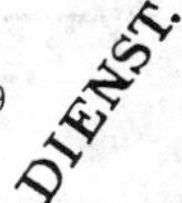

1911, Oct. 1 Unwmk. *Perf. 12½*
O1 A6 ½c violet 15 30
O2 A6 1c ol grn 15 15
O3 A6 2c yel brn 15 15
O4 A3 2½c yellow 55 55
O5 A6 2½c bl grn 1.00 1.10
O6 A6 3c orange 28 28
O7 A6 4c ultra 16 15
O8 A6 5c rose red 55 55
b. Double overprint *300.00*
O9 A6 7½c gray 2.50 2.75
O10 A9 10c slate 15 15
O11 A9 12½c dp bl 2.00 2.25
O12 A9 15c chocolate 48 48
a. Overprinted with two bars 27.50
b. As "a," "Dienst," inverted 52.50
O13 A9 17½c bister 2.50 2.25
O14 A9 20c ol grn 48 48
O15 A9 22½c brn & ol grn 3.25 2.75
O16 A9 25c violet 2.00 1.75
O17 A9 30c org brn 65 48
O18 A9 50c red brn 11.00 7.00
O19 A10 1g dull lilac 2.00 1.25
O20 A10 2½g slate blue 27.50 32.50
Nos. O1-O20 (20) 57.50

The overprint reads diagonally downward on Nos. O1-O3 and O5-O9.

Overprint Inverted
O1a A6 ½c 42.50 *130.00*
O2a A6 1c 3.00 *19.00*
O3a A6 2c 3.00 *20.00*
O5a A6 2½c 7.75 *30.00*
O6a A6 3c 115.00 *40.00*
O8a A6 5c 3.00 *20.00*
O10a A9 10c 3.00 *7.00*
O11a A9 12½c 32.50 *55.00*
O14a A9 20c 175.00 70.00
O16a A9 25c *1,250.* *850.00*
O17a A9 30c 225.00 140.00
O18a A9 50c 32.50 32.50
O19a A10 1g *525.00* *850.00*
O20a A10 2½g 225.00 *625.00*

Regular Issue of 1892-1894 Overprinted

1911, Oct. 1
O21 A4 10c org brn 1.00 60
O22 A4 12½c gray 2.25 4.50
O23 A4 15c bister 2.25 2.25
O24 A4 20c blue 1.50 80
O25 A4 25c lilac 8.00 8.00
O26 A4 50c carmine 1.00 80
O27 A4 2.50g org brn & bl 45.00 45.00
Nos. O21-O27 (7) 61.00 61.95

Inverted Overprints
O21a A4 10c 9.25 *32.50*
O22a A4 12½c 275.00 275.00
O23a A4 15c 300.00 300.00
O24a A4 20c 80.00 90.00
O25a A4 25c 425.00 425.00
O26a A4 50c 9.25 *85.00*
O27a A4 2.50g 500.00 800.00

OCCUPATION STAMPS

Issued under Japanese Occupation

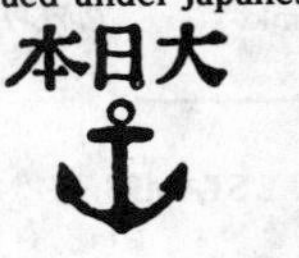

During the Japanese occupation of the Netherlands Indies, 1942-45, the occupation forces applied a great variety of overprints to supplies of Netherlands Indies stamps of 1933-42. A few typical examples are shown above.

Most of these overprinted stamps were for use in limited areas, such as Java, Sumatra, Bangka and Billiton, etc. The anchor overprints were applied by the Japanese naval authorities for areas under their control.

For a time, stamps of Straits Settlements and some of the Malayan states, with Japanese overprints, were used in Sumatra and the Riouw archipelago. Stamps of Japan without overprint were also used in the Netherlands Indies during the occupation.

For Use in Java and Sumatra

100 Sen (Cents) = 1 Rupee (Gulden)

Globe Showing Japanese Empire — OS1

Farmer Plowing Rice Field — OS2

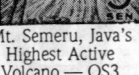

Mt. Semeru, Java's Highest Active Volcano — OS3

Bantam Bay, Northwest Java — OS4

Values in Sen

1943 Unwmk. Litho. *Perf. 12½*

N1	OS1	2s red brown	1.25	4.25
N2	OS2	3½s carmine	1.25	1.25
N3	OS3	5s green	1.25	1.25
N4	OS4	10s light blue	14.00	2.50

Issued to mark the anniversary of Japan's "Victory" in Java.

For Use in Java (also Sumatra, Borneo and Malaya)

Javanese Dancer — OS5

Javanese Puppet — OS6

Buddha Statue, Borobudur — OS7

Map of Java — OS8

Sacred Dancer of Djokja Palace, and Borobudur — OS9

Bird of Vishnu, Map of Java and Mt. Semeru — OS10

Plowing with Carabao — OS11

Terraced Rice Fields — OS12

Values in Cents, Sen or Rupees

1943-44 Unwmk. *Perf. 12½*

N5	OS5	3½c rose red	52	55
N6	OS6	5s yel grn	52	55
N7	OS7	10c dk bl	55	38
N8	OS8	20c gray olive	70	90
N9	OS9	40c rose lilac	1.75	2.25
N10	OS10	60c red org	2.50	1.10
N11	OS11	80s fawn ('44)	5.50	3.75
N12	OS12	1r vio ('44)	21.00	7.75
		Nos. N5-N12 (8)	33.04	17.23

Indies Soldier — OS13

1943

N13	OS13	3½c rose	9.00	9.25
N14	OS13	10c blue	45.00	5.75

Issued to commemorate reaching the postal savings goal of 5,000,000 gulden.

For Use in Sumatra

Batta Tribal House — OS14

Menangkabau House — OS15

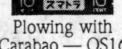

Plowing with Carabao — OS16

Nias Island Scene — OS17

Carabao Canyon — OS18

1943 Unwmk. *Perf. 12½*

N15	OS14	1c ol grn	38	28
N16	OS14	2c brt yel brn	38	28
N17	OS14	3c bluish grn	38	28
N18	OS15	3½c rose red	1.65	28
N19	OS15	4c ultra	1.90	55
N20	OS15	5c red org	52	28
N21	OS16	10c bl gray	52	28
N22	OS16	20c org brn	75	40
N23	OS17	30c red vio	75	80
N24	OS17	40c dl brn	6.75	2.50
N25	OS18	50c bis brn	6.75	2.50
N26	OS18	1r lt bl vio	35.00	10.50
		Nos. N15-N26 (12)	55.73	18.93

For Use in the Lesser Sunda Islands, Molucca Archipelago and Districts of Celebes and South Borneo Controlled by the Japanese Navy

Japanese Flag, Island Scene — OS19

Mt. Fuji, Kite, Flag, Map of East Indies — OS20

Values in Cents and Gulden

1943 Wmk. 257 Typo. *Perf. 13*

N27	OS19	2c brown	35	*15.00*
N28	OS19	3c yel grn	35	*15.00*
N29	OS19	3½c brn org	3.00	*15.00*
N30	OS19	5c blue	35	*15.00*
N31	OS19	10c carmine	35	*15.00*
N32	OS19	15c ultra	52	*15.00*
N33	OS19	20c dl vio	70	*15.00*
		Engr.		
N34	OS20	25c orange	5.00	*15.00*
N35	OS20	30c blue	7.00	*10.00*
N36	OS20	50c slate grn	8.50	*25.00*
N37	OS20	1g brn lil	42.50	*45.00*
		Nos. N27-N37 (11)	68.62	*200.00*

Issued under Nationalist Occupation

Menari Dancer of Amboina — OS21

Perf. 12½

1945, Aug. Photo. Unwmk.

N38	OS21	2c carmine	15	35

This stamp was prepared in 1941 or 1942 by Netherlands Indies authorities as an addition to the 1941 "dancers" set, but was issued in 1945 by the Nationalists (Indonesian Republic). It was not recognized by the Dutch. Exists imperforate.

NETHERLANDS NEW GUINEA

(Dutch New Guinea)

LOCATION — Western half of New Guinea, southwest Pacific Ocean
GOVT. — Former Overseas Territory of the Netherlands
AREA — 151,789 sq. mi.
POP. — 730,000 (est. 1958)
CAPITAL — Hollandia

Netherlands New Guinea came under temporary United Nations administration Oct. 1, 1962, when stamps of this territory overprinted "UNTEA" were introduced to replace issues of Netherlands New Guinea. See West New Guinea (West Irian) in Vol. 5.

100 Cents = 1 Gulden

Catalogue values for all unused stamps in this country are for Never Hinged items.

A1

Queen Juliana
A2 A3

Perf. 12½x13½

1950-52 Unwmk. Photo.

1	A1	1c slate blue	15	15
2	A1	2c deep org	15	15
3	A1	2½c olive brn	15	15
4	A1	3c deep plum	1.50	1.10
5	A1	4c blue grn	1.50	1.00
6	A1	5c ultra	3.00	15
7	A1	7½c org brown	32	15
8	A1	10c purple	1.65	15
9	A1	12½c crimson	1.65	1.25
		Perf. 13½x12½		
10	A2	15c brown org	1.10	50
11	A2	20c blue	32	15
12	A2	25c org red	32	15
13	A2	30c deep bl ('52)	3.25	24
14	A2	40c blue grn	65	15
15	A2	45c brown ('52)	3.00	50
16	A2	50c deep org	65	15
17	A2	55c brn blk ('52)	4.50	50
18	A2	80c purple	5.75	2.75
		Engr. ***Perf. 12½x12***		
19	A3	1g red	10.00	15
20	A3	2g yel brn ('52)	8.25	1.10
21	A3	5g dk ol grn	8.25	90
		Nos. 1-21 (21)	56.11	11.49

For surcharges see Nos. B1-B3.

Bird of Paradise — A4

Queen Victoria Crowned Pigeon — A5

Queen Juliana — A6

Designs: 10c, 15c and 20c, Bird of Paradise with raised wings.

Photo.; Litho. (Nos. 24, 26, 28)

1954-60 *Perf. 12½x12*

22	A4	1c ver & yel ('58)	15	15
23	A4	5c choc & yel	15	15
24	A5	7c org red, bl & brn vio ('59)	15	18
25	A4	10c aqua & red brn	15	15
26	A5	12c grn, bl & brn vio ('59)	15	18
27	A4	15c dp yel & red brn	15	15
28	A5	17c brn vio & bl ('59)	15	15
29	A4	20c lt bl grn & red brn ('56)	50	30
30	A6	25c red	15	15
31	A6	30c deep blue	15	15
32	A6	40c dp org ('60)	1.25	1.40
33	A6	45c dk olive ('58)	42	65
34	A6	55c dk blue grn	30	15
35	A6	80c dl gray vio	55	20
36	A6	85c dk vio brn ('56)	65	30
37	A6	1g plum ('59)	3.25	1.50
		Nos. 22-37 (16)	8.27	5.91

Stamps overprinted "UNTEA" are listed under West New Guinea in Vol. IV.
For surcharges see Nos. B4-B6.

Papuan Watching Helicopter — A7

Mourning Woman — A8

1959, Apr. 10 Photo. *Perf. 11½x11*

38 A7 55c red brown & blue 85 65

1959 expedition to the Star Mountains of New Guinea.

1960, Apr. 7 Unwmk. *Perf. 13x14*

39 A8 25c blue 38 38
40 A8 30c yellow bister 38 50

World Refugee Year, July 1, 1959-June 30, 1960.

Council Building A9

1961 Litho. *Perf. 11x11½*

41 A9 25c bluish green 18 25
42 A9 30c rose 18 25

Inauguration of the New Council.

School Children Crossing Street — A10

Design: 30c, Men looking at traffic sign.

1962, Mar. 16 Photo. *Perf. 14x13*

43 A10 25c dp bl & red 18 25
44 A10 30c brt grn & red 18 25

Need for road safety.

Queen Juliana and Prince Bernhard — A11

1962, Apr. 28 Unwmk. *Perf. 14x13*

45 A11 55c olive brown 25 30

Silver wedding anniv.

Tropical Beach A12

Design: 30c, Palm trees on beach.

1962, July 18 *Perf. 14x13*

46 A12 25c multi 18 28
47 A12 30c multi 18 28

5th So. Pacific Conf., Pago Pago, July 1962.

SEMI-POSTAL STAMPS

Regular Issue of 1950-52 Surcharged in Black

hulp nederland 1953 + 5 ct

Perf. 13½x12½, 12½x13½

1953, Feb. 9 Unwmk.

B1 A1 5c + 5c ultra 6.50 6.50
B2 A2 15c + 10c brn org 6.50 6.50
B3 A2 25c + 10c org red 6.50 6.50

The tax was for flood relief work in the Netherlands.

Nos. 23, 25, 27 Surcharged in Red

5

1955, Nov. 1 *Perf. 12½x12*

B4 A4 5c + 5c 90 90
B5 A4 10c + 10c 90 90
B6 A4 15c + 10c 90 90

The surtax was for the Red Cross.

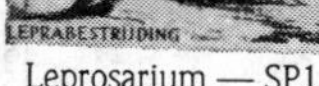
Leprosarium — SP1

Papuan Girl and Beach Scene — SP2

Design: 10c+5c, 30c+10c, Young Papuan and huts.

Perf. 12x12½

1956, Dec. 15 Unwmk. Photo.

B7 SP1 5c + 5c dk slate grn 75 75
B8 SP1 10c + 5c brn violet 75 75
B9 SP1 25c + 10c brt blue 75 75
B10 SP1 30c + 10c ocher 75 75

The surtax was for the fight against leprosy.

1957, Oct. 1 *Perf. 12½x12*

Design: 10c+5c, 30c+10c, Papuan boy and pile dwelling.

B11 SP2 5c + 5c maroon 65 65
B12 SP2 10c + 5c slate grn 65 65
B13 SP2 25c + 10c brown 65 65
B14 SP2 30c + 10c dark blue 65 65

The surtax was to fight infant mortality.

Ancestral Image, North Coast New Guinea — SP3

Bignonia — SP4

Design: 10c+5c, 30c+10c, Bowl in form of human figure, Asmat-Papua.

1958, Oct. 1 Litho. *Perf. 12½x12*

B15 SP3 5c + 5c bl, blk & red 75 75
B16 SP3 10c + 5c rose lake, blk, red & yel 75 75
B17 SP3 25c + 10c bl grn, blk & red 75 75
B18 SP3 30c + 10c ol gray, blk, red & yel 75 75

The surtax was for the Red Cross.

1959, Nov. 16 Photo. *Perf. 12½x13*

Flowers: 10c+5c, Orchid. 25c+10c, Rhododendron. 30c+10c, Gesneriacea.

B19 SP4 5c + 5c car rose & grn 48 35
B20 SP4 10c + 5c ol, yel & lil 48 35
B21 SP4 25c + 10c red, org & grn 48 45
B22 SP4 30c + 10c vio & grn 48 45

Birdwing — SP5

Various Butterflies.

Perf. 13x12½

1960, Sept. 1 Unwmk. Litho.

B23 SP5 5c + 5c lt bl, blk, emer & yel 65 65
B24 SP5 10c + 5c sal, blk & bl 65 65
B25 SP5 25c + 10c yel, blk & org red 75 70
B26 SP5 30c + 10c lt grn, brn & yel 75 70

Surtax for social care.

Rhinoceros Beetle and Coconut Palm Leaf — SP6

Beetles and leaves of host plants: 10c+5c, Ectocemus 10-maculatus Montri, a primitive weevil. 25c+10c, Stag beetle. 30c+10c, Tortoise beetle.

1961, Sept. 15 *Perf. 13x12½*

Beetles in Natural Colors

B27 SP6 5c + 5c deep org 20 22
B28 SP6 10c + 5c lt ultra 20 22
B29 SP6 25c + 10c citron 25 28
B30 SP6 30c + 10c green 32 35

Surtax for social care.

Crab — SP7

Designs: 10c+5c, Lobster, vert. 25c+10c, Spiny lobster, vert. 30c+10c, Shrimp.

Perf. 14x13, 13x14

1962, Sept. 17 Unwmk.

B31 SP7 5c + 5c red, grn, brn & yel 15 15
B32 SP7 10c + 5c Prus bl & yel 15 15
B33 SP7 25c + 10c multicolored 18 18
B34 SP7 30c + 10c bl, org red & yel 18 22

The surtax on Nos. B19-B34 went to various social works organizations.

POSTAGE DUE STAMPS

D1

Perf. 13½x12½

1957 Photo. Unwmk.

J1 D1 1c vermilion 15 15
J2 D1 5c vermilion 38 75
J3 D1 10c vermilion 1.10 1.50
J4 D1 25c vermilion 1.65 55
J5 D1 40c vermilion 1.65 65
J6 D1 1g blue 2.00 2.25
Nos. J1-J6 (6) 6.93 5.85

NEW CALEDONIA

LOCATION — Island in the South Pacific Ocean, east of Queensland, Australia
GOVT. — French Overseas Territory
AREA — 7,375 sq. mi.
POP. — 147,200 (est. 1984)
CAPITAL — Noumea

Dependencies of New Caledonia are the Loyalty Islands, Isle of Pines, Huon Islands and Chesterfield Islands.

100 Centimes = 1 Franc

Catalogue values for unused stamps in this country are for Never Hinged items, beginning with Scott 252 in the regular postage section, Scott B13 in the semi-postal section, Scott C14 in the airpost section, Scott J32 in the postage due section, and Scott O1 in the official section.

Napoleon III — A1

1859 Unwmk. Litho. *Imperf.*

Without Gum

1 A1 10c black 140.00

Fifty varieties. Counterfeits abound. See No. 315.

Type of French Colonies, 1877 Surcharged in Black:

NCE 5 — Nos. 2-5 **NCE 5** — Nos. 6-7

1881-83

2 A8 5c on 40c red, *straw* ('82) 225.00 200.00
a. Inverted surcharge 550.00 550.00
3 A8 05c on 40c red, *straw* ('83) 14.00 14.00
4 A8 25c on 35c dp vio, *yel* 85.00 90.00
a. Inverted surcharge 400.00 400.00
5 A8 25c on 75c rose car, *rose* ('82) 165.00 165.00
a. Inverted surcharge 400.00 400.00

1883-84

6 A8 5c on 40c red, *straw* ('84) 9.50 9.50
a. Inverted surcharge 10.00 10.00
7 A8 5c on 75c rose car, *rose* ('83) 19.00 19.00
a. Inverted surcharge 22.50 22.50

In type "a" surcharge, the narrower-spaced letters measure 14½mm, and an early printing of No. 4 measures 13½mm. Type "b" letters measure 18mm.

French Colonies No. 59 Surcharged in Black:

N.C.E. 5c. — No. 8 **N.C.E. 5c.** — Nos. 9-10

1886 *Perf. 14x13½*

8 A9 5c on 1fr 8.75 8.75
a. Inverted surcharge 12.00 12.00
9 A9 5c on 1fr 6.75 6.75
b. Inverted surcharge 20.00 20.00

French Colonies No. 29 Surcharged

Imperf

10 A8 5c on 1fr *7,000. 7,000.*

Types of French Colonies, 1877-86, Surcharged in Black:

Nos. 11, 13

No. 12

1891-92 *Imperf.*

11 A8 10c on 40c red, *straw* ('92) 13.00 12.00
a. Inverted surcharge 16.00 16.00
b. Double surcharge 30.00 30.00
c. No period after "10c" 13.00 12.00

Perf. 14x13½

12 A9 10c on 30c brn, *bis* 6.50 6.50
a. Inverted surcharge 7.50 7.50
b. Double surcharge 19.00 19.00
c. Double surcharge, inverted 19.00 19.00
13 A9 10c on 40c red, *straw* ('92) 6.50 6.50
a. Inverted surcharge 7.50 7.50
b. No period after "10c" 6.50 6.50
c. Double surcharge 19.00 19.00

Variety "double surcharge, one inverted" exists on Nos. 11-13. Value same as for "double surcharge."

Types of French Colonies, 1877-86, Handstamped in Black

g

1892 *Imperf.*

16 A8 20c red, *grn* 175.00 175.00
17 A8 35c vio, *org* 30.00 30.00
18 A8 40c red, *straw*
19 A8 1fr brnz grn, *straw* 130.00 130.00

The 1c, 2c, 4c and 75c of type A8 are believed not to have been officially made or actually used.

1892 *Perf. 14x13½*

23 A9 5c grn, *grnsh* 5.75 5.25
24 A9 10c blk, *lavender* 50.00 30.00
25 A9 15c blue 37.50 19.00
26 A9 20c red, *grn* 37.50 24.00
27 A9 25c yel, *straw* 7.50 6.50
28 A9 25c blk, *rose* 37.50 6.50
29 A9 30c brn, *bis* 30.00 25.00
30 A9 35c vio, *org* 100.00 82.50
32 A9 75c car, *rose* 82.50 60.00
33 A9 1fr brnz grn, *straw* 67.50 57.50

The note following No. 19 also applies to the 1c, 2c, 4c and 40c of type A9.

Surcharged in Blue or Black

h

1892-93 *Imperf.*

34 A8 10c on 1fr brnz grn, *straw* (Bl) *2,750. 2,000.*

Perf. 14x13½

35 A9 5c on 20c red, *grn* (Bk) 7.50 5.75
a. Inverted surcharge 50.00 47.50
b. Double surcharge inverted
36 A9 5c on 75c car, *rose* (Bk) 5.75 3.75
a. Inverted surcharge 50.00 47.50
37 A9 5c on 75c car, *rose* (Bl) 5.25 3.50
a. Inverted surcharge 50.00 47.50
38 A9 10c on 1fr brnz grn, *straw* (Bk) 5.25 3.75
a. Inverted surcharge 250.00 225.00
39 A9 10c on 1fr brnz grn, *straw* (Bl) 6.50 5.75
a. Inverted surcharge 50.00 47.50

Navigation and Commerce — A12

1892-1904 Typo. *Perf. 14x13½*
Name of Colony in Blue or Carmine

40 A12 1c blk, *blue* 35 28
41 A12 2c brn, *buff* 48 40
42 A12 4c claret, *lav* 85 70
43 A12 5c grn, *grnsh* 1.00 60
44 A12 5c yel grn ('00) 70 65
45 A12 10c blk, *lavender* 3.00 1.75
46 A12 10c rose red ('00) 3.50 70
47 A12 15c bl, quadrille paper 9.25 70
48 A12 15c gray ('00) 5.25 65
49 A12 20c red, *grn* 7.50 5.00
50 A12 25c blk, *rose* 8.50 3.00
51 A12 25c blue ('00) 7.00 4.00
52 A12 30c brn, *bis* 8.50 4.75
53 A12 40c red, *straw* 8.50 6.50
54 A12 50c car, *rose* 30.00 13.00
55 A12 50c brn, *az* (name in car) ('00) 47.50 40.00
56 A12 50c brn, *az* (name in bl) ('04) 30.00 25.00
57 A12 75c vio, *org* 14.00 10.00
58 A12 1fr brnz grn, *straw* 15.00 11.00
Nos. 40-58 (19) 200.88 128.68

Perf. 13½x14 stamps are counterfeits.
For overprints and surcharges see Nos. 59-87, 117-121.

Nos. 41-42, 52, 57-58, 53 Surcharged in Black:

N.C.E.
15
j

N.-C.E.
5
k

1900-01

59 A12 (h) 5c on 2c ('01) 3.50 3.00
a. Double surcharge 52.50 52.50
b. Inverted surcharge 52.50 52.50
60 A12 (h) 5c on 4c 75 75
a. Inverted surcharge 30.00 30.00
b. Double surcharge 30.00 30.00
61 A12 (j) 15c on 30c 75 75
a. Inverted surcharge 25.00 25.00
b. Double surcharge 25.00 25.00
62 A12 (j) 15c on 75c ('01) 3.00 2.00
a. Pair, one without surcharge
b. Inverted surcharge 52.50 52.50
c. Double surcharge 52.50 52.50
63 A12 (j) 15c on 1fr ('01) 4.50 4.25
a. Double surcharge 65.00 65.00
b. Inverted surcharge 65.00 65.00
Nos. 59-63 (5) 12.50 10.75

1902

64 A12 (k) 5c on 30c 4.00 3.50
a. Inverted surcharge 16.00 16.00
65 A12 (k) 15c on 40c 3.25 3.25
a. Inverted surcharge 16.00 16.00

Jubilee Issue

Samps of 1892-1900 Overprinted in Blue, Red, Black or Gold

1903

66 A12 1c blk, *lil bl* (Bl) 75 70
a. Inverted overprint 90.00 90.00
67 A12 2c brn, *buff* (Bl) 2.25 1.40
68 A12 4c cl, *lav* (Bl) 2.75 1.40
a. Double overprint 150.00 150.00
69 A12 5c dk grn, *grnsh* (R) 2.75 1.50
70 A12 5c yel grn (R) 3.75 3.00
71 A12 10c blk, *lav* (R) 7.25 5.00
72 A12 10c blk, *lav* (double G & Bk) 4.50 4.50
73 A12 15c gray (R) 4.75 2.75
74 A12 20c red, *grn* (Bl) 8.50 5.75
75 A12 25c blk, *rose* (Bl) 8.50 6.25
a. Double overprint
76 A12 30c brn, *bis* (R) 11.00 7.25
77 A12 40c red, *straw* (Bl) 15.00 9.50
78 A12 50c car, *rose* (Bl) 25.00 11.00
a. Pair, one without overprint
79 A12 75c vio, *org* (Bk) 37.50 27.50
a. Dbl. ovpt. in blk and red 250.00 250.00
80 A12 1fr brnz grn, *straw* (Bl) 45.00 37.50
a. Dbl. ovpt., one in red 250.00 250.00
Nos. 66-80 (15) 179.25 125.00

With Additional Surcharge of New Value in Blue

81 A12 1c on 2c #67 42 42
a. Numeral double 40.00 40.00
b. Numeral only
82 A12 2c on 4c #68 90 90
83 A12 4c on 5c #69 90 90
a. Small "4" 375.00 375.00
84 A12 4c on 5c #70 1.40 1.40
a. Pair, one without numeral
85 A12 10c on 15c #73 1.40 1.40
86 A12 15c on 20c #74 1.40 1.40
87 A12 20c on 25c #75 2.50 2.50
Nos. 81-87 (7) 8.92 8.92

50 years of French occupation.
Surcharge on Nos. 81-83, 85-86 is horizontal, reading down.
There are three types of numeral on No. 83. The numeral on No. 84 is identical with that of No. 83a except that its position is upright.
Nos. 66-87 are known with "I" of "TENAIRE" missing.

Kagu
A16

Landscape
A17

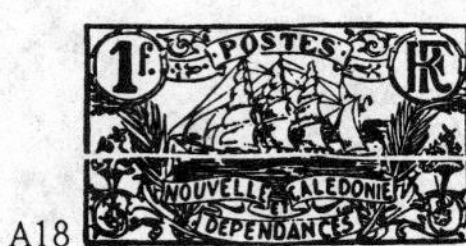

Ship — A18

1905-28 Typo. *Perf. 14x13½*

88 A16 1c blk, *green* 15 15
89 A16 2c red brn 15 15
90 A16 4c bl, *org* 15 15
91 A16 5c pale grn 15 15
92 A16 5c dl bl ('21) 15 15
93 A16 10c carmine 48 40
94 A16 10c grn ('21) 30 30
95 A16 10c red, *pink* ('25) 15 15
96 A16 15c violet 24 15
97 A17 20c brown 15 15
98 A17 25c bl, *grn* 15 15
99 A17 25c red, *yel* ('21) 15 15
100 A17 30c brn, *org* 15 15
101 A17 30c dp rose ('21) 60 60
102 A17 30c org ('25) 15 15
103 A17 35c blk, *yellow* 15 15
104 A17 40c car, *grn* 48 35
105 A17 45c vio brn, *lav* 30 30
106 A17 50c car, *org* 95 60
107 A17 50c dk bl ('21) 55 55
108 A17 50c gray ('25) 28 28
109 A17 65c dp bl ('28) 15 15
110 A17 75c ol grn, *straw* 15 15
111 A17 75c bl, *bluish* ('25) 15 15
112 A17 75c vio ('27) 30 30
113 A18 1fr bl, *yel grn* 38 15
114 A18 1fr dp bl ('25) 60 60
115 A18 2fr car, *bl* 85 70
116 A18 5fr blk, *straw* 2.50 2.50
Nos. 88-116 (29) 11.06 10.03

See Nos. 311, 317a. For surcharges see Nos. 122-135, B1-B3, Q1-Q3.

Stamps of 1892-1904 Surcharged in Carmine or Black

05 10

1912

117 A12 5c on 15c gray (C) 35 35
a. Inverted surcharge 60.00 60.00
118 A12 5c on 20c red, *grn* 45 45
119 A12 5c on 30c brn, *bis* (C) 45 45
120 A12 10c on 40c red, *straw* 85 85
121 A12 10c on 50c brn, *az* (C) 85 85
Nos. 117-121 (5) 2.95 2.95

Two spacings between the surcharged numerals are found on Nos. 117 to 121.

No. 96 Surcharged in Brown

5
CENTIMES

1918

122 A16 5c on 15c vio 60 60
a. Double surcharge 32.50 32.50
b. Inverted surcharge 17.50 17.50

The color of the surcharge on No. 122 varies from red to dark brown.

No. 96 Surcharged

0,05
=

1922

123 A16 5c on 15c vio (R) 28 28
a. Double surcharge 27.50 27.50

Stamps and Types of 1905-28 Surcharged New Value and Bars in Red or Black

60 =

1924-27

124 A16 25c on 15c vio 20 20
a. Double surcharge 27.50
125 A18 25c on 2fr car, *bl* 20 20
126 A18 25c on 5fr blk, *straw* 28 28
a. Double surcharge 45.00 45.00
127 A17 60c on 75c bl grn (R) 15 15
128 A17 65c on 45c red brn 55 55
129 A17 85c on 45c red brn 55 55
130 A17 90c on 75c dp rose 28 28
131 A18 1.25fr on 1fr dp bl (R) 20 20
132 A18 1.50fr on 1fr dp bl, *bl* 45 45
133 A18 3fr on 5fr red vio 48 48
134 A18 10fr on 5fr ol, *lav* (R) 3.00 3.00
135 A18 20fr on 5fr vio rose, *org* 6.25 6.25
Nos. 124-135 (12) 12.59 12.59

Issue years: Nos. 125-127, 1924. Nos. 124, 128-129, 1925. Nos. 131, 134, 1926. Nos. 130, 132-133, 135, 1927.

Bay of Palétuviers Point — A19

Landscape with Chief's House — A20

Admiral de Bougainville and Count de La Pérouse A21

1928-40 **Typo.**

136 A19 1c brn vio & ind 15 15
137 A19 2c dk brn & yel grn 15 15
137B A19 3c brn vio & ind 15 15
138 A19 4c org & Prus grn 15 15
139 A19 5c Prus bl & dp ol 15 15
140 A19 10c gray lil & dk brn 15 15
141 A19 15c yel brn & dp bl 15 15
142 A19 20c brn red & dk brn 15 15
143 A19 25c dk grn & dk brn 15 15
144 A20 30c gray grn & bl grn 15 15
145 A20 35c blk & brt vio 15 15
146 A20 40c brt red & olvn 15 15
147 A20 45c dp bl & red org 35 28
147A A20 45c bl grn & dl grn 28 28
148 A20 50c vio & brn 15 15
149 A20 55c vio bl & car 1.25 60
150 A20 60c vio bl & car 20 20
151 A20 65c org brn & bl 30 28
152 A20 70c dp rose & brn 15 15
153 A20 75c Prus bl & ol gray 60 28
154 A20 80c red brn & grn 30 15
155 A20 85c grn & brn 60 35
156 A20 90c dp red & brt red 30 28
157 A20 90c ol grn & rose red 28 28
158 A21 1fr dp ol & sal red 2.25 1.25
159 A21 1fr rose red & dk car 60 60
160 A21 1fr brn red & grn 15 15
161 A21 1.10fr dp grn & brn 5.50 5.00
162 A21 1.25fr brn red & grn 38 28
163 A21 1.25fr rose red & dk car 28 28
164 A21 1.40fr dk bl & red org 28 28
165 A21 1.50fr dp bl & bl 15 15
166 A21 1.60fr dp grn & brn 55 55
167 A21 1.75fr dk bl & red org 30 28
168 A21 1.75fr vio bl 28 28
169 A21 2fr red org & brn 22 15
170 A21 2.25fr vio bl 30 30
171 A21 2.50fr brn & lt brn 55 55
172 A21 3fr mag & brn 30 28
173 A21 5fr dk bl & brn 30 28

174	A21	10fr vio & brn, *pnksh*	60	48
175	A21	20fr red & brn, *yel*	1.00	70
		Nos. 136-175 (42)	20.55	16.92

The 35c in Prussian green and dark green without overprint is listed as Wallis and Futuna No. 53a.

Issue years: 35c, 70c, 85c, Nos. 162, 167, 1933. 55c, 80c, Nos. 159, 168, 1938. No. 157, 163, 2.25fr, 1939. 3c, 55c, 1.40fr, 1.60fr, 2.50fr, Nos. 147A, 160, 1940. Others, 1928.

For overprints see Nos. 180-207, 217-251, Q4-Q6.

Colonial Exposition Issue

Common Design Types

1931 **Engr.** ***Perf. 12½***

Country Name Typo. in Black

176	CD70	40c dp grn	1.75	1.75
177	CD71	50c violet	1.75	1.75
178	CD72	90c red org	1.75	1.75
179	CD73	1.50fr dl bl	1.75	1.75

Paris-Nouméa Flight Issue

Regular Issue of 1928 Overprinted:

1932 ***Perf. 14x13½***

180	A20	40c brt red & olvn	200.00	200.00
181	A20	50c vio & brn	200.00	200.00

Arrival on Apr. 5, 1932 at Nouméa, of the French aviators, Verneilh, Dévé and Munch.

Excellent forgeries exist of #180-181.

Types of 1928-33 Overprinted in Black or Red:

1933

182	A19	1c red vio & dl bl	3.75	3.75
183	A19	2c dk brn & yel grn	3.75	3.75
184	A19	4c dl org & Prus bl	3.75	3.75
185	A19	5c Prus grn & ol (R)	3.75	3.75
186	A19	10c gray lil & dk brn (R)	3.75	3.75
187	A19	15c yel brn & dp bl (R)	3.75	3.75
188	A19	20c brn red & dk brn	3.75	3.75
189	A19	25c dk grn & dk brn (R)	3.75	3.75
190	A20	30c gray grn & bl grn (R)	3.75	3.75
191	A20	35c blk & lt vio	3.75	3.75
192	A20	40c brt red & olvn	3.75	3.75
193	A20	45c dp bl & red org	3.75	3.75
194	A20	50c vio & brn	3.75	3.75
195	A20	70c dp rose & brn	3.75	3.75
196	A20	75c Prus bl & ol gray (R)	3.75	3.75
197	A20	85c grn & brn	3.75	3.75
198	A20	90c dp red & brt red	3.75	3.75
199	A21	1fr dp ol & sal red	3.75	3.75
200	A21	1.25fr brn red & grn	3.75	3.75
201	A21	1.50fr dp bl & bl (R)	4.00	4.00
202	A21	1.75fr dk bl & red org	4.00	4.00
203	A21	2fr red org & brn	4.25	4.25
204	A21	3fr mag & brn	4.25	4.25
205	A21	5fr dk bl & brn (R)	4.25	4.25
206	A21	10fr vio & brn, *pnksh*	4.25	4.25
207	A21	20fr red & brn, *yel*	4.25	4.25
		Nos. 182-207 (26)	100.50	100.50

1st anniv., Paris-Noumea flight. Plane centered on Nos. 190-207.

Paris International Exposition Issue

Common Design Types

1937 **Engr.** ***Perf. 13***

208	CD74	20c dp vio	60	60
209	CD75	30c dk grn	60	60
210	CD76	40c car rose	65	65
211	CD77	50c dk brn & bl	65	65
212	CD78	90c red	65	65
213	CD79	1.50fr ultra	65	65
		Nos. 208-213 (6)	3.80	3.80

Colonial Arts Exhibition Issue

Souvenir Sheet

Common Design Type

1937 ***Imperf.***

214	CD78	3fr sepia	2.50 2.50

New York World's Fair Issue

Common Design Type

1939 ***Perf. 12½x12***

215	CD82	1.25fr car lake	45	45
216	CD82	2.25fr ultra	45	45

Nouméa Roadstead and Marshal Pétain — A21a

1941 **Engr.** ***Perf. 12½x12***

216A	A21a	1fr bluish grn	30
216B	A21a	2.50fr dk bl	30

Nos. 216A-216B were issued by the Vichy government and were not placed on sale in the colony.

A 10c, type A19, without "RF," and a 60c, type A20, without "REPUBLIQUE FRANCAISE," were also issued by the Vichy government and not placed on sale in New Caledonia.

Types of 1928-40 Overprinted in Black **France Libre**

1941 ***Perf. 14x13½***

217	A19	1c red vio & dl bl	8.00	8.00
218	A19	2c dk brn & yel grn	8.00	8.00
219	A19	3c brn vio & ind	8.00	8.00
220	A19	4c dl org & Prus bl	8.00	8.00
221	A19	5c Prus bl & dp ol	8.00	8.00
222	A19	10c gray lil & dk brn	8.00	8.00
223	A19	15c yel brn & dp bl	8.00	8.00
224	A19	20c brn red & dk brn	8.00	8.00
225	A19	25c dk grn & dk brn	8.00	8.00
226	A20	30c gray grn & bl grn	8.00	8.00
227	A20	35c blk & brt vio	8.00	8.00
228	A20	40c brt red & olvn	8.00	8.00
229	A20	45c bl grn & dl grn	8.00	8.00
230	A20	50c vio & brn	8.00	8.00
231	A20	55c vio bl & car	8.00	8.00
232	A20	60c vio bl & car	8.00	8.00
233	A20	65c org brn & bl	8.00	8.00
234	A20	70c dp rose & brn	8.00	8.00
235	A20	75c Prus bl & ol gray	8.00	8.00
236	A20	80c red brn & grn	8.00	8.00
237	A20	85c grn & brn	9.00	9.00
238	A20	90c dp red & brt red	9.00	9.00
239	A21	1fr rose red & dk car	9.00	9.00
240	A21	1.25fr brn red & grn	9.00	9.00
241	A21	1.40fr dk bl & red org	9.00	9.00
242	A21	1.50fr dp bl & bl	9.00	9.00
243	A21	1.60fr dp grn & brn	9.00	9.00
244	A21	1.75fr dk bl & red org	9.00	9.00
245	A21	2fr red org & brn	9.00	9.00
246	A21	2.25fr vio bl	9.00	9.00
247	A21	2.50fr brn & lt brn	10.00	10.00
248	A21	3fr mag & brn	10.00	10.00
249	A21	5fr dk bl & brn	10.00	10.00
250	A21	10fr vio & brn, *pnksh*	10.00	10.00
251	A21	20fr red & brn, *yel*	10.00	10.00
		Nos. 217-251 (35)	300.00	300.00

Issued to note this colony's affiliation with the "Free France" movement.

Catalogue values for unused stamps in this section, from this point to the end of the section, are for Never Hinged items.

Kagu — A22

1942 **Photo.** ***Perf. 14½x14***

252	A22	5c brown	15	15
253	A22	10c dk gray bl	15	15
254	A22	25c emerald	15	15
255	A22	30c red org	15	15
256	A22	40c dk sl grn	15	15
257	A22	80c dl red brn	15	15
258	A22	1fr rose vio	15	15
259	A22	1.50fr red	15	15
260	A22	2fr gray blk	35	35
261	A22	2.50fr brt ultra	35	35
262	A22	4fr dl vio	28	28
263	A22	5fr bister	35	35
264	A22	10fr dp brn	50	50
265	A22	20fr dp grn	70	70
		Nos. 252-265 (14)	3.73	3.73

Stamps of 1942 Surcharged in Carmine or Black **60 c. ═**

1945-46 **Unwmk.** ***Perf. 14½x14***

266	A22	50c on 5c (C) ('46)	45	45
267	A22	60c on 5c (C)	45	45
268	A22	70c on 5c (C)	45	45
269	A22	1.20fr on 5c (C)	20	20
270	A22	2.40fr on 25c	20	20
271	A22	3fr on 25c ('46)	20	20
272	A22	4.50fr on 25c	45	45
273	A22	15fr on 2.50fr (C)	85	85
		Nos. 266-273 (8)	3.25	3.25

Eboue Issue

Common Design Type

1945 **Engr.** ***Perf. 13***

274	CD91	2fr black	28	28
275	CD91	25fr Prus grn	85	85

Kagus — A23

Ducos Sanatorium — A24

Porcupine Isle — A25

Nickel Foundry — A26

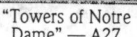

"Towers of Notre Dame" — A27

Chieftain's House — A28

1948 **Unwmk.** **Photo.** ***Perf. 13½x13***

276	A23	10c yel & brn	15	15
277	A23	30c grn & brn	15	15
278	A23	40c org & brn	15	15
279	A24	50c pink & brn	15	15
280	A24	60c yel & brn	15	15
281	A24	80c lt grn & bl grn	15	15
282	A25	1fr brn, pur & org	15	15
283	A25	1.20fr pale gray, brn & bl	20	15
284	A25	1.50fr cr, dk bl & yel	20	15
285	A26	2fr pck grn & brn	30	20
286	A26	2.40fr ver & dp rose	22	20
287	A26	3fr org & pur	2.50	60
288	A26	4fr bl & dk bl	48	28
289	A27	5fr ver & pur	60	35
290	A27	6fr yel & brn	75	45
291	A27	10fr org & dk bl	75	28
292	A28	15fr brn & gray	75	65
293	A28	20fr pur & yel	85	65
294	A28	25fr dk bl & org	1.25	95
		Nos. 276-294 (19)	9.90	5.96

Military Medal Issue

Common Design Type

1952 **Engr. & Typo.** ***Perf. 13***

295	CD101	2fr multi	2.00	2.00

Admiral Bruni d'Entrecasteaux and his Two Frigates — A29

Designs: 2fr, Msgr. Douarre and Cathedral of Nouméa. 6fr, Admiral Dumont d'Urville and map. 13fr, Admiral Auguste Febvrier-Despointes and Nouméa roadstead.

1953, Sept. 24 **Engr.**

296	A29	1.50fr org brn & dp cl	3.50	2.50
297	A29	2fr ind & aqua	2.50	1.75
298	A29	6fr dk brn, bl & car	5.25	2.75
299	A29	13fr bl grn & dk grnsh bl	5.50	4.00

Centenary of the presence of the French in New Caledonia.

"Towers of Notre Dame" — A30

Coffee — A31

1955, Nov. 21 **Unwmk.** ***Perf. 13***

300	A30	2.50fr dk brn, ultra & grn	35	30
301	A30	3fr grn, ultra & red brn	2.75	1.50
302	A31	9fr vio bl & indigo	55	30

FIDES Issue

Common Design Type

1956, Oct. 22 **Engr.** ***Perf. 13x12½***

303	CD103	3fr Dumbea Dam	60	45

Flower Issue

Common Design Type

Designs: 4fr, Xanthostemon. 15fr, Hibiscus.

1958, July 7 **Photo.** ***Perf. 12x12½***

304	CD104	4fr multi	1.10	45
305	CD104	15fr grn, red & yel	2.50	75

Imperforates

Most stamps of New Caledonia from 1958 onward exist imperforate, in trial colors, or in small presentation sheets in which the stamps are printed in changed colors.

Human Rights Issue

Common Design Type

1958, Dec. 10 **Engr.** ***Perf. 13***

306	CD105	7fr car & dk bl	60	45

Brachyrus Zebra — A32

Lienardella Fasciata — A33

Designs: 10fr, Claucus and Spirographe. 26fr, Fluorescent corals.

1959, Mar. 21 **Engr.** ***Perf. 13***

307	A32	1fr lil gray & red brn	38	28
308	A33	3fr bl, grn & red	45	24
309	A32	10fr dk brn, Prus bl & org brn	1.10	60
310	A33	26fr multi	2.50	1.75

Types of 1859, 1905 and

Girl Operating Check Writer — A34

Telephone Receiver and Exchange A35

Port-de-France (Nouméa) in 1859 — A36

Designs: 9fr, Wayside mailbox and mail bus, vert. 33fr, Like 19fr without stamps.

Perf. 13½x13, 13

1960, May 20 **Unwmk.**

311	A16	4fr red	45	30
312	A34	5fr cl & org brn	45	30
313	A36	9fr dk grn & brn	45	38
314	A35	12fr bl & blk	55	45
315	A1	13fr slate bl	1.75	90
316	A36	19fr bl grn, dl grn & red	1.75	65
317	A36	33fr Prus bl & dl red	1.90	1.25
a.		Souv. sheet of 3, #315, 311, 317 + label	4.50	4.50
		Nos. 311-317 (7)	7.30	4.23

Cent. of postal service and stamps in New Caledonia.

No. 317a has label between 4fr and 33fr stamps.

Melanesian Sailing Canoes A37

Designs: 4fr, Spear fisherman, vert. 5fr, Sail Rock and sailboats, Noumea.

1962, July 2 **Engr.** ***Perf. 13***

318	A37	2fr sl grn, ultra & brn	40	28
319	A37	4fr brn, car & grn	40	30
320	A37	5fr sepia, grn & bl	75	45

See Nos. C29-C32.

Map of Australia and South Pacific — A37a

1962, July 18 **Photo.** ***Perf. 13x12***

321	A37a	15fr multi	1.10	55

Fifth South Pacific Conf., Pago Pago, 1962.

Air Currents over Map of New Caledonia and South Pacific, Barograph and Compass Rose — A38

1962, Nov. 5 ***Perf. 12x12½***

322	A38	50fr multi	4.50	3.00

3rd regional assembly of the World Meteorological Association, Noumea, November 1962.

Wheat Emblem and Globe — A38a

1963, Mar. 21 **Engr.** ***Perf. 13***

323	A38a	17fr choc & dk bl	1.00	70

FAO "Freedom from Hunger" campaign.

Relay Race — A39

Perf. 12½

1963, Aug. 29 **Unwmk.** **Photo.**

324	A39	1fr shown	42	30
325	A39	7fr Tennis	75	42
326	A39	10fr Soccer	1.10	75
327	A39	27fr Javelin	2.25	1.75

Issued to publicize the South Pacific Games, Suva, Aug. 29-Sept. 7.

Red Cross Centenary Issue

Common Design Type

1963 Sept. 2 **Engr.** ***Perf. 13***

328	CD113	37fr bl, gray & car	2.75	2.25

Human Rights Issue

Common Design Type

1963, Dec. 10 **Unwmk.** ***Perf. 13***

329	CD117	50fr sl grn & dp cl	3.00	2.50

Bikkia Fritillarioides A40

Sea Squirts A41

Flowers: 1fr, Freycinettia Sp. 3fr, Xanthostemon Francii. 4fr, Psidiomyrtus locellatus. 5fr, Callistemon suberosum. 7fr, Montrouziera sphaeroidea, horiz. 10fr, Ixora collina, horiz. 17fr, Deplanchea speciosa.

Photogravure; Lithographed (2fr, 3fr)

1964-65 ***Perf. 13x12½***

330	A40	1fr multi	25	20
331	A40	2fr multi	32	20
332	A40	3fr multi	48	25
333	A40	4fr multi ('65)	80	40
334	A40	5fr multi ('65)	90	45
335	A40	7fr multi	2.00	70
336	A40	10fr multi	2.00	70
337	A40	17fr multi	3.25	1.90
		Nos. 330-337 (8)	10.00	4.80

1964-65 **Engr.** ***Perf. 13***

Design: 10fr, Alcyonium catalai. 17fr, Shrimp (hymenocera elegans).

338	A41	7fr dk bl, org & brn	75	60
339	A41	10fr dk red & dk vio bl ('65)	1.10	50
340	A41	17fr dk bl, mag & grn	1.90	1.40

Nouméa Aquarium. See Nos. C41-C43.

Philatec Issue

Common Design Type

1964, Apr. 9 **Unwmk.** ***Perf. 13***

341	CD118	40fr dk vio, grn & choc	3.50	3.50

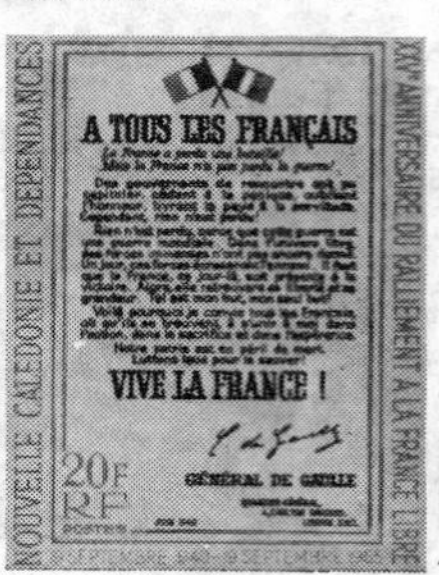

De Gaulle's 1940 Poster "A Tous les Francais" A42

1965, Sept. 20 **Engr.** ***Perf. 13***

342	A42	20fr red, bl & blk	4.00	2.75

25th anniversary of the rallying of the Free French.

Amedee Lighthouse A43

Games' Emblem A44

1965, Nov. 25

343	A43	8fr dk vio bl, bis & grn	65	35

Centenary of the Amedee lighthouse.

1966, Feb. 28 **Engr.** ***Perf. 13***

344	A44	8fr dk red, brt bl & blk	40	25

Issued to publicize the Second South Pacific Games, Nouméa, December, 1966.

Red-throated Parrot Finch — A45

Design: 3fr, Giant imperial pigeon.

1966, Oct. 10 **Litho.** ***Perf. 13x12½***

Size: 22x37mm

345	A45	1fr grn & multi	70	55
346	A45	3fr cit & multi	1.40	85

See #361-366, 380-381, C48-C49A, C70-C71.

Dancers and UNESCO Emblem A46

1966, Nov. 4 **Engr.** ***Perf. 13***

347	A46	16fr pur, ocher & grn	55	40

20th anniv. of UNESCO.

High Jump and Games' Emblem A47

Designs: 20fr, Hurdling. 40fr, Running. 100fr, Swimming.

1966, Dec. 8 **Engr.** ***Perf. 13***

348	A47	17fr mar, vio & grn	1.00	50
349	A47	20fr mar, lil & bl grn	1.65	85
350	A47	40fr mar, sl grn & vio	2.00	1.65
351	A47	100fr mar, bl grn & lil	4.00	2.75
a.		Souv. sheet of 4, #348-351 + label	12.00	12.00

2nd So. Pacific Games, Nouméa, Dec. 8-18.

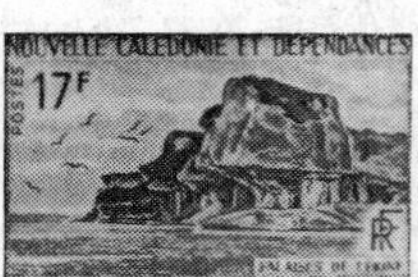

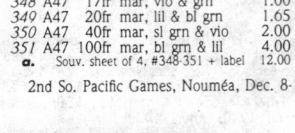

Lekine Cliffs — A48

1967, Jan. 14 **Engr.** ***Perf. 13***

352	A48	17fr brt grn, ultra & sl grn	75	40

Magenta Stadium, Nouméa A49

Design: 20fr, Fish hatchery, Nouméa.

1967, June 5 **Photo.** ***Perf. 12x13***

353	A49	10fr multi	65	40
354	A49	20fr multi	1.40	60

ITY Emblem, Beach at Nouméa A50

1967, June 19 **Engr.** ***Perf. 13***

355	A50	30fr multi	2.25	1.40

Issued for International Tourist Year, 1967.

19th Century Mailman A51

1967, July 12

356	A51	7fr dk car, bl grn & brn	50	40

Issued for Stamp Day.

Papilio Montrouzieri A52

Butterflies: 9fr, Polyura clitarchus. 13fr, 15fr, Hypolimnas bolina, male and female respectively.

1967-68 **Engr.** ***Perf. 13***

Size: 36x22mm

357	A52	7fr lt grn, blk & ultra	95	60
358	A52	9fr brn, lil & ind ('68)	1.40	85
359	A52	13fr vio bl, brn org & dk brn	2.00	1.25
360	A52	15fr dk brn, bl & yel	3.00	2.00
		Nos. 357-360,C51-C53 (7)	23.35	13.70

Issue dates: 9fr, Mar. 26, 1968. Others, Aug. 10, 1967.

Bird Type of 1966

Birds: 1fr, New Caledonian grass warbler. 2fr, New Caledonia whistler. 3fr, New Caledonia white-throated pigeon. 4fr, Kagus. 5fr, Crested parakeet. 10fr, Crow honey-eater.

1967-68 **Photo.** ***Perf. 13x12½***

Size: 22x37mm

361	A45	1fr multi ('68)	40	25
362	A45	2fr multi ('68)	55	32
363	A45	3fr multi ('68)	55	45

364	A45	4fr grn & multi	90	60
365	A45	5fr lt yel & multi	1.50	70
366	A45	10fr pink & multi	3.75	1.75
		Nos. 361-366 (6)	7.65	4.07

Issue dates: Nos. 364-366, Dec. 16, 1967. Others May 14, 1968.

WHO Anniversary Issue
Common Design Type

1968, May 4 **Engr.** ***Perf. 13***
367 CD126 20fr mar, vio & dk bl grn 1.25 90

Ferrying Mail Truck Across Tontouta River, 1900 — A53

1968, July 1 **Engr.** ***Perf. 13***
368 A53 9fr dk red brn, grn & ultra 1.00 50

Issued for Stamp Day, 1968.

Human Rights Year Issue
Common Design Type

1968, Aug. 10 **Engr.** ***Perf. 13***
369 CD127 12fr sl grn, dp car & org yel 75 55

Conus Geographus A54

1968, Nov. 9 **Engr.** ***Perf. 13***
Size: 36x22mm
370 A54 10fr dk brn, brt bl & gray 1.10 65

See Nos. C58-C60.

Car on Road — A55

1968, Dec. 26 **Engr.** ***Perf. 13***
371 A55 25fr dp bl, sl grn & hn brn 2.50 1.10

2nd Automobile Safari of New Caledonia.

Cattle Dip — A56

Design: 25fr, Cattle branding.

1969, May 10 **Engr.** ***Perf. 13***
Size: 36x22mm

372	A56	9fr sl grn, ultra & brn	70	55
373	A56	25fr grn, brn & lil	2.25	85

Issued to publicize cattle breeding in New Caledonia. See No. C64.

Murex Haustellum A57

Sea Shells: 5fr, Venus comb. 15fr, Murex ramosus.

1969, June 21 **Engr.** ***Perf. 13***
Size: 35½x22mm

374	A57	2fr ver, bl & brn	55	35
375	A57	5fr dl red, pur & beige	70	48
376	A57	15fr ver, dl grn & gray	2.50	1.00

See No. C65.

Judo — A58

1969, Aug. 7 **Engr.** ***Perf. 13***
Size: 36x22mm

377	A58	19fr shown	2.00	1.00
378	A58	20fr Boxers	2.00	1.00

3rd South Pacific Games, Port Moresby, Papua and New Guinea, Aug. 13-23. See Nos. C66-C67.

ILO Issue
Common Design Type

1969, Nov. 24 **Engr.** ***Perf. 13***
379 CD131 12fr org, brn vio & brn 60 40

Bird Type of 1966

Birds: 15fr, Friarbird. 30fr, Sacred kingfisher.

1970, Feb. 19 **Photo.** ***Perf. 13***
Size: 22x37mm

380	A45	15fr yel grn & multi	2.50	1.10
381	A45	30fr pale sal & multi	3.75	1.90

See Nos. C70-C71.

UPU Headquarters Issue
Common Design Type

1970, May 20 **Engr.** ***Perf. 13***
382 CD133 12fr brn, gray & dk car 70 55

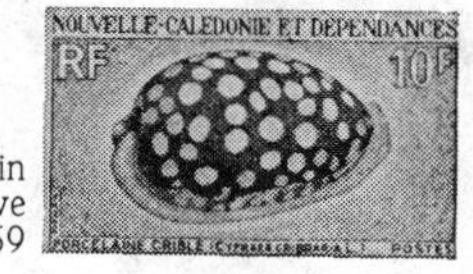
Porcelain Sieve Shell — A59

Designs: 1fr, Strombus epidromis linne, vert. No. 385, Strombus variabilis swainson, vert. 21fr, Mole porcelain shell.

1970
Size: 22x36mm, 36x22mm

383	A59	1fr brt grn & multi	55	28
384	A59	10fr rose & multi	1.40	55
385	A59	10fr blk & multi	1.40	55
386	A59	21fr bl grn, brn & dk brn	2.75	1.00
		Nos. 383-386,C73-C76 (8)	20.10	10.28

See Nos. 395-396, C89-C90.

Packet Ship "Natal," 1883 — A60

1970, July 23 **Engr.** ***Perf. 13***
387 A60 9fr Prus bl, blk & brt grn 80 45

Issued for Stamp Day.

Dumbea Railroad Post Office — A61

1971, Mar. 13 **Engr.** ***Perf. 13***
388 A61 10fr red, sl grn & blk 1.25 75

Stamp Day, 1971.

Racing Yachts — A62

1971, Apr. 17 **Engr.** ***Perf. 13***
389 A62 16fr bl, Prus bl & sl grn 3.25 1.75

Third sailing cruise from Whangarei, New Zealand, to Nouméa.

Morse Recorder, Communications Satellite — A63

1971, May 17 **Engr.** ***Perf. 13***
390 A63 19fr red, lake & org 85 40

3rd World Telecommunications Day.

Weight Lifting — A64

1971, June 24 **Engr.** ***Perf. 13***

391	A64	11fr shown	75	50
392	A64	23fr Basketball	1.50	75

4th South Pacific Games, Papeete, French Polynesia, Sept. 8-19. See Nos. C82-C83.

De Gaulle Issue
Common Design Type

Designs: 34fr, Gen. de Gaulle, 1940. 100fr, Pres. de Gaulle, 1970.

1971, Nov. 9

393	CD134	34fr dk pur & blk	3.00	1.25
394	CD134	100fr dk pur & blk	7.00	3.50

Sea Shell Type of 1970

Designs: 1fr, Scorpion conch, vert. 3fr, Common spider conch., vert.

1972, Mar. 4 **Engr.** ***Perf. 13***
Size: 22x36mm

395	A59	1fr vio & dk brn	28	20
396	A59	3fr grn & ocher	40	28

See Nos. C89-C90.

Carved Wooden Pillow — A66

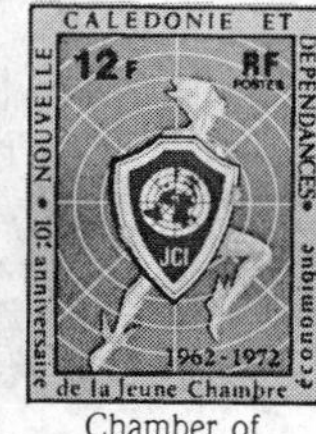
Chamber of Commerce Emblem — A67

1972-73 **Photo.** ***Perf. 12½x13***

397	A66	1fr Doorpost, Goa ('73)	35	22
398	A66	2fr shown	35	28
399	A66	5fr Monstrance	60	40
400	A66	12fr Tchamba mask	1.75	75
		Nos. 397-400,C102-C103 (6)	5.05	3.15

Objects from Nouméa Museum.

1972, Dec. 16
401 A67 12fr blk, yel & brt bl 80 50

10th anniversary of the Junior Chamber of Commerce.

Tchamba Mask — A68

Black-back Butterflyfish (Day) — A69

1973, Mar. 15 **Engr.** ***Perf. 13***
402 A68 12fr lilac 1.25 85
a. Booklet pane of 5 10.00

No. 402 issued in booklets only.
See No. C99.

1973, June 23 **Photo.** ***Perf. 13x12½***

403	A69	8fr shown	95	60
404	A69	14fr same fish (night)	1.40	85

Nouméa Aquarium. See No. C105.

Emblem A70

1973, July 21 ***Perf. 13***
405 A70 20fr grn, yel & vio bl 80 45

School Coordinating Office, 10th anniv.

"Nature Protection" — A72

1974, June 22 **Photo.** ***Perf. 13x12½***
406 A72 7fr multi 45 30

Scorched Landscape — A73

Calanthe Veratrifolia — A74

1975, Feb. 3 **Photo.** ***Perf. 13***
407 A73 20fr multi 60 50

"Prevent brush fires."

1975, May 30 Photo. *Perf. 13*

Design: 11fr, Liperanthus gigas.

408 A74 8fr pur & multi 70 40
409 A74 11fr dk bl & multi 85 48

Orchids. See Nos. 425-426, C125.

Festival Emblem — A75

1975, Sept. 6 Photo. *Perf. 12½x13*

410 A75 12fr ultra, org & yel 40 28

Melanesia 2000 Festival.

Birds in Flight A76

Georges Pompidou A77

1975, Oct. 18 Photo. *Perf. 13½x13*

411 A76 5fr ocher, yel & blk 32 18

Nouméa Ornithological Society, 10th anniversary.

1975, Dec. 6 Engr. *Perf. 13*

412 A77 26fr dk grn, blk & sl 90 45

Georges Pompidou (1911-1974), president of France.

Brown Booby — A78

Sea Birds: 2fr, Blue-faced booby. 8fr, Red-footed booby, vert.

Perf. 13x12½, 12½x13

1976, Feb. 21 Photo.

413 A78 1fr multi 18 15
414 A78 2fr multi 30 18
415 A78 8fr multi 75 40

Festival Emblem A79

1976, Mar. 13 Litho. *Perf. 12½*

416 A79 27fr bl, org & blk 80 45

Rotorua 1976, South Pacific Arts Festival, New Zealand.

Lion and Lions Emblem — A80

1976, Mar. 13 Photo. *Perf. 12½x13*

417 A80 49fr multi 1.40 1.10

Lions Club of Nouméa, 15th anniversary.

Music Pavilion — A81

Design: 30fr, Fountain, vert.

1976, July 3 Litho. *Perf. 12½*

418 A81 25fr multi 55 40
419 A81 30fr bl & multi 75 50

Old Nouméa.

Polluted Shore — A82

1976, Aug. 21 Photo. *Perf. 13*

420 A82 20fr dp bl & multi 60 45

Nature protection.

South Pacific People — A83

1976, Oct. 23 Photo. *Perf. 13*

421 A83 20fr bl & multi 75 45

16th South Pacific Commission Conference, Nouméa, Oct. 1976.

Giant Grasshopper A84

Design: 31fr, Beetle and larvae.

1977, Feb. 21 Engr. *Perf. 13*

422 A84 26fr multi 95 85
423 A84 31fr multi 95 85

Ground Satellite Station, Nouméa — A85

1977, Apr. 16 Litho. *Perf. 13*

424 A85 29fr multi 80 48

Orchid Type of 1975

Designs: 22fr, Phajus daenikeri. 44fr, Dendrobium finetianum.

1977, May 23 Photo. *Perf. 13*

425 A74 22fr brn & multi 75 60
426 A74 44fr bl & multi 1.50 85

Mask, Palms, "Stamps" — A86

1977, June 25 Photo. *Perf. 13*

427 A86 35fr multi 80 70

Philately in school, Philatelic Exhibition, La Perouse Lyceum, Nouméa.

Trees — A87

1977, July 16 Photo. *Perf. 13*

428 A87 20fr multi 85 55

Nature protection.

Congress Emblem — A88

1977, Aug. 6 Photo. *Perf. 13*

429 A88 200fr multi 5.25 3.50

French Junior Economic Chambers Congress, Nouméa.

Young Frigate Bird — A89

Designs: 22fr, Terns, horiz. 40fr, Sooty terns, horiz.

1977, Sept. 17 Photo. *Perf. 13*

430 A89 16fr multi 65 45
431 A89 22fr multi 85 60
432 A89 40fr multi 1.75 85

Issue dates: 16fr, Sept. 17, 1977. 22fr, 40fr, Feb. 11, 1978.

See No. C138.

Mare and Foal — A90

1977, Nov. 19 Engr. *Perf. 13*

433 A90 5fr multi 40 24

10th anniversary of the Society for Promotion of Caledonian Horses.

Araucaria Montana — A91

Halityle Regularis — A92

1978, Mar. 17 Photo. *Perf. 12½x13*

434 A91 16fr multi 55 35

See No. C149.

1978, May 20 Photo. *Perf. 13*

436 A92 10fr vio bl & multi 35 22

Nouméa Aquarium.

Stylized Turtle and Globe — A93

1978, May 20

437 A93 30fr multi 85 70

Protection of the turtle.

Flying Fox — A94

1978, June 10

438 A94 20fr multi 85 60

Nature protection.

Values quoted in this catalogue are for stamps graded at Fine-Very Fine and with no faults. An illustrated guide to grade is provided in introductory material, beginning on Page 5A.

Maurice Leenhardt — A95

Soccer Player, League Emblem — A96

1978, Aug. 16 **Engr.** ***Perf. 13***
439 A95 37fr multi 1.00 80

Pastor Maurice Leenhardt (1878-1954).

1978, Nov. 4 **Photo.** ***Perf. 13***
440 A96 26fr multi 70 42

New Caledonia Soccer League, 50th anniversary.

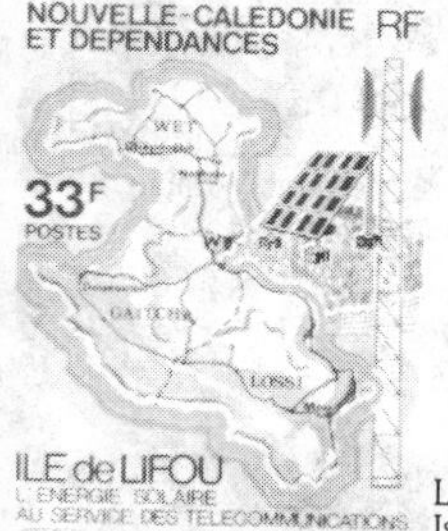

Lifu Island — A97

1978, Dec. 9 **Litho.** ***Perf. 13***
441 A97 33fr multi 1.00 65

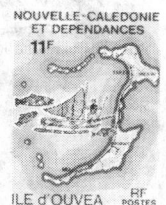

Petroglyph, Mère — A98

Map of Ouvea — A99

1979, Jan. 27 **Engr.** ***Perf. 13***
442 A98 10fr brick red 40 30

Perf. 12¹/₂x13, 13x12¹/₂
1979, Feb. 17 **Photo.**

Design: 31fr, Map of Mare Island, horiz.

443 A99 11fr multi 35 28
444 A99 31fr multi 60 45

Auguste Escoffier — A101

1979, July 21 **Engr.** ***Perf. 12¹/₂x13***
446 A101 24fr multi 65 48

Auguste Escoffier Hotel School.

Regatta and Games Emblem A102

1979, Aug. 11 **Photo.** ***Perf. 13***
447 A102 16fr multi 65 35

6th South Pacific Games, Suva, Fiji, Aug. 27-Sept. 8.

Agathis Ovata A103

1979, Oct. 6 **Photo.** ***Perf. 13x12¹/₂***
448 A103 5fr *shown* 24 15
449 A103 34fr *Cyathea intermedia* 70 48

Pouembout Rodeo A104

1979, Oct. 27 **Engr.** ***Perf. 13x12¹/₂***
450 A104 12fr multi 45 28

Bantamia Merleti A105

1979, Dec. 1 **Photo.** ***Perf. 13x11¹/₂***
451 A105 23fr multi 60 40

Fluorescent corals from Nouméa Aquarium.

Map of Pine Tree Island, Fishermen with Nets — A106

House at Artillery Point — A100

1979, Apr. 28 **Photo.** ***Perf. 13***
445 A100 20fr multi 65 48

1980, Jan. 12 **Photo.** ***Perf. 13x12¹/₂***
452 A106 23fr multi 45 28

Hibbertia Virotii A107

1980, Apr. 19 **Photo.** ***Perf. 13x12¹/₂***
453 A107 11fr shown 35 20
454 A107 12fr Grevillea meisneri 35 20

Philately at School — A108

1980, May 10 **Litho.** ***Perf. 12¹/₂***
455 A108 30fr multi 60 40

Prevention of Traffic Accidents A109

1980, July 5 **Photo.** ***Perf. 13x12¹/₂***
456 A109 15fr multi 35 20

Parribacus Caledonicus A110

Noumea Aquarium Crustacea: 8fr, Panulirus versicolor.

1980, Aug. 23 **Litho.** ***Perf. 13x13¹/₂***
457 A110 5fr multi 15 15
458 A110 8fr multi 22 15

Solar Energy A111

1980, Oct. 11 **Photo.** ***Perf. 13x12¹/₂***
459 A111 23fr multi 45 24

Manta Birostris A112

1981, Feb. 18 **Photo.** ***Perf. 13x12¹/₂***
460 A112 23fr shown 45 20
461 A112 25fr Carcharhinus amblyrhnchos 50 24

Belep Islands A113

1981, May 4
462 A113 26fr multi 55 28

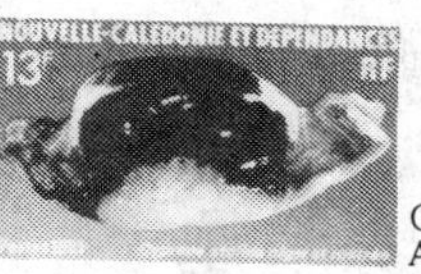

Cypraea Stolida A114

1981, June 17 **Photo.** ***Perf. 13***
463 A114 1fr Cymbiola rossiniana, vert. 15 15
464 A114 2fr Connus floccatus, vert. 15 15
465 A114 13fr shown 22 15
Set value 32 22

See Nos. 470-471.

Corvette Constantine, 1854 A115

1981, July 22 **Engr.** ***Perf. 13***
466 A115 10fr shown 22 15
467 A115 25fr Aviso le Phoque, 1853 45 18

See Nos. 476-477.

Intl. Year of the Disabled A116

1981, Sept. 2 **Litho.** ***Perf. 12¹/₂***
468 A116 45fr multi 85 48

Nature Preservation — A117

1981, Nov. 7 **Photo.** ***Perf. 13***
469 A117 28fr multi 50 24

Marine Life Type of 1981

1982, Jan. 20 **Photo.** ***Perf. 13x13¹/₂***
470 A114 13fr Calappa calappa 22 15
471 A114 25fr Etisus splendidus 45 18

Chalcantite A118

1982, Mar. 17 **Photo.** ***Perf. 13x13¹/₂***
472 A118 15fr shown 28 15
473 A118 30fr Anortnosite 55 20

Melaleuca Quinquenervia — A119

1982, June 23 Photo. *Perf. 13*

474 A119 20fr Savannah trees, vert. 38 18
475 A119 29fr shown 55 18

Ship Type of 1981

1982, July 7 Engr.

476 A115 44fr Barque Le Cher 75 35
477 A115 59fr Naval dispatch vessel Kersaint 1.00 55

Ateou Tribe Traditional House — A120

Grey's Ptilope — A121

1982, Oct. 13 Photo. *Perf. 13½x13*

478 A120 52fr multi 85 35

1982, Nov. 6

479 A121 32fr shown 60 24
480 A121 35fr Caledonian loriquet 65 24

Central Education Coordination Office — A122

1982, Nov. 27 Litho. *Perf. 13½x13*

481 A122 48fr Boat 75 28

Bernheim Library, Noumea — A123

1982, Dec. 15 Engr. *Perf. 13*

482 A123 36fr multi 60 28

Caledonian Orchids A123a

1983, Feb. 2 Photo. *Perf. 13x13½*

482A A123a 10fr Dendrobium oppositifolium 15 15
482B A123a 15fr Dendrobium munificum 20 15
482C A123a 29fr Dendrobium fractiflexum 40 20

Xanthostemon Aurantiacum — A124

1983, Mar. 23 Litho. *Perf. 13*

483 A124 1fr Crinum asiaticum 15 15
484 A124 2fr Xanthostemon aurantiacum 15 15
485 A124 4fr Metrosideros demonstrans, vert. 15 15
Set value 15 15

25th Anniv. of Posts and Telecommunications Dept. — A125

Telephones and post offices.

1983, Apr. 30 Litho. *Perf. 13*

486 A125 30fr multicolored 50 24
487 A125 40fr multicolored 60 28
488 A125 50fr multicolored 85 35
a. Souvenir sheet of 3 2.50 2.50

Nos. 486-488 se-tenant. No. 488a contains Nos. 486-488 with changed background colors.

Local Snakes — A126

1983, June 22 Photo. *Perf. 13*

489 A126 31fr Laticauda laticauda 55 24
490 A126 33fr Laticauda colubrina 60 28

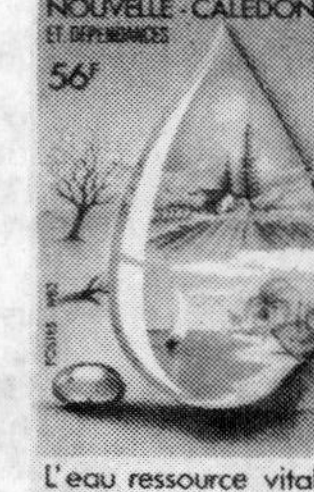

A127 A128

1983, Aug. 10 Engr.

491 A127 16fr Volleyball 25 15

7th South Pacific Games, Sept.

1983, Sept. 8 Photo. *Perf. 12½*

492 A128 56fr multi 70 40

Nature protection.

Birds of Prey A129

1983, Nov. 16 Litho. *Perf. 13*

493 A129 34fr Tyto Alba Lifuensis, vert. 40 26
494 A129 37fr Pandion Haliaetus 45 30

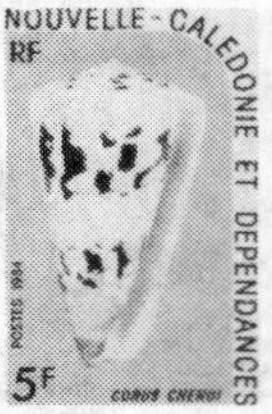

Local Shells — A130

Arms of Noumea — A132

Steamers A131

1984, Jan. 11 Litho. & Engr.

495 A130 5fr Conus chenui 15 15
496 A130 15fr Conus moluccensis 28 15
497 A130 20fr Conus optimus 30 28
Set value 36

See Nos. 521-522.

1984, Feb. 8 Engr.

498 A131 18fr St. Joseph 25 20
499 A131 31fr St. Antoine 45 32

1984, Apr. 11 Litho. *Perf. 12½x13*

500 A132 35fr multi 50 38

See No. 546, 607, C214.

Environmental Preservation — A133

1984, May 23 *Perf. 13*

501 A133 65fr Island scene 60 45

Orchids A134

1984, July 18 Litho. *Perf. 12*

502 A134 16fr Diplocaulobium ou-hinnae 22 15
503 A134 38fr Acianthus atepalus 48 30

Cent. of Public Schooling A135

Kagu A137

1984, Oct. 11 Litho. *Perf. 13½x13*

504 A135 59fr Schoolhouse 60 28

1985-86 Engr. *Perf. 13*

511 A137 1fr brt bl 15 15
512 A137 2fr green 15 15
513 A137 3fr brt org 15 15
514 A137 4fr brt grn 15 15
515 A137 5fr dp rose lil 15 15
516 A137 35fr crimson 28 15
517 A137 38fr vermilion 30 15
518 A137 40fr brt rose ('86) 40 20
Set value 1.20 70

Issue dates: 1fr, 2fr, 5fr, 38fr, May 22. 3fr, 4fr, 35fr, Feb. 13. 40fr, July 30.

See types A179, A179a.

Sea Shell Type of 1984

Lithographed and Engraved

1985, Feb. 27 *Perf. 13*

521 A130 55fr Conus bullatus 42 20
522 A130 72fr Conus lamberti 55 28

25th World Meteorological Day — A138

1985, Mar. 20 Litho.

523 A138 17fr Radio communication, storm 20 15

Red Cross, Medicine Without Frontiers — A139

1985, Apr. 10 *Perf. 12½*

524 A139 41fr multi 35 15

Electronic Railway Switching Center Inauguration — A140

1985, Apr. 24

525 A140 70fr E 10 B installation 70 38

Marguerite La Foa Suspension Bridge A141

1985, May 10 Engr. *Perf. 13*

526 A141 44fr brt bl & red brn 45 18

Historical Preservation Association.

Le Cagou Philatelic Society — A142

1985, June 15 Litho.

527 A142 220fr multi 1.75 85
a. Souvenir sheet, perf. 12½ 1.90 1.90

No. 527a sold for 230fr.

4th Pacific Arts Festival — A143

1985, July 3 *Perf. 13½*

Black Overprint

528 A143 55fr multi 52 25
529 A143 75fr multi 75 35

Not issued without overprint. Festival was transferred to French Polynesia.

Intl. Youth Year — A144

1985, July 24 **Litho.** *Perf. 13*

530 A144 59fr multi 60 30

Amedee Lighthouse Electrification A145

1985, Aug. 13

531 A145 89fr multi 85 42

Environmental Conservation A146

1985, Sept. 18

532 A146 100fr Planting trees 1.00 50

Birds — A147

1985, Dec. 18 *Perf. 12½*

533 A147 50fr Poule sultane 50 25
534 A147 60fr Merle caledonien 60 32

Noumea Aquarium A148

1986, Feb. 19 **Litho.** *Perf. 12½x13*

535 A148 10fr Pomacanthus imperator 15 15
536 A148 17fr Rhinopias aphanes 20 15
Set value 16

Kanumera Bay, Isle of Pines — A149

1986, Mar. 26 **Litho.** *Perf. 12½*

537 A149 50fr shown 60 30
538 A149 55fr Inland village 68 35

See Nos. 547-548, 617-618.

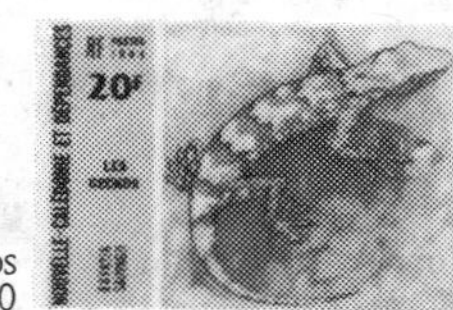
Geckos A150

1986, Apr. 16 *Perf. 12½x13*

539 A150 20fr Bavayia sauvagii 25 15
540 A150 45fr Rhacodactylus leachianus 55 30

1986 World Cup Soccer Championships, Mexico — A151

1986, May 28 *Perf. 13*

541 A151 60fr multi 75 38

1st Pharmacy in New Caledonia, 120th Anniv. — A152

1986, June 25 **Litho.** *Perf. 13*

542 A152 80fr multi 95 48

Orchids A153

1986, July 16 *Perf. 12½x13*

543 A153 44fr Coelogynae licastioides 45 22
544 A153 58fr Calanthe langei 60 30

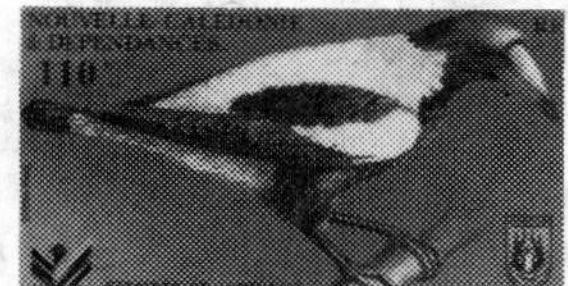
STAMPEX '86, Adelaide — A154

1986, Aug. 4 *Perf. 12½*

545 A154 110fr Bird 1.25 65

Arms Type of 1984

1986, Oct. 11 **Litho.** *Perf. 13½*

546 A132 94fr Mont Dore 1.10 55

Landscape Type of 1986

1986, Oct. 29 **Litho.** *Perf. 12½*

547 A149 40fr West landscape, vert. 45 24
548 A149 76fr South Landscape 95 52

Nature Protection Assoc. A156

Flowers: Niponthes vieillardi, Syzygium ngayense, Archidendropsis Paivana, Scavola balansae.

1986, Nov. 12 *Perf. 12½*

549 A156 73fr multi 90 45

A157 A159

A158

1986, Nov. 26 *Perf. 13x12½*

550 A157 350fr Emblem 4.25 2.00

Noumea Lions Club, 25th anniv.

1986, Dec. 23 **Litho.** *Perf. 13*

Paintings: 74fr, Moret Point, by A. Sisley. 140fr, Butterfly Chase, by B. Morisot.

551 A158 74fr multi 75 38
552 A158 140fr multi 1.40 70

1987, Jan. 28 *Perf. 13½*

553 A159 30fr Challenge France 38 18
554 A159 70fr French Kiss 90 45

America's Cup.

Plants, Butterflies A160

Designs: 46fr, Anona squamosa, Graphium gelon. 54fr, Albizzia granulosa, Polyura gamma.

1987, Feb. 25 **Litho.** *Perf. 13x12½*

555 A160 46fr multi 60 30
556 A160 54fr multi 65 32

Pirogues A161

1987, May 13 **Engr.** *Perf. 13x12½*

557 A161 72fr from Isle of Pines 80 40
558 A161 90fr from Ouvea 90 45

New Town Hall, Mont Dore — A162

1987, May 23 **Litho.** *Perf. 12½x13*

559 A162 92fr multi 1.10 55

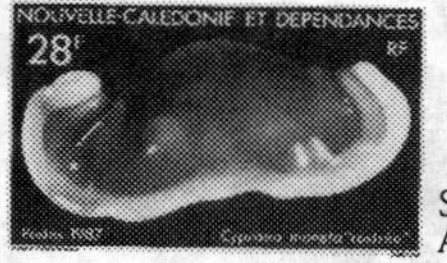
Seashells A163

1987, June 24 *Perf. 13*

560 A163 28fr Cypraea moneta 35 16
561 A163 36fr Cypraea martini 45 25

A164

A165

1987, July 8 *Perf. 12½x13*

562 A164 40fr multi 52 26

8th South Pacific Games.

1987, July 22 *Perf. 13½*

563 A165 270fr multi 3.50 1.75

Soroptimist Int'l. 13th Convention, Melbourne, July 26-31.

Birds — A166

1987, Aug. 26 *Perf. 13*

564 A166 18fr Zosterops xanthochroa 26 15
565 A166 21fr Falco peregrinus nesiotes, vert. 28 15
Set value 21

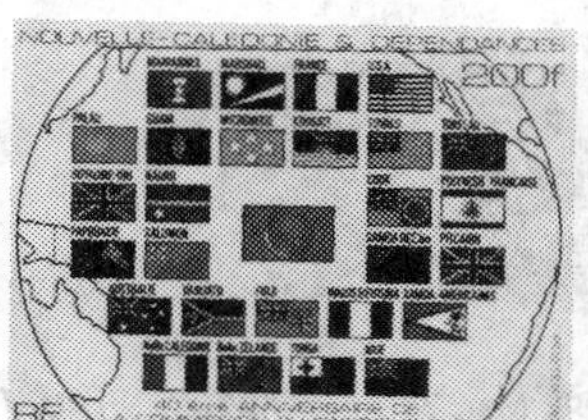
South Pacific Commission, 40th Anniv. — A167

1987, Oct. 14 **Litho.** *Perf. 13*

566 A167 200fr multi 2.75 1.40

Foreign postal stationery (stamped envelopes, postal cards and air letter sheets) lies beyond the scope of this Catalogue, which is limited to adhesive postage stamps.

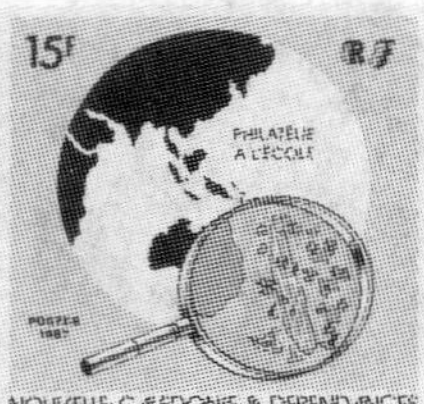

Philately at School
A168

1987, Oct. 21 *Perf. 12½*
567 A168 15fr multi 20 15

8th South Pacific Games, Noumea — A169

1987, Dec. 5 **Litho.** *Perf. 12½*
568 A169 20fr Golf 28 15
569 A169 30fr Rugby 40 20
570 A169 100fr Long jump 1.40 70

Map, Ships, La Perouse — A170

1988, Feb. 10 **Engr.** *Perf. 13*
571 A170 36fr dark rose lil 48 24

Disappearance of La Perouse expedition, 200th anniv., and Jean-Francois de Galaup (1741-1788), Comte de La Perouse.

French University of the South Pacific at Noumea and Papeete
A171

1988, Feb. 24 **Litho.** *Perf. 13x12½*
572 A171 400fr multi 5.25 2.75

Tropical Fish — A172

1988, Mar. 23 **Litho.** *Perf. 13*
573 A172 30fr Pomacanthus semicirculatus 38 20
574 A172 46fr Glyphidodontops cyaneus 60 30

Intl. Red Cross and Red Crescent Organizations, 125th Annivs.
A173

1988, Apr. 27
575 A173 300fr multi 3.75 1.50

Regional Housing
A174

Designs: 19fr, Mwaringou, Canala Region, vert. 21fr, Nathalo, Lifou.

1988, Apr. 13 **Engr.** *Perf. 13*
576 A174 19fr emer grn, brt blue & red brn 24 15
577 A174 21fr brt blue, emer grn & red brn 28 15

Medicinal Plants
A175

1988, May 18 **Litho.** *Perf. 13x12½*
578 A175 28fr *Ochrosia elliptica* 38 20
579 A175 64fr *Rauvolfia levenetii* 85 42

No. 579 is airmail.

Living Fossils — A176

1988, June 13 *Perf. 13*
580 A176 51fr *Gymnocrinus richeri* 70 35

Bourail Museum and Historical Soc. — A177

1988, June 25 **Litho.** *Perf. 13*
581 A177 120fr multi 1.50 75

SYDPEX '88 — A178

Designs: No. 582, La Perouse aboard *La Boussole*, gazing through spyglass at the First Fleet in Botany Bay, Jan. 24, 1788. No. 583, Capt. Phillip and crew ashore on Botany Bay watching the approach of La Perouse's ships *La Boussole* and *L'Astrolabe*.

1988, July 30 **Litho.** *Perf. 13x12½*
582 A178 42fr multi 50 25
583 A178 42fr multi 50 25
a. Souvenir sheet of 2, #582-583, perf. 13x13½ 1.40 1.40

Nos. 582-583 printed se-tenant with center label picturing SYDPEX '88 emblem.
No. 583a sold for 120fr.

Kagu
A179 A179a

1988-90 **Engr.** *Perf. 13*
584 A179 1fr bright blue 15 15
585 A179 2fr green 15 15
586 A179 3fr bright orange 15 15
587 A179 4fr bright green 15 15
588 A179 5fr deep rose lilac 15 15
589 A179 28fr orange 55 28
590 A179 40fr bright rose 50 25
Set value 1.35 75

Issue dates: 40fr, Aug. 11. 1fr, 4fr, Jan. 25, 1989. 2fr, 3fr, 5fr, Apr. 19, 1989. 28fr, Jan. 15, 1990.
See Type A137.

1990-93 **Engr.** *Perf. 13*
591 A179a 1fr bright blue 15 15
592 A179a 2fr bright green 15 15
593 A179a 3fr brt yel org 15 15
594 A179a 4fr dark green 15 15
595 A179a 5fr bright violet 15 15
596 A179a 9fr blue black 20 15
597 A179a 12fr orange 28 15
598 A179a 40fr lilac rose 95 48
599 A179a 50fr red 1.20 60
Nos. 591-599 (9) 3.38
Set value 1.50

Issue dates: 50fr, Sept. 6, 1990. 1fr-5fr, Jan. 9, 1991. 40fr, Jan. 16, 1992. 9fr, 12fr, Jan. 25, 1993.
This is an expanding set. Numbers will change if necessary.
See Type A137.

1988 Summer Olympics, Seoul — A180

1988, Sept. 15 *Perf. 12½x12*
600 A180 150fr multi 1.50 75

Pasteur Institute, Noumea, Cent. — A181

1988, Sept. 29 **Engr.** *Perf. 13*
601 A181 100fr blk, brt ultra & dark red 1.50 75

Writers — A182

1988, Oct. 15 **Engr.** *Perf. 13*
602 A182 72fr Georges Baudoux (1870-1949) 1.35 68
603 A182 73fr Jean Mariotti (1901-1975) 1.40 70

No. 603 is airmail.

WHO, 40th Anniv.
A183

1988, Nov. 16 **Litho.** *Perf. 13x12½*
604 A183 250fr multi 4.75 2.40

Art Type of 1984 Without "ET DEPENDANCES"

Paintings by artists of the Pacific: 54fr, *Land of Men*, by L. Bunckley. 92fr, *The Latin Quarter*, by Marik.

1988, Dec. 7
605 AP113 54fr multi 1.05 52
606 AP113 92fr multi 1.75 88

Arms Type of 1984 Without "ET DEPENDANCES"

1989, Feb. 22 **Litho.** *Perf. 13½*
607 A132 200fr Koumac 3.65 1.85

Indigenous Flora
A184

1989, Mar. 22 **Litho.** *Perf. 13½*
608 A184 80fr *Parasitaxus ustus*, vert. 1.55 78
609 A184 90fr *Tristaniopsis guillainii* 1.75 88

Marine Life — A185

1989, May 17 **Litho.** *Perf. 12½x13*
610 A185 18fr *Plesionika* 38 20
611 A185 66fr *Ocosia apia* 1.35 68
612 A185 110fr *Latiaxis* 2.25 1.25

See Nos. 652-653.

French Revolution, Bicent. — A186

1989, July 7 **Litho.** *Perf. 13½*
613 A186 40fr Liberty 72 35
614 A186 58fr Equality 1.05 52
615 A186 76fr Fraternity 1.35 68

Souvenir Sheet

616 A186 180fr Liberty, Equality, Fraternity 3.25 3.25

Nos. 614-616 are airmail.

Landscape Type of 1986 Without "ET DEPENDANCES"

1989, Aug. 23 **Litho.** *Perf. 13*
617 A149 64fr La Poule rookery, Hienghene 1.10 55
618 A149 180fr Ouaieme ferry 3.00 1.50

No. 617 is airmail.

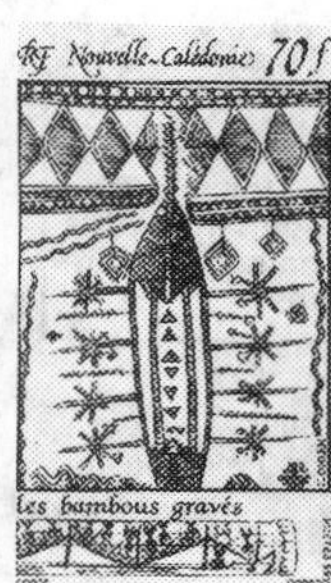

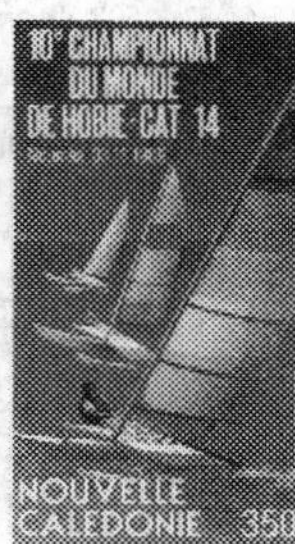

A187 A188

Perf. 12½x13

1989, Sept. 27 **Litho. & Engr.**
619 A187 70fr Carved bamboo 1.20 60

See No. C216.

1989, Oct. 25 **Litho.** ***Perf. 13***
620 A188 350fr multicolored 6.00 3.00

Hobie-Cat 14 10th World Championships, Nov. 3, Noumea.

Natl. Historical Soc., 20th Anniv. — A189

Cover of *Moeurs: Superstitions of New Caledonians,* cover of book on Melanesian oral literature and historians G. Pisier, R.P. Neyret and A. Surleau.

1989, Nov. 3 **Engr.**
621 A189 74fr brown & black 1.30 65

Ft. Teremba — A190

1989, Nov. 18 **Engr.**
622 A190 100fr bl grn & dk org 1.75 88

Marguerite Historical Preservation Soc.

Impressionist Paintings A191

Designs: 130fr, *The Escape of Rochefort,* by Manet. 270fr, *Self-portrait,* by Courbet.

1989, Dec. 6 **Litho.** ***Perf. 13½***
623 A191 130fr multicolored 2.25 1.15
624 A191 270fr multicolored 4.50 2.25

Fr. Patrick O'Reilly (1900-1988), Writer — A192

1990, Jan. 24 **Engr.** ***Perf. 13x13½***
625 A192 170fr blk & plum 3.25 1.65

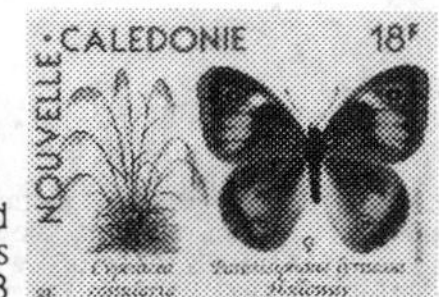

Grasses and Butterflies A193

Various *Cyperacea costularia* and *Paratisiphone lyrnessa:* 18fr, Female. 50fr, Female, diff. 94fr, Male.

1990, Jan. 21 **Litho.** ***Perf. 13½***
626 A193 18fr shown 35 18
627 A193 50fr multicolored 95 48
628 A193 94fr multicolored 1.75 88

Nos. 626 and 628 are airmail.

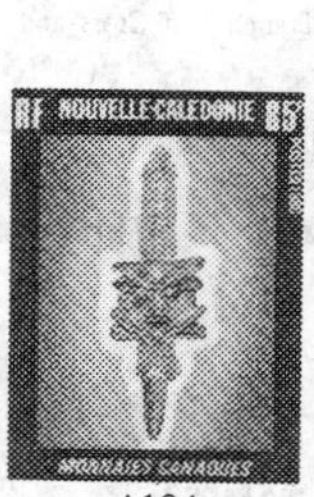

A194 A195

1990, Mar. 16 **Engr.** ***Perf. 12½x13***
629 A194 85fr Kanakan money 1.60 80
630 A194 140fr money, diff. 2.65 1.35

1990, Mar. 16 **Litho.** ***Perf. 13x13½***
631 A195 230fr multicolored 4.35 2.20

Jade and mother of pearl exhibition, New Caledonian Museum.

Noumea Aquarium A196

Perf. 13x12½, 12½x13

1990, Apr. 25
632 A196 10fr *Phyllidia ocellata* 20 15
633 A196 42fr *Chromodoris kuniei,* vert. 88 45

Petroglyphs — A197

1990, July 11 **Engr.** ***Perf. 13***
634 A197 40fr Neounda 78 40
635 A197 58fr Kassducou 1.10 55

No. 635 is airmail.

Meeting Center of the Pacific — A198

1990, July 25 **Litho.** ***Perf. 13***
636 A198 320fr multicolored 6.25 3.10

World Cup Soccer Championships, Italy — A199

1990, May 30 **Litho.** ***Perf. 13***
637 A199 240fr multicolored 5.25 2.60

Flowers A200

1990, Nov. 7 ***Perf. 13x12½***
638 A200 105fr Gardenia aubryi 1.00 50
639 A200 130fr Hibbertia baudouinii 1.20 60

La Maison Celieres by M. Petron A201

Design: 365fr, Le Mont-Dore de Jade by C. Degroiselle.

1990, Dec. 5 ***Perf. 12½***
640 A201 110fr multicolored 2.60 1.30
641 A201 365fr multicolored 8.75 4.35

No. 640 is airmail.

Writers — A202

Designs: #642, Louise Michel (1830-1905). #643, Charles B. Nething (1867-1947).

1991, Mar. 20 **Engr.** ***Perf. 13***
642 A202 125fr rose lil & bl 2.75 1.40
643 A202 125fr brn & bl 2.75 1.40
a. Pair, #642-643 + label 5.50 2.80

Native Huts — A203

1991, May 15 **Litho.** ***Perf. 12***
644 A203 12fr Houailou 25 15
645 A203 35fr Hienghene 75 38

Maps of the Provinces A204

1991, June 17 **Litho.** ***Perf. 13½***
646 A204 45fr Northern 95 48
647 A204 45fr Island 95 48
648 A204 45fr Southern 95 48
a. Strip of 3, #646-648 2.85 1.42

Orchids — A205

1991, July 24 **Litho.** ***Perf. 13***
649 A205 55fr Dendrobium biflorum 1.15 62
650 A205 70fr Dendrobium closterium 1.45 72

French Institute of Scientific Research — A206

1991, Aug. 26
651 A206 170fr multicolored 3.50 1.75

Marine Life Type of 1989

1991, Aug. 26 **Litho.** ***Perf. 12***
652 A185 60fr Monocentris japonicus 1.25 65
653 A185 100fr Tristigenys niphonia 2.10 1.05

9th South Pacific Games, Papua New Guinea A207

1991, Sept. 6 ***Perf. 12½***
654 A207 170fr multicolored 3.50 1.75

The lack of a value for a listed item does not necessarily indicate rarity.

Vietnamese in New Caledonia, Cent. — A208

1991, Sept. 8 Engr. *Perf. 13x12½*
655 A208 300fr multicolored 7.00 3.50

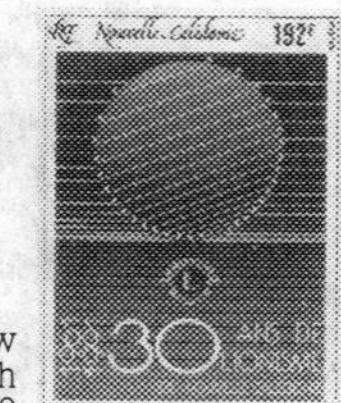
Lions Club of New Caledonia, 30th Anniv. — A209

1991, Oct. 5 Litho. *Perf. 12½*
656 A209 192fr multicolored 4.25 2.10

First Commercial Harvesting of Sandalwood, 150th Anniv. — A210

1991, Oct. 23 Engr. *Perf. 13*
657 A210 200fr multicolored 4.25 2.10

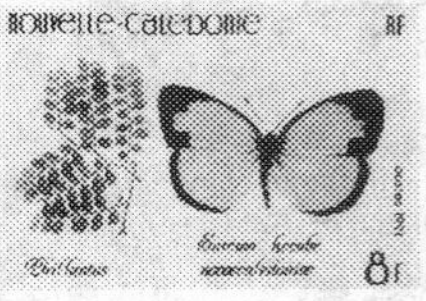
Phila Nippon '91 — A211

Plants and butterflies: 8fr, Phillantus, Eurema hecabe. 15fr, Pipturus incanus, Hypolimnas octocula. 20fr, Stachytarpheta urticaefolia, Precis villida. 26fr, Malaisia scandens, Cyrestis telamon.
Butterflies: No. 662a, Cyrestis telamon, vert. b, Hypolimnas octocula, vert. c, Eurema hecabe, vert. d, Precis villida, vert.

1991, Nov. 16 Litho. *Perf. 12½*
658 A211 8fr multicolored 20 15
659 A211 15fr multicolored 38 18
660 A211 20fr multicolored 50 25
661 A211 26fr multicolored 65 32
a. Strip of 4, #658-661 + label 1.70 85

Souvenir Sheet

662 A211 75fr Sheet of 4, #a.-d. 7.00 7.00

Central Bank for Economic Cooperation, 50th Anniv. — A212

Designs: No. 663, Nickel processing plant, dam. No. 664, Private home, tourist hotels.

1991, Dec. 2 Litho. *Perf. 13*
663 A212 76fr multicolored 2.60 1.30
664 A212 76fr multicolored 2.60 1.30
a. Pair, #663-664 + label 5.20 2.60

Preservation of Nature — A213

1992, Mar. 25 Litho. *Perf. 13*
665 A213 15fr Madeleine waterfalls 35 18
a. Souv. sheet, perf. 12½ 3.35 3.35

No. 665a sold for 150fr.

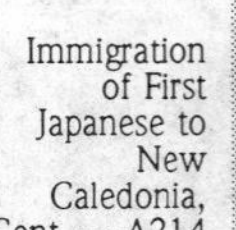
Immigration of First Japanese to New Caledonia, Cent. — A214

1992, May 11 Litho. *Perf. 13x12½*
666 A214 95fr yellow & multi 2.40 1.20
667 A214 95fr gray & multi 2.40 1.20
a. Pair, #666-667 + label 4.80 2.40

Arrival of American Armed Forces, 50th Anniv. — A215

1992, Aug. 13
668 A215 50fr multicolored 1.25 60

SEMI-POSTAL STAMPS

No. 93 Surcharged

1915 Unwmk. *Perf. 14x13½*
B1 A16 10c + 5c carmine 45 45
a. Inverted surcharge 17.50 17.50
b. Cross omitted 17.50 17.50

Regular Issue of 1905 Surcharged
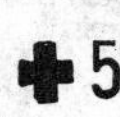

1917
B2 A16 10c + 5c rose 28 28
a. Double surcharge 30.00 30.00
B3 A16 15c + 5c violet 28 28

Curie Issue
Common Design Type

1938, Oct. 24 *Perf. 13*
B4 CD80 1.75fr + 50c brt ultra 5.75 5.75

French Revolution Issue
Common Design Type

1939, July 5 Photo.
Name and Value Typo. in Black
B5 CD83 45c + 25c grn 3.50 3.50
B6 CD83 70c + 30c brn 3.50 3.50
B7 CD83 90c + 35c red org 3.50 3.50
B8 CD83 1.25fr + 1fr rose pink 3.50 3.50
B9 CD83 2.25fr + 2fr blue 3.50 3.50
Nos. B5-B9 (5) 17.50 17.50

Common Design Type and

Dumont d'Urville's ship, "Zélée" — SP2

New Caledonian Militiaman SP3

1941 Photo. *Perf. 13½*
B10 SP2 1fr + 1fr red 50
B11 CD86 1.50fr + 3fr maroon 50
B12 SP3 2.50fr + 1fr dk blue 50

Nos. B10-B12 were issued by the Vichy government and were not placed on sale in the colony.
In 1944 Nos. 216A-216B were surcharged "OEUVRES COLONIALES" and surtax (including change of denomination of the 2.50fr to 50c). These were issued by the Vichy government and not placed on sale in New Caledonia.

Catalogue values for unused stamps in this section, from this point to the end of the section, are for Never Hinged items.

Red Cross Issue
Common Design Type

1944 *Perf. 14½x14*
B13 CD90 5fr + 20fr brt scar 45 45

The surtax was for the French Red Cross and national relief.

Tropical Medicine Issue
Common Design Type

1950, May 15 Engr. *Perf. 13*
B14 CD100 10fr + 2fr red brn & sepia 2.00 2.00

The surtax was for charitable work.

AIR POST STAMPS

Seaplane Over Pacific Ocean — AP1

1938-40 Unwmk. Engr. *Perf. 13*
C1 AP1 65c dp vio 38 38
a. "65c" omitted 67.50
C2 AP1 4.50fr red 55 55
C3 AP1 7fr dk bl grn ('40) 38 38
C4 AP1 9fr ultra 1.00 1.00
C5 AP1 20fr dk org ('40) 60 60
C6 AP1 50fr blk ('40) 1.25 1.25
Nos. C1-C6 (6) 4.16 4.16

V4

Stamps of type AP1, without "RF" monogram, and stamp of the design shown above were issued in 1942 to 1944 by the Vichy Government, but were not placed on sale in the colony.

Common Design Type

1942 Unwmk. *Perf. 14½x14*
C7 CD87 1fr dk org 28 24
C8 CD87 1.50fr brt red 28 24
C9 CD87 5fr brn red 30 24
C10 CD87 10fr black 50 40

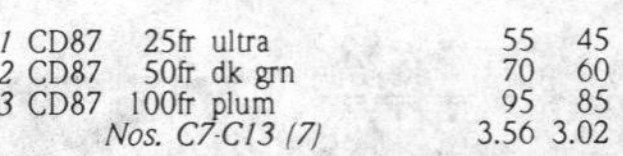
C11 CD87 25fr ultra 55 45
C12 CD87 50fr dk grn 70 60
C13 CD87 100fr plum 95 85
Nos. C7-C13 (7) 3.56 3.02

Catalogue values for unused stamps in this section, from this point to the end of the section, are for Never Hinged items.

Victory Issue
Common Design Type

1946, May 8 Engr. *Perf. 12½*
C14 CD92 8fr brt ultra 60 60

Chad to Rhine Issue
Common Design Types

1946, June 6
C15 CD93 5fr black 45 45
C16 CD94 10fr carmine 45 45
C17 CD95 15fr dk bl 48 48
C18 CD96 20fr org brn 48 48
C19 CD97 25fr ol grn 75 75
C20 CD98 50fr dk rose vio 1.10 1.10
Nos. C15-C20 (6) 3.71 3.71

St. Vincent Bay — AP2

Planes over Islands — AP3

View of Nouméa — AP4

Perf. 13x12½, 12½x13
1948, Mar. 1 Photo. Unwmk.
C21 AP2 50fr org & rose vio 1.90 1.50
C22 AP3 100fr bl grn & sl bl 4.25 2.00
C23 AP4 200fr brn & yel 9.00 4.50

UPU Issue
Common Design Type

1949, July 4 Engr. *Perf. 13*
C24 CD99 10fr multi 1.90 1.65

Liberation Issue
Common Design Type

1954, June 6
C25 CD102 3fr ind & ultra 1.90 1.65

Conveyor for Nickel Ore — AP5

1955, Nov. 21 Unwmk. *Perf. 13*
C26 AP5 14fr indigo & sepia 2.00 70

Rock Formations, Bourail — AP6

1959, Mar. 23
C27 AP6 200fr lt bl, brn & grn 20.00 7.50

Yaté Dam — AP7

1959, Sept. 20 **Engr.**
C28 AP7 50fr grn, brt bl & sep 4.00 2.75

Dedication of Yaté Dam.

Fisherman with Throw-net — AP8

Skin Diver Shooting Bumphead Surgeonfish — AP9

Designs: 20fr, Nautilus shell. 100fr, Yaté rock.

1962 **Unwmk.** ***Perf. 13***
C29 AP8 15fr red, Prus grn & sep 2.50 90
C30 AP9 20fr dk sl grn & org ver 3.50 1.50
C31 AP9 25fr red brn, gray & bl 5.00 1.50
C32 AP9 100fr dk brn, dk bl & sl grn 14.00 5.25

Telstar Issue
Common Design Type

1962, Dec. 4 **Unwmk.** ***Perf. 13***
C33 CD111 200fr dk bl, choc & grnsh bl 20.00 9.00

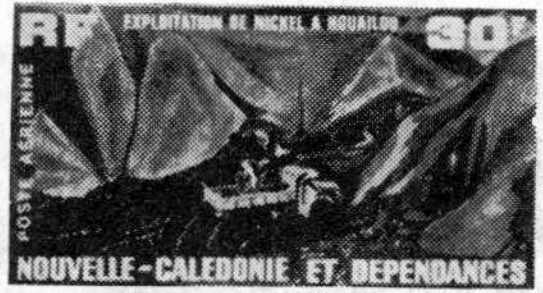

Nickel Mining, Houailou — AP10

1964, May 14 **Photo.**
C34 AP10 30fr multi 2.00 1.25

Isle of Pines AP11

1964, Dec. 7 **Engr.** ***Perf. 13***
C35 AP11 50fr dk bl, sl grn & choc 2.25 1.50

Phyllobranchus — AP12

Design: 27fr, Paracanthurus teuthis (fish).

1964, Dec. 17 **Photo.**
C36 AP12 27fr red brn, yel, dp bl & blk 3.00 1.50
C37 AP12 37fr bl, brn & yel 3.75 2.25

Issued to publicize the Nouméa Aquarium.

Greco-Roman Wrestling — AP13

1964, Dec. 28 **Engr.**
C38 AP13 10fr brt grn, pink & blk 12.50 10.00

18th Olympic Games, Tokyo, Oct. 10-25.

Nimbus Weather Satellite over New Caledonia — AP14

1965, Mar. 23 **Photo.** ***Perf. 13x12½***
C39 AP14 9fr multi 2.00 1.75

Fifth World Meteorological Day.

ITU Issue
Common Design Type

1965, May 17 **Engr.** ***Perf. 13***
C40 CD120 40fr lt bl, lil rose & lt brn 5.00 4.25

Coris Angulata (Young Fish) — AP15

Coris Angulata: 15fr, Adolescent fish. 25fr, Adult fish.

1965, Dec. 6 **Engr.** ***Perf. 13***
C41 AP15 13fr red org, ol bis & blk 1.10 40
C42 AP15 15fr ind, sl grn & bis 1.75 65
C43 AP15 25fr ind & yel grn 2.75 1.75

Issued to publicize the Nouméa Aquarium.

French Satellite A-1 Issue
Common Design Type

Designs: 8fr, Diamant rocket and launching installations. 12fr, A-1 satellite.

1966, Jan. 10 **Engr.** ***Perf. 13***
C44 CD121 8fr rose brn, ultra & Prus bl 2.00 1.10
C45 CD121 12fr ultra, Prus bl & rose brn 2.50 1.90
a. Strip of 2, #C44-C45 + label 4.50 3.00

French Satellite D-1 Issue
Common Design Type

1966, May 16 **Engr.** ***Perf. 13***
C46 CD122 10fr dl bl, ocher & sep 1.25 1.10

Port-de-France, 1866 — AP16

1966, June 2
C47 AP16 30fr dk red, bl & ind 2.25 1.90

Centenary of Port-de-France changing name to Nouméa.

Bird Type of Regular Issue

Designs: 27fr, Uvea crested parakeet. 37fr, Scarlet honey eater. 50fr, Two cloven-feathered doves.

1966-68 **Photo.** ***Perf. 13***
Size: 26x46mm
C48 A45 27fr pink & multi 3.25 2.00
C49 A45 37fr grn & multi 4.75 2.75
Size: 27x48mm
C49A A45 50fr multi ('68) 5.50 2.75

Issue dates: 50fr, May 14, 1968. Others, Oct. 10, 1966.

Sailboats and Map of New Caledonia-New Zealand Route — AP17

1967, Apr. 15 **Engr.** ***Perf. 13***
C50 AP17 25fr brt grn, dp ultra & red 2.25 1.50

2nd sailboat race from Whangarei, New Zealand, to Nouméa, New Caledonia.

Butterfly Type of Regular Issue

Butterflies: 19fr, Danaus plexippus. 29fr, Hippotion celerio. 85fr, Delias elipsis.

1967-68 **Engr.** ***Perf. 13***
Size: 48x27mm
C51 A52 19fr multi ('68) 3.00 1.75
C52 A52 29fr multi ('68) 3.50 2.50
C53 A52 85fr red, dk brn & yel 9.50 4.75

Issue dates: 85fr, Aug. 10. Others, Mar. 26.

Jules Garnier, Garnierite and Mine — AP18

1967, Oct. 9 **Engr.** ***Perf. 13***
C54 AP18 70fr bl gray, brn & yel grn 2.75 2.00

Centenary of the discovery of garnierite (nickel ore).

Lifu Island AP19

1967, Oct. 28 **Photo.** ***Perf. 13***
C55 AP19 200fr multi 6.00 4.00

Skier, Snowflake and Olympic Emblem — AP20

1967, Nov. 16 **Engr.** ***Perf. 13***
C56 AP20 100fr brn red, sl grn & brt bl 8.00 4.50

10th Winter Olympic Games, Grenoble, France, Feb. 6-18, 1968.

Sea Shell Type of Regular Issue

Designs: 39fr, Conus lienardi. 40fr, Conus cabriti. 70fr, Conus coccineus.

1968, Nov. 9 **Engr.** ***Perf. 13***
C58 A54 39fr bl grn, brn & gray 2.50 1.25
C59 A54 40fr blk, brn red & ol 2.50 1.25
C60 A54 70fr brn, pur & gray 6.00 3.00

Maré Dancers — AP21

1968, Nov. 20 **Engr.** ***Perf. 13***
C61 AP21 60fr grn, ultra & hn brn 3.50 2.25

World Map and Caudron C 600 "Aiglon" — AP22

1969, Mar. 24 **Engr.** ***Perf. 13***
C62 AP22 29fr lil, dk bl & dk car 2.00 1.40

Issued for Stamp Day and to commemorate the first flight from Nouméa to Paris of Henri Martinet and Paul Klein, March 24, 1939.

Concorde Issue
Common Design Type

1969, Apr. 17 **Engr.** ***Perf. 13***
C63 CD129 100fr sl grn & brt grn 14.00 10.00

Cattle Type of Regular Issue

Design: 50fr, Cowboy and herd.

1969, May 10 **Engr.** ***Perf. 13***
Size: 48x27mm
C64 A56 50fr sl grn, dk brn & red brn 3.00 2.00

Shell Type of Regular Issue, 1969

Design: 100fr, Black murex.

1969, June 21 **Engr.** ***Perf. 13***
Size: 48x27mm
C65 A57 100fr lake, bl & blk 13.00 7.00

Sports Type of 1969

Designs: 30fr, Woman diver. 39fr, Shot put, vert.

1969, Aug. 7 Engr. *Perf. 13*
Size: 48x27mm, 27x48mm

C66 A58 30fr dk brn, bl & blk 2.00 1.25
C67 A58 39fr dk ol, brt grn & ol 2.75 1.65

Napoleon in Coronation Robes, by Franois P. Gerard AP23

1969, Oct. 2 Photo. *Perf. 12½x12*

C68 AP23 40fr lil & multi 8.50 5.50

200th birth anniv. of Napoleon Bonaparte (1769-1821).

Air France Plane over Outrigger Canoe — AP24

1969, Oct. 2 Engr. *Perf. 13*

C69 AP24 50fr slate grn, sky bl & choc 2.50 2.00

20th anniversary of the inauguration of the Nouméa to Paris airline.

Bird Type of Regular Issue, 1966.

Birds: 39fr, Emerald doves. 100fr, Whistling kite.

1970, Feb. 19 Photo. *Perf. 13*
Size: 27x48mm

C70 A45 39fr multi 3.00 1.40
C71 A45 100r lt bl & multi 8.00 4.00

Planes Circling Globe and Paris-Nouméa Route — AP25

1970, May 6 Engr. *Perf. 13*

C72 AP25 200fr vio, org brn & grnsh bl 8.75 5.00

10th anniversary of the Paris to Nouméa flight: "French Wings Around the World."

Shell Type of Regular Issue

Designs: 22fr, Strombus sinautus humphrey, vert. 33fr, Argus porcelain shell. 34fr, Strombus vomer, vert. 60fr, Card porcelain shell.

1970 Engr. *Perf. 13*
Size: 27x48mm, 48x27mm

C73 A59 22fr bl & multi 2.00 1.40
C74 A59 33fr brn & gray bl 3.00 1.75
C75 A59 34fr pur & multi 3.00 1.75
C76 A59 60fr lt grn & brn 6.00 3.00

See Nos. C89-C90.

Bicyclists on Map of New Caledonia — AP26

1970, Aug. 20 Engr. *Perf. 13*

C77 AP26 40fr bl, ultra & choc 1.75 1.25

The 4th Bicycling Race of New Caledonia.

Mt. Fuji and Monorail Train — AP27

Design: 45fr, Map of Japan and Buddha statue.

1970, Sept. 3 Photo. *Perf. 13x12½*

C78 AP27 20fr blk, bl & yel grn 1.10 65
C79 AP27 45fr mar, lt bl & ol 1.90 90

EXPO '70 International Exposition, Osaka, Japan, Mar. 15-Sept. 13.

Racing Yachts AP28

1971, Feb. 23 Engr. *Perf. 13*

C80 AP28 20fr grn, blk & ver 1.25 65

First challenge in New Zealand waters for the One Ton Cup ocean race.

Lt. Col. Broche and Map of Mediterranean — AP29

1971, May 5 Photo. *Perf. 12½*

C81 AP29 60fr multi 3.00 2.25

30th anniversary of Battalion of the Pacific.

Pole Vault AP30

1971, June 24 Engr. *Perf. 13*

C82 AP30 25fr shown 1.40 90
C83 AP30 100fr Archery 3.75 2.25

4th South Pacific Games, Papeete, French Polynesia, Sept. 8-19.

Port de Plaisance, Nouméa — AP31

1971, Sept. 27 Photo. *Perf. 13*

C84 AP31 200fr multi 10.00 5.00

Golden Eagle and Pilot's Leaflet — AP32

1971, Nov. 20 Engr. *Perf. 13*

C85 AP32 90fr dk brn, org & ind 4.00 2.25

40th anniversary of the first flight from New Caledonia to Australia with Victor Roffey piloting the Golden Eagle.

Skiing and Sapporo '72 Emblem — AP33

1972, Jan. 22 Engr. *Perf. 13*

C86 AP33 50fr brt bl, car & sl grn 2.75 1.40

11th Winter Olympic Games, Sapporo, Japan, Feb. 3-13.

South Pacific Commission Headquarters, Nouméa — AP34

1972, Feb. 5 Photo.

C87 AP34 18fr bl & multi 70 45

South Pacific Commission, 25th anniv.

St. Mark's Basilica, Venice — AP35

1972, Feb. 5 Engr.

C88 AP35 20fr lt grn, bl & grn 1.40 65

UNESCO campaign to save Venice.

Shell Type of Regular Issue, 1970

Designs: 25fr, Orange spider conch, vert. 50fr, Chiragra spider conch, vert.

1972, Mar. 4 Engr. *Perf. 13*
Size: 27x48mm

C89 A59 25fr dp car & dk brn 2.25 1.10
C90 A59 50fr grn, brn & rose car 3.50 1.90

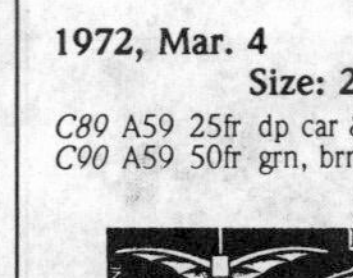

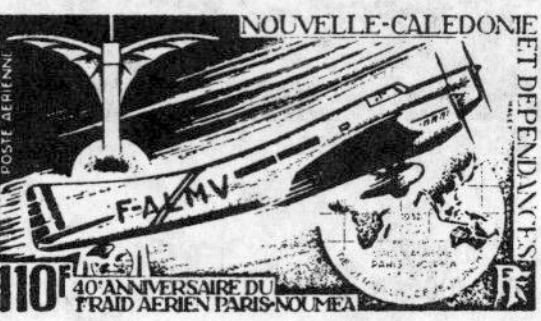

Breguet F-ALMV and Globe — AP36

1972, Apr. 5 Engr. *Perf. 13*

C91 AP36 110fr brt rose lil, bl & grn 6.50 4.50

40th anniversary of the first Paris-Nouméa flight, Mar. 9-Apr. 5, 1932.

Round House and Festival Emblem — AP37

1972, May 13

C92 AP37 24fr org, bl & brn 1.25 80

So. Pacific Festival of Arts, Fiji, May 6-20.

Hurdles and Olympic Rings AP38

1972, Sept. 2 Engr. *Perf. 13*

C93 AP38 72fr vio, bl & red lil 4.00 2.25

20th Olympic Games, Munich, Aug. 26-Sept. 11.

New Post Office, Noumea — AP39

1972, Nov. 25 Engr. *Perf. 13*

C94 AP39 23fr brn, brt bl & grn 1.25 55

Molière and Scenes from Plays — AP40

1973, Feb. 24 Engr. *Perf. 13*

C95 AP40 50fr multi 3.00 1.50

300th anniversary of the death of Molière (Jean Baptiste Poquelin, 1622-1673), French actor and playwright.

Woodlands — AP41

Designs: 18fr, Palm trees on coast, vert. 21fr, Waterfall, vert.

1973, Feb. 24 **Photo.**
C96 AP41 11fr gold & multi 75 50
C97 AP41 18fr gold & multi 1.50 60
C98 AP41 21fr gold & multi 2.00 75

Concorde — AP42

1973, Mar. 15 **Engr.** ***Perf. 13***
C99 AP42 23fr blue 2.75 2.00
a. Booklet pane of 5 25.00

No. C99 issued in booklets only.

El Kantara in Panama Canal — AP43

1973, Mar. 24 **Engr.** ***Perf. 13***
C100 AP43 60fr brn, yel grn & blk 3.50 2.00

50th anniversary of steamship connection Marseilles to Nouméa through Panama Canal.

Sun, Earth, Wind God and Satellite — AP44

1973, Mar. 24
C101 AP44 80fr multi 3.00 1.65

Centenary of international meteorological cooperation and 13th World Meteorological Day.

Museum Type of Regular Issue

Designs: 16fr, Carved arrows and arrowhead. 40fr, Carved entrance to chief's house.

1973, Apr. 30 **Photo.** ***Perf. 12½x13***
C102 A66 16fr multi 60 50
C103 A66 40fr multi 1.40 1.00

DC-10 over Map of Route Paris to Nouméa — AP45

1973, May 19 **Engr.** ***Perf. 13***
C104 AP45 100fr brn, ultra & sl grn 4.00 2.50

First direct flight by DC-10, Nouméa to Paris.

Fish Type of Regular Issue

Design: 32fr, Old and young olive surgeonfish.

1973, June 23 **Photo.** ***Perf. 13x12½***
C105 A69 32fr multi 3.00 1.75

Coach, 1880 — AP46

1973, Sept. 22 **Engr.** ***Perf. 13***
C106 AP46 15fr choc, bl & sl grn 85 55

Stamp Day 1973.

Landscape — AP47

West Coast Landscapes: 8fr, Rocky path, vert. 26fr, Trees on shore.

1974, Feb. 23 **Photo.** ***Perf. 13***
C107 AP47 8fr gold & multi 60 25
C108 AP47 22fr gold & multi 1.10 45
C109 AP47 26fr gold & multi 1.65 65

Anse-Vata, Scientific Center, Nouméa — AP48

1974, Mar. 23 **Photo.** ***Perf. 13x12½***
C110 AP48 50fr multi 1.75 80

Ovula Ovum AP49

1974, Mar. 23
C111 AP49 3fr *shown* 22 15
C112 AP49 32fr *Hydatina* 1.40 65
C113 AP49 37fr *Dolium perdix* 2.00 1.00

Nouméa Aquarium.

Capt. Cook, Map of Grande Terre and "Endeavour" — AP50

Designs: 25fr, Jean F. de la Perouse, his ship and map of Grande Terre. 28fr, French sailor, 18th century, on board ship, vert. 30fr, Antoine R. J. d'Entrecasteaux, ship and map. 36fr, Dumont d'Urville, ship and map of Loyalty Islands.

1974, Sept. 4 **Engr.** ***Perf. 13***
C114 AP50 20fr multi 65 25
C115 AP50 25fr multi 65 45
C116 AP50 28fr multi 85 45
C117 AP50 30fr multi 1.00 55
C118 AP50 36fr multi 1.10 85
Nos. C114-C118 (5) 4.25 2.55

Discovery and exploration of New Caledonia and Loyalty Islands.

UPU Emblem and Symbolic Design — AP51

1974, Oct. 9 **Engr.** ***Perf. 13***
C119 AP51 95fr multi 3.00 2.00

Centenary of Universal Postal Union.

Abstract Design — AP52

1974, Oct. 26 **Photo.** ***Perf. 13***
C120 AP52 80fr bl, blk & org 2.50 1.25

ARPHILA 75, Philatelic Exhibition, Paris, June 6-16, 1975.

Hôtel Chateau-Royal, Nouméa — AP53

1975, Jan. 20 **Photo.** ***Perf. 13***
C121 AP53 22fr multi 85 50

Cricket AP54

Designs: 25fr, Bougna ceremony (food offering). 31fr, Pilou dance.

1975, Mar. 24 **Photo.** ***Perf. 13***
C122 AP54 3fr bl & multi 32 15
C123 AP54 25fr ol grn & multi 65 35
C124 AP54 31fr yel grn & multi 1.00 45

Tourist publicity.

Orchid Type of 1975

Design: 42fr, Eriaxis rigida.

1975, May 30
C125 A74 42fr grn & multi 2.75 1.75

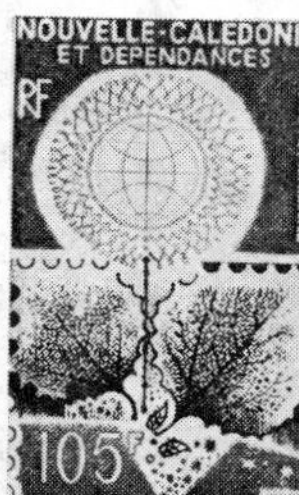

Globe as "Flower" with "Stamps" and leaves — AP55

1975, June 7 **Engr.** ***Perf. 13***
C126 AP55 105fr multi 3.25 2.00

ARPHILA 75 International Philatelic Exhibition, Paris, June 6-16.

Discus and Games' Emblem — AP56

Design: 50fr, Volleyball and Games' emblem.

1975, Aug. 23 **Photo.** ***Perf. 13x12½***
C127 AP56 24fr emer, pur & dk bl 50 40
C128 AP56 50fr multi 1.40 85

5th South Pacific Games, Guam, Aug. 1-10.

Concorde — AP57

1976, Jan. 21 **Engr.** ***Perf. 13***
C129 AP57 147fr car & ultra 5.50 4.00

First commercial flight of supersonic jet Concorde, Paris-Rio de Janeiro, Jan. 21.
For surcharge see No. C141.

Telephones 1876 and 1976, Satellite — AP58

1976, Mar. 10 **Photo.** ***Perf. 13***
C130 AP58 36fr multi 1.10 55

Centenary of first telephone call by Alexander Graham Bell, Mar. 10, 1876.

Battle Scene — AP59

1976, June 14 **Engr.** ***Perf. 13***
C131 AP59 24fr red brn & ver 75 55

American Bicentennial.

Runners and Maple Leaf — AP60

1976, July 24 **Engr.** ***Perf. 13***
C132 AP60 33fr car, vio & brn 1.10 55

21st Olympic Games, Montreal, Canada, July 17-Aug. 1.

Whimsical Bird as Student and Collector AP61

1976, Aug. 21 **Photo.**
C133 AP61 42fr multi 1.40 1.00

Philately in School, Philatelic Exhibition in La Perouse Lyceum, Nouméa.

Old City Hall, Nouméa — AP62

Design: 125fr, New City Hall, Nouméa.

1976, Oct. 22 **Photo.** ***Perf. 13***
C134 AP62 75fr multi 2.50 1.40
C135 AP62 125fr multi 3.50 2.00

Lagoon, Women and Festival Symbols AP63

1977, Jan. 15 **Photo.** ***Perf. 13x12½***
C136 AP63 11fr multi 45 28

Summer Festival 1977, Nouméa.

Training Children in Toy Cars — AP64

1977, Mar. 12 **Litho.** ***Perf. 13***
C137 AP64 50fr multi 1.40 1.00

Road safety training.

Bird Type of 1977

Design: 42fr, Male frigate bird, horiz.

1977, Sept. 17 **Photo.** ***Perf. 13***
C138 A89 42fr multi 2.25 1.10

Magenta Airport and Routes — AP65

Design: 57fr, La Tontouta airport.

1977, Oct. 22 **Litho.** ***Perf. 13***
C139 AP65 24fr multi 55 40
C140 AP65 57fr multi 1.65 65

No. C129 Surcharged in Violet Blue: "22.11.77 PARIS NEW YORK"

1977, Nov. 22 **Engr.** ***Perf. 13***
C141 AP57 147fr car & ultra 6.50 5.50

Concorde, 1st commercial flight Paris-NY.

Old Nouméa, by H. Didonna — AP66

Valley of the Settlers, by Jean Kreber — AP67

1977, Nov. 26 **Photo.** ***Perf. 13***
C142 AP66 41fr gold & multi 1.25 55

Engr.

C143 AP67 42fr yel brn & dk brn 1.25 55

"Underwater Carnival," Aubusson Tapestry — AP68

1978, June 17 **Photo.** ***Perf. 13***
C144 AP68 105fr multi 2.50 1.40

"The Hare and the Tortoise" — AP69

1978, Aug. 19 **Photo.** ***Perf. 13x13½***
C145 AP69 35fr multi 1.25 75

School philately.

Bourail School Children, Map and Conus Shell — AP70

1978, Sept. 30 **Engr.** ***Perf. 13***
C146 AP70 41fr multi 1.10 55

Promotion of topical philately in Bourail public schools.

Old and New Candles — AP71

1978, Oct. 21 **Photo.** ***Perf. 13***
C147 AP71 36fr multi 75 45

Third Caledonian Senior Citizens' Day.

Faubourg Blanchot, by Lacouture — AP72

1978, Nov. 25 **Photo.** ***Perf. 13***
C148 AP72 24fr multi 85 60

Type of 1978

Design: 42fr, Amyema scandens (horiz.).

1978, Mar. 17 ***Perf. 13x12½***
C149 A91 42fr multi 2.00 90

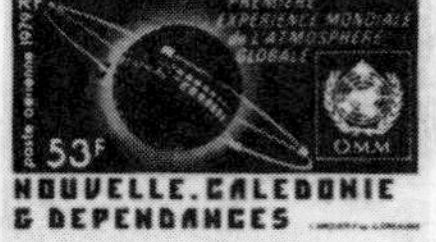

Orbiting Weather Satellites, WMO Emblem AP73

1979, Mar. 24 **Photo.** ***Perf. 13***
C150 AP73 53fr multi 90 55

First world-wide satellite system in the atmosphere.

Ships and Emblem — AP74

1979, Mar. 31 **Engr.**
C151 AP74 49fr multi 95 50

Chamber of Commerce and Industry, centenary.

Child's Drawing, IYC Emblem AP75

1979, Apr. 21 **Photo.** ***Perf. 13***
C152 AP75 35fr multi 80 52

International Year of the Child.

Surf Casting AP76

Design: 30fr, Swordfish fishing.

1979, May 26 **Litho.** ***Perf. 12½***
C153 AP76 29fr multi 85 55
C154 AP76 30fr multi 1.00 65

Port-de-France, 1854, and de Montravel — AP77

1979, June 16 **Engr.** ***Perf. 13***
C155 AP77 75fr multi 1.75 1.00

125th anniversary of Noumea, formerly Port-de-France, founded by L. Tardy de Montravel.

The Eel Queen, Kanaka Legend — AP78

1979, July 7 **Photo.** ***Perf. 13***
C156 AP78 42fr multi 1.50 1.00

Nature protection.

Map of New Caledonia, Postmark, Five Races — AP79

1979, Aug. 18 **Photo.** ***Perf. 13***
C157 AP79 27fr multi 50 30

New Caledonian youth and philately.

Orstom Center, Noumea, Orstom Emblem — AP80

1979, Sept. 17 Photo. *Perf. 13*
C158 AP80 25fr multi 45 28

Old Post Office, Noumea, New Caledonia No. 1, Hill — AP81

1979, Nov. 17 Engr.
C159 AP81 150fr multi 3.50 2.25

Sir Rowland Hill (1795-1879), originator of penny postage.

Pirogue AP82

1980, Jan. 26 Engr. *Perf. 13*
C160 AP82 45fr multi 1.00 70

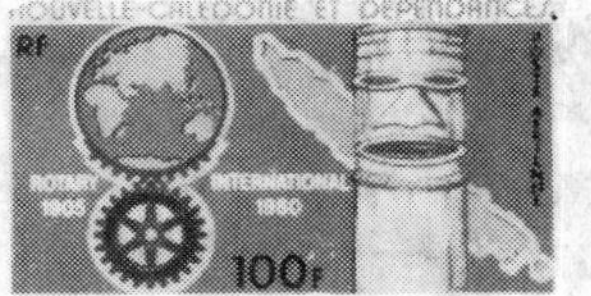
Rotary International, 75th Anniversary — AP83

1980, Feb. 23 Photo. *Perf. 13*
C161 AP83 100fr multi 2.50 1.75

Man Holding Dolphinfish AP84

1980, Oct. 11 Photo. *Perf. 13x12½*
C162 AP84 34fr shown 85 55
C163 AP84 39fr Fishermen, sail fish, vert. 1.00 65

Coral Seas Air Rally AP85

1980, June 7 Engr. *Perf. 13*
C164 AP85 31fr multi 85 65

Carved Alligator, Boat — AP86

1980, June 21 Photo.
C165 AP86 27fr multi 60 40

South Pacific Arts Festival, Port Moresby, Papua New Guinea.

New Caledonian Kiwanis, 10th Anniversary — AP87

1980, Sept. 10 Photo. *Perf. 13*
C166 AP87 50fr multi 1.00 65

View of Old Noumea — AP88

1980, Oct. 25 Photo. *Perf. 13½*
C167 AP88 33fr multi 65 48

Charles de Gaulle, 10th Anniversary of Death — AP89

1980, Nov. 15 Engr. *Perf. 13*
C168 AP89 120fr multi 3.00 2.00

Fluorescent Coral, Noumea Aquarium AP90

1980, Dec. 13 Photo. *Perf. 13x13½*
C169 AP90 60fr multi 1.25 70

Xeronema Moorei AP91

1981, Mar. 18 Photo. *Perf. 13x12½*
C170 AP91 38fr shown 75 40
C171 AP91 51fr Geissois pruinosa 95 40

Yuri Gagarin and Vostok I — AP92

20th Anniversary of First Space Flights: 155fr, Alan B. Shepard, Freedom 7.

1981, Apr. 8 Engr. *Perf. 13*
C172 AP92 64fr multi 1.40 85
C173 AP92 155fr multi 3.00 1.75
a. Souv. sheet of 2, #C172-C173 5.25 5.25

No. C173a sold for 225fr.

40th Anniv. of Departure of Pacific Batallion — AP93

1981, May 5 Photo. *Perf. 13*
C174 AP93 29fr multi 70 55

Ecinometra Mathaei AP94

1981, Aug. 5 Photo. *Perf. 13x13½*
C175 AP94 38fr shown 65 35
C176 AP94 51fr Prionocidaris verticillata 85 48

No. 4, Post Office Building AP95

1981, Sept. 16 Photo. *Perf. 13x13½*
C177 AP95 41fr multi 75 48

Stamp Day.

Old Noumea Latin Quarter — AP96

1981, Oct. 14 Photo. *Perf. 13½*
C178 AP96 43fr multi 75 48

New Caledonia to Australia Airmail Flight by Victor Roffey, 50th Anniv. AP97

1981, Nov. 21 Engr. *Perf. 13*
C179 AP97 37fr multi 70 40

Rousette AP98

1982, Feb. 17 Engr. *Perf. 13*
C180 AP98 38fr shown 65 35
C181 AP98 51fr Kagu 85 48

See Nos. C188B-C188C.

50th Anniv. of Paris-Noumea Flight — AP99

1982, Apr. 5 Engr. *Perf. 13*
C182 AP99 250fr Pilots, map, plane 4.50 2.50

Scouting Year — AP100

1982, Apr. 21 Photo. *Perf. 13½x13*
C183 AP100 40fr multi 70 40

PHILEXFRANCE '82 Intl. Stamp Show, Paris, June 11-21 — AP101

1982, May 12 Engr. *Perf. 13*
C184 AP101 150fr multi 2.50 2.00

1982 World Cup AP102

1982, June 9 Photo. *Perf. 13x13½*
C185 AP102 74fr multi 1.25 70

French Overseas Possessions Week, Sept. 18-25
AP103

1982, Sept. 17 *Perf. 13x12½*
C186 AP103 100fr Map, kagu, citizens 1.75 85

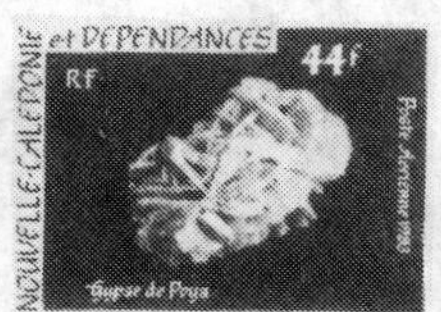

Gypsum, Poya Mines
AP104

1983, Jan. 15 Photo. *Perf. 13x13½*
C187 AP104 44fr shown 55 30
C188 AP104 59fr Silica gel, Kone mine 70 35

World Communications Year — AP104a

Design: WCY emblem, map, globe.

1983, Mar. 9 Litho. *Perf. 13*
C188A AP104a 170fr multi 2.25 1.10

Aircraft Type of 1982

1983, Jul. 6 Engr. *Perf. 13*
C188B AP98 46fr Pou-du-Ciel 80 50
C188C AP98 61fr L'Aiglon Caudron 85 60

Temple and Dancers — AP105

1983, July 20 Litho. *Perf. 12½x12*
C189 AP105 47fr multi 85 55

BANGKOK '83 Intl. Stamp Show, Aug. 4-13.

Oueholle Tribe, Straw Hut — AP106

1983, Sept. 8 Litho. *Perf. 13*
C190 AP106 76fr multi 1.10 75

Loyalty Islander by the Shore, by R. Mascart
AP107

Paintings: 350fr, The Guitarist from Mare Island, by P. Neilly.

1983, Dec. 7 Photo. *Perf. 13*
C191 AP107 100fr multi 1.10 75
C192 AP107 350fr multi 4.00 2.75

Noumea Aquarium Fish — AP108

1984, Mar. 7 Photo. *Perf. 13*
C193 AP108 46fr Amphiprion clarkii 50 35
C194 AP108 61fr Centropyge bicolor 70 50

Local Plants — AP109

1984, Apr. 25 Litho. *Perf. 12½x13*
C195 AP109 51fr Araucaria columnaris 65 32
C196 AP109 67fr Pritchardiopsis jeanneneyi 85 42

1984 Summer Olympics — AP110

1984, June 20 Photo. *Perf. 13½x13*
C197 AP110 50fr Swimming 55 40
C198 AP110 83fr Wind surfing 95 70
C199 AP110 200fr Running 2.25 1.40

Ausipex '84 — AP111

Army Day — AP112

1984, Sept. 21 Engr. *Perf. 13*
C200 AP111 150fr Exhibition Hall 1.75 1.40
a. Souvenir sheet 1.90 1.90

Se-tenant with label showing exhibition emblem. No. C200a contains No. C200 in changed colors.

1984, Oct. 28 Litho. *Perf. 13½x13*
C201 AP112 51fr multi 60 32

Woman Fishing for Crabs, by Mme. Bonnet de Larbogne — AP113

Painting: 300fr, Cook Discovering New Caledonia, by Pilioko.

1984, Nov. 8 Litho. *Perf. 13x12½*
C202 AP113 120fr multi 1.50 70
C203 AP113 300fr multi 3.50 1.75

See Nos. 605-606.

Transpac Dragon Rapide, Map
AP114

1985, Oct. 2 Litho. *Perf. 13½*
C204 AP114 80fr multi 80 40

Internal air services, 30th anniv.

UN, 40th Anniv.
AP115

Perf. 12½x13

1985, Oct. 25 **Wmk. 385**
C205 AP115 250fr multi 2.25 1.10

Jules Garnier High School
AP116

1985, Nov. 13 Unwmk. *Perf. 13*
C206 AP116 400fr multi 3.75 1.90

Paris-Noumea Scheduled Flights, 30th Anniv. — AP117

1986, Jan. 6
C207 AP117 72fr multi 75 38

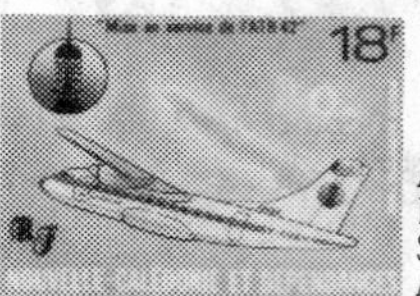

Nou Island Livestock Warehouse — AP118

1986, June 14 Engr. *Perf. 13*
C208 AP118 230fr Prus bl, sep & brn 2.75 1.40

ATR-42 Inaugural Service
AP119

1986, Aug. 13 Litho. *Perf. 12½x13*
C209 AP119 18fr multi 20 10

STOCKHOLMIA '86 — AP120

1986, Aug. 29 Engr. *Perf. 13*
C210 AP120 108fr No. 1 1.25 65

Natl. Assoc. of Amateur Radio Operators, 25th Anniv.
AP121

1987, Jan. 7 Litho. *Perf. 12½*
C211 AP121 64fr multi 80 40

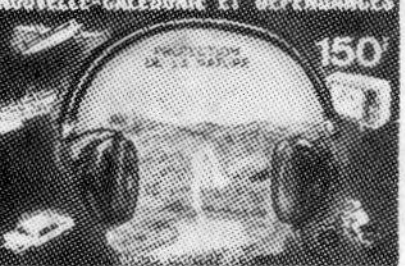

Nature Conservation, Fight Noise Pollution
AP122

1987, Mar. 25 Litho. *Perf. 13x12½*
C212 AP122 150fr multi 1.90 1.00

French Cricket Federation
AP123

1987, Nov. 25 Litho. *Perf. 12½*
C213 AP123 94fr multi 1.40 75

Arms Type of 1984

1988, Jan. 13 *Perf. 12½x13*
C214 A132 76fr Dumbea 1.00 50

Rotary Intl. Anti-Polio Campaign — AP124

1988, Oct. 26 Litho. *Perf. 13½*
C215 AP124 220fr multi 4.00 2.00

Bamboo Type of 1989

Perf. 12½x13

1989, Sept. 27 **Litho. & Engr.**
C216 A187 44fr multi 80 40

De Gaulle's Call For French Resistance, 50th Anniv.
AP125

1990, June 20 Litho. *Perf. 12½*
C217 AP125 160fr multicolored 3.50 1.75

Military Cemetery, New Zealand — AP126

Auckland 1990: C219, Brigadier William Walter Dove.

1990, Aug. 24 *Perf. 13*

C218 AP126 80fr multi 1.60 80
C219 AP126 80fr multi 1.60 80
a. Pair, #C218-C219 + label 3.25 1.60

Souvenir Sheet

New Zealand 1990 — AP126a

1990, Aug. 25 Litho. *Perf. $13x12\frac{1}{2}$*

C219B AP126a 150fr multi 3.50 1.75

Crustaceans — AP127

1990, Oct. 17 Litho. *Perf. $12\frac{1}{2}x13$*

C220 AP127 30fr Munidopsis sp. Orstom 60 30
C221 AP127 60fr Lyreidius tridentatus 1.20 60

30th South Pacific Conference — AP128

1990, Oct. 29 Litho. *Perf. 13*

C222 AP128 85fr multicolored 2.10 1.05

Gen. Charles de Gaulle (1890-1970) AP129

1990, Nov. 21 Engr. *Perf. 13*

C223 AP129 410fr dk blue 10.00 5.00

Scenic Views — AP130

1991, Feb. 13 Litho. *Perf. 13*

C224 AP130 36fr Fayawa-Ouvea Bay 90 45
C225 AP130 90fr shown 2.20 1.10

New Caledonian Cricket Players by Marcel Moutouh — AP131

Design: 435fr, Saint Louis by Janine Goetz.

1991, Dec. 18 *Perf. $13x12\frac{1}{2}$*

C226 AP131 130fr multicolored 3.00 1.50
C227 AP131 435fr multicolored 10.00 5.00

Blue River Nature Park — AP132

Illustration reduced.

1992, Feb. 6 Litho. *Perf. $12\frac{1}{2}$*

C228 AP132 400fr multicolored 9.25 4.65
a. Souvenir sheet of 1 10.50 5.25

No. C228a sold for 450fr.

Native Pottery — AP133

Photo. & Engr.

1992, Apr. 9 *Perf. $12\frac{1}{2}x13$*

C229 AP133 25fr black & orange 53 28

Expo '92, Seville AP134

1992, Apr. 25 Litho. *Perf. 13*

C230 AP134 10fr multicolored 25 15

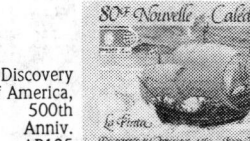

Discovery of America, 500th Anniv. AP135

Designs: No. C234a, Erik the Red, Viking longship. b, Columbus, coat of arms. c, Amerigo Vespucci.

1992, May 22 Litho. *Perf. $13\frac{1}{2}$*

C231 AP135 80fr Pinta 2.00 1.00
C232 AP135 80fr Santa Maria 2.00 1.00
C233 AP135 80fr Nina 2.00 1.00
a. Strip of 3, #C231-C233 6.00 3.00
b. Bklt. pane of 3, #C231-C233 6.00 3.00

Souvenir Sheet

Perf. $12\frac{1}{2}$

C234 AP135 110fr Sheet of 3, #a.-c. 9.00 4.50

World Columbian Stamp Expo '92, Chicago. No. C234 sold for 360fr.

1992 Summer Olympics, Barcelona — AP136

1992, July 25 *Perf. 13*

C235 AP136 260fr Synchronized swimming 6.35 3.20

Wahpa, by Paul Mascart AP137

1992, Sept. 28 Litho. *Perf. $12\frac{1}{2}x13$*

C236 AP137 205fr multicolored 5.00 2.50

Australian Bouvier — AP138

1992, Oct. 4 *Perf. 12*

C237 AP138 175fr multicolored 4.10 2.05

Exploration of New Caledonian Coast by Chevalier d'Entrecasteaux, Bicent. — AP139

1992, Nov. 18 Engr. *Perf. 13*

C238 AP139 110fr bl grn, ocher & olive grn 2.50 1.25

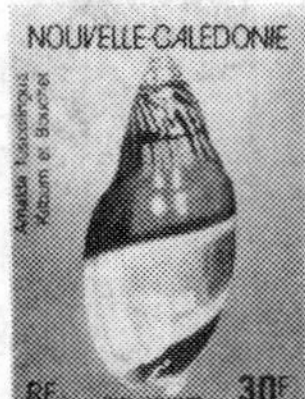

Shells — AP140

AP141

1992, Nov. 26 Litho. *Perf. $13\frac{1}{2}x13$*

C239 AP140 30fr Amalda fuscolingua 70 35
C240 AP140 50fr Cassis abbotti 1.15 58

The vignettes on Nos. C239-C240 were applied by a thermographic process, producing a shiny, raised effect.

1992, Dec. 9 Litho. *Perf. $13\frac{1}{2}$*

Comic Strip Characters from "La Brousse en Folie," by Bernard Berger: a, Dede. b. Torton Marcel in Mimine II. c, Tathan. d, Joinville.

C241 AP141 80fr Strip of 4, #a.-d. 7.20 3.60

AIR POST SEMI-POSTAL STAMP

French Revolution Issue

Common Design Type

Unwmk.

1939, July 5 Photo. *Perf. 13*

Name and Value Typo. in Orange

CB1 CD83 4.50fr + 4fr brn blk 12.00 12.00

V5

Stamps of the design shown above and stamp of Cameroun type V10 inscribed "Nlle Calédonie" were issued in 1942 by the Vichy Government, but were not placed on sale in the colony.

POSTAGE DUE STAMPS

For a short time in 1894, 5, 10, 15, 20, 25 and 30c postage stamps (Nos. 43, 45, 47, 49, 50 and 52) were overprinted with a "T" in an inverted triangle and used as Postage Due stamps.

French Colonies Postage Due Stamps Overprinted in Carmine, Blue or Silver

1903 Unwmk. *Imperf.*

J1	D1	5c blue (C)	75	65
J2	D1	10c brown (C)	4.00	2.50
J3	D1	15c yel grn (C)	7.50	3.75
J4	D1	30c carmine (Bl)	5.75	4.50
J5	D1	50c violet (Bl)	30.00	6.75
J6	D1	60c brn, *buff* (Bl)	95.00	24.00
J7	D1	1fr rose, *buff* (S)	15.00	6.00
J8	D1	2fr red brn (Bl)	525.00	525.00
		Nos. J1-J8 (8)	683.00	573.15

Nos. J1 to J8 are known with the "I" in "TENAIRE" missing.

Commemorating fifty years of French occupation.

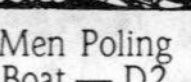
Men Poling Boat — D2

Malayan Sambar — D3

1906 Typo. Perf. 13½x14

No.	Type	Description	Unused	Used
J9	D2	5c ultra, *azure*	20	20
J10	D2	10c vio brn, *buff*	20	20
J11	D2	15c grn, *greenish*	35	35
J12	D2	20c blk, *yellow*	35	35
J13	D2	30c carmine	48	48
J14	D2	50c ultra, *buff*	60	60
J15	D2	60c brn, *azure*	60	60
J16	D2	1fr dk grn, *straw*	85	85
		Nos. J9-J16 (8)	3.63	3.63

Type of 1906 Issue Surcharged **2F. ═**

1926-27

No.	Type	Description	Unused	Used
J17	D2	2fr on 1fr vio	1.50	1.50
J18	D2	3fr on 1fr org brn	1.50	1.50

1928 Typo.

No.	Type	Description	Unused	Used
J19	D3	2c sl bl & dp brn	15	15
J20	D3	4c brn red & bl grn	15	15
J21	D3	5c red org & bl blk	15	15
J22	D3	10c mag & Prus bl	15	15
J23	D3	15c dl grn & scar	15	15
J24	D3	20c mar & ol grn	40	40
J25	D3	25c bis brn & sl bl	28	28
J26	D3	30c bl grn & ol grn	35	35
J27	D3	50c lt brn & dk red	60	60
J28	D3	60c mag & brt rose	60	60
J29	D3	1fr dl bl & Prus grn	70	70
J30	D3	2fr dk red & ol grn	70	70
J31	D3	3fr vio & brn	1.25	1.25
		Nos. J19-J31 (13)	5.63	5.63

Catalogue values for unused stamps in this section, from this point to the end of the section, are for Never Hinged items.

D4

Bat — D5

1948 Unwmk. Photo. Perf. 13

No.	Type	Description	Unused	Used
J32	D4	10c violet	15	15
J33	D4	30c brown	15	15
J34	D4	50c blue green	15	15
J35	D4	1fr orange	15	15
J36	D4	2fr red violet	15	15
J37	D4	3fr red brown	15	15
J38	D4	4fr dull blue	28	28
J39	D4	5fr henna brown	40	40
J40	D4	10fr slate green	60	60
J41	D4	20fr violet blue	1.25	1.25
		Nos. J32-J41 (10)	3.43	3.43

1983 Litho. Perf. 13

No.	Type	Description	Unused	Used
J42	D5	1fr multi	15	15
J43	D5	2fr multi	15	15
J44	D5	3fr multi	15	15
J45	D5	4fr multi	15	15
J46	D5	5fr multi	15	15
J47	D5	10fr multi	22	22
J48	D5	20fr multi	42	42
J49	D5	40fr multi	85	85
J50	D5	50fr multi	1.00	1.00
		Nos. J42-J50 (9)	3.24	3.24

MILITARY STAMPS

Stamps of the above types, although issued by officials, were unauthorized and practically a private speculation.

OFFICIAL STAMPS

Catalogue values for unused stamps in this section are for Never Hinged items.

Ancestor Pole — O1

Carved Wooden Pillow — O2

Various carved ancestor poles.

1959 Unwmk. Typo. Perf. 14x13

No.	Type	Description	Unused	Used
O1	O1	1fr org yel	28	15
O2	O1	3fr lt bl grn	28	15
O3	O1	4fr purple	35	20
O4	O1	5fr ultra	45	24
O5	O1	9fr black	50	35
O6	O1	10fr brt vio	65	35
O7	O1	13fr yel grn	75	48
O8	O1	15fr lt bl	85	70
O9	O1	24fr red lilac	1.00	85
O10	O1	26fr deep org	1.25	1.00
O11	O1	50fr green	3.00	1.50
O12	O1	100fr chocolate	6.00	3.00
O13	O1	200fr red	11.00	5.25
		Nos. O1-O13 (13)	26.36	14.22

1973-87 Photo. Perf. 13

Vignette: Green, Red Brown (2, 29, 31, 35, 38, 65, 76fr), Brown (40fr), Blue (58fr)

No.	Type	Description	Unused	Used
O14	O2	1fr yellow	15	15
O14A	O2	2fr green ('87)	15	15
O15	O2	3fr tan	20	15
O16	O2	4fr pale violet	20	15
O17	O2	5fr lilac rose	28	15
O18	O2	9fr light blue	35	20
O19	O2	10fr orange	35	24
O20	O2	11fr bright lilac	18	15
O21	O2	12fr bl grn ('76)	50	35
O22	O2	15fr green ('76)	24	15
O23	O2	20fr rose ('76)	28	15
O24	O2	23fr red ('80)	28	15
O25	O2	24fr Prus bl ('76)	32	15
O25A	O2	25fr gray ('81)	32	15
O26	O2	26fr yellow ('76)	35	18
O26A	O2	29fr dl grn ('83)	30	15
O26B	O2	31fr yellow ('82)	32	16
O26C	O2	35fr yellow ('84)	48	24
O27	O2	36fr dp lil rose ('76)	50	20
O27A	O2	38fr tan	28	15
O27B	O2	40fr blue ('87)	52	28
O28	O2	42fr bister ('76)	60	35
O29	O2	50fr blue ('76)	70	60
O29A	O2	58fr blue grn ('87)	75	48
O29B	O2	65fr lilac ('84)	75	30
O29C	O2	76fr brt yel ('87)	1.10	52
O30	O2	100fr red ('76)	1.40	1.00
O31	O2	200fr orange ('76)	2.75	1.50
		Nos. O14-O31 (28)	14.60	8.55

This is an expanding set. Numbers will change when complete.

PARCEL POST STAMPS

Type of Regular Issue of 1905-28 Surcharged or Overprinted

50

Colis Postaux

1926 Unwmk. Perf. 14x13½

No.	Type	Description	Unused	Used
Q1	A18	50c on 5fr ol, *lav*	50	50
Q2	A18	1fr deep blue	70	70
Q3	A18	2fr car, *bluish*	1.00	1.00

Regular Issue of 1928 Overprinted:

Colis Postaux

1930

No.	Type	Description	Unused	Used
Q4	A20	50c vio & brown	50	50
Q5	A21	1fr dp ol & sal red	60	60
Q6	A21	2fr red org & brn	85	85

NEW HEBRIDES

LOCATION — A group of islands in the South Pacific Ocean lying north of New Caledonia
GOVT. — Condominium under the joint administration of Great Britain and France
AREA — 5,790 sq. mi.
POP. — 100,000 (est. 1976)
CAPITAL — Port-Vila (Vila)

Postage stamps are issued by both Great Britain and France. In 1911 a joint issue was made bearing the coats of arms of both countries. The British stamps bore the coat of arms of Great Britain and the value in British currency on the right and the French coat of arms and values at the left. On the French stamps the positions were reversed. This resulted in some confusion when the value of the French franc decreased following World War I but the situation was corrected by arranging that both series of stamps be sold for their value as expressed in French currency.

12 Pence = 1 Shilling
100 Centimes = 1 Franc
New Hebrides Franc (FNH)--1977

Catalogue values for unused stamps in this country are for Never Hinged items, beginning with Scott 79 in the regular postage section, Scott J16 in the postage due section.

See Vol. I for British issues.

French Issues

Stamps of New Caledonia, 1905, Overprinted in Black or Red

NOUVELLES HÉBRIDES
Nos. 1-4

NOUVELLES-HEBRIDES
No. 5

1908 Unwmk. Perf. 14x13½

No.	Type	Description	Unused	Used
1	A16	5c green	1.50	1.50
2	A16	10c rose	1.75	1.75
3	A17	25c blue, *grnsh* (R)	2.50	2.50
4	A17	50c carmine, *org*	3.25	3.25
5	A18	1fr bl, *yel grn* (R)	6.50	6.50
		Nos. 1-5 (5)	15.50	15.50

For overprints and surcharges see #6-10, 33-35.

Stamps of 1908 with Additional Overprint **CONDOMINIUM**

1910

No.	Type	Description	Unused	Used
6	A16	5c green	60	60
7	A16	10c rose	80	80
8	A17	25c blue, *grnsh* (R)	1.00	1.00
9	A17	50c car, *orange*	2.75	2.75
10	A18	1fr bl, *yel grn* (R)	9.00	9.00
		Nos. 6-10 (5)	14.15	14.15

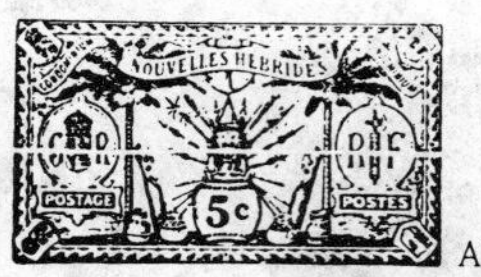
A2

Wmk. 3

1911, July 12 Engr. Perf. 14

No.	Type	Description	Unused	Used
11	A2	5c pale green	35	35
12	A2	10c red	35	35
13	A2	20c gray	1.10	1.10
14	A2	25c ultramarine	1.40	1.10
15	A2	30c vio, *yellow*	1.75	1.60
16	A2	40c red, *yellow*	1.75	1.60
17	A2	50c olive green	1.75	1.60
18	A2	75c brn orange	2.75	2.75
19	A2	1fr brn red, *bl*	1.50	1.50
20	A2	2fr violet	3.00	3.00
21	A2	5fr brn red, *grn*	6.50	6.50
		Nos. 11-21 (11)	22.20	21.45

For surcharges see Nos. 36-37, 43 and British issue No. 30.

1912 Wmk. R F in Sheet

No.	Type	Description	Unused	Used
22	A2	5c pale green	1.25	1.25
23	A2	10c red	1.25	1.25
24	A2	20c gray	1.65	1.65
25	A2	25c ultramarine	1.65	1.65
26	A2	30c vio, *yellow*	1.65	1.65
27	A2	40c red, *yellow*	10.00	10.00
28	A2	50c olive green	5.75	5.75
29	A2	75c brn orange	5.75	5.75
30	A2	1fr brn red, *bl*	3.25	3.25
31	A2	2fr violet	5.75	5.75
32	A2	5fr brn red, *grn*	10.00	10.00
		Nos. 22-32 (11)	47.95	47.95

In the watermark, "R F" (République Franaise initials) are large double-lined Roman capitals, about 120mm high. About one-fourth of the stamps in each sheet show parts of the watermark. The other stamps are without watermark.

For surcharge see Nos. 38-42 and British issue No. 31.

Nos. 9 and 8 Surcharged **5c.**

1920 Unwmk. Perf. 14x13½

No.	Type	Description	Unused	Used
33	A17	5c on 50c red, *org*	1.40	1.40
34	A17	10c on 25c bl, *grnsh*	65	65

Same Surcharge on No. 4

No.	Type	Description	Unused	Used
35	A17	5c on 50c red, *org*	650.00	650.00

British Issue No. 21 and French Issue No. 15 Surcharged **10c.**

1921 Wmk. 3 Perf. 14

No.	Type	Description	Unused	Used
36	A1	10c on 5p ol grn	6.25	6.25
37	A2	20c on 30c vio, *yel*	6.25	6.25

Nos. 27 and 26 Surcharged **05c.**

1921 Wmk. R F in Sheet

No.	Type	Description	Unused	Used
38	A2	5c on 40c red, *yel*	19.00	19.00
39	A2	20c on 30c vio, *yel*	7.00	7.00

Stamps of 1910-12 Surcharged with New Values as in 1920-21

1924

No.	Type	Description	Unused	Used
40	A2	10c on 5c pale grn	60	60
41	A2	30c on 10c red	60	60
42	A2	50c on 25c ultra	1.60	1.60

Wmk. 3

No.	Type	Description	Unused	Used
43	A2	50c on 25c ultra	4.50	4.50

A4

The values at the lower right denote the currency and amount for which the stamps were to be sold. The stamps could be purchased at the French post office and used to pay postage at the English rates.

1925 Engr. Wmk. R F in Sheet

No.	Type	Description	Unused	Used
44	A4	5c (½p) black	55	55
45	A4	10c (1p) green	40	40
46	A4	20c (2p) grnsh gray	40	40
47	A4	25c (2½p) brown	40	40
48	A4	30c (3p) carmine	40	40
49	A4	40c (4p) car, *org*	60	60
50	A4	50c (5p) ultra	70	70
51	A4	75c (7½p) bis brn	1.10	1.10
52	A4	1fr (10p) car, *blue*	1.90	1.90
53	A4	2fr (1sh 8p) gray vio	1.90	1.90
54	A4	5fr (4sh) car, *grnsh*	4.50	4.50
		Nos. 44-54 (11)	12.85	12.85

For overprints see Nos. J1-J5.

Beach Scene — A6

1938 *Perf. 12*

55	A6	5c green	40	40
56	A6	10c dark orange	40	40
57	A6	15c violet	40	40
58	A6	20c rose red	40	40
59	A6	25c brown	60	60
60	A6	30c dark blue	60	60
61	A6	40c olive grn	90	90
62	A6	50c brn violet	90	90
63	A6	1fr dk car, *grn*	2.00	2.00
64	A6	2fr blue, *grn*	4.00	4.00
65	A6	5fr red, *yellow*	14.00	14.00
66	A6	10fr vio, *blue*	27.50	27.50
		Nos. 55-66 (12)	52.10	52.10

For overprints see Nos. 67-78, J6-J15.

Stamps of 1938 Overprinted in Black

France Libre

1941

67	A6	5c green	6.00	6.00
68	A6	10c dark org	6.00	6.00
69	A6	15c violet	6.00	6.00
70	A6	20c rose red	6.50	6.50
71	A6	25c brown	6.75	6.75
72	A6	30c dark blue	6.75	6.75
73	A6	40c olive grn	6.75	6.75
74	A6	50c brn violet	6.75	6.75
75	A6	1fr dk car, *grn*	8.50	8.50
76	A6	2fr blue, *grn*	8.50	8.50
77	A6	5fr red, *yellow*	10.50	10.50
78	A6	10fr vio, *blue*	16.00	16.00
		Nos. 67-78 (12)	95.00	95.00

Catalogue values for unused stamps in this section, from this point to the end of the section, are for Never Hinged items.

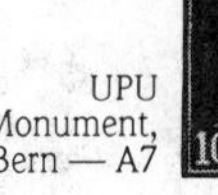

UPU Monument, Bern — A7

Wmk. RF in Sheet

1949 **Engr.** *Perf. 13½x14*

79	A7	10c red org	50	50
80	A7	15c violet	60	60
81	A7	30c vio bl	85	85
82	A7	50c rose vio	1.75	1.75

75th anniv. of the UPU.

Some stamps in each sheet show part of the watermark; others show none.

Outrigger Canoes with Sails — A8

Designs: 5c, 10c, 15c, 20c, Canoes with sails. 25c, 30c, 40c, 50c, Native carving. 1fr, 2fr, 5fr, Natives.

1953 *Perf. 12½*

83	A8	5c green	22	22
84	A8	10c red	35	35
85	A8	15c yellow	35	35
86	A8	20c ultramarine	60	60
87	A8	25c olive	60	60
88	A8	30c light brown	90	90
89	A8	40c black brown	90	90
90	A8	50c violet	1.10	1.10
91	A8	1fr deep orange	2.50	2.50
92	A8	2fr red violet	9.00	9.00
93	A8	5fr scarlet	14.00	14.00
		Nos. 83-93 (11)	30.52	30.52

For overprints see Nos. J16-J20.

Discovery of New Hebrides, 1606 — A9

Designs: 20c, 50c, Britannia, Marianne, Flags and Mask.

1956 Unwmk. Photo. *Perf. 14½x14*

94	A9	5c emerald	58	58
95	A9	10c crimson	58	58
96	A9	20c ultramarine	80	80
97	A9	50c purple	2.50	2.50

50th anniv. of the establishment of the Anglo-French Condominium.

Port Vila and Iririki Islet — A10

Designs: 25c, 30c, 40c, 50c, Tropical river and spear fisherman. 1fr, 2fr, 5fr, Woman drinking from coconut (inscribed: "Alliance Franco-Britannique 4 Mars 1947").

Wmk. RF in Sheet

1957 **Engr.** *Perf. 13½x13*

98	A10	5c green	28	28
99	A10	10c red	35	35
100	A10	15c orange yel	45	45
101	A10	20c ultramarine	45	45
102	A10	25c olive	45	45
103	A10	30c light brown	70	70
104	A10	40c sepia	80	80
105	A10	50c violet	1.25	1.25
106	A10	1fr orange	2.50	2.50
107	A10	2fr rose lilac	6.00	6.00
108	A10	5fr black	12.50	12.50
		Nos. 98-108 (11)	25.73	25.73

For overprints see Nos. J21-J25.

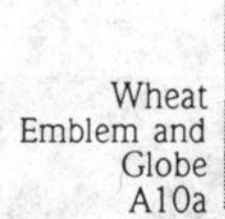

Wheat Emblem and Globe A10a

1963, Sept. 2 Unwmk. *Perf. 13*

109	A10a	60c org brn & sl grn	2.00	2.00

FAO "Freedom from Hunger" campaign.

Centenary Emblem — A11

1963, Sept. 2 Unwmk.

110	A11	15c org, gray & car	80	80
111	A11	45c bis, gray & car	1.50	1.50

Centenary of International Red Cross.

Copra Industry A12

Designs: 5c, Manganese loading, Forari Wharf. 10c, Cacao. 20c, Map of New Hebrides, tuna, marlin and ships. 25c, Striped triggerfish. 30c, Nautilus. 40c, 60c, Turkeyfish (pterois volitans). 50c, Lined tang (fish). 1fr, Cardinal honeyeater and hibiscus. 2fr, Buff-bellied flycatcher. 3fr, Thicket warbler. 5fr, White-collared kingfisher.

Perf. 12½ (10c, 20c, 40c, 60c); 14 (3fr); 13 (others)

Photo. (10c, 20c, 40c, 60c, 3fr); Engr. (others)

1963-67 Unwmk.

112	A12	5c Prus bl & cl ('66)	40	40
113	A12	10c brt grn, org brn & dk brn ("RF" at left) ('65)	1.40	90
114	A12	15c dk pur, yel & brn	28	28
115	A12	20c brt bl, gray & cit ("RF" at left) ('65)	1.90	1.40
116	A12	25c vio, rose lil & org brn ('66)	55	55
117	A12	30c lil, brn & cit	65	65
118	A12	40c dk bl & ver ('65)	3.25	2.25
119	A12	50c Prus bl, yel & grn	90	90
119A	A12	60c dk bl & ver ('67)	1.10	90
120	A12	1fr bl grn, blk & red ('66)	2.00	2.00
121	A12	2fr ol, blk & brn	4.50	4.50
122	A12	3fr org brn, brt grn & blk ("RF" at left) ('65)	9.00	6.50
123	A12	5fr ind, dp bl & gray ('67)	10.00	10.00
		Nos. 112-123 (13)	35.93	31.23

See #146-148. For surcharge see #160.

Telegraph, Syncom Satellite and ITU Emblem — A13

1965, May 17 Unwmk. *Perf. 13*

124	A13	15c dk red brn, brt bl & emer	1.00	75
125	A13	60c Prus grn, mag & sl	2.25	1.50

ITU, centenary.

ICY Emblem A14

1965, Oct. 24 Litho. *Perf. 14½*

126	A14	5c bl grn & cl	35	35
127	A14	55c lt vio & grn	90	90

International Cooperation Year.

Winston Churchill and St. Paul's, London, During Air Attack A15

1966, Jan. 24 Photo. *Perf. 14*

Design in Black, Gold and Carmine Rose

128	A15	5c brt blue	20	20
129	A15	15c green	25	25
130	A15	25c brown	55	55
131	A15	30c violet	1.00	1.00

Soccer Player and Rimet Cup A16

1966, July 1 Litho. *Perf. 14*

132	A16	20c multi	60	60
133	A16	40c multi	70	70

World Cup Soccer Championship, Wembley, England, July 11-30.

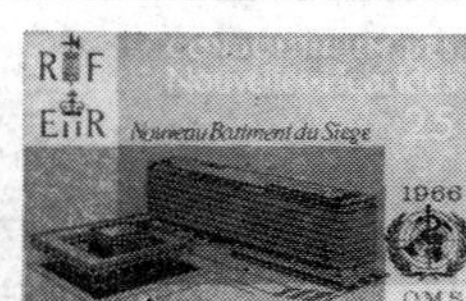

Inauguration of WHO Headquarters, Geneva — A17

1966, Sept. 20 Litho. *Perf. 14*

134	A17	25c multi	60	60
135	A17	60c multi	80	80

"Education" — A18

UNESCO, 20th anniv.: 30c, "Science" (retort and grain). 45c, "Culture" (lyre and columns).

1966, Dec. 1 Litho. *Perf. 14*

136	A18	15c dp org, yel & dl vio	40	40
137	A18	30c vio, dk ol grn & yel	65	65
138	A18	45c yel, mag & blk	90	90

US Marine, Australian Soldier and Map of South Pacific War Zone — A19

Designs: 15c, The coast watchers. 60c, Australian cruiser Canberra. 1fr, Flying fortress taking off from Bauer Field, and view of Vila.

Perf. 14x13

1967, Sept. 26 Photo. Unwmk.

139	A19	15c lt bl & multi	40	40
140	A19	25c yel & multi	55	55
141	A19	60c multi	80	80
142	A19	1fr pale sal & multi	1.50	1.50

25th anniv. of the Allied Forces' campaign in the South Pacific War Zone.

L. A. de Bougainville, Ship's Figurehead and Bougainvillea A20

Designs: 15c, Globe and world map. 25c, Ships La Boudeuse and L'Etoile and map of Bougainville Strait.

1968, May 23 Engr. *Perf. 13*

143	A20	15c ver, emer & dl vio	22	22
144	A20	25c ultra, ol & brn	45	45
145	A20	60c mag, grn & brn	80	80

200th anniv. of Louis Antoine de Bougainville's (1729-1811) voyage around the world.

Type of 1963-67 Redrawn, "E II R" at left, "RF" at Right

Designs as before.

1968, Aug. 5 Photo. *Perf. 12½*

146	A12	10c brt grn, org brn & dk brn	30	30
147	A12	20c brt bl, gray & cit	42	42

Perf. 14

148	A12	3fr org brn, brt grn & blk	3.50	3.50

On Nos. 113, 115 and 122 "RF" is at left and "E II R" is at right.

For surcharge see No. 160.

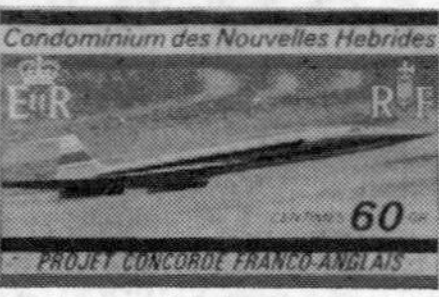

Concorde Supersonic Airliner A21

Design: 25c, Concorde seen from above.

1968, Oct. 9 Litho. *Perf. 14x13½*
149 A21 25c vio bl, red & lt bl 2.25 2.00
150 A21 60c red, ultra & blk 4.00 3.50

Development of the Concorde supersonic airliner, a joint Anglo-French project.

Kauri Pine — A22

Land Diver at Start, Pentecost Island — A24

Relay Race, British and French Flags A23

1969, June 30 *Perf. 14½x14*
151 A22 20c brn & multi 40 40

New Hebrides timber industry. Issued in sheets of 9 (3x3) on simulated wood grain background.

1969, Aug. 13 Photo. *Perf. 12½x13*
152 A23 25c shown 60 60
153 A23 1fr Runner at right 1.25 1.25

3rd South Pacific Games, Port Moresby, Papua and New Guinea, Aug. 13-23.

1969, Oct. 15 Litho. *Perf. 12½*
154 A24 15c shown 35 35
155 A24 25c Diver in mid-air 45 45
156 A24 1fr Diver near ground 2.00 2.00

Land divers of Pentecost Island.

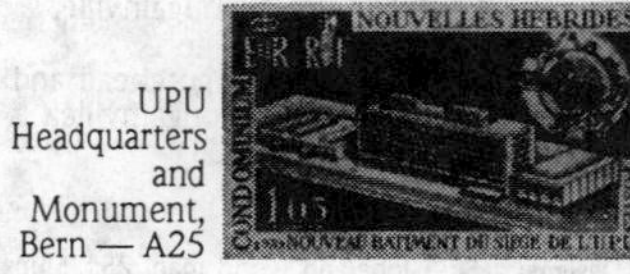

UPU Headquarters and Monument, Bern — A25

1970, May 20 Engr. *Perf. 13*
157 A25 1.05fr org, lil & slate 1.20 1.20

New UPU Headquarters, Bern.

Charles de Gaulle — A26

1970, July 20 Photo. *Perf. 13*
158 A26 65c brn & multi 1.20 1.20
159 A26 1.10fr dp bl & multi 2.25 2.25

Rallying of the Free French, 30th anniv.
For overprints see Nos. 163-164.

No. 147 Surcharged

35

1970, Oct. 15 Photo. *Perf. 12½*
160 A12 35c on 20c multi 80 80

Virgin and Child, by Giovanni Bellini — A27

Design: 50c, Virgin and Child, by Giovanni Cima.

1970, Nov. 30 Litho. *Perf. 14½x14*
161 A27 15c tan & multi 35 22
162 A27 50c lt grn & multi 62 45

Christmas. See Nos. 186-187.

Nos. 158-159 Overprinted "1890-1970 / IN MEMORIAM / 9-11-70" in Gold, 2 Vertical Bars in Black

1971, Jan. 19 Photo. *Perf. 13*
163 A26 65c brn & multi 80 80
164 A26 1.10fr dp bl & multi 2.00 2.00

In memory of Gen. Charles de Gaulle (1890-1970), President of France.

Soccer A28

Design: 65c, Basketball, vert.

1971, July 13 Photo. *Perf. 12½*
165 A28 20c multi 40 40
166 A28 65c multi 90 70

4th South Pacific Games, Papeete, French Polynesia, Sept. 8-19.

Breadfruit Tree and Fruit, Society Arms — A29

Perf. 14½x14
1971, Sept. 7 Litho. Unwmk.
167 A29 65c multi 80 65

Expedition of the Royal Society of London for the Advancement of Science to study vegetation and fauna, July 1-October.

Adoration of the Shepherds, by Louis Le Nain — A30

Christmas: 50c, Adoration of the Shepherds, by Jacopo Tintoretto.

1971, Nov. 23 *Perf. 14x13½*
168 A30 25c lt grn & multi 45 35
169 A30 50c lt bl & multi 65 60

Drover Mk III A31

Airplanes: 25c, Sandringham seaplane. 30c, Dragon Rapide. 65c, Caravelle.

1972, Feb. 29 Photo. *Perf. 13½x13*
170 A31 20c lt grn & multi 45 35
171 A31 25c ultra & multi 55 40
172 A31 30c org & multi 75 60
173 A31 65c dk bl & multi 2.25 1.75

Headdress, South Malekula — A32

Baker's Pigeon — A33

Artifacts; 15c, Slit gong and carved figure, North Ambrym. 1fr, Carved figures, North Ambrym. 3fr, Ceremonial headdress, South Malekula.
Birds: 20c, Red-headed parrot-finch. 35c, Chestnut-bellied kingfisher. 2fr, Green palm lorikeet.
Sea Shells: 25c, Cribraria fischeri. 30c, Oliva rubrolabiata. 65c, Strombus plicatus. 5fr, Turbo marmoratus.

1972, July 24 Photo. *Perf. 12½x13*
174 A32 5c plum & multi 15 15
175 A33 10c bl & multi 15 15
176 A32 15c red & multi 20 16
177 A33 20c org brn & multi 25 20
178 A32 25c dp bl & multi 30 25
179 A32 30c dk grn & multi 35 30
180 A33 35c gray bl & multi 55 45
181 A32 65c dk grn & multi 75 70
182 A32 1fr org & multi 1.50 1.25
183 A33 2fr multi 2.50 1.75
184 A32 3fr yel & multi 4.25 2.75
185 A32 5fr pink & multi 8.50 6.00
Nos. 174-185 (12) 19.45 14.11

For overprints see Nos. 200-201.

Christmas Type of 1970

Christmas: 25c, Adoration of the Magi (detail), by Bartholomaeus Spranger. 70c, Virgin and Child, by Jan Provoost.

1972, Sept. 25 Litho. *Perf. 14x13½*
186 A27 25c lt grn & multi 45 40
187 A27 70c lt bl & multi 65 62

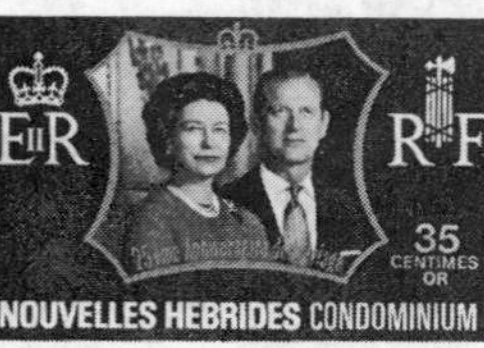

Queen Elizabeth II and Prince Philip — A34

Perf. 14x14½
1972, Nov. 20 Photo. Wmk. 314
188 A34 35c vio blk & multi 35 28
189 A34 65c olive & multi 65 45

25th anniversary of the marriage of Queen Elizabeth II and Prince Philip.

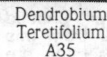

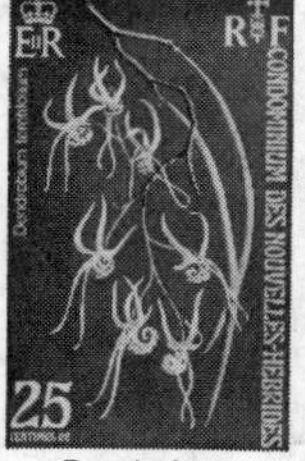

Dendrobium Teretifolium A35

New Wharf, Vila A36

Orchids: 30c, Ephemerantha comata. 35c, Spathoglottis petri. 65c, Dendrobium mohlianum.

Unwmk.

1973, Feb. 26 Litho. *Perf. 14*
190 A35 25c bl vio & multi 32 25
191 A35 30c multi 45 42
192 A35 35c vio & multi 65 50
193 A35 65c dk grn & multi 1.75 1.50

1973, May 14 Litho. *Perf. 14*
194 A36 25c shown 60 40
195 A36 70c New Wharf, horiz. 1.25 1.00

New wharf at Vila, completed Nov. 1972.

Wild Horses, Tanna — A37

Design: 70c, Yasur Volcano, Tanna.

1973, Aug. 13 Photo. *Perf. 13x13½*
196 A37 35c multi 65 60
197 A37 70c multi 1.40 1.10

Mother and Child, by Marcel Moutouh — A38

Christmas: 70c, Star over Lagoon, by Tatin D'Avesnieres.

1973, Nov. 19 Litho. *Perf. 14x13½*
198 A38 35c tan & multi 45 28
199 A38 70c lil rose & multi 65 60

Nos. 180, 183 Overprinted in Red or Black: "VISITE ROYALE / 1974"

1974, Feb. 11 Photo. *Perf. 12½x13*
200 A33 35c multi (R) 40 25
201 A33 2fr multi (B) 1.65 1.25

Visit of British Royal Family, Feb. 15-16.

Pacific Dove — A39

Designs: 35c, Night swallowtail. 70c, Green sea turtle. 1.15fr, Flying fox.

1974, Feb. 11 *Perf. 13x12½*

202	A39	25c gray & multi	42	40
203	A39	35c gray & multi	1.00	55
204	A39	70c gray & multi	1.65	1.25
205	A39	1.15fr gray & multi	2.25	1.75

Nature conservation.

Old Post Office, Vila A40

Design: 70c, New Post Office.

Unwmk.

1974, May 6 **Photo.** *Perf. 12*

206	A40	35c bl & multi	45	32
207	A40	70c red & multi	65	65
a.		Pair, #206-207	1.10	1.00

Opening of New Post Office, May, 1974.

Capt. Cook and Tanna Island A41

Designs: No. 209, William Wales and boat landing on island. No. 210, William Hodges painting islanders and landscape. 1.15fr, Capt. Cook, "Resolution" and map of New Hebrides.

1974, Aug. 1 **Litho.** *Perf. 13*

Size: 40x25mm

208	A41	35c multi	1.25	90
209	A41	35c multi	1.25	90
210	A41	35c multi	1.25	90
a.		Strip of 3, #208-210	3.75	2.75

Size: 58x34mm

Perf. 11

211	A41	1.15fr lil & multi	3.00	1.90

Bicentenary of the discovery of the New Hebrides by Capt. James Cook.

No. 210a has a continuous design.

Exchange of Letters, UPU Emblem A42

1974, Oct. 9 **Photo.** *Perf. 13x12½*

212	A42	70c multi	62	60

Centenary of Universal Postal Union.

Nativity, by Gerard Van Honthorst — A43

Christmas: 35c, Adoration of the Kings, by Velazquez, vert.

1974, Nov. 14 **Litho.** *Perf. 13½*

213	A43	35c multi	40	35
214	A43	70c multi	60	55

Charolais Bull — A44

1975, Apr. 29 **Engr.** *Perf. 13*

215	A44	10fr multi	10.00	10.00

Nordjamb Emblem, Kayaks A45

Pitti Madonna, by Michelangelo A46

1975, Aug. 5 **Litho.** *Perf. 14x13½*

216	A45	25c shown	42	30
217	A45	35c Camp cooks	45	42
218	A45	1fr Map makers	1.10	75
219	A45	5fr Fishermen	6.00	4.75

Nordjamb 75, 14th Boy Scout Jamboree, Lillehammer, Norway, July 29-Aug. 7.

1975, Nov. 11 **Litho.** *Perf. 14½x14*

Christmas (After Michelangelo): 70c, Bruges Madonna. 2.50fr, Taddei Madonna.

220	A46	35c multi	40	28
221	A46	70c brn & multi	62	45
222	A46	2.50fr bl & multi	2.25	1.90

Concorde, Air France Colors and Emblem — A47

1976, Jan. 30 **Typo.** *Perf. 13*

223	A47	5fr bl & multi	10.00	6.50

1st commercial flight of supersonic jet Concorde from Paris to Rio, Jan. 21.

Telephones, 1876 and 1976 — A48

Designs: 70c, Alexander Graham Bell. 1.15fr, Nouméa Earth Station and satellite.

1976, Mar. 31 **Photo.** *Perf. 13*

224	A48	25c blk, car & bl	35	28
225	A48	70c blk & multi	65	55
226	A48	1.15fr blk, org & vio bl	1.40	90

Centenary of first telephone call by Alexander Graham Bell, Mar. 10, 1876.

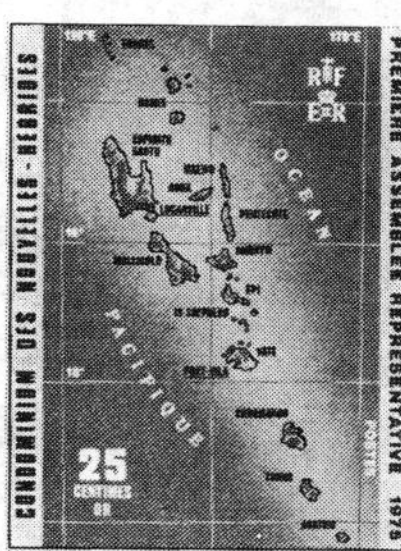
Map of New Hebrides A49

View of Luganville (Santo) — A50

Design: 2fr, View of Vila.

1976, June 29 **Unwmk.** *Perf. 13*

227	A49	25c blue & multi	45	28
228	A50	1fr multi	1.25	65
229	A50	2fr multi	3.00	1.60

Opening of first Representative Assembly, June 29, 1976 (25c); first Luganville (Santo) Municipal Council (1fr); first Vila Municipal Council (2fr).

Nos. 228-229 exist with lower inscription reading "Premiere Assemblée Representative 1975" instead of "Premiere Municipalite de Luganville" on 1fr and "Premiere Municipalite de Port-Vila" on 2fr.

Flight into Egypt, by Francisco Vieira Lusitano — A51

Portuguese 16th Century Paintings: 70c, Adoration of the Shepherds. 2.50fr, Adoration of the Kings.

1976, Nov. 8 **Litho.** *Perf. 14*

230	A51	35c pur & multi	45	35
231	A51	70c bl & multi	65	60
232	A51	2.50fr multi	2.50	2.00

Christmas 1976.

Queen's Visit, 1974 — A52

Designs: 70c, Imperial State crown. 2fr, The blessing.

1977, Feb. 7 **Litho.** *Perf. 14x13½*

233	A52	35c lt grn & multi	35	22
234	A52	70c bl & multi	60	40
235	A52	2fr pink & multi	1.60	1.40

Reign of Queen Elizabeth II, 25th anniv.

Nos. 174-185, 215 Surcharged with New Value, "FNH" and Bars

1977, July 1 **Photo.** *Perf. 12½x13*

236	A32	5fr on 5c multi	22	22
237	A33	10fr on 10c multi	35	35
238	A32	15fr on 15c multi	55	55
239	A33	20fr on 20c multi	60	50
240	A32	25fr on 25c multi	80	80
241	A32	30fr on 30c multi	1.10	1.10
242	A33	35fr on 35c multi	1.10	1.10
243	A32	40fr on 65c multi	1.50	1.50
244	A32	50fr on 1fr multi	2.50	2.50
245	A33	70fr on 2fr multi	4.50	4.50
246	A32	100fr on 3fr multi	6.25	6.25
247	A32	200fr on 5fr multi	11.00	11.00

Engr.

Perf. 13

248	A44	500fr on 10fr multi	25.00	25.00
		Nos. 236-248 (13)	55.47	55.37

Surcharged in Paris. Later all except 20fr were surcharged in Vila with slightly different letters and different bars. Of these 12, the 50fr, 70fr and 100fr were reported to have been sold only at the philatelic bureau.

Espiritu Santo and Cattle — A53

Tempi Madonna, by Raphael — A54

Designs: 5fr, Erromango Island and Kaori tree. 10fr, Archipelago and man making copra. 20fr, Efate Island and Post Office, Vila. 25fr, Malakula Island and headdresses. 30fr, Aoba and Maewo Islands and pig tusks. 35fr, Pentecost Island and land diving. 40fr, Tanna Island and Prophet John Frum's Red Cross. 50fr, Shepherd Island and canoe with sail. 70fr, Banks Island and dancers. 100fr, Ambrym Island and carvings. 200fr, Aneityum Island and decorated baskets. 500fr, Torres Islands and fishing with bow and arrow.

1977-78 **Litho.** *Perf. 14*

258	A53	5fr multi	20	20
259	A53	10fr multi	25	22
260	A53	15fr multi	32	28
261	A53	20fr multi	45	32
262	A53	25fr multi	50	35
263	A53	30fr multi	55	48
264	A53	35fr multi	65	50
265	A53	40fr multi	80	55
266	A53	50fr multi	90	70
267	A53	70fr multi	1.25	1.00
268	A53	100fr multi	2.25	1.50
269	A53	200fr multi	5.00	3.50
270	A53	500fr multi	11.00	8.75
		Nos. 258-270 (13)	24.12	18.35

Issue dates: 5fr, 20fr, 50fr, 100fr, 200fr, Sept. 7; 15fr, 25fr, 30fr, 40fr, Nov. 23, 1977; 10fr, 35fr, 70fr, 500fr, May 9, 1978.

1977, Dec. 8 **Litho.** *Perf. 12*

Christmas: 15fr, Virgin and Child, by Gerard David. 30fr, Virgin and Child, by Pompeo Batoni.

271	A54	10fr multi	30	25
272	A54	15fr multi	38	32
273	A54	30fr multi	80	70

British Airways Concorde over New York — A55

Designs: 20fr, British Airways Concorde over London. 30fr, Air France Concorde over Washington. 40fr, Air France Concorde over Paris.

1978, May 9 **Litho.** *Perf. 14*

274	A55	10fr multi	60	40
275	A55	20fr multi	1.00	70
276	A55	30fr multi	1.40	1.10
277	A55	40fr multi	2.00	1.50

Souvenir Sheet

White Horse of Hanover — A56

Elizabeth II — A57

Design: No. 278c, Gallic cock.

1978, June 2 Litho. *Perf. 15*

278		Sheet of 6	6.00	6.00
a.	A56	40fr greenish blue & multi	85	85
b.	A57	40fr greenish blue & multi	85	85
c.	A56	40fr greenish blue & multi	85	85

25th anniversary of coronation of Queen Elizabeth II. No. 278 contains 2 se-tenant strips of Nos. 278a-278c, separated by horizontal gutter with commemorative and descriptive inscriptions and showing central part of coronation procession with coach.

Virgin and Child, by Dürer — A58

Paintings by Albrecht Durer (1471-1528): 15fr, Virgin and Child with St. Anne. 30fr, Virgin and Child with Goldfinch. 40fr, Virgin and Child with Pear.

1978, Dec. 1 Litho. *Perf. 14x13½*

279	A58	10fr multi	25	25
280	A58	15fr multi	35	35
281	A58	30fr multi	60	55
282	A58	40fr multi	1.00	80

Christmas.

Type of 1976 Surcharged with New Value, Bars over Old Denomination and Inscription at Right. Longitude changed to "166E."

1979, Jan. 11 Photo. *Perf. 13*

283	A49	10fr on 25c bl & multi	40	28
284	A49	40fr on 25c lt grn & multi	1.10	80

First anniv. of Internal Self-Government.

New Hebrides No. 155 and Hill Statue A59

Rowland Hill and New Hebrides Stamps: 10fr, No. 55. 40fr, No. 46.

1979, Sept. 10 Litho. *Perf. 14*

285	A59	10fr multi	22	16
286	A59	20fr multi	45	35
287	A59	40fr multi	80	62

Sir Rowland Hill (1795-1879), originator of penny postage. A souvenir sheet containing No. 286 and British Issue No. 266 is listed as No. 266a in Volume I, New Hebrides, British Issues.

Arts Festival — A60

Designs: 10fr, Clubs and spears. 20fr, Ritual puppet. 40fr, Headdress.

1979, Nov. 16 Litho. *Perf. 14*

288	A60	5fr multi	20	20
289	A60	10fr multi	28	22
290	A60	20fr multi	50	38
291	A60	40fr multi	1.00	62

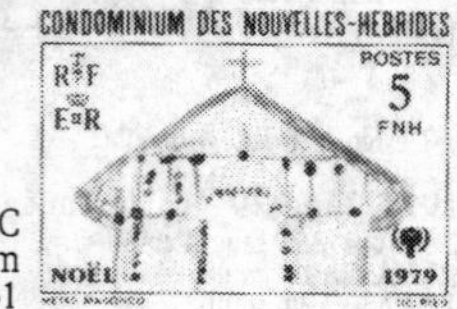

Church, IYC Emblem A61

IYC Emblem, Children's Drawings: 10fr, Father Christmas. 20fr, Cross and Bible, vert. 40fr, Stars, candle and Santa Claus, vert.

1979, Dec. 4 *Perf. 13x13½*

292	A61	5fr multi	20	20
293	A61	10fr multi	28	22
294	A61	20fr multi	50	35
295	A61	40fr multi	1.00	62

Christmas; Intl. Year of the Child.

White-bellied Honeyeater — A62

1980, Feb. 27 Litho. *Perf. 14*

296	A62	10fr shown	40	40
297	A62	20fr Scarlet robins	60	60
298	A62	30fr Yellow white-eyes	1.00	1.00
299	A62	40fr Fan-tailed brush cuckoo	1.50	1.50

Stamps of Vanuatu (Vol. 1) replaced those of New Hebrides in 1980.

POSTAGE DUE STAMPS

French Issues

Nos. 45-46, 48, 50, 52 Overprinted **CHIFFRE TAXE**

1925 Wmk. R F in Sheet *Perf. 14*

J1	A4	10c green	27.50	3.50
J2	A4	20c greenish gray	27.50	3.50
J3	A4	30c carmine	27.50	3.50
J4	A4	50c ultramarine	27.50	3.50
J5	A4	1fr carmine, *blue*	27.50	3.50
		Nos. J1-J5 (5)	137.50	17.50

Nos. 55-56, 58, 61, 63 Overprinted **CHIFFRE TAXE**

1938 *Perf. 12*

J6	A6	5c green	1.50	1.50
J7	A6	10c dark orange	1.50	1.50
J8	A6	20c rose red	2.25	2.25
J9	A6	40c olive green	6.25	6.25
J10	A6	1fr dark car, *green*	9.50	9.50
		Nos. J6-J10 (5)	21.00	21.00

Nos. J6-J10 Overprinted **France Libre**

1941

J11	A6	5c green	7.00	7.00
J12	A6	10c dark orange	7.00	7.00
J13	A6	20c rose red	7.00	7.00
J14	A6	40c olive green	7.00	7.00
J15	A6	1fr dk car, *green*	7.00	7.00
		Nos. J11-J15 (5)	35.00	35.00

Catalogue values for unused stamps in this section, from this point to the end of the section, are for Never Hinged items.

Nos. 83-84, 86, 89, 91 Overprinted "TIMBRE-TAXE"

1953 Unwmk. *Perf. 12½*

J16	A8	5c green	60	60
J17	A8	10c red	80	80
J18	A8	20c ultramarine	2.00	2.00
J19	A8	40c black brown	4.00	4.00
J20	A8	1fr deep orange	7.00	7.00
		Nos. J16-J20 (5)	14.40	14.40

Nos. 98-99, 101, 104, 106 Overprinted "TIMBRE-TAXE"

Wmk. R F in Sheet

1957 Engr. *Perf. 13½x13*

J21	A10	5c green	40	40
J22	A10	10c red	55	55
J23	A10	20c ultramarine	62	62
J24	A10	40c sepia	2.00	2.00
J25	A10	1fr orange	6.00	6.00
		Nos. J21-J25 (5)	9.57	9.57

NICARAGUA

LOCATION — Central America, between Honduras and Costa Rica
GOVT. — Republic
AREA — 57,143 sq. mi.
POP. — 2,908,000 (est. 1984)
CAPITAL — Managua

100 Centavos = 1 Peso
100 Centavos = 1 Córdoba (1913)

Catalogue values for unused stamps in this country are for Never Hinged items, beginning with Scott 689 in the regular postage section, Scott C261 in the airpost section, Scott CO37 in the airpost official section, and Scott RA60 in the postal tax section.

Watermarks

Wmk. 117- Liberty Cap

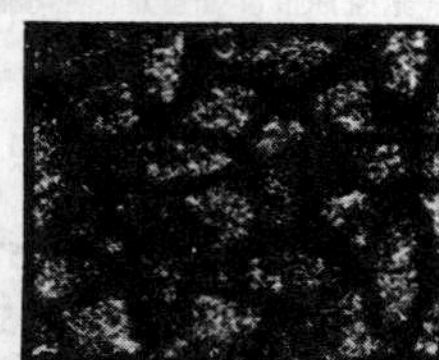
Wmk. 209- Multiple Ovals

Liberty Cap on Mountain Peak; From Seal of Country — A1

A2

A3

Unwmk.

1862, Dec. 2 Engr. *Perf. 12*

Yellowish Paper

1	A1	2c dark blue	75.00	20.00
2	A1	5c black	150.00	50.00

Values are for copies without gum. Copies with gum sell for more. Nos. 1-2 were canceled only by pen.

See No. C509.

1869-71

White Paper

3	A1	1c bister ('71)	2.50	1.25
4	A1	2c blue	2.50	1.25
5	A1	5c black	22.50	1.00
6	A2	10c vermilion	3.75	1.75
7	A3	25c green	6.25	4.00

1878-80 *Rouletted 8½*

8	A1	1c brown	2.00	1.25
9	A1	2c blue	2.00	1.25
10	A1	5c black	10.00	1.00
11	A2	10c ver ('80)	2.50	1.50
12	A3	25c grn ('79)	2.50	4.00

Nos. 3-12 were reprinted in 1892. The corresponding values of the two series are printed in the same shades which is not usually true of the originals. They are, however, similar to some of the original shades and the only certain test is comparison. Originals have thin white gum; reprints have rather thick yellowish gum. Value 50c each.

Seal of Nicaragua — A4

Locomotive and Telegraph Key — A5

1882 Engr. *Perf. 12*

13	A4	1c green	20	25
14	A4	2c carmine	20	25
15	A4	5c blue	20	25
16	A4	10c dl vio	25	*75*
17	A4	15c yellow	60	*2.50*
18	A4	20c slate gray	90	*5.00*
19	A4	50c dl vio	1.25	*10.00*
		Nos. 13-19 (7)	3.60	

Used Values

of Nos. 13-120 are for stamps with genuine cancellations applied while the stamps were valid. Various counterfeit cancellations exist.

1890 Engr.

20	A5	1c yel brn	20	25
21	A5	2c vermilion	20	25
22	A5	5c deep blue	20	25
23	A5	10c lilac gray	20	25
24	A5	20c red	20	*1.75*
25	A5	50c purple	20	*5.00*
26	A5	1p brown	25	*8.50*
27	A5	2p dk grn	25	*9.00*
28	A5	5p lake	25	
29	A5	10p orange	25	
		Nos. 20-29 (10)	2.20	

The issues of 1890-1899 were printed by the Hamilton Bank Note Co., New York, to the order of N. F. Seebeck who held a contract for stamps with the government of Nicaragua. Reprints were made, for sale to collectors, of the 1896, 1897 and 1898, postage, postage due and official stamps. See notes following those issues.

For overprints see Nos. O1-O10.

Goddess of Plenty — A6

Columbus Sighting Land — A7

1891 Litho.

30	A6	1c yel brn	25	35
31	A6	2c red	25	35
32	A6	5c dk bl	25	25
33	A6	10c slate	25	50
34	A6	20c plum	25	*2.00*
35	A6	50c purple	25	*5.00*

36	A6	1p blk brn	25	*5.00*
37	A6	2p green	25	*8.50*
38	A6	5p brn red	25	
39	A6	10p orange	25	
		Nos. 30-39 (10)	2.50	

For overprints see Nos. O11-O20.

1892 **Engr.**

40	A7	1c yel brn	20	25
41	A7	2c vermilion	20	20
42	A7	5c dk bl	20	20
43	A7	10c slate	20	25
44	A7	20c plum	20	*2.00*
45	A7	50c purple	20	*7.00*
46	A7	1p brown	20	*7.00*
47	A7	2p bl grn	20	*8.50*
48	A7	5p rose lake	20	
49	A7	10p orange	20	
		Nos. 40-49 (10)	2.00	

Commemorative of the 400th anniversary of the discovery of America by Columbus.

Stamps of the 1892 design were printed in other colors than those listed and overprinted "Telegrafos". The 1c blue, 10c orange, 20c slate, 50c plum and 2p vermilion are telegraph stamps which did not receive the overprint.

For overprints see Nos. O21-O30.

Arms
A8

"Victory"
A9

1893 **Engr.**

51	A8	1c yel brn	20	20
52	A8	2c vermilion	20	20
53	A8	5c dk bl	20	20
54	A8	10c slate	20	25
55	A8	20c dl red	20	*1.50*
56	A8	50c violet	20	*4.00*
57	A8	1p dk brn	20	*7.00*
58	A8	2p bl grn	20	*8.50*
59	A8	5p rose lake	20	
60	A8	10p orange	20	
		Nos. 51-60 (10)	2.00	

The 1c blue and 2c dark brown are telegraph stamps which did not receive the "Telegrafos" overprint.

For overprints see Nos. O31-O41.

1894 **Engr.**

61	A9	1c yel brn	20	25
62	A9	2c vermilion	20	30
63	A9	5c dp bl	20	25
64	A9	10c slate	20	30
65	A9	20c lake	20	*1.75*
66	A9	50c purple	20	*4.00*
67	A9	1p brown	20	*7.00*
68	A9	2p green	20	*12.50*
69	A9	5p brn red	20	*15.00*
70	A9	10p orange	20	
		Nos. 61-70 (10)	2.00	

Specialists believe the 25c yellow green, type A9, is a telegraph denomination never issued for postal purposes. Stamps in other colors are telegraph stamps without the usual "Telegrafos" overprint.

There was little use of No. 70. Canceled copies are c-t-o or faked cancels.

For overprints see Nos. O42-O51.

Coat of Arms
A10

Map of
Nicaragua
A11

1895 **Engr.**

71	A10	1c yel brn	20	30
72	A10	2c vermilion	20	30
73	A10	5c dp bl	20	25
74	A10	10c slate	20	25
75	A10	20c claret	20	*75*
76	A10	50c dl vio	3.00	*5.00*
77	A10	1p dk brn	20	*5.00*
78	A10	2p dp grn	20	*8.00*
79	A10	5p brn red	20	*11.00*
80	A10	10p orange	20	
		Nos. 71-80 (10)	4.80	

Frames of Nos. 71-80 differ for each denomination.

A 50c violet blue exists. Its status is questioned. Value 20c.

There was little use of No. 80. Canceled copies are c-t-o or faked cancels.

For overprints see Nos. O52-O71.

1896 **Engr.**

81	A11	1c violet	30	*1.00*
82	A11	2c bl grn	30	*50*
83	A11	5c brt rose	30	*30*
84	A11	10c blue	50	*50*
85	A11	20c bis brn	3.00	*4.00*
86	A11	50c bl gray	60	*8.00*
87	A11	1p black	75	*11.00*
88	A11	2p claret	75	*15.00*
89	A11	5p dp bl	75	*15.00*
		Nos. 81-89 (9)	7.25	

See italic note after No. 109M.

For overprints see Nos. O82-O117.

Wmk. 117

89A	A11	1c violet	3.75	90
89B	A11	2c bl grn	3.75	1.25
89C	A11	5c brt rose	15.00	30
89D	A11	10c blue	25.00	90
89E	A11	20c bis brn	3.75	4.25
89F	A11	50c bl gray	42.50	*9.00*
89G	A11	1p black	37.50	*12.50*
89H	A11	2p claret		*18.50*
89I	A11	5p dp bl		*40.00*

Same, dated 1897

1897 **Engr.** **Unwmk.**

90	A11	1c violet	50	50
91	A11	2c bl grn	50	62
92	A11	5c brt rose	50	32
93	A11	10c blue	6.25	75
94	A11	20c bis brn	2.50	*3.75*
95	A11	50c bl gray	9.00	*9.50*
96	A11	1p black	9.00	*15.00*
97	A11	2p claret	20.00	*19.00*
98	A11	5p dp bl	20.00	*42.50*
		Nos. 90-98 (9)	68.25	*91.94*

See italic note after No. 109M.

Wmk. 117

98A	A11	1c violet	14.00	50
98B	A11	2c bl grn	14.00	50
98C	A11	5c brt rose	20.00	38
98D	A11	10c blue	22.50	90
98E	A11	20c bis brn	3.75	4.25
98F	A11	50c bl gray	22.50	*8.00*
98G	A11	1p black	25.00	*16.00*
98H	A11	2p claret	25.00	*25.00*
98I	A11	5p dp bl	125.00	*50.00*
		Nos. 98A-98I (9)	271.75	*105.53*

Coat of Arms of "Republic of Central America" — A12

1898 **Engr.** **Wmk. 117**

99	A12	1c brown	25	38
100	A12	2c slate	25	38
101	A12	4c red brn	25	50
102	A12	5c ol grn	40.00	22.50
103	A12	10c violet	15.00	62
104	A12	15c ultra	40	1.50
105	A12	20c blue	10.00	2.00
106	A12	50c yellow	10.00	*9.50*
107	A12	1p vio bl	40	*16.00*
108	A12	2p brown	19.00	*22.50*
109	A12	5p orange	25.00	*32.50*
		Nos. 99-109 (11)	120.55	*108.38*

Unwmk.

109A	A12	1c brown	1.25	32
109B	A12	2c slate	1.25	
109D	A12	4c red brn	2.25	62
109E	A12	5c ol grn	25.00	15
109G	A12	10c violet	25.00	62
109H	A12	15c ultra	25.00	
109I	A12	20c blue	25.00	
109J	A12	50c yellow	25.00	
109K	A12	1p dp ultra	25.00	
109L	A12	2p ol brn	25.00	
109M	A12	5p orange	25.00	
		Nos. 109A-109M (11)	204.75	

The paper of Nos. 109A to 109M is slightly thicker and more opaque than that of Nos. 81 to 89 and 90 to 98. The 5c and 10c also exist on very thin, semi-transparent paper.

Many reprints of Nos. 81-98, 98F-98H, 99-109M are on thick, porous paper, with and without watermark. The watermark is sideways. Paper of the originals is thinner for Nos. 81-109 but thicker for Nos. 109A-109M. Value 15 cents each.

In addition, reprints of Nos. 81-89 and 90-98 exist on thin paper, but with shades differing slightly from those of originals.

For overprints see Nos. O118-O128.

"Justice"
A13

Mt. Momotombo
A14

1899 **Litho.**

110	A13	1c gray grn	15	*35*
111	A13	2c brown	15	*25*
112	A13	4c dp rose	35	*40*
113	A13	5c dp bl	20	*25*
114	A13	10c buff	20	*30*
115	A13	15c chocolate	20	*65*
116	A13	20c dk grn	35	*75*
117	A13	50c brt rose	20	*3.00*
118	A13	1p red	20	*8.50*
119	A13	2p violet	20	*20.00*
120	A13	5p lt bl	20	*25.00*
		Nos. 110-120 (11)	2.40	

Nos. 110-120 exist imperf. and in horizontal pairs imperf. between.

For overprints see Nos. O129-O139.

Imprint: "American Bank Note Co. NY"

1900, Jan. 1 **Engr.**

121	A14	1c plum	50	15
122	A14	2c vermilion	50	15
123	A14	3c green	75	25
124	A14	4c ol grn	1.00	25
125	A14	5c dk bl	4.00	20
126	A14	6c car rose	14.00	5.00
127	A14	10c violet	7.00	25
128	A14	15c ultra	8.00	65
129	A14	20c brown	8.00	65
130	A14	50c lake	7.00	1.10
131	A14	1p yellow	12.00	4.00
132	A14	2p salmon	10.00	2.25
133	A14	5p black	10.00	3.00
		Nos. 121-133 (13)	82.75	17.90

See Nos. 159-161. For overprints and surcharges see Nos. 134-136, 144-151, 162-163, 175-178, O150-O154, 1L1-1L13, 1L16-1L19, 1L20, 2L1-2L10, 2L16-2L24, 2L36-2L39.

Nos. 131-133 Surcharged in Black or Red

1901

2 Cent.

1901, Mar. 5

134	A14	2c on 1p yel	5.00	3.00
a.		Bar below date	14.00	8.00
b.		Inverted surcharge		16.50
c.		Double surcharge		27.50
135	A14	10c on 5p blk (R)	6.50	4.50
a.		Bar below date	14.00	8.00
136	A14	20c on 2p salmon	7.50	7.50
a.		Bar below date	14.00	10.00

A 2c surcharge on No. 121, the 1c plum, was not put on sale, nor postally used.

The 2c on 1p yellow without ornaments is a reprint.

Correos

Postage Due Stamps of 1900 Overprinted in Black or Gold

1901

1901, Mar.

137	D3	1c plum	4.50	3.50
138	D3	2c vermilion	4.50	3.50
139	D3	5c dk bl	6.00	3.50
140	D3	10c pur (G)	8.50	5.00
a.		Double overprint	14.00	14.00
141	D3	20c org brn	10.00	6.50
142	D3	30c dk grn	10.00	6.50
143	D3	50c lake	8.50	4.00
a.		"1091" for "1901"	16.00	16.00
b.		"Correo"	37.50	
		Nos. 137-143 (7)	52.00	32.50

In 1904 an imitation of this overprint was made to fill a dealer's order. The date is at top and "Correos" at bottom. The overprint is printed in black, sideways on the 1c and 2c and upright on the 5c and 10c. Some copies of the 2c were further surcharged "1 Centavo." None of these stamps was ever regularly used.

Nos. 126, 131-133 Surcharged

3 Cent.

1901

Black Surcharge

1901, Oct. 20

144	A14	3c on 6c rose	6.00	5.00
a.		Bar below value	7.00	5.50
b.		Inverted surcharge	8.00	8.00
c.		Double surcharge	8.00	8.00
d.		Double surch., one inverted	25.00	25.00
145	A14	4c on 6c rose	5.00	4.00
a.		Bar below value	5.50	4.50
b.		"1 cent" instead of "4 cent"	8.00	8.00
c.		Double surcharge	20.00	20.00
146	A14	5c on 1p yellow	5.00	4.00
a.		Three bars below value	6.00	4.50
b.		Ornaments at each side of "1901"	6.00	4.50
c.		Double surcharge, one in red	15.00	15.00
147	A14	10c on 2p salmon	5.50	4.00
a.		Inverted surcharge	12.50	12.50
b.		Double surcharge		

Blue Surcharge

148	A14	3c on 6c rose	6.00	4.50
a.		Bar below value	7.00	5.50
b.		Double surcharge	8.00	8.00
149	A14	4c on 6c rose	6.50	5.00
a.		Bar below value	7.50	7.50
b.		"1 cent" instead of "4 cent"	10.00	10.00
c.		Inverted surcharge	20.00	20.00

Red Surcharge

150	A14	5c on 1p yellow	7.50	6.50
a.		Three bars below value	9.00	7.00
b.		Ornaments at each side of "1901"	9.00	7.00
c.		Inverted surcharge	12.00	12.00
d.		Double surcharge, inverted	17.50	17.50
151	A14	20c on 5p black	5.00	3.50
a.		Inverted surcharge	16.00	16.00
b.		Double surcharge	22.50	22.50
c.		Triple surcharge		
		Nos. 144-151 (8)	46.50	36.50

In 1904 a series was surcharged as above, but with "Centavos" spelled out. About the same time No. 122 was surcharged "1 cent." and "1901," "1902" or "1904." All of these surcharges were made to fill a dealer's order and none of the stamps was regularly issued or used.

1901

Postage Due Stamps of 1900 Overprinted in Black

Correos

1901, Oct.

152 D3	1c red violet	1.00	40
a.	Ornaments at each side of the stamp	1.10	65
b.	Ornaments at each side of "1901"	1.10	65
c.	"Correos" in italics	1.50	1.50
d.	Double overprint	14.00	14.00
153 D3	2c vermilion	75	40
a.	Double overprint	8.50	5.50
154 D3	5c dark blue	1.00	60
a.	Double overprint, one inverted		
b.	Double overprint	7.00	7.00
155 D3	10c purple	1.00	60
b.	Double overprint	10.00	10.00
c.	Double overprint, one inverted	12.00	12.00
156 D3	20c org brn	1.25	1.25
b.	Double overprint	7.00	7.00
157 D3	30c dk grn	1.00	1.10
a.	Double overprint	9.00	9.00
b.	Inverted overprint	19.00	19.00
158 D3	50c lake	1.00	1.10
a.	Triple overprint	25.00	25.00
b.	Double overprint	16.50	16.50
	Nos. 152-158 (7)	7.00	5.45

One stamp in each group of 25 has the 2nd "o" of "Correos" italic. Value twice normal.

Momotombo Type of 1900 Without Imprint

1902 Litho. *Perf. 14*

159 A14	5c blue	50	25
a.	Imperf., pair	3.75	
160 A14	5c carmine	50	20
a.	Imperf., pair	3.75	
161 A14	10c violet	1.50	20
a.	Imperf., pair	3.75	

No. 161 was privately surcharged 6c, 1p and 5p in black in 1903.

15 cvos.

Nos. 121 and 122 Surcharged in Black

1902

1902, Oct. *Perf. 12*

162 A14	15c on 2c ver	2.00	75
a.	Double surcharge	32.50	
b.	Blue surcharge	90.00	
163 A14	30c on 1c plum	1.00	2.25
a.	Double surcharge	9.00	
b.	Inverted surcharge	27.50	

Counterfeits of No. 163 exist in slightly smaller type.

President José Santos Zelaya — A15

1903, Jan. **Engr.**

167 A15	1c emer & blk	35	50
168 A15	2c rose & blk	70	50
169 A15	5c ultra & blk	35	50
170 A15	10c yel & blk	35	85
171 A15	15c lake & blk	60	2.00
172 A15	20c vio & blk	60	2.00
173 A15	50c ol & blk	60	5.00
174 A15	1p red brn & blk	60	6.00
	Nos. 167-174 (8)	4.15	17.35

10th anniv. of 1st election of Pres. Zelaya.

The so-called color errors-1c orange yellow and black, 2c ultramarine and black, 5c lake and black and 10c emerald and black-were also delivered to postal authorities. They were intended for official use though not issued as such. Value, $4 each.

Vale ₵ 5

Nos. 175-176

15 Centcvos

No. 177

No. 161 Surcharged with New Values in Blue

1904-05

175 A14	5c on 10c vio ('05)	1.75	25
a.	Inverted surcharge	2.00	1.40
b.	Without ornaments	2.00	70
c.	Character for "cents" inverted	1.75	40
d.	As "b," inverted		
e.	As "c," inverted	2.75	2.75
f.	Double surcharge	8.00	8.00
g.	"5" omitted	2.75	2.75
176 A14	15c on 10c vio ('05)	30	30
a.	Inverted surcharge	1.40	1.40
b.	Without ornaments	1.40	1.40
c.	Character for "cents" inverted	1.10	1.10
d.	As "b," inverted		
e.	As "c," inverted	1.75	1.75
f.	Imperf.	6.50	
h.	As "a," imperf.	9.00	9.00
i.	Double surcharge	14.00	14.00
177 A14	15c on 10c vio	4.50	2.75
a.	Inverted surcharge	6.00	6.00
b.	"Centcvos"	6.00	4.50
c.	"5" of "15" omitted	7.50	
d.	As "b," inverted	8.50	8.50
e.	Double surcharge	11.00	11.00
f.	Double surcharge, inverted	13.00	13.00
g.	Imperf., pair	9.00	9.00

There are two settings of the surcharge on No. 175. In the 1st the character for "cents" and the figure "5" are 2mm apart and in the 2nd 4mm.

The 2c vermilion, No. 122, with surcharge "1 cent. / 1904" was not issued.

No. 161 Surcharged in Black

5 CENTS.

1905, June

178 A14	5c on 10c violet	60	35
a.	Inverted surcharge	2.75	2.75
b.	Double surcharge	4.50	4.50
c.	Surcharge in blue	13.00	

Coat of Arms — A18

Imprint: "American Bank Note Co. NY"

1905, July 25 Engr. *Perf. 12*

179 A18	1c green	30	20
180 A18	2c car rose	30	20
181 A18	3c violet	45	25
182 A18	4c org red	45	25
183 A18	5c blue	45	15
184 A18	6c slate	60	40
185 A18	10c yel brn	85	25
186 A18	15c brn olive	75	35
187 A18	20c lake	60	30
188 A18	50c orange	3.00	1.50
189 A18	1p black	1.50	1.50
190 A18	2p dk grn	1.50	2.00
191 A18	5p violet	1.75	2.50
	Nos. 179-191 (13)	12.50	9.85

See Nos. 202-208, 237-248. For overprints and surcharges see Nos. 193-201, 212-216, 235-236, 249-265, O187-O198, O210-O222, 1L21-1L62, 1L73-1L95, 1LO1-1LO3, 2L26-2L35, 2L42-2L46, 2L48-2L72, 2LO1-2LO4.

Nos. 179-184 and 191 Surcharged in Black or Red Reading Up or Down

Vale 10₵

1906-08

193 A18	10c on 2c car rose (up)	7.00	4.00
a.	Surcharge reading down	13.00	13.00
194 A18	10c on 3c vio (up)	60	20
a.	"¢" normal	2.75	1.35
b.	Double surcharge	4.50	4.50
c.	Double surch., up and down	7.00	5.00
d.	Pair, one without surcharge	9.50	
e.	Surcharge reading down	30	20
195 A18	10c on 4c org red (up) ('08)	*35.00*	*20.00*
a.	Surcharge reading down	*32.50*	*22.50*
196 A18	15c on 1c grn (up)	60	30
a.	Double surcharge	7.50	7.50
b.	Dbl. surch., one reading down	11.00	11.00
c.	Surcharge reading down	40	25
197 A18	20c on 2c car rose (down) ('07)	50	30
a.	Double surcharge	13.00	13.00
b.	Surcharge reading up	37.50	32.00
c.	"V" omitted	10.00	10.00
198 A18	20c on 5c bl (down)	75	50
a.	Surcharge reading up	35.00	
199 A18	50c on 6c sl (R) (down)	60	50
a.	Double surcharge		
b.	Surcharge reading up	30.00	30.00
c.	Yellow brown surcharge	60	40
200 A18	1p on 5p vio (down) ('07)	42.50	25.00

There are several settings of these surcharges and many varieties in the shapes of the figures, the spacing, etc.

Surcharged in Red Vertically Reading Up

Vale 35 cts.

1908, May

201 A18	35c on 6c slate	3.00	2.25
a.	Double surcharge (R)	25.00	
b.	Double surcharge (R + Bk)	65.00	
c.	Carmine surcharge	3.00	2.25

Arms Type of 1905

Imprint: "Waterlow & Sons, Ltd."

1907, Feb. *Perf. 14 to 15*

202 A18	1c green	70	40
203 A18	2c rose	80	25
204 A18	4c brn org	2.00	30
205 A18	10c yel brn	3.00	25
206 A18	15c brn olive	4.50	90
207 A18	20c lake	8.00	1.25
208 A18	50c orange	11.00	4.25
	Nos. 202-208 (7)	30.00	7.60

Nos. 202-204, 207-208 Surcharged in Black or Blue (Bl) Reading Down

Vale 10 ₵

1907-08

212 A18	10c on 2c rose	1.50	50
a.	Double surcharge		10.00
b.	"Vale" only		22.50
c.	Surcharge reading up	14.00	6.50
213 A18	10c on 4c brn org (up) ('08)	2.25	85
a.	Double surcharge		10.00
b.	Surcharge reading down		5.50
214 A18	10c on 20c lake ('08)	3.25	1.40
b.	Surcharge reading up		80.00
215 A18	10c on 50c org (Bl) ('08)	2.00	60
216 A18	15c on 1c grn ('08)	32.50	4.00
	Nos. 212-216 (5)	41.50	7.35

Several settings of this surcharge provide varieties of numeral font, spacing, etc.

Revenue Stamps Overprinted "CORREO-1908" — A19

1908, June

217 A19	5c yel & blk	60	40
a.	"CORROE"	2.75	2.75
b.	Overprint reading down		7.00
c.	Double overprint		13.00
218 A19	10c lt bl & blk	50	25
a.	Double overprint	4.50	4.50
b.	Overprint reading down	50	25
c.	Double overprint, up and down	13.00	13.00
219 A19	1p yel brn & blk	50	*2.00*
a.	"CORROE"	7.50	7.50
220 A19	2p pearl gray & blk	50	*2.50*
a.	"CORROE"	10.00	10.00

Remainders of Nos. 219-220 were sold.

Revenue Stamps Surcharged Vertically Reading Up in Red, Blue, Green or Orange

CORREO—1908
VALE 2 ₵

221 A19	1c on 5c yel & blk (R)	40	25
a.	"1008"	1.50	1.50
b.	"8908"	1.50	1.50
c.	Surcharge reading down	4.00	4.00
d.	Double surcharge	4.00	4.00
222 A19	2c on 5c yel & blk (Bl)	50	30
b.	"ORREO"	1.75	1.75
c.	"1008"	1.75	1.75
d.	"8908"	1.75	1.75
f.	Double surcharge	7.00	7.00
g.	Double surcharge, one inverted	7.00	7.00
h.	Surcharge reading down	9.00	9.00
223 A19	4c on 5c yel & blk (G)	65	35
a.	"ORREO"	2.50	2.50
b.	"1008"	2.00	2.00
c.	"8908"	2.00	2.00
224 A19	15c on 50c ol & blk (R)	60	40
a.	"1008"	4.00	4.00
b.	"8908"	4.00	4.00
c.	Surcharge reading down	10.00	10.00
225 A19	35c on 50c ol & blk (O)	4.00	1.00
a.	Double surcharge, one inverted	12.00	12.00
b.	Surcharge reading down	12.00	12.00
c.	Double surcharge, one in black		
	Nos. 221-225 (5)	6.15	2.30

For surcharges and overprints see Nos. 225D-225H, 230-234, 266-278, 1L63-1L72A, 1L96-1L106, 2L47.

Revenue Stamps Surcharged Vertically Reading Up in Blue, Black or Orange

CORREOS-1908
VALE 2 ₵

1908, Nov.

225D A19	2c on 5c yel & blk (Bl)	20.00	12.50
e.	"9c" instead of "2c"	75.00	75.00
225F A19	10c on 50c ol & blk (Bk)	*850.00*	*325.00*
g.	Double surcharge	*425.00*	
225H A19	35c on 50c ol & blk (O)	17.50	10.00

In this setting there are three types of the character for "cents".

CORREOS—1908
VALE 4 ₵
CORREOS—1908

Revenue Stamps Overprinted or Surcharged in Various Colors

1908, Dec.

226	2c org (Bk)	3.50	2.00
a.	Double overprint	6.00	6.00
b.	Overprint reading up	5.00	5.00
227	4c on 2c org (Bk)	1.75	90
a.	Surcharge reading up	5.00	5.00
b.	Blue surcharge	80.00	80.00
228	5c on 2c org (Bl)	1.50	60
a.	Surcharge reading up	6.00	6.00
229	10c on 2c org (G)	1.50	30
a.	"1988" for "1908"	4.00	3.00
b.	Surcharge reading up	5.00	5.00
c.	"¢" inverted	4.00	4.00
d.	Double surcharge	7.50	

Two printings of No. 229 exist. In the first, the initial of "VALE" is a small capital, and in the second a large capital.

The overprint "Correos-1908." 35mm long, handstamped on 1c blue revenue stamp of type A20, is private and fraudulent.

Revenue Stamps Surcharged in Various Colors

CORREOS 1909
VALE 10 ₵

1909, Feb.

Color: Olive & Black

230 A19	1c on 50c (V)	4.00	1.65
231 A19	2c on 50c (Br)	7.00	3.00
232 A19	4c on 50c (G)	7.00	3.00
233 A19	5c on 50c (C)	4.00	1.75
a.	Double surcharge	12.50	12.50
234 A19	10c on 50c (Bk)	1.10	75
	Nos. 230-234 (5)	23.10	10.15

Nos. 230 to 234 are found with three types of the character for "cents".

Nos. 190 and 191 Surcharged in Black

VALE 10 ¢

1909, Mar. *Perf. 12*

235 A18 10c on 2p dk grn 20.00 12.00
236 A18 10c on 5p vio *100.00 70.00*

There are three types of the character for "cents."

Arms Type of 1905
Imprint: "American Bank Note Co. NY"

1909, Mar.

237 A18 1c yel grn 35 20
238 A18 2c vermilion 35 20
239 A18 3c red org 35 20
240 A18 4c violet 35 20
241 A18 5c dp bl 35 20
242 A18 6c gray brn 3.00 1.50
243 A18 10c lake 85 15
244 A18 15c black 85 15
245 A18 20c brn olive 85 15
246 A18 50c dp grn 1.25 40
247 A18 1p yellow 1.25 40
248 A18 2p car rose 1.00 40
Nos. 237-248 (12) 10.80 4.15

Nos. 239 and 244, Surcharged in Black or Red

VALE 2 ¢

1910, July

249 A18 2c on 3c red org 2.75 1.10
250 A18 10c on 15c blk (R) 1.25 30
a. "VLEA" 3.50 2.00
b. Double surcharge 17.50 17.50

There are two types of the character for "cents."

Nos. 239, 244, 245 Surcharged in Black or Red

VALE 2 C

1910

252 A18 2c on 3c (Bk) 1.50 1.25
a. Double surcharge 6.00 6.00
b. Pair, one without surcharge
c. "Vale" omitted 10.00 10.00
254 A18 5c on 20c (R) 40 30
a. Double surcharge (R) 6.00 5.00
b. Inverted surcharge (R) 3.50 2.50
c. Black surcharge 100.00
d. Double surcharge (Bk) 135.00
e. Inverted surcharge (Bk) 110.00
255 A18 10c on 15c (Bk) 90 30
a. "c" omitted 2.00 1.10
b. "10c" omitted 2.50 1.50
c. Inverted surcharge 4.00 4.00
d. Double surcharge 6.00 6.00
e. Double surch., one inverted 12.00

There are several minor varieties in this setting, such as italic "L" and "E" and fancy "V" in "VALE", small italic "C", and italic "I" for "1" in "10".

Nos. 239, 244, 246 and 247, Surcharged in Black

Vale
2 cts.

1910, Dec. 10

256 A18 2c on 3c red org 90 50
a. Without period 1.00 75
b. Inverted surcharge 6.00 6.00
c. Double surcharge 6.00 6.00
257 A18 10c on 15c blk 2.00 75
a. Without period 3.50 1.25
b. Double surcharge 3.50 3.00
c. Inverted surcharge 5.00 5.00
258 A18 10c on 50c dp grn 1.25 40
a. Without period 1.50 75
b. Double surcharge 3.00 3.00
c. Inverted surcharge 3.00 3.00
259 A18 10c on 1p yel 90 40
a. Without period 1.25 75
b. Double surcharge 3.00 3.00

The 15c on 50c deep green is a telegraph stamp.

Nos. 240, 244-248 Surcharged in Black

Vale
2 cts.

Surcharge as on Nos. 256-259 but lines wider apart.

1911, Mar.

260 A18 2c on 4c vio 30 20
a. Without period 35 30
b. Double surcharge 3.50 3.00
c. Double surcharge, inverted 4.00 4.00
d. Double surcharge, one inverted 3.50 3.50
e. Inverted surcharge 7.50 7.50
261 A18 5c on 20c brn ol 30 20
a. Without period 60 50
b. Double surcharge 2.50 2.50
c. Inverted surcharge 2.50 2.00
d. Double surcharge, one inverted 6.00 6.00
262 A18 10c on 15c blk 40 20
a. Without period 1.00 50
b. "Yale" 12.00 12.00
c. Double surcharge 3.00 3.00
d. Inverted surcharge 3.00 3.00
e. Double surch., one inverted 5.00 4.00
f. Double surch., both inverted 12.00 12.00
263 A18 10c on 50c dp grn 25 20
a. Without period 1.00 50
b. Double surcharge 3.00 2.50
c. Double surcharge, one inverted 5.00 4.00
d. Inverted surcharge 5.00 5.00
264 A18 10c on 1p yel 1.50 40
a. Without period 2.00 1.50
b. Double surcharge 4.00 4.00
c. Double surcharge, one inverted 7.50
265 A18 10c on 2p car rose 60 50
a. Without period 2.00 1.50
b. Double surcharge 2.50 2.50
c. Double surcharge, one inverted 6.00 6.00
d. Inverted surcharge 6.00 6.00
Nos. 260-265 (6) 3.35 1.70

Revenue Stamps Surcharged in Black

Correos
02 cts
1911

1911, Apr. 10 *Perf. 14 to 15*

266 A19 2c on 5p dl bl 1.00 1.25
a. Without period 1.25 1.50
b. Double surcharge 2.50 *2.00*
267 A19 2c on 5p ultra 35 40
a. Without period 75 1.25
b. Double surcharge *3.50*
268 A19 5c on 10p pink 75 40
a. Without period 1.50 1.00
b. "cte" for "cts" 1.50 1.00
c. Double surcharge 4.00 4.00
d. Inverted surcharge 2.50 2.50
269 A19 10c on 25c lilac 40 25
a. Without period 1.00 75
b. "cte" for "cts" 1.25 1.00
c. Inverted surcharge 4.00 4.00
d. Double surcharge 2.50 2.50
e. Double surcharge, one inverted 4.00 4.00
270 A19 10c on 2p gray 40 25
a. Without period 1.00 75
b. "cte" for "cts" 1.25 1.00
c. Double surcharge 5.00 5.00
d. Double surcharge, one inverted 4.00 3.00
271 A19 35c on 1p brown 40 30
a. Without period 1.00 75
b. "cte" for "cts" 1.25 1.00
c. "Corre" 1.50 1.50
d. Double surcharge 2.50 2.50
e. Double surcharge, one inverted 2.50 2.50
f. Double surcharge inverted 3.00 3.00
g. Inverted surcharge *5.00*
Nos. 266-271 (6) 3.30 2.85

These surcharges are in settings of twenty-five. One stamp in each setting has a large square period after "cts" and two have no period. One of the 2c has no space between "02" and "cts" and one 5c has a small thin "s" in "Correos."

Surcharged in Black

CORREOS
05 cts.
1911

1911, June

272 A19 5c on 2p gray 1.50 1.00
a. Inverted surcharge 6.00 5.00

In this setting one stamp has a large square period and another has a thick up-right "c" in "cts."

Surcharged in Black

VALE
05 cts
POSTAL
de 1911

1911, June 12

273 A19 5c on 25c lilac 1.50 1.25
274 A19 5c on 50c ol grn 5.00 5.00
275 A19 5c on 5p blue 7.00 7.00
276 A19 5c on 5p ultra 6.00 6.00
a. Inverted surcharge
277 A19 5c on 50p ver 5.00 5.00
278 A19 10c on 50c ol grn 1.50 50
Nos. 273-278 (6) 26.00 24.75

This setting has the large square period and the thick "c" in "cts." Many of the stamps have no period after "cts." Owing to broken type and defective impressions letters sometimes appear to be omitted.

A21

Revenue Stamps Surcharged on the Back in Black:

vale
05 cts.
CORREO
DE 1911
a

Vale
05 cts
CORREO
DE 1911
b

Railroad coupon tax stamps (1st class red and 2nd class blue) are the basic stamps of Nos. 279-294. They were first surcharged for revenue use in 1903 in two types: I- "Timbre Fiscal" and "ctvs." II- "TIMBRE FISCAL" and "cents" (originally intended for use in Bluefields).

1911, July

279 A21 (a) 2c on 5c on 2 bl 25 30
a. New value in yellow on face 6.00 6.00
b. New value in black on face 5.00 5.00
c. New value in red on face 60.00
d. Inverted surcharge 75
e. Double surch., one inverted 7.50 7.50
f. "TIMBRE FISCAL" in blk 75 75
280 A21 (b) 2c on 5c on 2 bl 25 30
a. New value in yellow on face 3.00 3.00
b. New value in black on face 4.00 4.00
c. New value in red on face 60.00
d. Inverted surcharge 90 1.00
e. Double surch., one inverted 7.50 7.50
f. "TIMBRE FISCAL" in blk 1.00 1.00
281 A21 (a) 5c on 5c on 2 bl 20 15
a. Inverted surcharge 50 35
b. "TIMBRE FISCAL" in blk 1.00 1.00
c. New value in yellow on face
282 A21 (b) 5c on 5c on 2 bl 25 20
a. Inverted surcharge 40 35
b. "TIMBRE FISCAL" in blk 1.00 1.00
283 A21 (a) 10c on 5c on 2 bl 20 20
a. Inverted surcharge 75 50
b. "TIMBRE FISCAL" in blk 1.00 1.00
c. New value in yellow on face 60.00
284 A21 (b) 10c on 5c on 2 bl 20 20
a. Inverted surcharge 75 50
b. "TIMBRE FISCAL" in blk 1.00 1.00
c. Double surcharge 6.00 6.00
d. New value in yellow on face 65.00
285 A21 (a) 15c on 10c on 1 red 25 25
a. Inverted surcharge 1.00 1.25
b. "Timbre Fiscal" double 5.00
286 A21 (b) 15c on 10c on 1 red 35 35
a. Inverted surcharge 1.00 1.00
b. "Timbre Fiscal" double 5.00
Nos. 279-286 (8) 1.95 1.95

These surcharges are in settings of 20. For listing, they are separated into small and large figures, but there are many other varieties due to type and arrangement.

For overprints and surcharges see Nos. 287-294, O223-O244, 1L107-1L108.

Surcharged on the Face in Black

CORREO
02 centavos

1911, Oct.

287 A21 2c on 10c on 1 red 6.50 6.50
a. Inverted surcharge 1.40 1.40
b. Double surcharge 10.00 10.00
288 A21 20c on 10c on 1 red 4.50 4.50
a. Inverted surcharge 5.25 5.00
289 A21 50c on 10c on 1 red 5.25 4.50
a. Inverted surcharge 10.00 10.00

There are two varieties of the figures "2" and "5" in this setting.

Surcharged on the Back in Black

Vale
10 cts.
CORREO DE
1911

1911, Nov.

289B A21 5c on 10c on 1 red 37.50
c. Inverted surcharge 20.00
289D A21 10c on 10c on 1 red 12.50
e. Inverted surcharge 24.00

Surcharged on the Face

Correo
Vale
2 cts.
1911

1911, Dec.

Dark Blue Postal Surcharge

290 A21 2c on 10c on 1 red 25 20
a. Inverted surcharge 2.50 2.50
b. Double surcharge 5.00 5.00
291 A21 5c on 10c on 1 red 30 20
a. Double surcharge 2.50 2.50
b. Inverted surcharge 2.50 2.50
292 A21 10c on 10c on 1 red 35 20
a. Inverted surcharge 2.50 2.50
b. Double surcharge 2.50 2.50
c. "TIMBRE FISCAL" on back 3.50 3.50

Black Postal Surcharge

293 A21 10c on 10c on 1 red 1.50 1.00
a. Inverted surcharge 7.00 7.00
b. New value surch. on back 12.00 12.00

Red Postal Surcharge

293C A21 5c on 5c on 2 blue 1.40 1.25
d. "TIMBRE FISCAL" in blk 2.50 1.75
e. "5" omitted 3.75 3.75
f. Inverted surcharge 4.75 4.75
Nos. 290-293C (5) 3.80 2.85

Bar Overprinted on No. O234 in Dark Blue

Correo ~~oficial~~
Vale
10 cts.
1911

294 A21 10c on 10c on 1 red 1.25 1.00
a. Inverted surcharge 2.50 2.50
b. Bar at foot of stamp 5.00 5.00

Nos. 290-294 each have three varieties of the numerals in the surcharge.

"Liberty"
A22

Coat of Arms
A23

1912, Jan. **Engr.** *Perf. 14, 15*

295 A22 1c yel grn 30 15
296 A22 2c carmine 40 15
297 A22 3c yel brn 30 20
298 A22 4c brn vio 30 15
299 A22 5c blue & blk 25 15
300 A22 6c olive bister 30 80
301 A22 10c red brn 25 15
302 A22 15c vio 25 15
303 A22 20c red 25 15
304 A22 25c blue grn & blk 30 20
305 A23 35c grn & chnt 2.00 1.50
306 A22 50c lt blue 1.00 40
307 A22 1p org 1.40 2.00
308 A22 2p dark blue grn 1.50 2.25
309 A22 5p blk 3.50 3.50
Nos. 295-309 (15) 12.30 11.90

For overprints and surcharges see Nos. 310-324, 337A-348, 395-396, O245-O259.

No. 305 Surcharged in Violet

Vale 15 cts.
Correos-1913.

1913, Mar.

310 A23 15c on 35c 40 25
a. "ats" for "cts" 6.00 6.00

Stamps of 1912 Surcharged in Red or Black

VALE
medio
centavo
de córdoba
1913

1913-14

311 A22 ½c on 3c yel brn (R) 40 35
a. "Corooba" 2.50 2.50
b. "do" for "de" 2.50 2.50
c. Inverted surcharge 22.50
d. Black surcharge *50.00*
312 A22 ½c on 15c vio (R) 25 20
a. "Corooba" 1.00 1.00
b. "do" for "de" 1.25 1.25
c. Black surcharge *25.00*
313 A22 ½c on 1p org 25 20
a. "VALB" 1.50 1.00
b. "ALE" 4.00 3.50
c. "LE" 6.00 5.00
d. "VALE" omitted 3.50 3.50
314 A22 1c on 3c yel brn 75 60
315 A22 1c on 4c brn vio 25 20
316 A22 1c on 50c lt blue 25 20
317 A22 1c on 5p blk 25 20
318 A22 2c on 4c brn vio 35 25
a. "do" for "de" 1.25 1.25
319 A22 2c on 20c red 3.50 4.50
a. "do" for "de" 17.50 12.50
320 A22 2c on 25c blue grn & blk 35 20
a. "do" for "de" 3.50 2.50
321 A23 2c on 35c grn & chnt 25 40
a. "9131" 3.00 2.00
b. "do" for "de" 2.50 2.00
322 A22 2c on 50c lt blue 25 20
a. "do" for "de" 1.25 1.25
323 A22 2c on 2p dark blue grn 20 15
a. "VALB" 1.25 75
b. "ALE" 2.50 1.25
c. "VALE" omitted 6.00
d. "VALE" and "dos" omitted 6.00
324 A22 3c on 6c olive bis 20 15
a. "VALB" *35.00*

Surcharged on Zelaya Issue of 1912

325 Z2 ½c on 2c ver 60 45
a. "Corooba" 1.25 1.25
b. "do" for "de" 1.25 1.25
326 Z2 1c on 3c org brn 50 20
327 Z2 1c on 4c car 50 20
328 Z2 1c on 6c red brn 40 20
329 Z2 1c on 20c dark vio 50 20
330 Z2 1c on 25c grn & blk 50 20
331 Z2 2c on 1c yel grn ('14) 6.75 1.25
a. "Centavos" 7.50 1.50
332 Z2 2c on 25c grn & blk 2.25 *3.00*
333 Z2 5c on 35c brn & blk 40 20
334 Z2 5c on 50c ol grn 40 20
a. Double surcharge 22.50
335 Z2 6c on 1p org 40 20
336 Z2 10c on 2p org brn 40 20
337 Z2 1p on 5p dk bl grn 40 40
Nos. 325-337 (13) 14.00 6.90

On No. 331 the surcharge has a space of 2½mm between "Vale" and "dos".

Space between "Vale" and "dos" 2½mm instead of 1mm "de Cordoba" in different type.

1914, Feb.

337A A22 2c on 4c brn vio 27.50 4.00
b. "Ccntavos" 12.00
337C A22 2c on 20c red 13.00 1.25
d. "Ccntavos" 4.00
337E A22 2c on 25c bl grn & blk 6.00
f. "Ccntavos" 12.00
337G A23 2c on 35c grn & chnt 8.50
h. "Ccntavos" 15.00
337I A22 2c on 50c lt bl 22.00 4.00
j. "Ccntavos" 10.00

No. 310 with Additional Surcharge

medio
cvo. Córdoba

1913, Dec.

337K A23 ½c on 15c on 35c *200.00*

The word "Medio" is usually in heavy-faced, shaded letters. It is also in thinner, unshaded letters and in letters from both fonts mixed.

No. 310 Surcharged in Black and Violet

½ ct. Cordoba
Correos 1913.

338 A23 ½c on 15c on 35c 20 15
a. Double surcharge 3.50
b. Inverted surcharge 3.50
c. Surcharged on No. 305 12.00
339 A23 1c on 15c on 35c 25 20
a. Double surcharge 4.00

Official Stamps of 1912 Surcharged

VALE
₡ 0.01

1914, Feb.

340 A22 1c on 25c lt bl 40 25
a. Double surcharge 9.00
341 A23 1c on 35c lt bl 40 25
a. "0.10" for "0.01" 10.00 10.00
341B A22 1c on 50c lt bl *160.00*
342 A22 1c on 1p lt bl 25 20
342A A22 2c on 20c lt bl *160.00 110.00*
b. "0.12" for "0.02"
343 A22 2c on 50c lt bl 40 20
a. "0.12" for "0.02" 75.00
344 A22 2c on 2p lt bl 40 20
345 A22 2c on 5p lt bl *185.00*
346 A22 5c on 5p lt bl 25 20

Red Surcharge

347 A22 5c on 1p lt bl *55.00*
348 A22 5c on 5p lt bl *325.00*

National Palace, Managua — A24

León Cathedral — A25

Various Frames

1914, May 13 Engr. *Perf. 12*

349 A24 ½c lt bl 85 20
350 A24 1c dk grn 85 15
351 A25 2c red org 85 15
352 A24 3c red brn 1.25 30
353 A25 4c scarlet 1.25 40
354 A24 5c gray blk 45 15
355 A25 6c blk brn 9.00 5.50
356 A25 10c org yel 85 20
357 A24 15c dp vio 5.75 2.00
358 A25 20c slate 11.00 5.50
359 A24 25c orange 1.50 45
360 A25 50c pale blue 1.40 40
Nos. 349-360 (12) 35.00 15.40

In 1924 the 5c, 10c, 25c, 50c were issued in slightly larger size, 27x22¾mm. The original set was 26x22½mm.

No. 356 with overprint "Union Panamericana 1890-1940" in green is of private origin.

See Nos. 408-415, 483-495, 513-523, 652-664. For overprints and surcharges see Nos. 361-394, 397-400, 416-419, 427-479, 500, 540-548, 580-586, 600-648, 671-673, 684-685, C1-C3, C9-C13, C49-C66, C92-C105, C121-C134, C147-C149, C155-C163, C174-C185, CO1-CO24, O260-O294, O296-O319, O332-O376, RA1-RA5, RA10-RA11, RA26-RA35, RA39-RA40, RA44, RA47, RA52.

No. 355 Surcharged in Black

VALE
5 cts
de Córdoba
1915

1915, Sept.

361 A25 5c on 6c blk brn 1.50 40
a. Double surcharge 7.00 7.00

Stamps of 1914 Surcharged in Black or Red

Vale
1 centavo
de córdoba

New Value in Figures

1918-19

362 A24 1c on 3c red brn 6.50 2.25
a. Double surch., one invtd. 12.50
363 A25 2c on 4c scar 32.50 22.50
364 A24 5c on 15c dp vio (R) 7.50 1.50
a. Double surcharge 12.00
364C A24 5c on 15c dp vio 350.00

Surcharged in Black

VALE
por 2 centavos
de Córdoba

365 A25 2c on 20c sl 110.00 55.00
a. "ppr" for "por" *120.00*
b. Double surcharge 90.00 30.00
c. "Cordobo" 150.00 110.00
365D A25 5c on 20c sl 325.00 120.00
e. Double surch. (Bk + R) 250.00
f. "Cordobo" 200.00

The surcharge on No. 365 is in blue black, and that on No. 365D usually has an admixture of red.

Surcharged in Black, Red or Violet

Vale
medio centavo
de córdoba

New Value in Words

366 A25 ½c on 6c blk brn 4.00 1.50
a. "Meio" 15.00
b. Double surcharge 12.00
367 A25 ½c on 10c yel 2.50 30
a. "Val" for "Vale" 3.00
b. "Codoba" 3.00
c. Inverted surcharge 5.00
d. Double surch., one inverted 10.00
368 A24 ½c on 15c dp vio 2.50 60
a. Double surcharge 7.50
b. "Codoba" 4.00
c. "Meio" 6.00
369 A24 ½c on 25c org 5.00 2.00
a. Double surcharge 8.00
b. Double surch., one inverted 6.00
370 A25 ½c on 50c pale bl 2.50 30
a. "Meio" 6.00
b. Double surcharge 5.00
c. Double surch., one inverted 7.00
371 A25 ½c on 50c pale bl (R) 4.50 1.50
a. Double surcharge 10.00
372 A24 1c on 3c red brn 3.00 30
a. Double surcharge 3.50
373 A25 1c on 6c blk brn 12.50 3.50
a. Double surcharge 9.00
374 A25 1c on 10c yel 24.00 8.00
a. "nu" for "un" 22.50
375 A24 1c on 15c dp vio 4.50 75
a. Double surcharge 10.00
b. "Codoba" 6.00
376 A25 1c on 20c sl 110.00 55.00
a. Blk surch., normal and red surch. invtd. 80.00
b. Double surch., red & blk 90.00
c. Blue surcharge 110.00
377 A25 1c on 20c sl (V) 110.00 42.50
a. Double surcharge (V + Bk) 80.00
378 A25 1c on 20c sl (R) 2.50 30
a. Double surch., one inverted
b. "Val" for "Vale" 3.50 3.00
379 A24 1c on 25c org 4.50 1.00
a. Double surcharge 11.00
380 A25 1c on 50c pale bl 14.00 4.50
a. Double surcharge 17.50
381 A25 2c on 4c scar 3.50 30
a. Double surcharge 10.00
b. "centavo" 5.00
c. "Val" for "Vale"
382 A25 2c on 6c blk brn 24.00 8.00
a. "Centavoss"
b. "Cordobas"
383 A25 2c on 10c yel 24.00 4.50
a. "centavo"
384 A25 2c on 20c sl (R) 13.00 3.25
a. "pe" for "de" 15.00
b. Double surch., red & blk 27.50
c. "centavo" 12.00
d. Double surcharge (R) 17.50
385 A24 2c on 25c org 5.50 40
a. "Vle" for "Vale" 7.50
b. "Codoba" 7.50
c. Inverted surcharge 10.00
386 A25 5c on 6c blk brn 10.00 4.25
a. Double surcharge 13.50
387 A24 5c on 15c dp vio 3.50 60
a. "cincoun" for "cinco" 15.00
b. "Vle" for "Vale" 12.50
c. "Codoba" 12.50
Nos. 366-387 (22) 389.50 143.35

No. 378 is surcharged in light red and brown red: the latter color is frequently offered as the violet surcharge (No. 377).

Official Stamps of 1915 Surcharged in Black or Blue

Vale
dos centavos
de cordoba

1919-21

388 A24 1c on 25c lt bl 1.50 25
a. Double surcharge 10.00
b. Inverted surcharge 12.00
389 A25 2c on 50c lt bl 1.50 25
a. "centavo" 4.00 4.00
b. Double surcharge 12.00
390 A25 10c on 20c lt bl 1.40 40
a. "centovos" 5.00 5.00
b. Double surcharge 8.00
390F A25 10c on 20c lt bl (Bl) 65.00

There are numerous varieties of omitted, inverted and italic letters in the foregoing surcharges.

No. 358 Surcharged in Black

VALE
5 Centavos

Types of the numerals:

2 2 2
I II III

2 2 2 2 2
IV V VI VII VIII

5 5 5 5
I II III IV

5 5 5 5
V VI VII VIII

1919, May

391 A25 2c on 20c (I) 160.00 110.00
a. Type II
b. Type III
c. Type IV
d. Type VI
e. Type VIII
392 A25 5c on 20c (I) 110.00 40.00
a. Type II 110.00 45.00
b. Type III 120.00 50.00
c. Type IV 125.00 50.00
d. Type V 140.00 60.00
e. Type VI 140.00 60.00
f. Type VII 400.00 250.00
h. Double surch., one inverted

No. 358 Surcharged in Black

VALE
2 Cents

393 A25 2 Cents on 20c (I) 135.00
a. Type II
b. Type III
c. Type IV
d. Type V
e. Type VI
f. Type VII
393G A25 5 Cents on 20c sl, (VIII) 135.00 55.00

No. 351 Surcharged in Black

Vale
un centavo
de córdoba

1920, Jan.

394 A25 1c on 2c red org 1.50 25
a. Inverted surcharge
b. Double surcharge

Official Stamps of 1912 Overprinted in Carmine

«Particular»

1921, Mar.

395 A22 1c lt bl 1.50 60
a. "Particular" 5.00 5.00
b. Inverted overprint 10.00
396 A22 5c lt bl 1.50 40
a. "Particular" 5.00 5.00

Official Stamps of 1915 Surcharged in Carmine

Vale
un centavo
de córdoba

397 A25 ½c on 2c lt bl 50 20
a. "Mddio" 2.50 2.50
398 A25 ½c on 4c lt bl 1.25 20
a. "Mddio" 2.50 2.50
399 A24 1c on 3c lt bl 1.25 30

No. 354 Surcharged in Red

Vale
medio centavo

1921, Aug.

400 A24 ½c on 5c gray blk 75 75

Trial printings of this stamp were surcharged in yellow, black and red, and yellow and red. Some of these were used for postage.

Gen. Manuel José Arce — A26

José Cecilio del Valle — A27

Miguel Larreinaga A28

Gen. Fernando Chamorro A29

Gen. Máximo Jérez A30

Gen. Pedro Joaquín Chamorro A31

Rubén Darío — A32

1921, Sept. **Engr.**
401 A26 ½c lt bl & blk 1.00 1.00
402 A27 1c grn & blk 1.00 1.00
403 A28 2c rose red & blk 1.00 1.00
404 A29 5c ultra & blk 1.00 1.00
405 A30 10c org & blk 1.00 1.00
406 A31 25c yel & blk 1.00 1.00
407 A32 50c vio & blk 1.00 1.00
Nos. 401-407 (7) 7.00 7.00

Centenary of independence.
For overprints and surcharges see Nos. 420-421, RA12-RA16, RA19-RA23.

Types of 1914 Issue
Various Frames

1922
408 A24 ½c green 20 15
409 A24 1c violet 20 15
410 A25 2c car rose 20 15
411 A24 3c ol gray 30 15
411A A25 4c vermilion 35 25
412 A25 6c red brn 20 15
413 A24 15c brown 35 15
414 A25 20c bis brn 50 20
415 A25 1cor blk brn 90 50
Nos. 408-415 (9) 3.20 1.85

In 1924 Nos. 408-415 were issued in slightly larger size, 27x22¾mm. The original set was 26x22½mm.

Nos. 408, 410 exist with signature controls. See note before No. 600. Same values.

No. 356 Surcharged in Black — **Vale 0.01 de córdoba**

1922, Nov.
416 A25 1c on 10c org yel 1.00 35
417 A25 2c on 10c org yel 1.00 25

Nos. 354 and 356 Surcharged in Red — **Vale 2 centavos de córdoba**

1923, Jan.
418 A24 1c on 5c gray blk 1.25 20
419 A25 2c on 10c org yel 1.25 20
a. Inverted surcharge

Nos. 401 and 402 Overprinted in Red — **Sello Postal**

1923
420 A26 ½c lt bl & blk 7.50 7.50
421 A27 1c grn & blk 2.50 85
a. Double overprint 7.50

Francisco Hernández de Córdoba — A33

1924 **Engr.**
422 A33 1c dp grn 1.50 30
423 A33 2c car rose 1.50 30
424 A33 5c dp bl 1.00 30
425 A33 10c bis brn 1.00 60

400th anniversary of the founding of León and Granada.
For overprint and surcharges see Nos. 499, 536, O295.

Stamps of 1914-22 Overprinted — **Resello 1927**

Black, Red or Blue Overprint

1927, May 3
427 A24 ½c grn (Bk) 25 20
428 A24 1c vio (R) 20 15
a. Double overprint 3.00
428B A24 1c vio (Bk) 85.00 55.00
429 A25 2c car rose (Bk) 20 15
a. Inverted overprint 5.00
b. Double overprint 5.00
430 A24 3c ol gray (Bk) 1.25 1.25
a. Inverted overprint 5.00
b. Double overprint 6.00
c. Double ovpt., one inverted 9.00 7.00
430D A24 3c ol gray (Bl) 8.00 3.25
431 A25 4c ver (Bk) 16.00 13.00
a. Inverted overprint 30.00
432 A24 5c gray blk (R) 1.25 30
a. Inverted overprint 7.50
432B A24 5c gray blk (Bk) 75 25
c. Double ovpt., one inverted 8.00
d. Double overprint 8.00
433 A25 6c red brn (Bk) 13.00 11.00
a. Inverted overprint 17.50
b. Double overprint
434 A25 10c yel (Bl) 65 40
a. Double overprint 12.50
b. Double ovpt., one inverted 10.00
435 A24 15c brn (Bk) 6.00 2.50
436 A25 20c bis brn (Bk) 6.00 2.50
a. Double overprint 17.50
437 A24 25c org (Bk) 27.50 5.00
438 A25 50c pale bl (Bk) 7.50 3.00
439 A25 1cor blk brn (Bk) 15.00 9.00

Most stamps of this group exist with tall "1" in "1927." Counterfeits exist of normal stamps and errors of Nos. 427-478.

Violet Overprint

1927, May 19
440 A24 ½c green 15 15
a. Inverted overprint 2.00 2.00
b. Double overprint 2.00 2.00
441 A24 1c violet 20 15
a. Double overprint 2.00 2.00
442 A25 2c car rose 15 15
a. Double overprint 2.00 2.00
b. "1927" double 5.00
d. Double ovpt., one inverted 2.00 2.00
443 A24 3c ol gray 25 15
a. Inverted overprint 6.00
b. Overprinted "1927" only 12.00
c. Double ovpt., one inverted 9.00
444 A25 4c vermilion 37.50 27.50
a. Inverted overprint 75.00
445 A24 5c gray blk 1.00 25
a. Double overprint, one inverted 6.00
446 A25 6c red brn 37.50 27.50
a. Inverted overprint 75.00
447 A25 10c yellow 35 20
a. Double overprint 2.00 2.00
448 A24 15c brown 75 30
a. Double overprint 5.00
b. Double overprint, one inverted 8.00
449 A25 20c bis brn 35 20
a. Double overprint
450 A24 25c orange 40 20
451 A25 50c pale bl 40 20
a. Double ovpt., one inverted 4.00 4.00
452 A25 1cor blk brn 75 20
a. Double overprint 3.00
b. "1927" double 5.00
c. Double ovpt., one inverted 6.00
Nos. 440-452 (13) 79.75 57.15

Stamps of 1914-22 Overprinted in Violet — **Resello 1928**

1928, Jan. 3
453 A24 ½c green 25 20
a. Double overprint 3.00
b. Double overprint, one inverted 4.00
454 A24 1c violet 15 15
a. Inverted overprint 2.00
b. Double overprint 2.00
c. Double overprint, one inverted 2.00
d. "928" for "1928" 2.50
455 A25 2c car rose 20 15
a. Inverted overprint 2.00
b. Double overprint 2.00
c. "1928" omitted 5.00
d. "928" for "1928" 2.50
e. As "d," inverted
f. "19" for "1928"
456 A24 3c ol gray 40 15
457 A25 4c vermilion 20 15
458 A24 5c gray blk 20 15
a. Double overprint 5.00
b. Double overprint, one inverted 5.00
459 A25 6c red brn 20 15
460 A25 10c yellow 25 15
a. Double overprint 2.50
c. Inverted overprint
461 A24 15c brown 35 25
462 A25 20c bis brn 50 25
a. Double overprint
463 A24 25c orange 75 25
a. Double overprint, one inverted 4.00
464 A25 50c pale bl 1.25 15
465 A25 1cor blk brn 1.25 35
Nos. 453-465 (13) 5.95 2.50

Stamps of 1914-22 Overprinted in Violet — **Correos 1928**

1928, June 11
466 A24 ½c green 20 15
467 A24 1c violet 15 15
a. "928" omitted
469 A24 3c ol gray 75 25
a. Double overprint 6.00
470 A25 4c vermilion 35 15
471 A24 5c gray blk 25 20
a. Double overprint 4.00
472 A25 6c red brn 40 20
a. Double overprint 5.00
473 A25 10c yellow 50 20
474 A24 15c brown 1.75 20
a. Double overprint
475 A25 20c bis brn 2.00 20
476 A24 25c orange 2.00 25
a. Double overprint, one inverted 6.00
477 A25 50c pale bl 2.00 25
478 A25 1cor blk brn 5.00 2.50
a. Double overprint 10.00
Nos. 466-478 (12) 15.35 4.70

No. 410 with above overprint in black was not regularly issued.

No. 470 with Additional Surcharge in Violet — **Vale 2 Cts.**

1928
479 A25 2c on 4c ver 1.25 35
a. Double surcharge 9.00

A34

Inscribed: "Timbre Telegrafico"
Red Surcharge

1928
480 A34 1c on 5c bl & blk 30 20
a. Double surcharge 5.00
b. Double surcharge, one inverted
481 A34 2c on 5c bl & blk 30 20
a. Double surcharge 5.00
482 A34 3c on 5c bl & blk 30 20

Stamps similar to Nos. 481-482, but with surcharge in black and with basic stamp inscribed "Timbre Fiscal," are of private origin.
See designs A36, A37, A44, PT1, PT4, PT6, PT7.

Types of 1914 Issue
Various Frames

1928
483 A24 ½c org red 40 15
484 A24 1c orange 40 15
485 A25 2c green 40 15
486 A24 3c dp vio 40 25
487 A25 4c brown 40 25
488 A24 5c yellow 40 20
489 A25 6c lt bl 40 25
490 A25 10c dk bl 90 20
491 A24 15c car rose 1.40 50
492 A25 20c dk grn 1.40 50
493 A24 25c blk brn 27.50 6.00
494 A25 50c bis brn 3.25 1.00
495 A25 1cor dl vio 6.25 3.00
Nos. 483-495 (13) 43.50 12.60

No. 425 Overprinted in Violet — **Correos 1928**

1929
499 A33 10c bis brn 75 60

No. 408 Overprinted in Red

Correos 1929

1929
500 A24 ½c green (R) 25 20
a. Inverted overprint 2.50
b. Double overprint 2.50
c. Double overprint, one inverted 3.50

A36

A37

Ovptd. Horiz. in Black "R. de T."
Surcharged Vert. in Red

1929
504 A36 1c on 5c bl & blk (R) 25 20
a. Inverted surcharge 3.00
b. Surcharged "0.10" for "0.01" 3.00
c. "0.0" instead of "0.01" 5.00
509 A36 2c on 5c bl & blk (R) 20 15
a. Double surcharge 2.50
b. Double surcharge, one inverted 3.50
c. Inverted surcharge 5.00

Overprinted Horizontally in Black "R. de C." Surcharged Vertically in Red

510 A36 2c on 5c bl & blk (R) 22.50 1.25
a. Dbl. surcharge, one inverted 25.00

Surcharged in Red

511 A37 1c on 10c dk grn & blk (R) 25 20
a. Double surcharge
512 A37 2c on 5c bl & blk (R) 25 15

The varieties tall "1" in "0.01" and "O$" for "C$" are found in this surcharge.

Nos. 500, 504, 509-512 and RA38 were surcharged in red and sold in large quantities to the public. Surcharges in various other colors were distributed only to a favored few and not regularly sold at the post offices.

Types of 1914 Issue
Various Frames

1929-31
513 A24 1c ol grn 15 15
514 A24 3c lt bl 30 15
515 A25 4c dk bl ('31) 30 20
516 A24 5c ol brn 40 15
517 A25 6c bis brn ('31) 50 30
518 A25 10c lt brn ('31) 60 20
519 A24 15c org red ('31) 90 25
520 A25 20c org ('31) 1.20 35
521 A24 25c dk vio 25 15
522 A25 50c grn ('31) 50 20
523 A25 1cor yel ('31) 4.50 1.25
Nos. 513-523 (11) 9.60 3.35

Nos. 513-523 exist with signature controls. See note before No. 600. Same values.

New Post Office at Managua — A38

1930, Sept. 15 **Engr.**
525 A38 ½c olive gray 1.20 1.20
526 A38 1c carmine 1.20 1.20
527 A38 2c red org 90 90
528 A38 3c orange 1.75 1.75
529 A38 4c yellow 1.75 1.75
530 A38 5c ol grn 2.25 2.25
531 A38 6c bl grn 2.25 2.25

532 A38 10c black 2.75 2.75
533 A38 25c dp bl 5.50 5.50
534 A38 50c ultra 9.00 9.00
535 A38 1cor dp vio 25.00 25.00
Nos. 525-535 (11) 53.55 53.55

Opening of the new general post office at Managua. The stamps were on sale on day of issuance and for an emergency in April, 1931.

No. 499 Surcharged in Black and Red — ₡ 0.02 / 1931

1931, May 29

536 A33 2c on 10c bis brn 50 1.60
a. Red surcharge omitted 2.50
b. Red surcharge double 5.00
c. Red surcharge inverted 3.50
d. Red surcharge double, one invtd.

Surcharge exists in brown.

Types of 1914-31 Issue Overprinted — **1931**

1931, June 11

540 A24 ½c green 35 15
a. Double overprint 80
b. Double ovpt., one inverted 1.40
c. Inverted overprint 80
541 A24 1c ol grn 35 15
a. Double overprint 80
b. Double ovpt., one inverted 1.40
c. Inverted overprint
542 A25 2c car rose 35 15
a. Double overprint 80
b. Double ovpt., both inverted 2.50
c. Inverted overprint 1.40
543 A24 3c lt bl 35 15
a. Double overprint 80
b. Double ovpt., one inverted 1.40
c. Inverted overprint 1.40
544 A24 5c yellow 3.50 2.25
545 A24 5c ol brn 1.00 16
a. Double overprint 1.40
b. Inverted overprint 1.40
546 A24 15c org red 1.20 40
a. Double overprint 3.50
547 A24 25c blk brn 10.00 6.50
a. Double overprint 11.00 7.00
b. Inverted overprint 11.00 7.00
548 A24 25c dk vio 4.00 2.50
a. Double overprint 6.50
Nos. 540-548 (9) 21.10 12.41

Counterfeits exist of the scarcer values. The 4c brown and 6c light blue with this overprint are bogus.

Managua P.O. Before and After Earthquake A40

1932, Jan. 1 Litho. *Perf. 11½*
Soft porous paper, Without gum

556 A40 ½c emerald 1.50
557 A40 1c yel brn 1.90
558 A40 2c dp car 1.50
559 A40 3c ultra 1.50
560 A40 4c dp ultra 1.50
561 A40 5c yel brn 1.60
562 A40 6c gray brn 1.60
563 A40 10c yel brn 2.50
564 A40 15c dl rose 3.75
565 A40 20c orange 3.50
566 A40 25c dk vio 2.50
567 A40 50c emerald 2.50
568 A40 1cor yellow 6.25
Nos. 556-568 (13) 32.10

Issued in commemoration of the earthquake at Managua, Mar. 31, 1931. The stamps were on sale on Jan. 1, 1932, only. The money received from this sale was for the reconstruction of the Post Office building and for the improvement of the postal service. Many shades exist.

Sheets of 10.

Reprints are on thin hard paper and do not have the faint horiz. ribbing that is on the front or back of the originals. Fake cancels abound. Value 75 cents each.

See Nos. C20-C24. For overprints and surcharges see Nos. C32-C43, C47-C48.

Rivas Railroad Issue

"Fill" at El Nacascolo — A41

Designs: 1c, Wharf at San Jorge. 5c, Rivas Station. 10c, San Juan del Sur. 15c, Train at Rivas Station.

1932, Dec. 17 Litho. *Perf. 12*
Soft porous paper

570 A41 1c yellow 16.50
a. 1c ocher 18.00
571 A41 2c carmine 16.50
572 A41 5c blk brn 16.50
573 A41 10c chocolate 16.50
574 A41 15c yellow 16.50
a. 15c deep orange 18.00
Nos. 570-574 (5) 82.50

Inauguration of the railroad from San Jorge to San Juan del Sur. On sale only on Dec. 17, 1932.

Sheets of 4, without gum. See #C67-C71.

Reprints exist on thin hard paper and do not have the faint horiz. ribbing that is on the front or back of the originals. Value, $1 each.

Leon-Sauce Railroad Issue

Bridge No. 2 at Santa Lucia A42

Designs: 1c, Environs of El Sauce. 5c, Santa Lucia. 10c, Works at Km. 64. 15c, Rock cut at Santa Lucia.

1932, Dec. 30 *Perf. 12*
Soft porous paper

575 A42 1c orange 16.50
576 A42 2c carmine 16.50
577 A42 5c blk brn 16.50
578 A42 10c brown 16.50
579 A42 15c orange 16.50
Nos. 575-579 (5) 82.50

Inauguration of the railroad from Leon to El Sauce. On sale only on Dec. 30, 1932.

Sheets of 4, without gum. See #C72-C76.

Reprints exist on thin hard paper and do not have the faint horiz. ribbing that is on the front or back of the originals. Value $1 each.

Nos. 514-515, 543 Surcharged in Red — **Vale un centavo**

1932, Dec. 10

580 A24 1c on 3c lt bl (514) 35 15
a. Double surcharge 3.50
581 A24 1c on 3c lt bl (543) 4.00 3.50
582 A25 2c on 4c dk bl (515) 25 15
a. Double surcharge 2.50

Nos. 514, 516, 545 and 518 Surcharged in Black or Red — **Resello 1933 Vale Un Centavo**

1933

583 A24 1c on 3c lt bl (Bk) (514) 16 15
a. "Censavo" 4.00 2.25
b. Double surcharge, one inverted 4.00
584 A24 1c on 5c ol brn (R) (516) 16 15
a. Inverted surcharge
b. Double surcharge
585 A24 1c on 5c ol brn (R) (545) 6.50 5.00
a. Red surcharge double 12.00
586 A25 2c on 10c lt brn (Bk) (518) 16 15
a. Double surcharge 4.00 2.50
b. Inverted surcharge 3.50 3.50
c. Double surcharge, one inverted 4.00 2.50

On No. 586 "Vale Dos" measures 13mm and 14mm.

No. 583 with green surcharge and No. 586 with red surcharge are bogus.

Flag of the Race Issue

Flag with Three Crosses for Three Ships of Columbus — A43

1933, Aug. 3 Litho. *Rouletted 9*
Without gum

587 A43 ½c emerald 1.75 1.75
588 A43 1c green 1.50 1.50
589 A43 2c red 1.50 1.50
590 A43 3c dp rose 1.50 1.50
591 A43 4c orange 1.50 1.50
592 A43 5c yellow 1.75 1.75
593 A43 10c dp brn 1.75 1.75
594 A43 15c dk brn 1.75 1.75
595 A43 20c vio bl 1.75 1.75
596 A43 25c dl bl 1.75 1.75
597 A43 30c violet 4.50 4.50
598 A43 50c red vio 4.50 4.50
599 A43 1cor ol brn 4.50 4.50
Nos. 587-599 (13) 30.00 30.00

Commemorating the raising of the symbolical "Flag of the Race"; also the 441st anniversary of the sailing of Columbus for the New World, Aug. 3, 1492. Printed in sheets of 10.

See Nos. C77-C87, O320-O331.

In October, 1933, various postage, airmail and official stamps of current issues were overprinted with facsimile signatures of the Minister of Public Works and the Postmaster-General. These overprints are control marks.

Nos. 410 and 513 Overprinted in Black — **Resello 1935**

1935 *Perf. 12*

600 A24 1c ol grn 15 15
a. Inverted overprint 1.40 1.60
b. Double overprint 1.40 1.60
c. Double overprint, one inverted 1.60 1.60
601 A25 2c car rose 15 15
a. Inverted overprint 1.60
b. Double overprint 1.60
c. Double overprint, one inverted 1.60
d. Double overprint, both inverted 2.50 2.25
Set value 24 15

No. 517 Surcharged in Red as in 1932

1936, June

602 A25 ½c on 6c bis brn 35 15
a. "Ccentavo" 80 80
b. Double surcharge 3.50 3.50

Regular Issues of 1929-35 Overprinted in Blue — RESELLO-1935

1935, Dec.

603 A25 ½c on 6c bis brn 65 15
604 A24 1c ol grn (#600) 80 15
605 A25 2c car rose (#601) 80 15
a. Black overprint inverted 6.00
606 A24 3c lt bl 80 22
607 A24 5c ol brn 1.00 25
608 A25 10c lt brn 1.60 80
Nos. 603-608 (6) 5.65 1.72

Nos. 606-608 have signature control overprint. See note before No. 600.

Same Overprint in Red

1936, Jan.

609 A24 ½c dk grn 16 15
610 A25 ½c on 6c bis brn (602) 15 15
a. Double surch., one inverted 6.00 6.00
611 A24 1c ol grn (513) 22 15
612 A24 1c ol grn (600) 25 15
613 A25 2c car rose (410) 50 15
614 A25 2c car rose (601) 25 15
a. Black overprint inverted 2.50 2.50
b. Black ovpt. double, one invtd. 3.50 3.50
615 A24 3c lt bl 25 15
616 A25 4c dk bl 25 15
617 A24 5c ol brn 22 15
618 A25 6c bis brn 25 15
619 A25 10c lt brn 50 16
620 A24 15c org red 15 15
621 A25 20c orange 80 22
622 A24 25c dk vio 25 15
623 A25 50c green 35 20
624 A25 1cor yellow 40 25
Nos. 609-624 (16) 4.95
Set value 1.95

Red or blue "Resello 1935" overprint may be found inverted or double. Red and blue overprints on same stamp are bogus.

Nos. 615-624 have signature control overprint. See note before No. 600.

Regular Issues of 1922-29 Overprinted in Carmine

1936, May

625 A24 ½c green 15 15
626 A24 1c ol grn 16 15
627 A25 2c car rose 50 15
628 A24 3c lt bl 16 15
Set value 35

No. 628 has signature control overprint. See note before No. 600.

Nos. 514, 516 Surcharged in Black — **Resello 1936 Vale Un Centavo**

1936, June

629 A24 1c on 3c lt bl 15 15
a. "1396" for "1936" 1.00 1.00
b. "Un" omitted 1.40 1.40
c. Inverted surcharge 1.60 1.60
d. Double surcharge 1.60 1.60
630 A24 2c on 5c ol brn 15 15
a. "1396" for "1936" 1.40 1.40
b. Double surcharge 3.50 3.50
Set value 20

Regular Issues of 1929-31 Surcharged in Black or Red — **1936 Vale Un Centavo**

1936

631 A24 ½c on 15c org red (R) 16 15
a. Double surcharge 4.00
632 A25 1c on 4c dk bl (Bk) 22 15
633 A24 1c on 5c ol brn (Bk) 22 16
634 A25 1c on 6c bis brn (Bk) 40 16
a. "1939" instead of "1936" 2.50 1.60
635 A24 1c on 15c org red (Bk) 22 16
a. "1939" instead of "1936" 2.50 1.60
636 A25 1c on 20c org (Bk) 16 15
a. "1939" intead of "1936" 2.50 1.60
b. Double surcharge 4.00
637 A25 1c on 20c org (R) 16 15
638 A25 2c on 10c lt brn (Bk) 25 16
639 A24 2c on 15c org red (Bk) 1.00 80
640 A25 2c on 20c org (Bk) 50 25
641 A24 2c on 25c dk vio (R) 35 16
642 A24 2c on 25c dk vio (Bk) 35 16
a. "1939" instead of "1936" 2.50 1.60
643 A25 2c on 50c grn (Bk) 35 22
a. "1939" instead of "1936" 2.50 1.60
644 A25 2c on 1 cor yel (Bk) 35 22
a. "1939" instead of "1936" 2.50 1.60
645 A25 3c on 4c dk bl (Bk) 65 50
a. "1939" instead of "1936" 2.50 1.60
b. "s" of "Centavos" omitted and "r" of "Tres" inverted 2.50
Nos. 631-645 (15) 5.34 3.55

Nos. 634, 639, 643-644 exist with and without signature controls. Nos. 635-636, 642, 645 do not have signature controls. Others have signature controls. See note before No. 600. Same values for those that come both ways.

Regular Issues of 1929-31 Overprinted in Black — **Resello 1936**

1936, Aug.

646 A24 3c lt bl 35 20
647 A24 5c ol brn 25 15
648 A25 10c lt brn 50 35

No. 648 bears script control mark.

A44

Surcharged in Red

1936, Oct. 19

649 A44 1c on 5c grn & blk	20	15
650 A44 2c on 5c grn & blk	20	15
Set value		15

Types of 1914

1937, Jan. 1 **Engr.**

652 A24 ½c black	15	15
653 A24 1c car rose	15	15
654 A25 2c dp bl	15	15
655 A24 3c chocolate	15	15
656 A25 4c yellow	16	15
657 A24 5c org red	15	15
658 A25 6c dl vio	16	15
659 A25 10c ol grn	16	15
660 A24 15c green	15	15
661 A25 20c red brn	25	15
663 A25 50c brown	35	15
664 A25 1cor ultra	60	22
Nos. 652-664 (12)	2.58	
Set value		1.25

See note after No. 360.

Mail Carrier — A45

Designs: 1c, Mule carrying mail. 2c, Mail coach. 3c, Sailboat. 5c, Steamship. 7½c, Train.

1937, Dec. **Litho.** ***Perf. 11***

665 A45 ½c green	15	15
666 A45 1c magenta	15	15
667 A45 2c brown	15	15
668 A45 3c purple	15	15
669 A45 5c blue	15	15
670 A45 7½c red org	55	35
Nos. 665-670 (6)	1.30	
Set value		75

75th anniversary of the postal service in Nicaragua.

Nos. 665-670 were also issued in sheets of 4, value, set of sheets, $7.

The miniature sheets are ungummed, and also exist imperf. and part-perf.

Nos. 662, 663 and 664 Surcharged in Red

Vale Tres Centavos

1938

1938 ***Perf. 12***

671 A24 3c on 25c org	15	15
672 A25 5c on 50c brn	24	15
a. "e" of "Vale" omitted	1.60	1.00
673 A25 6c on 1cor ultra	15	15
Set value	48	25

No. 672 has a script signature control and the surcharge is in three lines.

Dario Park A46

1939, Jan. **Engr.** ***Perf. 12½***

674 A46 1½c yel grn	15	15
675 A46 2c dp rose	15	15
676 A46 3c brt bl	15	15
677 A46 6c brn org	15	15
678 A46 7½c dp grn	15	15
679 A46 10c blk brn	20	15
680 A46 15c orange	20	15
681 A46 25c lt vio	20	15
682 A46 50c brt yel grn	16	15
683 A46 1cor yellow	65	40
Nos. 674-683 (10)	2.16	
Set value		1.10

Nos. 660 and 661 Surcharged in Red

Vale un Centavo
1939

1939 ***Perf. 12***

684 A24 1c on 15c grn	15	15
a. Inverted surcharge	2.00	2.00
685 A25 1c on 20c red brn	15	15
Set value	17	15

No. C236 Surcharged in Carmine

Servicio ordinario
Vale Diez Centavos
de Córdoba

1941 **Unwmk.** ***Perf. 12***

686 AP14 10c on 1c brt grn	15	15
a. Double surcharge	10.00	2.50
b. Inverted surcharge	10.00	2.50

Rubén Darío A47

1941, Dec. **Engr.** ***Perf. 12½***

687 A47 10c red	35	15
Nos. 687,C257-C260 (5)	1.95	1.05

25th anniversary of the death of Rubén Darío, poet and writer.

No. C236 Surcharged in Carmine

Servicio Ordinario
Vale Diez Centavos

1943 ***Perf. 12***

688 AP14 10c on 1c brt grn	4.00	15
a. Inverted surcharge	10.00	
b. Double surcharge	10.00	

Catalogue values for unused stamps in this section, from this point to the end of the section, are for Never Hinged items.

"Victory" A48

Columbus and Lighthouse A49

1943, Dec. 8 **Engr.**

689 A48 10c vio & cerise	15	15
690 A48 30c org brn & cerise	15	15
Set value	21	15

2nd anniv. of Nicaragua's declaration of war against the Axis. See Nos. C261-C262.

1945, Sept. 1 **Unwmk.** ***Perf. 12½***

691 A49 4c dk grn & blk	20	20
692 A49 6c org & blk	25	25
693 A49 8c dp rose & blk	35	35
694 A49 10c bl & blk	40	40
Nos. 691-694,C266-C271 (10)	6.10	5.35

Issued in honor of the discovery of America by Columbus and the Columbus Lighthouse near Ciudad Trujillo, Dominican Republic.

Franklin D. Roosevelt, Philatelist A50

Roosevelt Signing Declaration of War Against Japan — A51

Designs: 8c, F. D. Roosevelt and Winston Churchill. 16c, Gen. Henri Giraud, Roosevelt, Gen. Charles de Gaulle and Churchill. 32c, Stalin, Roosevelt and Churchill. 50c, Sculptured head of Roosevelt.

Engraved, Center Photogravure

1946, June 15 **Unwmk.** ***Perf. 12½***

Frame in Black

695 A50 4c sl grn	16	16
696 A50 8c violet	28	28
697 A51 10c ultra	32	32
698 A50 16c rose red	40	40
699 A50 32c org brn	28	28
700 A51 50c gray	28	28
Nos. 695-700 (6)	1.72	1.72

Issued to honor US Pres. Franklin D. Roosevelt (1882-1945). See Nos. C272-C276.

Metropolitan Cathedral, Managua — A56

Designs: 5c, Sanitation Building. 6c, Municipal Building. 10c, Projected Provincial Seminary. 75c, Communications Building.

1947, Jan. 10

Frame in Black

701 A56 4c carmine	15	15
702 A56 5c blue	16	15
703 A56 6c green	20	16
704 A56 10c olive	20	16
705 A56 75c golden brn	28	28
Nos. 701-705 (5)	99	90

Issued to commemorate the centenary of the founding of the city of Managua. See Nos. C277-C282.

San Cristóbal Volcano — A61

Designs: 3c, Tomb of Rubén Dario. 4c, Grandstand. 5c, Soldiers' monument. 6c, Sugar cane. 8c, Tropical fruit. 10c, Cotton industry. 20c, Horse race. 30c, Nicaraguan coffee. 50c, Steer. 1cor, Agriculture.

Engraved, Center Photogravure

1947, Aug. 29

Frame in Black

706 A61 2c orange	16	15
707 A61 3c violet	15	15
708 A61 4c gray	22	15
709 A61 5c rose car	55	22
710 A61 6c green	32	15
711 A61 8c org brn	38	15
712 A61 10c red	55	22
713 A61 20c brt ultra	1.90	48
714 A61 30c rose lilac	1.50	48
715 A61 50c dp claret	3.25	95
716 A61 1cor brn org	1.10	48
Nos. 706-716 (11)	10.08	3.58

The frames differ for each denomination. For surcharge see No. 769.

Softball A62

Boy Scout, Badge and Flag — A63

Designs: 3c, Pole vault. 4c, Diving. 5c, Bicycling. 10c, Proposed stadium. 15c, Baseball. 25c, Boxing. 35c, Basketball. 40c, Regatta. 60c, Table tennis. 1 cor, Soccer. 2 cor, Tennis.

1949, July 15 **Photo.** ***Perf. 12***

717 A62 1c henna brn	15	15
718 A63 2c ultra	75	20
719 A63 3c bl grn	30	15
720 A62 4c dp claret	20	15
721 A63 5c orange	50	15
722 A62 10c emerald	50	15
723 A62 15c cerise	75	18
724 A63 25c brt bl	75	20
725 A63 35c ol grn	1.25	25
726 A62 40c violet	1.75	30
727 A62 60c ol gray	2.00	40
728 A62 1cor scarlet	2.50	1.25
729 A62 2cor red vio	4.50	2.50
Nos. 717-729 (13)	15.90	6.03

Issued to publicize the tenth World Series of Amateur Baseball, 1948.

Each denomination was also issued in a souvenir sheet containing four stamps and marginal inscriptions. Value, set of 13 sheets, $100.

See Nos. C296-C308.

Rowland Hill — A64

Designs: 25c, Heinrich von Stephan. 75c, UPU Monument. 80c, Congress medal, obverse. 4cor, as 80c, reverse.

1950, Nov. 23 **Engr.** ***Perf. 13***

Frame in Black

730 A64 20c car lake	15	15
731 A64 25c yel grn	15	15
732 A64 75c ultra	48	18
733 A64 80c green	22	22
734 A64 4cor blue	90	80
Nos. 730-734 (5)	1.90	1.50

75th anniv. (in 1949) of the UPU.

Each denomination was also issued in a souvenir sheet containing four stamps and marginal inscriptions. Size: 115x123mm. Value, set of 5 sheets, $30.

See Nos. C309-C315, CO45-CO50. For surcharge see No. 771.

Queen Isabella I — A65

Ships of Columbus — A66

Designs: 98c, Santa Maria. 1.20cor, Map. 1.76cor, Portrait facing left.

1952, June 25 *Perf. 11½*

735 A65 10c lil rose 15 15
736 A66 96c dp ultra 75 75
737 A65 98c carmine 75 75
738 A65 1.20cor brown 90 90
739 A65 1.76cor red vio 1.25 1.25
a. Souv. sheet of 5, #735-739 3.75 3.75
Nos. 735-739 (5) 3.80 3.80

500th anniversary of the birth of Queen Isabella I of Spain.

See Nos. C316-C320.

ODECA Flag — A67

Designs: 5c, Map of Central America. 6c, Arms of ODECA. 15c, Presidents of Five Central American Republics. 50c, ODECA Charter and Flags.

1953, Apr. 15 *Perf. 13½x14*

740 A67 4c dk bl 15 15
741 A67 5c emerald 15 15
742 A67 6c lt brn 15 15
743 A67 15c lt ol grn 15 15
744 A67 50c blk brn 15 15
Set value 55 35

Founding of the Organization of the Central American States (ODECA).

See #C326-C338. For surcharge see #767.

Pres. Carlos Solorzano — A68

Presidents: 6c, Diego Manuel Chamorro. 8c, Adolfo Diaz. 15c, Gen. Anastasio Somoza. 50c, Gen. Emiliano Chamorro.

Engr. (frames); Photo. (heads)
1953, June 25 *Perf. 12½*
Heads in Gray Black

745 A68 4c dk car rose 15 15
746 A68 6c dp ultra 15 15
747 A68 8c brown 15 15
748 A68 15c car rose 15 15
749 A68 50c bl grn 18 15
Set value 45 35

See Nos. C326-C338. For surcharges see Nos. 768, 853.

Sculptor and UN Emblem — A69

Capt. Dean L. Ray, USAF — A70

Designs: 4c, Arms of Nicaragua. 5c, Globe. 15c, Candle and Charter. 1cor, Flags of Nicaragua and UN.

Perf. 13½
1954, Apr. 30 Engr. Unwmk.

750 A69 3c olive 15 15
751 A69 4c ol grn 15 15
752 A69 5c emerald 18 15
753 A69 15c dp grn 90 18
754 A69 1cor bl grn 75 30
Nos. 750-754 (5) 2.13
Set value 70

Issued to honor the United Nations Organization. See Nos. C339-C345.

Engraved; Center Photogravure
1954, Nov. 5 *Perf. 13*

Designs: 2c, Sabre jet plane. 3c, Plane, type A-20. 4c, B-24 bomber. 5c, Plane, type AT-6. 15c, Gen. Anastasio Somoza. 1cor, Air Force emblem.

Frame in Black

755 A70 1c gray 15 15
756 A70 2c gray 15 15
757 A70 3c dk gray grn 15 15
758 A70 4c orange 15 15
759 A70 5c emerald 15 15
760 A70 15c aqua 15 15
761 A70 1cor purple 20 15
Set value 55 40

Issued to honor the National Air Force. See Nos. C346-C352.

Rotary Slogans and Wreath — A71

Map of the World and Rotary Emblem — A72

Designs: 20c, Handclasp, Rotary emblem and globe. 35c, Flags of Nicaragua and Rotary. 90c, Paul P. Harris.

1955, Aug. 30 Photo. *Perf. 11½*
Granite Paper.

762 A71 15c dp org 15 15
763 A71 20c dk olive grn 15 15
764 A71 35c red vio 15 15
765 A72 40c carmine 20 20
766 A71 90c blk & gray 35 35
a. Souv. sheet of 5, #762-766 4.25 4.25
Nos. 762-766 (5) 1.00 1.00

50th anniversary of Rotary International.

See Nos. C353-C362. For surcharges see Nos. 770, 772, 876.

Issues of 1947-55 Surcharged in Various Colors

Conmemoración
Exposición Nacional
Febrero 4-16, 1956
₵ 0.15

Perf. 13½x14, 12½, 11½, 13
Engraved, Photogravure
1956, Feb. 4 Unwmk.

767 A67 5c on 6c lt brn 15 15
768 A68 5c on 6c ultra & gray blk (Ult) 15 15
769 A61 5c on 8c blk & org brn 15 15
770 A71 15c on 35c red vio (G) 15 15
771 A64 15c on 80c blk & grn 15 15
772 A71 15c on 90c blk & gray (Bl) 15 15
Set value 62 48

Spacing of surcharge varies to fit shape of stamps.

Issued to commemorate the National Exhibition, Feb. 4-16, 1956. See Nos. C363-C366.

Gen. Máximo Jerez — A73

Battle of San Jacinto — A74

Designs: 10c, Gen. Fernando Chamorro. 25c, Burning of Granada. 50c, Gen. José Dolores Estrada.

Perf. 12½x12, 12, 12½
1956, Sept. 14 Engr.

773 A73 5c brown 15 15
774 A73 10c dk car rose 15 15
775 A74 15c bl gray 15 15
776 A74 25c brt red 25 18
777 A73 50c brt red vio 30 20
Set value 84 58

Issued to commemorate the centenary of the National War. See Nos. C367-C371.

Boy Scout — A75

Pres. Luis A. Somoza — A76

Designs: 15c, Cub Scout. 20c, Boy Scout. 25c, Lord Baden-Powell. 50c, Joseph A. Harrison.

Perf. 13½x14
1957, Apr. 9 Photo. Unwmk.

778 A75 10c vio & ol 15 15
779 A75 15c dp plum & gray blk 15 15
780 A75 20c ultra & brn 15 15
781 A75 25c dl red brn & dp bluish grn 15 15
782 A75 50c red & ol 20 16
a. Souv. sheet of 5, #778-782 2.50 2.50
Set value 65 45

Centenary of the birth of Lord Baden-Powell, founder of the Boy Scouts.

See #C377-C386. For surcharge see #C754.

1957, July 2 *Perf. 14x13½*
Portrait in Dark Brown

783 A76 10c brt red 15 15
784 A76 15c dp bl 15 15
785 A76 35c rose vio 22 15
786 A76 50c brown 30 18
787 A76 75c gray grn 65 55
Nos. 783-787 (5) 1.47
Set value 1.00

Issued to honor President Luis A. Somoza. See Nos. C387-C391.

Managua Cathedral A77

Bishop Pereira y Castellon — A78

Designs: 15c, Archbishop Lezcano y Ortega. 20c, Leon Cathedral. 50c, De la Merced Church, Granada. 1cor, Father Mariano Dubon.

Perf. 13½x14, 14x13½
1957, July 12
Centers in Olive Gray

788 A77 5c dl grn 15 15
789 A78 10c dk pur 15 15
790 A78 15c dk bl 15 15
791 A77 20c dk brn 15 15
792 A77 50c dk sl grn 16 15
793 A78 1cor dk vio 30 28
Set value 70 60

Issued in honor of the Catholic Church in Nicaragua. See Nos. C392-C397.

M. S. Honduras A79

Designs: 5c, Gen. Anastasio Somoza and freighter. 6c, M. S. Guatemala. 10c, M. S. Salvador. 15c, Ship between globes. 50c, Globes and ship.

1957, Oct. 15 Litho. *Perf. 14*

794 A79 4c grn, bl & blk 15 15
795 A79 5c multi 15 15
796 A79 6c red, bl & blk 15 15
797 A79 10c brn, bl grn & blk 15 15
798 A79 15c dk car, ultra & ol brn 24 15
799 A79 50c vio, bl & mar 40 26
Set value 1.00 65

Issued to honor Nicaragua's Merchant Marine. See Nos. C398-C403. For surcharge see No. C691.

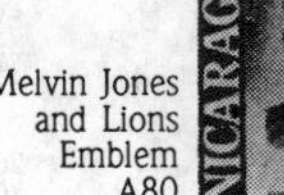
Melvin Jones and Lions Emblem A80

Designs: 5c, Arms of Central American Republics. 20c, Dr. Teodoro A. Arias. 50c, Edward G. Barry. 75c, Motto and emblem. 1.50 cor, Map of Central America.

1958, May 8 Unwmk. *Perf. 14*
Emblem in Yellow, Red and Blue

800 A80 5c bl & multi 15 15
801 A80 10c bl & org 15 15
802 A80 20c bl & olive 15 15
803 A80 50c bl & lilac 25 20
804 A80 75c bl & pink 35 25
805 A80 1.50cor bl, gray ol & sal 60 45
a. Souv. sheet of 6, #800-805 2.50 2.50
Nos. 800-805 (6) 1.65
Set value 1.10

17th convention of Lions Intl. of Central America, May, 1958.

See Nos. C410-C415. For surcharge see No. C686.

St. Jean Baptiste De La Salle — A81

UN Emblem and Globe — A82

Designs: 5c, Arms of La Salle. 10c, School, Managua, horiz. 20c, Bro. Carlos. 50c, Bro. Antonio. 75c, Bro. Julio. 1cor, Bro. Argeo.

1958, July 13 Photo. *Perf. 14*

806 A81 5c car, bl & yel 15 15
807 A81 10c emer, blk & ultra 15 15
808 A81 15c red brn, bis & blk 15 15
809 A81 20c car, bis & blk 15 15
810 A81 50c org, bis & brn blk 16 15
811 A81 75c bl, lt grn & dk brn 24 20
812 A81 1cor vio, bis & grnsh blk 32 32
Set value 95 85

Issued to honor the Christian Brothers. See Nos. C416-C423. For surcharges see Nos. C539A, C755-C756.

1958, Dec. 15 Litho. *Perf. 11½*

Designs: 15c, UNESCO building. 25c, 45c, "UNESCO." 40c, UNESCO building and Eiffel tower.

813 A82 10c brt pink & bl 15 15
814 A82 15c bl & brt pink 15 15
815 A82 25c grn & brn 15 15
816 A82 40c red org & blk 15 15
817 A82 45c dk bl & rose lil 15 15
818 A82 50c brn & grn 15 15
a. Min. sheet of 6, #813-818 45 45
Set value 45 35

Opening of UNESCO Headquarters in Paris, Nov. 3. See Nos. C424-C429.

Pope John XXIII and Cardinal Spellman — A83

Abraham Lincoln — A84

Designs: 10c, Spellman coat of arms. 15c, Cardinal Spellman. 20c, Human rosary and Cardinal, horiz. 25c, Cardinal with Ruben Dario order.

1959, Nov. 26 Unwmk. *Perf. 12½*

819	A83	5c	grnsh bl & brn	15	15
820	A83	10c	yel, bl & car	15	15
821	A83	15c	dk grn, blk & dk car	15	15
822	A83	20c	yel, dk bl & grn	15	15
823	A83	25c	ultra, vio & mag	15	15
a.			Min. sheet of 5, #819-823, perf. or imperf.	35	35
			Set value	30	25

Cardinal Spellman's visit to Managua, Feb. 1958. See Nos. C430-C436. For surcharges see Nos. C638, C747, C752.

1960, Jan. Engr. *Perf. 13x13½*

Center in Black

824	A84	5c	dp car	15	15
825	A84	10c	green	15	15
826	A84	15c	dp org	15	15
827	A84	1cor	plum	20	15
828	A84	2cor	ultra	35	30
a.			Souv. sheet of 5, #824-828, imperf.	90	90
			Set value	70	60

150th anniversary of the birth of Abraham Lincoln. See Nos. C437-C442. For surcharges see Nos. C637, C680, C753.

Nos. 824-828 Overprinted in Red

1960, Sept. 19

Center in Black

829	A84	5c	dp car	15	15
830	A84	10c	green	15	15
831	A84	15c	dp org	15	15
832	A84	1cor	plum	22	20
833	A84	2cor	ultra	50	42
			Set value	85	75

Issued for the Red Cross to aid earthquake victims in Chile. For overprints and surcharges see Nos. C446-C451, C500, C539.

Gen. Tomas Martinez and Pres. Luis A. Somoza — A85

Arms of Nueva Segovia — A86

Designs: 5c, Official decrees. 10c, Two envelopes.

Perf. 13½

1961, Aug. 29 Unwmk. Litho.

834	A85	5c	grnsh bl & lt brn	15	15
835	A85	10c	grn & lt brn	15	15
836	A85	15c	pink & brn	15	15
			Set value	17	15

Issued to commemorate the centenary (in 1960) of the postal rates regulation.

1962, Nov. 22 *Perf. 12½x13*

Coats of Arms: 3c, León. 4c, Managua. 5c, Granada. 6c, Rivas.

Arms in Original Colors; Black Inscriptions

837	A86	2c	pink	15	15
838	A86	3c	lt bl	15	15
839	A86	4c	pale lil	15	15
840	A86	5c	yellow	15	15
841	A86	6c	buff	15	15
			Set value	25	25

See #C510-C514. For surcharge see #854.

No. RA73 Overprinted in Red: "CORREOS"

1964 Photo. *Perf. 11½*

842	PT13	5c	gray, red & org	15	15
a.			Inverted overprint		

Nos. RA66-RA75 Overprinted: CAMPOREE SCOUT 1965

1965 Photo. *Perf. 11½*

Orchids in Natural Colors

843	PT13	5c	pale lil & grn	30
844	PT13	5c	yel & grn	30
845	PT13	5c	pink & grn	30
846	PT13	5c	pale vio & grn	30
847	PT13	5c	lt grnsh bl & red	30
848	PT13	5c	buff & lil	30
849	PT13	5c	yel grn & brn	30
850	PT13	5c	gray & red	30
851	PT13	5c	lt bl & dk bl	30
852	PT13	5c	lt grn & brn	30
			Nos. 843-852 (10)	3.00

7th Central American Scout Camporee at El Coyotete. This overprint was also applied to each stamp on souvenir sheet No. C386a.

Use of Nos. 843-852 for postage was authorized by official decree.

Nos. 746 and 841 Surcharged with New Value and "RESELLO"

1968, May Engr. *Perf. 12½*

853	A68	5c	on 6c dp ultra & gray blk	50	50

Litho. *Perf. 12½x13*

854	A86	5c	on 6c multi	50	50

Nos. RA66-RA67, RA69 and RA71 Overprinted: CORREO

1969 Photo. *Perf. 11½*

Orchids in Natural Colors

855	PT13	5c	pale lil & grn	50	50
856	PT13	5c	yel & grn	50	50
857	PT13	5c	pale vio & grn	50	50
858	PT13	5c	buff & lil	50	50

Nos. RA66-RA75 Overprinted: O. I. T. 1919 - 1969

1969 Photo. *Perf. 11½*

Orchids in Natural Colors

859	PT13	5c	pale lil & grn	20	20
860	PT13	5c	yel & grn	20	20
861	PT13	5c	pink & grn	20	20
862	PT13	5c	pale vio & grn	20	20
863	PT13	5c	lt grnsh bl & red	20	20
864	PT13	5c	buff & lil	20	20
865	PT13	5c	yel grn & brn	20	20
866	PT13	5c	gray & red	20	20
867	PT13	5c	lt & dk bl	20	20
868	PT13	5c	lt grn & brn	20	20
			Nos. 859-868 (10)	2.00	2.00

Issued to commemorate the 50th anniversary of the International Labor Organization.

Pelé, Brazil — A87

Soccer Players: 10c, Ferenc Puskás, Hungary. 15c, Sir Stanley Matthews, England. 40c, Alfredo di Stefano, Argentina. 2cor, Giacinto Facchetti, Italy. 3cor, Lev Yashin, USSR. 5cor, Franz Beckenbauer, West Germany.

1970, May 11 Litho. *Perf. 13½*

869	A87	5c	multi	15	15
870	A87	10c	multi	15	15
871	A87	15c	multi	15	15
872	A87	40c	multi	25	18
873	A87	2cor	multi	90	75
874	A87	3cor	multi	1.25	90
875	A87	5cor	multi	1.25	1.25
			Nos. 869-875,C712-C716 (12)	7.40	6.23

Issued to honor the winners of the 1970 poll for the International Soccer Hall of Fame. Names of players and their achievements printed in black on back of stamps.

For surcharges and overprint see Nos. 899-900, C786-C788.

No. 766 Surcharged with New Value and Overprinted "RESELLO" and Bar Through Old Denomination

1971, Mar. Photo. *Perf. 11*

876	A71	30c	on 90c blk & gray		

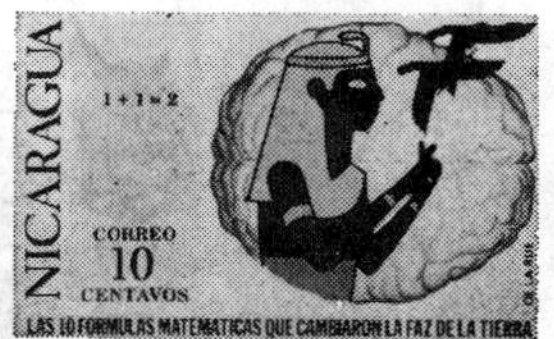

Egyptian Using Fingers to Count — A88

Symbolic Designs of Scientific Formulas: 15c, Newton's law (gravity). 20c, Einstein's theory (relativity). 1cor, Tsiolkovski's law (speed of rockets). 2cor, Maxwell's law (electromagnetism).

1971, May 15 Litho. *Perf. 13½*

877	A88	10c	lt bl & multi	15	15
878	A88	15c	lt bl & multi	15	15
879	A88	20c	lt bl & multi	20	20
880	A88	1cor	lt bl & multi	65	60
881	A88	2cor	lt bl & multi	1.50	1.25
			Nos. 877-881,C761-C765 (10)	4.83	3.96

Mathematical equations which changed the world. On the back of each stamp is a descriptive paragraph.

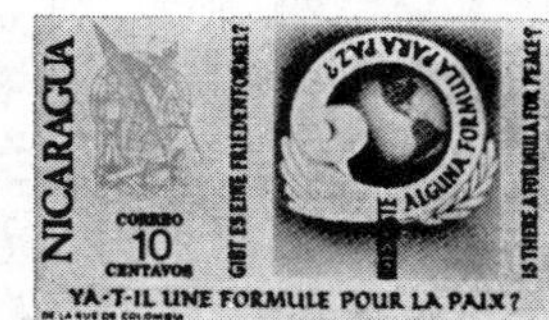

Symbols of Civilization, Peace Emblem with Globe — A89

1971, Sept. 6 Litho. *Perf. 14*

882	A89	10c	blk & bl	15	15
883	A89	15c	vio bl, bl & blk	15	15
884	A89	20c	brn bl & blk	20	20
885	A89	40c	emer, bl & blk	30	30
886	A89	50c	mag, bl & blk	40	40
887	A89	80c	org, bl & blk	60	60
888	A89	1cor	ol, bl & blk	75	75
889	A89	2cor	vio, bl & blk	1.50	1.50
			Nos. 882-889 (8)	4.05	4.05

"Is there a formula for peace?" issue.

Moses with Tablets of the Law, by Rembrandt A90

The Ten Commandments (Paintings): 15c, Moses and the Burning Bush, by Botticelli (I). 20c, Jephthah's Daughter, by Degas, (II, horiz.). 30c, St. Vincent Ferrer Preaching in Verona, by Domenico Morone (III). 35c, The Nakedness of Noah, by Michelangelo (IV, horiz.). 40c, Cain and Abel, by Francesco Trevisani (V, horiz.). 50c, Potiphar's wife, by Rembrandt (VI). 60c, Isaac Blessing Jacob, by Gerbrand van den Eeckhout (VII, horiz.). 75c, Susanna and the Elders, by Rubens (VIII, horiz.).

1971, Nov. 1 *Perf. 11*

890	A90	10c	ocher & multi	15	15
891	A90	15c	ocher & multi	15	15
892	A90	20c	ocher & multi	15	15
893	A90	30c	ocher & multi	18	18
894	A90	35c	ocher & multi	24	24
895	A90	40c	ocher & multi	24	24
896	A90	50c	ocher & multi	35	35
897	A90	60c	ocher & multi	48	48
898	A90	75c	ocher & multi	75	75
			Nos. 890-898,C776-C777 (11)	5.09	3.94

Descriptive inscriptions printed in gray on back of stamps.

Nos. 873-874 Surcharged

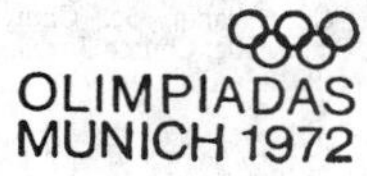

1972, Mar. 20 Litho. *Perf. 13½*

899	A87	40c	on 2cor multi	15	15
900	A87	50c	on 3cor multi	20	15
			Nos. 899-900,C786-C788 (5)	1.75	1.60

20th Olympic Games, Munich, Aug. 26-Sept. 10.

Nos. RA66-RA69, RA71-RA74 Overprinted in Blue: CORREO

1972, July 29 Photo. *Perf. 11½*

Granite Paper

901	PT13	5c	(#RA66)	25	25
902	PT13	5c	(#RA67)	25	25
903	PT13	5c	(#RA68)	25	25
904	PT13	5c	(#RA69)	25	25
905	PT13	5c	(#RA71)	25	25
906	PT13	5c	(#RA72)	25	25
907	PT13	5c	(#RA73)	25	25
908	PT13	5c	(#RA74)	25	25
			Nos. 901-908 (8)	2.00	2.00

Gown by Givenchy, Paris — A91

1973, July 26 Litho. *Perf. 13½*

909	A91	1cor	shown	30	24
910	A91	2cor	Hartnell, London	55	52
911	A91	5cor	Balmain, Paris	1.40	1.20
			Set value, #909-911, C839-C844	2.75	2.35

Gowns by famous designers, modeled by Nicaraguan women. Inscriptions on back printed on top of gum give description of gown in Spanish and English.

Nos. 909-911 in perf. 11, see No. C844a.

Christmas A92

Designs: 2c, 5c, Virginia O'Hanlon writing letter, father. 3c, 15c, letter. 4c, 20c, Virginia, father reading letter.

1973, Nov. 15 Litho. *Perf. 15*

No.	Type	Description	Value
912	A92	2c multicolored	15
913	A92	3c multicolored	15
914	A92	4c multicolored	15
915	A92	5c multicolored	15
916	A92	15c multicolored	15
917	A92	20c multicolored	15
		Set value, #912-917, C846-C848	2.30

Sir Winston Churchill (1874-1965) A93

Designs: 2c, Churchill speaking. 3c, Military planning. 4c, Cigar, lamp. 5c, Churchill with Roosevert and Stalin. 10c, Churchill walking ashore from landing craft.

1974, Apr. 30 *Perf. 14½*

No.	Type	Description	Value
918	A93	2c multicolored	15
919	A93	3c multicolored	15
920	A93	4c multicolored	15
921	A93	5c multicolored	15
922	A93	10c multicolored	15
		Set value, #918-922, C849-C850	3.25

World Cup Soccer Championships, Munich — A94

Scenes from previous World Cup Championships with flags and scores of finalists.

1974, May 8 *Perf. 14½*

No.	Type	Description	Value
923	A94	1c 1930	15
924	A94	2c 1934	15
925	A94	3c 1938	15
926	A94	4c 1950	15
927	A94	5c 1954	15
928	A94	10c 1958	15
929	A94	15c 1962	15
930	A94	20c 1966	15
931	A94	25c 1970	15
		Set value, #923-931, C853	3.25

For overprint see No. C856.

Hollyhocks — A95

Wild Flowers and Cacti: 3c, Paguira insignis. 4c, Morning glory. 5c, Pereschia autumnalis. 10c, Cultivated morning glory. 15c, Hibiscus. 20c, Pagoda tree blossoms.

1974, June 11 Litho. *Perf. 14*

No.	Type	Description	Unused	Used
932	A95	2c grn & multi	15	15
933	A95	3c grn & multi	15	15
934	A95	4c grn & multi	15	15
935	A95	5c grn & multi	15	15
936	A95	10c grn & multi	15	15
937	A95	15c grn & multi	15	15
938	A95	20c grn & multi	15	15
		Set value, #932-938, C854-C855	1.25	1.10

Nicaraguan Stamps — A96

1974, July 10 *Perf. 14½*

No.	Type	Description	Value
939	A96	2c No. 670	15
940	A96	3c No. 669	15
941	A96	4c No. C110, horiz.	15
942	A96	5c No. 667	15
943	A96	10c No. 666	15
944	A96	20c No. 665	15
		Set value, #934-944, C855A-C855C	2.75

UPU, Cent.

Four-toed Anteater A97

Designs: 2c, Puma. 3c, Raccoon. 4c, Ocelot. 5c, Kinkajou. 10c, Coypu. 15c, Peccary. 20c, Tapir.

1974, Sept. 10 Litho. *Perf. 14½*

No.	Type	Description	Unused	Used
946	A97	1c multi	15	15
947	A97	2c multi	15	15
948	A97	3c multi	15	15
949	A97	4c multi	15	15
950	A97	5c multi	15	15
951	A97	10c multi	15	15
952	A97	15c multi	15	15
953	A97	20c multi	15	15
		Set value, #946-953, C857-C858	2.10	1.85

Wild animals from San Diego and London Zoos.

Prophet Zacharias, by Michelangelo — A98

Works of Michelangelo: 2c, The Last Judgment. 3c, The Creation of Adam, horiz. 4c, Sistine Chapel. 5c, Moses. 10c, Mouscron Madonna. 15c, David. 20c, Doni Madonna.

1974, Dec. 15

No.	Type	Description	Unused	Used
954	A98	1c dp rose & multi	15	15
955	A98	2c yel & multi	15	15
956	A98	3c sal & multi	15	15
957	A98	4c bl & multi	15	15
958	A98	5c tan & multi	15	15
959	A98	10c multi	15	15
960	A98	15c multi	15	15
961	A98	20c bl & multi	15	15
		Set value, #954-961, C859-C862	1.50	1.40

Christmas 1974 and 500th birth anniversary of Michelangelo Buonarroti (1475-1564), Italian painter, sculptor and architect.

Giovanni Martinelli, Othello — A99

Opera Singers and Scores: 2c, Tito Gobbi, Simone Boccanegra. 3c, Lotte Lehmann, Der Rosenkavalier. 4c, Lauritz Melchior, Parsifal. 5c, Nellie Melba, La Traviata. 15c, Jussi Bjoerling, La Bohème. 20c, Birgit Nilsson, Turandot.

1975, Jan. 22 *Perf. 14x13½*

No.	Type	Description	Unused	Used
962	A99	1c rose lil & multi	15	15
963	A99	2c brt bl & multi	15	15
964	A99	3c yel & multi	15	15
965	A99	4c dl bl & multi	15	15
966	A99	5c org & multi	15	15
967	A99	15c lake & multi	15	15
968	A99	20c gray & multi	15	15
		Set value, #962-968, C863-C870	3.00	1.60

Famous opera singers.

Jesus Condemned A100

The Spirit of 76, by Archibald M. Willard A101

Stations of the Cross: 2c, Jesus Carries the Cross. 3c, Jesus falls the first time. 4c, Jesus meets his mother. 5c, Simon of Cyrene carries the Cross. 15c, St. Veronica wipes Jesus' face. 20c, Jesus falls the second time. 25c, Jesus meets the women of Jerusalem. 35c, Jesus falls the third time. Designs from Leon Cathedral.

1975, Mar. 20 *Perf. 14½*

No.	Type	Description	Unused	Used
969	A100	1c ultra & multi	15	15
970	A100	2c ultra & multi	15	15
971	A100	3c ultra & multi	15	15
972	A100	4c ultra & multi	15	15
973	A100	5c ultra & multi	15	15
974	A100	15c ultra & multi	15	15
975	A100	20c ultra & multi	15	15
976	A100	25c ultra & multi	15	15
977	A100	35c ultra & multi	15	15
		Set value, #969-977, C871-C875	1.80	1.60

Easter 1975.

1975, Apr. 16 *Perf. 14*

Designs: 2c, Pitt Addressing Parliament, by K. A. Hickel. 3c, The Midnight Ride of Paul Revere, horiz. 4c, Statue of George III Demolished, by W. Walcutt, horiz. 5c, Boston Massacre. 10c, Colonial coin and seal, horiz. 15c, Boston Tea Party, horiz. 20c, Thomas Jefferson, by Rembrandt Peale. 25c, Benjamin Franklin, by Charles Willson Peale. 30c, Signing Declaration of Independence, by John Trumbull, horiz. 35c, Surrender of Cornwallis, by Trumbull, horiz.

No.	Type	Description	Unused	Used
978	A101	1c tan & multi	15	15
979	A101	2c tan & multi	15	15
980	A101	3c tan & multi	15	15
981	A101	4c tan & multi	15	15
982	A101	5c tan & multi	15	15
983	A101	10c tan & multi	15	15
984	A101	15c tan & multi	15	15
985	A101	20c tan & multi	15	15
986	A101	25c tan & multi	15	15
987	A101	30c tan & multi	16	15
988	A101	35c tan & multi	20	18
		Set value, #978-988, C876-C879	4.20	3.80

American Bicentennial.

Scouts Saluting Flag, Scout Emblems A102

Designs (Scout and Nordjamb Emblems and): 2c, Two-men canoe. 3c, Scouts of various races shaking hands. 4c, Scout cooking. 5c, Entrance to Camp Nicaragua. 20c, Group discussion.

1975, Aug. 15 *Perf. 14½*

No.	Type	Description	Unused	Used
989	A102	1c multi	15	15
990	A102	2c multi	15	15
991	A102	3c multi	15	15
992	A102	4c multi	15	15
993	A102	5c multi	15	15
994	A102	20c multi	15	15
		Set value, #989-994, C880-C883	1.90	1.70

Nordjamb 75, 14th World Boy Scout Jamboree, Lillehammer, Norway, July 29-Aug. 7.

Pres. Somoza, Map and Arms of Nicaragua — A103

1975, Sept. 10 *Perf. 14*

No.	Type	Description	Unused	Used
995	A103	20c multi	15	15
996	A103	40c org & multi	15	15
		Nos. 995-996,C884-C886 (5)	6.50	5.28

Reelection of Pres. Anastasio Somoza D.

King's College Choir, Cambridge — A104

Famous Choirs: 2c, Einsiedeln Abbey. 3c, Regensburg. 4c, Vienna Choir Boys. 5c, Sistine Chapel. 15c, Westminster Cathedral. 20c, Mormon Tabernacle.

1975, Nov. 15 *Perf. 14½*

No.	Type	Description	Unused	Used
997	A104	1c silver & multi	15	15
998	A104	2c silver & multi	15	15
999	A104	3c silver & multi	15	15
1000	A104	4c silver & multi	15	15
1001	A104	5c silver & multi	15	15
1002	A104	15c silver & multi	15	15
1003	A104	20c silver & multi	15	15
		Set value, #997-1003, C887-C890	1.90	1.70

Christmas 1975.

The Chess Players, by Ludovico Carracci A105

History of Chess: 2c, Arabs Playing Chess, by Delacroix. 3c, Cardinals Playing Chess, by Victor Marais-Milton. 4c, Albrecht V of Bavaria and Anne of Austria Playing Chess, by Hans Muelich, vert. 5c, Chess Players, Persian manuscript, 14th century. 10c, Origin of Chess, Indian miniature, 17th century. 15c, Napoleon Playing Chess at Schönbrunn, by Antoni Uniechowski, vert. 20c, The Chess Game, by J. E. Hummel.

1976, Jan. 8 *Perf. 14½*

No.	Type	Description	Unused	Used
1004	A105	1c brn & multi	15	15
1005	A105	2c lt vio & multi	15	15
1006	A105	3c ocher & multi	15	15
1007	A105	4c multi	15	15
1008	A105	5c multi	15	15
1009	A105	10c multi	15	15
1010	A105	15c blue & multi	15	15
1011	A105	20c ocher & multi	15	15
		Set value, #1004-1011, C891-C893	2.90	2.30

Olympic Rings, Danish Crew, — A107

Winners, Rowing and Sculling Events: 2c, East Germany, 1972. 3c, Italy, 1968. 4c, Great Britain, 1936. 5c, France, 1952. 35c, United States, 1920, vert.

1976, Sept. 7 Litho. *Perf. 14*

No.	Type	Denom.	Color	Unused	Used
1022	A107	1c	blue & multi	15	15
1023	A107	2c	blue & multi	15	15
1024	A107	3c	blue & multi	15	15
1025	A107	4c	blue & multi	15	15
1026	A107	5c	blue & multi	15	15
1027	A107	35c	blue & multi	15	15
Nos. 1022-1027,C902-C905 (10)				5.98	5.13

The Smoke Signal, by Frederic Remington — A108

Designs (American Bicentennial Emblem and): No. 1029, Space Signal Monitoring Center. No. 1030, Candlelight. No. 1031, Edison's laboratory and light bulb. No. 1032, Agriculture, 1776. No. 1033, Agriculture, 1976. No. 1034, Harvard College, 1726. No. 1035, Harvard University, 1976. No. 1036, Horse-drawn carriage. No. 1037, Boeing 747.

1976, May 25 Litho. *Perf. 13½*

No.	Type	Denom.	Color	Unused	Used
1028	A108	1c	gray & multi	15	15
1029	A108	1c	gray & multi	15	15
1030	A108	2c	gray & multi	15	15
1031	A108	2c	gray & multi	15	15
1032	A108	3c	gray & multi	15	15
1033	A108	3c	gray & multi	15	15
1034	A108	4c	gray & multi	15	15
1035	A108	4c	gray & multi	15	15
1036	A108	5c	gray & multi	15	15
1037	A108	5c	gray & multi	15	15
Set value, #1028-1037, C907-C912				3.30	2.35

American Bicentennial, 200 years of progress. Stamps of same denomination printed se-tenant.

Mauritius No. 2 — A109

Rare Stamps: 2c, Western Australia #3a. 3c, Mauritius #1. 4c, Jamaica #83a. 5c, US #C3a. 10c, Basel #3L1. 25c, Canada #387a.

1976, Dec. *Perf. 14*

No.	Type	Denom.	Color	Unused	Used
1038	A109	1c	multi	15	15
1039	A109	2c	multi	15	15
1040	A109	3c	multi	15	15
1041	A109	4c	multi	15	15
1042	A109	5c	multi	15	15
1043	A109	10c	multi	15	15
1044	A109	25c	multi	15	15
Set value. #1038-1044, C913-C917				2.85	2.60

Back inscriptions printed on top of gum describe illustrated stamp.

Zeppelin in Flight A110

Designs: 1c, Zeppelin in hangar. 3c, Giffard's dirigible airship, 1852. 4c, Zeppelin on raising stilts coming out of hangar. 5c, Zeppelin ready for take-off.

1977, Oct. 31 Litho. *Perf. 14½*

No.	Type	Denom.	Color	Unused	Used
1045	A110	1c	multi	15	15
1046	A110	2c	multi	15	15
1047	A110	3c	multi	15	15
1048	A110	4c	multi	15	15
1049	A110	5c	multi	15	15
Nos. 1045-1049,C921-C924 (9)				4.23	
Set value					2.75

75th anniversary of Zeppelin.

Lindbergh, Map of Nicaragua A111

Designs: 2c, Spirit of St. Louis, map of Nicaragua. 3c, Lindbergh, vert. 4c, Spirit of St. Louis and New York-Paris route. 5c, Lindbergh and Spirit of St. Louis. 20c, Lindbergh, New York-Paris route and plane.

1977, Nov. 30

No.	Type	Denom.	Color	Unused	Used
1050	A111	1c	multi	15	15
1051	A111	2c	multi	15	15
1052	A111	3c	multi	15	15
1053	A111	4c	multi	15	15
1054	A111	5c	multi	15	15
1055	A111	20c	multi	15	15
Nos. 1050-1055,C926-C929 (10)				3.61	
Set value					2.40

Charles A. Lindbergh's solo transatlantic flight from New York to Paris, 50th anniversary.

Clara and Snowflakes — A112

Nutcracker Suite: 1c, Christmas party. 2c, Dancing dolls. 4c, Snowflake and prince. 5c, Snowflake dance. 15c, Sugarplum fairy and prince. 40c, Waltz of the flowers. 90c, Chinese tea dance. 1cor, Bonbonnière. 10cor, Arabian coffee dance.

1977, Dec. 12

No.	Type	Denom.	Color	Unused	Used
1056	A112	1c	multi	15	15
1057	A112	2c	multi	15	15
1058	A112	3c	multi	15	15
1059	A112	4c	multi	15	15
1060	A112	5c	multi	15	15
1061	A112	15c	multi	15	15
1062	A112	40c	multi	15	15
1063	A112	90c	multi	20	20
1064	A112	1cor	multi	28	20
1065	A112	10cor	multi	2.25	2.00
Set value				3.00	2.70

Christmas 1977. See No. C931.

Mr. and Mrs. Andrews, by Gainsborough — A113

Paintings: 2c, Giovanna Bacelli, by Gainsborough. 3c, Blue Boy by Gainsborough. 4c, Francis I, by Titian. 5c, Charles V in Battle of Muhlberg, by Titian. 25c, Sacred Love, by Titian.

1978, Jan. 11 Litho. *Perf. 14½*

No.	Type	Denom.	Color	Unused	Used
1066	A113	1c	multi	15	15
1067	A113	2c	multi	15	15
1068	A113	3c	multi	15	15
1069	A113	4c	multi	15	15
1070	A113	5c	multi	15	15
1071	A113	25c	multi	15	15
Set value, #1066-1071, C932-C933				3.25	2.75

Thomas Gainsborough (1727-1788), 250th birth anniversary; Titian (1477-1576), 500th birth anniversary.

Gothic Portal, Lower Church, Assisi — A114

Designs: 2c, St. Francis preaching to the birds. 3c, St. Francis, painting. 4c, St. Francis and Franciscan saints, 15th century tapestry. 5c, Portiuncola, cell of St. Francis, now in church of St. Mary of the Angels, Assisi. 15c, Blessing of St. Francis for Brother Leo (parchment). 25c, Stained-glass window, Upper Church of St. Francis, Assisi.

1978, Feb. 23 Litho. *Perf. 14½*

No.	Type	Denom.	Color	Unused	Used
1072	A114	1c	red & multi	15	15
1073	A114	2c	brt grn & multi	15	15
1074	A114	3c	bl grn & multi	15	15
1075	A114	4c	ultra & multi	15	15
1076	A114	5c	rose & multi	15	15
1077	A114	15c	yel & multi	15	15
1078	A114	25c	ocher & multi	15	15
Set value, #1072-1078, C935-C936				2.35	2.15

St. Francis of Assisi (1182-1266), 750th anniversary of his canonization, and in honor of Our Lady of the Immaculate Conception, patron saint of Nicaragua.

Passenger and Freight Locomotives — A115

Locomotives: 2c, Lightweight freight. 3c, American. 4c, Heavy freight Baldwin. 5c, Light freight and passenger Baldwin. 15c, Presidential coach.

1978, Apr. 7 Litho. *Perf. 14½*

No.	Type	Denom.	Color	Unused	Used
1079	A115	1c	lil & multi	15	15
1080	A115	2c	rose lil & multi	15	15
1081	A115	3c	bl & multi	15	15
1082	A115	4c	ol & multi	15	15
1083	A115	5c	yel & multi	15	15
1084	A115	15c	dp org & multi	15	15
Set value, #1079-1084, C938-C940				3.60	3.35

Centenary of Nicaraguan railroads.

Michael Strogoff, by Jules Verne — A116

Designs (Jules Verne Books): 2c, The Mysterious Island. 3c, Journey to the Center of the Earth (battle of the sea monsters). 4c, Five Weeks in a Balloon.

1978, Aug. Litho. *Perf. 14½*

No.	Type	Denom.	Color	Unused	Used
1085	A116	1c	multi	15	15
1086	A116	2c	multi	15	15
1087	A116	3c	multi	15	15
1088	A116	4c	multi	15	15
Nos. 1085-1088,C942-C943 (6)				2.55	
Set value					1.90

Jules Verne (1828-1905), science fiction writer.

Montgolfier Balloon — A117

Designs: 1c, Icarus, horiz. 3c, Wright Brothers' Flyer A, horiz. 4c, Orville Wright at control of Flyer, 1908.

1978, Sept. 29 Litho. *Perf. 14½*

No.	Type	Denom.	Color	Unused	Used
1089	A117	1c	multi	15	15
1090	A117	2c	multi	15	15
1091	A117	3c	multi	15	15
1092	A117	4c	multi	15	15
Set value, #1089-1092, C945-C946				1.70	1.30

History of aviation and 75th anniversary of first powered flight.

Ernst Ocwirk and Alfredo Di Stefano — A118

St. Peter, by Goya — A119

Soccer Players: 25c, Ralf Edstroem and Oswaldo Piazza.

1978, Oct. 25 Litho. *Perf. 13½x14*

No.	Type	Denom.	Color	Unused	Used
1093	A118	20c	multicolored	15	15
1094	A118	25c	multicolored	15	15
Set value				15	15

11th World Soccer Cup Championship, Argentina, June 1-25. See Nos. C948-C950.

1978, Dec. 12 Litho. *Perf. 13½x14*

Paintings: 15c, St. Gregory, by Goya.

No.	Type	Denom.	Color	Unused	Used
1095	A119	10c	multi	15	15
1096	A119	15c	multi	15	15
Set value				15	15

Christmas 1978. See Nos. C951-C953.

San Cristobal Volcano and Map — A120

Designs: No. 1098, Lake Cosiguina. No. 1099, Telica Volcano. No. 1100, Lake Jiloa.

1978, Dec. 29 *Perf. 14x13½*

No.	Type	Denom.	Color	Unused	Used
1097	A120	5c	multi	15	15
1098	A120	5c	multi	15	15
a.			Pair, #1097-1098	25	25
1099	A120	20c	multi	15	15
1100	A120	20c	multi	15	15
a.			Pair, #1099-1100	25	25
Nos. 1097-1100,C954-C961 (12)				5.42	
Set value					3.35

Volcanos, lakes and their locations.

1980 Overprints

The editors are still gathering data on the 1980 overprints for the listing of these issues.

Souvenir Sheet

Quetzal — A121

1981, May 18 **Litho.** ***Perf. 13***

1101 A121 10cor multi		1.75	1.25

WIPA 1981 Phil. Exhib., Vienna, May 22-31.

1982 World Cup A122

Designs: Various soccer players and stadiums.

1981, June 25 ***Perf. 12x12½***

1102 A122	5c	multi	15	15
1103 A122	20c	multi	15	15
1104 A122	25c	multi	15	15
1105 A122	30c	multi	15	15
1106 A122	50c	multi	15	15
1107 A122	4cor	multi	45	26
1108 A122	5cor	multi	52	32
1109 A122	10cor	multi	1.10	65
		Set value	2.30	1.30

Souvenir Sheet

Perf. 13

1110 A122 10cor multi		1.40	1.00

2nd Anniv. of Revolution — A123

1981, July 19 ***Perf. 12½x12***

1111 A123 50c Adult education		15	15

See Nos. C973-C975.

20th Anniv. of the FSLN A124

1981, July 23

1112 A124 50c Armed citizen		15	15

See No. C976.

Postal Union of Spain and the Americas, 12th Congress, Managua — A125

1981, Aug. 10

1113 A125 50c Mailman		15	15

See Nos. C977-C979.

Aquatic Flowers (Nymphaea...) A126

1981, Sept. 15 ***Perf. 12½***

1114 A126	50c	Capensis	15	15
1115 A126	1cor	Daubenyana	15	15
1116 A126	1.20cor	Marliacea	22	15
1117 A126	1.80cor	GT Moore	35	15
1118 A126	2cor	Lotus	35	15
1119 A126	2.50cor	BG Berry	50	28
		Nos. 1114-1119,C981 (7)	3.12	1.93

Tropical Fish A127

1981, Oct. 19

1120 A127	50c	Cheirodon axelrodi	15	15
1121 A127	1cor	Poecilia reticulata	18	15
1122 A127	1.85cor	Anostomus anostomus	35	18
1123 A127	2.10cor	Corydoras arcuatus	42	20
1124 A127	2.50cor	Cynolebias nigripinnis	48	28
		Nos. 1120-1124,C983-C984 (7)	2.61	1.54

Dryocopus Lineatus — A128

1981, Nov. 30 ***Perf. 12½***

1125 A128	50c	shown	15	15
1126 A128	1.20cor	Ramphastos sulfuratus, horiz.	26	15
1127 A128	1.80cor	Aratinga finschi, horiz.	40	22
1128 A128	2cor	Ara macao	40	26
		Nos. 1125-1128,C986-C988 (7)	3.29	1.97

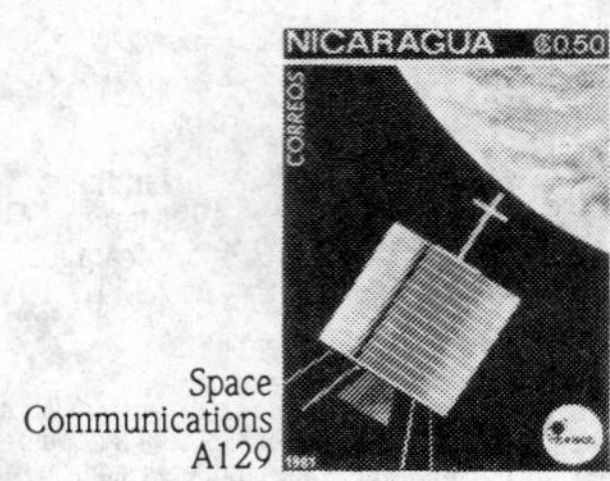

Space Communications A129

Designs: Various communications satellites.

1981, Dec. 15 ***Perf. 13x12½***

1129 A129	50c	multi	15	15
1130 A129	1cor	multi	15	15
1131 A129	1.50cor	multi	25	15
1132 A129	2cor	multi	30	20
		Nos. 1129-1132,C989-C991 (7)	2.30	1.50

Vaporcito 93 A130

1981, Dec. 30 ***Perf. 12½***

1133 A130	50c	shown	15	15
1134 A130	1cor	Vulcan Iron Works, 1946	20	15
1135 A130	1.20cor	1911	25	15
1136 A130	1.80cor	Hoist & Derriel, 1909	38	20
1137 A130	2cor	U-10B, 1956	38	25
1138 A130	2.50cor	Ferrobus, 1945	38	30
		Nos. 1133-1138,C992 (7)	2.74	1.75

1982 World Cup — A131

Designs: Various soccer players. 3.50cor horiz.

1982, Jan. 25

1139 A131	5c	multi	15	15
1140 A131	20c	multi	15	15
1141 A131	25c	multi	15	15
1142 A131	2.50cor	multi	42	34
1143 A131	3.50cor	multi	55	35
		Nos. 1139-1143,C993-C994 (7)	3.15	
		Set value		1.80

Cocker Spaniels A132

1982, Feb. 18

1144 A132	5c	shown	15	15
1145 A132	20c	German shepherds	15	15
1146 A132	25c	English setters	15	15
1147 A132	2.50cor	Brittany spaniels	45	28
		Nos. 1144-1147,C996-C998 (7)	2.73	
		Set value		1.40

Dynamine Myrrhina A133

1982, Mar. 26

1148 A133	50c	shown	15	15
1149 A133	1.20cor	Eunica alcmena	24	15
1150 A133	1.50cor	Callizona acesta	28	16
1151 A133	2cor	Adelpha leuceria	35	24
		Nos. 1148-1151,C1000-C1002 (7)	2.50	1.63

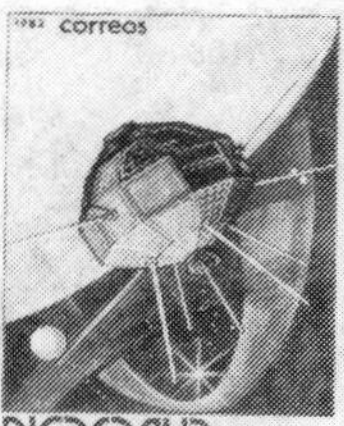

Satellite — A134

Designs: Various satellites. 5c, 50c, 1.50cor, 2.50cor horiz.

1982, Apr. 12

1152 A134	5c	multi	15	15
1153 A134	15c	multi	15	15
1154 A134	50c	multi	15	15
1155 A134	1.50cor	multi	26	16
1156 A134	2.50cor	multi	45	26
		Nos. 1152-1156,C1003-C1004 (7)	2.71	
		Set value		1.45

UPU Membership Centenary — A135

1982, May 1 **Litho.** ***Perf. 13***

1157 A135	50c	Mail coach	15	15
1158 A135	1.20cor	Ship	16	15
		Set value	23	15

See Nos. C1005-C1006.

14th Central American and Caribbean Games (Cuba '82) — A136

1982, May 13

1159 A136	10c	Bicycling, vert.	15	15
1160 A136	15c	Swimming	15	15
1161 A136	25c	Basketball, vert.	15	15
1162 A136	50c	Weight lifting, vert.	15	15
		Set value, #1159-1162, C1007-C1009	2.45	1.50

3rd Anniv. of Revolution — A137

1982, July 19

No.	Type	Description	Unused	Used
1163	A137	50c multi	15	15

See Nos. C1012-C1014.

George Washington (1732-1799) A138

19th Century Paintings. 1cor horiz. Size of 50c: 45x35mm.

Perf. 13x12½, 12½x13

1982, June 20 **Litho.**

No.	Type	Description	Unused	Used
1164	A138	50c Mount Vernon	15	15
1165	A138	1cor Signing the Constitution	20	15
1166	A138	2cor Riding through Trenton	38	25
		Nos. 1164-1166,C1015-C1018 (7)	3.23	2.10

Flower Arrangement, by R. Penalba — A139

Paintings: 50c, Masked Dancers, by M. Garcia, horiz. 1cor, The Couple, by R. Perez. 1.20cor, Canales Valley, by A. Mejias, horiz. 1.85cor, Portrait of Mrs. Castellon, by T. Jerez. 2cor, Street Vendors, by L. Cerrato. 10cor, Cock Fight, by Gallos P. Ortiz.

1982, Aug. 17 *Perf. 13*

No.	Type	Description	Unused	Used
1167	A139	25c multi	15	15
1168	A139	50c multi	15	15
1169	A139	1cor multi	18	15
1170	A139	1.20cor multi	20	15
1171	A139	1.85cor multi	32	20
1172	A139	2cor multi	32	20
		Nos. 1167-1172,C1019 (7)	2.57	
		Set value		1.45

Souvenir Sheet

No.	Type	Description	Unused	Used
1173	A139	10cor multi	1.65	1.00

No. 1173 contains one 36x28mm stamp.

George Dimitrov, First Pres. of Bulgaria — A140

1982, Sept. 9

No.	Type	Description	Unused	Used
1174	A140	50c Lenin, Dimitrov, 1921	15	15

See Nos. C1020-C1021.

26th Anniv. of End of Dictatorship — A141

1982, Sept. 21 *Perf. 13x12½*

No.	Type	Description	Unused	Used
1175	A141	50c Ausberto Narvaez	15	15
1176	A141	2.50cor Cornelio Silva	52	30
		Set value		36

See Nos. C1022-C1023.

Ruins, Leon Viejo A142

1982, Sept. 25 *Perf. 13*

No.	Type	Description	Unused	Used
1177	A142	50c shown	15	15
1178	A142	1cor Ruben Dario Theater and Park	15	15
1179	A142	1.20cor Independence Plaza, Granada	18	15
1180	A142	1.80cor Corn Island	28	16
1181	A142	2cor Santiago Volcano crater, Masaya	30	18
		Nos. 1177-1181,C1024-C1025 (7)	1.72	
		Set value		1.10

Karl Marx (1818-1883) — A143

1982, Oct. 4 *Perf. 12½*

No.	Type	Description	Unused	Used
1182	A143	1cor Marx, birthplace	18	15

Se-tenant with label showing Communist Manifesto titlepage. See No. C1026.

World Food Day (Oct. 16) A144

1982, Oct. 10 *Perf. 13*

No.	Type	Description	Unused	Used
1183	A144	50c Picking fruit	15	15
1184	A144	1cor Farm workers, vert.	15	15
1185	A144	2cor Cutting sugar cane	30	25
1186	A144	10cor Emblems	1.50	1.20

Discovery of America, 490th Anniv. A145

1982, Oct. 12 *Perf. 12½x13*

No.	Type	Description	Unused	Used
1187	A145	50c Santa Maria	15	15
1188	A145	1cor Nina	22	15
1189	A145	1.50cor Pinta	32	20
1190	A145	2cor Columbus, fleet	42	28
		Nos. 1187-1190,C1027-C1029 (7)	3.28	2.14

A146 A147

1982, Nov. 13 *Perf. 12½*

No.	Type	Description	Unused	Used
1191	A146	50c Lobelia laxiflora	15	15
1192	A146	1.20cor Bombacopsis quinata	25	15
1193	A146	1.80cor Mimosa albida	38	22
1194	A146	2cor Epidendrum alatum	38	25
		Nos. 1191-1194,C1031-C1033 (7)	2.81	1.76

1982, Dec. 10 *Perf. 13*

No.	Type	Description	Unused	Used
1195	A147	10c Coral snake	15	15
1196	A147	50c Iguana, horiz.	15	15
1197	A147	2cor Lachesis muta, horiz.	38	25
		Nos. 1195-1197,C1034-C1037 (7)	2.78	1.82

Telecommunications Day — A148

1982, Dec. 12 **Litho.** *Perf. 12½*

No.	Type	Description	Unused	Used
1198	A148	50c Radio transmission station	15	15
1199	A148	1cor Telcor building, Managua	16	15
		Set value	25	15

50c airmail.

Jose Marti, Cuban Independence Hero, 130th Birth Anniv. — A149

1983, Jan. 28 *Perf. 13*

No.	Type	Description	Unused	Used
1200	A149	1cor multi	25	15

Boxing — A150

Local Flowers — A151

1983, Jan. 31 *Perf. 12½*

No.	Type	Description	Unused	Used
1201	A150	50c shown	15	15
1202	A150	1cor Gymnast	15	15
1203	A150	1.50cor Running	20	15
1204	A150	2cor Weightlifting	25	16
1205	A150	4cor Women's discus	65	35
1206	A150	5cor Basketball	80	40
1207	A150	6cor Bicycling	1.00	50
		Nos. 1201-1207 (7)	3.20	1.86

Souvenir Sheet

Perf. 13

No.	Type	Description	Unused	Used
1208	A150	15cor Sailing	2.25	1.20

23rd Olympic Games, Los Angeles, July 28-Aug. 12, 1984. Nos. 1205-1208 airmail. No. 1208 contains one 31x39mm stamp.

1983, Feb. 5 *Perf. 12½*

No.	Type	Description	Unused	Used
1209	A151	1cor Bixa orellana	16	15
1210	A151	1cor Brassavola nodosa	16	15
1211	A151	1cor Cattleya lueddemanniana	16	15
1212	A151	1cor Cochlospermum spec.	16	15
1213	A151	1cor Hibiscus rosa-sinensis	16	15
1214	A151	1cor Laella spec.	16	15
1215	A151	1cor Malvaviscus arboreus	16	15
1216	A151	1cor Neomarica coerulea	16	15
1217	A151	1cor Plumeria rubra	16	15
1218	A151	1cor Senecio spec.	16	15
1219	A151	1cor Sobralia macrantha	16	15
1220	A151	1cor Stachytarpheta indica	16	15
1221	A151	1cor Tabebula ochraceae	16	15
1222	A151	1cor Tagetes erecta	16	15
1223	A151	1cor Tecoma stans	16	15
1224	A151	1cor Thumbergia alata	16	15
		Nos. 1209-1224 (16)	2.56	
		Set value		1.25

See Nos. 1515-1530, 1592-1607, 1828-1843.

Visit of Pope John Paul II A152

1983, Mar. 4 *Perf. 13*

No.	Type	Description	Unused	Used
1225	A152	50c Peace banner	15	15
1226	A152	1cor Map, girl picking coffee beans	24	15
1227	A152	4cor Pres. Rafael Rivas, Pope	95	60
1228	A152	7cor Pope, Managua Cathedral	1.65	95

Souvenir Sheet

No.	Type	Description	Unused	Used
1229	A152	15cor Pope, vert.	3.25	1.75

Nos. 1227-1229 airmail. No. 1229 contains one 31x39mm stamp.

Nocturnal Moths A153

1983, Mar. 10

No.	Type	Description	Unused	Used
1230	A153	15c Xilophanes chiron	15	15
1231	A153	50c Protoparce ochus	15	15
1232	A153	65c Pholus lasbruscae	15	15
1233	A153	1cor Amphypterus gannascus	16	15
1234	A153	1.50cor Pholus licaon	20	15
1235	A153	2cor Agrius cingulata	35	16
1236	A153	10cor Rothschildia jurulla, vert.	1.50	75
		Nos. 1230-1236 (7)	2.66	
		Set value		1.20

26th Anniv. of the Anti-Somoza Movement — A154

Various monuments and churches. 2cor, 4cor vert. 4cor airmail.

1983, Mar. 25 *Perf. 12½*

1237 A154 50c Church of Subtiava, Leon 15 15
1238 A154 1cor La Immaculata Castle, Rio San Juan 16 15
1239 A154 2cor La Recoleccion Church, Leon 35 16
1240 A154 4cor Ruben Dario monument, Managua 65 35
Set value 64

Railroad Cars A155

1983, Apr. 15

1241 A155 15c Passenger 15 15
1242 A155 65c Freight 15 15
1243 A155 1cor Tank 15 15
1244 A155 1.50cor Ore 20 15
1245 A155 4cor Passenger, diff. 55 30
1246 A155 5cor Flat 70 35
1247 A155 7cor Rail bus 95 48
Nos. 1241-1247 (7) 2.85
Set value 1.35

Nos. 1245-1247 airmail.

Red Cross Flood Rescue A156

1983, May 8 *Perf. 13*

1248 A156 50c shown 15 15
1249 A156 1cor Putting patient in ambulance 18 15
1250 A156 4cor 1972 earthquake & fire rescue 65 38
1251 A156 5cor Nurse examining soldier, 1979 Liberation War 70 42

4cor, 5cor airmail. 4cor vert.

World Communications Year — A157

1983, May 17

1252 A157 1cor multi 18 15

9th Pan-American Games, Aug. — A158

1983, May 30 **Litho.** *Perf. 13*

1253 A158 15c Baseball 15 15
1254 A158 50c Water polo 15 15
1255 A158 65c Running 15 15
1256 A158 1cor Women's basketball, vert. 16 15
1257 A158 2cor Weightlifting, vert. 35 16
1258 A158 7cor Fencing 1.10 55
1259 A158 8cor Gymnastics 1.20 65
Nos. 1253-1259 (7) 3.26
Set value 1.55

Souvenir Sheet

1260 A158 15cor Boxing 2.25 1.25

Nos. 1258-1260 airmail. No. 1260 contains one 39x31mm stamp.

4th Anniv. of Revolution — A159

1983, July 19 **Litho.** *Perf. 12½*

1261 A159 1cor Port of Corinto 16 15
1262 A159 2cor Telecommunications Bldg., Leon 38 16
Set value 25

Founders of FSLN (Sandinista Party) — A160

1983, July 23 **Litho.** *Perf. 13*

1263 A160 50c multi 15 15
1264 A160 1cor multi 16 15
1265 A160 4cor multi, vert. 60 35
Set value 48

No. 1265, airmail, 33x44mm.

Simon Bolivar, 200th Birth Anniv. A161

1983, July 24 **Litho.** *Perf. 12½*

1266 A161 50c Bolivar and Sandino 15 15
1267 A161 1cor Bolivar on horseback, vert. 15 15
Set value 24 15

14th Winter Olympic Games, Sarajevo, Yugoslavia, Feb. 8-19, 1984 — A162

1983, Aug. 5 **Litho.** *Perf. 13*

1268 A162 50c Speed skating 15 15
1269 A162 1cor Slalom 15 15
1270 A162 1.50cor Luge 20 15
1271 A162 2cor Ski jumping 35 16
1272 A162 4cor Ice dancing 60 35
1273 A162 5cor Skiing 70 40
1274 A162 6cor Biathlon 90 50
Nos. 1268-1274 (7) 3.05 1.86

Souvenir Sheet

1983, Aug. 25 **Litho.** *Perf. 13*

1275 A162 15cor Hockey 2.50 1.40

No. 1275 contains one 39x32mm stamp. Nos. 1272-1275 airmail.

Chess Moves — A163

Archaeological Finds — A164

1983, Aug. 20 **Litho.** *Perf. 13*

1276 A163 15c Pawn 15 15
1277 A163 65c Knight 15 15
1278 A163 1cor Bishop 15 15
1279 A163 2cor Castle 35 16
1280 A163 4cor Queen 60 35
1281 A163 5cor King 70 40
1282 A163 7cor Player 1.00 55
Nos. 1276-1282 (7) 3.10
Set value 1.60

Nos. 1280-1282 airmail.

1983, Aug. 20 *Perf. 13x12½*

1283 A164 50c Stone figurine 15 15
1284 A164 1cor Covered dish 15 15
1285 A164 2cor Vase 35 16
1286 A164 4cor Platter 60 35
Set value 64

No. 1286 airmail.

Madonna of the Chair, by Raphael (1483-1517) A165

Paintings: 1cor, The Eszterhazy Madonna. 1.50cor, Sistine Madonna. 2cor, Madonna of the Linnet. 4cor, Madonna of the Meadow. 5cor, La Belle Jardiniere. 6cor, Adoration of the Kings. 15cor, Madonna de Foligno. 4, 5, 6, 15cor airmail.

1983, Sept. 15

1287 A165 50c multi 15 15
1288 A165 1cor multi 15 15
1289 A165 1.50cor multi 20 15
1290 A165 2cor multi 35 16
1291 A165 4cor multi 60 35
1292 A165 5cor multi 70 40
1293 A165 6cor multi 90 48
Nos. 1287-1293 (7) 3.05 1.84

Souvenir Sheet

1984, Sept. 15 **Litho.** *Perf. 13*

1293A A165 15cor multi 2.25 1.25

Mining Industry Nationalization — A166

1983, Oct. 2 *Perf. 13*

1294 A166 1cor Pouring molten metal 16 15
1295 A166 4cor Mine headstock, workers 60 40

4cor airmail.

Ship-to-Shore Communications — A167

1983, Oct. 7 *Perf. 12½*

1296 A167 1cor shown 16 15
1297 A167 4cor Radio tower, view 60 40

FRACAP '83, Federation of Central American and Panamanian Radio Amateurs Cong., Oct. 7-9.

Agrarian Reform — A168

1983, Oct. 16

1298 A168 1cor Tobacco 15 15
1299 A168 2cor Cotton 35 15
1300 A168 4cor Corn 60 25
1301 A168 5cor Sugar cane 70 35
1302 A168 6cor Cattle 90 40
1303 A168 7cor Rice paddy 1.00 45
1304 A168 8cor Coffee beans 1.20 55
1305 A168 10cor Bananas 1.50 65
Nos. 1298-1305 (8) 6.40 2.95

See Nos. 1531-1538, 1608-1615.

Fire Engine A169

Various Fire Engines.

1983, Oct. 17 *Perf. 13*

1306 A169 50c multi 15 15
1307 A169 1cor multi 15 15
1308 A169 1.50cor multi 20 15
1309 A169 2cor multi 35 16
1310 A169 4cor multi 60 35
1311 A169 5cor multi 70 40
1312 A169 6cor multi 90 48
Nos. 1306-1312 (7) 3.05 1.84

Nos. 1308-1311 airmail.

Nicaraguan-Cuban Solidarity — A170

1983, Oct. 24

1313 A170 1cor José Marti, Gen. Sandino 16 15
1314 A170 4cor Education, health, industry 60 40

4cor airmail.

A171

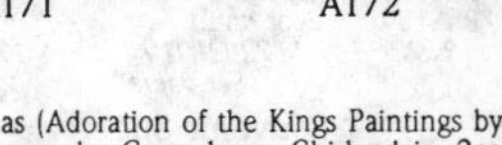

A172

Christmas (Adoration of the Kings Paintings by): 50c, Hugo van der Goes. 1 cor, Ghirlandaio. 2cor, El Greco. 7cor, Konrad von Soest. 7cor airmail.

1983, Dec. 1

1315 A171 50c multi 15 15
1316 A171 1cor multi 15 15
1317 A171 2cor multi 28 15
1318 A171 7cor multi 90 42
Set value 1.30 66

1984, Jan. 10

1319 A172 50c Biathlon 15 15
1320 A172 50c Bobsledding 15 15
1321 A172 1cor Speed skating 15 15
1322 A172 1cor Slalom 15 15
1323 A172 4cor Downhill skiing 65 35
1324 A172 5cor Ice dancing 80 40
1325 A172 10cor Ski jumping 1.40 75
Nos. 1319-1325 (7) 3.45
Set value 1.75

Souvenir Sheet

1326 A172 15cor Hockey 2.50 1.50

1984 Winter Olympics. No. 1326 contains one 31x39mm stamp. Nos. 1323-1326 airmail.

Domestic Cats A173

1984, Feb. 15 *Perf. 12½*

1327	A173	50c	Chinchilla	15	15
1328	A173	50c	Long-haired Angel	15	15
1329	A173	1cor	Red tabby	18	15
1330	A173	2cor	Tortoiseshell	38	18
1331	A173	3cor	Siamese	32	28
1332	A173	4cor	Blue Burmese	70	38
1333	A173	7cor	Silver long-haired	1.25	60
			Nos. 1327-1333 (7)	3.13	
			Set value		1.55

Nos. 1331, 1333 airmail.

Augusto Cesar Sandino (d. 1934) — A174

1984, Feb. 21

1334	A174	1cor	Arms	16	15
1335	A174	4cor	Portrait	60	40

4cor airmail.

Intl. Women's Day — A175

1984, Mar. 8

1336	A175	1cor	Blanca Arauz	15	15

Bee-pollinated Flowers — A176

1984, Mar. 20

1337	A176	50c	Poinsettia	15	15
1338	A176	50c	Sunflower	15	15
1339	A176	1cor	Antigonan leptopus	16	15
1340	A176	1cor	Cassia alata	16	15
1341	A176	3cor	Bidens pilosa	42	25
1342	A176	4cor	Althea rosea	60	35
1343	A176	5cor	Rivea corymbosa	70	40
			Nos. 1337-1343 (7)	2.34	
			Set value		1.25

Nos. 1341-1343 airmail.

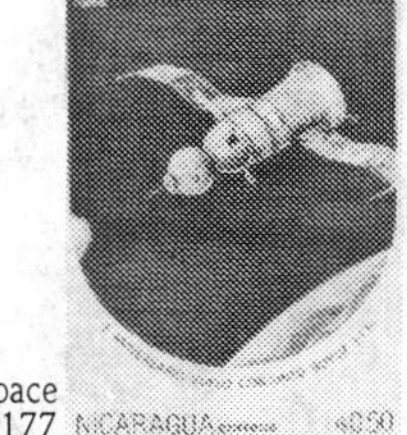

Space Annivs. — A177

1984, Apr. 20

1344	A177	50c	Soyuz 6,7,8, 1969	15	15
1345	A177	50c	Soyuz 6,7,8, diff.	15	15
1346	A177	1cor	Apollo 11, 1969	15	15
1347	A177	2cor	Luna 1, 1959	35	16
1348	A177	3cor	Luna 2, 1959	50	25
1349	A177	4cor	Luna 3, 1959	65	35
1350	A177	9cor	Painting by Koroliov, 1934	1.40	50
			Nos. 1344-1350 (7)	3.35	
			Set value		1.40

Nos. 1348-1350 airmail.

Noli Me Tangere, by Correggio — A178

1984, May 17 **Litho.** *Perf. 12½*

1351	A178	50c	shown	15	15
1352	A178	50c	Madonna of San Girolamo	15	15
1353	A178	1cor	Allegory of the Virtues	15	15
1354	A178	2cor	Allegory of Placer	35	16
1355	A178	3cor	Ganimedes	50	25
1356	A178	5cor	Danae	80	40
1357	A178	8cor	Leda	1.20	65
			Nos. 1351-1357 (7)	3.30	
			Set value		1.60

Souvenir Sheet

1358	A178	15cor	St. John the Evangelist	2.25	1.20

No. 1358 contains one 31x39mm stamp. Nos. 1355-1358 airmail.

Vintage Cars A179

1984, May 18

1359	A179	1cor	Abadal, 1914	15	15
1360	A179	1cor	Daimler, 1886, vert.	15	15
1361	A179	2cor	Ford, 1903, vert.	35	16
1362	A179	2cor	Renault, 1899, vert.	35	16
1363	A179	3cor	Rolls Royce, 1910	50	25
1364	A179	4cor	Metallurgique, 1907	65	35
1365	A179	7cor	Bugatti Mode 40	1.10	55
			Nos. 1359-1365 (7)	3.25	1.77

Birth sesquicentennial of Gottlieb Daimler. Nos. 1363-1365 airmail.

1984 Summer Olympics — A180

1984, July 6

1366	A180	50c	Volleyball	15	15
1367	A180	50c	Basketball	15	15
1368	A180	1cor	Field hockey	15	15
1369	A180	2cor	Tennis	35	16
1370	A180	3cor	Soccer	50	25
1371	A180	4cor	Water polo	65	35
1372	A180	9cor	Net ball	1.40	70
			Nos. 1366-1372 (7)	3.35	
			Set value		1.60

Souvenir Sheet

Perf. 13

1373	A180	15cor	Baseball	2.25	1.20

No. 1373 contains one 40x31mm stamp. Nos. 1370-1373 airmail and horiz.

5th Anniv. of Revolution A181

1984, July 19

1374	A181	50c	Construction	15	15
1375	A181	1cor	Transportation	16	15
1376	A181	4cor	Agriculture	65	35
1377	A181	7cor	Govt. building	1.20	55
			Set value		1.00

Nos. 1376-1377 airmail.

UNESCO Nature Conservation Campaign A182

1984, Aug. 3 *Perf. 12½x13, 13x12½*

1378	A182	50c	Children dependent on nature	15	15
1379	A182	1cor	Forest	15	15
1380	A182	2cor	River	35	16
1381	A182	10cor	Seedlings, field, vert.	1.50	80
			Set value		1.05

No. 1381 airmail.

Nicaraguan Red Cross, 50th Anniv. — A183

1984, Sept. 16 *Perf. 12½x12*

1382	A183	1cor	Air ambulance	16	15
1383	A183	7cor	Battle field	1.00	55

No. 1383 airmail.

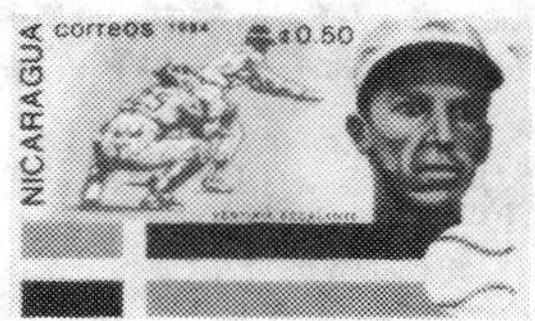

History of Baseball — A184

Portraits and national colors: No. 1384, Ventura Escalante, Dominican Republic. No. 1385, Daniel Herrera, Mexico. No. 1386, Adalberto Herrera, Venezuela. No. 1387, Roberto Clemente, Puerto Rico. No. 1388, Carlos Colas, Cuba. No. 1389, Stanley Cayasso, Nicaragua. No. 1390, Babe Ruth, US.

1984, Oct. 25 **Litho.** *Perf. 12½*

1384	A184	50c	multi	15	15
1385	A184	50c	multi	15	15
1386	A184	1cor	multi	16	15
1387	A184	1cor	multi	16	15
1388	A184	3cor	multi	50	20
1389	A184	4cor	multi	65	25
1390	A184	5cor	multi	80	35
			Nos. 1384-1390 (7)	2.57	
			Set value		1.00

Nos. 1388-1390 are airmail.

Tapirus Bairdii A185

1984, Dec. 28 *Perf. 13*

1391	A185	25c	In winter	15	15
1392	A185	25c	In field	15	15
1393	A185	3cor	Baring teeth	40	20
1394	A185	4cor	Female and young	55	25
			Set value	1.00	50

Wildlife conservation. Nos. 1393-1394 are airmail. Compare with type A202.

1986 World Cup Soccer Championships, Mexico — A186

Evolution of soccer.

1985, Jan. 20

1395	A186	50c	1314	15	15
1396	A186	50c	1500	15	15
1397	A186	1cor	1846	15	15
1398	A186	1cor	1872	15	15
1399	A186	2cor	1883	20	15
1400	A186	4cor	1890	40	20
1401	A186	6cor	1953	60	30
			Set value	1.50	75

Souvenir Sheet

Perf. 12½

1402	A186	10cor	1985	1.20	80

Nos. 1399-1402 are airmail. No. 1402 contains one 40x32mm stamp.

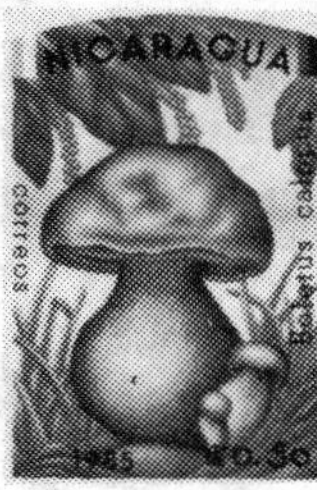

Mushrooms — A187

1985, Feb. 20

1403	A187	50c	Boletus calopus	15	15
1404	A187	50c	Strobilomyces retisporus	15	15
1405	A187	1cor	Boletus luridus	15	15
1406	A187	1cor	Xerocomus illudens	15	15
1407	A187	4cor	Gyrodon merulioides	50	20
1408	A187	5cor	Tylopilus plumbeoviolaceus	60	25
1409	A187	8cor	Gyroporus castaneus	1.00	40
			Nos. 1403-1409 (7)	2.70	
			Set value		1.00

Nos. 1406-1409 are airmail.

15-Cent Minimum Value
The minimum value for a single stamp is 15 cents. This value reflects the costs of the handlling of inexpensive stamps.

Postal Union of the Americas and Spain, 13th Congress A188

UPAE emblem and: 1cor, Chasqui, mail runner and map of Realejo-Nicaragua route. 7cor, Monoplane and Nicaraguan air network.

1985, Mar. 11 *Perf. 12½x13*
1410 A188 1cor multi 15 15
1411 A188 7cor multi 70 38

No. 1411 is airmail.

City Railway Engine A189

Various locomotives.

1985, Apr. 5 *Perf. 12½*
1412 A189 1cor Electric 15 15
1413 A189 1cor Steam 15 15
1414 A189 9cor shown 52 25
1415 A189 9cor shown 52 25
1416 A189 15cor steam, diff. 85 42
1417 A189 21cor steam, diff. 1.25 35
Nos. 1412-1417 (6) 3.44 1.57

Souvenir Sheet

Perf. 13

1418 A189 42cor steam, diff. 3.25 1.90

German Railroads, 150th Anniv. No. 1418 also for 100th anniv. of Nicaraguan railroads. No. 1418 contains one 40x32mm stamp. Nos. 1414-1418 are airmail.

Motorcycle Cent. — A190

1985, Apr. 30 **Litho.** *Perf. 12½*
1419 A190 50c F.N., 1928 15 15
1420 A190 50c Douglas, 1928 15 15
1421 A190 1cor Puch, 1938 15 15
1422 A190 2cor Wanderer, 1939 20 15
1423 A190 4cor Honda, 1949 40 20
1424 A190 5cor BMW, 1984 50 25
1425 A190 7cor Honda, 1984 70 38
Nos. 1419-1425 (7) 2.25
Set value 1.00

Nos. 1419-1425 se-tenant with labels picturing manufacturers' trademarks. Nos. 1422-1425 are airmail.

Flowers — A194

1985, May 20 **Litho.** *Perf. 13*
1454 A194 50c Metelea quirosii 15 15
1455 A194 50c Ipomea nil 15 15
1456 A194 1cor Lysichitum americanum 18 15
1457 A194 2cor Clusia sp. 36 18
1458 A194 4cor Vanilla planifolia 72 36
1459 A194 7cor Stemmadenia obovata 1.25 62
a. Min. sheet of 6, #1454-1459 2.75
Nos. 1454-1459 (6) 2.81
Set value 1.35

Nos. 1457-1459 are airmail.
Stamps in No. 1459a do not have white border.

End of World War II, 40th Anniv. — A195

1985, May *Perf. 12x12½, 12½x12*
1460 A195 9.50cor German army surrenders 38 18
1461 A195 28cor Nuremberg trials, horiz. 1.10 52

No. 1461 is airmail.

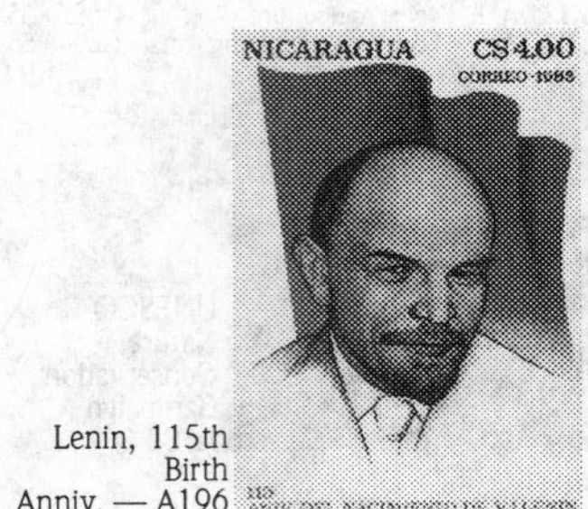

Lenin, 115th Birth Anniv. — A196

Design: 21cor, Lenin speaking to workers.

1985, June **Litho.** *Perf. 12x12½*
1462 A196 4cor multicolored 40 20
1463 A196 21cor multicolored 2.25 1.10

Souvenir Sheet

Argentina '85 — A197

1985, June 5 **Litho.** *Perf. 13*
1464 A197 75cor multicolored 4.25 2.00

World Stamp Exposition.

Birds — A198

1985, Aug. 25
1465 A198 50c Ring-neck pheasant 15 15
1466 A198 50c Chicken 15 15
1467 A198 1cor Guinea hen 20 15
1468 A198 2cor Goose 40 20
1469 A198 6cor Wild turkey 1.25 60
1470 A198 8cor Duck 1.65 80
Nos. 1465-1470 (6) 3.80 2.05

Intl. Music Year A199

1985, Sept. 1
1471 A199 1cor Luis A. Delgadillo, vert. 15 15
1472 A199 1cor shown 15 15
1473 A199 9cor Parade 60 30
1474 A199 9cor Managua Cathedral 60 30
1475 A199 15cor Masked dancer 95 48
1476 A199 21cor Parade, diff. 1.25 65
Nos. 1471-1476 (6) 3.70 2.03

Nos. 1473-1476 are airmail.

Natl. Fire Brigade, 6th Anniv. A200

1985, Oct. 18
1477 A200 1cor Fire station 15 15
1478 A200 1cor Fire truck 15 15
1479 A200 1cor shown 15 15
1480 A200 3cor Ambulance 20 15
1481 A200 9cor Airport fire truck 60 30
1482 A200 15cor Waterfront fire 1.00 50
1483 A200 21cor Hose team, fire 1.40 75
a. Min. sheet of 7, #1474-1483 + 2 labels 3.75
Nos. 1477-1483 (7) 3.65
Set value 1.70

Stamps from No. 1483a have orange borders. Nos. 1480-1483 are airmail.

Halley's Comet — A201

1985, Nov. 26
1484 A201 1cor Edmond Halley 15 15
1485 A201 3cor Map of comet's track, 1910 16 15
1486 A201 3cor Tycho Brahe's observatory 16 15
1487 A201 9cor Astrolabe, map 50 24
1488 A201 15cor Telescopes 80 40
1489 A201 21cor Telescope designs 1.25 60
Nos. 1484-1489 (6) 3.02 1.69

Nos. 1487-1489 are airmail.

Tapirus Bairdii A202

1985, Dec. 30
1490 A202 1cor Eating 15 15
1491 A202 3cor Drinking 32 16
1492 A202 5cor Grazing in field 50 25
1493 A202 9cor With young 95 45

Nos. 1491-1493 are airmail.

Roses — A203

1986, Jan. 15 *Perf. 12½*
1494 A203 1cor Spinosissima 15 15
1495 A203 1cor Canina 15 15
1496 A203 3cor Eglanteria 15 15
1497 A203 5cor Rubrifolia 15 15
1498 A203 9cor Foetida 20 15
1499 A203 100cor Rugosa 2.25 1.10
Nos. 1494-1499 (6) 3.05
Set value 1.25

Nos. 1497-1499 are airmail.

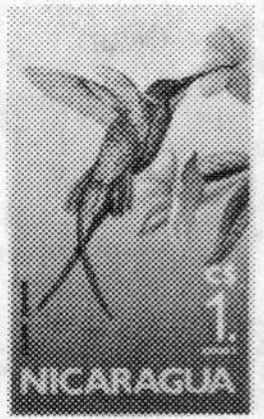

Birds — A204

A205

1986, Feb. 10 *Perf. 13x12½*
1500 A204 1cor Colibri topacio 15 15
1501 A204 3cor Paraulata picodorado 15 15
1502 A204 3cor Troupial 15 15
1503 A204 5cor Vereron pintado 15 15
1504 A204 10cor Tordo ruisenor 24 15
1505 A204 21cor Buho real 50 26
1506 A204 75cor Gran kiskadee 1.75 90
Nos. 1500-1506 (7) 3.09
Set value 1.45

Nos. 1504-1506 are airmail.

1986, Mar. 20 *Perf. 12½*

World Cup Soccer Championships, Mexico: Soccer players and pre-Columbian artifacts. No. 1514, Player's foot, ball.

Shirt Colors

1507 A205 1cor blue & yel 15 15
1508 A205 1cor yel & green 15 15
1509 A205 3cor blue & white 15 15
1510 A205 3cor red & white 15 15
1511 A205 5cor red 15 15
1512 A205 9cor blk & yel 15 15
1513 A205 100cor red & grn 2.00 1.10
Nos. 1507-1513 (7) 2.90
Set value 1.35

Souvenir Sheet

Perf. 13

1514 A205 100cor multicolored 2.50 1.25

Nos. 1509-1514 are airmail.

Flower Type of 1983

1986, Mar. **Litho.** *Perf. 12½*
1515 A151 5cor like #1209 35 15
1516 A151 5cor like #1210 35 15
1517 A151 5cor like #1211 35 15
1518 A151 5cor like #1212 35 15
1519 A151 5cor like #1213 35 15
1520 A151 5cor like #1214 35 15
1521 A151 5cor like #1215 35 15
1522 A151 5cor like #1216 35 15
1523 A151 5cor like #1217 35 15
1524 A151 5cor like #1218 35 15
1525 A151 5cor like #1219 35 15
1526 A151 5cor like #1220 35 15
1527 A151 5cor like #1221 35 15
1528 A151 5cor like #1222 35 15
1529 A151 5cor like #1223 35 15
1530 A151 5cor like #1224 35 15
Nos. 1515-1530 (16) 5.60
Set value 2.00

Agrarian Reform Type of 1983

1986, Apr. 15 *Perf. 12½*

1531 A168 1cor dk brown 15 15
1532 A168 9cor purple 20 15
1533 A168 15cor rose violet 32 16
1534 A168 21cor dk car rose 45 22
1535 A168 33cor orange 75 35
1536 A168 42cor green 95 45
1537 A168 50cor brown 1.10 55
1538 A168 100cor blue 2.25 1.10
Nos. 1531-1538 (8) 6.17 3.13

Writers
A207

1986, Apr. 23 *Perf. 12½x13*

1539 A207 1cor Alfonso Cortes 15 15
1540 A207 3cor Salomon de la Selva 15 15
1541 A207 3cor Azarias H. Pallais 15 15
1542 A207 5cor Ruben Dario 15 15
1543 A207 9cor Pablo Neruda 22 15
1544 A207 15cor Alfonso Reyes 35 18
1545 A207 100cor Pedro Henriquez Urena 2.25 1.10
Nos. 1539-1545 (7) 3.42
Set value 1.55

Nos. 1544-1545 are airmail.

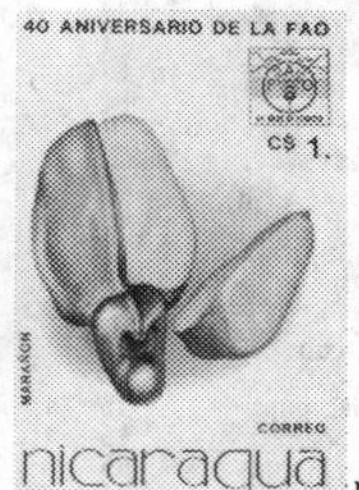

Nuts — A208

1986, June 20 *Perf. 12x12½*

1546 A208 1cor Maranon (cashew) 15 15
1547 A208 1cor Zapote 15 15
1548 A208 3cor Pitahaya 15 15
1549 A208 3cor Granadilla 15 15
1550 A208 5cor Anona 15 15
1551 A208 21cor Melocoton (star-fruit) 50 25
1552 A208 100cor Mamey 2.25 1.10
Set value 3.10 1.55

FAO, 40th Anniv. Nos. 1550-1552 are airmail.

Lockheed L-1011 Tristar
A209

Airplanes: No. 1554, YAK 40. No. 1555, BAC 1-11. No. 1556, Boeing 747. 9cor, A-300. 15cor, TU-154. No. 1559, Concorde, vert. No. 1560, Fairchild 340.

1986, Aug. 22 *Perf. 12½*

1553 A209 1cor multicolored 15 15
1554 A209 1cor multicolored 15 15
1555 A209 3cor multicolored 15 15
1556 A209 3cor multicolored 15 15
1557 A209 9cor multicolored 22 15
1558 A209 15cor multicolored 35 20
1559 A209 100cor multicolored 2.25 1.10
Set value 3.10 1.55

Souvenir Sheet

Perf. 13

1560 A209 100cor multicolored 2.50 1.25

Stockholmia '86. No. 1560 contains one 40x32mm stamp.

Nos. 1557-1560 airmail.

A210

A210a

Discovery of America, 500th Anniv. (in 1992) — A210b

1986, Oct. 12 *Perf. 12½x12*

1561 A210 1cor shown 15 15
1562 A210 1cor 2 of Columbus' ships 15 15
a. Pair, #1561-1562 15 15
b. Souv. sheet of 2, #1561-1562 15 15

Perf. 12x12½

1563 A210a 9cor Juan de la Cosa 20 15
1564 A210a 9cor Columbus 20 15
a. Pair, #1563-1564 40 20
1565 A210b 21cor Ferdinand, Isabella 50 25
1566 A210b 100cor Columbus before throne 2.25 1.10
a. Pair, #1565-1566 2.75 1.35
b. Souv. sheet of 4, #1563-1566 3.25 1.55
Nos. 1561-1566 (6) 3.45 1.95

Nos. 1563-1566 are airmail. Nos. 1564a, 1566a have continuous design.

Butterflies — A211

1986, Dec. 12 *Perf. 12½*

1567 A211 10cor Theritas coronata 24 15
1568 A211 15cor Charayes nitebis 35 18
1569 A211 15cor Salamis cacta 35 18
1570 A211 15cor Papilio maacki 35 18
1571 A211 25cor Euphaedro cyparissa 60 30
1572 A211 25cor Palaeochrysophonus hippothoe 60 30
1573 A211 30cor Ritra aurea 70 35
Nos. 1567-1573 (7) 3.19 1.64

Nos. 1568-1573 are airmail.

Ruben Dario Order of Cultural Independence
A212

Dario Order Winning Writers: No. 1574, Ernesto Mejia Sanchez. No. 1575, Fernando Gordillo C. No. 1576, Francisco Perez Estrada. 30cor, Julio Cortazar. 60cor, Enrique Fernandez Morales.

1987, Jan. 18 **Litho.** *Perf. 13*

1574 A212 10cor multicolored 22 15
1575 A212 10cor multicolored 22 15
1576 A212 10cor multicolored 22 15
1577 A212 15cor multicolored 32 16
1578 A212 30cor multicolored 65 32
1579 A212 60cor multicolored 1.25 65
a. Strip of 6, #1574-1579 2.90 1.50
b. Min. sheet of 6, #1574-1579 2.90 2.90
Nos. 1574-1579 (6) 2.88 1.58

1988 Winter Olympics, Calgary — A213

Designs: No. 1580, Speed skating. No. 1581, Ice hockey. No. 1582, Women's figure skating. No. 1583, Ski jumping. 20cor, Biathalon. 30cor, Slalom skiing. 40cor, Downhill skiing. 110cor, Ice hockey, diff., horiz.

1987, Feb. 3 *Perf. 13*

1580 A213 10cor multi 22 15
1581 A213 10cor multi 22 15
1582 A213 15cor multi 30 15
1583 A213 15cor multi 30 15
1584 A213 20cor multi 40 20
1585 A213 30cor multi 60 30
1586 A213 40cor multi 85 42
Nos. 1580-1586 (7) 2.89 1.52

Souvenir Sheet

Perf. 12½

1587 A213 110cor multi 2.25 2.25

Nos. 1582-1587 are airmail. No. 1587 contains one 40x32mm stamp.

Children's Welfare Campaign — A214

1987, Mar. 18 *Perf. 13*

1588 A214 10cor Growth & development 25 15
1589 A214 25cor Vaccination 60 30
1590 A214 30cor Rehydration 75 35
1591 A214 50cor Breastfeeding 1.25 60

Nos. 1589-1591 are airmail.

Flower Type of 1983

1987, Mar. 25 *Perf. 12½*

1592 A151 10cor Bixa orellana 20 15
1593 A151 10cor Brassavola nodosa 20 15
1594 A151 10cor Cattleya lueddemanniana 20 15
1595 A151 10cor Cochlospermum spec. 20 15
1596 A151 10cor Hibiscus rosa-sinensis 20 15
1597 A151 10cor Laella spec. 20 15
1598 A151 10cor Malvaviscus arboreus 20 15
1599 A151 10cor Neomarica coerulea 20 15
1600 A151 10cor Plumeria rubra 20 15
1601 A151 10cor Senecio spec. 20 15
1602 A151 10cor Sobralia macrantha 20 15
1603 A151 10cor Stachytarpheta indica 20 15
1604 A151 10cor Tabebula ochraceae 20 15
1605 A151 10cor Tagetes erecta 20 15
1606 A151 10cor Tecoma stans 20 15
1607 A151 10cor Thumbergia alata 20 15
Nos. 1592-1607 (16) 3.20
Set value 1.70

Agrarian Reform Type of 1983 Inscribed "1987"

Designs: No. 1608, Tobacco. No. 1609, Cotton. 15cor, Corn. 25cor, Sugar. 30cor, Cattle. 50cor, Coffee Beans. 60cor, Rice. 100cor, Bananas.

1987, Mar. 25 *Perf. 12½*

1608 A168 10cor dk brown 28 15
1609 A168 10cor purple 28 15
1610 A168 15cor rose violet 45 22
1611 A168 25cor dk car rose 70 35
1612 A168 30cor orange 85 45
1613 A168 50cor brown 1.40 65
1614 A168 60cor green 1.75 90
1615 A168 100cor blue 2.75 1.40
Nos. 1608-1615 (8) 8.46 4.27

77th Interparliamentary Conf., Managua — A215

1987, Apr. 27

1616 A215 10cor multicolored 18 15

Prehistoric Creatures — A216

1987, May 25 *Perf. 13*

1617 A216 10cor Mammoth 18 15
1618 A216 10cor Dimetrodon 18 15
1619 A216 10cor Triceratops 18 15
1620 A216 15cor Dinichthys 22 15
1621 A216 15cor Uintaterium 22 15
1622 A216 30cor Pteranodon 55 25
1623 A216 40cor Tilosaurus 75 32
Nos. 1617-1623 (7) 2.28 1.32

Nos. 1620-1623 are airmail.

CAPEX '87 — A217

Various tennis players in action.

1987, June 2 *Perf. 13*

1624 A217 10cor Male player 20 15
1625 A217 10cor Female player 20 15
1626 A217 15cor Player at net 30 15
1627 A217 15cor Female player, diff. 30 15
1628 A217 20cor multi 35 20
1629 A217 30cor multi 60 30
1630 A217 40cor multi 90 40
Nos. 1624-1630 (7) 2.85 1.50

Souvenir Sheet

Perf. 12½

1631 A217	110cor Doubles partners, vert.		2.25	2.25

Nos. 1626-1631 are airmail. No. 1631 contains one 32x40mm stamp.

Dogs — A218

1987, June 25 *Perf. 13*

1632	A218	10cor Doberman pinscher	20	15
1633	A218	10cor Bulldog	20	15
1634	A218	15cor Pekinese	30	15
1635	A218	15cor Chow	30	15
1636	A218	20cor Chihuahua	40	20
1637	A218	30cor St. Bernard	60	30
1638	A218	40cor West Gotha spitz	85	40
		Nos. 1632-1638 (7)	2.85	1.50

Nos. 1634-1638 are airmail.

Cacti A219

1987, July 25 *Perf. 12½*

1639	A219	10cor Lophocereus schottii	20	15
1640	A219	10cor Opuntia acanthocarpa	20	15
1641	A219	10cor Echinocereus engelmanii	20	15
1642	A219	20cor Lemaireocereus thurberi	40	20
1643	A219	20cor Saguaros	40	20
1644	A219	30cor Opuntia fulgida	60	30
1645	A219	50cor Opuntia ficus	1.00	50
		Nos. 1639-1645 (7)	3.00	1.65

Nos. 1642-1645 are airmail.

10th Pan American Games, Indianapolis — A220

1987, Aug. 7 *Perf. 13*

1646	A220	10cor High jump	20	15
1647	A220	10cor Volleyball	20	15
1648	A220	15cor Sprinter	30	22
1649	A220	15cor Gymnastics	30	22
1650	A220	20cor Baseball	42	30
1651	A220	30cor Synchronized swimming	60	45
1652	A220	40cor Weightlifting	85	60
		Nos. 1646-1652 (7)	2.87	2.09

Souvenir Sheet

1653	A220	110cor Rhythmic gymnastics	2.25	2.25

Nos. 1648-1653 are airmail. No. 1653 contains one 32x40mm stamp. Nos. 1651-1653 are vert.

Satellites A221

1987, Oct. 4

1654	A221	10cor Sputnik	20	15
1655	A221	10cor Cosmos	20	15
1656	A221	15cor Proton	30	15
1657	A221	25cor Meteor	50	22
1658	A221	25cor Luna	50	22
1659	A221	30cor Electron	60	30
1660	A221	50cor Mars 1	90	50
		Nos. 1654-1660 (7)	3.20	1.69

Cosmonauts' Day. Nos. 1656-1660 are airmail.

Fish — A222

Designs: No. 1661, Tarpon atlanticus. No. 1662, Cichlasoma managuense. No. 1663, Atractoteus tropicus. No. 1664, Astyana fasciatus. No. 1665, Cichlasoma citrimellum. 20cor, Cichlosoma dowi. 50cor, Caracharhinus nicaraguensis.

1987, Oct. 18 *Perf. 12½*

1661	A222	10cor multicolored	20	15
1662	A222	10cor multicolored	20	15
1663	A222	10cor multicolored	20	15
1664	A222	15cor multicolored	30	15
1665	A222	15cor multicolored	30	15
1666	A222	20cor multicolored	40	20
1667	A222	50cor multicolored	1.00	50
		Nos. 1661-1667 (7)	2.60	1.45

Nos. 1663-1667 are airmail.

October Revolution, 70th Anniv. — A223

Designs: 30cor, Cruiser Aurora, horiz. 50cor, USSR natl. arms.

1987, Nov. 7 *Perf. 13*

1668	A223	10cor multicolored	22	15
1669	A223	30cor multicolored	60	35
1670	A223	50cor multicolored	1.00	60

Nos. 1669-1670 are airmail.

Christmas Paintings by L. Saenz — A224

1987, Nov. 15 *Perf. 13*

1671	A224	10cor Nativity	15	15
1672	A224	20cor Adoration of the Magi	30	15
1673	A224	25cor Adoration of the Magi, diff.	35	18
1674	A224	50cor Nativity, diff.	75	35

1988 Winter Olymmpics, Calgary — A225

1988, Jan. 30 **Litho.** *Perf. 12½*

1675	A225	10cor Biathlon	18	15
1676	A225	10cor Cross-country skiing, vert.	18	15
1677	A225	15cor Hockey, vert.	35	15
1678	A225	20cor Women's figure skating, vert.	50	20
1679	A225	25cor Slalom skiing, vert.	65	30
1680	A225	30cor Ski jumping	75	40
1681	A225	40cor Men's downhill skiing, vert.	1.00	50
		Nos. 1675-1681 (7)	3.61	1.85

Souvenir Sheet

Perf. 13

1682	A225	100cor Pairs figure skating	2.00	2.00

Nos. 1675-1681 printed with se-tenant label showing Canadian flag and wildlife.

No. 1682 contains one 40x32mm stamp.

Nicaraguan Journalists Assoc., 10th Anniv. — A226

Design: 5cor, Churches of St. Francis Xavier and Fatima, and speaker addressing journalists, horiz.

1988, Feb. 10

1683	A226	1cor shown	15	15
1684	A226	5cor multicolored	75	40

No. 1684 is airmail.

1988 Summer Olympics, Seoul — A227

1988, Feb. 28

1685	A227	10cor Gymnastics	18	15
1686	A227	10cor Basketball	18	15
1687	A227	15cor Volleyball	35	15
1688	A227	20cor Long jump	50	20
1689	A227	25cor Soccer	65	25
1690	A227	30cor Water polo	75	40
1691	A227	40cor Boxing	1.00	50
		Nos. 1685-1691 (7)	3.61	1.80

Souvenir Sheet

1692	A227	100cor Baseball	2.00	2.00

No. 1692 contains one 40x32mm stamp.

European Soccer Championships, Essen — A228

Designs: Various soccer players in action.

Perf. 13x12½, 12½x13

1988, Apr. 14

1693	A228	50c multicolored	15	15
1694	A228	1cor multicolored	15	15
1695	A228	2cor multi, vert.	25	15
1696	A228	3cor multi, vert.	40	22
1697	A228	4cor multi, vert.	55	25
1698	A228	5cor multi, vert.	75	35
1699	A228	6cor multicolored	85	40
		Nos. 1693-1699 (7)	3.10	1.67

Souvenir Sheet

Perf. 13

1700	A228	15cor multi, vert.	2.00	2.00

Nos. 1695-1700 are airmail. No. 1700 contains one 32x40mm stamp.

Sandanista Revolution, 9th Anniv. — A229

1988, July 19 *Perf. 13*

1701	A229	1cor shown	15	15
1702	A229	5cor Volcanoes, dove	60	30

No. 1702 is airmail.

Animals — A230

1988, Mar. 3 *Perf. 13x12½*

1703	A230	10c Bear, cub	15	15
1704	A230	15c Lion, cubs	15	15
1705	A230	25c Spaniel, pups	15	15
1706	A230	50c Wild boars	15	15
1707	A230	4cor Cheetah, cubs	85	35
1708	A230	7cor Hyenas	1.25	70
1709	A230	8cor Fox, kit	1.50	80
		Nos. 1703-1709 (7)	4.20	2.45

Souvenir Sheet

Perf. 12½

1710	A230	15cor House cat, kittens, vert.	2.00	1.65

Nos. 1707-1710 are airmail. No. 1710 contains one 32x40mm stamp.

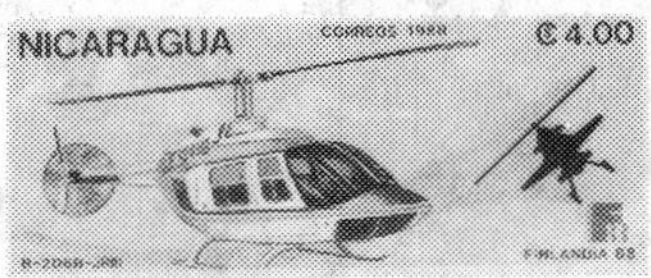

Helicopters — A231

Illustration reduced.

1988, June 1 *Perf. 12½x12*

1711	A231	4cor B-206B-JRIII	15	15
1712	A231	12cor BK-117A-3	20	15
1713	A231	16cor B-360	28	15
1714	A231	20cor 109-MRII	35	18
1715	A231	24cor S-61	42	20
1716	A231	28cor SA-365N-D2	50	25
1717	A231	56cor S-76	1.00	50
		Nos. 1711-1717 (7)	2.90	1.58

Souvenir Sheet

Perf. 13

1718	A231	120cor NH-90	2.50	2.50

Nos. 1712-1718 are airmail. No. 1718 contains one 40x32mm stamp.

Shells — A232

1988, Sept. 20 *Perf. 13*

No.	Type	Value	Description	Unused	Used
1719	A232	4cor	Strombus pugilis	15	15
1720	A232	12cor	Polymita picta	24	15
1721	A232	16cor	Architectonica maximum	32	16
1722	A232	20cor	Pectens laqueatus	40	20
1723	A232	24cor	Guildfordia triumphans	50	24
1724	A232	28cor	Ranella pustulosa	55	32
1725	A232	50cor	Trochus maculatus	1.00	50
			Nos. 1719-1725 (7)	3.16	1.72

Nos. 1720-1725 are airmail.

Insects — A233

1988, Nov. 10

No.	Type	Value	Description	Unused	Used
1726	A233	4cor	Chrysina macropus	15	15
1727	A233	12cor	Plusiotis victoriana	25	15
1728	A233	16cor	Ceratotrupes bolivari	35	16
1729	A233	20cor	Gymnetosoma stellata	45	20
1730	A233	24cor	Euphoria lineoligera	55	25
1731	A233	28cor	Euphoria candezei	60	30
1732	A233	50cor	Sulcophanaeus chryseicollis	1.10	50
			Nos. 1726-1732 (7)	3.45	1.71

Nos. 1727-1732 are airmail.

Heroes of the Revolution — A234

Designs: 4cor, Casimiro Sotelo Montenegro. 12cor, Ricardo Morales Aviles. 16cor, Silvio Mayorga Delgado. 20cor, Pedro Arauz Palacios. 24cor, Oscar A. Turcios Chavarrias. 28cor, Julio C. Buitrago Urroz. 50cor, Jose B. Escobar Perez. 100cor, Eduardo E. Contreras Escobar.

1988, Aug. 27 *Perf. $12^1/_2$x12*

No.	Type	Value	Description	Unused	Used
1733	A234	4cor	sky blue	15	15
1734	A234	12cor	red lilac	24	15
1735	A234	16cor	yel grn	32	16
1736	A234	20cor	org brown	40	20
1737	A234	24cor	brown	45	24
1738	A234	28cor	purple	55	32
1739	A234	50cor	henna brown	95	50
1740	A234	100cor	plum	1.90	95
			Nos. 1733-1740 (8)	4.96	2.67

Nos. 1734-1740 are airmail.

Flowers — A235

Designs: 4cor, Acacia baileyana. 12cor, Anigozanthos manglesii. 16cor, Telopia speciosissima. 20cor, Eucalyptus ficifolia. 24cor, Boronia heterophylla. 28cor, Callistemon speciosus. 30cor, Nymphaea caerulea, horiz. 50cor, Clianthus formosus.

1988, Aug. 30 *Perf. 13*

No.	Type	Value	Description	Unused	Used
1741	A235	4cor	multicolored	15	15
1742	A235	12cor	multicolored	24	15
1743	A235	16cor	multicolored	32	16
1744	A235	20cor	multicolored	40	20
1745	A235	24cor	multicolored	45	24
1746	A235	28cor	multicolored	55	48
1747	A235	30cor	multicolored	60	30
1748	A235	50cor	multicolored	1.00	45
			Nos. 1741-1748 (8)	3.71	2.13

Nos. 1742-1748 are airmail.

A236

A237

Pre-Columbian Art: 4cor, Zapotec funeral urn. 12cor, Mochica ceramic kneeling man. 16cor, Mochica ceramic head. 20cor, Taina ceramic vase. 28cor, Nazca cup, horiz. 100cor, Inca pipe, horiz. 120cor, Aztec ceramic vessel, horiz.

Perf. 12x$12^1/_2$, $12^1/_2$x12

1988, Oct. 12

No.	Type	Value	Description	Unused	Used
1749	A236	4cor	multicolored	15	15
1750	A236	12cor	multicolored	24	15
1751	A236	16cor	multicolored	32	16
1752	A236	20cor	multicolored	40	20
1753	A236	28cor	multicolored	55	28
1754	A236	100cor	multicolored	1.90	1.00
			Nos. 1749-1754 (6)	3.56	1.94

Souvenir Sheet

Perf. 13x$13^1/_2$

No.	Type	Value	Description	Unused	Used
1755	A236	120cor	multicolored	2.25	1.10

Discovery of America, 500th anniv. (in 1992). Nos. 1750-1755 are airmail. Nos. 1749-1754 printed with se-tenant label. No. 1755 contains one 40x32mm stamp.

1988, Oct. 12 *Perf. 12x$12^1/_2$*

No.	Type	Value	Description	Unused	Used
1756	A237	25cor	Ruben Dario	45	20

Publication of "Blue," centenary. Printed se-tenant with label.

Tourism A238

1989, Feb. 5 *Perf. $12^1/_2$x12*

No.	Type	Value	Description	Unused	Used
1757	A238	4cor	Pochomil	15	15
1758	A238	12cor	Granada	24	16
1759	A238	20cor	Olof Palme Convention Center	40	20
1760	A238	24cor	Masaya Volcano Natl. Park	45	24
1761	A238	28cor	La Boquita	55	25
1762	A238	30cor	Xiloa	60	25
1763	A238	50cor	Hotels of Managua	1.00	45
			Nos. 1757-1763 (7)	3.39	1.70

Souvenir Sheet

Perf. 13

No.	Type	Value	Description	Unused	Used
1764	A238	160cor	Montelimar	2.00	2.00

Nos. 1758-1764 are airmail. No. 1764 contains one 40x32mm stamp.

French Revolution, Bicentennial A240

Designs: 50cor, Procession of the Estates General, Versailles. 300cor, Oath of the Tennis Court. 600cor, 14th of July, vert. 1000cor, Dancing Around the Liberty Tree. 2000cor, Liberty Guiding the People, vert. 3000cor, Storming the Bastille. 5000cor, Lafayette Swearing Allegiance to the Constitution, vert. 9000cor, La Marseillaise, vert.

Perf. $12^1/_2$x13 (50cor), 13x$12^1/_2$ (600, 2000cor), $12^1/_2$

1989, July 14

Sizes: 50cor, 40x25mm

600cor, 2000cor, 33x44mm

No.	Type	Value	Description	Unused	Used
1773	A240	50cor	multicolored	15	15
1774	A240	300cor	shown	15	15
1775	A240	600cor	multicolored	16	15
1776	A240	1000cor	multicolored	28	15
1777	A240	2000cor	multicolored	55	28
1778	A240	3000cor	multicolored	90	42
1779	A240	5000cor	multicolored	1.40	65
			Nos. 1773-1779 (7)	3.59	1.95

Souvenir Sheet

Perf. $12^1/_2$

No.	Type	Value	Description	Unused	Used
1780	A240	9000cor	multicolored	2.25	2.25

Philexfrance '89. #1774-1780 are airmail. #1780 contains one 32x40mm stamp.

Currency Reform

Currency reform took place Mar. 4, 1990. Until stamps in the new currency were issued mail was to be handstamped "Franqueo Pagado," (Postage Paid). Stamps were not used again until Apr. 25, 1991. The following four sets were sold by the post office but were not valid for postage.

Ships

Stamp World London '90: 500cor, *Director.* 1000cor, *Independence.* 3000cor, *Orizaba.* 5000cor, SS *Lewis.* 10,000cor, *Golden Rule.* 30,000cor, *Santiago de Cuba.* 75,000cor, *Bahia de Corinto.* 100,000cor, *North Star.*

1990, Apr. 3 *Perf. $12^1/_2$x12*

500cor multi
1000cor multi
3000cor multi
5000cor multi
10,000cor multi
30,000cor multi
100,000cor multi

Souvenir Sheet

Perf. $12^1/_2$

75,000cor multi

World Cup Soccer Championships, Italy

Designs: Various soccer players in action.

1990, Apr. 30 *Perf. 13*

500cor multi
1000cor multi
3000cor multi
5000cor multi
10,000cor multi
30,000cor multi
100,000cor multi

Souvenir Sheet

Perf. $12^1/_2$

75,000cor multi

1992 Winter Olympics, Albertville

Designs: 500cor, Ski jumping. 1000cor, Downhill skiing. 3000cor, Figure skating, vert. 5000cor, Speed skating, vert. 10,000cor, Biathlon, vert. 30,000cor, Cross country skiing, vert. 75,000cor, Two-man bobsled, vert. 100,000cor, Ice hockey, vert.

1990, July 25 *Perf. 13*

500cor multi
1000cor multi
3000cor multi
5000cor multi
10,000cor multi
30,000cor multi
100,000cor multi

Souvenir Sheet

Perf. $12^1/_2$

75,000cor multi

1992 Summer Olympics, Barcelona

Designs: 500cor, Javelin. 1000cor, Steeplechase. 3000cor, Handball. 5000cor, Basketball. 10,000cor, Gymnastics. 30,000cor, Cycling. 75,000cor, Soccer. 100,000cor, Boxing, horiz.

1990, Aug. 10 *Perf. 13*

500cor multi
1000cor multi
3000cor multi
5000cor multi
10,000cor multi
30,000cor multi
100,000cor multi

Souvenir Sheet

75,000cor multi

Birds A245

Designs: No. 1813, Apteryx owenii. No. 1814, Notornis mantelli. 10c, Cyanoramphus novaezelandiae. 20c, Gallirallus australis. 30c, Rhynochetos jubatus, vert. 60c, Nestor notabilis. 70c, Strigops habroptilus. 1.50cor, Cygnus atratus.

1990, Aug. 14 **Litho.** *Perf. $12^1/_2$*

No.	Type	Value	Description	Unused	Used
1813	A245	5c	multicolored	15	15
1814	A245	5c	multicolored	15	15
1815	A245	10c	multicolored	20	15
1816	A245	20c	multicolored	42	20
1817	A245	30c	multicolored	65	32
1818	A245	60c	multicolored	1.30	65
1819	A245	70c	multicolored	1.50	75
			Nos. 1813-1819 (7)	4.37	2.37

Souvenir Sheet

No.	Type	Value	Description	Unused	Used
1820	A245	1.50cor	multicolored	3.25	1.60

New Zealand '90, Intl. Philatelic Exhibition.

Fauna A246

1990, Oct. 10
1821 A246 5c Panthera onca 15 15
1822 A246 5c Felis pardalis, vert. 15 15
1823 A246 10c Atelles geoffrogi, vert. 20 15
1824 A246 20c Tapirus bairdi 42 20
1825 A246 30c Dasypus novencintus 65 32
1826 A246 60c Canis latrans 1.30 65
1827 A246 70c Choloepus hoffmanni 1.50 75
Nos. 1821-1827 (7) 4.37 2.37

FAO, 45th anniv.

Flower Type of 1983 Redrawn Without Date

1991, Apr. 24 Litho. *Perf. 14x13½*

Size: 19x22mm

1828 A151 1cor like #1220 40 15
1829 A151 2cor like #1212 80 15
1830 A151 3cor like #1218 1.20 15
1831 A151 4cor like #1219 1.60 15
1832 A151 5cor like #1217 2.00 15
1833 A151 6cor like #1210 2.40 15
1834 A151 7cor like #1216 2.80 15
1835 A151 8cor like #1215 3.20 15
1836 A151 9cor like #1211 3.60 15
1837 A151 10cor like #1221 4.00 15
1838 A151 11cor like #1214 4.40 15
1839 A151 12cor like #1222 4.80 15
1840 A151 13cor like #1213 5.20 15
1841 A151 14cor like #1224 5.60 15
1842 A151 15cor like #1223 6.00 15
1843 A151 16cor like #1209 6.40 15
Nos. 1828-1843 (16) 54.40
Set value 1.25

Dr. Pedro Joaquin Chamorro — A247

1991, Apr. 25 *Perf. 14½x14*
1844 A247 2.25cor multicolored 90 45

1990 World Cup Soccer Championships, Italy — A248

Designs: No. 1845, Two players. No. 1846, Four players, vert. 50c, Two players, referee. 1cor, Germany, five players, vert. 1.50cor, One player, vert. 3cor, Argentina, five players, vert. 3.50cor, Italian players. 7.50cor, German team with trophy.

Perf. 14x14½, 14½x14

1991, July 16
1845 A248 25c multicolored 15 15
1846 A248 25c multicolored 15 15
1847 A248 50c multicolored 20 15
1848 A248 1cor multicolored 40 20
1849 A248 1.50cor multicolored 60 30
1850 A248 3cor multicolored 1.20 60
1851 A248 3.50cor multicolored 1.40 70
Nos. 1845-1851 (7) 4.10 2.25

Souvenir Sheet
1852 A248 7.50cor multicolored 3.00 1.50

Butterflies — A249

Designs: No. 1853, Prepona praeneste. No. 1854, Anartia fatima. 50c, Eryphanis aesacus. 1cor, Heliconius melpomene. 1.50cor, Chlosyne janais. 3cor, Marpesia iole. 3.50cor, Metamorpha epaphus. 7.50cor, Morpho peleides.

1991, July 16 *Perf. 14½x14*
1853 A249 25c multicolored 15 15
1854 A249 25c multicolored 15 15
1855 A249 50c multicolored 20 15
1856 A249 1cor multicolored 40 20
1857 A249 1.50cor multicolored 60 30
1858 A249 3cor multicolored 1.20 60
1859 A249 3.50cor multicolored 1.40 70
Nos. 1853-1859 (7) 4.10 2.25

Souvenir Sheet
1860 A249 7.50cor multicolored 3.00 1.50

Miniature Sheet

Fauna of Rainforest — A250

Designs: a, Yellow-headed amazon. b, Toucan. c, Scarlet macaw (lapa roja). d, Quetzal. e, Spider monkey (mono arana). f, Capuchin monkey. g, Sloth (cucala). h, Oropendola. i, Violet sabrewing (colibri violeta). j, Tamandua. k, Jaguarundi. l, Boa constrictor. m, Iguana. n, Jaguar. o, White-necked jacobin. p, Doxocopa clothilda. q, Dismorphia deione. r, Golden arrow-poison frog (rana venenosa). s, Callithomia hezia. t, Chameleon.

1991, Aug. 7 Litho. *Perf. 14x14½*
1861 A250 2.25cor Sheet of 20, #a.-t. 19.00 9.50

America Issue — A251

1991, Oct. 12 *Perf. 14½x14*
1862 A251 2.25cor Concepcion volcano 95 48

Orchids A252

Designs: No. 1863, Isochilus major. No. 1864, Cycnoches ventricosum. 50c, Vanilla odorata. 1cor, Helleriella nicaraguensis. 1.50cor, Barkeria spectabilis. 3cor, Maxillaria hedwigae. 3.50cor, Cattleya aurantiaca. 7.50cor, Psygmorchis pusilla, vert.

1991 Litho. *Perf. 14x14½*
1863 A252 25c multicolored 15 15
1864 A252 25c multicolored 15 15
1865 A252 50c multicolored 16 15
1866 A252 1cor multicolored 32 16
1867 A252 1.50cor multicolored 48 24
1868 A252 3cor multicolored 95 48
1869 A252 3.50cor multicolored 1.10 55
Nos. 1863-1869 (7) 3.31 1.88

Souvenir Sheet

Perf. 14½x14
1870 A252 7.50cor multicolored 3.00 1.50

Locomotives of South America — A253

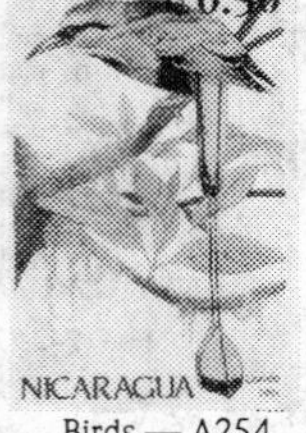

Birds — A254

Various steam locomotives.

1991, Apr. 21 *Perf. 14½x14*
1871 A253 25c Bolivia 15 15
1872 A253 25c Peru 15 15
1873 A253 50c Argentina 16 15
1874 A253 1.50cor Chile 48 24
1875 A253 2cor Colombia 65 32
1876 A253 3cor Brazil 95 48
1877 A253 3.50cor Paraguay 1.10 55
Nos. 1871-1877 (7) 3.64 2.04

Souvenir Sheets
1878 A253 7.50cor Nicaragua 2.50 1.25
1879 A253 7.50cor Guatemala 2.50 1.25

1991 *Perf. 14½x14, 14x14½*

Designs: 50c, Eumomota superciliosa. 75c, Trogon collaris. 1cor, Electron platyrhynchum. 1.50cor, Teleonema filicauda. 1.75cor, Tangara chilensis, horiz. No. 1885, Pharomachrus mocino. No. 1886, Phlegopsis nigromaculata. No. 1887, Hylophylax naevioides, horiz. No. 1888, Aulacorhynchus haematopygius, horiz.

1880 A254 50c multicolored 16 15
1881 A254 75c multicolored 24 15
1882 A254 1cor multicolored 32 16
1883 A254 1.50cor multicolored 48 24
1884 A254 1.75cor multicolored 55 28
1885 A254 2.25cor multicolored 75 35
1886 A254 2.25cor multicolored 75 35
Nos. 1880-1886 (7) 3.25 1.68

Souvenir Sheets
1887 A254 7.50cor multicolored 2.50 1.25
1888 A254 7.50cor multicolored 2.50 1.25

Paintings by Vincent Van Gogh — A255

Designs: No. 1889, Head of a Peasant Woman Wearing a Bonnet. No. 1890, One-Eyed Man. 50c, Self-Portrait. 1cor, Vase with Carnations and Other Flowers. 1.50cor, Vase with Zinnias and Geraniums. 3cor, Portrait of Pere Tanguy. 3.50cor, Portrait of a Man, horiz. 7.50cor, Path Lined with Poplars, horiz.

1991 *Perf. 14x13½, 13½x14*
1889 A255 25c multicolored 15 15
1890 A255 25c multicolored 15 15
1891 A255 50c multicolored 16 15
1892 A255 1cor multicolored 32 16
1893 A255 1.50cor multicolored 48 24
1894 A255 3cor multicolored 95 48
1895 A255 3.50cor multicolored 1.10 55
Nos. 1889-1895 (7) 3.31 1.88

Size: 128x102mm

Imperf
1896 A255 7.50cor multicolored 2.50 1.25

Phila Nippon '91 A256

Designs: 25c, Golden Hall. 50c, Phoenix Hall. 1cor, Bunraku puppet head. 1.50cor, Japanese cranes. 2.50cor, Himeji Castle. 3cor, Statue of the Guardian. 3.50cor, Kabuki warrior. 7.50cor, Vase.

1991 *Perf. 14x14½*
1897 A256 25c multicolored 15 15
1898 A256 50c multicolored 16 15
1899 A256 1cor multicolored 32 16
1900 A256 1.50cor multicolored 48 24
1901 A256 2.50cor multicolored 80 40
1902 A256 3cor multicolored 95 48
1903 A256 3.50cor multicolored 1.10 55
Nos. 1897-1903 (7) 3.96 2.13

Souvenir Sheet
1904 A256 7.50cor multicolored 2.50 1.25

Inscriptions are switched on 50c and 2.50cor.

Child's Drawing A257

1991
1905 A257 2.25cor multicolored 72 36

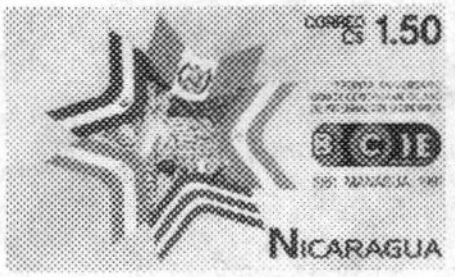

Central American Bank of Economic Integration, 30th Anniv. A258

1991 Litho. *Perf. 14*
1906 A258 1.50cor multicolored 65 52

No. 1906 printed with se-tenant label.

Discovery of America, 500th Anniv. (in 1992) — A259

1991 *Perf. 14½x14*
1907 A259 2.25cor Columbus' fleet 95 75

Swiss Confederation, 700th Anniv. (in 1991) — A260

1992 Litho. *Perf. 14x14½*
1908 A260 2.25cor black & red 95 75

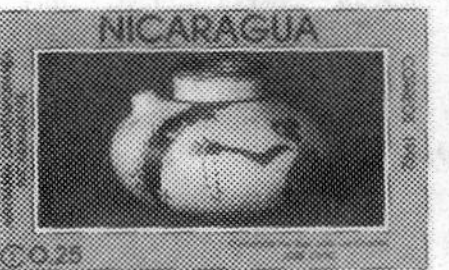

Contemporary Art — A261

Designs: No. 1909, Pitcher, by Jose Ortiz. No. 1910, Black jar, by Lorenza Pineda Cooperative, vert. 50c, Vase, by Elio Gutierrez, vert. 1cor, Christ on Cross, by Jose de Los Santos, vert. 1.50cor, Sculpture of family, by Erasmo Moya, vert. 3cor, Bird and fish, by Silvio Chavarria Cooperative. 3.50cor, Filigree jar, by Maria de Los Angeles Bermudez, vert. 7.50cor, Masks by Jose Flores.

1992 Litho. ***Perf. 14x14½, 14½x14***

1909 A261 25c multicolored 15 15
1910 A261 25c multicolored 15 15
1911 A261 50c multicolored 22 15
1912 A261 1cor multicolored 45 22
1913 A261 1.50cor multicolored 65 32
1914 A261 3cor multicolored 1.30 65
1915 A261 3.50cor multicolored 1.50 75
Nos. 1909-1915 (7) 4.42 2.39

Imperf

Size: 100x70mm

1916 A261 7.50cor multicolored 3.25 1.60

Miniature Sheet

Fauna and Flora of Rainforest — A262

Designs: a, Colibri magnifico (b). b, Aguila arpia (f). c, Orchids. d, Toucan, Mariposa morpho. e, Quetzal (i). f, Guardabarranco (g, k). g, Mono aullador (howler monkey). h, Perezoso (sloth). i, Mono ardilla (squirrel monkey). j, Guacamaya (macaw) (n). k, Boa esmeralda, Tanagra escarlata (emerald boa, scarlet tanager). l, Rana flecha venenosa (arrow frog). m, Jaguar. n, Oso hormiguero (anteater) (o). o, Ocelot. p, Coati.

1992 ***Perf. 14½x14***

1917 A262 1.50cor Sheet of 16, #a.-p. 10.00 5.00

1992 Winter Olympics, Albertville A263

1992 ***Perf. 14x14½, 14½x14***

1918 A263 25c Ice hockey 15 15
1919 A263 25c 4-man bobsled 15 15
1920 A263 50c Combined slalom, vert. 22 15
1921 A263 1cor Speed skating 45 22
1922 A263 1.50cor Cross-country skiing 65 32
1923 A263 3cor Double luge 1.35 65
1924 A263 3.50cor Ski jumping, vert. 1.50 75
Nos. 1918-1924 (7) 4.47 2.39

Imperf

Size: 100x70mm

1925 A263 7.50cor Slalom 3.15 1.60

1992 Summer Olympics, Barcelona A264

1992 Litho. ***Perf. 14x14½, 14½x14***

1926 A264 25c Javelin 15 15
1927 A264 25c Fencing 15 15
1928 A264 50c Basketball 22 15
1929 A264 1.50cor 1500-meter race 65 32
1930 A264 2cor Long jump 85 42
1931 A264 3cor Women's 10,000-meter race 1.25 65
1932 A264 3.50cor Equestrian 1.50 75
Nos. 1926-1932 (7) 4.77 2.59

Imperf

Size: 100x70mm

1933 A264 7.50cor Canoeing 3.15 1.60

Nos. 1927-1932 are vert. Dated 1991.

Father R. M. Fabretto and Children A265

1992 Litho. ***Perf. 14x14½***

1934 A265 2.25cor multicolored 95 48

Nicaraguan Natives, by Claudia Gordillo A266

1992

1935 A266 2.25cor black & brown 95 48

Nicaraguan Caciques, by Milton Jose Cruz A267

1992

1936 A267 2.25cor multicolored 95 48

Contemporary Paintings — A268

Paintings by: No. 1937, Alberto Ycaza, vert. No. 1938, Alejandro Arostegui, vert. 50c, Bernard Dreyfus. 1.50cor, Orlando Sobalvarro. 2cor, Hugo Palma. 3cor, Omar D'Leon. 3.50cor, Carlos Montenegro, vert. 7.50cor, Federico Nordalm.

1992 ***Perf. 14½x14, 14x14½***

1937 A268 25c multicolored 15 15
1938 A268 25c multicolored 15 15
1939 A268 50c multicolored 22 15
1940 A268 1.50cor multicolored 65 32
1941 A268 2cor multicolored 85 42
1942 A268 3cor multicolored 1.25 65
1943 A268 3.50cor multicolored 1.50 75
Nos. 1937-1943 (7) 4.77 2.59

Imperf

Size: 100x70mm

1944 A268 7.50cor multicolored 3.15 1.60

AIR POST STAMPS

Counterfeits exist of almost all scarce surcharges among Nos. C1-C66.

Regular Issues of 1914-28 Overprinted in Red

Correo Aéreo
1929
P.A.A.

1929, May 15 Unwmk. ***Perf. 12***

C1 A24 25c orange 1.75 1.75
a. Double overprint, one inverted 50.00
b. Inverted overprint 50.00
c. Double overprint 50.00
C2 A24 25c blk brn 2.25 2.25
a. Double overprint, one inverted 50.00
b. Double overprint 50.00
c. Inverted overprint 30.00

There are numerous varieties in the setting of the overprint. The most important are: Large "1" in "1929" and large "A" in "Aereo" and "P. A. A."

Similar Overprint on Regular Issue of 1929 in Red

C3 A24 25c dk vio 1.25 75
a. Double overprint 50.00
b. Inverted overprint 50.00
c. Double overprint, one inverted 50.00

The stamps in the bottom row of the sheet have the letters "P. A. A." larger than usual.

Airplanes over Mt. Momotombo AP1

1929, Dec. 15 **Engr.**

C4 AP1 25c olive blk 50 40
C5 AP1 50c blk brn 75 75
C6 AP1 1cor org red 1.00 1.00

See Nos. C18-C19, C164-C168. For surcharges and overprints see Nos. C7-C8, C14-C17, C25-C31, C106-C120, C135-C146, C150-C154, C169-C173, CO25-CO29.

No. C4 Surcharged in Red or Black

Vale
C$ 0.15

1930, May 15

C7 AP1 15c on 25c ol blk (R) 50 40
a. "$" inverted 3.50
b. Double surcharge (R + Bk) 7.00
c. As "b," red normal, blk invtd. 7.00
d. Double red surch., one inverted 7.00
C8 AP1 20c on 25c ol blk (Bk) 75 60
a. "$" inverted 7.00
b. Inverted surcharge 15.00

Nos. C1, C2 and C3 Surcharged in Green

Vale ₡ 0.15
1931

1931, June 7

C9 A24 15c on 25c org 50.00 50.00
C10 A24 15c on 25c blk brn 100.00 100.00
C11 A24 15c on 25c dk vio 15.00 15.00
c. Inverted surcharge 30.00
C12 A24 20c on 25c dk vio 10.00 10.00
c. Inverted surcharge 50.00
d. Double surcharge 50.00
C13 A24 20c on 25c blk brn *375.00*

No. C13 was not regularly issued.

"1391"

C9a A24 15c on 25c
C10a A24 15c on 25c
C11a A24 15c on 25c 60.00
d. As "a," inverted 400.00
C12a A24 20c on 25c 25.00
e. As "a," inverted 400.00
g. As "a," double 400.00
C13a A24 20c on 25c

"1921"

C9b A24 15c on 25c
C10b A24 15c on 25c 400.00
C11b A24 15c on 25c 60.00
e. As "b," inverted 400.00
C12b A24 20c on 25c 25.00
f. As "b," inverted 400.00
h. As "b," double 400.00
C13b A24 20c on 25c

Nos. C8, C4-C6 Surcharged in Blue

1931
₡ 0.15

1931, June

C14 AP1 15c on 20c on 25c 9.00 9.00
b. Blue surcharge inverted 25.00
c. "$" in blk, surch. invtd. 50.00
d. Blue surch. dbl., one invtd. 25.00
C15 AP1 15c on 25c 5.50 5.50
b. Blue surcharge inverted 25.00
c. Double surch., one invtd. 25.00
C16 AP1 15c on 50c 40.00 40.00
C17 AP1 15c on 1cor 100.00 100.00

"1391"

C14a AP1 15c on 20c on 25c 50.00
C15a AP1 15c on 25c 30.00
C16a AP1 15c on 50c 80.00
C17a AP1 15c on 1cor 225.00

Momotombo Type of 1929

1931, July 8

C18 AP1 15c deep violet 16 15
C19 AP1 20c deep green 42 38

Managua Post Office Before and After Earthquake AP2

Without gum, Soft porous paper

1932, Jan. 1 Litho. ***Perf. 11***

C20 AP2 15c lilac 1.50 *1.20*
a. 15c violet 22.50
b. Vert. pair, imperf. btwn. 22.50
C21 AP2 20c emerald 1.90
b. Horizontal pair, imperf. between 27.50
C22 AP2 25c yel brn 6.50
b. Vertical pair, imperf. between 60.00
C23 AP2 50c yel brn 8.00
C24 AP2 1cor dp car 12.00
a. Vert. or horiz. pair, imperf. btwn. 80.00
Nos. C20-C24 (5) 29.90

Sheets of 10. See note after No. 568.
For overprint and surcharges see #C44-C46.
Reprints: see note following No. 568. Value $1 each.

Nos. C5 and C6 Surcharged in Red or Black

Vale ₡ 0.30

1932, July 12 ***Perf. 12***

C25 AP1 30c on 50c (Bk) 1.50 1.50
a. "Valc" 25.00
b. Double surcharge 15.00
c. Double surch., one inverted 15.00
d. Period omitted after "O" 25.00
e. As "a," double 300.00
C26 AP1 35c on 50c (R) 1.50 1.50
a. "Valc" 30.00
b. Double surcharge 12.00
c. Double surch., one inverted 12.00
d. As "a," double 300.00
C27 AP1 35c on 50c (Bk) 35.00 35.00
a. "Valc" 250.00
C28 AP1 40c on 1cor (Bk) 1.75 1.75
a. "Valc" 25.00
b. Double surcharge 15.00
c. Double surch., one inverted 15.00
d. Inverted surcharge 15.00
e. As "a," inverted 300.00
f. As "a," double 300.00
C29 AP1 55c on 1cor (R) 1.75 1.75
a. "Valc" 25.00
b. Double surcharge 12.00
c. Double surch., one inverted 12.00
d. Inverted surcharge 12.00
e. As "a," inverted 300.00
f. As "a," double 300.00
Nos. C25-C29 (5) 41.50 41.50

No. C18 Overprinted in Red

Semana Correo Aéreo
Internacional
11-17 Septiembre 1932

1932, Sept. 11

C30 AP1 15c dp vio 70.00 70.00
a. "Aerreo" 150.00 150.00
b. Invtd. "m" in "Septiembre" 150.00

International Air Mail Week.

No. C6 Surcharged

Inauguracion Interior
12 Octubre 1932
Vale ₡ 0.08

1932, Oct. 12

C31 AP1 8c on 1 cor org red 20.00 20.00
a. "1232" 30.00 30.00
b. 2nd "u" of "Inauguration" invtd. 30.00 30.00

Issued for the inauguration of airmail service to the interior.

Regular Issue of 1932 Overprinted in Red

Correo Aéreo Interior
1932

1932, Oct. 24 *Perf. 11½*

Without Gum

C32 A40	1c yel brn	20.00	20.00
a.	Inverted overprint	125.00	125.00
C33 A40	2c carmine	20.00	20.00
a.	Inverted overprint	125.00	125.00
b.	Double overprint	100.00	100.00
C34 A40	3c ultra	9.50	9.50
a.	Inverted overprint	150.00	150.00
b.	As "a," vert. pair, imperf. btwn.	500.00	
C35 A40	4c dp ultra	9.50	9.50
a.	Inverted overprint	125.00	125.00
b.	Double overprint	100.00	100.00
c.	Vert. or horiz. pair, imperf. btwn.	300.00	
C36 A40	5c yel brn	9.50	9.50
a.	Inverted overprint	125.00	125.00
b.	Vert. pair, imperf. btwn.	75.00	
C37 A40	6c gray brn	9.50	9.50
a.	Inverted overprint	100.00	100.00
C38 A40	50c green	9.00	9.00
a.	Inverted overprint	125.00	125.00
C39 A40	1cor yellow	9.50	9.50
a.	Inverted overprint	125.00	125.00
b.	Horiz. pair, imperf. btwn.	200.00	
	Nos. C32-C39 (8)	96.50	96.50

Nos. C20 and C21 exist overprinted as C32-C39. The editors believe they were not regularly issued.

Surcharged in Red

Correo Aéreo Interior
1932
Vale ₡ 0.16

C40 A40	8c on 10c yel brn	9.00	9.00
a.	Inverted surcharge	125.00	125.00
C41 A40	16c on 20c org	9.00	9.00
a.	Inverted surcharge	125.00	125.00
C42 A40	24c on 25c dp vio	9.00	9.00
a.	Inverted surcharge	125.00	125.00
b.	Horiz. pair, imperf. vert.	300.00	

Surcharged in Red as No. C40 but without the word "Vale"

C43 A40	80c on 10c yel brn	45.00	45.00
a.	Inverted surcharge	125.00	125.00
b.	Horiz. pair, imperf. vert.	300.00	

No. C22 Overprinted in Red

Interior—1932

C44 AP2	25c yel brn	8.00	8.00
a.	Inverted overprint	125.00	125.00

Nos. C23 and C24 Surcharged in Red

Interior—1932

Vale ₡ 0.32

C45 AP2	32c on 50c yel brn	9.50	9.50
a.	Inverted surcharge	125.00	125.00
b.	"Interior-1932" inverted	150.00	150.00
c.	"Vale $0.32" inverted	150.00	150.00
d.	Horiz. pair, imperf. btwn.	200.00	
C46 AP2	40c on 1cor car	7.00	7.00
a.	Inverted surcharge	125.00	125.00
b.	"Vale $0.40" inverted	200.00	200.00

Nos. 557-558 Overprinted in Black like Nos. C32 to C39

1932, Nov. 16

C47 A40	1c yel brn	25.00	22.50
a.	"1232"	45.00	45.00
b.	Inverted overprint	125.00	125.00
c.	Double ovpt., one invtd.	125.00	125.00
d.	As "a," inverted	500.00	
C48 A40	2c dp car	20.00	17.50
a.	"1232"	45.00	45.00
b.	Inverted overprint	125.00	125.00
c.	As "a," inverted	500.00	

Excellent counterfeits exist of Nos. C27, C30-C48. Forged overprints and surcharges as on Nos. C32-C48 exist on reprints of Nos. C20-C24.

Regular Issue of 1914-32 Surcharged in Black

Correo Aéreo
Interior-1932
Vale ₡ 0.01

1932 *Perf. 12*

C49 A25	1c on 2c brt rose	35	30
C50 A24	2c on 3c lt bl	35	30
C51 A25	3c on 4c dk bl	35	30
C52 A24	4c on 5c gray brn	35	30
C53 A25	5c on 6c ol brn	35	30
C54 A25	6c on 10c lt brn	35	30
a.	Double surcharge	25.00	
C55 A24	8c on 15c org red	35	30
C56 A25	16c on 20c org	35	35
C57 A24	24c on 25c dk vio	1.40	1.00
C58 A24	25c on 25c dk vio	1.40	1.00
a.	Double surcharge	25.00	
C59 A25	32c on 50c grn	1.40	1.25
C60 A25	40vc on 50c grn	1.60	1.40
C61 A25	50c on 1cor yel	2.25	2.25
C62 A25	1cor on 1cor yel	3.00	3.00
	Nos. C49-C62 (14)	13.85	12.35

Nos. C49-C62 exist with inverted surcharge.

In addition to C49 to C62, four other stamps, Type A25, exist with this surcharge.

40c on 50c bister brown, black surcharge.
1cor on 2c bright rose, black surcharge.
1cor on 1cor yellow, red surcharge.
1cor on 1cor dull violet, black surcharge.

The editors believe they were not regularly issued.

Surcharged on Nos. 548, 547

1932

C65 A24	24c on 25c dk vio	45.00	45.00
C66 A24	25c on 25c blk brn	50.00	50.00

Counterfeits of Nos. C65 and C66 are plentiful.

Rivas Railroad Issue

La Chocolata Cut — AP3

El Nacascola — AP4

Designs: 25c, Cuesta cut. 50c, Mole of San Juan del Sur. 1cor, View of El Estero.

1932, Dec. **Litho.**

Soft porous paper

C67 AP3	15c dk vio	20.00
C68 AP4	20c bl grn	20.00
C69 AP4	25c dk brn	20.00
C70 AP4	50c blk brn	20.00
C71 AP4	1cor rose red	20.00
	Nos. C67-C71 (5)	100.00

Inauguration of the railroad from San Jorge to San Juan del Sur, Dec. 18, 1932. Printed in sheets of 4, without gum.

Reprints: see note following No. 574. Value, $6 each.

Leon-Sauce Railroad Issue

"Fill" at Santa Lucia River AP5

Designs: 15c, Bridge at Santa Lucia. 25c, Malpaicillo Station. 50c, Panoramic view. 1cor, San Andres.

1932, Dec. 30

Soft porous paper

C72 AP5	15c purple	20.00
C73 AP5	20c bl grn	20.00
C74 AP5	25c dk brn	20.00
C75 AP5	50c blk brn	20.00
C76 AP5	1cor rose red	20.00
	Nos. C72-C76 (5)	100.00

Inauguration of the railroad from Leon to El Sauce, Dec. 30, 1932. Sheets of 4, without gum.

Reprints: see note following No. 579. Value, $6 each.

Flag of the Race Issue

1933, Aug. 3 **Litho.** ***Rouletted 9***

Without gum

C77 A43	1c dk brn	1.50	1.50
C78 A43	2c red vio	1.50	1.50
C79 A43	4c violet	2.50	2.25
C80 A43	5c dl bl	2.25	2.25
C81 A43	6c vio bl	2.25	2.25
C82 A43	8c dp brn	70	70
C83 A43	15c ol brn	70	70
C84 A43	20c yellow	2.25	2.25
a.	Horiz. pair, imperf. btwn.	15.00	
b.	Horiz. pair, imperf. vert.	15.00	
C85 A43	25c orange	2.25	2.25
C86 A43	50c rose	2.25	2.25
C87 A43	1cor green	11.00	11.00
	Nos. C77-C87 (11)	29.15	28.90

See note after No. 599. Printed in sheets of 10. *Reprints exist, shades differ from postage and official stamps.*

Imperf., Pairs

C78a A43	2c	14.00
C79a A43	4c	10.00
C81a A43	6c	10.00
C82a A43	8c	10.00
C83a A43	15c	10.00
C87a A43	1cor	30.00

AP7

1933, Nov. ***Perf. 12***

C88 AP7	10c bis brn	1.50	1.50
a.	Vert. pair, imperf. between	35.00	
C89 AP7	15c violet	1.20	1.20
a.	Vert. pair, imperf. between	37.50	
C90 AP7	25c red	1.40	1.40
a.	Horiz. pair, imperf. between	22.50	
C91 AP7	50c dp bl	1.50	1.50

Intl. Air Post Week, Nov. 6-11, 1933. Printed in sheets of 4. Counterfeits exist.

Stamps and Types of 1928-31 Surcharged in Black

Correo Aéreo
Interior
Vale ₡ 0.01

1933, Nov. 3

C92 A25	1c on 2c grn	15	15
C93 A24	2c on 3c ol gray	15	15
C94 A25	3c on 4c car rose	15	15
C95 A24	4c on 5c lt bl	15	15
C96 A25	5c on 6c dk bl	15	15
C97 A25	6c on 10c ol brn	15	15
C98 A24	8c on 15c bis brn	20	15
C99 A25	16c on 20c brn	16	15
C100 A24	24c on 25c ver	15	15
C101 A24	25c on 25c org	22	16
C102 A25	32c on 50c vio	20	20
C103 A25	40c on 50c grn	20	15
C104 A25	50c on 1cor yel	16	15
C105 A25	1cor on 1cor org red	35	22
	Set value	2.20	1.75

Nos. C100, C102-C105 exist without script control overprint. Value, each $1.50.

Type of Air Post Stamps of 1929 Surcharged in Black

Vale ₡ 0.30

1933, Oct. 28

C106 AP1	30c on 50c org red	22	15
C107 AP1	35c on 50c lt bl	25	16
C108 AP1	40c on 1cor yel	40	16
C109 AP1	55c on 1cor grn	30	22

No. C19 Surcharged in Red

Servicio
Centroamericano
Vale 10 centavos

1934, Mar. 31

C110 AP1	10c on 20c grn	30	25
a.	Inverted surcharge	15.00	
b.	Double surcharge, one inverted	15.00	
c.	"Ceutroamericano"	10.00	

No. C110 with black surcharge is believed to be of private origin.

No. C4 Surcharged in Red

Servicio
Centroamericano
Vale 10 centavos

1935, Aug.

C111 AP1	10c on 25c ol blk	25	25
a.	Small "v" in "vale" (R)	5.00	
b.	"centrvos" (R)	5.00	
c.	Double surcharge (R)	25.00	
d.	Inverted surcharge (R)	25.00	
g.	As "a," inverted	400.00	
h.	As "a," double	400.00	

No. C111 with blue surcharge is believed to be private origin.

The editors do not recognize the Nicaraguan air post stamps overprinted in red "VALIDO 1935" in two lines and with or without script control marks as having been issued primarily for postal purposes.

Nos C4-C6, C18-C19 Overprinted Vertically in Blue, Reading Up:

1935-36

C112 AP1	15c dp vio	1.00	1.00
C113 AP1	20c dp grn	1.75	1.75
C114 AP1	25c ol blk	2.25	2.25
C115 AP1	50c blk brn	5.00	5.00
C116 AP1	1cor org red	40.00	40.00
	Nos. C112-C116 (5)	50.00	50.00

Same Overprint on Nos. C106-C109 Reading Up or Down

C117 AP1	30c on 50c org red	1.50	1.40
C118 AP1	35c on 50c lt bl	6.50	6.50
C119 AP1	40c on 1cor yel	6.50	6.50
C120 AP1	55c on 1cor grn	6.50	6.50

Same Overprint in Red on Nos. C92-C105

1936

C121 A25	1c on 2c grn	15	15
C122 A24	2c on 3c ol gray	16	16
C123 A25	3c on 4c car rose	16	16
C124 A24	4c on 5c lt bl	16	16
C125 A25	5c on 6c dk bl	16	16
C126 A25	6c on 10c ol brn	16	16
C127 A24	8c on 15c bis brn	16	16
C128 A25	16c on 20c brn	25	25
C129 A24	24c on 25c ver	35	28
C130 A24	25c on 25c org	22	22
C131 A25	32c on 50c vio	16	16
C132 A25	40c on 50c grn	55	50
C133 A25	50c on 1cor yel	40	25
C134 A25	1cor on 1cor org red	1.40	65
	Nos. C121-C134 (14)	4.44	3.42

Nos. C121 to C134 are handstamped with script control mark.

Overprint Reading Down on No. C110

C135 AP1	10c on 20c grn	*350.00*

This stamp has been extensively counterfeited.

Overprinted in Red on Nos. C4 to C6, C18 and C19

C136 AP1	15c dp vio	55	15
C137 AP1	20c dp grn	65	60
C138 AP1	25c ol blk	65	55
C139 AP1	50c blk brn	55	55
C140 AP1	1cor org red	1.10	55

On Nos. C106 to C109

C141 AP1	30c on 50c org red	65	60
C142 AP1	35c on 50c lt bl	65	42
C143 AP1	40c on 1cor yel	65	55
C144 AP1	55c on 1cor grn	65	50

Same Overprint in Red or Blue on No. C111 Reading Up or Down

C145 AP1	10c on 25c, down	55	45
a.	"Centrvos"	25.00	
C146 AP1	10c on 25c (Bl), up	1.20	1.00
a.	"Centrvos"	25.00	
	Nos. C136-C146 (11)	7.85	5.92

Overprint on No. C145 is at right, on No. C146 in center.

Nos. C92, C93 and C98 Overprinted in Black

Resello
1936

1936

C147 A25 1c on 2c grn 20 16
C148 A24 2c on 3c ol gray 15 15
a. "Resello 1936" dbl., one invtd. 2.50
C149 A24 8c on 15c bis brn 22 22

With script control handstamp.

Nos. C5 and C6 Surcharged in Red

1936
Vale
Quince Centavos

C150 AP1 15c on 50c blk brn 20 16
C151 AP1 15c on 1cor org red 20 16

Nos. C18 and C19 Overprinted in Carmine

RESELLO - 1935

C152 AP1 15c dp vio 35 16
C153 AP1 20c dp grn 35 25

Overprint reading up or down.

No. C4 Surcharged and Overprinted in Red

Servicio Centroamericano Vale diez centavos
and
RESELLO - 1935

C154 AP1 10c on 25c ol blk 30 30
a. Surch. and ovpt. inverted 3.50

Same Overprint in Carmine on Nos. C92 to C99

C155 A25 1c on 2c grn 15 15
C156 A24 2c on 3c ol gray 65 65
C157 A25 3c on 4c car rose 15 15
C158 A24 4c on 5c lt bl 15 15
C159 A25 5c on 6c dk bl 15 15
C160 A25 6c on 10c ol brn 15 15
C161 A24 8c on 15c bis brn 15 15
C162 A25 16c on 20c brn 15 15
Set value 1.40 1.40

No. 518 Overprinted in Black

Correo Aéreo Centro-Americano Resello 1936

C163 A25 10c lt brn 16 16
a. Overprint inverted 2.25
b. Double overprint 2.25

Two fonts are found in the sheet of #C163.

Momotombo Type of 1929

1937

C164 AP1 15c yel org 15 15
C165 AP1 20c org red 15 15
C166 AP1 25c black 15 15
C167 AP1 50c violet 22 15
C168 AP1 1cor orange 55 15
Nos. C164-C168 (5) 1.22
Set value 42

Surcharged in Black **Vale ₡ 0.30**

1937

C169 AP1 30c on 50c car rose 16 15
C170 AP1 35c on 50c ol grn 20 15
C171 AP1 40c on 1cor grn 22 15
C172 AP1 55c on 1cor bl 20 20
Set value 42

No. C168 Surcharged in Violet

Servicio
Centroamericano
Vale Diez Centavos

1937 Unwmk. *Perf. 12*

C173 AP1 10c on 1cor org 15 15
a. "Centauos" 10.00

No. C98 with Additional Overprint "1937"

C174 A24 8c on 15c bis brn 45 15
a. "1937" double 6.50

Nos. C92-C102 with Additional Overprint in Blue reading "HABILITADO 1937"

C175 A25 1c on 2c grn 15 15
a. Blue overprint double 2.50
C176 A24 2c on 3c ol gray 15 15
a. Double surch., one inverted 2.50
C177 A25 3c on 4c car rose 15 15
C178 A24 4c on 5c lt bl 15 15
C179 A25 5c on 6c dk bl 15 15
C180 A25 6c on 10c ol brn 15 15
C181 A24 8c on 15c bis brn 15 15
a. "Habilitado 1937" double 3.50
C182 A25 16c on 20c brn 16 16
a. Double surcharge 2.50
C183 A24 24c on 25c ver 16 16
C184 A24 25c on 25c org 22 20
C185 A25 32c on 50c vio 22 22
Set value, #C175-C185 1.25 1.10

Map of Nicaragua AP8

For Foreign Postage

1937, July 30 Engr.

C186 AP8 10c green 15 15
C187 AP8 15c dp bl 15 15
C188 AP8 20c yellow 20 16
C189 AP8 25c bl vio 20 16
C190 AP8 30c rose car 22 20
C191 AP8 50c org yel 35 20
C192 AP8 1cor ol grn 70 55
Nos. C186-C192 (7) 1.97 1.57

Presidential Palace AP9

For Domestic Postage

C193 AP9 1c rose car 15 15
C194 AP9 2c dp bl 15 15
C195 AP9 3c ol grn 15 15
C196 AP9 4c black 15 15
C197 AP9 5c dk vio 15 15
C198 AP9 6c chocolate 15 15
C199 AP9 8c bl vio 15 15
C200 AP9 16c org yel 22 20
C201 AP9 24c yellow 15 15
C202 AP9 25c yel grn 25 20
Set value 1.32 1.00

No. C201 with green overprint "Union Panamericana 1890-1940" is of private origin.

Managua AP10

Designs: 15c, Presidential Palace. 20c, Map of South America. 25c, Map of Central America. 30c, Map of North America. 35c, Lagoon of Tiscapa, Managua. 40c, Road Scene. 45c, Park. 50c, Another park. 55c, Scene in San Juan del Sur. 75c, Tipitapa River. 1cor, Landscape.

Wmk. 209

1937, Sept. 17 Typo. *Perf. 11*

Center in Dark Blue

C203 AP10 10c yel grn 1.60 1.20
C204 AP10 15c orange 1.60 1.40
C205 AP10 20c red 1.00 1.00
C206 AP10 25c vio brn 1.00 1.00
C207 AP10 30c bl grn 1.00 1.00
a. Great Lakes omitted 40.00 40.00
C208 AP10 35c lemon 50 45
C209 AP10 40c green 40 38
C210 AP10 45c brt vio 40 35
C211 AP10 50c rose lil 40 35
a. Vert. pair, imperf. btwn. 140.00
C212 AP10 55c lt bl 40 35
C213 AP10 75c gray grn 40 35

Center in Brown Red

C214 AP10 1cor dk bl 1.00 50
Nos. C203-C214 (12) 9.70 8.33

150th anniv. of the Constitution of the US.

Diriangen — AP11

Designs: 4c, 10c, Nicarao. 5c, 15c, Bartolomé de Las Casas. 8c, 20c, Columbus.

For Domestic Postage
Without gum

1937, Oct. 12 Unwmk. *Perf. 11*

C215 AP11 1c green 15 15
C216 AP11 4c brn car 15 15
C217 AP11 5c dk vio 15 15
a. Without imprint 40
C218 AP11 8c dp bl 15 15
a. Without imprint 50

For Foreign Postage
Wmk. 209
With Gum

C219 AP11 10c lt brn 15 15
C220 AP11 15c pale bl 15 15
a. Without imprint 1.00
C221 AP11 20c pale rose 16 15
Set value, #C215-C221 75 65

Nos. C215-C221 printed in sheets of 4.

Imperf., Pairs

C215a AP11 1c 16 16
C216a AP11 4c 20 20
C217b AP11 5c 20 20
C218b AP11 8c 20
C219a AP11 10c 20 20
C220b AP11 15c 22 22
C221a AP11 20c 35 35

Gen. Tomas Martinez — AP11a

Design: 10c, 15c, 25c, 50c, Gen. Anastasio Somoza.

For Domestic Postage
Without Gum
Perf. 11½, Imperf.

1938, Jan. 18 Typo. Unwmk.

Center in Black

C221B AP11a 1c orange 20 20
C221C AP11a 5c red vio 20 20
C221D AP11a 8c dk bl 22 22
C221E AP11a 16c brown 25 25
f. Sheet of 4, 1c, 5c, 8c, 16c 1.25 1.25

For Foreign Postage

C221G AP11a 10c green 22 20
C221H AP11a 15c dk bl 25 25
C221J AP11a 25c violet 42 40
C221K AP11a 50c carmine 50 45
m. Sheet of 4, 10c, 15c, 25c, 50c 2.00 2.00
Nos. C221B-C221K (8) 2.26 2.17

75th anniv. of postal service in Nicaragua. Printed in sheets of four.

Stamps of type AP11a exist in changed colors and with inverted centers, double centers and frames printed on the back. These varieties were private fabrications.

Lake Managua AP12

President Anastasio Somoza — AP13

For Domestic Postage

1939 Unwmk. Engr. *Perf. 12½*

C222 AP12 2c dp bl 15 15
C223 AP12 3c green 15 15
C224 AP12 8c pale lil 15 15
C225 AP12 16c orange 15 15
C226 AP12 24c yellow 15 15
C227 AP12 32c dk grn 16 15
C228 AP12 50c dp rose 16 15

For Foreign Postage

C229 AP13 10c dk brn 15 15
C230 AP13 15c dk bl 15 15
C231 AP13 20c org yel 15 16
C232 AP13 25c dk pur 15 15
C233 AP13 30c lake 16 16
C234 AP13 50c dp org 25 20
C235 AP13 1cor dk ol grn 40 35
Set value, #C222-C235 2.10 1.90

For Domestic Postage

Will Rogers and View of Managua AP14

Designs: 2c, Rogers standing beside plane. 3c, Leaving airport office. 4c, Rogers and US Marines. 5c, Managua after earthquake.

1939, Mar. 31 Engr. *Perf. 12*

C236 AP14 1c brt grn 15 15
C237 AP14 2c org red 15 15
C238 AP14 3c lt ultra 15 15
C239 AP14 4c dk bl 15 15
C240 AP14 5c rose car 15 15
Set value 28 25

Will Rogers' flight to Managua after the earthquake, Mar. 31, 1931.

For surcharges see Nos. 686, 688.

Pres. Anastasio Somoza in US House of Representatives — AP19

President Somoza and US Capitol AP20

President Somoza, Tower of the Sun and Trylon and Perisphere AP21

For Domestic Postage

1940, Feb. 1

C241 AP19 4c red brn 15 15
C242 AP20 8c blk brn 15 15
C243 AP19 16c grnsh bl 15 15
C244 AP20 20c brt plum 50 30
C245 AP21 32c scarlet 16 16

For Foreign Postage

C246 AP19 25c dp bl 20 15
C247 AP19 30c black 20 15
C248 AP20 50c rose pink 45 38
C249 AP21 60c green 50 30
C250 AP19 65c dk vio brn 50 20
C251 AP19 90c ol grn 65 30
C252 AP21 1cor violet 1.00 55
Nos. C241-C252 (12) 4.61
Set value 2.50

Visit of Pres. Somoza to US in 1939.

For surcharge see No. C636.

L. S. Rowe, Statue of Liberty, Nicaraguan Coastline, Flags of 21 American Republics, US Shield and Arms of Nicaragua — AP22

1940, Aug. 2 Engr. *Perf. 12½*

C253	AP22	1.25cor multi	65	60

50th anniversary of Pan American Union.
For overprint see No. C493.

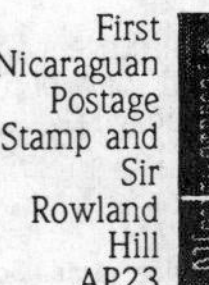

First Nicaraguan Postage Stamp and Sir Rowland Hill AP23

1941, Apr. 4

C254	AP23	2cor brown	2.50	80
C255	AP23	3cor dk bl	8.25	1.40
C256	AP23	5cor carmine	22.50	3.50

Centenary of the first postage stamp.
Nos. C254-C256 imperf. are proofs.

Rubén Darío AP24

1941, Dec. 23

C257	AP24	20c pale lil	25	18
C258	AP24	35c yel grn	30	20
C259	AP24	40c org yel	40	22
C260	AP24	60c lt bl	65	30

25th anniversary of the death of Rubén Dario, poet and writer.

Catalogue values for unused stamps in this section, from this point to the end of the section, are for Never Hinged items.

"Victory" — AP25

1943, Dec. 8 *Perf. 12*

C261	AP25	40c dk bl grn & cer	20	15
C262	AP25	60c lt bl & cer	30	15
		Set value		15

Issued to commemorate the second anniversary of Nicaragua's declaration of war against the Axis.

The Catalogue editors cannot undertake to appraise, identify or judge the genuineness or condition of stamps.

Red Cross — AP26 Cross and Globes — AP27

Red Cross Workers AP28

1944, Oct. 12 Engr.

C263	AP26	25c red lil & car	65	30
C264	AP27	50c ol brn & car	1.00	55
C265	AP28	1cor dk bl grn & car	2.00	2.00

80th anniversary of the International Red Cross Society.

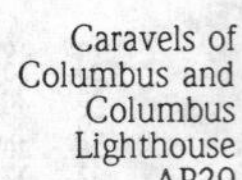

Caravels of Columbus and Columbus Lighthouse AP29

Landing of Columbus AP30

1945, Sept. 1 *Perf. 12½*

C266	AP29	20c dp grn & gray	15	15
C267	AP29	35c dk car & blk	35	30
C268	AP29	75c ol grn & rose pink	45	40
C269	AP29	90c brick red & aqua	80	75
C270	AP29	1cor blk & pale bl	90	30
C271	AP30	2.50cor dk bl & car rose	2.25	2.25
		Nos. C266-C271 (6)	4.90	4.15

Issued in honor of the discovery of America by Columbus and the Columbus Lighthouse near Ciudad Trujillo, Dominican Republic.

Franklin D. Roosevelt and Winston Churchill AP31

Roosevelt Signing Declaration of War Against Japan — AP32

Designs: 1cor, Gen. Henri Giraud, Roosevelt, Gen. Charles de Gaulle and Churchill. 3cor, Stalin, Roosevelt and Churchill. 5cor, Sculptured head of Roosevelt.

Engraved, Center Photogravure

1946, June 15 *Perf. 12½*

Frame in Black

C272	AP31	25c orange	15	15
a.		Horiz. pair, imperf. btwn.	225.00	
b.		Imperf., pair	175.00	
C273	AP32	75c carmine	25	25
a.		Imperf., pair	175.00	
C274	AP31	1cor dk grn	40	40
C275	AP31	3cor violet	3.75	3.75
C276	AP32	5cor grnsh bl	5.00	5.00
		Nos. C272-C276 (5)	9.55	9.55

Issued to honor Franklin D. Roosevelt.

Projected Provincial Seminary — AP36

Designs: 20c, Communications Building. 35c, Sanitation Building. 90c, National Bank. 1cor, Municipal Building. 2.50cor, National Palace.

1947, Jan. 10

Frame in Black

C277	AP36	5c violet	15	15
a.		Imperf., pair	125.00	
C278	AP36	20c gray grn	15	15
C279	AP36	35c orange	20	18
C280	AP36	90c red lil	40	30
C281	AP36	1cor brown	60	45
C282	AP36	2.50cor rose lil	1.75	1.50
		Nos. C277-C282 (6)	3.25	2.73

City of Managua centenary.

Rubén Darío Monument — AP42

Designs: 6c, Tapir. 8c, Stone Highway. 10c, Genizaro Dam. 20c, Detail of Dario Monument. 25c, Sulphurous Lake of Nejapa. 35c, Mercedes Airport. 50c, Prinzapolka River delta. 1cor, Tipitapa Spa. 1.50cor, Tipitapa River. 5cor, United States Embassy. 10cor, Indian fruit vendor. 25cor, Franklin D. Roosevelt Monument.

Engraved, Center Photogravure

1947, Aug. 29 Unwmk. *Perf. 12½*

C283	AP42	5c dk bl grn & rose car	15	15
C284	AP42	6c blk & yel	15	15
C285	AP42	8c car & ol	15	15
C286	AP42	10c brn & bl	18	15
C287	AP42	20c bl vio & org	30	30
C288	AP42	25c brn red & emer	35	35
C289	AP42	35c gray & bis	30	30
C290	AP42	50c pur & sep	25	25
C291	AP42	1cor blk & lil rose	75	75
C292	AP42	1.50cor red brn & aqua	80	80
C293	AP42	5cor choc & car rose	6.25	6.25
C294	AP42	10cor vio & dk brn	5.00	5.00
C295	AP42	25cor dk bl grn & yel	10.00	10.00
		Nos. C283-C295 (13)	24.63	24.60

The frames differ for each denomination.
For surcharge see No. C750.

Tennis — AP43

Designs: 2c, Soccer. 3c, Table tennis. 4c, Proposed stadium. 5c, Regatta. 15c, Basketball. 25c, Boxing. 30c, Baseball. 40c, Bicycling. 75c, Diving. 1cor, Pole vault. 2cor, Boy Scouts. 5cor, Softball.

1949, July Photo. *Perf. 12*

C296	AP43	1c cerise	15	15
C297	AP43	2c ol gray	15	15
C298	AP43	3c scarlet	15	15
C299	AP43	4c dk bl gray	15	15
C300	AP43	5c aqua	30	15
C301	AP43	15c bl grn	90	15
C302	AP43	25c red vio	2.00	30
C303	AP43	30c red brn	1.75	30
C304	AP43	40c violet	45	30
C305	AP43	75c magenta	4.50	2.75
C306	AP43	1cor lt bl	5.00	1.35
C307	AP43	2cor brn ol	2.00	1.75
C308	AP43	5cor lt grn	2.25	2.25
a.		Set of 13 souvenir sheets of 4	125.00	125.00
		Nos. C296-C308 (13)	19.75	9.90

Issued to publicize the tenth World Series of Amateur Baseball, 1948.

Rowland Hill — AP44

Designs: 20c, Heinrich von Stephan. 25c, First UPU Bldg. 30c, UPU Bldg., Bern. 85c, UPU Monument. 1.10cor, Congress medal, obverse. 2.14cor, as 1.10cor, reverse.

1950, Nov. 23 Engr. *Perf. 13*

Frames in Black

C309	AP44	16c cerise	15	15
C310	AP44	20c orange	15	15
C311	AP44	25c gray	20	20
C312	AP44	30c cerise	30	15
C313	AP44	85c dk bl grn	65	65
C314	AP44	1.10cor chnt brn	50	45
C315	AP44	2.14cor ol grn	2.25	2.25
		Nos. C309-C315 (7)	4.20	4.00

75th anniv. (in 1949) of the UPU.

Each denomination was also issued in a souvenir sheet containing four stamps and marginal inscriptions. Size: 126x114mm. Value, set of 7 sheets, $35.

For surcharges see Nos. C501, C758.

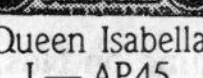

Queen Isabella I — AP45 Columbus' Ships — AP46

Designs: 2.80cor, Map. 3cor, Santa Maria. 3.60cor, Portrait facing right.

1952, June 25 Unwmk. *Perf. 11½*

C316	AP45	2.30cor rose car	2.00	2.00
C317	AP45	2.80cor red org	1.75	1.75
C318	AP45	3cor green	2.00	2.00
C319	AP46	3.30cor lt bl	2.00	2.00
C320	AP45	3.60cor yel grn	2.25	2.25
a.		Souv. sheet of 5, #C316-C320	10.00	10.00
		Nos. C316-C320 (5)	10.00	10.00

Issued to commemorate the 500th anniversary of the birth of Queen Isabella I of Spain.

For overprint see No. C445.

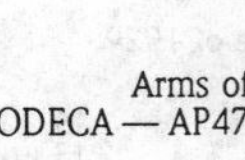

Arms of ODECA — AP47

Designs: 25c, ODECA Flag. 30c, Presidents of five Central American countries. 60c, ODECA Charter and Flags. 1cor, Map of Central America.

1953, Apr. 15 *Perf. 13½x14*

C321	AP47	20c red lil	15	15
C322	AP47	25c lt bl	15	15
C323	AP47	30c sepia	20	15
C324	AP47	60c dk bl grn	30	25
C325	AP47	1cor dk vio	70	65
		Nos. C321-C325 (5)	1.50	1.35

Founding of the Organization of Central American States (ODECA).

Leonardo Arguello — AP48

Presidents: 5c, Gen. Jose Maria Moncada. 20c, Juan Bautista Sacasa. 25c, Gen. Jose Santos Zelaya. 30c, Gen. Anastasio Somoza. 35c, Gen. Tomas Martinez. 40c, Fernando Guzman. 45c, Vicente Cuadra. 50c, Pedro Joaquin Chamorro. 60c, Gen. Joaquin Zavala. 85c, Adan Cardenas. 1.10cor, Evaristo Carazo. 1.20cor, Roberto Sacasa.

Engraved (frames); Photogravure (heads)

1953, June 25 *Perf. 12½*

Heads in Gray Black

C326 AP48 4c dp car 15 15
C327 AP48 5c dp org 15 15
C328 AP48 20c dk Prus bl 15 15
C329 AP48 25c blue 15 15
C330 AP48 30c red brn 15 15
C331 AP48 35c dp grn 18 18
C332 AP48 40c dk vio brn 22 18
C333 AP48 45c olive 22 22
C334 AP48 50c carmine 28 15
C335 AP48 60c ultra 30 22
C336 AP48 85c brown 38 35
C337 AP48 1.10cor purple 45 45
C338 AP48 1.20cor ol bis 45 45
Set value 2.80 2.40

For surcharges see Nos. C363-C364, C757.

Torch and UN Emblem — AP49

Capt. Dean L. Ray, USAF — AP50

Designs: 4c, Raised hands. 5c, Candle and charter. 30c, Flags of Nicaragua and UN. 2cor, Globe. 3cor, Arms of Nicaragua. 5cor, Type A69 inscribed "Aereo."

1954, Apr. 30 **Engr.** *Perf. 13½*

C339 AP49 3c rose pink 15 15
C340 AP49 4c dp org 15 15
C341 AP49 5c red 15 15
C342 AP49 30c cerise 1.00 20
C343 AP49 2cor magenta 1.35 1.00
C344 AP49 3cor org brn 2.50 1.75
C345 AP49 5cor brn vio 3.00 2.25
Nos. C339-C345 (7) 8.30 5.65

Honoring the United Nations.
For overprint and surcharge see Nos. C366, C443.

Engraved; Center Photogravure

1954, Nov. 5 *Perf. 13*

Designs: 15c, Sabre jet plane. 20c, Air Force emblem. 25c, National Air Force hangars. 30c, Gen. A. Somoza. 50c, AT-6's in formation. 1cor, Plane, type P-38.

Frame in Black

C346 AP50 10c gray 15 15
C347 AP50 15c gray 15 15
C348 AP50 20c claret 15 15
C349 AP50 25c red 15 15
C350 AP50 30c ultra 15 15
C351 AP50 50c blue 45 45
C352 AP50 1cor green 35 22
Set value 1.25 95

Issued to honor the National Air Force.

Paul P. Harris — AP51

Map of the World and Rotary Emblem — AP52

Designs: 2c, 50c, Handclasp, Rotary emblem and globe. 4c, 30c, Rotary slogans and wreath. 5c, 25c, Flags of Nicaragua and Rotary.

Perf. 11½

1955, Aug. 30 **Unwmk.** **Photo.**

Granite Paper

C353 AP51 1c vermilion 15 15
C354 AP51 2c ultra 15 15
C355 AP52 3c pck grn 15 15
C356 AP51 4c violet 15 15
C357 AP51 5c org brn 15 15
C358 AP51 25c brt grnsh bl 20 18
C359 AP51 30c dl pur 15 15
C360 AP52 45c lil rose 35 30
C361 AP51 50c lt bl grn 25 20
C362 AP51 1cor ultra 35 35
a. Souv. sheet of 5, #C358-C362 9.50 9.50
Set value 1.50 1.35

Rotary International, 50th anniversary.
For surcharge see No. C365.

Nos. C331, C333, C360, C345 Surcharged in Green or Black

Conmemoración
Exposición Nacional
Febrero 4-16, 1956
₵ 0.15

Engraved, Photogravure

1956, Feb. 4 *Perf. 13½x13, 11½*

C363 AP48 30c on 35c (G) 20 18
C364 AP48 30c on 45c (G) 20 18
C365 AP52 30c on 45c 20 15
C366 AP49 2cor on 5cor 80 75

National Exhibition, Feb. 4-16, 1956.
See note after No. 772.

Gen. Jose D. Estrada — AP53

The Stoning of Andres Castro — AP54

Designs: 1.50 cor, Emanuel Mongalo. 2.50 cor, Battle of Rivas. 10 cor, Com. Hiram Paulding.

1956, Sept. 14 **Engr.** *Perf. 12½*

C367 AP53 30c dk car rose 15 15
C368 AP54 60c chocolate 15 15
C369 AP53 1.50cor green 30 30
C370 AP54 2.50cor dk ultra 50 50
C371 AP53 10cor red org 2.00 2.00
Nos. C367-C371 (5) 3.10 3.10

Centenary of the National War.
For overprint and surcharge see #C444, C751.

President Somoza — AP55

1957, Feb. 1 **Photo.** *Perf. 14x13½*

Various Frames: Centers in Black

C372 AP55 15c gray blk 15 15
C373 AP55 30c indigo 20 20
C374 AP55 2cor purple 1.00 1.00
C375 AP55 3cor dk grn 2.00 2.00
C376 AP55 5cor dk brn 3.25 3.25
Nos. C372-C376 (5) 6.60 6.60

Issued in tribute to President Anastasio Somoza, 1896-1956.

Type of Regular Issue and

Handshake and Globe — AP56

Designs: 4c, Scout emblem, globe and Lord Baden-Powell. 5c, Cub Scout. 6c, Crossed flags and Scout emblem. 8c, Scout symbols. 30c, Joseph A. Harrison. 40c, Pres. Somoza receiving decoration at first Central American Camporee. 75c, Explorer Scout. 85c, Boy Scout. 1cor, Lord Baden-Powell.

1957, Apr. 9 **Unwmk.** *Perf. 13½x14*

C377 AP56 3c red org & ol 15 15
C378 A75 4c dk brn & dk Prus grn 15 15
C379 A75 5c grn & brn 15 15
C380 A75 6c pur & ol 15 15
C381 A75 8c grnsh blk & red 15 15
C382 A75 30c Prus grn & gray 15 15
C383 AP56 40c dk bl & grysh blk 15 15
C384 A75 75c mar & brn 20 20
C385 A75 85c red & gray 22 22
C386 A75 1cor dl red brn & sl grn 30 28
a. Souv. sheet of 5, #C382-C386, imperf. 2.50 2.50
Set value 1.50 1.45

Centenary of the birth of Lord Baden-Powell, founder of the Boy Scouts.
No. C386a with each stamp overprinted "CAMPOREE SCOUT 1965" was issued in 1965 along with Nos. 843-852.
For surcharge see No. C754.

Pres. Luis A. Somoza — AP57

1957, July 2 *Perf. 14x13½*

Portrait in Dark Brown

C387 AP57 20c dp bl 15 15
C388 AP57 25c lil rose 15 15
C389 AP57 30c blk brn 15 15
C390 AP57 40c grnsh bl 20 20
C391 AP57 2cor brt vio 1.25 1.25
Nos. C387-C391 (5) 1.90 1.90

Issued to honor President Luis A. Somoza.

Church Types of Regular Issue

Designs: 30c, Archbishop Lezcano y Ortega. 60c, Managua Cathedral. 75c, Bishop Pereira y Castellon. 90c, Leon Cathedral. 1.50cor, De la Merced Church, Granada. 2cor, Father Mariano Dubon.

1957, July 16 **Unwmk.**

Centers in Olive Gray

C392 A78 30c dk grn 15 15
C393 A77 60c chocolate 15 15
C394 A78 75c dk bl 20 20
C395 A77 90c brt red 28 28
C396 A77 1.50cor Prus grn 40 40
C397 A78 2cor brt pur 60 60
Nos. C392-C397 (6) 1.78 1.78

Merchant Marine Type of 1957

Designs: 25c, M. S. Managua. 30c, Ship's wheel and map. 50c, Pennants. 60c, M. S. Costa Rica. 1 cor, M. S. Nicarao. 2.50 cor, Flag, globe & ship.

1957, Oct. 24 **Litho.** *Perf. 14*

C398 A79 25c ultra grysh bl & gray 15 15
C399 A79 30c red brn, gray & yel 15 15
C400 A79 50c vio, ol gray & bl 30 30
C401 A79 60c lake, grnsh bl & blk 35 35
C402 A79 1cor crim, brt bl & blk 48 48
C403 A79 2.50cor blk, bl & red brn 1.50 1.50
Nos. C398-C403 (6) 2.93 2.93

For surcharge see No. C691.

Fair Emblem — AP58

Designs: 30c, 2cor, Arms of Nicaragua. 45c, 10cor, Pavilion of Nicaragua, Brussels.

1958, Apr. 17 **Unwmk.** *Perf. 14*

C404 AP58 25c bluish grn, blk & yel 15 15
C405 AP58 30c multi 15 15
C406 AP58 45c bis, bl & blk 15 15
C407 AP58 1cor pale brn, lt bl & blk 18 18
C408 AP58 2cor multi 32 32
C409 AP58 10cor pale bl, lil & brn 1.65 1.65
a. Souv. sheet of 6, #C404-C409 7.50 7.50
Nos. C404-C409 (6) 2.60 2.60

World's Fair, Brussels, Apr. 17-Oct. 19.

Lions Type of Regular Issue

Designs: 30c, Dr. Teodoro A. Arias. 60c, Arms of Central American Republics. 90c, Edward G. Barry. 1.25cor, Melvin Jones. 2cor, Motto and emblem. 3cor, Map of Central America.

1958, May 8 **Litho.**

Emblem in Yellow, Red and Blue

C410 A80 30c bl & org 15 15
C411 A80 60c multi 25 20
C412 A80 90c blue 35 30
C413 A80 1.25cor bl & ol 45 40
C414 A80 2cor bl & grn 80 70
C415 A80 3cor bl, lil & pink 1.25 1.10
a. Souv. sheet of 6, #C410-C415 4.25 4.25
Nos. C410-C415 (6) 3.25 2.85

For surcharge see No. C686.

Chrisyian Brothers Type of 1958

Designs: 30c, Arms of La Salle. 60c, School, Managua, horiz 85c, St. Jean Baptiste De La Salle. 90c, Bro. Carlos. 1.25cor, Bro. Julio. 1.50cor, Bro. Antonio. 1.75cor, Bro. Argeo. 2cor, Bro. Eugenio.

1958, July 13 **Photo.** *Perf. 14*

C416 A81 30c bl, car & yel 15 15
C417 A81 60c gray, brn & lil 28 24
C418 A81 85c red, bl & grnsh blk 32 28
C419 A81 90c ol grn, ocher & blk 40 36
C420 A81 1.25cor car, ocher & blk 55 52
C421 A81 1.50cor lt grn, gray & vio blk 65 55
C422 A81 1.75cor brn, bl & grnsh blk 70 65
C423 A81 2cor ol grn, gray & vio blk 1.00 1.00
Nos. C416-C423 (8) 4.05 3.75

For surcharges see Nos. C539A, C755-C756.

UNESCO Building, Paris — AP59

Designs: 75c, 5cor, "UNESCO." 90c, 3cor, UNESCO building and Eiffel tower. 1cor, Emblem and globe.

Perf. 11½

1958, Dec. 15 **Unwmk.** **Litho.**

C424 AP59 60c brt pink & bl 15 15
C425 AP59 75c grn & red brn 15 15
C426 AP59 90c lt brn & grn 18 15
C427 AP59 1cor ultra & brt pink 20 20
C428 AP59 3cor gray & org 65 65
C429 AP59 5cor rose lil & dk bl 1.00 95
a. Min. sheet of 6, #C424-C429 2.50 2.50
Nos. C424-C429 (6) 2.33 2.25

Opening of UNESCO Headquarters in Paris, Nov. 3.
For overprints see Nos. C494-C499.

Type of Regular Issue, 1959 and

Nicaraguan, Papal and US Flags AP60

Designs: 35c, Pope John XXIII and Cardinal Spellman. 1 cor, Spellman coat of arms. 1.05 cor, Cardinal Spellman. 1.50 cor, Human rosary and Cardinal, horiz. 2 cor, Cardinal with Ruben Dario order.

1959, Nov. 26 *Perf. 12½*

C430 AP60 30c vio bl, yel & red 15 15
C431 A83 35c dp org & grnsh blk 15 15
C432 A83 1cor yel, bl & car 22 22
C433 A83 1.05cor red, bk, bl & dk car 28 28
C434 A83 1.50cor dk bl & yel 30 30
C435 A83 2cor multi 40 40

C436 AP60 5cor multi 1.25 90
a. Min. sheet of 7, #C430-C436, perf. or imperf. 3.75 3.75
Nos. C430-C436 (7) 2.75 2.40

Visit of Cardinal Spellman to Managua, Feb. 1958.
For surcharges see #C538, C638, C747, C752.

Type of Lincoln Regular Issue and

AP61

Perf. 13x13½, 13½x13

1960, Jan. 21 Engr. Unwmk.

Portrait in Black

C437 A84 30c indigo 15 15
C438 A84 35c brt car 15 15
C439 A84 70c plum 15 15
C440 A84 1.05cor emerald 22 22
C441 A84 1.50cor violet 30 30
C442 AP61 5cor int blk & bis 90 90
a. Souv. sheet of 6, #C437-C442, imperf. 3.00 3.00
Nos. C437-C442 (6) 1.87 1.87

150th anniv. of the birth of Abraham Lincoln.
For overprints and surcharges see Nos. C446-C451, C500, C539, C637, C680, C753.

Nos. C343, C370 and C318 Overprinted: "X Aniversario Club Filatelico S.J.-C.R."

1960, July 4 Engr.

C443 AP49 2cor magenta 65 70
C444 AP54 2.50cor dk ultra 65 75
C445 AP45 3cor green 85 1.10

10th anniversary of the Philatelic Club of San Jose, Costa Rica.

Nos. C437-C442 Overprinted in Red

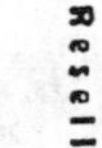

Resello

Perf. 13x13½, 13½x13

1960, Sept. 19 Unwmk.

Center in Black

C446 A84 30c indigo 20 16
C447 A84 35c brt car 16 15
C448 A84 70c plum 16 16
C449 A84 1.05cor emerald 22 22
C450 A84 1.50cor violet 38 35
C451 AP61 5cor int blk & bis 1.10 1.10
Nos. C446-C451 (6) 2.22 2.14

Issued for the Red Cross to aid earthquake victims in Chile. The overprint on No. C451 is horizontal and always inverted.

People and World Refugee Year Emblem AP62

Design: 5cor, Crosses, globe and WRY emblem.

1961, Jan. 2 Litho. *Perf. 11x11½*

C452 AP62 2cor multi 30 30
C453 AP62 5cor multi 65 65
a. Souv. sheet of 2, #C452-C453 2.50 2.50

World Refugee Year, July 1, 1959-June 30, 1960.

AP63

Consular Service Stamps Surcharged "Correo Aéreo" and New Denomination in Red, Black or Blue

Unwmk.

1961, Feb. 21 Engr. *Perf. 12*

Red Marginal Number

C454 AP63 20c on 50c dp bl (R) 15 15
C455 AP63 20c on 1cor grnsh blk (R) 15 15
C456 AP63 20c on 2cor grn (R) 15 15
C457 AP63 20c on 3cor dk car 15 15
C458 AP63 20c on 5cor org (Bl) 15 15
C459 AP63 20c on 10cor vio (R) 15 15
C460 AP63 20c on 20cor red brn (R) 15 15
C461 AP63 20c on 50cor brn (R) 15 15
C462 AP63 20c on 100cor mag 15 15
Set value 72 54

See Nos. CO51-CO59, RA63-RA64.

Charles L. Mullins, Anastasio Somoza and Franklin D. Roosevelt AP64

Standard Bearers with Flags of Nicaragua and Academy — AP65

Designs: 25c, 70c, Flags of Nicaragua and Academy. 30c, 1.05cor, Directors of Academy: Fred T. Cruse, LeRoy Bartlett, Jr., John F. Greco, Anastasio Somoza Debayle, Francisco Boza, Elias Monge. 40c, 2cor, Academy Emblem. 45c, 5cor, Anastasio Somoza Debayle and Luis Somoza Debayle.

Perf. 11x11½, 11½x11

1961, Feb. 24 Litho. Unwmk.

C463 AP64 20c rose lil, gray & buff 15 15
C464 AP65 25c bl, red & blk 15 15
C465 AP64 30c bl, gray & yel 15 15
C466 AP65 35c multi 15 15
C467 AP65 40c multi 15 15
C468 AP64 45c pink, gray & buff 15 15
a. Min. sheet of 6, #C463-C468, imperf. 40 40
C469 AP64 60c brn, gray & buff 15 15
C470 AP65 70c multi 15 15
C471 AP64 1.05cor lil, gray & yel 15 15
C472 AP65 1.50cor multi 18 18
C473 AP65 2cor multi 26 25
C474 AP64 5cor gray & buff 70 55
a. Min. sheet of 6, #C469-C474, imperf. 1.65 1.65
Set value 1.80 1.65

20th anniversary (in 1959) of the founding of the Military Academy of Nicaragua.
In 1977, Nos. C468a and C474a were overprinted in black: "1927-1977 50 ANIVERSARIO / Guardia Nacional de Nicaragua." Value, $4.
For surcharges see Nos. C692, C748, C759.

Emblem of Junior Chamber of Commerce — AP66

Designs: 2c, 15c, Globe showing map of Americas, horiz. 4c, 35c, Globe and initials, horiz. 5c, 70c, Chamber credo. 6c, 1.05cor, Handclasp. 10c, 5cor, Regional map.

Perf. 11x11½, 11½x11

1961, May 16 Unwmk.

C475 AP66 2c multi 15 15
C476 AP66 3c yel & blk 15 15
C477 AP66 4c multi 15 15
C478 AP66 5c crim & blk 15 15
C479 AP66 6c brn, yel & blk 15 15
C480 AP66 10c red org, blk & bl 15 15
C481 AP66 15c bl, blk & grn 15 15
C482 AP66 30c bl & blk 15 15
C483 AP66 35c multi 15 15
C484 AP66 70c yel, blk & crim 15 15
C485 AP66 1.05cor multi 15 15
C486 AP66 5cor multi 55 55
Set value 1.25 1.15

13th Regional Congress of the Junior Chamber of Commerce of Nicaragua and the Intl. Junior Chamber of Commerce.
The imperforates of Nos. C475-C486 were not authorized.
For overprints and surcharges see Nos. C504-C508, C537, C634, C687, C749.

Rigoberto Cabezas — AP67

Map of Mosquito Territory and View of Cartago AP68

Designs: 45c, Newspaper. 70c, Building. 2cor, Cabezas quotation. 10cor, Map of lower Nicaragua with Masaya area.

1961, Aug. 29 Litho. *Perf. 13½*

C487 AP67 20c org & dk bl 15 15
C488 AP68 40c lt bl & cl 15 15
C489 AP68 45c cit & brn 15 15
C490 AP68 70c beige & grn 15 15
C491 AP68 2cor pink & dk bl 32 22
C492 AP68 10cor grnsh bl & cl 1.40 1.10
Nos. C487-C492 (6) 2.32 1.92

Centenary of the birth of Rigoberto Cabezas, who acquired the Mosquito Territory (Atlantic Littoral) for Nicaragua.

No. C253 Overprinted in Red: "Convención Filatélica-Centro-América-Panama-San Salvador-27 Julio 1961"

1961, Aug. 23 Engr. *Perf. 12½*

C493 AP22 1.25cor multi 42 42
a. Inverted overprint 75.00

Central American Philatelic Convention, San Salvador, July 27.

Nos. C424-C429 Overprinted in Red: "Homenaje a Hammarskjold Sept. 18-1961"

1961 Litho. *Perf. 11½*

C494 AP59 60c brt pink & bl 25 25
C495 AP59 75c grn & red brn 28 28
C496 AP59 90c lt brn & grn 30 30
C497 AP59 1cor ultra & brt pink 32 32
C498 AP59 3cor gray & org 65 65
C499 AP59 5cor rose lil & dk bl 1.75 1.75
Nos. C494-C499 (6) 3.55 3.55

Issued in memory of Dag Hammarskjold, Secretary General of the United Nations, 1953-61.

RESELLO

Nos. C314 and C440 Surcharged in Red

₡ 1.00

Perf. 13x13½, 13

1962, Jan. 20 Engr.

C500 A84 1cor on 1.05cor 20 18
C501 AP44 1cor on 1.10cor 20 18

UNESCO Emblem and Crowd — AP69

Design: 5cor, UNESCO and UN Emblems.

Unwmk.

1962, Feb. 26 Photo. *Perf. 12*

C502 AP69 2cor multi 28 25
C503 AP69 5cor multi 70 70
a. Souv. sheet of 2, #C502-C503, imperf. 1.25 1.25

15th anniv. (in 1961) of UNESCO.

Nos. C480 and C483-C486 Overprinted

Perf. 11x11½, 11½x11

1962, July Litho.

C504 AP66 10c multi 22 20
C505 AP66 35c multi 30 20
C506 AP66 70c multi 38 30
C507 AP66 1.05cor multi 50 45
C508 AP66 5cor multi 85 1.40
Nos. C504-C508 (5) 2.25 2.55

WHO drive to eradicate malaria.

Souvenir Sheet

Stamps and Postmarks of 1862 — AP69a

1962, Sept. 9 Litho. *Imperf.*

C509 AP69a 7cor multi 2.50 2.50

Cent. of Nicaraguan postage stamps.

Arms Type of Regular Issue, 1962

Coats of Arms: 30c, Nueva Segovia. 50c, León. 1cor, Managua. 2cor, Granada. 5cor, Rivas.

1962, Nov. 22 *Perf. 12½x13*

Arms in Original Colors; Black Inscriptions

C510 A86 30c rose 15 15
C511 A86 50c salmon 15 15
C512 A86 1cor lt grn 15 15
C513 A86 2cor gray 32 28
C514 A86 5cor lt bl 85 75
Nos. C510-C514 (5) 1.62
Set value 1.25

Liberty Bell AP70

1963, May 15 Litho. *Perf. 13x12*

C515 AP70 30c lt bl, blk & ol bis 15 15

Issued to commemorate the sesquicentennial of the first Nicaraguan declaration of Independence (in 1961).

Paulist Brother Comforting Boy — AP71

Map of Central America — AP72

Designs: 60c, Nun comforting girl. 2cor, St. Vincent de Paul and St. Louisa de Marillac, horiz.

1963, May 15 Photo. Perf. 13½

C516 AP71 60c gray & ocher 15 15
C517 AP71 1cor sal & blk 25 22
C518 AP71 2cor crim & blk 50 50

300th anniv. of the deaths of St. Vincent de Paul and St. Louisa de Marillac (in 1960).

Lithographed and Engraved

1963, Aug. 2 Unwmk. Perf. 12

C519 AP72 1cor bl & yel 20 15

Issued to honor the Federation of Central American Philatelic Societies.

Cross over World AP73

Wheat and Map of Nicaragua AP74

1963, Aug. 6

C520 AP73 20c yel & red 15 15

Vatican II, the 21st Ecumenical Council of the Roman Catholic Church.

1963, Aug. 6

Design: 25c, Dead tree on parched earth.

C521 AP74 10c lt grn & grn 15 15
C522 AP74 25c yel & dk brn 15 15
Set value 15 15

FAO "Freedom from Hunger" campaign.

Boxing — AP75

Flags of Central American States — AP75a

Lithographed and Engraved

1963, Dec. 12 Unwmk. Perf. 12

C523 AP75 2c shown 15 15
C524 AP75 3c Running 15 15
C525 AP75 4c Underwater 15 15
C526 AP75 5c Soccer 15 15
C527 AP75 6c Baseball 15 15
C528 AP75 10c Tennis 15 15
C529 AP75 15c Bicycling 15 15
C530 AP75 20c Motorcycling 15 15
C531 AP75 35c Chess 22 22
C532 AP75 60c Deep-sea fishing 28 28
C533 AP75 1cor Table tennis 42 42
C534 AP75 2cor Basketball 80 80
C535 AP75 5cor Golf 2.00 2.00
Set value 4.25 4.25

Publicizing the 1964 Olympic Games.
For overprints and surcharge see Nos. C553-C558, C635.

Central American Independence Issue

1964, Sept. 15 Litho. Perf. 13x13½

Size: 27x43mm

C536 AP75a 40c multi 25 25

Nos. C479, C430, C437 and C416 Surcharged in Black or Red

Resello ₡ 0.15 — a

RESELLO ₡ 0.20 — b

1964 Litho. Perf. 11½x11

C537 AP66 5c on 6c 25 15

Perf. 12½

C538 AP60 10c on 30c 50 15

Engr.

Perf. 13x13½

C539 A84 15c on 30c (R) 65 15

Photo.

Perf. 14

C539A A81 20c on 30c 15 15
Set value 20

Floating Red Cross Station — AP76

Designs: 5c, Alliance for Progress emblem, vert. 15c, Highway. 20c, Plowing with tractors, and sun. 25c, Housing development. 30c, Presidents Somoza and Kennedy and World Bank Chairman Eugene Black. 35c, Adult education. 40c, Smokestacks.

1964, Oct. 15 Litho. Perf. 12

C540 AP76 5c yel, brt bl, grn & gray 15 15
C541 AP76 10c multi 15 15
C542 AP76 15c multi 15 15
C543 AP76 20c org brn, yel & blk 15 15
C544 AP76 25c multi 15 15
C545 AP76 30c dk bl, blk & brn 15 15
C546 AP76 35c lil rose, dk red & blk 18 15
C547 AP76 40c dp car, blk & yel 22 15
Set value 90 52

Alliance for Progress.
For surcharges see Nos. C677, C693.

Map of Central America and Central American States — AP77

Designs (Map of Central America and): 25c, Grain. 40c, Cogwheels. 50c, Heads of cattle.

1964, Nov. 30 Litho. Perf. 12

C548 AP77 15c ultra & multi 15 15
C549 AP77 25c multi 15 15
C550 AP77 40c multi 15 15
C551 AP77 50c multi 15 15
Set value 36 30

Central American Common Market.
For surcharge see No. C678.

Nos. C523-C525, C527 and C533-C534 Overprinted: "OLIMPIADAS / TOKYO-1964"

Lithographed and Engraved

1964, Dec. 19 Unwmk. Perf. 12

C553 AP75 2c multi 15 15
C554 AP75 3c multi 15 15
C555 AP75 4c multi 15 15
C556 AP75 6c multi 15 15
C557 AP75 1cor multi 2.00 2.00
C558 AP75 2cor multi 2.50 2.50
Nos. C553-C558 (6) 5.10 5.10

18th Olympic Games, Tokyo, Oct. 10-25.

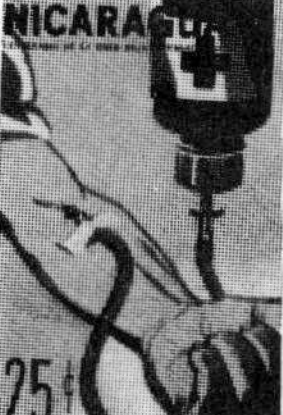

Blood Transfusion AP78

Stele AP79

Designs: 20c, Volunteers and priest rescuing wounded man. 40c, Landscape during storm. 10cor, Red Cross over map of Nicaragua.

1965, Jan. 28 Litho. Perf. 12

C559 AP78 20c yel, blk & red 15 15
C560 AP78 25c red, blk & ol bis 15 15
C561 AP78 40c grn, blk & red 15 15
C562 AP78 10cor multi 1.75 1.10
Set value 1.90 1.20

Centenary (in 1963) of the Intl. Red Cross.

Perf. 13½x13, 13x13½

1965, Mar. 24 Litho. Unwmk.

Antique Indian artifacts: 5c, Three jadeite statuettes, horiz. 15c, Dog, horiz. 20c, Talamanca pendant. 25c, Decorated pottery bowl and vase, horiz. 30c, Stone pestle and mortar on animal base. 35c, Three statuettes, horiz. 40c, Idol on animal pedestal. 50c, Decorated pottery bowl and vase. 60c, Vase and metate (tripod bowl), horiz. 1cor, Metate.

Black Margin and Inscription

C563 AP79 5c yel & multi 15 15
C564 AP79 10c multi 15 15
C565 AP79 15c multi 15 15
C566 AP79 20c sal & dk brn 15 15
C567 AP79 25c lil & multi 15 15
C568 AP79 30c lt grn & multi 15 15
C569 AP79 35c multi 15 15
C570 AP79 40c cit & multi 15 15
C571 AP79 50c ocher & multi 15 15
C572 AP79 60c multi 15 15
C573 AP79 1cor car & multi 30 15
Set value 95 55

For surcharges see Nos. C596-597, C679, C688-C690.

Pres. John F. Kennedy (1917-63) — AP80

Photogravure & Lithographed

1965, Apr. 28 Perf. 12½x13½

C574 AP80 35c blk & brt grn 20 15
C575 AP80 75c blk & brt pink 35 20
C576 AP80 1.10cor blk & dk bl 50 40
C577 AP80 2cor blk & yel brn 1.25 1.00
Set of 4 souvenir sheets 5.00 5.00

Nos. C574-C577 each exist in separate imperf. souvenir sheets, each containing one imperf. block of 4.
For surcharge see No. C760.

Andrés Bello — AP81

1965, Oct. 15 Litho. Perf. 14

C578 AP81 10c dk brn & red brn 15 15
C579 AP81 15c ind & lt bl 15 15
C580 AP81 45c blk & dl lil 15 15
C581 AP81 80c blk & yel grn 15 15
C582 AP81 1cor dk brn & yel 18 15
C583 AP81 2cor blk & gray 32 30
Set value 80 70

Issued to commemorate the centenary of the death of Andrés Bello (1780?-1864), Venezuelan writer and educator.

Winston Churchill AP82

Pope John XXIII AP83

Winston Churchill: 35c, 1cor, Broadcasting, horiz. 60c, 3cor, On military inspection. 75c, As young officer.

1966, Feb. 7 Unwmk. Perf. 14

C584 AP82 20c cer & blk 15 15
C585 AP82 35c dk ol grn & blk 15 15
C586 AP82 60c brn & blk 16 15
C587 AP82 75c rose red 20 16
C588 AP82 1cor vio blk 28 25
C589 AP82 2cor lil & blk 55 50
a. Souv. sheet of 4 1.40 1.40
C590 AP82 3cor ind & blk 85 70
Nos. C584-C590 (7) 2.34 2.06

Sir Winston Spencer Churchill (1874-1965), statesman and World War II leader.
No. C589a contains four imperf. stamps similar to Nos. C586-C589 with simulated perforations.

1966, Dec. 15 Litho. Perf. 13

Designs: 35c, Pope Paul VI. 1cor, Archbishop Gonzalez y Robleto. 2cor, St. Peter's, Rome. 3cor, Arms of Pope John XXIII and St. Peter's.

C591 AP83 20c multi 15 15
C592 AP83 35c multi 15 15
C593 AP83 1cor multi 22 18
C594 AP83 2cor multi 42 35
C595 AP83 3cor multi 65 50
Nos. C591-C595 (5) 1.59 1.33

Closing of the Ecumenical Council, Vatican II.

Nos. C571-C572 Surcharged in Red

RESELLO ₡ 0.10

1967 Perf. 13x13½, 13½x13

C596 AP79 10c on 50c multi 15 15
C597 AP79 15c on 60c multi 15 15
Set value 15 15

Rubén Dario and Birthplace — AP84

Portrait and: 10c, Monument, Managua. 20c, Leon Cathedral, site of Dario's tomb. 40c, Centaurs. 75c, Swans. 1cor, Roman triumphal march. 2cor, St. Francis and the Wolf. 5cor, "Faith" defeating "Death."

1967, Jan. 18 Litho. Perf. 13

C598 AP84 5c lt brn, tan & blk 15 15
C599 AP84 10c org, pale org & blk 15 15
C600 AP84 20c vio, lt bl & blk 15 15
C601 AP84 40c grn, dk grn & blk 15 15
a. Souv. sheet of 4, #C598-C601 50 50
C602 AP84 75c ultra, pale bl & blk 15 15
C603 AP84 1cor red, pale red & blk 18 15
C604 AP84 2cor rose pink, car & blk 32 28
C605 AP84 5cor dp ultra, vio bl, & blk 75 65
a. Souv. sheet of 4, #C602-C605 3.50 3.50
Set value 1.60 1.35

Rubén Dario (pen name of Felix Rubén Garcia Sarmiento, 1867-1916), poet, newspaper correspondent and diplomat.
Sheets were issued perf. and imperf.

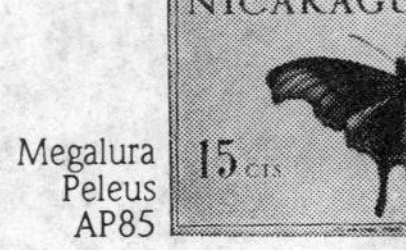

Megalura Peleus AP85

Designs: Various butterflies. 5c, 10c, 30c, 35c, 50c and 1cor are vertical.

1967, Apr. 20 **Litho.** ***Perf. 14***

C606 AP85	5c	multi	15	15
C607 AP85	10c	multi	15	15
C608 AP85	15c	multi	15	15
C609 AP85	20c	multi	15	15
C610 AP85	25c	multi	15	15
C611 AP85	30c	multi	15	15
C612 AP85	35c	multi	20	15
C613 AP85	40c	multi	20	15
C614 AP85	50c	multi	25	15
C615 AP85	60c	multi	25	15
C616 AP85	1cor	multi	40	22
C617 AP85	2cor	multi	75	45
		Set value	2.50	1.50

Com. James McDivitt and Maj. Edward H. White AP86

Gemini 4 Space Flight: 10c, 40c, Rocket launching and astronauts. 15c, 75c, Edward H. White walking in space. 20c, 1cor, Recovery of capsule.

1967, Sept. 20 **Litho.** ***Perf. 13***

C618 AP86	5c	red & multi	15	15
C619 AP86	10c	org & multi	15	15
C620 AP86	15c	multi	15	15
C621 AP86	20c	multi	15	15
C622 AP86	35c	ol & multi	15	15
C623 AP86	40c	ultra & multi	15	15
C624 AP86	75c	brn & multi	18	18
C625 AP86	1cor	multi	22	22
		Set value	75	75

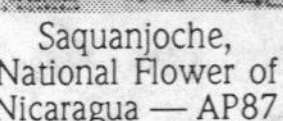

Saquanjoche, National Flower of Nicaragua — AP87

Presidents of Nicaragua and Mexico — AP88

National Flowers: No. C626, White nun orchid, Guatemala. No. C627, Rose, Honduras. No. C629, Maquilishuat, Salvador. No. C630, Purple guaria orchid, Costa Rica.

1967, Nov. 22 **Litho.** ***Perf. 13½***

C626 AP87	40c	multi	15	15
C627 AP87	40c	multi	15	15
C628 AP87	40c	multi	15	15
C629 AP87	40c	multi	15	15
C630 AP87	40c	multi	15	15
a.		Strip of 5, #C626-C630	75	50
		Nos. C626-C630 (5)	75	
		Set value		25

5th anniversary of the General Treaty for Central American Economic Integration.

1968, Feb. 28 **Litho.** ***Perf. 12½***

Designs: 40c Pres. Gustavo Diáz Ordaz of Mexico and Pres. René Schick of Nicaragua signing statement, horiz. 1cor, President Diáz.

C631 AP88	20c	black	15	15
C632 AP88	40c	slate grn	15	15
C633 AP88	1cor	dp brn	22	15
		Set value	40	22

Issued to commemorate the visit of the President of Mexico, Gustavo Diáz Ordaz.

Nos. C479, C527, C242, C440 and C434 Surcharged "Resello" and New Value in Black, Red or Yellow

1968, May **Litho.; Engr.**

C634 AP66	5c	on 6c multi	15	15
C635 AP75	5c	on 6c multi	15	15
C636 AP20	5c	on 8c blk brn	15	15
C637 A84	1cor	on 1.05cor emer & blk (R)	15	15
C638 A83	1cor	on 1.50cor dk bl & yel (Y)	15	15
		Set value	45	38

Mangos — AP89

1968, May 15 **Litho.** ***Perf. 14***

C639 AP89	5c	shown	15	15
C640 AP89	10c	Pineapples	15	15
C641 AP89	15c	Orange	15	15
C642 AP89	20c	Papaya	15	15
C643 AP89	30c	Bananas	15	15
C644 AP89	35c	Avocado	15	15
C645 AP89	50c	Watermelon	15	15
C646 AP89	75c	Cashews	25	15
C647 AP89	1cor	Sapodilla	38	22
C648 AP89	2cor	Cacao	75	45
		Set value	1.90	1.15

The Last Judgment, by Michelangelo AP90

Paintings: 10c, The Crucifixion, by Fra Angelo, horiz. 35c, Madonna with Child and St. John, by Raphael. 2cor, The Disrobing of Christ, by El Greco. 3cor, The Immaculate Conception, by Murillo. 5cor, Christ of St. John of the Cross, by Salvador Dali.

1968, July 22 **Litho.** ***Perf. 12½***

C649 AP90	10c	gold & multi	15	15
C650 AP90	15c	gold & multi	15	15
C651 AP90	35c	gold & multi	15	15
C652 AP90	2cor	gold & multi	45	40
C653 AP90	3cor	gold & multi	65	55
		Set value	1.25	1.10

Miniature Sheet

C654 AP90	5cor	gold & multi	2.75	2.75

Nos. C649-C652 Overprinted: "Visita de S.S. Paulo VI C.E. de Bogota 1968"

1968, Oct. 25 **Litho.** ***Perf. 12½***

C655 AP90	10c	gold & multi	15	15
C656 AP90	15c	gold & multi	15	15
C657 AP90	35c	gold & multi	15	15
C658 AP90	2cor	gold & multi	50	45
		Set value	68	60

Visit of Pope Paul VI to Bogota, Colombia, Aug. 22-24. The overprint has 3 lines on the 10c stamp and 5 lines on others.

Basketball — AP91

Sports: 15c, Fencing, horiz. 20c, Diving. 35c, Running. 50c, Hurdling, horiz. 75c, Weight lifting. 1cor, Boxing, horiz. 2cor, Soccer.

1968, Nov. 28 **Litho.** ***Perf. 14***

C659 AP91	10c	multi	15	15
C660 AP91	15c	org red, blk & gray	15	15
C661 AP91	20c	multi	15	15
C662 AP91	35c	multi	15	15
C663 AP91	50c	multi	15	15
C664 AP91	75c	multi	18	18
C665 AP91	1cor	yel & multi	30	30
C666 AP91	2cor	gray & multi	80	80
a.		Souv. sheet of 4, #C663-C666	1.75	1.75
		Set value	1.55	1.55

19th Olympic Games, Mexico City, Oct. 12-27.

Cichlasoma Citrinellum — AP92

Fish: 15c, Cichlasoma nicaraguensis. 20c, Carp. 30c, Gar (lepisosteus tropicus). 35c, Swordfish. 50c, Phylipnus dormitor, vert. 75c, Tarpon atlanticus, vert. 1cor, Eulamia nicaraguensis, vert. 2cor, Sailfish, vert. 3cor, Sawfish, vert.

Perf. 13½x13, 13x13½

1969, Mar. 12 **Litho.**

C667 AP92	10c	vio bl & multi	15	15
C668 AP92	15c	org & multi	15	15
C669 AP92	20c	grn & multi	15	15
C670 AP92	30c	pur & multi	15	15
C671 AP92	35c	yel & multi	15	15
C672 AP92	50c	brn & multi	15	15
C673 AP92	75c	ultra & multi	15	15
C674 AP92	1cor	org & multi	20	15
C675 AP92	2cor	dk bl & multi	40	25
C676 AP92	3cor	multi	65	42
a.		Min. sheet of 4, #C673-C676	1.75	1.75
		Set value	1.70	1.10

Nos. C544, C549, C567 and C439 Surcharged in Black or Red

RESELLO
C$ 0.10

1969, Mar. **Litho.** ***Perf. 12, 13½x13***

C677 AP76	10c	on 25c multi	15	15
C678 AP77	10c	on 25c multi	15	15
C679 AP79	15c	on 25c multi	15	15

Engr.

C680 A84	50c	on 70c (R)	15	15
		Set value	25	22

Size of 50c surcharge: 11½x9mm.

View, Exhibition Tower and Emblem — AP93

1969, May 30 **Litho.** ***Perf. 13½x13***

C681 AP93	30c	dk vio bl & red	15	15
C682 AP93	35c	blk & red	15	15
C683 AP93	75c	car rose & vio bl	15	15
C684 AP93	1cor	dp plum & blk	25	15
C685 AP93	2cor	dk brn & blk	45	35
a.		Souv. sheet of 4, #C681-C682, C684-C685	1.25	1.25
		Set value	92	65

HEMISFAIR 1968 Exhibition.

Nos. C410, C482, C567-C569, C399, C465, C546 Surcharged in Black or Red

RESELLO
C$ 0.20

1969 **Litho.** ***Perfs. as before***

C686 A80	10c	on 30c multi	15	15
C687 AP66	10c	on 30c bl & blk (R)	15	15
C688 AP79	10c	on 25c multi	15	15
C689 AP79	10c	on 30c multi	15	15
C690 AP79	15c	on 35c multi (R)	15	15
C691 A79	20c	on 30c multi	15	15
C692 AP64	20c	on 30c multi	15	15
C693 AP76	20c	on 35c multi	15	15
		Set value	40	40

Fishing AP94

Products of Nicaragua: 5c, Minerals (miner). 15c, Bananas. 20c, Timber (truck). 35c, Coffee. 40c, Sugar cane. 60c, Cotton. 75c, Rice and corn. 1cor, Tobacco. 2cor, Meat.

1969, Sept. 22 **Litho.** ***Perf. 13x13½***

C694 AP94	5c	gold & multi	15	15
C695 AP94	10c	gold & multi	15	15
C696 AP94	15c	gold & multi	15	15
C697 AP94	20c	gold & multi	15	15
C698 AP94	35c	gold & multi	15	15
C699 AP94	40c	gold & multi	15	15
C700 AP94	60c	gold & multi	15	15
C701 AP94	75c	gold & multi	15	15
C702 AP94	1cor	gold & multi	20	15
C703 AP94	2cor	gold & multi	42	25
		Set value	1.20	75

Woman Carrying Jar, Conference Emblem — AP95

1970, Feb. 26 **Litho.** ***Perf. 13½x14***

C704 AP95	10c	multi	15	15
C705 AP95	15c	grn & multi	15	15
C706 AP95	20c	ultra & multi	15	15
C707 AP95	35c	multi	15	15
C708 AP95	50c	multi	20	15
C709 AP95	75c	multi	25	18
C710 AP95	1cor	lil & multi	45	25
C711 AP95	2cor	multi	85	50
		Nos. C704-C711 (8)	2.35	
		Set value		1.20

Issued to publicize the 8th Inter-American Conference on Savings and Loans.

Soccer Type of Regular Issue and

Flags of Participating Nations, World Cup, 1970 — AP96

Soccer Players: 20c, Djalma Santos, Brazil. 80c, Billy Wright, England. 4cor, Jozef Bozsik, Hungary. 5cor, Bobby Charlton, England.

1970, May 11 **Litho.** ***Perf. 13½***

C712 A87	20c	multi	15	15
C713 A87	80c	multi	22	18
C714 AP96	1cor	multi	28	22
C715 A87	4cor	multi	1.25	90
C716 A87	5cor	multi	1.40	1.25
		Nos. C712-C716 (5)	3.30	2.70

Issued to honor the winners of the 1970 poll for the International Soccer Hall of Fame. No. C714 also publicizes the 9th World Soccer Championships for the Jules Rimet Cup, Mexico City, May 30-June 21, 1970.

Names of players and their achievements printed in black on back of stamps.

For overprint and surcharges see Nos. C786-788.

EXPO Emblem, Mt. Fuji and Torii — AP97

1970, July 5 Litho. *Perf.* 13½x14

C717 AP97 25c multi 15 15
C718 AP97 30c multi 15 15
C719 AP97 35c multi 15 15
C720 AP97 75c multi 22 15
C721 AP97 1.50cor multi 42 30
C722 AP97 3cor multi 75 75
a. Souv. sheet of 3, #C720-C722, imperf. 1.00 1.00
Nos. C717-C722 (6) 1.84
Set value 1.35

EXPO '70 International Exhibition, Osaka, Japan, Mar. 15-Sept. 13, 1970.

Moon Landing, Apollo 11 Emblem and Nicaragua Flag — AP98

Designs (Apollo 11 Emblem, Nicaragua Flag and): 40c, 75c, Moon surface and landing capsule. 60c, 1cor, Astronaut planting US flag.

1970, Aug. 12 Litho. *Perf.* 14

C723 AP98 35c multi 15 15
C724 AP98 40c multi 15 15
C725 AP98 60c pink & multi 18 15
C726 AP98 75c yel & multi 22 15
C727 AP98 1cor vio & multi 38 18
C728 AP98 2cor org & multi 65 38
Nos. C723-C728 (6) 1.73
Set value 90

Man's 1st landing on the moon, July 20, 1969. See note after US No. C76.

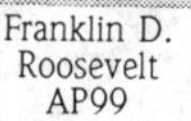

Franklin D. Roosevelt AP99

Annunciation, by Matthias Grunewald AP100

Roosevelt Portraits: 15c, 1cor, as stamp collector. 20c, 50c, 2cor, Full face.

1970, Oct. 12

C729 AP99 10c blk & bluish blk 15 15
C730 AP99 15c blk & brn vio 15 15
C731 AP99 20c blk & ol grn 15 15
C732 AP99 35c blk & brn vio 15 15
C733 AP99 50c brown 15 15
C734 AP99 75c blue 15 15
C735 AP99 1cor rose red 18 15
C736 AP99 2cor black 38 25
Set value 1.00 70

Franklin Delano Roosevelt (1882-1945).

1970, Dec. 1 Litho. *Perf.* 14

Paintings: No. C737, like 15c. No. C738, 20c, Nativity, by El Greco. No. C739, 35c, Adoration of the Magi, by Albrecht Dürer No. C740, 75c, Virgin and Child, by J. van Hemessen. No. C741, 1cor, Holy Shepherd, Portuguese School, 16th century.

C737 AP100 10c multi 15 15
C738 AP100 10c multi 15 15
C739 AP100 10c multi 15 15
C740 AP100 10c multi 15 15
C741 AP100 10c multi 15 15
C742 AP100 15c multi 15 15
C743 AP100 20c multi 15 15
C744 AP100 35c multi 15 15
C745 AP100 75c multi 18 15
C746 AP100 1cor multi 22 15
Set value 80 60

Christmas 1970. Nos. C737-C741 printed se-tenant.

Issues of 1947-67 Surcharged

RESELLO
C$ 0.15

1971, Mar.

C747 A83 10c on 1.05cor (#C433) 28 28
C748 AP64 10c on 1.05cor (#C471) 28 28
C749 AP66 10c on 1.05cor (#C485) 28 28
C750 AP42 15c on 1.50cor (#C292) 42 42
C751 AP53 15c on 1.50cor (#C369) 42 42
C752 A83 15c on 1.50cor (#C434) 42 42
C753 A84 15c on 1.50cor (#C441) 42 42
C754 A75 20c on 85c (#C385) 55 55
C755 A81 20c on 85c (#C418) 55 55
C756 A81 25c on 90c (#C419) 70 70
C757 AP48 30c on 1.10cor (#C337) 85 85
C758 AP44 40c on 1.10cor (#C314) 1.10 1.10
C759 AP65 40c on 1.50cor (#C472) 1.10 1.10
C760 AP80 1cor on 1.10cor (#C576) 2.75 2.75
Nos. C747-C760 (14) 10.12 10.12

The arrangement of the surcharge differs on each stamp.

Mathematics Type of Regular Issue

Symbolic Designs of Scientific Formulae: 25c, Napier's law (logarithms). 30c, Pythagorean theorem (length of sides of right-angled triangle). 40c, Boltzman's equation (movement of gases). 1cor, Broglie's law (motion of particles of matter). 2cor, Archimedes' principle (displacement of mass).

1971, May 15 Litho. *Perf.* 13½

C761 A88 25c lt bl & multi 15 15
C762 A88 30c lt bl & multi 18 16
C763 A88 40c lt bl & multi 25 20
C764 A88 1cor lt bl & multi 60 35
C765 A88 2cor lt bl & multi 1.00 75
Nos. C761-C765 (5) 2.18 1.61

On the back of each stamp is a descriptive paragraph.

Montezuma Oropendola — AP101

Birds: 15c, Turquoise-browed motmot. 20c, Magpie-jay. 25c, Scissor-tailed flycatchers. 30c, Spot-breasted oriole, horiz. 35c, Rufous-naped wren. 40c, Great kiskadee. 75c, Red-legged honeycreeper, horiz. 1cor, Great-tailed grackle, horiz. 2cor, Belted kingfisher.

1971, Oct. 15 Litho. *Perf.* 14

C766 AP101 10c multi 15 15
C767 AP101 15c multi 15 15
C768 AP101 20c gray & multi 15 15
C769 AP101 25c multi 15 15
C770 AP101 30c multi 15 15
C771 AP101 35c multi 15 15
C772 AP101 40c multi 15 15
C773 AP101 75c yel & multi 25 15
C774 AP101 1cor org & multi 30 18
C775 AP101 2cor org & multi 65 32
Set value 1.75 95

Ten Commandments Type of Regular Issue

Designs: 1cor, Bathsheba at her Bath, by Rembrandt (IX). 2cor, Naboth's Vineyard, by James Smetham (X).

1971, Nov. 1 *Perf.* 11

C776 A90 1cor ocher & multi 90 45
C777 A90 2cor ocher & multi 1.50 80

Descriptive inscriptions printed in gray on back of stamps.

U Thant, Anastasio Somoza, UN Emblem AP102

1972, Feb. 15 *Perf.* 14x13½

C778 AP102 10c pink & mar 15 15
C779 AP102 15c green 15 15
C780 AP102 20c blue 15 15
C781 AP102 25c rose cl 15 15
C782 AP102 30c org & brn 15 15
C783 AP102 40c gray & sl grn 15 15
C784 AP102 1cor ol grn 22 15
C785 AP102 2cor brown 45 25
Set value 1.00 65

25th anniv. of the United Nations (in 1970).

Nos. C713, C715, C716 Surcharged or Overprinted Like Nos. 899-900

1972, Mar. 20 Litho. *Perf.* 13½

C786 A87 20c on 80c multi 15 15
C787 A87 60c on 4cor multi 15 15
C788 A87 5cor multi 1.10 1.00

20th Olympic Games, Munich, Aug. 26-Sept. 11.

Ceramic Figure, Map of Nicaragua AP103

Designs: Pre-Columbian ceramics (700-1200A.D.) found at sites indicated on map of Nicaragua.

1972, Sept. 16 Litho. *Perf.* 14x13½

C789 AP103 10c bl & multi 15 15
C790 AP103 15c bl & multi 15 15
C791 AP103 20c bl & multi 15 15
C792 AP103 25c bl & multi 15 15
C793 AP103 30c bl & multi 15 15
C794 AP103 35c bl & multi 15 15
C795 AP103 40c bl & multi 15 15
C796 AP103 50c bl & multi 15 15
C797 AP103 60c bl & multi 15 15
C798 AP103 80c bl & multi 15 15
C799 AP103 1cor bl & multi 20 15
C800 AP103 2cor bl & multi 38 25
Set value 1.20 90

Lord Peter Wimsey, by Dorothy L. Sayers AP104

Designs (Book and): 10c, Philip Marlowe, by Raymond Chandler. 15c, Sam Spade, by Dashiell Hammett. 20c, Perry Mason, by Erle S. Gardner. 25c, Nero Wolfe, by Rex Stout. 35c, Auguste Dupin, by Edgar Allan Poe. 40c, Ellery Queen, by Frederick Dannay and Manfred B. Lee. 50c, Father Brown, by G. K. Chesterton. 60c, Charlie Chan, by Earl Derr Biggers. 80c, Inspector Maigret, by Georges Simenon. 1cor, Hercule Poirot, by Agatha Christie. 2cor, Sherlock Holmes, by A. Conan Doyle.

1972, Nov. 13 Litho. *Perf.* 14x13½

C801 AP104 5c bl & multi 15 15
C802 AP104 10c bl & multi 15 15
C803 AP104 15c bl & multi 15 15
C804 AP104 20c bl & multi 15 15
C805 AP104 25c bl & multi 16 16
C806 AP104 35c bl & multi 22 22
C807 AP104 40c bl & multi 25 25
C808 AP104 50c bl & multi 32 32
C809 AP104 60c bl & multi 38 38
C810 AP104 80c bl & multi 50 50
C811 AP104 1cor bl & multi 65 65
C812 AP104 2cor bl & multi 1.25 1.25
Nos. C801-C812 (12) 4.33 4.33

50th anniversary of INTERPOL, international police organization. Designs show famous fictional detectives. Inscriptions on back, printed on top of gum, give thumbnail sketch of character and author.

Shepherds Following Star — AP105

Legend of the Christmas Rose: 15c, Adoration of the kings and shepherds. 20c, Shepherd girl alone crying. 35c, Angel appears to girl. 40c, Christmas rose (Helleborus niger). 60c, Girl thanks angel. 80c, Girl and Holy Family. 1cor, Girl presents rose to Christ Child. 2cor, Adoration.

1972, Dec. 20

C813 AP105 10c multi 15 15
C814 AP105 15c multi 15 15
C815 AP105 20c multi 15 15
C816 AP105 35c multi 15 15
C817 AP105 40c multi 15 15
C818 AP105 60c multi 15 15
C819 AP105 80c multi 16 15
C820 AP105 1cor multi 18 16
C821 AP105 2cor multi 35 32
a. Souv. sheet of 9, #C813-C821 1.10 1.10
Set value 1.00 90

Christmas 1972.

No. C821a exists with red marginal overprint, "TERREMOTO DESASTRE," for the Managua earthquake of Dec. 22-23, 1972. It was sold abroad, starting in Jan. 1973.

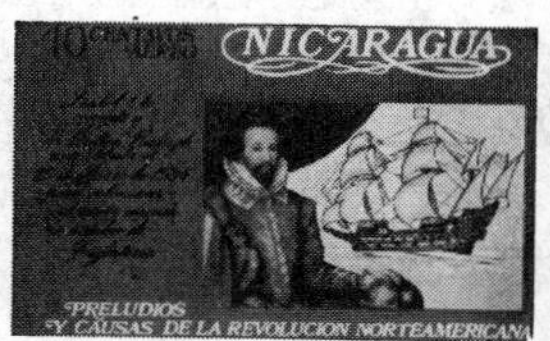

Sir Walter Raleigh, Patent to Settle New World — AP106

Events and Quotations from Contemporary Illustrations: 15c, Mayflower Compact, 1620. 20c, Acquittal of Peter Zenger, 1735, vert. 25c, William Pitt, 1766, vert. 30c, British revenue stamp for use in America No. RM31, vert. 35c, "Join or Die" serpent, 1768. 40c, Boston Massacre and State House, 1770, vert. 50c, Boston Tea Party and 3p coin, 1774. 60c, Patrick Henry, 1775, vert. 75c, Battle scene ("Our cause is just, our union is perfect," 1775). 80c, Declaration of Independence, 1776. 1cor, Liberty Bell, Philadelphia. 2cor, Seal of US, 1782, vert.

1973, Feb. 22 Photo. *Perf.* 13½

C822 AP106 10c ol & multi 15 15
C823 AP106 15c ol & multi 15 15
C824 AP106 20c ol & multi 15 15
C825 AP106 25c ol & multi 15 15
C826 AP106 30c ol & multi 20 15
C827 AP106 35c ol, gold & blk 35 20
C828 AP106 40c ol & multi 35 20
C829 AP106 50c ol & multi 35 35
C830 AP106 60c ol & multi 40 35
C831 AP106 75c ol & multi 50 40
C832 AP106 80c ol & multi 50 40
C833 AP106 1cor ol & multi 80 50
C834 AP106 2cor ol & multi 1.50 1.00
Nos. C822-C834 (13) 5.55 4.15

Inscriptions on back, printed on top of gum, give brief description of subject and event.

Baseball, Player and Map of Nicaragua — AP107

1973, May 25 Litho. *Perf.* 13½x14

C835 AP107 15c lil & multi 15 15
C836 AP107 20c multi 15 15
C837 AP107 40c multi 15 15

C838 AP107 10cor multi 1.75 1.50
a. Souvenir sheet of 4 2.50 2.50
Set value 1.65

20th International Baseball Championships, Managua, Nov. 15-Dec. 5, 1972. No. C838a contains 4 stamps similar to Nos. C835-C838 with changed background colors (15c, olive; 20c, gray; 40c, lt. green; 10cor, lilac), and 5 labels.

Fashion Type of 1973

1973, July 26 Litho. *Perf. 13½*
C839 A91 10c Lourdes Nicaragua 15 15
C840 A91 15c Halston, New York 15 15
C841 A91 20c Pino Lancetti, Rome 15 15
C842 A91 35c Madame Ges, Paris 15 15
C843 A91 40c Irene Galitzine, Rome 15 15
C844 A91 80c Pedro Rodriguez, Barcelona 18 15
a. Souv. sheet of 9, #909-911, C839-C844, perf. 11 + 3 labels 3.00 3.00
Set value 50 42

Inscriptions on back printed on top of gum give description of gown in Spanish and English.

Type of Air Post Semi-Postal Issue

Design: 2cor, Pediatric surgery.

1973, Sept. 25
C845 SPAP1 2cor multi 40 35
Set value, #C845, CB1-CB11 1.60 1.35

Planned Children's Hospital. Inscription on back, printed on top of gum gives brief description of subject shown.

Christmas Type

Designs: 1cor, Virginia O'Hanlon writing letter, father. 2cor, Letter. 4cor, Virginia, father reading letter.

1973, Nov. 15 Litho. *Perf. 15*
C846 A92 1cor multicolored 30
C847 A92 2cor multicolored 55
C848 A92 4cor multicolored 1.10
a. Souvenir sheet of 3, #C846-C848, perf. 14½ 3.75

Churchill Type

Designs: No. C851, Silhouette, Parliament. No. C852, Silhouette, #10 Downing St. 5cor, Showing "V" sign. 6cor, "Bulldog" Churchill protecting England.

1974, Apr. 30 *Perf. 14½*
C849 A93 5cor multicolored 1.40
C850 A93 6cor multicolored 1.70

Souvenir Sheets
Perf. 15
C851 A93 4cor blk, org, & bl 1.10
C852 A93 4cor blk, org, & grn 1.10

Nos. C851-C852 contain one 28x42mm stamp.

World Cup Type

Scenes from previous World Cup Championships with flags and scores of finalists.

1974, May 8 *Perf. 14½*
C853 A94 10cor Flags of participants 2.80

Souvenir Sheets
C853A A94 4cor like No. 928 1.10
C853B A94 5cor like No. 930 1.40

For overprint see No. C856.

Flower Type of 1974

Wild Flowers and Cacti: 1 cor, Centrosema. 3 cor, Night-blooming cereus.

1974, June 11 Litho. *Perf. 14*
C854 A95 1cor grn & multi 20 18
C855 A95 3cor grn & multi 65 55

Nicaraguan Stamps Type

1974, July 10 *Perf. 14½*
C855A A96 40c #835 20
C855B A96 3cor #C313, horiz. 90
C855C A96 5cor #734 1.40

Souvenir Sheet
Imperf
C855D Sheet of 3 2.05
e. A96 1cor #665 30
f. A96 2cor #C110, horiz. 55
g. A96 4cor Globe, stars 1.20

UPU, Cent.

No. C853 Ovptd. **TRIUMFADOR ALEMANIA OCCIDENTAL**

1974, July 12
C856 A94 10cor Flags 2.80

Animal Type of 1974

Designs: 3cor, Colorado deer. 5cor, Jaguar.

1974, Sept. 10 Litho. *Perf. 14½*
C857 A97 3cor multi 65 55
C858 A97 5cor multi 1.00 90

Christmas Type of 1974

Works of Michelangelo: 40c, Madonna of the Stairs. 80c, Pitti Madonna. 2cor, Pietà. 5cor, Self-portrait.

1974, Dec. 15
C859 A98 40c multi 15 15
C860 A98 80c multi 15 15
C861 A98 2cor multi 28 25
C862 A98 5cor multi 70 65

An imperf. souvenir sheet exists containing 2cor and 5cor stamps.

Opera Type of 1975

Opera Singers and Scores: 25c, Rosa Ponselle, Norma. 35c, Giuseppe de Luca, Rigoletto. 40c, Joan Sutherland, La Figlia del Reggimento. 50c, Ezio Pinza, Don Giovanni. 60c, Kirsten Flagstad, Tristan and Isolde. 80c, Maria Callas, Tosca. 2cor, Fyodor Chaliapin, Boris Godunov. 5cor, Enrico Caruso, La Juive.

1975, Jan. 22 *Perf. 14x13½*
C863 A99 25c grn & multi 15 15
C864 A99 35c multi 15 15
C865 A99 40c multi 15 15
C866 A99 50c org & multi 15 15
C867 A99 60c rose & multi 18 15
C868 A99 80c lake & multi 25 15
C869 A99 2cor sep & multi 50 25
C870 A99 5cor multi 1.25 65
a. Souvenir sheet of 3 2.50
Nos. C863-C870 (8) 2.78
Set value 1.25

No. C870a contains one each of Nos. C869-C870 and a 1cor with design and colors of No. C868. Exists imperf.

Easter Type of 1975

Stations of the Cross: 40c, Jesus stripped of his clothes. 50c, Jesus nailed to the Cross. 80c, Jesus dies on the Cross. 1cor, Descent from the Cross. 5cor, Jesus laid in the tomb.

1975, Mar. 20 *Perf. 14½*
C871 A100 40c ultra & multi 15 15
C872 A100 50c ultra & multi 15 15
C873 A100 80c ultra & multi 15 15
C874 A100 1cor ultra & multi 16 15
C875 A100 5cor ultra & multi 90 80
Nos. C871-C875 (5) 1.51
Set value 1.15

American Bicentennal Type of 1975

Designs: 40c, Washington's Farewell, 1783. 50c, Washington Addressing Continental Congress by J. B. Stearns. 2cor, Washington Arriving for Inauguration. 5cor, Statue of Liberty and flags of 1776 and 1976. 40c, 50c, 2cor, horiz.

1975, Apr. 16 *Perf. 14*
C876 A101 40c tan & multi 18 15
C877 A101 50c tan & multi 25 18
C878 A101 2cor tan & multi 80 75
C879 A101 5cor tan & multi 2.00 1.90

Perf. and imperf. 7cor souv. sheets exist.

Nordjamb 75 Type of 1975

Designs (Scout and Nordjamb Emblems and): 35c, Camp. 40c, Scout musicians. 1cor, Campfire. 10cor, Lord Baden-Powell.

1975, Aug. 15 *Perf. 14½*
C880 A102 35c multi 15 15
C881 A102 40c multi 15 15
C882 A102 1cor multi 15 15
C883 A102 10cor multi 1.40 1.25
Set value 1.45

Two airmail souvenir sheets of 2 exist. One, perf., contains 2cor and 3cor with designs of Nos. 992 and 990. The other, imperf., contains 2cor and 3cor with designs of Nos. 993 and C882. Size: 125x101mm.

Pres. Somoza Type of 1975

1975, Sept. 10 *Perf. 14*
C884 A103 1cor vio & multi 20 18
C885 A103 10cor bl & multi 2.00 1.80
C886 A103 20cor multi 4.00 3.00

Choir Type of 1975

Famous Choirs: 50c, Montserrat Abbey. 1cor, St. Florian Choir Boys. 2cor, Choir Boys of the Wooden Cross, vert. 5cor, Boys and Pope Paul VI (Pueri Cantores International Federation).

1975, Nov. 15 *Perf. 14½*
C887 A104 50c sil & multi 15 15
C888 A104 1cor sil & multi 20 16
C889 A104 2cor sil & multi 35 32
C890 A104 5cor sil & multi 1.00 85

A 10cor imperf. souvenir sheet exists (Obserndorf Memorial Chapel Choir and score of "Holy Night-Silent Night").

Chess Type of 1976

Designs: 40c, The Chess Players, by Thomas Eakins. 2cor, Bobby Fischer and Boris Spasski in Reykjavik, 1972. 5cor, Shakespeare and Ben Johnson Playing Chess, by Karel van Mander.

1976, Jan. 8 *Perf. 14½*
C891 A105 40c multi 16 15
C892 A105 2cor vio & multi 75 50
C893 A105 5cor multi 1.50 1.25

A souvenir sheet contains one each of Nos. C892-C893, perf. and imperf. Size: 143x67mm.

Olympic Winner Type 1976

Winners, Rowing and Sculling Events: 55c, USSR, 1956, 1960, 1964, vert. 70c, New Zealand, 1972, vert. 90c, New Zealand, 1968. 10cor, Women's rowing crew, US, 1976, vert. 20cor, US, 1956.

1976, Sept. 7 Litho. *Perf. 14*
C902 A107 55c bl & multi 18 15
C903 A107 70c bl & multi 18 15
C904 A107 90c bl & multi 22 18
C905 A107 20cor bl & multi 4.50 3.75

Souvenir Sheet
C906 A107 10cor multi 1.65

No. C906 for the 1st participation of women in Olympic rowing events, size of stamp: 37x50mm.

The overprint "Republica Democratica Alemana Vencedor en 1976" was applied in 1976 to No. C905 in black in 3 lines and to the margin of No. C906 in gold in 2 lines.

Bicentennial Type of 1976

Designs (American Bicentennial Emblem and): No. C907, Philadelphia, 1776. No. C908, Washington, 1976. No. C909, John Paul Jones' ships. No. C910, Atomic submarine. No. C911, Wagon train. No. C912, Diesel train.

1976, May 25 Litho. *Perf. 13½*
C907 A108 80c multi 18 15
C908 A108 80c multi 18 15
C909 A108 2.75cor multi 50 38
C910 A108 2.75cor multi 50 38
C911 A108 4cor multi 65 50
C912 A108 4cor multi 65 50
Nos. C907-C912 (6) 2.66 2.06

Stamps of same denomination printed se-tenant. A souvenir sheet contains two 10cor stamps showing George Washington and Gerald R. Ford with their families. Size: 140x111mm.

Rare Stamps Type of 1976

Rare Stamps: 40c, Hawaii #1. 1cor, Great Britain #1. 2cor, British Guiana #13. 5cor, Honduras #C12. 10cor, Newfoundland #C1.

1976, Dec. *Perf. 14*
C913 A109 40c multi 15 15
C914 A109 1cor multi 15 15
C915 A109 2cor multi 28 25
C916 A109 5cor multi 70 65
C917 A109 10cor multi 1.40 1.25
Nos. C913-C917 (5) 2.68 2.45

Inscriptions on back printed on top of gum give description of illustrated stamp. A 4cor imperf. souvenir sheet shows 1881 Great Britain-Nicaragua combination cover. Size: 140x101mm.

Olga Nuñez de Saballos — AP108

Designs: 1cor, Josefa Toledo de Aguerri. 10cor, Hope Portocarrero de Somoza.

1977, Feb. Litho. *Perf. 13½*
C918 AP108 35c multi 15 15
C919 AP108 1cor red & multi 20 18
C920 AP108 10cor multi 2.00 1.75

Famous Nicaraguan women and for International Women's Year (in 1975).

Zeppelin Type of 1977

Designs: 35c, Ville de Paris airship. 70c, Zeppelin "Schwaben." 3cor, Zeppelin in flight. 10cor, Vickers "Mayfly" before take-off. 20cor, Zeppelin with leadlines extended.

1977, Oct. 31 Litho. *Perf. 14½*
C921 A110 35c multi 15 15
C922 A110 70c multi 18 15
C923 A110 3cor multi 65 50
C924 A110 10cor multi 2.50 1.75

Souvenir Sheet
C925 A110 20cor multi 4.50 2.75

Lindbergh Type of 1977

Designs: 55c, Lindbergh's plane approaching Nicaraguan airfield, 1928. 80c, Spirit of St. Louis and map of New York-Paris route. 2cor, Plane flying off Nicaragua's Pacific Coast. 10cor, Lindbergh flying past Momotombo Volcano on way to Managua. 20cor, Spirit of St. Louis.

1977, Nov. 30
C926 A111 55c multi 15 15
C927 A111 80c multi 16 15
C928 A111 2cor multi 40 32
C929 A111 10cor multi 2.00 1.65

Souvenir Sheet
C930 A111 20cor multi 4.50 3.50

Christmas Type of 1977
Souvenir Sheet

Design: 20cor, Finale of Nutcracker Suite.

1977, Dec. 12
C931 A112 20cor multi 4.50 4.50

Painting Type of 1978

Rubens Paintings: 5cor, Hippopotamus and Crocodile Hunt. 10cor, Duke de Lerma on Horseback. 20cor, Self-portrait.

1978, Jan. 11 Litho. *Perf. 14½*
C932 A113 5cor multi 1.00 85
C933 A113 10cor multi 2.00 1.65

Souvenir Sheet
C934 A113 20cor multi 4.75 4.00

Peter Paul Rubens (1577-1640), 400th birth anniversary.

St. Francis Type of 1978

Designs: 80c, St. Francis and the wolf. 10cor, St. Francis, painting. 20cor, Our Lady of Conception, statue in Church of El Viejo.

1978, Feb. 23 Litho. *Perf. 14½*
C935 A114 80c lt brn & multi 16 15
C936 A114 10cor bl & multi 1.90 1.75

Souvenir Sheet
C937 A114 20cor multi 3.50

Railroad Type of 1978

Locomotives: 35c, Light-weight American. 4cor, Heavy Baldwin. 10cor, Juniata, 13-ton. 20cor, Map of route system.

1978, Apr. 7 Litho. *Perf. 14½*
C938 A115 35c lt grn & multi 15 15
C939 A115 4cor dp org & multi 90 75
C940 A115 10cor cit & multi 2.00 1.90

Souvenir Sheet
C941 A115 20cor multi 3.50

Jules Verne Type of 1978

Designs: 90c, 20,000 Leagues under the Sea. 10cor, Around the World in 80 Days. 20cor, From the Earth to the Moon.

1978, Aug. Litho. *Perf. 14½*
C942 A116 90c multi 20 15
C943 A116 10cor multi 1.75 1.50

Souvenir Sheet
C944 A116 20cor multi 5.00

Aviation History Type of 1978

Designs: 55c, Igor Sikorsky in his helicopter, 1913, horiz. 10cor, Space shuttle, horiz. 20cor, Flyer III, horiz.

1978, Sept. 29 Litho. *Perf. 14½*
C945 A117 55c multi 15 15

C946 A117 10cor multi 1.40 1.00

Souvenir Sheet

C947 A117 20cor multi 5.00

Soccer Type of 1978

Soccer Players: 50c, Denis Law and Franz Beckenbauer. 5cor, Dino Zoff and Pelé. 20cor, Dominique Rocheteau and Johan Neeskens.

1978, Oct. 25 Litho. *Perf. 13½x14*

C948 A118 50c multi 15 15

C949 A118 5cor multi 1.00 85

Souvenir Sheet

C950 A118 20cor multi 4.50

Christmas Type of 1978

Paintings: 3cor, Apostles John and Peter, by Dürer. 10cor, Apostles Paul and Mark, by Dürer. 20cor, Virgin and Child with Garlands, by Dürer.

1978, Dec. 12 Litho. *Perf. 13½x14*

C951 A119 3cor multi 42 35

C952 A119 10cor multi 1.40 1.00

Souvenir Sheet

C953 A119 20cor multi 3.50

Volcano Type of 1978

Designs: No. C954, Cerro Negro Volcano. No. C955, Lake Masaya. No. C956, Momotombo Volcano. No. C957, Lake Asososca. No. C958, Mombacho Volcano. No. C959, Lake Apoyo. No. C960, Concepcion Volcano. No. C961, Lake Tiscapa.

1978, Dec. 29 *Perf. 14x13½*

C954 A120 35c multi 15 15

C955 A120 35c multi 15 15

C956 A120 90c multi 16 15

C957 A120 90c multi 16 15

C958 A120 1cor multi 20 15

C959 A120 1cor multi 20 15

C960 A120 10cor multi 1.90 1.35

C961 A120 10cor multi 1.90 1.35

Nos. C954-C961 (8) 4.82 3.60

Stamps of same denomination printed se-tenant in sheets of 40.

Bernardo O'Higgins — AP109

1979, Mar. 7 Litho. *Perf. 14*

C962 AP109 20cor multi 4.25 3.25

Bernardo O'Higgins (1778-1842), Chilean soldier and statesman.

Red Ginger and Rubythroated Hummingbird — AP110

Designs: 55c, Orchid. 70c, Poinsettia. 80c, Flower and bees. 2cor, Lignum vitae and blue morpho butterfly. 4cor, Cattleya.

1979, Apr. 6 Litho. *Perf. 14x13½*

C963 AP110 50c multi 15 15

C964 AP110 55c multi 15 15

C965 AP110 70c multi 16 15

C966 AP110 80c multi 16 15

C967 AP110 2cor multi 35 28

C968 AP110 4cor multi 70 52

Nos. C963-C968 (6) 1.67

Set value 1.00

Revolution Type of 1981

1981, July 19 Litho. *Perf. 12½x12*

C973 A123 2.10cor March 30 15

C974 A123 3cor Construction 42 24

C975 A123 6cor Health programs 80 48

FSLN Type of 1981

1981, July 23

C976 A124 4cor Founder 55 35

Postal Union Type of 1981

1981, Aug. 10

C977 A125 2.10cor Pony express 22 15

C978 A125 3cor Headquarters 30 18

C979 A125 6cor Members' flags 60 35

1300th Anniv. of Bulgaria — AP112

1981, Sept. 2 *Imperf.*

C980 AP112 10cor multi 1.25 1.00

Size: 96x70mm.

Aquatic Flower Type of 1981

1981, Sept. 15 *Perf. 12½*

C981 A126 10cor Nymphaea gladstoniana 1.40 90

Souvenir Sheet

Panda Bear — AP113

1981, Oct. 9 *Perf. 13*

C982 AP113 10cor multi 1.25 1.00

Philatokyo Stamp Exhibition, Tokyo.

Tropical Fish Type of 1981

1981, Oct. 19 *Perf. 12½*

C983 A127 3.50cor Pterolebias longipinnis 48 28

C984 A127 4cor Xiphophorus helleri 55 30

Souvenir Sheet

Frigate — AP114

1981, Nov. 2 *Perf. 13*

C985 AP114 10cor multi 1.40 85

Espamer '81 Stamp Exhibition, Buenos Aires, Nov. 13-22.

Bird Type of 1981

1981, Nov. 30 *Perf. 12½*

C986 A128 3cor Trogon massena 48 26

C987 A128 4cor Campylo-pterus hemileucurus, horiz. 65 38

C988 A128 6cor Momotus momota 95 55

Satellite Type of 1981

1981, Dec. 15 *Perf. 13x12½*

C989 A129 3cor multi 35 22

C990 A129 4cor multi 50 28

C991 A129 5cor multi 60 35

Railroad Type of 1981

1981, Dec. 30 *Perf. 12½*

C992 A130 6cor Ferrobus, 1967 1.00 55

World Cup Type of 1982

1982, Jan. 25

C993 A131 4cor multi 48 30

C994 A131 10cor multi, horiz. 1.25 80

Souvenir Sheet

Perf. 13

C995 A131 10cor multi 1.65 1.10

No. C995 contains one 39x31mm stamp.

Dog Type of 1982

1982, Feb. 18

C996 A132 3cor Boxers 45 28

C997 A132 3.50cor Pointers 48 28

C998 A132 6cor Collies 90 50

Intl. ITU Congress AP115

1982, Mar. 12

C999 AP115 25cor multi 3.25 2.25

Butterfly Type of 1982

1982, Mar. 26

C1000 A133 3cor Parides iphidamas 45 28

C1001 A133 3.50cor Consul hippona 48 30

C1002 A133 4cor Morpho peleides 55 35

Satellite Type of 1982

1982, Apr. 12

C1003 A134 5cor multi, horiz. 65 40

C1004 A134 6cor multi 90 48

UPU Type of 1982

1982, May 1 Litho. *Perf. 13*

C1005 A135 3.50cor Train 38 22

C1006 A135 10cor Jet 1.10 70

Sports Type of 1982

1982, May 13

C1007 A136 2.50cor Women's volleyball, vert. 38 22

C1008 A136 3cor Boxing 45 30

C1009 A136 9cor Soccer 1.40 80

Souvenir Sheet

C1010 A136 10cor Baseball, vert. 1.50 80

No. C1010 contains one 29x36mm stamp.

Souvenir Sheet

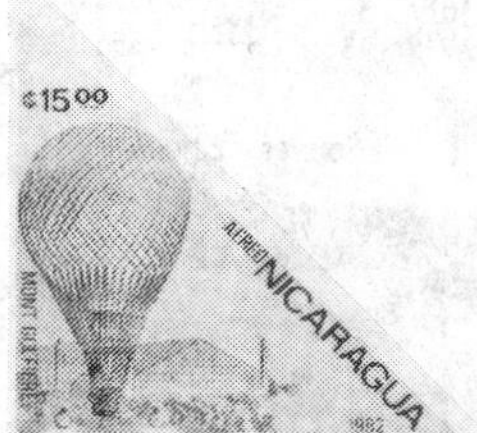

PHILEXFRANCE '82 Intl. Stamp Exhibition, Paris, June 11-21 — AP116

1982, June 9 *Perf. 13x12½*

C1011 AP116 15cor multi 1.65 1.00

Revolution Type of 1982

Designs: Symbolic doves. 2.50cor, 4cor vert.

1982, July 19 *Perf. 13*

C1012 A137 2.50cor multi 38 22

C1013 A137 4cor multi 60 38

C1014 A137 6cor multi 1.00 60

Washington Type of 1982

Perf. 12½x13, 13x12½

1982, June 20 Litho.

C1015 A138 2.50cor Crossing the Delaware, horiz. 38 22

C1016 A138 3.50cor At Valley Forge, horiz. 52 35

C1017 A138 4cor Battle of Trenton 60 38

C1018 A138 6cor Washington in Princeton 1.00 60

Painting Type of 1982

1982, Aug. 17 *Perf. 13*

C1019 A139 9cor Seated Woman, by A. Morales 1.25 80

Dimitrov Type of 1982

1982, Sept. 9

C1020 A140 2.50cor Dimitrov, Yikov, Sofia, 1946 38 24

C1021 A140 4cor Portrait, flag 60 38

Dictatorship Type of 1982

1982, Sept. 21 *Perf. 13x12½*

C1022 A141 4cor Rigoberto Lopez Perez 60 38

C1023 A141 6cor Edwin Castro 1.00 60

Tourism Type of 1982

1982, Sept. 25 *Perf. 13*

C1024 A142 2.50cor Coyotepe Fortress, Masaya 28 16

C1025 A142 3.50cor Velazquez Park, Managua 38 24

Marx Type of 1982

1982, Oct. 4 *Perf. 12½*

C1026 A143 4cor Marx, Highgate Monument 55 35

Discovery of America Type of 1982

1982, Oct. 12 *Perf. 12½x13*

C1027 A145 2.50cor Trans-atlantic voyage 42 24

C1028 A145 4cor Landing of Columbus 65 42

C1029 A145 7cor Death of Columbus 1.10 70

Souvenir Sheet

Perf. 13

C1030 A145 10cor Columbus' fleet 1.65 1.00

No. C1030 contains one 31x39mm stamp.

Flower Type of 1982

1982, Nov. 13 *Perf. 12½*

C1031 A146 2.50cor Pasiflora foetida 38 22

C1032 A146 3.50cor Clitoria sp. 52 32

C1033 A146 5cor Russelia sarmentosa 75 45

Reptile Type of 1982

1982, Dec. 10 *Perf. 13*

C1034 A147 2.50cor Turtle, horiz. 38 22

C1035 A147 3cor Boa constrictor 45 28

C1036 A147 3.50cor Crocodile, horiz. 52 32

C1037 A147 5cor Sistrurus catenatus, horiz. 75 45

Non-aligned States Conference, Jan. 12-14 — AP117

1983, Jan. 10 Litho. *Perf. 12½x13*

C1038 AP117 4cor multi 60 38

Geothermal Electricity Generating Plant, Momotombo Volcano — AP118

1983, Feb. 25 *Perf. 13*

C1039 AP118 2.50cor multi 38 22

Souvenir Sheet

TEMBAL '83 Philatelic Exhibition, Basel, Switzerland AP119

1983, May 21 **Litho.** ***Perf. 13***
C1040 AP119 15cor Chamoix 2.25 1.25

Souvenir Sheet

1st Nicaraguan Philatelic Exhibition AP120

1983, July 17 **Litho.** ***Perf. 13***
C1041 AP120 10cor Nicaragua Airlines jet 2.25 1.25

Armed Forces — AP121

1983, Sept. 2 **Litho.** ***Perf. 13***
C1042 AP121 4cor Frontier guards, watch dog 42 26

Souvenir Sheet

BRASILIANA '83 Intl. Stamp Show, Rio de Janeiro, July 29-Aug. 7 — AP122

1983
C1043 AP122 15cor Jaguar 2.25 1.25

Cuban Revolution, 25th Anniv. — AP122a

1984, Jan. 1 **Litho.** ***Perf. 13***
C1043A AP122a 4cor shown 60 32
C1043B AP122a 6cor Castro, Guevara, flag 95 45

An enhanced introduction to the Scott Catalogue begins on Page 5A. A thorough understanding of the material presented there will greatly aid your use of the catalogue itself.

Souvenir Sheet

Cardinal Infante Don Fernando, by Diego Velazquez — AP123

1984, May 2 **Litho.** ***Perf. 13***
C1044 AP123 15cor multi 1.75 1.00

ESPANA '84.

Souvenir Sheet

Hamburg '84 AP124

1984, June 19 **Litho.** ***Perf. 13***
C1045 AP124 15cor Dirigible 1.75 90

1984 UPU Congress AP125

1984, June 24 ***Perf. 12½***
C1046 AP125 15cor Mail transport 1.75 90

Souvenir Sheet

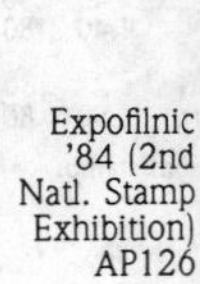

Expofilnic '84 (2nd Natl. Stamp Exhibition) AP126

1984, July 15
C1047 AP126 15cor Communications Museum 1.75 90

Souvenir Sheet

Ausipex '84 — AP127

1984, Sept. 21
C1048 AP127 15cor Explorer ship 1.75 90

Souvenir Sheet

OLYMPHILEX '85 — AP128

1985, Mar. 18 **Litho.** ***Perf. 12½***
C1049 AP128 15cor Bicycle race 1.10 60

Souvenir Sheet

ESPAMER '85, Havana, Mar. 19-24 — AP129

1985, Mar. 19
C1050 AP129 10cor Crocodylus rhombifer 75 38

Victory of Sandanista Revolution, 6th Anniv. AP134

1985, July 19 **Litho.** ***Perf. 12½***
C1125 AP134 9cor Soldier, flag 90 58
C1126 AP134 9cor Sugar mill 90 58

Benjamin Zeledon, Birth Cent. — AP135

1985, Oct. 4 **Litho.** ***Perf. 12½***
C1127 AP135 15cor multicolored 75 38

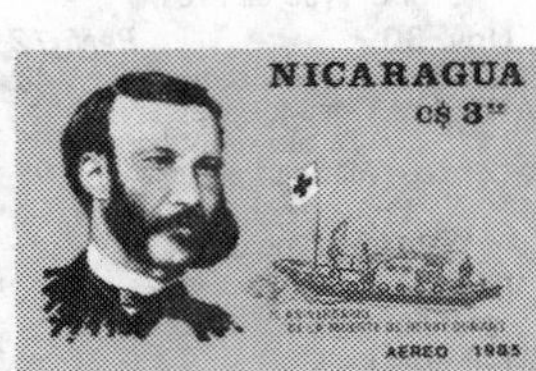

Henri Dunant (1828-1910), Founder of Red Cross — AP136

1985, Oct. 10 ***Perf. 12½x12***
C1128 AP136 3cor shown 18 15
C1129 AP136 15cor Dunant, air ambulance 90 45
a. Pair, #C1128-C1129 + label 1.10 55

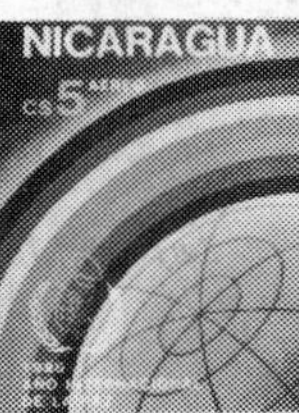

Nicaraguan Stamps, 125th Anniv. AP137

1986, May 22 ***Perf. 12½x13***
C1130 AP137 30cor No. C1 65 32
C1131 AP137 40cor No. 174 85 42
C1132 AP137 50cor No. 48 1.10 52
C1133 AP137 100cor No. 1 2.00 1.10

Intl. Peace Year — AP138

1986, July 19 ***Perf. 12½***
C1134 AP138 5cor shown 15 15
C1135 AP138 10cor Globe, dove 25 15
Set value 20

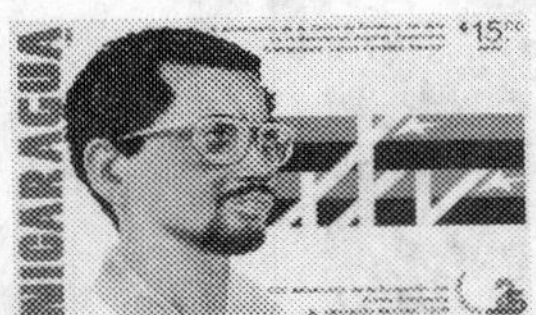

Carlos Fonseca, 10th Death Anniv. — AP139

1986, Aug. 11 **Litho.** ***Perf. 12½***
C1136 AP139 15cor multicolored 32 20

Formation of the Sandinista Front, 25th anniv.

AP140 AP141

1986, Nov. 20 ***Perf. 13***
C1137 AP140 15cor Rhinoceros 32 16
C1138 AP140 15cor Zebra 32 16
C1139 AP140 25cor Elephant 55 28
C1140 AP140 25cor Giraffe 55 28
C1141 AP140 50cor Mandrill 1.10 55
C1142 AP140 50cor Tiger 1.10 55
Nos. C1137-C1142 (6) 3.94 1.98

1986, Dec. 20 ***Perf. 13***

World Cup Soccer Championships, Mexico: Various soccer players and natl. flags.

Shirt Colors
C1143 AP141 10cor blue 22 15
C1144 AP141 10cor blk & white 22 15
C1145 AP141 10cor blue & white 22 15
C1146 AP141 15cor pink & white 35 18
C1147 AP141 15cor grn & blk 35 18
C1148 AP141 25cor blk & white, red 55 28

C1149 AP141 50cor grn & yel, red, horiz. 1.10 55
Nos. C1143-C1149 (7) 3.01 1.64

Souvenir Sheet

Perf. 12½

C1150 AP141 100cor blk & white, bl & white 2.75 1.10

Vassil Levski, 150th Birth Anniv. — AP142

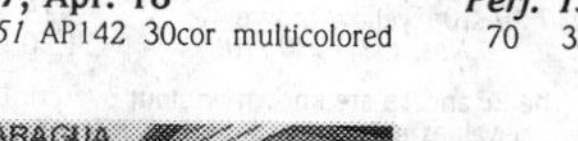

1987, Apr. 18 ***Perf. 13***
C1151 AP142 30cor multicolored 70 32

Intl. Year of Shelter for the Homeless AP143

1987, Aug. 2
C1152 AP143 20cor multicolored 45 22
C1153 AP143 30cor Housing, diff. 70 35

Souvenir Sheet

Berlin, 750th Anniv. — AP144

1987, Sept. 25 **Litho.** ***Perf. 13***
C1154 AP144 130cor multi 1.40 70

Discovery of America, 500th Anniv. (in 1992) — AP145

1987, Oct. 12 ***Perf. 13***
C1155 AP145 15cor Indian village 32 16
C1156 AP145 15cor Sailing ships 32 16
C1157 AP145 20cor Battle in village 42 22
C1158 AP145 30cor Battle, prisoners 65 32
C1159 AP145 40cor Spanish town 85 42
C1160 AP145 50cor Cathedral 1.00 52
a. Min. sheet of 6, #C1155-C1160 3.75 3.75
Nos. C1155-C1160 (6) 3.56 1.80

Cuban Revolution, 30th Anniv. AP146

1989, Jan. 1 ***Perf. 13***
C1161 AP146 20cor multicolored 45 22

AP147

AP148

Designs: Various soccer players in action.

1989, Feb. 20 ***Perf. 13x12½***
C1162 AP147 100cor multi 15 15
C1163 AP147 200cor multi 15 15
C1164 AP147 600cor multi 16 15
C1165 AP147 1000cor multi 26 15
C1166 AP147 2000cor multi 52 46
C1167 AP147 3000cor multi 80 40
C1168 AP147 5000cor multi 1.25 65
Nos. C1162-C1168 (7) 3.29 2.11

Souvenir Sheet

Perf. 13

C1169 AP147 9000cor multi 2.25 2.25

World Cup Soccer Championships, Italy. No. C1169 contains one 32x40mm stamp.

1989, July 19 ***Perf. 13***

Design: 9000cor, Concepcion Volcano.

C1170 AP148 300cor multi 15 15

Souvenir Sheet

C1171 AP148 9000cor multi 2.25 2.25

Sandinista Revolution, 10th Anniv. No. C1171 contains one 40x32mm stamp.

AP149

AP150

Birds: 100cor, Anhinga anhinga. 200cor, Elanoides forficatus. 600cor, Eumomota superciliosa. 1000cor, Setophaga picta. 2000cor, Taraba major, horiz. 3000cor, Onychorhynchus mexicanus. 5000cor, Myrmotherula axillaris, horiz. 9000cor, Amazona ochrocephala.

Perf. 13x12½, 12½x13

1989, July 18
C1172 AP149 100cor multi 15 15
C1173 AP149 200cor multi 15 15
C1174 AP149 600cor multi 18 15
C1175 AP149 1000cor multi 30 15
C1176 AP149 2000cor multi 60 30
C1177 AP149 3000cor multi 90 45
C1178 AP149 5000cor multi 1.50 75
Nos. C1172-C1178 (7) 3.78 2.10

Souvenir Sheet

Perf. 13

C1179 AP149 9000cor multi 1.65 1.65

Brasiliana '89. No. C1179 contains one 32x40mm stamp.

1989, Mar. 25 ***Perf. 13***

Designs: 50cor, Downhill skiing. 300cor, Ice hockey. 600cor, Ski jumping. 1000cor, Pairs figure skating. 2000cor, Biathalon. 3000cor, Slalom skiing. 5000cor, Cross country skiing. 9000cor, Two-man luge.

C1180 AP150 50cor multi 15 15
C1181 AP150 300cor multi 15 15
C1182 AP150 600cor multi 15 15
C1183 AP150 1000cor multi 15 15
C1184 AP150 2000cor multi 20 15
C1185 AP150 3000cor multi 30 15
C1186 AP150 5000cor multi 48 24
Set value 1.20 65

Souvenir Sheet

C1187 AP150 9000cor multi 88 45

1992 Winter Olympics, Albertville. No. C1187 contains one 32x40mm stamp.

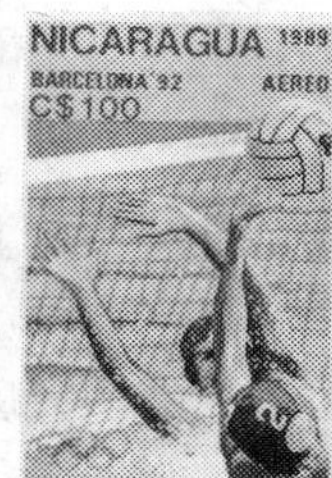

AP151

AP152

Designs: 100cor, Water polo. 200cor, Running. 600cor, Diving. 1000cor, Gymnastics. 2000cor, Weight lifting. 3000cor, Volleyball. 5000cor, Wrestling. 9000cor, Field hockey.

1989, Apr. 23
C1188 AP151 100cor multi 15 15
C1189 AP151 200cor multi 15 15
C1190 AP151 600cor multi 15 15
C1191 AP151 1000cor multi 15 15
C1192 AP151 2000cor multi 20 15
C1193 AP151 3000cor multi 30 15
C1194 AP151 5000cor multi 50 25
Set value 1.20 60

Souvenir Sheet

C1195 AP151 9000cor multi 88 45

1992 Summer Olympics, Barcelona. No. C1195 contains one 32x40mm stamp.

1989, Oct. 12
C1196 AP152 2000cor Vase 68 32

Discovery of America, 500th Anniv. (in 1992).

Currency Reform

Currency reform took place Mar. 4, 1990. Until stamps in the new currency were issued mail was to be handstamped "Franqueo Pagado," (Postage Paid). Stamps were not used again until Apr. 25, 1991. The following set was sold by the post office but was not valid for postage.

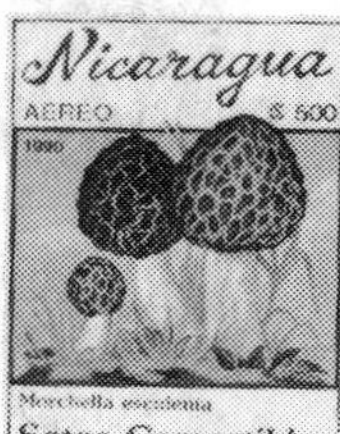

Mushrooms

Designs: 500cor, Morchella esculenta. 1000cor, Boletus edulis. 5000cor, Lactarius deliciosus. 10,000cor, Panellus stipticus. 20,000cor, Craterellus cornucopioides. 40,000cor, Cantharellus cibarius. 50,000cor, Armillariella mellea.

1990, July 15 ***Perf. 13***
500cor multi
1000cor multi
5000cor multi
10,000cor multi
20,000cor multi
40,000cor multi
50,000cor multi

AIR POST SEMI-POSTAL STAMPS

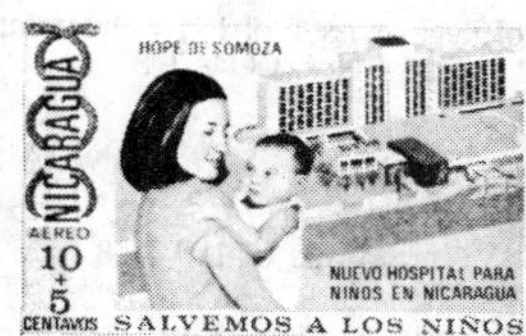

Mrs. Somoza and Children's Hospital — SPAP1

Designs: 5c+5c, Children and weight chart. 15c+5c, Incubator and Da Vinci's "Child in Womb." 20c+5c, Smallpox vaccination. 30c+5c, Water purification. 35c+5c, 1cor+50c, like 10c+5c. 50c+10c, Antibiotics. 60c+15c, Malaria control. 70c+10c, Laboratory. 80c+20c, Gastroenteritis (sick and well babies).

1973, Sept. 25 **Litho.** ***Perf. 13½x14***
CB1 SPAP1 5c + 5c multi 15 15
CB2 SPAP1 10c + 5c multi 15 15
CB3 SPAP1 15c + 5c multi 15 15
CB4 SPAP1 20c + 5c multi 15 15
CB5 SPAP1 30c + 5c multi 15 15
CB6 SPAP1 35c + 5c multi 15 15
CB7 SPAP1 50c + 10c multi 15 15
CB8 SPAP1 60c + 15c multi 15 15
CB9 SPAP1 70c + 10c multi 15 15
CB10 SPAP1 80c + 20c multi 20 18
CB11 SPAP1 1cor + 50c multi 30 25
Set value 1.20 1.00

The surtax was for hospital building fund. See No. C845. Inscriptions on back, printed on top of gum give brief description of subjects shown.

AIR POST OFFICIAL STAMPS

OA1

"Typewritten" Overprint on #O293

1929, Aug. **Unwmk.** ***Perf. 12***
CO1 OA1 25c orange 50.00 45.00

Excellent counterfeits of No. CO1 are plentiful.

Official Stamps of 1926 Overprinted in Dark Blue

Correo Aéreo

1929, Sept. 15
CO2 A24 25c orange 50 50
a. Inverted overprint 25.00
b. Double overprint 25.00
CO3 A25 50c pale bl 75 75
a. Inverted overprint 25.00
b. Double overprint 25.00
c. Double overprint, one inverted 25.00

Nos. 519-523 Overprinted in Black

Correo Aéreo
OFICIAL

1932, Feb.
CO4 A24 15c org red 40 40
a. Inverted overprint 25.00
b. Double overprint 25.00
c. Double overprint, one invtd. 25.00
CO5 A25 20c orange 45 45
a. Double overprint 25.00
CO6 A24 25c dk vio 45 45
CO7 A25 50c green 55 55
CO8 A25 1cor yellow 1.00 1.00
Nos. CO4-CO8 (5) 2.85 2.85

Nos. CO4-CO5, CO7-CO8 exist with signature control overprint. Value, each, $2.50.

Overprinted on Stamp No. 547
CO9 A24 25c blk brn 42.50 42.50

The varieties "OFICAL", "OFIAIAL" and "CORROE" occur in the setting and are found on each stamp of the series.

Counterfeits of No. CO9 are plentiful.

Stamp No. CO4 with overprint "1931" in addition is believed to be of private origin.

Type of Regular Issue of 1914 Overprinted Like Nos. CO4-CO8

1933

CO10	A24	25c olive	15	15
CO11	A25	50c ol grn	22	22
CO12	A25	1cor org red	40	40

On Stamps of 1914-28

CO13	A24	15c dp vio	15	15
CO14	A25	20c dp grn	15	15
		Nos. CO10-CO14 (5)	1.07	1.07

Nos. CO10-CO14 exist without signature control mark. Value, each $2.50.

Air Post Official Stamps of 1932-33 Overprinted in Blue

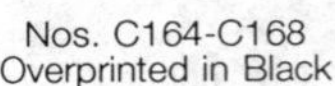

1935

CO15	A24	15c dp vio	1.00	80
CO16	A25	20c dp grn	2.00	1.60
CO17	A24	25c olive	3.00	2.50
CO18	A25	50c ol grn	35.00	30.00
CO19	A25	1cor org red	40.00	37.50
		Nos. CO15-CO19 (5)	81.00	72.40

Overprinted in Red

CO20	A24	15c dp vio	25	22
CO21	A25	20c dp grn	25	22
CO22	A24	25c olive	25	25
CO23	A25	50c ol grn	80	80
CO24	A25	1cor org red	80	80
		Nos. CO20-CO24 (5)	2.35	2.29

Nos. CO15 to CO24 are handstamped with script control mark. Counterfeits of blue overprint are plentiful.

The editors do not recognize the Nicaraguan air post Official stamps overprinted in red "VALIDO 1935" in two lines and with or without script control marks as having been issued primarily for postal purposes.

Nos. C164-C168 Overprinted in Black

1937

CO25	AP1	15c yel org	80	55
CO26	AP1	20c org red	80	60
CO27	AP1	25c black	80	70
CO28	AP1	50c violet	80	70
CO29	AP1	1cor orange	80	70
		Nos. CO25-CO29 (5)	4.00	3.25

Pres. Anastasio Somoza — OA2

1939, Feb. 7 Engr. *Perf. 12½*

CO30	OA2	10c brown	25	25
CO31	OA2	15c dk bl	25	25
CO32	OA2	20c yellow	25	25
CO33	OA2	25c dk pur	25	25
CO34	OA2	30c lake	25	25
CO35	OA2	50c dp org	65	65
CO36	OA2	1cor dk ol grn	1.20	1.20
		Nos. CO30-CO36 (7)	3.10	3.10

Catalogue values for unused stamps in this section, from this point to the end of the section, are for Never Hinged items.

Mercedes Airport OA3

Designs: 10c, Sulphurous Lake of Nejapa. 15c, Ruben Dario Monument. 20c, Tapir. 25c, Genizaro Dam. 50c, Tipitapa Spa. 1cor, Stone Highway. 2.50cor, Franklin D. Roosevelt Monument.

Engraved, Center Photogravure
1947, Aug. 29
Various Frames in Black

CO37	OA3	5c org brn	15	15
CO38	OA3	10c blue	20	20
CO39	OA3	15c violet	15	15
CO40	OA3	20c red org	20	15
CO41	OA3	25c blue	15	15
CO42	OA3	50c car rose	20	20
CO43	OA3	1cor slate	45	45
CO44	OA3	2.50cor red brn	1.25	1.25
		Nos. CO37-CO44 (8)	2.75	2.70

Rowland Hill — OA4

Designs: 10c, Heinrich von Stephan. 25c, 1st UPU Bldg. 50c, UPU Bldg., Bern. 1cor, UPU Monument. 2.60cor, Congress medal, reverse.

1950, Nov. 23 Engr. *Perf. 13*
Frames in Black

CO45	OA4	5c rose vio	15	15
CO46	OA4	10c dp grn	15	15
CO47	OA4	25c rose vio	15	15
CO48	OA4	50c dp org	15	15
CO49	OA4	1cor ultra	28	28
CO50	OA4	2.60cor gray blk	2.25	2.00
		Nos. CO45-CO50 (6)	3.13	2.88

75th anniv. (in 1949) of the UPU.

Each denomination was also issued in a souvenir sheet containing four stamps and marginal inscriptions. Size: 121x96mm. Value, set of 6 sheets, $35.

Consular Service Stamps Surcharged "Oficial Aéreo" and New Denomination in Red, Black or Blue

1961, Nov. Unwmk. Engr. *Perf. 12*
Red Marginal Number

CO51	AP63	10c on 1cor grnsh blk (R)	15	15
CO52	AP63	15c on 20cor red brn (R)	15	15
CO53	AP63	20c on 100cor mag	15	15
CO54	AP63	25c on 50c dp bl (R)	15	15
CO55	AP63	35c on 50cor brn (R)	15	15
CO56	AP63	50c on 3cor dk car	15	15
CO57	AP63	1cor on 2cor grn (R)	20	20
CO58	AP63	2cor on 5cor org (Bl)	42	42
CO59	AP63	5cor on 10cor vio (R)	1.00	1.00
		Set value	2.10	2.05

POSTAGE DUE STAMPS

D1

D2

1896 Unwmk. Engr. *Perf. 12*

J1	D1	1c orange	50	*1.25*
J2	D1	2c orange	50	*1.25*
J3	D1	5c orange	50	*1.25*
J4	D1	10c orange	50	*1.25*
J5	D1	20c orange	50	*1.25*
J6	D1	30c orange	50	*1.25*
J7	D1	50c orange	50	*1.50*
		Nos. J1-J7 (7)	3.50	*9.00*

Wmk. 117

J8	D1	1c orange	1.00	*1.50*
J9	D1	2c orange	1.00	*1.50*
J10	D1	5c orange	1.00	*1.50*
J11	D1	10c orange	1.00	*1.50*
J12	D1	20c orange	1.25	*1.50*
J13	D1	30c orange	1.00	*1.50*
J14	D1	50c orange	1.00	*1.50*
		Nos. J8-J14 (7)	7.25	*10.50*

1897 Unwmk.

J15	D1	1c violet	50	*1.50*
J16	D1	2c violet	50	*1.50*
J17	D1	5c violet	50	*1.50*
J18	D1	10c violet	50	*1.50*
J19	D1	20c violet	1.25	*2.00*
J20	D1	30c violet	50	*1.50*
J21	D1	50c violet	50	*1.50*
		Nos. J15-J21 (7)	4.25	*11.00*

Wmk. 117

J22	D1	1c violet	50	*1.50*
J23	D1	2c violet	50	*1.50*
J24	D1	5c violet	50	*1.50*
J25	D1	10c violet	50	*1.50*
J26	D1	20c violet	1.00	*2.00*
J27	D1	30c violet	50	*1.50*
J28	D1	50c violet	50	*1.50*
		Nos. J22-J28 (7)	4.00	*11.00*

Reprints of Nos. J8-J28 are on thick, porous paper. Color of 1896 reprints, reddish orange; or 1897 reprints, reddish violet. On watermarked reprints, liberty cap is sideways. Value 25c each.

1898 Litho. Unwmk.

J29	D2	1c blue green	15	*2.00*
J30	D2	2c blue green	15	*2.00*
J31	D2	5c blue green	15	*2.00*
J32	D2	10c blue green	15	*2.00*
J33	D2	20c blue green	15	*2.00*
J34	D2	30c blue green	15	*2.00*
J35	D2	50c blue green	15	*2.00*
		Nos. J29-J35 (7)	1.05	

1899

J36	D2	1c carmine	15	*2.00*
J37	D2	2c carmine	15	*2.00*
J38	D2	5c carmine	15	*2.00*
J39	D2	10c carmine	15	*2.00*
J40	D2	20c carmine	15	*2.00*
J41	D2	50c carmine	15	*2.00*
		Set value	60	

Some denominations are found in se-tenant pairs.

Various counterfeit cancellations exist on Nos. J1-J41.

D3

1900 Engr.

J42	D3	1c plum	1.00
J43	D3	2c vermilion	1.00
J44	D3	5c dk bl	1.00
J45	D3	10c purple	1.00
J46	D3	20c org brn	1.00
J47	D3	30c dk grn	2.00
J48	D3	50c lake	2.00
		Nos. J42-J48 (7)	9.00

Nos. J42-J48 were not issued without postage overprint. For overprints see Nos. 137-143, 152-158, O72-O81, 2L11-2L15, 2L25, 2L40-2L41.

OFFICIAL STAMPS

Types of Postage Stamps Overprinted in Red Diagonally Reading up

FRANQUEO OFICIAL

1890 Unwmk. Engr. *Perf. 12*

O1	A5	1c ultra	15	*35*
O2	A5	2c ultra	15	*35*
O3	A5	5c ultra	15	*35*
O4	A5	10c ultra	15	*40*
O5	A5	20c ultra	15	*75*
O6	A5	50c ultra	15	*75*
O7	A5	1p ultra	15	*1.25*
O8	A5	2p ultra	15	*1.50*
O9	A5	5p ultra	15	*2.50*
O10	A5	10p ultra	15	*3.25*
		Nos. O1-O10 (10)	1.50	

All values of the 1890 issue are known without overprint and most of them with inverted or double overprint, or without overprint and imperforate. There is no evidence that they were issued in these forms.

Official stamps of 1890-1899 are scarce with genuine cancellations. Forged cancellations are plentiful.

Overprinted Vertically Reading Up

1891 Litho.

O11	A6	1c green	15	*35*
O12	A6	2c green	15	*35*
O13	A6	5c green	15	*35*
O14	A6	10c green	15	*35*
O15	A6	20c green	15	*75*
O16	A6	50c green	15	*1.25*
O17	A6	1p green	15	*1.50*
O18	A6	2p green	15	*1.50*
O19	A6	5p green	15	*2.50*
O20	A6	10p green	15	*4.00*
		Nos. O11-O20 (10)	1.50	

All values of this issue except the 2c and 5p exist without overprint and several with double overprint. They are not known to have been issued in this form.

Many of the denominations may be found in se-tenant pairs.

Overprinted in Dark Blue

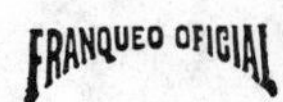

1892 Engr.

O21	A7	1c yellow brown	15	*35*
O22	A7	2c yellow brown	15	*35*
O23	A7	5c yellow brown	15	*35*
O24	A7	10c yellow brown	15	*35*
O25	A7	20c yellow brown	15	*75*
O26	A7	50c yellow brown	15	*1.00*
O27	A7	1p yellow brown	15	*1.50*
O28	A7	2p yellow brown	15	*2.00*
O29	A7	5p yellow brown	15	*3.00*
O30	A7	10p yellow brown	15	*4.00*
		Nos. O21-O30 (10)	1.50	

The 2c and 1p are known without overprint and several values exist with double or inverted overprint. These probably were not regularly issued.

Commemorative of the 400th anniversary of the discovery of America by Christopher Columbus.

Overprinted in Red

FRANQUEO OFICIAL

1893 Engr.

O31	A8	1c slate	15	*35*
O32	A8	2c slate	15	*35*
O33	A8	5c slate	15	*35*
O34	A8	10c slate	15	*35*
O35	A8	20c slate	15	*50*
O36	A8	25c slate	15	
O37	A8	50c slate	15	*85*
O38	A8	1p slate	15	*1.50*
O39	A8	2p slate	15	*2.00*
O40	A8	5p slate	15	*3.00*
O41	A8	10p slate	15	*4.00*
		Nos. O31-O41 (11)	1.65	

The 2, 5, 10, 20, 25, 50c and 5p are known without overprint but probably were not regularly issued. Some values exist with double or inverted overprints.

Overprinted in Black

FRANQUEO OFICIAL

1894

O42	A9	1c orange	15	*35*
O43	A9	2c orange	15	*35*
O44	A9	5c orange	15	*35*
O45	A9	10c orange	15	*35*
O46	A9	20c orange	15	*50*
O47	A9	50c orange	15	*75*
O48	A9	1p orange	15	*1.50*
O49	A9	2p orange	15	*2.00*
O50	A9	5p orange	15	*3.00*
O51	A9	10p orange	15	*4.00*
		Nos. O42-O51 (10)	1.50	

Reprints are yellow.

1895

Overprinted in Blue

O52	A10	1c green	15	*35*
O53	A10	2c green	15	*35*
O54	A10	5c green	15	*35*
O55	A10	10c green	15	*35*
O56	A10	20c green	15	*50*
O57	A10	50c green	15	*1.00*
O58	A10	1p green	15	*1.50*
O59	A10	2p green	15	*2.00*
O60	A10	5p green	15	*3.00*
O61	A10	10p green	15	*4.00*
		Nos. O52-O61 (10)	1.50	

Wmk. 117

O62	A10	1c green
O63	A10	2c green
O64	A10	5c green
O65	A10	10c green
O66	A10	20c green
O67	A10	50c green
O68	A10	1p green
O69	A10	2p green
O70	A10	5p green
O71	A10	10p green

Nos. O62-O71 probably exist only as reprints. Value, each 15 cents.

Postage Due Stamps of Same Date Handstamped in Violet

Franqueo Oficial

1896 **Unwmk.**

O72 D1 1c orange 7.00
O73 D1 2c orange 7.00
O74 D1 5c orange 5.00
O75 D1 10c orange 5.00
O76 D1 20c orange 5.00
Set value 29.00

Wmk. 117

O77 D1 1c orange 7.00
O78 D1 2c orange 7.00
O79 D1 5c orange 4.00
O80 D1 10c orange 4.00
O81 D1 20c orange 4.00
Set value 26.00

Nos. O72 to O81 were handstamped in rows of five. Several handstamps were used, one of which had the variety "Oftcial". Most varieties are known inverted and double.

Types of Postage Stamps Overprinted in Red

1896 **Unwmk.**

O82 A11 1c red 2.50 3.00
O83 A11 2c red 2.50 3.00
O84 A11 5c red 2.50 3.00
O85 A11 10c red 2.50 3.00
O86 A11 20c red 3.00 3.00
O87 A11 50c red 5.00 *5.00*
O88 A11 1p red 12.00 *12.00*
O89 A11 2p red 12.00 *12.00*
O90 A11 5p red 16.00 *16.00*
Nos. O82-O90 (9) 58.00 *60.00*

Wmk. 117

O91 A11 1c red 3.00 3.50
O92 A11 2c red 3.00 3.50
O93 A11 5c red 3.00 3.50
O94 A11 10c red 3.00 3.50
O95 A11 20c red 5.00 5.00
O96 A11 50c red 3.00 *5.00*
O97 A11 1p red 14.00 *14.00*
O98 A11 2p red 16.50 *16.50*
O99 A11 5p red 25.00 *25.00*
Nos. O91-O99 (9) 75.50 *79.50*

Same, Dated 1897

1897 **Unwmk.**

O100 A11 1c red 3.00 3.00
O101 A11 2c red 3.00 3.00
O102 A11 5c red 3.00 2.50
O103 A11 10c red 3.00 3.00
O104 A11 20c red 3.00 4.00
O105 A11 50c red 5.00 *5.00*
O106 A11 1p red 12.00 *12.00*
O107 A11 2p red 12.00 *12.00*
O108 A11 5p red 16.00 *16.00*
Nos. O100-O108 (9) 60.00 *60.50*

Wmk. 117

O109 A11 1c red 5.00 5.00
O110 A11 2c red 5.00 5.00
O111 A11 5c red 5.00 5.00
O112 A11 10c red 10.00 10.00
O113 A11 20c red 10.00 10.00
O114 A11 50c red 12.00 *12.00*
O115 A11 1p red 20.00 *20.00*
O116 A11 2p red 20.00 *20.00*
O117 A11 5p red 20.00 *20.00*
Nos. O109-O117 (9) 107.00 *107.00*

Overprinted in Blue

1898 **Unwmk.**

O118 A12 1c carmine 3.25 3.25
O119 A12 2c carmine 3.25 3.25
O120 A12 4c carmine 3.25 3.25
O121 A12 5c carmine 2.50 2.50
O122 A12 10c carmine 4.00 4.00
O123 A12 15c carmine 6.00 6.00
O124 A12 20c carmine 6.00 6.00
O125 A12 50c carmine 8.50 *8.50*
O126 A12 1p carmine 11.00 *11.00*
O127 A12 2p carmine 11.00 *11.00*
O128 A12 5p carmine 11.00 *11.00*
Nos. O118-O128 (11) 69.75 *69.75*

Stamps of this set with sideways watermark 117 or with black overprint are reprints. Value 25c each.

Reprints of Nos. O82-O117 are described in notes after No. 109M. Value 15c each.

Overprinted in Dark Blue

1899

O129 A13 1c gray grn 15 *1.00*
O130 A13 2c bis brn 15 *1.00*
O131 A13 4c lake 15 *1.00*
O132 A13 5c dk bl 15 *50*
O133 A13 10c buff 15 *1.00*
O134 A13 15c chocolate 15 *2.00*
O135 A13 20c dk grn 15 *3.00*
O136 A13 50c car rose 15 *3.00*
O137 A13 1p red 15 *10.00*
O138 A13 2p violet 15 *10.00*
O139 A13 5p lt bl 15 *15.00*
Set value 1.10

Counterfeit cancellations on Nos. O129-O139 are plentiful.

"Justice" — O5

1900 **Engr.**

O140 O5 1c plum 60 60
O141 O5 2c vermilion 50 50
O142 O5 4c ol grn 60 60
O143 O5 5c dk bl 1.25 45
O144 O5 10c purple 1.25 35
O145 O5 20c brown 90 35
O146 O5 50c lake 1.25 50
O147 O5 1p ultra 3.50 2.50
O148 O5 2p brn org 4.00 4.00
O149 O5 5p grnsh blk 5.00 5.00
Nos. O140-O149 (10) 18.85 14.85

For surcharges see Nos. O155-O157.

Nos. 123, 161 Surcharged in Black

1 1
OFICIAL
1 Centavo

1903 ***Perf. 12, 14***

O150 A14 1c on 10c violet 25 30
a. "Centovo" 1.00
b. "Contavo" 1.00
c. With ornaments 30
d. Inverted surcharge 1.00
e. "1" omitted at upper left 2.00
O151 A14 2c on 3c green 30 40
a. "Centovos" 1.00
b. "Contavos" 1.00
c. With ornaments 35
d. Inverted surcharge 1.00
O152 A14 4c on 3c green 1.25 1.25
a. "Centovos" 2.50
b. "Contavos" 2.50
c. With ornaments 2.50
d. Inverted surcharge
O153 A14 4c on 10c violet 1.25 1.25
a. "Centovos" 2.50
b. "Contavos" 2.50
c. With ornaments 2.00
d. Inverted surcharge
O154 A14 5c on 3c green 15 18
a. "Centovos" 1.00
b. "Contavos" 1.00
c. With ornaments 30
d. Double surcharge 2.00
e. Inverted surcharge
Nos. O150-O154 (5) 3.20 3.38

These surcharges are set up to cover 25 stamps. Some of the settings have bars or pieces of fancy border type below "OFICIAL." There are 5 varieties on #O150, 3 on #O151, 1 each on #O152, O153, O154.

In 1904 #O151 was reprinted to fill a dealer's order. This printing lacks the small figure at the upper right. It includes the variety "OFICILA." At the same time the same setting was printed in carmine on official stamps of 1900, 1c on 10c violet and 2c on 1p ultramarine. Also the 1, 2 and 5p official stamps of 1900 were surcharged with new values and the dates 1901 or 1902 in various colors, inverted, etc. It is doubtful if any of these varieties were ever in Nicaragua and certain that none of them ever did legitimate postal duty.

No. O145 Surcharged in Black

10 10
10 Ctvs.

1904 ***Perf. 12***

O155 O5 10c on 20c brn 20 20
a. No period after "Ctvs" 1.00 75
O156 O5 30c on 20c brn 20 20
O157 O5 50c on 20c brn 50 35
a. Lower "50" omitted 2.50 2.50
b. Upper figures omitted 2.50 2.50
c. Top left and lower figures omitted 3.50 3.50

Coat of Arms — O6

1905, July 25 **Engr.**

O158 O6 1c green 25 25
O159 O6 2c rose 25 25
O160 O6 5c blue 25 25
O161 O6 10c yel brn 25 25
O162 O6 20c orange 25 25
O163 O6 50c brn ol 25 25
O164 O6 1p lake 25 25
O165 O6 2p violet 25 25
O166 O6 5p gray blk 25 25
Nos. O158-O166 (9) 2.25 2.25

Surcharged Vertically Up or Down

Vale 10 c

1907

O167 O6 10c on 1c grn 75 75
O168 O6 10c on 2c rose 25.00 22.50
O169 O6 20c on 2c rose 22.50 17.50
O170 O6 50c on 1c grn 1.50 1.50
O171 O6 50c on 2c rose 22.50 12.50

Surcharged

Vale $1.00

O172 O6 1p on 2c rose 1.50 1.50
O173 O6 2p on 2c rose 1.50 1.50
O174 O6 3p on 2c rose 1.50 1.50
O175 O6 4p on 2c rose
O176 O6 4p on 5c blue 2.25 2.25

The setting for this surcharge includes various letters from wrong fonts, the figure "1" for "l" in "Vale" and an "l" for "1" in "$1.00."

Surcharged

Vale 20 cts

O177 O6 20c on 1c green 1.00 1.00
a. Double surcharge 5.00 5.00
Nos. O167-O174,O176-O177 (10) 80.00 62.50

The preceding surcharges are vertical, reading both up and down.

O7

Revenue Stamps Surcharged

1907 ***Perf. 14 to 15***

O178 O7 10c on 2c org (Bk) 15 15
O179 O7 35c on 1c bl (R) 15 15
a. Inverted surcharge 3.00 3.00
O180 O7 70c on 1c bl (V) 15 15
a. Inverted surcharge 3.00 3.00
O181 O7 70c on 1c bl (O) 15 15
a. Inverted surcharge 3.00 3.00
O182 O7 1p on 2c org (G) 15 15
a. Inverted surcharge 2.50 2.50
O183 O7 2p on 2c org (Br) 15 15
O184 O7 3p on 5c brn (Bl) 15 15
O185 O7 4p on 5c brn (G) 20 20
a. Double surcharge 3.00 3.00
O186 O7 5p on 5c brn (G) 20 20
a. Inverted surcharge 3.50 3.50
Nos. O178-O186 (9) 1.45 1.45

Letters and figures from several fonts were mixed in these surcharges.

See Nos. O199-O209.

No. 202 Surcharged

OFICIAL
— 10 cvs —

1907, Nov.

Black or Blue Black Surcharge

O187 A18 10c on 1c grn 15.00 13.00
O188 A18 15c on 1c grn 15.00 13.00
O189 A18 20c on 1c grn 15.00 13.00
O190 A18 50c on 1c grn 15.00 13.00

Red Surcharge

O191 A18 1(un)p on 1c grn 14.00 13.00
O192 A18 2(dos)p on 1c grn 14.00 13.00
Nos. O187-O192 (6) 88.00 78.00

No. 181 Surcharged

OFICIAL
VALE 10 c

1908 **Yellow Surcharge** ***Perf. 12***

O193 A18 10c on 3c vio 15.00 15.00
O194 A18 15c on 3c vio 15.00 15.00
O195 A18 20c on 3c vio 15.00 15.00
O196 A18 35c on 3c vio 15.00 15.00
O197 A18 50c on 3c vio 15.00 15.00
Nos. O193-O197 (5) 75.00 75.00

Black Surcharge

O198 A18 35c on 3c vio 60.00 60.00

Revenue Stamps Surcharged like 1907 Issue
Dated "1908"

1908 ***Perf. 14 to 15***

O199 O7 10c on 1c bl (V) 75 50
a. Inverted surcharge 3.50 3.50
O200 O7 35c on 1c bl (Bk) 75 50
a. Inverted surcharge 3.50 3.50
b. Double surcharge 4.00 4.00
O201 O7 50c on 1c bl (R) 75 50
O202 O7 1p on 1c bl (Br) 37.50 37.50
a. Inverted surcharge 65.00 65.00
O203 O7 2p on 1c bl (G) 90 75
O204 O7 10c on 2c org (Bk) 1.10 65
O205 O7 35c on 2c org (R) 1.10 65
a. Double surcharge 3.50
O206 O7 50c on 2c org (Bk) 1.10 65
O207 O7 70c on 2c org (Bl) 1.10 65
O208 O7 1p on 2c org (G) 1.10 65
O209 O7 2p on 2c org (Br) 1.10 65
Nos. O199-O209 (11) 47.25 43.65

There are several minor varieties in the figures, etc., in these surcharges.

Nos. 243-248 Overprinted in Black

OFICIAL

1909 ***Perf. 12***

O210 A18 10c lake 20 15
a. Double overprint 2.50 2.50
O211 A18 15c black 60 50
O212 A18 20c brn ol 1.00 75
O213 A18 50c dp grn 1.50 1.00
O214 A18 1p yellow 1.75 1.25
O215 A18 2p car rose 2.75 2.00
Nos. O210-O215 (6) 7.80 5.65

Overprinted in Black

OFICIAL

1910

O216 A18 15c black 1.50 1.25
a. Double overprint 4.00 4.00
O217 A18 20c brn ol 2.50 2.00
O218 A18 50c dp grn 2.50 2.00
O219 A18 1p yellow 2.75 2.50
a. Inverted overprint 7.50 7.50
O220 A18 2p car rose 4.00 3.00
Nos. O216-O220 (5) 13.25 10.75

Nos. 239-240 Surcharged in Black

OFICIAL
Vale 10 *cts.*

1911
O221 A18 5c on 3c red org 6.00 6.00
O222 A18 10c on 4c vio 5.00 5.00
a. Double surcharge 10.00 10.00
b. Pair, one without new value 20.00

Railroad Stamps Surcharged in Black

Correo oficial
Vale
10 cts.

1911, Nov. *Perf. 14 to 15*
O223 A21 10c on 1 red 3.00 3.00
a. Inverted surcharge 4.50
b. Double surcharge 4.50
O224 A21 15c on 1 red 3.00 3.00
a. Inverted surcharge 5.00
b. Double surcharge 4.50
O225 A21 20c on 1 red 3.00 3.00
a. Inverted surcharge 5.00
O226 A21 50c on 1 red 3.75 3.75
a. Inverted surcharge 4.50
O227 A21 1p on 1 red 5.00 7.00
a. Inverted surcharge 6.00
O228 A21 2p on 1 red 5.50 10.00
a. Inverted surcharge 7.50
b. Double surcharge 7.50
Nos. O223-O228 (6) 23.25 29.75

Surcharged in Black

CORREO
OFICIAL
15 centavos

1911, Nov.
O229 A21 10c on 1 red 22.50
O230 A21 15c on 1 red 22.50
O231 A21 20c on 1 red 22.50
O232 A21 50c on 1 red 16.00

Surcharged in Black

Correo oficial
Vale
5 cts.
1911

1911, Dec.
O233 A21 5c on 1 red 4.50 6.00
a. Double surcharge 7.50
b. Inverted surcharge 7.50
c. "5" omitted 6.00
O234 A21 10c on 1 red 5.50 7.00
O235 A21 15c on 1 red 6.00 7.50
O236 A21 20c on 1 red 6.50 8.50
O237 A21 50c on 1 red 7.50 10.00
Nos. O233-O237 (5) 30.00 39.00

Nos. O233 to O237 have a surcharge on the back like Nos. 285 and 286 with "15 cts" obliterated by a heavy bar.

Surcharged Vertically in Black

Correo Oficial
1912
35 cvs.

1912
O238 A21 5c on 1 red 8.00 8.00
O239 A21 10c on 1 red 8.00 8.00
O240 A21 15c on 1 red 8.00 8.00
O241 A21 20c on 1 red 8.00 8.00
O242 A21 35c on 1 red 8.00 8.00
O243 A21 50c on 1 red 8.00 8.00
O244 A21 1p on 1 red 8.00 8.00
Nos. O238-O244 (7) 56.00 56.00

Nos. O238 to O244 are printed on Nos. 285 and 286 but the surcharge on the back is obliterated by a vertical bar.

Types of Regular Issue of 1912 Overprinted in Black **OFICIAL**

1912 *Perf. 12*
O245 A22 1c light blue 15 15
O246 A22 2c light blue 15 15
O247 A22 3c light blue 15 15
O248 A22 4c light blue 15 15
O249 A22 5c light blue 15 15
O250 A22 6c light blue 15 15
O251 A22 10c light blue 15 15
O252 A22 15c light blue 15 15
O253 A22 20c light blue 15 15
O254 A22 25c light blue 20 20
O255 A22 35c light blue 25 25
O256 A22 50c light blue 1.50 1.50
O257 A22 1p light blue 30 30
O258 A22 2p light blue 35 35
O259 A22 5p light blue 50 50
Set value 3.85 3.85

On the 35c the overprint is 15½mm wide, on the other values it is 13mm.

Types of Regular Issue of 1914 Overprinted in Black **OFICIAL**

1915, May
O260 A24 1c light blue 15 15
O261 A25 2c light blue 15 15
O262 A24 3c light blue 20 15
O263 A25 4c light blue 15 15
O264 A24 5c light blue 15 15
O265 A25 6c light blue 15 15
O266 A25 10c light blue 15 15
O267 A24 15c light blue 20 20
O268 A25 20c light blue 20 20
O269 A24 25c light blue 30 30
O270 A25 50c light blue 60 60
Nos. O260-O270 (11) 2.40 2.35

Regular Issues of 1914-22 Overprinted in Red **Oficial**

1925
O271 A24 ½c dp grn 15 15
a. Double overprint 2.50 2.50
O272 A24 1c violet 15 15
O273 A25 2c car rose 15 15
O274 A24 3c ol grn 15 15
O275 A25 4c vermilion 15 15
a. Double overprint 2.50 2.50
O276 A24 5c black 15 15
a. Double overprint 2.50 2.50
O277 A25 6c red brn 25 25
O278 A25 10c yellow 35 35
a. Double overprint 3.50 3.50
O279 A24 15c red brn 40 40
O280 A25 20c bis brn 50 50
O281 A24 25c orange 60 60
a. Inverted overprint 4.00 4.00
O282 A25 50c pale bl 75 75
a. Double overprint 5.00 5.00
Nos. O271-O282 (12) 3.75 3.75

Type II overprint has "f" and "i" separated. Comes on Nos. O272-O274 and O276.

Regular Issues of 1914-22 Overprinted in Black **OFICIAL**

1926
O283 A24 ½c dk grn 15 15
O284 A24 1c dp vio 15 15
O285 A25 2c car rose 15 15
O286 A24 3c ol gray 15 15
O287 A25 4c vermilion 15 15
O288 A24 5c gray blk 15 15
O289 A25 6c red brn 15 15
O290 A25 10c yellow 15 15
O291 A24 15c dp brn 15 15
O292 A25 20c bis brn 15 15
O293 A24 25c orange 15 18
O294 A25 50c pale bl 25 25
Set value 1.30 1.30

No. 499 Surcharged in Black

OFICIAL
₵ 0.05
1931

1931
O295 A33 5c on 10c bis brn 20 20

Nos. 517-518 Overprinted in Red **OFICIAL**

1931
O296 A25 6c bis brn 20 20
O297 A25 10c lt brn 20 20

Nos. 541, 543, 545 With Additional Overprint in Black **1931**

O298 A24 1c ol grn 16 16
O299 A24 3c lt bl 16 16
a. "OFICIAL" inverted 80 80
O300 A24 5c gray brn 16 16
a. "1931" double 80 80

Regular Issues of 1914-31 Overprinted in Black **OFICIAL**

1932, Feb. 6
O301 A24 1c ol grn 15 15
a. Double overprint 1.40 1.40
O302 A25 2c brt rose 15 15
a. Double overprint 1.40 1.40
O303 A24 3c lt bl 15 15
a. Double overprint 50 50
O304 A25 4c dk bl 15 15
O305 A24 5c ol brn 15 15
O306 A25 6c bis brn 20 15
a. Double overprint 2.00 2.00
O307 A25 10c lt brn 30 20
O308 A24 15c org red 40 22
a. Double overprint 2.25 2.25
O309 A25 20c orange 65 35
O310 A24 25c dk vio 2.00 50
O311 A25 50c green 15 15
O312 A25 1cor yellow 20 20
Nos. O301-O312 (12) 4.65 2.52

With Additional Overprint in Black **1931**

1932, Feb. 6
O313 A24 1c ol grn 5.50 5.50
O314 A25 2c brt rose 6.50 6.50
a. Double overprint 8.25 8.25
O315 A24 3c lt bl 5.00 5.00
O316 A24 5c ol brn 5.00 5.00
O317 A24 15c org red 65 65
O318 A24 25c blk brn 65 65
O319 A24 25c dk vio 1.50 1.50
Nos. O313-O319 (7) 24.80 24.80

The variety "OFIAIAL" occurs once in each sheet of Nos. O301 to O319 inclusive.

Flag of the Race Issue

1933, Aug. 9 **Litho.** *Rouletted 9*
Without gum
O320 A43 1c orange 1.00 1.00
O321 A43 2c yellow 1.00 1.00
O322 A43 3c dk brn 1.00 1.00
O323 A43 4c dp brn 1.00 1.00
O324 A43 5c gray brn 1.00 1.00
O325 A43 6c dp ultra 1.20 1.20
O326 A43 10c dp vio 1.20 1.20
O327 A43 15c red vio 1.20 1.20
O328 A43 20c dp grn 1.20 1.20
O329 A43 25c green 2.00 2.00
O330 A43 50c carmine 2.50 2.50
O331 A43 1cor red 4.00 4.00
Nos. O320-O331 (12) 18.30 18.30

See note after No. 599.
Reprints of Nos. O320-O331 exist.
A 25c dull blue exists. Its status is questioned.

Regular Issue of 1914-31 Overprinted in Red **OFICIAL**

1933, Nov. *Perf. 12*
O332 A24 1c ol grn 15 15
O333 A25 2c brt rose 15 15
O334 A24 3c lt bl 15 15
O335 A25 4c dk bl 15 15
O336 A24 5c ol brn 15 15
O337 A25 6c bis brn 15 15
O338 A25 10c lt brn 15 15
O339 A24 15c red org 15 15
O340 A25 20c orange 15 15
O341 A24 25c dk vio 15 15
O342 A25 50c green 16 16
O343 A25 1cor yellow 35 20
Set value 1.00 90

Nos. O332-O343 exist with or without signature control overprint. Values are the same.

Official Stamps of 1933 Overprinted as Nos. CO15-CO19 in Blue

1935, Dec.
O344 A24 1c ol grn 65 42
O345 A25 2c brt rose 65 50
O346 A24 3c lt bl 1.60 50
O347 A25 4c dk bl 1.60 1.60
O348 A24 5c ol brn 1.60 1.60
O349 A25 6c bis brn 2.00 2.00
O350 A25 10c lt brn 2.00 2.00
O351 A24 15c org red 28.00 28.00
O352 A25 20c orange 28.00 28.00
O353 A24 25c dk vio 28.00 28.00
O354 A25 50c green 28.00 28.00
O355 A25 1cor yellow 28.00 28.00
Nos. O344-O355 (12) 150.10 148.62

Nos. O344-O355 have signature control overprints. Counterfeits of overprint abound.

Same Overprinted in Red

1936, Jan.
O356 A24 1c ol grn 15 15
O357 A25 2c brt rose 15 15
O358 A24 3c lt bl 15 15
a. Double overprint
O359 A25 4c dk bl 15 15
O360 A24 5c ol brn 15 15
O361 A25 6c bis brn 15 15
O362 A25 10c lt brn 15 15
O363 A24 15c org red 15 15
O364 A25 20c orange 15 15
O365 A24 25c dk vio 15 15
O366 A25 50c green 16 16
O367 A25 1cor yellow 35 35
Set value 1.35 1.35

Have signature control overprints.

Nos. 653 to 655, 657, 659 660, 662 to 664 Overprinted in Black

1937
O368 A24 1c car rose 20 16
O369 A25 2c dp bl 20 16
O370 A24 3c chocolate 25 22
O371 A24 5c org red 35 25
O372 A25 10c ol grn 65 40
O373 A24 15c green 80 50
O374 A24 25c orange 1.00 65
O375 A25 50c brown 1.40 80
O376 A25 1cor ultra 2.50 1.20
Nos. O368-O376 (9) 7.35 4.34

Islands of the Great Lake — O9

1939, Jan. **Engr.** *Perf. 12½*
O377 O9 2c rose red 15 15
O378 O9 3c lt bl 15 15
O379 O9 6c brn org 15 15
O380 O9 7½c dp grn 15 15
O381 O9 10c blk brn 15 15
O382 O9 15c orange 15 15
O383 O9 25c dk vio 25 25
O384 O9 50c brt yel grn 40 40
Set value 1.25 1.25

POSTAL TAX STAMPS

Official Stamps of 1915 Surcharged in Black

Vale
un centavo
R de C

1921, July **Unwmk.** *Perf. 12*
RA1 A24 1c on 5c lt bl 1.50 60
RA2 A25 1c on 6c lt bl 65 20
a. Double surcharge, one inverted
RA3 A25 1c on 10c lt bl 1.00 25
a. Double surcharge 3.50 3.50
RA4 A24 1c on 15c lt bl 1.50 25
a. Double surcharge, one inverted 5.00 5.00

"R de C" signifies "Reconstruccion de Comunicaciones." The stamps were intended to provide a fund for rebuilding the General Post Office which was burned in April, 1921. One stamp was required on each letter or parcel, in addition to the regular postage. In the setting of one hundred there are five stamps with antique "C" and twenty-one with "R" and "C" smaller than in the illustration. One or more stamps in the setting have a dotted bar, as illustrated over No. 388, instead of the double bar.

The use of the "R de C" stamps for the payment of regular postage was not permitted.

Official Stamp of 1915 Overprinted in Black

«Particular»
R de C

RA5 A24 1c light blue	6.00	1.75

This stamp is known with the dotted bar as illustrated over No. 388, instead of the double bar.

Coat of Arms — PT1

PT2

1921, Sept.

Red Surcharge

RA6 PT1 1c on 1c ver & blk	15	15
RA7 PT1 1c on 2c grn & blk	15	15
a. Double surcharge	3.00	3.00
b. Double surcharge, one inverted	4.00	4.00
RA8 PT1 1c on 4c org & blk	15	15
a. Double surcharge	4.00	4.00
RA9 PT1 1c on 15c dk bl & blk	15	15
a. Double surcharge	3.00	3.00
Set value		40

1922, Feb.

Black Surcharge

RA10 PT2 1c on 10c yellow	15	15
a. Period after "de"	50	40
b. Double surcharge	2.00	2.00
c. Double inverted surcharge	3.75	3.75
d. Inverted surcharge	3.00	3.00
e. Without period after "C"	1.00	1.00

No. 409 Overprinted in Black **R. de C.**

RA11 A24 1c violet	16	15
a. Double overprint	2.00	2.00

This stamp with the overprint in red is a trial printing.

Nos. 402, 404-407 Surcharged in Black **R. de C. Vale un centavo**

1922, June

RA12 A27 1c on 1c grn & blk	75	75
RA13 A29 1c on 5c ultra & blk	75	75
RA14 A30 1c on 10c org & blk	75	40
RA15 A31 1c on 25c yel & blk	75	30
a. Inverted surcharge	5.00	5.00
RA16 A32 1c on 50c vio & blk	30	25
a. Double surcharge	4.00	4.00
Nos. RA12-RA16 (5)	3.30	2.45

PT3

Surcharge in Red or Dark Blue

1922, Oct. *Perf. 11½*

RA17 PT3 1c yellow (R)	15	15
a. No period after "C"	1.00	1.00
RA18 PT3 1c violet (DBl)	15	15
a. No period after "C"	1.00	1.00
Set value	24	20

Surcharge is inverted on 22 out of 50 of No. RA17, 23 out of 50 of No. RA18.

Nos. 403-407 Surcharged in Black **R. de C. Vale un centavo de córdoba**

1923 *Perf. 12*

RA19 A28 1c on 2c rose red & ultra	50	45
RA20 A29 1c on 5c ultra & blk	55	15
RA21 A30 1c on 10c org & blk	25	20
RA22 A31 1c on 25c yel & blk	35	30
RA23 A32 1c on 50c vio & blk	25	15
Nos. RA19-RA23 (5)	1.90	1.25

The variety no period after "R" occurs twice on each sheet.

Red Surcharge

Wmk. Coat of Arms in Sheet

Perf. 11½

RA24 PT3 1c pale blue	15	15

Unwmk.

Type of 1921 Issue Without Surcharge of New Value

RA25 PT1 1c ver & blk	15	15
a. Double overprint, one inverted	3.00	3.00

No. 409 Overprinted in Blue **R. de C. 1924**

1924

RA26 A24 1c violet	20	15
a. Double overprint	8.00	8.00

There are two settings of the overprint on No. RA26, with "1924" 5½mm or 6½mm wide.

No. 409 Overprinted in Blue **R. de C. 1925**

1925

RA27 A24 1c violet	15	15

No. 409 Overprinted in Blue **R. de C.**

1926

RA28 A24 1c violet	25	15

No. RA28 Overprinted in Various Colors **Resello 1927**

1927

RA29 A24 1c vio (R)	15	15
a. Double overprint (R)	2.00	2.00
b. Inverted overprint (R)	3.00	3.00
RA30 A24 1c vio (V)	15	15
a. Double overprint	2.50	2.50
b. Inverted overprint	2.50	2.50
RA31 A24 1c vio (Bl)	15	15
a. Double overprint	5.00	5.00
RA32 A24 1c vio (Bk)	15	15
a. Double ovpt., one invtd.	4.25	4.25
b. Double overprint	4.25	4.25

Same Overprint on No. RA27

RA33 A24 1c vio (Bk)	15.00	10.00
Nos. RA29-RA33 (5)	15.60	10.60

No. RA28 Overprinted in Violet **Resello 1928**

1928

RA34 A24 1c violet	15	15
a. Double overprint	2.00	2.00
b. "928"	1.00	1.00

Similar to No. RA34 but 8mm space between "Resello" and "1928"

Black Overprint

RA35 A24 1c violet	40	15
a. "1828"	2.00	2.00

PT4

Inscribed "Timbre Telegrafico"
Horiz. Surch. in Black,
Vert. Surch. in Red

RA36 PT4 1c on 5c bl & blk	60	15
a. Comma after "R"	1.25	1.25
b. No period after "R"	1.25	1.25
c. No periods after "R" and "C"	1.25	1.25

("CORREOS" at right) — PT5

PT6

1928 **Engr.** *Perf. 12*

RA37 PT5 1c plum	25	15

See Nos. RA41-RA43. For overprints see Nos. RA45-RA46, RA48-RA51.

1929

Surcharged in Red

RA38 PT6 1c on 5c bl & blk	15	15
a. Inverted surcharge	3.00	3.00
b. Double surcharge	2.00	2.00
c. Double surcharge, one inverted	2.00	2.00
d. Period after "de"	1.25	1.25
e. Comma after "R"	1.25	1.25

See note after No. 512.

Regular Issue of 1928 Overprinted in Blue **R. de C.**

RA39 A24 1c red orange	15	15

No. RA39 exists both with and without signature control overprint.

An additional overprint, "1929" in black or blue on No. RA39, is fraudulent.

No. 513 Overprinted in Red **R. de C.**

1929

RA40 A24 1c ol grn	20	15
a. Double overprint	75	75

No. RA40 is known with overprint in black, and with overprint inverted. These varieties were not regularly issued, but copies have been canceled by favor.

Type of 1928 Issue
Inscribed at right "COMUNICACIONES"

1930-37

RA41 PT5 1c carmine	20	15
RA42 PT5 1c orange ('33)	15	15
RA43 PT5 1c green ('37)	15	15
Set value		18

No. RA42 has signature control. See note before No. 600.

No. RA39 Overprinted in Black **1931**

1931

RA44 A24 1c red orange	15	15
a. "1931" double overprint	35	35
b. "1931" double ovpt., one invtd.	42	42

No. RA44 exists with signature control overprint. See note before No. 600. Value is the same.

No. RA42 Overprinted Vertically, up or down, in Black **Resello 1935**

1935

RA45 PT5 1c orange	15	15
a. Double overprint	1.00	1.00
b. Double ovpt., one inverted		

No. RA45 and RA45a Overprinted Vertically, Reading Down, in Blue

RA46 PT5 1c orange	50	15
a. Black overprint double	2.00	2.00

Same Overprint in Red on Nos. RA39, RA42 and RA45

RA47 A24 1c red org (#RA39)	37.50	
RA48 PT5 1c org (#RA42)	20	15
RA49 PT5 1c org (#RA45)	20	15
a. Black overprint double	80	80

Overprint is horizontal on No. RA47 and vertical, reading down, on Nos. RA48-RA49.

No. RA48 exists with signature control overprint. See note before No. 600. Same values.

No. RA42 Overprinted Vertically, Reading Down, in Carmine

1935 **Unwmk.** *Perf. 12*

RA50 PT5 1c orange	20	15

No. RA45 with Additional Overprint "1936", Vertically, Reading Down, in Red

1936

RA51 PT5 1c orange	50	16

No. RA39 with Additional Overprint "1936" in Red

RA52 A24 1c red orange	50	16

No. RA52 exists only with script control mark.

PT7

Vertical Surcharge in Red

1936

RA53 PT7 1c on 5c grn & blk	15	15
a. "Cenavo"	1.40	1.40
b. "Centavos"	1.40	1.40

Horizontal Surcharge in Red

RA54 PT7 1c on 5c grn & blk	15	15
a. Double surcharge	1.40	1.40
Set value		16

Baseball Player — PT8

1937 **Typo.** *Perf. 11*

RA55 PT8 1c carmine	35	15
RA56 PT8 1c yellow	35	15
RA57 PT8 1c blue	35	15
RA58 PT8 1c green	35	15
b. Sheet of 4, #RA55-RA58	3.00	3.00
Set value		44

Issued for the benefit of the Central American Caribbean Games of 1937.

Control mark in red is variously placed. See dark oval below "OLIMPICO" in illustration.

Tête bêche Pairs

RA55a PT8 1c	75	75
RA56a PT8 1c	75	75
RA57a PT8 1c	75	75
RA58a PT8 1c	75	75

Catalogue values for unused stamps in this section, from this point to the end of the section, are for Never Hinged items.

Proposed Natl. Stadium, Managua — PT9

PT10

1949 **Photo.** ***Perf. 12***

RA60 PT9 5c greenish blue 25 15
a. Souvenir sheet of 4 3.75 3.75

10th World Series of Amateur Baseball, 1948. The tax was used toward the erection of a national stadium at Managua.

Type Similar to 1949, with "Correos" omitted

1952

RA61 PT9 5c magenta 25 15

The tax was used toward the erection of a national stadium at Managua.

1956 **Engr.** ***Perf. 12½x12***

RA62 PT10 5c deep ultra 15 15

The tax was used for social welfare.

PT11

Jesus and Children — PT12

Surcharged in Red or Black

1959 **Unwmk.** ***Perf. 12***

Red Marginal Number

RA63 PT11 5c on 50c vio bl (R) 15 15
RA64 PT11 5c on 50c vio bl (B) 15 15
Set value 24 15

Nos. RA63-RA64 are surcharged on consular revenue stamps. Surcharge reads "Sobre Tasa Postal CO.05." Vertical surcharge on No. RA63, horizontal on No. RA64.

1959 **Photo.** ***Perf. 16***

RA65 PT12 5c ultra 15 15

Hexisia Bidentata — PT13

Orchids: No. RA67, Schomburgkia tibicinus. No. RA68, Stanhopea ecornuta. No. RA69, Lycaste macrophylla. No. RA70, Maxillaria tenuifolia. No. RA71, Cattleya skinneri. No. RA72, Cycnoches egertonianum. No. RA73, Bletia roezlii. No. RA74, Sobralia pleiantha. No. RA75, Oncidium cebolleta and ascendens.

1962, Feb. **Photo.** ***Perf. 11½***

Granite Paper

Orchids in Natural Colors

RA66 PT13 5c pale lil & grn 15 15
RA67 PT13 5c yel & grn 15 15
RA68 PT13 5c pink & grn 15 15
RA69 PT13 5c pale vio & grn 15 15
RA70 PT13 5c lt grnsh bl & red 15 15
RA71 PT13 5c buff & lil 15 15
RA72 PT13 5c yel grn & brn 15 15
RA73 PT13 5c gray & red 15 15
RA74 PT13 5c lt bl & dk bl 15 15
RA75 PT13 5c lt grn & brn 15 15
Set value 80 80

For overprints see Nos. 842-852, 855-868, 901-908.

PROVINCE OF ZELAYA

(Bluefields)

A province of Nicaragua lying along the eastern coast. Special postage stamps for this section were made necessary because for a period two currencies, which differed materially in value, were in use in Nicaragua. Silver money was used in Zelaya and Cabo Gracias a Dios while the rest of Nicaragua used paper money. Later the money of the entire country was placed on a gold basis.

Dangerous counterfeits exist of most of the Bluefields overprints.

Regular Issues of 1900-05 Handstamped in Black (4 or more types)

B
Dpto Zelaya.

1904-05 **Unwmk.** ***Perf. 12, 14***

On Engraved Stamps of 1900

1L1 A14 1c plum 1.50 75
1L2 A14 2c vermilion 1.50 75
1L3 A14 3c green 1.90 1.50
1L4 A14 4c ol grn 11.00 11.00
1L5 A14 15c ultra 3.00 1.90
1L6 A14 20c brown 3.00 1.90
1L7 A14 50c lake 10.50 7.50
1L8 A14 1p yellow 21.00
1L9 A14 2p salmon 30.00
1L10 A14 5p black 37.50

On Lithographed Stamps of 1902

1L11 A14 5c blue 3.00 75
1L12 A14 5c carmine 1.90 90
1L13 A14 10c violet 1.50 75

On Postage Due Stamps Overprinted "1901 Correos"

1L14 D3 20c brn (No. 156) 4.50 1.90
1L15 D3 50c lake (No. 158)

On Surcharged Stamps of 1904-05

1L16 A16 5c on 10c (#175) 1.50 1.10
1L17 A14 5c on 10c (#178) 4.00 1.50
1L18 A16 15c on 10c vio 1.50 1.50
1L19 A17 15c on 10c vio 14.00 4.50

On Surcharged Stamp of 1901

1L20 A14 20c on 5p blk 18.00 3.00

On Regular Issue of 1905

1906-07 ***Perf. 12***

1L21 A18 1c green 30 30
1L22 A18 2c car rose 30 30
1L23 A18 3c violet 30 30
1L24 A18 4c org red 45 45
1L25 A18 5c blue 22 22
1L26 A18 10c yel brn 3.00 1.50
1L27 A18 15c brn ol 4.50 1.75
1L28 A18 20c lake 9.00 7.50
1L29 A18 50c orange 35.00 30.00
1L30 A18 1p black 30.00 27.50
1L31 A18 2p dk grn 37.50
1L32 A18 5p violet 45.00
Nos. 1L21-1L32 (12) 165.57

On Surcharged Stamps of 1906-08

1L33 A18 10c on 3c vio 38 38
1L34 A18 15c on 1c grn 52 52
1L35 A18 20c on 2c rose 3.50 3.50
1L36 A18 20c on 5c bl 1.50 1.50
1L37 A18 50c on 6c sl (R) 1.50 3.00
Nos. 1L33-1L37 (5) 7.40 8.90

B B

Dpto. Zelaya Dto. Zelaya

Stamps with the above overprints were made to fill dealers' orders but were never regularly issued or used. Stamps with similar overprints handstamped are bogus.

Surcharged Stamps of 1906 Overprinted in Red, Black or Blue

B
Dpto. Zelaya

1L38 A18 15c on 1c grn (R) 2.75 2.75
a. Red overprint inverted

1L39 A18 20c on 2c rose (Bk) 1.90 1.90
1L40 A18 20c on 5c bl (R) 3.00 3.00
1L41 A18 50c on 6c sl (Bl) 14.00 14.00

Stamps of the 1905 issue overprinted as above No. 1L38 or similarly overprinted but with only 2¼mm space between "B" and "Dpto. Zelaya" were made to fill dealers' orders but not placed in use.

No. 205 Handstamped in Black

B
Dpto Zelaya.

Perf. 14 to 15

1L42 A18 10c yel brn 24.00 24.00

Stamps of 1907 Overprinted in Red or Black

B
Dpto Zelaya

1L43 A18 15c brn ol (R) 3.00 3.00
1L44 A18 20c lake 90 90
a. Inverted overprint 11.00 11.00

With Additional Surcharge

5 cent.

1L45 A18 5c brn org 52 45
a. Inverted surcharge 7.50 7.50

With Additional Surcharge

5 cent.

1L46 A18 5c on 4c brn org 12.00 12.00

On Provisional Postage Stamps of 1907-08 in Black or Blue

1L47 A18 10c on 2c rose (Bl) 4.50 4.50
1L48 A18 10c on 2c rose
1L48A A18 10c on 4c brn org
1L49 A18 10c on 20c lake 3.00 3.00
1L50 A18 10c on 50c org (Bl) 3.00 2.25

Arms Type of 1907 Overprinted in Black or Violet

"COSTA ATLANTICA"
B.

1907

1L51 A18 1c green 30 22
1L52 A18 2c rose 30 22
1L53 A18 3c violet 38 38
1L54 A18 4c brn org 45 45
1L55 A18 5c blue 4.50 2.25
1L56 A18 10c yel brn 38 30
1L57 A18 15c brn ol 75 38
1L58 A18 20c lake 75 45
1L59 A18 50c orange 2.25 1.50
1L60 A18 1p blk (V) 2.25 1.50
1L61 A18 2p dk grn 2.25 1.90
1L62 A18 5p violet 3.75 2.25
Nos. 1L51-1L62 (12) 18.31 11.80

Nos. 217-225 Overprinted in Green

1908

1L63 A19 1c on 5c yel & blk (R) 45 38
1L64 A19 2c on 5c yel & blk (Bl) 45 38
1L65 A19 4c on 5c yel & blk (G) 45 38
a. Overprint reading down 11.00 11.00
b. Double overprint, reading up and down 18.00 18.00
1L66 A19 5c yel & blk 45 45
a. "CORROE" 4.50
b. Double overprint 11.00 11.00
c. Double overprint, reading up and down 19.00 19.00
d. "CORREO 1908" double 15.00 15.00
1L67 A19 10c lt bl & blk 45 45
a. Ovpt. reading down 52 52
b. "CORREO 1908" triple 37.50
1L68 A19 15c on 50c ol & blk (R) 90 90
a. "1008" 4.50
b. "8908" 4.50
1L69 A19 35c on 50c ol & blk 1.40 1.40
1L70 A19 1p yel brn & blk 1.90 1.90
a. "CORROE" 12.00 12.00
1L71 A19 2p pearl gray & blk 2.25 2.25
a. "CORROE" 15.00 15.00
Nos. 1L63-1L71 (9) 8.70 8.49

Overprinted Horizontally in Black or Green

1L72 A19 5c yel & blk 9.00 7.50
1L72A A19 2p pearl gray & blk (G)

On Nos. 1L72-1L72A, space between "B" and "Dpto. Zelaya" is 13mm.

Nos. 237-248 Overprinted in Black

B
Dpto. Zelaya

Imprint: "American Bank Note Co. NY"

1909 ***Perf. 12***

1L73 A18 1c yel grn 22 22
1L74 A18 2c vermilion 22 22
a. Inverted overprint
1L75 A18 3c red org 22 22
1L76 A18 4c violet 22 22
1L77 A18 5c dp bl 30 22
a. Inverted overprint 9.00 9.00
b. "B" inverted 7.50 7.50
c. Double overprint 12.00 12.00
1L78 A18 6c gray brn 4.50 3.00
1L79 A18 10c lake 30 28
a. "B" inverted 9.00 9.00
1L80 A18 15c black 45 38
a. "B" inverted 11.00 11.00
b. Inverted overprint 12.00 12.00
c. Double overprint 14.00 14.00
1L81 A18 20c brn ol 52 52
a. "B" inverted 19.00 19.00
1L82 A18 50c dp grn 1.50 1.50
1L83 A18 1p yellow 2.25 2.25
1L84 A18 2p car rose 3.00 3.00
a. Double overprint 27.50 27.50
Nos. 1L73-1L84 (12) 13.70 12.03

One stamp in each sheet has the "o" of "Dpto." sideways.

Overprinted in Black

B
Dpto. Zelaya

1910

1L85 A18 3c red org 38 38
1L86 A18 4c violet 38 38
a. Inverted overprint 14.00 14.00
1L87 A18 15c black 4.50 2.25
1L88 A18 20c brn ol 22 30
1L89 A18 50c dp grn 28 38
1L90 A18 1p yellow 30 45
a. Inverted overprint 7.50
1L91 A18 2p car rose 38 75
Nos. 1L85-1L91 (7) 6.44 4.89

Z1

Black Ovpt., Green Surch., Carmine Block-outs

1910

1L92 Z1 5c on 10c lake 3.75 3.00

There are three types of the letter "B". It is stated that this stamp was used exclusively for postal purposes and not for telegrams.

No. 247 Surcharged in Black

B
Vale
5 cts.

1911

1L93 A18 5c on 1p yellow 75 75
a. Double surcharge 14.00
1L94 A18 10c on 1p yellow 1.50 1.50
1L95 A18 15c on 1p yellow 75 75
a. Inverted surcharge 9.00
b. Double surcharge 9.00
c. Double surcharge, one invtd. 9.00

B
CORREOS
Revenue Stamps Surcharged in Black
05 cts.
1911

Perf. 14 to 15

1L96 A19 5c on 25c lilac 75 1.10
a. Without period 1.50 1.50
b. Inverted surcharge 9.00 9.00
1L97 A19 10c on 1p yel brn 1.10 75
a. Without period 1.90 1.90
b. "01" for "10" 9.00 7.50
c. Inverted surcharge 13.00 13.00

VALE
05 cts.
Surcharged in Black
POSTAL B
de 1911

1L98 A19 5c on 1p yel brn 1.50 1.50
a. Without period 2.25
b. "50" for "05" 14.00 14.00
c. Inverted surcharge 15.00 15.00
1L99 A19 5c on 10p pink 1.50 1.50
a. Without period 2.25 2.25
b. "50" for "05" 11.00 11.00
1L100 A19 10c on 1p yel brn 82.50 82.50
a. Without period 95.00 95.00
1L101 A19 10c on 25p grn 75 75
a. Without period 2.25 2.25
b. "1" for "10" 7.50
1L102 A19 10c on 50p ver 11.00 11.00
a. Without period 16.50
b. "1" for "10" 22.50
Nos. 1L98-1L102 (5) 97.25 97.25

With Additional Overprint "1904"

1L103 A19 5c on 10p pink 14.00 14.00
a. Without period 24.00 24.00
b. "50" for "05" 110.00 110.00
1L104 A19 10c on 2p gray 75 75
a. Without period 1.90
b. "1" for "10" 7.50
1L105 A19 10c on 25p grn 92.50
a. Without period 100.00
1L106 A19 10c on 50p ver 7.50 7.50
a. Without period 14.00
b. "1" for "10" 18.00
c. Inverted surcharge

The surcharges on Nos. 1L96 to 1L106 are in settings of twenty-five. One stamp in each setting has a large square period after "cts" and another has a thick upright "c" in that word. There are two types of "1904".

B
No. 293C Overprinted
Dpto. Zelaya

1911

1L107 A21 5c on 5c on 2c bl (R) 22.50
a. "5" omitted 27.50
b. Red overprint inverted 30.00
c. As "a" and "b" 37.50

Same Overprint
On Nos. 290, 291, 292 and 289D with Lines of Surcharge spaced 2 1/2mm apart Reading Down

1L107D A21 2c on 10c on 1c red
e. Overprint reading up
1L107F A21 5c on 10c on 1c red 92.50
1L107G A21 10c on 10c on 1c red (#292) 125.00
1L108 A21 10c on 10c on 1c red (#289D) 120.00

There is no evidence that Nos. 1L107D-1L108 were issued by the government.

Locomotive — Z2

1912 Engr. *Perf. 14*

1L109 Z2 1c yel grn 75 50
1L110 Z2 2c vermilion 50 25
1L111 Z2 3c org brn 75 45
1L112 Z2 4c carmine 75 30
1L113 Z2 5c dp bl 75 45
1L114 Z2 6c red brn 4.00 2.50
1L115 Z2 10c slate 75 30
1L116 Z2 15c dl lil 75 60
1L117 Z2 20c bl vio 75 60
1L118 Z2 25c grn & blk 1.00 80
1L119 Z2 35c brn & blk 1.25 1.00
1L120 Z2 50c ol grn 1.25 1.00
1L121 Z2 1p orange 1.75 1.50
1L122 Z2 2p org brn 4.00 3.00
1L123 Z2 5p dk bl grn 7.00 6.50
Nos. 1L109-1L123 (15) 26.00 19.75

The stamps of this issue were for use in all places on the Atlantic Coast of Nicaragua where the currency was on a silver basis.

For surcharges see Nos. 325-337.

OFFICIAL STAMPS

Regular Issue of 1909 Overprinted in Black
Oficial
B

1909 Unwmk. *Perf. 12*

1LO1 A18 20c brn ol 11.00 8.00
a. Double overprint 13.00

Official Stamp of 1909 Overprinted in Black B

1LO2 A18 15c black 11.00 6.50

Same Overprint on Official Stamp of 1911

1911

1LO3 A18 5c on 3c red org 16.00 13.00

CABO GRACIAS A DIOS

A cape and seaport town in the extreme northeast of Nicaragua. The name was coined by Spanish explorers who had great difficulty finding a landing place along the Nicaraguan coast and when eventually locating this harbor expressed their relief by designating the point "Cape Thanks to God." Special postage stamps came into use for the same reasons as the Zelaya issues. See Zelaya.

Dangerous counterfeits exist of most of the Cabo Gracias a Dios overprints.

Regular Issues of 1900-04 Handstamped in Violet CABO

On Engraved Stamps of 1900

1904-05 Unwmk. *Perf. 12, 14*

2L1 A14 1c plum 2.25 1.10
2L2 A14 2c vermilion 4.50 1.20
2L3 A14 3c green 6.00 4.50
2L4 A14 4c ol grn 9.75 9.75
2L5 A14 15c ultra 35.00 22.50
2L6 A14 20c brown 3.00 2.25
Nos. 2L1-2L6 (6) 60.50 41.30

On Lithographed Stamps of 1902

2L7 A14 5c blue 24.00 24.00
2L8 A14 10c violet 24.00 24.00

On Surcharged Stamps of 1904

2L9 A16 5c on 10c vio 22.50 22.50
2L10 A16 15c on 10c vio

On Postage Due Stamps
Violet Handstamp

2L11 D3 20c org brn (#141) 5.00 1.25
2L12 D3 20c org brn (#156) 3.50 1.25
2L13 D3 30c dk grn (#157) 14.00 14.00
2L14 D3 50c lake (#158) 3.75 75

Black Handstamp

2L15 D3 30c dk grn (#157) 24.00 24.00

Stamps of 1900-05 Handstamped in Violet Cabo

On Engraved Stamps of 1900

2L16 A14 1c plum 2.75 2.25
2L17 A14 2c vermilion 27.50 24.00
2L18 A14 3c green 37.50 27.50
2L19 A14 4c ol grn 40.00 37.50
2L20 A14 15c ultra 45.00 45.00
Nos. 2L16-2L20 (5) 152.75 136.25

On Lithographed Stamps of 1902

2L22 A14 5c dk bl 95.00 50.00
2L23 A14 10c violet 27.50 24.00

On Surcharged Stamp of 1904

2L24 A16 5c on 10c vio

On Postage Due Stamp

2L25 D3 20c org brn (#141)

Cabo

The editors have no evidence that stamps with this handstamp were issued. Copies were sent to the UPU and covers are known.

Stamps of 1900-08 Handstamped in Violet

1905

On Stamps of 1905

2L26 A18 1c green 1.10 1.10
2L27 A18 2c car rose 1.50 1.50
2L28 A18 3c violet 1.50 1.50
2L29 A18 4c org red 3.75 3.75
2L30 A18 5c blue 1.50 1.10
2L31 A18 6c slate 3.75 3.75
2L32 A18 10c yel brn 3.00 1.90
2L33 A18 15c brn ol 4.50 4.50
2L34 A18 1p black 20.00 20.00
2L35 A18 2p dk grn 35.00 35.00
Nos. 2L26-2L35 (10) 75.60 74.10

Magenta Handstamp

2L26a A18 1c 3.75 3.00
2L27a A18 2c 3.00 2.75
2L28a A18 3c 3.75 3.00
2L30a A18 5c 7.50 6.00
2L33a A18 15c 13.50 11.00

On Stamps of 1900-04

2L36 A16 5c on 10c vio 14.00 14.00
2L37 A14 10c violet
2L38 A14 20c brown 12.00 12.00
2L39 A14 20c on 5p blk 95.00

On Postage Due Stamps Overprinted "Correos"

2L40 D3 20c org brn (#141) 9.00 9.00
2L41 D3 20c org brn (#156) 5.00 4.50

On Surcharged Stamps of 1906-08

2L42 A18 10c on 3c vio
2L43 A18 20c on 5c blue 9.00 9.00
2L44 A18 50c on 6c slate 24.00 24.00

On Stamps of 1907
Perf. 14 to 15

2L44A A18 2c rose
2L45 A18 10c yel brn 100.00 75.00
2L46 A18 15c brn ol 90.00 75.00

On Provisional Stamp of 1908 in Magenta

2L47 A19 5c yel & blk 7.50 7.50

Stamps with the above large handstamp in black instead of violet, are bogus. There are also excellent counterfeits in violet.

The foregoing overprints being handstamped are found in various positions, especially the last type.

Stamps of 1907 Type A18, Overprinted in Black or Violet
"COSTA ATLANTICA"
C.

1907

2L48 A18 1c green 30 30
2L49 A18 2c rose 30 30
2L50 A18 3c violet 30 30
a. Vert. pair, imperf. btwn. 15.00
2L51 A18 4c brn org 38 38
2L52 A18 5c blue 50 50
2L53 A18 10c yel brn 38 38
2L54 A18 15c brn ol 75 75
2L55 A18 20c lake 75 75
2L56 A18 50c orange 1.90 1.50
2L57 A18 1p blk (V) 2.25 1.90
2L58 A18 2p dk grn 3.00 2.25
2L59 A18 5p violet 4.50 3.75
Nos. 2L48-2L59 (12) 15.31 13.06

Nos. 237-248 Overprinted in Black
C
Dpto. Zelaya

Imprint: American Bank Note Co.

1909 *Perf. 12*

2L60 A18 1c yel grn 35 38
2L61 A18 2c vermilion 35 38
2L62 A18 3c red org 35 38
2L63 A18 4c violet 35 38
2L64 A18 5c dp bl 35 60
2L65 A18 6c gray brn 6.00 6.00
2L66 A18 10c lake 60 75
2L67 A18 15c black 90 90
2L68 A18 20c brn ol 1.00 1.10
2L69 A18 50c dp grn 2.50 2.50
2L70 A18 1p yellow 4.00 4.00
2L71 A18 2p car rose 5.75 5.75
Nos. 2L60-2L71 (12) 22.50 23.12

No. 199 Overprinted Vertically CABO

2L72 A18 50c on 6c slate (R) 7.50 7.50

OFFICIAL STAMPS

Official Stamps of 1907 Overprinted in Red or Violet

1907

2LO1 A18 10c on 1c green 60.00
2LO2 A18 15c on 1c green 75.00
2LO3 A18 20c on 1c green 100.00
2LO4 A18 50c on 1c green 125.00

NIGER

LOCATION — Northern Africa, directly north of Nigeria
GOVT. — Republic
AREA — 458,075 sq. mi.
POP. — 6,265,000 (est. 1984)
CAPITAL — Niamey

The colony, formed in 1922, was originally a military territory. The Republic of the Niger was proclaimed December 19, 1955. In the period between issues of the colony and the republic, stamps of French West Africa were used.

100 Centimes = 1 Franc

Catalogue values for unused stamps in this country are for Never Hinged items, beginning with Scott 91 in the regular postage section, Scott B14 in the semi-postal section, Scott C14 in the airpost section, Scott J22 in the postage due section, and Scott O1 in the official section.

Camel and Rider — A1

Stamps of Upper Senegal and Niger Type of 1914, Overprinted

1921-26 Unwmk. *Perf. 13 1/2x14*

1 A1 1c brn vio & vio 15 15
2 A1 2c dk gray & dl vio 15 15
3 A1 4c blk & bl 15 15
4 A1 5c ol brn & dk brn 15 15
5 A1 10c yel grn & bl grn 40 40
6 A1 10c mag, *bluish* ('26) 15 15
7 A1 15c red brn & org 15 15
8 A1 20c brn vio & blk 15 15
9 A1 25c blk & bl grn 15 15
10 A1 30c red org & rose 35 35
11 A1 30c bl grn & red org ('26) 28 28

12 A1 35c rose & vio 20 20
13 A1 40c gray & rose 28 28
14 A1 45c bl & ol brn 28 28
15 A1 50c ultra & bl 35 35
16 A1 50c dk gray & bl vio ('25) 28 28
17 A1 60c org red ('26) 42 42
18 A1 75c yel & ol brn 40 40
19 A1 1fr dk brn & dl vio 50 50
20 A1 2fr grn & bl 55 55
21 A1 5fr vio & blk 1.00 1.00
Nos. 1-21 (21) 6.49 6.49

Stamps and Type of 1921 Surcharged New Value and Bars in Black or Red

60 = 60

1922-26

22 A1 25c on 15c red brn & org ('25) 20 20
a. Multiple surcharge 55.00
b. "25c" inverted 55.00
23 A1 25c on 2fr grn & bl (R) ('24) 28 28
24 A1 25c on 5fr vio & blk (R) ('24) 28 28
a. Double surcharge 55.00
25 A1 60c on 75c vio, *pnksh* 28 28
26 A1 65c on 45c bl & ol brn ('25) 1.10 1.10
27 A1 85c on 75c yel & ol brn ('25) 1.10 1.10
28 A1 1.25fr on 1fr dp bl & lt bl (R) ('26) 20 20
a. Surcharge omitted 90.00
Nos. 22-28 (7) 3.44 3.44

Nos. 22-24 are surcharged "25c," No. 28, "1f25." Nos. 25-27 are surcharged like illustration.

Drawing Water from Well — A2

Zinder Fortress — A4

Boat on Niger River — A3

Perf. 13x14, 13½x14, 14x13, 14x13½

1926-40 **Typo.**

29 A2 1c lilac rose & olive 15 15
30 A2 2c dk gray & dl red 15 15
31 A2 3c red vio & ol gray ('40) 15 15
32 A2 4c umber & gray 15 15
33 A2 5c ver & yel grn 15 15
34 A2 10c dp bl & Prus bl 15 15
35 A2 15c gray grn & yel grn 15 15
36 A2 15c gray lil & lt red ('28) 15 15
37 A3 20c Prus grn & ol brn 15 15
38 A3 25c blk & dl red 15 15
39 A3 30c bl grn & yel grn 22 20
40 A3 30c yel & red vio ('40) 15 15
41 A3 35c brn org & turq bl, *bluish* 15 15
42 A3 35c bl grn & dl grn ('38) 20 20
43 A3 40c red brn & sl 15 15
44 A3 45c yel & red vio 40 40
45 A3 45c bl grn & dl grn ('40) 15 15
46 A3 50c scar & grn, *grnsh* 15 15
47 A3 55c dk car & brn ('38) 40 40
48 A3 60c dk car & brn ('40) 15 15
49 A3 65c ol grn & rose 15 15
50 A3 70c ol grn & rose ('40) 40 40
51 A3 75c grn & vio, *pink* 55 52
52 A3 80c cl & ol grn ('38) 55 55
53 A3 90c brn red & ver 40 40
54 A3 90c brt rose & yel grn ('39) 40 40
55 A4 1fr rose & yel grn 3.50 2.50
56 A4 1fr dk red & red org ('38) 40 32
57 A4 1fr grn & red ('40) 15 15
58 A4 1.10fr ol brn & grn 2.00 1.50
59 A4 1.25fr grn & red ('33) 55 55
60 A4 1.25fr dk red & red org ('39) 20 20
61 A4 1.40fr red vio & dk brn ('40) 20 20
62 A4 1.50fr dp bl & pale bl 15 15
63 A4 1.60fr ol brn & grn ('40) 60 60
64 A4 1.75fr red vio & dk brn ('33) 1.20 1.00
65 A4 1.75fr dk bl & vio bl ('38) 40 40
66 A4 2fr red org & ol brn 15 15
67 A4 2.25fr dk bl & vio bl ('39) 30 30
68 A4 2.50fr blk brn ('40) 30 30
69 A4 3fr dl vio & blk ('27) 28 28
70 A4 5fr vio brn & blk, *pink* 28 28
71 A4 10fr chlky bl & mag 62 62
72 A4 20fr yel grn & red org 62 62
Nos. 29-72 (44) 17.97 16.14

For surcharges see Nos. B7-B10.

Colonial Exposition Issue
Common Design Types

1931 **Typo.** ***Perf. 12½***
Name of Country in Black

73 CD70 40c dp grn 1.60 1.60
74 CD71 50c violet 1.60 1.60
75 CD72 90c red org 2.00 2.00
76 CD73 1.50fr dl bl 2.00 2.00

Paris International Exposition Issue
Common Design Types

1937 ***Perf. 13***

77 CD74 20c dp vio 45 45
78 CD75 30c dk grn 45 45
79 CD76 40c car rose 45 45
80 CD77 50c dk brn 45 45
81 CD78 90c red 60 60
82 CD79 1.50fr ultra 60 60
Nos. 77-82 (6) 3.00 3.00

Colonial Arts Exhibition Issue
Souvenir Sheet
Common Design Type

1937 ***Imperf.***

83 CD74 3fr magenta 2.25 2.25

Caillie Issue
Common Design Type

1939 ***Perf. 12½x12***

84 CD81 90c org brn & org 40 40
85 CD81 2fr brt vio 40 40
86 CD81 2.25fr ultra & dk bl 40 40

New York World's Fair Issue
Common Design Type

1939, May 10

87 CD82 1.25fr car lake 40 40
88 CD82 2.25fr ultra 40 40

Zinder Fortress and Marshal Pétain — A5

1941 **Unwmk.** **Engr.** ***Perf. 12x12½***

89 A5 1fr green 28
90 A5 2.50fr dk bl 28

Nos. 89-90 were issued by the Vichy government and were not placed on sale in the colony.

Catalogue values for unused stamps in this section, from this point to the end of the section, are for Never Hinged items.

Republic of the Niger

Giraffes — A6

Designs: 1fr, 2fr, Crested cranes. 5fr, 7fr, Saddle-billed storks. 15fr, 20fr, Barbary sheep. 25fr, 30fr, Giraffes. 50fr, 60fr, Ostriches. 85fr, 100fr, Lion.

1959-60 **Unwmk.** **Engr.** ***Perf. 13***

91 A6 1fr multi 15 15
92 A6 2fr multi 15 15
93 A6 5fr blk, car & ol 15 15
94 A6 7fr grn, blk & red 15 15
95 A6 15fr grnsh bl & dk brn 18 15
96 A6 20fr vio, blk & ind 20 15
97 A6 25fr multi 22 15
98 A6 30fr multi 28 15
99 A6 50fr ind & org brn 50 25
100 A6 60fr dk brn & emer 60 35
101 A6 85fr org brn & bis 75 40
102 A6 100fr bis & yel grn 90 50
Nos. 91-102 (12) 4.23
Set value 2.00

Issue years: #97, 1959; others, 1960.
For surcharge see No. 103.

Imperforates

Most stamps of the republic exist imperforate in issued and trial colors, and also in small presentation sheets in issued color.

No. 102 Surcharged with New Value and: "Indépendance 3-8-60"

1960

103 A6 200fr on 100fr 4.00 4.00

Niger's independence.

C.C.T.A. Issue
Common Design Type

1960 **Engr.** ***Perf. 13***

104 CD106 25fr buff & red brn 35 30

Emblem of the Entente — A6a

Pres. Diori Hamani — A7

1960 **Photo.** ***Perf. 13x13½***

105 A6a 25fr multi 35 28

1st anniversary of the Entente (Dahomey, Ivory Coast, Niger and Upper Volta).

1960, Dec. 18 **Engr.** ***Perf. 13***

106 A7 25fr ol bis & blk 22 15

2nd anniversary of the proclamation of the Republic of the Niger.

Common Design Types pictured in section at front of book.

Manatee — A8

1962, Jan. 29 **Unwmk.** ***Perf. 13***

107 A8 50c grn & dk sl grn 15 15
108 A8 10fr red brn & dk grn 15 15
Set value 20 15

Abidjan Games Issue
Common Design Type

Designs: 25fr, Basketball and Soccer. 85fr, Track, horiz.

1962, May 26 **Photo.** ***Perf. 12x12½***

109 CD109 15fr multi 15 15
110 CD109 25fr multi 22 15
111 CD109 85fr multi 65 38

African-Malgache Union Issue
Common Design Type

1962, Sept. 8 ***Perf. 12½x12***

112 CD110 30fr multi 30 22

Pres. Diori Hamani and Map of Niger in Africa — A10

1962, Dec. 18 **Photo.** ***Perf. 12½x12***

113 A10 25fr multi 22 20

Woman Runner — A11

Woodworker — A12

Designs: 15fr, Swimming, horiz. 45fr, Volleyball.

Unwmk.

1963, Apr. 11 **Engr.** ***Perf. 13***

114 A11 15fr brt bl & dk brn 15 15
115 A11 25fr dk brn & red 22 15
116 A11 45fr grn & blk 38 25
Set value 46

Friendship Games, Dakar, Apr. 11-21.

Perf. 12x12½, 12½x12

1963, Aug. 30 **Photo.**

Designs: 10fr, Tanners, horiz. 25fr, Goldsmith. 30fr, Mat makers, horiz. 85fr, Decoy maker.

117 A12 5fr brn & multi 15 15
118 A12 10fr dk grn & multi 15 15
119 A12 25fr blk & multi 22 15
120 A12 30fr vio & multi 28 15
121 A12 85fr dk bl & multi 65 40
Nos. 117-121,C26 (6) 2.25
Set value 1.20

Berberi (Nuba) Woman's Costume — A13

Costume Museum, Niamey — A14

Costumes: 20fr, Hausa woman. 25fr, Tuareg woman. 30fr, Tuareg man. 60fr, Djerma woman.

Perf. 12x12½, 12½x12

1963, Oct. 15 **Photo.**

122 A13 15fr multi 15 15
123 A13 20fr blk & bl 18 15
124 A13 25fr multi 25 15
125 A13 30fr multi 28 15
126 A13 60fr multi 60 35
127 A14 85fr multi 70 40
Nos. 122-127 (6) 2.16 1.35

Man, Globe and Scales — A15

Parkinsonia Aculeata — A16

Unwmk.

1963, Dec. 10 Engr. *Perf. 13*

128 A15 25fr lt ol grn, ultra & brn org 25 18

Issued to commemorate the 15th anniversary of the Universal Declaration of Human Rights.

1964-65 Photo. *Perf. 13½x13*

Flowers: 10fr, Russelia equisetiformis. 15fr, Red sage (lantana). 20fr, Argyreia nervosa. 25fr, Luffa cylindrica. 30fr, Hibiscus rosa sinensis. 45fr, Red jasmine (frangipani). 50fr, Catharanthus roseus. 60fr, Caesalpinia pulcherrima.

129 A16	5fr dk red, grn & yel	25	15
130 A16	10fr multi	20	15
131 A16	15fr multi	28	15
132 A16	20fr multi	28	15
133 A16	25fr multi	28	15
134 A16	30fr multi	40	25
135 A16	45fr multi ('65)	48	25
136 A16	50fr dk red, brt pink & grn ('65)	48	25
137 A16	60fr multi ('65)	70	35
	Nos. 129-137 (9)	3.35	1.85

Solar Flares and IQSY Emblem — A17

1964, May 12 Engr. *Perf. 13*

138 A17 30fr dp org, vio & blk 30 22

International Quiet Sun Year, 1964-65.

Mobile Medical Unit — A18

Designs: 30fr, Mobile children's clinic. 50fr, Mobile women's clinic. 60fr, Outdoor medical laboratory.

1964, May 26

139 A18	25fr bl, org & ol	25	15
140 A18	30fr multi	28	15
141 A18	50fr vio, org & bl	40	18
142 A18	60fr grnsh bl, org & dk brn	48	22

Nigerian mobile health education organization, OMNES (Organisation Médicale Mobile Nigérienne d'Education Sanitaire).

Cooperation Issue

Common Design Type

1964, Nov. 7 Unwmk. *Perf. 13*

143 CD119 50fr vio, dk brn & org 40 25

Tuareg Tent of Azawak A19

Designs: 20fr, Songhai house. 25fr, Wogo and Kourtey tents. 30fr, Djerma house. 60fr, Huts of Sorkawa fishermen. 85fr, Hausa town house.

1964-65 Engr.

144 A19	15fr ultra, dl grn & red brn	15	15
145 A19	20fr multi	18	15
146 A19	25fr Prus bl, dk brn & org brn	20	15
147 A19	30fr multi ('65)	22	15
148 A19	60fr red, grn & bis ('65)	40	18
149 A19	85fr multi ('65)	60	30
	Nos. 144-149 (6)	1.75	1.08

Leprosy Examination A20

Abraham Lincoln A21

1964, Dec. 15 Photo. *Perf. 13x12½*

150 A20 50fr multi 35 28

Issued to publicize the fight against leprosy.

1965, Apr. 3 *Perf. 13x12½*

151 A21 50fr vio bl, blk, & ocher 40 35

Centenary of death of Abraham Lincoln.

Teaching with Radio and Pictures — A22

Designs: 25fr, Woman studying arithmetic: "A better life through knowledge." 30fr, Adult education class. 50fr, Map of Niger and 5 tribesmen, "Literacy for adults."

1965, Apr. 16 Engr. *Perf. 13*

152 A22	20fr dk bl, dk brn & ocher	20	15
153 A22	25fr sl grn, brn & ol brn	25	15
154 A22	30fr red, sl grn & vio brn	28	15
155 A22	50fr dp bl, brn & vio brn	45	20

Issued to promote adult education and "a better life through knowledge."

Ader Portable Telephone A23

Runner A24

Designs: 30fr, Wheatstone telegraph interrupter. 50fr, Early telewriter.

1965, May 17 Unwmk. *Perf. 13*

156 A23	25fr red brn, dk grn & ind	25	15
157 A23	30fr lil, sl grn & red	28	15
158 A23	50fr red, sl grn & pur	40	25

Issued to commemorate the centenary of the International Telecommunication Union.

1965, July 1 Engr. *Perf. 13*

Designs: 10fr, Hurdler, horiz. 20fr, Pole vaulter, horiz. 30fr, Long jumper.

159 A24	10fr brn, ocher & blk	15	15
160 A24	15fr gray, brn & red	18	15
161 A24	20fr dk grn, brn & vio bl	20	15
162 A24	30fr mar, brn & grn	28	15
	Set value		34

African Games, Brazzaville, July 18-25.

Radio Interview and Club Emblem A25

Designs (Club Emblem and): 45fr, Recording folk music, vert. 50fr, Group listening to broadcast, vert. 60fr, Public debate.

1965, Oct. 1 Engr. *Perf. 13*

163 A25	30fr brt vio, emer & red brn	25	15
164 A25	45fr blk, car & buff	35	15
165 A25	50fr dk car, bl & lt brn	38	18
166 A25	60fr bis, ultra & brn	45	22

Issued to promote radio clubs.

Water Cycle — A26

1966, Feb. 28 Engr. *Perf. 13*

167 A26 50fr vio, ocher & bl 40 22

Hydrological Decade, 1965-74.

Carvings, Mask and Headdresses A27

Designs: 50fr, Carvings and wall decorations. 60fr, Carvings and arch. 100fr, Architecture and handicraft.

1966, Apr. 12

168 A27	30fr red brn, blk & brt grn	25	15
169 A27	50fr brt bl, ocher & pur	40	20
170 A27	60fr car lake, dl pur & yel brn	50	25
171 A27	100fr brt red, bl & blk	80	35

International Negro Arts Festival, Dakar, Senegal, Apr. 1-24.

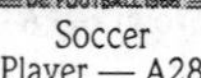
Soccer Player — A28

Color Guard — A29

Designs: 50fr, Goalkeeper, horiz. 60fr, Player kicking ball.

1966, June 17 Engr. *Perf. 13*

172 A28	30fr dk brn, brt bl & rose red	30	15
173 A28	50fr bl, choc & emer	40	15
174 A28	60fr bl, lil & brn	50	25

8th World Soccer Cup Championship, Wembley, England, July 11-30.

Perf. 12½x13, 13x12½

1966, Aug. 23 Photo.

Designs: 20fr, Parachutist, horiz. 45fr, Tanks, horiz.

175 A29	20fr multi	20	15
176 A29	30fr multi	25	15
177 A29	45fr multi	35	22
	Set value		44

Issued to commemorate the 5th anniversary of the National Armed Forces.

Cow Receiving Injection A30

1966, Sept. 26 Litho. *Perf. 12½x13*

178 A30 45fr org brn, bl & blk 35 18

Campaign against cattle plague.

UNESCO Emblem — A31

1966, Nov. 4 Litho. *Perf. 13x12½*

179 A31 50fr multi 48 18

20th anniversary of UNESCO.

Cement Works Malbaza A32

Designs: 10fr, Furnace, vert. 20fr, Electric center. 50fr, Handling of raw material.

1966, Dec. 17 Engr. *Perf. 13*

180 A32	10fr ind, brn & org	15	15
181 A32	20fr dk ol grn & dl bl	22	15
182 A32	30fr bl, gray & red brn	28	15
183 A32	50fr ind, bl & brn	40	15
	Set value		36

Redbilled Hornbill A33

Birds: 2fr, Pied kingfisher. 30fr, Barbary shrike. 45fr, 65fr, Little weaver and nest.

1967 Engr. *Perf. 13*

184 A33	1fr red, sl grn & dk brn	15	15
185 A33	2fr brn, brt grn & blk	15	15
186 A33	30fr multi	25	15
187 A33	45fr multi	30	15
188 A33	65fr multi ('81)	28	18
189 A33	70fr multi	42	30
	Set value	1.30	82

Issue dates: 45fr, 70fr, Nov. 18. Others, Feb. 8. See No. 237.

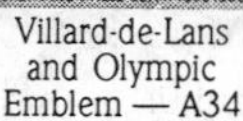
Villard-de-Lans and Olympic Emblem — A34

Lions Emblem and Family — A35

Olympic Emblem and Mountains: 45fr, Autrans and ski jump. 60fr, Saint Nizier du Moucherotte and ski jump. 90fr, Chamrousse and course for downhill and slalom races.

1967, Feb. 24

190 A34 30fr grn, ultra & brn 22 15
191 A34 45fr grn, ultra & brn 35 40
192 A34 60fr grn, ultra & brn 42 22
193 A34 90fr grn, ultra & brn 65 35

Issued to publicize the 10th Winter Olympic Games, Grenoble, 1968.

1967, Mar. 4

194 A35 50fr dk grn, brn red & ultra 40 22

Lions International, 50th anniversary.

ITY Emblem, Views, Globe and Plane — A36

1967, Apr. 28 **Engr.** ***Perf. 13***

195 A36 45fr vio, brt grn & red lil 35 22

International Tourist Year, 1967.

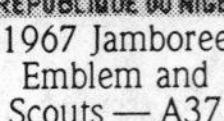

1967 Jamboree Emblem and Scouts — A37

Red Cross Aides Carrying Sick Man — A38

Designs (Jamboree Emblem and): 45fr, Scouts gathering from all directions, horiz. 80fr, Campfire.

1967, May 25 **Engr.** ***Perf. 13***

196 A37 30fr mar, Prus bl & ol 22 15
197 A37 45fr org, vio bl & brn ol 32 20
198 A37 80fr multi 60 35

Issued to publicize the 12th Boy Scout World Jamboree, Farragut State Park, Idaho, Aug. 1-9.

1967, July 13 **Engr.** ***Perf. 13***

Designs: 50fr, Nurse, mother and infant. 60fr, Physician examining woman.

199 A38 45fr blk, grn & car 32 15
200 A38 50fr grn, blk & car 38 18
201 A38 60fr blk, grn & car 42 20

Issued for the Red Cross.

Europafrica Issue, 1967

Map of Europe and Africa — A39

1967, July 20 **Photo.** ***Perf. 12½x12***

202 A39 50fr multi 40 20

Women and UN Emblem — A40

1967, Oct. 21 **Engr.** ***Perf. 13***

203 A40 50fr brn, brt bl & yel 38 22

UN Commission on Status of Women.

Monetary Union Issue

Common Design Type

1967, Nov. 4 **Engr.** ***Perf. 13***

204 CD125 30fr grn & dk gray 22 15

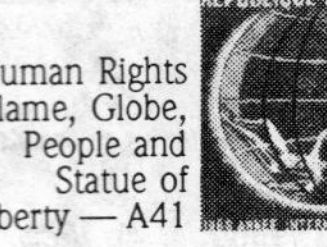

Human Rights Flame, Globe, People and Statue of Liberty — A41

1968, Feb. 19 **Engr.** ***Perf. 13***

205 A41 50fr brn, ind & brt bl 35 20

International Human Rights Year.

Woman Dancing and WHO Emblem — A42

1968, Apr. 8 **Engr.** ***Perf. 13***

206 A42 50fr brt bl, blk & red brn 35 22

20th anniv. of WHO.

Gray Hornbill A43

Birds: 10fr, Woodland kingfisher. 15fr, Senegalese coucal. 20fr, Rose-ringed parakeets. 25fr, Abyssinian roller. 50fr, Cattle egret.

Dated "1968"

1968, Nov. 15 **Photo.** ***Perf. 12½x13***

207 A43 5fr dk grn & multi 15 15
208 A43 10fr grn & multi 15 15
209 A43 15fr bl vio & multi 15 15
210 A43 20fr pink & multi 15 15
211 A43 25fr ol & multi 18 15
212 A43 50fr pur & multi 30 18
Set value 82 55

See Nos. 233-236, 316.

ILO Emblem and "Labor Supporting the World" — A44

1969, Apr. 22 **Engr.** ***Perf. 13***

213 A44 30fr yel grn & dk car 22 15
214 A44 50fr dk car & yel grn 35 22

50th anniv. of the World Labor Organization.

Red Crosses, Mother and Child — A45

Designs: 50fr, People, globe, red crosses, horiz. 70fr, Man with gift parcel and red crosses.

1969, May 5 **Engr.** ***Perf. 13***

215 A45 45fr bl, red & brn ol 30 18
216 A45 50fr dk grn, red & gray 35 18
217 A45 70fr ocher, red & dk brn 42 28

Issued to commemorate the 50th anniversary of the League of Red Cross Societies.

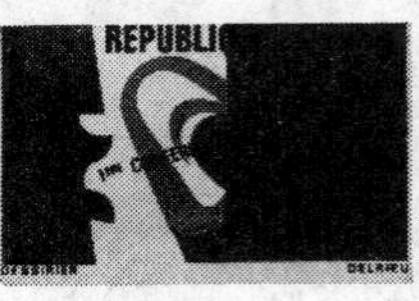

Mouth and Ear — A46

1969, May 20 **Photo.** ***Perf. 12½x12***

218 A46 100fr multi 65 40

First (cultural) Conference of French-speaking Community at Niamey.

National Administration College — A47

1969, July 8 **Photo.** ***Perf. 12½x12***

219 A47 30fr emer & dp org 18 15

Development Bank Issue

Common Design Type

1969, Sept. 10 **Engr.** ***Perf. 13***

220 CD130 30fr pur, grn & ocher 20 15

ASECNA Issue

Common Design Type

1969, Dec. 12 **Engr.** ***Perf. 12***

221 CD132 100fr car rose 65 40

Classical Pavilion, National Museum A48

Pavilions, National Museum: 45fr, Temporary exhibitions. 50fr, Audio-visual. 70fr, Nigerian musical instruments. 100fr, Craftsmanship.

1970, Feb. 23 **Engr.** ***Perf. 13***

222 A48 30fr brt bl, sl grn & brn 20 15
223 A48 45fr emer, Prus bl & brn 28 15
224 A48 50fr sl grn, vio bl & brn 32 15
225 A48 70fr brn, sl grn & lt bl 45 25
226 A48 100fr sl grn, vio bl & brn 65 35
Nos. 222-226 (5) 1.90 1.05

Map of Africa and Vaccination Gun — A49

1970, Mar. 31 **Engr.** ***Perf. 13***

227 A49 50fr ultra, dp yel grn & mag 30 18

Issued to commemorate the 100 millionth smallpox vaccination in West Africa.

Mexican Figurine and Soccer Player — A50

Designs: 70fr, Figurine, globe and soccer ball. 90fr, Figurine and 2 soccer players.

1970, Apr. 25

228 A50 40fr dk brn, red lil & emer 28 18
229 A50 70fr red brn, bl & plum 40 28
230 A50 90fr blk & red 60 40

9th World Soccer Championship for the Jules Rimet Cup, Mexico City, May 29-June 21.

UPU Headquarters Issue

Common Design Type

1970, May 20 **Engr.** ***Perf. 13***

231 CD133 30fr brn, dk gray & dk red 22 15
232 CD133 60fr vio bl, dk car & vio 35 18

Bird Types of 1967-68

Birds: 5fr, Gray hornbill. 10fr, Woodland kingfisher. 15fr, Senegalese coucal. 20fr, Rose-ringed parakeets. 40fr, Red bishop.

Dated "1970"

1970-71 **Photo.** ***Perf. 13***

233 A43 5fr multi ('71) 15 15
234 A43 10fr multi ('71) 15 15
235 A43 15fr multi ('71) 15 15
236 A43 20fr multi ('71) 20 15

Engr.

237 A33 40fr multi 30 22
Set value 75 50

Issue dates: 40fr, Dec. 9; others Jan. 4.

World Map with Niamey in Center — A51

1971, Mar. 3 **Photo.** ***Perf. 12½x12***

238 A51 40fr brn & multi 28 15

First anniversary of founding of the cooperative agency of French-speaking countries.

For overprint see No. 289.

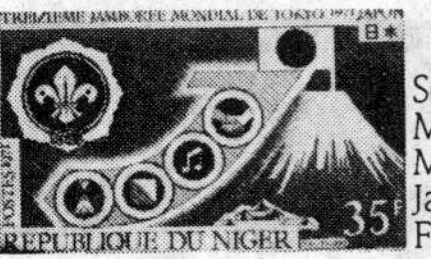

Scout Emblem, Merit Badges, Mt. Fuji, Japanese Flag — A52

Designs: 40fr, Boy Scouts and flags, vert. 45fr, Map of Japan, Boy Scouts and compass rose, vert. 50fr, Tent and "Jamboree."

1971, July 5 **Engr.** ***Perf. 13***

239 A52 35fr rose lil, dp car & org 22 15
240 A52 40fr dk pur, grn & mar 25 15
241 A52 45fr ultra, cop red & grn 28 18
242 A52 50fr multi 30 18

13th Boy Scout World Jamboree, Asagiri Plain, Japan, Aug. 2-10.

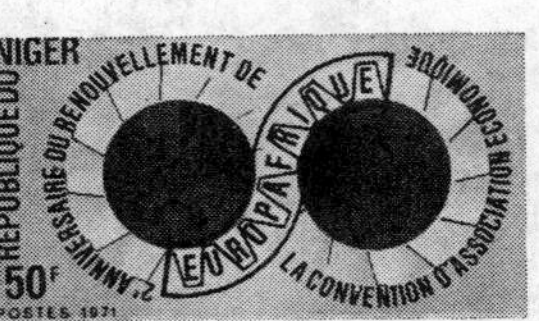

Maps of Europe and Africa — A53

1971, July 29 **Photo.** ***Perf. 13x12***

243 A53 50fr lt bl & multi 35 18

2nd anniversary of the renewal of the agreement on economic association between Europe and Africa.

Broad-tailed Whydah A54

1971, Aug. 17 ***Perf. 12½x12***

244 A54 35fr yel grn & multi 32 20

See No. 443.

Garaya, Haoussa — A55

UNICEF Emblem, Children of 4 Races — A56

Stringed Instruments of Niger: 25fr, Gouroumi, Haoussa. 30fr, Molo, Djerma. 40fr, Godjie, Djerma-Sonrai. 45fr, Inzad, Tuareg. 50fr, Kountigui, Sonrai.

1971-72 Engr. *Perf. 13*

245 A55 25fr red, emer & brn 18 15
246 A55 30fr emer, pur & brn 20 15
247 A55 35fr brn red, emer & ind 18 15
248 A55 40fr emer, org & dk brn 20 15
249 A55 45fr Prus bl, grn & bis 25 18
250 A55 50fr blk, red & brn 32 20
Nos. 245-250 (6) 1.33
Set value 78

Issue dates: 35fr, 40fr, 45fr, Oct. 13, 1971; others, June 16, 1972.

1971, Dec. 11 Photo. *Perf. 11*

251 A56 50fr multi 32 25

25th anniversary of UNICEF.

Star with Globe, Book, UNESCO Emblem A57

Design: 40fr, Boy reading, UNESCO emblem, sailing ship, plane, mosque.

1972, Mar. 27 Engr. *Perf. 13*

252 A57 35fr mag & emer 22 15
253 A57 40fr dk car & Prus bl 25 15
Set value 24

International Book Year 1972.

Cattle Egret — A58

1972, July 31 Photo. *Perf. 12½x12*

254 A58 50fr tan & multi 38 22

See No. 425.

Cattle at Salt Pond of In-Gall — A59

1972, Aug. 25 *Perf. 13*

255 A59 35fr shown 22 15
256 A59 40fr Cattle wading in pond 25 15
Set value 24

Salt cure for cattle.
For surcharge see No. 282.

Lottery Drum — A60

1972, Sept. 18

257 A60 35fr multi 22 15

6th anniversary of the national lottery.

West African Monetary Union Issue
Common Design Type

Design: 40fr, African couple, city, village and commemorative coin.

1972, Nov. 2 Engr. *Perf. 13*

258 CD136 40fr brn, lil & gray 25 15

Dromedary Race — A61

Design: 40fr, Horse race.

1972, Dec. 15 Engr. *Perf. 13*

259 A61 35fr brt bl, dk red & brn 22 15
260 A61 40fr sl grn, mar & brn 28 15

Pole Vault, Map of Africa — A62

Knight, Pawn, Chessboard — A63

Designs (Map of Africa and): 40fr, Basketball. 45fr, Boxing. 75fr, Soccer.

1973, Jan. 15 Engr. *Perf. 13*

261 A62 35fr cl & multi 20 15
262 A62 40fr grn & multi 22 15
263 A62 45fr red & multi 25 18
264 A62 75fr dk bl & multi 38 25

2nd African Games, Legos, Nigeria, Jan. 7-18.

1973, Feb. 16 Engr. *Perf. 13*

265 A63 100fr dl red, sl grn & bl 55 35

World Chess Championship, Reykjavik, Iceland, July-Sept. 1972.

Abutilon Pannosum A64

Interpol Emblem A65

Rare African Flowers: 45fr, Crotalaria barkae. 60fr, Dichrostachys cinerea. 80fr, Caralluma decaisneana.

1973, Feb. 26 Photo. *Perf. 12x12½*

266 A64 30fr dk vio & multi 18 15
267 A64 45fr red & multi 25 15
268 A64 60fr ultra & multi 32 22
269 A64 80fr ocher & multi 40 25

1973, Mar. 13 Typo. *Perf. 13x12½*

270 A65 50fr brt grn & multi 25 15

50th anniversary of International Criminal Police Organization (INTERPOL).

Dr. Hansen, Microscope and Petri Dish — A66

Nurse Treating Infant, UN and Red Cross Emblems — A67

1973, Mar. 29 Engr. *Perf. 13*

271 A66 50fr vio bl, sl grn & dk brn 28 15

Centenary of the discovery by Dr. Armauer G. Hansen of the Hansen bacillus, the cause of leprosy.

1973, Apr. 3 Engr. *Perf. 13*

272 A67 50fr red, bl & brn 25 15

25th anniversary of WHO.

Crocodile A68

Animals from W National Park: 35fr, Elephant. 40fr, Hippopotamus. 80fr, Wart hog.

1973, June 5 Typo. *Perf. 12½x13*

273 A68 25fr gray & blk 18 15
274 A68 35fr blk, gold & gray 22 15
275 A68 40fr red, lt bl & blk 25 15
276 A68 80fr multi 40 22
Set value 56

Eclipse over Mountains A69

1973, June 21 Engr. *Perf. 13*

277 A69 40fr dk vio bl 22 18

Solar eclipse, June 30, 1973.

Palominos — A70

Horses: 75fr, French trotters. 80fr, English thoroughbreds. 100fr, Arabian thoroughbreds.

1973, Aug. 1 Photo. *Perf. 13x12½*

278 A70 50fr ultra & multi 28 15
279 A70 75fr gray & multi 38 20
280 A70 80fr emer & multi 45 25
281 A70 100fr ocher & multi 55 30

No. 255 Surcharged with New Value, 2 Bars, and Overprinted in Ultramarine: "SECHERESSE/SOLIDARITE AFRICAINE"

1973, Aug. 16 *Perf. 13*

282 A59 100fr on 35fr multi 50 35

African solidarity in drought emergency.

Diesel Engine and Rudolf Diesel — A71

Designs: Various Diesel locomotives.

1973, Sept. 7 *Perf. 13x12½*

283 A71 25fr gray, choc & Prus bl 15 15
284 A71 50fr sl bl, gray & dk grn 25 15
285 A71 75fr red lil, sl bl & gray 38 28
286 A71 125fr brt grn, vio bl & car 60 38

Rudolf Diesel (1858-1913), inventor of an internal combustion engine, later called Diesel engine.

African Postal Union Issue
Common Design Type

1973, Sept. 12 Engr. *Perf. 13*

287 CD137 100fr ol, dk car & sl grn 55 35

TV Set, Map of Niger, Children A72

1973, Oct. 1 Engr. *Perf. 13*

288 A72 50fr car, ultra & brn 25 18

Educational television.

Type of 1971 Overprinted

3e CONFERENCE DE LA FRANCOPHONIE
LIEGE
OCTOBRE 1973

1973, Oct. 12 Photo. *Perf. 13*

289 A51 40fr red & multi 25 15

3rd Conference of French-speaking countries, Liège, Sept. 15-Oct. 14.

Apollo of Belvedère — A73

Classic Sculpture: No. 291, Venus of Milo. No. 292, Hercules. No. 293, Atlas.

1973, Oct. 15 Engr.

290 A73 50fr brn & sl grn 32 20
291 A73 50fr rose car & pur 32 20
292 A73 50fr red brn & dk brn 32 20
293 A73 50fr red brn & blk 32 20

Beehive, Bees and Globes — A74

1973, Oct. 31 Engr. *Perf. 13*
294 A74 40fr dl red, ocher & dl bl 22 15

World Savings Day.

Tcherka Songhai Blanket — A75

Design: 35fr, Kounta Songhai blanket (vert.).

Perf. 12½x13, 13x12½
1973, Dec. 17 Photo.
295 A75 35fr brn & multi 25 15
296 A75 40fr brn & multi 25 18

Textiles of Niger.

WPY Emblem, Infant and Globe — A76

1974, Mar. 4 Engr. *Perf. 13*
297 A76 50fr multi 25 15

World Population Year 1974.

Locomotives, 1938 and 1948 — A77

1974, May 24 Engr. *Perf. 13*
298 A77 50fr shown 25 18
299 A77 75fr Locomotive, 1893 35 22
300 A77 100fr Locomotives, 1866 and 1939 48 35
301 A77 150fr *Locomotives, 1829* 70 55

Map and Flags of Members A78

1974, May 29 Photo. *Perf. 13x12½*
302 A78 40fr bl & multi 20 15

15th anniversary of the Council of Accord.

Marconi Sending Radio Signals to Australia — A79

1974, July 1 Engr. *Perf. 13*
303 A79 50fr pur, bl & dk brn 25 18

Centenary of the birth of Guglielmo Marconi (1874-1937), Italian inventor and physicist.

Hand Holding Sapling — A80

Camel Saddle — A81

1974, Aug. 2 Engr. *Perf. 13*
304 A80 35fr multi 18 15

National Tree Week.

1974, Aug. 20 Engr. *Perf. 13*

Design: 50fr, 3 sculptured horses, horiz.

305 A81 40fr ol brn, bl & red 20 15
306 A81 50fr ol brn, bl & red 25 15
Set value 22

Chopin and Polish Eagle — A82

Design: No. 308, Ludwig van Beethoven and allegory of Ninth Symphony.

1974
307 A82 100fr multi 48 28
308 A82 100fr multi 48 28

125th anniversary of the death of Frederic Chopin (1810-1849), composer and 150th anniversary of Beethoven's Ninth Symphony, composed 1823.
Issue dates: #307, Sept. 4; #308, Sept. 19.

Don-Don Drum — A83

1974, Nov. 12 Engr. *Perf. 13*
309 A83 60fr multi 30 18

Tenere Tree, Compass Rose and Caravan — A84

1974, Nov. 24 Engr. *Perf. 13*
310 A84 50fr multi 30 20

Tenere tree, a landmark in Sahara Desert, first death anniversary.

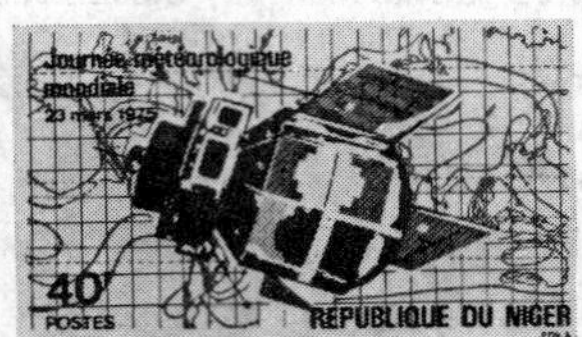

Satellite over World Weather Map — A85

1975, Mar. 23 Litho. *Perf. 13*
311 A85 40fr bl, blk & red 20 15

World Meteorological Day, Mar. 23, 1975.

"City of Truro," English, 1903 — A86

Locomotives and Flags: 75fr, "5.003," Germany, 1937. 100fr, "The General," United States, 1863. 125fr, "Electric BB 15.000," France, 1971.

1975, Apr. 24 Typo. *Perf. 13*
312 A86 50fr org & multi 25 18
313 A86 75fr yel grn & multi 35 22
314 A86 100fr lt bl & multi 48 32
315 A86 125fr multi 65 40

Bird Type of 1968 Dated "1975"

1975, Apr. Photo. *Perf. 13*
316 A43 25fr ol & multi 15 15

Zabira Leather Bag — A87

Handicrafts: 40fr, Damier tapestry. 45fr, Vase. 60fr, Gourd flask.

1975, May 28 Litho. *Perf. 12½*
317 A87 35fr dp bl & multi 18 15
318 A87 40fr dp grn & multi 20 15
319 A87 45fr brn & multi 22 30
320 A87 60fr dp org & multi 28 18

Mother and Child, IWY Emblem — A88

1975, June 9 Engr. *Perf. 13*
321 A88 50fr claret, brn & bl 25 18

International Women's Year 1975.

Dr. Schweitzer and Lambarene Hospital — A89

1975, June 23 Engr. *Perf. 13*
322 A89 100fr brn, grn & blk 42 28

Dr. Albert Schweitzer (1875-1965), medical missionary.

Peugeot, 1892 — A90

Early Autos: 75fr, Daimler, 1895. 100fr, Fiat, 1899. 125fr, Cadillac, 1903.

1975, July 16 Engr. *Perf. 13*
323 A90 50fr rose & vio bl 22 15
324 A90 75fr bl & vio brn 21 20
325 A90 100fr brt grn & mag 40 28
326 A90 125fr brick red & brt grn 55 30

Sun, Tree and Earth — A91

Boxing — A92

1975, Aug. 2 Engr. *Perf. 13*
327 A91 40fr multi 20 15

National Tree Week.

1975, Aug. 25 Engr. *Perf. 13*

Designs: 35fr, Boxing, horiz. 45fr, Wrestling, horiz. 50fr, Wrestling.

328 A92 35fr blk, org & brn 18 15
329 A92 40fr bl grn, brn & blk 20 15
330 A92 45fr blk, brt bl & brn 22 15
331 A92 50fr red, brn & blk 25 18

Lion's Head Tetradrachma, Leontini, 460 B.C. — A93

Greek Coins: 75fr, Owl tetradrachma, Athens, 500 B.C. 100fr, Crab diadrachma, Himera, 480 B.C. 125fr, Minotaur tetradrachma, Gela, 460 B.C.

1975, Sept. 12 Engr. *Perf. 13*

332 A93 50fr red, dl bl & blk 22 15
333 A93 75fr lil, brt bl & blk 32 22
334 A93 100fr bl, org & blk 42 28
335 A93 125fr grn, pur & blk 55 32

Starving Family — A94

Designs: 45fr, Animal skeletons. 60fr, Truck bringing food.

1975, Oct. 21 Engr. *Perf. 13x12½*

336 A94 40fr multi 20 18
337 A94 45fr ultra & brn 22 15
338 A94 60fr grn, org & dk bl 28 15

Fight against drought.

Niger River Crossing — A95

Designs: 45fr, Entrance to Boubon camp. 50fr, Camp building.

1975, Nov. 10 Litho. *Perf. 12½*

339 A95 40fr multi 18 15
340 A95 45fr multi 20 15
341 A95 50fr multi 22 15

Tourist publicity.

Teacher and Pupils — A96

Designs: Each stamp has different inscription in center.

1976, Jan. 12 Photo. *Perf. 13*

342 A96 25fr ol & multi 15 15
343 A96 30fr vio bl & multi 15 15
344 A96 40fr multi 18 15
345 A96 50fr multi 22 15
346 A96 60fr multi 25 18
Nos. 342-346 (5) 95
Set value 65

Literacy campaign 1976.
For overprints see Nos. 371-375.

12th Winter Olympic Games, Innsbruck — A97

1976, Feb. 20 Litho. *Perf. 14x13½*

347 A97 40fr Ice hockey 20 15
348 A97 50fr Luge 28 15
349 A97 150fr Ski jump 75 35
Nos. 347-349,C266-C267 (5) 3.73 1.70

Satellite, Telephone, ITU Emblem — A98

1976, Mar. 10 Litho. *Perf. 13*

350 A98 100fr org, bl & vio bl 42 28

Centenary of first telephone call by Alexander Graham Bell, Mar. 10, 1876.

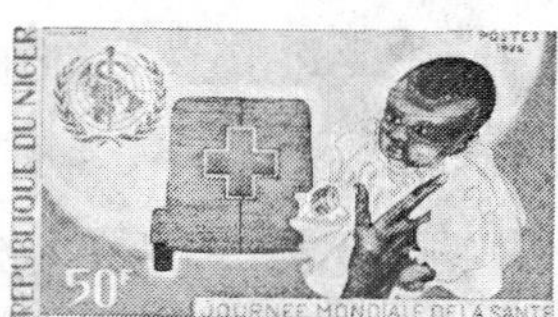

WHO Emblem, Red Cross Truck, Infant — A99

1976, Apr. 7 Engr. *Perf. 13*

351 A99 50fr multi 22 15

World Health Day 1976.

Statue of Liberty and Washington Crossing the Delaware — A100

Design: 50fr, Statue of Liberty and call to arms.

1976, Apr. 8 Litho. *Perf. 14x13½*

352 A100 40fr multi 20 15
353 A100 50fr multi 25 15
Nos. 352-353,C269-C271 (5) 3.55 1.80

American Bicentennial.

The Army Helping in Development — A101

Design: 50fr, Food distribution, vert.

Perf. 12½x13, 13x12½

1976, Apr. 15 Litho.

354 A101 50fr multi 22 15
355 A101 100fr multi 42 28

National Armed Forces, 2nd anniversary of take-over.

Europafrica Issue 1976

Maps, Concorde, Ship and Grain — A102

1976, June 9 Litho. *Perf. 13*

356 A102 100fr multi 42 28

Road Building A103

Design: 30fr, Rice cultivation.

1976, June 26 *Perf. 12½*

357 A103 25fr multi 15 15
358 A103 30fr multi 15 15
Set value 18

Community labor.

Motobecane 125, France — A104

Motorcycles: 75fr, Norton Challenge, England. 100fr, BMW 90 S, Germany. 125fr, Kawasaki 1000, Japan.

1976, July 16 Engr. *Perf. 13*

359 A104 50fr vio bl & multi 22 15
360 A104 75fr dp grn & multi 21 25
361 A104 100fr dk brn & multi 42 35
362 A104 125fr slate & multi 55 35

Boxing A105

Designs: 50fr, Basketball. 60fr, Soccer. 80fr, Cycling, horiz. 100fr, Judo, horiz.

1976, July 17 Litho. *Perf. 14*

363 A105 40fr multi 22 15
364 A105 50fr multi 28 15
365 A105 60fr multi 35 15
366 A105 80fr multi 40 18
367 A105 100fr multi 50 25
Nos. 363-367 (5) 1.75 88

21st Summer Olympic games, Montreal. See No. C279.

Map of Niger, Planting Seedlings A106

Designs: 50fr, Woman watering seedling, vert. 60fr, Women planting seedlings, vert.

1976, Aug. 1 Litho. *Perf. 12½x13*

368 A106 40fr org & multi 18 15
369 A106 50fr yel & multi 22 18
370 A106 60fr grn & multi 28 18

Reclamation of Sahel Region.

Nos. 342-346 Overprinted: "JOURNEE / INTERNATIONALE / DE L'ALPHABETISATION"

1976, Sept. 8 Photo. *Perf. 13*

371 A96 25fr ol & multi 15 15
372 A96 30fr vio bl & multi 15 15
373 A96 40fr multi 20 15
374 A96 50fr multi 22 15
375 A96 60fr multi 28 15
Nos. 371-375 (5) 1.00
Set value 55

Literacy campaign.

Hairdresser — A107

Designs: 40fr, Woman weaving straw, vert. 50fr, Women potters, vert.

1976, Oct. 6 *Perf. 13*

376 A107 40fr buff & multi 18 15
377 A107 45fr bl & multi 20 15
378 A107 50fr red & multi 22 15

Niger Women's Association.

Rock Carvings A108

Archaeology: 50fr, Neolithic sculptures. 60fr, Dinosaur skeleton.

1976, Nov. 15 Photo. *Perf. 13x12½*

379 A108 40fr blk, sl & yel 18 15
380 A108 50fr blk, red & bis 22 15
381 A108 60fr bis, blk & brn 28 15

Benin Head — A109

Weaver, Dancers and Musicians — A110

1977, Jan. 15 Engr. *Perf. 13*

382 A109 40fr dk brn 20 15
383 A110 50fr gray bl 22 15

2nd World Black and African Festival, Lagos, Nigeria, Jan. 15-Feb. 12.

First Aid, Student, Blackboard and Plow — A111

Midwife — A112

Designs: Inscriptions on blackboard differ on each denomination.

1977, Jan. 23 Photo. *Perf. 12½x13*

384 A111 40fr multi 18 15
385 A111 50fr multi 22 15
386 A111 60fr multi 28 15
Set value 38

Literacy campaign.

1977, Feb. 23 Litho. *Perf. 13*

Design: 50fr, Midwife examining newborn.

387 A112 40fr multi 18 15
388 A112 50fr multi 22 15
Set value 24

Village health service.

Titan Rocket Launch A113

Design: 80fr, Viking orbiter near Mars, horiz.

1977, Mar. 15 Litho. *Perf. 14*

389 A113 50fr multi 28 15
390 A113 80fr multi 40 20
Nos. 389-390,C283-C285 (5) 2.93 1.37

Viking Mars project.
For overprints see #497-498, C295-C297.

Marabous A114

Design: 90fr, Harnessed antelopes.

1977, Mar. 18 Engr. *Perf. 13*

391 A114 80fr multi 38 22
392 A114 90fr multi 40 25

Nature protection.

Weather Map, Satellite, WMO Emblem A115

1977, Mar. 23

393 A115 100fr multi 40 28

World Meteorological Day.

Group Gymnastics — A116

Designs: 50fr, High jump. 80fr, Folk singers.

1977, Apr. 7 Litho. *Perf. 13x12½*

394 A116 40fr dl yel & multi 20 15
395 A116 50fr bl & multi 22 15
396 A116 80fr org & multi 35 18

2nd Tahoua Youth Festival, Apr. 7-14.

Red Cross, WHO Emblems and Children — A117

1977, Apr. 25 Engr. *Perf. 13*

397 A117 80fr lil, org & red 35 22

World Health Day: "Immunization means protection of your children."

Eye with WHO Emblem, and Sword Killing Fly — A118

1977, May 7

398 A118 100fr multi 42 28

Fight against onchocerciasis, a roundworm infection, transmitted by flies, causing blindness.

Guirka Tahoua Dance A119

Dances: 50fr, Mailfilafili Gaya. 80fr, Naguihinayan Loga.

1977, June 7 Photo. *Perf. 13x12½*

399 A119 40fr multi 18 15
400 A119 50fr multi 22 15
401 A119 80fr multi 35 20

Popular arts and traditions.

Cavalry — A120

Designs: Traditional chief's cavalry, different groups.

1977, July 7 Litho. *Perf. 13x12½*

402 A120 40fr multi 18 15
403 A120 50fr multi 22 15
404 A120 60fr multi 28 15

Planting and Cultivating — A121

1977, Aug. 10

405 A121 40fr multi 18 15

Reclamation of Sahel Region.

Albert John Luthuli Peace — A122

Designs: 80fr, Maurice Maeterlinck, literature. 100fr, Allan L. Hodgkin, medicine. 150fr, Albert Camus, literature. 200fr, Paul Ehrlich, medicine.

1977, Aug. 20 Litho. *Perf. 14*

406 A122 50fr multi 28 15
407 A122 80fr multi 28 18
408 A122 100fr multi 50 20
409 A122 150fr multi 75 28
410 A122 200fr multi 1.00 40
Nos. 406-410 (5) 2.81 1.21

Nobel prize winners. See No. C287.

Mao Tse-tung — A123

1977, Sept. 9 Engr. *Perf. 13*

411 A123 100fr blk & red 42 28

Argentina '78 Emblem, Soccer Players and Coach, Vittorio Pozzo, Italy — A124

Designs (Argentina '78 emblem, soccer players and coach): 50fr, Vincente Feola, Spain. 80fr, Aymore Moreira, Portugal. 100fr, Sir Alf Ramsey, England. 200fr, Helmut Schoen, Germany. 500fr, Sepp Herberger, Germany.

1977, Oct. 12 Litho. *Perf. 13½*

412 A124 40fr multi 20 15
413 A124 50fr multi 28 15
414 A124 80fr multi 40 20
415 A124 100fr multi 55 25
416 A124 200fr multi 1.10 40
Nos. 412-416 (5) 2.53 1.15

Souvenir Sheet

417 A124 500fr multi 2.50 1.10

World Cup Soccer championship, Argentina '78.
For overprints see Nos. 453-458.

Horse's Head, Parthenon and UNESCO Emblem — A125

1977, Nov. 12 Engr. *Perf. 13*

418 A125 100fr multi 42 28

United Nations, Educational, Scientific and Cultural Organization.

Woman Carrying Water Pots — A126

Design: 50fr, Women pounding corn.

1977, Nov. 23 Photo. *Perf. 12½x13*

419 A126 40fr multi 18 15
420 A126 50fr red & multi 22 15
Set value 22

Niger Women's Association.

Crocodile's Skull, 100 Million Years Old — A127

Design: 80fr, Neolithic flint tools.

1977, Dec. 14 *Perf. 13*

421 A127 50fr multi 22 15
422 A127 80fr multi 35 22

Raoul Follereau and Lepers A128

Design: 40fr, Raoul Follereau and woman leper, vert.

1978, Jan. 28 Engr. *Perf. 13*

423 A128 40fr multi		18	15
424 A128 50fr multi		22	15

25th anniversary of Leprosy Day. Follereau (1903-1977) was "Apostle to the Lepers" and educator of the blind.

Bird Type of 1972 Redrawn

1978, Feb. Photo. *Perf. 13*

425 A58 50fr tan & multi	22	15

No. 425 is dated "1978" and has only designer's name in imprint. No. 254 has printer's name also.

Assumption, by Rubens A129

Rubens Paintings: 70fr, Rubens and Friends, horiz. 100fr, History of Marie de Medici. 150fr, Alathea Talbot and Family. 200fr, Marquise de Spinola. 500fr, Virgin and St. Ildefonso.

1978, Feb. 25 Litho. *Perf. 14*

426 A129 50fr multi	28	15
427 A129 70fr multi	32	18
428 A129 100fr multi	50	22
429 A129 150fr multi	75	35
430 A129 200fr multi	1.10	42
Nos. 426-430 (5)	2.95	1.32

Souvenir Sheet

Perf. 13½

431 A129 500fr gold & multi	2.50	1.10

Peter Paul Rubens (1577-1640), 400th birth anniversary.

Shot Put — A130

1978, Mar. 22 Photo. *Perf. 13*

432 A130 40fr shown	18	15
433 A130 50fr Volleyball	22	15
434 A130 60fr Long jump	28	15
435 A130 100fr Javelin	42	28

Natl. University Games' Championships.

First Aid and Red Crosses A131

1978, May 13 Litho.

436 A131 40fr red & multi	18	15

Niger Red Cross.

Goudel Earth Station A132

1978, May 23

437 A132 100fr multi	45	28

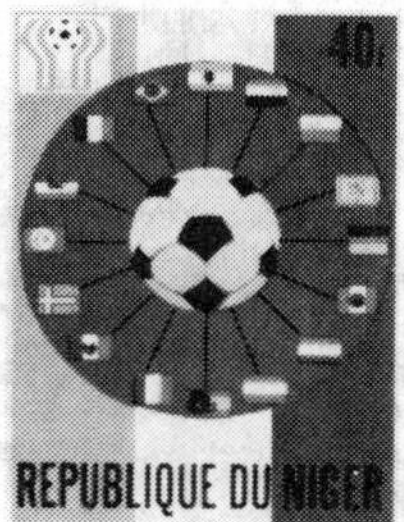
Soccer Ball, Flags of Participants A133

Designs (Argentina '78 Emblem and): 50fr, Ball in net. 100fr, Globe with South America, Soccer field. 200fr, Two players, horiz. 300fr, Player and globe.

1978, June 18 Litho. *Perf. 13½*

438 A133 40fr multi	20	15
439 A133 50fr multi	30	18
440 A133 100fr multi	50	35
441 A133 200fr multi	1.00	60

Souvenir Sheet

442 A133 300fr multi	1.60	90

11th World Cup Soccer Championship, Argentina, June 1-25.

Bird Type of 1971 Redrawn

1978, June Photo. *Perf. 13*

443 A54 35fr bl & multi	18	15

No. 443 has no year date, nor Delrieu imprint.

Post Office, Niamey — A134

Design: 60fr, Post Office, different view.

1978, Aug. 12 Litho.

444 A134 40fr multi	18	15
445 A134 60fr multi	28	15

The indexes in each volume of the Scott Catalogue contain many listings which help to identify stamps.

Goudel Water Works A135

1978, Sept. 25 Photo. *Perf. 13*

446 A135 100fr multi	42	28

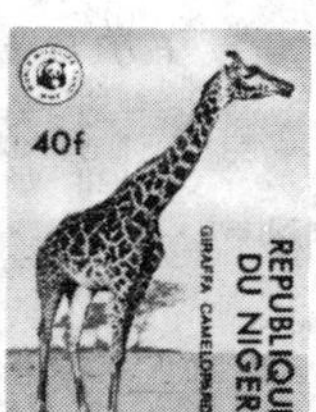
Giraffe — A136

Animals and Wildlife Fund Emblem: 50fr, Ostrich. 70fr, Cheetah. 150fr, Oryx, horiz. 200fr, Addax, horiz. 300fr, Hartebeest, horiz.

1978, Nov. 20 Litho. *Perf. 15*

447 A136 40fr multi	20	15
448 A136 50fr multi	28	15
449 A136 70fr multi	35	20
450 A136 150fr multi	75	40
451 A136 200fr multi	1.00	55
452 A136 300fr multi	1.50	80
Nos. 447-452 (6)	4.08	2.25

Endangered species.

Nos. 412-417 Overprinted in Silver
a. "EQUIPE QUATRIEME: ITALIE"
b. "EQUIPE TROISIEME: BRESIL"
c. "EQUIPE / SECONDE: / PAYS BAS"
d. "EQUIPE VAINQUEUR: ARGENTINE"
e. "ARGENTINE-PAYS BAS 3-1"

1978, Dec. 1 *Perf. 13½*

453 A124(a) 40fr multi	18	15
454 A124(b) 50fr multi	22	15
455 A124(c) 80fr multi	35	22
456 A124(d) 100fr multi	42	28
457 A124(e) 200fr multi	85	55
Nos. 453-457 (5)	2.02	1.35

Souvenir Sheet

458 A124(e) 500fr multi	2.25	90

Winners, World Soccer Cup Championship, Argentina, June 1-25.

Tinguizi — A137

Musicians: No. 460, Dan Gourmou. No. 461, Chetima Ganga, horiz.

1978, Dec. 11 Litho. *Perf. 13*

459 A137 100fr multi	42	28
460 A137 100fr multi	42	28
461 A137 100fr multi	42	28

Virgin Mary, by Dürer — A138

Paintings: 50fr, The Homecoming, by Honoré Daumier (1808-79). 150fr, 200fr, 500fr, Virgin and Child, by Albrecht Dürer (1471-1528) (different).

1979, Jan. 31 Litho. *Perf. 13½*

462 A138 50fr multi	30	15
463 A138 100fr multi	50	30
464 A138 150fr multi	75	40
465 A138 200fr multi	1.00	55

Souvenir Sheet

466 A138 500fr multi	2.50	1.10

Solar Panels and Tank — A139

Design: 40fr, Tank and panels on roof, vert.

Perf. 12½x12, 12x12½

1979, Feb. 28

467 A139 40fr multi	18	15
468 A139 50fr multi	22	15

Hot water from solar heat.

Children with Building Blocks — A140

Children and IYC Emblem: 100fr, Reading books. 150fr, With model plane.

1979, Apr. 10 Litho. *Perf. 13½*

469 A140 40fr multi	22	15
470 A140 100fr multi	50	28
471 A140 150fr multi	75	40

International Year of the Child.

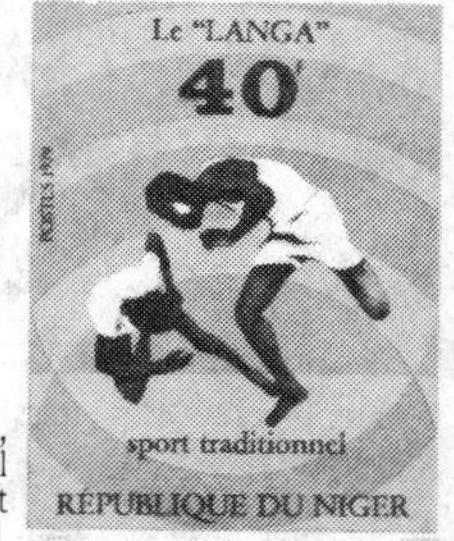
The Langa, Traditional Sport A141

Design: 50fr, The langa, diff.

1979, Apr. 10 Litho. *Perf. 12½x12*

472 A141 40fr multi	18	15
473 A141 50fr multi	22	15

Rowland Hill, Mail Truck and France No. 8 — A142

Designs (Hill and): 100fr, Canoes and Austria #P4. 150fr, Air Niger plane and US #122. 200fr, Streamlined mail train and Canada type A6. 400fr, Electric train and Niger #51.

1979, June 6 Litho. *Perf. 14*

474 A142	40fr multi	18	15
475 A142	100fr multi	42	28
476 A142	150fr multi	65	40
477 A142	200fr multi	85	55

Souvenir Sheet

478 A142	400fr multi	1.90	

Sir Rowland Hill (1795-1879), originator of penny postage.

Zabira Handbag and Niger No. 135 — A143

Design: 150fr, Heads with communications waves, world map, UPU emblem and satellite.

1979, June 8 Litho. *Perf. 12x12½*

479 A143	50fr multi	22	15

Engr. *Perf. 13*

480 A143	150fr brt red & ultra	65	80

Philexafrique II, Libreville, Gabon, June 8-17. Nos. 479, 480 each printed in sheets of 10 and 5 labels showing exhibition emblem.

Djermakoye Palace — A144

1979, Sept. 26 Litho. *Perf. 13x12½*

481 A144	100fr multi	42	28

Bororo Festive Headdress — A145

Design: 60fr, Bororo women's traditional costumes, vert.

Perf. 13x12½, 12½x13

1979, Sept. 26

482 A145	45fr multi	20	15
483 A145	60fr multi	25	18

Annual Bororo Festival.

Olympic Emblem, Flame and Boxers — A146

Designs: 100fr, 150fr, 250fr, 500fr, Olympic emblem, flame and boxers, diff.

1979, Oct. 6 *Perf. 13½*

484 A146	45fr multi	20	15
485 A146	100fr multi	42	28
486 A146	150fr multi	65	40
487 A146	250fr multi	1.10	65

Souvenir Sheet

488 A146	500fr multi	2.50	1.50

Pre-Olympic Year.

John Alcock, Arthur Whitten Brown, Vickers-Vimy Biplane — A147

1979, Sept. 3 *Perf. 13½*

489 A147	100fr multi	45	30

First Transatlantic flight, 60th anniversary.

Road and Traffic Safety — A148

1979, Nov. 20 Litho. *Perf. 12½*

490 A148	45fr multi	20	15

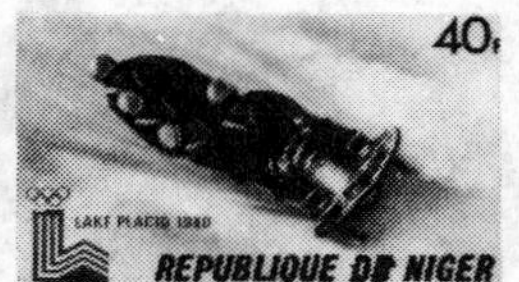

Four-Man Bobsledding, Lake Placid '80 Emblem — A149

Lake Placid '80 Emblem and: 60fr, Downhill skiing. 100fr, Speed skating. 150fr, Two-man bobsledding. 200fr, Figure skating. 300fr, Cross-country skiing.

1979, Dec. 10 *Perf. 14½*

491 A149	40fr multi	18	15
492 A149	60fr multi	25	18
493 A149	100fr multi	42	30
494 A149	150fr multi	65	40
495 A149	200fr multi	90	55
	Nos. 491-495 (5)	2.40	1.58

Souvenir Sheet

496 A149	300fr multi	1.40	90

13th Winter Olympic Games, Lake Placid, NY, Feb. 12-24, 1980.
For overprints see Nos. 501-506.

Nos. 389, 390 Overprinted in Silver or Black "alunissage/apollo XI/juillet 1969" and Emblem

1979, Dec. 20 Litho. *Perf. 14*

497 A113	50fr multi (S)	22	15
498 A113	80fr multi	35	22

Apollo 11 moon landing, 10th anniversary. See Nos. C295-C297.

Court of Sultan of Zinder — A150

1980, Mar. 25 Litho. *Perf. 13x12½*

499 A150	45fr shown	20	15
500 A150	60fr Sultan's court, diff.	25	18

Nos. 491-496 Overprinted
a. VAINQUEUR/R.D.A.
b. VAINQUEUR/STENMARK/SUEDE
c. VAINQUEUR/HEIDEN/Etats-Unis
d. VAINQUEURS/SCHAERER-BENZ/ Suisse
e. VAINQUEUR/COUSINS/ Grande Bretagne
f. VAINQUEUR/ZIMIATOV/U.R.S.S.

1980, Mar. 31 Litho. *Perf. 14½*

501 A149 (a)	40fr multi	18	15
502 A149 (b)	60fr multi	25	18
503 A149 (c)	100fr multi	45	28
504 A149 (d)	150fr multi	65	40
505 A149 (e)	200fr multi	90	55
	Nos. 501-505 (5)	2.43	1.56

Souvenir Sheet

506 A149 (f)	300fr multi	1.25	80

Javelin, Olympic Rings — A151

Man Smoking Cigarette, Runner — A152

1980, Apr. 17

507 A151	60fr shown	25	18
508 A151	90fr Walking	38	25
509 A151	100fr High jump, horiz.	42	28
510 A151	300fr Marathon runners, horiz.	1.25	80

Souvenir Sheet

511 A151	500fr High jump, diff.	2.25	1.40

22nd Summer Olympic Games, Moscow, July 19-Aug. 3.
For overprints see Nos. 527-531.

1980, Apr. 7 *Perf. 13*

512 A152	100fr multi	42	28

World Health Day; fight against cigarette smoking.

Health Year — A153

1980, May 15 Photo. *Perf. 13x12½*

513 A153	150fr multi	65	40

Shimbashi-Yokohama Locomotive — A154

1980, June Litho. *Perf. 12½*

514 A154	45fr shown	20	15
515 A154	60fr American type	25	18
516 A154	90fr German Reichsbahn series 61	40	25
517 A154	100fr Prussian Staatsbahn P2	42	28
518 A154	130fr L'Aigle	55	35
	Nos. 514-518 (5)	1.82	1.21

Souvenir Sheet

519 A154	425fr Stephenson's Rocket	1.80	1.10

For overprint see No. 674.

Steve Biko, 4th Anniversary of Death — A155

1980, Sept. 12 Litho. *Perf. 13*

520 A155	150fr org & blk	65	40

Soccer Players — A156

Designs: Various soccer scenes.

1980, Oct. 15 *Perf. 12½*

521 A156	45fr multi	20	15
522 A156	60fr multi	25	18
523 A156	90fr multi	38	25
524 A156	100fr multi	42	28
525 A156	130fr multi	55	35
	Nos. 521-525 (5)	1.80	1.21

Souvenir Sheet

526 A156	425fr multi	1.90	1.10

World Soccer Cup 1982.

Nos. 507-511 Overprinted in Gold with Winner's Name and Country

1980, Sept. 27 Litho. *Perf. 14½*

527 A151	60fr multi	25	18
528 A151	90fr multi	38	25
529 A151	100fr multi	45	30
530 A151	300fr multi	1.25	80

Souvenir Sheet

531 A151	500fr multi	2.25	1.40

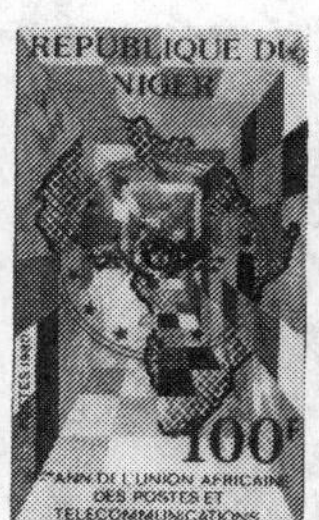

African Postal Union, 5th Anniversary A157

Terra Cotta Kareygorou Head A158

1980, Dec. 24 Photo. *Perf. 13½*

532	A157	100fr multi	45	30

1981, Jan. 23 Litho. *Perf. 13*

Designs: Terra Cotta Kareygorou Statues, 5th-12th cent. 45fr, 150fr, horiz.

533	A158	45fr multi	20	15
534	A158	60fr multi	25	18
535	A158	90fr multi	40	25
536	A158	150fr multi	65	40

Ostrich — A159

1981, Mar. 17 Litho. *Perf. 12½*

537	A159	10fr shown	15	15
538	A159	20fr Oryx	15	15
539	A159	25fr Gazelle	15	15
540	A159	30fr Great bustard	15	15
541	A159	60fr Giraffe	25	18
542	A159	150fr Addax	65	40
		Nos. 537-542 (6)	1.50	
		Set value		85

7th Anniv. of the F.A.N. — A160

1981, Apr. 14 Litho. *Perf. 13*

543	A160	100fr multi	45	30

One-armed Archer — A161

1981, Apr. 24 Engr.

544	A161	50fr shown	22	15
545	A161	100fr Draftsman	42	28

Intl. Year of the Disabled.

Scene from Mahalba Ballet, 1980 Youth Festival, Dosso — A162

1981, May 17 Litho.

546	A162	100fr shown	42	28
547	A162	100fr Ballet, diff.	42	28

Prince Charles and Lady Diana, Coach A163

Designs: Couple and coaches.

1981, July 15 Litho. *Perf. 14½*

548	A163	150fr multi	65	40
549	A163	200fr multi	85	55
550	A163	300fr multi	1.25	80

Souvenir Sheet

551	A163	400fr multi	1.75	1.10

Royal wedding.

For overprints see Nos. 595-598.

Hegira 1500th Anniv. A164

Alexander Fleming (1881-1955) A165

1981, July 15 *Perf. 13½x13*

552	A164	100fr multi	45	30

1981, Aug. 6 Engr. *Perf. 13*

553	A165	150fr multi	65	40

25th Intl. Letter Writing Week, Oct. 6-12 — A167

1981, Oct. 9 Surcharged in Black

554	A167	65fr on 40fr multi	30	18
555	A167	85fr on 60fr multi	35	25

Nos. 554-555 not issued without surcharge.

World Food Day — A168

1981, Oct. 16 Litho.

556	A168	100fr multi	42	30

Espana '82 World Cup Soccer A169

Designs: Various soccer players.

1981, Nov. 18 Litho. *Perf. 14x13½*

557	A169	40fr multi	18	15
558	A169	65fr multi	28	18
559	A169	85fr multi	35	22
560	A169	150fr multi	65	40
561	A169	300fr multi	1.25	80
		Nos. 557-561 (5)	2.71	1.75

Souvenir Sheet

562	A169	500fr multi	2.25	1.40

For overprints see Nos. 603-608.

75th Anniv. of Grand Prix A170

Designs: Winners and their cars.

1981, Nov. 30 *Perf. 14*

563	A170	20fr Peugeot, 1912	15	15
564	A170	40fr Bugatti, 1924	18	15
565	A170	65fr Lotus-Climax, 1962	28	18
566	A170	85fr Georges Boillot, 1912	35	22
567	A170	150fr Phil Hill, 1960	65	40
		Nos. 563-567 (5)	1.61	1.10

Souvenir Sheet

568	A170	450fr Race	2.00	1.25

For overprint see No. 675.

Christmas 1981 — A171

Designs: Virgin and Child paintings.

1981, Dec. 24

569	A171	100fr Botticelli	42	26
570	A171	200fr Botticini	85	55
571	A171	300fr Botticelli, diff.	1.25	80

School Gardens A172

1982, Feb. 19 Litho. *Perf. 13x13½*

572	A172	65fr shown	28	18
573	A172	85fr Garden, diff.	35	22

Fruit on a Table, by Edouard Manet (1832-1883) — A173

Anniversaries: 120fr, Arturo Toscanini (1867-1957), vert. 200fr, L'Estaque, by Georges Braque (1882-1963). 300fr, George Washington (1732-99), vert. 400fr, Goethe (1749-1832), vert. Nos. 579-580, 21st birthday of Diana, Princess of Wales (portraits), vert.

1982, Mar. 8 Litho. *Perf. 13*

574	A173	120fr multi	55	35
575	A173	140fr multi	65	38
576	A173	200fr multi	85	55
577	A173	300fr multi	1.25	80
578	A173	400fr multi	1.75	1.10
579	A173	500fr multi	2.25	1.40
		Nos. 574-579 (6)	7.30	4.58

Souvenir Sheet

580	A173	500fr multi	2.25	1.40

Palace of Congress — A174

1982, Mar. 17

581	A174	150fr multi	65	40

7th Youth Festival, Agadez — A175

Reafforestation Campaign — A176

1982, Apr. 7 *Perf. 12½*

582	A175	65fr Martial arts, horiz.	28	18
583	A175	100fr Wrestling	42	28

1982, Apr. 16 *Perf. 13*

584	A176	150fr Tree planting	65	40
585	A176	200fr Trees, Desert	85	55

For overprints see Nos. 668-669.

Scouting Year A177

1982, May 13

586	A177	65fr Canoeing	28	18
587	A177	85fr Scouts in rubber boat	35	22
588	A177	130fr Canoeing, diff.	55	35
589	A177	200fr Rafting	85	55

Souvenir Sheet

590	A177	400fr Beach scene	1.75	1.10

For overprint see No. 673.

13th Meeting of Islamic Countries Foreign Affairs Ministers, Niamey, Aug. 20-27 A178

1982, June 6

591	A178	100fr multi	42	28

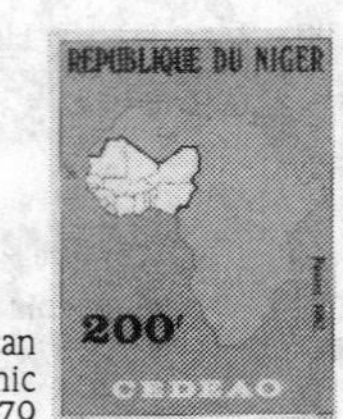

West African Economic Community — A179

1982, June 28

592 A179 200fr Map 85 55

Fishermen in Canoe A180

1982, July 18 *Perf. 13x12½*

593 A180 65fr shown 28 18
594 A180 85fr Bringing in nets 35 22

Nos. 548-551 Overprinted in Blue: "NAISSANCE ROYALE 1982"

1982, Aug. 4 *Perf. 14½*

595 A163 150fr multi 65 40
596 A163 200fr multi 85 55
597 A163 300fr multi 1.25 80

Souvenir Sheet

598 A163 400fr multi 1.75 1.10

Flautist, by Norman Rockwell A181

1982, Sept. 10 **Litho.** *Perf. 14*

599 A181 65fr shown 28 18
600 A181 85fr Clerk 35 22
601 A181 110fr Teacher and Pupil 48 30
602 A181 150fr Girl Shopper 65 40

Nos. 557-562 Overprinted with Past and Present Winners in Black on Silver

1982, Sept. 28 *Perf. 14x13½*

603 A169 40fr multi 18 15
604 A169 65fr multi 28 18
605 A169 85fr multi 35 22
606 A169 150fr multi 65 40
607 A169 300fr multi 1.25 80
Nos. 603-607 (5) 2.71 1.75

Souvenir Sheet

608 A169 500fr multi 2.25 1.40

Italy's victory in 1982 World Cup.

ITU Plenipotentiaries Conference, Nairobi, Sept. — A182

1982, Sept. 28 *Perf. 13*

609 A182 130fr black & blue 55 35

Laboratory Workers A183

Various laboratory workers.

1982, Nov. 9 **Litho.** *Perf. 13*

610 A168 65fr multi 30 18
611 A183 115fr multi 50 30

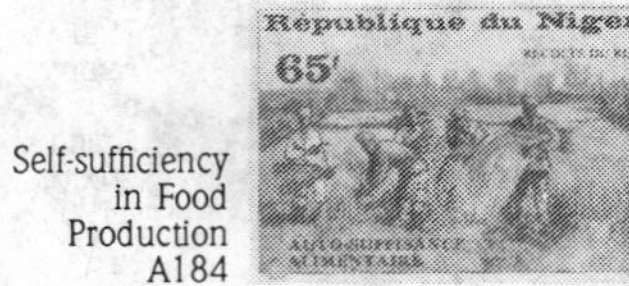

Self-sufficiency in Food Production A184

1983, Feb. 16 **Litho.** *Perf. 13½x13*

612 A184 65fr Rice harvest 28 18
613 A184 85fr Planting rice, vert. 35 22

Grand Ducal Madonna, by Raphael A185

Raphael Paintings: 65fr, Miraculous Catch of Fishes. 100fr, Deliverance of St. Peter. 150fr, Sistine Madonna. 200fr, Christ on the Way to Calvary. 300fr, Deposition. 400fr, Transfiguration. 500fr, St. Michael Slaying the Dragon. 65fr, 100fr, 300fr horiz.

1983, Mar. 30 **Litho.** *Perf. 14*

614 A185 65fr multi 28 18
615 A185 85fr multi 35 22
616 A185 100fr multi 42 26
617 A185 150fr multi 65 40
618 A185 200fr multi 85 55
619 A185 300fr multi 1.25 80
620 A185 400fr multi 1.75 1.10
621 A185 500fr multi 2.25 1.30
Nos. 614-621 (8) 7.80 4.81

African Economic Commission, 25th Anniv. — A186

1983, Mar. 18 *Perf. 12½x13*

622 A186 120fr multi 55 32
623 A186 200fr multi 85 55

Army Surveyors A187

1983, Apr. 14 *Perf. 13x12½*

624 A187 85fr shown 35 22
625 A187 150fr Road building 65 40

Agadez Court — A188

1983, Apr. 26 **Litho.** *Perf. 13x12½*

626 A188 65fr multi 28 18

Mail Van — A189

1983, June 25 **Litho.**

627 A189 65fr Van 28 18
628 A189 100fr Van, map 42 25

Palestine Solidarity — A190

1983, Aug. 21 **Litho.** *Perf. 12½*

629 A190 65fr multi 28 18

Intl. Literacy Year — A191

Various adult education classes. 65fr, 150fr vert.

Perf. 13½x14½, 14½x13½

1983, Sept. 8 **Litho.**

630 A191 40fr multi 15 15
631 A191 65fr multi 15 15
632 A191 85fr multi 18 15
633 A191 100fr multi 22 15
634 A191 150fr multi 32 18
Nos. 630-634 (5) 1.02
Set value 58

7th Ballet Festival of Dosso Dept. A192

Various dancers.

1983, Oct. 7 *Perf. 14½x13½*

635 A192 65fr multi 15 15
636 A192 85fr multi 18 15
637 A192 120fr multi 25 16
Set value 36

A193

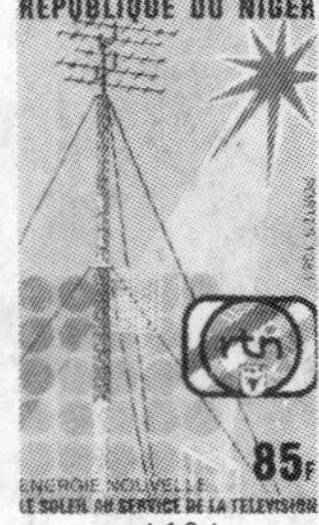

A194

Perf. 13x12½, 12½x13

1983, Oct. 18

638 A193 80fr Post Office, mail van 16 15
639 A193 120fr Sorting mail 25 16
640 A193 150fr Emblem, vert. 32 20

World Communications Year.

1983, Nov. 26 *Perf. 13*

641 A194 85fr Antenna 18 15
642 A194 130fr Car 28 18

Solar energy for television.

Local Butterflies — A195

1983, Dec. 9 *Perf. 12½*

643 A195 75fr Hypolimnas misippus 18 15
644 A195 120fr Papilio demodocus 32 16
645 A195 250fr Vanessa antiopa 70 35
646 A195 350fr Charesex jasius 90 45
647 A195 500fr Danaus chrisippus 1.40 65
Nos. 643-647 (5) 3.50 1.76

SAMARIYA Natl. Development Movement — A196

1984, Jan. 18 **Litho.** *Perf. 13x13½*

648 A196 80fr multi 16 15

Alestes Bouboni A197

1984, Mar. 28 **Litho.** *Perf. 13*

649 A197 120fr multi 32 15

Military Pentathlon A198

1984, Apr. 10

650 A198 120fr Hurdles 32 15
651 A198 140fr Shooting 36 16

Radio Broadcasting Building Opening
A199

1984, May 14 Litho. *Perf. 13*

652 A199 120fr multi 32 15

25th Anniv. of Council of Unity — A200

1984, May 29 *Perf. 12½*

653 A200 65fr multi 18 15
654 A200 85fr multi 22 15
Set value 18

Renault, 1902 — A201

Vintage cars (100fr, 140fr, 250fr, 400fr) and ships.

1984, June 12 *Perf. 12½*

655	A201	80fr	Paris	22	15
656	A201	100fr	Gottlieb Daimler	28	15
657	A201	120fr	Three-master Jacques Coeur	32	15
658	A201	140fr	shown	36	16
659	A201	150fr	Barque Bosphorus	38	18
660	A201	250fr	Delage D8	65	35
661	A201	300fr	Three-master Comet	80	36
662	A201	400fr	Maybach Zeppelin	1.10	48
			Nos. 655-662 (8)	4.11	1.98

1984 UPU Congress
A202

1984, June 20 Engr. *Perf. 13x12½*

663 A202 300fr Ship, emblems 80 35

Ayerou Market Place — A203

1984, July 18 Litho. *Perf. 12½*

664 A203 80fr shown 22 15
665 A203 120fr River scene 32 16

Vipere Echis Leucogaster — A204

1984, Aug. 16 *Perf. 13x12½*

666 A204 80fr multi 22 15

West African Union, CEAO, 10th Anniv.
A205

1984, Oct. 26 Litho. *Perf. 13½*

667 A205 80fr multi 18 15

UN Disarmament Campaign, 20th Anniv. — A205a

1984, Oct. 31 *Perf. 13*

667A A205a 400fr brt grn & blk 90 48
667B A205a 500fr brt bl & blk 1.25 60

Nos. 584-585 Overprinted "Aide au Sahel 84"

1984 Litho. *Perf. 13*

668 A176 150fr multi 32 18
669 A176 200fr multi 45 22

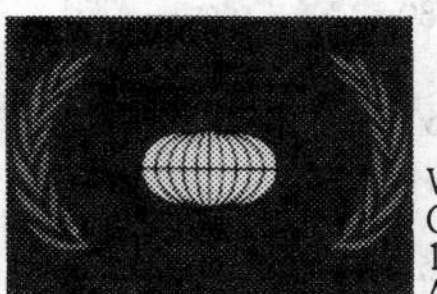

World Tourism Organization, 10th Anniv.
A206

1984, Jan. 2 Litho. *Perf. 12½*

670 A206 110fr WTO emblem 25 15

Infant Survival Campaign — A207

1985, Jan. 28 Litho. *Perf. 12½*

671 A207 85fr Breastfeeding 18 15
672 A207 110fr Weighing child, giving liquids 24 15
Set value 24

Nos. 590, 519 and 568 Overprinted with Exhibitions in Red

Souvenir Sheets

Perf. 13, 12½, 14

1985, Mar. 11 Litho.

673 A177 400fr MOPHILA '85 / HAMBOURG 90 50
674 A154 425fr TSUKUBA EXPO '85 90 50
675 A170 450fr ROME, ITALIA '85 emblem 1.10 55

See Nos. C356-C357.

Technical & Cultural Cooperation Agency, 15th Anniv. — A208

1985, Mar. 20 *Perf. 13*

676 A208 110fr vio, brn & car rose 24 15

8th Niamey Festival
A209

Gaya Ballet Troupe. No. 678 vert.

1985, Apr. 8 *Perf. 12½x13, 13x12½*

677 A209 85fr multi 18 15
678 A209 110fr multi 24 15
679 A209 150fr multi 32 16
Set value 38

Intl. Youth Year — A210

Authors and scenes from novels: 85fr, Jack London (1876-1916). 105fr, Joseph Kessel (1898-1979). 250fr, Herman Melville. 450fr, Rudyard Kipling.

1985, Apr. 29 *Perf. 13*

680 A210 85fr multi 18 15
681 A210 105fr multi 22 15
682 A210 250fr multi 55 30
683 A210 450fr multi 1.10 55

PHILEXAFRICA '85, Lome, Togo — A211

1985, May 6 *Perf. 13x12½*

684 A211 200fr Tree planting 45 22
685 A211 200fr Industry 45 22

Nos. 684-685 printed se-tenant with center label picturing map of Africa or the UAPT emblem.

Victor Hugo and His Son Francois, by A. de Chatillon — A212

1985, May 22 *Perf. 12½*

686 A212 500fr multi 1.10 55

Europafrica
A213

1985, June 3 *Perf. 13*

687 A213 110fr multi 24 15

World Wildlife Fund — A214

Designs: 50fr, 60fr, Addax. 85fr, 110fr, Oryx.

1985, June 15

688 A214 50fr Head, vert. 15 15
689 A214 60fr Grazing 15 15
690 A214 85fr Two adults 18 15
691 A214 110fr Head, vert. 24 15
Set value 35

Environ-destroying Species — A215

1985, July 1 *Perf. 13x12½, 12½x13*

692	A215	85fr	Oedaleus sp.	18	15
693	A215	110fr	Dysdercus volkeri	24	15
694	A215	150fr	Tolyposporium ehrenbergii, Sclerospora graminicola, horiz.	32	16
695	A215	210fr	Passer luteus	45	22
696	A215	390fr	Quelea quelea	80	40
			Nos. 692-696 (5)	1.99	1.08

Cross of Agadez — A216

1985, July Engr. *Perf. 13*

697 A216 85fr green 18 15
698 A216 110fr brown 24 15
Set value 22

Natl. Independence, 25th Anniv. — A217

1985, Aug. 3 Litho. *Perf. 13x12½*
707 A217 110fr multi 24 15

Protected Trees A218

Designs: 30fr, No. 711, Adansonia digitata and pod, vert. 85fr, 210fr, Acacia albida. No. 710, 390fr, Adansonia digitata, diff. Nos. 708-710 inscribed "DES ARBRES POUR LE NIGER."

1985 *Perf. 13x12½, 12½x13*
708 A218 30fr grn & multi 15 15
709 A218 85fr brn & multi 18 15
710 A218 110fr mag & multi 24 15
711 A218 110fr blk & multi 24 15
712 A218 210fr blk & multi 45 22
713 A218 390fr blk & multi 80 40
Nos. 708-713 (6) 2.06
Set value 1.00

Issue dates: Nos. 708-710, Oct. 1. Nos. 711-713, Aug. 19.

Niamey-Bamako Motorboat Race — A219

1985, Sept. 16 *Perf. 13½*
714 A219 110fr Boats on Niger River 24 15
715 A219 150fr Helicopter, competitor 32 16
716 A219 250fr Motorboat, map 55 28

Mushrooms A220

1985, Oct. 3
717 A220 85fr Boletus 24 15
718 A220 110fr Hypholma fasciculare 32 15
719 A220 200fr Coprinus comatus 55 22
720 A220 300fr Agaricus arvensis 85 32
721 A220 400fr Geastrum fimbriatum 1.25 48
Nos. 717-721 (5) 3.21 1.32

Nos. 717-719 vert.

PHILEXAFRICA '85, Lome, Togo — A221

1985, Oct. 21 *Perf. 13x12½*
722 A221 250fr Village water pump 55 30
723 A221 250fr Children playing dili 55 30

Nos. 722-723 printed se-tenant with center label picturing map of Africa or UAPT emblem.

61st World Savings Day — A222

1985, Oct. 31 *Perf. 12½x13*
724 A222 210fr multi 44 22

European Music Year — A223

Traditional instruments.

1985, Nov. 4 *Perf. 13½*
725 A223 150fr Gouroumi, vert. 32 16
726 A223 210fr Gassou 45 22
727 A223 390fr Algaita, vert. 80 40

Souvenir Sheet
Perf. 12½
728 A223 500fr Biti 1.10 55

Civil Statutes Reform — A224

1986, Jan. 2 Litho. *Perf. 13x12½*
729 A224 85fr Natl. identity card 35 18
730 A224 110fr Family services 45 22

Traffic Safety — A225

Artists — A226

1986, Mar. 26 Litho. *Perf. 12½x13*
731 A225 85fr Obey signs 35 18
732 A225 110fr Speed restriction 45 22

1986, Apr. 11 *Perf. 12½*

Designs: 60fr, Oumarou Ganda, filmmaker. 85fr, Ida Na Dadaou, entertainer. 100fr, Dan Gourmou, entertainer. 130fr, Koungoui, comedian.

733 A226 60fr multi 24 15
734 A226 85fr multi 35 18
735 A226 100fr multi 42 20
736 A226 130fr multi 45 26

Hunger Relief Campaign, Trucks of Hope — A227

1986, Aug. 27 Litho. *Perf. 12½*
737 A227 85fr Relief supply truck 35 18
738 A227 110fr Mother, child, vert. 45 22

Intl. Solidarity Day — A228

Designs: 200fr, Nelson Mandela and Walter Sisulu, Robben Island prison camp. 300fr, Mandela.

1986, Oct. 8 *Perf. 13½*
739 A228 200fr multi 80 42
740 A228 300fr multi 1.25 60

FAO, 40th Anniv. A229

1986, Oct. 16 *Perf. 13*
741 A229 50fr Cooperative peanut farm 20 15
742 A229 60fr Fight desert encroachment 24 15
743 A229 85fr Irrigation management 35 18
744 A229 100fr Breeding livestock 42 20
745 A229 110fr Afforestation 45 22
Nos. 741-745 (5) 1.66 90

Improved Housing for a Healthier Niger — A230

Insects Protecting Growing Crops — A231

1987, Feb. 26 Litho. *Perf. 13½*
746 A230 85fr Albarka 35 18
747 A230 110fr Mai Sauki 45 22

1987, Mar. 26 *Perf. 13x12½*
748 A231 85fr Sphodromantis 35 18
749 A231 110fr Delta 45 22
750 A231 120fr Cicindela 50 25

Liptako-Gourma Telecommunications Link Inauguration — A232

1987, Apr. 10 *Perf. 13½*
751 A232 110fr multi 45 22

A particular stamp may be scarce, but if few collectors want it, its market value may remain relatively low.

Samuel Morse — A233

1988 Seoul Summer Olympics — A234

1987, May 21 Litho. *Perf. 12x12½*
752 A233 120fr Telegraph key, operator, horiz. 50 25
753 A233 200fr shown 85 40
754 A233 350fr Receiver, horiz. 1.50 75

Invention of the telegraph, 150th anniv.

1987, July 15
755 A234 85fr Tennis 35 18
756 A234 110fr Pole vault 45 22
757 A234 250fr Soccer 1.10 52

Souvenir Sheet
758 A234 500fr Running 2.00 1.10

1988 Winter Olympics, Calgary — A235

1987, July 28 Litho. *Perf. 12½*
759 A235 85fr Ice hockey 35 18
760 A235 110fr Speed skating 45 22
761 A235 250fr Pairs figure skating 1.10 52

Souvenir Sheet
762 A235 500fr Downhill skiing 2.00 1.10

For overprints see Nos. 783-785.

African Games, Nairobi — A236

1987, Aug. 5 *Perf. 13*
763 A236 85fr Runners 35 18
764 A236 110fr High jump 45 22
765 A236 200fr Hurdles 85 40
766 A236 400fr Javelin 1.65 85

Natl. Tourism Office, 10th Anniv. A237

1987, Sept. 10 *Perf. 13½*
767 A237 85fr Chief's stool, scepter, vert. 45 22
768 A237 110fr Nomad, caravan, scepter 60 30
769 A237 120fr Moslem village 60 30
770 A237 200fr Bridge over Niger River 1.10 50

Aga Khan Architecture Prize, 1986 — A238

1987, Oct. 7 *Perf. 13*
771 A238 85fr Yaama Mosque, dawn 45 22
772 A238 110fr At night 60 30
773 A238 250fr In daylight 1.40 65

Niamey Court of Appeal A239

1987, Nov. 17 *Perf. 13x12½*
774 A239 85fr multi 45 22
775 A239 110fr multi 60 30
776 A239 140fr multi 75 38

Christmas 1987 — A240

Paintings: 110fr, The Holy Family with Lamb, by Raphael. 500fr, The Adoration of the Magi, by Hans Memling (c. 1430-1494).

Perf. 12½
1987, Dec. 24 Litho. Wmk. 385
777 A240 110fr multi 60 28

Souvenir Sheet
778 A240 500fr multi 2.50 1.40

No. 778 is airmail.

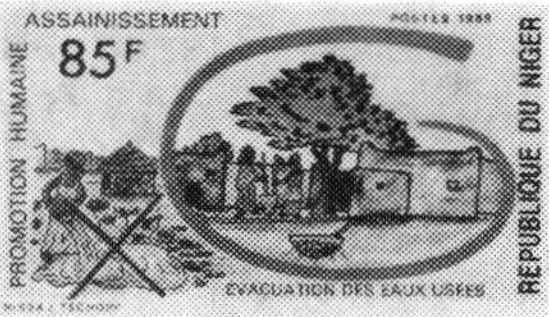

Modern Services for a Healthy Community — A241

1988, Jan. 21 *Perf. 13*
779 A241 85fr Water drainage 60 30
780 A241 110fr Sewage 78 40
781 A241 165fr Garbage removal 1.20 60

Dan-Gourmou Prize — A242

1988, Feb. 16 Litho. *Perf. 13½*
782 A242 85fr multi 60 30

Natl. modern music competition.

Nos. 759-761 Ovptd. "Medaille d'or" and Name of Winner in Gold

1988, Mar. 29 *Perf. 12½*
783 A235 85fr USSR 62 30
784 A235 110fr Gusafson, Sweden 80 40
785 A235 250fr Gordeeva and Grinkov, USSR 1.80 90

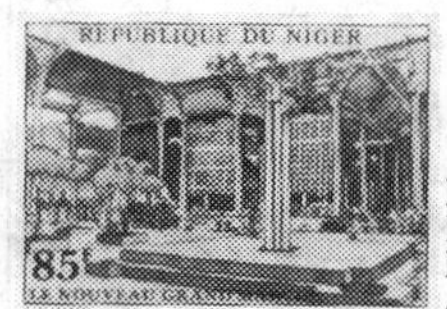

New Market Building, Niamey A243

1988, Apr. 9 Litho. *Perf. 13x12½*
786 A243 85fr multi 60 30

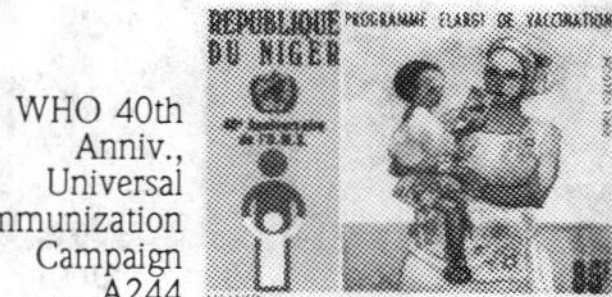

WHO 40th Anniv., Universal Immunization Campaign A244

1988, May 26 Litho. *Perf. 12½x13*
787 A244 85fr Mother and child 55 28
788 A244 110fr Visiting doctor 72 35

Organization for African Unity (OAU), 25th Anniv. — A245

1988, June 28 *Perf. 12½*
789 A245 85fr multi 55 28

Construction of a Sand Break to Arrest Desert Encroachment — A246

1988, Sept. 27 Litho. *Perf. 12½x13*
790 A246 85fr multi 55 28

Intl. Red Cross and Red Crescent Organizations, 125th Annivs. — A247

1988, Oct. 26 *Perf. 13x12½*
791 A247 85fr multi 55 28
792 A247 110fr multi 72 35

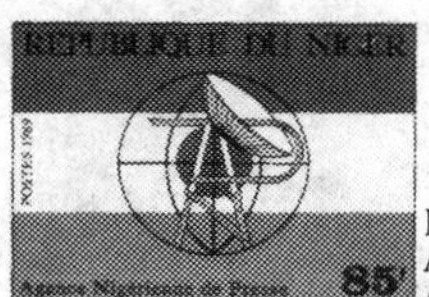

Niger Press Agency A248

1989, Jan. 31 Litho. *Perf. 12½*
793 A248 85fr blk, org & grn 55 28

Fight Against AIDS — A249

1989, Feb. 28 *Perf. 13½*
794 A249 85fr multi 55 28
795 A249 110fr multi 72 35

Intl. Maritime Organization, 30th Anniv. A250

1989, Mar. 29 Litho. *Perf. 12½x13*
796 A250 100fr multi 65 32
797 A250 120fr multi 78 35

FAN Seizure of Government, 15th Anniv. — A251

1989, Apr. 14
798 A251 85fr Gen. Ali Saibou 55 28
799 A251 110fr Raising of the flag 72 35

PHILEXFRANCE '89 — A252

1989, July 1 Litho. *Perf. 13*
800 A252 100fr Eiffel Tower 60 30
801 A252 200fr Simulated stamps 1.20 60

French Revolution, Bicent. — A253

1989, July 1
802 A253 250fr Planting a tree for liberty 1.50 75

> ***15-Cent Minimum Value***
> *The minimum catalogue value is 15 cents. Separating se-tenant pieces into individual stamps does not increase the "value" of the stamps... since demand for the separated stamps may be small.*

A254

A255

1989, Aug. 30 Litho. *Perf. 13½*
803 A254 100fr multi 65 32

African Development Bank, 25th anniv.

1989, July 3 Litho. *Perf. 13½*
804 A255 85fr multi 55 28

Communication and Postal Organization of West Africa (CAPTEAO), 30th anniv.

Verdant Field, Field After Locust Plague — A256

1989, Oct. 1 Litho. *Perf. 13*
805 A256 85fr multicolored 55 28

Lumiere Brothers, Film Pioneers A256a

Designs: 150fr, Auguste Lumiere (1862-1954). 250fr, Louis Lumiere (1864-1948).

1989, Nov. 21 Litho. *Perf. 13½*
805A A256a 150fr multicolored 1.05 52
805B A256a 250fr multicolored 1.75 85
805C A256a 400fr multicolored 2.75 1.38

Flora — A257

A258

1989, Dec. 12 Litho. *Perf. 13*
806 A257 10fr *Russelia equisetiformis* 15 15
807 A257 20fr *Argyreia nervosa* 15 15
808 A257 30fr *Hibiscus rosa-sinensis* 22 15
809 A257 50fr *Catharanthus roseus* 35 18
810 A257 100fr *Cymothoe sangaris*, horiz. 70 35
Nos. 806-810 (5) 1.57
Set value 75

1990, Jan. 18 *Perf. 12½*
811 A258 120fr multicolored 85 42

Pan-African Postal Union, 10th anniv.

Intl. Literacy Year — A259

OCI Emblem — A260

1990, Feb. 27 *Perf. 13½x13*

812 A259	85fr shown		60	30
813 A259	110fr Class, diff.		78	40

1990, Mar. 15 *Perf. 13x12½*

814 A260	85fr multicolored	60	30

Islamic Conference Organization, 20th anniv.

A261

A262

Mickey Leland, US Congressman.

1990, Mar. 29 Litho. *Perf. 13½*

815 A261	300fr multicolored	2.35	1.20
816 A261	500fr multicolored	4.00	2.00

Congressman Leland died Aug. 7, 1989 in a plane crash on a humanitarian mission.

1990, May 15 Litho. *Perf. 13½*

817 A262	85fr multicolored	60	30

Natl. Development Society, 1st anniv.

Multinational Postal School, 20th Anniv. — A263

1990, May 31 *Perf. 13x12½*

818 A263	85fr multicolored	60	30

1992 Summer Olympics, Barcelona — A263a

1990, June 4 Litho. *Perf. 13½*

818A A263a	85fr Gymnastics	65	32
818B A263a	110fr Hurdles	85	42
818C A263a	250fr Running	1.95	1.00
818D A263a	400fr Equestrian	3.10	1.55
818E A263a	500fr Long jump	4.00	2.00
	Nos. 818A-818E (5)	10.55	5.29

Souvenir sheet

819F A263a	600fr Cycling	4.65	2.30

Nos. 818D-818F are airmail.

Independence, 30th Anniv. A264

1990, Aug. 3 *Perf. 12½*

819 A264	85fr gray grn & multi	60	30
820 A264	110fr buff & multi	80	40

UN Development Program, 40th Anniv. — A265

1990, Oct. 24 Litho. *Perf. 13½*

821 A265	100fr multicolored	78	40

Butterflies and Mushrooms
A266 A266a

Designs: 85fr, Amanita rubescens. 110fr, Graphum pylades. 200fr, Pseudacraea hostilia. 250fr, Russula virescens. 400fr, Boletus impolitus. 500fr, Precis octavia. 600fr, Cantharellus cibarius & pseudacraea boisduvali.

1991, Jan. 15 Litho. *Perf. 13½*

822 A266	85fr multicolored	65	32
823 A266	110fr multicolored	85	42
824 A266	200fr multicolored	1.55	78
825 A266	250fr multicolored	1.95	1.00
826 A266	400fr multicolored	3.10	1.55
827 A266	500fr multicolored	4.00	2.00
	Nos. 822-827 (6)	12.10	6.07

Souvenir Sheet

828 A266a	600fr multicolored	4.65	2.30

Nos. 826-828 are airmail. No. 828 contains one 30x38mm stamp.

Palestinian Uprising — A267

1991, Mar. 30 Litho. *Perf. 12½*

829 A267	110fr multicolored	90	45

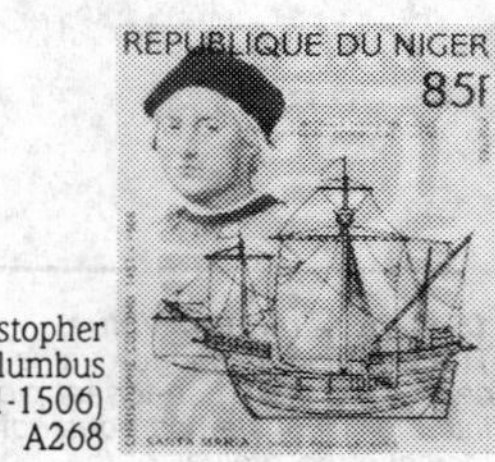

Christopher Columbus (1451-1506) A268

Hypothetical portraits and: 85fr, Santa Maria. 110fr, Frigata, Portuguese caravel, 15th cent. 200fr, Four-masted caravel, 16th cent. 250fr, Estremadura, Spanish caravel, 1511. 400fr, Vija, Portuguese caravel, 1600. 500fr, Pinta. 600fr, Nina.

1991, Mar. 19 Litho. *Perf. 13½*

830 A268	85fr multicolored	65	32
831 A268	110fr multicolored	85	42
832 A268	200fr multicolored	1.55	78
833 A268	250fr multicolored	1.95	1.00
834 A268	400fr multicolored	3.10	1.55
835 A268	500fr multicolored	4.00	2.00
	Nos. 830-835 (6)	12.10	6.07

Souvenir Sheet

835A A268	600fr multicolored	4.65	2.35

Nos. 834-835A are airmail.

Timia Falls — A269

African Tourism Year — A270

Designs: 85fr, Boubon Market, horiz. 130fr, Ruins of Assode, horiz.

1991, July 10

836 A269	85fr multicolored	65	32
837 A269	110fr multicolored	85	42
838 A269	130fr multicolored	1.00	50
839 A270	200fr multicolored	1.50	75

A271

A272

Women with various native hairstyles.

1991

840 A271	85fr multicolored	65	32
841 A271	110fr multicolored	85	42
842 A271	165fr multicolored	1.25	62
843 A271	200fr multicolored	1.50	75

1991, Dec. 17 Litho. *Perf. 12½*

844 A272	85fr multicolored	65	32

Natl. Conference of Niger

House Built Without Wood A273

1992, May 25 Litho. *Perf. 12½*

845 A273	85fr multicolored	75	38

World Population Day — A274

Designs: 85fr, Assembling world puzzle. 110fr, Globe on a kite string.

1992, July 11 Litho. *Perf. 12½*

846 A274	85fr multicolored	75	38
847 A274	110fr multicolored	95	48

Discovery of America, 500th Anniv. — A275

1992, Sept. 16 *Perf. 13*

848 A275	250fr multicolored	2.20	1.10

Hadjia Haoua Issa (1927-1990), Singer A276

1992, Sept. 23 *Perf. 12½x13*

849 A276	150fr multicolored	1.30	65

SEMI-POSTAL STAMPS

Curie Issue

Common Design Type

1938 Unwmk. Engr. *Perf. 13*

B1	CD80	1.75fr + 50c brt ultra	8.00	8.00

French Revolution Issue

Common Design Type

1939 Photo. *Perf. 13*

Name and Value Typo. in Black

B2	CD83	45c + 25c grn	3.75	3.75
B3	CD83	70c + 30c brn	3.75	3.75
B4	CD83	90c + 35c red org	3.75	3.75
B5	CD83	1.25fr + 1fr rose pink	3.75	3.75
B6	CD83	2.25fr + 2fr blue	3.75	3.75
		Nos. B2-B6 (5)	18.75	18.75

Stamps of 1926-38, Surcharged in Black

SECOURS
+ 1 fr.
NATIONAL

1941 *Perf. 14x13½, 13½x14*

B7	A3	50c + 1fr scar & grn, *grnsh*	45	45
B8	A3	80c + 2fr cl & ol grn	2.50	2.50
B9	A4	1.50fr + 2fr dp bl & pale bl	3.50	3.50
B10	A4	2fr + 3fr red org & ol brn	3.50	3.50

Common Design Type and

Colonial Cavalry — SP1

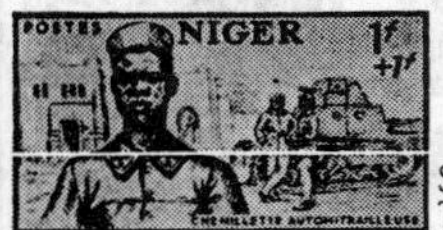

Soldiers and Tank — SP2

1941 Unwmk. Photo. *Perf. 13½*

B11 SP2 1fr + 1fr red 50
B12 CD86 1.50fr + 3fr claret 50
B13 SP1 2.50fr + 1fr blue 50

Nos. B11-B13 were issued by the Vichy government and were not placed on sale in the colony.
Nos. 89-90 were surcharged "OEUVRES COLONIALES" and surtax (including change of denomination of the 2.50fr to 50c). These were issued in 1944 by the Vichy government and were not placed on sale in the colony.

> **Catalogue values for unused stamps in this section, from this point to the end of the section, are for Never Hinged items.**

Republic of the Niger
Anti-Malaria Issue
Common Design Type
Perf. 12½x12

1962, Apr. 7 Engr. Unwmk.

B14 CD108 25fr + 5fr brn 38 38

Freedom from Hunger Issue
Common Design Type

1963, Mar. 21 *Perf. 13*

B15 CD112 25fr + 5fr gray ol, red lil & brn 45 45

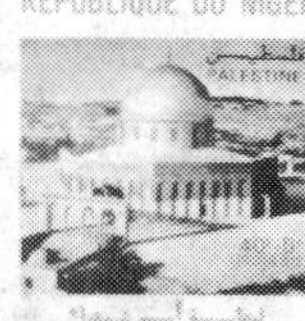

Dome of the Rock — SP3

1978, Dec. 11 Litho. *Perf. 12½*

B16 SP3 40fr + 5fr multi 15 15

Surtax was for Palestinian fighters and their families.

AIR POST STAMPS

Common Design Type

1940 Unwmk. Engr. *Perf. 12½x12*

C1	CD85	1.90fr ultra	28	16
C2	CD85	2.90fr dk red	28	16
C3	CD85	4.50fr dk gray grn	60	45
C4	CD85	4.90fr yel bis	40	32
C5	CD85	6.90fr dp org	40	32
		Nos. C1-C5 (5)	1.96	1.41

Common Design Types

1942

C6	CD88	50c car & bl	15
C7	CD88	1fr brn & blk	15
C8	CD88	2fr multi	15
C9	CD88	3fr multi	15
C10	CD88	5fr vio & brn red	15

Frame Engraved, Center Typographed

C11	CD89	10fr multi	28
C12	CD89	20fr multi	35
C13	CD89	50fr multi	65
		Nos. C6-C13 (8)	2.03

There is doubt whether Nos. C6-C13 were officially placed in use. They were issued by the Vichy government.

> **Catalogue values for unused stamps in this section, from this point to the end of the section, are for Never Hinged items.**

Republic of the Niger

Wild Animals, W National Park — AP1

1960, Apr. 11 Engr. *Perf. 13*

C14 AP1 500fr multi 6.50 3.25

For overprint see No. C112.

Nubian Carmine Bee-eater — AP2

1961, Dec. 18 Unwmk. *Perf. 13*

C15 AP2 200fr multi 1.75 1.00

UN Headquarters and Emblem, Niger Flag and Map — AP3

1961, Dec. 16

C20 AP3 25fr multi 22 15
C21 AP3 100fr multi 80 50

Niger's admission to the United Nations.
For overprints see Nos. C28-C29.

Air Afrique Issue
Common Design Type

1962, Feb. 17 Unwmk. *Perf. 13*

C22 CD107 100fr multi 80 48

Mosque at Agadez and UPU Emblem AP4

Designs: 85fr, Gaya Bridge. 100fr, Presidential Palace, Niamey.

1963, June 12 Photo. *Perf. 12½*

C23 AP4 50fr multi 48 18
C24 AP4 85fr multi 70 35
C25 AP4 100fr multi 80 55

2nd anniv. of Niger's admission to the UPU.

Type of Regular Issue, 1963

Design: 100fr, Building boats (kadei), horiz.

1963, Aug. 30 *Perf. 12½x12*
Size: 47x27mm

C26 A12 100fr multi 80 40

African Postal Union Issue
Common Design Type

1963, Sept. 8 *Perf. 12½*

C27 CD114 85fr multi 65 35

Nos. C20-C21 Overprinted "Centenaire de la Croix-Rouge" and Cross in Red

1963, Sept. 30 Engr. *Perf. 13*

C28 AP3 25fr multi 32 22
C29 AP3 100fr multi 1.00 55

Centenary of International Red Cross.

White and Black before Rising Sun — AP5

1963, Oct. 25 Photo. *Perf. 12x13*

C30 AP5 50fr multi 65 50

See note after Mauritania No. C28.

Peanut Cultivation — AP6

Designs: 45fr, Camels transporting peanuts to market. 85fr, Men closing bags. 100fr, Loading bags on truck.

1963, Nov. 5 Engr. *Perf. 13*

C31	AP6	20fr grn, bl & red brn	18	15
C32	AP6	45fr red brn, bl & grn	35	18
C33	AP6	85fr multi	65	30
C34	AP6	100fr red brn, ol bis & bl	90	40
a.		Souv. sheet of 4, #C31-C34	2.25	2.25

To publicize Niger's peanut industry.

1963 Air Afrique Issue
Common Design Type

1963, Nov. 19 Photo. *Perf. 13x12*

C35 CD115 50fr multi 40 28

Telstar and Capricornus and Sagittarius Constellations — AP7

Design: 100fr, Relay satellite and Leo and Virgo constellations.

1964, Feb. 11 Engr. *Perf. 13*

C36 AP7 25fr ol gray & vio 22 15
C37 AP7 100fr grn & rose cl 70 55

Ramses II Holding Crook and Flail, Abu Simbel — AP8

1964, Mar. 9

C38 AP8 25fr bis brn & dl bl grn 32 25
C39 AP8 30fr dk bl & org brn 36 28
C40 AP8 50fr dp cl & dk bl 65 48

Issued to publicize the UNESCO world campaign to save historic monuments in Nubia.

Tiros I Weather Satellite over Globe and WMO Emblem — AP9

1964, Mar. 23 Unwmk. *Perf. 13*

C41 AP9 50fr emer, dk bl & choc 65 40

4th World Meteorological Day, Mar. 23.

Rocket, Stars and "Stamp" — AP10

1964, June 5 Engr.

C42 AP10 50fr dk bl & magenta 55 35

Issued to publicize "PHILATEC," International Philatelic and Postal Techniques Exhibition, Paris, June 5-21, 1964.

Europafrica Issue, 1963
Common Design Type

Design: 50fr, European and African shaking hands, emblems of industry and agriculture.

1964, July 20 Photo. *Perf. 12x13*

C43 CD116 50fr multi 40 22

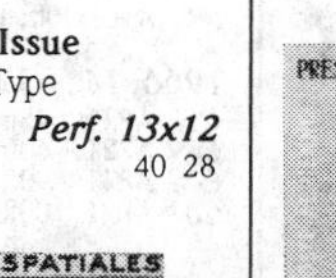

John F. Kennedy — AP11

Discobolus and Discus Thrower — AP12

Perf. 12½

1964, Sept. 25 Unwmk. Photo.

C44 AP11 100fr multi 80 60
a. Souvenir sheet of 4 3.25 2.75

Issued in memory of President John F. Kennedy (1917-1963).

1964, Oct. 10 Engr. *Perf. 13*

Designs: 60fr, Water polo, horiz. 85fr, Relay race, horiz. 250fr, Torch bearer and Pierre de Coubertin.

C45	AP12	60fr red brn & sl grn	40	30
C46	AP12	85fr ultra & red brn	65	35
C47	AP12	100fr brt grn, dk red & sl	70	45
C48	AP12	250fr yel brn, brt grn & sl	1.65	1.10
a.		Min. sheet of 4, #C45-C48	3.50	3.50

18th Olympic Games, Tokyo, Oct. 10-25.

Pope John XXIII (1881-1963) AP13

1965, June 3 Photo. *Perf. 12½x13*
C49 AP13 100fr multi 75 55

Hand Crushing Crab — AP14

Sir Winston Churchill — AP15

1965, July 15 Engr. *Perf. 13*
C50 AP14 100fr yel grn, blk & brn 80 42

Issued to publicize the fight against cancer.

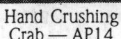

Perf. 12½x13
1965, Sept. 3 Photo. Unwmk.
C51 AP15 100fr multi 80 42

Sir Winston Spencer Churchill (1875-1965), statesman and World War II leader.

Symbols of Agriculture, Industry, Education — AP16

Flags and Niamey Fair — AP17

1965, Oct. 24 Engr. *Perf. 13*
C52 AP16 50fr hn brn, blk & ol 40 22

International Cooperation Year, 1965.

1965, Dec. 10 Photo. *Perf. 13x12½*
C53 AP17 100fr multi 75 42

International Fair at Niamey.

Dr. Schweitzer, Crippled Hands and Symbols of Medicine, Religion and Music — AP18

1966, Jan. 4 Photo. *Perf. 12½x13*
C54 AP18 50fr multi 40 24

Dr. Albert Schweitzer (1875-1965), medical missionary, theologian and musician.

Weather Survey Frigate and WMO Emblem — AP19

1966, Mar. 23 Engr. *Perf. 13*
C55 AP19 50fr brt rose lil, dl grn & dk vio bl 42 28

6th World Meteorological Day, Mar. 23.

Edward H. White Floating in Space and Gemini IV — AP20

Design: #C57, Alexei A. Leonov & Voskhod II.

1966, Mar. 30
C56 AP20 50fr dk red brn, blk & brt grn 42 28
C57 AP20 50fr pur, sl & org 42 28

Issued to honor astronauts Edward H. White and Alexei A. Leonov.

A-1 Satellite and Earth — AP21

Designs: 45fr, Diamant rocket and launching pad, vert. 90fr, FR-1 satellite. 100fr, D-1 satellite.

1966, May 12 Photo. *Perf. 13*
C58 AP21 45fr multi 36 24
C59 AP21 60fr multi 48 28
C60 AP21 90fr multi 70 36
C61 AP21 100fr multi 85 48

French achievements in space.

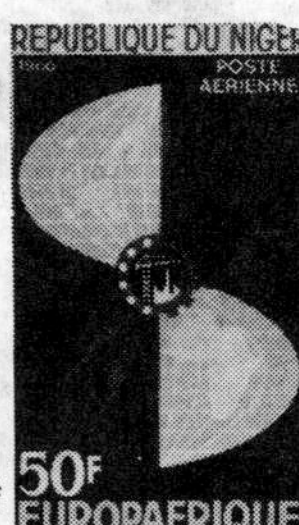

Maps of Europe and Africa and Symbols of Industry — AP22

1966, July 20 Photo. *Perf. 12x13*
C62 AP22 50fr multi 40 26

Third anniversary of economic agreement between the European Economic Community and the African and Malgache Union.

Air Afrique Issue, 1966
Common Design Type

1966, Aug. 31 Photo. *Perf. 13*
C63 CD123 30fr gray, yel grn & blk 22 15

Gemini 6 and 7 — AP23

Design: 50fr, Voskhod 1, vert.

1966, Oct. 14 Engr. *Perf. 13*
C64 AP23 50fr red brn, sl & ultra 40 22
C65 AP23 100fr red brn, bl & pur 80 38

Issued to commemorate Russian and American achievements in space.

Torii and Atom Destroying Crab — AP24

1966, Dec. 2 Photo. *Perf. 13*
C66 AP24 100fr dp cl, brn, vio & bl grn 75 42

Issued to commemorate the 9th International Anticancer Congress, Tokyo, Oct. 23-29.

New Mosque, Niamey — AP25

1967, Jan. 11 Engr. *Perf. 13*
C67 AP25 100fr grn & brt bl 70 35

Albrecht Dürer, Self-portrait AP26

Self-portraits: 100fr, Jacques Louis David. 250fr, Ferdinand Delacroix.

1967, Jan. 27 Photo. *Perf. 12½*
C68 AP26 50fr multi 45 30
C69 AP26 100fr multi 75 60
C70 AP26 250fr multi 1.90 1.10

See No. C98.

Demand, as well as supply, determines a stamp's market value. One is as important as the other.

Maritime Weather Station — AP27

1967, Apr. 28 Engr. *Perf. 13*
C71 AP27 50fr brt bl, dk car rose & blk 65 32

7th World Meteorological Day.

View of EXPO '67, Montreal — AP28

1967, Apr. 28 Engr. *Perf. 13*
C72 AP28 100fr lil, brt bl & blk 70 35

Issued for EXPO '67, International Exhibition, Montreal, Apr. 28-Oct. 27, 1967.

Audio-visual Center, Stylized Eye and People — AP29

1967, June 22 Engr. *Perf. 13*
C73 AP29 100fr brt bl, pur & grn 70 35

National Audio-Visual Center.

Konrad Adenauer — AP30

1967, Aug. 11 Photo. *Perf. 12½*
C74 AP30 100fr dk bl, gray & sep 75 40
a. Souv. sheet of 4 3.00 2.50

Konrad Adenauer (1876-1967), chancellor of West Germany (1949-63).

African Postal Union Issue, 1967
Common Design Type

1967, Sept. 9 Engr. *Perf. 13*
C75 CD124 100fr emer, red & brt lil 70 35

Jesus Teaching in the Temple, by Ingres — AP31

Design: 150fr, Jesus Giving the Keys to St. Peter, by Ingres, vert.

1967, Oct. 2 Photo. *Perf. 12½*

C76 AP31 100fr multi	1.00	65
C77 AP31 150fr multi	1.50	1.00

Jean Dominique Ingres (1780-1867), French painter.

Children and UNICEF Emblem — AP32

1967, Dec. 11 Engr. *Perf. 13*

C78 AP32 100fr bl, brn & grn	70	35

21st anniv. of UNICEF.

O.C.A.M. Emblem — AP33

1968, Jan. 12 Engr. *Perf. 13*

C79 AP33 100fr brt bl, grn & org	70	35

Issued to publicize the conference of the Organization Communitée Afrique et Malgache (OCAM) held in Niamey, January 1968.

Vincent van Gogh, Self-portrait AP34

Self-portraits: 50fr, Jean Baptiste Camille Corot. 150fr, Francisco de Goya.

1968, Jan. 29 Photo. *Perf. 12½*

C80 AP34 50fr multi	50	22
C81 AP34 150fr multi	1.20	55
C82 AP34 200fr multi	1.60	80

See No. C98.

Breguet 27 — AP35

Planes: 80fr, Potez 25 on the ground. 100fr, Potez 25 in the air.

1968, Mar. 14 Engr. *Perf. 13*

C83 AP35 45fr ind, car & dk grn	34	22
C84 AP35 80fr ind, bl & brn	60	28
C85 AP35 100fr sky bl, brn blk & dk grn	70	34

25th anniversary of air mail service between France and Niger.

Splendid Glossy Starling — AP36

Design: 100fr, Amethyst starling, vert.

1968-69 Photo. *Perf. 13*

C86 AP36 100fr gold & multi ('69)	65	28

Engr.

C87 AP36 250fr mag, sl grn & brt bl	1.40	70

See No. C255.

Dandy Horse, 1818, and Racer, 1968 — AP37

1968, May 17 Engr. *Perf. 13*

C88 AP37 100fr bl grn & red	65	35

Issued to commemorate the 150th anniversary of the invention of the bicycle.

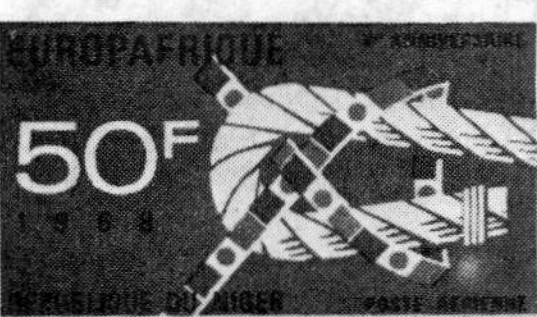
Sheet Bend Knot — AP37a

1968, July 20 Photo. *Perf. 13*

C89 AP37a 50fr gray, blk, red & grn	38	22

Fifth anniversary of economic agreement between the European Economic Community and the African and Malgache Union.

Fencing — AP38

Designs: 100fr, Jackknife dive, vert. 150fr, Weight lifting, vert. 200fr, Equestrian.

1968, Sept. 10 Engr. *Perf. 13*

C90 AP38 50fr pur & blk	32	18
C91 AP38 100fr choc, ultra & blk	65	28
C92 AP38 150fr choc & org	90	42
C93 AP38 200fr brn, emer & ind	1.25	65
a. Min. sheet of 4, #C90-C93	3.50	3.50

Issued to publicize the 19th Olympic Games, Mexico City, Oct. 12-27.

No. C93a is folded down the vertical gutter separating Nos. C90-C91 se-tenant at left and Nos. C92-C93 se-tenant at right.

Robert F. Kennedy — AP39

Designs: No. C94, John F. Kennedy. No. C95, Rev. Dr. Martin Luther King, Jr. No. C96, Mahatma Gandhi.

1968, Oct. 4 Photo. *Perf. 12½*

C94 AP39 100fr blk & dl org	65	30
C95 AP39 100fr blk & aqua	65	30
C96 AP39 100fr blk & gray	65	30
C97 AP39 100fr blk & yel	65	30
a. Souv. sheet of 4, #C94-C97	3.00	2.50

Issued to honor proponents of non-violence.

PHILEXAFRIQUE Issue
Painting Type of 1968

Design: 100fr, Interior Minister Paré, by J. L. La Neuville (1748-1826).

1968, Oct. 25 Photo. *Perf. 12½*

C98 AP34 100fr multi	80	80

Issued to publicize PHILEXAFRIQUE, Philatelic Exhibition in Abidjan, Feb. 14-23, 1969. Printed with alternating light blue label.

Arms and Flags of Niger AP40

1968, Dec. 17 Litho. *Perf. 13*

C99 AP40 100fr multi	65	30

10th anniv. of the proclamation of the Republic.

Bonaparte as First Consul, by Ingres AP41

Paintings: 100fr, Napoleon Visiting the Plague House in Jaffa, by Antoine Jean Gros. 150fr, Napoleon on the Imperial Throne, by Jean Auguste Dominique Ingres. 200fr, Napoleon's March Through France, by Jean Louis Ernest Meissonier, horiz.

Perf. 12½x12, 12x12½

1969, Jan. 20 Photo.

C100 AP41 50fr multi	80	60
C101 AP41 100fr grn & multi	1.30	1.40
C102 AP41 150fr pur & multi	1.75	1.25
C103 AP41 200fr brn & multi	2.50	1.75

Issued to commemorate the 200th anniversary of the birth of Napoleon Bonaparte (1769-1821).

2nd PHILEXAFRIQUE Issue
Common Design Type

Designs: 50fr, Niger No. 41 and giraffes.

1969, Feb. 14 Engr. *Perf. 13*

C104 CD128 50fr slate, brn & org	40	34

Weather Observation Plane in Storm and Anemometer — AP42

1969, Mar. 23 Engr. *Perf. 13*

C105 AP42 50fr blk, brt bl & grn	35	16

9th World Meteorological Day.

Panhard Levassor, 1900 — AP43

Early Automobiles: 45fr, De Dion Bouton 8, 1904. 50fr, Opel, 1909. 70fr, Daimler, 1910. 100fr, Vermorel 12/16, 1912.

1969, Apr. 15 Engr. *Perf. 13*

C106 AP43 25fr gray, lt grn & bl grn	18	15
C107 AP43 45fr gray, bl & vio	24	15
C108 AP43 50fr gray, yel bis & brn	40	20
C109 AP43 70fr gray, brt pink & brt lil	55	28
C110 AP43 100fr gray, lem & sl grn	70	35
Nos. C106-C110 (5)	2.07	1.13

Apollo 8 Trip around Moon AP44

Embossed on Gold Foil

1969, Mar. 31 *Die-cut Perf. 10½*

C111 AP44 1000fr gold	7.00	7.00

US Apollo 8 mission, which put the 1st men into orbit around the moon, Dec. 21-27, 1968.

No. C14 Overprinted in Red with Lunar Landing Module and: "L'HOMME / SUR LA LUNE / JUILLET 1969 / APOLLO 11"

1969, July 25 Engr. *Perf. 13*

C112 AP1 500fr multi	3.50	3.50

See note after Mali No. C80.

Toys — AP45

1969, Oct. 13 Engr. *Perf. 13*

C113 AP45 100fr bl, red brn & grn	65	28

International Nuremberg Toy Fair.

Europafrica Issue

Links AP46

1969, Oct. 30 **Photo.**

C114 AP46 50fr vio, yel & blk 35 16

Camels and Motor Caravan Crossing Desert — AP47

Designs: 100fr, Motor caravan crossing mountainous region. 150fr, Motor caravan in African village. 200fr, Map of Africa showing tour, Citroen B-2 tractor, African and European men shaking hands.

1969, Nov. 22 **Engr.** ***Perf. 13***

C115 AP47 50fr lil, pink & brn 32 15
C116 AP47 100fr dk car rose, lt bl & vio bl 65 28
C117 AP47 150fr multi 90 42
C118 AP47 200fr sl grn, bl & blk 1.20 60

Issued to commemorate the Black Tour across Africa from Colomb-Bechar, Algeria, to Mombassa, Dar es Salaam, Mozambique, Tananarive and the Cape of Good Hope.

EXPO '70 at Osaka — AP48

1970, Mar. 25 **Photo.** ***Perf. 12½***

C119 AP48 100fr multi 65 30

Issued to publicize EXPO '70 International Exhibition, Osaka, Japan, Mar. 15-Sept. 13.

Education Year Emblem and Education Symbols — AP49

1970, Apr. 6 **Engr.** ***Perf. 13***

C120 AP49 100fr plum, red & gray 65 30

Issued for International Education Year.

For unused stamps, more recent issues are valued as never hinged, with the beginning point determined on a country-by-country basis. Notes to show the beginning points are prominently placed in the text.

Rotary Emblem, Globe and Niamey Club Emblem — AP50

1970, Apr. 30 **Photo.** ***Perf. 12½***

C121 AP50 100fr gold & multi 65 30

65th anniversary of Rotary International.

Modern Plane, Clement Ader and his Flying Machine — AP51

Designs: 100fr, Joseph and Jacques Montgolfier, rocket and balloon. 150fr, Isaac Newton, planetary system and trajectories. 200fr, Galileo Galilei, spaceship and trajectories. 250fr, Leonardo da Vinci, his flying machine, and plane.

1970, May 11 **Engr.** ***Perf. 13***

C122 AP51 50fr bl, cop red & sl 32 15
C123 AP51 100fr cop red, bl & sl 60 30
C124 AP51 150fr brn, grn & ocher 85 45
C125 AP51 200fr dk car rose, dp vio & bis 1.20 60
C126 AP51 250fr cop red, gray & pur 1.60 80
Nos. C122-C126 (5) 4.57 2.30

Pioneers of space research.
For overprints and surcharges see Nos. C129-C130, C141-C142.

Bay of Naples, Buildings, Mt. Vesuvius and Niger No. 97 — AP52

1970, May 5 **Photo.** ***Perf. 12½***

C127 AP52 100fr multi 65 28

Issued to publicize the 10th Europa Philatelic Exhibition, Naples, Italy, May 2-10.

TV Tube, Books, Microscope, Globe and ITU Emblem — AP53

1970, May 16 **Engr.** ***Perf. 13***

C128 AP53 100fr grn, brn & red 65 28

Issued for World Telecommunications Day.

Nos. C123 and C125 Overprinted: "Solidarité Spatiale / Apollo XIII / 11-17 Avril 1970"

1970, June 6 **Engr.** ***Perf. 13***

C129 AP51 100fr multi 65 30
C130 AP51 200fr multi 1.10 55

Issued to commemorate the abortive flight of Apollo 13, Apr. 11-17, 1970.

UN Emblem, Man, Woman and Doves — AP54

1970, June 26 **Photo.** ***Perf. 12½***

C131 AP54 100fr brt bl, dk bl & org 60 28
C132 AP54 150fr multi 1.10 45

25th anniversary of the United Nations.

European and African Men, Globe and Fleur-de-lis — AP55

Lithographed; Embossed on Gold Foil

1970, July 22 ***Perf. 12½***

C133 AP55 250fr gold & ultra 1.60 1.60

French Language Cong., Niamey, Mar. 1970.

Europafrica Issue

European and African Women — AP56

1970, July 29 **Engr.** ***Perf. 13***

C134 AP56 50fr sl grn & dl red 32 18

EXPO Emblem, Geisha and Torii — AP57

Design: 150fr, EXPO emblem, exhibition at night and character from Noh play.

1970, Sept. 16 **Engr.** ***Perf. 13***

C135 AP57 100fr multi 60 28
C136 AP57 150fr bl, dk brn & grn 85 42

Issued to commemorate EXPO '70 International Exhibition, Osaka, Japan, Mar. 15-Sept. 13.

Gymnast on Parallel Bars — AP58

Beethoven and Piano — AP59

Sports: 100fr, Vaulting, horiz. 150fr, Flying jump, horiz. 200fr, Rings.

1970, Oct. 26 **Engr.** ***Perf. 13***

C137 AP58 50fr brt bl 35 20
C138 AP58 100fr brt grn 65 35
C139 AP58 150fr brt rose lil 1.00 50
C140 AP58 200fr red org 1.25 65

17th World Gymnastics Championships, Ljubljana, Oct. 22-27.

Nos. C124 and C126 Surcharged and Overprinted: "LUNA 16 - Sept. 1970 / PREMIERS PRELEVEMENTS / AUTOMATIQUES SUR LA LUNE"

1970, Nov. 5

C141 AP51 100fr on 150fr multi 65 30
C142 AP51 200fr on 250fr multi 1.25 55

Unmanned moon probe of the Russian space ship Luna 16, Sept. 12-24.

1970, Nov. 18 **Photo.** ***Perf. 12½***

Design: 150fr, Beethoven and dancers with dove, symbolic of Ode to Joy.

C143 AP59 100fr multi 65 26
C144 AP59 150fr multi 1.25 55

Ludwig van Beethoven (1770-1827), composer.

John F. Kennedy Bridge, Niamey — AP60

1970, Dec. 18 **Photo.** ***Perf. 12½***

C145 AP60 100fr multi 60 22

Proclamation of the Republic, 12th anniversary.

Gamal Abdel Nasser — AP61

Design: 200fr, Nasser with raised arm.

1971, Jan. 5 **Photo.** ***Perf. 12½***

C146 AP61 100fr blk, org brn & grn 55 22
C147 AP61 200fr grn, org & blk brn 1.10 60

In memory of Gamal Abdel Nasser (1918-70), President of Egypt.

Charles de Gaulle AP62

Embossed on Gold Foil

1971, Jan. 22 ***Die-cut Perf. 10***

C148 AP62 1000fr gold 14.00 14.00

In memory of Gen. Charles de Gaulle (1890-1970), President of France.

Olympic Rings and "Munich" — AP63

1971, Jan. 29 Engr. *Perf. 13*
C149 AP63 150fr dk bl, rose lil & grn 85 45

Publicity for 1972 Summer Olympic Games in Munich.

Landing Module over Moon — AP64

Masks of Hate — AP65

1971, Feb. 5 Engr. *Perf. 13*
C150 AP64 250fr ultra, sl grn & org 1.40 70

Apollo 14 mission, Jan. 31-Feb. 9.

1971, Mar. 20 Engr. *Perf. 13*

Design: 200fr, People and 4-leaf clover (symbol of unity).

C151 AP65 100fr red, sl & brt bl 65 30
C152 AP65 200fr sl, red & grn 1.10 55

Intl. Year against Racial Discrimination.

Map of Africa and Telecommunications System — AP66

1971, Apr. 6 Photo. *Perf. 12½*
C153 AP66 100fr grn & multi 60 22

Pan-African telecommunications system.

African Mask and Japan No. 580 — AP67

Design: 100fr, Japanese actors, stamps of Niger, No. 95 on cover and No. 170.

1971, Apr. 23 Engr. *Perf. 13*
C154 AP67 50fr dk brn, emer & blk 32 16
C155 AP67 100fr brn & multi 65 28

Philatokyo 71, Tokyo Philatelic Exposition, Apr. 19-29.

Longwood, St. Helena, by Carle Vernet — AP68

Design: 200fr, Napoleon's body on camp bed, by Marryat.

1971, May 5 Photo. *Perf. 13*
C156 AP68 150fr gold & multi 95 42
C157 AP68 200fr gold & multi 1.25 60

Sesquicentennial of the death of Napoleon Bonaparte (1769-1821).

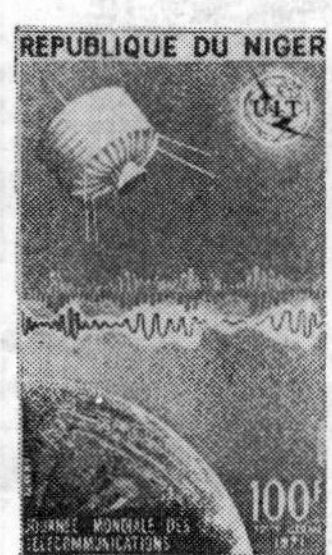

Satellite, Waves and Earth — AP69

Olympic Rings, Athletes and Torch — AP70

1971, May 17 Engr. *Perf. 13*
C158 AP69 100fr org, ultra & dk brn 60 28

3rd World Telecommunications Day.

1971, June 10

Designs: 50fr, Pierre de Coubertin, discus throwers, horiz. 150fr, Runners, horiz.

C159 AP70 50fr red & slate 32 15
C160 AP70 100fr sl, brn & grn 65 22
C161 AP70 150fr plum, bl & rose lil 95 42

75th anniv. of modern Olympic Games.

Astronauts and Landing Module on Moon — AP71

Charles de Gaulle — AP72

1971, July 26 Engr. *Perf. 13*
C162 AP71 150fr red brn, pur & sl 85 40

US Apollo 15 moon mission, July 26-Aug. 7, 1971.

1971, Nov. 9 Photo. *Perf. 12½x12*
C163 AP72 250fr multi 2.25 1.40

First anniversary of the death of Charles de Gaulle (1890-1970), president of France.

African Postal Union Issue, 1971

Common Design Type

Design: 100fr, Water carrier, cattle and UAMPT headquarters, Brazzaville, Congo.

1971, Nov. 13 Photo. *Perf. 13x13½*
C164 CD135 100fr bl & multi 60 28

Al Hariri Holding Audience, Baghdad, 1237 — AP73

Designs from Mohammedan Miniatures: 150fr, Archangel Israfil, late 14th century, vert. 200fr, Horsemen, 1210.

1971, Nov. 25 *Perf. 13*
C165 AP73 100fr multi 55 30
C166 AP73 150fr multi 80 45
C167 AP73 200fr multi 1.10 60

Louis Armstrong — AP74

Design: 150fr, Armstrong with trumpet.

1971, Dec. 6
C168 AP74 100fr multi 60 28
C169 AP74 150fr multi 85 42

Louis Armstrong (1900-1971), American jazz musician.

Adoration of the Kings, by Di Bartolo — AP75

Paintings: 150fr, Nativity, by Domenico Ghirlandaio, vert. 200fr, Adoration of the Shepherds, by Il Perugino.

1971, Dec. 24 Photo. *Perf. 13*
C170 AP75 100fr blk & multi 65 30
C171 AP75 150fr blk & multi 1.00 45
C172 AP75 200fr blk & multi 1.25 60

Christmas 1971. See Nos. C210-C212, C232-C234.

Presidents Pompidou and Diori Hamani, Flags of Niger and France — AP76

1972, Jan. 22
C173 AP76 250fr multi 2.25 1.50

Visit of President Georges Pompidou of France, Jan. 1972.

Snowflakes, Olympic Torch and Emblem — AP77

Design: 100fr, Torii made of ski poles and skis, and dwarf tree, vert.

1972, Jan. 27 Engr.
C174 AP77 100fr dk vio, grn & car 55 25
C175 AP77 150fr dk vio, lil & red 85 40
a. Souv. sheet of 2, #C174-C175 1.60 1.60

11th Winter Olympic Games, Sapporo, Japan, Feb. 3-13.

The Masked Ball, by Guardi — AP78

Designs: 50fr, 100fr, 150fr, Details from "The Masked Ball," by Francesco Guardi (1712-1793); all vertical.

1972, Feb. 7 Photo.
C176 AP78 50fr gold & multi 32 15
C177 AP78 100fr gold & multi 65 28
C178 AP78 150fr gold & multi 95 42
C179 AP78 200fr gold & multi 1.25 60

UNESCO campaign to save Venice.
See Nos. C215-C216.

Johannes Brahms and "Lullaby" — AP79

Scout Sign and Tents — AP80

1972, Mar. 17 Engr. *Perf. 13*
C180 AP79 100fr brt grn, car rose & sl grn 65 28

75th anniversary of death of Johannes Brahms (1833-1897), German composer.

1972, Mar. 22
C181 AP80 150fr pur, org & sl bl 80 30

World Boy Scout Seminar, Cotonou, Dahomey, March 1972.

Surgical Team, Heart-shaped Globe and Emblem — AP81

1972 Engr. *Perf. 13*
C182 AP81 100fr dp brn & car 65 28

"Your heart is your health," World Health Day.

Bleriot XI Crossing English Channel — AP82

Famous Aircraft: 75fr, Spirit of St. Louis crossing Atlantic. 100fr, First flight of Concorde supersonic jet.

1972, Apr. 24

C183	AP82	50fr dk vio bl, brn & mag	35	18
C184	AP82	75fr brn red, bl & ind	55	30
C185	AP82	100fr dp ultra, mag & grnsh bl	75	45

ITU Emblem, Satellite, Stars and Earth — AP83

1972, May 17 Engr. *Perf. 13*

C186	AP83	100fr pur, car & blk	60	28

4th World Telecommunications Day.

Boxing and Opera House — AP84

Designs: 100fr, Broad jump and City Hall, vert. 150fr, Soccer and Church of the Theatines, vert. 200fr, Running and Propylaeum.

1972, May 26

C187	AP84	50fr bl & grn	30	15
C188	AP84	100fr yel grn & dk brn	55	25
C189	AP84	150fr org red & dk brn	80	35
C190	AP84	200fr vio & dk brn	1.10	45
a.		Min. sheet of 4, #C187-C190	3.25	2.75

20th Olympic Games, Munich, Aug. 26-Sept. 10.
For overprints see Nos. C196-C199.

"Alexander Graham Bell," Telephone — AP85

1972, July 7

C191	AP85	100fr car, dk pur & sl	60	25

50th anniversary of the death of Alexander Graham Bell (1847-1922), inventor of the telephone. Stamp pictures Samuel F. B. Morse.

Europafrica Issue

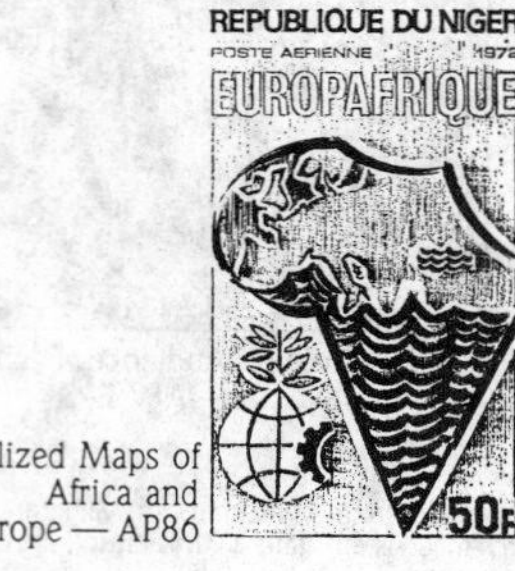

Stylized Maps of Africa and Europe — AP86

1972, July 29 Engr. *Perf. 13*

C192	AP86	50fr red brn, bl & grn	30	15

Mail Runner, UPU Emblem — AP87

Designs: 100fr, Mail truck, UPU emblem. 150fr, Mail plane, UPU emblem.

1972, Oct. 9 Engr. *Perf. 13*

C193	AP87	50fr red brn, sl grn & dk brn	30	18
C194	AP87	100fr red brn, ultra & Prus grn	60	30
C195	AP87	150fr red brn, pur & sl grn	85	45

Universal Postal Union Day.

Nos. C187-C190 Overprinted in Red or Violet Blue

a. WELTER / CORREA / MEDAILLE D'OR
b. TRIPLE SAUT / SANEEV / MEDAILLE D'OR
c. FOOTBALL / POLOGNE / MEDAILLE D'OR
d. MARATHON / SHORTER / MEDAILLE D'OR

1972, Nov. 10

C196	AP84(a)	50fr multi (R)	30	15
C197	AP84(b)	100fr multi (R)	60	24
C198	AP84(c)	150fr multi (VBl)	95	38
C199	AP84(d)	200fr multi (R)	1.40	50

Gold medal winners in 20th Olympic Games: Emilio Correa, Cuba, welterweight boxing; Victor Saneev, USSR, triple jump; Poland, soccer; Frank Shorter, US, marathon.

The Crow and The Fox AP88

Fables: 50fr, The Lion and the Mouse. 75fr, The Monkey and the Leopard.

1972, Nov. 23

C200	AP88	25fr emer, blk & brn	18	15
C201	AP88	50fr brt pink, bl grn & brn	32	15
C202	AP88	75fr lt brn, grn & dk brn	48	28

Jean de La Fontaine (1621-1695), French fabulist.

Astronauts on Moon — AP89

1972, Dec. 12 Photo. *Perf. 13*

C203	AP89	250fr multi	1.40	65

Apollo 17 US moon mission, Dec. 7-19.

Young Athlete AP90

Design: 100fr, Head of Hermes.

1973, Feb. 7 Engr. *Perf. 13*

C204	AP90	50fr dk car	28	15
C205	AP90	100fr purple	55	25

Treasures of antiquity.

Boy Scouts and Radio Transmission — AP91

Niger Boy Scouts: 50fr, Red Cross, first aid. 100fr, Scout and gazelle. 150fr, Scouts with gazelle and bird.

1973, Mar. 21 Engr. *Perf. 13*

C206	AP91	25fr sl grn, choc & dk red	15	15
C207	AP91	50fr grn, red & choc	28	15
C208	AP91	100fr mar, sl grn & choc	55	28
C209	AP91	150fr multi	80	35

For overprints see Nos. C217-C218.

Christmas Type of 1971

Paintings: 50fr, Crucifixion, by Hugo van der Goes, vert. 100fr, Burial of Christ, by Cima da Conegliano. 150fr, Pietà, by Giovanni Bellini.

1973, Apr. 20 Photo. *Perf. 13*

C210	AP75	50fr gold & multi	32	15
C211	AP75	100fr gold & multi	65	32
C212	AP75	150fr gold & multi	90	42

Easter 1973.

Air Afrique Plane and Mail Truck — AP92

1973, Apr. 30 Engr. *Perf. 13*

C213	AP92	100fr brt grn, choc & car	60	28

Stamp Day 1973.

WMO Emblem, Pyramids with Weather Symbols, Satellite — AP93

1973, May 7

C214	AP93	100fr ol brn, brt grn & brt mag	60	28

Cent. of intl. meteorological cooperation.

Painting Type of 1972

Paintings by Delacroix: 150fr, Prowling lioness. 200fr, Tigress and cub.

1973, May 22 Photo. *Perf. 13x12½*

C215	AP78	150fr blk & multi	85	40
C216	AP78	200fr blk & multi	1.20	60

175th anniversary of the birth of Ferdinand Delacroix (1798-1863), French painter.

Nos. C208-C209 Overprinted: "24 * Conference Mondiale / du Scoutisme / NAIROBI 1973"

1973, July 19 Engr. *Perf. 13*

C217	AP91	100fr multi	55	28
C218	AP91	150fr multi	80	35

Boy Scout 24th World Jamboree, Nairobi, Kenya, July 16-21.

Head and City Hall, Brussels — AP93a

1973, Sept. 17 Engr. *Perf. 13*

C219	AP93a	100fr dk pur, mag & vio bl	60	28

Africa Weeks, Brussels, Sept. 15-30, 1973.

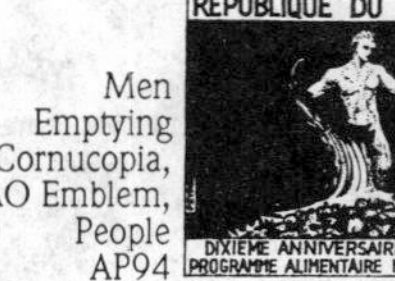

Men Emptying Cornucopia, FAO Emblem, People AP94

1973, Nov. 2 Engr. *Perf. 13*

C220	AP94	50fr ultra, pur & ver	30	15

10th anniversary of the World Food Program.

AP95

AP96

Copernicus, Sputnik 1, Heliocentric System.

1973, Nov. 12

C221	AP95	150fr mag, vio bl & brn	85	42

500th anniversary of the birth of Nicolaus Copernicus (1473-1543), Polish astronomer.

1973, Nov. 22 Photo. *Perf. 12½*

C222	AP96	100fr redsh brn & multi	60	30

Souvenir Sheet

Perf. 13

C223	AP96	200fr dp ultra & multi	1.10	1.10

10th anniversary of the death of Pres. John F. Kennedy (1917-63).

Barge on Niger River AP97

Design: 75fr, Tug Baban Maza.

1974, Jan. 18 Engr. *Perf. 13*
C224 AP97 50fr mar, vio bl & grn 24 15
C225 AP97 75fr yel grn, bl & lil rose 38 20

First anniversary of the upstream voyage of the Flotilla of Hope.

Lenin — AP98

1974, Jan. 21
C226 AP98 50fr dk red brn 25 15

50th anniversary of the death of Lenin (1870-1924), Russian Communist leader.

Skiers AP99

1974, Feb. 8 Engr. *Perf. 11½x11*
C227 AP99 200fr bl, sep & car 1.10 55

50th anniversary of the first Winter Olympic Games, Chamonix, France.

Soccer and Emblem — AP100

Designs: Various views of soccer game.

1974, Apr. 8 Engr. *Perf. 13*
C228 AP100 75fr vio & blk 30 18
C229 AP100 150fr brn, lt & sl grn 52 30
C230 AP100 200fr Prus bl, grn & brn 75 50

Souvenir Sheet

C231 AP100 250fr yel grn, brn & ol brn 1.10 1.10

World Soccer Championship, Munich, June 13-July 7.
For overprint see No. C239.

Christmas Type of 1971

Paintings: 50fr, Crucifixion, by Matthias Grunewald. 75fr, Avignon Pietà, attributed to Enguerrand Quarton. 125fr, Burial of Christ, by G. Isenmann.

1974, Apr. 12 Litho. *Perf. 13x12½*
C232 AP75 50fr blk & multi 26 15
C233 AP75 75fr blk & multi 38 18
C234 AP75 125r blk & multi 65 32

Easter 1974.

21st Chess Olympiad, Nice, June 6-30 — AP101

1974, June 3 Engr. *Perf. 13*
C235 AP101 50fr Knights 28 15
C236 AP101 75fr Kings 38 22

Astronaut and Apollo 11 Badge AP102

1974, July 20 Engr. *Perf. 13*
C237 AP102 150fr multi 70 40

5th anniversary of the first manned moon landing.

Europafrica Issue

The Rhinoceros, by Pietro Longhi AP103

1974, Aug. 10 Photo. *Perf. 12½x13*
C238 AP103 250fr multi 1.40 85

No. C231 Overprinted in Red: "R.F.A. 2 / HOLLANDE 1"

1974, Sept. 27 Engr. *Perf. 13*

Souvenir Sheet

C239 AP100 250fr multi 1.40 1.40

World Cup Soccer Championship, Munich, 1974, victory of German Federal Republic. No. C239 has additional red inscription in margin: "7 JUILLET 1974 / VAINQUEUR REPUBLIQUE FEDERALE ALLEMANDE."

Caucasian Woman, Envelope, UPU Emblem and Jets — AP104

Skylab over Africa — AP105

Designs (UPU emblem, Envelope and): 100fr, Oriental woman and trains. 150fr, Indian woman and ships. 200fr, Black woman and buses.

1974, Oct. 9 Engr. *Perf. 13*
C240 AP104 50fr multi 28 15
C241 AP104 100fr multi 48 28
C242 AP104 150fr bl & multi 70 40
C243 AP104 200fr multi 90 60

Centenary of Universal Postal Union.

1974, Nov. 4 Engr. *Perf. 13*
C244 AP105 100fr multi 48 28

Virgin and Child, by Correggio AP106

Paintings: 150fr, Virgin and Child with St. Hilary, by Filippo Lippi. 200fr, Virgin and Child, by Murillo.

1974, Dec. 24 Litho. *Perf. 12½x13*
C245 AP106 100fr multi 55 22
C246 AP106 150fr multi 75 40
C247 AP106 200fr multi 1.10 60

Christmas 1974. See Nos. C252-C254, C260-C262, C280-C282.

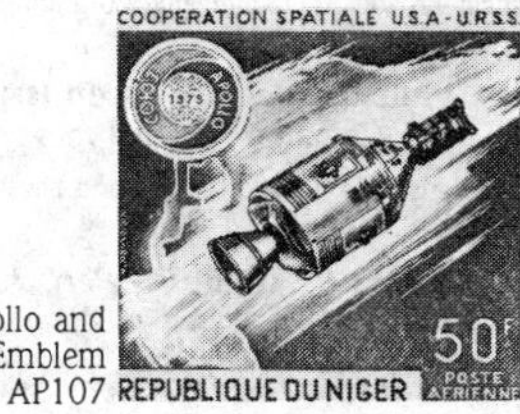

Apollo and Emblem AP107

Designs (Emblem of Soyuz-Apollo Space Docking): 100fr, Docking in space over earth. 150fr, Soyuz in space.

1975, Jan. 31 Engr. *Perf. 13*
C248 AP107 50fr bl & multi 25 15
C249 AP107 100fr multi 45 28
C250 AP107 150fr multi 75 40

Russo-American space cooperation.
For overprints see Nos. C263-C265.

Europafrica Issue

European and African Women, Globe — AP108

1975, Feb. 28 Engr. *Perf. 13*
C251 AP108 250fr brn, lil & red 1.20 70

Painting Type of 1974

Easter: 75fr, Jesus in Garden of Olives, by Delacroix, horiz. 125fr, Crucifixion, by El Greco. 150fr, Resurrection, by Leonard Limosin.

Perf. 13x12½, 12½x13

1975, Mar. 27 Litho.
C252 AP106 75fr multi 38 15
C253 AP106 125fr multi 60 32
C254 AP106 150fr multi 75 40

Bird Type of 1968-69 Dated "1975"

Design: 100fr, Cinnyricinclus leucogaster, vert.

1975, Apr. Photo. *Perf. 13*
C255 AP36 100fr gold & multi 42 25

Lt. Col. Seyni Kountche AP109

1975, Apr. 15 Litho. *Perf. 12½x13*
C256 AP109 100fr multi 42 28

Military Government, first anniversary.

Shot Put, Maple Leaf, Montreal Olympic Emblem AP110

Design: 200fr, Gymnast on rings, Canadian flag, Montreal Olympic emblem.

1975, Oct. 6 Engr. *Perf. 13*
C257 AP110 150fr blk & red 65 35
C258 AP110 200fr red & blk 85 55

Pre-Olympic Year 1975.

UN Emblem and Dove — AP111

1975, Nov. 26 Engr. *Perf. 13*
C259 AP111 100fr grn & bl 45 28

United Nations, 30th anniversary.

Painting Type of 1974

Paintings: 50fr, Virgin of Seville, by Murillo. 75fr, Adoration of the Shepherds, by Tintoretto, horiz. 125fr, Virgin with Angels, Florentine, 15th century.

1975, Dec. 24 Litho. *Perf. 12½x13*
C260 AP106 50fr multi 22 15
C261 AP106 75fr multi 32 25
C262 AP106 125fr multi 55 40

Christmas 1975.

Nos. C248-C250 Overprinted: "JONCTION / 17 Juillet 1975"

1975, Dec. 30 Engr. *Perf. 13*
C263 AP107 50fr bl & multi 22 15
C264 AP107 100fr multi 45 30
C265 AP107 150fr multi 65 42

Apollo-Soyuz link-up in space, July 17, 1975.

12th Winter Olympic Games Type, 1976

Designs: 200fr, Women's figure skating. 300fr, Biathlon. 500fr, Speed skating.

1976, Feb. 20 Litho. *Perf. 14x13½*
C266 A97 200fr multi 1.10 45

C267 A97 300fr multi 1.40 60

Souvenir Sheet

C268 A97 500fr multi 2.50 1.10

American Bicentennial Type, 1976

Design (Statue of Liberty and): 150fr, Joseph Warren, martyr at Bunker Hill. 200fr, John Paul Jones on the bridge of the "Bonhomme Richard." 300fr, Molly Pitcher, Monmouth battle heroine. 500fr, Start of the fighting.

1976, Apr. 8

C269 A100 150fr multi 70 30
C270 A100 200fr multi 90 50
C271 A100 300fr multi 1.50 70

Souvenir Sheet

C272 A100 500fr multi 2.50 1.10

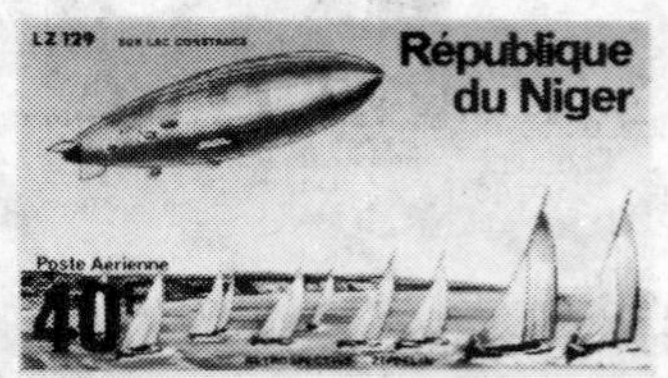

LZ-129 over Lake Constance — AP112

Designs: 50fr, LZ-3 over Würzburg. 150fr, LZ-9 over Friedrichshafen. 200fr, LZ-2 over Rothenburg, vert. 300fr, LZ-130 over Essen. 500fr, LZ-127 over the Swiss Alps.

1976, May 18 Litho. *Perf. 11*

C273 AP112 40fr multi 20 15
C274 AP112 50fr multi 30 15
C275 AP112 150fr multi 75 40
C276 AP112 200fr multi 1.00 40
C277 AP112 300fr multi 1.50 60
Nos. C273-C277 (5) 3.75 1.70

Souvenir Sheet

C278 AP112 500fr multi 2.50 1.10

75th anniversary of the Zeppelin.

Olympic Games Type, 1976
Souvenir Sheet

1976, July 17 Litho. *Perf. 14*

C279 A105 150fr Sprint 80 38

Christmas Type of 1974

Paintings: 50fr, Nativity, by Rubens. 100fr, Virgin and Child, by Correggio. 150fr, Adoration of the Kings, by Gerard David, horiz.

1976, Dec. 24 Litho. *Perf. 12½*

C280 AP106 50fr multi 22 15
C281 AP106 100fr multi 45 28
C282 AP106 150fr multi 65 35

Christmas 1976.

Viking Mars Project Type, 1977

Designs: 100fr, Viking lander and probe, horiz. 150fr, Descent phases of Viking lander. 200fr, Titan rocket start for Mars. 400fr, Viking orbiter in flight.

1977, Mar. 15 Litho. *Perf. 14*

C283 A113 100fr multi 50 25
C284 A113 150fr multi 75 32
C285 A113 200fr multi 1.00 45

Souvenir Sheet

C286 A113 400fr multi 2.25 80

For overprints see Nos. C295-C297.

Nobel Prize Type, 1977
Souvenir Sheet

Design: 500fr, Theodore Roosevelt, peace.

1977, Aug. 20 Litho. *Perf. 14*

C287 A122 500fr multi 3.00 1.10

Games' Emblem, Wheels and Colors AP113

Design: 150fr, Rings, colors and Games' emblem.

1978, July 13 Litho. *Perf. 12½x13*

C288 AP113 40fr multi 18 15
C289 AP113 150fr multi 65 40

Third African Games, Algiers, July 13-28.

Emblem AP114

1978, Oct. 6 Litho. *Perf. 13*

C290 AP114 150fr multi 65 40

Niger Broadcasting Company, 20th anniversary.

Philexafrique II - Essen Issue
Common Design Types

Designs: No. C291, Giraffes and Niger No. 92. No. C292, Eagle and Oldenburg No. 7.

1978, Nov. 1 Litho. *Perf. 13x12½*

C291 CD138 100fr multi 42 28
C292 CD139 100fr multi 42 28
a. Pair, #C291-C292 85 60

View of Campus and Laying Cornerstone — AP115

1978, Dec. 11 Litho. *Perf. 12½*

C293 AP115 100fr multi 42 28

Islamic University of Niger.

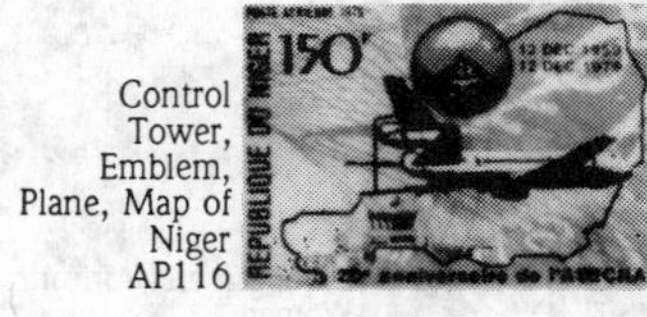

Control Tower, Emblem, Plane, Map of Niger AP116

1979, Dec. 12 Litho. *Perf. 12½*

C294 AP116 150fr multi 65 40

ASECNA (Air Safety Board), 20th anniversary.

Nos. C284-C286 Overprinted in Silver or Black: "alunissage / apollo XI / juillet 1969" and Emblem

1979, Dec. 20 Litho. *Perf. 14*

C295 A113 150fr multi 65 40
C296 A113 200fr multi (S) 85 55

Souvenir Sheet

C297 A113 400fr multi (S) 2.50 1.50

Apollo 11 moon landing, 10th anniversary.

Gaweye Hotel — AP117

1980, Jan. 10 Litho. *Perf. 13*

C298 AP117 100fr multi 45 28

Self-portrait, by Rembrandt AP118

Rembrandt Portraits: 90fr, Hendrickje at the Window. 100fr, Old Man. 130fr, Maria Trip. 200fr, Self-portrait, diff. 400fr, Saskia.

1981, Feb. 12 Litho. *Perf. 12½*

C299 AP118 60fr multi 25 18
C300 AP118 90fr multi 38 25
C301 AP118 100fr multi 42 28
C302 AP118 130fr multi 55 35
C303 AP118 200fr multi 85 55
C304 AP118 400fr multi 1.65 1.10
Nos. C299-C304 (6) 4.10 2.71

Apollo 11, 1969 — AP119

Space Conquest: Views of Columbia space shuttle, 1981.

1981, Mar. 30 Litho. *Perf. 12½*

C305 AP119 100fr multi 42 28
C306 AP119 150fr multi 65 40
C307 AP119 200fr multi 85 55
C308 AP119 300fr multi 1.20 80

Souvenir Sheet

C309 AP119 500fr multi 2.25 1.40

For overprint see No. C356.

Girl in a Room, by Picasso — AP120

Picasso Birth Centenary: 60fr, Olga in an Armchair. 90fr, Family of Acrobats. 120fr, Three Musicians. 200fr, Paul on a Donkey. All vert.

1981, June 25 Litho. *Perf. 12½*

C310 AP120 60fr multi 25 18
C311 AP120 90fr multi 38 25
C312 AP120 120fr multi 50 32
C313 AP120 200fr multi 85 55
C314 AP120 400fr multi 1.75 1.10
Nos. C310-C314 (5) 3.73 2.40

Christmas 1982 AP121

Rubens Paintings.

1982, Dec. 24 Litho. *Perf. 14*

C315 AP121 200fr Adoration of the Kings 65 42
C316 AP121 300fr Mystical Marriage of St. Catherine 1.10 80
C317 AP121 400fr Virgin and Child 1.40 90

Manned Flight Bicentenary AP122

1983, Jan. 24

C318 AP122 65fr Montgolfiere balloon, 1783, vert. 28 18
C319 AP122 85fr Hydrogen balloon, 1783, vert. 38 22
C320 AP122 200fr Zeppelin 85 55
C321 AP122 250fr Farman plane 1.10 65
C322 AP122 300fr Concorde 1.25 80
C323 AP122 500fr Apollo 11, vert. 2.25 1.40
Nos. C318-C323 (6) 6.11 3.80

Pre-Olympic Year — AP123

1983, May 25 Litho. *Perf. 13*

C324 AP123 85fr Javelin 38 22
C325 AP123 200fr Shot put 85 55
C326 AP123 250fr Hammer, vert. 1.10 70
C327 AP123 300fr Discus 1.25 80

Souvenir Sheet

C328 AP123 500fr Shot put, diff. 2.25 1.40

For overprint see No. C357.

Christmas 1983 — AP124

Botticelli Paintings. 120fr, 500fr vert.

Wmk. 385 Cartor

1983 Litho. *Perf. 13*

C329 AP124 120fr Virgin and Child with Angels 25 18
C330 AP124 350fr Adoration of the Kings 75 45
C331 AP124 500fr Virgin of the Pomegranate 1.10 65

1984 Summer Olympics — AP125

Unwmk.

1984, Feb. 22 Litho. *Perf. 13*

C332 AP125 80fr Sprint 18 15
C333 AP125 120fr Pole vault 30 18
C334 AP125 140fr High jump 35 22
C335 AP125 200fr Triple jump, vert. 48 30
C336 AP125 350fr Long jump 85 55
Nos. C332-C336 (5) 2.16 1.40

Souvenir Sheet

C337 AP125 500fr 110-meter hurdles 1.20 75

1984, Oct. 8 Litho.

Designs: Winners of various track events. Nos. C338-C341 vert.

C338 AP125 80fr Carl Lewis 22 15
C339 AP125 120fr J. Cruz 32 16
C340 AP125 140fr A. Cova 38 18
C341 AP125 300fr Al Joyner 80 40

Souvenir Sheet

C342 AP125 500fr D. Mogenburg, high jump 1.40 65

World Soccer Cup — AP126

1984, Nov. 19 Litho. *Perf. 13*

C345 AP126 150fr multi 32 16
C346 AP126 250fr multi 55 28
C347 AP126 450fr multi 95 50
C348 AP126 500fr multi 1.10 55

Christmas 1984 AP127

Paintings: 100fr, The Visitation, by Ghirlandajo. 200fr, Virgin and Child, by the Master of Santa Verdiana. 400fr, Virgin and Child, by J. Koning.

1984, Dec. 24 Litho. *Perf. 13*

C349 AP127 100fr multi 22 15
C350 AP127 200fr multi 42 22
C351 AP127 400fr multi 85 42

Audubon Birth Bicentennial — AP128

1985, Feb. 6 Litho. *Perf. 13*

C352 AP128 110fr Himantopus mexicanus 25 15
C353 AP128 140fr Phoenicopterus ruber, vert. 30 15
C354 AP128 200fr Fratercula arctica 42 22
C355 AP128 350fr Sterna paradisaea, vert. 75 38

Nos. C309, C328 Ovptd. in Silver with Exhibition Emblems

1985, Mar. 11 Litho. *Perf. 12½, 13*

C356 AP119 500fr ARGENTINA '85 BUENOS AIRES 1.10 55
C357 AP123 500fr OLYMPHILEX '85 LAUSANNE 1.10 55

Religious Paintings by Bartolome Murillo (1617-1682) AP129

1985, Dec. 19 Litho. *Perf. 13*

C358 AP129 110fr Virgin of the Rosary 32 16
C359 AP129 250fr The Immaculate Conception 65 35
C360 AP129 390fr Virgin of Seville 1.10 55

Christmas 1985.

Halley's Comet — AP130

1985, Dec. 26

C361 AP130 110fr Over Paris, 1910 32 16
C362 AP130 130fr Over New York 35 16
C363 AP130 200fr Giotto space probe 55 28
C364 AP130 300fr Vega probe 80 40
C365 AP130 390fr Planet A probe 1.10 55
Nos. C361-C365 (5) 3.12 1.55

Martin Luther King, Jr. (1929-1968), Civil Rights Activist — AP131

1986, Apr. 28 Litho. *Perf. 13½*

C366 AP131 500fr multi 2.00 1.00

1986 World Cup Soccer Championships, Mexico — AP132

Various soccer plays, stamps and labels.

1986, May 21 *Perf. 13*

C367 AP132 130fr No. 228 45 28
C368 AP132 210fr No. 229 90 42
C369 AP132 390fr No. 230 1.65 85
C370 AP132 400fr Aztec drawing 1.65 85

Souvenir Sheet

C371 AP132 500fr World Cup 2.00 1.00

Statue of Liberty, Cent. AP133

1986, June 19

C372 AP133 300fr Bartholdi, statue 1.25 55

1988 Summer Olympics, Seoul AP134

Olympic Rings, Pierre de Coubertin and: 85fr, One-man kayak, vert. 165fr, Crew racing. 200fr, Two-man kayak. 600fr, One-man kayak, diff., vert. 750fr, One-man kayak, diff., vert.

1988, June 22 Litho. *Perf. 13*

C373 AP134 85fr multi 58 30
C374 AP134 165fr multi 1.10 55
C375 AP134 200fr multi 1.35 68
C376 AP134 600fr multi 4.00 2.00

Souvenir Sheet

C377 AP134 750fr multi 5.00 5.00

First Moon Landing, 20th Anniv. AP135

1989, July 27 Litho. *Perf. 13*

C378 AP135 200fr Launch 1.30 65
C379 AP135 300fr Crew 1.90 95
C380 AP135 350fr Lunar experiments 2.25 1.15
C381 AP135 400fr Raising flag 2.55 1.30

1990 World Cup Soccer Championships, Italy — AP136

Various athletes and views or symbols of Italian cities.

1990, Mar. 6 Litho. *Perf. 13*

C382 AP136 130fr Florence 92 45
C383 AP136 210fr Verona 1.50 75
C384 AP136 500fr Bari 3.50 1.75
C385 AP136 600fr Rome 4.25 2.15

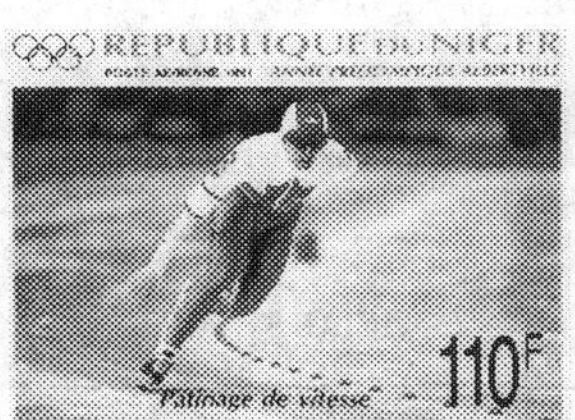

1992 Winter Olympics, Albertville — AP138

1991, Mar. 28 Litho. *Perf. 13*

C392 AP138 110fr Speed skating 80 40
C393 AP138 300fr Ice hockey 2.35 1.20
C394 AP138 500fr Downhill skiing 4.00 2.00
C395 AP138 600fr Luge 4.70 2.35

AIR POST SEMI-POSTAL STAMPS

Stamps of Dahomey types V1, V2, V3 and V4 inscribed "Niger" were issued in 1942 by the Vichy Government, but were not placed on sale in the colony.

POSTAGE DUE STAMPS

D1

D2

Postage Due Stamps of Upper Senegal and Niger, 1914, Overprinted

1921 Unwmk. *Perf. 14x13½*

J1 D1 5c green 35 35
J2 D1 10c rose 35 35
J3 D1 15c gray 40 40
J4 D1 20c brown 40 40
J5 D1 30c blue 40 40
J6 D1 50c black 45 45
J7 D1 60c orange 70 70
J8 D1 1fr violet 90 90
Nos. J1-J8 (8) 3.95 3.95

1927 Typo.

J9 D2 2c dk bl & red 15 15
J10 D2 4c ver & blk 15 15
J11 D2 5c org & vio 15 15
J12 D2 10c red brn & blk vio 15 15
J13 D2 15c grn & org 20 20
J14 D2 20c cer & ol brn 28 28
J15 D2 25c blk & ol brn 28 28
J16 D2 30c dl vio & blk 75 75
J17 D2 50c dp red, *grnsh* 35 35
J18 D2 60c gray vio & org, *bluish* 35 35
J19 D2 1fr ind & ultra, *bluish* 35 35
J20 D2 2fr rose red & vio 35 35
J21 D2 3fr org brn & ultra 65 65
Nos. J9-J21 (13) 4.16 4.16

Catalogue values for unused stamps in this section, from this point to the end of the section, are for Never Hinged items.

Republic of the Niger

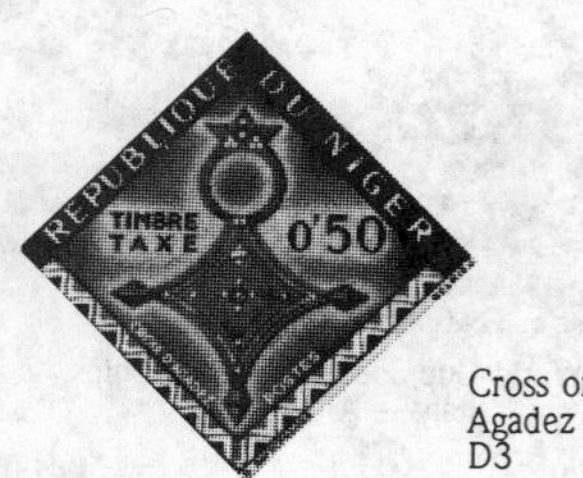

Cross of Agadez D3

Native Metalcraft: 3fr, 5fr, 10fr, Cross of Iferouane. 15fr, 20fr, 50fr, Cross of Tahoua.

Perf. 12½

1962, July 1		Unwmk.	Photo.	
J22	D3	50c emerald	15	15
J23	D3	1fr violet	15	15
J24	D3	2fr slate green	15	15
J25	D3	3fr lilac rose	15	15
J26	D3	5fr green	15	15
J27	D3	10fr orange	15	15
J28	D3	15fr deep blue	15	15
J29	D3	20fr carmine	15	15
J30	D3	50fr chocolate	28	28
		Set value	95	95

OFFICIAL STAMPS

Catalogue values for unused stamps in this section are for Never Hinged items.

Djerma Girl Carrying Jug
O1 O2

Perf. 14x13½

1962-71		Typo.	Unwmk.	
		Denomination in Black		
O1	O1	1fr dark purple	15	15
O2	O1	2fr yel grn	15	15
O3	O1	5fr brt blue	15	15
O4	O1	10fr deep red	15	15
O5	O1	20fr vio blue	16	15
O6	O1	25fr orange	18	15
O7	O1	30fr light blue ('65)	22	16
O8	O1	35fr pale grn ('71)	28	22
O9	O1	40fr brown ('71)	28	22
O10	O1	50fr black	32	22
O11	O1	60fr rose red	42	28
O12	O1	85fr blue green	58	28
O13	O1	100fr red lilac	65	28
O14	O1	200fr dark blue	1.40	65
		Nos. O1-O14 (14)	5.09	
		Set value		2.70

1988, Nov.		Typo.	*Perf. 13*	
O15	O2	5fr brt blue	15	15
O16	O2	10fr henna brn	15	15
O17	O2	20fr vio blue	15	15
O18	O2	50fr greenish blk	25	15

1989, Mar.				
O19	O2	15fr bright yellow	15	15
O20	O2	45fr orange	30	15
		Set value, #O15-O20	85	45

This is an expanding set. Numbers will change when complete.

NORTH INGERMANLAND

LOCATION — In Northern Russia lying between the River Neva and Finland
CAPITAL — Kirjasalo

In 1920 the residents of this territory revolted from Russian rule and set up a provisional government. The new State existed only a short period as the revolution was quickly quelled by Soviet troops.

100 Pennia = 1 Markka

Arms — A1

Perf. 11½

1920, Mar. 21		Unwmk.	Litho.	
1	A1	5p green	2.50	3.25
2	A1	10p rose red	2.50	3.25
3	A1	25p bister	2.50	3.25
4	A1	50p dark blue	2.50	3.25
5	A1	1m car & black	21.00	27.50
6	A1	5m lilac & black	90.00	100.00
7	A1	10m brown & blk	175.00	190.00
		Nos. 1-7 (7)	296.00	330.50

Imperf., Pairs

1a	A1	5p	17.50
2a	A1	10p	17.50
3a	A1	25p	17.50
4a	A1	50p	17.50
5a	A1	1m	70.00
6a	A1	5m	275.00
7a	A1	10m	625.00

Arms — A2

Peasant — A3

Plowing — A4

Milking — A5

Planting — A6

Ruins of Church — A7

Peasants Playing Zithers — A8

1920, Aug. 2				
8	A2	10p gray grn & ultra	3.25	*6.50*
9	A3	30p buff & gray grn	3.25	*6.50*
10	A4	50p ultra & red brn	3.25	*6.50*
11	A5	80p claret & slate	3.25	*6.50*
12	A6	1m red & slate	15.00	*32.50*
13	A7	5m dk vio & dl rose	9.00	*13.00*
14	A8	10m brn & violet	9.00	*13.00*
a.		Center inverted	700.00	
		Nos. 8-14 (7)	46.00	*84.50*

Counterfeits abound.
Nos. 8-14 exist imperf. Value for set in pairs, $200.

NORWAY

LOCATION — Western half of the Scandinavian Peninsula in northern Europe
GOVT. — Kingdom
AREA — 125,051 sq. mi.
POP. — 4,134,353 (1984)
CAPITAL — Oslo

120 Skilling = 1 Specie Daler
100 Ore = 1 Krone (1877)

Catalogue values for unused stamps in this country are for Never Hinged items, beginning with Scott 275 in the regular postage section, Scott B27 in the semi-postal section, and Scott O65 in the official section.

Watermarks

Wmk. 159- Lion

Wmk. 160- Post Horn

Coat of Arms — A1

King Oscar I — A2

1855	Typo.	Wmk. 159	*Imperf.*	
1	A1	4s blue	*4,000.*	100.00
a.		Double foot on right hind leg of lion		2,500.

Only a few genuine unused copies of No. 1 exist. Specimens often offered have had pen-markings removed. The unused catalogue value is for a specimen without gum. Copies with original gum sell for much more.

No. 1 was reprinted in 1914 and 1924 unwatermarked. Lowest value reprint, $75.

Roulletted Reprints

1963: Nos. 1, 2-5, 15. Value each $20.

1965: Nos. 57, 70a, 100, 152, J1, O1. Value each $10.

1969: Nos. 69, 92, 107, 114, 128, J12. Value each $10.

1856-57		Unwmk.	*Perf. 13*	
2	A2	2s yellow ('57)	425.00	125.00
3	A2	3s lilac ('57)	225.00	65.00
4	A2	4s blue	150.00	9.00
a.		Imperf.		*9,000.*
b.		Half used as 2s on cover		
5	A2	8s dull lake	800.00	27.50

Nos. 2-5 were reprinted in 1914 and 1924, perf. 13½. Lowest valued reprint, $60 each.

A3

A4

1863		Litho.	*Perf. 14½x13½*	
6	A3	2s yellow	450.00	150.00
7	A3	3s gray lilac	475.00	325.00
8	A3	4s blue	65.00	6.00
9	A3	8s rose	575.00	32.50
10	A3	24s brown	40.00	52.50

There are four types of the 2, 3, 8 and 24 skilling and eight types of the 4 skilling. See note on used value of No. 10 following No. 21.

1867-68			Typo.	
11	A4	1s black ('68)	75.00	35.00
12	A4	2s orange	20.00	15.00
13	A4	3s dl lil ('68)	250.00	65.00
14	A4	4s blue	45.00	6.00
15	A4	8s car rose	350.00	30.00
a.		8s rose, clear impression	750.00	300.00

See note on used value of No. 12 following No. 21.

For surcharges see Nos. 59-61, 149.

No. 15 was reprinted in 1914 and 1924, perf. 13½. Lowest valued reprint, $60.

Post Horn and Crown — A5

1872-75			Wmk. 160	
16	A5	1s yel grn ('75)	8.50	9.75
a.		1s deep green ('73)	135.00	45.00
b.		"E.EN"	22.50	27.50
17	A5	2s ultra ('74)	12.00	14.00
a.		2s Prussian blue ('74)	3,750.	3,000.
b.		2s gray blue	12.00	16.00
18	A5	3s rose	40.00	5.00
a.		3s carmine	40.00	5.00
b.		3s car, *bluish* thin paper	125.00	16.00
19	A5	4s lilac ('73)	12.00	14.00
a.		4s dark violet, *bluish* thin paper	375.00	125.00
b.		4s brown violet, *bluish* thin paper ('73)	375.00	125.00
20	A5	6s org brn ('75)	375.00	30.00
21	A5	7s red brn ('73)	30.00	30.00

In this issue there are 12 types each of Nos. 16, 17, 18 and 19; 15 types of No. 20 and 22 types of No. 21. The differences are in the words of value.

Used values of Nos. 10, 12, 16-17, 19 and 21 are for specimens canceled in later period, 1888-1908. Those canceled before 1888 are usually worth considerably more. These six stamps were used until Mar. 31, 1908.

No. 19 comes on thin and thick paper. Same value used. Unused, thick paper ten times given value.

For surcharges see Nos. 62-63.

Post Horn — A6

King Oscar II — A7

"NORGE" in Sans-serif Capitals, Ring of Post Horn Shaded

1877-78				
22	A6	1o drab	4.00	3.00
23	A6	3o orange	70.00	17.50
24	A6	5o ultra	30.00	4.50
a.		5o dull blue	60.00	7.00
b.		5o bright blue	90.00	14.00
c.		No period after "Postfrim"	50.00	8.00
d.		Retouched plate	55.00	8.00
e.		As "c," retouched plate	85.00	12.00
25	A6	10o rose	50.00	1.00
a.		No period after "Postfrim"	52.50	1.50
b.		Retouched plate	50.00	1.10
26	A6	12o lt green	85.00	13.00
27	A6	20o org brn	230.00	8.75
28	A6	25o lilac	225.00	95.00
29	A6	35o bl grn ('78)	16.00	8.00
a.		Retouched plate	100.00	70.00
30	A6	50o maroon	35.00	8.00
31	A6	60o dk bl ('78)	32.50	8.00
32	A7	1k gray grn & grn ('78)	22.50	6.00
33	A7	1.50k ultra & bl ('78)	60.00	30.00
34	A7	2k rose & mar ('78)	35.00	20.00

There are 6 types each of Nos. 22, 26 and 28 to 34; 12 types each of Nos. 23, 24, 25 and 27. The differences are in the numerals.

A 2nd plate of the 5o ultramarine has 100 types, the 10o, 200 types.

The retouch on 5o, 10o and 35o shows as a thin white line between crown and post horn.

Post Horn — A8

"NORGE" in Sans-serif Capitals, Ring of Horn Unshaded

1882-93		Wmk. 160	*Perf. 14½x13½*	
35	A8	1o blk brn ('86)	16.00	14.00
a.		No period after "Postfrim"	55.00	55.00
b.		Small "N" in "NORGE"	55.00	55.00
36	A8	1o gray ('93)	8.25	8.25
37	A8	2o brn ('90)	3.00	2.00

38 A8 3o org ('83) 47.50 2.75
a. 3o yellow ('89) 47.50 2.75
b. Perf. 13½x12½ ('89) 1,500.
39 A8 5o bl grn ('89) 40.00 1.10
a. 5o gray green ('86) 55.00 1.75
b. 5o emerald ('88) 150.00 6.00
c. 5o yellow green ('91) 35.00 1.10
d. Perf. 13½x12½ ('92) 800.00
40 A8 10o rose 40.00 85
a. 10o rose red ('86) 35.00 85
b. 10o carmine ('91) 47.50 85
c. As "b," imperf., pair 1,000. 1,000.
41 A8 12o green ('84) 1,400. 300.00
42 A8 12o yel brn ('84) 25.00 13.00
a. 12o bister brown ('83) 40.00 30.00
43 A8 20o brown 75.00 9.00
44 A8 20o blue ('86) 47.50 1.10
a. 20o ultramarine ('83) 105.00 6.50
b. No period after "Postfrim" ('85) 275.00 12.00
c. As "a," imperf., pair 1,100. 1,100.
45 A8 25o dl vio ('84) 12.50 9.00

Dies vary from 20 to 21mm high. Numerous types exist due to different production methods, including separate handmade dies for value figures. Many shades exist.

No. 42 and 42a Surcharged in Black **2 Øre.**

1888 *Perf. 14½x13½*

46 A8 2o on 12o yel brn 1.50 1.50
a. 2o on 12o bister brown 1.50 1.50

Post Horn — A10

"NORGE" in Roman instead of Sans-serif capitals

Perf. 14½x13½

1893-1908 **Wmk. 160**

Size: 16x20mm

47 A10 1o gray ('99) 2.00 1.10
48 A10 2o pale brn ('99) 2.00 1.10
49 A10 3o org yel 1.50 20
50 A10 5o dp grn ('98) 4.50 15
b. Booklet pane of 6
51 A10 10o car rose ('98) 11.50 15
b. Booklet pane of 6
52 A10 15o brn ('08) 42.50 4.00
53 A10 20o dp ultra 27.50 20
b. Booklet pane of 6
54 A10 25o red vio ('01) 52.50 2.00
55 A10 30o sl gray ('07) 45.00 1.50
56 A10 35o dk bl grn ('98) 12.50 3.50
57 A10 50o maroon ('94) 50.00 1.10
58 A10 60o dk bl ('00) 60.00 12.00
Nos. 47-58 (12) 311.50 27.00

Two dies exist of each except 2, 25 and 60o.

See Nos. 74-95, 162-166, 187-191, 193, 307-309, 325-326, 416-419, 606, 709-714, 960-967.

For overprints and surcharge see Nos. 99, 207-211, 220-224, 226, 329.

1893-98 **Wmk. 160** *Perf. 13½x12½*

47a A10 1o gray ('95) 10.50 10.50
49a A10 3o orange ('95) 45.00 4.00
50a A10 5o green 27.50 90
51a A10 10o carmine ('95) 27.50 90
c. 10o rose 42.50 90
53a A10 20o dull ultra ('95) 75.00 3.25
54a A10 25o red violet ('98) 75.00 20.00
56a A10 35o dark blue green ('95) 75.00 20.00
57a A10 50o maroon ('97) 110.00 13.00

No. 12 Surcharged in Green, Blue or Carmine **Kr. 1.00**

1905 **Unwmk.** *Perf. 14½x13½*

59 A4 1k on 2s org (G) 35.00 26.00
60 A4 1.50k on 2s org (Bl) 62.50 62.50
61 A4 2k on 2s org (C) 65.00 47.50

Nos. 19 and 21 Surcharged in Black **30 ØRE**

1906-08 **Wmk. 160** *Perf. 14½x13½*

62 A5 15o on 4s lilac ('08) 3.00 3.00
a. 15o on 4s violet ('08) 8.00 8.00
63 A5 30o on 7s red brown 5.50 5.50

King Haakon VII — A11

Die A - Background of ruled lines. The coils at the sides are ornamented with fine cross-lines and small dots. Stamps 20¼mm high.

Die B - Background of ruled lines. The coils are ornamented with large white dots and dashes. Stamps 21¼mm high.

Die C - Solid background. The coils are without ornamental marks. Stamps 20¾mm high.

1907 **Typo.** *Perf. 14½x13½*

Die A

64 A11 1k yel grn 35.00 30.00
65 A11 1.50k ultra 80.00 80.00
66 A11 2k rose 100.00 100.00

1909-10

Die B

67 A11 1k green 165.00 100.00
68 A11 1.50k ultra 180.00 *350.00*
69 A11 2k rose 180.00 4.00

1911-18

Die C

70 A11 1k light green 70 15
a. 1k dark green 62.50 1.75
71 A11 1.50k ultra 1.75 30
72 A11 2k rose ('15) 2.50 30
73 A11 5k dk vio ('18) 4.25 3.25

Post Horn Type Redrawn

Original Redrawn

In the redrawn stamps the white ring of the post horn is continuous instead of being broken by a spot of color below the crown. On the 3 and 30 ore the top of the figure "3" in the oval band is rounded instead of flattened.

1910-29 *Perf. 14½x13½*

74 A10 1o pale olive 35 18
75 A10 2o pale brown 35 18
76 A10 3o orange 35 18
77 A10 5o green 3.50 15
a. Booklet pane of 6 80.00
78 A10 5o magenta ('22) 70 15
79 A10 7o green ('29) 70 15
80 A10 10o car rose 4.50 15
a. Booklet pane of 6 100.00
81 A10 10o green ('22) 6.00 18
82 A10 12o purple ('17) 70 45
83 A10 15o brown 4.00 15
a. Booklet pane of 6 40.00
84 A10 15o indigo ('20) 4.00 18
85 A10 20o deep ultra 6.50 15
a. Booklet pane of 6 150.00
86 A10 20o ol grn ('21) 6.00 18
87 A10 25o red lilac 30.00 18
88 A10 25o car rose ('22) 6.00 80
89 A10 30o slate gray 7.00 24
90 A10 30o lt blue ('27) 10.00 3.00
91 A10 35o dk olive ('20) 10.00 28
92 A10 40o ol grn ('17) 3.00 28
93 A10 40o dp ultra ('22) 22.50 28
94 A10 50o claret 19.00 28
95 A10 60o deep blue 22.50 30
Nos. 74-95 (22) 167.65 8.07

Constitutional Assembly of 1814 — A12

1914, May 10 **Engr.** *Perf. 13½*

96 A12 5o green 1.00 42
97 A12 10o car rose 2.00 42
98 A12 20o deep blue 8.50 3.50

Centenary of Norway's Constitution of May 17, 1814.

No. 87 Surcharged **5 ØRE**

1922, Mar. 1 *Perf. 14½x13½*

99 A10 5o on 25o red lilac 35 35

Lion Rampant A13

Polar Bear and Airplane A14

"NORGE" in Roman capitals, Line below "Ore"

1922-24 **Typo.** *Perf. 14½x13½*

100 A13 10o dp grn ('24) 9.00 28
101 A13 20o dp vio 15.00 15
102 A13 25o scarlet ('24) 25.00 60
103 A13 45o blue ('24) 1.00 55

For surcharge see No. 129.

1925, Apr. 1

104 A14 2o yel brn 2.00 2.00
105 A14 3o orange 2.50 2.50
106 A14 5o magenta 5.00 5.00
107 A14 10o yel grn 6.50 6.50
108 A14 15o dark blue 6.50 6.50
109 A14 20o plum 12.00 12.00
110 A14 25o scarlet 1.75 1.75
Nos. 104-110 (7) 36.25 36.25
Set, never hinged 75.00

Issued to help finance Roald Amundsen's attempted flight to the North Pole.

A15

A16

1925, Aug. 19

111 A15 10o yel grn 4.00 4.00
112 A15 15o indigo 3.50 3.50
113 A15 20o plum 4.00 1.00
114 A15 45o dark blue 4.00 4.00
Set, never hinged 47.50

Annexation of Spitsbergen (Svalbard).

For surcharge see No. 130.

"NORGE" in Sans-serif Capitals, No Line below "Ore"

1926-34 **Wmk. 160**

Size: 16x19½mm

115 A16 10o yel grn 70 15
116 A16 14o dp org ('29) 1.50 1.50
117 A16 15o olive gray 70 15
118 A16 20o plum 20.00 15
119 A16 20o scar ('27) 70 15
a. Booklet pane of 6 80.00
120 A16 25o red 9.00 1.75
121 A16 25o org brn ('27) 1.00 16
122 A16 30o dull bl ('28) 1.00 16
123 A16 35o ol brn ('27) 50.00 16
124 A16 35o red vio ('34) 1.90 16
125 A16 40o dull blue 2.75 90
126 A16 40o slate ('27) 1.90 16
127 A16 50o claret ('27) 1.90 16
128 A16 60o Prus bl ('27) 1.90 16
Nos. 115-128 (14) 94.95 5.87
Set, never hinged 275.00

See Nos. 167-176, 192, 194-202A. For overprints and surcharges see Nos. 131, 212-219, 225, 227-234, 237-238, 302-303.

Nos. 103 and 114 Surcharged **30**

1927, June 13

129 A13 30o on 45o blue 11.00 95
130 A15 30o on 45o dk blue 2.50 2.50
Set, never hinged 35.00

No. 120 Surcharged **20**

1928

131 A16 20o on 25o red 1.50 95
Never hinged 5.75

See Nos. 302-303.

Henrik Ibsen — A17

Niels Henrik Abel — A18

1928, Mar. 20 **Litho.**

No.	Type	Description	Unused	Used
132	A17	10o yel grn	5.00	1.50
133	A17	15o chnt brn	2.50	1.75
134	A17	20o carmine	2.75	45
135	A17	30o dp ultra	3.25	2.75
		Set, never hinged	35.00	

Ibsen (1828-1906), dramatist.

Postage Due Stamps of 1889-1923 Overprinted

Post Frimerke — a

POST — b

1929, Jan.

No.	Type	Description	Unused	Used
136	D1 (a)	1o gray	38	30
137	D1 (a)	4o lilac rose	38	30
138	D1 (a)	10o green	1.50	1.50
139	D1 (b)	15o brown	2.00	2.00
140	D1 (b)	20o dull vio	1.10	50
141	D1 (b)	40o deep ultra	1.90	50
142	D1 (b)	50o maroon	6.50	6.25
143	D1 (a)	100o org yel	3.00	1.50
144	D1 (b)	200o dk vio	4.75	3.00
		Nos. 136-144 (9)	21.51	15.85
		Set, never hinged	40.00	

1929, Apr. 6 **Litho.** ***Perf. 14½x13½***

No.	Type	Description	Unused	Used
145	A18	10o green	1.75	70
146	A18	15o red brn	2.25	1.65
147	A18	20o rose red	1.40	35
148	A18	30o deep ultra	2.25	1.75
		Set, never hinged	14.00	

Abel (1802-1829), mathematician.

No. 12 Surcharged

Perf. 14½x13½

1929, July 1 **Unwmk.**

No.	Type	Description	Unused	Used
149	A4	14o on 2s orange	2.25	2.25
		Never hinged	4.00	

Saint Olaf A19

Trondheim Cathedral A20

Death of Olaf in Battle of Stiklestad A21

Typo.; Litho. (15o)
Perf. 14½x13½

1930, Apr. 1 **Wmk. 160**

No.	Type	Description	Unused	Used
150	A19	10o yel grn	7.50	35
151	A20	15o brn & blk	1.00	45
152	A19	20o scarlet	1.40	30

Engr.
Perf. 13½

No.	Type	Description	Unused	Used
153	A21	30o deep blue	3.00	3.00
		Set, never hinged	27.50	

King Olaf Haraldsson (995-1030), patron saint of Norway.

Björnson A22

Holberg A23

1932, Dec. 8 ***Perf. 14½x13½***

No.	Type	Description	Unused	Used
154	A22	10o yel grn	8.25	40
155	A22	15o blk brn	1.25	90
156	A22	20o rose red	1.10	30
157	A22	30o ultra	2.00	2.25
		Set, never hinged	27.50	

Björnstjerne Björnson (1832-1910), novelist, poet and dramatist.

1934, Nov. 23

No.	Type	Description	Unused	Used
158	A23	10o yel grn	1.25	35
159	A23	15o brown	60	60
160	A23	20o rose red	11.00	24
161	A23	30o ultra	2.50	2.25
		Set, never hinged	37.50	

Ludvig Holberg (1684-1754), Danish man of letters.

Types of 1893-1900, 1926-34
Second Redrawing
Perf. 13x13½

1937 **Wmk. 160** **Photo.**
Size: 17x21mm

No.	Type	Description	Unused	Used
162	A10	1o olive	70	50
163	A10	2o yel brn	70	50
164	A10	3o deep org	1.75	1.40
165	A10	5o rose lilac	55	15
a.		Booklet pane of 6	55.00	
166	A10	7o brt grn	70	20
167	A16	10o brt grn	45	15
a.		Booklet pane of 6	50.00	
168	A16	14o dp org	1.90	1.65
169	A16	15o olive bis	1.10	15
170	A16	20o scarlet	1.10	15
a.		Booklet pane of 6	50.00	
171	A16	25o dk org brn	5.50	25
172	A16	30o ultra	2.50	25
173	A16	35o brt vio	2.50	25
174	A16	40o dk slate grn	3.00	25
175	A16	50o deep claret	3.50	40
176	A16	60o Prussian bl	1.50	20
		Nos. 162-176 (15)	27.45	6.45
		Set, never hinged	55.00	

Nos. 162 to 166 have a solid background inside oval. Nos. 74, 75, 76, 78, 79 have background of vertical lines.

King Haakon VII — A24

1937-38

No.	Type	Description	Unused	Used
177	A24	1k dark green	15	18
178	A24	1.50k sapphire ('38)	65	70
179	A24	2k rose red ('38)	65	70
180	A24	5k dl vio ('38)	5.00	5.75
		Set, never hinged	11.00	

Nos. 177-180, 267, B19, B32-B34 and B38-B41 were demonetized from May 15, 1945 until Sept. 1, 1981. Used values are for stamps canceled after this period. Stamps with dated cancellations prior to May 15, 1945 sell for more. False cancellations exist.

Reindeer — A25

Borgund Church — A26

Jolster in Sunnfiord A27

Perf. 13x13½, 13½x13

1938, Apr. 20 **Wmk. 160**

No.	Type	Description	Unused	Used
181	A25	15o olive brn	60	42
182	A26	20o copper red	4.00	55
183	A27	30o brt ultra	3.75	1.65
		Set, never hinged	13.00	

1939 **Unwmk.**

No.	Type	Description	Unused	Used
184	A25	15o olive brn	38	22
185	A26	20o copper red	52	20
186	A27	30o brt ultra	52	28
		Set, never hinged	2.50	

Types of 1937
Perf. 13x13½

1940-49 **Unwmk.** **Photo.**
Size: 17x21mm

No.	Type	Description	Unused	Used
187	A10	1o ol grn ('41)	16	15
188	A10	2o yel brn ('41)	16	15
189	A10	3o dp org ('41)	16	15
190	A10	5o rose lil ('41)	32	15
a.		Booklet pane of 6, vert.	20.00	
b.		Booklet pane of 10, horiz.	8.00	
191	A10	7o brt grn ('41)	40	15
192	A16	10o brt grn	32	15
a.		Booklet pane of 6, vert.	24.00	
b.		Booklet pane of 10, horiz.	20.00	
193	A10	12o brt vio	80	1.10
194	A16	14o dp org ('41)	1.00	2.00
195	A16	15o olive bister	48	15
a.		Booklet pane of 10	40.00	
196	A16	20o red	45	15
a.		Booklet pane of 6, vert.	24.00	
b.		Booklet pane of 10, horiz.	25.00	
197	A16	25o dk org brn	1.25	15
197A	A16	25o scarlet ('46)	40	15
b.		Booklet pane of 10	24.00	
198	A16	30o brt ultra ('41)	1.25	20
198A	A16	30o gray ('49)	5.75	15
199	A16	35o brt vio ('41)	1.50	15
200	A16	40o dk sl grn ('41)	1.00	15
200A	A16	40o dp ultra ('46)	1.50	15
201	A16	50o dp claret ('41)	1.00	15
201A	A16	55o dp org ('46)	15.00	15
202	A16	60o Prus bl ('41)	1.00	15
202A	A16	80o dk org brn ('46)	12.50	15
		Nos. 187-202A (21)	46.40	
		Set value		4.90
		Set, never hinged	95.00	

Lion Rampant
A28 A29

1940 **Unwmk.** **Photo.** ***Perf. 13x13½***

No.	Type	Description	Unused	Used
203	A28	1k brt grn	80	15
204	A28	1½k dp blue	1.10	30
205	A28	2k brt red	1.25	90
206	A28	5k dull pur	3.00	2.50
		Set, never hinged	12.00	

For overprints see Nos. 235-236.

Stamps of 1937-41, Types A10, A16, A28, Overprinted "V" in Black

1941 **Wmk. 160** ***Perf. 13x13½***

No.	Type	Description	Unused	Used
207	A10	1o olive	40	*2.75*
208	A10	2o yel brn	40	*2.75*
209	A10	3o orange	2.00	*6.00*
210	A10	5o rose lil	50	*1.40*
211	A10	7o brt grn	50	*2.75*
212	A16	10o brt grn	7.50	*26.00*
213	A16	14o dp org	1.00	*6.00*
214	A16	15o olive bis	30	*95*
215	A16	30o ultra	1.00	*1.50*
216	A16	35o brt vio	75	70
217	A16	40o dk sl grn	7.50	*10.00*
218	A16	50o dp claret	200.00	*375.00*
		Never hinged	340.00	
219	A16	60o Prus bl	75	*95*
		Nos. 207-217,219 (12)	22.60	*61.75*
		Set, #207-217, 219, never hinged	35.00	

Unwmk.

No.	Type	Description	Unused	Used
220	A10	1o olive	35	*1.25*
221	A10	2o yel brn	35	*1.25*
222	A10	3o deep org	35	*1.25*
223	A10	5o rose lil	35	30
224	A10	7o brt grn	95	*3.25*
225	A16	10o brt grn	35	15
226	A10	12o brt vio	1.10	*6.50*
227	A16	15o ol bis	1.90	*8.75*
228	A16	20o red	35	15
a.		Inverted overprint	750.00	1,050.
a.		Never hinged	900.00	
229	A16	25o dk org brn	42	32
230	A16	30o brt ultra	70	*65*
231	A16	35o brt vio	70	50
232	A16	40o dk sl grn	70	50
233	A16	50o dp claret	80	*1.25*
234	A16	60o Prus bl	1.90	75
235	A28	1k brt grn	1.25	50
236	A28	1½k dp blue	3.75	*9.00*
237	A16	2k brt red	10.50	*30.00*
238	A16	5k dl pur	19.00	*50.00*

Coil Stamp

239 A29 10o brt grn	1.25	*7.00*
Nos. 220-239 (20)	47.02	*123.32*
Set, never hinged	72.50	

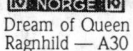

Dream of Queen Ragnhild — A30

Snorri Sturluson — A32

Einar Tambarskjelve in Fight at Svolder — A31

Designs: 30o, King Olaf sailing in wedding procession to Landmerket. 50o, Sypidag's sons and followers going to Hall of Seven Kings. 60o, Before Battle of Stiklestad.

1941 ***Perf. 13½x13, 13x13½***

240 A30 10o bright grn	35	20
241 A31 15o olive brn	38	55
242 A32 20o dark red	35	15
243 A31 30o blue	1.00	1.40
244 A31 50o dull violet	1.10	1.40
245 A31 60o Prussian bl	1.10	1.40
Nos. 240-245 (6)	4.28	5.10
Set, never hinged	6.50	

700th anniversary of the death of Snorri Sturluson, writer and historian.

University of Oslo — A36

1941, Sept. 2 ***Perf. 13x13½***

246 A36 1k dk ol grn	32.50	40.00
Never hinged	42.50	

Centenary of cornerstone laying of University of Oslo building.

Richard (Rikard) Nordraak (1842-66), Composer — A37

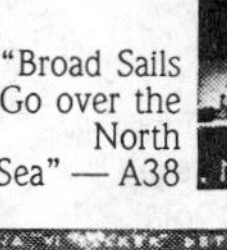

"Broad Sails Go over the North Sea" — A38

View of Coast and Lines of National Anthem A39

1942, June 12 ***Perf. 13***

247 A37 10o dp grn	1.25	1.25
248 A38 15o dp brn	1.25	1.25
249 A37 20o rose red	1.25	1.25
250 A39 30o sapphire	1.25	1.25
Set, never hinged	8.00	

Johan Herman Wessel (1742-1785), Author — A40

1942, Oct. 6

251 A40 15o dl brn	20	20
252 A40 20o henna	20	20
Set, never hinged	90	

Designs of 1942 and 1855 Stamps of Norway A41

1942, Oct. 12

253 A41 20o henna	25	55
254 A41 30o sapphire	35	1.10
Set, never hinged	90	

To commemorate the European Postal Congress at Vienna, October, 1942.

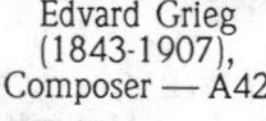

Edvard Grieg (1843-1907), Composer — A42

Destroyer Sleipner — A43

1943, June 15

255 A42 10o dp grn	25	25
256 A42 20o henna	25	25
257 A42 40o grnsh blk	25	25
258 A42 60o dk grnsh bl	25	25
Set, never hinged	1.50	

1943-45 Unwmk. Engr. ***Perf. 12½***

Designs: 5o, 10o, "Sleipner." 7o, 30o, Convoy under midnight sun. 15o, Plane and pilot. 20o, "We will win." 40o, Ski troops. 60o, King Haakon VII.

259 A43 5o rose vio ('45)	16	15
260 A43 7o grnsh blk ('45)	20	20
261 A43 10o dk bl grn	15	15
262 A43 15o dk ol grn	52	45
263 A43 20o rose red	15	15
264 A43 30o dp ultra	65	75
265 A43 40o olive black	55	55
266 A43 60o dark blue	55	55
Nos. 259-266 (8)	2.93	2.95
Set, never hinged	4.75	

Nos. 261-266 were used for correspondence carried on Norwegian ships until after the liberation of Norway, when they became regular postage stamps.

Nos. 261-266 exist with overprint "London 17-5-43" and serial number. Value for set, unused, $1,000; canceled $1,200.

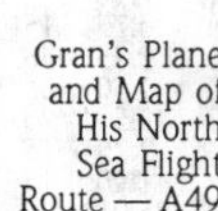

Gran's Plane and Map of His North Sea Flight Route — A49

1944, July 30 ***Perf. 13***

267 A49 40o dk grnsh bl	40	40
Never hinged	60	

20th anniv. of the 1st flight over the North Sea, made by Tryggve Gran on July 30, 1914.

For used value see note following No. 180.

New National Arms of 1943 — A50

1945, Feb. 15 Typo. ***Perf. 13***

268 A50 1½k dark blue	85	40
Never hinged	1.50	

Henrik Wergeland A51

Lion Rampant A52

1945, July 12 **Photo.**

269 A51 10o dk olive grn	30	30
270 A51 15o dark brown	85	1.00
271 A51 20o dark red	25	30
Set, never hinged	2.00	

Henrik Wergeland, poet and playwright, death cent.

1945, Dec. 19

272 A52 10o dk ol grn	35	30
273 A52 20o red	35	30
Set, never hinged	1.00	

Founding of the Norwegian Folklore Museum, 50th anniv.

Pilot and Mechanic — A53

King Haakon VII — A54

1946, Mar. 22 Engr. ***Perf. 12***

274 A53 15o brown rose	40	75
Never hinged	60	

Issued in honor of Little Norway, training center in Canada for Norwegian pilots.

> **Catalogue values for unused stamps in this section, from this point to the end of the section, are for Never Hinged items.**

1946, June 7 Photo. ***Perf. 13***

275 A54 1k bright grn	1.65	15
276 A54 1½k Prussian bl	4.75	15
277 A54 2k henna brn	35.00	15
278 A54 5k violet	21.00	40
Set value		60

Hannibal Sehested — A55

Designs: 10o, Letter carrier, 1700. 15o, Adm. Peter W. Tordenskjold. 25o, Christian Magnus Falsen. 30o, Cleng Peerson and "Restaurationen." 40o, Post ship "Constitution." 45o, First Norwegian locomotive. 50o, Sven Foyn and whaler. 55o, Fridtjof Nansen and Roald Amundsen. 60o, Coronation of King Haakon VII and Queen Maud, 1906. 80o, Return of King Haakon, June 7, 1945.

1947, Apr. 15 Photo. ***Perf. 13***

279 A55 5o red lilac	15	15
280 A55 10o green	65	15
281 A55 15o brown	65	15
282 A55 25o orange red	65	15
283 A55 30o gray	1.00	15
284 A55 40o blue	1.10	15
285 A55 45o violet	2.25	48
286 A55 50o orange brn	2.75	15
287 A55 55o orange	6.00	24
288 A55 60o slate gray	4.00	75
289 A55 80o dk brown	3.00	24
Nos. 279-289 (11)	22.20	
Set value		2.30

Establishment of the Norwegian Post Office, 300th anniv.

Petter Dass — A66

King Haakon VII — A67

1947, July 1 **Unwmk.**

290 A66 25o brt red	90	55

300th birth anniv. of Petter Dass, poet.

1947, Aug. 2

291 A67 25o org red	90	55

75th birthday of King Haakon.

Axel Heiberg — A68

Alexander L. Kielland — A69

1948, June 15

292 A68 25o dp carmine	1.10	32
293 A68 80o dp red brn	2.25	30

50th anniv. of the Norwegian Society of Forestry; birth cent. of Axel Heiberg, its founder.

1949, May 9

295 A69 25o rose brn	1.65	20
296 A69 40o greenish blue	1.65	50
297 A69 80o org brn	2.00	65

Birth cent. of Alexander L. Kielland, author.

Symbols of UPU Members — A70

Stylized Pigeons and Globe — A71

Symbolical of the UPU — A72

1949, Oct. 9 ***Perf. 13***

299 A70 10o dk grn & blk	75	60
300 A71 25o scarlet	52	25
301 A72 40o dull blue	55	52

75th anniv. of the formation of the UPU.

Nos. 196 and 200A Surcharged with New Value and Bar in Black

1949 ***Perf. 13x13½***

302 A16 25o on 20o red	45	15
303 A16 45o on 40o dp ultra	2.00	28
Set value		36

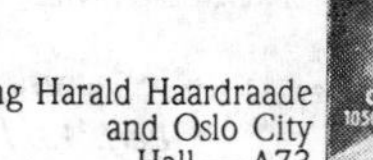

King Harald Haardraade and Oslo City Hall — A73

1950, May 15 Photo. *Perf. 13*

304 A73 15o green 90 1.00
305 A73 25o red 55 35
306 A73 45o ultramarine 90 75

900th anniversary of Oslo.

Redrawn Post Horn Type of 1937

1950-51 Photo. *Perf. 13x13½*
Size: 17x21mm

307 A10 10o grnsh gray 50 15
a. Booklet pane of 10 6.00
308 A10 15o dark green 2.00 40
a. Booklet pane of 10 22.50
309 A10 20o chnt brn ('51) 5.00 2.25

King Haakon VII — A74

Arne Garborg — A75

1950-51 Photo. *Perf. 13x13½*

310 A74 25o dk red ('50) 90 15
a. Booklet pane of 10 40.00
311 A74 30o gray 9.00 60
312 A74 35o red brn 19.00 15
313 A74 45o brt blue 1.75 85
314 A74 50o olive brn 1.75 15
315 A74 55o orange 1.75 85
316 A74 60o gray blue 10.00 15
317 A74 80o chnt brn 2.75 30
Nos. 310-317 (8) 46.90 3.20

See Nos. 322-324, 345-352. For surcharge see No. 321.

1951, Jan. 25 *Perf. 13*

318 A75 25o red 65 22
319 A75 45o dull blue 2.25 1.50
320 A75 80o brown 3.50 1.25

Birth cent. of Arne Garborg, poet.

No. 310 Surcharged with New Value in Black

1951 *Perf. 13x13½*

321 A74 30o on 25o dk red 60 15

Haakon Type of 1950-51

1951-52 Photo.

322 A74 25o gray 22.50 15
323 A74 30o dk red ('52) 90 15
a. Booklet pane of 10 35.00
324 A74 55o blue ('52) 1.75 40
Set value 52

Redrawn Post Horn Type of 1937

1952, June 3 *Perf. 13x13½*

325 A10 15o org brn 70 15
a. Booklet pane of 10 12.00
326 A10 20o green 70 15
Set value 15

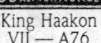

King Haakon VII — A76

Medieval Sculpture, Nidaros Cathedral — A77

1952, Aug. 3 Unwmk. *Perf. 13*

327 A76 30o red 50 15
328 A76 55o deep blue 1.10 1.00

80th birthday of King Haakon VII.

No. 308 Surcharged with New Value

1952, Nov. 18 *Perf. 13x13½*

329 A10 20o on 15o dk grn 60 15

1953, July 15 *Perf. 13*

330 A77 30o henna brn 60 40

800th anniv. of the creation of the Norwegian Archbishopric of Nidaros.

Train of 1854 and Horse-drawn Sled — A78

Carsten T. Nielsen — A79

Designs: 30o, Diesel train. 55o, Engineer.

1954, Apr. 30 Photo.

331 A78 20o green 85 30
332 A78 30o red 85 18
333 A78 55o ultra 2.00 1.25

Inauguration of the first Norwegian railway, cent.

1954, Dec. 10

Designs: 30o, Government radio towers. 55o, Lineman and telegraph poles in snow.

334 A79 20o ol grn & blk 40 20
335 A79 30o brt red 40 15
336 A79 55o blue 1.50 85

Centenary (in 1955) of the inauguration of the first Norwegian public telegraph line.

Norway No. 1 — A80

Stamp Reproductions: 30o, Post horn type A5. 55o, Lion type A13.

1955, Jan. 3 *Perf. 13*

337 A80 20o dp grn & gray bl 48 28
338 A80 30o red & carmine 18 15
339 A80 55o gray bl & dp bl 95 55

Centenary of Norway's first postage stamp.

Nos. 337-339 Overprinted in Black OSLO NORWEX

1955, June 4

340 A80 20o dp grn & gray bl 12.00 10.00
341 A80 30o red & carmine 12.00 10.00
342 A80 55o gray bl & dp bl 12.00 10.00

Norway Philatelic Exhibition, Oslo, 1955. Sold at exhibition post office for face value plus 1kr admission fee.

King Haakon VII and Queen Maud in Coronation Robes — A81

1955, Nov. 25 Photo. *Perf. 13*

343 A81 30o rose red 40 20
344 A81 55o ultra 60 48

Haakon's 50th anniv. as King of Norway.

Haakon Type of 1950-51

1955-57 Unwmk. *Perf. 13x13½*

345 A74 25o dk grn ('56) 1.10 15
346 A74 35o brn red ('56) 4.50 15
a. Booklet pane of 10 62.50
347 A74 40o pale pur 1.90 15
a. Booklet pane of 10 60.00
348 A74 50o bister ('57) 1.50 15
349 A74 65o ultra ('56) 1.65 40
350 A74 70o brn ol ('56) 11.00 15
351 A74 75o mar ('57) 2.25 15
352 A74 90o dp org 1.65 15
Nos. 345-352 (8) 25.55
Set value 1.00

Northern Countries Issue

Whooper Swans — A81a

1956, Oct. 30 Engr. *Perf. 12½*

353 A81a 35o rose red 95 60
354 A81a 65o ultra 95 85

Issued to emphasize the close bonds connecting the northern countries: Denmark, Finland, Iceland, Norway and Sweden.

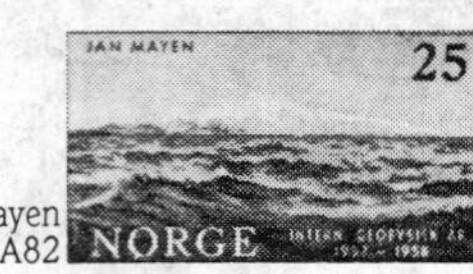

Jan Mayen Island — A82

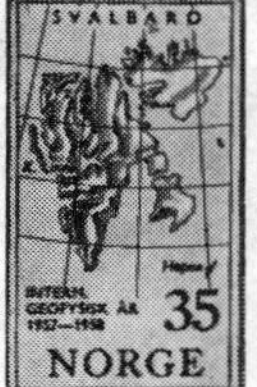

Map of Spitsbergen A83

King Haakon VII A84

Design: 65o, Map of South Pole with Queen Maud Land.

Perf. 12½x13, 13x12½

1957, July 1 Photo. Unwmk.

355 A82 25o slate grn 65 40
356 A83 35o dk red & gray 65 15
357 A83 65o dk grn & bl 65 50

Intl. Geophysical Year, 1957-58.

1957, Aug. 2 *Perf. 13*

358 A84 35o dk red 35 20
359 A84 65o ultra 85 85

85th birthday of King Haakon VII.

King Olav V
A85 A86

1958-60 Photo. *Perf. 13x13½*

360 A85 25o emerald 85 15
a. Booklet pane of 4 150.00
361 A85 30o pur ('59) 1.65 15
361A A85 35o brn car ('60) 1.25 15
362 A85 40o dk red 1.25 15
a. Booklet pane of 10 85.00
363 A85 45o scarlet 1.90 15
a. Booklet pane of 10 55.00
364 A85 50o bis ('59) 6.75 15
365 A85 55o dk gray ('59) 2.25 48
366 A85 65o blue 2.50 35
367 A85 80o org brn ('60) 12.50 20
368 A85 85o ol brn ('59) 2.25 15
369 A85 90o org ('59) 1.90 15
Nos. 360-369 (11) 35.05
Set value 1.55

See Nos. 408-412.

1959, Jan. 12

370 A86 1k green 1.10 15
371 A86 1.50k dark blue 3.50 15
372 A86 2k crimson 3.50 15
373 A86 5k lilac 50.00 15
374 A86 10k dp org 5.00 25
Nos. 370-374 (5) 63.10
Set value 60

See Phosphorescence note following No. 430.

Asbjörn Kloster — A87

Agricultural Society Medal — A88

1959, Feb. 2

375 A87 45o vio brn 70 25

Centenary of the founding of the Norwegian Temperance Movement; Asbjörn Kloster, its founder.

1959, May 26

376 A88 45o red & ocher 80 25
377 A88 90o blue & gray 2.25 1.65

150th anniversary of the Royal Agricultural Society of Norway.

Sower — A89

Society Seal — A90

Design: 90o, Grain, vert.

1959, Oct. 1 Photo. *Perf. 13*

378 A89 45o ocher & blk 80 25
379 A89 90o bl & blk 1.25 1.25

Agricultural College of Norway, cent.

1960, Feb. 26 Unwmk.

380 A90 45o carmine 75 25
381 A90 90o dk blue 2.00 1.40

Bicentenary of the Royal Norwegian Society of Sciences, Trondheim.

Viking Ship — A91

Designs: 25o, Caravel and fish. 45o, Sailing ship and nautical knot. 55o, Freighter and oil derricks. 90o, Passenger ship and Statue of Liberty.

1960, Aug. 27 *Perf. 12½x13*

382 A91 20o gray & blk 1.10 65
383 A91 25o yel grn & blk 1.50 1.00
384 A91 45o ver & blk 1.10 18
385 A91 55o ocher & blk 3.50 2.75
386 A91 90o Prus bl & blk 1.50 1.25
Nos. 382-386 (5) 8.70 5.83

Norwegian shipping industry.

Europa Issue, 1960
Common Design Type

1960, Sept. 19 *Perf. 13*
Size: 27x21mm

387 CD3 90o blue 75 75

The only foreign revenue stamps listed in this Catalogue are those authorized for prepayment of postage.

DC-8 Airliner — A91a

Javelin Thrower — A92

1961, Feb. 24 Photo. Perf. 13

388 A91a 90o dk bl 1.00 60

10th anniv. of the Scandinavian Airlines System, SAS.

Common Design Types pictured in section at front of book.

1961, Mar. 15

389 A92 20o shown 80 48
390 A92 25o Skater 80 48
391 A92 45o Ski jumper 80 15
392 A92 90o Sailboat 1.40 1.40

Norwegian Sports Federation centenary.

Haakonshallen A93

1961, May 25 Perf. 12½x13

393 A93 45o maroon & gray 70 22
394 A93 1k gray green & gray 1.10 24

700th anniv. of Haakonshallen, castle in Bergen.

Domus Media, Oslo University A94

1961, Sept. 2 Photo. Perf. 12½x13

395 A94 45o dk red 60 22
396 A94 1.50k Prus bl 1.25 24

150th anniversary of Oslo University.

Fridtjof Nansen — A95

1961, Oct. 10 Perf. 13

397 A95 45o org red & gray 50 20
398 A95 90o chlky bl & gray 1.10 85

Birth centenary of Fridtjof Nansen, explorer.

Roald Amundsen A96

Design: 90o, Explorers and tent at Pole.

1961, Nov. 10 Unwmk. Perf. 13

399 A96 45o dl red brn & gray 90 20
400 A96 90o dk & lt bl 1.40 70

50th anniversary of Roald Amundsen's arrival at the South Pole.

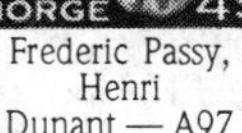

Frederic Passy, Henri Dunant — A97

Vilhelm Bjerknes — A98

1961, Dec. 9 Photo.

401 A97 45o henna brn 45 20
402 A97 1k yel grn 1.25 30

Winners of the first Nobel Peace prize. Frederic Passy, a founder of the Interparliamentary Union, and Henri Dunant, founder of the International Red Cross.

1962, Mar. 14 Perf. 13

403 A98 45o dk red & gray 35 24
404 A98 1.50k dk bl & gray 90 35

Vilhelm Bjerknes (1862-1951), physicist, mathematician, meteorologist, etc.

German Rumpler Taube over Oslo Fjord — A99

1962, June 1 Photo.

405 A99 1.50k dl bl & blk 1.90 70

50th anniversary of Norwegian aviation.

Fir Branch and Cone — A100

1962, June 15

406 A100 45o sal & blk 75 40
407 A100 1k pale grn & blk 6.75 28

Olav Type of 1958-60

1962 Unwmk. Perf. 13x13½

408 A85 25o slate grn 1.25 15
a. Booklet pane of 4 150.00
b. Booklet pane of 10 30.00
409 A85 35o emerald 4.25 15
410 A85 40o gray 4.25 75
411 A85 50o scarlet 9.50 15
a. Booklet pane of 10 125.00
412 A85 60o violet 4.75 42
Nos. 408-412 (5) 24.00
Set value 1.35

Europa Issue, 1962
Common Design Type

1962, Sept. 17 Photo. Perf. 13
Size: 37x21mm

414 CD5 50o dp rose & mar 42 28
415 CD5 90o bl & dk bl 1.40 1.00

Post Horn Type of 1893-1908 Redrawn and

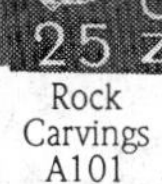

Rock Carvings A101

Boatswain's Knot A102

Designs: 30o, 55o, 85o, Rye and fish. 65o, 80o, Stave church and northern lights.

1962-63 Engr. Perf. 13x13½

416 A10 5o rose cl 15 15
a. Booklet pane of 4, vert. 1.65
b. Booklet pane of 10, horiz. 8.00
417 A10 10o slate 15 15
a. Booklet pane of 10 20.00
418 A10 15o org brn 15 15
419 A10 20o green 15 15
a. Booklet pane of 4 8.00
420 A101 25o gray grn ('63) 1.10 15
a. Booklet pane of 4 16.00
b. Booklet pane of 10 20.00
421 A101 30o ol brn ('63) 4.00 2.75
422 A102 35o brt grn ('63) 32 15
423 A101 40o lake ('63) 3.00 15
424 A102 50o vermilion 4.75 15
a. Booklet pane of 10 65.00
425 A101 55o org brn ('63) 50 45
426 A102 60o dk grnsh gray ('63) 8.50 15
427 A102 65o dk bl ('63) 3.50 15
a. Booklet pane of 10 62.50
428 A102 80o rose lake ('63) 7.25 2.00
429 A101 85o sepia ('63) 50 22
430 A101 90o blue ('63) 32 15
Nos. 416-430 (15) 34.34
Set value 6.00

Nos. 416-419 have been redrawn and are similar to 1910-29 issue, with vertical lines inside oval and horizontal lines in oval frame. See Nos. 462-470, 608-615.

Phosphorescence
Nos. 370-372, 416-419, 423, 425, 428, 430, 462, 466, O65-O68, O75, O78-O82, O83-O84 and O88 have been issued on both ordinary and phosphorescent paper.
Nos. 463-465, 467-468, 510 to last number assigned, O86 and O89-O93 have been issued only on phosphorescent paper.

Camilla Collett (1813-1895), Author — A103

1963, Jan. 23 Photo. Perf. 13

431 A103 50o red brn & tan 38 20
432 A103 90o slate & gray 1.50 1.10

Girl in Boat Loaded with Grain — A104

Still Life — A105

1963, Mar. 21 Unwmk. Perf. 13

433 A104 25o yel brn 35 25
434 A104 35o dk grn 60 45
435 A105 50o dk red 50 35
436 A105 90o dk bl 1.50 1.10

FAO "Freedom from Hunger" campaign.

River Boat — A106

Design: 90o, Northern sailboat.

1963, May 20 Unwmk. Perf. 13

437 A106 50o brn red 1.50 48
438 A106 90o blue 2.25 1.50

Tercentenary of regular postal service between Northern and Southern Norway.

Ivar Aasen — A107

1963, Aug. 5 Photo.

439 A107 50o dk red & gray 60 28
440 A107 90o dk bl & gray 1.25 75

150th birth anniv. of Ivar Aasen, poet and philologist.

Europa Issue, 1963
Common Design Type

1963, Sept. 14 Unwmk. Perf. 13
Size: 27x21½mm

441 CD6 50o dl rose & org 75 42
442 CD6 90o bl & yel grn 2.50 1.50

Patterned Fabric A108

1963, Sept. 24

443 A108 25o ol & ol grn 60 40
444 A108 35o Prus bl & dk bl 85 70
445 A108 50o dk car rose & plum 60 40

Norwegian textile industry, 150th anniv.

"Loneliness" — A109

Eilert Sundt — A110

Paintings by Edvard Munch (1863-1944): 25o, Self-portrait, vert. 35o, "Fertility." 90o, "Girls on Bridge," vert.

1963, Dec. 12 Litho. Perf. 13

446 A109 25o black 35 22
447 A109 35o dk grn 45 35
448 A109 50o dp claret 42 32
449 A109 90o gray bl & dk bl 1.25 1.00

1964, Feb. 17 Photo.

Design: 50o, Beehive, Workers' Society emblem.

450 A110 25o dk grn 40 45
451 A110 50o dk red brn 38 24

Centenary of the Oslo Workers' Society.

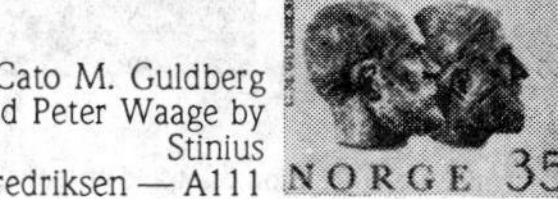

Cato M. Guldberg and Peter Waage by Stinius Fredriksen — A111

1964, Mar. 11 Unwmk. Perf. 13

452 A111 35o ol grn 90 45
453 A111 55o bister 2.00 1.75

Centenary of the presentation of the Law of Mass Action (chemistry) by Professors Cato M. Guldberg and Peter Waage in the Oslo Scientific Society.

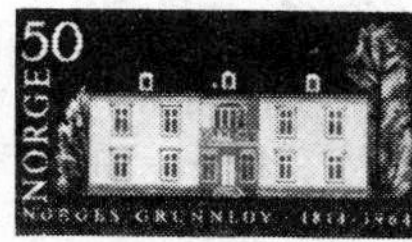

Eidsvoll Building A112

Design: 90o, Storting (Parliament House).

1964, May 11 Photo.

454 A112 50o hn brn & blk 45 30
455 A112 90o Prus bl & dk bl 1.25 1.10

150th anniv. of Norway's constitution.

Church and Ships in Harbor A113

1964, Aug. 17 Perf. 13

456 A113 25o dk sl grn & buff 48 40
457 A113 90o dk bl & gray 2.00 1.65

Centenary of the Norwegian Seamen's Mission, which operates 32 stations around the world.

Europa Issue, 1964
Common Design Type

1964, Sept. 14 Photo. *Perf. 13*
458 CD7 90o dark blue 2.00 1.25

Herman Anker and Olaus Arvesen A114

1964, Oct. 31 Litho. Unwmk.
459 A114 50o rose 65 30
460 A114 90o blue 2.75 1.90

Centenary of the founding of Norwegian schools of higher education (Folk High Schools).

Types of Regular Issue, 1962-63

Designs: 30o, 45o, Rye and fish. 40o, 100o, Rock carvings. 50o, 60o, 65o, 70o, Boatswain's knot.

Two types of 60o:
I - Four twists across bottom of knot.
II - Five twists.

1964-70 Engr. *Perf. 13x13½*
462 A101 30o dl grn 80 15
463 A101 40o lt bl grn ('68) 52 15
464 A101 45o lt yel grn ('68) 1.10 75
465 A102 50o indigo ('68) 52 15
466 A102 60o brick red, II ('75) 2.50 30
a. Booklet pane of 10 45.00
b. Type I 2.75 30
467 A102 65o lake ('68) 65 15
a. Booklet pane of 10 35.00
468 A102 70o brn ('70) 52 15
a. Booklet pane of 10 20.00
469 A101 100o vio bl ('70) 1.10 15
Nos. 462-469 (8) 7.71
Set value 1.60

See Phosphorescence note following #430.

Coil Stamp

1965 *Perf. 13½ Horiz.*
470 A101 30p dull grn 4.25 1.25

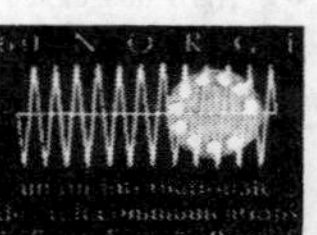

Telephone Dial and Waves — A115

Design: 90o, Television mast and antenna.

1965, Apr. 1 Engr. *Perf. 13*
471 A115 60o redsh brn 38 15
472 A115 90o slate 1.65 1.50

ITU, centenary.

Mountain Scene A116

Design: 90o, Coastal view.

1965, June 4 Unwmk. *Perf. 13*
473 A116 60o brn blk & car 52 35
474 A116 90o slate bl & car 3.75 3.25

Centenary of the Norwegian Red Cross.

Europa Issue, 1965
Common Design Type

1965, Sept. 25 Photo. *Perf. 13*
Size: 27x21mm
475 CD8 60o brick red 50 24
476 CD8 90o blue 1.50 1.40

St. Sunniva and Buildings of Bergen — A117

Rondane Mountains by Harold Sohlberg — A118

Design: 90o, St. Sunniva and stylized view of Bergen, horiz.

1965, Oct. 25 *Perf. 13*
477 A117 30o dk grn & blk 55 30
478 A117 90o bl & blk 1.65 1.25

Issued to commemorate the bicentenary of Bergen's philharmonic society "Harmonien."

1965, Nov. 29 Photo. *Perf. 13*
484 A118 1.50k dk bl 1.75 18

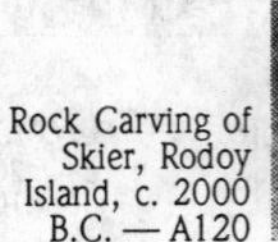

Rock Carving of Skier, Rodoy Island, c. 2000 B.C. — A120

Designs: 55o, Ski jumper. 60o, Cross country skier. 90o, Holmenkollen ski jump, vert.

1966, Feb. 8 Engr. *Perf. 13*
486 A120 40o sepia 75 70
487 A120 55o dl grn 1.50 1.40
488 A120 60o dl red 60 20
489 A120 90o blue 1.50 1.40

World Ski Championships, Oslo, Feb. 17-27.

Open Bible and Chrismon — A121

1966, May 20 Photo. *Perf. 13*
490 A121 60o dull red 40 15
491 A121 90o slate blue 1.40 1.00

150th anniv. of the Norwegian Bible Society.

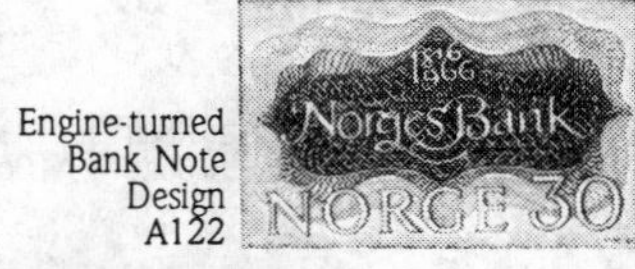

Engine-turned Bank Note Design A122

Bank of Norway — A123

1966, June 14 Engr.
492 A122 30o green 55 32
493 A123 60o dk car rose 55 15

150th anniversary of Bank of Norway.

Johan Sverdrup A124

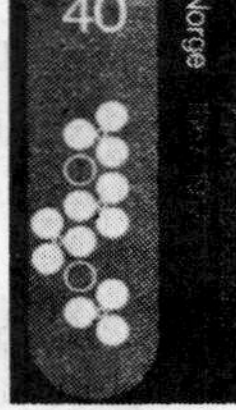

Nitrogen Molecule in Test Tube A125

1966, July 30 Photo. *Perf. 13*
494 A124 30o green 48 25
495 A124 60o rose lake 48 15
Set value 32

Johan Sverdrup (1816-92), Prime Minister of Norway (1884-89).

Canceled to Order
The Norwegian philatelic agency began in 1966 to sell commemorative and definitive issues canceled to order at face value.

Europa Issue, 1966
Common Design Type

1966, Sept. 26 Engr. *Perf. 13*
Size: 21x27mm
496 CD9 60o dark carmine 60 25
497 CD9 90o blue gray 1.75 1.25

1966, Oct. 29 Photo. *Perf. 13x12½*

Design: 55o, Wheat and laboratory bottle.

498 A125 40o bl & dp bl 1.25 95
499 A125 55o red, org & lil rose 2.25 1.65

Centenary of the birth of Kristian Birkeland (1867-1917), and of Sam Eyde (1866-1940), who together developed the production of nitrates.

EFTA Emblem — A126

1967, Jan. 16 Engr. *Perf. 13*
500 A126 60o rose red 52 18
501 A126 90o dark blue 2.25 1.65

European Free Trade Association. Tariffs were abolished Dec. 31, 1966, among EFTA members: Austria, Denmark, Finland, Great Britain, Norway, Portugal, Sweden, Switzerland.

Sabers, Owl and Oak Leaves — A127

1967, Feb. 16 Engr. *Perf. 13*
502 A127 60o chocolate 1.00 35
503 A127 90o black 3.00 2.00

150th anniversary of higher military training in Norway.

Europa Issue, 1967
Common Design Type

1967, May 2 Photo. *Perf. 13*
Size: 21x27mm
504 CD10 60o mag & plum 55 20
505 CD10 90o bl & dk vio bl 1.50 1.25

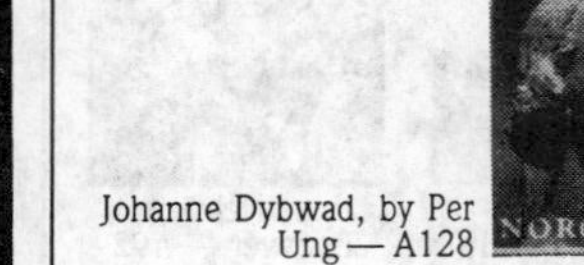

Johanne Dybwad, by Per Ung — A128

1967, Aug. 2 Photo. *Perf. 13*
506 A128 40o slate blue 52 45
507 A128 60o dk car rose 52 15

Johanne Dybwad (1867-1950), actress.

Missionary L.O. Skrefsrud A129

Ebenezer Church, Benagaria, Santal A130

1967, Sept. 26 Engr. *Perf. 13*
508 A129 60o red brown 55 15
509 A130 90o blue gray 1.25 1.10

Norwegian Santal (India) mission, cent.

Mountaineers A131

Designs: 60o, Mountain view. 90o, Glitretind mountain peak.

1968, Jan. 22 Engr. *Perf. 13*
510 A131 40o sepia 95 60
511 A131 60o brown red 52 20
512 A131 90o slate blue 1.25 1.10

Centenary of the Norwegian Mountain Touring Association.

Two Smiths A132

1968, Mar. 30 Photo. *Perf. 12½x13*
513 A132 65o dk car rose & brn 45 20
514 A132 90o bl & brn 1.10 1.10

Issued to honor Norwegian craftsmen.

A. O. Vinje — A133

Cross and Heart — A134

1968, May 21 Engr. *Perf. 13*
515 A133 50o sepia 55 35
516 A133 65o maroon 50 25

Aasmund Olafsson Vinje (1818-1870), poet, journalist and language reformer.

1968, Sept. 16 Photo.
517 A134 40o brt grn & brn red 3.25 1.25
518 A134 65o brn red & vio bl 45 25

Centenary of the Norwegian Lutheran Home Mission Society.

Cathinka Guldberg — A135

1968, Oct. 31 Engr. *Perf. 13*

519 A135 50o brt bl 50 35
520 A135 65o dl red 50 20

Nursing profession; centenary of Deaconess House in Oslo. Cathinka Guldberg was a pioneer of Norwegian nursing and the first deaconess.

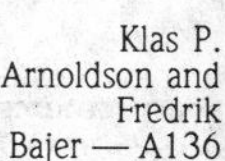

Klas P. Arnoldson and Fredrik Bajer — A136

1968, Dec. 10 Engr. *Perf. 13*

521 A136 65o red brn 42 28
522 A136 90o dk bl 1.00 80

60th anniv. of the awarding of the Nobel Peace prize to Klas P. Arnoldson (1844-1916), Swedish writer and statesman, and to Fredrik Bajer (1837-1922), Danish writer and statesman.

Nordic Cooperation Issue

Five Ancient Ships — A136a

1969, Feb. 28 Engr. *Perf. 13*

523 A136a 65o red 35 28
524 A136a 90o blue 1.25 1.00

Nordic Society's 50th anniversary and centenary of postal cooperation among the northern countries: Denmark, Finland, Iceland, Norway and Sweden.

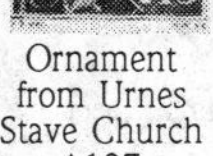

Ornament from Urnes Stave Church A137

Traena Island A138

1969 Engr. *Perf. 13*

526 A137 1.15k sepia 1.25 50
529 A138 3.50k bluish blk 1.00 20

Issue dates: 1.15k, Jan. 23, 3.50k, June 18.

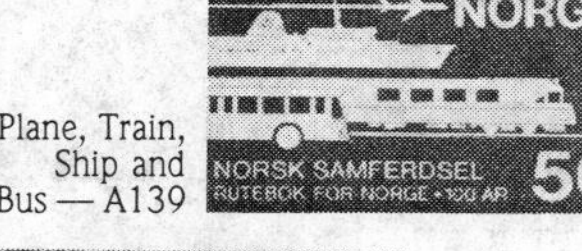

Plane, Train, Ship and Bus — A139

Child Crossing Street A140

1969, Mar. 24 Photo. *Perf. 13*

531 A139 50o green 60 30
532 A140 65o sl grn & dk red 42 25

No. 531 for the centenary of the publication of "Rutebok of Norway" (Communications of Norway); No. 532 publicizes traffic safety.

Europa Issue, 1969
Common Design Type

1969, Apr. 28

Size: 37x21mm

533 CD12 65o dk red & gray 65 25
534 CD12 90o chlky bl & gray 1.50 85

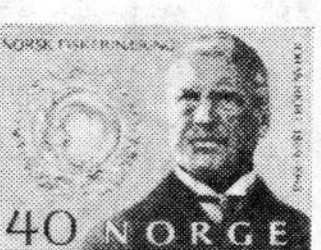

Johan Hjort — A141

King Olav V — A142

Design: 90o, different emblem.

1969, May 30 Engr. *Perf. 13*

535 A141 40o brn & bl 90 60
536 A141 90o bl & grn 1.50 1.50

Hjort (1869-1948), zoologist and oceanographer.

1969-83 Engr. *Perf. 13*

537 A142 1k lt ol grn ('70) 85 15
538 A142 1.50k dk bl ('70) 85 15
539 A142 2k dk red ('70) 85 15
540 A142 5k vio bl ('70) 1.75 15
541 A142 10k org brn ('70) 3.50 15
542 A142 20k brown 7.25 35
543 A142 50k dk ol grn ('83) 14.00 3.00
Nos. 537-543 (7) 29.05 4.10

Man, Woman and Child, by Vigeland A143

Design: 65o, Mother and Child, by Gustav Vigeland.

1969, Sept. 8 Photo. *Perf. 13*

545 A143 65o car rose & blk 45 35
546 A143 90o bl & blk 1.10 90

Gustav Vigeland (1869-1943), sculptor.

People A144

1969, Oct. 10

547 A144 65o Punched card 42 35
548 A144 90o shown 1.10 90

1st Norwegian census, 200th anniv.

Queen Maud — A145

Pulsatilla Vernalis — A146

1969, Nov. 26 Engr. *Perf. 13*

549 A145 65o dk car 45 25
550 A145 90o vio bl 1.10 90

Queen Maud (1869-1938), wife of King Haakon VII.

1970, Apr. 10 Photo. *Perf. 13*

European Nature Conservation Year: 40o, Wolf. 70o, Voringsfossen (waterfall). 100o, White-tailed sea eagle, horiz.

551 A146 40o sep & pale bl 1.25 60
552 A146 60o lt brn & gray 1.40 1.10
553 A146 70o pale bl & brn 1.40 48
554 A146 100o pale bl & brn 1.40 1.10

"V" for Victory A147

"Citizens" A148

Design: 100o, Convoy, horiz.

Perf. 13x12½, 12½x13

1970, May 8 Photo.

555 A147 70o red & lil 1.75 45
556 A147 100o vio bl & brt grn 1.75 1.25

Norway's liberation from the Germans, 25th anniv.

1970, June 23 Engr. *Perf. 13*

Designs: 70o, "The City and the Mountains." 100o, "Ships."

557 A148 40o green 1.25 65
558 A148 70o rose claret 2.50 35
559 A148 100o violet blue 1.90 1.75

City of Bergen, 900th anniversary.

Olive Wreath and Hands Upholding Globe A149

Georg Ossian Sars (1837-1927) A150

1970, Sept. 15 Engr. *Perf. 13*

560 A149 70o dk car rose 2.75 50
561 A149 100o steel blue 1.75 1.25

25th anniversary of the United Nations.

1970, Oct. 15 Engr. *Perf. 13*

Portraits: 50o, Hans Strom (1726-1797). 70o, Johan Ernst Gunnerus (1718-1773). 100o, Michael Sars (1805-1869).

562 A150 40o brown 90 90
563 A150 50o dl pur 1.10 65
564 A150 70o brn red 1.10 40
565 A150 100o brt bl 1.10 1.10

Issued to honor Norwegian zoologists.

Leapfrog — A151

1970, Nov. 17 Photo. *Perf. 13*

566 A151 50o Ball game 55 40
567 A151 70o shown 80 20

Central School of Gymnastics, Oslo, cent.

Seal of Tonsberg A152

1971, Jan. 20 Photo. *Perf. 13*

568 A152 70o dk red 48 35
569 A152 100o bl blk 95 65

City of Tonsberg, 1,100th anniversary.

Parliament A153

1971, Feb. 23

570 A153 70o red brn & lil 48 35
571 A153 100o dk bl & sl grn 95 65

Centenary of annual sessions of Norwegian Parliament.

Hand, Heart and Eye — A154

1971, Mar. 26 Photo. *Perf. 13*

572 A154 50o emer & blk 55 45
573 A154 70o scarlet & blk 55 30

Joint northern campaign for the benefit of refugees.

"Haugianerne" by Adolph Tiedemand — A155

1971, Apr. 27 Photo. *Perf. 13*

574 A155 60o dk gray 45 25
575 A155 70o brown 45 25

Hans Nielsen Hauge (1771-1824), church reformer.

Worshippers Coming to Church A156

Design: 70o, Building first church, vert.

1971, May 21

576 A156 70o blk & dk red 48 32
577 A156 1k blk & bl 1.90 1.25

900th anniversary of the Bishopric of Oslo.

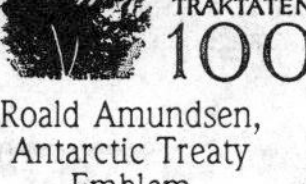

Roald Amundsen, Antarctic Treaty Emblem A157

The Farmer and the Woman A158

1971, June 23 Engr. *Perf. 13*

578 A157 100o bl & org red 3.00 2.50

Antarctic Treaty pledging peaceful uses of and scientific cooperation in Antarctica, 10th anniv.

1971, Nov. 17 Photo. *Perf. 13*

Designs: 50o, The Preacher and the King, vert. 70o, The Troll and the Girl. Illustrations for legends and folk tales by Erik Werenskiold.

579 A158 40o olive & blk 42 25
580 A158 50o blue & blk 42 25
581 A158 70o magenta & blk 85 25

Engine Turning A159

1972, Apr. 10 Photo. *Perf. 13*

582 A159 80o red & gold 80 35
583 A159 1.20k ultra & gold 80 75

Norwegian Savings Bank sesquicentennial.

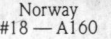

Norway #18 — A160

Dragon's Head, Oseberg Viking Ship — A161

1972, May 6 Engr. & Photo. *Perf. 12*

584 A160 80o shown 48 35
585 A160 1k Norway #17 70 50
a. Souvenir sheet of 2, #584-585 4.75 5.50

Centenary of the post horn stamps. No. 585a sold for 2.50k.

1972, June 7 Engr. *Perf. 13*

Ancient Artifacts: 50o, Horseman from Stone of Alstad. 60o, Horseman, wood carving, stave church, Hemsedal. 1.20k, Sword hilt, found at Lodingen.

586 A161 50o yel grn 60 55
587 A161 60o brown 1.10 1.00
588 A161 80o dl red 1.25 45
589 A161 1.20k ultra 1.10 1.00

1,100th anniversary of unification.

King Haakon VII (1872-1957) A162

"Joy" A163

1972, Aug. 3 Engr. *Perf. 13*

590 A162 80o brown org 90 35
591 A162 1.20k Prussian bl 80 70

1972, Aug. 15 Photo. *Perf. 13x13¹/₂*

Design: 1.20k, "Solidarity."

592 A163 80o brt mag 70 30
593 A163 1.20k Prussian bl 80 70

2nd Intl. Youth Stamp Exhib., INTERJUNEX 72, Kristiansand, Aug. 25-Sept. 3.

Same Overprinted "INTERJUNEX 72"

1972, Aug. 25

594 A163 80o brt mag 3.00 2.50
595 A163 1.20k Prussian bl 3.00 2.50

Opening of INTERJUNEX 72. Sold at exhibition only together with 3k entrance ticket.

"Maud" A164

"Little Man" A165

Polar Exploration Ships: 80o, "Fram." 1.20k, "Gjoa."

1972, Sept. 20 *Perf. 13¹/₂x13*

596 A164 60o ol & grn 1.25 70
597 A164 80o red & blk 1.75 35
598 A164 1.20k bl & red brn 1.75 1.50

1972, Nov. 15 Litho. *Perf. 13¹/₂x13*

Illustrations for folk tales by Theodor Kittelsen (1857-1914): 60o, The Troll who wondered how old he was. 80o, The princess riding the polar bear.

599 A165 50o green & blk 45 20
600 A165 60o blue & blk 45 35
601 A165 80o pink & blk 45 20

Dr. Armauer G. Hansen and Leprosy Bacillus Drawing — A166

Design: 1.40k, Dr. Hansen and leprosy bacillus, microscopic view.

1973, Feb. 28 Engr. *Perf. 13x13¹/₂*

602 A166 1k henna brn & bl 52 35
603 A166 1.40k dk bl & dp org 1.10 1.00

Centenary of the discovery of the Hansen bacillus, the cause of leprosy.

Europa Issue 1973

Common Design Type

1973, Apr. 30 Photo. *Perf. 12¹/₂x13*

Size: 37x20mm

604 CD16 1k red, org & lil 1.65 35
605 CD16 1.40k dk grn, grn & bl 1.10 75

Types of 1893 and 1962-63

Designs: 75o, 85o, Rye and fish. 80o, 140o, Stave church. 100o, 110o, 120o, 125o, Rock carvings.

1972-75 Engr. *Perf. 13x13¹/₂*

606 A10 25o ultra ('74) 15 15
a. Booklet pane of 4 3.00
608 A101 75o green ('73) 45 15
609 A102 80o red brn 75 15
a. Booklet pane of 10 35.00
610 A101 85o bister ('74) 60 25
611 A101 100o red ('73) 1.10 15
a. Booklet pane of 10 15.00
612 A101 110o rose car ('74) 75 15
613 A101 120o gray blue 85 50
614 A101 125o red ('75) 85 15
a. Booklet pane of 10 12.00
615 A102 140o dk bl ('73) 95 40
Nos. 606-615 (9) 6.45
Set value 1.55

Nordic Cooperation Issue

Nordic House, Reykjavik A167

1973, June 26 Engr. *Perf. 12¹/₂*

617 A167 1k multi 1.25 40
618 A167 1.40k multi 65 60

A century of postal cooperation among Denmark, Finland, Iceland, Norway and Sweden; Nordic Postal Conference, Reykjavik, Iceland.

King Olav V — A168

Jacob Aall — A169

1973, July 2 Engr. *Perf. 13*

619 A168 1k car & org brn 65 22
620 A168 1.40k bl & org brn 70 65

70th birthday of King Olav V.

1973, Aug. 22 Engr. *Perf. 13*

621 A169 1k dp claret 65 20
622 A169 1.40k dk bl gray 1.00 65

Jacob Aall (1773-1844), mill owner and industrial pioneer.

Blade Decoration A170

Viola Biflora A171

Handicraft from Lapland: 1k, Textile pattern. 1.40k, Decoration made of tin.

1973, Oct. 9 Photo. *Perf. 13x12¹/₂*

623 A170 75o blk brn & buff 40 40
624 A170 1k dp car & buff 65 30
625 A170 1.40k blk & dl bl 80 50

1973, Nov. 15 Litho. *Perf. 13*

626 A171 65o shown 48 18
627 A171 70o Speedwell 55 40
628 A171 1k Mountain heath 70 25

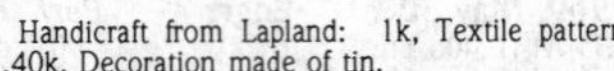

Surveyor in Northern Norway, 1907 — A172

Design: 1.40k, Map of South Norway Mountains, 1851.

1973, Dec. 14 Engr. *Perf. 13*

629 A172 1k red org 48 48
630 A172 1.40k slate blue 70 70

Geographical Survey of Norway, bicent.

Lindesnes — A173

Design: 1.40k, North Cape.

1974, Apr. 25 Photo. *Perf. 13*

631 A173 1k olive 80 50
632 A173 1.40k dark blue 1.50 1.50

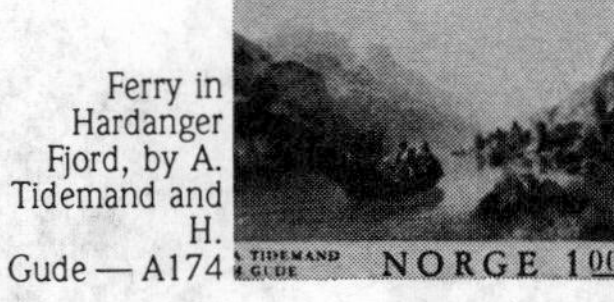

Ferry in Hardanger Fjord, by A. Tidemand and H. Gude — A174

Classical Norwegian paintings: 1.40k, Stugunoset from Filefjell, by Johan Christian Dahl.

1974, May 21 Litho. *Perf. 13*

633 A174 1k multi 60 20
634 A174 1.40k multi 80 60

Gulating Law Manuscript, 1325 A175

King Magnus VI Lagaböter A176

1974, June 21 Engr.

635 A175 1k red & brn 55 20
636 A176 1.40k ultra & brn 95 75

700th anniv. of the National Code given by King Magnus VI Lagaböter (1238-80).

Saw Blade and Pines — A177

J.H.L. Vogt — A178

Design: 1k, Cog wheel and guard.

1974, Aug. 12 Photo. *Perf. 13*

637 A177 85o grn, ol & dk grn 1.65 1.65
638 A177 1k org, plum & dk red 1.40 60

Safe working conditions.

1974, Sept. 4 Engr. *Perf. 13*

Geologists: 85o, V. M. Goldschmidt. 1k, Theodor Kjerulf. 1.40k, Waldemar C. Brogger.

639 A178 65o ol & red brn 30 20
640 A178 85o mag & red brn 90 75
641 A178 1k org & red brn 45 25
642 A178 1.40k bl & red brn 75 60

"Man's Work," Famous Buildings A179

Design: 1.40k, "Men, our brethren," people of various races.

1974, Oct. 9 Photo. *Perf. 13*

643 A179 1k grn & brn 52 20
644 A179 1.40k brn & grnsh bl 70 60

Centenary of Universal Postal Union.

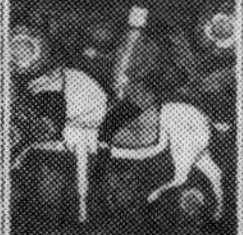

Horseback Rider A180

Flowers A181

1974, Nov. 15 Litho. *Perf. 13*

645 A180 85o multi 42 35
646 A181 1k multi 50 20

Norwegian folk art, rose paintings from furniture decorations.

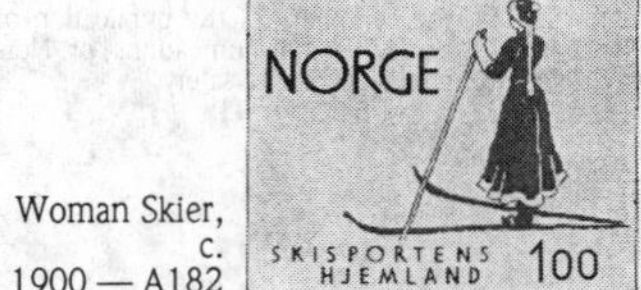

Woman Skier, c. 1900 — A182

1975, Jan. 15 Litho. *Perf. 13*

647 A182 1k shown 90 20
648 A182 1.40k Telemark turn 90 70

"Norway, homeland of skiing."

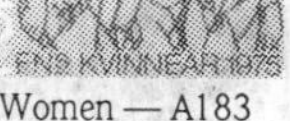

Women — A183

Nusfjord Fishing Harbor — A184

Design: Detail from wrought iron gates of Vigeland Park, Oslo.

1975, Mar. 7 Litho. *Perf. 13*

649 A183 1.25k brt rose lil & dk bl 65 25
650 A183 1.40k bl & dk bl 65 65

International Women's Year.

1975, Apr. 17 Litho. *Perf. 13*

Designs: 1.25k, Street in Stavanger. 1.40k, View of Roros.

651 A184 1k yel grn 85 40
652 A184 1.25k dl red 60 15
653 A184 1.40k blue 70 60

European Architectural Heritage Year.

Norwegian Krone, 1875 — A185

Ole Jacob Broch — A186

1975, May 20 Engr. *Perf. 13*

654 A185 1.25k dark car 48 70
655 A186 1.40k blue 70 60

Centenary of Monetary Convention of Norway, Sweden and Denmark (1.25k); and of Intl. Meter Convention, Paris, 1875. Ole Jacob Broch (1818-1889) was first director of Intl. Bureau of Weights and Measures.

Scouting in Summer A187

Design: 1.40k, Scouting in winter (skiers).

1975, June 19 Litho. *Perf. 13*

656 A187 1.25k multi 75 35
657 A187 1.40k multi 75 75

Nordjamb 75, 14th Boy Scout Jamboree, Lillehammer, July 29-Aug. 7.

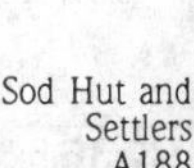

Sod Hut and Settlers A188

Cleng Peerson and Letter from America, 1874 A189

1975, July 4

658 A188 1.25k red brn 1.00 15
659 A189 1.40k bluish blk 70 65

Sesquicentennial of Norwegian emigration to America.

Templet, Tempelfjord, Spitsbergen — A190

Miners Leaving Coal Pit — A191

Design: 1.40k, Polar bear.

1975, Aug. 14 Engr. *Perf. 13*

660 A190 1k olive blk 80 50
661 A191 1.25k maroon 80 30
662 A191 1.40k Prus bl 2.25 1.75

50th anniversary of union of Spitsbergen (Svalbard) with Norway.

Microphone with Ear Phones — A192

Radio Tower and Houses — A193

Designs after children's drawings.

1975, Oct. 9 Litho. *Perf. 13*

663 A192 1.25k multi 40 35
664 A193 1.40k multi 60 50

50 years of broadcasting in Norway.

Annunciation A194

Nativity A195

Designs: 1k, Visitation. 1.40k, Adoration of the Kings. Designs are from painted vault of stave church of Al, 13th century.

1975, Nov. 14

665 A194 80o red & multi 30 20
666 A194 1k red & multi 42 20
667 A195 1.25k red & multi 42 20
668 A195 1.40k red & multi 70 45

Sigurd and Regin A196

Halling, Hallingdal Dance A197

1976, Jan. 20 Engr. *Perf. 13*

669 A196 7.50k brown 2.25 50

Norwegian folk tale, Sigurd the Dragon-killer. Design from portal of Hylestad stave church, 13th century.

1976, Feb. 25 Litho. *Perf. 13*

Folk Dances: 1k, Springar, Hordaland region. 1.25k, Gangar, Setesdal.

670 A197 80o blk & multi 45 30
671 A197 1k blk & multi 60 20
672 A197 1.25k blk & multi 60 15

Silver Sugar Shaker, Stavanger, c. 1770 — A198

Design: 1.40k, Goblet, Nostetangen glass, c. 1770.

1976, Mar. 25 Engr. *Perf. 13*

673 A198 1.25k multi 55 42
674 A198 1.40k multi 70 70

Oslo Museum of Applied Art, centenary.

Ceramic Bowl Shaped Like Bishop's Mitre A199

Europa: 1.40k, Plate and CEPT emblem. Both designs after faience works from Herrebo Potteries, c. 1760.

1976, May 3 Litho. *Perf. 13*

675 A199 1.25k rose mag & brn 80 60
676 A199 1.40k brt bl & vio bl 1.10 95

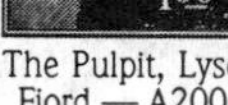

The Pulpit, Lyse Fjord — A200

Gulleplet (Peak), Sogne Fjord — A201

Perf. 13 on 3 Sides

1976, May 20 Litho.

677 A200 1k multi 80 40
  a. Booklet pane of 10 5.50
678 A201 1.25k multi 80 25
  a. Booklet pane of 10 8.00

Nos. 677-678 issued only in booklets.

Graph Paper, Old and New Subjects — A202

Design: 2k, Graph of national product.

1976, July 1 Engr. *Perf. 13*

679 A202 1.25k red brn 50 20
680 A202 2k dark blue 80 40

Central Bureau of Statistics, centenary.

Olav Duun on Dun Mountain A203

1976, Sept. 10 Engr. *Perf. 13*

681 A203 1.25k multi 65 20
682 A203 1.40k multi 70 60

Olav Duun (1876-1939), novelist.

"Birches" by Th. Fearnley (1802-1842) A204

Design: 1.40k, "Gamle Furutraer" (trees), by L. Hertervig (1830-1902).

1976, Oct. 8 Litho. *Perf. 13*

683 A204 1.25k multi 65 25
684 A204 1.40k multi 70 60

"April" — A205

"May" — A206

Baldishol Tapestry — A207

Design: 80o, 1k, Details from 13th century Baldishol tapestry, found in Baldishol stave church.

1976, Nov. 5 Litho. *Perf. 13*

685 A205 80o multi 45 25
686 A206 1k multi 45 25
687 A207 1.25k multi 60 25

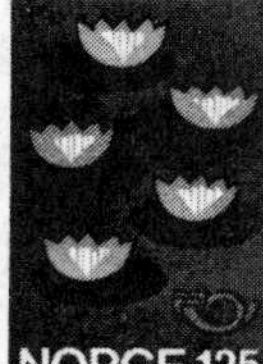

Five Water Lilies — A208

Photo. & Engr.

1977, Feb. 2 *Perf. 12½*

688 A208 1.25k multi 65 20
689 A208 1.40k multi 65 60

Nordic countries cooperation for protection of the environment and 25th Session of Nordic Council, Helsinki, Feb. 19.

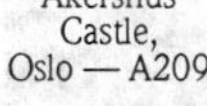

Akershus Castle, Oslo — A209

Steinviksholm Fort, Asen Fjord — A210

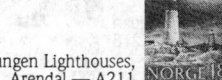

Torungen Lighthouses, Arendal — A211

1977, Feb. 24 Engr. *Perf. 13*

690 A209 1.25k red 45 15
691 A210 1.30k olive brn 50 15
692 A211 1.80k blue 65 20
Set value 35

See Nos. 715-724, 772-774.

Europa Issue

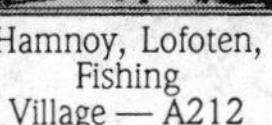

Hamnoy, Lofoten, Fishing Village — A212

Huldre Falls, Loen — A213

Perf. 13 on 3 Sides

1977, May 2 **Litho.**

693 A212 1.25k multi 70 15
a. Booklet pane of 10 8.00
694 A213 1.80k multi 1.00 60
a. Booklet pane of 10 6.00

Nos. 693-694 issued only in booklets.

Norwegian Trees — A214

1977, June 1 **Engr.** *Perf. 13*

695 A214 1k Spruce 38 25
696 A214 1.25k Fir 45 25
697 A214 1.80k Birch 65 60

"Constitutionen," Norway's 1st Steamship, at Arendal — A215

Designs: 1.25k, "Vesteraalen" off Bodo, 1893. 1.30k, "Kong Haakon," 1904 and "Dronningen," 1893, off Stavanger. 1.80k, "Nordstjernen" and "Harald Jarl" at pier, 1970.

1977, June 22

698 A215 1k brown 55 25
699 A215 1.25k red 65 25
700 A215 1.30k green 1.50 1.50
701 A215 1.80k blue 75 65

Norwegian ships serving coastal routes.

Fishermen and Boats — A216

Fish and Fishhooks — A217

1977, Sept. 22 **Engr.** *Perf. 13*

702 A216 1.25k buff, lt brn & dk brn 55 20
703 A217 1.80k lt bl, bl & dk bl 75 60

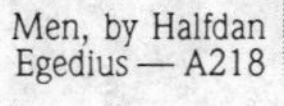

Men, by Halfdan Egedius — A218

Landscape, by August Cappelen A219

1977, Oct. 7 **Litho.** *Perf. 13*

704 A218 1.25k multi 55 20
705 A219 1.80k multi 75 60

Norwegian classical painting.

David with the Bells — A220

Christmas: 1k, Singing Friars. 1.25k, Virgin and Child, horiz. Designs from Bible of Bishop Aslak Bolt, 13th century.

1977, Nov. 10 **Litho.** *Perf. 13*

Size: 21x27mm

706 A220 80o multi 42 20
707 A220 1k multi 42 15

Size: 34x27mm

708 A220 1.25k multi 42 15

Post Horn Type of 1893 and Scenic Types of 1977

Designs: 1k, Austrat Manor, 1650. 1.10k, Trondenes Chruch, early 13th Century. 1.40k, Ruins of Hamar Cathedral, 12th Century. 1.75k, Seamen's Hall, Stavern, 1926, vert. 2k, Tofte Estate, Dovre, 16-17th cent., vert. 2.25k, Oscarhall, Oslofjord, 1847, vert. 2.50k, Log house, Breiland, 1785. 2.75k, Damsgard Building, Lakesvag, 1770. 3k, Selje Monastery, 11th cent. 3.50k, Lighthouse, Lindesnes, 1655.

1978 **Engr.** *Perf. 13x13½, 13½x13*

709 A10 40o olive 15 15
710 A10 50o dull pur 18 15
711 A10 60o vermilion 22 15
712 A10 70o orange 30 22
713 A10 80o red brn 28 15
714 A10 90o brown 35 22
715 A209 1k green 35 15
716 A209 1.10k rose mag 70 18
717 A209 1.40k dark pur 48 18
718 A211 1.75k green ('82) 55 18
719 A211 2k brn red ('82) 65 18
720 A211 2.25k dp vio ('82) 80 35
721 A209 2.50k brn red ('83) 80 18
722 A209 2.75k dp mag ('82) 1.00 65
723 A209 3k dk bl ('82) 90 35
724 A209 3.50k dp vio ('83) 1.10 45
Nos. 709-724 (16) 8.81
Set value 3.30

See Nos. 772-774.

Peer Gynt, and Reindeer by Per Krogh — A222

Henrik Ibsen, by Erik Werenskiold, 1895 — A223

1978, Mar. 10 **Litho.** *Perf. 13*

725 A222 1.25k buff & blk 60 28
726 A223 1.80k multi 70 70

Ibsen (1828-1906), poet and dramatist.

Heddal Stave Church, c. 1250 A224

Lenangstindene and Jaegervasstindene A225

Europa: 1.80k, Borgund stave church.

1978, May 2 **Engr.** *Perf. 13*

727 A224 1.25k dk brn & red 75 25
728 A224 1.80k sl grn & bl 95 70

Perf. 13 on 3 Sides

1978, June 1 **Litho.**

Design: 1.25k, Gaustatoppen, mountain, Telemark.

729 A225 1k multi 80 40
a. Booklet pane of 10 6.50
730 A225 1.25k multi 80 25
a. Booklet pane of 10 9.00

Nos. 729-730 issued only in booklets.

Olav V Sailing — A226

Design: 1.80k, King Olav delivering royal address in Parliament, vert.

1978, June 30 **Engr.** *Perf. 13*

731 A226 1.25k red brn 55 20
732 A226 1.80k vio bl 70 60

75th birthday of King Olav V.

Norway No. 107 — A227

Stamps: b, #108. c, #109. d, #110. e, #111. f, #112. g, #113. h, #114.

Perf. 13 on 3 Sides

1978, Sept. 19 **Litho.**

733 Booklet pane of 8 8.75 9.50
a.-h. A227 1.25k, any single 1.05 1.10

NORWEX '80 Philatelic Exhibition, Oslo, June 13-22, 1980. Booklet sold for 15k; the additional 5k went for financing the exhibition.

Willow Pipe Player — A228

Musical Instruments: 1.25k, Norwegian violin. 1.80k, Norwegian zither. 7.50k, Ram's horn.

1978, Oct. 6 **Engr.** *Perf. 13*

734 A228 1k deep grn 35 15
735 A228 1.25k dk rose car 55 15
736 A228 1.80k dk vio bl 60 30
737 A228 7.50k gray 2.25 30

Wooden Doll, 1830 — A229

Ski Jump, Huseby Hill, c. 1900 — A230

Christmas: 1k, Toy town 1896-97. 1.25k, Wooden horse from Torpo in Hallingdal.

1978, Nov. 10 **Litho.**

738 A229 80o multi 45 20
739 A229 1k multi 45 15
740 A229 1.25k multi 45 15

1979, Mar. 2 **Engr.** *Perf. 13*

Designs: 1.25k, Crown Prince Olav, Holmenkollen ski jump competition, 1922. 1.80k, Cross-country race, Holmenkollen, 1976.

741 A230 1k green 42 25
742 A230 1.25k red 52 25
743 A230 1.80k blue 70 60

Huseby Hills and Holmenkollen ski competitions, centenary.

Girl, by Mathias Stoltenberg A231

Road to Briksdal Glacier A232

Portrait: 1.80k, Boy, by H. C. F. Hosenfelder.

1979, Apr. 26 **Litho.** *Perf. 13*

744 A231 1.25k multi 52 25
745 A231 1.80k multi 70 60

International Year of the Child.

1979, June 13 *Perf. 13 on 3 Sides*

Design: 1.25k, Boat on Skjernoysund, near Mandal.

746 A232 1k multi 75 20
a. Booklet pane of 10 5.50
747 A232 1.25k multi 75 25
a. Booklet pane of 10 7.50

Nos. 746-747 issued only in booklets.

Johan Falkberget, by Harald Dal — A233

Kylling Bridge, Verma, 1923 — A234

Design: 1.80k, "Ann-Magritt and the Hovi Bullock" (by Falkberget), monument by Kristofer Leirdal.

1979, Sept. 4 **Engr.** *Perf. 13*

748 A233 1.25k dp claret 55 25
749 A233 1.80k Prussian bl 70 60

Johan Falkberget (1879-1967), novelist.

1979, Oct. 5

Norwegian Engineering: 2k, Vessingsjo Dam, Nea, 1960. 10k, Stratfjord A, oil drilling platform in North Sea.

750 A234 1.25k gray brn 65 15
751 A234 2k gray bl 1.00 25
752 A234 10k brn ol 3.25 65

Souvenir Sheet

Dornier Wal over Polar Map — A235

Arctic Aviation and Polar Maps: 2k, Dirigible Norge. 2.80k, Loening air yacht amphibian. 4k, Reidar Viking DC-7C.

1979, Oct. 5 Litho. *Perf. 13*

753 Sheet of 4 6.25 6.25
a. A235 1.25k multi 1.40 1.40
b. A235 2k multi 1.40 1.40
c. A235 2.80k multi 1.40 1.40
d. A235 4k multi 1.40 1.40

Norwex '80 Intl. Phil. Exhib., Oslo, June 13-22, 1980. No. 753 sold for 15k.

Buttercup — A236

Mountain Flowers: 1k, Cinquefoil. 1.25k, Twinleaf saxifrage.

1979, Nov. 22 Litho. *Perf. 13½*

754 A236 80o multi 35 15
755 A236 1k multi 55 25
756 A236 1.25k multi 55 15

See Nos. 770-771.

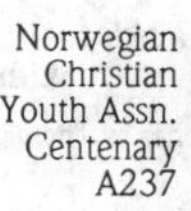

Norwegian Christian Youth Assn. Centenary A237

1980, Feb. 26 Litho. *Perf. 13*

757 A237 100o shown 40 15
758 A237 180o Emblems and doves 70 50

Oyster Catcher — A238

Perf. 13 on 3 Sides

1980, Apr. 18 Litho.

759 A238 100o shown 40 15
760 A238 100o Mallard 40 15
a. Bklt. pane of 10 (5 #759, 5 #760) 4.00
761 A238 125o Dipper 40 15
762 A238 125o Great tit 40 15
a. Bklt. pane of 10 (5 #761, 5 #762) 4.50
Set value 45

Nos. 759-762 issued in booklets only.

Dish Antenna, Old Phone — A239

National Telephone Service Centenary: 1.80k, Erecting telephone pole.

1980, May 9 Litho. *Perf. 13½*

763 A239 1.25k multi 48 25
764 A239 1.80k multi 70 52

Souvenir Sheet

Paddle Steamer "Bergen" A240

1980, June 13

765 Sheet of 4 6.00 6.00
a. A240 1.25k shown 1.40 1.40
b. A240 2k Train, 1900 1.40 1.40
c. A240 2.80k Bus, 1940 1.40 1.40
d. A240 4k Boeing 737 1.40 1.40

NORWEX '80 Stamp Exhibition, Oslo, June 13-22. Sold for 15k.

Nordic Cooperation Issue

Vulcan as an Armourer, by Henrich Bech, 1761 — A241

Henrich Bech Cast Iron Stove Ornament: 1.80k, Hercules at a Burning Altar, 1769.

1980, Sept. 9 Engr. *Perf. 13*

766 A241 1.25k dk vio brn 55 25
767 A241 1.80k dark blue 80 50

Self-Portrait, by Christian Skredsvig (1854-1924) A242

Paintings: 1.25k, Fire, by Nikolai Astrup.

1980, Nov. 14 Litho. *Perf. 13½x13*

768 A242 1.25k multi 50 25
769 A242 1.80k multi 75 50

Mountain Flower Type of 1979

1980, Nov. 14 *Perf. 13*

770 A236 80o Sorbus aucuparia 48 15
771 A236 1k Rosa canina 48 15
Set value 24

Scenic Type of 1977

Designs: 1.50k, Stavanger Cathedral, 13th cent. 1.70k, Rosenkrantz Tower, Bergen, 13th-16th cent. 2.20k, Church of Tromsdalen (Arctic Cathedral), 1965.

Perf. 13x13½, 13½x13

1981, Feb. 26 Engr.

772 A211 1.50k brn red 48 15
773 A211 1.70k ol grn 55 25
774 A209 2.20k dk blue 70 50

Lesser White-fronted Goose — A243

Nat'l Milk Producers Assn. Centenary — A244

Perf. 13 on 3 Sides

1981, Feb. 26 Litho.

775 A243 1.30k shown 35 20
776 A243 1.30k Peregrine falcon 35 20
a. Booklet pane of 10 (5 each) 3.50
777 A243 1.50k Black guillemot 42 18
778 A243 1.50k Puffin 42 18
a. Booklet pane of 10 (5 each) 4.25

Nos. 775-778 issued in booklets. See Nos. 800-801, 821-822.

1981, Mar. 24 Litho. *Perf. 13x13½*

779 A244 1.10k Cow 35 20
780 A244 1.50k Goat 65 15

A245

A246

Europa: 1.50k, The Mermaid, painted dish, Hol. 2.20k, The Proposal, painted box, Nes.

1981, May 4 Litho. *Perf. 13*

781 A245 1.50k multi 75 25
782 A245 2.20k multi 90 60

1981, May 4 Engr.

Designs: 1.30k, Weighing anchor. 1.50k, Climbing sail pole, vert. 2.20k, Training Ship Christian Radich.

783 A246 1.30k dk ol grn 48 25
784 A246 1.50k org red 65 25
785 A246 2.20k dark blue 70 60

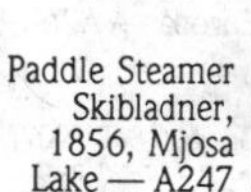

Paddle Steamer Skibladner, 1856, Mjosa Lake — A247

Lake Transportation: 1.30k, Victoria, 1882, Bandak Channel. 1.50k, Faemund II, 1905, Fermund Lake. 2.30k, Storegut, 1956, Tinnsjo Lake.

1981, June 11 Engr. *Perf. 13*

786 A247 1.10k dk brown 40 32
787 A247 1.30k green 48 25
788 A247 1.50k red 65 25
789 A247 2.30k dark blue 90 65

Group Walking Arm in Arm — A248

1981, Aug. 25 Engr.

790 A248 1.50k shown 50 25
791 A248 2.20k Group, diff. 75 60

Intl. Year of the Disabled.

A249

A250

Paintings: 1.50k, Interior in Blue, by Harriet Backer (1845-1932). 1.70k, Peat Moor on Jaeren, by Kitty Lange Kielland (1843-1914).

1981, Oct. 9 Litho. *Perf. 13*

792 A249 1.50k multi 48 25
793 A249 1.70k multi 65 40

1981, Nov. 25 Litho. *Perf. 13½*

Tapestries: 1.10k, One of the Three Kings, Skjak, 1625. 1.30k, Adoration of the Infant Christ, tapestry, Skjak, 1625. 1.50k, The Marriage of Cana, Storen, 18th cent.

794 A250 1.10k multi 40 15
795 A250 1.30k multi 40 15

Size: 29x37mm

796 A250 1.50k multi 55 15
Set value 36

1921 Nobel Prize Winners Christian L. Lange (1869-1938) and Hjalmar Branting (1860-1925) A251

1981, Nov. 25 Engr. *Perf. 13*

797 A251 5k black 1.75 40

World Skiing Championship, Oslo — A252

1982, Feb. 16 *Perf. 13½*

798 A252 2k Poles 65 25
799 A252 3k Skis 1.10 60

Bird Type of 1981

Perf. 13 on 3 Sides

1982, Apr. 1 Litho.

800 A243 2k Blue-throat 55 15
801 A243 2k Robin 55 15
a. Bklt. pane of 10 (5 each) 6.00

Nos. 800-801 issued only in booklets.

Fight Against Tuberculosis — A253

1982, Apr. 1 *Perf. 13*

802 A253 2k Nurse 70 20
803 A253 3k Microscope 1.10 60

Jew's Harp — A254

1982, May 3 Engr. *Perf. 13*

804 A254 15k sepia 4.00 65

Europa 1982 — A255

1982, May 3

805 A255 2k Haakon VII, 1905 85 25
806 A255 3k Prince Olav, King Haakon VII, 1945 1.40 60

Girls from Telemark, by Erik Werenskiold (1855-1938) A256

Design: 2k, Tone Veli at the Fence, by Henrik Sorensen (1882-1962), vert.

1982, June 23 Litho. *Perf. 13*

807 A256 1.75k multi 70 35
808 A256 2k multi 70 20

Consecration Ceremony, Nidaros Cathedral, Trondheim — A257

Sigrid Undset (1882-1949), Writer, by A.C. Svarstad — A258

1982, Sept. 2 Engr. *Perf. 13x13½*
809 A257 3k blue 1.10 55

Reign of King Olav, 25th anniv.

1982, Oct. 1 Litho. *Perf. 13*

Painting: 1.75k, Bjornstjerne Bjornson (1832-1910), writer, by Erik Werenskiold, horiz.

810 A258 1.75k multi 65 30
811 A258 2k multi 75 25

A souvenir sheet containing Nos. 810-811 was prepared by the Norwegian Philatelic Association.

Graphical Union of Norway Centenary A259

1982, Oct. 1
812 A259 2k "A" 65 15
813 A259 3k Type 1.00 42

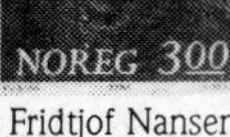

Fridtjof Nansen A260

Christmas A261

1982, Nov. 15 Engr. *Perf. 13½x13*
814 A260 3k dark blue 1.10 50

Fridtjof Nansen (1861-1930) polar explorer, 1922 Nobel Peace Prize winner.

Perf. 13 on 3 Sides
1982, Nov. 15 Litho.

Painting: Christmas Tradition, by Adolf Tidemand (1814-1876).

815 A261 1.75k multi 60 32
a. Booklet pane of 10 6.00

Farm Dog — A262

1983, Feb. 16 Litho. *Perf. 13x13½*
816 A262 2k shown 60 15
817 A262 2.50k Elk hound 80 15
818 A262 3.50k Hunting dog 1.10 50

Nordic Cooperation Issue — A263

1983, Mar. 24 Litho. *Perf. 13*
819 A263 2.50k Mountains 90 15
820 A263 3.50k Fjord 1.25 65

Bird Type of 1981

1983, Apr. 14 *Perf. 13 on 3 Sides*
821 A243 2.50k Goose 80 15
822 A243 2.50k Little auk 80 15
a. Bklt. pane of 10 (5 each) 8.00

Nos. 821-822 issued only in booklets.

Europa — A264

Designs: 2.50k, Edvard Grieg (1843-1907), composer and his Piano Concerto in A-minor. 3.50k, Niels Henrik Abel (1802-1829), mathematician, by Gustav Vigeland, vert.

1983, May 3 Engr. *Perf. 13*
823 A264 2.50k red org 1.10 15
824 A264 3.50k dk bl & grn 1.65 40

World Communications Year — A265

Symbolic arrow designs.

1983, May 3 Litho.
825 A265 2.50k multi 90 25
826 A265 3.50k multi 1.25 60

80th Birthday of King Olav V, July 2 — A266

1983, June 22 Engr. *Perf. 13x13½*
827 A266 5k green 1.65 40

Jonas Lie (1833-1908), Writer — A267

Northern Ships — A268

1983, Oct. 7 Engr. *Perf. 13½x13*
828 A267 2.50k red 90 15

1983, Oct. 7 Litho.
829 A268 2k Nordlandsfemboring 70 15
830 A268 3k Nordlandsjekt 1.10 50

Christmas 1983 — A269

Paintings: 2k, The Sleigh Ride by Axel Ender (1853-1920). 2.50k, The Guests are Arriving by Gustav Wenzel (1859-1927).

Perf. 13 on 3 sides
1983, Nov. 17 Litho.
831 A269 2k multi 60 15
a. Booklet pane of 10 6.00
832 A269 2.50k multi 90 15
a. Booklet pane of 10 9.00

Postal Services A270

1984, Feb. 24 Litho. *Perf. 13½x13*
833 A270 2k Counter service 70 20
834 A270 2.50k Sorting 85 15
835 A270 3.50k Delivery 1.10 45

Freshwater Fishing A271

Christopher Hansteen (1784-1873), Astronomer A272

1984, Apr. 10 Engr. *Perf. 13*
836 A271 2.50k shown 80 15
837 A271 3k Salmon fishing 1.00 45
838 A271 3.50k Ocean fishing 1.10 45

1984, Apr. 10
839 A272 3.50k Magnetic meridians, parallels, horiz. 1.10 45
840 A272 5k shown 1.50 45

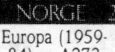

Europa (1959-84) — A273

Produce, Spices — A274

1984, June 4 Litho. *Perf. 13*
841 A273 2.50k multi 80 15
842 A273 3.50k multi 1.10 45

1984, June 4 *Perf. 13*
843 A274 2k shown 60 15
844 A274 2.50k Flowers 75 15
Set value 24

Horticultural Society centenary.

A275

A276

1984, June 4
845 A275 2.50k Worker bees 80 15
846 A275 2.50k Rooster 80 15
Set value 24

Centenaries: Beekeeping Society (No. 845); Poultry-breeding Society (No. 846).

1984, Oct. 5 Engr. *Perf. 13*
847 A276 2.50k lake 80 15

Ludvig Holberg (1684-1754), writer, by J.M. Bernigeroth.

A277

A278

1984, Oct. 5 Litho. & Engr.
848 A277 2.50k Children reading 70 15
849 A277 3.50k First edition 1.10 45

Norwegian Weekly Press sesquicentennial.

Perf. 13½x13 on 3 sides
1984, Nov. 15 Litho.

Illustrations from Children's Stories by Thorbjorn Egner.

850 A278 2k Karius & Baktus 60 15
851 A278 2k Tree Shrew 60 15
a. Bklt. pane of 10 (5 each #850-851) 6.00
852 A278 2.50k Cardamom Rovers 75 15
853 A278 2.50k Chief Constable Bastian 75 15
a. Bklt. pane of 10 (5 each #852-853) 7.50
Set value 48

Nos. 850-853 issued only in booklets.

Parliament Centenary A279

1984, Nov. 15 Engr. *Perf. 13½x13*
854 A279 7.50k Sverdrup Govt. parliament, 1884 2.25 80

Antarctic Mountains — A280

1985, Apr. 18 Litho. *Perf. 13*
855 A280 2.50k The Saw Blade 70 15
856 A280 3.50k The Chopping Block 1.10 45

Liberation from the German Occupation Forces, 40th Anniv. — A281

1985, May 8 Engr. *Perf. 13x13½*
857 A281 3.50k dk bl & red 1.00 45

Norwegian Artillery A282

Anniversaries: 3k, Norwegian Artillery, 300th. 4k, Artillery Officers Training School, 200th.

1985, May 22 Litho. *Perf. 13½x13*
858 A282 3k multi 80 55
859 A282 4k multi 1.10 70

Kongsten Fort, 300th Anniv. A283

1985, May 22
860 A283 2.50k multi 75 25

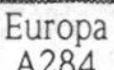

Europa A284 — Intl. Youth Year A285

Designs: 2.50k, Torgeir Augundsson (1801-1872), fiddler. 3.50k, Ole Bull (1810-1880), composer, violinist.

1985, June 19 **Engr.**
861 A284 2.50k brn lake 75 15
862 A284 3.50k dk bl 1.10 45

1985, June 19 **Litho.**

Stone and bronze sculptures: 2k, Boy and Girl, detail, Vigeland Museum, Oslo. 3.50k, Fountain, detail, Vigeland Park, Oslo.

863 A285 2k multi 60 25
864 A285 3.50k multi 1.10 70

Electrification of Norway, Cent. — A286

1985, Sept. 6 **Engr.** ***Perf. 13½x13***
865 A286 2.50k Glomfjord Dam penstock 75 20
866 A286 4k Linemen 1.25 70

Public Libraries, 200th Anniv. — A287

Designs; 2.50k, Carl Deichman (1705-1780), Public Libraries System founder. 10k, Modern library interior, horiz.

1985, Oct. 4
867 A287 2.50k hn brn & yel brn 65 20
868 A287 10k dk grn 2.50 1.00

Ship Navigation A288

Lithographed & Engraved

1985, Nov. 14 ***Perf. 13x13½***
869 A288 2.50k Dredger Berghavn, 1980 75 20
870 A288 5k Sextant and chart, 1791 1.50 70

Port Authorities 250th anniv., Hydrographic Services bicent.

Christmas Wreath A289 — Bullfinches A290

Booklet Stamps
Perf. 13½ on 3 Sides

1985, Nov. 14 **Litho.**
871 A289 2k multi 60 20
a. Booklet pane of 10 6.00
872 A290 2.50k multi 75 20
a. Booklet pane of 10 7.50

World Biathlon Championships, Feb. 18-23 — A290a

1986, Feb. 18 ***Perf. 13x13½***
873 A290a 2.50k shown 65 20
874 A291 3.50k Shooting upright 1.00 70

Ornaments A291 — Fauna A292

Mushrooms — A293

Perf. 13½x13

1986-90 **Litho. & Engr.**

No.	Type	Value	Design	Unused	Used
875	A291	2.10k	Sun	65	22
876	A291	2.30k	Fish	68	26
877	A292	2.60k	Fox	78	28
878	A291	2.70k	Flowers, wheat	78	28
879	A292	2.90k	Capercaillie	95	35
880	A292	3k	Ermine	90	35
881	A292	3.20k	Mute swan	1.00	38
882	A292	3.80k	Reindeer	1.20	45
883	A291	4k	Star	1.25	42
883A	A292	4k	Squirrel	1.20	45
883B	A292	4.50k	Beaver	1.40	55
			Nos. 875-883B (11)	10.79	3.99

Issue dates: 2.10k, No. 883, Feb. 18. 2.30k, 2.70k, Feb. 12, 1987. 2.90k, 3.80k, Feb. 18, 1988. 2.60k, 3k, No. 883A, Feb. 20, 1989. 3.20k, 4.50k, Feb. 23, 1990.

See Nos. 958-959.

Booklet Stamps
Perf. 13½x13 on 3 Sides

1987-89 **Litho.**
884 A293 2.70k Cantharellus tubaeformis 80 60
885 A293 2.70k Rozites caperata 80 60
a. Bklt. pane, 5 #884, 5 #885 8.00
886 A293 2.90k Lepista nuda 95 72
887 A293 2.90k Lactarius deterrimus 95 72
a. Bklt. pane, 5 #886, 5 #887 9.50
888 A293 3k Cantharellus cibarius 90 68
889 A293 3k Suillus luteus 90 68
a. Bklt. pane, 5 #888, 5 #889 9.00

Issue dates: 2.70k, May 8, 1987. 2.90k, Apr. 26, 1988. 3k, Feb. 20, 1989.

Natl. Federation of Craftsmen, Cent. — A294

1986, Apr. 11 **Engr.**
890 A294 2.50k Stone cutter 55 25
891 A294 7k Carpenter 1.65 1.00

Europa A295

1986, Apr. 11 **Litho.** ***Perf. 13***
892 A295 2.50k Bird, industry 55 30
893 A295 3.50k Acid rain 80 35

Nordic Cooperation Issue — A296

Sister towns.

1986, May 27 ***Perf. 13½x13***
894 A296 2.50k Moss 55 30
895 A296 4k Alesund 95 50

Famous Men — A297

Designs: 2.10k, Hans Poulson Egede (1686-1758), missionary, and map of Norway and Greenland. 2.50k, Herman Wildenvey (1886-1959), poet, and poem carved in Seaman's Commemoration Hall, Stavern. 3k, Tore Orjasaeter (1886-1968), poet, and antique cupboard, Skjak. 4k, Engebret Soot, engineer, and canal lock, Orje.

Engr., Litho. & Engr. (#897)

1986, Oct. 17 ***Perf. 13x13½***
896 A297 2.10k multi 48 45
897 A297 2.50k multi 55 52
898 A297 3k multi 65 65
899 A297 4k multi 95 88

NORGE 2.10
A298

FREDSÅRET 1986
NORGE 15kr
A299

Christmas (Stained glass windows by Gabriel Kielland, Nidaros Cathedral, Trondheim): 2.10k, Olav Kyrre Founding The Diocese in Nidaros. 2.50k, The King and the Peasant at Sul.

Perf. 13½ on 3 Sides

1986, Nov. 26 **Litho.**

Booklet Stamps
900 A298 2.10k multi 57 42
a. Booklet pane of 10 5.75
901 A298 2.50k multi 67 50
a. Booklet pane of 10 6.75

Lithographed & Engraved

1986, Nov. 26 ***Perf. 13½x13***
902 A299 15k brt grn, org & lt bl 3.75 3.00

Intl. Peace Year.

A300

1987, Feb. 12 **Litho.** ***Perf. 13½***
903 A300 3.50k red, yel & dk bl 1.00 75
904 A300 4.50k bl, yel & grn 1.30 1.00

Europa A301

Modern architecture: 2.70k, Wood. 4.50k, Glass and stone.

1987, Apr. 3 **Litho.** ***Perf. 13½x13***
905 A301 2.70k multi 80 60
906 A301 4.50k multi 1.30 1.00

Odelsting (Norwegian Assembly) Voting on Law Administering Local Councils, 150th Anniv. — A302

1987, Apr. 3 **Engr.** ***Perf. 13x13½***
907 A302 12k dk grn 3.50 2.65

Miniature Sheet

Red Crescent-Red Cross Rehabilitation Center, Mogadishu, Somalia — A303

Illustration reduced.

1987, May 8 **Litho.** ***Perf. 13½x13***
908 A303 4.50k multi 1.40 1.40

See Somalia Nos. 576-577.

Sandvig Collection, Maihaugen Open-air Museum A305

1987, June 10 **Engr.** ***Perf. 13x13½***
911 A305 2.70k Bjornstad Farm, Vaga 80 60
912 A305 3.50k Horse and Rider, by Christen E. Listad 1.05 80

Churchyard, Inspiration for Valen's Churchyard by the Sea — A306

Designs: 4.50k, Fartein Valen (1887-1952), Composer.

Perf. 13x13½, 13½x13

1987, Aug. 25 **Engr.**
913 A306 2.30k emer grn & dark blue 65 48
914 A306 4.50k dark brown 1.25 95

Tempest at Sea, by Christian Krogh (1852-1925) A307

Painting: 5k, The Farm, by Gerhard Munthe (1849-1929).

1987, Oct. 9 **Litho.** ***Perf. 13½x13***

915 A307 2.70k multi		85	65
916 A307 5k multi		1.60	1.20

Norwegian Horse Breeds — A308

Perf. 13x13½

1987, Nov. 12 **Litho. & Engr.**

917 A308 2.30k Dales	72	58
918 A308 2.70k Fjord	85	65
919 A308 4.50k Nordland	1.40	1.05

Christmas A309

Perf. 13½x13 on 3 sides

1987, Nov. 12 **Litho.**

Booklet Stamps

920 A309 2.30k Children making tree ornaments	72	58
a. Booklet pane of 10	7.25	
921 A309 2.70k Baking gingersnaps	85	65
a. Booklet pane of 10	8.50	

Salvation Army in Norway, Cent. — A310

1988, Feb. 18 ***Perf. 13½***

922 A310 2.90k multi	95	72
923 A310 4.80k multi	1.50	1.15

European North-South Solidarity Campaign A311

1988, Apr. 26 ***Perf. 13x13½***

924 A311 25k multi	8.00	6.00

Defense Forces Activities — A312

Defense Forces, 300th anniv.: 2.50k, Fortress construction. 2.90k, Army Signal Corps on duty. 4.60k, Pontoon bridge under construction, Corps of Engineers.

1988, Apr. 26 **Engr.**

925 A312 2.50k dark green	80	60
926 A312 2.90k car lake	95	72
927 A312 4.60k dark blue	1.50	1.15

Europa — A313

Transport: 2.90k, *Prinds Gustav* passing Lofoten Isls., 1st passenger steamer in northern Norway, sesquicent. 3.80k, Heroybrua Bridge, between Leinoy and Blankholm, 1976.

Perf. 13x13½

1988, July 1 **Litho. & Engr.**

928 A313 2.90k blue black & ver	95	72
929 A313 3.80k blue black, pink & ver	1.25	95

A souvenir sheet containing 2 No. 928 exists, though it is invalid for postage. Sold for 30k.

85th Birthday of King Olav V — A314

Reign of King Christian IV (1577-1648), 400th Anniv. — A315

Designs: No. 930, Portrait, c. 1988. No. 931a, Arrival in 1905 after Norway declared independence from Sweden. No. 931b, Olav in snowstorm at Holmenkollen.

1988, July 1 **Litho.** ***Perf. 13½x13***

930 A314 2.90k multi	95	72

Souvenir Sheet

931 Sheet of 3	2.85	2.85
a. A314 2.90k org red, black & ultra	95	95
b. A314 2.90k multi	95	95
c. A314 2.90k like No. 930, no date	95	95

Perf. 13½x13

1988, Oct. 7 **Litho. & Engr.**

Designs: 10k, Reverse of a rixdaler struck in Christiania (Oslo), 1628, and excerpt of a mining decree issued by Christian IV.

932 A315 2.50k black & buff	75	58
933 A315 10k multi	3.00	2.25

Miniature Sheet

Handball A316

Ball sports: b, Soccer. c, Basketball. d, Volleyball.

1988, Oct. 7 **Litho.** ***Perf. 13½x13***

934 Sheet of 4	4.50	4.50
a.-d. A316 2.90k any single	1.10	1.10

Stamp Day. No. 934 sold for 15k.

Christmas — A317

Ludvig, a cartoon character created by Kjell Aukrust: No. 935, With ski pole. No. 936, Reading letter.

Perf. 13½x13 on 3 sides

1988, Nov. 15 **Litho.**

Booklet Stamps

935 A317 2.90k multi	90	68
936 A317 2.90k multi	90	68
a. Bklt. pane of 10, 5 #935, 5 #936	9.00	

World Cross-Country Running Championships, Stavanger, Mar. 19 — A318

1989, Feb. 20 **Litho.** ***Perf. 13x13½***

937 A318 5k multi	1.50	1.15

Port City Bicentennials A319

Nordic Cooperation Issue A320

Perf. 13½x13

1989, Apr. 20 **Litho. & Engr.**

938 A319 3k Vardo	90	68
939 A319 4k Hammerfest	1.20	90

1989, Apr. 20 **Litho.** ***Perf. 13x13½***

Folk costumes.

940 A320 3k Setesdal (woman)	90	68
941 A320 4k Kautokeino (man)	1.20	90

Europa 1989 — A321

Public Primary Schools, 250th Anniv. — A322

Children's games.

1989, June 7 **Litho.** ***Perf. 13x13½***

942 A321 3.70k Building snowman	1.10	82
943 A321 5k Cat's cradle	1.50	1.15

Perf. 13½x13

1989, June 7 **Litho. & Engr.**

944 A322 2.60k shown	80	60

Engr.

945 A322 3k Child learning to write	90	68

Souvenir Sheet

Winter Olympic Gold Medalists from Norway A323

Portraits: a, Bjoerg Eva Jensen, women's 3000-meter speed skating, 1980. b, Eirik Kvalfoss, 10k biathlon, 1984. c, Tom Sandberg, combined cross-country and ski jumping, 1984. d, Women's Nordic ski team, 20k relay, 1984.

1989, Oct. 6 **Litho.** ***Perf. 13½x13***

946 Sheet of 4	5.60	5.60
a.-d. A323 4k any single	1.40	1.40

Sold for 20k to benefit Olympic sports promotion. See Nos. 984, 997, 1021.

Souvenir Sheet

Impression of the Countryside, 1982, by Jakob Weidemann — A324

Illustration reduced.

1989, Oct. 6

947 A324 Sheet of 4	4.20	4.20
a.-d. 3k any single	1.05	1.05

Stamp Day. Sold for 15k to benefit philatelic promotion.

Writers A325

Portraits: 3k, Arnulf Overland (1889-1968), poet. 25k, Hanna Winsnes (1789-1872), author.

Perf. 13x13½

1989, Nov. 24 **Litho. & Engr.**

948 A325 3k dk red & brt bl	85	62
949 A325 25k multi	7.00	5.25

Manors A326

1989, Nov. 24 **Engr.** ***Perf. 13***

950 A326 3k Manor at Larvik	85	62
951 A326 3k Rosendal Barony	85	62

A327

NORGE 5KR

A328

Christmas decorations.

Perf. 13 on 3 sides

1989, Nov. 24 **Litho.**

Booklet Stamps

952 A327 3k Star	85	62
953 A327 3k Round ornament	85	62
a. Bklt. pane of 10, 5 #952, 5 #953	8.50	

1990, Feb. 23 **Litho.** ***Perf. 13½***

954 A328 5k multicolored	1.55	1.15

Winter City events, Tromso.

Fauna Type of 1988

1991 **Litho. & Engr.** ***Perf. 13***

958 A292 5.50k Lynx	1.75	1.30
959 A292 6.40k Owl	2.00	1.50

Issue date: Feb. 21.

This is an expanding set. Numbers will change if necessary.

Posthorn Type of 1893

1991-92 Engr. *Perf. 12½x13*

960 A10 1k orange & black 32 25
961 A10 2k emerald & lake 65 50
962 A10 3k blue & green 1.00 75
963 A10 4k orange & henna brn 1.30 1.00
963A A10 5k green & dark blue 1.65 1.25
964 A10 6k grn & red vio 1.80 1.35
965 A10 7k red brn & bl 2.10 1.60
966 A10 8k red vio & grn 2.40 1.80
967 A10 9k ultra & red brn 2.65 2.00
Nos. 960-967 (9) 13.87 10.50

Issued: 1k, 2k, 3k, 4k, 5k, Nov. 23, 1992; others, Nov. 22.

This is an expanding set. Numbers may change.

A332

A334

Orchids.

Perf. 13½x13 on 3 Sides

1990-92 Litho. Booklet Stamps

970 A332 3.20k *Dactylorhiza fuchsii* 1.00 75
971 A332 3.20k *Epipactis atrorubens* 1.00 75
a. Bklt. pane, 5 #970, 5 #971 10.00
972 A332 3.30k Cypripedium calceolus 1.00 75
973 A332 3.30k Ophrys insectifera 1.00 75
a. Bklt. pane, 5 each #972-973 10.00

Issued: Nos. 970-971, Feb. 23. Nos. 972-973, Feb. 21, 1992.

This is an expanding set. Numbers will change if necessary.

1990, Apr. 9 Litho. *Perf. 13x13½*

German Invasion of Norway, 40th Anniv.: 3.20k, King Haakon VII's monogram, merchant navy, air force, Norwegian Home Guard and cannon Moses. 4k, Recapture of Narvik, May 28, 1940, by the Polish, British, Norwegian and French forces.

975 A334 3.20k shown 1.00 75
976 A334 4k multicolored 1.25 92

A335

A336

Souvenir Sheet

Stamps on stamps: b, Norway #1.

1990, Apr. 9 *Perf. 13½x13*

977 Sheet of 2 4.60 4.60
a.-b. A335 5k any single 2.30 2.30

Penny Black, 150th anniv. Sold for 15k.

1990, June 14 Litho. & Engr.

978 A336 3.20k Portrait 1.00 75
979 A336 5k Coat of arms 1.50 1.15

Tordenskiold (Peter Wessel, 1690-1720), naval hero.

A337

A338

Europa: Post offices.

1990, June 14 Litho. *Perf. 13x13½*

980 A337 3.20k Trondheim 1.00 75
981 A337 4k Longyearbyen 1.25 92

1990, Oct. 5 Litho. & Engr. *Perf. 13*

982 A338 2.70k Svendsen 85 62
983 A338 15k Monument by Fredriksen 4.65 3.50

Johan Severin Svendsen (1840-1911), composer.

Winter Olympic Type of 1989
Souvenir Sheet

Gold medal winners: a, Thorleif Haug, skier, 1924. b, Sonja Henie, figure skater, 1928, 1932, 1936. c, Ivar Ballangrud, speed skater, 1928, 1936. d, Hjalmar Andersen, speed skater, 1952.

1990, Oct. 5 Litho. *Perf. 13½x13*

984 Sheet of 4 6.25 6.25
a.-d. A323 4k any single 1.55 1.55

Sold for 20k to benefit Olympic sports promotion.

A339

A340

1990, Nov. 23 Litho & Engr. *Perf. 13*

985 A339 30k bl, brn & car rose 10.00 7.50

Lars Olof Jonathan Soderblom (1866-1931), 1930 Nobel Peace Prize winner.

Perf. 13 on 3 sides

1990, Nov. 23 Litho.

Christmas (Children's drawings): No. 987, Church, stars, and Christmas tree.

986 A340 3.20k multicolored 1.10 80
987 A340 3.20k multicolored 1.10 80
a. Bklt. pane, 5 each #986-987 11.00

Ship Building Industry A341

1991, Feb. 21 Litho. *Perf. 13½x13*

988 A341 5k multicolored 1.60 1.20

Europa — A342

1991, Apr. 16 Litho. *Perf. 13*

989 A342 3.20k ERS-1 90 70
990 A342 4k Andoya rocket range 1.15 85

City of Christiansand, 350th Anniv. — A343

1991, Apr. 16 Litho. & Engr. *Perf. 13*

991 A343 3.20k Early view 90 70
992 A343 5.50k Modern view 1.55 1.15

Lifeboat Service, Cent.
A344

Tourism
A345

Designs: 3.20k, Rescue boat, Skomvaer III, horiz. 27k, Sailboat Colin Archer.

1991, June 7 Litho & Engr. *Perf. 13*

993 A344 3.20k multicolored 90 70
994 A344 27k multicolored 7.50 5.65

1991, June 7 Litho. *Perf. 13½x13*

Designs: 3.20k, Fountain, Vigeland Park. 4k, Globe, North Cape.

995 A345 3.20k multicolored 90 70
996 A345 4k multicolored 1.10 85

Winter Olympics Type of 1989
Souvenir Sheet

Gold medal winners: a, Birger Ruud, ski jumping. b, Johan Grottumsbraten, cross country skiing. c, Knut Johannesen, speed skating. d, Magnar Solberg, biathlon.

1991, Oct. 11 Litho. *Perf. 13½x13*

997 Sheet of 4 5.60 5.60
a.-d. A323 4k any single 1.40 1.40

Sold for 20k to benefit Olympic sports promotion.

A346

A347

Natl. Stamp Day: a, Hands engraving. b, Magnifying glass above hands. c, View of hands through magnifying glass. d, Printed label being removed from plate.

1991, Oct. 11 *Perf. 13x13½*

Souvenir Sheet

998 Sheet of 4 5.60 5.60
a. A346 2.70k multicolored 1.25 1.25
b. A346 3.20k multicolored 1.00 1.00
c. A346 4k multicolored 1.40 1.40
d. A346 5k multicolored 2.00 2.00

Sold for 20k.

Perf. 13½x13 on 3 Sides

1991, Nov. 22 Litho.

Christmas: No. 1000, People with lantern.

Booklet Stamps

999 A347 3.20k multicolored 95 75
1000 A347 3.20k multicolored 95 75
a. Bklt. pane, 5 each #999-1000 9.50

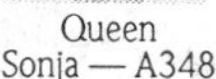

Queen Sonja — A348

King Harald — A349

King Harald V — A349a

Perf. 13x13½

1992-93 Litho. & Engr.

1004 A348 2.80k multicolored 85 65
1005 A348 3k multicolored 90 68
1007 A349 3.30k multicolored 1.00 75
1008 A349 3.50k multicolored 1.05 78
1011 A349 5.50k multicolored 1.70 1.25
1012 A349 5.60k multicolored 1.75 1.10
1015 A349 6.60k multicolored 2.00 1.50

Engr.

Perf. 13½x13

1020 A349a 50k olive black 18.00 13.50
Nos. 1004-1020 (8) 27.25 20.21

Issued: 2.80k, 3.30k, 5.60k, 6.60k, Feb. 21; 50k, June 12; 3k, 3.50k, 5.50k, Feb. 23, 1993.

This is an expanding set. Numbers may change.

Winter Olympics Type of 1989
Souvenir Sheet

Gold Medal winners: a, Hallgeir Brenden, cross-country skiing. b, Arnfinn Bergmann, ski jumping. c, Stein Eriksen, giant slalom. d, Simon Slattvik, Nordic combined.

1992, Feb. 21 Litho. *Perf. 13½x13*

1021 Sheet of 4 6.00 6.00
a.-d. A323 4k any single 1.50 1.50

Sold for 20k to benefit Olympic sports promotion.

Expo '92, Seville A350

Designs: 3.30k, Norwegian pavilion, ship. 5.20k, Mountains, boat and fish.

1992, Apr. 20 Litho. *Perf. 13x13½*

1022 A350 3.30k multicolored 1.00 75
1023 A350 5.20k multicolored 1.55 1.15

Discovery of America, 500th Anniv. — A351

Europa: 3.30k, Sailing ship Restauration at sea, 1825. 4,20k, Stavangerfjord in New York Harbor, 1918.

Perf. 13x13½

1992, Apr. 21 Litho. & Engr.

1024 A351 3.30k multicolored 1.00 75
1025 A351 4.20k multicolored 1.25 95

Kristiansund, 250th Anniv. — A352

1992, June 12 Litho. & Engr. *Perf. 13*

1026 A352 3.30k brn, bl & blk 1.20 90
1027 A352 3.30k View of Molde 1.20 90

Molde, 250th anniv. (#1027).

Souvenir Sheet

Glass — A353

Stamp Day: a, Decorated vase. b, Carafe with gold design. c, Cut glass salad bowl. d, Decorated cup.

1992, Oct. 9 Litho. *Perf. 13x13½*

1028 Sheet of 4 7.25 7.25
a. A353 2.80k multicolored 1.80 1.80
b. A353 3.30k multicolored 1.80 1.80
c. A353 4.20k multicolored 1.80 1.80
d. A353 5.20k multicolored 1.80 1.80

No. 1028 sold for 20k.

A354

A355

Designs: 3.30k, Flags, buildings in Lillehammer. 4.20k, Flag.

1992, Oct. 9 Litho. *Perf. 13x13½*

1029 A354 3.30k multicolored 1.20 90
1030 A354 4.20k multicolored 1.50 1.10

1994 Winter Olympics, Lillehammer.

Perf. 13 on 3 Sides

1992, Nov. 23 Litho.

Christmas: No. 1031, Elves in front of mailbox. No. 1032, One elf holding other on shoulders to mail letters.

Booklet Stamps

1031 A355 3.30k multicolored 1.10 80
1032 A355 3.30k multicolored 1.10 80
a. Pair, #1031-1032 2.20 1.60
b. Bklt. pane, 5 #1032a 11.00

SEMI-POSTAL STAMPS

North Cape Issue

North Cape — SP1

Perf. 13½x14

1930, June 28 Wmk. 160 Photo.

Size: 33¼x21½mm

B1 SP1 15o + 25o blk brn 1.65 1.65
B2 SP1 20o + 25o car 20.00 20.00
B3 SP1 30o + 25o ultra 65.00 65.00
Set, never hinged 140.00

The surtax was given to the Tourist Association. See Nos. B9-B10, B28-B30, B54-B56, B59-B61.

Radium Hospital SP2

1931, Apr. 1 *Perf. 14½x13½*

B4 SP2 20o + 10o carmine 8.50 2.75
Never hinged 25.00

The surtax aided the Norwegian Radium Hospital.

Fridtjof Nansen — SP3

Queen Maud — SP4

1935, Dec. 13 *Perf. 13½*

B5 SP3 10o + 10o green 1.25 1.50
B6 SP3 15o + 10o red brn 6.00 7.25
B7 SP3 20o + 10o crimson 95 1.20
B8 SP3 30o + 10o brt ultra 5.00 6.00
Set, never hinged 27.50

The surtax aided the International Nansen Office for Refugees.

North Cape Type of 1930

1938, June 20 *Perf. 13x13½*

Size: 27x21mm

B9 SP1 20o + 25o brn car 2.75 4.00
B10 SP1 30o + 25o dp ultra 11.00 13.00
Set, never hinged 22.50

Surtax given to the Tourist Assoc.

Perf. 13x13½

1939, July 24 Photo. Unwmk.

B11 SP4 10o + 5o brt grn 40 40
B12 SP4 15o + 5o red brn 40 40
B13 SP4 20o + 5o scarlet 40 40
B14 SP4 30o + 5o brt ultra 40 40
Set, never hinged 2.50

The surtax was used for charities.

Fridtjof Nansen — SP5

SP6

1940, Oct. 21

B15 SP5 10o + 10o dk grn 1.25 2.25
B16 SP5 15o + 10o henna brn 1.75 3.25
B17 SP5 20o + 10o dark red 42 1.10
B18 SP5 30o + 10o ultra 1.25 2.25
Set, never hinged 10.00

The surtax was used for war relief work.

1941, May 16

Ancient Sailing Craft off Lofoten Islands.

B19 SP6 15o + 10o deep blue 90 90
Never hinged 2.25

Haalogaland Exposition. Surtax for relief fund for families of lost fishermen.

Nos. 177-180, 267, B19, B32-B34 and B38-B41 were demonetized from May 15, 1945 until Sept. 1, 1981. Used values are for stamps canceled after this period. Stamps with dated cancellations prior to May 15, 1945 sell for more. False cancellations exist.

Colin Archer and Lifeboat — SP7

Lifeboat — SP8

1941, July 9 *Perf. 13x13½, 13½x13*

B20 SP7 10o + 10o yel grn 95 1.65
B21 SP7 15o + 10o dk ol brn 1.25 1.90
B22 SP8 20o + 10o brt red 38 55
B23 SP8 30o + 10o ultra 2.50 4.00
Set, never hinged 8.50

Norwegian Lifeboat Society, 50th anniv.

Legionary, Norwegian and Finnish Flags SP9

Vidkun Quisling SP10

1941, Aug. 1 *Perf. 13½x13*

B24 SP9 20o + 80o scar ver 50.00 80.00
Never hinged 72.50

The surtax was for the Norwegian Legion.

1942, Feb. 1

B25 SP10 20o + 30o henna 4.00 13.00
Never hinged 6.00

Overprinted in Red **1-2-1942**

B26 SP10 20o + 30o henna 4.00 13.00
Never hinged 6.00

Inauguration of Quisling as prime minister.

Catalogue values for unused stamps in this section, from this point to the end of the section, are for Never Hinged items.

Vidkun Quisling SP11

Frontier Guardsmen Emblem SP12

1942, Sept. 26 *Perf. 13*

B27 SP11 20o + 30o henna 45 3.00

8th annual meeting of Nasjonal Samling, Quisling's party. The surtax aided relatives of soldiers killed in action.

North Cape Type of 1930

1943, Apr. 1

Size: 27x21mm

B28 SP1 15o + 25o ol brn 1.25 1.25
B29 SP1 20o + 25o dk car 1.50 1.50
B30 SP1 30o + 25o chalky bl 2.25 2.25

The surtax aided the Tourist Association.

1943, Aug. 2 Unwmk.

B31 SP12 20o + 30o henna 75 3.25

The surtax aided the Frontier Guardsmen (Norwegian Nazi Volunteers).

Fishing Village — SP13

Drying Grain — SP14

Barn in Winter — SP15

1943, Nov. 10

B32 SP13 10o + 10o gray grn 1.50 1.00
B33 SP14 20o + 10o henna 1.50 1.00
B34 SP15 40o + 10o grnsh blk 1.50 1.00

The surtax was for winter relief.

The Baroy Sinking — SP16

Sanct Svithun Aflame — SP17

Design: 20o+10o, "Irma" sinking.

1944, May 20

B35 SP16 10o + 10o gray grn 1.40 *3.50*
B36 SP17 15o + 10o dk olive 1.40 *3.50*
B37 SP16 20o + 10o henna 1.40 *3.50*

The surtax aided victims of wartime ship sinkings, and their families.

Spinning SP19

Plowing SP20

Tree Felling — SP21

Child Care — SP22

1944, Dec. 1

B38 SP19 5o + 10o dp mag 90 90
B39 SP20 10o + 10o dk yel grn 90 90
B40 SP21 15o + 10o choc 90 90
B41 SP22 20o + 10o henna 90 90

The surtax was for National Welfare.

Red Cross Nurse — SP23

Crown Prince Olav — SP24

1945, Sept. 22

B42 SP23 20o + 10o red 1.00 1.10

80th anniv. of the founding of the Norwegian Red Cross. The surtax was for that institution.
For surcharge see No. B47.

1946, Mar. 4 Unwmk.

B43 SP24 10o + 10o ol grn 45 40
B44 SP24 15o + 10o ol brn 45 40
B45 SP24 20o + 10o dk red 45 40
B46 SP24 30o + 10o brt bl 2.00 1.50

The surtax was for war victims.

No. B42 Surcharged with New Value and Bar in Black

1948, Dec. 1

B47 SP23 25o + 5o on 20o+10o 85 85

The surtax was for Red Cross relief work.

Child Picking Flowers — SP25

1950, Aug. 15 Photo. *Perf. 13*

B48 SP25 25o + 5o brt red 1.90 1.10
B49 SP25 45o + 5o dp bl 5.75 3.50

The surtax was for poliomyelitis victims.

Skater — SP26

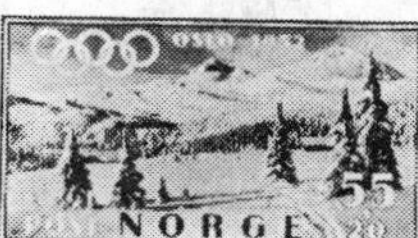

Winter Scene SP27

Design: 30o+10o, Ski jumper.

1951, Oct. 1

B50 SP26 15o + 5o ol grn 1.50 1.25
B51 SP26 30o + 10o red 1.50 1.25
B52 SP27 55o + 20o blue 9.00 7.25

Olympic Winter Games, Oslo, Feb. 14-29, 1952.

Kneeling Woman — SP28

Crown Princess Martha — SP29

1953, June 1 Photo. & Litho.

B53 SP28 30o + 10o red & cr 2.25 2.00

The surtax was for cancer research.

North Cape Type of 1930

1953, June 15 Photo.

Size: 27x21mm

B54 SP1 20o + 10o green 10.50 8.50
B55 SP1 30o + 15o red 10.50 8.50
B56 SP1 55o + 25o gray bl 17.00 13.00

The surtax aided the Tourist Association.

1956, Mar. 28 *Perf. 13*

B57 SP29 35o + 10o dk red 1.75 1.50
B58 SP29 65o + 10o dk bl 4.25 3.50

The surtax was for the Crown Princess Martha Memorial Fund.

North Cape Type of 1930

1957, May 6

Size: 27x21mm

B59 SP1 25o + 10o grn 4.75 4.00
B60 SP1 35o + 15o red 5.50 5.00
B61 SP1 65o + 25o gray bl 4.75 3.50

The surtax aided the Tourist Association.

White Anemone SP30

Mother, Child, WRY Emblem SP31

Design: 90o+10o, Hepatica.

1960, Jan. 12 Litho. *Perf. 13*

B62 SP30 45o + 10o brt red & grn 2.00 1.90
B63 SP30 90o + 10o bl, org & grn 5.75 5.50

The surtax was for anti-tuberculosis work.

1960, Apr. 7 Photo. Unwmk.

B64 SP31 45o + 25o rose & blk 5.00 3.75
B65 SP31 90o + 25o bl & blk 9.00 6.50

World Refugee Year, July 1, 1959-June 30, 1960. The surtax was for aid to refugees.

Severed Chain and Dove SP32

Design: 60o+10o, Norwegian flags.

1965, May 8 Photo. *Perf. 13*

B66 SP32 30o + 10o grn, blk & tan 75 70
B67 SP32 60o + 10o red & dk bl 75 75

20th anniversary of liberation from the Germans. The surtax was for war cripples.

Souvenir Sheet

Offshore Oil Drilling SP33

Designs: a, Ekofisk Center. b, Treasure Scout drilling rig and Odin Viking supply vessel at Tromsoflaket, 1982. c, Statfjord C oil platform, 1984. d, Men working on deck of Neptune Nordraug.

1985, Oct. 4 Litho. *Perf. 13½x13*

B68 Sheet of 4 2.75 3.50
a.-d. SP33 2k + 1k, any single 65 85

Stamp Day 1985. Surtax for philatelic promotion.

Souvenir Sheet

Paper Industry SP34

Paper mill: a, Wood aging containers. b, Boiling plant. c, Paper-making machine. d, Paper dryer.

1986, Oct. 17 Litho. *Perf. 13½*

B69 Sheet of 4 3.25 3.75
a.-d. SP34 2.50k + 1k, any single 80 90

Surtax for philatelic promotion. Nos. B69a-B69b and B69c-B69d printed in continuous designs.

Souvenir Sheet

Salmon Industry SP35

Designs: a, Eggs and milt pressed out of fish by hand. b, Cultivation of eggs in tanks. c, Outdoor hatchery. d, Market.

1987, Oct. 9 Litho. *Perf. 13½x13*

B70 Sheet of 4 3.75 3.75
a. SP35 2.30k +50o multi 65 65
b. SP35 2.70k +50o multi 75 75
c. SP35 3.50k +50o multi 95 95
d. SP35 4.50k +50o multi 1.25 1.25

AIR POST STAMPS

Airplane over Akershus Castle
AP1 AP2

Perf. 13½x14½

1927-34 Typo. Wmk. 160

C1 AP1 45o lt bl, strong frame line ('34) 5.00 2.00
Never hinged 15.00
a. Faint or broken frame line 13.00 3.75
Never hinged 75.00

1937, Aug. 18 Photo. *Perf. 13*

C2 AP2 45o Prussian blue 1.25 55
Never hinged 1.75

1941, Nov. 10 Unwmk.

C3 AP2 45o indigo 40 30
Never hinged 60

POSTAGE DUE STAMPS

Numeral of Value — D1

Perf. 14½x13½

1889-1914 Typo. Wmk. 160

Inscribed "at betale"

J1 D1 1o gray 52 50
J2 D1 4o magenta 1.00 50
J3 D1 10o carmine rose 4.00 50
a. 10o rose red 47.50 7.50
J4 D1 15o brown ('14) 1.10 50
J5 D1 20o ultra 2.00 50
a. Perf. 13½x12½ 150.00 75.00
J6 D1 50o maroon 4.00 1.75
Nos. J1-J6 (6) 12.62 4.25

See #J7-J12. For overprint see #136-144.

1922-23

Inscribed "a betale"

J7 D1 4o lilac rose 5.00 5.00
Never hinged 11.00
J8 D1 10o green 1.65 1.50
Never hinged 4.00
J9 D1 20o dull violet 3.50 3.25
Never hinged 7.50
J10 D1 40o deep ultra 5.50 50
Never hinged 12.50
J11 D1 100o orange yel 22.50 8.50
Never hinged 42.50
J12 D1 200o dark violet 55.00 18.00
Never hinged 85.00
Nos. J7-J12 (6) 93.15 36.75

OFFICIAL STAMPS

Coat of Arms
O1 O2

Perf. 14½x13½

1926 Typo. Wmk. 160

O1 O1 5o rose lilac 32 32
O2 O1 10o yellow green 32 15
O3 O1 15o indigo 1.40 1.40
O4 O1 20o plum 32 15
O5 O1 30o slate 4.00 4.00
O6 O1 40o deep blue 1.25 52
O7 O1 60o Prussian blue 4.00 4.00
Nos. O1-O7 (7) 11.61 10.54

Official Stamp of 1926 Surcharged **2 2**

1929, July 1

O8 O1 2o on 5o magenta 40 32

Perf. 14½x13½

1933-34 Litho. Wmk. 160

Size: 35x19¼mm

O9 O2 2o ocher 60 85
O10 O2 5o rose lilac 1.65 1.65
O11 O2 7o orange 8.00 5.00
O12 O2 10o green 16.00 65
O13 O2 15o olive 52 42
O14 O2 20o vermilion 16.00 42
O15 O2 25o yellow brn 52 42
O16 O2 30o ultra 52 42
O18 O2 40o slate 21.00 52
O19 O2 60o blue 6.50 52
O20 O2 70o olive brn 1.50 1.50
O21 O2 100o violet 2.00 1.10
Nos. O9-O16,O18-O21 (12) 74.81 13.47

On the lithographed stamps, the lion's left leg is shaded.

Typo.

Size: 34x18¾mm

O10a O2 5o rose lilac 85 1.10
O11a O2 7o orange 10.00 7.25
O12a O2 10o green 70 40
O13a O2 15o olive 10.00 12.00
O14a O2 20o vermilion 70 25
O17 O2 35o red violet ('34) 85 50
O18a O2 40o slate 85 50
O19a O2 60o blue 85 50
Nos. O10A-O14A,O17,O18A-O19A (8) 24.80 22.50

Coat of Arms — O3

Norwegian Nazi Party Emblem — O4

1937-38 Photo. *Perf. 13½x13*

O22 O3 5o rose lilac ('38) 65 60
O23 O3 7o dp orange 65 60
O24 O3 10o brt green 40 22
O25 O3 15o olive bister 52 52
O26 O3 20o carmine ('38) 52 15
O27 O3 25o red brown ('38) 1.00 70
O28 O3 30o ultra 1.00 60
O29 O3 35o red vio ('38) 1.00 60
O30 O3 40o Prus grn ('38) 85 40
O31 O3 60o Prus bl ('38) 1.00 60
O32 O3 100o dk vio ('38) 2.00 1.50
Nos. O22-O32 (11) 9.59 6.49
Set, never hinged 16.00

See Nos. O33-O43, O55-O56. For surcharge see No. O57.

1939-47 Unwmk.

O33 O3 5o dp red lil ('41) 40 15
O34 O3 7o dp org ('41) 40 32
O35 O3 10o brt grn ('41) 25 15
O36 O3 15o olive ('45) 40 22
O37 O3 20o carmine 25 15
O38 O3 25o red brn 2.00 3.00
O38A O3 25o scarlet ('46) 25 15
O39 O3 30o ultra 2.75 1.10
O39A O3 30o dk gray ('47) 65 52
O40 O3 35o brt lilac ('41) 52 22
O41 O3 40o grnsh blk ('41) 52 22
O41A O3 40o dp ultra ('46) 1.25 22
O42 O3 60o Prus blue ('41) 65 22
O43 O3 100o dk vio ('41) 65 22
Nos. O33-O43 (14) 10.94 6.86
Set, never hinged 18.00

1942-44

O44 O4 5o magenta 32 *85*
O45 O4 7o yellow org 32 *85*
O46 O4 10o emerald 15 15
O47 O4 15o olive ('44) 2.00 *5.00*
O48 O4 20o bright red 15 15
O49 O4 25o red brn ('43) 4.00 *8.50*
O50 O4 30o brt ultra ('44) 3.00 *10.00*
O51 O4 35o brt pur ('43) 3.00 *7.25*
O52 O4 40o grnsh blk ('43) 25 15
O53 O4 60o indigo ('43) 2.25 *5.00*
O54 O4 1k blue vio ('43) 2.25 *7.25*
Nos. O44-O54 (11) 17.69 45.15
Set, never hinged 32.50

Type of 1937

1947, Nov. 1

O55 O3 50o deep magenta 75 22
O56 O3 200o orange 3.00 45
Set, never hinged 6.50

No. O37 Surcharged with New Values and Bars in Black

1949, Mar. 15

O57 O3 25o on 20o carmine 25 35
Never hinged 35

Norway Coat of Arms
O5 O6

1951-52 Unwmk. Photo. *Perf. 13*

No.	Type	Description	Unused	Used
O58	O5	5o rose lilac	60	15
O59	O5	10o dk gray	60	15
O60	O5	15o dp org brn ('52)	60	15
O61	O5	30o scarlet	60	15
O62	O5	35o red brn ('52)	70	45
O63	O5	60o blue gray	70	15
O64	O5	100o vio bl ('52)	1.10	15
		Nos. O58-O64 (7)	4.90	1.35
		Set, never hinged	8.50	

Catalogue values for unused stamps in this section, from this point to the end of the section, are for Never Hinged items.

1955-61

No.	Type	Description	Unused	Used
O65	O6	5o rose lilac	18	15
O66	O6	10o slate	18	15
O67	O6	15o orange brn	1.65	1.10
O68	O6	20o bl grn ('57)	28	15
O69	O6	25o emer ('59)	70	15
O70	O6	30o scarlet	1.65	65
O71	O6	35o brown red	70	15
O72	O6	40o blue lilac	1.10	15
O73	O6	45o scar ('58)	90	15
O74	O6	50o gldn brn ('57)	2.50	22
O75	O6	60o grnsh bl	2.25	32
O76	O6	70o brn olive	3.25	1.10
O77	O6	75o maroon ('57)	8.00	6.00
O78	O6	80o org brn ('58)	3.50	70
O79	O6	90o org ('58)	1.10	20
O80	O6	1k vio ('57)	1.65	15
O81	O6	2k gray grn ('60)	1.75	15
O82	O6	5k red lil ('61)	6.25	85
		Nos. O65-O82 (18)	37.59	12.49

See Phosphorescence note after No. 430.

1962-74 Photo.

No.	Type	Description	Unused	Used
O83	O6	30o green ('64)	75	15
O84	O6	40o ol grn ('68)	25	15
O85	O6	50o scarlet	1.10	25
O86	O6	50o slate ('69)	18	15
O87	O6	60o dk red ('64)	1.10	15
O88	O6	65o dk red ('68)	1.10	15
O89	O6	70o dk red ('70)	30	15
O90	O6	75o lt grn ('73)	75	75
O91	O6	85o ocher ('74)	95	95
O92	O6	1k dp org ('73)	45	15
O93	O6	1.10k car lake ('74)	75	60
		Nos. O83-O93 (11)	7.68	3.60

Shades exist of several values of type O6.

1975-82 Litho.

No.	Type	Description	Unused	Used
O94	O6	5o rose lil ('80)	60	60
O95	O6	10o bluish gray ('82)	80	80
O96	O6	15o henna brn	1.25	1.25
O97	O6	20o green ('82)	80	80
O98	O6	25o yellow grn	40	15
O99	O6	40o ol grn ('79)	1.00	1.00
O100	O6	50o grnsh gray ('76)	40	15
O101	O6	60o dk grnsh bl	1.00	1.00
O102	O6	70o dk red ('82)	2.00	1.50
O103	O6	80o red brn ('76)	60	15
O104	O6	1k vio ('80)	1.40	35
O105	O6	1.10k red ('80)	1.25	60
O106	O6	1.25k dull red	60	15
O107	O6	1.30k lilac ('81)	1.00	1.00
O108	O6	1.50k red ('81)	70	20
O109	O6	1.75k dl bl grn ('82)	1.40	1.25
O110	O6	2k dk gray grn	1.00	20
O111	O6	2k cerise ('82)	1.40	30
O112	O6	3k purple ('82)	2.00	80
O113	O6	5k lt vio	12.00	2.50
O114	O6	5k blue ('77)	2.75	80
		Nos. O94-O114 (21)	34.35	15.55

In lithographed set, shield's background is dotted; on photogravure stamps it is solid color.

Official stamps invalid as of Apr. 1, 1986.

NOSSI-BE

LOCATION — Island in the Indian Ocean, off the northwest coast of Madagascar
GOVT. — A former French Protectorate
AREA — 130 sq. mi.
POP. — 9,000 (approx. 1900)
CAPITAL — Hellville

In 1896 the island was placed under the authority of the Governor-General of Madagascar and postage stamps of Madagascar were placed in use.

100 Centimes = 1 Franc

Stamps of French Colonies Surcharged in Blue:

25 a 25 c b 5 c c

On the following issues the colors of the Fench Colonies stamps, type A9, are: 5c, green, *greenish*; 10c, black, *lavender*; 15c, blue; 20c, red, *green*; 30c, brown, *bister*; 40c, vermilion, *straw*; 75c, carmine, *rose*; 1fr, bronze green, *straw*.

1889 Unwmk. *Imperf.*

No.	Type	Description	Unused	Used
1	A8(a)	25 on 40c red, *straw*	1,300.	400.00
a.		Double surcharge		*900.00*
2	A8(b)	25c on 40c red, *straw*	1,750.	1,000.

Perf. 14x13½

No.	Type	Description	Unused	Used
3	A9(b)	5c on 10c	1,750.	600.00
4	A9(b)	5c on 20c	1,750.	650.00
5	A9(c)	5c on 10c	1,600.	500.00
6	A9(c)	5c on 20c	1,750.	1,100.
7	A9(a)	15 on 20c	1,500.	600.00
a.		15 on 30c (error)	*17,500.*	*11,000.*
8	A9(a)	25 on 30c	1,500.	375.00
9	A9(a)	25 on 40c	1,500.	400.00

N S B 0 25 d

N S B 25 c. f

N S B 25 g

Black Surcharge

1890

No.	Type	Description	Unused	Used
10	A9(d)	0.25 on 20c	200.00	140.00
11	A9(d)	0.25 on 75c	200.00	140.00
12	A9(d)	0.25 on 1fr	200.00	140.00
a.		Without ornament		
16	A9(f)	25c on 20c	200.00	140.00
17	A9(f)	25c on 75c	200.00	140.00
18	A9(f)	25c on 1fr	200.00	140.00
19	A9(g)	25 on 20c	550.00	350.00
20	A9(g)	25 on 75c	550.00	350.00
21	A9(g)	25 on 1fr	550.00	350.00

The 25c on 20c with surcharge composed of "25 c." as in "f," "N S B" as in "d," and frame as in "g" is an essay.

Surcharged or Overprinted in Black, Carmine, Vermilion or Blue:

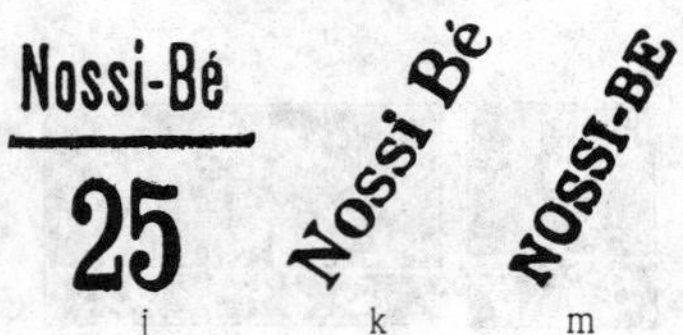

j k m

1893

No.	Type	Description	Unused	Used
23	A9(j)	25 on 20c (Bk)	20.00	16.00
24	A9(j)	50 on 10c (Bk)	22.50	16.00
a.		Inverted surcharge	150.00	110.00
25	A9(j)	75 on 15c (Bk)	150.00	100.00
26	A9(j)	1fr on 5c (Bk)	52.50	40.00
a.		Inverted surcharge	150.00	125.00
27	A9(k)	10c (C)	6.50	5.75
a.		Inverted overprint	45.00	42.50
28	A9(k)	10c (V)	6.50	5.75
29	A9(k)	15c (Bk)	6.50	5.75
a.		Inverted overprint	45.00	42.50
30	A9(k)	20c (Bk)	225.00	27.50
a.		Double overprint		
31	A9(m)	20c (Bl)	47.50	21.00
a.		Inverted overprint	65.00	62.50

Counterfeits exist of surcharges and overprints of Nos. 1-31.

Navigation and Commerce — A14

1894 Typo. *Perf. 14x13½*
Name of Colony in Blue or Carmine

No.	Type	Description	Unused	Used
32	A14	1c blk, *lil bl*	55	55
33	A14	2c brn, *buff*	65	62
34	A14	4c claret, *lav*	80	62
35	A14	5c grn, *greenish*	1.10	80
36	A14	10c blk, *lav*	2.50	1.40
37	A14	15c blue, quadrille paper	3.50	1.75
38	A14	20c red, *grn*	3.75	2.25
39	A14	25c blk, *rose*	5.00	3.75
40	A14	30c brn, *bister*	5.75	4.25
41	A14	40c red, *straw*	7.00	5.75
42	A14	50c carmine, *rose*	7.00	5.75
43	A14	75c dp vio, *orange*	16.00	16.00
44	A14	1fr brnz grn, *straw*	9.00	6.50
		Nos. 32-44 (13)	62.60	49.99

Perf. 13½x14 stamps are counterfeits.

POSTAGE DUE STAMPS

Stamps of French Colonies Surcharged in Black:

Nossi-Bé chiffre-taxe 0.20 A PERCEVOIR n

Nossi-Bé chiffre-taxe 0.35 A PERCEVOIR o

1891 Unwmk. *Perf. 14x13½*

No.	Type	Description	Unused	Used
J1	A9(n)	20 on 1c blk, *lil bl*	180.00	150.00
a.		Inverted surcharge	325.00	250.00
b.		Surcharged vertically	500.00	500.00
c.		Surcharge on back	375.00	375.00
J2	A9(n)	30 on 2c brn, *buff*	180.00	150.00
a.		Inverted surcharge	325.00	250.00
b.		Surcharge on back	400.00	400.00
J3	A9(n)	50 on 30c brn, *bister*	55.00	50.00
a.		Inverted surcharge	325.00	250.00
b.		Surcharge on back	400.00	400.00
J4	A9(o)	35 on 4c cl, *lav*	210.00	160.00
a.		Inverted surcharge	325.00	250.00
b.		Surcharge on back	400.00	400.00
c.		Pair, one without surcharge		
J5	A9(o)	35 on 20c red, *green*	225.00	160.00
a.		Inverted surcharge	325.00	250.00
J6	A9(o)	1fr on 35c vio, *orange*	135.00	90.00
a.		Inverted surcharge	325.00	250.00
b.		Surcharge on back	400.00	400.00

Nossi-Bé 5 c. A PERCEVOIR p

Nossi-Bé 5 c. A PERCEVOIR q

Nossi-Bé 0.10 A PERCEVOIR r

1891

No.	Type	Description	Unused	Used
J7	A9(p)	5c on 20c	120.00	120.00
J8	A9(q)	5c on 20c	140.00	140.00
J9	A9(r)	0.10c on 5c	9.00	8.00
J10	A9(p)	10c on 15c	120.00	120.00
J11	A9(q)	10c on 15c	140.00	140.00
J12	A9(p)	15c on 10c	80.00	80.00
J13	A9(q)	15c on 10c	90.00	90.00
J14	A9(r)	0.15c on 20c	9.00	9.00
a.		25c on 20c (error)	*20,000.*	*20,000.*
J15	A9(p)	25c on 5c	80.00	80.00
J16	A9(q)	25c on 5c	90.00	90.00
J17	A9(r)	0.25c on 75c	325.00	275.00

Inverted Surcharge

No.	Type	Description	Unused	Used
J7a	A9(p)	5c on 20c	175.00	175.00
J8a	A9(q)	5c on 20c	175.00	175.00
J10a	A9(p)	10c on 15c	190.00	190.00
J11a	A9(q)	10c on 15c	190.00	190.00
J12a	A9(p)	15c on 10c	190.00	190.00
J13a	A9(q)	15c on 10c	190.00	190.00
J15a	A9(p)	25c on 5c	190.00	190.00
J16a	A9(q)	25c on 5c	190.00	190.00
J17a	A9(r)	0.25c on 75c	625.00	600.00

Stamps of Nossi-Be were superseded by those of Madagascar.

Counterfeits exist of surcharges on #J1-J17.

NYASSA

LOCATION — In the northern part of Mozambique in southeast Africa
GOVT. — Part of Portuguese East Africa Colony
AREA — 73,292 sq. mi.
POP. — 3,000,000 (estimated)
CAPITAL — Porto Amelia

The district formerly administered by the Nyassa Company is now a part of Mozambique. Postage stamps of Mozambique are used.

1000 Reis = 1 Milreis
100 Centavos = 1 Escudo (1919)

Mozambique Nos. 24-35 Overprinted in Black

NYASSA

1898 Unwmk. *Perf. 11½, 12½*

No.	Type	Description	Unused	Used
1	A3	5r yellow	2.50	1.75
2	A3	10r redsh vio	2.50	1.75
3	A3	15r chocolate	2.50	1.75
4	A3	20r gray vio	2.50	1.75
5	A3	25r bl grn	2.50	1.75
6	A3	50r light blue	2.50	1.75
a.		Inverted overprint		
b.		Perf. 12½	8.00	6.50
7	A3	75r rose	3.25	2.25
8	A3	80r yel grn	3.25	2.25
9	A3	100r brn, *buff*	3.25	2.25
10	A3	150r car, *rose*	8.25	6.00
11	A3	200r dk bl, *blue*	5.25	3.25
12	A3	300r dk bl, *salmon*	6.25	3.25
		Nos. 1-12 (12)	44.50	29.75

Reprints of Nos. 1, 5, 8, 9, 10 and 12 have white gum and clean-cut perforation 13½. Value of No. 9, $15; others $3 each.

Same Overprint on Mozambique Issue of 1898

1898 *Perf. 11½*

No.	Type	Description	Unused	Used
13	A4	2½r gray	1.75	1.25
14	A4	5r orange	1.75	1.25
15	A4	10r light grn	1.75	1.25
16	A4	15r brown	2.00	1.50
17	A4	20r gray vio	2.00	1.50
18	A4	25r sea green	2.00	1.50
19	A4	50r blue	2.00	1.50
20	A4	75r rose	2.50	1.25
21	A4	80r violet	2.75	2.00
22	A4	100r dk bl, *bl*	2.75	2.00
23	A4	150r brn, *straw*	3.50	2.00
24	A4	200r red lil, *pnksh*	3.50	2.00
25	A4	300r dk blue, *rose*	3.50	2.00
		Nos. 13-25 (13)	31.75	21.00

Giraffe — A5

Camels — A6

Perf. 13½-15 & Compound

1901 Engr.

No.	Type	Description	Unused	Used
26	A5	2½r blk & red brn	75	45
27	A5	5r blk & violet	75	45
28	A5	10r blk & dp grn	75	45
29	A5	15r blk & org brn	75	45
30	A5	20r blk & org red	75	45
31	A5	25r blk & orange	75	45
32	A5	50r blk & dl bl	75	45
33	A6	75r blk & car lake	1.00	45
34	A6	80r blk & lilac	1.00	45
35	A6	100r blk & brn bis	1.00	50
36	A6	150r blk & dp org	1.25	95
37	A6	200r blk & grnsh bl	1.00	95
38	A6	300r blk & yel grn	1.00	1.10
		Nos. 26-38 (13)	11.50	7.55

Nos. 26 to 38 are known with inverted centers but are believed to be purely speculative and never regularly issued. Value $25 each.

For overprints and surcharges see Nos. 39-50, 63-80.

Nos. 34, 36, 38 Surcharged **65 REIS**

1903

39 A6 65r on 80r 70 65
40 A6 115r on 150r 70 65
41 A6 130r on 300r 70 65

Nos. 29, 31 Overprinted **PROVISORIO**

42 A5 15r blk & org brn 70 65
43 A5 25r blk & orange 70 65

Nos. 34, 36, 38 Surcharged **65 réis**

44 A6 65r on 80r 22.50 10.00
45 A6 115r on 150r 22.50 10.00
46 A6 130r on 300r 22.50 10.00

Nos. 29, 31 Overprinted **Provisorio**

47 A5 15r blk & org brn 650.00 200.00
48 A5 25r blk & org 325.00 125.00

Forgeries exist of Nos. 44-48.

Nos. 26, 35 Surcharged **5 REIS PROVISORIO**

1910

49 A5 5r on 2½r 85 75
50 A6 50r on 100r 85 75
a. "50 REIS" omitted 90.00

Reprints of Nos. 49-50, made in 1921, have 2mm space between surcharge lines, instead of 1½mm. Value, each 25 cents.

Zebra — A7

Vasco da Gama's Flagship "San Gabriel" — A8

Red Overprint

Designs: Nos. 51-53, Camels. Nos. 57-59, Giraffe and palms.

1911

51 A7 2½r blk & dl vio 1.00 55
52 A7 5r black 1.00 55
53 A7 10r blk & gray grn 1.00 55
54 A7 20r blk & car lake 1.00 55
55 A7 25r blk & vio brn 1.00 55
56 A7 50r blk & dp bl 1.00 55
57 A8 75r blk & brn 1.00 85
58 A8 100r blk & brn, *grn* 1.00 85
59 A8 200r blk & dp grn, *sal* 1.25 1.10
60 A8 300r blk, *blue* 2.00 1.90
61 A8 400r blk & dk brn 2.00 2.25
a. Pair, one without overprint
62 A8 500r ol & vio brn 2.50 2.50
Nos. 51-62 (12) 15.75 12.75

Nos. 51-62 exist without overprint but were not issued in that condition. Value $10 each.
For surcharges see Nos. 81-105.

REPUBLICA

Stamps of 1901-03 Surcharged **1½C.**

1918

On Nos. 26-38

63 A5 ¼c on 2½r 85.00 65.00
64 A5 ½c on 5r 85.00 65.00
65 A5 1c on 10r 85.00 65.00
66 A5 1½c on 15r 5.50 4.00
67 A5 2c on 20r 3.00 3.00
68 A5 3½c on 25r 3.00 3.00
69 A5 5c on 50r 3.00 3.00
70 A6 7½c on 75r 3.00 3.00
71 A6 8c on 80r 3.00 3.00
72 A6 10c on 100r 3.00 3.00
73 A6 15c on 150r 5.00 3.75
74 A6 20c on 200r 5.00 3.75
75 A6 30c on 300r 3.25 6.50

On Nos. 39-41

76 A6 40c on 65r on 80r 30.00 25.00
77 A6 50c on 115r on 150r 8.50 6.50
78 A6 1e on 130r on 300r 8.50 6.50

On Nos. 42-43

79 A5 1½c on 15r 37.50 30.00
80 A5 3½c on 25r 10.00 7.50
Nos. 63-80 (18) 386.25 306.50

On Nos. 70-78 there is less space between "REPUBLICA" and the new value than on the other stamps of this issue.

On Nos. 76-78 the 1903 surcharge is canceled by a bar.

The surcharge exists inverted on #64, 66-70, 72, 76, 78-80, and double on #64, 67, 69.

Nos. 51-62 Surcharged in Black or Red **7½ Centavos**

1921

Lisbon Surcharges

Numerals: The "1" (large or small) is thin, sharp-pointed, and has thin serifs. The "2" is italic, with the tail thin and only slightly wavy. The "3" has a flat top. The "4" is open at the top. The "7" has thin strokes.

Centavos: The letters are shaded, i.e., they are thicker in some parts than in others. The "t" has a thin cross bar ending in a downward stroke at the right. The "s" is flat at the bottom and wider than in the next group.

81 A7 ¼c on 2½r 13.00 13.00
83 A7 ½c on 5r (R) 13.00 13.00
a. ½c on 2½r (R) (error) 200.00 200.00
84 A7 1c on 10r 13.00 13.00
a. Pair, one without surcharge
85 A8 1½c on 300r (R) 18.00 18.00
86 A7 2c on 20r 13.00 13.00
87 A7 2½c on 25r 18.00 18.00
88 A8 3c on 400r 10.00 10.00
a. "Republica" omitted
89 A7 5c on 50r 18.00 18.00
90 A8 7½c on 75r 11.00 11.00
91 A8 10c on 100r 18.00 18.00
92 A8 12c on 500r 10.00 10.00
93 A8 20c on 200r 16.00 16.00
Nos. 81-93 (12) 171.00 171.00

The surcharge exists inverted on Nos. 83-85, 87-88 and 92, and double on Nos. 81, 83 and 86.
Forgeries exist of Nos. 81-93.

London Surcharges

Numerals: The "1" has the vertical stroke and serifs thicker than in the Lisbon printing. The "2" is upright and has a strong wave in the tail. The small "2" is heavily shaded. The "3" has a rounded top. The "4" is closed at the top. The "7" has thick strokes.

Centavos: The letters are heavier than in the Lisbon printing and are of even thickness throughout. The "t" has a thick cross bar with scarcely any down stroke at the end. The "s" is rounded at the bottom and narrower than in the Lisbon printing.

94 A7 ¼c on 2½r 1.25 1.25
95 A7 ½c on 5r (R) 1.25 1.25
96 A7 1c on 10r 1.25 1.25
97 A8 1½c on 300r (R) 1.25 1.25
98 A7 2c on 20r 1.25 1.25
99 A7 2½c on 25r 1.25 1.25
100 A8 3c on 400r 1.25 1.25
101 A7 5c on 50r 1.25 1.25
102 A8 7½c on 75r 1.25 1.25
a. Inverted surcharge
103 A8 10c on 100r 1.25 1.25
104 A8 12c on 500r 1.25 1.25
105 A8 20c on 200r 1.25 1.25
Nos. 94-105 (12) 15.00 15.00

A9

Zebra and Warrior — A10

Designs: 2c-5c, Vasco da Gama. 7½c-20c, "San Gabriel." 2e-5e, Dhow and warrior.

Perf. 12½, 13½-15 & Compound

1921-23 **Engr.**

106 A9 ¼c claret 80 80
107 A9 ½c steel blue 80 80
108 A9 1c grn & blk 80 80
109 A9 1½c blk & ocher 80 80
110 A9 2c red & blk 80 80
111 A9 2½c blk & ol grn 80 80
112 A9 4c blk & org 80 80
113 A9 5c ultra & blk 80 80
114 A9 6c blk & vio 80 80
115 A9 7½c blk & blk brn 80 80
116 A9 8c blk & ol grn 80 80
117 A9 10c blk & red brn 80 80
118 A9 15c blk & carmine 80 80
119 A9 20c blk & pale bl 1.00 1.00
120 A10 30c blk & bister 1.00 1.00
121 A10 40c blk & gray bl 1.00 1.00
122 A10 50c blk & green 1.00 1.00
123 A10 1e blk & red brn 1.00 1.00
124 A10 2e red brn & blk ('23) 5.50 5.50
125 A10 5e ultra & red brn ('23) 4.50 4.50
Nos. 106-125 (20) 25.40 25.40

POSTAGE DUE STAMPS

Giraffe — D1

Designs: ½c, 1c, Giraffe. 2c, 3c, Zebra. 5c, 6c, 10c, "San Gabriel." 20c, 50c, Vasco da Gama.

1924 **Unwmk.** **Engr.** ***Perf. 14***

J1 D1 ½c deep green 75 75
J2 D1 1c gray 75 75
J3 D1 2c red 75 75
J4 D1 3c red orange 75 75
J5 D1 5c dark brown 75 75
J6 D1 6c orange brown 75 75
J7 D1 10c brown violet 85 85
J8 D1 20c carmine 85 85
J9 D1 50c lilac gray 85 85
Nos. J1-J9 (9) 7.05 7.05

NEWSPAPER STAMP

Mozambique No. P6 Overprinted Like Nos. 1-25 in Black

1898 **Unwmk.** ***Perf. 13½***

P1 N3 2½r brown 1.00 85

Reprints have white gum and clean-cut perf. 13½. Value $1.

POSTAL TAX STAMPS

Pombal Issue

Mozambique Nos. RA1-RA3 Overprinted "NYASSA" in Red

1925 **Unwmk.** ***Perf. 12½***

RA1 CD28 15c brn & blk 2.50 2.50
RA2 CD29 15c brn & blk 2.50 2.50
RA3 CD30 15c brn & blk 2.50 2.50

POSTAL TAX DUE STAMPS

Pombal Issue

Mozambique Nos. RAJ1-RAJ3 Overprinted "NYASSA" in Red

1925 **Unwmk.** ***Perf. 12½***

RAJ1 CD31 30c brn & blk 30.00 27.50
RAJ2 CD32 30c brn & blk 30.00 27.50
RAJ3 CD33 30c brn & blk 30.00 27.50

OBOCK

LOCATION — A seaport in eastern Africa on the Gulf of Aden, directly opposite Aden.

Obock was the point of entrance from which French Somaliland was formed. The port was acquired by the French in 1862 but was not actively occupied until 1884 when Sagallo and Tadjoura were ceded to France. In 1888 Djibouti was made into a port and the seat of government moved from Obock to the latter city. In 1902 the name Somali Coast was adopted on the postage stamps of Djibouti, these stamps superseding the individual issues of Obock. See Somali Coast in Vol. 5.

100 Centimes = 1 Franc

Counterfeits exist of Nos. 1-31.

Stamps of French Colonies Handstamped in Black:

OBOCK — #1-11, J1-J4
OBOCK — #12-20, J5-J18

1892 **Unwmk.** ***Perf. 14x13½***

1 A9 1c blk, *lil bl* 15.00 12.50
2 A9 2c brn, *buff* 17.00 15.00
3 A9 4c claret, *lav* 225.00 225.00
4 A9 5c grn, *grnsh* 12.00 10.00
5 A9 10c blk, *lavender* 30.00 20.00
6 A9 15c blue 30.00 26.00
7 A9 25c blk, *rose* 40.00 35.00
8 A9 35c vio, *org* 210.00 210.00
9 A9 40c red, *straw* 175.00 175.00
10 A9 75c car, *rose* 200.00 200.00
11 A9 1fr brnz grn, *straw* 240.00 240.00

No. 3 has been reprinted. On the reprints the second "O" of "OBOCK" is 4mm high instead of 3½mm. Value $7.50.

1892

12 A9 4c claret, *lav* 10.00 9.00
13 A9 5c grn, *grnsh* 10.00 9.00
14 A9 10c blk, *lavender* 12.00 11.50
15 A9 15c blue 12.00 11.50
16 A9 20c red, *grn* 20.00 16.00
17 A9 25c blk, *rose* 9.00 8.00
18 A9 40c red, *straw* 25.00 22.50
19 A9 75c car, *rose* 190.00 150.00
20 A9 1fr brnz grn, *straw* 35.00 27.50

Exists inverted or double on all denominations.

Nos. 14, 15, 17, 20 with Additional Surcharge Handstamped in Red, Blue or Black:

Nos, 21-30

5F

No. 31

1892

21 A9 1c on 25c blk, *rose* 5.00 5.00
22 A9 2c on 10c blk, *lav* 32.00 21.00
23 A9 2c on 15c blue 6.25 6.00
24 A9 4c on 15c bl (Bk) 6.25 6.00
25 A9 4c on 25c blk, *rose* (Bk) 7.00 6.25
26 A9 5c on 25c blk, *rose* 10.00 7.00
27 A9 20c on 10c blk, *lav* 45.00 35.00
28 A9 30c on 10c blk, *lav* 60.00 50.00
29 A9 35c on 25c blk, *rose* 45.00 40.00
a. "3" instead of "35" 400.00 400.00
30 A9 75c on 1fr brnz grn, *straw* 62.50 52.50
b. "57" instead of "75" *4,500. 4,500.*
c. "55" instead of "75" *4,500. 4,500.*
31 A9 5fr on 1fr brnz grn, *straw*(Bl) 500.00 425.00

Exists inverted on most denominations.

Navigation and Commerce A4

Camel and Rider A5

1892 **Typo.** ***Perf. 14x13½***

Obock in Red (1c, 5c, 15c, 25c, 75c, 1fr) or Blue

32 A4 1c blk, *lil bl* 1.00 70
33 A4 2c brn, *buff* 60 60
34 A4 4c claret, *lav* 1.00 70
35 A4 5c grn, *grnsh* 1.50 70
36 A4 10c blk, *lavender* 2.75 1.25

No.	Type	Description	Unused	Used
37	A4	15c bl, quadrille paper	5.50	3.00
38	A4	20c red, *grn*	11.00	8.00
39	A4	25c blk, *rose*	10.50	8.00
40	A4	30c brn, *bis*	7.75	5.25
41	A4	40c red, *straw*	7.75	5.00
42	A4	50c car, *rose*	9.25	5.25
43	A4	75c vio, *org*	11.00	5.25
a.		Name double	140.00	140.00
b.		Name inverted	*1,400.*	*1,400.*
44	A4	1fr brnz grn, *straw*	14.00	11.00

Perf. 13½x14 stamps are counterfeits.

1893 *Imperf.*

Quadrille Lines Printed on Paper

Size: 32mm at base

No.	Type	Description	Unused	Used
44A	A5	2fr brnz grn	26.00	22.50

Size: 45mm at base

No.	Type	Description	Unused	Used
45	A5	5fr red	60.00	50.00

Somali Warriors A7

A8

1894 *Imperf.*

Quadrille Lines Printed on Paper

No.	Type	Description	Unused	Used
46	A7	1c blk & rose	1.10	1.10
47	A7	2c vio brn & grn	1.10	1.10
48	A7	4c brn vio & org	1.10	1.10
49	A7	5c bl grn & brn	1.25	1.10
50	A7	10c blk & grn	4.50	2.75
a.		Half used as 5c on cover		90.00
51	A7	15c bl & rose	3.25	2.25
52	A7	20c brn org & mar	4.50	2.50
a.		Half used as 10c on cover		70.00
53	A7	25c blk & bl	4.50	2.75
a.		Half used on cover		60.00
54	A7	30c bis & yel grn	10.00	6.00
a.		Half used as 15c on cover		850.00
55	A7	40c red & bl grn	7.00	3.50
56	A7	50c rose & bl	6.25	3.50
a.		Half used as 25c on cover		1,500.
57	A7	75c gray lil & org	7.25	4.00
58	A7	1fr ol grn & mar	7.25	5.25

Size: 37mm at base

No.	Type	Description	Unused	Used
60	A8	2fr vio & org	62.50	55.00

Size: 42mm at base

No.	Type	Description	Unused	Used
61	A8	5fr rose & bl	52.50	42.50

Size: 46mm at base

No.	Type	Description	Unused	Used
62	A8	10fr org & red vio	80.00	70.00
63	A8	25fr brn & bl	450.00	450.00
64	A8	50fr red vio & grn	500.00	500.00

Counterfeits exist of Nos. 63-64.

Stamps of Obock were replaced in 1901 by those of Somali Coast. The 5c on 75c, 5c on 25fr and 10c on 50fr of 1902 are listed under Somali Coast.

POSTAGE DUE STAMPS

Postage Due Stamps of French Colonies Handstamped Like #1-20

1892 **Unwmk.** *Imperf.*

No.	Type	Description	Unused	Used
J1	D1	5c black	*6,250.*	
J2	D1	10c black	100.00	110.00
J3	D1	30c black	165.00	190.00
J4	D1	60c black	210.00	225.00
J5	D1	1c black	21.00	21.00
J6	D1	2c black	16.00	16.00
J7	D1	3c black	16.00	16.00
J8	D1	4c black	13.00	13.00
J9	D1	5c black	5.50	5.50
J10	D1	10c black	13.00	13.00
J11	D1	15c black	8.00	8.00
J12	D1	20c black	11.00	11.00
J13	D1	30c black	13.50	13.50
J14	D1	40c black	21.00	21.00
J15	D1	60c black	32.50	32.50
J16	D1	1fr brown	100.00	100.00
J17	D1	2fr brown	100.00	100.00
J18	D1	5fr brown	210.00	210.00

These handstamped overprints may be found double or inverted on some values. Counterfeits exist of Nos. J1-J18.

No. J1 has been reprinted. The overprint on the original measures 12½x3¾mm and on the reprint 12x3¼mm. Value, $120.

OLTRE GIUBA

(Italian Jubaland)

LOCATION — A strip of land, 50 to 100 miles in width, west of and parallel to the Juba River in East Africa

GOVT. — Former Italian Protectorate

AREA — 33,000 sq. mi.

POP. — 12,000

CAPITAL — Kismayu

Oltre Giuba was ceded to Italy by Great Britain in 1924 and in 1926 was incorporated with Italian Somaliland. In 1936 it became part of Italian East Africa.

100 Centesimi = 1 Lira

Watermarks

Wmk. 140- Crown

Italian Stamps of 1901-26 Overprinted

OLTRE GIUBA On #1-15 — **OLTRE GIUBA** On #16-20

1925, July 29 **Wmk. 140** *Perf. 14*

No.	Type	Description	Unused	Used
1	A42	1c brown	1.25	1.00
a.		Inverted overprint	65.00	
2	A43	2c yel brown	1.10	1.00
3	A48	5c green	60	1.00
4	A48	10c claret	60	1.00
5	A48	15c slate	60	1.00
6	A50	20c brn orange	60	1.00
7	A49	25c blue	90	1.00
8	A49	30c org brown	90	1.00
9	A49	40c brown	1.10	1.00
10	A49	50c violet	1.10	1.00
11	A49	60c carmine	1.25	1.00
12	A46	1 l brn & green	3.00	2.50
13	A46	2 l dk grn & org	21.00	14.00
14	A46	5 l blue & rose	32.50	17.00
15	A51	10 l gray grn & red	4.50	*7.25*
		Nos. 1-15 (15)	71.00	*51.75*

1925-26

No.	Type	Description	Unused	Used
16	A49	20c green	2.00	*3.00*
17	A49	30c gray	3.00	*3.00*
18	A46	75c dk red & rose	16.00	*17.00*
19	A46	1.25 l bl & ultra	20.00	*21.00*
20	A46	2.50 l dk grn & org	25.00	*27.50*
		Nos. 16-20 (5)	66.00	*71.50*

Issue years: #18-20, 1926; others 1925.

Victor Emmanuel Issue

Italian Stamps of 1925 Overprinted

OLTRE GIUBA

1925-26 **Unwmk.** *Perf. 11*

No.	Type	Description	Unused	Used
21	A78	60c brown car	15	*2.00*
a.		Perf. 13½	*2,000.*	
22	A78	1 l dark blue	20	*2.00*
a.		Perf. 13½	80.00	*500.00*
23	A78	1.25 l dk bl ('26)	50	*6.00*
a.		Perf. 13½	50	*7.25*

Saint Francis of Assisi Issue

Italian Stamps and Type of 1926 Overprinted

OLTRE GIUBA

1926, Apr. 12 **Wmk. 140** *Perf. 14*

No.	Type	Description	Unused	Used
24	A79	20c gray green	95	*3.00*
25	A80	40c dark violet	95	*3.00*
26	A81	60c red brown	95	*3.00*

Overprinted in Red **Oltre Giuba**

Unwmk.

No.	Type	Description	Unused	Used
27	A82	1.25 l dk bl, perf. 11	95	*3.00*
28	A83	5 l + 2.50 l ol grn, perf. 13½	2.40	*5.50*
		Nos. 24-28 (5)	6.20	

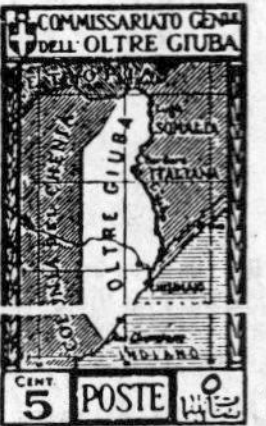

Map of Oltre Giuba — A1

1926, Apr. 21 **Typo.** **Wmk. 140**

No.	Type	Description	Unused	Used
29	A1	5c yellow brown	30	*1.65*
30	A1	20c blue green	30	*1.65*
31	A1	25c olive brown	30	*1.65*
32	A1	40c dull red	30	*1.65*
33	A1	60c brown violet	30	*1.65*
34	A1	1 l blue	30	*1.65*
35	A1	2 l dark green	30	*1.65*
		Nos. 29-35 (7)	2.10	

Oltre Giuba was incorporated with Italian Somaliland on July 1, 1926, and stamps inscribed "Oltre Giuba" were discontinued.

SEMI-POSTAL STAMPS

Note preceding Italy semi-postals applies to No. 28.

Colonial Institute Issue

"Peace" Substituting Spade for Sword — SP1

Wmk. 140

1926, June 1 **Typo.** *Perf. 14*

No.	Type	Description	Unused	Used
B1	SP1	5c + 5c brown	15	*1.65*
B2	SP1	10c + 5c olive green	15	*1.65*
B3	SP1	20c + 5c blue green	15	*1.65*
B4	SP1	40c + 5c brown red	15	*1.65*
B5	SP1	60c + 5c orange	15	*1.65*
B6	SP1	1 l + 5c blue	15	*1.65*
		Nos. B1-B6 (6)	90	

Surtax for Italian Colonial Institute.

SPECIAL DELIVERY STAMPS

Special Delivery Stamps of Italy Overprinted

OLTRE GIUBA

1926 **Wmk. 140** *Perf. 14*

No.	Type	Description	Unused	Used
E1	SD1	70c dull red	11.00	*10.00*
E2	SD2	2.50 l blue & red	14.00	*14.00*

POSTAGE DUE STAMPS

Italian Postage Due Stamps of 1870-1903 Overprinted Like Nos. E1-E2

1925, July 29 **Wmk. 140** *Perf. 14*

No.	Type	Description	Unused	Used
J1	D3	5c buff & magenta	5.75	3.50
J2	D3	10c buff & magenta	4.00	3.50
J3	D3	20c buff & magenta	4.00	3.50
J4	D3	30c buff & magenta	4.00	3.50
J5	D3	40c buff & magenta	5.00	4.00
J6	D3	50c buff & magenta	5.75	5.00
J7	D3	60c buff & brown	5.75	5.00
J8	D3	1 l blue & magenta	7.75	6.00
J9	D3	2 l blue & magenta	22.50	*20.00*
J10	D3	5 l blue & magenta	27.50	*27.50*
		Nos. J1-J10 (10)	92.00	

PARCEL POST STAMPS

These stamps were used by affixing them to the waybill so that one half remained on it following the parcel, the other half staying on the receipt given the sender. Most used halves are right halves. Complete stamps were obtainable canceled, probably to order. Both unused and used values are for complete stamps.

Italian Parcel Post Stamps of 1914-22 Overprinted

OLTRE GIUBA

1925, July 29 **Wmk. 140** *Perf. 13½*

No.	Type	Description	Unused	Used
Q1	PP2	5c brown	6.50	*3.00*
Q2	PP2	10c blue	1.40	*1.50*
Q3	PP2	20c black	1.40	*1.50*
Q4	PP2	25c red	1.40	*1.50*
Q5	PP2	50c orange	3.25	*2.50*
Q6	PP2	1 l violet	2.50	*2.50*
a.		Double overprint	65.00	
Q7	PP2	2 l green	2.50	*2.50*
Q8	PP2	3 l bister	3.25	3.00
Q9	PP2	4 l slate	4.25	4.00
Q10	PP2	10 l rose lilac	18.00	14.00
Q11	PP2	12 l red brown	57.50	50.00
Q12	PP2	15 l olive green	35.00	32.50
Q13	PP2	20 l brown violet	35.00	32.50
		Nos. Q1-Q13 (13)	171.95	

Halves Used

Nos.	Value
Q1,Q10	32
Q2-Q6	15
Q7-Q8	15
Q9	15
Q11,Q13	1.00
Q12	80

PANAMA

LOCATION — Central America between Costa Rica and Colombia
GOVT. — Republic
AREA — 30,134 sq. mi.
POP. — 1,970,000 (est. 1983)
CAPITAL — Panama

Formerly a department of the Republic of Colombia, Panama gained its independence in 1903. Dividing the country at its center is the Panama Canal.

100 Centavos = 1 Peso
100 Centesimos = 1 Balboa (1906)

Catalogue values for unused stamps in this country are for Never Hinged items, beginning with Scott 350 in the regular postage section, Scott C82 in the airpost section, Scott CB1 in the airpost semi-postal section, and Scott RA21 in the postal tax section.

Watermarks

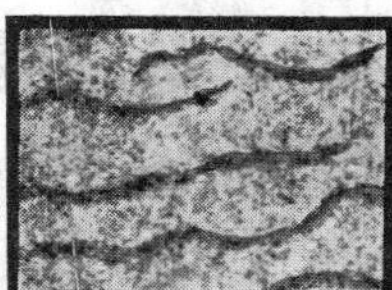

Wmk. 229- Wavy Lines

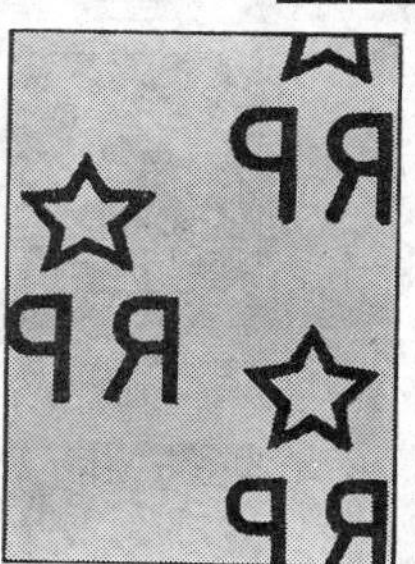

Wmk. 311- Star and RP Multiple

Wmk. 334- Rectangles

Wmk. 343- RP Multiple

Wmk. 365- Argentine Arms, Casa de Moneda de la Nacion & RA Multiple

Wmk. 377- Interlocking Circles

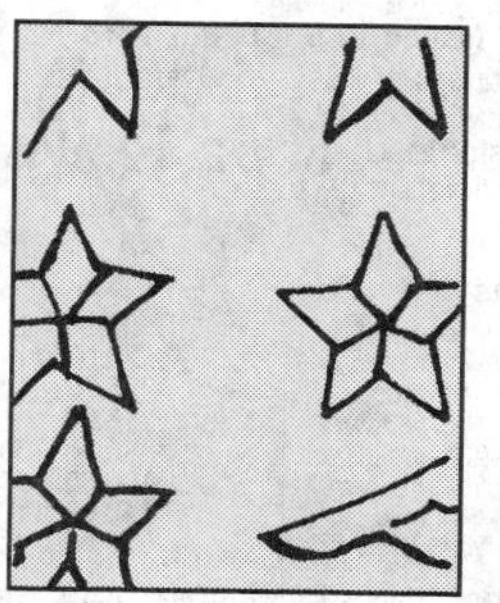

Wmk. 343- Stars

Wmk. 382 may be a sheet watermark. It includes stars with rays, wings and "Panama R de P."

Issues of the Colombian State of Panama

Valid only for domestic mail.

Coat of Arms
A1 A2

1878 Unwmk. Litho. *Imperf.*
Thin Wove Paper

1 A1 5c gray green 25.00 22.50
a. 5c yellow green 25.00 22.50
2 A1 10c blue 65.00 60.00
3 A1 20c rose red 40.00 35.00
4 A2 50c buff *1,500.*

All values of this issue are known rouletted unofficially.

Medium Thick Paper

5 A1 5c bl grn 25.00 22.50
6 A1 10c blue 65.00
7 A2 50c orange 13.00

Nos. 5-7 were printed before Nos. 1-4, according to Panamanian archives.

Values for used Nos. 1-5 are for handstamped postal cancellations.

These stamps have been reprinted in a number of shades, on thin to moderately thick, white or yellowish paper. They are without gum or with white, crackly gum. Some of the 50c stamps appear to have been reprinted from the original stone; they are all in a golden yellow shade, less brownish than the orange originals. All values have been reprinted from new stones made from retouched dies. The marks of retouching are plainly to be seen in the sea and clouds. On the original 10c the shield in the upper left corner has two blank sections; on the reprints the design of this shield is completed. The impression of these reprints is frequently blurred.

Issues of Colombia for use in the Department of Panama

Issued because of the use of different currency.

Map of Panama
A3 A4

1887-88 *Perf. 13½*

8 A3 1c blk, *green* 80 80
9 A3 2c blk, *pink* ('88) 1.65 1.25
a. 2c black, *salmon* 1.65 1.25
10 A3 5c blk, *blue* 80 35
11 A3 10c blk, *yellow* 80 40
a. Imperf., pair
12 A3 20c blk, *lilac* 90 52
13 A3 50c brn ('88) 2.00 1.00
a. Imperf.
Nos. 8-13 (6) 6.95 4.32

See No. 14. For surcharges and overprints see Nos. 24-30, 107-108, 115-116, 137-138.

1892 Pelure Paper

14 A3 50c brown 2.50 1.10

The stamps of this issue have been reprinted on papers of slightly different colors from those of the originals. These are: 1c yellow green, 2c deep rose, 5c bright blue, 10c straw, 20c violet. The 50c is printed from a very worn stone, in a lighter brown than the originals. The series includes a 10c on lilac paper. All these stamps are to be found perforated, imperforate, imperforate horizontally or imperforate vertically. At the same time that they were made, impressions were struck upon a variety of glazed and surface-colored papers.

Wove Paper

1892-96 Engr. *Perf. 12*

15 A4 1c green 25 22
16 A4 2c rose 40 25
17 A4 5c blue 1.50 50
18 A4 10c orange 35 25
19 A4 20c vio ('95) 50 35
20 A4 50c bis brn ('96) 50 35
21 A4 1p lake ('96) 6.50 4.00
Nos. 15-21 (7) 10.00 5.92

In 1903 Nos. 15-21 were used in Cauca and three other southern Columbia towns. Stamps canceled in these towns are worth much more.

For surcharges and overprints see Nos. 22-23, 51-106, 109-114, 129-136, 139, 151-162, 181-184, F12-F15, H4-H5.

Nos. 16, 12-14 Surcharged:

HABILITADO. 1894 1 CENTAVO. — a
HABILITADO. 1894 1 CENTAVO. — b
HABILITADO. 1894 5 CENTAVOS. — c
HABILITADO. 1894 5 CENTAVOS. — d
HABILITADO. 1894 5 CENTAVOS. — e
HABILITADO. 1894 10 CENTAVOS. — f
HABILITADO. 1894 10 CENTAVOS, — g

1894 Black Surcharge

22 (a) 1c on 2c rose 50 40
a. Inverted surcharge 2.50 2.50
b. Double surcharge
23 (b) 1c on 2c rose 40 50
a. "CCNTAVO" 2.50 2.50
b. Inverted surcharge 2.50 2.50
c. Double surcharge 5.50 5.50

Red Surcharge

24 (c) 5c on 20c blk, *lil* 2.50 1.50
a. Inverted surcharge 12.50 12.50
b. Double surcharge
c. Without "HABILITADO"
25 (d) 5c on 20c blk, *lil* 3.50 3.00
a. "CCNTAVOS" 7.50 7.50
b. Inverted surcharge 12.50 12.50
c. Double surcharge
d. Without "HABILITADO"
26 (e) 5c on 20c blk, *lil* 6.00 5.00
a. Inverted surcharge 12.50 12.50
b. Double surcharge
27 (f) 10c on 50c brn 3.00 3.00
a. "1894" omitted
b. Inverted surcharge
c. "CCNTAVOS" 15.00
28 (g) 10c on 50c brn 12.50 12.50
a. "CCNTAVOS" 32.50
b. Inverted surcharge

Pelure Paper

29 (f) 10c on 50c brn 4.00 3.00
a. "1894" omitted 7.50
b. Inverted surcharge 12.50 12.50
30 (g) 10c on 50c brn 10.00 10.00
a. "CCNTAVOS"
b. Without "HABILITADO"
c. Inverted surcharge 25.00 25.00
d. Double surcharge
Nos. 22-30 (9) 42.40 38.90

There are several settings of these surcharges. Usually the surcharge is about 15½mm high, but in one setting, it is only 13mm. All the types are to be found with a comma after "CENTAVOS". Nos. 24, 25, 26, 29 and 30 exist with the surcharge printed sideways. Nos. 23, 24 and 29 may be found with an inverted "A" instead of "V" in "CENTAVOS". There are also varieties caused by dropped or broken letters.

Issues of the Republic Issued in the City of Panama

Stamps of 1892-96 Overprinted — REPUBLICA DE PANAMA

1903, Nov. 16
Rose Handstamp

51 A4 1c green 2.00 1.50
52 A4 2c rose 5.00 3.00
53 A4 5c blue 2.00 1.25
54 A4 10c yellow 2.00 2.00
55 A4 20c violet 4.00 3.50
56 A4 50c bis brn 10.00 7.00
57 A4 1p lake 50.00 40.00
Nos. 51-57 (7) 75.00 58.25

Blue Black Handstamp

58 A4 1c green 2.00 1.25
59 A4 2c rose 1.00 1.00
60 A4 5c blue 7.00 6.00
61 A4 10c yellow 5.00 3.50
62 A4 20c violet 10.00 7.50
63 A4 50c bis brn 10.00 7.50
64 A4 1p lake 50.00 42.50
Nos. 58-64 (7) 85.00 69.25

The stamps of this issue are to be found with the handstamp placed horizontally, vertically or diagonally; inverted; double; double, one inverted; double, both inverted; in pairs, one without handstamp; etc.

This handstamp has been reprinted in brown rose on the 1, 5, 20 and 50c, in purple on the 1, 2, 50c and 1p, and in magenta on the 5, 10, 20 and 50c. Reprints were also made in rose and black when the handstamp was nearly worn out, so that the "R" of "REPUBLICA" appears to be shorter than usual, and the bottom part of "LI" has been broken off. The "P" of "PANAMA" leans to the left and the tops of "NA" are broken. Many of these varieties are found inverted, double, etc.

Overprinted

PANAMA PANAMA

1903, Dec. 3
Bar in Similar Color to Stamp
Black Overprint

65 A4 2c rose 2.50 2.50
a. "PANAMA" 15mm long 3.50
b. Violet bar 5.00
66 A4 5c blue 100.00
a. "PANAMA" 15mm long 100.00

67 A4 10c yellow 2.50 2.50
- ***a.*** "PANAMA" 15mm long 6.00
- ***b.*** Horizontal overprint 17.50

Gray Black Overprint

68 A4 2c rose 2.00 2.00
- ***a.*** "PANAMA" 15mm long 2.50

Carmine Overprint

69 A4 5c blue 2.50 2.50
- ***a.*** "PANAMA" 15mm long 3.50
- ***b.*** Bar only 35.00 35.00
- ***c.*** Double overprint

70 A4 20c violet 7.50 6.50
- ***a.*** "PANAMA" 15mm long 10.00
- ***b.*** Double overprint, one in black 40.00

Nos. 65,67-70 (5) 17.00 16.00

This overprint was set up to cover fifty stamps. "PANAMA" is normally 13mm long and 1 3/4mm high but, in two rows in each sheet, it measures 15 to 16mm. This word may be found with one or more of the letters taller than usual; with one, two or three inverted "V's" instead of "A's"; with an inverted "Y" instead of "A"; an inverted "N"; an "A" with accent; and a fancy "P." Owing to misplaced impressions, stamps exist with "PANAMA" once only, twice on one side, or three times.

Overprinted in Red

PANAMA PANAMA

1903, Dec.

71 A4 1c green 75 60
- ***a.*** "PANAMA" 15mm long 1.25
- ***b.*** "PANAMA" reading down 3.00 75
- ***c.*** "PANAMA" reading up and down 3.00
- ***d.*** Double overprint 8.00

72 A4 2c rose 50 40
- ***a.*** "PANAMA" 15mm long 1.00
- ***b.*** "PANAMA" reading down 75 50
- ***c.*** "PANAMA" reading up and down 4.00
- ***d.*** Double overprint 8.00

73 A4 20c violet 1.50 1.00
- ***a.*** "PANAMA" 15mm long 2.25
- ***b.*** "PANAMA" reading down
- ***c.*** "PANAMA" reading up and down 8.00 8.00
- ***d.*** Double overprint 18.00 18.00

74 A4 50c bis brn 3.00 2.50
- ***a.*** "PANAMA" 15mm long 5.00
- ***b.*** "PANAMA" reading up and down 12.00 12.00
- ***c.*** Double overprint 6.00 6.00

75 A4 1p lake 6.00 4.50
- ***a.*** "PANAMA" 15mm long 6.25
- ***b.*** "PANAMA" reading up and down 15.00 15.00
- ***c.*** Double overprint 15.00
- ***d.*** Inverted overprint 25.00

Nos. 71-75 (5) 11.75 9.00

This setting appears to be a re-arrangement (or two very similar re-arrangements) of the previous overprint. The overprint covers fifty stamps. "PANAMA" usually reads upward but sheets of the 1, 2 and 20c exist with the word reading upward on one half the sheet and downward on the other half.

In one re-arrangement one stamp in fifty has the word reading in both directions. Nearly all the varieties of the previous overprint are repeated in this setting excepting the inverted "Y" and fancy "P." There are also additional varieties of large letters and "PANAMA" occasionally has an "A" missing or inverted. There are misplaced impressions, as the previous setting.

Overprinted in Red

PANAMA PANAMA

1904-05

76 A4 1c green 20 18
- ***a.*** Both words reading up 1.50
- ***b.*** Both words reading down 2.75
- ***c.*** Double overprint
- ***d.*** Pair, one without overprint 7.50
- ***e.*** "PANAAM" 20.00
- ***f.*** Inverted "M" in "PANAMA" 75

77 A4 2c rose 20 18
- ***a.*** Both words reading up 2.50
- ***b.*** Both words reading down 2.50
- ***c.*** Double overprint 10.00
- ***d.*** Double overprint, one inverted 14.00
- ***e.*** Inverted "M" in "PANAMA" 75

78 A4 5c blue 25 20
- ***a.*** Both words reading up 3.00
- ***b.*** Both words reading down 4.25
- ***c.*** Inverted overprint 12.50
- ***d.*** "PANAMAM" 25.00
- ***e.*** "PANANA" 8.00
- ***f.*** "PAMANA" 5.00
- ***g.*** Inverted "M" in "PANAMA" 1.75
- ***h.*** Double overprint 20.00

79 A4 10c yellow 25 20
- ***a.*** Both words reading up 5.00
- ***b.*** Both words reading down 5.00
- ***c.*** Double overprint 15.00
- ***d.*** Inverted overprint 6.75
- ***e.*** "PAMANA" 8.00
- ***f.*** Inverted "M" in "PANAMA" 2.50
- ***g.*** Red brown overprint 7.50 3.50

80 A4 20c violet 2.00 1.00
- ***a.*** Both words reading up 5.00
- ***b.*** Both words reading down 10.00

81 A4 50c bis brn 2.00 1.65
- ***a.*** Both words reading up 10.50
- ***b.*** Both words reading down 10.00
- ***c.*** Double overprint

82 A4 1p lake 5.00 5.00
- ***a.*** Both words reading up 12.50
- ***b.*** Both words reading down 12.50
- ***c.*** Double overprint
- ***d.*** Double overprint, one inverted 20.00

Nos. 76-82 (7) 9.90 8.41

This overprint is also set up to cover fifty stamps. One stamp in each fifty has "PANAMA" reading upward at both sides. Another has the word reading downward at both sides, a third has an inverted "V" in place of the last "A" and a fourth has a small thick "N." In a resetting all these varieties are corrected except the inverted "V." There are misplaced overprints as before.

Later printings show other varieties and have the bar 2 1/2mm instead of 2mm wide. The colors of the various printings of Nos. 76-82 range from carmine to almost pink.

Experts consider the black overprint on the 50c to be bogus.

The 20c violet and 50c bister brown exist with bar 2 1/2mm wide, including the error "PAMANA," but are not known to have been issued. Some copies have been canceled "to oblige."

Issued in Colon

Handstamped in Magenta or Violet — REPUBLICA DE PANAMA

On Stamps of 1892-96

1903-04

101 A4 1c green 75 75
102 A4 2c rose 75 75
103 A4 5c blue 1.00 1.00
104 A4 10c yellow 3.50 3.00
105 A4 20c violet 8.00 6.50
106 A4 1p lake 80.00 70.00

On Stamps of 1887-92
Ordinary Wove Paper

107 A3 50c brown 25.00 20.00
Nos. 101-107 (7) 119.00 102.00

Pelure Paper

108 A3 50c brown 70.00

Handstamped in Magenta, Violet or Red — PANAMA

On Stamps of 1892-96

109 A4 1c green 5.50 5.00
110 A4 2c rose 5.50 5.00
111 A4 5c blue 5.50 5.00
112 A4 10c yellow 8.25 7.00
113 A4 20c violet 12.00 9.00
114 A4 1p lake 70.00 60.00

On Stamps of 1887-92
Ordinary Wove Paper

115 A3 5c brown 35.00 25.00
Nos. 109-115 (7) 141.75 116.00

Pelure Paper

116 A3 50c brown 50.00 37.50

The first note after No. 64 applies also to Nos. 101-116.

The handstamps on Nos. 109-116 have been counterfeited.

REPUBLICA DE PANAMA

Stamps with this overprint were a private speculation. They exist on cover.

Overprinted — *República de Panamá*

On Stamps of 1892-96

Carmine Overprint

129 A4 1c green 40 40
- ***a.*** Inverted overprint 6.00
- ***b.*** Double overprint 2.25
- ***c.*** Double overprint, one inverted 6.00

130 A4 5c blue 50 50

Brown Overprint

131 A4 1c green 12.00
- ***a.*** Double overprint, one inverted

Black Overprint

132 A4 1c green 40.00 30.00
- ***a.*** Vertical overprint 42.50
- ***b.*** Inverted overprint 42.50
- ***c.*** Double overprint, one inverted 42.50

133 A4 2c rose 50 50
- ***a.*** Inverted overprint

134 A4 10c yellow 50 50
- ***a.*** Inverted overprint 4.00
- ***b.*** Double overprint 16.00
- ***c.*** Double overprint, one inverted 6.00

135 A4 20c violet 50 50
- ***a.*** Inverted overprint 4.00
- ***b.*** Double overprint 5.50

136 A4 1p lake 16.00 14.00

On Stamps of 1887-88

Blue Overprint
Ordinary Wove Paper

137 A3 50c brown 3.00 3.00

Pelure Paper

138 A3 50c brown 3.00 3.00
- ***a.*** Double overprint 14.00

This overprint is set up to cover fifty stamps. In each fifty there are four stamps without accent on the last "a" of "Panama", one with accent on the "a" of "Republica" and one with a thick, upright "I".

Overprinted in Carmine — REPUBLICA DE PANAMA.

On Stamp of 1892-96

139 A4 20c violet 100.00 55.00
- ***a.*** Double overprint

Issued in Bocas del Toro

Stamps of 1892-96 Overprinted

Handstamped in Violet — R DE PANAMA

1903-04

151 A4 1c green 20.00 14.00
152 A4 2c rose 20.00 14.00
153 A4 5c blue 25.00 16.00
154 A4 10c yellow 15.00 8.25
155 A4 20c violet 50.00 30.00
156 A4 50c bis brn 100.00 55.00
157 A4 1p lake 140.00 110.00
Nos. 151-157 (7) 370.00 247.25

The handstamp is known double and inverted. Counterfeits exist.

Handstamped in Violet — Panama

158 A4 1c green *100.00*
159 A4 2c rose *70.00*
160 A4 5c blue *80.00*
161 A4 10c yellow *100.00*
162 A4 1p lake *225.00*

This handstamp was applied to these 5 stamps only by favor, experts state. Counterfeits are numerous.

General Issues

A5

1905, Feb. 4 **Engr.** ***Perf. 12***

179 A5 1c green 60 40
180 A5 2c rose 80 50

Panama's Declaration of Independence from the Colombian Republic, Nov. 3, 1903.

Surcharged in Vermilion on Stamps of 1892-96 Issue:

Panamá 1 ct. Panamá

1906

181 A4 1c on 20c violet 25 22
- ***a.*** "Panrma" 2.25 2.25
- ***b.*** "Pnnama" 2.25 2.25
- ***c.*** "Pauama" 2.25 2.25
- ***d.*** Inverted surcharge 4.00 4.00
- ***e.*** Double surcharge 3.50 3.50
- ***f.*** Double surcharge, one inverted

PANAMÁ 2 cts. PANAMÁ

182 A4 2c on 50c bis brn 25 22
- ***a.*** 3rd "A" of "PANAMA" inverted 2.25 2.25
- ***b.*** Both "PANAMA" reading down 4.00 4.00
- ***c.*** Double surcharge
- ***d.*** Inverted surcharge 2.50

The 2c on 20c violet was never issued to the public.

Carmine Surcharge

183 A4 5c on 1p lake 60 40
- ***a.*** Both "PANAMA" reading down 6.00 6.00
- ***b.*** "5" omitted
- ***c.*** Double surcharge
- ***d.*** Inverted surcharge
- ***e.*** 3rd "A" of "PANAMA" inverted 5.50 5.50

On Stamp of 1903-04, No. 75

184 A4 5c on 1p lake 60 40
- ***a.*** "PANAMA" 15mm long
- ***b.*** "PANAMA" reading up and down
- ***c.*** Both "PANAMA" reading down
- ***d.*** Inverted surcharge
- ***e.*** Double surcharge
- ***f.*** 3rd "A" of "PANAMA" inverted

National Flag — A6

Vasco Núñez de Balboa — A7

Fernández de Córdoba — A8

Coat of Arms — A9

Justo Arosemena A10

Manuel J. Hurtado A11

José de Obaldía — A12

Tomás Herrera — A13

José de Fábrega — A14

1906-07 **Engr.** ***Perf. 11 1/2***

185 A6 1/2c org & multi 45 35
186 A7 1c dk grn & blk 45 35
187 A8 2c scarlet & blk 60 35
188 A9 2 1/2c red orange 75 35
189 A10 5c blue & blk 1.75 35
- ***a.*** 5c ultramarine & black 2.00 50

190 A11 8c pur & blk 1.00 65
191 A12 10c vio & blk 1.00 50
192 A13 25c brn & blk 2.50 1.00
193 A14 50c black 6.50 3.50
Nos. 185-193 (9) 15.00 7.40

Inverted centers exist of Nos. 185-187, 189, 189a, 190-193, Value, each $25. Nos. 185-193 exist imperf.

For surcharge see No. F29.

Map — A17

Balboa — A18

Córdoba — A19

Arms — A20

Arosemena A21

Obaldía A23

1909-15 *Perf. 12*

195 A17 ½c org ('11) 60 32
a. Booklet pane of 6
196 A17 ½c rose ('15) 60 60
197 A18 1c dk grn & blk 80 35
a. Inverted center
b. Booklet pane of 6 *165.00*
198 A19 2c red & blk 60 20
a. Booklet pane of 6 *165.00*
199 A20 2½c red org 1.00 20
a. Booklet pane of 6
200 A21 5c bl & blk 1.65 20
a. Booklet pane of 6 *165.00*
201 A23 10c vio & blk 2.50 80
a. Booklet pane of 6
Nos. 195-201 (7) 7.75 2.67

For overprints and surcharges see #H23, I4-I7.

Balboa Sighting Pacific Ocean, His Dog "Leoncico" at His Feet — A24

1913, Sept.

202 A24 2½c dk grn & yel grn 80 65

400th anniv. of Balboa's discovery of the Pacific Ocean.

Panama Exposition Issue

Chorrera Falls — A25

Map of Panama Canal — A26

Balboa Taking Possession of the Pacific — A27

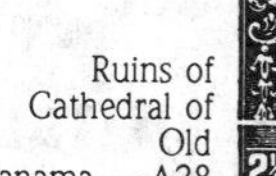

Ruins of Cathedral of Old Panama — A28

Palace of Arts — A29

Gatun Locks — A30

Culebra Cut — A31

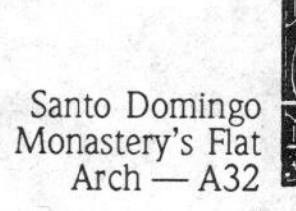
Santo Domingo Monastery's Flat Arch — A32

1915-16 *Perf. 12*

204 A25 ½c ol grn & blk 40 32
205 A26 1c dk grn & blk 90 32
206 A27 2c car & blk 70 32
a. 2c ver & blk ('16) 70 32
208 A28 2½c scar & blk 90 35
209 A29 3c vio & blk 1.50 55
210 A30 5c bl & blk 2.00 35
a. Center inverted 650.00 550.00
211 A31 10c org & blk 2.00 70
212 A32 20c brn & blk 10.00 3.25
a. Center inverted 475.00
Nos. 204-212 (8) 18.40 6.16

For surcharges and overprints see Nos. 217, 233, E1-E2.

Manuel J. Hurtado — A33

1916

213 A33 8c vio & blk 7.00 4.25

For surcharge see No. 30.

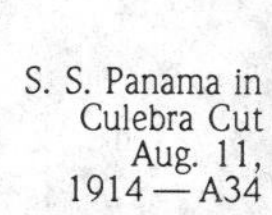

S. S. Panama in Culebra Cut Aug. 11, 1914 — A34

S. S. Panama in Culebra Cut Aug. 11, 1914 — A35

S. S. Cristobal in Gatun Lock — A36

1918

214 A34 12c pur & blk 15.00 5.75
215 A35 15c brt bl & blk 10.00 3.50
216 A36 24c yel brn & blk 15.00 3.50

No. 208 Surcharged in Dark Blue

1519 1919

2 CENTESIMOS 2

1919, Aug. 15

217 A28 2c on 2½c scar & blk 30 30
a. Inverted surcharge 10.00 8.25
b. Double surcharge 12.00 10.00

City of Panama, 400th anniversary.

Dry Dock at Balboa — A38

Ship in Pedro Miguel Lock — A39

1920 **Engr.**

218 A38 50c org & blk 20.00 12.00
219 A39 1b dk vio & blk 30.00 17.50

For overprint and surcharge see Nos. C6, C37.

Arms of Panama City A40

José Vallarino A41

"Land Gate" — A42

Simón Bolivar — A43

Statue of Cervantes A44

Bolívar's Tribute A45

Carlos de Ycaza — A46

Municipal Building in 1821 and 1921 — A47

Statue of Balboa — A48

Villa de Los Santos Church — A49

Herrera — A50

Fábrega — A51

1921, Nov.

220 A40 ½c orange 45 22
221 A41 1c green 55 18
222 A42 2c carmine 60 22
223 A43 2½c red 1.40 1.10
224 A44 3c dl vio 1.40 1.10
225 A45 5c blue 1.40 35
226 A46 8c ol grn 5.00 2.75
227 A47 10c violet 3.25 1.25
228 A48 15c lt bl 4.00 1.65
229 A49 20c ol brn 7.00 3.25
230 A50 24c blk brn 7.00 4.00
231 A51 50c black 12.00 6.00
Nos. 220-231 (12) 44.05 22.07

Centenary of independence.

For overprints and surcharges see Nos. 264, 275-276, 299, 304, 308-310, C35.

Hurtado — A52

Arms — A53

1921, Nov. 28

232 A52 2c dark green 50 50

Manuel José Hurtado (1821-1887), president and folklore writer.

For overprints see Nos. 258, 301.

No. 208 Surcharged in Black

1923

2 CENTESIMOS 2

1923

233 A28 2c on 2½c scar & blk 35 35

Surcharge varieties include wrong or omitted date, double surcharge and pair, one without surcharge. Value $2.50 each.

Two stamps in each sheet have a bar above "CENTESIMOS."

1924, May **Engr.**

234 A53 ½c orange 15 15
235 A53 1c dk grn 15 15
236 A53 2c carmine 18 15
237 A53 5c dk bl 35 15
238 A53 10c dk vio 50 15
239 A53 12c ol grn 60 32
240 A53 15c ultra 80 32
241 A53 24c yel brn 1.75 80
242 A53 50c orange 3.50 90
243 A53 1b black 5.25 2.00
Nos. 234-243 (10) 13.23 5.09

For overprints and surcharges see Nos. 277, 321A, 331-338, 352, C19-C20, C68, RA5, RA10-RA22.

Bolívar — A54

Statue of Bolívar — A55

Bolívar Hall — A56

1926, June 10 *Perf. 12½*

No.	Type	Description	Unused	Used
244	A54	½c orange	25	22
245	A54	1c dk grn	25	22
246	A54	2c scarlet	35	30
247	A54	4c gray	45	35
248	A54	5c dk bl	70	50
249	A55	8c lilac	1.10	80
250	A55	10c dl vio	80	80
251	A55	12c ol grn	1.25	1.00
252	A55	15c ultra	1.65	1.25
253	A55	20c brown	3.25	1.65
254	A56	24c blk vio	4.00	2.00
255	A56	50c black	6.50	5.00
		Nos. 244-255 (12)	20.55	14.09

Bolivar Congress.

For surcharges and overprints see Nos. 259-263, 266-267, 274, 298, 300, 302-303, 305-307, C33-C34, C36, C38-C39.

Lindbergh's Airplane, "The Spirit of St. Louis" — A57

Lindbergh's Airplane and Map of Panama A58

1928, Jan. 9 **Typo.** *Rouletted 7*

No.	Type	Description	Unused	Used
256	A57	2c dk red & blk, *sal*	30	25
257	A58	5c dk bl, *grn*	45	38

Visit of Colonel Charles A. Lindbergh to Central America by airplane.

No. 232 Overprinted in Red

1903

1928

1928, Nov. 1 *Perf. 12*

No.	Type	Description	Unused	Used
258	A52	2c dk grn	25	25

25th anniversary of the Republic.

No. 247 Surcharged in Black

1830 - 1930

UNCENTESIMO

1930, Dec. 17 *Perf. 12½, 13*

No.	Type	Description	Unused	Used
259	A54	1c on 4c gray	22	20

Centenary of the death of Simón Bolívar, the Liberator.

Nos. 244-246 Overprinted in Red or Blue

HABILITADA

1932 *Perf. 12½*

No.	Type	Description	Unused	Used
260	A54	½c org (R)	20	20
261	A54	1c dk grn (R)	35	20
a.		Double overprint	18.00	
262	A54	2c scar (Bl)	35	25

No. 252 Surcharged in Red

HABILITADA
10 c.

No.	Type	Description	Unused	Used
263	A55	10c on 15c ultra	1.00	50
a.		Double surcharge	55.00	

No. 220 Overprinted as in 1932 in Black

1933 *Perf. 12*

Overprint 19mm Long

No.	Type	Description	Unused	Used
264	A40	½c orange	35	20
a.		Overprint 17mm long		

Dr. Manuel Amador Guerrero — A60

1933, July 3 **Engr.** *Perf. 12½*

No.	Type	Description	Unused	Used
265	A60	2c dk red	50	20

Centenary of the birth of Dr. Manuel Amador Guerrero, founder of the Republic of Panama and its first President.

No. 251 Surcharged in Red

HABILITADA
10 c.

1933

No.	Type	Description	Unused	Used
266	A55	10c on 12c ol grn	1.25	65

No. 253 Overprinted in Red

HABILITADA

No.	Type	Description	Unused	Used
267	A55	20c brown	1.75	1.75

José Domingo de Obaldía — A61

Quotation from Emerson — A63

National Institute — A64

Designs: 2c, Eusebio A. Morales. 12c, Justo A. Facio. 15c, Pablo Arosemena.

1934, July **Engr.** *Perf. 14*

No.	Type	Description	Unused	Used
268	A61	1c dk grn	70	50
269	A61	2c scarlet	70	45
270	A63	5c dk bl	1.00	80
271	A64	10c brown	2.75	1.50
272	A61	12c yel grn	5.00	2.00
273	A61	15c Prus bl	6.75	2.50
		Nos. 268-273 (6)	16.90	7.75

25th anniv. of the First Natl. Institute.

Nos. 248, 227 Overprinted in Black or Red

HABILITADA

1935-36 *Perf. 12½, 12*

No.	Type	Description	Unused	Used
274	A54	5c dk bl	70	30
275	A47	10c vio (R) ('36)	1.00	60

No. 225 Surcharged in Red

HABILITADA
B. 0.01

1936 *Perf. 11½*

No.	Type	Description	Unused	Used
276	A45	1c on 5c blue	40	40
a.		Lines of surcharge 1½mm between	6.50	

No. 241 Surcharged in Blue

1836 1936

2 CENTESIMOS

1936, Sept. 24 *Perf. 12*

No.	Type	Description	Unused	Used
277	A53	2c on 24c yel brn	60	50
a.		Double surcharge	20.00	

Issued to commemorate the centenary of the birth of Pablo Arosemena, president of Panama in 1910-12. See Nos. C19-C20.

Ruins of Custom House, Portobelo A67

Designs: 1c, Panama Tree. 2c, "La Pollera." 5c, Simon Bolivar. 10c, Cathedral Tower Ruins. Old Panama. 15c, Francisco Garcia y Santos, 20c, Madden Dam, Panama Canal. 25c, Columbus. 50c, Gaillard Cut. 1b, Panama Cathedral.

1936, Dec. **Engr.** *Perf. 11½*

No.	Type	Description	Unused	Used
278	A67	½c yel org	40	25
279	A67	1c bl grn	40	20
280	A67	2c car rose	40	20
281	A67	5c blue	70	50
282	A67	10c dk vio	1.25	75
283	A67	15c turq bl	1.25	75
284	A67	20c red	1.60	1.50
285	A67	25c blk brn	2.50	2.00
286	A67	50c orange	6.50	5.00
287	A67	1b black	15.00	12.00
		Nos. 278-287 (10)	30.00	23.15

4th Postal Congress of the Americas and Spain. See Nos. C21-C26.

Stamps of 1936 Overprinted in Red or Blue

1937

No.	Type	Description	Unused	Used
288	A67	½c yel org (R)	30	30
a.		Inverted overprint	18.00	
289	A67	1c bl grn (R)	35	18
290	A67	2c car rose (Bl)	35	18
291	A67	5c bl (R)	50	22
292	A67	10c dk vio (R)	1.00	35
293	A67	15c turq bl (R)	4.50	3.25
294	A67	20c red (Bl)	1.65	1.25
295	A67	25c blk brn (R)	2.50	1.25
296	A67	50c org (Bl)	6.75	6.00
297	A67	1b blk (R)	12.00	10.00
		Nos. 288-297 (10)	29.90	22.98

See Nos. C27-C32.

Stamps of 1921-26 Overprinted in Red or Blue

1937-38

1937, July *Perf. 12, 12½*

No.	Type	Description	Unused	Used
298	A54	½c org (R)	80	80
a.		Inverted overprint	30.00	
299	A41	1c grn (R)	25	25
a.		Inverted overprint	30.00	
300	A54	1c dk grn (R)	25	25
301	A52	2c dk grn (R)	35	35
302	A54	2c scar (Bl)	35	35

Stamps of 1921-26 Surcharged in Red

1937-38
2¢

No.	Type	Description	Unused	Used
303	A54	2c on 4c gray	60	45
304	A46	2c on 8c ol grn	60	60
305	A55	2c on 8c lil	60	45
306	A55	2c on 10c dl vio	60	50
307	A55	2c on 12c ol grn	60	45
308	A48	2c on 15c lt bl	60	60
309	A50	2c on 24c blk brn	60	75
310	A51	2c on 50c blk	60	35
		Nos. 298-310 (13)	6.80	6.15

Ricardo Arango A77

Juan A. Guizado A78

La Concordia Fire — A79

Modern Fire Fighting Equipment A80

Firemen's Monument A81

David H. Brandon A82

Perf. 14x14½, 14½x14

1937, Nov. 25 **Photo.** **Wmk. 233**

No.	Type	Description	Unused	Used
311	A77	½c org red	40	35
312	A78	1c green	40	35
313	A79	2c red	40	25
314	A80	5c brt bl	80	50
315	A81	10c purple	1.50	1.25
316	A82	12c yel grn	2.50	2.00
		Nos. 311-316,C40-C42 (9)	9.25	7.05

50th anniversary of the Fire Department.

Old Panama Cathedral Tower and Statue of Liberty Enlightening the World, Flags of Panama and US — A83

Engr. & Litho.

1938, Dec. 7 **Unwmk.** *Perf. 12½*

Center in Black; Flags in Red and Ultramarine

No.	Type	Description	Unused	Used
317	A83	1c dp grn	30	25
318	A83	2c carmine	38	18
319	A83	5c blue	65	30
320	A83	12c olive	1.25	75
321	A83	15c brt ultra	1.50	1.25
		Nos. 317-321 (5)	4.08	2.73

150th anniv. of the US Constitution. See Nos. C49-C53.

No. 236 Overprinted in Black

NORMAL DE SANTIAGO JUNIO 5 1938

1938, June 5 *Perf. 12*

321A A53 2c carmine 25 25
b. Inverted overprint 22.50

Opening of the Normal School at Santiago, Veraguas Province, June 5, 1938. See Nos. C53A-C53B.

Gatun Lake — A84

Liberty — A93

Designs: 1c, Pedro Miguel Locks. 2c, Allegory. 5c, Culebra Cut. 10c, Ferryboat. 12c, Aerial View of Canal. 15c, Gen. William C. Gorgas. 50c, Dr. Manuel A. Guerrero. 1b, Woodrow Wilson.

1939, Aug. 15 **Engr.** *Perf. 12½*

322 A84 ½c yellow 22 15
323 A84 1c dp blue grn 40 15
324 A84 2c dull rose 50 15
325 A84 5c dull blue 80 15
326 A84 10c dk vio 1.00 35
327 A84 12c ol grn 1.00 50
328 A84 15c ultra 1.00 80
329 A84 50c orange 2.50 1.65
330 A84 1b dk brown 5.00 3.00
Nos. 322-330 (9) 12.42 6.90

25th anniversary of the opening of the Panama Canal. See Nos. C54-C61. For surcharges see Nos. C64, G2.

Stamps of 1924 Overprinted in Black or Red

1941, Jan. 2 *Perf. 12*

331 A53 ½c orange 25 25
332 A53 1c dk grn (R) 30 30
333 A53 2c carmine 30 15
334 A53 5c dk bl (R) 40 30
335 A53 10c dk vio (R) 65 50
336 A53 15c ultra (R) 1.40 65
337 A53 50c dp org 5.25 3.50
338 A53 1b blk (R) 12.00 6.00
Nos. 331-338 (8) 20.55 11.65

Issued to commemorate the new constitution of Panama which became effective Jan. 2, 1941. See Nos. C67-C71.

Black Overprint

1942, Feb. 19 **Engr.**

339 A93 10c purple 1.00 1.00

Surcharged with New Value

340 A93 2c on 5c dk bl 1.25 50

See No. C72.

Flags of Panama and Costa Rica A94

1942 **Engraved and Lithographed**

341 A94 2c rose red, dk bl & dp rose 30 22

1st anniv. of the settlement of the Costa Rica-Panama border dispute. See No. C73.

National Emblems — A95

Farm Girl in Work Dress — A96

Cart Laden with Sugar Cane (Inscribed "ACARRERO DE CAÑA") A97

Balboa Taking Possession of the Pacific A98

Golden Altar of San José — A99

San Blas Indian Woman and Child — A101

Santo Tomas Hospital A100

Modern Highway A102

1942 **Engr.; Flag on ½c Litho.**

342 A95 ½c dl vio, bl & car 15 15
343 A96 1c dk grn 15 15
344 A97 2c vermilion 16 15
345 A98 5c dp bl & blk 20 15
346 A99 10c car rose & org 35 20
347 A100 15c lt bl & blk 60 50
348 A101 50c org red & ol blk 1.40 1.00
349 A102 1b black 2.00 1.00
Nos. 342-349 (8) 5.01 3.30

See Nos. 357, 365, 376-377, 380, 395, 409.
For surcharges and overprints see Nos. 366-370, 373-375, 378-379, 381, 387-388, 396, C129-C130, RA23.

Catalogue values for unused stamps in this section, from this point to the end of the section, are for Never Hinged items.

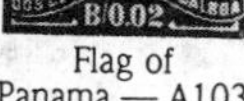
Flag of Panama — A103

Arms of Panama — A104

Engraved; Flag on 2c Lithographed

1947, Apr. **Unwmk.** *Perf. 12½*

350 A103 2c car, bl & red 15 15
351 A104 5c deep blue 16 16

Second anniversary of the National Constitutional Assembly of 1945.

No. 241 Surcharged in Black

Habilitada CORREOS B/. 0.50

1947 *Perf. 12*

352 A53 50c on 24c yel brn 1.00 1.00
a. "Habilitada" 2.00 2.00

Nos. C6C, C75, C74 and C87 Surcharged in Black or Carmine

HABILITADA CORREOS B/. 0.0½

353 AP5 ½c on 8c gray blk 15 15
a. "B/.0.0½ CORREOS" (transposed) 2.50 2.50
354 AP34 ½c on 8c dk ol brn & blk (C) 15 15
355 AP34 1c on 7c rose car 15 15
356 AP42 2c on 8c vio 16 15
Nos. 352-356 (5) 1.61
Set value 1.38

Flag Type of 1942

1948 **Engr. and Litho.**

357 A95 ½c car, org, bl & dp car 15 15

Monument to Firemen of Colon — A105

American-La France Fire Engine A106

Designs: 20c, Firemen and hose cart. 25c, New Central Fire Station, Colon. 50c, Maximino Walker. 1b, J. J. A. Ducruet.

1948 **Engr.**

Center in Black

358 A105 5c dp car 35 15
359 A106 10c orange 60 20
360 A106 20c gray bl 90 38
361 A106 25c chocolate 90 50
362 A105 50c purple 1.00 50
363 A105 1b dp grn 2.50 1.50
Nos. 358-363 (6) 6.25 3.23

50th anniversary of the founding of the Colon Fire Department.
For overprint see No. C125.

Cervantes — A107

1948 **Unwmk.** *Perf. 12½*

364 A107 2c car & blk 25 15

400th anniv. of the birth of Miguel de Cervantes Saavedra, novelist, playwright and poet. See Nos. C105-C106.

Oxcart Type of 1942 Redrawn
Inscribed: "ACARREO DE CANA"

1948 *Perf. 12*

365 A97 2c vermilion 60 15

No. 365 Surcharged or Overprinted in Black

1949, May 23

366 A97 1c on 2c ver 16 15
367 A97 2c vermilion 16 15
a. Inverted overprint 2.00 2.00
Nos. 366-367,C108-C111 (6) 3.63 3.61

Centenary of the incorporation of Chiriqui Province.

Stamps and Types of 1942-48 Issues Overprinted in Black or Red

1949, Sept. **Engr.**

368 A96 1c dk green 15 15
369 A97 2c ver (#365) 20 15
370 A98 5c blue (R) 30 18
Nos. 368-370,C114-C118 (8) 3.81 3.43

75th anniv. of the UPU.
Overprint on No. 368 is slightly different and smaller, 15½x12mm.

Francisco Javier de Luna — A108

Dr. Carlos J. Finlay — A109

1949, Dec. 7 *Perf. 12½*

371 A108 2c car & blk 22 15

200th anniversary of the founding of the University of San Javier. See No. C119.

1950, Jan. 12 **Unwmk.** *Perf. 12*

372 A109 2c car & gray blk 35 15

Issued to honor Dr. Carlos J. Finlay (1833-1915), Cuban physician and biologist who found that a mosquito transmitted yellow fever. See No. C120.

Nos. 343, 357 and 345, Overprinted or Surcharged in Carmine or Black

CENTENARIO del Gral. José de San Martín 17 de Agosto de 1950

1950, Aug. 17

373 A96 1c dk green 15 15
374 A95 2c on ½c car, org, bl & dp car (Bk) 16 15
375 A98 5c dp bl & blk 30 16
Nos. 373-375,C121-C125 (8) 4.21 3.51

Centenary of the death of Gen. José de San Martin.
The overprint is in four lines on No. 375.

Types of 1942

1950 **Engr.**

376 A97 2c ver & blk 15 15
377 A98 5c blue 25 15
Set value 15

No. 376 is inscribed "ACARREO DE CANA."

Nos. 376 and 377 Overprinted in Green or Carmine

Tercer Centenario del Natalicio de San Juan Bautista de La Salle.

1651-1951

1951, Sept. 26

378 A97 2c ver & blk (G) 15 15
379 A98 5c blue (C) 22 15

500th anniversary of the birth of St. Jean-Baptiste de la Salle.

The overprint exists (a) inverted on both stamps, (b) with top line omitted and second line repeated in its place. Value, each $12.50.

Altar Type of 1942

1952 Engr. *Perf. 12*

380 A99 10c pur & org 75 25

No. 357 Surcharged "1952" and New Value in Black

1952

381 A95 1c on ½c multi 15 15

Queen Isabella I and Arms — A110

1952, Oct. 20 Engr. *Perf. 12½*

Center in Black

382 A110 1c green 15 15
383 A110 2c carmine 15 15
384 A110 5c dk bl 20 15
385 A110 10c purple 30 30
Nos. 382-385,C131-C136 (10) 5.95 5.27

500th anniversary of the birth of Queen Isabella I of Spain.

No. 380 and Type of 1942 Surcharged "B/ .0.01 1953" in Black or Carmine

1953 *Perf. 12*

387 A99 1c on 10c pur & org 15 15
388 A100 1c on 15c black (C) 15 15
Set value 20 15

A similar surcharge on No. 346 was privately applied.

A111

A112

Designs: 2c, Baptism of the Flag. 5c, Manuel Amador Guerrero and Senora de Amador. 12c, Santos Jorge A. and Jeronimo de la Ossa. 20c, Revolutionary Junta. 50c, Old city hall. 1b, National coinage.

1953, Nov. 3 Engr. *Perf. 12*

389 A111 2c purple 15 15
390 A112 5c red orange 25 15
391 A112 12c dp red vio 50 15
392 A112 20c slate gray 1.00 22
393 A111 50c org yel 1.50 60
394 A112 1b blue 2.50 1.25
Nos. 389-394 (6) 5.90 2.52

50th anniversary of the founding of the Republic of Panama. See Nos. C140-C145. For surcharge see No. 413.

Farm Girl Type of 1942

1954 Unwmk. *Perf. 12*

395 A96 1c dp car rose 15 15

Surcharged with New Value

396 A96 3c on 1c dp car rose 15 15
Set value 15 15

Monument to Gen. Tomas Herrera — A113

1954 Litho. *Perf. 12½*

397 A113 3c purple 16 15

Centenary of the death of Gen. Tomas Herrera. See Nos. C148-C149.

Tocumen International Airport — A114

1955

398 A114 ½c org brn 15 15

For surcharges see Nos. 411-412.

Pres. José Antonio Remon Cantera, 1908-1955 — A115

1955, June 1

399 A115 3c lil rose & blk 15 15

See No. C153.

Victor de la Guardia y Ayala and Miguel Chiari A116

1955, Sept. 13

400 A116 5c violet 16 15

Centenary of province of Coclé.

Ferdinand de Lesseps — A117

First Excavation of Panama Canal A118

Design: 50c, Theodore Roosevelt.

1955, Nov. 16

401 A117 3c rose brn, *rose* 30 15
402 A118 25c vio bl, *lt bl* 75 75
403 A117 50c vio, *lt vio* 1.50 1.00
Nos. 401-403,C155-C156 (5) 4.71 4.05

150th anniversary of the birth of Ferdinand de Lesseps, French promoter connected with building of Panama Canal.

Imperforates exist, but were not sold at any post office.

Arms of Panama City A119

Carlos A. Mendoza A120

Perf. 12½

1956, Aug. 17 Litho. Unwmk.

404 A119 3c green 15 15

Issued to commemorate the sixth Inter-American Congress of Municipalities, Panama City, Aug. 14-19, 1956.

For souvenir sheet see C182a.

1956, Sept. 13 Wmk. 311

405 A120 10c rose red & dp grn 20 15

Issued to commemorate the centenary of the birth of Pres. Carlos A. Mendoza.

National Archives A121

1956, Nov. 27

406 A121 15c shown 40 20
407 A121 25c Pres. Belisario Porras 60 50

Centenary of the birth of Pres. Belisario Porras. See Nos. C183-C184. For surcharges see Nos. 446.

Pan-American Highway, Panama A122

1957, Aug. 1

408 A122 3c gray green 15 15

Issued to publicize the 7th Pan-American Highway Congress. See Nos. C185-C187.

Hospital Type of 1942

1957 Unwmk. Engr. *Perf. 12*

409 A100 15c black 60 45

Manuel Espinosa Batista — A123

Flags of 21 American Nations — A124

Perf. 12½

1957, Sept. 20 Litho. Wmk. 311

410 A123 5c grn & ultra 15 15

Centenary of the birth of Manuel Espinosa B., independence leader.

No. 398 Surcharged "1957" and New Value in Violet or Black

1957 Unwmk.

411 A114 1c on ½c org brn (V) 15 15
412 A114 3c on ½c org brn 15 15
Set value 15 15

No. 391 Surcharged "1958," New Value and Dots

1958 Engr. *Perf. 12*

413 A112 3c on 12c dp red vio 15 15

Perf. 12½

1958, July 10 Litho. Unwmk.

Center yellow & black; flags in national colors

414 A124 1c lt gray 15 15
415 A124 2c brt yel grn 15 15
416 A124 3c red org 15 15
417 A124 7c vio bl 22 15
Nos. 414-417,C203-C206 (8) 3.48
Set value 2.60

10th anniv. of the Organization of American States.

Brazilian Pavilion, Brussels Fair — A125

Pavilions: 3c, Argentina. 5c, Venezuela. 10c, Great Britain.

1958, Sept. 8 Wmk. 311

418 A125 1c org yel & emer 15 15
419 A125 3c lt bl & olive 15 15
420 A125 5c lt brn & slate 15 15
421 A125 10c aqua & redsh brn 20 16
Nos. 418-421,C207-C209 (7) 2.95 2.86

World's Fair, Brussels, Apr. 17-Oct. 19.

A souvenir sheet containing Nos. 418-421 and C207-C209 is listed as No. C209a.

Pope Pius XII as Young Man A126

Headquarters Building A127

Perf. 12½

1959, Jan. Wmk. 311 Litho.

422 A126 3c orange brown 15 15

Issued in memory of Pope Pius XII, 1876-1958. See Nos. C210-C212a.

1959, Apr. 14 Wmk. 311

Design: 15c, Humanity looking into sun.

423 A127 3c maroon & olive 15 15
424 A127 15c orange & emer 35 22
Nos. 423-424,C213-C217 (7) 3.25 2.92

10th anniv. (in 1958) of the signing of the Universal Declaration of Human Rights.

For overprints see Nos. 425-426, C219-C221.

Nos. 423-424 Overprinted in Dark Blue

**8A REUNION
C.E.P.A.L.
MAYO 1959**

1959, May 16

425 A127 3c maroon & olive 15 15
426 A127 15c orange & emer 35 20
Nos. 425-426,C218-C221 (6) 3.06 2.80

Issued to commemorate the 8th Reunion of the Economic Commission for Latin America.

Eusebio A. Morales A128

National Institute A129

Perf. 12½

1959, July 27 Litho. Wmk. 311

427 A128 3c shown		15	15
428 A128 13c Abel Bravo		25	25
429 A129 21c shown		40	25
Nos. 427-429,C222-C223 (5)		1.11	
Set value			70

50th anniversary, National Institute.

Soccer — A130 Fencing — A131

1959, Oct. 26

430 A130 1c shown	15	15
431 A130 3c Swimming	15	15
432 A130 20c Hurdling	45	40
Nos. 430-432,C224-C226 (6)	1.90	
Set value		1.35

Issued to commemorate the 3rd Pan American Games, Chicago, Aug. 27-Sept. 7, 1959.
For overprint and surcharge see #C289, C349.

Perf. 12½

1960, Sept. 22 Litho. Wmk. 343

433 A131 3c shown	15	15
434 A131 5c Soccer	16	15
Nos. 433-434,C234-C237 (6)	2.16	
Set value		1.30

17th Olympic Games, Rome, Aug. 25-Sept. 11.
For surcharges and overprints see Nos. C249-C250, C254, C266-C270, C290, C298, C350, RA40.

Agricultural Products and Cattle — A132

1961, Mar. 3 Wmk. 311 *Perf. 12½*

435 A132 3c blue green	15	15

Issued to publicize the second agricultural and livestock census, Apr. 16, 1961.

Children's Hospital — A133

1961, May 2

436 A133 3c greenish blue	15	15

25th anniv. of the Lions Club of Panama. See #C245-C247. For overprints see #C284-C286.

Flags of Panama and Costa Rica A134

1961, Oct. 2 Wmk. 343 *Perf. 12½*

437 A134 3c car & bl	15	15

Meeting of Presidents Mario Echandi of Costa Rica and Roberto F. Chiari of Panama at Paso Canoa, Apr. 21, 1961. See No. C251.

Arms of Colon — A135

Mercury and Cogwheel — A136

1962, Feb. 28 Litho. Wmk. 311

438 A135 3c car, yel & vio bl	15	15

Issued to publicize the third Central American Municipal Assembly, Colon, May 13-17. See No. C255.

1962, Mar. 16 Wmk. 343

439 A136 3c red org	15	15

First industrial and commercial census.

Social Security Hospital A137

1962, June 1 *Perf. 12½*

440 A137 3c vermilion & gray	15	15

Opening of the Social Security Hospital.
For surcharge see No. 445.

San Francisco de la Montana Church, Veraguas A138

Ruins of Old Panama Cathedral (1519-1671) — A139

Designs: 3c, David Cathedral. 5c, Natá Church. 10c, Don Bosco Church. 15c, Church of the Virgin of Carmen. 20c, Colon Cathedral. 25c, Greek Orthodox Temple. 50c, Cathedral of Panama. 1b, Protestant Church of Colon.

1962-64 Litho. Wmk. 343

Buildings in Black

441	A138	1c red & bl	15	15
441A	A139	2c red & yel	15	15
441B	A138	3c vio & yel	15	15
441C	A139	5c rose & lt grn	15	15
441D	A139	10c grn & yel	25	20
441E	A139	10c red & bl ('64)	25	15
441F	A139	15c ultra & lt grn	30	16
441G	A139	20c red & pink	40	25
441H	A138	25c grn & pink	50	45
441I	A139	50c ultra & pink	1.00	42
441J	A138	1b lilac & yel	2.00	1.50
		Nos. 441-441J (11)	5.30	3.73

Issued to publicize freedom of religion in Panama. Issue dates: No. 441E, June 4, 1964; others, July 20, 1962.
See #C256-C265; souvenir sheet #C264a.
For surcharges and overprints see Nos. 445A, 451, C288, C296-C297, C299.

Bridge of the Americas during Construction A140

1962, Oct. 12 *Perf. 12½*

442 A140 3c carmine & gray	15	15

Opening of the Bridge of the Americas (Thatcher Ferry Bridge), Oct. 12, 1962. See No. C273. For surcharge see No. 445B.

Fire Brigade Exercises, Inauguration of Aqueduct, 1906 — A141

Portraits of Fire Brigade Officials: 3c, Lt. Col. Luis Carlos Endara P., Col. Raul Arango N. and Major Ernesto Arosemena A. 5c, Guillermo Patterson Jr., David F. de Castro, Pres. T. Gabriel Duque, Telmo Rugliancich and Tomas Leblanc.

1963 Wmk. 311 *Perf. 12½*

443	A141	1c emer & blk	15	15
443A	A141	3c vio bl & blk	15	15
444	A141	5c mag & blk	15	15
		Nos. 443-444,C279-C281 (6)	1.45	
		Set value		1.05

75th anniversary (in 1962) of the Panamanian Fire Brigade.
For surcharge see No. 445C.

Nos. 440, 441A, 442, 443A and 407 Surcharged "VALE" and New Value in Black or Red

1963 Wmk. 343 *Perf. 12½*

445	A137	4c on 3c ver & gray	15	15
445A	A138	4c on 3c vio & yel	15	15
445B	A140	4c on 3c car & gray	15	15

Wmk. 311

445C	A141	4c on 3c vio bl & blk	15	15
446	A121	10c on 25c dk car rose & bluish blk (R)	35	15
		Nos. 445-446 (5)	95	
		Set value		58

1964 Winter Olympics, Innsbruck — A141a

Perf. 14x13½, 13½x14 (#447A, 447C)

1963, Dec. 20 Litho.

447	A141a	½c Mountains
447A	A141a	1c Speed skating
447B	A141a	3c like No. 447
447C	A141a	4c like No. 447A
447D	A141a	5c Slalom skiing
447E	A141a	15c like No. 447D
447F	A141a	21c like No. 447D
447G	A141a	31c like No. 447D
h.		Souv. sheet of 2, #447F-447G, perf. 13½x14

#447D-447G are airmail. #447h exists imperf., with background colors switched.

Pres. Francisco J. Orlich, Costa Rica — A142

Vasco Nuñez de Balboa — A143

Flags and Presidents: 2c, Luis A. Somoza, Nicaragua. 3c, Dr. Ramon Villeda M., Honduras. 4c, Roberto F. Chiari, Panama.

Perf. 12½x12

1963, Dec. 18 Litho. Unwmk.

Portrait in Slate Green

448	A142	1c lt grn, red & ultra	15	15
448A	A142	2c lt bl, red & ultra	15	15
448B	A142	3c pale pink, red & ultra	16	15
448C	A142	4c rose, red & ultra	20	16
		Set value		45

Issued to commemorate the meeting of Central American Presidents with Pres. John F. Kennedy, San José, Mar. 18-20, 1963. See Nos. C292-C294.

1964, Jan. 22 Photo. *Perf. 13*

449 A143 4c green, *pale rose*	15	15

450th anniv. of Balboa's discovery of the Pacific Ocean. See No. C295.

No. C231 Surcharged in Red: "Correos B/.0.10"

1964 Wmk. 311 Litho. *Perf. 12½*

450 AP74 10c on 21c lt bl	20	15

Type of 1962 Overprinted in Red: "HABILITADA"

1964 Wmk. 343

451 A138 1b red, bl & blk	2.00	2.00

1964 Summer Olympics, Tokyo — A144

1964, Apr. *Perf. 13½x14*

452	A144	½c shown
452A	A144	1c Torch bearer

Perf. 14x13½

452B	A144	5c Olympic stadium
452C	A144	10c like No. 452
452D	A144	21c like No. 452
452E	A144	50c like No. 452
f.		Souv. sheet of 1, perf. 13½x14

Nos. 452B-452E are airmail. No. 452f exists imperf. with different colors.

Space Conquest — A145

Designs: ½c, Projected Apollo spacecraft. 1c, Gemini, Agena spacecraft. 5c, Astronaut Walter M. Schirra. 10c, Astronaut L. Gordon Cooper. 21c, Schirra's Mercury capsule. 50c, Cooper's Mercury capsule.

1964, Apr. 21 *Perf. 14x14x13½*

453	A145	½c bl grn & multi
453A	A145	1c dk bl & multi
453B	A145	5c yel bis & multi
453C	A145	10c lil rose & multi

453D A145 21c bl & multi
453E A145 50c vio & multi
f. Souv. sheet of 1

Nos. 453B-453E are airmail. No. 453f exists imperf. with different colors.

Aquatic Sports A146

Perf. 14x13½, 13½x14

1964, Sept. 2

454 A146 ½c Water skiing
454A A146 1c Skin diving
454B A146 5c Fishing
454C A146 10c Sailing, vert.
454D A146 21c Hydroplane racing
454E A146 31c Water polo
f. Souv. sheet of 1

Nos. 454B-454E are airmail. Nos. 454-454f exist imperf. with different colors.

Eleanor Roosevelt — A147

Perf. 12x12½

1964, Oct. 9 Litho. Unwmk.

455 A147 4c car & blk, *grnsh* 15 15

Issued to honor Eleanor Roosevelt (1884-1962). See Nos. C330-C330a.

Canceled to Order
Canceled sets of new issues have been sold by the government. Postally used copies are worth more.

1964 Winter Olympics, Innsbruck — A147a

Olympic medals and winners: ½c, Women's slalom. 1c, Men's 500-meter speed skating. 2c, Four-man bobsled. 3c, Women's figure skating. 4c, Ski jumping. 5c, 15km cross country skiing. 6c, 50km cross country skiing. 7c, Women's 3000-meter speed skating. 10c, Men's figure skating. 21c, Two-man bobsled. 31c, Men's downhill skiing.

Litho. & Embossed
Perf. 13½x14

1964, Oct. 14 Unwmk.

456 A147a ½c bl grn & multi
456A A147a 1c dk bl & multi
456B A147a 2c brn vio & multi
456C A147a 3c lil rose & multi
456D A147a 4c brn lake & multi
456E A147a 5c brt vio & multi
456F A147a 6c grn bl & multi
456G A147a 7c dp vio & multi
456H A147a 10c emer grn & multi
456I A147a 21c ver & multi
456J A147a 31c ultra & multi
k. Souv. sheet of 3, #456H-456J

Nos. 456E-456J are airmail. No. 456k exists imperf.
See Nos. 458-458J.

Satellites — A147b

Designs: ½c, Telstar 1. 1c, Transit 2A. 5c, OSO 1 Solar Observatory. 10c, Tiros 2 weather satellite. 21c, Weather station. 50c, Syncom 3.

1964, Dec. 21 ***Perf. 14x14x13½***

457 A147b ½c ver & multi
457A A147b 1c vio & multi
457B A147b 5c lil rose & multi
457C A147b 10c bl & multi
457D A147b 21c bl grn & multi
457E A147b 50c grn & multi
f. Souv. sheet of 1

Nos. 457B-457E are airmail. No. 457f exists imperf. with different colors.
For overprints see Nos. 489-489b.

1964 Olympic Medals Type

Summer Olympic Medals and Winners: ½c, Parallel bars. 1c, Dragon-class sailing. 2c, Individual show jumping. 3c, Two-man kayak. 4c, Team road race cycling. 5c, Individual dressage. 6c, Women's 800-meter run. 7c, 3000-meter steeplechase. 10c, Men's floor exercises. 21c, Decathlon. 31c, Men's 100-meter freestyle swimming.

Litho. & Embossed

1964, Dec. 28 ***Perf. 13½x14***

458 A147a ½c org & multi
458A A147a 1c plum & multi
458B A147a 2c bl grn & multi
458C A147a 3c red brn & multi
458D A147a 4c lil rose & multi
458E A147a 5c dl grn & multi
458F A147a 6c bl & multi
458G A147a 7c dk vio & multi
458H A147a 10c ver & multi
458I A147a 21c dl vio & multi
458J A147a 31c dk bl grn & multi
k. Souv. sheet of 3, #458H-458J

Nos. 458E-458J are airmail. No. 458k exists imperf.

John F. Kennedy & Cape Kennedy — A147c

Designs: 1c, Launching of Titan II rocket, Gemini capsule. 2c, Apollo lunar module. 3c, Proposed Apollo command and service modules. 5c, Gemini capsule atop Titan II rocket. 6c, Soviet cosmonauts Komarov, Yegorov, Feoktistov. 11c, Ranger VII. 31c, Lunar surface.
Illustration reduced.

1965, Feb. 25 Litho. ***Perf. 14***

459 A147c ½c vio bl & multi
459A A147c 1c bl & multi
459B A147c 2c plum & multi
459C A147c 3c ol grn & multi
459D A147c 5c lil rose & multi
459E A147c 10c dl grn & multi
459F A147c 11c brt vio & multi
459G A147c 31c grn & multi
h. Souv. sheet of 1

Nos. 459D-459G are airmail. No. 459h exists imperf. with different color. For overprints see Nos. 491-491b.

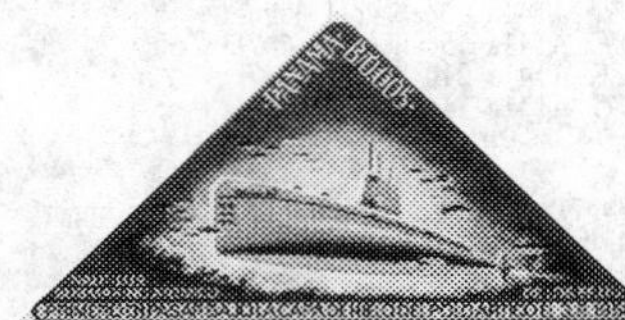

Atomic Power for Peace — A147d

Designs: ½c, Nuclear powered submarine *Nautilus.* 1c, Nuclear powered ship *Savannah.* 4c, First nuclear reactor, Calderhall, England. 6c, Nuclear powered icebreaker *Lenin.* 10c, Nuclear powered observatory. 21c, Nuclear powered space vehicle.
Illustration reduced.

1965, May 12

460 A147d ½c bl & multi
460A A147d 1c grn & multi
460B A147d 4c red & multi
460C A147d 6c dl bl grn & multi
460D A147d 10c bl grn & multi
460E A147d 21c dk vio & multi
f. Souv. sheet of 2, #460D-460E

Nos. 460B-460E are airmail. Nos. 460-460fa exist imperf. with different colors.

John F. Kennedy Memorial — A147e

Kennedy and: ½c, PT109. 1c, Space capsule. 10c, UN emblem. 21c, Winston Churchill. 31c, Rocket launch at Cape Kennedy.

1965, Aug. 23 ***Perf. 13½x13***

461 A147e ½c multicolored
461A A147e 1c multicolored
461B A147e 10c + 5c, multi
461C A147e 21c + 10c, multi
461D A147e 31c + 15c, multi
e. Souv. sheet of 2, #461A, 461D, perf. 12½x12

Nos. 461B-461D are airmail semipostal. Nos. 461-461e exist imperf. with different colors.
For overprints see Nos. C367A-C367B.

Keel-billed Toucan — A148

Song Birds: 2c, Scarlet macaw. 3c, Red-crowned woodpecker. 4c, Blue-gray tanager (horiz.).

1965, Oct. 27 Unwmk. ***Perf. 14***

462 A148 1c brt pink & multi	15	15
462A A148 2c multi	15	15
462B A148 3c brt vio & multi	15	15
462C A148 4c org yel & multi	15	15
Set value		38

Snapper — A149

1965, Dec. 7 Litho.

463 A149 1c shown	15	15
463A A149 2c Dorado	15	15
Nos. 463-463A,C339-C342 (6)	1.70	
Set value		1.00

Pope Paul VI, Visit to UN A149a

Designs: ½c, Pope on Balcony of St. Peters, Vatican City. 1c, Pope Addressing UN General Assembly. 5c, Arms of Vatican City, Panama, UN emblem. 10c, Lyndon Johnson, Pope Paul VI, Francis Cardinal Spellman. 21c, Ecumenical Council, Vatican II. 31c, Earlybird satellite.

1966 Apr. 4 ***Perf. 12x12½***

464 A149a ½c multicolored
464A A149a 1c multicolored
464B A149a 5c multicolored
464C A149a 10c multicolored
464D A149a 21c multicolored
464E A149a 31c multicolored
f. Souv. sheet of 2, #464B, 464E, perf. 13x13½

Nos. 464B-464E are airmail. No. 464f exists imperf. with different margin color.
For overprints see Nos. 490-490B.

Famous Men — A149b

Designs: ½c, William Shakespeare. 10c, Dante Alighieri. 31c, Richard Wagner.

1966, May 26 ***Perf. 14***

465 A149b ½c multicolored
465A A149b 10c multicolored
465B A149b 31c multicolored
c. Souv. sheet of 2, #465A-465B, perf. 13½x14

Nos. 465A-465B are airmail. No. 465c exists imperf. with different margin color.

Works by Famous Artists — A149c

Paintings: ½c, Elizabeth Tucher by Durer. 10c, Madonna of the Rocky Grotto by Da Vinci. 31c, La Belle Jardiniere by Raphael.

1966, May 26

466 A149c ½c multicolored
466A A149c 10c multicolored
466B A149c 31c multicolored
c. Souv. sheet of 2, #466A-466B

Nos. 466A-466B are airmail. No. 466c exists imperf. with different margin color.

No. 441H Surcharged

1966, June 27 Wmk. 343 ***Perf. 12½***

467 A138 13c on 25c grn & pink 40 25

The "25c" has not been obliterated.

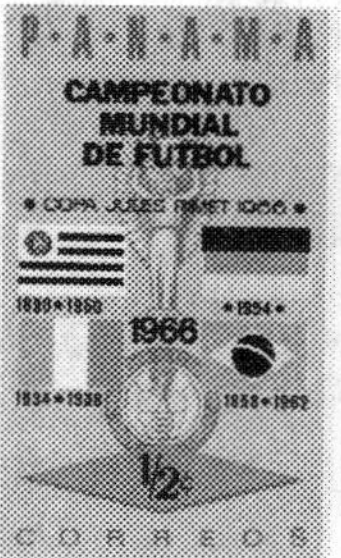

A149d

A149e

1966, July 11 *Perf. 14*

468 A149d 1/2c shown
468A A149d .005b Uruguay, 1930, 1950
468B A149d 10c Italy, 1934, 1938
468C A149d 10c Brazil, 1958, 1962
468D A149d 21c Germany, 1954
468E A149d 21c Great Britain
f. Souv. sheet of 2, #468B, 468D
g. Souv. sheet of 2, #468, 468E, imperf.

World Cup Soccer Championships, Great Britain. Nos. 468B-468E are airmail. Imperfs. are different colors than perforated issues.
For overprints see Nos. 470-470g.

Perf. 12x12 1/2, 12 1/2x12
1966, Aug. 12

Italian Contributions to Space Research: 1/2c, Launch of Scout rocket, San Marco satellite. 1c, San Marco in orbit, horiz. 5c, Italian scientists, rocket. 10c, Arms of Panama, Italy, horiz. 21c, San Marco boosted into orbit, horiz.

469 A149e 1/2c multicolored
469A A149e 1c multicolored
469B A149e 5c multicolored
469C A149e 10c multicolored
469D A149e 21c multicolored
e. Souv. sheet of 2, #469C-469D, imperf.

Nos. 469C-469D are airmail.

Nos. 468-468g Ovptd. **Inglaterra vs Alemania 4 2 Wembley, 7-30-1966**

1966, Sept. 28 *Perf. 14*

470 A149d 1/2c on #468
470A A149d .005b on #468A
470B A149d 10c on #468B
470C A149d 10c on #468C
470D A149d 21c on #468D
470E A149d 21c on #468E
f. on #468f
g. on #468g, imperf.

Nos. 470B-470E are airmail.

A149f

Religious Paintings A149g

Paintings: 1/2c, Coronation of Mary. 1c, Holy Family with Angel. 2c, Adoration of the Magi. 3c, Madonna and Child. No. 471D, The Annunciation. No. 471E, The Nativity. No. 471h, Madonna and Child.

1966, Oct. 24 *Perf. 11*
Size of No. 471D: 32x34mm

471 A149f 1/2c Velazquez
471A A149f 1c Saraceni
471B A149g 2c Durer
471C A149f 3c Orazio
471D A149g 21c Rubens
471E A149f 21c Boticelli

Souvenir Sheet
Perf. 14

471F Sheet of 2
g. A1 21c like No. 471E, black inscriptions
h. A1 31c Mignard

Nos. 471D-471F are airmail. All exist imperf. with different colors.

Sir Winston Churchill, British Satellites — A149h

Churchill and: 10c, Blue Streak, NATO emblem. 31c, Europa 1, rocket engine.

1966, Nov. 25 *Perf. 12x12 1/2*

472 A149h 1/2c shown
472A A149h 10c org & multi
472B A149h 31c dk bl & multi
c. Souv. sheet of 2, #472A-472B, perf. 13 1/2x14

Nos. 472A-472B are airmail. No. 472c exists imperf. with different colors.
For overprints see Nos. 492-492B.

John F. Kennedy, 3rd Death Anniv. — A149i

1966, Nov. 25 *Perf. 14*

473 A149i 1/2c shown
473A A149i 10c Kennedy, UN bldg.
473B A149i 31c Kennedy, satellites & map
c. Souv. sheet of 2, #473A-473B

Nos. 473A-473B are airmail. No. 473c exists imperf. with different colors.

Jules Verne (1828-1905), French Space Explorations — A149j

Designs: 1/2c, Earth, A-1 satellite. 1c, Verne, submarine. 5c, Earth, FR-1 satellite. 10c, Verne, telescope. 21c, Verne, capsule heading toward Moon. 31c, D-1 satellite over Earth.

1966, Dec. 28 *Perf. 13 1/2x14*

474 A149j 1/2c bl & multi
474A A149j 1c bl grn & multi
474B A149j 5c ultra & multi
474C A149j 10c lil, blk & red
474D A149j 21c vio & multi
f. Souv. sheet of 2, #474C, 474D, imperf.
474E A149j 31c dl bl & multi
g. Souvenir sheet of 1

Nos. 474B-474E are airmail. All imperfs. are in different colors.

Hen and Chicks A150

Domestic Animals: 3c, Rooster. 5c, Pig, horiz. 8c, Cow, horiz.

1967, Feb. 3 **Unwmk.** *Perf. 14*

475 A150 1c multi 15 15
475A A150 3c multi 15 15
475B A150 5c multi 15 15
475C A150 8c multi 25 15
Nos. 475-475C,C353-C356 (8) 3.00
Set value 1.55

Easter — A150a

Paintings: 1/2c, Christ at Calvary. 1c, The Crucifixion. 5c, Pieta, horiz. 10c, Body of Christ. 21c, The Arisen Christ. No. 476E, Christ Ascending into Heaven. No. 476F, Christ on the Cross. No. 476G, Madonna and Child.

Perf. 14x13 1/2, 13 1/2x14
1967, Mar. 13

476 A150a 1/2c Giambattista Tiepolo
476A A150a 1c Rubens
476B A150a 5c Sarto
476C A150a 10c Raphael Santi
476D A150a 21c Multscher
476E A150a 31c Grunewald

Souvenir Sheets
Perf. 12 1/2x12x12 1/2x13 1/2

476F A150a 31c Van der Weyden

Imperf

476G A150a 31c Rubens

Nos. 476B-476G are airmail.

1968 Summer Olympics, Mexico City — A150b

Indian Ruins at: 1/2c, Teotihuacan. 1c, Tajin. 5c, Xochicalco. 10c, Monte Alban. 21c, Palenque. 31c, Chichen Itza.

1967, Apr. *Perf. 12x12 1/2*

477 A150b 1/2c plum & multi
477A A150b 1c red lil & multi
477B A150b 5c bl & multi
477C A150b 10c ver & multi
477D A150b 21c grn bl & multi
477E A150b 31c grn & multi

Nos. 477B-477E are airmail.

New World Anhinga A151

Birds: 1c, Quetzals. 3c, Turquoise-browed motmot. 4c, Double-collared aracari, horiz. 5c, Macaw. 13c, Belted kingfisher. 50c, Hummingbird.

1967, July 20 *Perf. 14*

478 A151 1/2c lt bl & multi 15 15
478A A151 1c lt gray & multi 15 15
478B A151 3c pink & multi 15 15
478C A151 4c lt grn & multi 15 15
478D A151 5c buff & multi 20 15
478E A151 13c yel & multi 50 25
Nos. 478-478E (6) 1.30
Set value 75

Souvenir Sheet
Perf. 14 1/2

478F A151 50c Sheet of 1

No. 478A exists imperf. with blue background.

Works of Famous Artists A151a

Paintings: No. 479, Maiden in the Doorway. No. 479A, Blueboy. No. 479B, The Promise of Louis XIII. No. 479C, St. George and the Dragon. No. 479D, The Blacksmith's Shop, horiz. No. 479E, St. Hieronymus. Nos. 479F-479K, Self-portraits.

Perf. 14x13 1/2, 13 1/2x14
1967, Aug. 23

479 A151a 5c Rembrandt
479A A151a 5c Gainsborough
479B A151a 5c Ingres
479C A151a 21c Raphael
479D A151a 21c Velazquez
479E A151a 21c Durer

Souvenir Sheets
Various Compound Perfs.

479F A151a 21c Gainsborough
479G A151a 21c Rembrandt
479H A151a 21c Ingres
479I A151a 21c Raphael
479J A151a 21c Velazquez
479K A151a 21c Durer

Nos. 479C-479K are airmail.

Red Deer, by Franz Marc A152

Animal Paintings by Franz Marc: 3c, Tiger, vert. 5c, Monkeys. 8c, Blue Fox.

1967, Sept. 1 *Perf. 14*

480 A152 1c multi 15 15
480A A152 3c multi 15 15
480B A152 5c multi 15 15
480C A152 8c multi 25 15
Nos. 480-480C,C357-C360 (8) 2.15
Set value 1.25

Paintings by Goya
A152a

Designs: 2c, The Water Carrier. 3c, Count Floridablanca. 4c, Senora Francisca Sebasa y Garcia. 5c, St. Bernard and St. Robert. 8c, Self-portrait. 10c, Dona Isabel Cobos de Porcel. 13c, Clothed Maja, horiz. 21c, Don Manuel Osoria de Zuniga as a child. 50c, Cardinal Luis of Bourbon and Villabriga.

Perf. 14x13½, 13½x14

1967, Oct. 17

481 A152a 2c multicolored
481A A152a 3c multicolored
481B A152a 4c multicolored
481C A152a 5c multicolored
481D A152a 8c multicolored
481E A152a 10c multicolored
481F A152a 13c multi, horiz.
481G A152a 21c multicolored

Souvenir Sheet

481H A152a 50c multicolored

Nos. 481C-481H are airmail.

Life of Christ
A152b

Paintings: No. 482, The Holy Family. No. 482A, Christ Washing Feet. 3c, Christ's Charge to Peter. 4c, Christ and the Money Changers in the Temple, horiz. No. 482D, Christ's Entry into Jerusalem, horiz. No. 482E, The Last Supper. No. 482l, Pastoral Adoration. No. 482m, The Holy Family. No. 482n, Christ with Mary and Martha. No. 482o, Flight from Egypt. No. 482p, St. Thomas. No. 482q, The Tempest. No. 482r, The Transfiguration. No. 482s, The Crucification. No. 482J, The Baptism of Christ, by Guido Reni. No. 482K, Christ at the Sea of Galilee, by Tintoretto, horiz.

1968, Jan. 10 ***Perf. 14x13½x13½x14***

482 A152b 1c Michaelangelo
482A A152b 1c Brown
482B A152b 3c Rubens
482C A152b 4c El Greco
482D A152b 21c Van Dyck
482E A152b 21c de Juanes

Souvenir Sheets

Various Perfs.

482F Sheet of 2
l. A152b 1c Schongauer
m. A152b 21c Raphael
482G Sheet of 2
n. A152b 3c Tintoretto
o. A152b 21c Caravaggio
482H Sheet of 2
p. A152b 21c Anonymous, 12th cent.
q. A152b 31c multicolored
482I Sheet of 2
r. A152b 21c Raphael
s. A152b 31c Montanez

Imperf

482J A152b 22c Sheet of 1
482K A152b 24c Sheet of 1

Nos. 482C-482K are airmail.

A little time given to the study of the arrangement of the Scott Catalogue can make it easier to use effectively.

Butterflies — A152c

1968, Feb. 23 ***Perf. 14***

483 A152c ½c Apodemia albinus
483A A152c 1c Caligo ilioneus, vert.
483B A152c 3c Meso semia tenera
483C A152c 4c Pamphila epictetus
483D A152c 5c Entheus peleus
483E A152c 13c Tmetoglene drymo

Souvenir Sheet

Perf. 14½

483F A152c 50c Thymele chalco, vert.

Nos. 483D-483F are airmail. No. 483F exists imperf. with pink margin.

10th Winter Olympics, Grenoble — A152d

1968, May 7 ***Perf. 14x13½, 13½x14***

484 A152d ½c Emblem, vert.
484A A152d 1c Ski jumper
484B A152d 5c Skier
484C A152d 10c Mountain climber
484D A152d 21c Speed skater
484E A152d 31c Two-man bobsled

Souvenir Sheets

Perf. 14

484F Sheet of 2
h. A152d 10c Emblem, snowflake
i. A152d 31c Figure skater
484G Sheet of 2
j. A152d 31c Biathlon
k. A152d 10c Skier on ski lift

Nos. 484B-484G are airmail.

Sailing Ships
A152e

Paintings by: ½c, Gamiero, vert. 1c, Lebreton. 3c, Anonymous Japanese. 4c, Le Roi. 5c, Van de Velde. 13c, Duncan. 50c, Anonymous Portuguese, vert.

1968, May 7 ***Perf. 14***

485 A152e ½c multicolored
485A A152e 1c multicolored
485B A152e 3c multicolored
485C A152e 4c multicolored
485D A152e 5c multicolored
485E A152e 13c multicolored

Souvenir Sheet

Perf. 14½

485F A152e 50c multicolored

Nos. 485D-485E are airmail. No. 485F exists imperf. with light blue margin.

Tropical Fish — A152f

1968, June 26 ***Perf. 14***

486 A152f ½c Balistipus undulatus
486A A152f 1c Holacanthus ciliaris
486B A152f 3c Chaetodon ephippium
486C A152f 4c Epinephelus elongatus
486D A152f 5c Anisotremus verginicus
486E A152f 13c Balistoides conspicillum

Souvenir Sheet

Perf. 14½

486F A152f 50c Raja texana, vert.

Nos. 486D-486F are airmail. No. 486F exists imperf. with pink margin.

Olympic Medals and Winners, Grenoble — A152g

Olympic Medals and Winners: 1c, Men's giant slalom. 2c, Women's downhill. 3c, Women's figure skating. 4c, 5000-meter speed skating. 5c, 10,000-meter speed skating. 6c, Women's slalom. 8c, Women's 1000-meter speed skating. 13c, Women's 1500-meter speed skating. 30c, Two-man bobsled. 70c, Nordic combined.

Litho. & Embossed

1968, July 30 ***Perf. 13½x14***

487 A152g 1c pink & multi
487A A152g 2c vio & multi
487B A152g 3c grn & multi
487C A152g 4c plum & multi
487D A152g 5c red brn & multi
487E A152g 6c brt vio & multi
487F A152g 8c Prus bl & multi
487G A152g 13c bl & multi
487H A152g 30c rose lil & multi

Souvenir Sheet

487I A152g 70c red & multi

Nos. 487G-487H are airmail.

Miniature Sheet

Music
A152h

Paintings of Musicians, Instruments: 5c, Mandolin, by de la Hyre. 10c, Lute, by Caravaggio. 15c, Flute, by ter Bruggehen. 20c, Chamber ensemble, by Tourmer. 25c, Violin, by Caravaggio. 30c, Piano, by Vermeer. 40c, Harp, by Memling.

1968, Sept. 11 **Litho.** ***Perf. 13½x14***

488 Sheet of 6
a. A152h 5c multicolored
b. A152h 10c multicolored
c. A152h 15c multicolored
d. A152h 20c multicolored
e. A152h 25c multicolored
f. A152h 30c multicolored

Souvenir Sheet

Perf. 14

488A A152h 40c multicolored

Nos. 457, 457E Ovptd. in Black

OLIMPIADAS MEXICO
TRANSMITIDAS
VIA SATELITE
TELEVISION PANAMENA

1968, Oct. 17

489 A147b ½c on No. 457
489A A147b 50c on No. 457E
b. Souv. sheet of 1, on No. 457f

Nos. 489-489A exist with gold overprint. Overprint differs on No. 489b.

Nos. 464, 464D & 464f Ovptd. in Black or Gold

VISITA S. S. PAULO VI
CONGRESO EUCARISTICO
LATINOAMERICANO
TRANSMITIDA «ATS-3»

1968, Oct. 18 ***Perf. 12x12½***

490 A149a ½c on No. 464
490A A149a 21c on No. 464D

Souvenir Sheet

Perf. 13x13½

490B on No. 464f (G)

Nos. 490A-490B are airmail. No. 490B exists imperf. with different colored border. Overprint differs on No. 490B.

Nos. 459, 459G-459h Ovptd. in Black

1968, Oct. 21 ***Perf. 14***

491 A147c ½c on No. 459
491A A147c 31c on No. 459G
b. on souv. sheet, No. 459h

Nos. 491A-491b are airmail. Nos. 491-491A exist overprinted in gold, and imperf., overprinted in gold. No. 491b exists imperf. with different colors and black or gold overprints.

Nos. 472-472A, 472c Overprinted in Black or Gold

INAUGURACION
COMUNICACIONES
POR SATELITE
PANAMA, 5-OCT 1968

1968, Oct. 22 ***Perf. 12x12½***

492 A149h ½c on No. 472
492A A149h 10c on No. 472A

Souvenir Sheet

Perf. 13½x14

492B on No. 472c

Nos. 492A-492B are airmail. No. 492c exists imperf. with different colors.

Hunting on Horseback — A152i

Paintings and Tapestries: 1c, Koller. 3c, Courbet. 5c, Ancien. 10c, Gobelin, vert. 13c, Oudry. 30c, Rubens.

1968, Oct. 29 ***Perf. 14***

493 A152i 1c multicolored
493A A152i 3c multicolored
493B A152i 5c multicolored

493C A152i 10c multicolored
493D A152i 13c multicolored
493E A152i 30c multicolored

Nos. 493D-493E are airmail.

Miniature Sheet

Famous Race Horses — A152j

Horse Paintings: a, 5c, Lexington, by Edward Troye. b, 10c, American Eclipse, by Alvan Fisher. c, 15c, Plenipotentiary, by Abraham Cooper. d, 20c, Gimcrack, by George Stubbs. e, 25c, Flying Childers, by James Seymour. f, 30c, Eclipse, by Stubbs.

1968, Oct. 29 ***Perf. 13½x14***
494 A152j Sheet of 6, #a.-f.

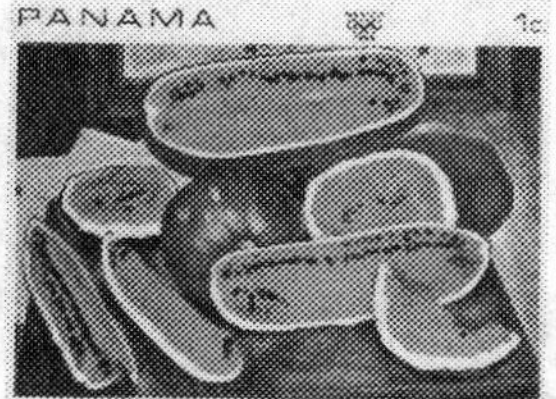

1968 Summer Olympics, Mexico City — A152k

Mexican art: 1c, Watermelons, by Diego Rivera. 2c, Women, by Jose Clemente Orozco. 3c, Flower Seller, by Miguel Covarrubias, vert. 4c, Nutall Codex, vert. 5c, Mayan statue, vert. 6c, Face sculpture, vert. 8c, Seated figure, vert. 13c. Ceramic angel, vert. 30c, Christ, by David Alfaro Siqueiros. 70c, Symbols of Summer Olympic events.

Perf. 13½x14, 14x13½
1968, Dec. 23
495 A152k 1c multicolored
495A A152k 2c multicolored
495B A152k 3c multicolored
495C A152k 4c multicolored
495D A152k 5c multicolored
495E A152k 6c multicolored
495F A152k 8c multicolored
495G A152k 13c multicolored
495H A152k 30c multicolored

Souvenir Sheet
Perf. 14
495I A152k 70c multicolored

Nos. 495G-495H are airmail.

First Visit of Pope Paul VI to Latin America A152l

Paintings: 1c-3c, 5c-6c, Madonna and Child. 4c, The Annunciation. 7c-8c, Adoration of the Magi. 10c, Holy Family. 50c, Madonna and Child, angel.

1969 ***Perf. 14***
496 A152l 1c Raphael
496A A152l 2c Ferruzzi
496B A152l 3c Bellini
496C A152l 4c Portuguese School, 17th cent.
496D A152l 5c Van Dyck
496E A152l 6c Albani
496F A152l 7c Viennese master
496G A152l 8c Van Dyck
496H A152l 10c Portuguese School, 16th cent.

Souvenir Sheet
Perf. 14½
496I A152l 50c Del Sarto

Nos. 496E-496I are airmail.

Map of Panama, People and Houses A153

Design: 10c, Map of Americas and people, vert.

1969, Aug. **Photo.** **Wmk. 350**
500 A153 5c violet blue 15 15
501 A153 10c bright rose lilac 30 15
Set value 20

Issued to publicize the 1970 census.

Cogwheel A154

1969, Aug.
502 A154 13c yel & dk bl gray 35 16

50th anniv. of Rotary International of Panama.

Cornucopia and Map of Panama — A155

Perf. 14½x15
1969, Oct. 10 **Litho.** **Unwmk.**
503 A155 10c lt bl & multi 25 15

First anniversary of the October 11 Revolution.

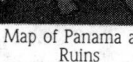

Map of Panama and Ruins A156

Natá Church A157

Designs: 5c, Farmer, wife and mule. 13c, Hotel Continental. 20c, Church of the Virgin of Carmen. 21c, Gold altar, San José Church. 25c, Del Rey bridge. 30c, Dr. Justo Arosemena monument. 34c, Cathedral of Panama. 38c, Municipal Palace. 40c, French Plaza. 50c, Thatcher Ferry Bridge (Bridge of the Americas). 59c, National Theater.

Perf. 14½x15, 15x14½
1969-70 **Litho.** **Unwmk.**
504 A156 3c org & blk 15 15
505 A156 5c lt bl grn ('70) 15 15
506 A157 8c dl brn ('70) 20 15
507 A156 13c emer & blk 30 15
508 A157 20c vio brn ('70) 50 22
509 A157 21c yellow ('70) 50 40
510 A156 25c lt bl grn ('70) 60 25
511 A157 30c black ('70) 75 40
512 A156 34c org brn ('70) 80 50
513 A156 38c brt bl ('70) 85 40
514 A156 40c org yel ('70) 1.00 60
515 A156 50c brt rose lil & blk 1.10 70
516 A156 59c brt rose lil ('70) 1.40 90
Nos. 504-516 (13) 8.30 4.97

For surcharges see Nos. 541, 543, 545-547, RA78-RA80.

Stadium and Discus Thrower A158

Flor del Espiritu Santo — A159

Perf. 13½
1970, Jan. 6 **Litho.** **Wmk. 365**
517 A158 1c ultra & multi 15 15
518 A158 2c ultra & multi 15 15
519 A158 3c ultra & multi 15 15
520 A158 5c ultra & multi 20 15
521 A158 10c ultra & multi 30 15
522 A158 13c ultra & multi 40 20
523 A159 13c pink & multi 40 20
524 A158 25c ultra & multi 85 50
525 A158 30c ultra & multi 1.00 75
Nos. 517-525,C368-C369 (11) 4.90 3.45

11th Central American and Caribbean Games, Feb. 28-Mar. 14.

Office of Comptroller General, 1970 — A160

Designs: 5c, Alejandro Tapia and Martin Sosa, first Comptrollers, 1931-34, horiz. 8c, Comptroller's emblem. 13c, Office of Comptroller General, 1955-70, horiz.

1971, Feb. 25 **Litho.** **Wmk. 365**
526 A160 3c yel & multi 15 15
527 A160 5c brn, buff & gold 15 15
528 A160 8c gold & multi 16 15
529 A160 13c blk & multi 25 15
Set value 56 32

Comptroller General's Office, 40th anniv.

Indian Alligator Design — A161

1971, Aug. 18 **Wmk. 343** ***Perf. 13½***
530 A161 8c multicolored 20 20

SENAPI (Servicio Nacional de Artesania y Pequeñas Industrias), 5th anniv.

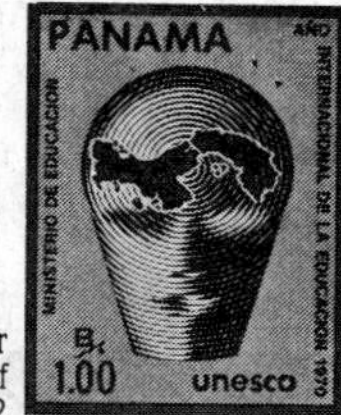

Education Year Emblem, Map of Panama — A162

1971, Aug. 19 **Litho.**
531 A162 1b multicolored 2.50 2.50

International Education Year, 1970.
For surcharge see No. 542.

Congress Emblem A163

1972, Aug. 25
532 A163 25c multicolored 75 60

9th Inter-American Conference of Saving and Loan Associations, Panama City, Jan. 23-29, 1971.

UPU Headquarters, Bern — A164

Design: 30c, Universal Postal Union Monument, Bern, vert.

1971, Dec. 14 **Wmk. 343**
533 A164 8c multicolored 20 15
534 A164 30c multicolored 80 60

Inauguration of Universal Postal Union Headquarters, Bern, Switzerland.
For surcharge see No. RA77.

Cow, Pig and Produce A165

1971, Dec. 15
535 A165 3c yel, brn & blk 15 15

3rd agricultural census.

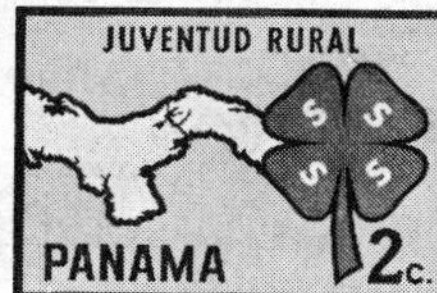

Map of Panama and "4-S" Emblem A166

1971, Dec. 16
536 A166 2c multicolored 15 15

Rural youth 4-S program.

UNICEF Emblem, Children A167

Perf. 13½

1972, Sept. 12 Litho. Wmk. 365

537 A167 1c yel & multi 15 15

25th anniv. (in 1971) of UNICEF. See Nos. C390-C392a.

Tropical Fruits A168

1972, Sept. 13

538 A168 1c shown 15 15
539 A168 2c Isla de Noche 15 15
540 A168 3c Carnival float, vert. 15 15
Set value, #538-540, C393-C395 1.10 65

Tourist publicity.
For surcharges see Nos. RA75-RA76.

VALE 10¢

Nos. 516, 531 and 511 Surcharged in Red

CONSEJO DE SEGURIDAD
15 · 21 Marzo 1973

Perf. 14½x15, 15x14½, 13½
Wmk. 343, Unwmkd.

1973, Mar. 16

541 A156 8c on 59c brt rose lil 15 15
542 A162 10c on 1b multi 20 20
543 A157 13c on 30c blk 25 25

UN Security Council Meeting, Panama City, Mar. 15-21. Surcharges differ in size and are adjusted to fit shape of stamp. See No. C402.

José Daniel Crespo, Educator — A169

Perf. 13½

1973, June 20 Litho. Wmk. 365

544 A169 3c lt bl & multi 15 15
Nos. 544,C403-C413 (12) 5.31 3.57

For overprints and surcharges see Nos. C414-C416, C418-C421, RA81-RA82, RA84.

Nos. 511-512 and 509 Surcharged in Red **VALE 13¢**

Perf. 15x14½, 14½x15

1974, Nov. 11 Unwmk.

545 A157 5c on 30c blk 15 15
546 A156 10c on 34c org brn 20 15
547 A157 13c on 21c yel 25 15
Set value, #545-547, C417-C421 1.25 75

Surcharge vertical on No. 546.

> ***Set Values***
> *A 15-cent minimum now applies to individual stamps and sets. Where the 15-cent minimum per stamp would increase the "value" of a set beyond retail, there is a "Set Value" notation giving the retail value of the set.*

Bolivar, Bridge of the Americas, Men with Flags — A170

Perf. 12½

1976, Mar. 30 Litho. Unwmk.

548 A170 6c multicolored 15 15

150th anniversary of Congress of Panama. See Nos. C426-C428.

Evibacus Princeps A171

Marine life: 3c, Ptitosarcus sinuosus, vert. 4c, Acanthaster planci. 7c, Starfish. 1b, Mithrax spinossimus.

Perf. 12½x13, 13x12½

1976, May 6 Litho. Wmk. 377

549 A171 2c multi 15 15
550 A171 3c multi 15 15
551 A171 4c multi 15 15
552 A171 7c multi 20 15
Nos. 549-552,C429-C430 (6) 1.55 1.30

Souvenir Sheet
Imperf

553 A171 1b multi 3.00

Flag Bearer from Bolivar Monument A172

Bolivar and Argentine Flag — A173

Designs: Stamps of type A172 show details of Bolivar Monument, Panama City; type A173 shows head of Bolivar and flags of Latin American countries.

Perf. 13½

1976, June 22 Unwmk. Litho.

554 A172 20c shown 40 40
555 A173 20c shown 40 40
556 A173 20c Bolivia 40 40
557 A173 20c Brazil 40 40
558 A173 20c Chile 40 40
559 A172 20c Battle scene 40 40
560 A173 20c Colombia 40 40
561 A173 20c Costa Rica 40 40
562 A173 20c Cuba 40 40
563 A173 20c Ecuador 40 40
564 A173 20c El Salvador 40 40
565 A173 20c Guatemala 40 40
566 A173 20c Guyana 40 40
567 A173 20c Haiti 40 40
568 A172 20c Assembly 40 40
569 A172 20c Liberated people 40 40
570 A173 20c Honduras 40 40
571 A173 20c Jamaica 40 40
572 A173 20c Mexico 40 40
573 A173 20c Nicaragua 40 40
574 A173 20c Panama 40 40
575 A173 20c Paraguay 40 40
576 A173 20c Peru 40 40
577 A173 20c Dominican Rep. 40 40
578 A172 20c Bolivar and flag bearer 40 40
579 A173 20c Surinam 40 40
580 A173 20c Trinidad-Tobago 40 40
581 A173 20c Uruguay 40 40
582 A173 20c Venezuela 40 40
583 A172 20c Indian delegation 40 40
Nos. 554-583 (30) 12.00 12.00

Souvenir Sheet

584 Sheet of 3 2.25 2.25
a. A172 30c Bolivar and flag bearer 50 50
b. A172 30c Monument, top 50 50
c. A172 40c Inscription tablet 65 65

Amphictyonic Congress of Panama, sesquicentennial. Nos. 554-583 printed se-tenant in sheets of 30 (6x5). No. 584 comes perf. and imperf.

Nicanor Villalaz, Designer of Coat of Arms — A174

National Lottery Building, Panama City — A175

1976, Nov. 12 Litho. *Perf. 12½*

585 A174 5c dk blue 15 15
586 A175 6c multicolored 15 15
Set value 22 15

Contadora Island A176

1976, Dec. 29 *Perf. 12½*

587 A176 3c multicolored 15 15

Pres. Carter and Gen. Omar Torrijos Signing Panama Canal Treaties — A177

Design: 23c, like No. 588. Design includes Alejandro Orfila, Secretary General of OAS.

1978, Jan. Litho. *Perf. 12*
Size: 90x40mm

588 A177 Strip of 3 2.00 2.00
a. 3c multicolored 15 15
b. 40c multicolored 80 50
c. 50c multicolored 1.00 75

Perf. 14
Size: 36x26mm

589 A177 23c multicolored 45 15

Signing of Panama Canal Treaties, Washington, DC, Sept. 7, 1977.

Pres. Carter and Gen. Torrijos Signing Treaties — A178

1978, Nov. 13 Litho. *Perf. 12*

590 A178 Strip of 3 2.00 2.00
a. 5c multi (30x40mm) 15 15
b. 35c multi (30x40mm) 70 35
c. 41c multi (45x40mm) 80 40

Size: 36x26mm

591 A178 3c Treaty signing 15 15

Signing of Panama Canal Treaties, Panama City, Panama, June 6, 1978.

World Trade Center, Colon A179

1978 Litho. *Perf. 12*

592 A179 6c multicolored 15 15

Free Zone of Colon, 30th anniversary.

Melvin Jones, Lions Emblem A180

1978, Dec. 5

593 A180 50c multicolored 1.00 75

Birth centenary of Melvin Jones, founder of Lions International.

Torrijos with Children, Ship, Flag — A181

"75," Coat of Arms — A182

Rotary Emblem, "75" — A183

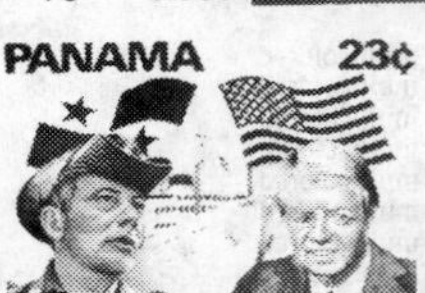

Gen. Torrijos and Pres. Carter, Flags, Ship — A184

UPU Emblem, Globe — A185

AÑO INTERNACIONAL DEL NIÑO
REPUBLICA DE PANAMA 1979 50¢

Boy and Girl Inside Heart — A186

1979, Oct. 1 Litho. *Perf. 14*

594 A181 3c multicolored 15 15
595 A182 6c multicolored 15 15
596 A183 17c multicolored 35 30
597 A184 23c multicolored 45 20
598 A185 35c multicolored 70 60
599 A186 50c multicolored 1.00 50
Nos. 594-599 (6) 2.80 1.90

Return of Canal Zone to Panama, Oct. 1 (3c, 23c); Natl. Bank, 75th anniv.; Rotary Intl., 75th anniv.; 18th UPU Cong., Rio, Sept.-Oct., 1979; Intl. Year of the Child.

Colon Station, St. Charles Hotel, Engraving — A187

Postal Headquarters, Balboa, Inauguration A188

Return of Canal Zone to Panama, Oct. 1, 1979 — A189

Census of the Americas A190

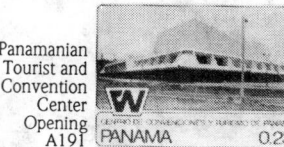

Panamanian Tourist and Convention Center Opening A191

Inter-American Development Bank, 25th Anniversary A192

Canal Centenary A193

Olympic Stadium, Moscow '80 Emblem A194

1980, June 17 Litho. *Perf. 12*

600 A187	1c rose violet	15	15
601 A188	3c multicolored	15	15
602 A189	6c multicolored	15	15
603 A190	17c multicolored	35	25
604 A191	23c multicolored	45	20
605 A192	35c multicolored	70	30
606 A193	41c pale rose & blk	90	45
607 A194	50c multicolored	1.00	50
	Nos. 600-607 (8)	3.85	
	Set value		1.80

Transpanamanian Railroad, 130th anniv. (1c); 22nd Summer Olympic Games, Moscow, July 19-Aug. 3 (50c).

La Salle Congregation, 75th Anniv. (1979) — A195

Louis Braille — A196

1981, May 15 Litho. *Perf. 12*

608 A195 17c multicolored 35 16

1981, May 15

609 A196 23c multicolored 45 20

Intl. Year of the Disabled.

Bull's Blood A197

1981, June 26 Litho. *Perf. 12*

610 A197	3c shown	15	15
611 A197	6c Lory, vert.	15	15
612 A197	41c Hummingbird, vert.	90	50
613 A197	50c Toucan	1.10	42
	Set value		1.00

Apparition of the Virgin to St. Catherine Laboure, 150th Anniv. — A198

1981, June 26 Litho. *Perf. 12*

614 A198 35c multicolored 70 35

Gen. Torrijos and Bayano Dam A199

Perf. 10½

1982, Mar. Litho. Wmk. 311

615 A199 17c multicolored 35 16

78th Anniv. of Independence Soldiers Institute — A200

1981, Nov. 30 Litho. *Perf. 10½*

616 A200 3c multicolored 15 15

First Death Anniv. of Gen. Omar Torrijos Herrera A201

1982, May 14 Litho. *Perf. 10½*

617 A201	5c Aerial view	15	15
618 A201	6c Army camp	15	15
619 A201	50c Felipillo Engineering Works	1.00	40
	Nos. 617-619,C433-C434 (5)	2.80	
	Set value		1.15

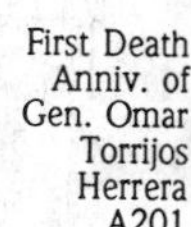

Ricardo J. Alfaro (1882-1977), Statesman — A202

Designs: Photos by Luiz Gutierrez Cruz.

1982, Aug. 18 Wmk. 382

620 A202 3c multicolored 15 15

See Nos. C436-C437.

1983 World Cup — A203

1982, Dec. 27 Litho. *Perf. 10½*

621 A203 50c Italian team 1.00 48

See Nos. C438-C440.

Chamber of Commerce Expo Comer '83, Jan. 12-16 A204

1983 Litho. Wmk. 382 *Perf. 10½*

622 A204 17c multicolored 40 30

Visit of Pope John Paul II — A205

Bank Emblem — A206

Various portraits of the Pope. 35c airmail.

Perf. 12x11

1983, Mar. 1 Litho. Wmk. 382

623 A205	6c multicolored	15	15
624 A205	17c multicolored	35	25
625 A205	35c multicolored	75	25

1983, Mar. 18

626 A206 50c multicolored 1.00 40

24th Council Meeting of Inter-American Development Bank, Mar. 21-23.

Simon Bolivar (1783-1830) — A207

1983, July 25 Litho. *Perf. 12*

627 A207 50c multicolored 1.00 50

Souvenir Sheet

Imperf

628 A207 1b like 50c 2.00 80

World Communications Year — A208

1983, Oct. 9 Litho. *Perf. 14*

629 A208	30c UPAE emblem	60	22
630 A208	40c WCY emblem	80	32
631 A208	50c UPU emblem	1.00	40
632 A208	60c Dove in flight	1.25	50

Souvenir Sheet

Imperf

633 A208 1b multicolored 2.00 2.00

No. 633 contains designs of Nos. 629-632 without denominations.

Freedom of Worship A209

1983, Oct. 21 Litho. *Perf. 11½*

634 A209	3c Panama Mosque	15	15
635 A209	5c Bahai Temple	15	15
636 A209	6c St. Francis Church	20	15
637 A209	17c Kol Shearit Israel Synagogue	45	25
	Set value	80	42

No. 637 incorrectly inscribed.

Ricardo Miro (1883-1940), Poet — A210

The Prophet, by Alfredo Sinclair — A211

Famous Men: 3c, Richard Newman (1883-1946), educator. 5c, Cristobal Rodriguez (1883-1943), politician. 6c, Alcibiades Arosemena (1883-1958), industrialist and financier. 35c, Cirilo Martinez (1883-1924), linguist.

1983, Nov. 8 Litho. *Perf. 14*

638 A210	1c multicolored	15	15
639 A210	3c multicolored	15	15
640 A210	5c multicolored	15	15
641 A210	6c multicolored	15	15
642 A210	35c multicolored	70	35
	Set value	1.00	65

1983, Dec. 12 *Perf. 12*

Paintings: No. 643, Village House, by Juan Manuel Cedeno. No. 644, Large Nude, by Manuel Chong Neto. 3c, On Another Occasion, by Spiros Vamvas. 6c, Punta Chame Landscape, by Guillermo Trujillo. 28c, Neon Light, by Alfredo Sinclair. 41c, Highland Girls, by Al Sprague. 1b, Bright Morning, by Ignacio Mallol Pibernat. Nos. 643-647, 650 horiz.

643 A211 1c multicolored 15 15
644 A211 1c multicolored 15 15
645 A211 3c multicolored 15 15
646 A211 6c multicolored 15 15
647 A211 28c multicolored 55 22
648 A211 35c multicolored 70 28
649 A211 41c multicolored 80 35
650 A211 1b multicolored 2.00 80
Nos. 643-650 (8) 4.65
Set value 1.80

Double Cup, Indian Period A212

Pottery: 40c, Raised dish, Tonosi period. 50c, Jug with face, Canazas period, vert. 60c, Bowl, Conte, vert.

1984, Jan. 16 Litho. *Perf. 12*
651 A212 30c multicolored 90 20
652 A212 40c multicolored 1.00 30
653 A212 50c multicolored 1.25 40
654 A212 60c multicolored 1.50 55

Souvenir Sheet
Imperf
655 A212 1b like 30c 2.00 2.00

Pre-Olympics A213

1984, June Litho. *Perf. 14*
656 A213 19c Baseball 40 35
657 A213 19c Basketball, vert. 40 35
658 A213 19c Boxing 40 35
659 A213 19c Swimming, vert. 40 35

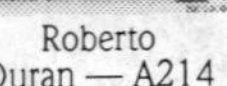

Roberto Duran — A214 Paintings — A215

1984 Olympic Games — A214a

1984, June 14 Litho. *Perf. 14*
660 A214 26c multicolored 60 25

1st Panamanian to hold 3 boxing championships.

1984 Litho. *Perf. 14*
660A A214a 6c Shooting 15 15
660B A214a 30c Weight lifting 60 20
660C A214a 37c Wrestling 75 30
660D A214a 1b Long jump 2.00 1.50

Souvenir Sheet
660E A214a 1b Running 2.00 80

Nos. 660B-660D are airmail. No. 660E contains one 45x45x64mm stamp.

1984, Sept. 17 Litho. *Perf. 14*

Paintings by Panamanian artists: 1c, Woman Thinking, by Manuel Chong Neto. 3c, The Child, by Alfredo Sinclair. 6c, A Day in the Life of Rumalda, by Brooke Alfaro. 30c, Highlands People, by Al Sprague. 37c, Intermission during the Dance, by Roberto Sprague. 44c, Punta Chame Forest, by Guillermo Trujillo. 50c, The Blue Plaza, by Juan Manuel Cedeno. 1b, Ira, by Spiros Vamvas.

661 A215 1c multi 15 15
662 A215 3c multi, horiz. 15 15
663 A215 6c multi, horiz. 15 15
664 A215 30c multi 60 20
665 A215 37c multi, horiz. 75 25
666 A215 44c multi, horiz. 90 35
667 A215 50c multi, horiz. 1.00 40
668 A215 1b multi, horiz. 2.00 1.50
Nos. 661-668 (8) 5.70 3.15

Postal Sovereignty A216

1984, Oct. 1 Litho. *Perf. 12*
669 A216 19c Pres. Torrijos, canal 40 25

Fauna A217

1984, Dec. 5 Engr. *Perf. 14*
670 A217 3c Manatee 15 15
671 A217 30c Gato negro 60 22
672 A217 44c Tigrillo congo 90 38
673 A217 50c Puerco de monte 1.00 40

Souvenir Sheet
674 A217 1b Perezoso de tres dedos, vert. 2.00 2.00

Nos. 671-673 are airmail.

Coins A218

1985, Jan. 17 Litho. *Perf. 11x12*
675 A218 3c 1935 1c 15 15
676 A218 3c 1904 10c 15 15
677 A218 6c 1916 5c 15 15
678 A218 30c 1904 50c 60 22
679 A218 37c 1962 half-balboa 75 35
680 A218 44c 1953 balboa 90 45
Nos. 675-680 (6) 2.70
Set value 1.20

Nos. 678-680 are airmail.

Contadora Type of 1985
Souvenir Sheet

1985, Oct. 1 Litho. *Perf. 13½x13*
680A AP108 1b Dove, flags, map 2.00 2.00

Cargo Ship in Lock — A219

1985, Oct. 16 *Perf. 14*
681 A219 19c multicolored 40 25

Panama Canal, 70th anniv. (1984).

UN 40th Anniv. A220

1986, Jan. 17 Litho. *Perf. 14*
682 A220 23c multicolored 45 35

Intl. Youth Year — A221

1986, Jan. 17
683 A221 30c multicolored 60 35

Waiting Her Turn, by Al Sprague (b.1938) — A222

Oil paintings: 5c, Aerobics, by Guillermo Trujillo (b. 1927). 19c, Cardboard House, by Eduardo Augustine (b. 1954). 30c, Door to the Homeland, by Juan Manuel Cedeno (b. 1914). 36c, Supper for Three, by Brooke Alfaro (b. 1949). 42c, Tenderness, by Alfredo Sinclair (b. 1915). 50c, Woman and Character, by Manuel Chong Neto (b. 1927). 60c, Cella lillies, by Maigualida de Diaz (b. 1950).

1986, Jan. 21
684 A222 3c multicolored 15 15
685 A222 5c multicolored 15 15
686 A222 19c multicolored 38 20
687 A222 30c multicolored 60 35
688 A222 36c multicolored 70 45
689 A222 42c multicolored 85 52
690 A222 50c multicolored 1.00 60
691 A222 60c multicolored 1.25 72
Nos. 684-691 (8) 5.08 3.14

Miss Universe Pageant A223

1986, July 7 Litho. *Perf. 12*
692 A223 23c Atlapa Center 45 28
693 A223 60c Emblem, vert. 1.25 72

Halley's Comet A224

Designs: 30c, Old Panama Cathedral tower, vert.

1986, Oct. 30 Litho. *Perf. 13½*
694 A224 23c multicolored 45 35
695 A224 30c multicolored 60 35

Size: 75x86mm
Imperf
695A A224 1b multicolored 2.00

A225 A226

1986 World Cup Soccer Championships, Mexico: Illustrations from Soccer History, by Sandoval and Meron.

1986, Oct. 30
696 A225 23c Argentina, winner 45 35
697 A225 30c Fed. Rep. of Germany, second 60 35
698 A225 37c Argentina, Germany 75 60

Souvenir Sheet
698A A225 1b Argentina, diff. 2.00

1986, Nov. 21
699 A226 20c shown 40 24
700 A226 23c Montage of events 45 35

15th Central American and Caribbean Games, Dominican Republic.

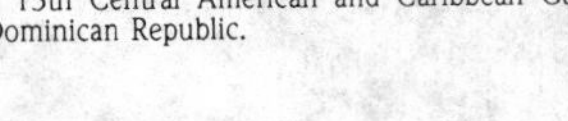

Christmas — A227

1986, Dec. 18 Litho.
701 A227 23c shown 45 30
702 A227 36c Green tree 70 48
703 A227 42c Silver tree 85 55

Intl. Peace Year — A228 Tropical Carnival, Feb.-Mar. — A229

1986, Dec. 30 *Perf. 13½*
704 A228 8c multicolored 16 15
705 A228 19c multicolored 38 25

1987, Jan. 27 Litho. *Perf. 13½*
706 A229 20c Diablito Sucio mask 40 30
707 A229 35c Sun 70 52

Size: 74x84mm
Imperf
708 A229 1b like 35c 2.00 1.50

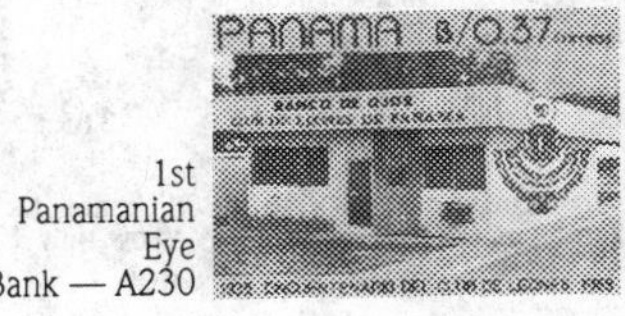

1st Panamanian Eye Bank — A230

1987, Feb. 17 Litho. *Perf. 14*
709 A230 37c multicolored 75 75

Panama Lions Club, 50th Anniv. (in 1985). Dated 1986.

Flowering Plants — A231

Birds — A232

1987, Mar. 5

710 A231	3c	Brownea macrophylla	15	15
711 A232	5c	Thraupis episcopus	15	15
712 A231	8c	Solandra grandiflora	16	15
713 A232	15c	Tyrannus melancholicus	30	22
714 A231	19c	Barleria micans	38	35
715 A232	23c	Pelecanus occidentalis	45	35
716 A231	30c	Cordia dentata	60	45
717 A232	36c	Columba cayennensis	75	55
		Nos. 710-717 (8)	2.94	2.37

Dated 1986.

Monument and Octavio Mendez Pereira, Founder A233

1987, Mar. 26 Litho. *Perf. 14*

718 A233 19c multicolored 38 28

University of Panama, 50th anniv. (in 1985). Stamp dated "1986."

UNFAO, 40th Anniv. (in 1985) A234

1987, Apr. 9 *Perf. 13½*

719 A234	10c	blk, pale ol & yel org	20	15
720 A234	45c	blk, dk grn & yel grn	90	70

Natl. Theater, 75th Anniv. A235

Baroque composers: 19c, Schutz (1585-1672). 37c, Bach. 60c, Handel. Nos. 721, 723-724 vert.

1987, Apr. 28 *Perf. 14*

721 A235	19c	multicolored	38	28
722 A235	30c	shown	60	45
723 A235	37c	multicolored	75	60
724 A235	60c	multicolored	1.20	90

A236

A237

1987, May 13 Litho. *Perf. 14*

725 A236 23c multicolored 50 45

Inter-American Development Bank, 25th anniv.

1987, Nov. 28 Litho. *Perf. 14*

726 A237	25c	Fire wagon, 1887, and modern ladder truck	55	42
727 A237	35c	Fireman carrying victim	80	60

Panama Fire Brigade, cent.

A238

A239

1987, Dec. 11

728 A238	15c	Wrestling, horiz.	35	26
729 A238	23c	Tennis	50	38
730 A238	30c	Swimming, horiz.	65	48
731 A238	41c	Basketball	90	70
732 A238	60c	Cycling	1.30	1.00
		Nos. 728-732 (5)	3.70	2.82

Souvenir Sheet

733 A238 1b Weight lifting 2.25 1.75

10th Pan American Games, Indianapolis.

1987, Dec. 17

Christmas (Religious paintings): 22c, Adoration of the Magi, by Albrecht Nentz (d. 1479). 35c, Virgin Adored by Angels, by Matthias Grunewald (d. 1528). 37c, The Virgin and Child, by Konrad Witz (c. 1400-1445).

734 A239	22c	multicolored	48	35
735 A239	35c	multicolored	80	60
736 A239	37c	multicolored	80	60

Intl. Year of Shelter for the Homeless A240

Designs: 45c, by A. Sinclair. 50c, Woman, boy, girl, shack, housing in perspective by A. Pulido.

1987, Dec. 29 *Perf. 14*

737 A240	45c	multicolored	1.00	75
738 A240	50c	multicolored	1.10	82

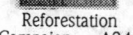

Reforestation Campaign — A241

Say No to Drugs — A242

1988, Jan. 14 Litho. *Perf. 14½x14*

739 A241	35c	dull grn & yel grn	78	60
740 A241	40c	red & pink	90	70
741 A241	45c	brn & lem	1.00	75

Dated 1987.

1988, Jan. 14

742 A242	10c	org lil rose	22	16
743 A242	17c	yel grn & lil rose	38	28
744 A242	25c	pink & sky blue	55	42

Child Survival Campaign A243

1988, Feb. 29 Litho. *Perf. 14*

745 A243	20c	Breast-feeding	45	35
746 A243	31c	Universal immunization	70	60
747 A243	45c	Growth and development, vert.	1.00	90

Fish — A244

1988, Mar. 14

748 A244	7c	Myripristis jacobus	16	15
749 A244	35c	Pomacanthus paru	80	60
750 A244	60c	Holocanthus tricolor	1.35	1.00
751 A244	1b	Equetus punctatus	2.25	1.70

The 7c actually shows the Holocanthus tricolor, the 60c the Myripristis jacobus.

Girl Guides, 75th Anniv. — A245

1988, Apr. 14

752 A245 35c multicolored 80 60

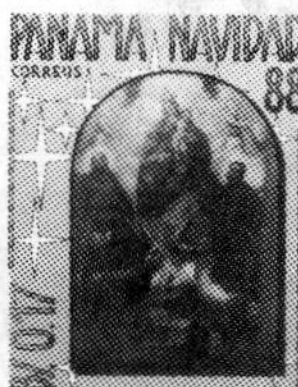

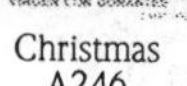

Christmas A246

St. John Bosco (1815-1888) A247

Paintings: 17c, *Virgin and Gift-givers.* 45c, *Virgin of the Rosary and St. Dominic.*

1988, Dec. 29 Litho. *Perf. 12*

753 A246	17c	multicolored	40	30
754 A246	45c	multicolored	1.00	75

See No. C446.

1989, Jan. 31

755 A247	10c	Portrait	22	16
756 A247	20c	Minor Basilica	48	35

1988 Summer Olympics, Seoul A248

Athletes and medals.

1989, Mar. 17 Litho. *Perf. 12*

757 A248	17c	Running	38	30
758 A248	25c	Wrestling	55	42
759 A248	60c	Weight lifting	1.30	1.00

Souvenir Sheet

760 A248 1b Swimming, vert. 2.25 1.65

See No. C447.

A249

A250

1989, Apr. 12 Litho. *Perf. 12*

761 A249	40c	red, blk & blue	1.00	75
762 A249	1b	Emergency and rescue services	2.40	1.80

Intl. Red Cross and Red Crescent organizations, 125th annivs.

1989, Oct. 12 Litho. *Perf. 12*

America Issue: Pre-Columbian artifacts.

767 A250	20c	Monolith of Barriles	50	38
768 A250	35c	Vessel	88	65

French Revolution, Bicent. A251

1989, Nov. 14 *Perf. 13½*

769 A251 25c multicolored 62 48

See Nos. C450-C451.

Christmas — A252

Designs: 17c, Holy family in Panamanian costume. 35c, Creche. 45c, Holy family, gift givers.

1989, Dec. 1

770 A252	17c	multicolored	42	32
771 A252	35c	multicolored	88	65
772 A252	45c	multicolored	1.15	85

A253

A254

1990, Jan. 16

773 A253 23c brown 58 45

Rogelio Sinan (b. 1902), writer.

1990, Mar. 14 Litho. *Perf. 13½*

774 A254	25c	blue & black	60	45
775 A254	35c	Experiment	82	60
776 A254	45c	Beakers, test tubes, books	1.00	75

Dr. Guillermo Patterson, Jr., chemist.

Fruits
A255

1990, May 15 ***Perf. 13½***

777 A255 20c Byrsonima crassifolia 48 35
778 A255 35c Bactris gasipaes 82 60
779 A255 40c Anacardium occidentale 95 68

Tortoises
A256

1990, July 17

780 A256 35c Pseudemys scripta 82 60
781 A256 45c Lepidochelys olivacea 1.00 75
782 A256 60c Geochelone carbonaria 1.40 1.00

Native
American
A257

1990, Oct. 12

783 A257 20c shown 65 40
784 A257 35c Native, vert. 1.15 85

Discovery of Isthmus of Panama, 490th Anniv. — A258

1991, Nov. 19 **Litho.** ***Perf. 12***

785 A258 35c multicolored 90 65

St. Ignatius of Loyola, 500th Birth Anniv. — A259

1991, Nov. 29

786 A259 20c multicolored 50 32

Society of Jesus, 450th anniv.

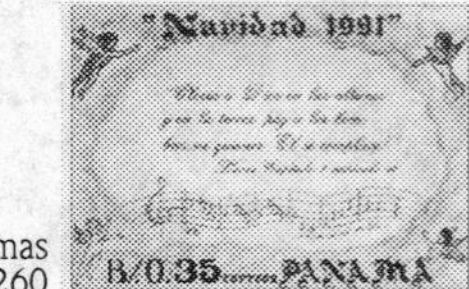

Christmas
A260

1991, Dec. 2

787 A260 35c Luke 2:14 90 65
788 A260 35c Nativity scene 90 65
a. Pair, #787-788 1.80 1.30

Social Security Administration, 50th Anniv. — A261

Design: No. 790, Dr. Arnulfo Arias Madrid (1901-1988), Constitution of Panama, 1941.

1991 **Litho.** ***Perf. 12***

789 A261 10c multicolored 24 15
790 A261 10c multicolored 24 15

Women's citizenship rights, 50th anniv. (No. 790).

Epiphany — A262

1992, Feb. 5 **Litho.** ***Perf. 12***

791 A262 10c multicolored 22 15

New Life Housing Project — A263

1992, Feb. 17

792 A263 5c multicolored 15 15

Border Treaty Between Panama and Costa Rica, 50th Anniv. — A264

Designs: a, 20c, Hands clasped. b, 40c, Map. c, 50c, Pres. Rafael A. Calderon, Costa Rica. and Pres. Arnulfo Arias Madrid, Panama.

1992, Feb. 20

793 A264 Strip of 3, #a.-c. 2.65 1.75

Causes of Hole in Ozone Layer — A265

1992, Feb. 24

794 A265 40c multicolored 1.00 70

Expocomer '92, Intl. Commercial Exposition — A266

1992, Mar. 11

795 A266 10c multicolored 25 18

A267 A268

Margot Fonteyn (1919-91), ballerina: a, 35c, Wearing dress. b, 45c, In costume.

1992, Mar. 12

796 A267 Pair, #a.-b. 1.95 1.40

1992, June 22 **Litho.** ***Perf. 12***

797 A268 10c multicolored 25 15

Maria Olimpia de Obaldia (1891-1985), poet.

1992 Summer Olympics, Barcelona — A269

1992, June 24 **Litho.** ***Perf. 12***

798 A269 10c multicolored 25 18
a. Tete-beche pair 50 36

Zion Baptist Church, Bocas del Toro, 1892 — A270

1992, Oct. 1 **Litho.** ***Perf. 12***

799 A270 20c multicolored 50 35

Baptist Church in Panama, Cent.

Discovery of America, 500th Anniv. — A271

Designs: a, 20c, Columbus' fleet. b, 35c, Coming ashore.

1992, Oct. 12

800 A271 Pair, #a.-b. 1.35 95

Endangered Wildlife — A272

Designs: a, 5c, Agouti paca. b, 10c, Harpia harpyja. c, 15c, Felis onca. d, 20c, Iguana iguana.

1992, Sept. 23

801 A272 Strip of 4, #a.-d. 1.25 90

Expo '92, Seville — A273

Worker's Health Year — A274

1992, Dec. 21 **Litho.** ***Perf. 12***

802 A273 10c multicolored 25 18

1992, Dec. 21

803 A274 15c multicolored 40 30

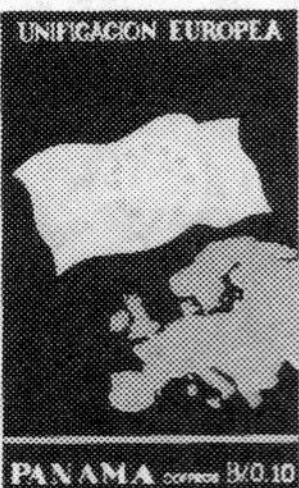

Unification of Europe — A275

1992, Dec. 21 **Litho.** ***Perf. 12***

804 A275 10c multicolored 28 15

Issued with se-tenant label.

Christmas — A276

Designs: a, 20c, Angel announcing birth of Christ. b, 35c, Mary and Joseph approaching city gate.

1992, Dec. 21

805 A276 Pair, #a.-b. 1.35 95

AIR POST STAMPS

Special Delivery Stamp No. E3 Surcharged in Dark Blue

CORREO AEREO

VEINTICINCO CENTESIMOS

1929, Feb. 8 Unwmk. *Perf. 12½*

C1	SD1 25c on 10c org	1.00	80
a.	Inverted surcharge	22.50	22.50

Nos. E3-E4 Overprinted in Blue

CORREO AEREO

1929

C2	SD1 10c orange	50	50
a.	Inverted overprint	16.00	14.00
b.	Double overprint	16.00	14.00

Some specialists claim the red overprint is a proof impression.

With Additional Surcharge of New Value

C3	SD1 15c on 10c org	50	50
C4	SD1 25c on 20c dk brn	1.10	1.00
a.	Double surcharge	14.00	14.00

No. E3 Surcharged in Blue

1930, Jan. 25

C5	SD1 5c on 10c org	50	50

No. 219 Overprinted in Red

1930, Feb. 28 *Perf. 12*

C6	A39 1b dk vio & blk	17.50	12.50

Airplane over Map of Panama
AP5 AP6

1930-41 Engr. *Perf. 12*

C6A	AP5 5c blue ('41)	15	15
C6B	AP5 7c rose car ('41)	22	15
C6C	AP5 8c gray blk ('41)	22	15
C7	AP5 15c dp grn	30	15
C8	AP5 20c rose	35	15
C9	AP5 25c deep blue	65	65
	Nos. C6A-C9 (6)	1.89	
	Set value		92

See No. C112.
For surcharges and overprints see Nos. 353, C16-C16A, C53B, C69, C82-C83, C109, C122, C124.

1930, Aug. 4 *Perf. 12½*

C10	AP6 5c ultra	15	15
C11	AP6 10c orange	35	20
C12	AP6 30c dp vio	5.50	4.00
C13	AP6 50c dp red	1.50	50
C14	AP6 1b black	5.50	4.00
	Nos. C10-C14 (5)	13.00	8.85

For surcharge and overprints see Nos. C53A, C70-C71, C115.

Amphibian — AP7

1931, Nov. 24 Typo.
Without Gum

C15	AP7 5c deep blue	80	1.00
a.	5c gray blue	80	1.00
b.	Horiz. pair, imperf. btwn.	50.00	

For the start of regular airmail service between Panama City and the western provinces, but valid only on Nov. 28-29 on mail carried by hydroplane "3 Noviembre."

Many sheets have a papermaker's watermark "DOLPHIN BOND" in double-lined capitals.

No. C9 Surcharged in Red 19mm long

HABILITADA
20 c.

1932, Dec. 14 *Perf. 12*

C16	AP5 20c on 25c dp bl	5.00	50

Surcharge 17mm long

C16A	AP5 20c on 25c dp bl	150.00	2.50

Special Delivery Stamp No. E4 Overprinted in Red or Black

CORREO AEREO

1934 *Perf. 12½*

C17	SD1 20c dk brn	1.00	50
C17A	SD1 20c dk brn (Bk)	75.00	55.00

Surcharged In Black

CORREO AEREO
10
CENTESIMOS

1935, June

C18	SD1 10c on 20c dk brn	80	50

Same Surcharge with Small "10"

C18A	SD1 10c on 20c dk brn	40.00	5.00
b.	Horiz. pair, imperf. vert.	100.00	

Nos. 234 and 242 Surcharged in Blue

1836 - 1936

5 CENTESIMOS

1936, Sept. 24

C19	A53 5c on ½c org	225.00	250.00
C20	A53 5c on 50c org	1.00	80
a.	Double surcharge	60.00	60.00

Centenary of the birth of President Pablo Arosemena.

It is claimed that No. C19 was not regularly issued.

Urracá Monument — AP8

Human Genius Uniting the Oceans AP9

Designs: 20c, Panama City. 30c, Balboa Monument. 50c, Pedro Miguel Locks. 1b, Palace of Justice.

1936, Dec. 1 Engr. *Perf. 12*

C21	AP8 5c blue	55	40
C22	AP9 10c yel org	70	60
C23	AP9 20c red	1.65	1.50
C24	AP8 30c dk vio	3.00	2.50
C25	AP9 50c car rose	6.75	5.75
C26	AP9 1b black	8.00	6.00
	Nos. C21-C26 (6)	20.65	16.75

4th Postal Congress of the Americas and Spain.

Nos. C21-C26 Overprinted in Red or Blue

1937, Mar. 29

C27	AP8 5c blue (R)	35	35
a.	Inverted overprint	35.00	
C28	AP9 10c yel org (Bl)	55	45
C29	AP9 20c red (Bl)	1.25	1.00
a.	Double overprint	35.00	
C30	AP8 30c dk vio (R)	3.25	3.25
C31	AP8 50c car rose (Bl)	13.00	13.00
a.	Double overprint	120.00	
C32	AP9 1b black (R)	16.00	13.00
	Nos. C27-C32 (6)	34.40	31.05

Regular Stamps of 1921-26 Surcharged in Red

CORREO
AEREO
5¢

1937, June 30 *Perf. 12, 12½*

C33	A55 5c on 15c ultra	75	75
C34	A55 5c on 20c brn	75	75
C35	A47 10c on 10c vio	1.75	1.50

Regular Stamps of 1920-26 Surcharged in Red

CORREO AEREO
5¢

C36	A56 5c on 24c blk vio	75	75
C37	A39 5c on 1b dk vio & blk	75	50
C38	A56 10c on 50c blk	2.25	2.00
a.	Inverted surcharge	18.00	

No. 248 Overprinted in Red

CORREO
AEREO

C39	A54 5c dark blue	75	75
a.	Double overprint	18.00	
	Nos. C33-C39 (7)	7.75	7.00

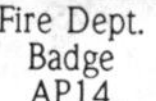

Fire Dept. Badge AP14

Florencio Arosemena AP15

José Gabriel Duque — AP16

Perf. 14x14½
1937, Nov. 25 Photo. Wmk. 233

C40	AP14 5c blue	75	60
C41	AP15 10c orange	1.00	1.00
C42	AP16 20c crimson	1.50	75

50th anniversary of the Fire Department.

Basketball — AP17

Baseball AP18

1938, Feb. 2 *Perf. 14x14½, 14½x14*

C43	AP17 1c shown	90	22
C44	AP18 2c shown	90	15
C45	AP18 7c Swimming	1.25	25
C46	AP18 8c Boxing	1.25	25
C47	AP17 15c Soccer	3.00	1.25
a.	Souv. sheet of 5, #C43-C47	6.00	8.00
b.	As "a," No. C43 omitted	*2,500.*	
	Nos. C43-C47 (5)	7.30	2.12

4th Central American Caribbean Games.

US Constitution Type
Engr. & Litho.
1938, Dec. 7 Unwmk. *Perf. 12½*
Center in Black, Flags in Red and Ultramarine

C49	A83 7c gray	25	18
C50	A83 8c brt ultra	35	18
C51	A83 15c red brn	45	45
C52	A83 50c orange	5.00	5.00
C53	A83 1b black	5.00	5.00
	Nos. C49-C53 (5)	11.05	10.81

Nos. C12 and C7 Surcharged in Red

1938, June 5 *Perf. 12½, 12*

C53A	AP6 7c on 30c dp vio	40	40
c.	Double surcharge	18.00	
d.	Inverted surcharge	27.50	
C53B	AP5 8c on 15c dp grn	40	40
e.	Inverted surcharge	22.50	

Opening of the Normal School at Santiago, Veraguas Province, June 5, 1938. The 8c surcharge has no bars.

Belisario Porras — AP23

Designs: 2c, William Howard Taft. 5c, Pedro J. Sosa. 10c, Lucien Bonaparte Wise. 15c, Armando Reclus. 20c, Gen. George W. Goethals. 50c, Ferdinand de Lesseps. 1b, Theodore Roosevelt.

1939, Aug. 15 Engr.

C54	AP23 1c dl rose	35	15
C55	AP23 2c dp bl grn	35	15
C56	AP23 5c indigo	50	15
C57	AP23 10c dk vio	60	18
C58	AP23 15c ultra	1.40	30
C59	AP23 20c rose pink	3.50	1.40
C60	AP23 50c dk brn	4.00	70
C61	AP23 1b black	6.00	3.75
	Nos. C54-C61 (8)	16.70	6.78

Opening of Panama Canal, 25th anniv.

For surcharges see Nos. C63, C65, G1, G3.

Flags of the 21 American Republics AP31

1940, Apr. 15 **Unwmk.**
C62 AP31 15c blue 42 35

Pan American Union, 50th anniversary.
For surcharge see No. C66.

Stamps of 1939-40 Surcharged in Black:

a **5 5**

b **AEREO SIETE**

c **SIETE**

d **8— 8**

1940, Aug. 12

C63 AP23 (a) 5c on 15c lt ultra		22	22
a.	"7 AEREO 7" on 15c	40.00	40.00
C64 A84 (b) 7c on 15c ultra		40	25
C65 AP23 (c) 7c on 20c rose pink		40	25
C66 AP31 (d) 8c on 15c blue		40	25

Stamps of 1924-30 Overprinted in Black or Red:

e **7 CONSTITUCION 7 CENTESIMOS 1941 CENTESIMOS AEREO**

f **CONSTITUCION 1941 AEREO 15**

g **CONSTITUCION 1941**

1941, Jan. 2 ***Perf. 12½, 12***

C67 SD1 (e) 7c on 10c org	80	80
C68 A53 (f) 15c on 24c yel brn (R)	2.00	2.00
C69 AP5 (g) 20c rose	1.65	1.65
C70 AP6 (g) 50c deep red	5.00	3.25
C71 AP6 (g) 1b blk (R)	11.00	8.00
Nos. C67-C71 (5)	20.45	15.70

New constitution of Panama which became effective Jan. 2, 1941.

Liberty — AP32

Black Overprint

1942, Feb. 19 **Engr.** ***Perf. 12***
C72 AP32 20c chestnut brn 3.00 2.50

Costa Rica - Panama Type

Engr. & Litho.

1942, Apr. 25 **Unwmk.**
C73 A94 15c dp grn, dk bl & dp rose 55 15

Swordfish AP34

J. D. Arosemena Normal School — AP35

Alejandro Meléndez G. — AP40

Designs: 8c, Gate of Glory, Portobelo. 15c, Taboga Island, Balboa Harbor. 50c, Firehouse. 1b, Gold animal figure.

1942, June 4 **Engr.** ***Perf. 12***

C74 AP34 7c rose car	50	16
C75 AP34 8c dk ol brn & blk	16	15
C76 AP34 15c dk vio	25	15
C77 AP35 20c red brn	35	15
C78 AP34 50c ol grn	65	35
C79 AP34 1b blk & org yel	1.60	80
Nos. C74-C79 (6)	3.51	
Set value		1.50

See Nos. C96-C99, C113, C126. For surcharges and overprints see Nos. 354-355, C84-C86, C108, C110-C111, C114, C116, C118, C121, C123, C127-C128, C137.

1943, Dec. 16

Design: 5b, Ernesto T. Lefevre.

C80 AP40 3b dk ol gray	4.50	4.50
C81 AP40 5b dk bl	7.00	7.00

For overprint and surcharge see Nos. C117, C128A.

Catalogue values for unused stamps in this section, from this point to the end of the section, are for Never Hinged items.

Nos. C6C and C7 Surcharged in Carmine

AEREO B/. 0.10 1947

1947, Mar. 8 ***Perf. 12***

C82 AP5 5c on 8c gray blk		15	15
a.	Double overprint	25.00	
C83 AP5 10c on 15c dp grn		50	40

Nos. C74 to C76 Surcharged in Black or Carmine

AEREO B/. 0.10 1947

C84 AP34 5c on 7c rose car (Bk)		16	16
a.	Double surcharge		375.00
C85 AP34 5c on 8c dk ol brn & blk		16	16
C86 AP34 10c on 15c dk vio		25	22
a.	Double surcharge	10.00	10.00

National Theater — AP42

1947, Apr. 7 **Engr.** **Unwmk.**
C87 AP42 8c violet 40 25

Natl. Constitutional Assembly of 1945, 2nd anniv.
For surcharge see No. 356.

Manuel Amador Guerrero AP43

Manuel Espinosa B. — AP44

Designs: 5c, José Agustin Arango. 10c, Federico Boyd. 15c, Ricardo Arias. 50c, Carlos Constantino Arosemena. 1b, Nicanor de Obarrio. 2b, Tomas Arias.

1948, Feb. 11 ***Perf. 12½***

Center in Black

C88 AP43 3c blue	30	18
C89 AP43 5c brown	30	18
C90 AP43 10c orange	30	18
C91 AP43 15c deep claret	30	18
C92 AP44 20c dp car	55	55
C93 AP44 50c dark gray	1.00	80
C94 AP44 1b green	3.00	2.50
C95 AP44 2b yellow	6.50	6.00
Nos. C88-C95 (8)	12.25	10.57

Issued to honor members of the Revolutionary Junta of 1903.

Types of 1942

1948, June 14 ***Perf. 12***

C96 AP34 2c carmine	50	15
C97 AP34 15c olive gray	25	15
C98 AP35 20c green	25	15
C99 AP34 50c rose carmine	4.00	3.00

Franklin D. Roosevelt and Juan D. Arosemena AP45

Four Freedoms AP46

Monument to F. D. Roosevelt AP47

Map showing Boyd-Roosevelt Trans-Isthmian Highway AP48

Franklin D. Roosevelt AP49

1948, Sept. 15 ***Perf. 12½***

C100 AP45 5c dp car & blk	16	15
C101 AP46 10c yel org	30	30
C102 AP47 20c dl grn	35	35
C103 AP48 50c dp ultra & blk	65	60
C104 AP49 1b gray blk	1.50	1.20
Nos. C100-C104 (5)	2.96	2.60

Franklin Delano Roosevelt (1882-1945).
For surcharges see Nos. RA28-RA29.

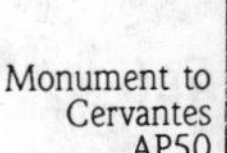

Monument to Cervantes AP50

Design: 10c, Don Quixote attacking windmill.

1948, Nov. 15

C105 AP50 5c dk bl & blk	16	15
C106 AP50 10c pur & blk	35	25

400th anniv. of the birth of Miguel de Cervantes Saavedra, novelist, playwright and poet.

No. C106 Overprinted in Carmine

"CENTENARIO DE JOSE GABRIEL DUQUE"

"18 de Enero de 1949"

1949, Jan.

C107 AP50 10c pur & blk		60	38
a.	Inverted overprint	8.00	

José Gabriel Duque (1849-1918), newspaper publisher and philanthropist.

Nos. C96, C6A, C97 and C99 Overprinted in Black or Red

h

i

1949, May

C108 AP34(h) 2c carmine		16	16
a.	Double overprint	5.00	
C109 AP5(i) 5c bl (R)		25	25
C110 AP34(h) 15c ol gray (R)		65	65
C111 AP34(h) 50c rose car		2.25	2.25

Issued to commemorate the centenary of the incorporation of Chiriqui Province.

Types of 1930-42

Design: 10c, Gate of Glory, Portobelo.

1949, Aug. 4 ***Perf. 12***

C112 AP5 5c orange	16	15
C113 AP34 10c dk bl & blk	20	15
Set value		22

For surcharge see No. C137.

Stamps of 1943-49 Overprinted or Surcharged in Black, Green or Red

1949, Sept. 9

C114 AP34 2c carmine		15	15
a.	Inverted overprint	14.00	
b.	Double overprint	14.00	
C115 AP5 5c org (G)		38	25
a.	Inverted overprint	8.00	
b.	Double overprint	20.00	
c.	Double ovpt., one inverted	20.00	
C116 AP34 10c dk bl & blk (R)		38	30
C117 AP40 25c on 3b dk ol gray (R)		50	50
C118 AP34 50c rose car		1.75	1.75
Nos. C114-C118 (5)		3.16	2.95

75th anniv. of the UPU.

No. C115 has small overprint, 15½x12mm, like No. 368. Overprint on Nos. C114, C116 and C118 as illustrated. Surcharge on No. C117 is arranged vertically, 29x18mm.

University of San Javier — AP51

1949, Dec. 7 **Engr.** ***Perf. 12½***
C119 AP51 5c dk bl & blk 35 15

See note after No. 371.

Mosquito — AP52

1950, Jan. 12 ***Perf. 12***
C120 AP52 5c dp ultra & gray blk 1.40 65

Issued to honor Dr. Carlos J. Finlay. See note after No. 372.

Nos. C96, C112, C113 and C9 Overprinted in Black or Carmine (5 or 4 lines)

CENTENARIO del Gral. José de San Martín 17 de Agosto de 1950

1950, Aug. 17 **Unwmk.**
C121 AP34 2c carmine 35 25
C122 AP5 5c orange 35 35
C123 AP34 10c dk bl & blk (C) 50 40
C124 AP5 25c dp bl (C) 80 80

Same on No. 362, Overprinted "AEREO"

C125 A105 50c pur & blk (C) 1.60 1.25
Nos. C121-C125 (5) 3.60 3.05

Issued to commemorate the centenary of the death of Gen. José de San Martin.

Firehouse Type of 1942

1950, Oct. 30 **Engr.**
C126 AP34 50c deep blue 2.00 1.00

Nos. C113 and C81 Surcharged in Carmine or Orange

AEREO

B/. 0.02

X 1952 X

1952, Feb. 20
C127 AP34 2c on 10c 16 15
a. Pair, one without surch. 250.00
C128 AP34 5c on 10c (O) 20 15
b. Pair, one without surch. 250.00
C128A AP40 1b on 5b 20.00 20.00

The surcharge on No. C128A is arranged to fit stamp, with four bars covering value panel at bottom, instead of crosses.

Nos. 376 and 380 Surcharged "AEREO 1952" and New Value in Carmine or Black

1952, Aug. 1
C129 A97 5c on 2c ver & blk (C) 15 15
a. Inverted surcharge 22.50
C130 A99 25c on 10c pur & org 1.00 1.00

Isabella Type of Regular Issue

Perf. 12½

1952, Oct. 20 **Unwmk.** **Engr.**

Center in Black

C131 A110 4c red orange 15 15
C132 A110 5c olive green 15 15
C133 A110 10c orange 20 25
C134 A110 25c gray blue 65 32
C135 A110 50c chocolate 1.00 65
C136 A110 1b black 3.00 3.00
Nos. C131-C136 (6) 5.15 4.52

Issued to commemorate the 500th anniversary of the birth of Queen Isabella I of Spain.

No. C113 Surcharged "5 1953" in Carmine

1953, Apr. 22 ***Perf. 12***
C137 AP34 5c on 10c dk bl & blk 35 15

Masthead of La Estrella — AP54

1953, July
C138 AP54 5c rose car 16 15
C139 AP54 10c blue 22 20

Panama's 1st newspaper, La Estrella de Panama, cent.
For surcharges see Nos. C146-C147.

Act of Independence — AP55

Senora de Remon and Pres. José A. Remon Cantera AP56

Designs: 7c, Pollera. 25c, National flower. 50c, Marcos A. Salazar, Esteban Huertas and Domingo Diaz A. 1b, Dancers.

1953, Nov.
C140 AP55 2c dp ultra 15 15
C141 AP56 5c dp grn 15 15
C142 AP56 7c gray 25 15
C143 AP56 25c black 1.50 65
C144 AP56 50c dk brn 1.00 65
C145 AP56 1b red org 2.50 1.00
Nos. C140-C145 (6) 5.55 2.75

Founding of republic, 50th anniversary.
For overprints see Nos. C227-C229.

Nos. C138-C139 Surcharged with New Value in Black or Red

1953-54
C146 AP54 1c on 5c rose car ('54) 15 15
C147 AP54 1c on 10c bl (R) 15 15
Set value 15 15

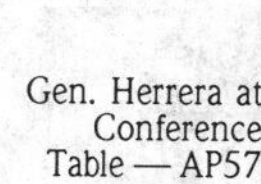

Gen. Herrera at Conference Table — AP57

Design: 1b, Gen. Herrera leading troops.

1954, Dec. 4 **Litho.** ***Perf. 12½***
C148 AP57 6c dp grn 15 15
C149 AP57 1b scar & blk 2.50 2.25

Death of Gen. Tomas Herrera, cent.
For surcharge see No. C198.

Rotary Emblem and Map — AP58

1955, Feb. 23
C150 AP58 6c rose vio 15 15
C151 AP58 21c red 50 35
C152 AP58 1b black 4.00 3.25
a. 1b violet black 4.50 4.50

Rotary International, 50th anniv.
For surcharge see No. C154.

Cantera Type

1955, June 1
C153 A115 6c rose vio & blk 16 15

Issued in tribute to Pres. José Antonio Remon Cantera, 1908-1955.
For surcharge see No. C188.

No. C151 Surcharged

B/.xxxxxxxx0.15

1955, Dec. 7
C154 AP58 15c on 21c red 40 35

Pedro J. Sosa — AP60

First Barge Going through Canal and de Lesseps AP61

Perf. 12½

1955, Nov. 22 **Unwmk.** **Litho.**
C155 AP60 5c grn, *lt grn* 16 15
C156 AP61 1b red lil & blk 2.00 2.00

150th anniversary of the birth of Ferdinand de Lesseps. Imperforates exist.

Pres. Dwight D. Eisenhower AP62

Statue of Bolivar AP63

Bolivar Hall AP64

Portraits-Presidents: C158, Pedro Aramburu, Argentina. C159, Dr. Victor Paz Estenssoro, Bolivia. C160, Dr. Juscelino Kubitschek O., Brazil. C161, Gen. Carlos Ibanez del Campo, Chile. C162, Gen. Gustavo Rojas Pinilla, Colombia. C163, Jose Figueres, Costa Rica. C164, Gen. Fulgencio Batista y Zaldivar, Cuba. C165, Gen. Hector B. Trujillo Molina, Dominican Rep. C166, José Maria Velasco Ibarra, Ecuador. C167, Col. Carlos Castillo Armas, Guatemala. C168, Gen. Paul E. Magloire, Haiti. C169, Julio Lozano Diaz, Honduras. C170, Adolfo Ruiz Cortines, Mexico. C171, Gen. Anastasio Somoza, Nicaragua. C172, Ricardo Arias Espinosa, Panama. C173, Gen. Alfredo Stroessner, Paraguay. C174, Gen. Manuel Odria, Peru. C175, Col. Oscar Osorio, El Salvador. C176, Dr. Alberto F. Zubiria, Uruguay. C177, Gen. Marcos Perez Jimenez, Venezuela. 1b, Simon Bolivar.

1956, July 18
C157 AP62 6c rose car & vio bl 40 35
C158 AP62 6c brt grnsh bl & blk 25 20
C159 AP62 6c bis & blk 25 20
C160 AP62 6c emer & blk 25 20
C161 AP62 6c lt grn & brn 25 20
C162 AP62 6c yel & grn 25 20
C163 AP62 6c brt vio & grn 25 20
C164 AP62 6c dl pur & vio bl 25 20
C165 AP62 6c red lil & sl grn 25 20
C166 AP62 6c cit & vio bl 25 20
C167 AP62 6c ap grn & brn 25 20
C168 AP62 6c brn & vio bl 25 20
C169 AP62 6c brt car & grn 25 20
C170 AP62 6c red & brn 35 25
C171 AP62 6c lt bl & grn 25 20
C172 AP62 6c vio bl & grn 25 20
C173 AP62 6c org & blk 25 20
C174 AP62 6c bluish gray & brn 25 20
C175 AP62 6c sal rose & blk 25 20
C176 AP62 6c dk grn & vio bl 25 20
C177 AP62 6c dk org brn & dk grn 25 20
C178 AP63 20c dk bluish gray 55 55
C179 AP64 50c green 1.00 1.00
C180 AP63 1b brown 2.00 1.25
Nos. C157-C180 (24) 9.05 7.20

Pan-American Conf., Panama City, July 21-22, 1956, and 130th anniv. of the 1st Pan-American Conf. Imperforates exist.

Ruins of First Town Council Building — AP65

Design: 50c, City Hall, Panama City.

1956, Aug. 17
C181 AP65 25c red 50 35
C182 AP65 50c black 1.00 90
a. Souv. sheet of 3, #404, C181-C182, imperf. 2.25 2.25

6th Inter-American Congress of Municipalities, Panama City, Aug. 14-19, 1956.
No. C182a sold for 85c.
For overprint see No. C187a.

Monument AP66

St. Thomas Hospital AP67

1956, Nov. 27 **Wmk. 311**
C183 AP66 5c green 15 15
C184 AP67 15c dk car 25 20
Set value 25

Issued to commemorate the centenary of the birth of Pres. Belisario Porras.

Highway Construction — AP68

Designs: 20c, Road through jungle, Darien project. 1b, Map of Americas showing Pan-American Highway.

Perf. 12½

1957, Aug. 1 **Wmk. 311** **Litho.**
C185 AP68 10c black 15 15
C186 AP68 20c lt bl & blk 50 50
C187 AP68 1b green 2.25 2.25
a. AP65 Souvenir sheet of 3, unwmkd. 5.00 5.00

Nos. C185-C187a were issued to publicize the 7th Pan-American Highway Congress.
No. C187a is No. C182a overprinted in black: "VII degree CONGRESSO INTERAMERICANO DE CARRETERAS 1957."

No. C153 Surcharged "1957" and New Value

1957, Aug. 13 **Unwmk.**
C188 AP59 10c on 6c rose vio & blk 20 16

Remon Polyclinic AP69 — Customs House, Portobelo AP70

Buildings: C191, Portobelo Castle. C192, San Jeronimo Castle. C193, Remon Hippodrome. C194, Legislature. C195, Interior and Treasury Department. C196, El Panama Hotel. C197, San Lorenzo Castle.

Perf. 12½
1957, Oct. **Wmk. 311** **Litho.**
Design in Black

C189 AP69 10c lt bl 22 15
C190 AP70 10c lilac 22 15
C191 AP70 10c gray 22 15
C192 AP70 10c lil rose 22 15
C193 AP70 10c ultra 22 15
C194 AP70 10c brn ol 22 15
C195 AP70 10c org yel 22 15
C196 AP70 10c yel grn 22 15
C197 AP70 1b red 2.25 1.60
Nos. C189-C197 (9) 4.01 2.80

No. C148 Surcharged with New Value and "1958" in Red

1958, Feb. 11 **Unwmk.**
C198 AP57 5c on 6c dp grn 20 15

United Nations Emblem — AP71

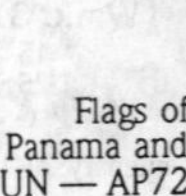

Flags of Panama and UN — AP72

1958, Mar. 5 **Litho.** **Wmk. 311**
C199 AP71 10c brt grn 15 15
C200 AP71 21c lt ultra 35 25
C201 AP71 50c orange 1.00 85
C202 AP72 1b gray, ultra & car 2.00 1.60
a. Souv. sheet of 4, #C199-C202, imperf. 4.50 4.50

10th anniv. of the UN (in 1955).
The sheet also exists with the 10c and 50c omitted.

OAS Type of Regular Issue, 1958

Designs: 10c, 1b, Flags of 21 American Nations. 50c, Headquarters in Washington.

1958, July 10 **Unwmk.** *Perf. 12½*
Center yellow and black; flags in national colors

C203 A124 5c lt bl 15 15
C204 A124 10c car rose 16 15
C205 A124 50c gray 60 60
C206 A124 1b black 1.90 1.60

Type of Regular Issue

Pavilions: 15c, Vatican City. 50c, United States. 1b, Belgium.

1958, Sept. 8 **Wmk. 311** *Perf. 12½*
C207 A125 15c gray & lt vio 25 20
C208 A125 50c dk gray & org brn 65 65
C209 A125 1b brt vio & bluish grn 1.40 1.40
a. Souv. sheet of 7, #418-421, C207-C209 3.50 3.50

No. C209a sold for 2b.

Pope Type of Regular Issue

Portraits of Pius XII: 5c, As cardinal. 30c, Wearing papal tiara. 50c, Enthroned.

1959, Jan. 21 **Litho.** **Wmk. 311**
C210 A126 5c violet 15 15
C211 A126 30c lilac rose 50 40
C212 A126 50c blue gray 80 65
a. Souv. sheet of 4, #422, C210-C212, imperf. 1.90 1.90

No. C212a is watermarked sideways and sold for 1b. The sheet also exists with 30c omitted. No. C212a with C.E.P.A.L. overprint is listed as No. C221a.

Human Rights Issue Type

Designs: 5c, Humanity looking into sun. 10c, 20c, Torch and UN emblem. 50c, UN Flag. 1b, UN Headquarters building.

1959, Apr. 14 *Perf. 12½*
C213 A127 5c emer & bl 15 15
C214 A127 10c gray & org brn 15 15
C215 A127 20c brn & gray 25 20
C216 A127 50c grn & ultra 70 65
C217 A127 1b red & bl 1.50 1.40
Nos. C213-C217 (5) 2.75 2.55

Nos. C213-C215, C212a Overprinted and C216 Surcharged in Red or Dark Blue

8A REUNION
C.E.P.A.L.
MAYO 1959

1959, May 16
C218 A127 5c emer & bl (R) 15 15
C219 A127 10c gray & org brn (Bl) 16 15
C220 A127 20c brn & gray (R) 35 25
C221 A127 1b on 50c grn & ultra (R) 1.90 1.90
a. Souvenir sheet of 4 4.00 4.00

8th Reunion of the Economic Commission for Latin America.
This overprint also exists on Nos. C216-C217. These have been disavowed by Panama's postmaster general.
No. C221a is No. C212a with two-line black overprint at top of sheet: "8a. REUNION DE LA C.E.P.A.L. MAYO 1959."

Type of Regular Issue, 1959

Portraits: 5c, Justo A. Facio, Rector. 10c, Ernesto de la Guardia, Jr., Pres. of Panama.

Perf. 12½
1959, July 27 **Wmk. 311** **Litho.**
C222 A128 5c black 15 15
C223 A128 10c black 16 15
Set value 24 15

Type of Regular Issue, 1959

1959, Oct. 26 **Wmk. 311** *Perf. 12½*
C224 A130 5c Boxing 15 15
C225 A130 10c Baseball 20 15
C226 A130 50c Basketball 80 65

For surcharge see No. C349.

Nos. C143-C145 Overprinted in Vermilion, Red or Black

NACIONES UNIDAS
AÑO MUNDIAL.
REFUGIADOS.
1959-1960

Unwmk.
1960, Feb. 6 **Engr.** *Perf. 12*
C227 AP56 25c blk (V) 75 20
C228 AP56 50c dk brn (R) 1.00 40
C229 AP56 1b red org 1.75 1.25

Issued to publicize World Refugee Year, July 1, 1959-June 30, 1960.
The revenues from the sale of Nos. C227-C229 went to the United Nations Refugee Fund.

Administration Building, National University AP74

Designs: 21c, Humanities building. 25c, Medical school. 30c, Dr. Octavio Mendez Pereria first rector of University.

Perf. 12½
1960, Mar. 23 **Litho.** **Wmk. 311**
C230 AP74 10c brt grn 20 15
C231 AP74 21c lt bl 40 20
C232 AP74 25c ultra 50 25
C233 AP74 30c black 60 35

25th anniv. of the founding of the National University.
For surcharges see Nos. 450, C248, C253, C287, C291.

Olympic Games Type

Designs: 5c, Basketball. 10c, Bicycling, horiz. 25c, Javelin thrower. 50c, Athlete with Olympic torch.

1960, Sept. 22 **Wmk. 343** *Perf. 12½*
C234 A131 5c org & red 15 15
C235 A131 10c ocher & blk 20 15
C236 A131 25c lt bl & dk bl 50 35
C237 A131 50c brn & blk 1.00 65
a. Souv. sheet of 2, #C236-C237 2.25 2.25

For surcharges see Nos. C249-C250, C254, C266-C270, C290, C350, RA40.

Citizens' Silhouettes AP75

Design: 10c, Heads and map of Central America.

1960 **Litho.** **Wmk. 229**
C238 AP75 5c black 15 15
C239 AP75 10c brown 20 15
Set value 20

6th census of population and the 2nd census of dwellings (No. C238), Dec. 11, 1960, and the All America Census, 1960 (No. C239).

Boeing 707 Jet Liner AP76

1960, Dec. 1 **Wmk. 343** *Perf. 12½*
C240 AP76 5c lt grnsh bl 15 15
C241 AP76 10c emerald 20 15
C242 AP76 20c red brn 40 25
Set value 45

1st jet service to Panama. For surcharge see No. RA41.

Souvenir Sheet

UN Emblem — AP77

Wmk. 311
1961, Mar. 7 **Litho.** *Imperf.*
C243 AP77 80c blk & car rose 1.60 1.60

15th anniv. (in 1960) of the UN.

No. C243 Overprinted in Blue with Large Uprooted Oak Emblem and "Ano de los Refugiados"

1961, June 2
C244 AP77 80c blk & car rose 2.50 2.50

World Refugee Year, July 1, 1959-June 30, 1960.

Lions International Type

Designs: 5c, Helen Keller School for the Blind. 10c, Children's summer camp. 21c, Arms of Panama and Lions emblem.

1961, May 2 **Wmk. 311** *Perf. 12½*
C245 A133 5c black 15 15
C246 A133 10c emerald 20 15
C247 A133 21c ultra, yel & red 40 25
Set value 40

For overprints see Nos. C284-C286.

Nos. C230 and C236 Surcharged in Black or Red

HABILITADA
en
B/. 0.01

1961 **Wmk. 311 (1c); Wmk. 343**
C248 AP74 1c on 10c 15 15
C249 A131 1b on 25c (Bk) 2.00 2.00
C250 A131 1b on 25c (R) 2.00 2.00

Pres. Roberto F. Chiari and Pres. Mario Echandi AP78

Perf. 12½
1961, Oct. 2 **Wmk. 343** **Litho.**
C251 AP78 1b blk & gold 2.00 1.25

Meeting of the Presidents of Panama and Costa Rica at Paso Canoa, Apr. 21, 1961.

Dag Hammarskjold — AP79

1961, Dec. 27 *Perf. 12½*
C252 AP79 10c black 20 15

Issued in memory of Dag Hammarskjold, Secretary General of the United Nations, 1953-61.

No. C230 Surcharged

Vale B/. 0.15

1962, Feb. 21 **Wmk. 311**
C253 AP74 15c on 10c brt grn 30 20

No. C236 Surcharged

XX
VALE
B/. 1.00

Wmk. 343
C254 A131 1b on 25c 2.00 1.25

City Hall, Colon — AP80

1962, Feb. 28 **Litho.** **Wmk. 311**
C255 AP80 5c vio bl & blk 15 15

Issued to publicize the third Central American Municipal Assembly, Colon, May 13-17.

Church Type of Regular Issue, 1962

Designs: 5c, Church of Christ the King. 7c, Church of San Miguel. 8c, Church of the Sanctuary. 10c, Saints Church. 15c, Church of St. Ann. 21c, Canal Zone Synagogue (Now used as USO Center). 25c, Panama Synagogue. 30c, Church of St. Francis. 50c, Protestant Church, Canal Zone. 1b, Catholic Church, Canal Zone.

Perf. 12½

1962-64 Wmk. 343 Litho.

Buildings in Black

C256 A138 5c pur & buff 15 15
C257 A138 7c lil rose & brt pink 15 15
C258 A138 8c pur & bl 16 15
C259 A139 10c lil & sal 20 15
C259A A139 10c grn & dl red brn ('64) 20 20
C260 A139 15c red & buff 30 20
C261 A138 21c brn & bl 40 40
C262 A138 25c bl & pink 50 35
C263 A139 30c lil rose & bl 60 42
C264 A138 50c lil & lt grn 1.00 65
a. Souv. sheet of 4, #441H-441J, C262, C264, imperf. 2.00 2.00
C265 A139 1b bl & sal 2.00 1.40
Nos. C256-C265 (11) 5.66 4.22

Freedom of religion in Panama. Issue dates: #C259A, June 4, 1964; others, July 20, 1962.

For overprints and surcharges see Nos. C288, C296-C297, C299.

Nos. C234 and C236 Overprinted and Surcharged "IX JUEGOS C.A. Y DEL CARIBE KINGSTON-1962" and Games Emblem in Black, Green, Orange or Red

1962 Wmk. 343 *Perf. 12½*

C266 A131 5c org & red 15 15
C267 A131 10c on 25c (G) 20 20
C268 A131 15c on 25c (O) 30 30
C269 A131 20c on 25c (R) 40 40
C270 A131 25c lt bl & dk bl 50 50
Nos. C266-C270 (5) 1.55 1.55

Issued to commemorate the Ninth Central American and Caribbean Games, Kingston, Jamaica, Aug. 11-25.

Nos. CB1-CB2 Surcharged

VALE .20 ¢ XX

1962, May 3 Wmk. 311

C271 SPAP1 10c on 5c + 5c 1.00 75
C272 SPAP1 20c on 10c + 10c 1.50 1.50

Type of Regular Issue, 1962

Design: 10c, Canal bridge completed.

1962, Oct. 12 Wmk. 343

C273 A140 10c bl & blk 20 15

John H. Glenn, "Friendship 7" Capsule — AP81

UPAE Emblem — AP82

Designs: 10c, "Friendship 7" capsule and globe, horiz. 31c, Capsule in space, horiz. 50c, Glenn with space helmet.

1962, Oct. 19 Wmk. 311 *Perf. 12½*

C274 AP81 5c rose red 15 15
C275 AP81 10c yellow 20 16
C276 AP81 31c blue 80 80
C277 AP81 50c emerald 1.00 1.00
a. Souv. sheet of 4, #C274-C277, imperf. 2.25 2.25

1st orbital flight of US astronaut Lt. Col. John H. Glenn, Jr., Feb. 20, 1962. No. C277a sold for 1b.

For surcharges see Nos. C290A-C290D, C367, CB4-CB7.

1963, Jan. 8 Litho. Wmk. 343

C278 AP82 10c multi 20 15

Issued to commemorate the 50th anniversary of the founding of the Postal Union of the Americas and Spain, UPAE.

Type of Regular Issue

Designs: 10c, Fire Engine "China", Plaza de Santa Ana. 15c, 14th Street team. 21c, Fire Brigade emblem.

1963, Jan. 22 Wmk. 311 *Perf. 12½*

C279 A141 10c org & blk 20 15
C280 A141 15c lil & blk 30 20
C281 A141 21c gold, red & ultra 50 50

"FAO" and Wheat Emblem — AP83

1963, Mar. 21 Litho.

C282 AP83 10c grn & red 20 16
C283 AP83 15c ultra & red 30 22

FAO "Freedom from Hunger" campaign.

No. C245 Overprinted in Yellow, Orange or Green: "XXII Convención / Leonística / Centroamericana / Panama, 18-21 / Abril 1963"

1963, Apr. 18 Wmk. 311 *Perf. 12½*

C284 A133 5c blk (Y) 15 15
C285 A133 5c blk (O) 15 15
C286 A133 5c blk (G) 15 15
Set value 30 30

22nd Central American Lions Congress, Panama, Apr. 18-21.

No. C230 Surcharged:

HABILITADO

Vale B/. 0.04

1963, June 11

C287 AP74 4c on 10c brt grn 15 15

Nos. 445 and 432 Overprinted "AEREO" Vertically

1963 Wmk. 343 *Perf. 12½*

C288 A139 10c grn, yel & blk 20 15

Wmk. 311

C289 A130 20c emer & red brn 40 22

No. C234 Overprinted: "LIBERTAD DE PRENSA 20-VIII-63"

1963, Aug. 20 Wmk. 343

C290 A131 5c org & red 15 15

Freedom of Press Day, Aug. 20, 1963.

Nos. C274, C277a Overprinted or Surcharged — a

"Visita Astronautas Glenn-Schirra Sheppard Cooper a Panamá"

HABILITADO

No. C274 Surcharged in Black — b

10¢

Perf. 12½

1963, Aug. 21 Litho. Wmk. 311

C290A AP81(a) 5c on #C274
C290B AP81(a) 10c on 5c #C274
C290C AP81(b) 10c on 5c #C274

Souvenir Sheet

Imperf.

C290D AP81(a) Sheet of 4, #C277a

Overprint on No. C290D has names in capital letters and covers all four stamps.

No. C232 Surcharged in Red: "VALE 10¢"

1963, Oct. 9 Wmk. 311 *Perf. 12½*

C291 AP74 10c on 25c ultra 20 15

Type of Regular Issue, 1963

Flags and Presidents: 5c, Julio A. Rivera, El Salvador. 10c, Miguel Ydigoras F., Guatemala. 21c, John F. Kennedy, US.

Perf. 12½x12

1963, Dec. 18 Litho. Unwmk.

Portrait in Slate Green

C292 A142 5c yel, red & ultra 15 30
C293 A142 10c bl, red & ultra 30 40
C294 A142 21c org yel, red & ultra 1.00 1.00

Balboa Type of Regular Issue, 1964

1964, Jan. 22 Photo. *Perf. 13*

C295 A143 10c dk vio, *pale pink* 20 16

No. C261 Surcharged in Red: "VALE B/.0.50"

1964 Wmk. 343 Litho. *Perf. 12½*

C296 A138 50c on 21c brn, bl & blk 1.00 70

Type of 1962 Overprinted: "HABILITADA"

C297 A139 1b emer, yel & blk 2.00 2.00

Nos. 434 and 444 Surcharged: "Aéreo B/.0.10"

1964 Wmk. 343 *Perf. 12½*

C298 A131 10c on 5c bl grn & emer 20 15
C299 A139 10c on 5c rose, lt grn & blk 20 15

St. Patrick's Cathedral, New York — AP84

Cathedrals: No. C301, St. Stephen's, Vienna. No. C302, St. Sofia's, Sofia. C303, Notre Dame, Paris. No. C304, Cologne. C305, St. Paul's, London. C306, Metropolitan, Athens. C307, St. Elizabeth's, Kosice, Czechoslovakia (inscr. Kassa, Hungary). No. C308, New Delhi. C309, Milan. C310, Guadalupe Basilica. C311, New Church, Delft, Netherlands. C312, Lima. C313, St. John's Poland. C314, Lisbon. C315, St. Basil's, Moscow. C316, Toledo. C317, Stockholm. C318, Basel. C319, St. George's Patriarchal Church, Istanbul. 1b, Panama City. 2b, St. Peter's Basilica, Rome.

Unwmk.

1964, Feb. 17 Engr. *Perf. 12*

Center in Black

C300 AP84 21c olive 60 60
C301 AP84 21c chocolate 60 60
C302 AP84 21c aqua 60 60
C303 AP84 21c red brn 60 60
C304 AP84 21c magenta 60 60
C305 AP84 21c red 60 60
C306 AP84 21c org red 60 60
C307 AP84 21c blue 60 60
C308 AP84 21c brown 60 60
C309 AP84 21c green 60 60
C310 AP84 21c vio bl 60 60
C311 AP84 21c dk sl grn 60 60
C312 AP84 21c violet 60 60
C313 AP84 21c black 60 60
C314 AP84 21c emerald 60 60
C315 AP84 21c dp vio 60 60
C316 AP84 21c ol grn 60 60
C317 AP84 21c car rose 60 60
C318 AP84 21c Prus grn 60 60
C319 AP84 21c dk brn 60 60
C320 AP84 1b dk bl 3.00 3.00
C321 AP84 2b yel grn 6.00 6.00
a. Souv. sheet of 6 7.50 7.50
Nos. C300-C321 (22) 21.00 21.00

Vatican II, the 21st Ecumenical Council of the Roman Catholic Church.

No. C321a contains 6 imperf. stamps similar to Nos. C300, C303, C305, C315, C320 and C321. Size: 198x138mm. Sold for 3.85b.

Six stamps of this set (Nos. C300, C305, C309, C319, C321a) were overprinted "1964." The overprint is olive bister on the stamps, yellow on the souvenir sheet. The overprint is reported to exist also in yellow gold on the same six stamps and in olive bister on the souvenir sheet.

World's Fair, New York AP84a

Designs: 5c, 10, 15c, Various pavilions. 21c, Unisphere.

1964, Sept. 14 Wmk. 311 *Perf. 12½*

C322 AP84a 5c yel & blk
C323 AP84a 10c red & blk
C324 AP84a 15c grn & blk
C325 AP84a 21c ultra & blk

Souvenir Sheet

Perf. 12

C326 AP84a 21c ultra & blk

No. C326 contains one 49x35mm stamp. Exists imperf.

Hammarskjold Memorial, UN Day — AP84b

Designs: No. C327, C329a, Dag Hammarskjold. No. C328, C329b, UN emblem.

Perf. 13½x14

1964, Sept. 24 Unwmk.

C327 AP84b 21c blk & bl
C328 AP84b 21c blk & bl

Souvenir Sheet

Imperf

C329 Sheet of 2
a.-b. AP84b 21c blk & grn, any single

Nos. C327-C328 exist imperf. in black and green.

Roosevelt Type of Regular Issue

Perf. 12x12½

1964, Oct. 9 Litho. Unwmk.

C330 A147 20c grn & blk, *buff* 40 30
a. Souv. sheet of 2, #455, C330, imperf. 55 55

Pope John XXIII (1881-1963) AP84c

1964 *Perf. 13½x14*

C331 AP84c 21c shown
C332 AP84c 21c Papal coat of arms
a. Souv. sheet of 2, #C331-C332

Nos. C331-C332 exist imperf. in different colors.

Galileo, 400th Birth Anniv. — AP84d

Design: 21c, Galileo, studies of gravity. (Illustration reduced).

1965 *Perf. 14*

C333 AP84d 10c bl & multi
C334 AP84d 21c grn & multi
a. Souv. sheet of 2, #C333-C334

Nos. C333-C334a exist imperf. with different colors.

Alfred Nobel (1833-1896), Founder of Nobel Prize — AP84e

Illustration reduced.

1965 **Litho. & Embossed**

C335 AP84e 10c Peace Medal, rev.
C336 AP84e 21c Peace Medal, obv.
a. Souv. sheet of 2, #C335-C336

Nos. C335-C336a exist imperf. with different colors.

Bird Type of Regular Issue, 1965

Song Birds: 5c, Common troupial, horiz. 10c, Crimson-backed tanager, horiz.

1965, Oct. 27 **Unwmk.** *Perf. 14*

C337 A148 5c dp org & multi 15 15
C338 A148 10c brt bl & multi 25 15
Set value 18

Fish Type of Regular Issue

Designs: 8c, Shrimp. 12c, Hammerhead. 13c, Atlantic sailfish. 25c, Seahorse, vert.

1965, Dec. 7 **Litho.**

C339 A149 8c multi 20 15
C340 A149 12c multi 30 20
C341 A149 13c multi 30 22
C342 A149 25c multi 60 40

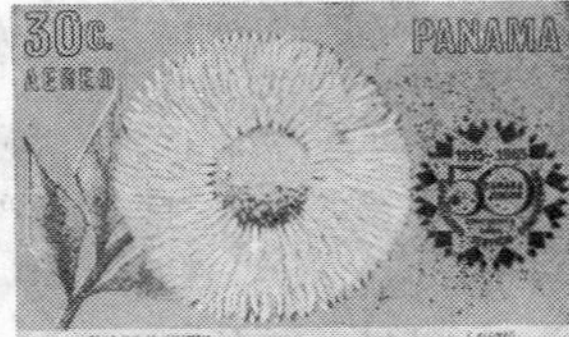

English Daisy and Emblem — AP85

Designs (Junior Chamber of Commerce Emblem and): No. C344, Hibiscus. No. C345, Orchid. No. C346, Water lily. No. C347, Gladiolus. No. C348, Flor del Espiritu Santo.

1966, Mar. 16

C343 AP85 30c brt pink & multi 75 35
C344 AP85 30c sal & multi 75 35
C345 AP85 30c pale yel & multi 75 35
C346 AP85 40c lt grn & multi 1.00 35
C347 AP85 40c bl & multi 1.00 35
C348 AP85 40c pink & multi 1.00 35
Nos. C343-C348 (6) 5.25 2.10

50th anniv. of the Junior Chamber of Commerce.

Nos. C224 and C236 Surcharged

1966, June 27 **Wmk. 311** *Perf. 12½*

C349 A130 3c on 5c blk & red brn 15 15

Wmk. 343

C350 A131 13c on 25c lt & dk bl 35 25

The old denominations are not obliterated on Nos. C349-C350.

ITU Cent. AP85a

1966, Aug. 12 *Perf. 13½x14*

C351 AP85a 31c multicolored

Sovenir Sheet

Perf. 14

C352 AP85a 31c multicolored

No. C352 exists imperf. with blue green background.

Animal Type of Regular Issue, 1967

Domestic Animals: 10c, Pekingese dog. 13c, Zebu, horiz. 30c, Cat. 40c, Horse, horiz.

1967, Feb. 3 **Unwmk.** *Perf. 14*

C353 A150 10c multi 25 16
C354 A150 13c multi 30 20
C355 A150 30c multi 75 45
C356 A150 40c multi 1.00 55

Young Hare, by Durer AP86

Designs: 10c, St. Jerome and the Lion, by Albrecht Durer. 20c, Lady with the Ermine, by Leonardo Da Vinci. 30c, The Hunt, by Delacroix, horiz.

1967, Sept. 1

C357 AP86 10c blk, buff & car 20 15
C358 AP86 13c lt yel & multi 25 16
C359 AP86 20c multi 40 22
C360 AP86 30c multi 60 40

Panama-Mexico Friendship — AP86a

Designs: 1b, Pres. Gustavo Diaz Ordaz of Mexico and Pres. Marco A. Robles of Panama, horiz.

1968, Jan. 20 *Perf. 14*

C361 AP86a 50c shown
C361A AP86a 1b multi
b. Souv. sheet of 2, #C361-C361A, imperf.

For overprints see Nos. C364-C364B.

Souvenir Sheet

Olympic Equestrian Events — AP86b

1968, Oct. 29 *Imperf.*

C362 Sheet of 2
a. AP86b 8c Dressage
b. AP86b 30c Show jumping

Intl. Human Rights Year — AP86c

1968, Dec. 18 *Perf. 14*

C363 AP86c 40c multicolored
a. Miniature sheet of 1

Nos. C361-C361b Ovptd. in Red or Black

"1A. EXPOSICION FILATELICA Y NUMISMA-TICA NAL. 29-8-68"

1969, Jan. 31

C364 AP86a 50c on #C361 (R)
C364A AP86a 1b on #C361A (B)

Souvenir Sheet

C364B on #C361a (R)

Intl. Philatelic and Numismatic Expo.
Overprint larger on No. C364A, larger and in different arrangement on No. C364B.

Intl. Space Exploration — AP86d

1969, Mar. 14

C365 Sheet of 6
a. AP86d 5c France, Diadem I
b. AP86d 10c Italy, San Marco II
c. AP86d 15c Great Britain, UK 3
d. AP86d 20c US, Saturn V/Apollo 7
e. AP86d 25c US, Surveyor 7
f. AP86d 30c Europe/US, Esro 2

Satellite Transmission of Summer Olympics, Mexico, 1968 — AP86e

1969, Mar. 14 *Perf. 14½*

C366 AP86e 1b multi
a. Min. sheet of 1

Decreto Nº 112 (de 6 de marzo de 1969)

Nos. CB4, 461B & 461C Overprinted

B/. 0.05

1969, Mar. 26 *Perf. 13½x13*

C367 AP81 5c on 5c+5c
C367A A147e 5c on 10c+5c
C367B A147e 10c on 21c+10c

Games Type of Regular Issue and

San Blas Indian Girl — AP87

Design: 13c, Bridge of the Americas.

1970, Jan. 6 **Litho.** *Perf. 13½*

C368 A158 13c multi 40 30
C369 AP87 30c multi 90 75
a. "AEREO" omitted *50.00 50.00*

See notes after No. 525.

Juan D. Arosemena and Arosemena Stadium AP88

Designs: 2c, 3c, 5c, like 1c. No. C374, Basketball. No. C375, New Panama Gymnasium. No. C376, Revolution Stadium. No. C377, Panamanian man and woman in Stadium. 30c, Stadium, eternal flame, arms of Mexico, Puerto Rico and Cuba.

1970, Oct. 7 **Wmk. 365** *Perf. 13½*

C370 AP88 1c pink & multi 15 15
C371 AP88 2c pink & multi 15 15
C372 AP88 3c pink & multi 15 15
C373 AP88 5c pink & multi 15 15
C374 AP88 13c lt bl & multi 30 15
C375 AP88 13c lil & multi 30 15
C376 AP88 13c yel & multi 30 15
C377 AP88 13c pink & multi 30 15
C378 AP88 30c yel & multi 85 50
a. Souv. sheet of 1, imperf. 1.50 1.50
Nos. C370-C378 (9) 2.65
Set value 1.45

11th Central American and Caribbean Games, Feb. 28-Mar. 14.

Astronaut on Moon — AP89

EXPO '70 Emblem and Pavilion — AP90

Design: No. C380, US astronauts Charles Conrad, Jr., Richard F. Gordon, Jr. and Alan L. Bean.

1971 Wmk. 343 *Perf. 13½*

C379 AP89 13c gold & multi 50 35
C380 AP89 13c lt grn & multi 50 35

Man's first landing on the moon, Apollo 11, July 20, 1969 (No. C379) and Apollo 12 moon mission, Nov. 14-24, 1969.
Issue dates: No. C379, Aug. 20; No. C380, Aug. 23.

1971, Aug. 24 Litho.

C381 AP90 10c pink & multi 25 25

EXPO '70 International Exposition, Osaka, Japan, Mar. 15-Sept. 13.

Flag of Panama AP91

Design: 13c, Map of Panama superimposed on Western Hemisphere, and tourist year emblem.

1971, Dec. 11 Wmk. 343

C382 AP91 5c multi 15 15
C383 AP91 13c multi 25 25
Set value 32

Proclamation of 1972 as Tourist Year of the Americas.

Mahatma Gandhi — AP92

1971, Dec. 17

C384 AP92 10c blk & multi 60 35

Centenary of the birth of Mohandas K. Gandhi (1869-1948), leader in India's fight for independence.

Central American Independence Issue

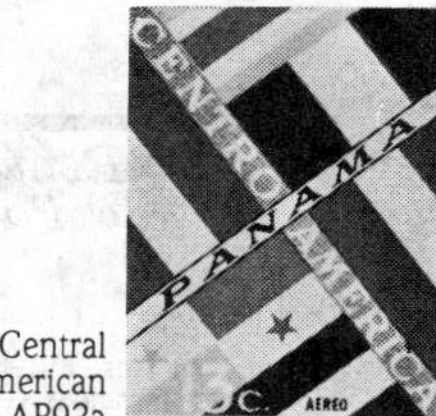

Flags of Central American States — AP92a

1971, Dec. 20

C385 AP92a 13c multi 35 25

160th anniv. of Central America independence.

AP93

AP94

1971, Dec. 21

C386 AP93 8c Panama #4 25 25

2nd National Philatelic and Numismatic Exposition, 1970.

1972, Sept. 7 Wmk. 365

C387 AP94 40c Natá Church 80 60

450th anniversary of the founding of Natá.
For surcharges see Nos. C402, RA85.

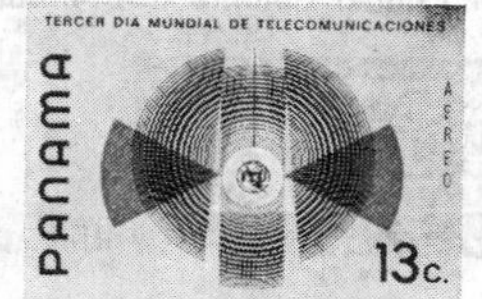

Telecommunications Emblem — AP95

1972, Sept. 8

C388 AP95 13c lt bl, dp bl & blk 40 40

3rd World Telecommunications Day (in 1971).

Apollo 14 — AP96

1972, Sept. 11

C389 AP96 13c tan & multi 75 50

Apollo 14 US moon mission, Jan. 1-Feb. 9, 1971.

Shoeshine Boy Counting Coins — AP97

1972, Sept. 12

C390 AP97 5c shown 15 15
C391 AP97 8c Mother & Child 25 25
C392 AP97 50c UNICEF emblem 1.00 50
a. Souv. sheet of 1, imperf. 1.20 1.20

25th anniv. (in 1971) of the UNICEF.

San Blas Cloth, Cuna Indians AP98

1972, Sept. 13

C393 AP98 5c shown 15 15
C394 AP98 8c Beaded necklace, Guaymi Indians 25 15
C395 AP98 25c View of Portobelo 60 45
a. Souv. sheet of 2, #C393, C395, imperf. 1.00 1.00
Set value 60

Tourist publicity.

For surcharges see Nos. C417, RA83.

Baseball and Games' Emblem AP99

Designs (Games' Emblem and): 10c, Basketball, vert. 13c, Torch, vert. 25c, Boxing. 50c, Map and flag of Panama, Bolivar. 1b, Medals.

Perf. 12½

1973, Feb. 9 Litho. Unwmk.

C396 AP99 8c rose red & yel 20 15
C397 AP99 10c blk & ultra 25 15
C398 AP99 13c bl & multi 35 16
C399 AP99 25c blk, yel grn & red 60 25
C400 AP99 50c grn & multi 1.20 60
C401 AP99 1b multi 2.25 1.00
Nos. C396-C401 (6) 4.85 2.31

7th Bolivar Games, Panama City, Feb. 17-Mar. 3.

No. C387 Surcharged in Red Similar to No. 542

1973, Mar. 16 Wmk. 365 *Perf. 13½*

C402 AP94 13c on 40c multi 30 30

UN Security Council Meeting, Panama City, Mar. 15-21.

Portrait Type of Regular Issue 1973

Designs: 5c, Isabel Herrera Obaldia, educator. 8c, Nicolas Victoria Jaén, educator. 10c, Forest Scene, by Roberto Lewis. No. C406, Portrait of a Lady, by Manuel E. Amador. No. C407, Ricardo Miró, poet. 20c, Portrait, by Isaac Benitez. 21c, Manuel Amador Guerrero, statesman. 25c, Belisario Porras, statesman. 30c, Juan Demostenes Arosemena, statesman. 34c, Octavio Mendez Pereira, writer. 38c, Ricardo J. Alfaro, writer.

1973, June 20 Litho. *Perf. 13½*

C403 A169 5c pink & multi 15 15
C404 A169 8c pink & multi 16 15
C405 A169 10c gray & multi 20 15
C406 A169 13c pink & multi 35 16
C407 A169 13c pink & multi 35 16
C408 A169 20c bl & multi 50 40
C409 A169 21c yel & multi 50 40
C410 A169 25c pink & multi 50 40
C411 A169 30c gray & multi 65 35
C412 A169 34c lt bl & multi 80 60
C413 A169 38c lt bl & multi 1.00 50
Nos. C403-C413 (11) 5.16 3.42

Famous Panamanians.
For overprints and surcharges see Nos. C414-C416, C418-C421.

Nos. C403, C410, and C412 Overprinted in Black or Red

1923
1973

Bodas de Oro
Escuela Profesional
Isabel Herrera Obaldía

1973, Sept. 14 Litho. *Perf. 13½*

C414 A169 5c pink & multi 20 20
C415 A169 25c pink & multi 60 45
C416 A169 34c bl & multi (R) 90 75

50th anniversary of the Isabel Herrera Obaldia Professional School.

Nos. C395, C408, C413, C412 and C409 Surcharged in Red

VALE 8¢

1974, Nov. 11 Litho. *Perf. 13½*

C417 AP98 1c on 25c multi 15 15
C418 A169 3c on 20c multi 15 15
C419 A169 5c on 38c multi 16 15
C420 A169 10c on 34c multi 20 20
C421 A169 13c on 21c multi 25 15
Set value 70 50

Women's Hands, Panama Map, UN and IWY Emblems — AP100

Victoria Sugar Plant, Sugar Cane, Map of Veraguas Province — AP101

Perf. 12½

1975, May 6 Litho. Unwmk.

C422 AP100 17c blue & multi 50 20
a. Souv. sheet, typo., imperf., no gum 1.00 1.00

International Women's Year 1975.

1975, Oct. 9 Litho. *Perf. 12½*

Designs: 17c, Bayano electrification project and map of Panama, horiz. 33c, Tocumen International Airport and map, horiz.

C423 AP101 17c bl, buff & blk 35 30
C424 AP101 27c ultra & yel grn 50 35
C425 AP101 33c bl & multi 65 45

Oct. 11, 1968, Revolution, 7th anniv.

Bolivar Statue and Flags — AP102

Bolivar Hall, Panama City AP103

Design: 41c, Bolivar with flag of Panama, ruins of Old Panama City.

1976, Mar.

C426 AP102 23c multi 50 20
C427 AP103 35c multi 70 28
C428 AP102 41c multi 80 60

150th anniversary of Congress of Panama.
Issue dates: 23c, Mar. 15; others Mar. 30.

Marine Life Type of 1976

Marine life: 17c, Diodon hystrix, vert. 27c, Pocillopora damicornis.

Perf. 13x12½, 12½x13

1976, May 6 Litho. Wmk. 377

C429 A171 17c multi 35 30
C430 A171 27c multi 55 40

Cerro Colorado AP104

1976, Nov. 12 Litho. *Perf. 12½*

C431 AP104 23c multi 45 20

Cerro Colorado copper mines, Chiriqui Province.

Gen. Omar Torrijos Herrera (1929-1981) AP105

1982, Feb. Litho. *Perf. 10½*

C432 AP105 23c multi 45 20

Torrijos Type of 1982

Perf. 10½

1982, May 14 Litho. Wmk. 311

C433 A201 35c Security Council reunion, 1973 70 28
C434 A201 41c Torrijos Airport 80 50

Souvenir Sheet

Imperf

C435 A201 23c like #C432 2.00 2.00

No. C435 sold for 1b.

Alfaro Type of 1982

Photos by Luiz Gutierrez Cruz.

1982, Aug. 18 Wmk. 382

C436 A202 17c multi 35 15
C437 A202 23c multi 45 18

World Cup Type of 1982

1982, Dec. 27 Litho. *Perf. 10½*

C438 A203 23c Map 60 18
C439 A203 35c Pele, vert. 80 28
C440 A203 41c Cup, vert. 1.00 40

1b imperf. souvenir sheet exists in design of 23c; black control number. Size; 85x75mm.

Nicolas A. Solano (1882-1943), Tuberculosis Researcher — AP106

Wmk. 382 (Stars)

1983, Feb. 8 Litho. *Perf. 10½*

C441 AP106 23c brown 45 20

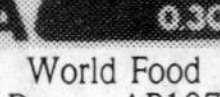

World Food Day — AP107

Contadora Group for Peace — AP108

1984, Oct. 16 Litho. *Perf. 12*

C442 AP107 30c Hand grasping fork 60 20

1985, Oct. 1 Litho. *Perf. 14*

C443 AP108 10c multi 20 15
C444 AP108 20c multi 40 16
C445 AP108 30c multi 60 22

See No. 680A.

Christmas Type of 1988

1988, Dec. 29 Litho. *Perf. 12*

C446 A246 35c *St. Joseph and the Infant* 80 40

Olympics Type of 1989

1989, Mar. 17 Litho. *Perf. 12*

C447 A248 35c Boxing 78 40

Opening of the Panama Canal, 75th Anniv. AP109

1989, Sept. 29 Litho. *Perf. 13½*

C448 AP109 35c *Ancon* in lock, 1914 88 65
C449 AP109 60c Ship in lock, 1989 1.50 1.15

Revolution Type of 1989

1989, Nov. 14 Litho.

C450 A251 35c Storming of the Bastille 88 65
C451 A251 45c Anniv. emblem 1.15 85

French revolution, bicent.

AIR POST SEMI-POSTAL STAMPS

Catalogue values for unused stamps in this section are for Never Hinged items.

"The World Against Malaria" — SPAP1

Perf. 12½

1961, Dec. 20 Wmk. 311 Litho.

CB1 SPAP1 5c + 5c car rose 50 50
CB2 SPAP1 10c + 10c vio bl 50 50
CB3 SPAP1 15c + 15c dk grn 50 50

WHO drive to eradicate malaria.
For surcharges see Nos. C271-C272.

Nos. C274-C276 Surcharged in Red

1863 1963

+10¢

Perf. 12½

1963, Mar. 4 Litho. Wmk. 311

CB4 AP81 5c +5c on #C274
CB5 AP81 10c +10c on #C275
CB6 AP81 15c +15c on #C276

Surcharge on No. CB4 differs to fit stamp. See No. CB7.

No. CB4 Surcharged in Black

"Centenario Cruz Roja Internacional"

XX

10¢

CB7 AP81 10c on 5c+5c

Intl. Red. Cross cent.

SPECIAL DELIVERY STAMPS

Nos. 211-212 Overprinted in Red **EXPRESO**

1926 Unwmk. *Perf. 12*

E1 A31 10c org & blk 7.50 3.25
a. "EXRPESO" 40.00
E2 A32 20c brn & blk 10.00 3.25
a. "EXRPESO" 40.00
b. Double overprint 35.00 35.00

Bicycle Messenger SD1

1929 Engr. *Perf. 12½*

E3 SD1 10c orange 1.25 1.00
E4 SD1 20c dk brn 4.75 2.50

For surcharges and overprints see Nos. C1-C5, C17-C18A, C67.

REGISTRATION STAMPS

Issued under Colombian Dominion

R1

1888 Unwmk. Engr. *Perf. 13½*

F1 R1 10c black, *gray* 8.00 5.25

Imperforate and part-perforate copies without gum and those on surface-colored paper are reprints.

R2

Magenta, Violet or Blue Black Handstamped Overprint

1898 *Perf. 12*

F2 R2 10c yellow 7.00 6.50

The handstamp on No. F2 was also used as a postmark.

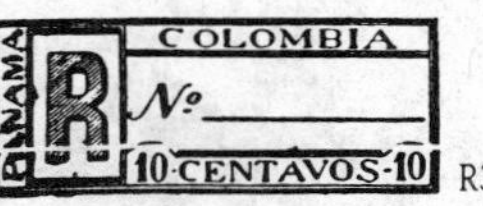

R3

1900 Litho. *Perf. 11*

F3 R3 10c blk, *lt bl* 4.00 3.50

1901

F4 R3 10c brown red 30.00 20.00

R4

Blue Black Surcharge

1902

F5 R4 20c on 10c brn red 20.00 16.00

Issues of the Republic Issued in the City of Panama

Registration Stamps of Colombia Handstamped

R9

Handstamped in Blue Black or Rose REPUBLICA DE PANAMA

1903-04 *Imperf.*

F6 R9 20c red brn, *bl* 45.00 42.50
F7 R9 20c blue, *blue* (R) 45.00 42.50

For surcharges and overprints see Nos. F8-F11, F16-F26.

Reprints exist of Nos. F6 and F7; see note after No. 64.

With Additional Surcharge in Rose **10.**

F8 R9 10c on 20c red brn, *bl* 60.00 55.00
b. "10" in blue black 60.00 55.00
F9 R9 10c on 20c bl, *bl* 60.00 45.00

Handstamped in Rose

Panamá

.10

F10 R9 10c on 20c red brn, *bl* 60.00 55.00
F11 R9 10c on 20c blue, *blue* 45.00 42.50

Issued in Colon

Regular Issues Handstamped "R/COLON" in Circle (as on F2) Together with Other Overprints and Surcharges

Handstamped **REPUBLICA DE PANAMA**

1903-04 *Perf. 12*

F12 A4 10c yellow 3.00 2.50

Handstamped **PANAMA**

F13 A4 10c yellow 22.50

Overprinted in Red

PANAMA PANAMA

F14 A4 10c yellow 3.00 2.50

Overprinted in Black ***República de Panamá.***

F15 A4 10c yellow 7.50 5.00

The handstamps on Nos. F12 to F15 are in magenta, violet or red; various combinations of these colors are to be found. They are struck in various positions, including double, inverted, one handstamp omitted, etc.

Colombia No. F13 Handstamped Like No. F12 in Violet

Imperf

F16 R9 20c red brn, *bl* 60.00 55.00

Overprinted Like No. F15 in Black

F17 R9 20c red brn, *bl* 6.00 5.75

No. F17 Surcharged in Manuscript

F18 R9 10c on 20c red brn, *bl* 60.00 55.00

No. F17 Surcharged in Purple **10**

F19 R9 10c on 20c 82.50 80.00

No. F17 Surcharged in Violet **10**

F20 R9 10c on 20c 82.50 80.00

The varieties of the overprint which are described after No. 138 are also to be found on the Registration and Acknowledgment of Receipt stamps. It is probable that Nos. F17 to F20 inclusive owe their existence more to speculation than to postal necessity.

Issued in Bocas del Toro
Colombia Nos. F17 and F13 Handstamped in Violet

R DE PANAMA

1903-04
F21 R9 20c blue, *blue* 125.00 120.00
F22 R9 20c red brn, *bl* 125.00 120.00

No. F21 Surcharged in Manuscript in Violet or Red
F23 R9 10c on 20c bl, *bl* 150.00 140.00

Colombia Nos. F13, F17 Handstamped in Violet

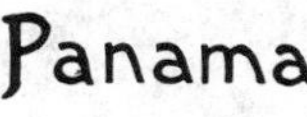

Surcharged in Manuscript (a) "10" (b) "10cs" in Red
F25 R9 10 on 20c red brn, *bl* 70.00 65.00
F26 R9 10cs on 20c bl, *bl* 55.00 50.00

No. F25 without surcharge is bogus, according to leading experts.

General Issue

R5

1904 **Engr.** *Perf. 12*
F27 R5 10c green 1.00 50

R

Nos. 190 and 213 Surcharged in Red

5 cts.

1916-17
F29 A11 5c on 8c pur & blk 3.00 2.25
a. "5" inverted 55.00
b. Large, round "5" 8.00
c. Inverted surcharge 12.50 11.00
d. Tête bêche surcharge
F30 A33 5c on 8c vio & blk ('17) 3.50 80
a. Inverted surcharge 10.00 8.25
b. Tête bêche surcharge
c. Double surcharge 40.00

Stamps similar to No. F30, overprinted in green were unauthorized.

INSURED LETTER STAMPS

Stamps of 1939 Surcharged in Black

0 05 0 05
SEGURO POSTAL
HABILITADO

1942 **Unwmk.** *Perf. 12½*
G1 AP23 5c on 1b blk 50 50
G2 A84 10c on 1b dk brn 80 80
G3 AP23 25c on 50c dk brn 2.00 2.00

ACKNOWLEDGMENT OF RECEIPT STAMPS

Issued under Colombian Dominion

Experts consider this handstamp-"A.R. / COLON / COLOMBIA"-to be a cancellation or a marking intended for a letter to receive special handling. It was applied at Colon to various stamps in 1897-1904 in different colored inks for philatelic sale. It exists on cover, usually with the bottom line removed by masking the handstamp.

Nos. 17-18 Handstamped in Rose

1902
H4 A4 5c blue 5.00 5.00
H5 A4 10c yellow 10.00 10.00

This handstamp was also used as a postmark.

Issues of the Republic
Issued in the City of Panama
Colombia No. H3 Handstamped

AR2

Handstamped in Rose REPUBLICA DE PANAMA

1903-04 **Unwmk.** *Imperf.*
H9 AR2 10c blue, *blue* 10.00 8.00

Reprints exist of No. H9, see note after No. 64.

No. H9 Surcharged with New Value
H10 AR2 5c on 10c bl, *bl* 5.00 5.00

Colombia No. H3 Handstamped in Rose Panamá

H11 AR2 10c blue, *blue* 17.50 14.00

Issued in Colon

Handstamped in Magenta or Violet REPUBLICA DE PANAMA

Imperf
H17 AR2 10c blue, *blue* 15.00 15.00

Handstamped PANAMA

H18 AR2 10c blue, *blue* 82.50 70.00

Overprinted in Black

República de Panamá

H19 AR2 10c blue, *blue* 11.00 8.00

No. H19 Surcharged in Manuscript
H20 AR2 10c on 5c on 10c 100.00 82.50

Issued in Bocas del Toro
Colombia No. H3 Handstamped in Violet and Surcharged in Manuscript in Red Like Nos. F25-F26

1904
H21 AR2 5c on 10c blue, *blue*

No. H21 without surcharge is bogus.

General Issue

AR3

1904 **Engr.** *Perf. 12*
H22 AR3 5c blue 1.00 80

No. 199 Overprinted in Violet A. R.

1916
H23 A20 2½c red orange 1.00 80
a. "R.A." for "A.R." 50.00
b. Double overprint 8.00
c. Inverted overprint 8.00

LATE FEE STAMPS

Issues of the Republic
Issued in the City of Panama

LF3

Colombia No. I4 Handstamped in Rose or Blue Black REPUBLICA DE PANAMA

1903-04 **Unwmk.** *Imperf.*
I1 LF3 5c pur, *rose* 12.50 9.00
I2 LF3 5c pur, *rose* (Bl Blk) 17.50 12.50

Reprints exist of #I1-I2; see note after #64.

General Issue

LF4

1904 **Engr.** *Perf. 12*
I3 LF4 2½c lake 1.00 65

No. 199 Overprinted with Typewriter Retardo

1910, Aug. 12
I4 A20 2½c red orange 120.00 100.00

Used only on Aug. 12-13.

Handstamped

1910
I5 A20 2½c red orange 60.00 50.00

No. 195 Surcharged in Green RETARDO UN CENTÉSIMO

1917
I6 A17 1c on ½c orange 80 80
a. "UN CENTESIMO" inverted 50.00
b. Double surcharge 10.00
c. Inverted surcharge 6.50 6.50

Same Surcharge on No. 196

1921
I7 A17 1c on ½c rose 25.00 20.00

POSTAGE DUE STAMPS

San Lorenzo Castle Gate, Portobelo
D1

Statue of Columbus
D2

Pedro J. Sosa — D4

D5

Design: 4c, Capitol, Panama City.

1915 **Unwmk.** **Engr.** *Perf. 12*
J1 D1 1c olive brown 3.00 75
J2 D2 2c olive brown 4.50 65
J3 D1 4c olive brown 6.00 1.25
J4 D4 10c olive brown 4.50 1.75

Type D1 was intended to show a gate of San Lorenzo Castle, Chagres, and is so inscribed.

1930 *Perf. 12½*
J5 D5 1c emerald 80 60
J6 D5 2c dark red 80 60
J7 D5 4c dark blue 1.20 80
J8 D5 10c violet 1.20 80

POSTAL TAX STAMPS

Pierre and Marie Curie — PT1

1939 **Unwmk.** **Engr.** *Perf. 12*
RA1 PT1 1c rose carmine 50 15
RA2 PT1 1c green 50 15
RA3 PT1 1c orange 50 15
RA4 PT1 1c blue 50 15

See Nos. RA6-RA18, RA24-RA27, RA30.

Stamp of 1924 Overprinted in Black

1940
RA5 A53 1c dark green 1.40 75

Inscribed 1940

1941
RA6 PT1 1c rose carmine 50 15
RA7 PT1 1c green 50 15
RA8 PT1 1c orange 50 15
RA9 PT1 1c blue 50 15
Set value 40

Inscribed 1942

1942

RA10 PT1 1c violet 40 15

Inscribed 1943

1943

RA11 PT1 1c rose carmine 40 15
RA12 PT1 1c green 40 15
RA13 PT1 1c orange 40 15
RA14 PT1 1c blue 40 15

Inscribed 1945

1945

RA15 PT1 1c rose carmine 40 16
RA16 PT1 1c green 40 16
RA17 PT1 1c orange 40 16
RA18 PT1 1c blue 40 16

Nos. 234 and 235 Surcharged in Black or Red

CANCER B/. 0.01 1947

1946 Unwmk. *Perf. 12*

RA19 A53 1c on 1/2c orange 60 15
RA20 A53 1c on 1c dk grn (R) 60 15

Catalogue values for unused stamps in this section, from this point to the end of the section, are for Never Hinged items.

Same Surcharged in Black on Nos. 239 and 241

1947

RA21 A53 1c on 12c ol grn 40 30
RA22 A53 1c on 24c yel brn 40 30

Surcharged in Red on No. 342

RA23 A95 1c on 1/2c dl vio, bl & car 40 15

Type of 1939
Inscribed 1947

1947

RA24 PT1 1c rose carmine 40 15
RA25 PT1 1c green 40 15
RA26 PT1 1c orange 40 15
RA27 PT1 1c blue 40 15
Set value 28

Nos. C100 and C101 Surcharged in Black

a

LUCHA CONTRA EL CANCER
1 CENTESIMO 1

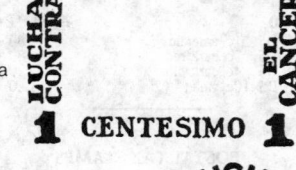

b

1 CENTESIMO 1

1949 Unwmk. *Perf. 12 1/2*

RA28 AP45 (a) 1c on 5c 35 15
a. Inverted surcharge 10.00
RA29 AP46 (b) 1c on 10c yel org 35 15
Set value 16

Type of 1939
Inscribed 1949

1949 *Perf. 12*

RA30 PT1 1c brown 50 15

The tax from the sale of Nos. RA1-RA30 was used for the control of cancer.

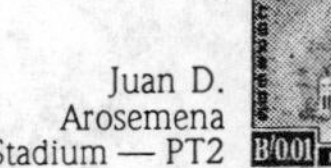

Juan D. Arosemena Stadium — PT2

Torch Emblem — PT3

Discobolus — PT4

Design: No. RA33, Adan Gordon Olympic Swimming Pool.

1951 Unwmk. Engr. *Perf. 12 1/2*

RA31 PT2 1c carmine & blk 65 16
RA32 PT3 1c dk bl & blk 65 16
RA33 PT2 1c grn & blk 65 16

1952

Design: No. RA34, Turners' emblem.

RA34 PT3 1c org & red 65 16
RA35 PT4 1c pur & blk 65 16

The tax from the sale of Nos. RA31-RA35 was used to promote physical education.

Boys Doing Farm Work — PT5

1958 Wmk. 311 Litho. *Perf. 12 1/2*
Size: 35x24mm

RA36 PT5 1c rose red & gray 15 15

Type of 1958
Inscribed 1959

1959 Size: 35x24mm

RA37 PT5 1c gray & emerald 15 15
RA38 PT5 1c vio bl & gray 15 15
Set value 16 15

Type of 1958
Inscribed 1960

1960 Litho. Wmk. 334 *Perf. 13 1/2*
Size: 32x23mm

RA39 PT5 1c carmine & gray 15 15

Nos. C235 and C241 Surcharged in Black or Red

XX

1¢

"Rehabilitación de Menores"

1961 Wmk. 343 *Perf. 12 1/2*

RA40 A131 1c on 10c ocher & blk 15 15
RA41 AP76 1c on 10c emer (R) 15 15
a. Inverted surcharge
Set value 20 15

Girl at Sewing Machine — PT6

Perf. 12 1/2

1961, Nov. 24 Litho. Wmk. 343

RA42 PT6 1c brt vio 15 15
RA43 PT6 1c rose lilac 15 15
RA44 PT6 1c yellow 15 15
RA45 PT6 1c blue 15 15
RA46 PT6 1c emerald 15 15
Set value 35 25

1961, Dec. 1

Design: Boy with hand saw.

RA47 PT6 1c red lilac 15 15
RA48 PT6 1c rose 15 15
RA49 PT6 1c orange 15 15

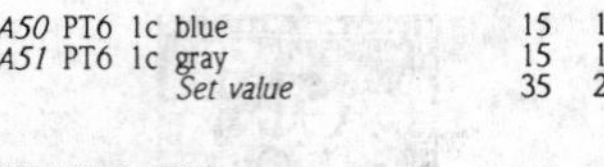

RA50 PT6 1c blue 15 15
RA51 PT6 1c gray 15 15
Set value 35 25

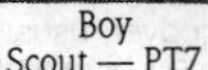

Boy Scout — PT7

Map of Panama, Flags — PT8

Designs: Nos. RA57-RA61, Girl Scout.

1964, Feb. 7 Wmk. 343

RA52 PT7 1c olive 15 15
RA53 PT7 1c gray 15 15
RA54 PT7 1c lilac 15 15
RA55 PT7 1c carmine rose 15 15
RA56 PT7 1c blue 15 15
RA57 PT7 1c bluish green 15 15
RA58 PT7 1c violet 15 15
RA59 PT7 1c orange 15 15
RA60 PT7 1c yellow 15 15
RA61 PT7 1c brn org 15 15
Set value 1.00 50

The tax from Nos. RA36-RA61 was for youth rehabilitation.

1973, Jan. 22 Unwmk.

RA62 PT8 1c black 15 15

7th Bolivar Sports Games, Feb. 17-Mar. 3, 1973. The tax was for a new post office in Panama City.

Farm Cooperative — PT9

Designs: No. RA64, 5b silver coin. No. RA65, Victoriano Lorenzo. No. RA66, RA69, Cacique Urraca. No. RA67-RA68, RA70, Post Office.

1973-75

RA63 PT9 1c brt yel grn & ver 15 15
RA64 PT9 1c gray & red 15 15
RA65 PT9 1c ocher & red 15 15
RA66 PT9 1c org & red 15 15
RA67 PT9 1c bl & red 15 15
RA68 PT9 1c blue ('74) 15 15
RA69 PT9 1c orange ('74) 15 15
RA70 PT9 1c vermilion ('75) 15 15
Set value 80 40

The tax was for a new post office in Panama City.

Stamps of 1969-1973 Surcharged in Violet Blue, Yellow, Black or Carmine

VALE 1¢
PRO EDIFICIO

1975

RA75 A168 1c on 1c (#538; VB) 15 15
RA76 A168 1c on 2c (#539; Y) 15 15
RA77 A164 1c on 30c (#534; B) 15 15
RA78 A157 1c on 30c (#511; B) 15 15
RA79 A156 1c on 40c (#514; B) 15 15
RA80 A156 1c on 50c (#515; B) 15 15
RA81 A169 1c on 20c (#C408; C) 15 15
RA82 A169 1c on 25c (#C410; B) 15 15
RA83 AP98 1c on 25c (#C395; B) 15 15
RA84 A169 1c on 30c (#C411; B) 15 15
RA85 AP94 1c on 40c (#C387; C) 15 15
Set value 1.10 85

The tax was for a new post office in Panama City. Surcharge vertical, reading down on No. RA75 and up on Nos. RA76, RA78 and RA83. Nos. RA75-RA85 were obligatory on all mail.

PT10

PT11

1980, Dec. 3 Litho. *Perf. 12*

RA86 PT10 2c Boys 15 15
RA87 PT10 2c Boy and chicks 15 15
RA88 PT10 2c Working in fields 15 15
RA89 PT10 2c Boys feeding piglet 15 15
a. Souv. sheet of 4, #RA86-RA89 2.00
Set value 20 20

Tax was for Children's Village (Christmas 1980). Nos. RA86-RA89 se-tenant and were obligatory on all mail. #RA89a sold for 1b.

1981, Nov. 1 Litho. *Perf. 12*

RA90 PT11 2c Boy, pony 15 15
RA91 PT11 2c Nativity 15 15
RA92 PT11 2c Tree 15 15
RA93 PT11 2c Church 15 15
Set value 20 20

Souvenir Sheet

RA94 Sheet of 4 7.50
a.-d. PT11 2c, Children's drawings

Tax was for Children's Village. Nos. RA90-RA93 se-tenant and were obligatory on all mail. No. RA94 sold for 5b.

PT12

1982, Nov. 1 Litho. *Perf. 13 1/2x12 1/2*

RA95 PT12 2c Carpentry 15 15
RA96 PT12 2c Beekeeping 15 15
RA97 PT12 2c Pig farming, vert. 15 15
RA98 PT12 2c Gardening, vert. 15 15
Set value 20 20

Tax was for Children's Village (Christmas 1982). Nos. RA95-RA96 and RA97-RA98 se-tenant and were obligatory on all mail.

Children's Drawings — PT13

Boy — PT14

1983, Nov. 1 Litho. *Perf. 14 1/2*

RA99 TP13 2c Annunciation 15 15
RA100 PT13 2c Bethlehem and Star 15 15
RA101 PT13 2c Church and Houses 15 15
RA102 PT13 2c Flight into Egypt 15 15
Set value 20 20

Souvenir sheets exist showing undenominated designs of Nos. RA99, RA101 and Nos. RA100, RA102 respectively. They sold for 2b each.

1984, Nov. 1 Litho. *Perf. 12x12 1/2*

RA103 PT14 2c White-collared shirt 15 15
RA104 PT14 2c T-shirt 15 15
RA105 PT14 2c Checked shirt 15 15
RA106 PT14 2c Scout uniform 15 15
Set value 20 20

Tax was for Children's Village. Obligatory on all mail. Issued se-tenant. An imperf. souvenir sheet sold for 2b, with designs similar to Nos. RA103-RA106, exists.

Christmas 1985 — PT15

Inscriptions: No. RA107, "Ciudad del Nino es . . . mi vida." No. RA108, "Feliz Navidad." No. RA109, "Feliz Ano Nuevo." No. RA110, "Gracias."

1985, Dec. 10 Litho. *Perf. 13 1/2x13*

RA107 PT15 2c multi 15 15
RA108 PT15 2c multi 15 15
RA109 PT15 2c multi 15 15
RA110 PT15 2c multi 15 15
Set value 20 20

Nos. RA107-RA110 obligatory on all mail: tax for Children's Village. A souvenir sheet, perf. and imperf., sold for 2b, with designs of Nos. RA107-RA110.

Children's Village, 20th Anniv. — PT16

Inscriptions and Embera, Cuna, Embera and Guaymies tribal folk figures: No. RA111, "1966-1986." No. RA112, "Ciudad del Nino es . . . mi vida." No. RA113, "20 anos de fundacion." No. RA114, "Gracias."

1986, Nov. 1 Litho. *Perf. 13½*

RA111	PT16 2c multi	15	15
RA112	PT16 2c multi	15	15
RA113	PT16 2c multi	15	15
RA114	PT16 2c multi	15	15
	Set value	20	20

Nos. RA111-RA114 obligatory on all mail through Nov., Dec. and Jan.; tax for Children's Village. Printed se-tenant. Sheets of 4 exist perf. and imperf. Sold for 2b.

PARAGUAY

LOCATION — South America, bounded by Bolivia, Brazil and Argentina
GOVT. — Republic
AREA — 157,042 sq. mi.
POP. — 3,477,000 (1983)
CAPITAL — Asuncion

10 Reales = 100 Centavos = 1 Peso
100 Centimos = 1 Guarani (1944)

Values of early Paraguay stamps vary according to condition. Quotations for Nos. 1-9 are for fine copies. Very fine to superb specimens sell at much higher prices, and inferior or poor copies sell at reduced prices, depending on the condition of the individual specimen.

Catalogue values for unused stamps in this country are for Never Hinged items, beginning with Scott 430 in the regular postage section, Scott B11 in the semi-postal section, and Scott C154 in the airpost section.

Watermarks

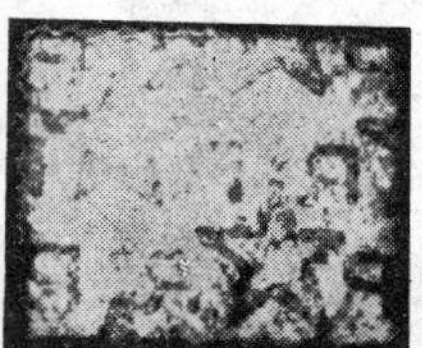

Wmk. 319 - Stars and R P Multiple

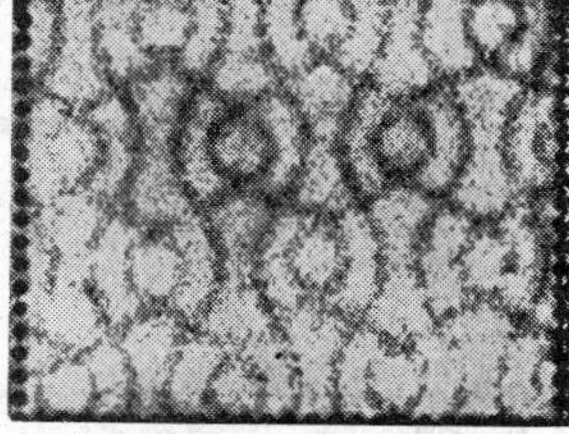

Wmk. 320 - Interlacing Lines

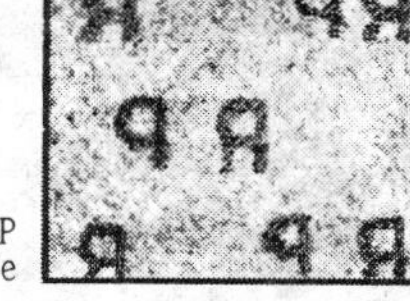

Wmk. 347 - RP Multiple

Vigilant Lion Supporting Liberty Cap
A1 A2

A3

Unwmk.

1870, Aug. 1 Litho. *Imperf.*

1	A1 1r rose	3.00	3.00
2	A2 2r blue	35.00	35.00
3	A3 3r black	85.00	85.00

Unofficial reprints of 2r in blue and other colors are on thicker paper than originals. They show a colored dot in upper part of "S" of "DOS" in upper right corner.

For surcharges see Nos. 4-9, 19.

Handstamp Surcharged

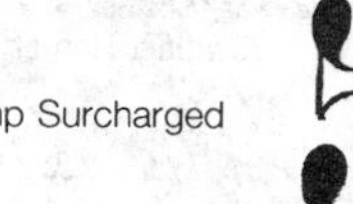

1878 Black Surcharge

4	A1 5c on 1r rose	32.50	32.50
5	A2 5c on 2r blue	150.00	140.00
5E	A3 5c on 3r black	250.00	200.00

Blue Surcharge

5F	A1 5c on 1r rose	32.50	32.50
5H	A2 5c on 2r blue	*500.00*	*500.00*
6	A3 5c on 3r black	150.00	150.00

The surcharge may be found inverted, double, sideways and omitted.

The originals are surcharged in dull black or dull blue. The reprints are in intense black and bright blue. The reprint surcharges are overinked and show numerous breaks in the handstamp.

Handstamp Surcharged

Black Surcharge

7	A2 5c on 2r blue	250.00	190.00
8	A3 5c on 3r black	200.00	160.00

Blue Surcharge

9	A3 5c on 3r black	110.00	110.00
a.	Dbl. surch., large & small "5"	*650.00*	*650.00*

The surcharge on Nos. 7, 8 and 9 is usually placed sideways. It may be found double or inverted on Nos. 8 and 9.

Nos. 4 to 9 have been extensively counterfeited.

A4 A4a

1879 Litho. *Perf. 12½*
Thin Paper

10	A4 5r orange		38
11	A4 10r red brown		45
a.	Imperf.		
b.	Horiz. pair, imperf. vert.		11.25

Nos. 10 and 11 were never placed in use.
For surcharges see Nos. 17-18.

1879-81 Thin Paper

12	A4a 5c orange brown	90	90
13	A4a 10c blue grn ('81)	1.25	1.25

Reprints of Nos. 10-13 are imperf., perf. 11½, 12, 12½ or 14. They have yellowish gum and the 10c is deep green.

A5 A6

A7

1881, Aug. Litho. *Perf. 11½-13½*

14	A5 1c blue	45	38
a.	Imperf., pair	1.75	1.75
15	A6 2c rose red	45	38
a.	2c dull orange red	45	38
b.	Imperf., pair	1.75	1.75
c.	Horiz. or vert. pair, imperf. btwn.	1.50	1.50
16	A7 4c brown	45	38
a.	Imperf., pair	1.75	1.75
b.	Horiz. or vert. pair, imperf. btwn.	1.50	1.50

No. 11 Surcharged

Handstamped in Black or Gray

1881, July *Perf. 12½*

17	A4 1c on 10c blue grn	4.50	4.50
18	A4 2c on 10c blue grn	4.50	4.50

No. 1 Surcharged

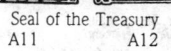

1884, May 8 Handstamped *Imperf.*

19	A1 1c on 1r rose	2.00	1.75

The surcharges on Nos. 17-19 exist double, inverted and in pairs with one omitted. Counterfeits exist.

Seal of the Treasury
A11 A12

1884, Aug. 3 Litho. *Perf. 11½, 12½*

20	A11 1c green	25	18
21	A11 2c rose red	25	18
22	A11 5c blue	25	18

Shades exist.
For overprints see Nos. O1, O8, O15.

Imperf., Pairs

20a	A11 1c green	1.00
21a	A11 2c rose red	1.75
22a	A11 5c blue	3.75

Perf. 11½, 11½x12, 12½x11½

1887 Typo.

23	A12 1c green	15	15
24	A12 2c rose	15	15
25	A12 5c blue	20	15
26	A12 7c brown	42	30
27	A12 10c lilac	30	18
28	A12 15c orange	30	18
29	A12 20c pink	30	18
	Nos. 23-29 (7)	1.82	
	Set value		1.10

See Nos. 42-45. For surcharges and overprints see Nos. 46, 49-50, 71-72, 167-170A, O20-O41, O49.

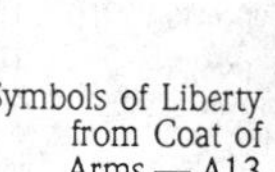

Symbols of Liberty from Coat of Arms — A13

1889, Feb. Litho. *Perf. 11½*

30	A13 15c red violet	1.25	1.25
a.	Imperf., pair	5.00	5.00

For overprints see Nos. O16-O19.

Overprint Handstamped in Violet

1892, Oct. 12 *Perf. 12x12½*

31	A15 10c violet blue	4.50	2.00

Discovery of America by Columbus, 400th anniversary. Overprint reads: "1492 / 12 DE OCTUBRE / 1892." Sold only on day of issue.

Cirilo A. Rivarola — A15

Designs: 2c, Salvador Jovellanos. 4c, Juan B. Gil. 5c, Higinio Uriarte. 10c, Cándido Bareiro. 14c, Gen. Bernardino Caballero. 20c, Gen. Patricio Escobar. 30c, Juan G. González.

1892-96 Litho. *Perf. 12x12½*

32	A15 1c gray (centavos)	15	15
33	A15 1c gray (centavo) ('96)	15	15
34	A15 2c green	15	15
a.	Chalky paper ('96)	15	15

35	A15	4c carmine	15	15
a.		Chalky paper ('96)	15	15
36	A15	5c violet ('93)	15	15
a.		Chalky paper ('96)	15	15
37	A15	10c vio bl (punched) ('93)	18	15
		Unpunched ('96)	4.00	1.50
38	A15	10c dull blue ('96)	15	15
39	A15	14c yellow brown	42	38
40	A15	20c red ('93)	65	38
41	A15	30c light green	1.00	65
		Nos. 32-41 (10)	3.15	
		Set value		1.90

The 10c violet blue (No. 37) was, until 1896, issued punched with a circular hole in order to prevent it being fraudulently overprinted as No. 31.
Nos. 33 and 38 are on chalky paper.
For surcharge see No. 70.

Seal Type of 1887

1892 **Typo.**

42	A12	40c slate blue	1.75	90
43	A12	60c yellow	75	38
44	A12	80c light blue	65	38
45	A12	1p olive green	65	38

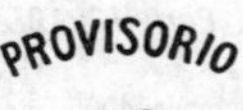

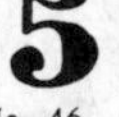

No. 46 Nos. 47-48

1895, Aug. 1 *Perf. 11½x12*

46	A12	5c on 7c brown, #26	25	15

Telegraph Stamps Surcharged

1896, Apr. **Engr.** *Perf. 11½*

Denomination in Black

47		5c on 2c brown & gray	38	25
a.		Inverted surcharge	10.00	10.00
48		5c on 4c yellow & gray	38	25
a.		Inverted surcharge	7.50	7.50

Nos. 28, 42 Surcharged — Provisorio 10 Centavos

1898-99 **Typo.**

49	A12	10c on 15c org ('99)	45	35
a.		Inverted surcharge	14.00	14.00
b.		Double surcharge	9.00	9.00
50	A12	10c on 40c slate bl	20	15

Surcharge on No. 49 has small "c."

Telegraph Stamps Surcharged

1900, May 14 **Engr.** *Perf. 11½*

50A		5c on 30c grn, gray & blk	1.25	90
50B		10c on 50c dl vio, gray & blk	3.00	2.00

The basic telegraph stamps are like those used for Nos. 47-48, but the surcharges on Nos. 50A-50B consist of "5 5" and "10 10" above a blackout rectangle covering the engraved denominations.
A 40c red, bluish gray and black telegraph stamp (basic type of A24) was used provisionally in August, 1900, for postage. Value, postally used, $5.

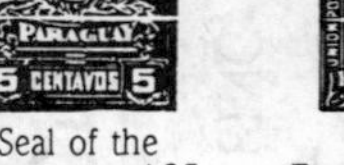

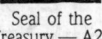

Seal of the Treasury — A25 J. B. Egusquiza — A26

1900, Sept. **Engr.** *Perf. 11½, 12*

51	A25	2c gray	15	15
52	A25	3c orange brown	15	15
53	A25	5c dark green	15	15
54	A25	8c dark brown	15	15
55	A25	10c carmine rose	15	15
56	A25	24c deep blue	30	15
		Nos. 51-56 (6)	1.05	
		Set value		60

See Nos. 57-67. For surcharges see Nos. 69, 74, 76, 156-157.

1901, Apr. **Litho.** *Perf. 11½*

Small Figures

57	A25	2c rose	15	15
58	A25	5c violet brown	15	15
59	A25	40c blue	65	22
		Set value		40

1901-02

Larger Figures

60	A25	1c gray green ('02)	15	15
61	A25	2c gray	15	15
a.		Half used as 1c on cover		38
62	A25	4c pale blue	15	15
63	A25	5c violet	15	15
64	A25	8c gray brown ('02)	15	15
65	A25	10c rose red ('02)	18	15
66	A25	28c orange ('02)	30	18
67	A25	40c blue	30	15
		Nos. 60-67 (8)	1.53	
		Set value		84

Perf. 12x12½

1901, Sept. 24 **Typo.** **Chalky Paper**

68	A26	1p slate	30	20

For surcharge see No. 73.

No. 56 Surcharged — Habilitado en 20 centavos

1902, Aug.

Red Surcharge

69	A25	20c on 24c dp blue	25	15
a.		Inverted surcharge	6.25	

Nos. 39, 43-44 Surcharged

Habilitado en un 1 cent. 1 — Habilitado en cinco 5 cent. 5

1902, Dec. 22 *Perf. 12x12½*

70	A15	1c on 14c yellow brn	18	15
a.		No period after "cent"	90	75
b.		Comma after "cent"	65	50
c.		Accent over "Un"	65	50

1903 *Perf. 11½*

71	A12	5c on 60c yellow	25	15
72	A12	5c on 80c lt blue	18	15

Nos. 68, 64, 66 Surcharged

Habilitado en un 1 cent. 1 (#73) — Habilitado en 5 cent 5 (#74) — Habilitado en cinco 5 cent. 5 (#76)

1902-03 *Perf. 12*

73	A26	1c on 1p slate ('03)	15	15
a.		No period after "cent"	1.65	1.50

Perf. 11½

74	A25	5c on 8c gray brown	25	15
a.		No period after "cent"	90	75
b.		Double surcharge	3.50	3.00
76	A25	5c on 28c orange	25	18
a.		No period after "cent"	90	75
b.		Comma after "cent"	38	30

The surcharge on Nos. 73 and 74 is found reading both upward and downward.

Sentinel Lion with Right Paw Ready to Strike for "Peace and Justice"
A32 A33

Perf. 11½

1903, Feb. 28 **Litho.** **Unwmk.**

77	A32	1c gray	15	15
78	A32	2c blue green	18	15
79	A32	5c blue	25	15
80	A32	10c orange brown	30	15
81	A32	20c carmine	30	15
82	A32	30c deep blue	38	15
83	A32	60c purple	1.00	65
		Nos. 77-83 (7)	2.56	1.55

For surcharges and overprints see Nos. 139-140, 166, O50-O56.

1903, Sept.

84	A33	1c yellow green	15	15
85	A33	2c red orange	15	15
86	A33	5c dark blue	15	15
87	A33	10c purple	20	15
88	A33	20c dark green	65	30
89	A33	30c ultramarine	75	20
90	A33	60c ocher	75	50
		Nos. 84-90 (7)	2.80	
		Set value		1.38

Nos. 84-90 exist imperf. Value for pairs, $3 each for 1c-20c, $4 for 30c, $5 for 60c.
The three-line overprint "Gobierno provisorio Ago. 1904" is fraudulent.

Sentinel Lion at Rest
A35 A36

Perf. 11½, 12, 11½x12

1905-10 **Engr.**

Dated "1904"

91	A35	1c orange	15	15
92	A35	1c vermilion ('07)	15	15
93	A35	1c grnsh bl ('07)	15	15
94	A35	2c vermilion ('06)	15	15
95	A35	2c olive grn ('07)	30.00	
96	A35	2c car rose ('08)	15	15
97	A35	5c dark blue	15	15
98	A35	5c slate blue ('06)	15	15
99	A35	5c yellow ('06)	15	15
100	A35	10c bister ('06)	15	15
101	A35	10c emerald ('07)	15	15
102	A35	10c dp ultra ('08)	15	15
103	A35	20c violet ('06)	30	20
104	A35	20c bister ('07)	30	20
105	A35	20c apple grn ('07)	25	15
106	A35	30c turq bl ('06)	30	15
107	A35	30c blue gray ('07)	30	15
108	A35	30c dull lilac ('08)	38	18
109	A35	60c chocolate ('07)	25	15
110	A35	60c org brn ('07)	3.50	1.25
111	A35	60c salmon pink ('10)	3.50	1.25
		Nos. 91-94,96-111 (20)	10.73	
		Set value		4.35

All but Nos. 92 and 104 exist imperf. Value for pair, $3 each, except No. 95 at $17.50 and Nos. 109-111 at $7.50 each pair.
For surcharges and overprints see Nos. 129-130, 146-155, 174-190, 266.

1904, Aug. **Litho.** *Perf. 11½*

112	A36	10c blue	25	15
a.		Imperf., pair	3.00	

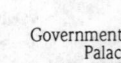

No. 112 Surcharged in Black — PAZ 12 Dic. 1904 30 centavos

1904, Dec.

113	A36	30c on 10c blue	38	25

Peace between a successful revolutionary party and the government previously in power.

Governmental Palace, Asunción — A37

Dated "1904"

1906-10 **Engr.** *Perf. 11½, 12*

Center in Black

114	A37	1p bright rose	1.25	75
115	A37	1p brown org ('07)	50	25
116	A37	1p ol gray ('07)	50	25
117	A37	2p turquoise ('07)	25	18
118	A37	2p lake ('09)	25	20
119	A37	2p brn org ('10)	30	20
120	A37	5p red ('07)	75	50
121	A37	5p ol grn ('10)	75	50
122	A37	5p dull bl ('10)	75	50
123	A37	10p brown org ('07)	70	50
124	A37	10p dp blue ('10)	70	50
125	A37	10p choc ('10)	75	50
126	A37	20p olive grn ('07)	1.75	1.65
127	A37	20p violet ('10)	1.75	1.65
128	A37	20p yellow ('10)	1.75	1.65
		Nos. 114-128 (15)	12.70	9.78

Nos. 94 and 95 Surcharged — Habilitado en 5 CENTAVOS

1907

129	A35	5c on 2c vermilion	20	15
a.		"5" omitted	1.00	1.00
b.		Inverted surcharge	1.25	1.25
c.		Double surcharge		
d.		Double surcharge, one inverted	1.00	1.00
e.		Double surcharge, both invtd.	6.00	6.00
130	A35	5c on 2c olive grn	25	15
a.		"5" omitted	1.00	1.00
b.		Inverted surcharge	1.00	1.00
c.		Double surcharge	2.00	2.00
d.		Bar omitted	2.00	2.00

Official Stamps of 1906-08 Surcharged — Habilitado en 5 CENTAVOS

1908

131	O17	5c on 10c bister	18	15
a.		Double surcharge	3.00	3.00
132	O17	5c on 10c violet	18	15
a.		Inverted surcharge	1.50	1.50
133	O17	5c on 20c emerald	18	15
134	O17	5c on 20c violet	18	15
a.		Inverted surcharge	1.50	1.50
135	O17	5c on 30c slate bl	65	65
136	O17	5c on 30c turq bl	65	65
a.		Inverted surcharge		
b.		Double surcharge	3.00	3.00
137	O17	5c on 60c choc	15	15
a.		Double surcharge	6.00	6.00
138	O17	5c on 60c red brown	20	15
a.		Inverted surcharge	38	38
		Nos. 131-138 (8)	2.37	2.20

Same Surcharge on Official Stamps of 1903

139	A32	5c on 30c dp blue	1.25	1.10
140	A32	5c on 60c purple	50	30
a.		Double surcharge	2.50	2.50

Official Stamps of 1906-08 Overprinted — Habilitado

141	O17	5c deep blue	20	15
a.		Inverted overprint	1.50	1.50
b.		Bar omitted	4.50	4.50
c.		Double overprint	2.00	2.00
142	O17	5c slate blue	25	20
a.		Inverted overprint	1.25	1.25
b.		Double overprint	1.75	1.75
c.		Bar omitted	4.50	4.50
143	O17	5c greenish blue	15	15
a.		Inverted overprint	1.25	1.25
b.		Bar omitted	3.75	3.75
144	O18	1p brown org & blk	25	22
a.		Double overprint	1.00	1.00
b.		Double overprint, one inverted	1.25	1.25
c.		Triple overprint, two inverted	2.25	2.25
145	O18	1p brt rose & blk	42	35
a.		Bar omitted		
		Nos. 141-145 (5)	1.27	1.07

Regular Issues of 1906-08 Surcharged — Habilitado en 5 CENTAVOS

1908

146 A35 5c on 1c grnsh bl 15 15
a. Inverted surcharge 50 50
b. Double surcharge 75 75
c. "5" omitted 1.50 1.50
147 A35 5c on 2c car rose 15 15
a. Inverted surcharge 50 50
b. "5" omitted 1.25 1.25
c. Double surcharge 75 75
d. Double surcharge, one invtd.
148 A35 5c on 60c org brn 15 15
a. Inverted surcharge 75 75
b. "5" omitted 1.00 1.00
149 A35 5c on 60c sal pink 15 15
a. Double surcharge 50 50
b. Double surcharge, one invtd. 3.50 3.50
150 A35 5c on 60c choc 15 15
a. Inverted surcharge 1.25 1.25
151 A35 20c on 1c grnsh bl 15 15
a. Inverted surcharge 1.50 1.50
152 A35 20c on 2c ver 6.00 5.00
153 A35 20c on 2c car rose 3.50 3.00
a. Inverted surcharge 12.50
154 A35 20c on 30c dl lil 20 18
a. Inverted surcharge 1.50 1.50
b. Double surcharge
155 A35 20c on 30c turq bl 1.50 1.50
Nos. 146-155 (10) 12.10 10.58

Same Surcharge on Regular Issue of 1901-02

156 A25 5c on 28c org 1.25 1.10
157 A25 5c on 40c dk bl 38 30
a. Inverted surcharge 1.50 1.50

Same Surcharge on Official Stamps of 1908

158 O17 5c on 10c emer 18 15
a. Double surcharge
159 O17 5c on 10c red lil 18 15
a. Double surcharge 2.00 2.00
b. "5" omitted 1.50 1.50
160 O17 5c on 20c bis 38 30
a. Double surcharge 1.25 1.25
161 O17 5c on 20c sal pink 38 30
a. "5" omitted 1.75 1.75
162 O17 5c on 30c bl gray 15 15
163 O17 5c on 30c yel 15 15
a. "5" omitted 1.50 1.50
b. Inverted surcharge 1.25 1.25
164 O17 5c on 60c org brn 20 15
a. Double surcharge 5.00 5.00
165 O17 5c on 60c dp ultra 15 15
a. Inverted surcharge 2.50 2.50
b. "5" omitted 1.50
Nos. 158-165 (8) 1.77
Set value 1.20

Same Surcharge on No. O52

166 A32 20c on 5c blue 1.25 1.00
a. Inverted surcharge 3.00 3.75

Surcharged

Habilitado en
20
CENTAVOS

1908

On Stamp of 1887

167 A12 20c on 2c car 2.50 2.00
a. Inverted surcharge 7.50

On Official Stamps of 1892

168 A12 1c on 15c org 2.50 1.75
169 A12 5c on 20c pink 40.00 32.50
170 A12 5c on 50c gray 17.50 12.50
170A A12 20c on 5c blue 1.50 1.25
b. Inverted surcharge 8.75 8.75

Nos. 151, 152, 153, 155, 167, 170A, while duly authorized, all appear to have been sold to a single individual, and although they paid postage, it is doubtful whether they can be considered as ever having been placed on sale to the public.

Nos. O82-O84 Surcharged (Date in Red)

Habilitado
1908
UN CENTAVO

1908-09

171 O18 1c on 1p brt rose & blk 20 15
172 O18 1c on 1p lake & blk 18 15
173 O18 1c on 1p brn org & blk ('09) 90 65

Varieties of surcharge on Nos. 171-173 include: "CETTAVO"; date omitted, double or inverted; third line double or omitted.

Types of 1905-1910 Overprinted

1908

1908, Mar. 5 *Perf. 11½*

174 A35 1c emerald 15 15
175 A35 5c yellow 15 15
176 A35 10c lilac brown 15 15
177 A35 20c yellow orange 15 15
178 A35 30c red 25 20
179 A35 60c magenta 20 18
180 A37 1p light blue 15 15
Set value 90 70

Overprinted

1909

1909, Sept.

181 A35 1c blue gray 15 15
182 A35 1c scarlet 15 15
183 A35 5c dark green 15 15
184 A35 5c deep orange 15 15
185 A35 10c rose 15 15
186 A35 10c bister brown 15 15
187 A35 20c yellow 15 15
188 A35 20c violet 15 15
189 A35 30c orange brown 30 20
190 A35 30c dull blue 30 20
Set value 1.35 95

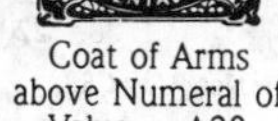

Coat of Arms above Numeral of Value — A38

"The Republic" — A39

1910-21 **Litho.** *Perf. 11½*

191 A38 1c gray black 15 15
192 A38 5c bright violet 15 15
a. Pair, imperf. between 1.00 1.00
193 A38 5c blue grn ('19) 15 15
194 A38 5c lt blue ('21) 15 15
195 A38 10c yellow green 15 15
196 A38 10c dp vio ('19) 15 15
197 A38 10c red ('21) 15 15
198 A38 20c red 15 15
199 A38 50c car rose 30 15
200 A38 75c deep blue 15 15
a. Diag. half perforated ('11) 15 15
Set value 1.05 60

Nos. 191-200 exist imperforate.
No. 200a was authorized for use as 20c.
For surcharges see Nos. 208, 241, 261, 265.

1911 **Engr.**

201 A39 1c olive grn & blk 15 15
202 A39 2c dk blue & blk 15 15
203 A39 5c carmine & indigo 15 15
204 A39 10c dp blue & brn 18 15
205 A39 20c olive grn & ind 18 15
206 A39 50c lilac & indigo 30 15
207 A39 75c ol grn & red lil 30 15
Nos. 201-207 (7) 1.41
Set value 72

Centenary of National Independence.
The 1c, 2c, 10c and 50c exist imperf. Value for pairs, $1.50 each.

No. 199 Surcharged

Habilitada
en
VEINTE

1912

208 A38 20c on 50c car rose 15 15
a. Inverted surcharge 1.00 1.00
b. Double surcharge 1.00 1.00
c. Bar omitted 1.75 1.75

National Coat of Arms — A40

1913 **Engr.** *Perf. 11½*

209 A40 1c gray 15 15
210 A40 2c orange 15 15
211 A40 5c lilac 15 15
212 A40 10c green 15 15
213 A40 20c dull red 15 15
214 A40 40c rose 15 15
215 A40 75c deep blue 15 15
216 A40 80c yellow 15 15
217 A40 1p light blue 15 15
218 A40 1.25p pale blue 15 15
219 A40 3p greenish blue 18 15
Set value 85 60

For surcharges see Nos. 225, 230-231, 237, 242, 253, 262-263, L3-L4.

Nos. J7-J10 Overprinted

HABILITADO
1918

1918

220 D2 5c yellow brown 15 15
221 D2 10c yellow brown 15 15
222 D2 20c yellow brown 15 15
223 D2 40c yellow brown 15 15

Nos. J10 and 214 Surcharged

HABILITADO
EN 0.05
1918

224 D2 5c on 40c yellow brn 15 15
225 A40 30c on 40c rose 15 15
Set value 44 38

Nos. 220-225 exist with surcharge inverted, double and double with one inverted.
The surcharge "Habilitado-1918-5 cents 5" on the 1c gray official stamps of 1914, is bogus.

No. J11 Overprinted

HABILITADO
1920

1920

229 D2 1p yellow brown 15 15
a. Inverted overprint 65 65
e. "AABILITADO" 75 75
f. "1929" for "1920" 75 75
g. Overprint lines 8mm apart 20 15

Nos. 216 and 219 Surcharged

HABILITADO
en 0.50
1920

230 A40 50c on 80c yellow 15 15
231 A40 1.75p on 3p grnsh bl 75 65

Same Surcharge on No. J12

232 D2 1p on 1.50p yel brn 22 15
Set value, #229-232 85

Nos. 229-232 exist with various surcharge errors, including inverted, double, double inverted and double with one inverted. Those that were issued are listed.

Parliament Building — A41

1920 **Litho.** *Perf. 11½*

233 A41 50c red & black 22 15
a. "CORRLOS" 1.50 1.50
234 A41 1p lt blue & blk 65 30
235 A41 1.75p dk blue & blk 15 15
236 A41 3p orange & blk 1.00 15

50th anniv. of the Constitution.
All values exist imperforate and Nos. 233, 235 and 236 with center inverted. It is doubtful that any of these varieties were regularly issued.

No. 215 Surcharged

50

1920

237 A40 50c on 75c deep blue 30 15

Nos. 200, 215 Surcharged

50

1921

241 A38 50c on 75c deep blue 15 15
242 A40 50c on 75c deep blue 15 15
Set value 15

A42

1922, Feb. 8 **Litho.** *Perf. 11½*

243 A42 50c car & dk blue 15 15
a. Imperf. pair 50
b. Center inverted 10.00 10.00
244 A42 1p dk blue & brn 15 15
a. Imperf. pair 50
b. Center inverted 12.50 12.50
Set value 20 16

For overprints see Nos. L1-L2.

Rendezvous of Conspirators A43

1922-23

245 A43 1p deep blue 15 15
246 A43 1p scar & dk bl ('23) 15 15
247 A43 1p red vio & gray ('23) 15 15
248 A43 1p org & gray ('23) 15 15
249 A43 5p dark violet 38 18
250 A43 5p dk bl & org brn ('23) 38 18
251 A43 5p dl red & lt bl ('23) 38 18
252 A43 5p emer & blk ('23) 38 18
Nos. 245-252 (8) 2.12
Set value 1.00

National Independence.

No. 218 Surcharged "Habilitado en $1:-1924" in Red

1924

253 A40 1p on 1.25p pale blue 15 15

This stamp was for use in Asunción. Nos. L3 to L5 were for use in the interior, as is indicated by the "C" in the surcharge.

Map of Paraguay — A44

1924 **Litho.** *Perf. 11½*

254 A44 1p dark blue 15 15
255 A44 2p carmine rose 15 15
256 A44 4p light blue 18 15
a. Perf. 12 38 15
Set value 38 20

#254-256 exist imperf. Value $3 each pair.
For surcharges and overprint see Nos. 267, C5, C15-C16, C54-C55, L7.

Gen. José E. Díaz — A45

Columbus — A46

1925-26 *Perf. 11½, 12*

257 A45 50c red	15	15
258 A45 1p dark blue	15	15
259 A45 1p emerald ('26)	15	15
Set value	26	18

#257-258 exist imperf. Value $1 each pair.
For overprints see Nos. L6, L8, L10.

1925 *Perf. 11½*

260 A46 1p blue	20	15
a. Imperf., pair	2.00	

For overprint see No. L9.

Nos. 194, 214-215, J12 Surcharged in Black or Red

Habilitado en 1 centavo

1926

261 A38 1c on 5c lt blue	15	15
262 A40 7c on 40c rose	15	15
263 A40 15c on 75c dp bl (R)	15	15
264 D2 1.50p on 1.50p yel brn	15	15
Set value	32	24

Nos. 194, 179 and 256 Surcharged "Habilitado" and New Values

1927

265 A38 2c on 5c lt blue	15	15
266 A35 50c on 60c magenta	15	15
a. Inverted surcharge	2.00	
267 A44 1.50p on 4p lt blue	15	15

Official Stamp of 1914 Surcharged "Habilitado" and New Value

268 O19 50c on 75c dp bl	15	15
Set value, #265-268	28	25

National Emblem A47

Pedro Juan Caballero A48

Map of Paraguay — A49

Fulgencio Yegros — A50

Ignacio Iturbe A51

Oratory of the Virgin, Asunción A52

Perf. 12, 11, 11½, 11x12

1927-38 **Typo.**

269 A47 1c lt red ('31)	15	15
270 A47 2c org red ('30)	15	15
271 A47 7c lilac	15	15
272 A47 7c emerald ('29)	15	15
273 A47 10c gray grn ('28)	15	15
a. 10c light green ('31)	15	15
274 A47 10c lil rose ('30)	15	15
275 A47 10c light bl ('35)	15	15
276 A47 20c dull bl ('28)	15	15
277 A47 20c lil brn ('30)	15	15
278 A47 20c lt vio ('31)	15	15
279 A47 20c rose ('35)	15	15
280 A47 50c ultramarine	15	15
281 A47 50c dl red ('28)	15	15
282 A47 50c orange ('30)	15	15
283 A47 50c gray ('31)	15	15
284 A47 50c brn vio ('34)	15	15
285 A47 50c rose ('36)	15	15
286 A47 70c ultra ('28)	15	15
287 A48 1p emerald	15	15
288 A48 1p org red ('30)	15	15
289 A48 1p brn org ('34)	15	15
290 A49 1.50p brown	15	15
291 A49 1.50p lilac ('28)	15	15

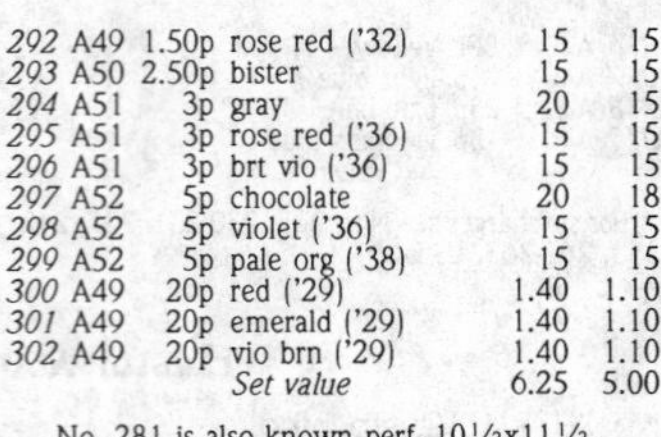

292 A49 1.50p rose red ('32)	15	15
293 A50 2.50p bister	15	15
294 A51 3p gray	20	15
295 A51 3p rose red ('36)	15	15
296 A51 3p brt vio ('36)	15	15
297 A52 5p chocolate	20	18
298 A52 5p violet ('36)	15	15
299 A52 5p pale org ('38)	15	15
300 A49 20p red ('29)	1.40	1.10
301 A49 20p emerald ('29)	1.40	1.10
302 A49 20p vio brn ('29)	1.40	1.10
Set value	6.25	5.00

No. 281 is also known perf. 10½x11½.

Papermaker's watermarks are sometimes found on No. 271 ("GLORIA BOND" in double-lined circle) and No. 280 ("Extra Vencedor Bond").

For surcharges and overprints see Nos. 312, C4, C6, C13-C14, C17-C18, C25-C32, C34-C35, L11-L30, O94-O96, O98.

Arms of Juan de Salazar de Espinosa A53

Columbus A54

1928, Aug. 15 *Perf. 12*

303 A53 10p violet brown	1.25	90

Issued in commemoration of Juan de Salazar de Espinosa, founder of Asunción.

A papermaker's watermark ("INDIAN BOND EXTRA STRONG S.&C") is sometimes found on Nos 303, 305-307.

1928 **Litho.**

304 A54 10p ultra	50	25
305 A54 10p vermilion	50	25
306 A54 10p dp red	50	25

For surcharge and overprint see Nos. C33, L37.

President Rutherford B. Hayes of US and Villa Occidental A55

1928, Nov. 20 *Perf. 12*

307 A55 10p gray brown	3.25	1.40
308 A55 10p red brown	3.25	1.40

50th anniv. of the Hayes' Chaco decision.

Portraits of Archbishop Bogarin — A56

1930, Aug. 15

309 A56 1.50p lake	1.00	75
310 A56 1.50p turq bl	1.00	75
311 A56 1.50p dl vio	1.00	75

Archbishop Juan Sinforiano Bogarin, first archbishop of Paraguay.
For overprints see Nos. 321-322.

No. 272 Surcharged

Habilitado en CINCO

1930

312 A47 5c on 7c emer	15	15

A57

1930-39 **Typo.** *Perf. 11½, 12*

313 A57 10p brown	50	20
314 A57 10p brn red, *bl* ('31)	50	20
315 A57 10p dk bl, *pink* ('32)	50	20
316 A57 10p gray brn ('36)	38	18
317 A57 10p gray ('37)	38	18
318 A57 10p blue ('39)	15	15
Nos. 313-318 (6)	2.41	1.11

1st Paraguayan postage stamp, 60th anniv.
For overprint see No. L31.

Gunboat "Humaitá" — A58

1931 *Perf. 12*

319 A58 1.50p purple	38	22

Constitution, 60th anniv. See Nos. C39-C53.
For overprint see No. L33.

View of San Bernardino — A59

1931, Aug.

320 A59 1p light green	25	15

Founding of San Bernardino, 50th anniv.
For overprint see No. L32.

Nos. 309-310 Overprinted in Blue or Red

FELIZ AÑO NUEVO 1932

1931, Dec. 31

321 A56 1.50p lake (Bl)	75	75
322 A56 1.50p turq blue (R)	75	75

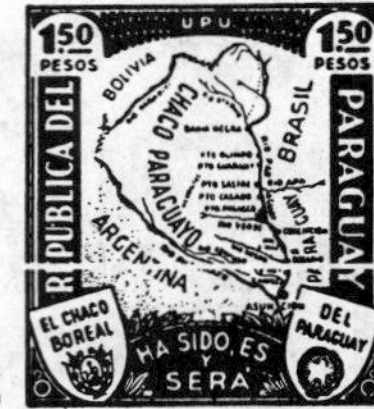

Map of the Gran Chaco — A60

1932-35 **Typo.** *Perf. 12*

323 A60 1.50p deep vio	15	15
324 A60 1.50p rose ('35)	15	15
Set value		18

For overprints see Nos. L34-L36, O97.

Nos. C74-C78 Surcharged

CORREOS 1 PESO FELIZ AÑO NUEVO 1933

1933 **Litho.**

325 AP18 50c on 4p ultra	25	20
326 AP18 1p on 8p red	50	38
327 AP18 1.50p on 12p bl grn	50	38
328 AP18 2p on 16p dk vio	50	38
329 AP18 5p on 20p org brn	1.25	1.00
Nos. 325-329 (5)	3.00	2.34

Flag of the Race Issue

Flag with Three Crosses: Caravels of Columbus — A61

1933, Oct. 10 **Litho.** *Perf. 11*

330 A61 10c multicolored	15	15
331 A61 20c multicolored	15	15
332 A61 50c multicolored	15	15
333 A61 1p multicolored	15	15
334 A61 1.50p multicolored	15	15
335 A61 2p multicolored	25	25
336 A61 5p multicolored	50	50
337 A61 10p multicolored	50	50
Set value	1.70	1.60

441st anniv. of the sailing of Christopher Columbus from the port of Palos, Aug. 3, 1492, on his first voyage to the New World.

Monstrance A62

Arms of Asunción A63

1937, Aug. **Unwmk.** *Perf. 11½*

338 A62 1p dk bl, yel & red	15	15
339 A62 3p dk bl, yel & red	15	15
340 A62 10p dk bl, yel & red	15	15
Set value	22	20

1st Natl. Eucharistic Congress, Asuncion.

1937, Aug.

341 A63 50c vio & buff	15	15
342 A63 1p bis & lt grn	15	15
343 A63 3p red & lt bl	15	15
344 A63 10p car rose & buff	15	15
345 A63 20p blue & drab	15	15
Set value	40	35

Founding of Asuncion, 400th anniv.

Oratory of the Virgin, Asunción — A64

Carlos Antonio Lopez — A65

José Eduvigis Diaz — A66

1938-39 Typo. Perf. 11, 12

346 A64	5p olive grn	18	15
347 A64	5p pale rose ('39)	25	15
348 A64	11p vio brown	18	15
	Set value		28

Founding of Asuncion, 400th anniv.

1939 Perf. 12

349 A65	2p lt ultra & pale brn	18	15
350 A66	2p lt ultra & brn	20	15

Reburial of ashes of Pres. Carlos Antonio Lopez (1790-1862) and Gen. José Eduvigis Diaz in the National Pantheon, Asuncion.

Pres. Patricio Escobar and Ramon Zubizarreta A67

Design: 5p, Pres. Bernardino Caballero and Senator José S. Decoud.

1939-40 Litho. Perf. 11½
Heads in Black

351 A67	50c dl org ('40)	15	15
352 A67	1p lt vio ('40)	15	15
353 A67	2p red brn ('40)	18	15
354 A67	5p lt ultra	25	15
	Nos. 351-354,C122-C123,O99-O104 (12)	9.03	8.85

Founding of the University of Asuncion, 50th anniv.

Varieties of this issue include inverted heads (50c, 1p, 2p); doubled heads; Caballero and Decoud heads in 50c frame: imperforates and part-perforates. Copies with inverted heads were not officially issued.

Coats of Arms — A69

Pres. Baldomir of Uruguay, Flags of Paraguay, Uruguay — A70

Designs: 2p, Pres. Benavides, Peru. 3p, US Eagle and Shield. 5p, Pres. Alessandri, Chile. 6p, Pres. Vargas, Brazil. 10p, Pres. Ortiz, Argentina.

1939 Engr.; Flags Litho. Perf. 12
Flags in National Colors

355 A69	50c vio blue	15	15
356 A70	1p olive	15	15
357 A70	2p blue grn	15	15
358 A70	3p sepia	25	18
359 A70	5p orange	20	15
360 A70	6p dull vio	50	40
361 A70	10p bister brn	38	25
	Nos. 355-361 (7)	1.78	
	Set value		1.20

First Buenos Aires Peace Conference. See Nos. C113-C121.

For overprint and surcharge see Nos. 387, B10.

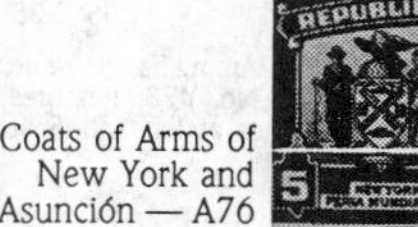
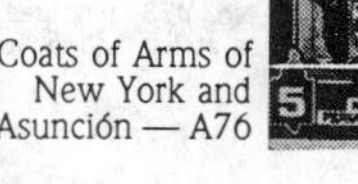

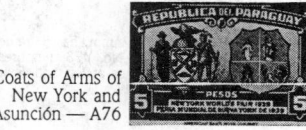

Coats of Arms of New York and Asunción — A76

1939, Nov. 30

362 A76	5p scarlet	15	15
363 A76	10p deep blue	25	18
364 A76	11p dk blue grn	35	30
365 A76	22p olive blk	45	38

New York World's Fair. See Nos. C124-C126.

Paraguayan Soldier — A77

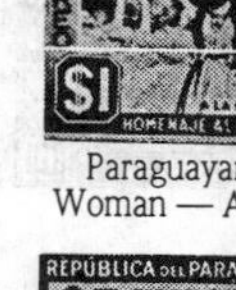

Paraguayan Woman — A78

Cowboys — A79

Plowing — A80

View of Paraguay River — A81

Oxcart A82

Pasture A83

Piraretá Falls — A84

1940, Jan. 1 Photo. Perf. 12½

366 A77	50c deep org	15	15
367 A78	1p brt red vio	15	15
368 A79	3p bright grn	15	15
369 A80	5p chestnut	16	15
370 A81	10p magenta	20	15
371 A82	20p violet	38	32
372 A83	50p cobalt blue	90	45
373 A84	100p black	1.90	1.40
	Nos. 366-373 (8)	3.99	2.92

Second Buenos Aires Peace Conference.
For surcharge see No. 386.

Map of the Americas — A85

1940, May Engr. Perf. 12

374 A85	50c red org	15	15
375 A85	1p green	15	15
376 A85	5p dark blue	15	15
377 A85	10p brown	38	38
	Nos. 374-377,C127-C130 (8)	4.21	3.41

Pan American Union, 50th anniversary.

Reproduction of Type A1 — A86

Sir Rowland Hill — A87

Designs: 6p, Type A2. 10p, Type A3.

1940, Aug. 15 Photo. Perf. 13½

378 A86	1p aqua & brt red vio	50	25
379 A87	5p dp yel grn & red brn	65	32
380 A86	6p org brn & ultra	1.50	65
381 A86	10p ver & black	1.50	1.00

Postage stamp centenary.

Dr. José Francia
A90 A91

1940, Sept. 20 Engr. Perf. 12

382 A90	50c car rose	15	15
383 A91	50c plum	15	15
384 A90	1p bright grn	15	15
385 A91	5p deep blue	15	15
	Set value	48	40

Centenary of the death of Dr. Jose Francia (1766-1840), dictator of Paraguay, 1814-1840.

No. 366 Surcharged in Black

1940, Sept. 7 Perf. 12½

386 A77	5p on 50c dp org	20	20

In honor of Pres. Jose F. Estigarribia who died in a plane crash Sept. 7, 1940.

No. 360 Overprinted in Black

Visita al Paraguay
Agosto de 1941

1941, Aug. Perf. 12

387 A70	6p multi	20	20

Visit to Paraguay of Pres. Vargas of Brazil.

Nos. C113-C115 Overprinted "HABILITADO" and Bars in Blue or Red

1942, Jan. 17 Perf. 12½

388 A69	1p multi (Bl)	15	15
389 A69	3p multi (R)	15	15
390 A70	5p multi (R)	18	15
	Set value		30

Coat of Arms — A92

1942-43 Litho. Perf. 11, 12, 11x12

391 A92	1p light green	15	15
392 A92	1p orange ('43)	15	15
393 A92	7p light blue	15	15
394 A92	7p yel brn ('43)	15	15
	Set value	24	20

The Indian Francisco — A93

Arms of Irala — A95

Domingo Martinez de Irala and His Vision — A94

1942, Aug. 15 Engr. Perf. 12

395 A93	2p green	65	30
396 A94	5p rose	65	30
397 A95	7p sapphire	65	25
	Nos. 395-397,C131-C133 (6)	7.95	5.85

400th anniversary of Asuncion.

Pres. Higinio Morinigo, Scenes of Industry & Agriculture A96

Christopher Columbus A97

1943, Aug. 15 Unwmk.

398 A96	7p blue	15	15

For surcharges see Nos. 404, 428.

1943, Aug. 15

399 A97	50c violet	18	15
400 A97	1p gray brn	15	15
401 A97	5p dark grn	45	15
402 A97	7p brt ultra	25	15
	Set value		46

Discovery of America, 450th anniv.
For surcharges see Nos. 405, 429.

No. 296 Surcharged in Black

Habilitado
en
un céntimo

1944 Perf. 12, 11, 11½, 11x12

403 A51	1c on 3p brt vio	15	15

Nos. 398 and 402 Surcharged "1944 / 5 Centimos 5" in Red

1944 Perf. 12

404 A96	5c on 7p blue	15	15
405 A97	5c on 7p brt ultra	15	15
	Set value	20	15

Imperforates
Starting with No. 406, many Paraguayan stamps exist imperf.

Primitive Postal Service among Indians — A98

Ruins of Humaitá Church — A99

Locomotive of early Paraguayan Railroad — A100

Early Merchant Ship — A102

Marshal Francisco S. Lopez — A101

Port of Asunción — A103

Birthplace of Paraguay's Liberation — A104

Monument to Heroes of Itororó — A105

1944-45 Unwmk. Engr. *Perf. 12½*

No.	Type	Value	Color	Unused	Used
406	A98	1c	black	15	15
407	A99	2c	copper brn ('45)	15	15
408	A100	5c	light olive	25	15
409	A101	7c	light blue ('45)	15	15
410	A102	10c	green ('45)	25	20
411	A103	15c	dark blue ('45)	25	20
412	A104	50c	black brown	45	45
413	A105	1g	dk rose car ('45)	90	50
			Nos. 406-413 (8)	2.55	1.95

See Nos. 435, 437, 439, 441, C134-C146, C158-C162.
For surcharges see Nos. 414, 427.

No. 409 Surcharged in Red

5 5

1945

No.	Type	Value	Color	Unused	Used
414	A101	5c on 7c	light blue	15	15

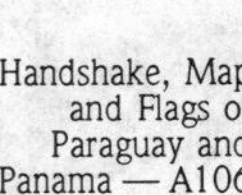

Handshake, Map and Flags of Paraguay and Panama — A106

Designs: 3c, Venezuela Flag. 5c, Colombia Flag. 2g, Peru Flag.

Engr.; Flags Litho. in Natl. Colors
1945, Aug. 15 Unwmk. *Perf. 12½*

No.	Type	Value	Color	Unused	Used
415	A106	1c	dark green	15	15
416	A106	3c	lake	15	15
417	A106	5c	blue blk	15	15
418	A106	2g	brown	1.10	75
			Set value	1.30	90

Goodwill visits of Pres. Higinio Morinigo during 1943. See Nos. C147-C153.

Nos. B6 to B9 Surcharged "1945" and New Value in Black

1945 Engr. *Perf. 12*

No.	Type	Value	Color	Unused	Used
419	SP4	2c on 7p + 3p	red brn	15	15
420	SP4	2c on 7p + 3p	purple	15	15
421	SP4	2c on 7p + 3p	car rose	15	15
422	SP4	2c on 7p + 3p	saph	15	15
423	SP4	5c on 7p + 3p	red brn	15	15
424	SP4	5c on 7p + 3p	purple	15	15
425	SP4	5c on 7p + 3p	car rose	15	15
426	SP4	5c on 7p + 3p	saph	15	15
			Set value	84	60

Similar Surcharge in Red on Nos. 409, 398 and 402

Perf. 12½, 12

No.	Type	Value	Color	Unused	Used
427	A101	5c on 7c	lt blue	15	15
428	A96	5c on 7p	blue	15	15
429	A97	5c on 7p	brt ultra	15	15
			Set value		30

Nos. 427-429 exist with black surcharge.

Catalogue values for unused stamps in this section, from this point to the end of the section, are for Never Hinged items.

Coat of Arms ("U.P.U." at bottom) — A110

1946 Litho. *Perf. 11, 12, 11x12*

No.	Type	Value	Color	Unused	Used
430	A110	5c	gray	15	15

See Nos. 459-463, 478-480, 498-506, 525-536, 646-658.
For overprints see Nos. 464-466.

Nos. B6 to B9 Surcharged "1946" and New Value in Black

1946 *Perf. 12*

No.	Type	Value	Color	Unused	Used
431	SP4	5c on 7p + 3p	red brn	32	25
432	SP4	5c on 7p + 3p	purple	32	25
433	SP4	5c on 7p + 3p	car rose	32	25
434	SP4	5c on 7p + 3p	saph	32	25

Types of 1944-45 and

First Telegraph in South America — A111

Colonial Jesuit Altar — A113

Monument to Antequera A112

1946, Sept. 21 Engr. *Perf. 12½*

No.	Type	Value	Color	Unused	Used
435	A102	1c	rose car	15	15
436	A111	2c	purple	15	15
437	A98	5c	ultra	15	15
438	A112	10c	org yel	15	15
439	A105	15c	brn olive	15	15
440	A113	50c	deep grn	30	20
441	A104	1g	brt ultra	65	38
			Set value	1.35	90

See Nos. C135-C138, C143.

Marshal Francisco Solano Lopez — A114

1947, May 15 *Perf. 12*

No.	Type	Value	Color	Unused	Used
442	A114	1c	purple	15	15
443	A114	2c	org red	15	15
444	A114	5c	green	15	15
445	A114	15c	ultra	15	15
446	A114	50c	dark grn	25	25
			Set value	48	48

See Nos. C163-C167.

Juan Sinforiano Bogarin, Archbishop of Asunción — A115

Archbishopric Coat of Arms — A116

Projected Monument of the Sacred Heart of Jesus A117

Vision of Projected Monument A118

1948, Jan. 6 Engr. *Perf. 12½*

No.	Type	Value	Color	Unused	Used
447	A115	2c	dark blue	15	15
448	A116	5c	deep car	15	15
449	A117	10c	gray blk	15	15
450	A118	15c	green	20	15
			Set value	40	30

Establishment of the Archbishopric of Asunción, 50th anniv.
See Nos. C168-C175.

"Political Enlightenment" A119

1948, Sept. 11 Engr. & Litho.

No.	Type	Value	Color	Unused	Used
451	A119	5c	car red & bl	15	15
452	A119	15c	red org, red & bl	15	15
			Set value	15	15

Issued to honor the Barefeet, a political group. See Nos. C176-C177.

C. A. Lopez, J. N. Gonzalez and Freighter Paraguari A120

1949 Litho.

Centers in Carmine, Black, Ultramarine and Blue

No.	Type	Value	Color	Unused	Used
453	A120	2c	orange	15	15
454	A120	5c	blue vio	15	15
455	A120	10c	black	15	15
456	A120	15c	violet	15	15
457	A120	50c	blue grn	15	15
458	A120	1g	dull vio brn	20	15
			Set value	58	40

Paraguay's merchant fleet centenary.

Type of 1946

1950 Unwmk. *Perf. 10½*

No.	Type	Value	Color	Unused	Used
459	A110	5c	red	15	15
460	A110	10c	blue	15	15
461	A110	50c	rose lilac	15	15
462	A110	1g	pale violet	15	15

1951

Coarse Impression

No.	Type	Value	Color	Unused	Used
463	A110	30c	green	15	15
			Set value, #459-463	28	25

Blocks of Four of Nos. 459, 460 and 463 Overprinted in Various Colors

Illustration reduced one-half.

1951, Apr. 18

No.	Type	Value	Color	Unused	Used
464	A110	5c	red (Bk), block	15	15
465	A110	10c	blue (R), block	25	18
466	A110	30c	green (V), block	38	30

1st Economic Cong. of Paraguay, Apr. 18, 1951.

Columbus Lighthouse A121

1952, Feb. 11 *Perf. 10*

No.	Type	Value	Color	Unused	Used
467	A121	2c	org brn	15	15
468	A121	5c	light ultra	15	15
469	A121	10c	rose	15	15
470	A121	15c	light blue	15	15
471	A121	20c	lilac	15	15
472	A121	50c	orange	15	15
473	A121	1g	bluish grn	18	18
			Set value	50	50

Silvio Pettirossi, Aviator — A122

1954, Mar. Litho. *Perf. 10*

No.	Type	Value	Color	Unused	Used
474	A122	5c	blue	15	15
475	A122	20c	rose pink	15	15
476	A122	50c	vio brn	15	15
477	A122	60c	lt vio	15	15
			Set value, #474-477, C201-C204	64	62

Arms Type of 1946

1954 *Perf. 11*

No.	Type	Value	Color	Unused	Used
478	A110	10c	vermilion	15	15

Perf. 10

No.	Type	Value	Color	Unused	Used
478A	A110	10c	ver, redrawn	15	15
479	A110	10g	orange	25	20
480	A110	50g	vio brn	1.25	1.00
			Set value	1.55	1.25

No. 478A measures 20½x24mm, has 5 frame lines at left and 6 at right. No. 478 measures 20x24½mm, has 6 frame lines at left and 5 at right.

Three National Heroes — A123

1954, Aug. 15 Litho. *Perf. 10*

No.	Type	Description	Unused	Used
481	A123	5c light vio	15	15
482	A123	20c light blue	15	15
483	A123	50c rose pink	15	15
484	A123	1g org brn	15	15
485	A123	2g blue grn	15	15
		Set value	30	30

Marshal Francisco S. Lopez, Pres. Carlos A. Lopez and Gen. Bernardino Caballero.
See Nos. C216-C220.

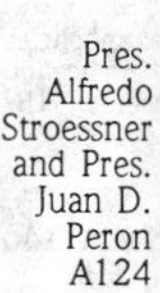

Pres. Alfredo Stroessner and Pres. Juan D. Peron A124

Photo. & Litho.
1955, Apr. Wmk. 90 *Perf. 13x13½*
Frames and Flags in Blue and Carmine

No.	Type	Description	Unused	Used
486	A124	5c brn, yel brn & sal pink	15	15
487	A124	10c lil rose, dp cl & cream	15	15
488	A124	50c gray, blk & cr	15	15
489	A124	1.30g rose lil, rose vio & cream	15	15
490	A124	2.20g ultra, dk bl & cr	15	15
		Set value, #486-490, C221-C224	75	66

Visit of Pres. Juan D. Peron of Argentina.

Jesuit Ruins, Trinidad Belfry A125

Santa Maria Cornice — A126

Jesuit Ruins: 20c, Corridor at Trinidad. 2.50g, Tower of Santa Rosa. 5g, San Cosme gate. 15g, Church of Jesus. 25g, Niche at Trinidad.

Perf. 12½x12, 12x12½
1955, June 19 Engr. Unwmk.

No.	Type	Description	Unused	Used
491	A125	5c org yel	15	15
492	A125	20c olive bister	15	15
493	A126	50c lt red brn	15	15
494	A126	2.50g olive	15	15
495	A125	5g yel brn	15	15
496	A125	15g blue grn	22	15
497	A126	25g deep grn	45	25
		Set value	92	64

25th anniv. of the priesthood of Monsignor Rodriguez. See Nos. C225-C232.
For surcharges see Nos. 545-551.

Arms Type of 1946
Perf. 10, 11 (No. 500)
1956-58 Litho. Unwmk.

No.	Type	Description	Unused	Used
498	A110	5c brown ('57)	15	15
499	A110	30c red brn ('57)	15	15
500	A110	45c gray olive	15	15
500A	A110	90c lt vio bl	15	15
501	A110	2g ocher	15	15
502	A110	2.20g lil rose	15	15
503	A110	3g ol bis ('58)	15	15
503A	A110	4.20g emer ('57)	15	15
504	A110	5g ver ('57)	15	15
505	A110	10g lt grn ('57)	15	15
506	A110	20g blue ('57)	30	22
		Set value	92	75

No. 500A exists with four-line, carmine overprint: "DIA N. UNIDAS 24 Octubre 1945-1956". It was not regularly issued and no decree authorizing it is known.

Soldiers, Angel and Asuncion Cathedral — A127

Design: Nos. 513-519, Soldier and nurse in medallion and flags.

Perf. 13½
1957, June 12 Photo. Unwmk.
Granite Paper
Flags in Red and Blue

No.	Type	Description	Unused	Used
508	A127	5c bl grn	15	15
509	A127	10c carmine	15	15
510	A127	15c ultra	15	15
511	A127	20c dp claret	15	15
512	A127	25c gray blk	15	15
513	A127	30c lt blue	15	15
514	A127	40c gray blk	15	15
515	A127	50c dark car	15	15
516	A127	1g bluish grn	15	15
517	A127	1.30g ultra	15	15
518	A127	1.50g dp claret	15	15
519	A127	2g brt grn	15	15
		Set value	60	55

Heroes of the Chaco war. See #C233-C245.

Statue of St. Ignatius (Guarani Carving) — A128

Blessed Roque Gonzales and St. Ignatius A129

Design: 1.50g, St. Ignatius and San Ignacio Monastery.

Wmk. 319
1958, Mar. 15 Litho. *Perf. 11*

No.	Type	Description	Unused	Used
520	A128	50c dk red brn	15	15
521	A129	50c lt bl grn	15	15
522	AP91	1.50g brt vio	15	15
523	A128	3g light bl	15	15
524	A129	6.25g rose car	15	15
		Set value	35	28

St. Ignatius of Loyola (1491-1556).
See Nos. 704-707.

Arms Type of 1946
1958-64 Litho. *Perf. 10, 11*

No.	Type	Description	Unused	Used
525	A110	45c gray olive	15	15
526	A110	50c rose vio	15	15
527	A110	70c lt brn ('59)	15	15
527A	A110	90c vio blue	15	15
528	A110	1g violet	15	15
529	A110	1.50g lilac ('59)	15	15
529A	A110	2g bister ('64)	15	15
530	A110	3g ol bis ('59)	15	15
531	A110	4.50g lt ultra ('59)	15	15
531A	A110	5g rose red ('59)	15	15
531B	A110	10g bl grn ('59)	15	15
532	A110	12.45g yel green	15	15
533	A110	15g dl orange	15	15
534	A110	30g citron	28	20
535	A110	50g brown red	42	30
536	A110	100g gray vio	85	65
		Set value	2.40	1.90

Pres. Alfredo Stroessner — A130

Perf. 13½
1958, Aug. 15 Litho. Wmk. 320
Center in Slate

No.	Type	Description	Unused	Used
537	A130	10c sal pink	15	15
538	A130	15c violet	15	15
539	A130	25c yel grn	15	15
540	A130	30c light fawn	15	15
541	A130	50c rose car	15	15
542	A130	75c light ultra	15	15
543	A130	5g lt bl grn	15	15
544	A130	10g brown	15	15
		Set value	50	45

Re-election of President General Alfredo Stroessner. See Nos. C246-C251.

Nos. 491-497 Surcharged in Red

Perf. 12½x12, 12x12½
1959, May 14 Engr. Unwmk.

No.	Type	Description	Unused	Used
545	A125	1.50g on 5c org yel	15	15
546	A125	1.50g on 20c ol bis	15	15
547	A126	1.50g on 50c lt red brn	15	15
548	A126	3g on 2.50g ol	15	15
549	A125	6.25g on 5g yel brn	15	15
550	A125	20g on 15g bl grn	25	25
551	A126	30g on 25g dp grn	38	38
		Set value	90	90

The surcharge is made to fit the stamps. See Nos. C252-C259.
Counterfeits of surcharge exist.

Goalkeeper Catching Soccer Ball A131

WRY Emblem A132

1960, Mar. 18 Photo. *Perf. 12½*

No.	Type	Description	Unused	Used
556	A131	30c brt red & bl grn	15	15
557	A131	50c plum & dk bl	15	15
558	A131	75c ol grn & org	15	15
559	A131	1.50g dk vio & bl grn	15	15
		Set value, #556-559, C262-C264	90	90

Olympic Games of 1960.

1960, Apr. 7 Litho. *Perf. 11*

No.	Type	Description	Unused	Used
560	A132	25c sal & yel grn	15	15
561	A132	50c lt yel grn & red org	15	15
562	A132	70c lt brn & lil rose	25	20
563	A132	1.50g lt bl & ultra	25	20
564	A132	3g gray & bis brn	50	45
		Nos. 560-564,C265-C268 (9)	5.15	4.43

World Refugee Year, July 1, 1959-June 30, 1960 (1st issue).

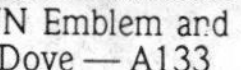

UN Emblem and Dove — A133

Flags of UN and Paraguay and UN Emblem — A134

UN Declaration of Human Rights: 3g, Hand holding seales. 6g, Hands breaking chains. 20g, Flame.

1960, Apr. 21 *Perf. 12½x13*

No.	Type	Description	Unused	Used
565	A133	1g dk car & bl	15	15
566	A133	3g blue & org	15	15
567	A133	6g gray grn & sal	15	15
568	A133	20g ver & yel	15	15
		Set value, #565-568, C269-C271	1.45	1.45

Miniature sheets exist, perf. and imperf., containing one each of Nos. 565-568, all printed in purple and orange.

Perf. 13x13½
1960, Oct. 24 Photo. Unwmk.

No.	Type	Description	Unused	Used
569	A134	30c lt bl, red & bl	15	15
570	A134	75c yel, red & bl	15	15
571	A134	90c pale lil, red & bl	15	15
		Set value, #569-571, C272-C273	25	25

15th anniversary of the United Nations.

International Bridge, Arms of Brazil, Paraguay — A135

Truck Carrying Logs — A136

1961, Jan. 26 Litho. *Perf. 14*

No.	Type	Description	Unused	Used
572	A135	15c green	15	15
573	A135	30c dull blue	15	15
574	A135	50c orange	15	15
575	A135	75c vio blue	15	15
576	A135	1g violet	15	15
		Set value, #572-575, C274-C277	1.05	95

Inauguration of the International Bridge between Paraguay and Brazil.

Unwmk.
1961, Apr. 10 Photo. *Perf. 13*

Designs: 90c, 2g, Logs on river barge. 1g, 5g, Radio tower.

No.	Type	Description	Unused	Used
577	A136	25c yel grn & rose car	15	15
578	A136	90c blue & yel	15	15
579	A136	1g car rose & org	15	15
580	A136	2g ol grn & sal	15	15
581	A136	5g lilac & emer	15	15
		Set value, #577-581, C278-C281	1.65	1.40

Paraguay's progress, "Paraguay en Marcha."

P. J. Caballero, José G. R. Francia, F. Yegros, Revolutionary Leaders A137

1961, May 16 Litho. *Perf. 14½*

No.	Type	Description	Unused	Used
582	A137	30c green	15	15
583	A137	50c lil rose	15	15
584	A137	90c violet	15	15
585	A137	1.50g Prus bl	15	15
586	A137	3g olive bis	15	15

587 A137	4g	ultra	15	15
588 A137	5g	brown	15	15
		Set value	36	35

150th anniv. of Independence (1st issue). See Nos. C282-C287.

"Chaco Peace"
A138

Puma
A139

1961, June 12 ***Perf. 14x14½***

589 A138	25c	vermilion	15	15
590 A138	30c	green	15	15
591 A138	50c	red brn	15	15
592 A138	1g	bright vio	15	15
593 A138	2g	dk bl gray	15	15
		Set value, #589-593, C288-C290	1.40	1.30

Chaco Peace; 150th anniv. of Independence (2nd issue).

1961, Aug. 16 **Unwmk.** ***Perf. 14***

594 A139	75c	dull vio	15	15
595 A139	1.50g	brown	15	15
596 A139	4.50g	green	15	15
597 A139	10g	Prus blue	15	15
		Nos. 594-597,C291-C293 (7)	3.15	3.00

150th anniv. of Independence (3rd issue).

University Seal — A140

Hotel Guarani — A141

1961, Sept. 18 ***Perf. 14x14½***

598 A140	15c	ultra	15	15
599 A140	25c	dk red	15	15
600 A140	75c	bl grn	15	15
601 A140	1g	orange	15	15
		Set value, #598-601, C294-C296	85	85

Founding of the Catholic University in Asuncion; 150th anniv. of Independence (4th issue).

1961, Oct. 14 **Litho.** ***Perf. 15***

602 A141	50c	slate bl	15	15
603 A141	1g	green	15	15
604 A141	4.50g	lilac	15	15
		Set value, #602-604, C297-C300	90	85

Opening of the Hotel Guarani; 150th anniv. of Independence (5th issue).

Tennis Racket and Balls in Flag Colors — A142

1961, Oct. 16 **Litho.** ***Perf. 11***

605 A142	35c	multi	15
606 A142	75c	multi	15
607 A142	1.50g	multi	15
608 A142	2.25g	multi	15
609 A142	4g	multi	15
		Set value	28

28th South American Tennis Championships, Asuncion, Oct. 15-23 (1st issue). Some specialists question the status of this issue. See Nos. C301-C303.

Imperforates exist in changed colors as well as two imperf. souvenir sheets with stamps in changed colors.

Limited Distribution Issues Beginning with No. 610, sets with limited distribution are not valued.

Alan B. Shepard, First US Astronaut
A143

Design: 18.15g, 36g, 50g, Shepard, Saturn, horiz.

1961, Dec. 22 **Litho.** ***Perf. 11***

610 A143	10c	blue & brown
611 A143	25c	blue & car rose
612 A143	50c	blue & yel org
613 A143	75c	blue & green
614 A143	18.15g	green & blue
615 A143	36g	orange & blue
616 A143	50g	car rose & blue
a.		Souvenir sheet of 1

Nos. 614-616a are airmail.

Uprooted Oak Emblem — A145

1961, Dec. 30 **Unwmk.** ***Perf. 11***

619 A145	10c	ultra & lt bl	15
620 A145	25c	maroon & org	15
621 A145	50c	car rose & pink	15
622 A145	75c	dk bl & yel grn	15
		Set value	20

World Refugee Year, 1959-60 (2nd issue). Imperforates in changed colors and souvenir sheets exist. Some specialists question the status of this issue.

See Nos. C307-C309.

Europa
A146

Design: 20g, 50g, Dove.

1961, Dec. 31

623 A146	50c	multicolored
624 A146	75c	multicolored
625 A146	1g	multicolored
626 A146	1.50g	multicolored
627 A146	4.50g	multicolored
a.		Souvenir sheet of 5, #623-627
628 A146	20g	multicolored
629 A146	50g	multicolored
a.		Souvenir sheet of 1

Nos. 628-629 are airmail.

Tennis Player — A147

1962, Jan. 5 ***Perf. 15x14½***

630 A147	35c	Prussian bl	15	15
631 A147	75c	dark vio	15	15
632 A147	1.50g	red brn	15	15
633 A147	2.25g	emerald	15	15
634 A147	4g	carmine	15	15
635 A147	12.45g	red lil	20	20
636 A147	20g	bl grn	35	35
637 A147	50g	org brn	55	55
		Set value	1.35	1.35

28th South American Tennis Championships, 1961 (2nd issue) and the 150th anniv. of Independence (6th issue).

Nos. 634-637 are airmail.

Scout Bugler
A148

Lord Baden-Powell
A148a

1962, Feb. 6 ***Perf. 11***

Olive Green Center

638 A148	10c	dp magenta	15
639 A148	20c	red orange	15
640 A148	25c	dk brown	15
641 A148	30c	emerald	15
642 A148	50c	indigo	15
643 A148a	12.45g	car rose & bl	25
644 A148a	36g	car rose & emer	75
645 A148a	50g	car rose & org yel	1.00
		Set value	2.25

Issued to honor the Boy Scouts. Imperfs. in changed colors exist and imperf. souvenir sheets exist. Some specialists question the status of this issue.

Nos. 643-645 are airmail.

Arms Type of 1946

1962-68 **Litho.** **Wmk. 347**

646 A110	50c	steel bl ('63)	15	15
647 A110	70c	dull lil ('63)	15	15
648 A110	1.50g	violet ('63)	15	15
649 A110	3g	dp bl ('68)	15	15
650 A110	4.50g	redsh brn ('67)	15	15
651 A110	5g	lilac ('64)	15	15
652 A110	10g	car rose ('63)	15	15
653 A110	12.45g	ultra	15	15
654 A110	15.45g	org ver	15	15
655 A110	18.15g	lilac	15	15
656 A110	20g	lt brn ('63)	15	15
657 A110	50g	dl red brn ('67)	35	18
658 A110	100g	bl gray ('63)	70	42
		Set value	1.85	1.25

Map and Laurel Branch
A149

UN Emblem
A150

Design: 20g, 50g, Hands holding globe.

Perf. 14x14½

1962, Apr. 14 **Unwmk.**

659 A149	50c	ocher	15	15
660 A149	75c	vio blue	15	15
661 A149	1g	purple	15	15
662 A149	1.50g	brt grn	15	15
663 A149	4.50g	vermilion	15	15
664 A149	20g	lil rose	18	18
665 A149	50g	orange	38	38
		Set value	80	80

Day of the Americas; 150th anniv. of Independence (7th issue).

Nos. 664-665 are airmail.

1962, Apr. 23 ***Perf. 15***

Design: #670-673, UN Headquarters, NYC.

666 A150	50c	bister brn	15	15
667 A150	75c	dp claret	15	15
668 A150	1g	Prussian bl	15	15
669 A150	2g	orange brn	15	15
670 A150	12.45g	dl vio	20	20
671 A150	18.15g	ol grn	30	30
672 A150	23.40g	brn red	45	45
673 A150	30g	carmine	50	50
		Set value	1.60	1.60

United Nations; 150th anniv. of Independence (8th issue).

Nos. 670-673 are airmail.

Malaria Eradication Emblem and Mosquito
A151

Design: 75c, 1g, 1.50g, Microscope, anopheles mosquito and eggs. 3g, 4g, Malaria eradication emblem. 12.45g, 18.15g, 36g, Mosquito, UN emblem and microscope.

Perf. 14x13½

1962, May 23 **Wmk. 346**

674 A151	30c	pink, ultra & blk	15
675 A151	50c	bis, grn & blk	15
676 A151	75c	rose red, blk & bis	15
677 A151	1g	brt grn, blk & bis	15
678 A151	1.50g	dl red brn, blk & bis	15
679 A151	3g	bl, red & blk	15
680 A151	4g	grn, red & blk	15
681 A151	12.45g	ol bis, grn & blk	18
682 A151	18.15g	rose lil, red & blk	38
683 A151	36g	rose red, vio bl & blk	1.00
		Set value	2.00

WHO drive to eradicate malaria. Imperforates exist in changed colors. Two souvenir sheets exist, one containing one copy of No. 683, the other an imperf. 36g in blue, red & black. Some specialists question the status of this issue.

Nos. 679-683 are airmail.

Stadium — A152

Soccer Players and Globe
A152a

Perf. 13½x14

1962, July 28 **Litho.** **Wmk. 346**

684 A152	15c	yel & dk brn	15
685 A152	25c	brt grn & dk brn	15
686 A152	30c	lt vio & dk brn	15
687 A152	40c	dl org & dk brn	15
688 A152	50c	brt yel grn & dk brn	15
689 A152a	12.45g	brt rose, blk & vio	38
690 A152a	18.15g	lt red brn, blk & vio	55
691 A152a	36g	gray grn, blk & brn	1.10
		Set value	2.25

World Soccer Championships, Chile, May 30-June 17. Some specialists question the status of this issue. Imperfs. exist. A souvenir sheet contains one No. 691.

Nos. 689-691 are airmail.

Freighter
A153

Ship's Wheel — A153a

Designs: Various merchantmen. 44g, Like 12.45g with diagonal colorless band in background.

Perf. 14½x15

1962, July 31 **Unwmk.**

692	A153	30c	bister brn	15	15
693	A153	90c	slate bl	15	15
694	A153	1.50g	brown red	15	15
695	A153	2g	green	15	15
696	A153	4.20g	vio blue	15	15

Perf. 15x14½

697	A153a	12.45g	dk red	15	15
698	A153a	44g	blue	38	32
			Set value	78	70

Issued to honor the merchant marine.
Nos. 697-698 are airmail.

Friendship 7 over South America — A154

Lt. Col. John H. Glenn, Jr., Lt. Cmdr. Scott Carpenter — A154a

Perf. 13½x14

1962, Sept. 4 **Litho.** **Wmk. 346**

699	A154	15c	dk bl & bis	15
700	A154	25c	vio brn & bis	15
701	A154	30c	dk sl grn & bis	15
702	A154	40c	dk gray & bis	15
703	A154	50c	dk vio & bis	15
704	A154a	12.45g	car lake & gray	15
705	A154a	18.15g	red lil & gray	20
706	A154a	36g	dl cl & gray	40
			Set value	1.00

US manned space flights. Imperfs. in changed colors and two souvenir sheets exist. Some specialists question the status of this issue.
Nos. 704-706 are airmail.

Discus Thrower — A155

Olympic flame and: 12.45g, Melbourne, 1956. 18.15g, Rome, 1960. 36g, Tokyo, 1964.

1962, Oct. 1 **Litho.**

707	A155	15c	blk & yel	15
708	A155	25c	blk & lt grn	15
709	A155	30c	blk & pink	15
710	A155	40c	blk & pale vio	15
711	A155	50c	blk & lt bl	15
712	A155	12.45g	brt grn, lt grn & choc	15
713	A155	18.15g	ol brn, yel & choc	20
714	A155	36g	rose red, pink & choc	40
			Set value	1.00

Olympic Games from Amsterdam 1928 to Tokyo 1964. Each stamp is inscribed with date and place of various Olympic Games. Imperfs. in changed colors and two souvenir sheets exist. Some specialists question the status of this issue.
Nos. 712-714 are airmail.

Peace Dove and Cross A156

Dove Symbolizing Holy Ghost A156a

Perf. 14½

1962, Oct. 11 **Litho.** **Unwmk.**

715	A156	50c	olive	15	15
716	A156	70c	dark blue	15	15
717	A156	1.50g	bister	15	15
718	A156	2g	violet	15	15
719	A156	3g	brick red	15	15
720	A156a	5g	vio bl	15	15
721	A156a	10g	brt grn	15	15
722	A156a	12.45g	lake	15	15
723	A156a	18.15g	orange	25	20
724	A156a	23.40g	violet	30	22
725	A156a	36g	rose red	50	35
			Set value	1.60	1.25

Vatican II, the 21st Ecumenical Council of the Roman Catholic Church, which opened Oct. 11, 1962.
Nos. 720-725 are airmail.

Europa A157

1962, Dec. 17 ***Perf. 11***

726 A157 4g yel, red & brn
727 A157 36g multi, diff.
a. Souvenir sheet of 2, #726-727

No. 727 is airmail.

Solar System A158

Designs: 12.45g, 36g, 50g, Inner planets, Jupiter and rocket.

Perf. 14x13½

1962, Dec. 17 **Wmk. 346**

728	A158	10c	org & purple
729	A158	20c	org & brn vio
730	A158	25c	org & dark vio
731	A158	30c	org & ultra
732	A158	50c	org & dull green
733	A158	12.45g	org & brown
734	A158	36g	org & blue
735	A158	50g	org & green
a.			Souvenir sheet of 1

Nos. 733-735 are airmail.

The following stamps exist imperf. in different colors: Nos. 736-743a, 744-751a, 752-759a, 760-766a, 775-782a, 783-790a, 791-798a, 799-805a, 806-813a, 814-821a, 828-835a, 836-843, 841a, 850-857a, 858-865a, 871-878, 876a, 887-894a, 895-902, 900a, 903-910a, 911-918a, 919-926a, 927-934a, 943-950a, 951-958a, 959-966a, 978-985a, 986-993a, 994-1001a, 1002-1003, 1003d, 1004-1007a, 1051-1059, B12-B19.

Pierre de Coubertin (1836-1937), Founder of Modern Olympic Games — A159

Summer Olympic Games sites and: Nos. 12.45g, 18.15g, 36g, Torch bearer in stadium.

Perf. 14x13½

1963, Feb. 16 **Wmk. 346**

736	A159	15c	Athens, 1896
737	A159	25c	Paris, 1900
738	A159	30c	St. Louis, 1904
739	A159	40c	London, 1908
740	A159	50c	Stockholm, 1912
741	A159	12.45g	No games, 1916
742	A159	18.15g	Antwerp, 1920
743	A159	36g	Paris, 1924
a.			Souvenir sheet of 1

Nos. 741-743a are airmail.

Walter M. Schirra, US Astronaut — A160

Design: 12.45g, 36g, 50g, Schirra.

1963, Mar. 16 ***Perf. 13½x14***

744	A160	10c	brn org & blk
745	A160	20c	car & blk
746	A160	25c	lake & blk
747	A160	30c	ver & blk
748	A160	50c	mag & blk
749	A160	12.45g	bl blk & lake
750	A160	36g	dl gray vio & lake
751	A160	50g	dk grn bl & lake
a.			Souvenir sheet of 1

Nos. 749-751a are airmail.

Winter Olympics A161

Games sites and: 12.45g, 36g, 50g, Snowflake.

1963, May 16 ***Perf. 14x13½***

752	A161	10g	Chamonix, 1924
753	A161	20c	St. Moritz, 1928
754	A161	25c	Lake Placid, 1932
755	A161	30c	Garmisch-Partenkirchen, 1936
756	A161	50c	St. Moritz, 1948
757	A161	12.45g	Oslo, 1952
758	A161	36g	Cortina d'Ampezzo, 1956
759	A161	50g	Squaw Valley, 1960
a.			Souvenir sheet of 1

Nos. 757-759a are airmail.

Freedom from Hunger A162

Perf. 13½x14, 14x13½

1963, May 31

760	A162	10c	yel grn & brn
761	A162	25c	lt bl & brn
762	A162	50c	lt grn bl & brn
763	A162	75c	lt lil & brn
764	A162	18.15g	yel org & brn
765	A162	36g	lt bl grn & brn
766	A162	50g	bis & brn
a.			Souvenir sheet of 1

#760-763 are vert. #764-766a are airmail.

Pres. Alfredo Stroessner — A163

1963, Aug. 6 **Wmk. 347** ***Perf. 11***

767	A163	50c	ol gray & sep	15	15
768	A163	75c	buff & sepia	15	15
769	A163	1.50g	lt lil & sep	15	15
770	A163	3g	emer & sepia	15	15
771	A163	12.45g	pink & claret	18	15
772	A163	18.15g	pink & grn	25	22
773	A163	36g	pink & vio	75	50
			Set value	1.45	1.00

Third presidential term of Alfredo Stroessner. A 36g imperf. souvenir sheet exists.
Nos. 771-773 are airmail.

MUESTRA
Illustrations may show the word "MUESTRA." This means specimen and is not on the actual stamps.

Souvenir Sheet

Dag Hammarskjold, UN Secretary General — A164

1963, Aug. 21 **Unwmk.** ***Imperf.***

774 A164 2g Sheet of 2

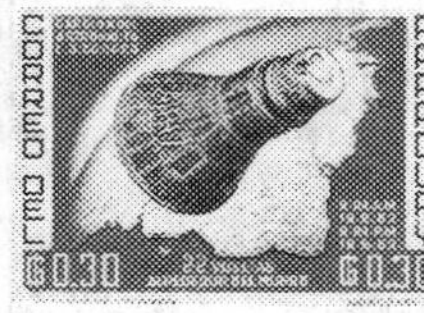
Project Mercury Flight of L. Gordon Cooper A165

Design: 12.45g, 18.15g, 50g, L. Gordon Cooper, vert.

Perf. 14x13½, 13½x14

1963, Aug. 23 **Litho.** **Wmk. 346**

775	A165	15c	brn & orange
776	A165	25c	brn & blue
777	A165	30c	brn & violet
778	A165	40c	brn & green
779	A165	50c	brn & red vio
780	A165	12.45g	brn & bl grn
781	A165	18.15g	brn & blue
782	A165	50g	brn & pink
a.			Souvenir sheet of 1

Nos. 780-782 are airmail.

1964 Winter Olympics, Innsbruck A166

Design: 12.45g, 18.15g, 50g, Innsbruck Games emblem, vert.

Perf. 14x13½, 13½x14

1963, Oct. 28 **Unwmk.**

783 A166 15c choc & red
784 A166 25c gray grn & red
785 A166 30c plum & red
786 A166 40c sl grn & red
787 A166 50c dp bl & red
788 A166 12.45g sep & red
789 A166 18.15g grn bl & red
790 A166 50g tan & red
a. Souvenir sheet of 1

Nos. 788-790 are airmail.

1964 Summer Olympics, Tokyo — A167

Design: 12.45g, 18.15g, 50g, Tokyo games emblem.

1964, Jan. 8 *Perf. 13½x14*

791 A167 15c blue & red
792 A167 25c org & red
793 A167 30c tan & red
794 A167 40c vio brn & red
795 A167 50c grn bl & red
796 A167 12.45g vio & red
797 A167 18.15g brn & red
798 A167 50g grn bl & red
a. Souvenir sheet of 1

Nos. 796-798 are airmail.

Intl. Red Cross, Cent. — A168

Designs: 10c, Helicopter. 25c, Space ambulance. 30c, Red Cross symbol, vert. 50c, Clara Barton, founder of American Red Cross, vert. 18.15g, Jean Henri Dunant, founder of Intl. Red Cross, vert. 36g, Red Cross space hospital, space ambulance. 50g, Plane, ship, ambulance, vert.

1964, Feb. 4 *Perf. 14x13½, 13½x14*

799 A168 10c vio brn & red
800 A168 25c bl grn & red
801 A168 30c dk bl & red
802 A168 50c ol blk & red
803 A168 18.15g choc, red, & pink
804 A168 36g grn bl & red
805 A168 50g vio & red
a. Souvenir sheet of 1

Nos. 803-805 are airmail.

Space Research A169

Designs: 15c, 25c, 30c, Gemini spacecraft rendezvous with Agena rocket. 40c, 50c, Future Apollo and Lunar Modules. 12.45g, 18.15g, 50g, Telstar communications satellite, Olympic rings, vert.

1964, Mar. 11

806 A169 15c vio & tan
807 A169 25c grn & tan
808 A169 30c bl & tan
809 A169 40c brt bl & red
810 A169 50c sl grn & red
811 A169 12.45g dk bl & tan
812 A169 18.15g dk grn bl & tan
813 A169 50g dp vio & tan
a. Souvenir sheet of 1

1964 Summer Olympic Games, Tokyo. Nos. 811-813a are airmail.

Rockets and Satellites A170

Designs: 15c, 25c, Apollo command module mock-up. 30c, Tiros 7 weather satellite, vert. 40c, 50c, Ranger 6. 12.45g, 18.15g, 50g, Saturn I lift-off, vert.

1964, Apr. 25

814 A170 15c brn & tan
815 A170 25c vio & tan
816 A170 30c Prus bl & lake
817 A170 40c ver & tan
818 A170 50c ultra & tan
819 A170 12.45g grn bl & choc
820 A170 18.15g bl & choc
821 A170 50g lil rose & choc
a. Souvenir sheet of 1

Nos. 819-821a are airmail.

Popes Paul VI, John XXIII and St. Peter's, Rome — A171

Design: 12.45g, 18.15g, 36g, Asuncion Cathedral, Popes Paul VI and John XXIII.

1964, May 23 **Wmk. 347**

822	A171	1.50g	claret & org	15	15
823	A171	3g	cl & dk grn	15	15
824	A171	4g	cl & bister	15	15
825	A171	12.45g	sl grn & lem	18	15
826	A171	18.15g	pur & lem	25	22
827	A171	36g	vio bl & lem	1.00	80
			Set value	1.55	1.25

National holiday of St. Maria Auxiliadora (Our Lady of Perpetual Help).
Nos. 825-827 are airmail.

United Nations — A172

Designs: 15c, John F. Kennedy. 25c, 12.45g, Pope Paul VI and Patriarch Atenagoras. 30c, Eleanor Roosevelt, Chairman of UN Commission on Human Rights. 40c, Relay, Syncom and Telstar satellites. 50c, Echo 2 satellite. 18.15g, U Thant, UN Sec. Gen. 50g, Rocket, flags of Europe, vert.

Perf. 14x13½, 14 (15c, 25c, 12.45g)

1964, July 30 **Unwmk.**

Size: 35x35mm (#830, 834), 40x29mm (#831-832, 835)

828 A172 15c blk & brn
829 A172 25c blk, bl & red
830 A172 30c blk & ver
831 A172 40c dk bl & sep
832 A172 50c vio & car
833 A172 12.45g blk, grn & red
834 A172 18.15g blk & grn

Perf. 13½x14

835 A172 50g multicolored
a. Souvenir sheet of 1

Nos. 833-835a are airmail.

Space Achievements — A173

Designs: 10c, 30c, Ranger 7, Moon, vert. 15c, 12.45+6g, Wernher von Braun looking through telescope, vert. 20c, 20+10g, John F. Kennedy, rockets, vert. 40c, 18.15+9g, Rockets, von Braun.

1964, Sept. 12 *Perf. 12½x12*

836 A173 10c bl & blk
837 A173 15c yel grn & brt pink
838 A173 20c yel org & bl
839 A173 30c mag & blk
840 A173 40c yel org, bl & blk
841 A173 12.45g +6g red & bl
a. Souvenir sheet of 2, #840-841
842 A173 18.15g +9g grn bl, brn & blk
843 A173 20g +10g red & bl

Nos. 841-843 are airmail.

Coats of Arms of Paraguay and France — A174

Designs: 3g, 12.45g, 36g, Presidents Stroessner and de Gaulle. 18.15g, Coats of Arms of Paraguay and France.

1964, Oct. 6 **Wmk. 347**

844	A174	1.50g	brown	15	15
845	A174	3g	ultramarine	15	15
846	A174	4g	gray	15	15
847	A174	12.45g	lilac	18	15
848	A174	18.15g	bl grn	25	22
849	A174	36g	magenta	1.00	80
			Set value	1.55	1.25

Visit of Pres. Charles de Gaulle of France.
Nos. 847-849 are airmail.

Boy Scout Jamborees — A175

Designs: 15c, 18.15g, Lord Robert Baden-Powell (1857-1941), Boy Scouts founder. 20c, 30c, 12.45g, Boy Scout emblem, map, vert.

1965, Jan. 15 **Unwmk.** *Perf. 14*

850 A175 10c Argentina, 1961
851 A175 15c Peru, canceled
852 A175 20c Chile, 1959
853 A175 30c Brazil, 1954
854 A175 50c Uruguay, 1957
855 A175 12.45g Brazil, 1960
856 A175 18.15g Venezuela, 1964
857 A175 30g Brazil, 1963
a. Souvenir sheet of 1, perf. 12x12½

Nos. 855-857a are airmail.

A176 A177

Olympic and Paraguayan Medals: 25c, John F. Kennedy. 30c, Medal of Peace and Justice, reverse. 40c, Gens. Stroessner and DeGaulle, profiles. 50c, 18.15g, DeGaulle and Stroessner, in uniform. 12.45g, Medal of Peace and Justice, obverse.

Litho. & Embossed

1965, Mar. 30 *Perf. 13½x13*

858 A176 15c multicolored
859 A176 25c multicolored
860 A176 30c multicolored

Perf. 12½x12

861 A176 40c multicolored
862 A176 50c multicolored
863 A176 12.45g multicolored
864 A176 18.15g multicolored
865 A176 50g multicolored
a. Souv. sheet of 1, perf. 13½x13

Nos. 863-865a are airmail. Medal on No. 865a is gold foil.

Overprint: "Centenario de la Epopeya Nacional 1.864-1.870"

Design: Map of Americas.

1965, Apr. 26 **Wmk. 347** *Perf. 11*

866	A177	1.50g	dull grn	15	15
867	A177	3g	car red	15	15
868	A177	4g	dark blue	15	15
869	A177	12.45g	brn & blk	15	15
870	A177	36g	brt lil & blk	50	35
			Set value	78	60

Centenary of National Epic. Not issued without overprint.
Nos. 869-870 are airmail.

Scientists — A178

Unwmk.

1965, June 5 **Litho.** *Perf. 14*

871 A178 10c Newton
872 A178 15c Copernicus
873 A178 20c Galileo
874 A178 30c like #871
875 A178 40c Einstein
876 A178 12.45g +6g like #873
a. Souvenir sheet of 2, #875-876
877 A178 18.15g +9g like #875
878 A178 20g +10g like #872

Nos. 876-878 are airmail.

Cattleya Warscewiczii A179

Ceibo Tree — A179a

1965, June 28 **Unwmk.** *Perf. 14½*

879	A179	20c	purple	15	15
880	A179	30c	blue	15	15
881	A179	90c	bright mag	15	15
882	A179	1.50g	green	15	15
883	A179a	3g	brn red	15	15
884	A179a	4g	green	15	15
885	A179	4.50g	orange	15	15
886	A179a	66g	brn org	75	50
			Set value	1.10	85

150th anniv. of Independence (1811-1961).
Nos. 883-884, 886 are airmail.

John F. Kennedy and Winston Churchill — A180

Designs: 15c, Kennedy, PT 109. 25c, Kennedy family. 30c, 12.45g, Churchill, Parliament building. 40c, Kennedy, Alliance for Progress emblem. 50c, 18.15g, Kennedy, rocket launch at Cape Canaveral. 50g, John Glenn, Kennedy, Lyndon Johnson examining Friendship 7.

1965, Sept. 4 *Perf. 12x12½*

887 A180 15c bl & brn
888 A180 25c red & brn
889 A180 30c vio & blk
890 A180 40c org & sep
891 A180 50c bl grn & sep
892 A180 12.45g yel & blk
893 A180 18.15g car & blk
894 A180 50g grn & blk
a. Souvenir sheet of 1

Nos. 892-894a are airmail.

ITU, Cent. A181

Satellites: 10c, 40c, Ranger 7 transmitting to Earth. 15c, 20g+10g, Syncom, Olympic rings. 20c, 18.15g+9g, Early Bird. 30c, 12.45g+6g, Relay, Syncom, Telstar, and Echo 2.

1965, Sept. 30

895 A181 10c dull bl & sep
896 A181 15c lilac & sepia
897 A181 20c ol grn & sep
898 A181 30c blue & sepia
899 A181 40c grn & sep
900 A181 12.45g +6g ver & sep
a. Souvenir sheet of 2, #899-900
901 A181 18.15g +9g org & sep
902 A181 20g +10g vio & sep

Nos. 900-902 are airmail.

Pope Paul VI, Visit to UN A182

Designs: 10c, 50c, Pope Paul VI, U Thant, A. Fanfani. 15c, 12.45g, Pope Paul VI, Lyndon B. Johnson. 20c, 36g, Early Bird satellite, globe, papal arms. 30c, 18.15g, Pope Paul VI, Unisphere.

1966, Nov. 19

903 A182 10c multicolored
904 A182 15c multicolored
905 A182 20c multicolored
906 A182 30c multicolored
907 A182 50c multicolored
908 A182 12.45g multicolored
909 A182 18.15g multicolored
910 A182 36g multicolored
a. Souvenir sheet of 1

Nos. 908-910a are airmail.

Astronauts and Space Exploration — A183

Designs: 15c, 50g, Edward White walking in space, June 3, 1965. 25c, 18.15g, Gemini 7 & 8 docking, Dec. 16-18, 1965. 30c, Virgil I. Grissom and John W. Young, Mar. 23, 1965. 40c, 50c, Edward White and James McDivitt, June 3, 1965. 12.45g, Photographs of lunar surface.

1966, Feb. 19 *Perf. 14*

911 A183 15c multicolored
912 A183 25c multicolored
913 A183 30c multicolored
914 A183 40c multicolored
915 A183 50c multicolored
916 A183 12.45g multicolored
917 A183 18.15g multicolored
918 A183 50g multicolored
a. Souvenir sheet of 1

Nos. 916-918a are airmail.

Events of 1965 — A184

Designs: 10c, Meeting of Pope Paul VI and Cardinal Spellman, Oct. 4, 1965. 15c, Intl. Phil. Exposition, Vienna. 20c, OAS, 75th anniv. 30c, 36g, Intl. Quiet Sun Year, 1964-65. 50c, 18.15g, Saturn rockets at NY World's Fair. 12.45g, UN Intl. Cooperation Year.

1965, Mar. 9

919 A184 10c multicolored
920 A184 15c multicolored
921 A184 20c multicolored
922 A184 30c multicolored
923 A184 50c multicolored
924 A184 12.45g multicolored
925 A184 18.15g multicolored
926 A184 36g multicolored
a. Souvenir sheet of 1

Nos. 924-926a are airmail.

1968 Summer Olympics, Mexico City — A185

Perf. 12½x12 (Nos. 927, 929, 931, 933), 13½x13

1966, Apr. 1

927 A185 10c shown
928 A185 15c God of Death
929 A185 20c Aztec calendar stone
930 A185 30c like No. 928
931 A185 50c Zapotec deity
932 A185 12.45g like No. 931
933 A185 18.15g like No. 927
934 A185 36g like No. 929
a. Souvenir sheet of 1

Nos. 932-934a are airmail.

St. Ignatius Type of 1958 and

St. Ignatius and San Ignacio Monastery A185a

1966, Apr. 20 **Wmk. 347** *Perf. 11*

935	A129	15c	ultramarine	15	15
936	A129	25c	ultramarine	15	15
937	A129	75c	ultramarine	15	15
938	A129	90c	ultramarine	15	15
939	A185a	3g	brown	15	15
940	A185a	12.45g	sepia	15	15
941	A185a	18.15g	sepia	15	15
942	A185a	23.40g	sepia	25	20
			Set value	75	62

350th anniv. of the founding of San Ignacio Guazu Monastery.
Nos. 939-942 are airmail.

German Contributors in Space Research — A186

Designs: 10c, 36g, Paraguay #835, C97, Germany #C40. 15c, 50c, 18.15g, 3rd stage of Europa 1 rocket, vert. 20c, 12.45g, Hermann Oberth, jet propulsion engineer, vert. 30c, Reinhold K. Tiling, builder of 1st German rocket, 1931, vert.

Perf. 12x12½ (Nos. 943, 950), 12½x12 (Nos. 945, 947, 949), 13½x13

1966, May 16 **Unwmk.**

943 A186 10c multicolored
944 A186 15c multicolored
945 A186 20c multicolored
946 A186 30c multicolored
947 A186 50c multicolored
948 A186 12.45g multicolored
949 A186 18.15g multicolored
950 A186 36g multicolored
a. Souvenir sheet of 1, perf. 12x13½x13x13½

Nos. 948-950a are airmail.

Writers — A187

1966, June 11 *Perf. 12x12½*

951 A187 10c Dante
952 A187 15c Moliere
953 A187 20c Goethe
954 A187 30c Shakespeare
955 A187 50c like #952
956 A187 12.45g like #953
957 A187 18.15g like #954
958 A187 36g like #951
a. Souvenir sheet of 1, perf. 13½x14

Nos. 956-958a are airmail.

Italian Contributors in Space Research — A188

Designs: 10c, 36g, Italian satellite, San Marco 1. 15c, 18.15g, Drafting machine, Leonardo Da Vinci. 20c, 12.45g, Map, Italo Balbo (1896-1940), aviator. 30c, 50c, Floating launch and control facility, satellite.

1966, July 11

959 A188 10c multicolored
960 A188 15c multicolored
961 A188 20c multicolored
962 A188 30c multicolored
963 A188 50c multicolored
964 A188 12.45g multicolored
965 A188 18.15g multicolored
966 A188 36g multicolored
a. Souvenir sheet of 1, perf. 13x13½

Nos. 964-966a are airmail.

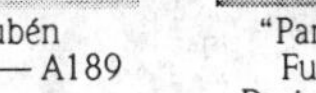

Rubén Dario — A189

"Paraguay de Fuego" by Dario — A189a

1966, July 16 **Wmk. 347**

967	A189	50c	ultramarine	15	15
968	A189	70c	bister brn	15	15
969	A189	1.50g	rose car	15	15
970	A189	3g	violet	15	15
971	A189	4g	greenish bl	15	15
972	A189	5g	black	15	15
973	A189a	12.45g	blue	15	15
974	A189a	18.15g	red lil	15	15
975	A189a	23.40g	org brn	25	15
976	A189a	36g	brt grn	38	18
977	A189a	50g	rose car	42	20
			Nos. 967-977 (11)	2.25	
			Set value		1.50

50th death anniv. of Ruben Dario (pen name of Felix Rubén Garcia Sarmiento, 1867-1916), Nicaraguan poet, newspaper correspondent and diplomat.
Nos. 973-977 are airmail.

Space Missions — A190

1966, Aug. 25 **Unwmk.**

978 A190 10c Gemini 8
979 A190 15c Gemini 9
980 A190 20c Surveyor 1 on moon
981 A190 30c Gemini 10
982 A190 50c like #981
983 A190 12.45g like #980
984 A190 18.15g like #979
985 A190 36g like #978
a. Souvenir sheet of 1, perf. 13x13½

Nos. 983-985a are airmail.

1968 Winter Olympics, Grenoble — A191

1966, Sept. 30 *Perf. 14*

986 A191 10c Figure skating
987 A191 15c Downhill skiing
988 A191 20c Speed skating
989 A191 30c 2-man luge
990 A191 50c like #989
991 A191 12.45g like #988

992 A191 18.15g like #987
993 A191 36g like #986
a. Souvenir sheet of 1

Nos. 987, 992, World Skiing Championships, Portillo, Chile, 1966. Nos. 991-993a are airmail.

Pres. John F. Kennedy, 3rd Death Anniv. — A192

Perf. 12x12½, 13½x14 (#997-998, 1001)

1966, Nov. 7

994 A192 10c Echo 1 & 2
995 A192 15c Telstar 1 & 2
996 A192 20c Relay 1 & 2
997 A192 30c Syncom 1, 2 & 3, Early Bird
998 A192 50c like #997
999 A192 12.45g like #996
1000 A192 18.15g like #995
1001 A192 36g like #994
a. Souvenir sheet of 1, perf. 13x14x13½x14

Nos. 999-1001a are airmail.

Paintings — A193

Portraits of women by: No. 1002a, 10c, De Largilliere. b, 15c, Rubens. c, 20c, Titian. d, 30c, Hans Holbein. e, 50c, Sanchez Coello.

Paintings: No. 1003a, 12.45g, Mars and Venus with United by Love by Veronese. b, 18.15g, Allegory of Prudence, Peace and Abundance by Vouet. c, 36g, Madonna and Child by Andres Montegna.

1966, Dec. 10 ***Perf. 14x13½***

1002 A193 Strip of 5, #a.-e.
1003 A193 Strip of 3, #a.-c.
d. Souvenir sheet of 1, #1003c

Nos. 1003a-1003d are airmail. No. 1003d has green pattern in border and is perf. 12½x12.

Holy Week Paintings A194

Life of Christ by: No. 1004a, 10c, Raphael. b, 15c, Rubens. c, 20c, Da Ponte. d, 30c, El Greco. e, 50c, Murillo, horiz.

12.45g, G. Reni. 18.15g, Tintoretto. 36g, Da Vinci, horiz.

Perf. 14x13½, 13½x14

1967, Feb. 28

1004 A194 Strip of 5, #a.-e.
1005 A194 12.45g multicolored
1006 A194 18.15g multicolored
1007 A194 36g multicolored
a. Souvenir sheet of 1

Nos. 1005-1007a are airmail. No. 1007a has salmon pattern in border and contains one 60x40mm, perf. 14 stamp.

Birth of Christ by Barocci A195

16th Cent. Paintings: 12.45g, Madonna and Child by Caravaggio. 18.15g, Mary of the Holy Family (detail) by El Greco. 36g, Assumption of the Virgin by Vasco Fernandes.

1967, Mar. 10 ***Perf. 14½***

1008 A195 10c lt bl & multi
1009 A195 15c lt grn & multi
1010 A195 20c lt brn & multi
1011 A195 30c lil & multi
1012 A195 50c pink & multi
1013 A195 12.45g lt bl grn & multi
1014 A195 18.15g brt pink & multi
1015 A195 36g lt vio & multi
a. Souv. sheet of 1, sep & multi

Nos. 1013-1015a are airmail.
Exist imperf. with changed borders.

Globe and Lions Emblem — A196

Medical Laboratory "Health" — A196a

Designs: 1.50g, 3g, Melvin Jones. 4g, 5g, Lions' Headquarters, Chicago. 12.45g, 18.15g, Library "Education."

1967, May 9 Litho. Wmk. 347

1016	A196	50c	light vio	15	15
1017	A196	70c	blue	15	15
1018	A196	1.50g	ultra	15	15
1019	A196	3g	brown	15	15
1020	A196	4g	Prussian grn	15	15
1021	A196	5g	ol gray	15	15
1022	A196a	12.45g	dk brn	15	15
1023	A196a	18.15g	violet	15	15
1024	A196a	23.40g	rose cl	15	15
1025	A196a	36g	Prus blue	30	18
1026	A196a	50g	rose car	35	20
			Set value	1.20	90

50th anniversary of Lions International.
Nos. 1022-1026 are airmail.

Vase of Flowers by Chardin A197

Still Life Paintings by: No. 1027b, 15c, Fontanesi, horiz. c, 20c, Cezanne. d, 30c, Van Gogh. e, 50c, Renoir.

Paintings: 12.45g, Cha-U-Kao at the Moulin Rouge by Toulouse-Lautrec. 18.15g, Gabrielle with Jean Renoir by Renoir. 36g, Patience Escalier, Shepherd of Provence by Van Gogh.

1967, May 16 ***Perf. 12½x12***

1027 A197 Strip of 5, #a.-e.
1028 A197 12.45g multicolored
1029 A197 18.15g multicolored
1030 A197 36g multicolored
a. Souvenir sheet of 1, perf. 14x12x14x13½

Nos. 1028-1030a are airmail. No. 1030a has a green pattern in border.

Exist imperf. with changed borders.

Famous Paintings — A198

1967, July 16 ***Perf. 12x12½***

1031 A198 10c Jan Steen

Perf. 14x13½, 13½x14

1032 A198 15c Frans Hals, vert.
1033 A198 20c Jordaens
1034 A198 25c Rembrandt
1035 A198 30c de Marees, vert.
1036 A198 50c Quentin, vert.
1037 A198 12.45g Nicolaes Maes, vert.
1038 A198 18.15g Vigee-Lebrun, vert.
1039 A198 36g Rubens, vert.

Souvenir Sheet

Perf. 12x12½

1040 A198 50g G. B. Tiepolo

Nos. 1037-1039 are airmail. An imperf. souvenir sheet of 3, #1037-1039 exists with dark green pattern in border.

John F. Kennedy, 50th Birth Anniv. A199

Kennedy and: 10c, Recovery of Alan Shepard's capsule, Lyndon Johnson, Mrs. Kennedy. 15c, John Glenn. 20c, Mr. and Mrs. M. Scott Carpenter. 25c, Rocket 2nd stage, Wernher Von Braun. 30c, Cape Canaveral, Walter Schirra. 50c, Syncom 2 satellite, horiz. 12.45g, Launch of Atlas rocket. 18.15g, Theorized lunar landing, horiz. 36g, Portrait of Kennedy by Torres. 50g, Apollo lift-off, horiz.

Perf. 14x13½, 13½x14

1967, Aug. 19

1041 A199 10c multicolored
1042 A199 15c multicolored
1043 A199 20c multicolored
1044 A199 25c multicolored
1045 A199 30c multicolored
1046 A199 50c multicolored
1047 A199 12.45g multicolored
1048 A199 18.15g multicolored
1049 A199 36g multicolored

Souvenir Sheet

1050 A199 50g multicolored

Nos. 1047-1050 are airmail. An imperf. souvenir sheet of 3 containing #1047-1049 exists with violet border.

Sculptures A200

1967, Oct. 16 ***Perf. 14x13½***

1051 A200 10c Head of athlete
1052 A200 15c Myron's Discobolus
1053 A200 20c Apollo of Belvedere
1054 A200 25c Artemis
1055 A200 30c Venus De Milo
1056 A200 50c Winged Victory of Samothrace
1057 A200 12.45g Laocoon Group
1058 A200 18.15g Moses
1059 A200 50g Pieta

Nos. 1057-1059 are airmail.

Mexican Art — A201

Designs: 10c, Bowl, Veracruz. 15c, Knobbed vessel, Colima. 20c, Mixtec jaguar pitcher. 25c, Head, Veracruz. 30c, Statue of seated woman, Teotihuacan. 50c, Vessel depicting a woman, Aztec. 12.45g, Mixtec bowl, horiz. 18.15g, Three-legged vessel, Teotihuacan, horiz. 36g, Golden mask, Teotihuacan, horiz. 50g, The Culture of the Totonac by Diego Rivera, 1950, horiz.

1967, Nov. 29 ***Perf. 14x13½***

1060 A201 10c multicolored
1061 A201 15c multicolored
1062 A201 20c multicolored
1063 A201 25c multicolored
1064 A201 30c multicolored
1065 A201 50c multicolored

Perf. 13½x14

1066 A201 12.45g multicolored
1067 A201 18.15g multicolored
1068 A201 36g multicolored

Souvenir Sheet

Perf. 14

1069 A201 50g multicolored

1968 Summer Olympics, Mexico City (#1065-1069).

Nos. 1066-1069 are airmail. An imperf. souvenir sheet of 3 containing #1066-1068 exists with green patter in border.

Paintings of the Madonna and Child A202

1968, Jan. 27 ***Perf. 14x13½,13½x14***

1070 A202 10c Bellini
1071 A202 15c Raphael
1072 A202 20c Correggio
1073 A202 25c Luini
1074 A202 30c Bronzino
1075 A202 50c Van Dyck
1076 A202 12.45g Vignon, horiz.
1077 A202 18.15g de Ribera
1078 A202 36g Botticelli

Nos. 1076-1078 are airmail and also exist as imperf. souvenir sheet of 3 with olive brown pattern in border.

Paintings of Winter Scenes — A203

1968 Winter Olympics Emblem A204

Perf. 13½x14, 14x13½

1968, Apr. 23

1079	A203	10c	Pissarro
1080	A203	15c	Utrillo, vert.
1081	A203	20c	Monet
1082	A203	25c	Breitner, vert.
1083	A203	30c	Sisley
1084	A203	50c	Brueghel, vert.
1085	A203	12.45g	Avercampe, vert.
1086	A203	18.15g	Brueghel, diff.
1087	A203	36g	P. Limbourg & brothers, vert.

Souvenir Sheet

1088 Sheet of 2
a. A204 50g multicolored

Nos. 1087-1088, 1088a are airmail. No. 1088 contains #1088a and #1087 with red pattern.

Paraguayan Stamps, Cent. (in 1970) — A205

Perf. 13½x14, 14x13½

1968, June 3 **Litho.**

1089	A205	10c	#1, 4
1090	A205	15c	#C21, 310, vert.
1091	A205	20c	#203, C140
1092	A205	25c	#C72, C61, vert.
1093	A205	30c	#638, 711
1094	A205	50c	#406, C38, vert.
1095	A205	12.45g	#B2, B7
1096	A205	18.15g	#C10, C11, vert.
1097	A205	36g	#828, C76, 616

Souvenir Sheet

Perf. 14

1098 Sheet of 2
a. A205 50g #929 & #379

Nos. 1095-1098a are airmail. No. 1098 contains No. 1098a and No. 1097 with light brown pattern in border.

Paintings A206

Designs: Nos. 1099-1106, paintings of children. Nos. 1107-1108, paintings of sailboats at sea.

1968, July 9 ***Perf. 14x13½, 13½x14***

1099	A206	10c	Russell
1100	A206	15c	Velazquez
1101	A206	20c	Romney
1102	A206	25c	Lawrence
1103	A206	30c	Caravaggio
1104	A206	50c	Gentileschi
1105	A206	12.45g	Renoir
1106	A206	18.15g	Copley
1107	A206	36g	Sessions, horiz.

Souvenir Sheet

Perf. 14

1108 Sheet of 2
a. A206 50g Currier & Ives, horiz.

1968 Summer Olympics, Mexico City (Nos. 1107-1108).

Nos. 1106-1108a are airmail. No. 1108 contains No. 1108a and No. 1107 with a red pattern in border.

WHO Emblem
A207 A207a

1968, Aug. 12 **Wmk. 347** ***Perf. 11***

1109	A207	3g	bluish grn	15	15
1110	A207	4g	brt pink	15	15
1111	A207	5g	bister brn	15	15
1112	A207	10g	violet	15	15
1113	A207a	30g	blk brn	30	18
1114	A207a	50g	rose claret	35	22
1115	A207a	100g	brt bl	75	45
			Set value	1.55	1.00

WHO, 20th anniv.; cent. of the natl. epic.

39th Intl. Eucharistic Congress A208

Paintings of life of Christ by various artists (except No. 1125a).

Perf. 14x13½

1968, Sept. 25 **Litho.** **Unwmk.**

1116	A208	10c	Caravaggio
1117	A208	15c	El Greco
1118	A208	20c	Del Sarto
1119	A208	25c	Van der Weyden
1120	A208	30c	De Patinier
1121	A208	50c	Plockhorst
1122	A208	12.45g	Bronzino
1123	A208	18.15g	Raphael
1124	A208	36g	Correggio

Souvenir Sheet

Perf. 14

1125 Sheet of 2
a. A208 36g Pope Paul VI
b. A208 50g Tiepolo

Pope Paul VI's visit to South America (No. 1125). Nos. 1122-1125b are airmail.

Events of 1968 A209

Designs: 10c, Mexican 25p Olympic coin. 15c, Rentry of Echo 1 satellite. 20c, Visit of Pope Paul VI to Fatima, Portugal. 25c, Dr. Christian Barnard, 1st heart transplant. 30c, Martin Luther King, assasination. 50c, Pres. Alfredo Stroessner laying wreath at grave of Pres. Kennedy, vert. 12.45g, Pres. Stroessner, Pres. Lyndon B. Johnson. 18.15g, John F. Kennedy, Abraham Lincoln, Robert Kennedy. 50g, Summer Olympics, Mexico City, satellite transmissions, vert.

Perf. 13½x14, 14x13½

1968, Dec. 21

1126	A209	10c	multicolored
1127	A209	15c	multicolored
1128	A209	20c	multicolored
1129	A209	25c	multicolored
1130	A209	30c	multicolored
1131	A209	50c	multicolored
1132	A209	12.45g	multicolored
1133	A209	18.15g	multicolored
1134	A209	50g	multicolored

Nos. 1132-1134 are airmail. Set exists imperf. in sheets of 3 in changed colors.

1968 Summer Olympics, Mexico City — A210

Olympic Stadium A210a

Gold Medal Winners: 10c, Felipe Munoz, Mexico, 200-meter breast stroke. 15c, Daniel Rebillard, France, 4000-meter cycling. 20c, David Hemery, England, 400-meter hurdles. 25c, Bob Seagren, US, pole vault. 30c, Francisco Rodriguez, Venezuela, light flyweight boxing. 50c, Bjorn Ferm, Sweden, modern pentathlon. 12.45g, Klaus Dibiasi, Italy, platform diving. 50g, Ingrid Becker, West Germany, fencing, women's pentathlon.

1969, Feb. 13 ***Perf. 14x13½***

1135	A210	10c	multicolored
1136	A210	15c	multicolored
1137	A210	20c	multicolored
1138	A210	25c	multicolored
1139	A210	30c	multicolored
1140	A210	50c	multicolored
1141	A210	12.45g	multicolored
1142	A210a	18.15g	multicolored
1143	A210	50g	multicolored

Nos. 1141-1143 are airmail. Set exists imperf. in sheets of 3 in changed colors.

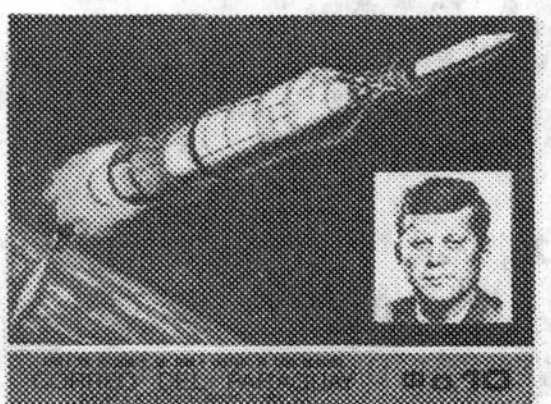

Space Missions — A211

Designs: 10c, Apollo 7, John F. Kennedy. 15c, Apollo 8, Kennedy. 20c, Apollo 8, Kennedy, diff. 25c, Study of solar flares, ITU emblem. 30c, Canary Bird satellite. 50c, ESRO satellite. 12.45g, Wernher von Braun, rocket launch. 18.15g, Global satellite coverage, ITU emblem. 50g, Otto Lilienthal, Graf Zeppelin, Hermann Oberth, evolution of flight.

1969, Mar. 10 ***Perf. 13½x14***

1144	A211	10c	multicolored
1145	A211	15c	multicolored
1146	A211	20c	multicolored
1147	A211	25c	multicolored
1148	A211	30c	multicolored
1149	A211	50c	multicolored
1150	A211	12.45g	multicolored
1151	A211	18.15g	multicolored
1152	A211	50g	multicolored

Nos. 1150-1152 are airmail. Set exists imperf. in sheets of 3 in changed colors.

"World United in Peace" — A212

1969, June 28 **Wmk. 347** ***Perf. 11***

1153	A212	50c	rose	15	15
1154	A212	70c	ultra	15	15
1155	A212	1.50g	light brn	15	15
1156	A212	3g	lil rose	15	15
1157	A212	4g	emerald	15	15
1158	A212	5g	violet	15	15
1159	A212	10g	brt lilac	15	15
			Set value	45	45

Peace Week.

Birds A213

Designs: 10c, Pteroglossus viridis. 15c, Phytotoma rutila. 20c, Porphyrula martinica. 25c, Oxyrunchus cristatus. 30c, Spizaetus ornatus. 50c, Phoenicopterus ruber. 75c, Amazona ochrocephala. 12.45g, Ara ararauna, Ara macao. 18.15g, Colibri coruscans.

Perf. 13½x14, 14x13½

1969, July 9 **Unwmk.**

1160	A213	10c	multicolored
1161	A213	15c	multicolored
1162	A213	20c	multicolored
1163	A213	25c	multicolored
1164	A213	30c	multicolored
1165	A213	50c	multicolored
1166	A213	75c	multicolored
1167	A213	12.45g	multicolored
1168	A213	18.15g	multicolored

Nos. 1167-1168 are airmail. Nos. 1161, 1164-1168 are vert.

Fauna A214

1969, July 9

1169	A214	10c	Porcupine
1170	A214	15c	Lemur, vert.
1171	A214	20c	3-toed sloth, vert.
1172	A214	25c	Puma
1173	A214	30c	Alligator
1174	A214	50c	Jaguar
1175	A214	75c	Anteater
1176	A214	12.45g	Tapir
1177	A214	18.15g	Capybara

Nos. 1176-1177 are airmail.

Olympic Soccer Champions, 1900-1968 A215

Designs: 10c, Great Britain, Paris, 1900. 15c, Canada, St. Louis, 1904. 20c, Great Britain, London, 1908 and Stockholm, 1912. 25c, Belgium, Antwerp, 1920. 30c, Uruguay, Paris, 1924 and Amsterdam, 1928. 50c, Italy, Berlin, 1936. 75c, Sweden, London, 1948; USSR, Melbourne, 1956. 12.45g, Yugoslavia, Rome, 1960. 18.15g, Hungary, Helsinki, 1952, Tokyo, 1964 and Mexico, 1968.

1969, Nov. 26 ***Perf. 14***

No.	Type	Value	Color
1178	A215	10c	multicolored
1179	A215	15c	multicolored
1180	A215	20c	multicolored
1181	A215	25c	multicolored
1182	A215	30c	multicolored
1183	A215	50c	multicolored
1184	A215	75c	multicolored
1185	A215	12.45g	multicolored
1186	A215	18.15g	multicolored

Nos. 1185-1186 are airmail.

A216

World Cup or South American Soccer Champions: 10c, Paraguay, 1953. 15c, Uruguay, 1930. 20c, Italy, 1934. 25c, Italy, 1938. 30c, Uruguay, 1950. 50c, Germany, 1954, horiz. 75c, Brazil, 1958. 12.45g, Brazil, 1962. 18.15g, England, 1966. No. 1198, Trophy.

1969, Nov. 26 ***Perf. 14***

No.	Type	Value	Color
1189	A216	10c	multicolored
1190	A216	15c	multicolored
1191	A216	20c	multicolored
1192	A216	25c	multicolored
1193	A216	30c	multicolored
1194	A216	50c	multicolored
1195	A216	75c	multicolored
1196	A216	12.45g	multicolored
1197	A216	18.15g	multicolored

Souvenir Sheet

Perf. 13½

1198 A216 23.40g multicolored

Nos. 1196-1198 are airmail. No. 1198 contains one 50x60mm stamp.

Paintings by Francisco de Goya (1746-1828) A217

Designs: 10c, Miguel de Lardibazal. 15c, Francisca Sabasa y Gracia. 20c, Don Manuel Osorio. 25c, Young Women with a Letter. 30c, The Water Carrier. 50c, Truth, Time and History. 75c, The Forge. 12.45g, The Spell. 18.15g, Duke of Wellington on Horseback. 23.40g, "La Maja Desnuda."

1969, Nov. 29 **Litho.** ***Perf. 14x13½***

No.	Type	Value	Color
1200	A217	10c	multicolored
1201	A217	15c	multicolored
1202	A217	20c	multicolored
1203	A217	25c	multicolored
1204	A217	30c	multicolored
1205	A217	50c	multicolored
1206	A217	75c	multicolored
1207	A217	12.45g	multicolored
1208	A217	18.15g	multicolored

Souvenir Sheet

Perf. 14

1209 A217 23.40g multicolored

Nos. 1207-1209 are airmail.

Christmas A218

Various paintings of The Nativity or Madonna and Child.

1969, Nov. 29 ***Perf. 14x13½***

No.	Type	Value	Design
1210	A218	10c	Master Bertram
1211	A218	15c	Procaccini
1212	A218	20c	Di Crediti
1213	A218	25c	De Flemalle
1214	A218	30c	Correggio
1215	A218	50c	Borgianni
1216	A218	75c	Botticelli
1217	A218	12.45g	El Greco
1218	A218	18.15g	De Morales

Souvenir Sheet

Perf. 13½

1219 A218 23.40g Isenheimer Altar

Nos. 1217-1219 are airmail.

Souvenir Sheet

European Space Program — A219

1969, Nov. 29 **Litho.** ***Perf. 14***

1220 A219 23.40g ESRO 1B

Imperf

1221 A219 23.40g Ernst Stuhlinger

Francisco Solano — A220

1970, Mar. 1 **Wmk. 347** ***Perf. 11***

No.	Type	Value	Color	Unused	Used
1222	A220	1g	bis brn	15	15
1223	A220	2g	violet	15	15
1224	A220	3g	brt pink	15	15
1225	A220	4g	rose claret	15	15
1226	A220	5g	blue	15	15
1227	A220	10g	bright grn	15	15
1228	A220	15g	lt Prus bl	15	15
1229	A220	20g	org brn	15	15
1230	A220	30g	gray grn	22	15
1231	A220	40g	gray brn	28	20
			Set value	1.00	80

Marshal Francisco Solano Lopez (1827-1870), President of Paraguay. Nos. 1228-1231 are airmail.

1st Moon Landing, Apollo 11 — A221

Designs: 10c, Wernher von Braun, lift-off. 15c, Eagle and Columbia in lunar orbit. 20c, Deployment of lunar module. 25c, Landing on Moon. 30c, First steps on lunar surface. 50c, Gathering lunar soil. 75c, Lift-off from Moon. 12.45g, Rendevouz of Eagle and Columbia. 18.15g, Pres. Kennedy, von Braun, splashdown. No. 1241, Gold medal of Armstrong, Aldrin and Collins. No. 1242, Moon landing medal, Kennedy, von Braun. No. 1243, Apollo 12 astronauts Charles Conrad and Alan Bean on moon, and Dr. Kurt Debus.

1970, Mar. 11 **Unwmk.** ***Perf. 14***

No.	Type	Value	Color
1232	A221	10c	multicolored
1233	A221	15c	multicolored
1234	A221	20c	multicolored
1235	A221	25c	multicolored
1236	A221	30c	multicolored
1237	A221	50c	multicolored
1238	A221	75c	multicolored
1239	A221	12.45g	multicolored
1240	A221	18.15g	multicolored

Souvenir Sheets

1241 A221 23.40g multicolored

Imperf

1242 A221 23.40g multicolored
1243 A221 23.40g multicolored

Nos. 1239-1243 are airmail. Nos. 1241-1242 contain one 50x60mm stamp, No. 1243 one 60x50mm stamp.

Easter A222

Designs: 10c, 15c, 20c, 25c, 30c, 50c, 75c, Stations of the Cross. 12.45g, Christ appears to soldiers, vert. 18.15g, Christ appears to disciples, vert. 23.40g, The sad Madonna, vert.

1970, Mar. 11

No.	Type	Value	Color
1244	A222	10c	multicolored
1245	A222	15c	multicolored
1246	A222	20c	multicolored
1247	A222	25c	multicolored
1248	A222	30c	multicolored
1249	A222	50c	multicolored
1250	A222	75c	multicolored
1251	A222	12.45g	multicolored
1252	A222	18.15g	multicolored

Souvenir Sheet

Perf. 13½

1253 A222 23.40g multicolored

Nos. 1251-1253 are airmail. No. 1253 contains one 50x60mm stamp.

Paraguay No. 2 — A223

Designs (First Issue of Paraguay): 2g, 10g, #1. 3g, #3. 5g, #2. 15g, #3. 30g, #2. 36g, #1.

1970, Aug. 15 **Litho.** **Wmk. 347**

No.	Type	Value	Color	Unused	Used
1254	A223	1g	car rose	15	15
1255	A223	2g	ultra	15	15
1256	A223	3g	org brn	15	15
1257	A223	5g	violet	15	15
1258	A223	10g	lilac	15	15
1259	A223	15g	vio brn	22	18
1260	A223	30g	dp grn	45	38
1261	A223	36g	brt pink	50	42
			Set value	1.40	1.20

Centenary of stamps of Paraguay.

1972 Summer Olympics, Munich A224

No. 1262: a, 10c, Discus. b, 15c, Cycling. c, 20c, Men's hurdles. d, 25c, Fencing. e, 30c, Swimming, horiz.

50c, Shotput. 75c, Sailing. 12.45, Women's hurdles, horiz. 18.15g, Equestrian, horiz. No. 1267, Flags, Olympic coins. No. 1268, Frauenkirche Church, Munich. No. 1269, Olympic Village, Munich, horiz.

1970, Sept. 28 **Unwmk.** ***Perf. 14***

No.	Type	Value	Color
1262	A224		Strip of 5, #a.-e.
1263	A224	50c	multicolored
1264	A224	75c	multicolored
1265	A224	12.45g	multicolored
1266	A224	18.15g	multicolored

Souvenir Sheets

Perf. 13½

1267 A224 23.40g multicolored

Imperf

1268 A224 23.40g multicolored
1269 A224 23.40g multicolored

Nos. 1265-1269 are airmail. Nos. 1267-1269 each contain one 50x60mm stamp.

Paintings, Pinakothek, Munich, 1972 A225

Nudes by: No. 1270a, 10c, Cranach. b, 15c, Baldung. c, 20c, Tintoretto. d, 25c, Rubens. e, 30c, Boucher, horiz. 50c, Baldung, diff. 75c, Cranach, diff.

12.45g, Self-portrait, Durer. 18.15g, Alterpiece, Altdorfer. 23.40g, Madonna and Child.

1970, Sept. 28 ***Perf. 14***

No.	Type	Value	Color
1270	A225		Strip of 5, #a.-e.
1271	A225	50c	multicolored
1272	A225	75c	multicolored
1273	A225	12.45g	multicolored
1274	A225	18.15g	multicolored

Souvenir Sheet

Perf. 13½

1275 A225 23.40g multicolored

Nos. 1273-1275 are airmail. No. 1275 contains one 50x60mm stamp.

Apollo Space Program — A226

No. 1276: a, 10c, Ignition, Saturn 5. b, 15c, Apollo 1 mission emblem, vert. c, 20c, Apollo 7, Oct. 1968. d, 25c, Apollo 8, Dec. 1968. e, 30c, Apollo 9, Mar. 1969.

50c, Apollo 10, May 1969. 75c, Apollo 11, July 1969. 12.45g, Apollo 12, Nov. 1969. 18.15g, Apollo 13, Apr. 1970. No. 1281, Lunar landing sites. No. 1282, Wernher von Braun, rockets. No. 1283, James A. Lovell, John L. Swigert, Fred W. Haise.

1970, Oct. 19 ***Perf. 14***

1276 A226 Strip of 5, #a.-e.
1277 A226 50c multicolored
1278 A226 75c multicolored
1279 A226 12.45g multicolored
1280 A226 18.15g multicolored

Souvenir Sheets

Perf. 13½

1281 A226 23.40g multicolored

Imperf

1282 A226 23.40g multicolored
1283 A226 23.40g multicolored

Nos. 1279-1283 are airmail. Nos. 1281-1283 each contain one 60x50mm stamp.

1970, Oct. 19 ***Perf. 14***

Future Space Projects: No. 1284a, 10c, Space station, 2000. b, 15c, Lunar station, vert. c, 20c, Space transport. d, 25c, Lunar rover. e, 30c, Skylab.

50c, Space station, 1971. 75c, Lunar vehicle. 12.45g, Lunar vehicle, diff., vert. 18.15g, Vehicle rising above lunar surface. 23.40g, Moon stations, transport.

1284 A226 Strip of 5, #a.-e.
1285 A226 50c multicolored
1286 A226 75c multicolored
1287 A226 12.45g multicolored
1288 A226 18.15g multicolored

Souvenir Sheet

Perf. 13½

1289 A226 23.40g multicolored

Nos. 1287-1289 are airmail. No. 1289 contains one 50x60mm stamp. For overprints see Nos. 2288-2290, C653.

EXPO '70, Osaka, Japan A228

Paintings from National Museum, Tokyo: No. 1288a, 10c, Buddha. b, 15c, Fire, people. c, 20c, Demon, Ogata Korin. d, 25c, Japanese play, Hishikawa Moronobu. e, 30c, Birds.

50c, Woman, Utamaro. 75c, Samurai, Wantabe Kazan. 12.45c, Women Beneath Tree, Kano Hideroi. 18.15g, Courtesans, Torrii Kiyonaga. 50g, View of Mt. Fuji, Hokusai, horiz. No. 1296, Courtesan, Kaigetsudo Ando. No. 1297, Emblem of Expo '70. No. 1298, Emblem of 1972 Winter Olympics, Sapporo.

1970, Nov. 26 **Litho.** ***Perf. 14***

1290 A228 Strip of 5, #a.-e.
1291 A228 50c multicolored
1292 A228 75c multicolored
1293 A228 12.45g multicolored
1294 A228 18.15g multicolored
1295 A228 50g multicolored

Souvenir Sheets

Perf. 13½

1296 A228 20g multicolored
1297 A228 20g multicolored
1298 A228 20g multicolored

Nos. 1293-1298 are airmail. Nos. 1296-1298 each contain one 50x60mm stamp.

Flower Paintings A229

Artists: No. 1299a, 10c, Von Jawlensky. b, 15c, Purrmann. c, 20c, De Vlaminck. d, 25c, Monet. e, 30c, Renoir.

50c, Van Gogh. 75, Cezanne. 12.45g, Van Huysum. 18.15g, Ruysch. 50g, Walscappelle. 20g, Bosschaert.

1970, Nov. 26 ***Perf. 14***

1299 A229 Strip of 5, #a.-e.
1300 A229 50c multicolored
1301 A229 75c multicolored
1302 A229 12.45g multicolored
1303 A229 18.15g multicolored
1304 A229 50g multicolored

Souvenir Sheet

Perf. 13½

1305 A229 20g multicolored

Nos. 1302-1305 are airmail. No. 1305 contains one 50x60mm stamp.

Paintings from The Prado, Madrid — A230

Nudes by: No. 1306a, 10c, Titian. b, 15c, Velazquez. c, 20c, Van Dyck. d, 25c, Tintoretto. e, 30c, Rubens.

50c, Venus and Sleeping Adonis, Veronese. 75c, Adam and Eve, Titian. 12.45g, The Holy Family, Goya. 18.15g, Shepherd Boy, Murillo. 50g, The Holy Family, El Greco.

1970, Dec. 16 ***Perf. 14***

1306 A230 Strip of 5, #a.-e.
1307 A230 50c multicolored
1308 A230 75c multicolored
1309 A230 12.45g multicolored
1310 A230 18.15g multicolored
1311 A230 50g multicolored

Nos. 1309-1311 are airmail. No. 1307-1311 are vert.

1970, Dec. 16

Paintings by Albrecht Durer (1471-1528): No. 1312a, 10c, Adam and Eve. b, 15c, St. Jerome in the Wilderness. c, 20c, St. Eustachius and George. d, 25c, Piper and drummer. e, 30c, Lucretia's Suicide.

50c, Oswald Krel. 75c, Stag Beetle. 12.45g, Paul and Mark. 18.15g, Lot's Flight. 50g, Nativity.

1312 A230 Strip of 5, #a.-e.
1313 A230 50c multicolored
1314 A230 75c multicolored
1315 A230 12.45g multicolored
1316 A230 18.15g multicolored
1317 A230 50g multicolored

No. 1315-1317 are airmail. See No. 1273.

Christmas A232

Paintings: No. 1318a, 10c, The Annunciation, Van der Weyden. b, 15c, The Madonna, Zeitblom. c, 20c, The Nativity, Von Soest. d, 25c, Adoration of the Magi, Mayno. e, 30c, Adoration of the Magi, Da Fabriano.

50c, Flight From Egypt, Masters of Martyrdom. 75c, Presentation of Christ, Memling. 12.45g, The Holy Family, Poussin, horiz. 18.15g, The Holy Family, Rubens. 20g, Adoration of the Magi, Giorgione, horiz. 50g, Madonna and Child, Batoni.

1971, Mar. 23

1318 A232 Strip of 5, #a.-e.
1319 A232 50c multicolored
1320 A232 75c multicolored
1321 A232 12.45g multicolored
1322 A232 18.15g multicolored
1323 A232 50g multicolored

Souvenir Sheet

Perf. 13½

1324 A232 20g multicolored

Nos. 1321-1324 are airmail. No. 1324 contains one 60x50mm stamp.

1972 Summer Olympics, Munich A233

Olympic decathlon gold medalists: No. 1325a, 10c, Hugo Wieslander, Stockholm 1912. b, 15c, Helge Lovland, Antwerp 1920. c, 20c, Harald M. Osborn, Paris 1924. d, 25c, Paavo Yrjola, Amsterdam 1928. e, 30c, James Bausch, Los Angeles 1932.

50c, Glenn Morris, Berlin 1936. 75c, Bob Mathias, London 1948, Helsinki 1952. 12.45g, Milton Campbell, Melbourne 1956. 18.15g, Rafer Johnson, Rome 1960. 50g, Willi Holdorf, Tokyo 1964. No. 1331, Bill Toomey, Mexico City 1968. No. 1332, Pole vaulter, Munich, 1972.

1971, Mar. 23 ***Perf. 14***

1325 A233 Strip of 5, #a.-e.
1326 A233 50c multicolored
1327 A233 75c multicolored
1328 A233 12.45g multicolored
1329 A233 18.15g multicolored
1330 A233 50g multicolored

Souvenir Sheets

Perf. 13½

1331 A233 20g multicolored
1332 A233 20g multicolored

Nos. 1328-1332 are airmail. Nos. 1331-1332 each contain one 50x60mm stamp.

Art A234

Paintings by: No. 1333a, 10c, Van Dyck. b, 15c, Titian. c, 20c, Van Dyck, diff. d, 25c, Walter. e, 30c, Orsi.

50c, 17th cent. Japanese artist, horiz. 75c, David. 12.45g, Huguet. 18.15g, Perugino. 20g, Van Eyck. 50g, Witz.

1971, Mar. 26 ***Perf. 14***

1333 A234 Strip of 5, #a.-e.
1334 A234 50c multicolored
1335 A234 75c multicolored
1336 A234 12.45g multicolored
1337 A234 18.15g multicolored
1338 A234 50g multicolored

Souvenir Sheet

Perf. 13½

1339 A234 20g multicolored

Nos. 1336-1339 are airmail. No. 1339 contains one 50x60mm stamp.

Paintings from the Louvre, Paris

Portraits of women by: No. 1340a, 10c, De la Tour. b, 15c, Boucher. c, 20c, Delacroix. d, 25c, 16th cent. French artist. e, 30c, Ingres.

50c, Ingres, horiz. 75c, Watteau, horiz. 12.45g, 2nd cent. artist. 18.15g, Renoir. 20g, Mona Lisa, Da Vinci. 50g, Liberty Guiding the People, Delacroix.

1971, Mar. 26 ***Perf. 14***

1340 A234 Strip of 5, #a.-e.
1341 A234 50c multicolored
1342 A234 75c multicolored
1343 A234 12.45g multicolored
1344 A234 18.15g multicolored
1345 A234 50g multicolored

Souvenir Sheet

Perf. 13½

1346 A234 20g multicolored

Nos. 1343-1346 are airmail. No. 1346 contains one 50x60mm stamp.

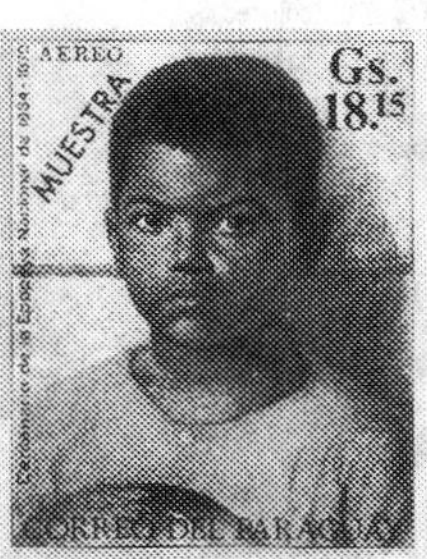

Paintings A236

Artist: No. 1347a, 10c, Botticelli. b, 15c, Titian. c, 20c, Raphael. d, 25c, Pellegrini. e, 30c, Caracci.

50c, Titian, horiz. 75c, Ricci, horiz. 12.45g, Courtines. 18.15g, Rodas. 50g, Murillo.

1971, Mar. 29 ***Perf. 14***

1347 A236 Strip of 5, #a.-e.
1348 A236 50c multicolored
1349 A236 75c multicolored
1350 A236 12.45g multicolored
1351 A236 18.15g multicolored
1352 A236 50g multicolored

Nos. 1350-1352 are airmail.

Hunting Scenes — A237

Different Paintings by: No. 1353a, 10c, Gozzoli, vert. b, 15c, Velazquez, vert. c, 20c, Brun. d, 25c, Fontainebleau School, 1550, vert. e, 30c, Uccello, vert.

50c, P. De Vos. 75c, Vernet. 12.45g, 18.15g, 50g, Alken & Sutherland. No. 1359, Paul & Derveaux. No. 1360, Degas.

1971, Mar. 29

1353 A237 Strip of 5, #a.-e.
1354 A237 50c multicolored
1355 A237 75c multicolored
1356 A237 12.45g multicolored
1357 A237 18.15g multicolored
1358 A237 50g multicolored

Souvenir Sheets

Perf. 13½

1359 A237 20g multicolored
1360 A237 20g multicolored

Nos. 1356-1360 are airmail. Nos. 1359-1360 each contain one 60x50mm stamp.

Philatokyo '71
A238

Designs: Nos. 1361a-1361e, 10c, 15c, 20c, 25c, 30c, Different flowers, Gukei. 50c, Birds, Lu Chi. 75c, Flowers, Sakai Hoitsu. 12.45g, Man and Woman, Utamaro. 18.15g, Tea Ceremony, from Tea museum. 50g, Bathers, Utamaro. No. 1367, Woman, Kamakura Period. No. 1368, Japan #1, #821, #904, #1023.

1971, Apr. 7 *Perf. 14*

1361 A238 Strip of 5, #a.-e.
1362 A238 50c multicolored
1363 A238 75c multicolored
1364 A238 12.45g multicolored
1365 A238 18.15g multicolored
1366 A238 50g multicolored

Souvenir Sheets

Perf. 13½

1367 A238 20g multicolored
1368 A238 20g multicolored

Nos. 1364-1368 are airmail. Nos. 1367-1368 each contain one 50x60mm stamp.
See Nos. 1375-1376.

1972 Winter Olympics, Sapporo
A239

Paintings of women by: No. 1369a, 10c, Harunobu. b, 15c, Hosoda. c, 20c, Harunobu, diff. d, 25c, Uemura Shoen. e, 30c, Ketao.

50c, Three Women, Torii. 75c, Old Man, Kakizahi. 12.45g, 2-man bobsled. 18.15g, Ice sculptures, horiz. 50g, Mt. Fuji, Hokusai, horiz. No. 1375, Skier, horiz. No. 1376, Sapporo Olympic emblems.

1971, Apr. *Perf. 14*

1369 A239 Strip of 5, #a.-e.
1370 A239 50c multicolored
1371 A239 75c multicolored
1372 A239 12.45g multicolored
1373 A239 18.15g multicolored
1374 A239 50g multicolored

Souvenir Sheets

Perf. 14½

1375 A239 20g multicolored

Perf. 13½

1376 A239 20g multicolored

Nos. 1372-1376 are airmail. No. 1375 contains one 35x25mm stamp with PhilaTokyo 71 emblem. No. 1376 contains one 50x60mm stamp.

For Japanese painting stamps with white border and Winter Olympics emblem, see Nos. 1409-1410.

UNESCO and Paraguay Emblems, Globe, Teacher and Pupil — A240

Wmk. 347

1971, May 18 **Litho.** *Perf. 11*

1377	A240	3g	ultra	15	15
1378	A240	5g	lilac	15	15
1379	A240	10g	emerald	15	15
1380	A240	20g	claret	15	15
1381	A240	25g	brt pink	18	15
1382	A240	30g	brown	20	15
1383	A240	50g	gray olive	35	25
			Set value	1.00	75

International Education Year.
Nos. 1380-1383 are airmail.

Paintings, Berlin-Dahlem Museum — A241

Artists: 10c, Caravaggio. No. 1385: a, 15c, b, 20c, Di Cosimo. 25c, Cranach. 30c, Veneziano. 50g, Holbein. 75c, Baldung. 12.45g, Cranach, diff. 18.15g, Durer. 50g, Schongauer.

1971, Dec. 24 **Unwmk.** *Perf. 14*

1384 A241 10c multicolored
1385 A241 Pair, #a.-b.
1386 A241 25c multicolored
1387 A241 30c multicolored
1388 A241 50c multicolored
1389 A241 75c multicolored
1390 A241 12.45g multicolored
1391 A241 18.15g multicolored
1392 A241 50g multicolored

Nos. 1390-1392 are airmail. No. 1385 has continuous design.

Napoleon I, 150th Death Anniv.
A242

Paintings: No. 1393a, 10c, Desiree Clary, Gerin. b, 15c, Josephine de Beauharnais, Gros. c, 20c, Maria Luisa, Gerard. d, 25c, Juliette Recamier, Gerard. e, 30c, Maria Walewska, Gerard.

50c, Victoria Kraus, unknown artist, horiz. 75c, Napoleon on Horseback, Chabord. 12.45g, Trafalgar, A. Mayer, horiz. 18.15g, Napoleon Leading Army, Gautherot, horiz.

50g, Napoleon's tomb.

1971, Dec. 24

1393 A242 Strip of 5, #a.-e.
1394 A242 50c multicolored
1395 A242 75c multicolored
1396 A242 12.45g multicolored
1397 A242 18.15g multicolored
1398 A242 50g multicolored

Nos. 1396-1398 are airmail.

Locomotives — A243

Designs: No. 1399a, 10c, Trevithick, Great Britain, 1804. b, 15c, Blenkinsops, 1812. c, 20c, G. Stephenson #1, 1825. d, 25c, Marc Seguin, France, 1829. e, 30c, "Adler," Germany, 1835.

50c, Sampierdarena #1, Italy, 1854. 75c, Paraguay #1, 1861. 12.45g, "Munich," Germany, 1841. 18.15g, US, 1875. 20g, Japanese locomotives, 1872-1972. 50g, Mikado D-50, Japan, 1923.

1972, Jan. 6

1399 A243 Strip of 5, #a.-e.
1400 A243 50c multicolored
1401 A243 75c multicolored
1402 A243 12.45g multicolored
1403 A243 18.15g multicolored
1404 A243 50g multicolored

Souvenir Sheet

Perf. 13½

1405 A243 20g multicolored

Nos. 1402-1405 are airmail. No. 1405 contains one 60x50mm stamp.
See Nos. 1476-1480.

1972 Winter Olympics, Sapporo — A244

Designs: Nos. 1406a, 10c, Hockey player. b, 15c, Jean-Claude Killy. c, 20c, Gaby Seyfert. d, 25c, 4-Man bobsled. e, 30c, Luge.

50c, Ski jumping, horiz. 75c, Slalom skiing, horiz. 12.45g, Painting, Kuniyoshi. 18.15g, Winter Scene, Hiroshige, horiz. 50g, Ski lift, man in traditional dress.

1972, Jan. 6 *Perf. 14*

1406 A244 Strip of 5, #a.-e.
1407 A244 50c multicolored
1408 A244 75c multicolored
1409 A244 12.45g multicolored
1410 A244 18.15g multicolored
1411 A244 50g multicolored

Souvenir Sheet

Perf. 13½

1412 A244 20g Skier
1413 A244 20g Flags

Nos. 1409-1413 are airmail. Nos. 1412-1413 each contain one 50x60mm stamp. For overprint see Nos. 2295-2297. For Winter Olympic stamps with gold border, see Nos. 1372-1373.

UNICEF, 25th Anniv. (in 1971) — A245

1972, Jan. 24

Granite Paper

1414	A245	1g	red brn	15	15
1415	A245	2g	ultra	15	15
1416	A245	3g	lil rose	15	15
1417	A245	4g	violet	15	15
1418	A245	5g	emerald	15	15
1419	A245	10g	claret	15	15
1420	A245	20g	brt bl	15	15
1421	A245	25g	lt ol	18	15
1422	A245	30g	dk brn	20	15
			Set value	82	65

Nos. 1420-1422 are airmail.

Race Cars — A246

Designs: No. 1423a, 10c, Ferrari. b, 15c, B.R.M. c, 20c, Brabham. d, 25c, March. e, 30c, Honda.

50c, Matra-Simca MS 650. 75c, Porsche. 12.45g, Maserati-8 CTF, 1938. 18.15g, Bugatti 35B, 1929. 20g, Lotus 72 Ford. 50g, Mercedes, 1924.

1972, Mar. 20 **Unwmk.** *Perf. 14*

1423 A246 Strip of 5, #a.-e.
1424 A246 50c multicolored
1425 A246 75c multicolored
1426 A246 12.45g multicolored
1427 A246 18.15g multicolored
1428 A246 50g multicolored

Souvenir Sheet

Perf. 13½

1429 A246 20g multicolored

Nos. 1426-1429 are airmail. No. 1429 contains one 60x50mm stamp.

Sailing Ships — A247

Paintings: No. 1430a, 10c, Holbein. b, 15c, Nagasaki print. c, 20c, Intrepid, Roux. d, 25c, Portuguese ship, unknown artist. e, 30c, Mount Vernon, US, 1798, Corne.

50c, Van Eertvelt, vert. 75c, Santa Maria, Van Eertvelt, vert. 12.45g, Royal Prince, 1679, Van Beecq. 18.15g, Van Bree. 50g, Book of Arms, 1497, vert.

1972, Mar. 29 *Perf. 14*

1430 A247 Strip of 5, #a.-e.
1431 A247 50c multicolored
1432 A247 75c multicolored
1433 A247 12.45g multicolored
1434 A247 18.15g multicolored
1435 A247 50g multicolored

Nos. 1433-1435 are airmail.

Paintings in Vienna Museum
A248

Nudes by: No. 1436a, 10c, Rubens. b, 15c, Bellini. c, 20c, Carracci. d, 25c, Cagnacci. e, 30c, Spranger.

50c, Mandolin Player, Strozzi. 75c, Woman in Red Hat, Cranach the elder. 12.45g, Adam and Eve, Coxcie. 18.15g, Legionary on Horseback, Poussin. 50g, Madonna and Child, Bronzino.

1972, May 22

1436 A248 Strip of 5, #a.-e.
1437 A248 50c multicolored
1438 A248 75c multicolored
1439 A248 12.45g multicolored
1440 A248 18.15g multicolored
1441 A248 50g multicolored

Nos. 1439-1441 are airmail.

Paintings in Asuncion Museum
A249

Designs: No. 1442a, 10c, Man in Straw Hat, Holden Jara. b, 15c, Portrait, Tintoretto. c, 20c,

Indians, Holden Jara. d, 25c, Nude, Bouchard. e, 30c, Italian School.

50c, Reclining Nude, Berisso, horiz. 75c, Carracci, horiz. 12.45g, Reclining Nude, Schiaffino, horiz. 18.15g, Reclining Nude, Lostow, horiz. 50g, Madonna and Child, 17th cent. Italian School.

1972, May 22

1442 A249		Strip of 5, #a.-e.	
1443 A249	50c	multicolored	
1444 A249	75c	multicolored	
1445 A249	12.45g	multicolored	
1446 A249	18.15g	multicolored	
1447 A249	50g	multicolored	

Nos. 1445-1447 are airmail.

Presidential Summit A250

Designs: No. 1448a, 10c, Map of South America. b, 15c, Brazil natl. arms. c, 20c, Argentina natl. arms. d, 25c, Bolivia natl. arms. e, 30c, Paraguay natl. arms.

50c, Pres. Emilio Garrastazu, Brazil. 75c, Pres. Alejandro Lanusse, Argentina. 12.45g, Pres. Hugo Banzer Suarez, Bolivia. 18.15, Pres. Stroessner, Paraguay, horiz. 23.40g, Flags.

1972, Nov. 18

1448 A250		Strip of 5, #a.-e.	
1449 A250	50c	multicolored	
1450 A250	75c	multicolored	
1451 A250	12.45g	multicolored	
1452 A250	18.15g	multicolored	

Souvenir Sheet

Perf. 13½

1453 A250 23.40g multicolored

Nos. 1451-1453 are airmail. No. 1453 contains one 50x60mm stamp. For overprint see No. 2144.

Pres. Stroessner's Visit to Japan A251

Designs: No. 1454a, 10c, Departure of first Japanese mission to US & Europe, 1871. b, 15c, First railroad, Tokyo-Yokahama, 1872. c, 20c, Samurai. d, 25c, Geishas. e, 30c, Cranes, Hiroshige.

50c, Honda race car. 75c, Pres. Stroessner, Emperor Hirohito, Mt. Fuji, bullet train, horiz. 12.45g, Rocket. 18.15g, Stroessner, Hirohito, horiz. No. 1459, Mounted samurai, Masanobu, 1740. No. 1460, Hirohito's speech, state dinner, horiz. No. 1461, Delegations at Tokyo airport, horiz.

1972, Nov. 18 ***Perf. 14***

1454 A251		Strip of 5, #a.-e.	
1455 A251	50c	multicolored	
1456 A251	75c	multicolored	
1457 A251	12.45g	multicolored	
1458 A251	18.15g	multicolored	

Souvenir Sheets

Perf. 13½

1459 A251 23.40g multicolored
1460 A251 23.40g multicolored

Imperf

1461 A251 23.40g multicolored

Nos. 1457-1461 are airmail. Nos. 1459-1460 each contain one 50x60mm stamp. No. 1461 contains one 85x42mm stamp with simulated perforations. For overprints see Nos. 2192-2194, 2267.

Wildlife — A252

Paintings: No. 1462a, 10c, Cranes, Botke. b, 15c, Tiger, Utamaro. c, 20c, Horses, Arenys. d, 25c, Pheasant, Dietzsch. e, 30c, Monkey, Brueghel, the Elder. All vert.

50c, Deer, Marc. 75c, Crab, Durer. 12.45g, Rooster, Jakuchu, vert. 18.15g, Swan, Asselyn.

1972, Nov. 18 ***Perf. 14***

1462 A252		Strip of 5, #a.-e.	
1463 A252	50c	multicolored	
1464 A252	75c	multicolored	
1465 A252	12.45g	multicolored	
1466 A252	18.15g	multicolored	

Nos. 1465-1466 are airmail.

Acaray Dam A253

Designs: 2g, Francisco Solano Lopez monument. 3g, Friendship Bridge. 5g, Tebicuary River Bridge. 10g, Hotel Guarani. 20g, Bus and car on highway. 25g, Hospital of Institute for Social Service. 50g, "Presidente Stroessner" of state merchant marine. 100g, "Electra C" of Paraguayan airlines.

Perf. 13½x13

1972, Nov. 16 **Wmk. 347**

Granite Paper

1467 A253	1g	sepia	15	15
1468 A253	2g	brown	15	15
1469 A253	3g	brt ultra	15	15
1470 A253	5g	brt pink	15	15
1471 A253	10g	dl grn	15	15
1472 A253	20g	rose car	15	15
1473 A253	25g	gray	18	15
1474 A253	50g	violet	35	25
1475 A253	100g	brt lil	70	50
		Set value	1.60	1.20

Tourism Year of the Americas.
Nos. 1472-1475 are airmail.

Locomotives Type

Designs: No. 1476a, 10c, Stephenson's Rocket, 1829. b, 15c, First Swiss railroad, 1847. c, 20c, 1st Spanish locomotive, 1848. d, 2c, Norris, US, 1850. e, 30c, Ansaldo, Italy, 1859.

50c, Badenia, Germany, 1863. 75c, 1st Japanese locomotive, 1895. 12.45g, P.L.M., France, 1924. 18.15g, Stephenson's Northumbrian.

1972, Nov. 25 **Unwmk.** ***Perf. 14***

1476 A243		Strip of 5, #a.-e.	
1477 A243	50c	multicolored	
1478 A243	75c	multicolored	
1479 A243	12.45g	multicolored	
1480 A243	18.15g	multicolored	

Nos. 1479-1480 are airmail.

South American Wildlife — A254

No. 1481a, 10c, Tetradactyla. b, 15c, Nasua socialis. c, 20c, Priodontes giganteus. d, 25c, Blastocerus dichotomus. e, 30c, Felis pardalis.

50c, Aotes, vert. 75c, Rhea americana. 12.45g, Desmodus rotundus. 18.15g, Urocyon cinereoargenteus.

1972, Nov. 25

1481 A254		Strip of 5, #a.-e.	
1482 A254	50c	multicolored	
1483 A254	75c	multicolored	
1484 A254	12.45g	multicolored	
1485 A254	18.15g	multicolored	

Nos. 1484-1485 are airmail.

OAS Emblem — A255

Perf. 13x13½

1973 **Litho.** **Wmk. 347**

Granite Paper

1486 A255	1g	multi	15	15
1487 A255	2g	multi	15	15
1488 A255	3g	multi	15	15
1489 A255	4g	multi	15	15
1490 A255	5g	multi	15	15
1491 A255	10g	multi	15	15
1492 A255	20g	multi	15	15
1493 A255	25g	multi	18	15
1494 A255	50g	multi	35	25
1495 A255	100g	multi	70	50
		Set value	1.65	1.20

Org. of American States, 25th anniv.
Nos. 1492-1495 are airmail.

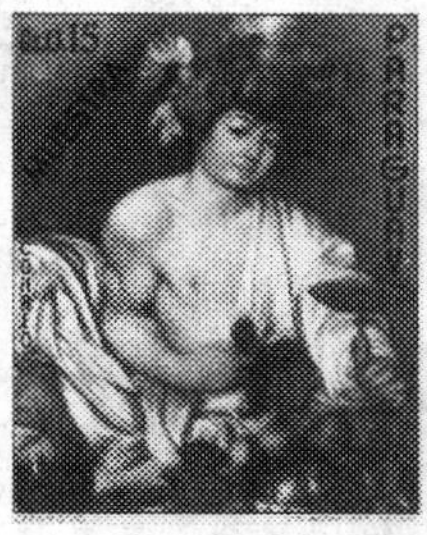

Paintings in Florence Museum A256

Artists: No. 1496a, 10c, Cranach, the Elder. b, 15c, Caravaggio. c, 20c, Fiorentino. d, 25c, Di Credi. e, 30c, Liss. f, 50c, Da Vinci. g, 75c, Botticelli.

No. 1497a, 5g, Titian, horiz. b, 10g, Del Piombo, horiz. c, 20g, De Michelino, horiz.

1973, Mar. 13 **Unwmk.** ***Perf. 14***

1496 A256 Strip of 7, #a.-g.
1497 A256 Strip of 3, #a.-c.

No. 1497 is airmail.

Butterflies — A257

Designs: No. 1498a, 10c, Catagramma patazza. b, 15c, Agrias narcissus. c, 20c, Papilio zagreus. d, 25c, Heliconius chestertoni. e, 30c, Metamorphadido. f, 50c, Catagramma astarte. g, 75c, Papilio brasiliensis.

No. 1499a, 5g, Agrias sardanapalus. b, 10g, Callithea saphhira. c, 20g, Jemadia hospita.

1973, Mar. 13

1498 A257 Strip of 7, #a.-g.
1499 A257 Strip of 3, #a.-c.

Nos. 1499 is airmail.

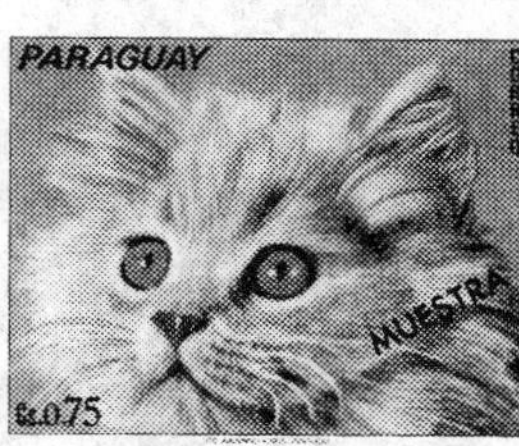

Cats A258

Faces of Cats: No. 1500a, 10c, b, 15c. c, 20c, d, 25c, e, 30c. f, 50c. g, 75c.

No. 1501a, 5g, Cat under rose bush, by Desportes. b, 10g, Two cats, by Marc, horiz. c, 20g, Man with cat, by Rousseau.

1973, June 29

1500 A258 Strip of 7, #a.-g.
1501 A258 Strip of 3, #a.-c.

Nos. 1500 is airmail. For other cat designs, see type A287.

Flemish Paintings A259

Nudes by: No. 1502a, 10c, Spranger. b, 15c, Jordaens. c, 20c, de Clerck. d, 25c, Spranger, diff. e, 30c, Goltzius. f, 50c, Rubens. g, 75c, Vase of flowers, J. Brueghel.

No. 1503a, 5g, Nude, de Clerck, horiz. b, 10g, Woman with mandolin, de Vos. c, 20g, Men, horses, Rubens, horiz.

1973, June 29 **Litho.** ***Perf. 14***

1502 A259 Strip of 7, #a.-g.
1503 A259 Strip of 3, #a.-c.

No. 1503 is airmail.

Hand Holding Letter — A260

EXPOPAR 73, Paraguayan Industrial Exhib. — A261

Wmk. 347

1973, July 10 **Litho.** ***Perf. 11***

1504 A260 2g lil rose & blk 15 15

No. 1504 was issued originally as a nonobligatory stamp to benefit mailmen, but its status was changed to regular postage.

1973, Aug. 11 ***Perf. 13x13½***

Granite Paper

1505 A261	1g	org brn	15	15
1506 A261	2g	vermilion	15	15
1507 A261	3g	blue	15	15
1508 A261	4g	emerald	15	15
1509 A261	5g	lilac	15	15
1510 A261	20g	lilac rose	15	15
1511 A261	25g	rose claret	18	15
		Set value	55	45

Nos. 1510-1511 are airmail.

1974 World Cup Soccer Championships, Munich — A262

No. 1512: a, 10c, Uruguay vs. Paraguay. b, 15c, Crerand, England and Eusebio, Portugal. c, 20c, Bobby Charlton, England. d, 25c, Franz Beckenbauer, Germany. e, 30c, Erler, Germany and McNab, England. f, 50c, Pele, Brazil and Willi Schulz, Germany. g, 75c, Arsenio Erico, Paraguay.

5g, Brian Labone, Gerd Mueller, Bobby Moore. No. 1514a, 10g, Luigi Riva, Italy. No. 1514b, 20g, World Cup medals. No. 1515, World Cup trophy.

1973 Litho. Unwmk. *Perf. 14*

1512 A262 Strip of 7, #a.-g.
1513 A262 5g multicolored
1514 A262 Pair, #a.-b.

Souvenir Sheet

Perf. 13½

1515 A262 25g multicolored

Nos. 1513-1515 are airmail. Issue dates: Nos. 1512-1514, Oct. 8. No. 1515, June 29. For overprint see No. 2131.

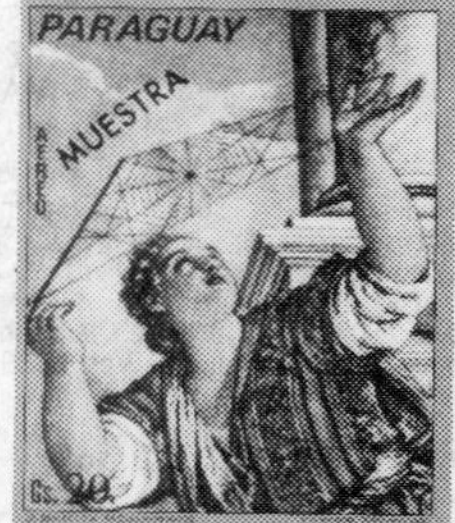

Paintings A263

Details from paintings, artist: No. 1517a, 10c, Lion of St. Mark, Carpaccio. b, 15c, Venus and Mars, Pittoni. c, 20c, Rape of Europa, Veronese. d, 25c, Susannah and the Elders, Tintoretto. e, 30c, Euphrosyne, Amigoni. f, 50c, Allegory of Moderation, Veronese. g, 75c, Ariadne, Tintoretto.

5g, Pallas and Mars, Tintoretto. No. 1519a, 10g, Portrait of Woman in Fur Hat, G.D. Tiepolo. b, 20g, Dialectic of Industry, Veronese.

1973, Oct. 8 ***Perf. 14***

1517 A263 Strip of 7, #a.-g.
1518 A263 5g multicolored
1519 A263 Pair, #a.-b.

Nos. 1518-1519 are airmail.

Birds A264

No. 1520: a, 10c, Tersina viridis. b, 15c, Pipile cumanensis. c, 20c, Pyrocephalus rubinus. d, 25c, Andigena laminirostris. e, 30c, Xipholena punicea. f, 50c, Tangara chilensis. g, 75, Polytmus guainumbi.

5g, Onychorhynchus mexicanus, vert. No. 1522a, 10g, Rhinocrypta lanceolata, vert. b, 20g, Trogon collaris, vert. 25g, Colibri florisuga mellivora, vert.

1973, Nov. 14

1520 A264 Strip of 7, #a.-g.
1521 A264 5g multicolored
1522 A264 Pair, #a.-b.

Souvenir Sheet

Perf. 13½

1523 A264 25g multicolored

Nos. 1521-1523 are airmail. No. 1523 contains one 50x60mm stamp.

Space Exploration — A265

Designs: No. 1524a, 10c, Apollo 11. b, 15c, Apollo 12. c, 20c, Apollo 13. d, 25c, Apollo 14. e, 30c, Apollo 15. f, 50c, Apollo 16. g, 75c, Apollo 17.

5g, Skylab. No. 1526a, 10g, Space shuttle. b, 20g, Apollo-Soyuz mission. No. 1527, Pioneer 11, Jupiter. No. 1528, Pioneer 10, Jupiter, vert.

1973, Nov. 14 ***Perf. 14***

1524 A265 Strip of 7, #a.-g.
1525 A265 5g multicolored
1526 A265 Pair, #a.-b.

Souvenir Sheet

Perf. 14½

1527 A265 25g multicolored

Perf. 13½

1528 A265 25g multicolored

#1525-1528 are airmail. #1527 contains on 35x25mm stamp, #1528 one 50x60mm stamp.

Souvenir Sheet

Women of Avignon, Pablo Picasso — A266

Illustration reduced.

1973, Nov. 14 ***Perf. 13½***

1529 A266 25g multicolored

Traditional Costumes A267

No. 1530: a, 25c, Indian girl. b, 50c, Bottle dance costume. c, 75c, Dancer balancing vase on head. d, 1g, Dancer with flowers. e, 1.50g, Weavers. f, 1.75g, Man, woman in dance costumes. g, 2.25g, Musicians in folk dress, horiz.

1973, Dec. 30 ***Perf. 14***

1530 A267 Strip of 7, #a.-g.

Flowers A268

Designs: No. 1531a, 10c Passion flower. b, 20c, Dahlia. c, 25c, Bird of paradise. d, 30c, Freesia. e, 40c, Anthurium. f, 50c, Water lily. g, 75c, Orchid.

1973, Dec. 31

1531 A268 Strip of 7, #a.-g.

Roses A269

Designs: No. 1532a, 10c, Hybrid perpetual. b, 15c, Tea scented. c, 20c, Japanese rose. d, 25c, Bouquet of roses and flowers. e, 30c, Rose of Provence. f, 50c, Hundred petals rose. g, 75c, Bouquet of roses, dragonfly.

1974, Feb. 2

1532 A269 Strip of 7, #a.-g.

Paintings in Gulbenkian Museum A270

Designs and artists: No. 1533a, 10c, Cupid and Three Graces, Boucher. b, 15c, Bath of Venus, Burne-Jones. c, 20c, Mirror of Venus, Burne-Jones. d, 25c, Two Women, Natoire. e, 30c, Fighting Cockerels, de Vos. f, 50c, Portrait of a Young Girl, Bugiardini. g, 75c, Madonna and Child, J. Gossaert.

5g, Outing on Beach at Enoshima, Utamaro. No. 1534a, 10g, Woman with Harp, Lowrence. b, 20g, Centaurs Embracing, Rubens.

1974, Feb. 4

1533 A270 Strip of 7, #a.-g.
1534 A270 5g multicolored
1535 A270 Pair, #a.-b.

Nos. 1534-1535 are airmail.

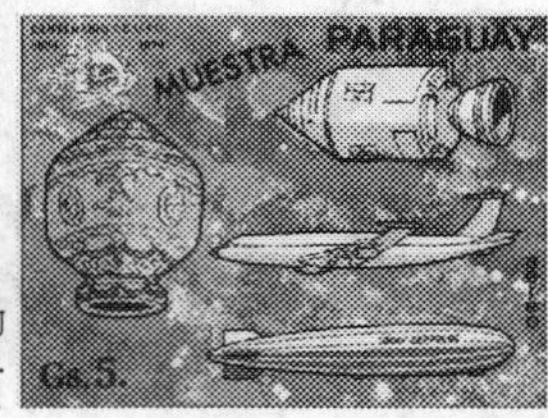

UPU Cent. A271

Horse-drawn mail coaches: No. 1536a, 10c, London. b, 15c, France. c, 20c, England. d, 25c, Bavaria. e, 30c, Painting by C.C. Henderson. f, 50c, Austria, vert. g, 75c, Zurich, vert.

5g, Hot air balloon, Apollo spacecraft, airplane, Graf Zeppelin. No. 1538a, 10g, Steam locomotive. b, 20g, Ocean liner, sailing ship. No. 1539, Airship, balloon. No. 1540, Mail coach crossing river.

1974, Mar. 20 ***Perf. 14***

1536 A271 Strip of 7, #a.-g.
1537 A271 5g multicolored
1538 A271 Pair, #a.-b.

Souvenir Sheets

Perf. 14½

1539 A271 15g multicolored

Perf. 13½

1540 A271 15g multicolored

Nos. 1537-1540 are airmail. No. 1539 contains one 50x35mm stamp, No. 1540 one 60x50mm stamp. Nos. 1539-1540 each include a 5g surtax for a monument to Francisco Solano Lopez. For overprint see No. 2127.

Paintings A272

Details from works, artist: No. 1541a, 10c, Adam and Eve, Mabuse. b, 15c, Portrait, Piero di Cosimo. c, 20c, Bathsheba in her Bath, Cornelisz. d, 25c, Toilet of Venus, Boucher. e, 30c, The Bathers, Renoir. f, 50c, Lot and his Daughters, Dix. g, 75c, Bouquet of Flowers, van Kessel.

5g, King's Pet Horse, Seele. No. 1543a, 10g, Woman with Paintbrushes, Batoni. b, 20g, Three Musicians, Flemish master.

1974, Mar. 20

1541 A272 Strip of 7, #a.-g.
1542 A272 5g multicolored
1543 A272 Pair, #a.-b.

Nos. 1542-1543 are airmail.

Sailing Ships — A272a

Designs: No. 1544a, 5c, Ship, map. b, 10c, English ship. c, 15c, Dutch ship. d, 20c, Whaling ships. e, 25c, Spanish ship. f, 35c, USS Constitution. g, 40c, English frigate. h, 50c, "Fanny," 1832.

1974, Sept. 13 ***Perf. 14½***

1544 A272a Strip of 8, #a.-h.

Strip price includes a 50c surtax.

Paintings in Borghese Gallery, Rome A273

Details from works and artists: No. 1545a, 5c, Portrait, Romano. b, 10c, Boy Carrying Fruit, Caravaggio. c, 15c, A Sybil, Domenichino. d, 20c, Nude, Titian. e, 25c, The Danae, Correggio. f, 35c, Nude, Savoldo. g, 40c, Nude, da Vinci. h, 50c, Nude, Rubens. 15g, Christ Child, Piero di Cosimo.

1975, Jan. 15 ***Perf. 14***
1545 A273 Strip of 8, #a.-h.

Souvenir Sheet
Perf. 14½
1546 A273 15g multicolored

No. 1546 is airmail and price includes a 5g surtax used for a monument to Francisco Solano Lopez.

Christmas A274

Paintings, artists: No. 1547a, 5c, The Annunciation, della Robia. b, 10c, The Nativity, G. David. c, 15c, Madonna and Child, Memling. d, 20c, Adoration of the Shepherds, Giorgione. e, 25c, Adoration of the Magi, French school, 1400. f, Madonna and Child with Saints, 35c, Pulzone. g, 40c, Madonna and Child, van Orley. h, 50c, Flight From Egypt, Pacher. 15g, Adoration of the Magi, Raphael.

1975, Jan. 17 ***Perf. 14***
1547 A274 Strip of 8, #a.-h.

Souvenir Sheet
Perf. 14½
1548 A274 15g multicolored

No. 1548 is airmail and price includes a 5g surtax for a monument to Francisco Solano Lopez.

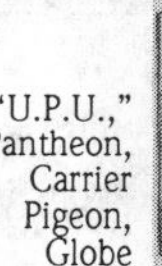

"U.P.U.," Pantheon, Carrier Pigeon, Globe A275

1975, Feb. Wmk. 347 ***Perf. 13½x13***

1549 A275	1g blk & lilac	15	15
1550 A275	2g blk & rose red	15	15
1551 A275	3g blk & ultra	15	15
1552 A275	5g blk & blue	15	15
1553 A275	10g blk & lil rose	15	15
1554 A275	20g blk & brn	15	15
1555 A275	25g blk & emer	18	15
	Set value	58	52

Centenary of Universal Postal Union.
Nos. 1554-1555 are airmail.

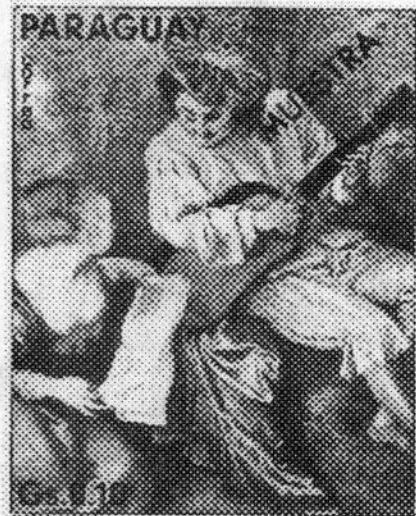

Paintings in National Gallery, London A276

Details from paintings, artist: 5c, The Rokeby Venus, Velazquez, horiz. 10c, The Range of Love, Watteau. 15c, Venus (The School of Love), Correggio. 20c, Mrs. Sarah Siddons, Gainsborough. 25c, Cupid Complaining to Venus, L. Cranach the Elder. 35c, Portrait, Lotto. 40c, Nude, Rembrandt. 50c, Origin of the Milky Way, Tintoretto. 15g, Rider and Hounds, Pisanello.

1975, Apr. 25 Unwmk. ***Perf. 14***
1556 A276 5c multicolored
1557 A276 10c multicolored
1558 A276 15c multicolored
1559 A276 20c multicolored
1560 A276 25c multicolored
1561 A276 35c multicolored
1562 A276 40c multicolored
1563 A276 50c multicolored

Souvenir Sheet
Perf. 13½
1564 A276 15g multicolored

No. 1564 is airmail, contains one 50x60mm stamp and price includes a 5g surtax for a monument to Francisco Solano Lopez.

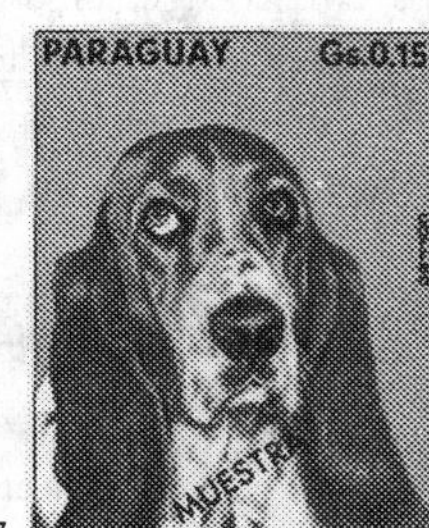

Dogs — A277

1975, June 7 ***Perf. 14***
1565 A277 5c Boxer
1566 A277 10c Poodle
1567 A277 15c Basset hound
1568 A277 20c Collie
1569 A277 25c Chihuahua
1570 A277 35c German shepherd
1571 A277 40c Pekinese
1572 A277 50c Chow

Souvenir Sheet
Perf. 13½
1573 A277 15g Fox hound, horse

No. 1573 is airmail, contains one 39x57mm stamp and price includes a 5g surtax for a monument to Francisco Solano Lopez.

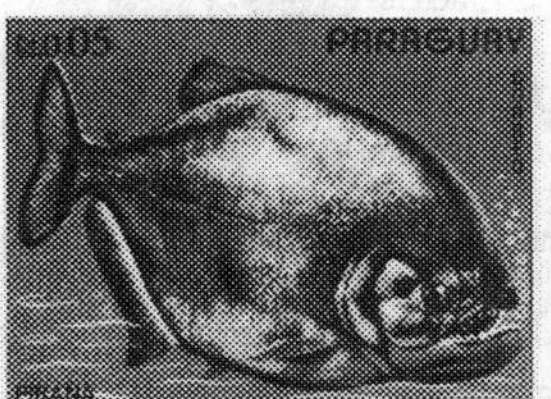

South American Fauna — A278

Designs: No. 1574a, 5c, Piranha (Pirana). b, 10c, Anaconda. c, 15c, Turtle (Tortuga). d, 20c, Iguana. e, 25c, Mono, vert. f, 35c, Mara. g, 40c, Marmota, vert. h, 50c, Peccary.

1975, Aug. 20 Litho. ***Perf. 14***
1574 A278 Strip of 8, #a.-h.

Souvenir Sheet
Perf. 13½
1575 A278 15g Aguara guazu

No. 1575 is airmail, contains and one 60x50mm stamp, and price includes a 5g surtax for a monument to Francisco Solano Lopez.
For overprints see Nos. 2197.

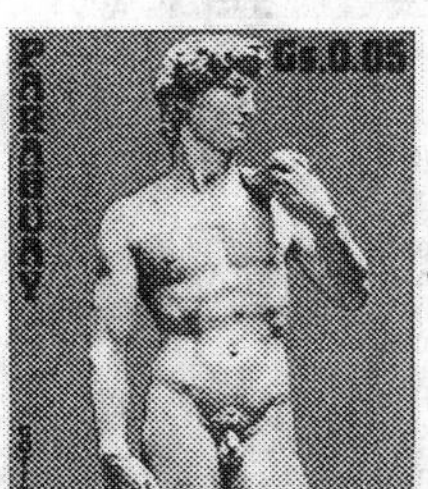

Michelangelo (1475-1564), Italian Sculptor and Painter A279

No. 1583: Statues, a, 5c, David. b, 10c, Aurora.

Paintings, c, 15c, Original Sin. d, 20c, The Banishment. e, 25c, The Deluge. f, 35c, Eve. g, 40c, Mary with Jesus and John. h, 50c, Judgement Day.
4g, Adam Receiving Life from God, horiz. No. 1585a, 5g, Libyan Sybil. b, 10g, Delphic Sybil. No. 1586, God Creating the Heaven and the Earth, horiz. No. 1587, The Holy Family.

1975, Aug. 23 Litho. ***Perf. 14***
1583 A279 Strip of 8, #a.-h.
1584 A279 4g multicolored
1585 A279 Pair, #a.-b.

Perf. 12
1586 A279 15g multicolored

Souvenir Sheet
Perf. 13½
1587 A279 15g multicolored

Nos. 1586-1587 sold for 20g with surtax for a monument to Francisco Solano Lopez. Nos. 1584-1587 are airmail.

Winter Olympics, Innsbruck, 1976 — A280

Designs: No. 1597a, 2g, Slalom skier. b, 3g, Cross country skier. c, 4g, Pair figure skating. d, 5g, Hockey.
No. 1598a, 10g, Speed skater. b, 15g, Downhill skier.

1975, Aug. 27 Litho. ***Perf. 14***
1596 A280 1g Luge
1597 A280 Strip of 4, #a.-d.
1598 A280 Pair, #a.-b.
1599 A280 20g 4-Man bobsled

Souvenir Sheet
Perf. 13½
1600 A280 25g Ski jumper
1601 A280 25g Woman figure skater

Nos. 1596, 1598-1601 are horiz. Nos. 1598-1601 are airmail. Nos. 1600-1601 each contain one 60x50mm stamp.

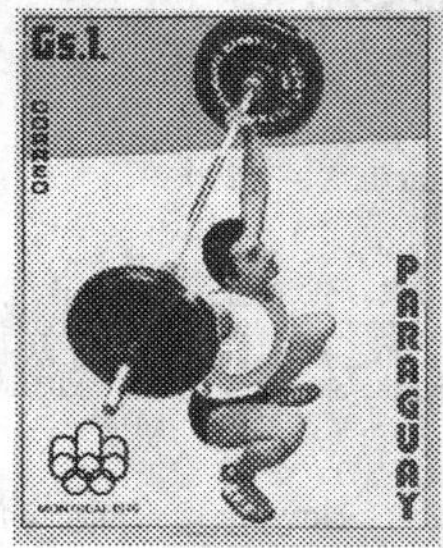

Summer Olympics, Montreal, 1976 A281

Designs: No. 1606a, 1g, Weightlifting. b, 2g, Kayak. c, 3g, Hildegard Flack, 800 meter run. d, Lasse Viren, 5,000 meter run. No. 1607a, 5g, Dieter Kottysch, boxing. b, 10g, Lynne Evans, archery. c, 15g, Akinori Kakayama, balance rings. 20g, Heide Rosendahl, broad jump. No. 1609, Decathlon. No. 1610, Liselott Linsenhoff, dressage, horiz.

1975, Aug. 28 ***Perf. 14***
1606 A281 Strip of 4, #a.-d.
1607 A281 Strip of 3, #a.-c.
1608 A281 20g multicolored

Souvenir Sheets
Perf. 14½
1609 A281 25g multicolored
1610 A281 25g multicolored

Nos. 1607b-1610 are airmail.

US, Bicent. — A282

Ships.

Unwmk.
1975, Oct. 20 Litho. ***Perf. 14***
1616 A282 5c Sachem, vert.
1617 A282 10c Reprisal, Lexington
1618 A282 15c Wasp
1619 A282 20c Mosquito, Spy
1620 A282 25c Providence, vert.
1621 A282 35c Yankee Hero, Milford
1622 A282 40c Cabot, vert.
1623 A282 50c Hornet, vert.

Souvenir Sheet
1624 A282 15g Montgomery

No. 1624 is airmail and contains one 50x70mm stamp.

US, Bicent. — A283

Details from paintings, artists: No. 1625a, 5c, The Collector, Kahill. b, 10c, Morning Interlude, Brackman, vert. c, 15c, White Cloud, Catlin, vert. d, 20c, Man From Kentucky, Benton, vert. e, 25c, The Emigrants, Remington. f, 35c, Spirit of '76, Willard, vert. g, John Paul Jones capturing Serapis, unknown artist. h, 50c, Declaration of Independence, Trumbull. 15g, George Washington, Stuart and Thomas Jefferson, Peale.

1975, Nov. 20 ***Perf. 14***
1625 A283 Strip of 8, #a.-h.

Souvenir Sheet
Perf. 13½
1625A A283 15g multicolored

No. 1625A is airmail, contains one 60x50mm stamp and price includes a 5g surtax for a monument to Francisco Solano Lopez.

Institute of Higher Education A284

Perf. 13½x13
1976, Mar. 16 Litho. Wmk. 347

1626 A284	5g vio, blk & red	15	15
1627 A284	10g ultra, blk & red	15	15
1628 A284	30g brn, blk & red	22	18
	Set value	34	28

Inauguration of Institute of Higher Education, Sept. 23, 1974.
No. 1628 is airmail.

The Scott Catalogue value is a retail price, what you could expect to pay for the stamp in a grade of Fine-Very Fine. The value listed is a reference which reflects recent actual dealer selling price.

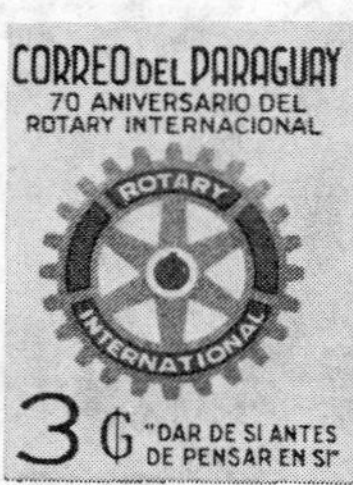

Rotary Intl., 70th Anniv. — A285

1976, Mar. 16 *Perf. 13x13½*

1629 A285	3g blk, bl & citron	15	15
1630 A285	4g car, bl & citron	15	15
1631 A285	25g emer, bl & lem	18	15
	Set value	28	22

No. 1631 is airmail.

IWY Emblem, Woman's Head — A286

1976, Mar. 16

1632 A286	1g ultra & brn	15	15
1633 A286	2g car & brn	15	15
1634 A286	20g grn & brn	15	15
	Set value	24	20

Intl Women's Year (1975).
No. 1634 is airmail.

Cats — A287

Various cats: No. 1635a, 5c. b, 10c. c, 15c. d, 20c. e, 25c. f, 35c. g, 40c. h, 50c. 15g.

1976, Apr. 2 Unwmk. *Perf. 14*

1635 A287 Strip of 8, #a.-h.

Souvenir Sheet

Perf. 13½

1636 A287 15g multicolored

No. 1636 is airmail, contains one 50x60mm stamp and price includes a 5g surtax for a monument to Francisco Solano Lopez.

See Nos. 2132-2133, 2201-2202, 2274-2275. For overprint see No. 2212.

Railroads, 150th Anniv. (in 1975) — A288

Locomotives: 1g, Planet, England, 1830. 2g, Koloss, Austria, 1844. 3g, Tarasque, France, 1846. 4g, Lawrence, Canada, 1853. 5g, Carlsruhe, Germany, 1854. 10g, Great Sagua, US, 1856. 15g, Berga, Spain. 20g, Encarnacion, Paraguay. 25g, English locomotive, 1825.

1976, Apr. 2 *Perf. 13x13½*

1637 A288 1g multicolored
1638 A288 2g multicolored
1639 A288 3g multicolored
1640 A288 4g multicolored
1641 A288 5g multicolored
1642 A288 10g multicolored
1643 A288 15g multicolored
1644 A288 20g multicolored

Souvenir Sheet

1645 A288 25g multicolored

Nos. 1642-1645 are airmail. No. 1645 contains one 40x27mm stamp.

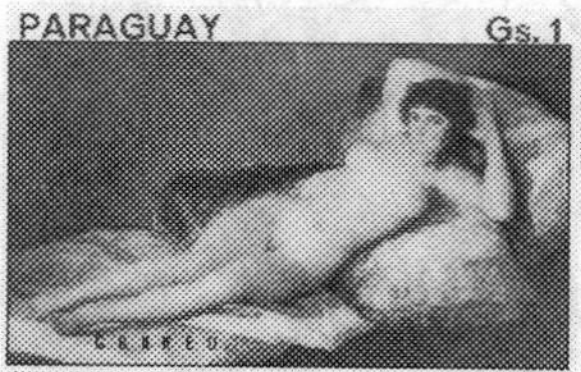

Painting by Spanish Artists — A289

Paintings: 1g, The Naked Maja by Goya. 2g, Nude by J. de Torres. 3g, Nude holding oranges by de Torres, vert. 4g, Woman playing piano by Z. Velazquez, vert. 5g, Knight on white horse by Esquivel. 10g, The Shepherd, by Murillo. 15g, The Immaculate Conception by Antolinez, vert. 20g, Nude by Zuloaga. 25g, Prince Baltasar Carlos on Horseback by D. Velasquez.

1976, Apr. 2 *Perf. 13x13½,13½x13*

1646 A289 1g multicolored
1647 A289 2g multicolored
1648 A289 3g multicolored
1649 A289 4g multicolored
1650 A289 5g multicolored
1651 A289 10g multicolored
1652 A289 15g multicolored
1653 A289 20g multicolored

Souvenir Sheet

1654 A289 25g multicolored

Nos. 1651-1654 are airmail. No. 1654 contains one 58x82mm stamp.

Butterflies — A290

Designs: No. 1655a, 5c, Prepona praeneste. b, 10c, Prepona proschion. c, 15c, Pereute leucodrosime. d, 20c, Agrias amydon. e, 25c, Morpho aegea gynandromorphe. f, 35c, Pseudatteria leopardina. g, 40c, Morpho helena. h, 50c, Morpho hecuba.

1976, May 12 Unwmk. *Perf. 14*

1655 A290 Strip of 8, #a.-h.

Farm Animals — A291

1976, June 15

1656 A291 1g Rooster, vert.
1657 A291 2g Hen, vert.
1658 A291 3g Turkey, vert.
1659 A291 4g Sow
1660 A291 5g Donkeys
1661 A291 10g Brahma cattle
1662 A291 15g Holstein cow
1663 A291 20g Horse

Nos. 1661-1663 are airmail.

US and US Post Office, Bicent. — A292

Designs: 1g, Pony Express rider. 2g, Stagecoach. 3g, Steam locomotive, vert. 4g, American steamship, Savannah. 5g, Curtiss Jenny biplane. 10g, Mail bus. 15g, Mail car, rocket train. 20g, First official missile mail, vert. No. 1672, First flight cover, official missile mail. No. 1673, US #C76 tied to cover by moon landing cancel.

1976, June 18

1664 A292 1g multicolored
1665 A292 2g multicolored
1666 A292 3g multicolored
1667 A292 4g multicolored
1668 A292 5g multicolored
1669 A292 10g multicolored
1670 A292 15g multicolored
1671 A292 20g multicolored

Souvenir Sheets

Perf. 14½

1672 A292 25g multicolored
1673 A292 25g multicolored

Nos. 1669-1673 are airmail and each contain one 50x40mm stamp.

Mythological Characters A293

Details from paintings, artists: No. 1674a, 1g, Jupiter, Ingres. b, 2g, Saturn, Rubens. c, 3g, Neptune, Tiepolo. d, 4g, Uranus and Aphrodite, Medina, horiz. e, 5g, Pluto and Prosperpine, Giordano, horiz. f, 10g, Venus, Ingres. g, 15g, Mercury, de la Hyre. 20g, Mars and Venus, Veronese.
25g, Viking Orbiter descending to Mars, horiz.

1976, July 18 *Perf. 14*

1674 A293 Strip of 7, #a.-g.
1675 A293 20g multicolored

Souvenir Sheet

Perf. 14½

1676 A293 25g multicolored

Nos. 1674f-1674g, 1675-1676 are airmail.

Sailing Ships A294

Paintings: No. 1677a, 1g, Venice frigate of the Spanish Armada, vert. b, 2g, Swedish war ship, Vasa, 1628, vert. c, 3g, Spanish galleon being attacked by pirates by Puget. d, 4g, Combat by Dawson. e, 5g, European boat in Japan, vert. f, 10g, Elizabeth Grange in Liverpool by Walters. g, 15g, Prussen, 1903, by Holst. 20g, Grand Duchess Elizabeth, 1902, by Bohrdt.

1976, July 15 *Perf. 14*

1677 A294 Strip of 7, #a.-g.
1678 A294 20g multicolored

Nos. 1677f-1678 are airmail.

German Sailing Ships — A295

Ship, artist: 1g, Bunte Kuh, 1402, Zeeden. 2g, Arms of Hamburg, 1667, Wichman, vert. 3g, Kaiser Leopold, 1667, Wichman, vert. 4g, Deutschland, 1848, Pollack, vert. 5g, Humboldt, 1851, Fedeler. 10g, Borussia, 1855, Seitz. 15g, Gorch Fock, 1958, Stroh, vert. 20g, Grand Duchess Elizabeth, 1902, Bohrdt. 25g, SS Pamir, Zeytline, vert.

Unwmk.

1976, Aug. 20 Litho. *Perf. 14*

1685 A295 1g multicolored
1686 A295 2g multicolored
1687 A295 3g multicolored
1688 A295 4g multicolored
1689 A295 5g multicolored
1690 A295 10g multicolored
1691 A295 15g multicolored
1692 A295 20g multicolored

Souvenir Sheet

Perf. 14½

1693 A295 25g multicolored

Intl. German Naval Exposition, Hamburg; NORDPOSTA '76 (No. 1693). Nos. 1690-1693 are airmail.

US Bicentennial A296

Western Paintings by: No. 1694a, 1g, E. C. Ward. b, 2g, William Robinson Leigh. c, 3g, A. J. Miller. d, 4g, Charles Russell. e, 5g, Frederic Remington. f, 10g, Remington, horiz. g, 15g, Carl Bodmer.

No. 1695, A. J. Miller. No. 1696, US #1, 2, 245, C76.

Unwmk.

1976, Sept. 9 Litho. *Perf. 14*

1694 A296 Strip of 7, #a.-g.
1695 A296 20g multicolored

Souvenir Sheet

Perf. 13x13½

1696 A296 25g multicolored

Nos. 1694f-1694g, 1695-1696 are airmail. No. 1696 contains one 65x55mm stamp.

1976 Summer Olympics, Montreal — A297

Gold Medal Winners: No. 1703a, 1g, Nadia Comaneci, Romania, gymnastics, vert. b, 2g, Kornelia Ender, East Germany, swimming. c, 3g, Luann Ryan, US, archery, vert. d, 4g, Jennifer Chandler, US, diving. e, 5g, Shirley Babashoff, US, swimming. f, 10g, Christine Stuckelberger, Switzerland, equestrian. g, 15g, Japan, volleyball, vert.
20g, Annegret Richter, W. Germany, running, vert. No. 1705, Bruce Jenner, US, decathlon. No. 1706, Alwin Schockemohle, equestrian. No. 1707, Medals list, vert.

Unwmk.

1976, Dec. 18 Litho. *Perf. 14*

1703 A297 Strip of 7, #a.-g.
1704 A297 20g multicolored

Souvenir Sheets

Perf. 14½

1705 A297 25g multicolored
1706 A297 25g multicolored
1707 A297 25g multicolored

Nos. 1703f-1703g, 1705-1707 are airmail. Nos. 1705-1706 each contain one 50x40mm stamp. No. 1707 contains one 50x70mm stamp.

Titian, 500th Birth Anniv. A298

Details from paintings: No. 1708a, 1g, Venus and Adonis. b, 2g, Diana and Callisto. c, 3g, Perseus and Andromeda. d, 4g, Venus of the Mirror. e, 5g, Venus Sleeping, horiz. f, 10g, Bacchanal, horiz. g, 15g, Venus, Cupid and the Lute Player. 20g, Venus and the Organist, horiz.

1976, Dec. 18 *Perf. 14*

1708 A298 Strip of 7, #a.-g.
1709 A298 20g multicolored

No. 1708f-1708g, 1709 are airmail.

Peter Paul Rubens, 400th Birth Anniv. A299

Paintings: No. 1710a, 1g, Adam and Eve. b, 2g, Tiger and Lion Hunt. c, 3g, Bathsheba Receiving David's Letter. d, 4g, Susanna in the Bath. e, 5g, Perseus and Andromeda. f, 10g, Andromeda Chained to the Rock. g, 15g, Shivering Venus. 20g, St. George Slaying the Dragon. 25g, Birth of the Milky Way, horiz.

1977, Feb. 18

1710 A299 Strip of 7, #a.-g.
1711 A299 20g multicolored

Souvenir Sheet

Perf. 14½

1712 A299 25g multicolored

Nos. 1710f-1710g, 1711-1712 are airmail.

US, Bicent. — A300

Space exploration: No. 1713a, 1g, John Glenn, Mercury 7. b, 2g, Pres. Kennedy, Apollo 11. c, 3g, Wernher von Braun, Apollo 17. d, 4g, Mercury, Venus, Mariner 10. e, 5g, Jupiter, Saturn, Jupiter 10/11. f, 10g, Viking, Mars. g, 15g, Viking A on Mars. 20g, Viking B on Mars. No. 1715, Future space projects on Mars, vert. No. 1716, Future land rover on Mars.

1977, Mar. 3 *Perf. 14*

1713 A300 Strip of 7, #a.-g.
1714 A300 20g multicolored

Souvenir Sheets

Perf. 13½

1715 A300 25g multicolored
1716 A300 25g multicolored

Nos. 1713f-1713g, 1714-1716 are airmail. No. 1715 contains one 50x60mm stamp, No. 1716 one 60x50mm stamp.

Olympic History A301

Designs: 1g, Spiridon Louis, marathon 1896, Athens, Pierre de Coubertin. 2g, Giuseppe Delfino, fencing 1960, Rome, Pope John XXIII. 3g, Jean Claude Killy, skiing 1968, Grenoble, Charles de Gaulle. 4g, Ricardo Delgado, boxing 1968, Mexico City, G. Diaz Ordaz. 5g, Hayata, gymnastics 1964, Tokyo, Emperor Hirohito. 10g, Klaus Wolfermann, javelin 1972, Munich, Avery Brundage. 15g, Michel Vaillancourt, equestrian 1976, Montreal, Queen Elizabeth II. 20g, Franz Klammer, skiing 1976, Innsbruck, Austrian national arms.

25g, Emblems of 1896 Athens games and 1976 Montreal games.

1977, June 7 *Perf. 14*

1717 A301 1g multicolored
1718 A301 2g multicolored
1719 A301 3g multicolored
1720 A301 4g multicolored
1721 A301 5g multicolored
1722 A301 10g multicolored
1723 A301 15g multicolored
1724 A301 20g multicolored

Souvenir Sheet

Perf. 13½

1725 A301 25g multicolored

Nos. 1722-1725 are airmail. No. 1725 contains one 49x60mm stamp.

LUPOSTA '77, Intl. Stamp Exhibition, Berlin A302

Graf Zeppelin 1st South America flight and: 1g, German girls in traditional costumes. 2g, Bull fighter, Seville. 3g, Dancer, Rio de Janeiro. 4g, Gaucho breaking bronco, Uruguay. 5g, Like #1530b. 10g, Argentinian gaucho. 15g, Ceremonial indian costume, Bolivia. 20g, Indian on horse, US.

No. 1734, Zeppelin over sailing ship. No. 1735, Ferdinand Von Zeppelin, zeppelin over Berlin, horiz.

1977, June 9 *Perf. 14*

1726 A302 1g multicolored
1727 A302 2g multicolored
1728 A302 3g multicolored
1729 A302 4g multicolored
1730 A302 5g multicolored
1731 A302 10g multicolored
1732 A302 15g multicolored
1733 A302 20g multicolored

Souvenir Sheets

Perf. 13½

1734 A302 25g multicolored
1735 A302 25g multicolored

Nos. 1731-1735 are airmail. No. 1734 contains one 49x60mm stamp, No. 1735 one 60x49mm stamp.

Mburucuya Flowers — A303

Weaver with Ostrich Feather Panel — A304

Designs: 1g, Ostrich feather panel. 2g, Black palms. 20g, Rose tabebuia. 25g, Woman holding ceramic pot.

Perf. 13x13½

1977 Litho. Wmk. 347

1736 A304	1g multicolored		15	15
1737 A303	2g multicolored		15	15
1738 A303	3g multicolored		15	15
1739 A304	5g multicolored		15	15
1740 A303	20g multicolored		25	18
1741 A304	25g multicolored		30	20
		Set value	75	55

Issue dates: 2g, 3g, 20g, Apr. 25; 1g, 5g, 25g, June 27.

Nos. 1740-1741 are airmail.

Aviation History — A305

Designs: No. 1742a, 1g, Orville and Wilbur Wright, Wright Flyer, 1903. b, 2g, Alberto Santos-Dumont, Canard, 1906. c, 3g, Louis Bleriot, Bleriot 11, 1909. d, 4g, Otto Lilienthal, Glider, 1891. e, 5g, Igor Sikorsky, Avion le Grande, 1913. f, 10g, Juan de la Cierva, Autogiro. g, 15g, Silvio Pettirossi, Deperdussin acrobatic plane. No. 1743, Concorde jet. No. 1744, Lindbergh, Spirit of St. Louis, Statue of Liberty, Eiffel Tower. No. 1745, Design of flying machine by da Vinci.

1977, July 18 Unwmk. *Perf. 14*

1742 A305 Strip of 7, #a.-g.
1743 A305 20g multicolored

Souvenir Sheet

Perf. 14½

1744 A305 25g multicolored
1745 A305 25g multicolored

Nos. 1742f-1745 are airmail. No. 1745 contains one label.

Francisco Solano Lopez — A306

Perf. 13x13½

1977, July 24 Litho. Wmk. 347

1752 A306	10g brown	15	15
1753 A306	50g dk vio	50	38
1754 A306	100g green	1.00	75

Marshal Francisco Solano Lopez (1827-1870), President of Paraguay.

Nos. 1753-1754 are airmail.

Paintings — A307

Paintings by: No. 1755a, 1g, Gabrielle Rainer Istvanffy. b, 2g, L. C. Hoffmeister. c, 3g, Frans Floris. d, 4g, Gerard de Lairesse. e, 5g, David Teniers I. f, 10g, Jacopo Zucchi. g, 15g, Pierre Paul Prudhon. 20g, Francois Boucher. 25g, Ingres. 5g-25g vert.

1977, July 25 *Perf. 14*

1755 A307 Strip of 7, #a.-g.
1756 A307 20g multicolored

Souvenir Sheet

Perf. 14½

1757 A307 25g multicolored

Nos. 1755f-1757 are airmail.

German Sailing Ships — A308

Designs: No. 1764a, 1g, De Beurs van Amsterdam. b, 2g, Katharina von Blankenese. c, 3g, Cuxhaven. d, 4g, Rhein. e, 5g, Churprinz and Marian. f, 10g, Bark of Bremen, vert. g, 15g, Elbe II, vert. 20g, Karacke. 25g, Admiral Karpeanger.

Unwmk.

1977, Aug. 27 Litho. *Perf. 14*

1764 A308 Strip of 7, #a.-g.
1765 A308 20g multicolored

Souvenir Sheet

Perf. 13½

1766 A308 25g multicolored

Nos. 1764f-1766 are airmail. No. 1766 contains one 40x30mm stamp.

Nobel Laureates for Literature — A309

Authors and scenes from books: No. 1773a, 1g, John Steinbeck, Grapes of Wrath, vert. b, 2g, Ernest Hemingway, Death in the Afternoon. c, 3g, Pearl S. Buck, The Good Earth, vert. d, 4g, George Bernard Shaw, Pygmalion, vert. e, 5g, Maurice Maeterlinck, Joan of Arc, vert. f, 10g, Rudyard Kipling, The Jungle Book. g, Henryk Sienkiewicz, Quo Vadis. 20g, C. Theodor Mommsen, History of Rome. 25g, Nobel prize medal.

1977, Sept. 5 *Perf. 14*

1773 A309 Strip of 7, #a.-g.
1774 A309 20g multicolored

Souvenir Sheet
Perf. 14½

1775 A309 25g multicolored

Nos. 1773f-1775 are airmail.

1978 World Cup Soccer Championships, Argentina — A310

Posters and World Cup Champions: No. 1782a, 1g, Uruguay, 1930. b, 2g, Italy, 1934. c, 3g, Italy, 1938. d, 4g, Uruguay, 1950. e, 5g, Germany, 1954. f, 10g, Soccer player by Fritz Genkinger. g, 15g, Soccer player, orange shirt by Genkinger.

No. 1783a, 1g, Brazil, 1958. b, 2g, Brazil, 1962. c, 3g, England, 1966. d, 4g, Brazil, 1970. e, 5g, Germany, 1974. f, 10g, Player #4 by Genkinger. g, 15g, Player #1 by Genkinger, horiz.

No. 1784, World Cup Trophy. No. 1785, German players, Argentina '78. No. 1786, The Loser, by Genkinger. No. 1787, The Defender, (player #11) by Genkinger.

1977, Oct. 28 Unwmk. *Perf. 14*

1782 A310 Strip of 7, #a.-g.
1783 A310 Strip of 7, #a.-g.
1784 A310 20g multicolored
1785 A310 20g multicolored

Souvenir Sheets
Perf. 14½

1786 A310 25g red & multi
1787 A310 25g black & multi

Nos. 1782f-1782g, 1783f-1783g, 1784-1787 are airmail.

Peter Paul Rubens, 400th Birth Anniv. A312

Details from paintings: No. 1788a, 1g, Rubens and Isabella Brant under Honeysuckle Bower. b, 2g, Judgment of Paris. c, 3g, Union of Earth and Water. d, 4g, Daughters of Kekrops Discovering Erichthonius. e, 5g, Holy Family with the Lamb. f, 10c, Adoration of the Magi. g, 15c, Philip II on Horseback.

20g, Education of Marie de Medici, horiz. 25g, Triumph of Eucharist Over False Gods.

1978, Jan. 19 Unwmk. *Perf. 14*

1788 A312 Strip of 7, #a.-g.
1789 A312 20g multicolored

Souvenir Sheet
Perf. 14½

1790 A312 25g multicolored

Nos. 1788f-1788g, 1789-1790 are airmail. No. 1790 contains one 50x70mm stamp and exists inscribed in gold or silver.

1978 World Chess Championships, Argentina — A313

Paintings of chess players: No. 1791a, 1g, De Cremone. b, 2g, L. van Leyden. c, 3g, H. Muehlich. d, 4g, Arabian artist. e, 5g, Benjamin Franklin playing chess, E. H. May. f, 10g, G. Cruikshank. g, 15g, 17th cent. tapestry. 20g, Napoleon playing chess on St. Helena. 25g, Illustration from chess book, Shah Name.

1978, Jan. 23 *Perf. 14*

1791 A313 Strip of 7, #a.-g.
1792 A313 20g multicolored

Souvenir Sheet
Perf. 14½

1793 A313 25g multicolored

Nos. 1791f-1791g, 1792-1793 are airmail. No. 1793 contains one 50x40mm stamp.

Jacob Jordaens, 300th Death Anniv. A314

Paintings: No. 1794a, 3g, Satyr and the Nymphs. b, 4g, Satyr with Peasant. c, 5g, Allegory of Fertility. d, 6g, Upbringing of Jupiter. e, 7g, Holy Family. f, 8g, Adoration of the Shepherds. g, 20g, Jordaens with his family. 10g, Meleagro with Atalanta, horiz. No. 1796, Feast for a King, horiz. No. 1797, Holy Family with Shepherds.

1978, Jan. 25 *Perf. 14*

1794 A314 Strip of 7, #a.-g.
1795 A314 10g multicolored
1796 A314 25g multicolored

Souvenir Sheet
Perf. 14½

1797 A314 25g multicolored

Nos. 1795-1797 are airmail. No. 1797 contains one 50x70mm stamp.

Albrecht Durer, 450th Death Anniv. A315

Monograms and details from paintings: No. 1804a, 3g, Temptation of the Idler. b, 4g, Adam and Eve. c, 5g, Satyr Family. d, 6g, Eve. e, 7g, Adam. f, 8g, Portrait of a Young Man. g, 20g, Squirrels and Acorn. 10g, Madonna and Child. No. 1806, Brotherhood of the Rosary (Lute-playing Angel). No. 1807, Soldier on Horseback with a Lance.

1978, Mar. 10 *Perf. 14*

1804 A315 Strip of 7, #a.-g.
1805 A315 10g multicolored
1806 A315 25g multicolored

Souvenir Sheet
Perf. 13½

1807 A315 25g blk, buff & sil

Nos. 1805-1807 are airmail. No. 1807 contains one 30x40mm stamp.

Francisco de Goya, 150th Death Anniv. A316

Paintings: No. 1814a, 3g, Allegory of the Town of Madrid. b, 4g, The Clothed Maja. c, 5g, The Parasol. d, 6g, Dona Isabel Cobos de Porcel. e, 7g, The Drinker. f, 8g, The 2nd of May 1908. g, 20g, General Jose Palafox on Horseback. 10g, Savages Murdering a Woman. 25g, The Naked Maja, horiz.

1978, May 11 *Perf. 14*

1814 A316 Strip of 7, #a.-g.
1815 A316 10g multicolored
1816 A316 25g multicolored

Nos. 1815-1816 are airmail.

Future Space Projects — A317

Various futuristic space vehicles and imaginary creatures: No. 1816a, 3g. b, 4g. c, 5g. d, 6g. e, 7g. f, 8g. g, 20g.

1978, May 16

1817 A317 Strip of 7, #a.-g.
1818 A317 10g multicolored
1819 A317 25g multi, diff.

Nos. 1818-1819 are airmail.

Racing Cars A318

Designs: No. 1820a, 3g, Tyrell Formula I. b, 4g, Lotus Formula 1, 1978. c, 5g, McLaren Formula I. d, 6g, Brabham Alfa Romeo Formula 1. e, 7g, Renault Turbo Formula 1. f, 8g, Wolf Formula 1. g, 20g, Porsche 935. 10g, Bugatti. 25g, Mercedes Benz W196, Stirling Moss, driver. No. 1823, Ferrari 312T.

1978, June 28 *Perf. 14*

1820 A318 Strip of 7, #a.-g.
1821 A318 10g multicolored
1822 A318 25g multicolored

Souvenir Sheet
Perf. 14½

1823 A318 25g multicolored

Nos. 1821-1823 are airmail. No. 1823 contains one 50x35mm stamp.

Paintings by Peter Paul Rubens A319

Designs: 3g, Holy Family with a Basket. 4g, Amor Cutting a Bow. 5g, Adam and Eve in Paradise. 6g, Crown of Fruit, horiz. 7g, Kidnapping of Ganymede. 8g, The Hunting of Crocodile and Hippopotamus. 10g, The Reception of Marie de Medici at Marseilles. 20g, Two Satyrs. 25g, Felicity of the Regency.

1978, June 30 *Perf. 14*

1824 A319 3g multicolored
1825 A319 4g multicolored
1826 A319 5g multicolored
1827 A319 6g multicolored
1828 A319 7g multicolored
1829 A319 8g multicolored
1830 A319 10g multicolored
1831 A319 20g multicolored
1832 A319 25g multicolored

Nos. 1830, 1832 are airmail.

National College A320

Perf. 13½x13

1978 Litho. Wmk. 347

1833	A320	3g	claret	15	15
1834	A320	4g	violet blue	15	15
1835	A320	5g	lilac	15	15
1836	A320	20g	brown	16	15
1837	A320	25g	violet black	20	15
1838	A320	30g	bright green	25	18
			Set value	75	60

Centenary of National College in Asuncion.
Nos. 1836-1838 are airmail.

José Estigarribia, Bugler, Flag of Paraguay A321

1978 Litho. *Perf. 13x13½*

1839	A321	3g	multi	15	15
1840	A321	5g	multi	15	15
1841	A321	10g	multi	15	15
1842	A321	20g	multi	16	15
1843	A321	25g	multi	20	15
1844	A321	30g	multi	25	18
			Set value	78	60

Induction of Jose Felix Estigarribia (1888-1940), general and president of Paraguay, into Salon de Bronce (National Heroes' Hall of Fame).
Nos. 1842-1844 are airmail.

Queen Elizabeth II Coronation, 25th Anniv. A322

Flowers and: 3g, Barbados #234. 4g, Tristan da Cunha #13. 5g, Bahamas #157. 6g, Seychelles #172. 7g, Solomon Islands #88. 8g, Cayman Islands #150. 10g, New Hebrides #77. 20g, St. Lucia #156. 25g, St. Helena #139.

No. 1854, Solomon Islands #368a-368c, Gilbert Islands #312a-312c. No. 1855, Great Britain #313-316.

1978, July 25 Unwmk. *Perf. 14*

1845 A322 3g multicolored
1846 A322 4g multicolored
1847 A322 5g multicolored
1848 A322 6g multicolored
1849 A322 7g multicolored
1850 A322 8g multicolored
1851 A322 10g multicolored
1852 A322 20g multicolored
1853 A322 25g multicolored

Souvenir Sheets

Perf. 13½

1854 A322 25g multicolored
1855 A322 25g multicolored

Nos. 1851, 1853-1855 are airmail. Nos. 1854-1855 each contain one 60x40mm stamp.

Intl. Philatelic Exhibitions A323

Various paintings, ship, nudes, etc. for: No. 1856a, 3g, Nordposta '78. b, 4g, Riccione '78. c, 5g, Uruguay '79. d, 6g, ESSEN '78. e, 7g, ESPAMER '79. f, 8g, London '80. g, 20g, PRAGA '78. 10g, EUROPA '78. No. 1858, Eurphila '78.

No. 1859, Francisco de Pinedo, map of his flight.

1978, July 19 *Perf. 14*

1856 A323 Strip of 7, #a.-g.
1857 A323 10g multicolored
1858 A323 25g multicolored

Souvenir Sheet

Perf. 13½x13

1859 A323 25g multicolored

No. 1859 for Riccione '78 and Eurphila '78 and contains one 54x34mm stamp. Nos. 1857-1859 are airmail. Nos. 1856b-1858 are vert.

Intl. Year of the Child — A324

Grimm's Snow White and the Seven Dwarfs: No. 1866a, 3g, Queen pricking her finger. b, 4g, Queen and mirror. c, 5g, Man with dagger, Snow White. d, 6g, Snow White in forest. e, 7g, Snow White asleep, seven dwarfs. f, 8g, Snow White dancing with dwarfs. g, 20g, Snow White being offered apple. 10g, Snow White in repose. 25g, Snow White, Prince Charming on horseback.

1978, Oct. 26

1866 A324 Strip of 7, #a.-g.
1867 A324 10g multicolored
1868 A324 25g multicolored

Nos. 1867-1868 are airmail.
See Nos. 1893-1896, 1916-1919.

Mounted South American Soldiers A325

No. 1869a, 3g, Gen. Jose Felix Bogado (1771-1829). b, 4g, Colonel, First Volunteer Regiment, 1806. c, 5g, Colonel wearing dress uniform, 1860. d, 6g, Soldier, 1864-1870. e, 7g, Dragoon, 1865. f, 8g, Lancer. g, 20g, Soldier, 1865. 10g, Gen. Bernardo O'Higgins, 200th birth anniv. 25g, Jose de San Martin, 200th birth anniv.

1978, Oct. 31

1869 A325 Strip of 7, #a.-g.
1870 A325 10g multicolored
1871 A325 25g multicolored

Nos. 1870-1871 are airmail.

1978 World Cup Soccer Championships, Argentina — A326

Soccer Players: No. 1872a, 3g, Paraguay, vert. b, 4g, Austria, Sweden. c, 5g, Argentina, Poland. d, 6g, Italy, Brazil. e, 7g, Netherlands, Austria. f, 8g, Scotland, Peru. g, 20g, Germany, Italy. 10g, Argentina, Holland. 25g, Germany, Tunisia.

No. 1875, Stadium.

1979, Jan. 9 *Perf. 14*

1872 A326 Strip of 7, #a.-g.
1873 A326 10g multicolored
1874 A326 25g multicolored

Souvenir Sheet

Perf. 13½

1875 A326 25g multicolored

Nos. 1873-1875 are airmail. No. 1875 contains one 60x40mm stamp.

For overprint see No. C610.

Christmas A327

Paintings of the Nativity and Madonna and Child by: No. 1876a, 3g, Giorgione, horiz. b, 4g, Titian. c, 5g, Titian, diff. d, 6g, Raphael. e, 7g, Schongauer. f, 8g, Muratti. g, 20g, Van Oost. 10g, Memling. No. 1878, Rubens.

No. 1879, Madonna and Child Surrounded by a Garland and Boy Angels, Rubens.

1979, Jan. 10 Litho. *Perf. 14*

1876 A327 Strip of 7, #a.-g.
1877 A327 10g multicolored
1878 A327 25g multicolored

Souvenir Sheet

Photo. & Engr.

Perf. 12

1879 A327 25g multicolored

Nos. 1877-1879 are airmail.

First Powered Flight, 75th Anniv. (in 1978) — A328

Airplanes: No. 1880a, 3g, Eole, C. Ader, 1890. b, 4g, Flyer III, Wright Brothers. c, 5g, Voisin, Henri Farman, 1908. d, 6g, Curtiss, Eugene Ely, 1910. e, 7g, Etrich-Taube A11. f, 8g, Fokker EIII. g, 20g, Albatros C, 1915. 10g, Boeing 747 carrying space shuttle. No. 1882, Boeing 707. No. 1883, Zeppelin flight commemorative cancels.

1979, Apr. 24 Litho. *Perf. 14*

1880 A328 Strip of 7, #a.-g.
1881 A328 10g multicolored
1882 A328 25g multicolored

Souvenir Sheet

Perf. 14½

1883 A328 25g blue & black

Nos. 1881-1883 are airmail. Nos. 1880-1883 incorrectly commemorate 75th anniv. of ICAO. No. 1883 contains one 50x40mm stamp.

Albrecht Durer, 450th Death Anniv. (in 1978) A329

Paintings: No. 1884a, 3g, Virgin with the Dove. b, 4g, Virgin Praying. c, 5g, Mater Dolorosa. d, 6g, Virgin with a Carnation. e, 7g, Madonna and Sleeping Child. f, 8g, Virgin Before the Archway. g, 20g, Flight Into Egypt. No. 1885, Madonna of the Haller family. No. 1886, Virgin with a Pear.

No. 1887, Lamentation Over the Dead Christ for Albrecht Glimm. No. 1888, Space station, horiz., with Northern Hemisphere of Celestial Globe in margin.

1979, Apr. 28 *Perf. 14*

1884 A329 Strip of 7, #a.-g.
1885 A329 10g multicolored
1886 A329 25g multicolored

Souvenir Sheets

Perf. 13½

1887 A329 25g multicolored
1888 A329 25g multicolored

Intl. Year of the Child (#1885-1886).

Nos. 1885-1886, 1888 are airmail. No. 1887 contains one 30x40mm stamp, No. 1888 one 40x30mm stamp.

Sir Rowland Hill, Death Cent. — A330

Hill and: No. 1889a, 3g, Newfoundland #C1, vert. b, 4g, France #C14. c, 5g, Spain #B106. d, 6g, Similar to Ecuador #C2, vert. e, 7g, US #C3a. f, 8g, Gelber Hund inverted overprint, vert. g, 20g, Switzerland #C20a.

10g, Privately issued Zeppelin stamp. No. 1891, Paraguay #C82, #C96, vert. No. 1892, Italy #C49. No. 1892A, France #C3-C4.

1979, June 11 *Perf. 14*

1889 A330 Strip of 7, #a.-g.
1890 A330 10g multicolored
1891 A330 25g multicolored

Souvenir Sheet

Perf. 13½x13

1892 A330 25g multicolored

Perf. 14½

1892A A330 25g multicolored

Issue dates: No. 1892A, Aug. 28. Others, June 11. Nos. 1890-1892A are airmail.

Grimm's Fairy Tales Type of 1978

Cinderella: No. 1893a, 3g, Two stepsisters watch Cinderella cleaning. b, 4g, Cinderella, father, stepsisters. c, 5g, Cinderella with birds while working. d, 6g, Finding dress. e, 7g, Going to ball. f, 8g, Dancing with prince. g, 20g, Losing slipper leaving ball.

10g, Prince Charming trying slipper on Cinderella's foot. No. 1895, Couple riding to castle. No. 1896, Couple entering ballroom.

1979, June 24 *Perf. 14*

1893 A324 Strip of 7, #a.-g.
1894 A324 10g multicolored
1895 A324 25g multicolored

Souvenir Sheet

Perf. 13½

1896 A324 25g multicolored

Intl. Year of the Child.

Congress Emblem — A331

1979, Aug. Litho. *Perf. 13x13½*

1897 A331 10g red, blue & black	15	15
1898 A331 50g red, blue & black	40	30

22nd Latin-American Tourism Congress, Asuncion. No. 1898 is airmail.

1980 Winter Olympics, Lake Placid — A332

Designs: No. 1899a, 3g, Monica Scheftschik, luge. b, 4g, E. Deufl, Austria, downhill skiing. c, 5g, G. Thoeni, Italy, slalom skiing. d, 6g, Canada Two-man bobsled. e, 7g, Germany vs. Finland, ice hockey. f, 8g, Hoenl, Russia, ski jump. g, 20g, Dianne De Leeuw, Netherlands, figure skating, vert.

10g, Hanni Wenzel, Liechtenstein, slalom skiing. No. 1901, Frommelt, Liechtenstein, slalom skiing, vert. No. 1902, Kulakova, Russia, cross country skier. No. 1903, Dorothy Hamill, US, figure skating, vert. No. 1904, Brigitte Totschning, skier.

1979 Unwmk. *Perf. 14*

1899 A332 Strip of 7, #a.-g.
1900 A332 10g multicolored
1901 A332 25g multicolored

Souvenir Sheets

Perf. 13½

1902 A332 25g multicolored
1903 A332 25g multicolored
1904 A332 25g multicolored

Nos. 1900-1904 are airmail. Issue dates: Nos. 1899-1902, Aug. 22. No. 1903, June 11. No, 1904, Apr. 24. Nos. 1902-1903 each contain one 40x30mm stamp, No. 1904, one 25x36mm stamp.

Sailing Ships A333

Designs: No. 1905a, 3g, Caravel, vert. b, 4g, Warship. c, 5g, Warship, by Jan van Beeck. d, 6g, H.M.S. Britannia, vert. e, 7g, Salamis, vert. f, 8g, Ariel, vert. g, 20g, Warship, by Robert Salmon.

1979, Aug. 28 *Perf. 14*

1905 A333 Strip of 7, #a.-g.
1906 A333 10g Lisette
1907 A333 25g Holstein, vert.

Nos. 1906-1907 are airmail.

Intl. Year of the Child — A334

Various kittens: No. 1908a, 3g. b, 4g. c, 5g. d, 6g. e, 7g. f, 8g. g, 20g.

1979, Nov. 29 *Perf. 14*

1908 A334 Strip of 7, #a.-g.
1909 A334 10g multicolored
1910 A334 25g multicolored

Nos. 1909-1910 are airmail.

Grimm's Fairy Tales Type of 1978

Little Red Riding Hood: No. 1916a, 3g, Leaving with basket. b, 4g, Meets wolf. c, 5g, Picks flowers. d, 6g, Wolf puts on Granny's gown. e, 7g, Wolf in bed. f, 8g, Hunter arrives. g, 20g, Saved by the hunter.

10g, Hunter enters house. No. 1918, Hunter leaves. No. 1919, Overall scene.

1979, Dec. 4 *Perf. 14*

1916 A324 Strip of 7, #a.-g.
1917 A324 10g multicolored
1918 A324 25g multicolored

Souvenir Sheet

Perf. 14½

1919 A324 25g multicolored

Intl. Year of the Child. No. 1919 contains one 50x70mm stamp.

Greek Athletes A335

Paintings on Greek vases: No. 1926a, 3g, 3 runners. b, 4g, 2 runners. c, 5g, Throwing contest. d, 6g, Discus. e, 7g, Wrestlers. f, 8g, Wrestlers, diff. g, 20g, 2 runners, diff.

10g, Horse and rider, horiz. 25g, 4 warriors with shields, horiz.

1979, Dec. 20 *Perf. 14*

1926 A335 Strip of 7, #a.-g.
1927 A335 10g multicolored
1928 A335 25g multicolored

Nos. 1927-1928 are airmail.

Electric Trains — A336

Designs: No. 1929a, 3g, First electric locomotive, Siemens, 1879, vert. b, 4g, Switzerland, 1897. c, 5g, Model E71 28, Germany. d, 6g, Mountain train, Switzerland. e, 7g, Electric locomotive used in Benelux countries. f, 8g, Locomotive "Rheinpfeil", Germany. g, 20g, Model BB-9004, France.

10g, 200-Km/hour train, Germany. 25g, Japanese bullet train.

1979, Dec. 24 **Litho.** *Perf. 14*

1929 A336 Strip of 7, #a.-g.
1930 A336 10g multicolored
1931 A336 25g multicolored

Nos. 1930-1931 are airmail.

Sir Rowland Hill, Death Cent. — A337

Hill and: No. 1938a, 3g, Spad S XIII, 1917-18. b, 4g, P-51 D Mustang, 1944-45. c, 5g, Mitsubishi A6M6c Zero-Sen, 1944. d, 6g, Depperdussin float plane, 1913. e, 7g, Savoia Marchetti SM 7911, 1936. f, 8g, Messerschmitt Me 262B, 1942-45. g, 20g, Nieuport 24bis, 1917-18.

10g, Zeppelin LZ 104-/159, 1917. No. 1940, Fokker Dr-1 Caza, 1917. No. 1941, Vickers Supermarine "Spitfire" Mk.IX, 1942-45.

1980, Apr. 8 *Perf. 14*

1938 A337 Strip of 7, #a.-g.
1939 A337 10g multicolored
1940 A337 25g multicolored

Souvenir Sheet

Perf. 13½

1941 A337 25g multicolored

Incorrectly commemorates 75th anniv. of ICAO. Nos. 1939-1941 are airmail. No. 1941 contains one 37x27mm stamp.

Sir Rowland Hill, Paraguayan Stamps A338

Hill and: No. 1948a, 3g, #1. b, 4g, #5. c, 5g, #6. d, 6g, #379. e, 7g, #381. f, 8g, #C384. f, 20g, #C389.

10g, #C83, horiz. No. 1950, #C92, horiz. No. 1951, #C54, horiz. No. 1952, #C1, horiz.

1980, Apr. 14 **Litho.** *Perf. 14*

1948 A338 Strip of 7, #a.-g.
1949 A338 10g multicolored
1950 A338 25g multicolored

Souvenir Sheets

Perf. 14½

1951 A338 25g multicolored
1952 A338 25g multicolored

Nos. 1949-1952 are airmail. No. 1951 contains one 50x40mm stamp. No. 1952 contains one 50x35mm stamp.

1980 Winter Olympics, Lake Placid A339

Designs: No. 1953a, 3g, Thomas Wassberg, Sweden, cross country skiing. b, 4g, Scharer & Benz, Switzerland, 2-man bobsled. c, 5g, Annemarie Moser-Proll, Austria, women's downhill skiing. d, 6g, Hockey team, US. e, 7g, Leonhard Stock, Austria, men's downhill skiing. f, 8g, Anton (Toni) Innauer, Austria, ski jump. g, 20g, Christa Kinshofer, Germany, slalom skiing.

10g, Ingemar Stenmark, slalom, Sweden. No. 1955, Robin Cousins, figure skating, Great Britain. No. 1956, Eric Heiden, speed skating, US, horiz.

1980, June 4 *Perf. 14*

1953 A339 Strip of 7, #a.-g.
1954 A339 10g multi, horiz.
1955 A339 25g multi, horiz.

Souvenir Sheet

Perf. 13½

1956 A339 25g multicolored

Nos. 1954-1956 are airmail. No. 1956 contains one 60x49mm stamp.

Composers and Paintings of Young Ballerinas A340

Paintings of ballerinas by Cydney or Degas and: No. 1957a, 3g, Gioacchino Rossini. b, 4g, Johann Strauss, the younger. c, 5g, Debussy. d, 6g, Beethoven. e, 7g, Chopin. f, 8g, Richard Wagner. g, 20g, Johann Sebastian Bach, horiz. 10g, Robert Stoltz. 25g, Verdi.

1980, July 1 *Perf. 14*

1957 A340 Strip of 7, #a.-g.
1958 A340 10g multicolored
1959 A340 25g multicolored

Birth and death dates are incorrectly inscribed on 4g, 8g, 10g. No. 1957f is incorrectly inscribed "Adolph" Wagner. Nos. 1958-1959 are airmail. For overprints, see Nos. 1998-1999.

Pilar City Bicentennial A341

Perf. 13½x13

1980, July 17 **Litho.** **Wmk. 347**

1966 A341 5g multi	15	15
1967 A341 25g multi	20	15
Set value	25	20

No. 1967 is airmail.

Christmas, Intl. Year of the Child — A342

Designs: No. 1968a, 3g, Christmas tree. b, 4g, Santa filling stockings. c, 5g, Nativity scene. d, 6g, Adoration of the Magi. e, 7g, Three children, presents. f, 8g, Children, dove, fruit. g, 20g, Children playing with toys. 10g, Madonna and Child, horiz. No. 1970, Children blowing bubbles, horiz. No. 1971, Five children, horiz.

1980, Aug. 4 **Unwmk.** *Perf. 14*

1968 A342 Strip of 7, #a.-g.
1969 A342 10g multicolored
1970 A342 25g multicolored

Souvenir Sheet

1971 A342 25g multicolored

Nos. 1969-1970 are airmail.

Ships A343

Emblems and ships: No. 1972a, 3g, ESPAMER '80, Spanish Armada. b, 4g, NORWEX '80, Viking longboat. c, 5g, RICCIONE '80, Battle of Lepanto. d, 6g, ESSEN '80, Great Harry of Cruickshank. e, 7g, US Bicentennial, Mount Vernon. f, 8g, LONDON '80, H.M.S. Victory. g, 20g, ESSEN '80, Hamburg III, vert. 10g, ESSEN '80, Gorch Fock. 25g, PHILATOKYO '81, Nippon Maru, horiz.

1980, Sept. 15 *Perf. 14*

1972 A343 Strip of 7, #a.-g.
1973 A343 10g multicolored
1974 A343 25g multicolored

Nos. 1973-1974 are airmail. For overprint see No. 2278.

Souvenir Sheet

King Juan Carlos A344

1980, Sept. 19 *Perf. 14½*

1975 A344 25g multicolored

Paraguay Airlines Boeing 707 Service Inauguration — A345

Perf. 13½x13

1980, Sept. 17 Litho. Wmk. 347

1976 A345	20g multi		16	15
1977 A345	100g multi		80	65

No. 1977 is airmail.

A346

World Cup Soccer Championships, Spain — A346a

Various soccer players, winning country: No. 1978a, 3g, Uruguay 1930, 1950. b, 4g, Italy 1934, 1938. c, 5g, Germany 1954, 1974. d, 6g, Brazil 1958, 1962, 1970. e, 7g, England, 1966. f, 8g, Argentina, 1978. g, 20g, Espana '82 emblem.

10g, World Cup trophy, flags. 25g, Soccer player from Uruguay.

1980, Dec. 10 Unwmk. *Perf. 14*

1978 A346 Strip of 7, #a.-g.
1979 A346 10g multicolored
1980 A346 25g multicolored

Souvenir Sheet

Perf. 14½

1981 A346a 25g Sheet of 1 + 2 labels

Nos. 1979-1981 are airmail.

1980 World Chess Championships, Mexico — A347

Illustrations from The Book of Chess: No. 1982a, 3g, Two men, chess board. b, 4g, Circular chess board, players. c, 5g, Four-person chess match. d, 6g, King Alfonso X of Castile and Leon. e, 7g, Two players, chess board, horiz. f, 8g, Two veiled women, chess board, horiz. g, 20g, Two women in robes, chess board, horiz.

10g, Crusader knights, chess board, horiz. 25g, Three players, chess board, horiz.

1980, Dec. 15 Litho. *Perf. 14*

1982 A347 Strip of 7, #a.-g.
1983 A347 10g multicolored
1984 A347 25g multicolored

Nos. 1983-1984 are airmail.

See Nos. C506-C510. Compare with illustration AP199.

1980 Winter Olympics, Lake Placid A348

Olympic scenes, gold medalists: No. 1985a, 25c, Lighting Olympic flame. b, 50c, Hockey team, US. c, 1g, Eric Heiden, US, speed skating. d, 2g, Robin Cousins, Great Britain, figure skating. e, 3g, Thomas Wassberg, Sweden, cross country skiing. f, 4g, Annie Borckinck, Netherlands, speed skating. g, 5g, Gold, silver, and bronze medals.

No. 1986, Irene Epple, silver medal, slalom, Germany. 10g, Ingemar Stenmark, slalom, giant slalom, Sweden. 30g, Annemarie Moser-Proll, downhill, Austria. 25g, Baron Pierre de Coubertin.

1981, Feb. 4 Litho. *Perf. 14*

1985 A348 Strip of 7, #a.-g.
1986 A348 5g multicolored
1987 A348 10g multicolored
1988 A348 30g multicolored

Souvenir Sheet

Perf. 13½

1988A A348 25g multicolored

No. 1985 exists in strips of 4 and 3. Nos. 1986-1988A are airmail. No. 1988A contains one 30x40mm stamp.

Locomotives — A349

Designs: No. 1989, 25c, Electric model 242, Germany. b, 50c, Electric, London-Midlands-Lancashire, England. c, 1g, Electric, Switzerland. d, 2g, Diesel-electric, Montreal-Vancouver, Canada. e, 3g, Electric, Austria. f, 4g, Electric inter-urban, Lyons-St. Etienne, France, vert. g, 5g, First steam locomotive in Paraguay.

No. 1991, Steam locomotive, Japan. 10g, Stephenson's steam engine, 1830 England. No. 1993, Crocodile locomotive, Switzerland. 30g, Stephenson's Rocket, 1829, England, vert.

1981, Feb. 9 Litho. *Perf. 14*

1989 A349 Strip of 7, #a.-g.
1990 A349 5g multicolored
1991 A349 10g multicolored
1992 A349 30g multicolored

Souvenir Sheet

Perf. 13½x13

1993 A349 25g multicolored

Electric railroads, cent. (#1989a-1989f), steam-powered railway service, 150th anniv. (#1989g, 1990-1991), Liverpool-Manchester Railway, 150th anniv. (#1992). Swiss Railways, 75th anniv. (#1993).

Nos. 1990-1993 are airmail. No. 1993 contains one 54x34mm stamp.

Intl. Year of the Child A350

Portraits of children with assorted flowers: No. 1994a, 10g. b, 25g. c, 50g. d, 100g. e, 200g. f, 300g. g, 400g.

1981, Apr. 13 Litho. *Perf. 14*

1994 A350 Strip of 7, #a.-g.
1995 A350 75g multicolored
1996 A350 500g multicolored
1997 A350 1000g multicolored

Nos. 1995-1997 are airmail.

Nos. 1958 and 1963 Overprinted in Red

1981, May 22

1998 A340 4g on #1958
1999 A340 10g on #1963

No. 1999 is airmail.

The following stamps were issued in sheets of 8 with 1 label: Nos. 2001, 2013, 2037, 2044, 2047, 2055, 2140.

The following stamps were issued in sheets of 6 with 3 labels: Nos. 2029, 2035, 2104, 2145.

The following stamps were issued in sheets of 3 with 6 labels: 2079, 2143.

The following stamps were issued in sheets of 5 with 4 labels: Nos. 2050-2051, 2057, 2059, 2061, 2067, 2069, 2077, 2082, 2089, 2092, 2107, 2117, 2120, 2121, 2123, 2125, 2129, 2135, 2138, 2142, 2146, 2148, 2151, 2160, 2163, 2165, 2169, 2172, 2176, 2179, 2182, 2190, 2196, 2202, 2204, 2214, 2222, 2224, 2232, 2244, 2246, 2248, 2261, 2263, 2265, 2271, 2273, 2275, 2277.

The following stamps were issued in sheets of 4 with 5 labels: Nos. 2307, 2310, 2313, 2316, 2324, 2329.

Royal Wedding of Prince Charles and Lady Diana Spencer — A351

Prince Charles, sailing ships: No. 2000a, 25c, Royal George. b, 50c, Great Britain. c, 1g, Taeping. d, 2g, Star of India. e, 3g, Torrens. f, 4g, Loch Etive. No. 2001, Medway.

No. 2002, Charles, flags, and Concorde. 10g, Flags, flowers, Diana, Charles. 25g, Charles, Diana, flowers, vert. 30g, Coats of arms, flags.

1981, June 27

2000 A351 Strip of 6, #a.-f.
2001 A351 5g multicolored
2002 A351 5g multicolored
2003 A351 10g multicolored
2004 A351 30g multicolored

Souvenir Sheet

Perf. 13½

2005 A351 25g multicolored

Nos. 2002-2005 are airmail. No. 2005 contains one 50x60mm stamp. For overprint see No. 2253.

Traditional Costumes and Itaipu Dam A352

Women in various traditional costumes: a, 10g. b, 25g. c, 50g. d, 100g. e, 200g. f, 300g. g, 400g, President Stroessner, Itaipu Dam.

1981, June 30 *Perf. 14*

2006 A352 Strip of 7, #a.-g.

For overprints see No. 2281.

UPU Membership Centenary — A353

1981, Aug. 18 Litho. *Perf. 13½x13*

2007 A353	5g	rose lake & blk	15	15
2008 A353	10g	lil & blk	15	15
2009 A353	20g	grn & blk	16	15
2010 A353	25g	lt red brn & blk	20	15
2011 A353	50g	bl & blk	40	30
		Set value	88	68

Peter Paul Rubens, Paintings A354

Details from paintings: No. 2012a, 25c, Madonna Surrounded by Saints. b, 50c, Judgment of Paris. c, 1g, Duke of Buckingham Conducted to the Temple of Virtus. d, 2g, Minerva Protecting Peace from Mars. e, 3g, Henry IV Receiving the Portrait of Marie de Medici. f, 4g, Triumph of Juliers. 5g, Madonna and Child Reigning Among Saints (Cherubs).

1981, July 9 Litho. *Perf. 14*

2012 A354 Strip of 6, #a.-f.
2013 A354 5g multicolored

Jean Auguste-Dominique Ingres (1780-1867), Painter — A355

Details from paintings: No. 2014a, 25c, c, 1g, d, 2g, f, 4g, The Turkish Bath. b, 50c, The Water

Pitcher. e, 3g, Oedipus and the Sphinx. g, 5g, The Bathing Beauty.

1981, Oct. 13
2014 A355 Strip of 7, #a.-g.

No. 2014f and 2014g exist in sheet of 8 (four each) plus label. For overprints see No. 2045.

Pablo Picasso, Birth Cent. — A356

Designs: No. 2015a, 25c, Women Running on the Beach. b, 50c, Family on the Beach. No. 2016a, 1g, Still-life. b, 2g, Bullfighter. c, 3g, Children Drawing. d, 4g, Seated Woman. 5g, Paul as Clown.

1981, Oct. 19
2015 A356 Pair, #a.-b.
2016 A356 Strip of 4, #a.-d.
2017 A356 5g multicolored

Nos. 2015-2016 Ovptd. in Silver

1981, Oct. 22
2018 A356 on Nos. 2015a-2015b
2019 A356 on Nos. 2016a-2016d

Philatelia '81, Frankfurt.

Nos. 2015-2016 Ovptd. in Gold

1981, Oct. 25
2020 A356 on Nos. 2015a-2015b
2021 A356 on Nos. 2016a-2016d

Espamer '81 Philatelic Exhibition.

Royal Wedding of Prince Charles and Lady Diana A357

Designs: No. 2022a-2022c, 25c, 50c, 1g, Diana, Charles, flowers. d, 2g, Couple. e, 3g, Couple leaving church. f, 4g, Couple, Queen Elizabeth II waving from balcony. g, 5g, Diana. No. 2023, Wedding party, horiz. 10g, Riding in royal coach, horiz. 30g, Yeomen of the guard, horiz.

1981, Dec. 4 Litho. *Perf. 14*
2022 A357 Strip of 7, #a.-g.
2023 A357 5g multicolored
2024 A357 10g multicolored
2025 A357 30g multicolored

Souvenir Sheets
Perf. 14½
2026 A357 25g like #2022d
2027 A357 25g Wedding portrait

No. 2022g exists in sheets of 8 plus label. Nos. 2023-2027 are airmail. Nos. 2026-2027 contain one each 50x70mm stamp.

Christmas A358

Designs: No. 2028a, 25c, Jack-in-the-box. b, 50c, Jesus and angel. c, 1g, Santa, angels. d, 2g, Angels lighting candle. e, 3g, Christmas plant. f, 4g, Nativity scene. 5g, Children singing by Christmas tree.

1981, Dec. 17 *Perf. 14*
2028 A358 Strip of 6, #a.-f.

Size: 28x45mm
Perf. 13½
2029 A358 5g multicolored

Intl. Year of the Child (Nos. 2028-2029). For overprints see No. 2042.

Intl. Year of the Child — A359

Story of Puss 'n Boots: No. 2030a, 25c, Boy, Puss. b, 50c, Puss, rabbits.

1g, Puss, king. 2g, Prince, princess, king. 3g, Giant ogre, Puss. 4g, Puss chasing mouse. 5g, Princess, prince, Puss.

1982, Apr. 16 Litho. *Perf. 14*
2030 A359 Pair, #a.-b.
2031 A359 1g multicolored
2032 A359 2g multicolored
2033 A359 3g multicolored
2034 A359 4g multicolored
2035 A359 5g multicolored

#2031-2034 printed se-tenant with label.

Scouting, 75th Anniv. and Lord Baden-Powell, 125th Birth Anniv. — A360

Designs: No. 2036a, 25c, Tetradactyla, Scout hand salute. b, 50c, Nandu (rhea), Cub Scout and trefoil. c, 1g, Peccary, Wolf's head totem. d, 2g, Coatimundi, emblem on buckle. e, 3g, Mara, Scouting's Intl. Communications emblem. f, 4g, Deer, boy scout.

No. 2037, Aotes, Den mother, Cub Scout. No. 2038, Ocelot, scouts cooking. 10g, Collie, boy scout. 30g, Armadillo, two scouts planting tree. 25g, Lord Robert Baden-Powell, founder of Boy Scouts.

1982, Apr. 21
2036 A360 Strip of 6, #a.-f.
2037 A360 5g multicolored
2038 A360 5g multicolored
2039 A360 10g multicolored
2040 A360 30g multicolored

Souvenir Sheet
Perf. 14½
2041 A360 25g multicolored

Nos. 2038-2041 are airmail. For overprint see No. 2140.

No. 2028 Overprinted with ESSEN 82 Emblem

1982, Apr. 28 *Perf. 14*
2042 A358 on #2028a-2028f

Essen '82 Intl. Philatelic Exhibition.

Cats and Kittens — A361

Various cats or kittens: No. 2043a, 25c. b, 50c. c, 1g. d, 2g. e, 3g. f, 4g.

1982, June 7 *Perf. 14*
2043 A361 Strip of 6, #a.-f.
2044 A361 5g multi, vert.

For overprints see Nos. 2054-2055.

Nos. 2014a-2014e Ovptd. PHILEXFRANCE 82 Emblem ans "PARIS 11-21.6.82" in Blue

1982, June 11
2045 A355 Strip of 5, #a.-e.

Philexfrance '82 Intl. Philatelic Exhibition. Size of overprint varies.

World Cup Soccer Championships, Spain — A362

Designs: 2046a, 25c, Brazilian team. b, 50c, Chilean team. c, 1g, Honduran team. d, 2g, Peruvian team. e, 3g, Salvadoran team. f, 4g, Globe as soccer ball, flags of Latin American finalists. No. 2047, Ball of flags. No. 2048, Austrian team. No. 2049, Players from Brazil, Austria. No. 2050, Spanish team. No. 2051, Two players from Argentina, Brazil, vert. No. 2052, W. German team. No. 2053, Players from Argentina, Brazil. No. 2053A, World Cup trophy, world map on soccer balls. No. 2053B, Players from W. Germany, Mexico, vert.

1982 Litho. *Perf. 14*
2046 A362 Strip of 6, #a.-f.
2047 A362 5g multicolored
2048 A362 5g multicolored
2049 A362 5g multicolored
2050 A362 10g multicolored
2051 A362 10g multicolored
2052 A362 30g multicolored
2053 A362 30g multicolored

Souvenir Sheets
Perf. 14½
2053A A362 25g multicolored
2053B A362 25g multicolored

Issue dates: Nos. 2049, 2051, 2053, 2053A, Apr. 19. Others, June 13.

Nos. 2047 exists in sheets of 8 plus label. Nos. 2048-2053B are airmail.

For overprints see Nos. 2086, 2286, C593.

Nos. 2043-2044 Overprinted in Silver With PHILATECIA 82 and Intl. Year of the Child Emblems

1982, Sept. 12 *Perf. 14*
2054 A361 Strip of 5, #a.-e.
2055 A361 5g on #2044

Philatelia '82, Hanover, Germany and Intl. Year of the Child.

Raphael, 500th Birth Anniv. A363

Details from paintings: No. 2056a, 25c, Adam and Eve (The Fall). b, 50c, Creation of Eve. c, 1g, Portrait of a Young Woman (La Fornarina). d, 2g The Three Graces. e, 3g, f, 4g, Cupid and the Three Graces. 5g, Leda and the Swan.

1982, Sept. 27
2056 A363 Strip of 6, #a.-f.
2057 A363 5g multicolored

Nos. 2056e-2056f have continuous design.

Christmas A364

Entire works or details from paintings by Raphael: No. 2058a, 25c, The Belvedere Madonna. b, 50c, The Ansidei Madonna. c, 1g, La Belle Jardiniere. d, 2g, The Aldobrandini (Garvagh) Madonna. e, 3g, Madonna of the Goldfinch. f, 4g, The Alba Madonna. No. 2059, Madonna of the Grand Duke. No. 2060, Madonna of the Linen Window. 10g, The Alba Madonna, diff. 25g, The Holy Family with St. Elizabeth and the Infant St. John and Two Angels. 30g, The Canigiani Holy Family.

1982 ***Perf. 14, 13x13½ (#2061)***
2058 A364 Strip of 6, #a.-f.
2059 A364 5g multicolored
2060 A364 5g multicolored
2061 A364 10g multicolored
2062 A364 30g multicolored

Souvenir Sheet
Perf. 14½
2063 A364 25g multicolored

Issue dates: Nos. 2058-2059, Sept. 30. Others, Dec. 17.

Nos. 2058a-2058f and 2059 exist perf. 13. Nos. 2060-2063 are airmail and have silver lettering. For overprint see No. 2087.

Life of Christ, by Albrecht Durer A365

Details from paintings: No. 2064a, 25c, The Flight into Egypt. b, 50c, Christ Among the Doctors. c, 1g, Christ Carrying the Cross. d, 2g, Nailing of Christ to the Cross. e, 3g, Christ on the Cross. f, 4g, Lamentation Over the Dead Christ. 5g, The Circumcision of Christ.

1982, Dec. 14 ***Perf. 14***
2064 A365 Strip of 6, #a.-f.

Perf. 13x13½
2065 A365 5g multicolored

For overprint see No. 2094.

South American Locomotives — A366

Locomotives from: No. 2066a, 25c, Argentina. b, 50c, Uruguay. c, 1g, Ecuador. d, 2g, Bolivia. e, 3g, Peru. f, 4g, Brazil. 5g, Paraguay.

1983, Jan. 17 **Litho.** ***Perf. 14***
2066 A366 Strip of 6, #a.-f.
2067 A366 5g multicolored

For overprint see No. 2093.

Race Cars A367

Designs: No. 2068a, 25c, ATS-Ford D 06. b, 50c, Ferrari 126 C 2. c, 1g, Brabham-BMW BT 50. d, 2g, Renault RE 30 B. e, 3g, Porsche 956. f, 4g, Talbot-Ligier-Matra JS 19. 5g, Mercedes Benz C-111.

1983, Jan. 19 ***Perf. 14***
2068 A367 Strip of 6, #a.-f.

Perf. 13½x13
2069 A367 5g multicolored

For overprint see No. 2118.

Itaipua Dam, Pres. Stroessner — A368

1983, Jan. 22 **Litho.** **Wmk. 347**

2070 A368	3g multi		15	15
2071 A368	5g multi		15	15
2072 A368	10g multi		15	15
2073 A368	20g multi		16	15
2074 A368	25g multi		20	15
2075 A368	50g multi		40	30
	Set value		92	70

25th anniv. of Stroessner City. Nos. 2073-2075 airmail.

1984 Winter Olympics, Sarajevo — A369

Ice skaters: No. 2076a, 25c, Marika Kilius, Hans-Jurgens Baumler, Germany, 1964. b, 50c, Tai Babilonia, Randy Gardner, US, 1976. c, 1g, Anett Poetzsch, E. Germany, 1980, vert. d, 2g, Tina Riegel, Andreas Nischwitz, Germany, 1980, vert. e, Dagmar Lurz, Germany, 1980, vert. f, 4g, Trixi Schuba, Austria, 1972, vert. 5g, Peggy Fleming, US, 1968, vert.

Perf. 13½x13, 13x13½

1983, Feb. 23 **Unwmk.**
2076 A369 Strip of 6, #a.-f.
2077 A369 5g multicolored

For overprints see Nos. 2177, 2266.

Pope John Paul II A370

Designs: 2078a, 25c, Virgin of Caacupe. b, 50c, Cathedral of Caacupe. c, 1g, Cathedral of Asuncion. d, 2g, Pope John Paul II holding crucifix. e, 3g, Our Lady of the Assumption. f, 4g, Pope giving blessing. 5g, Pope with hands clasped. 25g, Madonna and child.

1983, June 11 **Litho.** ***Perf. 14***
2078 A370 Strip of 6, #a.-f.
2079 A370 5g multicolored

Souvenir Sheet

Perf. 14½
2080 A370 25g multicolored

No. 2080 is airmail. For overprint see No. 2143.

Antique Automobiles — A371

Designs: No. 2081a, 25c, Bordino Steamcoach, 1854. b, 50c, Panhard & Levassor, 1892. c, 1g, Benz Velo, 1894. d, 2g, Peugeot-Daimler, 1894. e, 3g, 1st car with patented Lutzmann system, 1898. f, 4g, Benz Victory, 1891-92. No. 2082, Ceirano 5CV. No. 2083, Mercedes Simplex PS 32 Turismo, 1902. 10g, Stae Electric, 1909. 25g, Benz Velocipede, 1885. 30g, Rolls Royce Silver Ghost, 1913.

1983, July 18 ***Perf. 14***
2081 A371 Strip of 6, #a.-f.
2082 A371 5g multicolored
2083 A371 5g multicolored
2084 A371 10g multicolored
2085 A371 30g multicolored

Souvenir Sheet

Perf. 14½
2085A A371 25g Sheet of 1 + label

Nos. 2083-2085A are airmail.

No. 2046 Ovptd. in Red, No. 2058 Ovptd. in Black with "52o CONGRESO F.I.P." and Brasiliana 83 Emblem

1983, July 27 ***Perf. 14***
2086 A362 Strip of 6, #a.-f.
2087 A364 Strip of 6, #a.-f.

Brasiliana '83, Rio de Janiero and 52nd FIP Congress. No. 2087 exists perf. 13.

Aircraft Carriers — A372

Carriers and airplanes: No. 2088a, 25c, 25 de Mayo, A-4Q Sky Hawk, Argentina. b, 50c, Minas Gerais, Brazil. c, 1g, Akagi, A6M3 Zero, Japan. d, 2g, Guiseppe Miraglia, Italy. e, 3g, Enterprise, S-3A Viking, US. f, 4g, Dedalo, AV-8A Matador, Spain. 5g, Schwabenland, Dornier DO-18, Germany. No aircraft on Nos. 2088b, 2088d.

25g, US astronauts Donn Eisele, Walter Schirra & Walt Cunningham, Earth & Apollo 7.

1983, Aug. 29 ***Perf. 14***
2088 A372 Strip of 6, #a.-f.
2089 A372 5g multicolored

Souvenir Sheet

Perf. 13½
2090 A372 25g multicolored

No. 2090 is airmail and contains one 55x45mm stamp.

Birds A373

Designs: No. 2091a, 25c, Pulsatrix perspicillata. b, 50c, Ortalis ruficauda. c, 1g, Chloroceryle amazona. d, 2g, Trogon violaceus. e, 3g, Pezites militaris. f, 4g, Bucco capensis. 5g, Cyanerpes cyaneus.

1983, Oct. 22 ***Perf. 14***
2091 A373 Strip of 6, #a.-f.

Perf. 13
2092 A373 5g multicolored

No. 2066 Ovptd. for PHILATELICA 83 in Silver

1983, Oct. 28
2093 A366 Strip of 6, #a.-f.

Philatelia '83, Dusseldorf, Germany.

No. 2064 Overprinted in Silver for EXFIVIA - 83

1983, Nov. 5
2094 A365 Strip of 6, #a.-f.

Exfivia '83 Philatelic Exhibition, La Paz, Bolivia.

Re-election of President Stroessner — A374

Designs: 10g, Passion flower, vert. 25g, Miltonia phalaenopsis, vert. 50g, Natl. arms, Chaco soldier. 75g, Acaray hydroelectric dam. 100g, Itaipu hydroelectric dam. 200g, President Alfredo Stroessner, vert.

1983, Nov. 24 ***Perf. 14***
2095 A374 10g multicolored
2096 A374 25g multicolored
2097 A374 50g multicolored
2098 A374 75g multicolored

Perf. 13
2099 A374 100g multicolored
2100 A374 200g multicolored

#2099-2100 are airmail. #2096 exists perf 13. For overprint see #C577.

Montgolfier Brothers' 1st Flight, Bicent. — A375

Designs: No. 2101a, 25c, Santos-Dumont's Biplane, 1906. b, 50c, Airship. No. 2102a, 1g, Paulhan's biplane over Juvisy. b, 2g, Zeppelin LZ-3, 1907. No. 2103a, 3g, Biplane of Henri Farman. b, 4g, Graf Zeppelin over Friedrichshafen. 5g, Lebaudy's dirigible. 25g, Detail of painting, Great Week of Aviation at Betheny, 1910.

1984, Jan. 7 ***Perf. 13***
2101 A375 Pair, #a.-b.
2102 A375 Pair, #a.-b.
2103 A375 Pair, #a.-b.

Perf. 14
2104 A375 5g multicolored

Souvenir Sheet

Perf. 13½
2105 A375 25g multicolored

No. 2105 is airmail and contains one 75x55mm stamp. For overprint see No. 2145.

Dogs A376

Designs: No. 2106a, 25c, German Shepherd. b, 50c, Great Dane, vert. c, 1g, Poodle, vert. d, 2g, Saint Bernard. e, 3g, Greyhound. f, 4g, Dachshund. 5g, Boxer.

1984, Jan. 11 **Litho.** ***Perf. 14***
2106 A376 Strip of 6, #a.-f.
2107 A376 5g multicolored

Animals, Anniversaries — A377

1984, Jan. 24 ***Perf. 13***
2108 A377 10g Puma
2109 A377 25g Alligator
2110 A377 50g Jaguar

2111 A377 75g Peccary
2112 A377 100g Simon Bolivar, vert.
2113 A377 200g Girl scout, vert.

Simon Bolivar, birth bicent. and Girl Scouts of Paraguay, 76th anniv.
Nos. 2112-2113 are airmail.

Christmas A378

Designs: No. 2114a, 25c, Pope John Paul II. b, 50c, Christmas tree. c, 1g, Children. d, 2g, Nativity Scene. e, 3g, Three Kings. f, 4g, Madonna and Child. No. 2115, Madonna and Child by Raphael.

1984, Mar. 23 ***Perf. 13x13½***
2114 A378 Strip of 6, #a.-f.
2115 A378 5g multicolored

Troubadour Knights A379

Illustrations of medieval miniatures: No. 2116a, 25c, Ulrich von Liechtenstein. b, 50c, Ulrich von Gutenberg. c, 1g, Der Putter. d, 2g, Walther von Metz. e, 3g, Hartman von Aue. f, 4g, Lutok von Seuen. 5g, Werner von Teufen.

1984, Mar. 27 ***Perf. 14***
2116 A379 Strip of 6, #a.-f.
Perf. 13
2117 A379 5g multicolored

For overprint see No. 2121.

No. 2068 Ovptd. in Silver with ESSEN 84 Emblem

1984, May 10
2118 A367 Strip of 6, #a.-f.

Essen '84 Intl. Philatelic Exhibition.

Endangered Animals — A380

Designs: No. 2119a, 25c, Priodontes giganteus. b, 50c, Catagonus wagneri. c, 1g, Felis pardalis. d, 2g, Chrysocyon brachyurus. e, 3g, Burmeisteria retusa. f, 4g, Myrmecophaga tridactyla. 5g, Caiman crocodilus.

1984, June 16 ***Perf. 14***
2119 A380 Strip of 6, #a.-f.
Perf. 13
2120 A380 5g multicolored

For overprint see No. 2129.

No. 2117 Ovptd. in Silver with Emblems, etc., for U.P.U. 19th World Congress, Hamburg

1984, June 19 ***Perf. 13***
2121 A379 5g on #2117

UPU Congress, Hamburg '84 — A381

Sailing ships: No. 2122a, 25c, Admiral of Hamburg. b, 50c, Neptune. c, 1g, Archimedes. d, 2g, Passat. e, 3g, Finkenwerder cutter off Heligoland. f, 4g, Four-masted ship. 5g, Deutschland.

1984, June 19 ***Perf. 13***
2122 A381 Strip of 6, #a.-f.
2123 A381 5g multicolored

For overprints see Nos. 2146, 2279-2280.

British Locomotives — A382

Designs: No. 2124a, 25c, Pegasus 097, 1868. b, 50c, Pegasus 097, diff. c, 1g, Cornwall, 1847. d, 2g, Cornwall, 1847, diff. e, 3g, Patrick Stirling #1, 1870. f, 4g, Patrick Stirling #1, 1870, diff. 5g, Stepney Brighton Terrier, 1872.

1984, June 20 ***Perf. 14***
2124 A382 Strip of 6, #a.-f.
Perf. 13
2125 A382 5g multicolored

No. C486 Overprinted in Blue on Silver with UN emblem and "40o Aniversario de la / Fundacion de las / Naciones Unidas 26.6.1944"

1984, Aug. 1 **Litho.** ***Perf. 14½***
2126 AP161 25g on No. C486

No. 1536 Ovptd. in Orange (#a.-d.) or Silver (#e.-g.) with AUSIPEX 84 Emblem and:

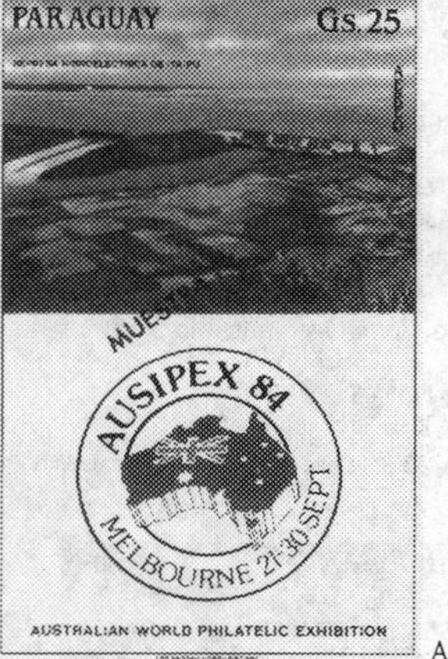

A383

1984, Aug. 21 ***Perf. 14***
2127 A271 Strip of 7, #a.-g.

Souvenir Sheet
Perf. 14½
2128 A383 25g multicolored

Ausipex '84 Intl. Philatelic Exhibition, Melbourne, Australia. No. 2128 is airmail.

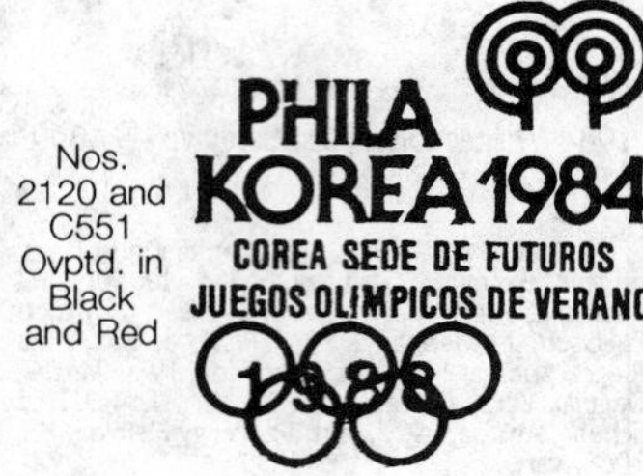

Nos. 2120 and C551 Ovptd. in Black and Red

1984 ***Perf. 13***
2129 A380 5g on #2120
Perf. 14
2130 AP178 30g on #C551

Issue dates: #2129, Sept. 20. #2130, Aug. 30.
No. 2130 is airmail.

No. 1512 Ovptd. "VER STUTTGART CAMPEON NACIONAL DE FUTBOL DE ALEMANIA 1984" and Emblem

1984, Sept. 5 ***Perf. 14***
2131 A263 Strip of 7, #a.-g.

VFB Stuttgart, 1984 German Soccer Champions.

Cat Type of 1976

Various cats: No. 2132a, 25c. b, 50c. c, 1g. d, 2g. e, 3g. f, 4g.

1984, Sept. 10 ***Perf. 13x13½***
2132 A287 Strip of 6, #a.-f.
2133 A287 5g multicolored

1984 Summer Olympics, Los Angeles — A384

Gold medalists: No. 2134a, 25c Michael Gross, W. Germany, swimming. b, 50c, Peter Vidmar, US, gymnastics. c, 1g, Fredy Schmidtke, W. Germany, cycling. d, 2g, Philippe Boisse, France, fencing. e, 3g, Ulrike Meyfarth, W. Germany, women's high jump. f, 4g, Games emblem. 5g, Mary Lou Retton, US, women's all-around gymnastics, vert. 30g, Rolf Milser, W. Germany, weight lifting, vert.

1985, Jan. 16 **Litho.** ***Perf. 13***
2134 A384 Strip of 6, #a.-f.
2135 A384 5g multicolored

Souvenir Sheet
Perf. 13½
2136 A384 30g multicolored

No. 2136 is airmail and contains one 50x60mm stamp. For overprints see Nos. 2174, 2199, 2200. Compare with type A399.

Mushrooms A385

Designs: No. 2137a, 25c, Boletus luteus. b, 50c, Agaricus campester. c, 1g, Pholiota spectabilis. d, 2g, Tricholoma terreum. e, 3g, Laccaria laccata. f, 4g, Amanita phalloides. 5g, Scleroderna verrucosum.

1985, Jan. 19 ***Perf. 14***
2137 A385 Strip of 6, #a.-f.
2138 A385 5g multicolored

See Nos. 2166-2167.

World Wildlife Fund — A386

Endangered or extinct species: No. 2139a, 25c, Capybara. b, 50c, Mono titi, vert. c, 1g, Rana cornuda adornada. d, 2g, Priodontes giganteus, digging. e, 3g, Priodontes giganteus, by water. f, 4g, Myrmecophaga tridactyla. g, 5g, Myrmecophaga tridactyla, with young.

1985, Mar. 13 ***Perf. 14***
2139 A386 Strip of 7, #a.-g.

See No. 2252.

No. 2037 Ovptd. in Red with ISRAPHIL Emblem

1985, Apr. 10
2140 A360 5g on No. 2037

Israel '85 Intl. Philatelic Exhibition.

John James Audubon, Birth Bicent. A387

Birds: No. 2141a, 25c, Piranga flava. b, 50c, Polyborus plancus. c, 1g, Chiroxiphia caudata. d, 2g, Xolmis irupero. e, 3g, Phloeoceastes leucopogon. f, 4g, Thraupis bonariensis. 5g, Parula pitiayumi, horiz.

1985, Apr. 18 ***Perf. 13***
2141 A387 Strip of 6, #a.-f.
2142 A387 5g multicolored

No. 2079 Ovptd. in Silver with Italia '85 Emblem

1985, May 20 ***Perf. 14***
2143 A370 5g on #2079

Italia '85 Intl. Philatelic Exhibition.

No. 1448e Ovptd. in Red on Silver

12 de Junio 1935 · 1985
Cincuentenario de la
PAZ del CHACO

1985, June 12
2144 A250 30c on #1448e

No. 2104 Ovptd. in Silver and Blue with LUPO 85 Congress Emblem

1985, July 5
2145 A375 5g on No. 2104

LUPO '85, Lucerne, Switzerland.

No. 2123 Ovptd. in Silver and Blue with MOPHILA 85 Emblem and "HAMBURGO 11-12. 9. 85"

1985, July 5 *Perf. 13*
2146 A381 5g on #2123

Mophila '85 Intl. Philatelic Exhibition, Hamburg.

Intl. Youth Year A388

Scenes from Tom Sawyer and Huckleberry Finn: No. 2147a, 25c, Mississippi riverboat. b, 50c, Finn. c, 1g, Finn and friends by campfire. d, 2g, Finn and Joe, sinking riverboat. e, 3g, Finn, friends, riverboat. f, 4g, Cemetery. 5g, Finn, Sawyer. 25g, Raft, riverboat.

1985, Aug. 5 *Perf. 13½x13*
2147 A388 Strip of 6, #a.-f.
2148 A388 5g multicolored

Souvenir Sheet

Perf. 14½

2149 A388 25g multicolored

No. 2149 is airmail. For overprint see No. C612.

German Railroads, 150th Anniv. — A389

Locomotives: No. 2150a, 25c, T3, 1883. b, 50c, T18, 1912. c, 1g, T16, 1914. d, 2g, #01 118, Historic Trains Society, Frankfurt. e, 3g, #05 001 Express, Nuremberg Transit Museum. f, 4g, #10 002 Express, 1957. 5g, Der Adler, 1835. 25g, Painting of 1st German Train, Dec. 7, 1835.

1985, Aug. 8 *Perf. 14*
2150 A389 Strip of 6, #a.-f.

Perf. 13

2151 A389 5g multicolored

Souvenir Sheet

Perf. 13½

2152 A389 25g multicolored

No. 2152 is airmail and contains one 75x53mm stamp. For overprint see No. 2165.

Development Projects — A390

Pres. Stroessner and: 10g, Soldier, map, vert. 25g, Model of Yaci Reta Hydroelectric Project. 50g, Itaipu Dam. 75g, Merchantman Lago Ipoa. 100g, 1975 Coin, vert. 200g, Asuncion Intl. Airport.

1985, Sept. 17 Litho. *Perf. 13*
2153 A390 10g multicolored
2154 A390 25g multicolored
2155 A390 50g multicolored
2156 A390 75g multicolored
2157 A390 100g multicolored
2158 A390 200g multicolored

Chaco Peace Agreement, 50th Anniv. (#2153, 2157). Nos. 2157-2158 are airmail. For overprints see Nos. 2254-2259.

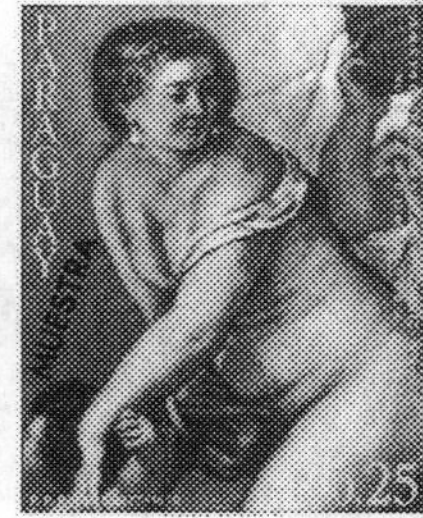

Nudes by Peter Paul Rubens A391

Details from paintings: No. 2159a, 25c, b, 50c, Venus in the Forge of Vulcan. c, 1g, Cimon and Iphigenia, horiz. d, 2g, The Horrors of War. e, 3g, Apotheosis of Henry IV and the Proclamation of the Regency. f, 4g, The Reception of Marie de Medici at Marseilles. 5g, Union of Earth and Water. 25g, Nature Attended by the Three Graces.

1985, Oct. 18 *Perf. 14*
2159 A391 Strip of 6, #a.-f.

Perf. 13x13½

2160 A391 5g multicolored

Souvenir Sheet

Perf. 14

2161 A391 25g multicolored

No. 2161 is airmail.

1986, Jan. 16 *Perf. 14*

Nudes by Titian: details from paintings. No. 2162a, 25c, Venus, an Organist, Cupid and a Little Dog. b, 50c, c, 1g, Diana and Actaeon. d, 2g, Danae. e, 3g, Nymph and a Shepherd. f, 4g, Venus of Urbino. 5g, Cupid Blindfolded by Venus, vert. 25g, Diana and Callisto, vert.

2162 A391 Strip of 6, #a.-f.

Perf. 13

2163 A391 5g multicolored

Souvenir Sheet

Perf. 13½

2164 A391 25g multicolored

No. 2164 is airmail and contains one 50x60mm stamp.

Nos. 2150 Ovptd. in Red **ESSEN 86**

1986, Feb. 25 *Perf. 14*
2165 A389 Strip of 6, #a.-f.

Essen '86 Intl. Philatelic Exhibition.

Mushrooms Type of 1985

Designs: No. 2166a, 25g, Lepiota procera. b, 50c, Tricholoma albo-brunneum. c, 1g, Clavaria. d, 2g, Volvaria. e, 3g, Licoperdon perlatum. f, 4g, Dictyophora duplicata. 5g, Polyporus rubrum.

1986, Mar. 17 *Perf. 14*
2166 A385 Strip of 6, #a.-f.

Perf. 13

2167 A385 5g multicolored

Automobile, Cent. — A393

Designs: No. 2168a, 25c, Wolseley, 1904. b, 50c, Peugeot, 1892. c, 1g, Panhard, 1895. d, 2g, Cadillac, 1903. e, 3g, Fiat, 1902. f, 4g, Stanley Steamer, 1898. 5g, Carl Benz Velocipede , 1885. 25g, Carl Benz (1844-1929), automotive engineer.

1986, Apr. 28 Litho. *Perf. 13½x13*
2168 A393 Strip of 6, #a.-f.
2169 A393 5g multicolored

Souvenir Sheet

Perf. 13½

2170 A393 25g multicolored

No. 2170 is airmail and contains one 30x40mm stamp.

World Cup Soccer Championships, Mexico City — A394

Various match scenes, Paraguay vs.: No. 2171a, 25c, b, 50c, US, 1930. c, 1g, d, 2g, Belgium, 1930. e, 3g, Bolivia, 1985. f, 4g, Brazil, 1985. 5g, Natl. Team, 1986. 25g, Player, vert.

1986, Mar. 12 *Perf. 13½x13*
2171 A394 Strip of 6, #a.-f.
2172 A394 5g multicolored

Souvenir Sheet

Perf. 14½

2173 A394 25g multicolored

No. 2173 is airmail. For overprints see Nos. 2283, 2287.

No. 2135 Ovptd. in Silver "JUEGOS / PANAMERICANOS / INDIANAPOLIS / 1987"

1986, June 9 *Perf. 13*
2174 A384 5g on No. 2135

1987 Pan American Games, Indianapolis.

Maybach Automobiles — A395

Designs: No. 2175a, 25c, W-6, 1930-36. b, 50c, SW-38 convertible. c, 1g, SW-38 hardtop, 1938. d, 2g, W-6/DSG, 1933. e, 3g, Zeppelin DS-8, 1931. f, 4g, Zeppelin DS-8, 1936. 5g, Zeppelin DS-8 aerodynamic cabriolet, 1936.

1986, June 19 *Perf. 13½x13*
2175 A395 Strip of 6, #a.-f.
2176 A395 5g multicolored

No. 2077 Overprinted in Bright Blue with Olympic Rings and "CALGARY 1988"

1986, July 9 *Perf. 13*
2177 A369 5g on #2077

1988 Winter Olympics, Calgary.

Statue of Liberty, Cent. — A396

Passenger liners: No. 2178a, 25c, City of Paris, England, 1867. b, 50c, Mauretania, England. c, 1g, Normandie, France, 1932. d, 2g, Queen Mary, England, 1938. e, 3g, Kaiser Wilhelm the Great II, Germany, 1897. f, 4g, United States, US, 1952. 5g, Bremen, Germany, 1928. 25g, Sailing ship Gorch Fock, Germany, 1976, vert.

1986, July 25 *Perf. 13*
2178 A396 Strip of 6, #a.-f.
2179 A396 5g multicolored

Souvenir Sheet

Perf. 14½

2180 A396 25g multicolored

No. 2180 is airmail and contains one 50x70mm stamp.

Dog Type of 1984

Designs: No. 2181a, 25c, German shepherd. b, 50c, Icelandic shepherd. c, 1g, Collie. d, 2g, Boxer. e, 3g, Scottish terrier. f, 4g, Welsh springer spaniel. 5g, Painting of Labrador retriever by Ellen Krebs, vert.

1986, Aug. 28 *Perf. 13x13½*
2181 A376 Strip of 6, #a.-f.

Perf. 13½x13

2182 A376 5g multicolored

Paraguay Official Stamps, Cent. — A397

Designs: Nos. 2183-2185, No. O1. Nos. 2186-2188, No. O4.

1986, Aug. 28 Litho. *Perf. 13x13½*

2183 A397	5g multi		15	15
2184 A397	15g multi		15	15
2185 A397	40g multi		15	15
2186 A397	65g multi		18	15
2187 A397	100g multi		25	18
2188 A397	150g multi		38	28
		Set value	1.00	75

Nos. 2186-2188 are airmail.

Tennis Players A398

Designs: No. 2189a, Victor Pecci, Paraguay. b, 50c, Jimmy Connors, US. c, 1g, Gabriela Sabatini, Argentina. d, 2g, Boris Becker, W. Germany. e, 3g, Claudia Kohde, E. Germany. f, 4g, Sweden, 1985 Davis Cup team champions, horiz. 5g, Steffi Graf, W. Germany. 25g, 1986 Wimbledon champions Martina Navratilova and Boris Becker, horiz.

Perf. 13x13½, 13½x13

1986, Sept. 17 **Unwmk.**
2189 A398 Strip of 6, #a.-f.
2190 A398 5g multicolored

Souvenir Sheet

Perf. 13½

2191 A398 25g multicolored

No. 2191 is airmail and contains one 75x55mm stamp. For overprints see No. 2229.

Nos. 1454-1456 Ovptd. in Red or Silver (#2192c, 2192d): "Homenage a la visita de Sus Altezas Imperiales los Principees Hitachi --28.9-3.10.86"

1986, Sept. 28 *Perf. 14*
2192 A251 Strip of 5, #a.-e.
2193 A251 50c on #1455
2194 A251 75c on #1456

1988 Summer Olympics, Seoul — A399

Athletes, 1984 Olympic medalists: No. 2195a, 25c, Runner. b, 50c, Boxer. c, 1g, Joaquim Cruz, Brazil, 800-meter run. d, 2g, Mary Lou Retton, US, individual all-around gymnastics. e, 3g, Carlos Lopes, Portugal, marathon. f, 4g, Fredy Schmidtke, W. Germany, 1000-meter cycling, horiz. 5g, Joe Fargis, US, equestrian, horiz.

1986, Oct. 29 *Perf. 13x13½,13½x13*
2195 A399 Strip of 6, #a.-f.
2196 A399 5g multicolored

For overprints see Nos. 2227-2228, 2230.

Nos. 1574c-1574g Ovptd. in Silver, Ship Type of 1983 Ovptd. in Red

1987, Mar. 20 **Litho.** *Perf. 14*
2197 A278 Strip of 5, #a.-e.
2198 AP176 10g multicolored

500th Anniv. of the discovery of America and the 12th Spanish-American Stamp & Coin Show, Madrid.

Olympics Type of 1985 Overprinted in Silver with Olympic Rings and 500th Anniv. of the Discovery of America Emblems and "BARCELONA 92 / Sede de las Olimpiadas en el ano del 500o Aniversario del Descubrimiento de America"

Designs like Nos. 2134a-2134f.

1987, Apr. 24 *Perf. 14*
2199 A384 Strip of 6, #a.-f.

1992 Summer Olympics, Barcelona and discovery of America, 500th anniv. in 1992.

No. 2135 Overprinted in Silver "ROMA / OLYMPHILEX" / Olympic Rings / "SEOUL / CALGARY / 1988"

1987, Apr. 30 *Perf. 13*
2200 A384 5g on No. 2135

Olymphilex '87 Intl. Philatelic Exhibition, Rome.

Cat Type of 1976

Various cats and kittens: No. 2201a, 1g. b, 2g. c, 3g. d, 5g. 60g, Black cat.

1987, May 22 *Perf. 13x13½*
2201 A287 Strip of 4, #a.-d.
2202 A287 60g multicolored

No. 2202 also exists perf. 14. For overprint see No. 2212.

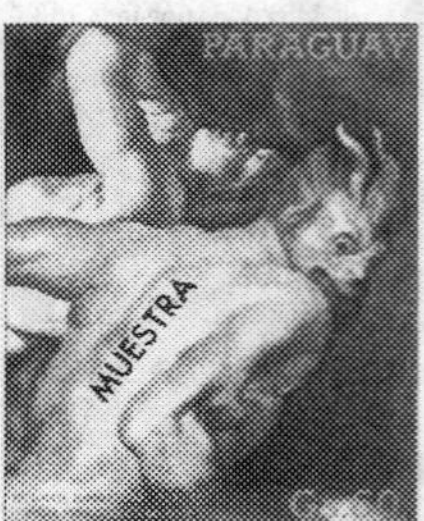

Paintings by Rubens A400

Designs: No. 2203a, 1g, The Four Corners of the World, horiz. b, 2g, Jupiter and Calisto. c, 3g, Susanna and the Elders. d, 5g, Marriage of Henry IV and Marie de Medici in Lyon.

60g, The Last Judgment. 100g, The Holy Family with St. Elizabeth and John the Baptist. No. 2205A, War and Peace.

1987 **Litho.** *Perf. 13x13½, 13½x13*
2203 A400 Strip of 4, #a.-d.
2204 A400 60g multicolored

Souvenir Sheets

2205 A400 100g multicolored
2205A A400 100g multicolored

Christmas 1986 (#2205).

Issue dates: No. 2204, May 25. No. 2205, May 26.

Nos. 2205-2205A are airmail and contain one 54x68mm stamp.

Places and Events A401

Designs: 10g, ACEPAR Industrial Plant. 25g, Franciscan monk, native, vert. 50g, Yaguaron Church altar, vert. 75g, Founding of Asuncion, 450th anniv. 100g, Paraguay Airlines passenger jet. 200g, Pres. Stoessner, vert.

1987, June 2 **Litho.** *Perf. 13*
2206 A401 10g multicolored
2207 A401 25g multicolored
2208 A401 50g multicolored
2209 A401 75g multicolored
2210 A401 100g multicolored
2211 A401 200g multicolored

Nos. 2210-2211 are airmail. For overprints see Nos. 2225-2226, C685, C722.

No. 2201 Ovptd. in Blue CAPEX 87

1987, June 12 *Perf. 13x13½*
2212 A287 Strip of 4, #a.-d.

Discovery of America, 500th Anniv. (in 1992) — A402

Discovery of America anniv. emblem and ships: No. 2213a, 1g, Spanish galleon, 17th cent. b, 2g, Victoria, 1st to circumnavigate the globe, 1519-22. c, 3g, San Hermenegildo. 5g, San Martin, c.1582. 60g, Santa Maria, c.1492, vert.

1987, Sept. 9 *Perf. 14*
2213 A402 Strip of 4, #a.-d.

Perf. 13x13½

2214 A402 60g multicolored

Colorado Party, Cent. A403

Bernardino Caballero (founder), President Stroessner and: 5g, 10g, 25g, Three-lane highway. 150g, 170g, 200g, Power lines.

Perf. 13½x13

1987, Sept. 11 **Wmk. 347**
2215 A403 5g multi 15 15
2216 A403 10g multi 15 15
2217 A403 25g multi 15 15
2218 A403 150g multi 35 26
2219 A403 170g multi 38 28
2220 A403 200g multi 45 35
Set value 1.30 1.00

Nos. 2218-2220 are airmail.

Berlin, 750th Anniv. A404

Berlin Stamps and Coins: No. 2221a, 1g, #9NB145. b, 2g, #9NB154. c, 3g, #9N57, vert. d, 5g, #9N170, vert. 60g, 1987 Commemorative coin, vert.

Perf. 13½x13, 13½x13

1987, Sept. 12 **Unwmk.**
2221 A404 Strip of 4, #a.-d.
2222 A404 60g multicolored

For overprints see Nos. 2239, 2294.

Race Cars A405

Designs: No. 2223a, 1g, Audi Sport Quattro. b, 2g, Lancia Delta S 4. c, 3g, Fiat 131. d, 5g, Porsche 911 4x4. 60g, Lancia Rally.

1987, Sept. 27 *Perf. 13*
2223 A405 Strip of 4, #a.-d.

Perf. 14

2224 A405 60g multicolored

Nos. 2209-2210 Ovptd. in Bright Blue

EXFIVIA 87
Bolivia
4 al 13.12.87

1987, Sept. 30 *Perf. 13*
2225 A401 75g on #2209
2226 A401 100g on #2210

EXFIVIA '87 Intl. Philatelic Exhibition, LaPaz, Bolivia. No. 2226 is airmail.

Nos. 2195d-2195f, 2196 Overprinted in Black or Silver

1987, Oct. 1 *Perf. 13½x13*
2227 A399 Strip of 3, #a.-c.
2228 A399 5g on No. 2196 (S)

Olymphilex '87 Intl. Phil. Exhib., Seoul.

No. 2189 Ovptd. with Emblem and "PHILATELIA '87," etc.

Perf. 13x13½, 13½x13

1987, Oct. 15
2229 A398 Strip of 6, #a.-f.

PHILATELIA '87 Intl. Phil. Exhib., Cologne. Size and configuration of overprint varies.

Nos. 2195a-2195b Ovptd. in Bright Blue for EXFILNA '87 and BARCELONA 92

1987, Oct. 24 *Perf. 13x13½*
2230 A399 Pair, #a.-b.

Exfilna '87 Intl. Philatelic Exhibition.

Ship Paintings A406

Designs: No. 2231a, 1g, San Juan Nepomuceno. b, 2g, San Eugenio. c, 3g, San Telmo. d, 5g, San Carlos. 60g, Spanish galleon, 16th cent. 100g, One of Columbus' ships.

1987 **Litho.** *Perf. 14*
2231 A406 Strip of 4, #a.-d.

Perf. 13x13½

2232 A406 60g multicolored

Souvenir Sheet

Perf. 13½

2233 A406 100g multicolored

Discovery of America, 500th anniv. in 1992 (#2233). Issue dates: Nos. 2231-2232, Dec. 10. No. 2233, Dec. 12.

No. 2233 is airmail and contains one 54x75mm stamp.

1988 Winter Olympics, Calgary — A407

Designs: No. 2237a, 5g, Joel Gaspoz. b, 60g, Peter Mueller.

1987, Dec. 31 *Perf. 14*
2234 A407 1g Maria Walliser
2235 A407 2g Erika Hess
2236 A407 3g Pirmin Zurbriggen

Miniature Sheet

Perf. 13½x13

2237 A407 Sheet of 4 each #2237a, 2237b+label

Souvenir Sheet

Perf. 14½

2238 A407 100g Walliser, Zurbriggen

No. 2238 is airmail. For overprints see Nos. 2240-2242.

No. 2221 Ovptd. in Silver "AEROPEX 88 / ADELAIDE"

1988, Jan. 29 ***Perf. 13***

2239 A404 Strip of 4, #a.-d.

Aeropex '88, Adelaide, Australia.

Nos. 2234-2236 Ovptd. in Gold with Olympic Rings and "OLYMPEX / CALGARY 1988"

1988, Feb. 13 ***Perf. 14***

2240 A407 1g on #2234
2241 A407 2g on #2235
2242 A407 3g on #2236

Olympex '88, Calgary. Size and configuration of overprint varies.

1988 Summer Olympics, Seoul — A408

Equestrians: No. 2243a, 1g, Josef Neckermann, W. Germany, on Venetia. b, 2g, Henri Chammartin, Switzerland. c, 3g, Christine Stueckelberger, Switzerland, on Granat. d, 5g, Liselott Linsenhoff, W. Germany, on Piaff. 60g, Hans-Guenter Winkler, W. Germany.

1988, Mar. 7 ***Perf. 13***

2243 A408 Strip of 4, #a.-d.

Perf. 13½x13

2244 A408 60g multicolored

For overprint see No. 2291.

Berlin, 750th Anniv. A409

Paintings: No. 2245a, 1g, Virgin and Child, by Jan Gossaert. b, 2g, Virgin and Child, by Rubens. c, 3g, Virgin and Child, by Hans Memling. d, 5g, Madonna, by Albrecht Durer. 60g, Adoration of the Shepherds, by Martin Schongauer.

1988, Apr. 8 ***Perf. 13***

2245 A409 Strip of 4, #a.-d.
2246 A409 60g multicolored

Christmas 1987. See Nos. C727-C731.

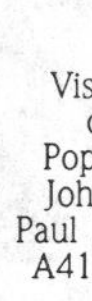

Visit of Pope John Paul II A410

Religious art: No. 2247a, 1g, Pope John Paul II, hands clasped. b, 2g, Statue of the Virgin. c, 3g, Czestochowa Madonna. d, 5g, Our Lady of Caacupe. Nos. 2247a-2247d are vert.

1988, Apr. 11 ***Perf. 13***

2247 A410 Strip of 4, #a.-d.
2248 A410 60g multicolored

Visit of Pope John Paul II — A411

Rosette window and crucifix.

1988, May 5 **Litho.** ***Perf. 13x13½***

2249 A411	10g blue & blk		15	15
2250 A411	20g blue & blk		15	15
2251 A411	50g blue & blk		22	16
	Set value		36	28

World Wildlife Fund Type of 1985

Endangered Animals: No. 2252a, 1g, like #2139g. b, 2g, like #2139f. c, 3g, like #2139d. d, 5g, like #2139e.

1988, June 14 **Unwmk.** ***Perf. 14***

2252 A386 Strip of 4, #a.-d.

Nos. 2252a-2252d have denomination and border in blue.

Nos. 2000a-2000d Ovptd. in Gold with Emblem and "Bicentenario de / AUSTRALIA / 1788-1988"

1988, June 17

2253 A351 Strip of 4, #a.-d.

Australia, bicent.

Types of 1985 Overprinted in 2 or 4 Lines in Gold "NUEVO PERIODO PRESIDENCIAL CONSTITUCIONAL 1988-1993"

1988, Aug. 12 ***Perf. 14***

2254 A390 10g like #2153
2255 A390 25g like #2154
2256 A390 50g like #2155
2257 A390 75g like #2156
2258 A390 100g like #2157
2259 A390 200g like #2158

Pres. Stroessner's new term in office. Nos. 2258-2259 are airmail.

Olympic Tennis, Seoul A412

Designs: No. 2260a, 1g, Steffi Graf, W. Germany. b, 2g, Olympic gold medal, horiz. c, 3g, Boris Becker, W. Germany. d, 5g, Emilio Sanchez, Spain. 60g, Steffi Graf, diff.

1988, Aug. 16 ***Perf. 13***

2260 A412 Strip of 4, #a.-d.
2261 A412 60g multicolored

1992 Summer Olympics, Barcelona — A413

Olympic medalists from Spain: No. 2262a, 1g, Ricardo Zamora, soccer, Antwerp, 1920, vert. b, 2g, Equestrian team, Amsterdam, 1928. c, 3g, Angel Leon, shooting, Helsinki, 1952. d, 5g, Kayak team, Montreal, 1976. 60g, Francisco Fernandez Ochoa, slalom, Sapporo, 1972, vert. 100g, Olympic Stadium, Barcelona, vert.

1989, Jan. 5 ***Perf. 14***

2262 A413 Strip of 4, #a.-d.

Perf. 13

2263 A413 60g multicolored

Souvenir Sheet

Perf. 13½

2264 A413 100g multicolored

Discovery of America 500th anniv. (in 1992). No. 2264 is airmail and contains one 50x60mm stamp. For overprint see No. 2293.

Columbus Space Station A414

1989, Jan. 7 **Litho.** ***Perf. 13x13½***

2265 A414 60g multicolored

Discovery of America 500th anniv. (in 1992).

No. 2076 Overprinted in Silver, Red and Blue with Olympic Rings, "1992" and Emblem

Perf. 13½x13, 13x13½

1989, Jan. 10

2266 A369 Strip of 6, #a.-f.

1992 Winter Olympics, Albertville. Location and configuration of overprint varies.

No. 1454 Ovptd. in Silver "HOMENAJE AL EMPERADOR HIROITO DE JAPON 29.IV,1901-6.1.1989"

1989, Feb. 8 ***Perf. 14***

2267 A251 Strip of 5, #a.-e.

Death of Emperor Hirohito of Japan.

Formula 1 Drivers, Race Cars — A415

Designs: No. 2268a, 1g, Stirling Moss, Mercedes W196. b, 2g, Emerson Fittipaldi, Lotus. c, 3g, Nelson Piquet, Lotus. d, 5g, Niki Lauda, Ferrari 312 B. 60g, Juan Manuel Fangio, Maserati 250F.

1989, Mar. 6 ***Perf. 13***

2268 A415 Strip of 4, #a.-d.
2269 A415 60g multicolored

Paintings by Titian A416

Details: No. 2270a, 1g, Bacchus and Ariadne (Bacchus). b, 2g, Bacchus and Ariadne (tutelary spirit). c, 3g, Death of Actaeon. d, 5g, Portrait of a Young Woman with a Fur Cape. 60g, Concert in a Field. 100g, Holy Family with Donor.

1989, Apr. 17 ***Perf. 13x13½***

2270 A416 Strip of 4, #a.-d.
2271 A416 60g multicolored

Souvenir Sheet

Perf. 13½

2271A A416 100g multicolored

No. 2271A is airmail and contains one 60x49mm stamp. Issue date: May 27.

1994 Winter Olympics, Lillehammer — A417

Athletes: No. 2272a, 1g, Torbjorn Lokken, 1987 Nordic combined world champion. b, 2g, Atle Skardal, skier, Norway. c, 3g, Geir Karlstad, Norway, world 10,000-meter speed skating champion, 1987. d, 5g, Franck Piccard, France, 1988 Olympic medalist, skiing. 60g, Roger Ruud, ski jumper, Norway.

1989, May 23 ***Perf. 13½x13***

2272 A417 Strip of 4, #a.-d.
2273 A417 60g multicolored

Cat Type of 1976

Various cats: #2274a, 1g. b, 2g. c, 3g. d, 5g.

1989, May 25 ***Perf. 13***

2274 A287 Strip of 4, #a.-d.
2275 A287 60g Siamese

Federal Republic of Germany, 40th Anniv. — A418

Famous men and automobiles: No. 2276a, 1g, Konrad Adenauer, chancellor, 1949-1963, Mercedes. b, 2g, Ludwig Erhard, chancellor, 1963-1966, Volkswagen Beetle. c, 3g, Felix Wankel, engine designer, 1963 NSU Spider. d, 5g, Franz Josef Strauss, President of Bavarian Cabinet, BMW 502. 60g, Pres. Richard von Weizsacker and Dr. Josef Neckermann.

1989, May 27 ***Perf. 13½x13***

2276 A418 Strip of 4, #a.-d.
2277 A418 60g multicolored

For overprints, see No. 2369.

Ship Type of 1980 Overprinted with Discovery of America, 500th Anniv. Emblem in Red on Silver

1989, May 29 *Perf. 14½*

Miniature Sheet

2278 A343 Sheet of 7+label, like #1972

Discovery of America 500th anniv. (in 1992).

No. 2122a Overprinted with Hamburg Emblem and Nos. 2122b-2122f, 2123 Ovptd. with Diff. Emblem in Red on Silver

1989, May 30 Litho. *Perf. 13½x13*

2279 A381 Strip of 6, #a.-f.
2280 A381 5g on #2123

City of Hamburg, 800th anniv.

Nos. 2006a-2006b Ovptd. "BRASILIANA / 89"

1989, July 5 *Perf. 14*

2281 A352 Pair, #a.-b.

No. 2171 Overprinted in Metallic Red and Silver with FIFA and Italia 90 Emblems and "PARAGUAY PARTICIPO EN 13 CAMPEONATOS MUNDIALES"

1989, Sept. 14 Litho. *Perf. 13½x13*

2283 A394 Strip of 6, #a.-f.

Size and configuration of overprint varies.

Nos. C738, C753 Overprinted in metallic red with Italia '90 emblem and "SUDAMERICA-GRUPO 2 / PARAGUAY-COLOMBIA / PARAGUAY-ECUADOR / COLOMBIA-PARAGUAY / ECUADOR-PARAGUAY" and in metallic red on silver with FIFA emblem

1989, Sept. 14 Litho. *Perf. 13*

2284 AP228 25g on #C738
2285 AP232 25g on #C753

Nos. 2046, 2172 Overprinted in Metallic Red and Silver "PARAGUAY CLASIFICADO EN 1930, 1950, 1958 Y 1986" and Emblems or "ITALIA '90"

1989, Sept. 15 Litho. *Perf. 14*

2286 A362 Strip of 6, #a.-f.

Perf. 13½x13

2287 A394 5g multicolored

1990 World Cup Soccer Championships, Italy. Location and size of overprint varies.

Nos. 1284-1286 Ovptd. in Gold "...BIEN ESTUVIMOS EN LA LUNA AHORA NECESITAMOS LOS MEDIOS PARA LLEGAR A LOS PLANETAS" Wernher von Braun's Signature and UN and Space Emblems

1989, Sept. 16 *Perf. 14*

2288 A226 Strip of 5, #a.-e.
2289 A226 50c multicolored
2290 A226 75c multicolored

Location, size and configuration of overprint varies.

Nos. 2243, C764 Overprinted in Silver or Gold with Emblem and "ATENAS 100 ANOS DE LOS JUEGOS OLIMPICOS 1896-1996"

1989, Sept. 18 *Perf. 13*

2291 A408 Strip of 4, #a.-d.
2292 AP233 25g on #C764 (G)

1992 Summer Olympics Barcelona, Spain. Size and location of overprint varies.

Nos. 2262a-2262d Ovptd. in Silver with Heads of Steffi Graf or Boris Becker and: "WIMBLEDON 1988 / SEUL 1988 / WIMBLEDON 1989 / EL TENIS NUEVAMENTE EN / LAS OLIMPIADAS 1988-1992" or Similar

1989, Sept. 19 *Perf. 14*

2293 A413 Strip of 4, #a.-d.

Addition of tennis as an Olympic sport in 1992. Size and configuration of overprint varies.

No. 2221 Ovptd. in Gold and Blue "PRIMER AEROPUERTO PARA / /COHETES, BERLIN 1930 OBERTH, / NEBEL, RITTER, VON BRAUN" space emblem and "PROF. DR. HERMANN / OBERTH 95o ANIV. / NACIMIENTO 25.6.1989"

Perf. 13½x13, 13x13½

1989, Sept. 20

2294 A404 Strip of 4, #a.-d.

Dr. Hermann Oberth, rocket scientist, 95th birth anniv. Overprint size, etc, varies.

Nos. 1406-1408 Ovptd. in Metallic Red and Silver with Emblems and "OLIMPIADAS / DE INVIERNO / ALBERTVILLE 1992" in 2 or 3 Lines

1989, Sept. 21 *Perf. 14*

2295 A244 Strip of 5, #a.-e.
2296 A244 50c multicolored
2297 A244 75c multicolored

1992 Winter Olympics, Albertville. Size and configuration of overprint varies.

Nos. 2251, C724 Overprinted **PARAFIL 89**

Perf. 13½, 13½x13

1989, Oct. 9 Litho. Wmk. 347

2298 A411 50g on #2251
2299 AP226 120g on #C724

Parafil '89, Paraguay-Argentina philatelic exhibition.

Birds Facing Extinction A419

Perf. 13½x13

1989, Dec. 19 Litho. Wmk. 347

2300	A419	50g	Ara chloroptera	15	15
2301	A419	100g	Mergus octosetaceus	16	15
2302	A419	300g	Rhea americana	50	40
2303	A419	500g	Ramphastos toco	80	65
2304	A419	1000g	Crax fasciolota	1.65	1.35
2305	A419	2000g	Ara araruna	3.25	2.60
			Nos. 2300-2305 (6)	6.51	5.30

Nos. 2302-2305 airmail. Nos. 2300 & 2305 vert. Frames and typestyles vary greatly. Watermark on 50g, 100g, 300g is 8mm high.

1992 Summer Olympics, Barcelona A420

Athletes: No. 2306a, 1g, A. Fichtel and S. Bau, W. Germany, foils, 1988. b, 2g, Spanish basketball team, 1984. c, 3g, Jackie Joyner-Kersee, heptathalon and long jump, 1988, horiz. d, 5g, L. Beerbaum, W. Germany, show jumping, team, 1988. 60g, W. Brinkmann, W. Germany, show jumping, team, 1988. 100g, Emilio Sanchez, tennis.

Unwmk.

1989, Dec. 26 Litho. *Perf. 14*

2306 A420 Strip of 4, #a.-d.

Perf. 13

2307 A420 60g multicolored

Souvenir Sheet

Perf. 13½

2308 A420 100g multicolored

No. 2308 is airmail and contains one 47x57mm stamp.

World Cup Soccer Championships, Italy — A421

1986 World Cup soccer players in various positions: No. 2309a, 1g, England vs. Paraguay. b, 2g, Spain vs. Denmark. c, 3g, France vs. Italy. d, 5g, Germany vs. Morocco. 60g, Mexico vs. Paraguay. 100g, Germany vs. Argentina.

1989, Dec. 29 *Perf. 14*

2309 A421 Strip of 4, #a.-d.

Perf. 13½

2310 A421 60g multicolored

Souvenir Sheet

Perf. 14½

2311 A421 100g multicolored

No. 2311 is airmail and contains one 40x50mm stamp.

For overprints, see Nos. 2355-2356.

1992 Summer Olympics, Barcelona — A422

Barcelona '92, proposed Athens '96 emblems and: No. 2312a, 1g, Greece #128. b, 2g, Greece #126, vert. c, 3g, Greece #127, vert. d, 5g, Greece #123, vert. 60g, Paraguay #736. 100g, Horse and rider, vert.

1990, Jan. 4 *Perf. 13½x13, 13x13½*

2312 A422 Strip of 4, #a.-d.
2313 A422 60g multicolored

Souvenir Sheet

Perf. 13½

2314 A422 100g multicolored

No. 2314 is airmail and contains one 50x60mm stamp and exists with either white or yellow border. Stamps inscribed 1989.

For overprints see No. 2357.

Swiss Confederation, 700th Anniv. — A423

Designs: No. 2315a, 3g, Monument to William Tell. b, 5g, Manship Globe, UN Headquarters, Geneva. 60g, 15th century messenger, Bern. No. 2317, First Swiss steam locomotive, horiz. No. 2318, Jean Henri Dunant, founder of the Red Cross, horiz.

1990, Jan. 25 *Perf. 14*

2315 A423 Pair, #a.-b.

Perf. 13

2316 A423 60g multicolored

Souvenir Sheets

Perf. 14½

2317 A423 100g multicolored
2318 A423 100g multicolored

Nos. 2317-2318 are airmail. For overprints see Nos. 2352-2354.

Wood Carving A424

Discovery of America, 500th anniversary emblem and: No. 2319a, 1g, First cathechism in Guarani. b, 2g, shown. No. 2319 has continuous design.

1990, Jan. 26 *Perf. 14*

2319 A424 Pair, #a.-b. + label

Organization of American States, Cent. — A425

Perf. 13½x13

1990, Feb. 9 Litho. Wmk. 347

2320	A425	50g	multicolored	15	15
2321	A425	100g	multicolored	30	25
2322	A425	200g	Map of Paraguay	60	48

1992 Winter Olympics, Albertville — A426

Calgary 1988 skiers: No. 2323a, 1g, Alberto Tomba, Italy, slalom and giant slalom. b, 2g, Vreni Schneider, Switzerland, women's slalom and giant slalom, vert. c, 3g, Luc Alphand, France, skier, vert. d, 5g, Matti Nykaenen, Finland, ski-jumping.

60g, Marina Kiehl, W. Germany, women's downhill. 100g, Frank Piccard, France, super giant slalom.

1990, Mar. 7 Unwmk. *Perf. 14*

2323 A426 Strip of 4, #a.-d.

Perf. 13

2324 A426 60g multicolored

Souvenir Sheet

Perf. 14½

2325 A426 100g multicolored

No. 2325 is airmail, contains one 40x50mm stamp and exists with either white or yellow border.

Pre-Columbian Art, Customs — A427

UPAE Emblem and: 150g, Pre-Columbian basket. 500g, Aboriginal ceremony.

1990, Mar. 8 Wmk. 347 *Perf. 13*

2326	A427	150g multicolored	45	38
2327	A427	500g multicolored	1.50	1.20

No. 2327 is airmail.
For overprints see Nos. 2345-2346.

First Postage Stamp, 150th Anniv. — A428

Penny Black, Mail Transportation 500th anniv. emblem and: No. 2328a, 1g, Penny Black on cover. b, 2g, Mauritius #1-2 on cover. c, 3g, Baden #4b on cover. d, 5g, Roman States #4 on cover. 60g, Paraguay #C38 and four #C54 on cover.

1990, Mar. 12 Unwmk. *Perf. 14*

2328 A428 Strip of 4, #a.-d.

Perf. 13¹/₂x13

2329 A428 60g multicolored

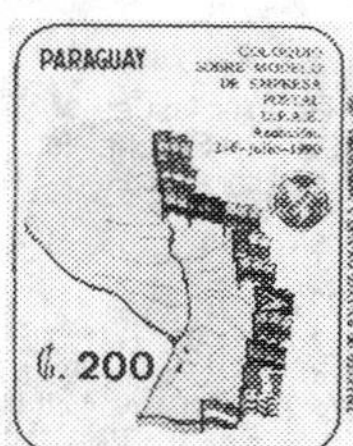

Postal Union of the Americas and Spain (UPAE) — A429

1990, July 2 *Perf. 13x13¹/₂*

2330	A429	200g Map, flags	35	30
2331	A429	250g Paraguay #1	40	35
2332	A429	350g FDC of #2326-2327, horiz.	60	45

National University, Cent. (in 1989) — A430

1990, Sept. 8

2333	A430	300g Future site	90	70
2334	A430	400g Present site	1.20	95
2335	A430	600g Old site	1.80	1.45

Franciscan Churches A431

Perf. 13¹/₂x13

1990, Sept. 25 Litho. Wmk. 347

2336	A431	50g Guarambare	15	15
2337	A431	100g Yaguaron	30	25
2338	A431	200g Ita	60	48

For overprints see Nos. 2366-2368.

Democracy in Paraguay A432

Designs: 100g, State and Catholic Church, vert. 200g, Human rights, vert. 300g, Freedom of the Press, vert. 500g, Return of the exiles. 3000g, People and democracy.

Perf. 13¹/₂x13, 13x13¹/₂

1990, Oct. 5 Litho. Wmk. 347

2339	A432	50g multicolored	15	15
2340	A432	100g multicolored	20	18
2341	A432	200g multicolored	40	36
2342	A432	300g multicolored	60	55
2343	A432	500g multicolored	1.00	90
2344	A432	3000g multicolored	6.00	5.50
		Nos. 2339-2344 (6)	8.35	7.64

Nos. 2343-2344 are airmail.

Nos. 2326-2327 Overprinted in Magenta

1990 Litho. Wmk. 347 *Perf. 13*

2345	A427	150g multicolored	45	38
2346	A427	500g multicolored	1.50	1.20

No. 2346 is airmail.

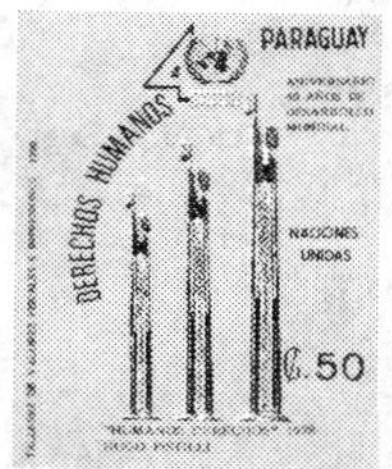

UN Development Program, 40th Anniv. A433

Designs: 50m, Human Rights, sculpture by Hugo Pistilli. 100m, United Nations, sculpture by Hermann Guggiari. 150m, Miguel de Cervantes Literature Award, won by Augusto Roa Bastos.

1990, Oct. 26

2347	A433	50g lilac & multi	15	15
2348	A433	100g gray & multi	30	25
2349	A433	150g green & multi	45	38

America A434

Designs: 50g, Banks of Paraguay River. 250g, Chaco land.

Perf. 13¹/₂x13

1990, Oct. 31 Wmk. 347

2350	A434	50g multicolored	15	15
2351	A434	250g multicolored	50	42

No. 2351 is airmail.

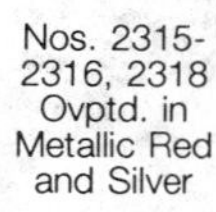
Nos. 2315-2316, 2318 Ovptd. in Metallic Red and Silver

Unwmk.

1991, Apr. 2 Litho. *Perf. 14*

2352 A423 Pair, #a.-b.

Perf. 13

2353 A423 60g on #2316

Souvenir Sheet

Perf. 14¹/₂

2354 A423 100g on #2318

Swiss Confederation, 700th anniv. and Red Cross, 125th anniv. No. 2354 is airmail. No. 2352 exists perf. 13. Location of overprint varies.

Nos. 2309-2310 Ovptd. in Silver

1991, Apr. 4 *Perf. 14*

2355 A421 Strip of 4, #a.-d.

Perf. 13x13¹/₂

2356 A421 60g on #2310

1994 World Cup Soccer Championships. Location of overprint varies.

Nos. 2312, C822, C766 Ovptd. in Silver

1991, Apr. 4 *Perf. 13*

2357 A422 Strip of 4, #a.-d.
2358 AP246 25g on #C822

Perf. 13x13¹/₂

2359 AP233 30g on #C766

Participation of reunified Germany in 1992 Summer Olympics. Nos. 2358-2359 are airmail. Location of overprint varies.

Professors — A435

Designs: 50g, Julio Manuel Morales, gynecologist. 100g, Carlos Gatti, clinician. 200g, Gustavo Gonzalez, geologist. 300g, Juan Max Boettner, physician and musician. 350g, Juan Boggino, pathologist. 500g, Andres Barbero, physician, founder of Paraguayan Red Cross.

Perf. 13x13¹/₂

1991, Apr. 5 Wmk. 347

2360	A435	50g multicolored	15	15
2361	A435	100g multicolored	20	18
2362	A435	200g multicolored	40	36
2363	A435	300g multicolored	60	55
2364	A435	350g multicolored	70	60
2365	A435	500g multicolored	1.00	90
		Nos. 2360-2365 (6)	3.05	2.74

Nos. 2364-2365 are airmail.

Nos. 2336-2338 Ovptd. in Black and Red

1991 Wmk. 347 *Perf. 13¹/₂x13*

2366	A431	50g on #2336	15	15
2367	A431	100g on #2337	20	18
2368	A431	200g on #2338	40	36

Espamer '91 Philatelic Exhibition.

Nos. 2276a-2276b Ovptd. in Silver

Unificación de Alemania
para la Paz del Mundo

200 Aniv. 1791-1991

Nos. 2276c-2276d Ovptd. in Silver

Unificación de Alemania
para la Paz del Mundo

100 Aniv.
Lilienthal

1991 **Unwmk.** ***Perf. 13***
2369 A418 Strip of 4, #a.-d.

Writers and Muscians — A436

Designs: 50g, Ruy Diaz de Guzman, historian. 100g, Maria Talavera, war correspondent, vert. 150g, Augusto Roa Bastos, writer, vert. 200g, Jose Asuncion Flores, composer, vert. 250g, Felix Perez Cardozo, harpist. 300g, Juan Carlos Moreno Gonzalez, composer.

Perf. 13½x13,13x13½
1991, Aug. 27 **Litho.** **Wmk. 347**
2373 A436 50g multicolored 15 15
2374 A436 100g multicolored 25 22
2375 A436 150g multicolored 38 35
2376 A436 200g multicolored 48 45
2377 A436 250g multicolored 60 55
2378 A436 300g multicolored 75 65
Nos. 2373-2378 (6) 2.61 2.37

Nos. 2376-2378 are airmail.

Paintings — A438

Designs: 50g, Compass of Life, by Alfredo Moraes. 100g, The Lighted Alley, by Michael Burt. 150g, Earring, by Lucy Yegros. 200g, Migrant Workers, by Hugo Bogado Barrios. 250g, Passengers Without a Ship, by Bernardo Ismachoviez. 300g, Native Guarani, by Lotte Schulz.

Perf. 13x13½
1991, Nov. 12 **Litho.** **Wmk. 347**
2381 A438 50g multicolored 15 15
2382 A438 100g multicolored 25 22
2383 A438 150g multicolored 38 35
2384 A438 200g multicolored 48 45
2385 A438 250g multicolored 60 55
2386 A438 300g multicolored 75 65
Nos. 2381-2386 (6) 2.61 2.37

Nos. 2384-2386 are airmail.

Tile Designs of Christianized Indians — A440

Perf. 13x13½
1992, Mar. 2 **Litho.** **Wmk. 347**
2391 A440 50g Geometric 15 15
2392 A440 100g Church 18 15
2393 A440 150g Missionary ship 28 25
2394 A440 200g Plant 38 35

Discovery of America, 500th anniv.

SEMI-POSTAL STAMPS

Red Cross Nurse — SP1

Unwmk.
1930, July 22 **Typo.** ***Perf. 12***
B1 SP1 1.50p + 50c gray violet 1.00 65
B2 SP1 1.50p + 50c deep rose 1.00 65
B3 SP1 1.50p + 50c dark blue 1.00 65

The surtax was for the benefit of the Red Cross Society of Paraguay.

College of Agriculture — SP2

1930
B4 SP2 1.50p + 50c blue, *pink* 25 25

Surtax for the Agricultural Institute.
The sheet of No. B4 has a papermaker's watermark: "Vencedor Bond."
A 1.50p+50c red on yellow was prepared but not regularly issued. Value, 20 cents.

Red Cross Headquarters — SP3
Our Lady of Asunción — SP4

1932
B5 SP3 50c + 50c rose 25 20

1941 **Engr.**
B6 SP4 7p + 3p red brown 30 25
B7 SP4 7p + 3p purple 30 25
B8 SP4 7p + 3p carmine rose 30 25
B9 SP4 7p + 3p sapphire 30 25

For surcharges see Nos. 419-426, 431-434.

No. 361 Surcharged in Black

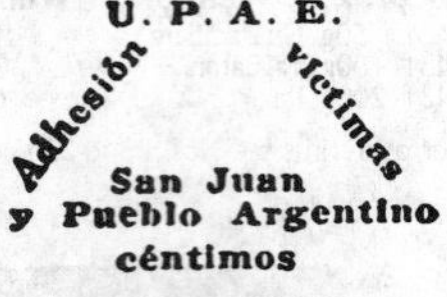

1944
B10 A70 10c on 10p multicolored 35 25

The surtax was for the victims of the San Juan earthquake in Argentina.

Catalogue values for unused stamps in this section, from this point to the end of the section, are for Never Hinged items.

No. C169 Surcharged in Carmine "AYUDA AL ECUADOR 5 + 5"

1949 **Unwmk.** ***Perf. 12½***
B11 A117 5c + 5c on 30c dk blue 15 15

Surtax for the victims of the Ecuador earthquake.

38th Intl. Eucharistic Congress, Bombay — SP5

Various coins and coat of arms.

Perf. 12x12½
1964, Dec. 11 **Litho. & Engr.**
B12 SP5 20g +10g multicolored
B13 SP5 30g +15g multicolored
B14 SP5 50g +25g multicolored
B15 SP5 100g +50g multicolored
a. Souvenir sheet of 4, #B12-B15

Buildings and Ancient Vatican Coins — SP6

1964, Dec. 12
B16 SP6 20g +10g multicolored
B17 SP6 30g +15g multicolored
B18 SP6 50g +25g multicolored
B19 SP6 100g +50g multicolored
a. Souvenir sheet of 4, #B16-B19

AIR POST STAMPS

Official Stamps of 1913 Surcharged

Correo
Aéreo
Habilitado
en $ 2:85

1929, Jan. 1 **Unwmk.** ***Perf. 11½***
C1 O19 2.85p on 5c lilac 75 65
C2 O19 5.65p on 10c grn 50 38
C3 O19 11.30p on 50c rose 75 50

Counterfeits of surcharge exist.

Regular Issues of 1924-27 Surcharged as in 1929

1929, Feb. 26 ***Perf. 12***
C4 A51 3.40p on 3p gray 1.75 1.10
a. Surch. "Correo / en $3.40 / Habilitado / Aereo" 8.75
b. Double surcharge 8.75
c. "Aéro" instead of "Aéreo"
C5 A44 6.80p on 4p lt bl 1.75 1.10
a. Surch. "Correo / Aereo / en $6.80 / Habilitado" 8.75
C6 A52 17p on 5p choc 1.75 1.10
a. Surch. "Correo / Habilitado / Habilitado / en 17p" 4.50
b. Double surcharge 8.75

Wings — AP1

Pigeon with Letter — AP2

Airplanes — AP3

1929-31 **Typo.** ***Perf. 12***
C7 AP1 2.85p gray green 50 45
a. Imperf., pair 37.50
C8 AP1 2.85p turq grn ('31) 25 20
C9 AP2 5.65p brown 75 38
C10 AP2 5.65p scar ('31) 38 25
C11 AP3 11.30p chocolate 50 38
a. Imperf., pair 37.50
C12 AP3 11.30p dp blue ('31) 25 25
Nos. C7-C12 (6) 2.63 1.91

Sheets of these stamps sometimes show portions of a papermaker's watermark "Indian Bond C. Extra Strong."
Excellent counterfeits are plentiful.

Regular Issues of 1924-28 Surcharged in Black or Red

Correo Aéreo
Habilitado
en $ 3.40

1929 ***Perf. 11½, 12***
C13 A47 95c on 7c lilac 20 15
C14 A47 1.90p on 20c dull bl 20 15
C15 A44 3.40p on 4p lt bl (R) 25 20
a. Double surcharge 2.00
C16 A44 4.75p on 4p lt bl (R) 45 38
a. Double surcharge 2.00
C17 A51 6.80p on 3p gray 50 50
a. Double surcharge 3.00
C18 A52 17p on 5p choc 1.50 1.50
a. Horiz. pair, imperf. between 25.00
Nos. C13-C18 (6) 3.10 2.88

Six stamps in the sheet of No. C17 have the "$" and numerals thinner and narrower than the normal type.

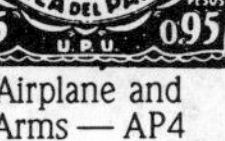

Airplane and Arms — AP4

Cathedral of Asunción — AP5

Airplane and Globe — AP6

1930 ***Perf. 12***
C19 AP4 95c dp red, *pink* 25 25
C20 AP4 95c dk bl, *blue* 25 25
C21 AP5 1.90p lt red, *pink* 25 25
C22 AP5 1.90p violet, *blue* 25 25

C23 AP6 6.80p blk, *lt bl*	25	25
C24 AP6 6.80p green, *pink*	25	30
Nos. C19-C24 (6)	1.50	1.55

Sheets of Nos. C19-C24 have a papermaker's watermark: "Extra Vencedor Bond."
Counterfeits exist.

Stamps and Types of 1927-28 Overprinted in Red **CORREO AEREO**

1930

C25 A47 10c olive green	15	15
a. Double overprint	2.50	
C26 A47 20c dull blue	15	15
a. "CORREO CORREO" instead of "CORREO AEREO"	2.50	
b. "AEREO AEREO" instead of "CORREO AEREO"	2.50	
C27 A48 1p emerald	50	50
C28 A51 3p gray	50	50

Nos. 273, 282, 286, 288, 300, 302, 305 Surcharged in Red or Black

CORREO AEREO CINCO #C29-C30, C32 — **CORREO AEREO VEINTE CENTAVOS** — **CORREO AEREO SEIS** #C33 — **CORREO AEREO DIEZ** #C34-C35

1930

Red or Black Surcharge

C29 A47 5c on 10c gray grn (R)	15	15
a. "AEREO" omitted	15.00	
C30 A47 5c on 70c ultra (R)	15	15
a. Vert. pair, imperf. between	20.00	
C31 A48 20c on 1p org red	18	18
a. "CORREO" double	3.00	3.00
b. "AEREO" double	3.00	3.00
C32 A47 40c on 50c org (R)	15	15
a. "AEREO" omitted	4.50	4.50
b. "CORREO" double	3.00	3.00
c. "AEREO" double	3.00	3.00
C33 A54 6p on 10p red	75	65
C34 A49 10p on 20p red	3.00	2.75
C35 A49 10p on 20p vio brn	3.00	2.75
Nos. C29-C35 (7)	7.38	6.78

Declaration of Independence AP11

1930, May 14 **Typo.**

C36 AP11 2.85p dark blue	25	25
C37 AP11 3.40p dark green	25	20
C38 AP11 4.75p deep lake	25	20

Natl. Independence Day, May 14, 1811.

Gunboat Type

Gunboat "Paraguay."

1931-39 ***Perf. 11½, 12***

C39 A58 1p claret	15	15
C40 A58 1p dk blue ('36)	15	15
C41 A58 2p orange	15	15
C42 A58 2p dk brn ('36)	15	15
C43 A58 3p turq green	24	24
C44 A58 3p lt ultra ('36)	25	25
C45 A58 3p brt rose ('39)	20	20
C46 A58 6p dk green	28	28
C47 A58 6p violet ('36)	35	32
C48 A58 6p dull bl ('39)	25	25
C49 A58 10p vermilion	70	60
C50 A58 10p bluish grn ('35)	1.00	1.00
C51 A58 10p yel brn ('36)	75	75
C52 A58 10p dk blue ('36)	50	50
C53 A58 10p lt pink ('39)	65	65
Nos. C39-C53 (15)	5.77	5.64

1st constitution of Paraguay as a Republic and the arrival of the "Paraguay" and "Humaita."
Counterfeits of #C39-C53 are plentiful.

Regular Issue of 1924 Surcharged

3 3 Correo Aéreo

"Graf Zeppelin"

1931, Aug. 22

C54 A44 3p on 4p lt bl	6.00	5.00

Overprinted **Correo Aêreo**

"Graf Zeppelin"

C55 A44 4p lt blue	4.50	3.75

On Nos. C54-C55 the Zeppelin is hand-stamped. The rest of the surcharge or overprint is typographed.

War Memorial — AP13

Orange Tree and Yerba Mate — AP14

Yerba Mate — AP15

Palms — AP16

Eagle — AP17

1931-36 **Litho.**

C56 AP13 5c lt blue	15	15
a. Horiz. pair, imperf. btwn.	6.25	
C57 AP13 5c dp grn ('33)	15	15
C58 AP13 5c lt red ('33)	15	15
C59 AP13 5c violet ('35)	15	15
C60 AP14 10c dp violet	15	15
C61 AP14 10c brn lake ('33)	15	15
C62 AP14 10c yel brn ('33)	15	15
C63 AP14 10c ultra ('35)	15	15
a. Imperf., pair	5.50	
C64 AP15 20c red	15	15
C65 AP15 20c dl blue ('33)	15	15
C66 AP15 20c emer ('33)	15	15
C67 AP15 20c yel brn ('35)	15	15
a. Imperf., pair	3.75	
C68 AP16 40c dp green	15	15
C69 AP16 40c slate bl ('35)	15	15
C70 AP16 40c red ('36)	15	15
C71 AP17 80c dull blue	15	15
C72 AP17 80c dl grn ('33)	15	15
C73 AP17 80c scar ('33)	15	15
Set value	1.60	1.25

Airship "Graf Zeppelin" — AP18

1932, Apr. **Litho.**

C74 AP18 4p ultra	85	85
a. Imperf., pair	5.00	
C75 AP18 8p red	1.40	1.00
C76 AP18 12p blue grn	1.10	85
C77 AP18 16p dk violet	2.25	1.50
C78 AP18 20p orange brn	2.25	2.00
Nos. C74-C78 (5)	7.85	6.20

For surcharges see Nos. 325-329.

"Graf Zeppelin" over Brazilian Terrain — AP19

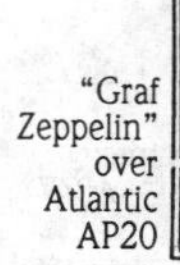

"Graf Zeppelin" over Atlantic AP20

1933, May 5

C79 AP19 4.50p dp blue	1.25	1.00
C80 AP19 9p dp rose	2.50	2.00
a. Horiz. pair, imperf. btwn.	150.00	
C81 AP19 13.50p blue grn	2.50	2.00
C82 AP20 22.50p bis brn	6.25	5.00
C83 AP20 45p dull vio	8.75	8.75
Nos. C79-C83 (5)	21.25	18.75

Excellent counterfeits are plentiful.
For overprints see Nos. C88-C97.

Posts and Telegraph Building, Asunción AP21

1934-37 ***Perf. 11½***

C84 AP21 33.75p ultra	1.50	1.25
C85 AP21 33.75p car ('35)	1.50	1.25
a. 33.75p rose ('37)	1.25	1.25
C86 AP21 33.75p emer ('36)	2.00	1.50
C87 AP21 33.75p bis brn ('36)	50	50

For surcharge see No. C107.

Nos. C79-C83 Overprinted in Black **1934**

1934, May 26

C88 AP19 4.50p deep bl	1.50	1.25
C89 AP19 9p dp rose	1.75	1.50
C90 AP19 13.50p blue grn	5.00	4.50
C91 AP20 22.50p bis brn	4.00	3.50
C92 AP20 45p dull vio	7.00	6.00
Nos. C88-C92 (5)	19.25	16.75

Types of 1933 Issue Overprinted in Black **1935**

1935

C93 AP19 4.50p rose red	2.00	1.10
C94 AP19 9p lt green	2.50	1.50
C95 AP19 13.50p brown	7.50	4.50
C96 AP20 22.50p violet	6.25	4.50
C97 AP20 45p blue	17.50	11.00
Nos. C93-C97 (5)	35.75	22.60

Tobacco Plant AP22

1935-39 **Typo.**

C98 AP22 17p lt brown	2.00	2.00
C99 AP22 17p carmine	3.75	3.75
C100 AP22 17p dark blue	2.50	2.50
C101 AP22 17p pale yel grn ('39)	1.50	1.50

Excellent counterfeits are plentiful.

Church of Incarnation AP23

1935-38

C102 AP23 102p carmine	3.00	2.25
C103 AP23 102p blue	3.00	2.25
C103A AP23 102p indigo ('36)	1.90	1.90
C104 AP23 102p yellow brn	2.00	2.00
a. Imperf., pair	15.00	
C105 AP23 102p violet ('37)	95	95
C106 AP23 102p brn org ('38)	85	85
Nos. C102-C106 (6)	11.70	10.20

Excellent counterfeits are plentiful.
For surcharges see Nos. C108-C109.

Types of 1934-35 Surcharged in Red **Habilitado en $ 24.—**

1937, Aug. 1

C107 AP21 24p on 33.75p sl bl	50	38
C108 AP23 65p on 102p ol bis	1.25	90
C109 AP23 84p on 102p bl grn	1.25	75

Plane over Asunción AP24

1939, Aug. 3 **Typo.** ***Perf. 10½, 11½***

C110 AP24 3.40p yel green	50	50
C111 AP24 3.40p orange brn	30	25
C112 AP24 3.40p indigo	30	25

Buenos Aires Peace Conference Type and

Map of Paraguay with New Chaco Boundary — AP28

Designs: 1p, Flags of Paraguay and Bolivia. 5p, Pres. Ortiz of Argentina, flags of Paraguay, Argentina. 10p, Pres. Vargas, Brazil. 30p, Pres. Alessandri, Chile. 50p, US Eagle and Shield. 100p, Pres. Benavides, Peru. 200p, Pres. Baldomir, Uruguay.

Engr.; Flags Litho.

1939, Nov. ***Perf. 12½***

Flags in National Colors

C113 A69 1p red brown	15	15
C114 A69 3p dark blue	15	15
C115 A70 5p olive blk	15	15
C116 A70 10p violet	15	15
C117 A70 30p orange	18	15
C118 A70 50p black brn	22	15
C119 A70 100p brt green	35	32
C120 A70 200p green	1.90	1.25
C121 AP28 500p black	5.00	5.00
Nos. C113-C121 (9)	8.25	7.47

For overprints see Nos. 388-390.

University of Asuncion Type

Pres. Bernardino Caballero and Senator José S. Decoud.

1939, Sept. **Litho.** ***Perf. 12***

C122 A67 28p rose & blk	3.25	3.25
C123 A67 90p yel grn & blk	4.00	4.00

Map with Asunción to New York Air Route — AP35

1939, Nov. 30 **Engr.**

C124 AP35	30p brown		1.90	1.50
C125 AP35	80p orange		2.25	2.25
C126 AP35	90p purple		4.00	4.00

New York World's Fair.

Pan American Union Type

1940, May ***Perf. 12***

C127 A85	20p rose car	18	15
C128 A85	70p violet bl	45	18
C129 A85	100p Prus grn	50	50
C130 A85	500p dk violet	2.25	1.75

Asuncion 400th Anniv. Type

1942, Aug. 15

C131 A93	20p deep plum	50	40
C132 A94	70p fawn	1.50	1.10
C133 A95	500p olive gray	4.00	3.50

Imperforates

Starting with No. C134, many Paraguayan air mail stamps exist imperforate.

Port of Asunción AP40

First Telegraph in South America — AP41

Early Merchant Ship — AP42

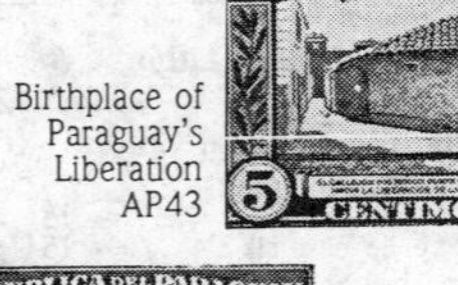
Birthplace of Paraguay's Liberation AP43

Monument to Antequera AP44

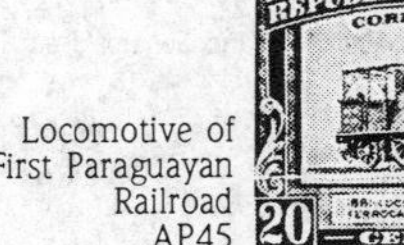

Locomotive of First Paraguayan Railroad AP45

Monument to Heroes of Itororó — AP46

Primitive Postal Service among Indians — AP48

Government House — AP47

Colonial Jesuit Altar — AP49

Ruins of Humaitá Church — AP50

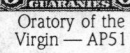

Oratory of the Virgin — AP51

Marshal Francisco S. Lopez — AP52

1944-45 **Unwmk.** ***Perf. 12½***

C134 AP40	1c blue	15	15
C135 AP41	2c green	15	15
C136 AP42	3c brown vio	15	15
C137 AP43	5c brt bl grn	15	15
C138 AP44	10c dk violet	15	15
C139 AP45	20c dk brown	18	15
C140 AP46	30c lt blue	15	15
C141 AP47	40c olive	18	18
C142 AP48	70c brown red	30	25
C143 AP49	1g orange yel	70	50
C144 AP50	2g copper brn	85	70
C145 AP51	5g black brn	1.90	1.90
C146 AP52	10g indigo	4.50	4.50
	Nos. C134-C146 (13)	9.51	9.08

See Nos. C158-C162. For surcharges see Nos. C154-C157.

Flags Type

Flags: 20c, Ecuador. 40c, Bolivia. 70c, Mexico. 1g, Chile. 2g, Brazil. 5g, Argentina. 10g, US.

Engr.; Flags Litho. in Natl. Colors

1945, Aug. 15

C147 A106	20c orange	15	15
C148 A106	40c olive	15	15
C149 A106	70c lake	16	15
C150 A106	1g slate bl	30	30
C151 A106	2g blue vio	40	40
C152 A106	5g green	60	60
C153 A106	10g brown	3.00	3.00
	Nos. C147-C153 (7)	4.76	4.75

Sizes: Nos. C147-C151, 30x26mm; 5g, 32x28mm; 10g, 33x30mm.

Catalogue values for unused stamps in this section, from this point to the end of the section, are for Never Hinged items.

Nos. C139-C142 Surcharged "1946" and New Value in Black

1946 **Engr.** ***Perf. 12½***

C154 AP45	5c on 20c dk brn	40	40
C155 AP46	5c on 30c lt blue	40	40
C156 AP47	5c on 40c olive	40	40
C157 AP48	5c on 70c brn red	40	40

Types of 1944-45

1946, Sept. 21 **Engr.**

C158 AP50	10c dp car	15	15
C159 AP40	20c emerald	15	15
C160 AP47	1g brown org	30	30
C161 AP52	5g purple	90	90
C162 AP51	10g rose car	2.50	2.50
	Nos. C158-C162 (5)	4.00	4.00

Marshal Francisco Solano Lopez Type

1947, May. 15 ***Perf. 12***

C163 A114	32c car lake	15	15
C164 A114	64c orange brn	18	18
C165 A114	1g Prus green	25	25
C166 A114	5g Prus grn & brn vio	75	75
C167 A114	10g dk car rose & dk yel grn	1.25	1.25
	Nos. C163-C167 (5)	2.58	2.58

Archbishopric of Asunción Types

1948, Jan. 6 **Unwmk.** ***Perf. 12½***

Size: 25½x31mm

C168 A116	20c gray blk	15	15
C169 A117	30c dark blue	15	15
C170 A118	40c lilac	15	15
C171 A115	70c orange red	15	15
C172 A112	1g brown red	18	18
C173 A118	2g red	50	50

Size: 25½x34mm

C174 A115	5g brt car & dk bl	90	90
C175 A116	10g dk grn & brn	1.25	1.25
	Nos. C168-C175 (8)	3.43	3.43

For surcharges see Nos. B11, C178.

Type of Regular Issue of 1948 Inscribed "AEREO"

1948, Sept. 11 **Engr. & Litho.**

C176 A119	69c dk grn, red & bl	50	50
C177 A119	5g dk bl, red & bl	2.00	1.75

The Barefeet, a political group.

No. C171 Surcharged in Black

DUELO NACIONAL
5 CENTIMOS 5

1949, June 29

C178 A115	5c on 70c org red	15	15

Archbishop Juan Sinforiano Bogarin (1863-1949).

Symbols of UPU AP65

Franklin D. Roosevelt AP66

1950, Sept. 4 **Engr.** ***Perf. 13½x13***

C179 AP65	20c green & violet	15	15
C180 AP65	30c rose vio & brn	15	15
C181 AP65	50c gray & green	15	15
C182 AP65	1g blue & brown	15	15
C183 AP65	5g rose & black	38	38
	Nos. C179-C183 (5)	98	98

UPU, 75th anniv. (in 1949).

Engr.; Flags Litho.

1950, Oct. 2 ***Perf. 12½***

Flags in Carmine & Violet Blue.

C184 AP66	20c red	15	15
C185 AP66	30c black	15	15
C186 AP66	50c claret	15	15
C187 AP66	1g dk gray grn	15	15
C188 AP66	5g deep blue	38	38
	Set value	78	78

Franklin D. Roosevelt (1882-1945).

Urn Containing Remains of Columbus AP67

1952, Feb. 11 **Litho.** ***Perf. 10***

C189 AP67	10c ultra	15	15
C190 AP67	20c green	15	15
C191 AP67	30c lilac	15	15
C192 AP67	40c rose	15	15
C193 AP67	50c bister brn	15	15
C194 AP67	1g blue	15	15
C195 AP67	2g orange	15	15
C196 AP67	5g red brown	30	30
	Set value	78	78

Queen Isabella I — AP68

1952, Oct. 12

C197 AP68	1g vio blue	15	15
C198 AP68	2g chocolate	15	15
C199 AP68	5g dull green	25	25
C200 AP68	10g lilac rose	55	55

500th birth anniv. of Queen Isabella I of Spain (in 1951).

Pettirossi Type

1954, Mar.

C201 A122	40c brown	15	15
C202 A122	55c green	15	15
C203 A122	80c ultra	15	15
C204 A122	1.30g gray blue	22	22
	Set value	38	38

Church of San Roque — AP70

1954, June 20 **Engr.** ***Perf. 12x13***

C205 AP70	20c carmine	15	15
C206 AP70	30c brown vio	15	15
C207 AP70	50c ultra	15	15
C208 AP70	1g red brn & bl grn	15	15
C209 AP70	1g red brn & lil rose	15	15
C210 AP70	1g red brn & blk	15	15
C211 AP70	1g red brn & org	15	15
a.	Min. sheet of 4, #C208-C211, perf. 12x12½	30	30
C212 AP70	5g dk red brn & vio	15	15
C213 AP70	5g dk red brn & ol grn	15	15
C214 AP70	5g dk red brn & org yel	15	15
C215 AP70	5g dk red brn & yel org	15	15
a.	Min. sheet of 4, #C212-C215, perf. 12x12½	65	65
	Set value	95	95

Centenary (in 1953) of the establishment of the Church of San Roque, Asuncion.

Nos. C211a and C215a issued without gum.

Heroes Type

Unwmk.

1954, Aug. 15 **Litho.** ***Perf. 10***

C216 A123	5g violet	15	15
C217 A123	10g olive green	25	25
C218 A123	20g gray brown	45	38
C219 A123	50g vermilion	1.00	1.00
C220 A123	100g blue	3.25	3.25
	Nos. C216-C220 (5)	5.10	5.03

Peron Visit Type

Photo. & Litho.

1955, Apr. **Wmk. 90** ***Perf. 13x13½***

Frames & Flags in Blue & Carmine

C221 A124	60c ol grn & cream	15	15
C222 A124	2g bl grn & cream	15	15
C223 A124	3g brn org & cream	15	15
C224 A124	4.10g brt rose pink & cr	18	15
	Set value	42	38

Monsignor Rodriguez Type

Jesuit Ruins: 3g, Corridor at Trinidad. 6g, Tower of Santa Rosa. 10g, San Cosme gate. 20g, Church of

Jesus. 30g, Niche at Trinidad. 50g, Sacristy at Trinidad.

Perf. 12½x12, 12x12½

1955, June 19 Engr. Unwmk.

C225	A125	2g aqua	15	15
C226	A125	3g olive grn	15	15
C227	A126	4g lt blue grn	15	15
C228	A126	6g brown	15	15
C229	A125	10g rose	15	15
C230	A125	20g brown ol	15	15
C231	A126	30g dk green	30	25
C232	A126	50g dp aqua	35	30
		Set value	1.00	90

For surcharges see Nos. C252-C259.

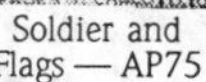

Soldier and Flags — AP75

"Republic" and Soldier — AP76

1957, June 12 Photo. *Perf. 13½*

Granite Paper

Flags in Red and Blue

C233	AP75	10c ultra	15	15
C234	AP75	15c dp claret	15	15
C235	AP75	20c red	15	15
C236	AP75	25c light blue	15	15
C237	AP75	50c bluish grn	15	15
C238	AP75	1g rose car	15	15
C239	AP76	1.30g dp claret	15	15
C240	AP76	1.50p light blue	15	15
C241	AP76	2g emerald	15	15
C242	AP76	4.10g red	15	15
C243	AP76	5g gray black	15	15
C244	AP76	10g bluish grn	15	15
C245	AP76	25g ultra	25	20
		Set value	90	80

Heroes of the Chaco war.

Stroessner Type of Regular Issue

1958, Aug. 16 Litho. Wmk. 320

Center in Slate

C246	A130	12g rose lilac	25	25
C247	A130	18g orange	30	30
C248	A130	23g orange brn	50	50
C249	A130	36g emerald	50	50
C250	A130	50g citron	65	65
C251	A130	65g gray	1.00	1.00
		Nos. C246-C251 (6)	3.20	3.20

Re-election of Pres. General Alfredo Stroessner.

Nos. C225-C232 Surcharged like #545-551 in Red

Perf. 12½x12, 12x12½

1959, May 26 Engr. Unwmk.

C252	A125	4g on 2g aqua	15	15
C253	A125	12.45g on 3g ol grn	18	15
C254	A126	18.15g on 6g brown	25	22
C255	A125	23.40g on 10g rose	35	28
C256	A125	34.80g on 20g brn ol	50	38
C257	A126	36g on 4g lt bl grn	55	40
C258	A126	43.95g on 30g dk grn	65	45
C259	A126	100g on 50g deep aqua	1.50	1.00
		Nos. C252-C259 (8)	4.13	3.03

The surcharge is made to fit the stamps. Counterfeits of surcharge exist.

UN Emblem — AP77

Unwmk.

1959, Aug. 27 Typo. *Perf. 11*

C260	AP77	5g ocher & ultra	50	40

Visit of Dag Hammarskjold, Secretary General of the UN, Aug. 27-29.

Map and UN Emblem AP78

Uprooted Oak Emblem AP79

1959, Oct. 24 Litho. *Perf. 10*

C261	AP78	12.45g blue & salmon	20	15

United Nations Day, Oct. 24, 1959.

Olympic Games Type of Regular Issue

Design: Basketball.

1960, Mar. 18 Photo. *Perf. 12½*

C262	A131	12.45g red & dk bl	15	15
C263	A131	18.15g lilac & gray ol	20	20
C264	A131	36g bl grn & rose car	40	40

The Paraguayan Philatelic Agency reported as spurious the imperf. souvenir sheet reproducing one of No. C264.

1960, Apr. 7 Litho. *Perf. 11*

C265	AP79	4g green & pink	45	38
C266	AP79	12.45g bl & yel grn	90	65
C267	AP79	18.15g car & ocher	1.25	75
C268	AP79	23.40g red org & bl	1.25	1.50

World Refugee Year, July 1, 1959-June 30, 1960 (1st issue).

Human Rights Type of Regular Issue, 1960

Designs: 40g, UN Emblem. 60g, Hands holding scales. 100g, Flame.

1960, Apr. 21 *Perf. 12½x13*

C269	A133	40g dk ultra & red	25	25
C270	A133	60g grnsh bl & org	30	30
C271	A133	100g dk ultra & red	65	65

An imperf. miniature sheet exists, containing one each of Nos. C269-C271, all printed in green and vermilion.

UN Type of Regular Issue

Perf. 13x13½

1960, Oct. 24 Photo. Unwmk.

C272	A134	3g orange, red & bl	15	15
C273	A134	4g pale grn, red & bl	15	15
		Set value	15	15

International Bridge, Paraguay-Brazil AP80

1961, Jan. 26 Litho. *Perf. 14*

C274	AP80	3g carmine	15	15
C275	AP80	12.45g brown lake	18	15
C276	AP80	18.15g Prus grn	20	18
C277	AP80	36g dk blue	38	35
a.		Souv. sheet of 4, #C274-C277, imperf.	75	75

Inauguration of the International Bridge between Paraguay and Brazil.

"Paraguay en Marcha" Type of 1961

Designs: 12.45g, Truck carrying logs. 18.15g, Logs on river barge. 22g, Radio tower. 36g, Jet plane.

1961, Apr. 10 Photo. *Perf. 13*

C278	A136	12.45g yel & vio bl	25	20
C279	A136	18.15g pur & ocher	30	25
C280	A136	22g ultra & ocher	38	30
C281	A136	36g brt grn & yel	40	38

Declaration of Independence AP81

1961, May 16 Litho. *Perf. 14½*

C282	AP81	12.45g dl red brn	15	15
C283	AP81	18.15g dk blue	20	18
C284	AP81	23.40g green	25	22
C285	AP81	30g lilac	30	28
C286	AP81	36g rose	40	38
C287	AP81	44g olive	50	45
		Nos. C282-C287 (6)	1.80	1.66

150th anniv. of Independence (1st issue).

"Paraguay" and Clasped Hands AP82

South American Tapir AP83

1961, June 12 *Perf. 14x14½*

C288	AP82	3g vio blue	15	15
C289	AP82	4g rose claret	15	15
C290	AP82	100g gray green	90	80

Chaco Peace; 150th anniv. of Independence (2nd issue).

1961, Aug. 16 Unwmk. *Perf. 14*

C291	AP83	12.45g claret	65	50
C292	AP83	18.15g ultra	65	65
C293	AP83	34.80g red brown	1.25	1.25

150th anniv. of Independence (3rd issue).

Catholic University Type of 1961

1961, Sept. 18 *Perf. 14x14½*

C294	A140	3g bister brn	15	15
C295	A140	12.45g lilac rose	20	20
C296	A140	36g blue	40	40

Hotel Guarani Type of 1961

Design: Hotel Guarani, different view.

1961, Oct. 14 Litho. *Perf. 15*

C297	A141	3g dull red brn	15	15
C298	A141	4g ultra	15	15
C299	A141	18.15g orange	25	22
C300	A141	36g rose car	40	38
		Set value	75	70

Tennis Type

1961, Oct. 16 Unwmk. *Perf. 11*

C301	A142	12.45g multi	25	
C302	A142	20g multi	45	
C303	A142	50g multi	1.00	

Some specialists question the status of this issue.

Two imperf. souvenir sheets exist containing four 12.45g stamps each in a different color with simulated perforations and black marginal inscription.

WRY Type

Design: Oak emblem rooted in ground, wavy-lined frame.

1961, Dec. 30

C307	A145	18.15g brn & red	20	
C308	A145	30g car & emer	45	
C309	A145	50g emer & org	65	

Imperforates in changed colors and souvenir sheets exist. Some specialists question the status of this issue.

Pres. Alfredo Stroessner and Prince Philip — AP84

1962, Mar. 9 Litho.

Portraits in Ultramarine

C310	AP84	12.45g grn & buff	15	15
C311	AP84	18.15g red & pink	18	18
C312	AP84	36g brn & yel	32	32

Visit of Prince Philip, Duke of Edinburgh. perf. and imperf. souvenir sheets exist.

Illustrations AP85-AP89, AP92-AP94, AP96-AP97, AP99-AP105, AP107-AP110, AP113-AP115, AP117, AP123, AP127a, AP132-AP133, AP136, AP138, AP140, AP142, AP144-AP145, AP149-AP150, AP152-AP153, AP156, AP158-AP159, AP165, AP167, AP171, AP180, AP183-AP184, AP187, AP196, AP202, AP205, AP208, AP211, AP221-AP222, AP224-AP225, AP229, AP234-AP235, AP237 and AP240 are reduced.

Souvenir Sheet

Abraham Lincoln (1809-1865), 16th President of US — AP85

1963, Aug. 21 Litho. *Imperf.*

C313	AP85	36g gray & vio brn	

Limited Distribution Issues

Beginning with No. C313, stamps with limited distribution are not valued.

Souvenir Sheet

1960 Summer Olympics, Rome — AP86

1963, Aug. 21 Litho. & Engr.

C314	AP86	50g lt bl, vio brn & sep	

MUESTRA

Illustrations may show the word "MUESTRA." This means specimen and is not on the actual stamps.

Buying Sets

Frequently it is less expensive to purchase complete sets rather than the individual stamps that make up the set. "Set Values" are provided for many such sets.

Souvenir Sheet

Cattleya Cigas — AP87

1963, Aug. 21 **Litho.**
C315 AP87 66g multicolored

Souvenir Sheet

Pres. Alfredo Stroessner — AP88

1964, Nov. 3
C316 AP88 36g multicolored

Souvenir Sheet

Saturn V Rocket, Pres. John F. Kennedy — AP89

1968, Jan. 27 ***Perf. 14***
C317 AP89 50g multicolored

Pres. Kennedy, 4th death anniv. (in 1967).

Torch, Book, Houses — AP90

1969, June 28 Wmk. 347 ***Perf. 11***

C318 AP90	36g blue	50
C319 AP90	50g bister brn	65
C320 AP90	100g rose car	1.25

National drive for teachers' homes.

Souvenir Sheets

US Space Program — AP91

John F. Kennedy, Wernher von Braun, moon and: No. C321, Apollo 11 en route to moon. No. C322, Saturn V lift-off. No. C323, Apollo 9. No. C324, Apollo 10.

1969, July 9 ***Perf. 14***
C321 AP91 23.40g multicolored
C322 AP91 23.40g multicolored

Imperf

C323 AP91 23.40g multicolored
C324 AP91 23.40g multicolored

Nos. C323-C324 each contain one 56x46mm stamp.

Souvenir Sheets

Events and Anniversaries — AP92

Designs: No. C325, Apollo 14. No. C326, Dwight D. Eisenhower, 1st death anniv. No. C327, Napoleon Bonaparte, birth bicent. No. C328, Brazil, winners of Jules Rimet World Cup Soccer Trophy.

1970, Dec. 16 ***Perf. 13½***
C325 AP92 20g multicolored
C326 AP92 20g multicolored
C327 AP92 20g multicolored
C328 AP92 20g multicolored

Souvenir Sheets

Paraguayan Postage Stamps, Cent. — AP93

Designs: No C329, Marshal Francisco Solano Lopez, Pres. Alfredo Stroessner, Paraguay #1. No. C330, #3, 1014, 1242. No. C331, #1243, C8, C74.

1971
C329 AP93 20g multicolored
C330 AP93 20g multicolored
C331 AP93 20g multicolored

Issue dates: No. C329, Mar. 23. No. C330-C331, Mar. 29.

Souvenir Sheets

Emblems of Apollo Space Missions — AP94

Designs: No. C332, Apollo 7, 8, 9, & 10. No. C333, Apollo 11, 12, 13, & 14.

1971, Mar. 26
C332 AP94 20g multicolored
C333 AP94 20g multicolored

Reserved #C334 AP95 for Charles de Gaulle Souv. sheet.

Souvenir Sheet

Taras Shevchenko (1814-1861), Ukrainian Poet — AP96

1971, Dec. 24 ***Perf. 13½***
C335 AP96 20g multicolored

Souvenir Sheets

Johannes Kepler (1571-1630), German Astronomer — AP97

Kepler and: No. C336, Apollo lunar module over moon. No. C337, Astronaut walking in space.

1971, Dec. 24
C336 AP97 20g multicolored
C337 AP97 20g multicolored

Reserved #C338 AP98 for American Space Explorations set.

Souvenir Sheet

Apollo 16 Moon Mission — AP99

1972, Mar. 29 **Litho.** ***Perf. 13½***
C339 AP99 20g multicolored

Souvenir Sheets

History of the Olympics — AP100

Designs: No. C340, French, Olympic flags. No. C341, Skier, Garmisch-Partenkirchen, 1936. No. C342, Olympic flame, Sapporo, 1972. No. C343, Pierre de Coubertin (1863-1937), founder of modern Olympics. No. C344, Javelin thrower, Paris, 1924. No. C345, Equestrian event.

1972, Mar. 29 ***Perf. 14½***
C340 AP100 20g multicolored
C341 AP100 20g multicolored
C342 AP100 20g multicolored
C343 AP100 20g multicolored
C344 AP100 20g multicolored
C345 AP100 20g multicolored

Souvenir Sheet

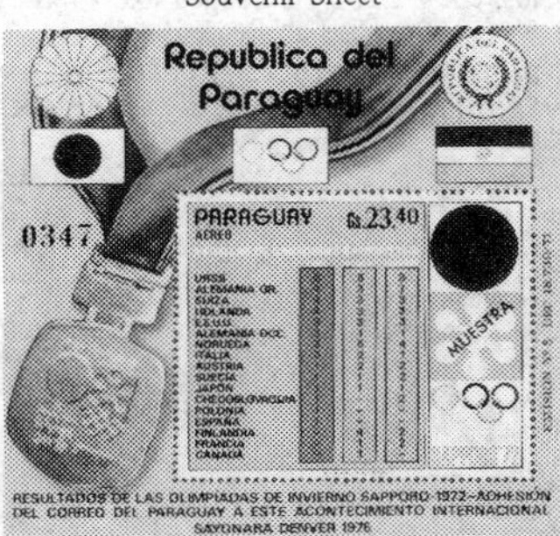

Medal Totals, 1972 Winter Olympics, Sapporo — AP101

1972, Nov. 18 ***Perf. 13½***
C346 AP101 23.40g multicolored

Souvenir Sheets

French Contributions to Aviation and Space Exploration — AP102

Georges Pompidou, Charles de Gaulle and: No. C347, Concorde. No. C348, Satellite D2A, Mirage G 8 jets.

1972, Nov. 25
C347 AP102 23.40g multicolored
C348 AP102 23.40g multicolored

Souvenir Sheets

Summer Olympic Gold Medals, 1896-1972 — AP103

1972, Nov. 25
C349 AP103 23.40g 9 medals, 1896-1932, vert.
C350 AP103 23.40g 8 medals, 1936-1972

Souvenir Sheet

Adoration of the Shepherds by Murillo — AP104

1972, Nov. 25
C351 AP104 23.40g multicolored

Christmas.

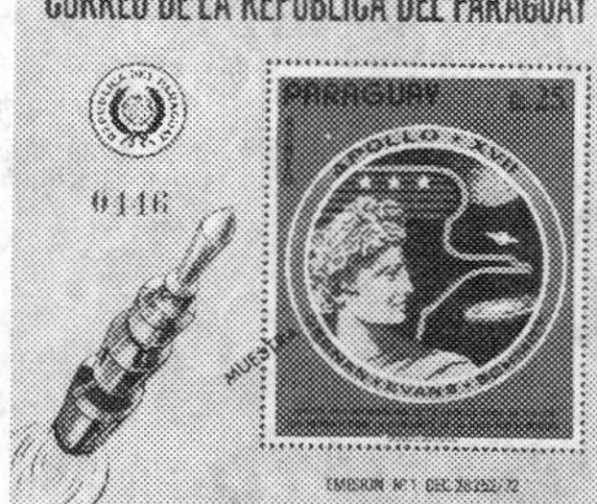

Apollo 17 Moon Mission — AP105

1973, Mar. 13
C352 AP105 25g multicolored

Reserved #C353 AP106 for Medal Winners of Summer Olympics, Munich.

Souvenir Sheets

The Holy Family by Peter Paul Rubens — AP107

Design: No. C355, In the Forest at Pierrefonds by Alfred de Dreux.

1973, Mar. 15
C354 AP107 25g multicolored
C355 AP107 25g multicolored

Souvenir Sheet

German Championship Soccer Team F.C. Bayern, Bavaria #2 — AP108

1973, June 29 *Imperf.*
C356 AP108 25g multicolored

IBRA '73 Intl. Philatelic Exhibition, Munich.

Souvenir Sheet

Copernicus, 500th Birth Anniv. and Space Exploration — AP109

Designs: No. C357, Lunar surface, Apollo 11. No. C358, Copernicus, position of Earth at soltices and equinoxes, vert. No. C359, Skylab space laboratory.

1973, June 29 *Perf. 13½*
C357 AP109 25g multicolored
C358 AP109 25g multicolored
C359 AP109 25g multicolored

Souvenir Sheets

Exploration of Mars — AP110

1973, Oct. 8
C360 AP110 25g Mariner 9
C361 AP110 25g Viking probe, horiz.

Pres. Stroessner's Visit to Europe and Morocco — AP111

Designs: No. C362a, 5g, Arms of Paraguay, Spain, Canary Islands. b, 10g, Gen. Franco, Stroessner, vert. c, 25g, Arms of Paraguay, Germany. d, 50g, Stroessner, Giovanni Leone, Italy, vert. No. C363, Itaipu Dam between Paraguay and Brazil.

1973, Dec. 30 *Perf. 14*
C362 AP111 Strip of 4, #a.-d.
C363 AP111 150g multicolored

Souvenir Sheet
Imperf

C364 AP111 100g Country flags

No. C364 contains one 60x50mm stamp.

1974 World Cup Soccer Championships, Munich — AP112

Abstract paintings of soccer players: No. C366a, 10g, Player seated on globe. b, 20g, Player as viewed from under foot. No. C367, Player kicking ball. No. C368, Goalie catching ball, horiz.

1974, Jan. 31 *Perf. 14*
C365 AP112 5g shown
C366 AP112 Pair, #a.-b.

Souvenir Sheets
Perf. 13½

C367 AP112 25g multicolored
C368 AP112 25g multicolored

Nos. C367-C368 each contain one 50x60mm stamp.

Souvenir Sheets

Tourism Year — AP113

Design: No. C370, Painting, Birth of Christ by Louis le Nain (1593-1648), horiz.

1974, Feb. 4 *Perf. 13½*
C369 AP113 25g multicolored
C370 AP113 25g multicolored

Christmas (No. C370).

Souvenir Sheets

Events and Anniversaries — AP114

1974, Mar. 20
C371 AP114 25g Rocket lift-off
C372 AP114 25g Solar system, horiz.
C373 AP114 25g Skylab 2 astronauts, horiz.

Souvenir Sheet

C374 AP114 25g Olympic Flame

UPU centennial (#C371-C372). 1976 Olympic Games (#C374).

President Stroessner Type of 1973

Designs: 100g, Stroessner, Georges Pompidou. 200g, Stroessner and Pope Paul VI.

1974, Apr. 25 *Perf. 14*
C375 AP111 100g multicolored

Souvenir Sheet
Perf. 13½

C376 AP111 200g multicolored

No. C376 contains one 60x50mm stamp.

Souvenir Sheet

Lufthansa Airlines Intercontinental Routes, 40th Anniv. — AP115

1974, July 13 *Perf. 13½*
C377 AP115 15g multicolored

No. C377 face value was 15g plus 5g extra for a monument to Francisco Solano Lopez.

Reserve #C378 (AP115) for Hermann Oberth, 80th birth anniv. souv. sheet.

1974 World Cup Soccer Championships, West Germany — AP116

1974, July 13 *Perf. 14*
C379 AP116 4g Goalie
C380 AP116 5g Soccer ball
C381 AP116 10g shown

Souvenir Sheet
Perf. 13½

C382 AP116 15g Soccer ball, diff.

No. C382 contains one 53x46mm stamp. No. C382 face value was 15g plus 5g extra for a monument for Francisco Solano Lopez.

Souvenir Sheet

First Balloon Flight over English Channel — AP117

1974, Sept. 13 *Imperf.*
C383 AP117 15g multicolored

No. C383 face value was 15g plus 5g extra for a monument for Francisco Solano Lopez.

Anniversaries and Events — AP118

Designs: 4g, US #C76 on covers that went to Moon. No. C385a, 5g, Pres. Pinochet of Chile. No. C385b, 10g, Pres. Stroessner's visit to South Africa. No. C386, Mariner 10 over Mercury, horiz. No. C387, Paraguay permanent member of UPU. No. C388, UPU cent., Rousseau's "Zeppelins."

1974, Dec. 2 *Perf. 14*
C384 AP118 4g multicolored
C385 AP118 Pair #a.-b.

Souvenir Sheets
Perf. 13½

C386 AP118 15g multicolored
C387 AP118 15g multicolored

Perf. 14½

C388 AP118 15g multicolored

Nos. C386-C387 contain one 60x50mm stamp, No. C388 one 50x35mm stamp. Face value was 15g plus 5g extra for a monument to Francisco Solano Lopez. Compare No. C386 with No. C392.

Anniversaries and Events AP119

Designs: 5g, 17th Congress, UPU, Lausanne. 10g, Intl. Philatelic Exposition, Montevideo, Uruguay. No. C392, Mariner 10 orbiting Mercury, horiz. No. C393, Figure skater, horiz. No. C394, Innsbruck Olympic emblem.

1974, Dec. 7 *Perf. 14*
C389 AP119 4g multicolored
C390 AP119 5g multicolored
C391 AP119 10g multicolored

Souvenir Sheets
Perf. 13½

C392 AP119 15g bl & multi
C393 AP119 15g multicolored
C394 AP119 15g multicolored

UPU centennial (#C389). Nos. C392-C394 each contain one 60x50mm stamp and face value was 15g plus 5g extra for a monument to Francisco Solano Lopez.

German World Cup Soccer Champions — AP120

1974, Dec. 20 *Perf. 14*
C395 AP120 4g Holding World Cup trophy, vert.
C396 AP120 5g Team on field
C397 AP120 10g Argentina '78 emblem, vert.

Souvenir Sheet
Perf. 13½

C398 AP120 15g Players holding trophy, vert.

No. C398 contains one 50x60mm stamp and face value was 15g plus 5g extra for a monument to Francisco Solano Lopez.

Expo '75 AP122

1975, Feb. 24 *Perf. 14*
C401 AP122 4g Ryukyumurasaki, vert.
C402 AP122 5g Hibiscus
C403 AP122 10g Ancient sailing ship

Souvenir Sheet
Perf. 14½

C404 AP122 15g Expo emblem, vert.

No. C404 face value was 15g plus 5g extra for a monument to Francisco Solano Lopez.

Souvenir Sheets

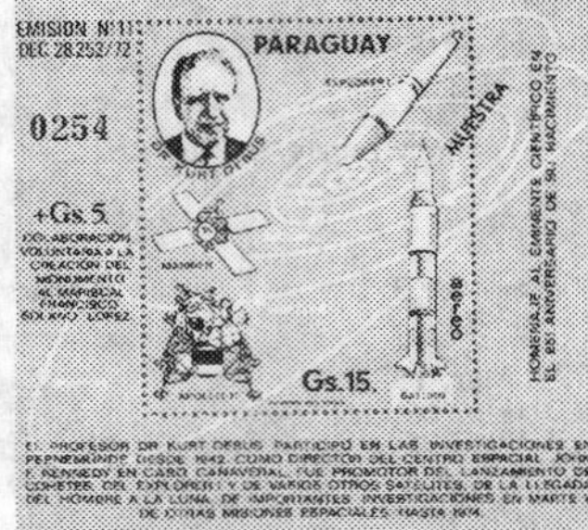

Anniversaries and Events — AP123

Designs: No. C405, Dr. Kurt Debus, space scientist, 65th birth anniv. No. C406, 1976 Summer Olympics, Montreal, horiz.

1975, Feb. 24 *Perf. 13½*
C405 AP123 15g multicolored
C406 AP123 15g multicolored

Nos. C405-C406 face value was 15g plus 5g extra for a monument to Francisco Solano Lopez.

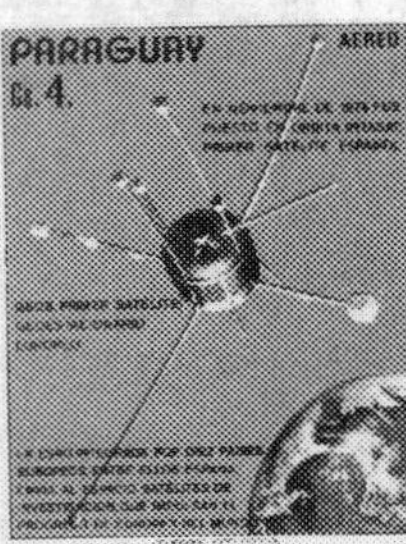

GEOS Satellite AP124

Designs: No. C408a, 5g, ESPANA 75. b, 10g, Mother and Child, Murillo.

1975, Aug. 21 *Perf. 14*
C407 AP124 4g shown
C408 AP124 Pair, #1.-b.

Souvenir Sheet
Perf. 13½

C409 AP124 15g Spain #1139, 1838, C167, charity stamp
C410 AP124 15g Zeppelin, plane, satellites

Perf. 14½

C411 AP124 15g Jupiter

Nos. C409-C411 face value was 15g plus 5g extra for a monument to Francisco Solano Lopez.
Size of stamps: No. C409, 45x55mm; C410, 55x45mm; C411, 32x22mm.

Souvenir Sheets

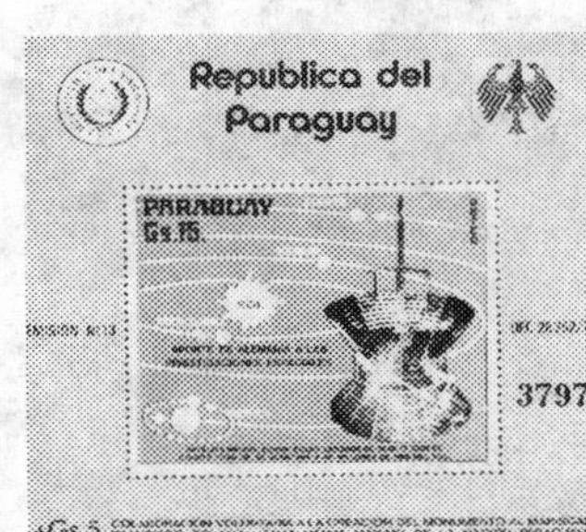

Anniversaries and Events — AP125

Designs: No. C413, UN emblem, Intl. Women's Year, vert. No. C414, Helios space satellite.

1975, Aug. 26 *Perf. 13½*
C413 AP125 15g multicolored
C414 AP125 15g multicolored

Nos. C413-C414 face value was 15g plus 5g extra for a monument to Francisco Solano Lopez.

Souvenir Sheets

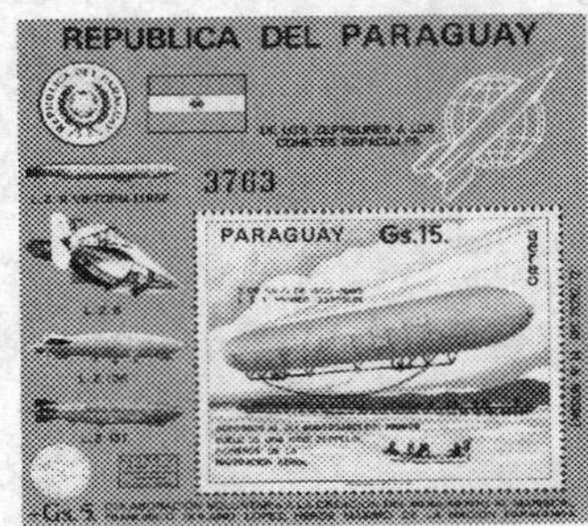

Anniversaries and Events — AP126

Designs: No. C418, Zeppelin, boats. No. C419, Soccer, Intelsat IV, vert. No. C420, Viking Mars landing.

1975, Oct. 13 *Perf. 13½*
C418 AP126 15g multicolored
C419 AP126 15g multicolored
C420 AP126 15g multicolored

Nos. C418-C420 face value was 15g plus 5g extra for a monument to Francisco Solano Lopez.

United States, Bicent. — AP127

Designs: No. C421a, 4g, Lunar rover. b, 5g, Ford Elite, 1975. c, 10g, Ford, 1896. No. C422, Airplanes and spacecraft. No. C423, Arms of Paraguay and United States.

1975, Nov. 28 **Litho.** *Perf. 14*
C421 AP127 Strip of 3, #a.-c.

Souvenir Sheets

Perf. 13½

C422 AP127 15g multicolored
C423 AP127 15g multicolored

Nos. C422-C423 each contain one 60x50mm stamp and face value was 15g plus 20g with 5g surtax for a monument to Francisco Solano Lopez.

Souvenir Sheet

La Musique by Francois Boucher — AP127a

1975, Nov. 28 *Perf. 13½*
C424 AP127a 15g multicolored

No. C424 face value was 15g plus 5g extra for a monument to Francisco Solano Lopez.

Anniversaries and Events — AP128

Designs: 4g, Flight of Concorde jet. 5g, JU 52/3M, Lufthansa Airlines, 50th anniv. 10g, EXFILMO '75 and ESPAMER '75. No. C428, Concorde, diff. No. C429, Dr. Albert Schweitzer, missionary and Konrad Adenauer, German statesman. No. C430, Ferdinand Porsche, auto designer, birth cent., vert.

1975, Dec. 20 *Perf. 14*
C425 AP128 4g multicolored
C426 AP128 5g multicolored
C427 AP128 10g multicolored

Souvenir Sheets

Perf. 13½

C428 AP128 15g multicolored
C429 AP128 15g multicolored
C430 AP128 15g multicolored

Nos. C428-C430 face value was 15g plus 5g extra for a monument to Francisco Solano Lopez. No. C428 contains one 54x34mm stamp, No. C429 one 60x50mm stamp, No. C430 one 30x40mm stamp.

Anniversaries and Events — AP129

Details: 4g, The Transfiguration by Raphael, vert. 5g, Nativity by Del Mayno. 10g, Nativity by Vignon. No. C434, Detail from Adoration of the Shepherds by Ghirlandaio. No. C435, Austria, 1000th anniv., Leopold I, natl. arms, vert. No. C436, Sepp Herberger and Helmut Schon, coaches for German soccer team.

1976, Feb. 2 **Litho.** *Perf. 14*
C431 AP129 4g multicolored
C432 AP129 5g multicolored
C433 AP129 10g multicolored

Souvenir Sheets

Perf. 13½

C434 AP129 15g multicolored
C435 AP129 15g multicolored

Perf. 13½x13

C436 AP129 15g multicolored

Nos. C434-C436 face value was 15g plus 5g extra for a monument to Francisco Solano Lopez. No. C434 contains one 40x30mm stamp, No. C435 one 30x40mm stamp, No. C436 one 54x34mm stamp.

Souvenir Sheet

Apollo-Soyuz — AP130

1976, Apr. 2 *Perf. 13½x13*
C437 AP130 25g multicolored

Souvenir Sheet

Lufthansa, 50th Anniv. — AP131

1976, Apr. 7 *Perf. 13½x13*
C438 AP131 25g multicolored

Souvenir Sheet

Interphil '76 — AP132

1976, May 12 *Perf. 13½*
C439 AP132 15g multicolored

No. C439 face value was 15g plus 5g extra for a monument to Francisco Solano Lopez.

Souvenir Sheets

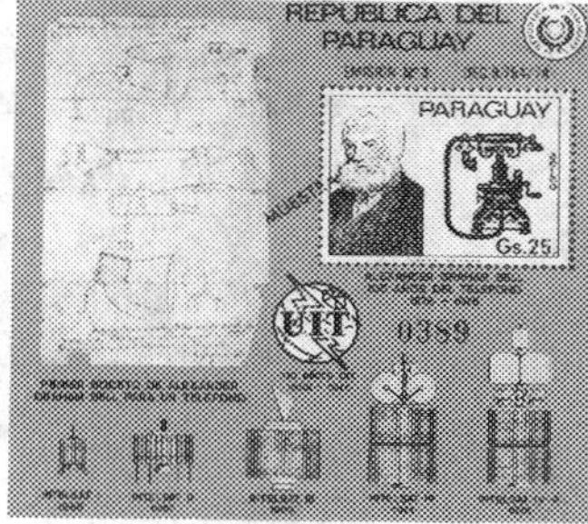

Anniversaries and Events — AP133

Designs: No. C440, Alexander Graham Bell, telephone cent. No. C441, Gold, silver, and bronze medals, 1976 Winter Olympics, Innsbruck. No. C442, Gold medalist Rosi Mittermaier, downhill and slalom, vert. No. C443, Viking probe on Mars. No. C444, UN Postal Administration, 25th anniv. and UPU, cent., vert. No. C445, Prof. Hermanm Oberth, Wernher von Braun. No. C446, Madonna and Child by Durer, vert.

1976 *Perf. 13½*
C440 AP133 25g multicolored
C441 AP133 25g multicolored
C442 AP133 25g multicolored

Perf. 14½

C443 AP133 25g multicolored
C444 AP133 25g multicolored
C445 AP133 25g multicolored
C446 AP133 25g multicolored

No. C442 contains one 35x54mm stamp, No. C443 one 46x36mm stamp, No. C444 one 25x35mm stamp.

Issue dates: Nos. C440-C441, June 15. No. C443, July 8. Nos. C442, C444, July 15. No. C445, Aug. 20. No. C446, Sept. 9.

Souvenir Sheet

UN Offices in Geneva #22, UN #42 — AP136

1976, Dec. 18 *Perf. 13½*
C447 AP136 25g multicolored

UN Postal Administration, 25th anniv. and telephone, cent.

Reserved #C448 AP137 for Ludwig Beethoven souvenir sheet.

Values quoted in this catalogue are for stamps graded at Fine-Very Fine and with no faults. An illustrated guide to grade is provided in introductory material, beginning on Page 5A.

Souvenir Sheet

Alfred Nobel, 80th Death Anniv. and First Nobel Prize, 75th Anniv. — AP138

1977, June 7 *Perf. 13½*
C449 AP138 25g multicolored

Souvenir Sheet

Coronation of Queen Elizabeth II, 25th Anniv. — AP139

1977, July 25 *Perf. 14½*
C450 AP139 25g multicolored

Souvenir Sheet

Uruguay '77 Intl. Philatelic Exhibition — AP140

1977, Aug. 27 **Litho.** *Perf. 13½*
C451 AP140 25g multicolored

Souvenir Sheets

Exploration of Mars — AP141

1977, Sept. 5 *Perf. 13½*
C452 AP141 25g Martian craters

1977, Oct. 28 Litho. *Perf. 13½*
C454 AP141 25g Projected Martian lander

Souvenir Sheet

Sepp Herberger, German Soccer Team Coach — AP142

1978, Jan. 23 Litho. *Perf. 13½*
C455 AP142 25g multicolored

Souvenir Sheet

Austria #B331, Canada #681, US #716, Russia #B66 — AP143

1978, Mar. 10 Litho. *Perf. 14½*
C456 AP143 25g multicolored

Inner perforations are simulated.

Souvenir Sheet

Alfred Nobel — AP144

1978, Mar. 15 Litho. *Perf. 13½*
C457 AP144 25g multicolored

Souvenir Sheets

Anniversaries and Events — AP145

Designs: No. C458, Queen Elizabeth II wearing St. Edward's Crown, holding orb and scepter. No. C459, Queen Elizabeth II presenting World Cup Trophy to English team captain. No. C460, Flags of nations participating in 1978 World Cup Soccer Championships. No. C461, Soccer action. No. C462, Argentina, 1978 World Cup Champions.

1978 *Perf. 14½, 13½ (#C461)*
C458 AP145 25g multicolored
C459 AP145 25g multicolored
C460 AP145 25g multicolored
C461 AP145 25g multicolored
C462 AP145 25g multicolored

Coronation of Queen Elizabeth II, 25th Anniv. (#C458-C459). 1978 World Cup Soccer Championships, Argentina (#C460-C462).

No. C460 contains one 70x50mm stamp, No. C461 one 39x57mm stamp.

Issue dates: No. C458, May 11. Nos. C459-C460, May 16. No. C461, June 30. No. C462, Oct. 26.

Souvenir Sheet

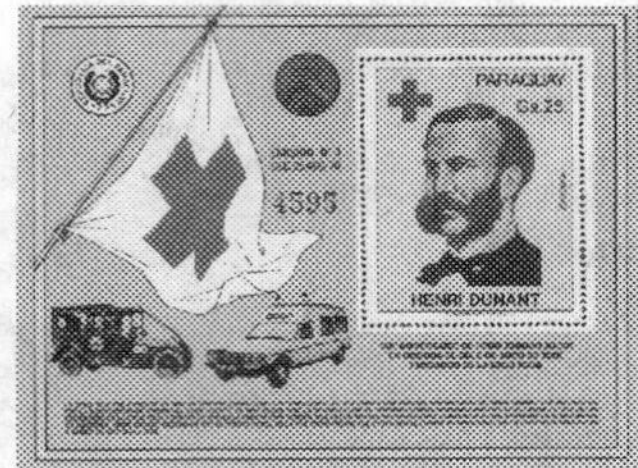

Jean-Henri Dunant, 150th Birth Anniv. — AP146

1978, June 28 *Perf. 14½*
C463 AP146 25g multicolored

Souvenir Sheet

Capt. James Cook, 250th Birth Anniv. — AP147

1978, July 19 *Perf. 13½*
C464 AP147 25g multicolored

Discovery of Hawaii, Death of Capt. Cook, bicentennial; Hawaii Statehood, 20th anniv.

Souvenir Sheet

Adoration of the Magi by Albrecht Durer — AP149

1978, Oct. 31 *Perf. 13½*
C468 AP149 25g multicolored

Souvenir Sheet

Prof. Hermann Oberth, 85th Birth Anniv. — AP150

1979, Aug. 28 *Perf. 14½*
C469 AP150 25g multicolored

Souvenir Sheet

World Cup Soccer Championships — AP151

1979, Nov. 29
C470 AP151 25g multicolored

Souvenir Sheet

Helicopters — AP152

1979, Nov. 29 Litho. *Perf. 13½*
C471 AP152 25g multicolored

Souvenir Sheet

1980 Summer Olympics, Moscow — AP153

1979, Dec. 20 *Perf. 14½*
C472 AP153 25g Two-man canoe

Souvenir Sheet

1982 World Cup Soccer Championships, Spain — AP154

1979, Dec. 24 Litho. *Perf. 13x13½*
C473 AP154 25g Sheet of 1+label

Souvenir Sheet

Maybach DS-8 "Zeppelin" — AP155

1980, Apr. 8 *Perf. 14½*
C474 AP155 25g multicolored

Wilhelm Maybach, 50th death anniv. Karl Maybach, 100th birth anniv.

Souvenir Sheet

Rotary Intl., 75th Anniv. — AP156

1980, July 1 Litho. *Perf. 14½*
C475 AP156 25g multicolored

Apollo 11 Type of 1970
Souvenir Sheet

Design: 1st steps on lunar surface.

1980, July 30 *Perf. 13½*
Size: 36x26mm
C476 A221 25g multicolored

Souvenir Sheet

Virgin Surrounded by Animals by Albrecht Durer AP158

Photo. & Engr.
1980, Sept. 24 *Perf. 12*
C477 AP158 25g multicolored

Souvenir Sheet

1980 Olympic Games — AP159

1980, Dec. 15 Litho. ***Perf. 14***
C478 AP159 25g multi

Metropolitan Seminary Centenary — AP160

1981, Mar. 26 Litho. Wmk. 347

C479 AP160	5g ultra		15	15
C480 AP160	10g red brn		15	15
C481 AP160	25g green		20	15
C482 AP160	50g gray		40	30
	Set value		72	55

Anniversaries and Events AP161

Designs: 5g, George Washington, 250th birth anniv. (in 1982). 10g, Queen Mother Elizabeth, 80th birthday (in 1980). 30g, Phila Tokyo '81.
No. C486, Emperor Hirohito, 80th birthday. No. C487, Washington Crossing the Delaware.

1981, July 10 Unwmk. ***Perf. 14***
C483 AP161 5g multicolored
C484 AP161 10g multicolored
C485 AP161 30g multicolored

Souvenir Sheets
Perf. 14½
C486 AP161 25g multicolored
C487 AP161 25g multicolored

No. C484 issued in sheets of 8 plus label. For overprints see Nos. 2126, C590-C591, C611.

First Space Shuttle Mission — AP162

Pres. Ronald Reagan and: 5g, Columbia in Earth orbit. 10g, Astronauts John Young and Robert Crippen. 30g, Columbia landing.

George Washington and: No. C491, Columbia re-entering atmosphere. No. C492, Columbia inverted above Earth.

1981, Oct. 9 ***Perf. 14***
C488 AP162 5g multicolored
C489 AP162 10g multicolored
C490 AP162 30g multicolored

Souvenir Sheets
Perf. 13½
C491 AP162 25g multicolored
C492 AP162 25g multicolored

Nos. C491-C492 each contain one 60x50mm stamp. Inauguration of Pres. Reagan, George Washington, 250th birth anniv. (in 1982) (#C491-C492).

World Cup Soccer, Spain, 1982 AP163

1981, Oct. 15 ***Perf. 14***
Color of Shirts
C493 AP163 5g yellow, green
C494 AP163 10g blue, white
C495 AP163 30g white & black, orange

Souvenir Sheet
Perf. 14½
C496 AP163 25g Goalie

No. C494 exists in sheets of 5 plus 4 labels.

Christmas AP164

Paintings: 5g, Virgin with the Child by Stefan Lochner. 10g, Our Lady of Caacupe. 25g, Altar of the Virgin by Albrecht Durer. 30g, Virgin and Child by Matthias Grunewald.

1981, Dec. 21 ***Perf. 14***
C497 AP164 5g multicolored
C498 AP164 10g multicolored
C499 AP164 30g multicolored

Souvenir Sheet
Perf. 13½
C500 AP164 25g multicolored

No. C500 contains one 54x75mm stamp.

Souvenir Sheet

Graf Zeppelin's First Flight to South America, 50th Anniv. — AP165

1981, Dec. 28 ***Perf. 14½***
C501 AP165 25g multicolored

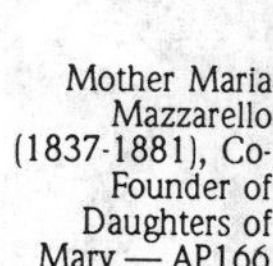

Mother Maria Mazzarello (1837-1881), Co-Founder of Daughters of Mary — AP166

Perf. 13x13½
1981, Dec. 30 Litho. Wmk. 347

C502 AP166	20g blk & grn	16	15
C503 AP166	25g blk & red brn	20	15
C504 AP166	50g blk & gray vio	40	30

Souvenir Sheet

The Magus (Dr. Faust) by Rembrandt — AP167

Litho. & Typo.
1982, Apr. 23 Unwmk. ***Perf. 14½***
C505 AP167 25g blk, buff & gold

Johann Wolfgang von Goethe, 150th death anniv.

The following stamps were issued 4 each in sheets of 8 with 1 label: Nos. C590-C591, C669-C670, C677-C678, C682-C683, C690-C691, C699-C700, C718-C719, C747-C748.
The following stamps were issued in sheets of 4 with 5 labels: Nos. C765-C766, C774, C779-C780, C785, C803, C813, C818, C823.
The following stamps were issued in sheets of 3 with 6 labels: Nos. C739, C754.
The following stamps were issued in sheets of 5 with 4 labels: Nos. C507, C512, C515, C519, C524, C529, C535, C539, C542, C547, C550, C559, C569, C572, C579, C582, C585, C588, C596, C598, C615, C622, C626, C634, C642, C647, C650, C656, C705, C711, C731, C791, C798, C808.
The following stamp was issued in sheets of 7 with 2 labels: No. C660.

World Chess Championships Type of 1980

Illustrations from The Book of Chess: 5g, The Game of the Virgins. 10g, Two gothic ladies. 30g, Chess game at apothecary shop.
No. C509, Christians and Jews preparing to play in garden. No. C510, Indian prince introducing chess to Persia.

1982, June 10 Litho. ***Perf. 14***
C506 A347 5g multicolored
C507 A347 10g multicolored
C508 A347 30g multicolored

Souvenir Sheets
Perf. 13½
C509 A347 25g multicolored
Perf. 14½
C510 A347 25g multicolored

No. C509 contains one 50x60mm stamp, No. C510 one 50x70mm stamp. For overprint see No. C665.

Italy, Winners of 1982 World Cup Soccer Championships — AP168

Players: 5g, Klaus Fischer, Germany. 10g, Altobelli holding World Cup Trophy. 25g, Forster, Altobelli, horiz. 30g, Fischer, Gordillo.

1982, Oct. 20 ***Perf. 14***
C511 AP168 5g multicolored
C512 AP168 10g multicolored
C513 AP168 30g multicolored

Souvenir Sheet
C513A AP168 25g multicolored

Christmas — AP169

Paintings by Peter Paul Rubens: 5g, The Massacre of the Innocents. 10g, The Nativity, vert. 25g, The Madonna Adored by Four Penitents and Saints. 30g, The Flight to Egypt.

1982, Oct. 23
C514 AP169 5g multicolored
C515 AP169 10g multicolored
C516 AP169 30g multicolored

Souvenir Sheet
Perf. 14½
C517 AP169 25g multicolored

No. C517 contains one 50x70mm stamp.

The Sampling Officials of the Draper's Guild by Rembrandt — AP170

Details from Rembrandt Paintings: 10g, Self portrait, vert. 25g, Night Watch, vert. 30g, Self portrait, diff., vert.

1983, Jan. 21 ***Perf. 14, 13 (10g)***
C518 AP170 5g multicolored
C519 AP170 10g multicolored
C520 AP170 30g multicolored

Souvenir Sheet
Perf. 13½
C521 AP170 25g multicolored

No. C521 contains one 50x60mm stamp.

Souvenir Sheet

1982 World Cup Soccer Championships, Spain — AP171

1983, Jan. 21 *Perf. 13½*

C522 AP171 25g Fuji blimp

German Rocket Scientists — AP172

Designs: 5g, Dr. Walter R. Dornberger, V2 rocket ascending. 10g, Nebel, Ritter, Oberth, Riedel, and Von Braun examining rocket mock-up. 30g, Dr. A. F. Staats, Cyrus B research rocket.

No. C526, Dr. Eugen Sanger, rocket design. No. C527, Fritz Von Opel, Opel-Sander rocket plane. No. C528, Friedrich Schmiedl, first rocket used for mail delivery.

1983 *Perf. 14*

C523 AP172 5g multicolored
C524 AP172 10g multicolored
C525 AP172 30g multicolored

Souvenir Sheets

Perf. 14½

C526 AP172 25g multicolored
C527 AP172 25g multicolored
C528 AP172 25g multicolored

Issue dates: No. C528, Apr. 13; others, Jan. 24.

First Manned Flight, 200th Anniv. AP173

Balloons: 5g, Montgolfier brothers, 1783. 10g, Baron von Lutgendorf's, 1786. 30g, Adorne's, 1784.

No. C532, Montgolfier brothers, diff. No. C533, Profiles of Montgolfier Brothers. No. C534, Bicentennial emblem, nova.

1983 *Perf. 14, 13 (10g)*

C529 AP173 5g multicolored
C530 AP173 10g multicolored
C531 AP173 30g multicolored

Souvenir Sheets

Perf. 13½

C532 AP173 25g multicolored
C533 AP173 25g multicolored
C534 AP173 25g multicolored

Nos. C532-C533 each contain one 50x60mm stamp, No. C534 one 30x40mm stamp.

Issue dates: Nos. C529-C533, Feb. 25; No. C534, Oct. 19.

1984 Summer Olympics, Los Angeles AP174

1932 Gold medalists: 5g, Wilson Charles, US, 100-meter dash. 10g, Ellen Preis, Austria, fencing. 25g, Rudolf Ismayr, Germany, weight lifting. 30g, John Anderson, US, discus.

1983, June 13 *Perf. 14*

C535 AP174 5g multicolored
C536 AP174 10g multicolored
C537 AP174 30g multicolored

Souvenir Sheet

Perf. 14½

C538 AP174 25g Sheet of 1 + label

No. C535 incorrectly credits Charles with gold medal.

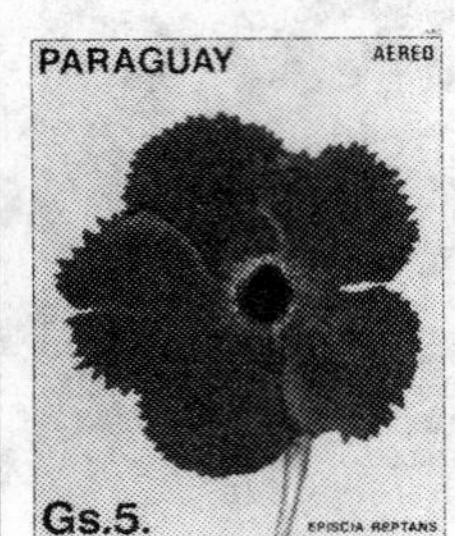

Flowers AP175

1983, Aug. 31 *Perf. 14*

C539 AP175 5g Episcia reptans
C540 AP175 10g Lilium
C541 AP175 30g Heliconia

Intl. Maritime Organization, 25th Anniv. AP176

Designs: 5g, Brigantine Undine. 10g, Training ship Sofia, 1881, horiz. 30g, Training ship Stein, 1879.

No. C545, Santa Maria. No. C546, Santa Maria and Telstar communications satellite.

Perf. 14, 13½x13 (10g)

1983, Oct. 24 **Litho.**

C542 AP176 5g multicolored
C543 AP176 10g multicolored
C544 AP176 30g multicolored

Souvenir Sheets

Perf. 14½

C545 AP176 25g multicolored

Perf. 13½

C546 AP176 25g multicolored

No. C546 contains one 90x57mm stamp. Discovery of America, 490th Anniv. (in 1982) (#C545-C546). For overprint see No. 2198.

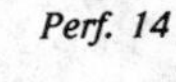

Space Achievements — AP177

Designs: 5g, Space shuttle Challenger. 10g, Pioneer 10, vert. 30g, Herschel's telescope, Cerro Tololo Obervatory, Chile, vert.

1984, Jan. 9 *Perf. 14*

C547 AP177 5g multicolored
C548 AP177 10g multicolored
C549 AP177 30g multicolored

Summer Olympics, Los Angeles AP178

Designs: 5g, 400-meter hurdles. 10g, Small bore rifle, horiz. 25g, Equestrian, Christine Stuckleberger. 30g, 100-meter dash.

1984, Jan. *Perf. 14*

C550 AP178 5g multicolored
C551 AP178 10g multicolored
C552 AP178 30g multicolored

Souvenir Sheet

Perf. 14½

C553 AP178 25g multicolored

For overprint see No. 2130.

1984 Winter Olympics, Sarajevo AP179

Perf. 14, 13x13½ (10g)

1984, Mar. 24

C554 AP179 5g Steve Podborski, downhill
C555 AP179 10g Olympic Flag
C556 AP179 30g Gaetan Boucher, speed skating

No. C555 printed se-tenant with label.

Souvenir Sheets

Cupid and Psyche by Peter Paul Rubens — AP180

Design: No. C558, Satyr and Maenad (copy of Rubens' Bacchanal) by Jean-Antoine Watteau (1684-1721).

1984, Mar. 26 *Perf. 13½*

C557 AP180 25g multicolored
C558 AP180 25g multicolored

No. C558 contains one 78x57mm stamp.

1982, 1986 World Cup Soccer Championships, Spain, Mexico City — AP181

Soccer players: 5g, Tardelli, Breitner. 10g, Zamora, Stielke. 30g, Walter Schachner, player on ground.

No. C562, Player from Paraguay. No. C563, World Cup Trophy, Spanish, Mexican characters, horiz.

1984, Mar. 29 *Perf. 14, 13 (10g)*

C559 AP181 5g multicolored
C560 AP181 10g multicolored
C561 AP181 30g multicolored

Souvenir Sheets

Perf. 14½

C562 AP181 25g multicolored
C563 AP181 25g multicolored

Souvenir Sheet

ESPANA '84 — AP182

1984, Mar. 31
C564 AP182 25g multicolored

No. C564 has one stamp and a label.

Souvenir Sheets

ESPANA '84 — AP183

Paintings: No. C565, Holy Family of the Lamb by Raphael. No. C566, Adoration of the Magi by Rubens.

1984, Apr. 16 *Perf. 13½*
C565 AP183 25g multicolored
C566 AP183 25g multicolored

Souvenir Sheet

19th UPU Congress — AP184

1984, June 9
C567 AP184 25g multicolored

Intl. Chess Federation, 60th Anniv. AP185

Perf. 14, 13x13½ (10g)
1984, June 18
C568 AP185 5g shown
C569 AP185 10g Woman holding chess piece
C570 AP185 30g Bishop, knight

First Europe to South America Airmail Flight by Lufthansa, 50th Anniv. — AP186

Designs: 5g, Lockheed Superconstellation. 10g, Dornier Wal. 30g, Boeing 707.

Perf. 14, 13½x13 (10g)
1984, June 22
C571 AP186 5g multicolored
C572 AP186 10g multicolored
C573 AP186 30g multicolored

For overprint see No. C592.

Souvenir Sheets

First Moon Landing, 15th Anniv. — AP187

1984, June 23 *Perf. 14½*
C574 AP187 25g Apollo 11 lunar module
C575 AP187 25g Prof. Hermann Oberth

Hermann Oberth, 90th Birthday (#C575).

Souvenir Sheet

The Holy Family with John the Baptist — AP188

1984, Aug. 3 Photo. & Engr. *Perf. 14*
C576 AP188 20g multicolored

Raphael, 500th Birth Anniv. (in 1983).

No. 2099 Overprinted in Red: ANIVERSARIO GOBIERNO CONSTRUCTIVO Y DE LA PAZ DEL PRESIDENTE CONSTITUCIONAL GRAL. DE EJERCITO ALFREDO STROESSNER 15 / 8 / 1964

1984, Aug. 15 *Perf. 13*
C577 A374 100g on No. 2099

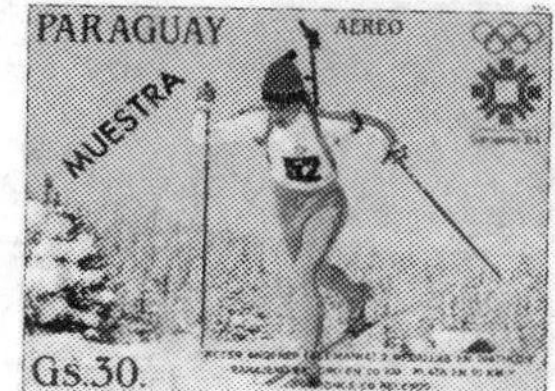

1984 Winter Olympics, Sarajevo — AP189

Gold medalists: 5g, Max Julen, giant slalom, Switzerland. 10g, Hans Stanggassinger, Franz Wembacher, luge, West Germany. 30g, Peter Angerer, biathlon, Germany.

Perf. 14, 13½x13 (10g)
1984, Sept. 12
C578 AP189 5g multicolored
C579 AP189 10g multicolored
C580 AP189 30g multicolored

For overprint see No. C596.

Motorcycles, Cent. — AP190

1984, Nov. 9 *Perf. 14, 13½x13 (10g)*
C581 AP190 5g Reitwagen, Daimler-Maybach, 1885
C582 AP190 10g BMW, 1980
C583 AP190 30g Opel, 1930

Christmas AP191

1985, Jan. 18 *Perf. 13*
C584 AP191 5g shown
C585 AP191 10g Girl playing guitar
C586 AP191 30g Girl, candle, basket

1986 World Cup Soccer Championships, Mexico — AP192

Various soccer players.

Perf. 13x13½, 13½x13
1985, Jan. 21

Color of Shirt

C587 AP192 5g red & white
C588 AP192 10g white & black, horiz.
C589 AP192 30g blue

No. C484 Ovptd. in Silver

1985, Feb. 6 *Perf. 14*
C590 AP161 10g INTERPEX / 1985
C591 AP161 10g STAMPEX / 1985

No. C572 Ovptd. in Vermilion

STUTTGART 85

1985, Feb. 16 *Perf. 13½x13*
C592 AP186 10g on No. C572

No. 2053A Ovptd. "FINAL / ALEMANIA 1 : 3 ITALIA"

1985, Mar. 7 *Perf. 14½*
C593 A362 25g multicolored

Souvenir Sheets

Rotary Intl., 80th Anniv. — AP193

Designs: No. C594, Paul Harris, founder of Rotary Intl. No. C595, Rotary Intl. Headquarters, Evanston, IL, horiz.

1985, Mar. 11

C594 AP193 25g multicolored
C595 AP193 25g multicolored

No. C579 Ovptd. "OLYMPHILEX 85" in Black and Olympic Rings in Silver

1985, Mar. 18 *Perf. 13½x13*

C596 AP189 10g on No. C579

Music Year AP194

Designs: 5g, Agustin Barrios (1885-1944), musician, vert. 10g, Johann Sebastian Bach, composer, score. 30g, Folk musicians.

Perf. 14, 13½x13 (10g)

1985, Apr. 16

C597 AP194 5g multicolored
C598 AP194 10g multicolored
C599 AP194 30g multicolored

1st Paraguayan Locomotive, 1861 — AP195

1985, Apr. 20 *Perf. 14*

C600 AP195 5g shown
C601 AP195 10g Transrapid 06, Germany
C602 AP195 30g TGV, France

Souvenir Sheet

Visit of Pope John Paul II to South America — AP196

1985, Apr. 22 **Litho.** *Perf. 13½*

C603 AP196 25g silver & multi

No. C603 also exists with gold inscriptions.

Inter-American Development Bank, 25th Anniv. — AP197

1985, Apr. 25 **Litho.** **Wmk. 347**

C604 AP197 3g dl red brn, org & yel 15 15
C605 AP197 5g vio, org & yel 15 15
C606 AP197 10g rose vio, org & yel 15 15
C607 AP197 50g sep, org & yel 15 15
C608 AP197 65g bl, org & yel 15 15
C609 AP197 95g pale bl grn, org & yel 15 15
Set value 42 35

No. 1875 Ovptd. in Black in Margin "V EXPOSICION MUNDIAL / ARGENTINA 85" and

1985, May 24 **Unwmk.** *Perf. 13½*

C610 A326 25g on No. 1875

No. C485 Ovptd. in Dark Blue with Emblem and:

1985, July 5 *Perf. 14*

C611 AP161 30g on No. C485

No. 2149 Ovptd. in Dark Blue in Margin with UN emblem and "26.6.1985 - 40- ANIVERSARIO DE LA / FUNDACION DE LAS NACIONES UNIDAS"

1985, Aug. 5 *Perf. 14½*

C612 A388 25g on No. 2149

Jean-Henri Dunant, Founder of Red Cross, 75th Death Anniv. — AP198

Dunant and: 5g, Enclosed ambulance. 10g, Nobel Peace Prize, Red Cross emblem. 30g, Open ambulance with passengers.

1985, Aug. 6 *Perf. 13*

C614 AP198 5g multicolored
C615 AP198 10g multicolored
C616 AP198 30g multicolored

World Chess Congress, Austria — AP199

Designs: 5g, The Turk, copper engraving, Book of Chess by Racknitz, 1789. 10g, King seated, playing chess, Book of Chess, 14th cent. 25g, Margrave Otto von Brandenburg playing chess with his wife, Great Manuscript of Heidelberg Songs, 13th cent. 30g, Three men playing chess, Book of Chess, 14th cent.

1985, Aug. 9 **Litho.** *Perf. 13*

C617 AP199 5g multicolored
C618 AP199 10g multicolored
C619 AP199 30g multicolored

Souvenir Sheet

Perf. 13½

C620 AP199 25g multicolored

No. C620 contains one 60x50mm stamp.

Discovery of America 500th Anniv. AP200

Explorers, ships: 5g, Marco Polo and ship. 10g, Vicente Yanez Pinzon, Nina, horiz. 25g, Christopher Columbus, Santa Maria. 30g, James Cook, Endeavor.

Perf. 14, 13½x13 (10g)

1985, Oct. 19 **Litho.**

C621 AP200 5g multicolored
C622 AP200 10g multicolored
C623 AP200 30g multicolored

Souvenir Sheet

Perf. 14½

C624 AP200 25g multicolored

Year of Cook's death is incorrect on No. C623. For overprint see No. C756.

ITALIA '85 — AP201

Nudes (details): 5g, La Fortuna, by Guido Reni, vert. 10g, The Triumph of Galatea, by Raphael. 25g, The Birth of Venus, by Botticelli, vert. 30g, Sleeping Venus, by Il Giorgione.

1985, Dec. 3 *Perf. 14*

C625 AP201 5g multicolored
C626 AP201 10g multicolored
C627 AP201 30g multicolored

Souvenir Sheet

Perf. 13½

C628 AP201 25g multicolored

No. C628 contains one 49x60mm stamp.

Souvenir Sheet

Maimonides, Philosopher, 850th Birth Anniv. — AP202

1985, Dec. 31 *Perf. 13½*

C629 AP202 25g multicolored

UN, 40th Anniv. — AP203

1986, Feb. 27 **Wmk. 392**

C630 AP203 5g bl & sepia 15 15
C631 AP203 10g bl & gray 15 15
C632 AP203 50g bl & grysh brn 15 15
Set value 24 22

For overprint see No. C726.

AMERIPEX '86 — AP204

Discovery of America 500th anniv. emblem and: 5g, Spain #424. 10g, US #233. 25g, Spain #426, horiz. 30g, Spain #421.

Perf. 14, 13½x13 (10g)

1986, Mar. 19 **Unwmk.**

C633 AP204 5g multicolored
C634 AP204 10g multicolored
C635 AP204 30g multicolored

Souvenir Sheet

Perf. 13½

C636 AP204 25g multicolored

No. C636 contains one 60x40mm stamp. For overprint see No. C755.

Souvenir Sheet

1984 Olympic Gold Medalist, Dr. Reiner Klimke on Ahlerich — AP205

1986, Mar. 20 *Perf. 14½*

C637 AP205 25g multicolored

Tennis Players AP206

Designs: 5g, Martina Navratilova, US. 10g, Boris Becker, W. Germany. 30g, Victor Pecci, Paraguay.

1986, Mar. 26 *Perf. 14, 13 (10g)*

C638 AP206 5g multicolored
C639 AP206 10g multicolored
C640 AP206 30g multicolored

Nos. C638-C640 exist with red inscriptions, perf. 13. For overprints see Nos. C672-C673.

Halley's Comet — AP207

Designs: 5g, Bayeux Tapestry, c. 1066, showing comet. 10g, Edmond Halley, comet. 25g, Comet, Giotto probe. 30g, Rocket lifting off, Giotto probe, vert.

Perf. 14, 13½x13 (10g)

1986, Apr. 30

C641 AP207 5g multicolored
C642 AP207 10g multicolored
C643 AP207 30g multicolored

Souvenir Sheet

Perf. 14½

C644 AP207 25g multicolored

Souvenir Sheet

Madonna by Albrecht Durer — AP208

1986, June 4 Typo. *Rough Perf. 11*

Self-Adhesive

C645 AP208 25g black & red

No. C645 was printed on cedar.

Locomotives — AP209

1986, June 23 Litho. *Perf. 13*

C646 AP209 5g #3038
C647 AP209 10g Canadian Pacific A1E, 1887
C648 AP209 30g 1D1 #483, 1925

1986 World Cup Soccer Championships — AP210

Paraguay vs.: 5g, Colombia. 10g, Chile. 30g, Chile, diff. 25g, Paraguay Natl. team.

Perf. 13, 13½x13 (10g)

1986, June 24

C649 AP210 5g multicolored
C650 AP210 10g multicolored
C651 AP210 30g multicolored

Souvenir Sheet

Perf. 14½

C652 AP210 25g multicolored

No. C652 contains one 81x75mm stamp. For overprints see Nos. C693-C695.

No. 1289 Ovptd. in Silver on Dark Blue with Mercury Capsule and "MERCURY / 5-V-1961 / 25 Anos Primer / Astronauta / Americano / Alan B. Shepard / 1986"

1986, July 11 ***Perf. 13½***

C653 A226 23.40g on No. 1289

Souvenir Sheet

Trajectory Diagram of Halley's Comet, Giotto Probe — AP211

1986, July 28

C654 AP211 25g multicolored

German Railroads, 150th Anniv. — AP212

Design: 25g, Christening of the First German Train, 1835, by E. Shilling and B. Goldschmidt.

1986, Sept. 1 ***Perf. 13½x13***

C655 AP212 5g VT 10 501DB, 1954
C656 AP212 10g 1st Electric, 1879
C657 AP212 30g Hydraulic diesel, class 218

Souvenir Sheet

Perf. 13½

C658 AP212 25g multicolored

No. C658 contains one 54x75mm stamp.

Intl. Peace Year AP213

Details from The Consequences of War by Rubens: 5g, Two women. 10g, Woman nursing child. 30g, Two men.

1986, Oct. 27 ***Perf. 13***

C659 AP213 5g multicolored
C660 AP213 10g multicolored
C661 AP213 30g multicolored

Japanese Emigrants in Paraguay, 50th Anniv. AP214

1986, Nov. 6 ***Perf. 13½x13, 13x13½***

C662 AP214	5g	La Colemna Vineyard	15	15
C663 AP214	10g	Cherry, lapacho flowers	15	15
C664 AP214	20g	Integration monument, vert.	15	15
		Set value	15	15

No. C507 Ovptd. in Silver "XXVII-DUBAI / Olimpiada de / Ajedrez - 1986"

1986, Dec. 30 Unwmk. *Perf. 14*

C665 A347 10g on No. C507

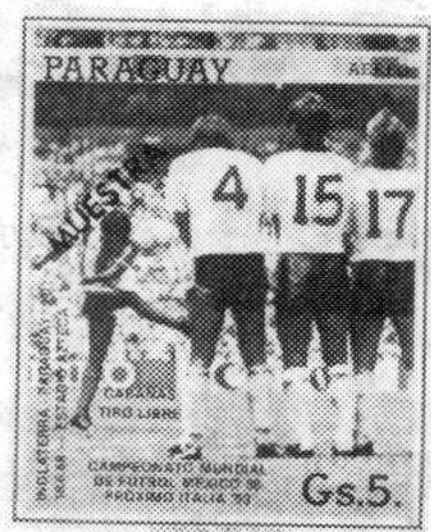

1986 World Cup Soccer Championships, Mexico — AP214a

Match scenes.

1987, Feb. 19 ***Perf. 14***

C666 AP214a 5g England vs. Paraguay
C667 AP214a 10g Larios catching ball
C668 AP214a 20g Trejo, Ferreira

Perf. 13½x13

C669 AP214a 25g Torales, Flores, Romero
C670 AP214a 30g Mendonza

Souvenir Sheet

Perf. 14½

C671 AP214a 100g Romero

Nos. C669-C670 are horiz. No. C671 contains one 40x50mm stamp.

Nos. C639-C640 Ovptd. in Silver including Olympic Rings and "NUEVAMENTE EL / TENIS EN LAS / OLYMPIADAS 1988 / SEOUL COREA"

1987, Apr. 15 ***Perf. 13***

C672 AP206 10g on No. C639
C673 AP206 30g on No. C640

Automobiles — AP215

1987, May 29 Litho. *Perf. 13½*

C674 AP215 5g Mercedes 300 SEL 6.3
C675 AP215 10g Jaguar Mk II 3.8
C676 AP215 20g BMW 635 CSI
C677 AP215 25g Alfa Romeo GTA
C678 AP215 30g BMW 1800 Tisa

1988 Winter Olympics, Calgary — AP216

Gold medalists or Olympic competitors: 5g, Michela Figini, Switzerland, downhill, 1984, vert. 10g, Hanni Wenzel, Liechtenstein, slalom and giant slalom, 1980. 20g, 4-Man bobsled, Switzerland, 1956, 1972. 25g, Markus Wasmeier, downhill. 30g, Ingemar Stenmark, Sweden, slalom and giant slalom, 1980. 100g, Pirmin Zurbriggen, Switzerland, vert. (downhill, 1988).

1987, Sept. 10 ***Perf. 14***

C679 AP216 5g multicolored
C680 AP216 10g multicolored
C681 AP216 20g multicolored

Perf. 13½x13

C682 AP216 25g multicolored
C683 AP216 30g multicolored

Souvenir Sheet

Perf. 13½

C684 AP216 100g multicolored

No. C684 contains one 45x57mm stamp.

Nos. 2211 and C467 Ovptd. in Red on Silver "11.IX.1887 - 1987 / Centenario de la fundacion de / la A.N.R. (Partido Colarado) / Bernardino Caballero Fundador / General de Ejercito / D. Alfredo Stroessner Continuador"

1987, Sept. 11 ***Perf. 13, 14***

C685 A401 200g on No. 2211
C686 AP148 1000g on No. C467

1988 Summer Olympics, Seoul — AP217

Medalists and competitors: 5g, Sabine Everts, West Germany, javelin. 10g, Carl Lewis, US, 100 and 200-meter run, 1984. 20g, Darrell Pace, US, archery, 1976, 1984. 25g, Juergen Hingsen, West Germany, decathalon, 1984. 30g, Claudia Losch, West Germany, shot put, 1984. 100g, Fredy Schmidtke, West Germany, cycling, 1984.

1987, Sept. 22 ***Perf. 14***

C687 AP217 5g multi
C688 AP217 10g multi, vert.
C689 AP217 20g multi

Perf. 13½x13

C690 AP217 25g multi, vert.
C691 AP217 30g multi, vert.

Souvenir Sheet

Perf. 14½

C692 AP217 100g multi, vert.

Nos. C650-C652 Ovptd. in Violet or Blue (#C694) with Soccer Ball and "ZURICH 10.VI.87 / Lanzamiento ITALIA '90 / Italia 3 - Argentina 1"

Perf. 13½x13, 13

1987, Oct. 19 Litho.

C693 AP210 10g on No. C650
C694 AP210 30g on No. C651

Souvenir Sheet

Perf. 14½

C695 AP210 25g on No. C652

Paintings by Rubens AP218

Details from: 5g, The Virtuous Hero Crowned. 10g, The Brazen Serpent, 1635. 20g, Judith with the Head of Holofernes, 1617. 25g, Assembly of the Gods of Olympus. 30g, Venus, Cupid, Bacchus and Ceres.

1987, Dec. 14 *Perf. 13*
C696 AP218 5g multicolored
C697 AP218 10g multicolored
C698 AP218 20g multicolored

Perf. 13x13½
C699 AP218 25g multicolored
C700 AP218 30g multicolored

Christmas AP219

Details from paintings: 5g, Virgin and Child with St. Joseph and St. John the Baptist, anonymous. 10g, Madonna and Child under the Veil with St. Joseph and St. John, by Marco da Siena. 20g, Sacred Conversation with the Donors, by Titian. 25g, The Brotherhood of the Rosary, by Durer. 30g, Madonna with Standing Child, by Rubens. 100g, Madonna and Child, engraving by Albrecht Durer.

1987 **Litho.** *Perf. 14*
C701 AP219 5g multicolored
C702 AP219 10g multicolored
C703 AP219 20g multicolored
C704 AP219 25g multicolored

Perf. 13x13½
C705 AP219 30g multicolored

Souvenir Sheet
Perf. 14½
C706 AP219 100g multi

Issue dates: Nos. C701-C705, Dec. 16. No. C706, Dec. 17.

Austrian Railways, Sesquicentennial — AP220

Locomotives: 5g, Steam #3669, 1899. 10g, Steam #GZ 44074. 20g, Steam, diff. 25g, Diesel-electric. 30g, Austria No. 1067. 100g, Steam, vert.

1988, Jan. 2 *Perf. 14*
C707 AP220 5g multicolored
C708 AP220 10g multicolored
C709 AP220 20g multicolored
C710 AP220 25g multicolored

Perf. 13½x13
C711 AP220 30g multicolored

Souvenir Sheet
Perf. 13½
C712 AP220 100g multicolored

No. C712 contains one 50x60mm stamp.

Souvenir Sheet

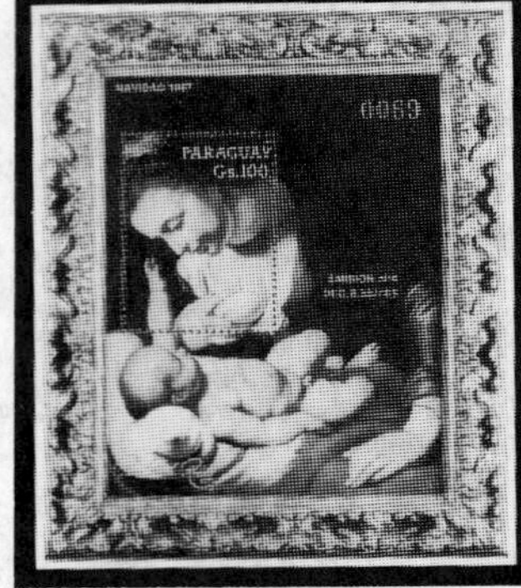
Christmas — AP221

1988, Jan. 4 *Perf. 13½*
C713 AP221 100g Madonna, by Rubens

Souvenir Sheet

1988 Summer Olympics, Seoul — AP222

1988, Jan. 18 *Perf. 14½*
C714 AP222 100g gold & multi

Exists with silver lettering and frame.

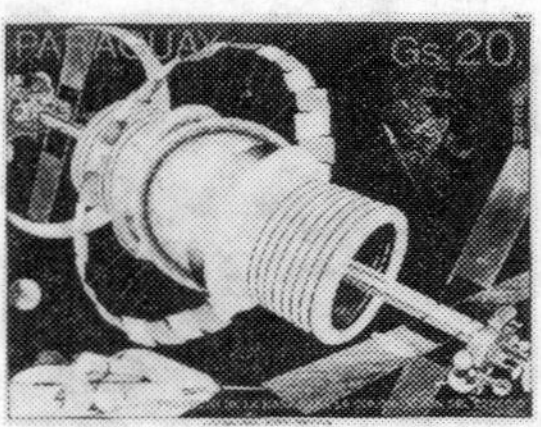
Colonization of Space — AP223

Designs: 5g, NASA-ESA space station. 10g, Eurospace module Columbus docked at space station. 20g, NASA space sation. 25g, Ring section of space station, vert. 30g, Space station living quarters in central core, vert.

1988, Mar. 9 **Litho.** *Perf. 13½x13*
C715 AP223 5g multicolored
C716 AP223 10g multicolored
C717 AP223 20g multicolored

Perf. 13x13½
C718 AP223 25g multicolored
C719 AP223 30g multicolored

Souvenir Sheet

Berlin, 750th Anniv. — AP224

1988, Mar. 10 **Litho.** *Perf. 14½*
C720 AP224 100g multicolored

LUPOSTA '87.

Souvenir Sheet

Apollo 15 Launch, 1971 — AP225

1988, Apr. 12
C721 AP225 100g multicolored

No. 2210 Ovptd. in Metallic Red with

1988, Apr. 28 *Perf. 13*
C722 A401 100g on No. 2210

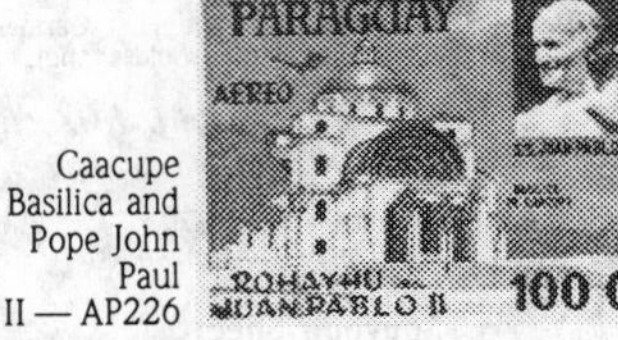

Caacupe Basilica and Pope John Paul II — AP226

Perf. 13½x13
1988, May 5 **Litho.** **Wmk. 347**

C723 AP226	100g multi		45	35
C724 AP226	120g multi		55	42
C725 AP226	150g multi		68	52

Visit of Pope John Paul II.

No. C631 Overprinted

*** 75º ANIVERSARIO**
DE FUNDACION
CENTRO FILATELICO
DEL PARAGUAY
15 JUNIO-1913 - 1988

Perf. 13x13½
1988, June 15 **Wmk. 392**

C726 AP203	10g blue & gray	15	15

Paraguay Philatelic Center, 75th Anniv.

Berlin, 750th Anniv. Paintings Type of 1988

Paintings: 5g, Venus and Cupid, 1742, by Francois Boucher. 10g, Perseus Liberates Andromeda, 1662, by Rubens. 20g, Venus and the Organist by Titian. 25g, Leda and the Swan by Correggio. 30g, St. Cecilia by Rubens.

1988, June 15 **Unwmk.** *Perf. 13*
C727 A409 5g multi, horiz.
C728 A409 10g multi, horiz.
C729 A409 20g multi, horiz.
C730 A409 25g multi, horiz.

Perf. 13x13½
C731 A409 30g multicolored

Founding of "New Germany" and 1st Cultivation of Herbal Tea, Cent. AP227

Perf. 13x13½, 13½x13
1988, June 18 **Litho.** **Wmk. 347**

C732 AP227	90g Cauldron, vert.	42	32
C733 AP227	105g Farm workers carrying crop	48	35
C734 AP227	120g like 105g	55	42

1990 World Cup Soccer Championships, Italy — AP228

Designs: 5g, Machine slogan cancel from Montevideo, May 21, 1930. 10g, Italy #324, vert. 20g, France #349. 25g, Brazil #696, vert. 30g, Paraguayan commemorative cancel for ITALIA 1990.

1988, Aug. 1 **Unwmk.** *Perf. 13*
C735 AP228 5g multicolored
C736 AP228 10g multicolored
C737 AP228 20g multicolored
C738 AP228 25g multicolored

Perf. 13½x13
C739 AP228 30g multicolored

For overprint see No. 2284.

Souvenir Sheet

Count Ferdinand von Zeppelin, Airship Designer, Birth Sesquicentennial — AP229

1988, Aug. 3 *Perf. 14½*
C740 AP229 100g multicolored

Government Palace and Pres. Stroessner AP230

Perf. 13½

1988, Aug. 5 Litho. Wmk. 347

C741 AP230	200g multi		40	30
C742 AP230	500g multi		1.00	1.00
C743 AP230	1000g multi		2.00	2.00

Pres. Stroessner's new term in office, 1988-1993. Size of letters in watermark on 200g, 1000g: 5mm. On 500g, 10mm.

1988 Winter Olympics, Calgary — AP231

Gold medalists: 5g, Hubert Strolz, Austria, Alpine combined. 10g, Alberto Tomba, Italy, giant slalom and slalom. 20g, Franck Piccard, France, super giant slalom. 25g, Thomas Muller, Hans-Peter Pohl and Hubert Schwarz, Federal Republic of Germany, Nordic combined team, vert. 30g, Vreni Schneider, Switzerland, giant slalom and slalom, vert. 100g, Marina Kiehl, Federal Republic of Germany, downhill, vert.

Perf. 13½x13

1988, Sept. 2 Unwmk.

C744 AP231 5g multicolored
C745 AP231 10g multicolored
C746 AP231 20g multicolored

Perf. 13x13½

C747 AP231 25g multicolored
C748 AP231 30g multicolored

Souvenir Sheet

Perf. 14½

C749 AP231 100g multicolored

1990 World Cup Soccer Championships, Italy — AP232

Designs: 5g, Mexico #C350. 10g, Germany #1146. 20g, Argentina #1147, vert. 25g, Spain #2211. 30g, Italy #1742.

1988, Oct. 4 *Perf. 13*

C750 AP232 5g multicolored
C751 AP232 10g multicolored
C752 AP232 20g multicolored
C753 AP232 25g multicolored

Perf. 14

C754 AP232 30g multicolored

For overprint see No. 2285.

No. C635 Ovptd. in Metallic Red:

1988, Nov. 25 *Perf. 14*

C755 AP204 30g on No. C635

No. C623 Ovptd. in Gold

1988, Nov. 25 *Perf. 14*

C756 AP200 30g on No. C623

1988 Summer Olympics, Seoul — AP233

Gold medalists: No. C757, Nicole Uphoff, individual dressage. No. C758, Anja Fichtel, Sabine Bau, Zita Funkenhauser, Anette Kluge and Christine Weber, team foil. No. C759, Silvia Sperber, smallbore standard rifle. No. C760, Mathias Baumann, Claus Erhorn, Thies Kaspareit and Ralph Ehrenbrink, equestrian team 3-day event. No. C761, Anja Fichtel, individual foil, vert. No. C762, Franke Sloothaak, Ludger Beerbaum, Wolfgang Brinkmann and Dirk Hafemeister, equestrian team jumping. No. C763, Arnd Schmitt, individual epee, vert. No. C764, Jose Luis Doreste, Finn class yachting. No. C765, Steffi Graf, tennis. No. C766, Michael Gross, 200-meter butterfly, vert. No. C767, West Germany, coxed eights. No. C768, Nicole Uphoff, Monica Theodorescu, Ann Kathrin Linsenhoff and Rainer Klimke, team dressage.

1989 *Perf. 13*

C757 AP233 5g multicolored
C758 AP233 5g multicolored
C759 AP233 10g multicolored
C760 AP233 10g multicolored
C761 AP233 20g multicolored
C762 AP233 20g multicolored
C763 AP233 25g multicolored
C764 AP233 25g multicolored

Perf. 13½x13

C765 AP233 30g multicolored
C766 AP233 30g multicolored

Souvenir Sheets

Perf. 14½

C767 AP233 100g multicolored
C768 AP233 100g multicolored

Nos. C767-C768 each contain one 80x50mm stamp.

Issue dates: Nos. C757, C759, C761, C763, C765, and C767, Mar. 3. Others, Mar. 20.

For overprints see Nos. 2292, 2359.

Souvenir Sheet

Intl. Red Cross, 125th Anniv. (in 1988) — AP234

1989, Apr. 17 Litho. *Perf. 13½*

C769 AP234 100g #803 in changed colors

No. C769 has perforated label picturing Nobel medal.

Olympics Type of 1989

1988 Winter Olympic medalists or competitors: 5g, Pirmin Zurbriggen, Peter Mueller, Switzerland, and Franck Piccard, France, Alpine skiing. 10g, Sigrid Wolf, Austria, super giant slalom, vert. 20g, Czechoslovakia vs. West Germany, hockey, vert. 25g, Piccard, skiing, vert. 30g, Piccard, wearing medal, vert.

1989, Apr. 17 *Perf. 13½x13*

C770 AP233 5g multicolored

Perf. 13x13½

C771 AP233 10g multicolored
C772 AP233 20g multicolored
C773 AP233 25g multicolored
C774 AP233 30g multicolored

Souvenir Sheet

1990 World Cup Soccer Championships, Italy — AP235

1989, Apr. 21 *Perf. 14½*

C775 AP235 100g Sheet of 1 + label

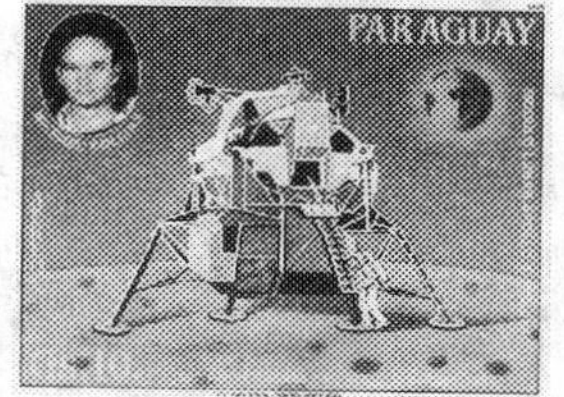

1st Moon Landing, 20th Anniv. — AP236

Designs: 5g, Wernher von Braun, Apollo 11 launch, vert. 10g, Michael Collins, lunar module on moon. 20g, Neil Armstrong, astronaut on lunar module ladder, vert. 25g, Buzz Aldrin, solar wind experiment, vert. 30g, Kurt Debus, splashdown of Columbia command module, vert.

1989, May 24 *Perf. 13*

C776 AP236 5g multicolored
C777 AP236 10g multicolored
C778 AP236 20g multicolored
C779 AP236 25g multicolored
C780 AP236 30g multicolored

Luis Alberto del Parana and the Paraguayans — AP237

1989, May 25 *Perf. 14½*

C780A AP237 100g multicolored

A clear plastic phonograph record is affixed to the souvenir sheet.

Hamburg, 800th Anniv. — AP238

Hamburg anniv. emblem, SAIL '89 emblem, and: 5g, Galleon and Icarus, woodcut by Pieter Brueghel. 10g, Windjammer, vert. 20g, Bark in full sail. 25g, Old Hamburg by A.E. Schliecker, vert. 30g, Commemorative coin issued by Federal Republic of Germany. 100g, Hamburg, 13th cent. illuminated manuscript, vert.

Perf. 13½x13, 13x13½

1989, May 26

C781 AP238 5g multicolored
C782 AP238 10g multicolored
C783 AP238 20g multicolored
C784 AP238 25g multicolored
C785 AP238 30g multicolored

Souvenir Sheet

Perf. 14½

C786 AP238 100g multicolored

No. C786 contains one 40x50mm stamp.

French Revolution, Bicent. — AP239

Details from paintings: 5g, Esther Adorns Herself for her Presentation to King Ahasuerus, by Theodore Chasseriau, vert. 10g, Olympia, by Manet, vert. 20g, The Drunker Erigone with a Panther, by Louis A. Reisener. 25g, Anniv. emblem and natl. coats of arms. 30g, Liberty Leading the People, by Delacroix, vert. 100g, The Education of Maria de Medici, by Rubens, vert.

Perf. 13x13½, 13½x13

1989, May 27

C787 AP239 5g multicolored
C788 AP239 10g multicolored
C789 AP239 20g multicolored
C790 AP239 25g multicolored
C791 AP239 30g multicolored

Souvenir Sheet

Perf. 14½

C792 AP239 100g multicolored

Souvenir Sheet

Railway Zeppelin, 1931 — AP240

1989, May 27 Litho. *Perf. 13½*

C793 AP240 100g multicolored

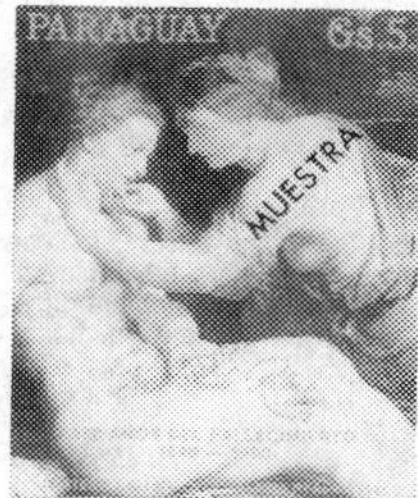

Jupiter and Calisto by Rubens AP241

Details from paintings by Rubens: 10g, Boreas Abducting Oreithyia (1619-20). 20g, Fortuna (1625). 25g, Mars with Venus and Cupid (1625). 30g, Virgin with Child (1620).

1989, Dec. 27 Litho. *Perf. 14*

C794 AP241 5g multicolored
C795 AP241 10g multicolored
C796 AP241 20g multicolored

C797 AP241 25g multicolored

Perf. 13

C798 AP241 30g multicolored

Death of Rubens, 350th anniversary.

Penny Black, 150th Anniv. AP242

Penny Black, 500 years of postal services emblem, Stamp World '90 emblem and: 5g, Brazil #1. 10g, British Guiana #2. 20g, Chile #1. 25g, Uruguay #1. 30g, Paraguay #1.

1989, Dec. 30 ***Perf. 14***

C799 AP242 5g multicolored
C800 AP242 10g multicolored
C801 AP242 20g multicolored
C802 AP242 25g multicolored

Perf. 13

C803 AP242 30g multicolored

Animals AP243

Designs: 5g, Martucha. 10g, Mara. 20g, Lobo de crin. 25g, Rana cornuda tintorera, horiz. 30g, Jaguar, horiz. Inscribed 1989.

1990, Jan. 8 ***Perf. 13x13¹/₂, 13¹/₂x13***

C804 AP243 5g multicolored
C805 AP243 10g multicolored
C806 AP243 20g multicolored
C807 AP243 25g multicolored
C808 AP243 30g multicolored

Columbus' Fleet AP244

Discovery of America 500th anniversary emblem and: 10g, Olympic rings, stylized basketball player, horiz. 20g, Medieval nave, Expo '92 emblem. 25g, Four-masted barkentine, Expo '92 emblem, horiz. 30g, Similar to Spain Scott 2571, Expo '92 emblem.

1990, Jan. 27 ***Perf. 14***

C809 AP244 5g multicolored
C810 AP244 10g multicolored
C811 AP244 20g multicolored
C812 AP244 25g multicolored

Perf. 13¹/₂x13

C813 AP244 30g multicolored

Postal Transportation, 500th Anniv. — AP245

500th Anniv. Emblem and: 5g, 10g, 20g, 25g, Penny Black and various post coaches, 10g, vert. 30g, Post coach.

1990, Mar. 9 ***Perf. 13¹/₂x13, 13x13¹/₂***

C814 AP245 5g multicolored
C815 AP245 10g multicolored
C816 AP245 20g multicolored
C817 AP245 25g multicolored
C818 AP245 30g multicolored

Fort and City of Arco by Durer AP246

Paintings by Albrecht Durer, postal transportation 500th anniversary emblem and: 10g, Trent Castle. 20g, North Innsbruck. 25g, Fort yard of Innsbruck, vert. 30g, Virgin of the Animals. No. C824, Madonna and Child, vert. No. C825, Postrider, vert.

1990, Mar. 14 ***Perf. 14***

C819 AP246 5g multicolored
C820 AP246 10g multicolored
C821 AP246 20g multicolored
C822 AP246 25g multicolored

Perf. 13

C823 AP246 30g multicolored

Souvenir Sheets

Perf. 14¹/₂

C824 AP246 100g multicolored
C825 AP246 100g multicolored

Nos. C824-C825 each contain one 40x50mm stamp.

For overprint see No. 2358.

POSTAGE DUE STAMPS

D1

D2

1904 Unwmk. Litho. ***Perf. 11¹/₂***

J1	D1	2c green	20	18
J2	D1	4c green	20	18
J3	D1	10c green	20	18
J4	D1	20c green	20	18

1913 **Engr.**

J5	D2	1c yellow brown	15	15
J6	D2	2c yellow brown	15	15
J7	D2	5c yellow brown	15	15
J8	D2	10c yellow brown	15	15
J9	D2	20c yellow brown	15	15
J10	D2	40c yellow brown	15	15
J11	D2	1p yellow brown	15	15
J12	D2	1.50p yellow brown	15	15
		Set value	55	40

For overprints and surcharges see Nos. 220-224, 229, 232, 264, L5.

INTERIOR OFFICE ISSUES

The "C" signifies "Campana" (rural). These stamps were sold by Postal Agents in country districts, who received a commission on their sales. These stamps were available for postage in the interior but not in Asunción or abroad.

Nos. 243-244 Overprinted in Red **C**

1922

L1	A42	50c car & dk bl	15	15
L2	A42	1p dk bl & brn	15	15
		Set value	22	15

The overprint on Nos. L1-L2 exists double or inverted. Counterfeits exist.

Nos. 215, 218, J12 Surcharged **C Habilitado en $ 1:— 1924**

1924

L3	A40	50c on 75c deep bl	15	15
L4	A40	1p on 1.25p pale bl	15	15
L5	D2	1p on 1.50p yel brn	15	15
		Set value	24	15

Nos. L3-L4 exist imperf.

Nos. 254, 257-260 Overprinted in Black or Red **C**

1924-26

L6	A45	50c red ('25)	15	15
L7	A44	1p dk blue (R)	15	15
L8	A45	1p dk bl (R) ('25)	15	15
L9	A46	1p blue (R) ('25)	15	15
L10	A45	1p emerald ('26)	15	15
		Set value	26	25

Nos. L6, L8-L9 exist imperf. Value $2.50 each pair.

Same Overprint on Stamps and Type of 1927-36 in Red or Black

1927-39

L11	A47	50c ultra (R)	15	15
L12	A47	50c dl red ('28)	15	15
L13	A47	50c orange ('29)	15	15
L14	A47	50c lt bl ('30)	15	15
L15	A47	50c gray (R) ('31)	15	15
L16	A47	50c bluish grn (R) ('33)	15	15
L17	A47	50c vio (R) ('34)	15	15
L18	A48	1p emerald	15	15
L19	A48	1p org red ('29)	15	15
L20	A48	1p lil brn ('31)	15	15
L21	A48	1p dk bl (R) ('33)	15	15
L22	A48	1p brt vio (R) ('35)	15	15
L23	A49	1.50p brown	15	15
	a.	Double overprint	1.50	
L24	A49	1.50p lilac ('28)	15	15
L25	A49	1.50p dull bl (R)	15	15
L26	A50	2.50p bister ('28)	15	15
L27	A50	2.50p vio (R) ('36)	15	15
L28	A51	3p gray (R)	15	15
L29	A51	3p rose red ('39)	15	15
L30	A52	5p vio (R) ('36)	15	15
L31	A57	10p gray brn (R) ('36)	30	25
		Set value	1.40	1.00

Types of 1931-35 and No. 305 Overprinted in Black or Red **C**

1931-36

L32	A59	1p light red	15	15
L33	A58	1.50p dp bl (R)	15	15
L34	A60	1.50p bis brn ('32)	15	15
L35	A60	1.50p grn (R) ('34)	15	15
L36	A60	1.50p bl (R) ('36)	15	15
L37	A54	10p vermilion	1.25	1.25
		Set value	1.50	1.40

OFFICIAL STAMPS

O1

O2

O3

O4

O5

O6

O7

Unwmk.

1886, Aug. 20 Litho. ***Imperf.***

O1	O1	1c orange	3.00	3.00
O2	O2	2c violet	3.00	3.00
O3	O3	5c red	3.00	3.00
O4	O4	7c green	3.00	3.00
O5	O5	10c brown	3.00	3.00
O6	O6	15c slate blue	3.00	3.00
	a.	Wavy lines on face of stamp		
	b.	"OFICIAL" omitted	1.25	
O7	O7	20c claret	3.00	3.00
		Nos. O1-O7 (7)	21.00	21.00

Nos. O1 to O7 have the date and various control marks and letters printed on the back of each stamp in blue and black.

The overprints exist inverted on all values.

Nos. O1 to O7 have been reprinted from new stones made from slightly retouched dies.

Types of 1886 With Overprint: **OFICIAL**

1886 ***Perf. 11¹/₂***

O8	O1	1c dark green	50	50
O9	O2	2c scarlet	50	50
O10	O3	5c dull blue	50	50
O11	O4	7c orange	50	50
O12	O5	10c lake	50	50
O13	O6	15c brown	50	50
O14	O7	20c blue	50	50
		Nos. O8-O14 (7)	3.50	3.50

The overprint exists inverted on all values. Value $1.50.

No. 20 Overprinted

1886, Sept. 1

O15	A11	1c dark green	1.50	1.50

Types of 1889 Regular Issue Surcharged

Handstamped Surcharge in Black

1889 *Imperf.*

O16 A13 3c on 15c violet 1.50 1.00
O17 A13 5c on 15c red brn 1.50 1.00

Perf. 11½

O18 A13 1c on 15c maroon 1.50 1.00
O19 A13 2c on 15c maroon 1.50 1.00

Counterfeits of Nos. O16-O19 abound.

Regular Issue of 1887 Handstamp Overprinted in Violet **OFICIAL**

Perf. 11½-12½ & Compounds

1890 **Typo.**

O20 A12 1c green 15 15
O21 A12 2c rose red 15 15
O22 A12 5c blue 15 15
O23 A12 7c brown 3.75 2.50
O24 A12 10c lilac 15 15
O25 A12 15c orange 45 25
O26 A12 20c pink 38 30
Nos. O20-O26 (7) 5.18 3.65

Nos. O20-O26 exist with double overprint and all but the 20c with inverted overprint.

Nos. O20-O22, O24-O26 exist with blue overprint. The status is questioned. Value, set $15.

Stamps and Type of 1887 Regular Issue Overprinted in Black **OFICIAL**

1892

O33 A12 1c green 15 15
O34 A12 2c rose red 15 15
O35 A12 5c blue 15 15
O36 A12 7c brown 1.75 1.00
O37 A12 10c lilac 65 22
O38 A12 15c orange 18 15
O39 A12 20c pink 22 15
O40 A12 50c gray 15 15
Nos. O33-O40 (8) 3.40
Set value 1.70

No. 26 Overprinted

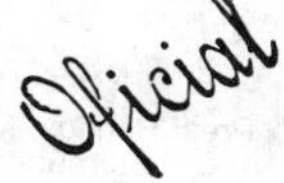

1893

O41 A12 7c brown 10.00 5.00

Counterfeits of No. O41 exist.

O16

1901, Feb. **Engr.** *Perf. 11½, 12½*

O42 O16 1c dull blue 20 20
O43 O16 2c rose red 15 15
O44 O16 4c dark brown 15 15
O45 O16 5c dark green 15 15
O46 O16 8c orange brn 15 15
O47 O16 10c car rose 15 15
O48 O16 20c deep blue 15 15
Set value 75 68

A 12c deep green, type O16, was prepared but not issued.

No. 45 Overprinted **Oficial**

1902 *Perf. 12x12½*

O49 A12 1p olive grn 15 15
a. Inverted overprint 10.00

Counterfeits of No. O49a exist.

Regular Issue of 1903 Overprinted

1903 *Perf. 11½*

O50 A32 1c gray 15 15
O51 A32 2c blue green 15 15
O52 A32 5c blue 15 15
O53 A32 10c orange brn 15 15
O54 A32 20c carmine 15 15
O55 A32 30c deep blue 15 15
O56 A32 60c purple 15 15
Set value 60 40

O17

O18

1905-08 **Engr.** *Perf. 11½, 12*

O57 O17 1c gray grn 15 15
O58 O17 1c ol grn ('05) 20 15
O59 O17 1c brn org ('06) 45 15
O60 O17 1c ver ('08) 25 15
O61 O17 2c brown org 15 15
O62 O17 2c gray grn ('05) 15 15
O63 O17 2c red ('06) 75 25
O64 O17 2c gray ('08) 38 20
O65 O17 5c deep bl ('06) 20 15
O66 O17 5c gray bl ('08) 1.50 1.00
O67 O17 5c grnsh bl ('08) 75 65
O68 O17 10c violet ('06) 15 15
O69 O17 20c violet ('08) 65 38
Nos. O57-O69 (13) 5.73
Set value 3.20

1908

O70 O17 10c bister 3.50
O71 O17 10c emerald 3.50
O72 O17 10c red lilac 4.50
O73 O17 20c bister 3.00
O74 O17 20c salmon pink 3.50
O75 O17 20c green 3.50
O76 O17 30c turquoise bl 3.35
O77 O17 30c blue gray 3.50
O78 O17 30c yellow 1.50
O79 O17 60c chocolate 3.50
O80 O17 60c orange brn 4.00
O81 O17 60c deep ultra 3.00
O82 O18 1p brt rose & blk 22.50
O83 O18 1p lake & blk 22.50
O84 O18 1p brn org & blk 22.50
Nos. O70-O84 (15) 107.85

Nos. O70-O84 were not issued, but were surcharged or overprinted for use as regular postage stamps. See Nos. 131-138, 141-145, 158-165, 171-173.

O19

1913 *Perf. 11½*

O85 O19 1c gray 15 15
O86 O19 2c orange 15 15
O87 O19 5c lilac 15 15
O88 O19 10c green 15 15
O89 O19 20c dull red 15 15
O90 O19 50c rose 15 15
O91 O19 75c deep blue 15 15
O92 O19 1p dull blue 15 15
O93 O19 2p yellow 15 15
Set value 50 50

For surcharges see Nos. 268, C1-C3.

Type of Regular Issue of 1927-38 Overprinted in Red **OFICIAL**

1935

O94 A47 10c light ultra 15 15
O95 A47 50c violet 15 15
O96 A48 1p orange 15 15
O97 A60 1.50p green 15 15
O98 A50 2.50p violet 15 15
Set value 30 25

Overprint is diagonal on 1.50p.

University of Asunción Type

1940 **Litho.** *Perf. 12*

O99 A67 50c red brn & blk 15 15
O100 A67 1p rose pink & blk 15 15
O101 A67 2p lt bl grn & blk 15 15
O102 A67 5p ultra & blk 15 15
O103 A67 10p lt vio & blk 15 15
O104 A67 50p dp org & blk 30 25
Set value 55 45

PERU

LOCATION — West coast of South America
GOVT. — Republic
AREA — 496,093 sq. mi.
POP. — 18,300,000 (est. 1982)
CAPITAL — Lima

8 Reales = 1 Peso (1857)
100 Centimos = 8 Dineros =
4 Pesetas = 1 Peso (1858)
100 Centavos = 1 Sol (1874)
100 Centimos = 1 Inti (1985)
100 Centimos = 1 Sol (1991)

Catalogue values for unused stamps in this country are for Never Hinged items, beginning with Scott 426 in the regular postage section, Scott B1 in the semi-postal section, Scott C78 in the airpost section, Scott CB1 in the airpost semi-postal section, and Scott RA31 in the postal tax section.

Values of early Peru stamps vary according to condition. Quotations for Nos. 1-15 are for fine copies. Very fine to superb specimens sell at much higher prices, and inferior or poor copies sell at reduced prices, depending on the condition of the individual specimen.

Sail and Steamship — A1

Design: 2r, Ship sails eastward.

1857, Dec. 1 **Unwmk.** **Engr.** ***Imperf.***

1 A1 1r blue, *blue* 1,200. 1,400.
2 A1 2r brn red, *blue* 1,300. 1,500.

The Pacific Steam Navigation Co. gave a quantity of these stamps to the Peruvian government so that a trial of prepayment of postage by stamps might be made.

Stamps of 1 and 2 reales, printed in various colors on white paper, laid and wove, were prepared for the Pacific Steam Navigation Co. but never put in use. Value $50 each on wove paper, $400 each on laid paper.

Coat of Arms

A2 A3

A4

Wavy Lines in Spandrels

1858, Mar. 1 **Litho.**

3 A2 1d deep blue 190.00 20.00
4 A3 1p rose red 800.00 120.00
5 A4 ½peso rose red *3,500.* *2,500.*
6 A4 ½peso buff *1,500.* 275.00
a. ½peso orange yellow *1,500.* 275.00

A5

A6

Large Letters

1858, Dec.

Double-lined Frame

7 A5 1d slate blue 225.00 25.00
8 A6 1p red 225.00 35.00

A7

A8

1860-61

Zigzag Lines in Spandrels

9 A7 1d blue 90.00 6.00
a. 1d Prussian blue 90.00 11.00
b. Cornucopia on white ground 200.00 42.50
c. Zigzag lines broken at angles 110.00 13.00
10 A8 1p rose 225.00 16.00
a. 1p brick red 225.00 16.00
b. Cornucopia on white ground 225.00 20.00

Retouched, 10 lines instead of 9 in left label

11 A8 1p rose 120.00 22.50
a. Pelure paper 180.00 22.50

A9

A10

1862-63 **Embossed**

12 A9 1d red 12.00 2.50
a. Arms embossed sideways 400.00 82.50
b. Thick paper 25.00 7.25
c. Diag. half used on cover 140.00
13 A10 1p brown ('63) 67.50 20.00
a. Diag. half used on cover 1,000.

Counterfeits of Nos. 13 and 15 exist.

A11

1868-72
14 A11 1d green 10.00 2.00
a. Arms embossed inverted *1,125.* *650.00*
b. Diag. half used on cover 350.00
15 A10 1p orange ('72) 82.50 25.00
a. Diag. half used on cover

Nos. 12-15, 19 and 20 were printed in horizontal strips. Stamps may be found printed on two strips of paper where the strips were joined by overlapping.

Llamas — A12

A13

A14

1866-67 **Engr.** ***Perf. 12***
16 A12 5c green 6.00 65
17 A13 10c vermilion 6.00 1.40
18 A14 20c brown 20.00 4.00
a. Diagonal half used on cover 375.00

See Nos. 109, 111, 113.

Locomotive and Arms — A15

Llama — A16

1871, Apr. **Embossed** ***Imperf.***
19 A15 5c scarlet 75.00 20.00
a. 5c pale red 75.00 20.00

20th anniv. of the first railway in South America, linking Lima and Callao.
The so-called varieties "ALLAO" and "CALLA" are due to over-inking.

1873, Mar. ***Rouletted Horiz.***
20 A16 2c dk ultra 30.00 *250.00*

Counterfeits are plentiful.

Sun God of the Incas — A17

Coat of Arms
A18 A19

A20

A21

A22

A23

Embossed with Grill

1874-84 **Engr.** ***Perf. 12***
21 A17 1c orange ('79) 50 40
22 A18 2c dk violet 65 50
23 A19 5c blue ('77) 85 25
24 A19 5c ultra ('79) 8.50 2.00
25 A20 10c green ('76) 25 22
a. Imperf., pair 25.00
26 A20 10c slate ('84) 2.00 25
a. Diag. half used as 5c on cover
27 A21 20c brown red 2.00 65
28 A22 50c green 9.00 2.50
29 A23 1s rose 1.50 1.50
Nos. 21-29 (9) 25.25 8.27

No. 25a lacks the grill.
No. 26 with overprint "DE OFICIO" is said to have been used to frank mail of Gen. A. A. Caceres during the civil war against Gen. Miguel Iglesias, provisional president. Experts question its status.

1880
30 A17 1c green 2.00
31 A18 2c rose 2.00

Nos. 30 and 31 were prepared for use but not issued without overprint.
See Nos. 104-108, 110, 112, 114-115.
For overprints see Nos. 32-103, 116-128, J32-J33, O2-O22, N11-N23, 1N1-1N9, 3N11-3N20, 5N1, 6N1-6N2, 7N1-7N2, 8N7, 8N10-8N11, 9N1-9N3, 10N3-10N8, 10N10-10N11, 11N1-11N5, 12N1-12N3, 13N1, 14N1-14N16, 15N5-15N8, 15N13-15N18, 16N1-16N22.

Stamps of 1874-80 Overprinted in Red, Blue or Black

Reduced illustration

1880, Jan. 5
32 A17 1c green (R) 50 40
a. Inverted overprint 10.00 10.00
b. Double overprint 13.50 13.50
33 A18 2c rose (Bl) 1.00 65
a. Inverted overprint 10.00 10.00
b. Double overprint 14.00 12.00
34 A18 2c rose (Bk) 45.00 35.00
a. Inverted overprint
b. Double overprint
35 A19 5c ultra (R) 2.00 1.00
a. Inverted overprint 10.00 10.00
b. Double overprint 14.00 14.00
36 A22 50c green (R) 27.50 17.50
a. Inverted overprint 45.00 45.00
b. Double overprint 55.00 55.00
37 A23 1s rose (Bl) 70.00 45.00
a. Inverted overprint 110.00 110.00
b. Double overprint 110.00 110.00

Stamps of 1874-80 Overprinted in Red or Blue

Reduced illustration

1881, Jan. 28
38 A17 1c green (R) 75 60
a. Inverted overprint 8.25 8.25
b. Double overprint 14.00 14.00
39 A18 2c rose (Bl) 14.00 9.00
a. Inverted overprint 17.50 15.00
b. Double overprint 25.00 20.00
40 A19 5c ultra (R) 1.50 75
a. Inverted overprint 14.00 14.00
b. Double overprint 20.00 20.00
41 A22 50c green (R) 450.00 250.00
a. Inverted overprint 600.00
42 A23 1s rose (Bl) 82.50 55.00
a. Inverted overprint 150.00

Reprints of Nos. 38 to 42 were made in 1884. In the overprint the word "PLATA" is 3mm high instead of $2^1/_2$mm. The cross bars of the letters "A" of that word are set higher than on the original stamps. The 5c is printed in blue instead of ultramarine.
For stamps of 1874-80 overprinted with Chilean arms or small UPU "horseshoe," see Nos. N11-N23.

Stamps of 1874-79 Handstamped in Black or Blue

1883
65 A17 1c orange (Bk) 85 65
66 A17 1c orange (Bl) 45.00
68 A19 5c ultra (Bk) 7.50 5.00
69 A20 10c green (Bk) 75 65
70 A20 10c green (Bl) 5.00 4.00
71 A22 50c green (Bk) 7.00 3.50
73 A23 1s rose (Bk) 10.00 6.00

This overprint is found in 11 types.
The 1c green, 2c dark violet and 20c brown red, overprinted with triangle, are fancy varieties made for sale to collectors and never placed in regular use.

Overprinted Triangle and "Union Postal Universal Peru" in Oval

1883
77 A22 50c grn (R & Bk) 120.00 60.00
78 A23 1s rose (Bl & Bk) 140.00 90.00

The 1c green, 2c rose and 5c ultramarine, over printed with triangle and "U. P. U. Peru" oval, were never placed in regular use.

Overprinted Triangle and "Union Postal Universal Lima" in Oval

1883
79 A17 1c grn (R & Bl) 50.00 37.50
80 A17 1c grn (R & Bk) 4.00 4.00
a. Oval overprint inverted
b. Double overprint of oval
81 A18 2c rose (Bl & Bk) 4.00 4.00
82 A19 5c ultra (R & Bk) 6.50 6.00
83 A19 5c ultra (R & Bl) 6.50 6.00
84 A22 50c grn (R & Bk) 140.00 90.00
85 A23 1s rose (Bl & Bk) 150.00 125.00

Some authorities question the status of No. 79.
Nos. 80, 81, 84, and 85 were reprinted in 1884. They have the second type of oval overprint with "PLATA" 3mm high.

Overprinted Triangle and

86 A17 1c grn (Bk & Bk) 1.00 80
a. Horseshoe inverted 10.00
87 A17 1c grn (Bl & Bk) 5.00 3.50
88 A18 2c ver (Bk & Bk) 1.00 75
89 A19 5c bl (Bk & Bk) 1.25 1.00
90 A19 5c bl (Bl & Bk) 7.00 6.50
91 A19 5c bl (R & Bk) *1,500.* *1,100.*

Overprinted Horseshoe Alone

1883, Oct. 23
95 A17 1c green 1.25 1.25
96 A18 2c vermilion 1.20 *4.00*
a. Double overprint
97 A19 5c blue 2.00 2.00
98 A19 5c ultra 20.00 15.00
99 A22 50c rose 57.50 57.50
100 A23 1s ultra 30.00 22.50

The 2c violet overprinted with the above design in red and triangle in black also the 1c green overprinted with the same combination plus the horseshoe in black, are fancy varieties made for sale to collectors.

No. 23 Overprinted in Black

1884, Apr. 28
103 A19 5c blue 65 40
a. Double overprint 5.00 5.00

Stamps of 1c and 2c with the above overprint, also with the above and "U. P. U. LIMA" oval in blue or "CORREOS LIMA" in a double-lined circle in red, were made to sell to collectors and were never placed in use.

Without Overprint or Grill

1886-95
104 A17 1c dull violet 50 16
105 A17 1c vermilion ('95) 40 22
106 A18 2c green 75 16
107 A18 2c dp ultra ('95) 35 22
108 A19 5c orange 60 30
109 A12 5c claret ('95) 1.25 50
110 A20 10c slate 40 15
111 A13 10c orange ('95) 60 35
112 A21 20c blue 5.00 65
113 A14 20c dp ultra ('95) 6.00 1.40
114 A22 50c red 1.50 65
115 A23 1s brown 1.25 50
Nos. 104-115 (12) 18.60 5.26

Overprinted Horseshoe in Black and Triangle in Rose Red

1889
116 A17 1c green 75 50
a. Horseshoe inverted 7.50

Nos. 30 and 25 Overprinted "Union Postal Universal Lima" in Oval in Red

1889, Sept. 1
117 A17 1c green 1.50 1.25
117A A20 10c green 1.50 1.50

The overprint on Nos. 117 and 117A is of the second type with "PLATA" 3mm high.

Stamps of 1874-80 Overprinted in Black

Pres. Remigio Morales Bermúdez

1894, Oct. 23
118 A17 1c orange 60 42
a. Inverted overprint 7.00 7.00
b. Double overprint 7.00 7.00
119 A17 1c green 40 35
a. Inverted overprint 3.50 3.50
b. Dbl. inverted ovpt. 5.00 5.00
120 A18 2c violet 40 35
a. Diagonal half used as 1c
b. Inverted overprint 7.00 7.00
c. Double overprint 7.00
121 A18 2c rose 40 35
a. Double overprint 7.00 7.00
b. Inverted overprint 7.00 7.00
122 A19 5c blue 2.50 1.75
122A A19 5c ultra 4.25 2.00
b. Inverted overprint 10.00 10.00
123 A20 10c green 40 35
a. Inverted overprint 7.00 7.00
124 A22 50c green 1.40 1.20
a. Inverted overprint 10.00 10.00
Nos. 118-124 (8) 10.35 6.77

Same, with Additional Overprint of Horseshoe

125 A18 2c vermilion 35 25
a. Head inverted 2.50 2.50
b. Head double 5.00 5.00
126 A19 5c blue 1.00 50
a. Head inverted 7.00 7.00
127 A22 50c rose 42.50 30.00
a. Head double 55.00 45.00
b. Head inverted
128 A23 1s ultra 100.00 90.00
a. Both overprints inverted 125.00 110.00
b. Head double 125.00 110.00

A23a

1895 **Vermilion Surcharge** ***Perf. $11^1/_2$***
129 A23a 5c on 5c grn 10.00 7.50
130 A23a 10c on 10c ver 8.00 6.00
131 A23a 20c on 20c brn 8.50 6.50

132	A23a	50c on 50c ultra	10.00	7.50
133	A23a	1s on 1s red brn	10.00	8.00
		Nos. 129-133 (5)	46.50	35.50

Nos 129-133 were used only in Tumbes. The basic stamps were prepared by revolutionaries in northern Peru.

"Liberty"

A23b A23c

1895, Sept. 8 **Engr.**

134	A23b	1c gray violet	1.25	80
135	A23b	2c green	1.25	65
136	A23b	5c yellow	1.25	65
137	A23b	10c ultra	1.25	65
138	A23c	20c orange	1.25	1.00
139	A23c	50c dark blue	7.25	4.50
140	A23c	1s car lake	37.50	25.00
		Nos. 134-140 (7)	51.00	33.25

Success of the revolution against the government of General Caceres and of the election of President Pierola.

Manco Capac, Founder of Inca Dynasty — A24

Francisco Pizarro Conqueror of the Inca Empire — A25

General José de La Mar — A26

1896-1900

141	A24	1c ultra	50	15
a.		1c blue (error)	40.00	35.00
142	A24	1c yel grn ('98)	50	15
143	A24	2c blue	50	15
144	A24	2c scar ('99)	50	15
145	A25	5c indigo	75	16
146	A25	5c green ('97)	75	15
147	A25	5c grnsh bl ('99)	50	15
148	A25	10c yellow	1.00	22
149	A25	10c gray blk ('00)	1.00	15
150	A25	20c orange	2.00	22
151	A26	50c car rose	5.00	80
152	A26	1s orange red	7.50	1.00
153	A26	2s claret	2.25	80
		Nos. 141-153 (13)	22.75	4.25

The 5c in black is a chemical changeling.
For surcharges and overprints see Nos. 187-188, E1, O23-O26.

Paucartambo Bridge — A27

Post and Telegraph Building, Lima — A28

Pres. Nicolás de Piérola — A29

1897, Dec. 31

154	A27	1c dp ultra	65	35
155	A28	2c brown	65	22
156	A29	5c bright rose	1.00	25

Opening of new P.O. in Lima.

A30 A31

1897, Nov. 8

157	A30	1c bister	50	45
a.		Inverted overprint	2.50	2.50
b.		Double overprint	10.00	10.00

1899

158	A31	5s orange red	1.65	1.65
159	A31	10s blue green	425.00	325.00

For surcharge see No. J36.

Pres. Eduardo de Romaña — A32

Admiral Miguel L. Grau — A33

Col. Francisco Bolognesi A33a

Pres. Romaña A33b

1900 **Frame Litho., Center Engr.**

160	A32	22c yel grn & blk	8.00	85

1901, Jan.

161	A33	1c green & blk	1.00	22
162	A33a	2c red & black	1.00	22
163	A33b	5c dull vio & blk	1.00	22

Advent of 20th century.

A34

Municipal Hygiene Institute Lima — A35

1902 **Engr.**

164	A34	22c green	35	20

1905

165	A35	12c dp blue & blk	1.00	22

For surcharges see Nos. 166-167, 186, 189.

Same Surcharged in Red or Violet

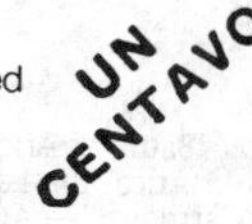

1907

166	A35	1c on 12c (R)	25	20
a.		Inverted surcharge	8.00	8.00
b.		Double surcharge	8.00	8.00
167	A35	2c on 12c (V)	50	35
a.		Double surcharge	8.00	8.00
b.		Inverted surcharge	8.00	8.00

Monument of Bolognesi — A36

Admiral Grau — A37

Llama — A38

Statue of Bolivar — A39

City Hall, Lima, formerly an Exhibition Building — A40

School of Medicine, Lima — A41

Post and Telegraph Building, Lima — A42

Grandstand at Santa Beatrix Race Track — A43

Columbus Monument — A44

1907

168	A36	1c yel grn & blk	35	15
169	A37	2c red & violet	35	15
170	A38	4c olive green	5.50	75
171	A39	5c blue & blk	60	15
172	A40	10c red brn & blk	1.00	22
173	A41	20c dk grn & blk	22.50	50
174	A42	50c black	22.50	1.00
175	A43	1s purple & grn	125.00	2.50
176	A44	2s dp bl & blk	120.00	100.00
		Nos. 168-176 (9)	297.80	105.42

For surcharges and overprint see #190-195, E2.

Manco Capac A45

Columbus A46

Pizarro — A47

San Martin — A48

Bolívar — A49

La Mar — A50

Ramón Castilla — A51

Grau — A52

Bolognesi — A53

1909

177	A45	1c gray	20	15
178	A46	2c green	20	15
179	A47	4c vermilion	30	15
180	A48	5c violet	20	15
181	A49	10c deep blue	50	15
182	A50	12c pale blue	1.00	15
183	A51	20c brown red	1.10	22
184	A52	50c yellow	5.00	35
185	A53	1s brn red & blk	10.00	35
		Nos. 177-185 (9)	18.50	
		Set value		1.45

See types A54, A78-A80, A81-A89.
For surcharges and overprint see Nos. 196-200, 208, E3.

No. 165 Surcharged in Red

1913, Jan.

186	A35	8c on 12c dp bl & blk	65	22

Stamps of 1899-1908 Surcharged in Magenta

UN CENTAVO 1915
a

UN CENTAVO 1915
b

2 CENTAVOS 1915
c

1915

On Nos. 142, 149

187	A24(a)	1c on 1c	16.50	12.00
a.		Inverted surcharge	22.50	18.00
188	A25(a)	1c on 10c	80	75

On No. 165

189	A35(c)	2c on 12c	22	20
a.		Inverted surcharge		

On Nos. 168-170, 172-174

190	A36(a)	1c on 1c	65	65
191	A37(a)	1c on 2c	1.00	1.00
192	A38(b)	1c on 4c	1.65	1.65
a.		Inverted surcharge	6.00	6.00
193	A40(b)	1c on 10c	35	30
a.		Inverted surcharge	2.50	2.50
193C	A40(c)	2c on 10c	100.00	80.00
194	A41(c)	2c on 20c	14.00	12.00
195	A42(c)	2c on 50c	2.00	2.00

Nos. 182-184, 179, 185 Surcharged in Red, Green or Violet

Vale 1 Centavo 1916

d

VALE 2 CENTAVOS 1916

e

VALE 10 CENTAVOS 1916

f

1916

No.	Type	Description	Unused	Used
196	A50(d)	1c on 12c (R)	16	15
a.		Double surcharge	2.00	2.00
b.		Green surcharge	4.50	4.50
197	A51(d)	1c on 20c (G)	16	15
198	A52(d)	1c on 50c (G)	16	15
a.		Inverted surcharge	2.00	2.00
199	A47(e)	2c on 4c (V)	16	15
200	A53(f)	10c on 1s (G)	50	25
a.		"VALF"	3.50	3.50
		Nos. 196-200 (5)	1.14	85

Official Stamps of 1909-14 Overprinted or Surcharged in Green or Red:

g

FRANQUEO VALE 2 Cts 1916

h

1916

No.	Type	Description	Unused	Used
201	O1	1c red (G)	15	15
202	O1	2c on 50c ol grn (R)	16	16
203	O1	10c bis brn (G)	20	15

Postage Due Stamps of 1909 Surcharged in Violet-Black

No.	Type	Description	Unused	Used
204	D7	2c on 1c brown	40	40
205	D7	2c on 5c brown	15	15
206	D7	2c on 10c brown	15	15
207	D7	2c on 50c brown	15	15
		Nos. 201-207 (7)	1.36	1.31

Many copies of Nos. 187 to 207 have a number of pin holes. It is stated that these holes were made at the time the surcharges were printed.

The varieties which we list of the 1915 and 1916 issues were sold to the public at post offices. Many other varieties which were previously listed are now known to have been delivered to one speculator or to have been privately printed by him from the surcharging plates which he had acquired.

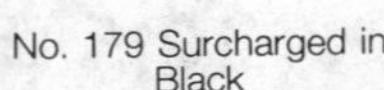

No. 179 Surcharged in Black

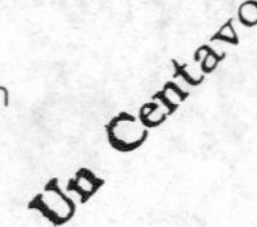

1917

No.	Type	Description	Unused	Used
208	A47	1c on 4c ver	22	16
a.		Double surcharge	4.00	4.00
b.		Inverted surcharge	4.00	4.00

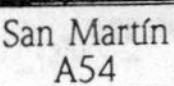

San Martín A54

Columbus at Salamanca A62

Funeral of Atahualpa — A63

Battle of Arica, "Arica, the Last Cartridge" — A64

Designs: 2c, Bolivar. 4c, José Gálvez. 5c, Manuel Pardo. 8c, Grau. 10c, Bolognesi. 12c, Castilla. 20c, General Cáceres.

1918 **Engr.**

Centers in Black

No.	Type	Description	Unused	Used
209	A54	1c orange	15	15
210	A54	2c green	20	15
211	A54	4c lake	30	15
212	A54	5c dp ultra	25	15
213	A54	8c red brn	75	25
214	A54	10c grnsh bl	35	15
215	A54	12c dl vio	1.00	16
216	A54	20c ol grn	1.25	16
217	A62	50c vio brn	5.00	35
218	A63	1s greenish bl	12.00	50
219	A64	2s deep ultra	21.00	65
		Nos. 209-219 (11)	42.25	
		Set value		2.40

For surcharges see Nos. 232-233, 255-256.

Augusto B. Leguía — A65

1919, Dec. **Litho.**

No.	Type	Description	Unused	Used
220	A65	5c bl & blk	16	16
a.		Imperf.	35	35
b.		Center inverted	11.00	11.00
221	A65	5c brn & blk	15	16
a.		Imperf.	35	35
b.		Center inverted	11.00	11.00

Constitution of 1919.

San Martín — A66

Thomas Cochrane — A70

Oath of Independence — A69

Designs: 2c, Field Marshal Arenales. 4c, Field Marshal Las Heras. 10c, Martin Jean Guisse. 12c, Vidal. 20c, Leguia. 50c, San Martin monument. 1s, San Martin and Leguia.

1921, July 28 **Engr.; 7c Litho.**

No.	Type	Description	Unused	Used
222	A66	1c ol brn & red brn	28	16
a.		Center inverted	350.00	325.00
223	A66	2c green	28	20
224	A66	4c car rose	80	60
225	A69	5c ol brn	40	15
226	A70	7c violet	65	28
227	A66	10c ultra	80	40
228	A66	12c blk & slate	2.50	60
229	A66	20c car & gray blk	2.50	80
230	A66	50c vio brn & dl vio	7.25	2.50
231	A69	1s car rose & yel grn	12.00	3.75
		Nos. 222-231 (10)	27.46	9.44

Centenary of Independence.

Nos. 213, 212 Surcharged in Black or Red Brown

CINCO Centavos 1923

CUATRO Centavos 1924

1923-24

No.	Type	Description	Unused	Used
232	A54	5c on 8c No. 213	50	25
233	A54	4c on 5c (RB) ('24)	35	16
a.		Inverted surcharge	5.00	5.00
b.		Double surcharge, one inverted	6.00	6.00

Simón Bolívar

A78 A79 A80

Perf. 14, 14x14½, 14½, 13½

1924 **Engr.; Photo. (4c, 5c)**

No.	Type	Description	Unused	Used
234	A78	2c olive grn	28	15
235	A79	4c yellow grn	52	15
236	A79	5c black	1.00	15
237	A80	10c carmine	60	15
238	A78	20c ultra	1.25	15
239	A78	50c dull violet	3.75	80
240	A78	1s yellow brn	10.00	2.50
241	A78	2s dull blue	20.00	10.00
		Nos. 234-241 (8)	37.40	14.05

Centenary of the Battle of Ayacucho which ended Spanish power in South America.

No. 237 exists imperf.

José Tejada Rivadeneyra A81

Mariano Melgar A82

Iturregui A83

Leguía A84

José de La Mar — A85

Monument of José Olaya — A86

Statue of María Bellido — A87

De Saco — A88

José Leguía — A89

1924-29 **Engr.** ***Perf. 12***

Size: 18½x23mm

No.	Type	Description	Unused	Used
242	A81	2c olive gray	20	15
243	A82	4c dk grn	20	15
244	A83	8c black	2.00	2.00
245	A84	10c org red	20	15
245A	A85	15c dp bl ('28)	60	16
246	A86	20c blue	80	15
247	A86	20c yel ('29)	1.50	16
248	A87	50c violet	5.00	32
249	A88	1s bis brn	9.00	80
250	A89	2s ultra	22.50	5.00
		Nos. 242-250 (10)	42.00	9.04

See Nos. 258, 260, 276-282.

For surcharges and overprint see Nos. 251-253, 257-260, 262, 268-271, C1.

No. 246 Surcharged in Red:

DOS Centavos 1925

a

DOS Centavos 1925

b

1925

No.	Type	Description	Unused	Used
251	A86(a)	2c on 20c blue	*350.00*	
252	A86(b)	2c on 20c blue	80	50
a.		Inverted surcharge	35.00	35.00
b.		Double surch., one inverted	50.00	50.00

No. 245 Overprinted **Plebiscito**

1925

No.	Type	Description	Unused	Used
253	A84	10c org red	1.00	1.00
a.		Inverted overprint	17.50	17.50

This stamp was for exclusive use on letters from the plebiscite provinces of Tacna and Arica, and posted on the Peruvian transport "Ucayali" anchored in the port of Africa.

No. 213 Surcharged

Habilitada 2 Cts. 1929

a

Habilitada 2 centavos 1929

b

1929

No.	Type	Description	Unused	Used
255	A54(a)	2c on 8c	75	75
256	A54(b)	2c on 8c	75	75

No. 247 Surcharged **Habilitada 15 cts. 1929**

No.	Type	Description	Unused	Used
257	A86	15c on 20c yellow	75	75
a.		Inverted surcharge	7.50	7.50

Stamps of 1924 Issue Coil Stamps

1929 ***Perf. 14 Horizontally***

No.	Type	Description	Unused	Used
258	A81	2c olive gray	40.00	20.00
260	A84	10c orange red	45.00	17.50

Postal Tax Stamp of 1928 Overprinted **Habilitada Franqueo**

1930 ***Perf. 12***

No.	Type	Description	Unused	Used
261	PT6	2c dark violet	35	35
a.		Inverted overprint	2.50	2.50

No. 247 Surcharged **Habilitada 2 Cts. 1930**

No.	Type	Description	Unused	Used
262	A86	2c on 20c yellow	22	22

Air Post Stamp of 1928 Surcharged

Habilitada Franqueo 2 Cts. 1930

No.	Description	Unused	Used
263	AP1 2c on 50c dk grn	20	15
a.	"Habitada"	1.00	1.00

Coat of Arms — A91

Lima Cathedral — A92

Designs: 10c, Children's Hospital. 50c, Madonna and Child.

Perf. 12x11½, 11½x12

1930, July 5 **Litho.**

No.	Description	Unused	Used
264	A91 2c green	70	70
265	A92 5c scarlet	1.65	1.25
266	A92 10c dark blue	1.10	1.00
267	A91 50c bister brown	18.00	12.00

6th Pan American Congress for Child Welfare. By error the stamps are inscribed "Seventh Congress."

Type of 1924 Overprinted in Black, Green or Blue

1930, Dec. 22 **Photo.** ***Perf. 15x14***

Size: 18¼x22mm

No.	Description	Unused	Used
268	A84 10c orange red (Bk)	20	15
a.	Inverted overprint	10.00	10.00
b.	Without overprint	6.50	6.50
c.	Double surcharge	5.00	5.00

Same with Additional Surcharge of Numerals in Each Corner

No.	Description	Unused	Used
269	A84 2c on 10c org red (G)	15	15
a.	Inverted surcharge	12.00	
270	A84 4c on 10c org red (G)	20	20
a.	Double surcharge	8.25	8.25

Engr.

Perf. 12

Size: 19x23½mm

No.	Description	Unused	Used
271	A84 15c on 10c org red (Bl)	30	15
a.	Inverted surcharge	10.00	10.00
b.	Double surcharge	10.00	10.00
	Set value, #268-271		44

Bolívar — A95

1930, Dec. 16 **Litho.**

No.	Description	Unused	Used
272	A95 2c buff	35	35
273	A95 4c red	65	50
274	A95 10c blue green	35	25
275	A95 15c slate gray	65	65

Death cent. of General Simón Bolivar. For surcharges see Nos. RA14-RA16.

Types of 1924-29 Issues
Size: 18x22mm

1931 **Photo.** ***Perf. 15x14***

No.	Description	Unused	Used
276	A81 2c olive green	25	15
277	A82 4c dark green	25	15
279	A85 15c deep blue	75	15
280	A86 20c yellow	1.25	20
281	A87 50c violet	1.25	25
282	A88 1s olive brown	2.00	35
	Nos. 276-282 (6)	5.75	
	Set value		1.00

Pizarro — A96

Old Stone Bridge, Lima — A97

1931, July 28 **Litho.** ***Perf. 11***

No.	Description	Unused	Used
283	A96 2c slate blue	1.65	1.40
284	A96 4c deep brown	1.65	1.40
285	A96 15c dark green	1.65	1.40
286	A97 10c rose red	1.65	1.40
287	A97 10c mag & lt grn	1.65	1.40
288	A97 15c yel & bl gray	1.65	1.40
289	A97 15c dk slate & red	1.65	1.40
	Nos. 283-289 (7)	11.55	9.80

1st Peruvian Phil. Exhib., Lima, July, 1931.

Manco Capac — A99

Sugar Cane Field — A102

Oil Refinery A100

Guano Deposits A104

Picking Cotton — A103

Mining — A105

Llamas — A106

Arms of Piura — A107

1931-32 ***Perf. 11, 11x11½***

No.	Description	Unused	Used
292	A99 2c olive black	25	15
293	A100 4c dark green	50	16
295	A102 10c red orange	1.00	15
a.	Vertical pair, imperf. between	30.00	
296	A103 15c turq blue	1.50	16
297	A104 20c yellow	5.00	25
298	A105 50c gray lilac	6.00	25
299	A106 1s brown olive	13.00	1.00
	Nos. 292-299 (7)	27.25	2.12

1932, July 28 ***Perf. 11½x12***

No.	Description	Unused	Used
300	A107 10c dark blue	6.00	6.00
301	A107 15c deep violet	6.00	6.00

400th anniv. of the founding of the city of Piura. On sale one day. Counterfeits exist. See No. C3.

Parakas A108

Chimu A109

Inca — A110

Perf. 11½, 12, 11½x12

1932, Oct. 15

No.	Description	Unused	Used
302	A108 10c dk vio	20	15
303	A109 15c brn red	40	15
304	A110 50c dk brn	90	16
	Set value		30

4th cent. of the Spanish conquest of Peru.

Arequipa and El Misti — A111

President Luis M. Sánchez Cerro — A112

Monument to Simón Bolívar at Lima A115

Statue of Liberty A116

1932-34 **Photo.** ***Perf. 13½***

No.	Description	Unused	Used
305	A111 2c black	16	15
306	A111 2c blue blk	16	15
307	A111 2c grn ('34)	16	15
308	A111 4c dk brn	16	15
309	A111 4c org ('34)	16	15
310	A112 10c vermilion	13.00	10.00
311	A115 15c ultra	35	15
312	A115 15c mag ('34)	35	15
313	A115 20c red brn	75	15
314	A115 20c vio ('34)	75	15
315	A115 50c dk grn ('33)	75	15
316	A115 1s dp org	6.00	22
317	A115 1s org brn	7.50	35
	Nos. 305-317 (13)	30.25	12.07

For overprint see No. RA24.

1934

No.	Description	Unused	Used
318	A116 10c rose	50	15

Pizarro — A117

The Inca — A119

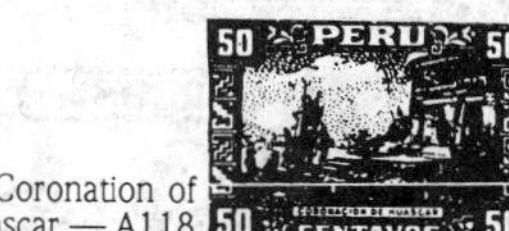

Coronation of Huascar — A118

1934-35 ***Perf. 13***

No.	Description	Unused	Used
319	A117 10c crimson	25	15
320	A117 15c ultra	75	15
321	A118 20c deep bl ('35)	1.25	15
322	A118 50c dp red brn	1.00	15
323	A119 1s dark vio	3.00	35
	Nos. 319-323 (5)	6.25	
	Set value		65

For surcharges and overprint see Nos. 354-355, J54, O32.

Pizarro and the Thirteen A120

Belle of Lima — A122

Francisco Pizarro — A123

Designs: 4c, Lima Cathedral. 1s, Veiled woman of Lima.

1935, Jan. 18 ***Perf. 13½***

No.	Description	Unused	Used
324	A120 2c brown	35	20
325	A120 4c violet	50	38
326	A122 10c rose red	50	20
327	A123 15c ultra	80	60
328	A120 20c slate gray	1.40	75
329	A122 50c olive grn	2.00	1.50
330	A122 1s Prus bl	4.50	3.00
331	A123 2s org brn	10.50	8.00
	Nos. 324-331 (8)	20.55	14.63

4th centenary of the founding of Lima. See Nos. C6-C12.

View of Ica — A125

Lake Huacachina, Health Resort A126

Grapes — A127

Cotton Boll — A128

Zuniga y Velazco and Philip IV — A129

Supreme God of the Nazcas — A130

Engr.; Photo. (10c)

1935, Jan. 17 ***Perf. 12½***

No.	Description	Unused	Used
332	A125 4c gray blue	80	80
333	A126 5c dark car	28	80
334	A127 10c magenta	3.25	1.65
335	A126 20c green	1.25	1.25
336	A128 35c dark car	6.50	4.00

337 A129	50c org & brn		4.50	4.00
338 A130	1s pur & red		13.00	10.00
	Nos. 332-338 (7)		29.58	22.50

Founding of the City of Ica, 300th anniv.

Pizarro and the Thirteen — A131

1935-36 Photo. *Perf. 13½*

339 A131	2c dp claret	25	15
340 A131	4c bl grn ('36)	25	15
	Set value		15

For surcharge and overprints see Nos. 353, J53, RA25-RA26.

"San Cristóbal," First Peruvian Warship — A132

Grand Marshal José de La Mar — A138

Naval College at Punta — A133

Independence Square, Callao A134

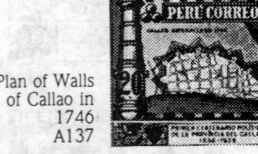

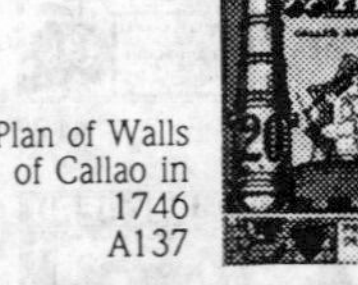
Aerial View of Callao A135

Plan of Walls of Callao in 1746 A137

Packetboat "Sacramento" A139

Viceroy José Antonio Manso de Velasco — A140

Fort Maipú — A141

Plan of Fort Real Felipe — A142

Design: 15c, Docks and Custom House.

1936, Aug. 27 Photo. *Perf. 12½*

341 A132	2c black	52	40
342 A133	4c bl grn	52	25
343 A134	5c yel brn	52	25
344 A135	10c bl gray	52	25
345 A135	15c green	52	25
346 A137	20c dk brn	52	25
347 A138	50c purple	1.10	50
348 A139	1s olive grn	9.50	2.00
	Engr.		
349 A140	2s violet	13.00	6.00
350 A141	5s carmine	18.00	14.00
351 A142	10s red org & brn	45.00	35.00
	Nos. 341-351 (11)	89.72	59.15

Founding of the Province of Callao, cent. See No. C13.

Nos. 340, 321 and 323 Surcharged in Black

Habilitado
S. 0.10 Cts.

1936 *Perf. 13½, 13*

353 A131	2c on 4c bl grn	15	15
a.	"0.20" for "0.02"	3.50	3.50
354 A118	10c on 20c dp bl	25	15
a.	Double surcharge	3.50	
b.	Inverted surcharge	3.50	
355 A119	10c on 1s dk vio	35	35
	Set value		54

Many varieties of the surcharge are found on these stamps: no period after "S," no period after "Cts," period after "2," "S" omitted, various broken letters, etc.

The surcharge on No. 355 is horizontal.

Peruvian Cormorants (Guano Deposits) — A143

Oil Well at Talara — A144

Avenue of the Republic, Lima — A146

San Marcos University at Lima — A148

Post Office, Lima — A149

Viceroy Manuel de Amat y Junyent — A150

Designs: 10c, "El Chasqui" (Inca Courier). 20c, Municipal Palace and Museum of Natural History. 5s, Joseph A. de Pando y Riva. 10s, Dr. José Dávila Condemarin.

1936-37 Photo. *Perf. 12½*

356 A143	2c lt brn	60	15
357 A143	2c grn ('37)	75	15
358 A144	4c blk brn	60	22
359 A144	4c int blk ('37)	35	15
360 A143	10c crimson	35	15
361 A143	10c ver ('37)	20	15
362 A146	15c ultra	65	15
363 A146	15c brt bl ('37)	35	15
364 A146	20c black	65	16
365 A146	20c blk brn ('37)	25	15
366 A148	50c org yel	2.50	50
367 A148	50c dk gray vio ('37)	75	16
368 A149	1s brn vio	5.00	65
369 A149	1s ultra ('37)	1.50	20
	Engr.		
370 A150	2s ultra	11.00	2.50
371 A150	2s dk vio ('37)	3.50	50
372 A150	5s slate bl	11.00	3.50
373 A150	10s dk vio & brn	60.00	22.50
	Nos. 356-373 (18)	100.00	32.09

No. 370 Surcharged in Black

Habilit.
Un Sol

1937

374 A150	1s on 2s ultra	2.50	2.50

Children's Holiday Center, Ancón — A153

Chavin Pottery — A154

Highway Map of Peru — A155

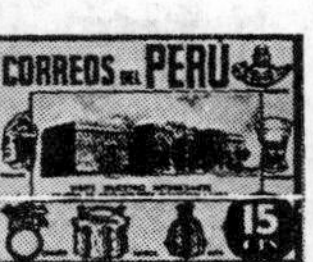
Archaeological Museum, Lima — A156

Industrial Bank of Peru — A157

Worker's Houses, Lima — A158

Toribio de Luzuriaga A159

Historic Fig Tree A160

Idol from Temple of Chavin — A161

Mt. Huascarán — A162

Imprint: "Waterlow & Sons Limited, Londres"

1938, July 1 Photo. *Perf. 12½, 13*

375 A153	2c emerald	15	15
376 A154	4c org brn	15	15
377 A155	10c scarlet	20	15
378 A156	15c ultra	24	15
379 A157	20c magenta	15	15
380 A158	50c greenish blue	40	15
381 A159	1s dp claret	1.00	15
382 A160	2s green	3.00	15
	Engr.		
383 A161	5s dl vio & brn	7.00	40
384 A162	10s blk & ultra	12.00	52
	Nos. 375-384 (10)	24.29	
	Set value		1.50

See Nos. 410-418, 426-433, 438-441.

For surcharges see Nos. 388, 406, 419, 445-446A, 456, 758.

Palace Square A163

Lima Coat of Arms — A164

Government Palace — A165

1938, Dec. 9 Photo. *Perf. 12½*

385 A163	10c slate green	50	30
	Engraved and Lithographed		
386 A164	15c blk, gold, red & bl	80	40
	Photo.		
387 A165	1s olive	2.00	1.00

8th Pan-American Conference at Lima, Dec. 1938. See Nos. C62-C64.

No. 377 Surcharged in Black

Habilitada
5
cts.

1940 *Perf. 13*

388 A155	5c on 10c scar	15	15
a.	Inverted surcharge		

National Radio Station — A166

Overprint: "FRANQUEO POSTAL"

1941 **Litho.** ***Perf. 12***

No.	Type	Value	Color	Unused	Used
389	A166	50c	dull yel	2.00	15
390	A166	1s	violet	2.00	20
391	A166	2s	dl gray grn	4.00	60
392	A166	5s	fawn	22.50	6.75
393	A166	10s	rose vio	35.00	5.25
			Nos. 389-393 (5)	65.50	12.95

Gonzalo Pizarro and Orellana A167

Francisco de Orellana A168

Francisco Pizarro — A169

Map of South America with Amazon as Spaniards Knew It in 1542 — A170

Gonzalo Pizarro A171

Discovery of the Amazon River A172

1943, Feb. ***Perf. 12½***

No.	Type	Value	Color	Unused	Used
394	A167	2c	crimson	15	15
395	A168	4c	slate	16	15
396	A169	10c	yel brn	20	15
397	A170	15c	vio blue	50	16
398	A171	20c	yel olive	16	16
399	A172	25c	dull org	1.65	40
400	A168	30c	dp magenta	40	20
401	A170	50c	blue grn	40	32
402	A167	70c	violet	2.25	80
403	A171	80c	lt bl	2.25	80
404	A172	1s	cocoa brn	4.00	60
405	A169	5s	intense blk	8.00	4.00
			Nos. 394-405 (12)	20.12	7.89

400th anniv. of the discovery of the Amazon River by Francisco de Orellana in 1542.

No. 377 Surcharged in Black

1943 ***Perf. 13***

No.	Type	Value	Color	Unused	Used
406	A155	10c	on 10c scar	15	15

Samuel Finley Breese Morse — A173

1944 ***Perf. 12½***

No.	Type	Value	Color	Unused	Used
407	A173	15c	light blue	16	15
408	A173	30c	olive gray	50	16

Centenary of invention of the telegraph.

Types of 1938
Imprint: "Columbian Bank Note Co."

1945-47 **Litho.** ***Perf. 12½***

No.	Type	Value	Color	Unused	Used
410	A153	2c	green	15	15
411	A154	4c	org brn ('46)	15	15
412	A156	15c	ultra	15	15
413	A157	20c	magenta	1.65	15
414	A158	50c	grnsh bl	15	15
415	A159	1s	vio brn	25	15
416	A160	2s	dl grn	65	15
417	A161	5s	dl vio & brn	4.00	50
418	A162	10s	blk & ultra ('47)	5.00	75
			Nos. 410-418 (9)	12.15	
			Set value		1.60

No. 415 Surcharged in Black

Habilitada
S|o. 0.20

1946

No.	Type	Value	Color	Unused	Used
419	A159	20c	on 1s vio brn	30	15
a.			Surcharge reading down	8.25	8.25

A174

A175

A176

A177

A178

Overprinted in Black
Perf. 12½

1947, Apr. 15 **Litho.** **Unwmk.**

No.	Type	Value	Color	Unused	Used
420	A174	15c	blk & car	25	15
421	A175	1s	olive brn	38	30
422	A176	1.35s	yel grn	38	35
423	A177	3s	Prus blue	80	75
424	A178	5s	dull grn	1.90	1.50
			Nos. 420-424 (5)	3.71	3.05

1st National Tourism Congress, Lima. The basic stamps were prepared, but not issued, for the 5th Pan American Highway Congress of 1944.

Catalogue values for unused stamps in this section, from this point to the end of the section, are for Never Hinged items.

Types of 1938
Imprint: "Waterlow & Sons Limited, Londres."
Perf. 13x13½, 13½x13

1949-51 **Photo.**

No.	Type	Value	Color	Unused	Used
426	A154	4c	chocolate	15	15
427	A156	15c	aquamarine	15	15
428	A157	20c	blue vio	15	15
429	A158	50c	red brn	25	15
430	A159	1s	blk brn	50	15
431	A160	2s	ultra	1.00	15

Engr.
Perf. 12½

No.	Type	Value	Color	Unused	Used
432	A161	5s	ultra & red brn ('50)	90	38
433	A162	10s	dk bl grn & blk ('51)	3.00	75
			Nos. 426-433 (8)	6.10	
			Set value		1.50

Monument to Admiral Miguel L. Grau — A179

1949, June 6 ***Perf. 12½***

No.	Type	Value	Color	Unused	Used
434	A179	10c	ultra & bl grn	15	15

Types of 1938
Imprint: "Inst. de Grav. Paris."

1951 ***Perf. 12½x12, 12x12½***

No.	Type	Value	Color	Unused	Used
438	A156	15c	peacock grn	15	15
439	A157	20c	violet	15	15
440	A158	50c	org brn	20	15
441	A159	1s	dark brn	30	15
			Set value		22

Nos. 375 and 438 Surcharged in Black

HABILITADA
S|. 0.01

1951-52 ***Perf. 12½, 12½x12***

No.	Type	Value	Color	Unused	Used
445	A153	1c	on 2c	15	15
446	A156	10c	on 15c	15	15
446A	A156	10c	on 15c ('52)	15	15
			Set value	30	15

On No. 446A "Sl. 0.10" is in smaller type measuring 11½mm. See No. 456.
Nos. 445-446A exist with surcharge double.

Water Promenade — A180

Post Boy — A181

Designs: 4c, 50c, 1s, 2s, Various buildings, Lima. 20c, Post Office Street, Lima. 5s, Lake Llangamuco, Ancachs. 10s, Ruins of Machu-Picchu.

Overprint: "V Congreso Panamericano de Carreteras 1951"

1951, Oct. 13 **Unwmk.** ***Perf. 12***
Black Overprint

No.	Type	Value	Color	Unused	Used
447	A180	2c	dk grn	15	15
448	A180	4c	brt red	15	15
449	A181	15c	gray	15	15
450	A181	20c	ol brn	20	15
451	A180	50c	dp plum	25	15
452	A180	1s	blue	30	15
453	A180	2s	deep blue	45	20
454	A180	5s	brn lake	1.25	1.25
455	A181	10s	chocolate	2.25	1.25
			Nos. 447-455 (9)	5.15	
			Set value		3.10

5th Pan-American Congress of Highways, 1951.

No. 438 Surcharged in Black

HABILITADA
S|o. 0.05

1952 **Unwmk.** ***Perf. 12½x12***

No.	Type	Value	Color	Unused	Used
456	A156	5c	on 15c pck grn	15	15

Tourist Hotel, Tacna — A182

Vicuña — A183

Contour Farming, Cuzco A184

Gen. Marcos Perez Jimenez A185

Designs: 5c, Fishing boat and principal fish. 10c, Matarani. 15c, Locomotive No. 80 and coaches. 25c, Engineering school. 30c, Ministry of Public Health and Social Assistance. 1s, Paramonga fortress. 2s, Monument to Native Farmer.

Imprint: "Thomas De La Rue & Co. Ltd."
Perf. 13, 12 (A184)

1952-53 **Litho.** **Unwmk.**

No.	Type	Value	Color	Unused	Used
457	A182	2c	red lil ('53)	15	15
458	A182	5c	green	15	15
459	A182	10c	yel grn ('53)	15	15
460	A182	15c	gray ('53)	15	15
461	A183	20c	red brn ('53)	38	15
462	A182	25c	rose red	15	15
463	A182	30c	indigo ('53)	15	15
464	A184	50c	green ('53)	45	15
465	A184	1s	brown	30	15
466	A184	2s	Prus grn ('53)	35	15
			Set value	2.00	62

See Nos. 468-478, 483-488, 497-501, C184-C185, C209.
For surcharges see Nos. C434, C437, C440-C441, C454, C494.

1956, July 25 **Engr.** ***Perf. 13½x13***

No.	Type	Value	Color	Unused	Used
467	A185	25c	brown	15	15

Visit of Gen. Marcos Perez Jimenez, Pres. of Venezuela, June 1955.

Types of 1952-53
Imprint: "Thomas De La Rue & Co. Ltd."
Designs as before.

1957-59 **Litho.** ***Perf. 13, 12***

No.	Type	Value	Color	Unused	Used
468	A182	15c	brown ('59)	40	15
469	A182	25c	green ('59)	40	15
470	A182	30c	rose red	20	15
471	A184	50c	dull pur	30	15
472	A184	1s	lt vio bl	40	15
473	A184	2s	gray ('58)	50	15
			Nos. 468-473 (6)	2.20	
			Set value		40

Types of 1952-53
Imprint: "Joh. Enschedé en Zonen-Holland"

Designs as before.

Perf. 12½x13½, 13½x12½, 13x14

1960	**Litho.**	**Unwmk.**	
474 A183	20c lt red brn	18	15
475 A182	30c lilac rose	15	15
476 A184	50c rose vio	15	15
477 A184	1s lt vio bl	20	15
478 A184	2s gray	42	15
	Nos. 474-478 (5)	1.10	
	Set value		30

No. 475 measures 33x22mm. No. 470 measures 32x22½mm.

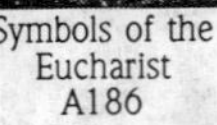

Symbols of the Eucharist A186

Trumpeting Angels A187

Design: 50c, Cross and "JHS."

1960, Aug. 10	**Photo.**	***Perf. 11½***	
479 A186	50c ultra, blk & dk red	15	15
480 A186	1s multi	25	25

Nos. 479-480 were intended for voluntary use to help finance the 6th National Eucharistic Congress at Piura, Aug. 25-28, 1960. Authorized for payment of postage on day of issue only, Aug. 10, but through misunderstanding within the Peruvian postal service they were accepted for payment of postage by some post offices until late in December. Reauthorized for postal use, they were again sold and used, starting in July, 1962. See Nos. RA37-RA38.

1961, Dec. 20	**Litho.**	***Perf. 10½***	
481 A187	20c bright blue	28	15

Christmas. Valid for postage for one day, Dec. 20. Used thereafter as a voluntary seal to benefit a fund for postal employees.

Centenary Cedar, Main Square, Pomabamba A188

Unwmk.

1962, Sept. 7	**Engr.**	***Perf. 13***	
482 A188	1s red & green	40	15

Cent. (in 1961) of Pomabamba province.

Types of 1952-53

Designs: 20c, Vicuña. 30c, Port of Matarani. 40c, Gunboat. 50c, Contour farming. 60c, Tourist hotel, Tacna. 1s, Paramonga, Inca fortress.

Imprint: "Thomas De La Rue & Co. Ltd."

Perf. 13x13½, 13½x13, 12 (A184)

1962, Nov. 19	**Litho.**	**Wmk. 346**	
483 A183	20c rose claret	15	15
484 A182	30c dark blue	15	15
485 AP49	40c orange	15	15
486 A184	50c lt bluish grn	15	15
487 A182	60c grnsh blk	16	15
488 A184	1s rose	22	15
	Nos. 483-488 (6)	98	
	Set value		38

Wheat Emblem and Symbol of Agriculture, Industry — A189

1963, July 23	**Unwmk.**	***Perf. 12½***	
489 A189	1s red org & ocher	15	15

FAO "Freedom from Hunger" campaign. See No. C190.

Alliance for Progress Emblem A190

Pacific Fair Emblem A191

1964, June 22	**Litho.**	***Perf. 12x12½***	
490 A190	40c multi	15	15

Alliance for Progress. See note after US No. 1234. See Nos. C192-C193.

1965, Oct. 30	**Litho.**	***Perf. 12x12½***	
491 A191	1.50s multi	15	15
492 A191	2.50s multi	20	15
493 A191	3.50s multi	25	20
	Set value		40

4th Intl. Pacific Fair, Lima, Oct. 30-Nov. 14.

Santa Claus and Letter — A192

1965, Nov. 2		***Perf. 11***	
494 A192	20c red & blk	15	15
495 A192	50c grn & blk	16	15
496 A192	1s bl & blk	35	15
	Set value		25

Christmas. Valid for postage for one day, Nov. 2. Used Nov. 3, 1965-Jan. 31, 1966, as voluntary seals for the benefit of a fund for postal employees. See Nos. 522-524. For surcharges see Nos. 641-643.

Types of 1952-62

Designs: 20c, Vicuña. 30c, Port of Matarani. 40c, Gunboat. 50c, Contour farming. 1s, Paramonga, Inca fortress.

Imprint: "I.N.A."

Perf. 12, 13½x14 (A184)

1966, Aug. 8	**Litho.**	**Unwmk.**	
497 A183	20c brn red	15	15
498 A182	30c dk bl	15	15
499 AP49	40c orange	15	15
500 A184	50c gray grn	15	15
501 A184	1s rose	15	15
	Set value	50	25

Postal Tax Stamps Nos. RA40, RA43 Surcharged

XHabilitadoX

XX Habilitado

S. 0.10 — a

S/. 0.10 — b

Perf. 14x14½, 12½x12

1966, May 9		**Litho.**	
501A PT11 (a)	10c on 2c lt brn	15	15
501B PT14 (b)	10c on 3c lt car	15	15

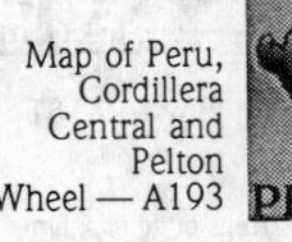

Map of Peru, Cordillera Central and Pelton Wheel — A193

1966, Nov. 24	**Photo.**	***Perf. 13½x14***	
502 A193	70c bl, blk & vio bl	15	15

Opening of the Huinco Hydroelectric Center. See No. C205.

Inca Wind Vane and Sun — A194

Perf. 13½x14

1967, Apr. 18	**Photo.**	**Unwmk.**	
503 A194	90c dp lil rose, blk & gold	15	15

6-year building program. See No. C212.

Pacific Fair Emblem A195

Indian and Wheat A197

Gold Alligator, Mochica Culture A196

1967, Oct. 9	**Photo.**	***Perf. 12***	
504 A195	1s gold, dk grn & blk	15	15

5th Intl. Pacific Fair, Lima, Oct. 27-Nov. 12. See No. C216.

1968, Aug. 16	**Photo.**	***Perf. 12***

Designs (gold sculptures of the pre-Inca Yunca tribes): 2.60s, Bird, vert. 3.60s, Lizard. 4.60s, Bird, vert. 5.60s, Jaguar.

Sculptures in Gold Yellow and Brown

505 A196	1.90s dp magenta	25	15
506 A196	2.60s black	35	20
507 A196	3.60s dp magenta	40	30
508 A196	4.60s black	50	35
509 A196	5.60s dp magenta	50	35
	Nos. 505-509 (5)	2.00	1.35

See Nos. B1-B5. For surcharge see No. 685.

1969, Mar. 3	**Litho.**	***Perf. 11***

Designs: 3s, 4s, Farmer digging in field.

Black Surcharge

510 A197	2.50s on 90c brn & yel	15	15
511 A197	3s on 90c lil & brn	16	15
512 A197	4s on 90c rose & grn	22	16
	Nos. 510-512,C232-C233 (5)	1.13	82

Agrarian Reform Law.
#510-512 were not issued without surcharge.

Flag, Worker Holding Oil Rig and Map — A198

1969, Apr. 9	**Litho.**	***Perf. 12***	
513 A198	2.50s multi	15	15
514 A198	3s gray & multi	16	15
515 A198	4s lil & multi	20	16
516 A198	5.50s lt bl & multi	25	20

Nationalization of the Brea Parinas oilfields, Oct. 9, 1968.

Kon Tiki Raft. Globe and Jet — A199

1969, June 17	**Litho.**	***Perf. 11***	
517 A199	2.50s dp bl & multi	15	15
	Nos. 517,C238-C241 (5)	83	
	Set value		55

1st Peruvian Airlines (APSA) flight to Europe.

Capt. José A. Quiñones Gonzales (1914-41), Military Aviator — A200

1969, July 23	**Litho.**	***Perf. 11***	
518 A200	20s red & multi	1.20	60

See No. C243.

Freed Andean Farmer A201

1969, Aug. 28	**Litho.**	***Perf. 11***	
519 A201	2.50s dk bl, lt bl & red	15	15

Enactment of the Agrarian Reform Law of June 24, 1969. See Nos. C246-C247.

Adm. Miguel Grau — A202

1969, Oct. 8	**Litho.**	***Perf. 11***	
520 A202	50s dk bl & multi	3.00	2.25

Issued for Navy Day.

Flags and "6" — A203

1969, Nov. 14			
521 A203	2.50s gray & multi	20	20

6th Intl. Pacific Trade Fair, Lima, Nov. 14-30. See Nos. C251-C252.

Santa Claus Type of 1965

Design: Santa Claus and letter inscribed "FELIZ NAVIDAD Y PROSPERO AÑO NUEVO."

1969, Dec. 1	**Litho.**	***Perf. 11***	
522 A192	20c red & blk	15	15
523 A192	20c org & blk	15	15
524 A192	20c brn & blk	15	15
	Set value	15	15

Christmas. Valid for postage for one day, Dec. 1, 1969. Used after that date as postal tax stamps.

Gen. Francisco Bolognesi and Soldier — A204

Puma-shaped Jug, Vicus Culture — A205

1969, Dec. 9

525 A204 1.20s lt ultra, blk & gold 15 15

Army Day, Dec. 9. See No. C253.

1970, Feb. 23 Litho. *Perf. 11*

526 A205 2.50s buff, blk & brn 20 20
Nos. 526,C281-C284 (5) 1.26 1.26

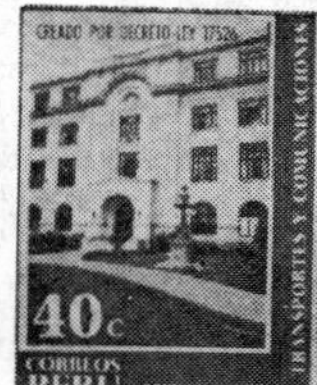

Ministry of Transport and Communications A206

1970, Apr. 1 Litho. *Perf. 11*

527 A206 40c org & gray 15 15
528 A206 40c gray & lt gray 15 15
529 A206 40c brick red & gray 15 15
530 A206 40c brt pink & gray 15 15
531 A206 40c org brn & gray 15 15
Set value 25 25

Ministry of Transport and Communications, 1st anniv.

Anchovy A207

Fish: No. 533, Pacific hake.

1970, Apr. 30 Litho. *Perf. 11*

532 A207 2.50s vio bl & multi 20 20
533 A207 2.50s vio bl & multi 20 20
a. Strip of 5, #532-533, C285-C287 1.10 1.10
Nos. 532-533,C285-C287 (5) 1.10 1.10

Composite Head; Soldier and Farmer — A208

1970, June 24 Litho. *Perf. 11*

534 A208 2.50s gold & multi 16 15

"United people and army building a new Peru." See Nos. C290-C291.

Cadets, Chorrillos College, and Arms A209

Coat of Arms and: No. 536, Cadets of La Punta Naval College. No. 537, Cadets of Las Palmas Air Force College.

1970, July 27 Litho. *Perf. 11*

535 A209 2.50s blk & multi 42 16
536 A209 2.50s blk & multi 42 16
537 A209 2.50s blk & multi 42 16
a. Strip of 3, #535-537 1.30 75

Peru's military colleges.

Courtyard, Puruchuco Fortress, Lima — A210

1970, Aug. 6

538 A210 2.50s multi 15 15
Nos. 538,C294-C297 (5) 1.28 1.28

Issued for tourist publicity.

Nativity, Cuzco School A211

Christmas paintings: 1.50s, Adoration of the Kings, Cuzco School. 1.80s, Adoration of the Shepherds, Peruvian School.

1970, Dec. 23 Litho. *Perf. 11*

539 A211 1.20s multi 15 15
540 A211 1.50s multi 15 15
541 A211 1.80s multi 15 15
Set value 22 15

St. Rosa of Lima — A212

1971, Apr. 12 Litho. *Perf. 11*

542 A212 2.50s multi 15 15

300th anniv. of the canonization of St. Rosa of Lima (1586-1617), first saint born in the Americas.

Tiahuanacoide Cloth — A213

Design: 2.50s, Chancay cloth.

1971, Apr. 19

543 A213 1.20s bl & multi 15 15
544 A213 2.50s yel & multi 20 15
Nos. 543-544,C306-C308 (5) 1.37
Set value 42

Nazca Sculpture, 5th Century, and Seriolella — A214

1971, June 7 Litho. *Perf. 11*

545 A214 1.50s multi 15 15
Nos. 545,C309-C312 (5) 2.03
Set value 62

Publicity for 200-mile zone of sovereignty of the high seas.

Mateo Garcia Pumacahua A215

Portraits: No. 547, Mariano Melgar. No. 548, Micaela Bastidas. No. 549, Jose Faustino Sanchez Carrion. No. 550, Francisco Antonia de Zela. No. 551, Jose Baquijano y Carrillo. No. 552, Martin Jorge Guise.

1971

546 A215 1.20s ver & blk 15 15
547 A215 1.20s gray & multi 15 15
548 A215 1.50s dk bl & multi 15 15
549 A215 2s dk bl & multi 15 15
550 A215 2.50s ultra & multi 20 15
551 A215 2.50s gray & multi 20 15
552 A215 2.50s dk bl & multi 20 15
Set value 1.00 85

150th anniv. of independence, and to honor the heroes of the struggle for independence.

Issue dates: Nos. 546, 550, May 10; Nos. 547, 551, July 5; Nos. 548-549, 552, July 27.

See Nos. C313-C325.

Gongora Portentosa — A216

Designs: Various Peruvian orchids.

1971, Sept. 27 *Perf. 13½x13*

553 A216 1.50s pink & multi 20 15
554 A216 2s pink & multi 25 15
555 A216 2.50s pink & multi 30 15
556 A216 3s pink & multi 35 15
557 A216 3.50s pink & multi 40 15
Nos. 553-557 (5) 1.50
Set value 32

"Progress of Liberation," by Teodoro Nuñez Ureta — A217

Design: 3.50s, Detail from painting by Teodoro Nuñez Ureta.

1971, Nov. 4 *Perf. 13x13½*

558 A217 1.20s multi 15 15
559 A217 3.50s multi 20 20
Set value 26 26

2nd Ministerial meeting of the "Group of 77." See No. C331.

Plaza de Armas, Lima, 1843 — A218

Design: 3.50s, Plaza de Armas, Lima, 1971.

1971, Nov. 6

560 A218 3s pale grn & blk 35 15
561 A218 3.50s lt brick red & blk 40 20

3rd Annual Intl. Stamp Exhibition, EXFILIMA '71, Lima, Nov. 6-14.

Army Coat of Arms — A219

1971, Dec. 9 Litho. *Perf. 13½x13*

562 A219 8.50s multi 75 20

Sesquicentennial of Peruvian Army.

Flight into Egypt A220

Old Stone Sculptures of Huamanga: 2.50s, Three Kings. 3s, Nativity.

1971, Dec. 18 *Perf. 13x13½*

563 A220 1.80s multi 18 15
564 A220 2.50s multi 25 15
565 A220 3s gray & multi 35 20

Christmas. See Nos. 597-599.

Fisherman, by J. M. Ugarte Elespuru — A221

Gold Statuette, Chimu, c. 1500 — A222

Paintings by Peruvian Workers: 4s, Threshing Grain in Cajamarca, by Camilo Blas. 6s, Huanca Highlanders, by José Sabogal.

1971, Dec. 30 *Perf. 13½x13*

566 A221 3.50s blk & multi 35 15
567 A221 4s blk & multi 42 15
568 A221 6s blk & multi 60 15

To publicize the revolution and change of order.

1972, Jan. 31 Litho. *Perf. 13½x13*

Ancient Jewelry: 4s, Gold drummer, Chimu. 4.50s, Quartz figurine, Lambayeque culture, 5th century. 5.40s, Gold necklace and pendant,

Mochiqua, 4th century. 6s, Gold insect, Lambayeque culture, 14th century.

No.	Type	Value	Description	Unused	Used
569	A222	3.90s	red, blk & ocher	40	15
570	A222	4s	red, blk & ocher	40	15
571	A222	4.50s	brt bl, blk & ocher	50	15
572	A222	5.40s	red, blk & ocher	60	15
573	A222	6s	red, blk & ocher	60	15
			Nos. 569-573 (5)	2.50	
			Set value		55

Popeye Catalufa A223

Fish: 1.50s, Guadara. 2.50s, Jack mackerel.

1972, Mar. 20 *Perf. 13x13½*

No.	Type	Value	Description	Unused	Used
574	A223	1.20s	lt bl & multi	25	15
575	A223	1.50s	lt bl & multi	25	15
576	A223	2.50s	lt bl & multi	25	15
			Nos. 574-576,C333-C334 (5)	1.55	75

Seated Warrior, Mochica — A224

"Bringing in the Harvest" (July) — A225

Painted pottery jugs of Mochica culture, 5th century: 1.50s, Helmeted head. 2s, Kneeling deer. 2.50s, Helmeted head. 3s, Kneeling warrior.

1972, May 8 *Perf. 13½x13*

Emerald Background

No.	Type	Value	Description	Unused	Used
577	A224	1.20s	multi	20	15
578	A224	1.50s	multi	25	15
579	A224	2s	multi	30	15
580	A224	2.50s	multi	35	15
581	A224	3s	multi	40	15
			Nos. 577-581 (5)	1.50	75

1972-73 **Litho.** *Perf. 13½x13*

Designs: Monthly woodcuts from Calendario Incaico.

Black Vignette & Inscriptions

No.	Type	Value	Description	Unused	Used
582	A225	2.50s	red brn *(July)*	35	15
583	A225	3s	grn *(Aug.)*	60	15
584	A225	2.50s	rose *(Sept.)*	35	15
585	A225	3s	lt bl *(Oct.)*	50	15
586	A225	2.50s	org *(Nov.)*	50	15
587	A225	3s	lil *(Dec.)*	50	15
588	A225	2.50s	brn *(Jan.)* ('73)	35	15
589	A225	3s	pale grn *(Feb.)* ('73)	50	15
590	A225	2.50s	bl *(Mar.)* ('73)	35	15
591	A225	3s	org *(Apr.)* ('73)	50	15
592	A225	2.50s	lil rose *(May)* ('73)	35	15
593	A225	3s	yel & blk *(June)* ('73)	50	15
			Nos. 582-593 (12)	5.35	
			Set value		85

400th anniversary of publication of the Calendario Incaico by Felipe Guaman Poma de Ayala.

Family Tilling Field — A226

Oil Derricks — A228

Sovereignty of the Sea (Inca Frieze) A227

Perf. 13½x13, 13x13½

1972, Oct. 31 **Litho.**

No.	Type	Value	Description	Unused	Used
594	A226	2s	multi	25	20
595	A227	2.50s	multi	25	20
596	A228	3s	gray & multi	25	20

4th anniversaries of land reforms and the nationalization of the oil industry and 15th anniv. of the claim to a 200-mile zone of sovereignty of the sea.

Christmas Type of 1971

Sculptures from Huamanga, 17-18th cent.: 1.50s, Holy Family, wood, vert. 2s, Holy Family with lambs, stone. 2.50s, Holy Family in stable, stone, vert.

1972, Nov. 30

No.	Type	Value	Description	Unused	Used
597	A220	1.50s	buff & multi	15	15
598	A220	2s	buff & multi	15	15
599	A220	2.50s	buff & multi	16	15
			Set value		30

Morning Glory — A228a

Mayor on Horseback, by Fierro — A229

1972, Dec. 29 **Litho.** *Perf. 13*

No.	Type	Value	Description	Unused	Used
600	A228a	1.50s	shown	15	15
601	A228a	2.50s	Amaryllis	25	15
602	A228a	3s	Liabum excelsum	30	15
603	A228a	3.50s	Bletia (orchid)	45	15
604	A228a	5s	Cantua buxifolia	35	15
			Nos. 600-604 (5)	1.50	75

1973, Aug. 13 **Litho.** *Perf. 13*

Paintings by Francisco Pancho Fierro (1803-1879): 2s, Man and Woman, 1830. 2.50s, Padre Abregu Riding Mule. 3.50s, Dancing Couple. 4.50s, Bullfighter Estevan Arredondo on Horseback.

No.	Type	Value	Description	Unused	Used
605	A229	1.50s	salmon & multi	15	15
606	A229	2s	salmon & multi	20	15
607	A229	2.50s	salmon & multi	25	15
608	A229	3.50s	salmon & multi	35	20
609	A229	4.50s	salmon & multi	55	20
			Nos. 605-609 (5)	1.50	85

Presentation in the Temple A230

Christmas Paintings of the Cuzqueña School: 2s, Holy Family, vert. 2.50s, Adoration of the Kings.

1973, Nov. 30 **Litho.** *Perf. 13x13½*

No.	Type	Value	Description	Unused	Used
610	A230	1.50s	multi	15	15
611	A230	2s	multi	15	15
612	A230	2.50s	multi	15	15
			Set value	32	16

The first value column gives the catalogue value of an unused stamp, the second that of a used stamp.

Peru No. 20 — A231

1974, Mar. 1 **Litho.** *Perf. 13*

No.	Type	Value	Description	Unused	Used
613	A231	6s	gray & dk bl	50	25

Peruvian Philatelic Assoc., 25th anniv.

Non-ferrous Smelting Plant, La Oroya A232

Colombia Bridge, San Martin A233

Designs: 8s, 10s, Different views, Santiago Antunez Dam, Tayacaja.

1974 **Litho.** *Perf. 13x13½*

No.	Type	Value	Description	Unused	Used
614	A232	1.50s	blue	15	15
615	A233	2s	multi	15	15
616	A232	3s	rose claret	20	15
617	A232	4.50s	green	25	15
618	A233	8s	multi	35	16
619	A233	10s	multi	45	20
			Nos. 614-619 (6)	1.55	
			Set value		65

"Peru Determines its Destiny."
Issue Dates: 2s, 8s, 10s, July 1. 1.50s, 3s, 4.50s, Dec. 6.

Battle of Junin, by Felix Yañez A234

Design: 2s, 3s, Battle of Ayacucho, by Felix Yañez.

1974 **Litho.** *Perf. 13x13½*

No.	Type	Value	Description	Unused	Used
620	A234	1.50s	multi	15	15
621	A234	2s	multi	20	15
622	A234	2.50s	multi	25	15
623	A234	3s	multi	30	15
			Set value		40

Sesquicentennial of the Battles of Junin and Ayacucho.
Issue dates: 1.50s, 2.50s, Aug. 6. 2s, 3s, Oct. 9.
See Nos. C400-C404.

Indian Madonna — A235

1974, Dec. 20 **Litho.** *Perf. 13½x13*

No.	Type	Value	Description	Unused	Used
624	A235	1.50s	multi	15	15

Christmas. See No. C417.

Maria Parado de Bellido A236

International Women's Year Emblem — A237

IWY Emblem, Peruvian Colors and: 2s, Micaela Bastidas. 2.50s, Juana Alarco de Dammert.

Perf. 13x13½, 13½x13

1975, Sept. 8 **Litho.**

No.	Type	Value	Description	Unused	Used
625	A236	1.50s	bl grn, red & blk	15	15
626	A237	2s	blk & red	15	15
627	A236	2.50s	pink, blk & red	20	15
628	A237	3s	red, blk & ultra	25	15
			Set value		20

International Women's Year.

St. Juan Macias — A238

1975, Nov. 14 *Perf. 13½x13*

No.	Type	Value	Description	Unused	Used
629	A238	5s	blk & multi	25	20

Canonization of Juan Macias in 1975.

Louis Braille A239

1976, Mar. 2 **Litho.** *Perf. 13x13½*

No.	Type	Value	Description	Unused	Used
630	A239	4.50s	gray, red & blk	20	20

Sesquicentennial of the invention of Braille system of writing for the blind by Louis Braille (1809-1852).

Peruvian Flag — A240

1976, Aug. 29 **Litho.** *Perf. 13x13½*

No.	Type	Value	Description	Unused	Used
631	A240	5s	gray, blk & red	20	20

Revolutionary Government, Phase II, 1st anniversary.

St. Francis, by El Greco — A241

Indian Mother — A242

1976, Dec. 9 Litho. *Perf. 13½x13*

632	A241	5s gold, buff & brn	25	20

St. Francis of Assisi, 750th death anniv.

1976, Dec. 23

633	A242	4s multi	25	15

Christmas.

Chasqui Messenger — A243

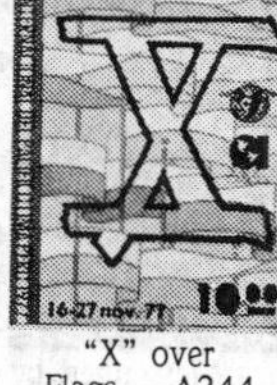

"X" over Flags — A244

1977 Litho. *Perf. 13½x13*

634	A243	6s grnsh bl & blk	25	20
635	A243	8s red & blk	25	20
636	A243	10s ultra & blk	50	35
637	A243	12s lt grn & blk	50	35

See Nos. C465-C467. For surcharge see No. C502.

1977, Nov. 25 Litho. *Perf. 13½x13*

638	A244	10s multi	20	20

10th Intl. Pacific Fair, Lima, Nov. 16-27.

Republican Guard Badge — A245

Indian Nativity — A246

1977, Dec. 1

639	A245	12s multi	25	25

58th anniversary of Republican Guard.

1977, Dec. 23

640	A246	8s multi	15	15

Christmas. See No. C484.

Nos. 495, 494, 496 Surcharged with New Value and Bar in Red, Dark Blue or Black: "FRANQUEO / 10.00 / RD-0161-77"

1977, Dec. *Perf. 11*

641	A192	10s on 50c (R)	25	15
642	A192	20s on 20c (DB)	50	30
643	A192	30s on 1s (B)	65	40

Inca Head — A247

1978 Litho. *Perf. 13½x13*

644	A247	6s bright green	15	15
645	A247	10s red	15	15
646	A247	16s red brown	20	20
		Nos. 644-646,C486-C489 (7)	3.37	2.75

For surcharges see Nos. C498-C499, C501.

Flags of Germany, Argentina, Austria, Brazil A248

Argentina '78 Emblem and Flags of Participants: No. 648, 652, Hungary, Iran, Italy, Mexico. No. 649, 653, Scotland, Spain, France, Netherlands. No. 650, 654, Peru, Poland, Sweden and Tunisia. No. 651, like No. 647.

1978 Litho. *Perf. 13x13½*

647	A248	10s blue & multi	30	20
648	A248	10s blue & multi	30	20
649	A248	10s blue & multi	30	20
650	A248	10s blue & multi	30	20
a.		Block of 4, #647-650	1.25	1.00
651	A248	16s blue & multi	30	20
652	A248	16s blue & multi	30	20
653	A248	16s blue & multi	30	20
654	A248	16s blue & multi	30	20
a.		Block of 4, #651-654	1.25	1.00
		Nos. 647-654 (8)	2.40	1.60

11th World Soccer Cup Championship, Argentina, June 1-25.
Issued: #647-650, June 28; #651-654, Dec. 4.

Thomas Faucett, Planes of 1928, 1978 A249

1978, Oct. 19 Litho. *Perf. 13*

655	A249	40s multi	40	25

Faucett Aviation, 50th anniversary.

Nazca Bowl, Huaco A250

1978-79 Litho. *Perf. 13x13½*

656	A250	16s vio bl ('79)	15	15
657	A250	20s green ('79)	16	15
658	A250	25s lt grn ('79)	20	20
659	A250	35s rose red ('79)	35	16
660	A250	45s dk brown	40	22
661	A250	50s black	50	25
662	A250	55s car rose ('79)	50	25
663	A250	70s lil rose ('79)	60	50
664	A250	75s blue	65	40
665	A250	80s salmon ('79)	65	40
667	A250	200s brt vio ('79)	1.65	1.25
		Nos. 656-667 (11)	5.81	3.93

For surcharge see No. 715.

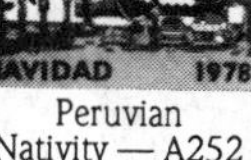

Peruvian Nativity — A252

Ministry of Education, Lima — A253

1978, Dec. 28 Litho. *Perf. 13½x13*

672	A252	16s multi	15	15

1979, Jan. 4

673	A253	16s multi	15	15

National Education Program.

Nos. RA40, B1-B5 and 509 Surcharged in Various Colors. No. RA40 Surcharged also:

Habilitado
Dif.-Porte
S/. **2.00**
a

SOBRE
TASA
OFICIAL
S/. **3.00**
b

Habilitado
R.D. Nº 0118
S/. **35.00**
c

1978, July-Aug.

674	PT11(a)	2s on 2c (O)	15	15
675	PT11(b)	3s on 2c (Bk)	15	15
676	PT11(a)	4s on 2c (G)	15	15
677	PT11(a)	5s on 2c (V)	15	15
678	PT11(b)	6s on 2c (DBl)	15	15
679	SP1	20s on 1.90s + 90c (G)	75	75
680	SP1	30s on 2.60s + 1.30s (Bl)	75	75
681	PT11(c)	35s on 2c (C)	30	30
682	PT11(c)	50s on 2c (LtBl)	2.00	2.00
683	SP1	55s on 3.60s + 1.80s (VBl)	1.00	1.00
684	SP1	65s on 4.60s + 2.30s (Go)	1.00	1.00
685	A196	80s on 5.60s (VBl)	75	75
686	SP1	85s on 20s + 10s (Bk)	1.50	1.50
		Nos. 674-686 (13)	8.80	8.80

Surcharge on Nos. 679-680, 683-684, 686 includes heavy bar over old denomination.

Battle of Iquique A254

Heroes' Crypt — A255

Col. Francisco Bolognesi — A256

War of the Pacific: No. 688, Col. Jose J. Inclan. No. 689, Corvette Union running Arica blockade. No. 690, Battle of Angamos, Aguirre, Miguel Grau (1838-1879), Perre. No. 690A, Lt. Col. Pedro Ruiz Gallo. 85s, Marshal Andres A. Caceres. No. 692, Naval Battle of Angamos. No. 697, Col. Bolognesi's Reply, by Angeles de la Cruz. No. 698, Col. Alfonso Ugarte on horseback.

Perf. 13½x13, 13x13½

1979-80 Litho.

687	A254	14s multi	15	15
688	A256	25s multi	35	20
689	A254	25s multi	16	20
690	A254	25s multi	22	20

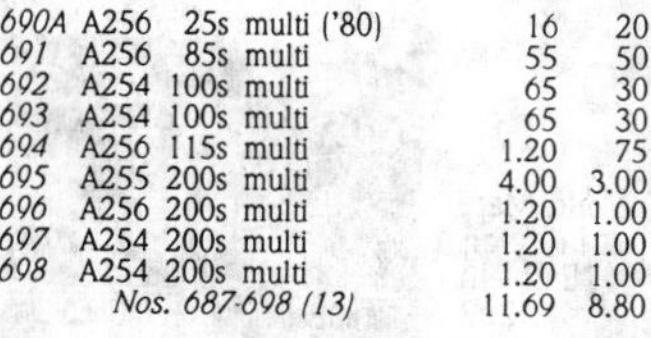

690A	A256	25s multi ('80)	16	20
691	A256	85s multi	55	50
692	A254	100s multi	65	30
693	A256	100s multi	65	30
694	A256	115s multi	1.20	75
695	A255	200s multi	4.00	3.00
696	A256	200s multi	1.20	1.00
697	A254	200s multi	1.20	1.00
698	A254	200s multi	1.20	1.00
		Nos. 687-698 (13)	11.69	8.80

For surcharge see No. 713.

Peruvian Red Cross, Cent. — A257

1979, May 4 *Perf. 13x13½*

699	A257	16s multi	15	15

Billiard Balls — A258

Arms of Cuzco — A259

1979, June 4 *Perf. 13½x13*

700	A258	34s multi	25	25

For surcharge see No. 714.

1979, June 24

701	A259	50s multi	35	20

Inca Sun Festival, Cuzco.

Peru Colors, Tacna Monument — A260

Telecom 79 — A261

1979, Aug. 28 Litho. *Perf. 13½x13*

702	A260	16s multi	15	15

Return of Tacna Province to Peru, 50th anniv.
For surcharge see No. 712.

1979, Sept. 20

703	A261	15s multi	15	15

3rd World Telecommunications Exhibition, Geneva, Sept. 20-26.

Caduceus — A262

Gold Jewelry — A264

World Map, "11," Fair Emblem A263

1979, Nov. 13

704 A262 25s multi	20	20

Stomatology Academy of Peru, 50th anniv.; 4th Intl. Congress.

1979, Nov. 24

705 A263 55s multi	38	25

11th Pacific Intl. Trade Fair, Lima, Nov. 14-25.

1979, Dec. 19 *Perf. 13½x13*

706 A264 85s multi	55	40

Larco Herrera Archaeological Museum.

Christmas A265

1979, Dec. 27 Litho. *Perf. 13x13½*

707 A265 25s multi	20	20

Queen Sofia and King Juan Carlos I, Visit to Peru — A266

1979 Litho. *Perf. 13x13½*

708 A266 75s multi	55	25

No. RA40 Surcharged in Black, Green or Blue

1979, Oct. 8

709 PT11 7s on 2c brn	15	15
710 PT11 9s on 2c brn (G)	15	15
711 PT11 15s on 2c brn (B)	20	15
Set value	42	35

Nos. 702, 687, 700, 663 Surcharged

Perf. 13½x13, 13x13½

1980, Apr. 14 Litho.

712 A260 20s on 16s multi	25	20
713 A254 25s on 14s multi	30	25
714 A258 65s on 34s multi	50	40
715 A250 80s on 70s lil rose	75	30
Nos. 712-715,C501-C502 (6)	2.50	1.70

Liberty Holding Arms of Peru — A267

Chimu Cult Cup — A268

Civic duties: 15s, Respect the Constitution. 20s, Honor country. 25s, Vote. 30s, Military service. 35s, Pay taxes. 45s, Contribute to national progress. 50s, Respect rights.

1980 Litho.

716 A267 15s greenish blue	15	15
717 A267 20s salmon pink	15	15
718 A267 25s ultra	16	16
719 A267 30s lilac rose	20	20
720 A267 35s black	22	16
721 A267 45s light bl grn	30	22
722 A267 50s brown	50	22
Nos. 716-722 (7)	1.68	1.26

1980, July 9 Litho.

723 A268 35s multi	22	16

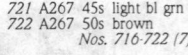

Map of Peru and Liberty — A269

Return to Civilian Government A270

Perf. 13½x13, 13x13½

1980, Sept. 9 Litho.

724 A269 25s multi	16	16
725 A270 35s multi	22	22

Machu Picchu A271

1980, Nov. 10 Litho. *Perf. 13x13½*

726 A271 25s multi	16	16

World Tourism Conf., Manila, Sept. 27.

Tupac Amaru Rebellion Bicent. — A272

150th Death Anniv. of Simon Bolivar (in 1980) — A274

Christmas A273

1980, Dec. 22 Litho. *Perf. 13½x13*

727 A272 25s multi	20	20

1980, Dec. 31 Litho. *Perf. 13*

728 A273 15s multi	15	15

1981, Jan. 28 Litho. *Perf. 13½x13*

729 A274 40s multi	30	22

Nos. 725, 667, 694 Surcharged

1981 Litho. *Perf. 13x13½*

730 A270 25s on 35s multi	20	20
731 A250 85s on 200s brt vio	65	50
732 A256 100s on 115s multi	75	60

Return to Constitutional Government, July 28, 1980 — A275

1981, Mar. 26 Litho. *Perf. 13½x13*

733 A275 25s multi	25	15

For surcharges see Nos. 736-737, 737C.

Tupac Amaru and Micaela Bastidas, Bronze Sculptures, by Miguel Baca-Rossi A276

1981, May 18 Litho. *Perf. 13x13½*

734 A276 60s multi	45	35

Rebellion of Tupac Amaru and Micaela Bastidas, bicentenary.

Nos. 733, RA41 and Voluntary Postal Tax Stamps of 1965 Surcharged in Black, Dull Brown or Lake

Cross, Unleavened Bread, Wheat — A276a

Chalice, Host — A276b

Perf. 13½x13, Rouletted 11 (#735, 737B), 11½ (#737A)

1981 Litho., Photo. (#737A-737B)

735	PT17	40s on 10c #RA41	15	15
736	A275	40s on 25s #733	15	15
737	A275	130s on 25s #733 (DB)	30	20
737A	A276a	140s on 50c brn, yel & red	32	20
737B	A276b	140s on 1s multi	32	20
737C	A275	140s on 25s #733 (L)	32	20
		Nos. 735-737C (6)	1.56	1.10

Issued: #735, Apr. 12. #736, 737, 737C, Apr. 6. #737A, Apr. 15. #737B, Apr. 28.

Carved Stone Head, Pallasca Tribe — A277

Designs: Nos. 739, 742, 749 Pottery vase, Inca, vert. No. 740, Head (diff. vert.). Nos. 743, 749A-749B, Huaco idol (fish), Nazca. 100s, Pallasca, vert. 140s, Puma.

Perf. 13½x13, 13x13½

1981-82 Litho.

738	A277	30s dp rose lil	25	25
739	A277	40s org ('82)	30	18
740	A277	40s ultra	30	18
742	A277	80s brn ('82)	75	50
743	A277	80s red ('82)	75	38
745	A277	100s lil rose	75	50
748	A277	140s lt bl grn	1.00	70
749	A277	180s grn ('82)	1.75	1.25
749A	A277	240s grnsh bl ('82)	1.00	70
749B	A277	280s vio ('82)	1.40	1.00
		Nos. 738-749B (10)	8.25	5.64

For surcharges see Nos. 789, 798-799, 1026.

A278

A279

1981, May 31 *Perf. 13½x13*

750 A278 130s multi	60	60

Postal and Philatelic Museum, 50th anniv.

1981, Oct. 7 Litho. *Perf. 13½x13*

751 A279 30s pur & gray	22	22

1979 Constitution Assembly President Victor Raul Haya de la Torre.

Inca Messenger, by Guaman Poma (1526-1613) A280

Intl. Year of the Disabled A280a

1981 Litho. *Perf. 12*

752 A280 30s lilac & blk	22	15
753 A280 40s ver & blk	18	38
754 A280 130s brt yel grn & blk	50	38
755 A280 140s brt bl & blk	50	50
756 A280 200s yel brn & blk	75	75
Nos. 752-756 (5)	2.15	2.16

Christmas. Issue dates: 30s, 40s, 200s, Dec. 21; others, Dec. 31.

1981 Litho. *Perf. 13½x13*

756A A280a 100s multi	60	38

Nos. 377, C130, C143, J56, O33, RA36, RA39, RA40, RA42, RA43 Surcharged in Brown, Black, Orange, Red, Green or Blue

1982

757	PT11	10s on 2c (#RA40, Br)	25	25
758	A155	10s on 10c (#377)	15	15
758A	AP60	40s on 1.25s (#C143	15	15
758B	PT15	70s on 5c (#RA36, R)	20	20
759	D7	80s on 10c (#J56)	18	18
760	O1	80s on 10c (#O33)	18	18
761	PT14	80s on 3c (#RA43, O)	18	18
762	PT17	100s on 10c (#RA42, R)	25	25
763	AP57	100s on 2.20s (#C130, R)	25	25
764	PT14	150s on 3c (#RA39, G)	35	35
765	PT14	180s on 3c (#RA43, R)	40	40
766	PT14	200s on 3c (#RA43, Bl)	50	50
767	AP60	240s on 1.25s (#C143, R)	60	60
768	PT15	280s on 5c (#RA36)	70	70
		Nos. 757-768 (14)	4.34	4.34

Nos. 758A, 763, 767 airmail. Nos. 759 and 760 surcharged "Habilitado / Franq. Postal / 80 Soles".

Jorge Basadre (1903-1908), Historian — A281

Julio C. Tello (1882-1947), Archaeologist A282

Perf. 13½x13, 13x13½

1982, Oct. 13 **Litho.**

769 A281 100s pale grn & blk	25	15
770 A282 200s lt grn & dk bl	50	30

9th Women's World Volleyball Championship, Sept. 12-26 — A283

Rights of the Disabled — A284

1982, Oct. 18 ***Perf. 12***

771 A283 80s blk & red 20 20

For surcharge see No. 791.

1982, Oct. 22

772 A284 200s bl & red 35 25

Brena Campaign Centenary A285

1982, Oct. 26 ***Perf. 13x13½***

773 A285 70s Andres Caceres medallion 15 15

For surcharge see No. 790.

1982 World Cup — A286

16th Intl. Congress of Latin Notaries, Lima, June — A287

1982, Nov. 2 ***Perf. 12***

774 A286 80s multi 15 15

For surcharge see No. 800.

1982, Nov. 6

775 A287 500s Emblem 90 60

Handicrafts Year — A288

1982, Nov. 24 ***Perf. 13x13½***

776 A288 200s Clay bull figurine 35 25

Christmas — A289

Pedro Vilcapaza — A290

1982 ***Perf. 13½x13***

777 A289 280s Holy Family 50 50

For surcharge see No. 797.

1982, Dec. 2 ***Perf. 13½x13***

778 A290 240s blk & lt brn 45 30

Death centenary of Indian leader against Spanish during Andes Rebellion.

For surcharges see Nos. 792.

Jose Davila Condemarin (1799-1882), Minister of Posts (1849-76) A291

1982, Dec. 10 ***Perf. 13x13½***

779 A291 150s bl & blk 25 25

10th Anniv. of Intl. Potato Study Center, Lima — A292

1982, Dec. 27 ***Perf. 13x13½***

780 A292 240s multi 45 30

For surcharge see No. 793.

450th Anniv. of City of San Miguel de Piura — A293

1982, Dec. 31 ***Perf. 13x13½***

781 A293 280s Arms 50 50

For surcharge see No. 795.

TB Bacillus Centenary A294

1983, Jan. 18 ***Perf. 12***

782 A294 240s Microscope, slide 45 45

For surcharge see No. 794.

St. Teresa of Jesus of Avila (1515-1582), by Jose Espinoza de los Monteros, 1682 — A295

1983, Mar. 1

783 A295 100s multi 18 15

10th Anniv. of State Security Service A296

1983, Mar. 8

784 A296 100s bl & org 18 15

Horseman's Ornamental Silver Shoe, 19th Cent. — A297

1983, Mar. 18

785 A297 250s multi 45 30

30th Anniv. of Santiago Declaration A298

75th Anniv. of Lima and Callao State Lotteries A300

25th Anniv. of Lima-Bogota Airmail Service A299

1983, Mar. 25

786 A298 280s Map 50 50

For surcharge see No. 796.

1983, Apr. 8

787 A299 150s Jet 28 18

1983, Apr. 26

788 A300 100s multi 18 18

Nos. 739, 773, 771, 778, 780, 782, 781, 786, 777, 749, 774 Surcharged in Black or Green

1983 **Litho.**

789 A277 100s on 40s org	18	15
790 A285 100s on 70s multi	18	15
791 A283 100s on 80s blk & red	18	15
792 A290 100s on 240s multi	18	15
793 A292 100s on 240s multi	18	18
794 A294 100s on 240s ol grn	18	18
795 A293 150s on 280s multi (G)	25	25
796 A298 150s on 280s multi	25	25
797 A289 200s on 280s multi	38	30
798 A277 300s on 180s grn	58	38
799 A277 400s on 180s grn	75	75
800 A286 500s on 80s multi	90	90
Nos. 789-800 (12)	4.19	3.79

Military Ships — A301

1983, May 2 ***Perf. 12***

801 A301 150s Cruiser Almirante Grau, 1907	25	18
802 A301 350s Submarine Ferre, 1913	65	40

Simon Bolivar Birth Bicentenary — A302

Christmas — A303

1983, Dec. 13 **Litho.** ***Perf. 14***

803 A302 100s blk & lt bl 18 15

1983, Dec. 16

804 A303 100s Virgin and Child 18 15

25th Anniv. of Intl. Pacific Fair — A304

Col. Leoncio Prado (1853-83) — A306

World Communications Year (in 1983) — A305

1983

805 A304 350s multi 65 40

1984, Jan. 27 **Litho.** ***Perf. 14***

806 A305 700s multi 1.25 90

1984, Feb. 3 **Litho.** ***Perf. 14***

807 A306 150s ol & ol brn 15 15

Postal Building A307

Pottery — A308

Arms of City of Callao — A310

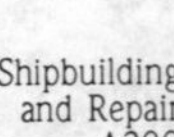

Shipbuilding and Repair A309

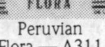

Peruvian Flora — A311 Peruvian Fauna — A312

1984 Litho. *Perf. 14*

808 A307 50s Ministry of Posts, Lima 15 15
809 A308 100s Water jar 15 15
810 A308 150s Llama 15 15
811 A308 200s Painted vase 15 15
812 A309 250s shown 16 15
813 A309 300s Mixed cargo ship 20 15
814 A310 350s shown 22 15
815 A310 400s Arms of Cajamarca 22 15
816 A310 500s Arms of Ayacucho 30 18
817 A311 700s Canna edulis ker 40 28
818 A312 1000s Lagothrix flavicauda 55 38
Nos. 808-818 (11) 2.65
Set value 1.60

Issue dates: 50s, Aug. 29; 100s-200s, May 9; 250s-300s, Feb. 22; 350s, Apr. 23; 400s, June 21; 500s, June 22; 700s, Sept. 12; 1000s, July 3.
See Nos. 844-853, 880-885.

A313 A315

Designs: 50s, Hipolito Unanue (1758-1833). 200s, Ricardo Palma (1833-1919), Writer.

1984 Litho. *Perf. 14*

819 A313 50s dl grn 15 15
820 A313 200s purple 15 15

Issue dates: 50s, Nov. 14; 200s, Mar. 20.
See No. 828.

1984, Mar. 30

821 A315 500s Shooting 35 22
822 A315 750s Hurdles 50 35

1984 Summer Olympics.

Independence Declaration Act — A316

1984, July 18 Litho. *Perf. 14*

823 A316 350s Signing document 20 15

Admiral Grau — A317

Naval Battle A318

1984, Oct. 8 Litho. *Perf. 12½*

824 Block of 4 1.10 75
a. A317 600s Knight of the Seas, by Pablo Muniz 28 18
b. A318 600s Battle of Angamos 28 18
c. A317 600s Congressional seat 28 18
d. A318 600s Battle of Iquique 28 18

150th Anniv. of the birth of Admiral Miguel Grau.

Peruvian Naval Vessels A319

1984, Dec. Litho. *Perf. 14*

825 A319 250s Destroyer Almirante Guise, 1934 15 15
826 A319 400s Gunboat America, 1905 18 15

Christmas A320

1984, Dec. 11 Litho. *Perf. 13x13½*

827 A320 1000s multi 45 30

Famous Peruvians Type of 1984

1984, Dec. 14 Litho. *Perf. 14*

828 A313 100s brown lake 22 15

Victor Andres Belaunde (1883-1967), Pres. of UN General Assembly, 1959-60.

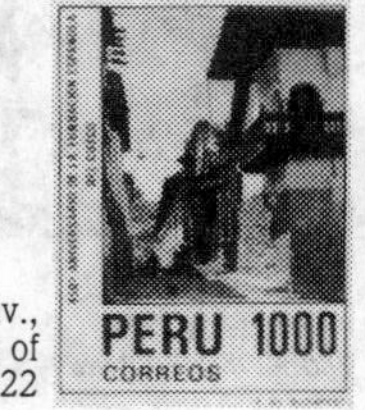

450th Anniv., Founding of Cuzco — A322

1984, Dec. 20 Litho. *Perf. 13½x13*

829 A322 1000s Street scene 42 28

15th Pacific Intl. Fair, Lima — A323

1984, Dec. 28 Litho. *Perf. 13x13½*

830 A323 1000s Llama 42 28

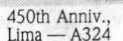

450th Anniv., Lima — A324 Visit of Pope John Paul II — A325

1985, Jan. 17 Litho. *Perf. 13½x13*

831 A324 1500s The Foundation of Lima, by Francisco Gamarra 50 35

1985, Jan. 31 Litho. *Perf. 13½x13*

832 A325 2000s Portrait 52 35

Microwave Tower — A326 Jose Carlos Mariategui (1894-1924), Author — A327

1985, Feb. 28 Litho. *Perf. 13½x13*

833 A326 1100s multi 20 15

ENTEL Peru, Natl. Telecommunications Org., 15th anniv.

1985-86 Photo. *Perf. 13½x13*

Designs: 500s, Francisco Garcia Calderon (1832-1905), president. No. 838, Oscar Miro Quesada (1884-1981), jurist. No. 839, Cesar Vallejo (1892-1938), author. No. 840, Jose Santos Chocano (1875-1934), poet.

836 A327 500s lt ol grn 15 15
837 A327 800s dl red 18 15
838 A327 800s dk ol grn 18 18
839 A327 800s Prus bl ('86) 15 15
840 A327 800s dk red brn ('86) 15 15
Set value 60 45

See Nos. 901-905.

American Air Forces Cooperation System, 25th Anniv. — A328

1985, Apr. 16

842 A328 400s Member flags, emblem 15 15

Jose A. Quinones Gonzales (1914-1941), Air Force Captain A329

1985, Apr. 22 *Perf. 13x13½*

843 A329 1000s Portrait, bomber 22 15

Types of 1984

Design: 200s, Entrance arch and arcade, Central PO admin. building, vert. No. 845, Spotted Robles Moqo bisque vase, Pacheco, Ica. No. 846, Huaura bisque cat. No. 847, Robles Moqo bisque llama head. No. 848, Huancavelica city arms. No. 849, Huanuco city arms. No. 850, Puno city arms. No. 851, Llama wool industry. No. 852, Hymenocallis amancaes. No. 853, Penguins, Antarctic landscape.

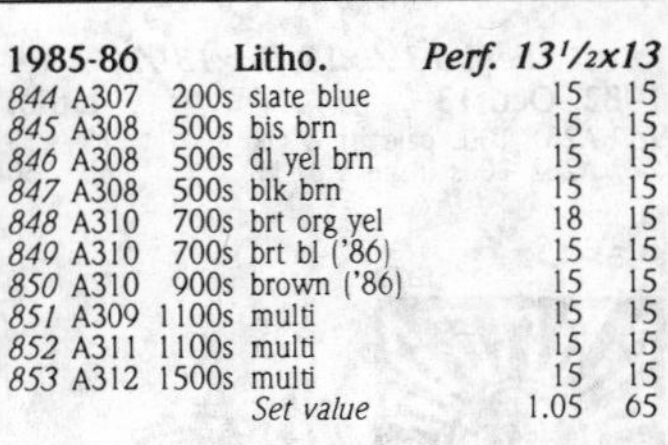

1985-86 Litho. *Perf. 13½x13*

844 A307 200s slate blue 15 15
845 A308 500s bis brn 15 15
846 A308 500s dl yel brn 15 15
847 A308 500s blk brn 15 15
848 A310 700s brt org yel 18 15
849 A310 700s brt bl ('86) 15 15
850 A310 900s brown ('86) 15 15
851 A309 1100s multi 15 15
852 A311 1100s multi 15 15
853 A312 1500s multi 15 15
Set value 1.05 65

Natl. Aerospace Institute Emblem, Globe — A330

1985, May 24 *Perf. 13x13½*

858 A330 900s ultra 20 15

14th Inter-American Air Defense Day.

Founding of Constitution City — A333

1985, July Litho. *Perf. 13½x13*

859 A333 300s Map, flag, crucifix 15 15

Natl. Radio Society, 55th Anniv. — A334

1985, July 24 *Perf. 13x13½*

860 A334 1300s bl & brt org 16 15

San Francisco Convent Church — A335 Doctrina Christiana Frontispiece, 1585, Lima — A336

1985, Oct. 12 *Perf. 13½x13*

861 A335 1300s multi 16 15

1985, Oct. 23

862 A336 300s pale buff & blk 15 15

1st printed book in South America, 400th anniv.

Intl. Civil Aviation Org., 40th Anniv. A337

1985, Oct. 31 *Perf. 13x13½*

863 A337 1100s 1920 Curtis Jenny 15 15

Christmas — A338

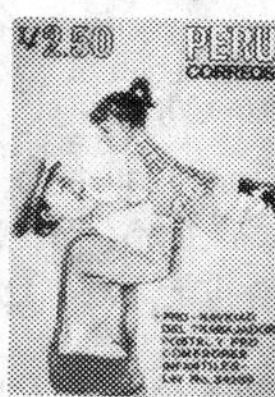
Postman, Child — A338a

1985, Dec. 30 Litho. *Perf. 13½x13*
864 A338 2.50i Virgin and child, 17th cent. 22 15

1985, Dec. 30 Litho. *Perf. 13½x13*
864A A338a 2.50i multi 28 22

Christmas charity for children's and postal workers' funds.

Founding of Trujillo, 450th Anniv. — A339

1986, Mar. 5 Litho. *Perf. 13½x13*
865 A339 3i City arms 40 25

Restoration of Chan Chan Ruins, Trujillo Province A340

1986, Apr. 5 Litho. *Perf. 13x13½*
866 A340 50c Bas-relief 15 15

Saint Rose of Lima, Birth Quadricent. A341

16th Intl. Pacific Fair A342

1986, Apr. 30 Litho. *Perf. 13½x13*
867 A341 7i multi 90 60

1986, May 20
868 A342 1i Natl. products symbols 15 15

Intl. Youth Year — A343

1986, May 23 *Perf. 13x13½*
869 A343 3.50i multi 42 28

A344

A346

A345

1986, June 27 Litho. *Perf. 13½x13*
870 A344 50c brown 15 15

Pedro Vilcapaza (1740-81), independence hero.

1986, Aug. 8 Litho. *Perf. 13x13½*
871 A345 3.50i multi 40 30

UN, 40th anniv.

1986, Aug. 11 *Perf. 13½x13*
872 A346 50c grysh brn 15 15

Fernando and Justo Albujar Fayaque, Manuel Guarniz Lopez, natl. heroes.

Peruvian Navy — A347

1986, Aug. 19 *Perf. 13x13½*
873 A347 1.50i R-1, 1926 18 15
874 A347 2.50i Abtao, 1954 30 22

Flora Type of 1984

1986 Litho. *Perf. 13½x13*
880 A311 80c Tropaeolum majus 15 15
881 A311 80c Datura candida 15 15
884 A312 2i Canis nudus 30 22
885 A312 2i Penelope albipennis 35 28

This is an expanding set. Numbers will change if necessary.

Canchis Province Folk Costumes — A348

1986, Aug. 26 Litho. *Perf. 13½x13*
890 A348 3i multi 35 25

Tourism Day — A349

1986, Aug. 29 *Perf. 13x13½*
891 A349 4i Sacsayhuaman 48 35

1986, Oct. 12 Litho. *Perf. 13x13½*
891A A349 4i Intihuatana, Cuzco 50 38

Interamerican Development Bank, 25th Anniv. A350

1986, Sept. 4
892 A350 1i multi 15 15

Beatification of Sr. Ana de Los Angeles A351

1986, Sept. 15
893 A351 6i Sr. Ana, Pope John Paul II 72 55

Jorge Chavez (1887-1910), Aviator, and Bleriot XI 1M — A352

VAN '86 — A353

1986, Sept. 23 *Perf. 13½x13*
894 A352 5i multi 60 45

Chavez's flight over the Alps, 75th anniv.

1986, Sept. 26
895 A353 50c light blue 15 15

Ministry of Health vaccination campaign, Sept. 27-28, Oct. 25-26, Nov. 22-23.

Natl. Journalism Day — A354

1986, Oct. 1
896 A354 1.50i multi 18 15

Peruvian Navy — A355

1986, Oct. 7 Litho. *Perf. 13x13½*
897 A355 1i Brigantine Gamarra, 1848 15 15
898 A355 1i Monitor Manco Capac, 1880 15 15
Set value 24

Institute of Higher Military Studies, 35th Anniv. — A356

1986, Oct. 31 Litho. *Perf. 13x13½*
899 A356 1i multi 18 15

Boy, Girl — A357

1986, Nov. 3 *Perf. 13½x13*
900 A357 2.50i red, brn & blk 38 30

Christmas charity for children and postal workers' funds.

Famous Peruvians Type of 1985

1986-87
901 A327 50c Carrion 15 15
902 A327 50c Barrenechea 15 15
904 A327 80c Jose de la Riva Aguero ('87) 15 15
905 A327 80c Barrenechea ('87) 15 15
Set value 28 22

Issue dates: No. 904, Oct. 22. No. 905, Nov. 9.
This is an expanding set. Numbers will change if necessary.

Christmas — A358

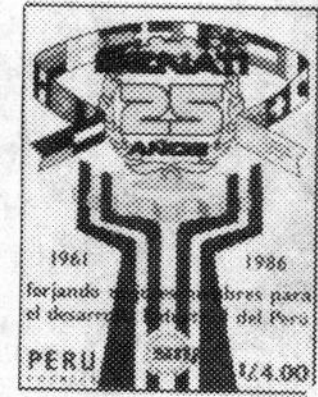
SENATI, 25th Anniv. — A359

1986, Dec. 3
908 A358 5i St. Joseph and Child 75 58

1986, Dec. 19 *Perf. 13½x13*
909 A359 4i multi 60 45

Shipibo Tribal Costumes — A360

World Food Day — A361

1987, Apr. 24 Litho. *Perf. 13½x13*
910 A360 3i multi 45 35

1987, May 26
911 A361 50c multi 15 15

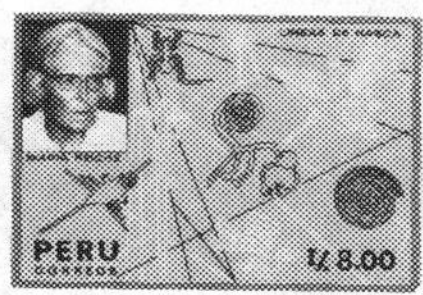
Preservation of the Nasca Lines — A362

Design: Nasca Lines and Dr. Maria Reiche (b. 1903), archaeologist.

1987, June 13 Litho. *Perf. 13x13½*
912 A362 8i multi 1.20 90

A363 A365

A364

1987, July 15 Litho. *Perf. 13½x13*
913 A363 50c vio 15 15

Mariano Santos (1850-1900), "The Hero of Tarapaca," 1879, Chilean war. Dated 1986.

1987, July 19 *Perf. 13x13½*
914 A364 3i multi 45 35

Natl. Horse Club, 50th anniv. Dated 1986.

1987, Aug 13 *Perf. 13½x13*
915 A365 2i multi 30 22

Gen. Felipe Santiago Salaverry (1806-1836), revolution leader. Dated 1986.

Colca's Canyon — A366 AMIFIL '87 — A367

1987, Sept. 8 Litho. *Perf. 13½x13*
916 A366 6i multi 52 38

10th Natl. Philatelic Exposition, Arequipa. Dated 1986.

1987, Sept. 10
917 A367 1i Nos. 1-2 15 15

Dated 1986.

Jose Maria Arguedas (b. 1911), Anthropologist, Author — A368

1987, Sept. 19
918 A368 50c brown 15 15

Arequipa Chamber of Commerce & Industry A369

1987, Sept. 23 *Perf. 13x13½*
919 A369 2i multi 22 16

Vaccinate Every Child Campaign A370

1987, Sept. 30 Litho. *Perf. 13x13½*
920 A370 50c org brn 15 15

Argentina, Winner of the 1986 World Cup Soccer Championships — A371

1987, Nov. 18
921 A371 4i multi 32 22

Restoration of Chan Chan Ruins, Trujillo Province A372

Design: Chimu culture (11th-15th cent.) bas-relief.

1987, Nov. 27
922 A372 50c multi 15 15

See No. 936.

Halley's Comet A373

1987, Dec. 7
923 A373 4i Comet, Giotto satellite 32 22

> ***15-Cent Minimum Value***
> *The minimum value for a single stamp is 15 cents. This value reflects the costs of the handlling of inexpensive stamps.*

Jorge Chavez Dartnell (1887-1910), Aviator — A374

Founding of Lima, 450th Anniv. (in 1985) — A375

1987, Dec. 15 *Perf. 13½x13*
924 A374 2i yel bis, cl brn & gold 16 15

1987, Dec. 18 Litho. *Perf. 13½x13*
925 A375 2.50i Osambela Palace 20 15

Dated 1985.

Discovery of the Ruins at Machu Picchu, 75th Anniv. (in 1986) A376

1987, Dec. *Perf. 13x13½*
926 A376 9i multi 65 48

Dated 1986.

St. Francis's Church, Cajamarca A377

1988, Jan. 23 Litho. *Perf. 13x13½*
927 A377 2i multi 16 15

Cultural Heritage. Dated 1986.

Participation of Peruvian Athletes in the Olympics, 50th Anniv. — A378

Design: Athletes on parade, poster publicizing the 1936 Berlin Games.

1988, Mar. 1 Litho. *Perf. 13½x13*
928 A378 1.50i multi 15 15

Dated 1986.

Ministry of Education, 150th Anniv. A379

1988, Mar. 10 *Perf. 13x13½*
929 A379 1i multi 15 15

Coronation of the Virgin of the Evangelization by Pope John Paul II — A380

1988, Mar. 14 Litho. *Perf. 13x13½*
930 A380 10i multi 48 24

Dated 1986.

Rotary Intl. Involvement in Anti-Polio Campaign A381

1988, Mar. 16
931 A381 2i org, gold & dark blue 15 15

Postman, Cathedral — A382

St. John Bosco (1815-1888), Educator — A384

Meeting of 8 Latin-American Presidents, Acapulco, 1st Anniv. — A383

1988, Apr. 29 Litho. *Perf. 13½x13*
932 A382 9i brt blue 28 15

Christmas charity for children and postal workers' funds.

1988, May 4 *Perf. 13x13½*
933 A383 9i multi 28 15

1988, June 1 *Perf. 13½x13*
934 A384 5i multi 15 15

1st Peruvian Scientific Expedition to the Antarctic A385

1988, June 2 *Perf. 13x13½*
935 A385 7i Ship Humboldt, globe 16 15

Restoration of Chan-Chan Ruins, Trujillo Province A386

1988, June 7
936 A386 4i Bas-relief 15 15

Cesar Vallejo (1892-1938), Poet — A387

Journalists' Fund — A388

1988, June 15 *Perf. 13½x13*
937 A387 25i buff, blk & brn 58 30

1988, July 12 Litho. *Perf. 13½x13*
938 A388 4i buff & deep ultra 15 15

Type A44 — A389

1988, Sept. 1 Litho. *Perf. 13½x13*
939 A389 20i blk, lt pink & ultra 16 15

EXFILIMA '88, discovery of America 500th anniv.

17th Intl. Pacific Fair — A390

1988, Sept. 6 *Perf. 13x13½*
940 A390 4i multi 15 15

Painting by Jose Sabogal (1888-1956) A391

1988, Sept. 7
941 A391 12i multi 15 15

Peru Kennel Club Emblem, Dogs — A392

1988, Sept. 9 *Perf. 13½x13*
942 A392 20i multi 16 15

CANINE '88 Intl. Dog Show, Lima.

Alfonso de Silva (1902-1934), Composer, and Score to Esplendido de Flores A393

1988, Sept. 27 Litho. *Perf. 13x13½*
943 A393 20i multi 16 15

2nd State Visit of Pope John Paul II — A394

1988 Summer Olympics, Seoul — A395

1988, Oct. 10 *Perf. 13½x13*
944 A394 50i multi 40 20

1988, Nov. 10 Litho. *Perf. 13½x13*
945 A395 25i Women's volleyball 20 15

Women's Volleyball Championships (1982) — A396

Chavin Culture Ceramic Vase — A397

1988, Nov. 16 *Perf. 12*

Surcharged in Red

946 A396 95i on 300s multi 78 40

No. 946 not issued without overprint.

Christmas charity for children's and postal workers' funds.

1988 Litho. *Perf. 12*

Surcharged in Henna or Black

947 A397 40i on 100s red brn 16 15
948 A397 80i on 10s blk 32 16
Set value 24

Nos. 947-948 not issued without surcharge. Issue dates: 40i, Dec. 15. 80i, Dec. 22.

Rain Forest Border Highway — A398

Codex of the Indian Kings, 1681 — A399

1989, Jan. 27 Litho. *Perf. 12*

Surcharged in Black

949 A398 70i on 80s multi 20 15

Not issued without surcharge.

1989, Feb. 10

Surcharged in Olive Brown

950 A399 230i on 300s multi 50 25

Not issued without surcharge.

Credit Bank of Peru, Cent. — A400

1989, Apr. 9 Litho. *Perf. 13x13½*
951 A400 500i Huari Culture weaving 70 35

Postal Services A401

1989, Apr. 20 *Perf. 13*
952 A401 50i SESPO, vert. 15 15
953 A401 100i CAN 15 15
Set value 18 15

El Comercio, 150th Anniv. — A402

1989, May 15
954 A402 600i multi 60 30

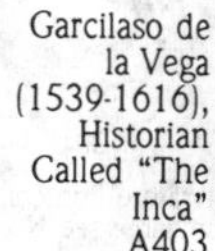

Garcilaso de la Vega (1539-1616), Historian Called "The Inca" A403

1989, July 11 Litho. *Perf. 12½*
955 A403 300i multi 32 16

Express Mail Service A404

1989, July 12
956 A404 100i dark red, org & dark blue 20 15

Federation Emblem and Roca A405

1989, Aug. 29 Litho. *Perf. 13*
957 A405 100i multi 21 15

Luis Loli Roca (1925-1988), founder of the Federation of Peruvian Newspaper Publishers.

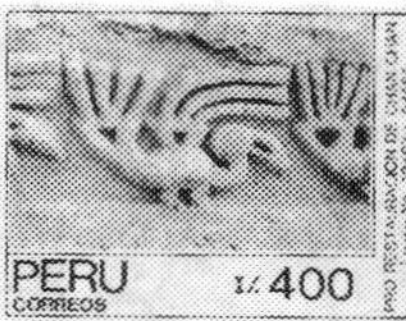

Restoration of Chan Chan Ruins, Trujillo Province A406

Design: Chimu culture (11th-15th cent.) bas-relief.

1989, Sept. 17 *Perf. 12½*
958 A406 400i multi 44 22

Geographical Society of Lima, Cent. — A407

1989, Sept. 18 *Perf. 13*
959 A407 600i Early map of So. America 65 32

Founders of Independence Soc. — A408

1989, Sept. 28 Litho. *Perf. 12½*
960 A408 300i multicolored 30 15

3rd Meeting of the Presidential Consultation and Planning Board — A409

1989, Oct. 12 *Perf. 13*
961 A409 1300i Huacachina Lake 1.40 70

For surcharge see No. 1017.

Children Mailing Letters — A410

1989, Nov. 29 Litho. *Perf. 12½*
962 A410 1200i multicolored 32

Christmas charity for children's and postal workers' funds.

Cacti A411

1989, Dec. 21 Litho. *Perf. 13*
963 A411 500i *Loxanthocereus acanthurus* 20
964 A411 500i *Corryocactus huincoensis* 20
965 A411 500i *Haageocereus clavispinus* 20
966 A411 500i *Trichocereus pervianus* 20
967 A411 500i *Matucana cereoides* 20
Nos. 963-967 (5) 1.00

Nos. 965-967 vert. For surcharges see Nos. 1028-1031

America Issue — A412

UPAE emblem and pre-Columbian medicine jars.

1989, Dec. 28 *Perf. 12½*
968 A412 5000i shown 2.00
969 A412 5000i multi, diff. 2.00

Belen Church, Cajamarca A413

1990, Feb. 1 Litho. *Perf. 12½*
970 A413 600i multicolored 20

Historic patrimony of Cajamarca and culture of the Americas.

Huascaran Natl. Park — A414

1990, Feb. 4 *Perf. 13*
971 A414 900i Llanganuco Lagoons 15
972 A414 900i Mountain climber, Andes, vert. 15
973 A414 1000i Alpamayo mountain 16
974 A414 1000i *Puya raimondi*, vert. 16
975 A414 1100i Condor and Quenual 17
976 A414 1100i El Huascaran 17
Nos. 971-976 (6) 96

Pope and Icon of the Virgin — A415

1990, Feb. 6 *Perf. 12½*
977 A415 1250i multicolored 38

Visit of Pope John Paul II. For surcharge see No. 1039.

Butterflies A416

1990, Feb. 11 *Perf. 13*
978 A416 1000i *Amydon* 15
979 A416 1000i *Agrias beata*, female 15
980 A416 1000i *Sardanapalus*, male 15
981 A416 1000i *Sardanapalus*, female 15
982 A416 1000i *Agrias beata*, male 15
Nos. 978-982 (5) 75

For surcharges see Nos. 1033-1037.

A417 A418

Victor Raul Haya de La Torre and Seat of Government.

1990, Feb. 24 *Perf. 12½*
983 A417 2100i multicolored 55

Return to constitutional government, 10th anniv.

1990, May 24 Litho. *Perf. 12½*
984 A418 300i multicolored 28

Peruvian Philatelic Assoc., 50th anniv. Dated 1989. For surcharge see No. 1038.

Prenfil '88 A419

1990, May 29
985 A419 300i multicolored 20

World Exposition of Stamp & Literature Printers, Buenos Aires. Dated 1989. For surcharge see No. 1032.

French Revolution, Bicentennial A420

Designs: No. 986, Liberty. No. 987, Storming the Bastille. No. 988, Lafayette celebrating the Republic. No. 989, Rousseau and symbols of the Revolution.

1990, June 5
986 A420 2000i multicolored 50
987 A420 2000i multicolored 50
988 A420 2000i multicolored 50
989 A420 2000i shown 50
a. Strip of 4, #986-989 + label 2.00

Dated 1989.

Arequipa, 450th Anniv. A421

1990, Aug. 15 Litho. *Perf. 13*
990 A421 50,000i multi 36

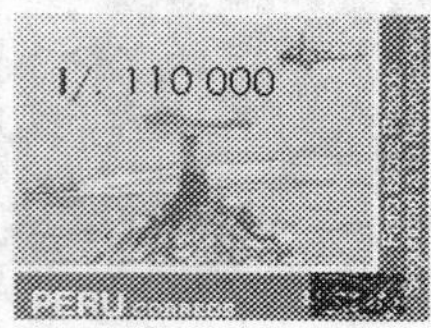

Lighthouse A422

Design: 230,000i, Hospital ship Morona.

1990, Sept. 19 *Perf. 12½*
Surcharged in Black
991 A422 110,000i on 200i blue 55
992 A422 230,000i on 400i blue 1.15

Not issued without surcharge.

A423 A424

1990-91 Litho. *Perf. 13*
993 A423 110,000i Torch bearer 55
994 A423 280,000i Shooting 1.40
995 A423 290,000i Running, horiz. 1.45
996 A423 300,000i Soccer 1.50
997 A423 560,000i Swimming, horiz. 2.30
998 A423 580,000i Equestrian 2.40
999 A423 600,000i Sailing 2.50
1000 A423 620,000i Tennis 2.55
Nos. 993-1000 (8) 14.65

4th South American Games, Lima. Issue dates: Nos. 993-996, Oct. 19. Nos. 997-1000, Feb. 5, 1991.

1990, Nov. 22 Litho. *Die Cut*
Self-Adhesive
1001 A424 250,000i No. 1 1.30
1002 A424 350,000i No. 2 1.80

Pacific Steam Navigation Co., 150th anniv.

Postal Workers' Christmas Fund A425

1990, Dec. 7 Litho. *Perf. 12½*
1003 A425 310,000i multi 1.70

Maria Jesus Castaneda de Pardo, First Woman President of Peruvian Red Cross — A426

1991, May 15 Litho. *Perf. 12½*
1004 A426 .15im on 2500i red & blk 60

Dated 1990. Not issued without surcharge.

2nd Peruvian Scientific Expedition to Antarctica — A427

Designs: .40im, Penguins, man. .45im, Peruvian research station, skua. .50im, Whale, map, research station.

1991, June 20
1005 A427 .40im on 50,000i 1.60
1006 A427 .45im on 80,000i 1.80
1007 A427 .50im on 100,000i 2.00

Not issued without surcharge.

A428 A429

St. Anthony Natl. Univ., Cuzco, 300th Anniv.: 10c, Siphoonandra ellipitica. 20c, Don Manuel de Mollinedo y Angulo, founder. 1s, University coat of arms.

1991, Sept. 26 Litho. *Perf. 13½x13*
1008 A428 10c multicolored 24
1009 A428 20c multicolored 48
1010 A428 1s multicolored 2.40

1991, Dec. 3 Litho. *Perf. 13½x13*

Paintings: No. 1011, Madonna and child. No. 1012, Madonna with lambs and angels.

1011 A429 70c multicolored 1.50
1012 A429 70c multicolored 1.50

Postal Workers' Christmas fund.

America Issue A430

1991, Dec. 23 *Perf. 13*
1013 A430 .50im Mangrove swamp 1.10
1014 A430 .50im Gera waterfall, vert. 1.10

Dated 1990.

Sir Rowland Hill and Penny Black A431

1992, Jan. 15 Litho. *Perf. 13*
1015 A431 .40im gray, blk & bl 85

Penny Black, 150th anniv. (in 1990).

A432 A433

1992, Jan. 28
1016 A432 .30im multicolored 65

Our Lady of Guadalupe College, 150th anniv. (in 1990)

1992, Jan. 30 *Perf. 13½x13*
1017 A433 10c multicolored 16

Entre Nous Society, 80th anniv.

Peru-Bolivia Port Access Agreement — A434

1992, Feb. 25 Litho. *Perf. 12½*
1018 A434 20c multicolored 32

Restoration of Chan-Chan Ruins — A435

1992, Mar. 17
1019 A435 .15im multicolored 35

Dated 1990.

Antonio Raimondi, Naturalist and Publisher, Death Cent. — A436

1992, Mar. 31
1020 A436 .30im multicolored 75

Dated 1990.

Newspaper "Diario de Lima", Bicent. (in 1990) — A437

1992, May 22 Litho. *Perf. 13*
1021 A437 .35im pale yel & black 65

Dated 1990.

Mariano Melgar (1790-1815), Poet A438

1992, Aug. 5 Litho. *Perf. 12½x13*
1022 A438 60c multicolored 85

8 Reales, 1568, First Peruvian Coinage A439

1992, Aug. 7 *Perf. 13x12½*
1023 A439 70c multicolored 1.00

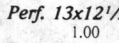

Catholic Univeristy of Peru, 75th Anniv. — A440

1992, Aug. 18 *Perf. 12½*
1024 A440 90c black & tan 1.30

Pan-American Health Organization, 90th Anniv. — A441

1992, Dec. 2 Litho. *Die Cut*
Self-Adhesive
1025 A441 3s multicolored 3.75

Nos. 749, 961 Surcharged

S/. 0.50

Perf. 13½x13, 13
1992, Nov. 18 Litho.
1026 A277 50c on 180s #749 65
1027 A409 1s on 1300i #961 1.25

Nos. 963, 965-967, 977-982, & 984-985 Surcharged

S/. 0.40 

1992, Dec. 24 Litho. *Perfs. as Before*
1028 A411 40c on 500i #963
1029 A411 40c on 500i #965
1030 A411 40c on 500i #966
1031 A411 40c on 500i #967
1032 A419 50c on 300i #985
1033 A416 50c on 1000i #978
1034 A416 50c on 1000i #979
1035 A416 50c on 1000i #980
1036 A416 50c on 1000i #981
1037 A416 50c on 1000i #982
1038 A418 1s on 300i #984
1039 A415 1s on 1250i #977

Virgin with a Spindle, by Urbina — A442

1993, Feb. 10 Litho. *Die Cut*
Self-Adhesive
1040 A442 80c multicolored 95

Sican Culture A443

Various artifacts.

1993, Feb. 10
Self-Adhesive
1041 A443 2s multicolored 2.35
1042 A443 5s multi, vert. 6.00

Evangelization in Peru, 500th Anniv. — A444

1993, Feb. 12
Self-Adhesive
1043 A444 1s multicolored 1.20

Fruit Sellers, by Angel Chavez — A445

Dancers, by Monica Rojas — A446

1993, Feb. 12
Self-Adhesive
1044 A445 1.50s multicolored 1.80
1045 A446 1.50s multicolored 1.80

SEMI-POSTAL STAMPS

Catalogue values for unused stamps in this section are for Never Hinged items.

Gold Funerary Mask SP1

Designs: 2.60s+1.30s, Ceremonial knife, vert. 3.60s+1.80s, Ceremonial vessel. 4.60s+2.30s, Goblet with precious stones, vert. 20s+10s, Earplug.

Perf. 12x12½, 12½x12
1966, Aug. 16 Photo. Unwmk.

B1	SP1	1.90s + 90c multi	40	40
B2	SP1	2.60s + 1.30s multi	50	50
B3	SP1	3.60s + 1.80s multi	75	75
B4	SP1	4.60s + 2.30s multi	1.00	1.00
B5	SP1	20s + 10s multi	4.00	4.00
		Nos. B1-B5 (5)	6.65	6.65

The designs show gold objects of the 12th-13th centuries Chimu culture. The surtax was for tourist publicity.

For surcharges see Nos. 679-680, 683-684, 686.

AIR POST STAMPS

No. 248 Overprinted in Black

Servicio Aéreo

1927, Dec. 10 Unwmk. *Perf. 12*
C1 A87 50c violet 37.50 20.00

Two types of overprint. Counterfeits exist.

An enhanced introduction to the Scott Catalogue begins on Page 5A. A thorough understanding of the material presented there will greatly aid your use of the catalogue itself.

President Augusto Bernardino Leguía — AP1

Coat of Arms of Piura — AP2

1928, Jan. 12 **Engr.**

C2	AP1	50c dk grn	65	35

For surcharge see No. 263.

1932, July 28 **Litho.**

C3	AP2	50c scarlet	20.00	19.00

400th anniv. of the city of Piura. On sale one day. Counterfeits exist.

Airplane in Flight — AP3

1934, Feb. **Engr.** ***Perf. 12½***

C4	AP3	2s blue	4.00	35
C5	AP3	5s brown	8.00	75

Funeral of Atahualpa AP4

Palace of Torre-Tagle — AP7

Designs: 35c, Mt. San Cristobal. 50c, Avenue of Barefoot Friars. 10s, Pizarro and the Thirteen.

1935, Jan. 18 **Photo.** ***Perf. 13½***

C6	AP4	5c emerald	22	15
C7	AP4	35c brown	32	30
C8	AP4	50c org yel	60	60
C9	AP4	1s plum	1.10	90
C10	AP7	2s red org	1.75	1.75
C11	AP4	5s dp claret	7.50	5.25
C12	AP4	10s dk blue	27.50	22.50
		Nos. C6-C12 (7)	38.99	31.45

4th centenary of founding of Lima.

Nos. C6-C12 overprinted "Radio Nacional" are revenue stamps.

"La Callao," First Locomotive in South America AP9

1936, Aug. 27 ***Perf. 12½***

C13	AP9	35c gray black	2.50	1.40

Founding of the Province of Callao, cent.

Nos. C4-C5 Surcharged "Habilitado" and New Value, like Nos. 353-355

1936, Nov. 4

C14	AP3	5c on 2s blue	35	15
C15	AP3	25c on 5s brown	65	35
a.		Double surcharge	13.50	13.50
b.		No period btwn. "O" & "25 Cts"	1.40	1.40
c.		Inverted surcharge	16.50	
		Set value		42

There are many broken letters in this setting.

La Mar Park, Lima — AP10

Jorge Chávez AP14

Aerial View of Peruvian Coast — AP16

View of the "Sierra" — AP17

St. Rosa of Lima — AP22

Designs: 15c, Mail Steamer "Inca" on Lake Titicaca. 20c, Native Queña (flute) Player and Llama. 30c, Ram at Model Farm, Puno. 50c, Mines of Peru. 1s, Train in Mountains. 1.50s, Jorge Chavez Aviation School. 2s, Transport Plane. 5s, Aerial View of Virgin Forests.

1936-37 **Photo.** ***Perf. 12½***

C16	AP10	5c brt grn	15	15
C17	AP10	5c emer ('37)	20	15
C18	AP10	15c lt ultra	40	15
C19	AP10	15c blue ('37)	25	15
C20	AP10	20c gray blk	1.10	15
C21	AP10	20c pale ol grn ('37)	70	22
C22	AP14	25c mag ('37)	32	15
C23	AP10	30c hn brn	3.50	80
C24	AP10	30c dk ol brn ('37)	1.00	15
C25	AP14	35c brown	2.00	1.75
C26	AP10	50c yellow	32	25
C27	AP10	50c brn vio ('37)	50	15
C28	AP16	70c Prus grn	4.25	3.75
C29	AP16	70c pck grn ('37)	70	55
C30	AP17	80c brn blk	5.00	3.75
C31	AP17	80c ol blk ('37)	1.00	38
C32	AP10	1s ultra	3.50	30
C33	AP10	1s red brn ('37)	1.75	20
C34	AP14	1.50s red brn	5.50	4.25
C35	AP14	1.50s org yel ('37)	3.50	32
		Engr.		
C36	AP10	2s dp bl	10.00	5.50
C37	AP10	2s yel grn ('37)	6.75	55
C38	AP16	5s green	12.50	2.75
C39	AP22	10s car & brn	100.00	80.00
		Nos. C16-C39 (24)	164.89	106.52

Nos. C23, C25, C28, C30, C36 Surcharged in Black or Red

Habilit.
Un Sol

1936, June 26

C40	AP10	15c on 30c hn brn	52	30
C41	AP14	15c on 35c brn	52	18
C42	AP16	15c on 70c Prus grn	3.25	2.75
C43	AP17	25c on 80c brn blk (R)	3.25	2.75
C44	AP10	1s on 2s dp bl	5.25	3.75
		Nos. C40-C44 (5)	12.79	9.73

Surcharge on No. C43 is vertical, reading down.

First Flight in Peru, 1911 AP23

Jorge Chávez AP24

Airport of Limatambo at Lima — AP25

Map of Aviation Lines from Peru — AP26

Designs: 10c, Juan Bielovucic (1889-?) flying over Lima race course, Jan. 14, 1911. 15c, Jorge Chavez-Dartnell (1887-1910), French-born Peruvian aviator who flew from Brixen to Domodossola in the Alps and died of plane-crash injuries.

1937, Sept. 15 **Engr.** ***Perf. 12***

C45	AP23	10c violet	35	15
C46	AP24	15c dk grn	50	15
C47	AP25	25c gray brn	35	15
C48	AP26	1s black	1.65	1.20

Inter-American Technical Conference of Aviation, Sept. 1937.

Government Restaurant at Callao — AP27

Monument on the Plains of Junin — AP28

Rear Admiral Manuel Villar — AP29

View of Tarma — AP30

Dam, Ica River — AP31

View of Iquitos — AP32

Highway and Railroad Passing — AP33

Mountain Road — AP34

Plaza San Martín, Lima — AP35

National Radio of Peru — AP36

Stele from Chavin Temple — AP37

Ministry of Public Works, Lima — AP38

Crypt of the Heroes, Lima — AP39

Imprint: "Waterlow & Sons Limited, Londres."

1938, July 1 **Photo.** ***Perf. 12½, 13***

C49	AP27	5c vio brn	15	15
C50	AP28	15c dk brn	15	15
C51	AP29	20c dp mag	32	15
C52	AP30	25c dp grn	15	15
C53	AP31	30c orange	15	15
C54	AP32	50c green	25	16
C55	AP33	70c sl bl	40	15
C56	AP34	80c olive	70	15
C57	AP35	1s sl grn	5.50	2.50
C58	AP36	1.50s purple	1.25	15
		Engr.		
C59	AP37	2s ind & org brn	2.00	50
C60	AP38	5s brown	10.00	1.00
C61	AP39	10s ol grn & ind	40.00	24.00
		Nos. C49-C61 (13)	61.02	29.36

See Nos. C73-C75, C89-C93, C103.

For surcharges see Nos. C65, C76-C77, C82-C88, C108C.

Torre-Tagle Palace — AP40

National Congress Building AP41

Manuel Ferreyros, José Gregorio Paz Soldán and Antonio Arenas AP42

1938, Dec. 9 **Photo.** ***Perf. 12½***

C62	AP40	25c brt ultra	65	45
C63	AP41	1.50s brn vio	1.75	1.50
C64	AP42	2s black	1.10	55

8th Pan-American Conference at Lima.

No. C52 Surcharged in Black

Habilit.
0.15

1942 *Perf. 13*

C65 AP30 15c on 25c dp grn	1.00	15

Types of 1938
Imprint: "Columbian Bank Note Co."

1945-46 Unwmk. Litho. *Perf. 12½*

C73 AP27 5c vio brn	15	15
C74 AP31 30c orange	20	15
C75 AP36 1.50s pur ('46)	32	25
Set value		35

Nos. C73 and C54 Overprinted in Black

1947, Sept. 25 *Perf. 12½, 13*

C76 AP27 5c vio brn	15	15
C77 AP32 50c green	15	15
Set value	15	15

1st Peru Intl. Airways flight from Lima to New York City, Sept. 27-28, 1947.

Catalogue values for unused stamps in this section, from this point to the end of the section, are for Never Hinged items.

Peru-Great Britain Air Route — AP43

Basketball Players — AP44

Designs: 5s, Discus thrower. 10s, Rifleman.

1948, July 29 Photo. *Perf. 12½*

C78 AP43 1s blue	1.50	1.50

Carmine Overprint, "AEREO"

C79 AP44 2s red brn	2.00	2.00
C80 AP44 5s yel grn	3.25	3.25
C81 AP44 10s yellow	4.00	4.00
a. Souvenir sheet, #C78-C81, perf. 13	13.00	13.00

Peru's participation in the 1948 Olympic Games held at Wembley, England, during July and August. Postally valid for four days, July 29-Aug. 1, 1948. Proceeds went to the Olympic Committee.

A surtax of 2 soles on No. C81a was for the Children's Hospital.

Remainders of Nos. C78-C81 and C81a were overprinted "Melbourne 1956" and placed on sale Nov. 19, 1956, at all post offices as "voluntary stamps" with no postal validity. Clerks were permitted to postmark them to please collectors, and proceeds were to help pay the cost of sending Peruvian athletes to Australia. On April 14, 1957, postal authorities declared these stamps valid for one day, April 15, 1957. The overprint was applied to 10,000 sets and 21,000 souvenir sheets. Value, set, $10; sheet, $10.

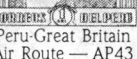

No. C55 Surcharged in Red

Habilitada.
S/. 0.10

1948, Dec. *Perf. 13*

C82 AP33 10c on 70c slate bl	15	15
C83 AP33 20c on 70c slate bl	15	15
C84 AP33 55c on 70c slate bl	16	15
Set value		15

Nos. C52, C55 and C56 Surcharged in Black

Habilitada
S/. 0.10

1949, Mar. 25

C85 AP30 5c on 25c dp grn	15	15
C86 AP30 10c on 25c dp grn	15	15
C87 AP33 15c on 70c slate bl	15	15
C88 AP34 30c on 80c olive	65	15
Set value	90	30

The surcharge is vertical, reading up, on No. C87.

Types of 1938
Imprint: "Waterlow & Sons Limited, Londres."

Perf. 13x13½, 13½x13

1949-50 Photo.

C89 AP27 5c ol bis	15	15
C90 AP31 30c red	15	15
C91 AP33 70c blue	25	15
C92 AP34 80c cerise	40	15
C93 AP36 1.50s vio brn ('50)	50	20
Nos. C89-C93 (5)	1.45	
Set value		50

Air View, Reserva Park, Lima — AP45

Flags of the Americas and Spain — AP46

Designs: 30c, National flag. 55c, Huancayo Hotel. 95c, Blanca-Ancash Cordillera. 1.50s, Arequipa Hotel. 2s, Coal chute and dock, Chimbote. 5s, Town hall, Miraflores. 10s, Hall of National Congress, Lima.

Overprinted "U. P. U. 1874-1949" in Red or Black

1951, Apr. 2 Engr. *Perf. 12*

C94 AP45 5c bl grn	15	15
C95 AP45 30c blk & car	15	15
a. Inverted overprint		
C96 AP45 55c yel grn (Bk)	15	15
C97 AP45 95c dk grn	15	15
C98 AP45 1.50s dp car (Bk)	16	15
C99 AP45 2s dp bl	20	16
C100 AP45 5s rose car (Bk)	2.50	2.50
C101 AP45 10s purple	3.25	3.50
C102 AP46 20s dk brn & ultra	5.50	5.50
Nos. C94-C102 (9)	12.21	12.41

UPU, 75th anniv. (in 1949).

Nos. C94-C102 exist without overprint, but were not regularly issued. Value, set, $200.

Type of 1938
Imprint: "Inst. de Grav. Paris."

1951, May Engr. *Perf. 12½x12*

C103 AP27 5c ol bis	15	15

Type of 1938 Surcharged in Black

HABILITADA
S|o. 0.25

1951

C108 AP31 25c on 30c rose red	15	15

Thomas de San Martin y Contreras and Jerónimo de Aliaga y Ramirez AP47

San Marcos University AP48

Designs: 50c, Church and convent of Santo Domingo. 1.20s, P. de Peralta Barnuevo, T. de San Martin y Contreras and J. Baquijano y Carrillo de Cordova. 2s, T. Rodriguez de Mendoza, J. Hipolito Unanue y Pavon and J. Cayetano Heredia y Garcia. 5s, Arms of the University, 1571 and 1735.

Perf. 11½x12½

1951, Dec. 10 Litho.

C109 AP47 30c gray	15	15
C110 AP48 40c ultra	15	15
C111 AP48 50c car rose	15	15
C112 AP47 1.20s emerald	15	15
C113 AP47 2s slate	25	15
C114 AP47 5s multi	1.10	15
Nos. C109-C114 (6)	1.95	
Set value		55

400th anniv. of the founding of San Marcos University.

River Gunboat Marañon AP49

Peruvian Cormorants AP50

National Airport, Lima — AP51

Tobacco Plant AP52

Manco Capac Monument AP54

Garcilaso de la Vega — AP53

Designs: 1.50s, Housing Unit No. 3. 2.20s, Inca Solar Observatory.

Imprint: "Thomas De La Rue & Co. Ltd."

1953-60 Unwmk. *Perf. 13, 12*

C115 AP49 40c yel grn	15	15
a. 40c blue green ('57)	15	15
C116 AP50 75c dk brn	75	15
C116A AP50 80c pale brn red ('60)	40	15
C117 AP51 1.25s blue	20	15
C118 AP49 1.50s cerise	20	15
C119 AP51 2.20s dk bl	80	25
C120 AP52 3s brown	90	22
C121 AP53 5s bister	75	15
C122 AP54 10s dl vio brn	1.75	35
Nos. C115-C122 (9)	5.90	
Set value		1.35

See Nos. C158-C162, C182-C183, C186-C189, C210-C211.

For surcharges see Nos. C420-C422, C429-C433, C435-C436, C438, C442-C443, C445-C450, C455, C471-C474, C476, C478-C479, C495.

Queen Isabella I — AP55

Fleet of Columbus AP56

Perf. 12½x11½, 11½x12½

1953, June 18 Engr. Unwmk.

C123 AP55 40c dp car	15	15
C124 AP56 1.25s emerald	20	16
C125 AP55 2.15s dp plum	42	30
C126 AP56 2.20s black	65	30

500th birth anniv. (in 1951) of Queen Isabella I of Spain.

For surcharge see No. C475.

Arms of Lima and Bordeaux AP57

Designs: 50c, Eiffel Tower and Cathedral of Lima. 1.25s, Admiral Dupetit-Thouars and frigate "La Victorieuse." 2.20s, Presidents Coty and Prado and exposition hall.

1957, Sept. 16 *Perf. 13*

C127 AP57 40c cl, grn & ultra	15	15
C128 AP57 50c grn, blk & hn brn	15	15
C129 AP57 1.25s bl, ind & dk grn	16	15
C130 AP57 2.20s bluish blk, bl & red brn	35	35
Set value	65	60

French Exposition, Lima, Sept. 15-Oct. 1.

For surcharges see Nos. 763, C503-C505.

Pre-Stamp Postal Markings — AP58

Designs: 10c, 1r Stamp of 1857. 15c, 2r Stamp of 1857. 25c, 1d Stamp of 1860. 30c, 1p Stamp of 1858. 40c, ½p Stamp of 1858. 1.25s, José Davila Condemarin. 2.20s, Ramon Castilla. 5s, Pres. Manuel Prado. 10s, Shield of Lima containing stamps.

Perf. 12½x13

1957, Dec. 1 Engr. Unwmk.

C131 AP58 5c sil & blk	15	15
C132 AP58 10c lil rose & bl	15	15
C133 AP58 15c grn & red brn	15	15
C134 AP58 25c org yel & bl	15	15
C135 AP58 30c vio brn & org brn	15	15
C136 AP58 40c blk & bis	15	15
C137 AP58 1.25s dk bl & dk brn	30	25
C138 AP58 2.20s red & sl bl	50	50
C139 AP58 5s lil rose & mar	1.25	1.00
C140 AP58 10s ol grn & lil	2.00	1.75
Set value	4.30	3.70

Centenary of Peruvian postage stamps. No. C140 issued to publicize the Peruvian Centenary Phil. Exhib. (PEREX).

Carlos Paz Soldan — AP59

Port of Callao and Pres. Manuel Prado — AP60

Design: 1s, Ramon Castilla.

Perf. 14x13½, 13½x14

1958, Apr. 7 Litho. Wmk. 116

C141 AP59	40c	brn & pale rose	15	15
C142 AP59	1s	grn & lt grn	15	15
C143 AP60	1.25s	dl pur & ind	20	15
		Set value		26

Centenary of the telegraph connection between Lima and Callao and the centenary of the political province of Callao.

For surcharge see No. 767.

Flags of France and Peru — AP61

Cathedral of Lima and Lady — AP62

Designs: 1.50s, Horseback rider and mall in Lima. 2.50s, Map of Peru showing national products.

Perf. 12½x13, 13x12½

1958, May 20 Engr. Unwmk.

C144 AP61	50c	dl vio, bl & car	15	15
C145 AP62	65c	multi	15	15
C146 AP62	1.50s	bl, brn vio & ol	20	15
C147 AP61	2.50s	sl grn, grnsh bl & claret	25	16
		Set value	62	40

Peruvian Exhib. in Paris, May 20-July 10.

Bro. Martin de Porres Velasquez AP63

First Royal School of Medicine (Now Ministry of Government and Police) — AP64

Designs: 1.20s, Daniel Alcides Carrion Garcia. 1.50s, Jose Hipolito Unanue Pavon.

Perf. 13x13½, 13½x13

1958, July 24 Litho. Unwmk.

C148 AP63	60c	multi	15	15
C149 AP63	1.20s	multi	15	15
C150 AP63	1.50s	multi	15	15
C151 AP64	2.20s	black	20	16
		Set value		38

Daniel A. Carrion (1857-85), medical martyr.

Gen. Ignacio Alvarez Thomas AP65

1958, Nov. 13 ***Perf. 13x12½***

C152 AP65	1.10s	brn lake, bis & ver	16	15
C153 AP65	1.20s	blk, bis & ver	20	16

General Thomas (1787-1857), fighter for South American independence.

"Justice" and Emblem — AP66

1958, Nov. 13

Star in Blue and Olive Bister

C154 AP66	80c	emerald	15	15
C155 AP66	1.10s	red orange	15	15
C156 AP66	1.20s	ultra	15	15
C157 AP66	1.50s	lilac rose	16	15
		Set value	46	36

Lima Bar Assoc., 150th anniv.

Types of 1953-57

Designs: 80c, Peruvian cormorants. 3.80s, Inca Solar Observatory.

Imprint: "Joh. Enschedé en Zonen-Holland"

Perf. 12½x14, 14x13, 13x14

1959, Dec. 9 Unwmk.

C158 AP50	80c	brn red	15	15
C159 AP52	3s	lt grn	60	22
C160 AP51	3.80s	orange	1.00	25
C161 AP53	5s	brown	60	25
C162 AP54	10s	org ver	1.20	40
		Nos. C158-C162 (5)	3.55	1.27

WRY Emblem, Dove, Rainbow and Farmer — AP67

Peruvian Cormorant Over Ocean — AP68

1960, Apr. 7 Litho. ***Perf. 14x13***

C163 AP67	80c	multi	25	25
C164 AP67	4.30s	multi	55	55
a.		Souv. sheet of 2, #C163-C164, imperf.	5.50	5.50

World Refugee Year, July 1, 1959-June 30, 1960. No. C164a sold for 15s.

1960, May 30 ***Perf. 14x13½***

C165 AP68	1s	multi	35	15

Intl. Pacific Fair, Lima, 1959.

Lima Coin of 1659 — AP69

1961, Jan. 19 Unwmk. ***Perf. 13x14***

C166 AP69	1s	org brn & gray	15	15
C167 AP69	2s	Prus bl & gray	20	16
		Set value		24

1st National Numismatic Exposition, Lima, 1959; 300th anniv. of the first dated coin (1659) minted at Lima.

The Earth — AP70

1961, Mar. 8 Litho. ***Perf. 13½x14***

C168 AP70	1s	multi	15	15

International Geophysical Year.

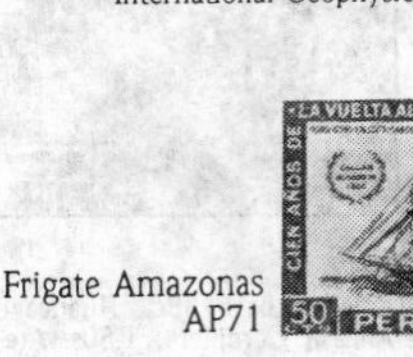

Frigate Amazonas AP71

1961, Mar. 8 Engr. ***Perf. 13½***

C169 AP71	50c	brn & grn	15	15
C170 AP71	80c	dl vio & red org	15	15
C171 AP71	1s	grn & sepia	20	20
		Set value	36	36

Centenary (in 1958) of the trip around the world by the Peruvian frigate Amazonas.

Machu Picchu Sheet

A souvenir sheet was issued Sept. 11, 1961, to commemorate the 50th anniversary of the discovery of the ruins of Machu Picchu, ancient Inca city in the Andes, by Hiram Bingham. It contains two bi-colored imperf. airmail stamps, 5s and 10s, lithographed in a single design picturing the mountaintop ruins. The sheet was valid for one day and was sold in a restricted manner. Value $7.50.

Olympic Torch, Laurel and Globe — AP72

Fair Emblem and Llama — AP73

1961, Dec. 13 Unwmk. ***Perf. 13***

C172 AP72	5s	gray & ultra	40	35
C173 AP72	10s	gray & car	80	60
a.		Souv. sheet of 2, #C172-C173, imperf.	2.25	2.25

17th Olympic Games, Rome, Aug. 25-Sept. 11, 1960.

1962, Jan. Litho. ***Perf. 10½x11***

C174 AP73	1s	multi	16	15

2nd International Pacific Fair, Lima, 1961.

Map Showing Disputed Border, Peru-Ecuador AP74

1962, May 25 ***Perf. 10½***

Gray Background

C175 AP74	1.30s	blk, red & car rose	16	16
C176 AP74	1.50s	blk, red & emer	20	20
C177 AP74	2.50s	blk, red & dk bl	25	25

20th anniversary of the settlement of the border dispute with Ecuador by the Protocol of Rio de Janeiro.

Cahuide and Cuauhtémoc AP75

Designs: 2s, Tupac Amaru (Jose G. Condorcanqui) and Miguel Hidalgo. 3s, Pres. Manuel Prado and Pres. Adolfo Lopez Mateos of Mexico.

1962, May 25 Engr. ***Perf. 13***

C178 AP75	1s	dk car rose, red & brt grn	15	15
C179 AP75	2s	grn, red & brt grn	20	15
C180 AP75	3s	brn, red & brt grn	25	16

Exhibition of Peruvian art treasures in Mexico.

Agriculture, Industry and Archaeology AP76

1962, Sept. 7 Litho. ***Perf. 14x13½***

C181 AP76	1s	blk & gray	15	15

Cent. (in 1961) of Pallasca Ancash province.

Types of 1953-60

Designs: 1.30s, Guanayes. 1.50s, Housing Unit No. 3. 1.80s, Locomotive No. 80 (like No. 460). 2s, Monument to Native Farmer. 3s, Tobacco plant. 4.30s, Inca Solar Observatory. 5s, Garcilaso de la Vega. 10s, Inca Monument.

Imprint: "Thomas De La Rue & Co. Ltd."

1962-63 Wmk. 346 Litho. ***Perf. 13***

C182 AP50	1.30s	pale yel	20	15
C183 AP49	1.50s	claret	22	15
C184 A182	1.80s	dark bl	25	15
		Perf. 12		
C185 A184	2s	emer ('63)	25	15
C186 AP52	3s	lil rose	35	16
C187 AP51	4.30s	orange	65	25
C188 AP53	5s	citron	65	35
		Perf. 13½x14		
C189 AP54	10s	vio bl ('63)	1.20	50
		Nos. C182-C189 (8)	3.77	1.86

Freedom from Hunger Type

1963, July 23 Unwmk. ***Perf. 12½***

C190 A189	4.30s	lt grn & ocher	50	50

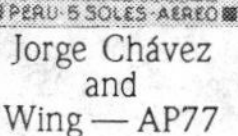
Jorge Chávez and Wing — AP77

Fair Poster — AP78

1964, Feb. 20 **Engr.** ***Perf. 13***
C191 AP77 5s org brn, dk brn & bl 65 35

50th anniversary of the first crossing of the Alps by air (Sept. 23, 1910) by the Peruvian aviator Jorge Chávez.

Alliance for Progress Type

Design: 1.30s, Same, horizontal.

Perf. 12½x12, 12x12½

1964, June 22 **Litho.**
C192 A190 1.30s multi 15 15
C193 A190 3s multi 25 22

1965, Jan. 15 **Unwmk.** ***Perf. 14½***
C194 AP78 1s multi 15 15

3rd International Pacific Fair, Lima 1963.

Basket, Globe, Pennant AP79

St. Martin de Porres AP80

1965, Apr. 19 ***Perf. 12x12½***
C195 AP79 1.30s vio & red 25 25
C196 AP79 4.30s bis brn & red 55 55

4th Women's Intl. Basketball Championship.
For surcharge see No. C493.

1965, Oct. 29 **Litho.** ***Perf. 11***

Designs: 1.80s, St. Martin's miracle: dog, cat and mouse feeding from same dish. 4.30s, St. Martin with cherubim in Heaven.

C197 AP80 1.30s gray & multi 15 15
C198 AP80 1.80s gray & multi 20 15
C199 AP80 4.30s gray & multi 50 50
Set value 68

Canonization of St. Martin de Porres Velasquez (1579-1639), on May 6, 1962.
For surcharges see Nos. C439, C496.

Victory Monument, Lima, and Battle Scene — AP81

Designs: 3.60s, Monument and Callao Fortress. 4.60s, Monument and José Galvez.

1966, May 2 **Photo.** ***Perf. 14x13½***
C200 AP81 1.90s multi 25 25
C201 AP81 3.60s brn, yel & bis 40 40
C202 AP81 4.60s multi 60 60

Centenary of Peru's naval victory over the Spanish Armada at Callao, May, 1866.

Civil Guard Emblem AP82

Design: 1.90s, Emblem and various activities of Civil Guard.

1966, Aug. 30 **Photo.** ***Perf. 13½x14***
C203 AP82 90c multi 15 15
C204 AP82 1.90s dp lil rose, gold & blk 16 15
Set value 24 22

Centenary of the Civil Guard.

Hydroelectric Center Type of Regular Issue

1966, Nov. 24 **Photo.** ***Perf. 13½x14***
C205 A193 1.90s lil, blk & vio bl 16 15

Sun Symbol, Ancient Carving — AP83

Designs: 3.60s, Map of Peru and spiral, horiz. 4.60s, Globe with map of Peru.

Perf. 14x13½, 13½x14

1967, Feb. 16 **Litho.**
C206 AP83 2.60s red org & blk 22 16
C207 AP83 3.60s dp bl & blk 35 22
C208 AP83 4.60s tan & multi 40 30

Photography exhibition "Peru Before the World" which opened simultaneously in Lima, Madrid, Santiago de Chile and Washington, Sept. 27, 1966.
For surcharges see Nos. C444, C470, C492.

Types of 1953-60

Designs: 2.60s, Monument to Native Farmer. 3.60s, Tobacco plant. 4.60s, Inca Solar Observatory.

Imprint: "I.N.A."

1967, Jan. ***Perf. 13½x14, 14x13½***
C209 A184 2.60s brt grn 22 16
C210 AP52 3.60s lil rose 35 20
C211 AP51 4.60s orange 40 25

Wind Vane and Sun Type of Regular Issue

1967, Apr. 18 **Photo.** ***Perf. 13½x14***
C212 A194 1.90s yel brn, blk & gold 16 16

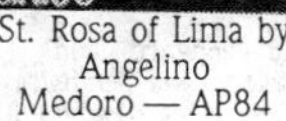

St. Rosa of Lima by Angelino Medoro — AP84

Lions Emblem — AP85

St. Rosa Painted by: 2.60s, Carlo Maratta. 3.60s, Cuzquena School, 17th century.

1967, Aug. 30 **Photo.** ***Perf. 13½***
C213 AP84 1.90s blk, gold & multi 25 15
C214 AP84 2.60s blk, gold & multi 42 16
C215 AP84 3.60s blk, gold & multi 60 22

350th death anniv. of St. Rosa of Lima.
For surcharge see No. C477.

Fair Type of Regular Issue

1967, Oct. 27 **Photo.** ***Perf. 12***
C216 A195 1s gold, brt red lil & blk 15 15

1967, Dec. 29 **Litho.** ***Perf. 14x13½***
C217 AP85 1.60s brt bl & vio bl, *grysh* 20 20

50th anniversary of Lions International.

Decorated Jug, Nazca Culture — AP86

Antarqui, Inca Messenger — AP87

Painted pottery jugs of pre-Inca Nazca culture: 2.60s, Falcon. 3.60s, Round jug decorated with grain-eating bird. 4.60s, Two-headed snake. 5.60s, Marine bird.

1968, June 4 **Photo.** ***Perf. 12***
C218 AP86 1.90s multi 15 15
C219 AP86 2.60s multi 16 15
C220 AP86 3.60s blk & multi 22 20
C221 AP86 4.60s brn & multi 30 25
C222 AP86 5.60s gray & multi 38 35
Nos. C218-C222 (5) 1.21 1.10

For surcharges see #C451-C453, C497, C500.

1968, Sept. 2 **Litho.** ***Perf. 12***

Design: 5.60s, Alpaca and jet liner.

C223 AP87 3.60s multi 30 30
C224 AP87 5.60s red, blk & brn 45 45

12th anniv. of Peruvian Airlines (APSA).
For surcharges see Nos. C480-C482.

Human Rights Flame — AP88

1968, Sept. 5 **Photo.** ***Perf. 14x13½***
C225 AP88 6.50s brn, red & grn 22 20

International Human Rights Year.

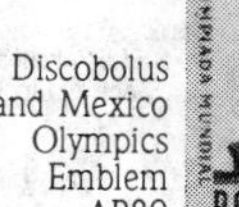
Discobolus and Mexico Olympics Emblem AP89

1968, Oct. 19 **Photo.** ***Perf. 13½***
C226 AP89 2.30s yel, brn & dk bl 15 15
C227 AP89 3.50s yel grn, sl bl & red 18 18
C228 AP89 5s brt pink, blk & ultra 25 16
C229 AP89 6.50s lt bl, mag & brn 38 30
C230 AP89 8s lil, ultra & car 40 25
C231 AP89 9s org, vio & grn 42 30
Nos. C226-C231 (6) 1.78 1.34

19th Olympic Games, Mexico City, Oct. 12-27.

Hand, Corn and Field — AP90

1969, Mar. 3 **Litho.** ***Perf. 11***
C232 AP90 5.50s on 1.90s grn & yel 25 16
C233 AP90 6.50s on 1.90s bl, grn & yel 35 20

Agrarian Reform Law. Not issued without surcharge.

Peruvian Silver 8-reales Coin, 1568 — AP91

1969, Mar. 17 **Litho.** ***Perf. 12***
C234 AP91 5s yel, gray & blk 20 15
C235 AP91 5s bl grn, gray & blk 20 15

400th anniv. of the first Peruvian coinage.

Ramon Castilla Monument — AP92

Design: 10s, Pres. Ramon Castilla.

1969, May 30 **Photo.** ***Perf. 13½***
Size: 27x40mm
C236 AP92 5s emer & indigo 35 15

Perf. 12
Size: 21x37mm
C237 AP92 10s plum & brn 65 30

Ramon Castilla (1797-1867), president of Peru (1845-1851 and 1855-1862), on the occasion of the unveiling of the monument in Lima.

Airline Type of Regular Issue

1969, June 17 **Litho.** ***Perf. 11***
C238 A199 3s org & multi 15 15
C239 A199 4s multi 15 15
C240 A199 5.50s ver & multi 18 15
C241 A199 6.50s vio & multi 20 16
Set value 48

First Peruvian Airlines (APSA) flight to Europe.

Radar Antenna, Satellite and Earth — AP93

1969, July 14 **Litho.** ***Perf. 11***
C242 AP93 20s multi 1.25 55
a. Souv. sheet 1.50 1.50

Opening of the Lurin satellite earth station near Lima.

No. C242a contains one imperf. stamp with simulated perforations similar to No. C242.

Gonzales Type of Regular Issue

1969, July 23 **Litho.** ***Perf. 11***
C243 A200 20s red & multi 1.20 55

WHO Emblem AP94

1969, Aug. 14 Photo. *Perf. 12*
C244 AP94 5s gray, red brn, gold & blk 16 15
C245 AP94 6.50s dl org, gray bl, gold & blk 20 16

WHO, 20th anniv.

Agrarian Reform Type of Regular Issue

1969, Aug. 28 Litho. *Perf. 11*
C246 A201 3s lil & blk 15 15
C247 A201 4s brn & buff 15 15
Set value 24 20

Garcilaso de la Vega — AP95

Designs: 2.40s, De la Vega's coat of arms. 3.50s, Title page of "Commemtarios Reales que tratan del origen de los Yncas," Lisbon, 1609.

1969, Sept. 18 Litho. *Perf. 12x12½*
C248 AP95 2.40s emer, sil & blk 15 15
C249 AP95 3.50s ultra, buff & blk 15 15
C250 AP95 5s sil, yel, blk & brn 20 15
a. Souv. sheet of 3, #C248-C250, imperf. 90 90
Set value 38

Garcilaso de la Vega, called "Inca" (1539-1616), historian of Peru.

Fair Type of Regular Issue, 1969

1969, Nov. 14 Litho. *Perf. 11*
C251 A203 3s bis & multi 20 15
C252 A203 4s multi 25 15
Set value 18

Bolognesi Type of Regular Issue

1969, Dec. 9 Litho. *Perf. 11*
C253 A204 50s lt brn, blk & gold 3.00 1.40

Arms of Amazonas — AP96

1970, Jan. 6 Litho. *Perf. 11*
C254 AP96 10s multi 50 50

ILO Emblem AP97

1970, Jan. 16
C278 AP97 3s dk vio bl & lt ultra 25 25

ILO, 50th anniv.

Motherhood and UNICEF Emblem AP98

1970, Jan. 16 Photo. *Perf. 13½x14*
C279 AP98 5s yel, gray & blk 22 15
C280 AP98 6.50s brt pink, gray & blk 35 20

Vicus Culture Type of Regular Issue

Ceramics of Vicus Culture, 6th-8th Centuries: 3s, Squatting warrior. 4s, Jug. 5.50s, Twin jugs. 6.50s, Woman and jug.

1970, Feb. 23 Litho. *Perf. 11*
C281 A205 3s buff, blk & brn 16 16
C282 A205 4s buff, blk & brn 20 20
C283 A205 5.50s buff, blk & brn 30 30
C284 A205 6.50s buff, blk & brn 40 40

Fish Type of Regular Issue

1970, Apr. 30 Litho. *Perf. 11*
C285 A207 3s Swordfish 20 20
C286 A207 3s Yellowfin tuna 20 20
C287 A207 5.50s Wolf fish 30 30

Telephone — AP99

UN Headquarters, NY — AP100

1970, June 12 Litho. *Perf. 11*
C288 AP99 5s multi 25 15
C289 AP99 10s multi 55 22

Nationalization of the Peruvian telephone system, Mar. 25, 1970.

Soldier-Farmer Type of Regular Issue

1970, June 24 Litho. *Perf. 11*
C290 A208 3s gold & multi 20 15
C291 A208 5.50s gold & multi 35 15
Set value 20

1970 June 26
C292 AP100 3s vio bl & lt bl 15 15

25th anniversary of United Nations.

Rotary Club Emblem AP101

1970, July 18
C293 AP101 10s blk, red & gold 70 50

Rotary Club of Lima, 50th anniversary.

Tourist Type of Regular Issue

Designs: 3s, Ruins of Sun Fortress, Trujillo. 4s, Sacsayhuaman Arch, Cuzco, vert. 5.50s, Arch and Lake Titicaca, Puno, vert. 10s, Machu Picchu, Cuzco, vert

1970, Aug. 6 Litho. *Perf. 11*
C294 A210 3s multi 15 15
C295 A210 4s multi 20 20
C296 A210 5.50s multi 28 28
C297 A210 10s multi 50 50
a. Souvenir sheet of 5 1.65 1.65

No. C297a contains 5 imperf. stamps similar to Nos. 538, C294-C297 with simulated perforations.

Procession, Lord of Miracles — AP102

Designs: 4s, Cockfight, by T. Nuñez Ureta. 5.50s, Altar of Church of the Nazarene, vert. 6.50s, Procession, by J. Vinatea Reinoso. 8s, Procession, by José Sabogal, vert.

1970, Nov. 30 Litho. *Perf. 11*
C298 AP102 3s blk & multi 15 15
C299 AP102 4s blk & multi 20 15
C300 AP102 5.50s blk & multi 25 15
C301 AP102 6.50s blk & multi 35 16
C302 AP102 8s blk & multi 40 20
Nos. C298-C302 (5) 1.35
Set value 66

October Festival in Lima.

"Tight Embrace" (from ancient monolith) AP103

1971, Feb. 8 Litho. *Perf. 11*
C303 AP103 4s ol gray, yel & red 22 15
C304 AP103 5.50s dk bl, pink & red 30 15
C305 AP103 6.50s sl, buff & red 35 16

Issued to express Peru's gratitude to the world for aid after the Ancash earthquake, May 31, 1970.

Textile Type of Regular Issue

Designs: 3s, Chancay tapestry, vert. 4s, Chancay lace. 5.50s, Paracas cloth, vert.

1971, Apr. 19 Litho. *Perf. 11*
C306 A213 3s multi 25 15
C307 A213 4s grn & multi 35 15
C308 A213 5.50s multi 42 15
Set value 30

Fish Type of Regular Issue

Fish Sculptures and Fish: 3.50s, Chimu Inca culture, 14th century and Chilean sardine. 4s, Mochica culture, 5th century, and engraulis ringens. 5.50s, Chimu culture, 13th century, and merluccios peruanos. 8.50s, Nazca culture, 3rd century, and brevoortis maculatachilcae.

1971, June 7 Litho. *Perf. 11*
C309 A214 3.50s multi 30 15
C310 A214 4s multi 38 15
C311 A214 5.50s multi 50 15
C312 A214 8.50s multi 70 20
Set value 52

Independence Type of 1971

Paintings: No. C313, Toribio Rodriguez de Mendoza. No. C314, José de la Riva Aguero. No. C315, Francisco Vidal. 3.50s, José de San Martin. No. C317, Juan P. Viscardo y Guzman. No. C318, Hipolito Unanue. 4.50s, Liberation Monument, Paracas. No. C320, José G. Condorcanqui-Tupac Amaru. No. C321, Francisco J. de Luna Pizarro. 6s, March of the Numancia Battalion, horiz. 7.50s, Peace Tower, monument for Alvarez de Arenales, horiz. 9s, Liberators' Monument, Lima, horiz. 10s, Independence Proclamation in Lima, horiz.

1971 Litho. *Perf. 11*
C313 A215 3s brt mag & blk 15 15
C314 A215 3s gray & multi 15 15
C315 A215 3s dk bl & multi 15 15
C316 A215 3.50s dk bl & multi 15 15
C317 A215 4s emer & blk 16 15
C318 A215 4s gray & multi 16 15
C319 A215 4.50s dk bl & multi 18 15
C320 A215 5.50s brn & blk 22 15
C321 A215 5.50s gray & multi 22 15
C322 A215 6s dk bl & multi 22 15
C323 A215 7.50s dk bl & multi 30 18
C324 A215 9s dk bl & multi 38 20
C325 A215 10s dk bl & multi 40 20
Nos. C313-C325 (13) 2.84
Set value 1.60

150th anniversary of independence, and to honor the heroes of the struggle for independence. Sizes: 6s, 10s, 45x35mm, 7.50s, 9s, 41x39mm. Others 31x49mm.

Issue dates: Nos. C313, C317, C320, May 10; Nos. C314, C318, C321, July 5; others July 27.

Canceled-to-order stamps are often from remainders. Most collectors of canceled stamps prefer postally used specimens.

Ricardo Palma — AP104

Weight Lifter — AP105

1971, Aug. 27 *Perf. 13*
C326 AP104 7.50s ol bis & blk 75 18

Sesquicentennial of National Library. Ricardo Palma (1884-1912) was a writer and director of the library.

1971, Sept. 15
C327 AP105 7.50s brt bl & blk 50 18

25th World Weight Lifting Championships, Lima.

Flag, Family, Soldier's Head — AP106

1971, Oct. 4
C328 AP106 7.50s blk, lt bl & red 50 18
a. Souv. sheet of 1, imperf. 1.00 1.00

3rd anniversary of the revolution of the armed forces.

"Sacramento" AP107

1971, Oct. 8
C329 AP107 7.50s lt bl & dk bl 38 18

Sesquicentennial of Peruvian Navy.

Peruvian Order of the Sun — AP108

1971, Oct. 8
C330 AP108 7.50s multi 40 40

Sequicentennial of the Peruvian Order of the Sun.

Liberation Type of Regular Issue

Design: 50s, Detail from painting "Progress of Liberation," by Teodoro Nuñez Ureta.

1971, Nov. 4 Litho. *Perf. 13x13½*
C331 A217 50s multi 3.00 1.50

2nd Ministerial meeting of the "Group of 77."

Fair Emblem — AP109

1971, Nov. 12 *Perf. 13*

C332 AP109 4.50s multi 30 15

7th Pacific International Trade Fair.

Fish Type of Regular Issue

Fish: 3s, Pontinus furcirhinus dubius. 5.50s, Hogfish.

1972, Mar. 20 Litho. *Perf. 13x13½*

C333 A223 3s lt bl & multi 30 15
C334 A223 5.50s lt bl & multi 50 15
Set value 22

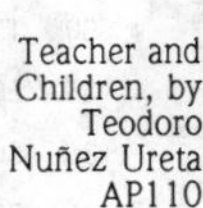

Teacher and Children, by Teodoro Nuñez Ureta AP110

1972, Apr. 10 Litho. *Perf. 13x13½*

C335 AP110 6.50s multi 50 16

Enactment of Education Reform Law.

White-tailed Trogon — AP111

1972, June 19 Litho. *Perf. 13½x13*

C336 AP111 2s shown 15 15
C337 AP111 2.50s Amazonian umbrella bird 18 15
C338 AP111 3s Peruvian cock-of-the-rock 22 15
C339 AP111 6.50s Cuvier's toucan 45 15
C340 AP111 8.50s Blue-crowned motmot 65 22
Nos. C336-C340 (5) 1.65
Set value 55

Quipu and Map of Americas — AP112

Inca Runner, Olympic Rings — AP113

1972, Aug. 21

C341 AP112 5s blk & multi 30 15

4th Interamerican Philatelic Exhibition, EXFILBRA, Rio de Janeiro, Aug. 26-Sept. 2.

1972, Aug. 28

C342 AP113 8s buff & multi 55 35

20th Olympic Games, Munich, Aug. 26-Sept. 11.

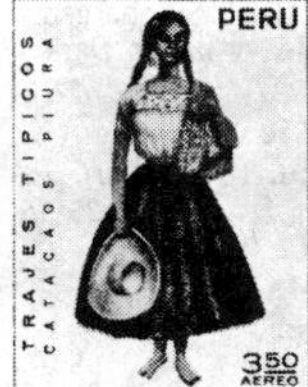

Woman of Catacaos, Piura — AP114

Funerary Tower, Sillustani, Puno — AP115

Regional Costumes: 2s, Tupe (Yauyos) woman of Lima. 4s, Indian with bow and arrow, from Conibo, Loreto. 4.50s, Man with calabash, Cajamarca. 5s, Moche woman, Trujillo. 6.50s, Man and woman of Ocongate, Cuzco. 8s, Chucupana woman, Ayacucho. 8.50s, Cotuncha woman, Junin. 10s, Woman of Puno dancing "Pandilla."

1972-73

C343 AP114 2s blk & multi 15 15
C344 AP114 3.50s blk & multi 30 30
C345 AP114 4s blk & multi 35 35
C346 AP114 4.50s blk & multi 40 40
C346A AP114 5s blk & multi 40 40
C347 AP114 6.50s blk & multi 50 50
C347A AP114 8s blk & multi 60 60
C347B AP114 8.50s blk & multi 65 65
C348 AP114 10s blk & multi 75 75
Nos. C343-C348 (9) 4.10 4.10

Issue dates: 3.50s, 4s and 6.50s, Sept. 29, 1972. 2s, 4.50s and 10s, Apr. 30, 1973. 5s, 8s and 8.50s, Oct. 15, 1973.

Perf. 13½x13, 13x13½

1972, Oct. 16 Litho.

Archaeological Monuments: 1.50s, Stone of the 12 angles, Cuzco. 3.50s, Ruins of Chavin, Ancash, horiz. 5s, Wall and gate, Chavin, Ancash, horiz. 8s, Ruins of Machu Picchu, horiz.

C349 AP115 1.50s multi 15 15
C350 AP115 3.50s multi 22 22
C351 AP115 4s multi 25 15
C352 AP115 5s multi 35 15
C353 AP115 8s multi 65 35
Nos. C349-C353 (5) 1.62 1.02

AP116

AP117

Designs: Inca ponchos, various textile designs.

1973, Jan. 29 Litho. *Perf. 13½x13*

C354 AP116 2s multi 15 15
C355 AP116 3.50s multi 20 15
C356 AP116 4s multi 20 15
C357 AP116 5s multi 25 20
C358 AP116 8s multi 50 25
Nos. C354-C358 (5) 1.30 90

1973, Mar. 19 Litho. *Perf. 13½x13*

Antique Jewelry: 1.50s, Goblets and Ring, Mochica, 10th cent. 2.50s, Golden hands and arms, Lambayeque, 12th cent. 4s, Gold male statuette, Mochica, 8th ceny. 5s, Two gold brooches, Nazca, 8th cent. 8s, Flayed puma, Mochica, 8th cent.

C359 AP117 1.50s multi 15 15
C360 AP117 2.50s multi 15 15
C361 AP117 4s multi 20 20
C362 AP117 5s multi 25 25
C363 AP117 8s multi 50 20
Nos. C359-C363 (5) 1.25 95

Andean Condor — AP118

Indian Guide, by José Sabogal — AP119

Protected Animals: 5s, Vicuña. 8s, Spectacled bear.

1973, Apr. 16 Litho. *Perf. 13½x13*

C364 AP118 4s blk & multi 20 15
C365 AP118 5s blk & multi 25 20
C366 AP118 8s blk & multi 42 20

See Nos. C372-C376, C411-C412.

1973, May 7 Litho. *Perf. 13½x13*

Peruvian Paintings: 8.50s, Portrait of a Lady, by Daniel Hernandez. 20s, Man Holding Figurine, by Francisco Laso.

C367 AP119 1.50s multi 15 15
C368 AP119 8.50s multi 38 30
C369 AP119 20s multi 90 50

Basket and World Map AP120

1973, May 26 *Perf. 13x13½*

C370 AP120 5s green 25 15
C371 AP120 20s lil rose 1.10 50

1st International Basketball Festival.

Darwin's Rhea — AP121

Orchid — AP122

1973, Sept. 3 Litho. *Perf. 13½x13*

C372 AP121 2.50s shown 20 20
C373 AP121 3.50s Giant otter 25 25
C374 AP121 6s Greater flamingo 40 40
C375 AP121 8.50s Bush dog, horiz. 55 55
C376 AP121 10s Chinchilla, horiz. 60 60
Nos. C372-C376 (5) 2.00 2.00

Protected animals.

1973, Sept. 27

Designs: Various orchids.

C377 AP122 1.50s blk & multi 15 15
C378 AP122 2.50s blk & multi 25 15
C379 AP122 3s blk & multi 30 20
C380 AP122 3.50s blk & multi 35 20
C381 AP122 8s blk & multi 75 20
Nos. C377-C381 (5) 1.80 90

Pacific Fair Emblem — AP123

1973, Nov. 14 Litho. *Perf. 13½x13*

C382 AP123 8s blk, red & gray 50 30

8th International Pacific Fair, Lima.

Cargo Ship ILO — AP124

Designs: 2.50s, Boats of Pescaperu fishing organization. 8s, Jet and seagull.

1973, Dec. 14 Litho. *Perf. 13*

C383 AP124 1.50s multi 15 15
C384 AP124 2.50s multi 30 30
C385 AP124 8s multi 60 16

Issued to promote government enterprises.

Lima Monument AP125

1973, Nov. 27 *Perf. 13*

C386 AP125 8.50s red & multi 50 16

50th anniversary of Air Force Academy. Monument honors Jorge Chavez, Peruvian aviator.

Bridge at Yananacu, by Enrique Camino Brant AP126

Paintings: 10c, Peruvian Birds, by Teodoro Nuñez Ureta, vert. 50s, Boats of Totora, by Jorge Vinatea Reinoso.

Perf. 13x13½, 13½x13

1973, Dec. 28

C387 AP126 8s multi 40 20
C388 AP126 10s multi 50 25
C389 AP126 50s multi 2.25 1.25

Moral House, Arequipa AP127

Landscapes: 2.50s, El Misti Mountain, Arequipa. 5s, Puya Raymondi (cacti), vert. 6s, Huascaran Mountain. 8s, Lake Querococha. Views on 5s, 6s, 8s are views in White Cordilleras Range, Ancash Province.

1974, Feb. 11

C390 AP127 1.50s multi 15 15
C391 AP127 2.50s multi 20 15
C392 AP127 5s multi 30 15
C393 AP127 6s multi 40 15
C394 AP127 8s multi 65 16
Nos. C390-C394 (5) 1.70
Set value 60

San Jeronimo's, Cuzco — AP128

Churches of Peru: 3.50s, Cajamarca Cathedral. 5s, San Pedro's, Zepita-Puno, horiz. 6s, Cuzco Cathedral. 8.50s, Santo Domingo, Cuzco.

1974, May 6

No.	Type	Denomination	Unused	Used
C395	AP128	1.50s multi	15	15
C396	AP128	3.50s multi	20	15
C397	AP128	5s multi	30	15
C398	AP128	6s multi	35	15
C399	AP128	8.50s multi	50	16
		Nos. C395-C399 (5)	1.50	
		Set value		60

Surrender at Ayacucho, by Daniel Hernandez AP129

Designs: 6s, Battle of Junin, by Felix Yañex. 7.50s, Battle of Ayachucho, by Felix Yañez.

1974 Litho. *Perf. 13x13½*

No.	Type	Denomination	Unused	Used
C400	AP129	3.50s multi	20	15
C401	AP129	6s multi	35	15
C402	AP129	7.50s multi	40	15
C403	AP129	8.50s multi	50	18
C404	AP129	10s multi	65	20
		Nos. C400-C404 (5)	2.10	
		Set value		70

Sesquicentennial of the Battles of Junin and Ayacucho and of the surrender at Ayacucho.

Issue dates: 7.50s, Aug. 6. 6s, Oct. 9. Others, Dec. 9.

Chavin Stone, Ancash AP130

Machu Picchu, Cuzco AP131

Designs: Nos. C407, C409, Different bas-reliefs from Chavin Stone. No. C408, Baths of Tampumacchay, Cuzco. No. C410, Ruins of Kencco, Cuzco.

Perf. 13½x13, 13x13½

1974, Mar. 25

No.	Type	Denomination	Unused	Used
C405	AP130	3s multi	20	15
C406	AP131	3s multi	20	15
C407	AP130	5s multi	30	15
C408	AP131	5s multi	30	15
C409	AP130	10s multi	60	20
C410	AP131	10s multi	60	20
		Nos. C405-C410 (6)	2.20	1.00

Cacajao Rubicundus AP132

1974, Oct. 21 *Perf. 13½x13*

No.	Type	Denomination	Unused	Used
C411	AP132	8s multi	40	25
C412	AP132	20s multi	1.00	40

Protected animals.

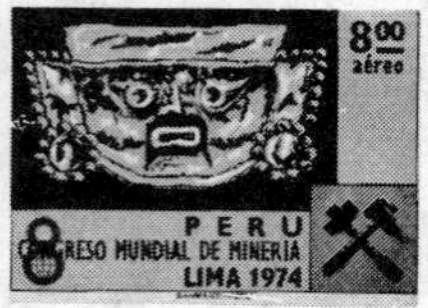

Inca Gold Mask AP133

1974, Nov. 8 *Perf. 13x13½*

No.	Type	Denomination	Unused	Used
C413	AP133	8s yel & multi	40	16

8th World Mining Congress, Lima.

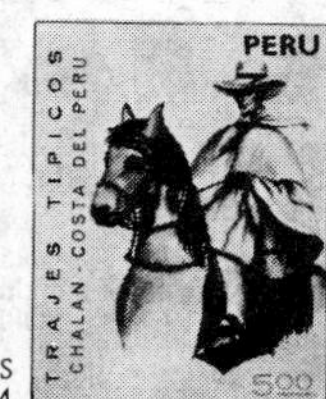

Chalan, Horseman's Cloak — AP134

1974, Nov. 11 Litho. *Perf. 13½x13*

No.	Type	Denomination	Unused	Used
C414	AP134	5s multi	25	15
C415	AP134	8.50s multi	50	25

Pedro Paulet and Aerial Torpedo AP135

1974, Nov. 28 Litho. *Perf. 13x13½*

No.	Type	Denomination	Unused	Used
C416	AP135	8s bl & vio	40	30

UPU, cent. Pedro Paulet, inventor of the mail-carrying aerial torpedo.

Christmas Type of 1974

Design: 6.50s, Indian Nativity scene.

1974, Dec. 20 *Perf. 13½x13*

No.	Type	Denomination	Unused	Used
C417	A235	6.50s multi	25	25

Andean Village, Map of South American West Coast AP136

1974, Dec. 30

No.	Type	Denomination	Unused	Used
C418	AP136	6.50s multi	35	25

Meeting of Communications Ministers of Andean Pact countries.

Map of Peru, Modern Buildings, UN Emblem — AP137

1975, Mar. 12 Litho. *Perf. 13x13*

No.	Type	Denomination	Unused	Used
C419	AP137	6s blk, gray & red	20	20

2nd United Nations Industrial Development Organization Conference, Lima.

Nos. C187, C211 and C160 Surcharged with New Value and Heavy Bar in Dark Blue

Wmk. 346

1975, April Litho. *Perf. 12*

No.	Type	Denomination	Unused	Used
C420	AP51	2s on 4.30s org	20	15

Perf. 13½x14, 13x14

Unwmk.

No.	Type	Denomination	Unused	Used
C421	AP51	2.50s on 4.60s org	25	15
C422	AP51	5s on 3.80s org	25	20

World Map and Peruvian Colors AP138

1975, Aug. 25 Litho. *Perf. 13x13½*

No.	Type	Denomination	Unused	Used
C423	AP138	6.50s lt bl, vio bl & red	25	20

Conference of Foreign Ministers of Nonaligned Countries.

Map of Peru and Flight Route AP139

1975, Oct. 23 Litho. *Perf. 13x13½*

No.	Type	Denomination	Unused	Used
C424	AP139	8s red, pink & blk	35	16

AeroPeru's first flights: Lima-Rio de Janeiro, Lima-Los Angeles.

Fair Poster — AP140

Col. Francisco Bolognesi — AP141

1975, Nov. 21 Litho. *Perf. 13½x13*

No.	Type	Denomination	Unused	Used
C425	AP140	6s blk, bis & red	50	25

9th International Pacific Fair, Lima, 1975.

1975, Dec. 23 Litho. *Perf. 13½x13*

No.	Type	Denomination	Unused	Used
C426	AP141	20s multi	80	50

160th birth anniv. of Col. Francisco Bolognesi.

Indian Mother and Child — AP142

Inca Messenger, UPAE Emblem — AP143

1976, Feb. 23 Litho. *Perf. 13½x13*

No.	Type	Denomination	Unused	Used
C427	AP142	6s gray & multi	35	25

Christmas 1975.

1976, Mar. 19 Litho. *Perf. 13½x13*

No.	Type	Denomination	Unused	Used
C428	AP143	5s red, blk & tan	40	25

11th Congress of the Postal Union of the Americas and Spain, UPAE.

Nos. C187, C211, C160, C209, C210 Surcharged in Dark Blue or Violet Blue (No Bar)

1976 As Before

No.	Type	Denomination	Unused	Used
C429	AP51	2s on 4.30s org	15	15
C430	AP51	3.50s on 4.60s org	16	15
C431	AP51	4.50s on 3.80s org	20	20
C432	AP51	5s on 4.30s org	25	20
C433	AP51	6s on 4.60s org	35	25
C434	A184	10s on 2.60s brt grn	50	20
C435	AP52	50s on 3.60s lil rose (VB)	2.00	1.75
		Nos. C429-C435 (7)	3.61	2.90

Stamps of 1962-67 Surcharged with New Value and Heavy Bar in Black, Red, Green, Dark Blue or Orange

1976-77 As Before

No.	Type	Denomination	Unused	Used
C436	AP52	1.50s on 3.60s (Bk) #C210	15	15
C437	A184	2s on 2.60s (R) #C209 ('77)	20	15
C438	AP52	2s on 3.60s (G) #C210	20	15
C439	AP80	2s on 4.30s (Bk) #C199	20	15
C440	A184	3s on 2.60s (Bk) #C209 ('77)	20	15
C441	A184	4s on 2.60s (DBl) #C209	25	15
C442	AP52	4s on 3.60s (DBl) #C210 ('77)	25	15
C443	AP51	5s on 4.30s (R) #C187	30	15
C444	AP83	6s on 4.60s (Bk) #C208 ('77)	35	20
C445	AP51	6s on 4.60s (DBl) #C211 ('77)	35	20
C446	AP51	7s on 4.30s (Bk) #C187 ('77)	25	20
C447	AP52	7.50s on 3.60s (DBl) #C210	45	25
C448	AP52	8s on 3.60s (O) #C210	50	16
C449	AP51	10s on 4.30s (Bk) #C187 ('77)	30	20
C450	AP51	10s on 4.60s (DBl) #C211	60	20
C451	AP86	24s on 3.60s (Bk) #C220 ('77)	1.75	60
C452	AP86	28s on 4.60s (Bk) #C221 ('77)	1.00	60
C453	AP86	32s on 5.60s (Bk) #C222 ('77)	1.00	60
C454	A184	50s on 2.60s (O) #C209 ('77)	2.50	1.00
C455	AP52	50s on 3.60s (G) #C210	2.00	1.25
		Nos. C436-C455 (20)	12.80	6.66

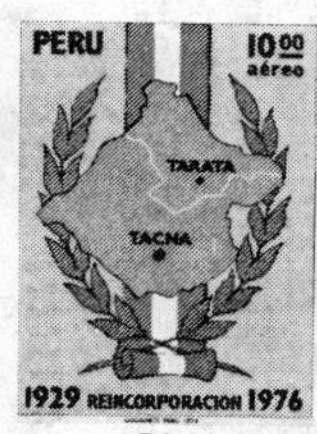

AP144

AP145

Map of Tacna and Tarata Provinces.

1976, Aug. 28 Litho. *Perf. 13½x13*

No.	Type	Denomination	Unused	Used
C456	AP144	10s multi	35	25

Re-incorporation of Tacna Province into Peru, 47th anniversary.

1976, Sept. 15 Litho. *Perf. 13½x13*

Investigative Police badge.

No.	Type	Denomination	Unused	Used
C457	AP145	20s multi	65	35

Investigative Police of Peru, 54th anniv.

AP146

AP147

"Declaration of Bogota."

1976, Sept. 22
C458 AP146 10s multi 35 25

Declaration of Bogota for cooperation and world peace, 10th anniversary.

1976, Nov. 2 Litho. *Perf. 13½x13*

Pal Losonczi and map of Hungary.

C459 AP147 7s ultra & blk 35 20

Visit of Pres. Pal Losonczi of Hungary, Oct. 1976.

Map of Amazon Basin, Colors of Peru and Brazil AP148

1976, Dec. 16 Litho. *Perf. 13*
C460 AP148 10s bl & multi 35 25

Visit of Gen. Ernesto Geisel, president of Brazil, Nov. 5, 1976.

Liberation Monument, Lima AP149

1977, Mar. 9 Litho. *Perf. 13x13½*
C461 AP149 20s red buff & blk 50 50

Army Day.

Map of Peru and Venezuela, South America AP150

1977, Mar. 14
C462 AP150 12s buff & multi 50 30

Meeting of Pres. Francisco Morales Bermudez Cerrutti of Peru and Pres. Carlos Andres Perez of Venezuela, Dec. 1976.

Electronic Tree — AP151

Map of Peru, Refinery, Tanker — AP152

1977, May 30 Litho. *Perf. 13½x13*
C463 AP151 20s gray, red & blk 65 35

World Telecommunications Day.

1977, July 13 Litho. *Perf. 13½x13*
C464 AP152 14s multi 42 30

Development of Bayovar oil complex.

Messenger Type of 1977

1977 Litho. *Perf. 13½x13*
C465 A243 24s mag & blk 65 40
C466 A243 28s bl & blk 1.40 50
C467 A243 32s rose brn & blk 80 60

Arms of Arequipa — AP153

Gen. Jorge Rafael Videla — AP154

1977, Sept. 3 Litho. *Perf. 13½x13*
C468 AP153 10s multi 20 15

Gold of Peru Exhibition, Arequipa 1977.

1977, Oct. 8 Litho. *Perf. 13½x13*
C469 AP154 36s multi 65 25

Visit of Jorge Rafael Videla, president of Argentina.

Stamps of 1953-67 Surcharged with New Value and Heavy Bar in Black, Dark Blue or Green

1977 As Before
C470 AP83 2s on 3.60s #C207 15 15
C471 AP51 2s on 4.60s (DB) #C211 15 15
C472 AP51 4s on 4.60s (DB) #C211 15 15
C473 AP51 5s on 4.30s #C187 35 15
C474 AP52 5s on 3.60s #C210 20 15
C475 AP55 10s on 2.15s #C125 40 20
C476 AP52 10s on 3.60s (DB) #C210 65 20
C477 AP84 10s on 3.60s #C215 50 20
C478 AP52 20s on 3.60s (DB) #C210 50 25
C479 AP51 100s on 3.80s (G) #C160 2.00 1.75
Nos. C470-C479 (10) 5.05 3.35

Nos. C223-C224 Surcharged with New Value, Heavy Bars and: "FRANQUEO"

1977 Litho. *Perf. 12*
C480 AP87 6s on 3.60s multi 40 30
C481 AP87 8s on 3.60s multi 50 35
C482 AP87 10s on 5.60s multi 50 40

Adm. Miguel Grau — AP155

1977, Dec. 15 Litho. *Perf. 13½x13*
C483 AP155 28s multi 38 25

Navy Day. Miguel Grau (1838-1879), Peruvian naval commander.

Christmas Type of 1977

1977, Dec. 23
C484 A246 20s Indian Nativity 50 20

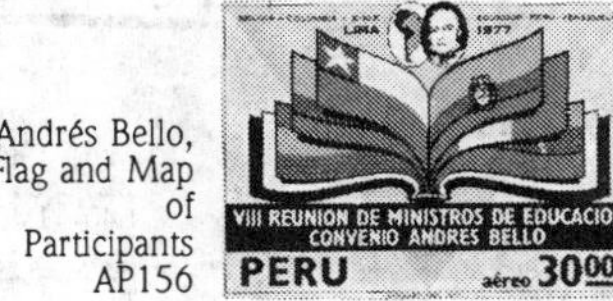

Andrés Bello, Flag and Map of Participants AP156

1978, Jan. 12 Litho. *Perf. 13*
C485 AP156 30s multi 40 30

8th Meeting of Education Ministers honoring Andrés Bello, Lima.

Inca Type of 1978

1978 Litho. *Perf. 13½x13*
C486 A247 24s dp rose lil 32 30
C487 A247 30s salmon 40 30
C488 A247 65s brt bl 90 65
C489 A247 95s dk bl 1.25 1.00

Antenna, ITU Emblem AP157

1978, July 3 Litho. *Perf. 13x13½*
C490 AP157 50s gray & multi 65 65

10th World Telecommunications Day.

San Martin, Flag Colors of Peru and Argentina — AP158

1978, Sept. 4 Litho. *Perf. 13½x13*
C491 AP158 30s multi 40 40

Gen. José de San Martin (1778-1850), soldier and statesman, protector of Peru.

Stamps of 1965-67 Surcharged "Habilitado / R.D. No. O118" and New Value in Red, Green, Violet Blue or Black

1978 Litho.
C492 AP83 34s on 4.60s multi (R) #C208 30 25
C493 AP79 40s on 4.30s multi (G) #C196 35 30
C494 A184 70s on 2.60s brt grn (VB) #C209 60 50
C495 AP52 110s on 3.60s lil rose (Bk) #C210 90 75
C496 AP80 265s on 4.30s gray & multi (Bk) #C199 2.25 2.00
Nos. C492-C496 (5) 4.40 3.80

Stamps and Type of 1968-78 Surcharged in Violet Blue, Black or Red

1978 Litho.
C497 AP86 25s on 4.60s (VB) #C221 25 25
C498 A247 45s on 28s dk grn (Bk) 40 22
C499 A247 75s on 28s dk grn (R) 65 40
C500 AP86 105s on 5.60s (R) #C222 1.25 1.00

Nos. C498-C499 not issued without surcharge.

Nos. C486, C467 Surcharged

1980, Apr. 14 Litho. *Perf. 13½x13*
C501 A247 35s on 24s dp rose lil 30 25
C502 A243 45s on 32s rose brn & blk 40 30

No. C130 Surcharged in Black

1981, Nov. Engr. *Perf. 13*
C503 AP57 30s on 2.20s multi 30 30
C504 AP57 40s on 2.20s multi 30 25

No. C130 Surcharged and Overprinted in Green: "12 Feria / Internacional / del / Pacifico 1981"

1981, Nov. 30
C505 AP57 140s on 2.20s multi 1.10 75

12th Intl. Pacific Fair.

AIR POST SEMI-POSTAL STAMPS

Catalogue values for unused stamps in this section are for Never Hinged items.

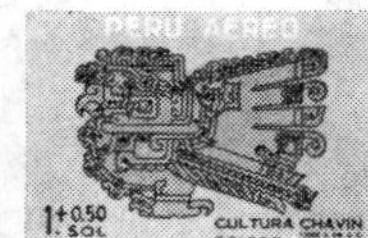

Chavin Griffin — SPAP1

Designs: 1.50s+1s, Bird. 3s+2.50s, Cat. 4.30s+3s, Mythological figure, vert. 6s+ 4s, Chavin god, vert.

Perf. 12½x12, 12x12½

1963, Apr. 18 Litho. Wmk. 346

Design in Gray and Brown

CB1 SPAP1 1s + 50c sal pink 20 20
CB2 SPAP1 1.50s + 1s blue 20 20
CB3 SPAP1 3s + 2.50s lt grn 50 50
CB4 SPAP1 4.30s + 3s green 80 80
CB5 SPAP1 6s + 4s citron 1.00 1.00
Nos. CB1-CB5 (5) 2.70 2.70

The designs are from ceramics found by archaeological excavations of the 14th century Chavin culture. The surtax was for the excavations fund.

Henri Dunant and Centenary Emblem — SPAP2

Perf. 12½x12

1964, Jan. 29 Unwmk.
CB6 SPAP2 1.30s + 70c multi 16 16
CB7 SPAP2 4.30s + 1.70s multi 42 42

Centenary of International Red Cross.

SPECIAL DELIVERY STAMPS

Regular Issue of 1900 Overprinted in Black

1908 Unwmk. *Perf. 12*
E1 A25 10c gray black 20.00 15.00

Regular Issue of 1907 Overprinted in Violet

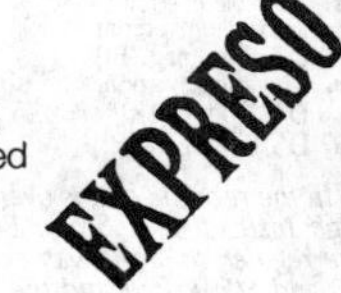

1909
E2 A40 10c red brn & blk 25.00 14.00

Regular Issue of 1909 Handstamped in Violet

EXPRESO

1910
E3 A49 10c deep blue 14.00 12.00

Two handstamps were used to make No. E2. Impressions from them measure 22½x6½mm and 24x6½mm.

Counterfeits exist of Nos. E1-3.

POSTAGE DUE STAMPS

Coat of Arms — D1

Steamship and Llama
D2 D3

D4 D5

1874-86 Unwmk. Engr. *Perf. 12*
With Grill

J1	D1	1c bister ('79)	25	15
J2	D2	5c vermilion	30	16
J3	D3	10c orange	35	25
J4	D4	20c blue	60	35
J5	D5	50c brown	9.00	3.50

A 2c green exists, but was not regularly issued.

For overprints and surcharges see Nos. J6-J31, J37-J38, 8N14-8N15, 14N18.

1886

Without Grill

J1a	D1	1c bister	15
J2a	D2	5c vermilion	15
J3a	D3	10c orange	20
J4a	D4	20c blue	35
J5a	D5	50c brown	3.50

Nos. J1-J5 Overprinted in Blue or Red

1881

"PLATA" 2 1/2mm High

J6	D1	1c bis (Bl)	3.50	2.50
J7	D2	5c ver (Bl)	6.50	6.00
a.		Double overprint		
b.		Inverted overprint	17.00	17.00
J8	D3	10c org (Bl)	6.50	6.50
a.		Inverted overprint	17.00	17.00
J9	D4	20c bl (R)	25.00	20.00
J10	D5	50c brn (Bl)	55.00	50.00

In the reprints of this overprint "PLATA" is 3mm high instead of 2 1/2mm. Besides being struck in the regular colors it was also applied to the 1, 5, 10 and 50c in red and the 20c in blue.

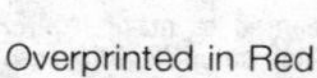

Overprinted in Red

1881

J11	D1	1c bister	5.00	5.00
J12	D2	5c vermilion	6.50	6.00
J13	D3	10c orange	8.00	6.50
J14	D4	20c blue	25.00	20.00
J15	D5	50c brown	80.00	65.00

Originals of Nos. J11 to J15 are overprinted in brick-red, oily ink; reprints in thicker, bright red ink. The 5c exists with reprinted overprint in blue.

Overprinted "Union Postal Universal Lima Plata", in Oval in first named color and Triangle in second named color

1883

J16	D1	1c bis (Bl & Bk)	5.00	3.50
J17	D1	1c bis (Bk & Bl)	7.50	7.00
J18	D2	5c ver (Bl & Bk)	7.50	7.00
J19	D3	10c org (Bl & Bk)	7.50	6.00
J20	D4	20c bl (R & Bk)	*450.00*	*450.00*
J21	D5	50c brn (Bl & Bk)	55.00	42.50

Reprints of Nos. J16 to J21 have the oval overprint with "PLATA" 3mm. high. The 1c also exists with the oval overprint in red.

Overprinted in Black

1884

J22	D1	1c bister	50	50
J23	D2	5c vermilion	50	50
J24	D3	10c orange	50	50
J25	D4	20c blue	1.00	50
J26	D5	50c brown	3.00	90
		Nos. J22-J26 (5)	5.50	2.90

The triangular overprint is found in 11 types.

Overprinted "Lima Correos" in Circle in Red and Triangle in Black

1884

J27	D1	1c bister	12.50	11.00

Reprints of No. J27 have the overprint in bright red. At the time they were made the overprint was also printed on the 5, 10, 20 and 50c Postage Due stamps.

Postage Due stamps overprinted with Sun and "CORREOS LIMA" (as shown above No. 103), alone or in combination with the "U. P. U. LIMA" oval or "LIMA CORREOS" in double-lined circle, are fancy varieties made to sell to collectors and never placed in use.

Overprinted

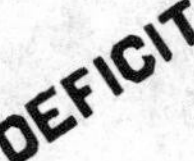

1896-97

J28	D1	1c bister	35	30
a.		Double overprint		
J29	D2	5c vermilion	45	25
a.		Double overprint		
b.		Inverted overprint		
J30	D3	10c orange	55	35
a.		Inverted overprint		
J31	D4	20c blue	65	50
a.		Double overprint		
J32	A22	50c red ('97)	75	50
J33	A23	1s brn ('97)	1.00	65
a.		Double overprint		
b.		Inverted overprint		
		Nos. J28-J33 (6)	3.75	2.55

Liberty — D6

1899 Engr.

J34	D6	5s yel grn	1.00	*5.00*
J35	D6	10s dl vio	900.00	900.00

For surcharge see No. J39.

DÉFICIT

UN CENTAVO **DEFICIT CINCO CENTAVOS**

1902

On No. 159

J36	A31	5c on 10s bl grn	1.00	80
a.		Double surcharge	12.00	12.00

On No. J4

J37	D4	1c on 20c blue	50	40
a.		"DEFICIT" omitted	6.50	2.00
b.		"DEFICIT" double	6.50	2.00
c.		"UN CENTAVO" double	6.00	2.00
d.		"UN CENTAVO" omitted	8.25	6.00

Surcharged Vertically

J38	D4	5c on 20c blue	1.50	1.00

On No. J35

J39	D6	1c on 10s dull vio	60	50

D7

1909 Engr. *Perf. 12*

J40	D7	1c red brown	50	15
J41	D7	5c red brown	50	15
J42	D7	10c red brown	60	16
J43	D7	50c red brown	90	20

1921

Size: 18 1/4x22mm

J44	D7	1c violet brown	25	16
J45	D7	2c violet brown	25	20
J46	D7	5c violet brown	35	20
J47	D7	10c violet brown	50	25
J48	D7	50c violet brown	1.65	75
J49	D7	1s violet brown	7.50	3.00
J50	D7	2s violet brown	12.00	3.50
		Nos. J44-J50 (7)	22.50	8.06

Nos. J49 and J50 have the circle at the center replaced by a shield containing "S/.", in addition to the numeral.

In 1929 during a shortage of regular postage stamps, some of the Postage Due stamps of 1921 were used instead.

See Nos. J50A-J52, J55-J56. For surcharges see Nos. 204-207, 757.

Type of 1909-22

Size: 18 3/4x23mm

J50A	D7	2c violet brown	75	16
J50B	D7	10c violet brown	75	16

Type of 1909-22 Issues

1932 Photo. *Perf. 14 1/2x14*

J51	D7	2c violet brown	75	25
J52	D7	10c violet brown	75	25

Regular Stamps of 1934-35 Overprinted in Black **"Deficit"**

1935 *Perf. 13*

J53	A131	2c deep claret	75	50
J54	A117	10c crimson	75	50

Type of 1909-32
Size: 19x23mm
Imprint: "Waterlow & Sons, Limited, Londres."

1936 Engr. *Perf. 12 1/2*

J55	D7	2c light brown	15	15
J56	D7	10c gray green	50	50

OFFICIAL STAMPS

Regular Issue of 1886 Overprinted in Red

a

1890, Feb. 2

O2	A17	1c dl vio	1.40	1.40
a.		Double overprint	8.25	8.25
O3	A18	2c green	1.40	1.40
a.		Double overprint		
b.		Inverted overprint	8.25	8.25
O4	A19	5c orange	2.00	1.65
a.		Inverted overprint	8.25	8.25
b.		Double overprint	8.25	8.25
O5	A20	10c slate	1.00	65
a.		Double overprint	8.25	8.25
b.		Inverted overprint	8.25	8.25
O6	A21	20c blue	3.00	2.00
a.		Double overprint	8.25	8.25
b.		Inverted overprint	8.25	8.25
O7	A22	50c red	4.00	2.00
a.		Inverted overprint	12.00	
b.		Double overprint		
O8	A23	1s brown	5.00	4.50
a.		Double overprint	17.00	17.00
b.		Inverted overprint	17.00	17.00

Nos. 118-124 (Bermudez Ovpt.) Overprinted Type "a" in Red

1894, Oct.

O9	A17	1c green	1.40	1.40
a.		"Gobierno" and head invtd.	6.50	5.50
b.		Dbl. ovpt. of "Gobierno"		
O10	A17	1c orange	22.50	20.00
O11	A18	2c rose	1.40	1.40
a.		Overprinted head inverted	10.00	10.00
b.		Both overprints inverted		
O12	A18	2c violet	1.40	1.40
a.		"Gobierno" double		
O13	A19	5c ultra	22.50	20.00
a.		Both overprints inverted		
O14	A19	5c blue	10.00	9.00
O15	A20	10c green	3.50	3.50
O16	A22	50c green	5.00	5.00

Nos. 125-126 ("Horseshoe" Ovpt.) Overprinted Type "a" in Red

O17	A18	2c vermilion	2.00	2.00
O18	A19	5c blue	2.00	2.00

Nos. 105, 107, 109, 113 Overprinted Type "a" in Red

1895, May

O19	A17	1c vermilion	8.25	8.25
O20	A18	2c dp ultra	8.25	8.25
O21	A12	5c claret	6.50	6.50
O22	A14	20c dp ultra	6.50	6.50

Nos. O2-O22 have been extensively counterfeited.

Nos. 141, 148, 149, 151 Overprinted in Black

1896-1901

O23	A24	1c ultra	15	15
O24	A25	10c yellow	1.00	50
a.		Double overprint		
O25	A25	10c gray blk ('01)	15	15
O26	A26	50c brt rose	40	25

O1

1909-14 Engr. *Perf. 12*

Size: 18 1/2x22mm

O27	O1	1c red	20	15
a.		1c brown red	20	15
O28	O1	1c orange ('14)	50	35
O29	O1	10c bis brn ('14)	20	15
a.		10c violet brown	20	15
O30	O1	50c ol grn ('14)	65	35
a.		50c blue green	1.00	35

Size: 18 3/4x23 1/2mm

O30B	O1	10c vio brn	50	16
		Nos. O27-O30B (5)	2.05	
		Set value		1.00

See Nos. O31, O33-O34. For overprints and surcharge see Nos. 201-203, 760.

1933 Photo. *Perf. 15x14*

O31	O1	10c violet brown	50	15

No. 319 Overprinted in Black **"Servicio Oficial"**

1935 Unwmk. *Perf. 13*

O32	A117	10c crimson	20	20

Type of 1909-33
Imprint: "Waterlow & Sons, Limited, Londres."

1936 Engr. *Perf. 12 1/2*

Size: 19x23mm

O33	O1	10c light brown	15	15
O34	O1	50c gray green	35	35

PARCEL POST STAMPS

PP1

PP2

PP3

1897 Typeset Unwmk. *Perf. 12*

Q1 PP1 1c dull lilac 2.25 1.90
Q2 PP2 2c bister 2.50 2.25
  a. 2c olive 2.50 2.25
  b. 2c yellow 2.50 2.25
  c. Laid paper 65.00 65.00
Q3 PP2 5c dk bl 10.00 6.50
  a. Tête bêche pair *375.00*
Q4 PP3 10c vio brn 14.00 10.00
Q5 PP3 20c rose red 17.00 14.00
Q6 PP3 50c bl grn 45.00 37.50
  Nos. Q1-Q6 (6) 90.75 72.15

Surcharged in Black **UN CENTAVO**

1903-04

Q7 PP3 1c on 20c rose red 12.00 10.00
Q8 PP3 1c on 50c bl grn 12.00 10.00
Q9 PP3 5c on 10c vio brn 80.00 65.00
  a. Inverted surcharge 120.00 110.00
  b. Double surcharge

POSTAL TAX STAMPS

Plebiscite Issues

These stamps were not used in Tacna and Arica (which were under Chilean occupation) but were used in Peru to pay a supplementary tax on letters, etc.

It was intended that the money derived from the sale of these stamps should be used to help defray the expenses of the plebiscite.

Morro Arica — PT1

Adm. Grau and Col. Bolognesi Reviewing Troops PT2

Bolognesi Monument — PT3

1925-26 Unwmk. Litho. *Perf. 12*

RA1 PT1 5c dp bl 1.50 35
RA2 PT1 5c rose red 80 22
RA3 PT1 5c yel grn 70 22
RA4 PT2 10c brown 3.00 80
RA5 PT3 50c bl grn 19.00 9.00
  Nos. RA1-RA5 (5) 25.00 10.59

PT4

1926

RA6 PT4 2c orange 30 15

PT5

1927-28

RA7 PT5 2c dp org 60 15
RA8 PT5 2c red brn 60 15
RA9 PT5 2c dk bl 60 15
RA10 PT5 2c gray vio 40 15
RA11 PT5 2c bl grn ('28) 40 15
RA12 PT5 20c red 2.50 1.00
  Nos. RA7-RA12 (6) 5.10 1.75

PT6

1928 Engr.

RA13 PT6 2c dk vio 20 15

The use of the Plebiscite stamps was discontinued July 26, 1929, after the settlement of the Tacna-Arica controversy with Chile.

For overprint see No. 261.

Unemployment Fund Issues

These stamps were required in addition to the ordinary postage, on every letter or piece of postal matter. The money obtained by their sale was to assist the unemployed.

Nos. 273-275 Surcharged **Habilitada Pro Desocupados 2 Cts.**

1931

RA14 A95 2c on 4c red 65 50
  a. Inverted surcharge 3.50 3.50
RA15 A95 2c on 10c bl grn 50 50
  a. Inverted surcharge 3.50 3.50
RA16 A95 2c on 15c sl gray 50 50
  a. Inverted surcharge 3.50 3.50

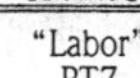

"Labor" PT7

Blacksmith PT8

Two types of Nos. RA17-RA18:
I - Imprint 15mm.
II - Imprint 13¾mm.

Perf. 12x11½, 11½x12

1931-32 Litho.

RA17 PT7 2c emer (I) 15 15
  a. Type II 15
RA18 PT7 2c rose car (I) ('32) 15 15
  a. Type II 15
  Set value 20 15

1932-34

RA19 PT8 2c dp gray 15 15
RA20 PT8 2c pur ('34) 15 15
  Set value 20 15

Monument of 2nd of May — PT9

Perf. 13, 13½, 13x13½

1933-35 Photo.

RA21 PT9 2c bl vio 20 15
RA22 PT9 2c org ('34) 20 15
RA23 PT9 2c brn vio ('35) 20 15
  Set value 18

For overprint see No. RA27.

No. 307 Overprinted in Black

a **Pro-Desocupados**

1934 *Perf. 13½*

RA24 A111 2c green 15 15
  a. Inverted overprint 2.00 2.00

No. 339 Overprinted in Black **Pro Desocupados**

1935

RA25 A131 2c deep claret 15 15

No. 339 Overprinted Type "a" in Black

1936 Unwmk. *Perf. 13½*

RA26 A131 2c deep claret 15 15

No. RA23 Overprinted in Black **"Ley 8310"**

1936 *Perf. 13x13½*

RA27 PT9 2c brn vio 15 15
  a. Double overprint 1.40
  b. Overprint reading down 1.40
  c. Overprint double, reading down 1.40

St. Rosa of Lima — PT10

"Protection" by John Q. A. Ward — PT11

1937 Engr. *Perf. 12*

RA28 PT10 2c car rose 15 15

Nos. RA27 and RA28 represented a tax to help erect a church.

Imprint: "American Bank Note Company"

1938 Litho.

RA29 PT11 2c brown 20 15

The tax was to help the unemployed.

See Nos. RA30, RA34, RA40. For surcharges see Nos. 501A, 674-678, 681-682, 709-711, 757.

Type of 1938 Redrawn
Imprint: "Columbian Bank Note Company."

1943 *Perf. 12½*

RA30 PT11 2c dl claret brn 20 15

See note above No. RA14. See Nos. RA34, RA40.

Catalogue values for unused stamps in this section, from this point to the end of the section, are for Never Hinged items.

PT12

PT13

1949 *Perf. 12½, 12*

Black Surcharge

RA31 PT12 3c on 4c vio bl 55 15
RA32 PT13 3c on 10c blue 55 15
  Set value 16

The tax was for an education fund.

Symbolical of Education PT14

Emblem of Congress PT15

1950 Typo. *Perf. 14*

Size: 16½x21mm

RA33 PT14 3c dp car 15 15

See Nos. RA35, RA39, RA43

For surcharges see Nos. 501B, 761, 764-766, RA45-RA48, RA58.

Type of 1938
Imprint: "Thomas De La Rue & Co. Ltd."

1951 Litho.

RA34 PT11 2c lt redsh brn 15 15

Type of 1950
Imprint: "Thomas De La Rue & Company, Limited."

1952 Unwmk. *Perf. 14, 13*

Size: 16½x21½mm

RA35 PT14 3c brn car 20 15

1954 *Rouletted 13*

RA36 PT15 5c bl & red 22 15

The tax was to help finance the National Marian Eucharistic Congress.

For surcharges see Nos. 758B, 768.

Piura Arms and Congress Emblem — PT16

1960 Litho. *Perf. 10½*

RA37 PT16 10c ultra, red, grn & yel 18 15
  a. Green ribbon inverted
RA38 PT16 10c ultra & red 25 15
  Set value 15

Nos. RA37-RA38 were used to help finance the 6th National Eucharistic Congress, Piura, Aug. 25-28. Obligatory on all domestic mail until Dec. 31, 1960. Both stamps exist imperf.

Type of 1950
Imprint: "Bundesdruckerei Berlin"

1961 *Perf. 14*

Size: 17½x22½mm

RA39 PT14 3c dp car 15 15

Type of 1938
Imprint: "Harrison and Sons Ltd"

1962, Apr. **Litho.** ***Perf. 14x14½***
RA40 PT11 2c lt brn 15 15

Symbol of Eucharist — PT17

1962, May 8 ***Rouletted 11***
RA41 PT17 10c bl & org 15 15

Issued to raise funds for the Seventh National Eucharistic Congress, Huancayo, 1964. Obligatory on all domestic mail.
See No. RA42. For surcharges and overprint see Nos. 735, 762, RA44.

1962
Imprint: "Iberia"
RA42 PT17 10c bl & org 15 15

Type of 1950
1965, Apr. **Litho.** ***Perf. 12½x12***
Imprint: "Thomas de La Rue"
Size: 18x22mm
RA43 PT14 3c light carmine 20 15

Type of 1962 Overprinted in Red with three "X," Bars and: "Periodista / Peruano / LEY / 16078"

1966, July 2 **Litho.** ***Pin Perf.***
Imprint: "Iberia"
RA44 PT17 10c vio & org 15 15

No. RA43 Surcharged in Green or Black

b	c
HABILITADO "Fondo del Periodista Peruano" Ley 16078 S/o. 0.10	Habilitado «Fondo del Periodista Peruano» Ley 16078 S/. 0.10

d
HABILITADO "Fondo del Periodista Peruano" Ley 16078 S/o. 0.10

1966-67 ***Perf. 12x12½***

RA45 PT14 (b) 10c on 3c (G)	80	15
RA46 PT14 (c) 10c on 3c (Bk)	80	15
RA47 PT14 (c) 10c on 3c (G)	20	15
RA48 PT14 (d) 10c on 3c (G)	25	15
Set value		46

The surtax of Nos. RA44-RA48 was for the Peruvian Journalists' Fund.

Pen Made of Newspaper
PT18

Temple at Chan-Chan
PT19

1967, Dec. **Litho.** ***Perf. 11***
RA49 PT18 10c dk red & blk 15 15

The surtax was for the Peruvian Journalists' fund.
For surcharges see Nos. RA56-RA57.

1967, Dec. 27

Designs: No. RA51, Side view of temple. Nos. RA52-RA55, Various stone bas-reliefs from Chan-Chan.

RA50 PT19 20c bl & grn	15	15
RA51 PT19 20c multi	15	15
RA52 PT19 20c brt bl & blk	15	15
RA53 PT19 20c emer & blk	15	15
RA54 PT19 20c sep & blk	15	15
RA55 PT19 20c lil rose & blk	15	15
Set value	42	30

The surtax was for the excavations at Chan-Chan, northern coast of Peru. (Mochica-Chimu pre-Inca period).

Type of 1967 Surcharged in Red: "VEINTE / CENTAVOS / R.S. 16-8-68"

Designs: No. RA56, Handshake. No. RA57, Globe and pen.

1968, Oct. **Litho.** ***Perf. 11***
RA56 PT18 20c on 50c multi 50 50
RA57 PT18 20c on 1s multi 50 50

Nos. RA56-RA57 without surcharge were not obligatory tax stamps.
No. C199 surcharged "PRO NAVIDAD/ Veinte Centavos/R.S. 5-11-68" was not a compulsory postal tax stamp.

#RA43 Surchd. Similar to Type "c"
1968, Oct. ***Perf. 12½x12***
RA58 PT14 20c on 3c lt car 15 15

Surcharge lacks quotation marks and 4th line reads: Ley 17050.

OCCUPATION STAMPS

Issued under Chilean Occupation

Stamps formerly listed as Nos. N1-N10 are regular issues of Chile canceled in Peru.

Stamps of Peru, 1874-80, Overprinted in Red, Blue or Black

1881-82 ***Perf. 12***

N11 A17 1c org (Bl)	50	1.00
a. Inverted overprint		
N12 A18 2c dk vio (Bk)	50	4.00
a. Inverted overprint	16.50	
b. Double overprint	22.50	
N13 A18 2c rose (Bk)	1.65	*18.00*
a. Inverted overprint		
N14 A19 5c bl (R)	55.00	62.50
a. Inverted overprint		
N15 A19 5c ultra (R)	90.00	100.00
N16 A20 10c grn (R)	50	*1.65*
a. Inverted overprint	6.50	6.50
b. Double overprint	12.00	12.00
N17 A21 20c brn red (Bl)	80.00	120.00

Reprints of No. N17 have the overprint in bright blue; on the originals it is in dull ultramarine. Nos. N11 and N12 exist with reprinted overprint in red or yellow. There are numerous counterfeits with the overprint in both correct and fancy colors.

Same, with Additional Overprint in Black

1882

N19 A17 1c grn (R)	50	80
a. Arms inverted	8.25	10.00
b. Arms double	5.50	6.50
c. Horseshoe inverted	12.00	13.50
N20 A19 5c bl (R)	80	80
a. Arms inverted	13.50	15.00
b. Arms double	13.50	15.00
N21 A22 50c rose (Bk)	1.65	2.00
a. Arms inverted	10.00	
N22 A22 50c rose (Bl)	1.65	2.75
N23 A23 1s ultra (R)	3.25	4.50
a. Arms inverted	13.50	
b. Horseshoe inverted	16.50	
c. Arms and horseshoe inverted	20.00	
d. Arms double	13.50	
Nos. N19-N23 (5)	7.85	10.85

PROVISIONAL ISSUES

Stamps Issued in Various Cities of Peru during the Chilean Occupation of Lima and Callao

During the Chilean-Peruvian War which took place in 1879 to 1882, the Chilean forces occupied the two largest cities in Peru, Lima & Callao. As these cities were the source of supply of postage stamps, Peruvians in other sections of the country were left without stamps and were forced to the expedient of making provisional issues from whatever material was at hand. Many of these were former canceling devices made over for this purpose. Counterfeits exist of many of the overprinted stamps.

ANCACHS

(See Note under "Provisional Issues")

Regular Issue of Peru, Overprinted in Manuscript in Black
Alerta

1884 **Unwmk.** ***Perf. 12***
1N1 A19 5c blue 57.50 55.00

Regular Issues of Peru, Overprinted in Black

Overprinted **FRANCA**

1N2 A19 5c blue 18.00 16.50

Overprinted

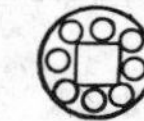

1N3 A19 5c blue	90.00	82.50
1N4 A20 10c green	55.00	40.00
1N5 A20 10c slate	55.00	35.00

Same, with Additional Overprint "FRANCA"
1N6 A20 10c green 82.50 42.50

Overprinted

1N7 A19 5c blue	30.00	25.00
1N8 A20 10c green	30.00	25.00

Same, with Additional Overprint "FRANCA"
1N9 A20 10c green

A1

Revenue Stamp of Peru, 1878-79, Overprinted in Black "CORREO Y FISCAL" and "FRANCA"
1N10 A1 10c yellow 37.50 37.50

APURIMAC

(See Note under "Provisional Issues")

Provisional Issue of Arequipa Overprinted in Black

ADMON. PRAL. DE
CORREOS DEL DEPTO DE
APURIMAC
ABANCAY

Overprint Covers Two Stamps
1885 **Unwmk.** ***Imperf.***
2N1 A6 10c gray 100.00 90.00

Some experts question the status of No. 2N1.

AREQUIPA

(See Note under "Provisional Issues")

Coat of Arms
A1 A2

Overprint ("PROVISIONAL 1881-1882") in Black

1881, Jan. **Unwmk.** ***Imperf.***

3N1 A1 10c blue	2.50	3.50
a. 10c ultramarine	2.50	4.00
b. Double overprint	12.00	13.50
c. Overprinted on back of stamp	8.25	10.00
3N2 A2 25c rose	2.50	6.00
a. "2" in upper left corner invtd.	8.25	
b. "Cevtavos"	8.25	10.00
c. Double overprint	12.00	13.50

The overprint also exists on 5s yellow.
The overprints "1883" in large figures or "Habilitado 1883" are fraudulent.
For overprints see Nos. 3N3, 4N1, 8N1, 10N1, 15N1-15N3.

With Additional Overprint Handstamped in Red

1881, Feb.
3N3 A1 10c blue 3.50 3.50
a. 10c ultramarine 13.50 8.25

A4

1883 **Litho.**
3N7 A4 10c dull rose 3.50 5.00
a. 10c vermilion 3.50 5.00

Overprinted in Blue like No. 3N3
3N9 A4 10c vermilion 5.00 4.00
a. 10c dull rose 5.00 4.00

See No. 3N10. For overprints see Nos. 8N2, 8N9, 10N2, 15N4.
Reprints of No. 3N9 are in different colors from the originals, orange, bright red, etc. They are printed in sheets of 20 instead of 25.

Redrawn
3N10 A4 10c brick red (Bl) 165.00

The redrawn stamp has small triangles without arabesques in the lower spandrels. The palm branch at left of the shield and other parts of the design have been redrawn.

Same Overprint in Black, Violet or Magenta On Regular Issues of Peru

1884 **Embossed with Grill** ***Perf. 12***

3N11 A17 1c org (Bk, V or M)	6.50	6.50
3N12 A18 2c dk vio (Bk)	6.50	6.50
3N13 A19 5c bl (Bk, V or M)	2.00	1.35
a. 5c ultramarine (Bk or M)	8.25	6.50
3N15 A20 10c sl (Bk)	3.50	2.50
3N16 A21 20c brn red (Bk, V or M)	25.00	25.00
3N18 A22 50c grn (Bk or V)	25.00	25.00
3N20 A23 1s rose (Bk or V)	35.00	35.00

A5

A6

Rear Admiral M. L. Grau
A7

Col. Francisco Bolognesi
A8

Same Overprint as on Previous Issues

1885 *Imperf.*

3N22 A5 5c olive (Bk) 5.25 5.25
3N23 A6 10c gray (Bk) 5.25 4.75
3N25 A7 5c blue (Bk) 5.25 4.75
3N26 A8 10c olive (Bk) 5.25 3.25

For overprints see Nos. 2N1, 8N5-8N6, 8N12-8N13, 10N9, 10N12, 15N10-15N12.

These stamps have been reprinted without overprint; they exist however with forged overprint. Originals are on thicker paper with distinct mesh, reprints on paper without mesh.

Without Overprint

3N22a A5 5c olive 5.25 5.25
3N23a A6 10c gray 4.00 3.25
3N25a A7 5c blue 4.00 3.25
3N26a A8 10c olive 4.00 3.25

AYACUCHO

(See Note under "Provisional Issues")

Provisional Issue of Arequipa Overprinted in Black

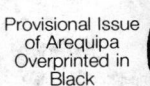

1881 **Unwmk.** *Imperf.*

4N1 A1 10c blue 82.50 70.00
a. 10c ultramarine 82.50 70.00

CHACHAPOYAS

(See Note under "Provisional Issues")

Regular Issue of Peru Overprinted in Black

1884 **Unwmk.** *Perf. 12*

5N1 A19 5c ultra 100.00 90.00

CHALA

(See Note under "Provisional Issues")

Regular Issues of Peru Overprinted in Black

1884 **Unwmk.** *Perf. 12*

6N1 A19 5c blue 8.25 6.50
6N2 A20 10c slate 10.00 8.25

CHICLAYO

(See Note under "Provisional Issues")

Regular Issue of Peru Overprinted in Black

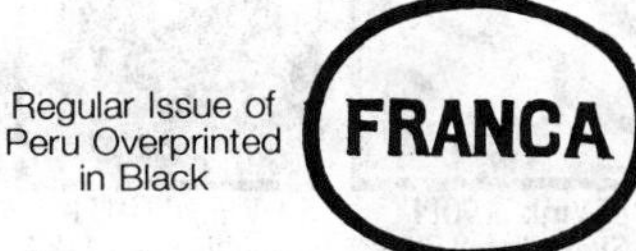

1884 **Unwmk.** *Perf. 12*

7N1 A19 5c blue 16.50 10.00

Same, Overprinted **FRANCA**

7N2 A19 5c blue 35.00 22.50

CUZCO

(See Note under "Provisional Issues")

Provisional Issues of Arequipa Overprinted in Black

1881-85 **Unwmk.** *Imperf.*

8N1 A1 10c blue 70.00 60.00
8N2 A4 10c red 70.00 60.00

Overprinted "CUZCO" in an oval of dots

8N5 A5 5c olive 110.00 100.00
8N6 A6 10c gray 80.00 75.00

Regular Issue of Peru Overprinted in Black "CUZCO" in a Circle

Perf. 12

8N7 A19 5c blue 50.00 50.00

Provisional Issues of Arequipa Overprinted in Black

1883 *Imperf.*

8N9 A4 10c red 10.00 10.00

Same Overprint in Black on Regular Issues of Peru

1884 *Perf. 12*

8N10 A19 5c blue 16.50 10.00
8N11 A20 10c slate 16.50 10.00

Same Overprint in Black on Provisional Issues of Arequipa

Imperf

8N12 A5 5c olive 27.50 27.50
8N13 A6 10c gray 8.00 8.00

Postage Due Stamps of Peru Surcharged in Black

Perf. 12

8N14 D1 10c on 1c bis 110.00 100.00
8N15 D3 10c on 10c org 110.00 100.00

HUACHO

(See Note under "Provisional Issues")

Regular Issues of Peru Overprinted in Black

1884 **Unwmk.** *Perf. 12*

9N1 A19 5c blue 8.00 8.00
9N2 A20 10c green 6.00 6.00
9N3 A20 10c slate 16.50 16.50

MOQUEGUA

(See Note under "Provisional Issues")

Provisional Issues of Arequipa Overprinted in Violet

Overprint 27mm wide (illustration reduced).

1881-83 **Unwmk.** *Imperf.*

10N1 A1 10c blue 42.50 40.00
10N2 A4 10c red ('83) 42.50 40.00

Same Overprint on Regular Issues of Peru in Violet

1884 *Perf. 12*

10N3 A17 1c orange 42.50 40.00
10N4 A19 5c blue 37.50 30.00

Red Overprint

10N5 A19 5c blue 30.00 20.00

Same Overprint in Violet on Provisional Issues of Peru of 1880

Perf. 12

10N6 A17 1c grn (R) 8.25 6.50
10N7 A18 2c rose (Bl) 10.00 10.00
10N8 A19 5c bl (R) 20.00 20.00

Same Overprint in Violet on Provisional Issue of Arequipa

1885 *Imperf.*

10N9 A6 10c gray 57.50 50.00

Regular Issues of Peru Overprinted in Violet **MOQUEA.**

Perf. 12

10N10 A19 5c blue 110.00 65.00
10N11 A20 10c slate 45.00 25.00

Same Overprint in Violet on Provisional Issue of Arequipa

Imperf

10N12 A6 10c gray 70.00 65.00

PAITA

(See Note under "Provisional Issues")

Regular Issues of Peru Overprinted

Black Overprint

1884 **Unwmk.** *Perf. 12*

11N1 A19 5c blue 22.50 22.50
a. 5c ultramarine
11N2 A20 10c green 15.00 15.00
11N3 A20 10c slate 22.50 22.50

Red Overprint

11N4 A19 5c blue 22.50 22.50

Overprint lacks ornaments on Nos. 11N4-11N5.

Violet Overprint. Letters 5 ½mm High

11N5 A19 5c ultra 22.50 22.50
a. 5c blue

PASCO

(See Note under "Provisional Issues")

Regular Issues of Peru Overprinted in Magenta or Black

1884 **Unwmk.** *Perf. 12*

12N1 A19 5c blue (M) 16.50 12.00
a. 5c ultramarine (M) 22.50 22.50
12N2 A20 10c green (Bk) 35.00 30.00
12N3 A20 10c slate (Bk) 65.00 57.50

PISCO

(See Note under "Provisional Issues")

Regular Issue of Peru Overprinted in Black

1884 **Unwmk.** *Perf. 12*

13N1 A19 5c blue 190.00 165.00

PIURA

(See Note under "Provisional Issues")

Regular Issues of Peru Overprinted in Black **PIURA**

1884 **Unwmk.** *Perf. 12*

14N1 A19 5c blue 20.00 10.00
a. 5c ultramarine 25.00 13.50
14N2 A21 20c brn red 82.50 82.50
14N3 A22 50c green 200.00 200.00

Same Overprint in Black on Provisional Issues of Peru of 1881

14N4 A17 1c grn (R) 22.50 22.50
14N5 A18 2c rose (Bl) 40.00 40.00
14N6 A19 5c ultra (R) 50.00 50.00

Regular Issues of Peru Overprinted in Violet, Black or Blue **PIURA**

14N7 A19 5c bl (V) 16.50 10.00
a. 5c ultramarine (V) 16.50 10.00
b. 5c ultramarine (Bk) 16.50 10.00
14N8 A21 20c brn red (Bk) 82.50 82.50
14N9 A21 20c brn red (Bl) 82.50 82.50

Same Overprint in Black on Provisional Issues of Peru of 1881

14N10 A17 1c grn (R) 20.00 20.00
14N11 A19 5c bl (R) 22.50 22.50
a. 5c ultramarine (R) 40.00 40.00

Regular Issues of Peru Overprinted in Black

14N13 A19 5c blue 4.00 3.50
14N14 A21 20c brn red 82.50 82.50

Regular Issues of Peru Overprinted in Black

14N15 A19 5c ultra 70.00 65.00
14N16 A21 20c brn red 135.00 120.00

Same Overprint on Postage Due Stamp of Peru

14N18 D3 10c orange 80.00 67.50

PUNO

(See Note under "Provisional Issues")

Provisional Issue of Arequipa Overprinted in Violet or Blue

Diameter of outer circle 20½mm, PUNO 11½mm wide, M 3½mm wide.

Other types of this overprint are fraudulent.

1882-83	**Unwmk.**		***Imperf.***
15N1 A1 10c blue (V)		16.50	16.50
a. 10c ultramarine (V)		20.00	20.00
15N3 A2 25c red (V)		25.00	20.00
15N4 A4 10c dl rose (Bl)		25.00	25.00
a. 10c vermilion (Bl)		25.00	25.00

The overprint also exists on 5s yellow of Arequipa.

Same Overprint in Magenta on Regular Issues of Peru

1884			***Perf. 12***
15N5 A17 1c orange		12.00	12.00
15N6 A18 2c violet		35.00	35.00
15N7 A19 5c blue		8.25	8.25

Violet Overprint

15N8 A19 5c blue		8.25	8.25
a. 5c ultramarine		12.00	12.00

Same Overprint in Black on Provisional Issues of Arequipa

1885			***Imperf.***
15N10 A5 5c olive		16.50	13.50
15N11 A6 10c gray		5.50	5.50
15N12 A8 10c olive		10.00	10.00

Regular Issues of Peru Overprinted in Magenta

1884			***Perf. 12***
15N13 A17 1c orange		10.00	8.25
15N14 A18 2c violet		13.50	12.00
15N15 A19 5c blue		5.50	5.50
a. 5c ultramarine		11.00	11.00
15N16 A20 10c green			
15N17 A21 20c brn red		82.50	82.50
15N18 A22 50c green			

YCA

(See Note under "Provisional Issues")

Regular Issues of Peru Overprinted in Violet

1884	**Unwmk.**		***Perf. 12***
16N1 A17 1c orange		40.00	40.00
16N3 A19 5c blue		12.00	6.75

Black Overprint

16N5 A19 5c blue		10.00	5.25

Magenta Overprint

16N6 A19 5c blue		10.00	5.25
16N7 A20 10c slate		30.00	30.00

Regular Issues of Peru Overprinted in Black

16N12 A19 5c blue		150.00	135.00
16N13 A21 20c brown		190.00	165.00

Regular Issues of Peru Overprinted in Carmine

16N14 A19 5c blue		150.00	135.00
16N15 A20 10c slate		190.00	165.00

Same, with Additional Overprint

16N21 A19 5c blue		165.00	150.00
16N22 A21 20c brn red		250.00	225.00

Various other stamps exist with the overprints "YCA" and "YCA VAPOR" but they are not known to have been issued. Some of them were made to fill a dealer's order and others are reprints or merely cancellations.

PHILIPPINES

LOCATION — Group of about 7,100 islands and islets in the Malay Archipelago, north of Borneo, in the North Pacific Ocean

GOVT. — Republic

AREA — 115,830 sq. mi.

POP. — 53,350,000 (est. 1984)

CAPITAL — Quezon City

The islands were ceded to the United States by Spain in 1898. On November 15, 1935, they were given their independence, subject to a transition period which ended July 4, 1946. On that date the Commonwealth became the Republic of the Philippines.

20 Cuartos = 1 Real
100 Centavos de Peso = 1 Peso (1864)
100 Centimos de Escudo = 1 Escudo (1871)
100 Centimos de Peseta = 1 Peseta (1872)
1000 Milesimas de Peso = 100 Centimos or Centavos = 1 Peso (1878)
100 Cents = 1 Dollar (1899)
100 Centavos = 1 Peso (1906)
100 Centavos (Sentimos) = 1 Peso (Piso) (1946)

Catalogue values for unused stamps in this country are for Never Hinged items, beginning with Scott 500 in the regular postage section, Scott B1 in the semi-postal section, Scott C64 in the air post section, Scott E11 in the special delivery section, Scott J23 in the postage due section, and Scott O50 in the officials section.

Values of early Philippine stamps vary according to condition. Quotations for Nos. 1-32 are for fine copies. Very fine to superb specimens sell at much higher prices, and inferior or poor copies sell at reduced prices, depending on the condition of the individual specimen.

Watermarks

Wmk. 104- Loops

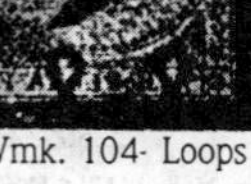
Wmk. 257- Curved Wavy Lines

Wmk. 190PI- Single-lined PIPS

Wmk. 191PI- Double-lined PIPS

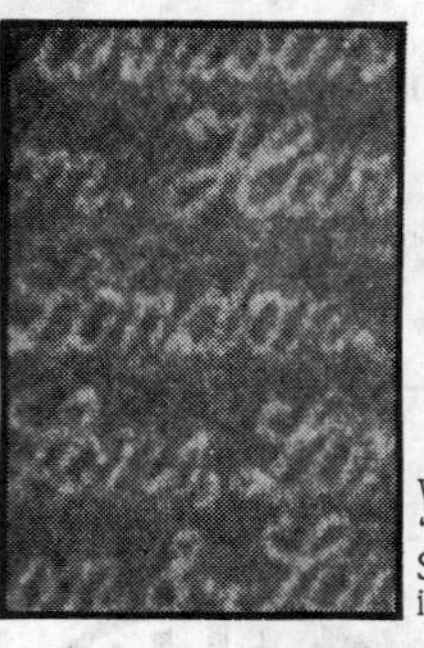
Wmk. 233- "Harrison & Sons, London." in Script

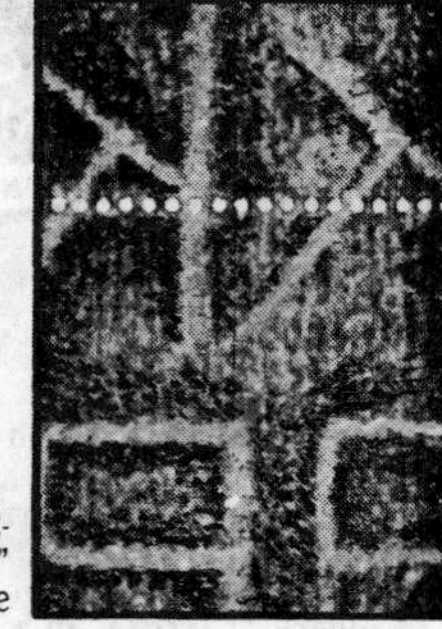
Wmk. 372- "K" and "P" Multiple

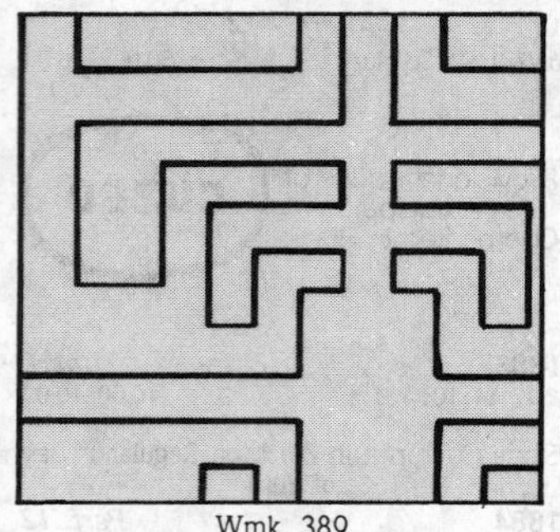
Wmk. 389

Wmk. 391- Natl. Crest, Rising Sun and Eagle

Issued under Spanish Dominion

The stamps of Philippine Islands punched with a round hole had been withdrawn from use and punched to indicate that they were no longer available for postage. In this condition they sell for only a trifle, as compared to postally used copies.

Queen Isabella II
A1 A2

1854	**Unwmk.**	**Engr.**	***Imperf.***
1 A1 5c orange		1,000.	150.00
a. 5c brown orange		1,100.	175.00
2 A1 10c carmine		300.00	110.00
a. 10c pale rose		425.00	175.00
4 A2 1r slate blue		300.00	140.00
a. 1r blue		375.00	190.00
b. 1r ultramarine		375.00	190.00
c. "CORROS"		*2,500.*	*1,500.*
5 A2 2r green		400.00	125.00
a. 2r yellow green		400.00	150.00

Forty varieties of each value.

For overprints see Nos. 25-25A.

A3

1855			**Litho.**
6 A3 5c pale vermilion		1,200.	275.00

Four varieties.

Redrawn

7 A3 5c vermilion		*8,000.*	*850.00*

In the redrawn stamp the inner circle is smaller and is not broken by the labels at top and bottom. Only one variety.

Queen Isabella II
A4 A5

1856	**Wmk. 104**		**Typo.**
8 A4 1r green, *blue*			85.00
9 A4 2r carmine, *blue*			80.00

Nos. 8 and 9 can be distinguished from the Cuban stamps of 1855 only by the cancellations.

For overprints see Nos. 26-27.

1859, Jan. 1	**Litho.**		**Unwmk.**
10 A5 5c vermilion		10.00	6.00
a. 5c scarlet		14.00	7.00
b. 5c orange		25.00	11.00
11 A5 10c rose		10.00	6.00

Four varieties of each value.

For overprint see No. 28.

Dot after CORREOS
A6 A7

1861-62			
12 A6 5c vermilion		15.00	7.75
13 A7 5c dull red ('62)		20.00	8.75

For overprint see No. 29.

Colon after CORREOS — A8

A8a

A9

A10

1863

14	A8	5c vermilion	8.00	6.50
15	A8	10c carmine	15.00	14.00
16	A8	1r violet	300.00	175.00
17	A8	2r blue	250.00	150.00
18	A8a	1r gray grn	85.00	65.00
20	A9	1r green	55.00	25.00
a.		1r emerald	37.50	25.00

No. 18 has "CORREOS" 10 1/2mm long, the point of the bust is rounded and is about 1mm from the circle which contains 94 pearls.

No. 20 has "CORREOS" 11mm long, and the bust ends in a sharp point which nearly touches the circle of 76 pearls.

For overprints see Nos. 30-34.

1864 **Typo.**

21	A10	3 1/8c blk, *buff*	2.00	1.25
22	A10	6 2/8c grn, *rose*	2.00	75
23	A10	12 4/8c blue, *sal*	4.50	75
24	A10	25c red, *buff*	4.50	2.50

For overprints see Nos. 35-38.

Preceding Issues Handstamped **HABILITADO POR LA NACION**

1868-74

25	A2	1r sl bl ('74)	*1,900.*	*800.00*
25A	A2	2r grn ('74)	*3,500.*	*775.00*
26	A4	1r grn, *bl* ('73)	120.00	55.00
27	A4	2r car, *bl* ('73)	165.00	50.00
28	A5	10c rose ('74)	50.00	35.00
29	A7	5c red ('73)	60.00	30.00
30	A8	5c ver ('72)	45.00	25.00
31	A8	1r vio ('72)	400.00	250.00
32	A8	2r bl ('72)	400.00	225.00
33	A8a	1r gray grn ('71)	42.50	15.00
34	A9	1r emer ('71)	8.00	3.00
35	A10	3 1/8c blk, *buff*	6.50	3.00
36	A10	6 2/8c grn, *rose*	6.00	3.00
37	A10	12 4/8c bl, *salmon*	25.00	12.00
38	A10	25c ver, *buff*	13.50	8.00

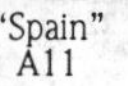
"Spain"
A11

King Amadeo
A12

1871 **Typo.** ***Perf. 14***

39	A11	5c blue	20.00	2.00
40	A11	10c deep green	5.00	2.00
41	A11	20c brown	25.00	10.00
42	A11	40c rose	35.00	6.50

1872

43	A12	12c rose	6.50	2.00
a.		Imperf.	40.00	
44	A12	16c blue	45.00	12.00
a.		16c ultramarine	65.00	40.00
45	A12	25c gray lilac	6.50	1.50
a.		25c lilac	11.00	6.50
46	A12	62c violet	15.00	3.00
47	A12	1p25c yel brn	30.00	8.00

"Peace"
A13

King Alfonso XII
A14

1874

48	A13	12c gray lilac	7.00	2.00
49	A13	25c ultra	2.50	75
50	A13	62c rose	22.50	2.00
51	A13	1p25c brown	85.00	15.00
a.		Imperf.	200.00	

1876-77

52	A14	2c rose	1.50	40
53	A14	2c dk bl ('77)	80.00	42.50
54	A14	6c org ('77)	6.00	1.50
55	A14	10c blue ('77)	2.50	50
56	A14	12c lilac	2.50	50
57	A14	20c vio brn	7.00	2.00
58	A14	25c dp grn	6.00	50

Imperforates of type A14 probably are from proof or trial sheets.

Nos. 52, 63 Handstamp Surcharged in Black or Blue

HABILITADO 12 C.S P.TA

1877-79

59	A14	12c on 2c rose (Bk)	27.50	8.25
60	A16	12c on 25m blk (Bk) ('79)	35.00	11.00
61	A16	12c on 25m blk (Bl) ('79)	110.00	77.50

Surcharge exists inverted and double.

A16

1878-79 **Typo.**

62	A16	0.0625 (62 1/2m) gray	25.00	5.00
62A	A16	0.0625 (62 1/2m) lil	25.00	5.00
63	A16	25m black	2.00	30
64	A16	25m grn ('79)	32.50	10.00
65	A16	50m dl lil	12.00	4.00
66	A16	100m car ('79)	45.00	15.00
67	A16	100m yel grn ('79)	4.50	1.50
68	A16	125m blue	3.00	35
69	A16	200m rose ('79)	12.00	4.00
70	A16	200m vio rose ('79)	120.00	60.00
71	A16	250m bis ('79)	5.00	1.00

Imperforates of type A16 probably are from proof or trial sheets.

For surcharges see Nos. 60-61, 72-75.

Stamps of 1878-79 Surcharged:

UNIVERSAL DE CONVENIO CORREOS HABILITADO 2 cént de peso
a

UNIVERSAL DE CONVENIO CORREOS HABILITADO 2 cént de peso
b

1879

72	A16 (a)	2c on 25m grn	27.50	5.50
a.		Double surcharge		
73	A16 (a)	8c on 100m car	27.50	5.50
a.		"COREROS"	65.00	50.00
74	A16 (b)	2c on 25m grn	65.00	19.00
75	A16 (b)	8c on 100m car	65.00	19.00

Inverts exist.

A19

Original state: The medallion is surrounded by a heavy line of color of nearly even thickness, touching the line below "Filipinas"; the opening in the hair above the temple is narrow and pointed.

1st retouch: The line around the medallion is thin, except at the upper right, and does not touch the horizontal line above it; the opening in the hair is slightly wider and rounded; the lock of hair above the forehead is shaped like a broad "V" and ends in a point; there is a faint white line below it, which is not found on the original. The shape of the hair and the width of the white line vary.

2nd retouch: The lock of hair is less pointed; the white line is much broader.

1880-86 **Typo.**

76	A19	2c rose	38	18
77	A19	2 1/2c brown	2.25	18
78	A19	2 4/8c ultra ('82)	32	18
79	A19	2 4/8c ultra, 1st retouch ('83)	28	18
80	A19	2 4/8c ultra, 2nd retouch ('86)	3.75	38
81	A19	5c gray ('82)	28	18
a.		5c gray blue	38	20
82	A19	6 2/8c dp grn ('82)	1.75	90
83	A19	8c yel brn	7.00	1.40
84	A19	10c green	175.00	100.00
85	A19	10c brn lil ('82)	1.25	22
a.		10c brown violet	2.00	1.00
86	A19	12 4/8c brt rose ('82)	65	22
87	A19	20c bis brn ('82)	1.25	22
88	A19	25c dk brn ('82)	1.90	22

See #137-139. For surcharges see #89-106.

Stamps and Type of 1880-86 Handstamp Surcharged in Black, Green or Red:

c

d

e

HABILITADO U. POSTAL UN CENTO
f

1881-88

Black Surcharge

89	A19 (c)	2c on 2 1/2c brn	2.75	1.10
91	A19 (f)	10c on 2 4/8c ultra (#80) ('87)	4.50	1.10
92	A19 (d)	20c on 8c brn ('83)	6.50	1.90
93	A19 (d)	1r on 2c car ('83)	32.50	18.00
94	A19 (d)	2r on 2 4/8c ultra ('83)	4.50	1.10

Green Surcharge

95	A19 (e)	8c on 2c car ('83)	4.50	1.65
96	A19 (d)	10c on 2c car ('83)	3.25	1.65
97	A19 (d)	1r on 2c car ('83)	65.00	22.50
98	A19 (d)	1r on 5c gray bl ('83)	4.50	1.65
99	A19 (d)	1r on 8c brn ('83)	5.50	1.65

Red Surcharge

100	A19 (f)	1c on 2 4/8c ultra (#79) ('87)	65	45
101	A19 (f)	1c on 2 4/8c ultra (#80) ('87)	2.00	1.00
102	A19 (d)	16c on 2 4/8c ultra ('83)	5.50	1.65
103	A19 (d)	1r on 2c car ('83)	4.50	1.65
104	A19 (d)	1r on 5c bl gray ('83)	12.50	3.50

Surcharges exist double or inverted on many of Nos. 89-104.

Handstamp Surcharged in Magenta

g

h

1887

105	A19 (g)	8c on 2 4/8c (#79)	60	30
106	A19 (g)	8c on 2 4/8c (#80)	65	65

1888

107	A19 (h)	2 4/8c on 1c gray grn	80	55
108	A19 (h)	2 4/8c on 5c bl gray	1.00	40
109	N1 (h)	2 4/8c on 1/8c grn	35	15
110	A19 (h)	2 4/8c on 50m bis	1.40	65
111	A19 (h)	2 4/8c on 10c grn	1.00	40

No. 109 is surcharged on a newspaper stamp of 1886-89 and has the inscriptions shown on cut N1.

On Revenue Stamps

R1

R2

R3

Handstamp Surcharged in Black, Yellow, Green, Red or Magenta:

j

HABILITADO CORREOS 6 2/8 CENS.
k

HABILITADO PARA CORREOS
m

1881-88

Black Surcharge

112	R1 (c)	2c on 10c bis	14.00	9.00
113	R1 (j)	2 4/8c on 10c bis	1.50	60
114	R1 (j)	2 4/8c on 2r bl	140.00	60.00
115	R1 (j)	8c on 10c bis	140.00	65.00
116	R1 (j)	8c on 2r bl	5.50	1.50
118	R1 (d)	1r on 12 4/8c gray bl ('83)	4.50	2.50

119 R1 (d) 1r on 10c bis ('82) 5.00 2.50

Yellow Surcharge

120 R2 (e) 2c on 200m grn ('82) 3.75 1.50
121 R1 (d) 16c on 2r bl ('83) 3.00 1.90

Green Surcharge

122 R1 (d) 1r on 10c bis ('83) 8.00 2.00

Red Surcharge

123 R1(d+e) 2r on 8c on 2r blue 25.00 10.00
a. On 8c on 2r blue (d+d)
124 R1(d) 1r on 12⁴/₈c gray bl ('83) 3.50 2.00
125 R1(k) 6²/₈c on 12⁴/₈c gray bl ('85) 3.50 1.65
126 R3(d) 1r on 10p bis ('83) 30.00 19.00
127 R1(m) 1r green 65.00 50.00
127A R1(m) 2r blue 140.00 80.00
128 R2(d) 1r on 1p grn ('83) 17.50 12.00
129 R2(d) 1r on 200m grn ('83) 55.00 30.00

Magenta Surcharge

130 R2(h) 2⁴/₈c on 200m grn ('88) 2.00 1.00
131 R2(h) 2⁴/₈c on 20c brn ('88) 8.00 4.00

On Telegraph Stamps

T1

T2

Surcharged in Red, or Black

1883-88

132 T1 (d) 2r on 250m ultra (R) 5.00 2.50
133 T1 (d) 20c on 250m ultra
134 T1 (d) 2r on 250m ultra 7.00 3.75
135 T1 (d) 1r on 20c on 250m ultra (R & Bk) 5.00 2.50

Magenta Surcharge

136 T2 (h) 2⁴/₈c on 1c bis ('88) 60 40

Most, if not all, copies of No. 133 are remainders with a punched hole.

Type of 1880-86 Redrawn

1887-88

137 A19 50m bister 50 25
138 A19 1c yel grn ('88) 50 20
139 A19 6c yel brn ('88) 7.00 1.50

King Alfonso XIII — A36

1890-97 **Typo.**

140 A36 1c violet ('92) 50 20
141 A36 1c rose ('95) 3.00 1.25
142 A36 1c bl grn ('96) 1.50 40
143 A36 1c claret ('97) 10.00 2.50
144 A36 2c claret 15 15
145 A36 2c violet ('92) 20 15
146 A36 2c dk brn ('94) 15 15
147 A36 2c ultra ('96) 25 25
148 A36 2c gray brn ('96) 15 15
149 A36 2⁴/₈c dl bl 30 15
150 A36 2⁴/₈c ol gray ('92) 20 15
151 A36 5c dk bl 30 15
152 A36 5c dk ol gray 60 20
153 A36 5c green ('92) 25 20
155 A36 5c vio brn ('96) 5.00 1.90
156 A36 5c bl grn ('96) 3.00 1.00
157 A36 6c brn vio ('92) 20 15
158 A36 6c red org ('94) 50 25
159 A36 6c car rose ('96) 3.00 1.50
160 A36 8c yel grn 15 15
161 A36 8c ultra ('92) 50 20
162 A36 8c red brn ('94) 25 15
163 A36 10c bl grn 1.00 15
164 A36 10c pale cl ('91) 60 15
165 A36 10c claret ('92) 25 15
166 A36 10c yel brn ('96) 25 15
167 A36 12⁴/₈c yel grn 20 15
168 A36 12⁴/₈c orange ('92) 60 15
169 A36 15c red brn ('92) 60 20
170 A36 15c rose ('94) 60 25
171 A36 15c bl grn ('96) 1.50 1.00
172 A36 20c rose 30.00 12.00
173 A36 20c salmon ('91) 8.00 2.50
174 A36 20c gray brn ('92) 1.50 25
175 A36 20c dk vio ('94) 3.00 1.20
176 A36 20c orange ('96) 2.25 1.00
177 A36 25c brown 3.75 1.00
178 A36 25c dl bl ('91) 1.50 20
179 A36 40c dk vio ('97) 9.00 2.50
180 A36 80c claret ('97) 16.50 5.50

The 5c lilac is a perforated proof. Many of Nos. 140-180 exist imperf.

Stamps of Previous Issues Handstamp Surcharged in Blue, Red, Black or Violet

1897

Blue Surcharge

181 A36 5c on 5c green 1.40 80
182 A36 15c on 15c red brn 1.65 80
183 A36 20c on 20c gray brn 5.00

Red Surcharge

185 A36 5c on 5c grn 1.65 1.00

Black Surcharge

187 A36 5c on 5c grn 16.00
188 A36 15c on 15c rose 2.25 1.40
189 A36 20c on 20c dk vio 13.00 7.75
190 A36 20c on 25c brn 7.00

Violet Surcharge

191 A36 15c on 15c rose 3.00 2.00

Inverted, double and other variations of this surcharge exist.

The 5c on 5c blue gray was released during US Administration. The surcharge is a mixture of red and black inks.

Impressions in violet black are believed to be reprints. The following varieties are known: 5c on 5c blue green, 15c on 15c rose, 15c on 15c red brown, 20c on 20c gray brown, 20c on 20c dark violet, 20c on 25c brown. These surcharges are to be found double, inverted, etc.

King Alfonso XIII — A39

1898 **Typo.**

192 A39 1m orange brn 15 15
193 A39 2m orange brn 15 15
194 A39 3m orange brn 15 15
195 A39 4m orange brn 1.75 65
196 A39 5m orange brn 15 15
197 A39 1c black vio 15 15
198 A39 2c dk bl grn 15 15
199 A39 3c dk brown 15 15
200 A39 4c orange 3.75
201 A39 5c car rose 15 15
202 A39 6c dk blue 40 25
203 A39 8c gray brn 20 15
204 A39 10c vermilion 60 40
205 A39 15c dull ol grn 60 35
206 A39 20c maroon 60 40
207 A39 40c violet 40 35
208 A39 60c black 1.75 90
209 A39 80c red brown 1.75 90
210 A39 1p yel green 4.00 2.75
211 A39 2p slate bl 8.00 3.00

Nos. 192-211 exist imperf. Value $1,000.

Issued under US Administration

Regular Issues of the United States Overprinted in Black

On US No. 260

1899-1900 **Unwmk.** ***Perf. 12***

212 A96 50c orange 375.00 225.00

On US Nos. 279, 279d, 267, 268, 281, 282C, 283, 284, 275 and 275a

Wmk. 191

213 A87 1c yel grn 2.50 50
a. Inverted overprint
214 A88 2c org red, III 90 50
a. 2c car, type III 1.50 75
b. Booklet pane of 6 ('00) 250.00 *90.00*
215 A89 3c purple 5.00 1.00
216 A91 5c blue 4.50 75
a. Inverted overprint *3,750.*
217 A94 10c brown, I 17.50 3.50
217A A94 10c org brn, II 200.00 25.00
218 A95 15c olive grn 30.00 7.00
219 A96 50c orange 110.00 30.00
a. 50c red orange *200.00*
Nos. 213-219 (8) 370.40 68.25

On US Nos. 280b, 282 and 272

1901

220 A90 4c orange brn 17.50 4.00
221 A92 6c lake 22.50 6.00
222 A93 8c violet brn 22.50 6.00

On US Nos. 276, 276A, 277a and 278

Red Overprint

223 A97 $1 blk, type I 425.00 240.00
223A A97 $1 blk, type II 2,250. 675.00
224 A98 $2 dk blue 475.00 250.00
225 A99 $5 dk green 850.00 575.00

On US Nos. 300-313 and shades

1903-04

226 A115 1c blue grn 3.50 25
227 A116 2c carmine 6.00 90
228 A117 3c brt vio 60.00 11.00
229 A118 4c brown ('04) 60.00 17.50
a. 4c orange brown 60.00 15.00
230 A119 5c blue 9.00 75
231 A120 6c brnsh lake ('04) 65.00 15.00
232 A121 8c vio blk ('04) 40.00 10.00
233 A122 10c pale red brn ('04) 20.00 1.75
a. 10c red brown 25.00 2.50
b. Pair, one without ovpt. *1,350.*
234 A123 13c pur blk 25.00 12.50
a. 13c brown violet 25.00 12.50
235 A124 15c olive grn 50.00 10.00
236 A125 50c orange 115.00 30.00
Nos. 226-236 (11) 453.50 *109.65*

Red Overprint

237 A126 $1 black 450.00 250.00
238 A127 $2 dk bl ('04) 1,000. 750.00
239 A128 $5 dk grn ('04) 1,250. 825.00

On US Nos. 319, 319c in Black

1904

240 A129 2c carmine 5.00 2.00
a. Booklet pane of 6 *1,000.*
b. 2c scarlet 5.75 2.50

José Rizal
A40

Arms of Manila
A41

Designs: 4c, McKinley. 6c, Magellan. 8c, Miguel Lopez de Legaspi. 10c, Gen. Henry W. Lawton. 12c, Lincoln. 16c, Adm. William T. Sampson. 20c, Washington. 26c, Francisco Carriedo. 30c, Franklin.

Each Inscribed "Philippine Islands / United States of America"

Wmk. 191PI

1906, Sept. 8 **Engr.** ***Perf. 12***

241 A40 2c dp green 20 15
a. 2c yellow green ('10) 35 15
b. Booklet pane of 6 275.00
242 A40 4c carmine 25 15
a. 4c carmine lake ('10) 50 15
b. Booklet pane of 6 400.00
243 A40 6c violet 1.00 15
244 A40 8c brown 2.00 50
245 A40 10c blue 1.50 15
246 A40 12c brown lake 4.00 1.50
247 A40 16c violet blk 3.00 16
248 A40 20c orange brn 3.25 25
249 A40 26c violet brn 5.00 1.65
250 A40 30c olive grn 4.00 1.10
251 A41 1p orange 22.50 5.50
252 A41 2p black 27.50 1.00
253 A41 4p dk blue 85.00 12.00
254 A41 10p dk green 175.00 55.00
Nos. 241-254 (14) 334.20 79.26

See Nos. 255-304, 326-353. For surcharges see Nos. 368-369, 450. For overprints see Nos. C1-C28, C36-C46, C54-C57, O5-O14.

Change of Colors

1909-13 ***Perf. 12***

255 A40 12c red org 7.00 2.00
256 A40 16c olive grn 2.75 50
257 A40 20c yellow 6.00 1.00
258 A40 26c blue grn 1.25 55
259 A40 30c ultra 8.00 2.50
260 A41 1p pale vio 24.00 4.00
260A A41 2p vio brn ('13) 65.00 2.00
Nos. 255-260A (7) 114.00 12.55

1911 **Wmk. 190PI** ***Perf. 12***

261 A40 2c green 50 15
a. Booklet pane of 6 350.00
262 A40 4c car lake 2.00 15
a. 4c carmine
b. Booklet pane of 6 350.00
263 A40 6c dp vio 1.50 15
264 A40 8c brown 6.50 35
265 A40 10c blue 2.50 15
266 A40 12c orange 2.00 35
267 A40 16c olive grn 2.00 15
268 A40 20c yellow 1.65 15
a. 20c orange 1.65 15
269 A40 26c blue grn 2.25 20
270 A40 30c ultra 2.75 35
271 A41 1p pale vio 17.50 40
272 A41 2p vio brn 22.50 60
273 A41 4p dp blue 475.00 60.00
274 A41 10p dp green 175.00 20.00
Nos. 261-274 (14) 713.65 83.15

1914

275 A40 30c gray 8.00 32

1914-23 ***Perf. 10***

276 A40 2c green 1.25 15
a. Booklet pane of 6 375.00
277 A40 4c carmine 1.25 15
a. Booklet pane of 6 375.00
278 A40 6c lt violet 30.00 7.50
a. 6c deep violet 35.00 4.50
279 A40 8c brown 32.50 8.25
280 A40 10c dk blue 20.00 16
281 A40 16c olive grn 60.00 3.50
282 A40 20c orange 17.50 65
283 A40 30c gray 45.00 2.25
284 A41 1p pale vio 95.00 2.50
Nos. 276-284 (9) 302.50 25.11

1918-26 ***Perf. 11***

285 A40 2c green 17.50 3.50
a. Booklet pane of 6 *450.00*
286 A40 4c carmine 22.50 2.00
a. Booklet pane of 6 *450.00*
287 A40 6c dp violet 32.50 1.40
287A A40 8c lt brown 175.00 25.00
288 A40 10c dk blue 45.00 1.25
289 A40 16c olive grn 80.00 5.50
289A A40 20c orange 50.00 6.50
289C A40 30c gray 47.50 10.00
289D A41 1p pale vio 60.00 11.00
Nos. 285-289D (9) 530.00 66.15

1917-25 **Unwmk.** ***Perf. 11***

290 A40 2c yellow grn 15 15
a. 2c dark green 15 15
b. Vert. pair, imperf. horiz. 1,500.
c. Horiz. pair, imperf. btwn. *1,500.*
d. Vertical pair, imperf. between *1,750.*
e. Booklet pane of 6 *20.00*
291 A40 4c carmine 15 15
a. 4c light rose 16 15
b. Booklet pane of 6 15.00
292 A40 6c dp violet 25 15
a. 6c lilac 28 15
b. 6c red violet 28 15
c. Booklet pane of 6 *300.00*
293 A40 8c yel brown 16 15
a. 8c orange brown 16 15
294 A40 10c dp blue 16 15
295 A40 12c red orange 25 15
296 A40 16c lt ol grn 40.00 16
a. 16c olive bister 40.00 35
297 A40 20c orange yel 20 15
298 A40 26c green 35 42
a. 26c blue green 45 25
299 A40 30 gray 40 15
300 A41 1p pale violet 27.50 85
a. 1p red lilac 27.50 85
b. 1p pale rose lilac 27.50 90
301 A41 2p violet brn 25.00 60
302 A41 4p blue 22.50 35
a. 4p dark blue 22.50 35
Nos. 290-302 (13) 117.07
Set value 2.85

1923-26

Design: 16c, Adm. George Dewey.

303 A40 16c olive bister 75 15
a. 16c olive green 1.10 16
304 A41 10p dp green ('26) 50.00 4.00

Legislative Palace — A42

1926, Dec. 20 **Unwmk.** ***Perf. 12***

319 A42 2c green & blk 40 25
a. Horiz. pair, imperf. btwn. *275.00*
b. Vert. pair, imperf. between *475.00*
320 A42 4c car & blk 40 32
a. Horiz. pair, imperf. btwn. *275.00*
b. Vert. pair, imperf. between *475.00*
321 A42 16c ol grn & blk 75 65
a. Horiz. pair, imperf. btwn. *350.00*
b. Vert. pair, imperf. between *525.00*
c. Double impression of center *575.00*
322 A42 18c lt brn & blk 1.00 60
a. Double impression of center *575.00*
b. Vert. pair, imperf. between *525.00*
323 A42 20c orange & blk 1.40 1.00
a. 20c orange & brown *400.00*
b. Imperf., pair *450.00* *450.00*
c. As "a," imperf., pair *525.00*
d. Vert. pair, imperf. between *525.00*
324 A42 24c gray & blk 1.00 65
a. Vert. pair, imperf. between *525.00*
325 A42 1p rose lil & blk 60.00 27.50
a. Vert. pair, imperf. between *575.00*
Nos. 319-325 (7) 64.95 30.97

Opening of the Legislative Palace.

For overprints see Nos. O1-O4.

Coil Stamp
Rizal Type of 1906

1928 ***Perf. 11 Vertically***
326 A40 2c green 6.50 15.00

Types of 1906-23

1925 **Unwmk.** ***Imperf.***
340 A40 2c yel grn ('31) 15 15
341 A40 4c car rose ('31) 15 15
342 A40 6c violet ('31) 1.00 1.00
343 A40 8c brown ('31) 90 90
344 A40 10c blue ('31) 1.00 1.00
345 A40 12c dp org ('31) 1.50 1.50
346 A40 16c ol grn *(Dewey)* ('31) 1.10 1.10
347 A40 20c org yel ('31) 1.10 1.10
348 A40 26c grn ('31) 1.10 1.10
349 A40 30c lt gray ('31) 1.25 1.25
350 A41 1p lt vio ('31) 4.00 4.00
351 A41 2p brn vio ('31) 10.00 10.00
352 A41 4p blue ('31) 30.00 30.00
353 A41 10p green ('31) 90.00 90.00
Nos. 340-353 (14) 143.25 143.25

Two imperforate issues were made, in 1925 and 1931. They differ in shade.

Mount Mayon, Luzon — A43

Post Office, Manila — A44

Pier No. 7, Manila Bay A45

(See footnote) A46

Rice Planting — A47

Rice Terraces — A48

Baguio Zigzag — A49

1932, May 3 ***Perf. 11***
354 A43 2c yellow green 45 20
355 A44 4c rose carmine 35 22
356 A45 12c orange 50 50
357 A46 18c red orange 17.50 8.25
358 A47 20c yellow 65 55
359 A48 24c dp violet 1.00 65
360 A49 32c olive brown 1.00 70
Nos. 354-360 (7) 21.45 11.07

The 18c vignette was intended to show Pagsanjan Falls in Laguna, central Luzon, and is so labeled. Through error the stamp pictures Vernal Falls in Yosemite National Park, California.
For overprints see #C29-C35, C47-C51, C63.

Nos. 302, 302a Surcharged in Orange or Red

1932
368 A41 1p on 4p blue (O) 1.65 35
a. 1p on 4p dark blue (O) 2.25 1.00
369 A41 2p on 4p dk bl (R) 3.00 65
a. 2p on 4p blue (R) 3.00 65

Baseball Players — A50

Tennis Player — A51

Basketball Players — A52

1934, Apr. 14 **Typo.** ***Perf. 11½***
380 A50 2c yellow brn *2.00 1.00*
381 A51 6c ultra 25 20
a. Vert. pair, imperf. btwn. *1,250.*
382 A52 16c violet brown 60 60
a. Vert. pair, imperf. horiz. *1,250.*

Tenth Far Eastern Championship Games.

José Rizal — A53

Woman and Carabao — A54

La Filipina — A55

Pearl Fishing — A56

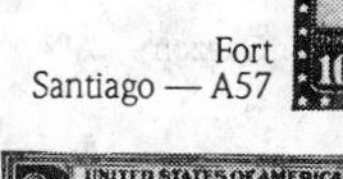
Fort Santiago — A57

Salt Spring — A58

Magellan's Landing, 1521 A59

"Juan de la Cruz" A60

Rice Terraces — A61

"Blood Compact," 1565 — A62

Barasoain Church, Malolos — A63

Battle of Manila Bay, 1898 — A64

Montalban Gorge — A65

George Washington — A66

1935, Feb. 15 **Engr.** ***Perf. 11***
383 A53 2c rose 15 15
384 A54 4c yellow grn 15 15
385 A55 6c dk brown 15 15
386 A56 8c violet 15 15
387 A57 10c rose car 16 15
388 A58 12c black 15 15
389 A59 16c dk blue 15 15
390 A60 20c lt ol grn 16 15
391 A61 26c indigo 22 22
392 A62 30c orange red 22 22
393 A63 1p red org & blk 1.65 1.25
394 A64 2p bister brn & blk 3.50 1.25
395 A65 4p blue & blk 3.50 2.50
396 A66 5p green & blk 7.50 1.50
Nos. 383-396 (14) 17.81 8.14

For overprints see Nos. 411-424, 433-446, 463-466, 468, 472-474, 478-484, 485-494, C52-C53, O15-O36, O38, O40-O43, N2-N3, NO6. For surcharges see Nos. 449, N4-N9, N28, NO2-NO5.

Commonwealth Issues

The Temples of Human Progress A67

1935, Nov. 15
397 A67 2c carmine rose 15 15
398 A67 6c dp violet 16 15
399 A67 16c blue 20 15
400 A67 36c yellow grn 35 30
401 A67 50c brown 55 55
Nos. 397-401 (5) 1.41 1.30

Inauguration of the Philippine Commonwealth, Nov. 15, 1935.

Jose Rizal — A68

President Manuel L. Quezon — A69

1936, June 19 ***Perf. 12***
402 A68 2c yellow brown 15 15
403 A68 6c slate blue 15 15
a. Horiz. pair, imperf. vert. *900.00*
404 A68 36c red brown 50 45
Set value 59

75th anniv. of the birth of José Rizal.

1936, Nov. 15 ***Perf. 11***
408 A69 2c orange brown 15 15
409 A69 6c yellow green 15 15
410 A69 12c ultra 15 15
Set value 27 24

1st anniversary of the Commonwealth.
For overprints see Nos. 467, 475.

Stamps of 1935 Overprinted in Black

COMMON-
WEALTH
a

COMMONWEALTH
b

1936-37 ***Perf. 11***
411 A53 (a) 2c rose 15 15
a. Booklet pane of 6 2.50 *65*
412 A54 (b) 4c yel grn ('37) 50
413 A55 (a) 6c dark brown 20 15
414 A56 (b) 8c vio ('37) 22 20
415 A57 (b) 10c rose car 16 15
a. "Commonwealt"
416 A58 (b) 12c black ('37) 16 15
417 A59 (b) 16c dk blue 16 15
418 A60 (a) 20c lt ol grn ('37) 60 35
419 A61 (b) 26c indigo ('37) 42 30
420 A62 (b) 30c orange red 28 15
421 A63 (b) 1p red org & blk 65 16
422 A64 (b) 2p bis brn & blk ('37) 4.50 2.50
423 A65 (b) 4p bl & blk ('37) 15.00 2.50
424 A66 (b) 5p grn & blk ('37) 1.50 1.25
Nos. 411-424 (14) 24.50 8.16

Map of Philippines A70

Arms of Manila A71

1937, Feb. 3
425 A70 2c yellow green 15 15
426 A70 6c lt brown 15 15
427 A70 12c sapphire 15 15
428 A70 20c dp orange 22 15
429 A70 36c dp violet 40 35
430 A70 50c carmine 45 28
Nos. 425-430 (6) 1.52
Set value 88

33rd Eucharistic Congress.

1937, Aug. 27 ***Perf. 11***
431 A71 10p gray 4.25 2.00
432 A71 20p henna brown 2.25 1.40

For overprints see Nos. 495-496. For surcharges see Nos. 451, C58.

Stamps of 1935 Overprinted in Black

COMMON-
WEALTH
a

COMMONWEALTH
b

1938-40 ***Perf. 11***
433 A53 (a) 2c rose ('39) 15 15
a. Booklet pane of 6 3.50 *65*
b. "WEALTH COMMON-" *3,500.*
c. Hyphen omitted
434 A54 (b) 4c yel grn ('40) 40
435 A55 (a) 6c dk brn ('39) 15 15
a. 6c golden brown 15 15
436 A56 (b) 8c violet ('39) 15 15
a. "Commonwealt" 65.00
437 A57 (b) 10c rose car ('39) 15 15
438 A58 (b) 12c black ('40) 15 15
439 A59 (b) 16c dk blue 15 15
440 A60 (a) 20c lt ol grn ('39) 15 15
441 A61 (b) 26c indigo ('40) 20 20
442 A62 (b) 30c org red ('39) 1.40 70
443 A63 (b) 1p red org & blk 40 16
444 A64 (b) 2p bis brn & blk 2.75 75
445 A65 (b) 4p bl & blk ('40) 55.00 42.50
446 A66 (b) 5p grn & blk ('40) 4.50 2.75
Nos. 433-446 (14) 65.70 48.11

Overprint "b" measures 18½x1¾mm. No. 433b occurs in booklet pane, No. 433a, position 5; all copies are straight-edged, left and bottom.

Stamps of 1917-37 Surcharged in Red, Violet or Black

FIRST FOREIGN
a

TRADE WEEK 2 CENTAVOS MAY 21-27,1939

FIRST FOREIGN TRADE WEEK 50CENTAVOS50

MAY 21-27, 1939 6CENTAVOS6
b

FIRST FOREIGN TRADE WEEK MAY 21-27,1939
c

1939, July 5

449 A54	2c on 4c yel grn (R)	15	15
450 A40	6c on 26c bl grn (V)	15	15
a.	6c on 20c green	65	30
451 A71	50c on 20p hn brn (Bk)	1.00	1.00

Foreign Trade Week.

Triumphal Arch — A72

Malacañan Palace — A73

1939, Nov. 15 *Perf. 11*

452 A72	2c yellow green	15	15
453 A72	6c carmine	15	15
454 A72	12c bright blue	16	15
	Set value	33	17

For overprints see Nos. 469, 476.

1939, Nov. 15

455 A73	2c green	15	15
456 A73	6c orange	15	15
457 A73	12c carmine	16	15
	Set value	33	17

Nos. 452-457 commemorate the 4th anniv. of the Commonwealth.
For overprint see No. 470.

Pres. Quezon Taking Oath of Office — A74

José Rizal — A75

1940, Feb. 8

458 A74	2c dk orange	15	15
459 A74	6c dk green	15	15
460 A74	12c purple	25	15
	Set value		23

4th anniversary of Commonwealth.
For overprints see Nos. 471, 477.

Rotary Press Printing

1941, Apr. 14 *Perf. 11x10½*

Size: 19x22½mm

461 A75	2c apple green	15	15

Flat Plate Printing

1941-43 Size: 18¾x22mm *Perf. 11*

462 A75	2c apple green ('43)	15	15
a.	2c pale apple green	16	15
b.	Bklt. pane of 6, #462 ('43)	1.25	*1.00*
c.	Bklt. pane of 6, #462A	2.50	*2.25*

No. 462 was issued only in booklet panes and all copies have straight edges.
Further printings were made in 1942 and 1943 in different shades from the first supply of stamps sent to the islands.
For type A75 overprinted see Nos. 464, O37, O39, N1, NO1.

Philippine Stamps of 1935-41, Handstamped in Violet

1944 *Perf. 11, 11x10½*

463 A53	2c rose (#411)		*260.00*	*95.00*
a.	Booklet pane of 6		*2,000.*	
463B A53	2c rose (#433)		*1,200.*	*1,200.*
464 A75	2c ap grn (#461)		2.50	2.25
465 A54	4c yel grn (#384)		*25.00*	*25.00*
466 A55	6c dk brn (#385)		*1,500.*	*1,350.*
467 A69	6c yel grn (#409)		*110.00*	*85.00*
468 A55	6c dk brn (#413)		*650.00*	*600.00*
469 A72	6c car (#453)		*135.00*	*110.00*
470 A73	6c org (#456)		*600.00*	*550.00*
471 A74	6c dk grn (#459)		*160.00*	*150.00*
472 A56	8c vio (#436)		15.00	20.00
473 A57	10c rose car (#415)		*110.00*	*75.00*
474 A57	10c rose car (#437)		*135.00*	*110.00*
475 A69	12c ultra (#410)		*350.00*	*175.00*
476 A72	12c brt bl (#454)		*3,500.*	*2,000.*
477 A74	12c pur (#460)		*190.00*	*135.00*
478 A59	16c dk bl (#389)		*700.00*	
479 A59	16c dk bl (#417)		*450.00*	*325.00*
480 A59	16c dk bl (#439)		*160.00*	*100.00*
481 A60	20c lt ol grn (#440)		27.50	27.50
482 A62	30c org red (#420)		*225.00*	*160.00*
483 A62	30c org red (#442)		*325.00*	*250.00*
484 A63	1p red org & blk (#443)		*5,500.*	*4,000.*

Types of 1935-37 Overprinted

VICTORY COMMON-WEALTH
a

VICTORY COMMONWEALTH
b

1945 *Perf. 11*

485 A53 (a)	2c rose	15	15
486 A54 (b)	4c yellow grn	15	15
487 A55 (a)	6c golden brn	15	15
488 A56 (b)	8c violet	15	15
489 A57 (b)	10c rose car	15	15
490 A58 (b)	12c black	20	15
491 A59 (b)	16c dk blue	25	15
492 A60 (a)	20c lt olive grn	30	15
493 A62 (b)	30c orange red	40	35
494 A63 (b)	1p red org & blk	1.10	25
	Nos. 485-494 (10)	3.00	
	Set value		1.30

Nos. 431-432 Overprinted in Black VICTORY

495 A71	10p gray	40.00	13.50
496 A71	20p henna brown	35.00	15.00

José Rizal — A76

Rotary Press Printing

1946, May 28 *Perf. 11x10½*

497 A76	2c sepia	15	15

For overprints see Nos. 503, O44.

Catalogue values for unused stamps in this section, from this point to the end of the section, are for Never Hinged items.

Republic

Philippine Girl Holding Flag of the Republic — A77

1946, July 4 Unwmk. Engr. *Perf. 11*

500 A77	2c carmine	20	20
501 A77	6c green	35	20
502 A77	12c blue	50	35

Issued to commemorate the independence of the Philippines, July 4, 1946.

No. 497 Overprinted in Brown

PHILIPPINES 50TH ANNIVERSARY MARTYRDOM OF RIZAL 1896 ~ 1946

1946, Dec. 30 *Perf. 11x10½*

503 A76	2c sepia	20	15

50th anniv. of the execution of José Rizal.

Rizal Monument A78

Bonifacio Monument A79

Jones Bridge — A80

Santa Lucia Gate — A81

Mayon Volcano — A82

Avenue of Palms — A83

1947 Engr. *Perf. 12*

504 A78	4c black brown	15	15
505 A79	10c red orange	16	15
506 A80	12c deep blue	22	15
507 A81	16c slate gray	1.35	80
508 A82	20c red brown	40	15
509 A83	50c dull green	1.00	65
510 A83	1p violet	2.00	50
	Nos. 504-510 (7)	5.28	
	Set value		2.20

For surcharges see Nos. 613-614, 809. For overprints see Nos. 609, O50-O52, O54-O55.

Manuel L. Quezon — A84

1947, May 1 **Typo.**

511 A84	1c green	15	15

See No. 515.

Pres. Manuel A. Roxas Taking Oath of Office — A85

1947, July 4 Unwmk. *Perf. 12½*

512 A85	4c carmine rose	20	15
513 A85	6c dk green	45	45
514 A85	16c purple	1.00	65

First anniversary of republic.

Quezon Type Souvenir Sheet

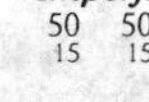

1947, Nov. 28 *Imperf.*

515	Sheet of 4	50	50
a.	A84 1c bright green	15	15

United Nations Emblem A87

1947, Nov. 24 *Perf. 12½*

516 A87	4c dk car & pink	1.40	1.20
a.	Imperf.	2.00	2.00
517 A87	6c pur & pale vio	2.00	2.00
a.	Imperf.	2.00	2.00
518 A87	12c dp bl & pale bl	2.25	2.25
a.	Imperf.	2.00	2.00

Issued to honor the conference of the Economic Commission in Asia and the Far East, held at Baguio.

Gen. Douglas MacArthur — A88

1948, Feb. 3 Engr. *Perf. 12*

519 A88	4c purple	45	20
520 A88	6c rose car	90	60
521 A88	16c brt ultra	1.40	60

Threshing Rice — A89

1948, Feb. 23 Typo. *Perf. 12½*

522 A89	2c grn & pale yel grn	75	50
523 A89	6c brown & cream	90	65
524 A89	18c dp bl & pale bl	2.50	2.00

Conf. of the FAO held at Baguio. No. 524 exists imperf. See No. C67.

Manuel A. Roxas A90

José Rizal A91

1948, July 15 Engr. *Perf. 12*

525 A90	2c black	20	15
526 A90	4c black	25	20

Issued in tribute to President Manuel A. Roxas who died April 15, 1948.

1948, June 19 **Unwmk.**

527 A91	2c bright green	15	15
a.	Booklet pane of 6	1.25	

For surcharges see Nos. 550, O56. For overprint see No. O53.

Scout Saluting — A92

Sampaguita, National Flower — A93

1948, Oct. 31 Typo. *Imperf.*

528 A92	2c chocolate & green	35	15
a.	Perf. 11½	1.00	50
529 A92	4c chocolate & pink	40	25
a.	Perf. 11½	1.20	70

25th anniversary of the foundation of the Boy Scouts of the Philippines.

No. 528 exists part perforate.

1948, Dec. 8 *Perf. 12½*
530 A93 3c blk, pale bl & grn 32 25

UPU Monument, Bern — A94

1949, Oct. 9 Unwmk. Engr. *Perf. 12*
531 A94 4c green 15 15
532 A94 6c dull violet 15 15
533 A94 18c blue gray 60 20
Set value 34

Souvenir Sheet

Imperf

534 Sheet of 3 55 45
a. A94 4c green 15 15
b. A94 6c dull violet 16 15
c. A94 18c blue 20 20

75th anniv. of the UPU.

In 1960 an unofficial, 3-line overprint ("President D. D. Eisenhower /Visit to the Philippines/June 14-16, 1960") was privately applied to No. 534.

For surcharge see No. 806. For overprint see No. 901.

Gen. Gregorio del Pilar at Tirad Pass — A95

1949, Dec. 2 *Perf. 12*
535 A95 2c red brown 15 15
536 A95 4c green 25 22

50th anniversary of the death of Gen. Gregorio P. del Pilar and fifty-two of his men at Tirad Pass.

Globe — A96

Red Lauan Tree — A97

1950, Mar. 1
537 A96 2c purple 15 15
538 A96 6c dk green 22 15
539 A96 18c dp blue 50 15
Nos. 537-539,C68-C69 (5) 1.90
Set value 58

5th World Cong. of the Junior Chamber of Commerce, Manila, Mar. 1-8, 1950.

For surcharge see No. 825.

1950, Apr. 14
540 A97 2c green 15 15
541 A97 4c purple 35 20
Set value 26

50th anniversary of the Bureau of Forestry.

F. D. Roosevelt with his Stamps — A98

Lions Club Emblem — A99

1950, May 22
542 A98 4c dark brown 22 18
543 A98 6c carmine rose 38 35
544 A98 18c blue 90 70

Honoring Franklin D. Roosevelt and for the 25th anniv. of the formation of the Philatelic Association of the Philippines. See No. C70.

1950, June 4 **Engr.**
545 A99 2c orange 42 42
546 A99 4c violet 55 55

Convention of the Lions Club, Manila, June 1950. See Nos. C71-C72.

Pres. Elpidio Quirino Taking Oath — A100

1950, July 4 Unwmk. *Perf. 12*
547 A100 2c car rose 15 15
548 A100 4c magenta 15 15
549 A100 6c blue green 20 15
Set value 38 35

4th anniversary of the Republic of the Philippines.

No. 527 Surcharged in Black

1950, Sept. 20
550 A91 1c on 2c bright green 15 15

Dove over Globe — A101

1950, Oct. 23
551 A101 5c green 25 20
552 A101 6c rose carmine 25 20
553 A101 18c ultra 55 42

Baguio Conference of 1950.

For surcharge see No. 828.

Headman of Barangay Inspecting Harvest A102

1951, Mar. 31 Litho. *Perf. 12½*
554 A102 5c dull green 16 15
555 A102 6c red brown 25 25
556 A102 18c violet blue 65 65

The government's Peace Fund campaign.

Imperf., Pairs
554a A102 5c dull green 16 16
555a A102 6c red brown 25 25
556a A102 18c violet blue 65 65

Arms of Manila A103

Arms of Cebu A104

Arms of Zamboanga A105

Arms of Iloilo A106

1951 Engr. *Perf. 12*

Various Frames
557 A103 5c purple 40 35
558 A103 6c gray 25 22
559 A103 18c bright ultra 40 35

Various Frames
560 A104 5c crimson rose 40 35
561 A104 6c bister brown 25 22
562 A104 18c violet 40 35

Various Frames
563 A105 5c blue green 45 38
564 A105 6c red brown 30 22
565 A105 18c light blue 45 38

Various Frames
566 A106 5c bright green 55 42
567 A106 6c violet 38 25
568 A106 18c deep blue 55 42
Nos. 557-568 (12) 4.78 3.91

Issue dates: A103, Feb. 3. A104, Apr. 27. A105, June 19. A106, Aug. 26.

For surcharges see Nos. 634-636.

UN Emblem and Girl Holding Flag — A107

Liberty Holding Declaration of Human Rights — A108

1951, Oct. 24 Unwmk. *Perf. 11½*
569 A107 5c red 55 25
570 A107 6c blue green 45 25
571 A107 18c violet blue 1.10 70

United Nations Day, Oct. 24, 1951.

1951, Dec. 10 *Perf. 12*
572 A108 5c green 40 22
573 A108 6c red orange 55 40
574 A108 18c ultra 1.00 60

Universal Declaration of Human Rights.

Students and Department Seal — A109

1952, Jan. 31
575 A109 5c orange red 40 32

50th anniversary (in 1951) of the Philippine Educational System.

Milkfish and Map — A111

1952, Oct. 27 *Perf. 12½*
578 A111 5c orange brown 90 55
579 A111 6c deep blue 55 45

Issued to publicize the 4th Indo-Pacific Fisheries Council Meeting, Quezon City, Oct. 23-Nov. 7, 1952.

Maria Clara — A112

1952, Nov. 16
580 A112 5c deep blue 40 15
581 A112 6c brown 40 15
Set value 20

Issued to publicize the first Pan-Asian Philatelic Exhibition, PANAPEX, Manila, Nov. 16-22, 1952. See also No. C73.

Wright Park, Baguio City — A113

Francisco Baltazar, Poet — A114

1952, Dec. 15 *Perf. 12*
582 A113 5c red orange 60 60
583 A113 6c dp blue green 90 75

Issued to publicize the third Lions District Convention, Baguio City.

1953, Mar. 27
584 A114 5c citron 35 30

National Language Week.

"Gateway to the East" — A115

Presidents Quirino and Sukarno — A116

1953, Apr. 30
585 A115 5c turq green 25 15
586 A115 6c vermilion 32 15
Set value 20

Philippines International Fair.

1953, Oct. 5 **Engr. & Litho.**
587 A116 5c multicolored 15 15
588 A116 6c multicolored 20 20
Set value 28

2nd anniversary of the visit of Indonesia's President Sukarno.

Marcelo H. del Pilar — A117

Portraits: 1c, Manuel L. Quezon. 2c, José Abad Santos (different frame). 3c, Apolinario Mabini (different frame). 10c, Father José Burgos. 20c, Lapu-Lapu. 25c, Gen. Antonio Luna. 50c, Cayetano Arellano. 60c, Andres Bonifacio. 2p, Graciano L. Jaena.

Perf. 12, 12½, 13, 14x13½

1952-60 **Engr.**
589 A117 1c red brn ('53) 15 15
590 A117 2c gray ('60) 15 15
591 A117 3c brick red ('59) 15 15
592 A117 5c crim rose 15 15
595 A117 10c ultra ('55) 15 15
597 A117 20c car lake ('55) 25 15
598 A117 25c yel grn ('58) 35 16
599 A117 50c org ver ('59) 65 22
600 A117 60c car rose ('58) 80 35
601 A117 2p violet 2.50 80
Nos. 589-601 (10) 5.30
Set value 1.80

For overprints see Nos. 608, 626, O57-O60. For surcharges see Nos. 641-642, 647, 830, 871, 875-877, O61.

Doctor Examining Boy — A118

1953, Dec. 16

603 A118 5c lilac rose	25	22
604 A118 6c ultra	32	30

50th anniversary of the founding of the Philippine Medical Association.

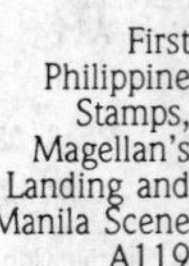

First Philippine Stamps, Magellan's Landing and Manila Scene A119

1954, Apr. 25 *Perf. 13*

Stamp of 1854 in Orange

605 A119 5c purple	50	32
606 A119 18c deep blue	1.00	85
607 A119 30c green	2.25	2.00
Nos. 605-607,C74-C76 (6)	9.90	8.37

Centenary of Philippine postage stamps.
For surcharge see No. 829.

Nos. 592 and 509 Overprinted or Surcharged in Black

1954, Apr. 23 *Perf. 12*

608 A117 5c crimson rose	1.00	85
609 A83 18c on 50c dull grn	1.75	1.25

1st National Boy Scout Jamboree, Quezon City, April 23-30, 1954.
The surcharge on No. 609 is reduced to fit the size of the stamp.

Discus Thrower and Games Emblem A120

1954, May 31 *Perf. 13*

610 A120 5c shown	70	50
611 A120 18c Swimmer	1.10	85
612 A120 30c Boxer	1.75	1.50

2nd Asian Games, Manila, May 1-9.

Nos. 505 and 508 Surcharged in Blue

5
MANILA CONFERENCE
OF
5 1954

1954, Sept. 6 *Perf. 12*

613 A79 5c on 10c red org	15	15
614 A82 18c on 20c red brn	55	52

Issued to publicize the Manila Conference, 1954.
The surcharge is arranged to obliterate the original denomination.

Allegory of Independence A121

"Immaculate Conception," by Murillo A122

1954, Nov. 30 *Perf. 13*

615 A121 5c dark carmine	22	16
616 A121 18c deep blue	65	40

56th anniversary of the declaration of the first Philippine Independence.
For surcharge see No. 826.

1954, Dec. 30 *Perf. 12*

617 A122 5c blue	38	25

Issued to mark the end of the Marian Year.

Mayon Volcano, Moro Vinta and Rotary Emblem A123

1955, Feb. 23 Engr. *Perf. 13*

618 A123 5c dull blue	20	15
619 A123 18c dk car rose	65	50

Rotary International, 50th anniversary. See No. C77. For surcharge see No. 827.

Allegory of Labor — A124

Pres. Ramon Magsaysay — A125

1955, May 26 *Perf. 13x12½*

620 A124 5c brown	35	25

Issued in connection with the Labor-Management Congress, Manila, May 26-28, 1955.

1955, July 4 *Perf. 12½*

621 A125 5c blue	16	15
622 A125 20c red	50	50
623 A125 30c green	80	80

9th anniversary of the Republic.

Village Well A126

1956, Mar. 16 *Perf. 12½x13½*

624 A126 5c violet	25	25
625 A126 20c dull green	60	55

Issued to publicize the drive for improved health conditions in rural areas.

No. 592 Overprinted

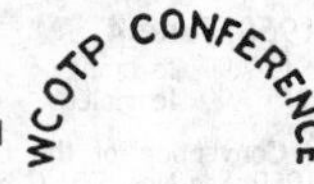

1956, Aug. 1 Unwmk. *Perf. 12*

626 A117 5c crimson rose	32	30

5th Annual Conf. of the World Confederation of Organizations of the Teaching Profession, Manila, Aug. 1-8, 1956.

Nurse and Disaster Victims — A127

Engraved; Cross Lithographed in Red

1956, Aug. 30

627 A127 5c violet	42	40
628 A127 20c gray brown	55	45

50 years of Red Cross Service in the Philippines.

Monument to US Landing, Leyte — A128

1956, Oct. 20 Litho. *Perf. 12½*

629 A128 5c carmine rose	15	15
a. Imperf. ('57)	42	42

Landing of US forces under Gen. Douglas MacArthur on Leyte, Oct. 20, 1944.
Issue date: No. 629a, Feb. 16.

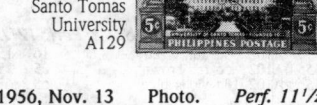

Santo Tomas University A129

1956, Nov. 13 Photo. *Perf. 11½*

630 A129 5c brown car & choc	32	22
631 A129 60c lilac & red brn	1.25	1.10

Issued in honor of the University of Santo Tomas.

Statue of Christ by Rizal — A130

1956, Nov. 28 Engr. *Perf. 12*

632 A130 5c gray olive	25	20
633 A130 20c rose carmine	55	52

2nd Natl. Eucharistic Cong., Manila, Nov. 28-Dec. 2, and for the centenary of the Feast of the Sacred Heart.

Nos. 561, 564 and 567 Surcharged with New Value in Blue or Black

1956 Unwmk. *Perf. 12*

634 A104 5c on 6c bis brn (Bl)	15	15
635 A105 5c on 6c red brn (Bl)	15	15
636 A106 5c on 6c vio (Bk)	15	15
Set value	36	36

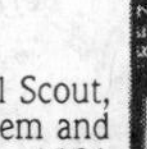

Girl Scout, Emblem and Tents — A131

1957, Jan. 19 Litho. *Perf. 12½*

637 A131 5c dark blue	32	32
a. Imperf.	42	42

Centenary of the Scout movement and for the Girl Scout World Jamboree, Quezon City, Jan. 19-Feb. 2, 1957.
Copies of Nos. 637 and 637a (No. 48 in sheet) exist with heavy black rectangular handstamps obliterating erroneous date at left, denomination and cloverleaf emblem.

Pres. Ramon Magsaysay (1907-57) — A132

1957, Aug. 31 Engr. *Perf. 12*

638 A132 5c black	15	15

"Spoliarium" by Juan Luna — A133

1957, Oct. 23 *Perf. 14x14½*

639 A133 5c rose carmine	15	15

Centenary of the birth of Juan Luna, painter.

Sergio Osmena and First National Assembly — A134

1957, Oct. 16 *Perf. 12½x13½*

640 A134 5c blue green	15	15

50th anniversary of the First Philippine Assembly and to honor Sergio Osmeña, Speaker of the Assembly.

Nos. 595 and 597 Surcharged in Carmine or Black

1957, Dec. 30 *Perf. 14x13½*

641 A117 5c on 10c ultra (C)	15	15
642 A117 10c on 20c car lake	22	22

Issued to commemorate the inauguration of Carlos P. Garcia as president and Diosdado Macapagal as vice-president, Dec. 30.

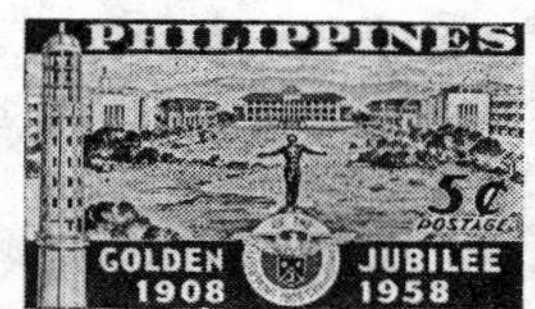

University of the Philippines — A135

1958 Engr. *Perf. 13½x13*
643 A135 5c dk carmine rose 30 15

50th anniversary of the founding of the University of the Philippines.

Pres. Carlos P. Garcia — A136

1958 Photo. *Perf. 11½*
Granite Paper
644 A136 5c multicolored 15 15
645 A136 20c multicolored 40 30
Set value 38

12th anniversary of Philippine Republic.

Manila Cathedral A137

Perf. 13x13½, 12
1958, Dec. 8 Engr.
646 A137 5c multicolored 20 15

Issued to commemorate the inauguration of the rebuilt Manila Cathedral, Dec. 8, 1958.

No. 592 Surcharged **OneCentavo**

1959 *Perf. 12*
647 A117 1c on 5c crim rose 15 15

Nos. B4-B5 Surcharged with New Values and Bars

1959 *Perf. 13*
648 SP4 1c on 2c + 2c red 15 15
649 SP5 6c on 4c + 4c vio 15 15
Set value 15 15

Issued on Feb. 3, 1959, the 14th anniversary of the liberation of Manila from the Japanese forces.

Philippine Flag — A138

1959, Feb. 8 Unwmk. *Perf. 13*
650 A138 6c dp ultra, yel & dp car 15 15
651 A138 20c dp car, yel & dp ultra 15 15
Set value 22 22

Seal of Bulacan Province — A139

Seal of Bacolod City — A140

1959 Engr. *Perf. 13*
652 A139 6c lt yellow grn 15 15
653 A139 20c rose red 22 15
Set value 22

Issued in conjunction with the 60th anniversary of the Malolos constitution.
For surcharge see No. 848.

1959

Design: 6c, 25c, Seal of Capiz Province and portrait of Pres. Roxas.

654 A139 6c lt brown 15 15
655 A139 25c purple 22 20
Set value 28 26

Issued on the 11th anniversary of the death of Pres. Manuel A. Roxas.

1959
656 A140 6c blue green 15 15
657 A140 10c rose lilac 15 15
Set value 16

Nos. 658-803 were reserved for the rest of a projected series showing seals and coats of arms of provinces and cities.

Camp John Hay Amphitheater, Baguio — A141

Perf. 13½ (6c, 25c), 12 (6c)
1959, Sept. 1
804 A141 6c bright green 15 15
805 A141 25c rose red 25 20

50th anniversary of the city of Baguio.

No. 533 Surcharged in Red

6¢

1959, Oct. 24 *Perf. 12*
806 A94 6c on 18c blue 15 15

Issued for United Nations Day, Oct. 24.

Maria Cristina Falls — A142

1959, Nov. 18 Photo. *Perf. 13½, 12*
807 A142 6c vio & dp yel grn 15 15
808 A142 30c green & brown 35 25
Set value 32

No. 504 Surcharged with New Value and Bars

1959 Engr. *Perf. 12*
809 A78 1c on 4c blk brn 15 15

Manila Atheneum Emblem A143

1959, Dec. 10 *Perf. 13½, 12*
810 A143 6c ultra 15 15
811 A143 30c rose red 35 25
Set value 42 32

Centenary of the Manila Atheneum (Ateneo de Manila), a school, and to mark a century of progress in education.

Manuel Quezon A144

José Rizal A145

1959-60 Engr. *Perf. 13*
812 A144 1c olive gray ('60) 15 15
Perf. 14x12
813 A145 6c gray blue 15 15
Set value 16 15

A146

Perf. 12½x13½
1960 Unwmk. Photo.
814 A146 6c brown & gold 15 15

25th anniversary of the Philippine Constitution. See No. C82.

Site of Manila Pact A147

1960 Engr. *Perf. 12½*
815 A147 6c emerald 15 15
816 A147 25c orange 30 22
Set value 36 28

5th anniversary (in 1959) of the Congress of the Philippines establishing the South-East Asia Treaty Organization (SEATO).
For overprints see Nos. 841-842.

Sunset at Manila Bay and Uprooted Oak Emblem A148

1960, Apr. 7 Photo. *Perf. 13½*
817 A148 6c multicolored 15 15
818 A148 25c multicolored 30 22
Set value 36 28

Issued to publicize World Refugee Year, July 1, 1959-June 30, 1960.

A149

1960, July 29 *Perf. 13½*
819 A149 5c lt grn, red & gold 15 15
820 A149 6c bl, red & gold 15 15
Set value 22 16

50th anniversary of the founding of the Philippine Tuberculosis Society.

Basketball A150

1960, Nov. 30 *Perf. 13x13½*
821 A150 6c shown 15 15
822 A150 10c Runner 15 15
Set value 16

17th Olympic Games, Rome, Aug. 25-Sept. 11. See Nos. C85-C86.

Presidents Eisenhower and Garcia and Presidential Seals — A151

1960, Dec. 30 *Perf. 13½*
823 A151 6c multi 15 15
824 A151 20c ultra, red & yel 40 20

Visit of Pres. Dwight D. Eisenhower to the Philippines, June 14, 1960.

Nos. 539, 616, 619, 553, 606 and 598 Surcharged with New Values and Bars in Red or Black

1960-61 Engr. *Perf. 12, 13, 12½*
825 A96 1c on 18c dp bl (R) 15 15
826 A121 5c on 18c dp bl (R) 15 15
827 A123 5c on 18c dp car rose 20 15
828 A101 10c on 18c ultra (R) 15 15
829 A119 10c on 18c dp bl & org (R) 20 15
830 A117 20c on 25c yel grn ('61) 20 15
Nos. 825-830 (6) 1.05
Set value 65

On No. 830, no bars are overprinted, the surcharge "20 20" serving to cancel the old denomination.

Mercury and Globe — A152

1961, Jan. 23 Photo. *Perf. 13½*
831 A152 6c red brn, bl, blk & gold 15 15

Issued to commemorate the Manila Postal Conference, Jan. 10-23. See also No. C87.

Nos. B10, B11 and B11a Surcharged "2nd National Boy Scout Jamboree Pasonanca Park" and New Value in Black or Red

1961, May 2 Engr. *Perf. 13*
Yellow Paper
832 SP8 10c on 6c + 4c car 15 15
833 SP8 30c on 25c + 5c bl (R) 32 32
a. Tete beche, *wht* (10c on 6c + 4c & 30c on 25c + 5c) (Bk) 50 50

Issued to publicize the Second National Boy Scout Jamboree, Pasonanca Park, Zamboanga City.

De la Salle College, Manila
A153

1961, June 16 Photo. *Perf. 11½*

834 A153 6c multi 15 15
835 A153 10c multi 15 15
Set value 22 16

50th anniversary of the founding of De la Salle College, Manila.

José Rizal as Student
A154

Designs: 6c, Rizal and birthplace at Calamba, Laguna. 10c, Rizal and parents. 20c, Rizal with Juan Luna and F. R. Hidalgo in Madrid. 30c, Rizal's execution.

1961 Unwmk. *Perf. 13½*

836 A154 5c multi 15 15
837 A154 6c multi 15 15
838 A154 10c grn & red brn 15 15
839 A154 20c brn red & grnsh bl 22 20
840 A154 30c vio, lil & org brn 32 25
Set value 84 72

Centenary of the birth of José Rizal.

Nos. 815-816 Overprinted

I
K
A
15 KAARAWAN
Republika ng Pilipinas
Hulyo 4, 1961

1961, July 4 Engr. *Perf. 12½*

841 A147 6c emerald 20 20
842 A147 25c orange 32 32

15th anniversary of the Republic.

Colombo Plan Emblem and Globe Showing Member Countries — A155

1961, Oct. 8 Photo. *Perf. 13x11½*

843 A155 5c multi 15 15
844 A155 6c multi 15 15
Set value 15 15

7th anniversary of the admission of the Philippines to the Colombo Plan.

Government Clerk
A156

1961, Dec. 9 Unwmk. *Perf. 12½*

845 A156 6c vio, bl & red 15 15
846 A156 10c gray bl & red 30 15
Set value 22

Issued to honor the Philippine government employees.

No. C83 Surcharged

6¢

PAAF
GOLDEN JUBILEE
1911 1961

1961, Nov. 30 Engr. *Perf. 14x14½*

847 AP11 6c on 10c car 15 15

50th anniversary of the Philippine Amateur Athletic Federation.

No. 655 Surcharged with New Value and: "MACAPAGAL-PELAEZ INAUGURATION DEC. 30, 1961"

1961, Dec. 30 *Perf. 12½*

848 A139 6c on 25c pur 15 15

Inauguration of President Diosdado Macapagal and Vice-President Emanuel Pelaez.

No. B8 Surcharged

6 s

1962, Jan. 23 Photo. *Perf. 13½x13*

849 SP7 6c on 5c grn & red 15 15

Vanda Orchids
A157

Apolinario Mabini
A158

Orchids: 6c, White mariposa. 10c, Sander's dendrobe. 20c, Sanggumay.

1962, Mar. 9 Photo. *Perf. 13½x14*

Dark Blue Background

850 A157 5c rose, grn & yel 15 15
851 A157 6c grn & yel 15 15
852 A157 10c grn, car & brn 15 15
853 A157 20c lil, brn & grn 25 25
a. Block of 4, #850-853 65 65
b. As "a," imperf. 90 90

Perf. 13½; 14 (1s); 13x12 (#857, 10s)

1962-69 Engr. Unwmk.

Portraits: 1s, Manuel L. Quezon. 5s, Marcelo H. del Pilar. 6s, José Rizal. No. 857A Rizal (wearing shirt). 10s, Father José Burgos. 20s, Lapu-Lapu. 30s, Rajah Soliman. 50s, Cayetano Arellano. 70s, Sergio Osmena. 1p (No. 863), Emilio Jacinto. 1p (No. 864), José M. Panganiban.

854 A158 1s org brn ('63) 15 15
855 A158 3s rose red 15 15
856 A158 5s car rose ('63) 15 15
857 A158 6s dk red brn 15 15
857A A158 6s pck bl ('64) 15 15
858 A158 10s brt pur ('63) 15 15
859 A158 20s Prus bl ('63) 15 15
860 A158 30s vermilion 24 15
861 A158 50s vio ('63) 40 15
862 A158 70s brt bl ('63) 50 22
863 A158 1p grn ('63) 1.00 20
864 A158 1p dp org ('69) 60 25
Set value 3.20 1.10

For surcharges see #873-874, 969, 1054, 1209.
For overprints see #946, 1119, O63-O69.

Pres. Macapagal Taking Oath of Office
A159

1962 Photo. *Perf. 13½*

Vignette Multicolored

865 A159 6s blue 15 15
866 A159 10s green 15 15
867 A159 30s violet 30 15
Set value 46 22

Issued to commemorate the swearing in of President Diosdado Macapagal, Dec. 30, 1961.

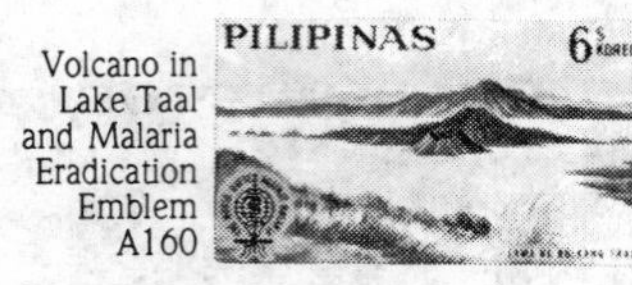

Volcano in Lake Taal and Malaria Eradication Emblem
A160

1962, Oct. 24 Unwmk. *Perf. 11½*

Granite Paper

868 A160 6s multi 15 15
869 A160 10s multi 15 15
870 A160 70s multi 70 50
Set value 86 64

Issued on UN Day for the WHO drive to eradicate malaria.

No. 598 Surcharged in Red

1762 1962
BICENTENNIAL
Diego Silang
Revolt
20

1962, Nov. 15 Engr. *Perf. 12*

871 A117 20s on 25c yel grn 20 15

Issued to commemorate the bicentennial of the Diego Silang revolt in Ilocos Province.

No. B6 Overprinted with Sideways Chevron Obliterating Surtax

1962, Dec. 23 *Perf. 12*

872 SP6 5c on 5c + 1c dp bl 15 15

Nos. 855, 857 Surcharged with New Value and Old Value Obliterated

1963 *Perf. 13½*

873 A158 1s on 3s rose red 15 15

Perf. 13x12

874 A158 5s on 6s dk red brn 15 15
Set value 15 15

No. 601 Surcharged

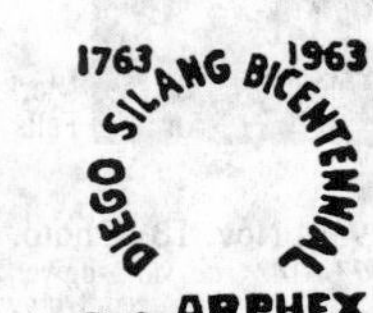

1963, June 12 *Perf. 12*

875 A117 6s on 2p vio 15 15
876 A117 20s on 2p vio 22 22
877 A117 70s on 2p vio 65 55

Issued to publicize the Diego Silang Bicentennial Art and Philatelic Exhibition, ARPHEX, Manila, May 28-June 30.

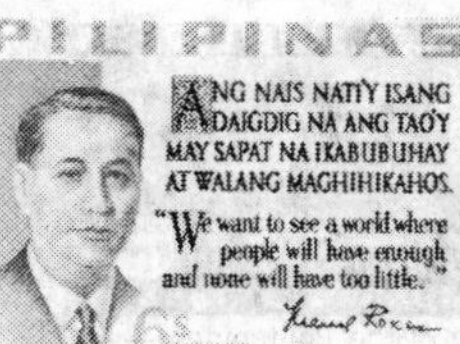

PILIPINAS
ANG NAIS NATIY ISANG DAIGDIG NA ANG TAO'Y MAY SAPAT NA IKABUBUHAY AT WALANG MAGHIHIKAHOS.
"We want to see a world where people will have enough and none will have too little."

Pres. Manuel Roxas
A161

1963-73 Engr. *Perf. 13½*

878 A161 6s brt bl & blk, *bluish* 15 15
879 A161 30s brn & blk 35 15

Pres. Ramon Magsaysay

880 A161 6s lil & blk 15 15
881 A161 30s yel grn & blk 30 15

Pres. Elpidio Quirino

882 A161 6s grn & blk ('65) 15 15
883 A161 30s rose lil & blk ('65) 30 15

Gen. (Pres.) Emilio Aguinaldo

883A A161 6s dp cl & blk ('66) 15 15
883B A161 30s bl & blk ('66) 30 15

Pres. José P. Laurel

883C A161 6s lt red brn & blk ('66) 15 15
883D A161 30s bl & blk ('66) 30 15

Pres. Manuel L. Quezon

883E A161 10s bl gray & blk ('67) 15 15
883F A161 30s lt vio & blk ('67) 30 15

Pres. Sergio Osmeña

883G A161 10s rose lil & blk ('70) 15 15
883H A161 40s grn & blk ('70) 30 15

Pres. Carlos P. Garcia

883I A161 10s multi ('73) 15 15
883J A161 30s multi ('73) 30 15
Set value, #878-883J 3.00 1.00

Nos. 878-883J honor former presidents.
For surcharges see Nos. 984-985, 1120, 1146, 1160-1161.

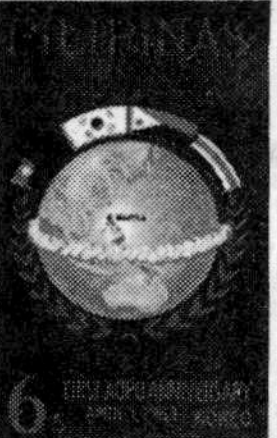

Globe, Flags of Thailand, Korea, China, Philippines
A162

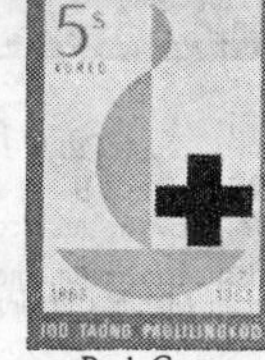

Red Cross Centenary Emblem
A163

1963, Aug. 26 Photo. *Perf. 13½x13*

884 A162 6s dk grn & multi 15 15
885 A162 20s dk grn & multi 18 15
Set value 26 16

Issued to commemorate the first anniversary of the Asian-Oceanic Postal Union.
For surcharge see No. 1078.

1963, Sept. 1 *Perf. 11½*

886 A163 5s lt vio, gray & red 15 15
887 A163 6s ultra, gray & red 15 15
888 A163 20s grn, gray & red 20 15
Set value 34 22

Centenary of the International Red Cross.

Bamboo Dance
A164

Folk Dances: 6s, Dance with oil lamps. 10s, Duck dance. 20s, Princess Gandingan's rock dance.

1963, Sept. 15 Unwmk. *Perf. 14*

889 A164 5s multi 15 15
890 A164 6s multi 15 15
891 A164 10s multi 15 15

892 A164 20s multi 22 22
a. Block of 4, #889-892 50 50
Set value 48 48

For surcharges and overprints see Nos. 1043-1046.

Pres. Macapagal and Filipino Family — A165

1963, Sept. 28 ***Perf. 14***

893 A165 5s bl & multi 15 15
894 A165 6s yel & multi 15 15
895 A165 20s lil & multi 15 15
Set value 30 22

Issued to publicize Pres. Macapagal's 5-year Socioeconomic Program.
For surcharge see No. 1181.

Presidents Lopez Mateos and Macapagal A166

1963, Sept. 28 **Photo.** ***Perf. 13½***

896 A166 6s multi 15 15
897 A166 30s multi 20 15
Set value 28 20

Issued to commemorate the visit of Pres. Adolfo Lopez Mateos of Mexico to the Philippines.
For surcharge see No. 1166.

Andres Bonifacio — A167

1963, Nov. 30 **Unwmk.** ***Perf. 12***

898 A167 5s gold, brn, gray & red 15 15
899 A167 6s sil, brn, gray & red 15 15
900 A167 25s brnz, brn, gray & red 24 22
Set value 38 32

Issued to commemorate the centenary of the birth of Andres Bonifacio, national hero and poet.
For surcharges see Nos. 1147, 1162.

No. 534 Overprinted: "UN ADOPTION/DECLARATION OF HUMAN RIGHTS/15TH ANNIVERSARY DEC. 10, 1963"

1963, Dec. 10 **Engr.** ***Imperf.***

Souvenir Sheet

901 A94 Sheet of 3 55 55

15th anniv. of the Universal Declaration of Human Rights.

Woman holding Sheaf of Rice — A168

1963, Dec. 20 **Photo.** ***Perf. 13½x13***

902 A168 6s brn & multi 15 15

FAO "Freedom from Hunger" campaign.
See Nos. C88-C89.

Bamboo Organ — A169

Apolinario Mabini — A170

1964, May 4 ***Perf. 13½***

903 A169 5s multi 15 15
904 A169 6s multi 15 15
905 A169 20s multi 20 15
Set value 34 22

The bamboo organ in the Church of Las Pinas, Rizal, was built by Father Diego Cera, 1816-1822.
For surcharge see No. 1055.

Perf. 14½

1964, July 23 **Photo.** **Wmk. 233**

906 A170 6s pur & gold 15 15
907 A170 10s red brn & gold 15 15
908 A170 30s brt grn & gold 22 15
Set value 38 26

Apolinario Mabini (1864-1903), national hero and a leader of the 1898 revolution.
For surcharge see No. 1056.

Flags Surrounding SEATO Emblem A171

Pres. Macapagal Signing Code A172

Unwmk.

1964, Sept. 8 **Photo.** ***Perf. 13***

Flags and Emblem Multicolored

909 A171 6s dk bl & yel 15 15
910 A171 10s dp grn & yel 15 15
911 A171 25s dk brn & yel 20 15
Set value 38 26

10th anniversary of the South-East Asia Treaty Organization (SEATO).
For surcharge see No. 1121.

1964, Dec. 21 **Wmk. 233** ***Perf. 14½***

912 A172 3s multi 15 15
913 A172 6s multi 15 15
Set value 15 15

Signing of the Agricultural Land Reform Code. See No. C90. For surcharges see Nos. 970, 1234.

Basketball — A173

Sport: 10s, Women's relay race. 20s, Hurdling. 30s, Soccer.

1964, Dec. 28 ***Perf. 14½x14***

915 A173 6s lt bl, dk brn & gold 15 15
916 A173 10s gold, pink & dk brn 15 15
b. Gold omitted
917 A173 20s gold, dk brn & yel 22 15
918 A173 30s emer, dk brn & gold 30 22
Set value 50

18th Olympic Games, Tokyo, Oct. 10-25.
For overprints see Nos. 962-965. For surcharge see No. 1079.

Imperf., Pairs

915a A173 6s 15 15
916a A173 10s 15 15
917a A173 20s 32 32
918a A173 30s 40 40

Presidents Lubke and Macapagal and Coats of Arms A174

1965, Apr. 19 **Unwmk.** ***Perf. 13½***

919 A174 6s ol grn & multi 15 15
920 A174 10s multi 15 15
921 A174 25s dp bl & multi 18 15
Set value 35 25

Issued to commemorate the visit of Pres. Heinrich Lubke of Germany, Nov. 18-23, 1964.
For surcharge see No. 1167.

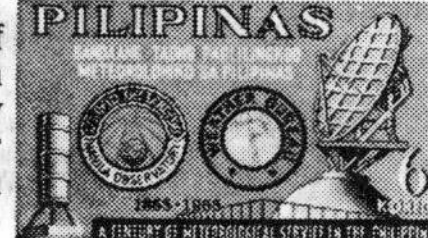

Emblems of Manila Observatory and Weather Bureau A175

1965, May 22 **Photo.** ***Perf. 13½***

922 A175 6s lt ultra & multi 15 15
923 A175 20s lt vio & multi 15 15
924 A175 50s bl grn & multi 40 25
Set value 60 38

Issued to commemorate the centenary of the Meteorological Service in the Philippines.
For surcharge see No. 1069.

Pres. John F. Kennedy (1917-63) — A176

Perf. 14½x14

1965, May 29 **Wmk. 233**

Center Multicolored

925 A176 6s gray 15 15
926 A176 10s brt vio 15 15
927 A176 30s ultra 35 20
Set value 32

Nos. 925-927 exist with ultramarine of tie omitted.
The 6s and 30s exist imperf. Value, each $30.
For surcharges see Nos. 1148, 1210.

King and Queen of Thailand, Pres. and Mrs. Macapagal — A177

Perf. 12½x13

1965, June 12 **Unwmk.**

928 A177 2s brt bl & multi 15 15
929 A177 6s bis & multi 15 15
930 A177 30s red & multi 22 15
Set value 34 22

Visit of King Bhumibol Adulyadej and Queen Sirikit of Thailand, July 1963.
For surcharge see No. 1122.

Princess Beatrix and Evangelina Macapagal A178

Perf. 13x12½

1965, July 4 **Photo.** **Unwmk.**

931 A178 2s bl & multi 15 15
932 A178 6s blk & multi 15 15
933 A178 10s multi 15 15
Set value 22 16

Issued to commemorate the visit of Princess Beatrix of the Netherlands, Nov. 21-23, 1962.
For surcharge see No. 1188.

Cross and Rosary Held Before Map of Philippines — A179

Design: 6s, Map of Philippines, cross and Legaspi-Urdaneta monument.

1965, Oct. 4 **Unwmk.** ***Perf. 13***

934 A179 3s multi 15 15
935 A179 6s multi 15 15
Set value 16 15

400th anniv. of the Christianization of the Philippines. See Nos. C91-C92 and souvenir sheet No. C92a. For overprint see No. C108.

Presidents Sukarno and Macapagal and Prime Minister Tunku Abdul Rahman A180

1965, Nov. 25 ***Perf. 13***

936 A180 6s multi 15 15
937 A180 10s multi 15 15
938 A180 25s multi 20 15
Set value 34 24

Signing of the Manila Accord (Mapilindo) by Malaya, Philippines and Indonesia.
For surcharge see No. 1182.

Bicyclists and Globe A181

1965, Dec. 5 ***Perf. 13½***

939 A181 6s multi 15 15
940 A181 10s multi 15 15
941 A181 25s multi 20 15
Set value 35 24

Second Asian Cycling Championship, Philippines, Nov. 28-Dec. 5.

Nos. B21-B22 Surcharged

10s

MARCOS-LOPEZ
INAUGURATION
DEC. 30, 1965

1965, Dec. 30 **Engr.** ***Perf. 13***

942 SP12 10s on 6s + 4s 15 15
943 SP12 30s on 30s + 5s 24 24

Inauguration of President Ferdinand Marcos and Vice-President Fernando Lopez.

Antonio Regidor — A182

1966, Jan. 21 *Perf. 12x11*

944	A182	6s blue	15	15
945	A182	30s brown	22	20
		Set value	28	25

Issued to honor Dr. Antonio Regidor, Secretary of the High Court of Manila and President of Public Instruction.

For surcharges see Nos. 1110-1111.

No. 857A Overprinted in Red: "HELP ME STOP / SMUGGLING / Pres. MARCOS"

1966, May 1 **Engr.** *Perf. 13½*

946	A158	6s pck bl	15	15

Issued to publicize the anti-smuggling drive of the government.

Exists with overprint inverted, double, double inverted and double with one inverted.

See No. 1209 for No. 946 with black 5s surcharge.

Girl Scout Giving Scout Sign A183

1966, May 26 **Litho.** *Perf. 13x12½*

947	A183	3s ultra & multi	15	15
948	A183	6s emer & multi	15	15
949	A183	20s brn & multi	20	15
		Set value	32	22

Philippine Girl Scouts, 25th anniversary.

For surcharge see No. 1019.

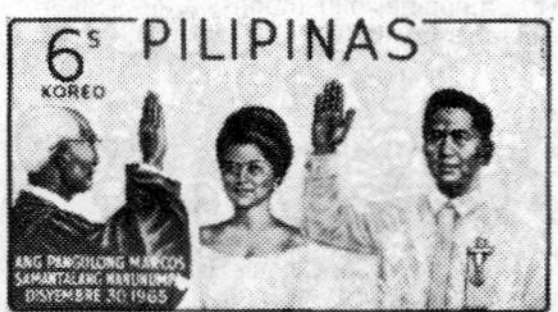

Pres. Marcos Taking Oath of Office — A184

1966, June 12 *Perf. 12½*

950	A184	6s bl & multi	15	15
951	A184	20s emer & multi	15	15
952	A184	30s yel & multi	22	20
		Set value	38	32

Issued to commemorate the inauguration of President Ferdinand E. Marcos, Dec. 30, 1965.

For overprints see Nos. 960-961. For surcharge see No. 1050.

Seal of Manila and Historical Scenes — A185

1966, June 24

953	A185	6s multi	15	15
954	A185	30s multi	20	15
		Set value	26	22

Adoption of the new seal of Manila.

For surcharges see Nos. 1070, 1118, 1235.

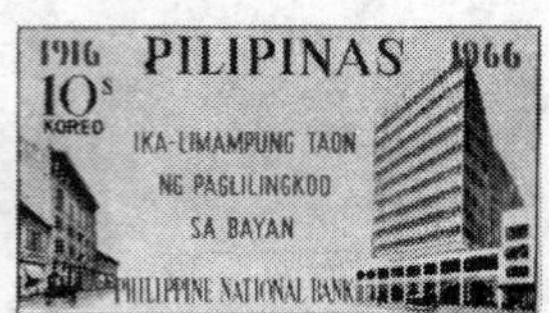

Old and New Philippine National Bank Buildings — A186

Designs: 6s, Entrance to old bank building and 1p silver coin.

1966, July 22 **Photo.** *Perf. 14x13½*

955	A186	6s gold, ultra, sil & blk	15	15
956	A186	10s multi	15	15
		Set value	22	15

50th anniv. of the Philippine Natl. Bank. See #C93. For surcharges see #1071, 1100, 1236.

Post Office, Annex Three A187

1966, Oct. 1 **Wmk. 233** *Perf. 14½*

957	A187	6s lt vio, yel & grn	15	15
958	A187	10s rose cl, yel & grn	15	15
959	A187	20s ultra, yel & grn	20	15
		Set value	35	22

60th anniversary of Postal Savings Bank.

For surcharges see Nos. 1104, 1112, 1189.

Nos. 950 and 952 Overprinted in Emerald or Black

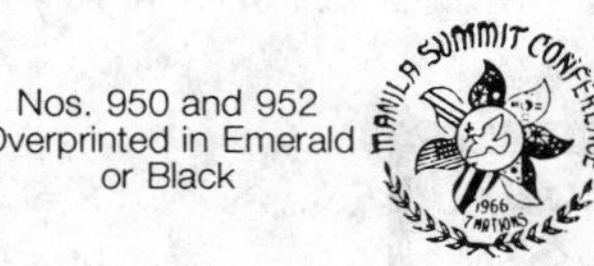

Perf. 12½

1966, Oct. 24 **Litho.** **Unwmk.**

960	A184	6s multi (E)	15	15
961	A184	30s multi	25	22
		Set value	32	28

Manila Summit Conference, Oct. 23-27.

Nos. 915a-918a Overprinted

50th ANNIVERSARY
LIONS INTERNATIONAL
1967

Wmk. 233

1967, Jan. 14 **Photo.** *Imperf.*

962	A173	6s lt bl, dk brn & gold	15	15
963	A173	10s gold, dk brn & pink	15	15
964	A173	20s gold, dk brn & yel	20	15
965	A173	30s emer, dk brn & gold	30	30
		Set value	68	55

50th anniversary of Lions International. The Lions emblem is in the lower left corner on the 6s, in the upper left corner on the 10s and in the upper right corner on the 30s.

"Succor" by Fernando Amorsolo — A188

Unwmk.

1967, May 15 **Litho.** *Perf. 14*

966	A188	5s sep & multi	15	15
967	A188	20s bl & multi	20	15
968	A188	2p grn & multi	1.75	1.00

25th anniversary of the Battle of Bataan.

Nos. 857A and 913 Surcharged

1967, Aug. **Engr.** *Perf. 13½*

969	A158	4s on 6s pck bl	15	15

Perf. 14½

Photo. **Wmk. 233**

970	A172	5s on 6s multi	15	15
		Set value	16	15

Issue dates: 4s, Aug. 10; 5s, Aug. 7.

Gen. Douglas MacArthur and Paratroopers Landing on Corregidor — A189

Unwmk.

1967, Aug. 31 **Litho.** *Perf. 14*

971	A189	6s multi	15	15
972	A189	5p multi	3.25	3.25

25th anniversary, Battle of Corregidor.

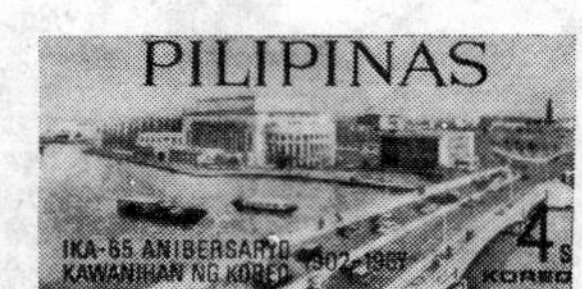

Bureau of Posts, Manila, Jones Bridge over Pasig River — A190

1967, Sept. 15 **Litho.** *Perf. 14x13½*

973	A190	4s multi & blk	15	15
974	A190	20s multi & red	15	15
975	A190	50s multi & vio	32	25
		Set value		44

65th anniversary of the Bureau of Posts.

For overprint see No. 1015.

Philippine Nativity Scene — A191

1967, Dec. 1 **Photo.** *Perf. 13½*

976	A191	10s multi	15	15
977	A191	40s multi	30	22

Christmas 1967.

Chinese Garden, Rizal Park, Presidents Marcos and Chiang Kai-shek — A192

Designs (Presidents' heads and scenes in Chinese Garden, Rizal Park, Manila): 10s, Gate. 20s, Landing pier.

1967-68 **Photo.** *Perf. 13½*

978	A192	5s multi	15	15
979	A192	10s multi ('68)	15	15
980	A192	20s multi	15	15
		Set value	25	20

Sino-Philippine Friendship Year 1966-67.

Makati Center Post Office, Mrs. Marcos and Rotary Emblem — A193

1968, Jan. 9 **Litho.** *Perf. 14*

981	A193	10s bl & multi	15	15
982	A193	20s grn & multi	15	15
983	A193	40s multi	30	30

Issued to commemorate the first anniversary of the Makati Center Post Office.

Nos. 882, 883C and B27 Surcharged with New Value and Two Bars

1968

984	A161	5s on 6s grn & blk	15	15
985	A161	5s on 6s lt red brn & blk	15	15
986	SP14	10s on 6s + 5s ultra & red	15	15
		Set value	20	15

Felipe G. Calderon, Barasoain Church and Malolos Constitution — A194

1968, Apr. 4 **Litho.** *Perf. 14*

987	A194	10s lt ultra & multi	15	15
988	A194	40s grn & multi	35	25
989	A194	75s multi	65	60

Calderon (1868-1909), lawyer and author of the Malolos Constitution.

Earth and Transmission from Philippine Station to Satellite A195

1968, Oct. 21 **Photo.** *Perf. 13½*

990	A195	10s blk & multi	15	15
991	A195	40s multi	45	35
992	A195	75s multi	75	60

Issued to commemorate the inauguration of the Philcomsat Station in Tany, Luzon, May 2, 1968.

Tobacco Industry and Tobacco Board's Emblem — A196

1968, Nov. 15 **Photo.** *Perf. 13½*

993	A196	10s blk & multi	15	15
994	A196	40s bl & multi	35	30
995	A196	70s crim & multi	60	50

Philippine tobacco industry.

Kudyapi A197

Philippine Musical Instruments: 20s, Ludag (drum). 30s, Kulintangan. 50s, Subing (bamboo flute).

1968, Nov. 22 Photo. *Perf. 13½*

996 A197 10s multi 15 15
997 A197 20s multi 15 15
998 A197 30s multi 28 25
999 A197 50s multi 45 40
Set value 82

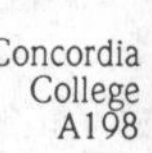

Concordia College A198

1968, Dec. 8 *Perf. 13x13½*

1000 A198 10s multi 15 15
1001 A198 20s multi 15 15
1002 A198 70s multi 40 32
Set value 60 50

Centenary of the Colegio de la Concordia, Manila, a Catholic women's school. Issued Dec. 8 (Sunday), but entered the mail Dec. 9.

Singing Children — A199

1968, Dec. 16 *Perf. 13½*

1003 A199 10s multi 15 15
1004 A199 40s multi 40 35
1005 A199 75s multi 75 60

Christmas 1968.

Animals A200

1969, Jan. 8 Photo. *Perf. 13½*

1006 A200 2s Tarsier 15 15
1007 A200 10s Tamarau 15 15
1008 A200 20s Carabao 15 15
1009 A200 75s Mouse deer 50 40
Set value 72 58

Opening of the hunting season.

Emilio Aguinaldo and Historical Building, Cavite — A201

1969, Jan. 23 Litho. *Perf. 14*

1010 A201 10s yel & multi 15 15
1011 A201 40s bl & multi 45 28
1012 A201 70s multi 75 60

Emilio Aguinaldo (1869-1964), commander of Filipino forces in rebellion against Spain.

Guard Turret, San Andres Bastion, Manila, and Rotary Emblem — A202

1969, Jan. 29 Photo. *Perf. 12½*

1013 A202 10s ultra & multi 15 15

Issued to commemorate the 50th anniversary of the Manila Rotary Club. See Nos. C96-C97.

Senator Claro M. Recto (1890-1960), Lawyer and Supreme Court Judge — A203

1969, Feb. 10 Engr. *Perf. 13*

1014 A203 10s brt rose lil 15 15

No. 973 Overprinted

PHILATELIC WEEK
NOV. 24-30, 1968

1969, Feb. 14 Litho. *Perf. 14x13½*

1015 A190 4s multi & blk 15 15

Issued to commemorate Philatelic Week, Nov. 24-30, 1968.

José Rizal College, Mandaluyong A204

1969, Feb. 19 Photo. *Perf. 13*

1016 A204 10s multi 15 15
1017 A204 40s multi 35 25
1018 A204 50s multi 45 38

Issued to commemorate the 50th anniversary of the founding of Rizal College.

No. 948 Surcharged in Red with New Value, 2 Bars and: "4th NATIONAL BOY / SCOUT JAMBOREE / PALAYAN CITY-MAY, 1969"

1969, May 12 Litho. *Perf. 13x12½*

1019 A183 5s on 6s multi 15 15

A205

A206

Map of Philippines, Red Crescent, Cross, Lion and Sun emblems.

1969, May 26 Photo. *Perf. 12½*

1020 A205 10s gray, ultra & red 15 15
1021 A205 40s lt ultra, dk bl & red 40 25
1022 A205 75s bis, brn & red 60 55

Issued to commemorate the 50th anniversary of the League of Red Cross Societies.

1969, June 13 Photo. *Perf. 14*

Pres. and Mrs. Marcos harvesting miracle rice.

1023 A206 10s multi 15 15
1024 A206 40s multi 40 30
1025 A206 75s multi 60 55

Issued to publicize the introduction of IR8 (miracle) rice, produced by the International Rice Research Institute.

Holy Child of Leyte and Map of Leyte A207

1969, June 30 *Perf. 13½*

1026 A207 5s emer & multi 15 15
1027 A207 10s crim & multi 15 15
Set value 16 15

Issued to commemorate the 80th anniversary of the return of the image of the Holy Child of Leyte to Tacloban. See No. C98.

Philippine Development Bank — A208

1969, Sept. 12 Photo. *Perf. 13½*

1028 A208 10s dk bl, blk & grn 15 15
1029 A208 40s rose car, blk & grn 50 25
1030 A208 75s brn, blk & grn 75 55

Issued to commemorate the inauguration of the new building of the Philippine Development Bank in Makati, Rizal.

Common Birdwing A209

Butterflies: 20s, Tailed jay. 30s, Red Helen. 40s, Birdwing.

1969, Sept. 15 Photo. *Perf. 13½*

1031 A209 10s multi 15 15
1032 A209 20s multi 15 15
1033 A209 30s multi 20 15
1034 A209 40s multi 30 18
Set value 68 42

World's Children and UNICEF Emblem A210

1969, Oct. 6

1035 A210 10s bl & multi 15 15
1036 A210 20s multi 15 15
1037 A210 30s multi 15 15
Set value 32 26

Issued for the 15th anniversary of Universal Children's Day.

Monument and Leyte Landing — A211

1969, Oct. 20 *Perf. 13½x14*

1038 A211 5s lt grn & multi 15 15
1039 A211 10s yel & multi 15 15
1040 A211 40s pink & multi 30 18
Set value 48 30

25th anniv. of the landing of the US forces under Gen. Douglas MacArthur on Leyte, Oct. 20, 1944.

Philippine Cultural Center, Manila A212

1969, Nov. 4 Photo. *Perf. 13½*

1041 A212 10s ultra 15 15
1042 A212 30s brt rose lil 20 15
Set value 28 22

Issued to publicize the Cultural Center of the Philippines, containing theaters, a museum and libraries.

Nos. 889-892 Surcharged or Overprinted: "1969 PHILATELIC WEEK"

1969, Nov. 24 Photo. *Perf. 14*

1043 A164 5s multi 15 15
1044 A164 5s on 6s multi 15 15
1045 A164 10s multi 15 15
1046 A164 10s on 20s multi 15 15
Set value 34 30

Philatelic Week, Nov. 23-29.

Melchora Aquino — A213

1969, Nov. 30 *Perf. 12½*

1047 A213 10s multi 15 15
1048 A213 20s multi 15 15
1049 A213 30s dk bl & multi 25 15
Set value 30

Issued to commemorate the 50th anniversary of the death of Melchora Aquino (Tandang Sora; 1812-1919), the Grand Old Woman of the Revolution.

No. 950 Surcharged with New Value, 2 Bars and: "PASINAYA, IKA -2 PANUNUNGKULAN / PANGULONG FERDINAND E. MARCOS / DISYEMBRE 30, 1969"

1969, Dec. 30 Litho. *Perf. 12½*

1050 A184 5s on 6s multi 20 15

Issued to commemorate the inauguration of Pres. Ferdinand E. Marcos and Vice Pres. Fernando Lopez for a second term, Dec. 30.

Footnotes often refer to other stamps of the same design.

Pouring Ladle and Iligan Steel Mills — A214

1970, Jan. 20 Photo. *Perf. 13½*

1051	A214	10s ver & multi	15	15
1052	A214	20s multi	15	15
1053	A214	30s ultra & multi	25	18
		Set value		36

Issued to publicize the Iligan Integrated Steel Mills, Northern Mindanao, the first Philippine steel mills.

Nos. 857A, 904 and 906 Surcharged with New Value and Two Bars

1970, Apr. 30 As Before

1054	A158	4s on 6s peacock bl	15	15
1055	A169	5s on 6s multi	15	15
1056	A170	5s on 6s pur & gold	15	15
		Set value	15	15

New UPU Headquarters and Monument, Bern — A215

Perf. 13½

1970, May 20 Unwmk. Photo.

1057	A215	10s bl, dk bl & yel	15	15
1058	A215	30s lt grn, dk bl & yel	32	18
		Set value		24

Opening of the new UPU Headquarters in Bern.

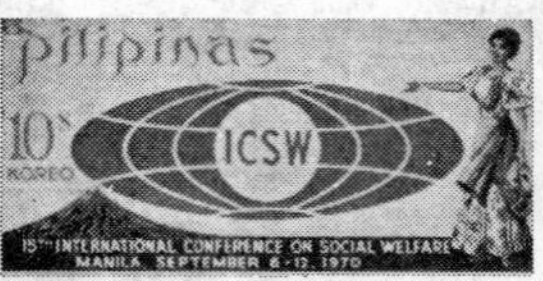

Emblem, Mayon Volcano and Filipina — A216

1970, Sept. 6 Photo. *Perf. 13½x14*

1059	A216	10s brt bl & multi	15	15
1060	A216	20s multi	18	15
1061	A216	30s multi	30	15
		Set value		36

Issued to publicize the 15th International Conference on Social Welfare, Manila, Sept. 6-12.

Crab, by Alexander Calder, and Map of Philippines A217

1970, Oct. 5 *Perf. 13x13½*

1062	A217	10s emer & multi	15	15
1063	A217	40s multi	35	20
1064	A217	50s ultra & multi	50	30

Campaign against cancer.

Scaled Tridacna — A218

Sea Shells: 10s, Royal spiny oyster. 20s, Venus comb. 40s, Glory of the sea.

1970, Oct. 19 Photo. *Perf. 13½*

1065	A218	5s blk & multi	15	15
1066	A218	10s dk grn & multi	15	15
1067	A218	20s multi	15	15
1068	A218	40s dk bl & multi	32	20
		Set value	60	38

Nos. 922, 953 and 955 Surcharged

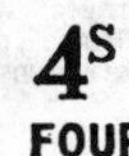

Photogravure; Lithographed

1970, Oct. 26 *Perf. 13½, 12½*

1069	A175	4s on 6s multi	15	15
1070	A185	4s on 6s multi	15	15
1071	A186	4s on 6s multi	15	15
		Set value	15	15

One line surcharge on No. 1071.

Map of Philippines and FAPA Emblem — A219

1970, Nov. 16 Photo. *Perf. 13½*

1072	A219	10s dp org & multi	15	15
1073	A219	50s lt vio & multi	40	20
		Set value		26

Issued to commemorate the opening of the 4th General Assembly of the Federation of Asian Pharmaceutical Associations (FAPA) and the 3rd Asian Congress of Pharmaceutical Sciences.

Hundred Islands of Pangasinan, Peddler's Cart — A220

Designs: 20s, Tree house in Pasonanca Park, Zamboanga City. 30s, Sugar industry, Negros Island, Mt. Kanlaon, Woman and Carabao statue, symbolizing agriculture. 2p, Miagao Church, Iloilo, and horse-drawn calesa.

1970, Nov. 12 *Perf. 12½x13½*

1074	A220	10s multi	15	15
1075	A220	20s multi	15	15
1076	A220	30s multi	18	16
1077	A220	2p multi	1.10	65

Tourist publicity. See Nos. 1086-1097.

No. 884 Surcharged: "UPU-AOPU / Regional Seminar / Nov. 23-Dec. 5, 1970 / TEN 10s"

1970, Nov. 22 Photo. *Perf. 13½x13*

1078	A162	10s on 6s multi	15	15

Universal Postal Union and Asian-Oceanic Postal Union Regional Seminar, Nov. 23-Dec. 5.

No. 915 Surcharged Vertically: "1970 PHILATELIC WEEK"

Perf. 14½x14

1970, Nov. 22 Wmk. 233

1079	A173	10s on 6s multi	15	15

Philatelic Week, Nov. 22-28.

Pope Paul VI, Map of Far East and Australia — A221

Perf. 13½x14

1970, Nov. 27 Photo. Unwmk.

1080	A221	10s ultra & multi	15	15
1081	A221	30s multi	18	15
		Set value	26	18

Visit of Pope Paul VI, Nov. 27-29, 1970. See No. C99.

Mariano Ponce — A222

1970, Dec. 30 Engr. *Perf. 14½*

1082	A222	10s rose car	15	15

Mariano Ponce (1863-1918), editor and legislator. See Nos. 1136-1137. For surcharges see Nos. 1190, 1231. For overprint see No. O70.

PATA Emblem A223

1971, Jan. 21 Photo. *Perf. 14½*

1083	A223	5s brt grn & multi	15	15
1084	A223	10s bl & multi	15	15
1085	A223	70s brn & multi	30	22
		Set value	46	35

Pacific Travel Association (PATA), 20th annual conference, Manila, Jan. 21-29.

Tourist Type of 1970

Designs: 10s, Filipina and Ang Nayong (7 village replicas around man-made lagoon). 20s, Woman and fisherman, Estancia. 30s, Pagsanjan Falls. 5p, Watch Tower, Punta Cruz, Boho.

Perf. 12½x13½

1971, Feb. 15 Photo.

1086	A220	10s multi	15	15
1087	A220	20s multi	15	15
1088	A220	30s multi	15	15
1089	A220	5p multi	1.25	1.25

1971, Apr. 19

Designs: 10s, Cultured pearl farm, Davao. 20s, Coral divers, Davao, Mindanao. 40s, Moslem Mosque, Zamboanga. 1p, Rice terraces, Banaue.

1090	A220	10s multi	15	15
1091	A220	20s multi	15	15
1092	A220	40s multi	15	15
1093	A220	1p multi	35	30
		Set value	68	55

1971, May 3

Designs: 10s, Spanish cannon, Zamboanga. 30s, Magellan's cross, Cebu City. 50s, Big Jar monument in Calamba, Laguna. 70s, Mayon Volcano, Legaspi.

1094	A220	10s multi	15	15
1095	A220	30s multi	15	15
1096	A220	50s multi	15	15
1097	A220	70s multi	32	20
		Set value	65	48

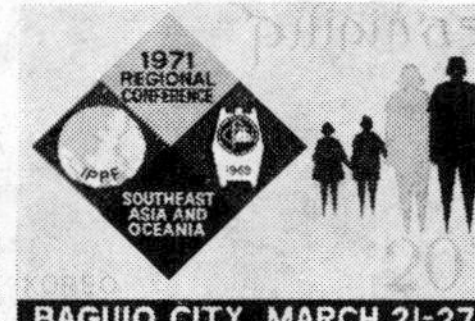

Family and Emblem A224

1971, Mar. 21 Photo. *Perf. 13½*

1098	A224	20s lt grn & multi	15	15
1099	A224	40s pink & multi	15	15
		Set value	22	18

Regional Conference of the International Planned Parenthood Federation for Southeast Asia and Oceania, Baguio City, March 21-27.

No. 955 Surcharged **FIVE 5s**

1971, June 10 Photo. *Perf. 14x13½*

1100	A186	5s on 6s multi	15	15

Allegory of Law A225

1971, June 15 Photo. *Perf. 13*

1101	A225	15s org & multi	15	15

60th anniversary of the University of the Philippines Law College. See No. C100.

Manila Anniversary Emblem — A226

1971, June 24

1102	A226	10s multi	15	15

400th anniversary of the founding of Manila. See No. C101.

Santo Tomas University, Arms of Schools of Medicine and Pharmacology — A227

1971, July 8 Photo. *Perf. 13½*

1103	A227	5s yel & multi	15	15

Centenary of the founding of the Schools of Medicine and Surgery, and Pharmacology at the University of Santo Tomas, Manila. See No. C102.

No. 957 Surcharged

1971, July 11 Wmk. 233 ***Perf. 14½***
1104 A187 5s on 6s multi 15 15

World Congress of University Presidents, Manila.

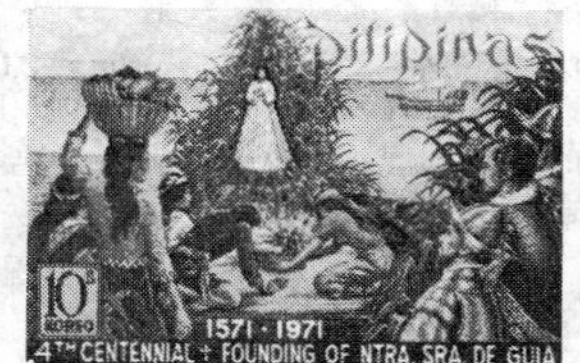

Our Lady of Guia Appearing to Filipinos and Spanish Soldiers — A228

1971, July 8 Photo. ***Perf. 13½***
1105 A228 10s multi 15 15
1106 A228 75s multi 32 30
Set value 38

4th centenary of appearance of the statue of Our Lady of Guia, Ermita, Manila.

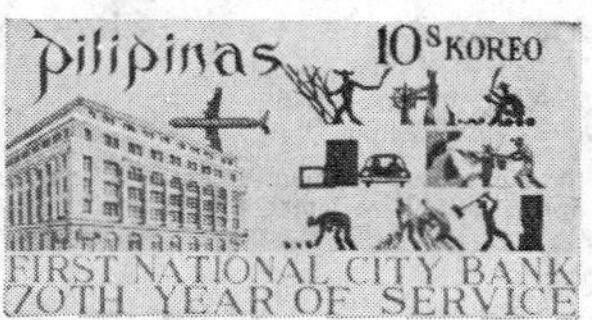

Bank Building, Plane, Car and Workers — A229

1971, Sept. 14 ***Perf. 12½***
1107 A229 10s bl & multi 15 15
1108 A229 30s lt grn & multi 18 15
1109 A229 1p multi 40 32
Set value 52

70th anniversary of the First National City Bank in the Philippines.

No. 944 Surcharged FOUR 4s

Perf. 12x11
1971, Nov. 24 Engr. Unwmk.
1110 A182 4s on 6s blue 15 15
1111 A182 5s on 6s blue 15 15
Set value 15 15

No. 957 Surcharged

5s FIVE

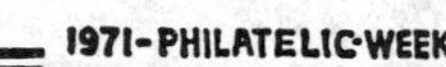

Perf. 14½
1971, Nov. 24 Wmk. 233 Photo.
1112 A187 5s on 6s multi 15 15

Philatelic Week, 1971.

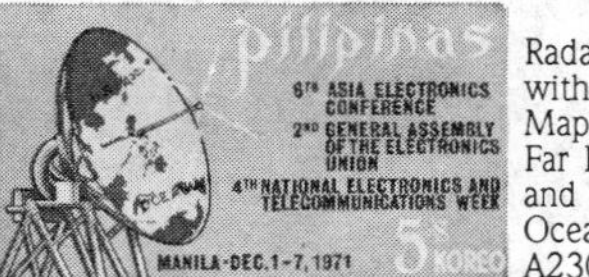

Radar with Map of Far East and Oceania A230

1972, Feb. 29 Photo. ***Perf. 14x14½***
1113 A230 5s org yel & multi 15 15
1114 A230 40s red org & multi 32 20
Set value 40 25

Electronics Conferences, Manila, Dec. 1-7, 1971.

Fathers Gomez, Burgos and Zamora — A231

1972, Apr. 3 ***Perf. 13x12½***
1115 A231 5s gold & multi 15 15
1116 A231 60s gold & multi 25 25
Set value 30 30

Centenary of the deaths of Fathers Mariano Gomez, José Burgos and Jacinto Zamora, martyrs for Philippine independence from Spain.

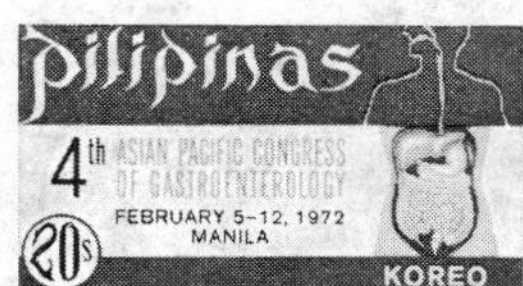

Digestive Tract — A232

1972, Apr. 11 Photo. ***Perf. 12½x13***
1117 A232 20s ultra & multi 15 15

4th Asian Pacific Congress of Gastroenterology, Manila, Feb. 5-12. See No. C103.

No. 953 Surcharged

5s FIVE

1972, Apr. 20 ***Perf. 12½***
1118 A185 5s on 6s multi 15 15

No. O69 with Two Bars over "G." and "O."

1972, May 16 Engr. ***Perf. 13½***
1119 A158 50s violet 25 15

Nos. 883A, 909 and 929 Surcharged with New Value and 2 Bars

1972, May 29
1120 A161 10s on 6s dp cl & blk 15 15
1121 A171 10s on 6s multi 15 15
1122 A177 10s on 6s multi 15 15
Set value 20 15

Independence Monument, Manila — A233

1972, May 31 Photo. ***Perf. 13x12½***
1123 A233 5s brt bl & multi 15 15
1124 A233 50s red & multi 50 15
1125 A233 60s emer & multi 65 20
Set value 38

Visit ASEAN countries (Association of South East Asian Nations).

"K," Skull and Crossbones — A234

Development of Philippine Flag: No. 1126, 3 "K's" in a row ("K" stands for Katipunan). No. 1127, 3 "K's" as triangle. No. 1128, One "K." No. 1130, 3 "K's," sun over mountain on white triangle. No. 1131, Sun over 3 "K's." No. 1132, Tagalog "K" in sun. No. 1133, Sun with human face. No. 1134, Tricolor flag, forerunner of present flag. No. 1135, Present flag. Nos. 1126, 1128, 1130-1131, 1133, 1135 inscribed in Tagalog.

1972, June 12 Photo. ***Perf. 13***
1126 A234 30s ultra & red 18 15
1127 A234 30s ultra & red 18 15
1128 A234 30s ultra & red 18 15
1129 A234 30s ultra & blk 18 15
1130 A234 30s ultra & red 18 15
1131 A234 30s ultra & red 18 15
1132 A234 30s ultra & red 18 15
1133 A234 30s ultra & red 18 15
1134 A234 30s ultra, red & blk 18 15
1135 A234 30s ultra, yel & red 18 15
a. Block of 10 1.90 1.50

Portrait Type of 1970

Portraits: 40s, Gen. Miguel Malvar. 1p, Julian Felipe.

1972 Engr. ***Perf. 14***
1136 A222 40s rose red 20 15
1137 A222 1p dp bl 55 20
Set value 25

Honoring Gen. Miguel Malvar (1865-1911), revolutionary leader, and Julian Felipe (1861-1944), composer of Philippine national anthem.
Issue dates: 40s, July 10; 1p, June 26.

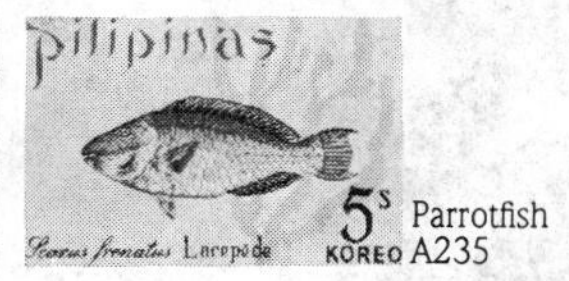

Parrotfish A235

1972, Aug. 14 Photo. ***Perf. 13***
1138 A235 5s shown 15 15
1139 A235 10s Sunburst butterflyfish 15 15
1140 A235 20s Moorish idol 15 15
Set value 28 18

Tropical fish. See No. C104.

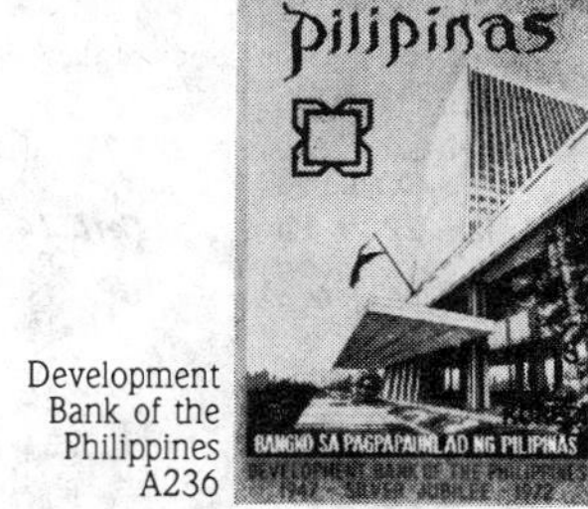

Development Bank of the Philippines A236

1972, Sept. 12
1141 A236 10s gray blue & multi 15 15
1142 A236 20s lilac & multi 15 15
1143 A236 60s tan & multi 32 20
Set value 50 32

25th anniversary of the Development Bank of the Philippines.

Pope Paul VI A237

1972, Sept. 26 Unwmk. ***Perf. 14***
1144 A237 10s lt grn & multi 15 15
1145 A237 50s lt vio & multi 25 20
Set value 30 25

First anniversary (in 1971) of the visit of Pope Paul VI to the Philippines, and for his 75th birthday. See No. C105.

Nos. 880, 899 and 925 Surcharged with New Value and 2 Bars

1972, Sept. 29 As Before
1146 A161 10s on 6s lil & blk 15 15
1147 A167 10s on 6s multi 15 15
1148 A176 10s on 6s multi 15 15
Set value 24 15

Charon's Bark, by Resurrección Hidalgo — A238

Paintings: 10s, Rice Workers' Meal, by F. Amorsolo. 30s, "Spain and the Philippines," by Juan Luna, vert. 70s, Song of Maria Clara, by F. Amorsolo.

Perf. 14x13
1972, Oct. 16 Unwmk. Photo.
Size: 38x40mm
1149 A238 5s sil & multi 15 15
1150 A238 10s sil & multi 15 15
Size: 24x56mm
1151 A238 30s sil & multi 15 15
Size: 38x40mm
1152 A238 70s sil & multi 32 32
Set value 58 58

25th anniversary of the organization of the Stamp and Philatelic Division.

Lamp, Nurse, Emblem — A239

1972, Oct. 22 ***Perf. 12½x13½***
1153 A239 5s vio & multi 15 15
1154 A239 10s bl & multi 15 15
1155 A239 70s org & multi 25 22
Set value 36 32

50th anniversary of the Philippine Nursing Association.

Heart, Map of Philippines A240

1972, Oct. 24 ***Perf. 13***
1156 A240 5s pur, emer & red 15 15
1157 A240 10s bl, emer & red 15 15
1158 A240 30s emer, bl & red 15 15
Set value 26 22

"Your heart is your health," World Health Month.

First Mass on Limasawa, by Carlos V. Francisco — A241

1972, Oct. 31 *Perf. 14*
1159 A241 10s brn & multi 15 15

450th anniversary of the first mass in the Philippines, celebrated by Father Valderama on Limasawa, Mar. 31, 1521. See No. C106.

Nos. 878, 882, 899 Surcharged: "ASIA PACIFIC SCOUT CONFERENCE NOV. 1972"

1972, Nov. 13 **As Before**
1160 A161 10s on 6s bl & blk 15 15
1161 A161 10s on 6s grn & blk 15 15
1162 A167 10s on 6s multi 15 15
Set value 30 20

Asia Pacific Scout Conference, Nov. 1972.

Torch, Olympic Emblems — A242

Perf. 12½x13½
1972, Nov. 15 **Photo.**
1163 A242 5s bl & multi 15 15
1164 A242 10s multi 15 15
1165 A242 70s org & multi 32 25
Set value 44 36

20th Olympic Games, Munich, Aug. 26-Sept. 11.
For surcharges see Nos. 1297, 1759-1760.

Nos. 896 and 919 Surcharged with New Value, Two Bars and: "1972 PHILATELIC WEEK"

1972, Nov. 23 **Photo.** *Perf. 13½*
1166 A166 10s on 6s multi 15 15
1167 A174 10s on 6s multi 15 15
Set value 15 15

Philatelic Week 1972.

Manunggul Burial Jar, 890-710 B.C. — A243

Designs: No. 1169, Ngipet Duldug Cave ritual earthenware vessel, 155 B.C. No. 1170, Metal age chalice, 200-600 A.D. No. 1171, Earthenware vessel, 15th century.

1972, Nov. 29
1168 A243 10s grn & multi 15 15
1169 A243 10s lil & multi 15 15
1170 A243 10s bl & multi 15 15
1171 A243 10s yel & multi 15 15
Set value 32 20

College of Pharmacy and Univ. of the Philippines Emblems — A244

1972, Dec. 11 *Perf. 12½x13½*
1172 A244 5s lt vio & multi 15 15
1173 A244 10s yel grn & multi 15 15
1174 A244 30s ultra & multi 20 15
Set value 35 22

60th anniversary of the College of Pharmacy of the University of the Philippines.

Christmas Lantern Makers, by Jorgé Pineda A245

1972, Dec. 14 **Photo.** *Perf. 12½*
1175 A245 10s dk bl & multi 15 15
1176 A245 30s brn & multi 15 15
1177 A245 50s grn & multi 25 22
Set value 46 36

Christmas 1972.

Red Cross Flags, Pres. Roxas and Mrs. Aurora Quezon — A246

1972, Dec. 21
1178 A246 5s ultra & multi 15 15
1179 A246 20s multi 15 15
1180 A246 30s brn & multi 15 15
Set value 30 25

25th anniv. of the Philippine Red Cross.

Nos. 894 and 936 Surcharged with New Value and 2 Bars

1973, Jan. 22 **Photo.** *Perf. 14, 13*
1181 A165 10s on 6s multi 15 15
1182 A180 10s on 6s multi 15 15
Set value 16 15

San Luis University, Luzon — A247

1973, Mar. 1 **Photo.** *Perf. 13½x14*
1183 A247 5s multi 15 15
1184 A247 10s yel & multi 15 15
1185 A247 75s multi 30 25
Set value 40 35

60th anniversary of San Luis University, Baguio City, Luzon.
For surcharge see No. 1305.

Jesus Villamor and Fighter Planes — A248

1973, Apr. 9 **Photo.** *Perf. 13½x14*
1186 A248 10s multi 15 15
1187 A248 2p multi 70 70

Col. Jesus Villamor (1914-1971), World War II aviator who fought for liberation of the Philippines.
For surcharge see No. 1230.

Nos. 932, 957, O70 Surcharged with New Values and 2 Bars

1973, Apr. 23 **As Before**
1188 A178 5s on 6s multi 15 15
1189 A187 5s on 6s multi 15 15
1190 A222 15s on 10s rose car 15 15
Set value 24 15

Two additional bars through "G.O." on No. 1190.

ITI Emblem, Performance and Actor Vic Silayan — A249

1973, May 15 **Photo.** *Perf. 13x12½*
1191 A249 5s bl & multi 15 15
1192 A249 10s yel grn & multi 15 15
1193 A249 50s org & multi 20 15
1194 A249 70s rose & multi 30 18
Set value 62 40

1st Third World Theater Festival, sponsored by the UNESCO affiliated International Theater Institute, Manila, Nov. 19-30, 1971.
For surcharge see No. 1229.

Josefa Llanes Escoda — A250

Designs: No. 1196, Gabriela Silang. No. 1197, Rafael Palma. 30s, Jose Rizal. 60s, Marcela Agoncillo. 90s, Teodoro R. Yangco. 1.10p, Dr. Pio Venezuela. 1.20p, Gregoria de Jesus. No. 1204, Pedro A. Paterno. No. 1205, Teodora Alonso. 1.80p, Edilberto Evangelista. 5p, Fernando M. Guerrero.

1973-78 **Engr.** *Perf. 14½*
1195 A250 15s sepia 15 15

Litho. *Perf. 12½*
1196 A250 15s vio ('74) 15 15
1197 A273 15s emer ('74) 15 15
1198 A250 30s vio bl ('78) 15 15
1199 A250 60s dl red brn 22 22
1200 A273 90s brt bl ('74) 30 15
1202 A273 1.10p brt bl ('74) 38 18
1203 A250 1.20p dl red ('78) 25 15
1204 A250 1.50p lil rose 50 42
1205 A273 1.50p brn ('74) 50 20
1206 A250 1.80p green 60 55
1208 A250 5p blue 1.65 1.65
Nos. 1195-1208 (12) 5.00 4.12

1973-74 ***Imperf.***
1196a A250 15s violet ('74) 15 15
1197a A273 15s emerald ('74) 15 15
1199a A250 60s dull red brown 30 30
1200a A273 90s bright blue ('74) 45 40
1202a A273 1.10p bright blue ('74) 52 52
1204a A250 1.50p lilac rose 60 52
1205a A273 1.50p brown ('74) 70 70
1206a A250 1.80p green 70 70
1208a A250 5p blue 2.00 2.00
Nos. 1196a-1208a (9) 5.57 5.44

Honoring: Escoda (1898-194?), leader of Girl Scouts and Federation of Women's Clubs. Silang (1731-63), "the Ilocana Joan of Arc". Palma (1874-1939), journalist, statesman, educator. Rizal (1861-96), natl. hero. Agoncillo (1859-1946), designer of 1st Philippine flag, 1898. Yangco (1861-1939), patriot and philanthropist. Valenzuela (1869-1956), physician and newspaperman.
Gregoria de Jesus, independence leader. Paterno (1857-1911), lawyer, writer, patriot. Alonso (1827-1911), mother of Rizal. Evangelista (1862-97), army engineer, patriot. Guerrero (1873-1929), journalist, political leader.
For overprint see No. 1277. For surcharges see Nos. 1311, 1470, 1518.

No. 946 surcharged with New Value

1973, June 4 **Engr.** *Perf. 13½*
1209 A158 5s on 6s peacock bl 15 15

Anti-smuggling campaign.

No. 925 Surcharged

1973, June 4 **Wmk. 233**
1210 A176 5s on 6s multi 15 15

10th anniversary of death of John F. Kennedy (1917-1963).

Pres. Marcos, Farm Family, Unfurling of Philippine Flag — A251

Perf. 12½x13½
1973, Sept. 24 **Photo.** **Unwmk.**
1211 A251 15s ultra & multi 15 15
1212 A251 45s red & multi 15 15
1213 A251 90s multi 32 32

75th anniversary of Philippine independence and 1st anniversary of proclamation of martial law.

Imelda Romualdez Marcos, First Lady of the Philippines A252

1973, Oct. 31 **Photo.** *Perf. 13*
1214 A252 15s dl bl & multi 15 15
1215 A252 50s multicolored 18 18
1216 A252 60s lil & multi 22 22
Set value 46 46

Presidential Palace, Manila, Pres. and Mrs. Marcos — A253

1973, Nov. 15 **Litho.** *Perf. 14*
1217 A253 15s rose & multi 15 15
1218 A253 50s ultra & multi 15 15
Set value 22 22

See No. C107.

INTERPOL Emblem — A254

1973, Dec. 18 Photo. *Perf. 13*

1219 A254 15s ultra & multi	15	15
1220 A254 65s lt grn & multi	30	15
Set value		22

50th anniversary of International Criminal Police Organization.

Cub and Boy Scouts — A255

Design: 15s, Various Scout activities; inscribed in Tagalog.

1973, Dec. 28 Litho. *Perf. 12½*

1221 A255 15s bis & emer	15	15
a. Imperf. ('74)	15	15
1222 A255 65s bis & brt bl	28	22
a. Imperf. ('74)	40	40
Set value	36	28

50th anniv. of Philippine Boy Scouts.

Nos. 1221a-1222a issued Feb. 4, although first day covers are dated Dec. 28, 1973.

Manila, Bank Emblem and Farmers — A256

Designs: 60s, Old bank building. 1.50p, Modern bank building.

1974, Jan. 3 Photo. *Perf. 12½x13½*

1223 A256 15s silver & multi	15	15
1224 A256 60s silver & multi	20	15
1225 A256 1.50p silver & multi	50	30
Set value		48

25th anniversary of the Central Bank of the Philippines.

UPU Emblem, Maria Clara Costume — A257

Filipino Costumes: 60s, Balintawak and UPU emblem. 80s, Malong costume and UPU emblem.

1974, Jan. 15 *Perf. 12½*

1226 A257 15s multicolored	15	15
1227 A257 60s multicolored	20	15
1228 A257 80s multicolored	30	18
Set value		36

Centenary of Universal Postal Union.

No. 1192 Surcharged in Red with New Value, 2 Bars and: "1973 / PHILATELIC WEEK"

1974, Feb. 4 Photo. *Perf. 13x12½*

1229 A249 15s on 10s multi	15	15

Philatelic Week, 1973. First day covers exist dated Nov. 26, 1973.

Nos. 1186 and 1136 Overprinted and Surcharged

PHILIPPINE LIONISM 1949-1974
LIONS INTERNATIONAL
45s

1974, Mar. 25 Photo. *Perf. 13½x14*

1230 A248 15s on 10s multi	15	15

Engr. *Perf. 14*

1231 A222 45s on 40s rose red	15	15
Set value	22	18

25th anniversary of Lions International of the Philippines. The overprint on No. 1230 arranged to fit shape of stamp.

Pediatrics Congress Emblem and Map of Participating Countries A258

1974, Apr. 30 Litho. *Perf. 12½*

1232 A258 30s brt bl & red	15	15
a. Imperf.	15	15
1233 A258 1p dl grn & red	32	20
a. Imperf.	42	32
Set value		28

Asian Congress of Pediatrics, Manila, Apr. 30-May 4.

Nos. 912, 954-955 Surcharged with New Value and Two Bars

1974, Aug. 1 As Before

1234 A172 5s on 3s multi	15	15
1235 A185 5s on 6s multi	15	15
1236 A186 5s on 6s multi	15	15
Set value	15	15

WPY Emblem A259

1974, Aug. 15 Litho. *Perf. 12½*

1237 A259 5s org & bl blk	15	15
a. Imperf.	15	15
1238 A259 2p lt grn & dk bl	60	32
a. Imperf.	65	50
Set value	65	36

World Population Year, 1974.

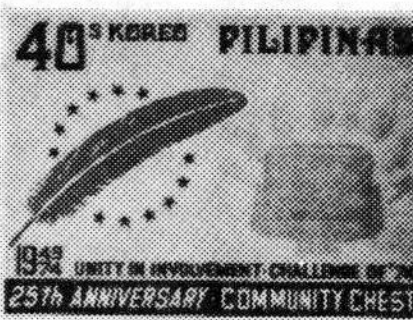

Red Feather Community Chest Emblem A260

Perf. 12½

1974, Sept. 5 Litho. Wmk. 372

1239 A260 15s brt bl & red	15	15
1240 A260 40s emer & red	15	15
1241 A260 45s red brn & red	20	15
Set value	42	25

25th anniversary of the Philippine Community Chest.

Imperf.

1239a A260 15s	15	15
1240a A260 40s	20	20
1241a A260 45s	20	20

Sultan Kudarat, Flag, Order and Map of Philippines — A261

Perf. 13½x14

1975, Jan. 13 Photo. Unwmk.

1242 A261 15s multicolored	15	15

Sultan Mohammad Dipatuan Kudarat, 16th-17th century ruler.

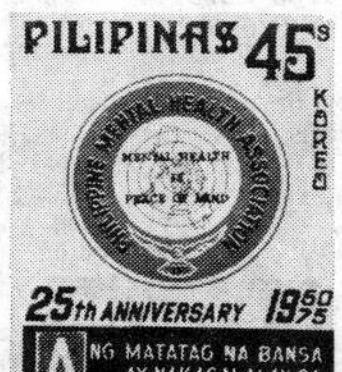

Mental Health Association Emblem — A262

Perf. 12½

1975, Jan. 20 Wmk. 372 Litho.

1243 A262 45s emer & org	15	15
a. Imperf.	20	20
1244 A262 1p emer & pur	25	20
a. Imperf.	32	32

Philippine Mental Health Association, 25th anniversary.

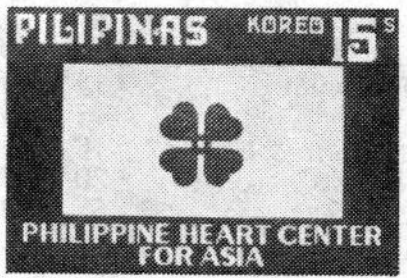

4-Leaf Clover — A263

1975, Feb. 14

1245 A263 15s vio bl & red	15	15
a. Imperf.	15	15
1246 A263 50s emer & red	15	15
a. Imperf.	18	18
Set value	20	16

Philippine Heart Center for Asia, inauguration.

Military Academy, Cadet and Emblem — A264

Perf. 13½x14

1975, Feb. 17 Unwmk.

1247 A264 15s grn & multi	15	15
1248 A264 45s plum & multi	24	15
Set value		22

Philippine Military Academy, 70th anniv.

Helping the Disabled — A265

Perf. 12½, Imperf.

1975, Mar. 17 Wmk. 372

1249 A265 Block of 10	1.65	1.25
a.-j. 45s grn, any single	15	15

25th anniversary (in 1974) of Philippine Orthopedic Association.

For surcharge see No. 1635.

Nos. B43, B50-B51 Surcharged with New Value and Two Bars

1975, Apr. 15 Unwmk.

1250 SP18 5s on 15s + 5s	15	15
1251 SP16 60s on 70s + 5s	22	20
1252 SP18 1p on 1.10p + 5s	25	22
Set value	52	46

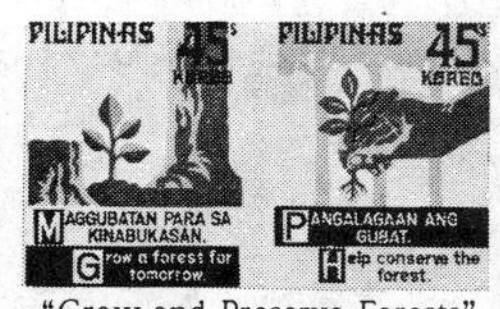

"Grow and Preserve Forests"
A266 A267

1975, May 19 Litho. *Perf. 14½*

1253 A266 45s blk, brn & grn	15	15
1254 A267 45s blk, brn & grn	15	15
Set value		20

Forest conservation. Nos. 1253-1254 printed se-tenant in sheets of 100.

Jade Vine — A268

1975, June 9 Photo. *Perf. 14½*

1255 A268 15s multicolored	15	15

Imelda R. Marcos, IWY Emblem — A269

Civil Service Emblem — A270

Perf. 12½

1975, July 2 Litho. Wmk. 372

1256 A269 15s bl & blk	15	15
a. Imperf.	15	15
1257 A269 80s pink, bl & grn	32	25
a. Imperf.	32	32
Set value	40	32

International Women's Year 1975.

For surcharges see Nos. 1500, 1505.

1975, Sept. 19 Litho. *Perf. 12½*

1258 A270 15s multicolored	15	15
a. Imperf.	15	15
1259 A270 50s multicolored	20	15
a. Imperf.	20	20
Set value	28	18

Dam and Emblem A271

1975, Sept. 30

1260 A271 40s org & vio bl 15 15
a. Imperf. 15 15
1261 A271 1.50p brt rose & vio bl 42 32
a. Imperf. 52 52

For surcharges see Nos. 1517, 1520.

Manila Harbor, 1875 A272

1975, Nov. 4 Unwmk. *Perf. 13x13½*

1262 A272 1.50p red & multi 42 25

Hong Kong and Shanghai Banking Corporation, centenary of Philippines service.

Norberto Romualdez (1875-1941), Scholar and Legislator — A273

Jose Rizal Monument, Luneta Park — A273a

Noted Filipinos: No. 1264, Rafael Palma (1874-1939), journalist, statesman, educator. No. 1265, Rajah Kalantiaw, chief of Panay, author of ethical-penal code (1443). 65s, Emilio Jacinto (1875-1899), patriot. No. 1269, Gen. Gregorio del Pilar (1875-1899), military hero. No. 1270, Lope K. Santos (1879-1963), grammarian, writer. 1.60p, Felipe Agoncillo (1859-1941), lawyer, cabinet member.

Perf. 12½

1975-81 Wmk. 372 Litho.

1264 A273 30s brn ('77) 15 15
1265 A273 30s dp rose ('78) 15 15
1266 A273a 40s yel & blk ('81) 15 15
1267 A273 60s violet 15 15
a. Imperf. 22 22
1268 A273 65s lilac rose 15 15
a. Imperf. 24 24
1269 A273 90s lilac rose 20 15
a. Imperf. 32 32
1270 A273 90s grn ('78) 15 15
1272 A273 1.60p blk ('76) 50 15
Nos. 1264-1272 (8) 1.60
Set value 60

See Nos. 1195-1208. For overprints see Nos. 1278. For surcharges see Nos. 1310, 1367, 1440, 1469, 1514, 1562, 1574, 1758-1760.

A274

1975, Nov. 22 Litho. *Perf. 12½*

1275 A274 60s multicolored 15 15
1276 A274 1.50p multicolored 40 32

40th anniversary of 1st landing of the Pan American World Airways China Clipper in the Philippines.

Nos. 1199 and 1205 Overprinted

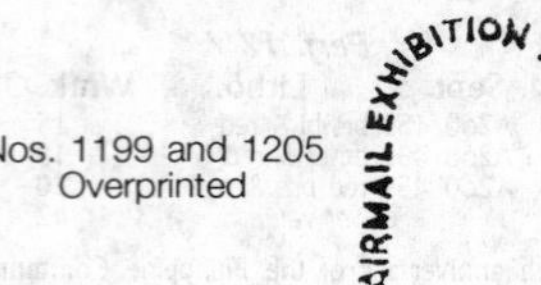

1975, Nov. 22 Unwmk.

1277 A250 60s dl red brn 15 15
1278 A273 1.50p brown 32 32

Airmail Exhibition, Nov. 22-Dec. 9.

APO Emblem — A275

1975, Nov. 24 Wmk. 372

1279 A275 5s ultra & multi 15 15
a. Imperf. 15 15
1280 A275 1p bl & multi 35 25
a. Imperf. 40 40
Set value 42 30

Amateur Philatelists' Organization, 25th anniversary.
For surcharge see No. 1338.

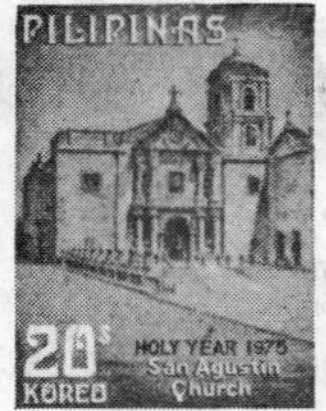

San Agustin Church — A276

Philippine Churches: 30s, Morong Church, horiz. 45s, Basilica of Taal, horiz. 60s, San Sebastian Church.

1975, Dec. 23 Litho. *Perf. 12½*

1281 A276 20s bluish grn 15 15
1282 A276 30s yel org & blk 15 15
1283 A276 45s rose, brn & blk 15 15
1284 A276 60s yel, bis & blk 20 15
Set value 52 40

Holy Year 1975.

Imperf.

1281a A276 20s 15 15
1282a A276 30s 15 15
1283a A276 45s 20 20
1284a A276 60s 32 32

Conductor's Hands — A277

1976, Jan. 27

1285 A277 5s org & multi 15 15
1286 A277 50s multicolored 20 15
Set value 25 20

Manila Symphony Orchestra, 50th anniversary.

PAL Planes of 1946 and 1976 A278

1976, Feb. 14

1287 A278 60s bl & multi 15 15
1288 A278 1.50p red & multi 42 32

Philippine Airlines, 30th anniversary.

National University — A279

1976, Mar. 30

1289 A279 45s bl, vio bl & yel 15 15
1290 A279 60s lt bl, vio bl & pink 20 15
Set value 22

National University, 75th anniversary.

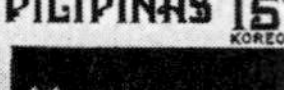

Eye Exam — A280

Book and Emblem — A281

1976, Apr. 7 Litho. *Perf. 12½*

1291 A280 15s multicolored 15 15

World Health Day: "Foresight prevents blindness."

1976, May 24 Unwmk.

1292 A281 1.50p grn & multi 45 40

National Archives, 75th anniversary.

Santo Tomas University, Emblems A282

1976, June 7 Wmk. 372

1293 A282 15s yel & multi 15 15
1294 A282 50s multicolored 15 15
Set value 22 16

Colleges of Education and Science, Santo Tomas University, 50th anniversary.

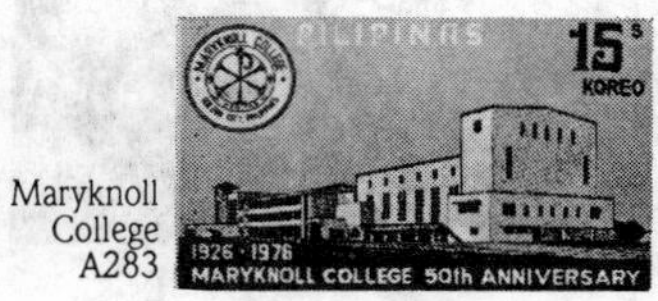

Maryknoll College A283

Perf. 12½

1976, July 26 Litho. Wmk. 372

1295 A283 15s lt bl & multi 15 15
1296 A283 1.50p bis & multi 42 32
Set value 36

Maryknoll College, Quezon City, 50th anniversary.

No. 1164 Surcharged in Dark Violet

15s ==
Montreal 1976
21st OLYMPICS CANADA

Perf. 12½x13½

1976, July 30 Photo.

1297 A242 15s on 10s multi 15 15

21st Olympic Games, Montreal, Canada, July 17-Aug. 1.

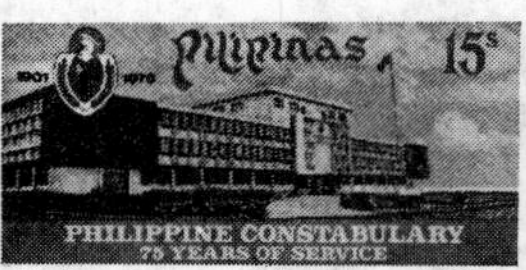

Police College, Manila — A284

1976, Aug. 8 Litho. *Perf. 12½*

1298 A284 15s multicolored 15 15
a. Imperf. 15 15
1299 A284 60s multicolored 20 15
a. Imperf. 32 32
Set value 28 20

Philippine Constabulary, 75th anniversary.

Surveyors — A285

1976, Sept. 2 Wmk. 372

1300 A285 80s multicolored 22 20

Bureau of Lands, 75th anniversary.

Monetary Fund and World Bank Emblems — A286

Virgin of Antipollo — A287

1976, Oct. 4 Litho. *Perf. 12½*

1301 A286 60s multicolored 15 15
1302 A286 1.50p multicolored 42 32

Joint Annual Meeting of the Board of Governors of the International Monetary Fund and the World Bank, Manila, Oct. 4-8.
For surcharge see No. 1575.

1976, Nov. 26 *Perf. 12½*

1303 A287 30s multicolored 15 15
1304 A287 90s multicolored 20 15
Set value 28 22

Virgin of Antipolo, Our Lady of Peace and Good Voyage, 350th anniversary of arrival of statue in the Philippines and 50th anniversary of the canonical coronation.

No. 1184 Surcharged with New Value and 2 Bars and Overprinted: "1976 PHILATELIC WEEK"

Perf. 13½x14

1976, Nov. 26 Photo. Unwmk.

1305 A247 30s on 10s multi 15 15

Philatelic Week 1976.

People Going to Church A288

Perf. 12½

1976, Dec. 1 Litho. Wmk. 372

1306 A288 15s bl & multi 15 15
1307 A288 30s bl & multi 15 15
Set value 16 15

Christmas 1976.

Symbolic Diamond and Book A289

Galicano Apacible A290

1976, Dec. 13

1308 A289 30s grn & multi 15 15
1309 A289 75s grn & multi 22 15
Set value 22

Philippine Educational System, 75th anniversary.

No. 1202 and 1208 Surcharged with New Value and 2 Bars

1977, Jan. 17 Unwmk.

1310 A273 1.20p on 1.10p bl 32 20
1311 A250 3p on 5p bl 65 60

1977 Litho. Wmk. 372 *Perf. 12½*

Design: 30s, José Rizal.

1313 A290 30s multicolored 15 15
1318 A290 2.30p multicolored 52 35
Set value 40

Dr. José Rizal (1861-1896) physician, poet and national hero (30s). Dr. Galicano Apacible (1864-1949), physician, statesman (2.30p).
Issue dates: 30s, Feb. 16; 2.30p, Jan. 24.

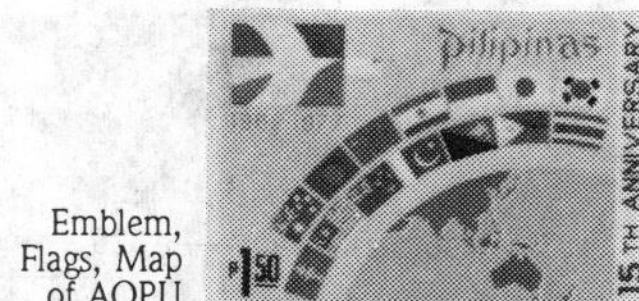

Emblem, Flags, Map of AOPU A291

1977, Apr. 1 Wmk. 372

1322 A291 50s multicolored 15 15
1323 A291 1.50p multicolored 32 25
Set value 32

Asian-Oceanic Postal Union (AOPU), 15th anniversary.

Cogwheels and Worker — A292

1977, Apr. 21 *Perf. 12½*

1324 A292 90s blk & multi 25 22
1325 A292 2.30p blk & multi 50 42

Asian Development Bank, 10th anniversary.

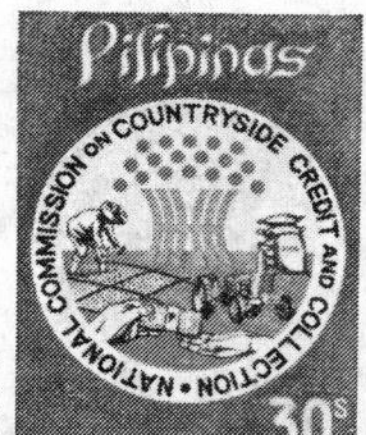

Farmer at Work and Receiving Money — A293

1977, May 14 Litho. Wmk. 372

1326 A293 30s org red & multi 15 15

National Commission on Countryside Credit and Collection, campaign to strengthen the rural credit system.

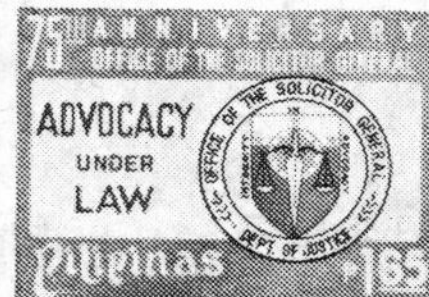

Solicitor General's Emblem A294

1977, June 30 Litho. *Perf. 12½*

1327 A294 1.65p multicolored 32 20

Office of the Solicitor General, 75th anniversary.
For surcharges see Nos. 1483, 1519.

Conference Emblem A295

1977, July 29 Litho. *Perf. 12½*

1328 A295 2.20p bl & multi 45 25

8th World Conference of the World Peace through Law Center, Manila, Aug. 21-26.
For surcharge see No. 1576.

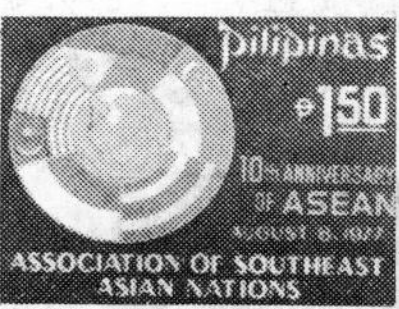

ASEAN Emblem A296

1977, Aug. 8

1329 A296 1.50p grn & multi 35 20

Association of South East Asian Nations (ASEAN), 10th anniversary.
For surcharge see No. 1559.

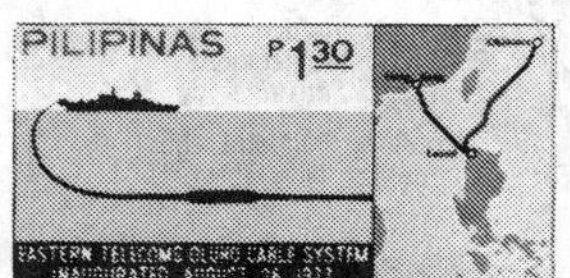

Cable-laying Ship, Map Showing Cable Route — A297

1977, Aug. 26 Litho. *Perf. 12½*

1330 A297 1.30p multicolored 30 20

Inauguration of underwater telephone cable linking Okinawa, Luzon and Hong Kong.

President Marcos A298

1977, Sept. 11 Wmk. 372

1331 A298 30s multicolored 15 15
1332 A298 2.30p multicolored 55 35
Set value 40

Ferdinand E. Marcos, president of the Philippines, 60th birthday.

People Raising Flag — A299

1977, Sept. 21 Litho. *Perf. 12½*

1333 A299 30s multicolored 15 15
1334 A299 2.30p multicolored 55 35
Set value 40

5th anniversary of "New Society."

Bishop Gregorio Aglipay — A300

1977, Oct. 1 Litho. *Perf. 12½*

1335 A300 30s multicolored 15 15
1336 A300 90s multicolored 22 15
Set value 28 16

Philippine Independent Aglipayan Church, 75th anniversary.

Fairchild FC-2 over World Map A301

1977, Oct. 28 Wmk. 372

1337 A301 2.30p multicolored 52 32

First scheduled Pan American airmail service, Key West to Havana, 50th anniversary.

No. 1280 Surcharged with New Value, 2 Bars and Overprinted in Red: "1977 / PHILATELIC / WEEK"

1977, Nov. 22 Litho. *Perf. 12½*

1338 A275 90s on 1p multi 20 15

Philatelic Week.

Children Celebrating and Star from Lantern — A302

1977, Dec. 1 Unwmk.

1339 A302 30s multicolored 15 15
1340 A302 45s multicolored 15 15
Set value 22 15

Christmas 1977.

Scouts and Map showing Jamboree Locations A303

1977, Dec. 27

1341 A303 30s multicolored 15 15

National Boy Scout Jamboree, Tumauini, Isabela; Capitol Hills, Cebu City; Mariano Marcos, Davao, Dec. 27, 1977-Jan. 5, 1978.

Far Eastern University Arms — A304

1978, Jan. 26 Litho. Wmk. 372

1342 A304 30s gold & multi 15 15

Far Eastern University, 50th anniversary.

Sipa A305

Designs: Various positions of Sipa ball-game.

1978, Feb. 28 *Perf. 12½*

1343 A305 5s bl & multi 15 15
1344 A305 10s bl & multi 15 15
1345 A305 40s bl & multi 15 15
1346 A305 75s bl & multi 24 15

Nos. 1343-1346 printed se-tenant with continuous design.

Arms of Meycauayan A306

1978, Apr. 21 Litho. *Perf. 12½*

1347 A306 1.05p multicolored 22 15

400th anniversary of Meycauayan, founded 1578-1579.
For surcharge see No. 1560.

Scott's editorial staff cannot undertake to identify, authenticate or appraise stamps and postal markings.

Moro Vinta and UPU Emblem — A307

Designs (UPU Emblem and): 2.50p, No. 1350b, Horse-drawn mail cart. No. 1350a, like 5p. No. 1350c, Steam locomotive. No. 1350d, Three-master.

1978, June 9 Litho. *Perf. 13½*

1348	A307	2.50p multicolored	60	40
1349	A307	5p multicolored	1.10	80

Souvenir Sheet

Perf. 12½x13

1350	Sheet of 4	10.00	
a.-d.	A307 7.50p, any single	2.00	2.00

CAPEX International Philatelic Exhibition, Toronto, Ont., June 9-18. No. 1350 contains 36½x25mm stamps.
No. 1350 exists imperf. in changed colors.

Andres Bonifacio Monument, by Guillermo Tolentino — A308

Perf. 12½

1978, July 10 Litho. Wmk. 372

1351 A308	30s multicolored	15	15

Rook, Knight and Globe A309

1978, July 17

1352 A309	30s vio bl & red	15	15
1353 A309	2p vio bl & red	42	30
	Set value	48	35

World Chess Championship, Anatoly Karpov and Viktor Korchnoi, Baguio City, 1978.

Miners A310

1978, Aug. 12 Litho. *Perf. 12½*

1354 A310	2.30p multicolored	45	25

75th anniversary of Benguet gold mining industry.

Manuel Quezon and Quezon Memorial — A311

1978, Aug. 19

1355 A311	30s multicolored	15	15
1356 A311	1p multicolored	22	15
	Set value	30	15

Manuel Quezon (1878-1944), first president of Commonwealth of the Philippines.

Law Association Emblem, Philippine Flag — A312

1978, Aug. 27 Litho. *Perf. 12½*

1357 A312	2.30p multicolored	45	32

58th International Law Conference, Manila, Aug. 27-Sept. 2.

Pres. Sergio Osmeña (1878-1961) A313

1978, Sept. 8

1358 A313	30s multicolored	15	15
1359 A313	1p multicolored	22	15
	Set value	30	15

For surcharge see No. 1501.

Map Showing Cable Route, Cablelaying Ship — A314

1978, Sept. 30

1360 A314	1.40p multicolored	30	18

ASEAN Submarine Cable Network, Philippines-Singapore cable system, inauguration.

Basketball, Games' Emblem A315

1978, Oct. 1

1361 A315	30s multicolored	15	15
1362 A315	2.30p multicolored	45	32
	Set value		36

8th Men's World Basketball Championship, Manila, Oct. 1-15.

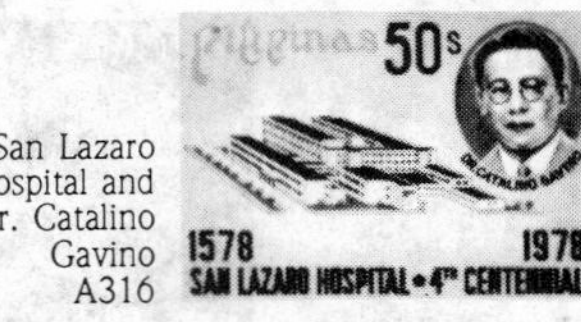

San Lazaro Hospital and Dr. Catalino Gavino A316

1978, Oct. 13 Litho. *Perf. 12½*

1363 A316	50s multicolored	15	15
1364 A316	90s multicolored	20	15
	Set value		16

San Lazaro Hospital, 400th anniversary.
For surcharge see No. 1512.

Nurse Vaccinating Child — A317

1978, Oct. 24

1365 A317	30s multicolored	15	15
1366 A317	1.50p multicolored	35	20
	Set value	42	25

Eradication of smallpox.

No. 1268 Surcharged

1978 PHILATELIC WEEK

60s

1978, Nov. 23

1367 A273	60s on 65s lil rose	15	15

Philatelic Week.

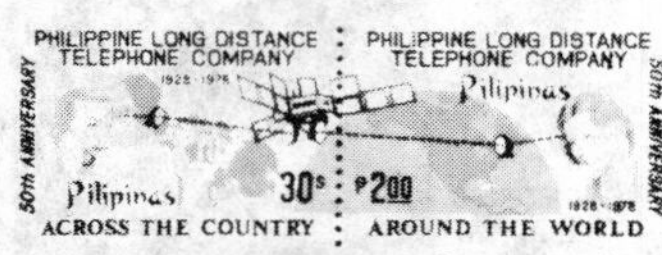

"The Telephone Across Country and World"
A318 A319

Perf. 12½

1978, Nov. 28 Litho. Wmk. 372

1368 A318	30s multicolored	15	15
1369 A319	2p multicolored	42	30
a.	Pair, #1368-1369	50	40
	Set value	48	35

Philippine Long Distance Telephone Company, 50th anniversary.

Traveling Family A320

1978, Nov. 28

1370 A320	30s multicolored	15	15
1371 A320	1.35p multicolored	32	15
	Set value	38	16

Decade of Philippine children.
For surcharges see Nos. 1504, 1561.

Church and Arms of Agoo — A321

1978, Dec. 7 Litho. *Perf. 12½*

1372 A321	30s multicolored	15	15
1373 A321	45s multicolored	15	15
	Set value	20	15

400th anniversary of the founding of Agoo.

Church and Arms of Balayan A322

1978, Dec. 8

1374 A322	30s multicolored	15	15
1375 A322	90s multicolored	22	15
	Set value	28	15

400th anniv. of the founding of Balayan.

Dr. Honoria Acosta Sison (1888-1970), 1st Philippine Woman Physician — A323

1978, Dec. 15

1376 A323	30s multicolored	15	15

Family, Houses, UN Emblem A324

1978, Dec. Litho. *Perf. 12½*

1377 A324	30s multicolored	15	15
1378 A324	3p multicolored	65	40
	Set value		45

30th anniversary of Universal Declaration of Human Rights.

Chaetodon Trifasciatus — A325

Fish: 1.20p, Balistoides niger. 2.20p, Rhinecanthus aculeatus. 2.30p, Chelmon rostratus. No. 1383, Chaetodon mertensi. No. 1384, Euxiphipops xanthometapon.

1978, Dec. 29 *Perf. 14*

1379 A325	30s multi	15	15
1380 A325	1.20p multi	25	15
1381 A325	2.20p multi	42	22
1382 A325	2.30p multi	45	25
1383 A325	5p multi	1.00	55
1384 A325	5p multi	1.00	55
	Nos. 1379-1384 (6)	3.27	1.87

Carlos P. Romulo, UN Emblem A326

1979, Jan. 14 Litho. *Perf. 12½*

1385 A326	30s multi	15	15
1386 A326	2p multi	50	25
	Set value		30

Carlos P. Romulo (1899-1985), pres. of UN General Assembly and Security Council.

Rotary Emblem and "60" A327 — Rosa Sevilla de Alvero A328

1979, Jan. 26 **Wmk. 372**

1387 A327 30s multi 15 15
1388 A327 2.30p multi 55 22
Set value 26

Rotary Club of Manila, 60th anniversary.

1979, Mar. 4 **Litho.** ***Perf. 12½***

1389 A328 30 rose 15 15

Rosa Sevilla de Alvero, educator and writer, birth centenary.

For surcharges see Nos. 1479-1482.

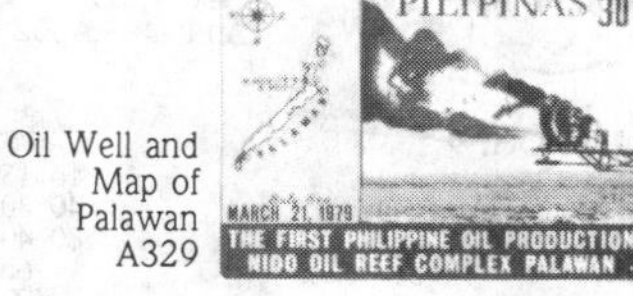

Oil Well and Map of Palawan A329

Perf. 12½

1979, Mar. 21 **Litho.** **Wmk. 372**

1390 A329 30s multi 15 15
1391 A329 45s multi 15 15
Set value 20 15

First Philippine oil production, Nido Oil Reef Complex, Palawan.

Merrill's Fruit Doves A330

Birds: 1.20p, Brown tit babbler. 2.20p, Mindoro imperial pigeons. 2.30p, Steere's pittas. No. 1396, Koch's and red-breasted pittas. No. 1397, Philippine eared nightjar.

Perf. 14x13½

1979, Apr. 16 **Unwmk.**

1392 A330 30s multi 15 15
1393 A330 1.20p multi 25 15
1394 A330 2.20p multi 42 22
1395 A330 2.30p multi 45 25
1396 A330 5p multi 1.00 55
1397 A330 5p multi 1.00 55
Nos. 1392-1397 (6) 3.27 1.87

Association Emblem and Reader A331

Perf. 12½

1979, Apr. 3 **Litho.** **Wmk. 372**

1398 A331 30s multi 15 15
1399 A331 75s multi 15 15
1400 A331 1p multi 22 15
Set value 44 20

Association of Special Libraries of the Philippines, 25th anniversary.

UNCTAD Emblem A332

Perf. 12½

1979, May 3 **Litho.** **Wmk. 372**

1401 A332 1.20p multi 22 15
1402 A332 2.30p multi 50 20

5th Session of United Nations Conference on Trade and Development, Manila, May 3-June 1.

Civet Cat A333

Philippine Animals: 1.20p, Macaque. 2.20p, Wild boar. 2.30p, Dwarf leopard. No. 1407, Asiatic dwarf otter. No. 1408, Anteater.

1979, May 14 ***Perf. 14***

1403 A333 30s multi 15 15
1404 A333 1.20p multi 25 15
1405 A333 2.20p multi 42 22
1406 A333 2.30p multi 45 25
1407 A333 5p multi 1.00 55
1408 A333 5p multi 1.00 55
Nos. 1403-1408 (6) 3.27 1.87

Dish Antenna — A334

Design: 1.30p, World map.

1979, May 17 ***Perf. 12½***

1409 A334 90s multi 18 15
1410 A334 1.30p multi 24 15
Set value 16

11th World Telecommunications Day, May 17.

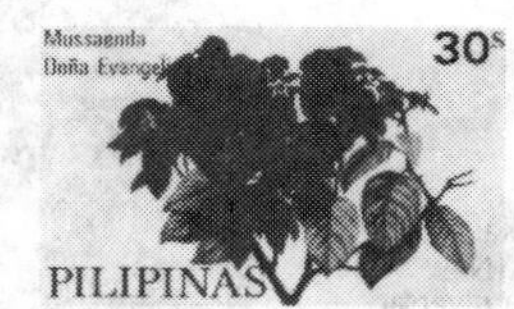

Mussaenda Donna Evangelina — A335

Philippine Mussaendas: 1.20p, Dona Esperanza. 2.20p, Dona Hilaria. 2.30p, Dona Aurora. No. 1415, Gining Imelda. No. 1416, Dona Trining.

1979, June 11 **Litho.** ***Perf. 14***

1411 A335 30s multi 15 15
1412 A335 1.20p multi 15 15
1413 A335 2.20p multi 42 22
1414 A335 2.30p multi 45 25
1415 A335 5p multi 1.00 55
1416 A335 5p multi 1.00 55
Nos. 1411-1416 (6) 3.17 1.87

Manila Cathedral, Coat of Arms — A336

1979, June 25 ***Perf. 12½***

1417 A336 30s multi 15 15
1418 A336 75s multi 15 15
1419 A336 90s multi 20 15
Set value 42 22

Archdiocese of Manila, 400th anniversary.

Patrol Boat, Naval Arms — A337

1979, June 26

1420 A337 30s multi 15 15
1421 A337 45s multi 15 15
Set value 16 15

Philippine Navy Day.

Man Breaking Chains, Broken Syringe — A338

1979, July 23 **Litho.** ***Perf. 12½***

1422 A338 30s multi 15 15
1423 A338 90s multi 20 15
1424 A338 1.05p multi 24 15
Set value 50 26

Fight drug abuse.

For surcharge see No. 1513.

Afghan Hound A339

Designs: 90s, Striped tabbies. 1.20p, Dobermann pinscher. 2.20p, Siamese cats. 2.30p, German shepherd. 5p, Chinchilla cats.

1979, Aug. 6 ***Perf. 14***

1425 A339 30s multi 15 15
1426 A339 90s multi 20 15
1427 A339 1.20p multi 24 15
1428 A339 2.20p multi 45 15
1429 A339 2.30p multi 50 42
1430 A339 5p multi 1.00 50
Nos. 1425-1430 (6) 2.54 1.52

Children Playing IYC Emblem A340

Designs: Children playing and IYC emblem, diff.

1979, Aug. 31 **Litho.** ***Perf. 12½***

1431 A340 15s multi 15 15
1432 A340 20s multi 15 15
1433 A340 25s multi 15 15
1434 A340 1.20p multi 20 15
Set value 40 25

International Year of the Child.

Hands Holding Emblem — A341

1979, Sept. 27 **Litho.** ***Perf. 12½***

1435 A341 30s multi 15 15
1436 A341 1.35p multi 25 15
Set value 32 15

Methodism in the Philippines, 80th anniversary.

Emblem and Coins A342

Perf. 12½

1979, Nov. 15 **Litho.** **Wmk. 372**

1437 A342 30s multi 15 15

Philippine Numismatic and Antiquarian Society, 50th anniversary.

Concorde over Manila and Paris A343

Design: 2.20p, Concorde over Manila.

1979, Nov. 22

1438 A343 1.05p multi 20 15
1439 A343 2.20p multi 45 32

Air France service to Manila, 25th anniversary.

No. 1272 Surcharged in Red

1979, Nov. 23

1440 A273 90s on 1.60 blk 20 15

Philatelic Week. Surcharge similar to No. 1367.

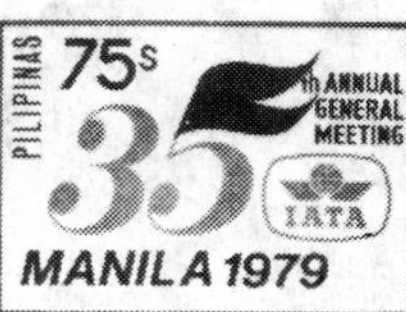

Transport Association Emblem A344

1979, Nov. 27

1441 A344 75s multi 18 15
1442 A344 2.30p multi 48 35

International Air Transport Association, 35th annual general meeting, Manila.

Local Government Year A345

Mother and Children, Ornament A346

1979, Dec. 14 Litho. *Perf. 12½*

1443 A345 30s multi 15 15
1444 A345 45s multi 15 15
Set value 20 15

1979, Dec. 17

1445 A346 30s shown 15 15
1446 A346 90s Stars 24 15
Set value 32 20

Christmas. For surcharge see No. 1515.

Rheumatic Pain Spots and Congress Emblem A347

Perf. 12½

1980, Jan. 20 Litho. Wmk. 372

1447 A347 30s multi 15 15
1448 A347 90s multi 32 15
Set value 20

Southeast Asia and Pacific Area League Against Rheumatism, 4th Congress, Manila, Jan. 19-24.

Gen. Douglas MacArthur — A348

Designs: 30s, MacArthur's birthplace (Little Rock, Ark) and burial place (Norfolk, Va.). 2.30p, MacArthur's cap, Sunglasses and pipe. 5p, MacArthur and troops wading ashore at Leyte, Oct. 20, 1944.

1980, Jan. 26 Wmk. 372 *Perf. 12½*

1449 A348 30s multi 15 15
1450 A348 75s multi 22 15
1451 A348 2.30p multi 70 50
Set value 66

Souvenir Sheet

1452 A348 5p multi 1.90 1.00

Gen. Douglas MacArthur (1880-1964).

Knights of Columbus of Philippines, 75th Anniversary A349

1980, Feb. 14

1453 A349 30s multi 15 15
1454 A349 1.35p multi 48 28
Set value 32

Philippine Military Academy, 75th Anniversary A350

Perf. 12½

1980, Feb. 17 Litho. Wmk. 372

1455 A350 30s multi 15 15
1456 A350 1.20p multi 42 20
Set value 25

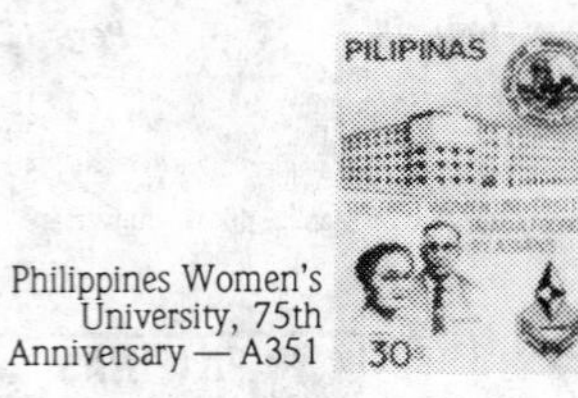

Philippines Women's University, 75th Anniversary — A351

1980, Feb. 21

1457 A351 30s multi 15 15
1458 A351 1.05p multi 38 18
Set value 22

Disaster Relief A352

Rotary International, 75th Anniversary (Paintings by Carlos Botong Francisco): Nos. 1459 and 1460 each in continuous design.

1980, Feb. 23 *Perf. 12½*

1459 Strip of 5 60 28
a. A352 30s single stamp 15 15
1460 Strip of 5 4.00 1.90
a. A352 2.30p single stamp 80 38

A353

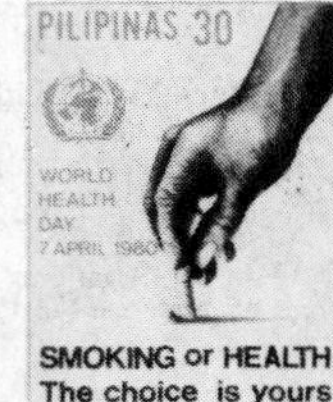

A354

Perf. 12½

1980, Mar. 28 Litho. Wmk. 372

1461 A353 30s multi 15 15
1462 A353 1.30p multi 45 20
Set value 25

6th centenary of Islam in Philippines.

1980, Apr. 14

Hand crushing cigarette, WHO emblem.

1463 A354 30s multi 15 15
1464 A354 75s multi 24 15
Set value 18

World Health Day (Apr. 17); anti-smoking campaign.

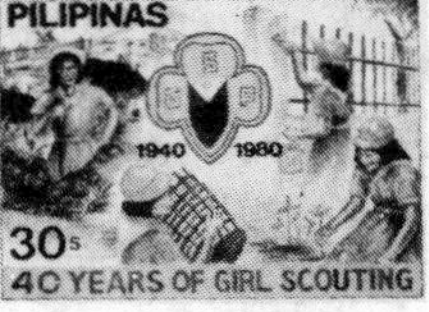

Philippine Girl Scouts, 40th Anniversary A355

Perf. 12½

1980, May 26 Litho. Wmk. 372

1465 A355 30s multi 15 15
1466 A355 2p multi 38 18
Set value 22

Jeepney (Public Jeep) — A356

1980, June 24 Litho. *Perf. 12½*

1467 A356 30s Jeepney, diff. 15 15
1468 A356 1.20p shown 40 20
Set value 25

For surcharge see No. 1503.

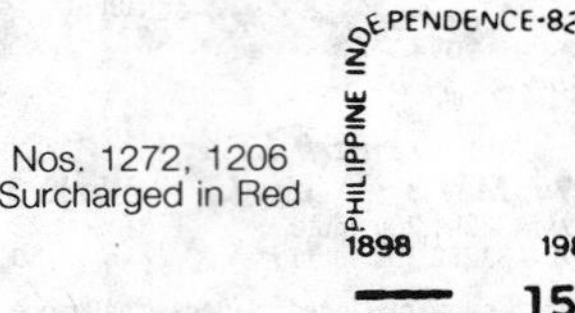

Nos. 1272, 1206 Surcharged in Red

Wmk. 372 (1.35p)

1980, Aug. 1 Litho. *Perf. 12½*

1469 A273 1.35p on 1.60p blk 52 26
1470 A250 1.50p on 1.80p grn 60 30

Independence, 82nd Anniversary.

Association Emblem — A357

1980, Aug. 1 Wmk. 372

1471 A357 30s multi 15 15
1472 A357 2.30p multi 80 75

International Association of Universities, 7th General Conference, Manila, Aug. 25-30.

Congress Emblem, Map of Philippines A358

Perf. 12½

1980, Aug. 18 Litho. Wmk. 372

1473 A358 30s lt grn & blk 15 15
1474 A358 75s lt bl & blk 28 16
1475 A358 2.30p sal & blk 90 48

International Federation of Library Associations and Institutions, 46th Congress, Manila, Aug. 18-23.

Kabataang Barangay (New Society), 5th Anniversary — A359

1980, Sept. 19 Litho. *Perf. 12½*

1476 A359 30s multi 15 15
1477 A359 40s multi 15 15
1478 A359 1p multi 38 20
Set value 32

Nos. 1389, 1422, 1443, 1445, 1327 Surcharged in Blue, Black or Red

Perf. 12½

1980, Sept. 26 Litho. Wmk. 372

1479 A328 40s on 30s rose (Bl) 16 15
1480 A338 40s on 30s multi 16 15
1481 A345 40s on 30s multi 16 15
1482 A346 40s on 30s multi (R) 16 15
1483 A294 2p on 1.65p multi (R) 80 40
Nos. 1479-1483 (5) 1.44
Set value 68

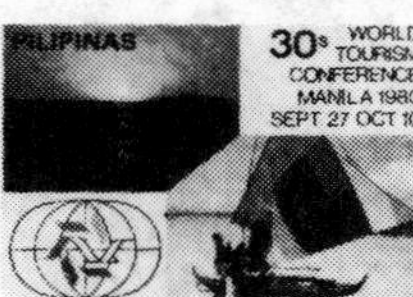

Catamaran, Conference Emblem A360

1980, Sept. 27

1484 A360 30s multi 15 15
1485 A360 2.30p multi 85 52
Set value 58

World Tourism Conf., Manila, Sept. 27.

Stamp Day — A361

UN, 35th Anniv. — A362

1980, Oct. 9

1486 A361 40s multi 16 15
1487 A361 1p multi 40 20
1488 A361 2p multi 80 40
Set value 66

1980, Oct. 20

Designs: 40s, UN Headquarters and Emblem, Flag of Philippines. 3.20p, UN and Philippine flags, UN headquarters.

1489 A362 40s multi 16 15
1490 A362 3.20p multi 1.25 85

Murex Alabaster A363

1980, Nov. 2

1491 A363 40s *shown* 16 15
1492 A363 60s *Bursa bubo* 22 15
1493 A363 1.20p *Homalocantha zamboi* 42 20
1494 A363 2p *Xenophora pallidula* 80 38

INTERPOL Emblem on Globe — A364

1980, Nov. 5 Litho. Wmk. 372

1495 A364 40s multi 16 15
1496 A364 1p multi 40 18
1497 A364 3.20p multi 1.25 85

49th General Assembly Session of INTERPOL (International Police Organization), Manila, Nov. 13-21.

Central Philippine University, 75th Anniversary A365

1980, Nov. 17 Unwmk.

1498 A365 40s multi 15 15
1499 A365 3.20p multi 1.25 80

No. 1257 Surcharged

Perf. 12½

1980, Nov. 21 Litho. Wmk. 372

1500 A269 1.20p on 80s multi 42 20

Philatelic Week 1980. Surcharge similar to No. 1367.

No. 1358 Surcharged

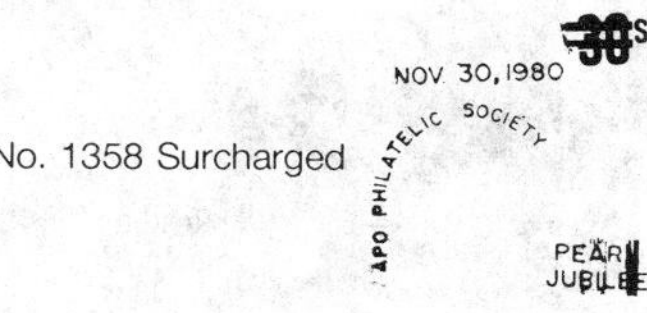

1980, Nov. 30
1501 A313 40s on 30s multi 16 15

APO Philatelic Society, 30th anniversary.

Christmas Tree, Present and Candy Cane — A366

Perf. 12½
1980, Dec. 15 Litho. Unwmk.
1502 A366 40s multi 16 15

Christmas 1980.

No. 1467 Surcharged

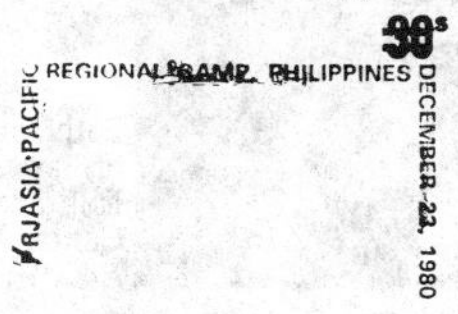

1981, Jan. 2
1503 A356 40c on 30s multi 16 15

Nos. 1370, 1257 Surcharged in Red or Black

1981
1504 A320 10s on 30s (R) multi 15 15
1505 A269 85s on 80s multi 32 16
Set value 36 20

Issue dates: 10s, Jan. 12; 85s, Jan. 2.

Heinrich Von Stephan, UPU Emblem — A367

1981, Jan. 30
1506 A367 3.20p multi 1.25 60

Heinrich von Stephan (1831-1897), founder of UPU, birth sesquicentennial.

Pope John Paul II Greeting Crowd — A368

Designs: 90s, Pope, signature, vert. 1.20p, Pope, cardinals, vert. 3p, Pope giving blessing, Vatican arms, Manila Cathedral. 7.50p, Pope, light on map of Philippines, vert.

Perf. 13½x14
1981, Feb. 17 Unwmk.
1507 A368 90s multi 35 16
1508 A368 1.20p multi 45 22
1509 A368 2.30p multi 90 42
1510 A368 3p multi 1.10 55

Souvenir Sheet
1511 A368 7.50p multi 3.00 1.40

Visit of Pope John Paul, Feb. 17-22.

Nos. 1364, 1423, 1268, 1446, 1261, 1206, 1327 Surcharged

1981 Litho. *Perf. 12½*
1512 A316 40s on 90s multi 16 15
1513 A338 40s on 90s multi 16 15
1514 A273 40s on 65s lil rose 16 15
1515 A346 40s on 90s multi 16 15
1517 A271 1p on 1.50p brt rose & vio bl 42 18
1518 A250 1.20p on 1.80p grn 45 22
1519 A294 1.20p on 1.65p multi 45 22
1520 A271 2p on 1.50p brt rose & vio bl 85 35
Nos. 1512-1520 (8) 2.81
Set value 1.25

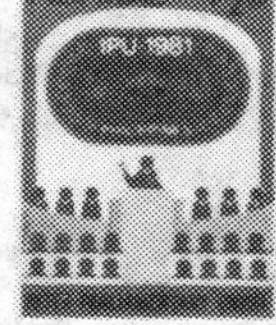

A369

A370

1981, Apr. 20 Wmk. 372
1521 A369 2p multi 80 38
1522 A369 3.20p multi 1.25 65

68th Spring Meeting of the Inter-Parliamentary Union, Manila, Apr. 20-25.

Unless otherwise stated, all issues on granite paper.

Perf. 12½
1981, May 22 Litho. Wmk. 372
1523 A370 40s Bubble coral 16 15
1524 A370 40s Branching coral 16 15
1525 A370 40s Brain coral 16 15
1526 A370 40s Table coral 16 15
Set value 28

Nos. 1523-1526 se-tenant.

Philippine Motor Assoc., 50th Anniv. — A371

Designs: Vintage cars. Nos. 1527-1530 se-tenant.

1981, May 25
1527 A371 40s Presidents car 16 15
1528 A371 40s 1930 16 15
1529 A371 40s 1937 16 15
1530 A371 40s shown 16 15
Set value 28

Re-inauguration of Pres. Ferdinand E. Marcos — A372

1981, June 30
1531 A372 40s multi 16 15

Souvenir Sheet
Imperf
1532 A372 5p multi 1.90 90

No. 1531 exists imperf.
For overprint see No. 1753.

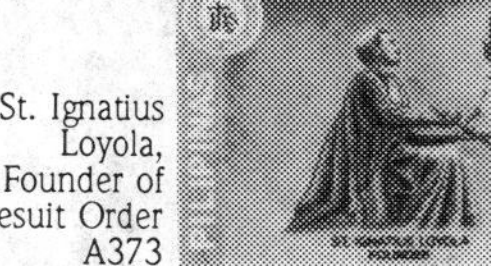

St. Ignatius Loyola, Founder of Jesuit Order A373

400th Anniv. of Jesuits in Philippines: No. 1534, Jose, Rizal, Ateneo University. No. 1535, Father Federico Faura, Manila Observatory. No. 1536, Father Saturnino Urios, map of Philippines. Nos. 1533-1536 se-tenant.

1981, July 31
1533 A373 40s multi 16 15
1534 A373 40s multi 16 15
1535 A373 40s multi 16 15
1536 A373 40s multi 16 15
Set value 28

Souvenir Sheet
Imperf
1537 A373 2p multi 90 35

No. 1537 contains vignettes of Nos. 1533-1536.
For surcharge see No. 1737.

A374

A375

Design: 40s, Isabelo de los Reyes (1867-1938), labor union founder. 1p, Gen. Gregorio del Pilar (1875-1899). No. 1540, Magsaysay. No. 1541, Francisco Dagohoy. No. 1543, Ambrosia R. Bautista, signer of Declaration of Independence, 1898. No. 1544, Juan Sumulong (1875-1942), statesman. 2.30p, Nicanor Abelardo (1893-1934), composer. 3.20p, Gen. Vicente Lim (1888-1945), first Philippine graduate of West Point.

Perf. 12½
1981-82 Litho. Wmk. 372
1538 A374 40s grnsh bl ('82) 16 15
1539 A374 1p blk & red brn 42 18
1540 A374 1.20p blk & lt red brn 45 22
1541 A374 1.20p brown ('82) 45 22
1543 A374 2p blk & red brn 85 35
1544 A374 2p rose lil ('82) 85 35
1545 A374 2.30p lt red brn ('82) 90 38
1546 A374 3.20p gray bl ('82) 1.25 65
Nos. 1538-1546 (8) 5.33 2.50

See Nos. 1672-1680, 1682-1683, 1685. For surcharges see Nos. 1668-1669.

1981, Sept. 2
1551 A375 40s multi 16 15

Chief Justice Fred Ruiz Castro, 67th birth anniv.

A376

A376a

Perf. 12½
1981, Oct. 24 Litho. Wmk. 372
1552 A376 40s multi 16 15
1553 A376 3.20p multi 1.25 65

Intl. Year of the Disabled.

1981, Nov. 7
1554 A376a 40s multi 15 15
1555 A376a 2p multi 80 35
1556 A376a 3.20p multi 1.20 60

24th Intl. Red Cross Conference, Manila, Nov. 7-14.

Intramuros Gate, Manila — A377

1981, Nov. 13
1557 A377 40s black 16 15

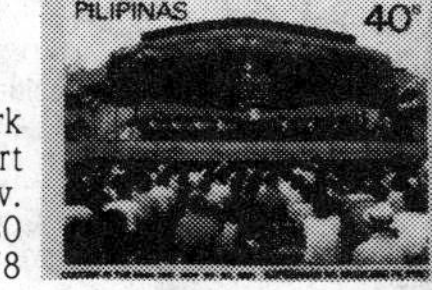

Manila Park Zoo Concert Series, Nov. 20-30 A378

1981, Nov. 20
1558 A378 40s multi 16 15

No. 1329 Overprinted "1981 Philatelic Week" and Surcharged

Perf. 12½
1981, Nov. 23 Litho. Wmk. 372
1559 A296 1.20p on 1.50p multi 45 22

Nos. 1205, 1347, 1371 Surcharged

1981, Nov. 25 Litho. *Perf. 12½*
1560 A306 40s on 1.05p multi 16 15
1561 A320 40s on 1.35p multi 16 15
1562 A273 1.20p on 1.50p brn 45 22
Set value 35

11th Southeast Asian Games, Manila, Dec. 6-15 — A379

1981, Dec. 3
1563 A379 40s Running 16 15
1564 A379 1p Bicycling 45 18
1565 A379 2p Pres. Marcos, Intl. Olympic Pres. Samaranch 90 35
1566 A379 2.30p Soccer 90 42
1567 A379 2.80p Shooting 1.10 50
1568 A379 3.20p Bowling 1.25 65
Nos. 1563-1568 (6) 4.76 2.25

Manila Intl. Film Festival, Jan. 18-29 A380

Perf. 12½
1982, Jan. 18 Litho. Wmk. 372
1569 A380 40s Film Center 16 15
1570 A380 2p Golden trophy, vert. 90 35
1571 A380 3.20p Trophy, diff., vert. 1.25 65

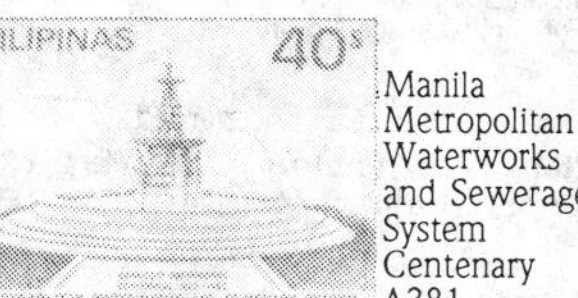

Manila Metropolitan Waterworks and Sewerage System Centenary A381

1982, Jan. 22
1572 A381 40s blue 16 15
1573 A381 1.20p brown 45 22
Set value 28

Nos. 1268, 1302, 1328 Surcharged

1982, Jan. 28
1574 A273 1p on 65s lil rose 45 20
1575 A286 1p on 1.50p multi 45 20
1576 A295 3.20p on 2.20p multi 1.25 65

Scouting Year — A382

1982, Feb. 22

1577 A382	40s	Portrait	16	15
1578 A382	2p	Scout giving salute	90	35
		Set value		42

25th Anniv. of Children's Museum and Library Foundation A383

1982, Feb. 25

1579 A383	40s	Mural	16	15
1580 A383	1.20p	Children playing	45	22
		Set value		28

77th Anniv. of Philippine Military Academy — A384

Perf. 12½

1982, Mar. 25 Litho. Wmk. 372

1581 A384	40s	multi	16	15
1582 A384	1p	multi	45	20
		Set value		26

40th Bataan Day — A385

1982, Apr. 9

1583 A385	40s	Soldier	16	15
1584 A385	2p	"Reunion for Peace"	90	35
		Set value		42

Souvenir Sheet

Imperf

1585 A385	3.20p	Cannon, flag	1.25	70

No. 1585 contains one 38x28mm stamp. No. 1585 comes on two different papers, the second being thicker with cream gum.

For surcharge see No. 2114.

No. B27 Surcharged

1982 Photo. *Perf. 13½*

1586 SP14	10s on 6 + 5s multi	15	15

15-Cent Minimum Value
The minimum catalogue value is 15 cents. Separating se-tenant pieces into individual stamps does not increase the "value" of the stamps... since demand for the separated stamps may be small.

A386

A387

1982, Apr. 28 Litho. *Perf. 12½*

1587 A386	1p rose pink	45	20

Aurora Aragon Quezon (1888-1949), former First Lady. See No. 1684.

1982, May 1

1588 A387	40s	Man holding award	16	15
1589 A387	1.20p	Award	45	22
		Set value		28

7th Towers Awards.

UN Conf. on Human Environment, 10th Anniv. A388

1982, June 5

1590 A388	40s	Turtle	16	15
1591 A388	3.20p	Philippine eagle	1.25	65

75th Anniv. of Univ. of Philippines College of Medicine A389

1982, June 10

1592 A389	40s	multi	16	15
1593 A389	3.20p	multi	1.25	65

Natl. Livelihood Movement A390

1982, June 12

1594 A390	40s multi	16	15

See No. 1681. For overprint see No. 1634.

Adamson Univ., 50th Anniv. — A391

1982, June 21

1595 A391	40s	bl & multi	16	15
1596 A391	1.20p	lt vio & multi	45	22
		Set value		28

Social Security, 25th Anniv. — A392

Pres. Marcos, 65th Birthday — A393

1982, Sept. 1 *Perf. 13½x13*

1597 A392	40s	multi	16	15
1598 A392	1.20p	multi	45	22
		Set value		28

1982, Sept. 11 *Perf. 13½x13*

1599 A393	40s	sil & multi	16	15
1600 A393	3.20p	sil & multi	1.25	65
a.		Souv. sheet of 2, #1599-1600, imperf.	1.40	70

For surcharge see No. 1666.

15th Anniv. of Assoc. of Southeast Asian Nations (ASEAN) — A394

1982, Sept. 22 Litho. *Perf. 12½*

1601 A394	40s Flags	16	15

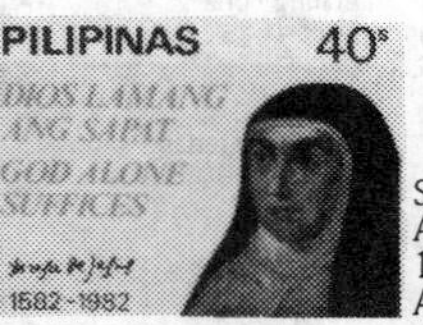
St. Teresa of Avila (1515-1582) A395

1982, Oct. 15 *Perf. 13x13½*

1602 A395	40s	Text	16	15
1603 A395	1.20p	Map	45	22
1604 A395	2p	like #1603	90	35

10th Anniv. of Tenant Farmers' Emancipation Decree — A396

Perf. 13x13½

1982, Oct. 21 Litho. Wmk. 372

1605 A396	40s Pres. Marcos signing law	16	15

See No. 1654.

350th Anniv. of St. Isabel College A397

1982, Oct. 22

1606 A397	40s	multi	16	15
1607 A397	1p	multi	45	20
		Set value		26

Reading Campaign A398

1982, Nov. 4

1608 A398	40s	yel & multi	16	15
1609 A398	2.30p	grn & multi	90	38

For surcharge see No. 1713.

42nd Skal Club World Congress, Manila, Nov. 7-12 A399

1982, Nov. 7

1610 A399	40s	Heads	16	15
1611 A399	2p	Chief	90	35
		Set value		42

25th Anniv. of Bayanihan Folk Arts Center A400

Designs: Various folk dances.

1982, Nov. 10 Litho. *Perf. 13x13½*

1612 A400	40s	multi	16	15
1613 A400	2.80p	multi	1.10	50

TB Bacillus Centenary A401

1982, Dec. 7 Wmk. 372

1614 A401	40s	multi	16	15
1615 A401	2.80p	multi	1.10	50

Christmas 1982 A402

1982, Dec. 10

1616 A402	40s	multi	16	15
1617 A402	1p	multi	45	20
		Set value		26

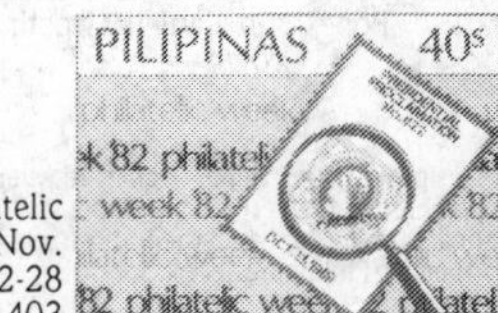
Philatelic Week, Nov. 22-28 A403

Perf. 13x13½

1982, Nov. 28 Litho. Wmk. 372

1618 A403	40s	yel & multi	16	15
1619 A403	1p	sil & multi	45	20
		Set value		26

For surcharge see No. 1667.

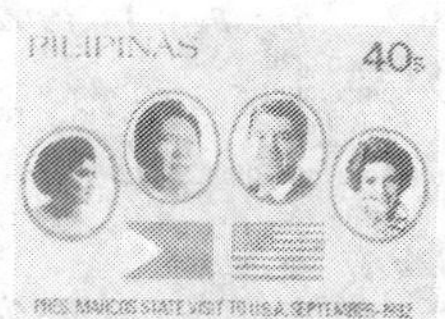

Visit of Pres. Marcos to the US, Sept. A404

1982, Dec. 18
1620 A404 40s multi 16 15
1621 A404 3.20p multi 1.25 60
a. Souv. sheet of 2, #1620-1621 1.50 70

UN World Assembly on Aging, July 26-Aug. 6 A405

Senate Pres. Eulogio Rodriguez, Sr. (1883-1964) A406

1982, Dec. 24
1622 A405 1.20p Woman 45 22
1623 A405 2p Man 90 35

1983, Jan. 21
1624 A406 40s grn & multi 16 15
1625 A406 1.20p org & multi 45 22
Set value 28

1983 Manila Intl. Film Festival, Jan. 24-Feb. 4 — A407

1983, Jan. 24
1626 A407 40s blk & multi 16 15
1627 A407 3.20p pink & multi 1.25 60

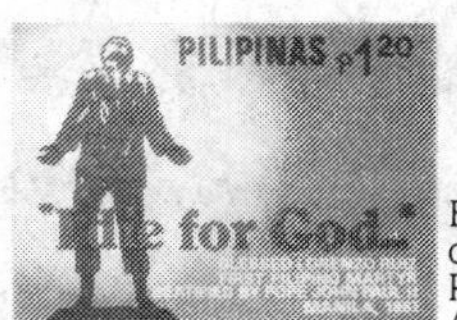

Beatification of Lorenzo Ruiz (1981) A408

Perf. 13x13½
1983, Feb. 18 Litho. Wmk. 372
1628 A408 40s multi 16 15
1629 A408 1.20p multi 45 22

400th Anniv. of Local Printing Press A409

1983, Mar. 14
1630 A409 40s blk & grn 16 15

Safety at Sea — A410

1983, Mar. 17 *Perf. 13½x13*
1631 A410 40s multi 16 15

25th anniv. of Inter-Governmental Maritime Consultation Org. Convention.

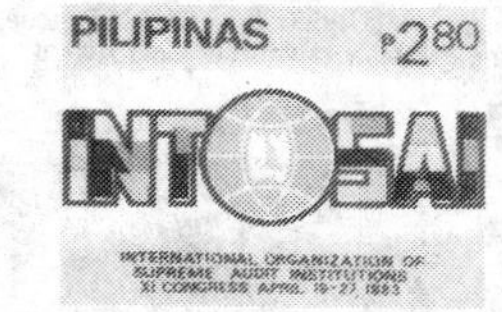

Intl. Org. of Supreme Audit Institutions, 11th Congress, Manila, Apr. 19-27 A411

Perf. 13x13½
1983, Apr. 8 Litho. Wmk. 372
1632 A411 40s Symbols 16 15
1633 A411 2.80p Emblem 1.10 50
a. Souv. sheet of 2, 1632-1633, imperf. 1.40 65

No. 1633a comes on two papers: cream gum, normal watermark; white gum, watermark made up of smaller letters.

Type of 1982 Overprinted in Red: "7th BSP NATIONAL JAMBOREE 1983"

1983, Apr. 13 *Perf. 12½*
1634 A390 40s multi 16 15

Boy Scouts of Philippines jamboree.

No. 1249 Surcharged

1983, Apr. 15
1635 Block of 10 1.65 70
a.-j. A265 40s on 45s, any single 16 15

A412 A413

Perf. 13½x13
1983, May 9 Litho. Wmk. 372
1636 A412 40s multi 16 15

75th anniv. of Dental Assoc.

Perf. 13½x13
1983, June 17 Litho. Wmk. 372
1637 A413 40s Statue 16 15
1638 A413 1.20p Statue, diff., diamond 45 22
Set value 28

75th anniv. of University of the Philippines.

Visit of Japanese Prime Minister Yasuhiro Nakasone, May 6-8 — A414

Perf. 13x13½
1983, June 20 Litho. Wmk. 372
1639 A414 40s multi 16 15

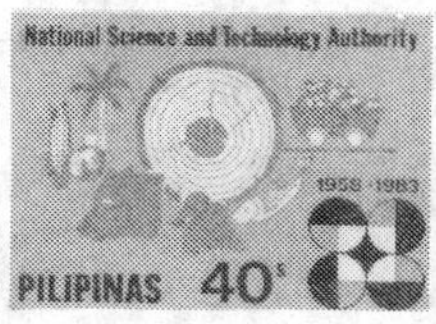

25th Anniv. of Natl. Science and Technology Authority A415

1983, July 11
1640 A415 40s Animals, produce 16 15
1641 A415 40s Heart, food, pill 16 15
1642 A415 40s Factories, windmill, car 16 15
1643 A415 40s Chemicals, house, book 16 15
a. Block of 4, #1640-1643 65 35
Set value 28

Science Week.

World Communications Year — A416

Perf. 12½
1983, Oct. 24 Litho. Wmk. 372
1644 A416 3.20p multi 1.25 60

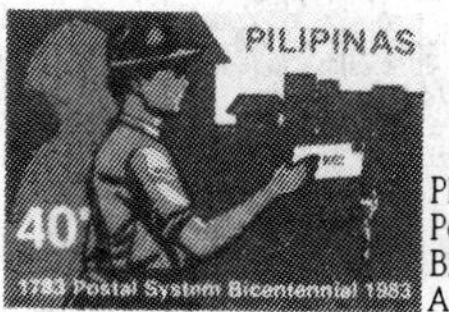

Philippine Postal System Bicentennial A417

1983, Oct. 31
1645 A417 40s multi 16 15

Christmas — A418

Star of the East and Festival Scene in continuous design.

1983, Nov. 15 Litho. *Perf. 12½*
1646 Strip of 5 80 35
a.-e. A418 40s single stamp 16 15
f. Souvenir sheet 80

Xavier University, 50th Anniv. A419

1983, Dec. 1 Litho. *Perf. 14*
1647 A419 40s multi 16 15
1648 A419 60s multi 24 15
Set value 16

A420 A421

1983, Dec. 8 Litho. *Perf. 12½*
1649 A420 40s brt ultra & multi 16 15
1650 A420 60s gold & multi 24 15
Set value 16

Ministry of Labor and Employment, golden jubilee.

1983, Dec. 7
1651 A421 40s multi 16 15
1652 A421 60s multi 24 15
Set value 16

50th anniv. of Women's Suffrage Movement.

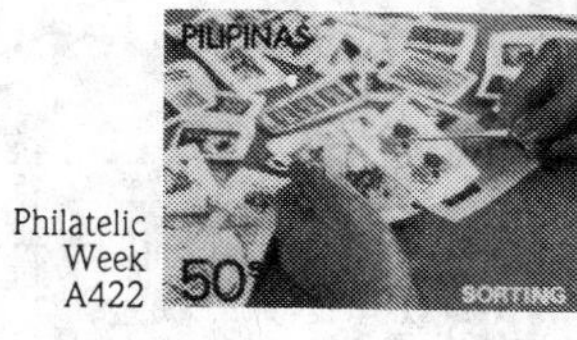

Philatelic Week A422

Stamp Collecting: a, Cutting. b, Sorting. c, Soaking. d, Affixing hinges. e, Mounting stamp.

1983, Dec. 20
1653 Strip of 5 1.00 40
a.-e. A422 50s any single 20 15

Emancipation Type of 1982

1983 Litho. *Perf. 13*
Size: 32x22mm
1654 A396 40s multi 15 15

Philippine Cockatoo — A423

Princess Tarhata Kiram — A424

1984, Jan. 9 Unwmk. *Perf. 14*
1655 A423 40s shown 15 15
1656 A423 2.30p Guaiabero 24 15
1657 A423 2.80p Crimson-spotted racket-tailed parrots 28 15
1658 A423 3.20p Large-billed parrot 32 15
1659 A423 3.60p Tanygnathus sumatranus 35 15
1660 A423 5p Hanging parakeets 50 20
Nos. 1655-1660 (6) 1.84
Set value 72

1984, Jan. 16 Wmk. 372 *Perf. 13*
1661 A424 3p grn & red 30 15

Order of Virgin Mary, 300th Anniv. A425

Dona Concha Felix de Calderon A426

1984, Jan. 23 *Perf. 13½x13*

1662 A425 40s blk & multi 15 15
1663 A425 60s red & multi 15 15
Set value 15 15

1984, Feb. 9 *Perf. 13*

1664 A426 60s blk & bl grn 15 15
1665 A426 3.60p red & bl grn 35 15
Set value 40 18

Nos. 1546, 1599, 1618 Surcharged

1984, Feb. 20

1666 A393 60s on 40s (R) 15 15
1667 A403 60s on 40s 15 15
1668 A374 3.60p on 3.20p (R) 35 15
Set value 46 24

No. 1685 Surcharged

1985, Oct. 21 **Litho.** *Perf. 12½*

1669 A374 3.60p on 4.20p rose lil 28 15

Portrait Type of 1981

Designs: No. 1672, Gen. Artemio Ricarte. No. 1673, Teodoro M. Kalaw. No. 1674, Pres. Carlos P. Garcia. No. 1675, Senator Quintin Paredes. No. 1676, Dr. Deogracias V. Villadolid (1896-1976), 1st director, Bureau of Fisheries. No. 1677, Santiago Fonacier (1885-1940), archbishop. No. 1678, 2p, Vicente Orestes Romualdez (1885-1970), lawyer. 3p, Francisco Dagohoy.

Perf. 13, 12½ (2p), 12½x13 (3p)

1984-85 **Litho.**

1672 A374 60s blk & lt brn 15 15
1673 A374 60s blk & pur 15 15
1674 A374 60s black 15 15
1675 A374 60s dull blue 15 15
1676 A374 60s brn blk ('85) 15 15
1677 A374 60s dk red ('85) 15 15
1678 A374 60s cobalt blue ('85) 15 15
1679 A374 2p brt rose ('85) 16 15
1680 A374 3p pale brn 25 15
Set value 95 55

Issue dates: No. 1672, Mar. 22; No. 1673, Mar. 31; No. 1674, June 14. No. 1675, Sept. 12. No. 1676, Mar. 22. No. 1677, May 21. No. 1678, 2p, July 3. 3p, Sept. 7.

Types of 1982

1984

1681 A390 60s green & multi 15 15
1681A A390 60s red & multi 15 15
1682 A374 1.80p #1546 18 15
1683 A374 2.40p #1545 25 15
1684 A386 3.60p Quezon 35 15
1685 A374 4.20p #1544 40 18
Nos. 1681-1685 (6) 1.48
Set value 60

Issue dates: 4.20p, Mar. 26; No. 1581A, 1984; others May 5.

Ayala Corp. Sesquicentenary — A427

Night Views of Manila.

1984, Apr. 25 **Litho.** *Perf. 13x13½*

1686 A427 70s multi 15 15
1687 A427 3.60p multi 35 15
Set value 42 18

ESPANA '84 — A428

Designs: 2.50p, No. 1690d, Our Lady of the Most Holy Rosary with St. Dominic, by C. Francisco. 5p, No. 1690a, Spoliarium, by Juan Luna. No. 1690b, Blessed Virgin of Manila as Patroness of Voyages, Galleon showing map of Panama-Manila. No. 1690c. Illustrations from The Monkey and the Turtle, by Rizal (first children's book published in Philippines, 1885.)

1984, Apr. 27 *Perf. 14*

1688 A428 2.50p multi 28 15
1689 A428 5p multi 55 25
a. Pair, #1688-1689 85 40

Souvenir Sheet

Perf. 14½x15, Imperf.

1690 Sheet of 4 3.50 1.55
a.-d. A428 7.50p, any single 85 38

Maria Pax Mendoza Guazon — A429

1984, May 26 *Perf. 13*

1691 A429 60s brt blue & red 15 15
1692 A429 65s brt blue, red & blk 15 15
Set value 15 15

Butterflies A430

1984, Aug. 2 **Litho.** *Perf. 14*

1693 A430 60s Adolias amlana 15 15
1694 A430 2.40p Papilio daedalus 20 15
1695 A430 3p Prothoe frankii semperi 25 15
1696 A430 3.60p Troides magellanus 28 15
1697 A430 4.20p Yoma sabina vasuki 35 18
1698 A430 5p Chilasa idaeoides 40 20
Nos. 1693-1698 (6) 1.63
Set value 78

Baguio City, 75th Anniv. A432

1984, Aug. 24 **Litho.** *Perf. 12½*

1706 A432 1.20p The Mansion 15 15

Light Rail Transit A433

1984, Sept. 10 *Perf. 13x13½*

1707 A433 1.20p multi 15 15

No. 1, Australia No. 59 and Koalas A434

1984, Sept. 21 *Perf. 14½x15*

1708 A434 3p multi 25 15
1709 A434 3.60p multi 28 15

Souvenir Sheet

1710 Sheet of 3 5.00 2.50
a. A434 20p multi 1.65 80

AUSIPEX '84. No. 1710 exists imperf.

No. 1609 Surcharged with 2 Black Bars and Ovptd. "14-17 NOV. 84 / R.I. ASIA REGIONAL CONFERENCE."

1984, Nov. 11 **Litho.** *Perf. 13x13½*

1713 A398 1.20p on 2.30p multi 15 15

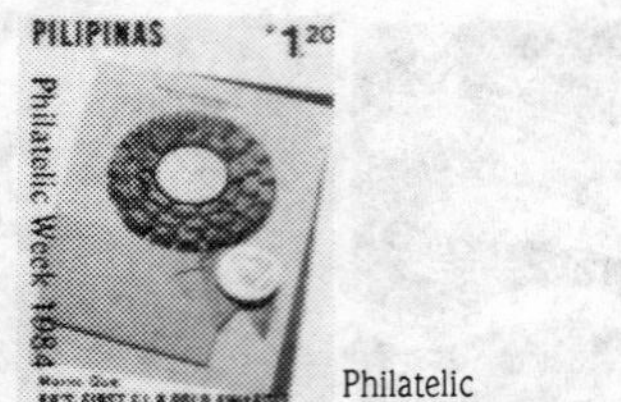

Philatelic Week — A435

1984, Nov. 22 *Perf. 13½x13*

1714 A435 1.20p Gold medal 15 15
1715 A435 3p Winning stamp exhibit 25 15
Set value 16

Se-tenant. AUSIPEX '84 and Mario Que, 1st Philippine exhibitor to win FIP Gold Award.

Ships A436

1984, Nov. **Litho.** *Perf. 13½x13*

1718 A436 60s Caracao canoes 15 15
1719 A436 1.20p Chinese junk 15 15
1720 A436 6p Spanish galleon 50 25
1721 A436 7.20p Casco 60 30
1722 A436 8.40p Steamboat 70 35
1723 A436 20p Cruise liner 1.65 80
Nos. 1718-1723 (6) 3.75 2.00

Ateneo de Manila University, 125th Anniv. A438

1984, Dec. 7 **Litho.** *Perf. 13x13½*

1730 A438 60s ultra & gold 15 15
1731 A438 1.20p dk ultra & sil 15 15
Set value 16 15

Christmas A439

Jaycees, Youth Development A440

1984, Dec. 8 *Perf. 13½x13*

1732 A439 60s Madonna and Child 15 15
1733 A439 1.20p Holy family 15 15
a. Pair, #1732-1733 16 15
Set value 16 15

1984, Dec. 19

Abstract painting by Raoul G. Isidro.

1734 Strip of 10 1.65 85
a.-e. A440 60s, any single 15 15
f.-j. A440 3p, any single 25 15

Natl. Jaycees Awards, 25th anniv.

Dried Tobacco Leaf and Plant A441

1985, Jan. 14 *Perf. 13x13½*

1735 A441 60s multicolored 15 15
1736 A441 3p multicolored 25 15
Set value 30 16

Philippine-Virginia Tobacco Admin., 25th anniv.

No. 1537 Surcharged

1985, Jan. **Litho.** *Imperf.*

1737 A373 3p on 2p multi 35 15

Comes with missing period ("p300").

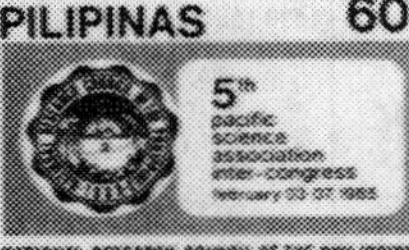

Natl. Research Council Emblem A442

1985, Feb. 3 **Litho.** *Perf. 13x13½*

1738 A442 60s bl, dk bl & blk 15 15
1739 A442 1.20p org, dk bl & blk 18 15
Set value 25 15

Pacific Science Assoc., 5th intl. congress, Manila, Feb. 3-7.

Medicinal Plants A443

1985, Mar. 15 *Perf. 12½*

1740 A443 60s Carmona retusa 15 15
1741 A443 1.20p Orthosiphon aristatus 15 15
1742 A443 2.40p Vitex negundo 20 15
1743 A443 3p Aloe barbadensis 25 15
1744 A443 3.60p Quisqualis indica 28 15
1745 A443 4.20p Blumea balsamifera 35 18
Nos. 1740-1745 (6) 1.38
Set value 62

INTELSAT, 20th Anniv. A444

1985, Apr. 6 *Perf. 13x13½*

1746 A444 60s multicolored 15 15
1747 A444 3p multicolored 25 15
Set value 30 16

Tax Research Institute, 25th Anniv. — A445

1985, Apr. 22 *Perf. 13½x13*

1748 A445 60s multicolored 15 15

Intl. Rice Research Institute, 25th Anniv. A446

1985, May 27 *Perf. 13x13½*

1749 A446 60s Planting 15 15
1750 A446 3p Paddies 15 15
Set value 16 15

1st Spain-Philippines Peace Treaty, 420th Anniv. — A447

Designs: 1.20p, Blessed Infant of Cebu, statue, shrine and basilica. 3.60p, King Tupas of Cebu and Miguel Lopez de Legaspi signing treaty, 1565.

1985, June 4 ***Perf. 12½***
1751 A447 1.20p multi 15 15
1752 A447 3.60p multi 28 15
a. Pair, #1751-1752 + label 45 45
Set value 18

No. 1532 Ovptd. "10th Anniversary Philippines and People's Republic of China Diplomatic Relations 1975-1985"

1985, June 8 ***Imperf.***
1753 A372 5p multi 40 20

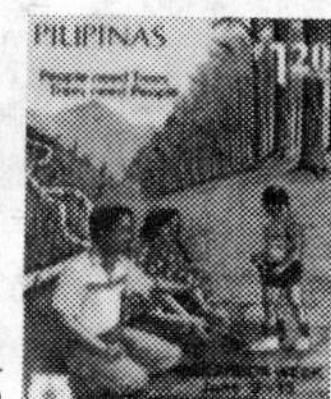

Arbor Week, June 9-15 — A448

1985, June 9 ***Perf. 13½x13***
1754 A448 1.20p multi 15 15

Battle of Bessang Pass, 40th Anniv. A449

1985, June 14 ***Perf. 13x13½***
1755 A449 1.20p multi 15 15

Natl. Tuberculosis Soc., 75th Anniv. A450

1985, July 29
1756 A450 60s Immunization, research 15 15
1757 A450 1.20p Charity seal 15 15
a. Pair, #1756-1757 18 16
Set value 18 15

No. 1297 Surcharged with Bars, New Value and Scout Emblem in Gold, Ovptd. "GSP" and "45th Anniversary Girl Scout Charter" in Black

Perf. 12½x13½

1985, Aug. 19 **Photo.**
1758 A242 2.40p on 15s on 10s 20 15
1759 A242 4.20p on 15s on 10s 35 18
1760 A242 7.20p on 15s on 10s 60 30

Virgin Mary Birth Bimillennium A451

Statues and paintings.

1985, Sept. 8 **Litho.** ***Perf. 13½x13***
1761 A451 1.20p Fatima 15 15
1762 A451 2.40p Beaterio 20 15
1763 A451 3p Penafrancia 25 15
1764 A451 3.60p Guadalupe 30 15
Set value 40

Intl. Youth Year — A452

Prize-winning children's drawings.

1985, Sept. 23 ***Perf. 13x13½***
1765 A452 2.40p Agriculture 20 15
1766 A452 3.60p Education 30 15
Set value 24

Girl and Rice Terraces A453

1985, Sept. 26
1767 A453 2.40p multi 20 15

World Tourism Organization, 6th general assembly, Sofia, Bulgaria, Sept. 17-26.

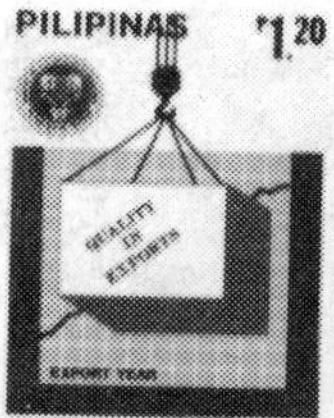

Export Year — A454

UN, 40th Anniv. — A455

1985, Oct. 8 ***Perf. 13½x13***
1768 A454 1.20p multi 15 15

1985, Oct. 24
1769 A455 3.60p multi 30 15

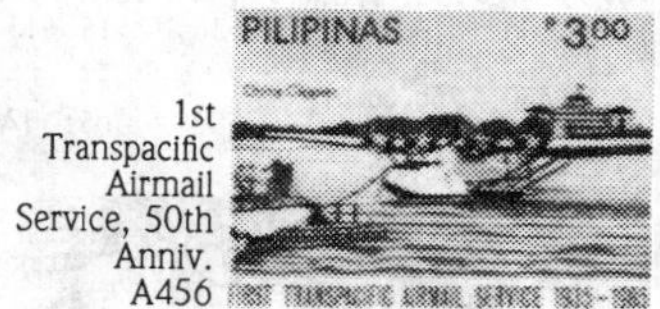

1st Transpacific Airmail Service, 50th Anniv. A456

1985, Nov. 22 ***Perf. 13x13½***
1770 A456 3p China Clipper on water 25 15
1771 A456 3.60p China Clipper, map 30 15

Natl. Bible Week A457

1985, Dec. 3 ***Perf. 12½***
1774 A457 60s multicolored 15 15
1775 A457 3p multicolored 25 15
Set value 30 16

Christmas 1985 A458

1985, Dec. 8 ***Perf. 13x13½***
1776 A458 60s Panuluyan 15 15
1777 A458 3p Pagdalaw 25 15
Set value 30 16

Scales of Justice A459

1986, Jan. 12
1778 A459 60s lilac rose & blk 15 15
1779 A459 3p brt grn, lil rose & blk 25 15

University of the Philippines, College of Law, 75th anniv.
See No. 1838.

Flores de Heidelberg, by Jose Rizal — A460

Design: 60s, Noli Me Tangere.

1986 **Litho.** **Wmk.** ***Perf. 13***
1780 A460 60s violet 15 15
1781 A460 1.20p bluish grn 15 15
1782 A460 3.60p redsh brn 28 15
Set value 42 24

Issue dates: 60s, 1.20p, Feb. 21. 3.60p, July 10.
For surcharges see Nos. 1834, 1913.

Philippine Airlines, 45th Anniv. — A461

Aircraft: No. 1783a, Douglas DC3, 1946. b, Douglas DC4 Skymaster, 1946. c, Douglas DC6, 1948. d, Vickers Viscount 784, 1957.
No. 1784a, Fokker Friendship F27 Mark 100, 1960. b, Douglas DC8 Series 50, 1962. c, Bac One Eleven Series 500, 1964. d, McDonnell Douglas DC10 Series 30, 1974.
No. 1785a, Beech Model 18, 1941. b, Boeing 747, 1980.

1986, Mar. 15 **Wmk.**
1783 Block of 4 25 20
a.-d. A461 60s, any single 15 15
1784 Block of 4 80 40
a.-d. A461 2.40p, any single 20 15
1785 Pair 60 28
a.-b. A461 3.60p, any single 30 15
Nos. 1783-1785 (3) 1.65 88

See No. 1842.

Bataan Oil Refining Corp., 25th Anniv. A462

Perf. 13½x13, 13x13½

1986, Apr. 12 **Wmk.**
1786 A462 60s Refinery, vert. 15 15
1787 A462 3p shown 25 15
Set value 30 16

EXPO '86, Vancouver A463

1986, May 2 **Wmk.** ***Perf. 13x13½***
1788 A463 60s multicolored 15 15
1789 A463 3p multicolored 25 15
Set value 30 16

Asian Productivity Organization, 25th Anniv. — A464

1986 **Wmk.**
1790 A464 60s multicolored 15 15
1791 A464 3p multicolored 25 15
Set value 30 16

Wmk. ***Perf. 13***
Size: 30x22mm
1792 A464 3p pale brown 25 15

Issue dates: Nos. 1790-1791, May 15. No. 1792, July 10.

AMERIPEX '86 — A465

Election of Corazon Aquino, 7th Pres. — A466

1986, May 22 **Wmk.** ***Perf. 13½x13***
1793 A465 60s No. 241 15 15
1794 A465 3p No. 390 25 15
Set value 30 16

See No. 1835.

1986, May 25 **Wmk.**

Portrait of Aquino and: 60s, Salvador Laurel, vice-president, and hands in symbolic gestures of peace and freedom. 1.20p, Symbols of communication and transportation. 2.40p, Parade. 3p, Military. 7.20p, Vice-president, parade, horiz.

1795 A466 60s multi 15 15
1796 A466 1.20p multi 15 15
1797 A466 2.40p multi 16 15
1798 A466 3p multi 20 15
Set value 48 28

Souvenir Sheet
Imperf
1799 A466 7.20p multi 45 22

For surcharge see No. 1939.

De La Salle University, 75th Anniv. A467

Designs: 60s, Statue of St. John the Baptist de la Salle, Paco buildings, 1911, and university, 1986. 2.40p, St. Miguel Febres Cordero, buildings, 1911. 3p, St. Benilde, buildings, 1986. 7.20p, Founding fathers.

1986, June 16 Wmk. *Perf. 13x13½*

1800 A467 60s grn, blk & pink 15 15
1801 A467 2.40p grn, blk & bl 20 15
1802 A467 3p grn, blk & yel 25 15
Set value 50 26

Souvenir Sheet

Imperf

1803 A467 7.20p grn & blk 55 28

For surcharge see No. 1940.

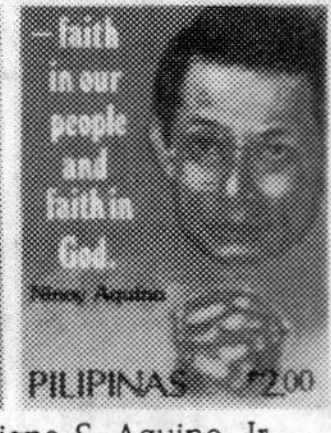

Memorial to Benigno S. Aquino, Jr. (1932-83)
A468 A469

Perf. 13½x13, 13x13½

1986, Aug. 21 Wmk.

1804 A468 60s dl bluish grn 15 15
1805 A469 2p shown 16 15
1806 A469 3.60p The Filipino is worth dying for, horiz. 30 15
Set value 52 26

Souvenir Sheet

Imperf

1807 A469 10p Hindi ka nag-iisa, horiz. 80 40

See No. 1836. For surcharge see No. 1914.

Indigenous Orchids — A470

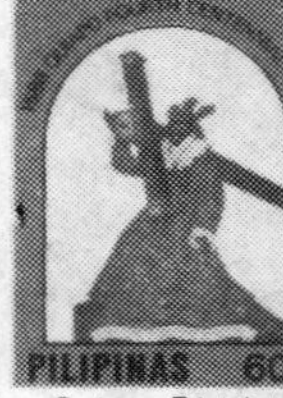

Quiapo District, 400th Anniv. — A471

1986, Aug. 28 Wmk. *Perf. 13½x13*

1808 A470 60s Vanda sanderiana 15 15
1809 A470 1.20p Epigeneium lyonii 15 15
1810 A470 2.40p Paphiopedilum philippinense 20 15
1811 A470 3p Amesiella philippinensis 25 15
Set value 60 32

For surcharge see No. 1941.

Perf. 13½x13, 13x13½

1986, Aug. 29 Wmk.

Designs: 60s, Our Lord Jesus the Nazarene, statue, Quiapo church. 3.60p, Quiapo church, 1930, horiz.

1812 A471 60s pink, blk & lake 15 15
1813 A471 3.60p pale grn, blk & dk ultra 30 15
Set value 36 18

For surcharge see No. 1915.

General Hospital, 75th Anniv. — A472

1986, Sept. 1 Wmk. *Perf. 13½x13*

1814 A472 60s bl & multi 15 15
1815 A472 3p grn & multi 25 15
Set value 30 16

See No. 1841. For surcharge see No. 1888.

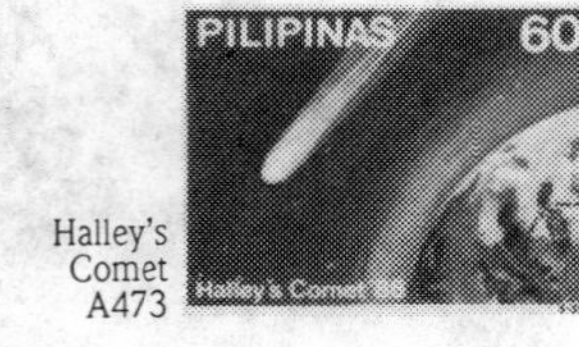

Halley's Comet A473

1986, Sept. 25 Wmk. *Perf. 13x13½*

1816 A473 60s Comet, Earth 15 15
1817 A473 2.40p Comet, Earth, Moon 20 15
Set value 26 15

For surcharge see No. 1942.

74th FDI World Dental Congress, Manila A474

Perf. 13x13½

1986, Nov. 10 Litho. Wmk.

1818 A474 60s Handshake 15 15
1819 A474 3p Jeepney bus 35 18
Set value 42 22

See Nos. 1837, 1840.

Insects A475

Intl. Peace Year — A476

Manila YMCA, 75th Anniv. — A477

Perf. 13x13½, 13½x13

1986, Nov. 21 Wmk.

1820 A475 60s Butterfly, beetles 15 15
1821 A476 1p bl & blk 15 15
1822 A475 3p Dragonflies 35 18
Set value 54 28

Philately Week.

1986, Nov. 28 Wmk. *Perf. 13x13½*

1823 A477 2p blue 25 15
1824 A477 3.60p red 42 20

See No. 1839. For surcharge see No. 1916.

Philippine Normal College, 85th Anniv. A478

Various arrangements of college crest and buildings, 1901-1986.

1986, Dec. 12 Wmk.

1825 A478 60s multi 15 15
1826 A478 3.60p buff, ultra & gldn brn 42 20
Set value 48 25

For surcharge see No. 1917.

Christmas A479

Perf. 13½x13, 13x13½

1986, Dec. 15 Wmk.

1827 A479 60s Holy family 15 15
1828 A479 60s Mother and child, doves 15 15
1829 A479 60s Child touching mother's face 15 15
1830 A479 1p Adoration of the shepherds 15 15
1831 A479 1p Mother, child signaling peace 15 15
1832 A479 1p Holy family, lamb 15 15
1833 A479 1p Mother, child blessing food 15 15
Set value 68 35

Nos. 1827-1829, vert.

No. 1780 Surcharged

1987, Jan. 6 Litho. Wmk. *Perf. 13*

1834 A460 1p on 60s vio 15 15

Types of 1986

Designs: 75s, No. 390, AMERIPEX '86. 1p, Benigno S. Aquino, Jr. 3.25p, Handshake, 74th World Dental Congress. 3.50p, Scales of Justice. 4p, Manila YMCA emblem. 4.75p, Jeepney bus. 5p, General Hospital. 5.50p, Boeing 747, 1980.

1987, Jan. 16 Wmk. Litho. *Perf. 13*
Size: 22x31mm, 31x22mm

1835 A465 75s brt yel grn 15 15
1836 A468 1p blue 15 15
1837 A474 3.25p dull grn 40 20
1838 A459 3.50p dark car 42 20
1839 A477 4p blue 45 22
1840 A474 4.75p dl yel grn 55 28
1841 A472 5p olive bister 65 32
1842 A461 5.50p dk bl gray 65 32
Nos. 1835-1842 (8) 3.42 1.84

All but 75s dated "1-1-87." No. 1838 exists without imprint.

Manila Hotel, 75th Anniv. A480

1987, Jan. 30 Wmk. *Perf. 13x13½*

1843 A480 1p Hotel, c. 1912 15 15
1844 A480 4p Hotel, 1987 45 22
1845 A480 4.75p Lobby 55 28
1846 A480 5.50p Foyer 65 32

Intl. Eucharistic Congress, Manila, 50th Anniv. A481

Perf. 13½x13, 13x13½

1987, Feb. 7 Wmk.

1847 A481 75s Emblem, vert. 15 15
1848 A481 1p shown 15 15
Set value 20 15

Pres. Aquino Taking Oath A482

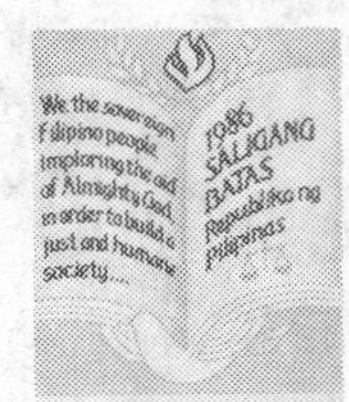

Text — A483

Perf. 13½x13, 13x13½

1987, Mar. 4 Wmk. 391

1849 A482 1p multi 15 15
1850 A483 5.50p blue & deep bister 70 35
Set value 40

Ratification of the new constitution.
See No. 1905. For surcharge see No. 2005.

Lyceum College and Founder, Jose P. Laurel A484

Perf. 13x13½

1987, May 7 Litho. Wmk.

1851 A484 1p multi 15 15
1852 A484 2p multi 16 15
Set value 24 15

Lyceum of the Philippines, 35th anniv.

Government Service Insurance System — A485

1987, June 1 *Perf. 13½x13*

1853 A485 1p Salary and policy loans 15 15
1854 A485 1.25p Disability, medicare 16 15
1855 A485 2p Retirement benefits 25 15
1856 A485 3.50p Life insurance 42 20
Set value 45

Davao City, 50th Anniv. A486

Perf. 13x13½

1987, Mar. 16 Litho. Wmk.

1857 A486 1p Falconer, woman planting, city seal 15 15

Salvation Army in the Philippines, 50th Anniv. — A487

Natl. League of Women Voters, 50th Anniv. — A488

Perf. 13½x13

1987, June 5 Photo. Wmk.

1858 A487 1p multi 15 15

1987, July 15 Wmk.

1859 A488 1p pink & blue 15 15

A489

A490

Designs: No. 1851, Gen. Vicente Lukban (1860-1916). No. 1862, Wenceslao Q. Vinzons (1910-1942). No. 1863, Brig.-gen. Mateo M. Capinpin (1887-1958). No. 1864, Jesus Balmori (1882-1948).

Perf. 13x13½, 12½ (#1862)

1987 Litho. Wmk.

1861 A489 1p olive grn 15 15
1862 A489 1p dull greenish blue 15 15
1863 A489 1p dull red brn 15 15
1864 A489 1p rose red & rose claret 15 15
Set value 36 22

Issue dates: No. 1861, July 31. No. 1862, Sept. 9. No. 1863, Oct. 15. No. 1864, Dec. 17.

This is an expanding set. Numbers will change if necessary.

Perf. 13½x13

1987, July 22 Litho. Wmk.

Nuns (1862-1987), children, Crucifix, Sacred Heart.

1881 A490 1p multi 15 15

Daughters of Charity of St. Vincent de Paul in the Philippines, 125th anniv.

Map of Southeast Asia, Flags of ASEAN Members A491

1987, Aug. 7 Wmk. *Perf. 13x13½*

1882 A491 1p multi 15 15

ASEAN, 20th anniv.

Exports Campaign A492

1987, Aug. 11 Wmk. *Perf. 13*

1883 A492 1p shown 15 15
1884 A492 2p Worker, gearwheel 16 15
Set value 24 15

See No. 1904.

Canonization of Lorenzo Ruiz by Pope John Paul II, Oct. 18 — A493

First Filipino saint: 1p, Ruiz, stained glass window showing Crucifixion. 5.50p, Ruiz at prayer, execution in 1637.

Perf. 13½x13

1987, Oct. 10 Litho. Wmk. 389

1885 A493 1p multi 15 15
1886 A493 5.50p multi 48 25

Size: 57x57mm

Imperf

1887 A493 8p like 5.50p 70 35
Set value 65

No. 1887 has denomination at LL.

No. 1841 Surcharged

1987, Oct. 12 Wmk. *Perf. 13*

1888 A472 4.75p on 5p olive bis 40 20

Order of the Good Shepherd Sisters in Philippines, 65th Anniv. A494

Perf. 13x13½

1987, Oct. 27 Wmk. 389

1889 A494 1p multi 15 15

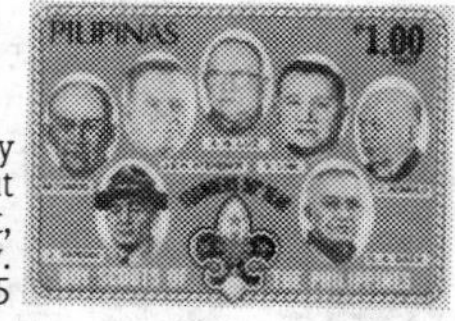

Natl. Boy Scout Movement, 50th Anniv. A495

Founders: J. Vargas, M. Camus, J.E.H. Stevenot, A.N. Luz, V. Lim, C. Romulo and G.A. Daza.

Perf. 13x13½

1987, Oct. 28 Litho. Wmk. 389

1890 A495 1p multi 15 15

Philippine Philatelic Club, 50th Anniv. A496

1987, Nov. 7 *Perf. 13x13½*

1891 A496 1p multi 15 15

Order of the Dominicans in the Philippines, 400th Anniv. A497

Designs: 1p, First missionaries shipwrecked, church and image of the Virgin, vert. 4.75p, J.A. Jeronimo Guerrero, Br., Diego de St. Maria and Letran Dominican College. 5.50p, Pope with Dominican representatives.

Perf. 13½x13, 13x13½

1987, Nov. 11

1892 A497 1p multi 15 15
1893 A497 4.75p multi 40 20
1894 A497 5.50p multi 48 25
Set value 50

3rd ASEAN Summit Meeting, Dec. 14-15 A498

Perf. 13x13½

1987, Dec. 5 Wmk. 389

1895 A498 4p multi 32 16

Christmas 1987 — A499

1987, Dec. 8 *Perf. 13½x13*

1896 A499 1p Postal service 15 15
1897 A499 1p 5-Pointed stars 15 15
1898 A499 4p Procession, church 32 16
1899 A499 4.75p Gift exchange 38 18
1900 A499 5.50p Bamboo cannons 42 20
1901 A499 8p Pig, holiday foods 60 32
1902 A499 9.50p Traditional foods 75 38
1903 A499 11p Serving meal 85 42
Nos. 1896-1903 (8) 3.62 1.96

Exports Type of 1987

Design: Worker, gearwheel.

Wmk. 391

1987, Dec. 16 Litho. *Perf. 13*

1904 A492 4.75p lt blue & blk 38 20

Constitution Ratification Type of 1987

1987, Dec. 16 Wmk. 391 *Perf. 13*

Size: 22x31½mm

1905 A483 5.50p brt yel grn & fawn 42 20

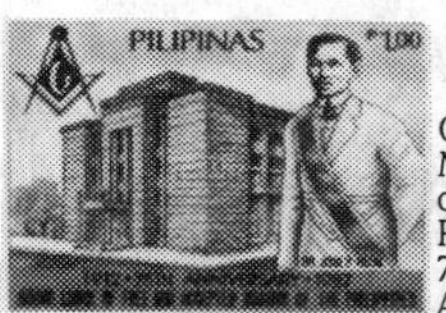

Grand Masonic Lodge of the Philippines, 75th Anniv. A500

Perf. 13x13½

1987, Dec. 19 Wmk. 389

1906 A500 1p multi 15 15

United Nations Projects A501

Designs: a, Intl. Fund for Agricultural Development (IFAD). b, Transport and Communications Decade for Asia and the Pacific. c, Intl. Year of Shelter for the Homeless (IYSH). d, World Health Day, 1987.

Perf. 13x13½

1987, Dec. 22 Litho. Wmk. 389

1907 Strip of 4 + label 32 20
a.-d. A501 1p, any single 15 15

Label pictures UN emblem.

7th Opening of Congress A502

Designs: 1p, Official seals of the Senate and Quezon City House of Representatives, gavel, vert. 5.50p, Congress in session.

Perf. 13½x13, 13x13½

1988, Jan. 25 Wmk. 389

1908 A502 1p multi 15 15
1909 A502 5.50p multi 58 30
Set value 36

St. John Bosco (1815-1888), Educator A503

1988, Jan. 31 *Perf. 13x13½*

1910 A503 1p multi 15 15
1911 A503 5.50p multi 58 30
Set value 36

Buy Philippine Goods — A504

Perf. 13½x13

1988, Feb. 1 Litho. Wmk. 389

1912 A504 1p buff, ultra, blk & scar 15 15

Nos. 1782, 1806, 1813, 1824, 1826 Surcharged

Wmk. (#1913, 1916) 389 (#1914, 1917), 391 (#1915)

Perf. 13 (#1782), 13x13½

1988, Feb. 14

1913 A460 3p on 3.60p redsh brn 32 16
1914 A469 3p on 3.60p multi 32 16
1915 A471 3p on 3.60p pale grn, blk & dark ultra 32 16
1916 A477 3p on 3.60p red 32 16
1917 A478 3p on 3.60p buff, ultra & golden brn 32 16
Nos. 1913-1917 (5) 1.60 80

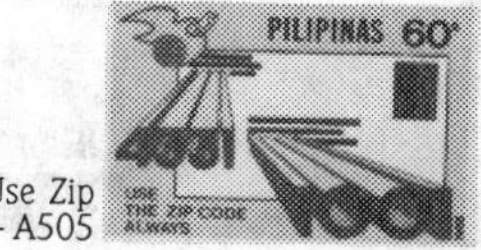

Use Zip Codes — A505

1988, Feb. 25 Wmk. *Perf. 13*

1918 A505 60s multi 15 15
1919 A505 1p multi 15 15
Set value 20 15

Insects That Prey on Other Insects — A506

1988, Mar. 11 Wmk. 390 *Perf. 13*

1920 A506 1p Vesbius purpureus 15 15
1921 A506 5.50p Campsomeris aurulenta 58 30
Set value 36

Solar Eclipse 1988 A507

Perf. 13x13½

1988, Mar. 18 Unwmk.

1922 A507 1p multi 15 15
1923 A507 5.50p multi 58 30
Set value 36

Toribio M. Teodoro (1887-1965), Shoe Manufacturer A508

1988, Apr. 27 Litho. Wmk. *Perf. 13*

1924 A508 1p buff, dark olive bister & brt rose 15 15

1925 A508 1.20p pale blue grn, blk & scar 15 15

Set value 26 15

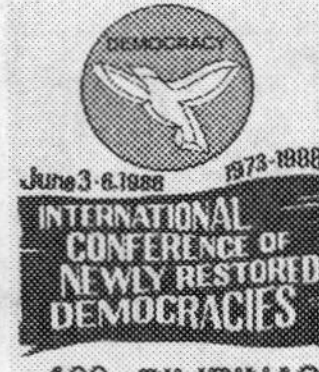

A509 A510

College of the Holy Spirit, 75th anniv.: 1p, Emblem and motto "Truth in Love." 4p, Arnold Janssen, founder, and Sr. Edelwina, director 1920-1947.

Perf. 13½x13

1988, May 22 Unwmk.

1926 A509 1p blk, maroon & gold 15 15

1927 A509 4p blk, olive grn & maroon 48 24

Set value 30

Perf. 13½x13

1988, June 4 Litho. Unwmk.

1928 A510 4p dark ultra, brt blue & blk 42 20

Intl. Conference of Newly Restored Democracies.

A511 A512

Juan Luna and Felix Hidalgo.

1988, June 15 Wmk. *Perf. 13*

1929 A511 1p multi 15 15

1930 A511 5.50p multi 45 22

Set value 26

First Natl. Juan Luna and Felix Resurreccion Hidalgo Commemorative Exhibition, June 15-Aug. 15. Artists Luna and Hidalgo won medals at the 1884 Madrid Fine Arts Exhibition.

Perf. 13½x13

1988, June 22 Litho. Wmk. 372

1931 A512 1p multi 15 15

1932 A512 5.50p multi 55 28

Set value 32

Natl. Irrigation Administration, 25th anniv.

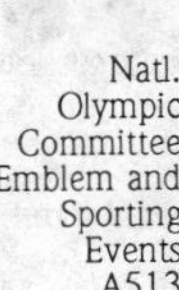

Natl. Olympic Committee Emblem and Sporting Events A513

Designs: 1p, Scuba diving, Siquijor Is. 1.20p, Big game fishing, Aparri, Cagayan Province. 4p, Yachting, Manila Central. 5.50p, Climbing Mt. Apo. 8p, Golf, Cebu, Cebu Is. 11p, Cycling through Marawi, Mindanao Is.

1988, July 11 *Perf. 13x13½*

1933 A513 1p multi 15 15

1934 A513 1.20p multi 15 15

1935 A513 4p multi 40 20

1936 A513 5.50p multi 55 28

1937 A513 8p multi 80 40

1938 A513 11p multi 1.10 55

Nos. 1933-1938 (6) 3.15

Set value 1.50

4p, 8p, 1p and 5.50p also exist in strips of 4 plus center label picturing torch and inscribed "Philippine Olympic Week, May 1-7, 1988."

Nos. 1797, 1801, 1810 and 1817 Surcharged with 2 Bars and New Value in Black or Gold

1988, Aug. 1 As Before

1939 A466 1.90p on 2.40p #1797 20 15

1940 A467 1.90p on 2.40p #1801 20 15

1941 A470 1.90p on 2.40p #1810 20 15

1942 A473 1.90p on 2.40p #1817 (G) 20 15

Set value 40

Land Bank of the Philippines, 25th Anniv. A514

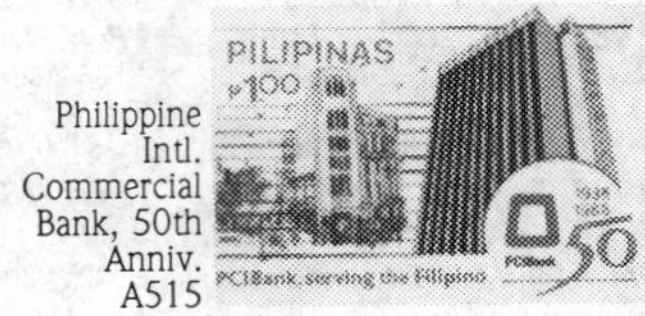

Philippine Intl. Commercial Bank, 50th Anniv. A515

Perf. 13x13½

1988, Aug. 8 Litho. Wmk. 372

1943 A514 1p shown 15 15

1944 A515 1p shown 15 15

1945 A514 5.50p like No. 1943 55 28

1946 A515 5.50p like No. 1944 55 28

Set value 65

Profile of Francisco Balagtas Baltasar (b. 1788), Tagalog Language Poet, Author — A516

1988, Aug. 8 Litho. Wmk. *Perf. 13*

1947 A516 1p Facing right 15 15

1948 A516 1p Facing left 15 15

Set value 20 15

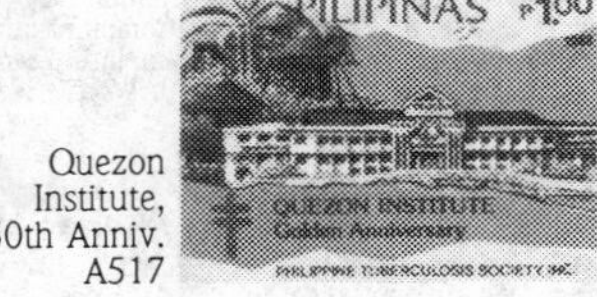

Quezon Institute, 50th Anniv. A517

Perf. 13x13½

1988, Aug. 18 Litho. Wmk. 372

1949 A517 1p multi 15 15

1950 A517 5.50p multi 55 28

Set value 32

Philippine Tuberculosis Soc.

Mushrooms A518 1988 Summer Olympics, Seoul A519

1988, Sept. 13 Wmk. 391 *Perf. 13*

1951 A518 60s Brown 15 15

1952 A518 1p Rat's ear fungus 15 15

1953 A518 2p Abalone 20 15

1954 A518 4p Straw 40 20

Set value 75 40

1988, Sept. 19 *Perf. 13½x13*

1955 A519 1p Women's archery 15 15

1956 A519 1.20p Women's tennis 15 15

1957 A519 4p Boxing 40 20

1958 A519 5.50p Women's running 55 28

1959 A519 8p Swimming 80 40

1960 A519 11p Cycling 1.10 55

Nos. 1955-1960 (6) 3.15 1.73

Souvenir Sheet

Imperf

1961 Sheet of 4 2.25 1.15

a. A519 5.50p Weight lifting 55 28

b. A519 5.50p Basketball, horiz. 55 28

c. A519 5.50p Judo 55 28

d. A519 5.50p Shooting, horiz. 55 28

Department of Justice, Cent. A520

1988, Sept. 26 *Perf. 13x13½*

1962 A520 1p multi 15 15

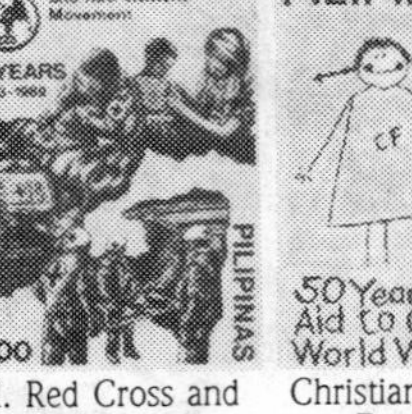

Intl. Red Cross and Red Crescent Organizations, 125th Annivs. — A521

Christian Children's Fund, 50th Anniv. — A522

1988, Sept. 30 *Perf. 13½x13*

1963 A521 1p multi 15 15

1964 A521 5.50p multi 55 28

Set value 32

1988, Oct. 6

1965 A522 1p multi 15 15

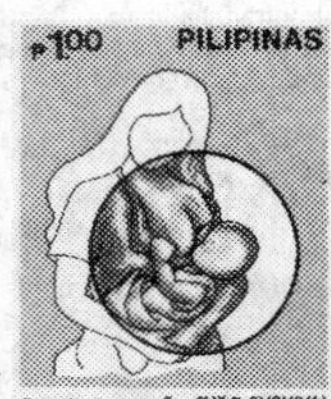

UN Campaigns — A523

Designs: a, Breast-feeding. b, Growth monitoring. c, Immunization. d, Oral rehydration. e, Oral rehydration therapy. f, Youth on crutches.

Perf. 13½x13

1988 Litho. Wmk. 392

1966 Strip of 5 50 25

a.-e. A523 1p any single 15 15

Child Survival Campaign (Nos. 1966a-1966d); Decade for Disabled Persons (No. 1966e).

Bacolod City Charter, 50th Anniv. A524

1988, Oct. 19 Litho. *Perf. 13x13½*

1967 A524 1p multi 15 15

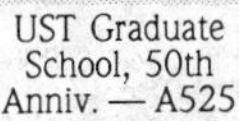

UST Graduate School, 50th Anniv. — A525

Dona Aurora Aragon Quezon (b. 1888) — A526

1988 Litho. Unwmk. *Perf. 13½x13*

1968 A525 1p multi 15 15

1988 Wmk. 391 *Perf. 13*

1969 A526 1p multi 15 15

1970 A526 5.50p multi 58 30

Set value 35

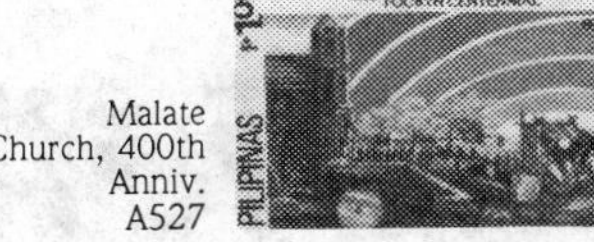

Malate Church, 400th Anniv. A527

Designs: a, Church, 1776. b, Statue and anniv. emblem. c, Church, 1880. d, Church, 1988. Printed se-tenant in a continuous design.

1988

1971 Block of 4 45 20

a.-d. A527 1p any single 15 15

UN Declaration of Human Rights, 40th Anniv. A528

1988 Wmk. *Perf. 13½x13*

1972 A528 1p shown 15 15

1973 A528 1p Commission on human rights 15 15

Set value 24 15

Long Distance Telephone Company — A529

Philatelic Week, Nov. 24-30 — A530

1988 **Wmk.**

1974 A529 1p Communications tower 15 15

1988 **Wmk. 391** ***Perf. 13***

Emblem and: a, Post Office, "1938." b, Stamp counter. c, Framed stamp exhibits, four people. d, Exhibits, 8 people. Has a continuous design.

1975 Block of 4 45 20
a.-d. A530 1p any single 15 15

Christmas
A531

Designs: 75s, Handshake, peave dove, vert. 1p, Children making ornaments. 2p, Boy carrying decoration. 3.50p, Tree, vert. 4.75p, Candle, vert. 5.50p, Man, star, heart.

1988, Dec. **Wmk. 391**

1976 A531 75s multi 15 15
1977 A531 1p multi 15 15
1978 A531 2p multi 20 15
1979 A531 3.50p multi 35 18
1980 A531 4.75p multi 50 25
1981 A531 5.50p multi 58 30
Nos. 1976-1981 (6) 1.93
Set value 90

Gen. Santos City, 50th Anniv.
A532

1989 **Litho.** **Wmk.** ***Perf. 13x13½***

1982 A532 1p multi 15 15

Guerrilla Fighters — A533

Oblates of Mary Immaculate, 50th Anniv. — A534

Emblem and: No. 1983, Miguel Z. Ver (1918-42). No. 1984, Eleuterio L. Adevoso (1922-75). Printed in continuous design.

1989 **Wmk. 391**

1983 A533 1p multi 15 15
1984 A533 1p multi 15 15
a. Pair, #1983-1984 24 20
Set value 24 15

1989 **Wmk.** ***Perf. 13½x13***

1985 A534 1p multicolored 15 15

Fiesta Islands '89 — A535

Perf. 13 (Nos. 1991, 1994, 1997), 13½x14

1989-90 **Litho.** **Wmk. 391**

1986 A535 60s Turumba 15 15
1987 A535 75s Pahiyas 15 15
1988 A535 1p Pagoda Sa Wawa 15 15
1989 A535 1p Masskara 15 15
1990 A535 3.50p Independence Day 35 18
1990A A535 4p like #1995 42 42
1991 A535 4.75p Sinulog 52 25
1992 A535 4.75p Cagayan de Oro 52 25
1993 A535 4.75p Grand Canao 50 25
1994 A535 5.50p Lenten festival 60 30
1995 A535 5.50p Penafrancia 60 30
1996 A535 5.50p Fireworks 60 30
1997 A535 6.25p Iloilo Paraw regatta 68 35
Nos. 1986-1997 (13) 5.39
Set value 2.35

Issue dates: Nos. 1991, 1994, 6.25p, Mar. 1. 60s, 75s, 3.50p, June 28. 4p, Aug. 6, 1990.

Great Filipinos — A536

Men and women: a, Don Tomas B. Mapua (1888-1989), educator. b, Camilo O. Osias (1889-1989), educator. c, Dr. Olivia D. Salamanca (1889-1989), physician. d, Dr. Francisco S. Santiago (1889-1989), composer. e, Leandro H. Fernandez (1889-1989), educator.

Perf. 14x13½

1989, May 18 **Litho.** **Unwmk.**

1998 Strip of 5 60 30
a.-e. A536 1p any single 15 15

See No. 2022, 2089, 2151.

26th World Congress of the Intl. Federation of Landscape Architects
A537

Designs: a, Adventure Pool. b, Paco Park. c, Beautification of Malacanang area streets. d, Erosion control at an upland farm.

1989, May 31 **Wmk. 391**

1999 Block of 4 45 20
a.-d. A537 1p any single 15 15

Printed in continuous design.

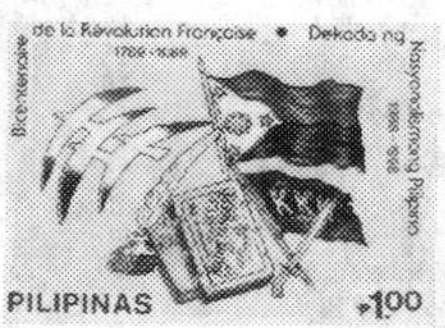

French Revolution, Bicent.
A538

1989, July 1 ***Perf. 14***

2000 A538 1p multi 15 15
2001 A538 5.50p multi 52 25
Set value 30

Supreme Court — A539

1989, June 11

2002 A539 1p multi 18 15

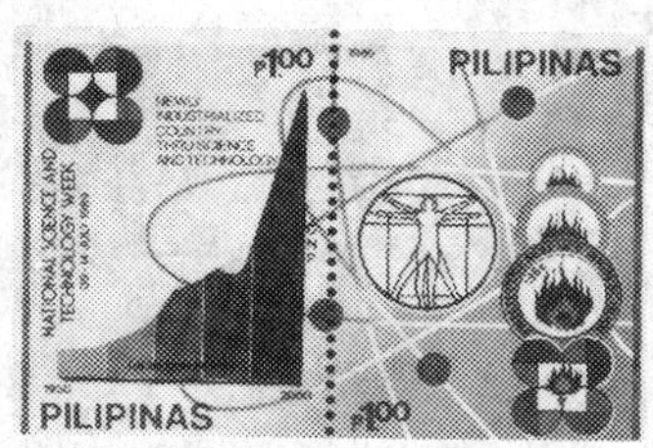

Natl. Science and Technology Week
A540 A541

1989, July 14

2003 A540 1p GNP chart 15 15
2004 A541 1p Science High School emblem 15 15
a. Pair, #2003-2004 24 20
Set value 24 15

No. 1905 Surcharged

1989 **Litho.** **Wmk. 391** ***Perf. 13***

2005 A483 4.75p on 5.50p 50 25

Philippine Environment Month
A542 A543

Wmk. 391

1989, June 5 **Litho.** ***Perf. 14***

2006 A542 1p Palawan peacock pheasant 15 15
2007 A543 1p Palawan bear cat 15 15
a. Pair, #2006-2007 24 20
Set value 24 15

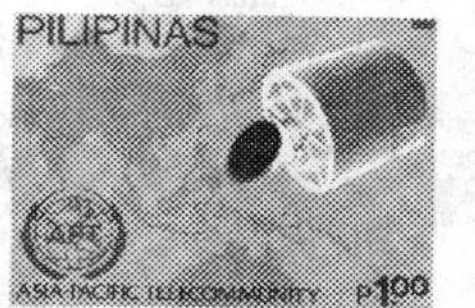

Asia-Pacific Telecommunity, 10th Anniv. — A544

1989 **Litho.** **Wmk. 372** ***Perf. 14***

2008 A544 1p multicolored 18 15

Dept. of Natl. Defense, 50th Anniv. — A545

1989

2009 A545 1p multicolored 18 15

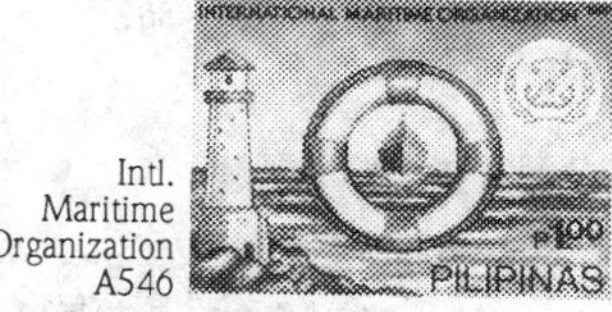

Intl. Maritime Organization
A546

1989 **Unwmk.** ***Perf. 14***

2010 A546 1p multicolored 16 15

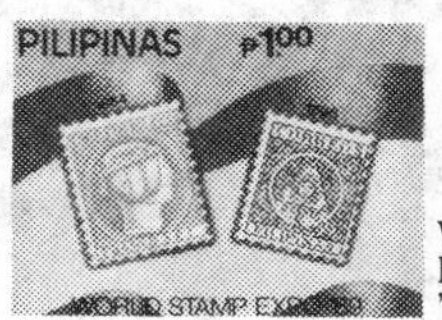

World Stamp Expo '89 — A546a

Unwmk.

1989, Nov. 17 **Litho.** ***Perf. 14***

2010A A546a 1p #1, Y1
2010B A546a 4p #219, 398
2010C A546a 5.50p #N1, 500

Nos. 2010A-2010C withdrawn from sale week of release.

Teaching Philately in the Classroom, Close-up of Youth Collectors
A547

1989 ***Perf. 14x13½***

2011 A547 1p shown 15 15
2012 A547 1p Class, diff. 15 15
Set value 28 15

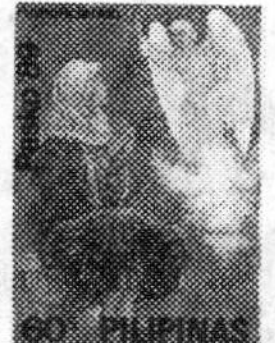

Christmas — A548

1989 ***Perf. 13½x14***

2013 A548 60s Annunciation 15 15
2014 A548 75s Visitation 15 15
2015 A548 1p Journey to Bethlehem 15 15
2016 A548 2p Search for the inn 22 15
2017 A548 4p Appearance of the star 42 22
2018 A548 4.75p Birth of Jesus Christ 52 25
Set value 1.40 70

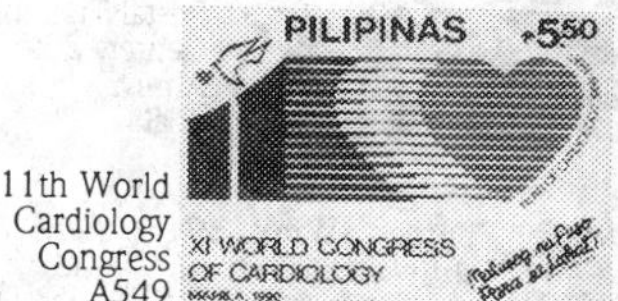

11th World Cardiology Congress
A549

1990 **Photo.** **Wmk.** ***Perf. 14***

2019 A549 5.50p black, dark red & deep blue 60 30

Beer Production, Cent.
A550

1990 **Wmk.**

2020 A550 1p multicolored 15 15
2021 A550 5.50p multicolored 60 30
Set value 35

Great Filipinos Type of 1989

Designs: a, Claro M. Recto (1890-1960), politician. b, Manuel H. Bernabe. c, Guillermo E. Tolentino. d, Elpidio R. Quirino (1890-1956), politician. e, Bienvenido Ma. Gonzalez.

Perf. 14x13½

1990, June 1 **Litho.** **Unwmk.**

2022 Strip of 5 60 30
a.-e. A536 1p any single 15 15

1990 Census — A551

Wmk. 391

1990, Apr. 30 **Photo.** ***Perf. 14***

Color of Buildings

2023 A551 1p light blue 15 15
2024 A551 1p beige 15 15
a. Pair, #2023-2024 24 15
Set value 24 15

No. 2024a printed in continuous design.

Legion of Mary, 50th Anniv. — A552

1990 Photo. Wmk. 391 *Perf. 14*

2025 A552 1p multicolored 15 15

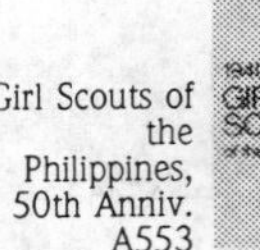

Girl Scouts of the Philippines, 50th Anniv. A553

1990, May 21

2026 A553 1p yellow & multi 15 15
2027 A553 1.20p lt lilac & multi 15 15
Set value 15

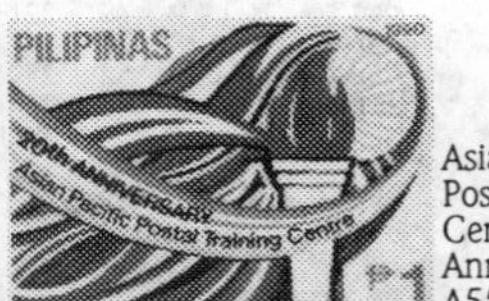

Asian Pacific Postal Training Center, 20th Anniv. A554

1990 Photo. Wmk. 391 *Perf. 14*

2028 A554 1p red & multi 15 15
2029 A554 4p blue & multi 45 34
Set value 40

Natl. Catechetical Year — A555

1990

2030 A555 1p blk & multi 15 15
2031 A555 3.50p grn & multi 40 20
Set value 26

Intl. Literacy Year — A556

1990 Photo. Wmk. 391 *Perf. 14*

2032 A556 1p blk, org & grn 15 15
2033 A556 5.50p blk, yel & grn 60 30
Set value 36

UN Development Program, 40th Anniv. A557

1990

2034 A557 1p yel & multi 15 15
2035 A557 5.50p orange & multi 60 30
Set value 36

Flowers — A558

1990 Photo. Wmk. 391 *Perf. 14*

2036 A558 1p Waling waling 15 15
2037 A558 4p Sampaguita 48 24
Set value 30

29th Orient and Southeast Asian Lions forum.

Christmas

A559 A560

Drawings of the Christmas star: a, Yellow star, pink beading. b, Yellow star, white beading. c, Green, blue, yellow and orange star. d, Red star, white outlines.

1990

2038 Strip of 4 48 24
a.-d. A559 1p any single 15 15
2039 A560 5.50p multicolored 60 30

Blind Safety Day — A561

1990 Photo. Wmk. 391 *Perf. 14*

2040 A561 1p bl, blk & yel 18 15

Publication of Rizal's "Philippines After 100 Years," Cent. A562

1990

2041 A562 1p multicolored 18 15

Philatelic Week A563

Paintings: 1p, Family by F. Amorsolo. 4.75p, The Builders by V. Edades. 5.50p, Laughter by A. Magsaysay-Ho.

1990

2042 A563 1p multicolored 18 15
2043 A563 4.75p multi, vert. 85 42
2044 A563 5.50p multi, vert. 1.00 50

2nd Plenary Council of the Philippines — A564

1991, Jan. 30 Wmk. 391

2045 A564 1p multicolored 18 15

Philippine Airlines, 50th Anniv. — A565

1991 Litho. Wmk. 391 *Perf. 14*

2046 A565 1p multicolored 15 15
2047 A565 5.50p multicolored 50 25

No. 2047 is airmail.

Flowers — A566

Flowers: 1p, 2p, Plumeria. 4p, 6p, Ixora. 4.75p, 7p, Bougainvillea. 5.50p, 8p, Hibiscus.

1991 Photo. *Perf. 14x13½*

2048	A566	60s	Gardenia	15	15
2049	A566	75s	Allamanda	15	15
2050	A566	1p	yellow	15	15
2051	A566	1p	red	15	15
2052	A566	1p	salmon	15	15
2053	A566	1p	white	15	15
a.			Block of 4, #2050-2053	35	18
2054	A566	1.20p	Nerium	15	15
2055	A566	1.50p	like #2048	15	15
2056	A566	2p	yellow	20	15
2057	A566	2p	red	20	15
2058	A566	2p	rose & yellow	20	15
2059	A566	2p	white	20	15
a.			Block of 4, #2055-2059	80	40
2060	A566	3p	like #2054	30	15
2061	A566	3.25p	Cananga	28	15
2062	A566	4p	dull rose	35	18
2063	A566	4p	pale yellow	35	18
2064	A566	4p	orange yel	35	18
2065	A566	4p	scarlet	35	18
a.			Block of 4, #2062-2065	1.40	75
2066	A566	4.75p	vermilion	40	20
2067	A566	4.75p	brt rose lil	40	20
2068	A566	4.75p	white	40	20
2069	A566	4.75p	lilac rose	40	20
a.			Block of 4, #2066-2069	1.60	80
2070	A566	5p	Canna	42	22
2071	A566	5p	like #2061	50	25
2072	A566	5.50p	red	48	24
2073	A566	5.50p	yellow	48	24
2074	A566	5.50p	white	48	24
2075	A566	5.50p	pink	48	24
a.			Block of 4, #2072-2075	2.00	1.00
2076	A566	6p	dull rose	60	30
2077	A566	6p	pale yellow	60	30
2078	A566	6p	orange yellow	60	30
2079	A566	6p	scarlet	60	30
a.			Block of 4, #2076-2079	2.40	1.20
2080	A566	7p	vermilion	70	35
2081	A566	7p	brt rose lilac	70	35
2082	A566	7p	white	70	35
2083	A566	7p	deep lil rose	70	35
a.			Block of 4, #2080-2083	2.80	1.40
2084	A566	8p	red	80	40
2085	A566	8p	yellow	80	40
2086	A566	8p	white	80	40
2087	A566	8p	deep pink	80	40
a.			Block of 4, #2084-2087	3.20	1.60
2088	A566	10p	like #2070	1.00	50
			Nos. 2048-2088 (41)	17.82	9.75

Issue dates: 60s, 75s, 1p, 5.50p, Mar. 30; 1.20p, 4p, 4.75p, May 17 (FDC, on sale June 7).

Great Filipinos Type of 1989

Designs: a, Jorge B. Vargas (1890-1980). b, Ricardo M. Paras (1891-1984). c, Jose P. Laurel (1891-1959), politician. d, Vincente Fabella (1891-1959). e, Maximo M. Kalaw (1891-1954).

Perf. 14x13½

1991, June 3 Litho. Wmk. 372

2089 A536 1p Strip of 5, #a.-e. 45 22

12th Asia-Pacific Boy Scout Jamboree A567

Perf. 14x13½

1991, Apr. 22 Wmk. 391

2090 A567 1p Square knot 15 15
2091 A567 4p Sheepshank knot 35 18
2092 A567 4.75p Granny knot 40 20
a. Souv. sheet of 3, #2090-2092, imperf. 1.75 90

No. 2092a sold for 16.50p and has simulated perfs.

Antipolo by Carlos V. Francisco A568

1991, June 23 Litho. Wmk. *Perf. 14*
Granite Paper

2093 A568 1p multicolored 18 15

Pithecophaga Jefferyi A569

1991, July 31 Photo. Wmk. 391

2094 A569 1p Head 15 15
2095 A569 4.75p Perched on limb 50 25
2096 A569 5.50p In flight 58 28
2097 A569 8p Feeding young 85 42

World Wildlife Fund.

Philippine Bar Association, Cent. — A570

Wmk. 391
1991, Aug. 20 Photo. *Perf. 14*

2098 A570 1p multicolored 18 15

A571

1991, Aug. 29

2099 A571 1p multicolored 18 15

Size: 82x88mm

Imperf

2100 A571 16p like #2099 1.70 85

Induction of Filipinos into USAFFE (US Armed Forces in the Far East), 50th Anniv. For overprint see No. 2193.

A572

A573

Independence Movement, cent.: a, Basil at graveside. b, Simon carrying lantern. c, Father Florentino, treasure chest. d, Sister Juli with rosary.

1991, Sept. 18
2101 A572 1p Block of 4, #a.-d. 45 22

Wmk. 391
1991, Oct. 15 Photo. *Perf. 14*
2102 A573 1p multicolored 18 15

Size: 60x60mm
Imperf
2103 A573 16p multicolored 1.70 85

St. John of the Cross, 400th death anniv.

United Nations Agencies A574

Designs: 1p, UNICEF, children. 4p, High Commissioner for Refugees, hands supporting boat people. 5.50p, Postal Administration, 40th anniv., UN #29, #C3.

1991, Oct. 24 *Perf. 14*
2104 A574 1p multicolored 15 15
2105 A574 4p multicolored 42 20
2106 A574 5.50p multicolored 60 30

Philatelic Week A575

Paintings: 2p, Bayanihan by Carlos Francisco. 7p, Sari-sari Vendor by Mauro Malang Santos. 8p, Give Us This Day by Vincente Manansala.

1991, Nov. 20
2107 A575 2p multicolored 22 15
2108 A575 7p multicolored 75 38
2109 A575 8p multicolored 85 42

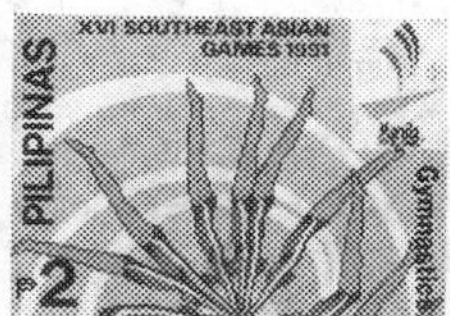

16th Southeast Asian Games, Manila A576

Designs: No. 2110, Gymnastics, games emblem at UR. No. 2111, Gymnastics, games emblem at LR. No. 2112, Martial arts, games emblem at LL, vert. No. 2113, Martial arts, games emblem at LR, vert.

Wmk. 391
1991, Nov. 22 Photo. *Perf. 14*
2110 A576 2p multicolored 18 15
2111 A576 2p multicolored 18 15
a. Pair, #2110-2111 36 18
2112 A576 6p multicolored 50 25
2113 A576 6p multicolored 50 25
a. Pair, #2112-2113 1.00 50
b. Souv. sheet of 2, #2112-2113, imperf. 1.40 70
c. Souv. sheet of 4, #2110-2113 1.05 52

No. 2113b has simulated perforations.

No. 1585 Surcharged in Red
Souvenir Sheet

1991, Nov. 27 Wmk. 372 *Imperf.*
2114 A385 4p on 3.20p 70 35

First Philippine Philatelic Convention.

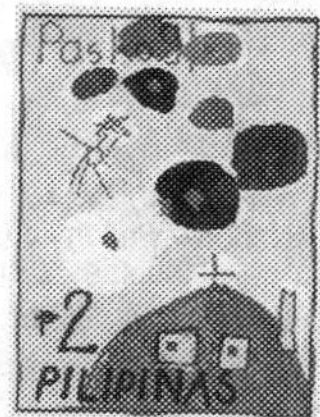

Children's Christmas Paintings — A577

1991, Dec. 4 Wmk. 391 *Perf. 14*
2115 A577 2p shown 18 15
2116 A577 6p Wrapped gift 50 25
2117 A577 7p Santa, tree 60 30
2118 A577 8p Tree, star 70 35

Insignias of Military Groups Inducted into USAFFE — A578

White background: No. 2119a, 1st Regular Div. b, 2nd Regular Div. c, 11th Div. d, 21st Div. e, 31st Div. f, 41st Div. g, 51st Div. h, 61st Div. i, 71st Div. j, 81st Div. k, 91st Div. l, 101st Div. m, Bataan Force. n, Philippine Div. o, Philippine Army Air Corps. p, Offshore Patrol.

Nos. 2120a-2120p, like #2119a-2119p with yellow background.

Perf. 14x13½
1991, Dec. 8 Photo. Wmk. 391
2119 A578 2p Block of 16, a.-p. 5.75 2.85
2120 A578 2p Block of 16, a.-p. 5.75 2.85
q. Block of 32, #2119-2120 11.50

Induction of Filipinos into USAFFE, 50th anniv.

Nos. 2119-2120 were printed in sheets of 200 containing 5 #2120q plus five blocks of 8.

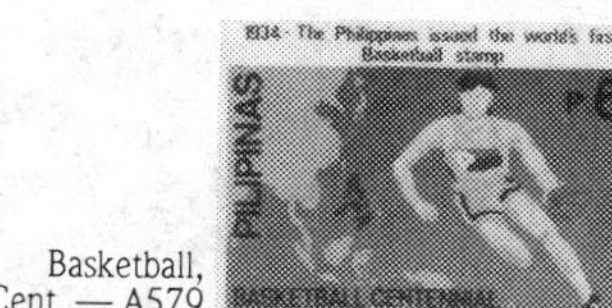

Basketball, Cent. — A579

Designs: 2p, PBA Games, vert. 6p, Map, player dribbling. 7p, Early players. 8p, Men shooting basketball, vert. 16p, Tip-off.

Wmk. 391
1991, Dec. 19 Litho. *Perf. 14*
2121 A579 2p multicolored 18 15
2122 A579 6p multicolored 50 25
2123 A579 7p multicolored 60 30
2124 A579 8p multicolored 70 35
a. Souv. sheet of 4, #2121-2124 2.00 1.05

Souvenir Sheet
Imperf
2125 A579 16p multicolored 1.45 72

No. 2125 has simulated perforations.

New Year 1992, Year of the Monkey A580

Wmk. 391
1991, Dec. 27 Litho. *Perf. 14*
2126 A580 2p violet & multi 18 15
2127 A580 6p green & multi 52 25
Set value 34

Services and Products A581

Wmk. 391
1992, Jan. 15 Litho. *Perf. 14*
2128 A581 2p Mailing center 18 15
2129 A581 6p Housing project 50 25
2130 A581 7p Livestock 60 30
2131 A581 8p Handicraft 70 35

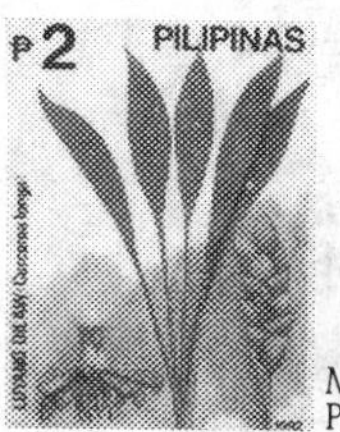

Medicinal Plants — A582

Wmk. 391
1992, Feb. 7 Litho. *Perf. 14*
2132 A582 2p Curcuma longa 18 15
2133 A582 6p Centella asiatica 52 25
2134 A582 7p Cassia alata 60 30
2135 A582 8p Ervatamia pandacaqui 70 35

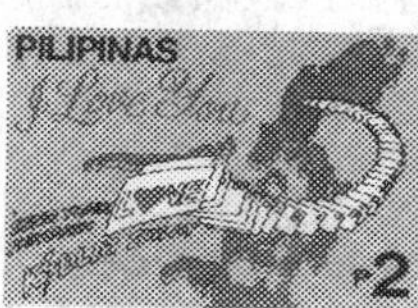

Love A583

"I Love You" in English on Nos. 2137a-2140a, in Filipino on Nos. 2137b-2140b with designs: No. 2137, Letters, map. No. 2138, Heart, doves. No. 2139, Bouquet of flowers. No. 2140, Map, Cupid with bow and arrow.

Wmk. 391
1992, Feb. 10 Photo. *Perf. 14*
2137 A583 2p Pair, #a.-b. 35 18
2138 A583 6p Pair, #a.-b. 1.05 52
2139 A583 7p Pair, #a.-b. 1.20 60
2140 A583 8p Pair, #a.-b. 1.40 70

A584 A585

Wmk. 391
1992, Apr. 12 Litho. *Perf. 14*
2141 A584 2p blue & multi 18 15
2142 A584 8p red vio & multi 70 35

Our Lady of Sorrows of Porta Vaga, 400th anniv.

1992, Mar. 27

Expo '92, Seville: 2p, Man and woman celebrating. 8p, Philippine discovery scenes. 16p, Pavilion, horiz.

2143 A585 2p multicolored 18 15
2144 A585 8p multicolored 70 35

Souvenir Sheet
Imperf
2145 A585 16p multicolored 1.40 70

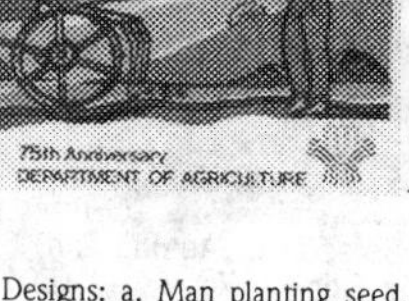

Department of Agriculture, 75th Anniv. A586

Designs: a, Man planting seed. b, Fish trap. c, Pigs.

1992, May 4
2146 A586 2p Strip of 3, #a.-c. 52 25

Manila Jockey Club, 125th Anniv. A588

Wmk. 391
1992, May 14 Litho. *Perf. 14*
2149 A588 2p multicolored 20 15

Souvenir Sheet
Imperf
2150 A588 8p multicolored 70 35

No. 2150 has simulated perfs.

Great Filipinos Type of 1989

Designs: a, Pres. Manuel A. Roxas (1892-1948). b, Justice Natividad Almeda-Lopez (1892-1977). c, Justice Roman A. Ozaeta (b. 1892). d, Engracia Cruz-Reyes (1892-1975). e, Fernando Amorsolo (1892-1972).

Perf. 14x13½
1992, June 1 Wmk. 391
2151 A536 2p Strip of 5, #a.-e. 90 45

30th Chess Olympiad, Manila A589

Designs: No. 2154a, like #2152. b, like #2153.

1992, June 7 *Perf. 14*
2152 A589 2p No. 1352 18 15
2153 A589 6p No. B21 52 25

Souvenir Sheet
Imperf
2154 A589 8p Sheet of 2, #a.-b. 1.40 70

No. 2154 has simulated perfs.

World War II, 50th Anniv. — A590

Designs: 2p, Bataan, cross. 6p, Insignia of defenders of Bataan and Corregidor. 8p, Corregidor, Monument. No. 2158, Cross, map of Bataan. No. 2159, Monument, map of Corregidor.

Wmk. 391
1992, June 12 Photo. *Perf. 14*
2155 A590 2p multicolored 18 15
2156 A590 6p multicolored 52 25
2157 A590 8p multicolored 70 35

Size: 63x76mm, 76x63mm
Imperf
2158 A590 16p multicolored 1.90 95
2159 A590 16p multicolored 1.90 95

Nos. 2158-2159 have simulated perforations.

President Corazon C. Aquino and President-Elect Fidel V. Ramos — A591

1992, June 30 *Perf. 14*
2160 A591 2p multicolored 22 15

Anniversary of Democracy.

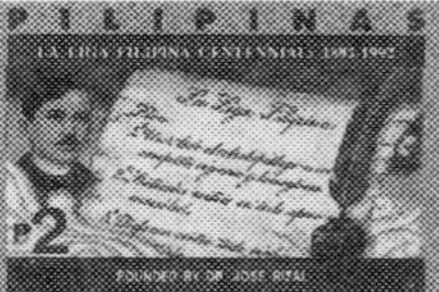

Jose Rizal's Exile to Dapitan, Cent. A592

1992, June 17
2161 A592 2p Dapitan shrine 18 15
2162 A592 2p Portrait, vert. 18 15
Set value 18

Philippine League, Cent. A595

Wmk. 391

1992, July 31 Photo. *Perf. 14*
2169 A595 2p multicolored 20 15

Religious of the Assumption in Philippines, Cent. A597

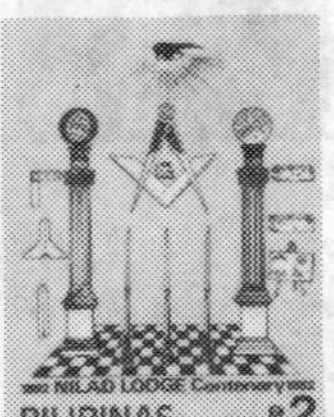

Cathedral of San Sebastian, Cent. — A597a

Wmk. 391

1992, Aug. 15 Photo. *Perf. 14*
2173 A597 2p multicolored 18 15
2174 A597a 2p multicolored 18 15
Set value 18

Founding of Nilad Masonic Lodge, Cent. — A598

Various Masonic symbols and: 6p, A. Luna. 8p, M.H. Del Pilar.

Wmk. 391

1992, Aug. 15 Photo. *Perf. 14*
2175 A598 2p green & black 18 15
2176 A598 6p yellow, black & brown 52 28
2177 A598 8p blue, black & violet 70 35

Pres. Fidel V. Ramos Taking Oath of Office, June 30, 1992 A599

1992, Aug. 30
2178 A599 2p Ceremony, people 18 15
2179 A599 8p Ceremony, flag 70 35
Set value 44

Freshwater Aquarium Fish — A600

Designs: No. 2180a, Red-tailed guppy. b, Tiger lacetail guppy. c, Flamingo guppy. d, Neon tuxedo guppy. e, King cobra guppy.

No. 2181a, Black moor. b, Bubble eye. c, Pearl scale goldfish. d, Red cap. e, Lionhead goldfish.

No. 2182, Golden arowana.

No. 2183a, Delta topsail variatus. b, Orange spotted hi-fin platy. c, Red lyretail swordtail. d, Bleeding heart hi-fin platy.

No. 2184a, 6p, Green discus. b, 6p, Brown discus. c, 7p, Red discus. d, 7p, Blue discus.

1992, Sept. 9 *Perf. 14*
2180 A600 1.50p Strip of 5, #a.-e. 65 32
2181 A600 2p Strip of 5, #a.-e. 90 45

Imperf

Size: 65x45mm

2182 A600 8p multicolored 70 35

Souvenir Sheets

Perf. 14

2183 A600 4p Sheet of 4, #a.-d. 1.40 70
2184 A600 Sheet of 4, #a.-d. 2.25 1.15

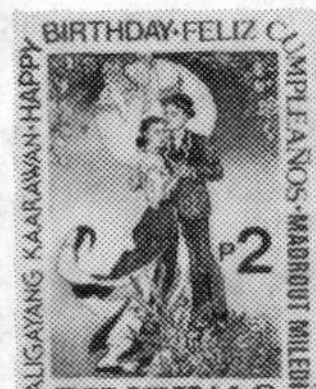

Birthday Greetings — A601

1992, Sept 28 *Perf. 14*
2185 A601 2p Couple dancing 18 15
2186 A601 6p like #2185 52 25
2187 A601 7p Cake, balloons 60 30
2188 A601 8p like #2187 70 35

Columbus' Discovery of America, 500th Anniv. A602

Various fruits and vegetables.

1992, Oct. 14
2189 A602 2p multicolored 18 15
2190 A602 6p multi, diff. 52 25
2191 A602 8p multi, diff. 70 35

Intl. Conference on Nutrition, Rome — A603

1992, Oct. 27
2192 A603 2p multicolored 18 15

No. 2100 Ovptd. in Blue "Second / National Philatelic Convention / Cebu, Philippines, Oct. 22-24, 1992"

Wmk. 391

1992, Oct. 15 Photo. *Imperf.*
2193 A571 16p multicolored 1.40 1.40

Christmas — A604

Various pictures of mother and child.

Wmk. 391

1992, Nov. 5 Litho. *Perf. 14*
2194 A604 2p multicolored 18 15
2195 A604 6p multicolored 52 25
2196 A604 7p multicolored 60 30
2197 A604 8p multicolored 70 35

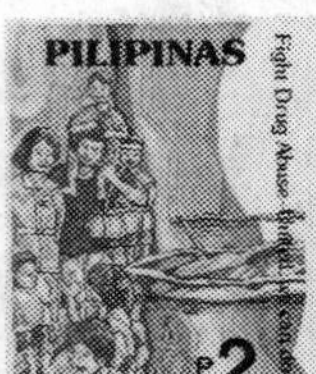

Fight Against Drug Abuse — A605

Wmk. 391

1992, Nov. 15 Litho. *Perf. 14*
2199 A605 2p People, boat 18 15
2200 A605 8p People, boat, diff. 70 35

Philatelic Week — A606

Paintings: 2p, Family, by Cesar Legaspi. 6p, Pounding Rice, by Nena Saguil. 7p, Fish Vendors, by Romeo V. Tabuena.

1992, Nov. 24
2201 A606 2p multicolored 18 15
2202 A606 6p multicolored 52 26
2203 A606 7p multicolored 60 30

Birds A607

Designs: No. 2204a, Black shama. b, Philippine cockatoo. c, Sulu hornbill. d, Mindoro imperial pigeon. e, Blue-headed fantail.

No. 2205a, Philippine trogon, vert. b, Rufous hornbill, vert. c, White-bellied woodpecker, vert. d, Spotted wood kingfisher, vert.

No. 2206a, Brahminy kite. b, Philippine falconet. c, Pacific reef egret. d, Philippine mallard.

1992 Litho. Wmk. 391 *Perf. 14*
2204 A607 2p Strip of 5, #a.-e. 1.05 52

Souvenir Sheets

2205 A607 2p Sheet of 4, #a.-d. 90 45
2206 A607 2p Sheet of 4, #a.-d. 90 45

No. 2204 printed in sheets of 10 with designs in each row shifted one space to the right from the preceding row. Two rows in each sheet are tete-beche.

New Year 1993, Year of the Rooster A608

1992
2207 A608 2p Native fighting cock 18 15
2208 A608 6p Legendary Maranao bird 52 25
a. Souvenir sheet of 2, #2207-2208 + 2 labels 90 45
b. As "a," ovptd. in sheet margin 90 45
Set value 34

Nos. 2208a and 2208b exist imperf. Overprint on No. 2208b reads: "PHILIPPINE STAMP EXHIBIT / TAIPEI, DECEMBER 1-3, 1992" in English and Chinese.

Issue dates: Nos. 2207-2208, 2208a, Nov. 27. No. 2208b, Dec. 1.

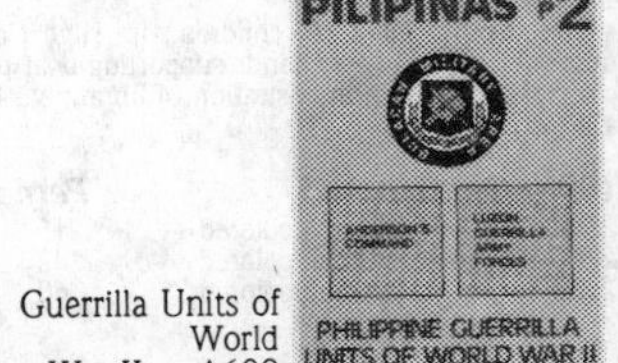

Guerrilla Units of World War II — A609

Units: a, Bulacan Military Area, Anderson's Command, Luzon Guerrilla Army Forces. b, Marking's Fil-American Guerrillas, Hunters ROTC Guerrillas, President Quezon's Own Guerrillas. c, 61st Division, 71st Division, Cebu Area Command. d, 48th Chinese Guerrilla Squadron, 101st Division, Vinzons Guerrillas.

1992, Dec. 7
2209 A609 2p Block of 4, #a.-d. 70 35

SEMI-POSTAL STAMPS

Catalogue values for unused stamps in this section are for Never Hinged items.

Republic

Epifanio de los Santos, Trinidad H. Pardo and Teodoro M. Kalaw SP1

Doctrina Christiana, Cover Page — SP2

"Noli Me Tangere," Cover Page — SP3

Unwmk.

1949, Apr. 1 Engr. *Perf. 12*

B1	SP1	4c + 2c sepia	80	60
B2	SP2	6c + 4c violet	2.50	1.65
B3	SP3	18c + 7c blue	3.00	2.75

The surtax was for restoration of war-damaged public libraries.

War Widow and Children — SP4

Disabled Veteran — SP5

1950, Nov. 30

B4	SP4	2c + 2c red	15	15
B5	SP5	4c + 4c violet	28	28
		Set value	35	36

The surtax was for war widows and children and disabled veterans of World War II.

For surcharges see Nos. 648-649.

Mrs. Manuel L. Quezon SP6

1952, Aug. 19 *Perf. 12*

B6	SP6	5c + 1c dp bl	15	15
B7	SP6	6c + 2c car rose	28	28

The surtax was used to encourage planting and care of fruit trees among Philippine children. For surcharge see No. 872.

Quezon Institute SP7

1958, Aug. 19 Photo. *Perf. 13½, 12*

Cross in Red

B8	SP7	5c + 5c grn	15	15
B9	SP7	10c + 5c dp vio	32	32

These stamps were obligatory on all mail from Aug. 19-Sept. 30.

For surcharges see Nos. 849, B12-B13, B16.

The surtax on all semi-postals from Nos. B8-B9 onward was for the Philippine Tuberculosis Society unless otherwise stated.

Scout Cooking — SP8

1959 Engr. *Perf. 13*

Yellow Paper

B10	SP8	6c + 4c shown	15	15
B11	SP8	25c + 5c Archery	42	42
a.		Nos. B10-B11 tête bêche, *white*	85	85
		Nos. B10-B11,CB1-CB3 (5)	2.42	2.42

Issued to publicize the 10th Boy Scout World Jamboree, Makiling National Park, July 17-26. The surtax was to finance the Jamboree.

For souvenir sheet see No. CB3a. For surcharges see Nos. 832-833, C111.

Nos. B8-B9 Surcharged in Red

HELP FIGHT TB

3+5

1959 Photo. *Perf. 13½, 12*

B12	SP7	3c + 5c on 5c + 5c	15	15
a.		"3 + 5" and bars omitted		
B13	SP7	6c + 5c on 10c + 5c	15	15
		Set value	24	20

Bohol Sanatorium — SP9

1959, Aug. 19 Engr. *Perf. 12*

Cross in Red

B14	SP9	6c + 5c yel grn	15	15
B15	SP9	25c + 5c vio bl	35	28

No. B8 Surcharged "Help Prevent TB" and New Value

1960, Aug. 19 Photo. *Perf. 13½, 12*

B16	SP7	6c + 5c on 5c + 5c	18	15

Roxas Memorial T.B. Pavilion SP10

Perf. 11½

1961, Aug. 19 Unwmk. Photo.

B17	SP10	6c + 5c brn & red	18	15

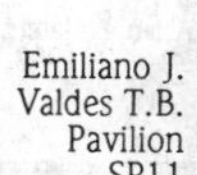

Emiliano J. Valdes T.B. Pavilion SP11

1962, Aug. 19

Cross in Red

B18	SP11	6s + 5s dk vio	15	15
B19	SP11	30s + 5s ultra	35	25
B20	SP11	70s + 5s brt bl	80	65

José Rizal Playing Chess SP12

Design: 30s+5s, Rizal fencing.

1962, Dec. 30 Engr. *Perf. 13*

B21	SP12	6s + 4s grn & rose lil	20	20
B22	SP12	30s + 5s brt bl & claret	42	42

Surtax for Rizal Foundation.

For surcharges see Nos. 942-943.

Map of Philippines and Cross — SP13

1963, Aug. 19 Unwmk. *Perf. 13*

B23	SP13	6s + 5s vio & red	15	15
B24	SP13	10s + 5s grn & red	15	15
B25	SP13	50s + 5s brn & red	52	35
		Set value		50

Negros Oriental T.B. Pavilion SP14

1964, Aug. 19 Photo. *Perf. 13½*

Cross in Red

B26	SP14	5s + 5s brt pur	15	15
B27	SP14	6s + 5s ultra	15	15
B28	SP14	30s + 5s brown	35	25
B29	SP14	70s + 5s green	65	60
		Set value		90

For surcharges see Nos. 986, 1586.

No. B27 Surcharged in Red with New Value and Two Bars

1965, Aug. 19

Cross in Red

B30	SP14	1s + 5s on 6s + 5s	15	15
B31	SP14	3s + 5s on 6s + 5s	18	15
		Set value	30	15

Stork-billed Kingfisher — SP15

Birds: 5s+5s, Rufous hornbill. 10s+5s, Monkey-eating eagle. 30s+5s, Great-billed parrot.

1967, Aug. 19 Photo. *Perf. 13½*

B32	SP15	1s + 5s multi	15	15
B33	SP15	5s + 5s multi	15	15
B34	SP15	10s + 5s multi	15	15
B35	SP15	30s + 5s multi	35	35
		Set value	58	58

1969, Aug. 15 Litho. *Perf. 13½*

Birds: 1s+5s, Three-toed woodpecker. 5s+5s, Philippine trogon. 10s+5s, Mt. Apo lorikeet. 40s+5s, Scarlet minivet.

B36	SP15	1s + 5s multi	15	15
B37	SP15	5s + 5s multi	15	15
B38	SP15	10s + 5s multi	18	15
B39	SP15	40s + 5s multi	35	25
		Set value	70	55

Julia V. de Ortigas and Tuberculosis Society Building — SP16

1970, Aug. 3 Photo. *Perf. 13½*

B40	SP16	1s + 5s multi	15	15
B41	SP16	5s + 5s multi	15	15
B42	SP16	30s + 5s multi	45	45
B43	SP16	70s + 5s multi	55	55

Mrs. Julia V. de Ortigas was president of the Philippine Tuberculosis Society, 1932-1969.

For surcharge see No. 1251.

Mabolo, Santol, Chico, Papaya SP17

Philippine Fruits: 10s+5s, Balimbing, atis, mangosteen, macupa, bananas. 40s+5s, Susong-kalabao, avocado, duhat, watermelon, guava, mango. 1p+5s, Lanzones, oranges, sirhuelas, pineapple.

1972, Aug. 1 Litho. *Perf. 13*

B44	SP17	1s + 5s multi	15	15
B45	SP17	10s + 5s multi	15	15
B46	SP17	40s + 5s multi	25	25
B47	SP17	1p + 5s multi	50	50
		Set value	86	86

Nos. B45-B46 Surcharged with New Value and 2 Bars

1973, June 15

B48	SP17	15s + 5s on 10s + 5s	15	15
B49	SP17	60s + 5s on 40s + 5s	32	32

Dr. Basilio J. Valdes and Veterans Memorial Hospital — SP18

1974, July 8 Litho. *Perf. 12½*

Cross in Red

B50	SP18	15s + 5s blue grn	15	15
a.		Imperf.	15	15
B51	SP18	1.10p + 5s vio blue	20	15
a.		Imperf.	25	25
		Set value	25	22
		Set value, imperf.	30	30

Dr. Valdes (1892-1970) was president of Philippine Tuberculosis Society.

For surcharges see Nos. 1250, 1252.

AIR POST STAMPS

Madrid-Manila Flight Issue

Regular Issue of 1917-26 Overprinted in Red or Violet

1926, May 13 Unwmk. *Perf. 11*

C1	A40	2c green (R)	5.50	2.50
C2	A40	4c carmine	7.25	3.00
a.		Inverted overprint	*1,600.*	
C3	A40	6c lilac (R)	35.00	10.00
C4	A40	8c org brn	35.00	10.00
C5	A40	10c dp bl (R)	35.00	10.00
C6	A40	12c red org	35.00	17.50
C7	A40	16c lt ol grn *(Sampson)*	*1,500.*	*1,350.*
C8	A40	16c ol bis *(Sampson)* (R)	*2,250.*	*2,000.*
C9	A40	16c ol grn *(Dewey)*	40.00	17.50
C10	A40	20c org yel	40.00	17.50
C11	A40	26c bl grn	40.00	20.00
C12	A40	30c gray	40.00	20.00
C13	A41	2p vio brn (R)	250.00	200.00
C14	A41	4p dk bl (R)	525.00	375.00
C15	A41	10p dp grn	750.00	500.00

Same Overprint on No. 269

Perf. 12

Wmk. 190PI

C16	A40	26c bl grn	*2,250.*	

Same Overprint on No. 284

Perf. 10

C17	A41	1p pale vio	135.00	85.00

Issued to commemorate the flight of Spanish aviators Gallarza and Loriga from Madrid to Manila.

London-Orient Flight Issue

Regular Issue of 1917-25 Overprinted in Red

L.O.F.
1928

1928, Nov. 9 Unwmk. *Perf. 11*

C18	A40	2c green	40	25
C19	A40	4c carmine	40	35
C20	A40	6c violet	1.50	1.25
C21	A40	8c org brn	1.65	1.50
C22	A40	10c dp bl	1.65	1.50
C23	A40	12c red org	2.25	2.00
C24	A40	16c ol grn *(Dewey)*	1.75	1.40
C25	A40	20c org yel	2.25	2.00
C26	A40	26c bl grn	6.50	5.00
C27	A40	30c gray	6.50	5.00

Same Overprint on No. 271

Perf. 12

Wmk. 190PI

C28	A41	1p pale vio	35.00	22.50
		Nos. C18-C28 (11)	59.85	42.75

Commemorating an airplane flight from London to Manila.

Nos. 354-360 Overprinted

1932, Sept. 27 Unwmk. *Perf. 11*

C29	A43	2c yel grn	30	30
C30	A44	4c rose car	30	30
C31	A45	12c orange	50	50
C32	A46	18c red org	3.00	3.00
C33	A47	20c yellow	1.50	1.50
C34	A48	24c dp vio	1.50	1.50
C35	A49	32c ol brn	1.50	1.50
		Nos. C29-C35 (7)	8.60	8.60

Visit of Capt. Wolfgang von Gronan on his round-the-world flight.

Regular Issue of 1917-25 Overprinted

F.REIN
MADRID-MANILA
FLIGHT-1933

1933, Apr. 11

C36	A40	2c green	30	30
C37	A40	4c carmine	35	35
C38	A40	6c dp vio	75	75
C39	A40	8c org brn	2.00	1.40
C40	A40	10c dk bl	1.50	90
C41	A40	12c orange	1.50	90
C42	A40	16c ol grn *(Dewey)*	1.50	90
C43	A40	20c yellow	1.50	1.00
C44	A40	26c green	2.00	1.40
a.		26c blue green	2.50	1.65
C45	A40	30c gray	2.25	1.50
		Nos. C36-C45 (10)	13.65	9.40

Commemorating the flight from Madrid to Manila of aviator Fernando Rein y Loring.

No. 290a Overprinted

1933, May 26 Unwmk. *Perf. 11*

C46	A40	2c green	45	40

Regular Issue of 1932 Overprinted

C47	A44	4c rose car	15	15
C48	A45	12c orange	25	15
C49	A47	20c yellow	25	16
C50	A48	24c dp vio	30	20
C51	A49	32c ol brn	40	30
		Nos. C46-C51 (6)	1.80	1.36

Nos. 387, 392 Overprinted in Gold

1935, Dec. 2

C52	A57	10c rose car	25	20
C53	A62	30c org red	40	35

Issued to commemorate the China Clipper flight from Manila to San Francisco, December 2-5, 1935.

Regular Issue of 1917-25 Surcharged in Various Colors

MANILA-MADRID
ARNACAL
FLIGHT-1936
2 CENTAVOS 2

1936, Sept. 6 *Perf. 11*

C54	A40	2c on 4c car (Bl)	15	15
C55	A40	6c on 12c red org (V)	15	15
C56	A40	16c on 26c bl grn (Bk)	20	20
a.		16c on 26c green	1.00	65
		Set value	35	35

Issued to commemorate the Manila-Madrid flight by aviators Antonio Arnaiz and Juan Calvo.

Regular Issue of 1917-37 Surcharged in Black or Red

FIRST
AIR MAIL EXHIBITION
Feb 17 to 19, 1939
8 CENTAVOS 8

1939, Feb. 17

C57	A40	8c on 26c bl grn (Bk)	60	38
a.		8c on 26c green (Bk)	1.40	50
C58	A71	1p on 10p gray (R)	2.50	2.00

Issued to commemorate the first Air Mail Exhibition, held Feb. 17-19, 1939.

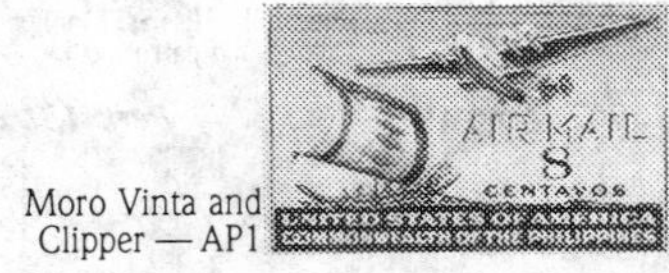

Moro Vinta and Clipper — AP1

1941, June 30

C59	AP1	8c carmine	1.00	60
C60	AP1	20c ultra	1.20	45
C61	AP1	60c bl grn	1.75	75
C62	AP1	1p sepia	70	42

For overprint see No. NO7. For surcharges see Nos. N10-N11, N35-N36.

No. C47 Handstamped in Violet

VICTORY

1944, Dec. 3 Unwmk. *Perf. 11*

C63	A44	4c rose car	*1,500.*	*1,500.*

Catalogue values for unused stamps in this section, from this point to the end of the section, are for Never Hinged items.

Republic

Manuel L. Quezon and Franklin D. Roosevelt AP2

Unwmk.

1947, Aug. 19 Engr. *Perf. 12*

C64	AP2	6c dk grn	52	52
C65	AP2	40c red org	1.00	1.00
C66	AP2	80c dp bl	2.75	2.75

Threshing Rice — AP3

1948, Feb. 23 Typo. *Perf. 12½*

C67	AP3	40c dk car & pink	12.50	6.50

FAO conf. held at Baguio.

Globe — AP4

1950, Mar. 1 Engr. *Perf. 12*

C68	AP4	30c dp org	38	15
C69	AP4	50c car rose	65	15

Issued to publicize the 5th World Congress of the Junior Chamber of Commerce, Manila, March 1-8, 1950.

F. D. Roosevelt Type of 1950
Souvenir Sheet

1950, May 22 *Imperf.*

C70	A98	80c dp grn	1.25	1.25

Lions Club Emblem — AP6

Maria Clara in 19th Century Costume — AP7

1950, June 2 *Perf. 12*

C71	AP6	30c emerald	60	45
C72	AP6	50c ultra	70	60
a.		Souv. sheet of 2, #C71-C72	1.40	1.40

Issued to commemorate the convention of the Lions Club, Manila, June 1950.

1952, Nov. 16 *Perf. 12½*

C73	AP7	30c rose car	85	70

Issued to publicize the first Pan-Asian Philatelic Exhibition, PANAPEX, Manila, Nov. 16-22, 1952.

First Philippine Stamp, Magellan's Landing and Manila Scene — AP8

1954, Apr. 25 *Perf. 13*

1854 Stamp in Orange

C74	AP8	10c dk brn	1.00	85
C75	AP8	20c dk grn	1.65	1.35
C76	AP8	50c carmine	3.50	3.00

Centenary of Philippine postage stamps.

Mayon Volcano, Moro Vinta and Rotary Emblem AP9

1955, Feb. 23

C77	AP9	50c bl grn	1.25	85

50th anniversary of the founding of Rotary International.

Lt. José Gozar AP10

Portraits: 20c, 50c, Lt. Gozar. 30c, 70c, Lt. Basa.

1955 Engr. *Perf. 13*

C78	AP10	20c dp vio	45	15
C79	AP10	30c red	52	15
C80	AP10	50c bluish grn	70	20
C81	AP10	70c blue	1.10	88

Issued in honor of Lt. José Gozar and Lt. Cesar Fernando Basa, Filipino aviators in World War II.

Constitution Type of Regular Issue

1960, Feb. 8 Photo. *Perf. 12½x13½*

C82	A146	30c brt bl & silver	32	25

Air Force Plane of 1935 and Saber Jet AP11

1960, May 2 Engr. *Perf. 14x14½*

C83	AP11	10c carmine	18	15
C84	AP11	20c ultra	35	25

25th anniversary of Philippine Air Force.
For surcharge see No. 847.

Olympic Type of Regular Issue

Designs: 30c, Sharpshooter. 70c, Woman swimmer.

1960, Nov. 30 Photo. *Perf. 13x13½*

C85	A150	30c org & brn	42	35
C86	A150	70c grnsh bl & vio brn	85	70

Postal Conference Type

1961, Feb. 23 *Perf. 13½x13*

C87	A152	30c multi	28	22

Freedom from Hunger Type

1963, Dec. 20 Photo.

C88	A168	30s lt grn & multi	28	20
C89	A168	50s multi	45	35

Land Reform Type

1964, Dec. 21 Wmk. 233 *Perf. 14½*

C90	A172	30s multi	25	20

Mass Baptism by Father Andres de Urdaneta, Cebu — AP12

Design: 70s, World map showing route of the Cross from Spain to Mexico to Cebu, and two galleons.

Unwmk.

1965, Oct. 4 Photo. *Perf. 13*

C91 AP12 30s multi 25 15

C92 AP12 70s multi 55 32

a. Souvenir sheet of 4 1.40 1.40

400th anniv. of the Christianization of the Philippines. No. C92a contains four imperf. stamps similar to Nos. 934-935 and C91-C92 with simulated perforation.

For surcharge see No. C108.

Souvenir Sheet

Family and Progress Symbols — AP13

1966, July 22 Photo. *Imperf.*

C93 AP13 70s multi 65 65

50th anniv. of the Philippine Natl. Bank. No. C93 contains one stamp with simulated perforation superimposed on a facsimile of a 50p banknote of 1916. Size of stamp: 55x27mm; sheet, 156x69mm.

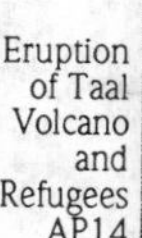

Eruption of Taal Volcano and Refugees AP14

1967, Oct. 1 Photo. *Perf. 13½x13*

C94 AP14 70s multi 52 45

Eruption of Taal Volcano, Sept. 28, 1965.

Eruption of Taal Volcano — AP15

1968, Oct. 1 Litho. *Perf. 13½*

C95 AP15 70s multi 52 52

Eruption of Taal Volcano, Sept. 28, 1965.

Rotary Type of 1969

1969, Jan. 29 Photo. *Perf. 12½*

C96 A202 40s grn & multi 25 18

C97 A202 75s red & multi 52 42

Holy Child Type of Regular Issue

1969, June 30 Photo. *Perf. 13½*

C98 A207 40s ultra & multi 28 20

Pope Type of Regular Issue

1970, Nov. 27 Photo. *Perf. 13½x14*

C99 A221 40s vio & multi 28 20

Law College Type of Regular Issue

1971, June 15 *Perf. 13*

C100 A225 1p grn & multi 45 42

Manila Type of Regular Issue

1971, June 24

C101 A226 1p multi & bl 65 45

Santo Tomas Type of Regular Issue

1971, July 8 Photo. *Perf. 13½*

C102 A227 2p lt bl & multi 90 80

Congress Type of Regular Issue

1972, Apr. 11 Photo. *Perf. 13½x13*

C103 A232 40s grn & multi 25 20

Tropical Fish Type of Regular Issue

1972, Aug. 14 Photo. *Perf. 13*

C104 A235 50s Dusky angelfish 42 20

Pope Paul VI Type of Regular Issue

1972, Sept. 26 Photo. *Perf. 14*

C105 A237 60s lt bl & multi 32 32

First Mass Type of Regular Issue

1972, Oct. 31 Photo. *Perf. 14*

C106 A241 60s multi 28 25

Presidential Palace Type of Regular Issue

1973, Nov. 15 Litho. *Perf. 14*

C107 A253 60s multi 20 20

No. C92a Surcharged and Overprinted with US Bicentennial Emblems and: "U.S.A. BICENTENNIAL / 1776-1976" in Black

Unwmk.

1976, Sept. 23 Photo. *Imperf.*

C108 Sheet of 4 45 45

a. A179 5s on 3s multi 15 15

b. A179 5s on 6s multi 15 15

c. AP12 15s on 30s multi 15 15

d. AP12 50s on 70s multi 25 25

American Bicentennial. Nos. C108a-C108d are overprinted with Bicentennial emblem and 2 bars over old denomination. Inscription and 2 Bicentennial emblems overprinted in margin. Overprint and surcharges exist in red.

Souvenir Sheet

Netherlands No. 1 and Philippines No. 1 and Windmill AP16

1977, May 26 Litho. *Perf. 14½*

C109 Sheet of 3 6.50 6.50

a. AP16 7.50p multi 1.90 1.90

AMPHILEX '77, International Stamp Exhibition, Amsterdam, May 26-June 5.

Exists imperf. Value $12.50.

Souvenir Sheet

Philippines and Spain Nos. 1, Bull and Matador AP17

1977, Oct. 7 Litho. *Perf. 12½x13*

C110 Sheet of 3 8.00 8.00

a. AP17 7.50p multi 2.00 2.00

ESPAMER '77 (Exposicion Filatelica de America y Europa), Barcelona, Spain, Oct. 7-13.

Exists imperf. Value $12.50.

Nos. B10 and CB3a Surcharged

50$

JULY 4-14, 1979
QUEZON CITY

1979, July 5 Engr. *Perf. 13*

C111 SP8 90s on 6c + 4c car, *yel* 18 18

Souvenir Sheet

White Paper

C112 Sheet of 5 70 70

a. SP8 50s on 6c + 4c carmine 15

b. SP8 50s on 25c + 5c blue 15

c. SP8 50s on 30c + 10c green 15

d. SP8 50s on 70c + 20c red brown 15

e. SP8 50s on 80c + 20c violet 15

First Scout Philatelic Exhibition, Quezon City, July 4-14, commemorating 25th anniversary of First National Jamboree.

Surcharge on No. C111 includes "AIRMAIL." Violet marginal inscriptions on No. C112 overprinted with heavy bars; new commemorative inscriptions and Scout emblem added.

AIR POST SEMI-POSTAL STAMPS

Catalogue values for unused stamps in this section are for Never Hinged items.

Type of Semi-Postal Issue, 1959

Designs: 30c+10c, Bicycling. 70c+20c, Scout with plane model. 80c+20c, Pres. Carlos P. Garcia and scout shaking hands.

Unwmk.

1959, July 17 Engr. *Perf. 13*

CB1 SP8 30c + 10c green 30 30

CB2 SP8 70c + 20c red brown 65 65

CB3 SP8 80c + 20c violet 90 90

a. Souvenir sheet of 5 2.75 2.75

Issued to publicize the 10th Boy Scout World Jamboree, Makiling National Park, July 17-26. The surtax was to finance the Jamboree.

No. CB3a measures 171x89mm. and contains one each of Nos. CB1-CB3 and types of Nos. B10-B11 on white paper. Sold for 4p.

For surcharge see No. C112.

SPECIAL DELIVERY STAMPS

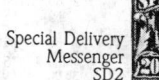

United States No. E5 Overprinted in Red PHILIPPINES

1901, Oct. 15 Wmk. 191 *Perf. 12*

E1 SD3 10c dk blue 90.00 80.00

Special Delivery Messenger SD2

1906 Engr. Wmk. 191PI

E2 SD2 20c ultra 25.00 6.50

b. 20c pale ultra 25.00 6.50

See Nos. E3-E6.

Special Printing

Overprinted in Red as No. E1 on United States No. E6

1907

E2A SD4 10c ultra *2,000.*

1911 Wmk. 190PI

E3 SD2 20c dp ultra 16.00 1.40

1916 *Perf. 10*

E4 SD2 20c dp ultra 150.00 40.00

1919 Unwmk. *Perf. 11*

E5 SD2 20c ultra 50 20

a. 20c pale blue 65 16

b. 20c dull violet 50 16

1925-31 *Imperf.*

E6 SD2 20c dl vio ('31) 17.50 *16.00*

Type of 1919 Overprinted in Black COMMONWEALTH

1939 *Perf. 11*

E7 SD2 20c blue violet 25 20

Nos. E5b and E7, Handstamped in Violet VICTORY

1944 *Perf. 11*

E8 SD2 20c dl vio (#E5b) *500.00 375.00*

E9 SD2 20c bl vio (#E7) *160.00 140.00*

Type SD2 Overprinted "VICTORY" As No. 486

1945

E10 SD2 20c blue violet 55 55

a. "IC" close together 2.75 2.75

Catalogue values for unused stamps in this section, from this point to the end of the section, are for Never Hinged items.

Republic

Manila Post Office and Messenger SD3

Unwmk.

1947, Dec. 22 Engr. *Perf. 12*

E11 SD3 20c rose lilac 52 38

Post Office Building, Manila, and Hands with Letter — SD4

1962, Jan. 23 *Perf. 13½x13*

E12 SD4 20c lilac rose 25 20

SPECIAL DELIVERY OFFICIAL STAMP

Type of 1906 Issue Overprinted O. B.

1931 Unwmk. *Perf. 11*

EO1 SD2 20c dull violet 55 40

a. No period after "B" 16.50 14.00

b. Double overprint

POSTAGE DUE STAMPS

Postage Due Stamps of the United States Nos. J38 to J44 Overprinted in Black

1899, Aug. 16 Wmk. 191 *Perf. 12*

J1 D2 1c deep claret 3.50 1.00

J2 D2 2c deep claret 3.50 90

J3 D2 5c deep claret 10.00 1.90

J4 D2 10c deep claret 10.00 3.50

J5 D2 50c deep claret 130.00 75.00

1901, Aug. 31

J6 D2 3c deep claret 10.00 5.00

J7 D2 30c deep claret 140.00 75.00

Nos. J1-J7 (7) 307.00 162.30

No. J1 was used to pay regular postage September 5-19, 1902.

Post Office Clerk — D3

Unwmk.

1928, Aug. 21 Engr. *Perf. 11*

J8 D3 4c brown red 15 15

J9 D3 6c brown red 15 15

J10 D3 8c brown red 15 15

J11 D3 10c brown red 15 15

J12 D3 12c brown red 15 15

J13 D3 16c brown red 16 16

J14 D3 20c brown red 15 15

Set value 88 88

For overprints see Nos. O16-O22, NJ1. For surcharge see No. J15.

No. J8 Surcharged in Blue 3 CVOS. 3

1937

J15 D3 3c on 4c brown red 16 15

Nos. J8 to J14 Handstamped in Violet VICTORY

1944

J16 D3 4c brown red *100.00*
J17 D3 6c brown red *65.00*
J18 D3 8c brown red *70.00*
J19 D3 10c brown red *65.00*
J20 D3 12c brown red *65.00*
J21 D3 16c brown red *70.00*
J22 D3 20c brown red *70.00*
Nos. J16-J22 (7) *505.00*

Catalogue values for unused stamps in this section, from this point to the end of the section, are for Never Hinged items.

Republic

D4

Unwmk.

1947, Oct. 20 **Engr.** *Perf. 12*

J23 D4 3c rose carmine 15 15
J24 D4 4c brt vio blue 30 25
J25 D4 6c olive green 38 38
J26 D4 10c orange 50 50

OFFICIAL STAMPS

Official Handstamped Overprints

"Officers purchasing stamps for government business may, if they so desire, overprint them with the letters 'O.B.' either in writing with black ink or by rubber stamps but in such a manner as not to obliterate the stamp that postmasters will be unable to determine whether the stamps have been previously used." C. M. Cotterman, Director of Posts, Dec. 26, 1905. Beginning with Jan. 1, 1906, all branches of the Insular Government used postage stamps to prepay postage instead of franking them as before. Some officials used manuscript, some utilized typewriters, some made press-printed overprints, but by far the larger number used rubber stamps. The majority of these read "O.B." but other forms were: "OFFICIAL BUSINESS" or "OFFICIAL MAIL" in two lines, with variations on many of these. These "O.B." overprints are known on US 1899-1901 stamps; on 1903-06 stamps in red and blue; on 1906 stamps in red, blue, black, yellow and green. "O.B." overprints were also made on the centavo and peso stamps of the Philippines, per order of May 25, 1907. Beginning in 1926 the stamps were overprinted and issued by the Government, but some post offices continued to handstamp "O.B."

Regular Issue of 1926 Overprinted in Red **OFFICIAL**

1926, Dec. 20 **Unwmk.** *Perf. 12*

O1 A42 2c green & blk 2.00 90
O2 A42 4c car & blk 2.00 1.10
a. Vert. pair, imperf. btwn. *375.00*
O3 A42 18c lt brn & blk 6.50 4.00
O4 A42 20c org & blk 6.00 1.40

Issued to commemorate the opening of the Legislative Palace.

Regular Issue of 1917-26 Overprinted **O. B.**

1931 *Perf. 11*

O5 A40 2c green 15 15
a. No period after "B" 15.00 5.00
b. No period after "O"
O6 A40 4c carmine 15 15
a. No period after "B" 15.00 5.00
O7 A40 6c dp violet 15 15
O8 A40 8c yel brn 15 15
O9 A40 10c dp blue 25 15
O10 A40 12c red org 16 15
a. No period after "B" 30.00
O11 A40 16c lt ol grn *(Dewey)* 16 15
a. 16c olive bister 1.00 20
O12 A40 20c org yel 20 15
a. No period after "B" 20.00 15.00
O13 A40 26c green 30 30
a. 26c blue green 80 65
O14 A40 30c gray 25 22
Nos. O5-O14 (10) 1.92
Set value 1.25

Same Overprint on Regular Issue of 1935

1935

O15 A53 2c rose 15 15
a. No period after "B" 15.00 5.00
O16 A54 4c yel grn 15 15
a. No period after "B" 15.00 10.00
O17 A55 6c dk brn 15 15
a. No period after "B" 20.00 20.00
O18 A56 8c violet 15 15
O19 A57 10c rose car 16 15
O20 A58 12c black 16 15
O21 A59 16c dark blue 16 15
O22 A60 20c lt ol grn 16 15
O23 A61 26c indigo 25 22
O24 A62 30c orange red 30 25
Set value 1.44 1.00

Same Overprint on Overprinted Issue of 1936-37

1937-38 *Perf. 11*

O25 A53 2c rose 15 15
a. No period after "B" 4.25 2.25
O26 A60 20c lt ol grn ('38) 65 50
Set value 70 55

Regular Issue of 1935, Overprinted in Black:

O. B.
COMMON-
WEALTH
a

O. B.
COMMONWEALTH
b

1938-40 *Perf. 11*

O27 A53(a) 2c rose 15 15
a. Hyphen omitted 20.00 20.00
b. No period after "B" 25.00 25.00
O28 A54(b) 4c yel grn 15 15
O29 A55(a) 6c dk brown 15 15
O30 A56(b) 8c violet 15 15
O31 A57(b) 10c rose car 15 15
a. No period after "O" 30.00 30.00
O32 A58(b) 12c black 15 15
O33 A59(b) 16c dark blue 16 15
O34 A60(a) 20c lt ol grn ('40) 22 22
O35 A61(b) 26c indigo 30 30
O36 A62(b) 30c org red 25 25
Set value 1.50 1.25

No. 461 Overprinted in Black — c **O. B.**

Perf. 11x10½

1941, Apr. 14 **Unwmk.**

O37 A75 2c apple green 15 15

Official Stamps Handstamped in Violet **VICTORY**

1944 *Perf. 11, 11x10½*

O38 A53 2c (#O27) *160.00 110.00*
O39 A75 2c (#O37) 5.00 3.00
O40 A54 4c (#O16) *30.00 20.00*
O40A A55 6c (#O29) *3,500.*
O41 A57 10c (#O31) *110.00*
O42 A60 20c (#O22) *5,000.*
O43 A60 20c (#O26) *1,400.*

No. 497 Overprinted Type "c" in Black

Perf. 11x10½

1946, June 19 **Unwmk.**

O44 A76 2c sepia 15 15

Catalogue values for unused stamps in this section, from this point to the end of the section, are for Never Hinged items.

Republic

Nos. 504, 505 and 507 Overprinted in Black — d **O. B.**

1948 **Unwmk.** *Perf. 12*

O50 A78 4c black brn 15 15
a. Inverted overprint 25.00
b. Double overprint 25.00
O51 A79 10c red orange 20 15
O52 A81 16c slate gray 1.40 52
Set value 62

The overprint on No. O51 comes in two sizes: 13mm, applied in Manila, and 12½mm, applied in New York.

Nos. 527, 508 and 509 Overprinted in Black — e **O. B.**

Overprint Measures 14mm

O53 A91 2c brt grn 38 15

1949

O54 A82 20c red brn 52 15

Overprint Measures 12mm

O55 A83 50c dl grn 90 52

No. 550 Overprinted Type "e" in Black
Overprint Measures 14mm

1950

O56 A91 1c on 2c brt grn 15 15

Nos. 589, 592, 595 and 597 Overprinted in Black — f **O. B.**

Overprint Measures 15mm

1952-55

O57 A117 1c red brn ('53) 15 15
O58 A117 5c crim rose 15 15
O59 A117 10c ultra ('55) 18 15
O60 A117 20c car lake ('55) 42 15
Set value 75 20

No. 647 Overprinted — g **O B**

1959 **Engr.** *Perf. 12*

O61 A117 1c on 5c crim rose 15 15

No. 813 Overprinted Type "f"
Overprint measures 16½mm

1959

O62 A145 6c gray bl 15 15

Nos. 856-861 Overprinted

G. O.
h

G. O.
j

G. O.
k

G.O.
l

1962-64 *Perf. 13½*

O63 A158(j) 5s car rose ('63) 15 15

Perf. 13x12

O64 A158(h) 6s dk red brn 15 15

Perf. 13½

O65 A158(k) 6s pck bl ('64) 15 15
O66 A158(j) 10s brt pur ('63) 15 15
O67 A158(j) 20s Prus bl ('63) 15 15
O68 A158(j) 30s vermilion 28 15
O69 A158(k) 50s violet ('63) 42 15
Set value 1.05 45

"G.O." stands for "Gawaing Opisyal," Tagalog for "Official Business."
On 6s overprint "k" is 10mm wide.
For overprint see No. 1119.

No. 1082 Overprinted Type "l"

1970, Dec. 30 **Engr.** *Perf. 14*

O70 A222 10s rose car 15 15

NEWSPAPER STAMPS

N1

N2

1886-89 **Unwmk.** **Typo.** *Perf. 14*

P1 N1 ⅛c yel grn 25 15
P2 N1 1m rose ('89) 25 15
P3 N1 2m blue ('89) 25 15
P4 N1 5m dk brn ('89) 25 15
Set value 40

1890-96

P5 N2 ⅛c dk vio 15 15
P6 N2 ⅛c grn ('92) 80 20
P7 N2 ⅛c org brn ('94) 15 15
P8 N2 ⅛c dl bl ('96) 60 35
P9 N2 1m dk vio 15 15
P10 N2 1m grn ('92) 1.65 40
P11 N2 1m ol gray ('94) 15 15
P12 N2 1m ultra ('96) 20 15
P13 N2 2m dk vio 15 15
P14 N2 2m grn ('92) 1.65 40
P15 N2 2m ol gray ('94) 15 15
P16 N2 2m brn ('96) 20 15
P17 N2 5m dk vio 15 15
P18 N2 5m grn ('92) 90.00 17.50
P19 N2 5m ol gray ('94) 15 15
P20 N2 5m dp bl grn ('96) 1.40 60

Imperfs. exist of Nos. P8, P9, P11, P12, P16, P17 and P20.

OCCUPATION STAMPS

Issued under Japanese Occupation

Nos. 461, 438 and 439 Overprinted with Bars in Black

1942-43 **Unwmk.** *Perf. 11x10½, 11*

N1 A75 2c apple green 15 15
a. Pair, one without overprint
N2 A58 12c black ('43) 15 15
N3 A59 16c dark blue 3.25 2.50

Nos. 435, 442, 443 and 423 Surcharged in Black

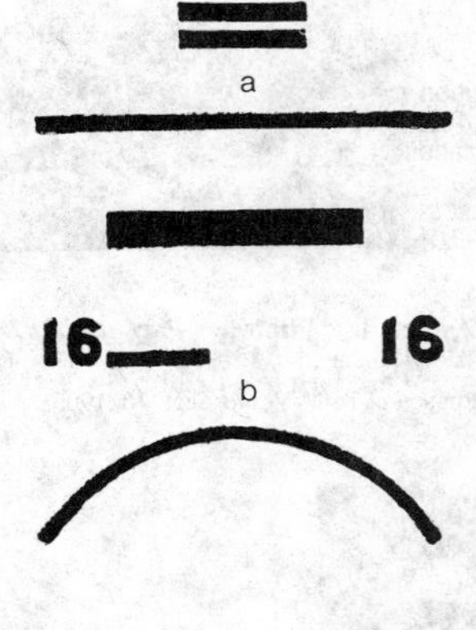

a

b

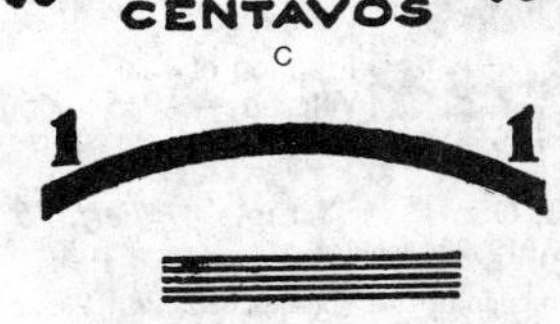

c

d

Perf. 11

N4 A55 5c on 6c gldn brn 15 15
a. Top bar shorter, thinner 20 20
b. 5(c) on 6c dk brn 20 20
c. As "b," top bar shorter and thinner 20 20
N5 A62 16c on 30c ('43) 25 25
N6 A63 50c on 1p ('43) 60 60
a. Double surcharge *250.00*
N7 A65 1p on 4p ('43) 65.00 52.50

On Nos. N4 and N4b, the top bar measures 1½x22½mm. On Nos. N4a and N4c, the top bar measures 1x21mm and the "5" is smaller and thinner.

No. 384 Surcharged in Black

CONGRATULATIONS
FALL OF
BATAAN AND
CORREGIDOR
1942

1942, May 18

N8 A54 2c on 4c yel grn 2.25 2.25

Issued to commemorate Japan's capture of Bataan and Corregidor. The American-Filipino forces finally surrendered May 7, 1942.

No. 384 Surcharged in Black

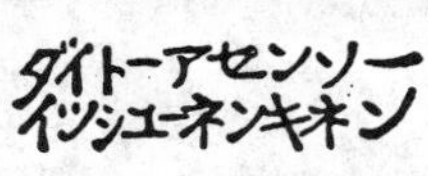

12-8-1942 5

1942, Dec. 8

N9 A54 5c on 4c yel grn 50 50

1st anniversary of the "Greater East Asia War".

Nos. C59 and C62 Surcharged in Black

ヒトー ギヨー セイフ
イツシユーオン キネン
1-23-43
2

1943, Jan. 23

N10 AP1 2c on 8c carmine 25 25
N11 AP1 5c on 1p sepia 50 50

1st anniversary of the Philippine Executive Commission.

Nipa Hut OS1

Rice Planting OS2

Mt. Mayon and Mt. Fuji — OS3

Moro Vinta — OS4

Engr., Typo. (2c, 6c, 25c)

1943-44 Wmk. 257 *Perf. 13*

N12 OS1	1c	dp org	15	15
N13 OS2	2c	brt grn	15	15
N14 OS1	4c	slate grn	15	15
N15 OS3	5c	org brn	15	15
N16 OS2	6c	red	15	15
N17 OS3	10c	bl grn	15	15
N18 OS4	12c	steel blue	65	65
N19 OS4	16c	dk brn	15	15
N20 OS1	20c	rose vio	70	70
N21 OS3	21c	violet	15	15
N22 OS2	25c	pale brn	15	15
N23 OS3	1p	dp car	15	15
N24 OS4	2p	dl vio	2.50	2.50
N25 OS4	5p	dark olive	6.00	5.00
		Nos. N12-N25 (14)	11.35	10.35

For surcharges see Nos. NB5-NB7.

Map of Manila Bay Showing Bataan and Corregidor OS5

1943, May 7 Photo. Unwmk.

N26 OS5 2c car red 15 15
N27 OS5 5c brt grn 25 25
Set value 34 34

1st anniversary of the fall of Bataan and Corregidor.

No. 440 Surcharged in Black

Limbagan
1593 - 1943
12 12

1943, June 20 Engr. *Perf. 11*

N28 A60 12c on 20c lt ol grn 20 20
a. Double surcharge

350th anniversary of the printing press in the Philippines. "Limbagan" is Tagalog for "printing press."

Rizal Monument, Filipina and Philippine Flag — OS6

1943, Oct. 14 Photo. *Perf. 12*

N29 OS6	5c	light blue	15	15
a.		Imperf.	15	15
N30 OS6	12c	orange	15	15
a.		Imperf.	15	15
N31 OS6	17c	rose pink	16	16
a.		Imperf.	15	15
		Set value	29	29
		Set value, imperf.	35	35

Issued to commemorate the "Independence of the Philippines." Japan granted "independence" Oct. 14, 1943, when the puppet republic was founded.

The imperforate stamps were issued without gum. See No. NB4.

José Rizal OS7

Rev. José Burgos OS8

Design: 17c, Apolinario Mabini

1944, Feb. 17 Litho. *Perf. 12*

N32 OS7	5c	blue	16	16
a.		Imperf.	16	16
N33 OS8	12c	carmine	15	15
a.		Imperf.	15	15
N34 OS7	17c	deep orange	15	15
a.		Imperf.	15	15
		Set value	33	33
		Set value, imperf.	33	33

See No. NB8.

Nos. C60 and C61 Surcharged in Black

REPÚBLIKA
NG PILIPINAS
5-7-44
5

1944, May 7 *Perf. 11*

N35 AP1 5c on 20c ultra 35 35
N36 AP1 12c on 60c bl grn 80 80

2nd anniv. of the fall of Bataan and Corregidor.

José P. Laurel — OS10

1945, Jan. 12 Litho. *Imperf.*

Without Gum

N37 OS10 5c dl vio brn 15 15
N38 OS10 7c blue green 15 15
N39 OS10 20c chalky blue 15 15
Set value 22 18

Issued belatedly on Jan. 12, 1945, to commemorate the first anniversary of the puppet Philippine Republic, Oct. 14, 1944. "S" stands for "sentimos."

OCCUPATION SEMI-POSTAL STAMPS

Woman, Farming and Cannery — OSP1

Unwmk.

1942, Nov. 12 Litho. *Perf. 12*

NB1 OSP1 2c + 1c pale vio 15 15
NB2 OSP1 5c + 1c brt grn 15 15
NB3 OSP1 16c + 2c org 10.00 8.00

Issued to promote the campaign to produce and conserve food. The surtax aided the Red Cross.

"Independence of the Philippines" Type Souvenir Sheet

1943, Oct. 14 *Imperf.*

Without Gum

NB4 Sheet of 3 19.00 *2.00*

Issued to commemorate the "Independence of the Philippines."

No. NB4 contains one each of Nos. N29a-N31a. Lower inscription from Rizal's "Last Farewell." Size: 127x177mm. Sold for 2.50p.

Nos. N18, N20 and N21 Surcharged in Black

BAHÂ
1943
+21

1943, Dec. 8 Wmk. 257 *Perf. 13*

NB5 OS4 12c + 21c steel blue 15 15
NB6 OS1 20c + 36c rose violet 15 15
NB7 OS3 21c + 40c violet 15 15
Set value 28 28

The surtax was for the benefit of victims of a Luzon flood. "Baha" is Tagalog for "flood."

Type of 1944 Souvenir Sheet

1944, Feb. 9 Unwmk. Litho. *Imperf.*

Without Gum

NB8 Sheet of 3 2.50 *2.50*

No. NB8 contains one each of Nos. N32a-N34a. Sheet sold for 1p, surtax going to a fund for the care of heroes' monuments.

OCCUPATION POSTAGE DUE STAMP

No. J15 Overprinted with Bar in Blue

1942, Oct. 14 Unwmk. *Perf. 11*

NJ1 D3 3c on 4c brown red 16.00 7.00

On copies of No. J15, two lines were drawn in India ink with a ruling pen across "United States of America" by employees of the Short Paid Section of the Manila Post Office to make a provisional 3c postage due stamp which was used from Sept. 1, 1942, (when the letter rate was raised from 2c to 5c) until Oct. 14 when No. NJ1 went on sale.

OCCUPATION OFFICIAL STAMPS

Nos. 461, 413, 435, 435a and 442 Overprinted or Surcharged in Black with Bars and

公用
(K. P.)

1943-44 Unwmk. *Perf. 11x10½, 11*

NO1 A75	2c apple green		15	15
a.	Double overprint			
NO2 A55	5(c) on 6c dk brn (#413) ('44)		15.00	15.00
NO3 A55	5(c) on 6c gldn brn (#435a)		15	15
a.	Narrower spacing between bars		15	15
b.	5(c) on 6c dark brown (#435)		15	15
c.	As "b," narrower spacing between bars		15	15
NO4 A62	16c on 30c org red		30	30
a.	Wider spacing between bars		30	30

On Nos. NO3 and NO3b, the bar deleting "United States of America" is 9¾mm to 10mm above the bar deleting "Common-." On Nos. NO3a and NO3c, the spacing is 8mm to 8½mm.

On No. NO4 the center bar is 19mm long, 3½mm below the top bar and 6mm above the Japanese characters. On No. NO4a, the center bar is 20½mm long, 9mm below the top bar and 1mm above the Japanese characters.

"K. P." stands for Kagamitang Pampamahalaan, "Official Business" in Tagalog.

Nos. 435 and 435a Surcharged in Black

5
REPUBLIKA NG
PILIPINAS
(K. P.)

1944 *Perf. 11*

NO5 A55 5c on 6c golden brown 15 15
a. 5c on 6c dark brown 15 15

Nos. O34 and C62 Overprinted in Black

a

REPUBLIKA NG PILIPINAS

(K. P.)

b

NO6 A60(a) 20c light olive green 22 22
NO7 AP1(b) 1p sepia 65 65

POLAND

LOCATION — Europe between Russia and Germany
GOVT. — Republic
AREA — 120,628 sq. mi.
POP. — 36,399,000 (est. 1983)
CAPITAL — Warsaw

100 Kopecks = 1 Ruble
100 Fenigi = 1 Marka (1918)
100 Halerzy = 1 Korona (1918)
100 Groszy = 1 Zloty (1924)

Catalogue values for unused stamps in this country are for Never Hinged items, beginning with Scott 566 in the regular postage section, Scott B63 in the semi-postal section, Scott C28 in the airpost section, Scott CB1 in the airpost semi-postal section, and Scott J146 in the postage due section.

Values for No. 1 are for fine copies. Very fine to superb specimens sell at much higher prices, and inferior or poor copies sell at reduced prices, depending on the condition of the individual specimen.

Watermarks

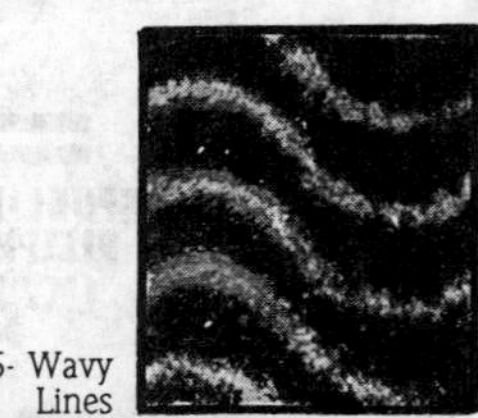

Wmk. 145- Wavy Lines

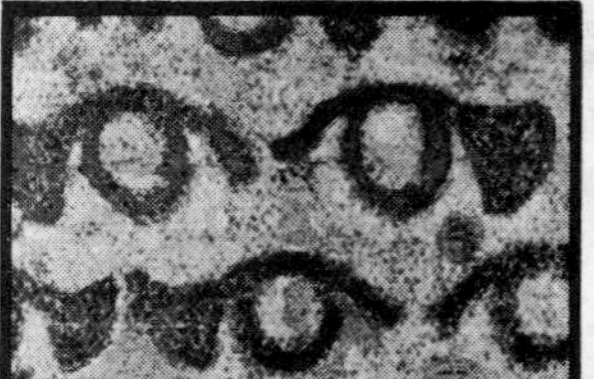

Wmk. 234- Multiple Post Horns

Wmk. 326- Post Horn Multiple

Issued under Russian Dominion

Coat of Arms — A1

Perf. 11½ to 12½

1860 Typo. Unwmk.

1	A1	10k blue & rose	500.00	175.00
a.		10k blue & carmine	650.00	250.00
b.		10k dark blue & rose	650.00	250.00
c.		Added blue frame for inner oval	975.00	425.00
d.		Imperf.		

Used for letters within the Polish territory and to Russia. Postage on all foreign letters was paid in cash.

These stamps were superseded by those of Russia in 1865.

Counterfeits exist.

Issues of the Republic

Local issues were made in various Polish cities during the German occupation. In the early months of the Republic many issues were made by overprinting the German occupation stamps with the words "Poczta Polska" and an eagle or bars often with the name of the city. These issues were not authorized by the Government but were made by the local authorities and restricted to local use. In 1914 two stamps were issued for the Polish Legion and in 1918 the Polish Expeditionary Force used surcharged Russian stamps. The regularity of these issues is questioned.

Warsaw Issues

Statue of Sigismund III — A2

Coat of Arms of Warsaw — A3

Polish Eagle — A4

Sobieski Monument — A5

Stamps of the Warsaw Local Post Surcharged

1918, Nov. 17 Wmk. 145 *Perf. 11½*

11	A2	5f on 2gr brn & buff	85	60
a.		Inverted surcharge	37.50	32.50
12	A3	10f on 6gr grn & buff	80	55
a.		Inverted surcharge	4.50	4.00
13	A4	25f on 10gr rose & buff	1.75	1.25
a.		Inverted surcharge	9.00	8.00
14	A5	50f on 20gr bl & buff	5.00	3.50
a.		Inverted surcharge	130.00	100.00

Counterfeits exist.

Occupation Stamps Nos. N6-N16 Overprinted or Surcharged:

5

Poczta Polska   Poczta Polska

a   b

1918-19 Wmk. 125 *Perf. 14, 14½*

15	A16	3pf brown ('19)	15.00	10.50
16	A22	5pf on 2½pf gray	25	25
17	A16	5pf on 3pf brn	2.75	1.90
18	A16	5pf green	52	45
19	A16	10pf carmine	15	15
20	A22	15pf dk vio	15	15
21	A16	20pf blue	16	18
a.		20pf ultramarine	*350.00*	*350.00*
23	A22	25pf on 7½pf org	25	15
24	A16	30pf org & blk, *buff*	15	15
25	A16	40pf lake & blk	35	38
26	A16	60pf magenta	52	55
		Nos. 15-26 (11)	20.25	14.81

There are two settings of this overprint. The first printing, issued Dec. 5, 1918, has space of 3½mm between the middle two bars. The second printing, issued Jan. 15, 1919, has space of 4mm. No. 15 comes only in the second setting; all others in both. The German overprint on No. 21a is very glossy.

Varieties of this overprint and surcharge are numerous: double; inverted; misspellings (Pocata, Poczto, Pelska); letters omitted, inverted or wrong font; 3 bars instead of 4, etc.

Counterfeits exist.

Lublin Issue

Austrian Military Semi-Postal Stamps of 1918 Overprinted

1918, Dec. 5 Unwmk. *Perf. 12½x13*

27	MSP7	10h gray green	6.50	6.00
a.		Inverted overprint	17.50	19.00
28	MSP8	20h magenta	6.50	6.00
a.		Inverted overprint	17.50	19.00
29	MSP7	45h blue	6.50	6.00
a.		Inverted overprint	17.50	19.00

Austrian Military Stamps of 1917 Surcharged

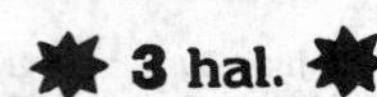

1918-19 *Perf. 12½*

30	M3	3hal on 3h ol gray	20.00	19.00
a.		Inverted surcharge	225.00	225.00
b.		Perf. 11½	30.00	21.00
c.		Perf. 11½x12½	40.00	40.00
31	M3	3hal on 15h brt rose	2.50	2.00
a.		Inverted surcharge	20.00	20.00

Surcharged in Black

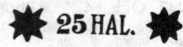

25HAL.

32	M3	10hal on 30h sl grn	2.75	1.75
a.		Inverted surcharge	20.00	20.00
b.		Brown surcharge (error)	60.00	50.00
34	M3	25hal on 40h ol bis	4.25	2.75
a.		Inverted surcharge	30.00	30.00
b.		Perf. 11½	15.00	9.00
35	M3	45hal on 60h rose	3.00	2.25
a.		Inverted surcharge	20.00	20.00
36	M3	45hal on 80h dl bl	5.00	4.25
a.		Inverted surcharge	30.00	30.00
37	M3	50hal on 60h rose	3.00	2.50
a.		Inverted surcharge	20.00	20.00

Similar surcharge with bars instead of stars over original value

38	M3	45hal on 80h dl bl	5.50	4.75
a.		Inverted surcharge	20.00	20.00

Overprinted

39	M3	50h dp grn	24.00	17.00
a.		Inverted overprint	80.00	80.00
40	M3	90h dk vio	3.75	2.75
a.		Inverted overprint	20.00	20.00
		Nos. 30-40 (10)	73.75	59.00

Cracow Issues

Austrian Stamps of 1916-18 Overprinted

POCZTA
POLSKA

1919, Jan. 17 Typo.

41	A37	3h brt vio	175.00	150.00
42	A37	5h lt grn	175.00	150.00
43	A37	6h dp org	17.50	15.00
a.		Inverted overprint	*2,000.*	
44	A37	10h magenta	175.00	160.00
45	A37	12h lt bl	17.50	14.00
46	A39	40h ol grn	12.00	11.00
a.		Inverted overprint	100.00	100.00
b.		Double overprint	400.00	
47	A39	50h bl grn	5.00	4.00
a.		Inverted overprint		*2,400.*
48	A39	60h dp bl	4.00	4.00
a.		Inverted overprint	100.00	75.00
49	A39	80h org brn	4.00	4.75
a.		Inverted overprint.	100.00	100.00
b.		Double overprint	*125.00*	*125.00*
50	A39	90h red vio	550.00	475.00
51	A39	1k car, *yel*	7.00	5.00

Engr.

52	A40	2k blue	4.00	4.00
53	A40	3k car rose	45.00	40.00
54	A40	4k yel grn	65.00	60.00
55	A40	10k dp vio	*3,150.*	*3,600.*

The 3k is on granite paper.

The overprint on Nos. 52-55 is litho. and slightly larger than illustration with different ornament between lines of type.

Same Overprint on Nos. 168-171

1919 Typo.

56	A42	15h dl red	6.00	5.00
57	A42	20h dk grn	60.00	55.00
58	A42	25h blue	650.00	650.00
59	A42	30h dl vio	110.00	100.00

Austria No. 157 Surcharged

POLSKA
POCZTA
25

1919, Jan. 24

60	A39	25h on 80h org brn	2.50	2.25
a.		Inverted surcharge	60.00	60.00

Excellent counterfeits of Nos. 27 to 60 exist.

Polish Eagle — A9

1919, Feb. 25 Litho. *Imperf.*

Without gum

Yellowish Paper

61	A9	2h gray	30	35
62	A9	3h dl vio	30	35
63	A9	5h green	15	15
64	A9	6h orange	12.50	16.00
65	A9	10h lake	15	15
66	A9	15h brown	15	15
67	A9	20h ol grn	30	35

Bluish Paper

68	A9	25h carmine	15	15
69	A9	50h indigo	15	15
70	A9	70h dp bl	30	35
71	A9	1k ol gray & car	55	95
		Nos. 61-71 (11)	15.00	19.10

Nos. 61-71 exist with privately applied perforations.

Counterfeits exist.

For surcharges see Nos. J35-J39.

Posen (Poznan) Issue

Germany Nos. 84-85, 87, 96, 98 Overprinted in Black

5 5 Poczta Polska   10 10 Poczta Polska

Perf. 14, 14½

1919, Aug. 5 Wmk. 125

72	A22	5pf on 2pf gray	18.00	15.00
73	A22	5pf on 7½pf org	1.90	1.25
a.		Inverted surcharge	100.00	
74	A16	5pf on 20pf bl vio	1.50	1.10
75	A16	10pf on 25pf org & blk, *yel*	3.75	3.00
76	A16	10pf on 40pf lake & blk	2.00	1.25
		Nos. 72-76 (5)	27.15	21.60

Counterfeits exist.

Germany Nos. 96 and 98 Surcharged in Red or Green

5   10

1919, Sept. 15
77 A22 5pf on 2pf (R) 150.00 115.00
a. Inverted surcharge 4,250.
78 A22 10pf on 7½pf (G) 125.00 85.00

Nos. 77-78 are a provisional issue for use in Gniezno. Counterfeit surcharges abound.

Eagle and Fasces, Symbolical of United Poland
A10 A11

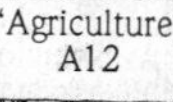

"Agriculture" A12 "Peace" A13

Polish Cavalryman — A14

For Northern Poland
Denominations as "F" or "M"

1919, Jan. 27 *Imperf.*
Wove or Ribbed Paper
81 A10 3f bis brn 15 15
82 A10 5f green 15 15
83 A10 10f red vio 15 15
84 A10 15f dp rose 15 15
85 A11 20f deep bl 15 15
86 A11 25f ol grn 15 15
87 A11 50f bl grn 15 15
88 A12 1m violet 1.75 1.25
89 A12 1.50m dp grn 3.25 1.75
90 A12 2m dk brn 2.75 1.75
91 A13 2.50m org brn 12.00 7.75
92 A14 5m red vio 15.00 7.75
Nos. 81-92 (12) 35.80 21.30

Perf. 10, 11, 11½, 10x11½, 11½x10
1919-20
93 A10 3f bis brn 15 15
94 A10 5f green 15 15
95 A10 10f red vio 15 15
96 A10 10f brn ('20) 15 15
97 A10 15f dp rose 15 15
98 A10 15f ver ('20) 15 15
99 A11 20f dp bl 15 15
100 A11 25f ol grn 15 15
101 A11 40f brt vio ('20) 15 15
102 A11 50f bl grn 15 15
103 A12 1m violet 40 20
105 A12 1.50m dp grn 80 40
106 A12 2m dk brn 80 40
107 A13 2.50m org brn 1.25 1.10
108 A14 5m red vio 2.00 1.10
Nos. 93-108 (15) 6.75
Set value 3.90

Several denominations among Nos. 81-132 are found with double impression or in pairs imperf. between.

See Nos. 109-132, 140-152C, 170-175. For surcharges and overprints see Nos. 153, 199-200, B1-B14, 2K1-2K10.

For Southern Poland
Denominations as "H" or "K"

1919, Jan. 27 *Imperf.*
109 A10 3h red brn 15 15
110 A10 5h emerald 15 15
111 A10 10h orange 15 15
112 A10 15h vermilion 15 15
113 A11 20h gray brn 15 15
114 A11 25h light bl 15 15
115 A11 50h org brn 15 15
116 A12 1k dk grn 15 15
117 A12 1.50k red brn 4.00 3.00
118 A12 2k dark bl 2.00 1.90
119 A13 2.50k dk vio 9.50 5.00
120 A14 5k slate bl 11.00 6.25
Nos. 109-120 (12) 27.70 17.35

Perf. 10, 11½, 10x11½, 11½x10
121 A10 3h red brn 15 15
122 A10 5h emerald 15 15
123 A10 10h orange 15 15
124 A10 15h vermilion 15 15
125 A11 20h gray brn 15 15
126 A11 25h light bl 15 15
127 A11 50h org brn 15 15
128 A12 1k dk grn 40 38
129 A12 1.50k red brn 1.10 52
130 A12 2k dark bl 1.10 52
131 A13 2.50k dk vio 1.25 65
132 A14 5k slate blue 2.00 1.25
Nos. 121-132 (12) 6.90
Set value 3.60

National Assembly Issue

A20

Ignacy Jan Paderewski — A21

Adalbert Trampczynski — A22

Eagle Watching Ship — A24

Designs: 25f, Gen. Josef Pilsudski. 1m, Griffin.

1919-20 *Perf. 11½*
Wove or Ribbed Paper
133 A20 10f red vio 15 15
134 A21 15f brn red 35 20
a. Imperf., pair 25.00
135 A22 20f dp brn (21x25mm) 28 24
136 A22 20f dp brn (17x20mm) ('20) 55 75
137 A21 25f ol grn 15 15
138 A24 50f Prus bl 22 15
139 A24 1m purple 28 24
Nos. 133-139 (7) 1.98 1.88

First National Assembly of Poland.

General Issue
1919 *Perf. 9 to 14½ and Compound*
Thin Laid Paper
140 A11 25f ol grn 15 15
141 A11 50f bl grn 15 15
142 A12 1m dk gray 28 15
143 A12 2m bis brn 85 15
144 A13 3m red brn 42 15
a. Pair, imperf. vert. 5.00 5.75
145 A14 5m red vio 15 15
146 A14 6m dp rose 15 15
a. Pair, imperf. vert. 6.50 6.50
147 A14 10m brn red 28 22
a. Horizontal pair, imperf. 6.50 6.50
148 A14 20m gray grn 52 42
Nos. 140-148 (9) 2.95
Set value 1.45

Type of 1919 Redrawn
Perf. 9 to 14½ and Compound
1920-22
Thin Laid or Wove Paper
149 A10 1m red 15 15
150 A10 2m gray grn 15 15
151 A10 3m light bl 15 15
152 A10 4m rose red 15 15
152A A10 5m dk vio 15 15
b. Horiz. pair, imperf. vert. 5.25 5.25
152C A10 8m gray brn ('22) 35 22
Set value 90 52

The word "POCZTA" is in smaller letters and the numerals have been enlarged.

The color of No. 152A varies from dark violet to red brown.

No. 101 Surcharged

3 Mk.

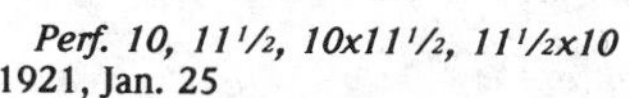

Perf. 10, 11½, 10x11½, 11½x10
1921, Jan. 25
Thick Wove Paper
153 A11 3m on 40f brt vio 15 15
a. Double surcharge 20.00 20.00
b. Inverted surcharge 20.00 20.00

Sower and Rainbow of Hope — A27

Perf. 9 to 14½ and Compound
1921 **Litho.**
Thin Laid or Wove Paper
Size: 28x22mm
154 A27 10m slate blue 15 15
155 A27 15m light brown 30 15
155A A27 20m red 15 15
Set value 35

Signing of peace treaty with Russia.
See No. 191. For surcharges see Nos. 196-198.

Sun (Peace) Breaking into Darkness (Despair) — A28

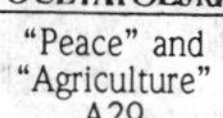

"Peace" and "Agriculture" A29

"Peace" A30

Perf. 11, 11½, 12, 12½, 13 and Compound
1921, May 2
156 A28 2m green 1.25 60
157 A28 3m blue 1.25 60
158 A28 4m red 85 60
a. 4m carmine rose (error) 200.00
159 A29 6m car rose 1.25 65
160 A29 10m slate blue 90 80
161 A30 25m dk vio 2.25 1.90
162 A30 50m sl bl & buff 1.40 1.10
Nos. 156-162 (7) 9.15 6.25

Issued to commemorate the Constitution.

Polish Eagle — A31

Perf. 9 to 14½ and Compound
1921-23
163 A31 25m vio & buff 15 15
164 A31 50m car & buff 15 15
a. Vert. pair, imperf. horiz.
165 A31 100m blk brn & org 15 15
166 A31 200m blk & rose ('23) 24 15
167 A31 300m ol grn ('23) 24 15
168 A31 400m brown ('23) 24 15
169 A31 500m brn vio ('23) 24 15
169A A31 1000m org ('23) 24 15
169B A31 2000m dull bl ('23) 24 15
Nos. 163-169B (9) 1.89 1.35

For surcharge see No. 195.

Type of 1919 and

Miner — A32

Perf. 9 to 14½ and Compound
1922-23
170 A10 5f blue 15 15
171 A10 10f lt vio 15 15
172 A11 20f pale red 15 15
173 A11 40f vio brn 15 15
174 A11 50f orange 15 15
175 A11 75f bl grn 15 15
176 A32 1m black 15 15
177 A32 1.25m dk grn 15 18
178 A32 2m dp rose 15 18
179 A32 3m emerald 15 18
180 A32 4m dp ultra 15 18
181 A32 5m yel brn 15 18
182 A32 6m red org 15 18
183 A32 10m lilac brn 15 18
184 A32 20m dp vio 15 22
185 A32 50m olive grn 18 25
187 A32 80m ver ('23) 38 75
188 A32 100m vio ('23) 38 75
189 A32 200m org ('23) 1.50 2.25
190 A32 300m pale bl ('23) 4.50 3.75
Nos. 170-190 (20) 9.19 10.28

This issue was to commemorate the union of Upper Silesia with Poland.

There were 2 printings of Nos. 176 to 190, the 1st being from flat plates, the 2nd from rotary press on thin paper, perf. 12½.

Nos. 173 and 175 are printed from new plates showing larger value numerals and a single "f."

Sower Type Redrawn
Size: 25x21mm
1922 **Thick or Thin Wove Paper**
191 A27 20m carmine 35 16

In this stamp the design has been strengthened and made more distinct, especially the ground and the numerals in the upper corners.

Nicolaus Copernicus — A33

Father Stanislaus Konarski — A34

1923 *Perf. 10 to 12½*
192 A33 1000m indigo 90 32
193 A34 3000m brown 50 32
a. "Konapski" 8.00 8.00
194 A33 5000m rose 90 32

Nicolaus Copernicus (1473-1543), astronomer (Nos. 192, 194); Stanislaus Konarski (1700-1773), educator, and the creation by the Polish Parliament of the Commission of Public Instruction (No. 193).

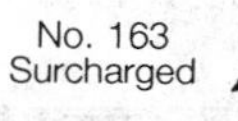

No. 163 Surcharged

1923 *Perf. 9 to 14½ and Compound*
195 A31 10000m on 25m 22 15
a. Double surcharge 5.00
b. Inverted surcharge 7.50

Stamps of 1921 Surcharged

MK MK
25,000

196 A27 25000m on 20m red 45 15
a. Double surcharge 5.00 5.00
b. Inverted surcharge 10.00
197 A27 50000m on 10m grnsh bl 22 15
a. Double surcharge 5.00 5.00
b. Inverted surcharge 7.50 7.50

No. 191 Surcharged

MK MK
25,000

198 A27 25000m on 20m car 35 15
a. Double surcharge 5.00 5.00
b. Inverted surcharge 7.50

No. 150 Surcharged with New Value
1924
199 A10 20000m on 2m gray grn 55 15
a. Inverted surcharge 7.50 7.50
b. Double surcharge 5.00 5.00

Type of 1919 Issue Surcharged with New Value
200 A10 100000m on 5m red brn 22 15
a. Double surcharge 5.00 5.00
b. Inverted surcharge 7.50 7.50
Set value, #195-200 60

Arms of Poland — A35

Perf. 10 to 14½ and Compound

1924 **Litho.**

Thin Paper

205 A35	10,000m lil brn	30	24
206 A35	20,000m ol grn	30	16
207 A35	30,000m scarlet	1.00	32
208 A35	50,000m ap grn	2.00	32
209 A35	100,000m brn org	60	28
210 A35	200,000m lt bl	30	15
211 A35	300,000m red vio	60	32
212 A35	500,000m brn	60	65
213 A35	1,000,000m pale rose	60	*2.75*
214 A35	2,000,000m dk grn	1.00	
	Nos. 205-214 (10)	7.30	

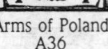

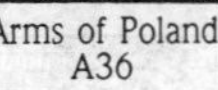
Arms of Poland A36

President Stanislaus Wojciechowski A37

Perf. 10 to 13½ and Compound

1924

215 A36	1g org brn	30	15
216 A36	2g dk brn	30	15
217 A36	3g orange	38	15
218 A36	5g ol grn	80	15
219 A36	10g bl grn	1.00	15
220 A36	15g red	1.00	15
221 A36	20g blue	2.00	16
222 A36	25g red brn	2.75	32
a.	25g indigo	*3,000.*	*4,250.*
223 A36	30g dp vio	19.00	24
a.	30g gray blue	*250.00*	
224 A36	40g indigo	3.75	32
225 A36	50g magenta	3.25	28

Perf. 11½, 12

226 A37	1z scarlet	20.00	1.10
	Nos. 215-226 (12)	54.53	
	Set value		2.90

For overprints see Nos. 1K1-1K11.

Holy Gate of Wilno (Vilnius) A38

Poznan Town Hall A39

Sigismund Monument, Warsaw — A40

Wawel Castle at Cracow — A41

Sobieski Statue at Lwow — A42

Ship of State — A43

1925-27 *Perf. 10 to 13*

227 A38	1g bis brn	35	15
228 A42	2g brn ol	42	22
229 A40	3g blue	1.65	15
230 A39	5g yel grn	1.65	15
231 A40	10g violet	1.65	15
232 A41	15g rose red	1.50	15
233 A43	20g dl red	1.75	15

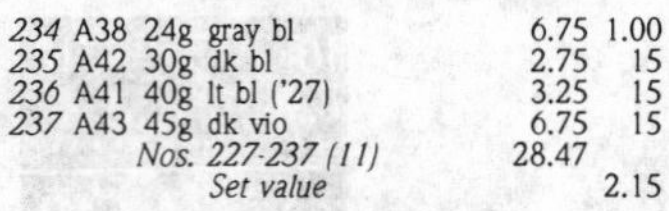

234 A38	24g gray bl	6.75	1.00
235 A42	30g dk bl	2.75	15
236 A41	40g lt bl ('27)	3.25	15
237 A43	45g dk vio	6.75	15
	Nos. 227-237 (11)	28.47	
	Set value		2.15

For overprints see Nos. 1K11A-1K17.

1926-27 **Redrawn**

238 A40	3g blue	2.50	42
239 A39	5g yel grn	3.00	18
240 A40	10g violet	4.50	18
241 A41	15g rose red	4.50	18

On Nos. 229 to 232 inclusive the lines representing clouds touch the numerals. On the redrawn stamps the numerals have white outlines, separating them from the cloud lines.

Marshal Pilsudski A44

Frederic Chopin A45

1927 **Typo.** *Perf. 12½, 11½*

242 A44	20g red brn	2.50	25
243 A45	40g dp ultra	15.00	1.75

See No. 250. For overprint see No. 1K18.

President Ignacy Moscicki — A46

1927, May 4 *Perf. 11½*

245 A46	20g red	5.25	45

Dr. Karol Kaczkowski A47

Julius Slowacki A48

1927, May 27 *Perf. 11½, 12½*

246 A47	10g gray grn	2.75	1.75
247 A47	25g carmine	6.50	2.50
248 A47	40g dk blue	8.75	2.50

4th Intl. Congress of Millitary Medicine and Pharmacy, Warsaw, May 30-June 4.

1927, June 28 *Perf. 12½*

249 A48	20g rose	6.00	50

Transfer from Paris to Cracow of the remains of Julius Slowacki, poet.

Pilsudski Type of 1927

Design Redrawn

1928 *Perf. 11½, 12x11½, 12½x13*

250 A44	25g yel brn	2.50	25

Souvenir Sheet

A49

1928, May 3 **Engr.** *Perf. 12½*

251 A49	Sheet of 2	225.00	300.00
a.	50g black brown	100.00	125.00
b.	1z black brown	100.00	125.00

1st Natl. Phil. Exhib., Warsaw, May 3-13.

Sold to each purchaser of a 1.50z ticket to the Warsaw Philatelic Exhibition.

Counterfeits exist.

Marshal Pilsudski A49a

Pres. Moscicki A50

Perf. 10½ to 14 and Compound

1928-31

Wove Paper

253 A49a	50g bluish slate	3.75	25
254 A49a	50g bl grn ('31)	11.00	25

See No. 315.

Perf. 12x12½, 11½ to 13½ and Compound

1928

Laid Paper

255 A50	1z black, *cream*	10.00	25
a.	Horizontally laid paper ('30)	65.00	2.50

See Nos. 305, 316. For surcharges and overprints see Nos. J92-J94, 1K19, 1K24.

General Josef Bem A51

Henryk Sienkiewicz A52

1928, May **Typo.** *Perf. 12½*

Wove Paper

256 A51	25g rose red	3.75	25

Return from Syria to Poland of the ashes of General Josef Bem.

1928, Oct.

257 A52	15g ultra	2.00	25

For overprint see No. 1K23.

Eagle Arms — A53

"Swiatowid," Ancient Slav God — A54

1928-29 *Perf. 12x12½*

258 A53	5g dk vio	30	15
259 A53	10g green	90	15
260 A53	25g red brn	50	15
	Set value		30

See type A58. For overprints see Nos. 1K20-1K22.

1928, Dec. 15 *Perf. 12½x12*

261 A54	25g brown	2.50	25

Poznan Agricultural Exhibition.

King John III Sobieski A55

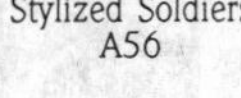
Stylized Soldiers A56

1930, July *Perf. 12x12½*

262 A55	75g claret	5.75	25

1930, Nov. 1 *Perf. 12½*

263 A56	5g vio brn	35	15
264 A56	15g dk bl	2.25	32
265 A56	25g red brn	1.25	15
266 A56	30g dl red	6.25	3.75

Centenary of insurrection of 1830.

Kosciuszko, Washington, Pulaski A57

1932, May 3 *Perf. 11½*

Laid Paper

267 A57	30g brown	3.00	25

200th birth anniv. of George Washington.

A58

A59

Perf. 12x12½

1932-33 **Typo.** **Wmk. 234**

268 A58	5g dl vio ('33)	32	15
269 A58	10g green	32	15
270 A58	15g red brn ('33)	32	15
271 A58	20g gray	65	15
272 A58	25g buff	85	15
273 A58	30g dp rose	3.00	15
274 A58	60g blue	19.00	45
	Nos. 268-274 (7)	24.46	
	Set value		75

For overprints and surcharge see Nos. 280-281, 284, 292, 1K25-1K27.

1933, Jan. 2 **Engr.** *Perf. 11½*

275 A59	60g Torun City Hall	35.00	75

700th anniversary of the founding of the City of Torun by the Grand Master of the Knights of the Teutonic Order.

See No. B28.

Altar Panel of St. Mary's Church, Cracow A60

Perf. 11½-12½ & Compound

1933, July 10 **Unwmk.**

Laid Paper

277 A60	80g red brn	15.00	1.25

400th death anniv. of Veit Stoss, sculptor and woodcarver.

For surcharge see No. 285.

John III Sobieski and Allies before Vienna, painted by Jan Matejko
A61

1933, Sept. 12 **Laid Paper**
278 A61 1.20z indigo 32.50 6.00

250th anniv. of the deliverance of Vienna by the Polish and allied forces under command of John III Sobieski, King of Poland, when besieged by the Turks in 1683.
For surcharge see No. 286.

Cross of Independence
A62

Josef Pilsudski
A63

Perf. 12½
1933, Nov. 11 **Typo.** **Wmk. 234**
279 A62 30g scarlet 7.50 50

15th anniversary of independence.

Type of 1932 Overprinted in Red or Black

Wyst. Filat.
1934
Katowice

1934, May 5 ***Perf. 12***
280 A58 20g gray (R) 26.00 21.00
281 A58 30g dp rose 26.00 21.00

Katowice Philatelic Exhibition. Counterfeits exist.

Perf. 11½ to 12½ and Compound
1934, Aug. 6 **Engr.** **Unwmk.**
282 A63 25g gray bl 1.10 22
283 A63 30g blk brn 2.75 32

Polish Legion, 20th anniversary.
For overprint see No. 293.

Nos. 274, 277-278 Surcharged in Black or Red

1934 **Wmk. 234** ***Perf. 12x12½***
284 A58 55g on 60g blue 5.75 50

Perf. 11½-12½ & Compound
Unwmk.
285 A60 25g on 80g red brn 6.50 50
286 A61 1z on 1.20z ind (R) 15.00 2.50
a. Figure "1" in surcharge 5mm high instead of 4½mm 15.00 2.50

Surcharge of No. 286 includes bars.

Pilsudski Mourning Issue

Marshal Pilsudski — A64

1935 ***Perf. 11 to 13 and Compound***
287 A64 5g black 80 15
288 A64 15g black 80 22
289 A64 25g black 1.65 18
290 A64 45g black 4.00 1.25
291 A64 1z black 8.00 4.00
Nos. 287-291 (5) 15.25 5.80

Nos. 287-288 are typo., Nos. 290-291 litho. No. 289 exists both typo. and litho.
See No. B35b.

Nos. 270, 282 Overprinted in Blue or Red

Kopiec Marszalka Pilsudskiego

1935 **Wmk. 234** ***Perf. 12x12½***
292 A58 15g red brown 1.00 45

Perf. 11½, 11½x12½
Unwmk.
293 A63 25g gray blue (R) 3.25 1.50

Issued in connection with the proposed memorial to Marshal Pilsudski, the stamps were sold at Cracow exclusively.

"The Dog Cliff"
A65

President Ignacy Moscicki
A75

Designs: 10g, "Eye of the Sea." 15g, M. S. "Pilsudski." 20g, View of Pieniny. 25g, Belvedere Palace. 30g, Castle in Mira. 45g, Castle at Podhorce. 50g, Cloth Hall, Cracow. 55g, Raczynski Library, Poznan. 1z, Cathedral, Wilno.

1935-36 **Typo.** ***Perf. 12½x13***
294 A65 5g vio bl 65 15
295 A65 10g yel grn 65 15
296 A65 15g Prus grn 2.00 15
297 A65 20g vio blk 1.00 15

Engr.
298 A65 25g myr grn 85 15
299 A65 30g rose red 2.25 28
300 A65 45g plum ('36) 1.10 28
301 A65 50g blk ('36) 1.10 28
302 A65 55g bl ('36) 10.00 55
303 A65 1z brn ('36) 4.00 1.50
304 A75 3z blk brn 2.50 2.50
Nos. 294-304 (11) 26.10 6.14

See Nos. 308-311. For overprints see Nos. 306-307, 1K28-1K32.

Type of 1928 inscribed "1926. 3. VI. 1936" on Bottom Margin

1936, June 3
305 A50 1z ultra 7.50 5.75

Presidency of Ignacy Moscicki, 10th anniv.

Nos. 299, 302 Overprinted in Blue or Red

GORDON-BENNETT 30.VIII. 1936

1936, Aug. 15
306 A65 30g rose red 12.00 6.00
307 A65 55g bl (R) 12.00 6.00

Gordon-Bennett Intl. Balloon Race. Counterfeits exist.

Scenic Type of 1935-36

Designs: 5g, Church at Czestochowa. 10g, Maritime Terminal, Gdynia. 15g, University, Lwow. 20g, Municipal Building, Katowice.

1937 **Engr.** ***Perf. 12½***
308 A65 5g vio bl 15 15
309 A65 10g green 42 15
310 A65 15g red brn 28 15
311 A65 20g org brn 42 15
Set value 30

For overprints see Nos. 1K31-1K32.

Marshal Smigly-Rydz
A80

President Moscicki
A81

1937 ***Perf. 12½x13***
312 A80 25g slate grn 22 15
313 A80 55g blue 55 15

For surcharges see Nos. N30, N32.

Types of 1928-37
Souvenir Sheets

1937
314 Sheet of 4 18.00 25.00
a. A80 25g, dark brown 3.00 2.75
315 Sheet of 4 18.00 25.00
a. A49a 50g, sdeep blue 3.00 2.75
316 Sheet of 4 18.00 25.00
a. A50 1z, gray black 3.00 2.75

Visit of King Carol of Romania to Poland, June 26-July 1.
See No. B35c.

1938, Feb. 1 ***Perf. 12½***
317 A81 15g slate green 15 15
318 A81 30g rose violet 60 15
Set value 25

71st birthday of President Moscicki.
For surcharge see No. N31.

Kosciuszko, Paine and Washington and View of New York City — A82

1938, Mar. 17 ***Perf. 12x12½***
319 A82 1z gray blue 1.25 1.75

150th anniv. of the US Constitution.

Boleslaus I and Emperor Otto III at Gnesen — A83

Marshal Pilsudski — A95

Designs: 10g, King Casimir III. 15g, King Ladislas II Jagello and Queen Hedwig. 20g, King Casimir IV. 25g, Treaty of Lublin. 30g, King Stephen Bathory commending Wielock, the peasant. 45g, Stanislas Zolkiewski and Jan Chodkiewicz. 50g, John III Sobieski entering Vienna. 55g, Union of nobles, commoners and peasants. 75g, Dabrowski, Kosciuszko and Poniatowski. 1z, Polish soldiers. 2z, Romuald Traugutt.

1938, Nov. 11 **Engr.** ***Perf. 12½***
320 A83 5g red org 15 15
321 A83 10g green 15 15
322 A83 15g fawn 28 15
323 A83 20g peacock blue 42 15
324 A83 25g dl vio 15 15
325 A83 30g rose red 65 15
326 A83 45g black 42 15
327 A83 50g brt red vio 2.75 15
328 A83 55g ultra 85 15
329 A83 75g dl grn 2.00 1.50
330 A83 1z orange 1.65 1.40
331 A83 2z car rose 10.50 8.00
332 A95 3z gray blk 8.50 14.00
Nos. 320-332 (13) 28.47 26.25

20th anniv. of Poland's independence. See No. 339. For surcharges see Nos. N33-N47.

Souvenir Sheet

Marshal Pilsudski, Gabriel Narutowicz, President Moscicki, Marshal Smigly-Rydz
A96

1938, Nov. 11 ***Perf. 12½***
333 A96 Sheet of 4 15.00 18.00
a. 25g dull violet (Pilsudski) 1.65 1.75
b. 25g dull violet (Narutowicz) 1.65 1.75
c. 25g dull violet (Moscicki) 1.65 1.75
d. 25g dull violet (Smigly-Rydz) 1.65 1.75

20th anniv. of Poland's independence.

Poland Welcoming Teschen People — A97

Skier — A98

1938, Nov. 11
334 A97 25g dull violet 1.50 45

Restoration of the Teschen territory ceded by Czechoslovakia.

1939, Feb. 6
335 A98 15g org brn 1.10 1.10
336 A98 25g dl vio 1.50 50
337 A98 30g rose red 2.25 1.10
338 A98 55g brt ultra 7.00 4.00

Intl. Ski Meet, Zakopane, Feb. 11-19.

Type of 1938

Design: 15g, King Ladislas II Jagello and Queen Hedwig.

Re-engraved

1939, Mar. 2 ***Perf. 12½***
339 A83 15g redsh brn 25 18

No. 322 with crossed swords and helmet at lower left. No. 339, swords and helmet have been removed.

Marshal Pilsudski Reviewing Troops — A99

1939, Aug. 1 **Engr.**
340 A99 25g dl rose vio 60 50

Polish Legion, 25th anniv. See No. B35a.

Polish Peoples Republic

Romuald Traugutt
A100

Tadeusz Kosciuszko
A101

Design: 1z, Jan Henryk Dabrowski.

Perf. 11½
1944, Sept. 7 **Litho.** **Unwmk.**
Without Gum
341 A100 25g crim rose 37.50 40.00
342 A101 50g dp grn 45.00 52.50
343 A101 1z dp ultra 40.00 52.50

Counterfeits exist.
For surcharges see Nos. 362-363.

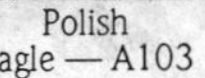

Polish Eagle — A103

Grunwald Monument, Cracow — A104

1944, Sept. 13 Photo. *Perf. 12½*

344 A103 25g deep red		60	35
a. 25g dull red, typo.		65	
345 A104 50g dk slate grn		45	15

No. 344a was not put on sale without surcharge. See Nos. 346, 349a. For surcharges see Nos. 345A-356, 364, B54, C19-C20.

No. 344 Surcharged in Black

— 1 zł —

31.XII.1943
K. R. N.
31.XII.1944

a

— 2 zł —

P. K. W. N.
31.XII.1944

b

— 3 zł —

31.XII.1944
R. T. R. P.

c

1944-45

345A A103 1z on 25g	1.90	2.00
345B A103 2z on 25g ('45)	1.90	2.00
345C A103 3z on 25g ('45)	1.90	2.00

Issued to honor Polish government agencies. K. R. N. - Krajowa Rada Narodowa (Polish National Council), P. K. W. N. - Polski Komitet Wyzwolenia Narodu (Polish National Liberation Committee) and R. T. R. P. - Rzad Tymczasowy Rzeczypospolitej Polskiej (Temporary Administration of the Polish Republic).

Counterfeits exist.

No. 344a Surcharged in Brown

1'50
ZL

1945, Sept. 1

346 A103 1.50z on 25g dl red	45	18
a. 1.50z on 25g dp red, #344	350.00	250.00

Counterfeits of No. 346a exist.

No. 344 Surcharged in Blue

— 3 zł —
Kielce
15. I. 1945

1945, Feb. 12

347 A103 3z on 25g	4.25	6.25
348 A103 3z on 25g *(Radom, 16. I. 1945)*	3.00	3.50
349 A103 3z on 25g *(Warszawa, 17. I. 1945)*	6.25	7.00
a. 3z on 25g dl red, #344a	110.00	125.00
350 A103 3z on 25g *(Czestochowa, 17. I. 1945)*	3.00	3.50
351 A103 3z on 25g *(Krakow, 19. I. 1945)*	3.00	3.50
352 A103 3z on 25g *(Lodz, 19. I. 1945)*	3.00	3.50
353 A103 3z on 25g *(Gniezno, 22. I. 1945)*	3.00	3.50
354 A103 3z on 25g *(Bydgoszcz, 23. I. 1945)*	3.00	3.50
355 A103 3z on 25g *(Kalisz, 24. I. 1945)*	3.00	3.50
356 A103 3z on 25g *(Zakopane, 29. I. 1945)*	3.00	3.50
Nos. 347-356 (10)	34.50	41.25

Dates overprinted are those of liberation for each city.

Counterfeits exist.

Grunwald Monument, Cracow — A105

Kosciuszko Statue, Cracow — A106

Cloth Hall, Cracow A107

Copernicus Memorial A108

Wawel Castle — A109

1945, Apr. 10 Photo. *Perf. 10½, 11*

357 A105 50g dk vio brn	15	15
a. 50g dark brown	45	35
358 A106 1z henna brn	30	24
359 A107 2z sapphire	45	35
360 A108 3z dp red vio	1.25	48
361 A109 5z bl grn	2.75	3.25
Nos. 357-361 (5)	4.90	4.47

Liberation of Cracow Jan. 19, 1945.

Nos. 357 to 361 exist imperforate.

No. 357a is a coarser printing from a new plate showing designer's name (J. Wilczyk) in lower left margin. No. 357 does not show his name.

Nos. 341 and 342 Surcharged in Black or Red:

5 zł 

22.I.1863.

d

5 zł. =

24. III. 1794

e

1945 *Perf. 11½*

362 A100(d) 5z on 25g	27.50	32.50
363 A101(e) 5z on 50g (R)	7.00	9.00

No. 362 was issued without gum.

No. 345 Surcharged in Brown

1 ZŁ

1945, Sept. 10 *Perf. 12½*

364 A104 1z on 50g dk sl grn	38	18

Lodz Skyline — A110

Kosciuszko Monument, Lodz — A111

Flag Bearer Carrying Wounded Comrade — A112

1945 Litho. *Perf. 11, 9 (3z)*

365 A110 1z dp ultra	55	15
366 A111 3z dl red vio	60	45
367 A112 5z dp car	2.00	1.90

Nos. 365 and 367 commemorate the liberation of Lodz and Warsaw.

Grunwald Battle Scene — A113

Eagle Breaking Fetters and Manifesto of Freedom — A114

1945, July 16

368 A113 5z deep blue	8.00	9.00

Battle of Grunwald (Tannenberg), July 15, 1410.

1945, July 22

369 A114 3z rose car	12.00	15.00

1st anniv. of the liberation of Poland.

Crane Tower, Gdansk A115

Stock Tower, Gdansk A116

Ancient High Gate, Gdansk — A117

1945, Sept. 15 Photo. Unwmk.

370 A115 1z olive	15	15
371 A116 2z sapphire	15	15
372 A117 3c dk vio	60	26

Recovery of Poland's access to the sea at Gdansk (Danzig).

Exist imperf. Value, set $25.

Civilian and Soldiers in Rebellion — A118

1945, Nov. 29

373 A118 10z black	7.75	7.50

115th anniv. of the "November Uprising" against the Russians, Nov. 29, 1830.

Warsaw Castle, 1939 and 1945 A119

Views of Warsaw, 1939 and 1945: 3z, Cathedral of St. John. 3.50z, City Hall. 6z, Post Office. 8z, Army General Staff Headquarters. 10z, Holy Cross Church.

1945-46 Unwmk. *Imperf.*

374 A119 1.50z crimson	20	15
375 A119 3z dk bl	38	15
376 A119 3.50z lt bl grn	95	42
377 A119 6z gray blk ('46)	38	22
378 A119 8z brn ('46)	1.90	42
379 A119 10z dk vio ('46)	80	22
Nos. 374-379 (6)	4.61	1.58

Nos. 374 to 379 Overprinted in Black

WARSZAWA
WOLNA
17 Styczeń
1945—1946

1946, Jan. 17

383 A119 1.50z crimson	1.25	1.75
384 A119 3z dk bl	1.25	1.75
385 A119 3.50z lt bl grn	1.25	1.75
386 A119 6z gray blk	1.25	1.75
387 A119 8z brown	1.25	1.75
388 A119 10z dk vio	1.25	1.75
Nos. 383-388 (6)	7.50	10.50

1st anniv. of the liberation of Warsaw, Jan. 17, 1945.

Counterfeits exist.

Polish Revolutionist A125

Infantry Advancing A126

1946, Jan. 22 *Perf. 11*

389 A125 6z slate blue	6.50	7.00

Revolt of Jan. 22, 1863.

1946, May 9

390 A126 3z brown	30	15

Polish freedom, first anniversary.

Premier Edward Osubka-Morawski Pres. Boleslaw Bierut and Marshal Michael Rola-Zymierski — A127

Perf. 11x10½

1946, July 22 **Unwmk.**
391 A127 3z purple 3.00 4.00

For surcharge see No. B53.

Bedzin Castle — A128

Duke Henry IV of Silesia, from Tomb at Wroclaw — A129

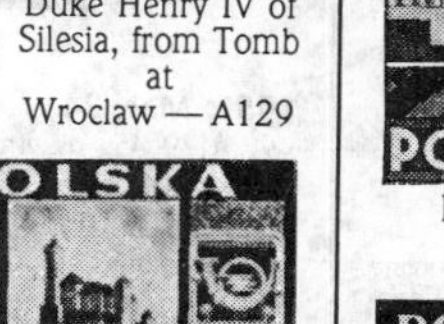

Lanckrona Castle — A130

1946, Sept. 1 **Photo.** ***Imperf.***
392 A128 5z olive gray 15 15
393 A128 5z brown 15 15

Perf. 10½

304 A129 6z gray blk 30 15

Imperf

395 A130 10z deep blue 65 20
Set value 50

Perforated copies of Nos. 392, 393 and 395 have been privately made.
For surcharge see No. 404.

Jan Matejko, Jacek Malczewski, Josef Chelmonski — A131

Adam Chmielowski (Brother Albert) — A132

Designs: 3z, Chopin. 5z, Wojciech Boguslawski, Helena Modjeska and Stefan Jaracz. 6z, Alexander Swietockowski, Stephen Zeromski and Boleslaw Prus. 10z, Marie Sklodowska Curie. 15z, Stanislaw Wyspianski, Juliusz Slowacki and Jan Kasprowicz. 20z, Adam Mickiewicz.

1947 ***Perf. 11, Imperf.***
396 A131 1z blue 20 15
397 A132 2z brown 40 18
398 A132 3z Prus grn 50 18
399 A131 5z ol grn 65 18
400 A131 6z gray grn 1.25 70
401 A132 10z gray brn 1.00 18
402 A131 15z sepia 1.50 55
403 A132 20z gray blk 1.50 75
Nos. 396-403 (8) 7.00 2.87

No. 394 Surcharged in Red

1947, Feb. 25 ***Perf. 10½***
404 A129 5z on 6z gray blk 25 15

Types of 1947

1947 **Photo.** ***Perf. 11, Imperf.***
405 A131 1z sl gray 16 15
406 A132 2z orange 16 15
407 A132 3z ol grn 1.10 35
408 A131 5z ol brn 24 15
409 A131 6z car rose 42 20
410 A132 10z blue 70 18
411 A131 15z chnt brn 55 32
412 A132 20z dk vio 42 50
a. Souv. sheet of 8, #405-412 175.00 165.00
Nos. 405-412 (8) 3.75 2.00

No. 412a sold for 500z.

Laborer A139

Farmer A140

Fisherman A141

Miner A142

1947, Aug. 20 **Engr.** ***Perf. 13***
413 A139 5z rose brn 70 15
414 A140 10z brt bl grn 16 15
415 A141 15z dk bl 75 15
416 A142 20z brn blk 50 15
Set value 50

Allegory of the Revolution A143

Insurgents A144

1948, Mar. 15 **Photo.** ***Perf. 11***
417 A143 15z brown 25 15

Centenary of the Revolution of 1848. See Nos. 430-432.

1948, Apr. 19
418 A144 15z gray blk 1.25 1.25

5th anniv. of the ghetto uprising, Warsaw, Apr. 19, 1943.

Decorated Bicycle Wheel — A145

1948, May 1
419 A145 15z brt rose & bl 2.25 1.00

1st Intl. Bicycle Peace Race, Warsaw-Prague-Warsaw.

Launching Ship — A146

Loading Freighter — A147

Design: 35z, Racing yacht "Gen. Mariusz Zaruski."

1948, June 22
420 A146 6z violet 1.10 1.25
421 A147 15z brn car 1.25 1.25
422 A147 35z sl gray 2.25 2.00

Polish Merchant Marine.

Cyclists — A148

A149

1948, June 22
423 A148 3z gray 1.75 1.40
424 A148 6z brown 1.75 2.50
425 A148 15z green 1.75 3.25

7th Circuit of Poland Bicycle Race, June 22-July 4.

1948, July 15
426 A149 6z blue 28 28
427 A149 15z red 65 30
428 A149 18z rose brn 55 15
429 A149 35z dk brn 55 30

Exhibition to commemorate the recovery of Polish territories, Wroclaw, 1948.

Gen. Henryk Dembinski and Gen. Josef Bem — A150

Symbolical of United Youth — A151

Designs: 35z, S. Worcell, P. Sciegienny and E. Dembowski. 60z, Friedrich Engels and Karl Marx.

1948, July 15
430 A150 30z dk brn 42 38
431 A150 35z ol grn 2.00 38
432 A150 60z brt rose 60 55

Revolution of 1848, cent. See No. 417.

1948, Aug. 8
433 A151 15z blue 42 25

Intl. Congress of Democratic Youth, Warsaw, Aug.

Stagecoach Leaving Torun Gate — A152

1948, Sept. 4
434 A152 15z brown 48 30

Philatelic Exhibition, Torun, Sept.

Clock Dial and Locomotive A153

Pres. Boleslaw Bierut A154

1948, Oct. 6 ***Perf. 11½***
435 A153 18z blue 3.75 4.00

European Railroad Schedule Conference, Cracow.

1948-49 **Unwmk.** ***Perf. 11, 11½***
436 A154 2z org ('49) 15 15
437 A154 3z bl grn ('49) 15 15
438 A154 5z brown 15 15
439 A154 6z slate 40 15
440 A154 10z vio ('49) 15 15
441 A154 15z dp car 15 15
442 A154 18z gray grn 45 25
443 A154 30z blue 75 15
444 A154 35z vio brn 2.00 35
Nos. 436-444 (9) 4.35
Set value 1.20

Workers Carrying Flag — A155

Designs: 15z, Marx, Engels, Lenin and Stalin. 25z, Ludwig Warynski.

Inscribed: "Kongres Jednosci Klasy Robotniczej 8. XII. 1948."

1948, Dec. 8 ***Perf. 11***
445 A155 5z crimson 50 15
446 A155 15z dl vio 50 45
447 A155 25z brown 1.25 38

Redrawn
Dated: "XII. 1948"

Designs as before.

1948, Dec. 15 ***Perf. 11½***
448 A155 5z brn car 1.75 1.10
449 A155 15z brt bl 1.75 1.10
450 A155 25z dk grn 2.50 2.00

Congress of the Union of the Working Class, Warsaw, Dec. 1948.

"Socialism" A156

Designs: 5z, "Labor." 15z, "Peace."

Perf. 11½

1949, May 31 **Unwmk.** **Photo.**
451 A156 3z car rose 1.00 1.00
452 A156 5z dp bl 1.00 1.00
453 A156 15z dp grn 1.40 1.40

8th Trade Union Congress, June 5, 1949.

Warsaw Scene — A157

Pres. Boleslaw Bierut — A158

Radio Station — A159

Perf. 13x12½, 12½x13

1949, July 22 **Litho.**

No.	Type	Value	Color	Unused	Used
454	A157	10z	gray blk	2.00	1.25
455	A158	15z	lil rose	1.25	1.40
456	A159	35z	gray bl	1.25	1.25

5th anniv. of "People's Poland."

A160

A161

UPU, 75th Anniv.: 6z, Stagecoach and world map. 30z, Ship and map. 80z, Plane and map.

1949, Oct. 10 **Engr.** ***Perf. 13x12½***

No.	Type	Value	Color	Unused	Used
457	A160	6z	gray pur	70	1.40
458	A160	30z	blue	1.75	1.40
459	A160	80z	dl grn	3.75	3.00

1949 ***Perf. 13½x13***

Symbolical of United Poland.

No.	Type	Value	Color	Unused	Used
460	A161	5z	brn red	85	15
461	A161	10z	rose red	22	15
462	A161	15z	green	22	15
463	A161	35z	dk brn	70	40
			Set value		70

Congress of the People's Movement for Unity.

Adam Mickiewicz A162

Frederic Chopin A163

Design: 35z, Juliusz Slowacki.

1949, Dec. 5 ***Perf. 12½***

No.	Type	Value	Color	Unused	Used
464	A162	10z	brn vio	2.25	1.40
465	A163	15z	brn rose	3.25	2.25
466	A162	35z	dp bl	2.25	1.40

Mail Delivery A164

Adam Mickiewicz and Pushkin A165

1950, Jan. 21

No.	Type	Value	Color	Unused	Used
467	A164	15z	red vio	2.25	1.50

3rd Congress of PTT Trade Unions, Jan. 21-23, 1950.

1949, Dec. 15

No.	Type	Value	Color	Unused	Used
468	A165	15z	lilac	2.00	1.25

Polish-Soviet friendship.

Pres. Boleslaw Bierut A166

Julian Marchlewski A167

1950, Feb. 25 **Engr.** ***Perf. 12x12½***

No.	Type	Value	Color	Unused	Used
469	A166	15z	red	28	15

See Nos. 478-484, 490-496. For surcharge see No. 522.

1950, Mar. 23 **Photo.** ***Perf. 11x10½***

No.	Type	Value	Color	Unused	Used
470	A167	15z	gray blk	55	30

25th death anniv. of Julian Marchlewski, author and political leader.

Reconstruction, Warsaw — A168

Perf. 11, 12 and Compounds of 13

1950, Apr. 15

No.	Type	Value	Color	Unused	Used
471	A168	5z	dark brn	15	15

See No. 497.

Worker Holding Hammer, Flag and Olive Branch — A169

Workers of Three Races with Flag — A170

1950, Apr. 26 ***Perf. 11½***

No.	Type	Value	Color	Unused	Used
472	A169	10z	dp lil rose	75	20
473	A170	15z	brn ol	75	15

60th anniversary of Labor Day.

Freedom Monument, Poznan A171

Dove on Globe A172

1950, Apr. 27

No.	Type	Value	Color	Unused	Used
474	A171	15z	chocolate	25	15

Poznan Fair, Apr. 29-May 14, 1950.

1950, May 15 **Unwmk.**

No.	Type	Value	Color	Unused	Used
475	A172	10z	dk grn	60	15
476	A172	15z	dk brn	30	15
			Set value		25

Day of Intl. Action for World Peace.

Polish Workers A173

Hibner, Kniewski and Rutkowski A174

1950, July 20 ***Perf. 12½x13***

No.	Type	Value	Color	Unused	Used
477	A173	15z	vio bl	15	15

Poland's 6-year plan. See Nos. 507A-510, 539.

Bierut Type of 1950, No Frame

1950 **Engr.** ***Perf. 12x12½***

No.	Type	Value	Color	Unused	Used
478	A166	5z	dl grn	15	15
479	A166	10z	dl red	15	15
480	A166	15z	dp bl	55	15
481	A166	20z	vio brn	15	15
482	A166	25z	yel brn	24	15
482A	A166	30z	rose brn	28	15
483	A166	40z	brown	20	15
484	A166	50z	olive	90	24
			Nos. 478-484 (8)	2.62	
			Set value		75

1950, Aug. 18 **Photo.** ***Perf. 11***

No.	Type	Value	Color	Unused	Used
485	A174	15z	gray blk	1.25	50

25th anniv. of the execution of three Polish revolutionists, Wladyslaw Hibner, Wladyslaw Kniewski and Henryk Rutkowski.

Worker and Dove — A175

Dove by Picasso — A176

1950, Aug. 31 **Engr.** ***Perf. 12½***

No.	Type	Value	Color	Unused	Used
486	A175	15z	gray grn	28	15

Polish Peace Congress, Warsaw, 1950.

"GROSZY"

To provide denominations needed as a result of the currency revaluation of Oct. 28, 1950, each post office was authorized to surcharge stamps of its current stock with the word "Groszy." Many types and sizes of this surcharge exist. The surcharge was applied to most of Poland's 1946-1950 issues. All stamps of that period could receive the surcharge upon request of anyone. Counterfeits exist.

1950, Nov. 13

No.	Type	Value	Color	Unused	Used
487	A176	40g	blue	1.00	30
488	A176	45g	brown red	32	15

2nd World Peace Congress.

Josef Bem and Battle Scene — A177

1950, Dec. 10

No.	Type	Value	Color	Unused	Used
489	A177	45g	blue	1.50	1.00

Death centenary of Gen. Josef Bem.

Type of 1950 with Frame Omitted

Perf. 12x12½

1950, Dec. 16 **Engr.** **Unwmk.**

No.	Type	Value	Color	Unused	Used
490	A166	5g	brn vio	15	15
491	A166	10g	bluish grn	15	15
492	A166	15g	dp yel grn	15	15
493	A166	25g	dk red	15	15
493A	A166	30g	red	20	15
494	A166	40g	vermilion	15	15
495	A166	45g	dp bl	85	18
496	A166	75g	brown	55	15
			Set value	2.00	76

Reconstruction Type of 1950

Perf. 11, 11x11½, 13x11

1950 **Photo.**

No.	Type	Value	Color	Unused	Used
497	A168	15g	green	15	15

Woman and Doves — A178

1951, Mar. 2 **Engr.** ***Perf. 12½***

No.	Type	Value	Color	Unused	Used
498	A178	45g	dk red	22	15

Congress of Women, Mar. 3-4, 1951.

Gen. Jaroslaw Dabrowski A179

1951, Mar. 24 ***Perf. 12x12½***

No.	Type	Value	Color	Unused	Used
499	A179	45g	dk grn	18	15

80th anniv. of the Insurrection of Paris and the death of Gen. Jaroslaw Dabrowski.

Dove Type of 1950 Surcharged

1951, Apr. 20 ***Perf. 12½***

No.	Type	Value	Color	Unused	Used
500	A176	45g on 15z	brn red	38	15

Worker and Flag — A180

Steel Mill, Nowa Huta — A181

1951, Apr. 25 **Photo.** ***Perf. 14x11***

No.	Type	Value	Color	Unused	Used
501	A180	45g	scarlet	35	15

Labor Day, May 1.

1951 **Engr.** ***Perf. 12½***

No.	Type	Value	Color	Unused	Used
502	A181	40g	dk bl	15	15
503	A181	45g	black	15	15
504	A181	60g	brown	15	15
505	A181	90g	dk car	30	15
			Set value	62	28

Pioneer Saluting A182

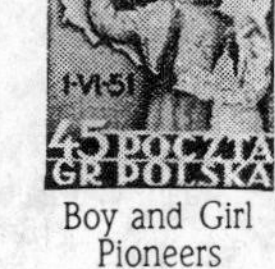
Boy and Girl Pioneers A183

1951, Apr. 1 **Photo.**

No.	Type	Value	Color	Unused	Used
506	A182	30g	ol brn	80	50
507	A183	45g	brt grnsh bl	6.75	70

Issued to publicize Children's Day, June 1, 1951.

Workers Type of 1950

1951 **Unwmk.** **Engr.** ***Perf. 12½x13***

No.	Type	Value	Color	Unused	Used
507A	A173	45g	vio bl	15	15
508	A173	75g	blk brn	15	15
509	A173	1.15z	dk grn	40	20
510	A173	1.20z	dk red	25	20
			Set value		54

Issued to publicize Poland's 6-year plan.

Stanislaw Staszyk — A184

Congress Emblem — A186

Z. F. von Wroblewski and Karol S. Olszewski A185

Portraits: 40g, Marie Sklodowska Curie. 60g, Marceli Nencki. 1.15z, Nicolaus Copernicus.

Perf. 12½, 14x11

1951, Apr. 25 **Photo.**

511 A184 25g car rose 1.90 1.40
512 A184 40g ultra 25 20
513 A185 45g purple 7.00 1.40
514 A184 60g green 55 20
515 A184 1.15z claret 1.90 70
516 A186 1.20z gray 1.40 55
Nos. 511-516 (6) 13.00 4.45

1st Congress of Polish Science.

Feliks E. Dzerzhinski — A187

1951, July 5 **Engr.** ***Perf. 12x12½***

517 A187 45g chnt brn 20 15

25th death anniv. of Feliks E. Dzerzhinski, Polish revolutionary, organizer of Russian secret police.

Pres. Boleslaw Bierut — A188

1951, July 22 ***Perf. 12½***

518 A188 45g dk car 55 15
519 A188 60g dp grn 13.00 6.75
520 A188 90g dp bl 1.10 40

7th anniv. of the formation of the Polish People's Republic.

Flag and Sports Emblem A189

Youths Encircling Globe A190

Perf. 12½, 14x11

1951, Sept. 8 **Photo.**

521 A189 45g green 85 50

National Sports Festival, 1951.

Type of 1950 with Frame Omitted Surcharged with New Value in Black

1951, Sept. 1 **Engr.** ***Perf. 12½x11½***

522 A166 45g on 35z org red 20 15

1951, Aug. 5 **Photo.** ***Perf. 12½x11***

523 A190 40g dp ultra 40 20

3rd World Youth Festival, Berlin, Aug. 5-19.

Joseph V. Stalin — A191

Frederic Chopin and Stanislaw Moniuszko — A192

1951, Oct. 30 **Engr.** ***Perf. 12½***

524 A191 45g lake 15 15
525 A191 90g gray blk 30 15
Set value 20

Month of Polish-Soviet friendship, Nov. 1951.

1951, Nov. 15 **Unwmk.**

526 A192 45g gray 20 15
527 A192 90g brnsh red 90 24
Set value 30

Festival of Polish Music, 1951.

Apartment House Construction A193

Coal Mining A194

Design: #529-530, Electrical installation.

1951-52

Inscribed: "Plan 6," etc.

528 A193 30g dl grn 15 15
529 A193 30g gray blk ('52) 15 15
530 A193 45g red ('52) 22 15
531 A194 90g chocolate 38 15
532 A193 1.15z vio brn ('52) 42 15
533 A194 1.20z dp bl ('52) 42 18
Nos. 528-533,B68-B69A (9) 2.99
Set value 1.38

Poland's 6-year plan.

Pawel Finder — A195

Flag, Workman, Mother and Child — A196

Portrait: 1.15z, Malgorzata Fornalska.

1952, Jan. 18

534 A195 90g chocolate 18 15
535 A195 1.15z red org 24 18
Set value 26

Polish Workers Party, 10th anniv.

1952, Mar. 8 ***Perf. 12½x12***

536 A196 1.20z dp car 28 15

Intl. Women's Day. See No. B64.

Gen. Karol Swierczewski-Walter A197

Pres. Boleslaw Bierut A198

1952, Mar. 28 ***Perf. 12½***

537 A197 90g bl gray 28 20

Gen. Karol Swierczewski-Walter (1896-1947). See No. B65.

1952, Apr. 18

538 A198 90g dull green 55 45

60th birth anniv. of Pres. Boleslaw Bierut. See Nos. B66-B67.

Souvenir Sheet

A199

1951, Nov. 15

539 A199 Sheet of 4 17.50 11.50
a. 45g red brown (A173) 1.25 1.00
b. 75g red brown (A173) 1.25 1.00
c. 1.15z red brown (A173) 1.25 1.00
d. 1.20z red brown (A173) 1.25 1.00

Polish Philatelic Association Congress, Warsaw, 1951. Sold for 5 zloty.

Workers with Flag A200

J. I. Kraszewski A201

1952, May 1 **Unwmk.** ***Perf. 12½***

540 A200 75g dp grn 25 15

Labor Day, May 1, 1952. See No. B70.

1952, May

Portraits: 1z, Hugo Kollontaj. 1.15z, Maria Konopnicka.

Various Frames

541 A201 25g brn vio 28 15
542 A201 1z yel grn 30 15
543 A201 1.15z red brn 60 35
Nos. 541-543,B71-B72 (5) 1.80

For unused stamps, more recent issues are valued as never hinged, with the beginning point determined on a country-by-country basis. Notes to show the beginning points are prominently placed in the text.

Nikolai Gogol A202

Gymnast A203

1952, June 5

544 A202 25g dp grn 60 38

100th death anniv. of Nikolai V. Gogol, writer.

1952, June 21 **Photo.** ***Perf. 13***

545 A203 1.15z Runners 1.40 90
546 A203 1.20z shown 60 52

See Nos. B75-B76.

Racing Cyclists — A204

Shipyard Worker and Collier — A205

1952, Apr. 25 ***Perf. 13½***

547 A204 40g blue 90 42

5th Intl. Peace Bicycle Race, Warsaw-Berlin-Prague.

1952, June 28 **Engr.** ***Perf. 12½***

548 A205 90g vio brn 60 32

Shipbuilders' Day, 1952. See Nos. B77-B78.

Concrete Works, Wierzbica — A206

Bugler — A207

1952, June 17

549 A206 3z gray 75 38
550 A206 10z brn red 1.25 25

1952, July 17 ***Perf. 12½x12***

551 A207 90g brown 40 15

Youth Festival, 1952. See Nos. B79-B80.

Celebrating New Constitution A208

Power Plant, Jaworzno A209

1952, July 22 **Photo.** ***Perf. 12½***

552 A208 3z vio & dk brn 30 24

Proclamation of a new constitution. See No. B81.

1952, Aug. 7 **Engr.**

553 A209 1z black 45 25
554 A209 1.50z dp grn 45 15

See No. B82.

Grywald — A210

Parachute Descent — A211

1952, Aug. 18

555 A210 60g dk grn 35 40
556 A210 1z red ("Niedzica") 60 15
a. 1z red ("Niedziga") 2.25 75

See No. B85.

1952, Aug. 23

557 A211 90g deep blue 55 45

Aviation Day, Aug. 23. See Nos. B86-B87.

Avicenna A212

Shipbuilding A213

Portrait: 90g, Victor Hugo.

1952, Sept. 1

558 A212 75g red brn 28 15
559 A212 90g sepia 20 15
Set value 20

Anniversaries of the births of Avicenna (1000th) and Victor Hugo (150th).

1952, Sept. 10

560 A213 5g dp grn 15 15
561 A213 15g red brn 15 15
Set value 20 15

Reconstruction of Gdansk shipyards.

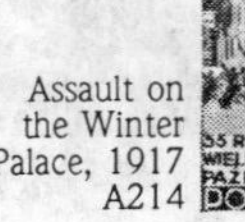

Assault on the Winter Palace, 1917 A214

1952, Nov. 7 *Perf. 12x12½*

562 A214 60g dk brn 50 32

35th anniv. of the Russian Revolution. See No. B92.

Exists imperf. Value $24.

Auto Assembly Plant, Zeran — A215

Dove — A216

1952, Dec. 12 *Perf. 12½*

563 A215 1.15z brown 35 15

See No. B99.

1952, Dec. 12 **Photo.**

564 A216 30g green 50 20
565 A216 60g ultra 1.10 52

Congress of Nations for Peace, Vienna, Dec. 12-19, 1952.

Catalogue values for unused stamps in this section, from this point to the end of the section, are for Never Hinged items.

Soldier with Flag — A217

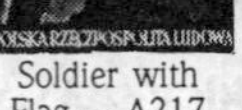

Karl Marx — A218

1953, Feb. 2 **Unwmk.** *Perf. 11*

Flag in Carmine

566 A217 60g ol gray 3.25 85
567 A217 80g bl gray 70 40

10th anniv. of the Battle of Stalingrad.

1953, Mar. 14 *Perf. 12½*

568 A218 60g dl bl 18.00 8.25
569 A218 80g dk brn 90 32

70th death anniv. of Karl Marx.

Cyclists and Arms of Warsaw — A219

Flag and Globe — A220

Arms: No. 571, Berlin. No. 572, Prague.

1953, Apr. 30

570 A219 80g dk brn 1.00 35
571 A219 80g dk grn 1.00 35
572 A219 80g red 12.00 8.75

6th Intl. Peace Bicycle Race, Warsaw-Berlin-Prague.

1953, Apr. 28

573 A220 60g vermilion 3.00 1.25
574 A220 80g carmine 50 15

Labor Day, May 1, 1953.

Boxer — A221

Design: 95g, Boxing match.

1953, May 17

575 A221 40g red brn 1.10 42
576 A221 80g orange 11.00 5.25
577 A221 95g vio brn 1.65 1.50

European Championship Boxing Matches, Warsaw, May 17-24, 1953.

Copernicus Watching Heavens, by Jan Matejko A222

Nicolaus Copernicus — A223

Perf. 12x12½, 12½x12

1953, May 22 **Engr.**

578 A222 20g brown 1.10 35
579 A223 80g dp bl 9.25 4.50

480th birth anniv. of Nicolaus Copernicus, astronomer.

Fishing Boat A224

Old Part of Warsaw A225

Design: 1.35z, Freighter "Czech."

1953, July 15 *Perf. 12½*

580 A224 80g dk grn 1.10 25
581 A224 1.35z dp bl 2.00 90

Issued for Merchant Marine Day.

1953, July 15 **Photo.**

582 A225 20g red brn 18 15
583 A225 2.35z blue 1.75 90

36th anniv. of the proclamation of "People's Poland."

Students of Two Races — A226

Schoolgirl and Dove — A227

Design: 1.35z, Congress badge (similar to AP7).

1953, Aug. 24

584 A226 40g dk brn 25 15
585 A227 1.35z green 60 15
586 A227 1.50z blue 1.40 1.25
Nos. 584-586,C32-C33 (5) 4.35 2.75

3rd World Congress of Students, Warsaw, 1953.

Nurse Feeding Baby — A228

Design: 1.75z, Nurse instructing mother.

1953, Nov. 21

587 A228 80g rose car 6.25 3.00
588 A228 1.75z dp grn 35 15

Poland's Social Health Service.

Mieczyslaw Kalinowski A229

Battle Scene, Polish and Soviet Flags A230

Portrait: 1.75z, Roman Pazinski.

1953, Oct. 10

589 A229 45g brown 3.00 2.00
590 A230 80g brn lake 48 15
591 A229 1.75z ol gray 48 16

10th anniv. of Poland's People's Army.

Jan Kochanowski A231

Courtyard, Wawel Castle A232

Portrait: 1.35z, Mikolaj Rej.

1953, Nov. 10 **Engr.**

592 A231 20g red brn 15 15
593 A232 80g dp plum 30 15
594 A231 1.35z gray blk 1.25 60
Set value 72

Issued for the "Renaissance Year."
For surcharges see Nos. 733-736.

Palace of Culture, Warsaw A233

Designs: 1.75z, Constitution Square. 2z, Old Section, Warsaw.

1953, Nov. 30 *Perf. 12x12½*

595 A233 80g vermilion 6.75 1.10
596 A233 1.75z dp bl 48 38
597 A233 2z vio brn 4.00 2.25

Issued for the reconstruction of Warsaw.

Ice Dancer — A236

Skier — A237

Design: 2.85z, Ice hockey player.

1953, Dec. 31 **Litho.** *Perf. 12½*

602 A236 80g blue 1.25 30
603 A237 95g bl grn 1.75 50
604 A236 2.85z dk red 4.75 2.00

Canceled to Order

The government stamp agency began late in 1951 to sell canceled sets of new issues. Values in the second ("used") column are for these canceled-to-order stamps. Postally used copies are worth more.

Children at Play — A238

Designs: 80g, Girls on the way to school. 1.50z, Two students in class.

1953, Dec. 31 **Photo.**

605 A238 10g violet 15 15
606 A238 80g red brn 60 25
607 A238 1.50z dk grn 4.00 1.65

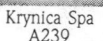

Krynica Spa
A239

Dunajec Canyon, Pieniny Mountains
A240

Designs: 80g, Morskie Oko, Tatra Mts. 2z, Windmill and framework, Ciechocinek.

1953, Dec. 16

608 A239 20g bl & rose brn 15 15
609 A240 80g bl grn & dk vio 1.65 90
610 A240 1.75z ol bis & dk grn 65 15
611 A239 2z brick red & blk 95 15

Electric Passenger Train
A241

Spinning Mill, Worker
A242

Design: 80g, Electric locomotive and cars.

1954, Jan. 26 **Engr.**

612 A241 60g deep bl 6.00 4.00
613 A241 80g red brn 52 18

1954, Mar. 24 **Photo.**

Designs: 40g, Woman letter carrier. 80g, Woman tractor driver.

614 A242 20g dp grn 1.25 45
615 A242 40g dp bl 52 15
616 A242 80g dk brn 35 15

Flags and May Flowers
A243

"Peace" Uniting Three Capitals
A244

1954, Apr. 28

617 A243 40g chocolate 60 22
618 A243 60g dp bl 60 15
619 A243 80g car rose 60 20

Labor Day, May 1, 1954.

1954, Apr. 29 ***Perf. 12½x12***

Design: No. 621, Dove, olive branch and wheel.

620 A244 80g red brn 50 15
621 A244 80g dp bl 52 15
Set value 24

7th Intl. Bicycle Tour, May 2-17, 1954.

A245

Glider and Framed Clouds — A246

1954, Apr. 30 **Engr.** ***Perf. 11½***

622 A245 25g gray 55 20
623 A245 80g brn car 20 15
Set value 26

3rd Trade Union Congress, Warsaw 1954.

1954, May 31 **Photo.** ***Perf. 12½***

Designs: 60g, Glider and flags. 1.35z, Glider and large cloud.

624 A246 45g dk grn 55 15
625 A246 60g purple 2.00 80
626 A246 60g brown 1.10 15
627 A246 1.35z blue 1.40 28

Intl. Glider Championships, Leszno.

Fencing — A247

Handstand on Horizontal Bars — A248

Design: 1z, Relay racers.

1954, July 17

628 A247 25g vio brn 1.40 30
629 A248 60g Prus bl 1.40 15
630 A247 1z vio bl 2.75 45

Javelin Throwers — A249

Studzianki Battle Scene — A250

1954, July 17 ***Perf. 12***

631 A249 60g rose brn & dk red brn 1.25 22
632 A249 1.55z gray & blk 1.10 35

Nos. 628-632 were issued to publicize the second Summer Spartacist Games, 1954.

1954, Aug. 24 ***Perf. 12½***

Design: 1z, Soldier and flag bearer.

633 A250 60g dk grn 1.50 40
634 A250 1z vio bl 6.50 1.25

10th anniversary, Battle of Studzianki.

Railway Signal — A251

Farmer Picking Fruit — A252

Design: 60g, Modern train.

1954, Sept. 9

635 A251 40g dl bl 2.00 70
636 A251 60g black 1.90 32

Issued to publicize Railwaymen's Day.

1954, Sept. 15

637 A252 40g violet 1.25 52
638 A252 60g black 55 15

Month of Polish-Soviet friendship.

View of Elblag — A253

Chopin and Piano — A254

Cities: 45g, Gdansk. 60g, Torun. 1.40z, Malbork. 1.55z, Olsztyn.

1954, Oct. 16 **Engr.** ***Perf. 12x12½***

639 A253 20g dk car, *bl* 1.75 70
640 A253 45g brn, *yel* 16 15
641 A253 60g dk grn, *cit* 20 15
642 A253 1.40z dk bl, *pink* 45 15
643 A253 1.55z dk vio brn, *cr* 65 15
Nos. 639-643 (5) 3.21
Set value 1.05

Pomerania's return to Poland, 500th anniv.
For overprint see No. 866.

1954, Nov. 8 **Photo.** ***Perf. 12½***

644 A254 45g dk brn 50 15
645 A254 60g dk grn 95 15
646 A254 1z dk bl 2.25 55

5th Intl. Competition of Chopin's Music.

Coal Mine — A255

Designs: 20g, Soldier, flag and map. 25g, Steel mill. 40g, Relaxing worker in deck chair. 45g, Building construction. 60g, Tractor in field. 1.15z, Lublin Castle. 1.40z, Books and publications. 1.55z, Loading ship. 2.10z, Attacking tank.

Photo.; Center Engr.

1954-55 ***Perf. 12½x12***

647 A255 10g red brn & choc 1.00 15
648 A255 20g rose & grnsh blk 55 30
649 A255 25g bis & blk 1.25 18
650 A255 40g yel org & choc 40 18
651 A255 45g cl & vio brn 80 18
652 A255 60g emer & red brn 80 22
653 A255 1.15z brt bl grn & sep 80 50
654 A255 1.40z org & choc 7.75 2.25
655 A255 1.55z bl & ind 1.50 65
656 A255 2.10z ultra & ind 2.50 1.40
Nos. 647-656 (10) 17.35 6.01

10th anniversary of "People's Poland."
Issue dates: 25g, 60g, 1955. Others, Dec. 23, 1954.

1954, Oct. 30 **Photo.; Center Litho.**

656A A255 25g bister & blk 2.00 1.40
656B A255 60g emer & red brn 1.10 90

Insurgents Attacking Russians — A256

Designs: 60g, Gen. Tadeusz Kosciuszko and insurgents. 1.40z, Kosciuszko leading attack in Cracow.

1954, Nov. 30 **Engr.** ***Perf. 12½***

657 A256 40g grnsh blk 35 15
658 A256 60g vio brn 52 16
659 A256 1.40z dk gray 1.40 70

160th anniv. of the Insurrection of 1794.

Bison — A257

Animals: 60g, European elk. 1.90z, Chamois. 3z, Beaver.

Engr.; Background Photo.

1954, Dec. 22

660 A257 45g yel grn & blk brn 35 15
661 A257 60g emer & dk brn 35 15
662 A257 1.90z bl & blk brn 50 15
663 A257 3z bl grn & dk brn 1.50 42

Exist imperf. Value, set $3.50.

Liberators Entering Warsaw — A258

Frederic Chopin — A259

Design: 60g, Allegory of freedom (Warsaw Mermaid).

1955, Jan. 17 **Photo.**

664 A258 40g red brn 48 32
665 A258 60g dull bl 1.25 65

Liberation of Warsaw, 10th anniversary.

1955, Feb. 22 **Engr.**

666 A259 40g dk brn 35 15
667 A259 60g indigo 65 20
Set value 26

5th Intl. Competition of Chopin's Music, Feb. 22-Mar. 21.

Brothers in Arms Monument
A260

Sigismund III
A261

Warsaw monuments: 5g, Mermaid. 10g, Feliks E. Dzerzhinski. 40g, Nicolaus Copernicus. 45g, Marie Sklodowska Curie. 60g, Adam Mickiewicz. 1.55z, Jan Kilinski.

1955, May 3 **Unwmk.** ***Perf. 12½***

668 A260 5g dk grn, *grnsh* 15 15
669 A260 10g vio brn, *yel* 15 15
670 A261 15g blk brn, *bluish* 15 15
671 A260 20g dk bl, *pink* 15 15
672 A260 40g vio, *vio* 35 15
673 A261 45g vio brn, *cr* 48 22
674 A260 60g dk bl, *gray* 35 15
675 A261 1.55z sl bl, *grysh* 95 32
Set value 2.30 90

See Nos. 737-739.

Palace of Culture and Flags of Poland and USSR — A262

Design: 60g, Monument.

Perf. 12½x12, 11

1955, Apr. 21 **Photo.**

676 A262 40g rose red 15 15
677 A262 40g lt brn 45 28
678 A262 60g Prus bl 20 15
679 A262 60g dk ol brn 20 15
Set value 48

10th anniv. of the Polish-USSR treaty of friendship.

Arms and Bicycle Wheels
A263

Poznan Town Hall and Fair Emblem
A264

Design: 60g, Three doves above road.

1955, Apr. 25 *Perf. 12*

680 A263 40g chocolate	35	15
681 A263 60g ultra	22	15
Set value		20

8th Intl. Peace Bicycle Race, Prague-Berlin-Warsaw.

1955, June 10 Photo. *Perf. 12½*

682 A264 40g brt ultra	30	15
683 A264 60g dl red	15	15
Set value		20

24th Intl. Fair at Poznan, July 3-24, 1955.

"Laikonik" Carnival Costume — A265

A265a

1955, June 16 Typo. *Perf. 12*
Multicolored Centers

684 A265 20g emer & hn	30	22
685 A265a 40g brt org & lil	42	15
686 A265 60g bl & car	1.25	30

Cracow Celebration Days.

Pansies — A266

Designs: 40g, 60g, (No. 690), Dove and Tower of Palace of Science and Culture. 45g, Pansies. 60g, (No. 691), 1z, "Peace" (POKOJ) and Warsaw Mermaid.

1955, July 13 Litho. *Perf. 12*

687 A266 25g vio brn, org & car	15	15
688 A266 40g gray bl & gray blk	15	15
689 A266 45g brn lake, yel & car	30	15
690 A266 60g sep & org	24	15
691 A266 60g ultra & lt bl	24	15
692 A266 1z pur & lt bl	75	50
Nos. 687-692 (6)	1.83	
Set value		1.00

5th World Festival of Youth, Warsaw, July 31-Aug. 14, 1955.
Exist imperf. Value, set $3.

Motorcyclists
A267

Stalin Palace of Culture and Science, Warsaw
A268

1955, July 20 Photo. *Perf. 12½*

693 A267 40g chocolate	30	20
694 A267 60g dk grn	24	15
Set value		26

13th Intl. Motorcycle Race in the Tatra Mountains, Aug. 7-9, 1955.

1955, July 21

695 A268 60g ultra	15	15
696 A268 60g gray	15	15
697 A268 75g bl grn	35	15
698 A268 75g brown	35	15
Set value		44

Polish National Day, July 22, 1955. Sheets contain alternating copies of the 60g values or the 75g values respectively.

Athletes
A269

Stadium
A270

Designs: 40g, Hammer throwing. 1z, Basketball. 1.35z, Sculling. 1.55z, Swimming.

1955, July 27 Unwmk. *Perf. 12½*

699 A269 20g chocolate	15	15
700 A269 40g plum	15	15
701 A270 60g dl bl	24	15
702 A269 1z org ver	45	15
703 A269 1.35z dl vio	60	15
704 A269 1.55z pck grn	1.00	50
Nos. 699-704 (6)	2.59	
Set value		95

2nd International Youth Games, 1955. Exist imperf. Value, set $3.50.

Town Hall, Szczecin (Stettin) — A271

Rebels with Flag — A272

Designs: 40g, Cathedral, Wroclaw (Breslau) 60g, Town Hall, Zielona Gora (Grunberg). 95g, Town Hall, Opole (Oppeln).

1955, Sept. 22 Engr. *Perf. 11½*

705 A271 25g dl grn	15	15
706 A271 40g red brn	16	15
707 A271 60g vio bl	40	15
708 A271 95g dk gray	60	24
Set value		50

10th anniv. of the acquisition of Western Polish Territories.

1955, Sept. 30 Photo. *Perf. 12x12½*

709 A272 40g dk brn	25	20
710 A272 60g dk car rose	22	15

Revolution of 1905, 50th anniversary.

Adam Mickiewicz
A273

Mickiewicz Monument, Paris — A274

Designs: 60g, Death mask. 95g, Statue, Warsaw.

1955, Oct. 10 *Perf. 12x12½, 12½*

711 A273 20g dk brn	15	15
712 A274 40g brn org & dk brn	18	15
713 A274 60g grn & brn	25	15
714 A274 95g brn red & blk	1.50	50
Set value		74

Death centenary of Adam Mickiewicz, poet, and to publicize the celebration of Mickiewicz year.

Teacher and Child — A275

Rook and Hands — A276

Design: 60g, Flame and open book.

Perf. 12½x13

1955, Oct. 21 Unwmk.

715 A275 40g brown	1.50	25
716 A275 60g ultra	2.50	85

50th anniv. of the Polish Teachers' Trade Union.

1956, Feb. 9 *Perf. 12½*

Design: 60g, Chess knight and hands.

717 A276 40g dk red	1.90	85
718 A276 60g blue	1.50	15

First World Chess Championship of the Deaf and Dumb, Feb. 9-23.

Captain and S. S. Kilinski
A277

Designs: 10g, Sailor and barges. 20g, Dock worker and S. S. Pokoj. 45g, Shipyard and worker. 60g, Fisherman, S. S. Chopin and trawlers.

1956, Mar. 16 Engr. *Perf. 12x12½*

719 A277 5g green	15	15
720 A277 10g car lake	15	15
721 A277 20g dp ultra	15	15
722 A277 45g rose brn	55	20
723 A277 60g vio bl	45	15
Set value	1.20	40

Snowflake and Ice Skates — A278

Cyclist — A279

Designs: 40g, Snowflake and Ice Hockey sticks. 60g, Snowflake and Skis.

1956, Mar. 7 Photo. *Perf. 12½*

724 A278 20g brt ultra & blk	3.50	1.50
725 A278 40g brt grn & vio bl	52	15
726 A278 60g lil & lake	52	15

XI World Students Winter Sport Championship, Mar. 7-13.

1956, Apr. 25

727 A279 40g dk bl	1.25	40
728 A279 60g dk grn	20	15

9th Intl. Peace Bicycle Race, Warsaw-Berlin-Prague, May 1-15.

Zakopane Mountains and Shelter — A280

Designs: 40g, Map, compass and knapsack. 60g, Map of Poland and canoe. 1.15z, Skis and mountains.

1956, May 25

729 A280 30g dk grn	25	15
730 A280 40g lt red brn	25	15
731 A280 60g blue	95	50
732 A280 1.15z dl pur	45	15
Set value		75

Polish Tourist industry.

No. 593 Surcharged with New Values

1956, July 6 Engr. *Perf. 12½*

733 A232 10g on 80g dp plum	18	15
734 A232 40g on 80g dp plum	15	15
735 A232 60g on 80g dp plum	28	15
736 A232 1.35z on 80g dp plum	70	32
Set value		55

The size and type of surcharge and obliteration of old value differ for each denomination.

Type of 1955

Warsaw Monuments: 30g, Ghetto Monument. 40g, John III Sobieski. 1.55z, Prince Joseph Poniatowski.

1956, July 10

737 A260 30g black	15	15
738 A260 40g red brn, *grnsh*	30	16
739 A260 1.55z vio brn, *pnksh*	42	16
Set value		36

No. 737 measures 22½x28mm, instead of 21x27mm.

Polish and Russian Dancers
A281

Design: 60g, Open book and cogwheels.

1956, Sept. 14 Litho. *Perf. 12*

740 A281 40g brn red & brn	30	20
741 A281 60g bis & red	15	15
Set value		28

Polish-Soviet Friendship month.

Ludwiga Warzynska and Children
A282

Bee on Clover and Beehive
A283

1956, Sept. 17 Photo. *Perf. 12½*

742 A282 40g dl red brn	70	20
743 A282 60g blue	32	15
Set value		26

Issued in honor of a heroic school teacher who saved three children from a burning house.

1956, Oct. 30 Litho. Unwmk.

Design: 60g, Father Jan Dzierzon.

744 A283	40g	org yel & brn	75	25
745 A283	60g	yel & brn	22	15
		Set value		32

50th death anniv. of Father Jan Dzierzon, the inventor of the modernized beehive.

"Lady with the Ermine" by Leonardo da Vinci — A284

Designs: 40g, Niobe. 60g, Madonna by Veit Stoss.

1956 Engr. *Perf. 11½x11*

746 A284	40g	dk grn	2.50	75
747 A284	60g	dk vio	80	24
748 A284	1.55z	chocolate	1.65	24

Intl. Museum Week (UNESCO), Oct. 8-14.

Fencer A285

Designs: 20g, Boxer. 25g, Sculling. 40g, Steeplechase racer. 60g, Javelin thrower. No. 755, Woman gymnast. No. 756, Woman broad jumper.

1956 Engr. *Perf. 11½*

750 A285	10g	slate & chnt	15	15
751 A285	20g	lt brn & dl vio	24	15
a.		Center inverted		
752 A285	25g	lt bl & blk	35	15
753 A285	40g	brt bl grn & redsh brn	28	15
754 A285	60g	rose car & ol brn	35	15
755 A285	1.55z	lt vio & sep	1.40	1.00
756 A285	1.55z	org & chnt	90	22
		Nos. 750-756 (7)	3.67	
		Set value		1.70

16th Olympic Games, Melbourne, Nov. 22-Dec. 8.

15th Century Mailman — A286

Lithographed and Engraved

1956, Nov. 30 Unwmk. *Perf. 12½*

757 A286	60g	lt bl & blk	1.10	80

Reopening of the Postal Museum in Wroclaw.

Skier and Snowflake A287

Ski Jumper and Snowflake A288

Design: 1z, Skier in right corner.

1957, Jan. 18 Photo. *Perf. 12½*

758 A287	40g	blue	30	15
759 A288	60g	dk grn	30	15
760 A287	1z	purple	55	30
		Set value		46

50 years of skiing in Poland.

Globe and Tree — A289

UN Emblem — A290

UN Building, NY — A291

1957, Feb. 26 Photo. *Perf. 12*

761 A289	5g	mag & brt grnsh bl	30	20
762 A290	15g	bl & gray	38	20
763 A291	40g	brt bl grn & gray	70	45

Issued in honor of the United Nations.
Exist imperf. Value, set $4.25.
An imperf. souvenir sheet exists, containing a 1.50z stamp in a redrawn design similar to A291. The stamp is blue and bright bluish green Value, $25 unused, $14 canceled.

Skier — A292

Sword, Foil and Saber on World Map — A293

1957, Mar. 22 *Perf. 12½*

764 A292	60g	blue	48	22
765 A292	60g	brown	65	28

12th anniv. of the death of the skiers Bronislaw Czech and Hanna Marusarzowna.

1957, Apr. 20 Unwmk. *Perf. 12½*

Designs: No. 767, Fencer facing right. No. 768, Fencer facing left.

766 A293	40g	dp plum	55	32
767 A293	60g	carmine	38	15
768 A293	60g	ultra	38	15
a.		Pair, Nos. 767-768	1.25	50
		Set value		45

World Youth Fencing Championships, Warsaw.
No. 768a has continuous design.

Dr. Sebastian Petrycy A294

Bicycle Wheel and Carnation A295

Doctors' Portraits: 20g Wojciech Oczko. 40g, Jedrzej Sniadecki. 60g, Tytus Chalubinski. 1z, Wladyslaw Bieganski. 1.35z, Jozef Dietl. 2.50z, Benedykt Dybowski. 3z, Henryk Jordan.

Portraits Engr., Inscriptions Typo.

1957 *Perf. 11½*

769 A294	10g	sep & ultra	15	15
770 A294	20g	emer & claret	15	15
771 A294	40g	gray & org red	15	15
772 A294	60g	bl & pale brn	35	16
773 A294	1z	org & dk bl	15	15
774 A294	1.35z	gray brn & grn	20	15
775 A294	2.50z	dl vio & lil rose	42	15
776 A294	3z	vio & ol brn	50	15
		Set value	1.75	55

1957, May 4 Photo. *Perf. 12½*

777 A295	60g	shown	55	20
778 A295	1.50z	Cyclist	18	15

10th Intl. Peace Bicycle Race, Warsaw-Berlin-Prague.

Poznan Fair Emblem A296

Turk's Cap A297

1957, June 8 Litho. Unwmk.

779 A296	60g	ultra	22	15
780 A296	2.50z	lt bl grn	30	15
		Set value		20

Issued to publicize the 26th Fair at Poznan.

1957, Aug. 12 Photo. *Perf. 12*

Flowers: No. 782, Carline Thistle. No. 783, Sea Holly. No. 784, Edelweiss. No. 785, Lady's-slipper.

781 A297	60g	bl grn & cl	18	15
782 A297	60g	gray, grn & yel	18	15
783 A297	60g	lt bl & grn	18	15
784 A297	60g	gray & yel grn	18	15
785 A297	60g	lt grn, mar & yel	75	25
		Nos. 781-785 (5)	1.47	
		Set value		52

Fire Fighter A298

Town Hall, Leipzig and Congress Emblem A299

Designs: 60g, Child and flames. 2.50z, Grain and flames.

1957, Sept. 11 *Perf. 12*

786 A298	40g	blk & red	15	15
787 A298	60g	dk grn & org red	15	15
788 A298	2.50z	vio & red	42	20
		Set value	55	30

Intl. Fire Brigade Conf., Warsaw.

1957, Sept. 25 Photo. *Perf. 12½*

789 A299	60g	violet	15	15

4th Intl. Trade Union Congress, Leipzig, Oct. 4-15.

The lack of a value for a listed item does not necessarily indicate rarity.

"Girl Writing Letter" by Fragonard — A300

Karol Libelt — A301

1957, Oct. 9 *Perf. 12*

790 A300	2.50z	dk bl grn	45	15

Issued for Stamp Day, Oct. 9.

1957, Nov. 15 Photo. *Perf. 12½*

791 A301	60g	car lake	16	15

Centenary of the Poznan Scientific Society and to honor Karol Libelt, politician and philosopher.

Broken Chain and Flag — A302

Jan A. Komensky (Comenius) — A303

Design: 2.50z, Lenin Statue, Poronin.

1957, Nov. 7

792 A302	60g	brt bl & red	15	15
793 A302	2.50z	blk & red brn	25	15
		Set value		20

40th anniv. of the Russian Revolution.

1957, Dec. 11 *Perf. 12*

794 A303	2.50z	brt car	25	15

300th anniv. of the publication of "Didactica Opera Omnia."

Henri Wieniawski A304

Andrzej Strug A305

1957, Dec. 2 *Perf. 12½*

795 A304	2.50z	blue	25	15

3rd Wieniawski Violin Competition in Poznan.

1957, Dec. 16 Unwmk. *Perf. 12½*

796 A305	2.50z	brown	18	15

20th death anniv. of Andrzej Strug, novelist.

Joseph Conrad and "Torrens" A306

1957, Dec. 30 Engr. *Perf. 12x12½*

797 A306	60g	brn, *grnsh*	15	15
798 A306	2.50z	dk bl, *pink*	42	18
		Set value		26

Birth cent. of Joseph Conrad, Polish-born English writer.

Postilion and Stylized Plane — A307

Town Hall at Biecz — A308

Designs: 40g, Tomb of Prosper Prowano, globe with plane and satellite. 60g, St. Mary's Church, Cracow, mail coach and plane. 95g, Mail coach and postal bus. 2.10z, Medieval postman and train. 3.40z, Medieval galleon and modern ships.

1958 Litho. *Perf. 12½*

799	A307	40g lt bl & vio brn	15	15
800	A307	60g pale vio & blk	15	15
801	A307	95g lem & vio	15	15
802	A307	2.10z gray & ultra	42	32
803	A307	2.50z brt bl & blk	30	15
804	A307	3.40z aqua & mar	30	15
		Set value	1.18	62

400th anniversary of the Polish posts. Imperfs. exist of all but No. 803.

1958, Mar. 29 Engr. *Perf. 12½*

Town Halls: 40g, Wroclaw. 60g, Tarnow, horiz. 2.10z, Danzig. 2.50z, Zamosc.

805	A308	20g green	15	15
806	A308	40g brown	15	15
807	A308	60g dk bl	15	15
808	A308	2.10z rose lake	24	15
809	A308	2.50z violet	35	15
		Set value	75	35

Giant Pike Perch — A309

Fishes: 60g, Salmon, vert. 2.10z, Pike, vert. 2.50z, Trout, vert. 6.40z, Grayling.

1958, Apr. 22 Photo. *Perf. 12*

810	A309	40g bl, blk, grn & yel	15	15
811	A309	60g yel grn, dk grn & bl	15	15
812	A309	2.10z dk bl, grn & yel	28	15
813	A309	2.50z pur, blk & yel grn	1.10	24
814	A309	6.40z bl grn, brn & red	65	30
		Nos. 810-814 (5)	2.33	
		Set value		78

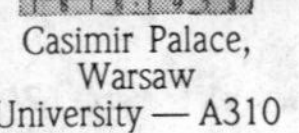

Casimir Palace, Warsaw University — A310

Stylized Glider and Cloud — A311

1958, May 14 Unwmk. *Perf. 12½*

815	A310	2.50z vio bl	20	15

140th anniv. of the University of Warsaw.

1958, June 14 Litho.

Design: 2.50z, Design reversed.

816	A311	60g gray bl & blk	15	15
817	A311	2.50z gray & blk	35	15
		Set value		20

7th Intl. Glider Competitions.

Fair Emblem A312

Armed Postman and Mail Box A313

1958, June 9

818	A312	2.50z blk & rose	20	15

27th Fair at Poznan.

1958, Sept. 1 Engr. *Perf. 11*

819	A313	60g dk bl	15	15

19th anniversary of the defense of the Polish post office at Danzig (Gdansk). Inscribed: "You were the first."

Letter, Quill and Postmark A314

Polar Bear A315

1958, Oct. 9 Litho.

820	A314	60g blk, bl grn & ver	42	25

Issued for Stamp Day. Exists imperf.

1958, Sept. 30 Photo. *Perf. 12½x12*

Design: 2.50z, Rocket and Sputnik.

821	A315	60g black	18	15
822	A315	2.50z dk bl	55	15
		Set value		20

Intl. Geophysical Year.

Partisan's Cross — A316

Designs: 60g, Virtuti Militari Cross. 2.50z, Grunwald Cross.

1958, Oct. 10 *Perf. 11*

823	A316	40g blk, grn & ocher	15	15
824	A316	60g blk, bl & yel	15	15
825	A316	2.50z multi	60	20
		Set value		34

Polish People's Army, 15th anniv.

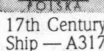

17th Century Ship — A317

UNESCO Building, Paris — A318

Design: 2.50z, Polish immigrants.

1958, Oct. 29 *Perf. 11*

826	A317	60g dk sl grn	15	15
827	A317	2.50z dk car rose	25	15
		Set value		18

350th anniversary of the arrival of the first Polish immigrants in America.

1958, Nov. 3 Unwmk.

828	A318	2.50z yel grn & blk	32	15

Opening of UNESCO Headquarters in Paris, Nov. 3.

Stagecoach — A319

Perf. 12½
1958, Oct. 26 Engr. Wmk. 326

829	A319	2.50z slate, *buff*	80	48
a.		Souvenir sheet of 6	6.75	6.75

Philatelic exhibition in honor of the 400th anniv. of the Polish post, Warsaw, Oct. 25-Nov. 10.

Souvenir Sheet
1958, Dec. 12 Unwmk. *Imperf.*
Printed on Silk

830	A319	50z dark blue	10.00	8.75

400th anniversary of the Polish posts.

Stanislaw Wyspianski A320

Kneeling Figure A321

Portrait: 2.50z, Stanislaw Moniuszko.

1958, Nov. 25 Engr. *Perf. 12½*

831	A320	60g dk vio	15	15
832	A320	2.50z dk sl grn	30	15
		Set value		20

Stanislaw Wyspianski, painter and poet, and Stanislaw Moniuszko, composer.

1958, Dec. 10 Litho.

833	A321	2.50z lt brn & red brn	28	15

Signing of the Universal Declaration of Human Rights, 10th anniv.

Red Flag — A322

Sailing — A323

1958, Dec. 16 Photo.

834	A322	60g plum & red	15	15

40th anniv. of the Communist Party of Poland.

1959, Jan. 3

Sports: 60g, Girl archer. 95g, Soccer. 2z, Horsemanship.

835	A323	40g lt bl & vio bl	20	15
836	A323	60g sal & brn vio	18	15
837	A323	95g grn & brn vio	30	20
838	A323	2z dp bl & lt grn	28	20

Hand at Wheel — A324

Wheat, Hammer and Flag — A325

1959, Mar. 10 Wmk. 326 *Perf. 12½*

839	A324	40gr shown	15	15
840	A325	60gr shown	15	15
841	A324	1.55z Factory	35	15
		Set value	50	24

3rd Workers Congress.

Amanita Phalloides — A326

Designs: Various mushrooms.

1959, May 8 Photo. *Perf. 11½*

842	A326	20g yel, grn & brn	1.25	55
843	A326	30g multi	18	15
844	A326	40g multi	55	15
845	A326	60g yel grn, brn & ocher	55	15
846	A326	1z multi	35	15
847	A326	2.50z bl, grn & brn	70	15
848	A326	3.40z multi	95	38
849	A326	5.60z dl yel, brn & grn	2.75	1.50
		Nos. 842-849 (8)	7.28	3.18

"Storks," by Jozef Chelmonski A327

Paintings by Polish Artists: 60g, Mother and Child, Stanislaw Wyspianski, vert. 1z, Mme. de Romanet, Henryk Rodakowski, vert. 1.50z, Old Man and Death, Jacek Malczewski, vert. 6.40z, River Scene, Aleksander Gierymski.

1959 Engr. *Perf. 12, 12½x12*

850	A327	40g gray grn	15	15
851	A327	60g dl pur	20	15
852	A327	1z int blk	25	15
853	A327	1.50z brown	40	22
854	A327	6.40z blue	1.65	55
		Nos. 850-854 (5)	2.65	
		Set value		1.05

Nos. 850 and 854 measure 36x28mm; Nos. 851 and 853, 28x36mm; No. 852, 28x37mm.

Miner and Globe — A328

Map of Poland and Symbol of Agriculture — A329

1959, July 1 Litho.

855	A328	2.50z multi	30	15

3rd Miners' Conf., Katowice, July 1959.

Perf. 12x12½
1959, July 21 Wmk. 326

Map of Poland and: 60g, Symbol of industry. 1.50z, Symbol of art and science.

856	A329	40g blk, bl & grn	15	15
857	A329	60g blk & ver	15	15
858	A329	1.50z blk & bl	15	15
		Set value	32	20

15 years of the Peoples' Republic of Poland.

Lazarus Ludwig Zamenhof
A330

Map of Austria and Flower
A331

Design: 1.50z, Star, globe and flag.

1959, July 24 *Perf. 12½*

859 A330 60g blk & grn, *ol* 15 15
860 A330 1.50z ultra, grn & red, *gray* 42 15
Set value 20

Centenary of the birth of Lazarus Ludwig Zamenhof, author of Esperanto, and in conjunction with the Esperanto Congress in Warsaw.

1959, July 27 **Litho.**

861 A331 60g sep, red & grn, *yel* 15 15
862 A331 2.50z bl, red, & grn, *gray* 45 20
Set value 26

7th World Youth Festival, Vienna, July 26-Aug. 14.

Symbolic Plane — A332

1959, Aug. 24 **Wmk. 326** *Perf. 12½*

863 A332 60g vio bl, grnsh bl & blk 15 15

30th anniv. of LOT, the Polish airline.

Sejm (Parliament) Building
A333

1959, Aug. 27 **Photo.** *Perf. 12x12½*

864 A333 60g lt grn, blk & red 15 15
865 A333 2.50z vio gray, blk & red 35 15
Set value 42 22

48th Interparliamentary Conf., Warsaw.

No. 640 Overprinted in Blue: "BALPEX I - GDANSK 1959"

1959, Aug. 30 **Engr.** **Unwmk.**

866 A253 45g brn, *yel* 50 28

Intl. Phil. Exhib. of Baltic States at Gdansk.

Stylized Dove and Globe — A334

Red Cross Nurse — A335

Perf. 12½

1959, Sept. 1 **Photo.** **Wmk. 326**

867 A334 60g bl & gray 15 15

World Peace Movement, 10th anniv.

1959, Sept. 21 **Litho.** *Perf. 12½*

Designs: 60g, Nurse. 2.50z, Henri Dunant.

Size: 21x26mm

868 A335 40g red, lt grn & blk 15 15
869 A335 60g bis brn, brn & red 15 15

Perf. 11

Size: 23x23mm

870 A335 2.50z red, pink & blk 45 32
Set value 62 48

40th anniversary of the Polish Red Cross and the centenary of the Red Cross.

Polish-Chinese Friendship Society Emblem — A336

Flower Made of Stamps — A337

Wmk. 326

1959, Sept. 28 **Litho.** *Perf. 11*

871 A336 60g multi 30 16
872 A336 2.50z multi 20 15

Polish-Chinese friendship.

1959, Oct. 9 *Perf. 12½*

873 A337 60g lt grnsh bl, grn & red 15 15
874 A337 2.50z red, grn & vio 28 16
Set value 24

Issued for Stamp Day, 1959.

Sputnik 3 — A338

Designs: 60g, Rocket. 2.50z, Earth, moon and Sputnik 2.

1959, Nov. 7 **Photo.** **Wmk. 326**

875 A338 40g Prus bl & gray 22 15
876 A338 60g mar & blk 32 20
877 A338 2.50z grn & dk bl 90 48

42nd anniv. of the Russian Revolution and the landing of the Soviet moon rocket.
Exist imperf. Value, set $3.

Child Doing Homework
A339

Charles Darwin
A340

Design: 60g, Three children leaving school.

Lithographed and Engraved

1959, Nov. 14 *Perf. 11½*

878 A339 40g grn & dk brn 15 15
879 A339 60g bl & red 15 15
Set value 16

"1,000 Schools" campaign for the 1,000th anniversary of Poland.

1959, Dec. 10 **Engr.** *Perf. 11*

Scientists: 10g, Dmitri I. Mendeleev. 60g, Albert Einstein. 1.50z, Louis Pasteur. 1.55z, Isaac Newton. 2.50z, Nicolaus Copernicus.

880 A340 20g dk bl 15 15
881 A340 40g ol gray 15 15
882 A340 60g claret 15 15
883 A340 1.50g dk vio brn 15 15
884 A340 1.55z dk grn 40 15
885 A340 2.50z violet 90 48
Set value 1.65 80

Man from Rzeszow — A341

Woman from Rzeszow — A342

Regional Costumes: 40g, Cracow. 60g, Kurpiow. 1z, Silesia. 2z, Lowicz. 2.50z, Mountain people. 3.10z, Kujawy. 3.40z, Lublin. 5.60z, Szamotuli. 6.50z, Lubuski.

Engraved and Photogravure

1959-60 **Wmk. 326** *Perf. 12, Imperf.*

886 A341 20g sl grn & blk 15 15
887 A342 20g sl grn & blk 15 15
888 A341 40g lt bl & rose car ('60) 15 15
889 A342 40g rose car & bl ('60) 15 15
890 A341 60g blk & pink 15 15
891 A342 60g blk & pink 15 15
892 A341 1z grnsh red & dk red 15 15
893 A342 1z grnsh bl & dk red 15 15
894 A341 2z yel & ultra ('60) 18 15
895 A342 2z yel & ultra ('60) 18 15
896 A341 2.50z grn & rose lil 26 18
897 A342 2.50z grn & rose lil 26 18
898 A341 3.10z yel grn & sl grn ('60) 32 25
899 A342 3.10z yel grn & sl grn ('60) 32 25
900 A341 3.40z gray grn & brn ('60) 40 28
901 A342 3.40z gray grn & brn ('60) 40 28
902 A341 5.60z yel grn & gray bl 95 52
903 A342 5.60z yel grn & gray bl 95 52
904 A341 6.50z vio & gray grn ('60) 95 52
905 A342 6.50z vio & gray grn ('60) 95 52
Nos. 886-905 (20) 7.32
Set value 4.25

The male and female costume stamps of each denomination were printed se-tenant in sheets of 56.

Piano — A343

Frederic Chopin — A344

Design: 1.50z, Musical note and manuscript.

1960, Feb. 22 **Litho.** *Perf. 12*

906 A343 60g brt vio & blk 35 32
907 A343 1.50z blk, gray & red 55 22

Perf. 12½x12

Engr.

908 A344 2.50z black 2.00 90

150th anniversary of the birth of Frederic Chopin and to publicize the Chopin music competition.

Stamp of 1860 — A345

Designs: 60g, Ski meet stamp of 1939. 1.35z, Design from 1860 issue. 1.55z, 1945 liberation stamp. 2.50z, 1957 stamp day stamp.

Litho. (40g, 1.35z); Litho. and Photo.

Perf. 11½x11

1960, Mar. 21 **Wmk. 326**

909 A345 40g multi 15 15
910 A345 60g vio, ultra & blk 28 15
911 A345 1.35z gray, red & bl 65 35
912 A345 1.55z grn, car & blk 65 20
913 A345 2.50z ap grn, dk grn & blk 85 35
Nos. 909-913 (5) 2.58 1.20

Centenary of Polish stamps. Nos. 909-913 were also issued in sheets of 4. Value, $275.
For overprint see No. 934.

Discus Thrower, Amsterdam 1928
A346

Polish Olympic Victories: No. 915, Runner. No. 916, Bicyclist. No. 917, Steeplechase. No. 918, Trumpeters. No. 919, Boxers. No. 920, Olympic flame. No. 921 Woman jumper.

Lithographed and Embossed

Perf. 12x12½

1960, June 15 **Unwmk.**

914 A346 60g bl & blk 15 15
915 A346 60g car rose & blk 15 15
916 A346 60g vio & blk 15 15
917 A346 60g bl grn & blk 15 15
918 A346 2.50z ultra & blk 45 25
919 A346 2.50z chnt & blk 45 25
920 A346 2.50z red & blk 45 25
921 A346 2.50z emer & blk 45 25
Nos. 914-921 (8) 2.40
Set value 1.40

17th Olympic Games, Rome, Aug. 25-Sept. 11.
Nos. 914-917 and Nos. 918-921 are printed se-tenant in the sheets. The oval lines of each set of 4 stamps form the stadium oval.
Nos. 914-921 exist imperf. Value, set $4.

Tomb of King Wladyslaw II Jagiello — A347

Battle of Grunwald by Jan Matejko — A348

Design: 90g, Detail from Grunwald monument.

Perf. 11x11½

1960 **Wmk. 326** **Engr.**

922 A347 60g vio brn 30 15
923 A347 90g ol gray 60 30

Size: 78x37mm

924 A348 2.50z dk gray 1.75 1.00

550th anniversary, Battle of Grunwald.

The Annunciation
A349

Carvings by Veit Stoss, St. Mary's Church, Cracow: 30g, Nativity. 40g, Adoration of the Kings. 60g, The Resurrection. 2.50z, The Ascension. 5.60z, Descent of the Holy Ghost. 10z, The Assumption of the Virgin, vert.

1960 **Wmk. 326** **Engr.** *Perf. 12*

925 A349 20g Prus bl 20 15
926 A349 30g lt red brn 15 15
927 A349 40g violet 22 15
928 A349 60g dl grn 22 15
929 A349 2.50z rose lake 70 22
930 A349 5.60z dk brn 4.50 2.75
Nos. 925-930 (6) 5.99 3.57

Miniature Sheet

Imperf

931 A349 10z black 4.50 4.00

No. 931 contains one vertical stamp which measures 72x95mm.

A350

A351

1960, Sept. 26 *Perf. 12½*

932	A350	2.50z black	25	15

Birth cent. of Ignacy Jan Paderewski, statesman and musician.

Engr. & Photo.

1960, Sept. 14 *Perf. 11*

Lukasiewicz and kerosene lamp.

933	A351	60g citron & blk	15	15

5th Pharmaceutical Congress; Ignacy Lukasiewicz, chemist-pharmacist.

No. 909 Overprinted: "DZIEN ZNACZKA 1960"

1960 Litho. *Perf. 11½x11*

934	A345	40g multi	75	55

Issued for Stamp Day, 1960.

Great Bustard A352

Birds: 20g, Raven. 30g, Great cormorant. 40g, Black stork. 50g, Eagle owl. 60g, White-tailed sea eagle. 75g, Golden eagle. 90g, Short-toed eagle. 2.50z, Rock thrush. 4z, European kingfisher. 5.60z, Wall creeper. 6.50z, European roller.

1960 Unwmk. Photo. *Perf. 11½*

Birds in Natural Colors

935	A352	10g gray & blk	15	15
936	A352	20g gray & blk	15	15
937	A352	30g gray & blk	15	15
938	A352	40g gray & blk	16	15
939	A352	50g pale grn & blk	22	15
940	A352	60g pale grn & blk	30	15
941	A352	75g pale grn & blk	30	15
942	A352	90g pale grn & blk	42	16
943	A352	2.50z pale ol gray & blk	2.75	1.65
944	A352	4z pale ol gray & blk	1.75	60
945	A352	5.60z pale ol gray & blk	3.00	65
946	A352	6.50z pale ol gray & blk	4.75	2.00
		Nos. 935-946 (12)	14.10	6.11

Gniezno A353

Front Page of "Merkuriusz" A354

Historic Towns: 10g, Cracow. 20g, Warsaw. 40g, Poznan. 50g, Plock. 60g, Kalisz. No. 952A, Tczew. 80g, Frombork. 90g, Torun. 95g, Puck (ships). 1z, Slupsk. 1.15z, Gdansk (Danzig). 1.35z, Wroclaw. 1.50z, Szczecin. 1.55z, Opole. 2z, Kolobrzeg. 2.10z, Legnica. 2.50z, Katowice. 3.10z, Lodz. 5.60z, Walbrzych.

1960-61 Engr. *Perf. 11½, 13x12½*

947	A353	5g red brn	15	15
948	A353	10g green	15	15
949	A353	20g dk brn	15	15
950	A353	40g vermilion	15	15
951	A353	50g violet	15	15
952	A353	60g rose claret	15	15
952A	A353	60g lt ultra ('61)	15	15
953	A353	80g blue	15	15
954	A353	90g brown ('61)	15	15
955	A353	95g ol gray	15	15

Engraved and Lithographed

956	A353	1z org & gray	15	15
957	A353	1.15z sl grn & sal	15	15
958	A353	1.35z lil rose & lt grn	15	15
959	A353	1.50z sep & pale grn	15	15
960	A353	1.55z car lake & buff	15	15
961	A353	2z dk bl & pink	15	15
962	A353	2.10z sep & yel	15	15
963	A353	2.50z dl vio & pale grn	20	15
964	A353	3.10z ver & gray	22	15
965	A353	5.60z sl grn & lt grn	55	15
		Set value	2.70	1.40

Lithographed and Embossed

1961 Wmk. 326 *Perf. 12*

Newspapers: 60g, "Proletaryat," first issue, Sept. 15, 1883. 2.50z, "Rzeczpospolita," first issue, July 23, 1944.

966	A354	40g blk, ultra & emer	45	20
967	A354	60g blk, org brn & yel	45	20
968	A354	2.50z blk, vio & bl	2.75	2.25

300th anniv. of the Polish newspaper Merkuriusz.

Ice Hockey A355

Part of Cogwheel A356

Sports: 60g, Ski jump. 1z, Soldiers on skis. 1.50z, Slalom.

1961, Feb. 1 Litho. Wmk. 326

969	A355	40g lt vio, blk & yel	35	15
970	A355	60g lt ultra, blk & car	1.00	50
971	A355	1z lt bl, ol & red	4.75	2.00
972	A355	1.50z grnsh bl, blk & yel	85	32

1st Winter Spartacist Games of Friendly Armies.

1961, Feb. 11 *Perf. 12½*

973	A356	60g red & blk	15	15

Fourth Congress of Polish Engineers.

Maj. Yuri A. Gagarin A357

Design: 60g, Globe and path of rocket.

1961, Apr. 27 Photo. *Perf. 12*

974	A357	40g dk red & blk	75	32
975	A357	60g ultra, blk & car	45	20

1st man in space, Yuri A. Gagarin, Apr. 12, 1961.

Emblem of Poznan Fair A358

1961, May 25 Litho. *Perf. 12½x12*

977	A358	40g brt bl, blk & red org	15	15
978	A358	1.50z red org, blk & brt bl	18	15
a.		Souv. sheet of 2	2.00	1.90
		Set value	26	16

30th Intl. Fair at Poznan.

No. 978a contains two of No. 978 with simulated perforation and blue marginal inscriptions. Sold for 4.50z. Issued July 29, 1961.

Tadeusz Kosciuszko A359

Famous Poles: No. 979, Mieszko I. No. 980, Casimir Wielki. No. 981, Casimir Jagiello. No. 982, Nicolaus Copernicus. No. 983, Andrzej Frycz-Modrzewski.

Photogravure and Engraved

1961, June 15 *Perf. 11x11½*

Black Inscriptions and Designs

979	A359	60g chalky bl	15	15
980	A359	60g dp rose	15	15
981	A359	60g slate	15	15
982	A359	60g dl vio	65	20
983	A359	60g lt brn	15	15
984	A359	60g olive gray	15	15
		Set value	1.18	54

See Nos. 1059-1064, 1152-1155.

Trawler — A360

Designs: Various Polish Cargo Ships.

Unwmk.

1961, June 24 Litho. *Perf. 11*

985	A360	60g multi	32	15
986	A360	1.55z multi	38	15
987	A360	2.50z multi	65	30
988	A360	3.40z multi	75	50
989	A360	4z multi	1.25	90
990	A360	5.60z multi	3.00	1.65
		Nos. 985-990 (6)	6.35	3.65

Issued to honor the Polish ship industry. Sizes (width): 60g, 2.50z, 54mm; 1.55z, 3.40z, 4z, 80mm; 5.60z, 108mm.

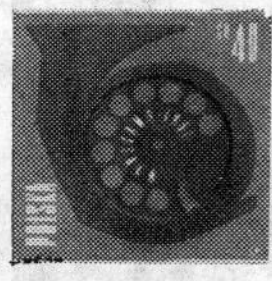
Post Horn and Telephone Dial — A361

Post horn and: 60g, Radar screen. 2.50z, Conference emblem, globe.

1961, June 26

991	A361	40g sl, gray & red org	15	15
992	A361	60g gray, yel & vio	15	15
993	A361	2.50z ol bis, brt bl & vio bl	35	25
a.		Souv. sheet of 3, #991-993	2.25	1.50
		Set value		40

Conference of Communications Ministers of Communist Countries, Warsaw.

No. 993a sold for 5z.

Seal of Opole, 13th Century A362

Cement Works, Opole A363

Designs: No. 996, Tombstone of Henry IV and seal, Wroclaw. No. 997, Apartment houses, Wroclaw. No. 998, Seal of Conrad II and Silesian eagle. No. 999, Steel works, Gorzow. No. 1000, Seal of Prince Barnim I. No. 1001, Seaport, Szczecin. No. 1002, Seal of Princess Elizabeth. No. 1003, Factory, Szczecinek. No. 1004, Seal of Unislaw. No. 1005, Shipyard, Gdansk. No. 1005A, Tower, Frombork Cathedral. No. 1005B, Chemical Laboratory, Kortowo.

1961-62 Wmk. 326 Engr. *Perf. 11*

Western Territories

994	A362	40g brn, *grysh*	15	15
995	A363	40g brn, *grysh*	15	15
996	A362	60g vio, *pink*	15	15
997	A363	60g vio, *pink*	15	15
998	A362	95g grn, *bluish*	15	15
999	A363	95g grn, *bluish*	15	15
1000	A362	2.50z ol grn, *grnsh*	32	15
1001	A363	2.50z ol grn, *grnsh*	32	15

Northern Territories

1002	A362	60g vio bl, *bluish*	15	15
1003	A363	60g vio bl, *bluish*	15	15
1004	A362	1.55z brn, *buff*	15	15
1005	A363	1.55z brn, *buff*	15	15
1005A	A362	2.50z sl bl, *grysh*	32	15
1005B	A363	2.50z sl bl, *grysh*	32	15
		Set value	2.40	1.30

Sheets of 56 with alternating rows of horizontal and vertical stamps. The horizontal stamps also alternate with a label with commemorative inscription. Each sheet contains 28 se-tenant pairs of types A362-A363 with label.

Issued: #994-997, 1000-1001, July 21; 85g, Feb. 23, 1962; #1002-1005B, 1308-1313, July 21, 1962.

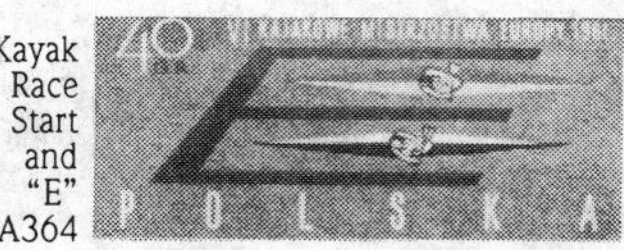

Kayak Race Start and "E" A364

Designs: 60g, Four-man canoes and "E". 2.50z, Paddle, Polish flag and "E," vert.

Perf. 12½

1961, Aug. 18 Wmk. 326 Litho.

1006	A364	40g bl grn, yel & red	15	15
1007	A364	60g multi	15	15
1008	A364	2.50z multi	90	35
		Set value		46

6th European Canoe Championships, Poznan, Aug. 18-20. Exist imperf. Value, set $1.75.

Maj. Gherman Titov, Star, Globe, Orbit A365

Dove and Earth A366

Perf. 12x12½

1961, Aug. 24 Photo. Unwmk.

1009	A365	40g pink, blk & red	25	15
1010	A366	60g bl & blk	25	15
		Set value		20

Manned space flight of Vostok 2, Aug. 6-7, in which Russian Maj. Gherman Titov orbited the earth 17 times.

Insurgents' Monument, St. Ann's Mountain — A367

Design: 1.55z, Cross of Silesian Insurgents.

Wmk. 326

1961, Sept. 15 Litho. *Perf. 12*

1011	A367	60g gray & emer	15	15
1012	A367	1.55z gray & bl	18	15
		Set value	26	20

40th anniv. of the third Silesian uprising.

"PKO," Initials of Polish Savings Bank — A368

Designs (Initials and): No. 1014, Bee and clover. No. 1015, Ant. No. 1016, Squirrel. 2.50z, Savings bankbook.

1961, Oct. 2 Wmk. 326 *Perf. 12*

1013	A368	40g	ver, blk & org	15	15
1014	A368	60g	bl, blk & brt pink	15	15
1015	A368	60g	bis brn, blk & ocher	15	15
1016	A368	60g	brt grn, blk & dl red	15	15
1017	A368	2.50z	car rose, gray & blk	1.75	1.40
			Nos. 1013-1017 (5)	2.35	
			Set value		1.70

Issued to publicize Savings Month.

Mail Cart, by Jan Chelminski A369

1961, Oct. 9 Engr. *Perf. 12x12½*

1018	A369	60g	dp grn	25	15
1019	A369	60g	vio brn	25	15
			Set value		18

40th anniv. of the Polish Postal Museum; Stamp Day.

Congress Emblem A370

1961, Nov. 20 Wmk. 326 *Perf. 12*

1020	A370	60g	black	15	15

Issued to publicize the Fifth World Congress of Trade Unions, Moscow, Dec. 4-16.

Seal of Kopasyni Family, 1284 A371

Child and Syringe A372

Designs: 60g, Seal of Bytom, 14th century. 2.50z, Emblem of International Miners Congress, 1958.

1961, Dec. 4 Litho. *Perf. 11x11½*

1021	A371	40g	multi	15	15
1022	A371	60g	bl, gray bl & vio bl	15	15
1023	A371	2.50z	yel grn, grn & blk	45	24
			Set value		38

1,000 years of the Polish mining industry.

Perf. 12½x12, 12x12½

1961, Dec. 11

Designs: 60g, Children of three races, horiz. 2.50z, Mother, child and milk bottle.

1024	A372	40g	lt bl & blk	15	15
1025	A372	60g	org & blk	15	15
1026	A372	2.50z	brt bl grn & blk	50	24
			Set value		38

15th anniversary of UNICEF.

Emblem A373

Design: 60g, Map with oil pipe line from Siberia to Central Europe.

1961, Dec. 12 Wmk. 326 *Perf. 12*

1027	A373	40g	dk red, yel & vio bl	15	15
1028	A373	60g	vio bl, bl & red	15	15
			Set value		18

15th session of the Council of Mutual Economic Assistance of the Communist States.

Ground Beetle — A374

Black Apollo Butterfly A375

Insects: 30g, Violet runner. 40g, Alpine longicorn beetle. 50g, Great oak capricorn beetle. 60g, Gold runner. 80g, Stag-horned beetle. 1.35z, Death's-head moth. 1.50z, Tiger-striped swallowtail butterfly. 1.55z, Apollo butterfly. 2.50z, Red ant. 5.60z, Bumble bee.

Perf. 12½x12

1961, Dec. 30 Photo. Unwmk.

Insects in Natural Colors

1029	A374	20g	bis brn	15	15
1030	A374	30g	pale gray grn	15	15
1031	A374	40g	pale yel grn	15	15
1032	A374	50g	bl grn	15	15
1033	A374	60g	dl rose lil	15	15
1034	A374	80g	pale grn	24	15

Perf. 11½

1035	A375	1.15z	ultra	32	15
1036	A375	1.35z	sapphire	32	15
1037	A375	1.50z	bluish grn	55	15
1038	A375	1.55z	brt pur	48	15
1039	A375	2.50z	brt grn	1.90	45
1040	A375	5.60z	org brn	9.00	3.50
			Nos. 1029-1040 (12)	13.56	5.45

Worker with Gun — A376

Women Skiers — A377

Designs: No. 1042, Worker with trowel and gun. No. 1043, Worker with hammer. No. 1044, Worker at helm. No. 1045, Worker with dove and banner.

Perf. 12½x12

1962, Jan. 5 Litho. Unwmk.

1041	A376	60g	red, blk & grn	15	15
1042	A376	60g	red, blk & sl	15	15
1043	A376	60g	blk & vio bl, *red*	15	15
1044	A376	60g	blk & bis, *red*	15	15
1045	A376	60g	blk & gray, *red*	15	15
			Set value	52	46

Polish Workers' Party, 20th anniversary.

Lithographed and Embossed

1962, Feb. 14 *Perf. 12*

Designs: 60g, Long distance skier. 1.50z, Ski jump, vert. 10z, FIS emblem, vert.

1046	A377	40g	gray, red & gray bl	15	15
a.			40g sepia, red & dull blue	40	15
1047	A377	60g	gray, red & gray bl	15	15
a.			60g sepia, red & dull blue	50	28
1048	A377	1.50z	gray, red & gray bl	25	18
a.			1.50z gray, lilac & red	1.50	80
			Set value		32

Souvenir Sheet

Imperf

1049	A377	10z	gray, red & gray bl	2.25	2.00

World Ski Championships at Zakopane (FIS).

No. 1049 contains one stamp with simulated perforation. The sheet sold for 15z.

Each of Nos. 1046-1048 exists in a souvenir sheet of four. Value, set of 3, $57.50.

Broken Flower and Prison Cloth (Auschwitz) — A378

Majdanek Concentration Camp — A379

Design: 1.50z, Proposed memorial, Treblinka concentration camp.

Perf. 11½

1962, Apr. 3 Wmk. 326 Engr.

1050	A378	40g	slate blue	15	15
1051	A379	60g	dk gray	24	15
1052	A378	1.50z	dk vio	52	22
			Set value		38

Issued during International Resistance Movement Month to commemorate the millions who died in concentration camps, 1940-45.

Bicyclist A380

Designs: 2.50z, Cyclists in race. 3.40z, Wheel and arms of Berlin, Prague and Warsaw.

Unwmk.

1962, Apr. 27 Litho. *Perf. 12*

1053	A380	60g	bl & blk	15	15
1054	A380	2.50z	yel & blk	35	15
1055	A380	3.40z	lil & blk	52	18
			Set value		36

15th Intl. Peace Bicycle Race, Warsaw-Berlin-Prague.

Size of Nos. 1053 and 1055: 36x22mm. No. 1054: 74x22mm.

Lenin in Bialy Dunajec A381

Karol Swierczewski-Walter A382

Designs: 60g, Lenin. 2.50z, Lenin and Cracow fortifications.

Engraved and Photogravure

Perf. 11x11½

1962, May 25 Wmk. 326

1056	A381	40g	pale grn & Prus grn	50	15
1057	A381	60g	pink & dp cl	15	15
1058	A381	2.50z	yel & dk brn	32	15
			Set value		36

50th anniv. of Lenin's arrival in Poland.

Famous Poles Type of 1961

Famous Poles: No. 1059, Adam Mickiewicz. No. 1060, Juliusz Slowacki. No. 1061, Frederic Chopin. No. 1062, Romuald Traugutt. No. 1063, Jaroslaw Dabrowski. No. 1064, Maria Konopnicka.

1962, June 20 Engr. & Photo.

Black Inscriptions and Designs

1059	A359	60g	dl grn	20	15
1060	A359	60g	brn org	15	15

Perf. 12x12½

Litho.

1061	A359	60g	dl bl	15	15
1062	A359	60g	brn ol	15	15
1063	A359	60g	rose lil	15	15
1064	A359	60g	bl grn	15	15
			Set value	80	52

Perf. 11x11½

1962, July 14 Engr. Unwmk.

1065	A382	60g	black	15	15

15th death anniv. of General Karol Swierczewski-Walter, organizer of the new Polish army.

Crocus A383

The Poisoned Well by Jacek Malczewski A384

Flowers: No. 1067, Orchid. No. 1068, Monkshood. No. 1069, Gas plant. No. 1070, Water lily. No. 1071, Gentian. No. 1072, Daphne mezereum. No. 1073, Cowbell. No. 1074, Anemone. No. 1075, Globeflower. No. 1076, Snowdrop. No. 1077, Adonis vernalis.

Unwmk.

1962, Aug. 8 Photo. *Perf. 12*

Flowers in Natural Colors

1066	A383	60g	dl yel & red	15	15
1067	A383	60g	redsh brn & vio	75	35
1068	A383	60g	pink & lil	15	15
1069	A383	90g	ol & grn	15	15
1070	A383	90g	yel grn & red	15	15
1071	A383	90g	lt ol grn & red	15	15
1072	A383	1.50z	gray bl & bl	25	15
1073	A383	1.50z	yel grn & dk grn	45	15
1074	A383	1.50z	Prus grn & dk bl	25	15
1075	A383	2.50z	gray grn & dk bl	60	38
1076	A383	2.50z	dk bl grn & dk bl	60	38
1077	A383	2.50z	gray bl & grn	95	45
			Nos. 1066-1077 (12)	4.60	
			Set value		2.40

1962, Aug. 15 Engr. Wmk. 326

1078	A384	60g	black, *buff*	30	15

Issued in sheets of 40 with alternating label for FIP Day (Federation Internationale de Philatelie), Sept. 1. Also issued in miniature sheet of 4. Value, $30.

Pole Vault — A385

Designs: 60g, Relay race. 90g, Javelin. 1z, Hurdles. 1.50z, High jump. 1.55z, Discus. 2.50z, 100m. dash. 3.40z, Hammer throw.

Unwmk.

1962, Sept. 12 Litho. *Perf. 11*

1079	A385	40g	multi	15	15
1080	A385	60g	multi	15	15
1081	A385	90g	multi	15	15
1082	A385	1z	multi	15	15
1083	A385	1.50z	multi	15	15
1084	A385	1.55z	multi	18	15
1085	A385	2.50z	multi	30	15
1086	A385	3.40z	multi	75	24
			Set value	1.70	78

7th European Athletic Championships, Belgrade, Sept. 12-16.

Exist imperf. Value, set $3.

Anopheles Mosquito A386

Pavel R. Popovich and Andrian G. Nikolayev A387

Designs: 1.50z, Malaria blood cells. 2.50z, Cinchona flowers. 3z, Anopheles mosquito.

1962, Oct. 1 Wmk. 326 *Perf. 13x12*

1087	A386	60g	ol blk, dk brn & bl grn	15	15
1088	A386	1.50z	red, gray & brt vio	16	15
1089	A386	2.50z	multi	38	16
			Set value		28

Miniature Sheet

Imperf

1090	A386	3z	multi	90	60

WHO drive to eradicate malaria.

1962, Oct. 6 *Perf. 12½x12*

Design: 2.50z, Two stars in orbit around earth. 10z, Two stars in orbit.

1091	A387	60g	vio, blk & cit	15	15
1092	A387	2.50z	Prus bl, blk & red	24	15
			Set value		22

Souvenir Sheet

Perf. 12x11

1093	A387	10z	sl bl, blk & red	1.65	1.50

1st Russian group space flight, Vostoks III and IV, Aug. 11-15, 1962.

Woman Mailing Letter Warsaw — A388

1962, Oct. 9 Engr. *Perf. 12½x12*

1094	A388	60g	black	15	15
1095	A388	2.50z	red brn	32	15
			Set value	40	20

Issued for Stamp Day, 1962. The design is from the painting "A Moment of Decision," by Anthony Kamienski.

Mazovian Princes' Mansion, — A389

1962, Oct. 13 Litho.

1096	A389	60g	red & blk	15	15

25th anniversary of the founding of the Polish Democratic Party.

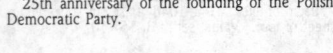

Cruiser "Aurora" — A390

Photo. & Engr.

1962, Nov. 3 *Perf. 11*

1097	A390	60g	red & dk bl	15	15

45th anniv. of the Russian October revolution.

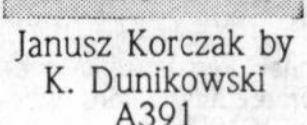

Janusz Korczak by K. Dunikowski A391

King on Horseback A392

Illustrations from King Matthew books: 90g, King giving fruit to Island girl. 1z, King handcuffed and soldier with sword. 2.50z, King with dead bird. 5.60z, King ice skating in moonlight.

Perf. 13x12

1962, Nov. 12 Unwmk. Litho.

1098	A391	40g	brn, bis & sep	15	15
1099	A392	60g	multi	15	15
1100	A392	90g	multi	25	15
1101	A392	1z	multi	25	15
1102	A392	2.50z	brn, yel & brt grn	50	32
1103	A392	5.60z	brn, dk bl & grn	1.75	80
			Nos. 1098-1103 (6)	3.05	
			Set value		1.45

20th anniversary of the death of Dr. Janusz Korczak (Henryk Goldszmit), physician, pedagogue and writer, in the Treblinka concentration camp, Aug. 5, 1942.

View of Old Warsaw — A393

1962, Nov. 26 Wmk. 326 *Perf. 11*

1104	A393	3.40z	multi	42	22
a.			Sheet of 4	3.00	2.50

5th Trade Union Congress, Warsaw, Nov. 26-Dec. 1.

Orphan Mary and the Dwarf — A394

Various Scenes from "Orphan Mary and the Dwarfs" by Maria Konopnicka.

Perf. 13x12

1962, Dec. 31 Unwmk. Litho.

1105	A394	40g	multi	30	15
1106	A394	60g	multi	2.00	1.00
1107	A394	1.50z	multi	50	15
1108	A394	1.55z	multi	50	15
1109	A394	2.50z	multi	60	35
1110	A394	3.40z	multi	2.00	1.25
			Nos. 1105-1110 (6)	5.90	3.05

120th anniversary of the birth of Maria Konopnicka, poet and fairy tale writer.

Romuald Traugutt A395

Perf. 11½x11

1963, Jan. 31 Wmk. 326

1111	A395	60g	aqua, blk & pale pink	15	15

Centenary of the 1863 insurrection and to honor its leader, Romuald Traugutt.

Tractor and Wheat — A396

Designs: 60g, Man reaping and millet. 2.50z, Combine and rice.

Perf. 12x12½

1963, Feb. 25 Litho. Wmk. 326

1112	A396	40g	gray, bl, blk & ocher	15	15
1113	A396	60g	brn red, blk, brn & grn	52	22
1114	A396	2.50z	yel, buff, blk & grn	42	15
			Set value		42

FAO "Freedom from Hunger" campaign.

Cocker Spaniel — A397

Dogs: 30g, Polish sheep dog. 40g, Boxer. 50g, Airedale terrier, vert. 60g, French bulldog, vert. 1z, Poodle, vert. 2.50z, Hunting dog. 3.40z, Sheep dog, vert. 6.50z, Great Dane.

1963, Mar. 25 Unwmk. *Perf. 12½*

1115	A397	20g	lil, blk & org brn	15	15
1116	A397	30g	rose car & blk	15	15
1117	A397	40g	lil, blk & yel grn	20	15
1118	A397	50g	multi	30	15
1119	A397	60g	lt bl & blk	38	15
1120	A397	1z	yel grn & blk	70	55
1121	A397	2.50z	org, blk & brn	1.25	52
1122	A397	3.40z	red org & blk	2.75	1.10
1123	A397	6.50z	brt yel & blk	4.75	3.00
			Nos. 1115-1123 (9)	10.63	5.92

Egyptian Ship — A398

Fighter and Ruins of Warsaw Ghetto — A399

Ancient Ships: 10g, Phoenician merchant ship. 20g, Greek trireme. 30g, 3rd century merchantman. 40g, Scandinavian "Gokstad." 60g, Frisian "Kogge." 1z, 14th century "Holk." 1.15z, 15th century "Caraca."

Photo. (Background) & Engr.

1963, Apr. 5 *Perf. 11½*

1124	A398	5g	brn, *tan*	15	15
1125	A398	10g	grn, *gray grn*	15	15
1126	A398	20g	ultra, *gray*	15	15
1127	A398	30g	blk, *gray ol*	15	15
1128	A398	40g	lt bl, *bluish*	15	15
1129	A398	60g	cl, *gray*	15	15
1130	A398	1z	blk, *bl*	15	15
1131	A398	1.15z	grn, *pale rose*	35	15
			Set value	85	50

See Nos. 1206-1213, 1299-1306.

Perf. 11½x11

1963, Apr. 19 Wmk. 326

1132	A399	2.50z	gray brn & gray	32	15

Warsaw Ghetto Uprising, 20th anniv.

Centenary Emblem — A400

Perf. 12½x12

1963, May 8 Litho. Unwmk.

1133	A400	2.50z	bl, yel & red	40	15

Intl. Red Cross, cent. Every other stamp in sheet inverted.

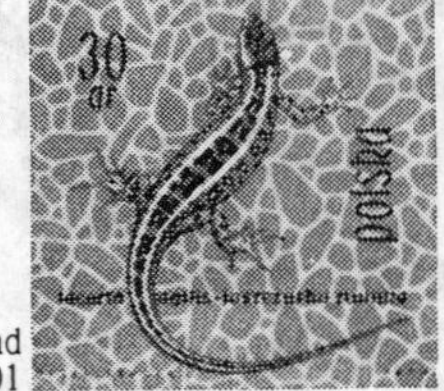

Sand Lizard — A401

Designs: 40g, Smooth snake. 50g, European pond turtle. 60g, Grass snake. 90g, Slow worm. 1.15z, European tree frog. 1.35z, Alpine newt. 1.50z, Crested newt. 1.55z, Green toad. 2.50z, Firebellied toad. 3z, Fire salamander. 3.40z, Natterjack.

Perf. 11½

1963, June 1 Unwmk. Photo.

Reptiles and Amphibians in Natural Colors

1134	A401	30g	grnsh gray & blk	15	15
1135	A401	40g	gray ol & blk	15	15
1136	A401	50g	bis brn & blk	15	15
1137	A401	60g	tan & blk	15	15
1138	A401	90g	gray grn & blk	15	15
1139	A401	1.15z	gray & blk	15	15
1140	A401	1.35z	gray bl & dk bl	30	15
1141	A401	1.50z	bluish grn & blk	38	20
1142	A401	1.55z	bluish gray & blk	30	15
1143	A401	2.50z	gray vio & blk	30	15
1144	A401	3z	gray grn & blk	65	28
1145	A401	3.40z	gray & blk	1.90	1.25
			Nos. 1134-1145 (12)	4.73	
			Set value		2.50

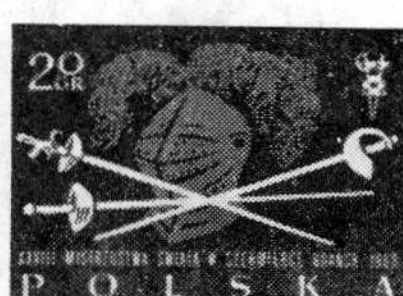

Foil, Saber, Sword and Helmet A402

Designs: 40g, Fencers and knights in armor. 60g, Fencers and dragoons. 1.15z, Contemporary and 18th cent. fencers. 1.55z, Fencers and old houses, Gdansk. 6.50z, Arms of Gdansk, vert.

Perf. 12x12½, 12½x12

1963, June 29 Litho. Unwmk.

1146	A402	20g	brn & org	15	15
1147	A402	40g	dk bl & bl	15	15
1148	A402	60g	red & dp org	15	15
1149	A402	1.15z	grn & emer	15	15
1150	A402	1.55z	vio & lil	32	15
1151	A402	6.50z	yel brn, mar & yel	1.10	45
			Nos. 1146-1151 (6)	2.02	
			Set value		88

28th World Fencing Championships, Gdansk, July 15-28. A souvenir sheet exists containing one each of Nos. 1147-1150. Value, $30.

Famous Poles Type of 1961

Famous Poles: No. 1152, Ludwik Warynski. No. 1153, Ludwik Krzywicki. No. 1154, Marie Sklodowska Curie. No. 1155, Karol Swierczewski-Walter.

Perf. 12x12½

1963, July 20 Wmk. 326

Black Inscriptions and Designs

1152	A359	60g	red brn	15	15
1153	A359	60g	gray brn	15	15
1154	A359	60g	blue	30	15
1155	A359	60g	green	15	15
			Set value	50	38

Valeri Bykovski — A403

Designs: 60g, Valentina Tereshkova. 6.50z, Rockets "Falcon" and "Mew" and globe.

Unwmk.

1963, Aug. 26 Litho. *Perf. 11*

1156	A403	40g	ultra, emer & blk	15	15
1157	A403	60g	grn, ultra & blk	15	15
1158	A403	6.50z	multi	75	30
			Set value		42

Space flights of Valeri Bykovski June 14-19, and Valentina Tereshkova, first woman cosmonaut, June 16-19, 1963.

For overprints see Nos. 1175-1177.

Basketball A404

Designs: Various positions of ball, hands and players. 10z, Town Hall, People's Hall and Arms of Wroclaw.

1963, Sept. 16 Unwmk. *Perf. 11½*

1159	A404	40g	multi	15	15
1160	A404	50g	fawn, grn & blk	15	15
1161	A404	60g	red, lt grn & blk	15	15
1162	A404	90g	multi	15	15
1163	A404	2.50z	multi	18	15
1164	A404	5.60z	multi	85	30
			Set value	1.28	68

Souvenir Sheet

Imperf

1165	A404	10z	multi	1.65	1.00

13th European Men's Basketball Championship, Wroclaw, Oct. 4-13. No. 1165 contains one stamp; inscription on margin also commemorates the simultaneous European Sports Stamp Exhibition. Sheet sold for 15z.

Eagle and Ground-to-Air Missile A405

Eagle and: 40g, Destroyer. 60g, Jet fighter plane. 1.15z, Radar. 1.35z, Tank. 1.55z, Self-propelled rocket launcher. 2.50z, Amphibious troop carrier. 3z, Swords and medieval and modern soldiers.

1963, Oct. 1 *Perf. 12x12½*

1166	A405	20g	multi	15	15
1167	A405	40g	vio, grn & red	15	15
1168	A405	60g	multi	15	15
1169	A405	1.15z	multi	15	15
1170	A405	1.35z	multi	15	15
1171	A405	1.55z	multi	15	15
1172	A405	2.50z	multi	18	15
1173	A405	3z	multi	40	18
			Set value	1.18	60

Polish People's Army, 20th anniversary.

"Love Letter" by Wladyslaw Czachórski — A406

Perf. 11½

1963, Oct. 9 Unwmk. Engr.

1174	A406	60g	dk red brn	20	15

Issued for Stamp Day.

Nos. 1156-1158 Overprinted: "23-28 X. 1963" and name of astronaut

1963 Litho. *Perf. 11*

1175	A403	40g	ultra, emer & blk	20	15
1176	A403	60g	grn, ultra & blk	28	15
1177	A403	6.50z	multi	1.25	65
			Set value		82

Visit of Valentina Tereshkova and Valeri Bykovski to Poland, Oct. 23-28. The overprints are: 40g, W. F. Bykowski / w Polsce; 60g, W. W. Tierieszkowa / w Polsce; 6.50z, W. F. BYKOWSKI I W. W. TIERIESZKOWA W POLSCE.

Konstantin E. Tsiolkovsky's Rocket and Rocket Speed Formula — A407

American and Russian Spacecrafts: 40g, Sputnik 1. 50g, Explorer 1. 60g, Lunik 2. 1z, Lunik 3. 1.50z, Vostok 1. 1.55z, Friendship 7. 2.50z, Vostoks 3 & 4. 5.60z, Mariner 2. 6.50z, Mars 1.

Perf. 12½x12

1963, Nov. 11 Litho. Unwmk.

Black Inscriptions

1178	A407	30g	dl bl grn & gray	15	15
1179	A407	40g	lt ol grn & gray	15	15
1180	A407	50g	vio bl & gray	15	15
1181	A407	60g	brn org & gray	15	15
1182	A407	1z	brt grn & gray	15	15
1183	A407	1.50z	org red & gray	15	15
1184	A407	1.55z	bl & gray	15	15
1185	A407	2.50z	lil & gray	15	15
1186	A407	5.60z	brt yel grn & gray	50	24
1187	A407	6.50z	grnsh bl & gray	85	30
			Set value	1.95	1.00

Conquest of space. A souvenir sheet contains 2 each of Nos. 1186-1187. Value $40.

Arab Stallion "Comet" — A408

Horses from Mazury Region — A409

Horses: 30g, Tarpans (wild horses). 40g, Horse from Sokolka. 50g, Arab mares and foals, horiz. 90g, Steeplechasers, horiz. 1.55z, Arab stallion "Witez II." 2.50z, Head of Arab horse, facing right. 4z, Mixed breeds, horiz. 6.50z, Head of Arab horse, facing left.

Perf. 11½x11 (A408); 12½x12, 12

1963, Dec. 30 Photo.

1188	A408	20g	blk, yel & car	15	15
1189	A408	30g	multi	16	15
1190	A408	40g	multi	16	15

Sizes: 75x26mm (50g, 90g, 4z); 28x38mm (60g, 1.55z, 2.50z, 6.50z)

1191	A409	50g	multi	20	15
1192	A409	60g	yel, dp rose & blk	20	15
1193	A409	90g	multi	28	15
1194	A409	1.55z	multi	48	18
1195	A409	2.50z	multi	60	18
1196	A409	4z	multi	1.40	48
1197	A409	6.50z	yel, dl bl & blk	2.50	1.50
			Nos. 1188-1197 (10)	6.13	3.24

Issued to publicize Polish horse breeding.

Ice Hockey A410

Sports: 30g, Slalom. 40g, Skiing. 60g, Speed skating. 1z, Ski jump. 2.50z, Tobogganing. 5.60z, Cross-country skiing. 6.50z, Figure skating pair.

1964, Jan. 25 Litho. *Perf. 12x12½*

1198	A410	20g	multi	15	15
1199	A410	30g	multi	15	15
1200	A410	40g	multi	15	15
1201	A410	60g	multi	18	15
1202	A410	1z	multi	18	15
1203	A410	2.50z	multi	30	15
1204	A410	5.60z	multi	48	28
1205	A410	6.50z	multi	85	55
			Set value	2.10	1.20

9th Winter Olympic Games, Innsbruck, Jan. 29-Feb. 9. A souvenir sheet contains 2 each of Nos. 1203, 1205. Value $32.50.

Ship Type of 1963

Sailing Ships: 1.35z, Caravel of Columbus, vert. 1.50z, Galleon. 1.55z, Polish warship. 1627, vert. 2z, Dutch merchant ship, vert. 2.10z, Line ship. 2.50z, Frigate. 3z, 19th century merchantman. 3.40z, "Dar Pomorza," 20th century school ship, vert.

1964, Mar. 19 Engr. *Perf. 12½*

1206	A398	1.35z	ultra	15	15
1207	A398	1.50z	claret	15	15
1208	A398	1.55z	black	15	15
1209	A398	2z	violet	15	15
1210	A398	2.10z	green	15	15
1211	A398	2.50z	car rose	22	15
1212	A398	3z	ol grn	35	15
1213	A398	3.40z	brown	50	15
			Set value	1.60	68

European Cat — A411

Designs: 40g, 60g, 1.55z, 2.50z, 6.50z, Various European cats. 50g, Siamese cat. 90g, 1.35z, 3.40z, Various Persian cats. 60g, 90g, 1.35z, 1.55z horizontal.

1964, Apr. 30 Litho. *Perf. 12½*

Cats in Natural Colors; Black Inscriptions

1216	A411	30g	yellow	15	15
1217	A411	40g	orange	15	15
1218	A411	50g	yellow	15	15
1219	A411	60g	brt grn	30	15
1220	A411	90g	lt brn	15	15
1221	A411	1.35z	emerald	15	15
1222	A411	1.55z	vio bl	45	18
1223	A411	2.50z	lilac	1.25	55
1224	A411	3.40z	rose	1.50	90
1225	A411	6.50z	violet	3.00	1.50
			Nos. 1216-1225 (10)	7.25	4.03

King Casimir III, the Great — A412

Designs: No. 1227, Hugo Kollataj. No. 1228, Jan Dlugosz. No. 1229, Nicolaus Copernicus. 2.50z, King Wladyslaw II Jagiello and Queen Jadwiga.

1964, May 5 Engr. *Perf. 11x11½*

Size: 22x35mm

1226	A412	40g	dull claret	15	15
1227	A412	40g	green	15	15
1228	A412	60g	violet	15	15
1229	A412	60g	dark blue	15	15

Size: 35½x37mm

1230	A412	2.50z	gray brown	35	15
			Set value	78	35

Jagiellonian University, Cracow, 600th anniv.

Lapwing A413

Waterfowl: 40g, White-spotted bluethroat. 50g, Black-tailed godwit. 60g, Osprey. 90g, Gray heron. 1.35z, Little gull. 1.55z, Shoveler. 5.60z, Arctic loon. 6.50z, Great crested grebe.

Perf. 11½

1964, June 5 Unwmk. Photo.

Birds in Natural Colors; Black Inscriptions

Size: 34x34mm

1231	A413	30g	chalky bl	15	15
1232	A413	40g	bister	15	15
1233	A413	50g	brt yel grn	15	15

Perf. 11½x11

Size: 34x48mm

1234	A413	60g	blue	15	15
1235	A413	90g	lemon	15	15
1236	A413	1.35z	green	26	15

Perf. 11½

Size: 34x34mm

1237 A413 1.55z olive	26	15
1238 A413 5.60z bl grn	75	35
1239 A413 6.50z brt grn	1.25	55
Nos. 1231-1239 (9)	3.27	
Set value		1.30

Hands Holding Red Flag — A414

Designs: No. 1241, Red and white ribbon around hammer. No. 1242, Hammer and rye. No. 1243, Brick wall under construction and red flag.

1964, June 15 Litho. *Perf. 11*

1240 A414 60g ol bis, red, blk & pink	15	15
1241 A414 60g red, gray & blk	15	15
1242 A414 60g mag, blk & yel	15	15
1243 A414 60g gray, red, sal & blk	15	15
Set value	36	32

4th congress of the Polish United Workers Party.

Symbols of Peasant-Worker Alliance — A415

Atom Symbol and Book — A416

Shipyard, Gdansk — A417

Designs: No. 1245, Stylized oak. No. 1247, Factory and cogwheel. No. 1248, Tractor and grain. No. 1249, Pen, brush, mask and ornament. No. 1251, Lenin Metal Works, Nowa Huta. No. 1252, Cement factory, Chelm. No. 1253, Power Station, Turoszow. No. 1254, Oil refinery, Plock. No. 1255, Sulphur mine, Tarnobrzeg.

1964 Litho. *Perf. 12x12½*

1244 A415 60g red, org & blk	15	15
1245 A415 60g grn, red, ocher, bl & blk	15	15

Photo.

Perf. 11

1246 A416 60g gray & dp vio bl	15	15
1247 A416 60g brt bl & blk	15	15
1248 A416 60g emer & blk	15	15
1249 A416 60g org & red	15	15

Photogravure and Engraved

1250 A417 60g dl bl grn & ultra	15	15
1251 A417 60g brt pink & pur	15	15
1252 A417 60g gray & gray brn	15	15
1253 A417 60g grn & slate grn	15	15
1254 A417 60g salmon & claret	15	15
1255 A417 60g citron & sepia	15	15
Set value	88	70

20th anniversary of the Polish People's Republic.

Warsaw Fighters, 1944 — A418

1964, Aug. 1 Litho. *Perf. 12½x12*

1256 A418 60g multi	15	15

20th anniv. of the Warsaw insurrection against German occupation.

Running — A419

Women's High Jump — A420

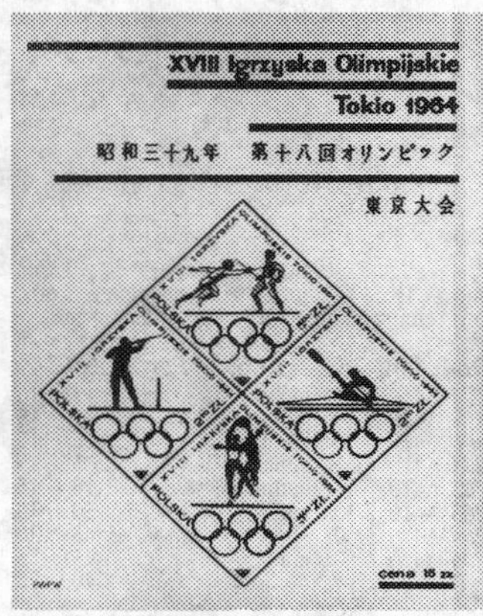

Olympic Sports — A421

Sport: 40g, Rowing (single). 60g, Weight lifting. 90g, Relay race (square). 1z, Boxing (square). 2.50z, Soccer (square). 6.50z, Diving.

Unwmk.

1964, Aug. 17 Litho. *Perf. 11*

1257 A419 20g multi	15	15
1258 A419 40g grnsh bl, bl & yel	15	15
1259 A419 60g vio bl, red & rose lil	15	15
1260 A419 90g dk brn, red & yel	18	15
1261 A419 1z dk vio, lil & gray	18	15
1262 A419 2.50z multi	38	20
1263 A420 5.60z multi	95	48
1264 A420 6.50z multi	1.50	80
Nos. 1257-1264 (8)	3.64	
Set value		1.80

Souvenir Sheet

Imperf

1265 A421 Sheet of 4	2.50	1.65
a. 2.50z Sharpshooting	32	22
b. 2.50z Canoeing	32	22
c. 5z Fencing	32	22
d. 5z Basketball	32	22

18th Olympic Games, Tokyo, Oct. 10-25. Size of stamps in No. 1265: 24x24mm. A souvenir sheet containing 2 each of Nos. 1263-1264 with black marginal inscription exists. Value $26.

Warsaw Mermaid and Stars A422

Stefan Zeromski by Monika Zeromska A423

1964, Sept. 7 *Perf. 12½x12*

1266 A422 2.50z vio & blk	28	15

15th Astronautical Congress, Warsaw, Sept. 7-12.

1964, Sept. 21 Photo. *Perf. 12½*

1267 A423 60g olive gray	18	15

Stefan Zeromski (1864-1925), writer.

Gun and Hand Holding Hammer — A424

Globe and Red Flag — A425

1964, Sept. 21 Litho. *Perf. 11*

1268 A424 60g brt grn, blk & red	15	15

Issued to commemorate the Third Miners' Militia Congress, Warsaw, Sept. 24-26.

1964, Sept. 28 Photo. *Perf. 12½*

1269 A425 60g blk & red org	15	15

First Socialist International, centenary.

Stagecoach by Jozef Brodowski — A426

1964, Oct. 9 Engr. *Perf. 11½*

1270 A426 60g green	15	15
1271 A426 60g lt brn	15	15
Set value		16

Issued for Stamp Day.

Eleanor Roosevelt (1884-1962) — A427

1964, Oct. 10 *Perf. 12½*

1272 A427 2.50z black	20	15

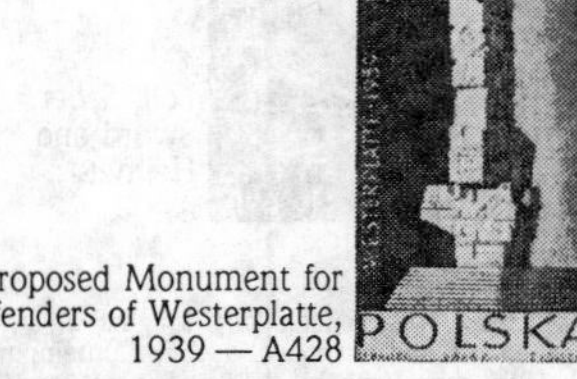

Proposed Monument for Defenders of Westerplatte, 1939 — A428

Polish Soldiers Crossing Oder River, 1945 A429

Designs: No. 1274, Virtuti Military Cross. No. 1275, Nike, proposed monument for the martyrs of Bydgoszcz (woman with sword and torch). No. 1277, Battle of Studzianki, 1944.

Perf. 12x11, 11x12

1964, Nov. 16 Engr. Unwmk.

1273 A428 40g bl vio	15	15
1274 A428 40g slate	15	15
1275 A428 60g dk bl	15	15
1276 A429 60g dk bl grn	15	15
1277 A429 60g grnsh blk	15	15
Set value	45	30

Struggle and martyrdom of the Polish people, 1939-45. The vertical stamps are printed in sheets of 56 stamps (8x7) with 7 labels in each outside vertical row. The horizontal stamps are printed in sheets of 50 stamps (5x10) with 10 labels in each outside vertical row. See Nos. 1366-1368.

Souvenir Sheet

Col. Vladimir M. Komarov, Boris B. Yegorov and Dr. Konstantin Feoktistov — A430

1964, Nov. 21 Litho. *Perf. 11½x11*

1278 A430 Sheet of 3	85	65
a. 60g red & black (Komarov)	25	15
b. 60g brt grn & blk (Feoktistov)	25	15
c. 60g ultra & blk (Yegorov)	25	15

Russian three-manned space flight in space ship Voskhod, Oct. 12-13, 1964. Size of stamps: 27x36mm.

Cyclamen A431

Garden Flowers: 30g, Freesia. 40g, Monique rose. 50g, Peony. 60g, Royal lily. 90g, Oriental poppy. 1.35z, Tulip. 1.50z, Narcissus. 1.55z, Begonia. 2.50z, Carnation. 3.40z, Iris. 5.60z, Camellia.

1964, Nov. 30 Photo. *Perf. 11*

Size: 35½x35½mm

Flowers in Natural Colors

1279 A431 20g violet	15	15
1280 A431 30g dp lil	15	15
1281 A431 40g blue	15	15
1282 A431 50g vio bl	15	15
1283 A431 60g lilac	15	15
1284 A431 90g dp grn	15	15

Size: 26x37½mm

1285 A431 1.35z dk bl	15	15
1286 A431 1.50z dp car	42	26
1287 A431 1.55z green	15	15
1288 A431 2.50z ultra	38	15
1289 A431 3.40z redsh brn	75	26
1290 A431 5.60z ol gray	1.40	65
Nos. 1279-1290 (12)	4.15	
Set value		1.75

Future Interplanetary Spacecraft — A432

Designs: 30g, Launching of Russian rocket. 40g, Dog Laika and launching tower. 60g, Lunik 3 photographing far side of the Moon. 1.55z, Satellite exploring the ionosphere. 2.50z, Satellite "Elektron 2" exploring radiation belt. 5.60z, "Mars 1" between Mars and Earth.

Perf. 12½x12

1964, Dec. 30 Litho. Unwmk.

1291	A432	20g	multi	15	15
1292	A432	30g	multi	15	15
1293	A432	40g	ol grn, blk & bl	15	15
1294	A432	60g	dk bl, blk & dk red	15	15
1295	A432	1.55z	gray & multi	25	15
1296	A432	2.50z	multi	52	15
1297	A432	5.60z	multi	90	40
			Nos. 1291-1297,B108 (8)	3.77	
			Set value		1.45

Issued to publicize space research.

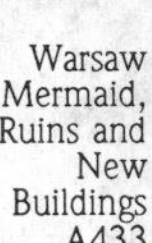

Warsaw Mermaid, Ruins and New Buildings A433

1965, Jan. 15 Engr. *Perf. 11x11½*

1298	A433	60g	slate green	15	15

Liberation of Warsaw, 20th anniversary.

Ship Type of 1963

Designs as before.

1965, Jan. 25 Engr. *Perf. 12½*

1299	A398	5g	dark brown	15	15
1300	A398	10g	slate grn	15	15
1301	A398	20g	slate blue	15	15
1302	A398	30g	gray olive	15	15
1303	A398	40g	dark blue	15	15
1304	A398	60g	claret	15	15
1305	A398	1z	red brown	15	15
1306	A398	1.15z	dk red brn	15	15
			Set value	58	48

Edaphosaurus — A434

Dinosaurs: 30g, Cryptocleidus, vert. 40g, Brontosaurus. 60g, Mesosaurus, vert. 90g, Stegosaurus. 1.15z, Brachiosaurus, vert. 1.35z, Styracosaurus. 3.40z, Corythosaurus, vert. 5.60z, Rhamphorhynchus, vert. 6.50z, Tyrannosaurus.

1965, Mar. 5 Litho. *Perf. 12½*

1307	A434	20g	multi	15	15
1308	A434	30g	multi	15	15
1309	A434	40g	multi	15	15
1310	A434	60g	multi	15	15
1311	A434	90g	multi	28	15
1312	A434	1.15z	multi	15	15
1313	A434	1.35z	multi	16	15
1314	A434	3.40z	multi	42	16
1315	A434	5.60z	multi	90	35
1316	A434	6.50z	multi	1.40	90
			Nos. 1307-1316 (10)	3.91	
			Set value		2.00

See Nos. 1395-1403.

Symbolic Wax Seal — A435

Russian and Polish Flags, Oil Refinery-Chemical Plant, Plock — A436

1965, Apr. 21 *Perf. 12½x12, 12½*

1317	A435	60g	multi	15	15
1318	A436	60g	multi	15	15
			Set value	20	16

20th anniversary of the signing of the Polish-Soviet treaty of friendship, mutual assistance and postwar cooperation.

Polish Eagle and Town Coats of Arms — A437

1965, May 8 Engr. *Perf. 11½*

1319	A437	60g	car rose	15	15

20th anniversary of regaining the Western and Northern Territories.

Dove — A438

1965, May 8 Litho. *Perf. 12x12½*

1320	A438	60g	red & blk	15	15

Victory over Fascism, 20th anniversary.

ITU Emblem — A439

"The People's Friend" and Clover — A440

Factory and Rye — A441

Perf. 12½x12

1965, May 17 Litho. Unwmk.

1321	A439	2.50z	brt bl, lil, yel & blk	28	15

ITU, cent.

1965, June 5 *Perf. 11*

1322	A440	40g	multi	15	15
1323	A441	60g	multi	15	15
			Set value	20	15

70th anniv. of the "Popular Movement" in Poland.

Finn Class Yachts A442

Yachts: 30g, Dragon class. 40g, 5.5-m. class. 50g, Group of Finn class. 60g, V-class. 1.35z, Group of Cadet class. 4z, Group of Star class. 5.60z, Two Flying Dutchmen. 6.50z, Two Amethyst class. 15z, Finn class race. (30g, 40g, 60g, 5.60z vertical.)

1965, June 14 Litho. *Perf. 12½*

1324	A442	30g	multi	15	15
1325	A442	40g	multi	15	15
1326	A442	50g	multi	15	15
1327	A442	60g	multi	15	15
1328	A442	1.35z	multi	15	15
1329	A442	4z	multi	50	22
1330	A442	5.60z	multi	90	42
1331	A442	6.50z	multi	1.40	70
			Nos. 1324-1331 (8)	3.55	
			Set value		1.75

Miniature Sheet

Perf. 11

1332	A442	15z	multi	1.65	1.25

World Championships of Finn Class Yachts, Gdynia, July 22-29. No. 1332 contains one stamp 48x22mm.

Marx and Lenin — A443

Photogravure and Engraved

1965, June 14 *Perf. 11½x11*

1333	A443	60g	blk, *ver*	15	15

6th Conference of Ministers of Post of Communist Countries, Peking, June 21-July 15.

Warsaw's Coat of Arms, 17th Cent. — A444

Old Town Hall, 18th Cent. — A445

Designs: 10g, Artifacts, 13th century. 20g, Tombstone of last Duke of Mazovia. 60g, Barbican, Gothic-Renaissance castle. 1.50z, Arsenal, 19th century. 1.55z, National Theater. 2.50z, Staszic Palace. 3.40z, Woman with sword from Heroes' Memorial and Warsaw Mermaid seal.

Perf. 11x11½, 11½x11, 12x12½, 12½x12

1965, July 21 Engr. Unwmk.

1334	A444	5g	car rose	15	15
1335	A444	10g	green	15	15
1336	A445	20g	vio bl	15	15
1337	A445	40g	brown	15	15
1338	A445	60g	orange	15	15
1339	A445	1.50z	black	15	15
1340	A445	1.55z	gray bl	15	15
1341	A445	2.50z	lilac	22	15

Perf. 11½

Photogravure and Engraved

1342	A444	3.40z	cit & blk	70	60
			Set value	1.35	1.05

700th anniversary of Warsaw.

No. 1342 is perforated all around, with lower right quarter perforated to form a 21x26mm stamp within a stamp. It was issued in sheets of 25 (5x5).

For surcharges see Nos. 1919-1926.

IQSY Emblem A446

Designs: 2.50z, Radar screen, Torun. 3.40z, Solar system.

1965, Aug. 9 Litho.

1343	A446	60g	vio, ver, brt grn & blk	15	15
a.			60g ultra, org, yel, bl & blk	15	15
1344	A446	2.50z	red, yel, pur & blk	25	15
a.			2.50z red brn, yel, gray & blk	25	15
1345	A446	3.40z	org & multi	32	15
a.			3.40z ol gray & multi	32	15
			Set value		26
			Set value, #1343a-1345a		26

International Quiet Sun Year, 1964-65.

Odontoglossum Grande — A447

Weight Lifting — A448

Orchids: 30g, Cypripedium hibridum. 40g, Lycaste skinneri. 50g, Cattleya. 60g, Vanda sanderiana. 1.35z, Cypripedium hibridum. 4z, Sobralia. 5.60z, Disa grandiflora. 6.50z, Cattleya labiata.

1965, Sept. 6 Photo. *Perf. 12½x12*

1346	A447	20g	multi	15	15
1347	A447	30g	multi	15	15
1348	A447	40g	multi	15	15
1349	A447	50g	multi	15	15
1350	A447	60g	multi	15	15
1351	A447	1.35z	multi	18	15
1352	A447	4z	multi	42	30
1353	A447	5.60z	multi	90	42
1354	A447	6.50z	multi	1.40	75
			Nos. 1346-1354 (9)	3.65	
			Set value		1.95

1965, Oct. 8 Photo. Unwmk.

Sport: 40g, Boxing. 50g, Relay race, men. 60g, Fencing. 90g, Women's 80-meter hurdles. 3.40z, Relay race, women. 6.50z, Hop, step and jump. 7.10z, Volleyball, women.

1355	A448	30g	gold & multi	15	15
1356	A448	40g	gold & multi	15	15
1357	A448	50g	sil & multi	15	15
1358	A448	60g	gold & multi	15	15
1359	A448	90g	sil & multi	15	15
1360	A448	3.40z	gold & multi	50	15
1361	A448	6.50z	gold & multi	85	42
1362	A448	7.10z	brnz & multi	1.00	60
			Nos. 1355-1362 (8)	3.10	
			Set value		1.50

Victories won by the Polish team in 1964 Olympic Games. Each denomination printed in sheets of eight stamps and two center labels showing medals.

Mail Coach, by Piotr Michalowski A449

Design: 2.50z, Departure of Coach, by Piotr Michalowski.

1965, Oct. 9 Engr. *Perf. 11x11½*

1363	A449	60g	brown	15	15
1364	A449	2.50z	sl grn	22	15
			Set value		15

Issued for Stamp Day, 1965. Sheets of 50 with labels se-tenant inscribed "Dzien Znaczka 1965 R."

UN Emblem
A450

Memorial, Plaszow
A451

1965, Oct. 24 Litho. *Perf. 12½x12*

1365	A450	2.50z	ultra	25	15

20th anniversary of United Nations.

Perf. 12x11, 11x12

1965, Nov. 29 Engr.

Designs: No. 1367, Kielce Memorial. No. 1368, Chelm Memorial, horiz.

1366	A451	60g	grnsh gray	15	15
1367	A451	60g	chocolate	15	15
1368	A451	60g	black	15	15
			Set value		18

Note after No. 1277 applies also to Nos. 1366-1368.

Wolf — A452

1965, Nov. 30 Photo. *Perf. 11½*

1369	A452	20g	shown	15	15
1370	A452	30g	Lynx	15	15
1371	A452	40g	Red fox	15	15
1372	A452	50g	Badger	15	15
1373	A452	60g	Brown bear	15	15
1374	A452	1.50z	Wild Boar	45	15
1375	A452	2.50z	Red deer	45	15
1376	A452	5.60z	European bison	1.00	45
1377	A452	7.10z	Moose	1.25	90
			Nos. 1369-1377 (9)	3.90	
			Set value		2.00

Gig — A453

Horse-drawn carriages, Lancut Museum: 40g, Coupé. 50g, Lady's basket. 60g, Vis-a-vis. 90g, Cab. 1.15z, Berlinka. 2.50z, Hunting break. 6.50z, Caleche àla Daumont. 7.10z, English break.

1965, Dec. 30 Litho. *Perf. 11*

Size: 50x23mm

1378	A453	20g	multi	15	15
1379	A453	40g	lil & multi	15	15
1380	A453	50g	org & multi	15	15
1381	A453	60g	fawn & multi	15	15
1382	A453	90g	yel & multi	15	15

Size: 76x23mm

1383	A453	1.15z	multi	15	15
1384	A453	2.50z	ol & multi	35	20
1385	A453	6.50z	multi	90	45

Size: 103x23mm

1386	A453	7.10z	bl & multi	1.65	90
			Nos. 1378-1386 (9)	3.80	
			Set value		1.90

Cargo Ship (No. 1389) — A454

Designs: No. 1387, Supervising Technical Organization (NOT) emblem, symbols of industry. No. 1388, Pit head and miners' badge, vert. No. 1390, Chemical plant, Plock. No. 1391, Combine. No. 1392, Railroad train. No. 1393, Building crane, vert. No. 1394, Pavilion and emblem of 35th International Poznan Fair.

1966 Litho. *Perf. 11*

1387	A454	60g	multi	15	15
1388	A454	60g	multi	15	15
1389	A454	60g	multi	15	15
1390	A454	60g	multi	15	15
1391	A454	60g	multi	15	15
1392	A454	60g	multi	15	15
1393	A454	60g	multi	15	15
1394	A454	60g	multi	15	15
			Set value	72	64

20th anniversary of the nationalization of Polish industry. No. 1394 also commemorates the 35th International Poznan Fair. Nos. 1387-1388 issued in connection with the 5th Congress of Polish Technicians, Katowice. Printed in sheets of 20 stamps and 20 labels with commemorative inscription within cogwheel on each label.

Issue dates: Nos. 1387-1388, Feb. 10; others, May 21.

Dinosaur Type of 1965

1966, Mar. 5 Litho. *Perf. 12½*

Prehistoric Vertebrates: 20g, Dinichthys. 30g, Eusthenopteron. 40g, Ichthyostega. 50g, Mastodonsaurus. 60g, Cynognathus. 2.50z, Archaeopteryx, vert. 3.40z, Brontotherium. 6.50z, Machairodus. 7.10z, Mammoth.

1395	A434	20g	multi	15	15
1396	A434	30g	multi	15	15
1397	A434	40g	multi	15	15
1398	A434	50g	multi	15	15
1399	A434	60g	multi	20	15
1400	A434	2.50z	multi	25	15
1401	A434	3.40z	multi	40	20
1402	A434	6.50z	multi	85	45
1403	A434	7.10z	multi	1.50	90
			Nos. 1395-1403 (9)	3.80	
			Set value		1.95

Henryk Sienkiewicz
A455

Photogravure and Engraved

1966, Mar. 30 *Perf. 11½*

1404	A455	60g	black, *dl yel*	15	15

Henryk Sienkiewicz (1846-1916), author and winner of 1905 Nobel Prize.

Soccer Game
A456

Peace Dove and War Memorial
A457

Designs: Various phases of soccer. Each stamp inscribed with the place and the result of final game in various preceding soccer championships.

1966, May 6 *Perf. 13x12*

1405	A456	20g	multi	15	15
1406	A456	40g	multi	15	15
1407	A456	60g	multi	15	15
1408	A456	90g	multi	15	15
1409	A456	1.50z	multi	25	15
1410	A456	3.40z	multi	40	15
1411	A456	6.50z	multi	85	38
1412	A456	7.10z	multi	1.10	60
			Nos. 1405-1412 (8)	3.20	
			Set value		1.50

World Cup Soccer Championship, Wembley, England, July 11-30. Each denomination printed in sheets of 10 (5x2).

See No. B109.

Typo. & Engr.

1966, May 9 *Perf. 11½*

1413	A457	60g	sil & multi	15	15

21st anniversary of victory over Fascism.

Women's Relay Race — A458

Designs: 20g, Start of men's short distance race, vert. 60g, Javelin, vert. 90g, Women's 80-meter hurdles. 1.35z, Discus, vert. 3.40z, Finish of men's medium distance race. 6.50z, Hammer throw, vert 7.10z, High jump.

Perf. 11½x11, 11x11½

1966, June 18 Litho.

1414	A458	20g	multi	15	15
1415	A458	40g	multi	15	15
1416	A458	60g	multi	15	15
1417	A458	90g	multi	15	15
1418	A458	1.35z	multi	15	15
1419	A458	3.40z	multi	35	15
1420	A458	6.50z	multi	48	32
1421	A458	7.10z	multi	60	50
			Set value	1.80	1.30

Souvenir Sheet

Design: 5z, Long distance race.

Imperf

1422	A458	5z	multi	1.00	55

European Athletic Championships, Budapest, August, 1966. No. 1422 contains one stamp 57x27mm.

Polish Eagle
A459

Flowers and Farm Produce
A460

Designs: Nos. 1424, 1426, Flag of Poland. No. 1425, Polish Eagle.

Photogravure and Embossed

Perf. 12½x12

1966, July 21 Unwmk.

1423	A459	60g	gold, red & blk	15	15
1424	A459	60g	gold, red & blk	15	15
1425	A459	2.50z	gold, red & blk	25	15
1426	A459	2.50z	gold, red & blk	25	15
			Set value	68	40

1000th anniversary of Poland. Nos. 1423-1424 and 1425-1426 printed in 2 sheets of 10 (5x2); top row in each sheet in eagle design, bottom row in flag design.

1966, Aug. 15 Photo. *Perf. 11*

Designs: 60g, Woman holding loaf of bread. 3.40z, Farm girls holding harvest wreath.

Size: 22x50mm

1427	A460	40g	gold & multi	22	15
1428	A460	60g	gold & multi	22	15

Size: 48x50mm

1429	A460	3.40z	vio bl & multi	55	35
			Set value		50

Issued to publicize the harvest festival.

Chrysanthemum — A461

Flowers: 20g, Poinsettia. 30g, Centaury. 40g, Rose. 60g, Zinnias. 90g, Nasturtium. 5.60z, Dahlia. 6.50z, Sunflower. 7.10z, Magnolia.

1966, Sept. 1 *Perf. 11½*

Flowers in Natural Colors

1430	A461	10g	gold & blk	15	15
1431	A461	20g	gold & blk	15	15
1432	A461	30g	gold & blk	15	15
1433	A461	40g	gold & blk	15	15
1434	A461	60g	gold & blk	15	15
1435	A461	90g	gold & blk	60	25
1436	A461	5.60z	gold & blk	75	25
1437	A461	6.50z	gold & blk	1.10	52
1438	A461	7.10z	gold & blk	85	65
			Nos. 1430-1438 (9)	4.05	
			Set value		1.90

Map Showing Tourist Attractions — A462

Designs: 20g, Lighthouse, Hel. 40g, Amethyst yacht on Masurian Lake. No. 1442, Poniatowski Bridge, Warsaw, and sailboat. No. 1443, Mining Academy, Kielce. 1.15z, Dunajec Gorge. 1.35z, Old oaks, Rogalin. 1.55z, Planetarium, Katowice. 2z, M.S. Batory and globe.

Perf. 12½x12, 11½x12

1966, Sept. 15 Engr.

1439	A462	10g	car rose	15	15
1440	A462	20g	ol gray	15	15
1441	A462	40g	grysh bl	15	15
1442	A462	60g	redsh brn	15	15
1443	A462	60g	black	15	15
1444	A462	1.15z	green	15	15
1445	A462	1.35z	vermilion	15	15
1446	A462	1.55z	violet	15	15
1447	A462	2z	dk gray	15	15
			Set value	74	55

Stableman with Percherons, by Piotr Michalowski — A463

Design: 2.50z, "Horses and Dogs" by Michalowski.

1966, Sept. 8 *Perf. 11x11½*

1448	A463	60g	gray brn	15	15
1449	A463	2.50z	green	18	15
			Set value		18

Issued for Stamp Day, 1966.

Capital of Romanesque Column from Tyniec and Polish Flag — A464

Engraved and Photogravure

1966, Oct. 7 *Perf. 11½*

1450	A464	60g	dk brn & rose	15	15

Polish Cultural Congress.

Soldier — A465

1966, Oct. 20 Litho. *Perf. 11x11½*

1451	A465	60g blk, ol grn, & dl red	15	15

Participation of the Polish Jaroslaw Dabrowski Brigade in the Spanish Civil War.

Green Woodpecker A466

Forest Birds: 10g, The eight birds of the set combined. 30g, Eurasian jay. 40g, European golden oriole. 60g, Hoopoe. 2.50z, European redstart. 4z, Siskin (finch). 6.50z, Chaffinch. 7.10z, Great tit.

1966, Nov. 17 Photo. *Perf. 11½*

Birds in Natural Colors; Black Inscription

1452	A466	10g	lt grn	15	15
1453	A466	20g	dl vio bl	15	15
1454	A466	30g	dl grn	15	15
1455	A466	40g	gray	15	15
1456	A466	60g	gray grn	15	15
1457	A466	2.50z	lt ol grn	25	15
1458	A466	4z	dl vio	90	35
1459	A466	6.50z	green	65	42
1460	A466	7.10z	gray bl	1.25	70
		Nos. 1452-1460 (9)		3.80	
		Set value			2.00

Ceramic Ram, c. 4000 B.C. — A467

Designs: No. 1462, Bronze weapons and ornaments, c. 3500 B.C., horiz. No. 1463, Biskupin, settlement plan, 2500 B.C.

1966, Dec. 10 Engr. *Perf. 11x11½*

1461	A467	60g dl vio bl	15	15
1462	A467	60g brown	15	15
1463	A467	60g green	15	15
		Set value	30	24

Polish Eagle, Hammer and Grain — A468

Designs: 60g, Eagle and map of Poland.

1966, Dec. 20 Litho. *Perf. 11*

1464	A468	40g brn, red & bluish lil	15	15
1465	A468	60g brn, red & ol grn	15	15
		Set value	16	15

Millenium of Poland.

Gemini, American Spacecraft — A469

Spacecraft: 20g, Vostok (USSR). 60g, Ariel 2 (Great Britain). 1.35z, Proton 1 (USSR). 1.50z, FR 1 (France). 3.40z, Alouette (Canada). 6.50z, San Marco 1 (Italy). 7.10z, Luna 9 (USSR).

1966, Dec. 20 *Perf. 11½x11*

1466	A469	20g	tan & multi	15	15
1467	A469	40g	brn & multi	15	15
1468	A469	60g	gray & multi	15	15
1469	A469	1.35z	multi	15	15
1470	A469	1.50z	multi	15	15
1471	A469	3.40z	multi	32	16
1472	A469	6.50z	multi	65	22
1473	A469	7.10z	multi	85	48
		Set value		2.20	1.15

Dressage — A470

Horses: 20g, Horse race. 40g, Jump. 60g, Steeplechase. 90g, Trotting. 5.90z, Polo. 6.60z, Stallion "Ofir." 7z, Stallion "Skowronek."

1967, Feb. 25 Photo. *Perf. 12½*

1474	A470	10g	ultra & multi	15	15
1475	A470	20g	org & multi	15	15
1476	A470	40g	ver & multi	15	15
1477	A470	60g	multi	15	15
1478	A470	90g	grn & multi	18	15
1479	A470	5.90z	multi	70	18
1480	A470	6.60z	multi	90	40
1481	A470	7z	vio & multi	1.75	90
		Nos. 1474-1481 (8)		4.13	
		Set value			1.80

Janov Podlaski stud farm, 150th anniv.

Memorial at Auschwitz (Oswiecim) A471

Emblem of Memorials Administration — A472

Memorials at: No. 1484, Oswiecim-Monowice. No. 1485, Westerplatte (Walcz). No. 1486, Lodz-Radugoszcz. No. 1487, Stutthof. No. 1488, Lambinowice-Jencom. No. 1489, Zagan.

1967 Engr. *Perf. 11½x11, 11x11½*

1482	A471	40g brn ol	15	15
1483	A472	40g dl vio	15	15
1484	A472	40g black	15	15
1485	A472	40g green	15	15
1486	A472	40g black	15	15
1487	A471	40g ultra	15	15
1488	A471	40g brown	15	15
1489	A472	40g dp plum	15	15
		Set value	64	40

Issued to commemorate the martyrdom and fight of the Polish people, 1939-45.

Issue dates: Nos. 1482-1484, Apr. 10. Nos. 1485-1487, Oct. 9. Nos. 1488-1489, Dec. 28.

See Nos. 1620-1624.

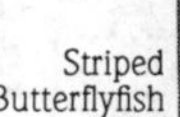

Striped Butterflyfish A473

Tropical fish: 10g, Imperial angelfish. 40g, Barred butterflyfish. 60g, Spotted triggerfish. 90g, Undulate triggerfish. 1.50z, Striped triggerfish. 4.50z, Black-eye butterflyfish. 6.60z, Blue angelfish. 7z, Saddleback butterflyfish.

1967, Apr. 1 Litho. *Perf. 11x11½*

1492	A473	5g	multi	15	15
1493	A473	10g	multi	15	15
1494	A473	40g	multi	15	15
1495	A473	60g	multi	15	15
1496	A473	90g	multi	15	15
1497	A473	1.50z	multi	15	15
1498	A473	4.50z	multi	50	28
1499	A473	6.60z	multi	65	42
1500	A473	7z	multi	1.10	70
		Nos. 1492-1500 (9)		3.15	
		Set value			1.80

Bicyclists — A474

1967, May 5 Litho. *Perf. 11*

1501	A474	60g multi	15	15

20th Warsaw-Berlin-Prague Bicycle Race.

Men's 100-meter Race A475

Sports and Olympic Rings: 40g, Steeplechase. 60g, Women's relay race. 90g, Weight lifter. 1.35z, Hurdler. 3.40z, Gymnast on vaulting horse. 6.60z, High jump. 7z, Boxing.

1967, May 24 Litho. *Perf. 11*

1502	A475	20g	multi	15	15
1503	A475	40g	multi	15	15
1504	A475	60g	multi	15	15
1505	A475	90g	multi	15	15
1506	A475	1.35z	multi	15	15
1507	A475	3.40z	multi	38	15
1508	A475	6.60z	multi	75	24
1509	A475	7z	multi	90	52
		Nos. 1502-1509 (8)		2.78	
		Set value			1.20

19th Olympic Games, Mexico City, 1968. Nos. 1502-1509 printed in sheets of 8, (2x4) with label showing emblem of Polish Olympic Committee between each two horizontal stamps. See No. B110.

Badge of Socialist Working Brigade A476

1967, June 2

1510	A476	60g multi	15	15

6th Congress of Polish Trade Unions. Printed in sheets of 20 stamps and 20 labels and in miniature sheets of 4 stamps and 4 labels.

Mountain Arnica — A477

Medicinal Plants: 60g, Columbine. 3.40z, Gentian. 4.50z, Ground pine. 5z, Iris sibirica. 10z, Azalea pontica.

1967, June 14 *Perf. 11½x11*

Flowers in Natural Colors

1511	A477	40g	blk & brn org	15	15
1512	A477	60g	blk & lt bl	15	15
1513	A477	3.40z	blk & dp org	30	15
1514	A477	4.50z	blk & lt vio	32	15
1515	A477	5z	blk & mar	35	15
1516	A477	10z	blk & bis	85	42
		Nos. 1511-1516 (6)		2.12	
		Set value			92

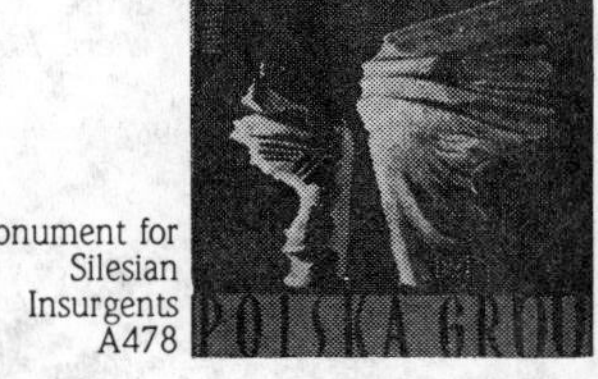

Monument for Silesian Insurgents A478

1967, July 21 Litho. *Perf. 11½*

1517	A478	60g multi	15	15

Unveiling of the monument for the Silesian Insurgents of 1919-21 at Katowice, July, 1967.

Marie Curie — A479

Designs: No. 1519, Curie statue, Warsaw. No. 1520, Nobel Prize diploma.

1967, Aug. 1 Engr. *Perf. 11½x11*

1518	A479	60g dk car rose	18	15
1519	A479	60g violet	15	15
1520	A479	60g sepia	18	15
		Set value		24

Marie Sklodowska Curie (1867-1934), discoverer of radium and polonium.

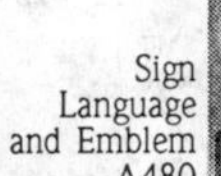

Sign Language and Emblem A480

1967, Aug. 1 Litho. *Perf. 11x11½*

1521	A480	60g brt bl & blk	15	15

5th Congress of the World Federation of the Deaf, Warsaw, Aug. 10-17.

Flowers of the Meadows A481

Flowers: 40g, Poppy. 60g, Morning glory. 90g, Pansy. 1.15z, Common pansy. 2.50z, Corn cockle. 3.40z, Wild aster. 4.50z, Common pimpernel. 7.90z, Chicory.

1967, Sept. 5 Photo. *Perf. 11½*

1522 A481	20g multi	15	15
1523 A481	40g multi	15	15
1524 A481	60g multi	15	15
1525 A481	90g multi	15	15
1526 A481	1.15z multi	15	15
1527 A481	2.50z multi	25	16
1528 A481	3.40z multi	38	16
1529 A481	4.50z multi	75	48
1530 A481	7.90z multi	95	48
	Nos. 1522-1530 (9)	3.08	
	Set value		1.60

Wilanow Palace, by Wincenty Kasprzycki A482

Engraved and Photogravure

1967, Oct. 9 *Perf. 11½*

1531 A482 60g ol blk & lt bl 15 15

Issued for Stamp Day, 1967.

Cruiser Aurora — A483

Designs: No. 1533, Lenin and library. No. 1534, Luna 10, earth and moon.

1967, Oct. 9 Litho. *Perf. 11*

1532 A483	60g gray, red & blk	15	15
1533 A483	60g gray, dl red & blk	15	15
1534 A483	60g gray, red & blk	15	15
	Set value		26

Russian Revolution, 50th anniv.

Tadeusz Kosciusko — A485

Engraved and Photogravure

1967, Oct. 14 *Perf. 12x11*

1540 A485	60g choc & ocher	15	15
1541 A485	2.50z sl grn & rose car	15	15
	Set value	22	22

Tadeusz Kosciusko (1746-1817), Polish patriot and general in the American Revolution.

Vanessa Butterfly A486

Designs: Various Butterflies.

1967, Oct. 14 Litho. *Perf. 11½*

Butterflies in Natural Colors

1542 A486	10g green	15	15
1543 A486	20g lt vio bl	15	15
1544 A486	40g yel grn	15	15
1545 A486	60g gray	15	15
1546 A486	2z lemon	15	15
1547 A486	2.50z Prus grn	18	15
1548 A486	3.40z blue	30	15
1549 A486	4.50z rose lil	1.00	40
1550 A486	7.90z bister	1.65	90
	Nos. 1542-1550 (9)	3.88	
	Set value		1.85

Polish Woman, by Antoine Watteau A487

Paintings from Polish Museums: 20g, Lady with the Ermine, by Leonardo da Vinci. 60g, Dog Fighting Heron, by Abraham Hondius. 2z, Guitarist after the Hunt, by J. Baptiste Greuze. 2.50z, Tax Collectors, by Marinus van Reymerswaele. 3.40z, Portrait of Daria Flodorowna, by Fiodor St. Rokotov. 4.50z, Still Life with Lobster, by Jean de Heem, horiz. 6.60z, Landscape (from the Good Samaritan), by Rembrandt, horiz.

Perf. 11½x11, 11x11½

1967, Nov. 15 Photo.

1551 A487	20g gold & multi	15	15
1552 A487	40g gold & multi	15	15
1553 A487	60g gold & multi	15	15
1554 A487	2z gold & multi	20	15
1555 A487	2.50z gold & multi	28	15
1556 A487	3.40z gold & multi	40	15
1557 A487	4.50z gold & multi	95	42
1558 A487	6.60z gold & multi	1.10	70
	Nos. 1551-1558 (8)	3.38	
	Set value		1.75

Printed in sheets of 5 + label.

Ossolinski Medal, Book and Flags — A488

1967, Dec. 12 Litho. *Perf. 11*

1559 A488 60g lt bl, red & lt brn 15 15

150th anniversary of the founding of the Ossolineum, a center for scientific and cultural activities, by Count Josef Maximilian Ossolinski.

Wladyslaw S. Reymont (1867-1924), Writer, Nobel Prize Winner — A489

1967, Dec. 12

1560 A489 60g dk brn, ocher & red 15 15

Ice Hockey A490

Designs: 60g, Skiing. 90g, Slalom. 1.35z, Speed skating. 1.55z, Long-distance skiing. 2z, Sledding. 7z, Biathlon. 7.90z, Ski jump.

1968, Jan. 10

1561 A490	40g multi	15	15
1562 A490	60g multi	15	15
1563 A490	90g multi	15	15
1564 A490	1.35z multi	15	15
1565 A490	1.55z multi	15	15
1566 A490	2z multi	20	15
1567 A490	7z multi	52	35
1568 A490	7.90z multi	85	52
	Nos. 1561-1568 (8)	2.32	
	Set value		1.30

10th Winter Olympic Games, Grenoble, France, Feb. 6-18, 1968.

Puss in Boots — A491

Fairy Tales: 40g, The Fox and the Raven. 60g, Mr. Twardowski (man flying on a cock). 2z, The Fisherman and the Fish. 2.50z, Little Red Riding Hood. 3.40z, Cinderella. 5.50z, Thumbelina. 7z, Snow White.

1968, Mar. 15 Litho. *Perf. 12½*

1569 A491	20g multi	15	15
1570 A491	40g lt vio & multi	15	15
1571 A491	60g multi	15	15
1572 A491	2z ol & multi	20	15
1573 A491	2.50z ver & multi	25	15
1574 A491	3.40z multi	45	16
1575 A491	5.50z multi	65	42
1576 A491	7z multi	1.10	70
	Nos. 1569-1576 (8)	3.10	
	Set value		1.70

Bird-of-Paradise Flower A492

Exotic Flowers: 10g, Clianthus dampieri. 20g, Passiflora quadrangularis. 40g, Coryphanta vivipara. 60g, Odontonia. 90g, Protea cynaroides.

1968, May 15 Litho. *Perf. 11½*

1577 A492	10g sep & multi	15	15
1578 A492	20g multi	15	15
1579 A492	30g brn & multi	15	15
1580 A492	40g ultra & multi	15	15
1581 A492	60g multi	15	15
1582 A492	90g multi	15	15
	Set value, #1577-1582, B111-B112	2.30	1.35

"Peace" by Henryk Tomaszewski A493

Design: 2.50z, Poster for Gounod's Faust, by Jan Lenica.

1968, May 29 Litho. *Perf. 11½x11*

1583 A493	60g gray & multi	15	15
1584 A493	2.50z gray & multi	18	15
	Set value		18

2nd Intl. Poster Biennial Exhibition, Warsaw.

Zephyr Glider A494

Polish Gliders: 90g, Storks. 1.50z, Swallow. 3.40z, Flies. 4z, Seal. 5.50z, Pirate.

1968, May 29 *Perf. 12½*

1585 A494	60g multi	15	15
1586 A494	90g multi	15	15
1587 A494	1.50z multi	15	15
1588 A494	3.40z multi	40	16
1589 A494	4z multi	52	28
1590 A494	5.50z multi	65	42
	Nos. 1585-1590 (6)	2.02	
	Set value		1.05

11th Intl. Glider Championships, Leszno.

Child Holding Symbolic Stamp A495

Sosnowiec Memorial A496

Design: No. 1592, Balloon over Poznan Town Hall.

1968, July 2 Litho. *Perf. 11½x11*

1591 A495	60g multi	15	15
1592 A495	60g multi	15	15
	Set value	24	15

75 years of Polish philately; "Tematica 1968" stamp exhibition in Poznan. Printed in sheets of 12 (4x3) se-tenant, arranged checkerwise.

Photogravure and Engraved

1968, July 20 *Perf. 11x11½*

1593 A496 60g brt rose lil & blk 15 15

The monument by Helena and Roman Husarski and Witold Ceckiewicz was unveiled Sept. 16, 1967, to honor the revolutionary deeds of Silesian workers and miners.

Relay Race and Sculptured Head — A497

Sports and Sculptures: 40g, Boxing. 60g, Basketball. 90g, Long jump. 2.50z, Women's javelin. 3.40z, Athlete on parallel bars. 4z, Bicycling. 7.90z, Fencing.

1968, Sept. 2 Litho. *Perf. 11x11½*

Size: 35x26mm

1594 A497	30g sep & multi	15	15
1595 A497	40g brn org, brn & blk	15	15
1596 A497	60g gray & multi	15	15
1597 A497	90g vio & multi	15	15
1598 A497	2.50z multi	20	15
1599 A497	3.40z brt grn, blk & lt ultra	30	15
1600 A497	4z multi	32	18
1601 A497	7.90z multi	65	35
	Nos. 1594-1601,B113 (9)	3.57	
	Set value		1.80

19th Olympic Games, Mexico City, Oct. 12-27.

Jewish Woman with Lemons, by Aleksander Gierymski
A498

Polish Paintings: 40g, Knight on Bay Horse, by Piotr Michalowski. 60g, Fisherman, by Leon Wyczolkowski. 1.35z, Eliza Parenska, by Stanislaw Wyspianski. 1.50z, "Manifest," by Wojciech Weiss. 4.50z, Stancyk (Jester), by Jan Matejko, horiz. 5z, Children's Band, by Tadeusz Makowski, horiz. 7z, Feast II, by Zygmunt Waliszewski, horiz.

Perf. 11½x11, 11x11½

1968, Oct. 10 **Litho.**

1602	A498	40g gray & multi	15	15
1603	A498	60g gray & multi	15	15
1604	A498	1.15z gray & multi	15	15
1605	A498	1.35z gray & multi	15	15
1606	A498	1.50z gray & multi	30	16
1607	A498	4.50z gray & multi	40	22
1608	A498	5z gray & multi	65	30
1609	A498	7z gray & multi	75	48
		Nos. 1602-1609 (8)	2.70	
		Set value		1.40

Issued in sheets of 4 stamps and 2 labels inscribed with painter's name.

"September, 1939" by M. Bylina — A499

Paintings: No. 1611, Partisans, by L. Maciag. No. 1612, Tank in Battle, by M. Bylina. No. 1613, Monte Cassino, by A. Boratynski. No. 1614, Tanks Approaching Warsaw, by S. Garwatowski. No. 1615, Battle on the Neisse, by M. Bylina. No. 1616, On the Oder, by K. Mackiewicz. No. 1617, "In Berlin," by M. Bylina. No. 1618, Warship "Blyskawica" by M. Mokwa. No. 1619, "Pursuit" (fighter planes), by T. Kulisiewicz.

Litho., Typo. & Engr.

1968, Oct. 12 *Perf. 11½*

1610	A499	40g pale yel, ol & vio	15	15
1611	A499	40g lil, red lil & ind	15	15
1612	A499	40g gray, dk bl & ol	15	15
1613	A499	40g pale sal, org brn & blk	15	15
1614	A499	40g pale grn, dk grn & plum	15	15
1615	A499	60g gray, vio bl & blk	15	15
1616	A499	60g pale grn, ol grn & vio brn	15	15
1617	A499	60g pink, car & grnsh blk	15	15
1618	A499	60g pink, brn & grn	15	15
1619	A499	60g lt bl, grnsh bl & blk	15	15
		Set value	1.00	65

Polish People's Army, 25th anniversary.

Memorial Types of 1967

Designs: No. 1620, Tomb of the Unknown Soldier, Warsaw. No. 1621, Nazi War Crimes Memorial, Zamosc. No. 1622, Guerrilla Memorial, Plichno. No. 1623, Guerrilla Memorial, Kartuzy. No. 1624, Polish Insurgents' Memorial, Poznan.

Perf. 11½x11, 11x11½

1968, Nov. 15 **Engr.**

1620	A471	40g slate	15	15
1621	A472	40g dl red	15	15
1622	A472	40g dk bl	15	15
1623	A471	40g sepia	15	15
1624	A472	40g sepia	15	15
		Set value	40	25

Issued to commemorate the martyrdom and fight of the Polish people, 1939-45.

Strikers, S. Lentz
A500

Paintings: No. 1626, "Manifesto," by Wojciech Weiss. No. 1627, Party members, by F. Kowarski, horiz.

Perf. 11½x11, 11x11½

1968, Nov. 11 **Litho.**

1625	A500	60g dk red & multi	15	15
1626	A500	60g dk red & multi	15	15
1627	A500	60g dk red & multi	15	15
		Set value	26	18

5th Congress of the Polish United Workers' Party.

Departure for the Hunt, by Wojciech Kossak — A501

Hunt Paintings: 40g, Hunting with Falcon, by Juliusz Kossak. 60g, Wolves' Raid, by A. Wierusz-Kowalski. 1.50z, Bear Hunt, by Julian Falat. 2.50z, Fox Hunt, by T. Sutherland. 3.40z, Boar Hunt, by Frans Snyders. 4.50z, Hunters' Rest, by W. G. Pierow. 8.50z, Lion Hunt in Morocco, by Delacroix.

1968, Nov. 20 *Perf. 11*

1628	A501	20g multi	15	15
1629	A501	40g multi	15	15
1630	A501	60g multi	15	15
1631	A501	1.50z multi	18	15
1632	A501	2.50z multi	16	15
1633	A501	3.40z multi	35	15
1634	A501	4.50z multi	70	40
1635	A501	8.50z multi	1.25	80
		Nos. 1628-1635 (8)	3.09	
		Set value		1.60

Afghan Greyhound
A502

Dogs: 20g, Maltese. 40g, Rough-haired fox terrier, vert. 1.50z, Schnauzer. 2.50z, English setter. 3.40z, Pekinese. 4.50z, German shepherd. 8.50z, Pointer.

1969, Feb. 2 *Perf. 11x11½, 11½x11*

Dogs in Natural Colors

1636	A502	20g gray & brt grn	15	15
1637	A502	40g gray & org	28	15
1638	A502	60g gray & lil	28	15
1639	A502	1.50z gray & blk	28	15
1640	A502	2.50z gray & brt pink	45	22
1641	A502	3.40z gray & dk grn	75	30
1642	A502	4.50z gray & ver	1.40	55
1643	A502	8.50z gray & vio	2.75	1.25
		Nos. 1636-1643 (8)	6.34	2.92

General Assembly of the Intl. Kennel Federation, Warsaw, May 1969.

Eagle-on-Shield House Sign — A503

1969, Feb. 23 **Litho.** *Perf. 11½x11*

1644	A503	60g gray, red & blk	15	15

9th Congress of Democratic Movement.

Sheaf of Wheat
A504

1969, Mar. 29 **Litho.** *Perf. 11½x11*

1645	A504	60g multi	15	15

5th Congress of the United Peasant Party, Warsaw, March 29-31.

Runner — A505

Olympic Rings and: 20g, Woman gymnast. 40g, Weight lifting. 60g, Women's javelin.

1969, Apr. 25 **Litho.** *Perf. 11½x11*

1646	A505	10g org & multi	15	15
1647	A505	20g ultra & multi	15	15
1648	A505	40g yel & multi	15	15
1649	A505	60g red & multi	15	15
		Set value, #1646-1649, B114-B117	2.20	1.00

50th anniv. of the Polish Olympic Committee, and the 75th anniv. of the Intl. Olympic Committee.

Sailboat and Lighthouse, Kolobrzeg Harbor — A506

Designs: 40g, Tourist map of Swietokrzyski National Park. 60g, Ruins of 16th century castle, Niedzica, vert. 1.50z, Castle of the Dukes of Pomerania and ship, Szczecin. 2.50z, View of Torun and Vistula. 3.40z, View of Klodzko, vert. 4z, View of Sulejow. 4.50z, Market Place, Kazimierz Dolny, vert.

1969, May 20 **Litho.** *Perf. 11*

1650	A506	40g multi	15	15
1651	A506	60g multi	15	15
1652	A506	1.35z multi	15	15
1653	A506	1.50z multi	15	15
1654	A506	2.50z multi	15	15
1655	A506	3.40z multi	18	15
1656	A506	4z multi	25	15
1657	A506	4.50z multi	42	18
		Set value	1.25	70

Issued for tourist publicity. Printed in sheets of 15 stamps and 15 labels. Domestic plants on labels of 40g, 60g and 1.35z, coats of arms on others.

See Nos. 1731-1735.

World Map and Sailboat Opty
A507

1969, June 21 **Litho.** *Perf. 11x11½*

1658	A507	60g multi	15	15

Leonid Teliga's one-man voyage around the world, Casablanca, Jan. 21, 1967, to Las Palmas, Apr. 16, 1969.

Nicolaus Copernicus, Woodcut by Tobias Stimer — A508

Designs: 60g, Copernicus, by Jeremias Falck, 15th century globe and map of constellations. 2.50z, Copernicus, painting by Jan Matejko and map of heliocentric system.

Photo., Engr. & Litho.

1969, June 26 *Perf. 11½*

1659	A508	40g dl yel, sep & dp car	15	15
1660	A508	60g grnsh gray, blk & dp car	15	15
1661	A508	2.50z lt vio brn, ol & dp car	42	16
		Set value		30

Copernicus (1473-1543), astronomer.

"Memory" Pathfinders' Cross and Protectors' Badge
A509

Frontier Guard and Embossed Arms of Poland
A510

Coal Miner — A511

Designs: No. 1663, "Defense," military eagle and Pathfinders' cross. No. 1664, "Labor," map of Poland and Pathfinders' cross.

Photo., Engr. & Litho.

1969, July 19 *Perf. 11x11½*

1662	A509	60g ultra, blk & red	15	15
1663	A509	60g grn, blk & red	15	15
1664	A509	60g car, blk & grn	15	15
		Set value	30	24

5th National Alert of Polish Pathfinders' Union.

1969, July 21 **Litho. & Embossed**

Designs: No. 1666, Oil refinery-chemical plant, Plock. No. 1667, Combine harvester. No. 1668, Rebuilt Grand Theater, Warsaw. No. 1669, Marie Sklodowska-Curie Monument and University, Lublin. No. 1671, Chemical industry (sulphur) worker. No. 1672, Steelworker. No. 1673, Ship builder and ship.

1665 A510	60g red & multi		15	15
1666 A510	60g red & multi		15	15
1667 A510	60g red & multi		15	15
1668 A510	60g red & multi		15	15
1669 A510	60g red & multi		15	15
a.	Strip of 5, #1665-1669		40	40

Perf. 11½x11

Litho.

1670 A511	60g gray & multi	15	15
1671 A511	60g gray & multi	15	15
1672 A511	60g gray & multi	15	15
1673 A511	60g gray & multi	15	15
a.	Strip of 4, #1670-1673	32	32
	Set value	72	45

25th anniv. of the Polish People's Republic.

Landing Module on Moon, and Earth — A512

1969, Aug. 21 Litho. *Perf. 12x12½*

1674 A512	2.50z multi	80	42

Man's first landing on the moon, July 20, 1969. US astronauts Neil A. Armstrong and Col. Edwin E. Aldrin, Jr., with Lieut. Col. Michael Collins piloting Apollo 11. Issued in sheets of 8 stamps and 2 tabs with decorative border. One tab shows Apollo 11 with lunar landing module, the other shows module's take-off from moon. Value, sheet. $22.50.

Motherhood, by Stanislaw Wyspianski — A513

Polish Paintings: 40g, "Hamlet," by Jacek Malczewski. 60g, Indian Summer (sleeping woman), by Jozef Chelmonski. 2z, Two Girls, by Olga Boznanska, vert. 2.50z, "The Sun of May" (Breakfast on the Terrace), by Jozef Mehoffer, vert. 3.40z, Woman Combing her Hair, by Wladyslaw Slewinski. 5.50z, Still Life, by Jozef Pankiewicz. 7z, The Abduction of the King's Daughter, by Witold Wojtkiewicz.

Perf. 11x11½, 11½x11

1969, Sept. 4 Photo.

1675 A513	20g gold & multi	15	15
1676 A513	40g gold & multi	15	15
1677 A513	60g gold & multi	15	15
1678 A513	2z gold & multi	20	15
1679 A513	2.50z gold & multi	20	15
1680 A513	3.40z gold & multi	32	15
1681 A513	5.50z gold & multi	80	32
1682 A513	7z gold & multi	1.25	52
	Nos. 1675-1682 (8)	3.22	
	Set value		1.35

Issued in sheets of 4 stamps and 2 labels inscribed with painter's name.

Nike — A514

1969, Sept. 19 Litho. *Perf. 11½x11*

1683 A514	60g gray, red & bis	15	15

4th Congress of the Union of Fighters for Freedom and Democracy.

Details from Memorial, Majdanek Concentration Camp — A515

1969, Sept. 20 *Perf. 11*

1684 A515	40g brt lil, gray & blk	15	15

Unveiling of a monument to the victims of the Majdanek concentration camp. The monument was designed by the sculptor Wiktor Tolkin.

Costumes from Krczonow, Lublin — A516

Regional Costumes: 60g, Lowicz, Lodz. 1.15z, Rozbark, Katowice. 1.35z, Lower Silesia, Wroclaw. 1.50z, Opoczno, Lodz. 4.50z, Sacz, Cracow. 5z, Highlanders, Cracow. 7z, Kurpiow, Warsaw.

1969, Sept. 30 Litho. *Perf. 11½x11*

1685 A516	40g multi	15	15
1686 A516	60g multi	15	15
1687 A516	1.15z multi	15	15
1688 A516	1.35z multi	15	15
1689 A516	1.50z multi	15	15
1690 A516	4.50z multi	40	24
1691 A516	5z multi	60	42
1692 A516	7z multi	48	30
	Set value	1.90	1.30

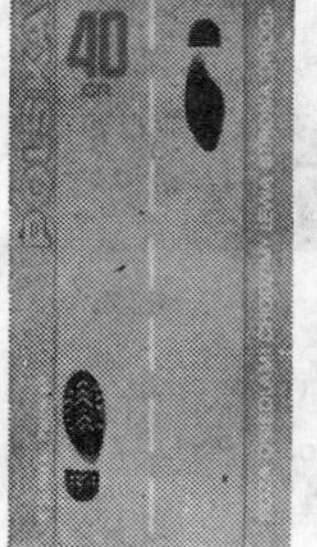

"Walk at Left" — A517

ILO Emblem and Welder's Mask — A518

Traffic safety: 60g, "Drive Carefully" (horses on road). 2.50z, "Lower your Lights" (automobile on road).

1969, Oct. 4 *Perf. 11*

1693 A517	40g multi	15	15
1694 A517	60g multi	15	15
1695 A517	2.50z multi	18	15
	Set value	30	16

1969, Oct. 20 *Perf. 11x11½*

1696 A518	2.50z vio bl & ol	15	15

ILO, 50th anniversary.

Bell Foundry A519

Miniatures from Behem's Code, completed 1505: 60g, Painter's studio. 1.35z, Wood carvers. 1.55z, Shoemaker. 2.50z, Cooper. 3.40z, Bakery. 4.50z, Tailor. 7z, Bowyer's shop.

1969, Nov. 12 Litho. *Perf. 12½*

1697 A519	40g gray & multi	15	15
1698 A519	60g gray & multi	15	15
1699 A519	1.35z gray & multi	15	15
1700 A519	1.55z gray & multi	15	15
1701 A519	2.50z gray & multi	20	15
1702 A519	3.40z gray & multi	28	15
1703 A519	4.50z gray & multi	40	22
1704 A519	7z gray & multi	85	40
	Set value	2.05	1.10

Angel — A520

Folk Art (Sculptures): 40g, Sorrowful Christ (head). 60g, Sorrowful Christ (seated figure). 2z, Crying woman. 2.50z, Adam and Eve. 3.40z, Woman with birds.

1969, Dec. 19 Litho. *Perf. 12½*

Size: 21x36mm

1705 A520	20g lt bl & multi	15	15
1706 A520	40g lil & multi	15	15
1707 A520	60g multi	15	15
1708 A520	2z multi	18	15
1709 A520	2.50z multi	20	15
1710 A520	3.40z multi	28	18
	Nos. 1705-1710,B118-B119 (8)	2.33	
	Set value		1.10

Leopold Staff (1878-1957) A521

Polish Writers: 60g, Wladyslaw Broniewski (1897-1962). 1.35z, Leon Kruczkowski (1900-1962). 1.50z, Julian Tuwim (1894-1953). 1.55z, Konstanty Ildefons Galczynski (1905-1953). 2.50z, Maria Dabrowska (1889-1965). 3.40z, Zofia Nalkowska (1885-1954).

Litho., Typo. & Engr.

1969, Dec. 30 *Perf. 11x11½*

1711 A521	40g ol grn & blk, *grnsh*	15	15
1712 A521	60g dp car & blk, *pink*	15	15
1713 A521	1.35z vio bl & blk, *grysh*	15	15
1714 A521	1.50z pur & blk, *pink*	15	15
1715 A521	1.55z dp grn & blk, *grnsh*	15	15
1716 A521	2.50z ultra & blk, *gray*	20	15
1717 A521	3.40z red brn & blk, *pink*	28	15
	Set value	1.00	50

Statue of Nike and Polish Colors A522

1970, Jan. 17 Photo. *Perf. 11½*

1718 A522	60g sil, gold, red & blk	15	15

Warsaw liberation, 25th anniversary.

Medieval Print Shop and Modern Color Proofs — A523

1970, Jan. 20 Litho. *Perf. 11½x11*

1719 A523	60g multi	15	15

Centenary of Polish printers' trade union.

Ringnecked Pheasant A524

Game Birds: 40g, Mallard drake. 1.15z, Woodcock. 1.35z, Ruffs (males). 1.50z, Wood pigeon. 3.40z, Black grouse. 7z, Gray partridges (cock and hen). 8.50z, Capercaillie cock giving mating call.

1970, Feb. 28 Litho. *Perf. 11½*

1720 A524	40g multi	15	15
1721 A524	60g multi	95	15
1722 A524	1.15z multi	15	15
1723 A524	1.35z multi	15	15
1724 A524	1.50z multi	28	15
1725 A524	3.40z multi	28	15
1726 A524	7z multi	1.25	65
1727 A524	8.50z multi	1.40	85
	Nos. 1720-1727 (8)	4.61	
	Set value		2.10

Lenin in his Kremlin Study, Oct. 1918, and Polish Lenin Steel Mill — A525

Designs: 60g, Lenin addressing 3rd International Congress in Leningrad, 1920, and Luna 13. 2.50z, Lenin with delegates to 10th Russian Communist Party Congress, Moscow, 1921, dove and globe.

Engr. & Typo.

1970, Apr. 22 *Perf. 11*

1728 A525	40g grnsh blk & dl red	15	15
1729 A525	60g sep & dp lil rose	15	15
a.	Souvenir sheet of 4	85	48
1730 A525	2.50z bluish blk & ver	18	15
	Set value	32	18

Lenin (1870-1924), Russian communist leader.

No. 1729a commemorates the Cracow Intl. Phil. Exhib.

Tourist Type of 1969

Designs: No. 1731, Townhall, Wroclaw, vert. No. 1732, Cathedral, Piast Castle tower and church towers, Opole. No. 1733, Castle, Legnica. No. 1734, Castle Tower, Bolkow. No. 1735, Town Hall, Brzeg.

1970, May 9 Litho. *Perf. 11*

1731 A506	60g Wroclaw	15	15
1732 A506	60g Opole	15	15
1733 A506	60g Legnica	15	15
1734 A506	60g Bolkow	15	15
1735 A506	60g Brzeg	15	15
	Nos. 1731-1735 (5)	75	
	Set value		40

Issued for tourist publicity. Printed in sheets of 15 stamps and 15 labels, showing coats of arms.

Polish and Russian Soldiers before Brandenburg Gate — A526

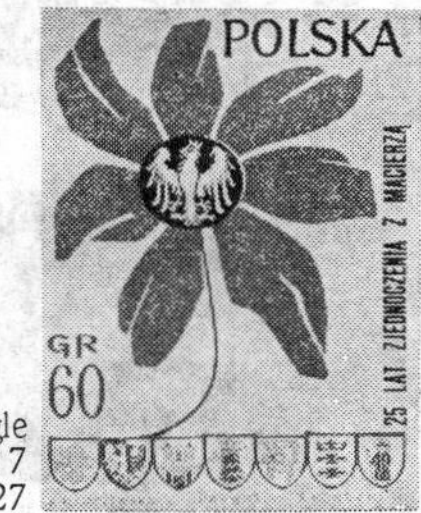

Flower, Eagle and Arms of 7 Cities — A527

Lithographed and Engraved

1970, May 9 *Perf. 11*
1736 A526 60g tan & multi 15 15

Perf. 11½
1737 A527 60g sil, red & sl grn 15 15
Set value 18 16

25th anniversary of victory over Germany and of Polish administration of the Oder-Neisse border area.

Peasant Movement Flag — A528

1970, May 15 Litho. *Perf. 11½*
1738 A528 60g ol & multi 15 15

Polish peasant movement, 75th anniv.

A529 A530

1970, May 20
1739 A529 2.50z bl & vio bl 15 15

Inauguration of new UPU headquarters, Bern.

1970, May 30 *Perf. 11½x11*
1740 A530 60g multi 20 15

European Soccer Cup Finals. Printed in sheets of 15 stamps and 15 se-tenant labels inscribed with the scores of the games.

Lamp of Learning — A531

1970, June 3 *Perf. 11½*
1741 A531 60g blk, bis & red 15 15

Plock Scientific Society, 150th anniversary.

Cross-country Race — A532

Designs: No. 1743, Runners from ancient Greek vase. No. 1744, Archer, drawing by W. Skoczylas.

1970, June 16 Photo. *Perf. 11x11½*
1742 A532 60g yel & multi 15 15
1743 A532 60g blk & multi 15 15
1744 A532 60g dk bl & multi 15 15
Set value 20

10th session of the Intl. Olympic Academy. See No. B120.

Copernicus, by Bacciarelli and View of Bologna — A533

Designs: 60g, Copernicus, by W. Lesseur and view of Padua. 2.50z, Copernicus, by Zinck Nora and view of Ferrara.

Photo., Engr. & Typo.

1970, June 26 *Perf. 11½*
1745 A533 40g org & multi 15 15
1746 A533 60g ol & multi 15 15
1747 A533 2.50z multi 38 15
Set value 54 28

Nicolaus Copernicus (1473-1543), Polish astronomer.

Aleksander Orlowski (1777-1832), Self-portrait A534

Miniatures: 40g, Jan Matejko (1838-1893), self-portrait. 60g, King Stefan Batory (1533-1586), anonymous painter. 2z, Maria Leszczynska (1703-1768), anonymous French painter. 2.50z, Maria Walewska (1789-1817), by Jacquotot Marie-Victoire. 3.40z, Tadeusz Kosciuszko (1746-1817), by Jan Rustem. 5.50z, Samuel Bogumil Linde (1771-1847), by G. Landolfi. 7z, Michal Oginski (1728-1800), by Windisch Nanette.

Litho. & Photo.

1970, Aug. 27 *Perf. 11½*
1748 A534 20g gold & multi 15 15
1749 A534 40g gold & multi 15 15
1750 A534 60g gold & multi 15 15
1751 A534 2z gold & multi 15 15
1752 A534 2.50z gold & multi 25 15
1753 A534 3.40z gold & multi 38 24
1754 A534 5.50z gold & multi 65 35
1755 A534 7z gold & multi 1.10 52
Nos. 1748-1755 (8) 2.98
Set value 1.60

Nos. 1748-1755 printed in sheets of 4 stamps and 2 labels. The miniatures show famous Poles and are from collections in the National Museums in Warsaw and Cracow.

Poster for Chopin Competition — A535

Photogravure and Engraved

1970, Sept. 8 *Perf. 11x11½*
1756 A535 2.50z blk & vio 18 15

8th Intl. Chopin Piano Competition, Warsaw, Oct. 7-25.

UN Emblem A536

1970, Sept. 8 Photo. *Perf. 11½*
1757 A536 2.50z multi 20 15

United Nations, 25th anniversary.

Poles — A537

Design: 60g, Family, home and Polish flag.

1970, Sept. 15 Litho. *Perf. 11½x11*
1758 A537 40g gray & multi 15 15
1759 A537 60g multi 15 15
Set value 20 16

National Census, Dec. 8, 1970.

Grunwald Cross and Warship Piorun (Thunderbolt) — A538

Grunwald Cross and Warship: 60g, Orzel (Eagle). 2.50z, Garland.

1970, Sept. 25 Engr. *Perf. 11½x11*
1760 A538 40g sepia 15 15
1761 A538 60g black 15 15
1762 A538 2.50z dp brn 45 15
Set value 28

Polish Navy during World War II.

Cellist, by Jerzy Nowosielski — A539

Paintings: 40g, View of Lodz, by Benon Liberski. 60g, Studio Concert, by Waclaw Taranczewski. 1.50z, Still Life, by Zbigniew Pronaszko. 2z, Woman Hanging up Laundry, by Andrzej Wroblewski. 3.40z, "Expressions," by Maria Jarema, horiz. 4z, Canal in the Forest, by Piotr Potworowski, horiz. 8.50z, "The Sun," by Wladyslaw Strzeminski, horiz.

1970, Oct. 9 Photo. *Perf. 11½*
1763 A539 20g multi 15 15
1764 A539 40g multi 15 15
1765 A539 60g multi 15 15
1766 A539 1.50z multi 15 15
1767 A539 2z multi 16 15
1768 A539 3.40z multi 24 15
1769 A539 4z multi 42 22
1770 A539 8.50z multi 90 48
Set value 2.00 1.15

Issued for Stamp Day.

Luna 16 Landing on Moon — A540 Stag — A541

1970, Nov. 20 Litho. *Perf. 11½x11*
1771 A540 2.50z multi 28 15

Luna 16 Russian unmanned, automatic moon mission, Sept. 12-24. Issued in sheets of 8 stamps and 2 tabs with bluish black commemorative inscription. One tab shows rocket launching; the other, parachute landing of capsule. Value, sheet $18.

1970, Dec. 23 Photo. *Perf. 11½x12*

Designs from 16th Century Tapestries in Wawel Castle: 1.15z, Stork. 1.35z, Leopard fighting dragon. 2z, Man's head. 2.50z, Child holding bird. 4z, God, Adam and Eve. 4.50z, Panel with monogram of King Sigismund Augustus. 5.50z, Poland's coat of arms.

1772 A541 60g multi 15 15
1773 A541 1.15z pur & multi 15 15
1774 A541 1.35z multi 15 15
1775 A541 2z sep & multi 18 15
1776 A541 2.50z dk bl & multi 22 15
1777 A541 4z grn & multi 52 22
1778 A541 4.50z multi 65 32
Nos. 1772-1778 (7) 2.02
Set value 95

Souvenir Sheet

Imperf
1779 A541 5.50z blk & multi 1.00 50

No. 1779 contains one 48x57mm stamp. See No. B121.

Transatlantic Liner Stefan Batory — A542

Polish Ships: 40g, School sailing ship Dar Pomorza. 1.15z, Ice breaker Perkun. 1.35z, Rescue ship R-1. 1.50z, Freighter Ziemia Szczecinska. 2.50z, Tanker Beskidy. 5z, Express freighter Hel. 8.50z, Ferry Gryf.

1971, Jan. 30 Photo. *Perf. 11*
1780 A542 40g ver & multi 15 15
1781 A542 60g multi 15 15
1782 A542 1.15z bl & multi 15 15
1783 A542 1.35z yel & multi 15 15
1784 A542 1.50z multi 18 15
1785 A542 2.50z vio & multi 24 15
1786 A542 5z multi 52 24
1787 A542 8.50z bl & multi 85 42
Set value 2.10 1.10

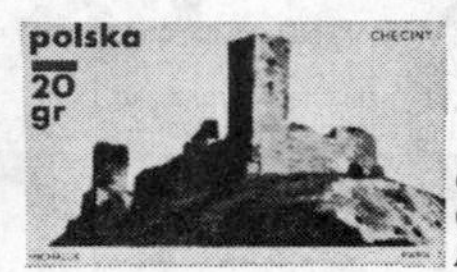

Checiny Castle A543

Polish Castles: 40g, Wisnicz. 60g, Bedzin. 2z, Ogrodzieniec. 2.50z, Niedzica. 3.40z, Kwidzyn. 4z, Pieskowa Skala. 8.50z, Lidzbark Warminski.

1971, Mar. 5 Litho. *Perf. 11*

1788 A543 20g multi 15 15
1789 A543 40g multi 15 15
1790 A543 60g multi 15 15
1791 A543 2z multi 15 15
1792 A543 2.50z multi 15 15
1793 A543 3.40z multi 25 15
1794 A543 4z multi 30 18
1795 A543 8.50z multi 65 42
Set value 1.65 1.00

Fighting in Pouilly Castle, Jaroslaw Dabrowski and Walery Wroblewski — A544

1971, Mar. 3 *Perf. 12½x12½*

1796 A544 60g vio bl, brn & red 15 15

Centenary of the Paris Commune.

Seedlings — A545 Bishop Marianos — A546

1971, Mar. 30 Photo. *Perf. 11½x11*
Sizes: 26x34mm (40g, 1.50z); 26x47mm (60g)

1797 A545 40g shown 15 15
1798 A545 60g Forest 15 15
1799 A545 1.50z Clearing 25 15
Set value 45 25

Proper forest management.

1971, Apr. 20

Frescoes from Faras Cathedral, Nubia, 8th-12th centuries: 60g, St. Anne. 1.15z, 1.50z, 7z, Archangel Michael (diff. frescoes). 1.35z, Hermit Anamon of Tuna el Gabel. 4.50z, Cross with symbols of four Evangelists. 5z, Christ protecting Nubian dignitary.

1800 A546 40g gold & multi 15 15
1801 A546 60g gold & multi 15 15
1802 A546 1.15z gold & multi 15 15
1803 A546 1.35z gold & multi 15 15
1804 A546 1.50z gold & multi 15 15
1805 A546 4.50z gold & multi 50 20
1806 A546 5z gold & multi 52 22
1807 A546 7z gold & multi 65 32
Nos. 1800-1807 (8) 2.42
Set value 1.10

Polish archaeological excavations in Nubia.

Silesian Insurrectionists — A547

1971, May 3 Photo. *Perf. 11*

1808 A547 60g dk red brn & gold 15 15
a. Souv. sheet of 3+3 labels 90 45

50th anniversary of the 3rd Silesian uprising. Printed in sheets of 15 stamps and 15 labels showing Silesian Insurrectionists monument in Katowice.

Peacock on the Lawn, by Dorota, 4 years old — A548

Children's Drawings and UNICEF Emblem: 40g, Our Army, horiz. 60g, Spring. 2z, Cat with Ball, horiz. 2.50z, Flowers in Vase. 3.40z, Friendship, horiz. 5.50z, Clown. 7z, The Unknown Planet, horiz.

Perf. 11½x11, 11x11½
1971, May 20

1809 A548 20g multi 15 15
1810 A548 40g multi 15 15
1811 A548 60g multi 15 15
1812 A548 2z multi 15 15
1813 A548 2.50z multi 15 15
1814 A548 3.40z multi 25 15
1815 A548 5.50z multi 40 22
1816 A548 7z multi 65 35
Set value 1.75 1.00

25th anniversary of UNICEF.

Fair Emblem — A549

1971, June 1 Photo. *Perf. 11½x11*

1817 A549 60g ultra, blk & dk car 15 15

40th International Poznan Fair, June 13-22.

Collegium Maius, Cracow — A550

Designs: 40g, Copernicus House, Torun, vert. 2.50z, Olsztyn Castle. 4z, Frombork Cathedral, vert.

1971, June Litho. *Perf. 11*

1818 A550 40g multi 15 15
1819 A550 60g blk, red brn & sep 15 15
1820 A550 2.50z multi 25 15
1821 A550 4z multi 45 18
Set value 42

Nicolaus Copernicus (1473-1543), astronomer. Printed in sheets of 15 with labels showing portrait of Copernicus, page from "Euclid's Geometry," astrolabe or drawing of heliocentric system, respectively.

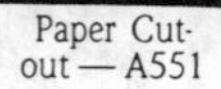

Paper Cut-out — A551

Worker, by Xawery Dunikowski — A552

Designs: Various paper cut-outs (folk art).

Photo., Engr. & Typo.
1971, July 12 *Perf. 12x11½*

1822 A551 20g blk & brt grn, *bluish* 15 15
1823 A551 40g sl grn & dk ol, *lt gray* 15 15
1824 A551 60g brn & bl, *gray* 15 15
1825 A551 1.15z plum & brn, *buff* 15 15
1826 A551 1.35z dk grn & ver, *yel grn* 15 15
Set value 38 34

1971, July 21 Photo. *Perf. 11½x12*

Sculptures: No. 1828, Founder, by Xawery Dunikowski. No. 1829, Miners, by Magdalena Wiecek. No. 1830, Woman harvester, by Stanislaw Horno-Poplawski.

1827 A552 40g sil & multi 15 15
1828 A552 40g sil & multi 15 15
1829 A552 60g sil & multi 15 15
1830 A552 60g sil & multi 15 15
a. Souv. sheet of 4, #1827-1830 1.00 60
Set value 40 28

Punched Tape and Cogwheel A553

1971, Sept. 2 Litho. *Perf. 11x11½*

1831 A553 60g pur & red 15 15

6th Congress of Polish Technicians, held at Poznan, February, 1971.

Angel, by Jozef Mehoffer, 1901 A554

Water Lilies, by Wyspianski A555

Stained Glass Windows: 60g, Detail from "The Elements" by Stanislaw Wyspianski. 1.35z, Apollo, by Wyspianski, 1904. 1.55z, Two Kings, 14th century. 3.40z, Flight into Egypt, 14th century. 5.50z, St. Jacob the Elder, 14th century.

1971, Sept. 15 Photo. *Perf. 11½x11*

1832 A554 20g gold & multi 15 15
1833 A555 40g gold & multi 15 15
1834 A555 60g gold & multi 15 15
1835 A555 1.35z gold & multi 15 15
1836 A554 1.55z gold & multi 15 15
1837 A554 3.40z gold & multi 24 15
1838 A554 5.50z gold & multi 35 18
Set value, #1832-1838, B122 1.75 1.00

Mrs. Fedorowicz, by Witold Pruszkowski (1846-1896) A556

Paintings of Women: 50g, Woman with Book, by Tytus Czyzewski (1885-1945). 60g, Girl with Chrysanthemums, by Olga Boznanska (1865-1940). 2.50z, Girl in Red Dress, by Jozef Pankiewicz (1866-1940), horiz. 3.40z, Nude, by Leon Chwistek (1884-1944), horiz. 4.50z, Strange Garden (woman), by Jozef Mehoffer (1869-1946). 5z, Artist's Wife with White Hat, by Zbigniew Pronaszko (1885-1958).

Perf. 11½x11, 11x11½
1971, Oct. 9 Litho.

1839 A556 40g gray & multi 15 15
1840 A556 50g gray & multi 15 15
1841 A556 60g gray & multi 15 15
1842 A556 2.50z gray & multi 20 15
1843 A556 3.40z gray & multi 28 15
1844 A556 4.50z gray & multi 42 22
1845 A556 5z gray & multi 55 32
Nos. 1839-1845,B123 (8) 2.60
Set value 1.25

Stamp Day, 1971. Printed in sheets of 4 stamps and 2 labels inscribed "Women in Polish Paintings."

Royal Castle, Warsaw A557

1971, Oct. 14 Photo. *Perf. 11x11½*

1846 A557 60g gold, blk & brt red 15 15

P-11C Dive Bombers A558

Planes and Polish Air Force Emblem: 1.50z, PZL 23-A Karas fighters. 3.40z, PZL Los bomber.

1971, Oct. 14

1847 A558 90g multi 15 15
1848 A558 1.50z bl, red & blk 15 15
1849 A558 3.40z multi 30 15
Set value 28

Martyrs of the Polish Air Force, 1939.

Lunar Rover and Astronauts A559

Design: No. 1851, Lunokhod 1 on moon, vert.

Perf. 11x11½, 11½x11
1971, Nov. 17

1850 A559 2.50z multi 24 15
1851 A559 2.50z multi 24 15
Set value 24

Apollo 15 US moon exploration mission, July 26-Aug. 7 (No. 1850); Luna 17 unmanned automated USSR moon mission, Nov. 10-17 (No. 1851). Printed in sheets of 6 stamps and 2 labels, with marginal inscriptions.

Worker at Helm — A560

Shipbuilding A561

Designs: No. 1853, Worker. No. 1855, Apartment houses under construction. No. 1856, "Bison" combine harvester. No. 1857, Polish Fiat 125. No. 1858, Mining tower. No. 1859, Chemical plant.

1971, Dec. 8 *Perf. 11½x11*

1852	A560	60g gray, ultra & red	15	15
1853	A560	60g red & gray	15	15
a.		Pair, #1852-1853 + label	20	16

Perf. 11x11½

1854	A561	60g red, gold & blk	15	15
1855	A561	60g red, gold & blk	15	15
1856	A561	60g red, gold & blk	15	15
1857	A561	60g red, gold & blk	15	15
1858	A561	60g red, gold & blk	15	15
1859	A561	60g red, gold & blk	15	15
a.		Souv. sheet of 6, #1854-1859	75	50
b.		Block of 6, #1854-1859	60	50
		Set value	80	64

6th Congress of the Polish United Worker's Party. No. 1859b has outline of map of Poland extending over the block.

Cherry Blossoms — A562

Blossoms: 20g, Niedzwiecki's apple. 40g, Pear. 60g, Peach. 1.15z, Japanese magnolia. 1.35z, Red hawthorne. 2.50z, Apple. 3.40z, Red chestnut. 5z, Acacia robinia. 8.50z, Cherry.

1971, Dec. 28 Litho. *Perf. 12½*

Blossoms in Natural Colors

1860	A562	10g dl bl & blk	15	15
1861	A562	20g grnsh bl & blk	15	15
1862	A562	40g lt vio & blk	15	15
1863	A562	60g grn & blk	15	15
1864	A562	1.15z Prus bl & blk	15	15
1865	A562	1.35z ocher & blk	15	15
1866	A562	2.50z grn & blk	20	15
1867	A562	3.40z ocher & blk	40	20
1868	A562	5z tan & blk	55	25
1869	A562	8.50z bis & blk	1.10	52
		Nos. 1860-1869 (10)	3.15	
		Set value		1.45

Fighting Worker, by J. Jarnuszkiewicz — A563

Photogravure and Engraved

1972, Jan. 5 *Perf. 11½*

1870	A563	60g red & blk	15	15

Polish Workers' Party, 30th anniversary.

Luge and Sapporo '72 Emblem — A564

Sapporo '72 Emblem and: 60g, Women's slalom, vert. 1.65z, Biathlon, vert. 2.50z, Ski jump.

1972, Jan. 12 Photo. *Perf. 11*

1871	A564	40g sil & multi	15	15
1872	A564	60g sil & multi	15	15
1873	A564	1.65z sil & multi	22	15
1874	A564	2.50z sil & multi	45	22
		Set value	85	48

11th Winter Olympic Games, Sapporo, Japan, Feb. 3-13. See No. B124.

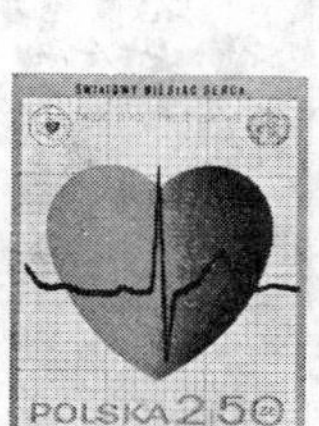

Heart and Electrocardiogram A565

Bicyclists Racing A566

1972, Mar. 28 Photo. *Perf. 11½x11*

1875	A565	2.50z bl, red & blk	18	15

"Your heart is your health," World Health Day.

1972, May 2 *Perf. 11*

1876	A566	60g sil & multi	15	15

25th Warsaw-Berlin-Prague Bicycle Race.

Berlin Monument — A567

Olympic Runner — A568

1972, May 9 Engr. *Perf. 11½x11*

1877	A567	60g grnsh blk	15	15

Unveiling of monument for Polish soldiers and German anti-Fascists in Berlin, May 14.

1972, May 20 *Perf. 11½x11*

Olympic Rings and "Motion" Symbol and: 30g, Archery. 40g, Boxing. 60g, Fencing. 2.50z, Wrestling. 3.40z, Weight lifting. 5z, Bicycling. 8.50z, Sharpshooting.

1878	A568	20g multi	15	15
1879	A568	30g multi	15	15
1880	A568	40g multi	15	15
1881	A568	60g gray & multi	15	15
1882	A568	2.50z multi	22	15
1883	A568	3.40z multi	40	18
1884	A568	5z bl & multi	52	24
1885	A568	8.50z multi	90	50
		Nos. 1878-1885 (8)	2.64	
		Set value		1.20

20th Olympic Games, Munich, Aug. 26-Sept. 10. See No. B125.

Vistula and Cracow — A569

1972, May 28 Photo. *Perf. 11½x11*

1886	A569	60g red, grn & ocher	15	15

50th anniversary of Polish Immigrants Society in Germany (Rodlo).

Knight of King Mieszko I — A570

1972, June 12

1887	A570	60g gold, red brn, yel & blk	15	15

Millennium of the Battle of Cedynia (Cidyny).

Zoo Animals — A571

1972, Aug. 20 Litho. *Perf. 12½*

1888	A571	20g Cheetah	15	15
1889	A571	40g Giraffe, vert	15	15
1890	A571	60g Toco toucan	15	15
1891	A571	1.35z Chimpanzee	18	15
1892	A571	1.65z Gibbon	22	15
1893	A571	3.40z Crocodile	30	18
1894	A571	4z Kangaroo	1.00	45
1895	A571	4.50z Tiger, vert	1.90	1.00
1896	A571	7z Zebra	2.25	1.25
		Nos. 1888-1896 (9)	6.30	3.63

Ludwik Warynski — A572

1972, Sept. 1 Photo. *Perf. 11*

1897	A572	60g multi	15	15

90th anniversary of Proletariat Party, founded by Ludwik Warynski. Printed in sheets of 25 stamps each se-tenant with label showing masthead of party newspaper "Proletariat."

Feliks Dzerzhinski A573

1972, Sept. 11 Litho. *Perf. 11x11½*

1898	A573	60g red & blk	15	15

Feliks Dzerzhinski (1877-1926), Russian politician of Polish descent.

> ***Set Values***
> *A 15-cent minimum now applies to individual stamps and sets. Where the 15-cent minimum per stamp would increase the "value" of a set beyond retail, there is a "Set Value" notation giving the retail value of the set.*

Congress Emblem — A574

1972, Sept. 15 Photo. *Perf. 11½x11*

1899	A574	60g multi	15	15

25th Congress of the International Cooperative Union, Warsaw, Sept. 1972.

"In the Barracks," by Moniuszko A575

Scenes from Operas or Ballets by Moniuszko: 20g, The Countess. 40g, The Frightful Castle. 60g, Halka. 1.15z, A New Don Quixote. 1.35z, Verbum Nobile. 1.55z, Ideal. 2.50z, Paria.

Photogravure and Engraved

1972, Sept. 15 *Perf. 11½*

1900	A575	10g gold & vio	15	15
1901	A575	20g gold & dk brn	15	15
1902	A575	40g gold & sl grn	15	15
1903	A575	60g gold & ind	15	15
1904	A575	1.15z gold & dk bl	15	15
1905	A575	1.35z gold & dk bl	15	15
1906	A575	1.55z gold & grnsh blk	15	15
1907	A575	2.50z gold & dk brn	32	18
		Set value	90	60

Stanislaw Moniuszko (1819-1872), composer.

"Amazon," by Piotr Michalowski A576

Paintings: 40g, Ostafi Daszkiewicz, by Jan Matejko. 60g, "Summer Rain" (dancing woman), by Wojciech Gerson. 2z, Woman from Naples, by Aleksander Kotsis. 2.50z, Girl Taking Bath, by Pantaleon Szyndler. 3.40z, Count of Thun (child), by Artur Grottger. 4z, Rhapsodist (old man), by Stanislaw Wyspianski. 60g and 2.50z inscribed "DZIEN ZNACZKA 1972."

1972, Sept. 28 Photo. *Perf. 10½x11*

1908	A576	30g gold & multi	15	15
1909	A576	40g gold & multi	15	15
1910	A576	60g gold & multi	15	15
1911	A576	2z gold & multi	15	15
1912	A576	2.50z gold & multi	15	15
1913	A576	3.40z gold & multi	30	15
1914	A576	4z gold & multi	65	40
		Nos. 1908-1914,B126 (8)	2.95	
		Set value		1.60

Stamp Day.

Copernicus, by Jacob van Meurs, 1654, Heliocentric System A577

Portraits of Copernicus: 60g, 16th century etching and Prussian coin, 1530. 2.50z, by Jeremiah Falck, 1645, and coat of arms of King of Prussia, 1520. 3.40z, Copernicus with lily of the valley, and page from Theophilactus Simocatta's "Letters on Customs."

1972, Sept. 28 Litho. *Perf. 11x11½*

1915 A577	40g	brt bl & blk	15	15
1916 A577	60g	ocher & blk	15	15
1917 A577	2.50z	red & blk	16	15
1918 A577	3.40z	yel grn & blk	35	20
		Set value	62	38

Nicolaus Copernicus (1473-1543), astronomer. See No. B127.

Nos. 1337-1338 Surcharged in Red or Black

50 GR X — a

═ 1 50 ZŁ — b

1972 Engr. *Perf. 11½x11*

1919 A445(a)	50g on 40g (R)	15	15
1920 A445(a)	90g on 40g (R)	15	15
1921 A445(a)	1z on 40g (R)	15	15
1922 A445(b)	1.50z on 60g	15	15
1923 A445(a)	2.70z on 40g (R)	16	15
1924 A445(b)	4z on 60g	24	15
1925 A445(b)	4.50z on 60g	25	15
1926 A445(b)	4.90z on 60g	30	15
	Set value	1.25	65

Issue dates: Nos. 1919-1920, Nov. 17; others, Oct. 2.

The Little Soldier, by E. Piwowarski A578

1972, Oct. 16 Litho. *Perf. 11½*

1927 A578 60g rose & blk 15 15

Children's health center "Centrum Zdrowia Dziecka," to be built as memorial to children killed during Nazi regime.

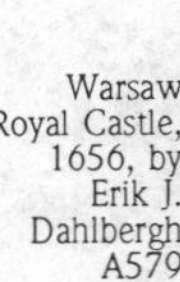

Warsaw Royal Castle, 1656, by Erik J. Dahlbergh A579

1972, Oct. 16 Photo. *Perf. 11x11½*

1928 A579 60g vio, bl & blk 15 15

Rebuilding of Warsaw Castle, destroyed during World War II.

Ribbons with Symbols of Trade Union Activities — A580

Mountain Lodge, Chocholowska Valley — A581

1972, Nov. 13 *Perf. 11½x11*

1929 A580 60g multi 15 15

7th and 13th Polish Trade Union congresses, Nov. 13-15.

1972, Nov. 13 *Perf. 11*

Mountain Lodges in Tatra National Park: 60g, Hala Ornak, West Tatra, horiz. 1.55z, Hala Gasienicowa. 1.65z, Pieciu Stawow Valley, horiz. 2.50z, Morskie Oko, Rybiego Potoku Valley

1930 A581	40g	multi	15	15
1931 A581	60g	multi	15	15
1932 A581	1.55z	multi	15	15
1933 A581	1.65z	multi	15	15
1934 A581	2.50z	multi	28	15
		Set value	72	40

Japanese Azalea — A582

Flowering Shrubs: 50g, Alpine rose. 60g, Pomeranian honeysuckle. 1.65z, Chinese quince. 2.50z, Viburnum. 3.40z, Rhododendron. 4z, Mock orange. 8.50z, Lilac.

1972, Dec. 15 Litho. *Perf. 12½*

1935 A582	40g	gray & multi	15	15
1936 A582	50g	bl & multi	15	15
1937 A582	60g	multi	15	15
1938 A582	1.65z	ultra & multi	16	15
1939 A582	2.50z	ocher & multi	24	15
1940 A582	3.40z	multi	30	20
1941 A582	4z	multi	55	22
1942 A582	8.50z	multi	1.10	52
		Nos. 1935-1942 (8)	2.80	
		Set value		1.30

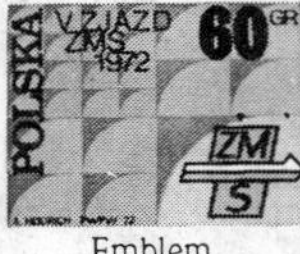
Emblem A583

Copernicus A584

1972, Dec. 15 Photo. *Perf. 11½*

1943 A583 60g red & multi 15 15

5th Congress of Socialist Youth Union.

Coil Stamps

1972, Dec. 28 Photo. *Perf. 14*

1944 A584	1z	deep claret	15	15
1945 A584	1.50z	yel brn	18	15
		Set value		16

Nicolaus Copernicus (1473-1543), astronomer. Black control number on back of every 5th stamp.

Piast Knight, 10th Century A585

Polish Cavalry: 40g, Knight, 13th century. 60g, Knight of Ladislas Jagello, 15th century, horiz. 1.35z, Hussar, 17th century. 4z, National Guard Uhlan, 18th century. 4.50z, Congress Kingdom Period, 1831. 5z, Light cavalry, 1939, horiz. 7z, Light cavalry, People's Army, 1945.

1972, Dec. 28 *Perf. 11*

1946 A585	20g	vio & multi	15	15
1947 A585	40g	multi	15	15
1948 A585	60g	org & multi	15	15
1949 A585	1.35z	org & multi	15	15
1950 A585	4z	org & multi	32	15
1951 A585	4.50z	org & multi	40	22
1952 A585	5z	brn & multi	65	32
1953 A585	7z	multi	90	50
		Nos. 1946-1953 (8)	2.87	
		Set value		1.40

Man and Woman, Sculpture by Wiera Muchina — A586

Design: 60g, Globe with Red Star.

1972, Dec. 30

1954 A586	40g	gray & multi	15	15
1955 A586	60g	blk, red & vio bl	15	15
		Set value	16	15

50th anniversary of the Soviet Union.

Nicolaus Copernicus, by M. Bacciarelli — A587

Portraits of Copernicus: 1.50z, painted in Torun, 16th century. 2.70z, by Zinck Nor. 4z, from Strasbourg clock. 4.90z, Copernicus in his Observatory, by Jan Matejko, horiz.

Perf. 11½x11, 11x11½

1973, Feb. 18 Photo.

1956 A587	1z	brn & multi	15	15
1957 A587	1.50z	multi	15	15
1958 A587	2.70z	multi	20	15
1959 A587	4z	multi	35	20
1960 A587	4.90z	multi	50	28
		Nos. 1956-1960 (5)	1.35	
		Set value		75

Copernicus (1473-1543), astronomer.

Piast Coronation Sword, 12th Century — A588

Lenin Monument, Nowa Huta — A589

Polish Art: No. 1962, Kruzlowa Madonna, c. 1410. No. 1963, Hussar's armor, 17th century. No. 1964, Wawel head, wood, 16th century. No. 1965, Cock, sign of Rifle Fraternity, 16th century. 2.70z, Cover of Queen Anna Jagiellonka's prayer book (eagle), 1582. 4.90z, Skarbimierz Madonna, wood, c. 1340. 8.50z, The Nobleman Tenczynski, portrait by unknown artist, 17th century.

1973, Mar. 28 Photo. *Perf. 11½x11*

1961 A588	50g	vio & multi	15	15
1962 A588	1z	lt bl & multi	15	15
1963 A588	1z	ultra & multi	15	15
1964 A588	1.50z	bl & multi	15	15
1965 A588	1.50z	grn & multi	15	15
1966 A588	2.70z	multi	18	15
1967 A588	4.90z	multi	35	15
1968 A588	8.50z	blk & multi	1.00	42
		Set value	1.92	1.00

1973, Apr. 28 Litho. *Perf. 11x11½*

1969 A589 1z multi 15 15

Unveiling of Lenin Monument at Nowa Huta.

Envelope Showing Postal Code — A590

1973, May 5 *Perf. 11x11½*

1970 A590 1.50z multi 15 15

Introduction of postal code system in Poland.

Wolf — A591

1973, May 21 Photo. *Perf. 11*

1971 A591	50g	shown	15	15
1972 A591	1z	Mouflon	15	15
1973 A591	1.50z	Moose	15	15
1974 A591	2.70z	Capercaillie	25	15
1975 A591	3z	Deer	30	15
1976 A591	4.50z	Lynx	42	20
1977 A591	4.90z	European hart	1.10	42
1978 A591	5z	Wild boar	1.25	70
		Nos. 1971-1978 (8)	3.77	
		Set value		1.65

Intl. Hunting Committee Congress and 50th anniv. of Polish Hunting Assoc.

US Satellite "Copernicus" over Earth — A592

Design: No. 1980, USSR satellite Salyut over earth.

1973, June 20

1979 A592	4.90z	multi	45	25
1980 A592	4.90z	multi	45	25

American and Russian astronomical observatories in space. No. 1979 issued in sheets of 6 stamps and 2 labels showing constellations and Nicolaus Copernicus. No. 1980 issued in sheets of 6 stamps and 2 labels showing astronauts and Soyuz 11.

Flame Rising from Book — A593

1973, June 26 Litho.

1981 A593 1.50z bl & multi 15 15

2nd Polish Science Congress, Warsaw, June 26-29.

Arms of Poznan on 14th Century Seal A594

Marceli Nowotko A595

Polska '73 Emblem and: 1.50z, Tombstone of Nicolas Tomicki, 1524. 2.70z, Kalisz paten, 12th century. 4z, Lion knocker from bronze gate, Gniezno, 12th century, horiz.

Perf. 11½x11, 11x11½

1973, June 30

1982 A594 1z pink & multi 15 15
1983 A594 1.50z org & multi 15 15
1984 A594 2.70z buff & multi 18 15
1985 A594 4z yel & multi 32 15
Set value 68 38

POLSKA '73 Intl. Phil. Exhib., Poznan, Aug. 19-Sept. 2. See No. B128.

1973, Aug. 8 Litho. *Perf. 11½x11*

1986 A595 1.50z red & blk 15 15

Marceli Nowotko (1893-1942), labor leader, member of Central Committee of Communist Party of Poland.

Emblem and Orchard — A596

Human Environment Emblem and: 90g, Grazing cows. 1z, Stork's nest. 1.50z, Pond with fish and water lilies. 2.70z, Flowers on meadow. 4.90z, Underwater fauna and flora. 5z, Forest scene. 6.50z, Still life.

1973, Aug. 30 Photo. *Perf. 11*

1987 A596 50g blk & multi 15 15
1988 A596 90g blk & multi 15 15
1989 A596 1z blk & multi 15 15
1990 A596 1.50z blk & multi 15 15
1991 A596 2.70z blk & multi 15 15
1992 A596 4.90z blk & multi 45 20
1993 A596 5z blk & multi 65 25
1994 A596 6.50z blk & multi 1.10 40
Nos. 1987-1994 (8) 2.95
Set value 1.20

Protection of the environment.

Motorcyclist — A597

1973, Sept. 2 *Perf. 11½*

1995 A597 1.50z sil & multi 15 15

Finals in individual world championship motorcycle race on cinder track, Chorzów, Sept. 2.

Tank A598

1973, Oct. 12 Litho. *Perf. 12½*

1996 A598 1z shown 15 15
1997 A598 1z Fighter plane 15 15
1998 A598 1.50z Missile 16 15
1999 A598 1.50z Warship 16 15
Set value 48 28

Polish People's Army, 30th anniversary.

Grzegorz Piramowicz — A599

Design: 1.50z, J. Sniadecki, Hugo Kollataj and Julian Ursyn Niemcewicz.

Photogravure and Engraved

1973, Oct. 13 *Perf. 11½x11*

2000 A599 1z buff & dk brn 15 15
2001 A599 1.50z gray & sl grn 15 15
Set value 25 16

Bicentenary of the National Education Commission.

Henryk Arctowski, and Penguins A600

Polish Scientists: No. 2003, Pawel Edmund Strzelecki and Kangaroo. No. 2004, Benedykt Tadeusz Dybowski and Lake Baikal. No. 2005, Stefan Rogozinski, sailing ship "Lucja-Malgorzata." 2z, Bronislaw Malinowski, Trobriand Island drummers. 2.70z, Stefan Drzewiecki and submarine. 3z, Edward Adolf Strasburger and plants. 8z, Ignacy Domeyko, geological strata.

1973, Nov. 30 Photo. *Perf. 10½x11*

2002 A600 1z gold & multi 15 15
2003 A600 1z gold & multi 15 15
2004 A600 1.50z gold & multi 15 15
2005 A600 1.50z gold & multi 15 15
2006 A600 2z gold & multi 15 15
2007 A600 2.70z gold & multi 18 15
2008 A600 3z gold & multi 25 15
2009 A600 8z gold & multi 85 42
Set value 1.70 90

Polish Flag — A601

1973, Dec. 15 Photo. *Perf. 11½x11*

2010 A601 1.50z dp ultra, red & gold 15 15

Polish United Workers' Party, 25th anniv.

Jelcz-Berliet Bus — A602

Designs: Polish automotives.

1973, Dec. 28 Photo. *Perf. 11x11½*

2011 A602 50g shown 15 15
2012 A602 90g Jelcz 316 15 15
2013 A602 1z Polski Fiat 126p 15 15
2014 A602 1.50z Polski Fiat 125p 15 15
2015 A602 4z Nysa M-521 bus 35 18
2016 A602 4.50z Star 660 truck 45 22
Set value 1.10 65

Iris — A603

Flowers: 1z, Dandelion. 1.50z, Rose. 3z, Thistle. 4z, Cornflowers. 4.50z, Clover. (Paintings by Stanislaw Wyspianski.)

1974, Jan. 22 Engr. *Perf. 12x11½*

2017 A603 50g lilac 15 15
2018 A603 1z green 15 15
2019 A603 1.50z red org 15 15
2020 A603 3z dp vio 28 15
2021 A603 4z vio bl 42 15
2022 A603 4.50z emerald 50 18
Set value 1.42 58

Cottage, Kurpie A604

Designs: 1.50z, Church, Sekowa. 4z, Town Hall, Sulmierzyce. 4.50z, Church, Lachowice. 4.90z, Windmill, Sobienie-Jeziory. 5z, Orthodox Church, Ulucz.

1974, Mar. 5 Photo. *Perf. 11x11½*

2023 A604 1z multi 15 15
2024 A604 1.50z yel & multi 15 15
2025 A604 4z pink & multi 28 15
2026 A604 4.50z lt bl & multi 30 15
2027 A604 4.90z multi 35 15
2028 A604 5z pink & multi 45 18
Nos. 2023-2028 (6) 1.68
Set value 74

Mail Coach and UPU Emblem — A605

Embroidery from Cracow — A606

1974, Mar. 30 *Perf. 11½x12*

2029 A605 1.50z multi 15 15

Centenary of Universal Postal Union.

1974, May 7 Photo. *Perf. 11½x11*

Embroideries from: 1.50z, Lowicz. 4z, Slask.

2030 A606 50g multi 15 15
2031 A606 1.50z multi 15 15
2032 A606 4z multi 38 18
a. Souvenir sheet of 3, #2030-2032, imperf. 1.75 1.25
b. As "a," perf. 11½x11 3.25 2.50
Set value 56 30

SOCPHILEX IV International Philatelic Exhibition, Katowice, May 18-June 2.

No. 2032a sold for 17z.

No. 2032b sold for 17z plus 15z for 4 envelopes.

Association Emblem A607

Soldier and Dove A608

1974, May 8 Litho. *Perf. 12x11½*

2033 A607 1.50z gray & red 15 15

5th Congress of the Assoc. of Combatants for Liberty & Democracy, Warsaw, May 8-9.

1974, May 9 *Perf. 11½x11*

2034 A608 1.50z org, lt bl & blk 15 15

29th anniversary of victory over Fascism.

Comecon Building, Moscow A609

1974, May 15 *Perf. 11x11½*

2035 A609 1.50z gray bl, bis & red 15 15

25th anniv. of the Council of Mutual Economic Assistance.

Soccer Ball and Games' Emblem A610

Design: No. 2037, Soccer players, Olympic rings and 1972 medal.

1974, June 15 Photo. *Perf. 11x11½*

2036 A610 4.90z ol & multi 42 20
a. Souvenir sheet of 4 + 2 labels 2.25 1.10
2037 A610 4.90z ol & multi 42 20
a. Souvenir sheet of 4, 2 each #2036-2037 14.00 5.00

World Cup Soccer Championship, Munich, June 13-July 7.

No. 2036a issued to commemorate Poland's silver medal in 1974 Championship.

Sailing Ship, 16th Century A611

Chess, by Jan Kochanowski A612

Polish Sailing Ships: 1.50z, "Dal," 1934. 2.70z, "Opty," sailed around the world, 1969. 4z, "Dar Pomorza," winner "Operation Sail," 1972. 4.90z, "Polonez," sailed around the world, 1973.

1974, June 29 Litho. *Perf. 11½x11*

2038 A611 1z multi 15 15
2039 A611 1.50z multi 15 15
2040 A611 2.70z multi 20 15
2041 A611 4z grn & multi 42 22
2042 A611 4.90z dp bl & multi 60 28
Nos. 2038-2042 (5) 1.52
Set value 74

1974, July 15 Litho. *Perf. 11½x11*

Design: 1.50z, "Education," etching by Daniel Chodowiecki.

2043	A612	1z	multi	15	15
2044	A612	1.50z	multi	22	15
			Set value		20

10th International Chess Festival, Lublin.

Man and Map of Poland — A613

Polish Eagle — A614

1974, July 21 Photo. *Perf. 11½x11*

2045	A613	1.50z	blk, gold & red	15	15
2046	A614	1.50z	sil & multi	15	15
2047	A614	1.50z	red & multi	15	15
			Set value	36	24

People's Republic of Poland, 30th anniv.

Lazienkowska Bridge Road — A615

1974, July 21 *Perf. 11x11½*

2048	A615	1.50z	multi	15	15

Opening of Lazienkowska Bridge over Vistula south of Warsaw.

Strawberries and Congress Emblem — A616

1974, Sept. 10 Photo. *Perf. 11½*

2049	A616	50g	shown	15	15
2050	A616	90g	Black currants	15	15
2051	A616	1z	Apples	15	15
2052	A616	1.50z	Cucumbers	15	15
2053	A616	2.70z	Tomatoes	15	15
2054	A616	4.50z	Peas	32	18
2055	A616	4.90z	Pansies	48	22
2056	A616	5z	Nasturtiums	1.00	40
			Set value	2.20	1.10

19th Intl. Horticultural Congress, Warsaw, Sept.

Civic Militia and Security Service Badge — A617

Polish Child, by Lukasz Orlowski — A618

1974, Oct. 3 Photo. *Perf. 11½x11*

2057	A617	1.50g	multi	15	15

30th anniv. of the Civic Militia and the Security Service.

1974, Oct. 9

Polish paintings of Children: 90g, Girl with Pigeon, Anonymous artist, 19th century. 1z, Girl, by Stanislaw Wyspianski. 1.50z, The Orphan from Poronin, by Wladyslaw Slewinski. 3z, Peasant Boy, by Kazimierz Sichulski. 4.50z, Florentine Page, by Aleksander Gierymski. 4.90z, The Artist's Son Tadeusz, by Piotr Michalowski. 6.50z, Boy with Doe, by Aleksander Kotsis.

2058	A618	50g	multi	15	15
2059	A618	90g	multi	15	15
2060	A618	1z	multi	15	15
2061	A618	1.50z	multi	15	15
2062	A618	3z	multi	24	15
2063	A618	4.50z	multi	35	15
2064	A618	4.90z	multi	42	22
2065	A618	6.50z	multi	55	28
			Set value	1.85	96

Children's Day. The 1z and 1.50z are inscribed "Dzien Znaczka (Stamp Day) 1974."

Cracow Manger — A619

King Sigismund Vasa — A620

Masterpieces of Polish art: 1.50z, Flight into Egypt, 1465. 4z, King Jan Olbracht.

1974, Dec. 2 Litho. *Perf. 11½x11*

2066	A619	1z	multi	15	15
2067	A620	1.50z	multi	15	15
2068	A620	2z	multi	18	15
2069	A619	4z	multi	45	20
			Set value		44

Angler — A621

Designs: 1.50z, Hunter with bow and arrow. 4z, Boy snaring geese. 4.50z, Beekeeper. Designs from 16th century woodcuts.

1974-77 Engr. *Perf. 11½x11*

2070	A621	1z	black	15	15
2071	A621	1.50z	indigo	15	15
2071A	A621	4z	sl grn	22	15
2071B	A621	4.50z	dk brn	25	15
			Set value	66	38

Issue dates: 1z, 1.50z, Dec. 30, 1974. 4z, 4.50z, Dec. 12, 1977.

Pablo Neruda, by Osvaldo Guayasamin — A622

1974, Dec. 31 Litho. *Perf. 11½x11*

2072	A622	1.50z	multi	15	15

Pablo Neruda (1904-1973), Chilean poet.

Nike Monument and Opera House, Warsaw — A623

1975, Jan. 17 Photo. *Perf. 11*

2073	A623	1.50z	multi	15	15

30th anniversary of the liberation of Warsaw.

Hobby Falcon A624

"Auschwitz" A625

1975, Jan. 23 *Perf. 11½x12*

2074	A624	1z	Lesser kestrel, male	15	15
2075	A624	1z	same, female	15	15
a.			Pair, #2074-2075	25	20
2076	A624	1.50z	Red-footed falcon, male	18	15
2077	A624	1.50z	same, female	18	15
a.			Pair, #2076-2077	36	25
2078	A624	2z	shown	35	15
2079	A624	3z	Kestrel	52	22
2080	A624	4z	Merlin	1.65	45
2081	A624	8z	Peregrine	2.25	90
			Nos. 2074-2081 (8)	5.43	
			Set value		2.00

Falcons.

Photogravure and Engraved

1975, Jan. 27 *Perf. 11½x11*

2082	A625	1.50z	red & blk	18	15

30th anniversary of the liberation of Auschwitz (Oswiecim) concentration camp.

Women's Hurdle Race A626

Designs: 1.50z, Pole vault. 4z, Hop, step and jump. 4.90z, Sprinting.

1975, Mar. 8 Litho. *Perf. 11x11½*

2083	A626	1z	multi	15	15
2084	A626	1.50z	ol & multi	15	15
2085	A626	4z	multi	35	15
2086	A626	4.90z	grn & multi	42	22
			Set value		48

6th European Indoor Athletic Championships, Katowice, Mar. 1975.

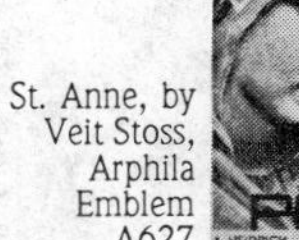

St. Anne, by Veit Stoss, Arphila Emblem A627

1975, Apr. 15 Photo. *Perf. 11x11½*

2087	A627	1.50z	multi	15	15

ARPHILA 75, International Philatelic Exhibition, Paris, June 6-10.

Amateur Radio Union Emblem, Globe A628

1975, Apr. 15 Litho. *Perf. 11½*

2088	A628	1.50z	multi	15	15

International Amateur Radio Union Conference, Warsaw, Apr. 1975.

Mountain Guides' Badge and Sudetic Mountains — A629

Designs: No. 2089, Pine, badge and Tatra Mountains, vert. No. 2090, Gentian and Tatra Mountains, vert. No. 2092, Yew branch with berries, and Sudetic Mountains. No. 2093, River, Beskids Mountains and badge, vert. No. 2094, Arnica and Beskids Mountains, vert.

1975, Apr. 30 Photo. *Perf. 11*

2089	A629	1z	multi	15	15
2090	A629	1z	multi	15	15
a.			Pair, #2089-2090	20	15
2091	A629	1.50z	multi	15	15
2092	A629	1.50z	multi	15	15
a.			Pair, #2091-2092	30	20
2093	A629	4z	multi	40	18
2094	A629	4z	multi	40	18
a.			Pair, #2093-2094	80	40
			Set value	1.10	60

Centenary of Polish Mountain Guides Organizations. Pairs have continuous design.

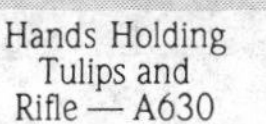

Hands Holding Tulips and Rifle — A630

Warsaw Treaty Members' Flags — A631

1975, May 9 *Perf. 11½x11*

2095	A630	1.50z	bl & multi	15	15

End of WWII, 30th anniv.; victory over Fascism.

1975, May 14

2096	A631	1.50z	bl & multi	15	15

20th anniversary of the signing of the Warsaw Treaty (Bulgaria, Czechoslovakia, German Democratic Rep., Hungary, Poland, Romania, USSR).

Cock and Hen, Congress Emblem — A632

1975, June 23 Photo. *Perf. 12x11½*

2097	A632	50g	shown	15	15
2098	A632	1z	Geese	15	15
2099	A632	1.50z	Cattle	15	15
2100	A632	2z	Cow	24	15
2101	A632	3z	Arabian stallion	38	15
2102	A632	4z	Wielkopolska horses	45	15
2103	A632	4.50z	Pigs	75	35
2104	A632	5z	Sheep	1.50	52
			Nos. 2097-2104 (8)	3.77	
			Set value		1.35

20th Congress of the European Zootechnical Federation, Warsaw.

Apollo and Soyuz Linked in Space — A633

1975, July 15 *Perf. 11x11½*

2105	A633	1.50z	shown	16	15
2106	A633	4.90z	Apollo	40	22
2107	A633	4.90z	Soyuz	40	22
a.			Souv. sheet of 6, 2 each #2106-2107 + 2 labels	7.50	4.00
b.			Pair, #2106-2107	80	50

Apollo Soyuz space test project (Russo-American cooperation), launching July 15; link-up, July 17.

Health Fund Emblem — A634

1975, July 12 *Perf. 11½x11*

2108	A634	1.50z	sil, blk & bl	15	15

National Fund for Health Protection.

"E" and Polish Flag — A635

1975, July 30 Litho. *Perf. 11x11½*

2109	A635	4z	lt bl, red & blk	32	15

European Security and Cooperation Conference, Helsinki, July 30-Aug. 1.

UN Emblem and Sunburst A636

1975, July 25

2110	A636	4z	bl & multi	32	15

30th anniversary of the United Nations.

Bolek and Lolek A637

Cartoon Characters and Children's Health Center Emblem: 1z, Jacek and Agatka. 1.50z, Reksio, the dog. 4z, Telesfor, the dragon.

1975, Aug. 30 Photo. *Perf. 11x11½*

2111	A637	50g	vio bl & multi	15	15
2112	A637	1z	multi	15	15
2113	A637	1.50z	multi	15	15
2114	A637	4z	multi	45	18
			Set value	70	40

Children's television programs.

Circular Bar Graph and Institute's Emblem — A638

IWY Emblem, White, Yellow and Brown Women — A639

1975, Sept. 1 Litho. *Perf. 11½x11*

2115	A638	1.50z	multi	15	15

International Institute of Statistics, 40th session, Warsaw, Sept. 1975.

1975, Sept. 8 Photo.

2116	A639	1.50z	multi	15	15

International Women's Year.

First Poles Arriving on "Mary and Margaret" 1608 A640

George Washington — A641

Designs: 1.50z, Polish glass blower and glass works, Jamestown, 1608. 2.70z, Helena Modrzejewska (1840-1909), Polish actress, came to US in 1877. 4z, Casimir Pulaski (1747-1779), and 6.40z, Tadeusz Kosciusko (1748-1817), heroes of American War of Independence.

1975, Sept. 24 Litho. *Perf. 11x11½*

2117	A640	1z	blk & multi	15	15
2118	A640	1.50z	blk & multi	15	15
2119	A640	2.70z	blk & multi	20	15
2120	A640	4z	blk & multi	32	15
2121	A640	6.40z	blk & multi	48	22
			Nos. 2117-2121 (5)	1.30	
			Set value		58

Souvenir Sheet

Perf. 12

2122			Sheet of 3+3 labels	1.75	1.50
a.	A641	4.90z	shown	55	30
b.	A641	4.90z	Kosciusko	55	30
c.	A641	4.90z	Pulaski	55	30

American Revolution, bicentenary.

Albatross Biplane, 1918-1925 A642

Design: 4.90z, IL 62 jet, 1975.

1975, Sept. 25 *Perf. 11x11½*

2123	A642	2.40z	buff & multi	15	15
2124	A642	4.90z	gray & multi	42	20
			Set value		26

50th anniversary of Polish air post stamps.

Frederic Chopin A643

Dunikowski, Self-portrait A644

1975, Oct. 7 Photo.

2125	A643	1.50z	gold, lt vio & blk	15	15

9th International Chopin Piano Competition, Warsaw, Oct. 7-28.

Printed in sheets of 50 stamps with alternating labels with commemorative inscription.

1975, Oct. 9 *Perf. 11½x11*

Sculptures: 1z, "Breath." 1.50z "Maternity."

2126	A644	50g	sil & multi	15	15
2127	A644	1z	sil & multi	15	15
2128	A644	1.50z	sil & multi	15	15
			Set value	26	20

Stamp Day; Xawery Dunikowski (1875-1964), sculptor. See No. B131.

Town Hall, Zamosc A645

Lodz, by Wladyslaw Strzeminski A646

Design: 1z, Arcades, Kazimierz Dolny, horiz.

Coil Stamps

1975, Nov. 11 Photo. *Perf. 14*

2129	A645	1z	ol grn	15	15
2130	A645	1.50z	rose brn	15	15
			Set value	20	15

European Architectural Heritage Year. Black control number on back of every fifth stamp of Nos. 2129-2130.

1975, Nov. 22 Litho. *Perf. 12½*

2131	A646	4.50z	multi	45	18
a.			Souvenir sheet	90	50

Lodz 75, 12th Polish Philatelic Exhibition, commemorating 25th anniversary of Polish Philatelists Union.

Piast Family Eagle A647

Designs: 1.50z, Seal of Prince Boleslaw of Legnica. 4z, Coin of Prince Jerzy Wilhelm (1660-1675).

1975, Nov. 29 Engr. *Perf. 11x11½*

2132	A647	1z	green	15	15
2133	A647	1.50z	brown	15	15
2134	A647	4z	dl vio	28	15
			Set value	46	26

Piast dynasty's influence on the development of Silesia.

"7" Inscribed "ZJAZD" and "PZPR" — A648

"VII ZJAZD PZPR" — A649

1975, Dec. 8 Photo. *Perf. 11½x11*

2135	A648	1z	lt bl & multi	15	15
2136	A649	1.50z	sil, red & ultra	15	15
			Set value	20	15

7th Congress of Polish United Workers' Party.

Ski Jump — A650

Designs (Winter Olympic Games Emblem and): 1z, Ice hockey. 1.50z, Slalom. 2z, Speed skating. 4z, Luge. 6.40z, Biathlon.

1976, Jan. 10 *Perf. 11x11½*

2137	A650	50g	sil & multi	15	15
2138	A650	1z	sil & multi	15	15
2139	A650	1.50z	sil & multi	15	15
2140	A650	2z	sil & multi	18	15
2141	A650	4z	sil & multi	38	15
2142	A650	6.40z	sil & multi	65	25
			Set value	1.45	64

12th Winter Olympic Games, Innsbruck, Austria, Feb. 4-15.

Engine by Richard Trevithick, 1803 — A651

Locomotives by: 1z, M. Murray and J. Blenkinsop, 1810. No. 2145, George Stephenson's Rocket, 1829. No. 2146, Polish electric locomotive, 1969. 2.70z, Stephenson, 1837. 3z, Joseph Harrison, 1840. 4.50z, Thomas Rogers, 1855. 4.90z, Chrzanow (Polish), 1922.

1976, Feb. 13 Photo. *Perf. 11½x12*

2143	A651	50g	multi	15	15
2144	A651	1z	multi	15	15
2145	A651	1.50z	multi	15	15
2146	A651	1.50z	multi	15	15
2147	A651	2.70z	multi	22	15
2148	A651	3z	multi	22	15
2149	A651	4.50z	multi	85	48
2150	A651	4.90z	multi	90	55
			Nos. 2143-2150 (8)	2.79	
			Set value		1.50

History of the locomotive.

Telephone, Radar and Satellites, ITU Emblem — A652

1976, Mar. 10 *Perf. 11*
2151 A652 1.50z multi 15 15

Centenary of first telephone call by Alexander Graham Bell, Mar. 10, 1876.

Atom Symbol and Flags of Communist Countries A653

1976, Mar. 10 Litho. *Perf. 11½*
2152 A653 1.50z multi 15 15

Joint Institute of Nuclear Research, Dubna, USSR, 20th anniversary.

Ice Hockey — A654

Design: 1.50z, Like 1z, reversed.

1976, Apr. 8 Photo. *Perf. 11½x11*
2153 A654 1z multi 15 15
2154 A654 1.50z multi 15 15
Set value 22 15

Ice Hockey World Championship 1976, Katowice.

Soldier and Map of Sinai A655

1976, Apr. 30 Photo. *Perf. 11x11½*
2155 A655 1.50z multi 15 15

Polish specialist troops serving with UN Forces in Sinai Peninsula.

No. 2155 printed se-tenant with label with commemorative inscription.

Sappers' Monument, by Stanislaw Kulow, Warsaw A656

Interphil 76, Philadelphia A657

Design: No. 2157, First Polish Army Monument, by Bronislaw Koniuszy, Warsaw.

1976, May 8 *Perf. 11½*
2156 A656 1z gold & multi 15 15
2157 A656 1z sil & multi 15 15
Set value 15 15

Memorials unveiled on 30th anniv. of WWII victory.

1976, May 20 Litho. *Perf. 11½x11*
2158 A657 8.40z gray & multi 52 32

Interphil 76, Intl. Phil. Exhib., Philadelphia, May 29-June 6.

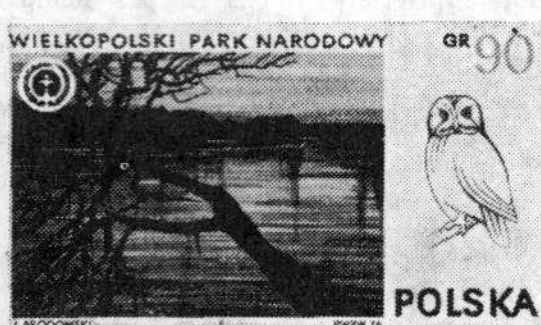
Wielkopolski Park and Owl — A658

National Parks: 1z, Wolinski Park and eagle. 1.50z, Slowinski Park and sea gull. 4.50z, Bieszczadzki Park and lynx. 5z, Ojcowski Park and bat. 6z, Kampinoski Park and elk.

1976, May 22 Photo. *Perf. 12x11½*
2159 A658 90g multi 15 15
2160 A658 1z multi 15 15
2161 A658 1.50z multi 15 15
2162 A658 4.50z multi 35 15
2163 A658 5z multi 38 18
2164 A658 6z multi 48 22
Set value 1.45 75

UN Headquarters, Dove-shaped Globe A659

1976, June 29 Litho. *Perf. 11x11½*
2165 A659 8.40z multi 52 32

UN postage stamps, 25th anniversary.

Fencing and Olympic Rings — A660

1976, June 30 **Photo.**
2166 A660 50g shown 15 15
2167 A660 1z Bicycling 15 15
2168 A660 1.50z Soccer 15 15
2169 A660 4.20z Boxing 32 15
2170 A660 6.90z Weight lifting 52 28
2171 A660 8.40z Running 60 35
Nos. 2166-2171 (6) 1.89
Set value 95

21st Olympic Games, Montreal, Canada, July 17-Aug. 1. See No. B132.

Polish Theater, Poznan — A662

1976, July 12 Litho. *Perf. 11x11½*
2173 A662 1.50z gray ol & org 15 15

Polish Theater in Poznan, centenary.

Czekanowski, Lake Baikal — A663

1976, Sept. 3 Photo. *Perf. 11x11½*
2174 A663 1.50z sil & multi 15 15

Aleksander Czekanowski (1833-1876), geologist, death centenary.

Siren A664

Designs: 1z, Sphinx, vert. 2z, Lion. 4.20z, Bull. 4.50z, Goat. Designs from Corinthian vases, 7th century B.C.

Perf. 11x11½, 11½x11

1976, Oct. 30 **Photo.**
2175 A664 1z gold & multi 15 15
2176 A664 1.50z gold & multi 15 15
2177 A664 2z gold & multi 15 15
2178 A664 4.20z gold & multi 28 16
2179 A664 4.50z gold & multi 30 18
Nos. 2175-2179,B133 (6) 2.13
Set value 1.05

Stamp Day.

Warszawa M20 — A665

Automobiles: 1.50z, Warszawa 223. 2z, Syrena 104. 4.90z, Polski Fiat 125.

1976, Nov. 6 Photo. *Perf. 11*
2180 A665 1z multi 15 15
2181 A665 1.50z multi 15 15
2182 A665 2z multi 15 15
2183 A665 4.90z multi 32 16
a. Souvenir sheet of 4 + 2 labels, #2180-2183 1.16 55
Set value 60 36

Zeran Automobile Factory, Warsaw, 25th anniv.

Pouring Ladle — A666

Virgin and Child, Epitaph, 1425 — A667

1976, Nov. 26 Litho. *Perf. 11*
2184 A666 1.50z multi 15 15

First steel production at Katowice Foundry.

1976, Dec. 15

Design: 6z, The Beautiful Madonna, sculpture, c. 1410.

2185 A667 1z multi 15 15
2186 A667 6z multi 40 20
Set value 26

Polish Trade Union Emblem — A668

1976, Dec. 29
2187 A668 1.50z multi 15 15

8th Polish Trade Union Congress.

Tanker Zawrat Unloading, Gdansk — A669

Polish Ports: No. 2189, Ferry "Gryf" and cars at pier, Gdansk. No. 2190, Loading containers, Gdynia. No. 2191, "Stefan Batory" and "People of the Sea" monument, Gdynia. 2z, Barge and cargoship "Ziemia Szczecinska", Szczecin. 4.20z, Coal loading installations, Swinoujscie. 6.90z, Liner, hydrofoil and lighthouse, Kolobrzeg. 8.40z, Map of Polish Coast with ports, ships and emblem of Union of Polish Ports.

1976, Dec. 29 Photo. *Perf. 11*
2188 A669 1z multi 15 15
2189 A669 1z multi 15 15
2190 A669 1.50z multi 15 15
2191 A669 1.50z multi 15 15
2192 A669 2z multi 15 15
2193 A669 4.20z multi 24 15
2194 A669 6.90z multi 45 24
2195 A669 8.40z multi 50 28
Set value 1.60 1.00

Nurse Helping Old Woman — A670

Civilian Defense Medal — A671

1977, Jan. 24 Litho. *Perf. 11½x11*
2196 A670 1.50z multi 15 15

Polish Red Cross.

1977, Feb. 26 Litho. *Perf. 11*
2197 A671 1.50z multi 15 15

Civilian Defense.

Ball on the Road — A672

1977, Mar. 12 **Photo.**
2198 A672 1.50z ol & multi 15 15

Social Action Committee (founded 1966), "Stop, Child on the Road!"

Forest Fruits — A673

1977, Mar. 17 *Perf. 11½x11*

2199	A673	50g	Dewberry	15	15
2200	A673	90g	Cranberry	15	15
2201	A673	1z	Wild strawberry	15	15
2202	A673	1.50z	Bilberry	15	15
2203	A673	2z	Raspberry	15	15
2204	A673	4.50z	Blueberry	32	15
2205	A673	6z	Dog rose	40	20
2206	A673	6.90z	Hazelnut	50	24
			Set value	1.70	88

Flags of USSR and Poland as Computer Tape — A674

Emblem and Graph — A675

1977, Apr. 4 **Litho.** *Perf. 11½x11*

2207	A674	1.50z	red & multi	15	15

Scientific and technical cooperation between Poland and USSR, 30th anniversary.

1977, Apr. 22

2208	A675	1.50z	red & multi	15	15

7th Congress of Polish Engineers.

Venus, by Rubens A676

Paintings by Flemish painter Peter Paul Rubens (1577-1640): 1.50z, Bathsheba. 5z, Helene Fourment. 6z, Self-portrait.

1977, Apr. 30 *Perf. 11½*

Frame in Gray Brown

2209	A676	1z	multi	15	15
2210	A676	1.50z	multi	15	15
2211	A676	5z	multi	38	18
2212	A676	6z	multi	40	22
			Set value		54

See No. B134.

Peace Dove A677

1977, May 6 *Perf. 11x11½*

2213	A677	1.50z	blk, ultra & yel	15	15

Congress of World Council of Peace, Warsaw, May 6-11.

Bicyclist A678

1977, May 6 **Photo.**

2214	A678	1.50z	gray & multi	15	15

30th International Peace Bicycling Race, Warsaw-Berlin-Prague.

Wolf A679

Violinist, by Jacob Toorenvliet A680

Wildlife Fund Emblem and: No. 2216, Great bustard. No. 2217, Kestrel. 6z, Otter.

1977, May 12 **Photo.** *Perf. 11½x11*

2215	A679	1z	sil & multi	15	15
2216	A679	1.50z	sil & multi	15	15
2217	A679	1.50z	sil & multi	15	15
2218	A679	6z	sil & multi	40	20
			Set value	72	42

Wildlife protection.

1977, May 16

2219	A680	6z	gold & multi	42	25

AMPHILEX '77 Intl. Phil. Exhib., Amsterdam, May 26-June 5. No. 2219 issued in sheets of 6.

Midsummer Bonfire A681

Folk Customs: 1z, Easter cock. 1.50z, Dousing the women on Easter Monday. 3z, Harvest festival. 6z, Christmas procession with crèche. 8.40z, Wedding dance. 1z, 1.50z, 3z, 6z vertical.

Perf. 11x11½, 11½x11

1977, June 13 **Photo.**

2220	A681	90g	multi	15	15
2221	A681	1z	multi	15	15
2222	A681	1.50z	multi	15	15
2223	A681	3z	multi	18	15
2224	A681	6z	multi	38	18
2225	A681	8.40z	multi	55	24
			Set value	1.35	65

Henryk Wieniawski and Musical Symbol — A682

1977, June 30 **Litho.** *Perf. 11½x11*

2226	A682	1.50z	gold, blk & red	15	15

Wieniawski Music Festivals, Poznan: 5th Intl. Lute Competition, June 30-July 10, and 7th Intl. Violin Competition, Nov. 13-27.

Parnassius Apollo — A683

Butterflies: No. 2228, Nymphalis polychloros. No. 2229, Papilio machaon. No. 2230, Nymphalis antiopa. 5z, Fabriciana adippe. 6.90z, Argynnis paphia.

1977, Aug. 22 **Photo.** *Perf. 11*

2227	A683	1z	multi	15	15
2228	A683	1z	multi	15	15
2229	A683	1.50z	multi	15	15
2230	A683	1.50z	multi	15	15
2231	A683	5z	multi	50	15
2232	A683	6.90z	multi	85	40
			Set value	1.65	75

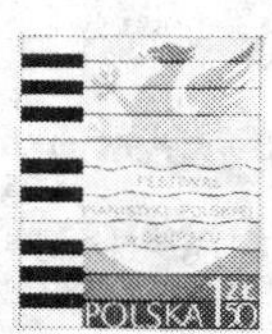

Arms of Slupsk, Keyboard A684

Feliks Dzerzhinski A685

1977, Sept. 3 *Perf. 11½*

2233	A684	1.50z	multi	15	15

Slupsk Piano Festival.

1977, Sept. 10 **Litho.** *Perf. 11½x11*

2234	A685	1.50z	ol bis & sepia	15	15

Feliks E. Dzerzhinski (1877-1926), organizer and head of Russian Secret Police (Cheka).

Earth and Sputnik — A686

1977, Oct. 1 **Litho.** *Perf. 11x11½*

2235	A686	1.50z	ultra & car	15	15
a.			Souvenir sheet of 3+3 labels	55	50

60th anniv. of the Russian Revolution and 20th anniv. of Sputnik space flight. Printed in sheets of 15 stamps and 15 carmine labels showing Winter Palace, Leningrad.

Boleslaw Chrobry's Denarius, 11th Century — A687

Silver Coins: 1z, King Kazimierz Wielki's Cracow groszy, 14th century. 1.50z, Legniza-Brzeg-Wolow thaler, 17th century. 4.20z, King Augustus III guilder, Gdansk, 18th century. 4.50z, 5z (ship), 1936. 6z, 100z, Poland's millenium, 1966.

1977, Oct. 9 **Photo.** *Perf. 11½x11*

2236	A687	50g	sil & multi	15	15
2237	A687	1z	sil & multi	15	15
2238	A687	1.50z	sil & multi	15	15
2239	A687	4.20z	sil & multi	32	15
2240	A687	4.50z	sil & multi	40	20
2241	A687	6z	sil & multi	65	25
			Set value	1.55	75

Stamp Day.

Monastery, Przasnysz A688

Architectural landmarks: No. 2242, Wolin Gate, vert. No. 2243, Church, Debno, vert. No. 2245, Cathedral, Plock. 6z, Castle, Kornik. 6.90z, Palace and Garden, Wilanow.

Perf. 11½x11, 11x11½

1977, Nov. 21 **Photo.**

2242	A688	1z	multi	15	15
2243	A688	1z	multi	15	15
2244	A688	1.50z	multi	15	15
2245	A688	1.50z	multi	15	15
2246	A688	6z	multi	35	15
2247	A688	6.90z	multi	45	22
			Set value	1.10	65

Vostok (USSR) and Mercury (USA) A689

1977, Dec. 28 **Photo.** *Perf. 11x11½*

2248	A689	6.90z	ultra & multi	48	28
a.			Souvenir sheet of 6	4.50	3.50

20 years of space conquest. No. 2248a contains 6 No. 2248 (2 tete-beche pairs) and 2 labels, one showing Sputnik 1 and "4.X.1957," the other Explorer 1 and "31.1.1958."

DN Class Iceboats — A690

Design: No. 2250, One iceboat.

1978, Feb. 6 **Litho.** *Perf. 11*

2249	A690	1.50z	lt ultra & blk	15	15
2250	A690	1.50z	lt ultra & blk	15	15
a.			Pair, #2249-2250 + label	25	20
			Set value	24	16

6th World Iceboating Championships, Feb. 6-11.

Electric Locomotive, Katowice Station, 1957 — A691

Locomotives in Poland: No. 2252, Narrow-gauge engine and Gothic Tower, Znin. No. 2253, Pm36 and Cegielski factory, Poznan, 1936. No. 2254, Electric train and Otwock Station, 1936. No. 2255, Marki Train and Warsaw Stalow Station, 1907. 4.50z, Ty51 coal train and Gdynia Station, 1933. 5z, Tr21 and Chrzanow factory, 1920. 6z, "Cockerill" and Vienna Station, 1848.

1978, Feb. 28 **Photo.** *Perf. 12x11½*

2251	A691	50g	multi	15	15
2252	A691	1z	multi	15	15
2253	A691	1z	multi	15	15
2254	A691	1.50z	multi	15	15
2255	A691	1.50z	multi	15	15
2256	A691	4.50z	multi	32	15
2257	A691	5z	multi	35	15
2258	A691	6z	multi	42	22
			Set value	1.50	75

Pierwsze Wzloty, 1896, and Czeslaw Tanski A692

Polish Sport Planes: 1z, Zwyciezcy-Challenge, 1932, F. Zwirko and S. Wigura, vert. 1.50z, RWD-5 bis over South Atlantic, 1933, and S. Skarzynski, vert. 4.20z, MI-2 helicopter over mountains, Pezetel emblem, vert. 6.90z, PZL-104 Wilga 35, Pezetel emblem. 8.40z, Motoszybowiec SZD-45 Ogar.

Perf. 11x11½, 11½x11

1978, Apr. 15

2259	A692	50g	multi	15	15
2260	A692	1z	multi	15	15
2261	A692	1.50z	multi	15	15
2262	A692	4.20z	multi	28	15
2263	A692	6.90z	multi	45	22
2264	A692	8.40z	multi	55	24
			Set value	1.50	75

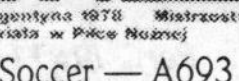

Soccer — A693

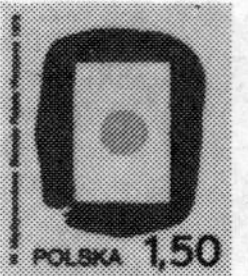

Poster — A694

Design: 6.90z, Soccer ball, horiz.

Perf. 11½x11, 11x11½

1978, May 12 **Litho.**

2265	A693	1.50z	multi	15	15
2266	A693	6.90z	multi	50	25
			Set value		32

11th World Cup Soccer Championships, Argentina, June 1-25.

1978, June 1 *Perf. 12x11½*

2267	A694	1.50z	multi	15	15

7th International Poster Biennale, Warsaw.

Fair Emblem — A695

1978, June 10 *Perf. 11*

2268	A695	1.50z	multi	15	15

50th International Poznan Fair.

Polonez Passenger Car — A696

1978, June 10 **Photo.** *Perf. 11*

2269	A696	1.50z	multi	15	15

Maj. Miroslaw Hermaszewski A697

Design: 6.90z, Hermaszewski, globe and trajectory, horiz.

Perf. 11½x11, 11x11½

1978, June 27 **Photo.**

2270	A697	1.50z	multi	15	15
a.			Without date	28	28
2271	A697	6.90z	multi	50	24
a.			Without date	1.00	1.00
			Set value		30

1st Polish cosmonaut on Russian space mission. Nos. 2270a, 2271a printed in sheets of 6 stamps and 2 labels.

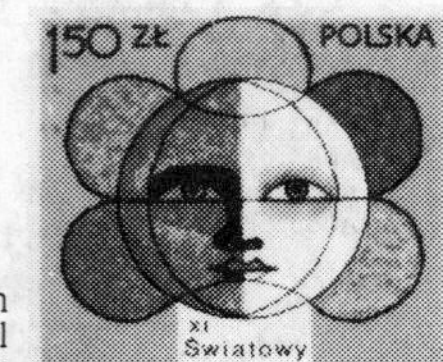

Youth Festival Emblem A698

1978, July 12 **Litho.** *Perf. 11½*

2272	A698	1.50z	multi	15	15

11th Youth Festival, Havana, July 28-Aug. 5.

Souvenir Sheet

Flowers — A699

Illustration reduced.

1978, July 20 *Perf. 11½x11*

2273	A699	1.50z	gold & multi	25	15

30th anniv. of Polish Youth Movement.

Anopheles Mosquito and Blood Cells — A700

Design: 6z, Tsetse fly and blood cells.

1978, Aug. 19 **Litho.** *Perf. 11½x11*

2274	A700	1.50z	multi	15	15
2275	A700	6z	multi	45	20
			Set value		28

4th International Parasitological Congress.

Norway Maple, Environment Emblem — A701

Jan Zizka, Battle of Grunwald, by Jan Matejko — A702

Human Environment Emblem and: 1z, English oak. 1.50z, White poplar. 4.20z, Scotch pine. 4.50z, White willow. 6z, Birch.

1978, Sept. 6 **Photo.** *Perf. 14*

2276	A701	50g	gold & multi	15	15
2277	A701	1z	gold & multi	15	15
2278	A701	1.50z	gold & multi	15	15
2279	A701	4.20z	gold & multi	30	15
2280	A701	4.50z	gold & multi	32	15
2281	A701	6z	gold & multi	42	18
			Set value	1.25	55

Protection of the environment.

Souvenir Sheet

1978, Sept. 8 *Perf. 11½x11*

2282	A702	6z	gold & multi	48	35

PRAGA '78 Intl. Phil. Exhib., Prague, Sept. 8-17.

Letter, Telephone and Satellite — A703

1978, Sept. 20 **Litho.** *Perf. 11*

2283	A703	1.50z	multi	15	15

20th anniversary of the Organization of Ministers of Posts and Telecommunications of Warsaw Pact countries.

Peace, by Andre le Brun — A704

1978-79 **Litho.** *Perf. 11½ (1z), 12½*

2284	A704	1z	violet	15	15
2285	A704	1.50z	steel blue ('79)	18	15
2286	A704	2z	brown ('79)	15	15
2287	A704	2.50z	ultra ('79)	20	15
			Set value		36

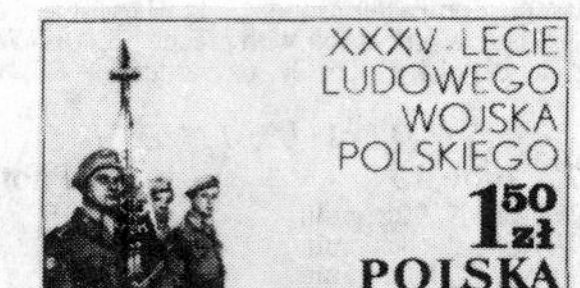

Polish Unit, UN Middle East Emergency Force — A706

Designs: No. 2289, Color Guard, Kosziusko Division (4 soldiers). No. 2290, Color Guard, field training (3 soldiers).

1978, Oct. 6 **Photo.** *Perf. 12x11½*

2289	A706	1.50z	multi	15	15
2290	A706	1.50z	multi	15	15
2291	A706	1.50z	multi	15	15
			Set value	36	24

35th anniversary of People's Army.

Young Man, by Raphael A707

1978, Oct. 9 *Perf. 11*

2292	A707	6z	multi	42	15

Stamp Day.

Dr. Korczak and Children — A708

1978, Oct. 11 **Litho.** *Perf. 11½x11*

2293	A708	1.50z	multi	15	15

Dr. Janusz Korczak, physician, educator, writer, birth centenary.

Wojciech Boguslawski (1757-1829) A709

Polish dramatists: 1z, Aleksander Fredro (1793-1878). 1.50z, Juliusz Slowacki (1809-1849). 2z, Adam Mickiewicz (1798-1855). 4.50z, Stanislaw Wyspianski (1869-1907). 6z, Gabriela Zapolska (1857-1921).

1978, Nov. 11 **Litho.** *Perf. 11½*

2294	A709	50g	multi	15	15
2295	A709	1z	multi	15	15
2296	A709	1.50z	multi	15	15
2297	A709	2z	multi	15	15
2298	A709	4.50z	multi	30	15
2299	A709	6z	multi	42	18
			Set value	1.05	50

Polish Combatants Monument, and Eiffel Tower, Paris A710

1978, Nov. 2 **Photo.** *Perf. 11x11½*

2300	A710	1.50z	brn, red & bl	15	15

Przewalski Mare and Colt A711

Animals: 1z, Polar bears. 1.50z, Indian elephants. 2z, Jaguars. 4.20z, Gray seals. 4.50z, Hartebeests. 6z, Mandrills.

1978, Nov. 10

2301	A711	50g	multi	15	15
2302	A711	1z	multi	15	15
2303	A711	1.50z	multi	15	15
2304	A711	2z	multi	15	15
2305	A711	4.20z	multi	24	15
2306	A711	4.50z	multi	30	15
2307	A711	6z	multi	42	15
			Set value	1.30	55

Warsaw Zoological Gardens, 50th anniv.

Adolf Warski (1868-1937) A712

Party Emblem A713

Portraits: No. 2309, Julian Lenski (1889-1937). No. 2310, Aleksander Zawadzki (1899-1964). No. 2311, Stanislaw Dubois (1901-1942).

Perf. 11½x11, 11x11½

1978, Dec. 15 **Photo.**

2308 A712 1.50z red & brn 15 15
2309 A712 1.50z red & blk 15 15
2310 A712 1.50z red & dk vio 15 15
2311 A712 1.50z red & dk bl 15 15
2312 A713 1.50z blk, red & gold 15 15
Set value 50 30

Polish United Workers' Party, 30th anniv.

LOT Planes, 1929 and 1979 A714

1979, Jan. 2 **Photo.** *Perf. 11x11½*

2313 A714 6.90z gold & multi 42 18

LOT, Polish airline, 50th anniversary.

POLSKA Gr 50

Train and IYC Emblem — A715

Children's Paintings: 1z, Children with toys. 1.50z, Children in meadow. 6z, Family.

1979, Jan. 13 *Perf. 11*

2314 A715 50g multi 15 15
2315 A715 1z multi 15 15
2316 A715 1.50z multi 15 15
2317 A715 6z multi 42 18
Set value 64 36

International Year of the Child.

Artist's Wife, by Karol Mondral — A716

Modern Polish Graphic Arts: 50g, "Lightning," by Edmund Bartlomiejcyk, horiz. 1.50z, Musicians, by Tadeusz Kulisiewicz. 4.50z, Portrait of a Brave Man, by Wladyslaw Skoczylas.

Perf. 11½x12, 12x11½

1979, Mar. 5 **Engr.**

2318 A716 50g brt vio 15 15
2319 A716 1z sl grn 15 15
2320 A716 1.50z bl gray 15 15
2321 A716 4.50z vio bl 30 15
Set value 52 28

Andrzej Frycz-Modrzewski, Stefan Batory, Jan Zamoyski — A717

Photogravure and Engraved

1979, Mar. 12 *Perf. 12x11½*

2322 A717 1.50z cream & sepia 15 15

Royal Tribunal in Piotrkow Trybunalski, 400th anniversary.

Pole Vault and Olympic Emblem — A718

Olympic Emblem and: 1.50z, High jump. 6z, Cross-country skiing. 8.40z, Equestrian.

1979, Mar. 26 **Photo.** *Perf. 12x11½*

2323 A718 1z multi 15 15
2324 A718 1.50z multi 15 15
2325 A718 6z multi 35 15
2326 A718 8.40z multi 50 20
Set value 1.00 46

1980 Olympic Games.

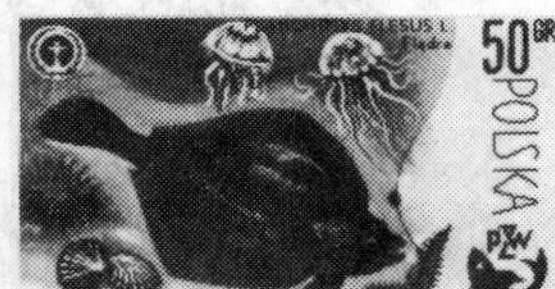

Flounder — A720

Fish and Environmental Protection Emblem: 90g, Perch. 1z, Grayling. 1.50z, Salmon. 2z, Trout. 4.50z, Pike. 5z, Carp. 6z, Catfish and frog.

1979, Apr. 26 **Photo.** *Perf. 11½x11*

2327 A720 50g multi 15 15
2328 A720 90g multi 15 15
2329 A720 1z multi 15 15
2330 A720 1.50z multi 15 15
2331 A720 2z multi 15 15
2332 A720 4.50z multi 30 15
2333 A720 5z multi 32 15
2334 A720 6z multi 40 18
Set value 1.40 70

Polish angling, centenary, and protection of the environment.

A721

1979, Apr. 30 **Litho.** *Perf. 11x11½*

2335 A721 1.50z multi 15 15

Council for Mutual Economic Aid of Socialist Countries, 30th anniversary.

Faces and Emblem — A722

1979, May 7 *Perf. 11*

2336 A722 1.50z red & blk 15 15

6th Congress of Association of Fighters for Liberty and Democracy, Warsaw, May 7-8.

St. George's Church, Sofia A722a

1979, May 15 **Photo.** *Perf. 11x11½*

2337 A722a 1.50z multi 15 15

Philaserdica '79 Phil. Exhib., Sofia, Bulgaria, May 18-27.

Pope John Paul II, Cracow Cathedral A723

Designs: 8.40z, Pope John Paul II, Auschwitz-Birkenau Memorial. 50z, Pope John Paul II.

1979, June 2 **Photo.** *Perf. 11x11½*

2338 A723 1.50z multi 15 15
2339 A723 8.40z multi 60 30
Set value 36

Souvenir Sheet

Perf. 11½x11

2340 A723 50z multi 2.75 2.50

Visit of Pope John Paul II to Poland, June 2-11. No. 2340 contains one 26x35mm stamp.

A variety of #2340 with silver margin exists.

Paddle Steamer Prince Ksawery and Old Warsaw — A724

Designs: 1.50z, Steamer Gen. Swierczewski and Gdansk, 1914. 4.50z, Tug Aurochs and Plock, 1960. 6z, Motor ship Mermaid and modern Warsaw, 1959.

1979, June 15 **Litho.** *Perf. 11*

2341 A724 1z multi 15 15
2342 A724 1.50z multi 15 15
2343 A724 4.50z multi 30 15
2344 A724 6z multi 42 18
Set value 42

Vistula River navigation, 150th anniversary.

Kosciuszko Monument, Philadelphia — A725

1979, July 1 **Photo.** *Perf. 11½*

2345 A725 8.40z multi 48 25

Gen. Tadeusz Kosziuszko (1746-1807), Polish soldier and statesman who served in American Revolution.

Mining Machinery A726

Eagle and People A727

Design: 1.50z, Salt crystals.

1979, July 14 **Photo.** *Perf. 14*

2346 A726 1z lt brn & blk 15 15
2347 A726 1.50z bl grn & blk 15 15
Set value 18 15

Wieliczka ancient rock-salt mines.

1979, July 21 *Perf. 11½x11*

Design: No. 2349, Man with raised hand and flag.

2348 A727 1.50z red, bl & gray 15 15
2349 A727 1.50z sil, red & blk 15 15
Set value 20 16

35 years of Polish People's Republic.

Souvenir Sheet

1979, Sept. 2 **Photo.** *Perf. 11½x11*

2350 A727 Sheet of 2, #2348-2349, plus label 48 35

13th National Philatelic Exhibition.

Poland No. 1, Rowland Hill (1795-1879), Originator of Penny Postage A728

1979, Aug. 16 **Litho.** *Perf. 11½x11*

2351 A728 6z multi 40 18

Souvenir Sheet

The Rape of Europa, by Bernardo Strozzi A729

1979, Aug. 20 **Photo.** *Perf. 11x11½*

2352 A729 10z multi 70 48

Europhil '79, Intl. Phil. Exhib.

Wojciech Jastrzebowski A730

1979, Aug. 27 *Perf. 11½x11*

2353 A730 1.50z multi 15 15

Economic Congress.

The Catalogue editors cannot undertake to appraise, identify or judge the genuineness or condition of stamps.

Postal Workers' Monument A731

1979, Sept. 1 *Perf. 11x11½*

2354	A731	1.50z	multi	15	15

40th anniversary of Polish postal workers' resistance to Nazi invaders. See No. B137.

ITU Emblem, Radio Antenna A732

1979, Sept. 24 *Perf. 11x11½*

2355	A732	1.50z	multi	15	15

Intl. Radio Consultative Committee (CCIR) of the ITU, 50th anniv.

Violin A733

1979, Sept. 25 **Litho.**

2356	A733	1.50z	dk bl, org, grn	15	15

Henryk Wieniawski Young Violinists' Competition, Lublin.

Pulaski Monument, Buffalo — A734

Gen. Franciszek Jozwiak — A735

1979, Oct. 1 **Photo.** *Perf. 11½x12*

2357	A734	8.40z	multi	48	22

Gen. Casimir Pulaski (1748-1779), Polish nobleman who served in American Revolutionary War.

1979, Oct. 3 *Perf. 11½x11*

2358	A735	1.50z	bl, gold	15	15

35th anniv. of Civil and Military Security Service, founded by Gen. Franciszek Jozwiak (1895-1966).

Drive-in Post Office — A736

Designs: 1.50z, Parcel sorting. 4.50z, Loading mail train. 6z, Mobile post office.

1979, Oct. 9 *Perf. 11½*

2359	A736	1z	multi	15	15
2360	A736	1.50z	multi	15	15
2361	A736	4.50z	multi	30	15
2362	A736	6z	multi	42	18
			Set value	78	44

Stamp Day.

Holy Family — A737

Design: 6.90z, Nativity, horiz.

Perf. 11½x11, 11x11½

1979, Dec. 4 **Photo.**

2363	A737	2z	multi	15	15
2364	A737	6.90z	multi	45	20
			Set value		28

A738 A739

Space Achievements: 1z, Soyuz 30 and Salyut 6. 1.50z, Kopernik 500 and Copernicus satellite. 2z, Lunik 2 and Ranger 7. 4.50z, Yuri Gagarin and Vostok. 6.90z, Neil Armstrong and Apollo 11.

1979, Dec. 28 **Photo.** *Perf. 11½x11*

2365	A738	1z	multi	15	15
2366	A738	1.50z	multi	15	15
2367	A738	2z	multi	15	15
2368	A738	4.50z	multi	30	15
2369	A738	6.90z	multi	40	18
a.			Souvenir sheet of 5	1.50	1.00
			Set value	98	50

No. 2369a contains Nos. 2365-2369, tete beche plus label.

1980, Jan. 31 **Photo.** *Perf. 11½x12*

Designs: Horse Paintings.

2370	A739	1z	Stagecoach	15	15
2371	A739	2z	Horse, trainer	15	15
2372	A739	2.50z	Trotters	15	15
2373	A739	3z	Fox hunt	15	15
2374	A739	4z	Sled	18	15
2375	A739	6z	Hay cart	30	16
2376	A739	6.50z	Pairs	32	16
2377	A739	6.90z	Hurdles	32	18
			Nos. 2370-2377 (8)	1.72	
			Set value		88

Sierakov horse stud farm, 150th anniv.

Party Slogan on Map of Poland — A740

Worker, by Janusz Stanny — A741

1980, Feb. 11 **Photo.** *Perf. 11½x11*

2378	A740	2.50z	multi	16	15
2379	A741	2.50z	multi	16	15
			Set value		18

Polish United Workers' Party, 8th Congress.

Equestrian, Olympic Rings — A742

1980, Mar. 31 *Perf. 12x11½*

2380	A742	2z	shown	15	15
2381	A742	2.50z	Archery	16	15
2382	A742	6.50z	Biathlon	42	20
2383	A742	8.40z	Volleyball	50	25
			Set value		62

13th Winter Olympic Games, Lake Placid, NY, Feb. 12-24 (6.50z); 22nd Summer Olympic Games, Moscow, July 19-Aug. 3. See No. B138.

Map and Old Town Hall, 1591, Zamosc A743

1980, Apr. 3 **Litho.** *Perf. 11½*

2384	A743	2.50z	multi	18	15

Zamosc, 400th anniversary.

Arms of Poland and Russia A744

1980, Apr. 21 **Litho.** *Perf. 11½*

2385	A744	2.50z	multi	18	15

Treaty of Friendship, Cooperation and Mutual Assistance between Poland and USSR, 35th anniversary.

Lenin, 110th Birth Anniversary A745

1980, Apr. 22 **Photo.** *Perf. 11*

2386	A745	2.50z	multi	18	15

Workers Marching — A746

Dove Over Liberation Date — A747

1980, May 1 *Perf. 11½x11*

2387	A746	2.50z	multi	18	15

Revolution of 1905, 75th anniversary.

1980, May 9 *Perf. 11½x12*

2388	A747	2.50z	multi	18	15

Victory over fascism, 35th anniversary.

Arms of Treaty-signing Countries — A748

1980, May 14 **Litho.** *Perf. 11½x11*

2389	A748	2z	red & blk	18	15

Signing of Warsaw Pact (Bulgaria, Czechoslovakia, German Democratic Rep., Hungary, Poland, Romania, USSR), 25th anniversary.

Caverns, (1961 Expedition) Map of Cuba — A749

1980, May 22 **Photo.** *Perf. 14*

2390	A749	2z	shown	15	15
2391	A749	2z	Seals, Antarctica, 1959	15	15
2392	A749	2.50z	Ethnology, Mongolia, 1963	15	15
2393	A749	2.50z	Archaeology, Syria, 1959	15	15
2394	A749	6.50z	Mountain climbing, Nepal, 1978	35	18
2395	A749	8.40z	Paleontology, Mongolia, 1963	42	22
			Nos. 2390-2395 (6)	1.37	
			Set value		72

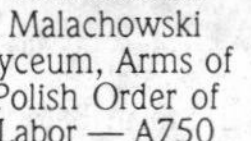

Malachowski Lyceum, Arms of Polish Order of Labor — A750

Xerocomus Parasiticus — A751

1980, June 7 **Photo.** *Perf. 11x12*

2396	A750	2z	blk & dl grn	15	15

Malachowski Lyceum (oldest school in Plock), 800th anniversary.

1980, June 30 *Perf. 11½x11*

2397 A751 2z shown 15 15
2398 A751 2z Clathrus ruber 15 15
2399 A751 2.50z Phallus hadriani 15 15
2400 A751 2.50z Strobilomyces floccopus 15 15
2401 A751 8z Sparassis crispa 42 22
2402 A751 10.50z Langermannia gigantea 55 28
Nos. 2397-2402 (6) 1.57
Set value 82

Sandomierz Millenium — A752

1980, July 12 **Photo.** *Perf. 11x11½*

2403 A752 2.50z dk brn 22 15

"Lwow," T. Ziolkowski — A753

Ships and Teachers: 2.50z, Antoni Garnuszewski, A. Garnuszewski. 6z, Zenit, A. Ledochowski. 6.50z, Jan Turlejski, K. Porebski. 6.90z, Horyzon, G. Kanski. 8.40z, Dar Pomorza, K. Maciejewicz.

1980, July 21 **Litho.** *Perf. 11*

2404 A753 2z multi 15 15
2405 A753 2.50z multi 18 15
2406 A753 6z multi 38 20
2407 A753 6.50z multi 45 22
2408 A753 6.90z multi 45 24
2409 A753 8.40z multi 52 30
Nos. 2404-2409 (6) 2.13 1.26

Marize Maritime High School.

A754

A755

Designs: Medicinal plants.

1980, Aug. 15 **Litho.** *Perf. 11½x11*

2410 A754 2z Atropa belladonna 16 15
2411 A754 2.50z Datura innoxia 20 15
2412 A754 3.40z Valeriana 22 15
2413 A754 5z Mentha piperita 40 18
2414 A754 6.50z Calendula 48 25
2415 A754 8z Salvia officinalis 52 28
Nos. 2410-2415 (6) 1.98
Set value 1.00

1980, Aug. 20 *Perf. 11*

2416 A755 2.50z multi 22 15

Jan Kochanowski (1530-1584), poet.

United Nations, 35th Anniversary A756

1980, Sept. 19 **Photo.** *Perf. 11x11½*

2417 A756 8.40z multi 60 32

Chopin Piano Competition A757

1980, Oct. 2 **Litho.** *Perf. 11½*

2418 A757 6.90z blk & tan 60 32

Mail Pick-up — A758

1980, Oct. 9 **Photo.** *Perf. 12x11½*

2419 A758 2z shown 15 15
2420 A758 2.50z Letter sorting 18 15
2421 A758 6z Loading mail plane 45 22
2422 A758 6.50z Mail boxes 45 24
a. Souvenir sheet of 4, #2419-2422 4.25 3.00
Set value 64

Stamp Day.

Girl Embracing Dove, UN Emblem A759

1980, Nov. 21 **Litho.** *Perf. 11x11½*

2423 A759 8.40z multi 70 35

UN Declaration on the Preparation of Societies for Life in Peace.

Battle of Olzynska Grochowska, by W. Kossak — A760

1980, Nov. 29 **Photo.** *Perf. 11*

2424 A760 2.50z multi 25 15

Battle of Olzynska Grochowska, 1830.

Horse-drawn Fire Engine — A761

Designs: Horse-drawn vehicles.

1980, Dec. 16

2425 A761 2z shown 18 15
2426 A761 2.50z Passenger coach 22 15
2427 A761 3z Beer wagon 24 15
2428 A761 5z Sled 45 18
2429 A761 6z Bus 50 25
2430 A761 6.50z Two-seater 55 25
Nos. 2425-2430 (6) 2.14 1.13

Honor to the Silesian Rebels, by Jan Borowczak A762

Pablo Picasso A763

1981, Jan. 22 **Engr.** *Perf. 11½*

2431 A762 2.50z gray grn 18 15

Silesian uprising, 60th anniversary.

1981, Mar. 10 **Photo.** *Perf. 11½x11*

2432 A763 8.40z multi 55 32
a. Miniature sheet of 2 + 2 labels 1.65 85

Pablo Picasso (1881-1973), artist, birth centenary. No. 2432 se-tenant with label showing A Crying Woman. Sold for 20.80z.

Balloon Flown by Pilatre de Rozier, 1783 — A764

Gordon Bennett Cup (Balloons): No. 2434, J. Blanchard, J. Jeffries, 1875. 2.50z, F. Godard, 1850. 3z, F. Hynek, Z. Burzynski, 1933. 6z, Z. Burzynski, N. Wysocki, 1935. 6.50z, B. Abruzzo, M. Anderson, P. Newman, 1978. 10.50z, Winners' names, 1933-1935, 1938.

1981, Mar. 25 **Photo.** *Perf. 11½x12*

2433 A764 2z multi 16 15
2434 A764 2z multi 16 15
2435 A764 2.50z multi 20 15
2436 A764 3z multi 22 15
2437 A764 6z multi 45 24
2438 A764 6.50z multi 48 25
Nos. 2433-2438 (6) 1.67
Set value 85

Souvenir Sheet

Imperf

2439 A764 10.50z multi 95 70

Iphegenia, by Franz Anton Maulbertsch (1724-1796), WIPA '81 Emblem A765

1981, May 11 **Litho.** *Perf. 11½*

2440 A765 10.50z multi 85 48

WIPA '81 Intl. Phil. Exhib., Vienna, May 22-31.

Wroclaw, 1493 A766

Gen. Wladyslaw Sikorski (1881-1943) A767

1981, May 15 **Photo.** *Perf. 14*

2441 A766 6.50z brown 50 22

See #2456-2459. For surcharge see #2526.

1981, May 20 *Perf. 11½x11*

2442 A767 6.50z multi 42 22

Kwan Vase, 18th Cent. — A768

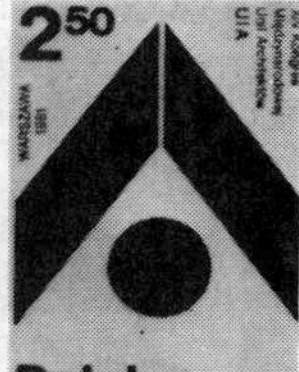

Intl. Architects Union, 14th Congress, Warsaw — A769

1981, June 15

2443 A768 1z shown 15 15
2444 A768 2z Cup, saucer, 1820 15 15
2445 A768 2.50z Jug, 1820 18 15
2446 A768 5z Portrait plate, 1880 38 15
2447 A768 6.50z Vase, 1900 45 20
2448 A768 8.40z Basket, 1840 52 24
Nos. 2443-2448 (6) 1.83
Set value 80

1981, July 15 **Litho.**

2449 A769 2.50z multi 18 15

Moose, Rifle and Pouch — A770

A770a

1981, July 30

2450 A770 2z shown 15 15
2451 A770 2z Boar 15 15
2452 A770 2.50z Fox 18 15
2453 A770 2.50z Elk 18 15
2454 A770 6.50z Greylag goose 45 20
2455 A770 6.50z Fen duck, horiz. 45 20
Nos. 2450-2455 (6) 1.56
Set value 72

City Type of 1981

Perf. 11x11½, 11½x13

1981, July 28 **Photo.**

2456 A766 4z Gdansk, 1652, vert. 30 15
2457 A766 5z Krakow, 1493, vert. 40 18
2458 A766 6z Legnica, 1744 50 22
2459 A766 8z Warsaw, 1618 65 28

1982, Nov. 2 **Photo.** *Perf. 11½*

2461 A770a 12z Vistula River 22 15
2463 A770a 17z Kasimierz Dolny 32 15
2466 A770a 25z Gdansk 45 22
Set value 44

Wild Bison — A771

1981, Aug. 27 *Perf. 11½x11*
2471 Strip of 5 2.25 1.10
a.-e. A771 6.50z, any single 42 20

60th Anniv. of Polish Tennis Federation A772

1981, Sept. 17 Photo. *Perf. 11x11½*
2472 A772 6.50z multi 50 22

Model Airplane — A773

1981, Sept. 24 *Perf. 14*
2473 A773 1z shown 15 15
2474 A773 2z Boats 15 15
2475 A773 2.50z Racing cars 18 15
2476 A773 4.20z Gliders 30 15
2477 A773 6.50z Radio-controlled racing cars 45 18
2478 A773 8z Yachts 48 22
Nos. 2473-2478 (6) 1.71
Set value 75

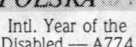

Intl. Year of the Disabled — A774

Stamp Day — A775

1981, Sept. 25 Litho. *Perf. 11½x11*
2479 A774 8.40z multi 52 28

1981, Oct. 9 Photo. *Perf. 14*
2480 A775 2.50z Pistol, 18th cent., horiz. 16 15
2481 A775 8.40z Sword, 18th cent. 50 24
Set value 32

A776

A777

1981, Oct. 10 *Perf. 11½x12*
2482 A776 2.50z multi 18 15

Henryk Wieniawski (1835-1880), violinist and composer.

1981, Oct. 15 **Litho.**

Working Movement Leaders: 50g, Bronislaw Wesolowski (1870-1919). 2z, Malgorzata Fornalska (1902-1944). 2.50z, Maria Koszutska (1876-1939). 6.50z, Marcin Kasprzak (1860-1905).

2483 A777 50g grn & blk 15 15
2484 A777 2z bl & blk 16 15
2485 A777 2.50z brn & blk 18 15
2486 A777 6.50z lil rose & blk 45 18
Set value 38

World Food Day — A778

1981, Oct. 16 *Perf. 11½x11*
2487 A778 6.90z multi 48 22

Old Theater, Cracow, 200th Anniv. — A779

Theater Emblem and: 2z, Helena Modrzejewska (1840-1909), actress. 2.50z, Stanislaw Kozmian (1836-1922), theater director, 1865-1885, founder of Cracow School. 6.50z, Konrad Swinarski (1929-1975), stage manager.

Photo. & Engr.

1981, Oct. 17 *Perf. 12x11½*
2488 A779 2z multi 16 15
2489 A779 2.50z multi 20 15
2490 A779 6.50z multi 40 20
2491 A779 8z multi 50 24

Souvenir Sheet

Vistula River Project — A780

1981, Dec. 20 Litho. *Perf. 11½x12*
2492 A780 10.50z multi 80 65

Flowering Succulent Plants — A781

1981, Dec. 22 Photo. *Perf. 13*
2493 A781 90g Epiphyllopsis gaertneri 15 15
2494 A781 1z Cereus tonduzii 15 15
2495 A781 2z Cylindropuntia leptocaulis 16 15
2496 A781 2.50z Cylindroppuntia fulgida 22 15
2497 A781 2.50z Caralluma lugardi 22 15
2498 A781 6.50z Nopalea cochenillifera 42 20
2499 A781 6.50z Lithopsps helmutii 42 20
2500 A781 10.50z Cylindropuntia spinosior 85 35
Nos. 2493-2500 (8) 2.59
Set value 1.10

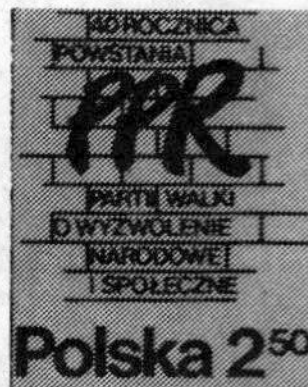

Polish Workers' Party, 40th Anniv. — A782

Stoneware Plate, 1890 — A783

1982, Jan. 5 Photo. *Perf. 11½x11*
2501 A782 2.50z multi 22 15

1982, Jan. 20

Porcelain or Stoneware: 2z, Plate, mug, 1790. 2.50z, Soup tureen, gravy dish, 1830. 6z, Salt and pepper dish, 1844. 8z, Stoneware jug, 1840. 10.50z, Stoneware figurine, 1740.

2502 A783 1z multi 15 15
2503 A783 2z multi 15 15
2504 A783 2.50z multi 16 15
2505 A783 6z multi 42 25
2506 A783 8z multi 55 32
2507 A783 10.50z multi 70 42
Nos. 2502-2507 (6) 2.13
Set value 1.20

Ignacy Lukasiewicz (1822-1882), Oil Lamp Inventor — A784

Designs: Various oil lamps.

1982, Mar. 22 Photo. *Perf. 11½x11*
2508 A784 1z multi 15 15
2509 A784 2z multi 15 15
2510 A784 2.50z multi 18 15
2511 A784 3.50z multi 25 15
2512 A784 9z multi 65 35
2513 A784 10z multi 70 40
Nos. 2508-2513 (6) 2.08
Set value 1.12

Karol Szymanowski (1882-1937), Composer — A785

1982, Apr. 8
2514 A785 2.50z dk brn & gold 15 15

Victory in Challenge Trophy Flights A786

1982, May 5 Photo. *Perf. 11x11½*
2515 A786 27z RWD-6 monoplane 95 55
2516 A786 31z RWD-9 1.40 70
a. Souv. sheet of 2, #2515-2516 2.50 1.25

Henryk Sienkiewicz (1846-1916), Writer — A787

1982 World Cup — A788

Polish Nobel Prize Winners: 15z, Wladyslaw Reymont (1867-1925), writer, 1924. 25z, Marie Curie (1867-1934), physicist 1903, 1911. 31z, Czeslaw Milosz (b. 1911), poet, 1980.

1982, May 10 Litho. *Perf. 11½x11*
2517 A787 3z blk & dk grn 15 15
2518 A787 15z blk & brn 55 24
2519 A787 25z black 90 40
2520 A787 31z blk & gray 1.00 52

Perf. 11½x11, 11x11½

1982, May 28 **Photo.**
2521 A788 25z Ball 80 50
2522 A788 27z Ball, ball, horiz. 1.00 55

Souvenir Sheet

Maria Kaziera Sobieska — A789

1982, June 11 Photo. *Perf. 11½x11*
2523 A789 65z multi 2.50 1.25

PHILEXFRANCE '82 Intl. Stamp Exhibition, Paris, June 11-21.

Assoc. Presidents Stanislaw Sierakowski and Boleslaw Domanski A790

1982, July 20 **Litho.**
2524 A790 4.50z multi 25 15

Assoc. of Poles in Germany, 60th anniv.

2nd UN Conference on Peaceful Uses of Outer Space, Vienna, Aug. 9-21 — A791

1982, Aug. 9 **Photo.**
2525 A791 31z Globe 1.25 65

No. 2441 Surcharged

1982, Aug. 20
2526 A766 10z on 6.50z brn 40 22

Black Madonna of Jasna Gora, 600th Anniv. — A792

Designs: 2.50z, Father Augustin Kordecki (1603-1673). 25z, Siege of Jasna Gora by Swedes, 1655, horiz.

1982, Aug. 26 *Perf. 11*

2527 A792 2.50z multi 15 15
2528 A792 25z multi 80 28
2529 A792 65z multi 2.50 1.10

A souvenir sheet of 2 No. 2529 exists.

Workers' Movement A793

1982, Sept. 3 *Perf. 11½x11*

2530 A793 6z multi 25 15

Norbert Barlicki (1880-1941) A794

Carved Head, Wawel Castle A795

Workers' Activists: 6z, Pawel Finder (1904-1944). 15z, Marian Buczek (1896-1939). 20z, Cezaryna Wojnarowska (1861-1911). 29z, Ignacy Daszynski (1866-1936).

1982, Sept. 10 *Perf. 12x11½*

2531 A794 5z multi 28 15
2532 A794 6z multi 30 15
2533 A794 15z multi 75 28
2534 A794 20z multi 95 32
2535 A794 29z multi 1.10 40
Nos. 2531-2535 (5) 3.38 1.30

1982, Sept. 25

2536 A795 60z Woman's head 2.75 1.00
2537 A795 100z Man's head 3.75 1.75

TB Bacillus Centenary A796

St. Maximilian Kolbe (1894-1941) A797

1982, Sept. 22 *Perf. 11½x11*

2538 A796 10z Koch 32 15
2539 A796 25z Oko Bujwid (1857-1942), bacteriologist 80 40

1982, Oct.

2540 A797 27z multi 85 40

50th Anniv. of Polar Research A798

1982, Oct. 25 Litho. *Perf. 11½*

2541 A798 27z multi 85 40

Stanislaw Zaremba (1863-1942), Mathematician — A799

Mathematicians: 6z, Waclaw Sierpinski (1882-1969). 12z, Zygmunt Janiszewski (1888-1920). 15z, Stefan Banach (1892-1945).

1982, Nov. 23 Photo. *Perf. 11x11½*

2542 A799 5z multi 15 15
2543 A799 6z multi 20 15
2544 A799 12z multi 40 28
2545 A799 15z multi 50 25

First Anniv. of Military Rule — A800

1982, Dec. 13 *Perf. 12x11½*

2546 A800 2.50z Medal obverse and reverse 15 15

Cracow Monuments Restoration A801

1982, Dec. 20 Litho. *Perf. 11½x11*

2547 A801 15z Deanery portal 50 25
2548 A801 25z Law College portal 80 40

Souvenir Sheet

Lithographed and Engraved

Imperf

2549 A801 65z City map 2.00 1.25

No. 2549 contains one stamp 22x27mm.
See Nos. 2593-2594, 2656-2657, 2717-2718, 2809, 2847.

Map of Poland, by Bernard Wapowski, 1526 A802

Maps: 6z, Warsaw, Polish Kingdom Quartermaster, 1839. 8z, Poland, Romer's Atlas, 1908. 25z, Krakow, by A. Buchowiecki, 1703, astrolabe, 17th cent.

1982, Dec. 28 Litho. *Perf. 11½*

2550 A802 5z multi 18 15
2551 A802 6z multi 24 15
2552 A802 8z multi 35 15
2553 A802 25z multi 1.00 40
Set value 72

120th Anniv. of 1863 Uprising — A803

1983, Jan. 22 Photo. *Perf. 12x11½*

2554 A803 6z The Battle, by Arthur Grottger (1837-67) 25 15

Warsaw Theater Sesquicentennial — A804

1983, Feb. 24 Photo. *Perf. 11*

2555 A804 6z multi 25 15

10th Anniv. of UN Conference on Human Environment, Stockholm — A805

1983, Mar. 24 Litho. *Perf. 11½*

2556 A805 5z Wild flowers 16 15
2557 A805 6z Swan, carp, eel 20 15
2558 A805 17z Hoopoe 52 32
2559 A805 30z Fish 90 50
2560 A805 31z Deer, fawn, buffalo 90 50
2561 A805 38z Fruit 1.00 60
Nos. 2556-2561 (6) 3.68 2.22

Karol Kurpinski (1785-1857), Composer — A806

Famous People: 6z, Maria Jasnorzewska Pawlikowska (1891-1945), poet. 17z, Stanislaw Szober (1879-1938), linguist. 25z, Tadeusz Banachiewicz (1882-1954), astronomer. 27z, Jaroslaw Iwaszkiewicz (1894-1980), writer. 31z, Wladyslaw Tatarkiewicz (1886-1980), philosopher, art historian.

1983, Mar. 25 Photo. *Perf. 11½x11*

2562 A806 5z tan & brn 20 15
2563 A806 6z pink & vio 25 15
2564 A806 17z dk grn & lt grn 55 28
2565 A806 25z bis & brn 85 42
2566 A806 27z lt bl & dk bl 95 45
2567 A806 31z vio & pur 1.10 55
Nos. 2562-2567 (6) 3.90 2.00

Polish Medalists in 22nd Olympic Games, 1980 A807

1983, Apr. 5 *Perf. 11x11½*

2568 A807 5z Steeplechase 15 15
2569 A807 6z Equestrian 20 15
2570 A807 15z Soccer, 1982 World Cup 50 25
2571 A807 27z + 5z Pole vault 1.00 50

Warsaw Ghetto Uprising, 40th Anniv. — A808

Customs Cooperation Council, 30th Anniv. — A809

1983, Apr. 19 Photo. *Perf. 11½x11*

2572 A808 6z Heroes' Monument, by Natan Rappaport 25 15

Se-tenant with label showing anniversary medal.

1983, Apr. 28

2573 A809 5z multi 15 15

Second Visit of Pope John Paul II — A810

Portraits of Pope. 31z vert.

1983, June 16 Photo. *Perf. 11*

2574 A810 31z multi 1.10 50
2575 A810 65z multi 2.25 1.10
a. Souvenir sheet 3.00 1.50

Army of King John III Sobieski — A811

1983, July 5 *Perf. 11½x11*

2576 A811 5z Dragoons 15 15
2577 A811 5z Knight in armor 15 15
2578 A811 6z Non-commissioned infantry officers 20 15
2579 A811 15z Light cavalryman 50 25
2580 A811 27z Hussars 90 45
Nos. 2576-2580 (5) 1.90
Set value 95

750th Anniv. of Torun Municipality — A812

1983, Aug. 25 Photo. *Perf. 11*
2581 A812 6z multi 25 15
a. Souv. sheet of 4 4.00 4.00

No. 2581a had limited distribution.

60th Anniv. of Polish Boxing Union — A813

1983, Nov. 4 Litho. *Perf. 11½x11*
2582 A813 6z multi 25 15

Enigma Decoding Machine, 50th Anniv. — A813a

Girl Near House — A813b

1983, Aug. 16 Litho. *Perf. 11½x11*
2582A A813a 5z multi 15 15

1983 Photo. *Perf. 11½x12*
2582B A813b 6z multi 25 15

Public courtesy campaign.

Portrait of King John III Sobieski A814

300th Anniv. of Victory over the Turks in Vienna (King's Portraits by): No. 2584, Unknown court painter. No. 2585, Sobieski on Horseback, by Francesco Trevisani (1656-1746). 25z, Jerzy Eleuter Szymonowicz-Siemiginowski (1660-1711). 65z+10z, Sobieski at Vienna, by Jan Matejko (1838-1893).

1983, Sept. 12 *Perf. 11*
2583 A814 5z multi 15 15
2584 A814 6z multi 20 15
2585 A814 6z multi 20 15
2586 A814 25z multi 80 40
Set value 68

Souvenir Sheet

Imperf

2587 A814 65z + 10z multi 2.25 1.50

Polish Peoples' Army, 40th Anniv. — A815

Designs: No. 2588, General Zygmunt Berling (1896-1980). No. 2589, Wanda Wasilewska (1905-1964). No. 2591, Troop formation.

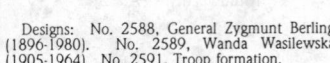

1983, Oct. 12 Photo. *Perf. 11*
2588 A815 5z multi 15 15
2589 A815 5z multi 15 15
2590 A815 6z multi 20 15
2591 A815 6z multi, horiz. 20 15
Set value 36

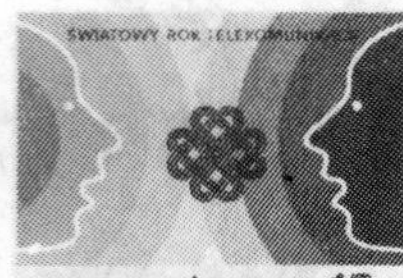

World Communications Year — A816

1983, Oct. 18 Photo. *Perf. 11*
2592 A816 15z multi 50 25

Cracow Restoration Type of 1982

1983, Nov. 25 Litho. *Perf. 11*
2593 A801 5z Cloth Hall, horiz. 18 15
2594 A801 6z Town Hall Tower 28 15
Set value 22

Traditional Hats — A818

Natl. People's Council, 40th Anniv. — A819

1983, Dec. 16 Photo. *Perf. 11½x11*
2595 A818 5z Biskupianski 15 15
2596 A818 5z Rozbarski 15 15
2597 A818 6z Warminsko-Mazurski 16 15
2598 A818 6z Cieszynski 16 15
2599 A818 25z Kurpiowski 65 38
2600 A818 38z Lubuski 1.00 55
Nos. 2595-2600 (6) 2.27
Set value 1.25

1983, Dec. 31
2601 A819 6z Hand holding sword (poster) 25 15

People's Army, 40th Anniv. A820

Musical Instruments A821

1984, Jan. 1 Litho. *Perf. 11½x11*
2602 A820 5z Gen. Bem Brigade badge 20 15

1984, Feb. 10 Photo.
2603 A821 5z Dulcimer 15 15
2604 A821 6z Drum, tambourine 15 15
2605 A821 10z Accordion 25 15
2606 A821 15z Double bass 30 20
2607 A821 17z Bagpipes 45 24
2608 A821 29z Figurines by Tadeusz Zak 85 38
Nos. 2603-2608 (6) 2.15
Set value 1.10

Wincenty Witos (1874-1945), Prime Minister — A822

1984, Mar. 2 Litho. *Perf. 11½x11*
2609 A822 6z grn & sepia 18 15

Local Flowers (Clematis Varieties) A823

1984, Mar. 26 Photo. *Perf. 11x11½*
2610 A823 5z Lanuginosa 16 15
2611 A823 6z Tangutica 20 15
2612 A823 10z Texensis 24 15
2613 A823 17z Alpina 52 24
2614 A823 25z Vitalba 70 35
2615 A823 27z Montana 80 38
Nos. 2610-2615 (6) 2.62
Set value 1.25

The Ecstasy of St. Francis, by El Greco A824

1984, Apr. 21 *Perf. 11*
2616 A824 27z multi 75 32

1984 Olympics A825

1984, Apr. 25 Litho. *Perf. 11x11½*
2617 A825 5z Handball 15 15
2618 A825 6z Fencing 18 15
2619 A825 15z Bicycling 45 20
2620 A825 16z Running 48 22
2621 A825 17z Running, diff. 52 24
a. Souv. sheet of 2, #2620-2621 1.10 75
2622 A825 31z Skiing 80 45
Nos. 2617-2622 (6) 2.58 1.41

No. 2621a sold for 43z.

Battle of Monte Cassino, 40th Anniv. — A826

1984, May 18 Photo. *Perf. 11½x11*
2623 A826 15z Memorial Cross 42 20

View of Warsaw from the Praga Bank, by Bernardo Belotto Canaletto — A827

Paintings of Vistula River views: 6z, Trumpet Festivity, by Aleksander Gierymski. 25z, The Vistula near the Bielany District, by Jozef Rapacki. 27z, Steamship Harbor in the Powisle District, by Franciszek Kostrzewski.

1984, June 20 Photo. *Perf. 11*
2624 A827 5z multi 15 15
2625 A827 6z multi 18 15
2626 A827 25z multi 75 35
2627 A827 27z multi 75 40
Set value 92

Warrior's Head, Wawel Castle — A828

Sculptures: 3.50z, Eastern ruler. No. 2628A, Woman wearing wreath. 10z, Man wearing hat.

1984-85 Photo. *Perf. 11½x12*
2628 A828 3.50z brown 15 15
2628A A828 5z dk claret 15 15
2628B A828 10z brt ultra 20 15
Set value 40 28

Coil Stamp

Perf. 13½x14

2629 A828 5z dk bl grn 20 15

Issue dates: 3.50z, Jan. 24, 1985. No. 2628A, 10z, July 8, 1985. No. 2629, July 10, 1984. No. 2629 has black control number on back of every fifth stamp.

See Nos. 2738-2744.

Order of Grunwald Cross — A829

Designs: 6z, Order of Revival of Poland. 10z, Order of the Banner of Labor, First Class. 16z, Order of Builders of People's Poland.

1984, July 21 Photo. *Perf. 11½*
2630 A829 5z multi 15 15
2631 A829 6z multi 20 15
2632 A829 10z multi 32 15
2633 A829 16z multi 52 24
a. Sheet of 4, #2630-2633, perf. 11½x12 3.25 3.00
Set value 56

40th anniversary of July Manifesto (Origin of Polish People's Republic).

Warsaw Uprising, 40th Anniv. A830

1984, Aug. 1

2634 A830 4z multi 15 15
2635 A830 5z multi 15 15
2636 A830 6z multi 18 15
2637 A830 25z multi 75 35
Set value 56

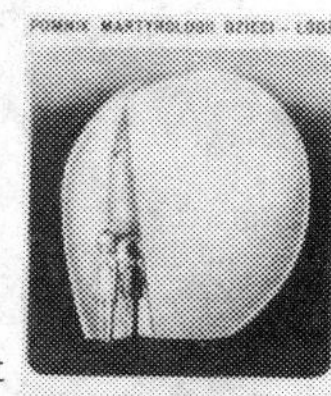

Broken Heart Monument, Lodz — A831

1984, Aug. 31

2638 A831 16z multi 48 22

Defense of Oksywie Holm, Col. S. Dabek — A832

1984, Sept. 1

2639 A832 5z shown 15 15
2640 A832 6z Bzura River battle, Gen. T. Kutrzeba 18 15
Set value 18

Invasion of Poland, 45th anniversary.
See Nos. 2692-2693, 2757, 2824-2826, 2864-2866, 2922-2925.

Polish Militia, 40th Anniv. A833

1984, Sept. 29 Photo. *Perf. 11½*

2641 A833 5z shown 15 15
2642 A833 6z Militiaman at Control Center 18 15
Set value 18

Polish Aviation A834

1984, Nov. 6 Photo. *Perf. 11x11½*

2643 A834 5z Balloon ascent, 1784 15 15
2644 A834 5z Powered flight, 1911 15 15
2645 A834 6z Balloon Polonez, 1983 15 15
2646 A834 10z Modern gliders 22 16
2647 A834 16z Wilga, 1983 35 30
2648 A834 27z Farman, 1914 60 48
2649 A834 31z Los and PZL P-7 65 48
Nos. 2643-2649 (7) 2.27 1.87

Protected Animals A835

1984, Dec. 4 Photo. *Perf. 11x11½*

2650 A835 4z Mustela nivalis 15 15
2651 A835 5z Martes foina 15 15
2652 A835 5z Mustela erminea 15 15

Perf. 11½x11

2653 A835 10z Castor fiber, vert. 22 15
2654 A835 10z Lutra lutra, vert. 22 15
2655 A835 65z Marmota marmota, vert. 1.25 65
Nos. 2650-2655 (6) 2.14
Set value 1.10

Cracow Restoration Type of 1982

Perf. 11½x11, 11x11½

1984, Dec. 10 Litho.

2656 A801 5z Royal Cathedral, Wawel 15 15
2657 A801 15z Royal Castle, Wawel, horiz. 32 15
Set value 22

Religious Buildings — A837

Perf. 11½x12, 12x11½

1984, Dec. 28 Photo.

2658 A837 5z Protestant Church, Warsaw 15 15
2659 A837 10z Saint Andrew Church, Cracow 22 15
2660 A837 15z Greek Orthodox Church, Rychwald 35 16
2661 A837 20z Orthodox Church, Warsaw 45 20
2662 A837 25z Tykocin Synagogue, horiz. 55 25
2663 A837 31z Tartar Mosque, Kruszyniany, horiz. 65 30
Nos. 2658-2663 (6) 2.37 1.21

Classic and Contemporary Fire Engines — A838

Designs: 4z, Horse-drawn fire pump, 19th cent. 10z, Polski Fiat, c. 1930. 12z, Jelcz 315, 1970s. 15z, Horse-drawn hand pump, 1899. 20z, Jelcz engine, Magirus power ladder, 1970s. 30z, Hand pump, 18th cent.

1985, Feb. 25 Photo. *Perf. 11x11½*

2664 A838 4z multi 15 15
2665 A838 10z multi 24 15
2666 A838 12z multi 28 15
2667 A838 15z multi 35 18
2668 A838 20z multi 48 22
2669 A838 30z multi 70 35
Nos. 2664-2669 (6) 2.20
Set value 1.00

Battle of Raclawice, April, 1794, by Jan Styka, 1894 — A839

1985, Apr. 4 *Perf. 11*

2670 A839 27z multi 55 30

Kosciuszko Insurrection cent.

A840 A841

1985, Apr. 11 Litho. *Perf. 11½*

2671 A840 10z sal rose & dk vio bl 22 15

Wincenty Rzymowski (1883-1950),Democratic Party founder.

1985, Apr. 25 Photo. *Perf. 11½x11*

2672 A841 15z Blue jeans, badge 32 15

Intl. Youth Year.

Prince Boleslaw Krzywousty (1085-1138) A842

Regional maps and: 5z, Shown. 10z, Wladyslaw Gomulka (1905-1982), sec.-gen. of the Polish Workers Party, prime minister 1945-49. 20z, Piotr Zaremba (b. 1910), president of Gdansk Province 1945-50.

1985, May 8 Litho. *Perf. 11½*

2673 A842 5z multi 15 15
2674 A842 10z multi 22 15
2675 A842 20z multi 45 20
Set value 38

Restoration of the Western & Northern Territories to Polish control, 40th anniv.

Victory Berlin 1945, by Jozef Mlynarski (b. 1925) — A843

Painting: Polish and Soviet soldiers at Brandenburg Gate, May 9, 1945.

1985, May 9 Photo. *Perf. 12x11½*

2676 A843 5z multi 15 15

Liberation from German occupation, 40th anniv.

Warsaw Treaty Org., 30th Anniv. — A844

1985, May 14 Litho. *Perf. 11½x11*

2677 A844 5z Emblem, member flags 15 15

World Wildlife Fund A845

Endangered Wildlife: Canis lupus.

1985, May 25 Photo. *Perf. 11x11½*

2678 A845 5z Wolves, winter landscape 15 15
2679 A845 10z Female, cubs 22 15
2680 A845 10z Wolf 22 15
2681 A845 20z Wolves, summer landscape 45 20
Set value 48

A846 A847

Folk instruments.

1985, June 25 *Perf. 11½x11*

2682 A846 5z Wooden rattle 15 15
2683 A846 10z Jingle 22 15
2684 A846 12z Clay whistles 24 15
2685 A846 20z Wooden fiddles 45 22
2686 A846 25z Tuned bells 52 24
2687 A846 31z Shepherd's flutes, ram's horn, ocarina 65 35
Nos. 2682-2687 (6) 2.23 1.26

Photogravure and Engraved

1985, June 29

Design: O.R.P. Iskra and emblem.

2688 A847 5z bluish blk & yel 15 15

Polish Navy, 40th anniv.

Tomasz Nocznicki (1862-1944) A848

Polish Labor Movement founders: 20z, Maciej Rataj (1884-1940).

1985, July 26 Engr. *Perf. 11x11½*

2689 A848 10z grnsh blk 24 15
2690 A848 20z brn blk 48 24

Natl. labor movement, 90th anniv.

Polish Field Hockey Assn., 50th Anniv. A849

1985, Aug. 22 Litho. *Perf. 11½x11*

2691 A849 5z multi 22 15

World War II Battles Type of 1984

Designs: 5z, Defense of Wizny, Capt. Wladyslaw Raginis. 10z, Attack on Mlawa, Col. Wilhelm Andrzej Liszka-Lawicz.

1985, Sept. 1 Photo. *Perf. 12x11½*

2692 A832 5z multi 15 15
2693 A832 10z multi 24 15
Set value 20

Pafawag Railway Rolling Stock Co. — A850

1985, Sept. 18 Litho. *Perf. 11½*

2694	A850	5z	Box car	15	15
2695	A850	10z	201 E locomotive	24	15
2696	A850	17z	Two-axle coal car	42	24
2697	A850	20z	Passenger car	52	28

Wild Ducks A851

1985, Oct. 21 Photo. *Perf. 11x11½*

2698	A851	5z	Anas crecca	15	15
2699	A851	5z	Anas querquedula	15	15
2700	A851	10z	Aythya fuligula	24	15
2701	A851	15z	Bucephala clangula	35	18
2702	A851	25z	Somateria mollissima	60	30
2703	A851	29z	Netta rufina	70	35
			Nos. 2698-2703 (6)	2.19	
			Set value		1.05

UN, 40th Anniv. A852

1985, Oct. 24 Litho. *Perf. 11½x11*

2704	A852	27z	multi	55	28

Polish Ballet, 200th Anniv. — A853

1985, Dec. 4

2705	A853	5z	Prima ballerina	15	15
2706	A853	15z	Male dancer	35	18
			Set value		24

Paintings by Stanislaw Ignacy Witkiewicz (1885-1939) — A854

Designs: 5z, Marysia and Burek in Ceylon. No. 2708, Woman with a Fox. No. 2709, Self-portrait, 1931. 20z, Compositions, 1917. 25z, Portrait of Nena Stachurska, 1929. Nos. 2707, 2709-2711 vert.

Perf. 11½x11, 11x11½

1985, Dec. 6 Photo.

2707	A854	5z	multi	15	15
2708	A854	10z	multi	24	15
2709	A854	10z	multi	24	15
2710	A854	20z	multi	48	24
2711	A854	25z	multi	60	30
			Nos. 2707-2711 (5)	1.71	
			Set value		84

Souvenir Sheet

Johann Sebastian Bach — A855

1985, Dec. 30 *Perf. 11½x11*

2712	A855	65z	multi	1.75	1.00
a.			With inscription	7.50	7.50

No. 2712a inscribed "300 Rocznica Urodzin Jana Sebastiana Bacha." Distribution was limited.

Profile, Emblem, Sigismond III Column, Royal Castle Tower — A856

Intl. Peace Year — A858

Halley's Comet A857

1986, Jan. 16 *Perf. 11½x11*

2713	A856	10z	lt ultra, brt ultra & ultra	25	15

Congress of Intellectuals for World Peace, Warsaw.

1986, Feb. 7 Photo. *Perf. 11½*

Designs: No. 2714, Michal Kamienski (1879-1973), astronomer, orbit diagram. No. 2715, Comet, Vega, Giotto, Planet-A, ICE-3 space probes.

2714	A857	25z	multi	50	30
2715	A857	25z	multi	50	30

1986, Mar. 20 Photo. *Perf. 11½x11*

2716	A858	25z	turq bl, yel & ultra	60	38

Cracow Restoration Type of 1982

Designs: 5z, Collegium Maius, Jagiellonian Museum. 10z, Town Hall, Kazimierz.

1986, Mar. 20 Litho. *Perf. 11½*

2717	A801	5z	multi	15	15
2718	A801	10z	multi	25	15

Wildlife A859

1986, Apr. 15 Photo. *Perf. 11½x11*

2719	A859	5z	Perdix perdix	15	15
2720	A859	5z	Oryctolagus cuniculus	15	15
2721	A859	10z	Dama dama	20	15
2722	A859	10z	Phasianus colchicus	20	15
2723	A859	20z	Lepus europaeus	42	20
2724	A859	40z	Ovis ammon	80	35
			Nos. 2719-2724 (6)	1.92	
			Set value		86

Nos. 2719-2720, 2723-2724 vert.

Stanislaw Kulczynski (1895-1975), Scientist, Party Leader — A860

Photogravure and Engraved

1986, May 3 *Perf. 11½x11*

2725	A860	10z	buff & choc	22	15

Warsaw Fire Brigade, 150th Anniv. — A861

Painting detail: The Fire Brigade on the Cracow Outskirts on Their Way to a Fire, 1871, by Josef Brodowski (1828-1900).

1986, May 16 *Perf. 11*

2726	A861	10z	dl brn & dk brn	22	15

Paderewski — A862

1986, May 22 *Perf. 11½x11*

2727	A862	65z	multi	1.25	70

AMERIPEX'86.

1986 World Cup Soccer Championships, Mexico — A863

1986, May 26 *Perf. 11½*

2728	A863	25z	multi	48	22

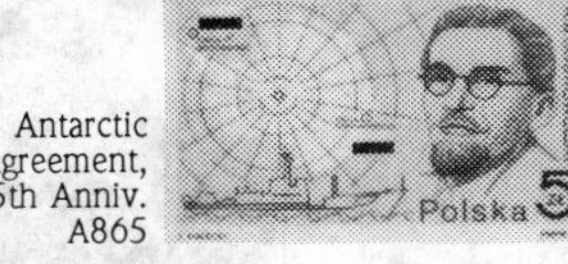

Ferryboats — A864

1986, June 18 Photo. *Perf. 11*

2729	A864	10z	Wilanow	20	15
2730	A864	10z	Wawel	20	15
a.			Souv. sheet of 2, #2729-2730	1.40	1.00
2731	A864	15z	Pomerania	30	15
2732	A864	25z	Rogalin	55	25
a.			Souv. sheet of 2, #2731-2732	2.75	1.90

Nos. 2729-2732 printed se-tenant with labels picturing historic sites from the names of cities serviced. No. 2730a sold for 30z; No. 2732a for 55z. Surtax for the Natl. Assoc. of Philatelists.

Antarctic Agreement, 25th Anniv. A865

Map of Antarctica and: 5z, A. B. Dobrowolski, Kopernik research ship. 40z, H. Arctowski, Professor Siedlecki research ship.

1986, June 23 Litho. *Perf. 11½x11*

2733	A865	5z	ver, pale grn & blk	15	15
2734	A865	40z	org, pale vio & dk vio	80	40
			Set value		45

PZPR JEDNOCZY WSZYSTKIE SIŁY TWÓRCZE NARODU
POLSKA 10zł

Polish United Workers' Party, 10th Congress A866

1986, July 29 Photo. *Perf. 11x11½*

2735	A866	10z	red & dk gray bl	20	15

Wawel Heads Type of 1984-85

Designs: 15z, Woman wearing a wreath (like No. 2628A). No. 2739, Thinker. No. 2740, Eastern ruler. 40z, Youth wearing beret. 60z, Warrior. 200z, Man's head.

Perf. 11½x12, 14 (15z, No. 2740, 60z)

Engr., Photo. (15z, No. 2740, 60z)

1986-89

2738	A828	15z	rose brown	18	15
2739	A828	20z	green	38	18
2740	A828	20z	peacock blue	20	15
2742	A828	40z	gray	75	35
2743	A828	60z	dark green		
2744	A828	200z	dark gray	3.75	1.75

Issue dates: 15z, Sept. 22, 1988. Nos. 2739, 2742, July 30, 1986. No. 2740, Mar. 31, 1989. 60z, Dec. 15, 1989. No. 2744, Nov. 11, 1986.

No. 2740 and 60z are coil stamps, have black control number on back of every 5th stamp.

For surcharge see No. 2954.

This is an expanding set. Numbers will change if necessary.

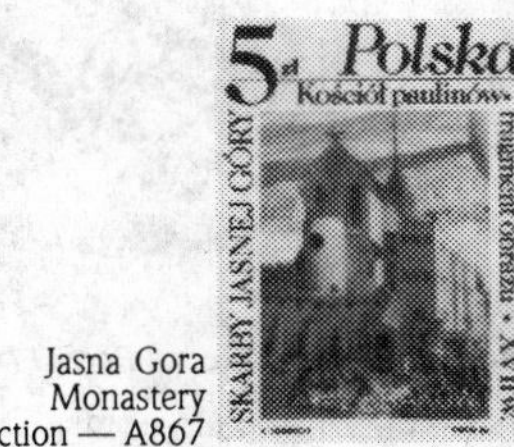

Jasna Gora Monastery Collection — A867

Designs: No. 2746, The Paulinite Church on Skalka in Cracow, oil painting detail, circa 1627. No. 2747, Jesse's Tree, oil on wood, 17th cent. No. 2748, Gilded chalice, 18th cent. No. 2749, Virgin Mary embroidery, 15th cent.

1986, Aug. 15 Photo. *Perf. 11½x11*

2746	A867	5z	multi	15	15
2747	A867	5z	multi	15	15
2748	A867	20z	multi	40	20
2749	A867	40z	multi	80	40
			Set value		72

Victories of Polish Athletes at 1985 World Championships — A868

Designs: No. 2750, Precision Flying, Kissimmee, Florida, won by Waclaw Nycz. No. 2751, Wind Sailing. Tallinn, USSR, won by Malgorzata Palasz-Piasecka. No. 2752, Glider Acrobatics, Vienna, won by Jerzy Makula. No. 2753, Greco-Roman Wrestling (82kg), Kolboten, Norway, won by Bogdan Daras. No. 2754, Road Cycling, Giavera del Montello, Italy, won by Lech Piasecki. No. 2755, Women's Modern Pentathlon, Montreal, won by Barbara Kotowska.

1986, Aug. 21 *Perf. 11½*

2750 A868	5z multi		15	15
2751 A868	10z multi		20	15
2752 A868	10z multi		20	15
2753 A868	15z multi		30	15
2754 A868	20z multi		48	20
2755 A868	30z multi		60	28
	Nos. 2750-2755 (6)		1.93	
	Set value			88

STOCKHOLMIA '86 — A869

1986, Aug. 28 *Perf. 11x11½*

2756 A869	65z multi	1.40	70
a.	Souvenir sheet	1.40	70

World War II Battles Type of 1984

Design: Battle of Jordanow, Col. Stanislaw Maczek, motorized cavalry 10th brigade commander-in-chief.

1986, Sept. 1 *Perf. 12x11½*

2757 A832 10z multi 20 15

Albert Schweitzer A870

World Post Day A871

Photogravure and Engraved

1986, Sept. 26 *Perf. 12x11½*

2758 A870 5z pale bl vio, sep & buff 15 15

1986, Oct. 9 Litho. *Perf. 11x11½*

2759 A871	40z org, ultra & sep	75	35
a.	— Souv. sheet of 2	8.00	4.00

No. 2759a sold for 120z.

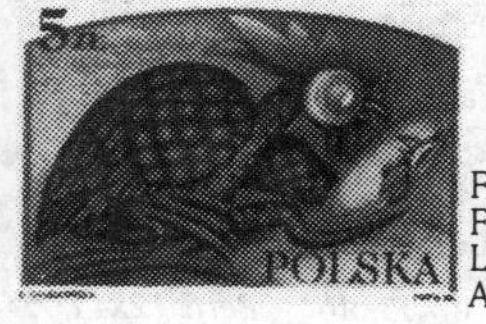

Folk and Fairy Tale Legends A872

Designs: No. 2760, Basilisk. No. 2761, Duke Popiel, vert. No. 2762, Golden Duck. No. 2763, Boruta, the Devil, vert. No. 2764, Janosik the Thief, vert. No. 2765, Lajkonik, conqueror of the Tartars, 13th cent., vert.

1986, Oct. 28 Photo. *Perf. 11½x11*

2760 A872	5z multi	15	15
2761 A872	5z multi	15	15
2762 A872	10z multi	20	15
2763 A872	10z multi	20	15
2764 A872	20z multi	35	18
2765 A872	50z multi	95	42
	Nos. 2760-2765 (6)	2.00	
	Set value		88

Prof. Tadeusz Kotarbinski (1886-1981) — A873

1986, Nov. 19 Litho. *Perf. 11½*

2766 A873 10z sep, buff & brn blk 28 15

17th-20th Cent. Architecture A874

Designs: No. 2767, Church, Baczal Dolny. No. 2768, Windmill, Zygmuntow. 10z, Oravian cottage, Zubrzycza Gorna. 15z, Kashubian Arcade cottage, Wazydze. 25z, Barn, Grzawa. 30z, Water mill, Molkowice Stare.

Perf. 11x11½, 11½x11

1986, Nov. 26 Photo.

2767 A874	5z multi	15	15
2768 A874	5z multi, vert.	15	15
2769 A874	10z multi	20	15
2770 A874	15z multi	28	15
2771 A874	25z multi	50	22
2772 A874	30z multi	55	28
	Nos. 2767-2772 (6)	1.83	
	Set value		80

Royalty A875

Photogravure and Engraved

1986, Dec. 4 *Perf. 11*

2773 A875	10z Mieszko I	20	15
2774 A875	25z Dobrava	50	25

See Nos. 2838-2839, 2884-2885, 2932-2933, 3033-3034, 3068-3069. For surcharges see Nos. 3016-3017.

New Year 1987 — A876

1986, Dec. 12 Photo. *Perf. 11x11½*

2775 A876 25z multi 48 22

Warsaw Cyclists Soc., Cent. A877

Designs: No. 2776, First trip to Bielany, uniformed escort, 1887. No. 2777, Jan Stanislaw Skrodzki (1867-1957), 1895 record-holder. No. 2778, Dynasy Society building, 1892-1937. No. 2779, Mieczyslaw Baranski, champion, 1896. No. 2780, Karolina Kociecka (b. 1875), female competitor. No. 2781, Henryk Weiss (d. 1912), Dynasy champion, 1904-1908.

Perf. 13x12½, 12½x13

1986, Dec. 19 Litho.

2776 A877	5z multi	15	15
2777 A877	5z multi	15	15
2778 A877	10z multi	20	15
2779 A877	10z multi	20	15
2780 A877	30z multi	55	28
2781 A877	50z multi	95	45
	Nos. 2776-2781 (6)	2.20	
	Set value		1.00

Nos. 2777-2781 vert.

Henryk Arctowski Antarctic Station, King George Island, 10th Anniv. A878

Wildlife and ships: No. 2782, Euphausia superba, training freighter Antoni Garnuszewski. No. 2783, Notothenia rossi, Dissostichus mawsoni, Zulawy transoceanic ship. No. 2784, Fulmarus glacialoides, yacht Pogoria. No. 2785, Pigoscelis adeliae, yacht Gedania. 30z, Arctocephalus, research boat Dziunia. 40z, Hydrurga leptonyx, ship Kapitan Ledochowski.

1987, Feb. 13 Litho. *Perf. 11½*

2782 A878	5z multi	15	15
2783 A878	5z multi	15	15
2784 A878	10z multi	20	15
2785 A878	10z multi	20	15
2786 A878	30z multi	60	28
2787 A878	40z multi	85	38
	Nos. 2782-2787 (6)	2.15	
	Set value		98

Paintings by Leon Wyczolkowski (1852-1936) — A879

1987, Mar. 20 Photo. *Perf. 11*

2788 A879	5z Cineraria Flowers, 1924	15	15
2789 A879	10z Portrait of a Woman, 1883	20	15
2790 A879	10z Wood Church, 1910	20	15
2791 A879	25z Harvesting Beetroot, 1910	50	25
2792 A879	30z Wading Fishermen, 1891	60	30
2793 A879	40z Self-portrait, 1912	80	40
	Nos. 2788-2793 (6)	2.45	
	Set value		1.20

Nos. 2789 and 2791 vert.

The Ravage, 1866, by Artur Grottger (1837-1867) — A880

1987, Mar. 26 Photo. *Perf. 11*

2794 A880 15z dark brn & buff 22 15

Gen. Karol Swierczewski-Walter (1897-1947) — A881

1987, Mar. 27 Engr. *Perf. 11½x12*

2795 A881 15z olive grn 22 15

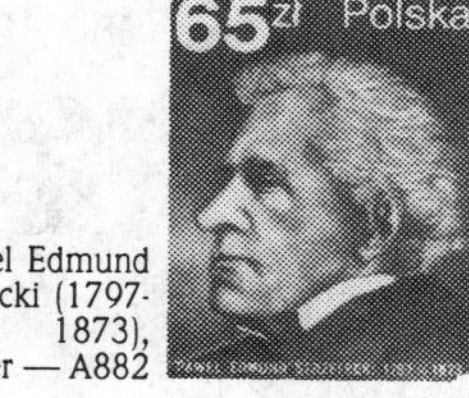

Pawel Edmund Strzelecki (1797-1873), Explorer — A882

1987, Apr. 23 Photo. *Perf. 11½x11*

2796 A882 65z olive blk 1.10 65

Colonization of Australia, bicentennial.

2nd PRON Congress A883

1987, May 8 Litho. *Perf. 11½*

2797 A882 10z pale gray, brn, red & brt ultra 20 15

Patriotic Movement of the National Renaissance Congress.

Motor Vehicles A884

1987, May 19 Photo. *Perf. 12x11½*

2798 A884	10z 1936 Saurer-Zawrat	20	15
2799 A884	10z 1928 CWS T-1	20	15
2800 A884	15z 1928 Ursus-A	30	15
2801 A884	15z 1936 Lux-Sport	30	15
2802 A884	25z 1939 Podkowa 100	50	25
2803 A884	45z 1935 Sokol 600 RT	90	45
	Nos. 2798-2803 (6)	2.40	1.30

Royal Castle, Warsaw — A885

1987, June 5

2804 A885 50z multi 90 50

A souvenir sheet of 1 exists.

A886

State Visit of Pope John Paul II — A887

1987, June 8 *Perf. 11*

2805 A886 15z shown 30 15
2806 A886 45z Portrait, diff. 90 45
a. Pair, #2805-2806 1.20 60

Souvenir Sheet
Perf. 12x11½

2807 A887 50z shown 1.00 1.00

No. 2806a has continuous design.

Cracow Restoration Type of 1982

1987, July 6 Litho. *Perf. 11½*

2809 A801 10z Barbican Gate, Wawel, horiz. 20 15

Esperanto Language, Cent. A890

1987, July 25 Litho. *Perf. 11½*

2811 A890 45z Ludwig L. Zamenhof 80 38

A891

A892

Poznan and Town Hall, by Stanislaw Wyspianski.

1987, Aug. 3

2812 A891 15z blk & pale sal 22 15

POZNAN '87, Aug. 8-16.

1987, Aug. 20 Photo. *Perf. 11½x11*

2813 A892 10z Queen 16 15
2814 A892 10z Worker 16 15
2815 A892 15z Drone 25 15
2816 A892 15z Box hive, orchard 25 15
2817 A892 40z Bee collecting pollen 70 40
2818 A892 50z Beekeeper collecting honey 85 50
Nos. 2813-2818 (6) 2.37 1.50

31st World Apiculture Congress, Warsaw.

Success of Polish Athletes at World Championship Events — A894

1987, Sept. 24 Litho. *Perf. 14*

2820 A894 10z Acrobatics, France 16 15
2821 A894 15z Kayak, Canada 24 15
2822 A894 20z Marksmanship, E. Germany 32 16
2823 A894 25z Wrestling, Hungary 40 20
Set value 56

World War II Battles Type of 1984

Designs: No. 2824, Battle of Mokra, Julian Filipowicz. No. 2825, Battle scene near Oleszycami, Brig.-Gen. Josef Rudolf Kustron. 15z, Air battles over Warsaw, pilot Stefan Pawlikowski.

1987, Sept. 1 Photo. *Perf. 12x11½*

2824 A832 10z multi 20 15
2825 A832 10z multi 20 15
2826 A832 15z multi 30 15
Set value 35

Jan Hevelius (1611-1687), Astronomer, and Constellations — A895

1987, Sept. 15 Litho. *Perf. 11½*

2827 A895 15z Hevelius, sextant, vert. 24 15
2828 A895 40z shown 65 35

Souvenir Sheet

1st Artificial Satellite, Sputnik, 30th Anniv. — A896

1987, Oct. 2 Photo. *Perf. 11½x11*

2829 A896 40z Stacionar 4 satellite 1.00 1.00

World Post Day — A897

Design: Ignacy Franciszek Przebendowski (1730-1791), postmaster general, and post office building, 19th cent., Krakowskie Przedmiescie, Warsaw.

1987, Oct. 9 **Litho.**

2830 A897 15z lt olive grn & rose claret 22 15

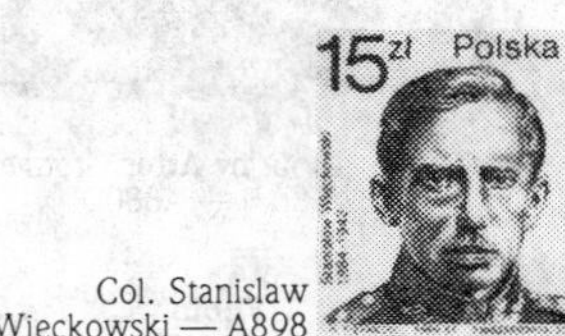

Col. Stanislaw Wieckowski — A898

Photo. & Engr.

1987, Oct. 16 *Perf. 12x11½*

2831 A898 15z deep blue & blk 22 15

Col. Wieckowski (1884-1942), physician and social reformer executed by the Nazis at Auschwitz.

HAFNIA '87 — A899

Fairy tales by Hans Christian Andersen (1805-1875): No. 2832, The Little Mermaid. No. 2833, The Nightingale. No. 2834, The Wild Swan. No. 2835, The Match Girl. 30z, The Snow Queen. 40z, The Brave Toy Soldier.

1987, Oct. 16 Photo. *Perf. 11x11½*

2832 A899 10z multi 20 15
2833 A899 10z multi 20 15
2834 A899 20z multi 40 20
2835 A899 20z multi 40 20
2836 A899 30z multi 60 30
2837 A899 40z multi 80 40
Nos. 2832-2837 (6) 2.60 1.40

Royalty Type of 1986

1987, Dec. 4 Photo. & Engr. *Perf. 11*

2838 A875 10z Boleslaw I Chrobry 20 15
2839 A875 15z Mieszko II 30 15

No. 2838 exists with label.

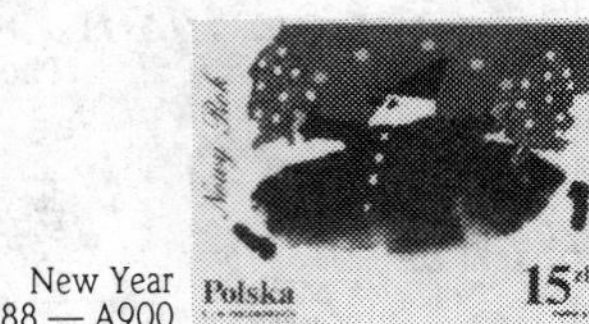

New Year 1988 — A900

1987, Dec. 14 Photo. *Perf. 11x11½*

2840 A900 15z multi 30 15

Dragonflies A901

Perf. 11x11½, 11½x11

1988, Feb. 23 **Photo.**

2841 A901 10z Anax imperator 20 15
2842 A901 15z Libellula quadrimaculata, vert. 30 15
2843 A901 15z Calopteryx splendens 30 15
2844 A901 20z Cordulegaster annulatus, vert. 40 20
2845 A901 30z Sympetrum pedemontanum 60 30
2846 A901 50z Aeschna viridis, vert. 1.00 50
Nos. 2841-2846 (6) 2.80 1.45

Cracow Restoration Type of 1982

1988, Mar. 8 Litho. *Perf. 11½x11*

2847 A801 15z Florianska Gate, 1300 30 15

Intl. Year of Graphic Design A903

1988, Apr. 28 Photo. *Perf. 11x11½*

2848 A903 40z multi 80 40

Antique Clocks — A904

Clocks in the Museum of Artistic and Precision Handicrafts, Warsaw, and clockworks: No. 2849, Frisian wall clock, 17th cent., vert. No. 2850, Anniversary clock and rotary pendulum, 20th cent. No. 2851, Carriage clock, 18th cent., vert. No. 2852, Louis XV rococo bracket clock, 18th cent., vert. 20z, Pocket watch, 19th cent. 40z, Gdansk six-sided clock signed by Benjamin Zoll, 17th cent.

Perf. 11½x12, 12x11½

1988, May 19 **Photo.**

2849 A904 10z lt grn & multi 20 15
2850 A904 10z pur & multi 20 15
2851 A904 15z dl org & multi 30 15
2852 A904 15z brn & multi 30 15
2853 A904 20z multi 40 20
2854 A904 40z multi 80 40
Nos. 2849-2854 (6) 2.20 1.20

1988 Summer Olympics, Seoul — A905

1988, June 27 Photo. *Perf. 11x11½*

2855 A905 15z Triple jump 30 15
2856 A905 20z Wrestling 40 20
2857 A905 20z Two-man kayak 40 20
2858 A905 25z Judo 50 25
2859 A905 40z Shooting 80 40
2860 A905 55z Swimming 1.10 55
Nos. 2855-2860 (6) 3.50 1.75

See No. B148.

Natl. Industry A906

1988, Aug. 23 Photo. *Perf. 11x11½*
Size: 35x27mm

2861 A906 45z Los "Elk" aircraft 90 45

State Aircraft Works, 60th anniv.
See Nos. 2867, 2871, 2881-2883.

16th European Regional FAO Conference, Cracow — A907

Designs: 15z, Computers and agricultural growth. 40z, Balance between industry and nature.

1988, Aug. 22 *Perf. 11½x11*

2862 A907 15z multi 30 15
2863 A907 40z multi 80 40

World War II Battles Type of 1984

Battle scenes and commanders: 15z, Modlin, Brig.-Gen. Wiktor Thommee. No. 2865, Warsaw, Brig.-Gen. Walerian Czuma. No. 2866, Tomaszow Lubelski, Brig.-Gen. Antoni Szylling.

1988, Sept. 1 Photo. *Perf. 12x11½*

2864 A832 15z multi 30 15
2865 A832 20z multi 40 20
2866 A832 20z multi 40 20

Natl. Industries Type of 1988

Design: Stalowa Wola Ironworks, 50th anniv.

1988, Sept. 5 *Perf. 11x11½*
Size: 35x27mm

2867 A906 15z multi		30	15

World Post Day — A909

Design: Postmaster Tomasz Arciszewski (1877-1955), Post and Telegraph Administration emblem used from 1919 to 1927.

1988, Oct. 9 **Litho.** *Perf. 11½x11*

2868 A909 20z multi		40	20

Also printed in sheet of 12 plus 12 labels.

World War II Combat Medals — A910

1988, Oct. 12 **Photo.**

2869 A910 20z Battle of Lenino Cross		40	20
2870 A910 20z shown		40	20

See Nos. 2930-2931.

Natl. Industries Type of 1988

Design: Air Force Medical Institute, 60th anniv.

1988, Oct. 12 *Perf. 11x11½*
Size: 38x27mm

2871 A906 20z multi		40	20

Stanislaw Malachowski, Kazimierz Nestor Sapieha — A912

1988, Oct. 16 *Perf. 11*

2872 A912 20z multi		40	20

Four Years' Sejm (Parliament) (1788-1792), bicent.

National Leaders — A913

1988, Nov. 11 *Perf. 12x11½*

2873 A913 15z Wincenty Witos		30	15
2874 A913 15z Ignacy Daszynski		30	15
2875 A913 20z Wojciech Korfanty		40	20
2876 A913 20z Stanislaw Wojciechowski		40	20
2877 A913 20z Julian Marchlewski		40	20
2878 A913 200z Ignacy Paderewski		4.00	2.00
2879 A913 200z Jozef Pilsudski		4.00	2.00
2880 A913 200z Gabriel Narutowicz		4.00	2.00
a. Souvenir sheet of 3, #2878-2880		12.00	12.00
Nos. 2873-2880 (8)		13.80	6.90

Natl. independence, 70th anniv.

Natl. Industry Types of 1988

Designs: 15z, Wharf, Gdynia. 20z, Industrialist Hipolit Cegielski, 1883 steam locomotive. 40z, Poznan fair grounds, Upper Silesia Tower.

1988 **Photo.** *Perf. 11x11½*
Size: 39x27mm

2881 A906 15z multi		30	15
2882 A906 20z multi		40	20

Size: 35x27mm

2883 A906 40z multi		80	40

70th anniv. of Polish independence. Gdynia Port, 65th anniv (15z); Metal Works in Poznan, 142nd anniv. (20z); and Poznan Intl. Fair 60th anniv. (40z).

Issue dates: 15z, Dec. 12; 20z, Nov. 28; 40z, Dec. 21.

Royalty Type of 1986

1988, Dec. 4 **Photo. & Engr.** *Perf. 11*

2884 A875 10z Rycheza		20	15
2885 A875 15z Kazimierz I Odnowiciel		30	15

New Year 1989 A914

1988, Dec. 9 **Photo.** *Perf. 11x11½*

2886 A914 20z multi		40	20

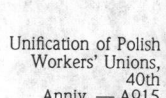

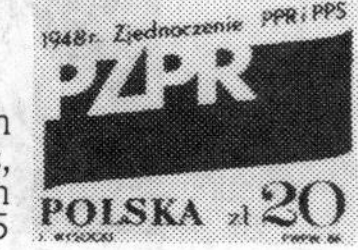
Unification of Polish Workers' Unions, 40th Anniv. — A915

1988, Dec. 15 *Perf. 11½x12*

2887 A915 20z blk & ver		40	20

Fire Boats — A916

1988, Dec. 29 **Litho.** *Perf. 14*

2888 A916 10z Blysk		20	15
2889 A916 15z Zar		30	15
2890 A916 15z Plomien		30	15
2891 A916 20z Strazak 4		40	20
2892 A916 20z Strazak 11		40	20
2893 A916 45z Strazak 25		90	45
Nos. 2888-2893 (6)		2.50	1.30

Horses — A917

1989, Mar. 6 **Photo.** *Perf. 11*

2894 A917 15z Lippizaner		30	15
2895 A917 15z Arden, vert.		30	15
2896 A917 20z English		40	20
2897 A917 20z Arabian, vert.		40	20
2898 A917 30z Wielkopolski		60	30
2899 A917 70z Polish, vert.		1.40	70
Nos. 2894-2899 (6)		3.40	1.70

Dogs — A918

Battle of Monte Cassino, 45th Anniv. — A919

1989, May 3 **Photo.** *Perf. 11½x11*

2900 A918 15z Wire-haired dachshund		15	15
2901 A918 15z Cocker spaniel		15	15
2902 A918 20z Czech fousek pointer		16	15
2903 A918 20z Welsh terrier		16	15
2904 A918 25z English setter		20	15
2905 A918 45z Pointer		38	20
Nos. 2900-2905 (6)		1.20	
Set value			58

1989, May 18 *Perf. 11½x12*

Design: 165z, Battle of Falaise, General Stanislaw Maczek, horiz. 210z, Battle of Arnhem, Gen. Stanislaw Sosabowski, vert.

2906 A919 80z Gen. W. Anders		45	22
2907 A919 165z multi		85	42
2907A A919 210z multi		1.20	60

1st Armored Division at the Battle of Falaise, 45th anniv. Battle of Arnhem, 45th anniv.

See No. 2968.

Woman Wearing a Phrygian Cap — A920

1989, July 3 **Litho.** *Perf. 11½x11*

2908 A920 100z blk, dark red & dark ultra		58	30
a. Souv. sheet of 2+2 labels		2.00	2.00

French revolution bicent., PHILEXFRANCE '89. No. 2908 printed se-tenant with inscribed label picturing exhibition emblem. No. 2908a sold for 270z. Surcharge benefited the Polish Philatelic Union.

Polonia House, Pultusk — A921

1989, July 16 **Photo.** *Perf. 11½*

2909 A921 100z multi		60	30

First Moon Landing, 20th Anniv. A922

1989, July 21 *Perf. 11x11½*

2910 A922 100z multi		60	30
a. Souv. sheet of 1		60	30

No. 2910a exists imperf.

Polish People's Republic, 45th Anniv. — A923

Winners of the Order of the Builders of People's Poland: No. 2911, Ksawery Dunikowski (1875-1964), artist. No. 2912, Stanislaw Mazur (1897-1964), agriculturist. No. 2913, Natalia Gasiorowska (1881-1964), historian. No. 2914, Wincenty Pstrowski (1904-1948), coal miner.

1989, July 21 *Perf. 11½x11*

2911 A923 35z multi		22	15
2912 A923 35z multi		22	15
2913 A923 35z multi		22	15
2914 A923 35z multi		22	15
Set value			44

Security Service and Militia, 45th Anniv. A924

1989, July 21 *Perf. 11x11½*

2915 A924 35z dull brn & slate blue		24	15

World Fire Fighting Congress, July 25-30, Warsaw — A925

1989, July 25 *Perf. 11½x11*

2916 A925 80z multi		55	28

Daisy — A926

Designs: 60z, Juniper. 150z, Daisy. 500z, Wild rose. 1000z, Blue corn flower.

1989 **Photo.** *Perf. 11x12*

2917 A926 40z slate green		24	15
2918 A926 60z violet blue		35	18
2919 A926 150z rose lake			
2920 A926 500z bright violet			
2921 A926 1000z bright blue			

Issue dates: 40z, 60z, Aug. 25. 150z, Dec. 4; 500z, 1000z, Dec. 19.

See Nos. 2978-2979, 3026. For surcharge see No. 2970.

World War II Battles Type of 1984

Battle scenes and commanders: No. 2922, Westerplatte, Capt. Franciszek Dabrowski. No. 2923, Hel, Artillery Capt. B. Przybyszewski. No. 2924, Kock, Brig.-Gen. Franciszek Kleeberg. No. 2925, Lwow, Brig.-Gen. Wladyslaw Langner.

1989, Sept. 1 *Perf. 12x11½*

2922 A832 25z multi		15	15
2923 A832 25z multi		15	15
2924 A832 35z multi		20	15
2925 A832 35z multi		20	15
Set value			34

Nazi invasion of Poland, 50th anniv.

Caricature Museum — A927

1989, Sept. 15 Photo. ***Perf. 11½x11***
2926 A927 40z multi 24 15

Teaching Surgery at Polish Universities, Bicent., and Surgeon's Soc. Cent. — A928

Surgeons: 40z, Rafal Jozef Czerwiakowski (1743-1813), 1st professor of surgery and founder of the 1st surgical department, Jagellonian University, Cracow. 60z, Ludwik Rydygier (1850-1920), founder of the Polish Surgeons Society.

1989, Sept. 18 ***Perf. 11½x12***
2927 A928 40z blk & brt ultra 24 15
2928 A928 60z blk & brt grn 35 18

World Post Day — A929

Design: Emil Kalinski (1890-1973), minister of the Post and Telegraph from 1933-1939.

1989, Oct. 9 ***Perf. 12x11½***
2929 A929 60z multi 35 18

Printed se-tenant with label picturing postal emblem of the second republic.

A similar 50z stamp for Gen. Grzegorz Korczynski was prepared but not issued.

WWII Decorations Type of 1988

Medals: No. 2930, Participation in the Struggle for Control of the Nation. No. 2931, Defense of Warsaw, 1939-45.

1989, Oct. 12 Photo. ***Perf. 11½x11***
2930 A910 60z multicolored 24 15
2931 A910 60z multicolored 24 15

Royalty Type of 1986

Photo. & Engr.

1989, Oct. 18 ***Perf. 11***
2932 A875 20z Boleslaw II Szczodry 15 15
2933 A875 30z Wladyslaw I Herman 15 15

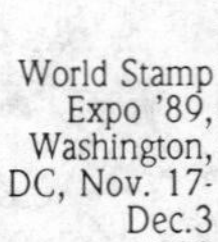
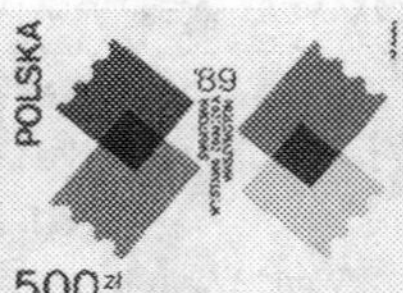

World Stamp Expo '89, Washington, DC, Nov. 17-Dec.3 A930

1989, Nov. 14 Photo. ***Perf. 11x11½***
2934 A930 500z multicolored

Exists imperf.

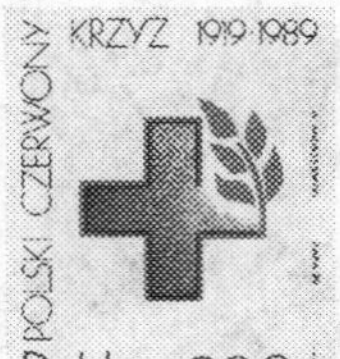

Polish Red Cross Soc., 70th Anniv. — A931

1989, Nov. 17 ***Perf. 11½x11***
2935 A931 200z blk, brt yel grn & scar

Treaty of Versailles, 70th Anniv. A932

Design: State arms and representatives of Poland who signed the treaty, including Ignacy Jan Paderewski (1860-1941), pianist, composer, statesman, and Roman Dmowski (1864-1939), statesman.

1989, Nov. 21 ***Perf. 11x11½***
2936 A932 350z multicolored

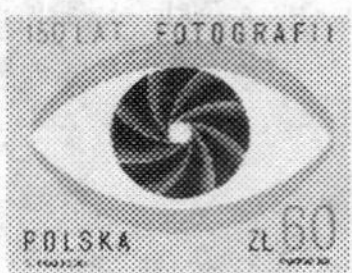

Camera Shutter as the Iris of the Eye — A933

Designs: 40z, Photographer in silhouette, Maksymilian Strasz (1804-1870), pioneer of photography in Poland.

Perf. 11½x12, 12x11½

1989, Nov. 27
2937 A933 40z multicolored
2938 A933 60z shown

Photography, 150th anniv.

No. 2456 Surcharged

1989, Nov. 30 Photo. ***Perf. 11x11½***
2939 A766 500z on 4z dark violet

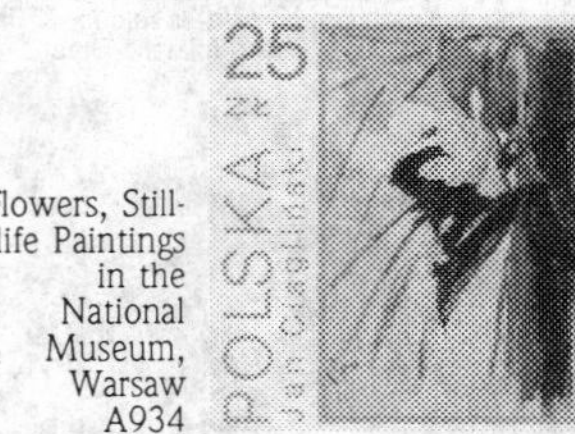

Flowers, Still-life Paintings in the National Museum, Warsaw A934

1989, Dec. 18 ***Perf. 13***
2940 A934 25z Jan Ciaglinski
2941 A934 30z Wojciech Weiss
2942 A934 35z Antoni Kolasinski
2943 A934 50z Stefan Nacht-Samborski
2944 A934 60z Jozef Pankiewicz
2945 A934 85z Henryka Beyer
2946 A934 110z Wladyslaw Slewinski
2947 A934 190z Czeslaw Wdowiszewski

Religious Art — A935

1989, Dec. 21 ***Perf. 11½x11***
2948 A935 50z Jesus, shroud
2949 A935 60z Two saints
2950 A935 90z Three saints

Perf. 11x11½
2951 A935 150z Jesus, Mary, Joseph
2952 A935 200z Madonna and Child Enthroned
2953 A935 350z Holy Family with angels

Nos. 2951-2953 vert.

No. 2738 Surcharged

1990, Jan. 31 Photo. ***Perf. 11½x12***
2954 A828 350z on 15z rose brn

Opera Singers — A936

Portraits: 100z, Krystyna Jamroz (1923-1986). 150z, Wanda Werminska (1900-1988). 350z, Ada Sari (1882-1968). 500z, Jan Kiepura (1902-1966).

1990, Feb. 9 ***Perf. 12x11½***
2955 A936 100z multicolored
2956 A936 150z multicolored
2957 A936 350z multicolored
2958 A936 500z multicolored

Yachting A937

1990, Mar. 29 ***Perf. 11x11½***
2959 A937 100z shown
2960 A937 200z Rugby
2961 A937 400z High jump
2962 A937 500z Figure skating
2963 A937 500z Diving
2964 A937 1000z Rhythmic gymnastics

Roman Kozlowski (1889-1977), Paleontologist A938

1990, Apr. 17 Photo. ***Perf. 11x11½***
2965 A938 500z red & olive bis

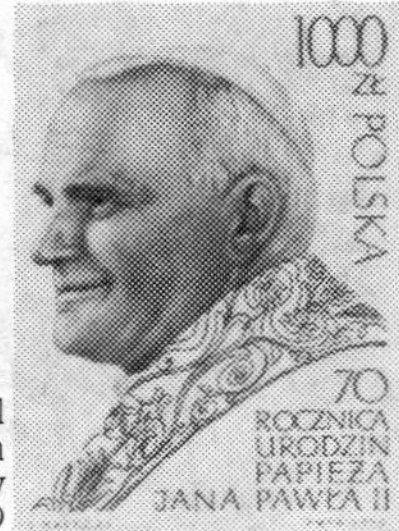

Pope John Paul II, 70th Birthday A939

1990, May 18 ***Perf. 11***
2966 A939 1000z multicolored

Souvenir Sheet

First Polish Postage Stamp, 130th Anniv. — A940

Design includes No. 1 separated by simulated perforations from 1000z commemorative version at right.

1990, May 25 ***Perf. 11½***
2967 A940 1000z multicolored

Battle Type of 1989

Design: Battle of Narvik, 1940, General Z. Bohusz-Szyszko.

1990, May 28 ***Perf. 11½x12***
2968 A919 1500z multicolored

World Cup Soccer Championships, Italy — A941

1990, June 8 ***Perf. 11½x11***
2969 A941 1000z multicolored

No. 2918 Surcharged in Vermilion

700 zł

1990, June 18 Photo. ***Perf. 11x12***
2970 A926 700z on 60z vio bl

Memorial to Victims of June 1956 Uprising, Poznan — A942

1990, June 28 Photo. ***Perf. 12x11½***
2971 A942 1500z multicolored

Social Insurance Institution, 70th Anniv. — A943

1990, July 5 ***Perf. 11x11½***
2972 A943 1500z multicolored

Shells — A944

Designs: No. 2973, Mussel. No. 2974, Fresh water snail.

1990, July 16 *Perf. 14*
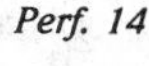
2973 A944 B (500z) dk pur
2974 A944 A (700z) olive grn

Katyn Forest Massacre, 50th Anniv. — A945

1990, July 20
2975 A945 1500z gray, red & blk

Polish Meteorological Service — A946

1990, July 27 *Perf. 11x11½*
2976 A946 500z shown
2977 A946 700z Thermometer

Flower Type of 1989

Designs: 2000z, Nuphar. 5000z, German iris.

1990, Aug. 13 *Die Cut*
Self Adhesive
2978 A926 2000z olive grn
2979 A926 5000z violet

World Kayaking Championships, Poznan — A947

Design: 1000z, One-man kayak.

1990, Aug. 22 Photo. *Perf. 11x11½*
2980 A947 700z multicolored
2981 A947 1000z multicolored
a. Souv. sheet of 1 + label

A948

A949

1990, Aug. 31 *Perf. 11½x11*
2982 A948 1500z blk, red & gray

Solidarity, 10th anniv.

1990, Sept. 24 Photo. *Perf. 11½x11*

Flowers.

2983 A949 200z Polemonium coeruleum
2984 A949 700z Nymphoides peltata
2985 A949 700z Dracocephalum ruyschiana
2986 A949 1000z Helleborus purpurascens
2987 A949 1500z Daphne cneorum
2988 A949 1700z Dianthus superbus

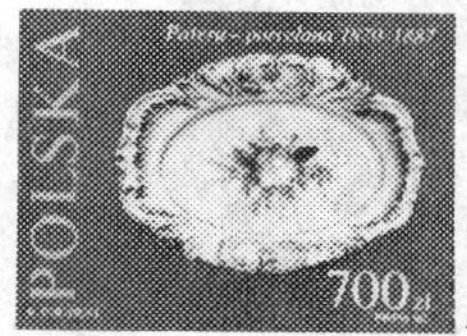

Cmielow Porcelain Works, Bicentennial A950

Designs: 700z, Platter, 1870-1887. 800z, Plate, 1887-1890, vert. No. 2991, Figurine, 1941-1944, vert. No. 2992, Cup, saucer, c. 1887. 1500z, Candy box, 1930-1990. 2000z, Vase, 1979, vert.

1990, Oct. 31 Photo. *Perf. 11*
2989 A950 700z multicolored
2990 A950 800z multicolored
2991 A950 1000z multicolored
2992 A950 1000z multicolored
2993 A950 1500z multicolored
2994 A950 2000z multicolored

Owls — A951

1990, Nov. 6 Litho. *Perf. 14*
2995 A951 200z Athene noctua
2996 A951 500z shown
2997 A951 500z Strix aluco, winter
2998 A951 1000z Asio flammeus
2999 A951 1500z Asio otus
3000 A951 2000z Tyto alba

Pres. Lech Walesa, 1983 Nobel Peace Prize Winner A952

1990, Dec. 12 Litho. *Perf. 11x11½*
3001 A952 1700z multicolored

A953 A954

1990, Dec. 21 Photo. *Perf. 11½x11*
3002 A953 1500z multicolored

Polish participation in Battle of Britain, 50th anniv.

1990, Dec. 28 Litho. *Perf. 11½*

Architecture: 700z, Collegiate Church, 12th cent., Leczyca. 800z, Castle, 14th cent., Reszel. 1500z, Town Hall, 16th cent., Chelmno. 1700z, Church of the Nuns of the Visitation, 18th cent., Warsaw.

3003 A954 700z multicolored
3004 A954 800z multicolored
3005 A954 1500z multicolored
3006 A954 1700z multicolored

No. 3006 printed with se-tenant label for World Philatelic Exhibition, Poland '93.

Art Treasures of the Natl. Gallery, Warsaw A955

Paintings: 500z, King Sigismund Augustus. 700z, The Adoration of the Magi, Pultusk Codex. 1000z, St. Matthew, Pultusk Codex. 1500z, Christ Removing the Moneychangers by Mikolaj Haberschrack. 1700z, The Annunciation. 2000z, The Three Marys by Haberschrack.

1991, Jan. 11 Photo. *Perf. 11*
3007 A955 500z multicolored
3008 A955 700z multicolored
3009 A955 1000z multicolored
3010 A955 1500z multicolored
3011 A955 1700z multicolored
3012 A955 2000z multicolored

Pinecones — A956

1991, Feb. 22 *Perf. 12x11½*
3013 A956 700z Abies alba
3014 A956 1500z Pinus strobus

Radziwill Palace A957

1991, Mar. 3 Photo. *Perf. 11x12*
3015 A957 1500z multicolored

Admission to CEPT.

Royalty Type of 1986 Surcharged in Red

Designs: 1000z, Boleslaw III Krzywousty. 1500z, Wladyslaw II Wygnaniec.

Photo. & Engr.
1991, Mar. 25 *Perf. 11*
3016 A875 1000z on 40z, grn & blk
3017 A875 1500z on 50z, red vio & gray blk

Not issued without surcharge.

Brother Albert (Adam Chmielowski, 1845-1916) — A958

1991, Mar. 29 Photo. *Perf. 12x11½*
3018 A958 2000z multicolored

Battle of Legnica, 750th Anniv. A959

Photo. & Engr.
1991, Apr. 9 *Perf. 14½x14*
3019 A959 1500z multicolored 38

See Germany No. 1635.

Polish Icons — A960

Designs: 500z, 1000z, 1500z, Various paintings of Madonna and Child. 700z, 2000z, 2200z, Various paintings of Jesus.

1991, Apr. 22 Photo. *Perf. 11*
3020 A960 500z multicolored 22
3021 A960 700z multicolored 30
3022 A960 1000z multicolored 44
3023 A960 1500z multicolored 66
3024 A960 2000z multicolored 88
3025 A960 2200z multicolored 98
Nos. 3020-3025 (6) 3.48

Flower Type of 1989

Design: 700z, Lily of the Valley.

1991, Apr. 26 Litho. *Perf. 14*
3026 A926 700z dk bl grn 32

Royalty Type of 1986

Designs: 1000z, Boleslaw IV Kedzierzawy. 1500z, Mieszko III Stary.

Photo. & Engr.
1991, Apr. 30 *Perf. 11x11½*
3033 A875 1000z brn red & black 45
3034 A875 1500z brt bl & bluish blk 68

A961

A962

Designs: 2000z, Title page of act. 2500z, Debate in the Sejm. 3000z, Adoption of Constitution, May 3, 1791, by Jan Matejko (1838-1893).

1991, May 2 Litho. *Perf. 11½*
3035 A961 2000z brn & ver 88
3036 A961 2500z brn & ver 98

Souvenir Sheet

3037 A961 3000z multicolored 1.35

May 3, 1791 Polish constitution, bicent.

1991, May 6 Litho. *Perf. 11½x11*
3038 A962 1000z multicolored 45

Europa.

European Conference for Protection of Cultural Heritage, Cracow — A963

1991, May 27 Litho. *Perf. 11½*
3039 A963 2000z bl & lake 75

Sinking of the Bismarck, 50th Anniv. — A964

1991, May 27
3040 A964 2000z multicolored 75

A965 A966

Designs: 1000z, Pope John Paul II. 2000z, Pope wearing white.

1991, June 1 Litho. *Perf. 11½x11*
3041 A965 1000z multicolored 38
3042 A965 2000z multicolored 75

1991, June 21 Litho. *Perf. 11½*
3043 A966 2000z multicolored 90

Antarctic Treaty, 30th anniv.

Polish Paper Industry, 500th Anniv. A967

1991, July 8
3044 A967 2500z lake & gray 98

Victims of Stalin — A968

1991, July 29 Litho. *Perf. 11½x12*
3045 A968 2500z blk & red 98

Souvenir Sheet

Pope John Paul II — A969

1991, Aug. 15 Photo. *Perf. 11½x11*
3046 A969 3500z multicolored 1.45

Basketball, Cent. A970

1991, Aug. 19 Litho. *Perf. 11x11½*
3047 A970 2500z multicolored 98

Leon Wyczolkowski (1852-1936), painter — A971

1991, Sept. 7 Photo. *Perf. 11½x12*
3048 A971 3000z olive brown 1.15
a. Sheet of 4 4.75

16th Polish Philatelic Exhibition, Bydgoszcz '91.

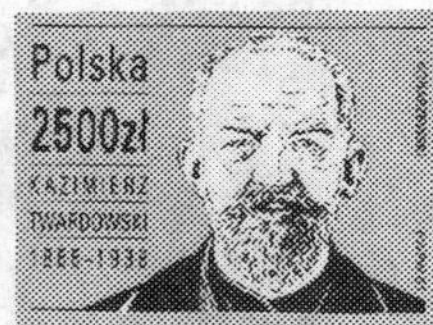

Kazimierz Twardowski (1866-1938) — A972

1991, Oct. 10 *Perf. 11x11½*
3049 A972 2500z sepia & blk 95

Butterflies — A973

1991, Nov. 16 Litho. *Perf. 12½*
3050 A973 1000z Papilio machaon 40
3051 A973 1000z Mormonia sponsa 40
3052 A973 1500z Vanessa cardui 60
3053 A973 1500z Iphiclides podalirius 60
3054 A973 2500z Panaxia dominula 1.00
3055 A973 2500z Nymphalis io 1.00
a. Block of 6, #3050-3055 4.00
Nos. 3050-3055 (6) 4.00

Souvenir Sheet

3056 A973 15,000z Aporia crataegi 6.00

No. 3056 has a holographic image that may be affected by soaking in water and also contains Phila Nippon '91 label.

Nativity Scene, by Francesco Solimena A974

1991, Nov. 25 Photo. *Perf. 11*
3057 A974 1000z multicolored 40

Polish Armed Forces at Tobruk, 50th Anniv. — A975

1991, Dec. 10 Photo. *Perf. 11½*
3058 A975 2000z Gen. Stanislaw Kopanski 75

A976 A977

World War II Commanders: 2000z, Brig. Gen. Michal Tokarzewski-Karaszewicz (1893-1964). 2500z, Gen. Kazimierz Sosukowski (1885-1969). 3000z, Gen. Stefan Rowecki (1895-1944). 5000z, Gen. Tadeusz Komorowski (1895-1966). 6500z, Brig. Gen. Leopold Okulicki (1898-1946).

1991, Dec. 20 Litho.
3059 A976 2000z ver & blk 75
3060 A976 2500z vio bl & lake 95
3061 A976 3000z mag & dk bl 1.15
3062 A976 5000z ol & brn 1.90
3063 A976 6500z brn org & brn 2.50
Nos. 3059-3063 (5) 7.25

1991, Dec. 30 Photo. *Perf. 12x11½*

Boy Scouts in Poland, 80th anniv.: 1500z, Lord Robert Baden-Powell, founder of Boy Scouts. 2000z, Andrzej Malkowski (1889-1919), founder of Boy Scouts in Poland. 2500z, Scout standing guard, 1920. 3500z, Soldier scout, 1944.

3064 A977 1500z multicolored 35
3065 A977 2000z multicolored 45
3066 A977 2500z multicolored 55
3067 A977 3500z multicolored 78

Royalty Type of 1986

Designs: 1500z, Kazimierz II Sprawiedliwy. 2000z, Leszek Bialy.

1992, Jan. 15 Photo. & Engr. *Perf. 11*
3068 A875 1500z olive green & brn 22
3069 A875 2000z gray blue & blk 30

Paintings A978

Paintings (self-portraits except for 2200z) by: 700z, Sebastien Bourdon. 1000z, Sir Joshua Reynolds. 1500z, Sir Gottfried Kneller. 2000z, Murillo. 2200z, Rubens. 3000z, Diego de Silva y Velazquez.

1992, Jan. 16 Photo.
3070 A978 700z multicolored 15
3071 A978 1000z multicolored 15
3072 A978 1500z multicolored 22
3073 A978 2000z multicolored 30
3074 A978 2200z multicolored 32
3075 A978 3000z multicolored 45
Nos. 3070-3075 (6) 1.59

1992 Winter Olympics, Albertville A979

1992, Feb. 8 Litho. *Perf. 11x11½*
3076 A979 1500z Skiing 22
3077 A979 2500z Hockey 35

See Nos. 3095-3098.

Tadeusz Manteuffel (1902-1970), Historian — A980

1992, Mar. 5 Photo. *Perf. 11½x11*
3078 A980 2500z brown 95

Famous Poles — A981

Designs: 1500z, Nicolaus Copernicus, astronomer. 2000z, Frederic Chopin, composer. 2500z, Henryk Sienkiewicz, novelist. 3500z, Marie Sklodowska Curie, scientist. 5000z, Casimir Funk, biochemist.

1992, Mar. 5 Litho. *Perf. 11x11½*

3079	A981	1500z	multicolored	60
3080	A981	2000z	multicolored	75
3081	A981	2500z	multicolored	95
3082	A981	3500z	multicolored	1.30

Souvenir Sheet

3083	A981	5000z	multicolored	1.90

Expo '92, Seville (#3083).

Discovery of America, 500th Anniv. — A982

1992, May 5

3084	A982	1500z	Columbus, chart	65
3085	A982	3000z	Chart, Santa Maria	1.35
a.			Pair, #3084-3085	2.00

Europa.

Waterfalls — A983

1992, June 1 Litho. *Perf. 11½*

3086	A983	2000z	Pstrag (trout)	30
3087	A983	2500z	Zimorodek (kingfisher)	38
3088	A983	3000z	Jelec (whiting)	45
3089	A983	3500z	Pluszcz	52

Order of Virtuti Militari, Bicent. A984

Designs: 1500z, Prince Jozef Poniatowski (1763-1813). 3000z, Marshal Jozef Pilsudski (1867-1935). No. 3092, Black Madonna of Czestochowa.

1992, June 18 *Perf. 11*

3090	A984	1500z	multi	22
3091	A984	3000z	multi	45

Souvenir Sheet

Imperf

3092	A984	20,000z	multi	3.00

No. 3092 contains one 39x60mm stamp.

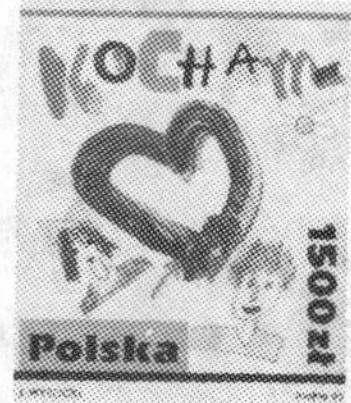

Children's Drawings of Love — A985

Designs: 1500z, Heart between woman and man. 3000z, Butterfly, animals with sun and rain.

1992, June 26 Litho. *Perf. 11½x11*

3093	A985	1500z	multicolored	22
3094	A985	3000z	multicolored	45
a.			Pair, #3093-3094	67

Olympics Type of 1992

1992, July 25 Litho. *Perf. 11x11½*

3095	A979	1500z	Fencing	50
3096	A979	2000z	Boxing	65
3097	A979	2500z	Sprinting	85
3098	A979	3000z	Cycling	1.00

1992 Summer Olympics, Barcelona.

Souvenir Sheet

OLYMPHILEX '92, Barcelona — A986

1992, July 29

3099	A986	20,000z	Runners	6.50

Exists imperf.

Janusz Korczak (1879-1942), Physician, Concentration Camp Victim — A987

1992, Aug. 5 Photo. *Perf. 11x11½*

3100	A987	1500z	multicolored	50

Polish Emigrants Assoc. World Meeting — A988

1992, Aug. 19 *Perf. 12x11½*

3101	A988	3000z	multicolored	1.00

World War II Combatants World Meeting — A989

1992, Aug. 14 *Perf. 11½x11*

3102	A989	3000z	multicolored	1.00

Stefan Cardinal Wyszynski (1901-1981) — A990

Design: 3000z, Pope John Paul II embracing person.

1992, Aug. 15 Litho.

3103	A990	1500z	multicolored	50
3104	A990	3000z	multicolored	1.00
a.			Block of 2, #3103-3104 + 2 labels	1.50

6th World Youth Cong., Czestochowa (#3104).

Adampol, Polish Village in Turkey, 150th Anniv. A991

1992, Sept. 15 Photo. *Perf. 11x11½*

3105	A991	3500z	multicolored	1.15

World Post Day — A992

1992, Oct. 9 *Perf. 11½x11*

3106 A992 3500z multicolored 1.15

Bruno Schulz (1892-1942), Author — A993

1992, Oct. 26 Litho. *Perf. 11x11½*

3107 A993 3000z multicolored 1.00

Polish Sculptures, Natl. Museum, Warsaw A994

Designs: 2000z, Seated Girl, by Henryk Wicinski. 2500z, Portrait of Tytus Czyzewski, by Zbigniew Pronaszko. 3000z, Polish Nike, by Edward Wittig. 3500z, The Nude, by August Zamoyski.

1992, Oct. 29 *Perf. 11½*

3108 A994 2000z multicolored 65
3109 A994 2500z multicolored 85
3110 A994 3000z multicolored 1.00
3111 A994 3500z multicolored 1.15
a. Souvenir sheet of 4, #3108-3111 3.65

Polska '93 (#3111a).

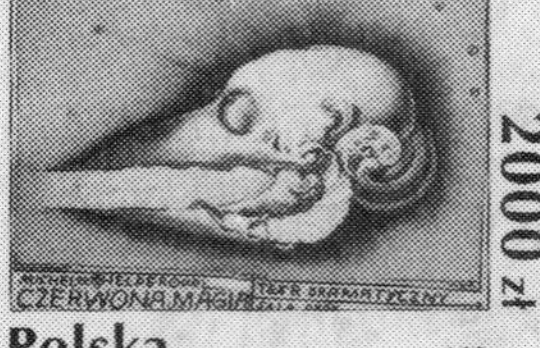
Posters — A995

Designs: 1500z, 10th Theatrical Summer in Zamosc, by Jan Mlodozeniec, vert. 2000z, Red Magic, by Franciszek Starowieyski. 2500z, Circus, by Waldemar Swierzy, vert. 3500z, Mannequins, by Henryk Tomaszewski.

1992, Oct. 30 *Perf. 13½*

3112 A995 1500z multicolored 50
3113 A995 2000z multicolored 65
3114 A995 2500z multicolored 85
3115 A995 3500z multicolored 1.15

The indexes in each volume of the Scott Catalogue contain many listings which help to identify stamps.

Illustrations by Edward Lutczyn A996

Designs: 1500z, Girl using snake as jump rope. 2000z, Boy on rocking horse with rockers reversed. 2500z, Boy using bird as arrow. 3500z, Girl with ladder, wind-up giraffe with keys on back.

1992, Nov. 16 Photo. *Perf. 11*

3116 A996 1500z multicolored 28
3117 A996 2000z multicolored 38
3118 A996 2500z multicolored 48
3119 A996 3500z multicolored 65

Polska '93.

Home Army A997

1992, Nov. 20 Litho. *Perf. 13½*

3120 A997 1500z shown 28
3121 A997 3500z Soldiers, diff. 65
a. Pair, #3120-3121 95

Souvenir Sheet

3122 A997 20,000z +500z "WP AK," vert. 4.00

Christmas A998

1992, Nov. 25 Photo. *Perf. 11½*

3123 A998 1000z multicolored 22

A999 A1000

1992, Dec. 5 Photo. *Perf. 11½x11*

3124 A999 1500z Wheat stalks 50
3125 A999 3500z Food products 1.15

Intl. Conference on Nutrition, Rome.

1992, Dec. 10 **Litho.**

3126 A1000 3000z multicolored 1.00

Postal Agreement with the Sovereign Military Order of Malta, Aug. 1, 1991.

Natl. Arms — A1001

1992, Dec. 14 Photo. *Perf. 12x11½*

3127 A1001 2000z 1295 65
3128 A1001 2500z 15th cent. 85
3129 A1001 3000z 18th cent. 1.00
3130 A1001 3500z 1919 1.15
3131 A1001 5000z 1990 1.65
Nos. 3127-3131 (5) 5.30

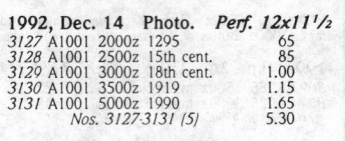

Polish Philatelic Society, Cent. A1002

1993, Jan. 6 Photo. *Perf. 11½*

3132 A1002 1500z multicolored 50

A1003 A1004

1993, Feb. 5 *Perf. 11½x11*

3133 A1003 3000z multicolored 1.00

1993 Winter University Games, Zakopane.

1993, Feb. 14

Design: I Love You.

3134 A1004 1500z shown 50
3135 A1004 3000z Heart on envelope 1.00

SEMI-POSTAL STAMPS

Regular Issue of 1919 Surcharged in Violet

I POLSKA WYSTAWA MAREK 5F + F5
a

I POLSKA WYSTAWA MAREK 5 + 5
b

1919, May 3 Unwmk. *Imperf.*

B1 A10(a) 5f + 5f grn 16 20
B2 A10(a) 10f + 5f red vio 2.00 1.40
B3 A10(a) 15f + 5f dp red 38 20
B4 A11(b) 25f + 5f ol grn 38 20
B5 A11(b) 50f + 5f bl grn 60 32

Perf. 11½

B6 A10(a) 5f + 5f grn 25 16
B7 A10(a) 10f + 5f red vio 50 16
B8 A10(a) 15f + 5f dp red 25 16
B9 A11(b) 25f + 5f ol grn 30 16
B10 A11(b) 50f + 5f bl grn 1.00 42
Nos. B1-B10 (10) 5.82 3.38

Commemorative of the First Polish Philatelic Exhibition. The surtax benefited the Polish White Cross Society.

Regular Issue of 1920 Surcharged in Carmine 30MK

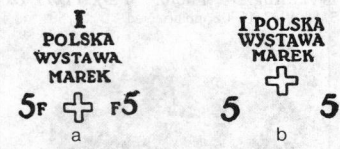

1921, Mar. 5 *Perf. 9*

Thin Laid Paper

B11 A14 5m + 30m red vio 4.50 6.50
B12 A14 6m + 30m dp rose 4.50 6.50
B13 A14 10m + 30m lt red 11.00 10.50
B14 A14 20m + 30m gray grn 35.00 32.50

Counterfeits, differently perforated, exist of Nos. B11-14.

SP1

Light of Knowledge — SP2

1925, Jan. 1 Typo. *Perf. 12½*

B15 SP1 1g org brn 10.00 13.00
B16 SP1 2g dk brn 10.00 13.00
B17 SP1 3g orange 10.00 13.00
B18 SP1 5g ol grn 10.00 13.00
B19 SP1 10g bl grn 10.00 13.00
B20 SP1 15g red 10.00 13.00
B21 SP1 20g blue 10.00 13.00
B22 SP1 25g red brn 10.00 13.00
B23 SP1 30g dp vio 10.00 13.00
B24 SP1 40g indigo 30.00 13.00
B25 SP1 50g magenta 10.00 13.00
Nos. B15-B25 (11) 130.00 143.00

"Na Skarb" means "National Funds". These stamps were sold at a premium of 50 groszy each, for charity.

1927, May 3 *Perf. 11½*

B26 SP2 10g + 5g choc & grn 7.50 3.50
B27 SP2 20g + 5g dk bl & buff 7.50 3.50

"NA OSWIATE" means "For Public Instruction". The surtax aided an Association of Educational Societies.

Torun Type of 1933

1933, May 21 **Engr.**

B28 A59 60g (+40g) red brn, *buff* 16.00 12.00

Philatelic Exhibition at Torun, May 21-28, 1933, and sold at a premium of 40g to aid the exhibition funds.

Souvenir Sheet

Stagecoach and Wayside Inn — SP3

1938, May 3 Engr. *Perf. 12, Imperf.*

B29 SP3 Sheet of 4 72.50 62.50
a. 45g green 7.50 7.50
b. 55g blue 7.50 7.50

5th Phil. Exhib., Warsaw, May 3-8. The sheet contains two 45g and two 55g stamps. Sold for 3z.

Souvenir Sheet

Stratosphere Balloon over Mountains — SP4

1938, Sept. 15 *Perf. 12½*

B31 SP4 75g dp vio, sheet 55.00 50.00

Issued in advance of a proposed Polish stratosphere flight. Sold for 2z.

Winterhelp Issue

SP5

1938-39

B32 SP5 5g + 5g red org	55	95
B33 SP5 25g + 10g dk vio ('39)	90	1.40
B34 SP5 55g + 15g brt ultra ('39)	1.75	2.25

For surcharges see Nos. N48-N50.

Souvenir Sheet

SP6

1939, Aug. 1

B35 SP6 Sheet of 3, dark blue gray	20.00	20.00
a. 25g Marshal Pilsudski Reviewing Troops	3.50	3.50
b. 25g Marshal Pilsudski	3.50	3.50
c. 25g Marshal Smigly-Rydz	3.50	3.50

25th anniv. of the founding of the Polish Legion. The sheets sold for 1.75z, the surtax going to the National Defense fund.

See types A64, A80, A99.

Polish People's Republic

Polish Warship SP7

Sailing Vessel — SP8

Polish Naval Ensign and Merchant Flag — SP9

Crane and Crane Tower, Gdansk SP10

1945, Apr. 24 Typo. *Perf. 11*

B36 SP7 50g + 2z red	2.50	2.50
B37 SP8 1z + 3z dp bl	2.50	2.50
B38 SP9 2z + 4z dk car	2.50	2.50
B39 SP10 3z + 5z ol grn	2.50	2.50

Polish Maritime League, 25th anniv.

City Hall, Poznan SP11

1945, June 16 Photo.

B40 SP11 1z + 5z green	15.00	15.00

Postal Workers' Convention, Poznan, June 16, 1945. Exists imperf.

Last Stand at Westerplatte — SP12

1945, Sept. 1

B41 SP12 1z + 9z steel blue	12.00	12.00

Polish army's last stand at Westerplatte, Sept. 1, 1939. Exists imperf.

"United Industry" — SP13

1945, Nov. 18 Unwmk. *Perf. 11*

B42 SP13 1.50z + 8.50z sl blk	5.00	5.00

Trade Unions Congress, Warsaw, Nov. 18.

Polish Volunteers in Spain — SP14

1946, Mar. 10

B43 SP14 3z + 5z red	3.25	3.00

Participation of the Jaroslaw Dabrowski Brigade in the Spanish Civil War.

14th Century Piast Eagle and Soldiers — SP15

"Death" Spreading Poison Gas over Majdanek Prison Camp — SP16

1946, May 2

B44 SP15 3z + 7z brn	60	50

Silesian uprisings of 1919-21, 1939-45.

1946, Apr. 29

B45 SP16 3z + 5z Prus grn	2.50	2.75

Issued to recall Majdanek, a concentration camp of World War II near Lublin.

Bydgoszcz (Bromberg) Canal — SP17

Map of Polish Coast and Baltic Sea — SP18

1946, Apr. 19 Unwmk. *Perf. 11*

B46 SP17 3z + 2z ol blk	2.25	3.00

600th anniv. of Bydgoszcz (Bromberg).

1946, July 21

B47 SP18 3z + 7z dp bl	1.25	1.00

Maritime Holiday of 1946. The surtax was for the Polish Maritime League.

Salute to P.T.T. Casualty and Views of Gdansk — SP19

1946, Sept. 14

B48 SP19 3z + 12z slate	1.50	1.50

Issued in honor of Polish postal employees killed in the German attack on Danzig (Gdansk), Sept. 1939.

School Children — SP20

Designs: 6z+24z, Courtyard of Jagiellon University, Cracow. 11z+19z, Gregor Piramowicz (1735-1801), founder of Education Commission.

1946, Oct. 10 Unwmk. *Perf. 11½*

B49 SP20 3z + 22z dk red	22.50	35.00
B49A SP20 6z + 24z dk bl	22.50	35.00
B49B SP20 11z + 19z dk grn	22.50	35.00
c. Souvenir sheet of 3, #B49-B49B	315.00	375.00

Polish educational work. Surtax was for International Bureau of Education.

No. B49c sold for 100z.

Stanislaw Stojalowski, Jakob Bojko, Jan Stapinski and Wincenty Witos — SP21

1946, Dec. 1

B50 SP21 5z + 10z bl grn	1.00	90
B51 SP21 5z + 10z dull blue	1.00	90
B52 SP21 5z + 10z dk olive	1.00	90

50th anniv. of the Peasant Movement. The surtax was for education and cultural improvement among the Polish peasantry.

No. 391 Surcharged in Red

SEJM
USTAWODAWCZY
19.I 1947

1947, Feb. 4 *Perf. 11x10½*

B53 A127 3z + 7z pur	5.75	6.00

Opening of the Polish Parliament, Jan. 19, 1947.

No. 344 Surcharged in Blue

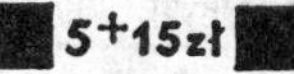

XXII
MISTRZOSTWA
NARCIARSKIE
POLSKI
1947

1947, Feb. 21 *Perf. 12½*

B54 A103 5z + 15z on 25g	1.10	3.50

Ski Championship Meet, Zakopane. Counterfeits exist.

Emil Zegadlowicz SP22

1947, Mar. 1 Photo. *Perf. 11*

B55 SP22 5z + 15z dl gray grn	1.10	75

Nurse and War Victims SP23

Adam Chmielowski SP24

1947, June 1 *Perf. 10½*

B56 SP23 5z + 5z ol blk & red	2.50	2.25

The surtax was for the Red Cross.

1947, Dec. 21 *Perf. 11*

B57 SP24 2z + 18z dk vio	1.25	75

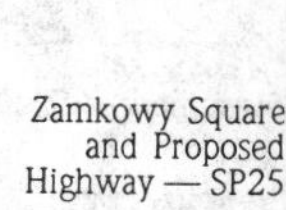

Zamkowy Square and Proposed Highway — SP25

1948, Nov. 1

B58 SP25 15z + 5z green	30	20

The surtax was to aid in the reconstruction of Warsaw.

Infant and TB Crosses SP26

Marceli Nowotko SP27

Various Portraits of Children

1948, Dec. 16 *Perf. 11½*

B59 SP26 3z + 2z dl grn 2.00 1.50
B60 SP26 5z + 5z brn 2.00 1.50
B61 SP26 6z + 4z vio 1.65 1.50
B62 SP26 15z + 10z car lake 1.65 1.50

Alternate vertical rows of stamps was ten different labels. The surtax was for anti-tuberculosis work among children.

Catalogue values for unused stamps in this section, from this point to the end of the section, are for Never Hinged items.

Perf. 12½

1952, Jan. 18 Engr. Unwmk.

B63 SP27 45g + 15g dk car 18 15

Polish Workers Party, 10th anniv.

Women's Day Type of 1952

1952, Mar. 8 *Perf. 12½x12*

B64 A196 45g + 15g chocolate 22 15

Swierczewski-Walter Type of 1952

1952, Mar. 28 *Perf. 12½*

B65 A197 45g + 15g chocolate 28 15

Bierut Type of 1952

1952, Apr. 18

B66 A198 45g + 15g red 40 20
B67 A198 1.20z + 15g ultra 40 18

Type of Regular Issue of 1951-52 Inscribed "Plan 6," etc.

Design: 45g+15g, Electrical installation.

1952

B68 A193 30g + 15g brn red 35 18
B69 A193 45g + 15g chocolate 60 30
B69A A194 1.20z + 15g red org 30 22

Labor Day Type of Regular Issue of 1952

1952, May 1

B70 A200 45g + 15g car rose 15 15

Similar to Regular Issue of 1952

Portraits: 30g+15g, Maria Konopnicka. 45g+15g, Hugo Kollataj.

1952, May

Different Frames

B71 A201 30g + 15g blue green 42 15
B72 A201 45g + 15g brown 20 15
Set value 24

Issued: No. B71, May 10. No. B72, May 20.

Leonardo da Vinci — SP28

Swimmers — SP30

Pres. Bierut and Children — SP29

1952, June 1

B73 SP28 30g + 15g ultra 85 50

500th birth anniv. of Leonardo da Vinci.

1952, June 1 Photo. *Perf. 13½x14*

B74 SP29 45g + 15g blue 2.50 60

Intl. Children's Day, June 1.

1952, June 21 *Perf. 13*

Design: 45g+15g, Soccer players and trophy.

B75 SP30 30g + 15g blue 3.75 1.40
B76 SP30 45g + 15g purple 1.75 35

Yachts SP31

"Dar Pomorza" SP32

1952, June 28 Engr. *Perf. 12½*

B77 SP31 30g + 15g dp bl grn 1.75 60
B78 SP32 45g + 15g dp ultra 45 22

Shipbuilders' Day, 1952.

Workers on Holiday — SP33

Students SP34

Perf. 12½x12, 12x12½

1952, July 17

B79 SP33 30g + 15g dp grn 28 20
B80 SP34 45g + 15g red 60 15

Issued to publicize the Youth Festival, 1952.

Constitution Type of Regular Issue

1952, July 22 Photo. *Perf. 11*

B81 A208 45g + 15g lt bl grn & dk brn 75 24

Power Plant Type of Regular Issue

1952, Aug. 7 Engr. *Perf. 12½*

B82 A209 45g + 15g red 45 15

Ludwik Warynski SP36

Church of Frydman SP37

1952, July 31

B83 SP36 30g + 15g dk red 30 15
B84 SP36 45g + 15g blk brn 28 20

70th birth anniv. of Ludwik Warynski, political organizer.

1952, Aug. 18

B85 SP37 45g + 15g vio brn 70 25

Aviator Watching Glider SP38

Henryk Sienkiewicz SP39

Design: 45g+15g, Pilot entering plane.

1952, Aug. 23

B86 SP38 30g + 15g grn 45 30
B87 SP38 45g + 15g brn red 1.75 90

Aviation Day, Aug. 23.

1952, Oct. 25

B88 SP39 45g + 15g vio brn 35 22

Henryk Sienkiewicz (1846-1916), author of "Quo Vadis" and other novels, Nobel prizewinner (literature, 1905).

Revolution Type of Regular Issue

1952, Nov. 7 *Perf. 12x12½*

B92 A214 45g + 15g red brn 65 15

Exists imperforate.

Lenin — SP42

Miner — SP43

1952, Nov. 7 *Perf. 12½*

B93 SP42 30g + 15g vio brn 22 15
B94 SP42 45g + 15g brn 55 28
a. "LENIN" omitted 20.00

Month of Polish-Soviet friendship, Nov. 1952.

1952, Dec. 4

B95 SP43 45g + 15g blk brn 18 15
B96 SP43 1.20z + 15g brn 52 20

Miners' Day, Dec. 4.

Henryk Wieniawski and Violin — SP44

Truck Factory, Lublin — SP45

1952, Dec. 5 **Photo.**

B97 SP44 30g + 15g dk grn 45 28
B98 SP44 45g + 15g pur 2.25 55

Henryk Wieniawski; 2nd Intl. Violin Competition.

Type of Regular Issue of 1952

1952, Dec. 12 **Engr.**

B99 A215 45g + 15g dp grn 20 15

1953, Feb. 20

B100 SP45 30g + 15g dp bl 20 16
B101 SP45 60g + 20g vio brn 40 15
Set value 24

Souvenir Sheet

Town Hall in Poznan — SP46

1955, July 7 Photo. & Litho. *Imperf.*

B102 SP46 2z pck grn & ol grn 3.50 1.75
B103 SP46 3z car rose & ol blk 19.00 10.00

6th Polish Philatelic Exhibition in Poznan. Sheets sold for 3z and 4.50z respectively.

Souvenir Sheet

"Peace" (POKOJ) and Warsaw Mermaid — SP47

Design: 1z, Pansies (A266) and inscription on map of Europe, Africa and Asia.

1955, Aug. 3

B104 SP47 1z bis, rose vio & yel 2.75 1.50
B105 SP47 2z ol gray, ultra & lt bl 13.00 7.50

Intl. Phil. Exhib., Warsaw, Aug. 1-14, 1955. Sheets sold for 2z and 3z respectively.

Souvenir Sheet

Chopin and Liszt — SP48

1956, Oct. 25 Photo. *Imperf.*

B106 SP48 4z dk bl grn 30.00 16.00

Day of the Stamp; Polish-Hungarian friendship. The sheet sold for 6z.

A particular stamp may be scarce, but if few collectors want it, its market value may remain relatively low.

Souvenir Sheet

Stamp of 1860 SP49

Wmk. 326

1960, Sept. 4 Litho. *Perf. 11*
B107 SP49 Sheet of 4 37.50 30.00
a. 10z + 10z blue, red & black 9.00 7.00

Intl. Phil. Exhib. "POLSKA 60" Warsaw, Sept. 3-11.
No. B107 sold only with 5z ticket to exhibition.

Type of Space Issue, 1964

Design: Yuri A. Gagarin in space capsule.

Perf. 12½x12
1964, Dec. 30 Unwmk.
B108 A432 6.50z + 2z Prus grn & multi 1.50 65

Miniature Sheet

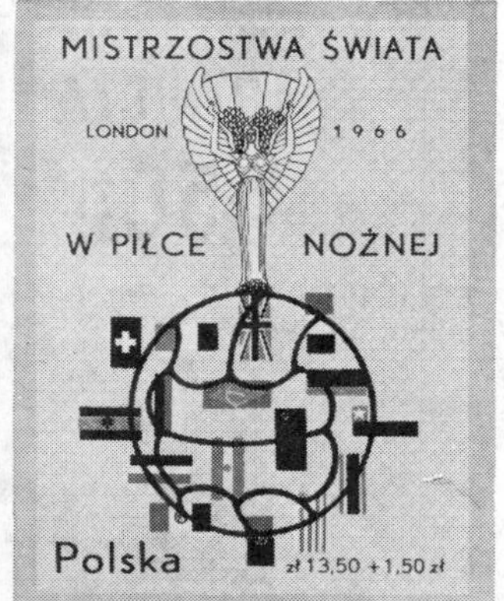

Jules Rimet Cup and Flags of Participating Countries — SP50

1966, May 9 Litho. *Imperf.*
B109 SP50 13.50z + 1.50z multi 1.90 1.00

World Cup Soccer Championship, Wembley, England, July 11-30.

Souvenir Sheet

J. Kusocinski, Olympic Winner 10,000-Meter Race, 1932 — SP51

1967, May 24 Litho. *Imperf.*
B110 SP51 10z + 5z multi 1.50 1.00

19th Olympic Games, Mexico City, 1968. Simulated perforations.

Flower Type of Regular Issue

Flowers: 4z+2z, Abutilon. 8z+4z, Rosa polyantha hybr.

1968, May 15 Litho. *Perf. 11½*
B111 A492 4z + 2z vio & multi 60 30
B112 A492 8z + 4z lt vio & multi 1.25 65

Olympic Type of Regular Issue, 1968

Design: 10z+5z, Runner with Olympic torch and Chin cultic carved stone disc showing Mayan ball player and game's scoreboard.

1968, Sept. 2 Litho. *Perf. 11½*
Size: 56x45mm
B113 A497 10z + 5z multi 1.50 85

19th Olympic Games, Mexico City, Oct. 12-27. The surtax was for the Polish Olympic Committee.

Olympic Type of Regular Issue, 1969

Olympic Rings and: 2.50z+50g, Women's discus. 3.40z+1z, Running. 4z+1.50z, Boxing. 7z+2z, Fencing.

1969, Apr. 25 Litho. *Perf. 11½x11*
B114 A505 2.50z + 50g multi 25 15
B115 A505 3.40z + 1z multi 32 15
B116 A505 4z + 1.50z multi 50 20
B117 A505 7z + 2z multi 85 40

Folk Art Type of Regular Issue

Designs: 5.50z+1.50z, Choir. 7z+1.50z, Organ grinder.

1969, Dec. 19 Litho. *Perf. 11½x11*
Size: 24x36mm
B118 A520 5.50z + 1.50z multi 52 24
B119 A520 7z + 1.50z multi 70 30

Sports Type of Regular Issue
Souvenir Sheet

Design: 10z+5z, "Horse of Glory," by Z. Kaminski.

1970, June 16 Photo. *Imperf.*
B120 A532 10z + 5z multi 1.50 90

The surtax was for the Polish Olympic Committee. No. B120 contains one imperf. stamp with simulated perforations.

Tapestry Type of Regular Issue
Souvenir Sheet

Design: 7z+3z, Satyrs holding monogram of King Sigismund Augustus.

1970, Dec. 23 Photo. *Imperf.*
B121 A541 7z + 3z multi 1.75 1.00

Type of Regular Issue

Design: 8.50z+4z, Virgin Mary, 15th century stained glass window.

1971, Sept. 15 *Perf. 11½x11*
B122 A555 8.50z + 4z multi 75 45

Painting Type of Regular Issue

Design: 7z+1z, Nude, by Wojciech Weiss (1875-1950).

1971, Oct. 9 Litho.
B123 A556 7z + 1z multi 70 35

Winter Olympic Type of Regular Issue
Souvenir Sheet

Design: 10z+5z, Slalom and Sapporo '72 emblem (vert.).

1972, Jan. 12 Photo. *Imperf.*
B124 A564 10z + 5z multi 1.40 90

No. B124 contains one stamp with simulated perforations, 27x52mm.

Summer Olympic Type of Regular Issue
Souvenir Sheet

Design: 10z+5z, Archery (like 30g).

1972, May 20 Photo. *Perf. 11½x11*
B125 A568 10z + 5z multi 1.65 1.00

Painting Type of Regular Issue, 1972

Design: 8.50z+4z, Portrait of a Young Lady, by Jacek Malczewski, horiz.

1972, Sept. 28 Photo. *Perf. 11x10½*
B126 A576 8.50z + 4z multi 1.25 65

Souvenir Sheet

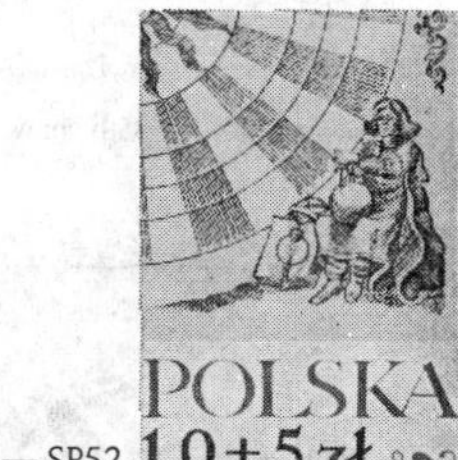

Copernicus — SP52

Engraved and Photogravure
1972, Sept. 28 *Perf. 11½*
B127 SP52 10z + 5z vio bl, gray & car 1.50 85

Nicolaus Copernicus (1473-1543), astronomer. No. B127 shows the Ptolemaic and Copernican concepts of solar system from L'Harmonica Microcosmica, by Cellarius, 1660.

Souvenir Sheet

Poznan, 1740, by F. B. Werner — SP53

1973, Aug. 19 *Imperf.*
B128 SP53 10z + 5z ol & dk brn 1.50 90
a. 10z + 5z pale lil & dk brn 4.50 4.00

POLSKA 73 Intl. Phil. Exhib., Poznan, Aug. 19-Sept. 2. No. B128 contains one stamp with simulated perforations.
No. B128a was sold only in combination with an entrance ticket.

Copernicus, by Marcello Baciarelli — SP54

1973, Sept. 27 Photo. *Perf. 11x11½*
B129 SP54 4z + 2z multi 50 28

Stamp Day. The surtax was for the reconstruction of the Royal Castle in Warsaw.

Souvenir Sheet

Montreal Olympic Games Emblem — SP55

Photo. & Engr.
1975, Mar. 8 *Perf. 12*
B130 SP55 10z + 5z sil & grn 1.50 1.00

21st Olympic Games, Montreal, July 17-Aug. 8, 1976.

Dunikowski Type of 1975

Design: 8z+4z, Mother and Child, from Silesian Insurrectionist Monument, by Dunikowski.

1975, Oct. 9 Photo. *Perf. 11½x11*
B131 A644 8z + 4z multi 1.00 45

Souvenir Sheet

Volleyball — SP56

Engraved and Photogravure
1976, June 30 *Perf. 11½*
B132 SP56 10z + 5z blk & car 1.25 70

21st Olympic Games, Montreal, Canada, July 17-Aug. 1. No. B132 contains one perf. 11½ stamp and is perf. 11½ all around.

Corinthian Art Type 1976

Design: 8z+4z, Winged Sphinx, vert.

1976, Oct. 30 Photo. *Perf. 11½x11*
B133 A664 8z + 4z multi 1.10 50

Souvenir Sheet

Stoning of St. Stephen, by Rubens — SP57

1977, Apr. 30 Engr. *Perf. 12x11½*
B134 SP57 8z + 4z sepia 1.10 65

Peter Paul Rubens (1577-1640), Flemish painter. No. B134 is arranged similar to type SP55 but with sheet margins perforated all around and stamp on top.

Souvenir Sheet

Kazimierz Gzowski — SP58

1978, June 6 Photo. *Perf. 11½x11*
B135 SP58 8.40z + 4z multi 1.10 55

CAPEX, '78 Canadian Intl. Phil. Exhib., Toronto, June 9-18.
K. S. Gzowski (1813-1898), Polish engineer and lawyer living in Canada, built International Bridge over Niagara River.

Souvenir Sheet

Olympic Rings — SP59

1979, May 19 Engr. *Imperf.*
B136 SP59 10z + 5z blk 1.00 75

1980 Olympic Games.

Monument Type of 1979
Souvenir Sheet

1979, Sept. 1 Photo. *Imperf.*
B137 A731 10z + 5z multi 1.25 75

Surtax was for monument.

Summer Olympic Type of 1980
Souvenir Sheet

1980, Mar. 31 Photo. *Perf. 11x11½*
B138 A742 10.50z + 5z Kayak 1.00 75

No. B138 contains one stamp 42x30mm.

Souvenir Sheet

Intercosmos Cooperative Space Program — SP60

1980, Apr. 12 *Perf. 11½x11*
B139 SP60 6.90z + 3z multi 85 75

SP61 SP62

1970 Uprising Memorial: 2.50z + 1z, Triple Crucifix, Gdansk (27x46mm). 6.50z + 1z, Monument, Gdynia.

1981, Dec. 16 Photo. *Perf. 11½x12*
B140 SP61 2.50 + 1z blk & red 70 32
B141 SP61 6.50 + 1z blk & lil 1.00 70

1984, May 15 Photo. *Perf. 11½x12*

Portrait of a German Princess, by Lucas Cranach

B142 SP62 27z + 10z multi 1.50 80

1984 UPU Congress, Hamburg. No. B142 issued se-tenant with multicolored label showing UPU emblem and text.

Souvenir Sheet

Madonna with Child, St. John and the Angel, by Sandro Botticelli (1445-1510), Natl. Museum, Warsaw SP63

1985, Sept. 25 Photo. *Perf. 11*
B143 SP63 65z + 15z multi 2.00 1.25
a. Inscribed: 35 LAT POLSKIEGO . . . 4.50 4.50

ITALIA '85. Surtax for Polish Association of Philatelists.
No. B143a was for the 35th anniv. of the Polish Philatelic Union. Distribution was limited.

Joachim Lelewel (1786-1861), Historian — SP64

1986, Dec. 22 Photo. *Perf. 11½x12*
B144 SP64 10z + 5z multi 30 18

Surtax for the Natl. Committee for School Aid.

Polish Immigrant Settling in Kasubia, Ontario — SP65

1987, June 13 Photo. *Perf. 12x11½*
B145 SP65 50z + 20z multi 1.40 70

CAPEX '87, Toronto, Canada. Surtaxed for the Polish Philatelists' Union.

Souvenir Sheet

OLYMPHILEX '87, Rome — SP66

1987, Aug. 28 Litho. *Perf. 14*
B146 SP66 45z + 10z like #2617 1.10 1.10

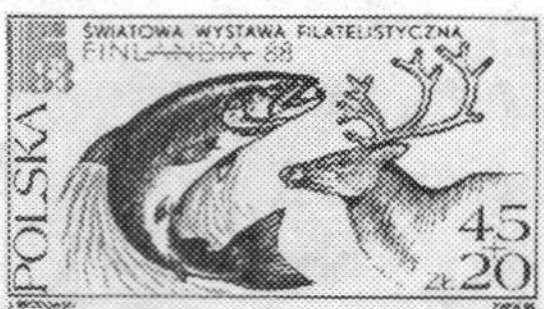

FINLANDIA '88 — SP67

1988, June 1 Photo. *Perf. 12x11½*
B147 SP67 45z +20z Salmon, reindeer 1.30 65

Souvenir Sheet

Jerzy Kukuczka, Mountain Climber Awarded Medal by the Intl. Olympic Committee for Climbing the Himalayas — SP68

1988, Aug. 17 Photo. *Perf. 11x11½*
B148 SP68 70z +10z multi 1.60 80

Surtax for the Polish Olympic Fund.

AIR POST STAMPS

Biplane — AP1

Perf. 12½

1925, Sept. 10 Typo. Unwmk.

C1	AP1	1g lt bl	60	1.75
C2	AP1	2g orange	60	1.75
C3	AP1	3g yel brn	60	1.75
C4	AP1	5g dk brn	60	70
C5	AP1	10g dk grn	1.50	60
C6	AP1	15g red vio	2.25	70
C7	AP1	20g ol grn	9.50	3.50
C8	AP1	30g dl rose	6.00	1.25
C9	AP1	45g dk vio	7.75	3.50
		Nos. C1-C9 (9)	29.40	15.50

Counterfeits exist.
For overprint see No. C11.

Capt. Franciszek Zwirko and Stanislaus Wigura AP2

Perf. 11½ to 12½ and Compound

1933, Apr. 15 Engr. Wmk. 234
C10 AP2 30g gray grn 13.00 90

Winning of the circuit of Europe flight by two Polish aviators in 1932. The stamp was available for both air mail and ordinary postage.
For overprint see No. C12.

Nos. C7 and C10 Overprinted in Red

Challenge 1934

1934, Aug. 28 Unwmk. *Perf. 12½*
C11 AP1 20g olive grn 12.50 6.00

Wmk. 234
Perf. 11½

C12 AP2 30g gray grn 7.00 2.00

Polish People's Republic

Douglas Plane over Ruins of Warsaw — AP3

Unwmk.

1946, Mar. 5 Photo. *Perf. 11*

C13	AP3	5z grnsh blk	35	15
a.		Without control number	4.00	40
C14	AP3	10z dk vio	35	15
C15	AP3	15z blue	1.10	25
C16	AP3	20z rose brn	70	15
C17	AP3	25z dk bl grn	1.40	38
C18	AP3	30z red	2.25	55
		Nos. C13-C18 (6)	6.15	1.63

The 10z, 20z and 30z were issued only with control number in lower right stamp margin. The 15z and 25z exist only without number. The 5z comes both ways.
Nos. C13-C18 exist imperforate.

Nos. 345, 344 and 344a Surcharged in Red or Black

a
Zł 40 Zł
LOTNICZA

b
LOTNICZA
Zł 50 Zł

1947, Sept. 10 *Perf. 12½*
C19 A104(a) 40z on 50g (R) 1.65 90
C20 A103(b) 50z on 25g dl red 1.90 1.75
a. 50z on 25g deep red 2.50 1.75

Counterfeits exist.

Centaur — AP4

1948 *Perf. 11*

C21	AP4	15z dk vio	1.25	22
C22	AP4	25z dp bl	65	15
C23	AP4	30z brown	50	35
C24	AP4	50z dk grn	1.10	35
C25	AP4	75z gray blk	1.25	45
C26	AP4	100z red org	1.25	35
		Nos. C21-C26 (6)	6.00	1.87

Pres. F. D. Roosevelt AP5

Airplane Mechanic and Propeller AP5a

Designs: 100z, Casimir Pulaski. 120z, Tadeusz Kosciusko.

1948, Dec. 30 Photo. *Perf. 11½*
Granite Paper

C26A AP5 80z bl blk 13.00 18.00
C26B AP5 100z purple 14.00 15.00
C26C AP5 120z dp bl 14.00 15.00
d. Souvenir sheet of 3 140.00 190.00

No. C26d contains stamps similar to Nos. C26A-C26C with colors changed: 80z ultramarine, 100z carmine rose, 120z dark green. Sold for 500z.

1950, Feb. 6 Engr. *Perf. 12½*
C27 AP5a 500z rose lake 3.00 2.50

Catalogue values for unused stamps in this section, from this point to the end of the section, are for Never Hinged items.

Seaport AP6

Designs: 90g, Mechanized farm. 1.40z, Warsaw. 5z, Steel mill.

1952, Apr. 10 *Perf. 12x12½*
C28 AP6 55g intense blue 15 15
C29 AP6 90g dull green 20 15
C30 AP6 1.40z vio brn 30 15
C31 AP6 5z gray black 1.10 40
Set value 68

Nos. C28-C31 exist imperf. Value $10.

Congress Badge — AP7

1953, Aug. 23 Photo. *Imperf.*
C32 AP7 55g brown lilac 85 30
C33 AP7 75g brn org 1.25 90

3rd World Congress of Students, Warsaw 1953.

Souvenir Sheet

AP8

1954, May 23 Engr. *Perf. 12x12½*
C34 AP8 5z gray green 27.50 20.00

3rd congress of the Polish Phil. Assoc., Warsaw, 1954. Sold for 7.50 zlotys. A similar sheet, imperf. and in dark blue, was issued but had no postal validity.

Paczkow Castle, Luban
AP9

Plane over "Peace" Steelworks
AP10

Designs: 80g, Kazimierz Dolny. 1.15z, Wawel castle, Cracow. 1.50z, City Hall, Wroclaw. 1.55z, Lazierskу Square, Warsaw. 1.95z, Cracow gate, Lublin.

1954, July 9 *Perf. 12½*
C35 AP9 60g dk gray grn 15 15
C36 AP9 80g red 15 15
C37 AP9 1.15z black 90 38
C38 AP9 1.50z rose lake 35 18
C39 AP9 1.55z dp gray bl 35 15
C40 AP9 1.95z chocolate 70 30
Nos. C35-C40 (6) 2.60 1.31

Wmk. 326 ('58 Values); Unwmkd.
1957-58 Engr. & Photo. *Perf. 12½*

Plane over: 1.50z, Castle Square, Warsaw. 3.40z, Old Market, Cracow. 3.90z, King Boleslaw Chrobry Wall, Szczecin. 4z, Karkonosze mountains. 5z, Gdansk. 10z, Ruins of Liwa Castle. 15z, Old City, Lublin. 20z, Kasprowy Wierch Peak and cable car. 30z, Porabka dam. 50z, M. S. Batory and Gdynia harbor.

C41 AP10 90g blk & pink 15 15
C42 AP10 1.50z brn & salmon 15 15
C43 AP10 3.40z sep & buff 28 15
C44 AP10 3.90z dk brn & cit 48 42
C45 AP10 4z ind & lt grn 22 15
C46 AP10 5z mar & gray 40 15
C47 AP10 10z sep & grn 80 22
C48 AP10 15z vio bl & pale bl 1.00 45
C49 AP10 20z vio blk & lem 2.00 60
C50 AP10 30z ol gray & bis 2.75 1.25
C51 AP10 50z dk bl & gray 4.50 1.65
Nos. C41-C51 (11) 12.73 5.34

Issue dates: 5z, 10z, 20z, 30z, 50z, Dec. 15, 1958. Others, Dec. 6, 1957.

1959, May 23 Litho. Wmk. 326
C52 AP10 10z sepia 1.75 1.50
a. With 5z label 2.00 2.00

65th anniv. of the Polish Philatelic Society. Sheet of 6 stamps and 2 each of 3 different labels. Each label carries an added charge of 5z for a fund to build a Society clubhouse in Warsaw.

Jantar Glider — AP11

Contemporary aviation: 10z, Mi6 transport helicopter. 20z, PZL-106 Kruk, crop spraying plane. 50z, Plane over Warsaw Castle.

1976-78 Unwmk. Engr. *Perf. 11½*
C53 AP11 5z dk bl grn 40 25
C54 AP11 10z dk brn 80 50
C55 AP11 20z grnsh blk 1.50 75
C56 AP11 50z claret 3.00 1.90

Issue dates: 5z, 10z, Mar. 27, 1976. 20z, Feb. 15, 1977. 50z, Feb. 2, 1978.

AIR POST SEMI-POSTAL STAMP

Catalogue values for unused stamps in this section are for Never Hinged items.

Polish People's Republic

Wing of Jet Plane and Letter — SPAP1

Perf. 11½
1957, Mar. 28 Unwmk. Photo.
CB1 SPAP1 4z + 2z blue 2.75 3.50
a. Souv. sheet of 1, ultra, imperf. 10.00 4.50

7th Polish National Philatelic Exhibition, Warsaw. Sheet of 12 with 4 diagonally arranged gray labels.

POSTAGE DUE STAMPS

Cracow Issues

Postage Due Stamps of Austria, 1916, Overprinted in Black or Red

POCZTA
◇
POLSKA

1919, Jan. 10 Unwmk. *Perf. 12½*
J1 D4 5h rose red 7.00 6.00
J2 D4 10h rose red *1,750. 1,750.*
J3 D4 15h rose red 3.75 3.00
a. Inverted overprint 150.00
J4 D4 20h rose red 275.00 275.00
J5 D4 25h rose red 17.50 15.00
J6 D4 30h rose red *800.00 750.00*
J7 D4 40h rose red 250.00 200.00
J8 D5 1k ultra (R) *2,400. 2,400.*
J9 D5 5k ultra (R) *2,400. 2,400.*
J10 D5 10k ultra (R) *10,000. 9,000.*
a. Black overprint *14,000. 16,000.*

Overprint on Nos. J1-J7, J10a is type. Overprint on Nos. J8-J10 is slightly larger than illustration, has a different ornament between lines of type and is litho.

D6

Type of Austria, 1916-18, Surcharged in Black

1919, Jan. 10
J11 D6 15h on 36h vio 300.00 200.00
J12 D6 50h on 42h choc 30.00 30.00
a. Double surcharge 275.00 275.00

Counterfeits exist of Nos. J1 to J12.

Regular Issues

Numerals of Value
D7 D8

1919 Typo. *Perf. 11½*
For Northern Poland
J13 D7 2f red orange 38 32
J14 D7 4f red orange 16 18
J15 D7 5f red orange 15 15
J16 D7 10f red orange 15 15
J17 D7 20f red orange 15 15
J18 D7 30f red orange 15 15
J19 D7 50f red orange 15 15
J20 D7 100f red orange 75 45
J21 D7 500f red orange 1.75 1.25

For Southern Poland
J22 D7 2h dark blue 15 15
J23 D7 4h dark blue 15 15
J24 D7 5h dark blue 15 15
J25 D7 10h dark blue 15 15
J26 D7 20h dark blue 15 15
J27 D7 30h dark blue 15 15
J28 D7 50h dark blue 15 15
J29 D7 100h dark blue 32 22
J30 D7 500h dark blue 1.40 1.10
Nos. J13-J30 (18) 6.56
Set value 4.50

Counterfeits exist.

1920 *Perf. 9, 10, 11½*
Thin Laid Paper
J31 D7 20f dark blue 70 48
J32 D7 100f dark blue 35 24
J33 D7 200f dark blue 60 48
J34 D7 500f dark blue 35 24

Regular Issue of 1919 Surcharged

6 Mk.
dopłata

1921, Jan. 25 *Imperf.*
Wove Paper
J35 A9 6m on 15h brown 45 42
J36 A9 6m on 25h car 45 42
J37 A9 20m on 10h lake 1.25 1.10
J38 A9 20m on 50h indigo 1.40 1.40
J39 A9 35m on 70h dp bl 12.00 12.00
Nos. J35-J39 (5) 15.55 15.34

Counterfeits exist.

Perf. 9 to 14½ and Compound
1921-22 Typo.
Thin Laid or Wove Paper
Size: 17x22mm
J40 D8 1m indigo 32 15
J41 D8 2m indigo 32 15
J42 D8 4m indigo 32 15
J43 D8 6m indigo 32 15
J44 D8 8m indigo 32 15
J45 D8 20m indigo 32 15
J46 D8 50m indigo 32 15
J47 D8 100m indigo 60 18
Nos. J40-J47 (8) 2.84
Set value 1.00

Nos. J44-J45, J41 Surcharged
Perf. 9 to 14½ and Compound
1923, Nov.
J48 D8 10,000(m) on 8m ind 35 15
J49 D8 20,000(m) on 20m ind 35 15
J50 D8 50,000(m) on 2m ind 2.25 70

Type of 1921-22 Issue
1923 Typo. *Perf. 12½*
Size: 19x24mm
J51 D8 50m indigo 15 15
J52 D8 100m indigo 15 15
J53 D8 200m indigo 15 15
J54 D8 500m indigo 15 15
J55 D8 1000m indigo 15 15
J56 D8 2000m indigo 15 15
J57 D8 10,000m indigo 15 15
J58 D8 20,000m indigo 15 15
J59 D8 30,000m indigo 15 15
J60 D8 50,000m indigo 38 15
J61 D8 100,000m indigo 38 15
J62 D8 200,000m indigo 45 15
J63 D8 300,000m indigo 45 32
J64 D8 500,000m indigo 65 18
J65 D8 1,000,000m indigo 1.50 60
J66 D8 2,000,000m indigo 2.75 60
J67 D8 3,000,000m indigo 3.00 85
Nos. J51-J67 (17) 10.91
Set value 3.80

D9

D10

Perf. 10 to 13½ and Compound
1924
Size: 20x25½mm
J68 D9 1g brown 28 22
J69 D9 2g brown 28 22
J70 D9 4g brown 28 22
J71 D9 6g brown 55 22
J72 D9 10g brown 3.25 22
J73 D9 15g brown 2.50 40
J74 D9 20g brown 6.00 40
J75 D9 25g brown 5.00 40
J76 D9 30g brown 1.10 40
J77 D9 40g brown 1.10 40
J78 D9 50g brown 1.10 40
J79 D9 1z brown 1.00 55
J80 D9 2z brown 1.00 55
J81 D9 3z brown 1.90 2.25
J82 D9 5z brown 1.90 85
Nos. J68-J82 (15) 27.24 7.70

Nos. J68-J69 and J72-J75 exist measuring 19½x24½mm.
For surcharges see Nos. J84-J91.

1930, July *Perf. 12½*
J83 D10 5g olive brown 70 20

Postage Due Stamps of 1924 Surcharged

50 groszy

Perf. 10 to 13½ and Compound

1934-38

No.	Type	Description	Unused	Used
J84	D9	10g on 2z brown ('38)	40	28
J85	D9	15g on 2z brown	40	28
J86	D9	20g on 1z brown	40	28
J87	D9	20g on 5z brown	2.00	55
J88	D9	25g on 40g brown	1.25	55
J89	D9	30g on 40g brown	85	55
J90	D9	50g on 40g brown	85	70
J91	D9	50g on 3z brown ('35)	1.75	1.00
		Nos. J84-J91 (8)	7.90	4.19

No. 255a Surcharged in Red or Indigo

DOPŁATA 25 GR

1934-36 **Laid Paper**

No.	Type	Description	Unused	Used
J92	A50	10g on 1z (R) ('36)	80	15
a.		Vertically laid paper (No. 255)	25.00	18.00
J93	A50	20g on 1z (R) ('36)	2.50	80
J94	A50	25g on 1z (I)	80	30
a.		Vertically laid paper (No. 255)	30.00	18.00

D11

1939, Nov. 25 **Typo.** *Perf. 12½x12*

No.	Type	Description	Unused	Used
J95	D11	5g dark blue green	15	15
J96	D11	10g dark blue green	15	15
J97	D11	15g dark blue green	15	15
J98	D11	20g dark blue green	60	20
J99	D11	25g dark blue green	15	16
J100	D11	30g dark blue green	42	20
J101	D11	50g dark blue green	80	1.25
J102	D11	1z dark blue green	2.50	1.65
		Nos. J95-J102 (8)	4.92	3.91

For surcharges see Nos. N51-N55.

Polish People's Republic

Post Horn with Thunderbolts
D12

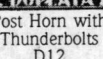

Polish Eagle
D13

Perf. 11x10½

1945, May 20 **Litho.** **Unwmk.**

Size: 25½x19mm

No.	Type	Description	Unused	Used
J103	D12	1z orange brown	15	15
J104	D12	2z orange brown	20	15
J105	D12	3z orange brown	25	20
J106	D12	5z orange brown	35	30

Type of 1945

Perf. 11, 11½ (P) or Imperf. (I)

1946-49 **Photo.**

Size: 29x21½mm

No.	Type	Description	Unused	Used
J106A	D12	1z org brn (P) ('49)	20	15
J107	D12	2z org brn (P,I)	20	15
J108	D12	3z org brn (P,I)	20	15
J109	D12	5z org brn (I)	20	15
J110	D12	6z org brn (I)	20	15
J111	D12	10z org brn (I)	25	20
J112	D12	15z org brn (P,I)	35	30
J113	D12	25z org brn (P,I)	50	45
J114	D12	100z brn (P) ('49)	1.00	50
J115	D12	150z brn (P) ('49)	1.75	50
		Nos. J106A-J115 (10)	4.85	2.70

1950 **Engr.** *Perf. 12x12½*

No.	Type	Description	Unused	Used
J116	D13	5z red brown	15	15
J117	D13	10z red brown	15	15
J118	D13	15z red brown	15	15
J119	D13	20z red brown	28	15
J120	D13	25z red brown	32	18
J121	D13	50z red brown	48	35
J122	D13	100z red brown	1.00	70
		Nos. J116-J122 (7)	2.53	
		Set value		1.55

1951-52

No.	Type	Description	Unused	Used
J123	D13	5g red brown	15	15
J124	D13	10g red brown	15	15
J125	D13	15g red brown	15	15
J126	D13	20g red brown	15	15
J127	D13	25g red brown	16	15
J128	D13	30g red brown	22	15
J129	D13	50g red brown	25	20
J130	D13	60g red brown	30	20
J131	D13	90g red brown	38	25
J132	D13	1z red brown	60	45
J133	D13	2z red brown	95	75
J134	D13	5z brown violet	2.00	1.75
		Nos. J123-J134 (12)	5.46	4.50

1953, Apr. **Photo.** **Without imprint**

No.	Type	Description	Unused	Used
J135	D13	5g red brown	15	15
J136	D13	10g red brown	15	15
J137	D13	15g red brown	15	15
J138	D13	20g red brown	15	15
J139	D13	25g red brown	16	15
J140	D13	30g red brown	25	15
J141	D13	50g red brown	42	25
J142	D13	60g red brown	50	30
J143	D13	90g red brown	60	50
J144	D13	1z red brown	80	50
J145	D13	2z red brown	1.50	1.25
		Nos. J135-J145 (11)	4.83	3.70

Catalogue values for unused stamps in this section, from this point to the end of the section, are for Never Hinged items.

1980, Sept. 2 **Litho.** *Perf. 12½*

No.	Type	Description	Unused	Used
J146	D13	1z lt red brown	15	15
J147	D13	2z gray olive	18	15
J148	D13	3z dull violet	28	15
J149	D13	5z brown	45	20
		Set value		46

OFFICIAL STAMPS

O1

Perf. 10, 11½, 10x11½, 11½x10

1920, Feb. 1 **Litho.** **Unwmk.**

No.	Type	Description	Unused	Used
O1	O1	3f vermilion	15	15
O2	O1	5f vermilion	15	18
O3	O1	10f vermilion	15	18
O4	O1	15f vermilion	15	18
O5	O1	25f vermilion	15	18
O6	O1	50f vermilion	15	18
O7	O1	100f vermilion	28	25
O8	O1	150f vermilion	28	38
O9	O1	200f vermilion	52	38
O10	O1	300f vermilion	28	38
O11	O1	600f vermilion	52	38
		Nos. O1-O11 (11)	2.78	2.82

Numerals Larger
Stars inclined outward

1920, Nov. 20 *Perf. 11½*

Thin Laid Paper

No.	Type	Description	Unused	Used
O12	O1	5f red	15	15
O13	O1	10f red	50	45
O14	O1	15f red	35	35
O15	O1	25f red	1.10	1.10
O16	O1	50f red	65	65
		Nos. O12-O16 (5)	2.75	2.70

Polish Eagle
O3 O4

Perf. 12x12½

1933, Aug. 1 **Typo.** **Wmk. 234**

No.	Type	Description	Unused	Used
O17	O3	(30g) vio (Zwyczajna)	95	15
O18	O3	(80g) red (Polecona)	2.25	30

1935, Apr. 1

No.	Type	Description	Unused	Used
O19	O4	(25g) bl vio (Zwyczajna)	15	15
O20	O4	(55g) car (Polecona)	30	15

Stamps inscribed "Zwyczajna" or "Zwykla" were for ordinary official mail. Those with "Polecona" were for registered official mail.

Polish People's Republic

Polish Eagle — O5

Perf. 11, 14

1945, July 1 **Photo.** **Unwmk.**

No.	Type	Description	Unused	Used
O21	O5	(5z) bl vio (Zwykla)	35	15
a.		Imperf.	1.00	1.00
O22	O5	(10z) red (Polecona)	65	18
a.		Imperf.	1.65	1.25
		Set value		25

Control number at bottom right: M-01705 on No. O21; M-01706 on No. O22.

Type of 1945 Redrawn

1946, July 31

No.	Type	Description	Unused	Used
O23	O5	(5z) dl bl vio (Zwykla)	30	15
O24	O5	(10z) dl rose red (Polecona)	50	22

The redrawn stamps appear blurred and the eagle contains fewer lines of shading.

Control number at bottom right: M-01709 on Nos. O23-O26.

Redrawn Type of 1946

1946, July 31 *Imperf.*

No.	Type	Description	Unused	Used
O25	O5	(60g) dl bl vio (Zwykla)	35	15
O26	O5	(1.55z) dl rose red (Polecona)	35	20

Type of 1945, 2nd Redrawing
No Control Number at Lower Right

Perf. 11, 11½, 11x12½

1952 **Unwmk.**

No.	Type	Description	Unused	Used
O27	O5	(60g) blue (Zwykla)	22	15
O28	O5	(1.55z) red (Polecona)	38	20

Redrawn Type of 1952

1954 *Perf. 13x11, 11½, 14*

No.	Type	Description	Unused	Used
O29	O5	(60g) slate gray (Zwykla)	1.10	50

O6

Perf. 11x11½, 12x12½

1954, Aug. 15 **Engr.**

No.	Type	Description	Unused	Used
O30	O6	(60g) dark blue (Zwykla)	25	15
O31	O6	(1.55z) red (Polecona)	45	24

Polish People's Republic, 10th anniversary.

NEWSPAPER STAMPS

Austrian Newspaper Stamps of 1916 Overprinted

POCZTA POLSKA

1919, Jan. 10 **Unwmk.** *Imperf.*

No.	Type	Description	Unused	Used
P1	N9	2h brown	7.00	6.50
P2	N9	4h green	3.00	2.50
P3	N9	6h dark blue	3.00	2.50
P4	N9	10h orange	35.00	35.00
P5	N9	30h claret	5.00	4.00
		Nos. P1-P5 (5)	53.00	50.50

OCCUPATION STAMPS

Issued under German Occupation

German Stamps of 1905 Overprinted

Perf. 14, 14½

1915, May 12 **Wmk. 125**

No.	Type	Description	Unused	Used
N1	A16	3pf brown	1.00	45
N2	A16	5pf green	1.25	55
N3	A16	10pf carmine	1.25	55
N4	A16	20pf ultra	1.90	80
N5	A16	40pf lake & blk	10.50	4.25
		Nos. N1-N5 (5)	15.90	6.60

German Stamps of 1905-17 Overprinted

Gen.-Gouv. Warschau

1916-17

No.	Type	Description	Unused	Used
N6	A22	2½pf gray	22	26
N7	A16	3pf brown	90	38
N8	A16	5pf green	90	85
N9	A22	7½pf orange	70	15
N10	A16	10pf carmine	90	26
N11	A22	15pf yel brn	4.25	1.75
N12	A22	15pf dk vio ('17)	55	26
N13	A16	20pf ultra	1.40	55
N14	A16	30pf org & blk, *buff*	6.25	3.00
N15	A16	40pf lake & blk	2.25	15
N16	A16	60pf magenta	3.00	1.20
		Nos. N6-N16 (11)	21.32	8.81

For overprints and surcharges see Nos. 15-26.

6 Groschen 6

German Stamps of 1934 Surcharged in Black

Deutsche Post OSTEN

1939, Dec. 1 **Wmk. 237** *Perf. 14*

No.	Type	Description	Unused	Used
N17	A64	6g on 3pf bister	30	30
N18	A64	8g on 4pf dl bl	30	32
N19	A64	12g on 6pf dk grn	30	30
N20	A64	16g on 8pf vermilion	75	90
N21	A64	20g on 10pf choc	30	30
N22	A64	24g on 12pf dp car	30	30
N23	A64	30g on 15pf maroon	90	85
N24	A64	40g on 20pf brt bl	75	40
N25	A64	50g on 25pf ultra	75	70
N26	A64	60g on 30pf ol grn	75	40
N27	A64	80g on 40pf red vio	90	85
N28	A64	1z on 50pf dk grn & blk	2.25	1.25
N29	A64	2z on 100(pf) org & blk	4.25	2.75
		Nos. N17-N29 (13)	12.80	9.62

Stamps of Poland 1937, Surcharged in Black or Brown

24 GR. 24

1940 **Unwmk.** *Perf. 12½, 12½x13*

No.	Type	Description	Unused	Used
N30	A80	24g on 25g sl grn	1.10	1.75
N31	A81	40g on 30g rose vio	40	65
N32	A80	50g on 55g blue	35	52

Similar Surcharge on Stamps of 1938-39

No.	Type	Description	Unused	Used
N33	A83	2g on 5g red org	22	35
N34	A83	4(g) on 5g red org	22	35
N35	A83	6(g) on 10g grn	22	35
N36	A83	8(g) on 10g grn (Br)	28	45
N37	A83	10(g) on 10g grn	22	35
N38	A83	12(g) on 15g redsh brn (#339)	22	35
N39	A83	16(g) on 15g redsh brn (#339)	28	45
N40	A83	24g on 25g dl vio	22	35
N41	A83	30(g) on 30g rose red	28	45
N42	A83	50(g) on 50g brt red vio	35	55
N43	A83	60(g) on 55g ultra	7.50	9.25
N44	A83	80(g) on 75g dl grn	7.50	9.25
N45	A83	1z on 1z org	7.50	9.25
N46	A83	2z on 2z car rose	5.00	5.50
N47	A95	3z on 3z gray blk	5.00	5.50

Similar Surcharge on Nos. B32-B34

No.	Type	Description	Unused	Used
N48	SP5	30g on 5g+5g	35	55
N49	SP5	40g on 25g+10g	35	55
N50	SP5	1z on 55g+15g	7.25	6.50

Similar Surcharge on Nos. J98-J102

Perf. 12½x12

No.	Type	Description	Unused	Used
N51	D11	50(g) on 20g	65	1.10
N52	D11	50(g) on 25g	13.00	13.00
N53	D11	50(g) on 30g	40.00	35.00
N54	D11	50(g) on 50g	65	90
N55	D11	50(g) on 1z	1.10	90
		Nos. N30-N55 (26)	100.21	104.17

The surcharge on Nos. N30 to N55 is arranged to fit the shape of the stamp and obliterate the original denomination. On some values, "General Gouvernement" appears at the bottom. Counterfeits exist.

St. Florian's Gate, Cracow — OS1

Palace, Warsaw — OS13

Designs: 8g, Watch Tower, Cracow. 10g, Cracow Gate, Lublin. 12g, Courtyard and statue of Copernicus. 20g, Dominican Church, Cracow. 24g, Wawel Castle, Cracow. 30g, Church, Lublin. 40g, Arcade, Cloth Hall, Cracow. 48g, City Hall, Sandomierz. 50g, Court House, Cracow. 60g, Courtyard, Cracow. 80g, St. Mary's Church, Cracow.

1940-41 Unwmk. Photo. *Perf. 14*

N56	OS1	6g brown	28	50
N57	OS1	8g brn org	28	50
N58	OS1	8g bl blk ('41)	28	35
N59	OS1	10g emerald	15	22
N60	OS1	12g dk grn	3.00	28
N61	OS1	12g dp vio ('41)	28	15
N62	OS1	20g dk ol brn	15	15
N63	OS1	24g hn brn	15	15
N64	OS1	30g purple	15	15
N65	OS1	30g vio brn ('41)	15	30
N66	OS1	40g slate blk	15	15
N67	OS1	48g chnt brn ('41)	60	75
N68	OS1	50g brt bl	15	15
N69	OS1	60g slate grn	15	22
N70	OS1	80g dull pur	25	28
N71	OS13	1z rose lake	2.00	1.00
N72	OS13	1z Prus grn ('41)	55	50
		Nos. N56-N72 (17)	8.72	5.80

For surcharges see Nos. NB1-NB4.

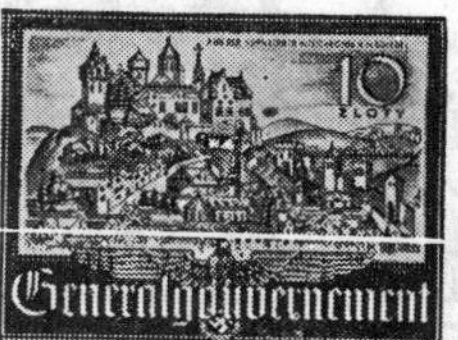

Cracow Castle and City, 15th Century OS14

1941, Apr. 20 Engr. *Perf. 14½*

N73	OS14	10z red & ol blk	2.00	2.00

Printed in sheets of 8.

Rondel and Florian's Gate, Cracow OS15

Design: 4z, Tyniec Monastery, Vistula River.

1941 *Perf. 13½x14*

N74	OS15	2z dk ultra	35	45
N75	OS15	4z slate grn	48	60

Adolf Hitler — OS17

1941-43 Unwmk. Photo. *Perf. 14*

N76	OS17	2g gray blk	15	16
N77	OS17	6g golden brn	15	16
N78	OS17	8g slate blue	15	16
N79	OS17	10g green	15	15
N80	OS17	12g purple	15	15
N81	OS17	16g org red	50	48
N82	OS17	20g blk brn	15	16
N83	OS17	24g henna	15	15
N84	OS17	30g rose vio	45	16
N85	OS17	32g dk bl grn	50	38
N86	OS17	40g brt blue	15	16
N87	OS17	48g chestnut	55	42
N88	OS17	50g vio bl ('43)	15	16
N89	OS17	60g dk olive ('43)	15	16
N90	OS17	80g dk vio ('43)	15	16
		Nos. N76-N90 (15)	3.65	3.17

A 20g black brown exists with head of Hans Frank substituted for that of Hitler. It was printed and used by Resistance movements.

Nos. N76-N80, N82-N90 exist imperf.

1942-44 Engr. *Perf. 12½*

N91	OS17	50g vio bl	40	48
N92	OS17	60g dk ol	40	48
N93	OS17	80g dk red vio	40	48
N94	OS17	1z slate grn	40	48
a.		Perf. 14 ('44)	52	60
N95	OS17	1.20z dk brn	45	55
a.		Perf. 14 ('44)	60	80
N96	OS17	1.60z bl vio	50	60
a.		Perf. 14 ('44)	75	1.10
		Nos. N91-N96 (6)	2.55	3.07

Exist imperf.

Rondel and Florian's Gate, Cracow OS18

Designs: 4z, Tyniec Monastery, Vistula River. 6z, View of Lwow. 10z, Cracow Castle and City, 15th Century.

1943-44 *Perf. 13½x14*

N100	OS18	2z slate grn	15	15
N101	OS18	4z dk gray vio	28	35
N102	OS18	6z sepia ('44)	48	50
N103	OS18	10z org brn & gray blk	52	60

OCCUPATION SEMI-POSTAL STAMPS

Issued under German Occupation

Types of 1940 Occupation Postage Stamps Surcharged in Red

Unwmk.

1940, Aug. 17 Photo. *Perf. 14*

NB1	OS1	12g + 8g olive gray	3.25	4.00
NB2	OS1	24g + 16g olive gray	3.25	4.00
NB3	OS1	50g + 50g olive gray	4.00	4.50
NB4	OS1	80g + 80g olive gray	4.00	4.50

German Peasant Girl in Poland — OSP1

Designs: 24g+26g, Woman wearing scarf. 30g+20g, Similar to type OSP4.

1940, Oct. 26 Engr. *Perf. 14½*

Thick Paper

NB5	OSP1	12g + 38g dk sl grn	2.25	2.75
NB6	OSP1	24g + 26g cop red	2.25	2.75
NB7	OSP1	30g + 20g dk pur	2.75	3.75

1st anniversary of the General Government.

German Peasant — OSP4

1940, Dec. 1 *Perf. 12*

NB8	OSP4	12g + 8g dk grn	1.00	90
NB9	OSP4	24g + 16g rose red	1.65	1.65
NB10	OSP4	30g + 30g vio brn	2.00	2.00
NB11	OSP4	50g + 50g ultra	2.75	2.50

The surtax was for war relief.

Adolf Hitler — OSP5

Unwmk.

1942, Apr. 20 Engr. *Perf. 11*

Thick Cream Paper

NB12	OSP5	30g + 1z brn car	30	35
NB13	OSP5	50g + 1z dk ultra	30	35
NB14	OSP5	1.20z + 1z brown	30	35

To commemorate Hitler's 53rd birthday. Printed in sheets of 25.

Ancient Lublin — OSP6

Designs: 24g+6g, 1z+1z, Modern Lublin.

1942, Aug. 15 Photo. *Perf. 12½*

NB15	OSP6	12g + 8g rose vio	15	15
NB16	OSP6	24g + 6g henna	15	15
NB17	OSP6	50g + 50g dp bl	18	25
NB18	OSP6	1z + 1z dp grn	40	55
		Set value	78	

600th anniversary of Lublin.

Veit Stoss — OSP8

Adolf Hitler — OSP13

Designs: 24g+26g, Hans Durer. 30g+30g, Johann Schuch. 50g+50g, Joseph Elsner. 1z+1z, Nicolaus Copernicus.

1942, Nov. 20 Engr. *Perf. 13½x14*

NB19	OSP8	12g + 18g dl pur	18	20
NB20	OSP8	24g + 26g dl henna	18	20
NB21	OSP8	30g + 30g dl rose vio	18	20
NB22	OSP8	50g + 50g dl bl vio	22	25
NB23	OSP8	1z + 1z dl myr grn	52	45
		Nos. NB19-NB23 (5)	1.28	1.30

For overprint see No. NB27.

1943, Apr. 20

NB24	OSP13	12g + 1z purple	15	22
NB25	OSP13	24g + 1z rose car	15	22
NB26	OSP13	84g + 1z myr grn	38	42

To commemorate Hitler's 54th birthday.

Type of 1942 Overprinted in Black

24. MAI 1543

24. MAI 1943

1943, May 24

NB27	OSP8	1z + 1z rose lake	80	1.10

To commemorate the 400th anniversary of the death of the astronomer, Nicolaus Copernicus (1473-1543).

Printed in sheets of 10, with marginal inscription in rose lake.

Poland German Occupation stamps can be mounted in Scott's Germany Part II Album.

Cracow Gate, Lublin — OSP14

Adolf Hitler — OSP19

Designs: 24g+76g, Cloth Hall, Cracow. 30g+70g, New Government Building, Radom. 50g+1z, Bruhl Palace, Warsaw. 1z+2z, Town Hall, Lwow.

The center of the designs is embossed with the emblem of the National Socialist Party.

1943 Photogravure, Embossed

NB28	OSP14	12g + 38g dk grn	15	15
NB29	OSP14	24g + 76g red	15	15
NB30	OSP14	30g + 70g rose vio	15	15
NB31	OSP14	50g + 1z brt bl	15	15
NB32	OSP14	1z + 2z bl blk	22	35
		Set value	70	

3rd anniversary of the National Socialist Party in Poland.

1944, Apr. 20 Photo. *Perf. 14x13½*

NB33	OSP19	12g + 1z green	15	18
NB34	OSP19	24g + 1z brn red	15	18
NB35	OSP19	84g + 1z dk vio	15	18
		Set value	35	

To commemorate Hitler's 55th birthday. Printed in sheets of 25.

Conrad Celtis — OSP20

Designs: 24g+26g, Andreas Schluter. 30g+30g, Hans Boner. 50g+50g, Augustus II. 1z+1z, Georg Gottlieb Pusch.

1944, July 15 Engr. *Perf. 13½x14*

NB36	OSP20	12g + 18g dk grn	15	15
NB37	OSP20	24g + 26g dk red	15	15
NB38	OSP20	30g + 30g rose vio	15	15
NB39	OSP20	50g + 50g ultra	15	32
NB40	OSP20	1z + 1z dl red brn	15	32
		Set value	54	88

Cracow Castle OSP25

1944, Oct. 26 *Perf. 14½*

NB41	OSP25	10z + 10z red & blk	7.50	12.00
a.		Imperf.	9.00	
b.		10z + 10z car & grnsh blk	16.00	18.00

5th anniv. of the General Government, Oct. 26, 1944. Printed in sheets of 8.

OCCUPATION RURAL DELIVERY STAMPS

Issued under German Occupation

OSD1

Perf. 13½

1940, Dec. 1 Photo. Unwmk.

NL1	OSD1	10g red orange	45	*65*
NL2	OSD1	20g red orange	45	*1.00*
NL3	OSD1	30g red orange	45	*1.00*
NL4	OSD1	50g red orange	1.10	*2.00*

OCCUPATION OFFICIAL STAMPS

Issued under German Occupation

Eagle and Swastika OOS1

Perf. 12, 13½x14

1940, Apr. Photo. Unwmk.

Size: 31x23mm

NO1	OOS1	6g lt brn	1.10	1.50
NO2	OOS1	8g gray	1.10	1.50
NO3	OOS1	10g green	1.10	1.50
NO4	OOS1	12g dk grn	1.25	1.90
NO5	OOS1	20g dk brn	1.25	3.25
NO6	OOS1	24g hn brn	20.00	50
NO7	OOS1	30g rose lake	1.75	2.75
NO8	OOS1	40g dl vio	1.75	4.50
NO9	OOS1	48g dl ol	7.25	4.75
NO10	OOS1	50g royal bl	1.50	2.75
NO11	OOS1	60g dk ol grn	1.10	1.90
NO12	OOS1	80g rose vio	1.10	1.90

Size: 35x26mm

NO13	OOS1	1z gray blk & brn vio	3.50	4.75
NO14	OOS1	3z gray blk & chnt	3.50	4.50
NO15	OOS1	5z gray blk & org brn	4.75	6.25
		Nos. NO1-NO15 (15)	52.00	44.20

1940 *Perf. 12*

Size: 21¼x16¼mm

NO16	OOS1	6g brown	65	1.10
NO17	OOS1	8g slate	1.10	1.75
NO18	OOS1	10g dp grn	1.75	2.00
NO19	OOS1	12g slate grn	1.75	2.00
NO20	OOS1	20g blk brn	90	1.10
NO21	OOS1	24g cop brn	65	1.10
NO22	OOS1	30g rose lake	1.10	1.75
NO23	OOS1	40g dl pur	1.75	2.00
NO24	OOS1	50g royal blue	1.75	2.00
		Nos. NO16-NO24 (9)	11.40	14.80

Nazi Emblem and Cracow Castle — OOS2

1943 Photo. *Perf. 14*

NO25	OOS2	6g brown	15	15
NO26	OOS2	8g slate blue	15	15
NO27	OOS2	10g green	15	15
NO28	OOS2	12g dk vio	35	24
NO29	OOS2	16g red org	15	15
NO30	OOS2	20g dk brn	18	15
NO31	OOS2	24g dk red	35	15
NO32	OOS2	30g rose vio	18	15
NO33	OOS2	40g blue	18	15
NO34	OOS2	60g olive grn	18	15
NO35	OOS2	80g dull claret	28	15
NO36	OOS2	100g slate blk	35	60
		Nos. NO25-NO36 (12)	2.65	2.34

POLISH OFFICES ABROAD

OFFICES IN DANZIG

Poland Nos. 215-225 Overprinted **PORT GDAŃSK**

1925, Jan. 5 Unwmk. *Perf. 11½x12*

1K1	A36	1g org brn	45	1.00
1K2	A36	2g dk brn	60	2.75
1K3	A36	3g orange	60	1.00
1K4	A36	5g ol grn	15.00	6.50
1K5	A36	10g bl grn	5.00	2.00
1K6	A36	15g red	30.00	5.00
1K7	A36	20g blue	1.75	1.00
1K8	A36	25g red brn	1.75	1.00
1K9	A36	30g dp vio	2.00	1.00
1K10	A36	40g indigo	2.00	1.00
1K11	A36	50g magenta	5.50	1.40
		Nos. 1K1-1K11 (11)	64.65	23.65

Same Ovpt. on Poland Nos. 230-231

1926 *Perf. 11½, 12*

1K11A	A39	5g yel grn	52.50	37.50
1K12	A40	10g violet	12.50	15.00

Counterfeit overprints are known on Nos. 1K1-1K32.

No. 232 Overprinted **PORT GDAŃSK**

1926-27

1K13	A41	15g rose red	45.00	40.00

Same Overprint on Redrawn Stamps of 1926-27

Perf. 13

1K14	A39	5g yel grn	2.00	1.75
1K15	A40	10g violet	2.00	1.75
1K16	A41	15g rose red	4.00	3.75
1K17	A43	20g dl red	3.25	2.25

Same Ovpt. on Poland Nos. 250, 255

1928-30 *Perf. 12½*

1K18	A44	25g yel brn	4.75	1.50

Laid Paper

Perf. 11½x12, 12½x11½

1K19	A50	1z blk, *cr* ('30)	30.00	30.00

Poland Nos. 258-260 Overprinted **PORT GDAŃSK**

1929-30 *Perf. 12x12½*

1K20	A53	5g dk vio	1.65	1.40
1K21	A53	10g grn ('30)	1.65	1.40
1K22	A53	25g red brn	2.75	1.40

Same Overprint on Poland No. 257

1931, Jan. 5 *Perf. 12½*

1K23	A52	15g ultra	3.00	4.00

Poland No. 255 Overprinted in Dark Blue **PORT GDAŃSK**

1933, July 1 *Perf. 11½*

Laid Paper

1K24	A50	1z blk, *cream*	82.50	100.00

Poland Nos. 268-270 Overprinted in Black **PORT GDAŃSK**

1934-36 Wmk. 234 *Perf. 12x12½*

1K25	A58	5g dl vio	3.25	3.75
1K26	A58	10g grn ('36)	35.00	*72.50*
1K27	A58	15g red brn	3.25	3.75

Poland Nos. 294, 296, 298 Overprinted in Black in one or two lines **PORT GDAŃSK**

1935-36 Unwmk. *Perf. 12½x13*

1K28	A65	5g vio bl	3.50	3.00
1K29	A65	15g Prus grn	3.50	4.75
1K30	A65	25g myr grn	3.50	2.00

Same Overprint in Black on Poland Nos. 308, 310

1937, June 5

1K31	A65	5g vio bl	1.10	1.75
1K32	A65	15g red brn	1.10	1.75

Polish Merchants Selling Wheat in Danzig, 16th Century — A2

1938, Nov. 11 Engr. *Perf. 12½*

1K33	A2	5g red org	60	95
1K34	A2	15g red brn	60	95
1K35	A2	25g dl vio	60	1.65
1K36	A2	55g brt ultra	1.40	3.00

OFFICES IN THE TURKISH EMPIRE

Stamps of Poland 1919, Overprinted in Carmine

LEVANT

1919, May Unwmk. *Perf. 11½*

Wove Paper

2K1	A10	3f bis brn	27.50	24.00
2K2	A10	5f green	27.50	24.00
2K3	A10	10f red vio	27.50	24.00
2K4	A10	15f red	27.50	24.00
2K5	A11	20f dp bl	27.50	24.00
2K6	A11	25f ol grn	27.50	24.00
2K7	A11	50f bl grn	27.50	24.00

Overprinted **LEVANT**

2K8	A12	1m violet	27.50	24.00
2K9	A12	1.50m dp grn	27.50	24.00
2K10	A12	2m dk brn	27.50	24.00
2K11	A13	2.50m org brn	27.50	24.00
2K12	A14	5m red vio	27.50	24.00
		Nos. 2K1-2K12 (12)	330.00	

Counterfeit cancellations are plentiful.

Counterfeits exist of Nos. 2K1-2K12.

Reissues are lighter, shiny red. Value, set $17.50.

Polish stamps with "P.P.C." overprint (Poste Polonaise Constantinople) were used on consular mail for a time.

Seven stamps with these overprints were not issued. Value, set $20.

EXILE GOVERNMENT IN GREAT BRITAIN

These stamps were issued by the Polish government in exile for letters posted from Polish merchant ships and warships.

United States Embassy Ruins, Warsaw — A1

Polish Ministry of Finance Ruins, Warsaw — A2

Destruction of Mickiewicz Monument, Cracow — A3

Polish Submarine "Orzel" — A8

Ruins of Warsaw A4

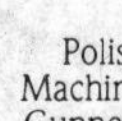

Polish Machine Gunners A5

Armored Tank — A6

Polish Planes in Great Britain A7

Perf. 12½, 11½x12

1941, Dec. 15 Engr. Unwmk.

3K1	A1	5g rose violet	35	52
3K2	A2	10g dk bl grn	75	70
3K3	A3	25g black	1.25	1.25
3K4	A4	55g dark blue	1.50	1.50
3K5	A5	75g olive grn	3.75	3.75
3K6	A6	80g dk car rose	3.75	3.75
3K7	A7	1z slate blue	3.75	3.75
3K8	A8	1.50z copper brn	3.75	4.25
		Nos. 3K1-3K8 (8)	18.85	19.47

These stamps were used for correspondence carried on Polish ships and, on certain days, in Polish Military camps in Great Britain.

For surcharges see Nos. 3K17-3K20.

Polish Air Force in Battle of the Atlantic — A9

Polish Army in France, 1939-40 — A11

Polish Merchant Navy A10

Polish Army in Narvik, Norway, 1940 — A12

The Homeland Fights On — A15

Polish Army in Libya, 1941-42 A13

General Sikorsky and Polish Soldiers in the Middle East, 1943 A14

The Secret Press in Poland A16

1943, Nov. 1

3K9	A9	5g rose lake	32	65
3K10	A10	10g dk bl grn	65	1.00
3K11	A11	25g dk vio	65	1.00
3K12	A12	55g sapphire	1.00	1.65
3K13	A13	75g brn car	1.65	2.25
3K14	A14	80g rose car	2.25	2.75
3K15	A15	1z olive blk	2.25	2.75
3K16	A16	1.50z black	3.00	3.25
		Nos. 3K9-3K16 (8)	11.77	15.30

Nos. 3K5 to 3K8 Surcharged in Blue

MONTE CASSINO

18. V. 1944

Perf. 12½, 11½x12

1944, June 27 **Unwmk.**

3K17	A5	45g on 75g	6.00	6.00
3K18	A6	55g on 80g	6.00	6.00
3K19	A7	80g on 1z	6.00	6.00
3K20	A8	1.20z on 1.50z	6.00	6.00

Capture of Monte Cassino by the Poles, May 18, 1944.

EXILE GOVERNMENT IN GREAT BRITAIN SEMI-POSTAL STAMP

Heroic Defenders of Warsaw — SP1

Perf. 11½

1945, Feb. 3 **Unwmk.** **Engr.**

3KB1	SP1	1z + 2z slate green	3.75	5.00

Warsaw uprising, Aug. 1-Oct. 3, 1944.

PONTA DELGADA

LOCATION — Administrative district of the Azores comprising the islands of Sao Miguel and Santa Maria
GOVT. — A district of Portugal
AREA — 342 sq. mi.
POP. — 124,000 (approx.)
CAPITAL — Ponta Delgada

1000 Reis = 1 Milreis

King Carlos
A1 A2

Perf. 11½, 12½, 13½

1892-93 **Typo.** **Unwmk.**

1	A1	5r yellow	50	50
a.		Diagonal half used as 2½r on piece		2.50
b.		Perf. 11½	5.00	4.25
2	A1	10r reddish vio	1.40	85
3	A1	15r chocolate	2.25	1.25
4	A1	20r lavender	2.00	1.25
a.		Perf. 13½	3.75	2.25
5	A1	25r deep green	1.50	50
6	A1	50r ultra	3.50	1.25
7	A1	75r carmine	7.75	7.50
8	A1	80r yel grn	10.50	8.50
9	A1	100r brn, *yel*	6.25	4.50
10	A1	150r car, *rose*	35.00	30.00
11	A1	200r dk bl, *bl*	30.00	27.50
12	A1	300r dk bl, *salmon*	42.50	35.00
		Nos. 1-12 (12)	143.15	118.60

The reprints are on paper slightly thinner that that of the originals, and unsurfaced. They have white gum and clean-cut perf. 13½ or 11½. Lowest valued, Nos. 1-9, $4 each, Nos. 10-12, $20 each.

1897-1905 *Perf. 11½*

Name and Value in Black except Nos. 25 and 34

13	A2	2½r gray	22	16
14	A2	5r orange	25	16
15	A2	10r lt grn	25	16
16	A2	15r brown	5.00	3.50
17	A2	15r gray grn ('99)	85	60
18	A2	20r dl vio	95	70
19	A2	25r sea grn	1.65	60
20	A2	25r rose red ('99)	60	22
21	A2	50r blue	1.50	1.10
22	A2	50r ultra ('05)	12.50	14.00
23	A2	65r slate blue ('98)	55	38
a.		Imperf.		
24	A2	75r rose	3.50	2.25
25	A2	75r brn & car, *yel* ('05)	10.50	11.00
26	A2	80r violet	1.65	85
27	A2	100r dk bl, *bl*	1.65	1.25
28	A2	115r org brn, *rose* ('98)	1.50	1.10
29	A2	130r gray brn, *buff* ('98)	1.50	1.10
30	A2	150r lt brn, *buff*	1.50	1.25
31	A2	180r sl, *pnksh* ('98)	1.50	1.10
32	A2	200r red vio, *pnksh*	6.00	4.25
33	A2	300r blue, *rose*	6.00	4.25
a.		Perf. 12½	35.00	27.50
34	A2	500r blk & red, *bl*	12.00	8.50
a.		Perf. 12½	16.00	10.50
		Nos. 13-34 (22)	71.62	58.48

The stamps of Ponta Delgada were superseded by those of the Azores, which in 1931 were replaced by those of Portugal.

PORTUGAL

LOCATION — Southern Europe, on the western coast of the Iberian Peninsula
GOVT. — Republic
AREA — 35,516 sq. mi.
POP. — 9,930,000 (est. 1983)
CAPITAL — Lisbon

Figures for area and population include the Azores and Madeira, which are integral parts of the republic. The republic was established in 1910. See Azores, Funchal, Madeira.

1000 Reis = 1 Milreis
10 Reis = 1 Centimo
100 Centavos = 1 Escudo (1912)

Catalogue values for unused stamps in this country are for Never Hinged items, beginning with Scott 662 in the regular postage section, Scott C11 in the airpost section, Scott J65 in the postage due section, and Scott O2 in the officials section.

Values of early Portugal stamps vary according to condition. Quotations for Nos. 1-51 are for fine copies. Very fine to superb specimens sell at much higher prices, and inferior or poor copies sell at reduced prices, depending on the condition of the individual specimen.

Queen Maria II
A1 A2

A3 A4

Typo. & Embossed

1853 **Unwmk.** ***Imperf.***

1	A1	5r orange brown	1,350.	175.00
2	A2	25r blue	500.00	3.00
3	A3	50r deep yel grn	1,800.	190.00
a.		50r blue green	2,200.	300.00
4	A4	100r lilac	8,000.	600.00

The stamps of the 1853 issue were reprinted in 1864, 1885, 1905 and 1953. Many stamps of subsequent issues were reprinted in 1885 and 1905. The reprints of 1864 are on thin white paper with white gum. The originals have brownish gum which often stains the paper. The reprints of 1885 are on a stout, very white paper. They are usually ungummed, but occasionally have a white gum with yellowish spots. The reprints of 1905 are on creamy white paper of ordinary quality with shiny white gum.

When perforated the reprints of 1885 have a rather rough perforation 13½ with small holes; those of 1905 have a clean-cut perforation 13½ with large holes making sharp pointed teeth.

The colors of the reprints usually differ from those of the originals, but actual comparison is necessary.

The reprints are often from new dies which differ slightly from those used for the originals.

5 reis: There is a defect in the neck which makes the Adam's apple appear very large in the first reprint. The later ones can be distinguished by the paper and the shades and by the absence of the pendant curl.

25 reis: The burelage of the ground work in the original is sharp and clear, while in the 1864 reprints it is blurred in several places; the upper and lower right hand corners are very thick and blurred. The central oval is less than ½mm from the frame at the sides in the originals and fully ¾mm in the 1885 and 1905 reprints.

50 reis: In the reprints of 1864 and 1885 there is a small break in the upper right hand diagonal line of the frame, and the initials of the engraver (F. B. F.), which in the originals are plainly discernible in the lower part of the bust, do not show. The reprints of 1905 have not the break in the frame and the initials are distinct.

100 reis: The small vertical lines at top and bottom at each side of the frame are heavier in the reprints of 1864 than in the originals. The reprints of 1885 and 1905 can be distinguished only by the paper, gum and shades.

Reprints of 1953 have thick paper, no gum and dates "1853/1953" on back.

Values of lowest-cost reprints (1885) of Nos. 1-3, $50 each; of No. 4, $100.

King Pedro V
A5 A6

A7 A8

1855 **With Straight Hair**

TWENTY-FIVE REIS:
Type I - Pearls mostly touch each other and oval outer line.
Type II - Pearls are separate from each other and oval outer line.

5	A5	5r red brown	1,800.	225.00
6	A6	25r blue, type II	425.00	5.00
a.		25r blue, type I	600.00	10.00
7	A7	50r green	200.00	20.00
8	A8	100r lilac	400.00	25.00

Several types of No. 5 exist, differing in number of pearls encircling head (74 to 89) and other details.

All values were reprinted in 1885 and 1905. Value for lowest-cost, $15 each.

1856 **With Curled Hair**

TWENTY-FIVE REIS:
Type I - The network is fine (single lines).
Type II - The network is coarse (double lines).

9	A5	5r brown (shades)	140.00	12.00
10	A6	25r blue, type II	140.00	4.00
a.		25r blue, type I	*1,650.*	13.00

1858

11	A6	25r rose, type II	100.00	1.00

The 5r dark brown, formerly listed and sold at about $1, is now believed by the best authorities to be a reprint made before 1866. It is printed on thin yellowish white paper with yellowish white gum and is known only unused. The same remarks will apply to a 25r blue which is common unused but not known used. It is printed from a die which was not used for the issued stamps but the differences are slight and can only be told by expert comparison.

Nos. 9 and 10, also 10a in rose, were reprinted in 1885 and Nos. 9, 10, 10a and 11 in 1905. Value of lowest-cost reprints, $15 each.

King Luiz
A9 A10

A11 A12

A13

1862-64

FIVE REIS:
Type I - The distance between "5" and "reis" is 3mm.
Type II - The distance between "5" and "reis" is 2mm.

12	A9	5r brown, type I	30.00	2.75
a.		5r brown, type II	55.00	8.25

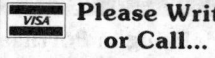

13	A10	10r orange	37.50	10.00
14	A11	25r rose	37.50	1.65
15	A12	50r yellow grn	265.00	20.00
16	A13	100r lilac ('64)	315.00	20.00

All values were reprinted in 1885 and all except the 25r in 1905. Value of lowest-cost reprints, $10 each.

King Luiz
A14 A15

1866-67 *Imperf.*

17	A14	5r black	45.00	3.75
18	A14	10r yellow	82.50	30.00
19	A14	20r bister	62.50	25.00
20	A14	25r rose ('67)	90.00	2.00
21	A14	50r green	110.00	25.00
22	A14	80r orange	110.00	25.00
23	A14	100r dk lil ('67)	120.00	30.00
24	A14	120r blue	130.00	25.00

Some values with unofficial percé en croix (diamond) perforation were used in Madeira.

All values were reprinted in 1885 and 1905. Value $10 each.

Typographed & Embossed

1867-70 *Perf. 12½*

25	A14	5r black	57.50	10.00
26	A14	10r yellow	110.00	35.00
27	A14	20r bister ('69)	135.00	35.00
28	A14	25r rose	27.50	1.00
29	A14	50r green ('68)	135.00	35.00
30	A14	80r orange ('69)	160.00	40.00
31	A14	100r lilac ('69)	135.00	35.00
32	A14	120r blue	145.00	20.00
33	A14	240r pale vio ('70)	390.00	150.00

Two types each of 5r and 100r differ in the position of the "5" at upper right and the "100" at lower right in relation to the end of the label.

Nos. 25-33 were reprinted in 1885 and 1905. Some of the 1885 reprints were perforated 12½ as well as 13½. Value of the lowest-cost reprints, $10 each.

1870-84 *Perf. 12½, 13½*

34	A15	5r black	10.00	4.00
a.		Imperf.	*350.00*	
b.		Perf. 11		150.00
c.		Perf. 14	65.00	24.00
35	A15	10r yel ('71)	27.50	8.50
a.		Imperf.	*350.00*	
b.		Perf. 11		150.00
c.		Perf. 14	120.00	65.00
36	A15	10r bl grn ('79)	95.00	47.50
37	A15	10r yel grn ('80)	40.00	7.25
38	A15	15r lil brn ('75)	32.50	6.00
39	A15	20r bister	24.00	3.50
a.		Imperf.	*350.00*	
b.		Perf. 11		150.00
40	A15	20r rose ('84)	125.00	15.00
41	A15	25r rose	9.50	75
a.		Imperf.	350.00	
b.		Perf. 11		150.00
c.		Perf. 14	120.00	3.50
42	A15	50r pale grn	47.50	3.50
b.		Perf. 11		175.00
43	A15	50r blue ('79)	95.00	9.00
44	A15	80r orange	35.00	1.75
a.		Perf. 14	165.00	110.00
b.		Perf. 11		175.00
45	A15	100r pale lil ('71)	22.50	1.50
a.		Perf. 14	210.00	110.00
46	A15	120r bl, perf. 12½ ('71)	115.00	27.50
a.		Perf. 13½		
47	A15	150r pale bl ('76)	135.00	42.50
b.		Perf. 13½	275.00	70.00
48	A15	150r yellow ('80)	47.50	3.00
49	A15	240r pale vio ('73)	600.00	200.00
b.		Perf. 11		
50	A15	300r dl vio ('76)	47.50	6.00
51	A15	1000r black ('84)	90.00	20.00

Two types each of 15r, 20r and 80r differ in the distance between the figures of value.

For overprints and surcharges see Nos. 86-87, 94-96.

All values of the issues of 1870-84 were reprinted in 1885 and 1905. Value of the lowest-cost reprints, $10 each.

King Luiz
A16 A17

A18 A19

1880-81 **Typo.** *Perf. 12½, 13½*

52	A16	5r black	9.00	90
53	A17	25r bluish gray	100.00	6.00
54	A18	25r gray	9.00	85
55	A18	25r brn vio ('81)	9.00	85
56	A19	50r blue ('81)	100.00	4.00

All values were reprinted in 1885 and 1905. Value of the lowest-cost reprints, $5 each.

A20 A21

King Luiz
A22 A23

A24 A24a

1882-87 *Perf. 11½, 12½, 13½*

57	A20	2r black ('84)	4.00	3.25
58	A21	5r black ('83)	4.25	45
59	A22	10r green ('84)	10.50	85
60	A23	25r brown	7.25	55
61	A24	50r blue	11.00	45
62	A24a	500r black ('84)	175.00	100.00
63	A24a	500r vio, perf. 12½ ('87)	100.00	15.00
a.		Perf. 13½	150.00	50.00

For overprints see Nos. 79-82, 85, 88-89, 93.

The stamps of the 1882-87 issues were reprinted in 1885, 1893 and 1905. Value of the lowest-cost reprints, $5 each.

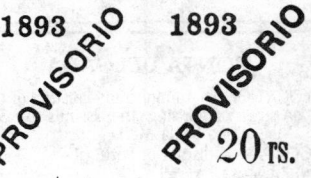

A25 A26

1887 *Perf. 11½*

64	A25	20r rose	18.00	4.00
65	A26	25r violet	10.50	35
66	A26	25r lilac rose	10.50	35

For overprints see Nos. 83-84, 90-92.

Nos. 64-66 were reprinted in 1905. Value $5 each.

King Carlos — A27

1892-93 *Perf. 11½, 12½, 13½*

67	A27	5r orange	4.00	40
68	A27	10r redsh vio	9.25	40
69	A27	15r chocolate	4.75	1.25
70	A27	20r lavender	8.00	1.50
71	A27	25r dk green	9.25	40
72	A27	50r blue	12.00	1.00
73	A27	75r car ('93)	25.00	1.50
a.		Perf. 11½	80.00	3.50
74	A27	80r yellow grn	27.50	10.00
75	A27	100r brn, *buff* ('93)	21.00	1.00
a.		Perf. 11½	100.00	3.50
76	A27	150r car, *rose* ('93)	47.50	10.00
77	A27	200r dk bl, *bl* ('93)	47.50	12.50
78	A27	300r dk bl, *sal* ('93)	52.50	14.00

Nos. 76-78 were reprinted in 1900 (perf. 11½), and all values in 1905 (perf. 13½). Values of the lowest-cost reprints of Nos. 67-75, $6 each; of Nos. 76-78, $12 each.

Stamps and Types of Previous Issues Overprinted in Black or Red:

PROVISORIO
a

PROVISORIO
b

PROVISORIO
c

1892

79	A21 (a)	5r gray blk	7.00	2.00
a.		Double overprint	240.00	90.00
80	A22 (b)	10r green	7.00	2.75
a.		Inverted overprint		
b.		Double overprint	240.00	100.00

1892-93

81	A21 (c)	5r gray blk (R)	4.75	3.00
82	A22 (c)	10r green (R)	5.75	3.25
a.		Inverted overprint	80.00	80.00
83	A25 (c)	20r rose	10.50	4.75
84	A26 (c)	25r rose lilac	5.25	2.00
85	A24 (c)	50r bl (R) ('93)	25.00	20.00

1893

86	A15 (c)	15r bis brn (R)	4.00	3.00
87	A15 (c)	80r yellow	35.00	30.00

Nos. 86-87 are found in two types each. See note below No. 51.

Some of Nos. 79-87 were reprinted in 1900 and all values in 1905. Value of lowest-cost reprint, $10.

Stamps and Types of Previous Issues Overprinted or Surcharged in Black or Red:

1893 PROVISORIO
d

1893 PROVISORIO 20 rs.
e

1893 *Perf. 11½, 12½*

88	A21 (d)	5r gray blk (R)	7.50	5.25
89	A22 (d)	10r green (R)	9.00	7.00
a.		"1938"	85.00	62.50
b.		"1863"	85.00	62.50
90	A25 (d)	20r rose	20.00	10.00
a.		Inverted overprint		
91	A26 (e)	20r on 25r lil rose	16.00	14.00
92	A26 (d)	25r lilac rose	45.00	30.00
a.		Inverted overprint	100.00	100.00
93	A24 (d)	50r blue (R)	40.00	25.00

Perf. 12½

94	A15 (e)	50r on 80r yel	50.00	40.00
95	A15 (e)	75r on 80r yel	30.00	25.00
96	A15 (d)	80r yellow	35.00	27.50

Nos. 94-96 are found in two types each. See note below No. 51.

Some of Nos. 88-96 were reprinted in 1900 and all values in 1905. Value of lowest-cost reprint, $10 each.

Prince Henry on his Ship — A46

Prince Henry Directing Fleet Maneuvers — A47

Symbolic of Prince Henry's Studies — A48

1894 Litho. Perf. 14

No.	Type	Description	Unused	Used
97	A46	5r orange	2.00	60
98	A46	10r magenta	2.50	60
99	A46	15r red brown	3.75	1.40
100	A46	20r dull vio	4.75	2.00
101	A47	25r gray grn	3.75	80
102	A47	50r blue	8.00	2.00
103	A47	75r car rose	15.00	4.75
104	A47	80r yellow grn	18.00	6.50
105	A47	100r lt brn, *pale buff*	13.00	4.75

Engr.

No.	Type	Description	Unused	Used
106	A48	150r lt car, *pale rose*	35.00	8.00
107	A48	300r dk bl, *sal buff*	45.00	12.00
108	A48	500r dp vio, *pale lil*	100.00	30.00
109	A48	1000r gray blk, *grysh*	125.00	37.50
		Nos. 97-109 (13)	375.75	110.90

5th centenary of the birth of Prince Henry the Navigator.

King Carlos — A49

1895-1905 Typo. Perf. 11½
Value in Black or Red (#122, 500r)

No.	Type	Description	Unused	Used
110	A49	2½r gray	15	15
a.		Imperf.		
111	A49	5r orange	15	15
112	A49	10r lt green	20	15
113	A49	15r brown	32.50	1.10
114	A49	15r gray grn ('99)	16.00	95
115	A49	20r gray vio	22	18
116	A49	25r sea green	25.00	16
117	A49	25r car rose ('99)	15	15
118	A49	50r blue	32.50	25
119	A49	50r ultra ('05)	20	15
120	A49	65r slate bl ('98)	20	15
121	A49	75r rose	35.00	1.50
122	A49	75r brn, *yel* ('05)	45	38
123	A49	80r violet	75	55
124	A49	100r dk bl, *bl*	32	25
125	A49	115r org brn, *pink* ('98)	1.65	1.25
126	A49	130r gray brn, *straw* ('98)	1.10	55
127	A49	150r lt brn, *straw*	37.50	7.50
128	A49	180r sl, *pnksh* ('98)	4.75	4.50
129	A49	200r red lil, *pnksh*	1.10	40
130	A49	300r blue, *rose*	1.25	40
131	A49	500r blk, *bl* ('96)	2.75	1.90
a.		Perf. 12½	47.50	10.00
		Nos. 110-131 (22)	193.89	22.72

Several values of the above type exist without figures of value, also with figures inverted or otherwise misplaced but they were not regularly issued.

St. Anthony and his Vision — A50

St. Anthony Ascends to Heaven — A52

St. Anthony Preaching to Fishes — A51

St. Anthony, from Portrait — A53

Perf. 11½, 12½ and Compound

1895 Typo.

No.	Type	Description	Unused	Used
132	A50	2½r black	3.75	65

Litho.

No.	Type	Description	Unused	Used
133	A51	5r brown org	4.25	85
134	A51	10r red lilac	7.75	3.25
135	A51	15r chocolate	10.50	3.50
136	A51	20r gray vio	10.50	3.50
137	A51	25r grn & vio	7.75	65
138	A52	50r blue & brn	22.50	6.75
139	A52	75r rose & brn	32.50	16.00
140	A52	80r lt grn & brn	37.50	20.00
141	A52	100r choc & blk	35.00	12.00
142	A53	150r carmine & bis	92.50	42.50
143	A53	200r blue & bis	82.50	40.00
144	A53	300r slate & bis	100.00	50.00
145	A53	500r vio brn & grn	225.00	110.00
146	A53	1000r violet & grn	325.00	150.00
		Nos. 132-146 (15)	997.00	459.65

7th centenary of the birth of Saint Anthony of Padua. Stamps have eulogy in Latin printed on the back.

Vasco da Gama Issue
Common Design Types

1898 Engr. Perf. 12½ to 16

No.	Type	Description	Unused	Used
147	CD20	2½r blue grn	50	20
148	CD21	5r red	50	20
149	CD22	10r red vio	3.00	65
150	CD23	25r yellow grn	2.25	22
151	CD24	50r dk blue	3.75	1.65
152	CD25	75r violet brn	14.00	4.75
153	CD26	100r bister brn	12.00	4.00
154	CD27	150r bister	20.00	12.00
		Nos. 147-154 (8)	56.00	23.67

For overprints and surcharges see Nos. 185-192, 199-206.

King Manuel II
A62 A63

1910 Typo. Perf. 14½x15

No.	Type	Description	Unused	Used
156	A62	2½r violet	20	15
157	A62	5r black	20	15
158	A62	10r gray grn	28	15
159	A62	15r lilac brn	1.25	80
160	A62	20r carmine	60	45
161	A62	25r violet brn	28	15
162	A62	50r dk blue	65	30
163	A62	75r bister brn	3.75	2.25
164	A62	80r slate	1.25	1.10
165	A62	100r brn, *lt grn*	5.25	1.65
166	A62	200r dk grn, *sal*	2.75	1.90
167	A62	300r blk, *azure*	3.50	2.75
168	A63	500r ol grn & vio brn	6.75	5.75
169	A63	1000r dk bl & blk	16.00	14.00
		Nos. 156-169 (14)	42.71	31.55

For overprint see No. RA1.

Preceding Issue Overprinted in Carmine or Green

1910

No.	Type	Description	Unused	Used
170	A62	2½r violet	25	15
171	A62	5r black	24	15
172	A62	10r gray grn	1.40	38
173	A62	15r lilac brn	35	30
174	A62	20r car (G)	1.75	90
175	A62	25r violet brn	45	15
176	A62	50r dk blue	3.25	1.00
177	A62	75r bister brn	4.50	2.00
178	A62	80r slate	1.40	1.00
179	A62	100r brn, *lt grn*	75	35
180	A62	200r dk grn, *sal*	1.25	90
181	A62	300r blk, *azure*	1.90	1.75
182	A63	500r ol grn & vio brn	4.50	4.25
183	A63	1000r dk bl & blk	9.75	8.50
		Nos. 170-183 (14)	31.74	21.78

The numerous inverted and double overprints on this issue were unofficially and fraudulently made. The 50r with blue overprint is a fraud.

Vasco da Gama Issue Overprinted or Surcharged:

REPUBLICA
a

REPUBLICA **REPUBLICA**

REIS 15 REIS
b

1$000
c

1911 Perf. 12½ to 16

No.	Type	Description	Unused	Used
185	CD20(a)	2½r blue grn	20	15
a.		Inverted overprint	14.00	14.00
186	CD21(b)	15r on 5r red	28	15
a.		Inverted surcharge	14.00	14.00
187	CD23(a)	25r yel grn	28	15
188	CD24(a)	50r dk blue	1.50	55
a.		Inverted overprint	22.50	22.50
189	CD25(a)	75r vio brn	18.00	13.00
190	CD27(b)	80r on 150r bis	2.50	1.65
191	CD26(a)	100r bis brn	2.50	1.00
a.		Inverted overprint	25.00	25.00
192	CD22(c)	1000r on 10r red vio	20.00	14.00
		Nos. 185-192 (8)	45.26	30.65

Common Design Types pictured in section at front of book.

Postage Due Stamps of 1898 Overprinted or Surcharged for Regular Postage:

REPUBLICA

REPUBLICA
d

Rs 300 Rs
e

1911 Perf. 12

No.	Type	Description	Unused	Used
193	D1(d)	5r black	24	15
a.		Double ovpt., one inverted	16.00	16.00
194	D1(d)	10r magenta	35	22
195	D1(d)	20r orange	1.50	90
196	D1(d)	200r brn, *buff*	21.00	14.00
197	D1(e)	300r on 50r slate	15.00	10.50
198	D1(e)	500r on 100r car, *pink*	7.75	5.25
a.		Inverted surcharge	37.50	32.50
		Nos. 193-198 (6)	45.84	31.02

Vasco da Gama Issue of Madeira Overprinted or Surcharged Types "a," "b" and "c"

1911 Perf. 12½ to 16

No.	Type	Description	Unused	Used
199	CD20(a)	2½r blue grn	1.10	85
a.		Double overprint		
200	CD21(b)	15r on 5r red	1.00	85
a.		Inverted surcharge	12.50	12.50
201	CD23(a)	25r yellow grn	2.50	2.00
202	CD24(a)	50r dk blue	4.25	3.00
a.		Inverted overprint	25.00	25.00
203	CD25(a)	75r violet brn	3.25	2.25
a.		Inverted overprint	18.00	18.00
204	CD27(b)	80r on 150r bis	4.25	2.50
a.		Inverted surcharge	25.00	25.00
205	CD26(a)	100r bister brn	9.00	3.00
a.		Inverted overprint	25.00	25.00
206	CD22(c)	1000r on 10r red vio	9.00	8.50
		Nos. 199-206 (8)	34.35	22.95

Ceres — A64

With Imprint

1912-31 Typo. Perf. 15x14, 12x11½

No.	Type	Description	Unused	Used
207	A64	¼c dk olive	15	15
208	A64	½c black	15	15
209	A64	1c dp green	60	15
210	A64	1c choc ('18)	15	15
211	A64	1½c chocolate	2.00	70
212	A64	1½c dp grn ('18)	15	15
213	A64	2c carmine	2.25	65
214	A64	2c org ('18)	15	15
215	A64	2c yel ('24)	15	15
216	A64	2c choc ('26)	16	*20.00*
217	A64	2½c violet	15	15
218	A64	3c car rose ('17)	15	15
219	A64	3c ultra ('21)	15	15
220	A64	3½c lt grn ('18)	15	15
221	A64	4c lt grn ('19)	15	15
222	A64	4c org ('26)	16	20
223	A64	5c dp bl	1.50	20
224	A64	5c yel brn ('18)	42	15
225	A64	5c ol brn ('23)	15	15
226	A64	5c blk brn ('31)	15	15
227	A64	6c pale rose ('20)	15	15
228	A64	6c brown ('24)	15	15
229	A64	6c red brn ('30)	15	15
230	A64	7½c yel brn	2.50	50
231	A64	7½c dp bl ('18)	15	15
232	A64	8c slate	20	15
233	A64	8c bl grn ('22)	15	15
234	A64	8c org ('24)	15	15
235	A64	10c orange brn	15	15
236	A64	10c red ('31)	15	15
237	A64	12c bl gray ('20)	75	40
238	A64	12c dp grn ('21)	25	15
239	A64	13½c chlky bl ('20)	35	22
240	A64	14c dk bl, *yel* ('20)	65	90
241	A64	14c brt vio ('21)	16	50
242	A64	15c plum	90	35
243	A64	15c black ('23)	15	15
244	A64	16c brt ultra ('24)	24	55
245	A64	20c vio brn, *grn*	6.00	85
246	A64	20c brn, *buff* ('20)	6.00	1.00
247	A64	20c dk brn ('21)	20	15
248	A64	20c dp grn ('23)	15	15
249	A64	20c gray ('24)	15	15
250	A64	24c grnsh bl ('21)	20	15
251	A64	25c sal pink ('23)	15	15
252	A64	25c lt gray ('26)	35	15
253	A64	25c bl grn ('30)	35	15
254	A64	30c brn, *pink*	47.50	4.00
255	A64	30c lt brn, *yel* ('17)	2.50	85
256	A64	30c gray brn ('21)	20	15
257	A64	30c dk brn ('24)	4.25	1.50
258	A64	32c dp grn ('24)	24	15
259	A64	36c red ('21)	24	15
260	A64	40c dk bl ('23)	22	22
261	A64	40c choc ('24)	15	25
262	A64	40c grn ('26)	20	15
263	A64	48c rose ('24)	90	60
264	A64	50c org, *sal*	5.00	65
265	A64	50c yel ('21)	35	15
266	A64	50c bis ('30)	90	40
267	A64	50c red brn ('30)	90	25
268	A64	60c blue ('21)	45	22
269	A64	64c pale ultra ('24)	1.10	1.25
270	A64	75c dl rose ('23)	3.25	2.50
271	A64	75c car rose ('30)	90	32
272	A64	80c brn rose ('21)	70	32
273	A64	80c vio ('24)	22	20
274	A64	80c dk grn ('30)	90	32
275	A64	90c chalky bl ('21)	60	22
276	A64	96c dp rose ('26)	8.50	10.00
277	A64	1e dp grn, *bl*	6.00	85
278	A64	1e vio ('21)	1.40	60
a.		Perf. 15x14	52.50	8.00
279	A64	1e dk bl ('23)	1.25	85
280	A64	1e gray vio ('24)	38	22
281	A64	1e brn lake ('30)	3.25	50
282	A64	1.10e yel brn ('21)	1.40	52
283	A64	1.20e yel grn ('21)	75	42
284	A64	1.20e buff ('24)	15.00	13.00
285	A64	1.20e pur brn ('31)	1.25	50
286	A64	1.25e dk bl ('31)	1.10	50
287	A64	1.50e blk vio ('23)	2.50	1.10
288	A64	1.50e lilac ('24)	3.50	1.65
289	A64	1.60e dp bl ('24)	2.50	65
290	A64	2e sl grn ('21)	21.00	1.00
291	A64	2e red vio ('31)	11.00	3.50
292	A64	2.40e ap grn ('26)	52.50	47.50
293	A64	3e pink ('26)	50.00	47.50
294	A64	3.20e gray grn ('24)	5.50	4.75
295	A64	4.50e org ('31)	30.00	17.00
296	A64	5e emer ('24)	5.00	2.00
297	A64	10e pink ('24)	37.50	14.00
298	A64	20e pale turq ('24)	100.00	75.00
		Nos. 207-298 (92)	462.89	290.40

For surcharges and overprints see Nos. 453-495, RA2.

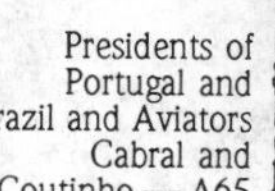

Presidents of Portugal and Brazil and Aviators Cabral and Coutinho — A65

1923 Litho. Perf. 14

No.	Type	Description	Unused	Used
299	A65	1c brown	15	*30*
300	A65	2c orange	15	*30*
301	A65	3c ultra	15	*30*
302	A65	4c yellow grn	15	*30*
303	A65	5c bister brn	15	*30*
304	A65	10c brown org	15	*30*
305	A65	15c black	15	*30*
306	A65	20c blue grn	15	*30*
307	A65	25c rose	15	*30*
308	A65	30c olive brn	42	*1.25*
309	A65	40c chocolate	15	*22*
310	A65	50c yellow	15	*35*
311	A65	75c violet	15	*45*
312	A65	1e dp blue	25	*55*
313	A65	1.50e olive grn	42	*1.25*
314	A65	2e myrtle grn	70	*2.00*
		Set value	2.75	

Flight of Sacadura Cabral and Gago Coutinho from Portugal to Brazil.

Camoens at Ceuta — A66

Camoens Saving the Lusiads — A67

Luis de Camoens — A68

First Edition of the Lusiads — A69

Monument to Camoens — A72

Camoens Dying — A70

Tomb of Camoens A71

Engr.; Values Typo. in Black

1924, Nov. 11 *Perf. 14, 14½*

315	A66	2c	lt blue	15	15
316	A66	3c	orange	15	15
317	A66	4c	dk gray	15	15
318	A66	5c	yellow grn	15	15
319	A66	6c	lake	15	15
320	A67	8c	org brn	15	15
321	A67	10c	gray vio	15	15
322	A67	15c	olive grn	15	15
323	A67	16c	vio brn	15	15
324	A67	20c	dp orange	15	15
325	A68	25c	lilac	15	15
326	A68	30c	dk brown	15	15
327	A68	32c	dk green	22	22
328	A68	40c	ultra	15	15
329	A68	48c	red brn	50	70
330	A69	50c	red org	60	65
331	A69	64c	green	60	65
332	A69	75c	dk violet	60	65
333	A69	80c	bister	50	60
334	A69	96c	lake	50	60
335	A70	1e	slate	40	45
336	A70	1.20e	lt brown	90	65
337	A70	1.50e	red	55	60
338	A70	1.60e	dk blue	55	65
339	A70	2e	apple grn	1.00	70
340	A71	2.40e	green, *grn*	1.50	90
341	A71	3e	dk bl, *bl*	60	65
a.			Value double	60.00	
b.			Value omitted		
342	A71	3.20e	blk, *green*	60	65
343	A71	4.50e	blk, *orange*	1.50	1.25
344	A71	10e	dk brn, *pnksh*	2.75	2.75
345	A72	20e	dk vio, *lil*	3.50	2.75
			Nos. 315-345 (31)	19.32	18.02

400th anniversary of the birth of Luis de Camoens, poet.

For overprints see Nos. 1S6-1S71.

Castello-Branco's House at Sao Miguel de Seide — A73

Castello-Branco's Study — A74

Camillo Castello-Branco A75

Teresa de Albuquerque A76

Mariana and Joao de Cruz — A77

Simao de Botelho — A78

1925, Mar. 26 *Perf. 12½*

346	A73	2c	orange	15	15
347	A73	3c	green	15	15
348	A73	4c	ultra	15	15
349	A73	5c	scarlet	15	15
350	A73	6c	brown vio	15	15
a.			"6" and "C" omitted		
351	A73	8c	blk brn	15	15
352	A74	10c	pale bl	15	15
353	A75	15c	ol grn	15	15
354	A74	16c	red org	18	15
355	A74	20c	dk vio	15	15
356	A75	25c	car rose	18	15
357	A74	30c	bis brn	18	15
358	A74	32c	green	40	55
359	A75	40c	grn & blk	18	15
360	A74	48c	red brn	70	1.10
361	A76	50c	bl grn	30	30
362	A76	64c	org brn	1.10	1.65
363	A76	75c	gray blk	40	55
364	A75	80c	brown	40	55
365	A76	96c	car rose	60	85
366	A76	1e	gray vio	40	40
367	A76	1.20e	yel grn	60	65
368	A77	1.50e	dk bl, *bl*	5.25	7.00
369	A75	1.60e	indigo	1.75	2.00
370	A77	2e	dk grn, *grn*	2.25	2.00
371	A77	2.40e	red, *org*	16.00	15.00
372	A77	3e	lake, *bl*	22.50	25.00
373	A77	3.20e	*green*	10.50	15.00
374	A75	4.50e	red & blk	5.25	2.00
375	A77	10e	brn, *yel*	5.25	2.00
376	A78	20e	*orange*	5.75	60
			Nos. 346-376 (31)	81.47	79.15

Centenary of the birth of Camillo Castello-Branco, novelist.

First Independence Issue

Alfonso the Conqueror, First King of Portugal — A79

Batalha Monastery and King John I — A80

Battle of Aljubarrota — A81

Filipa de Vilhena Arming her Sons — A82

King John IV (The Duke of Braganza) A83

Independence Monument, Lisbon A84

1926, Aug. 13 *Perf. 14, 14½*

Center in Black

377	A79	2c	orange	15	*24*
378	A80	3c	ultra	15	*24*
379	A79	4c	yellow grn	15	*24*
380	A80	5c	black brn	15	*24*
381	A79	6c	ocher	15	*24*
382	A80	15c	dk green	15	*24*
383	A79	16c	dp blue	28	*90*
384	A81	20c	dull vio	30	*90*
385	A82	25c	scarlet	30	*1.10*
386	A81	32c	dp green	38	*80*
387	A82	40c	yellow brn	15	*24*
388	A80	46c	carmine	70	*1.75*
389	A82	50c	olive bis	70	*1.75*
390	A83	64c	blue grn	1.10	*2.00*
391	A82	75c	red brn	1.10	*2.00*
392	A84	96c	dull red	1.50	*3.00*
393	A83	1e	black vio	1.75	*4.00*
394	A81	1.60e	myrtle grn	2.50	*4.00*
395	A84	3e	plum	8.00	*12.00*
396	A84	4.50e	olive grn	9.00	*16.00*
397	A81	10e	carmine	10.00	*20.00*
			Nos. 377-397 (21)	38.66	*71.88*

The use of these stamps instead of the regular issue was obligatory on Aug. 13th and 14th, Nov. 30th and Dec. 1st, 1926.

Surcharged with Bars and

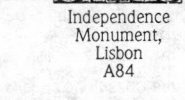

2 C.

1926

Center in Black

397A	A80	2c on 5c blk brn	50	*1.10*
397B	A80	2c on 46c car	60	*1.10*
397C	A83	2c on 64c bl grn	50	*80*
397D	A82	3c on 75c red brn	50	*80*
397E	A84	3c on 96c dl red	75	*1.25*
397F	A83	3c on 1e blk vio	55	*90*
397G	A81	4c on 1.60e myr grn	3.50	*5.50*
397H	A84	4c on 3e plum	1.65	*4.00*
397J	A84	6c on 4.50e ol grn	1.65	*4.00*
397K	A81	6c on 10e car	1.65	*4.00*
		Nos. 397A-397K (10)	11.85	*23.45*

There are two styles of the ornaments in these surcharges.

Ceres — A85

Without Imprint

1926, Dec. 2 **Typo.** *Perf. 13½x14*

398	A85	2c	chocolate	15	15
399	A85	3c	brt blue	15	15
400	A85	4c	dp orange	15	15
401	A85	5c	dp brown	15	15
402	A85	6c	orange brn	15	15
403	A85	10c	orange red	15	15
404	A85	15c	black	15	15
405	A85	16c	ultra	15	15
406	A85	25c	gray	15	15
407	A85	32c	dp green	15	25
408	A85	40c	blue grn	15	15
409	A85	48c	rose	40	45
410	A85	50c	ocher	32	40
411	A85	64c	dp blue	35	50
412	A85	80c	violet	85	22
413	A85	96c	car rose	50	55
414	A85	1e	red brown	2.75	22
415	A85	1.20e	yel brn	3.00	22
416	A85	1.60e	dk blue	38	15
417	A85	2e	green	4.75	32
418	A85	3.20e	olive grn	1.40	55
419	A85	4.50e	yellow	1.25	22
420	A85	5e	brn olive	30.00	35
421	A85	10e	red	1.75	28
			Nos. 398-421 (24)	49.35	
			Set value		5.00

Second Independence Issue

Gonalo Mendes da Maia — A86

Dr. Joao das Regras — A88

Guimaraes Castle — A87

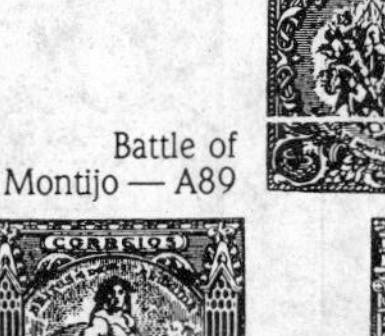

Battle of Montijo — A89

Brites de Almeida — A90

Joao Pinto Ribeiro — A91

1927, Nov. 29 **Engr.** *Perf. 14*

Center in Black

422	A86	2c	brown	15	15
423	A87	3c	ultra	15	15
424	A86	4c	orange	15	15
425	A88	5c	olive brn	15	15
426	A89	6c	orange brn	15	15
427	A87	15c	black brn	15	15
428	A88	16c	dp blue	24	*50*
429	A86	25c	gray	24	*50*
430	A89	32c	blue grn	60	*85*
431	A90	40c	yellow grn	18	*30*
432	A86	48c	brown red	2.75	*5.00*
433	A87	80c	dk violet	2.25	*5.00*
434	A90	96c	dull red	3.25	*7.00*
435	A88	1.60e	myrtle grn	4.00	*7.50*
436	A91	4.50e	bister	5.00	*9.00*
			Nos. 422-436 (15)	19.41	*36.55*

The use of these stamps instead of the regular issue was compulsory on Nov. 29-30, Dec. 1-2, 1927. The money derived from their sale was used for the purchase of a palace for a war museum, the organization of an international exposition in Lisbon, in 1940, and for fêtes to be held in that year in commemoration of the 8th cent. of the founding of Portugal and the 3rd cent. of its restoration.

Third Independence Issue

Gualdim Paes — A93

The Siege of Santarem — A94

Battle of Rolica — A95

Battle of Atoleiros — A96

Joana de Gouveia — A97

Matias de Albuquerque — A98

1928, Nov. 28

Center in Black

No.	Type	Denom.	Color	Unused	Used
437	A93	2c	lt blue	15	15
438	A94	3c	lt green	15	15
439	A95	4c	lake	15	15
440	A96	5c	olive grn	15	15
441	A97	6c	orange brn	15	15
442	A94	15c	slate	20	*45*
443	A95	16c	dk violet	20	*45*
444	A93	25c	ultra	24	*50*
445	A97	32c	dk green	1.00	*2.50*
446	A96	40c	olive brn	16	*25*
447	A95	50c	red org	3.00	*4.00*
448	A94	80c	lt gray	2.50	*5.50*
449	A97	96c	carmine	5.25	*13.00*
450	A96	1e	claret	8.50	*16.00*
451	A93	1.60e	dk blue	3.25	*7.50*
452	A98	4.50e	yellow	3.25	*7.50*
			Nos. 437-452 (16)	28.30	*58.40*

Obligatory Nov. 27-30. See note after No. 436.

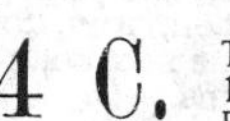

Type of and Stamps of 1912-28 Surcharged in Black

1928-29 *Perf. 12x11½, 15x14*

No.	Type	Denom.	Description	Unused	Used
453	A64	4c	on 8c orange	15	15
454	A64	4c	on 30c dk brn	15	15
455	A64	10c	on ¼c dk ol	15	15
a.			Inverted surcharge	5.00	
456	A64	10c	on ½c blk (R)	20	15
a.			Perf. 15x14	50	30
457	A64	10c	on 1c choc	15	15
a.			Perf. 15x14	*30.00*	*30.00*
458	A64	10c	on 4c grn	15	15
a.			Perf. 15x14	*40.00*	*55.00*
459	A64	10c	on 4c org	15	15
460	A64	10c	on 5c ol brn	15	15
461	A64	15c	on 16c blue	15	20
462	A64	15c	on 16c ultra	50	50
463	A64	15c	on 20c brn	15.00	15.00
464	A64	15c	on 20c gray	15	20
465	A64	15c	on 24c grnsh bl	65	32
466	A64	15c	on 25c gray	15	15
467	A64	15c	on 25c sal pink	15	15
468	A64	16c	on 32c dp grn	25	40
469	A64	40c	on 2c orange	15	15
470	A64	40c	on 2c yellow	1.25	3.25
471	A64	40c	on 2c choc	15	15
472	A64	40c	on 3c ultra	15	15
473	A64	40c	on 50c yellow	15	15
474	A64	40c	on 60c dl bl	25	22
a.			Perf. 15x14	4.00	3.25
475	A64	40c	on 64c pale ultra	25	25
476	A64	40c	on 75c dl rose	25	25
477	A64	40c	on 80c violet	22	22
478	A64	40c	on 90c chlky bl	2.00	1.50
a.			Perf. 15x14	3.25	3.00
479	A64	40c	on 1e gray vio	22	32
480	A64	40c	on 1.10e yel brn	22	32
481	A64	80c	on 6c pale rose	22	32
482	A64	80c	on 6c choc	22	25
483	A64	80c	on 48c rose	32	42
484	A64	80c	on 1.50e lilac	50	42
485	A64	96c	on 1.20e yel grn	1.25	1.10
486	A64	96c	on 1.20e buff	1.65	1.50
487	A64	1.60e	on 2e slate grn	8.00	8.00
488	A64	1.60e	on 3.20e gray grn	3.50	3.25
489	A64	1.60e	on 20e pale turq	4.50	4.00
			Nos. 453-489 (37)	43.67	44.31

Stamps of 1912-26 Overprinted in Black or Red

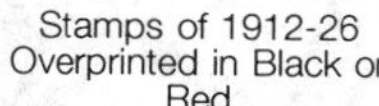

1929 *Perf. 12x11½*

No.	Type	Denom.	Color	Unused	Used
490	A64	10c	orange brn	15	15
a.			Perf. 15x14	70.00	70.00
491	A64	15c	black (R)	15	15
492	A64	40c	lt green	15	15
493	A64	40c	chocolate	15	15
494	A64	96c	dp rose	1.65	1.25
495	A64	1.60e	brt blue	4.00	4.00
a.			Double overprint		
			Nos. 490-495 (6)	6.25	5.85

Liberty A100

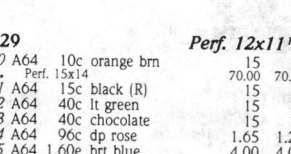

"Portugal" Holding Volume of "Lusiads" A101

1929, May *Perf. 12x11½*

No.	Type	Denom.	Description	Unused	Used
496	A100	1.60e	on 5c red brn	2.25	2.50

1931-38 **Typo.** *Perf. 14*

No.	Type	Denom.	Color	Unused	Used
497	A101	4c	bister brn	15	15
498	A101	5c	olive gray	15	15
499	A101	6c	lt gray	15	15
500	A101	10c	dk violet	15	15
501	A101	15c	gray blk	15	15
502	A101	16c	brt blue	35	18
503	A101	25c	deep green	1.25	15
a.			Imperf.		
504	A101	25c	brt bl ('33)	1.25	18
505	A101	30c	dk grn ('33)	52	18
506	A101	40c	org red	3.00	15
507	A101	48c	fawn	32	25
508	A101	50c	lt brown	15	15
509	A101	75c	car rose	1.50	55
510	A101	80c	emerald	15	15
511	A101	95c	car rose ('33)	4.50	2.50
512	A101	1e	claret	13.00	15
513	A101	1.20e	ol grn	85	55
514	A101	1.25e	dk blue	65	15
515	A101	1.60e	dk bl ('33)	9.25	1.50
516	A101	1.75e	dk bl ('38)	15	15
517	A101	2e	dull vio	22	15
518	A101	4.50e	orange	52	15
519	A101	5e	yellow grn	52	15
			Nos. 497-519 (23)	38.90	8.14

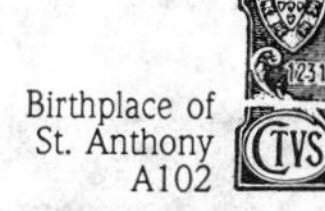

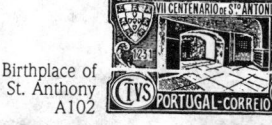

Birthplace of St. Anthony A102

Font where St. Anthony was Baptized A103

Lisbon Cathedral A104

St. Anthony with Infant Jesus A105

Santa Cruz Cathedral A106

St. Anthony's Tomb at Padua A107

1931, June **Typo.** *Perf. 12*

No.	Type	Denom.	Color	Unused	Used
528	A102	15c	plum	15	15

Litho.

No.	Type	Denom.	Color	Unused	Used
529	A103	25c	gray & pale grn	30	18
530	A104	40c	gray brn & buff	18	15
531	A105	75c	dl rose & pale rose	7.25	5.25
532	A106	1.25e	gray & pale bl	14.00	7.50
533	A107	4.50e	gray vio & lil	7.25	1.25
			Nos. 528-533 (6)	29.13	14.48

7th centenary of the death of St. Anthony of Padua and Lisbon.

For surcharges see Nos. 543-548.

Nuno Alvares Pereira (1360-1431), Portuguese Warrior and Statesman — A108

1931, Nov. 1 **Typo.** *Perf. 12x11½*

No.	Type	Denom.	Color	Unused	Used
534	A108	15c	black	42	42
535	A108	25c	gray grn & blk	42	40
536	A108	40c	orange	85	40
a.			Value omitted	30.00	30.00
537	A108	75c	car rose	6.50	5.50
538	A108	1.25e	dk bl & pale bl	10.00	6.00
539	A108	4.50e	choc & lt grn	47.50	24.00
a.			Value omitted	105.00	105.00
			Nos. 534-539 (6)	65.69	36.72

For surcharges see Nos. 549-554.

Nos. 528-533 Surcharged **40 C.**

1933 *Perf. 12*

No.	Type	Denom.	Description	Unused	Used
543	A104	15c	on 40c	32	20
544	A102	40c	on 15c	85	55
545	A103	40c	on 25c	60	25
546	A105	40c	on 75c	3.25	2.00
547	A106	40c	on 1.25e	3.25	2.00
548	A107	40c	on 4.50e	3.25	2.00
			Nos. 543-548 (6)	11.52	7.00

Nos. 534-539 Surcharged **15 C.**

1933 *Perf. 12x11½*

No.	Type	Denom.	Description	Unused	Used
549	A108	15c	on 40c	30	22
550	A108	40c	on 15c	1.25	1.10
551	A108	40c	on 25c	40	32
552	A108	40c	on 75c	3.25	2.75
553	A108	40c	on 1.25e	3.25	2.75
554	A108	40c	on 4.50e	3.25	2.75
			Nos. 549-554 (6)	11.70	9.89

President Carmona A109

Head of a Colonial A110

1934, May 28 **Typo.** *Perf. 11½*

No.	Type	Denom.	Color	Unused	Used
556	A109	40c	brt violet	5.00	15

1934, July *Perf. 11½x12*

No.	Type	Denom.	Color	Unused	Used
558	A110	25c	dk brown	65	22
559	A110	40c	scarlet	3.75	15
560	A110	1.60e	dk blue	9.25	5.00

Colonial Exposition.

Roman Temple, Evora A111

Prince Henry the Navigator A112

"All for the Nation" A113

Coimbra Cathedral A114

1935-41 *Perf. 11½x12*

No.	Type	Denom.	Color	Unused	Used
561	A111	4c	black	15	15
562	A111	5c	blue	15	15
563	A111	6c	choc ('36)	15	15

Perf. 11½, 12x11½ (1.75e)

No.	Type	Denom.	Color	Unused	Used
564	A112	10c	turq grn	24	15
565	A112	15c	red brown	15	15
a.			Booklet pane of 4		
566	A113	25c	dp blue	2.75	15
a.			Booklet pane of 4		
567	A113	40c	brown	55	15
a.			Booklet pane of 4		
568	A113	1e	rose red	2.75	20
568A	A114	1.75e	blue	10.00	52
568B	A113	10e	gray blk ('41)	3.80	75
569	A113	20e	turq grn ('41)	4.75	60
			Nos. 561-569 (11)	25.44	
			Set value		2.65

For overprint see No. O1.

Queen Maria — A115

Rod and Bowl of Aesculapius — A116

Typographed, Head Embossed

1935, June 1 *Perf. 11½*

No.	Type	Denom.	Color	Unused	Used
570	A115	40c	scarlet	50	15

First Portuguese Philatelic Exhibition.

1937, July 24 **Typo.** *Perf. 11½x12*

No.	Type	Denom.	Color	Unused	Used
571	A116	25c	blue	2.50	50

Centenary of the establishment of the School of Medicine in Lisbon and Oporto.

Gil Vicente A117

Grapes A118

1937

No.	Type	Denom.	Color	Unused	Used
572	A117	40c	dark brown	4.00	15
573	A117	1e	rose red	55	15
			Set value		20

400th anniversary of the death of Gil Vicente (1465-1536), Portuguese playwright. Design shows him in cowherd role in his play, "Auto do Vaqueiro."

1938 *Perf. 11½*

575	A118	15c	brt purple	35	30
576	A118	25c	brown	50	70
577	A118	40c	dp red lilac	3.25	20
578	A118	1.75e	dp blue	5.25	6.00

Issued in connection with the International Vineyard and Wine Congress.

Emblem of Portuguese Legion — A119

1940, Jan. 27 **Unwmk.** *Perf. 11½*

579	A119	5c	dull yellow	15	15
580	A119	10c	violet	15	15
581	A119	15c	brt blue	15	15
582	A119	25c	brown	3.00	20
583	A119	40c	dk green	6.25	15
584	A119	80c	yellow grn	25	15
585	A119	1e	brt red	8.25	60
586	A119	1.75e	dk blue	1.40	60
a.			Souvenir sheet of 8, #579-586	100.00	125.00
			Nos. 579-586 (8)	19.60	
			Set value		1.80

Issued in honor of the Portuguese Legion.
No. 586a sold for 5.50e, the proceeds going to various charities.

Portuguese World Exhibition A120

King John IV — A121

Discoveries Monument, Belém — A122

King Alfonso I — A123

1940 **Engr.** *Perf. 12x11½, 11½x12*

587	A120	10c	brown vio	15	15
588	A121	15c	dk grnsh bl	15	15
589	A122	25c	dk slate grn	30	15
590	A121	35c	yellow grn	25	16
591	A123	40c	olive bis	60	15
592	A120	80c	dk violet	1.50	15
593	A122	1e	dark red	3.00	48
594	A123	1.75e	ultra	1.65	60
a.			Souv. sheet of 8, #587-594 ('41)	19.00	27.50
			Nos. 587-594 (8)	7.60	
			Set value		1.65

Portuguese Intl. Exhibition, Lisbon (10c, 80c); restoration of the monarchy, 300th anniv (15c, 35c); Portuguese independence, 800th anniv (40c, 1.75e).
No. 594a sold for 10e.

Demand, as well as supply, determines a stamp's market value. One is as important as the other.

Sir Rowland Hill — A124

1940, Aug. 12 **Typo.** *Perf. 11½x12*

595	A124	15c	dk vio brn	15	15
596	A124	25c	dp org brn	15	15
597	A124	35c	green	15	15
598	A124	40c	brown vio	24	15
599	A124	50c	turq green	4.00	90
600	A124	80c	lt blue	40	42
601	A124	1e	crimson	4.25	85
602	A124	1.75e	dk blue	1.50	90
a.			Souv. sheet of 8, #595-602 ('41)	15.00	30.00
			Nos. 595-602 (8)	10.84	3.67

Postage stamp centenary.
No. 602a sold for 10e.

Fisherwoman of Nazare A126

Native of Coimbra A127

Native of Saloio — A128

Fisherwoman of Lisbon — A129

Native of Olhao — A130

$40 PORTUGAL
Native of Aveiro — A131

Native of Madeira A132

Native of Viana do Castelo A133

Rancher of Ribatejo A134

Peasant of Alentejo A135

1941, Apr. 4 **Typo.** *Perf. 11½*

605	A126	4c	sage grn	15	15
606	A127	5c	orange brn	15	15
607	A128	10c	red vio	70	35
608	A129	15c	lt yel grn	15	15
609	A130	25c	rose vio	50	20
610	A131	40c	yellow grn	15	15
611	A132	80c	lt blue	90	60
612	A133	1e	rose red	2.25	65
613	A134	1.75e	dull blue	2.75	1.50
614	A135	2e	red orange	10.50	10.50
a.			Sheet of 10, #605-614	32.50	87.50
			Nos. 605-614 (10)	18.20	14.40

No. 614a sold for 10e.

Ancient Sailing Vessel — A136

1943 *Perf. 14*

615	A136	5c	black	15	15
616	A136	10c	fawn	15	15
617	A136	15c	lilac gray	15	15
618	A136	20c	dull vio	15	15
619	A136	30c	brown vio	15	15
620	A136	35c	dk blue grn	15	15
621	A136	50c	plum	15	15
622	A136	1e	deep rose	1.90	15
623	A136	1.75e	indigo	8.00	25
624	A136	2e	dull claret	60	15
625	A136	2.50e	crim rose	85	15
626	A136	3.50e	grnsh bl	4.00	35
627	A136	5e	dp orange	50	15
628	A136	10e	blue gray	60	15
629	A136	15e	blue grn	10.00	35
630	A136	20e	olive gray	27.50	20
631	A136	50e	salmon	85.00	30
			Nos. 615-631 (17)	140.00	
			Set value		2.00

See Nos. 702-710.

Farmer A137

Postrider A138

1943, Oct. *Perf. 11½*

632	A137	10c	dull blue	22	20
633	A137	50c	red	25	20

Congress of Agricultural Science.

1944, May **Unwmk.**

634	A138	10c	dk vio brn	15	15
635	A138	50c	purple	15	15
636	A138	1e	cerise	50	28
637	A138	1.75e	brt blue	42	60
a.			Sheet of 4, #634-637	8.00	19.00
			Set value		1.00

3rd Philatelic Exhibition, Lisbon.
No. 637a sold for 7.50e.

Portrait of Avellar Brotero — A139

Statue of Brotero — A140

1944, Nov. 23 **Typo.** *Perf. 11½x12*

638	A139	10c	chocolate	15	15
639	A140	50c	dull green	32	15
640	A140	1e	carmine	1.10	32
641	A139	1.75e	dk blue	1.00	65
a.			Sheet of 4,#638-641 ('45)	10.00	20.00
			Set value		1.10

200th anniv. of the birth of Avellar Brotero, botanist.
No. 641a sold for 7.50e.

Gil Eannes — A141

Designs: 30c, Joao Goncalves Zarco. 35c, Bartolomeu Dias. 50c, Vasco da Gama. 1e, Pedro Alvares Cabral. 1.75e, Fernando Magellan. 2e, Goncalo Velho. 3.50e, Diogo Cao.

1945, July 29 **Engr.** *Perf. 13½*

642	A141	10c	vio brn	15	15
643	A141	30c	yel brn	15	15
644	A141	35c	bl grn	15	15
645	A141	50c	dk ol grn	20	15
646	A141	1e	vermilion	90	20
647	A141	1.75e	slate blue	1.00	70
648	A141	2e	black	1.25	50
649	A141	3.50e	car rose	2.50	1.10
a.			Sheet of 8, #642-649	12.50	18.00
			Nos. 642-649 (8)	6.30	3.10

Portuguese navigators of 15th and 16th centuries.
No. 649a sold for 15e.

Pres. Antonio Oscar de Fragoso Carmona A149

Astrolabe A150

Perf. 11½
1945, Nov. 12 **Photo.** **Unwmk.**

650	A149	10c	bright vio	15	15
651	A149	30c	copper brn	15	15
652	A149	35c	dark green	15	15
653	A149	50c	dark olive	20	15
654	A149	1e	dark red	2.75	60
655	A149	1.75e	dark blue	2.50	1.00
656	A149	2e	deep claret	13.00	1.90
657	A149	3.50e	slate black	6.25	2.75
a.			Sheet of 8, #650-657	67.50	85.00
			Nos. 650-657 (8)	25.15	6.85

No. 657a sold for 15e.

1945, Dec. 27 **Litho.**

658	A150	10c	light brown	15	15
659	A150	50c	gray green	15	15
660	A150	1e	brown red	1.10	25
661	A150	1.75e	dull chalky blue	85	1.10
a.			Sheet of 4, #658-661 ('46)	15.00	22.50

Centenary of the Portuguese Naval School.
No. 661a, issued Apr. 29, sold for 7.50e.

Catalogue values for unused stamps in this section, from this point to the end of the section, are for Never Hinged items.

Silves Castle A151

Almourol Castle A152

Designs-Castles: 30c, Leiria. 35c, Feira. 50c, Guimaraes. 1.75e, Lisbon. 2e, Braganca. 3.50e, Ourem.

1946, June 1 **Engr.**

662	A151	10c	brn vio	15	15
663	A151	30c	brn red	15	15
664	A151	35c	ol grn	15	15
665	A151	50c	gray blk	25	15
666	A152	1e	brt car	7.50	40
667	A152	1.75e	dk bl	6.00	1.00
a.			Sheet of 4	60.00	80.00
668	A152	2e	dk gray grn	16.00	1.25
669	A152	3.50e	org brn	10.00	1.40
			Nos. 662-669 (8)	40.20	4.65

No. 667a printed on buff granite paper, size 135x102mm, sold for 12.50e.

Figure with Tablet and Arms — A153

Madonna and Child — A154

1946, Nov. 19 *Perf. 12x11½*

No.	Type	Value	Color	Unused	Used
670	A153	50c	dark blue	32	15
a.			Sheet of 4	52.50	70.00

Issued to commemorate the centenary of the establishment of the Bank of Portugal.

No. 670a measures 155x143½mm and sold for 7.50e.

1946, Dec. 8 **Unwmk.** *Perf. 13½*

No.	Type	Value	Color	Unused	Used
671	A154	30c	gray blk	15	15
672	A154	50c	dp grn	15	15
673	A154	1e	rose car	1.10	32
674	A154	1.75e	brt bl	1.75	65
a.			Sheet of 4, #671-674 ('47)	30.00	42.50
			Set value		1.10

300th anniv. of the proclamation making the Virgin Mary patroness of Portugal.

No. 674a sold for 7.50e.

Shepherdess, Caramullo A155

Surrender of the Moors, 1147 A163

Designs: 30c, Timbrel player, Malpique. 35c, Flute player, Monsanto. 50c, Woman of Avintes. 1e, Field laborer, Maia. 1.75e, Woman of Algarve. 2e, Bastonet player, Miranda. 3.50e, Woman of the Azores.

1947, Mar. 1 **Photo.** *Perf. 11½*

No.	Type	Value	Color	Unused	Used
675	A155	10c	rose vio	15	15
676	A155	30c	dk red	15	15
677	A155	35c	dk ol grn	15	15
678	A155	50c	dk brn	20	15
679	A155	1e	red	3.50	25
680	A155	1.75e	slate bl	4.00	1.75
681	A155	2e	peacock bl	19.00	1.25
682	A155	3.50e	slate blk	9.25	2.00
a.			Sheet of 8, #675-682	145.00	160.00
			Nos. 675-682 (8)	36.40	5.85

No. 682a sold for 15e.

1947, Oct. 13 **Engr.** *Perf. 12½*

No.	Type	Value	Color	Unused	Used
683	A163	5c	bl grn	15	15
684	A163	20c	dk car	15	15
685	A163	50c	violet	20	15
686	A163	1.75e	dk bl	2.25	2.25
687	A163	2.50e	chocolate	3.25	4.00
688	A163	3.50e	slate blk	5.50	6.50
			Nos. 683-688 (6)	11.50	13.20

Issued to commemorate the 800th anniversary of the conquest of Lisbon from the Moors.

St. John de Britto
A164 A165

1948, May 28 *Perf. 11½x12*

No.	Type	Value	Color	Unused	Used
689	A164	30c	green	15	15
690	A165	50c	dk brn	15	15
691	A164	1e	rose car	3.75	60
692	A165	1.75e	blue	4.50	70

Issued to commemorate the 300th anniversary of the birth of St. John de Britto.

Architecture and Engineering — A166

King John I — A167

1948, May 28 *Perf. 13x12½*

No.	Type	Value	Color	Unused	Used
693	A166	50c	vio brn	15	15

Exposition of public Works and Natl. Congress of Engineering and Architecture, 1948.

Perf. 11½

1949, May 6 **Unwmk.** **Photo.**

Designs: 30c, Philippa of Lancaster. 35c, Prince Ferdinand. 50c, Prince Henry the Navigator. 1e, Nuno Alvarez Pereira. 1.75e, John das Regras. 2e, Fernao Lopes. 3.50e, Affonso Domingues.

No.	Type	Value	Color	Unused	Used
694	A167	10c	brn vio & cr	15	15
695	A167	30c	dk bl grn & cr	15	15
696	A167	35c	dk ol grn & cr	15	15
697	A167	50c	dp bl & cr	38	15
698	A167	1e	dk red & cr	38	15
699	A167	1.75e	dk gray & cr	7.50	4.00
700	A167	2e	dk gray bl & cr	4.00	55
701	A167	3.50e	dk brn & gray	12.50	10.00
a.			Sheet of 8, #694-701	20.00	25.00
			Nos. 694-701 (8)	25.21	15.30

No. 701a sold for 15e.

Ship Type of 1942

1948-49 **Typo.** *Perf. 14*

No.	Type	Value	Color	Unused	Used
702	A136	80c	dp grn	2.75	15
703	A136	1e	dp cl ('48)	1.65	15
704	A136	1.20e	dp car	2.75	15
705	A136	1.50e	olive	18.00	15
706	A136	1.80e	yel org	18.00	90
707	A136	2e	dp bl	3.50	20
708	A136	4e	orange	22.50	60
709	A136	6e	yel grn	40.00	65
710	A136	7.50e	grnsh gray	18.00	90
			Nos. 702-710 (9)	127.15	3.85

Angel, Coimbra Museum A168

Symbols of the UPU A169

1949, Dec. 20 **Engr.** *Perf. 13x14*

No.	Type	Value	Color	Unused	Used
711	A168	1e	red brn	4.50	15
712	A168	5e	ol brn	60	15

Issued to publicize the 16th International Congress of History and Art.

1949, Dec. 29

No.	Type	Value	Color	Unused	Used
713	A169	1e	brn vio	15	15
714	A169	2e	dp bl	25	15
715	A169	2.50e	dp grn	1.40	32
716	A169	4e	brn red	4.25	2.00

75th anniv. of the UPU.

Madonna of Fatima A170

St. John of God Helping Ill Man A171

1950, May 13 *Perf. 11½x12*

No.	Type	Value	Color	Unused	Used
717	A170	50c	dk grn	22	15
718	A170	1e	dk brn	95	15
719	A170	2e	blue	1.90	85
720	A170	5e	lilac	27.50	10.00

Holy Year, 1950, and to honor "Our Lady of the Rosary" at Fatima.

1950, Oct. 30 **Engr.** **Unwmk.**

No.	Type	Value	Color	Unused	Used
721	A171	20c	gray vio	15	15
722	A171	50c	cerise	18	15
723	A171	1e	ol grn	32	15
724	A171	1.50e	dp org	4.00	1.10
725	A171	2e	blue	3.00	32
726	A171	4e	chocolate	14.00	2.00
			Nos. 721-726 (6)	21.65	3.87

400th anniv. of the death of St. John of God.

Guerra Junqueiro — A172

Fisherman and Catch — A173

1951, Mar. 2 **Litho.** *Perf. 13½*

No.	Type	Value	Color	Unused	Used
727	A172	50c	dk brn	1.50	30
728	A172	1e	dk slate gray	38	20

Birth centenary of Guerra Junqueiro, poet.

1951, Mar. 9

No.	Type	Value	Color	Unused	Used
729	A173	50c	gray grn, *buff*	1.50	30
730	A173	1e	rose lake, *buff*	38	15

3rd National Congress of Fisheries.

Dove — A174

Pope Pius XII — A175

1951, Oct. 11

No.	Type	Value	Color	Unused	Used
731	A174	20c	dk brn & buff	15	15
732	A174	90c	dk ol grn & cr	1.90	50
733	A175	1e	dp cl & pink	1.65	15
734	A175	2.30e	dk bl grn & bl	2.25	45
			Set value		1.05

End of the Holy Year.

15th Century Colonists, Terceira — A176

1951, Oct. 24 *Perf. 13x13½*

No.	Type	Value	Color	Unused	Used
735	A176	50c	dk bl, *salmon*	1.00	25
736	A176	1e	dk brn, *cream*	45	25

500th anniversary (in 1950) of the colonizing of the island of Terceira.

Student, Soldiers and Workers — A177

1951, Nov. 22 *Perf. 13½x13*

No.	Type	Value	Color	Unused	Used
737	A177	1e	vio brn	1.25	15
738	A177	2.30e	dk bl	1.00	28
			Set value		35

25th anniversary of the national revolution.

16th Century Coach — A178

Designs: Various coaches.

Perf. 13x13½

1952, Jan. 8 **Engr.** **Unwmk.**

No.	Type	Value	Color	Unused	Used
739	A178	10c	purple	15	15
740	A178	20c	olive gray	15	15
741	A178	50c	steel blue	25	15
742	A178	90c	green	80	90
743	A178	1e	red orange	40	15
744	A178	1.40e	rose pink	2.00	2.50
745	A178	1.50e	rose brown	2.50	1.50
746	A178	2.30e	deep ultra	80	85
			Nos. 739-746 (8)	7.05	6.35

Issued to honor the National Museum of Coaches.

Symbolical of NATO — A179

1952, Apr. 4 **Litho.** *Perf. 12½*

No.	Type	Value	Color	Unused	Used
747	A179	1e	grn & blk	7.25	32
748	A179	3.50e	gray & vio bl	110.00	15.00

3rd anniv. of the signing of the North Atlantic Treaty.

Value of set hinged, $55.

Hockey Players on Roller Skates — A180

1952, June 28 *Perf. 13x13½*

No.	Type	Value	Color	Unused	Used
749	A180	1e	dk bl & gray	2.00	15
750	A180	3.50e	dk red brn	3.00	1.75

Issued to publicize the 8th World Championship Hockey-on-Skates matches.

Francisco Gomes Teixeira — A181

St. Francis and Two Boys — A182

1952, Nov. 25 *Perf. 14x14½*

No.	Type	Value	Color	Unused	Used
751	A181	1e	cerise	38	15
752	A181	2.30e	dp bl	2.50	1.75

Centenary of the birth of Francisco Gomes Teixeira (1851-1932), mathematician.

1952, Dec. 23 *Perf. 13½*

No.	Type	Value	Color	Unused	Used
753	A182	1e	dk grn	30	15
754	A182	2e	dp claret	55	25
755	A182	3.50e	chalky blue	8.75	5.00
756	A182	5e	dark pur	16.00	1.10

Issued to commemorate the 400th anniversary of the death of St. Francis Xavier.

Marshal Carmona Bridge A183

Designs: 1.40e, "28th of May" Stadium. 2e, University City, Coimbra. 3.50e, Salazar Dam.

1952, Dec. 10 Unwmk. *Perf. 12½*
Buff Paper

757	A183	1e	red brn	25	20
758	A183	1.40e	dl pur	3.75	3.00
759	A183	2e	dk grn	2.75	1.00
760	A183	3.50e	dk bl	4.50	2.50

Issued to commemorate the centenary of the foundation of the Ministry of Public Works.

Equestrian Seal of King Diniz — A184

1953-56 Litho.

761	A184	5c	grn, *citron*	15	15
762	A184	10c	ind, *salmon*	15	15
763	A184	20c	org red, *cit*	15	15
763A	A184	30c	rose lil, *cr* ('56)	15	15
764	A184	50c	gray	15	15
765	A184	90c	dk grn, *cit*	4.75	20
766	A184	1e	vio brn, *rose*	18	15
767	A184	1.40e	rose red	4.75	35
768	A184	1.50e	red, *cream*	18	15
769	A184	2e	gray	18	15
770	A184	2.30e	blue	7.75	25
771	A184	2.50e	gray blk, *sal*	25	15
772	A184	5e	rose vio, *cr*	25	15
773	A184	10e	blue, *citron*	80	15
774	A184	20e	bis brn, *cit*	1.75	15
775	A184	50e	rose vio	2.25	15
			Nos. 761-775 (16)	23.84	
			Set value		1.50

St. Martin of Braga A185

Guilherme Gomes Fernandes A186

Perf. 13x13½
1953, Feb. 26 Unwmk.

776	A185	1e	gray blk & gray	45	15
777	A185	3.50e	dk brn & yel	4.00	3.50

14th centenary of the arrival of St. Martin of Dume on the Iberian peninsula.

1953, Mar. 28 *Perf. 13*

778	A186	1e	red vio	38	15
779	A186	2.30e	dp bl	3.75	3.00

Birth of Guilherme Gomes Fernandes, General Inspector of the Firemen of Porto.

Emblems of Automobile Club A187

1953, Apr. 15 *Perf. 12½*

780	A187	1e	dk grn & yel grn	45	15
781	A187	3.50e	dk brn & buff	4.75	2.75

Issued to commemorate the 50th anniversary of the Portuguese Automobile Club.

Princess St. Joanna — A188

Queen Maria II — A189

Perf. 14½x14
1953, May 14 Litho. Unwmk.

782	A188	1e	blk & gray grn	65	15
783	A188	3.50e	dk bl & bl	4.50	3.75

Issued to commemorate the 500th anniversary of the birth of Princess St. Joanna.

1953, Oct. 3 Photo. *Perf. 13½*
Background of Lower Panel in Gold

784	A189	50c	red brown	15	15
785	A189	1e	claret brn	15	15
786	A189	1.40e	dk vio	70	45
787	A189	2.30e	dp bl	1.50	1.25
788	A189	3.50e	vio bl	1.50	1.25
789	A189	4.50e	dk bl grn	1.40	55
790	A189	5e	dk ol grn	2.50	45
791	A189	20e	red vio	25.00	6.25
			Nos. 784-791 (8)	32.90	10.50

Issued to commemorate the centenary of Portugal's first postage stamp.

Allegory — A190

1954, Sept. 22 *Perf. 13*

792	A190	1e	bl & dk grnsh bl	52	15
793	A190	1.50e	buff & dk brn	1.00	30

Issued to commemorate the 150th anniversary of the founding of the State Secretariat for Financial Affairs.

Open Textbook — A191

Cadet and College Arms — A192

1954, Oct. 15 Litho.

794	A191	50c	blue	15	15
795	A191	1e	red	15	15
796	A191	2e	dk grn	7.50	25
797	A191	2.50e	org brn	6.50	48
			Set value		82

National literacy campaign.

1954, Nov. 17

798	A192	1e	choc & lt grn	60	15
799	A192	3.50e	dk bl & gray grn	2.00	1.25

150th anniversary of the Military College.

Manuel da Nobrega and Crucifix — A193

King Alfonso I — A194

1954, Dec. 17 Engr. *Perf. 14x13*

800	A193	1e	brown	28	15
801	A193	2.30e	dp bl	12.00	6.50
802	A193	3.50e	gray grn	4.75	1.00
803	A193	5e	green	11.00	1.50

Issued to commemorate the 400th anniversary of the founding of Sao Paulo, Brazil.

1955, Mar. 17 *Perf. 13½x13*

Kings: 20c, Sancho I. 50c, Alfonso II. 90c, Sancho II. 1e, Alfonso III. 1.40e, Diniz. 1.50e, Alfonso IV. 2e, Pedro I. 2.30e, Ferdinand I.

804	A194	10c	rose vio	15	15
805	A194	20c	dk ol grn	15	15
806	A194	50c	dk bl grn	15	15
807	A194	90c	green	60	60
808	A194	1e	red brn	24	15
809	A194	1.40e	car rose	1.65	1.50
810	A194	1.50e	ol brn	70	50
811	A194	2e	dp org	2.00	1.40
812	A194	2.30e	vio bl	2.00	1.25
			Nos. 804-812 (9)	7.64	5.85

Telegraph Pole — A195

A. J. Ferreira da Silva — A196

1955, Sept. 16 Litho. *Perf. 13½*

813	A195	1e	ocher & hn brn	25	15
814	A195	2.30e	gray grn & Prus bl	4.25	1.40
815	A195	3.50e	lem & dp grn	4.25	75

Issued to commemorate the centenary of the telegraph system in Portugal.

1956, May 8 Photo. Unwmk.

816	A196	1e	bl & dk bl	28	15
817	A196	2.30e	grn & dk grn	3.00	1.75

Centenary of the birth of Prof. Antonio Joaquim Ferreira da Silva, chemist.

Steam Locomotive, 1856 A197

Madonna, 15th Century A198

Design: 1.50e, 2e, Electric train, 1956.

1956, Oct. 28 Litho. *Perf. 13*

818	A197	1e	lt & dk ol grn	20	15
819	A197	1.50e	Prus bl & lt grnsh bl	80	15
820	A197	2e	dk org brn & bis	6.00	45
821	A197	2.50e	choc & brn	7.00	60

Centenary of the Portuguese railways.

1956, Dec. 8 Photo.

822	A198	1e	dp grn & lt ol grn	22	15
823	A198	1.50e	dk red brn & ol bis	42	25
			Set value		32

Mothers' Day, Dec. 8.

J. B. Almeida Garrett A199

1957, Mar. 7 Engr. *Perf. 13½x14*

824	A199	1e	sepia	20	15
825	A199	2.30e	lt pur	6.50	3.00
826	A199	3.50e	dl grn	1.25	48
827	A199	5e	rose car	10.50	4.00

Issued in honor of Joao Baptista da Silva Leitao de Almeida Garrett, poet.

Cesario Verde A200

Exhibition Emblems A201

1957, Dec. 12 Litho. *Perf. 13½*

828	A200	1e	citron & brn	35	15
829	A200	3.30e	gray grn, yel grn & dk ol	95	60

Issued in honor of Jose Joaquim de Cesario Verde (1855-1886), poet.

1958, Apr. 7

830	A201	1e	multi	20	15
831	A201	3.30e	multi	75	55
			Set value		60

Issued for the Universal and International Exposition at Brussels.

Queen St. Isabel — A202

Institute for Tropical Medicine — A203

Design: 2e, 5e, St. Teotonio.

Perf. 14½x14
1958, July 10 Photo. Unwmk.

832	A202	1e	rose brn & buff	15	15
833	A202	2e	dk grn & buff	15	15
834	A202	2.50e	pur & buff	65	18
835	A202	5e	brn & buff	1.00	20
			Set value		58

1958, Sept. 4 Litho. *Perf. 13*

836	A203	1e	dk grn & lt gray	55	15
837	A203	2.50e	bl & pale bl	1.75	35
			Set value		40

Issued to publicize the 6th International Congress for Tropical Medicine and Malaria, Lisbon, Sept. 1958, and the opening of the new Tropical Medicine Institute.

Cargo Ship and Loading Crane — A204

1958, Nov. 27 Unwmk. *Perf. 13*

838	A204	1e	brn & dk brn	1.25	15
839	A204	4.50e	vio bl & dk bl	1.00	55
			Set value		60

2nd Natl. Cong. of the Merchant Marine, Porto.

Queen Leonor — A205

1958, Dec. 17

840	A205	1e	multi	15	15
841	A205	1.50e	bis, blk, bl & dk bis brn	1.10	15
a.			Dark bister brown omitted		
842	A205	2.30e	multi	90	20
843	A205	4.10e	multi	85	24
			Set value		58

500th anniv. of the birth of Queen Leonor.

Arms of Aveiro — A206

Symbols of Hope and Peace — A207

1959, Aug. 30 Litho. *Perf. 13*

844 A206 1e ol bis, brn, gold & sil 25 15

845 A206 5e grnsh gray, gold & sil 1.90 35

Set value 44

Millennium of Aveiro.

1960, Mar. 2 *Perf. 12½*

846 A207 1e lt vio & blk 40 15

847 A207 3.50e gray & dk grn 1.75 1.75

10th anniversary (in 1959) of NATO.

Open Door to "Peace" and WRY Emblem A208

Glider A209

1960, Apr. 7 Unwmk. *Perf. 13*

848 A208 20c multi 15 15

849 A208 1e multi 32 15

850 A208 1.80e yel grn, org & blk 35 42

Set value 58

Issued to publicize World Refugee Year, July 1, 1959-June 30, 1960.

1960, May 2

Designs: 1.50e, Plane. 2e, Plane and parachutes. 2.50e, Model plane.

851 A209 1e yel, gray & blue 15 15

852 A209 1.50e multi 52 22

853 A209 2e bl grn, yel & blk 75 35

854 A209 2.50e grnsh bl, ocher & red 1.40 45

Issued to commemorate the 50th anniversary (in 1959) of the Aero Club of Portugal.

Father Cruz — A210

University of Evora Seal — A211

1960, July 18 Unwmk. *Perf. 13*

855 A210 1e dp brn 15 15

856 A210 4.30e Prus bl & blk 2.50 2.50

Issued to honor Father Cruz, "father of the poor."

1960, July 18 Litho.

857 A211 50c vio bl 15 15

858 A211 1e red brn & yel 15 15

859 A211 1.40e rose cl & rose 85 50

Set value 1.00 62

400th anniversary of the founding of the University of Evora.

Arms of Prince Henry — A212

Arms of Lisbon and Symbolic Ship — A213

Designs: 2.50e, Caravel. 3.50e, Prince Henry. 5e, Prince Henry's motto. 8e, Prince Henry's sloop. 10e, Old chart of Sagres region of Portugal.

1960, Aug. 4 Photo. *Perf. 12x12½*

860 A212 1e gold & multi 15 15

861 A212 2.50e gold & multi 85 30

862 A212 3.50e gold & multi 1.00 1.00

863 A212 5e gold & multi 1.75 38

864 A212 8e gold & multi 40 38

865 A212 10e gold & multi 2.75 1.50

Nos. 860-865 (6) 6.90 3.71

Issued to commemorate the 500th anniversary of the death of Prince Henry the Navigator.

Europa Issue, 1960

Common Design Type

1960, Sept. 16 Litho. *Perf. 13*

Size: 31x21mm

866 CD3 1e ultra & gray bl 16 15

867 CD3 3.50e brn red & rose red 1.65 1.65

1960, Nov. 17 *Perf. 13*

868 A213 1e gray ol, blk & vio bl 28 15

869 A213 3.30e bl, blk & ultra 2.50 2.50

Issued to commemorate the Fifth National Philatelic Exhibition, Lisbon, part of the Prince Henry the Navigator festivities. (The ship in the design is in honor of Prince Henry).

Flag and Laurel — A214

1960, Dec. 20 Litho. *Perf. 13*

870 A214 1e multi 22 20

50th anniversary of the Republic.

King Pedro V — A215

1961, Aug. 3 Engr. *Perf. 13*

871 A215 1e gray brn & dk grn 22 15

872 A215 6.50e dk bl & blk 95 45

Issued to commemorate the centenary of the founding of the Faculty of Letters, Lisbon University.

Setubal Sea Gate and Ships — A216

1961, Aug. 24 Litho. *Perf. 12x11½*

873 A216 1e gold & multi 20 15

874 A216 4.30e gold & multi 4.25 3.00

Centenary of the city of Setubal.

Clasped Hands and CEPT Emblem — A217

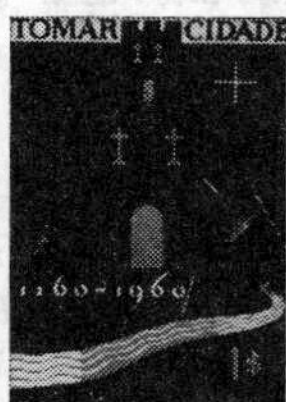

Tomar Castle and River Nabao — A218

Europa Issue, 1961

1961, Sept. 18 *Perf. 13½x13*

875 A217 1e bl & lt bl 15 15

876 A217 1.50e grn & brt grn 60 60

877 A217 3.50e brn, pink & red 90 90

1962, Jan. 26 *Perf. 11½x12*

878 A218 1e gold & multi 15 15

879 A218 3.50e gold & multi 95 90

800th anniversary of the city of Tomar.

National Guardsman A219

Archangel Gabriel A220

1962, Feb. 20 Unwmk. *Perf. 13½*

880 A219 1e multi 15 15

881 A219 2e multi 1.10 30

882 A219 2.50e multi 90 25

Set value 60

Issued to commemorate the 50th anniversary of the Republican National Guard.

1962, Mar. 24 Litho. *Perf. 13*

883 A220 1e ol, pink & red brn 50 15

884 A220 3.50e ol, pink & dk grn 30 30

Set value 36

Issued for St. Gabriel's Day. St. Gabriel is patron of telecommunications.

Tents and Scout Emblem — A221

1962, June 11 Unwmk. *Perf. 13*

885 A221 20c gray, bis, yel & blk 15 15

a. Double impression of gray frame lettering

886 A221 50c multi 15 15

887 A221 1e multi 32 15

888 A221 2.50e multi 1.50 25

889 A221 3.50e multi 35 30

890 A221 6.50e multi 35 30

Nos. 885-890 (6) 2.82

Set value 1.08

50th anniv. of the Portuguese Boy Scouts and the 18th Boy Scout World Conference, Sept. 19-24, 1961.

Children Reading — A222

Designs: 1e, Vaccination. 2.80e, Children playing ball. 3.50e, Guarding sleeping infant.

1962, Sept. 10 Litho. *Perf. 13½*

891 A222 50c bluish grn, yel & blk 15 15

892 A222 1e pale bl, yel & blk 42 15

893 A222 2.80e dp org yel & blk 85 50

894 A222 3.50e dl rose, yel & blk 1.25 85

Set value 1.45

Tenth International Congress of Pediatrics, Lisbon, Sept. 9-15.

19-Cell Honeycomb A223

1962, Sept. 17

895 A223 1e bl, dk bl & gold 15 15

896 A223 1.50e lt & dk grn & gold 52 40

897 A223 3.50e dp rose, mar & gold 50 65

Europa. The 19 cells represent the 19 original members of the Conference of European Postal and Telecommunications Administrations, C.E.P.T.

St. Zenon, the Courier A224

European Soccer Cup and Emblem A225

1962, Dec. 1 Unwmk. *Perf. 13½*

898 A224 1e multi 15 15

899 A224 2e multi 52 50

900 A224 2.80e multi 1.00 1.00

Issued for Stamp Day.

1963, Feb. 5 *Perf. 13½*

901 A225 1e multi 38 15

902 A225 4.30e multi 75 75

Victories of the Benfica Club of Lisbon in the 1961 and 1962 European Soccer Championships.

Wheat Emblem — A226

1963, Mar. 21 Litho.

903 A226 1e multi 15 15

904 A226 3.30e multi 60 70

905 A226 3.50e multi 70 50

FAO "Freedom from Hunger" campaign.

Stagecoach A227

1963, May 7 *Perf. 12x11½*

906 A227 1e gray, lt & dk bl 15 15

907 A227 1.50e bis, dk brn & lil rose 80 25

908 A227 5e org brn, dk brn & rose lil 18 22

1st Intl. Postal Conference, Paris, 1863.

St. Vincent de Paul by Monsaraz — A228

1963, July 10 Photo. *Perf. 13½x14*

Gold Inscription

909 A228 20c lt bl & ultra 15 15

a. Gold inscription omitted 55.00

910 A228 1e gray & sl 16 15

911 A228 2.80e grn & sl 80 80

a. Gold inscription omitted 65.00

912 A228 5e dp rose car & sl 80 38

Set value 1.30

Issued to commemorate the tercentenary of the death of St. Vincent de Paul.

Emblem of Order and Knight A229

1963, Aug. 13 Litho. *Perf. 11½*

913 A229 1e multi 15 15

914 A229 1.50e multi 18 15

915 A229 2.50e multi 1.25 32

Set value 46

800th anniv. of the Military Order of Avis.

Europa Issue, 1963

Stylized Bird — A230

1963, Sept. 16 *Perf. 13½*

916 A230 1e lt bl, gray & blk 16 15
917 A230 1.50e grn, gray & blk 1.10 48
918 A230 3.50e red, gray & blk 1.40 1.10

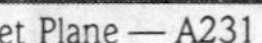
Jet Plane — A231

Apothecary Jar — A232

1963, Dec. 1 **Unwmk.** *Perf. 13½*

919 A231 1e dk bl & lt bl 15 15
920 A231 2.50e dk grn & yel grn 65 28
921 A231 3.50e org brn & org 85 55

Issued to commemorate the 10th anniversary of Transportes Aéreos Portugueses, TAP.

1964, Apr. 9 **Litho.**

922 A232 50c brn ol, dk brn & blk 15 15
923 A232 1e rose brn, dp cl & blk 15 15
924 A232 4.30e dk gray, sl & blk 3.25 3.25

4th centenary of the publication (in Goa, Apr. 10, 1563) of "Coloquios Dos Simples e Drogas" (Herbs and Drugs in India) by Garcia D'Orta.

Emblem of National Overseas Bank — A233

Mt. Sameiro Church — A234

1964, May 19 **Unwmk.** *Perf. 13½*

925 A233 1e bis, yel & dk bl 15 15
926 A233 2.50e ocher, yel & grn 1.00 38
927 A233 3.50e bis, yel & brn 70 50

Centenary of National Overseas Bank.

1964, June 5 **Litho.**

928 A234 1e red brn, bis & dl brn 15 15
929 A234 2e brn, bis & dl brn 52 30
930 A234 5e dk vio bl, bis & gray 75 48

Centenary of the Shrine of Our Lady of Mt. Sameiro, Braga.

Europa Issue, 1964
Common Design Type

1964, Sept. 14 **Unwmk.** *Perf. 13½*
Size: 19x32mm.

931 CD7 1e bl, lt bl & dk bl 20 15
932 CD7 3.50e rose brn, buff & dk brn 90 55
933 CD7 4.30e grn, yel grn & dk grn 1.40 2.00

Partial Eclipse of Sun — A235

Olympic Rings, Emblems of Portugal and Japan — A236

1964

934 A235 1e multi 18 15
935 A235 8e multi 70 45
Set value 50

International Quiet Sun Year, 1964-65.

1964, Dec. 1 **Unwmk.** *Perf. 13½*
Black Inscriptions; Olympic Rings in Pale Yellow

936 A236 20c tan, red & vio bl 15 15
937 A236 1e ultra, red & vio bl 15 15
938 A236 1.50e yel grn, red & vio bl 90 45
939 A236 6.50e rose lil, red & vio bl 1.00 1.00

18th Olympic Games, Tokyo, Oct. 10-25.

Eduardo Coelho — A237

Traffic Signs and Signals — A238

1964, Dec. 28 **Litho.** *Perf. 13½*

940 A237 1e multi 15 15
941 A237 5e multi 85 65

Centenary of the founding of Portugal's first newspaper, "Diario de Noticias," and to honor the founder, Eduardo Coelho, journalist.

1965, Feb. 15 **Litho.**

942 A238 1e yel, red & emer 15 15
943 A238 3.30e multi 1.75 2.00
944 A238 3.50e red, yel & emer 85 45

Issued to publicize the First National Traffic Congress, Lisbon, Feb. 15-19.

Ferdinand I, Duke of Braganza — A239

Coimbra Gate, Angel with Censer and Sword — A240

1965, Mar. 16 **Unwmk.** *Perf. 13½*

945 A239 1e rose brn & blk 15 15
946 A239 10e Prus grn & blk 90 65

500th anniv. of the city of Braganza (in 1964).

1965, Apr. 27 *Perf. 11½x12*

947 A240 1e bl & multi 15 15
948 A240 2.50e multi 90 40
949 A240 5e multi 1.00 65

9th centenary (in 1964) of the capture of the city of Coimbra from the Moors.

ITU Emblem — A241

1965, May 17 *Perf. 13½*

950 A241 1e bis brn, ol grn & ol 15 15
951 A241 3.50e ol, rose cl & dp cl 80 40
952 A241 6.50e yel grn, dl bl & sl bl 45 35

Issued to commemorate the centenary of the International Telecommunication Union.

Calouste Gulbenkian A242

1965, July 20 **Litho.** *Perf. 13½*

953 A242 1e multi 35 15
954 A242 8e multi 35 30
Set value 36

Gulbenkian (1869-1955), oil industry pioneer and sponsor of the Gulbenkian Foundation.

Red Cross — A243

1965, Aug. 17 **Unwmk.** *Perf. 13½*

955 A243 1e grn, red & blk 15 15
956 A243 4e ol, red & blk 75 60
957 A243 4.30e lt rose brn, red & blk 4.50 4.50

Centenary of the Portuguese Red Cross.

Europa Issue, 1965
Common Design Type

1965, Sept. 27 **Litho.** *Perf. 13*
Size: 31x24mm

958 CD8 1e saph, grnsh bl & dk bl 15 15
959 CD8 3.50e rose brn, sal & brn 1.00 1.00
960 CD8 4.30e grn, yel grn & dk grn 2.75 2.00

Military Plane — A244

1965, Oct. 20 *Perf. 13½*

961 A244 1e ol grn, red & dk grn 15 15
962 A244 2e sepia, red & dk grn 65 30
963 A244 5e chlky bl, red & dk grn 1.10 60

50th anniversary of the founding of the Portuguese Air Force.

Woman — A245

Chrismon with Alpha and Omega — A246

Designs: Characters from Gil Vicente Plays.

1965, Dec. 1 **Litho.** *Perf. 13½*

964 A245 20c ol, pale yel & blk 15 15
965 A245 1e brn, pale yel & blk 15 15
966 A245 2.50e dk red, buff & blk 1.25 22
967 A245 6.50e bl, gray & blk 25 22
Set value 58

Issued to commemorate the 500th anniversary of the birth of Gil Vicente (1465?-1536?).

1966, Mar. 28 **Litho.** *Perf. 13½*

968 A246 1e ol bis, gold & blk 18 15
969 A246 3.30e gray, gold & blk 1.75 1.50
970 A246 5e rose cl, gold & blk 1.00 45

Congress of the International Committee for the Defense of Christian Civilization, Lisbon.

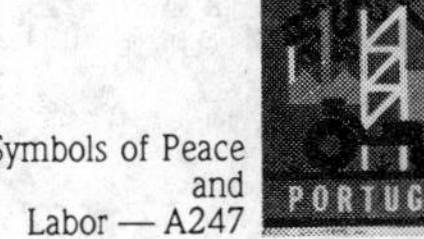

Symbols of Peace and Labor — A247

1966, May 28 **Litho.** *Perf. 13½*

971 A247 1e dk bl, sl bl & lt sl bl 15 15
972 A247 3.50e ol, ol brn, & lt ol 75 42
973 A247 4e dk brn, brn car & dl rose 60 35

40th anniversary of National Revolution.

Knight Giraldo on Horseback A248

1966, June 8

974 A248 1e multi 30 15
975 A248 8e multi 35 35
Set value 42

Issued to commemorate the 800th anniversary of the conquest of Evora from the Moors.

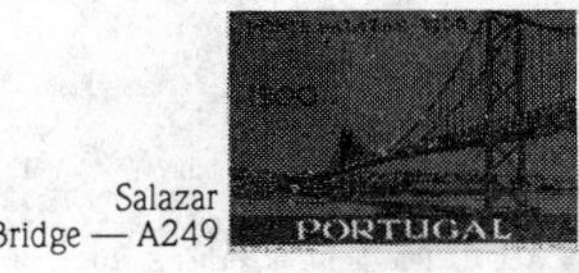

Salazar Bridge — A249

Designs: 2.80e, 4.30e, View of bridge, vert.

1966, Aug. 6 **Litho.** *Perf. 13½*

976 A249 1e gold & red 16 15
977 A249 2.50e gold & ultra 1.00 35
978 A249 2.80e sil & dp ultra 1.10 90
979 A249 4.30e sil & dk grn 1.10 90

Issued to commemorate the opening of the Salazar Bridge over the Tejo River, Lisbon.

Europa Issue, 1966
Common Design Type

1966, Sept. 26 **Litho.** *Perf. 11½x12*
Size: 26x32mm

980 CD9 1e bl & blk 15 15
981 CD9 3.50e red brn & blk 1.65 1.65
982 CD9 4.30e yel grn & blk 1.65 1.65

Pestana A250

Bocage A251

Portraits: 20c, Camara Pestana (1863-1899), bacteriologist. 50c, Egas Moniz (1874-1955), neurologist. 1e, Antonio Pereira Coutinho (1851-1939), botanist. 1.50e, José Corrêa da Serra (1750-1823), botanist. 2e, Ricardo Jórge (1858-1938), hygienist and anthropologist. 2.50e, J. Liete de Vasconcelos (1858-1941), ethnologist. 2.80e, Maximiano Lemos (1860-1923), medical historian. 4.30e, José Antonio Serrano, anatomist.

1966, Dec. 1 **Litho.** *Perf. 13½*
Portrait and Inscription in Dark Brown and Bister

983 A250 20c gray grn 15 15
984 A250 50c orange 15 15
985 A250 1e lemon 15 15
986 A250 1.50e bister brn 15 15
987 A250 2e brn org 85 15
988 A250 2.50e pale green 1.10 15
989 A250 2.80e salmon 1.25 1.25
990 A250 4.30e Prus bl 1.65 1.40
Nos. 983-990 (8) 5.45
Set value 3.10

Issued to honor Portuguese scientists.

1966, Dec. 28 Litho. *Perf. 11½x12*

991	A251	1e bis, grnsh gray & blk	15	15
992	A251	2e brn org, grnsh gray & blk	35	20
993	A251	6e gray, grnsh gray & blk	60	48

200th anniversary of the birth of Manuel Maria Barbosa du Bocage (1765-1805), poet.

Europa Issue, 1967
Common Design Type

1967, May 2 Litho. *Perf. 13*
Size: 21½x31mm

994	CD10	1e lt bl, Prus bl & blk	15	15
995	CD10	3.50e sal, brn red & blk	1.10	1.10
996	CD10	4.30e yel grn, ol grn & blk	1.65	1.65

Apparition of Our Lady of Fatima — A252

Statues of Roman Senators — A253

Designs: 2.80e, Church and Golden Rose. 3.50e, Statue of the Pilgrim Virgin, with lilies and doves. 4e, Doves holding crown over Chapel of the Apparition.

1967, May 13 *Perf. 11½x12*

997	A252	1e multi	15	15
998	A252	2.80e multi	48	80
999	A252	3.50e multi	20	20
1000	A252	4e multi	26	25

Issued to commemorate the 50th anniversary of the apparition of the Virgin Mary to 3 shepherd children at Fatima.

1967, June 1 Litho. *Perf. 13*

1001	A253	1e gold & rose claret	15	15
1002	A253	2.50e gold & dull blue	90	42
1003	A253	4.30e gold & gray green	52	52

Introduction of a new civil law code.

Shipyard, Margueira, Lisbon — A254

Design: 2.80e, 4.30e, Ship's hull and map showing location of harbor.

1967, June 23

1004	A254	1e aqua & multi	15	15
1005	A254	2.80e multi	40	45
1006	A254	3.50e multi	40	24
1007	A254	4.30e multi	50	48

Issued to commemorate the inauguration of the Lisnave Shipyard at Margueira, Lisbon.

Symbols of Healing A255

Flags of EFTA Nations A256

1967, Oct. 8 Litho. *Perf. 13½*

1008	A255	1e multi	15	15
1009	A255	2e multi	52	20
1010	A255	5e multi	85	60

Issued to publicize the 6th European Congress of Rheumatology, Lisbon, Oct. 8-13.

1967, Oct. 24 Litho. *Perf. 13½*

1011	A256	1e bister & multi	15	15
1012	A256	3.50e buff & multi	50	50
1013	A256	4.30e gray & multi	1.50	1.50

Issued to publicize the European Free Trade Association. See note after Norway No. 501.

Tables of the Law — A257

1967, Dec. 27 Litho. *Perf. 13½*

1014	A257	1e olive	15	15
1015	A257	2e red brown	45	20
1016	A257	5e green	75	55

Centenary of abolition of death penalty.

Bento de Goes — A258

1968, Feb. 14 Engr. *Perf. 12x11½*

1017	A258	1e olive, indigo & dk brn	40	15
1018	A258	8e org brn, dl pur & ol grn	65	48

Issued to commemorate the 360th anniversary (in 1967) of the death of Bento de Goes (1562-1607), Jesuit explorer of the route to China.

Europa Issue, 1968
Common Design Type

1968, Apr. 29 Litho. *Perf. 13*
Size: 31x21mm

1019	CD11	1e multi	15	15
1020	CD11	3.50e multi	1.25	1.25
1021	CD11	4.30e multi	2.75	2.75

Mother's and Child's Hands — A259

1968, May 26 Litho. *Perf. 13½*

1022	A259	1e lt gray, blk & red	15	15
1023	A259	2e salmon, blk & red	60	25
1024	A259	5e lt bl, blk & red	85	65

Issued to commemorate the 30th anniversary of the Mothers' Organization for National Education.

"Victory over Disease" and WHO Emblem A260

1968, July 10 Litho. *Perf. 12½*

1025	A260	1e multi	15	15
1026	A260	3.50e multi	40	28
1027	A260	4.30e tan & multi	3.00	3.00

20th anniv. of WHO.

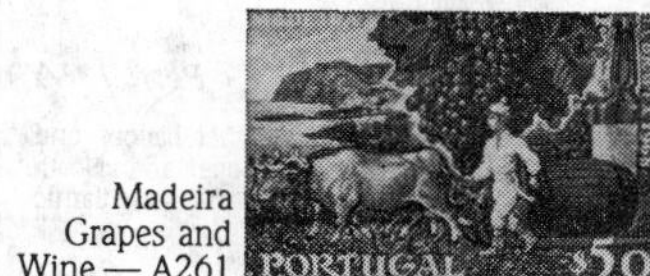

Madeira Grapes and Wine — A261

Joao Fernandes Vieira — A262

Designs: 1e, Fireworks on New Year's Eve. 1.50e, Mountains and valley. 3.50e, Woman doing Madeira embroidery. 4.30e, Joao Gonalves Zarco. 20e, Muschia aurea (flower.)

Perf. 12x11½, 11½x12
1968, Aug. 17 Litho.

1028	A261	50c multi	15	15
1029	A261	1e multi	15	15
1030	A261	1.50e multi	18	15
1031	A262	2.80e multi	1.40	1.40
1032	A262	3.50e multi	95	50
1033	A262	4.30e multi	4.00	4.00
1034	A262	20e multi	2.25	70
		Nos. 1028-1034 (7)	9.08	7.05

Issued to publicize Madeira and the Lubrapex 1968 stamp exhibition.

Design descriptions in Portuguese, French and English printed on back of stamps.

Pedro Alvares Cabral A263

Cabral's Fleet A264

Design: 3.50e, Cabral's coat of arms, vert.

Perf. 12x12½, 12½x12
1969, Jan. 30 Engr.

1035	A263	1e vio bl, bl & gray bl	15	15
1036	A263	3.50e dp claret	1.50	1.00

Litho.

1037	A264	6.50e grn & multi	1.10	1.10

5th cent. of the birth of Pedro Alvarez Cabral (1468-1520), navigator, discoverer of Brazil. Nos. 1035-1037 have description of the designs printed on the back in Portuguese, French and English.

Europa Issue, 1969
Common Design Type

1969, Apr. 28 Litho. *Perf. 13*
Size: 31x22½mm

1038	CD12	1e dp bl & multi	15	15
1039	CD12	3.50e multi	1.25	1.00
1040	CD12	4.30e grn & multi	2.00	1.50

King José I and Arms of National Press — A265

1969, May 14 Litho. *Perf. 11½x12*

1041	A265	1e multi	15	15
1042	A265	2e multi	55	20
1043	A265	8e multi	42	42

Bicentenary of the National Press.

ILO Emblem — A266

1969, May 28 *Perf. 13*

1044	A266	1e bluish grn, blk & sil	15	15
1045	A266	3.50e red, blk & sil	60	30
1046	A266	4.30e brt bl, blk & sil	1.00	85

50th anniversary of the ILO.

Juan Cabrillo Rodriguez — A267

Vianna da Motta, by Columbano Bordalo Pinheiro — A268

1969, July 16 Litho. *Perf. 11½x12*

1047	A267	1e multi	15	15
1048	A267	2.50e multi	75	25
1049	A267	6.50e multi	55	55

Bicentenary of San Diego, Calif., and honoring Juan Cabrillo Rodriguez, explorer of California coast.

Backs inscribed. See note below No. 1034.

1969, Sept. 24 Litho. *Perf. 12*

1050	A268	1e multi	40	15
1051	A268	9e gray & multi	42	55

Centenary of the birth of Vianna da Motta (1868-1948), pianist and composer.

Gago Coutinho and 1922 Seaplane A269

Design: 2.80e, 4.30e, Adm. Coutinho and Coutinho sextant.

1969, Oct. 22

1052	A269	1e grnsh gray, dk & lt brn	15	15
1053	A269	2.80e yel bis, dk & lt brn	65	65
1054	A269	3.30e gray bl, dk & lt brn	1.00	1.00
1055	A269	4.30e lt rose brn, dk & lt brn	1.40	1.25

Admiral Carlos Viegas Gago Coutinho (1869-1959), explorer and aviation pioneer.

Vasco da Gama — A270

Designs: 2.80e, Da Gama's coat of arms. 3.50e, Map showing route to India and compass rose, horiz. 4e, Da Gama's fleet, horiz.

Perf. 12x11½, 11½x12
1969, Dec. 30 Litho.

1056	A270	1e multi	15	15
1057	A270	2.80e multi	1.65	1.65
1058	A270	3.50e multi	1.25	70
1059	A270	4e multi	1.00	42

Vasco da Gama (1469-1525), navigator who found sea route to India.

Design descriptions in Portuguese, French and English printed on back of stamps.

Europa Issue, 1970

Common Design Type

1970, May 4 Litho. *Perf. 13½*

Size: 31x22mm

No.	Type	Value	Description	Unused	Used
1060	CD13	1e	dk bl & pale yel	25	25
1061	CD13	3.50e	red brn & pale yel	1.65	1.65
1062	CD13	4.30e	ol & pale yel	2.50	2.25

Distillation Plant — A271

Design: 2.80e, 6e, Catalytic cracking tower.

1970, June 5 Litho. *Perf. 13*

No.	Type	Value	Description	Unused	Used
1063	A271	1e	dk bl & dl bl	15	15
1064	A271	2.80e	sl grn & pale grn	75	75
1065	A271	3.30e	dk ol grn & ol	60	55
1066	A271	6e	dk brn & dl ocher	50	35

Opening of the Oporto Oil Refinery.

Marshal Carmona and Oak Leaves A272

Designs: 2.50e, Carmona, Portuguese coat of arms and laurel. 7e, Carmona and ferns.

Perf. 12x12½

1970, July 1 Litho. & Engr.

No.	Type	Value	Description	Unused	Used
1067	A272	1e	ol grn & blk	15	15
1068	A272	2.50e	red, ultra & blk	60	30
1069	A272	7e	slate bl & blk	55	55

Centenary of the birth of Marshal Antonio Oscar de Fragoso Carmona (1869-1951), President of Portugal, 1926-1951.

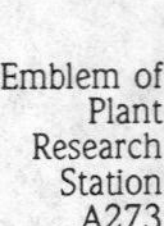

Emblem of Plant Research Station A273

1970, July 29 Litho.

No.	Type	Value	Description	Unused	Used
1070	A273	1e	multi	15	15
1071	A273	2.50e	multi	60	22
1072	A273	5e	multi	85	45

Issued to commemorate the 25th anniversary of the Plant Research Station at Elvas.

Compass Rose and EXPO Emblem — A274

Designs: 5e, Monogram of Christ (IHS) and EXPO emblem. 6.50e, "Portugal and Japan" as written in old manuscripts, and EXPO emblem.

1970, Sept. 16 Litho. *Perf. 13*

No.	Type	Value	Description	Unused	Used
1073	A274	1e	gold & multi	15	15
1074	A274	5e	silver & multi	65	22
1075	A274	6.50e	multi	1.25	1.25

EXPO '70 International Exhibition, Osaka, Japan, Mar. 15-Sept. 13. See No. C11.

Castle (from Arms of Santarem) A275

Designs: No. 1077, Star and wheel, from Covilha coat of arms. 2.80e, Ram and Covilha coat of arms. 4e, Knights on horseback and Santarem coat of arms.

1970, Oct. 7 Litho. *Perf. 12x11½*

No.	Type	Value	Description	Unused	Used
1076	A275	1e	multi	15	15
1077	A275	1e	ultra & multi	15	15
1078	A275	2.80e	red & multi	1.10	1.10
1079	A275	4e	gray & multi	45	35

Nos. 1076, 1079 for the centenary of the City of Santarem; Nos. 1077-1078 the centenary of the City of Covilha.

Paddlesteamer Great Eastern Laying Cable — A276

Designs: 2.80e, 4e, Cross section of cable.

1970, Nov. 21 Litho. *Perf. 14*

No.	Type	Value	Description	Unused	Used
1080	A276	1e	multi	15	15
1081	A276	2.50e	multi	90	35
1082	A276	2.80e	multi	1.25	1.25
1083	A276	4e	multi	90	65

Centenary of the Portugal-Great Britain submarine telegraph cable.

Grapes and Woman Filling Baskets A277

Designs: 1e, Worker carrying basket of grapes, and jug. 3.50e, Glass of wine, and barge with barrels on River Douro. 7e, Wine bottle and barrels.

1970, Dec. 20 Litho. *Perf. 12x11½*

No.	Type	Value	Description	Unused	Used
1084	A277	50c	multi	15	15
1085	A277	1e	multi	15	15
1086	A277	3.50e	multi	50	15
1087	A277	7e	multi	50	45
			Set value		68

Publicity for port wine export.

Mountain Windmill, Bussaco Hills — A278

Francisco Franco (1885-1955) — A279

Windmills: 50c, Beira Litoral Province. 1e, Estremadura Province. 2e, St. Miguel, Azores. 3.30e, Porto Santo, Madeira. 5e, Pico, Azores.

1971, Feb. 24 Litho. *Perf. 13*

No.	Type	Value	Description	Unused	Used
1088	A278	20c	multi	15	15
1089	A278	50c	lt bl & multi	15	15
1090	A278	1e	gray & multi	15	15
1091	A278	2e	multi	40	15
1092	A278	3.30e	ocher & multi	1.10	1.10
1093	A278	5e	multi	90	30
			Nos. 1088-1093 (6)	2.85	
			Set value		1.60

Backs inscribed. See note below No. 1034.

Europa Issue, 1971

Common Design Type

1971, May 3 Photo. *Perf. 14*

Size: 32x22mm

No.	Type	Value	Description	Unused	Used
1094	CD14	1e	dk bl, lt grn & blk	18	18
1095	CD14	3.50e	red brn, yel & blk	1.25	1.10
1096	CD14	7.50e	ol, yel & blk	1.90	1.90

Perf. 11½x12½; 13½ (2.50e, 4e)

1971, July 7 Engr.

Portuguese Sculptors: 1e, Antonio Teixeira Lopes (1866-1942). 1.50e, Antonio Augusto da Costa Mota (1862-1930). 2.50e, Rui Roque Gameiro (1906-1935). 3.50e, José Simoes de Almedia (nephew; 1880-1950). 4e, Francisco dos Santos (1878-1930).

No.	Type	Value	Description	Unused	Used
1097	A279	20c	black	15	15
a.			Perf. 13½	1.10	22
1098	A279	1e	claret	15	15
1099	A279	1.50e	sepia	20	15
1100	A279	2.50e	dk bl	45	15
1101	A279	3.50e	car rose	48	18
1102	A279	4e	gray grn	95	80
			Nos. 1097-1102 (6)	2.38	
			Set value		1.35

Pres. Antonio Salazar — A280

1971, July 27 Engr. *Perf. 13½*

No.	Type	Value	Description	Unused	Used
1103	A280	1e	multi	15	15
a.			Perf. 12½x12	35.00	1.10
1104	A280	5e	multi	52	20
1105	A280	10e	multi	85	40
a.			Perf. 12½x12	18.00	65

Wolframite Crystals A281

Minerals: 2.50e, Arsenopyrite (gold). 3.50e, Beryllium. 6.50e, Chalcopyrite (copper).

1971, Sept. 24 Litho. *Perf. 12*

No.	Type	Value	Description	Unused	Used
1106	A281	1e	multi	15	15
1107	A281	2.50e	car & multi	75	28
1108	A281	3.50e	grn & multi	30	15
1109	A281	6.50e	bl & multi	45	30

Spanish-Portuguese-American Economic Geology Congress.

Town Gate, Castelo Branco — A282

Weather Recording Station and Barograph Charts — A283

Designs: 3e, Memorial column. 12.50e, Arms of Castelo Branco, horiz.

1971, Oct. 7 *Perf. 14*

No.	Type	Value	Description	Unused	Used
1110	A282	1e	multi	15	15
1111	A282	3e	multi	75	32
1112	A282	12.50e	multi	60	30

Bicentenary of Castelo Branco as a town.

1971, Oct. 29 *Perf. 13½*

Designs: 4e, Stratospheric weather balloon and weather map of southwest Europe and North Africa. 6.50e, Satellite and aerial map of Atlantic Ocean off Portugal.

No.	Type	Value	Description	Unused	Used
1113	A283	1e	buff & multi	15	15
1114	A283	4e	multi	1.10	52
1115	A283	6.50e	blk, dl red brn & org	48	30

25 years of Portuguese meteorological service.

Missionaries and Ship — A284

1971, Nov. 24

No.	Type	Value	Description	Unused	Used
1116	A284	1e	gray, ultra & blk	15	15
1117	A284	3.30e	dp bis, lil & blk	75	75
1118	A284	4.80e	ol, grn & blk	75	75

400th anniv. of the martyrdom of a group of Portuguese missionaries on the way to Brazil.

"Man" A285

Nature Conservation: 3.30e, "Earth" (animal, vegetable, mineral). 3.50e, "Air" (birds). 4.50e, "Water" (fish).

1971, Dec. 22 Litho. *Perf. 12*

No.	Type	Value	Description	Unused	Used
1119	A285	1e	brn & multi	15	15
1120	A285	3.30e	lt bl, yel & grn	28	20
1121	A285	3.50e	lt bl, rose & vio	30	15
1122	A285	4.50e	lt bl, grn & ultra	1.10	75

City Hall, Sintra — A286

Designs: 5c, Aqueduct, Lisbon. 50c, University, Coimbra. 1e, Torre dos Clerigos, Porto. 1.50e, Belem Tower, Lisbon. 2.50e, Castle, Vila da Feira. 3e, Misericordia House, Viana do Castelo. 3.50e, Window, Tomar Convent. 8e, Ducal Palace, Guimaraes. 10e, Cape Girao, Madeira. 20e, Episcopal Garden, Castelo Branco. 100e, Lakes of Seven Cities, Azores.

1972-73 Litho. *Perf. 12½*

Size: 22x17½mm

No.	Type	Value	Description	Unused	Used
1123	A286	5c	gray, grn & blk	28	28
1124	A286	50c	gray bl, blk & org	16	15
1125	A286	1e	grn, blk & brn	15	15
1126	A286	1.50e	bl, bis & blk	15	15
1127	A286	2.50e	brn, dk brn & gray	28	15
1128	A286	3e	yel, blk & brn	40	15
1129	A286	3.50e	dp org, sl & brn	28	15
1130	A286	8e	blk, ol & grn	2.75	28

Perf. 13½

Size: 31x22mm

No.	Type	Value	Description	Unused	Used
1131	A286	10e	gray & multi	85	25
1132	A286	20e	grn & multi	5.50	35
1133	A286	50e	gray bl, ocher & blk	1.65	35
1134	A286	100e	grn & multi	3.75	1.10
			Nos. 1123-1134 (12)	16.20	
			Set value		3.00

"CTT" and year date printed in minute gray multiple rows on back of stamps.

Issue dates: 1e, 1.50e, 50e, 100e, Mar. 1; 50c, 3e, 10e, 20e, Dec. 6, 1972; 5c, 2.50e, 3.50e, 8e, Sept. 5, 1973.

See Nos. 1207-1214.

Tagging

Starting in 1975, phosphor (bar or L-shape) was applied to the face of most definitives and commemoratives.

Stamps issued both with and without tagging include Nos. 1124-1125, 1128, 1130-1131, 1209, 1213-1214, 1250, 1253, 1257, 1260, 1263.

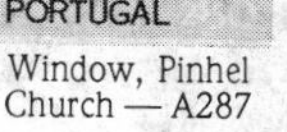

Window, Pinhel Church — A287

Heart and Pendulum — A288

Designs: 1e, Arms of Pinhel, horiz. 7.50e, Stone lantern.

1972, Mar. 29 *Perf. 13½*

1135 A287 1e bl & multi 15 15
a. Perf. 11½x12½ 16.00 45
1136 A287 2.50e multi 60 20
1137 A287 7.50e bl & multi 50 40

Bicentenary of Pinhel as a town.

1972, Apr. 24

Designs: 4e, Heart and spiral pattern. 9e, Heart and continuing coil pattern.

1138 A288 1e vio & red 15 15
1139 A288 4e grn & red 1.25 80
1140 A288 9e brn & red 52 48

"Your heart is your health," World Health Day.

Europa Issue 1972
Common Design Type

1972, May 1 *Perf. 13½*
Size: 21x31mm

1141 CD15 1e gray & multi 15 15
1142 CD15 3.50e sal & multi 65 65
1143 CD15 6e grn & multi 1.25 1.25

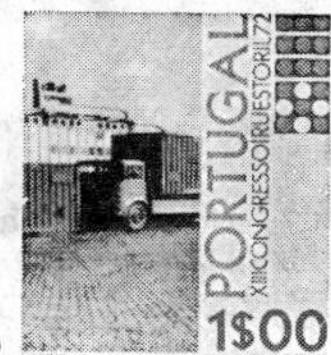

Trucks — A289

1972, May 17 **Litho.** *Perf. 13½*

1144 A289 1e shown 15 15
1145 A289 4.50e Taxi 75 45
1146 A289 8e Autobus 60 40

13th Congress of International Union of Road Transport (I.R.U.), Estoril, May 15-18.

Soccer, Olympic Rings — A290

1972, July 26 **Litho.** *Perf. 14*

1147 A290 50c shown 15 15
1148 A290 1e Running 15 15
1149 A290 1.50e Equestrian 15 15
1150 A290 3.50e Swimming, women's 38 18
1151 A290 4.50e Yachting 52 50
1152 A290 5e Gymnastics, women's 90 38
Nos. 1147-1152 (6) 2.25
Set value 1.25

20th Olympic Games, Munich, Aug. 26-Sept. 11.

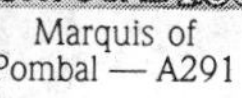

Marquis of Pombal — A291

Tomé de Sousa — A292

1972, Aug. 28 *Perf. 13½*

1153 A291 1e shown 15 15
1154 A291 2.50e Scientific apparatus 75 28
1155 A291 8e Seal of Univ. of Coimbra 60 45

Bicentenary of the Pombaline reforms of University of Coimbra.

1972, Oct. 5 **Litho.** *Perf. 13½*

Designs: 2.50e, José Bonifacio. 3.50e, Dom Pedro IV. 6e, Allegory of Portuguese-Brazilian Community.

1156 A292 1e gray & multi 15 15
1157 A292 2.50e grn & multi 32 15
1158 A292 3.50e multi 32 18
1159 A292 6e bl & multi 60 30

150th anniv. of Brazilian independence.

Sacadura Cabral, Gago Coutinho and Plane — A293

Designs: 2.50e, 3.80e, Map of flight from Lisbon to Rio de Janeiro. 2.80e, Like 1e.

1972, Nov. 15 *Perf. 11½x12½*

1160 A293 1e bl & multi 15 15
a. Perf. 13½ 10.50 1.25
1161 A293 2.50e multi 52 15
1162 A293 2.80e multi 60 60
1163 A293 3.80e multi 70 70
a. Perf. 13½ 25.00 16.00

50th anniversary of the Lisbon to Rio de Janeiro flight by Commander Arturo de Sacadura Cabral and Adm. Carlos Viegas Gago Coutinho, Mar. 30-June 5, 1922.

Luiz Camoens A294

Designs: 3e, Hand saving manuscript from sea. 10e, Symbolic of man's questioning and discovering the unknown.

1972, Dec. 27 **Litho.** *Perf. 13*

1164 A294 1e org brn, buff & blk 15 15
1165 A294 3e dl bl, lt grn & blk 65 24
1166 A294 10e red brn, buff & yel 90 42

4th centenary of the publication of The Lusiads by Luiz Camoens (1524-1580).

Graphs and Sequence Count — A295

1973, Apr. 11 **Litho.** *Perf. 14½*

1167 A295 1e shown 15 15
1168 A295 4e Odometer 65 28
1169 A295 9e Graphs 48 25

Productivity Conference '72, Jan. 17-22, 1972.

Europa Issue 1973
Common Design Type

1973, Apr. 30 *Perf. 13*
Size: 31x29mm

1170 CD16 1e multi 15 15
1171 CD16 4e brn red & multi 1.50 1.90
1172 CD16 6e grn & multi 2.50 2.50

Gen. Medici, Arms of Brazil and Portugal A296

Designs: 2.80e, 4.80e, Gen. Medici and world map.

Lithographed and Engraved

1973, May 16 *Perf. 12x11½*

1173 A296 1e dk grn, blk & sep 15 15
1174 A296 2.80e olive & multi 40 35
1175 A296 3.50e dk bl, blk & buff 40 30
1176 A296 4.80e multi 32 25

Visit of Gen. Emilio Garrastazu Medici, President of Brazil, to Portugal.

Child and Birds — A297

Designs: 4e, Child and flowers. 7.50e, Child.

1973, May 28 **Litho.** *Perf. 13*

1177 A297 1e ultra & multi 15 15
1178 A297 4e multi 60 20
1179 A297 7.50e bister & multi 75 45

To pay renewed attention to children.

Transportation, Weather Map — A298

Designs: 3.80e, Communications: telegraph, telephone, radio, satellite. 6e, Postal service: mailbox, truck, mail distribution diagram.

1973, June 25

1180 A298 1e multi 15 15
1181 A298 3.80e multi 22 18
1182 A298 6e multi 52 40
Set value 62

Ministry of Communications, 25th anniv.

Pupil and Writing Exercise — A299

Designs: 4.50e, Illustrations from 18th century primer. 5.30e, School and children, by 9-year-old Marie de Luz, horiz. 8e, Symbolic chart of teacher-pupil link, horiz.

1973, Oct. 24 **Litho.** *Perf. 13*

1183 A299 1e bl & multi 15 15
1184 A299 4.50e brn & multi 55 20
1185 A299 5.30e lt bl & multi 48 35
1186 A299 8e grn & multi 90 55

Primary state school education, bicent.

Oporto Streetcar, 1910 A300

Designs: 1e, Horse-drawn streetcar, 1872. 3.50e, Double-decker Leyland bus, 1972.

1973, Nov. 7
Size: 31½x34mm

1187 A300 1e brn, yel & blk 15 15
1188 A300 3.50e choc & multi 1.00 60

Size: 37½x27mm
Perf. 12½

1189 A300 7.50e buff & multi 90 55

Cent. of public transportation in Oporto.

Servicemen's League Emblem A301

Death of Nuño Gonzalves A302

Designs: 2.50e, Sailor, soldier and aviator. 11e, Military medals.

1973, Nov. 28 **Litho.** *Perf. 13*

1190 A301 1e multi 15 15
1191 A301 2.50e multi 95 45
1192 A301 11e dk bl & multi 65 52

50th anniv. of the Servicemen's League.

1973, Dec. 19

1193 A302 1e slate bl & org 15 15
1194 A302 10e vio brn & org 55 42

600th anniv. of the heroism of Nuno Gonzalves, alcaide of Faria Castle.

Damiao de Gois, by Dürer (?) — A303

"The Exile," by Soares dos Reis — A304

Designs: 4.50e, Title page of Cronica de Principe D. Joao. 7.50e, Lute and score of Dodecachordon.

1974, Apr. 5 **Litho.** *Perf. 12*

1195 A303 1e multi 15 15
1196 A303 4.50e multi 80 30
1197 A303 7.50e multi 90 35

400th anniversary of the death of Damiao de Gois (1502-1574), humanist, writer, composer.

Europa Issue 1974

1974, Apr. 29 **Litho.** *Perf. 13*

1198 A304 1e multi 32 32
1199 A304 4e dk red & multi 5.00 2.00
1200 A304 6e dk grn & multi 5.75 4.00

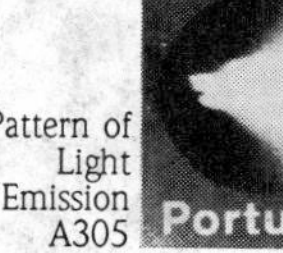

Pattern of Light Emission A305

Designs: 4.50e, Spiral wave radiation pattern. 5.30e, Satellite and earth.

1974, June 26 **Litho.** *Perf. 14*

1201 A305 1.50e gray olive 15 15
1202 A305 4.50e dark blue 1.00 45
1203 A305 5.30e brt rose lil 32 30

Establishment of satellite communications network via Intelsat among Portugal, Angola and Mozambique.

Diffusion of Hertzian Waves A306

Designs (Symbolic): 3.30e, Messages through space. 10e, Navigation help.

1974, Sept. 4 Litho. *Perf. 12*

1204	A306	1.50e	multi	15	15
1205	A306	3.30e	multi	50	45
1206	A306	10e	multi	1.10	60

Guglielmo Marconi (1874-1937), Italian electrical engineer and inventor.

Buildings Type of 1972-73

Designs: 10c, Ponte do Lima (Roman bridge). 30c, Alcobaa Monastery, interior. 2e, City Hall, Bragana. 4e, New Gate, Braga. 4.50e, Dolmen of Carrazeda. 5e, Roman Temple, Evora. 6e, Leca do Balio Monastery. 7.50e, Almourol Castle.

1974, Sept. 18 Litho. *Perf. 12½*
Size: 22x17½mm

1207	A286	10c	multi	15	15
1208	A286	30c	multi	15	15
1209	A286	2e	multi	15	15
1210	A286	4e	multi	35	15
1211	A286	4.50e	multi	60	15
1212	A286	5e	multi	6.25	15
1213	A286	6e	multi	1.75	18
1214	A286	7.50e	multi	90	15
			Nos. 1207-1214 (8)	10.30	
			Set value		75

"CTT" and year date printed in minute gray multiple rows on back of stamps.

Postilion, Truck and Letter A307

Designs: 2e, Hand holding letter. 3.30e, Packet and steamship. 4.50e, Pigeon and letters. 5.30e, Hand holding sealed letter. 20e, Old and new locomotives.

1974, Oct. 9 Litho. *Perf. 13*

1220	A307	1.50e	brn & multi	15	15
1221	A307	2e	multi	45	15
1222	A307	3.30e	ol & multi	15	15
1223	A307	4.50e	multi	45	42
1224	A307	5.30e	multi	35	30
1225	A307	20e	multi	1.25	1.00
a.			Souv. sheet of 6	4.50	4.50
			Nos. 1220-1225 (6)	2.80	2.17

Centenary of Universal Postal Union. No. 1225a contains one each of Nos. 1220-1225, arranged to show a continuous design with a globe in center. Sold for 50e.

Luisa Todi, Singer (1753-1833) A308

Marcos Portugal, Composer (1762-1838) A309

Portuguese Musicians: 2e, Joao Domingos Bomtempo (1775-1842). 2.50e, Carlos Seixas (1704-1742). 3e, Duarte Lobo (1565-1646). 5.30e, Joao de Sousa Carvalho (1745-1798).

1974, Oct. 30 Litho. *Perf. 12*

1226	A308	1.50e	brt pink	15	15
1227	A308	2e	vermilion	60	22
1228	A308	2.50e	brown	50	15
1229	A308	3e	bluish blk	35	22
1230	A308	5.30e	slate grn	38	35
1231	A309	11e	rose lake	38	35
			Nos. 1226-1231 (6)	2.36	1.44

Coat of Arms of Beja — A310

2,000th Anniv. of Beja: 3.50e, Men of Beja in costumes from Roman times to date. 7e, Moorish Arches and view across plains.

1974, Nov. 13

1232	A310	1.50e	multi	15	15
1233	A310	3.50e	multi	60	50
1234	A310	7e	multi	1.00	50

Annunciation A311

Rainbow and Dove A312

Christmas: 4.50e, Adoration of the Shepherds. 10e, Flight into Egypt. Designs show Portuguese costumes from Nazare township.

1974, Dec. 4 Litho. *Perf. 13*

1235	A311	1.50e	red & multi	15	15
1236	A311	4.50e	multi	1.25	30
1237	A311	10e	bl & multi	85	42

1974, Dec. 18 *Perf. 12*

1238	A312	1.50e	multi	15	15
1239	A312	3.50e	multi	1.50	42
1240	A312	5e	multi	1.00	25

Armed Forces Movement of Apr. 25, 1974.

Egas Moniz — A313

Soldier as Farmer, Farmer as Soldier — A314

Designs: 3.30e, Lobotomy probe and Nobel Prize medal, 1949. 10e, Cerebral angiograph, 1927.

1974, Dec. 27 Engr. *Perf. 11½x12*

1241	A313	1.50e	yel & multi	15	15
1242	A313	3.30e	brn & ocher	22	35
1243	A313	10e	gray & ultra	1.00	35

Egas Moniz (1874-1955), brain surgeon, birth centenary.

1975, Mar. 21 Litho. *Perf. 12*

1244	A314	1.50e	grn & multi	15	15
1245	A314	3e	gray & multi	85	20
1246	A314	4.50e	multi	1.10	40

Cultural progress and citizens' guidance campaign.

Hands and Dove — A315

Designs: 4.50e, Brown hands reaching for dove. 10e, Dove with olive branch and arms of Portugal.

1975, Apr. 23 Litho. *Perf. 13½*

1247	A315	1.50e	red & multi	15	15
1248	A315	4.50e	brn & multi	95	35
1249	A315	10e	grn & multi	1.10	48

Movement of April 25th, first anniversary. Slogans in Portuguese, French and English printed on back of stamps.

God's Hand Reaching Down — A316

Designs: 4.50e, Jesus' hand holding up cross. 10e, Dove (Holy Spirit) descending.

1975, May 13 Litho. *Perf. 13½*

1250	A316	1.50e	multi	15	15
1251	A316	4.50e	plum & multi	1.25	42
1252	A316	10e	blue & multi	1.25	55

Holy Year 1975.

Horseman of the Apocalypse, 12th Century — A317

Europa: 10e, The Poet Fernando Pessoa, by Almada Negreiros (1893-1970).

1975, May 26

1253	A317	1.50e	multi	25	15
1254	A317	10e	multi	4.50	3.50

Assembly Building A318

1975, June 2 Litho. *Perf. 13½*

1255	A318	2e	red, blk & yel	15	15
1256	A318	20e	emer, blk & yel	1.75	1.00

Opening of Constituent Assembly.

Hikers — A319

Designs: 4.50e, Campsite on lake. 5.30e, Mobile homes on the road.

1975, Aug. 4 Litho. *Perf. 13½*

1257	A319	2e	multi	50	15
1258	A319	4.50e	multi	90	35
1259	A319	5.30e	multi	35	45

36th Rally of the International Federation of Camping and Caravanning, Santo Andre Lake.

People and Sapling — A320

Designs (UN Emblem and): 4.50e, People and dove. 20e, People and grain.

1975, Sept. 17 Litho. *Perf. 13½*

1260	A320	2e	grn & multi	20	15
1261	A320	4.50e	vio & multi	90	20
1262	A320	20e	multi	2.00	55

United Nations, 30th anniversary.

Icarus and Rocket — A321

Designs: 4.50e, Apollo and Soyuz in space. 5.30e, Robert H. Goddard, Robert Esnault-Pelterie, Hermann Oberth and Konstantin Tsiolkovski. 10e, Sputnik, man in space, moon landing module.

1975, Sept. 26 Litho. *Perf. 13½*
Size: 30½x26½mm

1263	A321	2e	grn & multi	20	15
1264	A321	4.50e	brn & multi	90	30
1265	A321	5.30e	lil & multi	30	30

Size: 65x28mm

1266	A321	10e	bl & multi	2.00	52

26th Congress of International Astronautical Federation, Lisbon, Sept. 1975.

Land Survey A322

Designs: 8e, Ocean survey. 10e, People of many races and globe.

1975, Nov. 19 Litho. *Perf. 12x12½*

1267	A322	2e	ocher & multi	20	15
1268	A322	8e	blue & multi	60	52
1269	A322	10e	dk vio & multi	1.40	55

Centenary of Lisbon Geographical Society.

Arch and Trees — A323

Designs: 8e, Plan, pencil and ruler. 10e, Hand, old building and brick tower.

1975, Nov. 28 *Perf. 13½*

1270	A323	2e	dk bl & gray	18	15
1271	A323	8e	dk car & gray	1.50	1.40
1272	A323	10e	ocher & multi	1.65	1.50

European Architectural Heritage Year 1975.

Nurse and Hospital Ward — A324

Designs (IWY Emblem and): 2e, Farm workers. 3.50e, Secretary. 8e, Factory worker.

1975, Dec. 30 Litho. *Perf. 13½*

1273	A324	50c	multi	15	15
1274	A324	2e	multi	55	15
1275	A324	3.50e	multi	55	28
1276	A324	8e	multi	60	55
a.			Souvenir sheet of 4	2.50	2.50

International Women's Year 1975. No. 1276a contains 4 stamps similar to Nos. 1273-1276 in slightly changed colors. Sold for 25e.

Pen Nib as Plowshare A325

1976, Feb. 6 Litho. *Perf. 12*
1277 A325 3e dk bl & red org 22 15
1278 A325 20e org, ultra & red 2.00 95

Portuguese Society of Writers, 50th anniversary.

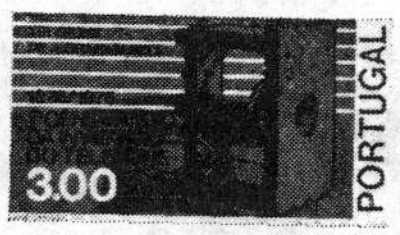

Telephones, 1876, 1976 — A326

Design: 10.50e, Alexander Graham Bell and telephone.

1976, Mar. 10 Litho. *Perf. 12x12½*
1279 A326 3e yel grn, grn & blk 60 15
1280 A326 10.50e rose, red & blk 1.65 52

Centenary of first telephone call by Alexander Graham Bell, March 10, 1876.

Industry and Shipping — A327

Design: 1e, Garment, food and wine industries.

1976, Apr. 7 Litho. *Perf. 12½*
1281 A327 50c red brn 20 15
1282 A327 1e slate 30 15
Set value 24

Support of national production.

Carved Spoons, Olive Wood — A328

Europa: 20e, Gold filigree pendant, silver box and CEPT emblem.

1976, May 3 Litho. *Perf. 12x12½*
1283 A328 3e olive & multi 35 15
1284 A328 20e tan & multi 6.75 5.25

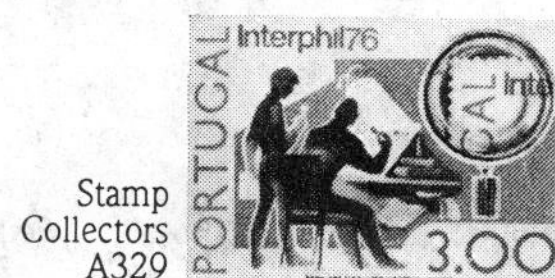

Stamp Collectors A329

Designs: 7.50e, Stamp exhibition and hand canceler. 10e, Printing and designing stamps.

1976, May 29 Litho. *Perf. 14½*
1285 A329 3e multi 15 15
1286 A329 7.50e multi 42 30
1287 A329 10e multi 1.10 30

Interphil 76, International Philatelic Exhibition, Philadelphia, Pa., May 29-June 6.

King Ferdinand I — A330

Designs: 5e, Plowshare, farmers chasing off hunters. 10e, Harvest.

1976, July 2 Litho. *Perf. 12*
1288 A330 3e lt bl & multi 15 15
1289 A330 5e yel grn & multi 75 52
1290 A330 10e multi 80 75
a. Souv. sheet of 3, #1288-1290 2.50 2.50

Agricultural reform law (compulsory cultivation of uncultivated lands), 600th anniversary. No. 1290a sold for 30e.

Torch Bearer A331

Designs (Montreal Games' Emblem, Maple Leaf and): 7e, Women's relay race. 10.50e, Olympic flame.

1976, July 16 *Perf. 13½*
1291 A331 3e red & multi 15 15
1292 A331 7e red & multi 75 52
1293 A331 10.50e red & multi 1.00 48

21st Olympic Games, Montreal, Canada, July 17-Aug. 1.

Farm A332

1976, Sept. 15 Litho. *Perf. 12*
1294 A332 3e shown 48 15
1295 A332 3e Ship 48 15
1296 A332 3e City 48 15
1297 A332 3e Factory 80 15
b. Souv. sheet of 4, #1294-1297 5.00 5.00

Fight against illiteracy. #1297b sold for 25e.

Perf. 13½
1294a A332 3e *30.00* *15.00*
1295a A332 3e 1.50 1.10
1296a A332 3e *35.00* *18.00*
1297a A332 3e 60 45

Azure-winged Magpie — A333

Designs: 5e, Lynx. 7e, Portuguese laurel cherry. 10.50e, Little wild carnations.

1976, Sept. 30 Litho. *Perf. 12*
1298 A333 3e multi 24 15
1299 A333 5e multi 70 15
1300 A333 7e multi 70 52
1301 A333 10.50e multi 90 70

Portucale 77, 2nd International Thematic Exhibition, Oporto, Oct. 29-Nov. 6, 1977.

Exhibition Hall — A334

Design: 20e, Symbolic stamp and emblem.

1976, Oct. 9 Litho. *Perf. 13½*
1302 A334 3e bl & multi 18 15
1303 A334 20e ocher & multi 1.75 1.10
a. Souv. sheet of 2, #1302-1303 2.50 2.50

6th Luso-Brazilian Philatelic Exhibition, LUBRAPEX 76, Oporto, Oct. 9. No. 1303a sold for 30e.

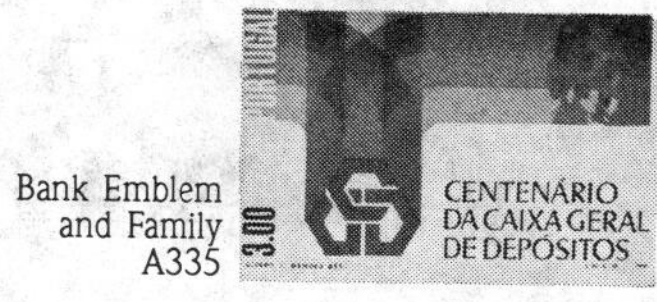

Bank Emblem and Family A335

Designs: 7e, Emblem and grain. 15e, Emblem and cog wheels.

1976, Oct. 29 *Perf. 12*
1304 A335 3e org & multi 15 15
1305 A335 7e grn & multi 95 45
1306 A335 15e bl & multi 1.10 55

Trust Fund Bank centenary.

Sheep Grazing on Marsh A336

Designs: 3e, Drainage ditches. 5e, Fish in water. 10e, Ducks flying over marsh.

1976, Nov. 24 Litho. *Perf. 14*
1307 A336 1e multi 18 15
1308 A336 3e multi 45 18
1309 A336 5e multi 95 30
1310 A336 10e multi 1.25 45

Protection of wetlands.

"Liberty" — A337

1976, Nov. 30 Litho. *Perf. 13½*
1311 A337 3e gray, grn & ver 45 15

Constitution of 1976.

Mother Examining Child's Eyes — A338

Designs: 5e, Welder with goggles. 10.50e, Blind woman reading Braille.

1976, Dec. 13
1312 A338 3e multi 15 15
1313 A338 5e multi 65 15
1314 A338 10.50e multi 95 65

World Health Day and campaign against blindness.

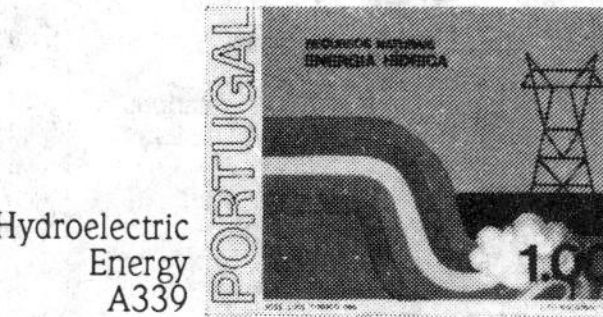

Hydroelectric Energy A339

Abstract Designs: 4e, Fossil fuels. 5e, Geothermal energy. 10e, Wind power. 15e, Solar energy.

1976, Dec. 30
1315 A339 1e multi 16 15
1316 A339 4e multi 30 15
1317 A339 5e multi 32 15
1318 A339 10e multi 60 40
1319 A339 15e multi 1.10 70
Nos. 1315-1319 (5) 2.48 1.55

Sources of energy.

Map of Council of Europe Members A340

1977, Jan. 28 Litho. *Perf. 12*
1320 A340 8.50e multi 40 40
1321 A340 10e multi 40 40

Portugal's joining Council of Europe.

Alcoholic and Bottle — A341

Designs (Bottle and): 5e, Symbolic figure of broken life. 15e, Bars blotting out the sun.

1977, Feb. 4 *Perf. 13*
1322 A341 3e multi 15 15
1323 A341 5e ocher & multi 38 20
1324 A341 15e org & multi 90 70

Anti-alcoholism Day and 10th anniversary of Portuguese Anti-alcoholism Society.

Trees Tapped for Resin — A342

Designs: 4e, Trees stripped for cork. 7e, Trees and logs. 15e, Trees at seashore as windbreakers.

1977, Mar. 21 Litho. *Perf. 13½*
1325 A342 1e multi 15 15
1326 A342 4e multi 24 15
1327 A342 7e multi 90 35
1328 A342 15e multi 1.00 65

Forests, a natural resource.

"Suffering" A343

Designs: 6e, Man exercising. 10e, Group exercising. All designs include emblems of World Health Organization and Portuguese Institute for Rheumatology.

1977, Apr. 13 Litho. *Perf. 12x12½*
1329 A343 4e blk, brn & ocher 15 15
1330 A343 6e blk, bl & vio 60 52
1331 A343 10e blk, pur & red 52 24

International Rheumatism Year.

Southern Plains Landscape A344

Europa: 8.50e, Northern mountain valley.

1977, May 2

1332 A344 4e multi 38 25
1333 A344 8.50e multi 1.65 1.10
a. Min. sheet, 2 each #1332-1333 11.00 11.00

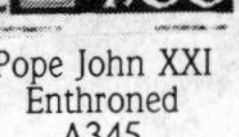

Pope John XXI Enthroned A345

Petrus Hispanus, the Physician A346

1977, May 20 Litho. *Perf. 13½*

1334 A345 4e multi 25 15
1335 A346 15e multi 60 60

Pope John XXI (Petrus Hispanus), only Pope of Portuguese descent, 7th death centenary.

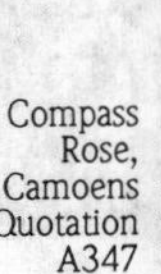

Compass Rose, Camoens Quotation A347

1977, June 8 *Perf. 12*

1336 A347 4e multi 18 15
1337 A347 8.50e multi 55 52

Camoens Day and to honor Portuguese overseas communities.

Student, Computer and Book — A348

Designs (Book and): No. 1339, Folk dancers, flutist and boat. No. 1340, Tractor drivers. No. 1341, Atom and people.

1977, July 20 Litho. *Perf. 12x12½*

1338 A348 4e multi 22 18
1339 A348 4e multi 22 18
1340 A348 4e multi 22 18
1341 A348 4e multi 22 18
a. Souv. sheet of 4, #1338-1341 2.50 2.50

Continual education. #1341a sold for 20e.

Pyrites, Copper, Chemical Industry A349

Designs: 5e, Marble, statue, public buildings. 10e, Iron ore, girders, crane. 20e, Uranium ore, atomic diagram.

1977, Oct. 4 Litho. *Perf. 12x11½*

1342 A349 4e multi 15 15
1343 A349 5e multi 42 16
1344 A349 10e multi 45 22
1345 A349 20e multi 1.25 55

Natural resources from the subsoil.

Alexandre Herculano A350

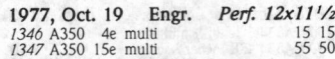

1977, Oct. 19 Engr. *Perf. 12x11½*

1346 A350 4e multi 15 15
1347 A350 15e multi 55 50

Alexandre Herculano de Carvalho Araujo (1810-1877), historian, novelist, death centenary.

Maria Pia Bridge A351

Design: 4e, Arrival of first train, ceramic panel by Jorge Colaco, St. Bento railroad station.

1977, Nov. 4 Litho. *Perf. 12x11½*

1348 A351 4e multi 16 15
1349 A351 10e multi 80 80

Centenary of extension of railroad across Douro River.

Poveiro Bark — A352

Coastal Fishing Boats: 3e, Do Mar bark. 4e, Nazaré bark. 7e, Algarve skiff. 10e, Xavega bark. 15e, Bateira de Buarcos.

1977, Nov. 19 *Perf. 12*

1350 A352 2e multi 32 15
1351 A352 3e multi 16 15
1352 A352 4e multi 16 16
1353 A352 7e multi 24 16
1354 A352 10e multi 40 40
1355 A352 15e multi 90 65
a. Souv. sheet of 6, #1350-1355 3.00 3.00
Nos. 1350-1355 (6) 2.18 1.67

PORTUCALE 77, 2nd International Topical Exhibition. Oporto, Nov. 19-20. No. 1355a sold for 60e.

Nativity A353

Children's Drawings: 7e, Nativity. 10e, Holy Family, vert. 20e, Star and Christ Child, vert.

Perf. 12x11½, 11½x12

1977, Dec. 12 Litho.

1356 A353 4e multi 15 15
1357 A353 7e multi 45 32
1358 A353 10e multi 45 35
1359 A353 20e multi 1.65 75

Christmas 1977.

Old Desk and Computer — A354

Designs: Work tools, old and new.

1978-83 Litho. *Perf. 12½*

Size: 22x17mm

1360 A354 50c Medical 15 15
1361 A354 1e Household 15 15
1362 A354 2e Communications 15 15
1363 A354 3e Garment making 15 15
1364 A354 4e Office 15 15
1365 A354 5e Fishing craft 15 15
1366 A354 5.50e Weaving 15 15
1367 A354 6e Plows 16 15
1368 A354 6.50e Aviation 15 15
1369 A354 7e Printing 20 15
1370 A354 8e Carpentry 18 15
1371 A354 8.50e Potter's wheel 20 15
1372 A354 9e Photography 20 15
1373 A354 10e Saws 20 15
1373A A354 12.50e Compasses ('83) 18 15
1373B A354 16e Mail processing ('83) 18 15

Perf. 13½

Size: 31x22mm

1374 A354 20e Construction 55 35
1375 A354 30e Steel industry 65 32
a. Incomplete arch 65 32
1376 A354 40e Transportation 75 70
1377 A354 50e Chemistry 1.10 55
1378 A354 100e Shipbuilding 2.00 90
1379 A354 250e Telescopes 4.75 2.75
Nos. 1360-1379 (22) 12.50
Set value 7.00

Red Mediterranean Soil — A355

Designs: 5e, Stone formation. 10e, Alluvial soil. 20e, Black soil.

1978, Mar. 6 Litho. *Perf. 12*

1380 A355 4e multi 16 15
1381 A355 5e multi 20 15
1382 A355 10e multi 32 32
1383 A355 20e multi 1.25 55

Soil, a natural resource.

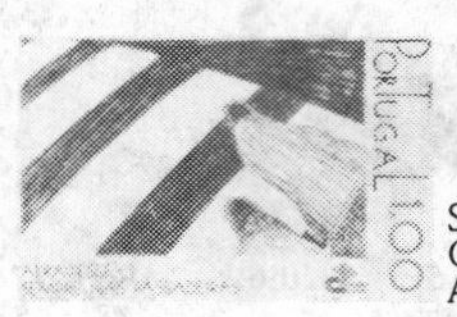

Street Crossing A356

Designs: 2e, Motorcyclist. 2.50e, Children in back seat of car. 5e, Hands holding steering wheel. 9e, Driving on country road. 12.50e, "Avoid drinking and driving."

1978, Apr. 19 Litho. *Perf. 12*

1384 A356 1e multi 15 15
1385 A356 2e multi 15 15
1386 A356 2.50e multi 22 15
1387 A356 5e multi 38 15
1388 A356 9e multi 55 30
1389 A356 12.50e multi 65 60
Nos. 1384-1389 (6) 2.10
Set value 1.20

Road safety campaign.

Roman Tower, Belmonte A357

Europa: 40e, Belém Monastery of Hieronymite monks (inside).

1978, May 2

1390 A357 10e multi 40 40
1391 A357 40e multi 1.65 1.65
a. Souvenir sheet, 2 each #1390-1391, imperf. 8.00 8.00

No. 1391a sold for 120e.

Trajan's Bridge — A358

Roman Tablet from Bridge — A359

1978, June 14 Litho. *Perf. 13½*

1392 A358 5e multi 16 15
1393 A359 20e multi 95 95

1900th anniv. of Chaves (Aquae Flaviae).

Running A360

1978, July 24 Litho. *Perf. 12*

1394 A360 5e shown 15 15
1395 A360 10e Bicycling 30 18
1396 A360 12.50e Watersport 45 45
1397 A360 15e Soccer 45 30

Sport for all the people.

Pedro Nunes A361

Design: 20e, "Nonio" navigational instrument and diagram from "Tratado da Rumaao do Globo."

1978, Aug. 9 Litho. *Perf. 12x11½*

1398 A361 5e multi 15 15
1399 A361 20e multi 75 50

Nunes (1502-78), navigator and cosmographer.

Trawler, Frozen Fish Processing, Can of Sardines A362

Fishing Industry: 9e, Deep-sea trawler, loading and unloading at dock. 12.50e, Trawler with radar and instruction in use of radar. 15e, Trawler with echo-sounding equipment, microscope and test tubes.

1978, Sept. 16 Litho. *Perf. 12x11½*

1400 A362 5e multi 15 15
1401 A362 9e multi 18 15
1402 A362 12.50e multi 45 40
1403 A362 15e multi 55 30

Natural resources.

Postrider A363

Designs: No. 1405, Carrier pigeon. No. 1406, Envelopes. No. 1407, Pen.

1978, Oct. 30 Litho. *Perf. 12*

1404 A363 5e yel & multi 24 18
1405 A363 5e bl gray & multi 24 18
1406 A363 5e grn & multi 24 18
1407 A363 5e red & multi 24 18

Introduction of Postal Code.

Human Figure, Flame Emblem A364

Design: 40e, Human figure pointing the way and flame emblem.

1978, Dec. 7 Litho. *Perf. 12*

1408	A364	14e multi	25	25
1409	A364	40e multi	1.10	1.10
a.		Souv. sheet, 2 each #1408-1409	3.75	3.75

Universal Declaration of Human Rights, 30th anniversary and 25th anniversary of European Declaration.

Sebastiao Magalhaes Lima A365

1978, Dec. 7

1410	A365	5e multi	20	15

Sebastiao Magalhaes Lima (1850-1928), lawyer, journalist, statesman.

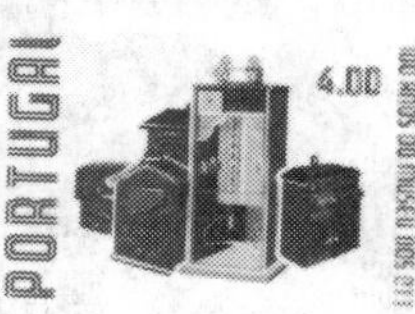
Mail Boxes and Scale — A366

Designs: 5e, Telegraph and condenser lens. 10e, Portugal Nos. 2-3 and postal card printing press, 1879. 14e, Book and bookcases, 1879, 1979.

1978, Dec. 20

1411	A366	4e multi	16	15
1412	A366	5e multi	20	15
1413	A366	10e multi	32	16
1414	A366	14e multi	75	65
a.		Souv. sheet of 4, #1411-1414	1.65	1.65

Centenary of Postal Museum and Postal Library; 125th anniversary of Portuguese stamps (10e). No. 1414a sold for 40e.

Emigrant at Railroad Station A367

Designs: 14e, Farewell at airport. 17e, Emigrant greeting child at railroad station.

1979, Feb. 21 Litho. *Perf. 12*

1415	A367	5e multi	15	15
1416	A367	14e multi	30	30
1417	A367	17e multi	75	65

Portuguese emigration.

Automobile Traffic — A368

Combat noise pollution: 5e, Pneumatic drill. 14e, Man with bull horn.

1979, Mar. 14 *Perf. 13 1/2*

1418	A368	4e multi	15	15
1419	A368	5e multi	15	15
1420	A368	14e multi	35	35

NATO Emblem A369

1979, Apr. 4 Litho. *Perf. 12*

1421	A369	5e multi	15	15
1422	A369	50e multi	1.40	1.25
a.		Souv. sheet, 2 each #1421-1422	3.25	3.25

NATO, 30th anniv.

Mail Delivery, 16th Century A370

Europa: 40e, Mail delivery, 19th century.

1979, Apr. 30 Litho. *Perf. 12*

1423	A370	14e multi	32	32
1424	A370	40e multi	80	80
a.		Souv. sheet, 2 each #1423-1424	5.25	5.25

Mother, Infant, Dove — A371

Designs (IYC Emblem and): 5.50e, Children playing ball. 10e, Child in nursery school. 14e, Black and white boys.

1979, June 1 Litho. *Perf. 12x12 1/2*

1425	A371	5.50e multi	15	15
1426	A371	6.50e multi	18	15
1427	A371	10e multi	25	18
1428	A371	14e multi	45	35
a.		Souv. sheet of 4, #1425-1428	1.50	1.50
		Set value		72

Intl. Year of the Child. No. 1428a sold for 40e.

Salute to the Flag — A372

1979, June 8

1429	A372	6.50e multi	22	18
a.		Souvenir sheet of 9	2.00	2.00

Portuguese Day.

Pregnant Woman A373

Designs: 17e, Boy sitting in a cage. 20e, Face, and hands using hammer.

1979, June 6 Litho. *Perf. 12x12 1/2*

1430	A373	6.50e multi	20	20
1431	A373	17e multi	48	48
1432	A373	20e multi	52	52

Help for the mentally retarded.

Children Reading Book, UNESCO Emblem A374

Design: 17e, Teaching deaf child, and UNESCO emblem.

1979, June 25

1433	A374	6.50e multi	20	15
1434	A374	17e multi	48	48

Intl. Bureau of Education, 50th anniv.

Water Cart, Brasiliana '79 Emblem A375

Brasiliana '79 Philatelic Exhibition: 5.50e, Wine sledge. 6.50e, Wine cart. 16e, Covered cart. 19e, Mogadouro cart. 20e, Sand cart.

1979, Sept. 15 Litho. *Perf. 12*

1435	A375	2.50e multi	15	15
1436	A375	5.50e multi	15	15
1437	A375	6.50e multi	18	18
1438	A375	16e multi	35	35
1439	A375	19e multi	40	35
1440	A375	20e multi	45	30
		Nos. 1435-1440 (6)	1.68	1.48

Antonio Jose de Almeida (1866-1929) — A376

Republican Leaders: 6.50e, Afonso Costa (1871-1937). 10e, Teofilo Braga (1843-1924). 16e, Bernardino Machado (1851-1944). 19.50e, Joao Chagas (1863-1925). 20e, Elias Garcia (1830-1891).

1979, Oct. 4 *Perf. 12 1/2x12*

1441	A376	5.50e multi	15	15
1442	A376	6.50e multi	15	15
1443	A376	10e multi	20	15
1444	A376	16e multi	30	30
1445	A376	19.50e multi	35	60
1446	A376	20e multi	35	30
		Nos. 1441-1446 (6)	1.50	1.65

See Nos. 1454-1459.

Red Cross and Family — A377

Red Cross and: 20e, Doctor examining elderly man.

1979, Oct. 26 *Perf. 12x12 1/2*

1447	A377	6.50e multi	15	15
1448	A377	20e multi	55	55

National Health Service Campaign.

Holy Family, 17th Century Mosaic — A378

Mosaics, Lisbon Tile Museum: 6.50e, Nativity, 16th century. 16e, Flight into Egypt, 18th century.

1979, Dec. 5 Litho. *Perf. 12x12 1/2*

1449	A378	5.50e multi	15	15
1450	A378	6.50e multi	18	18
1451	A378	16e multi	45	45

Christmas 1979.

Rotary International, 75th Anniversary A379

1980, Feb. 22 *Perf. 12x11 1/2*

1452	A379	16e shown	42	42
1453	A379	50e Emblem, torch	1.10	1.10

Portrait Type of 1979

Leaders of the Republican Movement: 3.50e, Alvaro de Castro (1878-1928). 5.50e, Antonio Sergio (1883-1969). 6.50e, Norton de Matos (1867-1955). 11e, Jaime Cortesao (1884-1960). 16e, Teixeira Gomes (1860-1941). 20e, Jose Domingues dos Santos (1885-1958). Nos. 1454-1459 horizontal.

1980, Mar. 19

1454	A376	3.50e multi	15	15
1455	A376	5.50e multi	18	15
1456	A376	6.50e multi	18	15
1457	A376	11e multi	35	35
1458	A376	16e multi	48	38
1459	A376	20e multi	48	32
		Nos. 1454-1459 (6)	1.82	1.50

Europa Issue

Serpa Pinto (1864-1900), Explorer of Africa — A380

1980, Apr. 14

1460	A380	16e shown	20	20
1461	A380	60e Vasco da Gama (1468-1524)	85	85
a.		Souv. sheet, 2 each #1460-1461	3.00	3.00

Barn Owl — A381

1980, May 6 Litho. *Perf. 12x11 1/2*

1462	A381	6.50e shown	25	18
1463	A381	16e Red fox	52	52
1464	A381	19.50e Timber wolf	60	50
1465	A381	20e Golden eagle	60	52
a.		Souv. sheet of 4, #1462-1465	2.25	2.25

European Campaign for the Protection of Species and their Habitat (Lisbon Zoo animals); London 1980 International Stamp Exhibition, May 6-14.

Luiz Camoens — A382

Lithographed & Engraved

1980, June 9 *Perf. 11 1/2x12*

1466	A382	6.50e multi	15	15
1467	A382	20e multi	50	50

Luiz Camoens (1524-1580), 400th death anniversary. Nos. 1466-1467 each se-tenant with label showing poetry text.

Mendes Pinto and Chinese Men
A383

1980, June 30 Litho. ***Perf. 12x11½***

1468 A383 6.50e shown 20 18
1469 A383 10e Battle at sea 28 28

A Peregrinacao (The Peregrination,) by Fernao Mendes Pinto (1509-1583), written in 1580, published in 1614.

St. Vincent and Old Lisbon — A384

Designs: 8e, Lantern Tower, Evora Cathedral. 11e, Jesus with top hat, Miranda do Douro Cathedral, and mountain. 16e, Our Lady of the Milk, Braga Cathedral, and Canicada Dam. 19.50e, Pulpit, Santa Cruz Monastery, Coimbra, and Aveiro River. 20e, Algarve chimney, and Rocha Beach.

1980, Sept. 17 Litho. ***Perf. 12x12½***

1470 A384 6.50e multi 16 15
1471 A384 8e multi 20 16
1472 A384 11e multi 25 20
1473 A384 16e multi 35 35
1474 A384 19.50e multi 42 42
1475 A384 20e multi 42 32
Nos. 1470-1475 (6) 1.80 1.60

World Tourism Conf., Manila, Sept. 27.

Caravel, Lubrapex '80 Emblem
A385

1980, Oct. 18 Litho. ***Perf. 12x11½***

1476 A385 6.50e shown 18 15
1477 A385 8e Three-master Nau 22 16
1478 A385 16e Galleon 42 42
1479 A385 19.50e Paddle steamer 48 32
a. Souv. sheet of 4, #1476-1479 3.00 3.00

Lubrapex '80 Stamp Exhib., Lisbon, Oct. 18-26.

Car Emitting Gas Fumes
A386

1980, Oct. 31

1480 A386 6.50e Light bulbs 20 15
1481 A386 16e shown 40 40

Energy conservation.

Student, School and Sextant
A387

1980, Dec. 19 Litho. ***Perf. 12x11½***

1482 A387 6.50e Founder, book, emblem 16 15
1483 A387 19.50e shown 42 40

Lisbon Academy of Science bicentennial.

Man with Diseased Heart and Lungs, Hand Holding Cigarette
A388

1980, Dec. 19 ***Perf. 13½***

1484 A388 6.50e shown 18 15
1485 A388 19.50e Healthy man rejecting cigarette 48 48

Anti-smoking campaign.

Census Form and Houses
A389

1981, Jan. 1 Litho. ***Perf. 13½***

1486 A389 6.50e Form, head 20 15
1487 A389 16e shown 40 40

Fragata on Tejo River — A390

1981, Feb. 23 Litho. ***Perf. 12x12½***

1488 A390 8e shown 20 15
1489 A390 8.50e Rabelo, Douro River 20 15
1490 A390 10e Moliceiro, Aveiro River 20 15
1491 A390 16e Barco, Lima River 32 28
1492 A390 19.50e Carocho, Minho River 35 32
1493 A390 20e Varino, Tejo River 35 24
Nos. 1488-1493 (6) 1.62 1.29

Rajola Tile, Valencia, 15th Century — A391

Designs: No. 1495, Moresque tile, Coimbra 16th cent. No. 1496, Arms of Duke of Braganza, 1510. No. 1497, Pisanos design, 1595.

1981 Litho. ***Perf. 11½x12***

1494 A391 8.50e multi 22 15
a. Miniature sheet of 6 1.90 1.90
1495 A391 8.50e multi 22 15
a. Miniature sheet of 6 1.90 1.90
1496 A391 8.50e multi 22 15
a. Miniature sheet of 6 1.90 1.90
1497 A391 8.50e multi 22 15
a. Miniature sheet of 6 1.90 1.90
b. Souv. sheet of 4, #1494-1497 1.50 1.50

Issued: #1494, Mar. 16; #1495, June 13; #1496, Aug. 28; #1497, Dec. 16. See Nos. 1528-1531, 1563-1566, 1593-1596, 1617-1620.

Perdigueiro
A392

1981, Mar. 16 ***Perf. 12***

1498 A392 7e Cao de agua 16 15
1499 A392 8.50e Serra de aires 24 15
1500 A392 15e shown 35 18
1501 A392 22e Podengo 50 35
1502 A392 25.50e Castro laboreiro 55 35
1503 A392 33.50e Serra da estrela 75 35
Nos. 1498-1503 (6) 2.55 1.53

Portuguese Kennel Club, 50th anniversary.

Workers and Rainbow
A393

1981, Apr. 30 Litho. ***Perf. 12x12½***

1504 A393 8.50e shown 22 22
1505 A393 25.50e Rainbow, demonstration 50 50

International Workers' Day.

Europa Issue

Dancer in National Costume — A394

1981, May 11 ***Perf. 13½***

1506 A394 22e shown 28 28
1507 A394 48e Painted boat, horiz. 75 75
a. Souv. sheet, 2 each #1506-1507 2.50 2.50

St. Anthony Writing
A395

St. Anthony of Lisbon, 750th Anniversary of Death: 70e, Blessing people.

1981, June 13 ***Perf. 12x11½***

1508 A395 8.50e multi 20 20
1509 A395 70e multi 1.40 1.40

500th Anniv. of King Joao II — A396

1981, Aug. 28 ***Perf. 12x11½***

1510 A396 8.50e shown 30 30
1511 A396 27e Joao II leading army 95 95

125th Anniv. of Portuguese Railroads
A397

Designs: Locomotives.

1981, Oct. 28 Litho. ***Perf. 12x11½***

1512 A397 8.50e Dom Luis, 1862 22 15
1513 A397 19e Pacific 500, 1925 38 35
1514 A397 27e ALCO 1500, 1948 55 45
1515 A397 33.50e BB 2600 ALSTHOM, '74 75 38

Pearier Pump Fire Engine, 1856 — A398

1981, Nov. 18 Litho. ***Perf. 12x12½***

1516 A398 7e shown 16 15
1517 A398 8.50e Ford, 1927 22 15
1518 A398 27e Renault, 1914 55 40
1519 A398 33.50e Snorkel, Ford 1978 70 50

A399 A400

Christmas: Clay creches.

1981, Dec. 16 ***Perf. 12½x12***

1520 A399 7e multi 20 15
1521 A399 8.50e multi 22 15
1522 A399 27e multi 70 48
Set value 65

1982, Jan. 20 Litho. ***Perf. 12½x12***

1523 A400 8.50e With animals 22 15
1524 A400 27e Building church 60 45

800th birth anniv. of St. Francis of Assisi.

Centenary of Figueira da Foz — A401

1982, Feb. 24 Litho. ***Perf. 13½***

1525 A401 10e St. Catherine Fort 22 15
1526 A401 19e Tagus Bridge, ships 40 30
Set value 38

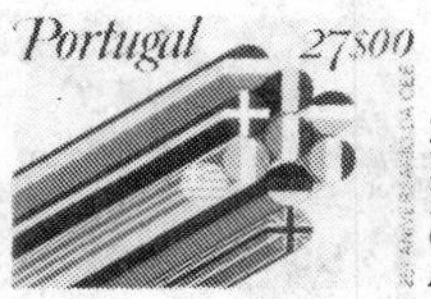

25th Anniv. of European Economic Community
A402

1982, Feb. 24 ***Perf. 12x11½***

1527 A402 27e multi 65 42
a. Souvenir sheet of 4 2.75 2.75

Tile Type of 1981

Designs: No. 1528, Italo-Flemish pattern, 17th cent. No. 1529, Oriental fabric pattern altar frontal, 17th cent. No. 1530, Greek cross, 1630-1640. No. 1531, Blue and white design, Mother of God Convent, Lisbon, 1670.

1982 Litho. ***Perf. 12x11½***

1528 A391 10e multi 22 15
a. Miniature sheet of 6 1.65 1.65
1529 A391 10e multi 20 15
a. Miniature sheet of 6 1.65 1.65
1530 A391 10e multi 18 15
a. Miniature sheet of 6 1.65 1.65
1531 A391 10e red & bl 18 15
a. Miniature sheet of 6 1.65 1.65
b. Souv. sheet of 4, #1528-1531 1.40 1.40

Issued: No. 1528, Mar. 24; No. 1529, June 11; No. 1530, Sept. 22; No. 1531, Dec. 15.

A403

A404

Major Sporting Events of 1982: 27e, Lisbon Sail. 33.50e, 25th Roller-hockey Championships, Lisbon and Barcelos, May 1-16. 50e, Intl. 470 Class World Championships, Cascais Bay. 75e, Espana '82 World Cup Soccer.

1982, Mar. 24 *Perf. 12x12½*
1532 A403 27e multi 60 35
1533 A403 33.50e multi 70 45
1534 A403 50e multi 1.10 65
1535 A403 75e multi 1.65 1.00

1982, Apr. 14 Litho. *Perf. 11½x12*
1536 A404 10e Phone, 1882 20 15
1537 A404 27e 1887 55 42

Telephone centenary.

Europa 1982 — A405

Design: Embassy of King Manuel to Pope Leo X, 1514.

1982, May 3 *Perf. 12x11½*
1538 A405 33.50e multi 65 42
a. Miniature sheet of 4 3.00 3.00

Visit of Pope John Paul II — A406

Designs: Pope John Paul and cathedrals.

1982, May 13 *Perf. 14*
1539 A406 10e Fatima 32 20
1540 A406 27e Sameiro 85 52
1541 A406 33.50e Lisbon 1.00 65
a. Min. sheet, 2 each #1539-1541 4.75 4.75

Tejo Estuary Nature Reserve Birds — A407

1982, June 11 *Perf. 11½x12*
1542 A407 10e Dunlin 22 15
1543 A407 19e Red-crested pochard 45 28
1544 A407 27e Greater flamingo 65 40
1545 A407 33.50e Black-winged stilt 85 48

PHILEXFRANCE '82 Stamp Exhibition, Paris, June 11-21.

TB Bacillus Centenary A408

1982, July 27 *Perf. 12x11½*
1546 A408 27e Koch 55 32
1547 A408 33.50e Virus, lungs 70 25

Don't Drink and Drive! — A409

1982, Sept. 22 *Perf. 12*
1548 A409 10e multi 22 15

Boeing 747 A410

Lubrapex '82 Stamp Exhibition (Historic Flights): 10e, South Atlantic crossing, 1922. 19e, South Atlantic night crossing, 1927. 33.50e, Lisbon-Rio de Janeiro discount fare flights, 1960-1967. 50e, Portugal-Brazil service, 10th anniv.

1982, Oct. 15 *Perf. 12x11½*
1549 A410 10e Fairey III D MK2 22 15
1550 A410 19e Dornier DO 40 22
1551 A410 33.50e DC-7C 65 40
1552 A410 50e shown 1.00 60
a. Souv. sheet of 4, #1549-1552 2.75 2.75

Marques de Pombal, Statesman, 200th Anniv. of Death — A411

1982, Nov. 24 Litho. *Perf. 12x11½*
1553 A411 10e multi 22 15

75th Anniv. of Port Authority of Lisbon — A412

1983, Jan. 5 *Perf. 12½*
1554 A412 10e Ships 22 15

French Alliance Centenary A413

1983, Jan. 5 *Perf. 12x11½*
1555 A413 27e multi 55 35

Export Effort A414

1983, Jan. 28
1556 A414 10e multi 20 15

World Communications Year — A415

1982, Feb. 23 Litho. *Perf. 11½x12*
1557 A415 10e bl & multi 20 15
1558 A415 33.50e lt brn & multi 65 40

Naval Uniforms and Ships — A416

1983, Feb. 23 *Perf. 13½*
1559 A416 12.50e Midshipman, 1782, Vasco da Gama 24 15
1560 A416 25e Sailor, 1845, Estefania 45 30
1561 A416 30e Sergeant, 1900, Adamastor 60 35
1562 A416 37.50e Midshipman, 1892, Comandante Joao Belo 75 45
a. Bklt. pane of 4, #1559-1562 3.00

See Nos. 1589-1592.

Tile Type of 1981

Design: No. 1563, Hunting scene, 1680. No. 1564, Birds, 18th cent. No. 1565, Flowers and Birds, 18th cent. No. 1566, Figurative tile, 18th cent.

1983 *Perf. 12x11½*
1563 A391 12.50e multi 25 15
a. Miniature sheet of 6 1.75 1.75
1564 A391 12.50e multi 28 18
a. Miniature sheet of 6 1.75 1.75
1565 A391 12.50e multi 22 15
a. Miniature sheet of 6 1.75 1.75
1566 A391 12.50e multi 22 15
a. Miniature sheet of 6 1.75 1.75
b. Souv. sheet of 4, #1563-1566 1.25 1.25

Issued: No. 1563, Mar. 16; No. 1563, June 16; No. 1563, Oct. 19; No. 1563, Nov. 23.

17th European Arts and Sciences Exhibition, Lisbon — A417

Portuguese Discoveries and Renaissance Europe: 11e, Helmet, 16th cent. 12.50e, Astrolabe. 25e, Ships, Flemish tapestry. 30e, Column capital, 12th cent. 37.50e, Hour glass. 40e, Chinese panel painting.

1983, Apr. 6
1567 A417 11e multi 25 16
1568 A417 12.50e multi 28 18
1569 A417 25e multi 55 32
1570 A417 30e multi 65 40
1571 A417 37.50e multi 85 50
1572 A417 40e multi 90 52
a. Souv. sheet of 6, #1567-1572 3.75 3.75
Nos. 1567-1572 (6) 3.48 2.08

Europa Issue

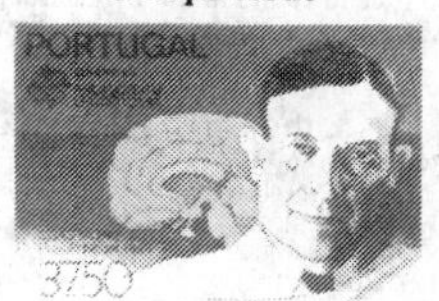
Egas Moniz (1874-1955), Cerebral Angiography and Pre-frontal Leucotomy Pioneer A418

1983, May 5 Litho. *Perf. 12½*
1573 A418 37.50e multi 60 60
a. Souvenir sheet of 4 2.50 2.50

European Conference of Ministers of Transport — A419

1983, May 16
1574 A419 30e multi 85 38

Endangered Sea Mammals A420

1983, July 29 Litho. *Perf. 12x11½*
1575 A420 12.50e Sea wolf 18 15
1576 A420 30e Dolphin 45 28
1577 A420 37.50e Killer whale 55 35
1578 A420 80e Humpback whale 1.25 75
a. Souv. sheet of 4, #1575-1578 3.25 3.25

BRASILIANA '83 Intl. Stamp Exhibition, Rio de Janeiro, July 29-Aug. 7.

600th Anniv. of Revolution of 1383 — A421

1983, Sept. 14 *Perf. 13½*
1579 A421 12.50e Death of Joao Fernandes Andeiro 25 15
1580 A421 30e Rebellion 60 32

First Manned Balloon Flight A422

Designs: 16e, Bartolomeu Lourenco de Gusmao, Passarola flying machine. 51e, Montgolfier Balloon, first flight.

1983, Nov. 9 Litho. *Perf. 12x11½*
1581 A422 16e multi 28 18
1582 A422 51e multi 85 52

Christmas 1983 — A423

Stained Glass Windows, Monastery at Batalha: 12.50e, Adoration of the Magi. 30e, Flight to Egypt.

1983, Nov. 23 *Perf. 12½*
1583 A423 12.50e multi 22 15
1584 A423 30e multi 52 32

Lisbon Zoo Centenary A424

1984, Jan. 18 Litho. *Perf. 12x11½*

1585 A424 16e Siberian tigers 50 30
1586 A424 16e White rhinoceros 50 30
1587 A424 16e Damalisco Albifronte 50 30
1588 A424 16e Cheetahs 50 30
a. Strip of 4, #1585-1588 2.00 1.25

Military Type of 1983

Air Force Dress Uniforms and Planes: 16e, 1954; Hawker Hurricane II, 1943. 35e, 1960; Republic F-84G Thunderjet. 40e, Paratrooper, 1966; 2502 Nord Noratlas, 1960. 51e, 1966; Corsair II, 1982.

1984, Feb. 5 Litho. *Perf. 13½*

1589 A416 16e multi 25 15
1590 A416 35e multi 55 35
1591 A416 40e multi 65 40
1592 A416 51e multi 80 48
a. Bklt. pane of 4, #1589-1592 2.90

Tile Type of 1981

Design: No. 1593, Royal arms, 19th cent. No. 1594, Pombal Palace wall tile, 19th cent. No. 1595, Facade covering, 19th cent. No. 1596, Grasshoppers, by Rafael Bordaro Pinhiero, 19th cent.

1984, Mar. 8 Litho. *Perf. 12x11½*

1593 A391 16e multi 25 15
a. Miniature sheet of 6 1.65 1.65
1594 A391 16e multi 25 15
a. Miniature sheet of 6 1.65 1.65
1595 A391 16e multi 25 15
a. Miniature sheet of 6 1.65 1.65
1596 A391 16e multi 24 15
a. Miniature sheet of 6 1.65 1.65
b. Souv. sheet of 4, #1593-1596 1.25 1.25

Issued: No. 1593, Mar. 8; No. 1594, July 18; No. 1595, Aug. 3; No. 1596, Oct. 17 .

25th Lisbon Intl. Fair, May 9-13 A425

Events: 40e, World Food Day. 51e, 15th Rehabilitation Intl. World Congress, Lisbon, June 4-8, vert.

1984, Apr. 3

1597 A425 35e multi 75 35
1598 A425 40e multi 90 40
1599 A425 51e multi 1.10 48

April 25th Revolution, 10th Anniv. — A426

1984, Apr. 25 *Perf. 13½*

1600 A426 16e multi 40 18

Europa (1959-84) A427

1984, May 2 *Perf. 12x11½*

1601 A427 51e multi 80 48
a. Souvenir sheet of 4 3.75 3.75

LUBRAPEX '84 and Natl. Early Art Museum Centenary A428

Paintings: 16e, Nun, 15th cent. 40e, St. John, by Master of the Retable of Santiago, 16th cent. 51e, View of Lisbon, 17th cent. 66e, Cabeca de Jovem, by Domingos Sesqueira, 19th cent.

1984, May 9 Litho. *Perf. 12x11½*

1602 A428 16e multi 30 18
1603 A428 40e multi 70 40
1604 A428 51e multi 95 52
1605 A428 66e multi 1.10 60
a. Souv. sheet of 4, #1602-1605 3.75 2.75

1984 Summer Olympics A429

1984, June 5

1606 A429 35e Fencing 52 32
1607 A429 40e Gymnastics 60 38
1608 A429 51e Running 75 45
1609 A429 80e Pole vault 1.25 75

Souvenir Sheet

1610 A429 100e Hurdles 2.25 1.50

Historical Events A430

Designs: 16e, Gil Eanes, explorer who reached west coast of Africa, 1434. 51e, King Peter I of Brazil and IV of Portugal.

1984, Sept. 24 *Perf. 12x11½*

1611 A430 16e multi 32 18
1612 A430 51e multi 85 45

See Brazil No. 1954.

Infantry Grenadier, 1740 — A431

1985, Jan. 23 Litho. *Perf. 13½*

1613 A431 20e shown 30 15
1614 A431 46e 5th Cavalry Regiment Officer, 1810 70 35
1615 A431 60e Artillery Corporal, 1892 90 45
1616 A431 100e Engineering Soldier, 1985 1.50 75
a. Bklt. pane of 4, #1613-1616 3.50

Tile Type of 1981

Designs: No. 1617, Tile from entrance hall of Lisbon's Faculdade de Letras, by Jorge Barradas, 20th cent.; No. 1618, Explorer and sailing ship, detail from tile panel by Maria Keil, Avenida Infante Santo, Lisbon; No. 1619, Profile and key, detail from a 20th century tile mural by Querubim Lapa; No. 1620, Geometric designs and flowers, by Manuel Cargaleiro.

1985 Litho. *Perf. 12x11½*

1617 A391 20e multi 30 15
a. Miniature sheet of 6 1.80 1.80
1618 A391 20e multi 25 15
a. Miniature sheet of 6 1.50 1.50
1619 A391 20e multi 28 15
a. Miniature sheet of 6 1.75 1.75
1620 A391 20e multi 25 15
a. Miniature sheet of 6 1.50 1.50
b. Souv. sheet of 4, #1617-1620 1.00 1.00

Issued: No. 1617, Feb. 13; No. 1617, June 11; No. 1617, Aug. 20; No. 1617, Nov. 15.

Kiosks — A432

1985, Mar. 19 Litho. *Perf. 11½x12*

1621 A432 20e Green kiosk 50 15
1622 A432 20e Red kiosk 50 15
1623 A432 20e Gray kiosk 50 15
1624 A432 20e Blue kiosk 50 15
a. Strip of 4, #1621-1624 2.00

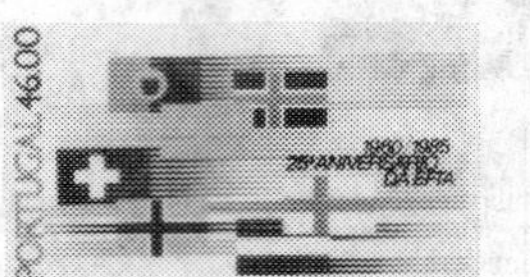

25th Anniv., European Free Trade Association — A433

1985, Apr. 10 Litho. *Perf. 12x11½*

1625 A433 46e Flags of members 80 30

Intl. Youth Year — A434

1985, Apr. 10 Litho.

1626 A434 60e Heads of boy and girl 1.10 40

Europa 1985-Music — A435

1985, May 6 Litho. *Perf. 11½x12*

1627 A435 60e Woman playing tambourine 80 40
a. Souvenir sheet of 4 3.25 3.25

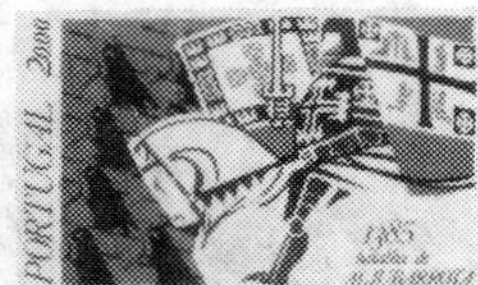

Historic Anniversaries — A436

Designs: 20e, King John I at the Battle of Aljubarrota, 1385. 46e, Queen Leonor (1458-1525) founding the Caldas da Rainha Hospital. 60e, Cartographer Pedro Reinel, earliest Portuguese map, c. 1483.

1985, July 5 Litho. *Perf. 12x11½*

1628 A436 20e multi 28 15
1629 A436 46e multi 60 30
1630 A436 60e multi 80 40

See Nos. 1678-1680.

Traditional Architecture — A437

1985-89 Litho. *Perf. 12*

1631 A437 50c Saloia, Estremadura 15 15
1632 A437 1e Beira interior 15 15
1633 A437 1.50e Ribatejo 15 15
1634 A437 2.50e Transmontanas 15 15
1635 A437 10e Minho and Douro Litoral 15 15
1636 A437 20e Farm house, Minho 28 15
1637 A437 22.50e Alentejo 32 16
1638 A437 25e African Sitio, Algarve 35 18
1639 A437 27e Beira Interior 45 22
1640 A437 29e Hill country 45 22
1641 A437 30e Algarve 50 25
1642 A437 40e Beira Interior 62 30
1643 A437 50e Private home, Beira Litoral 70 35
1644 A437 55e Tras-os-Montes 90 45
1645 A437 60e Beira Litoral 95 48
1646 A437 70e Estremadura Sul and Alentejo 1.10 55
1647 A437 80e Estremadura 1.10 55
1648 A437 90e Minho 1.25 62
1649 A437 100e Adobe Monte, Alentejo 1.30 65
1650 A437 500e Algarve 7.40 3.70
Nos. 1631-1650 (20) 18.42 9.58

Issue dates: 20e, 25e, 50e, 100e, Aug. 20, 1985. 2.50e, 22.50e, 80e, 90e, Mar. 10, 1986. 10e, 40e, 60e, 70e, Mar. 6, 1987. 1.50e, 27e, 30e, 55e, Mar. 15, 1988. 50c, 1e, 29e, 500e, Mar. 8, 1989.

Aquilino Ribeiro (1885-1963), Author — A438

Writers: 46c, Fernando Pessoa (1888-1935), poet.

1985, Oct. 2 Litho. *Perf. 12*

1651 A438 20e multi 25 15
1652 A438 46e multi 60 30

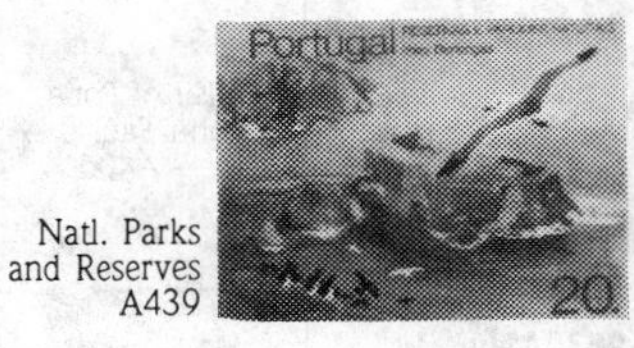

Natl. Parks and Reserves A439

1985, Oct. 25

1653 A439 20e Berlenga Island 25 15
1654 A439 40e Estrela Mountain Chain 52 25
1655 A439 46e Boquilobo Marsh 60 30
1656 A439 80e Formosa Lagoon 1.00 50

Souvenir Sheet

1657 A439 100e St. Jacinto Dunes 1.25 1.25

ITALIA '85.

Christmas 1985 — A440

Illuminated codices from The Prayer Times Book, Book of King Manuel, 1517-1538.

1985, Nov. 15 *Perf. 11½x12*

1658 A440 20e The Nativity 25 15
1659 A440 46e Adoration of the Magi 60 30

Postrider — A441

1985, Dec. 13 **Litho.** ***Perf. 13½***
1660 A441 A(22.50e) lt yel grn & dp yel grn 32 16

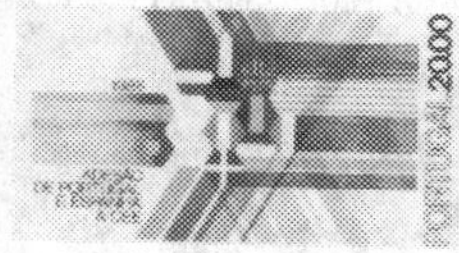
Flags of EEC Member Nations A442

Design: 57.50e, Map of EEC, flags.

1986, Jan. 7 **Litho.** ***Perf. 12***
1661 A442 20e multi 25 15
1662 A442 57.50e multi 75 38
a. Souv. sheet, 2 each #1661-1662 2.25 2.25

Admission of Portugal and Spain to the European Economic Community, Jan. 1. See Spain Nos. 2463-2466.
No. 1662a contains 2 alternating pairs of Nos. 1661-1662.

Castles A443

1986, Feb. 18 **Litho.** ***Perf. 12***
1663 A443 22.50e Beja 32 16
a. Bklt. pane of 4 1.30
1664 A443 22.50e Feira 32 16
a. Bklt. pane of 4 1.30

1986, Apr. 10
1665 A443 22.50e Guimaraes 32 16
a. Bklt. pane of 4 1.30
1666 A443 22.50e Braganca 32 16
a. Bklt. pane of 4 1.30

1986, Sept. 18
1667 A443 22.50e Montemor-o-Velho 32 16
a. Bklt. pane of 4 1.30
1668 A443 22.50e Belmonte 32 16
a. Bklt. pane of 4 1.30

See Nos. 1688-1695, 1723-1726.

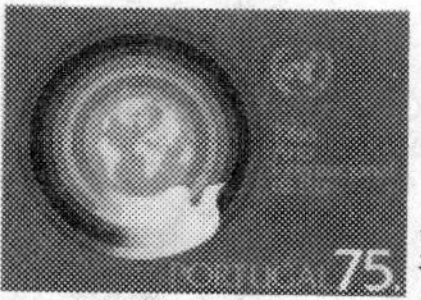
Intl. Peace Year — A445

1986, Feb. 18 **Litho.** ***Perf. 12***
1669 A445 75e multicolored 1.00 50

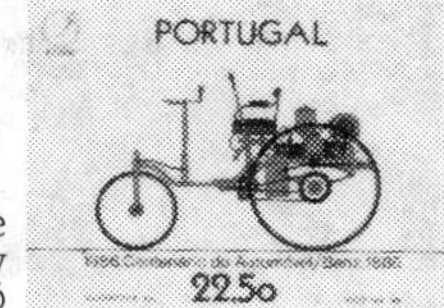
Automobile Centenary A446

1986, Apr. 10 **Litho.** ***Perf. 12***
1670 A446 22.50e 1886 Benz 32 16
1671 A446 22.50e 1886 Daimler 32 16
a. Pair, #1670-1671 65 40

Europa 1986 — A447

1986, May 5 **Litho.**
1672 A447 68.50e Shad 1.05 52
a. Souvenir sheet of 4 4.25 4.25

Horse Breeds A448

1986, May 22 **Litho.** ***Perf. 12***
1673 A448 22.50e Alter 32 16
1674 A448 47.50e Lusitano 68 35
1675 A448 52.50e Garrano 75 38
1676 A448 68.50e Sorraia 1.00 50

Souvenir Sheet

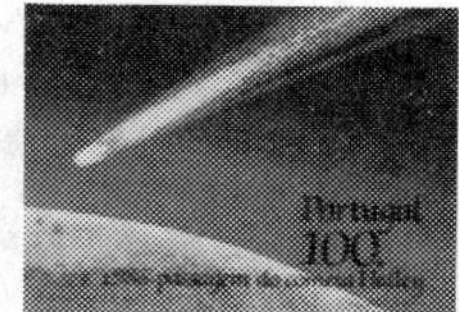
Halley's Comet A449

1986, June 24
1677 A449 100e multi 1.50 1.50

Anniversaries Type of 1985

Designs: 22.50e, Diogo Cao, explorer, heraldic pillar erected at Cape Lobo, 1484, 1st expedition. No. 1679, Manuel Passos, Corinthian column. No. 1680, Joao Baptista Ribeiro, painter, Oporto Academy director, c. 1836, and musicians.

1986, Aug. 28 **Litho.**
1678 A436 22.50e multi 32 16
1679 A436 52.50e multi 75 38
1680 A436 52.50e multi 75 38

Diogo Cao's voyages, 500th anniv. Academies of Fine Art, 150th anniv.

Stamp Day — A450

Natl. Guard, 75th Anniv. — A451

Order of Engineers, 50th Anniv. — A452

Anniversaries and events: No. 1681, Postal card, 100th anniv.

1986, Oct. 24 **Litho.**
1681 A450 22.50e multi 32 16
1682 A451 47.50e multi 68 35
1683 A452 52.50e multi 75 38

Watermills A453

1986, Nov. 7
1684 A453 22.50e Duoro 32 15
1685 A453 47.50e Coimbra 68 35
1686 A453 52.50e Gerez 75 38
1687 A453 90e Braga 1.25 62
a. Souv. sheet of 4, #1684-1687 3.00 3.00

LUBRAPEX '86. #1687a issued Nov. 21.

Castle Type of 1986

1987-88 **Litho.**
1688 A443 25e Silves 35 18
a. Bklt. pane of 4 1.40
1689 A443 25e Evora Monte 35 18
a. Bklt. pane of 4 1.40
1690 A443 25e Leiria 38 20
a. Bklt. pane of 4 + label 1.55
1691 A443 25e Trancoso 38 20
a. Bklt. pane of 4 + label 1.55
1692 A443 25e St. George 38 20
a. Bklt. pane of 4 + label 1.55
1693 A443 25e Marvao 38 20
a. Bklt. pane of 4 + label 1.55
1694 A443 27e Fernando's Walls of Oporto 45 22
a. Bklt. pane of 4 + label 1.80
1695 A443 27e Almourol 45 22
a. Bklt. pane of 4 + label 1.80
Nos. 1688-1695 (8) 3.12 1.60

Issued: Nos. 1688-1689, Jan. 16; Nos. 1690-1691, Apr. 10; Nos. 1692-1693, Sept. 15; Nos. 1694-1695, Jan. 19, 1988.

Natl. Tourism Organization, 75th Anniv. A454

1987, Feb. 10 **Litho.** ***Perf. 12***
1696 A454 25e Beach houses, Tocha 40 20
1697 A454 57e Boats, Espinho 90 45
1698 A454 98e Chafariz Fountain, Arraioles 1.50 75

European Nature Conservation Year — A455

1987, Mar. 20 ***Perf. 12x12½***
1699 A455 25e shown 40 20
1700 A455 57e Hands, flower, map 90 45
1701 A455 74.50e Hands, star, rainbow 1.15 58

Europa 1987 — A456

Modern architecture: Bank Borges and Irmao Agency, 1986, Vila do Conde.

1987, May 5 **Litho.** ***Perf. 12***
1702 A456 74.50e multi 1.25 62
a. Souv. sheet of 4 5.00 5.00

Lighthouses — A457

A458

1987, June 12 ***Perf. 11½x12***
1703 A457 25e Aveiro 40 20
1704 A457 25e Berlenga 40 20
1705 A457 25e Cape Mondego 40 20
1706 A457 25e Cape St. Vincente 40 20
a. Strip of 4, #1703-1706 1.60 80

1987, Aug. 27 **Litho.** ***Perf. 12***
1707 A458 74.50e multi 1.10 55

Amadeo de Souza-Cardoso (1887-1919), painter.

Portguese Royal Library, Rio de Janeiro, 150th anniv. A459

1987, Aug. 27 ***Perf. 12x11½***
1708 A459 125e multi 2.00 1.00

Paper Currency of Portugal, 300th Anniv. A460

1987, Aug. 27 ***Perf. 12x11½***
1709 A460 100e multi 1.50 75

Voyages of Bartolomeu Dias (d. 1499), 500th Anniv. A461

1987, Aug. 27 ***Perf. 12x11½***
1710 A461 25e Departing from Lisbon, 1487 38 20
1711 A461 25e Discovering the African Coast, 1488 38 20
a. Pair, #1710-1711 80 50

No. 1711a has continuous design.
See Nos. 1721-1722.

Souvenir Sheet

Phonograph Record, 100th Anniv. A462

1987, Oct. 9 **Litho.** ***Perf. 12***
1712 Sheet of 2 3.00 3.00
a. A462 75e Compact-disc player 1.10 1.10
b. A462 125e Gramophone 1.90 1.90

Christmas A463

Various children's drawings, Intl. Year of the Child emblem.

1987, Nov. 6
1713 A463 25e Angels, magi, tree 38 20
1714 A463 57e Friendship circle 88 45
1715 A463 74.50e Santa riding dove 1.10 58
a. Souv. sheet of 3, #1713-1715 2.40 2.40

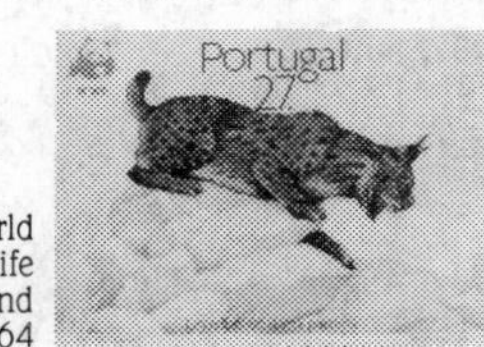

World Wildlife Fund A464

Lynx, *Lynx pardina.*

1988, Feb. 3 Litho. *Perf. 12*

1716	A464 27e Stalking		45	22
1717	A464 27e Carrying prey		45	22
1718	A464 27e Two adults		45	22
1719	A464 27e Adult, young		45	22
	a. Strip of 4, Nos. 1716-1719		1.80	1.80

Printed in a continuous design.

Journey of Pero da Covilha to the East, 500th Anniv. A465

1988, Feb. 3

1720	A465 105e multi	1.65	82

Bartolomeu Dias Type of 1987

Discovery of the link between the Atlantic and Indian Oceans by Dias, 500th Anniv.: No. 1721, Tidal wave, ship. No. 1722, Henricus Martelus Germanus's map (1489), picturing the African coast and linking the two oceans.

1988, Feb. 3

1721	A461 27e multi	45	22
1722	A461 27e multi	45	22
a.	Bklt. pane of 4, Nos. 1710-1711, 1721-1722	1.70	
b.	Pair, #1721-1722	1.00	60

No. 1722b has continuous design.

Castle Type of 1986

1988, Mar. 15 Litho. *Perf. 12*

1723	A443 27e Vila Nova de Cerveira	45	22
a.	Bklt. pane of 4 + label	1.80	
1724	A443 27e Palmela	45	22
a.	Bklt. pane of 4 + label	1.80	

1988, July 1

1725	A443 27e Chaves	45	22
a.	Bklt. pane of 4 + label	1.80	
1726	A443 27e Penedono	45	22
a.	Bklt. pane of 4 + label	1.80	

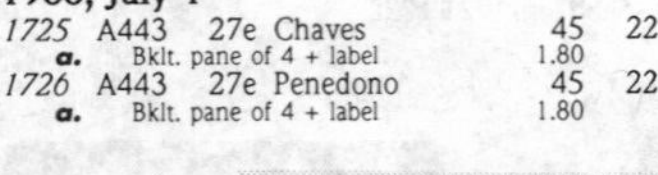

Europa 1988 — A466

Transportation: Mail coach, Lisbon-Oporto route, 1855-1864.

1988, Apr. 21 Litho. *Perf. 12*

1735	A466 80e multi	1.35	68
a.	Souv. sheet of 4	5.40	5.40

Jean Monnet (1888-1979), Economist A467

1988, May 9 Litho.

1736	A467 60e multi	98	50

Souvenir Sheet

National Heritage (Patrimony) — A468

Design: 150e, Belvedere of Cordovil House and Fountain of Porta de Moura reflected in the Garcia de Resende balcony window, Evora, 16th cent.

1988, May 13 *Perf. $13^1/_2$x$12^1/_2$*

1737	A468 150e multi	2.50	2.50

No. 1737 has inscribed margin picturing LUBRAPEX '88 and UNESCO emblems.

20th Cent. Paintings by Portuguese Artists — A469

Designs: 27e, *Viola,* c. 1916, by Amadeo de Souza-Cardoso (1887-1918). 60e, *Jugglers and Tumblers Do Not Fall,* 1949, by Jose de Almada Negreiros (1893-1970). 80e, *Still-life with Guitar,* c. 1940, by Eduardo Viana (1881-1967).

1988, Aug. 23 Litho. *Perf. $11^1/_2$x12*

1738	A469 27e multi	42	20
1739	A469 60e multi	90	45
1740	A469 80e multi	1.20	60
a.	Min. sheet of 3, #1738-1740	2.55	2.55

See Nos. 1748-1750, 1754-1765.

1988 Summer Olympics, Seoul — A470

1988, Sept. 16 Litho. *Perf. 12x$11^1/_2$*

1741	A470 27e Archery	40	20
1742	A470 55e Weight lifting	82	40
1743	A470 60e Judo	90	45
1744	A470 80e Tennis	1.20	60

Souvenir Sheet

1745	A470 200e Yachting	3.00	3.00

Remains of the Roman Civilization in Portugal A471

Mozaics: 27e, "Winter Image," detail of *Mosaic of the Four Seasons,* limestone and glass, 3rd cent., House of the Waterworks, Coimbra. 80e, *Fish in Marine Water,* limestone, 3rd-4th cent., cover of a tank wall, public baths, Faro.

1988, Oct. 18 Litho. *Perf. 12*

1746	A471 27e multi	40	20
1747	A471 80e multi	1.15	58

20th Cent. Art Type of 1988

Paintings by Portuguese artists: 27e, *Burial,* 1938, by Mario Eloy. 60e, *Lisbon Roofs,* c. 1936, by Carlos Botelho. 80e, *Avejao Lirico,* 1939, by Antonio Pedro.

1988, Nov. 18 Litho. *Perf. $11^1/_2$x12*

1748	A469 27e multi	42	20
1749	A469 60e multi	92	45
1750	A469 80e multi	1.25	62
a.	Souv. sheet of 3, #1748-1750	2.60	2.60
b.	Souv. sheet of 6, #1738-1740, 1748-1750	5.25	5.25

Braga Cathedral, 900th Anniv. A472

1989, Jan. 20 *Perf. 12*

1751	A472 30e multi	45	22

INDIA '89 — A473

Designs: 55e, Caravel, Sao Jorge da Mina Fort, 1482. 60e, Navigator using astrolabe, 16th cent.

1989, Jan. 20

1752	A473 55e multi	85	42
1753	A473 60e multi	92	45

20th Cent. Art Type of 1988

Paintings by Portuguese artists: 29e, *Antithesis of Calm,* 1940, by Antonio Dacosta. 60c, *Lunch of the Unskilled Mason,* c. 1926, by Julio Pomar. 87e, *Simums,* 1949, by Vespeira.

1989, Feb. 15 Litho. *Perf. $11^1/_2$x12*

1754	A469 29e multi	40	20
1755	A469 60e multi	82	40
1756	A469 87e multi	1.20	60
a.	Souv. sheet of 3, #1754-1756	2.50	2.50

1989, July 7

Paintings by Portuguese artists: 29e, *046-72,* 1972, by Fernando Lanhas. 60e, *Les Spirales,* 1954, by Nadir Afonso. 87e, *Sim,* 1987, by Carlos Calvet.

1757	A469 29e multi	35	18
1758	A469 60e multi	75	38
1759	A469 87e multi	1.10	55
a.	Souv. sheet of 3, #1757-1759	2.20	2.20
b.	Souv. sheet of 6, #1754-1759	4.75	4.75

1990, Feb. 14

Paintings by Portuguese artists: 32e, *Aluenda-Tordesillas* by Joaquim Rodrigo. 60e, *Pintura* by Noronha da Costa. 95e, *Pintura* by Vasco Costa (1917-1985).

1760	A469 32e multicolored	42	22
1761	A469 60e multicolored	78	40
1762	A469 95e multicolored	1.25	65
a.	Souv. sheet of 3, #1760-1762	2.50	2.50

1990, Sept. 21

Paintings by Portuguese artists: 32e, Costa Pinheiro. 60e, Paula Rego. 95e, Jose De Guimaraes.

1763	A469 32e multicolored	42	22
1764	A469 60e multicolored	80	40
1765	A469 95e multicolored	1.30	65
a.	Min. sheet of 3, #1763-1765	2.50	2.50
b.	Min. sheet of 6, #1760-1765	5.00	5.00

Special Occasions — A474

1989, Feb. 15 Litho. *Perf. 12*

1772	A474 29e multi	40	20
a.	Bklt. pane of 8	3.25	
1773	A474 60e With love	80	40
a.	Bklt. pane of 8	6.40	

European Parliament Elections — A475

1989, Mar. 8 Litho. *Perf. $11^1/_2$x12*

1774	A475 60e multi	90	45

Europa 1989 — A476

Children's toys.

1989, Apr. 26 Litho. *Perf. 12*

1775	A476 80e Top	1.20	60

Souvenir Sheet

1776	Sheet of 4, 2 each #1775, 1776a	4.80	4.80
a.	A476 80e Tops	1.20	1.20

Surface Transportation, Lisbon — A477

Designs: 29e, Carris Co. elevated railway, Bica Street. 65e, Carris electric tram. 87e, Carmo Elevator, Santa Justa Street. 100e, Carris doubledecker bus. 250e, Transtejo Co. riverboat *Cacilheiro,* horiz.

1989, May 22 Litho.

1777	A477 29e multi	45	22
1778	A477 65e multi	98	50
1779	A477 87e multi	1.30	65
1780	A477 100e multi	1.50	75

Souvenir Sheet

1781	A477 250e multi	3.75	3.75

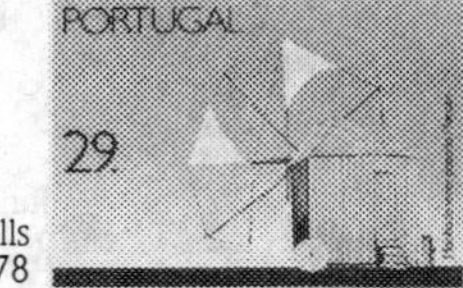

Windmills A478

1989, June 14 Litho.

1782	A478 29e Ansiao	45	22
1783	A478 65e Santiago do Cacem	98	50
1784	A478 87e Afife	1.30	65
1785	A478 100e Caldas da Rainha	1.50	75
a.	Bklt. pane of 4, #1782-1785	4.25	

Souvenir Sheet

French Revolution, 200th Anniv. — A479

1989, July 7 Litho. *Perf. 11½x12*
1786 A479 250e Drummer 3.00 3.00

No. 1786 has multicolored inscribed margin picturing the PHILEXFRANCE '89 emblem and the storming of the Bastille.

Natl. Palaces A480

1989, Oct. 18 Litho. *Perf. 12*
1787 A480 29e Ajuda, Lisbon, and King Luiz I 35 18
1788 A480 60e Queluz 75 38

Death cent. of King Luiz.

Exhibition Emblem and Wildflowers — A481

1989, Nov. 17 Litho.
1789 A481 29e *Armeria pseudarmeria* 38 20
1790 A481 60e *Santolina impressa* 75 38
1791 A481 87e *Linaria lamarckii* 1.10 55
1792 A481 100e *Limonium multiforum* 1.25 62
a. Bklt. pane of 4, #1789-1792 3.50

World Stamp Expo '89, Washington, DC.

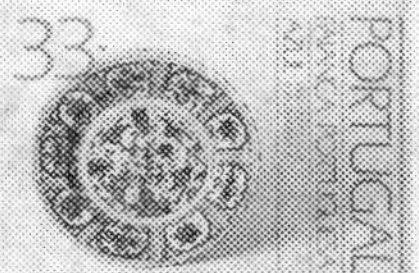

Portuguese Faience, 17th Cent. A482

1990, Jan. 24 Litho. *Perf. 12x11½*
1793 A482 33e shown 45 22
1794 A482 33e Nobleman (plate) 45 22
1795 A482 35e Urn 48 24
1796 A482 60e Fish (pitcher) 80 40
1797 A482 60e Crown, shield (plate) 80 40
1798 A482 60e Lidded bowl 80 40
Nos. 1793-1798 (6) 3.78 1.88

Souvenir Sheet

Perf. 12

1799 A482 250e Plate 3.35 3.35

No. 1799 contains one 52x45mm stamp. See Nos. 1829-1835, 1890-1896.

Score, Alfred Keil and Henrique Lopes de Mondonca A483

1990, Mar. 6 *Perf. 12x11½*
1804 A483 32e multicolored 42 22

A Portuguesa, the Natl. Anthem, cent. (32e).

University Education in Portugal, 700th Anniv. — A484

1990, Mar. 6 *Perf. 11½x12*
1805 A484 70e multicolored 95 48

Europa 1990 A485

1990, Apr. 11 *Perf. 12x11½*
1806 A485 80e Santo Tirso P.O. 1.10 55

Souvenir Sheet

1807 Sheet of 4, 2 each #1806, 1807a 4.40 4.40
a. A485 80e Mala Posta P.O. 1.10 1.10

Souvenir Sheet

Gentleman Using Postage Stamp, 1840 — A486

1990, May 3
1808 A486 250e multicolored 3.35 3.35

Stamp World London '90 and 150th anniv. of the Penny Black.

Greetings Issue — A487

"FELICITACOES" and street scenes.

1990, June 5 Litho. *Perf. 12*
1809 A487 60e Stairway 80 40
1810 A487 60e Automobile 80 40
1811 A487 60e Man in street 80 40
1812 A487 60e shown 80 40

Perf. 13 Vert.

1809a A487 60e 80 40
1810a A487 60e 80 40
1811a A487 60e 80 40
1812a A487 60e 80 40
b. Bklt. pane of 4, #1809a-1812a 3.25

Camilo Castelo Branco (1825-1890), Writer A488

Designs: 70e, Friar Bartolomeu dos Martires (1514-1590), theologian.

1990, July 11 Litho. *Perf. 12x11½*
1813 A488 65e multicolored 90 45
1814 A488 70e multicolored 95 48

Ships — A489

1990, Sept. 21 Litho. *Perf. 12*
1815 A489 32e Barca 42 22
1816 A489 60e Caravela Pescareza 80 40
1817 A489 70e Barinel 95 48
1818 A489 95e Caravela 1.30 65

Perf. 13½ Vert.

1815a A489 32e 42 22
1816a A489 60e 80 40
1817a A489 70e 95 48
1818a A489 95e 1.30 65
b. Bklt. pane of 4, #1815a-1818a 3.45

National Palaces — A490

1990, Oct. 11
1819 A490 32e Pena 45 22
1820 A490 60e Vila 82 40
1821 A490 70e Mafra 95 48
1822 A490 120e Guimaraes 1.65 82

Francisco Sa Carneiro (1934-1980), Politician A491

1990, Nov. 7
1823 A491 32e ol brn & blk 45 22

Rossio Railway Station, Cent. — A492

Various locomotives.

1990, Nov. 7
1824 A492 32e Steam, 1887 45 22
1825 A492 60e Steam, 1891 82 40
1826 A492 70e Steam, 1916 95 48
1827 A492 95e Electric, 1956 1.30 65

Souvenir Sheet

1828 A492 200e Railway station 2.90 1.45

Ceramics Type of 1990

1991, Feb. 7 Litho. *Perf. 12*
1829 A482 35e Lavabo 50 25
1830 A482 35e Tureen and plate 50 25
1831 A482 35e Flower vase 50 25
1832 A482 60e Finger bowl 85 45
1833 A482 60e Coffee pot 85 45
1834 A482 60e Mug 85 45
Nos. 1829-1834 (6) 4.05 2.10

Souvenir Sheet

1835 A482 250e Plate 3.90 1.95

No. 1835 contains one 52x44mm stamp.

European Tourism Year — A494

1991, Mar. 6 Litho. *Perf. 12*
1836 A494 60e Flamingos 95 48
1837 A494 110e Chameleon 1.70 85

Souvenir Sheet

1838 A494 250e Deer 3.90 1.95

Portuguese Navigators — A495

1990-92 Litho. *Perf. 12x11½*
1841 A495 2e Joao Goncalves Zarco 15 15
1842 A495 5e Tristao Vaz Teixeira 15 15
1843 A495 6e Pedro Alvares Cabral 15 15
1846 A495 32e Bartolomeu Perestrelo 42 22
1847 A495 35e Gil Eanes 50 25
1848 A495 38e Vasco da Gama 58 28
1851 A495 60e Nuno Tristao 85 45
1852 A495 65e Joao da Nova 1.00 50
1854 A495 80e Diogo Gomes 1.15 60
1856 A495 100e Diogo de Silves 1.35 68
1857 A495 250e Diogo Cao 3.60 1.80
1858 A495 350e Bartolomeu Dias 5.30 2.65
Nos. 1841-1858 (12) 15.20 7.88

Issued: 2e, 5e, 32e, 100e, Mar. 6, 1991; 6e, 38e, 65e, 350e, Mar. 6, 1992. 35e, 60e, 80e, 250e, Mar. 6, 1992. This is an expanding set. Numbers may change.

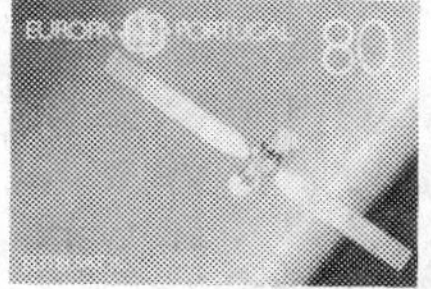

Europa A496

1991, Apr. 11 Litho. *Perf. 12*
1859 A496 80e Eutelsat II 1.15 60

Souvenir Sheet

1860 Sheet, 2 each #1859, 1860a 4.60 2.40
a. A496 80e Olympus I 1.15 60

Souvenir Sheet

Princess Isabel & Philip le Bon — A497

1991, May 27 Litho. *Perf. 12½*
1861 A497 300e multicolored 4.00 4.00

Europalia '91. See Belgium No. 1402.

Discovery Ships — A498

1991, May 27 Litho. *Perf. 12*

1862 A498 35e Caravel 50 25
1863 A498 75e Nau 1.10 55
1864 A498 80e Nau, stern 1.15 60
1865 A498 110e Galleon 1.70 85

Perf. 13½ Vert.

1862a A498 35e 50 25
1863a A498 75e 1.10 55
1864a A498 80e 1.15 60
1865a A498 110e 1.70 85
b. Bklt. pane of 4, #1862a-1865a 4.50

Portuguese Crown Jewels — A499

Designs: 35e, Running knot, diamonds & emeralds, 18th cent. 60e, Royal scepter, 19th cent. 70e, Sash of the Grand Cross, ruby & diamonds, 18th cent. 80e, Court saber, gold & diamonds in hilt, 19th cent. 140e, Royal crown, 19th cent.

1991, July 8 Litho. *Perf. 12*

1866 A499 35e multicolored 50 25
1867 A499 60e multicolored 88 44
1868 A499 80e multicolored 1.15 62
1869 A499 140e multicolored 2.00 1.00

Perf. 13½ Vert.

1870 A499 70e multicolored 1.00 50
a. Booklet pane of 5 5.00

See Nos. 1898-1902.

Antero de Quental (1842-1891), Poet — A500

First Missionaries to Congo, 500th Anniv. A501

1991, Aug. 2 *Perf. 12*

1871 A500 35e multicolored 50 25
1872 A501 110e multicolored 1.70 85

Architectural Heritage A502

Designs: 35e, School of Architecture, Oporto University, by Siza Vieira. 60e, Torre do Tombo, by Ateliers Associates of Arsenio Cordeiro. 80e, Railway Bridge over Douro River, by Edgar Cardoso. 110e, Setubal-Braga highway bridge.

1991, Sept. 4 Litho. *Perf. 12*

1873 A502 35e multicolored 50 25
1874 A502 60e multicolored 88 44
1875 A502 80e multicolored 1.15 62
1876 A502 110e multicolored 1.70 85

1992 Summer Olympics, Barcelona A503

1991, Oct. 9 Litho. *Perf. 12*

1877 A503 35e Equestrian 55 28
1878 A503 60e Fencing 90 45
1879 A503 80e Shooting 1.15 60
1880 A503 110e Sailing 1.70 85

History of Portuguese Communications — A504

Designs: 35e, King Manuel I appointing first Postmaster, 1520. 60e, Mailbox, telegraph, 1881. 80e, Automobile, telephone, 1911. 110e, Airplane, mail truck, 1991.

1991, Oct. 9

1881 A504 35e multicolored 55 28
1882 A504 60e multicolored 90 45
1883 A504 80e multicolored 1.15 60

Souvenir Sheet

1884 A504 110e multicolored 1.70 85

Automobile Museum, Caramulo A505

Designs: No. 1889a, Mercedes 380K, 1934. b, Hispano-Suiza, 1924.

1991, Nov. 15

1885 A505 35e Peugeot, 1899 55 28
1886 A505 60e Rolls Royce, 1911 90 45
1887 A505 80e Bugatti 35B, 1930 1.15 60
1888 A505 110e Ferrari 195 Inter, 1950 1.70 85

Souvenir Sheet

1889 Sheet, 2 each #1889a-1889b 4.20 2.10
a.-b. A505 70e any single 1.05 55

Phila Nippon '91 (No. 1889). See Nos. 1903-1906A.

Ceramics Type of 1990

1992, Jan. 24 Litho. *Perf. 12*

1890 A482 40e Tureen with lid 60 30
1891 A482 40e Plate 60 30
1892 A482 40e Pitcher with lid 60 30
1893 A482 65e Violin 95 48
1894 A482 65e Bottle in form of woman 95 48
1895 A482 65e Man seated on barrel 95 48
Nos. 1890-1895 (6) 4.65 2.34

Souvenir Sheet

1896 A482 260e Political caricature 3.85 3.85

No. 1896 contains one 51x44mm stamp.

Portuguese Presidency of the European Community Council of Ministers A506

1992, Jan. 24

1897 A506 65e multicolored 95 48

Crown Jewels Type of 1991

Designs: 38e, Coral flowers, 19th cent. 65e, Clock of gold, enamel, ivory and diamonds, 20th cent. 70e, Tobacco box encrusted with diamonds and emeralds, 1755. 85e, Royal scepter, 1828. 125e, Eighteen star necklace with diamonds, 1863.

1992, Feb. 7 Litho. *Perf. 11½x12*

1898 A499 38e multicolored 58 28
1899 A499 70e multicolored 1.05 58
1900 A499 85e multicolored 1.30 65
1901 A499 125e multicolored 1.90 95

Perf. 13½ Vert.

1902 A499 65e multicolored 1.00 50
a. Booklet pane of 5 5.00

Automobile Museum Type of 1991

Designs: 38e, Citroen Torpedo, 1922. 65e, Rochet Schneider, 1914. 85e, Austin Seven, 1933. 120e, Mercedes Benz 770, 1938. No. 1906b, Renault, 1911. c, Ford Model T, 1927.

1992, Mar. 6 Litho. *Perf. 12*

1903 A505 38e multicolored 58 28
1904 A505 65e multicolored 1.00 50
1905 A505 85e multicolored 1.30 65
1906 A505 120e multicolored 1.80 90

Souvenir Sheet

1906A Sheet of 2 each, #b.-c. 4.25 2.10
b.-c. A505 70e any single 1.05 55

Automobile Museum, Oeiras.

Portuguese Arrival in Japan, 450th Anniv. A508

Granada '92: 120e, Three men with gifts, Japanese.

1992, Apr. 24 Litho. *Perf. 12*

1907 A508 38e shown 58 30
1908 A508 120e multicolored 1.80 90

Portuguese Pavilion, Expo '92, Seville — A509

1992, Apr. 24 Litho. *Perf. 11½x12*

1909 A509 65e multicolored 1.10 55

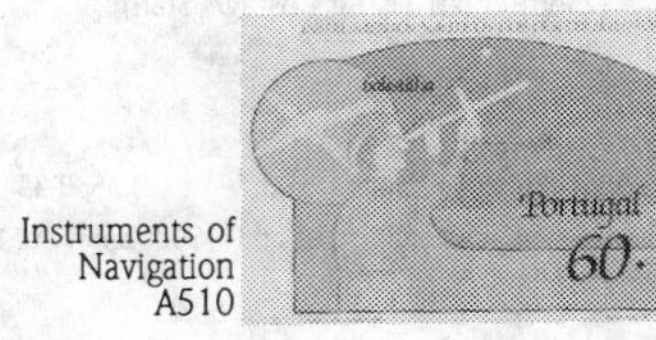

Instruments of Navigation A510

1992, May 9 Litho. *Perf. 12x11½*

1910 A510 60e Cross staff 95 48
1911 A510 70e Quadrant 1.10 55
1912 A510 100e Astrolabe 1.60 80
1913 A510 120e Compass 1.90 95
a. Souv. sheet of 4, #1910-1913 5.75 5.75

Lubrapex '92 (#1913a).

Royal Hospital of All Saints, 500th Anniv. A511

1992, May 11

1914 A511 38e multicolored 60 30

Apparitions of Fatima, 75th Anniv. A512

1992, May 11

1915 A512 70e multicolored 1.10 55

Port of Leixoes, Cent. — A513

1992, May 11

1916 A513 120e multicolored 1.90 95

A514

Voyages of Columbus — A515

Designs: 85e, King John II with Columbus. No. 1918, Columbus in sight of land. No. 1919, Landing of Columbus. No. 1920, Columbus soliciting aid from Queen Isabella. No. 1921, Columbus welcomed at Barcelona. No. 1922, Columbus presenting natives. No. 1923, Columbus.

Nos. 1918-1923 are similar in design to US Nos. 230-231, 234-235, 237 & 245.

1992, May 22 Litho. *Perf. 12x11½*

1917 A514 85e gold & multi 1.40 70

Souvenir Sheets

Perf. 12

1918 A515 260e blue 4.10 4.10
1919 A515 260e brown violet 4.10 4.10
1920 A515 260e brown 4.10 4.10
1921 A515 260e violet black 4.10 4.10
1922 A515 260e black 4.10 4.10
1923 A515 260e black 4.10 4.10

Europa.

See US Nos. 2624-2629, Italy Nos. 1883-1888, and Spain Nos. 2677-2682.

UN Conference on Environmental Development — A516

Designs: 70e, Bird flying over polluted water system. 120e, Clean water system, butterfly, bird, flowers.

1992, June 12 Litho. *Perf. 12x11½*

1924 A516 70e multicolored 1.15 58
1925 A516 120e multicolored 2.00 1.00
a. Pair, #1924-1925 3.15 1.58

1992 Summer Olympics, Barcelona — A517

1992, July 29 Litho. *Perf. 11½x12*
1926 A517 38e Women's running 65 32
1927 A517 70e Soccer 1.15 58
1928 A517 85e Hurdles 1.40 70
1929 A517 120e Roller hockey 2.00 1.00

Souvenir Sheet
Perf. 12
1930 A517 250e Basketball 4.10 4.10

Olymphilex '92 (#1930).

Campo Pequeno Bull Ring, Lisbon, Cent. — A518

Various scenes of picadors.

1992, Aug. 18 *Perf. 12x11½*
1931 A518 38e multicolored 65 32
1932 A518 65e multicolored 1.10 55
1933 A518 70e multicolored 1.15 58
1934 A518 155e multicolored 2.55 1.30

Souvenir Sheet
Perf. 13½x12½
1935 A518 250e Bull ring, vert. 4.10 4.10

No. 1935 contains one 35x50mm stamp.

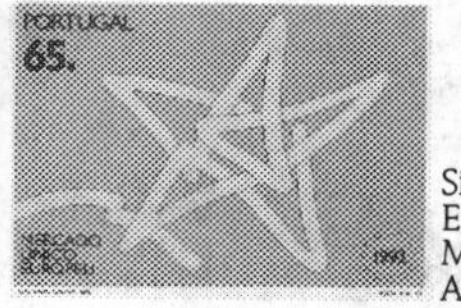

Single European Market A519

1992, Nov. 4 Litho. *Perf. 12x11½*
1936 A519 65e multicolored 95 48

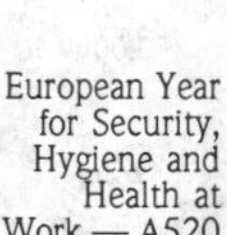

European Year for Security, Hygiene and Health at Work — A520

1992, Nov. 4 *Perf. 12x11½*
1937 A520 120e multicolored 1.80 90

AIR POST STAMPS

Symbol of Aviation AP1

Perf. 12x11½
1936-41 Unwmk. Typo.
C1 AP1 1.50e dk bl 35 35
C2 AP1 1.75e red org 55 35
C3 AP1 2.50e rose red 70 35
C4 AP1 3e brt bl ('41) 4.00 5.00
C5 AP1 4e dp yel grn ('41) 6.25 7.25
C6 AP1 5e car lake 90 35
C7 AP1 10e brn lake 1.40 30
C8 AP1 15e org ('41) 4.00 4.50
C9 AP1 20e blk brn 4.25 1.25
C10 AP1 50e brn vio ('41) 60.00 30.00
Nos. C1-C10 (10) 82.40 49.70

Nos. C1-C10 exist imperf.

Catalogue values for unused stamps in this section, from this point to the end of the section, are for Never Hinged items.

EXPO Type of Regular Issue

1970, Sept. 16 Litho. *Perf. 13*
C11 A274 3.50e silver & multi 35 20

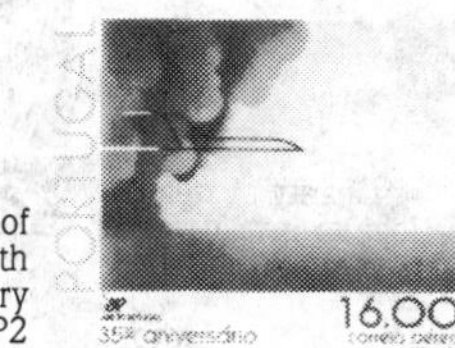

TAP-Airline of Portugal 35th Anniversary AP2

Design: 19e, Jet flying past sun.

1979, Sept. 21 Litho. *Perf. 12x11½*
C12 AP2 16e multi 35 35
C13 AP2 19e multi 45 45

POSTAGE DUE STAMPS

Vasco da Gama Issue

The Zamorin of Calicut Receiving Vasco da Gama — D1

Unwmk.
1898, May 1 Typo. *Perf. 12*
Denomination in Black
J1 D1 5r black 2.25 1.65
a. Value and "Continente" omitted 3.75 2.25
J2 D1 10r lilac & blk 3.75 2.25
J3 D1 20r orange & blk 5.50 3.00
J4 D1 50r slate & blk 15.00 6.00
J5 D1 100r car & blk, *pink* 45.00 22.50
J6 D1 200r brn & blk, *buff* 55.00 27.50

For overprints and surcharges see Nos. 193-198.

D2

D3

1904 *Perf. 11½x12*
J7 D2 5r brown 50 40
J8 D2 10r orange 1.50 50
a. Imperf.
J9 D2 20r lilac 6.00 3.00
J10 D2 30r gray grn 2.50 1.65
J11 D2 40r gray vio 5.00 1.65
J12 D2 50r carmine 20.00 4.25
a. Imperf.
J13 D2 100r dull blue 5.00 2.50
a. Imperf.
Nos. J7-J13 (7) 40.50 13.95

Preceding Issue Overprinted in Carmine or Green

1910
J14 D2 5r brown 40 30
J15 D2 10r orange 40 30
J16 D2 20r lilac 80 30
J17 D2 30r gray grn 55 30
J18 D2 40r gray vio 55 30
J19 D2 50r car (G) 2.75 1.40
J20 D2 100r dull blue 2.75 1.40
Nos. J14-J20 (7) 8.20 4.30

See note after No. 183.

1915, Mar. 18 Typo.
J21 D3 ½c brown 30 30
J22 D3 1c orange 30 30
J23 D3 2c claret 30 30
J24 D3 3c green 30 30
J25 D3 4c gray vio 30 30
J26 D3 5c carmine 30 30
J27 D3 10c dark blue 30 30
Nos. J21-J27 (7) 2.10 2.10

1921-27
J28 D3 ½c gray green ('22) 15 15
J29 D3 4c gray green ('27) 15 15
J30 D3 8c gray green ('23) 15 15
J31 D3 10c gray green ('22) 20 22
J32 D3 12c gray green 15 22
J33 D3 16c gray green ('23) 15 15
J34 D3 20c gray green 15 22
J35 D3 24c gray green 20 22
J36 D3 32c gray green ('23) 20 22
J37 D3 36c gray green 50 45
J38 D3 40c gray green ('23) 50 45
J39 D3 48c gray green ('23) 20 30
J40 D3 50c gray green 20 30
J41 D3 60c gray green 20 30
J42 D3 72c gray green 20 30
J43 D3 80c gray green ('23) 2.50 90
J44 D3 1.20e gray green 85 90
Nos. J28-J44 (17) 6.65 5.60

D4

D5

1932-33
J45 D4 5c buff 32 25
J46 D4 10c lt blue 15 25
J47 D4 20c pink 35 40
J48 D4 30c blue grn 45 50
J49 D4 40c lt green 45 50
J50 D4 50c gray 45 50
J51 D4 60c rose 70 80
J52 D4 80c vio brn 4.50 80
J53 D4 1.20e gray ol ('33) 5.00 4.00
Nos. J45-J53 (9) 12.37 8.00

1940, Feb. 1 Unwmk. *Perf. 12½*
J54 D5 5c bister, perf. 14 15 22
J55 D5 10c rose lilac 15 22
J56 D5 20c dk car rose 15 22
J57 D5 30c purple 15 22
J58 D5 40c cerise 15 22
J59 D5 50c brt bl 15 22
J60 D5 60c yel grn 15 22
J61 D5 80c scarlet 18 15
J62 D5 1e brown 35 15
J63 D5 2e dk rose vio 50 15
J64 D5 5e org yel, perf. 14 1.40 1.40
a. Perf. 12½
Nos. J54-J64 (11) 3.48 3.39

Nos. J54-J64 were first issued perf. 14. In 1955 all but the 5c were reissued in perf. 12½.

Catalogue values for unused stamps in this section, from this point to the end of the section, are for Never Hinged items.

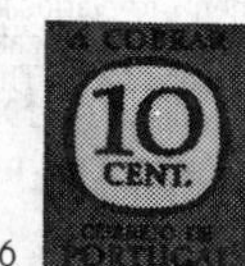

D6

1967-84 Litho. *Perf. 11½*
J65 D6 10c dp org, red brn & yel 15 15
J66 D6 20c bis, dk brn & yel 15 15
J67 D6 30c org, red brn & yel 15 15
J68 D6 40c ol bis, dk brn & yel 15 15
J69 D6 50c ultra, dk bl & bl 15 15
J70 D6 60c grnsh bl, dk grn & lt bl 15 15
J71 D6 80c bl, dk bl & lt bl 15 15
J72 D6 1e vio bl, dk bl & lt bl 15 15
J73 D6 2e grn, dk grn & lt grn 15 15
J74 D6 3e lt grn, grn & yel ('75) 15 15
J75 D6 4e bl grn, dk grn & yel ('75) 15 15
J76 D6 5e cl, dp cl & pink 15 15
J77 D6 9e vio, dk vio & pink ('75) 28 28
J78 D6 10e lil, pur & pale vio ('75) 28 28
J79 D6 20e red, brn & pale vio ('75) 52 52
J80 D6 40e dp red lil, rose vio & bluish lil ('84) 1.05 1.05
J81 D6 50e lil, brn & pale gray ('84) 1.35 1.35
Set value 4.25 4.25

OFFICIAL STAMPS

No. 567 Overprinted in Black **OFICIAL**

1938 Unwmk. *Perf. 11½*
O1 A113 40c brown 18 15

Catalogue values for unused stamps in this section, from this point to the end of the section, are for Never Hinged items.

O1

1952, Sept. Litho. *Perf. 12½*
O2 O1 black & cream 15 15

1975, June
O3 O1 black & yellow 55 40

NEWSPAPER STAMPS

N1

Perf. 11½, 12½, 13½
1876 Typo. Unwmk.
P1 N1 2½r bister 5.75 65
a. 2½r olive green 5.75 65

Various shades.

PARCEL POST STAMPS

Mercury and Commerce PP1

1920-22 Unwmk. Typo. *Perf. 12*
Q1 PP1 1c lil brn 15 15
Q2 PP1 2c orange 15 15
Q3 PP1 5c lt brn 15 15
Q4 PP1 10c red brn 15 15
Q5 PP1 20c gray bl 25 15
Q6 PP1 40c car rose 25 22
Q7 PP1 50c black 35 30
Q8 PP1 60c dk bl ('21) 35 30
Q9 PP1 70c gray brn ('21) 1.25 1.25
Q10 PP1 80c ultra ('21) 1.65 1.40
Q11 PP1 90c lt vio ('21) 1.50 1.40
Q12 PP1 1e lt grn 1.50 60
Q13 PP1 2e pale lil ('22) 4.25 1.50
Q14 PP1 3e olive ('22) 5.00 2.00
Q15 PP1 4e ultra ('22) 14.00 3.75
Q16 PP1 5e gray ('22) 15.00 2.50
Q17 PP1 10e choc ('22) 30.00 4.00
Nos. Q1-Q17 (17) 75.95 19.97

Parcel Post Package PP2

1936 *Perf. 11½*

Q18 PP2 50c ol brn 15 16
Q19 PP2 1e bis brn 15 16
Q20 PP2 1.50e purple 15 16
Q21 PP2 2e car lake 1.10 16
Q22 PP2 2.50e ol grn 1.10 16
Q23 PP2 4.50e brn lake 1.40 16
Q24 PP2 5e violet 3.25 24
Q25 PP2 10e orange 4.25 70
Nos. Q18-Q25 (8) 11.55 1.90

POSTAL TAX STAMPS

These stamps represent a special fee for the delivery of postal matter on certain days in each year. The money derived from their sale is applied to works of public charity.

Regular Issues Overprinted in Carmine **ASSISTENCIA**

1911, Oct. 4 Unwmk. *Perf. 14½x15*

RA1 A62 10r gray green 2.00 85

The 20r carmine of this type was for use on telegrams.

1912, Oct. 4 *Perf. 15x14½*

RA2 A64 1c deep green 1.65 75

The 2c carmine of this type was for use on telegrams.

"Lisbon" — PT1

"Charity" — PT2

1913, June 8 Litho. *Perf. 12x11½*

RA3 PT1 1c dark green 45 32

The 2c dark brown of this type was for use on telegrams.

1915, Oct. 4 **Typo.**

RA4 PT2 1c carmine 25 21

The 2c plum of this type was for use on telegrams.
See No. RA6.

No. RA4 Surcharged **15 ctvs.**

1924, Oct. 4

RA5 PT2 15c on 1c dull red 50 25

The 30c on 2c claret of this type was for use on telegrams.

Charity Type of 1915 Issue

1925, Oct. 4 *Perf. 12½*

RA6 PT2 15c carmine 25 20

The 30c brown violet of this type was for use on telegrams.

Comrades of the Great War Issue

Muse of History with Tablet — PT3

1925, Apr. 8 Litho. *Perf. 11*

RA7 PT3 10c brown 45 40
RA8 PT3 10c green 45 40
RA9 PT3 10c rose 45 40
RA10 PT3 10c ultra 45 40

The use of these stamps, in addition to the regular postage, was obligatory on certain days of the year. If the tax represented by these stamps was not prepaid, it was collected by means of Postal Tax Due Stamp No. RAJ1.

Pombal Issue

Common Design Types

Engraved; Value and "Continente" Typographed in Black

1925, May 8 *Perf. 12½*

RA11 CD28 15c ultra 15 15
RA12 CD29 15c ultra 35 45
RA13 CD30 15c ultra 35 45

Olympic Games Issue

Hurdler — PT7

1928 Litho. *Perf. 12*

RA14 PT7 15c dl red & blk 3.75 *6.00*

The use of this stamp, in addition to the regular postage, was obligatory on May 22-24, 1928. 10% of the money thus obtained was retained by the Postal Administration; the balance was given to a Committee in charge of Portuguese participation in the Olympic games at Amsterdam.

POSTAL TAX DUE STAMPS

PTD1

PTD2

Comrades of the Great War Issue

1925 Unwmk. Typo. *Perf. 11x11½*

RAJ1 PTD1 20c brn org 90 1.00

See Note after No. RA10.

Pombal Issue

Common Design Types

1925 *Perf. 12½*

RAJ2 CD31 30c ultra 50 60
RAJ3 CD32 30c ultra 50 60
RAJ4 CD33 30c ultra 50 60

When the compulsory tax was not paid by the use of stamps Nos. RA11 to RA13, double the amount was collected by means of Nos. RAJ2 to RAJ4.

Olympic Games Issue

1928 Litho. *Perf. 11½*

RAJ5 PTD2 30c lt red & blk 1.65 *3.00*

FRANCHISE STAMPS

These stamps are supplied by the Government to various charitable, scientific and military organizations for franking their correspondence. This franking privilege was withdrawn in 1938.

FOR THE RED CROSS SOCIETY

F1

Perf. 11½

1889-1915 Unwmk. Typo.

1S1 F1 rose & blk ('15) 1.50 32
a. Vermilion & black ('08) 2.50 1.00
b. Red & black, perf. 12½ 30.00 3.00

No. 1S1 Overprinted in Green

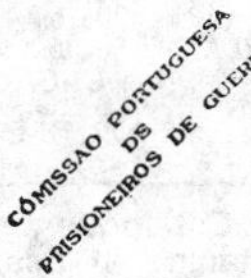

1917

1S3 F1 rose & black 45.00 35.00
a. Inverted overprint 150.00 150.00

"Charity" Extending Hope to Invalid — F1a

1926 Litho. *Perf. 14*

Inscribed "LISBOA"

1S4 F1a black & red 2.50 3.50

Inscribed "DELEGACOES"

1S5 F1a black & red 2.50 3.50

No. 1S4 was for use in Lisbon. No. 1S5 was for the Red Cross chapters outside Lisbon.
For overprints see Nos. 1S72-1S73.

Camoens Issue of 1924 Overprinted in Black or Red **CRUZ VERMELHA Porte franco 1927**

1927

1S6 A68 40c ultra 50 *75*
1S7 A68 48c red brn 50 *75*
1S8 A69 64c green 50 *75*
1S9 A69 75c dk violet 50 *75*
1S10 A71 4.50e blk, *org* (R) 50 *75*
1S11 A71 10e dk brn, *pnksh* 50 *75*
Nos. 1S6-1S11 (6) 3.00 *4.50*

Camoens Issue of 1924 Overprinted in Red

1928

1S12 A67 15c olive grn 75 *1.00*
1S13 A67 16c violet brn 75 *1.00*
1S14 A68 25c lilac 75 *1.00*
1S15 A68 40c ultra 75 *1.00*
1S16 A70 1.20e lt brown 75 *1.00*
1S17 A70 2e apple grn 75 *1.00*
Nos. 1S12-1S17 (6) 4.50 *6.00*

Camoens Issue of 1924 Overprinted in Red **Porte franco**

1929

1S18 A68 30c dk brown 60 *75*
1S19 A68 40c ultra 60 *75*
1S20 A69 80c bister 60 *75*
1S21 A70 1.50e red 60 *75*
1S22 A70 1.60e dk blue 60 *75*
1S23 A71 2.40e grn, *grn* 60 *75*
Nos. 1S18-1S23 (6) 3.60 *4.50*

Same Overprint Dated "1930"

1930

1S24 A68 40c ultra 60 *75*
1S25 A69 50c red org 60 *75*
1S26 A69 96c lake 60 *75*
1S27 A70 1.60e dk bl 60 *75*
1S28 A71 3e dk bl, *bl* 60 *75*
1S29 A72 20e dk vio, *lil* 60 *75*
Nos. 1S24-1S29 (6) 3.60 *4.50*

Camoens Issue of 1924 Overprinted in Red **Porte franco**

1931

1931

1S30 A68 25c lilac 65 *75*
1S31 A68 32c dk green 65 *75*
1S32 A68 40c ultra 65 *75*
1S33 A69 96c lake 65 *75*
1S34 A70 1.60e dk blue 65 *75*
1S35 A71 3.20e blk, *green* 65 *75*
Nos. 1S30-1S35 (6) 3.90 *4.50*

Same Overprint Dated "1932"

1931

1S36 A67 20c dp orange 65 *1.10*
1S37 A68 40c ultra 65 *1.10*
1S38 A68 48c red brn 65 *1.10*
1S39 A69 64c green 65 *1.10*
1S40 A70 1.60e dk blue 65 *1.10*
1S41 A71 10e dk brn, *pnksh* 65 *1.10*
Nos. 1S36-1S41 (6) 3.90 *6.60*

Nos. 1S6-1S11 Overprinted in Red

1932

1S42 A68 40c ultra 80 *1.40*
1S43 A68 48c red brn 80 *1.40*
1S44 A69 64c green 80 *1.40*
1S45 A69 75c dk violet 80 *1.40*
1S46 A71 4.50e blk, *orange* 80 *1.40*
1S47 A71 10e dk brn, *pnksh* 80 *1.40*
Nos. 1S42-1S47 (6) 4.80 *8.40*

Dated "1934"

1933

1S48 A68 40c ultra 80 *1.40*
1S49 A68 48c red brn 80 *1.40*
1S50 A69 64c green 80 *1.40*
1S51 A69 75c dk violet 80 *1.40*
1S52 A71 4.50e blk, *orange* 80 *1.40*
1S53 A71 10e dk brn, *pnksh* 80 *1.40*
Nos. 1S48-1S53 (6) 4.80 *8.40*

Dated "1935"

1935

1S54 A68 40c ultra 1.10 *1.90*
1S55 A68 48c red brn 1.10 *1.90*
1S56 A69 64c green 1.10 *1.90*
1S57 A69 75c dk violet 1.10 *1.90*
1S58 A71 4.50e blk, *orange* 1.10 *1.90*
1S59 A71 10e dk brn, *pnksh* 1.10 *1.90*
Nos. 1S54-1S59 (6) 6.60 *11.40*

Camoens Issue of 1924 Overprinted in Black or Red **Cruz Vermelha Porte Franco 1936**

1935

1S60 A68 25c lilac 50 *75*
1S61 A68 40c ultra (R) 50 *75*
1S62 A69 50c red org 50 *75*
1S63 A70 1e slate 50 *75*
1S64 A70 2e apple grn 50 *75*
1S65 A72 20e dk vio, *lil* 50 *75*
Nos. 1S60-1S65 (6) 3.00 *4.50*

Camoens Issue of 1924 Overprinted in Red

1936

1S66 A68 30c dk brown 50 *75*
1S67 A68 32c dk green 50 *75*
1S68 A69 80c bister 50 *75*
1S69 A70 1.20e lt brown 50 *75*
1S70 A71 3e dk bl, *bl* 50 *75*
1S71 A71 4.50e blk, *yel* 50 *75*
Nos. 1S66-1S71 (6) 3.00 *4.50*

No. 1S4 Overprinted "1935"

1936 Unwmk. *Perf. 14*

1S72 F1a black & red 2.75 5.00

Same Stamp with Additional Overprint "Delegacoes"

1S73 F1a black & red 2.75 5.00

After the government withdrew the franking privilege in 1938, the Portuguese Red Cross Society distributed charity labels which lacked postal validity.

FOR CIVILIAN RIFLE CLUBS

Rifle Club Emblem — F2

Perf. 11½x12

1899-1910 Typo. Unwmk.

2S1	F2	bl grn & car ('99)	5.00	4.00
2S2	F2	brn & yel grn ('00)	5.00	4.00
2S3	F2	car & buff ('01)	2.50	2.50
2S4	F2	bl & org ('02)	2.50	2.50
2S5	F2	grn & org ('03)	2.50	2.50
2S6	F2	lt brn & car ('04)	2.50	2.50
2S7	F2	mar & ultra ('05)	2.50	2.50
2S8	F2	ultra & buff ('06)	2.50	2.50
2S9	F2	choc & yel ('07)	2.50	2.50
2S10	F2	car & ultra ('08)	2.50	2.50
2S11	F2	bl & yel grn ('09)	2.50	2.50
2S12	F2	bl grn & brn, *pink* ('10)	2.50	2.50
		Nos. 2S1-2S12 (12)	35.00	33.00

FOR THE GEOGRAPHICAL SOCIETY OF LISBON

Coat of Arms
F3 F4

1903-34 Unwmk. Litho. *Perf. 11½*

3S1	F3	blk, rose, bl & red	14.00	3.25
3S2	F3	bl, yel, red & grn ('09)	16.00	4.00
3S3	F4	blk, org, bl & red ('11)	2.00	75
3S4	F4	blk & brn org ('22)	3.50	2.75
3S5	F4	blk & bl ('24)	8.50	4.50
3S6	F4	blk & rose ('26)	3.25	2.25
3S7	F4	blk & grn ('27)	3.25	2.25
3S8	F4	bl, yel & red ('29)	2.75	1.50
3S9	F4	bl, red & vio ('30)	2.75	1.50
3S10	F4	dp bl, lil & red ('31)	2.75	1.50
3S11	F4	bis brn & red ('32)	2.75	1.50
3S12	F4	lt grn & red ('33)	2.75	1.50
3S13	F4	blue & red ('34)	2.75	1.50
		Nos. 3S1-3S13 (13)	67.00	28.75

No. 3S12 with three-line overprint, "C.I.C.I. Portugal 1933," was not valid for postage and was sold only to collectors.

No. 3S2 was reprinted in 1933. Green vertical lines behind "Porte Franco" omitted. Value $7.50.

F5

1934 Litho. *Perf. 11½*

3S15	F5	blue & red	1.50	1.25

1935-38 *Perf. 11*

3S16	F5	blue	6.00	6.00
3S17	F5	dk bl & red ('36)	2.50	2.00
3S18	F5	lil & red ('37)	2.50	1.00
3S19	F5	blk, grn & car ('38)	2.50	1.00

The inscription in the inner circle is omitted on No. 3S16.

FOR THE NATIONAL AID SOCIETY FOR CONSUMPTIVES

F10

Perf. 11½x12

1904, July Typo. Unwmk.

4S1	F10	brown & green	4.00	3.00
4S2	F10	carmine & yellow	4.00	3.00

AZORES

Starting in 1980, stamps inscribed Azores and Madeira were valid and sold in Portugal.

Azores No. 2 — A33

Design: 19.50e, Azores No. 6.

1980, Jan. 2 Litho. *Perf. 12*

314	A33	6.50e multi	15	15
315	A33	19.50e multi	50	20
a.		Souvenir sheet of 2, #314-315	90	90
		Set value		25

No. 315a exists overprinted for Capex 87.

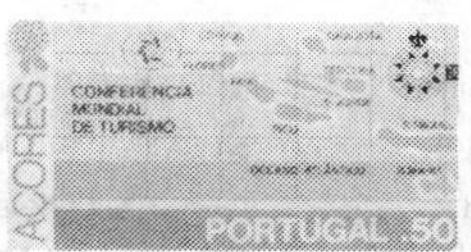

Map of Azores A34

1980, Sept. 17 Litho. *Perf. 12x11½*

316	A34	50c shown	15	15
317	A34	1e Cathedral	15	15
318	A34	5e Windmill	15	15
319	A34	6.50e Local women	15	15
320	A34	8e Coastline	20	15
321	A34	30e Ponta Delgada	60	32
		Set value	1.15	65

World Tourism Conf., Manila, Sept. 27.

Europa Issue 1981

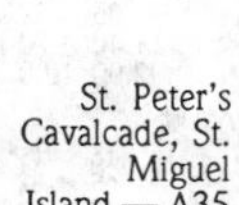

St. Peter's Cavalcade, St. Miguel Island — A35

1981, May 11 Litho. *Perf. 12*

322	A35	22e multicolored	52	25
a.		Souvenir sheet of 2	1.10	1.10

Bulls Attacking Spanish Soldiers A36

Battle of Salga Valley, 400th Anniv.: 33.50e, Friar Don Pedro leading citizens.

1981, July 24 Litho. *Perf. 12x11½*

323	A36	8.50e multi	18	15
324	A36	33.50e multi	80	45

Tolpis Azorica — A37

Designs: Local flora.

1981, Sept. 21 Litho. *Perf. 12½x12*

325	A37	7e shown	16	15
326	A37	8.50e Ranunculus azoricus	20	15
327	A37	20e Platanthera Micranta	38	15
328	A37	50e Laurus azorica	1.00	32
a.		Booklet pane of 4, #325-328	1.90	
		Set value		64

1982, Jan. 29

329	A37	4e Myosotis azorica	15	15
330	A37	10e Lactuca Watsoniana	24	16
331	A37	27e Vicia dennesiana	60	22
332	A37	33.50e Azorina vidalii	75	25
a.		Booklet pane of 4	1.90	
		Set value		68

See Nos. 338-341.

Europa Type of Portugal

Design: Heroes of Mindelo embarkation, 1832.

1982, May 3 Litho. *Perf. 12x11½*

333	A405	33.50e multi	65	32
a.		Souvenir sheet of 3	2.00	2.00

Chapel of the Holy Ghost — A39

Designs: Various Chapels of the Holy Ghost.

1982, Nov. 24 Litho. *Perf. 12½x12*

334	A39	27e multi	75	25
335	A39	33.50e multi	95	40

Europa 1983 — A40

1983, May 5 Litho. *Perf. 12½*

336	A40	37.50e Geothermal energy	70	35
a.		Souvenir sheet of 3	2.50	2.50

Flag of the Autonomous Region — A41

1983, May 23 Litho. *Perf. 12x11½*

337	A41	12.50e multi	30	15

Flower Type of 1981

1983, June 16 *Perf. 12½x12*

338	A37	12.50e St. John's wort	25	15
339	A37	30e Prickless bramble	60	30
340	A37	37.50e Romania bush	75	38
341	A37	100e Common juniper	1.90	1.00
a.		Booklet pane of 4, #338-341	3.50	

Woman Wearing Terceira Cloaks — A42

1984, Mar. 8 Litho. *Perf. 13½*

342	A42	16e Jesters costumes, 18th cent.	30	15
343	A42	51e shown	90	45

Europa Type of Portugal

1984, May 2 *Perf. 12x11½*

344	A427	51e multicolored	90	40
a.		Souvenir sheet of 3	2.75	2.75

Megabombus Ruderatus A44

1984, Sept. 3 Litho. *Perf. 12x11½*

345	A44	16e shown	24	15
346	A44	35e Pieris brassicae azorensis	52	26
347	A44	40e Chrysomela banksi	60	30
348	A44	51e Phlogophora interrupta	75	38

Perf. 12, Vert.

345a	A44	16e	24	15
346a	A44	35e	52	26
347a	A44	40e	60	30
348a	A44	51e	75	38
b.		Bklt. pane of 4, #345a-348a	2.50	

1985, Feb. 13

349	A44	20e Polyspilla polyspilla	30	15
350	A44	40e Sphaerophoria nigra	65	32
351	A44	46e Colias croceus	75	38
352	A44	60e Hipparchia azorina	1.00	50

Perf. 12, Vert.

349a	A44	20e	30	15
350a	A44	40e	65	32
351a	A44	46e	75	38
352a	A44	60e	1.00	50
b.		Bklt. pane of 4, #349a-352a	3.00	

Europa Type of Portugal

1985, May 6 Litho. *Perf. 11½x12*

353	A435	60e Man playing folia drum	1.00	40
a.		Souvenir sheet of 3	3.00	3.00

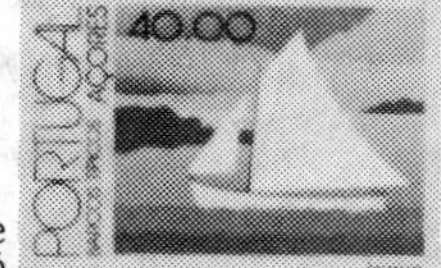

Native Boats — A46

1985, June 19 Litho. *Perf. 12x12½*

354	A46	40e Jeque	60	25
355	A46	60e Bote	90	38

Europa Type of Portugal

1986, May Litho.

356	A447	68.50e Pyrrhula murina	1.05	52
a.		Souvenir sheet of 3	3.25	3.25

Regional Architecture — A48

19th Century fountains: 22.50e, Alto das Covas, Angra do Heroismo. 52.50e, Faja de Baixo, San Miguel. 68.50e, Gates of St. Peter, Terceira. 100e, Agua d'Alto, San Miguel.

1986, Sept. 18 Litho. *Perf. 12*

357	A48	22.50e multi	35	18
358	A48	52.50e multi	80	40
359	A48	68.50e multi	1.05	52
360	A48	100e multi	1.50	75
a.		Booklet pane of 4, #357-360	3.75	

Traditional Modes of Transportation A49

1986, Nov. 7 Litho.

361	A49	25e Isle of Santa Maria ox cart	35	18
362	A49	75e Ram cart	1.05	52

Europa Type of Portugal

Modern architecutre: Regional Assembly, Horta, designed by Manuel Correia Fernandes and Luis Miranda.

1987, May 5 Litho. *Perf. 12*
363 A456 74.50e multicolored 1.20 60
a. Souvenir sheet of 4 5.00 5.00

Windows and Balconies A51

1987, July 1 *Perf. 12*
364 A51 51e Santa Cruz, Graciosa 80 40
365 A51 74.50e Ribiera Grande, San Miguel 1.15 58

Aviation History A52

Seaplanes.

1987, Oct. 9 *Perf. 12x11½*
366 A52 25e NC-4 Curtiss Flyer, 1919 38 20
367 A52 57e Dornier DO-X, 1932 88 45
368 A52 74.50e Savoia-Marchetti S 55-X, 1933 1.15 58
369 A52 125e Lockheed Sirius, 1933 1.90 95

Perf. 12, Vert.
366a A52 25e 38 20
367a A52 57e 88 45
368a A52 74.50e 1.15 58
369a A52 125e 1.90 95
b. Bklt. pane of 4, #366a-369a 4.25

Europa Type of Portugal

1988, Apr. 21 Litho. *Perf. 12*
370 A466 80e multicolored 1.35 68
a. Souvenir sheet of 4 5.40 5.40

Birds — A54

1988, Oct. 18 Litho.
371 A54 27e Columba palambus azorica 40 20
372 A54 60e Scolopax rusticola 88 45
373 A54 80e Sterna dougallii 1.15 58
374 A54 100e Buteo buteo 1.45 72
a. Booklet pane of 4, #371-374 3.90

Coats of Arms — A55

1988, Nov. 18 Litho.
375 A55 55e Dominion of Azores 85 42
376 A55 80e Bettencourt family 1.20 60

Wildlife Conservation A56

Various kinglets, *Regulus regulus.*

1989, Jan. 20 Litho.
377 A56 30e Adult on branch 45 22
378 A56 30e Two adults 45 22
379 A56 30e Adult, nest 45 22
380 A56 30e Bird in flight 45 22
a. Strip of 4, Nos. 377-380 1.80 88

See Nos. 385-388.

Europa Type of Portugal

Children's toys.

1989, Apr. 26 Litho.
381 A476 80e Tin boat 1.20 60

Souvenir Sheet
382 Sheet of 4, 2 each Nos. 381, 382a 4.80 4.80
a. A476 80e Tin boat, diff. 1.20 1.20

Settlement of the Azores, 550th Anniv. — A58

1989, Sept. 20 Litho.
383 A58 29e Friar Goncalho Velho 38 20
384 A58 87e Settlers farming 1.10 55

Bird Type of 1989 With World Wildlife Fund Emblem

Various *Pyrrhula murina.*

1990, Feb. 14 Litho. *Perf. 12 /*
385 A56 32e Adult on branch 45 22
386 A56 32e Two adults 45 22
387 A56 32e Brooding 45 22
388 A56 32e Bird in flight 45 22
a. Strip of 4, #385-388 1.80 88

No. 388a has continuous design.

Europa Type of Portugal

1990, Apr. 11 Litho. *Perf. 12x11½*
389 A486 80e Vasco da Gama P.O. 1.10 55

Souvenir Sheet
390 Sheet of 4, 2 each #389, 390a 4.40 4.40
a. A486 80e Maia P.O. 1.10 1.10

Professions A61

1990, July 11 Litho. *Perf. 12*
391 A61 5e Cart maker 15 15
392 A61 32e Potter 44 44
393 A61 60e Metal worker 80 80
394 A61 100e Cooper 1.35 1.35

Perf. 13½ Vert.
391a A61 5e 15 15
392a A61 32e 44 44
393a A61 60e 80 80
394a A61 100e 1.35 1.35
b. Bklt. pane of 4, #391a-394a 2.85

See Nos. 397-400, 406-409.

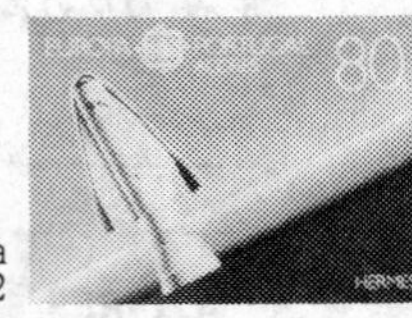

Europa A62

1991, Apr. 11 Litho. *Perf. 12*
395 A62 80e Hermes space shuttle 1.15 60

Souvenir Sheet
396 Sheet, 2 each #395, 396a 4.60 2.40
a. A62 80e Sanger 1.15 60

Professions Type of 1990

1991, Aug. 2 Litho. *Perf. 12x11½*
397 A61 35e Tile makers 50 25
398 A61 65e Mosaic artists 95 48
399 A61 70e Quarrymen 1.00 50
400 A61 110e Stonemasons 1.60 80

Perf. 13½ Vert.
397a A61 35e 50 25
398a A61 65e 95 48
399a A61 70e 1.00 50
400a A61 110e 1.60 80
b. Bklt. pane of 4, #397a-400a 4.05

Transportation in the Azores — A63

Ships and Planes: 35e, Schooner Helena, 1918. 60e, Beechcraft CS, 1947. 80e, Yacht, Cruzeiro do Canal, 1987. 110e, British Aerospace ATP, 1991.

1991, Nov. 15 Litho. *Perf. 12x11½*
401 A63 35e multicolored 52 25
402 A63 60e multicolored 90 45
403 A63 80e multicolored 1.20 60
404 A63 110e multicolored 1.65 80

See Nos. 410-413.

Europa Type of Portugal

Europa: 85e, Columbus aboard Santa Maria.

1992, May 22 Litho. *Perf. 12x11½*
405 A514 85e gold & multi 1.40 70

Professions Type of 1990

1992, June 12 Litho. *Perf. 12x11½*
406 A61 10e Guitar maker 16 15
407 A61 38e Carpenter 65 32
408 A61 85e Basket maker 1.40 70
409 A61 120e Boat builders 2.00 1.00

Perf. 13½ Vert.
406a A61 10e 16 15
407a A61 38e 65 32
408a A61 85e 1.40 70
409a A61 120e 2.00 1.00
b. Bklt. pane of 4, #406a-409a 4.25

Transportation Type of 1991

Ships.

1992, Oct. 7 Litho. *Perf. 12x11½*
410 A63 38e Insulano 58 28
411 A63 65e Carvalho Araujo 1.00 50
412 A63 85e Funchal 1.25 65
413 A63 120e Terceirense 1.80 90

MADEIRA

Type of Azores, 1980

Designs: 6.50e, Madeira No. 2. 19.50e, Madeira No. 5.

1980, Jan. 2 Litho. *Perf. 12*
66 A33 6.50e multi 15 15
67 A33 19.50e multi 50 20
a. Souvenir sheet of 2, #66-67 90 90
Set value 25

No. 67a exists overprinted for Capex 87.

Grapes and Wine — A7

1980, Sept. 17 Litho. *Perf. 12x11½*
68 A7 50c Bullock cart 15 15
69 A7 1e shown 15 15
70 A7 5e Produce map of Madeira 15 15
71 A7 6.50e Basket and lace 16 15
72 A7 8e Orchid 20 15
73 A7 30e Madeira boat 55 35
Set value 1.10 70

World Tourism Conf., Manila, Sept. 27.

Europa Issue 1981

O Bailinho Folk Dance — A8

1981, May 11 Litho. *Perf. 12*
74 A8 22e multi 42 22
a. Souvenir sheet of 2 1.50 1.10

Explorer Ship — A9

1981, July 1 Litho. *Perf. 12x11½*
75 A9 8.50e shown 15 15
76 A9 33.50e Map 60 20
Set value 26

Discovery of Madeira anniv.

A10

A12

Designs: Local flora.

1981, Oct. 6 Litho. *Perf. 12½x12*
77 A10 7e Dactylorhiza foliosa 15 15
78 A10 8.50e Echium candicans 18 15
79 A10 20e Geranium maderense 40 15
80 A10 50e Isoplexis sceptrum 95 35
a. Booklet pane of 4, #77-80 1.90

See Nos. 82-85, 90-93.

Europa Type of Portugal

1982, May 3 Litho. *Perf. 12x11½*
81 A405 33.50e Sugar mills, 15th cent. 60 30
a. Souvenir sheet of 3 2.00 2.00

1982, Aug. 31 Litho. *Perf. 12½x12*
82 A10 9e Goodyera macrophylla 15 15
83 A10 10e Armeria maderensis 18 15
84 A10 27e Viola paradoxa 35 20
85 A10 33.50e Scilla maderensis 90 45
a. Booklet pane of 4, #82-85 1.65
Set value 80

1982, Dec. 15 Litho. *Perf. 13½*
86 A12 27e Brinco dancing dolls 65 40
87 A12 33.50e Dancers 85 50

Europa 1983 — A13

1983, May 5 Litho. *Perf. 12½*

88 A13 37.50e Levadas irrigation system 70 32
a. Souvenir sheet of 3 2.25 2.25

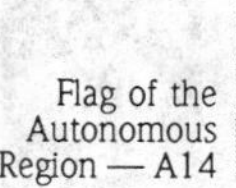

Flag of the Autonomous Region — A14

1983, July 1 Litho. *Perf. 12x11½*

89 A14 12.50e multi 30 30

Flower Type of 1981

1983, Oct. 19 Litho. *Perf. 12½x12*

90 A10 12.50e Matthiola maderensis 30 30
91 A10 30e Erica maderensis 65 30
92 A10 37.50e Cirsium latifolium 75 30
93 A10 100e Clethra arborea 2.00 1.00
a. Booklet pane of 4, #90-93 3.75

Europa Type of Portugal

1984, May 2 Litho. *Perf. 12x11½*

94 A427 51e multi 80 40
a. Souvenir sheet of 3 3.00 3.00

Madeira Rally (Auto Race), 25th Anniv. — A16

Various cars.

1984, Aug. 3 Litho. *Perf. 11½x12*

95 A16 16e multicolored 40 20
96 A16 51e multicolored 1.00 50

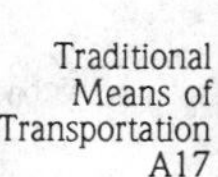

Traditional Means of Transportation A17

1984, Nov. 22 *Perf. 12*

97 A17 16e Mountain sledge 25 15
98 A17 35e Hammock 52 25
99 A17 40e Winebag carriers' procession 60 30
100 A17 51e Carreira Boat 75 38
a. Booklet pane of 4, Nos. 97-100 2.15

See Nos. 104-107.

Europa Type of Portugal

1985, May 6 Litho. *Perf. 11½x12*

101 A435 60e Man playing guitar 1.00 40
a. Souvenir sheet of 3 4.00 4.00

Marine Life — A19

1985, July 5 Litho. *Perf. 12*

102 A19 40e Aphanopus carbo 52 28
103 A19 60e Lampris guttatus 80 40

See Nos. 108-109.

Transportation type of 1984

1985, Sept. 11 Litho. *Perf. 12x11½*

104 A17 20e Ox-drawn sledge 35 16
105 A17 40e Mountrain train 65 32
106 A17 46e Fish vendors 75 38
107 A17 60e Coastal steamer 1.00 50
a. Booklet pane of 4, Nos. 104-107 2.20

Marine Life Type of 1985

1986, Jan. 7 Litho.

108 A19 20e Thunnus obesus 25 15
109 A19 75e Beryx decadactylus 1.00 50

Europa Type of Portugal

1986, May 5 Litho.

110 A447 68.50e Great Shearwater 1.05 52
a. Souvenir sheet of 3 3.25 3.25

Forts in Funchal and Machico A21

1986, July 1 Litho. *Perf. 12*

111 A21 22.50e Sao Lourenco, 1583 32 16
112 A21 52.50e Sao Joao do Pico, 1611 75 38
113 A21 68.50e Sao Tiago, 1614 1.00 50
114 A21 100e Sao do Amparo, 1706 1.45 75
a. Booklet pane of 4, #111-114 3.75

A22

A24

Indigenous birds.

1987, Mar. 6 Litho.

115 A22 25e Regulus ignicapillus madeirensis 40 20
116 A22 57e Columba trocaz 90 45
117 A22 74.50e Tyto alba schmitzi 1.15 58
118 A22 125e Pterodroma madeira 1.95 1.00
a. Booklet pane of 4, #115-118 4.50

See Nos. 123-126.

Europa Type of Portugal

Modern Architecture: Social Services Center, Funchal, designed by Raul Chorao Ramalho.

1987, May 5 Litho. *Perf. 12*

119 A456 74.50e multicolored 1.20 60
a. Souvenir sheet of 4 5.00 5.00

1987, July 1 *Perf. 12x12½*

Natl. monuments.

120 A24 51e Funchal Castle, 15th cent. 80 40
121 A24 74.50e Old Town Hall, Santa Cruz, 16th cent. 1.15 58

Europa Type of Portugal

Transportation Modern mail boat PS 13 TL.

1988, Apr. 21 Litho. *Perf. 12*

122 A466 80e multicolored 1.35 68
a. Souvenir sheet of 4 5.40 5.40

Bird Type of 1987

1988, June 15 Litho.

123 A22 27e Erithacus rubecula 45 22
124 A22 60e Petronia 98 50
125 A22 80e Fringilla coelebs 1.30 65
126 A22 100e Accipiter nisus 1.65 82
a. Booklet pane of 4, #123-126 4.40

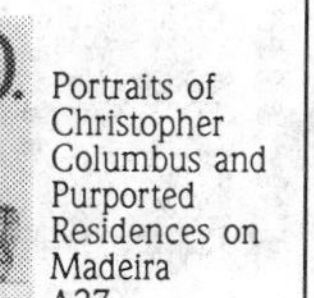

Portraits of Christopher Columbus and Purported Residences on Madeira A27

1988, July 1 Litho.

127 A27 55e Funchal, 1480-1481, vert. 88 45
128 A27 80e Porto Santo 1.30 65

Europa Type of Portugal

Children's toys.

1989, Apr. 26 Litho.

129 A476 80e Kite 1.20 60

Souvenir Sheet

130 Sheet, 2 each #129, 130a 4.80 4.80
a. A476 80e Kite, diff. 1.20 1.20

Monuments — A29

Churches: 29e, Church of the Colegio (St. John the Evangelist Church). 87e, Santa Clara Church and convent.

1989, July 28 Litho.

131 A29 29e multi 35 18
132 A29 87e multi 1.05 52

Fish — A30

1989, Sept. 20 Litho.

133 A30 29e *Argyropelecus aculeatus* 38 20
134 A30 60e *Pseudolepidaplois scrofa* 78 40
135 A30 87e *Coris julis* 1.10 55
136 A30 100e *Scorpaena maderensis* 1.30 65
a. Booklet pane of 4, #133-136 3.60

Europa Type of Portugal

1990, Apr. 11 Litho. *Perf. 12x11½*

137 A486 80e Zarco P.O. 1.10 55

Souvenir Sheet

138 Sheet, 2 each #137, 138a 4.40 4.40
a. A486 80e Porto da Cruz P.O. 1.10 1.10

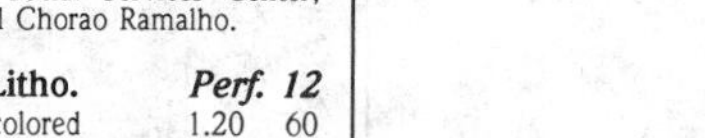

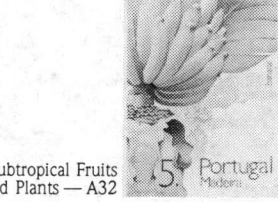

Subtropical Fruits and Plants — A32

1990, June 5 Litho. *Perf. 12*

139 A32 5e Banana 15 15
140 A32 32e Avocado 42 20
141 A32 60e Sugar apple 80 40
142 A32 100e Passion fruit 1.35 68

Perf. 13½ Vert.

139a A32 5e 15 15
140a A32 32e 42 42
141a A32 60e 80 80
142a A32 100e 1.35 1.35
b. Bklt. pane of 4, #139a-142a 2.65

See Nos. 153-160.

Boats of Madeira A33

1990, Aug. 24

143 A33 32e Tuna 42 20
144 A33 60e Desert islands 80 40
145 A33 70e Maneiro 95 48
146 A33 95e Chavelha 1.25 64

See Nos. 162-165.

Columba Trocaz Heineken — A34

1991, Jan. 23 Litho. *Perf. 12*

147 A34 35e shown 50 25
148 A34 35e On branch 50 25
149 A34 35e In flight 50 25
150 A34 35e On nest 50 35
a. Strip of 4, #147-150 2.00 1.00

Europa A35

1991, Apr. 11 Litho. *Perf. 12*

151 A35 80e ERS-1 1.15 60

Souvenir Sheet

152 Sheet, 2 each #151, 152a 4.60 2.40
a. A35 80e SPOT 1.15 60

Subtropical Fruits Type of 1990

1991, June 7 Litho. *Perf. 12*

153 A32 35e Mango 50 25
154 A32 65e Surinam cherry 90 45
155 A32 70e Brazilian guava 95 48
156 A32 110e Papaya 1.50 75

Perf. 13½Vert.

153a A32 35e 50 25
154a A32 65e 90 45
155a A32 70e 95 48
156a A32 110e 1.50 75
b. Bklt. pane of 4, #153a-156a 3.85

1992, Feb. 21 Litho. *Perf. 11½x12*

157 A32 10e Prickly pear 15 15
158 A32 38e Tree tomato 42 22
159 A32 85e Ceriman 1.30 65
160 A32 125e Guava 1.90 95

Perf. 13½ Vert.

157a A32 10e 15 15
158a A32 38e 42 22
159a A32 85e 1.30 65
160a A32 125e 1.90 95
b. Bklt. pane of 4, #157a-160a 3.80

Europa Type of Portugal

Europa: 85e, Columbus at Funchal.

1992, May 22 Litho. *Perf. 12x11½*

161 A514 85e gold & multi 1.40 70

Ships Type of 1990

1992, Sept. 18 Litho. *Perf. 12x11½*

162 A33 38e Gaviao 65 32
163 A33 65e Independencia 1.10 55
164 A33 85e Madeirense 1.40 70
165 A33 120e Funchalense 2.00 1.00

Portugal Regional Issues of Madeira can be mounted in Scott's annual Portugal Supplement.

PORTUGUESE AFRICA

For use in any of the Portuguese possessions in Africa.

1000 Reis = 1 Milreis
100 Centavos = 1 Escudo

Vasco da Gama Issue

Common Design Types

Perf. 13½ to 15½

1898, Apr. 1 — Engr. — Unwmk.

No.	Type	Description	Unused	Used
1	CD20	2½r bl grn	1.00	1.00
2	CD21	5r red	1.00	1.00
3	CD22	10r red vio	1.00	1.00
4	CD23	25r yel grn	1.00	1.00
5	CD24	50r dark blue	1.25	1.25
6	CD25	75r vio brn	6.75	6.75
7	CD26	100r bister brn	5.00	5.00
8	CD27	150r bister	7.25	6.75
		Nos. 1-8 (8)	24.25	23.75

Commemorating Vasco da Gama's voyage to India.

POSTAGE DUE STAMPS

D1

1945 — Unwmk. — Typo. — *Perf. 11½x12*

Denomination in Black

No.	Type	Description	Unused	Used
J1	D1	10c claret	40	70
J2	D1	20c purple	40	70
J3	D1	30c deep blue	40	70
J4	D1	40c chocolate	40	70
J5	D1	50c red violet	75	1.25
J6	D1	1e orange brown	1.50	3.75
J7	D1	2e yellow green	3.25	5.00
J8	D1	3e bright carmine	8.00	8.50
J9	D1	5e orange yellow	13.00	14.00
		Nos. J1-J9 (9)	28.10	35.30

Common Design Types pictured in section at front of book.

WAR TAX STAMPS

Liberty WT1

Perf. 12x11½, 15x14

1919 — Typo. — Unwmk.

Overprinted in Black, Orange or Carmine

No.	Type	Description	Unused	Used
MR1	WT1	1c green (Bk)	50	75
MR2	WT1	4c green (O)	50	75
MR3	WT1	5c green (C)	50	75

Some authorities consider No. MR2 a revenue stamp.

PORTUGUESE CONGO

LOCATION — The northernmost district of the Portuguese Angola Colony on the southwest coast of Africa

CAPITAL — Cabinda

Stamps of Angola replaced those of Portuguese Congo.

1000 Reis = 1 Milreis
100 Centavos = 1 Escudo (1913)

King Carlos
A1 A2

Perf. 11½, 12½, 13½

1894, Aug. 5 — Typo. — Unwmk.

No.	Type	Description	Unused	Used
1	A1	5r yellow	75	60
a.		Perf. 13½	15.00	12.50
2	A1	10r redsh vio	1.40	80
a.		Perf. 13½	17.50	14.00
3	A1	15r chocolate	2.50	2.00
4	A1	20r lavender	2.00	1.75
5	A1	25r green	1.25	80
6	A1	50r light blue	2.75	2.00
7	A1	75r rose	4.00	3.00
a.		Perf. 12½	17.50	15.00
8	A1	80r yellow grn	7.00	6.00
a.		Perf. 12½	17.50	12.50
9	A1	100r brown, *yel*	5.25	3.25
a.		Perf. 13½	22.50	15.00
10	A1	150r car, *rose*	10.00	9.00
11	A1	200r dk blue, *bl*	10.00	9.00
12	A1	300r dk bl, *salmon*	12.50	11.00
		Nos. 1-12 (12)	59.40	49.20

For surcharges and overprints see Nos. 36-47, 127-131.

1898-1903 — *Perf. 11½*

Name & Value in Black except 500r

No.	Type	Description	Unused	Used
13	A2	2½r gray	25	20
14	A2	5r orange	25	20
15	A2	10r lt green	40	35
16	A2	15r brown	1.65	1.25
17	A2	15r gray grn ('03)	75	60
18	A2	20r gray vio	75	65
19	A2	25r sea grn	1.10	75
20	A2	25r car rose ('03)	80	45
21	A2	50r deep blue	1.65	1.25
22	A2	50r brown ('03)	2.50	1.50
23	A2	65r dull bl ('03)	8.25	7.25
24	A2	75r rose	2.75	2.50
25	A2	75r red lil ('03)	2.75	2.50
26	A2	80r violet	3.00	2.50
27	A2	100r dk bl, *bl*	2.25	2.00
28	A2	115r org brn, *pink* ('03)	6.00	5.50
29	A2	130r brn, *straw* ('03)	12.50	12.50
30	A2	150r brn, *buff*	3.25	2.75
31	A2	200r red lil, *pnksh*	4.25	3.00
32	A2	300r dk bl, *rose*	3.25	2.75
33	A2	400r dl bl, *straw* ('03)	9.00	9.00
34	A2	500r blk & red, *bl* ('01)	16.00	10.00
35	A2	700r vio, *yelsh* ('01)	25.00	17.50
		Nos. 13-35 (23)	108.35	86.95

For overprints and surcharges see Nos. 49-53, 60-74, 117-126, 136-138.

Surcharged in Black

1902 — *Perf. 11½, 12½, 13½*

On Issue of 1894

No.	Type	Description	Unused	Used
36	A1	65r on 15r choc	3.50	3.00
a.		Perf. 11½	13.00	7.50
37	A1	65r on 20r lav	4.00	3.00
38	A1	65r on 25r grn	4.00	3.00
a.		Perf. 11½	15.00	9.00
39	A1	65r on 300r bl, *sal*	4.50	4.50
40	A1	115r on 10r red vio	4.00	3.00
41	A1	115r on 50r lt bl	3.00	2.50
42	A1	130r on 5r yel	3.50	2.75
a.		Inverted surcharge	27.50	27.50
43	A1	130r on 75r rose	3.50	3.00
a.		Perf. 12½	7.00	6.00
44	A1	130r on 100r brn, *yel*	4.00	3.00
a.		Inverted surcharge	40.00	35.00
b.		Perf. 11½	16.00	12.50
45	A1	400r on 80r yel grn	1.75	1.00
46	A1	400r on 150r car, *rose*	1.25	1.10
47	A1	400r on 200r bl, *bl*	1.25	1.10

On Newspaper Stamp of 1894

No.	Type	Description	Unused	Used
48	N1	115r on 2½r brn	3.75	2.75
a.		Inverted surcharge	25.00	25.00
		Nos. 36-48 (13)	42.00	33.70

Nos. 16, 19, 21 and 24 Overprinted in Black PROVISORIO

1902 — *Perf. 11½*

No.	Type	Description	Unused	Used
49	A2	15r brown	2.00	1.40
50	A2	25r sea green	2.00	1.40
51	A2	50r blue	2.00	1.40
52	A2	75r rose	4.00	2.75

No. 23 Surcharged 50 RÉIS

1905

No.	Type	Description	Unused	Used
53	A2	50r on 65r dull blue	3.50	2.25

Angola Stamps of 1898-1903 (Port. Congo type A2) Overprinted or Surcharged:

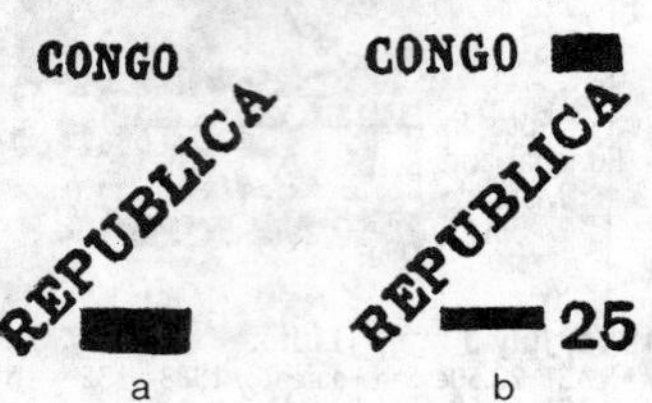

a b

1911

No.	Type	Description	Unused	Used
54	(a)	2½r gray	1.00	90
55	(a)	5r orange	1.40	1.25
56	(a)	10r lt grn	1.40	1.25
a.		"REPUBLICA" inverted	17.50	17.50
57	(a)	15r gray grn	1.40	1.25
a.		"REPUBLICA" inverted	17.50	17.50
58	(b)	25r on 200r red vio, *pnksh*	2.25	2.00
a.		"REPUBLICA" inverted	17.50	17.50
b.		"CONGO" double	17.50	17.50

Thin Bar and "CONGO" as Type "b"

No.	Type	Description	Unused	Used
59	(a)	2½r gray	1.10	90
		Nos. 54-59 (6)	8.55	7.55

Issue of 1898-1903 Overprinted in Carmine or Green — c

1911

No.	Type	Description	Unused	Used
60	A2	2½r gray	15	15
a.		Inverted overprint	*15.00*	*11.00*
61	A2	5r orange	22	20
62	A2	10r lt grn	22	20
63	A2	15r gray grn	28	25
64	A2	20r gray vio	28	25
65	A2	25r car rose (G)	30	25
a.		Inverted overprint	17.50	13.00
66	A2	50r brown	30	30
67	A2	75r red lilac	60	50
68	A2	100r dk bl, *bl*	60	55
69	A2	115r org brn, *pink*	1.40	1.00
70	A2	130r brn, *straw*	1.40	1.00
71	A2	200r red vio, *pnksh*	2.00	1.75
72	A2	400r dl bl, *straw*	2.00	1.75
73	A2	500r blk & red, *bl*	2.75	2.00
74	A2	700r vio, *yelsh*	2.75	2.00
		Nos. 60-74 (15)	15.25	12.15

Vasco da Gama Issue of Various Portuguese Colonies Surcharged REPUBLICA CONGO ¼ C.

1913

On Stamps of Macao

No.	Type	Description	Unused	Used
75	CD20	¼c on ½a bl grn	1.40	1.40
76	CD21	½c on 1a red	1.40	1.40
77	CD22	1c on 2a red vio	1.40	1.40
78	CD23	2½c on 4a yel grn	1.40	1.40
79	CD24	5c on 8a dk bl	1.40	1.40
80	CD25	7½c on 12a vio brn	2.75	2.75
81	CD26	10c on 16a bis brn	2.00	2.00
82	CD27	15c on 24a bis	2.00	2.00
		Nos. 75-82 (8)	13.75	13.75

On Stamps of Portuguese Africa

No.	Type	Description	Unused	Used
83	CD20	¼c on 2½r bl grn	90	90
84	CD21	½c on 5r red	90	90
85	CD22	1c on 10r red vio	90	90
86	CD23	2½c on 25r yel grn	90	90
87	CD24	5c on 50r dk bl	1.25	1.25
88	CD25	7½c on 75r vio brn	2.25	2.25
89	CD26	10c on 100r bis brn	1.40	1.40
a.		Inverted surcharge	22.50	22.50
90	CD27	15c on 150r bis	1.75	1.50
		Nos. 83-90 (8)	10.25	10.00

On Stamps of Timor

No.	Type	Description	Unused	Used
91	CD20	¼c on ½a bl grn	1.40	1.40
92	CD21	½c on 1a red	1.40	1.40
93	CD22	1c on 2a red vio	1.40	1.40
94	CD23	2½c on 4a yel grn	1.40	1.40
95	CD24	5c on 8a dk bl	1.40	1.40
a.		Double surcharge	22.50	22.50
96	CD25	7½c on 12a vio brn	2.75	2.75
97	CD26	10c on 16a bis brn	2.50	2.50
98	CD27	15c on 24a bis	2.50	2.50
		Nos. 91-98 (8)	14.75	14.75
		Nos. 75-98 (24)	38.75	38.50

Ceres — A3

1914 — Typo. — *Perf. 15x14*

Name and Value in Black

No.	Type	Description	Unused	Used
99	A3	¼c olive brn	30	*45*
a.		Inscriptions inverted		
100	A3	½c black	55	*90*
101	A3	1c blue grn	2.75	*3.75*
102	A3	1½c lilac brn	1.10	*1.25*
103	A3	2c carmine	1.10	*1.25*
104	A3	2½c lt violet	35	*80*
105	A3	5c dp blue	65	*1.25*
106	A3	7½c yellow brn	90	*1.25*
107	A3	8c slate	1.50	*3.00*
108	A3	10c orange brn	1.50	*3.00*
109	A3	15c plum	1.75	*3.00*
110	A3	20c yel grn	2.00	*3.00*
111	A3	30c brn, *grn*	2.50	*4.50*
112	A3	40c brn, *pink*	3.50	*6.00*
113	A3	50c org, *salmon*	3.50	*6.00*
114	A3	1e green, *blue*	5.00	*8.00*
		Nos. 99-114 (16)	28.95	*49.15*

Issue of 1898-1903 Overprinted Locally in Green or Red

1914-18 — *Perf. 11½*

No.	Type	Description	Unused	Used
117	A2	50r brn (G)	65	60
118	A2	75r rose (G)	*250.00*	
119	A2	75r red lil (G)	70	65
120	A2	100r bl, *bl* (R)	70	65
121	A2	200r red vio, *pink* (G)	1.10	1.00
122	A2	400r dl bl, *straw* (R) ('18)	72.50	50.00
123	A2	500r blk & red, *bl* (R)	57.50	37.50

Same on Nos. 51-52

No.	Type	Description	Unused	Used
124	A2	50r blue (R)	75	65
125	A2	75r rose (G)	1.40	1.00

Same on No. 53

No.	Type	Description	Unused	Used
126	A2	50r on 65r dl bl (R)	1.10	1.00
		Nos. 117,119-126 (9)	136.40	93.05

No. 118 was not regularly issued.

Provisional Issue of 1902 Overprinted Type "c" in Red

1915 — *Perf. 11½, 12½, 13½*

No.	Type	Description	Unused	Used
127	A1	115r on 10r red vio	25	20
a.		Perf. 13½	15.00	12.50
128	A1	115r on 50r lt bl	25	20
a.		Perf. 11½	1.75	60
129	A1	130r on 5r yellow	30	25
130	A1	130r on 75r rose	1.40	60
131	A1	130r on 100r brn, *buff*	40	35
135	N1	115r on 2½r brn	40	35

Nos. 49, 51 Overprinted Type "c"

No.	Type	Description	Unused	Used
136	A2	15r brown	40	35
137	A2	50r blue	40	35

No. 53 Overprinted Type "c"

No.	Type	Description	Unused	Used
138	A2	50r on 65r dull blue	50	35
		Nos. 127-138 (9)	4.30	3.00

NEWSPAPER STAMP

N1

Perf. 12½, 13½

1894, Aug. 5 — Typo. — Unwmk.

No.	Type	Description	Unused	Used
P1	N1	2½r brown	60	40

For surcharge and overprint see Nos. 48, 135.

PORTUGUESE GUINEA

LOCATION — On the west coast of Africa between Senegal and Guinea
GOVT. — Former Portuguese Overseas Territory
AREA — 13,944 sq. mi.
POP. — 560,000 (est. 1970)
CAPITAL — Bissau

The territory, including the Bissagos Islands, became an independent republic on Sept. 10, 1974. See Guinea-Bissau in Vol. 3.

1000 Reis = 1 Milreis
100 Centavos = 1 Escudo (1913)

Catalogue values for unused stamps in this country are for Never Hinged items, beginning with Scott 273 in the regular postage section, Scott J40 in the postage due section, and Scott RA17 in the postal tax section.

Values of early Portuguese Guinea stamps vary according to condition. Quotations for Nos. 1-7 are for fine copies. Very fine to superb specimens sell at much higher prices, and inferior or poor copies sell at reduced prices, depending on the condition of the individual specimen.

Stamps of Cape Verde, 1877-85 Overprinted in Black **GUINÉ**

1881 Unwmk. *Perf. 12½*
Without Gum (Nos. 1-7)

1 A1 5r black *1,000. 800.00*
1A A1 10r yellow *1,200. 800.00*
2 A1 20r bister *450.00 225.00*
3 A1 25r rose *1,100. 700.00*
4 A1 40r blue *1,000. 800.00*
a. Cliché of Mozambique in Cape Verde plate *5,500. 5,500.*
4B A1 50r green *1,250. 650.00*
5 A1 100r lilac 275.00 150.00
6 A1 200r orange *475.00 350.00*
7 A1 300r brown *475.00 425.00*

Overprinted in Red or Black **GUINÉ**

1881-85 *Perf. 12½, 13½*

8 A1 5r blk (R) 2.50 2.00
9 A1 10r yellow 125.00 100.00
10 A1 10r grn ('85) 6.00 5.50
11 A1 20r bister 2.00 1.75
12 A1 20r rose ('85) 6.00 5.50
a. Double overprint
13 A1 25r carmine 1.40 1.25
a. Perf. 13½ 62.50 30.00
14 A1 25r vio ('85) 2.00 1.75
a. Double overprint
15 A1 40r blue 125.00 75.00
a. Cliché of Mozambique in Cape Verde plate *1,250. 800.00*
16 A1 40r yel ('85) 1.10 1.25
a. Cliché of Mozambique in Cape Verde plate 30.00 27.50
b. Imperf.
c. As "a," imperf.
d. Double overprint
17 A1 50r green 150.00 75.00
18 A1 50r blue ('85) 4.50 2.25
a. Imperf.
b. Double overprint
19 A1 100r lilac 5.00 4.00
a. Inverted overprint
20 A1 200r orange 9.50 6.50
21 A1 300r yel brn 13.00 10.00
a. 300r lake brown 13.00 10.00

Varieties of this overprint may be found without accent on "E" of "GUINE," or with grave instead of acute accent.

Stamps of the 1879-85 issues were reprinted on a smooth white chalky paper, ungummed, and on thin white paper with shiny white gum and clean-cut perforation 13½.

King Luiz — A3

1886 Typo. *Perf. 12½, 13½*

22 A3 5r gray blk 2.50 2.00
a. Imperf.
23 A3 10r green 5.00 3.25
a. Perf. 13½ 5.00 4.50
b. Imperf.
24 A3 20r carmine 5.50 4.25
25 A3 25r red lilac 6.75 4.25
a. Imperf.
26 A3 40r chocolate 6.00 5.00
a. Perf. 12½ 70.00 45.00
27 A3 50r blue 8.50 3.00
a. Imperf.
28 A3 80r gray 11.00 11.00
a. Perf. 12½ 62.50 50.00
29 A3 100r brown 12.00 12.00
a. Perf. 12½ 30.00 20.00
30 A3 200r gray lilac 30.00 20.00
31 A3 300r orange 37.50 30.00
a. Perf. 13½ 165.00 165.00

For surcharges and overprints see Nos. 67-76, 180-183.

Reprinted in 1905 on thin white paper with shiny white gum and clean-cut perforation 13½.

King Carlos
A4 A5

1893-94 *Perf. 11½*

32 A4 5r yellow 1.50 .90
a. Perf. 12½ 2.00 1.25
33 A4 10r red vio 1.50 .90
34 A4 15r chocolate 1.75 1.25
35 A4 20r lavender 1.75 1.25
36 A4 25r bl grn 1.75 1.25
37 A4 50r lt blue 3.25 2.00
a. Perf. 12½ 7.50 4.50
38 A4 75r rose 10.00 7.50
39 A4 80r lt green 10.00 7.50
40 A4 100r brn, *buff* 10.00 7.50
41 A4 150r car, *rose* 10.00 8.00
42 A4 200r dk bl, *bl* 11.00 8.00
43 A4 300r dk bl, *sal* 15.00 12.00
Nos. 32-43 (12) 77.50 58.05

Almost all of Nos. 32-43 were issued without gum.

For surcharges and overprints see #77-88, 184-188, 203-205.

1898-1903 *Perf. 11½*
Name & Value in Black except 500r

44 A5 2½r gray .35 .30
45 A5 5r orange .35 .30
46 A5 10r lt grn .35 .30
47 A5 15r brown 2.75 1.75
48 A5 15r gray grn ('03) 1.25 1.10
49 A5 20r gray vio 1.10 1.00
50 A5 25r sea grn 1.65 1.00
51 A5 25r car ('03) .65 .60
52 A5 50r dk bl 2.50 1.25
53 A5 50r brn ('03) 2.00 1.40
54 A5 65r dl bl ('03) 7.00 6.00
55 A5 75r rose 15.00 8.00
56 A5 75r lilac ('03) 3.00 2.00
57 A5 80r brt vio 2.50 1.75
58 A5 100r dk bl, *bl* 2.25 1.75
a. Perf. 12½ 45.00 20.00
59 A5 115r org brn, *pink* ('03) 7.00 5.50
60 A5 130r brn, *straw* ('03) 8.00 5.50
61 A5 150r lt brn, *buff* 8.00 3.00
62 A5 200r red lil, *pnksh* 8.00 3.00
63 A5 300r bl, *rose* 7.00 3.75
64 A5 400r dl bl, *straw* ('03) 8.00 6.00
65 A5 500r blk & red, *bl* ('01) 10.00 7.00
66 A5 700r vio, *yelsh* ('01) 15.00 9.00
Nos. 44-66 (23) 113.70 71.25

Stamps issued in 1903 were without gum.

For overprints and surcharges see Nos. 90-115, 190-194, 197.

Issue of 1886 Surcharged in Black or Red

1902, Oct. 20 *Perf. 12½, 13½*

67 A3 65r on 10r grn 5.00 4.00
68 A3 65r on 20r car 5.00 4.00
69 A3 65r on 25r red lil 5.00 4.00
70 A3 115r on 40r choc 4.50 4.00
a. Perf. 13½ 10.00 7.50
71 A3 115r on 50r bl 4.50 4.00
72 A3 115r on 300r org 6.00 5.25
73 A3 130r on 80r gray 6.00 5.25
74 A3 130r on 100r brn 6.00 5.25
a. Perf. 13½ 14.00 12.00
75 A3 400r on 200r gray lil 11.00 10.00
76 A3 400r on 5r gray blk (R) 22.00 20.50
Nos. 67-76 (10) 75.00 66.25

Reprints of No. 76 are in black and have clean-cut perforation 13½.

Same Surcharge on Issue of 1893-94
Perf. 11½, 12½, 13½

77 A4 65r on 10r red vio 4.00 3.25
78 A4 65r on 15r choc 4.00 3.25
79 A4 65r on 20r lav 4.00 3.25
80 A4 65r on 50r lt bl 2.50 2.25
81 A4 115r on 5r yel 3.25 2.75
a. Inverted surcharge 40.00 45.00
b. Perf. 12½ 22.50 18.00
82 A4 115r on 25r bl grn 3.50 3.00
83 A4 130r on 150r car, *rose* 4.50 4.00
84 A4 130r on 200r dk bl, *bl* 4.50 4.00
85 A4 130r on 300r dk bl, *sal* 4.50 4.00
86 A4 400r on 75r rose 2.00 1.50
87 A4 400r on 80r lt grn 2.00 1.50
88 A4 400r on 100r brn, *buff* 2.00 1.50

Same Surcharge on No. P1

89 N1 115r on 2½r brn 4.00 3.50
Nos. 77-89 (13) 44.75 37.75

Issue of 1898 Overprinted in Black **PROVISORIO**

1902, Oct. 20 *Perf. 11½*

90 A5 15r brown 1.40 1.10
91 A5 25r sea green 2.00 1.25
92 A5 50r dark blue 2.00 1.25
93 A5 75r rose 4.00 3.50

No. 54 Surcharged in Black **50 RÉIS**

1905

94 A5 50r on 65r dull blue 4.00 2.25

Issue of 1898-1903 Overprinted in Carmine or Green

1911 *Perf. 11½*

95 A5 2½r gray .35 .30
a. Inverted overprint 17.50 17.50
96 A5 5r orange .35 .30
97 A5 10r lt grn .65 .45
98 A5 15r gray grn .65 .45
99 A5 20r gray vio .65 .45
100 A5 25r car (G) .65 .45
a. Double overprint 14.00 14.00
101 A5 50r brown .40 .35
102 A5 75c lilac .40 .35
103 A5 100r dk bl, *bl* 1.40 .70
104 A5 115r org brn, *pink* 1.40 .70
105 A5 130r brn, *straw* 1.40 .70
106 A5 200r red lil, *pink* 6.00 3.00
107 A5 400r dl bl, *straw* 2.25 1.35
108 A5 500r blk & red, *bl* 2.50 1.35
109 A5 700r vio, *yelsh* 3.75 2.00
Nos. 95-109 (15) 22.80 12.90

Issued without gum: Nos. 101-102, 104-105, 107.

Issue of 1898-1903 Overprinted in Red

1913 *Perf. 11½*
Without Gum (Nos. 110-115)

110 A5 15r gray grn 6.75 6.00
111 A5 75r lilac 6.75 6.00
a. Inverted overprint
112 A5 100r bl, *bl* 5.00 4.00
a. Inverted overprint
113 A5 200r red lil, *pnksh* 22.50 22.50
a. Inverted overprint

Same Overprint on Nos. 90, 93 in Red

114 A5 15r brown 8.00 6.50
a. "REPUBLICA" double
b. "REPUBLICA" inverted *27.50 27.50*
115 A5 75r rose 8.00 6.00
a. "REPUBLICA" inverted
Nos. 110-115 (6) 57.00 51.00

Vasco da Gama Issue of Various Portuguese Colonies Surcharged **REPUBLICA GUINE ¼ C.**

1913

On Stamps of Macao

116 CD20 ¼c on ½a bl grn 1.50 1.50
117 CD21 ½c on 1a red 1.50 1.50
118 CD22 1c on 2a red vio 1.50 1.50
119 CD23 2½c on 4a yel grn 1.50 1.50
120 CD24 5c on 8a dk bl 1.50 1.50
121 CD25 7½c on 12a vio brn 3.00 3.00
122 CD26 10c on 16a bis brn 1.50 1.50
a. Inverted surcharge 27.50 27.50
123 CD27 15c on 24a bis 2.50 2.50
Nos. 116-123 (8) 14.50 14.50

On Stamps of Portuguese Africa

124 CD20 ¼c on 2½c bl grn 1.25 1.25
125 CD21 ½c on 5r red 1.25 1.25
126 CD22 1c on 10r red vio 1.25 1.25
127 CD23 2½c on 25r yel grn 1.25 1.25
128 CD24 5c on 50r dk bl 1.25 1.25
129 CD25 7½c on 75r vio brn 3.25 3.25
130 CD26 10c on 100r bis brn 1.25 1.25
131 CD27 15c on 150r bis 3.50 3.50
Nos. 124-131 (8) 14.25 14.25

On Stamps of Timor

132 CD20 ¼c on ½a bl grn 1.50 1.50
133 CD21 ½c on 1a red 1.50 1.50
134 CD22 1c on 2a red vio 1.50 1.50
135 CD23 2½c on 4a yel grn 1.50 1.50
136 CD24 5c on 8a dk bl 1.50 1.50
137 CD25 7½c on 12a vio brn 2.75 2.75
138 CD26 10c on 16a bis brn 1.50 1.50
139 CD27 15c on 24a bis 2.75 2.75
Nos. 132-139 (8) 14.50 14.50
Nos. 116-139 (24) 43.25 43.25

Ceres — A6

1914-26 *Perf. 15x14, 12x11½*

Name and Value in Black

No.	Type	Description	Unused	Used
140	A6	¼c ol brn	20	15
141	A6	½c black	20	15
142	A6	1c bl grn	1.25	1.10
143	A6	1c yel grn ('22)	15	15
144	A6	1½c lil brn	20	15
145	A6	2c carmine	20	15
146	A6	2c gray ('25)	20	*1.50*
147	A6	2½c lt vio	15	15
148	A6	3c org ('22)	20	*1.50*
149	A6	4c dp red ('22)	20	*1.50*
150	A6	4½c gray ('22)	20	*1.50*
151	A6	5c dp bl	60	50
152	A6	5c brt bl ('22)	20	15
153	A6	6c lilac ('22)	20	*1.50*
154	A6	7c ultra ('22)	30	*1.50*
155	A6	7½c yel brn	20	15
156	A6	8c slate	20	15
157	A6	10c org brn	15	15
158	A6	12c bl grn ('22)	60	35
159	A6	15c plum	7.50	5.50
160	A6	15c brn rose ('22)	45	30
161	A6	20c yel grn	20	15
162	A6	24c ultra ('25)	1.75	1.50
163	A6	25c brn ('25)	2.25	2.00
164	A6	30c brn, *grn*	6.25	5.50
165	A6	30c gray grn ('22)	80	25
166	A6	40c brn, *pink*	3.25	3.00
167	A6	40c turq bl ('22)	60	35
168	A6	50c org, *salmon*	3.25	3.00
169	A6	50c violet ('25)	1.50	70
170	A6	60c dk bl ('22)	1.50	70
171	A6	60c dp rose ('26)	2.25	1.40
172	A6	80c brt rose ('22)	1.50	90
173	A6	1e green, *blue*	3.50	3.25
174	A6	1e pale rose ('22)	2.25	1.10
175	A6	1e indigo ('26)	2.75	2.25
176	A6	2e dk vio ('22)	2.75	1.10
177	A6	5e buff ('25)	10.50	7.25
178	A6	10e pink ('25)	22.50	13.00
179	A6	20e pale turq ('25)	52.50	27.50
		Nos. 140-179 (40)	135.40	93.15

For surcharges see Nos. 195-196, 211-213.

Provisional Issue of 1902 Overprinted in Carmine

REPUBLICA

1915 *Perf. 11½, 12½, 13½*

No.	Type	Description	Unused	Used
180	A3	115r on 40r choc	65	60
a.		Perf. 13½	8.25	5.75
181	A3	115r on 50r blude	80	70
182	A3	130r on 80r gray	2.75	1.75
a.		Perf. 12½	25.00	20.00
183	A3	130r on 100r brn	2.25	1.75
a.		Perf. 13½	11.00	8.50
184	A4	115r on 5r yellow	75	60
a.		Perf. 11½	4.50	4.00
185	A4	115r on 25r bl grn	70	60
186	A4	130r on 150r car, *rose*	1.10	75
187	A4	130r on 200r bl, *bl*	75	65
188	A4	130r on 300r dk bl, *sal*	1.00	75
189	N1	115r on 2½r brn	1.10	80
a.		Perf. 13½	25.00	25.00
b.		Inverted overprint	16.00	16.00

On Nos. 90, 92, 94

Perf. 11½

No.	Type	Description	Unused	Used
190	A5	15r brown	75	65
191	A5	50r dark blue	75	65
192	A5	50r on 65r dl bl	75	65
		Nos. 180-192 (13)	14.10	10.90

Nos. 64, 66 Overprinted **REPUBLICA**

1919 **Without Gum** *Perf. 11½*

No.	Type	Description	Unused	Used
193	A5	400r dl bl, *straw*	22.50	19.00
194	A5	700r vio, *yelsh*	8.25	5.75

Nos. 140, 141 and 59 Surcharged:

$04 centavos
a

$12 CENTAVOS
b

1920, Sept. *Perf. 15x14, 11½*

Without Gum

No.	Type	Description	Unused	Used
195	A6(a)	4c on ¼c ol brn	3.50	2.50
196	A6(a)	6c on ½c blk	3.50	2.50
197	A5(b)	12c on 115r org brn, *pink*	5.00	4.00

Nos. 86-88 Surcharged

República
40 C.

1925 *Perf. 11½*

No.	Type	Description	Unused	Used
203	A4	40c on 400r on 75r	1.00	70
204	A4	40c on 400r on 80r	65	50
205	A4	40c on 400r on 100r	65	50

Nos. 171-172, 176 Surcharged

70 C.

1931 *Perf. 12x11½*

No.	Type	Description	Unused	Used
211	A6	50c on 60c dp rose	2.00	1.50
212	A6	70c on 80c pink	2.25	1.75
213	A6	1.40e on 2e dk vio	4.50	3.50

Ceres — A7

1933 **Wmk. 232** *Perf. 12 x 11½*

No.	Type	Description	Unused	Used
214	A7	1c bister	15	15
215	A7	5c ol brn	15	15
216	A7	10c violet	15	15
217	A7	15c black	15	15
218	A7	20c gray	15	15
219	A7	30c dk grn	15	15
220	A7	40c red org	35	20
221	A7	45c lt bl	75	50
222	A7	50c lt brn	75	50
223	A7	60c ol grn	75	50
224	A7	70c org brn	75	60
225	A7	80c emerald	1.10	75
226	A7	85c dp rose	2.25	1.25
227	A7	1e red brn	1.10	80
228	A7	1.40e dk bl	4.25	2.00
229	A7	2e red vio	3.25	1.75
230	A7	5e ap grn	8.25	4.50
231	A7	10e ol bis	16.00	7.50
232	A7	20e orange	50.00	20.00
		Nos. 214-232 (19)	90.45	41.75

Common Design Types

Engr.; Name & Value Typo. in Black

1938 **Unwmk.** *Perf. 13½x13*

No.	Type	Description	Unused	Used
233	CD34	1c gray grn	15	15
234	CD34	5c org brn	15	15
235	CD34	10c dk car	15	15
236	CD34	15c dk vio brn	15	15
237	CD34	20c slate	35	20
238	CD35	30c rose vio	40	25
239	CD35	35c brt grn	50	30
240	CD35	40c brown	50	30
241	CD35	50c brt red vio	50	30
242	CD36	60c gray blk	50	30
243	CD36	70c brn vio	50	30
244	CD36	80c orange	1.10	65
245	CD36	1e red	1.15	45
246	CD37	1.75e blue	1.40	90
247	CD37	2e brn car	4.25	1.25
248	CD37	5e ol grn	5.00	2.00
249	CD38	10e bl vio	6.25	2.50
250	CD38	20e red brn	22.50	4.00
		Nos. 233-250 (18)	45.50	14.30

Fort of Cacheu — A8

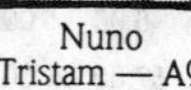

Nuno Tristam — A9

Ulysses S. Grant — A10

Designs: 3.50e, Teixeira Pinto. 5e, Honorio Barreto. 20e, Bissau Church.

Unwmk.

1946, Jan. 12 **Litho.** *Perf. 11*

No.	Type	Description	Unused	Used
251	A8	30c gray & lt gray	60	50
252	A9	50c blk & pink	50	30
253	A9	50c gray grn & lt grn	50	30
254	A10	1.75e bl & lt bl	2.00	1.25
255	A10	3.50e red & pink	3.50	2.00
256	A10	5e lt brn & buff	7.75	4.25
257	A8	20e vio & lt vio	11.00	5.50
a.		Sheet of 7, #251-257 ('47)	60.00	60.00
		Nos. 251-257 (7)	25.85	14.10

Discovery of Guinea, 500th anniversary. No. 257a sold for 40 escudos.

Guinea Village — A11

UPU Symbols — A12

Designs: 10c, Crowned crane. 20c, 3.50e, Tribesman 35c, 5e, Woman in ceremonial dress. 50c, Musician. 70c, Man. 80c, 20e, Girl. 1e, 2e, Drummer. 1.75e, Antelope.

1948, Apr. **Photo.** *Perf. 11½*

No.	Type	Description	Unused	Used
258	A11	5c chocolate	15	15
259	A11	10c lt vio	75	75
260	A11	20c dl rose	28	25
261	A11	35c green	28	25
262	A11	50c dp org	18	15
263	A11	70c dp gray bl	22	25
264	A11	80c dk ol grn	55	30
265	A11	1e rose red	50	40
266	A11	1.75e ultra	3.00	1.50
267	A11	2e blue	7.25	1.00
268	A11	3.50e org brn	1.00	80
269	A11	5e slate	1.50	1.25
270	A11	20e violet	5.50	3.00
a.		Sheet of 13, #258-270 + 2 labels	60.00	60.00
		Nos. 258-270 (13)	21.16	10.05

No. 270a sold for 40 escudos.

Lady of Fatima Issue

Common Design Type

1948, Oct. **Litho.** *Perf. 14½*

No.	Type	Description	Unused	Used
271	CD40	50c dp grn	2.75	2.25

1949, Oct. *Perf. 14*

No.	Type	Description	Unused	Used
272	A12	2e dp org & cream	2.75	2.25

Universal Postal Union, 75th anniversary.

Catalogue values for unused stamps in this section, from this point to the end of the section, are for Never Hinged items.

Holy Year Issue

Common Design Types

1950, May *Perf. 13x13½*

No.	Type	Description	Unused	Used
273	CD41	1e brn lake	1.25	1.00
274	CD42	3e bl grn	1.90	1.40

Holy Year Extension Issue

Common Design Type

1951, Oct. *Perf. 14*

No.	Type	Description	Unused	Used
275	CD43	1e choc & pale brn	90	60

Medical Congress Issue

Common Design Type

Design: Physical examination.

1952 *Perf. 13½*

No.	Type	Description	Unused	Used
276	CD44	50c pur & choc	40	30

Exhibition Entrance A13

Stamp of Portugal and Arms of Colonies A14

1953, Jan. **Litho.** *Perf. 13*

No.	Type	Description	Unused	Used
277	A13	10c brn lake & ol	15	15
278	A13	50c dk bl & bister	48	22
279	A13	3e blk, dk brn & sal	1.50	75

Issued to commemorate the Exhibition of Sacred Missionary Art held at Lisbon in 1951.

1953 **Photo.** **Unwmk.**

No.	Type	Description	Unused	Used
280	A14	50c multi	60	50

Centenary of Portugal's first postage stamps.

Analeptes Trifasciata — A15

1953 *Perf. 11½*

Various Beetles in Natural Colors

No.	Type	Description	Unused	Used
281	A15	5c yellow	15	15
282	A15	10c blue	15	15
283	A15	30c org vermilion	15	15
284	A15	50c yel grn	15	15
285	A15	70c gray brn	28	22
286	A15	1e orange	35	22
287	A15	2e pale ol grn	80	22
288	A15	3e lilac rose	1.10	60
289	A15	5e lt bl grn	2.00	65
290	A15	10e lilac	2.75	90
		Nos. 281-290 (10)	7.88	3.41

Sao Paulo Issue

Common Design Type

1954 **Litho.** *Perf. 13½*

No.	Type	Description	Unused	Used
291	CD46	1e lil rose, bl gray & blk	30	15

Belem Tower, Lisbon, and Colonial Arms — A16

1955, Apr. 14

No.	Type	Description	Unused	Used
292	A16	1e blue & multi	25	15
293	A16	2.50e gray & multi	55	20

Issued to publicize the visit of Pres. Francisco H. C. Lopes.

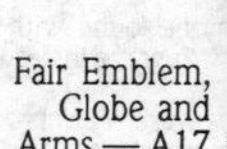

Fair Emblem, Globe and Arms — A17

1958 **Unwmk.** *Perf. 12x11½*

No.	Type	Description	Unused	Used
294	A17	2.50e multi	60	50

World's Fair at Brussels.

Tropical Medicine Congress Issue

Common Design Type

Design: Maytenus senegalensis.

1958 *Perf. 13½*

No.	Type	Description	Unused	Used
295	CD47	5e multi	1.90	1.00

Honorio Barreto A18 — Nautical Astrolabe A19

1959, Apr. 29 Litho. Perf. 13½

296	A18	2.50e multi	25	20

Centenary of the death of Honorio Barreto, governor of Portuguese Guinea.

1960, June 25 Perf. 13½

297	A19	2.50e multi	25	20

500th anniversary of the death of Prince Henry the Navigator.

Traveling Medical Unit — A20

1960 Unwmk. Perf. 14½

298	A20	1.50e multi	25	20

10th anniv. of the Commission for Technical Cooperation in Africa South of the Sahara (C.C.T.A.).

Sports Issue
Common Design Type

1962, Jan. 18 Litho. Perf. 13½

299	CD48	50c Automobile race	15	15
300	CD48	1e Tennis	60	22
301	CD48	1.50e Shot put	22	15
302	CD48	2.50e Wrestling	45	15
303	CD48	3.50e Trapshooting	45	18
304	CD48	15e Volleyball	1.40	80
		Nos. 299-304 (6)	3.27	1.65

Anti-Malaria Issue
Common Design Type

Design: Anopheles gambiae.

1962 Unwmk. Perf. 13½

305	CD49	2.50e multi	60	30

African Spitting Cobra — A21

Snakes: 35c, African rock python. 70c, Boomslang. 80c, West African mamba. 1.50e, Smythe's water snake. 2e, Common night adder, horiz. 2.50e, Green swamp snake. 3.50e, Brown house snake. 4e, Spotted wolf snake. 5e, Common puff adder. 15e, Striped beauty snake. 20e, African egg-eating snake, horiz.

1963, Jan. 17 Litho. Perf. 13½

306	A21	20c multi	15	15
307	A21	35c multi	15	15
308	A21	70c multi	35	25
309	A21	80c multi	35	25
310	A21	1.50e multi	55	25
311	A21	2e multi	40	15
312	A21	2.50e multi	1.25	25
313	A21	3.50e multi	45	20
314	A21	4e multi	45	25
315	A21	5e multi	45	25
316	A21	15e multi	80	50
317	A21	20e multi	1.25	60
		Nos. 306-317 (12)	6.60	3.25

For overprints see Guinea-Bissau Nos. 696-703.

Airline Anniversary Issue
Common Design Type

1963 Litho. Perf. 14½

318	CD50	2.50e lt brn & multi	60	30

National Overseas Bank Issue
Common Design Type

Design: 2.50e, Joao de Andrade Córvo.

1964, May 16 Perf. 13½

319	CD51	2.50e multi	60	35

ITU Issue
Common Design Type

1965, May 17 Unwmk. Perf. 14½

320	CD52	2.50e lt bl & multi	1.75	70

Soldier, 1548 — A22 — Sacred Heart of Jesus Monument and Chapel of the Apparition — A23

Designs: 40c, Rifleman, 1578. 60c, Rifleman, 1640. 1e, Grenadier, 1721. 2.50e, Fusiliers captain, 1740. 4.50e, Infantryman, 1740. 7.50e, Sergeant major, 1762. 10e, Engineers' officer, 1806.

1966, Jan. 8 Litho. Perf. 13½

321	A22	25c multi	18	15
322	A22	40c multi	20	15
323	A22	60c multi	28	15
324	A22	1e multi	35	18
325	A22	2.50e multi	1.00	35
326	A22	4.50e multi	1.75	1.00
327	A22	7.50e multi	1.75	1.25
328	A22	10e multi	2.25	1.50
		Nos. 321-328 (8)	7.76	4.73

National Revolution Issue
Common Design Type

Design: 2.50e, Berta Craveiro Lopes School and Central Pavilion of Bissau Hospital.

1966, May 28 Litho. Perf. 11½

329	CD53	2.50e multi	50	30

Navy Club Issue
Common Design Type

Designs: 50c, Capt. Oliveira Muzanty and cruiser Republica. 1e, Capt. Afonso de Cerqueira and torpedo boat Guadiana.

1967, Jan. 31 Litho. Perf. 13

330	CD54	50c multi	30	15
331	CD54	1e multi	70	50

1967, May 13 Perf. 12½x13

332	A23	50c multi	20	15

50th anniv. of the appearance of the Virgin Mary to three shepherd children at Fatima.

Pres. Rodrigues Thomas — A24 — Cabral's Coat of Arms — A25

1968, Feb. 2 Litho. Perf. 13½

333	A24	1e multi	20	15

Issued to commemorate the 1968 visit of Pres. Americo de Deus Rodrigues Thomaz.

1968, Apr. 22 Litho. Perf. 14

334	A25	2.50e multi	50	20

500th anniversary, birth of Pedro Alvares Cabral, navigator who took possession of Brazil for Portugal.

Admiral Coutinho Issue
Common Design Type

Design: 1e, Adm. Coutinho and astrolabe.

1969, Feb. 17 Litho. Perf. 14

335	CD55	1e multi	30	20

Da Gama Coat of Arms — A26 — Arms of King Manuel I — A27

Vasco da Gama Issue

1969, Aug. 29 Litho. Perf. 14

336	A26	2.50e multi	30	15

Vasco da Gama (1469-1524), navigator.

Administration Reform Issue
Common Design Type

1969, Sept. 25 Litho. Perf. 14

337	CD56	50c multi	20	15

King Manuel I Issue

1969, Dec. 1 Litho. Perf. 14

338	A27	2e multi	30	20

Pres. Ulysses S. Grant and View of Bolama — A28

1970, Oct. 25 Litho. Perf. 13½

339	A28	2.50e multi	40	20

Centenary of Pres. Grant's arbitration in 1868 of Portuguese-English dispute concerning Bolama.

Marshal Carmona Issue
Common Design Type

Design: 1.50e, Antonio Oscar Carmona in general's uniform.

1970, Nov. 15 Litho. Perf. 14

340	CD57	1.50e multi	30	20

Luiz Camoens — A29

1972, May 25 Litho. Perf. 13

341	A29	50c brn org & multi	20	15

4th centenary of publication of The Lusiads by Luiz Camoens (1524-1580).

Olympic Games Issue
Common Design Type

Design: 2.50e, Weight lifting, hammer throw and Olympic emblem.

1972, June 20 Perf. 14x13½

342	CD59	2.50e multi	40	20

Lisbon-Rio de Janeiro Flight Issue
Common Design Type

Design: 1e, "Lusitania" taking off from Lisbon.

1972, Sept. 20 Litho. Perf. 13½

343	CD60	1e multi	20	15

WMO Centenary Issue
Common Design Type

1973, Dec. 15 Litho. Perf. 13

344	CD61	2e lt brn & multi	30	20

AIR POST STAMPS

Common Design Type
Perf. 13½x13

1938, Sept. 19 Engr. Unwmk.
Name and Value in Black

C1	CD39	10c scarlet	38	30
C2	CD39	20c purple	38	30
C3	CD39	50c orange	45	30
C4	CD39	1e ultra	55	38
C5	CD39	2e lilac brown	4.75	3.25
C6	CD39	3e dark green	1.25	85
C7	CD39	5e red brown	3.00	95
C8	CD39	9e rose carmine	3.50	2.00
C9	CD39	10e magenta	8.50	2.75
		Nos. C1-C9 (9)	22.76	11.08

No. C7 exists with overprint "Exposicao Internacional de Nova York, 1939-1940" and Trylon and Perisphere.

POSTAGE DUE STAMPS

D1

D2

1904 Unwmk. Typo. Perf. 12
Without Gum

J1	D1	5r yellow green	40	32
J2	D1	10r slate	40	32
J3	D1	20r yellow brown	40	32
J4	D1	30r red orange	1.25	1.00
J5	D1	50r gray brown	1.25	1.00
J6	D1	60r red brown	2.50	1.75
J7	D1	100r lilac	2.50	1.65
J8	D1	130r dull blue	2.50	1.65
J9	D1	200r carmine	4.00	3.25
J10	D1	500r violet	8.75	4.00
		Nos. J1-J10 (10)	23.95	15.26

Same Overprinted in Carmine or Green

1911
Without Gum

J11	D1	5r yellow green	22	18
J12	D1	10r slate	22	18
J13	D1	20r yellow brown	32	28
J14	D1	30r red orange	32	28
J15	D1	50r gray brown	32	28
J16	D1	60r red brown	90	65
J17	D1	100r lilac	1.75	90
J18	D1	130r dull blue	1.75	90
J19	D1	200r carmine (G)	1.75	1.40
J20	D1	500r violet	1.00	90
		Nos. J11-J20 (10)	8.55	5.95

Nos. J2-J10 Overprinted **REPUBLICA**

1919
Without Gum

J21	D1	10r slate	5.00	5.00
J22	D1	20r yellow brown	5.50	5.50
J23	D1	30r red orange	4.00	3.50
J24	D1	50r gray brown	1.50	1.25
J25	D1	60r red brown	300.00	200.00
J26	D1	100r lilac	1.50	1.25
J27	D1	130r dull blue	20.00	17.50
J28	D1	200r carmine	2.25	2.00
J29	D1	500r violet	17.00	15.00
		Nos. J21-J24,J26-J29 (8)	56.75	51.00

No. J25 was not regularly issued but exists on genuine covers.

1921

J30	D2	½c yellow green	15	15
J31	D2	1c slate	15	15
J32	D2	2c orange brown	15	15
J33	D2	3c orange	15	15
J34	D2	5c gray brown	15	15
J35	D2	6c light brown	15	15
J36	D2	10c red violet	25	25
J37	D2	13c dull blue	25	25
J38	D2	20c carmine	30	30
J39	D2	50c gray	30	30
		Nos. J30-J39 (10)	2.00	
		Set value		1.70

Catalogue values for unused stamps in this section, from this point to the end of the section, are for Never Hinged items.

Common Design Type

Photogravure and Typographed

1952 Unwmk. *Perf. 14*

Numeral in Red, Frame Multicolored

J40	CD45	10c olive green	15	15
J41	CD45	30c purple	15	15
J42	CD45	50c dark green	15	15
J43	CD45	1e violet blue	20	20
J44	CD45	2e olive black	30	30
J45	CD45	5e brown red	65	65
		Set value	1.25	1.25

WAR TAX STAMPS

WT1

Perf. 11½x12

1919, May 20 Typo. Unwmk.

MR1	WT1	10r brn, buff & blk	40.00	25.00
MR2	WT1	40r brn, buff & blk	35.00	20.00
MR3	WT1	50r brn, buff & blk	37.50	22.50

The 40r is not overprinted "REPUBLICA."

Some authorities consider Nos. MR2-MR3 to be revenue stamps.

NEWSPAPER STAMP

N1

Perf. 12½, 13½

1893 Typo. Unwmk.

P1	N1	2½r brown	65	60

For surcharge and overprint see Nos. 89, 189.

POSTAL TAX STAMPS

Pombal Issue

Common Design Types

1925 Unwmk. Engr. *Perf. 12½*

RA1	CD28	15c red & black	65	60
RA2	CD29	15c red & black	65	60
RA3	CD30	15c red & black	65	60

Coat of Arms PT7

1934, Apr. 1 Typo. *Perf. 11½*

Without Gum

RA4	PT7	50c red brn & grn	7.25	4.00

Coat of Arms
PT8 PT9

1938-40

Without Gum

RA5	PT8	50c ol bis & citron	6.25	4.25
RA6	PT8	50c lt grn & ol brn ('40)	6.25	4.25

1942 *Perf. 11*

Without Gum

RA7	PT9	50c black & yellow	2.00	80

1959, July Unwmk.

Without Gum

RA8	PT9	30c dark ocher & blk	20	20

See Nos. RA24-RA26.

Lusignian Cross
PT10 PT11

1967 Typo. *Perf. 11x11½*

Without Gum

RA9	PT10	50c pink, red & blk	1.25	1.25
RA10	PT10	1e grn, red & blk	1.25	1.25
RA11	PT10	5e gray, red & blk	2.00	2.00
RA12	PT10	10e lt bl, red & blk	4.00	4.00

The tax was for national defense.

A 50e was used for revenue only.

1967, Aug. Typo. *Perf. 11*

Without Gum

RA13	PT11	50c pink, blk & red	95	95
RA14	PT11	1e pale grn, blk & red	95	95
RA15	PT11	5e gray, blk & red	1.65	1.65
RA16	PT11	10e lt bl, blk & red	2.50	2.50

The tax was for national defense.

Catalogue values for unused stamps in this section, from this point to the end of the section, are for Never Hinged items.

Carved Figurine — PT12

Art from Bissau Museum: 1e, Tree of Life, with 2 birds, horiz. #RA19, Man wearing horned headgear ("Vaca Bruto"). #RA20, as #RA19, inscribed "Tocador de Bombolon." 2.50e, The Magistrate. 5e, Man bearing burden on head. 10e, Stylized pelican.

1968 Litho. *Perf. 13½*

RA17	PT12	50c gray & multi	15	15
a.		Yellow paper	50	
RA18	PT12	1e multi	15	15
RA19	PT12	2e *(Vaca Bruto)*	16	15
RA20	PT12	2e *(Tocador de Bombolon)*	*10.00*	
RA21	PT12	2.50e multi	28	20
RA22	PT12	5e multi	42	35
RA23	PT12	10e multi	90	70
		Nos. RA17-RA19,RA21-RA23 (6)	2.06	1.70

Obligatory on all inland mail Mar. 15-Apr. 15 and Dec. 15-Jan. 15, and all year on parcels.

A souvenir sheet embracing Nos. RA17-RA19 and RA21-RA23 exists. The stamps have simulated perforations. Value $3.50.

For surcharges see Nos. RA27-RA28.

Arms Type of 1942

1968 Typo. *Perf. 11*

Without Gum

RA24	PT9	2.50e lt bl & blk	40	40
RA25	PT9	5e grn & blk	75	75
RA26	PT9	10e dp bl & blk	1.50	1.50

No. RA20 Surcharged

$50

1968 Litho. *Perf. 13½*

RA27	PT12	50c on 2e multi	45	45
RA28	PT12	1e on 2e multi	45	45

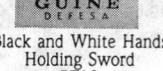

Black and White Hands Holding Sword PT13 — Mother and Children PT14

1968 Litho. *Perf. 13½*

RA29	PT13	50c pink & multi	15	15
RA30	PT13	1e multi	15	15
RA31	PT13	2e yel & multi	30	30
RA32	PT13	2.50e buff & multi	45	45
RA33	PT13	3e multi	50	50
RA34	PT13	4e gray & multi	55	55
RA35	PT13	5e multi	75	75
RA36	PT13	10e multi	1.75	1.75
		Nos. RA29-RA36 (8)	4.60	4.60

The surtax was for national defense. Other denominations exist: 8e, 9e, 15e.

1971, June Litho. *Perf. 13½*

RA37	PT14	50c multi	15	15
RA38	PT14	1e multi	15	15
RA39	PT14	2e multi	20	20
RA40	PT14	3e multi	30	30
RA41	PT14	4e multi	35	35
RA42	PT14	5e multi	60	60
RA43	PT14	10e multi	1.10	1.10
		Nos. RA37-RA43 (7)	2.85	2.85

A 20e exists.

POSTAL TAX DUE STAMPS

Pombal Issue

Common Design Types

1925 Unwmk. *Perf. 12½*

RAJ1	CD31	30c red & black	60	50
RAJ2	CD32	30c red & black	60	50
RAJ3	CD33	30c red & black	60	50

PORTUGUESE INDIA

LOCATION — West coast of the Indian peninsula
GOVT. — Former Portuguese colony
AREA — 1,537 sq. mi.
POP. — 649,000 (1958)
CAPITAL — Panjim (Nova-Goa)

The colony was seized by India on Dec. 18, 1961, and annexed by that republic.

1000 Reis = 1 Milreis
12 Reis = 1 Tanga (1881-82)
(Real = singular of Reis)
16 Tangas = 1 Rupia
100 Centavos = 1 Escudo (1959)

Catalogue values for unused stamps in this country are for Never Hinged items, beginning with Scott 490 in the regular postage section, Scott J43 in the postage due section, and Scott RA6 in the postal tax section.

Values of early Portuguese India stamps vary according to condition. Quotations for Nos. 1-55 are for fine copies. Perfs generally are rough. Stamps frequently were cut apart because of the irregular and missing perforations so that trimmed copies are considered normal.

Numeral of Value
A1 A2

A1: Large figures of value.
"REIS" in Roman capitals. "S" and "R" of "SERVICO" smaller and "E" larger than the other letters. 33 lines in background. Side ornaments of four dashes.

A2: Large figures of value.
"REIS" in block capitals. "S," "E" and "R" same size as other letters of "SERVICO." 44 lines in background. Side ornaments of five dots.

Handstamped from a Single Die

Perf. 13 to 18 & Compound

1871, Oct. 1 Unwmk.

Thin Transparent Brittle Paper

1	A1	10r black	700.00	300.00
2	A1	20r dk carmine	1,500.	300.00
3	A1	40r Prus blue	525.00	350.00
4	A1	100r yellow grn	625.00	400.00
5	A1	200r ocher yel	800.00	450.00

1872

Thick Soft Wove Paper

5A	A1	10r black	*1,700.*	300.00
6	A1	20r dk car	*1,800.*	250.00
7	A1	20r org ver	*1,800.*	250.00
8	A1	200r ocher yel	*1,700.*	550.00
9	A1	300r dp red vio		*2,250.*

The 600r and 900r of type A1 are bogus.

See Nos. 24-28. For surcharges see Nos. 70-71, 73, 83, 94, 99, 104, 108.

Perf. 12½ to 14½ & Compound

1872

10	A2	10r black	250.00	100.00
11	A2	20r vermilion	250.00	90.00
a.		"20" omitted		*1,100.*
12	A2	40r blue	90.00	70.00
a.		Tête bêche pair	*6,000.*	
13	A2	100r dp grn	80.00	60.00
14	A2	200r yellow	300.00	275.00
15	A2	300r red vio	300.00	225.00
a.		Imperf.		
16	A2	600r red vio	175.00	125.00
a.		"600" double	*600.00*	
17	A2	900r red vio	190.00	200.00

An unused 100r blue green exists with watermark of lozenges and gray burelage on back. Experts believe it to be a proof.

White Laid Paper

18	A2	10r black	32.50	20.00
a.		Tête bêche pair		*7,000.*
19	A2	20r vermilion	40.00	20.00
20	A2	40r blue	50.00	30.00
a.		"40" double	*350.00*	
b.		Tête bêche pair	*1,600.*	*1,600.*
21	A2	100r green	60.00	40.00
a.		"100" double	*400.00*	
22	A2	200r yellow	200.00	185.00

See No. 23. For surcharges see Nos. 72, 82, 95-96, 100-101, 105-106, 109-110.

1873
Re-issues
Thin Bluish Toned Paper

No.	Type	Description	Unused	Used
23	A2	20r vermilion	200.00	175.00
24	A1	10r black	10.00	7.00
a.		"1" inverted	150.00	125.00
b.		"10" double	450.00	
25	A1	20r vermilion	8.00	6.00
a.		"20" double	450.00	
b.		"20" inverted		
26	A1	300r dp violet	75.00	70.00
a.		"300" double	500.00	
27	A1	600r dp violet	85.00	80.00
a.		"600" double	550.00	
b.		"600" inverted	700.00	
28	A1	900r dp violet	85.00	80.00
a.		"900" double	550.00	
b.		"900" triple	1,100.	

Nos. 23 to 26 are re-issues of Nos. 11, 5A, 7, and 9. The paper is thinner and harder than that of the 1871-72 stamps and slightly transparent. It was originally bluish white but is frequently stained yellow by the gum.

A3

A4

A3: Same as A1 with small figures.
A4: Same as A2 with small figures.

1874
Thin Bluish Toned Paper

No.	Type	Description	Unused	Used
29	A3	10r black	37.50	30.00
30	A3	20r vermilion	625.00	300.00
a.		"20" double		700.00

For surcharge see No. 84.

1875

No.	Type	Description	Unused	Used
31	A4	10r black	35.00	25.00
32	A4	15r rose	11.00	10.00
a.		"15" inverted	500.00	
b.		"15" double		
33	A4	20r vermilion	50.00	30.00
a.		"0" missing	750.00	
b.		"20" sideways	750.00	
c.		"20" double		

For surcharges see Nos. 74, 78, 85.

A5

A6

A5: Re-cutting of A1.
Small figures. "REIS" in Roman capitals. Letters larger. "V" of "SERVICO" barred. 33 lines in background. Side ornaments of five dots.
A6: First re-cutting of A2.
Small figures. "REIS" in block capitals. Letters re-cut. "V" of "SERVICO" barred. 41 lines above and 43 below "REIS." Side ornaments of five dots.

Perf. 12½ to 13½ & Compound
1876

No.	Type	Description	Unused	Used
34	A5	10r black	18.00	14.00
35	A5	20r vermilion	15.00	12.00
a.		"20" double		
36	A6	10r black	5.50	3.50
a.		Double impression		
b.		"10" double	500.00	
37	A6	15r rose	375.00	340.00
a.		"15" omitted	*1,100.*	
38	A6	20r vermilion	18.00	15.00
39	A6	40r blue	105.00	95.00
40	A6	100r green	150.00	125.00
a.		Imperf.		
41	A6	200r yellow	900.00	700.00
42	A6	300r violet	600.00	500.00
a.		"300" omitted		
43	A6	600r violet	900.00	750.00
44	A6	900r violet	1,100.	850.00

For surcharges see Nos. 75-76, 78C-80, 86-87, 91-92, 98, 102, 107, 111.

A7

A8

A9

A7: Same as A5 with addition of a star above and a bar below the value.
A8: Second re-cutting of A2. Same as A6 but 41 lines both above and below "REIS." Star above and bar below value.
A9: Third re-cutting of A2. 41 lines above and 38 below "REIS." Star above and bar below value. White line around central oval.

1877

No.	Type	Description	Unused	Used
45	A7	10r black	30.00	21.00
46	A8	10r black	37.50	30.00
47	A9	10r black	30.00	21.00
a.		"10" omitted		
48	A9	15r rose	35.00	30.00
49	A9	20r vermilion	8.00	6.00
50	A9	40r blue	17.50	15.00
a.		"40" omitted		
51	A9	100r green	47.50	40.00
a.		"100" omitted		
52	A9	200r yellow	60.00	50.00
53	A9	300r violet	100.00	75.00
54	A9	600r violet	100.00	80.00
55	A9	900r violet	100.00	80.00

No. 47, 20r, 40r and 200r exist imperf.
For surcharges see Nos. 77, 81, 88-90, 93, 112.

Portuguese Crown — A10

Perf. 12½, 13½
1877, July 15 — Typo.

No.	Type	Description	Unused	Used
56	A10	5r black	3.50	2.75
57	A10	10r yellow	9.00	7.75
a.		Imperf.		
58	A10	20r bister	9.00	6.75
59	A10	25r rose	10.00	9.00
60	A10	40r blue	15.00	12.50
a.		Perf. 12½	175.00	135.00
61	A10	50r yel grn	32.50	22.50
62	A10	100r lilac	15.00	13.00
63	A10	200r orange	20.00	15.00
64	A10	300r yel brn	32.50	27.50

1880-81

No.	Type	Description	Unused	Used
65	A10	10r green	7.50	6.75
66	A10	25r slate	42.50	30.00
a.		Perf. 12½	85.00	60.00
67	A10	25r violet	27.50	19.00
68	A10	40r yellow	35.00	27.50
69	A10	50r dk blue	21.00	17.00

For surcharges see Nos. 113-161.

The stamps of the 1877-81 issues were reprinted in 1885, on stout very white paper, ungummed and with rough perforation 13½. They were again reprinted in 1905 on thin white paper with shiny white gum and clean-cut perforation 13½ with large holes. Value of the lowest-cost reprint, $1 each.

Stamps of 1871-77 Surcharged with New Values
Black Surcharge

1881

No.	Type	Description	Unused	Used
70	A1	1½r on 20r (#2)		*600.00*
71	A1	1½r on 20r (#7)		*500.00*
72	A2	1½r on 20r (#11)		*400.00*
73	A1	1½r on 20r (#25)	225.00	200.00
74	A4	1½r on 20r (#33)	135.00	125.00
a.		Inverted surcharge		
75	A5	1½r on 20r (#35)	110.00	80.00
76	A6	1½r on 20r (#38)	125.00	110.00
77	A9	1½r on 20r (#49)	200.00	140.00
78	A4	5r on 15r (#32)	2.50	2.50
a.		Double surcharge		
b.		Inverted surcharge		
78C	A6	5r on 15r (#37)	160.00	160.00
79	A5	5r on 20r (#35)	2.75	2.75
a.		Double surcharge		
b.		Inverted surcharge		
80	A6	5r on 20r (#38)	2.00	2.00
a.		Double surcharge		
b.		Inverted surcharge		
81	A9	5r on 20r (#49)	5.00	4.00
a.		Double surcharge		
b.		Invtd. surcharge		

Red Surcharge

No.	Type	Description	Unused	Used
82	A2	5r on 10r (#18)	*375.00*	*250.00*
83	A1	5r on 10r (#24)	*475.00*	*275.00*
84	A3	5r on 10r (#29)	*1,600.*	
85	A4	5r on 10r (#31)	*110.00*	*110.00*
86	A5	5r on 10r (#34)	5.50	5.50
a.		Double surcharge		
87	A6	5r on 10r (#36)	7.50	6.25
a.		Inverted surcharge		
88	A7	5r on 10r (#45)	85.00	50.00
a.		Inverted surcharge		
89	A8	5r on 10r (#46)	175.00	75.00
90	A9	5r on 10r (#47)	30.00	25.00
a.		Inverted surcharge		
b.		Double surcharge		

Similar Surcharge, Handstamped
Black Surcharge

1883

No.	Type	Description	Unused	Used
91	A5	1½r on 10r (#34)		*750.00*
92	A6	1½r on 10r (#36)		*750.00*
93	A9	1½r on 10r (#47)	*750.00*	*550.00*
94	A1	4½r on 40r (#3)		*700.00*
95	A2	4½r on 40r (#12)	27.50	27.50
96	A2	4½r on 40r (#20)	27.50	27.50
98	A6	4½r on 40r (#39)	27.50	27.50
99	A1	4½r on 100r (#4)		*700.00*
100	A2	4½r on 100r (#13)	35.00	35.00
101	A2	4½r on 100r (#21)	35.00	35.00
102	A6	4½r on 100r (#40)	35.00	35.00
104	A1	6r on 100r (#4)		*1,100.*
105	A2	6r on 100r (#13)		*250.00*
106	A2	6r on 100r (#21)	*200.00*	*150.00*
107	A6	6r on 100r (#40)	*275.00*	*200.00*
108	A1	6r on 200r (#5)	*750.00*	*550.00*
109	A2	6r on 200r (#14)		*200.00*
110	A2	6r on 200r (#22)	*200.00*	*200.00*
111	A6	6r on 200r (#41)		*400.00*
112	A9	6r on 200r (#52)	*500.00*	*500.00*

Stamps of 1877-81 Surcharged in Black **1½**

1881-82

No.	Type	Description	Unused	Used
113	A10	1½r on 5r blk	1.00	85
a.		With additional surcharge "4½" in blue	75.00	60.00
114	A10	1½r on 10r grn	1.00	90
a.		With additional surch. "6"	100.00	80.00
115	A10	1½r on 20r bis	8.50	6.75
a.		Inverted surcharge		
b.		Double surcharge		
c.		Pair, one without surcharge		
116	A10	1½r on 25r slate	35.00	27.50
117	A10	1½r on 100r lil	55.00	37.50
118	A10	4½r on 10r grn	165.00	150.00
119	A10	4½r on 20r bis	3.50	2.50
a.		Inverted surcharge		
120	A10	4½r on 25r vio	10.50	8.50
121	A10	4½r on 100r lil	105.00	85.00
122	A10	6r on 10r yel	42.50	35.00
123	A10	6r on 10r grn	9.25	6.75
124	A10	6r on 20r bis	15.00	11.00
125	A10	6r on 25r slate	30.00	21.00
126	A10	6r on 25r vio	2.00	1.65
127	A10	6r on 40r blue	75.00	62.50
128	A10	6r on 40r yel	37.50	30.00
129	A10	6r on 50r grn	42.50	32.50
130	A10	6r on 50r blue	60.00	50.00

Surcharged in Black **1 T**

No.	Type	Description	Unused	Used
131	A10	1t on 10r grn	200.00	110.00
a.		With additional surch. "6"		
132	A10	1t on 20r bis	42.50	37.50
133	A10	1t on 25r slate	32.50	22.50
134	A10	1t on 25r vio	12.00	7.75
135	A10	1t on 40r blue	17.00	12.00
136	A10	1t on 50r grn	50.00	37.50
137	A10	1t on 50r blue	22.50	17.00
138	A10	1t on 100r lil	21.00	12.00
139	A10	1t on 200r org	42.50	37.50
140	A10	2t on 25r slate	32.50	30.00
a.		Small "T"	50.00	35.00
141	A10	2t on 25r vio	12.50	10.50
142	A10	2t on 40r blue	37.50	30.00
143	A10	2t on 40r yel	47.50	37.50
144	A10	2t on 50r grn	14.00	12.00
a.		Inverted surcharge		
145	A10	2t on 50r blue	80.00	67.50
146	A10	2t on 100r lil	10.50	8.50
147	A10	2t on 200r org	35.00	30.00
148	A10	2t on 300r brn	30.00	27.50
149	A10	4t on 10r grn	12.50	10.50
a.		Inverted surcharge		
150	A10	4t on 50r grn	12.00	9.25
a.		With additional surch. "2"	150.00	95.00
151	A10	4t on 200r org	35.00	30.00
152	A10	8t on 20r bis	30.00	21.00
153	A10	8t on 25r rose	165.00	150.00
154	A10	8t on 40r blue	42.50	35.00
155	A10	8t on 100r lil	35.00	30.00
156	A10	8t on 200r org	30.00	27.50
157	A10	8t on 300r brn	42.50	35.00

1882
Blue Surcharge

No.	Type	Description	Unused	Used
158	A10	4½r on 5r black	7.75	6.75

Similar Surcharge, Handstamped

1883

No.	Type	Description	Unused	Used
159	A10	1½r on 5r black	22.50	10.00
160	A10	1½r on 10r grn	22.50	7.00
161	A10	4½r on 100r lil	*190.00*	*165.00*

The "2" in "½" is 3mm high, instead of 2mm as on Nos. 113, 114 and 121.
The handstamp is known double on #159-161.

A12

1882-83 — Typo.
With or Without Accent on "E" of "REIS"

No.	Type	Description	Unused	Used
162	A12	1½r black	45	40
a.		"½" for "1½"		
163	A12	4½r olive bister	45	40
164	A12	6r green	60	40
165	A12	1t rose	60	40
166	A12	2t blue	60	40
167	A12	4t lilac	2.75	2.50
168	A12	8t orange	2.75	2.50

There were three printings of the 1882-83 issue. The first had "REIS" in thick letters with acute accent on the "E." The second had "REIS" in thin letters with accent on the "E." The third had the "E" without accent. In the first printing the "E" sometimes had a grave or circumflex accent.

The third printing may be divided into two sets, with or without a small circle in the cross of the crown.

Stamps doubly printed or with value omitted, double, inverted or misplaced are printer's waste.

Nos. 162-168 were reprinted on thin white paper, with shiny white gum and clean-cut perforation 13½. Value of lowest-cost reprint, $1 each.

"REIS" no serifs — A13

"REIS" with serifs — A14

1883 — Litho. — *Imperf.*

No.	Type	Description	Unused	Used
169	A13	1½r black	1.25	1.00
a.		Tête bêche pair		
b.		"1½" double	*375.00*	*300.00*
170	A13	4½r ol grn	12.50	11.00
a.		"4½" omitted	375.00	300.00
171	A13	6r green	12.50	11.00
a.		Tête bêche pair	1,250.	
b.		"6" omitted	400.00	325.00
172	A14	1½r black	65.00	16.00
a.		"1½" omitted	375.00	325.00
173	A14	6r green	57.50	40.00
a.		"6" omitted	425.00	375.00

Nos. 169-171 exist with unofficial perf. 12.

King Luiz — A15

King Carlos — A16

Perf. 12½, 13½
1886, Apr. 29 — Embossed

No.	Type	Description	Unused	Used
174	A15	1½r black	1.65	85
a.		Perf. 13½	105.00	62.50
175	A15	4½r bister	1.90	95
a.		Perf. 13½	27.50	12.50
176	A15	6r dp green	1.90	1.25
a.		Perf. 13½	30.00	14.00
177	A15	1t brt rose	3.75	1.65
178	A15	2t deep blue	6.00	2.75
179	A15	4t gray vio	6.00	3.75
180	A15	8t orange	6.00	3.75
		Nos. 174-180 (7)	27.20	14.95

For surcharges and overprints see Nos. 224-230, 277-278, 282, 317-323, 354, 397.

Nos. 178-179 were reprinted. Originals have yellow gum. Reprints have white gum and clean-cut perforation 13½. Value, $4 each.

Perf. 11½, 12½, 13½
1895-96 — Typo.

No.	Type	Description	Unused	Used
181	A16	1½r black	90	40
182	A16	4½r pale orange	90	40
a.		Perf. 13½	6.00	1.50
183	A16	6r green	90	40
a.		Perf. 12½	2.75	1.00
184	A16	9r gray lilac	3.50	2.75
185	A16	1t lt blue	1.25	50
a.		Perf. 12½	4.00	1.65
186	A16	2t rose	90	50
a.		Perf. 12½	3.75	2.00

187 A16 4t dk blue 1.50 75
a. Perf. 12½ 3.75 2.00
188 A16 8t brt violet 3.00 2.00
Nos. 181-188 (8) 12.85 7.70

For surcharges and overprints see Nos. 231-238,275-276, 279-281, 324-331, 352.

No. 184 was reprinted. Reprints have white gum, and clean-cut perforation 13½. Value $10.

Vasco da Gama Issue
Common Design Types

1898, May 1 Engr. ***Perf. 14 to 15***

189 CD20 1½r blue green 90 80
190 CD21 4½r red 90 80
191 CD22 6r red violet 90 70
192 CD23 9r yellow green 90 90
193 CD24 1t dk blue 1.50 1.50
194 CD25 2t violet brn 2.00 1.75
195 CD26 4t bister brn 2.00 1.75
196 CD27 8t bister 4.00 3.50
Nos. 189-196 (8) 13.10 11.70

For overprints and surcharges see Nos. 290-297, 384-389.

King Carlos — A17

1898-1903 Typo. ***Perf. 11½***
Name and Value in Black except No. 219

197 A17 1r gray ('02) 30 15
198 A17 1½r orange 25 15
199 A17 1½r slate ('02) 25 20
200 A17 2r orange ('02) 25 20
201 A17 2½r yel brn ('02) 30 25
202 A17 3r dp blue ('02) 25 15
203 A17 4½r lt green 60 40
204 A17 6r brown 60 45
205 A17 6r gray grn ('02) 25 15
206 A17 9r dull vio 75 45
a. 9r gray lilac 1.25 1.25
208 A17 1t sea green 75 45
209 A17 1t car rose ('02) 40 20
210 A17 2t blue 1.00 40
a. Perf. 13½ 25.00 7.00
211 A17 2t brown ('02) 2.00 1.25
212 A17 2½t dull bl ('02) 6.50 5.00
213 A17 4t blue, *blue* 2.00 1.25
214 A17 5t brn, *straw* ('02) 2.00 1.25
215 A17 8t red lil, *pnksh* 2.00 1.25
216 A17 8t red vio, *pink* ('02) 4.50 2.25
217 A17 12t blue, *pink* 3.00 1.50
218 A17 12t grn, *pink* ('02) 4.50 2.50
219 A17 1rp blk & red, *bl* 7.00 4.00
220 A17 1rp dl bl, *straw* ('02) 9.00 5.00
221 A17 2rp vio, *yelsh* 10.00 6.00
222 A17 2rp gray blk, *straw* ('03) 15.00 10.00
Nos. 197-222 (25) 73.45 44.85

Several stamps of this issue exist without value or with value inverted but they are not known to have been issued in this condition. The 1r and 6r in carmine rose are believed to be color trials.

For surcharges and overprints see Nos. 223, 239-259, 260C-274, 283-289, 300-316, 334-350, 376-383, 390-396, 398-399.

No. 210 Surcharged in Black — **1½ Reis**

1900

223 A17 1½r on 2t blue 2.75 60
a. Inverted surcharge
b. Perf. 13½ 32.50 20.00

Stamps of 1885-96 Surcharged in Black or Red — **1 REAL**

On Stamps of 1886

1902 ***Perf. 12½, 13½***

224 A15 1r on 2t blue 85 45
225 A15 2r on 4½r bis 30 25
a. Inverted surcharge 20.00 20.00
b. Double surcharge
226 A15 2½r on 6r green 30 25
227 A15 3r on 1t rose 30 25
228 A15 2½t on 1½r blk (R) 1.65 1.25
229 A15 2½t on 4t gray vio 2.00 1.25
230 A15 5t on 8t orange 1.00 60
a. Perf. 12½ 25.00 15.00

On Stamps of 1895-96
Perf. 11½, 12½, 13½

231 A16 1r on 6r green 30 25
232 A16 2r on 8t brt vio 30 25
233 A16 2½r on 9r gray vio 30 30
234 A16 3r on 4½r yel 1.25 90
a. Inverted surcharge 17.50 17.50
235 A16 3r on 1t lt bl 1.25 80
236 A16 2½t on 1½r blk (R) 2.00 75
237 A16 5t on 2t rose 2.00 75
a. Perf. 12½ 32.50 20.00
238 A16 5t on 4t dk bl 2.00 75
a. Perf. 12½ 32.50 20.00
Nos. 224-238 (15) 15.80 9.05

Nos. 224, 229, 231, 233, 234, 235 and 238 were reprinted in 1905. They have whiter gum than the originals and very clean-cut perf. 13½. Value $2.50 each.

Nos. 204, 208, 210 Overprinted — PROVISORIO

1902 ***Perf. 11½***

239 A17 6r brown 1.10 90
a. Inverted overprint
240 A17 1t sea green 1.50 90
241 A17 2t blue 1.50 90
a. Perf. 13½ 135.00 90.00

No. 212 Surcharged in Black — **2 TANGAS**

1905

243 A17 2t on 2½t dull blue 1.75 1.50

Stamps of 1898-1903 Overprinted in Lisbon in Carmine or Green

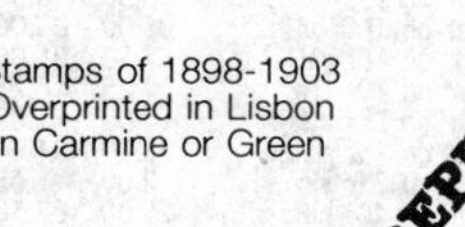

1911

244 A17 1r gray 15 15
a. Inverted overprint 10.00 10.00
245 A17 1½r slate 15 15
a. Double overprint 10.00 10.00
246 A17 2r orange 25 20
a. Double overprint
b. Inverted overprint 10.00 10.00
247 A17 2½r yel brn 25 15
248 A17 3r dp bl 25 15
249 A17 4½r light grn 30 20
250 A17 6r gray green 20 15
251 A17 9r gray lilac 30 20
252 A17 1t car rose (G) 30 20
253 A17 2t brown 30 20
254 A17 4t blue, *blue* 1.10 95
255 A17 5t brn, *straw* 1.10 95
256 A17 8t vio, *pink* 3.50 2.00
257 A17 12t grn, *pink* 3.50 2.00
258 A17 1rp dl bl, *straw* 4.75 3.75
259 A17 2rp gray blk, *straw* 7.25 5.50
Nos. 244-259 (16) 23.65 16.90

A18

Values are for pairs, both halves.

1911 **Perforated Diagonally**

260 A18 1r on 2r orange 75 65
a. Without diagonal perf. 4.00 3.50
b. Cut diagonally instead of perf. 3.25 3.00

Stamps of Preceding Issues Perforated Vertically through the Middle and Each Half Surcharged with New Value:

3 REIS — **3 REIS** (a) — **6 REIS** — **6 REIS** (b)

Values are for pairs, both halves of the stamp.

1912-13

On Issue of 1898-1903

260C A17(a) 1r on 2r org 25 20
261 A17(a) 1r on 1t car 25 20
262 A17(a) 1r on 5t brn, *straw* 95.00 65.00
263 A17(b) 1r on 5t brn, *straw* 3.50 2.75
264 A17(a) 1½r on 2½r yel brn 70 60
264C A17(a) 1½r on 4½r lt grn 8.00 4.00
265 A17(a) 1½r on 9r gray lil 50 40
266 A17(a) 1½r on 4t bl, *bl* 50 40
267 A17(a) 2r on 2½r yel brn 65 40
268 A17(a) 2r on 4t bl, *bl* 90 65
269 A17(a) 3r on 2½r yel brn 65 40
270 A17(a) 3r on 2t brown 65 45
271 A17(a) 6r on 4½r lt grn 65 55
272 A17(a) 6r on 9r gray lil 65 50
273 A17(b) 6r on 9r dull vio 4.00 3.25
274 A17(b) 6r on 8t red vio, *pink* 1.50 90

On Nos. 237-238, 230, 226, 233

275 A16(b) 1r on 5t on 2t 16.00 12.50
276 A16(b) 1r on 5t on 4t 6.00 5.75
277 A15(b) 1r on 5t on 8t 2.25 1.50
278 A15(a) 2r on 2½r on 6r 2.50 2.00
279 A16(a) 2r on 2½r on 9r 22.50 21.00
280 A16(b) 3r on 5t on 2t 7.00 5.75
281 A16(b) 3r on 5t on 4t 7.00 5.75
282 A15(b) 3r on 5t on 8t 2.25 1.50

On Issue of 1911

283 A17(a) 1r on 1r gray 25 25
283B A17(a) 1r on 2r org 25 25
284 A17(a) 1r on 1t car 30 25
285 A17(a) 1r on 5t brn, *straw* 30 25
285A A17(b) 1r on 5t brn, *straw*
285B A17(a) 1½r on 4½r lt grn 40 30
286 A17(a) 3r on 2t brown 9.00 6.75
289 A17(a) 6r on 9r gray lil 50 40

There are several settings of these surcharges and many minor varieties of the letters and figures, notably a small "6." Nos. 260-289 were issued mostly without gum.

More than half of Nos. 260C-289 exist with inverted or double surcharge, or with bisecting perforation omitted. The legitimacy of these varieties is questioned. Price of inverted surcharges, $3-$15; double surcharges, $1-$4; perf. omitted, $1.50-$15.

Similar surcharges made without official authorization on stamps of type A17 are: 2r on 2½r, 3r on 2½r, 3r on 5t, and 6r on 4½r.

Vasco da Gama Issue Overprinted — **REPUBLICA**

1913

290 CD20 1½r blue green 30 25
291 CD21 4½r red 30 25
a. Double overprint
292 CD22 6r red violet 40 35
a. Double overprint
293 CD23 9r yellow grn 40 35
294 CD24 1t dark blue 90 50
295 CD25 2t violet brown 2.00 1.10
296 CD26 4t orange brn 1.10 90
297 CD27 8t bister 2.00 1.25
Nos. 290-297 (8) 7.40 4.95

Issues of 1898-1913 Overprinted Locally in Red

1913-15

On Issues of 1898-1903

300 A17 2r orange 4.50 4.00
301 A17 2½r yellow brn 50 45
302 A17 3r dp blue 8.00 7.00
303 A17 4½r lt green 1.75 1.50
304 A17 6r gray grn 20.00 16.00
305 A17 9r gray lilac 1.75 1.25
306 A17 1t sea green 20.00 16.00
307 A17 2t blue 26.00 14.00
309 A17 4t blue, *blue* 19.00 12.50
310 A17 5t brn, *straw* 25.00 16.00
311 A17 8t red vio, *pink* 27.50 22.50
312 A17 12t grn, *pink* 3.50 2.50
313 A17 1rp blk & red, *bl* 30.00 22.50
314 A17 1rp dl bl, *straw* 20.00 12.50
315 A17 2rp gray blk, *straw* 22.50 14.00
316 A17 2rp vio, *yelsh* 17.50 10.00
Nos. 300-316 (16) 247.50 172.70

Inverted or double overprints exist on 2½r, 4½r, 9r, 1rp and 2rp.

Nos. 300-316 were issued without gum except 4½r and 9r.

Nos. 302, 304, 306, 307, 310, 311 and 313 were not regularly issued. Nor were the 1½r, 2t brown and 12t blue on pink with preceding overprint.

Same Overprint in Red or Green
On Provisional Issue of 1902

317 A15 1r on 2t blue 14.00 10.00
a. "REPUBLICA" inverted
318 A15 2r on 4½r bis 14.00 10.00
a. "REPUBLICA" inverted
319 A15 2½r on 6r grn 70 60
a. "REPUBLICA" inverted 17.00 17.00
320 A15 3r on 1t rose (R) 10.00 8.00
321 A15 2½t on 4t gray vio 40.00 19.00
323 A15 5t on 8t org (G) 10.00 7.50
a. Red overprint 10.00 7.50
324 A16 1r on 6r grn 10.00 7.50
325 A16 2r on 8t vio 10.00 7.50
a. Inverted surcharge
327 A16 3r on 4½r yel 30.00 25.00
328 A16 3r on 1t lt bl 30.00 25.00
329 A16 5t on 2t rose (G) 3.25 2.75
330 A16 5t on 4t bl (G) 3.25 2.75
331 A16 5t on 4t bl (R) 3.75 3.75
a. "REPUBLICA" inverted
b. "REPUBLICA" double
Nos. 317-331 (13) 178.95 129.35

The 2½r on 1½r of types A15 and A16, the 3r on 1t (A15) and 2½r on 9r (A16) were clandestinely printed.

Some authorities question the status of No. 317-318, 320-321, 324, 327-328.

Same Overprint on Nos. 240-241

1913-15

334 A17 1t sea green 7.00 5.00
335 A17 2t blue 6.50 6.00

This overprint was applied to No. 239 without official authorization.

On Issue of 1912-13 Perforated through the Middle

Values are for pairs, both halves of the stamp.

336 A17(a) 1r on 2r org 6.00 5.50
340 A17(a) 1½r on 4½r lt grn 6.00 5.50
341 A17(a) 1½r on 9r gray lil 6.00
342 A17(a) 1½r on 4t bl, *bl* 7.50
343 A17(a) 2r on 2½r yel brn 5.50
344 A17(a) 2r on 4t bl, *bl* 7.50 6.50
345 A17(a) 3r on 2½r yel brn 6.00
346 A17(a) 3r on 2t brn 5.00 4.75
347 A17(a) 6r on 4½r lt grn 1.00 80
348 A17(a) 6r on 9r gray lil 1.50 1.50
350 A17(b) 6r on 8t red vio, *pink* 1.50 1.50
352 A16(b) 1r on 5t on 4t bl 37.50
354 A15(a) 2r on 2½r on 6r grn 9.00
Nos. 334-354 (15) 113.50

The 1r on 5t (A15), 1r on 1t (A17), 1½r on 2½r (A17), 3r on 5t on 8t (A15), and 6r on 9r (A17) were clandestinely printed.

Nos. 336, 347 exist with inverted surcharge.

Some authorities question the status of Nos. 341-345, 352 and 354.

Ceres — A21

1913-21 Typo. ***Perf. 12x11½, 15x14***
Name and Value in Black

357 A21 1r olive brn 30 25
358 A21 1½r yellow grn 30 25
a. Imperf.
359 A21 2r black 35 30
360 A21 2½r olive grn 35 40
361 A21 3r lilac 35 20
362 A21 4½r orange brn 35 20
363 A21 5r blue green 65 45
364 A21 6r lilac brown 35 20
365 A21 9r ultra 55 25
366 A21 10r carmine 85 50
367 A21 1t lt violet 40 25
368 A21 2t deep blue 75 30
369 A21 3t yellow brown 1.75 60
370 A21 4t slate 2.00 90
371 A21 8t plum 4.00 3.50
372 A21 12t brown, *green* 3.50 3.00
373 A21 1rp brown, *pink* 21.00 14.00
374 A21 2rp org, *salmon* 14.00 10.00
375 A21 3rp green, *blue* 19.00 12.50
Nos. 357-375 (19) 70.80 48.05

The 1, 2, 2½, 3, 4½r, 1, 2, and 4t exist with the black inscriptions inverted and the 2½r with them double, one inverted, but it is not known that any of these were regularly issued.

See Nos. 401-410. For surcharges see Nos. 400, 420, 423.

Nos. 249, 251-253, 256-259 Surcharged in Black

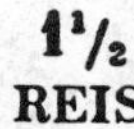

1914

376	A17	1½r on 4½r grn	30	25
377	A17	1½r on 9r gray lil	40	30
378	A17	1½r on 12t grn, *pink*	50	45
379	A17	3r on 1t car rose	40	35
380	A17	3r on 2t brn	3.00	2.50
381	A17	3r on 8t red vio, *pink*	2.25	2.00
382	A17	3r on 1rp dl bl, *straw*	65	40
383	A17	3r on 2rp gray blk, *straw*	75	60

There are 3 varieties of the "2" in "1½." Nos. 376-377 exist with inverted surcharge.

Vasco da Gama Issue Surcharged in Black

REPUBLICA 1½ REIS

384	CD21	1½r on 4½r red	35	28
385	CD23	1½r on 9r yel grn	45	30
386	CD24	3r on 1t dk bl	35	28
387	CD25	3r on 2t vio brn	55	45
388	CD26	3r on 4t org brn	28	22
389	CD27	3r on 8t bister	1.20	1.10
		Nos. 376-389 (14)	11.43	9.48

Double, inverted and other surcharge varieties exist on Nos. 384-386, 389.

Stamps of 1898-1903 Surcharged in Red

1½ REIS

1915

390	A17	1½r on 4½r grn	27.50	20.00
a.		"REPUBLICA" omitted	*42.50*	*42.50*
b.		"REPUBLICA" inverted		
391	A17	1½r on 9r gray lil	10.00	7.50
a.		"REPUBLICA" omitted		
392	A17	1½r on 12t grn, *pink*	1.25	1.00
396	A17	3r on 2rp gray blk, *straw*	5.00	4.00

Nos. 390, 390a, 390b, 391, and 391a were not regularly issued. The 3r on 2½r (A17) was surcharged without official authorization.

Common Design Types pictured in section at front of book.

Preceding Issues Overprinted in Carmine

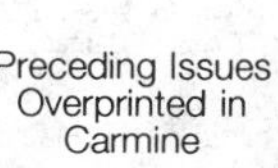

1915

On No. 230

397	A15	5t on 8t org	1.50	1.40

On Nos. 241, 243

398	A17	2t blue	90	90
399	A17	2t on 2½t dl bl	1.50	90

No. 359 Surcharged in Carmine

1½ REAL

1922

400	A21	1½r on 2r blk	50	42

Ceres Type of 1913-21

1922-25 Typo. *Perf. 12x11½*

Name and Value in Black

401	A21	4r blue	1.25	1.10
402	A21	1½t gray green	1.25	85
403	A21	2½t turq blue	1.25	90
404	A21	3t4r yellow brn	5.00	3.50
405	A21	4t gray ('25)	1.75	75
406	A21	8t dull rose	7.00	5.00
407	A21	1rp gray brn	16.50	15.00
408	A21	2rp yellow	20.00	15.00
409	A21	3rp bluish grn	30.00	22.50
410	A21	5rp carmine rose	35.00	25.00
		Nos. 401-410 (10)	119.00	89.60

Vasco da Gama and Flagship — A22

1925, Jan. 30 Litho.

Without Gum

411	A22	6r brown	3.50	2.50
412	A22	1t red violet	5.00	3.00

400th anniv. of the death of Vasco da Gama (1469?-1524), Portuguese navigator.

Monument to St. Francis — A23

Image of St. Francis — A25

Autograph of St. Francis A24

Image of St. Francis — A26

Tomb of St. Francis — A28

Church of Bom Jesus at Goa — A27

1931, Dec. 3 *Perf. 14*

414	A23	1r gray green	50	45
415	A24	2r brown	50	45
416	A25	6r red violet	1.50	50
417	A26	1½t yellow brn	5.25	2.50
418	A27	2t deep blue	6.25	3.75
419	A28	2½t light red	10.50	3.75
		Nos. 414-419 (6)	24.50	11.40

Exposition of St. Francis Xavier at Goa, in December, 1931.

Nos. 371 and 404 Surcharged

2½ T.

1931-32 *Perf. 15x14, 12x11½*

420	A21	1½r on 8t plum ('32)	1.40	1.00
423	A21	2½t on 3t4r yel brn	25.00	20.00

"Portugal" and Vasco da Gama's Flagship "San Gabriel" — A29

Perf. 11½x12

1933 Typo. Wmk. 232

424	A29	1r bister	15	15
425	A29	2r olive brn	15	15
426	A29	4r violet	15	15
427	A29	6r dk green	15	15
428	A29	8r black	20	15
429	A29	1t gray	25	15
430	A29	1½t dp rose	30	15
431	A29	2t brown	35	20
432	A29	2½t dk blue	1.75	40
433	A29	3t brt blue	1.75	40
434	A29	5t red orange	1.75	40
435	A29	1rp olive grn	9.00	2.50
436	A29	2rp maroon	15.00	5.00
437	A29	3rp orange	22.50	6.00
438	A29	5rp apple grn	40.00	25.00
		Nos. 424-438 (15)	93.45	40.95

For surcharges see Nos. 454-463, 472-474, J34-J36.

Common Design Types

Perf. 13½x13

1938, Sept. 1 Engr. Unwmk.

Name and Value in Black

439	CD34	1r gray grn	15	15
440	CD34	2r orange brn	15	15
441	CD34	3r dk vio brn	15	15
442	CD34	6r brt green	15	15
443	CD35	10r dk carmine	35	22
444	CD35	1t brt red vio	35	22
445	CD35	1½t red	40	22
446	CD37	2t orange	40	22
447	CD37	2½t blue	40	22
448	CD37	3t slate	80	28
449	CD36	5t rose vio	1.40	45
450	CD36	1rp brown car	4.00	80
451	CD36	2rp olive grn	6.25	2.50
452	CD38	3rp blue vio	10.00	6.00
453	CD38	5rp red brown	22.50	3.25
		Nos. 439-453 (15)	47.45	14.98

For surcharges see Nos. 492-495, 504-505.

Stamps of 1933 Surcharged in Black

1 tanga

1941, June Wmk. 232 *Perf. 11½x12*

454	A29	1t on 1½t dp rose	2.00	1.40
455	A29	1t on 1rp olive grn	2.00	1.40
456	A29	1t on 2rp maroon	2.00	1.40
457	A29	1t on 5rp apple grn	2.00	1.40

Nos. 430-431 Surcharged

3 RÉIS

1943

458	A29	3r on 1½t dp rose	1.00	75
459	A29	1t on 2t brown	2.50	2.00

Nos. 434, 428, 437 and 432 Surcharged in Dark Blue or Carmine

1 REAL
a

6 Réis
b

1945-46 Wmk. 232 *Perf. 11½x12*

460	A29(a)	1r on 5t red org (DB)	65	45
461	A29(b)	2r on 8r blk (C)	50	40
462	A29(b)	3r on 3rp org (DB) ('46)	1.75	1.50
463	A29(b)	6r on 2½t dk bl (C)	1.75	1.75

St. Francis Xavier A30

Luis de Camoens A31

Garcia de Orta — A32

St. John de Britto — A33

Arch of the Viceroy A34

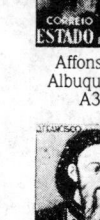

Affonso de Albuquerque A35

Vasco da Gama — A36

Francisco de Almeida — A37

Perf. 11½

1946, May 28 Litho. Unwmk.

464	A30	1r black & gray blk	45	25
465	A31	2r rose brn & pale rose brn	45	25
466	A32	6r ocher & dl yel	45	25
467	A33	7r vio & pale vio	2.00	50
468	A34	9r sepia & buff	2.00	50
469	A35	1t dk sl grn & sl grn	2.00	50
470	A36	3½t ultra & pale ultra	2.25	1.10
471	A37	1rp choc & bis brn	5.50	1.40
a.		Miniature sheet of 8, #464-471	17.50	17.50
		Nos. 464-471 (8)	15.10	4.75

No. 471a sold for 1½ rupias.

See No. 476. For surcharges see Nos. 595, J43-J46.

No. 428, 431 and 433 Surcharged in Carmine or Black

1 Real

1946 Wmk. 232 *Perf. 11½x12*

472	A29 (c)	1r on 8r blk (C)	60	50
473	A29 (b)	3r on 2t brn	60	55
474	A29 (b)	6r on 3t brt bl	2.00	1.75

Type of 1946 and

Joao de Castro — A38

José Vaz — A39

Luis de Ataide — A40

Duarte Pacheco Pereira — A41

1948 Unwmk. Litho. *Perf. 11½*

475 A38 3r brt ultra & lt bl 90 50
476 A30 1t dk grn & yel grn 1.25 60
477 A39 1½t dk pur & dl vio 2.00 1.10
478 A40 2½t brt ver 2.25 1.65
479 A41 7½t dk brn & org brn 4.00 2.25
a. Miniature sheet of 5 18.00 18.00
Nos. 475-479 (5) 10.40 6.10

No. 476 measures 21x31mm.

No. 479a measures 106x146mm. and contains one each of Nos. 475-479. Marginal inscriptions in gray. The sheet sold for 1 rupia.

For surcharge see No. 591.

Lady of Fatima Issue
Common Design Type

1948 *Perf. 14½*

480 CD40 1t dk blue green 2.25 1.90

Our Lady of Fatima — A42 UPU Symbols — A42a

1949 Litho. *Perf. 14*

481 A42 1r blue 60 50
482 A42 3r orange yel 60 50
483 A42 9r dk car rose 1.10 70
484 A42 2t green 2.75 1.10
485 A42 9t orange red 3.00 1.25
486 A42 2rp dk vio brn 5.75 2.75
487 A42 5rp olive grn 12.00 3.00
488 A42 8rp vio blue 27.50 9.25
Nos. 481-488 (8) 53.30 19.05

Issued to honor Our Lady of the Rosary at Fatima, Portugal.

1949, Oct.

489 A42a 2½t scarlet & pink 2.25 1.50

UPU, 75th anniversary.

Catalogue values for unused stamps in this section, from this point to the end of the section, are for Never Hinged items.

Holy Year Issue
Common Design Types

1950, May *Perf. 13x13½*

490 CD41 1r olive bister 60 55
491 CD42 2t dk gray green 1.00 55

See Nos. 496-503.

No. 443 Surcharged in Black

1 Real

1950 *Perf. 13½x13*

492 CD35 1r on 10r dk car 25 25
493 CD35 2r on 10r dk car 25 25

Similar Surcharge on No. 447 in Black or Red

494 CD37 1r on 2½t blue 25 25
495 CD37 3r on 2½t blue (R) 25 25

Letters with serifs, small (lower case) "r" in "real" and "réis."

Holy Year Issue
Common Design Types

1951 Litho. *Perf. 13½*

496 CD41 1r dp car rose 22 22
497 CD41 2r emerald 30 25
498 CD42 3r red brn 30 25
499 CD41 6r gray 35 35
500 CD42 9r brt pink 75 55
501 CD41 1t blue vio 50 45
502 CD42 2t yellow 85 55
503 CD41 4t violet brn 85 55
Nos. 496-503 (8) 4.12 3.17

No. 447 with Surcharge Similar to Nos. 492-493 in Red

1951 *Perf. 13½x13*

504 CD37 6r on 2½t blue 30 30
505 CD37 1t on 2½t blue 25 25

Letters with serifs, small (lower case) "r" in "réis."

Holy Year Extension Issue
Common Design Type

1951 Litho. *Perf. 14*

506 CD43 1rp bl vio & pale vio 1.50 1.00

José Vaz — A43

Ruins of Sancoale Church — A44

Design: 12t, Altar.

1951 Litho. *Perf. 14½*
Dated: "1651-1951"

507 A43 1r Prus bl & pale bl 15 15
508 A44 2r ver & red brn 15 15
509 A43 3r gray blk & gray 40 25
510 A44 1t vio bl & ind 15 15
511 A43 2t dp cl & cl 25 15
512 A44 3t ol grn & blk 40 20
513 A43 9t indigo & ultra 50 40
514 A44 10t lilac & vio 85 50
515 A44 12t blk brn & brn 1.25 75
Nos. 507-515 (9) 4.10 2.70

300th anniversary of the birth of José Vaz.

Medical Congress Issue
Common Design Type

Design: Medical School, Goa.

1952 Unwmk. *Perf. 13½*

516 CD44 4½t blk & lt blue 3.00 1.65

St. Francis Xavier Issue

Statue of Saint Francis Xavier — A44a

A45

St. Francis Xavier and his Tomb, Goa — A46

Designs: 2t, Miraculous Arm of St. Francis. 4t, 5t, Tomb of St. Francis.

1952, Oct. 25 Litho. *Perf. 14*

517 A44a 6r aqua & multi 25 20
518 A44a 2t cream & multi 2.00 55
519 A44a 5t pink & silver 3.50 1.25

Souvenir Sheets
Perf. 13

520 A45 9t brn & dk brn 8.50 8.50
521 A46 Sheet of 2 8.50 8.50
a. 4t orange buff & black 2.50 2.50
b. 8t slate & black 2.50 2.50

400th anniv. of the death of St. Francis Xavier.

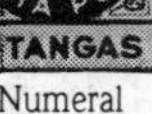

Numeral A47

St. Francis Xavier A48

1952, Dec. 4 Litho. *Perf. 13½*

522 A47 3t black 3.00 3.00
523 A48 5t dk violet & blk 3.00 3.00
a. Strip of 2 + label 7.00 7.00

Issued to publicize Portuguese India's first stamp exhibition, Goa, 1952.

No. 523a consists of a tête bêche pair of Nos. 522-523 separated by a label publicizing the exhibition.

Statue of Virgin Mary — A49

Stamp of Portugal and Arms of Colonies — A49a

1953, Jan.

524 A49 6r dk & lt blue 15 15
525 A49 1t brown & buff 75 50
526 A49 3t dk pur & pale ol 2.50 1.25

Exhibition of Sacred Missionary Art held at Lisbon in 1951.

For surcharge see No. 594.

Stamp Centenary Issue

1953 Typo.

527 A49a 1t multicolored 60 50

Centenary of Portugal's first postage stamps.

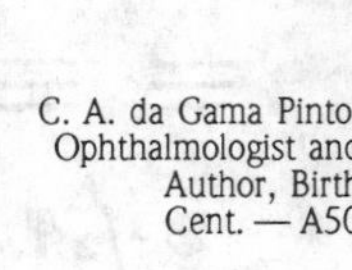

C. A. da Gama Pinto, Ophthalmologist and Author, Birth Cent. — A50

1954, Apr. 10 Litho. *Perf. 11½*

528 A50 3r gray & ol grn 25 20
529 A50 2t black & gray blk 15 15

Sao Paulo Issue
Common Design Type

1954, Oct. 2 Unwmk. *Perf. 13½*

530 CD46 2t dk Prus bl, bl & blk 25 25

For surcharge see No. 593.

Affonso de Albuquerque School — A51

Msgr. Sebastiao Rodolfo Dalgado — A52

1955, Feb. 26

531 A51 9t multicolored 85 60

Centenary (in 1954) of the founding of the Affonso de Albuquerque National School.

1955, Nov. 15 Unwmk. *Perf. 13½*

532 A52 1r multicolored 20 20
533 A52 1t multicolored 50 25

Centenary of the birth of Msgr. Sebastiao Rodolfo Dalgado.

Francisco de Almeida — A53

Manuel Antonio de Susa — A54

Map of Bassein by Pedro Barreto de Resendo, 1635 — A55

Portraits: 9r, Affonso de Albuquerque. 1t, Vasco da Gama. 1½t, Filipe Nery Xavier. 3t, Nuno da Cunha. 4t, Agostino Vicente Lourenco. 8t, Jose Vaz. 9t, Manuel Godinho de Heredia. 10t, Joao de Castro. 2rp, Antonio Caetano Pacheco. 3rp, Constantino de Braganca.

Maps of ancient forts, drawn in 1635: 2½t, Mombaim (Bombay). 3½t, Damao (Daman). 5t, Diu. 12t, Cochin. 1rp, Goa.

Inscribed: "450 Aniversario da Fundacao do Estado da India 1505-1955."

Perf. 11½x12 (A53), 14½ (A54), 12½ (A55)

1956, Mar. 24 Unwmk.

534 A53 3r multicolored 15 15
535 A54 6r multicolored 15 15
536 A53 9r multicolored 32 30
537 A53 1t multicolored 32 30
538 A54 1½t multicolored 15 15
539 A55 2t multicolored 1.90 1.40
540 A55 2½t multicolored 1.25 90
541 A53 3t multicolored 32 15
542 A55 3½t multicolored 1.40 90
543 A54 4t multicolored 15 15
544 A55 5t multicolored 60 40
545 A54 8t multicolored 50 38
546 A54 9t multicolored 50 38
547 A53 10t multicolored 48 35
548 A55 12t multicolored 1.10 80
549 A55 1rp multicolored 2.00 1.40
550 A54 2rp multicolored 1.90 1.10
551 A53 3rp multicolored 2.50 1.50
Nos. 534-551 (18) 15.69 10.86

450th anniversary of the Portuguese settlements in India.

For surcharges see Nos. 575-577, 579-581, 592.

Map of Damao and Nagar Aveli — A56

Arms of Vasco da Gama — A57

1957 **Litho.** ***Perf. 11½***

Map and Inscriptions in Black, Red, Ocher and Blue

No.	Type	Description	Unused	Used
552	A56	3r gray & buff	15	15
553	A56	6r bl grn & pale lem	15	15
554	A56	3t pink & lt gray	15	15
555	A56	6t blue	35	35
556	A56	11t ol bis & lt vio gray	75	55
557	A56	2rp lt vio & pale gray	1.75	1.10
558	A56	3rp citron & pink	2.00	1.50
559	A56	5rp magenta & pink	2.25	1.75
		Nos. 552-559 (8)	7.55	5.70

For surcharges see Nos. 571, 578, 584-585, 588-590.

1958, Apr. 3 **Unwmk.** ***Perf. 13x13½***

Arms of: 6r, Lopo Soares de Albergaria. 9r, Francisco de Almeida. 1t, Garcia de Noronha. 4t, Alfonso de Albuquerque. 5t, Joao de Castro. 11t, Luis de Ataide. 1r, Nuno da Cunha.

Arms in Original Colors
Inscriptions in Black and Red

No.	Type	Description	Unused	Used
560	A57	2r buff & ocher	15	15
561	A57	6r gray & ocher	15	15
562	A57	9r pale blue & emer	15	15
563	A57	1t pale citron & brn	20	15
564	A57	4t pale bl grn & lil	25	15
565	A57	5t buff & blue	30	20
566	A57	11t pink & lt brn	50	40
567	A57	1rp pale grn & maroon	80	60
		Nos. 560-567 (8)	2.50	1.95

For surcharges see Nos. 570, 572-574, 582-583, 586-587.

Exhibition Emblem and View — A58

1958, Dec. 15 **Litho.** ***Perf. 14½***

No.	Type	Description	Unused	Used
568	A58	1rp multicolored	50	40

World's Fair, Brussels, Apr. 17-Oct. 19.
For surcharge see No. 597.

Tropical Medicine Congress Issue
Common Design Type

Design: Holarrhena antidysenterica.

1958, Dec. 15 ***Perf. 13½***

No.	Type	Description	Unused	Used
569	CD47	5t gray, brn, grn & red	1.00	40

For surcharge see No. 596.

Stamps of 1955-58 Surcharged with New Values and Bars

1959, Jan. 1 **Litho.** **Unwmk.**

No.	Type	Description	Unused	Used
570	A57	5c on 2r (#560)	15	15
571	A56	10c on 3r (#552)	15	15
572	A57	15c on 6r (#561)	15	15
573	A57	20c on 9r (#562)	15	15
574	A57	30c on 1t (#563)	15	15
575	A55	40c on 2t (#539)	15	15
576	A55	40c on 2½t (#540)	40	32
577	A55	40c on 3½t (#542)	15	15
578	A56	50c on 3t (#554)	15	15
579	A53	80c on 3t (#541)	15	15
580	A53	80c on 10t (#547)	85	75
581	A53	80c on 3rp (#551)	1.00	85
582	A57	1e on 4t (#564)	15	15
583	A57	1.50e on 5t (#565)	15	15
584	A56	2e on 6t (#555)	38	32
585	A56	2.50e on 11t (#556)	45	25
586	A57	4e on 11t (#566)	60	50
587	A57	4.50e on 1rp (#567)	65	50
588	A56	5e on 2rp (#557)	65	50
589	A56	10e on 3rp (#558)	2.00	1.50
590	A56	30e on 5rp (#559)	4.50	2.00
		Nos. 570-590 (21)	13.13	9.14

Types of 1946-1958 Surcharged with New Values, Old Values Obliterated

1959 **Litho.** **Unwmk.**

No.	Type	Description	Unused	Used
591	A39	40c on 1½t dl pur	38	15
592	A54	40c on 1½t multi	38	15
593	CD46	40c on 2t bl & gray	1.00	75
594	A49	80c on 3t blk & pale citron	38	15
595	A36	80c on 3½t dk bl	55	15
596	CD47	80c on 5t gray, brn, grn & red	55	40
597	A58	80c on 1rp multi	1.25	65
		Nos. 591-597 (7)	4.49	2.40

Coin, Manuel I — A59

Arms of Prince Henry — A60

Various Coins from the Reign of Manuel I (1495-1521) to the Republic.

Perf. 13½x13

1959, Dec. 1 **Litho.** **Unwmk.**

Inscriptions in Black and Red

No.	Type	Description	Unused	Used
598	A59	5c lt bl & gold	15	15
599	A59	10c pale brn & gold	15	15
600	A59	15c pale grn & gray	15	15
601	A59	30c sal & gray	15	15
602	A59	40c pale yel & gray	15	15
603	A59	50c lilac & gray	15	15
604	A59	60c pale yel grn & gray	15	15
605	A59	80c lt bl & gray	15	15
606	A59	1e ocher & gray	15	15
607	A59	1.50e blue & gray	15	15
608	A59	2e pale bl & gold	15	15
609	A59	2.50e pale gray & gold	20	15
610	A59	3e citron & gray	22	18
611	A59	4e pink & gray	30	20
612	A59	4.40e pale bis & vio brn	35	30
613	A59	5e pale dl vio & gray	45	40
614	A59	10e brt yel & gray	80	70
615	A59	20e beige & gray	1.65	1.40
616	A59	30e brt yel grn & lt cop brn	2.50	2.00
617	A59	50e lt gray & gray	4.00	3.50
		Nos. 598-617 (20)	12.12	10.48

1960, June 25 ***Perf. 13½***

No.	Type	Description	Unused	Used
618	A60	3e multi	50	40

500th anniversary of the death of Prince Henry the Navigator.

Portugal continued to print special-issue stamps for its lost colony after its annexation by India Dec. 18, 1961. Stamps of India were first used on Dec. 29. Stamps of Portuguese India remained valid until Jan. 5, 1962.

AIR POST STAMPS

Common Design Type
Perf. 13½x13

1938, Sept. 1 **Engr.** **Unwmk.**

Name and Value in Black

No.	Type	Description	Unused	Used
C1	CD39	1t scarlet	50	25
C2	CD39	2½t purple	60	25
C3	CD39	3½t orange	60	25
C4	CD39	4½t ultra	1.50	42
C5	CD39	7t lilac brown	1.65	50
C6	CD39	7½t dark green	2.25	75
C7	CD39	9t red brown	4.00	1.10
C8	CD39	11t magenta	4.50	1.10
		Nos. C1-C8 (8)	15.60	4.62

No. C4 exists with overprint "Exposicao Internacional de Nova York, 1939-1940" and Trylon and Perisphere.

POSTAGE DUE STAMPS

D1

1904 **Unwmk.** **Typo.** ***Perf. 11½***

Name and Value in Black

No.	Type	Description	Unused	Used
J1	D1	2r gray green	30	30
J2	D1	3r yellow grn	30	30
J3	D1	4r orange	30	30
J4	D1	5r slate	30	30
J5	D1	6r gray	30	30
J6	D1	9r yellow brn	40	40
J7	D1	1t red orange	70	50
J8	D1	2t gray brown	1.50	1.00
J9	D1	5t dull blue	2.25	2.00
J10	D1	10t carmine	3.00	2.75
J11	D1	1rp dull vio	9.00	5.00
		Nos. J1-J11 (11)	18.35	13.15

Nos. J1-J11 Overprinted in Carmine or Green

1911

No.	Type	Description	Unused	Used
J12	D1	2r gray grn	15	15
J13	D1	3r yellow grn	15	15
J14	D1	4r orange	15	15
J15	D1	5r slate	15	15
J16	D1	6r gray	20	20
J17	D1	9r yellow brn	30	20
J18	D1	1t red org	35	30
J19	D1	2t gray brn	60	50
J20	D1	5t dull blue	1.25	1.10
J21	D1	10t carmine (G)	2.00	1.50
J22	D1	1rp dull violet	3.00	2.00
		Nos. J12-J22 (11)	8.30	6.40

Nos. J1-J11 Overprinted

1914

No.	Type	Description	Unused	Used
J23	D1	2r gray grn	25	25
J24	D1	3r yellow grn	25	25
J25	D1	4r orange	25	25
J26	D1	5r slate	25	25
J27	D1	6r gray	50	40
J28	D1	9r yellow brn	50	50
J29	D1	1t red org	75	50
J30	D1	2t gray brn	3.25	1.50
J31	D1	5t dull blue	3.25	2.00
J32	D1	10t carmine	7.00	2.50
J33	D1	1rp dull violet	14.00	4.25
		Nos. J23-J33 (11)	30.25	12.65

Nos. 432, 433 and 434 Surcharged In Red or Black

3
RÉIS
Porteado

1943 **Wmk. 232** ***Perf. 11½x12***

No.	Type	Description	Unused	Used
J34	A29	3r on 2½t dk bl (R)	60	40
J35	A29	6r on 3t brt bl (R)	80	80
J36	A29	1t on 5t red org (Bk)	1.75	1.50

D2

1945 **Typo.** **Unwmk.**

Country Name and Denomination in Black

No.	Type	Description	Unused	Used
J37	D2	2r brt carmine	90	90
J38	D2	3r blue	90	90
J39	D2	4r orange yel	90	90
J40	D2	6r yellow grn	90	90
J41	D2	1t bister brn	90	90
J42	D2	2t chocolate	90	90
		Nos. J37-J42 (6)	5.40	5.40

Catalogue values for unused stamps in this section, from this point to the end of the section, are for Never Hinged items.

Nos. 467 and 471 Surcharged in Carmine or Black

Porteado
2 Réis

1951, Jan. 1 ***Perf. 11½***

No.	Type	Description	Unused	Used
J43	A33	2r on 7r vio & pale vio (C)	55	45
J44	A33	3r on 7r vio & pale vio (C)	55	45
J45	A37	1t on 1rp choc & bis brn	55	45
J46	A37	2t on 1rp choc & bis brn	55	45

Common Design Type
Photogravure and Typographed

1952 ***Perf. 14***

Numeral in Red; Frame Multicolored

No.	Type	Description	Unused	Used
J47	CD45	2r olive	15	15
J48	CD45	3r black	15	15
J49	CD45	6r dark blue	15	15
J50	CD45	1t dk carmine	30	20
J51	CD45	2t orange	50	50
J52	CD45	10t violet blue	2.00	2.00
		Nos. J47-J52 (6)	3.25	3.15

Nos. J47-J49 and J51-J52 Surcharged with New Value and Bars

1959, Jan.

Numeral in Red; Frame Multicolored

No.	Type	Description	Unused	Used
J53	CD45	5c on 2r olive	15	15
J54	CD45	10c on 3r black	15	15
J55	CD45	15c on 6r dk blue	25	20
J56	CD45	60c on 2t orange	90	90
J57	CD45	60c on 10t vio blue	1.75	1.75
		Nos. J53-J57 (5)	3.20	3.15

WAR TAX STAMPS

WT1

Overprinted in Black or Carmine
Perf. 15x14

1919, Apr. 15 **Typo.** **Unwmk.**

Denomination in Black

No.	Type	Description	Unused	Used
MR1	WT1	0:00:05,48rp grn	1.40	1.10
MR2	WT1	0:01:09,94rp grn	4.00	2.25
MR3	WT1	0:02:03,43rp grn (C)	4.00	2.25

Some authorities consider No. MR2 a revenue stamp.

POSTAL TAX STAMPS

Pombal Issue
Common Design Types

1925 **Unwmk.** ***Perf. 12½***

No.	Type	Description	Unused	Used
RA1	CD28	6r rose & black	45	45
RA2	CD29	6r rose & black	45	45
RA3	CD30	6r rose & black	45	45

Mother and Child — PT1

1948 **Litho.** ***Perf. 11***

No.	Type	Description	Unused	Used
RA4	PT1	6r yellow green	2.75	2.50
RA5	PT1	1t carmine	2.75	2.50

See Nos. RA7-RA7A, RA9, RA12. For surcharge and overprint see Nos. RA6, RA8.

Catalogue values for unused stamps in this section, from this point to the end of the section, are for Never Hinged items.

Type of 1948 Surcharged with New Value and Bar in Black

1951

No.	Type	Description	Unused	Used
RA6	PT1	1t on 6r carmine	2.50	2.00

Type of 1948

1952-53

No.	Type	Description	Unused	Used
RA7	PT1	1t gray	2.25	1.65
RA7A	PT1	1t red orange ('53)	2.25	1.50

No. RA5 Overprinted in Black **«Revalidado» P. A. P.**

1953			
RA8 PT1	1t carmine	6.25	5.50

Type of 1948

1954	**Typo.**		
RA9 PT1	6r pale bister	3.50	3.00

Mother and Child
PT2 PT3

Surcharged in Black

1956	**Typo.**	*Perf. 11*	
RA10 PT2	1t on 4t light bl	11.00	10.00
	Litho.	*Perf. 13*	
RA11 PT3	1t blk, pale grn & red	1.25	60

See No. RA14. For surcharges see Nos. RA13, RA15-RA16.

Type of 1948 Redrawn

1956	**Without Gum**	*Perf. 11*	
RA12 PT1	1t bluish green	3.25	3.00

Denomination in white oval at left.

No. RA11 Surcharged with New Value and Bars in Red

1957		*Perf. 13½*	
RA13 PT3	6r on 1t	90	60

Type of 1956

1958	**Unwmk.**	*Perf. 13*	
RA14 PT3	1t dk bl, sal & grn	90	60

No. RA14 Surcharged with New Values and Four Bars

1959, Jan.	**Litho.**	*Perf. 13*	
RA15 PT3	20c on 1t	55	55
RA16 PT3	40c on 1t	55	55

Arms and People Seeking Help — PT4

1960		*Perf. 13½*	
RA17 PT4	20c brown & red	25	25

POSTAL TAX DUE STAMPS

Pombal Issue
Common Design Types

1925	**Unwmk.**	*Perf. 12½*	
RAJ1 CD31	1t rose & black	60	60
RAJ2 CD32	1t rose & black	60	60
RAJ3 CD33	1t rose & black	60	60

See note after Portugal No. RAJ4.

PUERTO RICO

(Porto Rico)

LOCATION — A large island in the West Indies, east of Hispaniola
GOVT. — Former Spanish Colony
AREA — 3,435 sq. mi.
POP. — 953,243 (1899)
CAPITAL — San Juan

The island was ceded to the United States by the Treaty of 1898.

100 Centimes = 1 Peseta
1000 Milesimas = 100 Centavos = 1 Peso (1881)
100 Cents = 1 Dollar (1898)

Issued under Spanish Dominion

Puerto Rican stamps of 1855-73, a part of the Spanish colonial period, were also used in Cuba. They are listed as Cuba Nos. 1-4, 9-14, 18-21, 32-34, 35A-37, 39-41, 43-45, 47-49, 51-53, 55-57.

Stamps of Cuba Overprinted in Black:

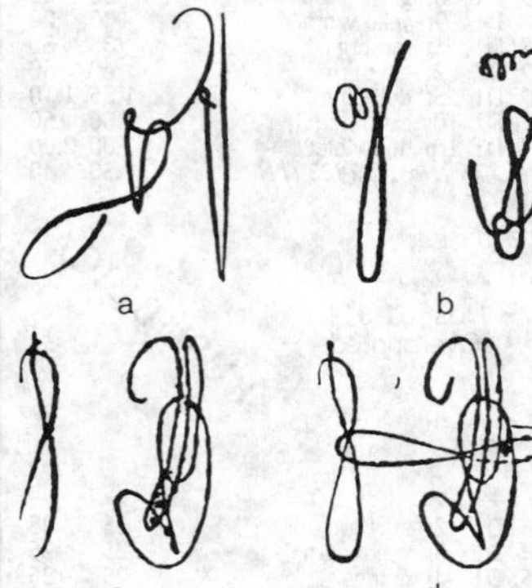

a b c d

1873	**Unwmk.**		*Perf. 14*	
1	A10 (a)	25c gray	22.50	1.50
2	A10 (a)	50c brown	60.00	4.50
3	A10 (a)	1p red brn	125.00	12.50
1874				
4	A11 (b)	25c ultra	15.00	2.00
1875				
5	A12 (b)	25c ultra	13.00	2.00
6	A12 (b)	50c green	24.00	2.00
a.		Inverted overprint	135.00	67.50
7	A12 (b)	1p brown	67.50	11.00
1876				
8	A13 (c)	25c bl gray	3.25	1.50
9	A13 (c)	50c ultra	7.50	2.00
10	A13 (c)	1p black	30.00	6.75
11	A13 (d)	25c bl gray	13.00	1.00
12	A13 (d)	1p black	37.50	6.75

Varieties of overprint on Nos. 8-11 include: inverted, double, partly omitted.

King Alfonso XII
A5 A6

1877			**Typo.**	
13	A5	5c yel brn	3.75	1.00
a.		5c carmine (error)	150.00	120.00
14	A5	10c carmine	10.00	1.65
a.		10c brown (error)	150.00	120.00
15	A5	15c dp grn	15.00	5.50
16	A5	25c ultra	7.75	1.00
17	A5	50c bister	10.00	2.75

Same, Dated "1878"

1878				
18	A5	5c ol bister	9.50	9.50
19	A5	10c red brn	110.00	45.00
20	A5	25c dp grn	1.40	85
21	A5	50c ultra	5.50	1.40
22	A5	1p bister	8.00	3.50

Same, Dated "1879"

1879				
23	A5	5c lake	6.75	2.00
24	A5	10c dk brn	6.75	2.00
25	A5	15c dk ol grn	6.75	2.00
26	A5	25c blue	2.00	85
27	A5	50c dk grn	6.75	2.00
28	A5	1p gray	25.00	5.50

Imperforates of type A5 are from proof or trial sheets.

1880				
29	A6	¼c dp grn	22.50	8.00
30	A6	½c brt rose	4.00	1.50
31	A6	1c brn lilac	8.50	4.00
32	A6	2c gray lilac	3.25	2.00
33	A6	3c buff	3.25	2.00
34	A6	4c black	3.25	2.75
35	A6	5c gray green	2.00	1.25
36	A6	10c rose	3.00	1.25
37	A6	15c yel brn	4.00	1.50
38	A6	25c gray blue	2.00	1.00
39	A6	40c gray	6.00	1.00
40	A6	50c dk brn	15.00	4.00
41	A6	1p olive bister	37.50	6.75

Same, Dated "1881"

1881				
42	A6	½m lake	24	15
43	A6	1m violet	25	15
44	A6	2m pale rose	35	25
45	A6	4m brt grn	50	20
46	A6	6m brn lil	50	38
47	A6	8m ultra	1.25	85
48	A6	1c gray grn	2.25	85
49	A6	2c lake	3.00	1.90
50	A6	3c dk brn	5.00	2.75
51	A6	5c gray bl	1.50	25
52	A6	8c brown	1.50	85
53	A6	10c slate	12.00	4.75
54	A6	20c ol bis	19.00	6.75

Alfonso XII — A7 Alfonso XIII — A8

1882-86				
55	A7	½m rose	25	15
a.		½m salmon rose	30	24
56	A7	½m lake ('84)	50	40
57	A7	1m pale lake	50	40
58	A7	1m brt rose ('84)	25	15
59	A7	2m violet	25	15
60	A7	4m brn lil	25	15
61	A7	6m brown	40	15
62	A7	8m yel grn	40	15
63	A7	1c gray grn	25	15
64	A7	2c rose	1.00	15
65	A7	3c yellow	3.00	1.25
a.		Cliché of 8c in plate of 3c	110.00	
66	A7	3c yel brn ('84)	3.00	50
a.		Cliché of 8c in plate of 3c	22.50	
67	A7	5c gray bl	11.00	60
68	A7	5c gray bl, 1st retouch ('84)	11.00	2.50
69	A7	5c gray bl, 2nd retouch ('86)	95.00	4.00
70	A7	8c gray brn	3.00	15
71	A7	10c dk grn	3.00	25
72	A7	20c gray lilac	4.00	25
a.		20c olive brown (error)	*50.00*	
73	A7	40c blue	27.50	7.50
74	A7	80c olive bister	27.50	8.75

For differences between the original and the retouched stamps see note on the 1883-86 issue of Cuba.

1890-97				
75	A8	½m black	24	15
76	A8	½m ol gray ('92)	15	15
77	A8	½m red brn ('94)	15	15
78	A8	½m dl vio ('96)	15	15
79	A8	1m emerald	28	15
80	A8	1m dk vio ('92)	15	15
81	A8	1m ultra ('94)	15	15
82	A8	1m dp brn ('96)	15	15
83	A8	2m lilac rose	24	15
84	A8	2m vio brn ('92)	15	15
85	A8	2m red org ('94)	15	15
86	A8	2m yel grn ('96)	15	15
87	A8	4m dk ol grn	9.00	4.50
88	A8	4m ultra ('92)	15	15
89	A8	4m yel brn ('94)	15	15
90	A8	4m bl grn ('96)	45	24
91	A8	6m dk brn	21.00	9.00
92	A8	6m pale rose ('92)	15	15
93	A8	8m olive bister	21.00	18.00
94	A8	8m yel grn ('92)	15	15
95	A8	1c yel brn	24	15
96	A8	1c bl grn ('91)	45	15
97	A8	1c vio brn ('94)	2.75	15
98	A8	1c claret ('96)	28	15
99	A8	2c dk vio	90	70
100	A8	2c red brn ('92)	70	15
101	A8	2c lilac ('94)	1.10	15
102	A8	2c org brn ('96)	28	15
103	A8	3c slate blue	6.00	70
104	A8	3c org ('92)	55	15
105	A8	3c ol gray ('94)	1.90	15
106	A8	3c blue ('96)	9.00	24
107	A8	3c cl brn ('97)	18	15
108	A8	4c slate bl ('94)	45	15
109	A8	4c gray brn ('96)	38	15
110	A8	5c brn vio	9.00	38
111	A8	5c yel grn ('94)	1.90	28
112	A8	5c bl grn ('92)	55	15
113	A8	5c blue ('96)	18	15
114	A8	6c org ('94)	28	15
115	A8	6c vio ('96)	18	15
116	A8	8c ultra	8.50	1.40
117	A8	8c gray brn ('92)	15	15
118	A8	8c dl vio ('94)	5.25	90
119	A8	8c car rose ('96)	90	60
120	A8	10c rose	3.75	60
a.		10c salmon rose	6.75	2.10
121	A8	10c lil rose ('92)	70	15
122	A8	20c red org	3.50	3.00
123	A8	20c lilac ('92)	85	24
124	A8	20c car rose ('94)	60	15
125	A8	20c ol gray ('96)	2.50	70
126	A8	40c orange	57.50	24.00
127	A8	40c sl bl ('92)	2.25	1.40
128	A8	40c claret ('94)	2.75	2.10
129	A8	40c salmon ('96)	2.50	1.40
130	A8	80c yel grn	175.00	90.00
131	A8	80c orange ('92)	6.00	3.75
132	A8	80c black ('97)	15.00	7.25

Imperforates of type A8 were not issued and are variously considered to be proofs or printer's waste.
For overprints see Nos. 154A-170, MR1-MR13.

Landing of Columbus on Puerto Rico
A9
Alfonso XIII
A10

1893	**Litho.**		*Perf. 12*	
133	A9	3c dk grn	80.00	27.50

400th anniversary, landing of Columbus on Puerto Rico. Counterfeits exist.

1898			**Typo.**	
135	A10	1m org brn	15	15
136	A10	2m org brn	15	15
137	A10	3m org brn	15	15
138	A10	4m org brn	85	38
139	A10	5m org brn	15	15
140	A10	1c blk vio	15	15
a.		Tête bêche pair	*900.00*	
141	A10	2c dk bl grn	15	15
142	A10	3c dk brn	15	15
143	A10	4c orange	1.00	55
144	A10	5c brt rose	15	15
145	A10	6c dk bl	52	15
146	A10	8c gray brn	15	15
147	A10	10c vermilion	15	15
148	A10	15c dl ol grn	15	15
149	A10	20c maroon	1.25	38
150	A10	40c violet	70	60
151	A10	60c black	70	60
152	A10	80c red brn	2.50	2.25
153	A10	1p yel grn	5.00	4.75
154	A10	2p slate blue	14.00	6.00
		Nos. 135-154 (20)	28.17	17.31

Nos. 135-154 exist imperf. Value, set $1,000.

Stamps of 1890-97 Handstamped in Rose or Purple

Habilitado PARA 1898 y 99.

1898				
154A	A8	½m dl vio	8.00	4.00
155	A8	1m dp brn	1.25	1.25
156	A8	2m yel grn	28	28
157	A8	4m bl grn	28	28
158	A8	1c claret	50	70
159	A8	2c org brn	50	70
160	A8	3c blue	14.00	6.75
161	A8	3c claret brn	35	35
162	A8	4c gray brn	35	35
163	A8	4c slate bl	8.50	5.75
164	A8	5c yel grn	5.00	5.00
165	A8	5c blue	30	30
166	A8	6c violet	30	28
167	A8	8c car rose (P)	50	30
a.		Rose overprint	4.75	4.75
168	A8	20c olive gray	85	85
169	A8	40c salmon	2.50	2.50
170	A8	80c black	12.00	10.00

As usual with handstamps there are many inverted, double and similar varieties. Counterfeits of Nos. 154A-170 abound.

Issued under US Administration

A11

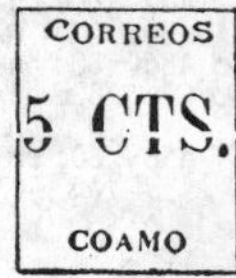

A12

Ponce Issue

1898 Unwmk. ***Imperf.***

200 A11 5c vio, *yelsh* 6,500.

Counterfeits exist of Nos. 200-201.

Coamo Issue

1898 Unwmk. ***Imperf.***

201 A12 5c black 425.00 500.00

There are ten varieties in the setting. The stamps bear the control mark "F. Santiago" in violet.

United States Nos. 279, 267, 281, 272 and 282C Overprinted in Black at 36 degree angle

1899 Wmk. 191 ***Perf. 12***

210 A87 1c yel grn 4.50 1.25
a. Ovpt. at 25 degree angle 6.50 2.00
211 A88 2c car, type III 3.75 1.00
a. Ovpt. at 25 degree angle 5.00 2.00
212 A91 5c blue 8.00 2.25
213 A93 8c vio brn 25.00 15.00
a. Ovpt. at 25 degree angle 30.00 16.00
c. "PORTO RIC" 100.00 100.00
214 A94 10c brn, type I 15.00 5.00
Nos. 210-214 (5) 56.25 24.50

Misspellings of the overprint, actually broken letters (PORTO RICU, PORTU RICO, FORTO RICO), are found on 1c, 2c, 8c and 10c.

United States Nos. 279 and 267 Overprinted Diagonally in Black

1900

215 A87 1c yellow green 5.00 1.25
216 A88 2c carmine 4.00 1.00
a. 2c orange red 4.50 1.00

Stamps of Puerto Rico were replaced by those of the United States.

POSTAGE DUE STAMPS

United States Nos. J38, J39 and J42 Overprinted in Black at 36 degree angle

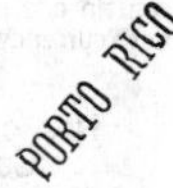

1899 Wmk. 191 ***Perf. 12***

J1 D2 1c deep claret 16.00 5.00
a. Ovpt. at 25 degree angle 20.00 7.00
J2 D2 2c deep claret 10.00 5.50
a. Ovpt. at 25 degree angle 14.00 6.50
J3 D2 10c deep claret 120.00 50.00
a. Ovpt. at 25 degree angle 150.00 75.00

WAR TAX STAMPS

Stamps of 1890-94 Overprinted or Surcharged by Handstamp

IMPUESTO
DE GUERRA

1898 Unwmk. ***Perf. 14***

Purple Overprint or Surcharge

MR1 A8 1c yel brn 5.50 4.00
MR2 A8 2c on 2m org 2.00 1.90
MR3 A8 2c on 5c bl grn 3.00 2.50
MR4 A8 2c dk vio 30 20
MR5 A8 2c lilac 60 60
MR6 A8 2c red brn 30 20
MR7 A8 5c bl grn 30 20
MR8 A8 5c on 5c bl grn 3.50 2.50

Rose Surcharge

MR9 A8 2c on 2m org 1.25 1.25
MR10 A8 5c on 1m dk vio 20 20
MR11 A8 5c on 1m dl bl 30 30

Magenta Surcharge

MR12 A8 5c on 1m dk vio 20 20
MR13 A8 5c on 1m dl bl 1.75 1.75

Nos. MR2-MR13 were issued as War Tax Stamps (2c on letters or sealed mail; 5c on telegrams) but, during the early days of the American occupation, they were accepted for ordinary postage.

Double, inverted and similar varieties of overprints are numerous in this issue.

QATAR

LOCATION — A peninsula in eastern Arabia
GOVT. — Independent state
AREA — 4,575 sq. mi.
POP. — 260,000 (est. 1982)
CAPITAL — Doha

Qatar was a British protected sheikdom until Sept. 1, 1971, when it declared its independence. Stamps of Muscat were used until 1957.

100 Naye Paise = 1 Rupee
100 Dirhams = 1 Riyal (1967)

Catalogue values for all unused stamps in this country are for Never Hinged items.

Great Britain Nos. 317-325, 328, 332-333 and 309-311 Surcharged "QATAR" and New Value in Black

Perf. 14½x14

1957, Apr. 1 Photo. Wmk. 308

1 A129 1np on 5p lt brn 15 15
2 A126 3np on ½p red org 15 15
3 A126 6np on 1p ultra 15 15
4 A126 9np on 1½p grn 15 15
5 A126 12np on 2p red brn 16 15
6 A127 15np on 2½p scarlet 20 20
7 A127 20np on 3p dk pur 20 20
8 A128 25np on 4p ultra 42 42
9 A129 40np on 6p lil rose 42 42
10 A130 50np on 9p dp ol grn 85 50
11 A132 75np on 1sh3p dk grn 2.25 1.00
12 A131 1r on 1sh6p dk bl 3.00 1.00

Engr. ***Perf. 11x12***

13 A133 2r on 2sh6p dk brn 6.00 2.25
14 A133 5r on 5sh crimson 14.00 6.50
15 A133 10r on 10sh brt ultra 30.00 13.50
Nos. 1-15 (15) 58.10 26.74

Both typeset and stereotyped overprints were used on Nos. 13-15. The typeset have bars close together and thick, bold letters. The stereotyped have bars wider apart and thinner letters.

Scout Jamboree Issue

Great Britain Nos. 334-336 Surcharged "QATAR," New Value and Square of Dots in Black

Perf. 14½x14

1957, Aug. 1 Photo. Wmk. 308

16 A138 15np on 2½p scarlet 45 35
17 A138 25np on 4p ultra 90 75
18 A138 75np on 1sh3p dk grn 1.40 1.25

50th anniv. of the Boy Scout movement and the World Scout Jubilee Jamboree, Aug. 1-12.

Great Britain Nos. 353-358, 362 Surcharged "QATAR" and New Value

1960 Wmk. 322 ***Perf. 14½x14***

19 A126 3np on ½p red org 90 2.00
20 A126 6np on 1p ultra 1.50 3.00
21 A126 9np on 1½p grn 1.25 1.25
22 A126 12np on 2p red brn 6.00 10.00
23 A127 15np on 2½p scar 40 35
24 A127 20np on 3p dk pur 40 35
25 A129 40np on 6p lil rose 1.00 60
Nos. 19-25 (7) 11.45 17.55

Sheik Ahmad bin Ali al Thani — A1

Peregrine Falcon — A2

Oil Derrick — A3

Designs: 75np, Dhow. 5r, 10r, Mosque.

Perf. 14½

1961, Sept. 2 Unwmk. Photo.

26 A1 5np rose car 15 15
27 A1 15np brn blk 15 15
28 A1 20np claret 15 15
29 A1 30np dp grn 20 15
30 A2 40np red 30 15
31 A2 50np sepia 40 30
32 A2 75np ultra 60 40

Engr. ***Perf. 13***

33 A3 1r rose red 70 40
34 A3 2r blue 1.40 1.00
35 A3 5r green 3.50 2.50
36 A3 10r black 7.50 4.50
Nos. 26-36 (11) 15.05 9.85

Nos. 31-32, 34-36 Overprinted or Surcharged

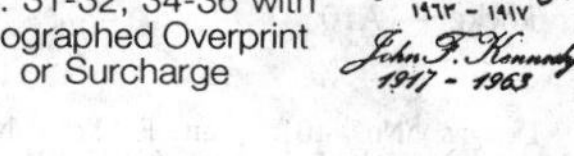

1964, Oct. 25 Photo. ***Perf. 14½***

37 A2 50np sepia 65 90
38 A2 75np ultra 90 1.40

Engr. ***Perf. 13***

39 A3 1r on 10r black 1.75 1.40
40 A3 2r blue 4.25 2.75
41 A3 5r green 10.00 6.25
Nos. 37-41 (5) 17.55 12.70

18th Olympic Games, Tokyo, Oct. 10-25.
For surcharges see Nos. 110-110D.

Nos. 31-32, 34-36 with Typographed Overprint or Surcharge

John F. Kennedy
1917 - 1963

1964, Nov. 22 Photo. ***Perf. 14½***

42 A2 50np sepia 70 50
43 A2 75np ultra 90 75

Engr. ***Perf. 13***

44 A3 1r on 10r blk 1.75 1.50
45 A3 2r blue 4.25 4.00
46 A3 5r green 10.00 8.25
Nos. 42-46 (5) 17.60 15.00

Pres. John F. Kennedy (1917-63).
For surcharges see Nos. 111-111D.

Column — A4

Designs: 2np, 1.50r, Isis Temple and Colonnade, Philae. 3np, 1r, Trajan's kiosk, Philae.

Perf. 14½x14

1965, Jan. 17 Photo. Unwmk.

47 A4 1np multi 50 15
48 A4 2np multi 50 15
49 A4 3np multi 50 15
50 A4 1r multi 75 40
51 A4 1.50r multi 1.40 60
52 A4 2r multi 50 50
Nos. 47-52 (6) 4.15
Set value 1.65

UNESCO world campaign to save historic monuments in Nubia.

Qatar Scout Emblem, Tents and Sheik Ahmad — A5

Scouts Saluting and Sheik Ahmad — A6

Designs: 1np, 4np, Qatar scout emblem.

Perf. 14 (A5), 14½x14 (A6)

1965, May 22 Photo. Unwmk.

53 A5 1np ol grn & dk red brn 20 15
54 A5 2np sal & dk vio bl 20 15
55 A5 3np dk vio bl & grn 20 15
56 A5 4np bl & dk red brn 20 15
57 A5 5np dk vio bl & grnsh bl 20 15
58 A6 30np multi 65 45
59 A6 40np multi 80 60
60 A6 1r multi 2.00 1.25
Nos. 53-60 (8) 4.45
Set value 2.50

Issued to honor the Qatar Boy Scouts. Perf. and imperf. souvenir sheets contain one each of Nos. 58-60 with red brown marginal inscription. Size: 108x76mm.
For surcharges see Nos. 113-113G.

Eiffel Tower, Telstar, ITU Emblem and "Qatar" in Morse Code — A7

Designs: 2np, 1r, Tokyo Olympic Games emblem and Syncom III. 3np, 40np, Radar tracking station and Relay satellite. 4np, 50np, Post Office Tower, London, and Echo II, Syncom III, Telstar and Relay satellites around globe.

Perf. 13½x14

1965, Oct. 16 Photo. Unwmk.

61 A7 1np dk bl & red brn 20 15
62 A7 2np bl & dk red brn 20 15
63 A7 3np dp yel grn & brt pur 20 15
64 A7 4np org brn & brt bl 20 15
65 A7 5np dl vio & dk ol bis 20 15
66 A7 40np dk car rose & blk 60 40
67 A7 50np sl grn & bis 75 50
68 A7 1r emer & car 1.50 1.00
a. Souv. sheet of 2, #67-68 5.00 3.50
Nos. 61-68 (8) 3.85
Set value 2.15

Cent. of the ITU. #68a also exists imperf.
For overprints and surcharges see Nos. 91-98, 114-114G, 117-117G.

Triggerfish — A8

Various Fish, including: 2np, 50np, Clown grunt. 2np, 10r, Saddleback butterflyfish. 4np, 5r, Butterflyfish. 15np, 3r, Paradisefish. 20np, 1r, Rio Grande perch. 75np, Triggerfish.

1965, Oct. 18 ***Perf. 14x14½***

69 A8 1np multi & black 15 15
70 A8 2np multi & black 15 15
71 A8 3np multi & black 15 15

72 A8 4np multi & black 15 15
73 A8 5np multi & black 15 15
74 A8 15np multi & black 20 15
75 A8 20np multi & black 25 15
76 A8 30np multi & black 30 22
77 A8 40np multi & black 40 25
78 A8 50np multi & gold 50 35
79 A8 75np multi & gold 80 50
80 A8 1r multi & gold 1.00 65
81 A8 2r multi & gold 2.25 1.25
82 A8 3r multi & gold 3.25 1.90
83 A8 4r multi & gold 4.00 2.50
84 A8 5r multi & gold 6.00 3.50
85 A8 10r multi & gold 12.50 6.50
Nos. 69-85 (17) 32.20 18.67

Basketball — A9

Sports: No. 87, Horse jumping. No. 88, Running. No. 89, Soccer. No. 90, Weight lifting.

1966, Jan. 10 Photo. *Perf. 11½*

Granite Paper

86 A9 1r gray, blk & dk red 1.00 60
87 A9 1r brn & ol grn 1.00 60
88 A9 1r dull rose & blue 1.00 60
89 A9 1r grn & blk 1.00 60
90 A9 1r bl & brn 1.00 60
Nos. 86-90 (5) 5.00 3.00

4th Pan Arab Games, Cairo, Sept. 2-11. Nos. 86-90 are printed in one sheet of 25 in horizontal rows of five.

Nos. 61-68 Overprinted

1966, Feb. 9 Photo. *Perf. 13½x14*

91 A7 1np dk bl & red brn 18 15
92 A7 2np bl & dk red brn 18 15
93 A7 3np dp yel grn & brt pur 18 15
94 A7 4np org brn & brt bl 18 15
95 A7 5np dl vio & dk ol bis 18 15
96 A7 40np dk car rose & blk 65 25
97 A7 50np slate grn & bis 75 30
98 A7 1r emer & car 1.50 60
Nos. 91-98 (8) 3.80
Set value 1.40

Issued to commemorate the rendezvous in space of Gemini 6 and 7, Dec. 15, 1965.
Exist overprinted in blue.
For surcharges see Nos. 117-117G.

Sheik Ahmad A9a

Designs: 3np, 5np, 40np, 80np, 2r, 10r, Reverse of coin with Arabic inscription.

Litho. & Embossed Gold or Silver Foil

1966, Feb. 24 *Imperf.*

99 A9a 1np ol & lil (S)
99A A9a 3np blk & org (S)
99B A9a 4np pur & red
99C A9a 5np brt grn & red brn

Diameter: 55mm

99D A9a 10np brn & brt vio (S)
99E A9a 40np org red & bl (S)
99F A9a 70np Prus bl & bl vio
99G A9a 80np car & grn

Diameter: 65mm

99H A9a 1r red vio & blk (S)
99J A9a 2r bl grn & cl (S)
99K A9a 5r red lil & ver
99L A9a 10r bl vio & brn car

John F. Kennedy, UN Headquarters, NY, and ICY Emblem — A10

Designs (ICY emblem and): No. 99, UN emblem. No. 101, Dag Hammarskjold and UN General Assembly. No. 102, Jawaharlal Nehru and dove.

1966, Mar. 8 *Perf. 11½*

Granite Paper

100 A10 40np brt bl, vio bl & red brn 1.50 1.00
100A A10 40np brt grn, vio & brn 1.50 1.00
100B A10 40np red brn, brt bl & blk 1.50 1.00
100C A10 40np dk vio & brt grn 1.50 1.00
d. Block of 4, #100-100C 6.00 4.00

UN Intl. Cooperation Year, 1965. Printed in sheets of 16 + 9 lables in shape of a cross.
An imperf. souvenir sheet of 4 contains one each of Nos. 100-100C.

Nos. 100-100C Overprinted in Black

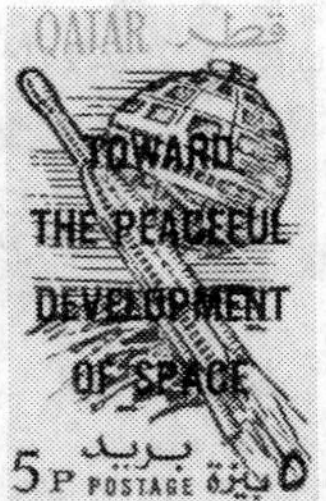

U.N. 20th ANNIVERSARY

Telstar, Rocket — A10a

Designs: No. 101, John F. Kennedy, "In Memoriam / John F. Kennedy / 1917-1963." No. 101A, Olive branches, Churchill quote and "In Memoriam / 1874-1965." No. 101B, like #101 portrait facing left, no overprint. No. 101C, Eternal flame, Arabic inscription.

1966, Mar. 8

Granite Paper

101 A10a 5np bl grn, car & blk
101A A10a 5np bl grn, rose & blk
101B A10a 5np bl grn & blk
101C A10a 5np bl grn, rose & blk
101D A10a 5np bl brn, car & blk
101E A10 40np on No. 101
101F A10 40np on No. 101A
101G A10 40np on No. 101B
101H A10 40np on No. 101C

Nos. 101-101H were made from the sheets of Nos. 100-100C. The 4 outer labels and the center label were surcharged to create Nos. 101-101D. The other 4 labels were overprinted but have no denomination. Exists with red overprints. The imperf. souvenir sheet exists with overprint in margin:"IN VICTORY, / MAGNAMIMITY. / IN PEACE / GOODWILL / WINSTON CHURCHILL." The margin overprint overlaps onto No. 101A on upper left quarter of stamp.
exist imperf.
For surcharges see Nos. 118-118C.

John F. Kennedy (1917-1963) — A10b

Kennedy and: #102c, 10np, #102f, 70np, NYC. #102d, 30np, #102g, 80np, Rocket lifting off at Cape Kennedy. #102e, 60np, #102h, 1r, Statue of Liberty. No. 102B, Statue of Liberty.

1966, July 18 *Perf. 13½*

102 A10b Strip of 3, #c.-e.
102A A10b Strip of 3, #f.-h.

Souvenir Sheet

Imperf

102B A10b 50np multicolored

Nos. 102-102A exist imperf. For surcharges see Nos. 119-119B.

1968 Summer Olympics, Mexico City A10c

Designs: #103c, 1np, #103f, 70np, #103B, Equestrian. #103d, 4np, #103g, 80np, Running. #103e, 5np, #103h, 90np, Javelin.

1966, July 20 *Perf. 13½*

103 A10c Strip of 3, #c.-e.
103A A10c Strip of 3, #f.-h.

Souvenir Sheet

Imperf

103B A10c 50np multicolored

Nos. 103-103A exist imperf. For surcharges see Nos. 120-120B.

A10d

American Astronauts — A10e

Astronaut and space vehicle: No. 104c, 5np, James A. Lovell. d, 10np, Thomas P. Stafford. e, 15np, Alan B. Shepard.
No. 104f, 20np, John H. Glenn. g, 30np, M. Scott Carpenter. h, 40np, Walter M. Schirra. i, 50np, Virgil I. Grissom. j, 60np, L. Gordon Cooper, Jr.
No. 104B, Stafford, Schirra, Frank Borman, Lovell and diagram of space rendezvous.

1966, Aug. 20 *Perf. 12*

104 A10d Strip of 3, #c.-e.
104A A10e Strip of 5, #f.-j.

Souvenir Sheet

Imperf

Size: 115x75mm

104B A10e 50np multicolored

The name of James A. Lovell is spelled "Lovel" on No. 104c. Nos. 104-104A exist imperf. For surcharges see Nos. 121-121B.

1966 World Cup Soccer Championships, London
A10h A10i

Designs: 1np-4np, Jules Rimet Cup. 60np, #107H, Hands holding Cup, soccer ball. 70np, #107J, Cup, soccer ball. 80np, #107K, Soccer players, ball. 90np, #107L, Wembley Stadium.

1966, Nov. 27 Photo. *Perf. 13½*

107 A10h 1np blue
107A A10h 2np blue
107B A10h 3np blue
107C A10h 4np blue
m. Block of 4, #107-107C
107D A10i 60np multicolored
107E A10i 70np multicolored
107F A10i 80np multicolored
107G A10i 90np multicolored
n. Block of 4, #107D-107G

Souvenir Sheets

Imperf

107H A10i 25np multicolored
107J A10i 25np multicolored
107K A10i 25np multicolored
107L A10i 25np multicolored

Nos. 107-107C are airmail. Issued in sheets of 36 containing 5 #107m and 4 #107n. Nos. 107-107G exist imperf.

Nos. 37-41 Surcharged with New Currency in Gray or Red

1966 Photo. *Perf. 14½*

110 A2 50d on 50np #37 (Gray)
110A A2 75d on 75np #38

Engr.

Perf. 13

110B A3 1r on 1r on 10r #39
110C A3 2r on 2r #40
110D A3 5r on 5r #41

Nos. 42-46 Surcharged with New Currency in Gray or Red

1966 Photo. *Perf. 14½*

111 A2 50d on 50np #42 (Gray)
111A A2 75d on 75np #43

Engr.

Perf. 13

111B A3 1r on 1r on 10r #44
111C A3 2r on 2r #45
111D A3 5r on 5r #46

Nos. 53-60 Surcharged with New Currency

Perf. 14 (A5), 14½x14 (A6)

1966 Photo.

113 A5 1d on 1np #53
113A A5 2d on 2np #54
113B A5 3d on 3np #55
113C A5 4d on 4np #56
113D A5 5d on 4np #57
113E A6 30d on 30r #58
113F A6 40d on 40r #59
113G A6 1r on 1r #60

Exist imperf. Perf and imperf souvenir sheets contain one each of #113E-113G surcharged with new currency.

Nos. 61-68 Surcharged with New Currency in Black or Red

1966 *Perf. 13½x14*

114 A7 1d on 1np #61
114A A7 2d on 2np #62
114B A7 3d on 3np #63
114C A7 4d on 4np #64
114D A7 5d on 5np #65
114E A7 40d on 40np #66
114F A7 50d on 50np #67
114G A7 1r on 1r #68

Exist imperf.

Nos. 91-95 Surcharged with New Currency

1966 Photo. *Perf. 13½x14*

117 A7 1d on 1np #91
117A A7 2d on 2np #92
117B A7 3d on 3np #93
117C A7 4d on 4np #94
117D A7 5d on 5np #95

Numbers have been reserved for additional values in this set.

Nos. 101E-101H with Red Overprint Surcharged with New Currency

1966 Photo. *Perf. 11½*

Granite Paper

118 A10a 40d on 40np #101E
118A A10a 40d on 40np #101F
118B A10a 40d on 40np #101G
118C A10a 40d on 40np #101H
d. Block of 4, #118-118C

Exist imperf. Imperf. souvenir sheets mentioned after Nos. 100C, 101H exist surcharged with new currency.

Nos. 102-102B Surcharged with New Currency

1966 *Perf. 13½*

119 Strip of 3
- **c.** A10b 10d on 10np #102c
- **d.** A10b 30d on 30np #102d
- **e.** A10b 60d on 60np #102e

119A Strip of 3
- **f.** A10b 70d on 70np #102f
- **g.** A10b 80d on 80np #102g
- **h.** A10b 1r on 1r #102h

Souvenir Sheet

Imperf

119B A10b 50d on 50np #102B

Nos. 119-119A exist imperf.

Nos. 103-103B Surcharged with New Currency

1966 *Perf. 13½*

120 Strip of 3
- **c.** A10c 1d on 1np #103c
- **d.** A10c 4d on 4np #103d
- **e.** A10c 5d on 5np #103e

120A Strip of 3
- **f.** A10c 70d on 70np #103f
- **g.** A10c 80d on 80np #103g
- **h.** A10c 90d on 90np #103h

Souvenir Sheet

Imperf

120B A10c 50d on 50np #103

Nos. 120-120 exist imperf.

Nos. 104-104B Surcharged with New Currency

1966 *Perf. 12*

121 Strip of 3
- **c.** A10d 5d on 5np #104c
- **d.** A10d 10d on 10np #104d
- **e.** A10d 15d on 15np #104e

121A Strip of 5
- **f.** A10e 20d on 20np #104f
- **g.** A10e 30d on 30np #104g
- **h.** A10e 40d on 40np #104h
- **i.** A10e 50d on 50np #104i
- **j.** A10e 60d on 60np #104j

Souvenir Sheet

Imperf

121B A10e 50d on 50np #104B

Nos. 121-121A printed se-tenant with five labels showing Arabic inscription.

Arab Postal Union Emblem A11

Traffic Light and Intersection A12

Apollo Project A11a

1967, Apr. 15 Photo. *Perf. 11x11½*

122	A11	70d magenta & sepia	1.10	28
122A	A11	80d dull blue & sepia	1.40	32

Qatar's joining the Arab Postal Union.

1967, May 1 *Perf. 12½*

Designs: 5d, 70d, Two astronauts on Moon. 10d, 80d, Command and lunar modules in lunar orbit. 20d, 1r, Lunar module on Moon. 30d, 1.20r, Lunar module ascending from Moon. 40d, 2r, Saturn 5 rocket.

123	A11a	5d multicolored
123A	A11a	10d multicolored
123B	A11a	20d multicolored
123C	A11a	30d multicolored
123D	A11a	40d multicolored
123E	A11a	70d multicolored
123F	A11a	80d multicolored
123G	A11a	1r multicolored
123H	A11a	1.20r multicolored
123J	A11a	2r multicolored

#123J exists in an imperf. souvenir sheet of one.

1967, May 24 Litho. *Perf. 13½*

124	A12	20d vio & multi	30	15
124A	A12	30d multi	50	15
124B	A12	50d multi	80	20
124C	A12	1r ultra & multi	1.65	40

Issued for Traffic Day.

Boy Scouts and Sheik Ahmad — A13

Designs: 1d, First Boy Scout camp, Brownsea Island, 1907, and tents, Idaho, US, 1967. 2d, Lord Baden-Powell. 5d, Boy Scout canoeing. 15d, Swimming. 75d, Mountain climbing. 2r, Boy Scout saluting flag and emblem of 12th World Jamboree. 1d and 2d lack head of Sheik Ahmad.

1967, Sept. 15 Litho. *Perf. 11½x11*

125	A13	1d multi	35	15
125A	A13	2d buff & multi	35	15

Litho. and Engr.

125B	A13	3d rose & multi	35	15
125C	A13	5d lilac & multi	35	15
125D	A13	15d multi	55	25
125E	A13	75d green & multi	1.10	80
125F	A13	2r sepia & multi	5.00	3.25
		Nos. 125-125F (7)	8.05	4.90

Nos. 125-125A for 60th anniv. of the Boy Scouts, Nos. 125B-125F for 12th Boy Scout World Jamboree, Farragut State Park, Idaho, Aug. 1-9.

Viking Ship (from Bayeux Tapestry) A14

Famous Ships: 2d, Santa Maria (Columbus). 3d, San Gabriel (Vasco da Gama). 75d, Victoria (Ferdinand Magellan). 1r, Golden Hind (Sir Francis Drake). 2r, Gipsy Moth IV (Sir Francis Chichester).

1967, Nov. 27 Litho. *Perf. 13½*

126	A14	1d org & multi	25	15
126A	A14	2d lt bl, tan & blk	25	15
126B	A14	3d lt bl & multi	25	15
126C	A14	75d fawn & multi	80	60
126D	A14	1r gray, yel grn & red	1.50	1.25
126E	A14	2r multi	3.50	2.50
		Nos. 126-126E (6)	6.55	4.80

Professional Letter Writer — A15

Designs: 2d, Carrier pigeon and man releasing pigeon, vert. 3d, Postrider. 60d, Mail transport by rowboat, vert. 1.25r, Mailman riding camel, jet plane and modern buildings. 2r, Qatar No. 1, hand holding pen, paper, envelopes and inkwell.

1968, Feb. 14

127	A15	1d multi	22	15
127A	A15	2d multi	22	15
127B	A15	3d multi	22	15
127C	A15	60d multi	1.10	70
127D	A15	1.25r multi	2.25	1.40
127E	A15	2r multi	3.75	2.25
		Nos. 127-127E (6)	7.76	4.80

Ten years of Qatar postal service.

Human Rights Flame and Barbed Wire A16

Designs (Human Rights Flame and): 2d, Arab refugee family leaving concentration camp. 3d, Scales of Justice. 60d, Hands opening gates to the sun. 1.25r, Family and sun, vert. 2r, Stylized family groups.

1968, Apr. 10

128	A16	1d gray & multi	20	15
129	A16	2d multi	20	15
130	A16	3d brt grn, org & blk	20	15
131	A16	60d org, brn & blk	1.00	70
132	A16	1.25r brt grn, blk & yel	1.75	1.40
133	A16	2r multi	3.00	2.25
		Nos. 128-133 (6)	6.35	4.80

International Human Rights Year.

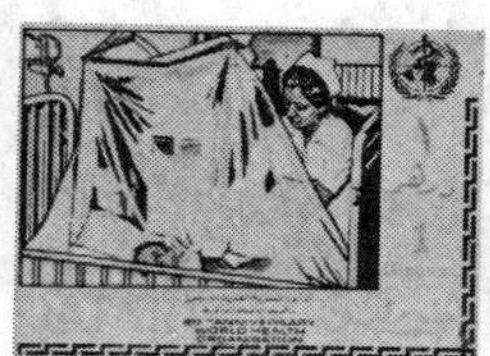
Nurse Attending Premature Baby A17

Designs (WHO Emblem and): 2d, Operating room. 3d, Dentist. 60d, X-ray examination. 1.25r, Medical laboratory. 2r, State Hospital.

1968, June 20

134	A17	1d multi	20	15
135	A17	2d multi	20	15
136	A17	3d multi	20	15
137	A17	60d multi	1.00	70
138	A17	1.25r multi	2.00	1.40
139	A17	2r multi	3.50	2.25
		Nos. 134-139 (6)	7.10	4.80

20th anniv. of the World Health Organization.

Olympic Rings and Gymnast A18

Designs (Olympic Rings and): 1d, Discobolus and view of Mexico City. 2d, Runner and flaming torch. 60d, Weight lifting and torch. 1.25r, Olympic flame as a mosaic, vert. 2r, Mythological bird.

1968, Aug. 24

140	A18	1d multi	18	15
141	A18	2d red yel & dk grn	18	15
142	A18	3d dk brn gray grn & ocher	18	15
143	A18	60d org brn pink & bl grn	90	65
144	A18	1.25r multi	1.75	1.25
145	A18	2r yel & multi	3.00	2.00
		Nos. 140-145 (6)	6.19	4.35

Issued to publicize the 19th Olympic Games, Mexico City, Oct. 12-27.

Sheik Ahmad bin Ali al Thani
A19 A21

Dhow A20

Designs: 40d, Desalination plant. 60d, Loading platform and oil tanker. 70d, Qatar Mosque. 1r, Clock Tower, Market Place, Doha. 1.25r, Doha Fort. 1.50r, Falcon.

1968 Litho. *Perf. 13½*

146	A19	5d blue & green	15	15
147	A19	10d brt bl & red brn	18	15
148	A19	20d blk & vermilion	25	15
149	A19	25d brt mag & brt grn	35	15

Lithographed and Engraved

Perf. 13

150	A20	35d grn & brt pink	55	30
151	A20	40d pur, lt bl & org	55	35
152	A20	60d lt bl, brn & lil	80	50
153	A20	70d blk, lt bl & brt grn	1.00	60
154	A20	1r vio bl, yel & brt grn	1.40	90
155	A20	1.25r ind, brt bl & ocher	1.90	1.10
156	A20	1.50r lt bl, dk grn & rose lil	2.00	1.25

Perf. 11½

157	A21	2r brn, ocher & bl gray	2.25	1.75
158	A21	5r grn, lt grn & pur	6.50	4.50
159	A21	10r ultra, lt bl & sep	19.00	9.00
		Nos. 146-159 (14)	36.88	20.85

UN Headquarters, NY, and Flags — A22

Designs (UN Emblem and): 1d, Flags. 4d, World map and dove. 60d, Classroom. 1.50r, Farmers, wheat and tractor. 2r, Sec. Gen. U Thant and General Assembly Hall.

1968, Oct. 24 Litho. *Perf. 13½x13*

160	A22	1d multi	15	15
161	A22	4d multi	15	15
162	A22	5d multi	15	15
163	A22	60d multi	90	55
164	A22	1.50r multi	2.00	1.25
165	A22	2r multi	2.50	1.75
		Nos. 160-165 (6)	5.85	4.00

United Nations Day, Oct. 24, 1968.

Fishing Vessel Ross Rayyan A23

Progress in Qatar: 4d, Elementary School and children playing. 5d, Doha Intl. Airport. 60d, Cement factory and road building. 1.50r, Power station. 2r, Housing development.

1969, Jan. 13

166	A23	1d brt bl & multi	15	15
167	A23	4d grn & multi	15	15
168	A23	5d dl org & multi	18	15
169	A23	60d lt brn & multi	90	50
170	A23	1.50r brt lil & multi	2.25	1.25
171	A23	2r buff & multi	2.50	1.50
		Nos. 166-171 (6)	6.13	3.70

Armored Cars A24

Designs: 2d, Traffic police. 3d, Military helicopter. 60d, Military band. 1.25r, Field gun. 2r, Mounted police.

1969, May 6 Litho. *Perf. 13½*

No.	Type	Denom.	Description	Unused	Used
172	A24	1d	multi	15	15
173	A24	2d	lt bl & multi	15	15
174	A24	3d	gray & multi	15	15
175	A24	60d	multi	50	35
176	A24	1.25r	multi	1.50	1.00
177	A24	2r	bl & multi	2.25	1.50
			Nos. 172-177 (6)	4.70	3.30

Issued to honor the public security forces.

Oil Tanker A25

Designs: 2d, Research laboratory. 3d, Off-shore oil rig and helicopter. 60d, Oil rig and storage tanks. 1.50r, Oil refinery. 2r, Oil tankers, 1890-1968.

1969, July 4

No.	Type	Denom.	Description	Unused	Used
178	A25	1d	gray & multi	15	15
179	A25	2d	olive & multi	15	15
180	A25	3d	ultra & multi	15	15
181	A25	60d	lilac & multi	90	60
182	A25	1.50r	red brn & multi	2.25	1.50
183	A25	2r	brn & multi	3.00	2.00
			Nos. 178-183 (6)	6.60	4.55

Qatar oil industry.

Boy Scouts Building Boats A26

Designs: 2d, Scouts at work and 10 symbolic candles. 3d, Parade. 60d, Gate to camp interior. 1.25r, Main camp gate. 2r, Hoisting Qatar flag, and Sheik Ahmad.

1969, Sept. 18 Litho. *Perf. 13½x13*

No.	Type	Denom.	Description	Unused	Used
184	A26	1d	multi	15	15
185	A26	2d	multi	15	15
186	A26	3d	multi	15	15
187	A26	60d	multi	1.00	65
a.			Souv. sheet of 4, #184-187	4.00	3.00
188	A26	1.25r	multi	2.00	1.25
189	A26	2r	multi	3.25	2.00
			Nos. 184-189 (6)	6.70	4.35

10th Qatar Boy Scout Jamboree. No. 187a sold for 1r.

Neil A. Armstrong — A27

Designs: 2d, Col. Edwin E. Aldrin, Jr. 3d, Lt. Col. Michael Collins. 60d, Astronaut walking on moon. 1.25r, Blast-off from moon. 2r, Capsule and raft in Pacific, horiz.

1969, Dec. 6 *Perf. 13x13½, 13½x13*

No.	Type	Denom.	Description	Unused	Used
190	A27	1d	bl & multi	15	15
191	A27	2d	multi	15	15
192	A27	3d	grn & multi	20	15
193	A27	60d	multi	85	50
194	A27	1.25r	pur & multi	1.90	1.10
195	A27	2r	multi	2.75	1.60
			Nos. 190-195 (6)	6.00	3.65

See note after US No. C76.

UPU Emblem, Boeing Jet Loading in Qatar A28

Designs (UPU Emblem and): 2d, Transatlantic ocean liner. 3d, Mail truck and mail bags. 60d, Qatar Post Office. 1.25r, UPU Headquarters, Bern. 2r, UPU emblem.

1970, Jan. 31 Litho. *Perf. 13½x13*

No.	Type	Denom.	Description	Unused	Used
196	A28	1d	multi	15	15
197	A28	2d	multi	15	15
198	A28	3d	multi	20	15
199	A28	60d	multi	85	50
200	A28	1.25r	multi	1.75	1.10
201	A28	2r	brt yel grn, blk & lt brn	2.75	1.90
			Nos. 196-201 (6)	5.85	3.95

Qatar's admission to the UPU.

Map of Arab League Countries, Flag and Emblem A28a

1970, Mar. *Perf. 13x13½*

No.	Type	Denom.	Description	Unused	Used
202	A28a	35d	yel & multi	50	38
203	A28a	60d	bl & multi	70	50
204	A28a	1.25r	multi	1.50	1.10
205	A28a	1.50r	vio & multi	2.00	1.50

25th anniversary of the Arab League.

VC10 Touching down for Landing A29

Designs: 2d, Hawk, and VC10 in flight. 3d, VC10 and airport. 60d, Map showing route Doha to London. 1.25r, VC10 over Gulftown. 2r, Tail of VC10 with emblem of Gulf Aviation.

1970, Apr. 5 *Perf. 13½x13*

No.	Type	Denom.	Description	Unused	Used
206	A29	1d	multi	15	15
207	A29	2d	multi	15	15
208	A29	3d	multi	15	15
209	A29	60d	multi	75	50
210	A29	1.25r	multi	1.40	1.00
211	A29	2r	multi	2.50	1.50
			Nos. 206-211 (6)	5.10	3.45

Issued to publicize the first flight to London from Doha by Gulf Aviation Company.

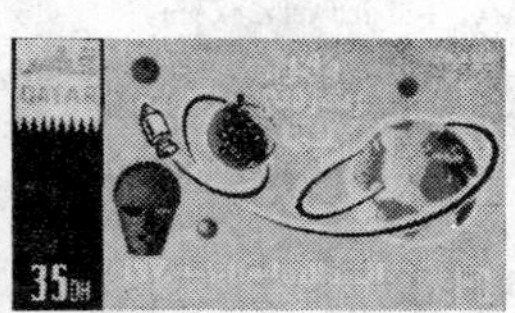

Education Year Emblem, Spaceship Trajectory, Koran Quotation — A30

1970, May 24 *Perf. 13x12½*

No.	Type	Denom.	Description	Unused	Used
212	A30	35d	bl & multi	60	35
213	A30	60d	bl & multi	1.40	75

Issued for International Education Year, 1970. Translation of Koran quotation: "And say, O God, give me more knowledge."

The only foreign revenue stamps listed in this Catalogue are those authorized for prepayment of postage.

Flowers — A31

1970, July 2 *Perf. 13x13½*

No.	Type	Denom.	Description	Unused	Used
214	A31	1d	Freesia	18	15
215	A31	2d	Azalea	18	15
216	A31	3d	Ixia	22	18
217	A31	60d	Amaryllis	75	60
218	A31	1.25r	Cineraria	1.60	1.25
219	A31	2r	Rose	2.75	1.75
			Nos. 214-219 (6)	5.68	4.08

For surcharges see Nos. 287-289.

EXPO Emblem and Fisherman on Shikoku Beach — A32

Designs (EXPO Emblem and): 1d, Toyahama fishermen honoring ocean gods, horiz. 2d, Map of Japan, horiz. 60d, Mt. Fuji. 1.50r, Camphorwood torii, horiz. 2r, Tower of Motherhood, EXPO Tower and Mt. Fuji.

Perf. 13½x13, 13x13½

1970, Sept. 29

No.	Type	Denom.	Description	Unused	Used
220	A32	1d	multi	15	15
221	A32	2d	multi	15	15
222	A32	3d	multi	16	15
223	A32	60d	multi	70	50
a.			Souvenir sheet of 4	4.00	3.00
224	A32	1.50r	multi	2.00	1.50
225	A32	2r	multi	2.50	2.00
			Nos. 220-225 (6)	5.66	4.45

EXPO '70 Intl. Exhib., Osaka, Japan, Mar. 15-Sept. 13. No. 223a contains 4 imperf. stamps similar to Nos. 220-223 with simulated perforations. Sold for 1r.

Globe and UN Emblem — A33

UN, 25th anniv.: 2d, Cannon used as flower vase. 3d, Birthday cake and dove. 35d, Emblems of UN agencies forming wall. 1.50r, Trumpet and emblems of UN agencies. 2r, Two men, black and white, embracing, and globe.

1970, Dec. 7 Litho. *Perf. 14x13½*

No.	Type	Denom.	Description	Unused	Used
226	A33	1d	bl & multi	15	15
227	A33	2d	multi	15	15
228	A33	3d	brt pur & multi	15	15
229	A33	35d	grn & multi	30	20
230	A33	1.50r	multi	1.50	1.00
231	A33	2r	brn red & multi	1.90	1.25
			Nos. 226-231 (6)	4.15	2.90

Al Jahiz and Old World Map A34

Designs: 2d, Sultan Saladin and palace. 3d, Al Farabi, sailboat and musical instruments. 35d, Iben al Haithum and palace. 1.50r, Al Motanabbi and camels. 2r, Avicenna and old world map.

1971, Feb. 20 *Perf. 13½x14*

No.	Type	Denom.	Description	Unused	Used
232	A34	1d	brt pink & multi	15	15
233	A34	2d	pale bl & multi	15	15
234	A34	3d	dl yel & multi	16	15
235	A34	35d	lt bl & multi	50	32
236	A34	1.50r	yel grn & multi	2.00	1.40
237	A34	2r	pale grn & multi	3.00	2.00
			Nos. 232-237 (6)	5.96	4.17

Famous men of Islam.

Cormorant A35

Designs: 2d, Lizard and prickly pear. 3d, Flamingos and palms. 60d, Oryx and yucca. 1.25r, Gazelle and desert dandelion. 2r, Camel, palm and bronzed chenopod.

1971, Apr. 14 Litho. *Perf. 11x12*

No.	Type	Denom.	Description	Unused	Used
238	A35	1d	multi	18	15
239	A35	2d	multi	18	15
240	A35	3d	multi	18	15
241	A35	60d	multi	90	60
242	A35	1.25r	multi	1.75	1.10
243	A35	2r	multi	3.00	1.75
			Nos. 238-243 (6)	6.19	3.90

Goonhilly Satellite Tracking Station A36

Designs: 2d, Cable ship, and section of submarine cable. 3d, 35d, London Post Office Tower, and television control room. 4d, Various telephones. 5d, 75d, Video telephone. 3r, Telex machine and tape.

1971, May 17 *Perf. 13½x13*

No.	Type	Denom.	Description	Unused	Used
244	A36	1d	vio bl & multi	15	15
245	A36	2d	multi	15	15
246	A36	3d	rose red & multi	15	15
247	A36	4d	magenta & multi	15	15
248	A36	5d	rose red & multi	15	15
249	A36	35d	multi	38	16
250	A36	75d	magenta & multi	75	35
251	A36	3r	ocher & multi	3.50	1.50
			Nos. 244-251 (8)	5.38	
			Set value		2.25

3rd World Telecommunications Day.

State of Qatar

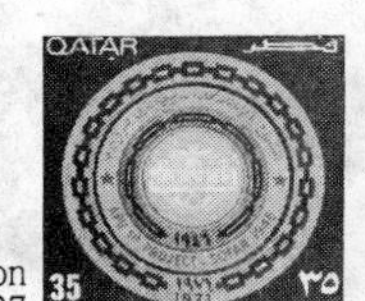

Arab Postal Union Emblem — A37

1971, Sept. 4 *Perf. 13*

No.	Type	Denom.	Description	Unused	Used
252	A37	35d	red & multi	60	25
253	A37	55d	blue & multi	75	40
254	A37	75d	brn & multi	1.25	55
255	A37	1.25r	vio & multi	2.00	90

25th anniv. of the Conf. of Sofar, Lebanon, establishing the Arab Postal Union.

Boy Reading — A38

1971, Aug. 10 *Perf. 13x13½*

256	A38	35d	brn & multi	45	25
257	A38	55d	ultra & multi	70	40
258	A38	75d	grn & multi	85	50

International Literacy Day, Sept. 8.

Men Splitting Racism A39

Designs: 2d, 3r, People fighting racism. 3d, Soldier helping war victim. 4d, Men of 4 races rebuilding, vert. 5d, Children on swing, vert. 35d, Wave of racism engulfing people. 75d, like 1d.

Perf. 13½x13, 13x13½

1971, Oct. 12 **Litho.**

259	A39	1d	multi	15	15
260	A39	2d	multi	15	15
261	A39	3d	multi	15	15
262	A39	4d	multi	15	15
263	A39	5d	multi	15	15
264	A39	35d	multi	20	20
265	A39	75d	multi	50	50
266	A39	3r	multi	2.25	2.25
			Set value	3.25	3.25

Intl. Year Against Racial Discrimination.

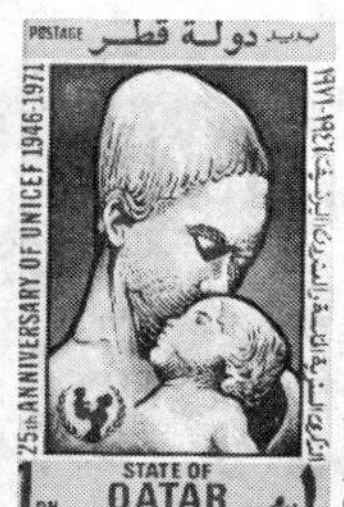

UNICEF Emblem, Mother and Child — A40

UNICEF, 25th anniv.: 2d, Child's head, horiz. 3d, 75d, Child with book. 4d, Nurse and child, horiz. 5d, Mother and child, horiz. 35d, Woman and daffodil. 3r, like 1d.

1971, Dec. 6 *Perf. 14x13½, 13½x14*

267	A40	1d	bl & multi	15	15
268	A40	2d	lil rose & multi	15	15
269	A40	3d	bl & multi	15	15
270	A40	4d	yel & multi	15	15
271	A40	5d	bl & multi	15	15
272	A40	35d	lil rose & multi	25	25
273	A40	75d	yel & multi	40	40
274	A40	3r	multi	2.00	1.40
			Set value	3.00	2.35

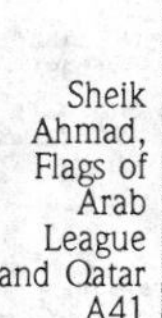

Sheik Ahmad, Flags of Arab League and Qatar A41

"International Cooperation" A42

Designs: 75d, Sheik Ahmad, flags of United Nations and Qatar. 1.25r, Sheik Ahmad bin Ali al Thani.

Perf. 13½x13, 13x13½

1972, Jan. 17

275	A41	35d	blk & multi	35	20
276	A41	75d	blk & multi	75	45
277	A42	1.25r	lt brn & blk	1.00	65
278	A42	3r	multi	3.00	1.75
	a.		Souvenir sheet	3.75	3.00

Independence 1971. No. 278a contains one stamp with simulated perforations.

European Roller — A43

Birds: 2d, European kingfisher. 3d, Rock thrush. 4d, Caspian tern. 5d, Hoopoe. 35d, European bee-eater. 75d, European golden oriole. 3r, Peregrine falcon.

1972, Mar. 1 **Litho.** *Perf. 12x11*

279	A43	1d	sepia & multi	15	15
280	A43	2d	emerald & multi	15	15
281	A43	3d	bister & multi	15	15
282	A43	4d	lt bl & multi	15	15
283	A43	5d	yellow & multi	15	15
284	A43	35d	vio bl & multi	45	20
285	A43	75d	pink & multi	1.10	50
286	A43	3r	blue & multi	4.50	2.00
			Nos. 279-286 (8)	6.80	
			Set value		2.90

Nos. 217-219 Surcharged

1972, Mar. 7 *Perf. 13x13½*

287	A31	10d on 60d	multi	15	15
288	A31	1r on 1.25r	multi	90	60
289	A31	5r on 2r	multi	4.00	2.75

Sheik Khalifa bin Hamad al Thani — A44

1972, Mar. 7 *Perf. 14*

Size: 23x27mm

290	A44	5d	pur & ultra	15	15
291	A44	10d	brn & rose red	15	15
292	A44	35d	org & dl grn	30	24
293	A44	55d	brt grn & lil	45	38
294	A44	75d	vio & lil rose	60	50

Size: 26½x32mm

295	A44	1r	bis & blk	90	75
296	A44	1.25r	ol & blk	1.00	80
297	A44	5r	bl & blk	4.25	3.50
298	A44	10r	red & blk	8.50	7.00
			Nos. 290-298 (9)	16.30	13.47

Book Year Emblem A45

1972, Apr. 23 *Perf. 13½x13*

299	A45	35d	lt ultra & blk	30	30
300	A45	55d	lt brn & blk	50	50
301	A45	75d	grn & blk	70	70
302	A45	1.25r	vio & blk	1.00	1.00

International Book Year 1972.

Olympic Rings, Soccer A46

Designs (Olympic Rings and): 2d, 3r, Running. 3d, Bicycling. 4d, Gymnastics. 5d, Basketball. 35d, Discus. 75d, Like 1d.

1972, June 12 *Perf. 13½x13*

303	A46	1d	grn & multi	15	15
304	A46	2d	yel grn & multi	15	15
305	A46	3d	bl & multi	15	15
306	A46	4d	lil & multi	15	15
307	A46	5d	bl & multi	15	15
308	A46	35d	gray & multi	28	16
	a.		Souvenir sheet of 6	2.50	1.50
309	A46	75d	grn & multi	60	35
310	A46	3r	multi	2.50	1.40
			Set value	3.60	2.10

20th Olympic Games, Munich, Aug. 26-Sept. 10. No. 308a contains stamps with simulated perforations similar to Nos. 303-308.

Installation of Underwater Pipe Line — A47

1972, Aug. 8 **Litho.** *Perf. 13x13½*

311	A47	1d	Drilling for oil, vert.	15	15
312	A47	4d	shown	15	15
313	A47	5d	Drilling platform	16	15
314	A47	35d	Ship searching for oil	40	30
315	A47	75d	like 1d, vert.	90	68
316	A47	3r	like 5d	3.50	2.50
			Nos. 311-316 (6)	5.26	3.93

Oil from the sea.

Government Palace — A48

Designs: 35d, Clasped hands, Qatar flag. 75d, Clasped hands, UN flag. 1.25r, Sheik Khalifa bin Hamad al-Thani, vert.

Perf. 13½x13, 13x13½

1972, Sept. 3

317	A48	10d	yel & multi	15	15
318	A48	35d	blk & multi	40	25
319	A48	75d	blk & multi	85	50
320	A48	1.25r	gold & multi	1.25	75
	a.		Souvenir sheet of 1	4.00	3.00

Independence Day, 1st anniv. of independence.

No. 320a contains one stamp with simulated perforations similar to No. 320.

Qatar Flag, Council Emblem and Flag — A49

1972, Dec. 4 **Litho.** *Perf. 14x13½*

321	A49	25d	bl & multi	60	45
322	A49	30d	vio bl & multi	80	60

Civil Aviation Council of Arab States, 10th session.

Tracking Station, Satellite, Telephone, ITU and UN Emblems A50

Designs (Agency and UN Emblems): 2d, Surveyor, artist; UNESCO. 3d, Tractor, helicopter, fish, grain and fruit; FAO. 4d, Reading children, teacher; UNICEF. 5d, Weather satellite and map; WMO. 25d, Workers and crane; ILO. 55d, Health clinic; WHO. 1r, Mail plane and post office; UPU.

1972, Oct. 24 *Perf. 13½x14*

323	A50	1d	multi	15	15
324	A50	2d	multi	15	15
325	A50	3d	multi	15	15
326	A50	4d	multi	15	15
327	A50	5d	multi	15	15
328	A50	25d	multi	38	20
329	A50	55d	multi	85	45
330	A50	1r	multi	1.40	75
			Nos. 323-330 (8)	3.38	
			Set value		1.75

United Nations Day, Oct. 24, 1972. Each stamp dedicated to a different UN agency.

Road Building A51

1973, Feb. 22 **Litho.** *Perf. 13x13½*

331	A51	2d	shown	15	15
332	A51	3d	Housing development	15	15
333	A51	4d	Operating room	15	15
334	A51	5d	Telephone operators	15	15
335	A51	15d	School, classroom	15	15
336	A51	20d	Television studio	25	15
337	A51	35d	Sheik Khalifa	35	28
338	A51	55d	New Gulf Hotel	60	40
339	A51	1r	Fertilizer plant	90	80
340	A51	1.35r	Flour mill	1.65	1.10
			Nos. 331-340 (10)	4.50	
			Set value		3.00

1st anniv. of the accession of Sheik Khalifa bin Hamad al Thani as Emir of Qatar.

Aerial Pest Control — A52

WHO, 25th anniv.: 3d, Medicines. 4d, Poliomyelitis prevention. 5d, Malaria control. 55d, Mental health. 1r, Pollution control.

1973, May 14 Litho. *Perf. 14*

341 A52 2d blue & multi 15 15
342 A52 3d blue & multi 15 15
343 A52 4d blue & multi 15 15
344 A52 5d blue & multi 15 15
345 A52 55d blue & multi 1.00 65
346 A52 1r blue & multi 1.50 1.50
Nos. 341-346 (6) 3.10
Set value 2.45

Weather Ship A53

Designs (WMO Emblem and): 3d, Launching of radiosonde balloon. 4d, Plane and meteorological data checking. 5d, Cup anemometers and meteorological station. 10d, Weather plane in flight. 1r, Nimbus I weather satellite. 1.55r, Launching of rocket carrying weather satellite.

1973, July Litho. *Perf. 14x13*

347 A53 2d multi 15 15
348 A53 3d multi 15 15
349 A53 4d multi 15 15
350 A53 5d multi 15 15
351 A53 10d multi 15 15
352 A53 1r multi 1.00 65
353 A53 1.55r multi 1.50 1.00
Nos. 347-353 (7) 3.25
Set value 2.00

Cent. of intl. meteorological cooperation.

Sheik Khalifa — A54

Clock Tower, Doha — A55

1973-74 Litho. *Perf. 14*

Size: 18x27mm

354 A54 5d grn & multi 15 15
355 A54 10d lt bl & multi 15 15
356 A54 20d ver & multi 15 15
357 A54 25d org & multi 20 15
358 A54 35d pur & multi 30 20
359 A54 55d dk gray & multi 45 30

Engr.

Perf. 13½

360 A55 75d lil, bl & yel grn 65 45

Photo.

Perf. 13

Size: 27x32mm

360A A54 1r multi 90 60
360B A54 5r multi 4.50 3.00
360C A54 10r multi 9.00 6.00
Nos. 354-360C (10) 16.45 11.15

Issue dates: 20d, 75d, July 3, 1973; 1r-10r, July 1974; others, Jan. 27, 1973.

Flag of Qatar, Handclasp, Sheik Khalifa — A56

Designs (Flag, Sheik and): 35d, Harvest. 55d, Government Building. 1.35r, Market and Clock Tower, Doha. 1.55r, Illuminated fountain.

1973, Oct. 4 Litho. *Perf. 13*

361 A56 15d red & multi 15 15
362 A56 35d buff & multi 20 16
363 A56 55d multi 38 30
364 A56 1.35r vio & multi 1.00 80
365 A56 1.55r multi 1.25 1.00
Nos. 361-365 (5) 2.98 2.41

2nd anniversary of independence.

Planting Tree, Qatar and UN Flags, UNESCO Emblem — A57

Designs (Qatar and UN Flags and): 4d, UN Headquarters and flags. 5d, Pipe laying, cement mixer, helicopter and ILO emblem. 35d, Nurse, patient and UNICEF emblem. 1.35r, Telecommunications and ITU emblem. 3r, Cattle, wheat disease analysis and FAO emblem.

1973, Oct. 24

366 A57 2d multi 15 15
367 A57 4d multi 15 15
368 A57 5d multi 15 15
369 A57 35d multi 25 16
370 A57 1.35r multi 1.00 60
371 A57 3r multi 2.50 1.40
Nos. 366-371 (6) 4.20
Set value 2.30

United Nations Day.

Prison Gates Opening — A58

Designs (Human Rights Flame and): 4d, Marchers with flags. 5d, Scales of Justice. 35d, Teacher and pupils. 1.35r, UN General Assembly. 3r, Human Rights flame, vert.

1973, Dec. Litho. *Perf. 13x13½*

372 A58 2d yel & multi 15 15
373 A58 4d pale lil & multi 15 15
374 A58 5d rose & multi 15 15
375 A58 35d ocher & multi 32 25
376 A58 1.35r lt bl & multi 1.40 1.00
377 A58 3r citron & multi 2.50 2.00
Nos. 372-377 (6) 4.67 3.70

25th anniversary of the Universal Declaration of Human Rights.

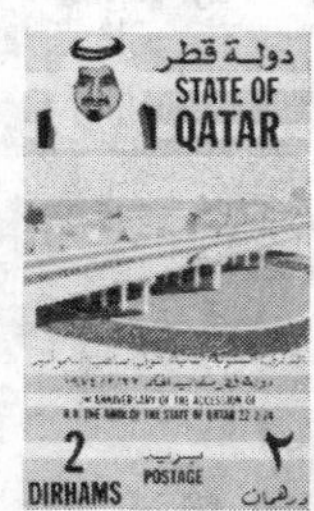

Highway Overpass — A59

1974, Feb. 22 *Perf. 14x13½*

378 A59 2s shown 15 15
379 A59 3d Symbol of learning 15 15
380 A59 5d Oil field 15 15
381 A59 35d Gulf Hotel, Doha 25 20
382 A59 1.55r Radar station 1.40 1.00
383 A59 2.25r Sheik Khalifa 2.00 1.50
Nos. 378-383 (6) 4.10 3.15

2nd anniversary of the accession of Sheik Khalifa as Emir.

Mail Truck, Camel Caravan and UPU Emblem A60

UPU cent.: 3d, Old and new trains, Arab Postal Union emblem. 10d, Old and new ships and Qatar coat of arms. 35d, Old and new planes. 75d, Mail sorting by hand and computer, and Arab Postal Union emblem. 1.25r, Old and new post offices, and Qatar coat of arms.

1974, May 22 Litho. *Perf. 13½*

384 A60 2d brt yel & multi 15 15
385 A60 3d lt bl & multi 15 15
386 A60 10d dp org & multi 15 15
387 A60 35d slate & multi 40 30
388 A60 75d yel & multi 80 60
389 A60 1.25r lt bl & multi 1.40 1.00
Nos. 384-389 (6) 3.05
Set value 2.10

Doha Hospital A61

1974, July 13 Litho. *Perf. 13½*

390 A61 5d shown 15 15
391 A61 10d WPY emblem and people 15 15
392 A61 15d WPY emblem 15 15
393 A61 35d World map 22 20
394 A61 1.75r Clock and infants 1.10 1.00
395 A61 2.25r Family 1.40 1.25
Nos. 390-395 (6) 3.17 2.90

World Population Year 1974.

Television Station — A62

1974, Sept. 2 *Perf. 13½x13*

399 A62 5d shown 15 15
400 A62 10d Palace of Doha 15 15
401 A62 15d Teachers'College 15 15
402 A62 75d Clock Tower and Mosque 65 50
403 A62 1.55r Traffic circle, Doha 1.00 75
404 A62 2.25r Sheik Khalifa 1.60 1.25
Nos. 399-404 (6) 3.70 2.95

3rd anniversary of independence.

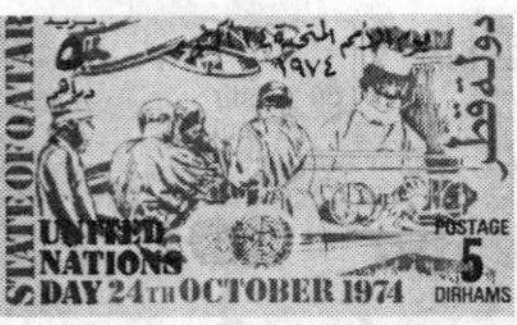

Operating Room and WHO Emblem — A63

United Nations Day: 10d, Satellite earth station and ITU emblem. 20d, Tractor, UN and FAO emblems. 25d, School children, UN and UNESCO emblems. 1.75r, Open air court, UN Headquarters, emblems. 2r, UPU and UN emblems.

1974, Oct. 24 Litho. *Perf. 13x13½*

405 A63 5d multi 15 15
406 A63 10d multi 15 15
407 A63 20d multi 15 15
408 A63 25d multi 16 15
409 A63 1.75r multi 1.10 1.00
410 A63 2r multi 1.40 1.25
Nos. 405-410 (6) 3.11 2.85

VC-10, Gulf Aviation Airliner A64

Arab League and Qatar Flags, Civil Aviation Emblem A65

Design: 25d, Doha Airport.

1974, Dec. 1 Litho. *Perf. 13½*

411 A64 20d multi 25 20
412 A64 25d yel & dk bl 32 25
413 A65 30d multi 40 30
414 A65 50d multi 65 50

Arab Civil Aviation Day.

Caspian Terns, Hoopoes and Shara'o Island A66

Dhow by Moonlight — A67

Designs: 5d, Clock Tower, Doha, vert. 15d, Zubara Fort. 35d, Gulf Hotel and sailboats. 75d, Arabian oryx. 1.25r, Khor Al-Udein. 1.75r, Ruins, Wakrah.

1974, Dec. 21 Litho. *Perf. 13½*

415 A66 5d multi 15 15
416 A66 10d multi 15 15
417 A66 15d multi 15 15
418 A66 35d multi 25 18
419 A67 55d multi 45 35
420 A66 75d multi 65 50
421 A67 1.25r multi 1.20 90
422 A66 1.75r multi 1.75 1.25
Nos. 415-422 (8) 4.75 3.63

Traffic Circle, Doha A68

Sheik Khalifa — A69

Designs: 35d, Pipe line from offshore platform. 55d, Laying underwater pipe line. 1r, Refinery.

1975, Feb. 22 Litho. *Perf. 13½*

423 A68 10d multi 15 15
424 A68 35d multi 55 40
425 A68 55d multi 80 60
426 A68 1r multi 1.75 1.20
427 A69 1.35r sil & multi 2.00 1.50
428 A69 1.55r gold & multi 2.50 1.75
Nos. 423-428 (6) 7.75 5.60

3rd anniversary of the accession of Sheik Khalifa.

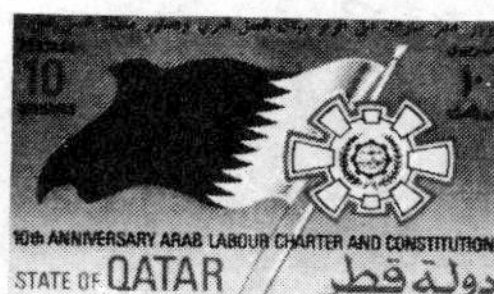

Qatar Flag and Arab Labor Charter Emblem A70

1975, May 28 **Litho.** ***Perf. 13***

429	A70	10d bl red brn & blk	15	15
430	A70	35d multi	42	35
431	A70	1r grn & multi	1.20	1.00

Arab Labor Charter and Constitution, 10th anniversary.

Flintlock Pistol with Ornamental Grip — A71

Designs: 3d, Ornamental mosaic. 35d, View of museum. 75d, Arch and museum, vert. 1.25r, Flint arrowheads and tool. 3r, Gold necklace, vert.

1975, June 23 ***Perf. 13***

432	A71	2d multi	15	15
433	A71	3d ver blk & gold	16	15
434	A71	35d bis & multi	40	25
435	A71	75d ver & multi	90	55
436	A71	1.25r vio & multi	1.50	90
437	A71	3r fawn & multi	3.50	2.00
		Nos. 432-437 (6)	6.61	4.00

Opening of Qatar National Museum.

Traffic Signs, Policeman, Doha — A72

Designs: 15d, 55d, Cars, arrows, traffic lights, Doha Clock Tower. 35d, like 5d.

1975, June 24

438	A72	5d lt grn & multi	15	15
439	A72	15d lt bl & multi	30	18
440	A72	35d lem & multi	70	45
441	A72	55d lt vio & multi	1.10	75

Traffic Week.

Constitution, Arabic Text — A73

Designs: 5d, Government buildings, horiz. 1 5d, Museum and Clock Tower, horiz. 55d, 1.25r, Sheik Khalifa and Qatar flag. 75d, Constitution, English text.

1975, Sept. 2

442	A73	5d multi	15	15
443	A73	15d multi	28	25
444	A73	35d multi	32	30
445	A73	55d multi	50	45
446	A73	75d multi	65	60
447	A73	1.25r multi	1.10	1.00
		Nos. 442-447 (6)	3.00	2.75

4th anniversary of independence.

Satellite over Globe, ITU Emblem A74

UN, 30th anniv.: 15d, UN Headquarters, NY and UN emblem. 35d, UPU emblem over Eastern Arabia, UN emblem. 1r, Nurses and infant, WHO emblem. 1.25r, Road building equipment, ILO emblem. 2r, Students, UNESCO emblem.

1975, Oct. 25 **Litho.** ***Perf. 13x13½***

448	A74	5d multi	15	15
449	A74	15d multi	20	15
450	A74	35d multi	25	18
451	A74	1r multi	65	50
452	A74	1.25r multi	80	60
453	A74	2r multi	1.40	1.00
		Nos. 448-453 (6)	3.45	2.58

Fertilizer Plant A75

Designs: 10d, Flour mill, vert. 35d, Natural gas plant. 75d, Oil refinery. 1.25r, Cement works. 1.55r, Steel mill.

1975, Dec. 6

454	A75	5d sal & multi	15	15
455	A75	10d yel & multi	18	15
456	A75	35d multi	42	25
457	A75	75d multi	90	60
458	A75	1.25r mag & multi	1.60	1.00
459	A75	1.55r multi	2.25	1.40
		Nos. 454-459 (6)	5.50	3.55

Modern Building, Doha A76

Designs: 10d, 35d, 1.55r, Various modern buildings. 55d, 75d, Sheik Khalifa and Qatar flag (diff. designs).

1976, Feb. 22 **Litho.** ***Perf. 13***

460	A76	5d multi	15	15
461	A76	10d multi	15	15
462	A76	35d multi	25	20
463	A76	55d multi	38	30
464	A76	75d multi	55	45
465	A76	1.55r multi	1.10	90
		Nos. 460-465 (6)	2.58	2.15

4th anniversary of accession of Sheik Khalifa.

Satellite Earth Station — A77

Designs: 55d, 1r, Satellite. 75d, Like 35d.

1976, Mar. 1

466	A77	35d multi	40	22
467	A77	55d dp bis & multi	55	30
468	A77	75d vermilion & multi	80	45
469	A77	1r vio & multi	1.00	60

Inauguration of satellite earth station in Qatar.

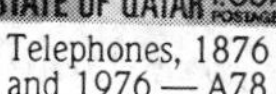

Telephones, 1876 and 1976 — A78

Arabian Soccer League Emblem — A79

1976, Mar. 10

470	A78	1r rose & multi	1.00	75
471	A78	1.35r lt bl & multi	1.40	1.00

Centenary of first telephone call by Alexander Graham Bell, Mar. 10, 1876.

1976, Mar. 25 **Litho.** ***Perf. 13½x13***

Designs: 10d, 1.25r, Stadium, Doha. 35d, Like 5d. 55d, Players. 75d, One player.

472	A79	5d lil & multi	15	15
473	A79	10d pink & multi	15	15
474	A79	35d bl grn & multi	30	25
475	A79	55d multi	48	40
476	A79	75d multi	72	60
477	A79	1.25r multi	1.25	1.00
		Nos. 472-477 (6)	3.05	2.55

4th Arabian Gulf Soccer Cup Tournament, Doha, Mar. 22-Apr.

Dhow A80

Designs: Various dhows.

1976, Apr. 19 ***Perf. 13½x14***

478	A80	10d blue & multi	15	15
479	A80	35d blue & multi	28	20
480	A80	80d blue & multi	60	45
481	A80	1.25r blue & multi	1.00	75
482	A80	1.50r blue & multi	1.20	90
483	A80	2r blue & multi	2.00	1.40
		Nos. 478-483 (6)	5.23	3.85

Soccer — A81

Designs (Olympic Rings and): 10d, Yachting. 35d, Steeplechase. 80d, Boxing. 1.25r, Weight lifting. 1.50r, Basketball.

1976, May 15 **Litho.** ***Perf. 14x13½***

484	A81	5d multi	15	15
485	A81	10d bl & multi	15	15
486	A81	35d org & multi	22	20
487	A81	80d bis & multi	45	40
488	A81	1.25r lil & multi	85	75
489	A81	1.50r rose & multi	1.10	1.00
		Nos. 484-489 (6)	2.92	2.65

21st Olympic Games, Montreal, Canada, July 17-Aug. 1.

Village and Emblems — A82

Designs (UN and Habitat Emblems): 35d, Emblems. 80d, Village. 1.25r, Sheik Khalifa.

1976, May 31 ***Perf. 13½x14***

490	A82	10d org & multi	15	15
491	A82	35d yel & multi	28	20
492	A82	80d citron & multi	60	45
493	A82	1.25r dp bl & multi	1.00	75

Habitat, UN Conf. on Human Settlements, Vancouver, Canada, May 31-June 11.

Snowy Plover A83

Birds: 10d, Great cormorant. 35d, Osprey. 80d, Flamingo. 1.25r, Rock thrush. 2r, Saker falcon. 35d, 80d, 1.25r, 2r, vertical.

Perf. 13½x14, 14x13½

1976, July 19 **Litho.**

494	A83	5d multi	15	15
495	A83	10d multi	22	15
496	A83	35d multi	60	28
497	A83	80d multi	1.10	65
498	A83	1.25r multi	1.90	1.10
499	A83	2r multi	2.25	1.60
		Nos. 494-499 (6)	6.22	3.93

Sheik Khalifa and Qatar Flag — A84

Government Building — A85

Designs: 10d, like 5d. 80d, Government building. 1.25r, Offshore oil platform. 1.50r, UN emblem and Qatar coat of arms.

Perf. 14x13½, 13½x14

1976, Sept. 2

500	A84	5d gold & multi	15	15
501	A84	10d silver & multi	15	15
502	A85	40d multi	32	25
503	A85	80d multi	65	50
504	A85	1.25r multi	1.00	75
505	A85	1.50r multi	1.25	90
		Nos. 500-505 (6)	3.52	2.70

5th anniversary of independence.

Qatar Flag and UN Emblem A86

1976, Oct. 24 **Litho.** ***Perf. 13½x14***

506	A86	2r multi	2.50	1.25
507	A86	3r multi	3.50	1.75

United Nations Day 1976.

A87 Sheik Khalifa — A88 Sheik Khalifa

1977, Feb. 22 Litho. *Perf. 14x13½*

508 A87 20d silver & multi 20 15
509 A87 1.80r gold & multi 1.90 1.40

5th anniversary of the accession of Sheik Khalifa.

1977, Mar. 1 Litho. *Perf. 14x14½*

Size: 22x27mm

510 A88 5d multi 15 15
511 A88 10d aqua & multi 15 15
512 A88 35d org & multi 28 15
513 A88 80d multi 60 32

Perf. 13½

Size: 25x30mm

514 A88 1r vio bl & multi 1.00 45
515 A88 5r yel & multi 3.75 2.25
516 A88 10r multi 9.50 4.50
Nos. 510-516 (7) 15.43 7.97

Letter, APU Emblem, Flag — A89

1977, Apr. 12 *Perf. 14x13½*

517 A89 35d blue & multi 25 25
518 A89 1.35r blue & multi 1.00 1.00

Arab Postal Union, 25th anniversary.

Waves and Sheik Khalifa A90

1977, May 17 Litho. *Perf. 13½x14*

519 A90 35d multi 25 25
520 A90 1.80r multi 1.50 1.50

World Telecommunications Day.

Sheik Khalifa — A90a

Perf. 13½x13

1977, June 29 Litho. Wmk. 368

520A A90a 5d multi 15 15
520B A90a 10d multi 15 15
520C A90a 35d multi 20 20
520D A90a 80d multi 45 45
e. Bklt. pane of 10 (4 5d, 3 10d, 2 35d, 80d) 6.00 6.00
Set value 75 75

Issued in booklets only.

Parliament, Clock Tower, Minaret — A91

Designs: No. 522, Main business district, Doha. No. 523, Highway crossings, Doha.

1977, Sept. 1 Litho. *Perf. 13x13½*

521 A91 80d multi 80 65
522 A91 80d multi 80 65
523 A91 80d multi 80 65

6th anniversary of independence.

UN Emblem, Flag — A92

1977, Oct. 24 Litho. *Perf. 13½x14*

524 A92 20d grn & multi 15 15
525 A92 1r bl & multi 75 75

United Nations Day.

Surgery A93

Designs: 20d, Steel mill. 1r, Classroom. 5r, Sheik Khalifa.

1978, Feb. 22 Litho. *Perf. 13½x14*

526 A93 20d multi 15 15
527 A93 80d multi 40 40
528 A93 1r multi 50 50
529 A93 5r multi 2.50 2.50

6th anniversary of the accession of Sheik Khalifa.

Oil Refinery — A94

Designs: 80d, Office buildings, Doha. 1.35r, Traffic Circle, Doha. 1.80r, Sheik Khalifa and flag.

1978, Aug. 31 Litho. *Perf. 13½x14*

530 A94 35d multi 24 20
531 A94 80d multi 60 50
532 A94 1.35r multi 90 75
533 A94 1.80r multi 1.25 1.00

7th anniversary of independence.

Man Learning to Read A95

1978, Sept. 8 Litho. *Perf. 13½x14*

534 A95 35d multi 24 20
535 A95 80d multi 75 65

International Literacy Day.

Flag and UN Emblem A96

1978, Oct. 14 *Perf. 13x13½*

536 A96 35d multi 24 20
537 A96 80d multi 75 65

United Nations Day.

Human Rights Emblem — A97

IYC Emblem — A98

Designs: 80d, like 35d. 1.25r, 1.80r, Scales and Human Rights emblem.

1978, Dec. 10 Litho. *Perf. 14x13½*

538 A97 35d multi 22 22
539 A97 80d multi 60 60
540 A97 1.25r multi 80 80
541 A97 1.80r multi 1.25 1.25

30th anniversary of Universal Declaration of Human Rights.

Wmk. JEZ Multiple (368)

1979, Jan. 1 Litho. *Perf. 13½x13*

542 A98 35d multi 25 25
543 A98 1.80r multi 1.25 1.25

International Year of the Child.

Sheik Khalifa

A99 — A100

1979, Jan. 15 Unwmk. *Perf. 14*

544 A99 5d multi 15 15
545 A99 10d multi 15 15
546 A99 20d multi 15 15
547 A99 25d multi 16 15
548 A99 35d multi 20 16
549 A99 60d multi 40 30
550 A99 80d multi 55 40

Size: 27x32mm

551 A99 1r multi 65 50
552 A99 1.25r multi 80 60
553 A99 1.35r multi 1.00 75
554 A99 1.80r multi 1.20 90
555 A99 5r multi 3.25 2.50
556 A99 10r multi 6.50 5.00
Nos. 544-556 (13) 15.16 11.71

1979, Feb. 22 Wmk. 368

557 A100 35d multi 20 20
558 A100 80d multi 50 50
559 A100 1r multi 60 60
560 A100 1.25r multi 75 75

7th anniv. of accession of Sheik Khalifa.

Cables and People — A101

1979, May 17 Litho. *Perf. 14x13½*

561 A101 2r multi 1.10 1.10
562 A101 2.80r multi 1.40 1.40

World Telecommunications Day.

Children Holding Globe, UNESCO Emblem A102

Perf. 13x13½

1979, July 15 Litho. Unwmk.

563 A102 35d multi 24 20
564 A102 80d multi 75 60

International Bureau of Education, Geneva, 50th anniversary.

Rolling Mill — A103 UN Day — A104

Perf. 13½

1979, Sept. 2 Litho. Wmk. 368

565 A103 5d shown 15 15
566 A103 10d Doha, aerial view 15 15
567 A103 1.25r Qatar flag 75 75
568 A103 2r Sheik Khalifa 1.00 1.00

Independence, 8th anniversary.

1979, Oct. 24 Litho. *Perf. 13½x13*

569 A104 1.25r multi 75 75
570 A104 2r multi 1.25 1.25

Conference Emblem — A105

1979, Nov. 24 *Perf. 13x13½*

571 A105 35d multi 32 25
572 A105 1.80r multi 1.60 1.25

Hegira (Pilgrimage Year); 3rd World Conference on Prophets.

Sheik Khalifa, 8th Anniversary of Accession — A106

1980, Feb. 22 Litho. *Perf. 13x13½*

573 A106 20d multi 15 15
574 A106 60d multi 35 35
575 A106 1.25r multi 65 65
576 A106 2r multi 1.25 1.25

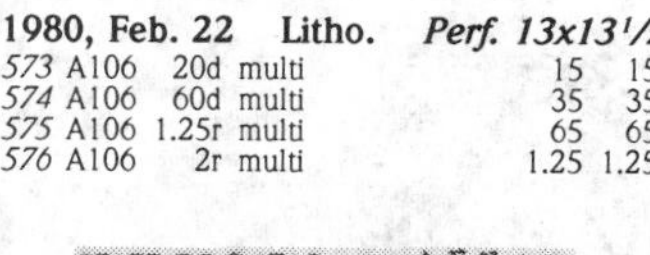

Map of Arab Countries — A107

1980, Mar. 1 Litho. *Perf. 13½x14*

577 A107 2.35r multi 1.50 95
578 A107 2.80r multi 1.75 1.15

6th Congress of Arab Town Organization, Doha, Mar. 1-4.

Oil Refinery A108

1980, Sept. 2 Litho. *Perf. 14½*

579 A108 10d shown 15 15
580 A108 35d View of Doha 32 25
581 A108 2r Oil rig 1.50 1.10
582 A108 2.35r Hospital 1.75 1.65

9th anniversary of independence.

Men Holding OPEC Emblem — A109

United Nations Day 1980 — A110

1980, Sept. 15 *Perf. 14x13½*

583 A109 1.35r multi 90 60
584 A109 2r multi 1.40 90

OPEC, 20th anniversary.

1980, Oct. 24

585 A110 1.35r multi 90 60
586 A110 1.80r multi 1.10 80

Hegira (Pilgrimage Year) — A111

1980, Nov. 8 Litho. *Perf. 14½*

587 A111 10d multi 15 15
588 A111 35d multi 24 24
589 A111 1.25r multi 80 80
590 A111 2.80r multi 1.90 1.90

International Year of the Disabled — A112

1981, Jan. 5 Photo. *Perf. 11½*
Granite Paper

591 A112 2r multi 1.40 1.00
592 A112 3r multi 2.00 1.50

Education Day — A113

Sheik Khalifa, 9th Anniversary of Accession — A114

Perf. 14x13½

1981, Feb. 22 Litho. Wmk. 368

593 A113 2r multi 1.20 80
594 A113 3r multi 1.90 1.25

1981, Feb. 22

595 A114 10d multi 15 15
596 A114 35d multi 20 15
597 A114 80d multi 50 35
598 A114 5r multi 3.50 2.25

A115

A116

1981, May 17 Litho. *Perf. 13½x13*

599 A115 2r multi 1.50 95
600 A115 2.80r multi 1.90 1.25

13th World Telecommunications Day.

1981, June 11 Litho. *Perf. 14x13½*

Championship emblem.

601 A116 1.25r multi 1.10 55
602 A116 2.80r multi 2.50 1.25

30th Intl. Military Soccer Championship, Doha.

10th Anniv. of Independence — A117

Perf. 13½x14

1981, Sept. 2 Litho. Wmk. 368

603 A117 5d multi 15 15
604 A117 60d multi 50 32
605 A117 80d multi 65 40
606 A117 5r multi 3.75 2.75

World Food Day A118

1981, Oct. 16 Litho. *Perf. 13*

607 A118 2r multi 1.25 80
608 A118 2.80r multi 1.75 1.15

Red Crescent Society — A119

1982, Jan. 16 Litho. *Perf. 14x13½*

609 A119 20d multi 20 15
610 A119 2.80r multi 2.75 2.00

10th Anniv. of Sheik Khalifa's Accession — A120

Perf. 13½x14

1982, Feb. 22 Litho. Wmk. 368

611 A120 10d multi 15 15
612 A120 20d multi 15 15
613 A120 1.25r multi 1.00 65
614 A120 2.80r multi 2.00 1.40

Sheik Khalifa A121

Oil Refinery A122

Designs: 5r, 10r, 15r, Hoda Clock Tower.

1982, Mar. 1 Photo. *Perf. 11½x12*
Granite Paper

615 A121 5d multi 15 15
616 A121 10d multi 15 15
617 A121 15d multi 15 15
618 A121 20d multi 15 15
619 A121 25d multi 15 15
620 A121 35d multi 20 15
621 A121 60d multi 32 25
622 A121 80d multi 45 35
623 A122 1r multi 60 45
624 A122 1.25r multi 75 55
625 A122 2r multi 1.20 90
626 A122 5r multi 3.00 2.25
627 A122 10r multi 6.00 4.50
628 A122 15r multi 8.50 6.50
Nos. 615-628 (14) 21.77 16.65

Hamad General Hospital A123

1982, Mar. Litho. *Perf. 13x13½*

629 A123 10d multi 15 15
630 A123 2.35r multi 1.90 1.40

6th Anniv. of United Arab Shipping Co. A124

1982, Mar. 6 Litho. *Perf. 13x13½*

631 A124 20d multi 15 15
632 A124 2.35r multi 1.90 1.40

A125

A126

1982, Apr. 12 Litho. *Perf. 13½x13*

633 A125 35d yel & multi 25 18
634 A125 2.80r bl & multi 2.00 1.40

30th anniv. of Arab Postal Union.

1982, Sept. 2 Litho. *Perf. 13½x13*

635 A126 10d multi 15 15
636 A126 80d multi 55 40
637 A126 1.25r multi 90 65
638 A126 2.80r multi 2.00 1.40

11th anniv. of Independence.

World Communications Year — A127

1983, Jan. 10 Litho. *Perf. 13½x13*

639 A127 35d multi 30 15
640 A127 2.80r multi 2.25 1.15

Gulf Postal Org., 2nd Conference, Doha, Apr. — A128

1983, Apr. 9 Litho. *Perf. 13½x14*

641 A128 1r multi 75 40
642 A128 1.35r multi 1.00 55

A129

A130

1983, Sept. 2 Litho. *Perf. 14*

643 A129 10d multi 15 15
644 A129 35d multi 25 15
645 A129 80d multi 60 32
646 A129 2.80r multi 2.25 1.15

12th anniv. of Independence.

1983, Nov. 7 Litho. *Perf. 13½x14*

647 A130 35d multi 30 15
648 A130 2.80r multi 2.25 1.10

GCC Supreme Council, 4th regular session.

35th Anniv. of UN Declaration of Human Rights — A131

1983, Dec. 10 Litho. *Perf. 13½x14*

649 A131 1.25r Globe, emblem 1.40 68
650 A131 2.80r Scale 2.50 1.50

A132 A133

1984, Mar. 1 Litho. *Perf. 13x13½*

651 A132 15d multi 15 15
652 A132 40d multi 28 25
653 A132 50d multi 35 32

Perf. 14½x13½

654 A133 1r multi 65 60
655 A133 1.50r multi 1.00 90
656 A133 2.50r multi 1.65 1.50
657 A133 3r multi 1.90 1.75
658 A133 5r multi 3.25 3.00
659 A133 10r multi 6.50 6.00
Nos. 651-659 (9) 15.73 14.47

See Nos. 707-709.

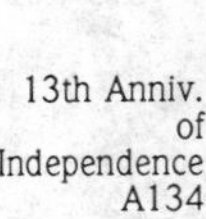

13th Anniv. of Independence A134

1984, Sept. 2 Photo. *Perf. 12*

660 A134 15d multi 15 15
661 A134 1r multi 80 54
662 A134 2.50r multi 1.75 1.35
663 A134 3.50r multi 2.50 1.90

Literacy Day, 1984 — A135

40th Anniv., ICAO — A136

1984, Sept. 8 Litho. *Perf. 14x13½*

664 A135 1r lilac & multi 75 54
665 A135 1r orange & multi 75 54

1984, Dec. 7 Litho. *Perf. 13½x13*

666 A136 20d multi 22 15
667 A136 3.50r multi 3.50 1.90

League of Arab States, 40th Anniv. A137

1985, Mar. 22 Photo. *Perf. 11½*

668 A137 50d multi 38 25
669 A137 4r multi 3.00 2.00

Intl. Youth Year — A138

Traffic Crossing — A139

Perf. 11½x12

1985, Mar. 4 Granite Paper

670 A138 50d multi 75 25
671 A138 1r multi 1.60 50

1985, Mar. 9 *Perf. 14x13½*

672 A139 1r lt bl & multi 90 50
673 A139 1r pink & multi 90 50

Gulf Cooperation Council Traffic Safety Week, Mar. 16-22.

Natl. Independence, 14th Anniv. — A140

Perf. 11½x12

1985, Sept. 2 Granite Paper

674 A140 40d Doha 28 20
675 A140 50d Earth satellite station 32 25
676 A140 1.50r Oil refinery 1.00 75
677 A140 4r Storage facility 2.75 2.00

Org. of Petroleum Exporting Countries, 25th Anniv. — A141

1985, Sept. 14 *Perf. 13½x14*

678 A141 1r brt yel grn & multi 75 50
679 A141 1r salmon rose & multi 75 50

UN, 40th Anniv. A142

1985, Oct. 24 Litho. *Perf. 13½x14*

680 A142 1r multi 65 50
681 A142 3r multi 2.00 1.50

Population and Housing Census — A143

1986, Mar. 1 Photo. *Perf. 11½x12*

682 A143 1r multi 80 55
683 A143 3r multi 2.25 1.65

United Arab Shipping Co., 10th Anniv. — A144

1986, May 30 Litho. *Perf. 13½x14*

684 A144 1.50r Qatari ibn al Fuja'a 1.00 85
685 A144 4r Al Wajba 2.75 2.25

Natl. Independence, 15th Anniv. — A145

Perf. 13x13½

1986, Sept. 2 Litho. Unwmk.

686 A145 40d multi 28 22
687 A145 50d multi 40 30
688 A145 1r multi 80 58
689 A145 4r multi 3.00 2.25

Sheik Khalifa — A146

1987, Jan. 1 Photo. *Perf. 11½x12*

Granite Paper

690 A146 15r multi 8.50 8.50
691 A146 20r multi 11.00 11.00
692 A146 30r multi 17.00 17.00

15th Anniv. of Sheik Khalifa's Accession A147

1987, Feb. 22 *Perf. 12x11½*

Granite Paper

693 A147 50d multi 35 30
694 A147 1r multi 65 58
695 A147 1.50r multi 1.00 85
696 A147 4r multi 2.75 2.25

Arab Postal Union, 35th Anniv. — A148

Perf. 14x13½

1987, Apr. 12 Litho. Unwmk.

697 A148 1r multi 58 58
698 A148 1.50r multi 85 85

Natl. Independence, 16th Anniv. — A149

1987, Sept. 2 Litho. *Perf. 13x13½*

699 A149 25d Housing complex 15 15
700 A149 75d Water tower, city 42 42
701 A149 2r Modern office building 1.15 1.15
702 A149 4r Oil refinery 2.25 2.25

A150 A151

Perf. 13½x13

1987, Sept. 8 Litho. Unwmk.

703 A150 1.50r multi 85 85
704 A150 4r multi 2.25 2.25

Intl. Literacy Day.

Perf. 14x13½

1987, Apr. 24 Litho. Wmk. 368

705 A151 1r multicolored 80 58
706 A151 4r multicolored 3.00 2.25

Gulf Environment Day.

Sheik Type of 1984

1988, Jan. 1 *Perf. 13x13½*

Size of 25d, 75d: 22x27mm

707 A133 25d multicolored 20 15
708 A133 75d multicolored 60 45

Perf. 14½x13

709 A133 2r multicolored 1.50 1.15

This is an expanding set. Numbers will change if necessary.

WHO, 40th Anniv. — A152

1988, Apr. 7 *Perf. 14x13½*

714 A152 1.50r multicolored 1.15 88
715 A152 2r multicolored 1.50 1.15

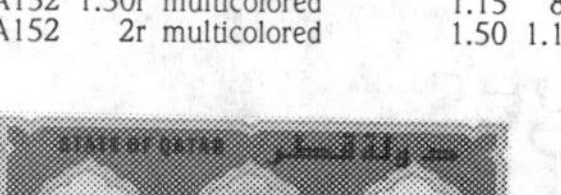

Independence, 17th Anniv. — A153

Perf. 11½x12
1988, Sept. 2 Litho. Unwmk.
Granite Paper

716 A153 50d multicolored 40 30
717 A153 75d multicolored 60 45
718 A153 1.50r multicolored 1.15 88
719 A153 2r multicolored 1.50 1.15

Opening of the Doha General P.O. — A154

1988, Sept. 3 *Perf. 13x13½*

720 A154 1.50r multicolored 1.15 88
721 A154 4r multicolored 3.00 2.30

Arab Housing Day — A155

Perf. 11½x12
1988, Oct. 3 Granite Paper

722 A155 1.50r multicolored 1.15 88
723 A155 4r multicolored 3.00 2.30

A156

A157

Perf. 14x13½
1988, Dec. 10 Wmk. 368

724 A156 1.50r multicolored 1.15 88
725 A156 2r multicolored 1.50 1.15

Declaration of Human Rights, 40th anniv.

Perf. 12x11½
1989, May 17 Unwmk.
Granite Paper

726 A157 2r multicolored 1.50 1.15
727 A157 4r multicolored 3.00 2.30

World Telecommunications Day.

Qatar Red Crescent Soc., 10th Anniv. — A158

Perf. 13½x14
1989, Aug. 8 Wmk. 368

728 A158 4r multicolored 3.00 2.30

Natl. Independence, 18th Anniv. — A159

Perf. 13x13½
1989, Sept. 2 Unwmk.

729 A159 75d multicolored 60 45
730 A159 1r multicolored 80 60
731 A159 1.50r multicolored 1.15 88
732 A159 2r multicolored 1.50 1.15

Gulf Air, 40th Anniv. A160

1990, Mar. 24 Litho. *Perf. 13x13½*

733 A160 50d multicolored 30 20
734 A160 75d multicolored 45 30
735 A160 4r multicolored 2.40 1.60

Independence, 19th Anniv. A161

Designs: 75d, Map, sunburst. 1.50r, 2r, Swordsman, musicians.

1990, Sept. 2 *Perf. 14x13½*

736 A161 50d multicolored 30 20
737 A161 75d multicolored 45 30
738 A161 1.50r multicolored 90 60
739 A161 2r multicolored 1.20 80

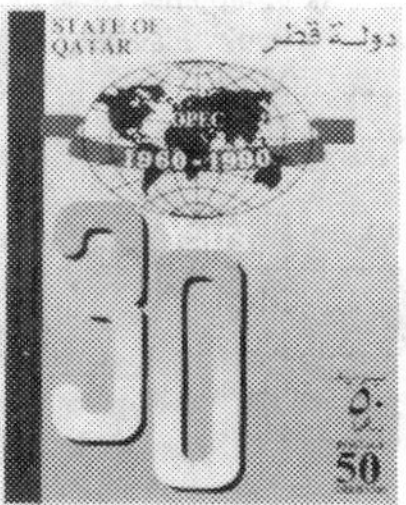

Organization of Petroleum Exporting Countries (OPEC), 30th Anniv. A162

1990, Sept. 14

740 A162 50d shown 30 20
741 A162 1.50r Flags 90 60

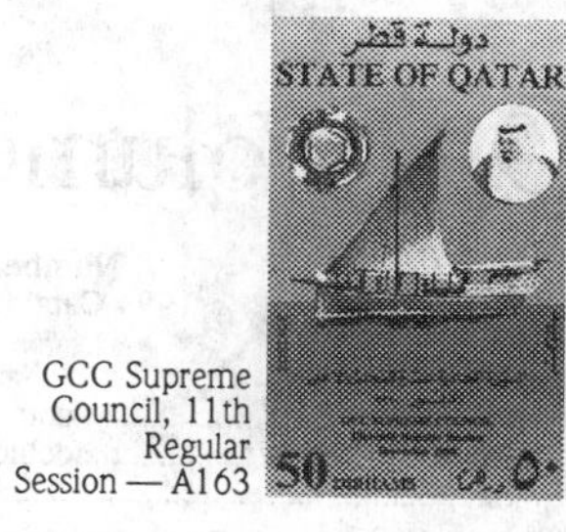

GCC Supreme Council, 11th Regular Session — A163

Designs: 1r, Leaders of member nations. 1.50r, Flag, council emblem. 2r, State seal, emblem.

Perf. 14x13½
1990, Dec. Litho. Wmk. 368

742 A163 50d multicolored 30 20
743 A163 1r multicolored 55 40
744 A163 1.50r multicolored 85 60
745 A163 2r multicolored 55 40

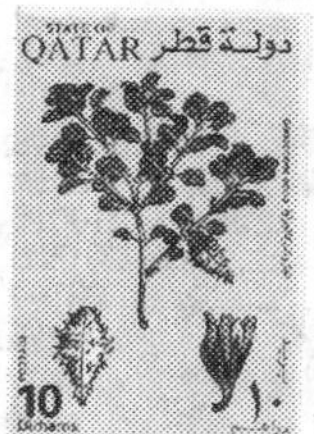

Plants — A164

Perf. 12½x13½
1991, June 20 Litho. Wmk. 368

747 A164 10d Glossonema edule 15 15
750 A164 25d Lycium shawii 22 15
752 A164 50d Acacia tortilis 45 30
754 A164 75d Acacia ehrenbergiana 68 45
756 A164 1r Capparis spinosa 90 60
759 A164 4r Cymhopogon parkeri 3.60 2.40
Nos. 747-759 (6) 6.00 4.05

This is an expanding set. Numbers may change.

Independence, 20th Anniv. — A165

1991, Aug. 15 Litho. *Perf. 14x14½*
Granite Paper

762 A165 25d shown 15 15
763 A165 75d red vio & multi 42 28

Perf. 14½x14

764 A165 1r Doha skyline, horiz. 58 38
765 A165 1.50r Palace, horiz. 90 58

Fish A166

Various species of fish.

1991, Dec. 1 *Perf. 14x13½*

767 A166 10d multicolored 15 15
768 A166 15d multicolored 15 15
770 A166 25d multicolored 15 15
772 A166 50d multicolored 28 20
773 A166 75d multicolored 42 28
774 A166 1r multicolored 58 38
775 A166 1.50r multicolored 90 58
776 A166 2r multicolored 1.15 78
Nos. 767-776 (8) 3.78 2.67

This is an expanding set. Numbers may change.

Sheik Khalifa, 20th Anniv. of Accession
A167 A168

Perf. 14x13½
1992, Feb. 22 Litho. Wmk. 368

781 A167 25d multicolored 15 15
782 A167 50d multicolored 30 18
783 A168 75d multicolored 45 28
784 A168 1.50r multicolored 90 58

World Health Day A169

1992, Apr. 7 *Perf. 14x13½, 13½x14*

785 A169 50d Heart with face, vert. 30 18
786 A169 1.50r shown 90 58

Children's Paintings A170

1992, June 15 Unwmk. *Perf. 11½*

787 A170 25d Girls dancing 15 15
788 A170 50d Children playing 30 18
789 A170 75d Ships 45 28
790 A170 1.50r Fishing from boats 90 58

QUELIMANE

LOCATION — A district of the Mozambique Province in Portuguese East Africa
GOVT. — Part of the Portuguese East Africa Colony
AREA — 39,800 sq. mi.
POP. — 877,000 (approx.)
CAPITAL — Quelimane

This district was formerly a part of Zambezia. Quelimane stamps were replaced by those of Mozambique.

100 Centavos = 1 Escudo

Vasco da Gama Issue of Various Portuguese Colonies Surcharged as

REPUBLICA
QUELIMANE
¼ C.

1913 Unwmk. *Perf. 12½ to 16*
On Stamps of Macao

1 CD20 ¼c on ½a bl grn 1.75 3.50
2 CD21 ½c on 1a red 1.75 3.00
3 CD22 1c on 2a red vio 1.75 3.00
4 CD23 2½c on 4a yel grn 1.75 3.00
5 CD24 5c on 8a dk bl 1.75 3.00
6 CD25 7½c on 12a vio brn 2.50 4.50
7 CD26 10c on 16a bis brn 1.75 3.00
a. Inverted surcharge 22.50
8 CD27 15c on 24a bis 1.75 3.00
Nos. 1-8 (8) 14.75 26.00

On Stamps of Portuguese Africa

9	CD20	¼c on 2½r bl grn	1.75	3.00
10	CD21	½c on 5r red	1.75	3.00
11	CD22	1c on 10r red vio	1.75	3.00
12	CD23	2½c on 25r yel grn	1.75	3.00
13	CD24	5c on 50r dk bl	2.00	3.25
14	CD25	7½c on 75r vio brn	2.50	4.50
15	CD26	10c on 100r bis	1.75	3.00
16	CD27	15c on 150r bis	1.75	3.00
		Nos. 9-16 (8)	15.00	25.75

On Stamps of Timor

17	CD20	¼c on ½a bl grn	1.75	3.00
18	CD21	½c on 1a red	1.75	3.00
19	CD22	1c on 2a red vio	1.75	3.00
20	CD23	2½c on 4a yel grn	1.75	3.00
21	CD24	5c on 8a dk bl	1.75	3.00
22	CD25	7½c on 12a vio brn	2.50	4.50
23	CD26	10c on 16a bis brn	1.75	3.00
24	CD27	15c on 24a bis	1.75	3.00
		Nos. 17-24 (8)	14.75	25.50
		Nos. 1-24 (24)	44.50	77.25

Ceres — A1

1914 **Typo.** ***Perf. 15x14***

Name and Value in Black

25	A1	¼c	olive brn	80	*3.00*
26	A1	½c	black	1.25	*3.00*
27	A1	1c	blue green	1.10	*3.00*
a.	Imperf.				
28	A1	1½c	lilac brn	1.65	*3.00*
29	A1	2c	carmine	1.75	*3.00*
30	A1	2½c	lt vio	50	*1.50*
31	A1	5c	deep blue	1.25	*3.00*
32	A1	7½c	yel brn	1.25	*3.00*
33	A1	8c	slate	1.35	*3.00*
34	A1	10c	org brn	1.25	*3.00*
35	A1	15c	plum	3.00	*5.00*
36	A1	20c	yel grn	1.50	*2.50*
37	A1	30c	brn, *grn*	4.00	*8.50*
38	A1	40c	brn, *pink*	4.00	*8.50*
39	A1	50c	org, *salmon*	4.00	*9.50*
40	A1	1e	green, *blue*	5.00	*11.00*
			Nos. 25-40 (16)	33.65	*73.50*

1994 Volume 4 Number Changes

Number in 1993 Catalogue	Number in 1994 Catalogue
Korea	
3-5	footnoted
35a, 36a, 36c, 37c, 37f	footnoted
957	963
969	966
Laos	
C56a	C57a
C57a	C56a
Liberia	
944-945	945-946
Macao	
638a	deleted
Madagascar	
985	C193
1000A	1001A
1001A	1001B
1001B-1001H	1001C-1001I
C193	C194
Mexico	
1579	1583
1581	1584
1583	1585
1587	1586
1589-1590	1587-1588
1592-1592A	1589-1590
1593-1598	1591-1596
1600-1600A	1597-1598
1601-1601A	1599-1600
1602-1602A	1601-1602
1769-1772	1765-1768
1774	1769
1776	1770
Montenegro	
J15a	footnoted
Netherlands	
545a	541a
Netherlands Antilles	
48a, 49a	deleted
Nicaragua	
1781-1812	deleted
C1197-C1203	deleted
Philippines	
154	footnoted
2058-2065B	2061-2070
2066-2069	2072-2075
Poland	
2K13-2K19	footnoted
Portugal	
1800-1801	1841-1842
1802	1846
1803	1856
Qatar	
99-102	100-100C
103-104	122-122A
105-108	124-125C
109-115	125-125F
116-121	126-126E
122-127	127-127E

Numerical Index of Volume 4 Watermark Illustrations

Watermark	Country
3	New Hebrides
104	Philippines
108	Latvia
109	Lithuania
110	Luxembourg
108	Latvia
109	Lithuania
110	Luxembourg
117	Nicaragua
125	Marshall Islands
140	Oltre Giuba
141	Manchukuo
141-142	Japan
143	Liberia
144-147	Lithuania
145	Latvia
145	Poland
148	Lubeck
149	Luxembourg
150-155	Mexico
156	Mexico
157	Modena
158	Netherlands
159-160	Norway
162	Prussia
170	Mongolia
181	Latvia
183	Liechtenstein
190-191	Philippines
195	Libya
197	Latvia
198	Lithuania
202	Netherlands
	Netherlands Antilles
	Netherlands Indies
212	Latvia
213, 216	Luxembourg
229	Panama
232	Macao
233	Philippines
234	Poland
238	Lithuania
239	Manchukuo
242	Manchukuo
246-247	Luxembourg
248	Mexico
257	Japan
	Korea
257	Philippines
	Ryukyu Islands
260	Mexico
265	Latvia
272	Mexico
279	Mexico
296	Liechtenstein
300	Mexico
305	Jordan
308	Qatar
310	Libya
311	Panama
312	Korea
313	German Dem. Rep.
314	New Hebrides
317	Korea
319-320	Paraguay
322	Qatar
326	Poland
328	Jordan
334	Panama
	Thailand
343	Panama
347	Paraguay
350	Mexico
365	Panama
372	Philippines
377	Panama
389	Philippines
391	Philippines

Notes

Notes

Notes

Notes

Index and Identifier

A & T ovptd. on French Colonies .Vol. 2
Aberdeen, Miss. ....Vol. 1
Abingdon, Va. ....Vol. 1
Abu Dhabi ....Vol. 2
Abyssinia (Ethiopia) ....Vol. 3
A Certo ovptd. on stamps of Peru 758
Acores ....Vol. 2
Aden ....Vol. 1
AEF ....Vol. 3
Aegean Islands (Greek Occupation) ....Vol. 3
Aegean Islands (Italian Occupation) ....Vol. 3
Aeroport International de Kandahar ....Vol. 2
Afars and Issas ....Vol. 2
Afghanistan ....Vol. 2
Africa Occidental Espanola ....Vol. 5
Africa, British Offices ....Vol. 1
Africa, German East ....Vol. 3
Africa, German South-West ....Vol. 3
Africa, Italian East ....Vol. 3
Africa, Orientale Italiana ....Vol. 3
Africa, Portuguese 886
Afrique Equatoriale Francaise ....390, Vol. 3, Vol. 5
Afrique Francaise ....Vol. 3
Afrique Occidentale Francaise ....Vol. 3
Aguera, La ....Vol. 2
Aitutaki ....Vol. 1
Ajman ....Vol. 2
Aland Islands ....Vol. 3
Alaouites ....Vol. 2
Albania ....Vol. 2
Albania, Greek Occupation ....Vol. 3
Albania, Italian Offices ....Vol. 3
Albany, Ga. ....Vol. 1
Alderney ....Vol. 1
Alerta ovptd. on stamps of Peru 758
Alexandretta ....Vol. 2, Vol. 3
Alexandria, French Offices ....Vol. 3
Alexandria, Va. ....Vol. 1
Alexandroupolis ....Vol. 3
Algeria, Algerie ....Vol. 2
Allemagne Duitschland ....Vol. 3
Allenstein ....Vol. 2
Allied Military Government (Austria) ..Vol. 2
Allied Military Government (France) ....Vol. 3
Allied Military Gov. (Germany) ....Vol. 3
Allied Military Government (Italy) ....Vol. 3
Allied Military Government (Trieste) ..Vol. 3
Allied Occupation of Azerbaijan ....Vol. 2
Allied Occupation of Thrace ....Vol. 5
Alsace and Lorraine ....Vol. 3
Alwar ....Vol. 1
A.M.G. ....Vol. 2, Vol. 3
A.M.G./F.T.T. ....Vol. 3
A.M.G./V.G. ....Vol. 3
AM Post ....Vol. 3
Anatolia ....Vol. 5
Ancachs 758
Andalusia ....Vol. 5
Anderson Court House, S.C. ....Vol. 1
Andorra, Andorre ....Vol. 2
Angola ....Vol. 2
Angra ....Vol. 2
Anguilla ....Vol. 1
Anhwei ....Vol. 2
Anjouan ....Vol. 2
Anna surcharged on France ....Vol. 3
Annam ....Vol. 3
Annam and Tonkin ....Vol. 2
Annapolis, Md. ....Vol. 1
Antigua ....Vol. 1
Antioquia ....Vol. 2
A.O. ovptd. on Congo ....Vol. 3
AOF on France ....Vol. 3
A.O.I. ....Vol. 3
A percevoir (see Belgium, France, French colonies, postage due) ....Vol. 2, Vol. 3
Apurimac 758
A R 461
A.R. ovptd. on stamps of Colombia 677
Arabie Saoudite ....Vol. 5
Arad ....Vol. 3
A receber (See Portugal or Portuguese Colonies) 881
Arequipa 758
Argentina ....Vol. 2
Argyrokastron ....Vol. 3
Arica 732, 757
Armenia ....Vol. 2, Vol. 5
Armenian stamps ovptd. ....Vol. 5
Army of the North ....Vol. 5
Army of the Northwest ....Vol. 5
Aruba ....Vol. 2
Arwad ....Vol. 5
Ascension ....Vol. 1
Assistencia Nacionalaos Tuberculosos 883
Assistencia Publica 499
Asturias ....Vol. 5
Athens, Ga. ....Vol. 1
Atlanta, Ga. ....Vol. 1
Augusta, Ga. ....Vol. 1
Aunus, ovptd. on Finland ....Vol. 5
Austin, Miss. ....Vol. 1
Austin, Tex. ....Vol. 1
Australia ....Vol. 1
Australia, Occupation of Japan ....Vol. 1
Australian Antarctic Territory ....Vol. 1
Austria ....Vol. 2
Austria, Allied Military Govt. ....Vol. 2
Austria, Adm. of Liechtenstein 210
Austria, Lombardy-Venetia ....Vol. 2
Austria-Hungary ....Vol. 2
Austrian Occupation of Italy ....Vol. 3
Austrian Occupation of Montenegro 461
Austrian Occupation of Romania ....Vol. 5
Austrian Occupation of Serbia ....Vol. 5
Austrian Offices Abroad ....Vol. 2
Austrian stamps surcharged (See Western Ukraine) ....Vol. 5
Autaugaville, Ala. ....Vol. 1
Autopaketti ....Vol. 3
Avisporto ....Vol. 3
Ayacucho 759
Azerbaijan ....Vol. 2, Vol. 5
Azores ....883, Vol. 2

B ....606, Vol. 2
B ovptd. on Straits Settlements ....Vol. 1
Baden ....Vol. 3
Baghdad ....Vol. 1
Bahamas ....Vol. 1
Bahawalpur ....Vol. 1
Bahrain ....Vol. 1
Bajar Porto ....Vol. 3
Baku ....Vol. 2
Baltimore, Md. ....Vol. 1
Bamra ....Vol. 1
Banat, Bacska ....Vol. 3
Bangkok ....Vol. 1
Bangladesh ....Vol. 1
Bani ovptd. on Hungary ....Vol. 3
Baranya ....Vol. 3
Barbados ....Vol. 1
Barbuda ....Vol. 1
Barcelona ....Vol. 5
Barranquilla ....Vol. 2
Barwani ....Vol. 1
Basel ....Vol. 5
Bashahr ....Vol. 1
Basutoland ....Vol. 1
Bataan, Corregidor, Manila ....797, Vol. 1
Batavia 543
Baton Rouge, La. ....Vol. 1
Batum (British Occupation) ....Vol. 1
Bavaria ....Vol. 3
Bayar Porto ....Vol. 3
Bayer., Bayern ....Vol. 3
B.C.A. ovptd. on Rhodesia ....Vol. 1
B.C.M. ....Vol. 1
B.C.O.F. ....Vol. 1
Beaumont, Tex. ....Vol. 1
Bechuanaland ....Vol. 1
Bechuanaland Protectorate ....Vol. 1
Behie ....Vol. 5
Belarus ....Vol. 2
Belgian Congo ....Vol. 2
Belgian East Africa ....Vol. 5
Belgian Occ. of German East Africa ....Vol. 3
Belgian Occupation of Germany ....Vol. 3
Belgien ....Vol. 2
Belgique ....Vol. 2
Belgium ....Vol. 2
Belgium (German Occupation) ....Vol. 2
Belize ....Vol. 1
Belize, Cayes of ....Vol. 1
Benadir ....Vol. 5
Bengasi ....Vol. 3
Benin ....Vol. 2
Bequia ....Vol. 1
Bergedorf ....Vol. 3
Berlin ....Vol. 3
Berlin-Brandenburg ....Vol. 3
Bermuda ....Vol. 1
Besetztes Gebiet Nordfrankreich ....Vol. 3
Beyrouth, French Offices ....Vol. 3
Beyrouth, Russian Offices ....Vol. 5
B. Guiana ....Vol. 1
Bhopal ....Vol. 1
Bhor ....Vol. 1
Bhutan ....Vol. 2
Bijawar ....Vol. 1
B.I.O.T. ovptd. on Seychelles ....Vol. 1
Blagoveshchensk ....Vol. 3
Bluefields 606
B.M.A. Eritrea ....Vol. 1
B.M.A. Somalia ....Vol. 1
B.M.A. Tripolitania ....Vol. 1
Bocas del Toro 654
Boer Occupation ....Vol. 1
Bogota ....Vol. 2
Bohemia and Moravia ....Vol. 2
Bohmen and Mahren ....Vol. 2
Bolivar ....Vol. 2
Bolivia ....Vol. 2
Bolletta, Bollettino ....Vol. 3, Vol. 5
Bollo ....Vol. 3
Bollo Postale ....Vol. 5
Bophuthatswana ....Vol. 1
Borneo 544
Boscawen, N.H. ....Vol. 1
Bosna i Hercegovina ....Vol. 5
Bosnia and Herzegovina ....Vol. 2, Vol. 5
Boston, Mass. ....Vol. 1
Botswana ....Vol. 1
Boyaca ....Vol. 2
Brattleboro, Vt. ....Vol. 1
Braunschweig ....Vol. 3
Brazil, Brasil ....Vol. 2
Bremen ....Vol. 3
Bridgeville, Ala. ....Vol. 1
British Antarctic Territory ....Vol. 1
British Bechuanaland ....Vol. 1
British Central Africa ....Vol. 1
British Colonies - Dies I and II ....Vol. 1
British Columbia & Vancouver Is. ....Vol. 1
British Consular Mail ....Vol. 1
British East Africa ....Vol. 1
British Guiana ....Vol. 1
British Honduras ....Vol. 1
British Indian Ocean Territory ....Vol. 1
British Levant ....Vol. 1
British New Guinea ....Vol. 1
British North Borneo ....Vol. 1
British Occupation of Batum ....Vol. 1
British Occupation of Bushire ....Vol. 1
British Occupation of Cameroons (Cameroun) ....Vol. 1, Vol. 2
British Occupation of Crete ....Vol. 1, Vol. 2
British Occ. of German East Africa ....Vol. 1
British Occupation of Iraq ....Vol. 1
British Occupation of Mesopotamia ....Vol. 1
British Occupation of Orange River Colony ....Vol. 1
British Occupation of Palestine ....Vol. 1
British Occupation of Persia ....Vol. 1
British Occupation of Togo ....Vol. 1
British Occ. of Transvaal ....Vol. 1
British Off. in the Turkish Empire ....Vol. 1
British Offices in Africa ....Vol. 1
British Offices in China ....Vol. 1
British Offices in Morocco ....Vol. 1
British Offices in Tangier ....Vol. 1
British Samoa ....Vol. 1
British Solomon Islands ....Vol. 1
British Somaliland (Somaliland Protectorate) ....Vol. 1
British South Africa (Rhodesia) ....Vol. 1
British Vice-Consulate ....Vol. 1
British Virgin Islands ....Vol. 1
British Zone (Germany) ....Vol. 3
Brunei ....Vol. 1
Brunei (Japanese Occupation) ....Vol. 1
Brunswick ....Vol. 3
Buchanan 182
Buenos Aires ....Vol. 2
Bulgaria ....Vol. 2
Bulgarian Occupation of Romania ....Vol. 5
Bundi ....Vol. 1
Bureau International ....Vol. 5
Burgenland ....Vol. 2
Burgos ....Vol. 5
Burkina Faso ....Vol. 2
Burma ....Vol. 1
Burma (Japanese Occupation) ....Vol. 1
Burundi ....Vol. 2
Bushire ....Vol. 1
Bussahir ....Vol. 1
Buu-Chinh ....Vol. 5
Byelorussia ....Vol. 2

Cabo, Cabo Gracias a Dios 607
Cabo Juby, Jubi ....Vol. 2
Cabo Verde ....Vol. 2
Cadiz ....Vol. 5
Caicos ....Vol. 1
Calchi ....Vol. 3
Calino, Calimno ....Vol. 3
Callao 730, 758
Camb. Aust. Sigillum Nov. ....Vol. 1
Cambodia, (Int. Com., India) ....Vol. 1
Cambodia, Cambodge ....Vol. 2, Vol. 3
Cameroons (British Occ.) ....Vol. 1, Vol. 2
Cameroons (U.K.T.T.) ....Vol. 1
Cameroun (Republique Federale) ....Vol. 2
Campeche 389
Canada ....Vol. 1
Canal Zone ....Vol. 1
Canary Islands ....Vol. 5
Candia ....Vol. 1, Vol. 2
Canton, French Offices ....Vol. 3
Canton, Miss. ....Vol. 1
Cape Juby ....Vol. 2
Cape of Good Hope stamps surchd. (see Griqualand West) ....Vol. 1
Cape of Good Hope ....Vol. 1
Cape Verde ....Vol. 2
Carchi ....Vol. 3
Carinthia ....Vol. 2, Vol. 5
Carlist ....Vol. 5
Carolina City, N.C. ....Vol. 1
Caroline Islands ....Vol. 2
Carpatho-Ukraine ....Vol. 2
Cartagena ....Vol. 2
Carupano ....Vol. 5
Caso ....Vol. 3
Castellorizo ....Vol. 2
Castelrosso ....Vol. 2
Cataluna ....Vol. 5
Cauca ....Vol. 2
Cavalla (Greek) ....Vol. 3
Cavalle, Cavalla (French) ....Vol. 3
Cayes of Belize ....Vol. 1
Cayman Islands ....Vol. 1
CCCP ....Vol. 5
C.CH on French Colonies ....Vol. 2
C.E.F. ovptd. on Cameroun ....Vol. 1, Vol. 2
C.E.F. ovptd. on India ....Vol. 1
Cefalonia ovptd. on Greece ....Vol. 3
Celebes 544
Centenary 1st Postage Stamp 1852-1952 ....Vol. 1
Centesimi overprinted on Austria or Bosnia ....Vol. 3
Centesimi di corona ....Vol. 2, Vol. 3
Centimos (no country name) ....Vol. 5
Centimos ovptd. on France ....Vol. 3
Centimos ovptd. on Germany ....Vol. 3
Central Africa (Centrafricaine) ....Vol. 2
Central China ....Vol. 2
Central Lithuania ....Vol. 2
Cephalonia ....Vol. 3
Cerigo ....Vol. 3
Cervantes ....Vol. 5
Ceskoslovenska, Ceskoslovensko ....Vol. 2
Ceylon ....Vol. 1
CFA ovptd. On France ....Vol. 3
C.G.H.S. ....Vol. 5
Ch ....Vol. 3
Chachapoyas 759
Chad ....Vol. 2
Chahar ....Vol. 2
Chala 759
Chamba ....Vol. 1
Chapel Hill, N.C. ....Vol. 1
Charkhari ....Vol. 1
Charleston, S.C. ....Vol. 1

Chattanooga, Tenn. ....Vol. 1
Chekiang ....Vol. 2
Chiapas 389
Chiclayo 759
Chiffre ....(see France and French colonies, postage due)
Chihuahua 389
Chile ....Vol. 2
Chilean Occupation of Peru 758
Chimarra ....Vol. 3
China ....Vol. 2
China (Japanese Occupation) ....Vol. 2
China Expeditionary Force (India) ....Vol. 1
China, Formosa ....Vol. 2
China, British Offices ....Vol. 1
China, French Offices ....Vol. 3
China, German Offices ....Vol. 3
China, Italian Offices ....Vol. 3
China, Japanese Offices 57
China, Northeastern Provinces ....Vol. 2
China, Offices in Manchuria ....Vol. 2
China, Offices in Tibet ....Vol. 2
China, People's Republic ....Vol. 2
China, People's Republic Regional Issues ....Vol. 2
China, Russian Offices ....Vol. 5
China, United States Offices ....Vol. 1
Chine ....Vol. 3
Chios ....Vol. 3
Chita ....Vol. 3
Chosen 77
Christiansburg, Va. ....Vol. 1
Christmas Island ....Vol. 1
Chungking ....Vol. 3
C.I.H.S. ....Vol. 5
Cilicia ....Vol. 2
Cincinnati, O. ....Vol. 1
Cirenaica ....Vol. 2
Ciskei ....Vol. 1
Cleveland, O. ....Vol. 1
Cluj ....Vol. 3
C.M.T. ....Vol. 5
Coamo ....896, Vol. 1
Cochin ....Vol. 1
Cochin China ....Vol. 2
Cochin, Travancore ....Vol. 1
Co. Ci. ovptd. on Yugoslavia ....Vol. 5
Cocos Islands ....Vol. 1
Colaparchee, Ga. ....Vol. 1
Colis Postaux ....Vol. 2
Colombia ....653, 676, Vol. 2
Colombian Dominion of Panama 653
Colon 654
Colonie (Coloniale) Italiane ....Vol. 3
Colonies de l'Empire Francaise ....Vol. 3
Columbia, S.C. ....Vol. 1
Columbia, Tenn. ....Vol. 1
Columbus Archipelago ....Vol. 3
Columbus, Ga. ....Vol. 1
Comayagua ....Vol. 3
Common Designs ....28A, Vol. 1, Vol. 2, Vol. 3, Vol. 5
Communicaciones ....Vol. 5
Communist China ....Vol. 2
Comores, Archipel des ....Vol. 2
Comoro Islands (Comorien) ....Vol. 2
Compania Colombiana ....Vol. 2
Confederate States ....Vol. 1
Congo, Congo Democratic Republic ....Vol. 2
Congo People's Republic (ex-French) ....Vol. 2
Congo, Belgian (Belge) ....Vol. 2
Congo, Francais ....Vol. 3
Congo, Indian U.N. Force ....Vol. 1
Congo, Portuguese 886
Congreso ....Vol. 5
Conseil de l'Europe ....Vol. 3
Constantinople, Italian Offices ....Vol. 3
Constantinople, Romanian Offices ....Vol. 5
Constantinople, Russian Offices ....Vol. 5
Constantinople, Turkey ....Vol. 5
Contribucao Industrial 258
Convention States (India) ....Vol. 1
Coo ....Vol. 3
Cook Islands ....Vol. 1
Cordoba ....Vol. 2
Corea, Corean, Coree 77
Corfu ....Vol. 2
Corona ....Vol. 3
Correio, Correios e Telegraphos 857, 858
Correo Submarino ....Vol. 5
Correo, Correos (no country name) ....760, 896, Vol. 1, Vol. 2, Vol. 3, Vol. 5
Correspondencia Urgente ....Vol. 5
Corrientes ....Vol. 2
Cos ....Vol. 3
Costa Atlantica 607
Costa Rica ....Vol. 2
Costantinopoli ....Vol. 3
Cote d'Ivoire ....Vol. 3
Cote des Somalis ....Vol. 5
Council of Europe ....Vol. 3
Cour Permanente de Justice Internationale 523
Courtland, Ala. ....Vol. 1
Cracow 798
Crete ....Vol. 2, Vol. 3
Crete (British Occupation) ....Vol. 1
Crete, Austrian Offices ....Vol. 2
Crete, French Offices ....Vol. 3
Crete, Italian Offices ....Vol. 3
Crimea ....Vol. 5
Croatia ....Vol. 2, Vol. 5
Croatia-Slavonia ....Vol. 5
Cuautla 389
Cuba ....Vol. 1, Vol. 2
Cuba, U.S. Administration ....Vol. 1, Vol. 2
Cucuta ....Vol. 2
Cuernavaca 389
Cundinamarca ....Vol. 2
Curacao 524
Cuzco 759
C.X.C. on Bosnia and Herzegovina ....Vol. 5
Cyprus ....Vol. 1
Cyprus, Turkish Republic of Northern ....Vol. 5
Cyrenaica ....Vol. 2
Czechoslovakia ....Vol. 2
Czechoslovak Legion Post ....Vol. 2

Dahomey ....Vol. 3
Dakar-Abidjan ....Vol. 3
Dalmatia ....Vol. 3, Vol. 5
Dalton, Ga. ....Vol. 1
Danish West Indies ....Vol. 1, Vol. 3
Danmark ....Vol. 3
Dansk-Vestindien ....Vol. 1, Vol. 3
Dansk-Vestindiske ....Vol. 1, Vol. 3
Danville, Va. ....Vol. 1
Danzig ....Vol. 3
Danzig, Polish Offices 856
Dardanelles ....Vol. 5
Datia (Duttia) ....Vol. 1
D.B.L. ovptd. on Far Eastern Republic and Russia ....Vol. 3
D.B.P. (Dalni Vostochini Respoublika) ....Vol. 3
DDR ....Vol. 3
Debrecen ....Vol. 3
Deccan (Hyderabad) ....Vol. 1
Dedeagatch (Greek) ....Vol. 3
Dedeagh (French) ....Vol. 3
Deficit 755
Demopolis, Ala. ....Vol. 1
Den Waisen ovptd. on Italy ....Vol. 5
Denikin ....Vol. 5
Denmark ....Vol. 3
Denmark stamps surcharged ....Vol. 3
Denver Issue, Mexico 342
Deutsch-Neu-Guinea ....Vol. 1, Vol. 3
Deutsch-Ostafrika ....Vol. 3
Deutsch-Sudwest Afrika ....Vol. 3
Deutsche Bundespost ....Vol. 3
Deutsche Demokratische Republik ....Vol. 3
Deutsche Nationalversammlung ....Vol. 3
Deutsche Post ....Vol. 3
Deutsche (Deutsches) Reich ....Vol. 3
Deutsches Reich, Nr. 21, Nr. 16 ....Vol. 3
Deutschosterreich ....Vol. 2
Dhar ....Vol. 1
Diego-Suarez ....Vol. 3
Dienftmarke (Dienstmarke) ....Vol. 3
Dies I and II, British Colonies ....Vol. 1
Diligencia ....Vol. 5
Distrito ovptd. on Arequipa 759
DJ ovptd. on Obock ....Vol. 5
Djibouti (Somali Coast) ....Vol. 3, Vol. 5
Dodecanese Islands ....Vol. 3
Dominica ....Vol. 1
Dominican Republic ....Vol. 3
Don Government ....Vol. 5
Drzava SHS ....Vol. 5
Dubai ....Vol. 3
Durazzo ....Vol. 3
Dutch Guiana (Surinam) ....Vol. 5
Dutch Indies 539
Dutch New Guinea 544
Duttia ....Vol. 1

E.A.F. overprinted on stamps of Great Britain ....Vol. 1
East Africa (British) ....Vol. 1
East Africa, (German) ....Vol. 1, Vol. 3
East Africa and Uganda Protectorates ....Vol. 1
East Africa Forces ....Vol. 1
East China ....Vol. 2
Eastern Rumelia ....Vol. 3
Eastern Silesia ....Vol. 3
Eastern Szechwan ....Vol. 2
Eastern Thrace ....Vol. 5
East India Co. ....Vol. 1
East Saxony ....Vol. 3
Eatonton, Ga. ....Vol. 1
Ecuador ....Vol. 3
E.E.F. ....Vol. 1
Eesti ....Vol. 3
Egeo ....Vol. 3
Egypt, Egypte, Egyptiennes ....Vol. 3
Egypt, French Offices ....Vol. 3
Eire (Ireland) ....Vol. 1
Ekaterinodar ....Vol. 5
Elobey, Annobon and Corisco ....Vol. 3
El Salvador ....Vol. 5
Elsas ....Vol. 3
Emory, Va. ....Vol. 1
Empire, Franc, Francais ....Vol. 3
Epirus ....Vol. 3
Equateur ....Vol. 3
Equatorial Guinea ....Vol. 3
Eritrea ....Vol. 3
Eritrea (British Military Administration) ....Vol. 1
Escuelas ....Vol. 5
Espana, Espanola ....Vol. 5
Estado da India 893
Est Africain Allemand overprinted on Congo ....Vol. 3
Estensi ....Vol. 3
Estero ....Vol. 3
Estonia ....Vol. 3
Etablissments Francais dans l'Inde ....Vol. 3
Ethiopia, Ethiopie, Etiopia ....Vol. 3
Ethiopia (Italian Occupation) ....Vol. 3
Eupen ....Vol. 3

Falkland Dependencies ....Vol. 1
Falkland Islands ....Vol. 1
Far Eastern Republic ....Vol. 3
Far Eastern Republic surcharged or ovptd. ....Vol. 5
Faridkot ....Vol. 1
Faroe Islands ....Vol. 3
FCFA ovptd. on France ....Vol. 3
Federacion ....Vol. 5
Federal Republic (Germany) ....Vol. 3
Federata Demokratike Mderkombetare e Grave ....Vol. 2
Federated Malay States ....Vol. 1
Fen (Manchukuo) 313
Fernando Po, Fdo. Poo ....Vol. 3
Feudatory States ....Vol. 1
Fezzan, Fezzan-Ghadames 209, 210
Fiera Campionaria Tripoli 184
15 August 1947 ....Vol. 1
Fiji ....Vol. 1
Filipinas, Filipas. 761
Fincastle, Va. ....Vol. 1
Finland ....Vol. 3
Finnish Occupation of Karelia 76
Finnish Occupation of Russia ....Vol. 5
Fiume, Fivme ....Vol. 3
Fiume-Kupa Zone (Fiumano Kupa) ....Vol. 5
Florida ....Vol. 5
Foochow, Chinese ....Vol. 2
Foochow, German ....Vol. 3
Formosa 58
Foroyar ....Vol. 3
Forsyth, Ga. ....Vol. 1
Franc ....Vol. 3
Franca ovptd. on stamps of Peru 758, 759
Francais, Francaise ....(see France and French colonies)
France ....Vol. 3
France (Allied Military Gov't.) ....Vol. 3
France (German occupation) ....Vol. 3
Franco Bollo ....Vol. 3
Franco Marke ....Vol. 3
Franco Scrisorei ....Vol. 5
Franklin, N.C. ....Vol. 1
Franqueo 758
Franquicia ....Vol. 5
Fredericksburg, Va. ....Vol. 1
Frei Durch Ablosung ....Vol. 3
Freimarke (No Country Name) ....Vol. 3
French Administration of Andorra ....Vol. 2
French Colonies ....Vol. 3
French Colonies surcharged ....265, 650, Vol. 3, Vol. 5
French Commemoratives Index ....Vol. 3
French Congo ....Vol. 3
French Equatorial Africa ....Vol. 3
French Guiana ....Vol. 3
French Guinea ....Vol. 3
French India ....Vol. 3
French Levant ....Vol. 3, Vol. 5
French Mandate of Alaouites ....Vol. 2
French Mandate of Lebanon 143
French Morocco ....Vol. 3
French Occupation of Cameroun ....Vol. 2
French Occupation of Castellorizo ....Vol. 2
French Occupation of Crete ....Vol. 2
French Occupation of Germany ....Vol. 3
French Occupation of Hungary ....Vol. 3
French Occupation of Libya 209, 210
French Occupation of Syria ....Vol. 5
French Occupation of Togo ....Vol. 5
French Oceania ....Vol. 3
French Offices Abroad ....Vol. 3
French Offices in China ....Vol. 3
French Offices in Crete ....Vol. 3
French Offices in Egypt ....Vol. 3
French Offices in Madagascar 265
French Offices in Morocco ....Vol. 3
French Offices in Tangier ....Vol. 3
French Offices in Turkish Empire ....Vol. 3
French Offices in Zanzibar ....Vol. 3
French Polynesia ....Vol. 3
French Saar ....Vol. 5
French Southern and Antarctic Territories ....Vol. 3
French Sudan ....Vol. 3
French West Africa ....Vol. 3
French Zone (Germany) ....Vol. 3
Frimarke, Frmrk (No Country Name) ....632, Vol. 5
Fujeira ....Vol. 3
Fukien ....Vol. 2
Funafuti ....Vol. 1
Funchal ....Vol. 3

G or GW overprinted on Cape of Good Hope ....Vol. 1
GAB on French Colonies ....Vol. 3
Gabon, Gabonaise ....Vol. 3
Gainesville, Ala. ....Vol. 1
Galapagos Islands ....Vol. 3
Galveston, Tex. ....Vol. 1
Gambia ....Vol. 1
Gaza ....Vol. 1
G.E.A. ovptd. on East Africa & Uganda; Tanganyika ....Vol. 1
General Gouvernement (Poland) 854
Geneva ....Vol. 5
Georgetown, S.C. ....Vol. 1
Georgia ....Vol. 3, Vol. 5
Georgienne, Republique ....Vol. 3
Germany (Allied Military Govt.) ....Vol. 3
German Administration of Danzig ....Vol. 3
German Administration of Saar ....Vol. 5
German Democratic Republic ....Vol. 3
German Dominion of Cameroun ....Vol. 2
German Dominion of Mariana Is. 315
German Dominion of Marshall Is. 316
German Dominion of Samoa ....Vol. 5
German Dominion of Togo ....Vol. 5
German East Africa ....Vol. 3
German East Africa (Belgian occ.) ....Vol. 3
German East Africa (British occ.) ....Vol. 1

German New Guinea ....Vol. 3
German New Guinea (New Britain)....Vol. 1
German Occupation of Belgium....Vol. 2
German Occupation of Estonia ....Vol. 3
German Occupation of France ....Vol. 3
German Occupation of Guernsey....Vol. 1
German Occupation of Ionian Is. ....Vol. 3
German Occupation of Jersey ....Vol. 1
German Occupation of Latvia 142
German Occupation of Lithuania 233
German Occupation of Ljubljana ....Vol. 5
German Occupation of Luxembourg....256
German Occupation of Montenegro....462
German Occupation of Poland 854
German Occupation of Romania ....Vol. 5
German Occupation of Russia....Vol. 5
German Occupation of Serbia ....Vol. 5
German Occupation of Ukraine ....Vol. 5
German Occupation of Yugoslavia ....Vol. 5
German Occupation of Zante....Vol. 3
German Offices in China ....Vol. 3
German Offices in Morocco....Vol. 3
German Offices in Turkish Empire....Vol. 3
German Protectorate of Bohemia and Moravia ....Vol. 2
German South-West Africa ....Vol. 3
German stamps surchd. ....77, 798, Vol. 3
German States....Vol. 3
Germany....Vol. 3
Germany (Allied Military Govt.) ....Vol. 3
Gerusalemme....Vol. 3
Ghadames....210
Ghana....Vol. 1
Gibraltar ....Vol. 1
Gilbert and Ellice Islands ....Vol. 1
Gilbert Islands....Vol. 1
Giumulzina District....Vol. 5
Gniezno....799
Gold Coast....Vol. 1
Golfo del Guinea ....Vol. 5
Goliad, Tex. ....Vol. 1
Gonzales, Tex. ....Vol. 1
Gorny Slask....Vol. 5
Governo Militare Alleato ....Vol. 3
G.P.E. ovptd. on French Colonies....Vol. 3
Graham Land ....Vol. 1
Granadine Confederation ....Vol. 2
Grand Comoro ....Vol. 3
Grand Liban....143
Great Britain ....Vol. 1
Great Britain, Gaelic ovpt. ....Vol. 1
Great Britain, Offices in Africa ....Vol. 1
Great Britain, Offices in China....Vol. 1
Great Britain, Offices in Morocco....Vol. 1
Great Britain, Offices in Turkish Empire....Vol. 1
Greater Rajasthan Union....Vol. 1
Greece ....Vol. 3
Greek Occ. of Turkey in Asia....Vol. 5
Greek Occupation of Albania, North Epirus, Dodecanese Islands ....Vol. 3
Greek Occupation of Epirus....Vol. 3
Greek Occupation of the Aegean Islands....Vol. 3
Greek Occupation of Thrace....Vol. 5
Greek Occupation of Turkey....Vol. 3
Greek stamps overprinted....Vol. 5
Greenland....Vol. 3
Greensboro, Ala. ....Vol. 1
Greensboro, N.C. ....Vol. 1
Greenville 182
Greenville, Ala. ....Vol. 1
Greenville Court House, S.C. ....Vol. 1
Greenwood Depot, Va....Vol. 1
Grenada....Vol. 1
Grenadines of Grenada....Vol. 1
Grenadines of St. Vincent ....Vol. 1
G.R.I. overprinted on German New Guinea ....Vol. 1
G.R.I. overprinted on German Samoa .Vol. 1
G.R.I. overprinted on Marshall Is. ....Vol. 1
Griffin, Ga....Vol. 1
Griqualand West ....Vol. 1
Grodno District 233
Gronland ....Vol. 3
Grossdeutsches Reich ....Vol. 3
Groszy....804
Grove Hill, Ala. ....Vol. 1
Guadalajara 389
Guadeloupe ....Vol. 3
Guam ....Vol. 1
Guanacaste ....Vol. 2
Guatemala ....Vol. 3
Guayana ....Vol. 5
Guernsey ....Vol. 1
Guernsey, German Occupation....Vol. 1
Guiana, British ....Vol. 1
Guiana, Dutch ....Vol. 5
Guiana, French ....Vol. 3
Guine 887
Guinea....Vol. 3, Vol. 5
Guinea, French ....Vol. 3
Guinea, Spanish ....Vol. 5
Guinea-Bissau ....Vol. 3
Guinee....Vol. 3
Guipuzcoa ....Vol. 5
Gultig 9, Armee ....Vol. 5
Guyana ....Vol. 1
Guyane, Guy. Franc. ....Vol. 3
Gwalior....Vol. 1

Habilitado on Telegrafos, Derechos de Firma 761, 762
Hadhramaut....Vol. 1
Hainan Island....Vol. 2
Haiti ....Vol. 3
Hallettsville, Tex. ....Vol. 1
Hamburg....Vol. 3
Hamburgh, S.C. ....Vol. 1
Hanover, Hannover ....Vol. 3
Harper 182
Hatay....Vol. 3
Haute Silesie ....Vol. 5
Haute Volta....Vol. 2
Haut Senegal-Niger....Vol. 5
Hawaii ....Vol. 1
H B A ovptd. on Russia....Vol. 5
H.E.H. The Nizam's ....Vol. 1
Heilungkiang....Vol. 2
Hejaz ....Vol. 5
Hejaz and Nejd ....Vol. 5
Helena, Tex. ....Vol. 1
Heligoland ....Vol. 1
Hellas ....Vol. 3
Helsinki (Helsingfors) ....Vol. 3
Helvetia, Helvetica (Switzerland)....Vol. 5
Heraklion....Vol. 1, Vol. 2
Herzegovina....Vol. 2
H.H. Nawabshah Jahanbegam ....Vol. 1
H.I. Postage ....Vol. 1
Hillsboro, N.C. ....Vol. 1
Hoi Hao, French Offices ....Vol. 3
Holkar (Indore) ....Vol. 1
Holland (Netherlands) 499
Holstein ....Vol. 3
Honan....Vol. 2
Honda....Vol. 2
Honduras....Vol. 3
Honduras, British ....Vol. 1
Hong Kong ....Vol. 1, Vol. 2
Hong Kong (Japanese Occupation)....Vol. 1
Hong Kong ovptd. China ....Vol. 1
Hopeh....Vol. 2
Hopei....Vol. 2
Horta ....Vol. 3
Houston, Tex. ....Vol. 1
Hrvatska ....Vol. 2, Vol. 5
Hrzgl. ....Vol. 3
Huacho 759
Hunan ....Vol. 2
Hungary....Vol. 2, Vol. 3
Hungary (French Occupation)....Vol. 3
Hungary (Romanian Occupation)....Vol. 3
Hungary (Serbian Occupation)....Vol. 3
Huntsville, Tex....Vol. 1
Hupeh ....Vol. 2
Hyderabad (Deccan)....Vol. 1

I.B. (West Irian)....Vol. 5
Icaria ....Vol. 3
ICC ovptd. on India....Vol. 1
Iceland....Vol. 3
Idar....Vol. 1
I.E.F. ovptd. on India....Vol. 1
I.E.F. (D(ovptd. on Turkey ....Vol. 1
Ierusalem....Vol. 5
Ifni....Vol. 3
Ile Rouad ....Vol. 5
Imperio Colonial Portugues 886
Impuesto de Guerra ....Vol. 5
Independence, Tex....Vol. 1
Index of U.S. Issues....Vol. 1
India....893, Vol. 1
India, China Expeditionary Force....Vol. 1
India, Convention States....Vol. 1
India, Feudatory States ....Vol. 1
India, French....Vol. 3
India, Portuguese 890
Indian Custodial Unit, Korea ....Vol. 1
Indian Expeditionary Force....Vol. 1
Indian U.N. Force, Congo....Vol. 1
Indian U.N. Force, Gaza....Vol. 1
Indies, Dutch (see Netherlands Indies)...539
Indo-China, Indo-chine....Vol. 3
Indo-China, Int. Commission....Vol. 1
Indonesia ....541, Vol. 3
Indore....Vol. 1
Industrielle Kriegswirschaft....Vol. 5
Inhambane....Vol. 3
Inini....Vol. 3
Inland 160
Inner Mongolia (Meng Chiang) ....Vol. 2
Instruccion....Vol. 5
International Bureau of Education ....Vol. 5
International Court of Justice....523
International Labor Bureau....Vol. 5
International Refugee Organization....Vol. 5
International Telecommunication Union....Vol. 5
Ionian Islands, IONIKON KPATOE....Vol. 1, Vol. 3
I.O.V.R. ....Vol. 5
Iran, Iraniennes....Vol. 3
Iran (see Bushire) ....Vol. 1
Iraq....Vol. 3
Iraq (British Occupation) ....Vol. 1
Ireland ....Vol. 1
Ireland, Northern ....Vol. 1
Irian Barat....Vol. 5
Island....Vol. 3
Isle of Man....Vol. 1
Isole Italiane dell'Egeo....Vol. 3
Isole Jonie ....Vol. 3
Israel....Vol. 3
Istria ....Vol. 5
Ita-Karjala....76
Itaca ovptd. on Greece ....Vol. 3
Italia, Italiana, Italiane, Italiano....Vol. 3
Italian Colonies ....Vol. 3
Italian Dominion of Albania....Vol. 2
Italian Dominion of Castellorizo ....Vol. 2
Italian East Africa ....Vol. 3
Italian Jubaland 652
Italian Occ. of Aegean Islands....Vol. 3
Italian Occupation of Austria ....Vol. 2
Italian Occupation of Corfu ....Vol. 2
Italian Occupation of Crete....Vol. 2
Italian Occupation of Dalmatia ....Vol. 3
Italian Occupation of Ethiopia....Vol. 3
Italian Occupation of Fiume-Kupa....Vol. 5
Italian Occupation of Ionian Islands....Vol. 3
Italian Occupation of Ljubljana ....Vol. 5
Italian Occupation of Montenegro 461
Italian Occupation of Yugoslavia ....Vol. 5
Italian Offices Abroad ....Vol. 3
Italian Offices in Africa ....Vol. 3
Italian Offices in Albania....Vol. 3
Italian Offices in China....Vol. 3
Italian Offices in Constantinople ....Vol. 3
Italian Offices in Crete....Vol. 3
Italian Offices in the Turkish Empire...Vol. 3
Italian Social Republic ....Vol. 3
Italian Somaliland....Vol. 5
Italian Somaliland (E.A.F.)....Vol. 1
Italian stamps surcharged ....Vol. 3
Italian States....Vol. 3
Italy (Allied Military Govt.)....Vol. 3
Italy (Austrian Occupation)....Vol. 3
Italy....Vol. 3
Ithaca ....Vol. 3
Iuka, Miss. ....Vol. 1
Ivory Coast ....Vol. 3

J. ovptd. on stamps of Peru 760
Jackson, Miss. ....Vol. 1
Jacksonville, Ala. ....Vol. 1
Jaffa ....Vol. 5
Jaipur....Vol. 1
Jamaica ....Vol. 1
Jamhuri....Vol. 1
Jammu....Vol. 1
Jammu and Kashmir....Vol. 1
Janina ....Vol. 3
Japan 1
Japan (Australian Occ.)....Vol. 1
Japan (Taiwan)....58
Japanese Offices Abroad....57
Japan Occupation of Brunei ....Vol. 1
Japan Occupation of Burma ....Vol. 1
Japan Occupation of China ....Vol. 2
Japan Occupation of Dutch Indies....544
Japan Occupation of Hong Kong ....Vol. 1
Japan Occupation of Johore ....Vol. 1
Japan Occupation of Kedah....Vol. 1
Japan Occupation of Kelantan....Vol. 1
Japan Occupation of Malacca....Vol. 1
Japan Occupation of Malaya ....Vol. 1
Japan Occupation of Negri Sembilan...Vol. 1
Japan Occupation of North Borneo ....Vol. 1
Japan Occupation of Pahang ....Vol. 1
Japan Occupation of Penang ....Vol. 1
Japan Occupation of Perak....Vol. 1
Japan Occupation of Philippines..796, Vol. 1
Japan Occupation of Sarawak ....Vol. 1
Japan Occupation of Selangor ....Vol. 1
Japan Occupation of Sts. Settlements ..Vol. 1
Japan Occ. of Trengganu ....Vol. 1
Jasdan....Vol. 1
Java....539, 544
Jedda ....Vol. 5
Jeend ....Vol. 1
Jehol ....Vol. 2
Jersey....Vol. 1
Jersey, German Occupation ....Vol. 1
Jerusalem, Italian Offices ....Vol. 3
Jerusalem, Russian Offices ....Vol. 5
Jetersville, Va. ....Vol. 1
Jhalawar....Vol. 1
Jhind, Jind ....Vol. 1
Johore....Vol. 1
Jonesboro, Tenn. ....Vol. 1
Jordan....58
Jordan (Palestine Occ.) 75
Journaux....Vol. 3
Juan Fernandez Islands (Chile) ....Vol. 2
Jubile de l'Union Postale Universelle...Vol. 5
Jugoslavia, Jugoslavija....Vol. 5
Junagarh ....Vol. 1

K ....Vol. 2
КАЗАКСТАН....77
Kabul....Vol. 2
Kamerun....Vol. 1, Vol. 2
Kansu ....Vol. 2
Karelia, Karjala....75
Karki....Vol. 3
Karolinen....Vol. 2
Kashmir....Vol. 1
Katanga....76
Kathiri State of Seiyun ....Vol. 1
Kaunas....228, 233, 336
Kazakhstan, Kazahstan 76
Kedah....Vol. 1
Keeling Islands....Vol. 1
Kelantan....Vol. 1
Kentta Postia....Vol. 3
Kenya....Vol. 1
Kenya and Uganda ....Vol. 1
Kenya, Uganda and Tanzania....Vol. 1
Kenya, Uganda, Tanganyika....Vol. 1
Kenya, Uganda, Tanganyika and Zanzibar ....Vol. 1
Kerassunde ....Vol. 5
K.G.C.A. ovptd. on Yugoslavia....Vol. 5
K.G.L. ....Vol. 1, Vol. 3
Khmer Republic ....Vol. 2
Khor Fakkan ....Vol. 5
Kiangsi ....Vol. 2
Kiangsu....Vol. 2
Kiauchau, Kiautschou....77
Kibris....Vol. 5
Kilis ....Vol. 5
King Edward VII Land ....Vol. 1
Kingston, Ga. ....Vol. 1
Kionga....77
Kirghizia 119

Kiribati....Vol. 1
Kirin....Vol. 2
Kishangarh....Vol. 1
Kithyra....Vol. 3
K.K. Post Stempel....Vol. 2
Klaipeda....336
Knoxville, Tenn....Vol. 1
Kolomyya....Vol. 5
Kolozsvar....Vol. 3
Kongeligt....Vol. 3
Kop Koh....Vol. 3
Korca, Korce (Albania)....Vol. 2
Korea....77
Korea (Japanese Offices)....57
Korea, Indian Custodial Unit....Vol. 1
Koritsa....Vol. 3
Kos....Vol. 3
Kouang Tcheou-Wan....Vol. 3
KPHTH (Crete)....Vol. 2
Kr.....Vol. 3
Kr., Kreuzer....Vol. 2
Kraljevstvo, Kraljevina....Vol. 5
K.S.A.....Vol. 5
Kuban Government....Vol. 5
K.U.K.....Vol. 2, Vol. 3, Vol. 5
Kunming....Vol. 3
Kupa Zone....Vol. 5
Kurland....143, 233
Kuwait....Vol. 1
Kwangchowan....Vol. 3
Kwangsi....Vol. 2
Kwangtung....Vol. 2
Kweichow....Vol. 2
K. Wurtt. Post....Vol. 3
Kyrgyzstan....119

La Aguera....Vol. 2
Labuan....Vol. 1
La Canea....Vol. 3
Lady McLeod....Vol. 1
La Georgie....Vol. 3
Lagos....Vol. 1
La Grange, Tex.....Vol. 1
Laibach....Vol. 5
Lake City, Fla.....Vol. 1
Land Post....Vol. 3
Laos....119
Laos (Int. Com., India)....Vol. 1
L.A.R.....189
Las Bela....Vol. 1
Latakia, Lattaquie....137
Latvia, Latvija....137
Laurens Court House, S.C.....Vol. 1
League of Nations....Vol. 5
Lebanon....143
Leeward Islands....Vol. 1
Lefkas....Vol. 3
Lemnos....Vol. 3
Lenoir, N.C.....Vol. 1
Lero, Leros....Vol. 3
Lesbos....Vol. 3
Lesotho....Vol. 1
Lesser Sundas....539, 544
Lettland, Lettonia....137
Levant, British....Vol. 1
Levant, French....Vol. 3, Vol. 5
Levant, Italian....Vol. 3
Levant, Polish....856
Levant, Romanian....Vol. 5
Levant, Russian....Vol. 5
Levant, Syrian (on Lebanon)....Vol. 5
Lexington, Miss.....Vol. 1
Liaoning....Vol. 2
Liban, Libanaise....143
Libau ovptd. on German....142
Liberia....160
Liberty, Va.....Vol. 1
Libya, Libia....184
Liechtenstein....210
Lietuva, Lietuvos....228
Ligne Aeriennes de la France Libre....Vol. 5
Lima....730, 758
Limestone Springs, S.C.....Vol. 1
Linja-Autorahti Bussfrakt....Vol. 3
Lipso, Lisso....Vol. 3
Lisboa....883
Lithuania....228
Lithuania, Central....Vol. 2
Lithuanian Occupation of Memel....336
Litwa Srodkowa, Litwy Srodkowej....Vol. 2
Livingston, Ala.....Vol. 1
Livonia....Vol. 5
Ljubljana....Vol. 5
L McL....Vol. 1
Lockport, N.Y.....Vol. 1
Lombardy-Venetia....Vol. 2
Lorraine....Vol. 3
Losen....Vol. 5
Lothringen....Vol. 3
Louisville, Ky.....Vol. 1
Lourenco Marques, L. Marques....234
Lower Austria....Vol. 2
LTSR on Lithuania....233
Lubeck, Luebeck....Vol. 3
Lubiana....Vol. 5
Lublin....798
Luminescence....Vol. 1
Luxembourg....235
Lydenburg....Vol. 1
Lynchburg, Va.....Vol. 1

Macao, Macau....257
Macon, Ga.....Vol. 1
Madagascar....265
Madagascar (British)....Vol. 1
Madeira....288, 884
Madrid....Vol. 5
Madura....539
Mafeking....Vol. 1
Magdalena....Vol. 2
Magyar, Magyarorszag,....Vol. 3
Magy. Kir.....Vol. 3
Majunga....265
Malacca....Vol. 1
Malaga....Vol. 5
Malagasy Republic....265
Malawi....Vol. 1
Malaya....Vol. 1
Malaya (Japanese Occ.)....544, Vol. 1
Malaya (Thai occ.)....Vol. 1
Malaya, Federation of....Vol. 1
Malaysia....Vol. 1
Malay States....Vol. 1
Maldive Islands, Maldives....Vol. 1
Malgache Republic....267
Mali....289
Malmedy....Vol. 3
Malta....Vol. 1
Maluku Selatan (So. Moluccas)....Vol. 5
Man, Isle of....Vol. 1
Manchukuo....313
Manchuria....Vol. 2
Manizales....Vol. 2
Mariana Islands, Marianen, Marianas....315
Marienwerder....315
Marietta, Ga.....Vol. 1
Marion, Va.....Vol. 1
Markka, Markkaa....Vol. 3
Maroc, Marocco, Marokko....462, Vol. 3
Marruecos....480, Vol. 5
Marshall Islands, Marschall, Marshall-Inseln....316, Vol. 1
Marshall Islands (G.R.I. surch.)....Vol. 1
Martinique....316
Mauritania, Mauritanie....318
Mauritius....Vol. 1
Mayotte....335
Mecklbg-Vorpomm....Vol. 3
Mecklenburg-Schwerin....Vol. 3
Mecklenburg-Strelitz....Vol. 3
Mecklenburg-Vorpommern....Vol. 3
Medellin....Vol. 2
Medina....Vol. 5
M.E.F. ovptd on Great Britain....Vol. 1
Melaka....Vol. 1
Memel, Memelgebiet....335
Memphis, Tenn.....Vol. 1
Meng Chiang....Vol. 2
Menge....428
Mengtsz....Vol. 3
Merida....389
Mesopotamia (British Occupation)....Vol. 1
Metelin....Vol. 5
Mexico, Mexicano....337
Micanopy, Fla.....Vol. 1
Micronesia....Vol. 1
Middle Congo....390
Middle East Forces....Vol. 1
Militarpost....Vol. 2
Millbury, Mass.....Vol. 1
Milledgeville, Ga.....Vol. 1
Miller, Gen.....Vol. 5
Mitau....143
M. Kir.....Vol. 3
Mobile, Ala.....Vol. 1
Mocambique....480, 496
Modena....Vol. 3
Moheli....391
Moldavia....391, Vol. 5
Moldova....391
Moluccas....539, 544
Monaco....391
Monastir....Vol. 5
Mongolia....428
Mongtseu (Mongtze)....Vol. 3
Monrovia....182
Mont Athos....Vol. 5
Montenegro....460, Vol. 5
Monterrey....390
Montevideo....Vol. 5
Montgomery, Ala.....Vol. 1
Montserrat....Vol. 1
Moquea, Moquegua....759
Morelia....390
Morocco....462
Morocco (German Offices)....Vol. 3
Morocco, French....Vol. 3
Morocco, Spanish....Vol. 5
Morvi....Vol. 1
Mosul....Vol. 1
Mount Athos (Turkey)....Vol. 5
Mount Athos, Russian Offices....Vol. 5
Mount Lebanon, La.....Vol. 1
Moyen-Congo....390
Mozambique....480
Mozambique Co.....496
MQE ovptd. on French Colonies....316
Muscat and Oman....Vol. 1
M.V.iR....Vol. 5
Myanmar (Burma)....Vol. 1
Mytilene....Vol. 3

Nabha....Vol. 1
Nagyvarad....Vol. 3
Namibia....Vol. 1
Nandgaon....Vol. 1
Nanking....Vol. 2
Nanumaga....Vol. 1
Nanumea....Vol. 1
Naples, Napoletana....Vol. 3
Nashville, Tenn.....Vol. 1
Natal....Vol. 1
Nations Unies....Vol. 1
Native Feudatory States, India....Vol. 1
Nauru....Vol. 1
Navanagar....Vol. 1
N.C.E. ovptd. on French Colonies....545
Neapolitan Provinces....Vol. 3
Ned. (Nederlandse) Antillen....524
Ned. (Nederl., Nederlandsch) Indie....539
Nederland....499
Negeri Sembilan....Vol. 1
Negri Sembilan....Vol. 1
Nejd....Vol. 5
Nejd-Hejaz....Vol. 5
Nepal....Vol. 1
Netherlands....499
Netherlands Antilles....524
Netherlands Indies....539
Netherlands New Guinea....544
Nevis....Vol. 1
New Britain....Vol. 1
New Brunswick....Vol. 1
New Caledonia....545
Newfoundland....Vol. 1
New Greece....Vol. 3
New Guinea....Vol. 1
New Guinea, British....Vol. 1
New Guinea, West....Vol. 5
New Haven, Conn.....Vol. 1
New Hebrides....Vol. 1
New Hebrides (French)....564
New Orleans, La.....Vol. 1
New Republic....Vol. 1
New Smyrna, Fla.....Vol. 1
New South Wales....Vol. 1
New York....Vol. 1
New Zealand....Vol. 1
Nezavisna....Vol. 2
N.F. overprinted on Nyasaland Protectorate....Vol. 1
Nicaragua....568
Nicaria....Vol. 3
Nieuwe Republiek....Vol. 1
Nieuw Guinea....544
Niger....607
Niger and Senegambia....Vol. 5
Niger and Upper Senegal....Vol. 5
Niger Coast Protectorate (Oil Rivers)..Vol. 1
Nigeria....Vol. 1
Nikolaevsk....Vol. 5
Ningsia....Vol. 2
Nippon....21
Nisiro, Nisiros....Vol. 3
Niuafo'ou....Vol. 1
Niue....Vol. 1
Niutao....Vol. 1
Nlle. Caledonie....545
Norddeutscher Postbezirk....Vol. 3
Noreg....636
Norfolk Island....Vol. 1
Norge....632
North Borneo....Vol. 1
North China....Vol. 2
Northeast China....Vol. 2
Northeastern Provinces (China)....Vol. 2
North Epirus (Greek Occupation)....Vol. 3
Northern Cyprus, Turkish Republic of.Vol. 5
Northern Ireland....Vol. 1
Northern Kiangsu....Vol. 2
Northern Nigeria....Vol. 1
Northern Poland....799
Northern Rhodesia....Vol. 1
Northern Zone, Morocco....480
North German Confederation....Vol. 3
North Ingermanland....632
North Korea....119
North Viet Nam....Vol. 5
Northwest China....Vol. 2
North West Pacific Islands....Vol. 1
Norway....632
Nossi-Be....650
Nouvelle Caledonie....546
Nouvelles Hebrides....564
Nova Scotia....Vol. 1
Novocherkassk....Vol. 5
Nowa Bb ovptd. on Bulgaria....Vol. 5
Nowanuggur....Vol. 1
Noyta....Vol. 3, Vol. 5
Nr. 21, Nr. 16....Vol. 3
N S B ovptd. on French Colonies....650
N. Sembilan....Vol. 1
N.S.W.....Vol. 1
Nueva Granada....Vol. 2
Nui....Vol. 1
Nukufetau....Vol. 1
Nukulaelae....Vol. 1
Nyasaland (Protectorate)....Vol. 1
Nyasaland and Rhodesia....Vol. 1
Nyassa....650
N.Z.....Vol. 1

Oakway, S.C.....Vol. 1
Oaxaca....342
Obock....651
Ob. Ost ovptd. on Germany (Lithuania).233
Oceania, Oceanie....Vol. 3
Oesterr. Post....Vol. 2
Offentlig Sak, Off. Sak....649
Oil Rivers....Vol. 1
O K C A (Russia)....Vol. 5
Oldenburg....Vol. 3
Oltre Giuba....652
Oman, Sultanate of....Vol. 1
Oradea....Vol. 3
Orange River Colony....Vol. 1
Oranje Vrij Staat....Vol. 1
Orchha....Vol. 1
Orense....Vol. 5
Organisation Mondiale....Vol. 5
Oriental....Vol. 5
Orts-Post....Vol. 5
O.S.....650
Osten....854
Osterreich....Vol. 2
Ostland....Vol. 5

Ottoman....Vol. 3, Vol. 5
Oubangi Chari....Vol. 5
Outer Mongolia....428

Pacchi Postali....Vol. 3, Vol. 5
Pacific Steam Navigation Co....729
Packhoi (Pakhoi)....Vol. 3
Pahang....Vol. 1
Paita....759
Pakistan....Vol. 1
Pakke-porto....Vol. 3
Palau....Vol. 1
Palestine....Vol. 3
Palestine (British Administration)....Vol. 1
Palestine (Jordan Occ.)....75
Panama....653
Panama (Colombian Dom.)....653, Vol. 2
Panama Canal Zone....Vol. 1
Papua....Vol. 1
Papua New Guinea....Vol. 1
Para....Vol. 3
Para ovptd. on Austria....Vol. 2
Para ovptd. on Germany....Vol. 3
Para ovptd. on Italy....Vol. 3
Paraguay....679
Paras ovptd. on France....Vol. 3
Paras ovpt. on Romania....Vol. 5
Parma, Parm., Parmensi....Vol. 3
Pasco....759
Patiala....Vol. 1
Patmo, Patmos....Vol. 3
Patzcuaro....390
Paxos....Vol. 2, Vol. 3
PD....Vol. 5
P.E....Vol. 3
Pechino, Peking....Vol. 3
Pen....Vol. 3
Penang....Vol. 1
Penrhyn Island....Vol. 1
Pensacola, Fla....Vol. 1
People's Republic of China....Vol. 2
Perak....Vol. 1
Perlis....Vol. 1
Persekutuan Tanah Melayu (Malaya)....Vol. 1
Persia (British Occupation)....Vol. 1
Persia, Persanes....Vol. 3
Peru....729
Pesa ovpt. on Germany....Vol. 3
Peshawar....Vol. 2
Petersburg, Va....Vol. 1
Pfennig....Vol. 3
P.G.S. (Perak)....Vol. 1
Philadelphia, Pa....Vol. 1
Philippines....760
Philippines (US Admin.)....762, Vol. 1
Philippines (Japanese Occ.)....796, Vol. 1
Piast., Piaster ovptd. on Austria....Vol. 2
Piaster ovptd. on Germany....Vol. 3
Piaster ovptd. on Romania....Vol. 5
Piastre, Piastra ovptd. on Italy....Vol. 3
Piastre, Piastres ovptd. on France....Vol. 3
Pietersburg....Vol. 1
Pilipinas....768, Vol. 1
Pisco....759
Piscopi....Vol. 3
Pitcairn Islands....Vol. 1
Pittsylvania C.H., Va....Vol. 1
Piura....759
Pleasant Shade, Va....Vol. 1
Poczta Polska....798
Pohjois Inkeri....632
Pokutia....Vol. 5
Poland....798
Poland, exile government in Great Britain....856
Polish Offices in Danzig....856
Polish Offices in Turkish Empire....856
Polska....798
Polynesia, French....Vol. 3
Ponce....897, Vol. 1
Ponta Delgada....857
Poonch....Vol. 1
Port Arthur and Dairen....Vol. 2
Porte de Conduccion....757
Porte de Mar....387
Porte Franco....729, 882
Port Gdansk....856
Port Hood, Nova Scotia....Vol. 1
Port Lagos....Vol. 3
Port Lavaca, Tex....Vol. 1
Porto....Vol. 2
Porto Gazetei....Vol. 5
Porto Pflichtige....Vol. 3
Porto Rico....896, Vol. 1
Port Said, French Offices....Vol. 3
Portugal, Portuguesa, Portugueza....857
Portuguese Africa....886
Portuguese Congo....886
Portuguese East Africa (Mozambique)....480
Portuguese Guinea....887
Portuguese India....890
Posen (Poznan)....798
Post....Vol. 3
Posta....Vol. 5
Postas le hioc....Vol. 1
Poste Locale....Vol. 5
Postes....235, Vol. 2, Vol. 3, Vol. 5
Postes Serbes ovptd. on France....Vol. 5
Postgebiet Ob. Ost....233
Postzegel....499
Poul, Pul....Vol. 2
P.P. ovptd. on French postage dues....Vol. 3
P.P.C. ovptd. on Poland....856
Preussen....Vol. 3
Priamur....Vol. 5
Prince Edward Island....Vol. 1
Pristina....Vol. 5
Providence, R.I....Vol. 1
Prussia....Vol. 3
PS....Vol. 2
P.S.N.C. (Peru)....729
Puerto Principe....Vol. 1, Vol. 2
Puerto Rico, Pto. Rico....896, Vol. 1
Puerto Rico (US Admin.)....896, Vol. 1
Pulau Pinang....Vol. 1
Puno....760
Puttialla State....Vol. 1

Qatar....897
Qu'aiti State in Hadhramaut....Vol. 1
Qu'aiti State of Shihr and Mukalla....Vol. 1
Queensland....Vol. 1
Quelimane....907

R (Jhind)....Vol. 1
R ovptd. on French Colonies....Vol. 3
Rajasthan....Vol. 1
Rajpeepla, Rajpipla....Vol. 1
Raleigh, N.C....Vol. 1
Rappen....Vol. 5
Rarotonga....Vol. 1
Ras Al Khaima....Vol. 5
R.A.U....Vol. 5
Rayon....Vol. 5
Republique Arab Unie....Vol. 5
Regatul....Vol. 3
Reichspost....Vol. 3
Reis (Portugal)....857
Repubblica Sociale Italiana....Vol. 3
Rethymnon, Retymno....Vol. 2
Reunion....Vol. 3
R.F....(see France or French Colonies)
R H....Vol. 3
Rheatown, Tenn....Vol. 1
Rheinland-Pfalz....Vol. 3
Rhine Palatinate....Vol. 3
Rhodes (Rodi)....Vol. 3
Rhodesia....Vol. 1
Rhodesia (formerly So. Rhodesia)....Vol. 1
Rhodesia and Nyasaland....Vol. 1
Riau, Riouw Archipelago....Vol. 3
Ricevuta....Vol. 3, Vol. 5
Richmond, Tex....Vol. 1
Rigsbank Skilling....Vol. 3
Ringgold, Ga....Vol. 1
Rio de Oro....Vol. 5
Rio Muni....Vol. 5
RIS on Netherlands Indies....Vol. 3
Rizeh....Vol. 5
Robertsport....182
Rodi (Rhodes)....Vol. 3
Romagna, Romagne....Vol. 3
Romana....Vol. 5
Romania....Vol. 5
Romania, Occupation, Offices....Vol. 5
Romanian Occupation of Hungary....Vol. 3
Romanian Occupation of Western Ukraine....Vol. 5
Roman States....Vol. 3
Romina....Vol. 5
Ross Dependency....Vol. 1
Rossija....Vol. 5
Rostov....Vol. 5
Rouad....Vol. 5
Roumelie orientale, RO....Vol. 3
RSA....Vol. 1
R S M (San Marino)....Vol. 3
Ruanda ovptd. on Congo....Vol. 3
Ruanda-Urundi....Vol. 5
Rumania....Vol. 5
Rumanien on Germany....Vol. 5
Russia....Vol. 5
Russia (Finnish Occupation)....Vol. 5
Russia (German Occupation)....Vol. 5
Russian Dominion of Poland....798
Russian Occupation of Crete....Vol. 2
Russian Occupation of Germany....Vol. 3
Russian Occupation of Latvia....143
Russian Occupation of Lithuania....233
Russian Offices....Vol. 5
Russian stamps surcharged or overprinted....Vol. 2, Vol. 3, Vol. 5
Russian Turkestan....Vol. 5
Russisch-Polen ovptd. on Germany....854
Rustenburg....Vol. 1
Rutherfordton, N.C....Vol. 1
Rwanda, Rwandaise....Vol. 5
Ryukyu Islands....Vol. 5

S A, S.A.K. (Saudi Arabia)....Vol. 5
Saar, Saargebiet....Vol. 5
Sabah....Vol. 1
Sachsen....Vol. 3
Sahara Occidental (Espanol)....Vol. 5
Saint....see St.
Salamanca....Vol. 5
Salem, N.C....Vol. 1
Salem, Va....Vol. 1
Salisbury, N.C....Vol. 1
Salonicco, Salonika....Vol. 3
Salonika (Turkish)....Vol. 5
Salonique....Vol. 5
Salvador, El....Vol. 5
Salzburg....Vol. 2
Samoa....Vol. 1, Vol. 5
Samos....Vol. 3
San Antonio, Tex....Vol. 1
San Marino....Vol. 5
San Sebastian....Vol. 5
Santa Cruz de Tenerife....Vol. 5
Santa Maura....Vol. 3
Santander....Vol. 2
Sao Tome and Principe....Vol. 5
SAR....Vol. 5
Sarawak....Vol. 1
Sardinia....Vol. 3
Sarre overprinted on Germany and Bavaria....Vol. 5
Saseno....Vol. 5
Saudi Arabia....Vol. 5
Saurashtra....Vol. 1
Savannah, Ga....Vol. 1
Saxony....Vol. 3
SCADTA....Vol. 2, Vol. 3
Scarpanto....Vol. 3
Schleswig....Vol. 3, Vol. 5
Schleswig-Holstein....Vol. 3
Schweizer Reneke....Vol. 1
Scinde....Vol. 1
Scotland....Vol. 1
Scutari, Italian Offices....Vol. 3
Segnatassa, Segnatasse....Vol. 3
Seiyun....Vol. 1
Selangor....Vol. 1
Selma, Ala....Vol. 1
Semenov....Vol. 3
Sen....1
Senegal....Vol. 5
Senegambia and Niger....Vol. 5
Serbia, Serbien....Vol. 5
Serbian Occupation of Hungary....Vol. 3
75 iNCi Yil Donumu....Vol. 5
Seville, Sevilla....Vol. 5
Seychelles....Vol. 1
S. H....Vol. 3
Shanghai....Vol. 2, Vol. 5
Shanghai (U.S. Offices)....Vol. 1
Shanghai and Nanking....Vol. 2
Shansi....Vol. 2
Shantung....Vol. 2
Sharjah....Vol. 5
Shensi....Vol. 2
Shihr and Mukalla....Vol. 1
Shqipenia, Shqiptare, Shqiperija, Shqiperise (Albania)....Vol. 2
Shri Lanka....Vol. 1
S. H. S. on Bosnia and Herzegovina....Vol. 5
S. H. S. on Hungary....Vol. 5
Siam (Thailand)....Vol. 5
Siberia....Vol. 5
Sicily, Sicilia....Vol. 3
Siege de la Ligue Arabe....463
Sierra Leone....Vol. 1
Sikang....Vol. 2
Silesia, Upper....Vol. 5
Simi....Vol. 3
Sinai....Vol. 5
Sinaloa....390
Singapore....Vol. 1
Sinkiang....Vol. 2
Sirmoor (Sirmur)....Vol. 1
Sld....Vol. 2
Slesvig....Vol. 5
Slovakia....Vol. 2, Vol. 5
Slovene Coast....Vol. 5
Slovenia, Slovenija....Vol. 5
Slovenia, Italian....Vol. 5
Slovensko....Vol. 5
S. Marino....Vol. 5
Smirne, Smyrna....Vol. 3
Smyrne....Vol. 5
S O ovptd. on Czechoslovakia or Poland....Vol. 3
Sobreporte....Vol. 2
Sociedad Colombo-Alemana....Vol. 2, Vol. 3
Sociedade de Geographia de Lisboa....883
Societe des Nations....Vol. 5
Soldi....Vol. 2
Solomon Islands....Vol. 1
Somali, Somalia, Somaliya....Vol. 5
Somalia, B.M.A....Vol. 1
Somalia, E.A.F....Vol. 1
Somali Coast (Djibouti)....Vol. 5
Somaliland Protectorate....Vol. 1
Sonora....341
Soomaaliya, Soomaliyeed....Vol. 5
Soruth, Sorath....Vol. 1
Soudan....Vol. 1, Vol. 3
Sourashtra....Vol. 1
South Africa....Vol. 1
South African Republic (Transvaal)....Vol. 1
South Arabia....Vol. 1
South Australia....Vol. 1
South Bulgaria....Vol. 3
South China....Vol. 2
Southern Cameroons....Vol. 1
Southern Nigeria....Vol. 1
Southern Poland....799
Southern Rhodesia....Vol. 1
Southern Yemen....Vol. 5
South Georgia....Vol. 1
South Georgia and the South Sandwich Islands....Vol. 1
South Kasai....Vol. 5
South Korea....79
South Lithuania....233
South Moluccas....Vol. 5
South Orkneys....Vol. 1
South Russia....Vol. 5
South Shetlands....Vol. 1
South Viet Nam....Vol. 5
South West Africa....Vol. 1
Southwest China....Vol. 2
Soviet Union (Russia)....Vol. 5
Sowjetische Besatzungs Zone....Vol. 3
Spain....Vol. 5
Spain, Dominion of Cuba....Vol. 2
Spanish Administration of Andorra....Vol. 2
Spanish Dominion of Mariana Islands....315
Spanish Dominion of Philippines....760
Spanish Dominion of Puerto Rico....896
Spanish Guinea....Vol. 5
Spanish Morocco....Vol. 5
Spanish Sahara....Vol. 5
Spanish West Africa....Vol. 5
Spanish Western Sahara....Vol. 5

Sparta, Ga. ....Vol. 1
Spartanburg, S.C. ....Vol. 1
SPM ovptd. on French Cols. ....Vol. 5
Sri Lanka ....Vol. 1
Srodkowa Litwa ....Vol. 2
Stamp ....Vol. 5
Stampalia ....Vol. 3
Stanislav ....Vol. 5
Statesville, N.C. ....Vol. 1
St. Christopher ....Vol. 1
St. Christopher-Nevis-Anguilla ....Vol. 1
Ste. Marie de Madagascar ....Vol. 5
Stellaland ....Vol. 1
Stempel ....Vol. 2
St. Helena ....Vol. 1
St. Kitts ....Vol. 1
St. Kitts-Nevis ....Vol. 1
St. Louis, Mo. ....Vol. 1
St. Lucia ....Vol. 1
St. Pierre and Miquelon ....Vol. 5
Straits Settlements ....Vol. 1
St. Thomas and Prince Islands ....Vol. 5
STT Vuja ....Vol. 5
St. Vincent ....Vol. 1
St. Vincent Grenadines ....Vol. 1
Styria ....Vol. 2
S.U. on Straits Settlements ....Vol. 1
Submarine mail (Correo Submarino) ....Vol. 5
Sudan ....Vol. 1
Sudan, French ....Vol. 3
Suid Afrika ....Vol. 1
Suidwes-Afrika ....Vol. 1
Suiyuan ....Vol. 2
Sultanate of Oman ....Vol. 1
Sumatra 539, 544
Sumter, S.C. ....Vol. 1
Sunda Islands 539, 544
Sungei Ujong ....Vol. 1
Suomi (Finland) ....Vol. 3
Supeh ....Vol. 2
Surinam, Suriname ....Vol. 5
Suvalki 233
Sverige ....Vol. 5
S.W.A. ....Vol. 1
Swaziland ....Vol. 1
Sweden ....Vol. 5
Switzerland ....Vol. 5
Switzerland, Administration of Liechtenstein 211
Syria, Syrienne ....Vol. 5
Syria (Arabian Government) ....Vol. 5
Syrie-Grand Liban ....Vol. 5
Szechwan ....Vol. 2
Szechwan Province ....Vol. 2
Szeged ....Vol. 3

T ....Vol. 2, Vol. 3
T ovptd. on stamps of Peru 759
Tacna 732, 757
Tadjikistan, Tadzikistan ....Vol. 5
Tae Han (Korea) 77
Tahiti ....Vol. 5
Taiwan (Formosa) ....Vol. 2
Taiwan, Japanese ....58, Vol. 2
Talbotton, Ga. ....Vol. 1
Talca ....Vol. 2
Tanganyika ....Vol. 1
Tanganyika and Zanzibar ....Vol. 1
Tangier, British Offices ....Vol. 1
Tangier, French Offices ....Vol. 3
Tangier, Spanish Offices ....Vol. 5
Tannu Tuva ....Vol. 5
Tanzania ....Vol. 1
Tartu ....Vol. 3
Tasmania ....Vol. 1
Tassa Gazzette ....Vol. 3
Taxa de Guerra 264, 886, 890, 895
Tchad ....Vol. 2
Tchongking ....Vol. 3
T.C., Postalari ....Vol. 5
Te Betalen ....523, 538, 543, Vol. 2, Vol. 5
Tegucigalpa ....Vol. 3
Teheran ....Vol. 3
Tellico Plains, Tenn. ....Vol. 1
Temesvar ....Vol. 3
T.E.O. ovptd. on Turkey or France ....Vol. 2
Terres Australes et Antarctiques Francaises ....Vol. 3
Territorio Insular Chileno ....Vol. 2
Teruel ....Vol. 5
Tete ....Vol. 5
Tetuan ....Vol. 5
Thailand, Thai ....Vol. 5
Thailand (Occupation of Malaya) ....Vol. 1
Thessaly ....Vol. 5
Thomasville, Ga. ....Vol. 1
Thrace ....Vol. 5
Thuringia, Thuringen ....Vol. 3
Thurn and Taxis ....Vol. 3
Tibet ....Vol. 5
Tibet (Chinese province) ....Vol. 2
Tibet, Chinese Offices ....Vol. 2
Tical ....Vol. 5
Tientsin (German) ....Vol. 3
Tientsin (Italian) ....Vol. 3
Tiflis ....Vol. 3
Timbre ovptd. on France ....Vol. 3
Timor ....Vol. 5
Tin Can Island ....Vol. 1
Tjedan Solidarnosti ....Vol. 5
Tjenestefrimerke ....649, Vol. 3
Tlacotalpan 390
Tobago ....Vol. 1
Toga ....Vol. 1
Togo ....Vol. 5
Togo (British Occupation) ....Vol. 1
Tokelau Islands ....Vol. 1
Tolima ....Vol. 2
Tonga ....Vol. 1
Tongareva ....Vol. 1
To Pay ....Vol. 1
Toscano ....Vol. 3
Tou ....Vol. 3
Touva ....Vol. 5
Transcaucasian Federated Republics ....Vol. 5
Trans-Jordan 58
Trans-Jordan (Palestine Occ.) 75
Transkei ....Vol. 1
Transvaal ....Vol. 1
Transylvania ....Vol. 3
Trasporto Pacchi ....Vol. 3
Travancore ....Vol. 1
Travancore-Cochin, State of ....Vol. 1
Trebizonde ....Vol. 5
Trengganu ....Vol. 1
Trentino ....Vol. 2
Trieste ....Vol. 2, Vol. 3, Vol. 5
Trinidad ....Vol. 1
Trinidad and Tobago ....Vol. 1
Tripoli di Barberia ....Vol. 3
Tripoli, Fiera Campionaria 184
Tripolitania ....Vol. 5
Tripolitania (B.M.A.) ....Vol. 1
Tristan da Cunha ....Vol. 1
Trucial States ....Vol. 1
Tsinghai ....Vol. 2
Tsingtau 77
T. Ta. C ....Vol. 5
Tullahoma, Tenn. ....Vol. 1
Tunisia, Tunisie, Tunis ....Vol. 5
Turkestan, Russian ....Vol. 5
Turkey, Turkiye ....Vol. 5
Turkey (Greek Occupation) ....Vol. 3
Turkey in Asia ....Vol. 5
Turk Federe Devleti ....Vol. 5
Turkish Empire, Austrian Offices ....Vol. 2
Turkish Empire, British Offices ....Vol. 1
Turkish Empire, French Offices ....Vol. 3
Turkish Empire, German Offices ....Vol. 3
Turkish Empire, Italian Offices ....Vol. 3
Turkish Empire, Polish Offices 856
Turkish Empire, Romanian Offices ....Vol. 5
Turkish Empire, Russian Offices ....Vol. 5
Turkish Republic of Northern Cyprus ....Vol. 5
Turkish stamps surcharged or overprinted ....Vol. 3, Vol. 5
Turkmenistan ....Vol. 5
Turks and Caicos Islands ....Vol. 1
Turks Islands ....Vol. 1
Tuscaloosa, Ala ....Vol. 1
Tuscany ....Vol. 3
Tuscumbia, Ala. ....Vol. 1
Tuva Autonomous Region ....Vol. 5
Tuvalu ....Vol. 1
Two Sicilies ....Vol. 3
Tyosen (Korea) 77
Tyrol ....Vol. 2

UAE ovptd. on Abu Dhabi ....Vol. 5
U.A.R. ....Vol. 3, Vol. 5
Ubangi, Ubangi-Shari ....Vol. 5
Uganda, U.G. ....Vol. 1
Uganda, and Kenya ....Vol. 1
Ukraine (Ukrainia) ....Vol. 5
Ukraine (German Occupation) ....Vol. 5
Uku Leta ....Vol. 1
Umm al Qiwain ....Vol. 5
UNEF ovptd. on India ....Vol. 1
UNESCO ....Vol. 3
U.N. Force in Congo (India) ....Vol. 1
Union City, Tenn. ....Vol. 1
Union Island, St. Vincent ....Vol. 1
Union Islands ....Vol. 1
Union of South Africa ....Vol. 1
Union of Soviet Socialist Republics ....Vol. 5
Uniontown, Ala ....Vol. 1
Unionville, S.C. ....Vol. 1
United Arab Emirates ....Vol. 5
United Arab Republic (UAR) ....Vol. 3, Vol. 5
United Arab Republic, Egypt ....Vol. 3
United Arab Republic Issues for Palestine ....Vol. 3
United Arab Republic Issues for Syria ....Vol. 5
United Kingdom ....Vol. 1
United Kingdom of Libya 185
United Nations ....Vol. 1
United Nations European Office ....Vol. 5
United Nations Offices in Geneva ....Vol. 1
United Nations Offices in Vienna ....Vol. 1
United State of Saurashtra ....Vol. 1
United States Admin. of Canal Zone ....Vol. 1
United States Admin. of Cuba ....Vol. 1, Vol. 2
United States Admin. of Guam ....Vol. 1
United States Administration of Philippines ....762, Vol. 1
United States Administration of Puerto Rico ....896, Vol. 1
United States of America ....Vol. 1
United States of Indonesia ....Vol. 3
United States of New Granada ....Vol. 2
United States, Offices in China ....Vol. 1
Universal Postal Union, International Bureau ....Vol. 5
UNTEA ovptd. on Netherlands New Guinea ....Vol. 5
UPHA ROPA 460
Upper Austria ....Vol. 2
Upper Senegal and Niger ....Vol. 5
Upper Silesia ....Vol. 5
Upper Volta ....Vol. 2
U.R.I. ovptd. on Yugoslavia ....Vol. 5
Uruguay ....Vol. 5
Urundi ovptd. on Congo ....Vol. 3
Uskub ....Vol. 5
U.S. Military Rule, Korea 78
U.S. Zone (Germany) ....Vol. 3
Uzbekistan ....Vol. 5

Vaitupu ....Vol. 1
Valdosta, Ga. ....Vol. 1
Valladolid ....Vol. 5
Valona ....Vol. 3
Vancouver Island ....Vol. 1
Van Diemen's Land (Tasmania) ....Vol. 1
Vanuatu ....Vol. 1
Varldspost Kongress ....Vol. 5
Vasa ....Vol. 3
Vathy (Samos) ....Vol. 3
Vatican City, Vaticane ....Vol. 5
Venda ....Vol. 1
Venezia Giulia ....Vol. 2, Vol. 3
Venezia Tridentina ....Vol. 2
Venezuela, Veneza., Venezolana ....Vol. 5
Venizelist Government ....Vol. 3
Vereinte Nationen ....Vol. 1
Victoria ....Vol. 1
Victoria, Texas ....Vol. 1
Victoria Land ....Vol. 1
Vienna ....Vol. 2
Viet Nam ....Vol. 5
Viet Nam, (Int. Com., India) ....Vol. 1
Viet Nam, North ....Vol. 5
Vilnius 228, 233
Virgin Islands ....Vol. 1
Vladivostok ....Vol. 3
Vojna Uprava ....Vol. 5
Volksrust ....Vol. 1
Vom Empfanger ....Vol. 3
Vorarlberg ....Vol. 2
V.R. ovptd. on Transvaal ....Vol. 1
Vryburg ....Vol. 1
Vuja-STT ....Vol. 5

Wadhwan ....Vol. 1
Walachia ....Vol. 5
Wales & Monmouthshire ....Vol. 1
Wallis and Futuna Islands ....Vol. 5
Walterborough, S.C. ....Vol. 1
War Board of Trade ....Vol. 5
Warrenton, Ga. ....Vol. 1
Warsaw 798
Washington, Ga. ....Vol. 1
Weatherford, Texas ....Vol. 1
Wenden ....Vol. 5
Western Australia ....Vol. 1
Western Samoa ....Vol. 1
Western Szechwan ....Vol. 2
Western Thrace (Greek Occupation) ....Vol. 5
Western Ukraine ....Vol. 5
West Irian ....Vol. 5
West New Guinea ....Vol. 5
West Saxony ....Vol. 3
Wet and dry printings ....Vol. 1
White Russia ....Vol. 5
Wiederaufbauspende ....Vol. 3
Wilayah Persekutuan ....Vol. 1
Winnsborough, S.C. ....Vol. 1
Wir sind frei ....Vol. 2
Wolmaransstad ....Vol. 1
World Health Organization ....Vol. 5
World Intellectual Property Organization ....Vol. 5
World Meteorological Organization ....Vol. 5
Wrangel Issues ....Vol. 5
Wurttemberg ....Vol. 3
Wytheville, Va. ....Vol. 1

Xeimappa ....Vol. 3

Y.A.R. ....Vol. 5
Yca 760
Yemen ....Vol. 5
Yemen Arab Republic ....Vol. 5
Yemen People's Republic ....Vol. 5
Yemen, People's Democratic Republic ....Vol. 5
Ykp. H.P. ....Vol. 5
Yksi Markka ....Vol. 3
Yuan ....Vol. 2
Yucatan 390
Yudenich, Gen. ....Vol. 5
Yugoslavia ....Vol. 5
Yugoslavia (German Occupation) ....Vol. 5
Yugoslavia (Italian Occupation) ....Vol. 5
Yugoslavia (Trieste) ....Vol. 5
Yugoslavia (Zone B) ....Vol. 5
Yugoslavia Offices Abroad ....Vol. 5
Yunnan (China) ....Vol. 2
Yunnan Fou, Yunnan Sen ....Vol. 3

Za Crveni Krst ....Vol. 5
Z. Afr. Republiek ....Vol. 1
Zaire ....Vol. 5
Zambezia ....Vol. 5
Zambia ....Vol. 1
Zante ....Vol. 3
Zanzibar ....Vol. 1
Zanzibar (French Offices) ....Vol. 3
Zanzibar-Tanzania ....Vol. 1
Z.A.R. ovptd. on Cape of Good Hope ....Vol. 1
Zelaya 606
Zentraler Kurierdienst ....Vol. 3
Zil Eloigne Sesel ....Vol. 1
Zil Elwagne Sesel ....Vol. 1
Zil Elwannyen Sesel ....Vol. 1
Zimbabwe ....Vol. 1
Zimska Pomoc ovptd. on Italy ....Vol. 5
Zone A (Trieste) ....Vol. 3
Zone B (Istria) ....Vol. 5
Zone B (Trieste) ....Vol. 5
Zone Francaise ....Vol. 3
Zuidwest Afrika ....Vol. 1
Zululand ....Vol. 1
Zurich ....Vol. 5

INDEX TO ADVERTISERS - 1994 VOLUME 4

ADVERTISER PAGE

– A –

Adirondack Stamps 257
Adirondack Stamps 857
Almaz Co .... Yellow Pages
American Topical Association 41A
Araz Stamp Company 143

– B –

Bexar Stamp Auctions .... Auction House Directory
Bexar Stamp Auction 339
Bieniecki International Inc 847
Roman J. Burkiewicz 847

– C –

City Hall Stamp Co., Inc .... Yellow Pages
The Classic Collector 3
The Classic Collector 338
The Classic Collector 569
The Classic Collector 679
The Classic Collector 729
The Classic Collector 858
The Classic Collector 887
County Stamp Center .... Yellow Pages

– E –

Erocole–Gloria .... Yellow Pages

– F –

Filatelia–Numismatica Madiera 858

– G –

Frank P. Gieger Philatelists 512
Frank P. Gieger Philatelists .... Yellow Pages
Henry Gitner Philatelists, Inc 55
Henry Gitner Philatelists, Inc 211
Henry Gitner Philatelists, Inc 525
David Grossblatt 425
Rolf Gummesson AB 634

– I –

Swamy Iyer 4

ADVERTISER PAGE

– J –

International Society for Japanese Philately 1
Jensen & Faurschou 633

– K –

Kenmore .... Yellow Pages

– L –

Kwan Lee, Inc 54
Kwan Lee, Inc 117
Linn's Stamp News 1A

– M –

Macau Post Office 263
The Matterhorn Mail 226
E. Joseph McConnell, Inc 422
Modlow–Arvai Stamps and Collectables .. Yellow Pages

– N –

Namchong Stamps & Coins 117
Gregg Nelson 338
Northland Co 633

– O –

Victor R. Ostolaza 747

– P –

Pacific–Midwest Company 4
Pacific–Midwest Company 78
Philstamps 761
Podiaolympic 711

– R –

Rebo Stamp Company 499
Manson Rideout Philatelist Ltd .... Yellow Pages
Rising Sun Stamps 54
Robin Philatelics 79
Michael Rogers, Inc 78

ADVERTISER PAGE

– S –

Jacques C. Schiff, Jr., Inc .... Auction House Directory
Jacques C. Schiff, Jr., Inc .... Yellow Pages
Bill Shelton Philatelics 339
Shull Service 1
Jay Smith 634
Superior Galleries 2A
Superior Galleries .... Auction House Directory

– T –

Gary Tanaka 57

– U –

Union Stamp Company 3

– V –

Vidiforms, Co., Inc .... Yellow Pages
J.O. Vadeboncoeur 372

– W –

Wallace .... Yellow Pages
The Washington Press .... Back Cover
Warren A. Wasson .... Yellow Pages
Westminster Stamp Gallery Ltd .... Yellow Pages
R. E. "Bob" Wilson 2
Winter Park Stamp Shop .... Yellow Pages

– Y –

Jack & Carol Yao 2

– Z –

Gregorio Zuskis .... Yellow Pages

MENTION SCOTT WHEN RESPONDING TO ADVERTISEMENTS!

SCOTT CATALOGUE PHILATELIC MARKETPLACE

1994 VOLUME 4

This "Yellow Pages" section of your Scott Catalogue contains advertisements to help you find what you need, when you need it...conveniently!

TOPICALS

CITY HALL STAMP CO., INC.
The TOPICAL Market SPECIALIST

TOPICALS • TOPICALS • TOPICALS • TOPICALS

* Want lists filled on all topics.
* Always ready to buy topical collections.
* Absolute satisfaction guaranteed.

City Hall Stamp Co., Inc.

Wholesale-Retail
P.O. Box 52, East Station
Yonkers, N.Y. 10704

Ph. 914-969-3554, 969-2023 * FAX: 914-969-3104
Cable — Alkastamp, Yonkers, N.Y. * Telex #497 2032

TOPICALS - ALL TOPICS

For many years (first as Filatelia Pampa) we have been a leader in this field. ANY sub-topic is Not Strange for us!

VERY LARGE WORLDWIDE STOCK
...including varieties, cancels, covers, etc.

WANT LISTS WELCOME
...any Catalogue #, any main language.

ERCOLE GLORIA - Gregorio Zuskis
Piazza Pio Xi 1, 20123 Milan, ITALY
PH. +39-2-804106 • FAX +39-2-864217

ALSO, BUYING AND SELLING TELEPHONE CARDS!

SCOTT STAMP MONTHLY AND CATALOGUE UPDATE.
Write for advertising information.
P.O. Box 828, Sidney, OH 45365.

SCOTT PUBLISHING COMPANY
Are you interested in advertising in the 1995 Scott Catalogues? Let us know and we'll send you information when it is available.
P.O. Box 828, Sidney, OH 45365.

SUBSCRIBE TO SCOTT STAMP MONTHLY
INCLUDING CATALOGUE UPDATE

LIVELY, ENGAGING ARTICLES THAT CAPTURE THE SPECIAL FASCINATION STAMPS HOLD, PLUS THE LATEST INFORMATION ON NEW ISSUES, INCLUDING SCOTT NUMBERS.

ONE YEAR, 12 ISSUES – $16.95
TWO YEARS, 24 ISSUES – $28.95

CALL TODAY... 1-800-5-SCOTT-5

OR WRITE TODAY TO: SCOTT PUBLISHING CO., P.O. BOX 828, SIDNEY, OH 45365